D0090626

BAKER'S BIOGRAPHICAL DICTIONARY *of* MUSICIANS

FIFTH EDITION

Completely Revised by
NICOLAS SLONIMSKY

with 1971 Supplement

G. SCHIRMER
New York/London

Printed in U.S.A.
38421cx x124
Library of Congress Catalog Card No. 78-183534
ISBN 0-911320-62-8

PREFACE

TO THE 1971 EDITION

There is no greater glory in the world of scholarship than to become a footnote, or a parenthesis. I have achieved both. I am an erudite footnote in the entry on Carl Maria von Weber in Grove's *Dictionary of Music and Musicians* and an honorific parenthesis in *Die Musik in Geschichte und Gegenwart* for correcting the birth date of Lully. Such flattering references carry a responsibility. There is a sense of finality; one feels like a scarab embedded in a piece of millennial amber, immutable and incapable of alteration. I experience painful remorse of conscience every time I find some of my own errors trustingly reproduced as the last word in a new European or American dictionary.

Corrections made in the Supplements 1965 and 1971 to the Fifth Edition of Baker's *Biographical Dictionary of Musicians* of 1958 must therefore represent an act of contrition. I had no right to confer knighthood on the English violist William Primrose who is a mere Commander of the British Empire. I was acting without authority in creating the English pianist Harriet Cohen, Dame. True, she was Dame of the Order of Merit of Spain, but in England she was, like Primrose, a Commander of the British Empire. I was careless in my report that Pablo Sarasate received his Stradivarius violin as a gift from the Queen of Spain. He purchased it with his own hard-earned pesetas, as I could easily have found out from a book on him in the bibliography listed in my own article on Sarasate in Baker 1958.

I still shudder at my reckless charge that Glenn Gould is a jazz addict. His manager was quick in denouncing the slanderous imputation, and demanded retraction. I had to confess that I had confused Glenn Gould with the Austrian pianist Friedrich Gulda, who is indeed a jazz enthusiast.

A mischievous poltergeist must have been at work on my typewriter during my labors on the Fifth Edition of Baker, juggling dates and transposing letters. Charles de Bériot (1802-1870) procreated a son in 1833, not in 1883, for posthumous artificial insemination had not yet been perfected in the nineteenth century. "Der alte Ries" did not become a father at the age of nine in 1784. He was 29 at the time of the happy event, for he was born in 1755, not in 1775, as my outrageous poltergeist caused it to appear. Reinken, who was born in 1623, could not have studied with Sweelinck who died in 1621; but he may have studied with Sweelinck's son. An assimilation to a famous name moved my overweening poltergeist to compress the name of Fritz Kreisler's teacher Auber to Auer. And so it goes.

The present Supplement 1971 absorbs, with necessary emendations, the entire content of Supplement 1965. Numerous new biographies, mostly of the youngest crop of avant-garde composers and performing Wunderkinder, have been added. Great masters naturally command most space, but opaque luminaries of the past — Bibl, Kittl, Lickl, Titl *et al.* — have not been neglected.

PREFACE

Shocked by the inclusion of an eccentric contemporary figure, an élitist American composer, who himself rates 34 lines in the 1971 Supplement, in addition to solid columns of space in the 1958 edition of Baker, exclaimed: "But he stinks! I know him!" Yet the very fact that the subject's olfactory emanations are powerful enough to reach and irritate the distant nostrils of a sensitive recipient justifies giving him a niche.

It has been heretofore considered *infra dignitatem* to offer lexicographical accommodations to unlettered, untutored and often ill-mannered purveyors of popular music — the Beatles and kindred musical coleoptera, crooners, country music balladiers, electric guitar strummers, and rock 'n' roll shouters. But European lexica have long accorded them full recognition and a generous amount of space. A biographical dictionary of musicians published in America can do no less. The 1971 Supplement contains a goodly number of them. No test of musical literacy has been applied in the selection; anyway, the popularity index is in inverse ratio to academic qualifications. But even institutions of learning are beginning to yield to mass appeal: a popular singer has recently been awarded an honorary doctorate by one of the iviest universities of the Ivy League.

A great effort has been made in the preparation of Baker's Dictionary and its supplements to check on long accepted biographical facts and fancies. Many a cherished legend crumbled in the process. Sweelinck never went to Venice for study; he stuck it out at the organ of his old Amsterdam church throughout his adult life. Corelli never made a trip to Paris to challenge the supremacy of Lully. It was Mozart's father, not Haydn, who composed the children's classic, *Toy Symphony,* although its best-known arrangement may have been made by Haydn's brother Michael. Beethoven was not the author of the notorious 'Jena Symphony'; it was the work of one Friedrich Witt. Purcell never wrote the trumpet voluntary that became famous under his name; it was written by his contemporary Jeremiah Clarke, and its original title was *The Prince of Denmark's March.* Wagner did not invent the *Leitmotiv;* nor did Hans von Wolzogen, the Wagnerian to whom the credit is often given; the term occurs for the first time in the introduction to an annotated catalogue of Weber's works compiled by Friedrich Wilhelm Jähns, published in 1871. Bizet did not compose the famous *Habanera* in *Carmen;* he borrowed it — melody, harmony, tonality, dynamics, and all — from a song collection by Sebastian Yradier. The common misspelling, *Habañera,* with a tilde over the *n,* is an illiteracy, regrettably popularized by Ravel and some other French composers; the Spanish name of the place is Habana, not Habaña. And what is a Cuban song doing in an opera with a locale in southern Spain anyway?

By and large, autobiographers and family chronicles are suspect. In the story of his life, Wagner devotes several pages to the trials and tribulations befallen his dog, but fails to mention the rather interesting episode of his incarceration for debt in the Clichy prison in Paris from October 28 to November 17, 1840. The autobiography of Berlioz is notable for self-dramatization and omission of essential facts. Modest Tchaikovsky's life of his brother makes no mention of the seminal matter of his homosexuality. After Tchaikovsky's death of cholera, somehow a false rumor spread that he had committed suicide by vibrion, and deliberately drank a glass of contaminated water during a raging epidemic in St. Petersburg. A still more fantastic version of Tchaikovsky's death was circulated quite recently by some Soviet writers, who were careful, however, not to publicize it in print. According to it, Tchaikovsky had a deviant liaison with a Romanov princeling; when Tsar Alexander III got wind of it, he served Tchaikovsky an ultimatum, either to kill himself or be publicly disgraced. Tchaikovsky took poison; the family physician was induced by relatives to sign a certificate of death by cholera. To bolster up the suicide theory, its proponents point out that cholera victims were usually buried in hermetically sealed zinc-lined caskets to prevent contagion, whereas Tchaikovsky's coffin was left open during the funeral services (photographs of Tchaikovsky in death exist) and mourners were allowed to approach and kiss him on the lips, according to the old Russian custom. *Se non è vero è ben trovato. . . .*

When death occurs dramatically it behooves a conscientious lexicographer to report it briefly, but it is not advisable to emulate the example of an obituary of Sir Armine Woodhouse in *The Annual Register* of London for the year 1777, noting that his death "was occasioned by a fishbone sticking in his throat."

Is it germane to the life and bookish habits of the French pianist and composer Alkan that he was crushed to death by a falling bookcase? The point is moot. But the self-defenestration of the Hungarian author of the suicidogenic song *Gloomy Sunday* Rezsö Seress should by right be included in any account of his life, for it illustrates the possibility of a composer's being subconsciously affected by the feeling of despair generated by his own music. (Seress jumped out of the window on a gloomy Monday, however, not on a gloomy Sunday.) It is indicative of the perturbed psyche of a musicologist under fire that Arthur Eaglefield Hull, distressed by the accusations of plagiarism levelled at him, threw himself under a train; and the circumstances are duly recorded in Baker 1958.

Musical murders are understandably prized by lexicographers whose own lives are usually drab. They salivate profusely over Gesualdo's adventure in assassination, although the story of his having his errant wife killed by proxy is sadly lacking in hard evidence. The execution of the German ethnomusicologist Kurt Huber by Hitler's axe is a matter of grisly history. Jean Marie Leclair was stabbed to death in his house, and circumstantial evidence points to his estranged wife as the culprit, for she was a professional engraver (she printed most of Leclair's music) skilled in handling the sharp tools of her trade, which were peculiarly suitable for stabbing. The theory has a certain degree of plausibility, and I offer it in the entry on Leclair for what it is worth, despite its curt dismissal by the foremost Leclairist Marc Pincherle.

Destructive afflictions are integral parts of musical biography. The insanity of Schumann, Smetana, Hugo Wolf and MacDowell must certainly be cited in their life stories. Modern biographers have a tendency to trace most maladies of their subjects to venereal infection. The suspicion that Beethoven's deafness was of syphilitic origin is a favorite theory with some, but recent otological studies rule it out. The sad probability is that Beethoven never knew a woman. It is hardly worth mentioning that Paganini suffered from some form of *Morbus gallicus*. But in the pathetic story of Delius the causes of his paralysis and blindness are of the essence. (In his book on Delius, Sir Thomas Beecham remarks ruefully that the goddess Aphrodite Pandemos repaid Delius with cruel ingratitude for his lifelong worship at her altar.)

PREFACE

Among medical wonders, the marriage of the castrato singer Tenducci, who eloped with a 16-year-old girl, requires a technical clarification. (He was a triorchis.)

Romantically inclined musicians often encourage speculation about their illegitimate birth. Self-spermed progeny of Liszt are numerous. Music dictionaries (including Baker) flatly state that the French cello player François Servais was Liszt's natural son, but despite all my research I could neither prove nor disprove it. Sigismond Thalberg apparently condoned the story of his being a bastard of Count Moritz Dietrichstein and Baroness von Wetzlar. There is even a letter in circulation, allegedly written by his alleged mother to his alleged father in which she suggests that their son be named Thalberg, so that he would grow as peaceful as a Thal (valley, in old German spelling), and would tower over the common lot of humanity like a Berg (mountain). But Thalberg was his real name! A dismissive footnote in the entry on Thalberg in Grove's Dictionary declares that his registry of birth is lost, but I obtained a copy without any difficulty, and it certifies that Thalberg was a perfectly legitimate son of Joseph Thalberg and Fortunée Stein, both of Frankfurt-am-Main, and that he was born in Geneva on January 8, 1812.

Ironically, when the authentically illegitimate daughter of Wagner, Isolde, petitioned the Bavarian Civil Court in 1914 for a share in Wagner's royalties, her claim was rejected on the ground that her mother Cosima, although admittedly cohabiting with Wagner for quite a while before Isolde's birth on April 10, 1865, had not ceased to communicate with her lawful husband Hans von Bülow within the maximum legal period of gestation of ten months, so that he could conceivably be Isolde's father after all, and this despite the evidence adduced by Isolde's lawyer husband as to her phrenological and hemological Wagnerian characteristics.

Mistaken identities between siblings are a lexicographer's nightmare. The bicentennial of Giovanni Battista Viotti was widely observed in 1953. But the Viotti thus commemorated died in infancy on May 23, 1753. When another male child was born to the bereaved parents on May 12, 1755, he was given the same first Christian names as his dead brother, following a frequent custom in Catholic families. This was the Viotti who lived to become famous.

Similar brotherly confusion occurred in the case of Giacomo Insanguine. His year of birth is variously given as 1712 and 1728, but the earlier date is that of his elder brother who died in 1726. Insanguine was born on March 22, 1728.

Angelo Mariani was very much upset, reading in a contemporary biographical compilation that he was born on October 11, 1821. Not so, he protested; he was born on the same day and month three years later. It was his elder brother who was born exactly three years before him. But his birth certificate, of which I obtained a copy, confirms the 1821 date, and there was no Mariani by any cognomen born in 1824.

Beethoven, no less vain for all his greatness, took pains to make himself two years younger than he was. Indeed, early encyclopedias list the year of his birth as 1772 instead of 1770. Beethoven insisted that he had an older brother born in 1770 with whom he was confused. There was a Ludwig Maria van Beethoven who was born on April 1, 1769, but he died a few days later. Beethoven was born in the following year and was given the baptismal name Ludwig in memory of the first-born.

Johann Jakob Froberger declared in a statement to his physician that he was born on May 18, 1620, but according to his baptism certificate he was christened on May 19, 1616. The probability is that he was born on the day before, May 18, four years earlier than his preferred date.

In a notice written for Mattheson's *Grundlage einer Ehrenpforte,* great Telemann gives his year of birth as 1682, whereas he was really born in 1681; but he set down the correct day and month, March 14, of his birth. Self-rejuvenating musicians usually retain the month and the day and alter only the year of birth.

Astrology helps sometimes. True believers do not lie to the stars. The date of birth of Kaspar Othmayr, March 12, 1515, must be accurate, for it figures in the astrological chart drawn for him.

The Polish conductor Artur Rodzinski was born during the night following New Year's Eve, 1892, but for professional reasons he gave his date of birth (even to his own wife) as 1894. The confusion was compounded by Rodzinski's father who registered his birth as January 2, 1892, instead of January 1st, as an extra safety margin against his being drafted into the Austro-Hungarian Army (he was born in Dalmatia) a year early.

An interesting calendar problem is presented by the birth on two consecutive days of the Bulgarian twins Pantcho and Luben Vladigerov. Distrustful of Bulgarian obstetricians, their mother rushed to Zürich as soon as she found out that she was going to have a multiple birth. There, Luben was born at 10:20 P.M. on March 12, 1899, and Pantcho at 2:10 P.M. on March 13, 1899.

In an autobiographical sketch, written for the 1925 *Tonkunst-Kalender,* Leo Slezak, noted equally for his trenchant wit as for the excellence of his singing, made capital fun of musical vanity in the matter of age. "I was born on August 18," he wrote. "I will not say in what year, because I will not be believed anyway, and in the supposition that I am not telling the truth, the editors will add three or four years to my age. My modesty forbids me to state that I am phenomenal and a star of the first magnitude on the artistic firmament." He volunteered, in response to my inquiry, the information that he was born in 1873, the date easily confirmed by his birth certificate. A fine soul, Leo Slezak! May his kind proliferate not only as a bright star in high heavens, but in musical lexicography as well!

The date of birth of Caruso probably will never be known. I received 13 birth certificates for 13 Enrico Carusos from the Demographic Office of Naples, roughly contemporaneous with the great Caruso, but none of them matched the known names of his parents. He was one of 18 children, and it may well be that his birth was simply overlooked.

There are inevitable disappointments. In the 1958 edition of Baker I proudly cited the exact date of birth of Jacob Obrecht, which I reconstructed from an entry of his enrollment in the registries of the University of Louvain under the date of August 17, 1470. It is known that Obrecht was born on St. Cecilia Day, November 22, and since the average age of University entrants at the time was between 17 and 18, I calculated that Obrecht was born on November 22, 1452. Alas, an *inébranlable* footnote in the revised edition of Gustave Reese's monumental *Music of the Renaissance* demolished my chronological construction by proving that the names of the fathers of my putative Obrecht and of the real Obrecht were not the same.

Another disillusionment was the wrong identification of the Portuguese musician Duarte Lobo whose baptism certificate, found in a learned Portuguese monograph, indicated the date of his birth on or shortly before he was baptized on September 19, 1565. It was a false Lobo, and I am now regretfully compelled to relegate the true Lobo to the lexicographical purgatory of unbaptized souls.

Until recently, the date of birth of Antonio Vivaldi was adorned in music dictionaries with an exasperating question mark. Following a false scent, thrown into my path by an Italian music historian, I tentatively listed Vivaldi's birth as June 11, 1669. My efforts to locate Vivaldi's baptismal entry in one of the thirty-odd churches that existed in Venice in the second half of the seventeenth century led to nothing. Gian Francesco Malipiero, the learned editor of Vivaldi's collected works, told me in 1949 that further search would be useless. But the elusive church entry of Vivaldi's baptism did come to light eventually, proving that Vivaldi was born in Venice on March 4, 1678. I have since obtained a facsimile copy of it, and the date is duly listed in the 1971 Supplement to Baker.

Then there are deliberate mystifications. The most notorious of these is one of which the expert Italian musicologist Raffaele Casimiri was a victim. He acquired from one Telemaco Bratti a notebook purporting to contain a notation by Palestrina dated September 19, 1578, stating that he was then 53 years, 4 months and 10 days old. This made it possible by simple calculation to deduce the exact date of Palestrina's birth as May 9, 1525, a *nunc dimittis* of heavenly delight to a devout Palestrinologist. Casimiri published the document with a suitable self-congratulatory fanfare in a bibliographical journal. To his dismay and chagrin, he was immediately attacked and derided for gullibility in endorsing a transparent fabrication. But who would forge a document of this nature? *Cui prodest?* The obvious answer is: another Palestrinologist. Brooding over his disgrace, the harassed Casimiri noticed that the name of the man who foisted the spurious notebook on him, Telemaco Bratti, was an anagram of the name of the eminent Italian music scholar Alberto Cametti! The rest is hidden in the thickets of intramural musicological strife. (It was thanks to a knowledgeable friend that I myself did not fall into the same trap.)

Mikhail Goldstein, a reputable Russian violinist and composer, produced a sensation in Soviet musical circles by announcing the discovery of a symphony by a totally unknown early Russian composer named Ovsianiko-Kulikovsky. The score was hailed as a major landmark in the history of symphonic music in Russia. A noted Soviet musicologist wrote a learned dissertation on the subject. The work was published, performed and recorded. I too, welcomed the discovery in a review in 'The Musical Quarterly.' Then Goldstein exploded a musicological stink bomb. Ovsianiko-Kulikovsky never existed, he declared. The score was his own creation. He perpetrated his hoax in retaliation for the systematic rejection of his own works by the Soviet Music Publishing House. Incredibly, his confession was dismissed as an attempt to appropriate for personal advantage an authentic Russian work of historic significance. Trouble threatened, and Goldstein deemed it wise to leave Russia. But the ghost of Ovsianiko-Kulikovsky continues to haunt music librarians. Recently, The Library of Congress had a request from a befuddled Ph.D. aspirant for more information on the mysterious Russian. Fortunately, the music librarians there, who had been tipped off by me about the non-existence of Ovsianiko-Kulikovsky, could refer the correspondent to the article on Goldstein in Baker's Supplement 1971, in which the whole tale is told, and of which they had a set of advance galley proofs.

A story which would be piquant if it were true concerns the German composer Egk whose unusual name gave rise to the conjecture that it was a self-aggrandizing acronym for "ein grosser Künstler." Eric Blom, the editor of the Fifth Edition of Grove's *Dictionary of Music and Musicians,* queried me regarding its authenticity, before committing it to an informative footnote. Conveniently, I managed to produce a copy of Egk's birth certificate proving that he was indeed Egk and not an acronym. My most embarrassing lexicographical moment came when I had to ask Blom himself about the place of his birth, which had been unaccountably omitted from entries on Blom in reference works. "I wish you had never asked this question," Blom wrote back, explaining that, although British to the core (with some scattered Danish blood cells in his veins), he was accidentally born in Bern, Switzerland, owing exclusively to his mother's unforeseen presence there at the time.

A persistent rumor, hard to kill, has it that Leopold Stokowski's last name is really Stokes, and that he changed it to Stokowski, following the vogue of Polish-sounding pseudonyms that swept the music world early in the century. This is a fantasy. He was born Leopold Anthony Stokowski in the All Souls subdistrict of Greater London on April 18, 1882, a son of Kopernik Joseph Boleslaw Stokowski, a cabinet maker, and Annie Marion Moore-Stokowski. Stokowski himself contributed to lexicographical confusion when he filled out *manu propria* a questionnaire for Riemann's *Musik-Lexikon,* stating therein that his full name was Leopold Boleslawowicz (an impossible patronymic in Polish) Stokowski, and that he was born in Cracow in 1887.

Charles Ives said once that his seemingly prosaic occupation as an insurance man gave him greater understanding of the people, and so enriched his philosophy of life and enhanced his musical ideas. Similar considerations are valid for lexicographical pursuits. My correspondence with musicians has greatly enlarged my psychological vistas. Their reactions varied from a sincere reluctance to have one's name inserted in a dictionary to uninhibited effusions about one's greatness, from petulant complaints about insufficient space vouchsafed to the subject, to heartfelt gratitude for the honor.

The American composer Walter Stockhoff (whose music was praised by Busoni as a "fresh voice from the New World that could revitalize the tired art of Europe") was overwhelmed by my interest in his music. "As pure, cool, crystal-clear water," he wrote me, "revives one thirsting in the desert, so intelligence, understanding, sympathy and sense of values come to brighten one's pathway. There is a noble generosity in your giving thought to my work. Through the greatness of your nature you strengthen others."

A response of a quite different order came to me in reply to my inquiry from that unique figure in modern music, Kaikhosru Sorabji. He administered a sharp rebuke to me for calling him an Indian composer. "Do not dare to call me an Indian," he thundered. "We are Parsi, Persians, followers of Zarathustra." He flatly declined to give me any biographical information, but he admitted that his *Opus Clavicembalisticum* is the greatest polyphonic work since Bach's *Kunst der Fuge*. This wrathful outburst pales in comparison with the icy invective he poured on Percy A. Scholes for publishing what he regarded as an inadequate entry on him in the *Oxford Companion to Music*. Scholes reproduced Sorabji's letter in part, and forwarded the full text to me with the inscription, "For your delectation." It is worth quoting *in toto:*

> Corfe Castle, Dorset, XXII.II.MCMLII A.D.
>
> My Good Sir:
>
> A valued friend draws my attention to a lucubration of yours under the entry of my name in a recently published book of reference. One is hard put to it at which to marvel the more, the exiguity of your sense of proportion or the poverty of your taste in devoting double the amount of space to cheap impertinences regarding the place and date of my birth (which is as little business of yours as of any other prying nosey busybody) to that which is devoted to my work, which is all that concerns anyone and which carefully conveys inaccurate and false information by leaving out material facts. Formerly I used to consider it enough when dealing with these stupid and impudent enquiries from lexicographical persons, deliberately to mislead them as to dates and places. This is a mistake: their enquiries should either be ignored or refused. And the sooner folk of their kidney grasp the fact that one is under no moral obligation to provide them with accurate, or indeed any information at all just because they choose to ask for it, the very much better for all concerned.
>
> I have the honour to be, Sir, Yours very faithfully,
> Kaikhosru Shapurji Sorabji

Later Sorabji complained that Scholes "slapped on" some years to his age. Actually, Scholes made him three years younger in the early editions of *The Oxford Companion to Music*. He was born Leon Dudley Sorabji in Chingford, England, on August 14, 1892.

One of the most bizarre cases in my files is that of the English composer Edward Maryon, who had dropped out of sight, lexicographically speaking, somewhere in the early editions of Baker. The American publishers of his curious pamphlet *Marcotone* told me that he had died. In my efforts to get more definite information, I wrote to his last known London address, but the house in which he lived was blitzed during World War II. Acting on a wild surmise, I sent an inquiry to Scotland Yard, which replied that, since there was no evidence of crime, the case was out of police jurisdiction. Then suddenly I received a letter from Maryon himself, who was very much alive and still living in London. A voluminous correspondence followed: then he really died. Shortly after his death, a large trunk arrived for me from England. It contained manuscripts of several of Maryon's many operas, and also family documents dating back to the reign of Henry VIII. (Maryon was of noble stock and bore the nobiliary second name d'Aulby.) Apparently, his executors decided to let me be the keeper of Maryon's musical legacy, for I was one of the few, if not the only one, who showed interest in his compositions.

High on my list of missing persons is Aloysius Ludwig Minkus, an Austrian ballet composer who was attached to the Imperial Theaters in St. Petersburg, Russia, until 1891, when he was pensioned off and promptly vanished. Not a year passes without my getting a request for information about Minkus. I went through the usual motions, trying to trace him to the place of his final rest, in Russia and in Austria, but to no avail. He was *spurlos versunken*. Anyone reading these lines know what happened to Minkus?

PREFACE

My gallery of characters is brightened by the presence of Baron Gabriel Wajditsch Verbovac von Dönhoff, Hungarian-born American composer of fourteen operas, some of them very long. His name first came to my attention at a meeting of the Music Panel of the Office of Cultural Presentations at the State Department, of which I was a member. His son, a New York tax accountant, wrote in, denouncing the panel for its failure to promote his father's music, adding, "I curse the Administration for its inhumanity." Naturally, I was fascinated. Anyone cursing the government out of filial piety has my sympathy. I wrote to the Baron, volunteering to include his name in my Supplement to Baker as the first step on the road to recognition. This initiated a flood of correspondence, mostly with Wajditsch-fils. In one of the letters, Baron Wajditsch himself added a revealing postscript: "I heard a piece by Stravinsky, and I think this man has no talent." In Supplement 1971 I had to add the date of his death.

Philanthropic impulses do not always pay off. Some years back I received a request from a Russian woman refugee asking me to find out whether her father, the violinist Vassili Bezekirsky, who came to America early in the century, was still living. Leapfrogging through a series of music schools and colleges in which he had been employed, I tracked him down to a town in upstate New York. Never in my lexicographical pursuits had I experienced such an elevating sense of unselfish duty well done as then. What can be nobler than to restore a father to a daughter already mourning his loss? I dispatched the happy tidings to both. To my consternation, I received a chilling reply from Bezekirsky: "Yes, your mission was successful," he wrote in longhand on a postcard, "if you call several unpleasant and demanding letters from my daughter a success. I am in no position to help her in any way." I never heard from the daughter.

The ultimate in lexicographical folly is the scenario enacted by the German writer on music Walter Dahms. Reference works leave him in suspended animation somewhere in Europe about 1923. Dahms became missing person No. 1 on my list, and I often brought up his name in conversation. By a lucky chance, a much traveled lady ethnomusicologist who had known Dahms personally told me that she saw him in Lisbon, that he had changed his name, but continued to publish books on music. Her identification seemed solid, and I inserted a brief item to that effect in Supplement 1965. This innocuous bit of factual information unleashed, unbeknownst to me, a most extraordinary chain of events. The editors of Riemann's *Musik-Lexikon* asked a German musicologist resident in Lisbon (*nomina sunt odiosa* but *sapienti sat*) to check on Dahms, but inquiries in the rather small circle of German musicians and writers in Lisbon led nowhere; even the German consul had never heard of Dahms. "Do you swear by Baker?" the Lisbon man asked, reporting the negative results to Riemann. "No," came the obvious reply, "nor do we swear by Riemann; but Baker (*eigentlich,* Slonimsky) has proved a highly reliable source, which we value greatly, and anyway such a definite statement could not have been conjured up out of thin air." The only German in Lisbon who could conceivably be Dahms was a Berlin-born musician who carried a passport of the Republic of Honduras and whose name was Portuguese in its phonetic structure. (Between wars and revolutions Honduran citizenship could easily be obtained in consideration of the sum of $100 payable directly to the President of Honduras, and the magic document enabled a stateless person in exile to get visas to most European countries and even, the prize of prizes, to the United States.) Taking a long chance, the mediator wrote to the suspect asking him point blank whether he was Dahms. He received a devastating reply. "I learn to my amazement," it ran, "that you have meddled in my affairs and importuned outsiders by asking questions about me. I have no idea what your purpose might be in that, and I am at a loss for a proper word to describe your conduct. I am identical with no one except myself. As for Herr W. D. [initials only in the original letter] whom you mention, I know nothing about him." Furious, the investigator fired off a letter to the editors of Riemann, calling the presumptive Dahms a rectal orifice (an epithet beloved by Mozart), and figuratively washed his hands of the whole feculent mess. When another emissary, representing another German music encyclopedia, confronted the mystery man of Lisbon with cumulative evidence of his true identity, the latter refused to engage in further discussion, and demanded that his name in any form be removed from the encyclopedia altogether. His wish was respected. But the editors of Riemann's *Musik-Lexikon* blew his cover and definitely identified him with Dahms. As to my own Supplement 1971, I decided to resort to tortuous circumlocution with some carefully planted cryptographic clues. Since Dahms, according to Dahms, does not exist, there can be no legal or moral restraint against my publishing the facts about Dahms as long as I do not disclose his present *nom de machine à écrire.*

Actuarial tables indicate a significant rise of longevity among musicians in the twentieth century. Supplement 1971 lists a number of nonagenarians who are not only technically alive, but even, some of them, spectacularly active in their professions. Pablo Casals, conducting and appearing on television in the middle of his tenth decade, is a supreme exemplar of gerontology *in excelsis.* Stokowski is going strong as a symphonic conductor on the eve of his 90th birthday. At 95 the British composer Havergal Brian is still composing symphonies now numbering thirty-two. Carl Ruggles stopped composing but keeps his faculties in splendid shape at 95. The Norwegian folklorist Ole Mörk Sandvik was still making his regular rounds in the Oslo Public Library at the age of 96. The German musician Heinrich Hammer married his young Hollywood pupil, age 22, when he was 91. The Russian-French singer Marie Olénine d'Alheim lived to be 100. Going over the list of *morituri,* I came upon the name of Victor Küzdö, a Hungarian-American violinist born, or so Baker said, in 1869. I addressed a discreet inquiry to his last known residence in Glendale, California, and was overjoyed to receive from him a dictated postcard, bearing the news that he was still alive. He took this opportunity to correct the date of his birth; he was born in 1863, not in 1869, and just celebrated his 100th anniversary at the time. This was immediately followed by a letter from a lifelong friend of the family, gently chiding Küzdö for diminishing his age and affirming that he was actually born in 1860, and that it was his 103rd birthday that he celebrated in 1963 — "over a glass of champagne." How could he be so sure? Simple: he was a practicing numerologist. Men are mortal; Küzdö is a man; ergo, Küzdö is mortal, the classical syllogism runs. But when the inevitable *dies mortis* came on February 24, 1966, Küzdö's death certificate revealed that he was born not in 1869, not in 1863, not in 1860, but in 1859, and that he was 106 years old at the time of his death!

PREFACE

Rudolf Friml was amazingly agile as performer on television, playing the piano arrangement of his perennial favorite, *Indian Love Call,* at the age of 91. Rudolph Ganz continued his activities as a writer of essays on musical pedagogy at 94. And the grande dame of piano teaching Mme Rosina Lhévinne was still conducting master classes in Los Angeles and New York at 91.

French musicians are holding their collective breaths in anticipation of the centennial of Henri-Paul Busser coming up on January 16, 1972, in the hope that he will be well enough to conduct one of his operas in person. As of summer 1971, the Boston composeress Margaret Ruthven Lang, aged 103, was still alive. In the earlier years of her eleventh decade she was still attending Boston Symphony concerts, traveling by subway.

Statistically speaking, organists live the longest lives, perhaps because their sedentary occupation keeps them from expending their physical energies unnecessarily. Ethnomusicologists come next in longevity; music scholars and pedagogues follow close in their determination to live indefinitely. Among singers, tenors dissipate their vitality quickly and are apt to die a sudden death. In all musical categories mediocrities outlive geniuses by a large margin.

The dating of births and deaths must follow local time zones. For men and women who died around midnight, the difference of a few minutes means a difference of a calendar day. Schoenberg died in Los Angeles on the night of July 13, 1951, when it was already the dawn of a new day in the East. In his case the date is of peculiar significance, for he had an unfeigned case of triskaidecaphobia; he seriously believed that there was something ominous in the circumstance of his birth on the 13th of the month of September in 1874. He was genuinely perturbed when a friend jocularly reminded him that the sum of the digits of his age on his 76th birthday, his last, was 13. That the symbol preoccupied him to the end is apparent from his remark that all would be well if he lived through July 13. He died on that day 13 minutes before midnight.

Dame Melba died in Sydney, Australia, in the early morning of February 23, 1931, local time, but her death was announced in New York newspapers which were on the streets on February 22, New York time. This paradox is explained, of course, by the fact that Australia is on the future side of the International Dateline.

Melba's case apart, daily newspapers often lag behind in death announcements; obituaries are sometimes updated a day or two to give an appearance of immediacy in reporting. There are, furthermore, frequent errors in the reported place of death, particularly if it is outside a major metropolitan center. The death of the Swedish composer Karl-Birger Blomdahl was reported in the daily press, including 'The New York Times' as having taken place in Stockholm on June 16, 1968, whereas he actually died in Kungsängen, quite a distance from Stockholm, on June 14. (His ashes were strewn over the nearby Lake Mälaren.) Even Swedish sources released inaccurate data, and it was only after I reached Blomdahl's family for information that I could establish the facts.

Personal preferences for lucky numbers backfire sometimes. Gregor Piatigorsky, who likes round numbers, changed his real birthday, April 17, to April 20, and kept the correct year 1903. To his horror he discovered that April 20 was also the birthday of

Hitler! He wasted no time to exorcise the hideous coincidence and to restore the correct date to the dictionaries.

Rudolf Friml likes the magic number 7, and therefore allows the world to celebrate his birthdays on December 7, but he agrees in private that the date given in his birth certificate, December 2, 1879, is the correct one.

Russians born in the nineteenth century have three birthdays: one according to the Greek Orthodox calendar, one according to the corresponding date of the Gregorian calendar in the nineteenth century and one that they celebrate in the twentieth century, when the difference between the two calendars grew from 12 days to 13, owing to the fact that 1900 was bissextile in Russia but not in the West. I was born on three dates (April 15, April 27 and April 28, 1894), and in three different cities into the bargain: St. Petersburg, Petrograd and Leningrad.

Quite a little controversy was stirred up in the press at the time of Stravinsky's eightieth birthday in 1962. Should it be celebrated on June 17 (corresponding to the nineteenth-century date, June 5, of his Russian birth) or June 18 (in twentieth-century concordance)? A columnist in the music section of 'The New York Times' hinted that the faces of some lexicographers would be red on June 18, which was Stravinsky's preferred date for his birthday, whereas the dictionaries, including mine, say it should be June 17. As one of the lexicographers involved, I felt it incumbent upon myself to reject the suggestion of my physiognomy being incarnadined, and I dispatched a letter to the editor of 'The New York Times' giving my reasons in favor of June 17. It was published with the caption, "It Is All Clear Now." To this Stravinsky demurred in an angry telegram. He was going to observe his birthday according to the calendar of his choice, he vowed; in the twenty-first century, he warned, he would celebrate it on June 19. This would obviously be supererogatory, inasmuch as the year 2000 will be a leap-year both in the Russian Orthodox Church and in the West, so that there will be no increase in the difference between the two calendars.

In planning the format of the Fifth Edition of Baker's *Biographical Dictionary of Musicians* and its two supplements, I made a special effort to establish exact dates of first performance of major works by all composers listed in Baker. I encountered some epistemological problems in dealing with works of indeterminate duration by avant-garde composers. They may last, according to their own specifications, a fleeting moment, or an eternity, a chiliad, a hebdomad, a circadian period, a quadrillion of milliseconds or a sextillion of infinitudes, each performance being both first and last, the alpha and omega. Clearly, no definite date can be assigned to such illusionist presentations, languorously evolving in misty improvisations.

Pedantry is the soul of a dictionary, but sciolistic outrecuidance is not recommended. Too close a study of an admired subject may lead to aberrations, exemplified by an editor's footnote to Goethe's avowal in his autobiography that he had never loved anyone as much as Lili Schönemann: "Here the great Goethe errs; his greatest love was Frederike Drion."

When I arrived at the final biography of the Fifth Edition of Baker, rosy-fingered

PREFACE

Aurora was already spreading its promissory rays over the town, but I could not stop. *Similia similibus curantur,* and I decided to add an ultimate Z. In feverish excitement I excogitated a model biographicai entry. This was the result:

> **Zyžík, Krsto,** Czech composer; b. Pressburg, Feb. 29, 1900. [1900 was not a leap-year.] He traveled widely to Pozsony and Bratislava as a child [Pozsony and Bratislava are respectively the Hungarian and Slovak names of Pressburg.] He studied singing and composition; attracted attention with his oratorio *Dieta Wormsová* written for the quadricentennial of the Diet of Worms in a vermicular counterpoint (Prague, Jan. 29, 1921); then brought out a bel canto voice poem *Strč prst skrz krk* (*Put Your Finger on Your Throat*), using only consonants in consonant harmony. His other works are *Pinč mj šuga* (*Pinch me, Sugar,* or *Pinch Mishuga* in phonetical transcription), a madrigal opera (1927); *Smyčkovy Kvartet* for woodwind quintet (1930); *Pták* for non-ornithological birds (1950); *Sappho LXIX* for 2 female participants in mixed media (Lesbos Festival, 1955). Cf. E. F. Burian, *Zyžík a jehó Prst Skrz Krk* (Prague, 1957).

I sent Zyžík in, gleefully anticipating a jolly response to my joke. To my surprise, the thing was automatically set in type, and presently I received the proofs. I made a hurried call to the publishers and told them to kill Zyžík forthwith, lest he should become a Slonimsky monster.

I owe a global debt of gratitude to a legion of librarians, registrars, clerks, keepers of archives of all nations, and other members of the intellectual International for their cooperation in supplying me with essential data. Nathan Broder, whose death was a great loss for his many friends and to the community of musical scholarship in general, read over the entire manuscript of the 1958 edition of Baker in minute detail, and corrected a number of dangerous mistakes.

No adjectives, adverbs or other parts of speech can adequately express the depth of my appreciation for the help I received from William Lichtenwanger, Reference Librarian in the Music Division of The Library of Congress, in preparing for publication the 1958 edition of Baker. He is one of those rare spirits to whom no musician is too obscure for tender care, no subject too trivial for thorough investigation, no bibliographical minutiae too small for weighing; add to this his familiarity with a dozen or so languages, including Turkish and Japanese (he served as a cryptanalyst during World War II). For the 1971 Supplement I was fortunate to have the assistance of Wayne Shirley, also of the Reference Department of the Music Division of the Library of Congress, a person of wide culture, himself a composer, and a performing singer to boot. He was particularly helpful in drawing a list of avant-garde composers for inclusion.

Per Olof Lundahl of the Swedish Music Information Center in Stockholm, and Bjarne Kortsen, foremost authority on Norwegian music, enabled me to cover musical Scandinavia in Supplement 1971. Boris Steinpress and Gregory Schneerson, eminent in the field of Soviet music, kept me informed about new works of Russian composers. Professor Klaus Pringsheim of Japan periodically sent me reports on new Japanese music. Claude Gitteau of the Société des Auteurs, Compositeurs et Éditeurs de Musique in Paris provided biographies of young French composers. Pierre Debièvre cleared up for me some discrepancies in vital statistics of French musical biography. Oliver Daniel, of Broadcast Music, Inc., gave me detailed information on a number of contemporary American composers. Out of his formidable arsenal of knowledge about the musical theater, Herbert Weinstock supplied precious corrections of long dormant errors in the chronology of Italian opera. Horst Adams of the editorial staff of Riemann's *Musik-Lexikon* and Dr. Ruth Blume of *Die Musik in Geschichte und Gegenwart* generously shared with me advance information they had collected for the supplements to their respective encyclopedias. Graham Hatton of London has helped me to untangle the intricate chronology of Havergal Brian's multitudinous symphonies, and also managed to get for me biographies of contemporary British composers which I had despaired of ever receiving either from themselves or from their publishers. Samuel Sprince of Boston, a fanatic of musical chronology, figured out for me some tough particulars regarding musicians of New England. When the question arose about the exact calendar date of death of a composer, which occurred about midnight in York, Maine, Sprince made some telephone calls and not only settled the exact hour (12:20 A.M.) of his death, but in addition checked with the State Bureau of Records to make sure that the official date is reckoned according to the local daylight saving time then in force.

At the last moment, when the galley proofs of Supplement 1971 were already being gathered in, there descended from the lexicographical empyrean James Lyons, the Protean intellectual whose knowledge embraces such disparate subjects as Asian philosophy, ballet, psychology, socialist economics, general esthetics, multilingual bibliography, musicology in the widest sense of the word and all there is to know about phonograph recordings. He went through the galleys with both speed and efficiency, weeding out annoying redundancies, insidious solecisms and just plain typos. If there still remains here a single palpable error of commission or omission after this capital job of fumigation, then it is Fate.

In conclusion, I want to quote my favorite passage from a letter I received from Alfred Einstein shortly before his death, in which he wondered, "... ob wir — und natürlich vor allem Sie — im Himmel einmal dafür belohnt werden, dass wir einige Ungenauigkeiten aus der Welt geschafft haben ..." But what — oh horrid thought! — if even at the Pearly Gates the book of arrivals contains faulty registrations and wrong dates?

NICOLAS SLONIMSKY
September, 1971

BIOGRAPHICAL DICTIONARY

OF

MUSICIANS

A

Aaron, abbot of the monasteries of St. Martin and St. Pantaleon at Cologne, where he died on Dec. 14, 1052. He was the author of two historically important treatises: *De utilitate cantus vocalis et de modo cantandi atque psallendi* and *De regulis tonorum et symphoniarum.* He is believed to be the first cleric to introduce the Gregorian evening service *(nocturns)* into Germany.

Aaron, Pietro, Italian theorist; b. Florence 1480; d. Venice 1545. He was cantor at the cathedral of Imola in 1521; at the Rimini cathedral in 1523. In 1525 he was 'maestro di casa' in a Venetian house; in 1536 entered the Order of Jerusalem. He published *Libri tres de institutione harmonica* (Bologna, 1516); *Il Toscanello in musica* (Venice, 1523; 4 reprints, 1525-62); *Trattato della natura et cognitione di tutti gli tuoni di canto figurato* (Venice, 1525; reproduced in part, in an English translation, in O. Strunk's *Source Readings in Music History,* N.Y., 1950); *Lucidario in musica di alcune opinione antiche e moderne* (Venice, 1545); *Compendiolo di molti dubbi, segreti, et sentenze intorno al canto fermo et figurato . . .* (Milan, posthumous; title page bears the inscription: 'In memoria eterna erit Aron').

Aavik, Juhan, composer; born Reval (Estonia), Jan. 29, 1884. He studied at the St. Petersburg Cons.; was a conductor in Dorpat (1911-25); settled again in Reval (1928-44) as prof. and dir. of the Conservatory; in 1944 he went to Sweden.

Abaco, Evaristo Felice dall', Italian composer, b. Verona, July 12, 1675; d. Munich, July 12, 1742. He was in Modena from 1696-1701. In 1704, he was at the Bavarian Court in Munich; then he followed the Duke of Bavaria to Belgium and France, where he became acquainted with French music, which left some influence on his later works. In 1715 he returned to Munich, and was active as leader of the Court orchestra. He wrote 12 violin sonatas, with cello or cembalo, op. 1 (1706); *Concerti da chiesa* for 4 string instruments, op. 2 (1714); *6 Sonate da chiesa* and *6 Sonate da camera* for 3 string instruments, op. 3 (1715); *12 Sonate da camera* for violin and cello, op. 4 (1716; arranged by Chédeville for musette, flute, oboe and continuo); *6 Concerti* for 7 instruments (4 violins, viola, bassoon or cello and bass), op. 5 (1717); concerto for violin solo with instruments, op. 6 (1730), his most important work. Sandberger published a biographical sketch and a selection from op. 1-4 in vol. I of 'Denkmäler der Tonkust in Bayern,' and a second selection in vol. IX, 1; Riemann edited 3 trio-sonatas. Bibl.: R. Brenzon, *Un grande musicista veronese, Ev. Fel. Dall' Abaco* ('Note d' Archivio' XII, 1935). See also K. G. Fellerer's article in 'Die Musik in Geschichte und Gegenwart.'

Abaco, Joseph Marie Clément, Belgian violoncellist; son of Evariste Felice dall' Abaco; b. Brussels, March 1710 (baptized March 27); d. at Arbizzano di Volpolicella, near Verona, Aug. 31, 1805. He studied with his father; as a small boy played in the orchestra of the Prince Elector at Bonn; in 1738 he was appointed music director there. He was in England in 1740; in 1753 he went to Verona; was given the title of baron by Prince Maximilian of Bavaria (1766). His works comprise 29 cello sonatas and other compositions.

Abbadia, Natale, Italian composer; b. Genoa, March 11, 1792; d. Milan, Dec. 25, 1861. He composed the opera *Giannina di Pontieu* (1812), the musical farce *L'imbrog-*

lione ed il castigamatti; masses, motets and other religious music.

Abbado, Marcello, pianist and composer; b. Milan, Oct. 7, 1926. He studied at the Cons. in Milan with Gavazzeni (piano) and Ghedini (composition), graduating in 1947. In 1951 he was appointed instructor at the Cons. of Venice. He has written a cantata *Ciapo* (1945); *Lento e Rondo* for violin and piano (1949) and piano pieces.

Abbatini, Antonio Maria, Italian composer; b. Tiferno (Città di Castello) c. 1595; d. there, Jan., 1680. He was maestro di cappella at the Lateran (1626-28), and other Roman churches; was at the church of Loreto from March, 1667. He wrote 3 operas, *Dal male al bene* (Rome, 1654; one of the earliest comic operas, and historically important as introducing the final ensemble); *Ione* (Vienna, 1666); *La comica del cielo* or *La Baltasara* (Rome, 1668); and a dramatic cantata *Il Pianto di Rodomonte* (Orvieto, 1633). He published 3 books of masses, 4 books of psalms, various antiphons (1630, 1638, 1677) and 5 books of motets (1635). Bibl.: H. Goldschmidt, *Studien zur Geschichte der italianischen Oper im 17. Jahrhundert* (Leipzig, 1901-04); F. Coradini, *A. M. Abbatini* (Arezzo, 1922).

Abbey, John, noted English organ-builder; b. Whilton, Northamptonshire, Dec. 22, 1785; d. Versailles, Feb. 19, 1859. He went to Paris in 1826 at the invitation of Sébastien Erard to construct an organ for the Paris Exposition. He remained in France and built organs for the cathedrals of many French cities. In 1831 he installed an organ at the Paris Opéra. His innovations in the English type of bellows were adopted by many French organ builders. His sons, E. and J. Abbey, inherited the business, situated at Versailles.

Abbott, Emma, American soprano; b. Chicago, Dec. 9, 1850; d. Salt Lake City, Jan. 5, 1891. She was taken to Peoria as a child; studied music with her father who was a singer, and played the guitar with him and her brother, a violinist, at hotels and clubs. Her first regular employment was with Chapin's choir in New York (1870-72) at a salary of $1500 a year. In March, 1872 she went to Europe where she studied with Sangiovanni in Milan and with Delle Sedie in Paris. From then on, she rapidly advanced as an opera singer. Her London debut was on May 2, 1876. Returning to America, she made her first appearance in New York on Feb. 8, 1877, and sang thereafter with great acclaim in the U.S. and in Europe. In 1875 she married E. Wetherell of New York (d. 1889). Bibl.: Sadie E. Martin, *The Life and Professional Career of Emma Abbott* (Minneapolis, 1891).

Abe, Komei, Japanese conductor and composer; b. Hiroshima, Sept. 1, 1911. He studied composition with Klaus Pringsheim at the Tokyo Academy of Music; conducting with Joseph Rosenstock; then became prof. at the Elizabeth Music College at Kyoto. Among his works are a cello concerto (Tokyo, March 31, 1940); piano concerto (Tokyo, March 27, 1947); 8 string quartets (1935-52); clarinet quintet (1943); divertimento for 9 instruments (1955), songs and piano pieces.

Abeille, Johann Christian Ludwig, German organist and composer; b. Bayreuth, Feb. 20, 1761; d. Stuttgart, March 2, 1838. He was educated in Stuttgart, and was leader of the private orchestra of the Duke of Württemberg; in 1802 became court music director, retiring in 1832. He published several albums of songs which found their way into vocal anthologies and wrote 2 light operas *Amor und Psyche* (1801) and *Peter und Ännchen* (1809); also composed concerted music for small groups, and harpsichord pieces.

Abel, Karl Friedrich, German viola da gamba player and composer; b. Cöthen, Dec. 22, 1723; d. London, June 20, 1787. He studied with his father; then with J. S. Bach at the Thomasschule in Leipzig. He was a member of the Royal Polish Band at Dresden (1748-58). Settling in London in 1759, he became a friend of John Christian Bach. With the Duke of York's assistance, he was appointed chamber-musician to Queen Charlotte (1765). He composed two operas: *Love in a Village* (London, 1760) and *Berenice* (London, 1764); several symphonies, many overtures, quartets and harpsichord sonatas. Abel is generally regarded as the last great virtuoso on the viola da gamba.

Abel, Ludwig, German violinist; b. Eckartsberg, Thuringia, Jan. 14, 1834; d. Neu-Pasing, Bavaria, Aug. 13, 1895. He studied with Ferdinand David; played in the Gewandhaus orch. in Leipzig, and was later violinist in Weimar and Munich. He published a method of violin playing.

Abell, Arthur M., American music critic; b. Norwich, Conn., April 6, 1868. He studied in Weimar with Carl Halir (violin), Wilhelm Saal (piano), and Fritz Hartmann (theory); remained in Europe for 28 years

(1890-1918) as a correspondent for 'The Musical Courier' and other publications. He knew Brahms, and was a friend of Richard Strauss, Max Bruch, Joseph Joachim and other celebrated musicians. Upon his return to the U.S., he lived in retirement in Hastings-on-Hudson. In 1955 he published a book of memoirs, *Talks With Great Composers*.

Abell, John, celebrated Scottish lute player; b. Aberdeenshire, 1652; d. Cambridge, 1724. He was a chorister in the Chapel Royal in London; in 1679 received a stipend from Charles II which enabled him to study in Italy. He returned to London in 1681; suspected of Roman Catholic adherence, he was compelled to seek employment on the continent; served as intendant of music at Kassel (1698-99); was back in London shortly afterwards, able to resume his career (he was described in a contemporary report as "a harmonious vagabond"). He gave his last London concert in 1716. Abell published 'A Collection of Songs in Several Languages' and 'A Collection of Songs in English'; also 'A Choice Collection of Italian Ayres.' — Cf. H. G. Farmer, *John Abell* in 'Hinrichsen's Music Book' (vol. VII, 1952).

Abendroth, Hermann, conductor and pedagogue; b. Frankfurt, Jan. 19, 1883; d. Jena, May 29, 1956. He studied in Munich (1900-1905); was active in Lübeck (1905-11); Essen (1911-15); Cologne (1915-34); also conducted at the Berlin State Opera (1923-34). From 1934-42 he was director of the Leipzig Cons. and conductor of the Gewandhaus Concerts. In 1947 he was appointed director of the Musikhochschule in Weimar; in 1949, music director of the Leipzig Radio.

Aber, Adolf, musicologist; b. Apolda, Germany, Jan. 28, 1893. He studied with Kretzschmar, Stumpf and Wolf in Berlin; was music critic in Leipzig (1918-33). In 1936 he settled in London and became connected with the Novello publishing firm. Publications: *Handbuch der Musikliteratur* (1922); *Die Musikinstrumente und ihre Sprache* (1924); *Die Musik im Schauspiel, Geschichtliches und Ästhetisches* (1926); *Verzeichnis der Werke von Brahms* (1928); also articles in various journals.

Abert, Anna Amalie, musicologist; b. Halle, Sept. 19, 1906. She studied at Berlin Univ. (Ph. D., 1934). In 1943 was appointed instructor at the Univ. of Kiel; 1950, prof. there; became assistant editor of the musical encyclopedia 'Die Musik in Geschichte und Gegenwart.' She edited several collections of German choral music; published an important book on Monteverdi, *Claudio Monteverdi und das musikalische Drama* (1953).

Abert, Hermann, German music scholar; b. Stuttgart, March 25, 1871; d. there, Aug. 13, 1927. He studied with his father, Johann Joseph Abert; then at Tübingen Univ. (*Dr. phil.*, 1897). He was Dozent of musical science at Halle Univ. (1902); prof. there (1909). In 1919 he was appointed prof. at Heidelberg Univ; 1920, at Leipzig Univ. (succeeding Hugo Riemann); 1923, at Berlin Univ. (succeeding Kretzschmar). — Publications: *Die Lehre vom Ethos in der griechischen Musik* (1899); *Die Musikanschauung des Mittelalters und ihre Grundlagen* (Halle, 1905); *Nic. Jommelli als Opern-Komponist* (Halle, 1908); *Nic. Piccinni als Buffo-Komponist* (1913); biography of his father, Johann Jos. Abert (1916); revision of Otto Jahn's biography of Mozart (1919-21); *Goethe und die Musik* (1922); *Luther und die Musik* (1924); *Illustriertes Musiklexikon* (1927). His collected writings were posthumously edited by F. Blume *(Gesammelte Schriften,* 1929).

Abert, Johann Joseph, German composer; b. Kochowitz, Sept. 20, 1832; d. Stuttgart, April 1, 1915. He was a choir-boy until 15 at Gastdorf and Leipa monasteries; then studied double-bass and composition at the Prague Cons. (1846-53). In 1853 he was engaged as double-bass player in the court orchestra at Stuttgart; in 1867 he became its conductor and also led the Stuttgart Opera. He produced several of his operas in Stuttgart: *Anna von Landskron* (1859); *König Enzio* (1862) and the 'romantic opera' *Astorga,* on the life of the composer Astorga (May 27, 1866; very successful at the time). His 5-act opera *Ekkehard* (Berlin, Oct. 11, 1878) also attracted considerable attention, as did his 'musical sea picture' *Columbus,* in the form of a symphony (1864). He also wrote 6 symphonies, several overtures and chamber music, and pieces for double-bass. Abert's style, influenced by Mendelssohn, Schumann, and to some extent Liszt, follows the romantic tradition. His son, Hermann Abert, wrote a detailed biography: *Johann Joseph Abert, sein Leben und seine Werke* (Leipzig, 1916).

Abos, Girolamo (baptismal name Geronimo), Maltese composer; b. Valetta, Nov. 16, 1715; d. Naples, May, 1760. He studied with Leonardo Leo and Francesco Durante in Naples. In 1756 he went to London as 'maestro al cembalo' at the Italian Theater. Returning to Naples in 1758 he taught at the Cons. della Pietà de' Turchini. Among his pupils was Paisiello. Abos wrote 14 operas which were produced in Naples, Rome and London; of these, *Tito Manlio* (Naples, May 30, 1751) was successful; also composed 7 masses and other church music. He is often confused with his contemporary, the Neapolitan opera composer, Giuseppe Avossa (1716-96).

Abraham, Gerald, eminent English musicologist; b. Newport, Isle of Wight, March 9, 1904. He studied piano; became interested in philology; has mastered the Russian language and made a profound study of Russian music which has become his specialty. From 1935-47 he was connected with the B.B.C. in London; then was appointed prof. of music at Liverpool Univ. He has publ. the following books: *Borodin* (1927); *This Modern Stuff* (1933; revised edition under the title *This Modern Music,* 1952); *Masters of Russian Music* (in collaboration with M. D. Calvocoressi, 1936); *A Hundred Years of Music* (1938); *On Russian Music* (1939); *Chopin's Musical Style* (1939); *Beethoven's Second-Period Quartets* (1942); *8 Soviet Composers* (1943); *Rimsky-Korsakov: A Short Biography* (1945); also edited collections of articles on Tchaikovsky (1945), Schubert (1946), Sibelius (1947), Schumann (1952), Handel (1954). Abraham has contributed important biographical articles to the 5th edition of Grove's Dictionary (1954).

Abraham, Max, German publisher; **b. Danzig, June 3,** 1831; d. Leipzig, Dec. 8, 1900. He became a partner in C. F. Peters' 'Bureau de Musique' in 1863, and sole proprietor in 1880. On Jan. 1, 1894, his nephew, Heinrich Hinrichsen, of Hamburg, entered the firm and, upon Abraham's death, became its head. The famous 'Edition Peters' was inaugurated by Abraham.

Abraham, Otto, German specialist in tone psychology; b. Berlin, May 31, 1872; d. there, Jan. 24, 1926. He studied medicine; became an associate of Stumpf at the Berlin Psychological Institute from 1894; then collaborated with Hornbostel in building up the Archive of Phonographic Recordings in Berlin. He published several valuable treatises on acoustics and primitive music, among them *Wahrnehmung kürzester Töne und Geräusche* (1898); *Studien über das Tonsystem und die Musik der Japaner* (1904); *Phonographierte Indianermelodien aus Britisch-Columbia* (1905; with Hornbostel). He also wrote studies on recorded Turkish, Siamese and Hindu melodies; a paper on Chinese musical notation, etc.

Ábrányi, Cornelius, Hungarian pianist, composer and writer on music; grandfather of Emil Ábrányi; b. Szentgyörgy-Ábrányi, Oct. 15, 1822; d. Budapest, Dec. 20, 1903. He came of an ancient Magyar family whose name was originally Eördögh. He was first destined to a legal profession, but in 1834 a meeting with the Hungarian national composer, Erkel, made him decide to study music. In 1843 Ábrányi went abroad; in Munich he met Liszt, and became his lifelong friend. He went to Paris and took lessons with Chopin and Kalkbrenner for a short time, returning to Hungary in 1845. He took a leading part in the formation and encouragement of the Hungarian national school of composition during the second half of the nineteenth century. His compositions (130 opus numbers) emphasize the Hungarian national elements; the most ambitious of these works being his *Hungarian Millennial Sonata,* op. 103. His books (all in Hungarian) include: *Art and Revolution* (1867); *Biography of Franz Liszt and Survey of his Oratorio Christus* (1873); *General History of Music* (1886); *History of Hungarian Music in the Nineteenth Century* (1900). He also wrote an autobiography, *From My Life and Memories* (1897).

Ábrányi, Emil, composer and conductor; b. Budapest, Sept. 22, 1882. His father was Emil Ábrányi, the poet, and his grandfather, Cornelius Ábrányi. In 1902 he went to Germany and studied under Nikisch in Leipzig. He was engaged as conductor to the Municipal Theater at Cologne (1904) and at Hanover (1907). Returning to Budapest (1911) he became conductor at the Royal Opera House; he was also active as music critic. He was director of the Budapest Municipal Theater (1921-26); conducted various orchestras in the provinces. As a composer, Ábrányi follows the tradition of Wagner. The following stage works were performed at the Royal Hungarian Opera House, Budapest: *The King of the Mist,* ballet (Oct. 17, 1903); the operas *Monna Vanna* (March 2, 1907); *Paolo e Francesca* (Jan. 13, 1912); *Don Quixote* (Nov. 30, 1917); *Ave Maria* (1922). Other operas are *Singing Dervishes* (1935); *The Prince with the Lilies* (1938); *Byzantium* (1942); *Sorceress Eve* (1944); *The Tale of Balaton* (1945) and *The Cantor of St. Thomas Church* (1947; the first opera written on the life of J. S. Bach).

Abravanel, Maurice, conductor; b. Saloniki (Greece), Jan. 6, 1903. He studied at Lausanne Univ., and later in Berlin. Leaving Germany in 1933 he conducted ballet in Paris and London; toured Australia with the British National Opera Co. (1934-35). Conducted at Metropolitan Opera (1936-38) and the Chicago Opera Co. (1940-41). In 1947 he became conductor of the Utah State Symph. Orch. at Salt Lake City.

Absil, Jean, Belgian composer; b. Peruwelz, Oct. 23, 1893. He studied organ and composition at the Brussels Cons.; later with Gilson. He won the Prix Agniez for his 1st symphony (1921); in 1922 won a second Prix de Rome for the cantata *La Guerre;* also received Prix Rubens and Prix Ysaÿe. Appointed music dir. of the Academy of Eterbeek (1923); from 1931, teaching at the Brussels Cons.; is also one of the founders of the 'Revue Internationale de Musique.' Absil has evolved an individual style, characterized by rhythmic variety, free tonality and compact counterpoint. Works: *Fanson,* musical comedy (1945); 2 ballets, *Le Miracle de Pan* (1949) and *Epouvantail* (1951); 4 cantatas: *La Guerre* (1922); *Philatélie* for 4 voices and 15 instruments (1940); *Les Bénédictions* (1941) and *Le Zodiaque* (1949). For orch.: 3 symphonies (1921, 1936, 1943); *La mort de Tintagiles,* symph. poem (1926); *Rapsodie sur des thèmes populaires flamands* (1928); violin concerto (1933); piano concerto (1937); *Chants des Morts* for chorus and orch. (1941); concertino for cello and orch. (1942); viola concerto (1942); *Rapsodie roumaine* for violin and orch. (1943); *Jeanne d'Arc,* symph. poem (1945). Chamber music: 4 string quartets (1929, 1934, 1935, 1941); wind quintet (1934); 2 string trios (1935, 1939); *Fantaisie* for string quartet and piano (1939); *Phantasmes* for contralto, saxophone, piano, viola and percussion (1950). Bibl.: J. Dopp, *Jean Absil* in 'La Revue Musicale' (Oct.-Dec., 1937).

Abt, Franz, German song writer and conductor; b. Eilenburg, Dec. 22, 1819; d. Wiesbaden, March 31, 1885. His father being a clergyman, he was sent to Leipzig Thomasschule to study theology; later obtained an excellent musical education both there and at the Univ. He became a choral conductor in Zürich (1841). In 1852 he was appointed second conductor at the Brunswick Court; in 1855 became first conductor. In 1869 he traveled, as a choral conductor, to Paris, London and Russia; in 1872 he made a highly successful tour in America. He retired on a pension from Brunswick in 1882. Abt wrote over 600 works, comprising more than 3,000 numbers; the largest are the 7 secular cantatas. His popularity as a song writer is due chiefly to the flowing, easy and elegant style of his vocal melodies, some of which (*Wenn die Schwalben heimwärts zieh'n, Gute Nacht, du mein herziges Kind, So viele Tausend Blumen,* etc.) have become so well known as to be mistaken for genuine folksongs. See B. Rost, *Vom Meister des volkstümlichen deutschen Liedes, Franz Abt* (Chemnitz, 1924).

Achron, Isidor, pianist and composer; b. Warsaw, Nov. 24, 1892; d. New York, May 12, 1948. He studied at the St. Petersburg Cons. with Liadov (composition) and Mme. Essipov (piano). After the Russian Revolution he came to the U.S. and was active in New York as teacher. He was the soloist in his Piano Concerto with the N. Y. Philh. Orch. (Dec. 9, 1937); he also wrote *Suite Grotesque* for orch. (St. Louis, Jan. 30, 1942) and solo pieces for piano.

Achron, Joseph, violinist and composer; b. Lozdzieje, Lithuania, May 13, 1886; d. Hollywood, Calif., April 29, 1943. He studied at the St. Petersburg Cons. with Auer (violin) and Liadov (theory), graduating in 1904. From 1913-16 he taught at Kharkov Cons., then was drafted into the Russian Army. Between 1918-22 he gave popular concerts in the Petrograd area; left Russia and toured in Europe and the Near East, coming to the U.S. in 1925. He lived in New York until 1939, when he settled in Hollywood. He wrote 3 violin concertos which he played with the Boston Symph. Orch. (Jan. 24, 1927) and the Los Angeles Philharm. (Dec. 19, 1936; March 31, 1939). His other works are: *Hebrew Melody* for violin and orch. (1911; his most famous composition, also published for violin and piano); *Hazan* for cello and orch. (1912); *2 Hebrew Pieces* (1913); *Shar* for clarinet and orch. (1917); and *Golem Suite* for orch. (1932) the last section of which is the exact retrograde movement of the first section to symbolize the undoing of the monster Golem. His chamber music includes *Chromatic String Quartet; Elegy* for string quartet; 3 suites and *Suite bizarre* for violin and piano; 2 violin sonatas. During his American period Achron adopted a highly advanced idiom of composition using atonal and polytonal devices.

Ackté (real name, Achté), **Aïno,** Finnish dramatic soprano; b. Helsinki, April 23, 1876; d. there, Aug. 8, 1944. She studied at the Paris Cons. and made her debut at the

Paris Opéra as Marguerite (Oct. 8, 1897). She sang the same role at her first appearance in America at the Metropolitan Opera (Feb. 22, 1904). Her performance of Salomé in Strauss's opera at Covent Garden (1913) led to an invitation from Richard Strauss to sing the part in Dresden and Paris. Her other roles were Juliette, Ophélie, Gilda, Nedda, Elsa, Elisabeth and Sieglinde. Her memoirs are published in Finnish, Swedish and German.

Adam (ăh-dăhn), **Adolphe-Charles,** celebrated French opera composer; b. Paris, July 24, 1803; d. there, May 3, 1856. He entered the Paris Cons. in 1817 and studied with Boieldieu, whose influence was a determining factor in his career. His first opera was *Pierre et Catherine* (Opéra-Comique, Feb. 9, 1829). The one-act comic opera, *Le Chalet* (Opéra-Comique, Sept. 25, 1834), marked his first success (1400 performances of this opera were given before 1899). With the production of *Le Postillon de Longjumeau* (Opéra-Comique, Oct. 13, 1836) Adam achieved international fame. Of his other operas (he wrote 53 in all), the following, all produced at the Opéra-Comique, are the most important: *Le Fidèle Berger* (Jan. 6, 1838); *Le Brasseur de Preston* (Oct. 31, 1838); *Régine, ou Les Deux Nuits* (Jan. 17, 1839); *La Reine d'un jour* (Sept. 19, 1839); *Le Roi d'Yvetot* (Oct. 13, 1842); *Cagliostro* (Feb. 10, 1844); *Le Toréador, ou L'Accord parfait* (May 18, 1849); *Giralda, ou La Nouvelle Psyché* (July 20, 1850); *Le Farfadet* (March 19, 1852); *Le Sourd, ou L'Auberge pleine* (Feb. 2, 1853). His comic opera *Si j'étais roi* (Théâtre-Lyrique, Sept. 4, 1852) was also very popular; his tragic opera *Richard en Palestine* was produced at the Paris Opéra (Oct. 7, 1854) with considerable success, but was not retained in the repertoire. Adam was also a very successful ballet composer; his *Giselle,* produced at the Paris Opéra (June 28, 1841) became one of the most celebrated and enduring choreographic scores. His song *Cantique de Noël,* in numerous arrangements, enjoyed great popularity. In 1847 Adam ventured into the field of management with an operatic enterprise, the Théâtre National; the revolutionary outbreak of 1848, however, brought financial ruin to his undertaking. In 1849 he was appointed prof. of composition at the Paris Cons. He traveled widely in Europe, visiting London, Berlin and St. Petersburg. As one of the creators of French comic opera, Adam ranks with Boieldieu and Auber in the expressiveness of his melodic material if not in originality or inventive power. Adam's memoirs were published posthumously in 2 volumes under the titles *Souvenirs d'un musicien* (1857), and *Derniers souvenirs d'un musicien* (1859). A. Pougin wrote his biography (Paris, 1877).

Adam, Claus, American cellist and composer; born of Austrian parents in Sumatra, Nov. 5, 1917. He was taken to Europe as a child (1923); studied in Germany and Austria. In 1931 he came to the U.S.; has appeared in concerts as a cellist. His piano sonata was performed at the Salzburg Festival in 1952.

Adam, Jenö, Hungarian conductor, composer and writer on music; b. Szigetszentmiklós, Dec. 13, 1896. He studied with Kodály, and was later associated with him in a program reorganizing the system of musical education; conducted several choirs in Budapest, and in 1938 was appointed prof. of choral singing at the Academy of Music there. He has written 2 operas, *Hungarian Christmas* (Budapest, Dec. 22, 1931) and *Mária Veronika* (Budapest, 1938); a symph. cantata *Man on the Road* (1946); 2 string quartets; a cello sonata and unaccompanied choral works. He has also published a number of musical text books for schools.

Adam, Louis; Alsatian pianist, teacher and composer; father of Adolphe-Charles Adam; b. Müttersholz, Dec. 3, 1758; d. Paris, April 8, 1848. He went to Paris in 1775; was later prof. of piano at the Paris Cons. (1797-1842). He was the teacher of Kalkbrenner and Hérold; was also known as composer of virtuoso piano pieces, some of which (especially variations on *Le Roi Dagobert)* were very popular. He was the author of two standard manuals for piano: *Méthode générale du doigté* (Paris, 1798) and *Méthode nouvelle pour le Piano* (5 editions, 1802-32), which he wrote for his pupils at the Paris Conservatory.

Adam de la Hale (or **Halle**), called 'Le Bossu d'Arras' (Hunchback of Arras); b. Arras, c. 1240; d. Naples, 1287. A famous trouvère, many of whose works have been preserved (publ. 1872 by Coussemaker as *Oeuvres complètes du Trouvère Adam de la Hale);* the most interesting is a dramatic pastoral *Le jeu de Robin et de Marion* (1285), written for the Aragonese court at Naples resembling an opéra comique in its plan. He was gifted in the dual capacity of poet and composer. Both monodic and polyphonic works of his survive. His rondeaux, etc., are reprinted by Fr. Gennrich, in *Rondeaux, Virelais und Balladen* (I, 1921).—

Cf. E. Langlois, *Le jeu de Robin et de Marion* (Paris, 1896); H. Guy, *Essai sur la vie et les œuvres littéraires d'Adam de la Hale* (Paris, 1898); J. Tiersot, *Sur le Jeu de Robin et Marion* (1897); A. Guesnon, *Une édition allemande des chansons d'Adam de la Hale* (1900); E. Langlois, *Le jeu de la feuillée* (1911); practical edition of *Le Jeu de Robin et Marion* by J. Beck (Philadelphia, 1928; 1939).

Adam von Fulda, German theorist and composer; b. Fulda, c. 1440; d. (of the plague) Wittenberg, 1505. His tract on music theory is published in Gerbert's 'Scriptores ecclesiastici'; his works were highly prized in their day. — Bibl.: H. Riemann in 'Kirchenmusikalisches Jahrbuch' (Regensburg, 1879); W. Niemann (ibid., 1902); W. Gurlitt in 'Luther Jahrbuch' (1932); W. Ehmann, *Adam von Fulda* (1936).

Adamowski (ăh-dăh-mov'-skē), **Joseph,** cellist; b. Warsaw, July 4, 1862; d. Cambridge, Mass., May 8, 1930. He studied at the Warsaw Cons. (1873-77) with Goebelt; and at the Moscow Cons. with Fitzenhagen; also attended Tchaikovsky's classes there. He gave concerts from 1883-89 in Warsaw. In 1889 joined the Boston Symph. Orch. In 1896 he married the pianist, Antoinette Szumowska. With his wife and brother, Timothée, he formed the Adamowski Trio. From 1903 he taught at the New England Cons.

Adamowski, Timothée, violinist; b. Warsaw, March 24, 1857; d. Boston, April 18, 1943. He studied in Warsaw and at the Paris Cons.; in 1879 gave concerts in the U.S. with Maurice Strakosch and Clara Louise Kellogg, and settled in Boston, where he taught at the New England Cons. (until 1933). In 1888 he organized the Adamowski String Quartet which gave about 30 concerts annually; he also conducted several summer seasons of popular concerts given by the Boston Symph. Orch. (1890-94 and 1900-07). He published songs and violin pieces *(Barcarolle, Polish Dance,* etc.)

Adams, Charles, American dramatic tenor; b. Charlestown, Mass., Feb. 9, 1834; d. West Harwich, Mass., July 4, 1900. He studied in Vienna with Barbieri; was engaged for three years by the Royal Opera, Berlin, and for nine years by the Imperial Opera, Vienna; sang at La Scala, at Covent Garden, and in the U.S. He settled in Boston as a teacher in 1879.

Adams, Suzanne, American soprano; b. Cambridge, Mass., Nov. 28, 1872; d. London, Feb. 5, 1953. She studied with J. Bouhy in New York; went to Paris in 1889; made her debut at the Paris Opéra as Juliette (Jan. 9, 1895), and subsequently was engaged to sing there for 3 more seasons; appeared at the Metropolitan Opera House as Juliette on Jan. 4, 1899.

Adams, Thomas, eminent English organist; b. London, Sept. 5, 1785; d. there, Sept. 15, 1858. He studied with Dr. Busby; was organist at various London churches. His publ. organ works include fugues, voluntaries, 90 interludes, and variations on popular airs; he also wrote anthems, hymns, and sacred songs.

Adaskin, Harry, Canadian violinist; b. Riga, Latvia, Sept. 17, 1901. He was brought to Toronto at the age of two, and studied at the Toronto Cons. (1912-18). He then entered the Chicago Musical College and later studied in Paris. From 1923-38 he was second violinist of the Hart House String Quartet, which toured in Europe and America. In 1946 he was appointed violin teacher at the Univ. of British Columbia, Vancouver. His brother, **Murray Adaskin** (b. Toronto, March 28, 1906) is also a violinist; another brother, **John Adaskin** (b. Toronto, June 4, 1908) is a cellist.

Addinsell, Richard, English composer of theater music; b. Oxford, Jan. 13, 1904. He studied law at Oxford Univ.; later entered the Royal College of Music; then studied music in Berlin and Vienna. He was commissioned in 1933 by Eva Le Gallienne to write the music for her production of *Alice in Wonderland;* later wrote for the films in Hollywood. Among his cinema scores are *Fire over England, Dark Journey, Goodbye, Mr. Chips* and *Dangerous Moonlight.* The score for the latter includes the *Warsaw Concerto,* which became enormously popular as a concert piece for piano and orch. During World War II Addinsell wrote music for a number of documentary films (*Siege of Tobruk, We Sail at Midnight,* etc.).

Adelburg, August Ritter von, Hungarian violinist and composer; b. Constantinople, Nov. 1, 1830; d. Vienna, Oct. 20, 1873. He studied the violin with Mayseder in Vienna (1850-54), and composition with Hoffmann; then toured Europe as violinist. He wrote 3 operas: *Zrinyi* (Budapest, June 23, 1868; his most successful work); *Martinuzzi* (1870) and *Wallenstein* (on Schiller's drama); an oratorio *War and Peace;* 5 string quartets and *School of Velocity* for violin.

Adgate, Andrew, American church organist and choral conductor; b. Philadelphia c. 1750; d. there of yellow fever, Sept. 30, 1793. In 1784 he organized, in Philadelphia, an Institution for the Encouragement of Church Music; in 1785 he founded there a 'Free School for Spreading the Knowledge of Vocal Music,' reorganized in 1787 as 'The Uranian Academy,' the purpose of which was to urge the incorporation of musical study with general education. On May 4, 1786, he presented in Philadelphia 'A Grand Concert of Sacred Music,' with a chorus of 230 voices and an orchestra of 50, featuring works by Handel, Billings and others. Adgate compiled several publications: *Lessons for the Uranian Society* (1785); *Select Psalms and Hymns* (1787); *Rudiments of Music* (1788); *Selection of Sacred Harmony* (1788).

Adler, Clarence, American pianist; b. Cincinnati, March 10, 1886. He studied at the Cincinnati College of Music (1898-1904); then in Berlin with Godowsky (1905-09). He toured in Europe as pianist in the Hekking Trio. Returning to America in 1913, he settled in New York; made his American debut with the N.Y. Symph. Orch. (Feb. 8, 1914). In 1941 he broadcast all of Mozart's 28 piano concertos. He has published an album of piano pieces; also arrangements of works by Dvořák and Franck.

Adler, F. Charles, conductor; b. London, July 2, 1889. He studied piano with August Halm in Munich, theory with Beer-Walbrunn, and conducting with Mahler. He was assistant to Felix Mottl at the Royal Opera in Munich (1908-11); in 1913 he became first conductor of the Municipal Opera, Düsseldorf. Conducted symphonic concerts in Europe (1919-33). He was owner of 'Edition Adler' in Berlin until 1933 when he came to America. In 1937 he founded the Saratoga Springs Music Festivals, N. Y.

Adler, Guido, musicologist; b. Eibenschütz, Moravia, Nov. 1, 1855; d. Vienna, Feb. 15, 1941. He studied at the Vienna Cons. under Bruckner and Dessoff; entered Vienna Univ. in 1874 and founded, in coöperation with Felix Mottl and K. Wolf, the academical Wagner Society; took the degree of *Dr. jur.* in 1878, and in 1880 that of *Dr. phil.* (dissertation on *Die historischen Grundklassen der christlich-abendländischen Musik bis 1600),* and in 1881 qualified as instructor, lecturing on musical science (thesis, *Studie zur Geschichte der Harmonie).* With Chrysander and Spitta he founded, in 1884, the 'Vierteljahrsschrift für Musikwissenschaft.' In 1885 he was appointed prof. of musical science at the German Univ. at Prague. In 1892 he was elected President of the Central Committee of the 'Internationale Ausstellung für Musik und Theater.' In 1895 he succeeded Hanslick as prof. of music history at the Univ. of Vienna, retiring in 1927. Important books by Adler are *Methode der Musikgeschichte* (1919); *Der Stil in der Musik* (1911; 2nd ed., 1929); *Gustav Mahler* (1914); *Handbuch der Musikgeschichte* (1 vol., 1924; 2nd ed. in 2 vols., 1930); *Wollen und Wirken* (memoirs; Vienna, 1935). He was also editor of the monumental collection 'Denkmäler der Tonkunst in Österreich' from its inception (the first volume appeared in 1894) to its completion (in 1938; 83 vols. in all). He contributed many articles to periodic music publications. Bibl.: C. Engel, *Guido Adler in Retrospect* in the 'Mus. Quarterly' (July, 1941).

Adler, Kurt, pianist and conductor; b. Neuhaus, Czechoslovakia, March 1, 1907. He was educated in Vienna; studied musicology with Guido Adler and Robert Lach at the Vienna Univ.; was assistant conductor of the Berlin State Opera (1927-29) and of the German Opera in Prague (1929-32). In 1933, with the advent of the Nazis to power, he went to Russia, where he was chief conductor at the Kiev State Opera (1933-35); organized and conducted the Philh. Orch. of Stalingrad (1935-37). In 1938 he came to the U.S.; first appeared as concert pianist; then conducted in Canada and Mexico. In 1943 he joined the staff of the Metropolitan Opera as choirmaster and assistant conductor; edited the collections *Operatic Anthology, The Prima Donna Album, Arias from Light Operas, Famous Operatic Choruses,* etc. He is no relation to Kurt Herbert Adler (q.v.).

Adler, Kurt Herbert, opera conductor; b. Vienna, April 2, 1905. He studied at the Vienna Cons.; was a theater conductor in Vienna (1925-28), in Prague and in Germany. He served as assistant to Toscanini at the Salzburg Festival in 1936; then settled in the U.S.; was with the Chicago Opera Company (1938-43); in 1943 joined the staff of the San Francisco Opera; in 1953 he became its artistic director. He is no relation to Kurt Adler (q.v.).

Adler, Larry (Lawrence), harmonica player; b. Baltimore, Feb. 10, 1914. He won a harmonica contest at 13 for the best rendition of Beethoven's Minuet in G. He has appeared in numerous revues; also gave concerts as soloist with piano and with orchestra, as well as command performances for King George VI, King Gustav of Sweden and Presidents Roosevelt and Truman. In 1940, determined to learn to read music, he took lessons with Ernst Toch. Darius Milhaud wrote a Suite for harmonica and orch. for Adler, which he played on Nov. 16, 1945 with the Philadelphia Orch.

Adler, Peter Herman, conductor; b. Jablonec, Czechoslovakia, Dec. 2, 1899. He studied in Prague with Fidelio Finke, Vitězlav Novák, and Alexander von Zemlinsky; conducted opera in Brno (1923); later was first conductor of the Bremen State Theater (1928-31). In 1932 he went to Russia; was chief conductor of the Ukrainian State Orch. in Kiev (1932-37) and taught conducting at the Kiev Cons.; also conducted symph. concerts in Moscow and Leningrad. He was in Prague in 1938; then settled in the U.S.; made his American debut as conductor at a concert for Czech relief in N. Y., Jan. 24, 1940; appeared as guest conductor with the Cleveland Orch., Detroit Symph., and other organizations. He then became active in the opera; in 1949 he became musical director of the N.B.C. Opera Theater.

Adler, Samuel, composer; b. Mannheim, Germany, March 4, 1928. He studied at Boston Univ. with Karl Geiringer, and at Harvard Univ. with Walter Piston, Randall Thompson and Paul Hindemith; also worked with Aaron Copland and Koussevitzky at Tanglewood. In 1950 he joined the U.S. Army; was sent to Germany, and there organized the Seventh Army Symph. Orch.; this group toured Germany and Austria. Was awarded the Medal of Honor for this work. While in Germany he appeared as guest conductor with numerous orchestras and opera companies. In 1953 he was appointed music director at the Temple Emanu-El in Dallas, Texas. Works: *American Comedy Overture* (1946); *Kinnereth,* symph. poem (1947); symphony (1953); concertino for flute, bassoon and string orch. (1949-50); *Two Poems* for viola and string orch. (1953); sonata for horn and piano (1948); 3 string quartets (1945-1955); a cantata *The Vision of Isaiah* (1949); several pieces for brass ensemble, choruses, etc.

Adlgasser, Anton Cajetan, organist and composer; b. Inzell, Bavaria, Oct. 1, 1729; d. Salzburg, Dec. 23, 1777. He studied with Johann Eberlin in Salzburg; on Dec. 11, 1750, was appointed organist at Salzburg Cathedral, and held this post until his death (he died of a stroke while playing the organ). Adlgasser enjoyed a great reputation as a musical scholar, and was admired by the young Mozart. He wrote an opera *Nitteti* (Salzburg, 1767); several oratorios and sacred dramas; 7 symphonies; piano sonatas and church works. Bibl.: C. Schneider, *Die Oratorien und Schuldramen A. C. Adlgassers* (Vienna, 1923); C. Schneider, *Musikgeschichte von Salzburg* (1936).

Adlung, Jakob, German music scholar; b. Bindersleben, near Erfurt, Jan. 14, 1699; d. Erfurt, July 5, 1762. He studied with Christian Reichardt; in 1727 became organist at the Erfurt Lutheran Church; in 1741 was named prof. at the town school. A man of wide erudition, Adlung gave language lessons as well as musical instruction. He built 16 clavichords with his own hands. Among his writings, three have historical value: *Anleitung zu der musikalischen Gelahrtheit* (Erfurt, 1758; 2nd ed., revised by J. A. Hiller, 1783; facsimile ed. by H. J. Moser, Kassel, 1953); *Musica mechanica organoedi* (1768; facsimile ed. by Chr. Mahrenholz, Kassel, 1931); *Musikalisches Siebengestirn* (1768). His autobiographical sketch was publ. by Marpurg (*Kritische Briefe,* II). See E. Valentin's article in 'Die Musik in Geschichte und Gegenwart.'

Adorno, Theodor (real name Wiesengrund), music theorist; b. Frankfurt, Sept. 11, 1903. He studied with Sekles in Frankfurt and Alban Berg in Vienna. Was music critic in Frankfurt; then instructor at the Univ. there. He emigrated to the U.S. in 1934; was connected with radio research at Princeton (1938-41); then lived in California. In 1950 he returned to Frankfurt and resumed his professorship there. Adorno published *Philosophie der neuen Musik* (Tübingen, 1949) and numerous articles on music in relation to society (radio, jazz, etc.); in his early writings he used the name Wiesengrund-Adorno.

Adriaensen, Emanuel (called Hadrianus), Flemish lutenist, born in Antwerp; flourished in the 16th century. In 1584 he published *Pratum musicum,* a collection of songs and dances for 2, 3, and 4 lutes; in 1592 he brought out another collection entitled *Novum pratum musicum,* containing canzonets, dances, fantasias, madrigals, motets and preludes by Cipriano de Rore, Orlando di Lasso, J. de Berchem, H. Waelrant and others, freely arranged by him for lute in tablature.

Adriano di Bologna. See **Banchieri.**

Adrio, Adam, German musicologist; b. Essen, April 4, 1901. He studied at Berlin Univ. (1927-34) and took his Ph. D. there. In 1951, appointed prof. at the Univ. of Berlin-West. Contributor to 'Die Musik in Geschichte und Gegenwart.' Author of *Die Anfänge des geistlichen Konzerts* (Berlin, 1935), and editor of collections of old German music.

Aerde, Raymond Van. See **Van Aerde, Raymond.**

Aerts (ahrts), **Egide,** Belgian flutist; b. Boom, near Antwerp, March 1, 1822; d. Brussels, June 9, 1853. A precocious musician, he studied as a child at the Brussels Cons.; gave a concert in Paris at the age of 15. In 1847 he was appointed teacher of flute at the Brussels Cons. He wrote numerous works for flute, most of which remain in manuscript.

Aeschbacher, Adrian, Swiss pianist; b. Langenthal, May 10, 1912. He studied at the Zürich Cons. with Emil Frey and Andreae; later took lessons with Schnabel in Berlin. He toured in Europe from 1934 to 1939; then taught and gave concerts in Switzerland.

Aeschbacher, Niklaus, Swiss conductor; b. Trogen, April 30, 1917. He studied in Zürich and Berlin. Was active as theater conductor in Germany; appointed conductor of the Municipal Theater in Bern in 1949. He wrote a radio opera *Die roten Schuhe* (1943) and chamber music.

Aeschbacher, Walther, Swiss conductor and composer; b. Bern, Oct. 2, 1901; studied music theory with Ernst Kurth, and conducting in Munich and then settled in Basel. He has written much choral music and several orchestral pieces in old forms.

Afanassiev (ăh-făh-nah'-syĕv), **Nikolay Yakovlevitch,** Russian composer; b. Tobolsk, 1821; d. St. Petersburg, June 3, 1898. He studied violin with his father, an amateur musician, and joined the orchestra of the Moscow Opera at the age of 17. Later he conducted Italian opera in Moscow and St. Petersburg. He traveled in Europe in 1857. Afanassiev was regarded as the first Russian composer to write a string quartet (1860), but this is refuted by the discovery of 3 string quartets by Aliabiev. He further wrote a cantata, *The Feast of Peter the Great,* and an opera *Ammalat-Bek,* which was produced at the Imperial Opera in St. Petersburg on Dec. 5, 1870, and three more operas, *Stenka Razin, Vakula the Smith,* and *Taras Bulba,* which were never performed; also wrote some children's songs.

Afranio de Pavia (family name **Albonese**), Italian theologian, reputed inventor of the bassoon; b. Pavia, 1480; d. Ferrara, c. 1560 as canon of Ferrara. His claim to the invention of the bassoon is based on the attribution to him of the instrument Phagotus, in the book by his nephew Teseo Albonese, *Introductio in chaldaicam linguam* (Pavia, 1539).

Agazzari (ăh-găht-săh'-rē), **Agostino,** Italian composer; b. Siena, Dec. 2, 1578; d. there April 10, 1640. He entered the service of Emperor Matthias as a professional musician; proceeding to Rome, he was in turn maestro di cappella at the German College there (1602-06), the church of St. Apollinaris, and the 'seminario romano'; intimacy with Viadana led to his adoption of the latter's innovations in sacred vocal music (writing church concerti for one or two voices with instrumental harmonic support). From 1630 he was maestro di cappella at Siena Cathedral. His works, variously reprinted in Germany and Holland, were in great favor and very numerous (madrigals, psalms, motets and other church music). His treatise *La musica ecclesiastica* (Siena, 1638) is a theoretical endeavor to bring the practice of church music into accord with the Resolution of the Council of Trent; he was also among the first to give written instructions for performing the basso continuo, presented in the tract *Del sonare sopra il basso con tutti gli strumenti e del loro uso nel concerto* (Siena, 1607; in English, O. Strunk, *Source Readings in Music History,* N. Y., 1950). His pastoral drama, *Eumelio* (1606) is one of the earliest operas. See A. Adrio's article in 'Die Musik Geschichte und Gegenwart.'

Agnew, Roy, Australian composer and pianist; b. Sydney, Aug. 23, 1893; d. there, Nov. 12, 1944. He went to London and studied with Gerrard Williams (1923-28); gave concerts in England (1931-34). He then returned to Australia; was appointed dir. of the Australian radio (1938-43) and taught at the Sydney Cons. Compositions: *Breaking of the Drought* for mezzo-soprano and orch. (1928); many piano works, including *Dance of the Wild Men* (1920); *Fantasia Sonata* (1927); *Sonata Poem*

(1935); *Sonata Ballade* (1936) and *Sonata Legend "Capricornia"* (1940).

Agostini, Lodovico, Italian composer and poet; b. Ferrara, 1534; d. there Sept. 20, 1590. He served as maestro di cappella to Alphonso II of Este, Duke of Ferrara. A number of his sacred and secular vocal works (madrigals, motets, masses, vespers, etc.) were published in Milan, Ferrara and Venice (1567-86).

Agostini, Mezio, Italian composer and theorist; b. Fano, Aug. 12, 1875; d. there, April 22, 1944. He studied with his father and with Carlo Pedrotti at the Liceo Rossini in Pesaro (1885-92); later became a harmony teacher there. He succeeded Wolf-Ferrari as director of the Liceo Benedetto Marcello in Venice (1909-40). Agostini wrote the following operas: *Iovo e Maria* (1896); *Il Cavaliere del Sogno* (1897); *La penna d'Airone* (1898); *Alcibiade* (1902); *America* (1904); *Ombra* (1907); *L'Anello del sogno* (1928). He also wrote a symphony, 4 orchestral suites, a string quartet, 2 piano trios, a cantata *A Rossini,* piano pieces and songs.

Agostini, Paolo, Italian organist and composer; b. Vallerano, 1593; d. Rome, Oct. 3, 1629. He studied with Giovanni Bernardino Nanino in Rome; was organist at S. Maria in Trastevere, in Rome, and at S. Lorenzo in Damaso. He succeeded Vincenzo Ugolini as maestro di cappella at the Vatican in 1626. Agostini's published works, 7 books of psalms (1619), 2 books of magnificats and antiphons (1620) and 5 books of masses (1624-28) are only a small portion of his total output. Most of his manuscripts are preserved in various Roman libraries. His music displays great ingenuity of contrapuntal structure; some of his choral works are written in 48 independent parts.

Agostini, Pietro Simone, Italian composer; b. Rome, c. 1650. He was in the service of the Duke of Parma as maestro di cappella. He wrote 6 operas: *Tolemeo* (Venice, 1668); *Ippolita* (Milan, 1670); *La costanza di Rosmonda* (Genoa, 1670); *Adelinda* (Aricia, 1673); *Il Ratto delle Sabine* (Venice, 1680); and *Floridea* (Venice, 1687). Some of his operas were written in collaboration with Busca, Ziani and others. He also wrote oratorios, motets and secular cantatas.

Agrell, Johan Joachim, Swedish composer; b. Löth, Feb. 1, 1701; d. Nuremberg, Jan. 19, 1765. He studied at Uppsala Univ.; later he was active in Kassel (1723-46) and in Nuremberg (from 1746). Among his published works are 5 concertos for cembalo and strings, 2 sonatas for violin and cembalo, 6 sonatas for cembalo solo, and pieces for cembalo in dance forms. His symphonies and cantatas are preserved in various European libraries (Stockholm, Uppsala, Brussels, Berlin, Königsberg, Munich and Darmstadt).

Agricola, Alexander, composer of the Netherland school; sometimes said to have been of German extraction, but referred to as a Belgian in his epitaph; b. Flanders, c. 1446; d. 1506 at Valladolid, Spain. He was in the service of the Duke of Milan from 1472-74; then went to Cambrai; in 1476 he is mentioned as "petit vicaire" at Cambrai Cathedral. He later traveled in Italy; entered the service of Philip I of Burgundy in 1500 and followed him to Spain in 1502, returning to Belgium in 1505. He went to Spain again in January, 1506 and died shortly afterward. Thirty-one of Agricola's songs and motets were printed by Petrucci (Venice, 1501-03) who also published a volume of 5 masses based on chanson material: *Le Serviteur, Je ne demande, Malheur me bat, Primi toni, Secundi toni* (Venice 1503). Modern reprints of examples of his works are found in O. Gombosi, *Jacob Obrecht, eine stilkritische Studie* (1925; includes discussion of Agricola's style). See also A. Schering, *Geschichte der Musik in Beispielen* (1931) and G. Reese, *Music in the Renaissance* (N.Y., 1954).

Agricola, Johann Friedrich, German organist and composer; b. Dobitzschen, near Altenburg, Jan. 4, 1720; d. Berlin, Dec. 2, 1774. He entered the Univ. of Leipzig as a law student in 1738, studying music meanwhile with J. S. Bach, and later (1741) with Johann Quantz in Berlin. In 1751 Agricola was appointed court composer to Frederick the Great, and in 1759 he succeeded Karl Graun as director of the Royal Chapel. Agricola wrote 8 operas (produced between 1750-1772 at Berlin and Potsdam) and church music; he also made arrangements of the King's compositions. He taught singing and translated (1757) Pier Tosi's *Opinioni de' cantori.* Under the pseudonym 'Olibrio' Agricola printed some polemical pamphlets directed against the theorist Friedrich Marpurg; he was also a collaborator with Jakob Adlung in the latter's *Musica mechanica organoedi* (1768).

Agricola, Martin, a very important German music theorist and writer; b. Schwiebus (Brandenburg), Jan. 6, 1486; d. Magdeburg, June 10, 1556. His real name wa[s] Sore, but he adopted the Latin name Ag[ricola]

cola to indicate his peasant origin. Mattheson says that he was the first to abandon the old tablature for modern notation, but this is not quite accurate; Agricola merely proposed an improved system for lute tablature. From 1510 he was a private music teacher in Magdeburg. In 1527 was cantor at the first Lutheran church there. His friend and patron, Rhaw of Wittenberg, published most of Agricola's works, the magnum opus being *Musica instrumentalis deudsch* (i.e., 'set in German'; 1st ed., Wittenberg, 1529; 4th ed., considerably revised, 1545; modern reprint, Leipzig, 1896). This work, although derived from Virdung's *Musica getutscht,* contains much new material and is set in couplet verse in the German vernacular. Further works are: *Ein kurtz deudsche Musica* (1529; 3d ed. as *Musica choralis deudsch,* 1533); *Musica figuralis,* with a supplement *Von den proportionibus* (1532); *Scholia in musicam planam Venceslai Philomatis* (1538); *Rudimenta musices* (1539); *Quaestiones vulgatiores in musicam* (1543); *Duo libri musices* (posthumous; Wittenberg, 1561; includes reprints of *Musica choralis* and *Musica figuralis;* and 54 *Instrumentische Gesänge* as a supplement). Compositions: *Ein Sangbüchlein aller Sonntags-Evangelien* (1541); *Neue deutsche geistliche Gesänge* (1544); *Hymni aliquot sacri* (1552); *Melodiae scholasticae* (1557).—Cf. Heinz Funck, *Martin Agricola* (Wolfenbüttel, 1933).

Aguado, Dionisio, Spanish guitar virtuoso and composer; b. Madrid, April 8, 1784; d. there, Dec. 29, 1849. He studied with Manuel Garcia; went to Paris in 1825; gave numerous concerts there, attracting the attention of Rossini and Paganini. Returning to Madrid in 1838, he became a teacher of guitar. He wrote *Estudio para la guitarra* (Madrid, 1820); *Escuela o método de guitarra* (Madrid, 1825); also 45 waltzes; 6 minuets, etc.

Aguilar (ăh-ghē-lăhr'), **Emanuel Abraham,** English pianist and composer of Spanish descent; b. London, Aug. 23, 1824; d. there Feb. 18, 1904. He wrote a collection of canons and fugues as preparatory exercises for the playing of Bach; also composed 3 symphonies, 2 overtures, much chamber music and the operas, *Wave King* (1855) and *The Bridal Wreath* (1863).

Aguilera de Heredia, Sebastian, b. in [illegible]gon, c. 1565; d. in Saragossa after 1620. [illegible] organist at Huesca (1585-1603) [illegible] 'maestro de musica' at Saragossa [illegible] He published there his collection [illegible] *Beatissimae Virginis Deiparae Mariae octo modis seu tonis compositum, quaternisque vocibus, quinis, senis et octonis concionandum* (1618). It contains sacred choruses in 4, 5, 6 & 8 parts, derived from 8 church models. A 'magnificat' by him can be found in Eslava's 'Lira Sacro-Hispana'; an 'ensalada' is in J. Bonnet's Historical Organ Recitals, vol. VI (N. Y., 1940). His music is notable for skillful use of dissonances ('falsas').—Bibl.: H. Anglès, *Orgelmusik der Schola Hispanica von XV.-XVII. Jahrhunderte* in 'Peter Wagner-Festschrift' (Leipzig, 1926).

Aguirre (ăh-gēr'-rĕ), **Julián,** Argentine composer; b. Buenos Aires, Jan. 28, 1868; d. there, Aug. 13, 1924. He was taken to Spain as a child; studied at the Madrid Cons., returning to Buenos Aires in 1887. His works are mostly miniatures for piano in the form of stylized Argentine dances and songs. He wrote 61 opus numbers; *Gato* and *Huella* (op. 49), his most popular pieces, were orchestrated by Ansermet, who performed them in Buenos Aires (April 6, 1930); the *Huella* was also arranged for violin and piano by Jascha Heifetz. Other notable works are *Aires nacionales argentinos* (op. 17) and *Zamba* (op. 40). Bibl.: J. F. Giacobbe, *Julián Aguirre* (Buenos Aires, 1945).

Agujari (ăh-goo-yăh'-rē), **Lucrezia** (known as La Bastardina, or Bastardella, being the natural daughter of a nobleman), a brilliant Italian singer; b. Ferrara, 1743; d. Parma, May 18, 1783. Her father entrusted her instruction to P. Lambertini; in 1764 she made a triumphant debut at Florence, followed by a succession of brilliant appearances in Milan and other Italian cities; also in London. Mozart wrote of her, that she had "a lovely voice, a flexible throat, and an incredibly high range." In 1780 she married the Italian composer, Giuseppe Colla, whose songs she constantly performed at her concerts. Her compass was phenomenal, embracing 3 octaves (C^1-C^4).

Ahle, Johann Georg, German organist and composer (son of Johann Rudolf Ahle); b. Mühlhausen, June, 1651 (baptized June 12); d. there, Dec. 1, 1706. He succeeded his father as organist in Mühlhausen, and was made poet laureate by Emperor Leopold I. Among Ahle's works published during his lifetime are *Musikalische Frühlings-, Sommer-, Herbst-, und Wintergespräche* (1695-1701; written to illustrate his method of composition); *Instrumentalische Frühlingsmusik* (1676); *Anmuthige zehn vierstimmige Viol-di-gamba Spiele* (1681) and many volumes of dances, sacred and secular songs.

Ahle, Johann Rudolf, German composer; b. Mühlhausen, Dec. 24, 1625; d. there July 9, 1673. From 1646 he was cantor in Erfurt. He was organist of St. Blasius, Mühlhausen, in 1654, and in 1661 was elected burgomaster of the town. Ahle was a diligent composer of church music and writer of theoretical works. His *Compendium pro tonellis* (1648) ran through 4 editions; 2nd (1673) as *Brevis et perspicua introductio in artem musicum;* 3rd and 4th (1690 and 1704) as *Kurze und deutliche Anleitung.* His principal compositions include: *Geistliche Dialoge,* songs in several parts (1648); *Thüringischer Lustgarten* (1657); *Geistliche Fest- und Communionandachten* (posthumous). Many of his songs are still popular in Thuringia. A selection from his works was published by J. Wolf in 'Denkmäler deutscher Tonkunst' (vol. V).—Bibl.: J. Wolf, *Johann Rudolf Ahle* in 'Sammelbände der Internationalen Musik-Gesellschaft' (Leipzig, 1920, II, 3); A. Adrio in 'Die Musik in Geschichte und Gegenwart.'

Ahna. See **De Ahna.**

Ahrens, Joseph, German composer; b. Sommersell, Westphalia, April 17, 1904. He studied with his father; in 1925 became a church organist in Berlin; since 1950 prof. of church music at the Berlin Musikhochschule. He has written a great number of organ works in a modern baroque style (toccatas, partitas, fugues, etc.) which are highly esteemed by organists; also motets and solo cantatas and 5 masses with organ: *Missa gregoriana, Missa dorica, Missa choralis, Missa gotica* and *Missa hymnica.* He published a handbook on improvisation as a basic science in music pedagogy.

Aibl (ibl), **Joseph,** founder of a music publishing firm, established at Munich in 1824; his successors were Eduard Spitzweg (from 1836), and his sons, Eugen and Otto. In 1904 'Universal Edition' bought the Aibl firm.

Aiblinger, Johann Kaspar, German conductor and composer; b. Wasserburg, Bavaria, Feb. 23, 1779; d. Munich, May 6, 1867. He studied music in Munich, then at Bergamo under Simon Mayr (1802); lived at Vicenza (1803-11), then became second maestro di cappella to the viceroy at Milan; founded the 'Odeon' (a society for the cultivation of classical vocal music) at Venice, in collaboration with Abbé Trentino; was engaged (1819) for the Italian opera in Munich as maestro al cembalo; returned in 1833 to Bergamo, and made the fine collection of ancient classical music, now in the Staatsbibliothek at Munich. He wrote many sacred compositions (masses, requiems, liturgies, psalms, etc.), which were very popular. He also wrote an opera, *Rodrigo e Ximene* (Munich, 1821), and 3 ballets.

Aichinger, Gregor, important German church composer; b. Regensburg, 1564; d. Augsburg, Jan. 21, 1628. At the age of 13 he went to Munich where he was under the tutelage of Orlando Lasso; then entered the Univ. of Ingolstadt. He made two journeys to Rome; visited Venice where he mastered the art of Venetian polyphony. He eventually settled in Augsburg as choir master and vicar of the Cathedral. He wrote almost exclusively for voices, to Latin texts; his sacred works are remarkable for their practical value and for the excellence of their musical content. Among his many published works are 3 books of *Sacrae cantiones* (Venice, 1590; Augsburg, 1595; Nuremberg, 1597); *Tricinia Mariana* (Innsbruck, 1598); *Divinae laudes* (Augsburg, 1602) etc. His *Cantiones ecclesiasticae cum basso generali et continuo* (Dillingen, 1607) are noteworthy as one of the earliest works in which the term 'basso continuo' appears in the title. A selection of Aichinger's works is included in vol. X of 'Denkmäler der Tonkunst in Bayern,' prefaced with a biographical article by the editor, Th. Kroyer. See also E. Fr. Schmid's article in 'Die Musik in Geschichte und Gegenwart.'

Aitken, Webster, American pianist; b. Los Angeles, June 17, 1908. He studied in Europe with Sauer and Schnabel; made his professional debut in Vienna (1929). Returning to America, he played a concert in New York (Nov. 17, 1935); in 1938 gave a series of recitals in New York in programs comprising all of Schubert's piano works. He has also appeared with chamber music ensembles.

Akeroyde, Samuel, English composer of songs; b. Yorkshire, about 1650; d. London, after 1706. He was in the service of James II in 1687 as 'Musician in Ordinary,' and wrote songs for at least eight plays produced in London between 1685 and 1706. His songs were printed in several contemporary collections: Durfey's 'Third Collection of Songs' (1685); 'The Theatre of Musick' (1685-87); 'Vinculum Societatis' (1687); 'Comes Amoris' (1687-94); 'The Banquet of Musick' (1688); 'Thesaurus Musicus' (1693-96).

Akimenko (ah-kē-mĕn'-koh) **Fyodor Stepanovitch,** Russian composer; b. Kharkov, Feb. 20, 1876; d. Paris, Jan 8, 1945. He studied with Rimsky-Korsakov at the St. Petersburg Cons. (1886-90); then lived in Moscow and Kharkov. After the Russian revolution he settled in Paris. He wrote an opera *The Queen of the Alps* (unperformed); *Poème lyrique* for orch.; *Pastorale* for oboe and piano; *Petite ballade* for clarinet and piano, 2 Sonata-fantasias and numerous character pieces for piano, many of which were published by Belaiev.

Akses, Necil Kâzim, Turkish composer; b. Istanbul, May 6, 1908. He studied cello and theory at the Istanbul Cons. In 1926 he studied in Vienna with Joseph Marx; in Prague, with Alois Hába and Josef Suk (1931). Returning to Turkey in 1935, he became instructor at the Teachers' College in Ankara; he also took lessons with Hindemith, who was teaching there at the time. In 1936 Akses was appointed prof. of composition at the Ankara State Cons., and was its director in 1948-49. His music, derived from Turkish folk rhythms, is in the modern idiom. Works: *Mete,* one-act opera (1933); *Bayönder,* opera (Ankara, Dec. 27, 1934); incidental music to *Antigone* and *King Oedipus* (Sophocles); *Çiftetelli,* dance for orch. (1933); *Ankara Castle,* tone-poem (Ankara, Oct. 22, 1942); *Poem* for cello and orch. (Ankara, June 29, 1946); *Ballade* for orch. (Ankara, April 14, 1948); string quartet (1946); *Allegro feroce* for saxophone and piano (1931); flute sonata (1939) and piano pieces.

Akutagawa, Yasushi, Japanese composer; b. Tokyo, July 10, 1925. He studied at the Tokyo Academy of Music; has been particularly successful in writing for the ballet. The following ballets were produced in Tokyo: *The Dream of the Lake* (Nov. 6, 1950); *Paradise Lost* (March 17, 1951); *Kappa* (July 21, 1951). He has also written a symphonic triptych, which he conducted in Tokyo (Sept. 26, 1948).

Alain, Jehan, French composer, b. Paris, Feb. 3, 1911; killed in action at Petits-Puis, near Saumur, June 20, 1940. He composed his first piece *Etude sur un thème de quatre notes* at the age of 8; studied with his father, an organist; later with Marcel Dupré, Paul Dukas and Roger-Ducasse. Alain wrote 127 opus numbers, mostly for organ or piano. Bibl.: B. Gavoty, *Jehan Alain, Musicien Français* (Paris, 1945).

Alaleona, Domenico, Italian theorist and composer; b. Montegiorgio, Nov. 16, 1881; d. there, Dec. 28, 1928. He studied organ and clarinet in his native town; in 1901 went to Rome where he studied piano with Sgambati, organ with Renzi and theory with De Sanctis at Santa Cecilia; was then active as choral conductor in Leghorn and Rome; in 1911 obtained the post of prof. of musical esthetics at Santa Cecilia. He wrote an opera *Mirra* (1912; produced in Rome, March 31, 1920, with critical acclaim, but not revived); a *Requiem; Sinfonia italiana;* 12 *Canzoni italiane* and 4 *Laudi italiane* for various instrumental groups; a cycle of 18 songs *Melodie Pascoliane* and other works. However, his importance lies in his theoretical writings. His valuable book *Studii sulla storia dell' oratorio musicale in Italia* (Turin, 1908) was reprinted in Milan (1945) as *Storia dell' oratorio musicale in Italia,* and is now a standard work. A believer in musical progress, he contributed several original ideas to the theory of modern music, notably in his article *L'armonia modernissima* ('Rivista Musicale,' 1911), and originated the term 'dodecafonia.' He also contributed articles on Italian composers to Eaglefield-Hull's *Dictionary of Modern Music and Musicians* (London, 1924). The entry on Alaleona in that dictionary contains a complete list of his works and bibliography.

Alard (ăh-lăr'), **Jean-Delphin,** a distinguished violinist of the French school; b. Bayonne, March 8, 1815; d. Paris, Feb. 22, 1888. A pupil of Habeneck at Paris Cons. (1827), his celebrity dates from 1831; he succeeded Baillot as prof. in 1843, and as leader of the royal orchestra, teaching in the Cons. till 1875. A fine instructor (Sarasate was his pupil), he publ. a *Violin School* of high merit, a selection from 18th-century classics *(Les maîtres classiques du violon),* and numerous brilliant and popular pieces for violin (concertos, études, fantasias, etc.).

Alary, Jules (Giulio) Eugène Abraham, Italian-French composer; b. Mantua, March 16, 1814; d. Paris, April 17, 1891. He studied at the Cons. of Milan; then played the flute at La Scala. In 1838 he settled in Paris as a successful voice teacher and composer. He wrote numerous operas, among them *Rosamunda* (Florence, June 10, 1840); *Le tre nozze* (Paris, March 29, 1851; a polka-duet from it, sung by Henrietta Sontag and Lablache, was highly popular), and *Sardanapalo* (St. Petersburg, Feb. 16, 1852). His opera *La voix humaine* had the curious distinction of being staged at the Paris Opéra (Dec. 30, 1861) with the sole purpose of making use of the scenery left over after the fiasco of *Tannhäuser* (the action of Alary's opera takes place in Wartburg, as in *Tannhäuser).* It held the stage for 13 performances *(Tannhäuser* had three). Alary also wrote a mystery play *Redemption* (Paris, April 14, 1850), much sacred music and some chamber works.

Alayrac, d.' See **Dalayrac.**

Albanese, Licia, Italian-American soprano; b. Bari, July 22, 1913. She studied with Giuseppina Baldassare-Tedeschi; made her opera debut at Parma in *Madama Butterfly* (Dec. 10, 1935); sang the same role in her first appearance with the Metropolitan Opera (Feb. 9, 1940). She lived in Italy during World War II; returning to America in 1945, she sang with Toscanini and the NBC Symphony; also continued to appear with the Metropolitan Opera.

Albani (ăhl-băh'-nē), **Emma,** (stage name of Marie Louise Cecilia Emma Lajeunesse) Canadian dramatic soprano; b. Chambly, near Montreal, Nov. 1, 1847; d. London, April 3, 1930. She sang in a Catholic church in Albany, N.Y. in 1864; was then sent to Europe for study, first with Duprez in Paris, and then with Lamperti in Milan (Lamperti dedicated to her his treatise on the trill). She made her debut as Amina in *La Sonnambula* in Messina in 1870, under the name of Albani, in honor of the American city that gave her the first start. After further appearances in Italy, she made her London debut, again as Amina (Covent Garden, April 2, 1872). In 1873 she sang in Moscow and St. Petersburg. Her American operatic debut was in the same role at the New York Academy of Music, in Max Strakosch's company (Oct. 21, 1874). It paved the way for later successes with the Metropolitan Opera, where she made her first appearance as Gilda (Dec. 23, 1891). Her last important operatic engagement was as Isolde at Covent Garden (June 26, 1896). She sang in concerts, however, for several years longer. Her repertoire included Marguerite, Mignon, Ophelia, Elsa, Elisabeth, Lucia and Desdemona. Albani married Ernest Gye, the lessee of Covent Garden, in 1878. In her singing, she combined high technical skill with profound feeling. She was equally successful on the operatic stage and in oratorio. In appreciation of her services to British art, she was made a Dame of the British Empire (1925). She published her memoirs, *Emma Albani: Forty Years of Song* (London, 1911).

Albani, Mattia (real name Mathias Alban), violin maker; b. S. Niccolo di Kaltern (Alto Adige) March, 1621 (baptized March 28); d. Bolzano, Feb. 7, 1712. Pupil of Jakob Stainer. Violins of his are extant dating from as early as the end of 1644. His best examples date from 1680 onward. Owing to the great vogue his violins enjoyed, many Albani forgeries are in existence. A son, Giuseppe, his pupil, worked from 1680 to 1722 at Bolzano, and another son, Michele (1677-1730) at Graz. Other violin makers named Albani, or at least using the name on their instruments (perhaps for its commercial value) are the following, none appearing to have been connected with the family of the original Mattia: Mattia (Rome, c. 1650-1715); Nicola (worked at Mantua, c. 1763); Filippo (active c. 1773); Francesco (active at Graz, c. 1724); Michele (at Palermo, 18th cent.); and Paolo (at Palermo and Cremona, 1630-70).

Albéniz, Isaac, eminent Spanish composer; b. Camprodón, May 29, 1860; d. Cambo-Bains (Pyrénées), May 18, 1909. He exhibited precocious musical ability. When he was six, his mother took him to Paris, where he had a few private lessons with Marmontel. Upon his return to Spain, he gave concerts with his sister Clementine, also a child prodigy. In 1868 the family moved to Madrid, and Albéniz entered the Conservatory there. Possessed by a spirit of adventure, he ran away from home at the age of 13, and traveled in Spain, giving concerts. He then stowed away on a ship for Puerto Rico; from there he went to Cuba and to the U.S., supporting himself by playing concerts in private and in public. He returned to Spain in June, 1875, and was befriended in Madrid by Count Guillermo Morphy, who enabled him to undertake serious study, first at the Brussels Cons. with Brassin (piano) and Dupont and Gevaert (composition); and then at the Leipzig Cons. with Jadassohn and Reinecke. He went to Budapest in 1878 to meet Liszt, but it is doubtful that he actually became Liszt's pupil. Albéniz married Rosita Jordana in 1883; their daughter, Laura Albéniz, became a well known painter. In 1893 he settled in Paris; he also gave frequent piano recitals in Spain, and visited London. His early works were for the theater; he wrote several operas: *The Magic Opal* (London, Jan 19, 1893); *Enrico Clifford* (Barcelona, May 8, 1895); *San Antonio de la Florida* (Madrid, Oct. 26, 1894; also staged in Brussels, Jan. 3, 1905 under the title *Ermitage fleuri): Pepita Jiménez* (Barcelona, Jan. 5, 1896). He undertook the composition of an operatic trilogy *King Arthur,* of which only the first part, *Merlin,* was completed. In the meantime he met Felipe

Pedrell, and was greatly influenced by Pedrell's passionate championship of national Spanish music. Albéniz's first nationalistically inspired composition was the rhapsody *Catalonia* for piano and orch. (1899). In 1906-09 he wrote his most remarkable national work *Iberia,* a set of 12 piano pieces: *Evocación, El Puerto, Fête-Dieu à Seville, Rondeña, Almería, Triana, El Albaicín, El Polo, Lavapiés, Málaga, Jérez, Eritaña.* In this suite, which is a brilliant example of virtuoso writing for the instrument, Albéniz applied the impressionistic technique as developed by Debussy. He left unfinished two other piano works, *Azulejos* (completed by Granados) and *Navarra* (completed by D. de Sévérac; orchestrated by Fernández Arbós). Arbós also made effective orchestral transcriptions of *Evocación, Triana,* and *Fête-Dieu à Séville* (also orchestrated by Stokowski). Among Albéniz's smaller piano pieces, the *Seguidillas, Córdova,* and the Tango in D have attained wide popularity. Bibl.: J. de Marliave, *Etudes musicales* (Paris, 1917); G. Jean-Aubry, *Isaac Albéniz,* in the 'Musical Times' (Dec. 1917); H. Klein, *Albéniz's Opera, Pepita Jiménez,* in the 'Musical Times' (March, 1918); G. Jean-Aubry, *La Musique et les Nations* (Paris, 1922; English translation, 1923); Henri Collet, *Albéniz et Granados* (1925); E. Istel, *Albéniz,* in the 'Mus. Quarterly' (Jan., 1929); A. de las Heras, *Vida de Albéniz* (Barcelona, 1940); M. Raux Deledicque, *Albéniz, su vida inquieta y ardorosa* (Buenos Aires, 1950); A. Sagardia, *Isaac Albéniz* (Buenos Aires, 1951).

Albéniz, Mateo (Antonio Perez de), Spanish composer; date of birth unknown; d. St. Sebastian, June 23, 1831; was a church organist; published *Instrucción melódica especulativa y practica para enseñar a cantar y a tañer la música antigua* (S. Sebastian, 1802). His sonata for piano was published by Joaquín Nín in *16 Sonates anciennes d'auteurs espagnols* (Paris, 1925).

Albéniz, Pedro, Spanish organist and composer; son of Mateo Albéniz; b. Logroño, April 14, 1795; d. Madrid, April 12, 1855. He studied with his father; from his early youth played the organ in various Spanish towns; later studied piano in Paris with Kalkbrenner and Henri Herz. In 1830 he was appointed prof. of piano at the Madrid Cons.; in 1834 became court organist. He was an energetic promoter of modern methods of piano playing in Spain. He published a manual (1840) which was adopted at the Madrid Cons.; also wrote some 70 piano pieces in a highly developed technical style (rondos, variations, medleys, etc.).

Albergati, Pirro Capacelli, Conte d', Italian composer; b. Carrati, Sept. 20, 1663; d. Bologna, June 22, 1735. He wrote 2 operas, *Gli amici* (Bologna, Aug. 16, 1699) and *Il Principe selvaggio* (Bologna, 1712), and numerous oratorios which were regularly performed at various churches in Bologna (1686-1732): *Nabuccodonosor; Giobbe; S. Orsola; Il convito di Baldassarre; L'innocenza di S. Eufemia; S. Catarina; S. Eustachio; Maria annunciata dall' angelo; La morte di Cristo;* etc. Besides these works, Albergati published during his lifetime 15 opus numbers, consisting of vocal and instrumental music, among them *Balletti, Correnti, Cantate morali, Cantate spirituali, Messa e salmi, Cantate da camera, Motetti et antifone, Capricci,* 12 sonatas for 2 violins and bass, etc.

Alberghetti, Anna Maria, Italian soprano; b. Rodi, May 5, 1936. She first sang in public at the age of 6; gave recitals in Milan at 9. She came to America in 1950; made her debut in Carnegie Hall; has also appeared in films.

Albert, Heinrich, German composer; b. Lobenstein, Saxony, July 8, 1604; d. Königsberg, Oct. 6, 1651. In 1622 he went to Dresden to study music with his cousin Heinrich Schütz; then studied law at the Univ. of Leipzig; traveled to Warsaw with a peace delegation in 1627, but was seized as a prisoner of war by the Swedes; upon his release in 1628 he settled in Königsberg; was appointed cathedral organist in 1631; took courses with Johann Stobäus. He publ. in Königsberg 8 books of arias (1638-50); a cantata *Musikalische Kürbs-Hütte* (1645) consisting of a cycle of 12 terzets to Albert's own texts (a modern reprint was issued by J. M. Müller-Blattau in 1932). A selection of his songs is found in the 'Neudrucke deutscher Litteraturwerke' (Halle, 1883); the arias in volumes XII and XIII of 'Denkmäler deutscher Tonkunst.' Bibl.: L. H. Fischer, *Gedichte des Königsberger Dichterkreises* (Halle, 1883); H. J. Moser, *Corydon* (1933).

d'Albert (dahl-bär'), **Eugène (Francis Charles),** British-born German pianist and composer; b. Glasgow, April 10, 1864; d. Riga, March 3, 1932. His father, Charles Louis Napoleon d'Albert (b. Nienstetten, near Hamburg, Feb. 25, 1809; d. London, May 26, 1886), was a dancing master who wrote popular music; it was from him that d'Albert received his early instruction in music. At the age of 12 he entered the National Training School in London, where he studied piano with Pauer and theory with Stainer, Prout and Sir Arthur Sullivan. He made extraordinary progress both as pianist and composer, and after several appearances at the Popular Concerts, was the soloist in Schumann's concerto at the Crystal Palace, London (Feb. 5, 1881). On Oct. 24, 1881, when only 17, he played his own piano concerto at one of Hans Richter's concerts, arousing great enthusiasm; the press compared him to Mozart and Mendelssohn. He received a Mendelssohn fellowship, and went to Vienna; later he studied with Liszt, who was greatly impressed by his technique and often referred to him as 'the young Tausig.' In 1895, d'Albert was appointed conductor at Weimar; in 1907, became director of the High School for Music in Berlin. In the wake of his success, he repudiated his English birth, adopting German citizenship, and made repeated statements derogatory to English culture and even to his former English teachers. He was vocal in his enmity to England during the first World War, which led in turn to an understandable repugnance among British musicians to accept his music. D'Albert composed industriously. He published two piano concertos (in B minor and E); a cello concerto in C; 2 overtures (*Hyperion* and *Esther);* a symphony in F; an orchestral suite in 5 movements (1924); a piano sonata, a piano suite in 5 movements; 2 string quartets; *Der Mensch und das Leben* for 6-part chorus and orch. (op. 14); 4 piano pieces, op. 16 *(Waltz, Scherzo, Intermezzo, Ballade),* minor piano pieces and songs. However, his main interest was in the field of opera. Of his 20 operas, the most successful were: *Tiefland,* first staged at the German opera in Prague (Nov. 15, 1903), and *Die toten Augen* (Dresden, March 5, 1916). The list of his other operas includes: *Der Rubin* (Karlsruhe, Oct. 12, 1893); *Ghismonda* (Dresden, Nov. 28, 1895); *Gernot* (Mannheim, April 11, 1897); *Die Abreise* (Frankfurt, Oct. 20, 1898); *Kain* (Berlin, Feb. 17, 1900); *Der Improvisator* (Berlin, Feb. 20, 1902); *Flauto solo* (Prague, Nov. 12, 1905); *Tragaldabas* (or *Der geborgte Ehemann;* Hamburg, Dec. 3, 1907); *Izeyl* (Hamburg, Nov. 6, 1909); *Die verschenkte Frau* (Vienna, Feb. 6, 1912); *Liebesketten* (Vienna, Nov. 12, 1912); *Der Stier von Olivera* (Leipzig, March 10, 1918); *Revolutionshochzeit* (Leipzig, Oct. 26, 1919); *Sirocco* (Darmstadt, May 18, 1921); *Mareike von Nymwegen* (Hamburg, Oct. 31, 1923); *Der Golem* (Frankfurt, Nov. 14 1926); *Die schwarze Orchidee* (Leipzig, Dec. 1, 1928); *Mister Wu* (unfinished; completed by Leo Blech; Dresden, Sept. 29, 1932). Despite a brilliant beginning, Eugène d'Albert did not justify his early promise, and his operas and other works are rarely revived. His musical idiom oscillates between the Italian melodic style and German contrapuntal writing, and fails to achieve originality. Eugène d'Albert's personal life was a stormy one. He was married six times; his first wife was Teresa Carreño (1892-95); his second was the singer, Hermine Finck. — Cf. W. Raupp, *Eugen d'Albert: ein Künstler- und Menschenschicksal* (Leipzig, 1930).

Albert, Karel, Belgian composer; b. Antwerp, April 16, 1901. He studied at the Cons. of Antwerp; conducted a traveling theater company (1926-31); later was active as music critic. He has written a ballet *The Magic Lantern* (1943); a number of scores of incidental music; 4 symphonies; several symph. poems and smaller works.

Albert, Prince Consort of Queen Victoria, b. Rosenau, Coburg, Aug. 26, 1819; d. Windsor, Dec. 14, 1861. He married Queen Victoria on Feb. 10, 1840; lent energetic support to musical activities in England, sponsoring orchestras and choral societies. He studied organ and theory, and acquired an estimable technique of composition; wrote *Invocazione alla armonia* for chorus and orch. His songs were published in 1881 under the title *The Collected Compositions of his Royal Highness the Prince Consort.* They reveal a romantic musical temper, influenced by Mendelssohn.

Alberti, Domenico, Venetian composer; b. Venice, 1710; d. Formio, or Rome, c. 1740. He studied with Lotti, and won considerable renown as singer and harpsichord player; wrote 3 operas, *Endimione, Galatea,* and *Olimpiade.* In 1737 he was a member of the Venetian Embassy in Rome, and made several appearances there as singer and player. His fame in music history rests on his reputed invention of the arpeggio style of keyboard accompaniment, which became known as the 'Alberti Bass'. His set of 8 sonatas, published by Walsh in London, gives many illustrations of this device.

Albertsen, Per Hjort, Norwegian composer; b. Trondheim, July 27, 1919. He studied architecture, then turned to music; was church organist in Trondheim; later studied with Tarp in Copenhagen. He has written a concertino for flute and orch.; an oratorio *Bendik og Arolilja;* choruses and piano pieces.

Albini, Srecko, Croatian composer and conductor; b. Zupanja, Dec. 10, 1869; d. Zagreb, April 18, 1933. He studied music in Vienna; then was theater conductor in Graz and Zagreb. He composed an opera *Maricon;* a ballet *The Lake of Plotvice;* the operettas *Nabob, Madame Troubadour, Baron Trenk* (1908; achieved considerable popularity); piano pieces and songs.

Albinoni, Tomaso, Italian violinist and composer; b. Venice, June 8, 1671; d. there, Jan. 17, 1750. Between 1694 and 1740 he produced 45 operas, most of them in Venice. He rarely absented himself from Venice, but it is known that he attended the premiere of his opera *Griselda* in Florence (1703); in 1722 he was in Munich where he presented his festive opera *I veri amici.* It is, however, as a composer of instrumental music that he is significant; Bach, his close contemporary, admired Albinoni's music; made arrangements of two fugues from Albinoni's trio-sonatas (Bach Gesellschaft, Nos. 437, 438). The following works are available in modern editions: violin concerto (ed. by Vieweg); 2 violin sonatas and a trio-sonata (ed. by Nagel); organ transcriptions of 2 violin concertos (ed. by Walther); flute sonata (ed. by Schäffler); 3 oboe concertos (ed. by B. Paumgartner, London, 1948). A detailed catalogue of Albinoni's works and a thematic analysis are given by R. Giazotto in his exhaustive monograph, *Tomaso Albinoni* (Milan, 1945).

Albonese, Afranio. See **Afranio.**

Alboni, Marietta (real name, Maria Anna Marzia Alboni), famous Italian contralto; b. Cesena, March 6, 1823; d. Ville d'Avray, France, June 23, 1894. She studied in Bologna with Monbelli; in 1841 was introduced to Rossini who agreed to give her lessons. She made her debut in Bologna, in Pacini's opera *Saffo* (Oct. 3, 1842); shortly afterwards, sang at La Scala in Rossini's *Assedio di Corinto* (Dec. 30, 1842). She then sang in Russia, and obtained great success during the season of 1844-45 in St. Petersburg, appearing at the Italian opera with Tamburini, Rubini and Mme. Viardot. After appearances in Prague, Berlin and Hamburg, she appeared in the spring of 1847 in Rome and at Covent Garden where she became a rival of Jenny Lind with the public. So successful were her London appearances that her fees were increased to 2,000 pounds a season. She gave four 'concerts-spectacles' in Paris in Oct., 1847; made her Paris opera debut in Rossini's *Semiramide* (Dec. 2, 1847). Auber wrote the opera *Zerlinda* for her, and she sang at its premiere (May 16, 1851). She made an American tour from June, 1852, till May, 1853, in concert and opera, appearing in New York, Boston and other cities. On July 21, 1853, Alboni married Count Pepoli (d. Oct. 10, 1867); on Jan. 22, 1877 she married Charles Ziéger, a French officer, and settled in France. Suffering from excessive obesity, she gradually retired from the stage, but continued to appear occasionally in concert, singing while sitting in a large chair. Her vocal range was exceptional, from the contralto G to high soprano C, enabling her to sing soprano parts. She bequeathed a large sum of money to the City of Paris. In appreciation, the City Council, on Oct. 15, 1895, named a street in Passy after her. Arthur Pougin's monograph *Marietta Alboni* (Paris, 1912) quotes many of her autobiographical notes and presents a documented outline of her career.

Albrecht, Evgeny Karlovitch, Russian conductor; son of Karl Albrecht and brother of Konstantin Albrecht; b. St. Petersburg, July 16, 1842; d. there, Feb. 9, 1894. He studied violin with Ferdinand David at the Leipzig Cons. (1857-60). Upon his return to Russia he conducted the Italian opera in St. Petersburg (1860-77); was also musical director of military schools there (1872-77). In 1877 he became inspector of the Imperial Orchestras; in 1892 was music librarian of the Imperial Theaters. He published 3 albums of Russian folksongs and a book of 128 children's songs.

Albrecht, Hans, German musicologist; b. Magdeburg, March 31, 1902. He studied at the Univ. of Berlin (1921-25); then taught music in Essen (1925-37). During World War II was prof. at the State Institute in Berlin (1939-45); from 1947 prof. at the Univ. of Kiel. He has publ. a valuable monograph *Kaspar Othmayr, Leben und Werke* (Kassel, 1943); several other papers of documentary significance remain in manuscript.

Albrecht, Johann Lorenz, German music scholar; b. Görmar (Thuringia), Jan. 8, 1732; d. Mühlhausen, 1773. He studied at Leipzig; edited Adlung's *Musica mechanica* and *Siebengestirn* (Berlin, 1768); wrote an essay *Abhandlung über die Frage: ob die Musik beim Gottesdienst zu dulden sei oder nicht* (1764), a manual *Gründliche Einleitung in die Anfangslehren der Tonkunst* (1761), and a treatise *Vom Hasse der Musik* (1765); contributed articles to Marpurg's 'Kritische Beiträge,' etc. He also composed several cantatas.

Albrecht, Karl, German-Russian conductor; father of Konstantin and Evg. Albrecht; b. Posen, Aug. 27, 1807; d. Gatchina, Feb. 24, 1863. He came to Russia in 1838; for 12 years (1838-50) was conductor at the Imperial Theaters, and gave the first performance of Glinka's opera *Russlan and Ludmilla* (1842).

Albrecht, Konstantin Karlovitch, Russian cellist; son of Karl Albrecht and brother of Evgeny Albrecht; b. Elberfeld, Oct. 4, 1836; d. Moscow, June 26, 1893. He was brought to Moscow by his father at the age of 2 and received his musical education from him. In 1854 he became a member of the orch. of the Moscow Opera. In 1860 he collaborated with Nicholas Rubinstein in organizing the Moscow Cons.; in 1866 he was appointed inspector there; also taught elementary theory. He was an intimate friend of Tchaikovsky and was a notable figure in the Moscow musical world. He published a manual on solfeggio and compiled several collections of choral works.

Albrecht, Max, German composer and conductor; b. Chemnitz, March 14, 1890. He studied in Leipzig with Reger; conducted opera in Chemnitz (1911-13), and in Neisse (1914-15); then lived in Dresden. He wrote the operas *Neros Ende* (1927); *Rama und Sita* (1929); *Amosa* (1930); *Die Brücke* (1932); a cantata *Marathon;* 2 symph. poems, and a number of songs.

Albrecht, Otto Edwin, American musicologist; b. Philadelphia, July 8, 1899. He studied at the Univ. of Pennsylvania (A.B., 1921; M.A., 1925; Ph.D., 1931); then became lecturer in music and curator of the Music Library there and in 1941 vice-pres. of the Music Library Association. His writings include *Four Latin Plays of St. Nicholas* (Philadelphia and London, 1935); *Brahms and von Bülow; 18th-century Music in the Univ. Library; Francis Hopkinson* (Univ. of Pennsylvania Library 'Chronicle,' 1934, 1936, 1938); *Microfilm Archives and Musicology* (American Musicological Soc. *Papers, 1938*); *A Census of Autograph Music Manuscripts of European Composers in American Libraries* (Philadelphia, 1953).

Albrechtsberger, Johann Georg, famous Austrian theoretical writer, composer and teacher; b. Klosterneuburg, near Vienna, Feb. 3, 1736; d. Vienna, March 7, 1809. After holding positions as organist and music-master in smaller towns (especially 12 years in Melk, where his fine playing attracted the Emperor Joseph's notice), in 1772 he was engaged in Vienna as 'Regens chori' to the Carmelites; app. court organist in the same year, and, in 1792, Kapellm. At St. Stephen's cathedral. His important theoretical writings (complete ed. publ. by Seyfried) are: *Gründliche Anweisung zur Composition* (1790 and 1818; French ed., 1814); *Kurzgefasste Methode, den Generalbass zu erlernen* (1792; also in French); *Clavierschule für Anfänger* (1808); and some lesser essays. Of his 244 compositions, only 27 have been printed (fugues; piano quartet; a *Concerto léger* for piano, 2 violins and bass; organ preludes; quartets, quintets, sextets, octets for strings); the MS. scores (in the possession of Prince Esterhazy-Galantha) comprise 26 masses, 43 graduals, 34 offertories, 6 oratorios; 28 trios, 42 quartets, and 38 quintets for strings; besides a great variety of church music. A selection from his instrumental works was publ. in 'Denkmäler der Tonkunst in Österreich,' vol. XVI, 2. He had many celebrated pupils, among whom was Beethoven (from Jan., 1794 to March, 1795). Scholars regard the quality of instruction he gave to Beethoven as of a very high order. Cf. A. Weissenbäck, *J. G. Albrechtsberger als Kirchenkomponist,* in 'Studien zur Musikwissenschaft' (vol. 14, 1927); R. Oppell, *Albrechtsberger als Bindeglied zwischen Bach und Beethoven,* in 'Neue Zeitschrift für Musik' (May 18, 1911).

Alcock, John, Sr., English organist; b. London, April 11, 1715; d. Lichfield, Feb. 23, 1806. He was a chorister at St. Paul's Cathedral; then studied with the blind organist, Stanley. Subsequently he held positions as organist at St. Andrew's Church, Plymouth (1737), St. Lawrence's Church, Reading (1742), Lichfield Cathedral (1750), etc. In 1761 he took the degree of D. Mus. at Oxford. He published several suites for harpsichord, and collections of anthems and other sacred choral works. He wrote numerous glees, for which he obtained prizes from the Catch Club. His son, also named **John** (b. Plymouth, 1740; d. Walsall, Staffs., March 30, 1791) was organist at various churches and author of anthems.

Alda, Frances (real name Frances Davies), lyric soprano; b. Christchurch, New Zealand, May 31, 1883; d. Venice, Sept. 18, 1952. She studied with Marchesi in Paris, and made her debut as Manon at the Opéra-Comique (April 15, 1904). She later sang in Brussels, London, Milan, Warsaw and Buenos Aires. Her debut at the Metropolitan Opera was on Dec. 7, 1908 (opposite Caruso in *Rigoletto);* her farewell appearance there, on Dec. 28, 1929 in *Manon*

Lescaut. She also made numerous recital tours in the U.S. Her principal roles included Louise, Mimi, Manon, Marguerite, Juliette, Gilda, Violetta and Aida. She married Giulio Gatti-Casazza, manager of the Metropolitan Opera, on April 3, 1910; divorced, 1928; married Ray Vir Den in 1941. In 1939 she became an American citizen. She wrote an autobiography *Men, Women and Tenors* (Boston, 1937).

Alden, John Carver, American pianist and teacher; b. Boston, Sept. 11, 1852; d. Cambridge, Mass., Oct. 20, 1935. He studied with Carl Faelten and was later associated with him at the New England Cons.; also took lessons with Plaidy at the Leipzig Cons. He wrote a piano concerto and several songs to German texts.

Alderighi, Dante, Italian composer and pianist; b. Taranto, July 7, 1898. He went to Rome as a child and studied with Giovanni Sgambati; from 1911-14 he was in Leipzig, studying piano with Teichmüller and theory with Krehl. Returning to Italy, he took lessons in composition with Malipiero; gave many recitals and began to write music criticism. In 1936 he was appointed prof. of piano at Santa Cecilia in Rome. He has written two piano concertos; *Fantasia* for piano and chamber orch. (1932); *Rococo Suite* for band (1932; revised 1952); oratorio, *Maria a Nazareth* (1949); *Divertimento* for piano and strings (1952); also many choral works.

Aldrich, Henry, English music scholar; b. Westminster, 1647; d. Oxford, Dec. 14, 1710. A man of versatile talents, excelling in music, but also distinguished as an architect, theologian, linguist and logician. He was educated at Christ Church, Oxford, receiving the degree of M.A. in 1669; in 1681 he became a canon, and in 1689, Dean of Christ Church, and exercised decisive influence on the teaching of music and other arts. He wrote the learned works: *On the Commencement of Greek Music; Theory of Organ-building; Theory of Modern Instruments;* composed several services (one of which, in G, is still sung); and, in a lighter vein, glees and catches (among them the popular *Catches on Tobacco).* The collections of Boyce, Arnold and Page contain numerous pieces by Aldrich.

Aldrich, Perley Dunn, American vocal teacher; b. Blackstone, Mass., Nov. 6, 1863; d. Philadelphia, Nov. 20, 1933. He studied at the New England Cons. (1883-86); then took singing lessons with William Shakespeare in London (1892-95) and with Sbriglia in Paris (1903); acted as Sbriglia's assistant in the summer classes in 1904 and 1908. He settled as vocal teacher in Philadelphia; was the first head of the vocal dept. at the Curtis Inst. He published a volume *Vocal Economy* (1895); composed several choruses, among them *The Sleeping Wood Nymph* for mixed voices (1896).

Aldrich, Putnam (Calder), American harpsichord player and musicologist; b. South Swansea, Mass., July 14, 1904. He studied at Yale Univ. (B.A., 1926); then went to Europe and took piano lessons with Tobias Matthay in London (1926-27) and harpsichord with Wanda Landowska in Paris (1929-33); later took his Ph. D. at Harvard Univ. (1942). He has given harpsichord recitals and played harpsichord solos with the Boston Symph. Orch.; in 1950 he was appointed associate prof. at Stanford Univ., California. He published a brief treatise, *Ornamentation in J. S. Bach's Organ Works* (New York, 1950) which is part of an important and much larger work (his Harvard dissertation) on 17th- and 18th-century ornamentation, which has not yet been published.

Aldrich, Richard, American music critic; b. Providence, July 31, 1863; d. Rome, June 2, 1937. He studied with Paine at Harvard Univ., graduating in 1885. He then was music critic of the 'Providence Journal' (1885-89) and 'Evening Star' (1889-91). From 1891-1901 he was assistant to H. E. Krehbiel on the 'N. Y. Tribune,' then became music editor of the 'N. Y. Times' (1902-23). A selection of his articles from the 'N. Y. Times' were published in *Musical Discourse* (1928) and, posthumously, in *Concert Life in New York,* 1902-1923 (1941). He also wrote *Guide to Parsifal* (1904) and *Guide to the Ring of the Nibelung* (1905). His critical writings were urbane and witty; while liberal-minded in regard to milder types of modern music, he vehemently opposed its extreme trends.

Aldrovandini, Giuseppe (Antonio Vincenzo), Italian composer; b. Bologna, 1665; d. there, Feb. 9, 1707, when, under the influence of alcohol, he fell into a canal and was drowned. He studied with Giacomo Perti at the Bologna Philharmonic Academy, taught there from 1695, and in 1702 became its head ('principe'). Among his 15 operas, the following were produced in Bologna: *Gli inganni amorosi* (Jan. 28, 1696); *Dafni* (Aug. 10, 1696); *Le due Auguste* (Aug. 16, 1700); *I tre rivali in soglio* (posthumously, Jan. 2, 1711). He also wrote a 'sinfonia' and much church music (6 oratorios, motets, etc.), some published in his lifetime.

d'Alembert (dăh-lăhn-băr'), **Jean-le Rond,** French philosopher and encyclopedist; b. Paris, Nov. 16, 1717; d. there, Oct. 29, 1783. He was the illegitimate child of one Mme. de Tencin and an artillery officer named Destouches; his mother abandoned him on the steps of the church of St. Jean-le-Rond, which name was subsequently attached to him. Later, his father acknowledged him, and enabled him to study. He was sent to the Mazarin College, and progressed rapidly in mathematics. He also was interested in theoretical musical subjects, and published several treatises on acoustics and on the theory of music: *Recherches sur la courbe, que forme une corde tendue mise en vibration* (1749); *Recherches sur les vibrations des cordes sonores* and *Recherches sur la vitesse du son* (both in 'Opuscules mathématiques,' Paris, 1761-80). He contributed several articles on music to the famous 'Encyclopédie,' which he edited with Diderot. He publ. further, *Reflexions sur la musique en général et sur la musique française en particulier* (1754); *Reflexions sur la théorie de la musique* (1777). His best known work on music was *Éléments de musique, théorique et pratique, suivant les principes de M. Rameau* (1752), which went into 6 editions. Bibl.: J. Bertrand, *d'Alembert* (Paris, 1889).

Alessandrescu, Alfred, Rumanian composer and conductor; b. Bucharest, Aug. 14, 1893. He studied with Vincent d'Indy at the Schola Cantorum in Paris, graduating in 1914. He was director of the Bucharest Philh. Orch. (1926-40); music director of the Bucharest Radio (1933-47). He has written a symph. poem *Acteon* (Paris, 1920; New York, 1938); an overture *Didon;* chamber music and songs.

Alessandri, Felice, Italian opera composer; b. Rome, Nov. 24, 1742; d. Casinalbo, Aug. 15, 1798. He studied music in Naples; then lived in Paris (1765-68) and in London (1768). From 1784-89 he was in Russia; then in Berlin as a second conductor at the Royal Opera (1789-92), finally returning to Italy. Alessandri wrote about 30 operas in all. Two were produced in London: *La Moglie fedele* (1768) and *Il re alla caccia* (1769); and two at La Scala in Milan: *Calliroe* (Dec. 26, 1778) and *Ezio* (Feb. 1, 1782). In Potsdam he produced *Il ritorno di Ulisse* (Jan. 25, 1790); *Dario* (1791), and the comic opera *La compagnia d'opera a Nanchino* (1790), which exhibited the colorful effects of pseudo-Chinese music. His opera *Virginia* was given in Venice (Dec. 26, 1793). He also wrote an oratorio *Betulia liberata* (1781); *6 sinfonie* in 8 parts; 6 trio-sonatas for 2 violins and basso continuo, etc., all in the then prevalent Italian manner. Cf. L. Valdrighi, *Felice Alessandri* (1896).

d'Alessandro, Rafaele, Swiss composer; b. Gallen, March 17, 1911. He studied with Victor Schlatter and Willi Schuh in Zürich; then with Nadia Boulanger and Marcel Dupré in Paris. Gave concerts as organist in Switzerland; eventually settled in Lausanne. He has written a symphony (1948); *Concerto Grosso* for string orch. (1950); 3 piano concertos; 2 string quartets, etc.

Alessandro, Victor, American conductor; b. Waco, Texas, Nov. 27, 1915. He studied the French horn with his father; composition with Howard Hanson and Bernard Rogers at the Eastman School of Music, Rochester, N. Y. He went to Italy and took courses at the Santa Cecilia in Rome (1938). Returning to the U.S. he became conductor of the Oklahoma Symph. Orch. (1938-51) and of the San Antonio Orch. (1952).

Alexander, Josef, American composer; b. Boston, May 15, 1910. He studied at the New England Cons. of Music and at Harvard Univ.; was active as a pianist; then devoted himself to composition. He has written 2 symphonies; a piano concerto; *Epitaphs* for orch.; *Dialogue Spirituel* for soprano, chorus and orch.; *Clockwork* for string orch.; *Campus Suite* for band; piano quintet; string quartet; piano trio, etc.

Alexandre, Jacob, French organ builder; b. Paris, 1804; d. there, June 11, 1876. In 1829 he established a firm of harmonium manufacturers, which introduced the 'Alexandre' organ, a development of the so-called 'American organ' (1874).

Alexandrov, Alexander Vasilievitch, Russian composer; b. Plakhino (Riazan Govt.), April 1, 1883; d. Berlin, during a concert tour, July 8, 1946. He studied with Rimsky-Korsakov and Glazunov at the St. Petersburg Cons. (1899-1901) and later at the Moscow Cons. with Vassilenko (1909-1913). In 1928 he organized the Red Army Ensemble and conducted it on numerous tours in Russia and abroad. His song *Hymn of the Bolshevik Party,* with a new set of words, was proclaimed as the Soviet national anthem on March 15, 1944.

Alfano, Franco, eminent Italian composer; b. Posilippo (Naples), March 8, 1876; d. San Remo, Oct. 26, 1954. He studied composition with Paolo Serrao in Naples, and with Jadassohn and Hans Sitt in Leipzig. From the beginning of his musical career, Alfano was interested in opera. His first stage work *Miranda* was produced in Leipzig when he was barely 20; another opera, *La Fonte di Enscir,* followed (Breslau, Nov. 8, 1898). In 1900 he went to Paris and became fascinated by light theater music. While in Paris he wrote a folk ballet *Napoli* which was staged at Folies-Bergères (Jan. 28, 1901), proving so successful that it ran for 160 successive performances. Returning to Italy, he began work on an opera after Tolstoy's novel *Resurrection.* It was produced as *Risurrezione,* in Turin (Nov. 4, 1904) with sensational acclaim; the American premiere (Chicago, Dec. 31, 1925) was equally successful; there were also numerous performances in Germany and France. The opera was widely praised for its dramatic power and melodic richness in the best tradition of realistic Italian opera. Alfano continued to compose industriously for another half-century, but his later operas failed to equal the success of *Risurrezione.* They are: *Il Principe Zilah* (Genoa, Feb. 3, 1909); *L'ombra di Don Giovanni* (La Scala, Milan, April 3, 1914); *La Leggenda di Sakuntala* (Bologna, Dec. 10, 1921); *Madonna Imperia,* lyric comedy (Turin, May 5, 1927; Met. Opera, N. Y., Feb. 8, 1928); *L'Ultimo Lord* (Naples, April 19, 1930); *Cyrano de Bergerac* (Rome, Jan. 22, 1936); *Il Dottor Antonio* (Rome, April 30, 1949). Alfano also wrote 3 symphonies (1909; 1932; 1934); 3 string quartets, a violin sonata, a cello sonata, and a ballet *Vesuvius* (1938; a symphonic poem was drawn from it in 1946). One of Alfano's signal achievements was that he completed Puccini's last opera, *Turandot,* adding the last scene. His *Hymn to Bolivar,* for chorus and orch., written for the centennial of Bolivar's death, was performed in Caracas, Venezuela, on Dec. 22, 1930. He was also active in the field of musical education; was successively director of the 'Liceo musicale' in Bologna (1919-23); of the Turin Cons. (1923-39); superintendent of the Teatro Massimo in Palermo (1940-42), and from 1947, director of the Rossini Cons. in Pesaro. — Bibl.: G. M. Gatti, *Franco Alfano* in 'Musicisti moderni d'Italia e di fuori,' (Bologna, 1920; also in the 'Musical Times,' March, 1921); G. Cesàri, *La leggenda di Sakuntala di Franco Alfano* in the 'Rivista Musicale Italiana' (Turin, 1921); Andrea della Corte, *Rittrato di Franco Alfano* (Turin, 1935). Ettore Desderi published a list of Alfano's works in 'Bolletino bibliografico musicale' (Milan, 1931).

Alfarabi, or **Alpharabius,** properly Al Farabi (abbr. Farabi) so named from his birthplace Farab (now transoxine Othrâx), Arabian music theorist; b. c. 870; d. Damascus, c. 950. Of Turkish descent, he became renowned through his writings on philosophy, political science and the arts. He was a Greek scholar and attempted unsuccessfully to introduce the Greek musical system into his country. His principal work is *Kitab al-musiqi al-kabir* ('Greater Book about Music') dealing with acoustics, intervals, scales, instruments and rhythm. The 2nd volume of this work was lost. Excepts from this book are contained in Kosegarten's *Alii Ispahanis Liber Cantilenarum Magnus* (1840) and in J. Land's *Recherches sur l'histoire de la gamme arabe* (Leyden, 1884). See also M. Steinschneider, *Al-Farabi* (St. Petersburg, 1869); Baron d'Erlanger, *La Musique arabe,* vol. I (Paris, 1930); E. A. Beichert, *Die Wissenschaft der Musik bei Al-Farabi* (Regensburg, 1931); H. G. Farmer, *Al-Farabi's Arabic-Latin Writings on Music* (Glasgow, 1934).

Alferaky, Achilles Nikolayevitch, Russian composer of Greek origin; b. Taganrog, July 3, 1846; d. Petrograd, 1920. He studied in Moscow with V. Suk (1884); wrote an opera *St. John's Eve* and numerous songs and piano pieces of considerable merit, in a romantic Russian style mainly influenced by Tchaikovsky; most of these were published by Belaiev.

Alfieri, Pietro, Italian music scholar; b. Rome, June 29, 1801; d. there, June 12, 1863. He was a member of the Camaldolese Order; taught Gregorian music at the English College in Rome. His major work is *Raccolta di musica sacra* (1841-46), a collection of 16th-century church music in 7 vols., which includes virtually all representative works of Palestrina; other collections are *Excerpta ex celebrioribus de musica viris* (Rome, 1840), containing works by Palestrina, Victoria and Allegri; *Raccolta di motetti* (1841), etc. His essays on Gregorian chant are very valuable: *Ristabilimento del canto e della musica ecclesiastica* (1843); *Saggio storico del canto gregoriano* (1855); *Prodromo sulla restaurazione de' libri di canto ecclesiastico detto gregoriano* (1857), etc.; he also publ. a biography of N. Jommelli (1845) and contributed articles on musical subjects to Italian periodicals.

Alford, Violet, English writer and lecturer on folk dancing; b. Bristol, March, 1881. She studied at London Univ., and at the Royal Academy of Music. She has published valuable compendia on folk music and dance: *English Folk Dances* (1923); *The Traditional Dance* (with Rodney Gallop; 1935); *Pyrenean Festivals* (1937); *Introduction to English Folklore* (1952). She also composed *A Folk Masque,* showing origins and development of the folk dance.

Alfvén, Hugo, outstanding Swedish composer; b. Stockholm, May 1, 1872. He studied at the Stockholm Cons., and played the violin in the Court Orch. He was then sent by the government to Belgium where he studied violin with César Thomson (1896-99). In 1900 he received the Jenny Lind stipend for three years. In 1910 he became musical director at the Univ. of Uppsala and conductor of the student chorus there until 1939 when he retired. His best known work is *Midsommarvaka (Midsummer Vigil,* 1904), the first of his three Swedish rhapsodies for orch. It was produced as a ballet, *La Nuit de Saint-Jean* (Ballets Suédois, Paris, Oct. 25, 1925) and had over 250 performances in four years. He has written 5 symphonies: I in F minor (Stockholm, Feb. 9, 1897); II in E major (Stockholm, May 2, 1899); III in E major (Göteborg, Dec. 5, 1906); IV in C minor (Stockholm, Nov. 16, 1918); V in A minor (Stockholm, April 30, 1952); contributed a number of festive cantatas on various occasions, patriotic anniversaries and the like, among them a cantata celebrating the 450th year since the founding of Uppsala Univ. (1927) and another on the 500th jubilee of the Swedish Parliament (1935). He also wrote a ballad on Gustaf Vasa (1920) for soloists, mixed chorus and organ; and numerous male choruses. He published 3 volumes of memoirs: *Tempo furioso* (Stockholm, 1948); *I dur och moll* (1949); *Finale* (1952). In Swedish music Alfvén occupies the position of a late romantic composer, representing the best traits of Scandinavian national art, along the lines of Grieg and Sibelius. — Bibl.: S. E. Svensson, *Hugo Alfvén, som människa och konstnär* (Uppsala, 1946).

Algarotti, Francesco, Italian musician and scholar; b. Venice, Dec. 11, 1712; d. Pisa, May 3, 1764. The fame of his great knowledge reached Frederick the Great who invited him to Berlin in 1740 and gave him the title of Count; and, in 1747, that of 'Chevalier de l'ordre pour le mérite.' In 1753 Algarotti returned to Italy. His musical monument is the *Saggio sopra l'opera in musica,* published in 1755; also in many later editions, including German and French translations. The English text of the *Saggio . . .* is reproduced in part in O. Strunk's *Source Readings in Music History* (N. Y., 1950). Bibl.: D. Michelessi, *Memorie intorno alla vita ed agli scritti del Francesco Algarotti* (Venice, 1770); R. Northcott, *Francesco Algarotti, A Reprint of His 'Saggio . . .' and a Sketch of His Life* (London, 1917).

Aliabiev (ăhl-yăh'-byĕv), **Alexander Nikolayevitch,** Russian song composer; b. Tobolsk, Siberia, Aug. 15, 1787; d. Moscow, March 6, 1851. He left Tobolsk at the age of nine; served in the cavalry during the War of 1812 and participated in the entry of the Russian Army into Dresden and Paris. Returning to Russia, he lived in Moscow. In 1825, he was arrested on suspicion of murder after a card game, and was exiled (on the express order of the Czar Nicholas I) to his birthplace in Siberia (1828). In 1831, he was allowed to return to European Russia, and lived in the Caucasus, Orenburg, and in the Crimea, before settling in Moscow. He wrote more than 100 songs, of which *The Nightingale* became extremely popular; it is often used in the music lesson scene in the *Barber of Seville.* Glinka and Liszt made piano arrangements of it. In exile, Aliabiev wrote a symphony (1830), 3 string quartets and a violin sonata. His opera *The Prisoner of the Caucasus* was very popular in Russia. He also set to music the stage ballads *The Village Philosopher* (to Zagoskin's text) and *The Moon Night;* with Verstovsky and Maurer he contributed the music to Chmelnitsky's comedy *A Novel Prank, or Theatrical Combat.* Bibl.: Dobrohotov, *Alexander Aliabiev* in 'Sovietskaya Musica' (April, 1951); Ilyin, *Aliabiev in Siberia* (with a facsimile reproduction of the registry of Aliabiev's birth), ibid. (Aug., 1952).

Alió, Francisco, Spanish composer; b. Barcelona, March 21, 1862; d. there, March 31, 1908. He studied piano with Vidiella and composition with Anselmo Barba. As a composer, he was a determined believer in the Spanish national type of music, and in his piano pieces and songs brought out native rhythms and melodies. He published several albums of Catalan folk songs.

Aliprandi, Bernardo, Italian cellist and composer; b. Milan, c. 1710; d. Munich, c. 1785. He became a member of the Court Orchestra in Munich (1732); then was concertmaster (1750); retired in 1780. He wrote 3 operas: *Mitridate* (1738), *Ifigenia* (1739), *Semiramide* (1740); a divertimento *Apollo tra le Muse in Parnasso* (1737), and a *Stabat Mater* (1749).

Alkan (ăhl-kăhn) (real name Morhange); **Charles-Henri Valentin,** French pianist and composer of Jewish extraction; b. Paris, Nov. 30, 1813; d. there, March 29, 1888. His three brothers were also musicians; his father was the founder of a school for Jewish children. Alkan's talent was precocious; he was accepted at the Paris Cons. at the age of six and studied piano with Zimmermann. In 1833 he visited London, then returned to Paris, where his main activities were playing concerts in the fashionable salons and teaching piano. He entered the brilliant circle of musicians and littérateurs, among whom were Chopin, George Sand, Hugo and Liszt. He died as a result of injuries sustained when a heavy bookcase fell on him as he tried to reach for a book. Like Chopin, Alkan wrote almost exclusively for piano; the list of his works includes 76 opus numbers, in addition to many pieces not numbered by opus. His pieces are programmatic, bearing such titles as *Désir;* a set of variations, *Les Omnibus; Le vent* (op. 15); *Le Tambour bat aux Champs* (op. 50); he was the first composer to write a piece descriptive of the railroad (*Le Chemin de fer,* op. 27). His 2 sets of études, in all major and minor keys (op. 35 and 39), of transcendent difficulty, present great interest as examples of modern piano technique. Other works are *3 Études de bravoure* (op. 16); *Le preux, étude de concert* (op. 17); *3 pièces poétiques* (op. 18); *Bourrée d'Auvergne* (op. 29); a sonata (op. 33, subtitled *Les quatre âges*); *Les mois* (op. 8, 74), comprising 12 pieces, etc. He also wrote 2 piano concertos, a piano trio, a cello sonata and vocal music. César Franck arranged several of his pieces for organ. For a long time Alkan's music was completely forgotten, but his significance as an inventive composer became more evident in the 20th century. Chapters dealing with Alkan are found in Sorabji's book *Around Music* (London, 1932), and in Bernard van Dieren's *Down Among the Dead Men* (London, 1935).

Allegri, Domenico, Italian composer; b. Rome, 1585; d. there, Sept. 5, 1629. He was maestro di cappella at S. Maria Maggiore from 1610-29, and was one of the first to provide vocal music with an independent instrumental accompaniment. A few of his *Mottetti* are extant (a soprano solo with violins, a tenor duet and a bass solo, each accompanied by 2 violins).

Allegri, Gregorio, Italian composer; b. Rome, c. 1582; d. there, Feb. 17, 1652. He was a choir boy in Rome from 1591-96; then studied with Giovanni Maria Nanino (1600-07). He entered the Papal Chapel in 1629, after serving for some years as chorister and composer for the cathedral at Fermo. He is chiefly known as the composer of the celebrated *Miserere* in 9 parts (i.e., for two choirs singing 4 and 5 parts respectively), regularly sung during Holy Week at the Sistine Chapel, and surreptitiously written out by Mozart after hearing it twice, though its publication was forbidden on pain of excommunication; since then it has been frequently published. Many other works by Allegri are preserved in MS.; 2 books of *Concertini* and 2 of *Mottetti* have been printed, also a 4-part sonata for strings which might be regarded as the prototype of the string quartet. See A. Cametti, *La scuola dei pueri cantus di S. Luigi dei Francesi in Roma,* in 'Rivista Musicale Italiana' (1915); J. Amann, *Allegris Miserere und die Aufführungspraxis in der Sixtina* (Regensburg, 1935); A. Eaglefield-Hull, *The Earliest Known String Quartet,* in the 'Mus. Quarterly' (Jan., 1929).

Allen, Creighton, American pianist and composer; b. Macon, Miss., March 26, 1900. He made his first public appearance at the age of nine; studied with Hutcheson in New York; then settled there as teacher and composer. He has written a piano concerto, a violin concerto, 17 settings of the poems of Edgar Allan Poe, piano pieces and many songs, some of which have acquired considerable popularity.

Allen, George Benjamin, English singer and composer; b. London, April 21, 1822; d. Brisbane, Queensland, Nov. 30, 1897. He was active successively as chorister, conductor, and organist in England, Ireland, and Australia; managed a light opera company, producing several of Sullivan's operas. He composed the operas: *Castle Grim* (London, 1865); *The Viking* (not performed); *The Wicklow Rose* (Manchester, 1882); 3 cantatas and songs.

Allen, Sir Hugh Percy, eminent English organist and educator; b. Reading, Dec. 23, 1869; d. Oxford, Feb. 20, 1946. He studied with Dr. F. Read in Reading, and at Oxford Univ. (Mus. Doc., 1898). At the age of 11 he acted as church organist in Reading. Thereafter he was organist at various churches and cathedrals until the turn of the century. He was appointed organist at New College, Oxford (1901-18), and later

(1908-18) director of music at University College, Reading. In 1918 he succeeded Sir Walter Parratt as prof. of music at Oxford, and in the same year became director of the Royal College of Music, London, from which he resigned in 1937 (succeeded by George Dyson). He was knighted in 1920. For many years he conducted the London and the Oxford Bach Choirs; he was an ardent promoter of British music. — Cf. C. Bailey, *Hugh Percy Allen* (London, 1948).

Allen, Nathan H., American organist and choral conductor; b. Marion, Mass., April 14, 1848; d. Hartford, Conn., May 9, 1925. He studied organ in Berlin; was active as church organist and teacher in Hartford, Conn. From 1906-11 he was organist at Worcester, Mass., then returned to Hartford. He wrote church music (including a cantata, *The Apotheosis of St. Dorothy*), and concert pieces for organ, violin and piano.

Allen, Paul Hastings, American composer; b. Hyde Park, Mass., Nov. 28, 1883; d. Boston, Sept. 28, 1952. He studied at Harvard Univ. (A.B., 1903), then in Italy. During World War I was in the American diplomatic service there; returning to the U. S. in 1920 and settling in Boston. A prolific composer, he wrote 12 operas, mostly in Italian, several of which were performed in Italy. They include *Il Filtro* (Genoa, Oct. 26, 1912); *Milda* (Venice, June 14, 1913); *L'Ultimo dei Mohicani* (Florence, Feb. 24, 1916); *Cleopatra* (1921); *La piccola Figaro* (1931). His *Pilgrim Symphony* received the Paderewski prize (1910); other orchestral works are largely unperformed. Allen wrote much chamber music, some for unusual combinations, such as a quartet for 2 clarinets, basset-horn and bass-clarinet; several piano sonatas and a great number of other piano pieces; choral works and songs. His writing is marked by technical mastery in a romantic style.

Allen, Warren D., American musicologist; b. San José, Cal., Aug. 3, 1885. He studied at the Univ. of Cal.; later with Fielitz in Berlin and with Widor in Paris. From 1913-19 he was dean of music at the College of the Pacific, San José. In 1918 he became choral director at Stanford Univ.; from 1940 till 1949, on the faculty there; 1949-55, prof. at Florida State Univ.; retired in 1955 and settled in Seattle. — Books: *Philosophies of Music History* (1939) and *Our Marching Civilization* (1943).

Allende (ah-yĕn-dā) **Sarón, (Pedro) Humberto,** eminent Chilean composer; b. Santiago, June 29, 1885. He studied violin and theory at the National Cons. in Santiago (1899-1908); then taught in public schools there. Elected member of the Chilean Folklore Soc. in 1911. He was in France and Spain (1922-23); appointed Chilean delegate to the Congress of Popular Arts in Prague, under the auspices of the League of Nations (1928); in 1929 he took part in the Festival of Ibero-American Music in Barcelona. He was prof. of composition at the National Cons. in Santiago from 1928-45. In 1945 he received the Chilean Government Prize. In his music, Allende combines authentic national sentiment with a modern treatment, often in an impressionistic manner. He has written a Symphony in B Flat (1910; awarded Chilean Centennial Prize); *Campesinas Chilenas* for orch. (1913); cello concerto (1915); *La Voz de las Calles,* symphonic poem utilizing street cries of Chilean cities (Santiago, May 20, 1921); *La Despedida* for 2 sopranos, contralto and orch. (Santiago, May 7, 1934); violin concerto (Santiago, Nov. 27, 1942); string quartet (1947); 3 piano sonatas (1909-15); *12 Tonadas de carácter popular chileno* for piano (1918-22; his most distinctive work in a national style; also arranged for orch.) and songs. He also published a teaching manual *Método Original de Iniciación Musical* (Santiago, 1937). — Cf. special issue of 'Revista Musical Chilena' (Sept., 1945); N. Slonimsky, *Humberto Allende, First Modernist of Chile,* in 'Musical America,' (Aug. 1942); V. S. Viu, *La Creación Musical en Chile,* pp. 115-129 (Santiago, 1952).

Allihn, Heinrich (Max), German music scholar; b. Halle-on-Saale, Aug. 31, 1841; d. there Nov. 15, 1910; from 1885 pastor and school inspector at Allenstedt; edited the 2nd edition (1888) of Töpfer's *Lehrbuch der Orgelbaukunst* (*Theorie und Praxis des Orgelbaues*); publ. *Die Hausinstrumente Klavier und Harmonium* (1892), and *Die Pflege des musikalisches Teils des Gottesdienstes* (1906); contributed many essays to De Wit's 'Zeitschrift für Instrumentenbau.'

d'Almeida, Fernando, Portuguese composer; b. Lisbon, c. 1618; d. Thomar, March 21, 1660. Distinguished pupil of Duarte Lobo; in 1638, entered the Order of Christ at Thomar. Of his many church compositions, only one folio vol. in MS. is known: *Lamentacões, Responsorias e Misereres das tres officias da Quarta, Quinta e Sexta-feria da Semana Santa.*

Almeida, Renato, Brazilian music historian; b. S. Antonio de Jesus, Bahia, Dec. 6, 1895. He studied law; worked as a journalist in Rio de Janeiro. He is the author of the standard work on Brazilian music: *Historia da musica brasileira* (1926; new enlarged ed., 1942).

Almenräder, Karl, German bassoon virtuoso; b. Ronsdorf, near Düsseldorf, Oct. 3, 1786; d. Biebrich, Sept. 14, 1843. Was prof. of bassoon at Cologne, theater conductor in Frankfurt and regimental bandmaster; started a factory for wind instruments (1820) at Cologne, but gave it up in two years, entering the Nassau Court Orch. at Biebrich. He materially improved the bassoon, wrote a treatise on it (Mainz, 1824), and a method for it; publ. a bassoon concerto; variations for bassoon and quartet; Duettinos for 2 bassoons, etc.; and the popular ballad, *Des Hauses letzte Stunde.*

Almquist, Carl Jonas Love, Swedish composer and writer on music; b. Stockholm, Nov. 28, 1793; d. Bremen, Sept. 26, 1866. He studied at Uppsala Univ.; wrote songs to his own words, but refused to study music for fear that his instinct for simple melody might be destroyed by learning. He published these songs in a collection *Törnrosens bok* (1838); he also published 11 albums of piano pieces under the title *Fria Fantasier* (1848). Almquist's life was an adventurous one; he was forced to leave Sweden, where he was accused of forgery; lived in America (1851-65); then went to Germany, where he died.

Alnaes, Eyvind, Norwegian composer; b. Fredriksstad, April 29, 1872; d. Oslo, Dec. 24, 1932. He studied in Oslo with Ivar Holter (1889-92) and in Leipzig with Carl Reinecke (1892-95). From 1895 he occupied various positions as church organist in Norway. His works include 2 symphonies (1898 and 1923); *Variations Symphoniques* (1898); piano concerto (Oslo, Feb. 7, 1914); *Marche symphonique* for 2 pianos, and several choruses and songs. He also published a collection of Norwegian folk songs (1922).

Alnar, Hasan Ferid, Turkish composer; b. Istanbul, March 11, 1906. As a child he played native instruments; at 16 composed an operetta in oriental style. In 1927 he went to Vienna, where he studied with Joseph Marx (composition) and Oswald Kabasta (conducting). Returning to Istanbul in 1932, he taught at the Municipal Cons. He was associate conductor of the Presidential Philh. Orch. in Ankara from 1936-49, and its director from 1949-52. He also taught composition at the Ankara Cons. (1937-46). Alnar's music is mostly of native inspiration. He has written *Prelude and Two Dances* for orch. (1935); *Istanbul Suite* for orch. (1938); cello concerto (Ankara, Feb. 15, 1943); concerto for Kanun (Turkish psaltery) and orch. (1951); etc.

Alpaerts, Flor, Belgian composer; b. Antwerp, Sept. 12, 1876; d. there, Oct. 5, 1954. He studied with Benoit and Blockx at the Royal Flemish Cons. in Antwerp; in 1903 he became prof. there; was its director from 1934-41. From 1919 he conducted the local orchestra at the Zoological Gardens, also conducted in France and Holland. His music is influenced by early impressionism, without venturing into the field of modern harmony. He wrote the opera *Shylock* (Antwerp, Nov. 22, 1913); *Symphonie du printemps;* symph. poems *Psyché* (1900); *Renouveau* (1904); *Cyrus* (1905); *Pallieter* (1921); *Poème symphonique* for flute and orch. (1903; revised 1940); incidental music to various plays; a violin concerto (1948) and several school manuals in Flemish. Cf. A. Corbet, *Flor Alpaerts* (Antwerp, 1941).

Alpaerts, Jef, Belgian conductor and pianist; son of Flor Alpaerts; b. Antwerp, July 17, 1904. He studied in Paris with Isidor Philipp and Cortot (piano) and with Vincent d'Indy (comp.). In 1936 he was appointed prof. at the Antwerp Cons.; in 1938 he inaugurated the Collegium Musicum Antverpiense for performances of old music.

Alsleben, Julius, German pianist and pedagogue; b. Berlin, March 24, 1832; d. there, Dec. 8, 1894. He studied piano with Zech, and theory with S. Dehn. In 1865 he became president of the Berlin 'Tonkünstlerverein'; in 1879 he was president of the 'Musiklehrerverein' of which he was also a founder. From 1874 he edited the periodical "Harmonie." Alsleben published 12 *Vorlesungen über Musikgeschichte* (1862); *Über die Entwickelung des Klavierspiels* (1870), *Licht- und Wendepunkte in der Entwickelung der Musik* (1880). He wrote a Requiem, a liturgy, choral pieces and some orchestral overtures.

Alsted, Johann Heinrich, German music scholar; b. Bellersbach, Nassau, in 1588; d. Weissenburg, Transylvania, Nov. 8, 1638. He taught philosophy and theology in Weissenburg. His articles on music are found in his *Encyclopädie der gesammten Wissenschaften* (1610) and in his *Elemen-*

tale mathematicum (1611), translated into English by Birchensha (1644).

Altar, Cevat, Turkish writer on music; b. Constantinople, Sept. 14, 1902. He studied in Leipzig (1922-27); taught music theory in Ankara (1927-35), and was a founder of the Ankara State Cons. (1936). In 1951 he was appointed director of Turkish theaters; in 1954 he visited the U.S. under the Educational Exchange Program. He has translated several German books into Turkish; wrote several essays on Beethoven's use of so-called Turkish music, and initiated a 6-volume edition of musical biography.

Altenburg, Johann Ernst, German trumpet player and composer; b. Weissenfels, June 15, 1734; d. Bitterfeld, May 14, 1801. He was field-trumpeter during the 7 Years' War; then became organist at Bitterfeld. He wrote the first special manual on playing the trumpet and kettledrums, *Versuch einer Anleitung zur heroisch-musikalischen Trompeter- und Paukerkunst* (Halle, 1795; reprinted, Dresden, 1911); also pieces for 2, 4, 6, and 8 trumpets, and a concerto for 7 trumpets and kettle-drums. Cf. A. Werner, *Johann Ernst Alternburg* ('Zeitschrift für Musikwissenschaft,' 1933).

Altenburg, Michael, German church musician; b. Alach, near Erfurt, May 27, 1584; d. Erfurt, Feb. 12, 1640. He studied theology at Halle (1601); became pastor at Tröchtelborn (1611), then at Gröss-Sommerda (1621), and finally in Erfurt (1637). He published a Wedding Motet in 7 parts; a collection of songs 'for Church and Home' in 6, 7, 8, and 9 voices (3 vols.; Erfurt, 1620-21); 16 instrumental *Intraden* in 6 parts (Erfurt, 1620) and numerous church anthems some of which have been permanently incorporated in the Lutheran service. For a detailed list of works, see Adrio's article in 'Die Musik in Geschichte und Gegenwart.'

Altès, Ernest-Eugène, French violinist and conductor; brother of Joseph-Henri Altès; b. Paris, March 28, 1830; d. St.-Dyé, near Blois, July 8, 1899. He studied with Habeneck at the Paris Cons., where he won first prize for violin playing in 1848. In 1871 he joined the staff of the Paris Opéra as conductor, retiring in 1887. He composed a symphony, chamber music, and an orchestral *Divertissement* on ballet airs by Auber on the occasion of Auber's centennial (1882).

Altès, Joseph-Henri, French flutist; brother of Ernest-Eugène Altès; b. Rouen, Jan. 18, 1826; d. Paris, July 24, 1895. He studied at the Paris Cons.; then became flutist at the Paris Opéra. He was appointed prof. of flute at the Paris Cons. in 1868, holding this post to the end of his life. He published a number of flute pieces.

Altglass, Max, lyric tenor; b. Warsaw, Feb. 16, 1886; d. New York, Feb. 15, 1952. He studied at the Berlin Cons.; sang in Berlin and Prague, and made his American debut with the Metropolitan Opera in 1924. Later he was active as vocal teacher in New York.

Althouse, Paul, American tenor; b. Reading, Pa., Dec. 2, 1889; d. New York, Feb. 6, 1954. He studied with O. Saenger, and made his debut as Dimitri in the American premiere of *Boris Godunov* at the Metropolitan Opera on March 19, 1913; later undertook Wagnerian tenor roles there; was also for a time a member of the Chicago Civic Opera and of the San Francisco Opera. He sang with Toscanini and the N. Y. Philh. as soloist in Beethoven's Ninth Symphony; also appeared with other U.S. orchestras. He gave two recital tours in Australia and New Zealand. In the last years of his life Althouse was mostly active as vocal teacher in New York.

Altmann, Wilhelm, German music bibliographer, b. Adelnau, near Posen, April 4, 1862; d. Hildesheim, March 25, 1951. He studied philology and government in Marburg and Berlin, and in 1885 received his *Dr. phil.* He served as librarian in Greifswald (1889-1900). In 1900 he was appointed a librarian of the Prussian State Library in Berlin; in 1915 he became director of the music dept., retiring in 1927. In 1906 he founded, in cooperation with Breitkopf & Härtel, the 'Deutsche Musiksammlung,' at the Berlin library. From 1945 he lived in Hildesheim. Altmann compiled a number of valuable bibliographical works; among them *Chronik des Berliner Philh. Orchesters* (1902); *Richard Wagners Briefe* (1905; a list of 3143 letters with brief synopses); *Brahms Briefwechsel* (1908); *Wagners Briefwechsel mit seinen Verlegern* (2 vols., 1911); *Kammermusik-Literatur-Verzeichnis* (1910; a list of chamber music published since 1841; 6 revisions up to 1945); *Max-Reger-Katalog* (1917 and 1923); catalogue of music for viola and viola d'amore (1937) and a catalogue of piano music for 4 and 6 hands and 2 pianos (1943). Altmann also edited Paul Frank's *Tonkünstler-Lexikon* (1926, 1927, 1936, 1949). Furthermore, he published bibliographies of books on instruments; also made arrangements of classical works.

Altnikol, Johann Christoph, German organist and composer; b. Berna (Silesia) in December 1719 (baptized Jan. 1, 1720); d. Naumburg, July 25, 1759. In 1744-48 he studied with J. S. Bach; was then organist at St. Wenzel's Church in Naumburg. On Jan. 20, 1749 Altnikol married Bach's daughter, Elisabeth. In a letter of recommendation Bach describes him as "quite skillful in composition." As Bach's copyist, Altnikol established authentic texts of many of Bach's works. See *(passim)* H. David and A. Mendel, *The Bach Reader* (N.Y., 1945); also F. Blume's article in 'Die Musik in Geschichte und Gegenwart.'

Altschuler (ahlt-shoo'-lĕr), **Modest,** Russian conductor; b. Mogilev, Russia, Feb. 15, 1873. He studied cello at the Warsaw Cons. (1884-86), and later took courses at the Moscow Cons. with Arensky and Taneyev (comp.) and Safonov (piano and cond.), graduating in 1890. After touring Russia as a cellist, he emigrated to America. In 1903 he organized in New York the Russian Symph. Soc. and conducted its first concert on Jan. 7, 1904. This organization became an important cultural medium for performances of Russian music in America; Altschuler obtained from Scriabin the right of the world premiere of *The Poem of Extasy* and conducted it in New York on Dec. 10, 1908. At the same concert Mischa Elman made his American debut. Altschuler also gave the first American perf. of Scriabin's *Prometheus,* employing the 'color organ' prescribed in the score, which was built especially for this performance (N. Y., March 20, 1915); among other Russian composers whose works were presented by him for the first time in America were Ippolitov-Ivanov, Liadov, Rachmaninov and Vassilenko. Eventually Altschuler settled in Los Angeles as a teacher. In 1956 he was writing his memoirs.

Alvarado, Alberto, Mexican composer; b. Durango, Dec. 10, 1864; d. there, June 18, 1939. He wrote nearly 1000 pieces of various types ranging from waltzes to symphonic works, mostly of a descriptive nature: *(El principe de Asturias; Angel Mujer; Almas Destrozadas; La Fiesta encantadora; Suite Tropical, Corazón latino).*

Alvarez (ahl-vah-rā'), **Albert Raymond** (real name Albert Gourron), French tenor; b. Bordeaux, 1861; d. Nice, Feb. 26, 1933. He sang at various opera houses and at the Paris Opéra; made his American debut at the Metropolitan Opera, on Dec. 18, 1899, as Romeo. He remained there for three seasons, then appeared in London, and again in France. His repertoire comprised about 60 roles.

Alvary, Max (real name Achenbach), German tenor; b. Düsseldorf, May 3, 1856; d. near Gross-Tabarz, Thuringia, Nov. 7, 1898. His father was a well known painter. Alvary studied with Stockhausen; made his debut at Weimar. On Nov. 25, 1885 he made his American debut at the Metropolitan Opera as Don José singing in German; later he specialized in Wagnerian roles, in which he was eminently successful in America and in Germany.

Alwin, Karl, German conductor and composer; b. Königsberg, April 15, 1891; d. Mexico City, Oct. 15, 1945. He studied in Berlin with Humperdinck and Hugo Kaun; then became Karl Muck's assistant (Berlin and Bayreuth, 1912). He conducted in Halle (1913); Posen (1914); Düsseldorf (1915-17) and Hamburg (1917-20). From 1920-38 he was conductor of the Vienna Staatsoper, and guest conductor in England, France and Spain. He left Austria permanently in 1938. He was conductor at the Opera Nacional in Mexico from 1941 until his death in 1945. In 1920 he married Elisabeth Schumann (divorced 1936).

Alwyn, William, English composer, b. Northampton, Nov. 7, 1905. He studied at the Royal Academy with McEwen; in 1928 became teacher there. In 1937 he was elected a member of the Worshipful Company of Musicians. He wrote a piano concerto (1930); violin concerto (1938); oboe concerto (1944); a symphony (1949); the oratorio *The Marriage of Heaven and Hell* (1936); several orchestral suites; *Lyra Angelica* for harp and string orch. (1954); some chamber music; piano sonata and songs. Alwyn has achieved his greatest success as composer of film music *(Desert Victory, Odd Man Out,* etc.) to which his ability to write effective music in a moderately advanced idiom is eminently suited.

Alypios, Greek musical theorist, who flourished in the middle of the 4th century. His 'Introduction to Music' is the chief source of specific information regarding ancient Greek notation; it contains a summary of Greek scales in all their transpositions, both for voices and instruments. This treatise was published by Meursius (Leyden, 1616); by Meibom in his *Antiquae musicae auctores septem* (Amsterdam, 1652); and reprinted by F. Bellermann in *Die Tonleitern und Musiknoten der Griechen* (Berlin, 1847). A new critical edition is found in Jan's *Musici scriptores graeci* (1895). A graphic explanation of the notation of Alypios is presented by A. Samoiloff in his article *Die Alypiusschen Reihen der altgriechischen Tonbezeichnung* in 'Archiv für Musikwissenschaft' (1924; pp. 383-400).

Amadei, Filippo, Italian opera composer; b. Reggio, 1683; place and date of death unknown. His claim to attention arises from the circumstance that he, under the name of Signor Pippo (diminutive of Filippo), was the real author of the first act of the opera *Muzio Scevola,* for which Bononcini wrote the second act, and Handel the third, and which was produced at the Royal Academy of Music in London, April 15, 1721. Amadei's name was erroneously converted into Filippo Mattei by Mattheson in his *Critica musica* and the mistake was carried into reference works and Handel's biographies.

Amalia, the name of three German princesses who were musicians. See **Anna Amalia** (Princess of Prussià), **Anna Amalia** (Duchess of Saxe-Weimar) and **Amalia Friederike.**

Amalia Friederike, Princess of Saxony who wrote comedies under the name of Amalie Heiter; b. Dresden, Aug. 10, 1794; d. there, Sept. 18, 1870. She composed several light operas *(Una donna, Le tre cinture, Die Siegesfahne, Der Kanonenschuss,* etc.) and church music.

Amani, Nikolay Nikolayevitch, Russian composer; b. St. Petersburg, April 4, 1872; d. Yalta, Oct. 4, 1904. He studied at the St. Petersburg Cons. with Rimsky-Korsakov and Liadov (1890-1900); then went to Italy and played a concert of his piano works at Naples (July 29, 1900); in 1901-02 he traveled in Germany. Tuberculosis forced him to stop working; he lived his last two years in the Crimea. Amani's music is close in style to Tchaikovsky; but he wrote only in small forms.

Amar, Licco, Hungarian violinist; b. Budapest, Dec. 4, 1891. He studied with Henri Marteau in Berlin, and later joined the Marteau Quartet as second violinist. He was subsequently concertmaster of the Berlin Philharmonic (1916-20) and at the National Theater in Mannheim (1920-23). In 1922 he organized the Amar Quartet (with Walter Caspar, Paul Hindemith and Maurits Frank); toured Europe with this group until 1929. He left Germany in 1933; lived in Paris, and eventually settled in Turkey as prof. at the Ankara Cons.

Amat, Juan Carlos, Spanish physician and writer on guitar playing; b. Monistrol, 1572; d. there, Feb. 10, 1642. His book *Guitarra Española en cinco ordenes* (Barcelona, 1596) has been reprinted many times. See E. Pujol, *Significación de Juan Carlos Amat (1572-1642) en la historia de la guitarra* in 'Anuario Musical,' vol. V (Barcelona, 1950).

Amati, a renowned family of violin makers at Cremona, Italy. (1) **Andrea,** b. 1530 (?), d. 1611 (?), was the first violin maker of the family; his violins were usually of small pattern, but show a marked advance over the Brescia instrs. His two sons, (2) **Antonio,** b. 1550, d. 1638, and (3) **Girolamo,** b. 1556; d. Nov. 2, 1630, worked together for a time, producing violins of nearly the same style of their father. (4) **Niccolò,** b. Dec. 3, 1596; d. April 12, 1684, the most celebrated of the Amatis, improved the model in several respects, and, though generally working with a small pattern, built some so-called 'grand Amatis'—large violins of powerful tone, clearer, purer, and more sonorous than in those of his predecessors. His label is 'Nicolaus Amati Cremonens. Hieronimi filius Antonii nepos. Fecit anno 16—.' In his workshop were trained both Andrea Guarneri and Antonio Stradivari. (5) Niccolò's son, **Girolamo,** b. Feb. 26, 1649; d. Feb. 21, 1740, the last of the family, was far inferior to his father as a workman.—See Lütgendorff, *Die Geigen- und Lautenmacher vom Mittelalter bis zur Gegenwart* (Frankfurt, 1904; 4th ed. 1922, in dictionary form); G. de Piccolellis, *Genealogia degli Amati e Guarneri* (1866).

Amato, Pasquale, Italian baritone; b. Naples, March 21, 1878; d. New York, Aug. 12, 1942. He studied at the Cons. of Naples (1896-99); made his debut in *La Traviata* in Naples in 1900. He later sang at leading European opera houses, and in Russia, England, Egypt and Argentina. He made his American debut at the Metropolitan Opera in *La Traviata* (Nov. 20, 1908) with Sembrich and Caruso. Amato remained a member of the Metropolitan Opera until 1921 and then settled in New York as voice teacher.

Ambros, August Wilhelm, eminent musical historiographer; b. Mauth, near Prague, Nov. 17, 1816; d. Vienna, June 28, 1876. He studied law and music; rapidly rose in the legal profession; was appointed Public Prosecutor in Prague (1850), but continued to devote much time to music; published his *Die Grenzen der Musik und Poesie* (Leipzig,

1856; English translation, N. Y., 1893) as a reply to Hanslick's views on esthetics; followed by a brilliant collection of essays under the title, *Culturhistorische Bilder aus dem Musikleben der Gegenwart* (Leipzig, 1860); also published two collections of articles, *Bunte Blätter* (1872-74; 2nd ed. by E. Vogel, 1896). In 1869 Ambros was appointed prof. of music at Prague Univ. and Prague Cons.; in 1872 received a post in the Ministry of Justice in Vienna; he also taught at Vienna Cons. His major work was the monumental *Geschichte der Musik* commissioned by the publisher Leuckart in 1860. Ambros spent many years of research in the libraries of Munich, Vienna, and several Italian cities for this work, but died before completing the 4th volume, which was edited from his notes by C. F. Becker and G. Nottebohm; a 5th volume was published in 1882 by O. Kade from newly collected materials. W. Langhans wrote a sequel in a more popular style under the title *Die Geschichte der Musik des 17., 18. und 19. Jahrhunderts,* bringing the work up to date (2 volumes, 1882-86). A list of names and general index were issued by W. Bäumker (1882). A 2nd edition of the original 4 volumes (Leipzig, 1880) contained the following: Vol. I, The Beginnings of Music; Vol. II, From the Christian Era to the First Flemish School; Vol. III, From the Netherlands Masters to Palestrina; Vol. IV, Palestrina, his contemporaries and immediate successors. Volume I has been rewritten, not always for the better, by B. Sokolovsky; 2nd volume was reprinted in a new revision by Riemann (1892); volume IV by Leichtentritt (1909); volume V was revised and enlarged by O. Kade (1911). Ambros was also an excellent practical musician, a proficient pianist, and composer. He wrote an opera in Czech, *Bretislaw a Jitka;* overtures to *Othello* and the *Magico prodigioso,* numerous songs, and religious music. Cf. Guido Adler, *August Wilhelm Ambros* in the 'Mus. Quarterly' (July, 1931).

Ambrose (Ambrosius), Christian saint and creator of 'Ambrosian Chant;' b. Trier (Trèves), c. 333; d. Milan, April 4, 397. He was elected Bishop of Milan in 374; canonized after his death. In 384 he was made responsible for the regulation and development of singing in the Western Church, by the introduction and cultivation of ritual song (antiphonal and congregational) as practiced at the time in the Eastern Church. His indisputable authorship of several sacred songs has earned him the title of 'Father of Christian Hymnology,' but his reputed composition of the 'Ambrosian Chant,' *Te Deum laudamus* (said to have been sung by St. Ambrose and St. Augustine at the baptism of the latter) is mythical. — Bibl.: Biraghi, *Inni sinceri e carmi di S. Ambrogio* (Milan, 1862); G. M. Dreves, *Aurelius Ambrosius, der Vater des Kirchengesanges* (Freiburg, 1893); A. Mocquereau, *Notes sur l'influence de l'accent et du cursus tonique latins dans le chant ambrosien* (Paris, 1897); A. Steier, *Untersuchungen über die Echtheit der Hymnen des Ambrosius* (Leipzig, 1903); P. Wagner, *Introduction to the Gregorian melodies,* part 1, *Origin and Development of the Forms of Liturgical Chant.* (London, 1907); E. Garbagnati, *Riviste sull' antica salmodia ambrosiana* (Rome, 1912); A. S. Parodi, *S. Ambrogio e la sua età* (Milan, 1941).

Ambrose, Paul, organist; b. Hamilton, Ontario, Oct. 11, 1868; d. there, June 1, 1941. He studied with his father; was organist at various churches in New York (1886-1917); then taught in New Jersey. He was four times president of the National Association of Organists.

d'Ambrosio, Alfredo, Italian violinist and composer; b. Naples, June 13, 1871; d. Nice, Dec. 29, 1914. He studied with E. Bossi at the Cons. of Naples (comp.); violin with Sarasate in Madrid and with Wilhelmj in London. Settled in Nice as teacher, and leader of a string quartet. He wrote an opera *Pia de Tolomei;* a ballet *Ersilia;* a string quintet; a string quartet; 2 violin concertos, and many smaller compositions for violin *(Romanza, Canzonetta,* etc.).

Ambrosius, Hermann, German composer; b. Hamburg, July 25, 1897. He studied at the Univ. of Leipzig; took master courses with Pfitzner in Berlin (1921-24). From 1924-45 he was active in Leipzig as teacher and lecturer. After World War II he settled at Engen. A prolific composer of symphonies, instrumental concertos, chamber music and songs.

Ameller, André-Charles, French composer; b. Arnaville, Jan. 2, 1912. He studied composition with Roger-Ducasse and Gaubert at the Paris Cons.; also violin and double-bass. He was a prisoner of war in Germany in 1940; then resumed his studies. He has written an opera *Sampiero Corso; Ouverture solennelle* for orch.; *Fresques symphoniques* (Paris Radio, 1949); a ballet, *La coupe de sang* (1950); *Jeux de table* for saxophone and piano (1955); *Terre secrète,* 6 poems for voice and orch. (1956).

Amengual, René, Chilean composer; b. Santiago, Sept. 2, 1911; d. there, Aug. 2, 1954. He studied with Humberto Allende at the National Cons. in Santiago. His compositions are few, and mostly in small forms; their style shows influences of the modern French school. He wrote a piano sonatina (1938); *Introduction and Allegro* for 2 pianos (1939); piano concerto (Santiago, June 30, 1942); *El Vaso* for voice and chamber orch. (Santiago, Aug. 25, 1944), etc. His *Burlesca* for piano is included in the album 'Latin American Art Music for the Piano' (N. Y., 1942).

Amfiteatrov, Daniele, composer and conductor; b. St. Petersburg, Russia, Oct. 29, 1901; studied composition in St. Petersburg with Wihtol, in Prague with Krička, and in Rome with Respighi. He stayed in Italy until 1937 when he came to America as assistant conductor of the Minneapolis Symph. Orch. (1938-41). In 1941 he settled in Hollywood as composer of film music; became an American citizen in 1944. He has written for orch. *Poema del Mare* (1925), *Miracolo delle Rose* (1927); *American Panorama* (1934), and some chamber music, as well as numerous film scores.

Amiot (ah-myoh'), **Joseph Marie,** French ecclesiastic; b. Toulon, Feb. 8, 1718: d. Peking, Oct. 8, 1793. He was Jesuit missionary to China; while there, he translated Li Koang Ti's work on Chinese music; *Commentaire sur le livre classique touchant la musique des anciens;* also wrote *Mémoires sur la musique des Chinois, tant anciens que modernes* (vol. VI of 'Mémoires concernant l'histoire, les sciences, les arts, etc., des Chinois'; Paris, 1780, edited by Abbé Rouffier).

Amirov, Fikret Dzhamil, Azerbaidzhan composer; b. Kirovabad, Nov. 22, 1922. He played native instruments; also studied composition. His music reflects native folkways. He has written a symph. poem *To the Memory of the Heroes of the Greek National War* (1944); several symph. poems on national modes 'mugamas'; double concerto for violin, piano and orch. (1948); *The Pledge of the Korean Guerilla Fighter* for voice and orch. (1951); variations for piano (1940), many arrangements of folk songs.

Ammann, Benno, Swiss composer and conductor; b. Gersau, June 14, 1904. He studied at the Leipzig Cons. and with Honegger, Milhaud and Roussel in Paris. He was choirmaster at the State Theater in Basel (1936-39); at the Teatro Reale in Rome (1939-42); then, conductor in Switzerland and France. Among his works are a mass *Defensor Pacis* (Rome, 1947), a string quartet and a saxophone sonata.

Ammerbach, Elias Nikolaus, German organist and contrapuntist; b. Naumberg, c. 1530; d. Leipzig, Jan. 1597 (buried Jan. 29). From 1560 he was organist of the Thomaskirche, Leipzig. He published *Orgel oder Instrument Tabulatur* (Leipzig, 1571), a work of importance regarding progress and development in the practice of tuning, the fingering of keyboard instruments, execution of graces, etc. (described by Becker in *Die Hausmusik in Deutschland,* Leipzig, 1840); and *Ein neu künstlich Tabulaturbuch* (1575; 2nd ed., 1583). He also published numerous compositions for organ and clavichord.

Ammon, Blasius, contrapuntist; b. 1560 at Imst, Tirol; d. Vienna, June, 1590. He was a choir boy in the service of Archduke Ferdinand of Austria, who sent him to Venice for his musical education. In 1578 he returned to Innsbruck and joined the Franciscan Order. In 1587 he went to the Franciscan monastery in Vienna, where he entered the priesthood. He printed a book of 5-part Introits (Vienna, 1582); a book of 4-part masses (Vienna, 1588); 2 books of 4, 5 and 6-part motets (Munich, 1590). A number of works in MS are in the libraries of Munich and Vienna. A volume containing his church music was published by Caecilianus Huigens in 'Denkmäler der Tonkunst in Österreich' (38, I).

Amon, Johann (Andreas), German musician; b. Bamberg, 1763; d. Wallerstein, Bavaria, March 29, 1825. He studied horn with Giovanni Punto and traveled with him on tours in France and Germany. From 1789 till 1817 he was music director at Heilbronn; then became court conductor to the Prince of Öttingen-Wallerstein. He wrote 2 operas, 3 Requiems (one of which he intended for performance at his funeral), and many pieces of chamber music.

Ancina, Giovanni Giovenale, Italian choral composer; b. Fossano, Oct. 19, 1545; d. Saluzzo, Aug. 31, 1604. He studied medicine and theology; became interested in music when he met Filippo Neri; in 1578 he joined the Congregazione dell' Oratorio, founded by Neri. Ancina wrote church music; published *Tempio armonico della beata Vergine* (Rome, 1599). — Cf. J. Bacci, *Vita di G. G. Ancina* (Rome, 1671); also Pietro Damilano, *G. G. Ancina e la lauda cinquecentesca* (Milan, 1953).

Ancona, Mario, Italian baritone, b. Leghorn, Feb. 28, 1860; d. Florence, Feb. 22, 1931. He studied social science and law, and started as a diplomat. He soon turned to the study of singing, however, and made his debut at Trieste; then sang at the principal opera houses of Italy. He appeared as Tonio at both the London (1892) and New York (1894) premieres of *Pagliacci;* for nine seasons he was a member of Covent Garden; he spent five seasons at the Metropolitan Opera, and two at the Manhattan Opera House. He also appeared in Spain, Portugal, Russia and Argentina. His repertoire included such various roles as Amonasro, Sachs, Wolfram, etc. After retiring from opera he was active as vocal teacher in Italy.

Ancot (ahn-koh'), a family of musicians at Bruges. **Jean** *(père),* b. Bruges, Oct. 22, 1779; d. there July 12, 1848; violin virtuoso, pianist and composer; studied (1799-1804) in Paris under Baillot, Kreutzer, and Catel; then settled in Bruges as teacher. Publ. 4 violin concertos; overtures, marches, sacred music, etc.; most of his works are still in MS. Taught his sons: (1) **Jean** *(fils);* b. Bruges, July 6, 1799; d. Boulogne, June 5, 1829; finished his mus. education at the Paris Cons. under Pradher and Berton; an accomplished pianist, he was successful in London (1823-25); eventually settled in Boulogne. He was an astonishingly prolific composer (225 works; a piano concerto, sonatas, etudes, 4-hand fantasias, also violin concertos); and (2) **Louis**; b. Bruges, June 3, 1803; d. there, 1836; for a time pianist to the Duke of Sussex, London; made extended continental tours, taught at Boulogne and Tours, and finally returned to Bruges. He wrote piano music in salon style.

Anda, Geza, Hungarian pianist; b. Budapest, Nov. 19, 1921. He studied with Dohnányi at the Royal Music Academy in Budapest; won the Liszt Prize. During World War II he escaped from Hungary and settled in Switzerland. He appeared with major symphony orchestras in Europe; made his American debut with the Philadelphia Orch. in Oct. 1955. He has also given numerous recitals in Europe and America; his programs are built on contrasts of romantic and modern music; he is especially successful in the works of Brahms, Liszt and Bartók.

Andersen, (Carl) Joachim, Danish flute player and composer; b. Copenhagen, April 29, 1847; d. there, May 7, 1909; son and pupil of the flutist Christian Joachim Andersen. From 1869-77, member of the Royal Orch.; 1881 in Berlin, where he was co-founder, and for 10 years first flutist and assistant conductor of the Philh. Orch.; from 1893, cond. of the Palace Orch. at Copenhagen. He wrote solo works for the flute; also pieces with orch.: *Hungarian Fantasia, Ballade; Dance of the Sylphs;* 24 easy and 24 difficult etudes, etc. His brother, Vigo, was an eminent flute player; b. Copenhagen, April 21, 1852; d. by suicide at Chicago, Jan. 29, 1895. He was first flutist in the Thomas Orch. in Chicago.

Andersen, Karl August, Norwegian composer and cellist; b. Oslo, Sept. 29, 1903. He studied cello in Oslo and later with Hugo Becker in Berlin. Since 1924, cellist in the Oslo Philh. Orch. He has written a string quartet (1934); chamber symph. (1936); suite for orch. (1937); trio for flute, clarinet and cello (1939); and choral works.

Andersen, Stell, American pianist; b. Linn Grove, Iowa, Feb. 28, 1897, of Norwegian parentage. She studied at the American Cons., Chicago, with Josef Lhévinne in New York, and with Isidor Philipp in Paris. She made her New York debut at Town Hall in 1921; then gave recitals in Europe. Returning to America in 1939, she was active as teacher (American Cons., Chicago) as well as performer; she later settled in St. Paul, Minn.; after 1946 made several European tours.

Anderson, Arthur, American bass; b. Harvey, Ill., Aug. 16, 1898. He studied at Cincinnati Cons. and later in Italy. He made his debut in Malta; then toured Italy. Upon his return to America he made his debut at the Metropolitan Opera as Donner in *Das Rheingold* (Feb. 26, 1932). Eventually he settled in New York as vocal teacher.

Anderson, Marian, American contralto; b. Philadelphia, Pa., Feb. 17, 1902. She studied voice with Giuseppe Boghetti; won a vocal competition against 300 entrants and was soloist at the Lewisohn Stadium with the N. Y. Philh., on Aug. 27, 1925. She later appeared in programs with Roland Hayes. In 1930 she made her European debut in Berlin. 1930-32, she gave 52 concerts in Scandinavia and again in 1933-34 (142 concerts); in 1934 she sang in Paris, London, Holland and Belgium; in 1934-35, made a tour of Poland, Russia, Latvia, Switzerland, Belgium, Austria, Hungary, Italy and Spain. From 1935-36 she toured America, giving a concert in Carnegie Hall on Jan. 30, 1936; another European tour followed including Vienna, Budapest and The Hague. From Jan. to May, 1938, she gave 70 concerts in the U.S. and South America, and again in Europe (1938-39). In Feb., 1939, Marian Anderson became a center of national attention when she was forbidden to sing at Constitution Hall in Washington. In protest against this case of racial discrimination, a distinguished group of citizens, headed by Mrs. Franklin D. Roosevelt, sponsored her concert at the Lincoln Memorial (April 9, 1939), which was attended by 75,000 persons. She was the first Negro singer to be engaged as a permanent member of the Metropolitan Opera Co., making her debut as Ulrica in *The Masked Ball* (Jan. 7, 1955). She received the honorary degree of Mus. Doc. from Howard Univ., Washington, D. C. in June, 1938. Cf. Kosti Vehanen, *Marian Anderson* (N. Y., 1941).

Anderson, Thomas, English organist; b. Birmingham, April 15, 1836; d. there, Sept. 18, 1903. He served as organist in Birmingham churches; was also music critic there. He composed several cantatas: *The Song of Deborah and Barak; The Wise and Foolish Virgins; The Wreck of the Hesperus; John Gilpin; The Three Jovial Huntsmen; The Norman Baron;* and *Yuletide;* an *English Requiem* and instrumental music.

Anderssen, Alfred, Finnish composer; b. Helsinki, July 4, 1887; d. there, Sept. 10, 1940. He studied in Helsinki and in Munich; settled in Abo as a choral conductor and music critic. In 1926 he married the singer, Karin Limnell. He wrote an opera *Kohtalo* (1932), 2 symphonies, 15 cantatas, and many choral works.

d'Andrade (dăhn-drăh'-dĕ), **Francesco,** Portuguese baritone; b. Lisbon, Jan. 11, 1859; d. Berlin, Feb. 8, 1921. He studied in Italy; made his debut in San Remo (1882); then lived in Berlin. He was well known as a successful singer in Europe; his most famous role was that of Don Giovanni.

Andrade, Mario de, Brazilian poet and writer on music; b. S. Paulo, Oct. 9, 1893; d. there, Feb. 25, 1945. He studied at S. Paulo Cons.; in 1935 he was appointed director of the S. Paulo Dept. of Culture. Andrade spent much time on special research and reconstruction of Brazilian folk songs and dances; he was also active as music critic. Among his publications are *Carlos Gomes* (Rio de Janeiro, 1939); *Musica do Brasil* (1941); *Pequeña Historia de Música* (1942).

André, Johann, German composer, publisher, and father of a musical family; b. Offenbach, March 28, 1741; d. there, June 18, 1799. He founded (Sept. 1, 1774) at Offenbach a music publishing house under his name and had publ. 1,200 compositions by the time of his death. For seven years (1777-84) he was Kapellmeister at Döbblelin's Theater in Berlin. He was a prolific composer, author of 19 Singspiele and 14 miscellaneous scores for the stage, among them *Der Töpfer* (Hanau, Jan. 22, 1773) and *Der Liebhaber als Automat* (Berlin, Sept. 11, 1782). Bretzner wrote the libretto of *Die Entführung aus dem Serail,* or *Belmont und Constanze* for him; the opera was produced in Berlin, May 25, 1781. The same text was used the following year by Mozart for his celebrated work, which elicited Bretzner's haughty protest against "a certain man named Mozart" for the unauthorized use of his libretto. Among André's songs, the *Rheinweinlied* ('Bekränzt mit Laub') was widely performed. André is credited with being the composer of the first 'durchkomponierte Ballade,' *Die Weiber von Weinsberg* (1783).

André, (Johann) Anton, third son of Johann André; b. Offenbach, Oct. 6, 1775; d. there April 6, 1842. A precocious talent, he studied with Vollweiler in Mannheim (1793-96); was a fine pianist, violinist and composer before entering the Univ. of Jena; after completing his studies he made extensive travels, and on his father's death took charge of the business, adding particular lustre to its good name by the purchase (1800) of Mozart's entire musical remains. He publ. Mozart's autograph thematic catalogue, and supplemented it by a list of the works so acquired. By accepting the application of the lithographic process to music-engraving (1779), he took another long stride towards placing his firm in the front rank. He was also a composer (2 operas, symphonies, songs, etc.), a successful teacher, and a noteworthy theorist. He wrote 2 vols. on harmony, counterpoint, canon and fugue, (1832-43; new revised ed. 1875); and *Anleitung zum Violinspiele.*—His sons were: (1) **Carl August,** b. Offenbach, June 15, 1806; d. Frankfurt, Feb. 15, 1887; head (from 1835) of the Frankfurt branch opened in 1828, and founder of a piano factory ('Mozartflügel'); author of *Der Klavierbau und seine Geschichte* (1855).—(2) **Julius,** b. Frankfurt, June 4, 1808; d. there, April 17, 1880; a fine organist and pianist, pupil of Aloys Schmitt (his grandfather's pupil), author of a *Praktische Orgelschule,* composer of several interesting organ compositions, and arranger of Mozart's works for piano, 4 hands.—(3) **Johann August, b.**

Offenbach, March 2, 1817; d. there, Oct. 29, 1887; his father's successor (1839) in the publishing establishment. His two sons, **Karl** (b. Aug. 24, 1853; d. June 29, 1914) and **Adolf** (b. April 10, 1855; d. Sept. 10, 1910), succeeded to the business.—(4) **Jean Baptiste** *(de St.-Gilles),* b. Offenbach, March 7, 1823; d. Frankfurt, Dec. 9, 1882; pianist, and composer of various pieces for piano and voice, was a pupil of A. Schmitt, Taubert (piano), and Kessler and Dehn (harmony); lived for years in Berlin; had the honorary title of 'Herzoglich Bernbergischer Hofkapellmeister.'

Andreae, Volkmar, Swiss conductor and composer; b. Bern, July 5, 1879. He studied music with Karl Munzinger in Bern, and later at the Cologne Cons. with Wüllner. From 1901 on, he devoted himself mainly to conducting; was conductor at the Munich Opera (1901); then chorus leader at Winterthur and Zürich, where he settled in 1902. He was director of the Zürich Cons. from 1914 till 1939. He distinguished himself particularly by his performances of oratorios and became known as one of the best conductors of Bruckner's music. In his compositions Andreae reflects the post-romantic tendencies of German music. He wrote 2 operas: *Ratcliff* (Duisburg, May 25, 1914) and *Abenteuer des Casanova* (Dresden, June 17, 1924); several choral works *(Der Göttliche, Charons Nachen, Magentalied,* etc.); 2 symphonies, a violin concerto, a concertino for oboe and orch.; 8 Chinese songs for tenor, *Li-Tai-Po;* 2 string quartets; 2 piano trios; a string trio, a violin sonata and piano pieces. See F. Seiler, *Dr. Volkmar Andreae . . . zum Jubiläum seiner 25 jährigen Tätigkeit* (Zürich, 1931).

Andrée, Elfrida, Swedish organist and composer; b. Visby, Feb. 19, 1841; d. Stockholm, Jan. 11, 1929. She studied at the Stockholm Cons. and with Gade in Copenhagen; at the same time studied telegraphy, and was the first woman telegrapher in Sweden. In 1867 she obtained the post of organist at the Göteborg Cathedral. She established a series of popular concerts, and presented about 800 programs. She was a member of the Swedish Academy of Music. A pioneer among women musicians, she was the first Swedish woman to write an organ symphony, and wrote a Swedish Mass, which had frequent performances, and chamber music.

Andreis, Josip, Croatian music historian; b. Split, March 19, 1909. He studied philosophy in Zagreb; then music at the Zagreb Cons. He was subsequently appointed prof. there. He has written a music history in 3 volumes (Zagreb, 1951-54); monographs on Berlioz and on several Yugoslav composers; became editor of a musical encyclopedia in 2 volumes (Zagreb, 1957).

Andrevi, Francisco, prominent Spanish church composer; b. Sanahuja, near Lérida, Nov. 16, 1786; d. Barcelona, Nov. 23, 1853. He started as choir boy, and from his earliest years devoted himself to the study of church music. At the age of 22 he became director of music at the Cathedral of Segorbe; then held similar posts at the churches at Barcelona, Valencia and Seville. During the civil war in Spain he was in Bordeaux (1832-42); later in Paris (1845-49), where he published his *Traité d'Harmonie et de Composition* (1848); in the same year it was also published in Spanish. Andrevi returned to Barcelona in 1849. He wrote a sacred drama *Juicio universal;* also much choral music, most of which is in MS.; two of his sacred choruses *(Nunc dimittis* and *Salve regina)* are included in Eslava's 'Lira Sacra-Hispana.'

Andrico, Michal, Rumanian composer; b. Bucharest, Sept. 22, 1894. He studied at the Bucharest Cons.; won the Enesco Prize (1924); later taught at the Academy of Music. He has written a *Suite pittoresque* for orch.; piano quintet; a string quartet and piano pieces.

Andries, Jean, Belgian musician; b. Ghent, April 25, 1798; d. there, Jan. 21, 1872. He played violin in a local theater from 1813 till 1848, at the same time taught at the Ghent Cons.; in 1851 became director, retiring in 1859. He published the following treatises: *Aperçu historique de tous les instruments de musique actuellement en usage* (1856); *Précis de l'histoire de la musique depuis les temps les plus reculés* (1862); *Instruments à vent: La Flûte* (1866); *Remarques sur les cloches et les carillons* (1868).

Andriessen, Hendrik, Dutch organist and composer (brother of Willem); b. Haarlem, Sept. 17, 1892. He studied with his brother; then with Zweers (composition) at the Amsterdam Cons.; taught harmony there (1928-34). He was organist at Utrecht Cathedral (1934-42) and director of the Utrecht Cons. (1937-49); director of the Royal Cons. at The Hague (1949). His works include 3 symphonies (1930, 1937, 1946); *Ricercare* for orch. (1949); *Missa Simplex* (1928); *Missa Sponsa Christi* (1933); *Missa Dia-*

tonica (1935); *Psalm 47* (1945); cello sonata (1926); violin sonata (1933); *Sonata da Chiesa* for organ (1927); *Miroir de Peine,* song cycle (1923). His opera *Philomela* attracted a great deal of attention when it was produced at the Holland Festival, in Amsterdam, on June 23, 1950.

Andriessen, Jurriaan, Dutch composer; son of Hendrik Andriessen; b. Haarlem, Nov. 15, 1925. He studied with his father, and later in Paris, returning to Holland in 1948. He has written many scores for the theater; a piano concerto; *Dutch Rhapsody* for 2 pianos; a violin sonata and other chamber music for various combinations. His style reflects the neo-classical trend, in which Stravinsky's influence is much in evidence.

Andriessen, Willem, Dutch pianist and composer; brother of Hendrik Andriessen; b. Haarlem, Oct. 25, 1887. He studied at the Amsterdam Cons.; received a prize for excellence, having performed his own concerto at the graduation ceremony (1908). He was prof. of piano at The Hague Cons. (1901-18); later at the Rotterdam Cons.; in 1937 he was appointed director of the Amsterdam Cons. He was also active as a concert pianist, notable for his performances of the classics. As a composer, he has written mainly for piano (sonata, sonatina, etc.).

Anerio, Felice, Italian composer; brother of Giovanni Francesco Anerio; b. Rome, c. 1560; d. there, Sept. 27, 1614. He studied with G. M. Manni; was a chorister at Santa Maria Maggiore in Rome (1568-75); then sang at St. Peter's under Palestrina (from May, 1575 to March, 1579). In 1584 he became maestro di cappella of the English College in Rome. After Palestrina's death, Anerio was appointed by Clement VIII to succeed him as composer to the Papal Chapel (April 3, 1594). His eminence as composer is best attested by the fact that several of his compositions were for a long time supposed to be Palestrina's own. Besides MSS. in Roman libraries, many of Anerio's works are extant in printed collections. They include: *Madrigali spirituali a 5* (1585, reprinted 1598); *Canzonette a 4* (1586, reprinted 1603, 1607); *Madrigali a 5* (1587); *Madrigali a 6,* book I (1590, reprinted 1599); *Concerti spirituali a 4* (1593); *Sacri hymni e cantica a 8,* book I (1596); *Madrigali a 3* (1598); *Madrigali a 6,* book II (1602); *Responsorii per la Settimana Santa a 4* (1602); *Sacri hymni e cantica a 8,* book II (1602) and *Responsoria a 4* (1606). Bibl.: L. Torri, *Nei parentali di Felice Anerio* ('Rivista Musicale Italiana,' 1914): A. Cametti, *Nuovi contributi alle biografie di Felice Anerio* ('Rivista Musicale Italiana,' 1915).

Anerio, Giovanni Francesco, Italian composer; younger brother of Felice Anerio; b. Rome, c. 1567; d. June, 1630, on his way from Poland to Italy (buried in Graz, June 12, 1630). He was a chorister at St. Peter's (1575-79) and sang with his brother under Palestrina; later he became maestro di cappella at the Lateran Church (1600-1603). He was at the court of King Sigismund III of Poland in Cracow (1607); in 1608 he returned to Rome; then became choirmaster at Verona cathedral (1609); at the Seminario Romano (1611-12) and at the Jesuit church of S. Maria dei Monti in Rome (1613-20). He became a priest in 1616; visited Treviso (near Venice) in 1624. He was a prolific composer in all forms of sacred music; many of his works were printed by leading Italian publishers. He also arranged Palestrina's 6-part *Missa Papae Marcelli* for 4 voices (Rome, 1600). Bibl.: G. Liberali, *Giovanni Francesco Anerio,* in 'Note d'Archivio' (Dec., 1940).

Anet (ăh-nā'), **Jean-Baptiste,** French violinist, known as Baptiste; b. c. 1661; d. Lunéville, Aug. 14, 1755. He was a pupil of Corelli in Rome; returning to France, became a member of the Royal Chapel in Paris; in 1736 he went to Lunéville as musician to the former Polish King Stanislas Leszczynski. Anet publ. 3 sets of sonatas for violin with basso continuo (1729) and 3 albums of duos for musettes (1726, 1730, 1734. Cf. L. de La Laurencie, *L'école française de violin* (vol. 1, Paris, 1922).

Anfossi, Pasquale, prolific Italian opera composer; b. Taggia, near Naples, April 25, 1727; d. Rome, Feb., 1797. Originally a violinist, he studied composition under Piccinni, and brought out two unsuccessful operas, but with his third opera, *L'incognita perseguitata* (Rome, 1773) won popular approval. This opera was written on the same subject as Piccinni's previously staged opera and Anfossi had a greater success, backed by a powerful clique hostile to Piccinni. Anfossi then proceeded to bring out opera after opera. He wrote 76, which were successful in Rome for a time; later he sought new fields: in Paris (1779), London (1781-83, as director of the Italian Opera); then in Prague, Dresden and Berlin. Returning to Italy in 1784 he was appointed maestro di cappella at the Lateran in 1791, and turned his attention to sacred composition (12 oratorios, masses, psalms, etc.). Mozart wrote two arias for use in Anfossi's opera *Il curioso indiscreto* (Vienna, 1783) and for *Le Gelosie fortunate* (Vienna, 1788).

Angeles, Victoria de Los. See **De Los Angeles.**

d'Angeli, Andrea, Italian composer and writer on music; b. Padua, Nov. 9, 1868; d. S. Michele, near Verona, Oct. 28, 1940. He studied at the Univ. of Padua; then was instructor at the Liceo Rossini in Pesaro. He wrote several operas: *L'Innocente; Il Negromante; Al Ridotto di Venezia; Fiori e Colombi; Maurizio e Lazzaro;* also a number of libretti. He published monographs on Verdi (Milan, 1924) and Benedetto Marcello (Milan, 1930), and numerous essays on music in 'La Cronaca Musicale' of which he was editor (1907-14).

Angelini, Bontempi Giovanni Andrea. See **Bontempi, Giovanni Andrea.**

d'Angelo, Louis, baritone; b. Naples, May 6, 1888; brought to the U.S. as a child; first apprenticed as a glove cutter in Gloversville, N. Y., then sang in a local church. He went to New York at 18 and appeared in vaudeville; then sang with the Savage Opera Co.; joined the staff of the Metropolitan Opera during the 1917-18 season, retiring in 1946. He had more than 300 operatic roles in his repertoire and was particularly successful as Bartolo in *The Barber of Seville.*

Angeloni, Carlo, Italian composer; b. Lucca, July 16, 1834; d. there, Jan. 13, 1901. He wrote the following operas, all performed at Lucca: *Carlo di Viana* (1855); *Asraele degli Abenceragi* (1871); *Dramma in montagna* (perf. posthumously, 1902). Bibl.: L. Landucci, *Carlo Angeloni* (Lucca, 1905).

Angeloni, Luigi, Italian writer on music; b. Frosione, Papal States, 1759; d. London, Feb. 5, 1842. He wrote a valuable monograph, *Sopra la vita, le opere ed il sapere di Guido d'Arezzo, restauratore della scienza e dell' arte musica* (Paris, 1811).

d'Anglebert, Jean-Henri, French clavecin player; b. Paris, probably in 1628; d. there, April 23, 1691. He studied with Champion de Chambonnières; in 1664 he succeeded his teacher as clavecinist to Louis XIV. In 1689 he published a collection, *Pièces de clavecin avec la manière de les jouer,* containing original suites, arrangements of airs from Lully's operas and also 22 variations on *Folies d'Espagne* (the theme later used by Corelli); the same volume contains instruction on figured bass. D'Anglebert contributed greatly to the establishment of the French method of performance on the clavecin. His extant compositions were published in 1934 by Marguerite Roesgen-Champion in 'Publications de la Société Française de Musicologie,' also containing biographical information. His son **Jean-Baptiste Henri** (b. Paris, Sept. 5, 1661; d. there, March 9, 1747) succeeded his father as court musician. Cf. Ch. Bouvet, *Les deux d'Anglebert* in 'La Revue de Musicologie' (May, 1928).

Anglès, Higini (Catalan form; in Spanish, **Higinio Anglés**), distinguished musicologist; b. Maspujols, Catalonia, Jan. 1, 1888. He studied philosophy at Tarragona (1900-13); musicology with Felipe Pedrell and composition with V. M. Gibert in Barcelona (1913-19). In 1917 he became head of the Music Dept. of the Barcelona library. In 1923 he went to Germany and studied with W. Gurlitt at Freiburg and F. Ludwig at Göttingen. In 1924 he returned to Barcelona and in 1927, became prof. of music history at the Cons. With the outbreak of the Spanish Civil War in 1936, he went to Munich; returned to Barcelona in 1939. In 1943 he was appointed director of the Instituto Español de Musicologia; in 1947 he became director of the Pontifical Institute of Sacred Music in Rome. His most important publication is *El Códex Musical de Las Huelgas* (3 vols., 1928-31), containing facsimiles and transcriptions of Spanish music of the 13th and 14th centuries. Part of the text of this edition was published in the 'Mus. Quarterly' (Oct., 1940). He has published the following books: *Cantigas del Rei N'Anfos el Savi* (Barcelona, 1927); *Historia de la musica española* (Barcelona, 1935); *La música a Catalunya fins al segle XIII* (Barcelona, 1935); *La música española desde la edad media hasta nuestros días* (Barcelona, 1941), and many smaller works. He edited the collected works of J. Pujol (1925); the organ works of Cabanilles (1926); *La Música en la Corte de los Reyes Católicos* (2 vols.; Madrid, 1941, Barcelona, 1947); *Recopilación de Sonetos,* etc. by Juan Vásquez (Barcelona, 1946); *El cancionero musical de Palacio* (Barcelona, 1947). Anglès has contributed to many music journals and has written articles on Spanish music for 'Die Musik in Geschichte und Gegenwart.' He is regarded as an outstanding expert on Spanish music of the Middle Ages.

Anglès, Rafael, Spanish organist and composer; b. Rafales (Teruel), 1731; d. Valencia, Feb. 19, 1816; was organist at Valencia Cathedral from 1762-72. He devoted his life to liturgical music; also wrote keyboard pieces, four of which are printed by J. Nín in his collection, *17 Sonates et pièces anciennes d'auteurs espagnols* (Paris, 1929).

Animuccia (ăh-nē-moo'-tchăh), **Giovanni,** Italian composer of sacred music; b. Florence, c. 1500; d. Rome, March 25, 1571. In 1555 he was appointed maestro di cappella at St. Peter's as successor to Palestrina (who resumed that post after Animuccia's death in 1571). In 1570 Animuccia joined Neri in the oratory of S. Filippo; his *Laudi spirituali* were used by Neri, who expressed his admiration for Animuccia's ability and devout spirit. These *Laudi* were contrapuntal songs in several parts, interspersed with occasional strophes or lines sung by a solo voice for variety's sake; the first book of the *Laudi* was printed by Dorici (1563), the second by Blado (1570). Other published works are a book of masses (1567), 2 of magnificats, a 4-part *Credo,* 4 books of madrigals. Modern reprints of a mass and a 5-part madrigal are in Torchi's 'L'Arte musicale in Italia' (vol. I). Animuccia's compositions show a gradual emancipation from the involved formalism of the Flemish school in the direction of a more practical style, which is in some respects similar to Palestrina's. That Animuccia possessed great skill in purely contrapuntal writings is shown by his intricate canons. His association with Neri undoubtedly played a role in the formation of the oratorio. See G. Reese, *Music in the Renaissance* (N. Y., 1954; pp. 453-55).

d'Ankerts. See **Danckerts, Ghiselin.**

Anna Amalia, Princess of Prussia, sister of Frederick the Great; b. Berlin, Nov. 9, 1723; d. there, March 30, 1787. She received her general musical training from her brother; then studied with the cathedral organist, Gottlieb Hayne, and with Joh. Ph. Kirnberger. She wrote music to Ramler's *Tod Jesu* which was later set also by Graun; she also composed some instrumental works and many chorales. Her sonata for flute, a trio sonata and 4 military marches have been published. She assembled a great library of manuscripts, including some of Bach; a catalogue was published by Eitner (Berlin, 1884).

Anna Amalia, Duchess of Saxe-Weimar; b. Wolfenbüttel, Oct. 24, 1739; d. Weimar, April 10, 1807. She was the mother of the Grand Duke Charles Augustus, who was Goethe's protector. Goethe supplied her with a libretto for *Erwin und Elmire,* a 'Singspiel'; first performed at the Weimar Court (May 24, 1776), it had numerous revivals. Max Friedländer publ. its vocal score in 1921. She also wrote some instrumental music *(Divertimento* for piano, clarinet, viola and cello, etc.). See W. Bode, *Amalie, Herzogin von Weimar* (3 vols., Berlin, 1908); O. Heuschele, *Herzogin Anna Amalia* (Munich, 1947).

Annibale (Il Padovano, from his birthplace, Padua); Italian organist and composer; b. Padua, c. 1527; d. Graz, March 15, 1575. He was organist at San Marco, (1552-66); from 1566 Kapellmeister ('Obrister Musicus') to the Archduke Carl at Graz. His published works include: a book of Ricercari *a* 4 (1556; modern ed. by N. Pierront and J. P. Hennebains, 1934); a book of madrigals *a* 5 (1564); a book of motets *a* 5-6 (1567); a book of masses *a* 5 (1573); a book of *Toccate e Ricercari* for organ (1604). Two *Ricercari* for organ are reprinted in vol. III of Torchi's 'L'Arte musicale in Italia.' — Cf. G. del Valle de Paz, *Annibale Il Padovano, nella storia della musica del cinquecento* (Turin, 1933; contains complete bibliography and musical examples).

Anrooy (properly **Anrooij**), **Peter van,** Dutch conductor and composer; b. Zalt-Bommel, Oct. 13, 1879. He studied with Johan Wagenaar; later went to Moscow, where he took lessons with Willem Kes and Taneyev. He played the violin in the orchestras of Glasgow and Zürich; then was engaged as conductor in Holland (Groningen, Arnhem). In 1917 he became conductor of the Residentie Orch. at The Hague. He retired in 1935. Anrooy has written an orchestral rhapsody on native themes *Piet Hein* (1911), a ballade for violin and orch., and chamber music.

Anschütz, Johann Andreas, German musician; father of Karl Anschütz; b. Koblenz, March 19, 1772; d. there, Dec. 26, 1856. In 1808 he founded a school for vocal music at Koblenz. He was a lawyer by profession, but was also a pianist and conductor, and composed numerous vocal works.

Anschütz, Karl, German conductor; son of Johann Andreas; b. Koblenz, Feb., 1815; d. New York, Dec. 30, 1870. He studied with Friedrich Schneider. In 1844 he assumed the directorship of the music school founded by his father, in 1848 went to London (where he conducted the Wednesday Concerts for a time). In 1857 he went to America and settled in New York as opera conductor. He was a cultivated musician; apart from his activity as conductor he published several piano pieces.

Ansermet, Ernest, celebrated Swiss conductor; b. Vevey, Nov. 11, 1883. He first studied mathematics with his father, who was a teacher of geometry; received his first musical training from his mother; after obtaining a degree from a college in Lausanne, Ansermet taught mathematics at the High School (1906-10). At the same time he pursued his musical studies with Denéréaz, Barblan and Ernest Bloch; later with Gédalge in Paris. He also studied conducting with Mottl in Munich and with Nikisch in Berlin. He conducted popular concerts in Montreux (1911-14), where he met Stravinsky who recommended him to Diaghilev. Subsequently, Ansermet conducted Diaghilev's Ballets Russes in Europe and America (1915-23). On Sept. 28, 1918, he presented in Lausanne the world premiere of Stravinsky's *Histoire du Soldat;* in 1918 he became permanent conductor of the newly founded Orchestre de la Suisse Romande in Geneva. He has made numerous successful appearances in the U. S. with major American orchestras. His specialty is modern French and Russian music; he is regarded as one of the greatest interpreters of Debussy, Ravel and Stravinsky. He has composed a symphonic poem *Feuilles de Printemps,* a ballade for piano and orch.; has also orchestrated Debussy's *6 epigraphes antiques,* and 2 Argentinian dances by Julian Aguirre. He published *Le geste du chef d'orchestre* (Lausanne, 1943).

Ansorge, Conrad (Eduard Reinhold), German pianist; b. Buchwald, near Löbau, Silesia, Oct. 15, 1862; d. Berlin, Feb. 13, 1930. He studied at the Leipzig Cons. (1880-82) and was one of the last pupils of Liszt in Weimar (1885). He toured in Russia and America; then lived in Weimar (1893-95) and in Berlin (from 1895). From 1898 he taught at the Klindworth-Scharwenka Cons. In 1920 he gave courses at the German Cons. in Prague. Ansorge excelled as an interpreter of romantic compositions; he was called "a metaphysician among pianists" for his insight into the inner meaning of the music of Beethoven, Schubert and Schumann. He wrote a piano concerto, a string sextet, 2 string quartets and a cello sonata; *Ballade, Traumbilder, Polish Dances,* and 3 sonatas for piano, and a Requiem.

Ansorge, Joachim, German pianist, son of Conrad; b. Weimar, July 24, 1893; d. Vienna, July 22, 1947. He studied with his father and his mother, Margarethe Ansorge (b. Halle, Dec. 14, 1872; d. Berlin, Oct. 4, 1944). He taught at the Cons. of Königsberg; in 1933 became prof. at the Hochschule für Musik in Berlin; then went to Vienna.

Antcliffe, Herbert, English writer on music; b. Sheffield, July 30, 1875. He studied organ with a local church organist; as a young man began writing music criticism; in 1916 became music critic of 'The Evening Standard.' In 1925 he went to Holland as correspondent for 'The Daily Mail'; in 1939 was elected President of the Foreign Press Association; in 1948 returned to England. During his long sojourn in Holland, he became an authority on Dutch music and contributed many articles on contemporary events in Holland to music magazines. He also published miniature biographies of Brahms (1905) and Schubert (1910); brief manuals *Living Music* (1912) and *How to Enjoy Music* (1921), etc.

Antegnati (ahn-tā-ñah'-tē), **Costanzo,** Italian organist and composer; b. Brescia, c. 1549; d. there, Nov. 16, 1624. He was descended from a family of organ builders, and served as apprentice to his father. In 1584 he became organist at Brescia cathedral. His madrigals and sacred compositions (masses, motets, psalms and canzoni) were published in Venice (1571-1608) with pieces in organ tablature; he also published an important treatise, *L'Arte organica* (Brescia, 1608; new ed. by Renato Lunelli, Mainz, 1938). His *3 Ricercari* for organ are reprinted in vol. III of Luigi Torchi's 'L'Arte musicale in Italia.' Bibl.: D. Muoni, *Gli Antegnati* (Milan, 1883).

Antes, John, 'Moravian' minister; b. Frederickstownship, Pa., March 24, 1740; d. Bristol, England, Dec. 17, 1811. He left America in 1764, and was a missionary in Egypt where he was beaten and crippled by order of a bey who tried to extort money from him. He spent the rest of his life in England. Watchmaker by trade, he was an inventive artisan. He constructed several string instruments; one violin, made by him in Bethlehem in 1759, is preserved in the Museum of the Moravian Historical Society at Nazareth, Pa. A contribution by Antes to the 'Allegemeine Musikalische Zeitung' in 1806 describes a device for better violin tuning, as well as improvements of the violin bow and of the keyboard hammer. Antes also invented a machine with which one could turn pages while playing. He wrote about 25 melodious short anthems to German or English words for chorus, winds, strings, and organ. All of his MS compositions are in the Archives of the Moravian Church at Bethlehem, Pa. and

Winston-Salem, N. C. His three string trios were discovered in 1949. They are the earliest chamber works by a native American. His interesting autobiography was publ. in 'Nachrichten aus der Brüder-Gemeine' (1845).—Cf. D. M. McCorkle, *John Antes, "American Dilettante"* in the 'Mus. Quarterly' (Oct., 1956).

Antheil, George, American composer; b. Trenton, N. J., July 8, 1900. He studied with Constantin von Sternberg and Ernest Bloch; also with Clark Smith at the Philadelphia Cons. In 1920 he went to Europe, where he played concerts of his piano works, in an ultra-modern vein, with titles such as *Mechanisms, Airplane Sonata, Sonate sauvage.* This emphasis on modernism culminated in his *Ballet mécanique,* performed as an orchestral piece by Golschmann (Paris, June 19, 1926). Upon his return to New York, Antheil staged a spectacular production of the *Ballet mécanique* at Carnegie Hall (April 10, 1927) with the use of airplane propellers, which created an uproar in the audience. A revival of this work in a new version (with 4 pianos instead of 8) and using a recording of the noise of a jet plane (Composer's Forum, N. Y., Feb. 20, 1954), passed without incident, almost as a period piece. In Europe, Antheil composed *Zingareska* for orch. (1921); *Jazz Symphony* for chamber orch. (1925); Symphony in F major, No. 1 (Paris, 1926) and a piano concerto (1926). His first opera *Transatlantic* (to his own libretto), employing jazz rhythms, was staged for the first time in Frankfurt (May 25, 1930) and aroused considerable attention as a curiosity of American modern music. A second opera, *Helen Retires* (libretto by John Erskine), was produced in New York (Feb. 28, 1934). In 1936 Antheil settled in Hollywood. In the meantime he had abandoned the extreme modernism of his early music, and adopted an effective style comprising elements of classicism, romanticism and impressionism, with moderately advanced harmonies. A number of works followed: 'American' Symphony No. 2 (1937); Symphony No. 3 (1942); Symphony No. 4 (NBC Symph. Orch., Stokowski conducting, Feb. 13, 1944); Violin concerto (Dallas, Feb. 9, 1947); Symphony No. 5 (Philadelphia, Dec. 31, 1948); Symphony No. 6 (San Francisco, Feb. 10, 1949); *Volpone,* opera after Ben Jonson (Los Angeles, Jan. 9, 1954); ballet, *The Capital of the World* (N. Y., Dec. 27, 1953); and two short operas, *The Brothers* (Denver, July 28, 1954) and *The Wish* (commissioned by the Louisville Orch.; first perf., Louisville, April 2, 1955). Antheil has also written 3 string quartets, 2 violin sonatas, 4 piano sonatas, a concerto for flute, bassoon and piano, and many flute scores. He married Boski Markus on Nov. 4, 1925. He is the author of an autobiographical volume *Bad Boy of Music* (N. Y., 1945). The poet Ezra Pound published a pamphlet entitled *Antheil and the Treatise on Harmony, with Supplementary Notes* (Chicago, 1927), which, however, has little bearing on Antheil's work as composer.

Antill, John Henry, Australian composer; b. Sydney, April 8, 1904. He studied music at Sydney Cons., and began to compose very early. He has worked for the Australian Broadcasting Commission; his compositions have been mainly for the stage. His ballet, *Corrobboree* (Sydney, Aug. 18, 1946) is based on the rhythms of Australian aboriginal music.

Antipov, Konstantin Afanasievitch, Russian composer; b. St. Petersburg, Jan. 18, 1859; date of death unknown. He was a minor composer whose works (mostly miniatures for piano) were published by Belaiev. They include: 3 Etudes; 3 Waltzes; *Variations* on an original Russian theme; 5 Pieces (of which No. 1, *Romance,* is the best); 2 Preludes; 3 Miniatures, etc.; also an *Allegro symphonique* for orchestra.

Antiquus, Andreas (also **A. de Antiquiis Venetus,** or **Andrea Antico**); Italian music-printer and composer; b. Montona (Istria) in the latter half of the 15th century. He printed music in Rome and Venice (1520), and was probably one of the earliest in his trade after Petrucci, who himself published many of Antiquus's *Frottole* (Venice, 1504-08). His collection of *Canzoni, Sonetti, Strambotti e Frottole, libro tertio,* was edited by A. Einstein (Northampton, Mass, 1941).

Antoine, Georges, Belgian composer; b. Liège, April 28, 1892; d. Bruges, Nov. 15, 1918 (of an ailment acquired during World War I). He studied at the Cons. of Liège (1902-13) with Sylvain Dupuis; joined the Belgian Army in 1914. He wrote a piano concerto (1914); *Vendanges* for voice and orch. (1914); *Veillée d'Armes,* symph. poem (1918); a piano quartet (1916); a violin sonata (1912-15) and songs. — Cf. M. Paquot, *Georges Antoine* (Brussels, 1935).

Antoine, Josephine, American coloratura soprano; b. Denver, Colorado, Oct. 27, 1908. She studied with Marcella Sembrich at the Juilliard Graduate School (1931-35). After singing with the Philadelphia Opera

(1935), she made her debut, Jan. 4, 1936, as Philine in *Mignon* at the Metropolitan Opera, of which she became a member. She also sang with the Chicago Opera Co. during the 1936-37 season.

Antoine, Paul. Pen-name of **Ernest Closson.**

Anton, Karl, German writer on liturgical music; b. Worms, June 2, 1887. He studied theology and music at Halle Univ.; took the degree of *Dr. Phil.* with the thesis *Beiträge zur Biographie Carl Loewes* (Halle, 1912). From 1918 he taught music history at the Mannheim Hochschule für Musik. He published a number of treatises on church music, among them *Luther und die Musik* (1917); *Angewandte Liturgik* (1918) and *Erneuerung der Kirchenmusik* (1932).

Anton, Max, German conductor and pedagogue; b. Bornstedt, Aug. 2, 1877; d. Bonn, Aug. 18, 1939. He studied with Stavenhagen in Munich and James Kwast in Frankfurt; then taught at Gladbach and Detmold. From 1922 was active in Bonn as choral conductor until his retirement in 1934. A prolific composer, he wrote an opera *Die Getreuen;* an oratorio *Ekkehard;* several instrumental concertos, piano pieces and songs. He published *Versuch einer Kunstanschauung* (1922).

Antony, Franz Joseph, German organist and writer on music; b. Münster, Westphalia, Feb. 1, 1790; d. there, Jan. 7, 1837. He was appointed music director at Münster cathedral in 1819; in 1832, succeeded his father Joseph Antony (1758-1836) as organist. He published *Archäologisch-liturgisches Gesangbuch des Gregorianischen Kirchengesangs* (1829) and *Geschichtliche Darstellung der Entstehung und Vervollkommnung der Orgel* (1832).

Apel, Johann August, German scholar; b. Leipzig, Sept. 17, 1771; d. there, Aug. 9, 1816. He is important in music history for his collection *Gespensterbuch* (1810-14), dealing with supernatural tales, which was the inspiration for Weber's *Der Freischütz.* Apel also published several treatises on music, among them a series of articles on rhythm (in 'Allgemeine musikalische Zeitung,' 1807-8) and a large work in 2 volumes, *Metrik* (1814-16).

Apel, Willi, musicologist; b. Konitz, Germany, Oct. 10, 1893. He studied mathematics at Bonn Univ. (1912), Munich (1913), and Berlin (1918-21), and took piano lessons. He taught mathematics and music in Germany; in 1935 he came to the U.S. He gave lectures at Harvard Univ. (1938-42); in 1950 he was engaged as prof. of musicology at Indiana Univ., Bloomington. While in Germany he edited 2 volumes of early music, *Musik aus früher Zeit* (Mainz, 1934), and published 2 treatises: *Die Fuge* (1932) and *Accidentien und Tonalität in den Musikdenkmälern des 15. und 16. Jahrhunderts* (Strasbourg, 1936); he also contributed to German music magazines. In America he published the extremely valuable compilations, *The Notation of Polyphonic Music, 900-1600* (Cambridge, Mass, 1942); *The Harvard Dictionary of Music* (ibid., 1944); *Historical Anthology of Music,* 2 vols. (with A. T. Davison; ibid., 1946 and 1949); *Masters of the Keyboard* (ibid., 1947). *The Harvard Dictionary of Music,* comprising only articles on forms and terms, has established itself as a prime reference work of musical terminology.

Apostel, Hans Erich, Austrian composer; b. Karlsruhe, Jan. 22, 1901. He studied with Schoenberg and Berg in Vienna; adopted the 12-tone method in some of his works. He has written a Symphony, a Requiem (to Rilke's text), string quartet, wind quartet, *Sonata ritmica* for piano, etc.

Appel, Richard Gilmore, music librarian and organist; b. Lancaster, Pa., April 25, 1889. He studied with Wallace Goodrich in Boston and Karl Straube in Germany. He received his M.A. from Harvard Univ. (1912); was active as organist at various churches in Boston and vicinity. He was appointed head of the music dept. of the Boston Public Library in 1922; retired in 1954.

Appeldoorn, Dina, Dutch composer; b. Rotterdam, Feb. 26, 1884; d. The Hague, Dec. 4, 1938. She was the composer of several works in romantic style, including 2 symphonic poems, *Noordzee* and *Volkfeest;* she also wrote chamber music and songs, and taught piano at The Hague.

Appenzeller (Appencellers; Appenzelder; Appenzelders), Benedictus, Franco-Flemish composer of the first half of the 16th century. Possibly a pupil of Josquin, he served Mary of Hungary as court musician and master of the choir boys at her chapel in Brussels (1539—c. 1554) and probably accompanied her on her visit to Spain (1551). Appenzeller's works were formerly attributed to Benedictus Ducis, a German composer whose identity was confused with his. Among Appenzeller's extant compositions are a book of chansons (1542; two of the chansons from this collection had been published by Attaingnant in 1529 without being ascribed to Appenzeller); a lament on the death of Josquin (1521) which uses half of the *Musae Jovis* text; and a double-canon on *Sancta Maria* embroidered on a tablecloth for Mary of Hungary (1548). Pieces by him are included in the second *Musyckboexken* of Susato; the *Hortus Musarum*, part I (1552), published by Phalese, contains a transcription for two lutes of a piece by him. Bibl.: E. van der Straeten, *La Musique aux Pays-Bas* (Brussels, 1867-8; volumes 3, 7, and 8); D. Bartha, *Benedictus Ducis und Appenzeller* (Wolfenbüttel, 1930); G. Reese, *Music in the Renaissance* (N. Y., 1954).

Aprile, Giuseppe, Italian male contralto; b. Martinafranca, Apulia, Oct. 28, 1731; d. there, Jan. 11, 1813. From c. 1763 he sang at the principal theaters of Italy and Germany; then settled in Naples as teacher; among his pupils was Cimarosa. Aprile's vocal treatise, *The Modern Italian Method of Singing, with 36 Solfeggi*, first published by Broderip in London (1791), has been reprinted in many editions and several languages.

Apthorp, William Foster, American music critic; b. Boston, Mass., Oct. 24, 1848; d. Vevey, Switzerland, Feb. 19, 1913. A graduate of Harvard Univ. (1869), he studied music with Paine. He taught music at the New England Cons. and lectured on music history at Boston Univ. He wrote music criticism for the 'Atlantic Monthly' (1872-77); was music and drama critic on the 'Boston Evening Transcript' (1881-1903). In his criticisms Apthorp violently opposed new Russian, French and German music (his intemperate attacks on Tchaikovsky elicited protests from his readers). Apthorp was also the annotator of the Boston Symph. programs (1892-1901). He published several books: *Musicians and Music Lovers* (N. Y., 1894); *By the Way*, a collection of short essays in 2 vols.: I. *About Music*, II. *About Musicians* (Boston, 1898); *The Opera, Past and Present* (N. Y., 1901). He was co-editor of Scribner's 'Cyclopedia of Music and Musicians' (N. Y., 1888-90).

Aptommas. See **Thomas, John.**

Ara, Ugo, Italian violinist; member of the Flonzaley Quartet; b. Venice, July 19, 1876; d. Lausanne, Switzerland, Dec. 10, 1936. He studied violin with Tirindelli in Venice; at the age of 13 played in theater orchs. In 1894 he went to Liège where he studied with César Thomson; he then took lessons in composition with R. Fuchs at the Vienna Cons. When the Flonzaley Quartet was established, he joined it as a viola player, (1903-17). He later returned to Italy.

Araja (ăh-ri'-ăh), **Francesco**, Italian composer; b. Naples, c. 1700; d. c. 1770. He produced his first opera *Lo matremmonejo pe' mennetta* in the Neapolitan dialect (Naples, 1729); his subsequent operas were *Berenice* (Florence, 1730); *La forza dell' amore e dell' odio* (Milan, 1734); *Lucio Vero* (Venice, Jan. 4, 1735). In 1735 he was engaged as musical director and court composer in St. Petersburg. There he wrote annual pieces for court occasions, beginning with the cantata *La gara dell' amore e del zelo* (April 28, 1736). Among his operas given at the Russian court were *La Semiramide riconosciuta* (Feb. 9, 1737); *Artaserse* (1738); *Seleuco* (1744); *Scipione* (1745); *Mitridate* (1747); *L'asilo della pace* (1748); *Bellerofonte* (1750); *Eudossa incoronata* (1751). He wrote 22 operas; *La Clemenza di Tito*, attributed to him by some, was the work of Hasse. On Feb. 27, 1755, Araja presented in St. Petersburg the first opera ever composed to a Russian text, *Céphale et Procris* (libretto by the famous Russian dramatist Sumarokov). He was in Italy in 1741-42 and 1759-61; in 1762 he revisited Russia briefly at the summons of Peter III, his great admirer, returning to Italy after the Czar's death. Nothing is known of Araja's last years. Bibl.: A. Mooser, *Annales de la musique et des musiciens en Russie au XVIII siècle*, vol. I, pp. 121-131 (Geneva, 1951).

Arakishvili (ăh-răh-kē-shvē'-lē), **Dmitri**, Russian composer; b. Vladikavkaz, Georgia, Feb. 23, 1873; d. Tiflis, Aug. 13, 1953. He studied composition at the Moscow Philharmonic Institute, graduating in 1901. He lived mostly in the Caucasus; compiled native songs for the Musical Ethnographic Committee of Moscow Univ. (1901-08). From 1917 on, he was prof. of music at the Tiflis Cons. He composed *The Legend of Shota Rustaveli* (first national opera of Georgia, performed in Tiflis, 1919); 3 symphonies; symph. poem *Hymn to the New East* (1933); many choral works and arrangements of native songs.

d'Aranyi, Adila. See **Fachiri, Adila.**

Aranyi, Francis, violinist; b. Budapest, March 21, 1893. He studied at the Royal Academy in Budapest, and later in Berlin with Willy Hess and Henri Marteau. He was a concert player and orchestral violinist in Europe; in Vienna (1912-14), in Budapest (1914-17); later in Stockholm (1921-

22), and Zagreb (1924-26). In 1935 he came to America; was violin teacher at Duquesne Univ., Pittsburgh, Pa. (1935-40); at Michigan State College (1940-41); concertmaster of the Seattle Symphony Orch. (1941-42). In 1942 he organized the Youth Symph. Orch. of the Pacific Northwest, in Seattle, where he settled.

d'Aranyi, Yelly, violinist; grandniece of Joachim, and sister of the violinist, Adila Fachiri; b. Budapest, May 30, 1895. She studied with Hubay in Budapest; made her concert debut in New York on Nov. 26, 1927; made her second American tour in 1932. She has frequently appeared in joint recitals with Myra Hess. A pioneer in modern music, she has given first performances of many new works. Béla Bartók's violin sonatas, Ravel's *Tzigane* and Vaughan Williams' violin concerto are dedicated to her. In 1937 she attracted considerable attention by proclaiming that Schumann's spirit appeared to her and revealed the secret of his unpublished violin concerto; the MS of the concerto, long known to have been preserved at the Berlin State Library, was made available to her, but the concerto was given its first performance by another violinist in Germany in 1937; Yelly d'Aranyi played it on Feb. 16, 1938 with the B.B.C. orch. in London.

Arauxo (or **Araujo**). See **Correa de Araujo.**

Arbatsky, Yury, composer and music scholar; b. Moscow, April 15, 1911. His family left Russia in 1924; he studied with Lopatnikov in Berlin, and also took lessons with Rachmaninoff in Dresden; he graduated from Leipzig Cons. in 1932; in 1933 he settled in Yugoslavia where he was active as conductor and teacher. He accumulated numerous materials on Balkan folk music, most of which were destroyed during the bombardment of Belgrade in 1941. In 1942-45, he was in Prague where he continued his work on Slavic folk music; in 1944 he received his doctorate from the Charles Univ. In 1949 Arbatsky came to the U.S.A., and settled in Chicago. In 1954 he transferred his valuable collection of folk music and deposited it at the Newberry Library, Chicago. Despite constant changes of residence, due to political upheavals, Arbatsky has composed a great number of works: 8 symphonies, chamber and choral music, etc. The Newberry Library published his paper *Beating the Tupan in the Central Balkans* (Chicago, 1953), and several of his sacred works. Cf. 'The Arbatsky Collection,' in the 'Bulletin of the Newberry Library' (July, 1954).

Arbeau (ăhr-bŏh), **Thoinot** (anagram of real name Jehan Tabourot), French writer; b. Dijon, c. 1519; d. Langres, c. 1595. He owes his fame to his unique treatise in dialogue form, *Orchésographie, et traité en forme de dialogue par lequel toutes personnes peuvent facilement apprendre et pratiquer l'honnête exercise des danses* (Langres, 1589; 2nd ed., 1596), which contains not only instruction for dancing (indicating dance steps by a simple system of initial letters) but also valuable observations on the dance music of his time. It was publ. in English translations by C. W. Beaumont (London, 1925) and M. Evans (N. Y., 1948).

Arbo, Jens, Norwegian music critic; b. Kristiansand, Aug. 20, 1885; d. Oslo, Jan. 8, 1944. He studied in Oslo; then in Germany (1911-14). He was music critic of 'Musikbladet' (1917-24) and of 'Morgenbladet' (1924-43).

Arbós, Enrique Fernández, Spanish violinist and conductor; b. Madrid, Dec. 24, 1863; d. San Sebastian, June 2, 1939. He studied violin with Monasterio in Madrid, with Vieuxtemps in Brussels, and with Joachim in Berlin. After successful tours in Europe he returned to Spain in 1888; taught violin at the Madrid Cons. In 1889 he was concertmaster of the Glasgow Symph. Orch.; from 1894-1916 he held the post of honorary prof. at the Royal College of Music in London. He was appointed conductor of the new Madrid Symph. Orch. in 1904; conducted in the U.S. (1928-31); then in Europe. At the outbreak of the Spanish Civil War in 1936 he retired to San Sebastian. Arbós was the author of a comic opera *El Centro de la Tierra* (Madrid, Dec. 22, 1895). He was a brilliant orchestrator; his arrangement of the music from *Iberia* by Albéniz is very popular. Bibl.: V. Espinós Moltó, *El Maestro Arbós* (Madrid, 1942).

Arbuckle, Matthew, American cornet player and bandmaster; b. 1828; d. New York, May 23, 1883. He published a manual under the title *Complete Cornet Method.*

Arbuthnot, John, British physician and musical amateur; b. Arbuthnot, Scotland, in 1667; d. London, Feb. 27, 1735. He was one of the founders of the Scriblerus Club in London (1714), and was friendly with Handel during the composer's difficulties with his opera company. Arbuthnot's publication entitled *Miscellaneous Works* throws sharp sidelights on various persons of interest at the time. He wrote several anthems, glees, etc.

Arcadelt, Jacob (or **Jachet Arkadelt, Archadet, Arcadet, Harcadelt**), great Flemish composer; b. probably in Liège, c. 1505; d. Paris, c. 1560. He was 'magister puerorum' to the Papal Chapel (1539), and choirmaster (1540). In 1544 he held the office of 'Camerlingo.' He went to France in 1546; returned to Rome in May, 1547. In 1555 he again went to France, this time with the Duc de Guise. Arcadelt is mentioned in Paris as 'Regis musicus,' in 1557. In the domain of secular music, his Roman period was, in the main, devoted to the madrigal; his Paris period to the French chanson. He wrote 20 motets, about 120 French chansons and 200 madrigals. Of his extant works, the most important are 6 books of 5-part madrigals (Venice, 1538-56; his finest and most characteristic compositions) and 3 books of masses in 3-7 parts (Paris, 1557). Modern reprints include the 4-part 'Madrigale parlando' *Il ciel che rado* (Riemann, *Handbuch der Musikgeschichte,* Part II); the 4-part madrigal *Il bianco e dolce cigno* (W. B. Squire's 'Ausgewählte Madrigale'); others in Eitner (vol. XXIII); Schering's 'Geschichte der Musik in Beispielen'; Maldeghem's 'Trésor Musical.' See also *The Chansons of Jacob Arcadelt,* ed. by E. B. Helm ('Smith College Music Archives,' vol. V, 1942). — Bibl.: W. Klefisch, *Arcadelt als Madrigalist* (Cologne, 1938); A. Einstein, *The Italian Madrigal* (Princeton, 1949).

d'Archambeau (dar-shăhn-boh'), **Iwan,** Belgian cellist; member of the Flonzaley Quartet; b. Hervé, Sept. 28, 1879; d. Villefranche-sur-Mer, France, Dec. 29, 1955. He studied music at home; played in a family quartet with his father and two brothers. He then studied cello with A. Massau in Verviers and with Hugo Becker in Frankfurt. In 1903 he became a member of the Flonzaley Quartet, until it disbanded in 1929; in 1935 he joined the Stradivarius Quartet in New York. From 1939 until 1950 he lived in Cambridge, Mass.; then returned to Belgium.

Archangelsky (ar-hahn'-gĕl-skē), **Alexander,** Russian choral conductor; b. near Penza, Oct. 23, 1846; d. Prague, Nov. 16, 1924. He studied singing and theory of music at the Court Chapel in St. Petersburg; in 1880 organized a chorus there, toured Russia with it in 1899-1900, presenting 110 concerts; also gave concerts with his chorus in Western Europe (1907 and 1912). Archangelsky was the first choir leader in Russia to include women's voices in performances of sacred works. He supported (with Gretchaninov) the reform movement in Russian church music; wrote a number of choral pieces for his organization and made transcriptions of Russian church hymns. In 1923 he went to Prague as conductor of a students' choir, and died there the following year.

Archer, Frederick, English-American organist, conductor and composer; b. Oxford, June 16, 1838; d. Pittsburgh, Oct. 22, 1901. He studied organ in Leipzig, and in 1873 was appointed organist of Alexandra Palace in London; then became conductor of a Glasgow choir (1878-80). In 1881 he came to America; was active as church organist in Brooklyn and, from 1895, at Carnegie Institute in Pittsburgh. He was the first conductor of the newly organized Pittsburgh Symphony Orchestra, from Feb. 27, 1896, to 1898, when he was succeeded by Victor Herbert. A prolific composer, he published a cantata, *King Witlaf's Drinking-horn;* organ and piano pieces and songs. The bulk of his music remains in MS. He was the author of the manuals *The Organ* (1875) and *A Complete Method for the American Reed Organ* (1899), and founder and editor of the music magazine 'The Keynote' (1883).

Ardévol, José, Spanish-Cuban composer; b. Barcelona, March 13, 1911. In 1930 he went to Havana, Cuba, settling there as composer and teacher and conducting a chamber music society. He has written a ballet *Forma,* with chorus (Havana, May 18, 1943, composer conducting); 3 concerti grossi (1937-46); concerto for 3 pianos (1938); 3 symphonies (1943; 1945; 1946); 6 sonatas for 3 instruments (1937-46) and 3 piano sonatas (1944). Bibl.: O. Mayer-Serra, *Música y Músicos de Latino-América* (Mexico, 1947, I, pp. 44-54).

Arditi, Luigi, Italian composer and conductor; b. Crescentino, Piedmont, July 22, 1822; d. Hove, near Brighton, England, May 1, 1903. He studied violin, piano and composition at the Milan Cons., where he also produced his first opera, *I Briganti* (1841). He then embarked on a career as operatic conductor. From 1846 he traveled in Cuba (where he produced his opera *Il Corsaro,* Havana, 1846), and visited New York and Philadelphia. In New York he produced his opera *La Spia* (March 24, 1856). He finally settled in London (1858) as conductor and vocal teacher, while making annual tours with the Italian Opera in Germany and Austria. He conducted in St. Petersburg in 1871 and 1873. His operas and other works were never revived, but he created a perennial success with his vocal waltz *Il Bacio*. He wrote his autobiography *My Reminiscences* (N. Y., 1896).

Arel, Bülent, Turkish composer and pianist; b. Constantinople, April 23, 1918. He studied composition with Necil Kâzim Akses. Since 1951, musical dir. of Radio Ankara. Among his works are 2 symphonies (1951 and 1952); *Cain and Abel,* music for radio; piano concerto (1946); *Suite Intime* for orch. (1949) and chamber music.

Arens, Franz Xavier, German-American composer; b. Neef (Rhenish Prussia), Oct. 28, 1856; d. Los Angeles, Jan. 28, 1932. His family came to the U.S. and settled in Milwaukee when he was very young; he studied with his father and later in Germany with Rheinberger. Upon his return to America he was active as conductor of various choral and instrumental groups. He led the Gesangverein in Cleveland (1885-88); from 1890-92 he was again in Europe; he was the first to present complete programs of orchestral works by American composers in Germany. He was president of the Indianapolis College of Music (1892-96), and later settled in New York as vocal teacher. In 1900 he established a series of People's Symph. Concerts, with low admission prices (from 5¢ to 50¢). He wrote orchestral music, a string quartet and numerous songs.

Arensky, Anton Stepanovitch, Russian composer; b. Novgorod, Aug. 11, 1861; d. Terijoki, Finland, Feb. 25, 1906. He studied at the St. Petersburg Cons. with Johanssen and Rimsky-Korsakov (1879-82); then taught harmony at the Moscow Cons. (1882-94). Returning to St. Petersburg, he conducted the choir of the Imperial Chapel (1895-1901); a victim of tuberculosis, he spent his last years in a sanatorium in Finland. In his music he followed Tchaikovsky's lyric style. Arensky wrote 3 operas: *A Dream on the Volga* (Moscow, Jan. 2, 1891); *Raphael* (Moscow, May 6, 1894); *Nal and Damayanti* (Moscow, Jan. 22, 1904); and 2 symphonies. He conducted the first performances of both in Moscow (Nov. 24, 1883 and Dec. 21, 1889). He was more successful in his works for smaller forms. His *Variations* for string orch. on Tchaikovsky's song, *The Christ Child had a Garden* (originally the *Variations* formed the slow movement of Arensky's quartet, op. 35, in A minor for violin, viola and 2 cellos) became a standard work. His piano trio in memory of Tchaikovsky also retains its popularity. His 4 suites for 2 pianos, expertly written, are often heard; he also arranged these suites for orch. Some of his songs are included in vocal anthologies. Other works are: music to Pushkin's poem *The Fountain of Bakhtchissaray;* ballet *Egyptian Nights* (St. Petersburg, 1900); *The Diver,* ballad for voices and orch.; *Coronation Cantata; Marche solennelle* for orch.; *Intermezzo* for string orch.; piano concerto; violin concerto in A minor; a fantasy on epic Russian songs, for piano and orch.; piano quintet in D; string quartet (op. 11, in G); pieces for cello, for violin, and many pieces for piano solo. He also published a *Manual of Harmony* (translated into German) and *Handbook of Musical Forms.*

d'Arezzo, Guido. See **Guido d'Arezzo.**

Argenta, Ataulfo, Spanish conductor; b. Castro Urdiales, Santander, Nov. 19, 1913. He first sang in a church choir; in 1926 he entered the Madrid Cons., studying piano, violin and composition. He continued his musical education in Germany and studied conducting. Returning to Spain in 1939, he conducted various small groups; in 1945 became director of the National Orch. in Madrid.

Aria, Cesare, Italian singing teacher; b. Bologna, Sept. 21, 1820; d. there, Jan. 30, 1894. He studied at the Bologna Cons. with Mattei. Rossini helped him in his career. For a number of years he was a voice teacher in France and England. He composed some church music; his *Dies irae* is particularly noteworthy.

Aribon (Aribo Scholasticus), medieval scholar, known also as **Aribon de Liège, Aribon de Freising** and **Aribon d'Orléans;** b. probably in Liège, about the year 1000; d. in Orléans, about 1078. In 1024 he was chancellor to the Bishop of Liège; after a short period of service he went to Italy, where he acquired a knowledge of the methods of Guido d'Arezzo. From 1060-70 he was again in Liège as preceptor at the Cathedral school; then went to Orléans. Aribon was the author of the important treatise *De Musica,* written by him in Liège about 1065. It is reproduced in Gerbert's 'Scriptores,' vol. II, pp. 197-230; and by J. Smits van Waesberghe ('Corpus Scriptorum de Musica,' vol. II, Rome, 1951). See also Waesberghe's *Muziekgeschiedenis der Middeleeuwen* (1936).

d'Arienzo, Nicola, Italian composer; b. Naples, Dec. 22, 1842; d. there April 25, 1915. He composed an opera in the Neapolitan dialect at the age of 18; a series of Italian operas followed: *I due mariti* (Naples, Feb. 1, 1866); *Il cacciatore delle Alpi* (Naples, June 23, 1870); *Il cuoco* (Naples, June 11, 1873); *I Viaggi* (Milan, June 28, 1875); *La figlia del diavolo* (Naples, Nov. 16, 1879; his most successful opera which aroused considerable controversy for its realistic tendencies); *I tre coscritti* (Naples, Feb. 10, 1880), etc. He also wrote 2 symphonies and much choral music. He published a treatise *Introduzione del sistema tetracordale nella moderna musica,* favoring pure intonation; a historical essay, *Dell'opera comica dalle origini a Pergolesi* (1887; German translation, 1902), several monographs on Italian composers and numerous articles in periodicals.

Ariosti, Attilio, Italian opera composer; b. Bologna, Nov. 5, 1666; d. c. 1740. He joined the Servite Order in 1688, but later abandoned it. He served as organist in Bologna in 1693; in 1697 he was in Berlin as court musician. From 1703 till 1711 he was in Vienna, then returned to Bologna. He was in London in 1716 and again from 1723-27. A volume of his cantatas and 'lessons' for the viola d'amore, on which he was an accomplished performer, was publ. in London in 1728. Ariosti then disappeared, the most probable conjecture being that he returned to Italy and died there in obscurity. Burney's attribution to Ariosti of one act of the opera *Muzio Scevola* (produced in London on April 15, 1721) is an anachronism, for Ariosti was not in London at the time. A list of his known operas includes the following: *Tirsi* (erroneously named *Dafne* by many music historians; Venice, 1696, in collaboration with Lotti and Caldara); *Mars und Irene* (Berlin, July 12, 1703); *Marte placato* (Vienna, March 19 1707); *Artaserse* (London, Dec. 1, 1724); *Dario* (London, April 5, 1725); *Lucio Vero, imperator di Roma* (London, Jan. 7, 1727). He also wrote 5 oratorios, some instrumental works and numerous cantatas (many of which are preserved in various European libraries), etc.

Aristides Quintilianus, Greek writer on music; lived about 200 A.D. in Smyrna. His treatise *De Musica libri VII* was printed in Meibom's 'Antiquae Musicae Auctores Septem' (1652) and by A. Jahn (1882); R. Schäfke published it in German (1937) with a commentary. Despite the dubious authenticity of some of his descriptions of Greek scales, the work is one of the basic sources of our knowledge of ancient Greek music.

Aristotle, famous Greek philosopher, pupil of Plato; b. Stagira, 384 B.C.; d. Chalcis, 322 B.C. The 19th section of the *Problems,* once ascribed to him, is the product of a much later follower of his theories; the English translation, by E. S. Forster, is found in *The Works of Aristotle,* vol. 7 (Oxford, 1927); the Greek text with French translation and commentary by F. A. Gevaert and C. Vollgraff is published in *Les problèmes musicaux d'Aristote* (3 vols., 1899-1902). Aristotle's actual writings on music are reproduced by K. von Jan in his *Musici Scriptores Graeci* (1895). The name Aristotle was also used by a writer on mensurable music of the 12th-13th centuries, whose treatise is published by E. de Coussemaker in his *Scriptores,* vol. I.

Aristoxenos, one of the earliest Greek writers on music; b. Tarentum, 354 B.C. His *Harmonic Elements* (complete) and *Rhythmical Elements* (fragmentary) are among the most important treatises on Greek musical theory that have come down to us. They have been published by R. Westphal and F. Saran (2 vols., 1883, 1893); also by H. S. Macran, with English and Greek text and a commentary (1902). The *Harmonic Elements* are included, in an English translation, in O. Strunk's *Source Readings in Music History* (N. Y., 1950). See also L. Laloy, *Aristoxène de Tarente* (1904); C. F. A. Williams, *The Aristoxenian Theory of Musical Rhythm* (Cambridge, 1911).

Arkwright, Godfrey Edward Pellew, English music editor; b. Norwich, April 10, 1864; d. Highclere, near Newbury, Aug. 16, 1944. He studied at Eton and at Oxford. His most important publication is 'The Old English Edition' in 25 volumes (1889-1902) containing masques, ballets, motets and madrigals by English composers of the 17th and 18th centuries. He also edited Purcell's church music published by the Purcell Society. He was the editor of 'The Musical Antiquary' from 1909-13.

Arlen, Harold (real name Hyman Arluck), American composer of popular music; b. Buffalo, Feb. 15, 1905. He received his elementary music training from his father, a cantor of the Buffalo Synagogue. As a youth, he went to New York, where he earned his living by playing and singing in nightclubs. He began to compose songs in the course of his professional occupation; his greatest success was *Stormy Weather*

(1932), a song that has achieved enormous popularity. From 1943-55 Arlen lived in Hollywood as composer of film music; in 1955 settled again in New York.

Arma, Paul (real name, Imre Weisshaus), composer; b. Budapest, Oct. 22, 1904. He studied with Béla Bartók at the Budapest Academy of Music (1921-24). He then went to New York (1925-30); later settled in Paris, where he assumed the pseudonym Paul Arma, under which he published a *Nouveau Dictionnaire de Musique* (Paris, 1947). A composer of empiric music exploring the ultimate in complexity, he has developed a compromise method evocative of folk songs in an advanced rhythmic style. Among his works are a concerto for string quartet (1947); sonatina for solo flute (1947); violin sonata (1949); 5 movements for solo viola; *31 instantanés* for woodwind, percussion, celesta, xylophone and piano (1951).

Armbruster, Karl, conductor; b. Andernach-on-Rhine, Germany, July 13, 1846; d. London, June 10, 1917. He studied piano in Cologne; at the age of 17 settled in London, where he made propaganda for Wagner by means of numerous lectures. He was Hans Richter's assistant at the Wagner concerts in London in 1884; later conducted operas at London theaters. He was also one of the conductors of the Wagner cycles at Bayreuth (1884-94).

Armes, Philip, English organist and composer; b. Norwich, Aug. 15, 1836; d. Durham, Feb. 10, 1908. He received his early musical education from his father, a singer; was chorister at the Cathedrals of Norwich (1846) and Rochester (1848); for his work as a boy soloist he received the gift of a grand piano. He subsequently was organist in London, Chichester and Durham, retiring shortly before his death. He wrote the oratorios *Hezekiah* (1877), *St. John the Evangelist* (1881), *Barnabas* (1891). His madrigal *Victoria* won the first prize of the Madrigal Society in 1897.

Armin, Georg (real name Hermann), German singer and pedagogue; b. Brunswick, Nov. 10, 1871. He studied architecture; then turned to singing. He settled in Berlin as voice teacher; from 1925 he edited the periodical 'Der Stimmwart.' His home was destroyed in Berlin during an air raid in World War II; in 1949 he settled in Denmark. He published several papers on voice production, among them *Das Stauprinzip* (1905) and *Von der Urkraft der Stimme* (1921). Cf. J. Berntsen, *Ein Meister der Stimmbildungskunst* (Leipzig, 1936).

Armingaud (ahr-măn-goh'), **Jules,** French violinist; b. Bayonne, May 3, 1820; d. Paris, Feb. 27, 1900. He began his career as a member of the orch. at the Paris Opéra. In 1855 he organized a string quartet, which he later enlarged by adding wind instruments, and named the 'Société classique.' He published some violin pieces, and 2 musico-philosophical books of essays: *Consonances et dissonances* and *Modulations.*

Armstrong, William Dawson, American organist and composer; b. Alton, Ill., Feb. 11, 1868; d. there, July 9, 1936. He studied with Clarence Eddy; occupied posts at various churches in Alton and St. Louis from 1890-1908; established a music school at Alton. He was active in local pedagogical groups. He wrote an opera *The Specter Bridegroom* (St. Louis, 1899); published some church music and many pieces for organ, and songs. He was the author of *The Romantic World of Music* (N.Y., 1922) and *Rudiments of Musical Notation, an Elementary Handbook.* Cf. W. T. Norton, *W. D. Armstrong* (N.Y., 1916).

Arne (ahrn), **Michael,** English opera composer (natural son of T. A. Arne); b. London, 1741; d. there Jan. 14, 1786. He was trained in his youth as an actor and a singer, and made his debut in London on April 2, 1750. He also acquired considerable skill as a harpsichord player. He wrote much stage music; among his operas (all produced at Drury Lane or at Covent Garden) are: *Hymen* (Jan. 20, 1764); *Cymon* (Jan. 2, 1767); *The Artifice* (April 14, 1780); *The Choice of Harlequin* (Dec. 26, 1781) and *Vertumnus and Pomona* (Feb. 21, 1782). He collaborated with other composers in the music of 14 other productions. In 1771-72 he traveled in Germany as conductor; from 1776 he was in Dublin; from 1784 again in London. He was an eccentric person, and among his vagaries was a preoccupation with alchemy, and a search for the philosopher's stone to convert base metals into gold.

Arne, Thomas Augustine, famous English dramatic composer; b. London, March 12, 1710; d. there, March 5, 1778. His father, an upholsterer, sent him to Eton College; he then spent three years in a solicitor's office. He studied music on the side, much against his father's wishes, and acquired considerable skill on the violin. He soon began to write musical settings "after the Italian manner," to various plays. His first production was Addison's *Rosamond* (March 7, 1733). He renamed Fielding's *Tragedy of Tragedies* as *Opera of Operas,* and produced it at the Haymarket Theatre (May 31, 1733); a masque *Dido and Aeneas* followed (Jan. 12, 1734). His most important work was the score of *Comus* (Drury Lane, March 4, 1738). On Aug. 1, 1740, he produced at Clivedon, Bucks., the masque *Alfred,* the finale of which contains the celebrated song *Rule Britannia,* which became a national patriotic song of Great Britain. In the meantime Arne married Cecilia Young (March 15, 1737), daughter of the organist Charles Young, and herself a fine singer. In 1742 he went with her to Dublin, where he also stayed in 1755 and 1758. Of his many dramatic productions the following were performed at Drury Lane, London: *The Temple of Dullness* (Jan. 17, 1745); *Harlequin Incendiary* (March 3, 1746); *The Triumph of Peace* (Feb. 21, 1749); *Britannia* (May 9, 1755); *Beauty and Virtue* (Feb. 26, 1762); *The Rose* (Dec. 2, 1772). The following were staged at Covent Garden: *Harlequin Sorcerer* (Feb. 11, 1752); *The Prophetess* (Feb. 1, 1758); *Thomas and Sally* (Nov. 28, 1760); *Love in a Village* (Dec. 8, 1762); *The Fairy Prince* (Nov. 12, 1771). He further contributed separate numbers to 28 theatrical productions, among them songs to Shakespeare's *As You Like It*; 'Where the Bee Sucks' in *The Tempest,* etc. He wrote 2 oratorios: *Abel* (Dublin, Feb. 18, 1744); and *Judith* (Drury Lane, Feb. 27, 1761), the latter remarkable for the introduction of female voices into the choral parts. He also wrote numerous glees and catches, and miscellaneous instrumental music. He received the honorary degree of Doc. of Mus. from Oxford Univ. (July 6, 1759), which accounts for his familiar appellation of 'Dr. Arne'.

d'Arneiro, (José Augusto) Ferreira Veiga, Viscount, distinguished Portuguese composer; b. Macao, China, Nov. 22, 1838; d. San Remo, July, 1903. He studied with Botelho, Schira and Soares in Lisbon. The production of his ballet *Gina* (Lisbon, 1866) attracted attention; he then produced an opera *L'Elisire di Giovinezza* (Lisbon, March 31, 1876), followed by *La Derelitta* (Lisbon, 1885). *Te Deum,* performed in Lisbon and in London in 1871 was very successful; it was later given in Paris under the somewhat affected title of 'Symphonie-Cantate.'

Arnell, Richard, English composer; b. London, Sept. 15, 1917. He studied with John Ireland at the Royal College of Music (1935-38). He was in New York from 1939-47; was active as conductor there. He composed *Prelude and Flourish* for brass, performed for the reception of Winston Churchill at Columbia University in 1946. He wrote 3 ballets: *Punch and the Child; Harlequin in April;* and *The Great Detective* (about Sherlock Holmes); 4 symphonies; a symph. poem, *Lord Byron;* a violin concerto; *Abstract Forms* for string orchestra; 2 string quartets, piano pieces and several film scores. Since 1948 he has been living in London.

Arnold, Byron, American composer; b. Vancouver, Washington, Aug. 15, 1901. He studied at Willamette Univ. (B.A., 1924); taught music at Oregon State College (1934-35); then went to the Eastman School of Music, where he took lessons in theory and composition with Rogers and Hanson (1935-37). He became asst. prof. of music at the Univ. of Alabama (1938-48). He has written *Five Incapacitated Preludes for Orchestra* (Rochester, N.Y., April 19, 1937, Hanson conducting); *Three Fanaticisms for Orchestra;* piano pieces and songs. He has published *Folk Songs of Alabama* (1950).

Arnold, Frank Thomas, English music scholar; b. Rugby, Sept. 6, 1861; d. Bath, Sept. 24, 1940. He studied at Trinity College, Cambridge, and was lecturer in German literature at the University College of South Wales at Cardiff (1886-1926). He wrote a valuable book, *The Art of Accompaniment from a Thorough-Bass, as Practiced in the 17th and 18th Centuries* (London, 1931), and contributed numerous papers on Bach, Viadana, Corelli, etc. to various music journals. He was also a collector of rare editions. Cf. D. R. Wakeling, 'An Interesting Music Collection' ('Music & Letters,' July, 1945).

Arnold, Georg, Hungarian composer; b. Paks, June 5, 1781; d. Subotica, Oct. 25, 1848. Adopting an operatic method in religious music, he created some unusual effects. His 3 operas were never performed, and the MSS seem to be lost, but his church music is extant. Arnold completed a music dictionary (1826) which, however, was never published. His songs, in the Hungarian style, were once very popular. See K. Isoz, *Georg Arnold* (Budapest, 1908).

Arnold, Gustav, Swiss organist and composer; b. Altdorf, Uri, Sept. 1, 1831; d. Lucerne, Sept. 28, 1900. He studied at Innsbruck; in 1850 he went to England, where he was choirmaster and organist at various churches. He returned to Switzerland in 1865 and settled in Lucerne as organizer of choral festivals and conductor. He wrote some sacred music and piano pieces.

Arnold, Johann Gottfried, German violoncellist and composer; b. Niederhall, near Öhringen, Feb. 15, 1773; d. Frankfurt, July 26, 1806. He studied with Willmann and Bernhard Romberg; after a brief concert career he became a theater cellist in Frankfurt. He wrote a *Symphonie concertante* for 2 flutes and orch.; several cello concertos; 6 sets of variations for cello, and various pieces for the guitar and other instruments.

Arnold, Karl, German pianist; b. Neukirchen, near Mergentheim, Württemberg, March 6, 1794; d. Christiania (Oslo), Norway, Nov. 11, 1873. He studied with J. A. André and Karl Vollweiler in Frankfurt; then occupied various positions in St. Petersburg (1819), Berlin (1824), and Münster (1835). In 1849 he settled in Norway, where he conducted the Philharmonic Society in Christiania, and was also active as church organist. He wrote an opera *Irene* (Berlin, 1832), a piano sextet, and numerous works for piano solo.

Arnold, Malcolm, English composer; b. Northampton, Oct. 21, 1921. He studied at the Royal College of Music in London; has written a symph. poem *Larch Trees* (1943); concerto for horn and orch. (1946); symphony for strings (1947); *Festival Overture* (1948); concerto for clarinet and strings (1948); Symphony No. 2 (Bournemouth, May 25, 1953); ballet, *Homage to the Queen* (London, June 2, 1953); Concerto for oboe and string orch. (London, June 9, 1953); harmonica concerto (London, Promenade Concert, Aug. 14, 1954, Larry Adler soloist); violin sonata; viola sonata and songs.

Arnold, Maurice (real name Maurice Arnold Strothotte), American violinist and composer; b. St. Louis, Jan. 19, 1865; d. New York, Oct. 23, 1937. He studied in Cincinnati; then in Germany with several teachers, including Max Bruch. The performance of his orchestral work *American Plantation Dances* (New York, 1894) aroused the interest of Dvořák, because of the Negro melodies used in it, and he engaged Arnold to teach at the National Cons. of which Dvořák was then head. Arnold subsequently was active as conductor of light opera, and as violin teacher. He wrote a comic opera *The Merry Benedicts* (Brooklyn, 1896); a grand opera *Cleopatra;* a symphony; a cantata *The Wild Chase; Minstrel Serenade* for violin and piano; and a fugue for piano-8 hands.

Arnold, Richard, German-American violinist; b. Eilenberg, Prussia, Jan. 10, 1845; d. New York, June 21, 1918. He emigrated to the U.S. in 1853, but returned to Germany in 1864 to study with Ferdinand David in Leipzig. He was a violinist in the Theodore Thomas Orch. (1869-76), and concertmaster of the New York Philharmonic Orch. (1880-1909). Then lived in New York as violin teacher.

Arnold, Samuel, celebrated English composer, organist and music scholar; b. London, Aug. 10, 1740; d. there, Oct. 22, 1802. He received his musical training from Gates and Nares as a chorister of the Chapel Royal. He early showed a gift for composition, and was commissioned to arrange the music for a play *The Maid of the Mill;* for this he selected songs by some 20 composers, including Bach, and added several numbers of his own; the resulting pasticcio was produced with success at Covent Garden (Jan. 31, 1765). This was the first of his annual productions for Covent Garden and other theaters in London, of which the following were composed mainly by Arnold: *Harlequin Dr. Faustus* (Nov. 18, 1766); *The Royal Garland* (Oct. 10, 1768); *The Magnet* (June 27, 1771); *A Beggar on Horseback* (June 16, 1785); *The Gnome* (Aug. 5, 1788); *New Spain, or Love in Mexico* (July 16, 1790); *The Surrender of Calais* (July 30, 1791); *The Enchanted Wood* (July 25, 1792); *The Sixty-Third Letter* (July 18, 1802). He also wrote several oratorios, among them *The Cure of Saul* (1767); *Abimelech; The Resurrection; The Prodigal Son;* and *Elisha* (1795; his last oratorio). On the occasion of a performance of *The Prodigal Son* at Oxford Univ. in 1773, Arnold was given the degree of D. Mus. In 1783, he became the successor of Nares as composer to the Chapel Royal, for which he wrote several odes and anthems. In 1789 Arnold was engaged as conductor of the Academy of Ancient Music; in 1793 he became organist of Westminster Abbey. He was buried in Westminster Abbey, near to Purcell and Blow. Arnold's edition of Handel's works, begun in 1786, was carried out by him in 36 volumes, embracing about 180 numbers; it is, however, incomplete and inaccurate in many respects. His principal work is *Cathedral Music* (1790, 4 vols.); its subtitle describes its contents: "A collection in score of the most valuable and useful compositions for that Service by the several English Masters of the last 200 years." It forms a sequel to Boyce's work of the same name. A new edition of Arnold's *Cathedral Music* was issued by Rimbault (1847).

Arnold, Youri von (Yury Karlovitch), Russian opera composer and theorist; b. St. Petersburg, Nov. 13, 1811; d. Karakash, Crimea, July 20, 1898. He studied in Dresden; and later at the German Univ. of Dorpat, Estonia; went to Germany in 1855; from 1870-94 was in Moscow, where he founded a music school; in 1894 he settled in St. Petersburg. He wrote a vaudeville-opera *Treasure Trove* (St. Petersburg, Feb. 1, 1853), the MS of which was lost in the fire at the Imperial Theater in 1859, together with the MS of his other opera *St. John's Eve.* He also wrote an overture, *Boris Godunov.* Arnold was the author of the first book in Russian dealing with the theory of composition (1841); he also published *Theory of Old Russian Religious Chants* (Moscow, 1886), and many articles in the German press. In 1867 he published, in Leipzig, the periodical 'Neue Allgemeine Zeitschrift für Theater und Musik.' Two of his papers from that journal were issued separately: *Der Einfluss des Zeitgeistes auf die Entwickelung der Tonkunst* and an essay on *Der Freischütz* in *24 auserlesene Opern-Charactere.* He also translated into German the libretti of operas by Tchaikovsky, Cui and others. He was friendly with Glinka and many other celebrated composers, and published historically valuable *Reminiscences* (3 volumes; Moscow, 1892).

Arnoldson, Sigrid, Swedish dramatic soprano; b. Stockholm, March 20, 1861; d. there, Feb. 7, 1943. She was the daughter of the celebrated tenor Oscar Arnoldson (b. 1830; d. Carlsbad, July 8, 1881). She studied with Maurice Strakosch and Désirée Artôt; made her debut in Moscow in 1886 as Rosina in *Il Barbiere di Siviglia;* then sang as prima donna in London (June 20, 1887), at the Opéra-Comique in Paris, in Nice and Rome with brilliant success. In 1888 she was engaged at Covent Garden as successor to Patti. On Nov. 29, 1894, she made her debut at the Metropolitan Opera. In 1910 she was elected member of the Stockholm Academy; in 1922 settled in Vienna as a singing teacher; later taught in Berlin. On June 16, 1888, she married the Austrian impresario, Alfred Fischhof, a nephew of Maurice Strakosch.

Arnould (ar-noold'), **(Madeleine) Sophie,** French operatic soprano; b. Paris, Feb. 14, 1740; d. there Oct. 18, 1802. She studied singing with Mme. Fel and acting with Mlle. Clairon; made her debut at the Paris Opéra on Dec. 15, 1757. She created the title role in Gluck's *Iphigénie en Aulide* (April 19, 1774), and after a highly successful career retired in 1778 with a pension of 2,000 livres. Bibl.: *Arnouldiana,* a large collection of anecdotes, published anonymously (Paris, 1813; real author, A. Deville); E. and J. de Goncourt, *Sophie Arnould d'après sa correspondance et ses mémoires* (Paris, 1877); R. B. Douglas, *Sophie Arnould, Actress and Wit* (Paris, 1898). Gabriel Pierné wrote a one-act 'lyric comedy' *Sophie Arnould* (1926), based on incidents of her life.

Aron, Pietro. See **Aaron.**

Arquier (ahr-kyā), **Joseph,** French opera composer; b. Toulon, 1763; d. Bordeaux, Oct., 1816. He played the cello in a theater at Lyon; then lived in Marseilles and Paris. After 1800 he went to New Orleans as director of an opera troupe, but failed and returned to France in 1804, holding various positions in Paris, Toulouse, Marseilles and Perpignan; he died in poverty. Arquier wrote about 16 comic operas.

Arrau, Claudio, Chilean pianist; b. Chillán, Feb. 6, 1903. He played in public at the age of five, and in 1910 was sent by the Chilean government to Berlin where he studied with Martin Krause. In 1914-15 he played recitals in Germany and Scandinavia, attracting a great deal of attention by his precocious talent. He made an extensive European tour after World War I, returning to South America in 1921. His U.S. debut was in 1923. Between 1925-40 he lived chiefly in Berlin, where he taught at Stern's Cons. He won the Grand Prix International des Pianistes at Geneva in 1927. In 1941 he settled in the U.S., making frequent European and South American tours. In his playing Arrau combines a classical purity of style with the rhapsodic breadth requisite for romantic music.

Arregui Garay (ahr-rā-gē-gah-ri'), **Vicente,** Spanish composer; b. Madrid, July 3, 1871; d. there, Dec. 1, 1925. He studied in Paris and Rome; was active in Madrid as music critic; wrote a symph. poem *Historia de una madre* (after H. C. Andersen, 1910); *Sinfonia vasca* for orch.; the operas *Yolanda, La Maya* and *El Cuento de Barba Azul;* a cantata *El Lobo ciego;* chamber music and choral works. His music follows the romantic school of programmatic writing.

Arriaga, Juan Crisóstomo, precocious composer; b. Rigoitia, near Bilbao, Jan. 27, 1806; d. Paris, Jan. 17, 1826 (ten days before his 20th birthday). He was an exceptionally gifted musician. While still in Bilbao, at the age of 13, he composed a 2-act opera *Los esclavos felices* (1819). He then went to Paris, where he studied at the Cons. with Baillot and Fétis, arousing their admiration for his talent. In Paris he wrote a symphony, a biblical scene *Agar,* 3 string quartets, several fugues, piano pieces and songs. On Aug. 13, 1933, a monument was unveiled to him in Bilbao, and a 'Comisión Permanente Arriaga' was formed there. The vocal scores of *Los esclavos felices* and *Ensayo en octeto,* subtitled *Nada o mucho* (scored for strings, trumpet, guitar and piano), were published in Bilbao in 1935 with extensive bio-bibliographical notes by Juan de Eresalde; the full score of a symphony was also publ. (Bilbao, 1953).

Arrieta y Corera, Pascual Juan Emilio, Spanish composer; b. Puente la Reina, Oct. 21, 1823; d. Madrid, Feb. 11, 1894. He studied at the Milan Cons. (1842-45) with Vaccai; returned to Spain in 1848; was prof. at the Madrid Cons. in 1857; became its director in 1868. He wrote more than 50 zarzuelas and several grand operas in Italian. Of these productions the most important is *La conquista de Granada,* produced in Madrid (Oct. 10, 1850) with Arrieta himself conducting, and revived five years later under the title *Isabel la Católica* (Madrid, Dec. 18, 1855). Other successful zarzuelas and operas are *Ildegonda* (Milan, Feb. 28, 1845); *El Domino Azul* (Madrid, Feb. 19, 1853); *El Grumete* (Madrid, June 17, 1853; its sequel, *La Vuelta del Corsario* was performed in Madrid, Feb. 18, 1863); *Marina* (Madrid, Sept. 21, 1855; revised and produced as a grand opera, Madrid, Oct. 4, 1871); *S. Francesco da Siena* (Madrid, Oct. 27, 1883).

Arrigoni, Carlo, Italian composer; b. Florence, Dec. 5, 1697; d. there, Aug. 19, 1744. He left Italy as a young man; in 1728 he was in Brussels. In 1732 he was invited to London by a group favorable to Italian composers in opposition to Handel; there he produced an opera *Fernando* (Feb. 8, 1734). Arrigoni then went back to Italy through Vienna, where he produced an oratorio *Esther* (1737); returning to Florence, he staged his new operas *Sirbace* and *Scipione nelle Spagne* (1739). His 10 *Cantate da camera* were published in London (1732). Several airs from his opera *Fernando* are preserved in the British Museum; Burney mistakenly attributed the music of this opera to Porpora.

l'Arronge, Adolf, German conductor and composer; b. Hamburg, March 8, 1838; d. Berlin, Dec. 25, 1908. He studied at the Leipzig Cons.; then conducted opera in Cologne, Danzig, Berlin, Breslau and Budapest. He wrote a number of light operas which, however, failed to obtain any degree of success.

Arroyo, João Marcellino, eminent Portuguese composer, writer and statesman; b. Oporto, Oct. 4, 1861; d. there, May 18, 1930. A member of a musical family, he first took lessons with his father; at the same time he studied law. From 1884-1904 he was a member of the Portuguese parliament; in 1900-01 he held the posts of minister of foreign affairs and public education. A royalist, he abandoned politics after the revolution of 1910, and received a professorship of law at the Univ. of Coimbra. He wrote two operas: *Amor de Perdição* (Lisbon, March 2, 1907; Hamburg, Jan. 25, 1910), which is regarded as the first modern Portuguese opera, and *Leonor Teles;* two symphonic poems; several choral works and songs; also compiled a manual of solfeggio for primary schools. See article on him in E. Amorim, *Dicionário biográfico de músicos do Norte de Portugal* (Oporto, 1941); also C. A. Dos Santos, *João Arroyo* (Lisbon, 1941).

Artaria, music publishing house in Vienna, founded by the cousins Carlo A. (1747-1808) and Francesco A. (1744-1808). They opened a music shop on Kohlmarkt in 1769, and in 1778 began printing music; they introduced the method of zinc plating for the first time in Vienna. In 1779, the firm acquired some of Haydn's works, which brought fame to them; music of Clementi, Salieri and Boccherini was published later. Artaria publ. Mozart's 6 violin sonatas (K. 296, 376-80), the *Haffner-Sinfonie* and 6 string quartets dedicated to Haydn, among other works, thus becoming Mozart's most important publisher in his lifetime. Other first editions in Artaria's catalogue were several songs by Schubert, Beethoven's C major quintet, op. 29, and string quartet, op. 131. The last owners were Carl August Artaria (d. 1919); Dominik Artaria (d. 1936) and Franz Artaria (d. 1942). After 1932, the old house became an art gallery and an auction bureau, preserving the name Artaria.—Cf. F. Artaria and Hugo Botstiber, *Joseph Haydn und das Verlagshaus Artaria* (Vienna, 1909); D. MacArdle, *Beethoven, Artaria, and the C major Quintet* ('Mus. Quarterly,' Oct., 1948); A. Weinmann, *Vollständiges Verlagsverzeichnis, Artaria & Comp.* (Vienna, 1952).

Arteaga, Esteban de, Spanish writer on music; b. Moraleja de Coca, Segovia, Dec. 26, 1747; d. Paris, Oct. 30, 1799. He joined the Jesuit Order at 16, and was banished to Corsica when they were proscribed in Spain. He left the Order in 1769; from 1773-78 he studied philosophy at the Univ. of Bologna; there he formed a friendship with Padre Martini, and at his behest undertook a history of the musical theater in Italy. The resulting work, *Le rivoluzioni del teatro musicale italiano dalla sua origine fino al presente,* was published in 3 volumes in Bologna and Venice (1783-86; the materials in the Bologna edition partly overlap, partly supplement those in the Venice edition); it was brought out in German by J. Forkel (2 vols., Leipzig, 1789); a summary was published in French (1802). Arteaga's strong and often critical opinions expressed in this work antagonized many Italian writers who resented the intrusion of a foreigner into their own field. A polemical exchange of considerable acrimony followed; Arteaga's views were attacked by Matteo Borsa in a tract *Del gusto presente in letteratura italiana . . .* and by Vincenzo Manfredini in *Difesa della musica moderna . . .* (Bologna, 1786). After a sojourn in Venice (1785), Arteaga lived in Rome (1786-87); in 1796 he went to Florence and later to Paris. In addition to his magnum opus, he published a book on esthetics, *Investigaciones filosóficas sobre la belleza ideal . . .* (Madrid, 1789; new ed., Madrid, 1943). A book of essays *Lettere musico-filologiche* and the treatise *Del ritmo sonoro e del ritmo muto nella musica degli antichi* (long regarded as lost) were published in Madrid in 1944, with an extensive biographical account by the editor Miguel Batllori, who also gives the bibliographical synopsis of the Bologna and Venice editions of *Rivoluzioni.*

Artemovsky. See Gulak-Artemovsky.

Arthur, Alfred, American composer and choral conductor; b. Pittsburgh, Pa., Oct. 8, 1844; d. Lakewood, Ohio, Nov. 20, 1918. He studied with Eichberg at the Boston Cons.; sang at Boston churches; then moved to Cleveland where he was conductor of the Vocal Society (from 1873) and director of the Cleveland School of Music. He wrote 3 operas which remained unperformed and unpublished: *The Water-carrier* (1876); *The Roundheads and Cavaliers* (1878) and *Adaline* (1879); brought out *Progressive Vocal Studies* (1887) and other manuals on singing.

Artôt (ahr-toh'), **Alexandre-Joseph Montagney,** Belgian violinist; b. Brussels, Jan. 25, 1815; d. Ville-d'Avray, July 20, 1845. He studied with his father, Maurice Artôt, and with Snel; then took lessons from Rodolphe and Auguste Kreutzer at the Paris Cons., obtaining first prize (1828). He then played concerts on the continent; made his debut in London (June 3, 1839) in his own *Fantaisie* for violin and orch. In 1843 he embarked on an American concert tour. He wrote a violin concerto, several sets of variations for violin, and some chamber music.

Artôt, (Jean) Désiré Montagney, Belgian horn player and composer; b. Paris, Sept. 23, 1803; d. Brussels, March 25, 1887. He was a pupil and successor of his father, Maurice Artôt. From 1843 he taught at the Brussels Cons.; also played in the Court Orch. He published fantasias and études for horn and quartets for cornets.

Artôt, (Marguerite-Joséphine) Désirée Montagney, Belgian mezzo soprano (daughter of Jean-Désiré Artôt); b. Paris, July 21, 1835; d. Berlin, April 3, 1907. She studied with Mme. Viardot-Garcia; sang in Belgium, Holland and England (1857). Meyerbeer engaged her to sing in *Le Prophète* at the Paris Opera (Feb. 5, 1858); she was greatly praised by Berlioz and other Paris musicians and critics. In 1858 she went to Italy; then made appearances in London. In 1868 she was in Russia, where she was briefly engaged to Tchaikovsky; however, this engagement was quickly disrupted by her marriage (on Sept. 15, 1869) to the Spanish singer Padilla y Ramos (1842-1906). Their daughter is Lola Artôt de Padilla (q.v.).

Artôt, Maurice Montagney, ancestor of a celebrated line of musicians (the true family name being Montagney); b. Gray (Haute-Saône), Feb. 3, 1772; d. Brussels, Jan. 8, 1829. He was a bandmaster in the French Army; then went to Brussels where he became first horn player at the Théâtre de la Monnaie. A versatile musician, he also played the guitar and taught singing.

Artsÿbushev (ar-tsē-boo'-shef), **Nikolay Vassilievitch,** Russian composer; b. Tsarskoe-Selo, March 7, 1858; d. Paris, April 15, 1937. He studied with Soloviev and Rimsky-Korsakov; in 1908 was president of the St. Petersburg Royal Music Society; in 1920 settled in Paris where he was active as representative of Belaiev's publishing house. Artsÿbushev is chiefly known for his melodic piano pieces and songs, which were published by Belaiev; he also wrote a *Valse-Fantasia* for orch., and was one of the composers to contribute to a collection of variations on a Russian song for string quartet, other variations being by Rimsky-Korsakov, Glazunov, Liadov, Scriabin, etc.

Artusi, Giovanni Maria, Italian contrapuntist and writer on music; b. Bologna, c. 1540; d. there, Aug. 18, 1613. He became canon-in-ordinary at S. Salvatore in Bologna in Feb., 1562. A capable musician and writer, a pupil of Zarlino, Artusi was reactionary in his musical philosophy. His first publication, *L'Arte del contrappunto* (in 2 parts, Venice, 1586 and 1589) has considerable theoretical value. He then published several polemical essays directed mainly against the innovations of Monteverdi and others: the characteristically named volume *L'Artusi, ovvero delle imperfettioni della moderna musica* (Venice, 1600; reproduced in part in English by O. Strunk in *Source Readings in Music History,* N. Y., 1950), followed by a posthumous attack on his teacher Zarlino in *Impresa del R. P. Gioseffo Zarlino* (Bologna, 1604); *Considerazioni musicali* (1603; as part II of *L'Artusi,* etc.); *Discorso musicale . . .* (1606); *Discorso secondo musicale* (both attacking Monteverdi); and further polemical essays against Bottrigari and Vincenzo Galileo. Monteverdi replied to Artusi in a leaflet entitled *Ottuso accademico,* and in the preface to his 5th book of madrigals; this reply is reproduced in Strunk's *Source Readings in Music History.* Bottrigari replied in a pamphlet entitled *Ant' Artusi.* As a composer, Artusi followed the old school; he published a set of 4-part *Canzonette* (1598), and an 8-part motet *Cantate Domino* (1599). Cf. H. Redlich, *Claudio Monteverdi, Life and Works* (London, 1952).

Artzibuschew. See **Artsÿbushev, Nikolay Vassilievitch.**

Arutunian, Alexander, Armenian composer; b. Erivan, Sept. 23, 1920. He studied piano with Igumnov and composition with Litinsky. He has written a piano concerto (1941); concert overture (1944); *Cantata for the Fatherland* (1948); trumpet concerto (1950), etc.

Asafiev, Boris Vladimirovitch, Russian composer and writer on music; b. St. Petersburg, July 29, 1884; d. Moscow, Jan. 27, 1949. He studied with Kalafati and Liadov at the St. Petersburg Cons. (grad. in 1910); at the same time he studied philology and history at St. Petersburg Univ. (grad. in 1908). He then became a ballet coach at the Opera. In 1914 he began writing music criticism under the pseudonym Igor Glebov. Subsequently he published his literary writings under that name, sometimes indicating his real name as well. He always signed his musical works, however, with the name Asafiev. In 1920 he was appointed Dean of the dept. of music of the Institute of History of Arts in Petrograd. He was also an editor of the journal 'Novaya Musica' (1924-28); within a few years he published brief monographs on Mussorgsky, Scriabin, Rimsky-Korsakov, Liszt, Chopin, etc.; translated articles from German, French and Italian. At the same time he continued to compose, mostly for the stage. The following ballets by him were performed in Leningrad: *Flames of Paris* (June 23, 1923); *The Fountain of Bakhtchisaray,* after Pushkin (Sept. 28, 1934; very popular); *The Partisan Days* (Sept. 12, 1937) and *The Prisoner of the Caucasus* (April 14, 1938). Altogether he wrote 9 operas, 27 ballets, works for orch. and chamber music. But it is as a historian of Russian music that Asafiev-Glebov is especially important. He continued the tradition of Vladimir Stasov in his ardent advocacy of the national Russian style. He published *The Russian Poets in Russian Music* (with a valuable catalogue of Russian vocal works; 1921); *Symphonic Études* (an account of the evolution of the Russian operatic style; 1922); *Stravinsky* (a comprehensive analysis of Stravinsky's works; Leningrad, 1929; later he repudiated the favorable view of Stravinsky expressed in this book); *Russian Music from the Beginning of the Nineteenth Century* (1930; English transl. by A. Swan; American Council of Learned Societies, 1953); *Musical Form as a Process* (2 vols., 1930 and 1947) and *Glinka* (Moscow, 1947; the only book on music to receive the Stalin Prize). A 7-volume edition of Asafiev's collected writings was begun in Moscow in 1952.

Aschaffenburg, Walter, composer; b. Essen, May 20, 1927. He came to America at the age of 11. He was with the U.S. Army in Germany in 1947; then studied at Oberlin with Elwell and at the Eastman School of Music with B. Rogers. In 1953 he was appointed instructor at the Oberlin Cons. He has written *Ozymandias,* 'symphonic reflections after Shelley' (Rochester, April 22, 1952); an overture *Oedipus Rex;* 3 string quartets; Divertimento for trumpets, horn and trombone; a piano trio and a cello sonata.

Aschenbrenner, Christian Heinrich, German violinist and composer; b. Altstettin, Dec. 29, 1654; d. Jena, Dec. 13, 1732. He studied with Schütz; was active as violinist at Zeitz (1677-81) and Merseburg (1683-

90); then served as music director to the Duke of Zeitz (1695-1713) and later to the Duke of Merseburg (1713-19); finally retired on a pension to Jena. His only known work is *Gast- und Hochzeitsfreude, bestehend in Sonaten, Präludien, Allemanden, Couranten, Balletten, Arien, Sarabanden mit 3, 4 und 5 Stimmen, nebst dem Basso continuo* (1673).

Ascher, Joseph, Dutch pianist and composer; b. Groningen, June 4, 1829; d. London, June 20, 1869. He studied with Moscheles; went to Paris in 1849 and was Court pianist to the Empress Eugénie. He wrote numerous pieces of salon music (études, nocturnes, galops, etc.).

Ascher, Leo, Austrian composer of light operas; b. Vienna, Aug. 17, 1880; d. New York, Feb. 25, 1942. His first successful operetta was *Vergeltsgott* (Vienna, Oct. 14, 1905); *Soldat der Marie* and *Hoheit tanzt Walzer* followed. Altogether he composed some 50 stage works, and film music. In 1938 he left Austria to live in New York.

Ashdown, Edwin, London music publisher; successor (1884) of Ashdown & Parry, who were the successors (1860) of Wessel & Co. (founded 1825). Two grandsons of Edwin Ashdown inherited the company, and incorporated into it the catalogue of Enoch & Co., and also of J. H. Larway & Co. (1936), the official name of the enlarged business remaining Edwin Ashdown, Ltd. Their list of publications contains mostly pedagogical works.

Ashton, Algernon (Bennet Langton), English composer; b. Durham, Dec. 9, 1859; d. London, April 10, 1937. His family moved to Leipzig and he studied at the Leipzig Cons. with Reinecke and Jadassohn (1875-79); later took lessons with Raff in Frankfurt (1880). Returning to England, he obtained the post of piano teacher at the Royal College of Music (1885-1910). He was a prolific composer, having written more than 160 opus numbers, mostly in a conventional German style: 5 symphonies, 3 overtures, a piano concerto, a violin concerto, 3 piano quintets, 3 piano quartets, 3 piano trios, trio for clarinet, viola and bassoon, trio for piano, horn and viola, 5 violin sonatas, 5 cello sonatas, a viola sonata, and more than 200 piano works (among them a sonata, 3 fantasias, and various picturesque pieces such as *Idyls; Roses and Thorns,* etc.); also more than 200 songs, choral pieces and organ works. Many of his chamber music compositions were published, but he was never given recognition as a composer; however, he acquired notoriety by his curious letters in the English press dealing with a variety of subjects. Many of these letters he collected in his volumes *Truth, Wit and Wisdom* (London, 1904) and *More Truth, Wit and Wisdom* (London, 1905).

Ashton, Hugh. See **Aston.**

Asioli, Bonifazio, Italian composer; b. Correggio, Aug. 30, 1769; d. there, May 18, 1832. A precocious talent, he began writing music at a very early age. He studied with Angelo Merighi in Parma (1780-82); then lived in Bologna and Venice as a harpsichord player. His first opera *La Volubile* was produced in Correggio (1785) with marked success; it was followed by *Le nozze in villa* (Correggio, 1786); *Cinna* (Milan, 1793); and *Gustavo al Malabar* (Turin, 1802). From 1796-99 he was private maestro to the Marquis Gherardini in Turin; then went to Milan and taught at the Cons. (1808-14). Asioli wrote 7 operas in all, an oratorio *Giacobbe in Galaad,* many cantatas, instrumental music and sacred choral works, etc. He was the author of several textbooks: *Principi elementari di musica* (Milan, 1809; also in English, German and French); *Trattato d'armonia e d'accompagnamento* (1813); also manuals for harpsichord, voice and double-bass. His theoretical book *Il maestro di composizione* was published posthumously (1836). Bibl.: A. Coli, *Vita di Bonifazio Asioli* (Milan, 1834), also O. S. Ancarani, *Sopra alcune parole di Carlo Botta intorno al metodo musicale di Bonifazio Asioli* (1836); A. Amadei, *Intorno allo stile della moderna musica di chiesa* (1841).

Asola (Latin, **Asula**), **Giovanni Matteo,** Italian composer; b. Verona, c. 1550; d. Venice, Oct. 1, 1609. He was ordained priest; was at Treviso in 1578; then at Vicenza (1581). Later he lived in Venice. Asola's importance in music history lies in his early use of a basso continuo for the organ accompaniment of sacred vocal music. He composed a great deal of church music; his two books of madrigals were published in Venice (1587; 1596; also later editions). See F. Caffi, *Della vita e delle opere di Giammateo Asola* (Padua, 1862).

Asow, Erich H. Müller von. See **Müller von Asow, Erich H.**

Aspa, Mario, Italian opera composer; b. Messina, 1799, d. there, Dec. 14, 1868. He studied with Zingarelli in Naples. He produced 42 operas, of which the most successful were *Paolo e Virginia* (Rome, April

29, 1843) and *Il muratore di Napoli* (Naples, Oct. 16, 1850). His last opera *Piero di Calais* was produced posthumously in his native town (Messina, March 6, 1872).

Aspestrand, Sigwart, Norwegian opera composer; b. Fredrikshald, Nov. 13, 1856; d. Oslo, Dec. 31, 1941. He studied at Leipzig and Berlin and spent 30 years of his life (1885-1915) in Germany. Of his 7 operas *Die Seemansbraut,* produced in Gotha (March 29, 1894) and later in Oslo (March 18, 1907) was the most successful. His other operas, all in German, are: *Der Recke von Lyrskovsheid; Freyas Alter; Die Wette; Der Kuss auf Sicht; Robin Hood* and *Pervonte.*

Asplmayr, Franz, Austrian composer; b. 1728; d. Vienna, July 29, 1786. He was composer of ballets at the Austrian Court; the scores of his ballets *Agamemnon, Iphigenia, Flora, Acis and Galatea* and others have been preserved. He also wrote the Singspiel, *Die Kinder der Natur* and the music for two of Shakespeare's plays: *Macbeth* (1777) and *The Tempest* (1781). Historically, Asplmayr was important as one of the earliest Austrian composers to adopt the instrumental style established by the Mannheim school. He composed *6 Serenate,* op. 1; *6 Quatuors concertants,* op. 2; 6 trios, op. 5; *6 Quatuors,* op. 6. A trio (op. 5, No. 1) and a quartet (op. 6, No. 2) were published by Riemann in 'Collegium Musicum.'

Assmayer, Ignaz, Austrian composer; b. Salzburg, Feb. 11, 1790; d. Vienna, Aug. 31, 1862. He studied with Michael Haydn; in 1808 became organist at Salzburg. In 1815 he moved to Vienna, where he studied additionally with Eybler. In 1825 was appointed Imperial organist; in 1838 was made one of the court conductors. He wrote the oratorios *Saul und David, Sauls Tod* and *Das Gelübde,* and performed them with the Vienna Tonkünstler Society. He further wrote 15 Masses, 2 Requiems, other church works, and some 60 instrumental compositions, many of which were published.

Aston, Hugh, English composer; b. 1480 (?); d. York, Dec. 9, 1522 (?). The dates given above apply to the son of a certain Richard Aston of Mawdesley in Lancashire, assumed to be the composer. After obtaining his B.A. (1505-6) and M.A. (Oct. 30, 1507) from Oxford, he moved to Cambridge to study canon law; he was throughout his life associated with St. John's College, Cambridge. On May 27, 1509, he became Prebend of St. Stephen's, Westminster, and in 1515, Archdeacon of York. Among Aston's authentic works are 2 Masses (*Te Deum* for 5 voices and *Videte manus meas* for 6 voices); two other vocal works for 5 voices (*Gaude Virgo Mater Christi* and *Te Deum laudamus*) and 3 fragments published in Tudor Church Music (vol. X). More unusual for the time is Aston's *Hornpipe* for virginals, which is preserved in a manuscript at the British Museum and printed in J. Wolf's *Sing- und Spielmusik aus alter Zeit* (Leipzig, 1926). It is the earliest known piece for the instrument. Of the ten other dances in this manuscript, some, notably *Lady Carey's Dompe* (printed in S. Smith's 'Musica Antiqua') may also be Aston's work. Bibl.: W. H. Grattan Flood, *Early Tudor Composers* (London, 1925, pp. 30-33).

d'Astorga, Emanuele (Gioacchino Cesare Rincón), Italian composer of operas; b. Augusta, Sicily, March 20, 1680; d. probably in Madrid, after 1757. Of a noble Spanish family which had settled in Augusta, Sicily, early in the 17th century; he was a baron in his own right, from his estate Ogliastro, nearby. Later in life he moved to Palermo; during the revolution of 1708 he was an officer in the municipal guard. In 1712 he went to Vienna; and was in Znaim in 1713. He was in London in 1714-15; and returned to Palermo where he became senator. It is known that he sold his Sicilian estate in 1744 and went to Spain, where he was in the service of the king. D'Astorga was widely known as a versatile and highly educated person; he was also adept as a singer and a cembalo player, but never regarded music as his primary profession. He composed at least 3 operas: the first, *La moglie nemica,* was produced at Palermo in 1698; the 2nd and most notable, *Dafni,* was staged at Genoa on April 21, 1709; it was probably also heard in Barcelona (1709) and in Breslau (1726); the third, *Amor tirannico,* was given in Venice in 1710. He also wrote numerous chamber cantatas and published himself 12 of them in one volume (Lisbon, 1726). His best known work is *Stabat Mater* for 4 voices; it was first heard in Oxford in 1752; a new edition of it was published by R. Franz in 1878. In his 2-volume biography of d'Astorga (Leipzig, 1911 and 1919), Hans Volkmann refutes the unsupported statement of R. Pohl in the 1st edition of Grove's Dictionary, that d'Astorga died at Raudnitz on Aug. 21, 1736; Volkmann also exposes the romantic account of d'Astorga's life published by Rochlitz in volume II of 'Für Freunde der Tonkunst' (1825) as a fanciful invention. An opera *Astorga,* based on his life, was written by J. J. Abert (1866). See also O. Tiby, *E. D'Astorga* in 'Acta Musicologica' (1953).

Atanasov, Georgi, Bulgarian composer; b. Plovdiv, May 6, 1881; d. Rome, Nov. 1, 1931. He studied in Italy; was one of the first Bulgarian composers to be fully equipped with the technique of composition. He wrote the early national Bulgarian operas *Borislav* (Sofia, March 4, 1911) and *Gergana* (Stara Zagora, July 1, 1925); other operas are *Zapustialata Vodenitza* (The Abandoned Mill); *Altzek; Tzveta;* also 2 children's operas: *The Sick Teacher* and *About Birds.*

Atherton, Percy Lee, American composer; b. Boston, Mass., Sept. 25, 1871; d. Atlantic City, N. J., March 8, 1944. He studied music at Harvard Univ.; then with Rheinberger in Munich, with Sgambati in Rome and with Widor in Paris. Returning to America he served on various advisory boards in Boston. He wrote 2 operas *The Heir Apparent* (1890) and *Maharajah* (1900), a symph. poem, *Noon in the Forest,* and numerous songs.

Attaignant (ăt-tä-ñan'), **Pierre** (also **Attaingnant, Atteignant**), French printer of music who lived during the first half of the 16th century; d. 1552. He was probably the earliest printer in France to employ movable type in music printing. His first publication was a *Breviarium Noviomense* (1525). He continued to publish a great many works, including 18 dances in tablature for the lute (1529); 25 pavans (1530); a folio edition of 7 books of masses (1532); 13 books of motets (1535) and a series of 35 books of chansons (1539-49) containing 927 part songs by French and Flemish composers. E. Bernoulli issued a facsimile edition of 4 books, under the title *Chansons und Tänze* (Munich, 1914); 31 chansons are found in Henry Expert's edition, *Les Maîtres musiciens de la Renaissance française* (1894-1908). Cf. Yvonne Rihouet (Rokseth), *Note bibliographique sur Attaignant* in 'Revue de Musicologie' (1924, No. 10); F. Lesure, *Pierre Attaignant, Notes et Documents* in 'Musica Disciplina' (Rome, 1949).

Attenhofer, Karl, Swiss conductor and composer; b. Wettingen, May 5, 1837; d. Zürich, May 22, 1914. He studied in his native city and later at the Leipzig Cons. (1857-58) with Richter and Dreyschock. Returning to Switzerland he developed vigorous activity as choral conductor and teacher. He settled in Zürich in 1867; was appointed director of the Cons. in 1896. Attenhofer wrote mainly for chorus; his cantatas *Hegelingenfahrt* (1890), *Frühlingsfeier,* and *Der deutsche Michel* for men's voices have achieved great popularity. For women's voices he wrote *Beim Rattenfänger im Zauberberg, Das Kind der Wüste, Prinzessin Wunderhold* and *Rütlifahrt;* he also compiled a manual *Liederbuch für Männergesang* (1882). See Ernst Isler, *Karl Attenhofer* (Zürich, 1915).

Atterberg, Kurt, Swedish composer; b. Göteborg, Dec. 12, 1887. He studied engineering and was employed in the wireless service; then studied at the Stockholm Cons. with Hallén, and in Berlin with Schillings (1910-12). From 1913-22 he conducted at the Dramatic Theater in Stockholm; from 1919 he wrote music criticism, and also served in the Swedish patent office. In 1940 he was named secretary of the Royal Academy of Music in Stockholm. His 6th symphony was the winner of the first prize of $10,000 given by the Columbia Phonograph Co. (1928) for the Schubert centennial contest. Atterberg subsequently declared that he had consciously imitated the style of some composers on the jury (Glazunov, Alfano and Nielsen) in order to ingratiate himself in their judgment. His other symphonies are, however, marked with the same expansive, romantic qualities as the winning work. They are: No. 1 (1911); No. 2 (1913); No. 3 (1916); No. 4, *Sinfonia piccola* (1918); No. 5, *Sinfonia funebre* (1922); No. 6 (1928); No. 7, *Sinfonia romantica* (Frankfurt, Feb. 14, 1943); No. 8 (Helsinki, Feb. 9, 1945). His orchestral rhapsody on Northern Swedish folk tunes, *Värmlandsrhapsodi,* written in honor of Selma Lagerlöf's 75 birthday (broadcast over the Swedish Radio, Nov. 20, 1933), became one of his most popular works. Atterberg is the author of 5 operas, all produced in Stockholm: *Härvard Harpolekare* (Sept. 29, 1919; revised as *Härvard der Harfner,* and produced in German at Chemnitz, 1936); *Bäckhästen* (Jan. 23, 1925); *Fanal* (Jan. 27, 1934); *Aladdin* (March 18, 1941); *Stormen,* after Shakespeare's *Tempest* (Sept. 19, 1949). Other works: 9 suites for orch.; symph. poem, *The River; Rondeau rétrospectif* for orch.; concertos for violin, cello, piano, and horn; 2 string quartets.

Attwood, Thomas, English organist and composer; b. London, Nov. 23, 1765; d. Chelsea, March 24, 1838. He was a chorister at the Chapel Royal under Nares and Ayrton from the age of nine. Following a performance before the Prince of Wales (afterwards George IV), he was sent to Italy for further study; there he received instruction in Naples from Filippo Cinque and Gaetano Latilla. He then went to Vienna, where Mozart accepted him as a pupil. In 1787 he returned to London and held various posts as organist. He was also music tutor to the Duchess of York (1791) and to the Princess of Wales (1795). A founder of the London Philharmonic Society (1813), he conducted some of its concerts. He occupied an important position in the English musical world; when Mendelssohn came to London as a young man, Attwood lent him enthusiastic support. Attwood was a prolific composer of operas, of which many were produced in London, including *The Prisoner* (Oct. 18, 1792); *The Mariners* (May 10, 1793); *The Packet Boat* (May 13, 1794); *The Smugglers* (April 13, 1796); *The Fairy Festival* (May 13, 1797); *The Irish Tar* (Aug. 24, 1797); *The Devil of a Lover* (March 17, 1798); *The Magic Oak* (Jan. 29, 1799); *True Friends* (Feb. 19, 1800); *The Sea-Side Story* (May 12, 1801); *The Curfew* (Feb. 19, 1807). In all, Attwood wrote 32 operas, in some of which he used material from other composers (he included music by Mozart in *The Prisoner* and *The Mariners).* He also wrote church music, piano sonatas, songs and glees.

Auber (oh-bär'), **Daniel-François-Esprit,** prolific French composer of comic operas; b. Caen (Normandy), Jan. 29, 1782; d. Paris, May 12, 1871. His father, an art dealer in Paris, sent him to London to acquire knowledge of business. Auber learned music as well as trade and wrote several songs for social entertainment in London. Political tension between France and England, however, forced him to return to Paris in 1804; there he devoted himself exclusively to music. His pasticcio *L'Erreur d'un moment,* a resetting of an old libretto, was produced by an amateur group in Paris in 1806; his next theatrical work was *Julie,* performed privately, with an accompaniment of 6 string instruments, in 1811. Cherubini, who was in the audience, was attracted by Auber's talent and subsequently gave him some professional advice. Auber's first opera to be given publicly in Paris was *Le Séjour Militaire* (1813). Six years later the Opéra-Comique produced his new work *Le Testament et les billets-doux* (1819). These operas passed without favorable notice, but his next production, *La Bergère châtelaine* (1820) was a definite success. From that time until nearly the end of his life, hardly a year elapsed without the production of a new opera. Not counting amateur performances, 45 operas from Auber's pen were staged in Paris between 1813 and 1869. He was fortunate in having the collaboration of the best librettist of the time, Scribe, who wrote (alone, or with other writers) no fewer than 37 libretti for Auber's operas. Auber's fame reached its height with *Masaniello, ou la Muette de Portici,* produced at the Opéra, Feb. 29, 1828. Its success was enormous. Historically, it laid the foundation of French grand opera with Meyerbeer's *Robert le Diable* and Rossini's *Guillaume Tell.* Its vivid portrayal of popular fury stirred French and Belgian audiences; revolutionary riots followed its performance in Brussels (Aug. 25, 1830). Another popular success was achieved by him with his romantic opera *Fra Diavolo* (Opéra-Comique, Jan. 28, 1830), which became a standard work. Despite these successes with grand opera, Auber may be rightfully regarded as a founder of the French comic opera, a worthy successor of Boieldieu and at least an equal of Adam and Hérold. The influence of Rossini was noted by contemporary critics, but on the whole, Auber's music preserves a distinctive quality of its own. Rossini himself remarked that although Auber's music is light, his art is profound. Auber was greatly appreciated by the successive regimes in France; in 1829 he succeeded Gossec at the Academy; in 1842 he was appointed director of the Paris Cons. by Louis Philippe, and retained this post until his death. In 1857 Napoleon III made him imperial 'maître de chapelle.' At the age of 87 he produced his last opera *Rêves d'amour.* Auber lived virtually all his life in Paris, remaining there even during the siege by the Germans. He died, during the days of the Paris Commune, in his 90th year. His memory was honored by the Academy. Among his operas (most of which were produced at the Opéra-Comique) are also the following: *Le Cheval de bronze* (March 23, 1835); *Le Domino noir* (Dec. 2, 1837); *Les Diamants de la couronne* (March 6, 1841); *Manon Lescaut* (Feb. 23, 1856); *Le premier jour de bonheur* (Feb. 15, 1868), etc. Bibl.: A. Pougin, *Auber* (Paris, 1873); A. Kohut, *Auber* (Leipzig, 1895); Ch. Malherbe, *Auber* (Paris, 1911).

Aubert (oh-bär'), **Jacques** (called 'le vieux'), celebrated French violinist; b. Paris, Sept. 30, 1689; d. Belleville, near Paris, May (buried May 19), 1753. He was a pupil of Senaillé; in 1719 he became band leader to the Duke of Bourbon; in 1727 was one of the King's 24 violinists; he played in the orch. of the Grand Opéra as first violinist from 1728-52, and took part in the Concerts Spirituels (1729-40). He published 33 separate instrumental works; was also the first in France to write instrumental concertos (scored for 4 violins and a bass). His music, distinguished by elegance, contributed to the formation of the French 'style galant.' Bibl.: L. La Laurencie, *L'École française de violon de Lully à Viotti* (Paris, 1922-23).

Aubert, Louis-François-Marie, French composer; b. Paramé, Ille-et-Vilaine, Feb. 19, 1877. Of precocious talent, he entered the Paris Cons. as a child, and studied piano with Diémer, theory with Lavignac and advanced composition with Gabriel Fauré; he also sang in church choirs. His song, *Rimes tendres* was published when he was 19. His *Fantaisie* for piano and orch. was performed in Paris by the Colonne Orch. with his teacher Diémer as soloist (Nov. 17, 1901). His *Suite brève* for 2 pianos was presented at the Paris Exposition, 1900; an orchestral version of it was performed for the first time in Paris on April 27, 1916. Aubert's major work is an operatic fairy tale *La Forêt bleue* (Geneva, Jan. 7, 1913); an American production was staged in Boston, March 8, 1913, attracting considerable attention. The Paris production of *La Forêt bleue,* delayed by the war, took place on June 10, 1924, at the Opéra-Comique. Aubert's style is largely determined by the impressionistic currents of the early 20th century; like Debussy and Ravel, he was attracted by the music of Spain and wrote several pieces in the Spanish idiom, of which the symph. poem *Habanera* (Paris, March 22, 1919) was particularly successful. The list of Aubert's works further includes: *La Légende du sang* for narrator, chorus and orch. (1902); 3 ballets, *La Momie* (1903); *Chrysothémis* (1904) and *La Nuit ensorcélée* (1922); *6 poèmes arabes* for voice and orch. (1907); a song cycle *Crépuscules d'automne* (Paris, Feb. 20, 1909); *Nuit mauresque* for voice and orch. (1911); *Dryade* for orch. (1921); *Caprice* for violin and orch. (1925); *Feuilles d'images,* symph. suite (Paris, March 7, 1931); *Saisons* for chorus and orch. (1937); *Offrande aux victimes de la guerre* for orch. (1947); *Le Tombeau de Châteaubriand* for orch. (1948); *Cinéma,* ballet (1953); a set of 3 piano pieces *Sillages* (1913); a piano quintet, songs etc. Bibl.: L. Vuillemin, *Louis Aubert et son œuvre* (Paris, 1921); E. B. Hill, *Modern French Music* (1924); R. Bernard, *Louis Aubert* in 'La Revue Musicale' (Feb. 1927).

Aubéry du Boulley (boo-lā'), **Prudent-Louis,** French composer; b. Verneuil, Eure, Dec. 9, 1796; d. there, Jan. 28, 1870. He studied at the Paris Cons. with Momigny, Méhul and Cherubini. He wrote much chamber music, in which he used the guitar; published a guitar method and a text book *Grammaire musicale* (Paris, 1830). He was an active teacher in his native province, and contributed much to the cultivation of music there. See J. de L'Avre, *Aubéry du Boulley* (Paris, 1896).

Aubin, Tony, French composer; b. Paris, Dec. 8, 1907. He studied at the Paris Cons. with Paul Dukas; won the Prix de Rome in 1930. In 1944 he became a radio conductor; in 1946 was engaged as prof. of composition at the Paris Cons. He has written 2 symphonies (1937, 1951); *Suite danoise* for orch. (1945); a string quartet, a piano sonata, and incidental music. A utilitarian composer par excellence, Aubin cultivates a neo-classical style designed for immediate effect.

Aubry, Pierre, French music scholar; b. Paris, Feb. 14, 1874; d. (following a fencing accident) Dieppe, Aug. 31, 1910. He began his education as a philologist; studied oriental languages, and traveled to Turkestan on a research project. He then became interested in medieval music; was, for a time, lecturer on music history at the École des hautes études sociales. His theories of notation are based on a plausible interpretation of medieval writers. His many publications, distinguished by profound scholarship, include: *Huits Chants héroiques de l'ancienne France* (1896); *Mélanges de Musicologie critique,* in 4 vols.: I. *La Musicologie médiévale* (1899); II. *Les Proses d'Adam de Saint-Victor* (1900, with Abbé Misset); III. *Lais et Descorts français du XIIIe siècle* (1901, with Jeanroy and Brandin); *IV. Les plus anciens monuments de la musique française* (1903, with 24 facsimiles); *Essais de musicologie comparée,* 2 vols.: I. *Le rhythme tonique dans la poésie liturgique et dans le chant des églises chrétiennes au moyen-âge* (1903); II. *Esquisse d'une bibliographie de la chanson populaire en Europe* (1905); *Les caractères de la danse. Histoire d'un divertissement pendant la première moitié du XVIIIe siècle* (1905); *Au Turkestan. Notes sur quelques habitudes musicales chez les Tadjikes et chez les Sartes* (1905); *La Musique et les musiciens d'église en Normandie au XIIIe siècle* (1906); *Estampies et danses royales. Les plus anciens textes de musique instrumentale au moyen-âge* (1907); *Recherches sur les ténors français* *dans les motets du XIIIe siècle* (1907); *Recherches sur les ténors latins dans les motets du XIIIe siècle* (1907; facsimile ed. of the Parisian MS., with index and editorial explanations); *Cent Motets du XIIIe siècle* (1908; 3 vols.; photographic facsimile of Bamberg Codex E. d. IV. 6, with annotations; a most important work); *Refrains et Rondeaux du XIIIe siècle* (1909, in the Riemann 'Festschrift'); *Trouvères et Troubadours* (1909; English ed. N. Y., 1914); and a number of essays on kindred topics, publ. in the 'Mercure musical' (1903-8).

Auda (oh-dah'), **Antoine,** French-Belgian organist and music scholar; b. at St. Julien-en-Jarez (Loire), Oct. 28, 1879. He studied music at Marseilles; then established himself at Liège as organist; published important studies on the musical history of the city: *Etienne de Liège* (1923); *La Musique et les Musiciens de l'ancien pays de Liège* (1930); and the valuable theoretical works: *Les Modes et les Tons* (1931); and *Les Gammes musicales* (1947).

Audran (oh-drahn'), **Edmond,** French composer of light opera; son of Marius Audran; b. Lyons, April 12, 1840; d.Tierceville, Aug. 17, 1901. He studied at the École Niedermayer in Paris (grad. in 1859). In 1861 he was appointed organist at St. Joseph's Church in Marseilles where he produced his first operetta *L'Ours et le Pacha* (1862). He wrote a funeral march on Meyerbeer's death (1864). After the production of *Le Grand Mogol* (Marseilles, Feb. 24, 1877), he returned to Paris, and staged *Les Noces d'Olivette* (Nov. 13, 1879). With the production of *La Mascotte* (Bouffes-Parisiens, Dec. 28, 1880), Audran achieved fame; this operetta became immensely popular; thousands of performances were given in Paris and all over the world. He continued to produce new operettas almost annually; of these, the following were successful: *Gillette de Narbonne* (1882); *La Cigale et la fourmi* (1886); *Miss Hélyett* (1891); *Sainte Freya* (1892); *Madame Suzette* (1893); *Mon Prince* (1893); *La Duchesse de Ferrare* (1895); *Photis* (1896); *La Poupée* (1896); *Monsieur Lohengrin* (1896); *Les petites femmes* (1897).

Audran, Marius-Pierre, French operatic tenor and composer of songs; father of Edmond Audran; b. Aix, Provence, Sept. 26, 1816; d. Marseilles, Jan. 9, 1887. He began his career in the provinces (Marseilles, Bordeaux, Lyons); then became first tenor at the Opéra-Comique, Paris. After a period of travel (1852-61), he settled in Marseilles and in 1863 became prof. of voice and dir. of the Marseilles Cons.

Auer, Leopold, celebrated Hungarian violinist and pedagogue; b. Veszprém, June 7, 1845; d. Loschwitz, near Dresden, July 15, 1930. He studied with Ridley Kohnel in Budapest and with Dont in Vienna; later lessons with Joachim. From 1863-65 he was in Düsseldorf as concertmaster of the orchestra; in 1866 in Hamburg. In 1868 he was called to St. Petersburg as soloist in the Imperial Orch., and prof. of violin at the newly founded Cons. He became one of the most famous violin teachers in Russia; among his pupils were Elman, Zimbalist, Heifetz and many other virtuosos. Tchaikovsky originally dedicated his violin concerto to Auer, but was offended when he suggested some revisions and changed the dedication to Brodsky. Nevertheless, the concerto became Auer's favorite work, and he made it a *pièce de résistance* for all his pupils. After the revolution he left Russia. On March 23, 1918, he played a concert in New York City; settling permanently in America, he devoted himself exclusively to teaching. He published the manuals *Violin Playing as I Teach it* (N. Y., 1921), *Violin Master Works and Their Interpretation* (1925), and an autobiography *My Long Life in Music* (1923).

Auer, Max, Austrian writer on music; b. Vöcklabruck, May 6, 1880. He studied in Vienna; later taught in provincial public schools; settled in Bad Ischl. He is the foremost authority on Bruckner; published *Anton Bruckner; Sein Leben und Werk* (Vienna, 1923); *Anton Bruckner als Kirchenmusiker* (Regensburg, 1927); completed vols. 2-4 (1928, 1932, 1937) of Göllerich's monumental biography, *Anton Bruckner; Ein Lebens- und Schaffensbild.*

Augener, George, English publisher, founder of Augener & Co.; b. Germany, 1830; d. London, Aug. 25, 1915. He organized the firm in 1853 (incorporated Oct. 11, 1904), and was its head until he retired in 1910. In 1870, Augener started publishing the music periodical 'The Monthly Musical Record.' In 1896 the firm purchased the catalogue of Robert Cocks & Co.

Augustine (Augustinus), Aurelius, known as **St. Augustine;** b. Tagaste, Numidia, Nov. 13, 354; d. as bishop, at Hippo (now Bona), Algeria, Aug. 28, 430. St. Augustine was one of the four great fathers of the Latin Church. He was educated at Madaura and Carthage. He became a Christian in 387, receiving his baptism from St. Ambrose. His writings contain valuable information concerning Ambrosian song; the book entitled *De Musica* treats largely of metre. It is printed in Migne, *Patrologiae cursus* (vol. 32); German translation by C. J. Perl (Strasbourg, 1937); English translation by R. Catesby Taliaferro in 'The Classics of the St. John's Program' (1939). A synopsis of *De Musica* in English (with commentaries and translated by W. F. Jackson Knight) was published by the Orthological Institute (London, 1949). Cf. J. Huré *Saint Augustin Musicien* (1924); H. Edelstein *Die Musikanschauung Augustins* (Freiburg, 1928); W. Hoffmann, *Philosophische Interpretation der Augustin-Schrift De Musica* (Freiburg, 1930); H. Davenson, *Traité de la musique selon l'esprit de Saint Augustin* (Neuchâtel, 1944).

Aulin, Tor, Swedish violinist and composer; b. Stockholm, Sept. 10, 1866; d. there, March 1, 1914. He studied with C. J. Lindberg in Stockholm (1877-83) and with Sauret and Scharwenka in Berlin (1884-86). In 1887 he established the Aulin String Quartet, and traveled with it in Germany and Russia. He was concertmaster at the Stockholm Opera from 1889 till 1902, but continued his concert career, and was considered the greatest Scandinavian violinist since Ole Bull. Aulin was appointed conductor of the Stockholm Philharmonic Soc. in 1902; became leader of the Göteborg Orch. in 1909. As conductor and violinist, he made determined propaganda for Swedish composers. He wrote incidental music to Strindberg's *Mäster Olof,* 3 violin concertos, several suites of Swedish dances for orch., violin sonata, a violin method and songs. His sister **Laura Aulin** (b. Gävle, Jan. 9, 1860; d. Örebro, Jan. 11, 1928), was a well known pianist; she also composed chamber and piano music.

Aurelianus Reomensis, French scholar; monk at Réomé in the 9th century. His treatise *Musica disciplina* (published by Gerbert in 'Scriptores,' Vol. I) contains the earliest information on the melodic character of the church modes. See H. Riemann, *Handbuch der Musikgeschichte* (Leipzig, 1919, vol. I).

Auric (oh-rēk), **Georges,** French composer; b. Lodève, Feb. 15, 1899. He studied in Paris with Vincent d'Indy and Roussel, but began to compose even before receiving formal tuition. Between the ages of 12 and 16 he wrote some 300 songs and piano pieces; at 18 he wrote the ballet *Les Noces de Gamache;* at 20 a comic opera *La Reine de cœur,* but destroyed the MS. Influenced mainly by Erik Satie, he pursued the type of composition that would, in his own words, produce "auditory pleasure without demanding a disproportionate effort from the listener." Auric became associated with Milhaud, Poulenc, Honegger and others in the celebrated group "Les Six." He wrote music for Diaghilev's Ballets Russes, and later for other ballet companies. In 1931 he composed a highly successful score for the film *A nous la liberté;* another effective film score was *Moulin Rouge* (1952). He has also been active as music critic in 'Paris Soir' and 'Nouvelles littéraires.' Works: Ballets: *Les Fâcheux* (Monte Carlo, Jan. 19, 1924); *Les Matelots* (Paris, June 17, 1925); *La Pastorale* (Paris, May 26, 1926); *Les Enchantements d'Alcine* (Paris, May 21, 1929); *Les Imaginaires* (Paris, May 31, 1934); *Le Peintre et son modèle* (Paris, Nov. 16, 1949); *La Pierre enchantée* (Paris, June 23, 1950); *Chemin de Lumière* (Munich, March 27, 1952); *Coup de feu* (Paris, May 7, 1952). — Bibl.: Boris de Schloezer, *Georges Auric,* in 'La Revue Musicale' (Jan., 1926).

Aus der Ohe, Adele, German pianist; b. Hanover, Dec. 11, 1864; d. Berlin, Dec. 7, 1937. She studied as a child with Kullak in Berlin; at the age of 12 became a pupil of Liszt for seven years. She then played concerts in Europe; made her American debut with Liszt's 1st piano concerto in New York (Dec. 23, 1886) and continued her American tours for 17 consecutive years. She played 51 times with the Boston Symph. Orch. between 1887 and 1906. One of the highlights of her career was her appearance as soloist in Tchaikovsky's 1st piano concerto under Tchaikovsky's own direction at his last concert (St. Petersburg, Oct. 28, 1893). Because of a crippling illness, she was forced to abandon her concert career; she lost her accumulated earnings in the German currency inflation in the 1920's, and from 1928 till her death, subsisted on a pension from the Bagby Music Lovers Foundation of New York.

Austin, Ernest, English composer, brother of Frederick Austin; b. London, Dec. 31, 1874; d. Wallington, Surrey, July 24, 1947. He had no formal musical education; began to compose at the age of 33 after a business career. His compositions, therefore, acquired an experimental air; he was particularly interested in a modern treatment of old English tunes. — Works (about 90 in all): *The Vicar of Bray* for string orch. (1910); *Hymn of Apollo* for chorus and orch. (Leeds, 1918); *Stella Mary Dances* (London, 1918); *Ode on a Grecian Urn,* after Keats (1922); 14 Sonatinas on English folk songs for children; a cycle of organ works in 12 parts (inspired by Bunyan's *Pilgrim's Progress)*; chamber music and songs. He published a book, *The Fairyland of Music* (1922).

Austin, Florence, American violinist; b. Galesburg, Mich., March 11, 1884; d. (in a railroad accident) Fairchild, Wis., Aug., 1926. She studied with Schradieck in New York, and with Musin at Liège Cons., winning first prize (for the first time by an American). Upon her return to New York (1901) she appeared in recitals, then settled in Newark, N. J., as violin teacher.

Austin, Frederick, English baritone and composer; brother of Ernest Austin; b. London, March 30, 1872; d. there, April 10, 1952. He studied with his uncle, Dr. W. H. Hunt; became an organist and also taught music at Liverpool. In 1902 he appeared as a singer in London, and participated in many choral festivals in later years. He sang in opera at Covent Garden, and with the Beecham Opera Co. At the same time he became known in England as a composer. He wrote a symphony, a symph. poem *Isabella,* a choral work *Pervigilium Veneris,* and an overture *The Sea Venturers* and composed incidental music for the stage.

Austin, Henry Richter, English-American music publisher and editor; b. London, May 17, 1882. He was organist at the English Royal Church in Berlin (1904-06); then settled in the U.S., occupying positions as church organist in and around Boston until 1948. He has conducted experiments with the acoustical characteristics of non-tempered scales and devised a keyboard *Novaton,* of 16 keys (8 white, 8 black) providing the true seventh partial tone. Became president of the Arthur P. Schmidt Co. in 1954 (after many years with the firm).

Austin, John Turnell, English-American organist; b. Poddington, Bedfordshire, May 16, 1869; d. Hartford, Conn., Sept. 17, 1948. He came to the U.S. in 1889 and worked for various organ building firms. On March 3, 1899 he founded an organ company under his own name at Hartford, Conn., retiring in 1935. He patented the Austin Universal Air Chest. The Austin Organ Co. supplied organs for many concert halls in the U.S.

Austin, Richard, English conductor; son of Frederick Austin; b. Birkenhead, Dec. 26, 1903. He studied conducting with Sir Adrian Boult and Sir Malcolm Sargent at the Royal College of Music; then conducted the Carl Rosa Opera Co. From 1934-40 he led the Bournemouth Orch. During World War II he was Music Advisor in the British Army. In 1946, was appointed prof. at the Royal College of Music. In 1947 he established in London the New Era Concert Society for performances of unusual works.

Austin, Sumner, English baritone; b. London, Sept. 24, 1888. He studied at Oxford; went to Germany in 1914 and was interned there during World War I. He was a member of the Carl Rosa Opera Co. in 1919; in later years he became an operatic producer in London.

Austral, Florence, Australian soprano (real name Florence Wilson); b. Melbourne April 26, 1894. She studied at the Melbourne Cons. (1914-18) and in New York (1918). She made her operatic debut as Brünnhilde at Covent Garden (May 16, 1922); later she sang the roles of Isolde and Aida. She toured in the U.S. between 1925 and 1931 with her husband, the flutist John Amadio.

Auteri Manzocchi (man-tsŏh-kē), **Salvatore,** Italian opera composer; b. Palermo, Dec. 25, 1845; d. Parma, Feb. 22, 1924. He studied in Palermo with Platania, and with Mabellini in Florence. His first opera *Marcellina* was never performed; his second, *Dolores* (Florence, Feb. 23, 1875) enjoyed considerable success, as did *Stella* (Piacenza, May 22, 1880). His other operas are *Il Negriero* (Milan, 1878); *Il Conte de Gleichen* (Milan, 1887); *Graziella* (Milan, Oct. 23, 1894) and *Severo Torelli* (Bologna, April 25, 1903).

d'Auvergne, Antoine. See **Dauvergne, Antoine.**

Aventinus, Johannes (real name Turmair), German theorist; b. Abensberg (whence Aventinus), July 4, 1477; d. there, Jan. 9, 1534. His treatise *Annales Boiorum* (1554) contains considerable information (not always trustworthy) about musical matters. He also edited Nicolaus Faber's *Musica rudimenta admodum brevia* (1516).

Averkamp, Anton, Dutch choral conductor and composer; b. Willige Langerak, Feb. 18, 1861; d. Bussum, June 1, 1934. He studied with Daniel de Lange in Amsterdam, with Friedrich Kiel in Berlin, and with Rheinberger in Munich. In 1890 he founded the famous chorus, 'Amsterdam A Cappella Coor,' with which he traveled in Europe, presenting programs of early polyphonic music. He led this group until 1918; then was appointed director of the Music School of Tonal Art in Utrecht. In 1927 he was elected chairman of the 'Vereeniging voor Nederlandsche Muziekgeschiedenis.' Averkamp wrote an opera *De Heidebloem* (not produced); a symph. poem *Elaine and Lancelot;* 2 choral works with orch., *Decora Lux* and *Die versunkene Burg;* a symphony; a *Te Deum;* a violin sonata and songs. He contributed numerous historical articles to music periodicals, and published a manual for singers, *Uit mijn practijk* (Groningen, 1916).

Avidom, Menahem (real name, Mahler-Kalkstein), Israeli composer; b. Stanislawow, Poland, Jan. 6, 1908. He studied in Beirut and Paris; since 1935 settled in Tel-Aviv as teacher and composer. For several years, managed the Israeli Philharmonic Orch. Among his works are a *Folk Symphony* (Tel-Aviv, March 5, 1947); *David Symphony* (Tel-Aviv, Dec. 1, 1949); chamber music and songs.

Avison, Charles, English organist and composer; b. Newcastle-on-Tyne 1709 (baptized Feb. 16); d. there, May 9, 1770. After studying with Geminiani in London, he became organist at St. John's Church, Newcastle (1736). He wrote a large number of chamber works, among them 26 concertos *a* 7 (4 violins, viola, cello, bass), 12 piano concertos with string quartet, 18 quartets for piano with 2 violins and cello, and 3 volumes of sonatas for harpsichord with 2 violins. He also published *An Essay on Musical Expression* (London, 1752) and (with J. Garth), Marcello's *Psalm-Paraphrases* (1757; with English words). Bibl.: A. Milner, *C. Avison* in the 'Musical Times' (Jan., 1954).

Avshalomov (ăhv-shăh-loh'-mov), **Aaron,** Russian-American composer; b. Nikolayevsk, Siberia, Nov. 11, 1894. He studied at the Zürich Cons.; in 1914 went to China; there he made a profound study of native music, and wrote a number of works based on Chinese subjects, often utilizing authentic Chinese melodies. On April 24, 1925, he conducted his first opera *Kuan Yin* in Peking. His 2nd opera, *The Great Wall,* was staged in Shanghai on Nov. 26, 1945, and also successfully presented in Nanking under the sponsorship of Madame Chiang Kai-Shek. His other works written in China (all performed in Shanghai) are: *Peiping Hutungs,* symph. sketch (Feb. 7, 1933; also perf. by Stokowski in Philadelphia, Nov. 8, 1935); *The Soul of the Ch'in,* ballet (May 21, 1933); *Incense Shadows,* pantomime (March 13, 1935); piano concerto (Jan. 19, 1936); violin concerto (Jan. 16, 1938); 1st Symphony (March 17, 1940, composer conducting); (March 17, 1940, composer conducting); *Buddha and the Five Planetary Deities,* choreographic tableau (April 18, 1942). Avshalomov came to America in 1947, and settled in New York; works composed since then are: 2nd Symphony (Cincinnati, Dec. 30, 1949); 3rd Symphony (1950); 4th Symphony (1951).

Avshalomov, Jacob, American composer, son of Aaron Avshalomov; b. Tsingtao, China, March 28, 1919; his mother was American; his father, Russian. He studied music in Peking; in 1936 he was in Shanghai, where material circumstances forced him to work for a time in a slaughterhouse. In 1937 he came to U.S.; studied with Ernst Toch in Los Angeles; then with Bernard Rogers in Rochester, N.Y. From 1943-45 he was in the U.S. Army as interpreter. From 1947-54 he was instructor at Columbia Univ.; received a Guggenheim Fellowship in 1952; in 1954 he was appointed permanent conductor of the Portland Junior Symphony. His music reflects the many cultures with which he was in contact; while the form is cohesive, the materials are multifarious, with tense chromatic harmonies and quasi-oriental inflections. — Compositions: *Sinfonietta* (1946); *Evocations* for clarinet and chamber orch. (1947); Sonatina for viola and piano (1947); *Prophecy* for chorus, tenor and organ (1948); *Taking of T'ung Kuan* for orch. (1948); *Tom o'Bedlam* for chorus (N. Y., Dec. 15, 1953; received the N. Y. Music Critics Award); *The Plywood Age* for orch., commissioned for the 50th anniversary of the Fir Plywood Corp. (Portland, June 20, 1955); *Psalm 100* for chorus and wind instruments (1956); *Inscriptions at the City of Brass* for chorus, narrator, and large orch., to a text from the *Arabian Nights* (1956).

Axman, Emil, Czech composer; b. Rataje, June 3, 1887; d. Prague, Jan. 5, 1949. Of a musical family, he began to compose at an early age. He later studied with Nejedlý at the Prague Univ., obtaining his Ph. D. in 1912; he also took private lessons with Novák. In 1913 he was appointed keeper of the musical archives at the National Museum in Prague. He participated in the modern musical movement but was not attracted by the spirit of experimentation. Axman was a prolific composer; he wrote 6 symphonies between 1920 and 1942 (his 2nd symphony was performed at the Frankfurt Festival, July 3, 1927); the cantatas *My Mother* (1926) and *The Cemetery of Sobotka* (1933); symph. poem *Mourning and Hope*; violin concerto (1936);

piano concerto (1939); cello concerto (1944); 4 string quartets, wind quintet, violin sonata, piano sonata; several song cycles.

Ayala, Daniel, Mexican (Indian) composer; b. Abalá, Yucatán, July 21, 1908. He studied violin with Revueltas; played at night clubs in Mexico City. In 1940 he became conductor of the band (later symphony orch.) in Mérida. His music, inspired by Mayan legends, has a strong rhythmic undercurrent. Among his works are the symphonic suites *Un Antiguo Cemeterio* (Mexico City, Oct. 13, 1933); *Tribú* (ibid., Oct. 18, 1935); *Paisaje* (ibid., June 2, 1936); *El Hombre Maya* (ibid., Nov. 21, 1940); *Panoramas de Mexico* (Dallas, Dec. 1, 1940). They have also been used for ballet productions in Mexico.

Ayestarán, Lauro, Uruguayan musicologist; b. Montevideo, July 9, 1913. He studied voice and music history; became instructor of choral music in municipal schools in Montevideo. He is the author of the important monograph *Domenico Zipoli, el gran compositor y organista romano en el Rio de la Plata* (Montevideo, 1941).

Ayres, Frederic (real name, Frederick Ayres Johnson), American composer; b. Binghamton, N. Y., March 17, 1876; d. Colorado Springs, Nov. 23, 1926. He studied with Edgar S. Kelley (1897-1901) and Arthur Foote (1899). His works include an overture *From the Plains;* 2 string quartets, 2 piano trios, 2 violin sonatas, a cello sonata and numerous songs. In his later music he showed a tendency towards impressionism, and used moderately complex harmonic combinations. Bibl.: Wm. T. Upton, *Frederic Ayres,* in the 'Mus. Quarterly' (1932).

Ayrton, Edmund, English organist and composer; father of William Ayrton; b. Ripon, Yorkshire, 1734; d. London, May 22, 1808. He studied organ with Nares; from 1754 he was organist in various churches; in 1764 was appointed a Gentleman of the Chapel Royal in London; in 1780 became Master of the Children. His anthem *Begin unto my God with Timbrels* was presented in St. Paul's Cathedral (July 28, 1784); he also wrote 2 morning and evening services.

Ayrton, William, English organist; son of Edmund Ayrton; b. London, Feb. 24, 1777; d. there, March 8, 1858. He received a fine education; was one of the original founders of the London Philharmonic Soc. in 1813; wrote music criticism for 'The Morning Chronicle' (1813-26) and for 'The Examiner' (1837-51). In 1823 he started the publication of the historically important London music periodical 'The Harmonicon,' and was its editor; from 1834-37 edited 'The Musical Library,' which published vocal and instrumental music. He also compiled a practical collection, 'Sacred Minstrelsy' (2 vols., 1835).

Azantchevsky, Mikhail Pavlovitch, Russian music scholar and composer; b. Moscow, 1838; d. there, Jan. 24, 1881. He studied music with Hauptmann and Richter at the Leipzig Cons. (1861-62) and took some lessons with Liszt in Rome. During his sojourn in Paris (1866-70) he purchased the important music library of Anders; later he presented it, together with other acquisitions, to the St. Petersburg Cons. of which he was director (1870-76). He wrote a concert overture, 2 string quartets, a piano trio, a cello sonata, some choral works and a *Festival Polonaise* for 2 pianos, as well as solo piano pieces.

Azevedo (ah-zĕ-vĕ-doh'), **Alexis-Jacob,** French writer on music; b. Bordeaux, March 18, 1813; d. Paris, Dec. 21, 1875. He was a prolific contributor to 'Le Ménestrel' and other French music magazines; published monographs on Félicien David (1863) and Rossini (1864); a pamphlet, *La verité sur Rouget de Lisle et la Marseillaise* (Dieppe, 1864); *La transposition par les nombres* (Paris, 1874); a collection of articles *Les doubles-croches malades* (1874), etc.

Azkué, Resurrección María, Spanish composer and musicologist; b. Lequeitio, Aug. 5, 1864; d. Bilbao, Nov. 9, 1951. He studied theology in Spain, then went to Paris and studied music at the Schola Cantorum. He wrote 2 operas: *Ortzuri* (Bilbao, 1911) and *Urlo* (Bilbao, 1913) to Basque texts; an oratorio *Daniel* and a *Te Deum;* also several zarzuelas. He published a valuable collection *Cancionero Vasco* (11 vols.) and *Literatura popular del país Vasco* (4 vols., the last containing musical examples).

Azzopardi, Francesco, Italian (Maltese) music theorist and composer; b. Rabat, Malta, May 5, 1748; d. there, Feb. 6, 1809. His fame rests on the school manual *Il musico prattico* (1760), published by Framéry in French translation (Paris, 1786) and quoted by Cherubini in his course on counterpoint and fugue, and by Grétry. He also composed sacred music, including an oratorio *La Passione di Cristo.* Cf. P. Pullicino, *Notizia biografica di Francesco Azzopardi* (1876).

B

Babbitt, Milton, American composer; b. Philadelphia, May 10, 1916. He studied at Princeton Univ. and in 1938 became an instructor there; also taught mathematics. His music is couched in an abstract style; the titles of his works are indicative of this tendency: *Composition for 4 instruments* (1948); *Composition for Viola and Piano* (1950); *Composition for 4 wood wind instruments* (1953), etc. In 1948 he adopted the 12-tone method of composition, expanding it into the domain of rhythm (12 basic rhythmic values in a theme) and into instrumentation (themes of 12 notes played successively by 12 different instruments).

Babin, Victor, pianist and composer; b. Moscow, Dec. 13, 1908; studied at the Riga Cons.; then with Schnabel in Berlin (1928-31). He married Vitya Vronsky (q.v.) on Aug. 31, 1933; they came to the U.S. in 1937; have toured widely as a two-piano team. Babin has written a concerto for 2 pianos and orch. and etudes for 2 pianos.

Babini, Matteo, famous Italian tenor; b. Bologna, Feb. 19, 1754; d. there, Sept. 22, 1816. He studied with Cortoni; made his debut in 1780; then toured England, Russia, Germany and Austria with great acclaim. He settled in Paris as a court favorite until the Revolution forced him to leave France; he was in Berlin in 1792 and in Trieste in 1796. Brighenti published an 'Elogio' in his memory (Bologna, 1821).

Babitz, Sol, American violinist; b. Brooklyn, Oct. 11, 1911. He studied in Los Angeles; then in Berlin with Paul Juon and Carl Flesch. Returning to America he became violinist in the Los Angeles Philh. Orch. (1933-37). Since 1947 on the staff of the 20th Century-Fox Studios in Hollywood; also teaching at the Los Angeles Cons. He has written numerous articles dealing with violin technique and edited many violin works by contemporary composers.

Bacarisse, Salvador, Spanish composer; b. Madrid, Sept. 12, 1898. He studied with Conrado del Campo at the Madrid Cons. and won three national prizes for music (1923, 1930, 1934). He was associated with the Loyalist Government during the Spanish Civil War, and after its defeat in 1939, settled in France. He has written *La Tragedia de Donna Ajada* for orch. (1929); piano concerto (1933); *Tres Movimientos Concertantes* for string trio and orch. (1934); cantata, *Por la Paz y Felicidad de las Naciones* (1950); concerto for guitar and orch. (Paris, Oct. 22, 1953); 2 string quartets, piano pieces and songs.

Baccaloni, Salvatore, Italian bass; b. Rome, April 14, 1900. He first studied to be an architect; then turned to singing; was engaged by Toscanini to sing at La Scala in Milan (1926); sang with the Chicago Opera during the season of 1930-31; became a member of the Metropolitan Opera in 1940, producing a fine impression as Bartolo in *The Marriage of Figaro* at his debut in Philadelphia (Dec. 3, 1940). He has specialized in comic roles, and his appearances in the *Barber of Seville* (as Bartolo) and in *Falstaff* were highly successful. His repertory is very large, comprising some 150 roles in several languages.

Bacchius (Senior), Greek theorist who flourished c. 350 A. D. His treatise, *Isagoge musicae artis,* was publ. by Mersenne (1623); with Latin translation and commentary by Morellus (1623); also by Meibom (1652) and Carl von Jan (with German translation and analysis in the Program of the Strasbourg Lyceum, 1890; Greek text alone in Jan's 'Scriptores,' 1895). French translations have been publ. by Mersenne (in Book I of his *Harmonie universelle,* 1627) and Ruelle (1896). The work is a musical catechism in dialogue form. Another treatise attributed to Bacchius, having no dialogue, and edited by Bellermann (in German, 1841) and Vincent (in French, 1847) is not by Bacchius, but by his contemporary, Dionysios.

Baccusi, Ippolito, Italian composer; b. Mantua, c. 1530; d. Verona, 1609. He served as maestro di cappella at Mantua cathedral (1587-92) and then at Verona cathedral. He publ. 3 masses (with instrumental accompaniment in unison) in Venice (1596) and several collections of other sacred works and madrigals. His music shows the influence of the Venetian school; his motets have considerable expressive power.

Bacewicz, Grazyna, Polish composer, b. Lodz, Feb. 5, 1913. She studied violin and theory at the Warsaw Cons., and composition with Nadia Boulanger in Paris. She gave concerts in France, Spain and Russia; taught at the Lodz Cons. (1934-35). She was in Paris again in 1939; after 1945 returned to her post in Poland at the Lodz Cons. In 1951 she received first prize for her 4th string quartet at the International Competition in Liège. A prolific composer, she writes in a neo-classical style, with a firm rhythmic pulse, in crisp dissonant harmonies (based on fourths and fifths). Her compositions include 4 symphonies; 4 violin concertos; cello concerto; *Overture* (1946); piano concerto (1949; received Chopin Centennial award); concerto for string orch. (1950); piano quintet (1952); 4 string quartets, 6 violin sonatas; many solo violin pieces.

Bacfarc (or **Bakfark, Bekwark,** etc.), **Valentin,** celebrated Hungarian lutenist; b. Kronstadt, 1507; d. Padua, Aug. 13, 1576. He was brought up by the family of his brother's wife, Greff (or Graew), and used that name in conjunction with his own. As a youth he was in the service of the King of Hungary in Buda, where he studied lute; evidence does not support the belief that he was a pupil of Antonio Rotta of Padua. He was later at the court of Sigismund Augustus of Poland (1549-66); traveled in Germany, France and Italy, eventually settling in Padua, where he died of the plague. He published works for the lute in tablature: *Intabulatura* (Lyons, 1552; reprinted as *Premier Livre de Tablature de Luth,* Paris 1564); *Harmonicarum Musicarum . . . Tomus Primus* (Cracow, 1565); some of his works are printed in 'Denkmäler der Tonkunst in Österreich,' (vol. XVIII, 2). Bibl.: H. Opienski, *Bekwark lutinista* (Warsaw, 1906; also in German as *Valentin Greff-Bekwark,* Leipzig, 1914); Otto Gombosi, *Walenty Bakfark à Pologne* in 'Muzyka' (Warsaw, Oct. 1929); id., *Der Lautenist Valentin Bakfark, Leben und Werke* (Budapest, 1935).

Bach, Albert (real family name Bak), Hungarian singer; b. Gyula, March 24, 1844; d. Edinburgh, Nov. 19, 1912. He studied at the Vienna Cons.; gave his first concert there in 1871; continued his studies in Italy. He sang opera in Italy, Russia, Germany and England. In his recitals he always performed Loewe's songs. He was a member of the Loewe-Verein in Berlin and edited three volumes of Loewe's ballades with English translations; also published several papers on music.

Bach, August Wilhelm, German organist; b. Berlin, Oct. 4, 1796; d. there April 15, 1869. After a period of organ playing in churches and in concert, he became teacher and later director (1832) of the Royal Institute for Church Music in Berlin. Mendelssohn was his pupil in organ playing.

Bach, Leonhard Emil, German pianist and composer; b. Posen, March 11, 1849; d. London, Feb. 15, 1902. He studied with Th. Kullak (piano) and with Kiel (theory); in 1869 became teacher at Kullak's Academy in Berlin. He settled in London; from 1882 taught at the Guildhall School of Music. He wrote several short operas: *Irmengard* (London, 1892); *The Lady of Longford* (London, 1894); *Des Königs Garde* (Cologne, 1895) which were fairly successful at their first productions.

Bach is the name of the illustrious family which, during two centuries, supplied the world with a number of musicians and composers of distinction. History possesses few records of such remarkable examples of hereditary art, which culminated in Johann Sebastian.

The genealogy of the family is traced to **Johannes** or **Hans Bach,** mentioned in 1561 as one of the guardians of the municipality of Wechmar, a little town near Gotha. **Veit Bach** (d. March 8, 1619), the presumed son of this Hans, and Caspar, a town-musician ('Stadtpfeifer') at Gotha, are the first of the family concerning whose musical tendencies we have any information. Veit was a baker by trade, and emigrated to Hungary; returning to Wechmar, he settled there as a miller and baker. His chief recreation consisted in playing the zither. His son, **Hans** (b. c. 1580, d. Dec. 26, 1626), was known as 'the minstrel' ('der Spielmann'), although he followed the supplementary occupation of carpet-weaver. He received instruction from the above-mentioned Caspar, possibly his uncle. On numerous occasions he was called to various places in Thuringia to assist the town-musicians. His three sons **Hans, Christoph** and **Heinrich,** inherited his ability. (See W. Wolffheim, *Hans Bach, der Spielmann,* in 'Bach-Jahrbuch,' 1910.) The Bach genealogy mentions a second son of Veit, presumably **Lips Bach** (d. Oct. 10, 1620), who had three sons, who were sent to Italy, by the Count of Schwarzburg-Arnstadt, to study music. From Hans and Lips, the two sons of Veit, sprang the main branches of the Bach family, whose male members filled so many positions as 'Stadtpfeifer' throughout Thuringia, that, in some instances, even after there had ceased to be any member of the family among them, the town-musicians were known as 'the Bachs.' When the family became numerous and widely dispersed, they agreed to assemble on a fixed date each year. Erfurt, Eisenach and Arnstadt were the places chosen for these meetings, which are said to have continued until the middle of the 18th century, as many as 120 persons of the name of Bach then assembling. At these meetings, a cherished pastime was the singing of 'quodlibets,' comic polyphonic potpourris of popular songs. An amusing example attributed to J. S. Bach, is publ. in 'Veröffentlichungen der Neuen Bach-Gesellschaft' (vol. XXXII, 2).

Johann Sebastian was very interested in the history of his family. A collection of notes on members of the family, entitled *Ursprung der musikalisch-Bachischen Familie,* and known as 'the genealogy,' was, according to Karl Philipp Emanuel, who made additions to the copy preserved (written in 1735), started by Johann Sebastian. This 'genealogy' is reproduced in 'Veröffentlichungen der Neuen Bach-Gesellschaft' (vol. XVII, 3). It has also been edited and translated by C. S. Terry as *The Origin of the Family of Bach Musicians* (Oxford, 1929).

A valuable collection of compositions by **Hans Bach** (1), his sons and grandsons, possibly also begun by J. S. Bach, is partly preserved. The remainders of this collection were edited by M. Schneider as 'Altbachisches Archiv' in *Das Erbe deutscher Musik, Reichsdenkmale* (vols. I and II, Breitkopf & Härtel, 1935). See also *Die Familie Bach,* a collection of excerpts from works by 12 Bachs, edited by Karl Geiringer (Vienna, 1936); also his books *The Bach Family* (N. Y., 1954) and *Music of the Bach Family* (Cambridge, Mass., 1955).

The principal members of the Bach family are enumerated below, in alphabetical order, with their list numbers according to the family tree.

2. Christoph
5. Georg Christoph
1. Hans
3. Heinrich
6. Johann Ambrosius
10. Johann Bernhard
19. Johann Christian
8. Johann Christoph
7. Johann Christoph
11. Johann Christoph
18. Johann Christoph Friedrich
4. Johann Egidius
15. Johann Ernst
14. Johann Ludwig
9. Johann Michael
13. Johann Nikolaus
12. Johann Sebastian
17. Karl Philipp Emanuel
16. Wilhelm Friedemann
20. Wilhelm Friedrich Ernst

1. **Bach, Hans** (eldest son of Hans, the 'Spielmann'), b. Wechmar, Nov. 26, 1604; d. Erfurt, May 13, 1673. Apprentice to an organist at Suhl; then organist at Schweinfurt. In 1635, director of the 'Raths-Musikanten' of Erfurt; 1647, also organist of an Erfurt church. 3 of his works are in the Bach Archives.

2. **Bach, Christoph** (2nd son of Hans, and grandfather of Johann Sebastian), b. Wechmar, April 19, 1613; d. Arnstadt, Sept. 12, 1661; instrumentalist, serving as town-musician at Weimar, Erfurt and Arnstadt. No compositions by him seem to be preserved.

3. **Bach, Heinrich** (3rd son of Hans), b. Wechmar, Sept. 16, 1615; d. Arnstadt, July 10, 1692. From 1641, organist at Arnstadt for 51 years. M. Schneider publ. a thematic index of his works in 'Bach-Jahrbuch' (1907, pp. 105-9). A cantata of his is found in the Bach Archives.

4. **Bach, Johann Egidius** (2nd son of Hans, 1), b. Erfurt, Feb. 9, 1645; d. there, 1716. Succeeded his father as municipal music director; was organist of an Erfurt church.

5. **Bach, Georg Christoph** (eldest son of Christoph, 2), b. Eisenach, Sept. 6, 1642; d. April 24, 1697, at Schweinfurt, where he was cantor. A cantata is in the Bach Archives.

6. **Bach, Johann Ambrosius** (2nd son of Christoph, 2), father of Johann Sebastian, b. Erfurt, Feb. 22, 1645; d. Eisenach, Feb. 20, 1695. (Exact date of death is found in his widow's petition for support, 'Bach Jahrbuch,' 1927.) At the age of nine, he was taken to Arnstadt where he was trained as a town piper ('Stadtpfeifer'). In 1667 he was engaged at Erfurt to play the viola ('Altgeige') in the town band; in 1671, he moved to Eisenach, where he was active as town-musician. He was married twice: on April 8, 1668, to Elisabeth Lämmerhirt (b. Feb. 24, 1644; d. May 3, 1694), who was the mother of Johann Sebastian; and on Nov. 27, 1694 to the widow of his cousin, Johann Günther Bach. Bibl.: F. Rollberg, *J. A. Bach* in 'Bach Jahrbuch' (1927).

7. **Bach, Johann Christoph,** twin brother of Johann Ambrosius; b. Erfurt, Feb. 22, 1645; d. Arnstadt, Aug. 25, 1693. He entered the town service at Arnstadt as 'Stadtpfeifer' in 1671. The physical resemblance between him and his twin brother (father of Johann Sebastian) was such that, according to the testimony of Ph. Emanuel Bach, even their wives had difficulty distinguishing between them.

8. **Bach, Johann Christoph** (eldest son of Heinrich, 3), organist and instrumental and vocal composer of the highest rank among the earlier Bachs; b. Arnstadt, Dec. 8, 1642; d. Eisenach, March 31, 1703.

From 1665, town organist of Eisenach; from 1700, court musician. A thematic catalogue of his compositions was publ. by M. Schneider in 'Bach-Jahrbuch' (1907, pp. 132-77). K. Ph. E. Bach described him as a 'great and expressive composer'; his works are printed in the Bach Archives and separate editions; several of his motets were publ. by V. Junk (Breitkopf & Härtel, 1922); his *Choräle zum Praeambulieren* by M. Fischer ('Bärenreiter-Verlag,' 1929). Cf. F. Rollberg, *Johann Christoph Bach,* in 'Zeitschrift für Musikwissenschaft' (vol. XI, pp. 549-61); M. Fischer, *Die organistische Improvisation . . .*, in 'Königsberger Studien zur Musikwissenschaft' (1919).

9. **Bach, Johann Michael,** brother of the preceding Bach, and father of Maria Barbara, first wife of Johann Sebastian; b. Arnstadt, Aug. 9, 1648; d. Gehren, May 1694. Organist and town clerk of Gehren from 1673; also maker of clavichords, violins, etc. His works are listed in 'Bach-Jahrbuch' (1907, pp. 109-32); many of them are included in the Bach Archives; also represented by motets publ. in 'Denkmäler deutscher Tonkunst' (vols. 49-50). Organ compositions are found in *Das Erbe deutscher Musik, Reichsdenkmale* (vol. IX). A published work consisting of sonatas for 2 groups of instruments is not preserved.

10. **Bach, Johann Bernhard** (son of Johann Egidius, 4), organist and organ composer, one of the best of his generation; b. Erfurt, Nov. 23, 1676; d. Eisenach, June 11, 1749. Organist at Erfurt, Magdeburg, and the successor of Johann Christoph (8), at Eisenach (1703); also served the Duke of Saxe-Eisenach. He wrote harpsichord pieces; several organ-chorales, a few of which are published; and 4 orchestral suites, one of which was published by A. Fareanu (1920).

11. **Bach, Johann Christoph** (brother of Johann Sebastian, and eldest son of Johann Ambrosius, 6), b. Erfurt, June 16, 1671; d. Ohrdruf, Feb. 22, 1721. He was a pupil of Pachelbel; then organist at Erfurt, for a short time at Arnstadt, and finally at Ohrdruf, where Johann Sebastian stayed with him for almost five years.

12. **Bach, Johann Sebastian,** the most famous of the family, and one of the great masters of music; b. Eisenach, March 21 (bapt. March 23), 1685; d. Leipzig, July 28, 1750. He first learned the violin from his father (Joh. Ambrosius [6]). His mother, Elisabeth, *née* Lämmerhirt, was a native of Erfurt. Both parents dying in his tenth year, he went to Ohrdruf to live with his brother, Johann Christoph [11], who taught him to play on keyboard instruments; but the boy's genius soon outstripped his brother's skill, and, if we may trust the somewhat fanciful tale first appearing in the 'Nekrolog', led to somewhat harsh treatment by the latter. Unable to obtain the loan of a MS. volume of works by composers of the day, Sebastian secretly obtained possession of the work, and, by the light of the moon, painfully and laboriously copied the music within six months, only to have it taken from him, when his brother accidentally found him practicing from it. He recovered it only after his brother's death.

In 1700 J. S. went to Lüneburg with a fellow-student named Erdmann, and both were admitted as choristers at St. Michael's Church, also receiving gratuitous scholastic education. The fame of the family had preceded Sebastian, for in the choice collections of printed and MS. music of the church were to be found the compositions of Heinrich [3] and J. Christoph Bach [8]. A fellow-Thuringian, Georg Böhm, was the organist of St. John's Church, and Bach attentively studied his compositions. He also went, occasionally, on foot to Hamburg to hear the famous old organist, J. A. Reinken, and to Celle, where the court music adhered completely to the French style.

In 1703 Bach became violinist in the orch. of a brother of the Duke of Saxe-Weimar, but the following year left the post for the more congenial one of organist of the new church at Arnstadt. In 1705 he obtained leave of absence, and walked to Lübeck, to make the acquaintance of the famous organist Dietrich Buxtehude. He was so impressed with this master's work that he trebled his leave of absence, and returned only after a peremptory summons from the church consistory of Arnstadt. In 1707, Bach accepted the appointment as organist of St. Blasius' Church at Mühlhausen. On Oct. 17 he married his cousin Maria Barbara Bach, daughter of Johann Michael [9]. The following year he went to Weimar, played before the reigning duke, and was offered the post of court organist and 'Kammermusicus'. In 1714 he was made 'Concertmeister'. A considerable series of compositions and arrangements, especially for organ, date from his Weimar period. Almost annually he made tours as an organ inspector and virtuoso. In 1714 he visited Kassel, Halle and Leipzig (where he furnished the music for a service in the Thomaskirche, including a cantata), Halle again in 1716, and Dresden in 1717. In this town his challenge to J. L. Marchand, a French clavecinist and organist of high reputation, was evaded by the latter's failure to appear. In 1717 Bach was app. Kapellmeister and director of the 'Kammermusik' to Prince Leopold of Anhalt, at Cöthen, and this period is especially rich in the production of orchestral and chamber music. In 1718 he revisited Halle, hoping to meet Handel; but the latter had just left for England. In 1720, during his absence at Carlsbad, his wife died suddenly. In November of the same year he applied, though (owing to bribery) without success, for the organistship of the Jacobikirche, Hamburg. Here he again met the aged Reinken, whose admiration he excited by his brilliant playing. In 1721 he married his second wife Anna Magdalena Wülken, a daughter of a court trumpeter at Weissenfels. Thirteen children were born to them. Of highly-cultured musical taste, she participated in his labors, and wrote out the parts of many of his cantatas. She also left 2 books of music in which her own hand appears as well as her husband's. In May, 1723 Bach succeeded Johann Kuhnau as cantor at the Thomasschule, Leipzig, becoming also organist and director of music at the two principal churches, the Thomaskirche and the Nicolaikirche, and continuing in the service of Prince Leopold of Anhalt as 'Kapellmeister von Haus aus.' He further received the appointment of honorary Kapellmeister to the Duke of Weissenfels, and in 1736, that of court composer to the King of Poland, Elector of Saxony. He remained in his post at Leipzig for 27 years, and there composed most of his religious music. Several times, he visited Dresden, where his eldest son, Wilhelm Friedemann, was appointed in 1733 organist of the Sophienkirche. On these occasions he attended the Italian opera, then conducted by Hasse. His second son, Karl Philipp Emanuel, was appointed in 1740 chamber musician to Frederick II of Prussia. He communicated to his father the king's oft-expressed wish to see and hear him; and on May 7, 1747, with his son Wilhelm Friedemann, Bach arrived at Potsdam. Here at the king's request, he improvised upon the various Silbermann pianos in the different rooms of the palace, to the admiration of his royal host, and of the musicians who followed them from room to room. Among Bach's improvisations was a fugue, presumably in 3 parts, on a theme proposed by the king, and a fugue in 6 parts on a theme by Bach himself. The next day Bach tried also the principal organs in Potsdam. On his return to Leipzig he used the king's theme for a Ricercare in 3 parts, a Ricercare in 6 parts, a series of ten canons and a Trio for flute, violin and basso continuo, dedicating the whole to Frederick as a *Musikalisches Opfer*. Bach was nearsighted from childhood, and later his eyes showed symptoms of weakness; in 1749 an unsuccessful operation resulted in total blindness, and his hitherto robust health also declined. His sight was suddenly restored on July 18, 1750; but immediately afterwards he was stricken by apoplexy, and ten days later he died. He worked to the end, dictating the chorale prelude *Vor deinen Thron tret' ich hiermit,* his last composition, a few days before his death.

Clearness and acuteness of intellect, strength of will, a love of order, and a high sense of duty, were Bach's leading characteristics. His home life was always of the happiest. Among the long list of his distinguished pupils were Johann Friedrich Agricola, Johann Christoph Altnikol, Heinrich Nikolaus Gerber, Johann Theophilus Goldberg, Gottfried August Homilius, Philipp Kirnberger, Johann Christian Kittel, Johann Tobias Krebs and his son Johann Ludwig; also his own sons Wilhelm Friedemann, Karl Philipp Emanuel and Johann Christoph Friedrich, and his nephew Bernhard, son of Johann Christoph [11]. Many of Bach's works were written with educational intent, among them the 2- and 3-part inventions which first appear in the *Clavierbüchlein für Wilhelm Friedemann Bach* (now at Yale Univ.). Only a small number of works were publ. during Bach's life; among them are 4 parts of the *Clavierübung,* including 6 Partitas, Overture in the French manner and the Italian Concerto; music for organ; the Goldberg Variations; Musical Offering; Canonic Variations upon *Vom Himmel hoch;* and six chorale preludes. A few pages of these publications were evidently engraved by Bach himself. (See G. Kinsky, *Die Originalausgaben der Werke J. S. Bachs,* 1937.)

Bach invented the 'viola pomposa' (a viola, or rather violoncello with 5 strings tuned C G D A E) and a certain type of 'Lauten-Clavicymbel' (a harpsichord, mostly with catgut strings). He promoted the adoption of the tempered system of tuning keyboard instruments; and introduced the style of fingering which, with comparatively few modifications, is still in use.

Bach's compositions mark an epoch. His originality and fecundity of thematic invention are astounding; the mastery of his polyphonic art remains a marvel of the ages. His style is elevated, and of sustained harmony; the momentum of his grand fugues is inexorable as the march of Fate. Bach's importance was but meagerly appreciated by his contemporaries, and for half a century after his death he was practically ignored. Some works were then occasionally performed, or even published; but Mendelssohn, by a performance of the St. Matthew Passion at Berlin, in 1829, first drew general attention to the great value of Bach's music. The centenary of Bach's death (1850) was marked by the formation, at Leipzig, of the 'Bach-Gesellschaft,' a society founded by K. F. Becker, M. Hauptmann, O. Jahn, R. Schumann and the publishers Härtel, in order to publish a complete edition of Bach's works. When the purpose of this society had been fulfilled, a 'Neue Bach-Gesellschaft' was founded in 1900. It seeks to popularize Bach's works through Bach festivals, the 'Bach-Jahrbuch' (begun 1904) and practical editions. A 'Bach-Society' was active in London from 1849 to 1870; numerous 'Bach Vereine' and similar institutions aiming at the cultivation and production of Bach's music existed, or exist, in many European and American cities. The most famous of such societies in the U. S. is the 'Bach Choir' at Bethlehem, Pa. (See R. Walters, *Bach at Bethlehem, Pa.,* in the 'Mus. Quart.' April 1935).

WORKS: VOCAL: Bach wrote 5 sets of sacred compositions for every Sunday and feast-day of the year, and not less than 5 Passions. Many of these works are lost. We have approximately 190 sacred 'concertos' or 'cantatas' (now all called cantatas); the *St. Matthew* and *St. John* Passions (the *St. Luke* is probably spurious); 'oratorios' for Christmas, Easter and Ascension (the latter known as Cantata No. 11); 2 Magnificats; a Grand Mass in B m.; several short masses; 5 Sanctus; motets; vocal works written for special occasions, e.g., the 'motetto' *Gott ist mein König* (written for the inauguration of the new council members of Mühlhausen in 1708; the only one among the works now called cantatas which was printed during Bach's life) and the *Tombeau de S. M., la Reine de Pologne;* many secular cantatas, including the *Dramma per musica, Der Streit zwischen Phoebus und Pan,* the 'Coffee' Cantata and the *Cantate en burlesque,* known as the 'Peasant' Cantata.—INSTRUMENTAL: Numerous pieces for organ, including a collection of chorale settings entitled *Orgelbüchlein;* many other chorale fantasias, preludes and fugues, toccatas; a set of 6 'trios'; Passacaglia, Canzona and Pastorale; numerous pieces for keyboard instruments, (mostly for harpsichord or clavichord; a few definitely require a harpsichord with 2 keyboards), including the 2 collections of 24 Preludes and Fugues in all keys entitled *Das Wohltemperierte Klavier* (i.e., the well-tempered keyboard; the common translation, 'clavichord', is wrong), the series of 15 Inventions and 15 'Sinfonias' (now known as 3-part inventions), the 6 English suites, the secular works contained in the *Clavierübung,* a number of suites, 6 of which became known as French suites, toccatas and various other works.—Among Bach's chamber-music works are a number for obbligato harpsichord and another instrument (violin, flute, or viola da gamba); a set of 6 suites for cello alone; a set of 3 sonatas and 3 partitas for violin alone. He dedicated a set of 6 'Concertos pour plusieurs instruments' to a Margrave of Brandenburg, whence they became known as Brandenburg Concertos. He wrote 4 'overtures' or orchestral suites, concertos for 1 and 2 violins, violin and oboe, violin, flute and harpsichord, and for from 1 to 3 harpsichords; also a concerto for 4 harpsichords which is an arrangement of a work by Vivaldi.

The monumental edition of Bach's works, published by the 'Bach-Gesellschaft', is in 47 volumes, including a volume of facsimile reproductions of original MS. pages. Bach's instrumental works were also completely publ. by C. F. Peters. There are innumerable reprints of many of his works. Deserving of special mention are the following: the edition of organ works, by C. M. Widor and A. Schweitzer with voluminous notes and directions for playing (G. Schirmer); that of the *Well-tempered Clavier,* in score, annotated by F. Stade (Steingräber); the *Kunst der Fuge* by H. T. David (Peters, 1928); the same work by Roy Harris and M. D. Herter Norton (G. Schirmer, N. Y., 1936); and Bach's 4-part chorales by C. S. Terry (5 vols., London, 1929). The 'Goldberg Variations' have been published in an edition by Ralph Kirkpatrick (G. Schirmer, N.Y., 1938).

Several works, including the *St. Matthew Passion,* the cantatas *Ach Herr, mich armen Sünder, Ich will den Kreuzstab gerne tragen,* the 'Coffee' Cantata, and Prelude and Fugue in B m. for organ, are publ. in facsimile reproduction of the original MSS.

A thematic catalogue of Bach's instrumental works was publ. by A. Dörffel in 1882, one of his vocal works by C. Tamme in 1890. A thematic index to 120 cantatas is included in vol. 27 of the 'Bach-Gesellschaft' ed., such an index to Bach's other works in vol. 46 of the same edition. A valuable systematic *Melodic Index to the Works of J. S. Bach* was publ. by May de Forest Payne (N. Y., 1938). A complete thematic catalogue of Bach's works was drawn up by W. Schmieder: *Thematisch - systematisch*

Verzeichnis der musikalischen Werke von Johann Sebastian Bach (Leipzig, 1950).

BIBLIOGRAPHY. — A. BIOGRAPHICAL: Bach's earliest biographers were his son, K. P. E. Bach, and J. F. Agricola in Mizler's 'Musikalische Bibliothek' (Leipzig, 1754; reprint in 'Bach-Jahrbuch,' 1920, pp. 13-29); J. N. Forkel, *Über J. S. Bachs Leben, Kunst und Kunstwerke* (a very lively account of Bach's career, and an invaluable source; Leipzig, 1802; Engl. transl., London, 1820; transl. with notes by C. S. Terry, 1920); C. L. Hilgenfeldt, *Bachs Leben, Wirken und Werke* (Leipzig, 1850); C. H. Bitter, *J. S. Bach* (2 vols., Berlin, 1865; 2nd ed., 4 vols., 1880); Ph. Spitta, *J. S. Bach* (the standard work on Bach's life and work, and one of the masterpieces of musical biography; 2 vols., Leipzig, 1873-80; rigidly shortened ed. in 1 vol., ib., 1935; Engl. transl. by C. Bell and J. A. Fuller Maitland, 3 vols., with many additions, London, 1884-5; 2nd ed., 1899; reissued, N. Y., 1951). There are numerous other biographies of Bach, all based on Spitta. Most widely known is A. Schweitzer's book, originally publ. as *J. S. Bach, le musicien-poète* (Paris, 1905; augm. German editions, 1908, 1915; English transl. by E. Newman, 2 vols., London, 1911; new Engl. ed., 1923). Other biographies in English: R. L. Poole, *J. S. Bach* (London, 1882; 2nd ed., 1890); C. F. Abdy Williams, *Bach* (ib., 1900; rev. ed., 1934); C. H. H. Parry, *J. S. Bach: The Story of the Development of a Great Personality* (N. Y. and London, 1909; new ed., 1934); Rutland Boughton, *Bach, the Master. A New Interpretation of His Genius* (N. Y. and London, 1930); T. Scott Buhrmann, *Bach's Life Chronologically as he lived it* (illustr. chronological tables; N. Y., 1935); H. T. David and A. Mendel, *The Bach Reader,* a life of Bach in letters and documents (N. Y., 1945); K. Geiringer, *The Bach Family,* (N. Y., 1954). A work based on original research is C. S. Terry's *Bach, a Biography* (the finest and most thorough description of Bach's life; London, 1928; new ed., 1933; Ger. ed., prefaced by K. Straube, Leipzig, 1929). Of German biographies the following deserve mention: Ph. Wolfrum, *J. S. Bach,* (2 vols., Leipzig, 1910); H. Kretzschmar, *Bach-Kolleg* (ib., 1922; Ital. transl., 1935); R. Steglich, *J. S. Bach* (Potsdam, 1935; richly illustr.); H. J. Moser, *Bach* (Berlin, 1935); W. Gurlitt, *Bach* (ib., 1935); H. and E. H. Müller von Asow, *J. S. Bachs Briefe* (Regensburg, 1950). Biographies in French: A. Pirro, *Bach* (Paris, 1906); T. Gérold, *Bach* (ib., 1925); J. Tiersot, *Bach* (ib., 1934); P. Collaer, *Bach* (Brussels, 1936); W. Cart, *J. S. Bach* (Lausanne, 1946). Of special interest are W. Dahms, *J. S. Bach, Ein Bild seines Lebens* (a collection of original documents; Munich, 1924) and W. Hitzig's *J. S. Bach, Sein Leben in Bildern* (Leipzig, 1935). See also W. His, *J. S. Bach, Forschungen über dessen Grabstätte, Gebeine und Antlitz* (Leipzig, 1895; dealing with the state of Bach's remains and his grave, including striking photographs of Bach's skull at the time of his exhumation and reinterment).

B. CRITICAL, ANALYTICAL: F. Rochlitz, *Wege zu Bach* (ed. from 'Für Freunde der Tonkunst', Leipzig, 1824-37, by J. M. Müller-Blattau, Augsburg, 1926); A. Pirro, *L'esthétique de J. S. Bach* (Paris, 1907); E. Kurth, *Grundlagen des linearen Kontrapunkts. Einführung in Stil und Technik von Bachs melodischer Polyphonie* (Berlin, 1917); C. S. Terry, *Bach: The Historical Approach* (London, 1930); id., *The Music of Bach* (ib., 1933); A. E. F. Dickinson, *The Art of J. S. Bach* (ib., 1936).—M. Hauptmann, *Erläuterungen in J. S. Bachs Kunst der Fuge* (Leipzig, 1841); H. Riemann, *Handbuch der Fugenkomposition* (vols. I and II, analysis of *Das wohltemperierte Klavier* [Berlin, 1890-91; 3rd ed., 1914; Engl. transl. by J. S. Shedlock, 2 vols., London, 1893, several eds.]; vol. III, analysis of the *Kunst der Fuge* [Berlin, 1894; 3rd ed., 1921]); F. Iliffe, *The 48 Preludes and Fugues of J. S. Bach* (London, 1897); W. Werker, *Bachstudien* (2 vols., Leipzig, 1922); D. F. Tovey, *A Companion to the Art of Fugue* (London, 1931); also various vols. of the 'Musical Pilgrim Series'.—R. Wustmann, *J. S. Bachs Kantatentexte* (Leipzig, 1913); C. S. Terry, *Bach's Chorals* (3 vols., Cambridge, 1915, 1917, 1921); id., *J. S. Bach's Original Hymn-Tunes for Congregational Use* (1922); id., *Bach's Mass in B minor;* id., *A Bach Hymnbook of 16th-Century Melodies* (1923); W.G. Whittaker, *Fugitive Notes on Certain Cantatas and the Motets of J.S. Bach* (London, 1924); C. S. Terry, *J. S. Bach's Cantata Texts, Sacred and Secular* (ib., 1926); id., *Bach's Four-Part Chorals* (complete ed., with German and English words, 1928); A. Eaglefield Hull, *Bach's Organ Works* (London, 1929); C. S. Terry, *Bach's Orchestra* (London, 1932); Cecil Gray, *Bach's 'Forty-Eight'* (ib., 1937); H. T. David, *Zu Bachs Kunst der Fuge* (Peters Jahrbuch, 1928); H. T. David, *Zur Gesamtgestalt von Bachs H-moll Messe* ('Festschrift für Johannes Wolf', 1929); J. Schreyer, *Beiträge zur Bach-Kritik* (2 vols., Leipzig, 1911-13); H. E. Huggler, *J. S. Bachs Orgelbüchlein* (Bern, 1930); L. Landshoff,

Urtextausgabe der Inventionen und Sinfonien J. S. Bachs (Leipzig, 1933; with Revisionsbericht); G. Herz, *J. S. Bach im Zeitalter des Rationalismus und der Frühromantik* (Würzburg, 1935); L. Landshoff, *Musikalisches Opfer* (Leipzig, 1936); A. Schering, *J. S. Bachs Leipziger Kirchenmusik* (ib. 1936); E. Thiele, *Die Chorfugen J. S. Bachs* (Bern, 1936); A. Schering, *Das Zeitalter J. S. Bachs und Johann Adam Hillers* (Leipzig, 1940); H. Rutters, *J. S. Bach en onze tijd* (Amsterdam, 1941); H. T. David, *J. S. Bach's Musical Offering* (N. Y., 1945); Marie M. Meyer, *J. P. Rameau; J. S. Bach* (Chambéry, 1946); N. Dufourcq, *J. S. Bach, le maître de l'orgue* (Paris, 1948); H. Besseler and G. Kraft, *J. S. Bach in Thüringen* (Weimar, 1950); A. Dürr, *Studien über die frühen Kantaten J. S. Bachs* (Leipzig, 1951); F. Hamel, *J. S. Bach: Geistige Welt* (Göttingen, 1951); Paul Hindemith, *J. S. Bach* (N.Y., 1952); F. Rothschild, *The Lost Tradition in Music: Rhythm and Tempo in J. S. Bach's Time* (N. Y., 1953); many special studies in the 'Bach-Jahrbuch.'

13. **Bach, Johann Nikolaus** (eldest son of Johann Christoph, 8), b. Eisenach, Oct. 10, 1669; d. there, Nov. 4, 1753. In 1695, appointed organist of the city and university at Jena. He was an expert on organ-building and also made keyboard instruments for secular use, especially lute-clavicymbals. J. Adlung highly praises him. Works: A fine *Missa* (Kyrie and Gloria), edited by A. Fareanu and V. Junk (Breitkopf & Härtel, 1920); a comic cantata, *Der Jenaische Wein- und Bier-Rufer,* a scene from Jena college life (ed. by F. Stein, 1920); suites for a keyboard instrument, which are not preserved, and organ chorales, of which only one is known.

14. **Bach, Johann Ludwig** (son of Jakob, a grandson of Lips, and cantor at Steinbach and Ruhle), b. Steinbach, 1677; d. 1741; was Court Kapellmeister at Saxe-Meiningen.

15. **Bach, Johann Ernst** (only son of Johann Bernhard, 10), b. Eisenach, Sept. 1, 1722; d. there, Jan. 28, 1777. Attended the Thomasschule and then the Leipzig Univ. He studied law, and, after his return to Eisenach, practiced as advocate. In 1748 he was appointed assistant, and then successor, to his father, organist of St. George's Church; 1756, appointed Kapellmeister at Weimar. Publ. a 'Sammlung auserlesener Fabeln mit Melodeyen' (ed. by H. Kretzschmar in 'Denkmäler deutscher Tonkunst,' vol. 42) and other works; prefaced one of J. Adlung's books, and left a number of compositions in manuscript.

16. **Bach, Wilhelm Friedemann** ('Bach of Halle'), eldest son of J. Sebastian; b. Weimar, Nov. 22, 1710; d. Berlin, July 1, 1784. Pupil of his father and, at 15 years of age, J. G. Graun at Merseburg. Also studied at the Thomasschule, and at the Univ. of Leipzig, taking courses, among others, in mathematics. Organist of the Sophienkirche, Dresden (1733-47); and at the Marienkirche, Halle (1747-64). A composer of superior gifts, he unfortunately gave way to dissipation, lost his positions, and died in misery. An edition of selected works was started by the Abteilung für Musik der Preussischen Akademie der Künste; vol. I contains 4 trios (Leipzig, 1934). Among other compositions available in modern editions are an impressive Sinfonia ('Wunderhorn Verlag,' 1910) and a collection of fugues and polonaises edited by W. Niemann (1914); also, piano compositions in *Die Söhne Bachs,* ed. by W. Rehberg (1933); three excerpts in Karl Geiringer, *Music of the Bach Family* (Cambridge, Mass., 1955). Cf. K. H. Bitter, *K. P. E. Bach und W. Friedemann Bach und deren Brüder* (2 vols., Berlin, 1868); M. Falck, *W. F. Bach; sein Leben und seine Werke* (Leipzig, 1913); K. Stabenow, *J. S. Bachs Sohn* (Leipzig, 1935); K. Geiringer, *The Bach Family* (N. Y., 1954).

17. **Bach, Karl Philipp Emanuel** (the Berlin or Hamburg Bach), 3rd (and 2nd surviving) son of J. Sebastian; b. Weimar, March 8, 1714; d. Hamburg, Dec. 14, 1788. He studied philosophy and law at Leipzig and Frankfurt-on-the-Oder; but the inherited passion for music, and completeness of musical study under his father, decided his profession. He conducted a singing society at Frankfurt, for which he also composed. In 1738 he went to Berlin, and, in 1740, was appointed chamber musician and clavecinist to Frederick the Great. In 1767 he went to Hamburg, succeeding Telemann as 'Musikdirector' of the principal church there, a position he held until death. He was one of the most brilliant performers of his day, creator of the modern expressive school of piano writing, and the outstanding master of 'Empfindsamkeit' (intimate expressiveness), the North German counterpart of the rococo; his work was of great significance in the establishment of the style as well as the forms of the classical school; Haydn and Mozart were indebted to him. His *Versuch über die wahre Art, das Clavier zu spielen* (2 parts, 1753-62, clumsily reedited by Schelling in 1857; new, but not complete, ed. by W. Niemann, 1906) is an important theoretical work and yields much informa-

tion about musical practice of the time. An English translation of the *Versuch* . . ., entitled *Essay on the True Art of Playing Keyboard Instruments,* was made by W. J. Mitchell (N. Y., 1948). His compositions are voluminous (thematic list by A. Wotquenne, Leipzig, 1905); for clavier they comprise 210 solo pieces; 52 concertos with orch.; quartets; trios, duets; also 18 orchestral symphonies; 34 miscellaneous pieces for wind instruments; trios for flute, violin and bass; flute, oboe, cello concertos; soli for flute, viola da gamba, oboe, cello, harp; duets for flute and violin; for 2 violins; also for clarinets. Vocal works: 2 oratorios, *Die Israeliten in der Wüste,* and *Die Auferstehung und Himmelfahrt Jesu;* 22 Passions; cantatas; etc. Reprints of sonatas for clavier have been edited by Bülow, C. F. Baumgart ('für Kenner und Liebhaber', 6 vols.), H. Schenker (9 sonatas), R. Steglich and others. There are also reprints of concertos and chamber music works. Bibl.: K. H. Bitter, *K. P. E. Bach und W. Friedemann Bach und deren Brüder* (2 vols., Berlin, 1868); M. Fleuler, *Die norddeutsche Symphonie zur Zeit Friedrichs des Grossen, und besonders die Werke Ph. E. Bachs* (Berlin, 1908); O. Vrieslander, *K. P. E. Bach* (Munich, 1923); H. Wien-Claudi, *Zum Liedschaffen K. P. E. Bachs* (Reichenberg, 1928); H. Miesner, *P. E. Bach in Hamburg* (Leipzig, 1929); E. F. Schmid, *K. P. E. Bach und seine Kammermusik* (Kassel, 1931). See also H. Schenker, *Ein Beitrag zur Ornamentik; Als Einführung zu P. E. Bachs Klavierwerke* (Vienna, 1904); Karl Geiringer, *The Bach Family* (N.Y., 1954). K. P. E. Bach's Autobiography was reprinted by Willi Kahl in *Selbst-Biographien Deutscher Musiker* (Cologne, 1948).

18. **Bach, Johann Christoph Friedrich** ('the Bückeburg Bach'), 9th son of J. Sebastian; b. Leipzig, June 21, 1732; d. Bückeburg, Jan. 26, 1795. He studied law at Leipzig, but adopted the profession of music, and, presumably in 1750, was appointed 'Kammermusicus' at Bückeburg. Although less brilliant in composition than his brothers, he was an excellent musician and thorough composer. An exhaustive biographical study was publ. by G. Schünemann in the 'Bach-Jahrbuch' (1914, pp. 45-165). The same author also prepared an edition of selected works by Johann Christoph Friedrich Bach, sponsored by the Fürstliches Institut für musikwissenschaftliche Forschung, in 1920, but abandoned after the publication of 2 motets, 4 piano sonatas and 4 chamber-music works. Schünemann also edited 3 oratorios by J. C. F. Bach in the 'Denkmäler deutscher Tonkunst' (vol. 56; contains a thematic index of his compositions). G. A. Walter edited the cantata *Die Amerikanerin* (1920) and L. Duttenhofer a set of 6 quartets (Paris, 1922).

19. **Bach, Johann (John) Christian** (the 'London Bach'), 11th and youngest surviving son of Sebastian; b. Leipzig, Sept. 5, 1735 (bapt. Sept. 7); d. London, Jan. 1, 1782. He went to Berlin to study with his brother, Karl Philipp Emanuel Bach, after the death of his father in 1750. He became music director to Count Antonio Litta in Milan in 1754; was organist at the cathedral there (1760-62); studied with Padre Martini in Bologna. He traveled through Italy; his opera *Alessandro nell'Indie* was produced at Naples (Jan. 20, 1762). In 1762 he went to England; and in London, produced his most successful opera *Orione* (Feb. 19, 1763); shortly afterwards he was appointed music master to the Queen. Beginning in 1764 he gave, together with K. F. Abel, a famous series of London concerts. Christian Bach was a prolific composer, and immensely popular in his day; he was master of the light and charming 'rococo' style; his music was an important source of the classical idiom, and influenced Mozart's development. His surviving works, many of them reprinted, include symphonies, concertos, operas, piano compositions and chamber music. Among his 13 operas are *Lucio Silla* (Mannheim, Nov. 20, 1776); *La Clemenza di Scipione* (London, April 4, 1778); *Amadis des Gaules* (Paris, Dec. 14, 1779), etc. His quintets for flute, oboe, violin, viola, and thoroughbass are reprinted in *Das Erbe deutscher Musik, Reichsdenkmale* (vol. I). Bibl.: C. S. Terry, *Johann Christian Bach* (London, 1929); H. P. Schökel, *Johann Christian Bach und die Instrumentalmusik seiner Zeit* (Wolfenbüttel, 1926); F. Tutenberg, *Die Sinfonik Johann Christian Bachs* (Kiel, 1926); G. de Saint-Foix, *A propos de J. Ch. Bach* in the 'Revue de Musicologie' (1926); A. Wenk, *Beiträge zur Kenntnis des Opernschaffens von Johann Christian Bach* (Frankfurt, 1932); see also Karl Geiringer, *The Bach Family* (N. Y., 1954).

20. **Bach, Wilhelm Friedrich Ernst** (son of Johann Christoph Friedrich, 18, and grandson and last male descendant of J. Sebastian), b. Bückeburg, May 23, 1759; d. Berlin, Dec. 25, 1845. Studied with his father, and his uncle Johann Christian (19), in London. After his uncle's death, he traveled giving concerts. In 1787 he is mentioned as music director at Minden; later, became Kapellmeister to the Queen of Prus-

sia, consort of Friedrich Wilhelm III, and also music master to the royal princes. He was pensioned after the Queen's death. Few of his compositions have been published.

Bachauer, Gina, Greek pianist; b. Athens, May 21, 1913, of Austrian parents. She studied at the Athens Cons.; then in Paris with Cortot. In 1933 she won the medal of honor at the International Contest in Vienna; from 1933-35, received occasional instruction from Rachmaninoff in France and Switzerland. In 1935 she made her professional debut with the Athens Symph. Orch., under Mitropoulos. She played with Monteux in Paris in 1937; during World War II she lived in Alexandria, Egypt and gave over 600 concerts for the Allied forces in the Middle East. On Jan. 21, 1946 she made her London debut playing with the New London Orch. under the direction of Alec Sherman, who became her second husband (Nov. 21, 1951). Her first American appearance was in New York on Oct. 29, 1950. The vigor of her technique has suggested comparisons with Teresa Carreño; her repertoire ranges from Mozart to Stravinsky.

Bache (bātch), **Constance,** English writer and musician; b. Birmingham, March 11, 1846; d. Montreux, Switzerland, June 28, 1903. She was the sister of the English pianists Francis Edward Bache (1833-1858) and Walter Bache (1842-1888). She studied at the Munich Cons. and later with Klindworth; planned a piano career, but was forced to abandon it owing to an accident to her hand. In 1883 she settled in London. She published a vivid book of memoirs *Brother Musicians* (London, 1901), describing the lives of her brothers; translated the letters of Hans von Bülow and Heintz's analyses of Wagner's operas; also translated the libretto of Humperdinck's *Hänsel und Gretel.*

Bachelet (bah-shā-lā'), **Alfred,** French composer; b. Paris, Feb. 26, 1864; d. Nancy, Feb. 10, 1944. He studied at the Paris Cons.; received the Grand Prix de Rome for his cantata, *Cléopatre* (1890). From his earliest works, Bachelet devoted himself mainly to opera. In his youth, he was influenced by Wagnerian ideas, but later adopted a more national French style. During World War I he conducted at the Paris Opéra; in 1919 became director of the Nancy Cons.; in 1939, elected a member of the Académie des Beaux Arts. Works: lyric drama *Scémo* (Paris Opéra, May 6, 1914); *Quand la cloche sonnera,* one-act music drama, his most successful work (Opéra-Comique, Nov. 6, 1922); lyric drama *Un jardin sur l'Oronte* (Paris Opéra, Nov. 7, 1931); Ballets: *La fête chez la Pouplinière; Castor et Pollux* by Rameau (adapted and rewritten); orchestral works with voices: *L'amour des Ondines, Joie, Le Songe de la Sulamith, Noël; Surya* for tenor, chorus and orch. (1940); *Ballade* for violin and orch.; songs.

Bachmann, Alberto Abraham, violinist; b. Geneva, March 20, 1875. He studied violin at the Cons. of Lille, then took courses in succession with Ysaÿe, Thomson, Hubay and Brodsky. He was in the U.S. from 1916-26; since then living near Paris. He is the author of three violin concertos (the last of which is called 'American Concerto'); 12 improvisations for solo violin; about 250 various pieces and as many transcriptions for violin. He published *Le violon* (1906); *Les grands violonistes du passé* (1913); *Gymnastique à l'usage des violonistes* (1914); *Le piano, ses origines et ses maîtres; L'école du violoniste* (in 4 parts); and *Encyclopedia of the Violin* (N. Y., 1925).

Bachner, Louis, American singing teacher; b. New York, April 17, 1882; d. there, Dec. 26, 1945. He studied voice in Boston, Paris and Berlin; taught at the Peabody Cons. in Baltimore (1908-10), and at various music schools in Berlin (1917-33); returned to the U.S. in 1935, and resumed his teaching activities in New York. He was the teacher of many well known singers, among them Sigrid Onegin; published a manual, *Dynamic Singing* (1945).

Bachrich, Sigismund, violinist and composer; b. Zsambokreth, Hungary, Jan. 23, 1841; d. Vienna, July 16, 1913. He studied violin with Böhm in Vienna; after several years in Paris, played with the Hellmesberger and Rosé quartets; was first violist of the Vienna Philh.; taught at the Vienna Cons. until 1899. His memoirs were posthumously published under the title *Aus verklungenen Zeiten* (Vienna, 1914). He wrote the comic operas *Muzzedin* (1883); *Heini von Steier* (1884); *Der Fuchs-Major* (1889); the ballet *Sakuntala* and other theatrical works.

Bäck, Knut, Swedish pianist and composer; b. Stockholm, April 22, 1868; d. Göteborg, Oct. 27, 1953. He studied music in Stockholm; later took lessons with Max Bruch in Berlin. He eventually settled in Göteborg as a music critic and teacher. Among his works are songs and piano pieces.

Bäck, Sven-Erik, Swedish violinist and composer; b. Stockholm, Sept. 16, 1919. He entered the Stockholm Cons. where he studied with Hilding Rosenberg (1940-44); later studied in Basel. Returning to Sweden he became the viola player in a local quartet. He has written several motets, 2 string quartets (1945; 1947); string quintet (1948); flute sonata, etc.

Backer-Grøndahl, Agathe, Norwegian composer and pianist; b. Holmestrand, Dec. 1, 1847; d. Ormöen, near Oslo, June 4, 1907. She studied in Norway with Kjerulf and Lindemann, in Florence with Hans von Bülow, and in Weimar with Liszt; married the singing teacher Grøndahl (1875). Among her piano works, *Études de Concert, Romantische Stücke,* and *Trois Morceaux* became well-known and have been frequently reprinted. She also wrote a song cycle, *Des Kindes Frühlingstag.*—Cf. Ole M. Sandvik, *Agathe Backer-Grøndahl* (Oslo, 1948), a centennial biography.

Backers, Cor, Dutch composer and music historian; b. Rotterdam, June 5, 1910. He studied at the Rotterdam Cons. with Dirk Schäfer; later took a course in conducting with Weingartner. Returning to Holland, he played piano recitals, specializing in duo piano concerts; was also active in radio broadcasting. He has written several choral works; a set of melodeclamations for speaking voice with piano; songs; etc. His book *Nederlandse Componisten van 1400 tot op onze Tijd* (Amsterdam, 1942; 2nd enlarged ed., 1949) is a valuable account of music history in the Netherlands, with particular emphasis on modern Dutch composers.

Backhaus, Wilhelm, German pianist; b. Leipzig, March 26, 1884. He studied with A. Reckendorf (1891-98); then with Eugene d'Albert. He made concert tours with great acclaim, in Europe (from 1900); the U.S. (1912-14), South America, Australia and the Far East. Eventually he settled in Switzerland as teacher. In 1954, at the age of 70, he undertook a return tour in the U.S., showing undiminished powers as a virtuoso; made another American tour in 1956. He is particularly distinguished as an interpreter of Beethoven.

Bacon, Ernst, American composer, b. Chicago, May 26, 1898. He studied at the Univ. of Chicago; later in Vienna; took courses with Ernest Bloch and Eugene Goossens (conducting) in Rochester, N. Y.; became assistant conductor of the Rochester Opera Co.; then held various posts as teacher of piano and theory. He won the Pulitzer Prize for music (1932) and a Guggenheim Fellowship (1939). Settling in Syracuse, N. Y., he became director of the Music School at Syracuse Univ. At the age of 19 he publ. a brochure *Our Musical Idiom* (Chicago, 1917), on new harmonies; developed an individual style of composition without abandoning tradition; later became interested in national American subjects and folk songs. Works: Symph. No. 1 for piano and orch. (1932); Symph. No. 2 (1937; Chicago, Feb. 5, 1940); orchestral suites; *Ford's Theatre* (1943); *From Emily's Diary* (1944; to words by Emily Dickinson); a musical play, *A Tree on the Plains* (Spartanburg, S. C., May 2, 1942); a folk opera, *A Drumlin Legend* (N. Y., May 4, 1949); chamber music.

Bacon, Richard Mackenzie, English writer on music; b. Norwich, May 1, 1776; d. Cossey, Nov. 27, 1844. He publ. *Elements of Vocal Science* (London, 1824); *Art of Improving the Voice and Ear* (London, 1825); was the founder and editor (1812-28) of the 'Quarterly Music Magazine and Review', the first music periodical in England; and the organizer of the triennial Music Festivals at Norwich.

Badarzewska (băh-dăhr-zhĕv'-skăh), **Thekla,** Polish composer of salon music; b. Warsaw, 1838; d. there Sept. 29, 1861. At the age of 18 she published in Warsaw a piano piece, *Prière d'une vierge* which became enormously successful after its publication as a supplement to the Paris 'Revue et Gazette Musicale' (1859). About 100 editions appeared in Europe and America in the 19th century, not counting innumerable transcriptions for various instruments. She wrote 34 more piano pieces, none of which achieved popularity.

Badings, Henk, eminent Dutch composer; b. Bandoeng (Java), Jan. 17, 1907. He first studied mining engineering; then took a course in composition with Pijper (1919-24). In 1937 he was appointed prof. of music at the Rotterdam Cons.; in 1941, became director of the Royal Cons. at The Hague. After the end of World War II, on charges of cultural collaboration with the Germans during the occupation, he was temporarily barred from professional activities, but regained his status in 1947. He is married to the violinist Olly Folge Fonden. A highly prolific composer, Badings has written in every genre. His style may be described as romantic modernism; his harmonies approach polytonality; in his melodic material he often uses a scale of alternating whole tones and semitones. His works include the opera *The Night Watch* (1942; Antwerp,

May 13, 1950); *Orpheus and Eurydice,* ballet (1941); *Apocalypse,* oratorio (Rotterdam, Nov. 25, 1949); 6 symphonies: No. 1 (1930); No. 2 (1932); No. 3 (1934); No. 4 (Rotterdam, Oct. 13, 1947); No. 5 (Amsterdam, Dec. 7, 1949); No. 6 ('Symphony of Psalms,' with chorus; Holland Festival, Haarlem, June 25, 1953); also *The Louisville Symphony* (commissioned work; Louisville, Feb. 26, 1955); 4 violin concertos (1928, 1935, 1944, 1946); 2 cello concertos (1939); piano concerto (1939); *Tragic Overture* (1937); *Symphonic Variations* for orch. (1937); *Dance suite* for small orch.; *Ballade* for orch. (Maastricht, Sept. 22, 1950); incidental music to the plays *Colportage* by Georg Kaiser and *Gysbreght van Aemstel* by Vondel (Amsterdam Festival, 1938); concertino for violin, cello, piano and chamber orch. (1942); woodwind quintet; 2 string quartets (1931, 1937); brass quartet (1947); piano trio (Paris Music Festival, 1937); trio for oboe, clarinet and bassoon (1943); trio for 2 oboes and English horn (1945); string trio (1945); piano sonata (1934); 2 suites for piano; 2 violin sonatas; 2 cello sonatas; organ toccata; piano pieces and songs. Badings is the author of a book on contemporary Dutch music, *De Hedendaagsche Nederlandsche Muziek* (Amsterdam, 1936). Bibl.: Cor Backers, *Nederlandse Componisten* (Amsterdam, 1949).

Badura-Skoda, Paul, Austrian pianist; b. Vienna, Oct. 6, 1927. He was brought up by his stepfather Skoda, whose name he adopted professionally. He studied mathematics and engineering as well as music; his piano teacher in Vienna was Viola Therns. He won first prize at the Austrian Music Competition in 1947; graduated from the Vienna College of Music in 1948; also won prizes at the International Music Contest in Budapest (1948) and Paris (1949). He married Eva Halfer on Sept. 19, 1951. Toured Europe, Australia (1952), Canada and the U.S. (1953). He made his New York debut on Jan. 10, 1953.

Bagby, Albert Morris, American pianist and concert manager; b. Rushville, Illinois, April 29, 1859; d. New York, Feb. 26, 1941. He studied in Berlin, and with Liszt in Weimar. Returning to America in 1891, he organized in New York the Bagby Morning Musicales, presenting 428 concerts; directed them until a few weeks before his death.

Bagge, Selmar, composer and music pedagogue; b. Coburg, June 30, 1823; d. Basel, July 16, 1896. He studied at the Prague Cons. and in Vienna with Sechter; later taught at the Vienna Cons. (1851-55); was editor of the 'Allgemeine Musikzeitung' in Leipzig (1863-66). Became director in 1868 of the Basel Music School, and retained this post until his death. He publ. several books: *Lehrbuch der Tonkunst* (1873); *Die geschichtliche Entwickelung der Sonate* (1880); *Die Symphonie in ihrer historischen Entwickelung* (1884); wrote a symphony, piano pieces, and other works. His biographical sketch (by Eglinger) was publ. in Basel (1897).

Bagier, Guido, German musicologist; b. Berlin, June 20, 1888. He studied at the Univ. of Leipzig with Max Reger and Riemann; taught at the State Academy of Arts in Düsseldorf; settled in Berlin, where he was connected with a motion picture company. He published a biography of Max Reger (Stuttgart, 1923).

Bai (bah-ē), **Tommaso,** Italian musician; b. Crevalcore, near Bologna, c. 1660; d. Rome, Dec. 22, 1714. He was a tenor at the Vatican where he became maestro di cappella Nov. 19, 1713. A follower of Palestrina, Bai's best known composition is a five-part *Miserere* sung during Holy Week in the Papal Chapel alternately with those by Allegri and Baini. It is reprinted in various collections (Choron, Burney, Peters); Bai's other compositions are included in C. Proske's *Musica Divina* (1853-63).

Baïf, Jean-Antoine de, French composer and poet; b. Venice, Feb. 19, 1532; d. Paris, Sept. 19, 1589. He was brought to Paris as a child, and formed a friendship with Ronsard and other eminent poets. In 1570 he founded the Académie de Poésie et de Musique, with the aim of reviving the music and poetry of ancient Greece. He developed a system of 'musique mesurée' which he believed would possess a moral force similar to the Greek ideas of 'ethos'. Settings of his poems were composed by Jacques Maudit in *26 Chansonettes mesurées* (1586) for 4 voices; and by Claude Le Jeune, in *Le Printemps* (1603). Both of these collections have been reprinted in Henri Expert's *Maîtres Musiciens* (1899-1901; vols. X, XII, XIII and XIV). Baïf's musical works comprise 12 sacred songs and several works in lute tablature.

Bailey, Parker, American composer; nephew of Horatio Parker; b. Kansas City, Mo., March 1, 1902; studied at Yale (1919-23) with D. S. Smith; also took courses with Ernest Bloch in Cleveland; piano with B. Rubinstein; studied law at Cornell Univ.

(LL.B., 1934); was on the legal staff of the Securities and Exchange Commission in Washington (1939-42); then settled in New York as a lawyer; became advisor to the Society for the Publication of American Music (1947) and to the Edward MacDowell Association (1952). —— Works: flute sonata (1929; Soc. for the Publ. of Amer. Music award); *Variations symphoniques* on a theme of Chambonnières (1930); *Toccata-Ricercare-Finale* on a Bach chorale (1933; honorable mention in the World's Fair Contest, 1939); several choruses and solo songs.

Baillot (bi-yoh'), **Pierre - Marie - François de Sales,** celebrated French violinist, b. Passy, near Paris, Oct. 1, 1771; d. Paris, Sept. 15, 1842. The son of a schoolmaster, he received an excellent education; at the age of nine he became a pupil of the French violinist, Saint-Marie; he later was sent to Rome where he studied under Pollani; returned to Paris in 1791. He met Viotti who obtained for him a position in the orchestra of the Théâtre Feydeau; later he served as a clerk in the Ministry of Finance. In 1795 he received the important appointment as violin teacher at the newly opened Paris Cons.; but continued to study comp. with Cherubini, Reicha and Catel. In 1802 he joined Napoleon's private instrumental ensemble; toured Russia with the cellist Lamarre (1805-1808). Upon his return to Paris, he organized chamber music concerts which enjoyed excellent success; also gave concerts in Belgium, Holland and England. In 1821 he became first violinist at the Paris Opéra; from 1825 he was also solo violinist in the Royal Orch. Baillot's musical compositions, rarely performed, comprise 10 violin concertos, 3 string quartets, 15 trios, a symphonie concertante for 2 violins with orch.; 6 violin duos, etc. Baillot's name is chiefly remembered through his manual *L'Art du Violon* (1834); with Rode and Kreutzer he wrote a *Méthode du Violon,* adopted by the Paris Cons., and republished in numerous editions and languages; he also edited the *Méthode de Violoncelle* by Levasseur, Catel and Baudiot.

Bailly (bah-yē), **Louis,** French-American violist; b. Valenciennes, June 13, 1882. He received the first prize when he graduated from the Paris Cons. (1899); played viola in the Capet, Flonzaley (1917-24), Elman and Curtis quartets; became head of the viola and chamber music departments at the Curtis Institute of Music in Philadelphia.

Baines, William, English composer; b. Horbury, near Wakefield, Yorkshire, Mar. 26, 1899; d. York, Nov. 6, 1922. He received a few lessons from Albert Jowett of Leeds, but was mainly self-taught. His untimely death at 23, of a lung ailment contracted during World War I, deprived contemporary British music of a great talent. Among Baines' works are several effective impressionist piano pieces *(Paradise Gardens, Tides, Milestones, Silverpoints, Colored Leaves,* etc.); and a symphony. For a latter-day appreciation, see R. Carpenter, *Baines and Britten: Some Affinities* in 'The Mus. Times' (April, 1956).

Baini, Giuseppe (also known as **Abbate Baini**), Italian writer on music and composer; b. Rome, Oct. 21, 1775; d. there, May 21, 1844. He received rudimentary training from his uncle, Lorenzo Baini; then entered the Seminario Romano, where his instructor, Stefano Silveyra, indoctrinated him with the spirit of Palestrina's music. In 1795 he became a member of the papal choir at St. Peter's; he continued his studies there with Bianchini; in 1802 he took courses with Jannaconi, whom he succeeded as maestro di cappella at St. Peter's (1818). In 1821 he wrote his masterpiece, a 10-part *Miserere,* which was accepted for singing at the Sistine Chapel during Holy Week, in alternation with the *Misereres* of Allegri and Bai. He also wrote many psalms, hymns, masses and motets. His great ambition was to publish a complete edition of Palestrina's works, but he was able to prepare only two volumes for publication. The monument of his devotion to Palestrina was his exhaustive biography *Memorie storico-critiche della vita e delle opere di Giovanni Pierluigi da Palestrina* (Rome, 1828; German translation by Kandler, with notes by Kiesewetter, 1834), which remains extremely valuable despite its occasional inaccuracies. He also wrote a *Saggio sopra l'identità de' ritmi musicali e poetici* (1820). Haberl published an essay on Baini in the 'Kirchenmusikalisches Jahrbuch' (1894).

Bainton, Edgar Leslie, English composer; b. London, Feb. 14, 1880. He studied with Walford Davies and Stanford; was appointed prof. of piano and composition at the Cons. of Newcastle-on-Tyne (1901), became director in 1912. He subsequently appeared as guest conductor with various European orchestras, and in 1934 was appointed director of the State Cons. at Sydney, Australia. Bainton's compositions include the operas *The Crier by Night* and *Oithona* (Glastonbury, Aug. 11, 1915); orchestral pieces *Pompilia* (1903) and *Paracelsus* (1921); a symphony; an overture, *Prometheus; Concerto-Fantasia* for piano and orch. (Carnegie Award, 1917; London, Jan. 26, 1922); choral works with orch. (*The Blessed Damozel, Before Sunrise, Sunset at Sea, The Vindictive Staircase, A Song of Freedom and Joy, The Tower*); a string quartet; viola sonata; songs.

Baird, Tadeusz, Polish composer; b. Grodzisk, July 26, 1928. During World War II he was sent by the Germans to a labor camp; returned to Warsaw in 1948. He has written a *Sinfonietta* (1949); Piano concerto (1949); Symphony No. 1 (1950); *Colas Breugnon* for flute and string orch. (1951); *Ouverture giocosa* (1952); Symphony No. 2 (1953).

Bairstow, Sir Edward Cuthbert, English organist and composer; b. Huddersfield, Aug. 22, 1874; d. York, May 1, 1946. He received his Mus. B. at Durham Univ. in 1894; his Mus. D. in 1900; was organist at Wigan (1899-1906), Leeds (1906-13) and at the York Minster. He composed church music, anthems, part songs, and an organ sonata (1937); author of *Counterpoint and Harmony* (1937) and *The Evolution of Musical Form* (1943). See E. Bradbury, *A Birthday Tribute* in the 'Mus. Times' (Aug. 1944).

Bakala, Břetislav, Czech conductor; b. Fryšták, Feb. 12, 1897. He studied at the Brno Cons. and in Prague with Janáček. He was conductor of the Brno radio orchestra (1926-40); since 1940, conductor of the Brno Symphony; also conducted abroad. He has written a Scherzo for orch. (1923); *Fantasy* for string quartet (1933); several choral works and songs. He has done much to make Janáček's music known and edited his posthumous opera *From the House of the Dead.*

Bakaleinikov (bah-kah-lā'-nē-kov), **Vladimir Romanovitch,** Russian viola player and conductor; b. Moscow, Oct. 12, 1885; d. Pittsburgh, Nov. 5, 1953. He studied with Michael Press; graduated from the Moscow Cons. in 1907; played the viola in the Grand Duke Mecklenburg-Strelitz Quartet (1910-20); taught at the Cons. of St. Petersburg (1913-20); conducted opera at the Music Drama Theater (1914-16). Returning to Moscow, he taught at the Moscow Cons. (1920-24); was in charge of the opera branch of the Moscow Art Theatre (1920-27). He came to America in 1927; was associate conductor of the Cincinnati Symph. Orch.; gave conducting courses in various American cities; settled in Pittsburgh as conductor and teacher. He wrote a viola concerto (1937) and 2 oriental dances for orch.; made arrangements of Bach, and a symph. transcription of Beethoven's Septet; published a manual *Elementary Rules of Conducting* (1937); *The Instruments of the Band and Orchestra* (with M. Rosen, N. Y., 1940), and an autobiography *A Musician's Notes* (N. Y., 1943; in Russian).

Baker, Benjamin Franklin, American music pedagogue; b. Wenham, Mass., July 10, 1811; died Boston, March 11, 1889. He was a singer in various churches in Salem, Boston and Portland; in 1841 he succeeded Lowell Mason as teacher of music in the public schools; sang with the Handel and Haydn Society. He founded the Boston Music School (1851-68) and edited the 'Boston Musical Journal'; composed 3 cantatas: *The Storm King, The Burning Ship* and *Camillus;* also published a text book *Thorough-Bass and Harmony* (1870).

Baker, George, English organist; b. Exeter 1768; d. Rugeley, Feb. 19, 1847. He studied in Exeter with William Jackson; was organist at Stafford (1795), Derby (1810) and Rugeley, Staffordshire (1824). The opera *The Caffres, or Buried Alive* (produced at Covent Garden in London, June 2, 1802) is often listed as a work by Baker but was really written by John Davy. Among Baker's own works are numerous anthems and glees.

Baker, Theodore, American writer on music, and the compiler of the 1st edition of the present dictionary; b. New York, June 3, 1851; d. Dresden, Germany, Oct. 13, 1934. As a young man, he was trained for business; in 1874, decided to study music; went to Leipzig, became a pupil of Oskar Paul and received his *Dr. phil.* there in 1882 (thesis: *Über die Musik der nordamerikanischen Wilden,* the first serious study of American Indian music); lived in Germany until 1890; returned to the U.S. in 1891, and became literary editor and translator for the publishing house of G. Schirmer, Inc. (1892); retired in 1926 and returned to Germany. Books: *A Dictionary of Musical Terms* (1895; highly popular: 25 editions before 1939); *A Pronouncing Pocket Manual of Musical Terms* (1905); *The Musician's Calendar and Birthday Book* (1915-17). *Baker's Biographical Dictionary of Musicians* was first published in 1900 by G. Schirmer, Inc. It included the names of many American musicians, theretofore not represented in musical reference works; 2nd edition was published in 1905; the 3d edition, revised and enlarged by Alfred Remy, in 1919; the 4th edition in 1940, under the general editorship of Carl Engel; a supplement (1949) was compiled by Nicolas Slonimsky, the editor of the present edition.

Bakfark. See **Bacfarc.**

Baklanov, George, Russian baritone; b. St. Petersburg, Jan. 18, 1882; d. Basel, Dec. 6, 1938. He made his debut in St. Petersburg (1905); then sang at various European opera houses; was a member of the Boston Opera Co. (1909) and the Chicago Opera Co. (1917). He was particularly successful in dramatic roles (Scarpia, Boris Godunov, Rigoletto).

Balaban, Emanuel, American pianist and conductor; b. N. Y., Jan. 27, 1895. He studied piano with Stojowski; served as Mischa Elman's accompanist; conducted at the Dresden Opera; returning to the U.S., was conductor of the opera department at the Eastman School of Music in Rochester, N.Y. (1927-53); then was active as theater conductor in New York.

Balakirev (băh-lăh'-kē-rev), **Mily Alexeyevitch,** celebrated Russian composer; b. Nizhny-Novgorod, Jan. 2, 1837 (new style); d. St. Petersburg, May 29, 1910. He received his musical training from his mother; then with Alexander Dubuque in Moscow; he further studied with a German house musician at the estate of Oulibishev (author of a book on Mozart). In 1853 Balakirev entered the Univ. of Kazan and studied mathematics. He accompanied Oulibishev to St. Petersburg (1855) and was introduced to Glinka who encouraged him. He made his public debut as composer and pianist playing a movement from his piano concerto (St. Petersburg, Feb. 24, 1856); his *Overture on Russian Themes* was given in 1859. In 1862 he opened a school of music with Lomakin; his *Second Overture on Russian Themes* was performed at a school concert (April 18, 1865); this *Overture* was published as *One Thousand Years* to commemorate the national millennium (Russia as a state was formed in 862); revised in 1882, it was renamed *Russia.* Balakirev became greatly interested in collecting Russian folksongs; he selected, harmonized and published a number of these songs in 1866. This coincided with the development of Slavophile tendencies in Russia. Balakirev visited Prague in the summer of 1866; he invited several Czech musicians to present their works at a concert in St. Petersburg; this Slavic concert took place at Balakirev's school on May 24, 1867; works of Balakirev, Borodin, Cui, Mussorgsky and Rimsky-Korsakov were presented; this event led Stassov to describe the new Russian composers as a 'Mighty Heap' (usually simplified to 'Mighty Five') which went down in history as a descriptive phrase. Under the influence of his several trips to the Caucasus, Balakirev began to exploit oriental musical elements in his works; the most brilliant of these is *Islamey,* an oriental fantasy for piano, of transcendental difficulty in performance. Although Balakirev was regarded as a mentor by Borodin, Mussorgsky and others, his own activity slackened considerably. His middle life was entirely unproductive. It took him many years to complete his symph. poem, *Tamara* (perf. St. Petersburg, March 19, 1883). His symphony in C took 32 years to compose (1866-98); he wrote his second symphony in D minor at the age of 70 (1907-08); it was perf. in St. Petersburg on April 23, 1909. His first piano concerto was written in 1855; he began his 2nd piano concerto in 1861, but laid it aside until 1909. It was completed after his death by S. Liapunov. Of smaller works, his Song Albums (45 songs in all) are remarkable in their expressiveness; he made brilliant piano arrangements of works by Berlioz, Chopin and others; his transcription of Glinka's song *The Lark* has become a standard piece in the piano repertory. He published 40 Russian folksongs in 1866, and 30 songs in 1898. —— Bibl.: M. D. Calvocoressi and Gerald Abraham, *Masters of Russian Music* (1936); M. D. Calvocoressi, *Mily Balakirev,* in the 'Mus. Quarterly' (centennial article, Jan. 1937); G. Kiselev, *Balakirev* (Moscow, 1938), containing a complete bibl. in Russian; V. Muzalevsky, *Balakirev* (Leningrad, 1938); G. Fedorova, *Balakirev* (Moscow, 1951). Balakirev's correspondence with Tchaikovsky was ed. by Liapunov (St. Petersburg, 1912); that with Stassov, by V. Karenin (Moscow, 1935).

Balantchivadze, Andrey, Georgian-Russian composer (brother of the choreographer George Balanchine); b. St. Petersburg, June 1, 1906. He studied with his father, the Georgian composer Meliton Balantchivadze, and with Ippolitov-Ivanov at the Tiflis Cons. and at the Leningrad Cons. In 1931 he settled in Tiflis as prof. at the Cons. In his music he utilizes elements of Georgian folksongs. He has written an opera *Mzia* (1950); a ballet *The Heart of the Mountains* (1938); a symphony (1946); 2 piano concertos (the 2nd of which was awarded the Stalin Prize for 1947); several symph. poems; choruses and songs.

Balart, Gabriel, Spanish composer; b. Barcelona, June 8, 1824; d. there, July 5,

1893. He studied at the Paris Cons.; composed various pieces of salon music, which enjoyed some success. In 1849 he went to Milan as theater conductor; in 1853 appointed musical director of the Teatro del Liceo in Barcelona. He wrote 5 symphonies in a romantic vein, which he conducted in Spain; for a time his light opera *Amore y Arte* enjoyed considerable success.

Balatka, Hans, conductor and composer; b. Hoffnungsthal, Moravia, March 5, 1827; d. Chicago, April 17, 1899. He was a choirboy in Olmütz Cathedral; studied in Vienna with Proch and Sechter (1846-48). He emigrated to America in 1849, settling in Milwaukee, where he founded a German Musikverein (1851), and was its conductor until 1860. He appeared at the Chicago music festival with considerable success (1857); was appointed conductor of the Chicago Philh. Soc. (1860). His concerts were extremely popular for several seasons; in 1869 his orchestra was superseded by that of Theodore Thomas. Balatka subsequently made concert tours with Mme. Pappenheim (1870); led various choral organizations in Milwaukee; in 1873 settled again in Chicago, where he founded the Liederkranz and the Mozart Club. He was an important bearer of musical culture in the American Midwest; he introduced the public to complete performances of Beethoven and Schubert symphonies. He composed *The Power of Song* for double male chorus (1856); *Festival Cantata* for soprano and orch. (1869); about 30 songs; many transcriptions of various works for orch.; also fantasias and potpourris.

Balbastre (Balbâtre), Claude, French organist and composer; b. Dijon, Dec. 8, 1729; d. Paris, April 9, 1799. He was a pupil of Rameau (1760); organist at the Church of Saint-Roche in Paris; later alternated with Couperin, Daquin, and Séjan as organist of Notre-Dame. He wrote four piano suites of variations on French *noëls;* also many pieces for organ and harpsichord.

Balbi (Latin, **Balbus**), **Lodovico,** Italian composer; b. probably Venice, 1545; d. there, 1604. He was a pupil of Costanzo Porta; sang in the choir of San Marco in Venice (1570); then was maestro di cappella at the Franciscan monastery there (1578), and at San Antonio in Padua (1585-91); later returned to Venice. He published masses, motets, canzoni, madrigals, sacred songs, etc.; compiled a collection of graduals and antiphons by celebrated Italian masters, publ. by Gardano (Venice, 1591).

Balbi, Melchiore, Italian theorist and composer; b. Venice, June 4, 1796; d. Padua, June 21, 1879. He was a pupil of Nini, Valeri, and Calegari in Padua; was theater conductor there (1818-53); from 1854 was maestro di cappella at the basilica San Antonio. He wrote 3 operas, all produced in Padua: *La Notte perigliosa* (1820); *L'Abitator del bosco* (1821); *L'Alloggio militare* (1825); a requiem (for Rossini, 1868); masses; psalms; edited Calegari's *Trattato del sistema armonico* (Padua, 1829); and wrote a *Grammatica ragionata della musica considerata sotto l'aspetto di lingua* (Milan, 1845), and *Nuova scuola basata sul sistema semitonato equabile* (1872).

Baldwin, Samuel Atkinson, American organist and composer; b. Lake City, Minn., Jan. 25, 1862; d. New York, Sept. 15, 1949. He studied in Dresden (1880-84); returned to America, and was organist in churches in Chicago (1885-89), New York (1895-1902) and Brooklyn (1902-11); taught at the College of the City of New York (1907-32). He was one of the founders of the American Guild of Organists; gave nearly 1500 organ recitals. Among his compositions are a piano trio; 2 string quartets; Psalm XVIII for soloists, chorus and orch. (1884); a concert overture, *A Journey in Norway* (1887); a cantata, *The Triumph of Love* (1892); a suite for orch., *A Summer Idyl* (1895); 2 symphonies; 4 symphonic rhapsodies; etc. His anthem *Tarry with Me* has attained wide popularity.

Bales, Richard, American conductor; b. Alexandria, Virginia, Feb. 3, 1915. He studied at the Eastman School of Music in Rochester; then under Koussevitzky (conducting) at the Berkshire Music Center (1940). In 1943 became conductor of the National Gallery Orch. in Washington, D.C. He has presented many scores by contemporary American composers; compiled and arranged an ingenious potpourri of Southern songs, *The Confederacy* (1954; very popular).

Balfe (balf), **Michael William,** Irish composer; b. Dublin, May 15, 1808; d. Rowney Abbey, Hertfordshire, Oct. 20, 1870. He was the son of a dancing-master; at the age of six played the violin for his father's dancing classes; subsequently studied violin with O'Rourke. After his father's death (Jan. 6, 1823), Balfe went to London where he studied with Charles Edward Horn (violin) and Carl Friedrich Horn (composition); in 1824 was violinist at the Drury Lane Theatre; also sang in London and the provinces.

His patron, Count Mazzara, took him to Italy (1825); he studied in Milan with Federici (counterpoint) and Filippo Galli (singing); his ballet, *La Pérouse,* was produced there in 1826. Acting on the advice of Rossini, Balfe further studied singing with Bordogni; then was engaged as principal baritone at the Italian Opera, Paris (1828); also sang in various Italian theaters until 1833. In Italy, he married the Hungarian vocalist Lina Rosa (b. 1808; d. London, June 8, 1888). Returning to England in 1835, he began his brilliant career as a composer of English operas with *The Siege of Rochelle* (Drury Lane Theatre, London, Oct. 29, 1835); he was then manager of the Lyceum Theatre in London (1841); went to Paris, where he composed the operas *Le Puits d'amour* (Opéra-Comique, Paris, April 20, 1843; in English as *Geraldine,* Princess's Theatre, London, Aug. 8, 1843), and *Les Quatres Fils Aymon* (Opéra-Comique, Paris, July 15, 1844; in English as *The Castle of Aymon,* Princess's Theatre, London, Nov. 20, 1844); returned to England in 1843 and produced his most famous opera, *The Bohemian Girl* (Drury Lane Theatre, London, Nov. 27, 1843), which was subsequently translated into French, German and Italian, and performed on the chief continental stages with great success. Excepting visits to Vienna (1846), Berlin (1848), to St. Petersburg and to Trieste (1852-6), he stayed in England; retired to his country seat at Rowney Abbey in 1864. His daughter, Victoire, made her debut as a singer in 1857 at the Lyceum Theatre, London. The further list of his operas includes three in Italian: *I rivali di se stesso* (Palermo, 1829); *Un avvertimento ai gelosi* (Pavia, 1830); *Enrico IV al Passo della Marna* (Milan, Feb. 19, 1833); and one in French: *L'Étoile de Séville* (Opéra, Paris, Dec. 17, 1845). The following operas were produced in London at Drury Lane, Covent Garden, and other theaters: *The Maid of Artois* (May 27, 1836); *Catherine Grey* (May 27, 1837); *Joan of Arc* (Nov. 30, 1837); *Diadeste, or The Veiled Lady* (May 17, 1838); *Falstaff* (in Italian, July 19, 1838); *Këolanthe, or The Unearthly Bride* (March 9, 1841); *The Daughter of St. Mark* (Nov. 27, 1844); *The Enchantress* (May 14, 1845); *The Bondman* (Dec. 11, 1846); *The Maid of Honour* (Dec. 20, 1847); *The Sicilian Bride* (March 6, 1852); *The Devil's In It* (July 26, 1852); *Moro, the Painter of Antwerp* (Jan. 28, 1882; originally produced as *Pittore e duca,* Trieste, Nov. 21, 1854); *The Rose of Castille* (Oct. 29, 1857); *Satanella, or The Power of Love* (Dec. 20, 1858); *Bianca, or The Bravo's Bride* (Dec. 6, 1860); *The Puritan's Daughter* (Nov. 30, 1861); *The Armourer of Nantes* (Feb. 12, 1863); *Blanche de Nevers* (Nov. 21, 1863); *The Sleeping Queen,* operetta (Sept. 8, 1864); *The Knight of the Leopard* (Liverpool, Jan. 15, 1891; originally produced in London as *Il Talismano,* June 11, 1874); also *Mazeppa,* a cantata, and 2 other cantatas; ballads, glees, songs, etc. Bibl.: Charles Lamb Kenney, *A Memoir of Michael William Balfe* (London, 1875); W. A. Barrett, *Balfe: His Life and Work* (London, 1882).

Balfoort, Dirk Jacobus, Dutch musicologist; b. Utrecht, July 19, 1886. He studied with Evert Cornelis; played violin in various German orchestras; then held teaching posts in Holland; also organized concerts of old music by Dutch composers. He published valuable books (in Dutch) on music making in Holland: *De Hollandsche vioolmakers* (Amsterdam, 1931); *Het Muziekleven in Nederland in de 17e en 18e eeuw* (Amsterdam, 1938); a monograph on Stradivarius (Amsterdam, 1945; also in German and English); etc.

Balfour, Henry Lucas, English organist; b. London, Oct. 28, 1859; d. Croydon, Surrey, Dec. 27, 1946. He studied music in London with Arthur Sullivan; later in Leipzig; was organist at Croydon (1872-1902). In 1902 he became organist at the Church of the Holy Trinity.

Ball, Ernest R., American composer of popular songs; b. Cleveland, July 21, 1878; d. Santa Ana, California, May 3, 1927. He studied at Cleveland Cons.; moved to N. Y., where he earned his living as a vaudeville pianist. His first success came with the song *Will You Love Me in December as You Do in May?* to the words of James J. Walker (later, Mayor of N. Y.). No less successful were his sentimental songs *Mother Machree, When Irish Eyes are Smiling, Little Bit of Heaven, Dear Little Boy of Mine, Till the Sands of the Desert Grow Cold, Love Me and the World is Mine,* etc., sung by John McCormack and other famous artists. Ball was a charter member of ASCAP (1914).

Ballantine, Edward, American composer; b. Oberlin, Ohio, August 6, 1886. He studied with Walter Spalding at Harvard Univ.; graduated with highest honors in 1907; took piano courses with Artur Schnabel and Rudolph Ganz in Berlin (1907-09). In 1912 he was appointed instructor at Harvard; became assistant prof. in 1926; associate prof.

in 1932; retired in 1947. His first published work was a musical play, *The Lotos Eaters* (1907); three of his orchestral pieces were performed by the Boston Symph. Orch.: *From the Garden of Hellas* (Feb. 9, 1923); *Prelude to The Delectable Forest* (Dec. 10, 1914); *The Eve of St. Agnes* (Jan. 19, 1917); a piece in lighter vein, *By a Lake in Russia,* was perf. at the Boston Pops (June 27, 1922). He has also written a violin sonata and songs. His most striking work is a set of piano variations on *Mary Had a Little Lamb* (1924) in the styles of 10 composers; a second series of variations on the same tune (1943) includes stylizations of Stravinsky, Gershwin and others. These sets have become highly popular in concert programs.

Ballard (băh-lahr'), a family of French music printers. The establishment was founded by Robert Ballard in 1552, whose patent from Henri II made him "Seul imprimeur de la musique de la chambre, chapelle, et menus plaisirs du roy"; the patent was renewed to various members of the family until 1776, when it expired. The firm enjoyed a virtual monopoly on French music printing, and continued under the management of the Ballard family until 1788. Until c. 1750, the movable types invented in 1540 by Guillaume le Bé were used; the Ballards printed Lully's operas in this style (from 1700); later printings were from engraved copper-plates.

Balling (băhl'-ling), **Michael,** German conductor; b. Heidingsfeld, near Würzburg, Aug. 28, 1866; d. Darmstadt, Sept. 1, 1925. He won a scholarship to the Königliche Musikschule in Würzburg, where he studied viola under Hermann Ritter; began his career as violist in the Municipal Orch. at Mainz; then played in the court orchestra at Schwerin; in 1886 was appointed first violist in the Festival Theater Orch. at Bayreuth; on various occasions played chamber music with Rubinstein and Brahms. He went to Nelson, New Zealand and established the first music school there (1892), organized an orchestra and a choral society; toured England as music director for F. R. Benson's production of *A Midsummer Night's Dream* (1895); was appointed assistant conductor at Bayreuth (1896). He was chorusmaster at the Stadttheater in Hamburg for a year; then at Lübeck, where he gave Wagner's *Nibelungen Ring* (complete) and later at Breslau; in 1903 succeeded Mottl as chorusmaster at the Karlsruhe opera and conductor of symphony concerts. He visited Spain in 1906 and conducted the first performances of *Die Meistersinger* in Barcelona; directed *Tristan* and the *Ring* at Bayreuth; in 1910 toured England as principal conductor of Denhof's Opera Company, and conducted the first performance of the *Ring* in English, at Edinburgh, Scotland; succeeded Richter (1911) as conductor of the Hallé Orch. in Manchester; settled in Darmstadt (1919) as general music director; from 1912 until his death was editor of the monumental edition of Wagner's works begun by Breitkopf & Härtel in 1912.

Balmer, Luc, Swiss conductor and composer; b. Munich, July 13, 1898. He studied with Hans Huber at the Basel Cons. and later in Berlin with Busoni. Returning to Switzerland in 1923, he occupied various posts as theater conductor. In 1941 he became conductor at the Musical Society of Berne. He has written two symphonies; violin concerto; piano concerto; variations for oboe, bassoon and strings (1951). His musical fairy tale *Die Verzauberte Blume* was performed in Berne in 1926.

Balogh, Ernö, Hungarian pianist and composer; b. Budapest, April 4, 1897. A precocious musician, he played in public as an infant; at seven entered the Royal Academy of Music in Budapest; at twelve took courses with Bartók (piano) and Kodály (comp.); graduated with honors at 17. He was 15 when he received the Liszt prize. He continued his studies in Berlin with Leonid Kreutzer; made his Berlin debut, Sept. 13, 1920. He then traveled as accompanist with celebrated artists; emigrated to America in 1924; became a U.S. citizen in 1929. His first orchestral works, written when he was 17, *Rêverie* and *Danse du Mi-Carême,* were performed by the Budapest Philharmonic (1915); he also wrote *Divertissement* for string orch.; violin pieces *Caprice Antique* and *Arabesque* (played by Kreisler) and numerous piano compositions.

Baloković (bah-loh'-koh-vitch), **Zlatko,** eminent violinist; b. Zagreb, Yugoslavia, March 21, 1895. He was a pupil of Vaclav Huml at the Zagreb Cons. (1905); then of Sevčik at the Meisterschule in Vienna; won the Australian State Prize (which included a Guarnerius violin) in 1913; has toured Europe and the U.S. many times as soloist with all the major orchestras, and in recital; gave the first performance of John Alden Carpenter's violin concerto in Chicago (Chicago Symph. Orch., Nov. 18, 1937); also performed it in Cleveland, Los Angeles, Boston and New York; since 1939 has been living mainly in N. Y.

Baltzell, Winton James, American music editor; b. Shiremanstown, Pa., Dec. 18, 1864; d. New York, Jan. 10, 1928. He was educated at Lebanon College (A.B., 1884); New England Cons. (1888-9); Univ. of Pennsylvania (Mus. Bac., 1896); also studied in London (1890) with Sir John Frederick Bridge (composition) and William Shakespeare (singing); was assistant editor of 'The Etude' in Philadelphia (1887); taught theory and the history of music at Wesleyan Univ. (1900-07); from 1907-18 was secretary of the National Academy of Music in New York. He published *A Complete History of Music for Schools* (1905), and a *Dictionary of Musicians* (1912); also edited the 'University Course of Music Study' at Wesleyan; composed choral and orchestral works, chamber music, numerous songs and anthems.

Bal y Gay, Jesús, Spanish composer and musicologist; b. Lugo, June 23, 1905. He studied at the Madrid Cons. From 1935-38 he lived in Cambridge, England, where he taught Spanish; then settled in Mexico City. In 1947 he became chief of the Section of Musical Research at the Instituto Nacional de Bellas Artes. He married the Spanish pianist, Rosita Garcia Ascot. Bal y Gay has written mostly in small forms; several of his piano pieces and songs have been published; he has made transcriptions of old Spanish romances; edited collections of Spanish lute music.

Bamberger, Carl, conductor; b. Vienna, Feb. 21, 1902. He studied theory and piano with Schenker; musicology at the Univ. of Vienna. He conducted opera at Danzig and Darmstadt (1924-30); in Russia (1931-35) and Egypt (1937). In 1937 he came to the U. S.; in 1939 was appointed director of the Orchestral and Opera Depts. at the Mannes Music School, N. Y. He founded and conducted the New Choral Group of Manhattan and the Brooklyn Oratorio Society (1940-45); guest conductor of the NBC Symph. Orch., CBS Symph. Orch., N. Y. Philh. Orch., Detroit Symph. Orch., Havana Philh. Orch. and at the Lewisohn Stadium Concerts.

Bamboschek, Giuseppe, conductor; b. Trieste, June 12, 1890. A precocious musician, he was organist at the San Giacomo Church in Trieste at the age of thirteen; studied piano, theory, and conducting at the Trieste Cons. (graduated 1907); made operatic debut as a conductor in Trieste (1908); came to the U. S. as accompanist for Pasquale Amato (1913); in 1916 was appointed conductor and music secretary at the Metropolitan Opera; conducted there for thirteen years, specializing in Italian repertory; has also conducted at various European cities, in New York, Philadelphia, and St. Louis. Since 1929, in addition to guest appearances as opera conductor, Bamboschek has been conducting for radio and motion pictures.

Bampton, Rose, American opera singer; b. Cleveland, Nov. 28, 1909. She studied at the Curtis Institute in Philadelphia (B.A.); made her operatic debut with the New York Chautauqua Opera as Siebel, under Albert Stoessel (1929); subsequently sang Schoenberg's *Gurre-Lieder,* with the Philadelphia Orch., under Stokowski's direction; also sang in the Bach Festival, Bethlehem, Pa., and was soloist with many major American orchestras; made her debut at the Metropolitan Opera as Laura in *La Gioconda* (Nov. 28, 1932). She first appeared as a mezzo-soprano; then retrained voice as a soprano; made her debut as a soprano at the Metropolitan Opera House in 1937, as Leonore in *Il Trovatore;* has sung dramatic soprano roles in *Norma* and *Don Giovanni;* in 1939 sang the role of Sieglinde in Chicago.

Banchieri (băn-kyā'-rē), **Adriano,** Italian organist and composer; b. Bologna, Sept. 3, 1568; d. there, 1634. He studied with Lucio Barbieri and Giuseppe Guami. On Sept. 8, 1589 he took holy orders and entered the monastery of Monte Oliveto. In 1592 he was at the Monastery of S. Bartolomeo in Lucca; 1593, in Siena; was organist at Santa Maria in Regola di Imola in 1600. In 1608 he returned to Bologna, remaining there until his death. Despite his clerical rank (he became abbot in 1620) Banchieri never abandoned music, and was active at the Accademia Filarmonica in Bologna (where he was known as 'Il dissonante'). He wrote numerous stage works, historically important in the evolution of early opera. Among these dramatic works were *La Pazzia senile* (1598); *Il zabaione musicale* (1604); *La barca da Venezia per Padova* (1605); *La prudenza giovanile* (1607); *Tirsi, Filli e Clori* (1614). He wrote a number of masses for 3 to 8 voices, and other sacred vocal works; also several groups of instrumental works: *I canzoni alla francese a 4 voci per sonar* (1595); *Dialoghi, concentus e sinfonie* (1625); *Il virtuoso ritrovato accademico* (1626), etc. As a theorist, he advocated the extension of the hexachord and proposed to name the 7th degree of the scale by the syllables *ba* and *bi* (corresponding to B flat and B). Banchieri's theoretical work *L'organo suonarino* (Venice, 1605) gives instructions for accompaniment with figured bass; his *Moderna prattica musicale* (Venice, 1613) contains further elaborations of the subject. Banchieri was the first to use the signs *f* and *p* for loudness and softness (in his *Libro III di nuovi pensieri ecclesiastici,* 1613). He also wrote dramatic plays under the name of Camillo Scaliggeri della Fratta. A reprint of his *Sinfonia d'istromenti* (1607) is found in A. Schering's *Geschichte der Musik in Beispielen* (No. 151); the organ pieces from *L'organo suonarino* are reprinted in Torchi's *Arte musicale in Italia* (vol. III). Banchieri further publ.: the treatises *Cartella musicale del canto figurato, fermo e contrappunto* (Venice, 1614); *Direttorio monastico di canto fermo* (Bologna, 1615); and *Lettere armoniche* (Bologna, 1628). Bibl.: Max Schneider, *Die Anfänge des Basso continuo* (1918); F. Vatielli, *Il Madrigale drammatico e Adriano Banchieri,* in *Arte e vita musicale a Bologna* (1927); F. T. Arnold, *The Art of Accompaniment from a Thorough Bass* (London, 1931); Gustave Reese, *Music in the Renaissance* (N. Y., 1954). See also E. Capaccioli, *Precisazioni biografiche su Adriano Banchieri* in 'Rivista Musicale' (Oct.-Dec., 1954).

Band, Erich, German conductor; b. Berlin, May 10, 1876; d. Waidhofen, May 13, 1945. He studied at the Hochschule für Musik in Berlin; was conductor at the Stuttgart Hoftheater (1905); chief of the opera at Halle (1924-32), and later at Berlin. He adapted Auber's *Le Domino noir* for the German stage; also wrote a manual, *Zur Entwickelungsgeschichte des modernen Orchesters* (1910); composed chamber music and songs.

Bang, Maia (Mrs. Hohn), Norwegian-American violinist and teacher; b. Tromsö, April 24, 1879; d. New York, Jan. 3, 1940. She was graduated from the Leipzig Cons. (1897); then studied with Leopold Auer in St. Petersburg. She came to the U. S. in 1919 and became Auer's assistant in New York. She was the author of several violin methods; at the time of her death, she was engaged in writing a biography of Paganini. Her collection of Paganini materials was given to the Library of Congress.

Banister, Henry Charles, English music theorist and teacher: b. London, June 13, 1831; d. Streatham, near London, Nov. 20, 1897. He studied music with his father, a cellist; then with Cipriani Potter at the Royal Academy of Music, where he twice gained the King's scholarship (1846-48); was appointed assistant prof. (1853) of harmony and composition at the Royal Academy; taught harmony at Guildhall School (from 1880) and at the Royal Normal College for the Blind (from 1881). He published a *Textbook of Music* (London, 1872, and 15 editions since); *Some Musical Ethics and Analogies* (1884); *Lectures on Musical Analysis* (1887); *Musical Art and Study* (1888); *George Alexander Macfarren* (1892); *Helpful Papers for Harmony Students.* (1895); *The Harmonising of Melodies* (1897); and *The Art of Modulating* (1901). A collection of his lectures, *Interludes,* edited by Macpherson, appeared in 1898. Banister composed 4 symphonies and 5 overtures, chamber music, cantatas, piano pieces, and songs.

Banister, Henry Joshua, English cellist; b. London, 1803; d. there, 1847. He was a skilled performer, and the author of several books on cello technique. His father, **Charles William Banister** (1768-1831), was a composer who published a *Collection of Vocal Music* (London, 1803).

Banister, John, English violinist and composer; b. London, 1630; d. there, Oct. 3, 1679. After he had received some musical instruction from his father, his skill earned him the patronage of King Charles II, who sent him to France for further study; was later a member of Charles' band, until an outspoken preference for the English over the French musicians playing in it caused his expulsion. Banister was director of a music school, and established the first public concerts in London (1672-78); was a prominent figure in the English musical life of his day. He wrote music for Davenant's *Circe* and Shakespeare's *The Tempest* (both 1676); composed *New Ayres and Dialogues for voices and viols* (London, 1678); contributed to Playford's *Courtly Masquing Ayres* (1662), and to Lock's *Melothesia* (1673); also wrote music for plays by Dryden, Shadwell and Wycherley. Cf. J. Pulver, *A Biographical Dictionary of Old English Music* (1927).

Banister, John (Jr.), English violinist, son of preceding; b. London, c. 1663; d. there, 1735. He studied violin with his father; was a member of the private band under Charles II, James II and Queen Anne; was concert master at the Italian Opera in London. He composed some music for the theater; contributed to Playford's *Division Violin* (1685), the first violin manual published in England.

Bannister, Rev. **Henry Marriott,** English

music editor and bibliographer; b. Oxford, March 18, 1854; d. there Feb. 16, 1919. He studied theology; was ordained priest in 1878; publ. the valuable editions, *Monumenti Vaticani di Paleografia Musicale Latina* (Leipzig, 1913; also in Italian transl. by R. Baralli), a catalogue of the music MSS. in the Vatican Library, including 141 plates; *Anglo-French Sequelae* (ed. by Dom Anselm Hughes and publ. by The Plainsong and Medieval Music Society in 1934); co-editor of vols. 47, 49, 53 and 54 of *Analecta Hymnica Medii Aevi* (1886-1922); also publ. some MSS. of the Abbey of Coupar-Angus in Scotland, with a brief description (Rome, 1910); ed. a Gallican sacramentary, *Missale Gothicum,* with introduction and liturgical notes (London, 1917-19). He was for many years librarian of the Bodleian Library in Oxford.

Banti-Giorgi, Brigida, famous Italian soprano; b. Monticelli d'Ongina (Piacenza), 1759; d. Bologna, Feb. 18, 1806. She sang in Parisian cafés where she was heard by de Vismes, the director of the Opera. Her engagement by him was the beginning of a brilliant career which took her to England, Italy and Germany. She studied with Sacchini, Piozzi and Abel; her abilities were greatly appreciated by composers; Paisiello wrote for her his opera *Giuochi di Agrigento,* and she sang at its premiere (Venice, May 16, 1792). She married the dancer, Zaccaria Banti; her son wrote her biography. Bibl.: Giuseppe Banti, *Vita di B. Banti-Giorgi* (Bologna, 1869); Carlo Lozzi, *Brigida Banti* ('Rivista Musicale Italiana', 1904).

Bantock, Sir Granville, eminent English composer; b. London, Aug. 7, 1868; d. there, Oct. 16, 1946. He studied at the Royal Academy of Music, graduating in 1892; was the first holder of the Macfarren Scholarship. His earliest works were presented at the Academy concerts: an Egyptian ballet suite *Rameses II;* overture *The Fire Worshippers;* and a short opera *Caedmar,* which was later presented at the Crystal Palace (Oct. 18, 1893). He then developed varied activities; he was founder and editor of 'The New Quarterly Mus. Review' (1893-96); toured as a musical comedy conductor (1894-95); organized and conducted concerts devoted to works by young British composers; conducted a military band and later a full orchestra at New Brighton (1897-1901). At the same time he was engaged in teaching activities; in 1907 he succeeded Sir Edward Elgar as prof. of music at Birmingham Univ., a post which he retained until 1934, when he became Chairman of the Board of Trinity College of Music. In 1938, at the age of 70, he undertook a journey to India and Australia, returning to England on the eve of World War II. He was married in 1898 to Helen von Schweitzer, daughter of the poet, Hermann von Schweitzer. Bantock was knighted in 1930. As a composer, Bantock was attracted to exotic subjects with mystical overtones; his interests were cosmopolitan and embraced all civilizations, with particular predilection for the Celtic and oriental cultures; however, his music was set in western terms. He was a strong believer in the programmatic significance of musical images, and most of his works bear titles relating to literature, mythology or legend. Yet he was a typically British composer in the treatment of his materials. His works are brilliantly scored and effective in performance, but few of them have been retained in the repertory of musical organizations. He wrote 3 Celtic operas: *Caedmar* (1892); *The Pearl of Iran* (1894); and *The Seal-Woman* (Birmingham, Sept. 27, 1924); ballets: *Egypt* (1892); *Lalla Rookh* (1902); *The Great God Pan* (1902); 6 tone poems: *Thalaba the Destroyer* (1900); *Dante* (1901; revised, 1910); *Fifine at the Fair* (1901); *Hudibras* (1902); *The Witch of Atlas* (1902); *Lalla Rookh* (from the ballet of that name, 1902); overture, *The Pierrot of the Minute* (1908); *Hebridean Symphony* (Glasgow, Jan. 17, 1916); *Pagan Symphony* (1923-28); *Celtic Symphony* for strings and 6 harps (1940); *2 Heroic Ballads* (1944); *The Funeral* (1946); choral works with orch.: *The Time Spirit* (1902); *Sea Wanderers* (1906); *Omar Khayyám* (in 3 parts; 1906-09; Bantock's most ambitious work); *The Pilgrim's Progress* (1928); *Prometheus Unbound* (1936); numerous works for unaccompanied chorus, among them 3 'choral symphonies': *Atalanta in Calydon* (1911); *Vanity of Vanities* (1913); *A Pageant of Human Life* (1913); also *The Golden Journey to Samarkand* (1922); choral suites to words from the Chinese; children's songs to the poems of Helen Bantock; works for brass band, cello and orch., voice and orch.; 2 string quartets; 3 violin sonatas; viola sonatas; cello sonatas; several sets of piano pieces; *Songs of the East* (6 cycles of 6 songs each); several sets of *Songs from the Chinese Poets;* sets of Celtic songs, etc. Bantock also edited albums of keyboard pieces by Byrd, Bull, etc. Bibl.: H. O. Anderton, *Granville Bantock* (London, 1915); H. Antcliffe, *A Brief Survey of the Works of Granville Bantock,* in the 'Mus. Quarterly' (July, 1918).

Baranović (bah-rah'-no-vitch), **Krešimir,** Croatian composer and conductor; b. Sibenik, July 25, 1894. He studied music in Vienna; then conducted opera in Zagreb and Belgrade. He conducted Anna Pavlova's ballet group (1927-28); became professor at the Belgrade Academy of Music (1945); was appointed conductor of the Serbian State Symph. Orch. (1951). He wrote 2 operas: *Striženo-Košeno (Clipped and Mowed)* and *The Turks are Coming,* and several ballets of which *The Gingerbread Heart* was produced at the Edinburgh Festival in 1951. Baranović employs native folk melodies and rhythms in his music; he is regarded as the foremost ballet composer of Yugoslavia.

Barati, George, Hungarian-American cellist composer and conductor; b. Györ, Hungary, April 3, 1913. He studied at the Budapest Cons.; was first cellist at the Budapest Opera (1936-38); then came to America. He taught at Princeton (1939-43); served as band leader with the U. S. Army (1943-46); was cellist in the San Francisco Symph. Orch. (1946-49). In 1950 he was appointed conductor of the Honolulu Symph. Orch., Hawaii. Works: String quartet (1944); *Scherzo* for orch. (1946); *Cantabile e ritmico* for viola and piano (1947); *The Love of Don Perlimplin,* ballet (1947); *Configurations* for orch. (1947).

Barbaja (bahr-bah'-yah), **Domenico,** celebrated Italian impresario; b. Naples, c. 1775; d. Posillipo, near Naples, Oct. 16, 1841. He was a waiter; then became a financial speculator; had a concession for gambling in Naples (1808-21); became so powerful that he was nicknamed 'Viceroy of Naples.' Under the influence of his mistress, the singer Isabella Colbran, he entered the theatrical business, and obtained enormous success with his undertakings in opera. He was impresario of San Carlo and other theaters in Naples (1809-24), two theaters in Vienna (1821-28); also managed La Scala (1829-32). He was a friend of Rossini, Bellini and Donizetti, from whom he commissioned operas. Emil Lucka wrote a novel *Der Impresario* (Vienna, 1937) on his life. See G. Monaldi, *Impresari celebri del Secolo XIX* (Milan, 1918).

Barber, Samuel, eminent American composer; b. West Chester, Pa., March 9, 1910. He came of a musical family; his mother's sister was the well known singer, Louise Homer. Barber began studying piano at the age of six; at ten he attempted to write an opera, *The Rose Tree.* He played the organ in a local church for a time, until, in 1924, he entered the newly founded Curtis Institute of Music in Philadelphia where he studied piano with Isabelle Vengerova and composition with Rosario Scalero. In 1928 he won a prize of $1200 for his violin sonata. His first work to attract general attention was the *Overture to The School for Scandal,* after Sheridan (Philadelphia, Aug. 30, 1933), which earned him another prize of $1200. His *Music for a Scene from Shelley* was performed by the N. Y. Philharmonic (March 23, 1935). He traveled extensively in Europe from 1928 on; received a Pulitzer Traveling Scholarship for 1935-6 and went to Rome; also won the American Prix de Rome (1935) for his cello sonata and *Music for a Scene from Shelley.* In Rome he wrote a *Symphony in One Movement,* which was performed there by Molinari (Dec. 13, 1936); Rodzinski conducted its American premiere in Cleveland (Jan. 21, 1937), and also at the Salzburg Festival (July 25, 1937) where it was the first American work to be given a performance. On Nov. 5, 1938, Toscanini, with the NBC Symphony Orch., gave two new works by Barber in New York: *Essay for Orchestra No. I* and *Adagio for Strings.* The *Adagio* (arranged from Barber's string quartet) has become one of the most popular American works for a string ensemble. From 1939-42 Barber was on the faculty of the Curtis Institute, teaching orchestration and conducting a chorus. In the autumn of 1942 he joined the Army Air Forces, by whom he was commissioned to write a symphony, his second. It was performed in Boston by Koussevitzky (March 3, 1944); the original score included a special electronic instrument to imitate radio signals. Another wartime work was *Commando March* for band (1943). In 1945, Barber was discharged from the Air Forces, and settled at Mt. Kisco, N. Y., in a house which he had purchased with Gian-Carlo Menotti in 1943. In 1947 he received a Guggenheim fellowship. Barber has written a ballet *The Serpent Heart* for Martha Graham, performed by her group in New York (May 10, 1946); it was later revised and produced under the title *Cave of the Heart* (N. Y., Feb. 27, 1947); an orchestral suite *Medea,* drawn from this ballet, was first played by the Philadelphia Orch. (Dec. 5, 1947). In his *Prayers of Kierkegaard* for soprano, chorus and orch. (Boston Symph., Dec. 3, 1954) Barber essayed the style of modern oratorio with impressive results. In 1956 he undertook the composition of an opera, *Vanessa,* to a libretto by Gian-Carlo Menotti. For piano he wrote an effective suite *Excursions* (1945) and a highly elaborate sonata (1949), making full use of the resources of modern piano technique and reaching a high degree of rhapsodic eloquence. His other works are: violin concerto (Philadelphia, Feb. 7, 1941); *Essay No. 2* for orch. (N. Y., April 16, 1942); *Capricorn Concerto* for flute, oboe, trumpet, and strings (N. Y., Oct. 8, 1944); cello concerto (Boston, April 5, 1946); *Knoxville: Summer of 1915* for soprano and orch. (Boston, April 9, 1948); *Souvenirs,* ballet suite (Chicago, Nov. 13, 1953). Vocal works: *Dover Beach* for voice and string quartet (1931); 3 Songs to poems by James Joyce (1936); *A Stopwatch and an Ordnance Map* for chorus (1940); *Mélodies passagères* (5 songs to Rilke's words; 1951); *Hermit Songs* to texts translated from the Irish (1953), etc. Chamber music: *Serenade* for string quartet (1929); cello sonata (1932); string quartet (1936); *Summer Music* for woodwind quintet (Detroit, March 20, 1956). Barber's style is distinguished by striking lyricism; his melodies are basically tonal, but he makes free use of chromatic techniques verging on atonality in his later works. His harmonic textures are often polytonal while his contrapuntal writing contains strong canonic and fugal elements; his orchestration is rich and full; his treatment of solo instruments is idiomatic but requires virtuoso performance. Bibl.: N. Broder, *Samuel Barber* (N. Y., 1954), containing a detailed biography and musical analysis.

Barberá, José, Catalan music theorist; b. Barcelona, Jan. 27, 1874; d. there, Feb. 19, 1947. He studied in Barcelona with Pedrell; in 1924 was appointed prof. at the Cons. there. He publ. several textbooks, among them *Curso de Melódica;* his pedagogical work *4 Lecciones de Alta Teoria Música* was publ. posthumously (1948). He also composed several symph. pieces and arrangements of folk songs.

Barbi, Alice, Italian mezzo-soprano; b. Modena, June 1, 1862; d. Rome, Sept. 4, 1948. She studied with Zamboni and Vannuccini; made her debut in Milan (April 2, 1882). She sang in London in 1884, and also appeared in Germany and Russia. At her concert in Vienna on Dec. 21, 1893, Brahms played the accompaniments to his songs. She married Pietro Della Torretta in 1920, and spent her last years in Rome.

Barbier, Jules Paul, French librettist and dramatist; b. Paris, March 8, 1822; d. there Jan. 16, 1901. Joint author (with Carré) of several librettos for famous operas, among them Gounod's *Faust* and *Roméo et Juliette, Hamlet* by Ambroise Thomas, etc.

Barbier, René (Auguste-Ernest), Belgian composer; b. Namur, July 12, 1890. He studied with Dupuis at the Liège Cons. He received the Premier Prix de Rome for his cantata *Légende de sœur Béatrice* (1920). He has also written 2 operas: *Yvette* (1910) and *La fête du vieux Tilleul* (1912); an oratorio *La Tour de Babel* (1932); symph. poem *La musique de perdition* (1947); a violin concerto; clarinet concerto and chamber music.

Barbieri, Carlo Emmanuele di, conductor and composer; b. Genoa, Oct. 22, 1822; d. Budapest, Sept. 28, 1867. He was a pupil of Mercadante and Crescentini; was orchestra conductor in numerous Italian theaters; then in Vienna (1845), Berlin (1847), Hamburg (1851) and Rio de Janeiro (1853); from 1856-62 he again conducted in Vienna; then settled in Budapest as director of the National Theater. He wrote 5 operas: *Cristoforo Colombo* (Berlin, 1848); *Nisida, la Perla di Procida* (1851); *Carlo und Carlin* (1859); *Arabella* (Budapest, 1862); and *Perdita, ein Wintermärchen* (Leipzig, 1865); church music; German and Italian songs.

Barbieri, Francisco Asenjo, Spanish composer; b. Madrid, Aug. 3, 1823; d. there, Feb. 17, 1894. After academic study at the Madrid Cons. with Carnicer, he played clarinet in military bands; also appeared as pianist and singer in various theaters. He developed a flair for writing zarzuelas, and wrote 77 of them. The following were particularly successful (all produced in Madrid): *Gloria y peluca* (March 9, 1850); *Jugar con fuego* (Oct. 6, 1851); *Los diamantes de la corona* (Sept. 15, 1854); *Pan y Toros* (Dec. 22, 1864) and *El Barberillo de Lavapiés* (Dec. 18, 1874). Barbieri was also a scholar; he published the music essays: *Ultimos Amores de Lope de Vega Carpio* (1876); *Sobre el Canto de Ultreja* (1883); *La Música religiosa* (1889); he also edited a valuable collection *Cancionero musical de los siglos XV y XVI* (1890), and a MS. novel by Eximeneo, *Don Lazaro Viscardi* (1872). Bibl.: A. Peña y Goñi, *La Opera Española en el siglo XIX* (Madrid, 1881); A. Salazar, *La Música contemporánea en España* (Madrid, 1930); J. Subirá, *Manuscritos de Barbieri, existentes en la Biblioteca Nacional* (Madrid, 1936); G. Chase, *Barbieri and the Spanish Zarzuela,* in 'Music & Letters' (Jan., 1939); A. Martínez Olmedilla, *El maestro Barbieri y su tiempo* (Madrid, 1950).

Barbireau (or **Barbirau, Barbarieu, Barbyrianus, Barberau, Barbingaut, Barbacola**), **Jacques,** Flemish composer; b. Mons, c. 1408; d. Antwerp, Aug. 8, 1491. He was choirmaster at the Antwerp Cathedral from 1447 until his death; Okeghem was one of his pupils. Barbireau enjoyed a great reputation in his time; his opinions are copiously cited by Tinctoris. Works: Mass for 5 voices, *Virgo parens Christi;* for 4 voices: *Missa Pascale; Faulx perverse;* antiphons, psalms, etc. Cf. H. du Saar, *Het Leven en de composities van Jacobus Barbireau* (Utrecht, 1946). See also G. Reese, *Music in the Renaissance* (N. Y., 1954).

Barbirolli, Sir John, eminent English conductor; b. London, Dec. 2, 1899, of Italian-French parentage. He studied at Trinity College (1911-12) and at the Royal Academy of Music (1912-17); made his concert debut in Queen's Hall as a cellist at the age of eleven; became cellist in the Queen's Hall Orch. (1915). He then held various positions as a conductor: with the Chenil Orch., Chelsea (1925); British National Opera Co. (1926); achieved recognition when he substituted for Beecham with the London Symph. (1926); in 1933 was appointed conductor of the Scottish Orch., Glasgow, and Leeds Symph. Orch. He made his American debut with the New York Philh. (Nov. 5, 1936) and produced such an excellent impression that he was selected to succeed Toscanini in 1937. He was chief conductor of the N. Y. Philh. until 1943, when he went back to England and was appointed conductor of the Hallé Orch., Manchester. He was knighted in 1949. As a conductor, Barbirolli shows a fine pragmatic sense of shaping the music according to its inward style, without projecting his own personality upon it; however, this lack of subjective interpretation was responsible for the somewhat lukewarm reception he obtained with the New York audiences accustomed to virtuoso conductors. While not by temperament a propagandist of modern music, he introduced several contemporary works during his conductorship with the N. Y. Philh., among them Benjamin Britten's *Sinfonia da Requiem.* He made transcriptions for string orch. and French horns of 5 pieces from the Fitzwilliam Virginal Book (performed by him under the title *Elizabethan Suite,* Los Angeles, Dec. 4, 1941); wrote an oboe concerto on themes by Pergolesi (dedicated to his wife, Evelyn Rothwell, the oboist). See Charles Rigby, *John Barbirolli* (Altrincham, 1948).

Barblan (bar-blahn), **Otto,** Swiss organist and composer; b. Scanfs, Switzerland, March 22, 1860; d. Geneva, Dec. 19, 1943. He studied at the Stuttgart Cons. (1878-84); made his debut as organist at Augsburg (1885); taught at Chur (1885-87); then became organist at the Cathedral of Geneva; prof. at the Cons. and conductor of the 'Société de Chant Sacré' (1887). He wrote an *Ode Patriotique* (1896); a *Festspiel* (Chur, May 28, 1899) commemorating the 400th anniversary of the battle of Calven, and containing the chorus *Terre des Monts* which has attained great popularity, placing it next to the national anthem as a patriotic song; *Post Tenebras Lux,* cantata for the Calvin jubilee (1909); string quartet; variations and triple fugue on B-A-C-H; Passion according to St. Luke (Geneva, April 9, 1919). Bibl.: A.-E. Cherbuliez in the 'Schweizerische Musikzeitung' (1925, and on Barblan's 70th birthday, 1930); see also his autobiographical note (ibidem, 1929).

Barbot (bahr-boh'), **Joseph-Théodore-Désiré,** French tenor; b. Toulouse, April 12, 1824; d. Paris, Jan. 1, 1897. He studied with Garcia at the Paris Cons.; was engaged to sing at the Paris Opéra in 1848; sang Faust at the premiere of Gounod's opera (March 19, 1859). In 1875 he became prof. at the Paris Cons. succeeding Mme. Viardot.

Barbour, Florence Newell, American composer and pianist; b. Providence, Aug. 4, 1866; d. there, July 24, 1946. She received her education in the U. S.; then traveled through Europe and the Far East. Her works include the piano suites *Holland, Venice, Forest Sketches, A Day in Arcady, At Chamonix* (orch. version was performed at a Boston Pops Concert); piano duets; children's piano pieces and songs; compositions for women's chorus; etc. She wrote *Childland in Song and Rhythm* (1921).

Barbour, J. Murray, American composer and musicologist; b. Chambersburg, Pa., March 31, 1897; studied musicology with Kinkeldey at Cornell Univ.; Ph.D., 1932 (first doctorate in musicology awarded by an American univ.). From 1932-39 taught English and music at Ithaca College; in 1939 appointed Prof. of Musicology at Michigan State College. He publ. a book *Tuning and Temperament* (1951); contributed various learned essays to music magazines; has composed a symph. poem, *Childe Rowland* (1928); a *Requiem;* chamber music; also incidental music to Shakespeare's plays.

Barclay, Arthur (real name, Arthur Barclay Jones); English choral conductor; b. London, Dec. 16, 1869; d. Purley, Surrey, Oct. 12, 1943. He studied at the Guildhall School of Music, where he later taught piano; served as musical director of the Brompton Oratory Choir (1893-1935). He changed his name from Arthur Barclay Jones to Arthur Barclay about 1900. He wrote a symphony (1896); violin sonata; hymns for children and miscellaneous pieces for organ.

Bardi, Benno, conductor and composer; b. Königsberg, April 16, 1890; later settled in England. He studied in Berlin with Humperdinck and Stumpf; was active as an opera coach and later became a conductor at the State Opera. In 1933 he left Germany; spent some time in the U. S., eventually settling in London. He has written incidental music to several of Shakespeare's plays, 3 sinfoniettas and 2 oratorios.

Bardi, Giovanni de', Count of Vernio, Italian nobleman, patron of music and art and composer; b. Florence, Feb. 5, 1534; d. Rome, c. 1612. He was the founder of the Florentine Camerata, a group of musicians who met at his home (1576—c. 1582) to discuss the music of Greek antiquity; this led to the beginnings of opera. Count Bardi was descended from an old Guelph banking family; he was a philologist, mathematician, neo-Platonic philosopher and lover of Dante. He was a member of the Crusca Academy, a literary group founded in 1583 whose ideas had great influence on the Camerata. Bardi is known to have been in Rome in 1567; he lent support to Vincenzo Galilei, a member of the Camerata. In 1580 Bardi married Lucrezia Salvati. The masques of 1589, commemorating the marriage of Grand Duke Ferdinand, were conceived largely by Bardi. In 1592 he left for Rome to become chamberlain at the court of Pope Clement VIII. Caccini was his secretary in 1592. Bardi's writings are: *Discorso sopra il giuoco del calzio fiorentino* (Florence, 1580); *Ristretto delle grandezze di Roma* (Rome, 1600); *Discorso mandato a Caccini sopra la musica antica* in Doni's *Lyra Barberina* (Florence, 1763). Among his compositions are a madrigal in 4 voices *Misere habitator* in Malvezzi's *Intermedi e concerti . . .* (Venice, 1591); the madrigal *Lauro ohime Lauro* in *Il Lauro secco, lib. I . . .* (Ferrara, 1582). Among contemporary documents which refer to him are Vincenzo Galilei's *Dialogo della musica antica e della moderna* (translated in part in O. Strunk's *Source Readings in Music History,* N. Y., 1951; also included is a letter from Bardi's son to G. B. Doni commenting on Bardi's ideas). Bibl.: G. Gasperini, *Intorno alle origini del melodramma* (Rome, 1902); Henriette Martin, *La Camerata du comte Bardi et la musique florentine du XVIe siècle* in the 'Revue de musicologie' (Nov., 1932); Nino Pirrotta, *Temperaments and Tendencies in the Florentine Camerata* in the 'Mus. Quarterly' (April, 1954).

Barge, Wilhelm, German flute player and composer; b. Wulfsahl, Nov. 23, 1836; d. there July 16, 1925. He played in a military band before his appointment as first flutist at the Gewandhaus Orch. in Leipzig; retired on pension in 1895. He publ. a method for flute, 4 sets of orch. flute studies based on passages in classical symph. works; also publ. flute arrangements of various famous works *(Sammlung beliebter Stücke);* edited the flute concertos of Frederick the Great.

Bargiel (bar'-gē-el), **Woldemar,** German composer; b. Berlin, Oct. 3, 1828; d. there Feb. 23, 1897. He was a half-brother of Clara Schumann. As a boy, he sang at the Berlin Cathedral and studied counterpoint with Dehn; and at the Leipzig Cons. (1846-50) with Hauptmann, Moscheles and Gade. He was teacher and conductor in Rotterdam from 1865-74; then returned to Berlin. He was greatly admired by Schumann and Brahms, and his works, in a romantic vein, were frequently performed; almost all of his music was publ. during his lifetime. He wrote a symphony; 3 overtures; string octet; 4 string quartets; 3 piano trios; violin sonatas; numerous piano pieces and songs. Cf. E. Rudorff, *Aus den Tagen der Romantik; Bildnis einer deutschen Familie* (Leipzig, 1938).

Barilli, Bruno, Italian writer on music; b. Fano, Dec. 14, 1880; d. Rome, April 15, 1952. He studied in Parma and later in Munich; his collections of essays are published under the titles *Il sorcio nel violino* and *Il paese del melodramma.* He also wrote 2 operas; *Medusa* (1914; first performed, Bergamo, Sept. 11, 1938) and *Emiral* (Rome, March 11, 1924).

Barini, Giorgio, Italian musicologist; b. Turin, Aug. 23, 1864; d. Rome, Sept. 22, 1944. He is noted for his editions of operas by Paisiello and Cimarosa; was also music critic of various newspapers in Rome. He published *La Donna e L'Artista: Musicisti innamorati* (Rome, 1927) and several essays on Wagner's operas.

Barlow, Harold, American composer of popular songs, bandleader and musical lexicographer; b. Boston, May 15, 1915. He studied violin at Boston Univ., and later played in various orchestras; also led a U. S. Army band. He has compiled two valuable reference works for which he designed an original method of indexing melodic themes by numbers: *A Dictionary of Musical Themes* (with Sam Morgenstern; N. Y., 1948); and *A Dictionary of Vocal Themes* (N. Y., 1950).

Barlow, Howard, American conductor; b. Plain City, Ohio, May 1, 1892. He studied at the Univ. of Colorado and at Columbia Univ. He conducted the American National Orch., N. Y. (1923-25), at the Neighborhood Playhouse (1925-27); was conductor of the C.B.S. Symph. Orch. (1927-43), with which he presented numerous new works. In 1943 he became conductor of the Firestone Hour on NBC Radio.

Barlow, Samuel, American composer; b. N. Y., June 1, 1892; studied music at Harvard Univ. (B.A., 1914); then took lessons with Respighi in Rome. His one-act opera, *Mon ami Pierrot,* was the first by an American composer to be given at the Opéra-Comique in Paris (Jan. 11, 1935); he wrote also 2 more operas, *Eugénie* and *Amanda.* His 'symphonic concerto' *Babar* (1935) employs magic lantern slides. Other works: piano concerto (Rochester, Jan. 23, 1931, composer-soloist); a suite of *Biedermeier Waltzes* for orch. (Rome, 1935); *Sousa ad Parnassum* for orch. (1939); several songs and choruses. A believer in mass education, Barlow has been active in various civic groups formed to promote music; has organized rural festivals; also has lectured and written about music and politics.

Barlow, Wayne, American composer; b. Elyria, Ohio, Sept. 6, 1912. He studied with Hanson and Rogers at the Eastman School of Music, Rochester, N. Y.; later with Schoenberg in Los Angeles; teaching composition at the Eastman School since 1937. He has written a ballet *The Black Madonna* (1941); *The Winter's Passed* for oboe and strings (Rochester, Oct. 18, 1938); *Three Moods* for orch. (1940); *Lyrical Piece* for clarinet and strings (1945); *Nocturne* for 18 instruments (1946); *Sinfonia* in C (1950); mass in G (1951) and a piano quintet (1951). Also publ. an appreciation book, *Foundations of Music* (N. Y., 1953).

Bärmann, Heinrich Joseph, German clarinetist; b. Potsdam, Feb. 14, 1784; d. Munich, June 11, 1847. He was a renowned performer; made extensive tours, and finally settled in Munich as first clarinetist of the court orchestra; his friends, Weber and Mendelssohn, wrote clarinet works for him. He composed concertos, fantasias, quintets, quartets, sonatas, etc. for his instrument, about 90 works in all; 38 have been published, and are still favorites with clarinetists.

Bärmann, Carl, German clarinetist, son of Heinrich Joseph Bärmann; b. Munich, Oct. 24, 1811; d. there, May 23, 1885. He was a pupil of his father, whom he accompanied on his tours; later succeeded him at the Munich court orchestra. He wrote a method for clarinet, with a supplement entitled *Materalien zur weiteren technischen Ausbildung.*

Bärmann (Baermann), Karl (Jr.), pianist and music pedagogue, son of the preceding; b. Munich, July 9, 1839; d. Boston, Jan. 17, 1913. He studied piano with Wanner, Wohlmuth and Liszt; and composition with Franz Lachner; was appointed teacher at the Munich Cons., but emigrated to the U. S. in 1881. He settled in Boston.

Barmas, Issaye, Russian violinist and pedagogue; b. Odessa, May 1, 1872; d. London, July 3, 1946. He studied in Moscow and with Joachim in Berlin; toured in Europe; settled in London. Among his publications are *Die Lösung des Geigentechnischen Problems* (1913); *Tonleiter-Spezialstudien; Doppelgriff Spezialstudien;* and many editions of classical works.

Barnard, Charlotte (née **Alington**), English song writer (pen name Claribel); b. Dec. 23, 1830; d. Dover, Jan. 30, 1869. Her ballad *Come Back to Erin* and numerous others in a similar vein were once extremely popular. She also published verses.

Barnby, Sir Joseph, English conductor, organist, and composer; b. York, Aug. 12, 1838; d. London, Jan. 28, 1896. He came from a musical family; sang in the choir of the York Minster at the age of seven; was organist and chorusmaster there at the age of twelve; then studied at the Royal Academy in London with Cipriani Potter (1854); held the post of organist at St. Michael's, St. James the Less, the Sacred Harmonic Society, at St. Andrews (1863-71), and St. Anne's (1871). In 1864 he organized Barnby's Choir, which gave five annual series of oratorio concerts in London; then became director of the Royal Albert Hall Choral Society; conducted at the Cardiff Festival (1892; 1895), and at the South Wales Festival. In 1874 he inaugurated a series of daily concerts at Albert Hall; conducted the London Music Society (1878-86), and with it performed Dvořák's *Stabat Mater* for the first time in England (March 10, 1883). In 1875 he was appointed precentor and director of music at Eton; in 1892 succeeded Thomas Weist-Hill as Principal of the Guildhall School of Music. He was knighted on Aug. 5, 1892. Barnby composed the sacred works *Rebekah,* an oratorio (1870); *Psalm 97* (1883); a service in 3 parts (morning, noon, and evening); a *Magnificat* and *Nunc dimittis* for chorus, organ, and orch. (1881); *King all-glorious* (motet for soli, chorus, organ and orch.); 45 anthems; 246 hymn-tunes (complete collection, 1897); organ pieces; piano pieces.

Barnekow, Christian, composer; b. St. Sauveur, France, July 28, 1837; d. Copenhagen, March 20, 1913. He adapted many songs by K. Ph. E. Bach, J. Chr. Fr. Bach, Schulz, etc.; also composed chamber music, organ works and much sacred music.

Barnes, Edward Shippen, American organist and composer; b. Seabright, N. J., Sept. 14, 1887. He studied at Yale Univ. with David Stanley Smith and Horatio Parker (comp.) and with Harry B. Jepson (organ); later took lessons with Louis Vierne in Paris. He was organist and choirmaster at Rutgers Presbyterian Church, N. Y., at St. Stephen's Episcopal Church in Santa Monica, Cal.; retired in 1954, after 45 years of service as organist. He wrote 2 organ symphonies; the cantatas *The Comforter, Remember Now Thy Creator* and *Christmas;* an Episcopal Service; several sacred songs, and the manuals: *School of Organ Playing; Modulation in Theory and Practice,* and *Bach for Beginners in Organ Playing.* He also published several collections of choral works for schools.

Barnett, Alice, American song composer; b. Lewiston, Ill., May 26, 1886; studied with Borowski and Ganz in Chicago and with Hugo Kaun in Berlin; in 1917 settled in San Diego. She wrote a number of agreeable songs in a romantic manner. —— Cf. W. T. Upton, *Art-Song in America* (N. Y., 1930; pp. 214-224).

Barnett, John, English composer; b. Bedford, July 1, 1802; d. Cheltenham, April 17, 1890. He was a pupil of Charles Edward Horn and Ferdinand Ries; brought out an operetta, *Before Breakfast* (London, 1825); then many small pieces. His most successful opera was *The Mountain Sylph* (Lyceum Theatre, London, Aug. 25, 1834); he subsequently produced the operas *Fair Rosamond* (London, Feb. 28, 1837) and *Farinelli* (London, Feb. 8, 1839). In 1841 he settled in Cheltenham as a singing teacher. Among his other works are a symphony, 2 string quartets, and nearly 4,000 songs; he also published a *School for the Voice* (1844).

Barnett, John Francis, English composer; nephew of the preceding; b. London, Oct. 16, 1837; d. there, Nov. 24, 1916. He studied piano with Dr. Wylde (1849); twice won the Queen's Scholarship at the Royal Academy of Music (1850; 1852); gave his first piano recital at the New Philharmonic Concerts in London (July 4, 1853); later studied at the Leipzig Cons. (1856-9) with Moscheles, Plaidy and Hauptmann; then settled in London as teacher, concert pianist, and conductor; was appointed prof. at the Royal College of Music (1883). Works: a symphony (1864); *Ouverture symphonique* (London, 1868); overture to Shakespeare's *A Winter's Tale* (1873); *The Lay of the Last Minstrel* for orch. (after Scott; Liverpool, 1874); orchestral suite, *The Harvest Festival* (Norwich, 1881); 4 sketches for orch.: *Ebbing Tide* and *Elfland* (Crystal Palace, London, 1883); *Flowing Tide* and *Fairyland* (Crystal Palace, London, 1891); also for orch. *Pastoral Suite* (1892); *Liebeslied* and *Im alten Styl* (1895); *Pensée mélodique* and *Gavotte* (1899); the cantatas *The Ancient Mariner,* after Coleridge (Birmingham, 1867); *Paradise and the Peri,* after Moore (Birmingham, 1870); *The Building of the Ship* (Leeds, 1880); *The Wishing-Bell* (Norwich, 1881); *The Triumph of Labour* (Crystal Palace, London, 1888); *The Eve of St. Agnes,* after Keats (London, 1913); oratorios, *The Raising of Lazarus* (Hereford, 1876); *The Good Shepherd,* (Brighton, 1876); *The Golden Gate,* scena for contralto; a piano concerto; flute concerto; chamber music; piano pieces; songs; published *Musical Reminiscences and Impressions* (London, 1906).

Barnett, John Manley, American conductor; b. N. Y., Sept. 3, 1917. He studied piano, violin and trumpet at the Manhattan School of Music (1930-36); conducting with Leon Barzin in New York, and with Bruno Walter, Weingartner, Enesco and Malko in Europe (1936-37). Returning to America, he became conductor of the Stamford Symph. Orch (1939-42) and of the N. Y. City Symphony (1940-42); then a U. S. Army bandleader (1942-46). Since 1946, assistant conductor of the Los Angeles Philh.; since 1952 has directed the summer concerts at the Hollywood Bowl.

Barns, Ethel, English violinist and composer; b. London, 1880; d. Maidenhead, Dec. 31, 1948. She studied at the Royal Academy in London; made her debut at the Crystal Palace (1896); toured England (1897) and America (1913). Her compositions include a *Concertstück* for violin and orch.; 2 trios; *Phantasy* for 2 violins and piano; 5 violin sonatas.

Baron (bah-rohn'), **Ernst Gottlieb,** German lutenist; b. Breslau, Feb. 17, 1696; d. Berlin, April 12, 1760. He was a court musician in Gotha (1727); theorbist to the Prussian Crown Prince (later Frederick II) in 1734; wrote *Historisch-theoretische und praktische Untersuchung des Instruments der Laute* (1727); an Appendix (on the lute) to Marpurg's *Historisch-kritische Beiträge,* vol. II; an *Abhandlung von dem Notensystem der Laute und der Theorbe;* other theoretical pamphlets; composed many works for the lute, which remain in MS.

Baron (băh-rŏhn'), **Maurice,** composer and conductor; b. Lille, France, Jan. 1, 1889. He studied in France; emigrated to the U. S. and conducted stage shows in New York. He has published numerous pieces of light music under his own name and the whimsical *noms de plume:* Francis Delille (i.e., "de Lille," a native of Lille); Morris Aborn (anagram of Baron); also used the name of his wife Alice Tremblay. Also wrote: choreographic suite *Susan at the Zoo;* symphonic paean *Blood, Sweat and Tears; Ode to Democracy* for narrator, chorus and orch. (N. Y. Philh., Jan. 23, 1949); etc., totalling more than 300 works. From 1933-43 he was arranger and staff composer at Radio City Music Hall, N. Y.

Baronius. See **Baron, Ernst Gottlieb.**

Barraine, Elsa, French composer; b. Paris, Feb. 13, 1910. Her father was a cellist, her mother a singer. She studied at the Paris Cons. with Dukas and Vidal; received 2nd Prix de Rome (1928) and then 1st Prix de Rome (1929). She has written Symphony No. 1 (1931); *Trois esquisses* for orch. (1931); *Pogromes,* symph. poem (1933; Paris, March 11, 1939); *Fantaisie concertante* for piano and orch. (1933); *Fête des Colonies* (1937); Symphony No. 2 (1938); *Le Fleuve Rouge,* symph. variations (1945); Symphony No. 3 (1947); *Suite astrologique* for orch. (1947); chamber music; piano pieces and songs.

Barraud, Henry, French composer; b. Bordeaux, April 23, 1900. He taught himself music while engaged in the family wine business in Bordeaux; in 1926, entered the Paris Cons. and studied composition with Aubert. In 1937 Barraud was in charge of the music for the International Exposition in Paris. He served in the French Army during World War II; after demobilization he lived in Marseilles, returning to Paris in 1943. In 1945 he was appointed musical director of Radiodiffusion Française, Paris. Works: *Finale dans le mode rustique* (Paris, 1932); *Poème* for orch. (1934); *Concerto da Camera* for 30 instruments (1936); *Le Diable à la Kermesse,* ballet (1943; a symph. suite from it was broadcast by Paris Radio, April 26, 1945); piano concerto (N. Y. Philh., Dec. 5, 1946); *Offrande à une ombre* (in memory of a brother killed by the Germans as a member of the Resistance; first U. S. performance, St. Louis, Jan. 10, 1947); *La Farce du Maître Pathelin* (Paris, June 24, 1948); *Symphonie de Numance* (Baden-Baden, Dec. 3, 1950); trio for oboe, clarinet and bassoon; *Préludes* for piano (2 series) and songs. He also wrote a book on Berlioz (Paris, 1955).

Barrère (băh-rär'), **Georges,** French flute virtuoso; b. Bordeaux, Oct. 31, 1876; d. Kingston, N. Y., June 14, 1944. He studied at the Paris Cons. (1889-95), graduating with first prize; was solo flutist at Colonne Concerts and at the Paris Opéra (1897-1905). He came to America in 1905; played flute with the N. Y. Symph. Orch. (1905-28); taught at the Institute of Musical Art, N. Y., and at the Juilliard School of Music. He was the founder of the 'Barrère Little Symphony' (1914); composed a *Nocturne* for flute; *Chanson d'automne* for voice; also edited classical works for flute.

Barret (bah-rā'), **Apollon (Marie-Rose),** French oboist; b. Paris, 1803; d. London, March 8, 1879. He studied at the Paris Cons.; played in the orchestras at opera houses; in 1874 went to London with the Italian Opera. Barret is the author of a standard manual, 'Complete Method for the Oboe Comprising All The New Fingerings, New Tables of Shakes, Scales, Exercises'.

Barrett, Reginald, English organist; b. London, Jan. 12, 1861; d. St. Petersburg, Florida, Feb. 7, 1940. He studied at the Guildhall School of Music and at Darmstadt Cons.; came to the U. S. in 1888; was organist in Kansas City until 1898, when he settled in New York City as organist at St. James Church, Fordham. From 1917 until 1925 he played the organ in motion picture theaters. He composed some 100 preludes and interludes for organ, sacred songs, choruses, etc.

Barrett, William Alexander, English writer on music; b. London, Oct. 15, 1834; d. there Oct. 17, 1891. As a boy, he was a chorister in St. Paul's Cathedral; then studied at Oxford (B. Mus., 1871). From 1881 he occupied various positions as inspector of music; was music critic of 'The Morning Post' from 1867 until his death; was editor of 'The Monthly Musical Record' (1877) and of 'The Musical Times.' He publ. *English Glee and Madrigal Writers* (1877); *English Church Composers* (1882); *Balfe: His Life and Work* (1882); etc.; was co-editor with Sir John Stainer of the *Dictionary of Musical Terms* (1875; new edition, 1898). His son, **Francis Barrett** (b. London, Nov. 14, 1869; d there Jan. 19, 1925), was also a music critic.

Barrientos, Maria, celebrated Spanish coloratura soprano; b. Barcelona, March 10, 1884; d. Ciboure, France, Aug. 8, 1946. She studied voice with Bonet; made her operatic debut at the age of 15 as Selika in the Teatro de las Novedades, Barcelona (March 4, 1899); toured Europe and South America (1899-1913). She made her first appearance at the Metropolitan Opera House as Lucia (Jan. 31, 1916), and remained with it until 1920; then settled in France, where she gave song recitals.

Barrington, Daines, English lawyer; b. London, 1727; d. there, March 14, 1800. He was the author of the famous account of Mozart as a child prodigy ('Philosophical Transactions', 1770), reprinted in his *Miscellanies* (1781); also wrote essays on Crotch, Mornington, the Wesleys (father and son); *Experiments and Observations on the Singing of Birds* (London, 1773); a description of the ancient Welsh crwth and pibcorn; etc.

Barrows, John, American composer and horn player; b. Glendale, Calif., February 12, 1913. He studied at the Eastman School in Rochester, and later at Yale with Donovan and Smith. Among his works are 2 string quartets, a wind trio, several sonatas for various instruments with piano, etc.

Barrozo Netto, Joaquim Antonio, Brazilian composer; b. Rio de Janeiro, Jan. 30, 1881; d. there, Sept. 1, 1941. He studied with Braga, Nepomuceno and others; appeared as pianist in public at an early age; his compositions, in a mildly romantic manner, are mostly for piano. He enjoyed a fine reputation in Brazil as a teacher; was prof. at the Instituto Nacional de Musica from 1906.

Barry, Charles Ainslie, English organist, and music editor; b. London, June 10, 1830; d. there, March 21, 1915. He studied with Walmisley; later at the Cologne Cons.; also with Moscheles, Plaidy and Richter at the Leipzig Cons. Returning to England, he wrote for various music magazines; was editor of 'The Monthly Musical Record' (1875-79); also served as an annotator for orchestral programs conducted by Richter in England.

Barsanti, Francesco, Italian flutist and composer; b. Lucca, c. 1690; d. c. 1760. He was flutist and, later, oboist at the Italian Opera in London; lived in Scotland for a time, and was engaged (1750) as a viola player in London. Works: 6 overtures; 12 violin concertos; 6 flute solos with bass; 6 sonatas for 2 violins with bass; 6 antiphons in Palestrina style; numerous pieces for various instruments. He published *A Collection of old Scots Tunes* (Edinburgh, 1742). Cf. Henry Farmer, *A History of Music in Scotland* (London, 1947).

Barsotti, Tommaso Gasparo Fortunato, Italian music teacher; b. Florence, Sept. 4, 1786; d. Marseilles, April, 1868. He founded the Free School of Music in Marseilles (1821), and was its director until 1852; wrote a number of pieces for piano and voice; published a *Méthode de Musique* (1828).

Barstow, Vera, American violinist; b. Celina, Ohio, June 3, 1893; studied in Pittsburgh with Luigi von Kunits; made her debut in Vienna (Jan. 2, 1912); returning to America, appeared with the Boston Symph. Orch., Philadelphia Orch., etc. She settled in Los Angeles as a teacher.

Bartay (bar'-ti), **Andreas,** Hungarian composer; b. Szeplak, 1798; d. Mainz, Oct. 4, 1856. He was director of the National Theater in Budapest (1838); gave concerts in Paris (1848); then settled in Hamburg. He wrote three operas: *Aurelia; Csel;* and *The Hungarians in Naples;* oratorios; masses; ballets.

Bartay, Ede, Hungarian composer, son of Andreas Bartay; b. Oct. 6, 1825; d. Budapest, Aug. 31, 1901. He was director of the National Music Academy in Budapest; founded the Hungarian pension-fund for musicians; wrote an overture, *Pericles,* and other works.

Bartels, Wolfgang von, German composer; b. Hamburg, July 21, 1883; d. Munich, April 19, 1938. He studied with Beer-Walbrunn in Munich and with Gédalge in Paris; then became a music critic in Munich. His early works show impressionist influences; later he adopted an eclectic style. Works: melodramas, *The Little Dream,* after Galsworthy (Manchester, 1911); *The Spanish Lovers,* after Rojas (London, 1912); *Li-I-Lan* (Kassel, 1918); song cycles *(Li-Tai-Pe, Baltic Songs, Minnesänge);* violin concerto; viola concerto, etc.

Barth, Christian Samuel, German oboist and composer; b. Glauchau, Jan. 13, 1735; d. Copenhagen, July 8, 1809. He was a student at the Thomasschule in Leipzig at the time of Bach; played the oboe in various court orchestras: in Rudolfstadt (1753); Weimar (1762); Hanover (1768) and Kassel (1772). In 1786 he joined the court chapel at Copenhagen where he remained until his death. Although he wrote a great number of instrumental works, particularly for the oboe, most of them remain in manuscript.

Barth, Hans, pianist and composer; b. Leipzig, June 25, 1897. When a small child, he won a scholarship at the Leipzig Cons. and studied under Carl Reinecke; came to the U. S. in 1907, but made frequent trips to Germany. His meeting with Busoni inspired him to experiment with new scales; with the aid of George L. Weitz, he perfected a portable quarter-tone piano (1928), on which he played in Carnegie Hall (Feb. 3, 1930); composed a piano concerto for this instrument, with a string orchestra also tuned in quarter-tones (perf. by him with Stokowski and the Philadelphia Orch., March 28, 1930). Other works using quarter-tones: suite for strings, brass and kettledrums; piano quintet; also a piano concerto for normal tuning (1928) and two piano sonatas; an operetta *Miragia* (1938); a piano manual, *Technic* (1935); various essays, etc. Barth has held numerous teaching positions in New York City.

Barth, Karl Heinrich, German pianist and teacher; b. Pillau, near Königsberg, July 12, 1847; d. Berlin, Dec. 23, 1922. He was a pupil of Hans von Bülow in Berlin; also studied with Bronsart and Tausig. He became teacher at Stern Cons., Berlin, in 1868; then at the Hochschule für Musik (1871); established the Barth Trio with de Ahna and Hausmann, which enjoyed considerable success.

Barthe (bahrt), **Grat-Norbert,** French composer; b. Bayonne, June 7, 1828; d. Asnières (Seine), Aug. 13, 1898. He was a pupil of Leborne at the Paris Cons.; won the Grand Prix de Rome (1854) with the cantata *Francesca da Rimini;* wrote the operas *Don Carlos* and *La Fiancée d'Abydos;* an oratorio, *Judith;* etc.

Barth, Richard, German left-handed violin virtuoso; b. Grosswanzleben, June 5, 1850; d. Marburg, Dec. 25, 1923. He studied with Joachim in Hanover; attracted considerable attention when he gave concerts using the left hand for the bow; was also conductor in Münster, Krefeld and Hamburg. He wrote chamber music in the style of Brahms; edited the correspondence between Brahms and J. O. Grimm (1908); was author of *Johannes Brahms und seine Musik* (1904). Bibl.: E. Deggeller-Engelke, *Richard Barth* (Marburg, 1949).

Barthélemon (băhr-tāl-mohn'), **François-Hippolyte,** French violinist and dramatic composer; b. Bordeaux, July 27, 1741; d. London, July 20, 1808. His father was French and his mother Irish. He held posts as violinist in various theater orchestras in London; became intimately acquainted with Haydn during Haydn's London visit in 1792. He was greatly praised as a violinist; Burney speaks of his tone as being "truly vocal." Barthélemon wrote mostly for the stage; among his operas, the most notable are *Pelopida* (London, May 24, 1766); *The Judgement of Paris* (London, Aug. 24, 1768); *Le Fleuve Scamandre* (Paris, Dec. 22, 1768); *The Maid of the Oaks* (London, Nov. 5, 1774); *Belphegor* (London, March 16, 1778). In addition he wrote a violin concerto; 2 sets of duos for violins; 6 string quartets; catches and glees to English words (many of them published). He was married to Mary Young, a descendant of Anthony Young; his daughter contributed a biographical memoir as a preface to a posthumous edition (London, 1827) of selections from Barthélemon's oratorio, *Jefte in Masfa.*

Bartholomew, Marshall, American choral conductor; b. Belleville, Ill., March 3, 1885. He studied at Yale University (B. A. 1907) with Horatio Parker and David Stanley Smith, and later in Berlin. Returning to America, he devoted himself mainly to choral conducting and arranging. In 1921 he founded the Yale Glee Club, which he conducted until 1928, and again from 1939-48; also during its South American tour in 1940-41. He publ. choral arrangements of American folk music; the *Yale Glee Club Series* for male voices (32 numbers); *Songs of*

Yale (a book of 128 college songs); *Mountain Songs of North Carolina;* various songs for solo voice and piano; *100 Original Songs for Young Voices* (educational).

Bartholomew, William, English violinist, writer and painter; b. London, 1793; d. there Aug. 18, 1867. A versatile artisan, he was proficient in chemistry, painting and languages. He was a friend of Mendelssohn and translated the texts of his oratorios (including *Elijah*) into English; also wrote the English text for Spohr's *Jessonda,* etc. During the last years of his life he was incapacitated by paralysis.

Bartlett, Ethel, English pianist; b. London, June 6, 1900; studied at the Royal Academy of Music with Tobias Matthay, and later with Schnabel. She specialized as piano duet player with her husband, Rae Robertson; made annual tours in Europe and the U.S. She edited, with her husband, the *Two Piano Series* (publ. by the Oxford Univ. Press).

Bartlett, Homer Newton, American pianist, organist and composer; b. Olive, N. Y., Dec. 28, 1845; d. Hoboken, N. J., April 3, 1920. He studied with Max Braun and Jacobsen; was organist at the Madison Avenue Baptist Church, N. Y., for 31 years. He was one of the founders of the American Guild of Organists. His published works include a cantata, *The Last Chieftain* (Boston, Jan. 29, 1891); a sextet for flute and strings; quartets, anthems, carols, etc.; about 80 songs and piano pieces. The following are in manuscript: opera, *La Vallière;* unfinished Japanese opera *Hinotito;* oratorio, *Samuel;* symph. poem, *Apollo;* a violin concerto; a cello concerto; etc. His first opus number, a *Grand Polka de Concert,* was very popular.

Bartmuss, Richard, German organist and composer; b. Schleesen, Dec. 23, 1859; d. Dessau, Dec. 25, 1910. He studied with Grell and Löschhorn; in 1885 became court organist in Dessau. He wrote numerous organ works that enjoyed considerable popularity, among them 2 organ concertos, 4 sonatas, 2 chorale-fantasias, etc.; also an oratorio *Der Tag der Pfingsten,* a cantata *Die Apostel in Philippi,* motets and songs. His sacred work *Liturgische Vespern* represents a partial formulation of his attempt to modernize the Lutheran musical service.

Bartók, Béla, foremost Hungarian composer; b. Nagy Szent Miklós, Transylvania, March 25, 1881; d. New York, Sept. 26, 1945. He studied with L. Erkel at Pozsony (Bratislava) and with Koessler at the Royal Academy of Music in Budapest; in 1907 he was appointed instructor. After World War I he was a member of the Music Directorate with Dohnányi and Kodály. Although a brilliant pianist, he confined his appearances mostly to his own music; also gave concerts with his second wife, Ditta Pasztory, playing works for 2 pianos. From his earliest steps as composer he was attracted both by folk music of eastern Europe and by modern devices in composition. His early works bear the influence of French impressionism. As he began to feel the fascination of primitive rhythms and melodies, his style gradually became more terse and acrid. The basic texture of his music remained true to tonality, while freely tolerating discordant harmonic combinations; in his instrumental works the melodic line is often atonal, but he never used the integral technique of the 12-tone method. He traveled widely in Europe; made his first tour in the United States in 1927-28, playing with orchestras and in concerts from coast to coast. Upon his return to Europe he continued to teach and compose in Budapest; in the fall of 1940 he went to America, where he remained till his death. The influence of Bartók's music on young composers in Hungary and elsewhere is very great, and has continued to increase since his death. The dual aspect of his style, embodying elements of Hungarian folk music and modern devices of polytonality and atonality, presents a solution for those modernists who are reluctant to abandon national melodic expression. Posthumous honors were given to Bartók in Hungary by naming one of the Budapest streets after him. Works: *Kossuth,* symph. poem (Budapest, Jan. 13, 1904); *Scherzo* for orch. (Budapest, Feb. 29, 1904); Rhapsody for piano (1904; also for orch.); Suite No. 1 for orch. (1905); 20 Hungarian folksongs (1906); Suite No. 2 for orch. (1907; revised 1943); *2 Portraits* for orch. (1908); 14 Bagatelles for piano (1908); string quartet No. 1 (1910); 2 Elegies for piano (1908); 7 Sketches for piano (1910; revised 1945); 2 Rumanian Dances for piano (1909); *Deux images* for orch. (1910; Budapest, Feb. 26, 1913); 3 Burlesques for piano (1910); *The Castle of Duke Bluebeard,* opera in 1 act (1911; Budapest, May 24, 1918); *Allegro barbaro* for piano (1911; very popular); 4 Pieces for orch. (1912); *The Wooden Prince,* ballet in 1 act (Budapest, May 12, 1917); string quartet No. 2 (1917); 3 Etudes for piano (1918); *The Miraculous Mandarin,* ballet (1919; Cologne, Nov. 27, 1926);

violin sonata No. 1 (1921); violin sonata No. 2 (1922); dance suite for orch. (1923); piano sonata (1926); piano concerto No. 1 (Frankfurt, July 1, 1927, composer as soloist); string quartet No. 3 (1927); 2 Rhapsodies for violin and piano (1928); string quartet No. 4 (1928); *Cantata Profana* (BBC, London, May 25, 1934); piano concerto No. 2 (1931); string quartet No. 5 (1934); *Music for String Instruments, Percussion and Celesta* (Basel, Jan. 21, 1937; one of Bartók's most successful works); Sonata for 2 pianos and percussion (Basel, Jan. 16, 1938; transcribed as Concerto for 2 pianos and orch.; perf. in this form by Béla and Ditta Bartók with the N. Y. Philh., Jan. 21, 1943; also an enduring work); *Mikrokosmos,* 153 progressive pieces for piano (1926-37; publ. in 6 vols.; a unique attempt to write simply in a modern idiom with varying meters and dissonant counterpoint); *Contrasts* for violin, clarinet and piano (1938); violin concerto (Amsterdam, April 23, 1939; has become a standard piece in the modern repertory); *Divertimento* for string orch. (Basel, June 11, 1940); string quartet No. 6 (1939); Concerto for orch. (commissioned by Koussevitzky; perf. by him, Boston, Dec. 1, 1944; highly successful); sonata for solo violin (1944); piano concerto No. 3 (1945; unfinished); viola concerto (1945; unfinished; orchestrated by Tibor Serly; first perf., Minneapolis, Dec. 2, 1949). In addition to these Bartók made numerous arrangements of folksongs and dances, of which a set of Rumanian dances, available in various instrumental transcriptions, is particularly popular; further to be noted are: 40 Hungarian folksongs; 15 Hungarian peasant songs; 9 Slovak folksongs; 8 improvisations on Hungarian peasant songs for piano; also arrangements for orch. of many of these songs. Scholarly editions and research publications; *Rumanian Folksongs from the Bihor District* (Bucharest, 1913); *Transylvanian Folksongs* (Budapest, 1923; in Hungarian, French and English; with Kodály); *A magyar népdal* (Budapest, 1924; in German as *Das ungarische Volkslied,* Berlin, 1925; in English as *Hungarian Folk Music,* London, 1931); *Our Folk Music* (Budapest, 1934; in Hungarian, German and French); *Die Melodien der rumänischen Colinde* (Vienna, 1935); *Serbo-Croatian Folk Songs* (with Albert B. Lord; N. Y., 1951); articles in various musical magazines, among them *Hungarian Peasant Music,* in the 'Mus. Quarterly' (July, 1933). An entire literature exists dealing with Bartók's life and music; the most comprehensive biography is by Halsey Stevens, *The Life and Music of Béla Bartók* (N. Y., 1953). See also E. Haraszti, *Béla Bartók* (Budapest, 1930; in English, 1938); A. Molnár, *The Art of Bartók* (Budapest, 1948, in Hungarian); S. Moreux, *Béla Bartók, sa vie, ses oeuvres, son langage* (Paris, 1949; in German, Zürich, 1950; in English, London, 1953); B. Rondi, *Bartók* (Rome, 1950); M. Seiber, *The String Quartets of Béla Bartók* (London, 1945). A memorial collection of articles on Bartók was issued by his publishers, Boosey & Hawkes (N. Y., 1950); a special Bartók number of 'La Revue Musicale' appeared in 1955.

Bartoš (bahr-tosh), **František,** Moravian music editor; b. Mlatcová, March 16, 1837; d. there, June 11, 1906. He was a school teacher; published important collections of Moravian folk songs between 1873 and 1901; also wrote essays on Moravian folklore.

Bartoš (bahr-tosh), **Jan Zdeněk,** Czech composer; b. Králové Dvur nad Labem, June 4, 1908. He began to study music rather late; took courses with Jirák and Kricka in Prague; in 1945 he entered government service. He has written 2 operas, a ballet, 2 cantatas, many choral works, 3 string quartets; and a quintet for flute, violin, viola, cello and guitar.

Bartoš (bahr-tosh), **Josef,** Czech writer on music; b. Vysoké Mýto, March 4, 1887. He studied with Hostinsky at the Univ. of Prague (1905-9); was active as a teacher and writer; published monographs on Dvořák (1913), Fibich (1914), J. B. Foerster (1922), and Otakar Ostrčil (1936); also an important work on the National Opera of Prague (1938).

Barvik, Miroslav, Czech composer; b. Lužiča, Sept. 14, 1919. He studied with V. Kaprál at the Brno Cons., and with Novák in Prague. Since 1948, instructor in composition at the Prague Cons. Among his works are a Symphony (1944); 2 string quartets (1940, 1944); and the patriotic and political cantatas: *Song of the Fatherland* (1944); *Thanks to the Soviet Union* (1946); *Hands Off Korea* (1950).

Bary, Alfred Erwin von, opera singer; b. La Valetta, Malta, Jan. 18, 1873; d. Munich, Sept. 13, 1926. He studied medicine at Munich Univ. (Dr. med., 1898); later developed his dramatic tenor voice, and was engaged at the Dresden Court Opera (1902-12); then at the Court Opera in Munich; sang the roles of Parsifal, Siegmund and Tristan at Bayreuth.

Barzin (bahr-zahn'), **Leon,** conductor; b. Brussels, Nov. 27, 1900. He was brought to the U.S. in 1902; his father was first viola player in the orchestra of the Metropolitan Opera; his mother was a ballerina. He studied violin with his father, and later with Henrotte, Deru and Eugène Ysaÿe. He settled in New York; played the violin in various orchestras there; in 1925 he was appointed first viola player of the New York Philharmonic, retaining this position until 1929, when he was engaged as assistant conductor of the American Orchestral Society; it was reorganized the following year as the National Orchestral Association, with Barzin as principal conductor and musical director. He has appeared as guest conductor with the N. Y. Philh. at the Lewisohn Stadium; was conductor of the Hartford Symph. Orch. (1938-40); also conducted in Europe. He is particularly successful in training semi-professional orchestral ensembles.

Barzun, Jacques, French-American educator and author of books on music; b. Paris, Nov. 30, 1907. He came to the U.S. in 1919; studied at Columbia Univ. (A.B., 1927; Ph.D., 1932); became lecturer in history there in 1927; professor in 1945. Among his writings concerned with music are *Darwin, Marx, Wagner* (Boston, 1941); and *Berlioz and the Romantic Century* (Boston, 1950; 2 vols. with exhaustive documentation). He is also editor and translator of *New Letters of Berlioz* (N.Y., 1954); publ. a new translation of Berlioz's *Evenings with the Orchestra* (N. Y., 1956); also wrote a survey, *Music in American Life* (N. Y., 1956).

Bas, Giulio, Italian organist and music editor; b. Venice, April 21, 1874; d. Vobbia, near Genoa, July 27, 1929. He studied in Munich with Rheinberger and in Venice with Bossi; was organist and conductor at churches in Venice, Calvi, Teano and Rome (S. Luigi de' Francesi); after 1908 taught at the Milan Cons.; composed church music and many pieces for organ. He contributed to musical publications, and was editor of 'Musica d'oggi'; wrote textbooks on formal analysis, harmony and counterpoint, including *Metodo per l'accompagnamento del canto gregoriano e per la composizione negli otto modi* (translated into French and Dutch); *Manuale di canto gregoriano* (also in Spanish); *Trattato di forma musicale,* etc.

Baselt, Fritz (Friedrich Gustav Otto), composer; b. Oels, Silesia, May 26, 1863; d. there, Nov. 12, 1931. He studied with Emil Kohler in Breslau and with Ludwig Bussler in Berlin; was musician, music-dealer, composer, teacher and conductor in Breslau, Essen and Nuremberg; after 1894 he settled in Frankfurt-on-Main, where he conducted the Philharmonischer Verein and the Frankfurt Sängervereinigung. He wrote many light operas: *Der Fürst von Sevilla* (Nuremberg, 1888); *Don Alvaro* (Ansbach, 1892); *Der Sohn des Peliden* (Kassel, 1893); *Die Annaliese* (Kassel, 1896); *Die Musketiere im Damenstift* (Kassel, 1896); *Die Circusfee* (Berlin, 1897); also 2 ballets: *Die Altweibermühle* (Frankfurt, 1906), and *Rokoko* (Frankfurt, 1907); some 100 male choruses; many instrumental pieces; songs.

Basevi, Abramo, Italian composer and writer on music; b. Leghorn, Dec. 29, 1818; d. Florence, Nov. 25, 1885. His 2 operas, *Romilda ed Ezzelino* (Florence, Aug. 11, 1840) and *Enrico Odoardo* (Florence, 1847), were unsuccessful, and he turned to musical journalism; founded the periodical 'Harmonia'; publ. a *Studio sulle opere di G. Verdi* (1859); *Studi sul armonia* (1865); *Compendio della storia della musica* (1866); etc.

Basil (Saint) the Great; b. 329 at Caesarea, Cappadocia; d. there in 379. He was a bishop in Caesarea; is reputed to have introduced congregational (antiphonal) singing into the Eastern Church, thus being the forerunner of St. Ambrose in the Western.

Basili, Francesco, Italian composer; b. Loreto, Feb., 1767; d. Rome, March 25, 1850. He was a pupil of his father, **Andrea Basili** (1720-1777); later of Jannaconi at Rome; was conductor at Foligno, Macerata and Loreto; produced 14 operas and several 'dramatic oratorios' in Rome, Naples, Florence, Milan and Venice; appointed to the faculty of the Milan Cons. (1827); in 1837 became conductor at St. Peter's in Rome. He wrote a Requiem (for Jannaconi, 1816); several symphonies; much sacred music; piano sonatas; songs; etc.

Bassani, Geronimo, Italian singer and composer; b. Padua, late in the 17th century. He studied with Lotti; was a fine contrapuntist, singer and singing teacher; produced 2 operas at Venice: *Bertoldo* (1718) and *Amor per forza* (1721); also wrote masses, motets and vespers.

Bassani (Bassano), Giovanni, Italian composer, singer and violinist. He was a singer at San Marco, Venice, in 1585; singing teacher at the Seminary of San Marco (1595); first violin soloist at the Chapel of the Basilica (1615). The following instrumental works by him are extant: *Fantasie a tre voci per cantar e sonar* (1585); *Il fiore dei capricci musicali a 4 voci* (1588); *Motetti, madrigali e canzoni francesi di diversi auttori . . . diminuiti per sonar con ogni sorti di stromenti* (1591; reprinted in 1602 in an arrangement for one voice with organ ad lib.; containing works of Clemens non Papa, Créquillon, Palestrina and others; the term *diminuiti* refers to ornamentation of the original vocal compositions); 2 volumes of *Motetti per concerti ecclesiastici* for 5-12 voices (1598-99); a volume of *Canzonette* for 4 voices (1587); etc.

Bassani (Bassano; Bassiani), Giovanni Battista, Italian composer, organist and violinist; b. Padua c. 1657; d. Bergamo, Oct. 1, 1716. He studied in Venice with Castrovillari; was maestro di cappella to the Duke of Mirandola (1678); at the chapel of the Accademia della Morte in Ferrara (1684); at the cathedral of Ferrara (1688) and at the Basilica Maria in Bergamo (1712), where he remained until his death. He was also a member of the Accademia dei Filarmonici in Bologna from 1677. His extant works include the following operas: *Amorosa Preda di Paride* (Bologna, 1683); *Falaride tiranno d'Agrigento* (1684); *Alarico re de Goti* (Ferrara, 1685); *Ginevra, infante di Scozia* (Ferrara, 1690); oratorios: *La morte delusa* (1686); *Giona* (1689); *Nella luna celestiale* (1687); *Il Conte di Bacheville* (1696); *Mosè risorto dalle acque* (1698); *Gl'Impegni del divino amore* (1703); *Il trionfo della fede* (1707). He also wrote numerous masses, and other sacred music. Of his instrumental works, several suites and trio-sonatas are reprinted in Torchi's *L'Arte musicale in Italia* (vol. VII) and in J. W. Wasielewski's *Instrumentalsätze vom Ende des XVI. bis Ende des XVII. Jahrhunderts* (1874). A cantata is included in Riemann's *Kantaten-Frühling* (vol. II); some vocal works are published by G. F. Malipiero in *Classici della musica italiana.* Bibl.: J. W. Wasielewski, *Die Violine und ihre Meister* (1883); A. Moser, *Geschichte des Violinspiels* (1923); A. Schering, *Geschichte des Oratoriums* (1911). See also F. Pasini, *Notes sur la vie de G. B. Bassani* in 'Sammelbände der Internationalen Musik-Gesellschaft' (vol. VII, 1906); R. Haselbach, *G. B. Bassani* (Kassel, 1955).

Bassford, William Kipp, American pianist, b. New York, April 23, 1839; d. there, Dec. 22, 1902. He was a church organist in New York; also gave piano concerts; composed an opera *Cassilda.* He completed Vincent Wallace's unfinished opera, *Estrella.*

Bassevi, Giacomo. See **Cervetto.**

Bassi, Amadeo (Vittorio), Italian operatic tenor; b. Florence, July 20, 1874; d. there, January 14, 1949. His sole teacher was the Marchese Pavese Negri in Florence, where he made his debut in *Ruy Blas* (1899). He toured South America (1902-7); sang at the Manhattan Opera House, N. Y. (1906-8) and at the Chicago Opera Co. (1910-12). His repertoire included more than 50 operas, mostly Italian; he created the following roles: Angel Clare in d'Erlanger's *Tess;* Federico in Franchetti's *Germania;* Giorgio in Mascagni's *L'Amica;* and Lionello in Cilea's *Gloria.*

Bassi, Luigi, Italian opera baritone; b. Pesaro, Sept. 4, 1766; d. Dresden, Sept. 13, 1825. He studied with Pietro Morandi of Bologna; made his debut in Pesaro at the age of thirteen; he then sang in Florence; went to Prague in 1784, where he soon became greatly appreciated. Mozart wrote the part of Don Giovanni for him and heeded his advice in matters of detail. Bassi was in Vienna from 1806-14; then briefly in Prague; in 1815 he joined an Italian opera company in Dresden.

Bastiaans, Johannes Gijsbertus, Dutch organist; b. Wilp, Oct. 31, 1812; d. Haarlem, Feb. 16, 1875. He was a pupil of Schneider at Dessau, and Mendelssohn at Leipzig; was organist at the Zuiderkerk, Amsterdam, and at St. Bavo's, Haarlem (1868); succeeded at St. Bavo's by his son, **Johann** (1854-1885). Bastiaans published a book of chorales and numerous songs.

Baston, Josquin, Flemish composer of the mid-16th century. It is known that from May 1552 to Oct. 1553 he was at the Polish Court of Sigismond Augustus at Cracow. Motets and chansons by Baston appeared between 1542 and 1559 in various collections: Susato's *Het ierste musyck boexken* (Antwerp, 1551); Salbinger's *Concertus* (Augsburg, 1545); also in Louvain (published by Phalèse). His *Lament* has 2 middle voices singing the *Requiem aeternam* in canon 6 times while the other voices have fresh parts. See R. van Maldeghem (ed.), *Trésor musical* (1865-93; vol. XII).

Bate, Stanley Richard, English composer; b. Plymouth, Dec. 12, 1911. He studied at the Royal College of Music (1931-35) with Vaughan Williams (composition) and Arthur Benjamin (piano); won a travelling scholarship enabling him to go to Paris where he studied with Nadia Boulanger, and to Berlin where he took some lessons with Hindemith. Returning to England in 1937, he was commissioned to write a concertino for piano and chamber orch., which he performed at the Eastbourne Festival of Music (Feb. 8, 1938). He also wrote several ballets: *Goyescas* (1937), *Perseus* (1938), *Cap Over Mill* (1938), etc. On Nov. 7, 1938, he married Peggy Glanville-Hicks (divorced 1948). During World War II he toured Australia as pianist, composer and lecturer (1940-41). In 1942 he went to the U.S. and played the solo part in his 2nd piano concerto with the New York Philh., under Beecham (Feb. 8, 1942); in 1945 he was in Brazil where he gave several concerts of his works on the radio. In 1946 he was in New York; then returned to London in 1950. He has written 4 symphonies; the 3rd symphony (1940) was first performed fourteen years after its composition (Cheltenham Festival, July 14, 1954), obtaining remarkable success. His 4th symphony was given in London, on Nov. 20, 1955. Other works: 2 sinfoniettas, 3 violin concertos, a viola concerto, 3 piano concertos, a cello concerto, a harpsichord concerto, 2 string quartets, sonata for recorder and piano, violin sonata, oboe sonata, 9 piano sonatinas; music for the films.

Bates, Joah, British conductor; b. Halifax, March (baptized March 8), 1741; d. London, June 8, 1799. He studied organ in Manchester; was a tutor of King's College in Cambridge (1760); received his B.A. in 1764, and M.A. in 1767. He then went to London, and established and conducted the series known as 'Concerts of Ancient Music' (1776); also conducted the famous Handel Commemoration Festivals (1784-87; 1791).

Bates, William, English composer who flourished in the second half of the 18th century. He wrote popular ballad operas for the Marylebone and Vauxhall Gardens, London: *The Jovial Crew* (1760, altered to *The Ladies Frolick* in 1770); *Flora, or Hob in the Well* (1767); *The Theatrical Candidates* (1775); *The Device, or The Marriage Officer* (1777); *Second Thought Is Best* (1778); also a grand opera, *Pharnaces* (London, Nov. 15, 1765).

Bateson, Thomas, English composer; b. probably at Cheshire c. 1570; d. Dublin, March or April, 1630. According to Rimbault, he was organist at Chester Cathedral in 1599. In 1609 he became vicar choral and organist of the Cathedral of the Holy Trinity in Dublin. He is said to have been the first music graduate of Trinity College, earning his Mus. B. in 1612 and his M.A. in 1622. As a composer, Bateson is especially noted for his madrigals, although they are regarded as inferior to those by Morley or Weelkes. In 1604 he published a collection of 29 madrigals for 3 to 6 voices; it included the madrigal *When Oriana walked to take the ayre* originally intended for publication in Morley's *Triumphs of Oriana.* A second set of 30 madrigals was published in 1618. Both sets are reprinted in *The English Madrigal School* edited by E. H. Fellowes (volumes XXI and XXII).

Bath, Hubert, English composer; b. Barnstaple, Nov. 6, 1883; d. Harefield, April 24, 1945. He studied piano and composition at the Royal Academy of Music; won a scholarship with his short opera based on Longfellow's *Spanish Student;* conducted Thomas Quinlan's opera troupe on its world tour (1912-13); returning to England, devoted himself chiefly to theatrical music. His works include several short operas: *Young England* (1915); *Bubbles* (Belfast, Nov. 26, 1923); *The Sire de Maletroit's Door; The Three Strangers;* and the grand opera *Trilby.* He also wrote incidental music to *Hannele* (1908; later expanded into a symph. poem); *African Suite* for orch., and 6 cantatas: *Legend of Nerbudda* (1908), *The Wedding of Shon MacLean* (Leeds Festival, 1910), *The Jackdaw of Rheims* (1911), *Look at the Clock* (1911), *The Men on the Line* (1913), *The Wake of O'Connor* (1914); a piece for brass band, *Freedom* (1922); more than 150 songs, and various instrumental compositions.

Bathe, William, Irish writer on musical subjects; b. Ireland, April 2, 1564; d. Madrid, June 17, 1614. He was the son of Judge John Bathe; studied at Oxford; remained in England (1584-90); taught mnemonics to Queen Elizabeth and presented her with a harp of his own design. He was in Spain in 1591; went to Flanders where he became a Jesuit and entered his novitiate in 1596; was ordained a priest at Padua in 1599; returned to Spain in 1601; in 1604 was appointed spiritual director of the Irish College at Lisbon; was in Salamanca in 1606 and 1612. As a theorist, his chief contributions lay in the establishment of fixed rules for the placing of accidentals and in the transition from the hexachordal system to the system of scales based on the octave. He was the author of one of the earliest theoretical works on music in English, *Introduction to the True Art of Musicke* (London, 1584); also published *A Brief Introduction to the Skill of Song* (London, 1600). His best known work was not on music but on linguistics, *Janua linguarum* (*Portal of Tongues;* Salamanca, 1611). Bibl.: J. Pulver, *The English Theorists: William Bathe,* in the 'Mus. Times' (October, 1934).

Batiste, Antoine-Edouard, French organist; b. Paris, March 28, 1820; d. there, Nov. 9, 1876. He studied at the Paris Cons. with Halévy; won 2d Grand Prix de Rome with the cantata *Héloïse de Montfort* (1840); subsequently was organist of St.-Nicolas-des-Champs (1842-54), then of St. Eustache. He composed organ music, piano pieces and songs; also edited the official *Solfèges du Conservatoire* (12 vols.), and published a *Petit solfège harmonique.*

Batistin. See **Stuck, Johann Baptist.**

Batka, Richard, music editor; b. Prague, Dec. 14, 1868; d. Vienna, April 24, 1922. He received his *Dr. phil.* from the Univ. of Prague; from 1896-8 was co-editor, with Teibler, of the 'Neue musikalische Rundschau'; also wrote for the 'Neue Revue' and the 'Prager Tageblatt'; settled in Vienna (1908), where he was music editor of the 'Wiener Fremdenblatt' and other musical publications. He wrote the librettos of many modern German operas (almost all of Blech's), and translated the texts of numerous foreign operas. Writings: Biographies of Bach and Schumann (in Reclam's ed., Leipzig, 1892); *Aus der Musik und Theaterwelt* (Prague, 1894); *Martin Plüddemann: Eine kritische Studie* (Prague, 1896); *Musikalische Streifzüge* (Leipzig, 1899); *Die Musik der Griechen* (1900); *Die mehrstimmige Kunstmusik des Mittelalters* (1901); with P. Runge, *Die Lieder Mülichs von Prag* (in 'Denkmäler deutscher Tonkunst aus Böhmen', 1905); *Die Musik in Böhmen* (Berlin, 1906); *Geschichte der Musik in Böhmen* (Vol. I: *Böhmen unter deutschem Einfluss,* Prague, 1906); *Aus der Opernwelt* (1907); *Allgemeine Geschichte der Musik* (2 vols., Stuttgart, 1909-11); a monograph on Wagner (Berlin, 1912); etc.

Batta, Alexandre, cellist; b. Maastricht, July 9, 1816; d. Versailles, Oct. 8, 1902. He was a pupil of Platel at the Brussels Cons.; settled in Paris (1835); made successful concert tours on the continent; wrote many melodious pieces and transcriptions for cello with piano accompaniment.

Battaille (bah-tah'-y), **Charles-Aimable,** French bass; b. Nantes, Sept. 30, 1822; d. Paris, May 2, 1872. He was originally a medical student; then studied music; sang at the Opéra-Comique in Paris (1848-57), until a throat disorder ended his public career; taught singing at the Paris Cons. (1851). He published an extensive method of singing in 2 vols.: I. *Nouvelles recherches sul la phonation* (1861); II. *De la physiologie appliquée au mécanisme du chant* (1863).

Battanchon (ba-tahn-shohn'), **Félix,** French cellist and composer; b. Paris, April 9, 1814; d. there, July, 1893. He studied with Vaslin and Norblin at the Paris Cons.; member of the Grand Opera Orch. (1840). In 1846 he invented, and vainly tried to popularize, a small type of cello called a Baryton.

Batten, Adrian, English organist and composer, b. c. 1585; d. London, 1637. He studied at Winchester with the Cathedral organist John Holmes; in 1614 went to London as vicar choral of Westminster Abbey. In 1624 he became vicar choral and organist at St. Paul's Cathedral. A prolific composer, he left 15 services and 47 anthems in manuscript. Some of his pieces are included in Boyce's 'Cathedral Music'. A modern reprint of one of his services is included in *The Choir;* several anthems have been published by Novello. Batten also transcribed into organ score numerous sacred choral works, some of which have come down to us only through his transcriptions. His organ book is described in *Tudor Church Music* (1922, vol. II).

Battishill, Jonathan, English organist and composer; b. London, May, 1738; d. Islington, Dec. 10, 1801. He was a chorister in St. Paul's (1747); later apprenticed to William Savage; was deputy organist under Boyce at the Chapel Royal; then harpsichordist at Covent Garden and organist in several London parishes. He wrote an opera with Michael Arne: *Almena* (Drury Lane Theatre, Nov. 2, 1764); a pantomime, *The Rites of Hecate* (1764); many popular anthems, glees and songs. Cf. J. B. Trend, *Jonathan Battishill* in 'Music and Letters' (1932).

Battista, Vincenzo, Italian composer; b. Naples, Oct. 5, 1823; d. there, Nov. 14, 1873. He studied at the Naples Cons.; wrote 13 operas, eleven of which were produced at Naples (1844-69).

Battistini, Gaudenzio, Italian composer, grandson of Giacomo Battistini; b. Novara, June 30, 1722; d. there, Feb. 25, 1800. He succeeded his father, Giuseppe Battistini, in 1747 as organist of the chapel of San Gaudenzio in Novara, and served for more than 50 years until his death. He wrote numerous church works in a highly developed polyphonic style (15 motets, a Requiem, etc.). A biographical sketch and examples of his music are found in Vito Fedeli, 'Le Cappelle musicali di Novara' in vol. III of 'Istituzioni e monumenti dell' arte musicale italiana' (Milan, 1933).

Battistini, Giacomo, Italian composer; b. 1665; d. Novara, Feb. 5, 1719. He was organist at the Novara Cathedral (1694-1706); then at the church of San Gaudenzio. He is reputed to have been the first to introduce the violoncello into instrumental accompaniment. He composed several masses, motets, organ works; also contributed music to the third act of the drama *Antemio in Roma* (1695; with A. Besozzi and D. Erba). See Vito Fedelli, 'Le cappelle musicali di Novara' in vol. III of 'Istituzioni e monumenti dell' arte musicale italiana' (Milan, 1933), containing musical illustrations from Battistini's works.

Battistini, Mattia, Italian baritone; b. Rome, Feb. 27, 1856; d. Collebaccaro, near Rome, Nov. 7, 1928. He made his debut in Donizetti's *La Favorita* (Teatro Argentina, Rome, 1878); subsequently appeared for a season with the Italian Opera in Buenos Aires; sang on all the principal stages of Italy, Spain and Portugal; gave recitals in many European cities, including London, Berlin and St. Petersburg, until 1927. Cf. G. Monaldi, *Cantanti celebri,* vol. II (Rome, 1929).

Battke, Max, German teacher and writer; b. Schiffuss, near Wandlacken, Sept. 15, 1863; d. Berlin, Oct. 4, 1916. He studied at Königsberg and Berlin, where he later taught at various conservatories. He founded a music seminary in Berlin (1900), which became (1910) the famous 'Seminar für Schulgesang'; also founded (1902) the first concerts for young people. He wrote numerous textbooks on music and methods for voice production; edited (with Humperdinck) new collections of folksongs and piano pieces.

Battmann, Jacques-Louis, organist and composer; b. Maasmünster, Alsace, Aug. 25, 1818; d. Dijon, July 7, 1886. He was organist at Belfort (1840); wrote masses, motets, choral music, many pieces for harmonium, a treatise on harmony, etc.

Batton (bah-tohn'), **Désiré-Alexandre,** French composer; b. Paris, Jan. 2, 1798; d. Versailles, Oct. 15, 1855. He was a pupil of Cherubini at the Paris Cons.; won the Prix de Rome (1816) for his cantata, *La mort d'Adonis;* was inspector of the branch schools of the Cons. from 1842, and teacher of a vocal class at the Cons. from 1849. His most successful opera, *La Marquise de Brinvilliers* (1832), was written jointly with Auber, Hérold and others; his own operas were *La fenêtre secrète* (Paris, Nov. 17, 1818); *Ethelvina* (1827); and *Le prisonnier d'état* (1828).

Battu (bah-tü'), **Pantaléon,** French violinist; b. Paris, 1799; d. there, Jan. 17, 1870. He studied with R. Kreutzer at the Paris Cons.; member of the orchestra of the Opéra and the court until his retirement in 1859; wrote 3 violin concertos; 3 violin duos; etc.

Bätz, Karl, German music editor; b. Sömmerda, Thuringia, March 17, 1851; d. Berlin, 1902. He lived in America (1871-86); then settled in Berlin, where he founded the 'Musikinstrumenten-Zeitung' in 1890; published *Die Musikinstrumente der Indianer* (1876); also various pamphlets on instrument-making.

Baudiot (boh-d'yoh'), **Charles-Nicolas,** French cellist; b. Nancy, March 29, 1773; d. Paris, Sept. 26, 1849. He was a pupil of the elder Janson, whom he succeeded as cello professor at the Paris Cons. (1802); from 1816 was first cellist in the royal orchestra; retired in 1832. With Levasseur and Baillot he wrote the cello method used at the Paris Cons.; also wrote *Instruction pour les compositeurs* (a guide to composers for cello); composed 2 cello concertos; 2 cello concertinos; a great variety of chamber music for cello.

Baudrier, Yves, French composer; b. Paris, Feb. 11, 1906. He was originally a law student; then turned to music. In 1936 he, together with Messiaen, Jolivet and Daniel-Lesur, formed in Paris 'La Jeune France', a group dedicated to propaganda for a new, purely national French music, neither ultramodern nor academic. In 1946 Baudrier visited the U.S., giving lectures on new French music. He has written the orchestral works *Raz de Sein; Chant de Jeunesse; Le musicien dans la Cité; Eleonora* (after Poe), a suite for string orch. (1938); *Le grand voilier,* symph. poem (1939-41); string quartet (1942); symphony (1945).

Bauer, Harold, distinguished pianist; b. Kingston-on-Thames, near London, of an English mother and German father, April 28, 1873; d. Miami, March 12, 1951. He studied violin with his father and Adolf Politzer; made his debut as a violinist in

London; in 1892 he went to Paris and studied piano for a year with Paderewski; in 1893 made his first tour as a pianist in Russia; gave piano recitals throughout Europe; in 1900 made his U.S. debut with the Boston Symph. Orch.; appeared as soloist with other U.S. orchestras, with eminent chamber music groups, and as a recitalist. He founded the Beethoven Association in New York (1918); was president of the Friends of Music in the Library of Congress, Washington, D.C.; Knight of the Legion of Honor; Mus. Doc. (honorary), Lawrence College, Appleton, Wisconsin (1938). Among his writings are: *Self-Portrait of the Artist as a Young Man* in the 'Mus. Quarterly' (October, 1947); *Harold Bauer, His Book* (N.Y., 1948). He also made arrangements and transcriptions of Beethoven's *Grosse Fuge,* op. 133; Kuhnau's *David and Goliath;* and Bach's *Concerto in C* for 2 pianos and string orchestra; edited works by Schubert and Brahms, and Mussorgsky's *Pictures at an Exhibition.*

Bauer, Marion Eugenie, American composer and writer; b. Walla Walla, Wash., Aug. 15, 1887; d. South Hadley, Mass., Aug. 9, 1955. Her parents were of French extraction; her father was an amateur musician. She was educated at schools in Portland, Oregon; in 1932 received an honorary M.A. from Whitman College in Walla Walla; studied music in Paris with André Gédalge, Nadia Boulanger and Campbell-Tipton; also in Berlin with Paul Ertel, and in America with Walter Henry Rothwell, Eugene Heffley and Henry Holden Huss. She was visiting professor at Mills College (1935), and at the Carnegie Institute of Technology in Pittsburgh (1936; 1939); annual lecturer at the Chautauqua Institute from 1928; later lived in New York; was associate prof. of music at New York Univ. and instructor at the Juilliard Summer School; joined the faculty of the Institute of Musical Art in 1940. She was active in music societies; was a founder of the American Music Guild in N.Y. (1921); a member of the Executive Board of the League of Composers, etc. Her compositions are distinguished by fine texture, in a fairly advanced modern manner. She was highly esteemed as a teacher of music history and composition. Works: *Up the Ocklawaha,* tone poem (1913); *From New Hampshire Woods* for piano (1921); string quartet (1928); *Fantasia quasi una sonata* for violin and piano (1928); *Indian Pipes* (orchestrated by Martin Bernstein; Chautauqua Festival, 1928); *Three Noëls* for chorus (1929); incidental music to Aeschylus' *Prometheus Bound* (1930); *Sun Splendor,* for piano (1926; also for orch.; perf. by Stokowski with the N. Y. Philh., Oct. 25, 1947); *Dance Sonata* for piano (1932); suite for oboe and clarinet (1932); viola sonata (1936); 4 songs with string quartet (1936); *Pan,* choreographic sketch for 7 instruments and piano (1937); *A Garden is a Lovesome Thing* for chorus (1938); *The Thinker* for chorus (1938); symphony-suite for strings (1940); *Concertino* for oboe, clarinet and string quartet (1940); sonatina for oboe and piano (1940); *American Youth Concerto* for piano and orch. (1943); *Trio Sonata* for flute, cello and piano (1944); *China* for chorus with orch. (Worcester Festival, Oct. 12, 1945). Writings: *How Music Grew* (1925; with Ethel Peyser); *Music Through The Ages* (1932; with Ethel Peyser); *Twentieth Century Music* (1933); *Musical Questions and Quizzes* (1941); *How Opera Grew* (1955; with Ethel Peyser).

Bauer, Moritz, German teacher and writer on music; b. Hamburg, April 8, 1875; d. Frankfurt, Dec. 31, 1932. He first studied medicine; then turned to music (Mus. Doc., Zürich, 1904); taught at the Hoch Cons. (1926) and at the Univ. of Frankfurt. He published *Die Lieder Franz Schuberts* (1915); *Iwan Knorr* (1916); *Formprobleme des späten Beethoven* (1927); also edited songs by Zelter. Cf. F. Szymichowski, *Moritz Bauer* in 'Zeitschrift für Musikwissenschaft' (1933).

Bäuerle, Hermann, German music editor and composer of sacred choruses; b. Ebersberg, Oct. 24, 1869; d. Ulm, May 21, 1936. He studied theology at Tübingen and music with E. Kauffmann; took holy orders; from 1899-1908, was court chaplain at Thurn and Taxis. In 1906, he became Papal Privy Chamberlain, with the title 'Monsignore'. He took the degree of *Dr. Phil.* in Leipzig (1906) with the thesis, *Eine musik-philologische Studie über die 7 Busspsalmen Lassos;* in 1917 was organist and director of music in Schwäbisch-Gmünd; in 1921 founded a conservatory at Ulm. Among his published writings are: *Palestrina muss populärer werden* (1903); *Der Vatikanische Choral in Reformnotation* (1907); *Liturgie* (1908; a manual of the Roman Catholic liturgy); *Gesangslehre für Oberstimmen* (1918); *Musikalische Grammatik* (1919); and *Allgemeine Erziehungs- und Unterrichtslehre* (1931). His chief work, however, was the editing of sacred music of the 16th century in practical form for performance; from 1903 on he edited the series *Bibliothek altklassischer Kirchenmusik in moderner Notation.* The following numbers appeared: Palestrina, Vol. I, 10 masses for 4 voices (1903); Vol. II, 52 motets (1904); Vol. III, masses for 4 voices (1905); Vol. IV, 10 masses for 5 voices; Lassus, *Septem psalmi poenitentiales* (1906); Victoria, motets for 4 voices, and 6 masses for 4 voices (1904-7); J. J. Fux, *Missa canonica* and *Missa Quadragesimalis*. He also edited works of Anerio, Nanino, and others.

Bauldewijn (Baudoin; Bauldewyn; Bauldeweyn; Balduin; Bauldoin), Noël (Natalis Balduinus), Flemish composer, d. Antwerp c. 1529. From Aug. 31, 1509, to July 29, 1513, he was choir director at the church of Saint-Rombaut at Mechlin. On Nov. 16, 1513 he was appointed choir director at the Cathedral of Antwerp where he probably remained until his death. Two motets by Bauldewijn were included by Petrucci in his collection *Motetti della Corona* (1519); 3 motets were published by Proske; and a chanson was included in Tylman Susato's *Le sixième livre contenant trente et une chansons . . .* (Antwerp, 1545). In addition 10 motets and 6 masses by Bauldewijn are also known.

Baumbach, Friedrich August, German composer and conductor; b. 1753; d. Leipzig, Nov. 30, 1813. He was conductor at the Hamburg opera (1778-89); then settled in Leipzig; wrote many pieces for various instruments; also contributed musical articles to the *Kurzgefasstes Handwörterbuch über die schönen Künste* (Leipzig, 1794).

Baume, Émile, French pianist; b. Toulon, March 14, 1903. He first studied music with his father, who was a piano pupil of Marmontel and Diémer; then at the Paris Cons. with Samuel-Rousseau and Widor; won the Prix Diémer in 1927; studied conducting with Weingartner; lived for a number of years in the U.S., where he gave more than 200 concerts; subsequently continued his career in Europe.

Baumfelder, Friedrich, German pianist and composer; b. Dresden, May 28, 1836; d. there, Aug. 8, 1916. He studied at the Leipzig Cons. with Moscheles, Wenzel and Hauptmann; was conductor of the Schumann Singakademie at Dresden. He wrote a cantata *Der Geiger zu Gmünd,* a collection of piano studies, *Tirocinium musicae,* and a great number of piano pieces in the salon style (totalling more than 300 opus numbers).

Baumgart, Expedit (Friedrich), German music teacher; b. Grossglogau, Jan. 13, 1817; d. Warmbrunn, Sept. 15, 1871. He was music director at Breslau Univ., and teacher in the Royal Institute for Church Music; edited K. Ph. E. Bach's *Clavier-Sonaten*. Cf. monograph by H. Palm (1872).

Baumgarten, Gotthilf von, German composer; b. Berlin, Jan. 12, 1741; d. Gross-Strehlitz, Silesia, Oct. 1, 1813. He wrote 3 operas, produced in Breslau: *Zemire und Azor* (1775), *Andromeda* (1776), and *Das Grab des Mufti* (1778).

Baumgarten, Karl Friedrich, composer; b. Lübeck, 1740; d. London, 1824. He was conductor of the Covent Garden opera orchestra (1780-94); wrote many operas and pantomimes, the best known being *Robin Hood* (London, 1786) and *Blue Beard* (1792).

Baumgartner, August, German composer and writer on music; b. Munich, Nov. 9, 1814; d. there, Sept. 29, 1862. He was choirmaster at the Church of St. Anna in Munich; wrote articles on 'musical shorthand' for the 'Stenographische Zeitschrift' (1852); published a *Kurzgefasste Anleitung zur musikalischen Stenographie oder Tonzeichenkunst* (1853), and a *Kurzgefasste Geschichte der musikalischen Notation* (1856); composed an instrumental mass; a requiem; psalms; many choruses and piano pieces.

Baumgartner, Wilhelm, Swiss composer; b. Rorschach, Nov. 15, 1820; d. Zürich, March 17, 1867. He studied with Alexander Müller; in 1842 was a piano teacher in St. Gall and in Zürich; conducted choruses; wrote pieces on Swiss folk themes. His patriotic song, *O mein Heimatland* (1846) has acquired tremendous popularity in Switzerland, and is regarded as a second national anthem. See C. Widmer, *Wilhelm Baumgartner, ein Liebensbild* (Zürich, 1868); L. Gross, *Wilhelm Baumgartner, sein Leben und sein Schaffen* (Munich, 1930).

Bäumker, Wilhelm, German writer on music; b. Elberfeld, Oct. 25, 1842; d. Rurich, March 3, 1905. He studied theology and philology at Münster and Bonn; from 1892 was a priest at Rurich. His great work is *Das katholische deutsche Kirchenlied in seinen Singweisen von den frühesten Zeiten bis gegen Ende des 17. Jahrhunderts* (4 vols., Freiburg, 1883-1911). Vol. II (1883) and vol. III (1891) appeared originally as continuation of the work begun by K. S. Meister, who published vol. I in 1862; Bäumker revised this volume in 1886; vol. IV (1911) was edited by J. Gotzen from Bäumker's notes, and also contains supplements to the preceding volumes. Other works by Bäumker are: *Palestrina, ein Beitrag, etc.* (1877); *Orlandus de Lassus, ein historisches Bildniss* (1878); *Zur Geschichte der Tonkunst in Deutschland* (1881); *Der Todtentanz* (1881); *Niederländische geistliche Lieder nebst ihren Singweisen aus Handschriften des 15. Jahrhunderts* (1888); and *Ein deutsches geistliches Liederbuch,* melodies from the 15th century (Leipzig, 1896). He also contributed to many musical publications, including the 'Allgemeine deutsche Biographie' and the 'Monatshefte für Musikgeschichte'.

Bausch, Ludwig Christian August, celebrated violin maker; b. Naumburg, Jan. 15, 1805; d. Leipzig, May 26, 1871. He established shops for making and repairing violins in Dresden (1826), Dessau (1828), Wiesbaden (1862) and Leipzig (1863). His son, **Ludwig** (b. Dessau, Nov. 10, 1829; d. Leipzig, April 7, 1871) first lived in New York, later establishing his own violin shop in Leipzig. **Otto,** a younger son (b. Leipzig, Aug. 6, 1841; d. there, Dec. 30, 1875), inherited the business, which then passed to A. Paulus at Markneukirchen.

Baussnern, Waldemar von, German composer and conductor; b. Berlin, Nov. 29, 1866; d. Potsdam, Aug. 20, 1931. He was a pupil of Kiel and Bargiel at the Musik Hochschule in Berlin (1882-8); was conductor of the 'Musikverein' and 'Lehrergesangverein' at Mannheim (1891); then conductor of the Dresden 'Liedertafel' (1895) and of the Dresden 'Bachverein' (1896); taught at the Cologne Cons. (1903-8); taught at conservatories in Weimar, Frankfurt, and Berlin (1908-23); from 1923 was secretary of the Berlin Academy of Arts and Letters. Works: 6 operas: *Dichter und Welt* (Weimar, 1897); *Dürer in Venedig* (Weimar, 1901); *Herbort und Hilde* (Mannheim, 1902); *Der Bundschuh* (Frankfurt, 1904); *Satyros* (after Goethe; Basel, 1922); *Hafis* (1926); 8 symphonies: the 3d, *Leben,* with choral finale; the 5th, *Es ist ein Schnitter, heisst der Tod,* with choral finale; the 6th, *Psalm der Liebe,* with soprano; the 7th, *Die Ungarische; Himmlische Idyllen* for strings and organ; a ballade for orch.; *Champagner,* overture; *Das hohe Lied vom Leben und Sterben* for soli, chorus, orch. and organ; *Die Geburt Jesu,* a Christmas cantata; *Die himmlische Orgel* for baritone and orch.; *Dem Lande meiner Kindheit,* orchestral suite; 4 string quartets; 4 piano quintets; 3 trio-sonatas; 2 piano trios; *Das klagende Lied,* a ballad cycle for baritone and piano; songs for solo voice with orch.; mixed choruses; etc. For the complete edition of Peter Cornelius' works, Baussnern revised his *Barbier von Bagdad* and *Cid,* and finished and edited *Gunlöd* (Cologne, 1906). Cf. G. Wehle, *Baussnerns Sinfonisches Schaffen* (Regensburg, 1931).

Bautista, Julian, Spanish composer; b. Madrid, April 21, 1901. He studied at the Madrid Cons. with Conrado del Campo (1915); won national prizes in composition (1923, 1926, 1932); later appointed prof. of harmony at the Madrid Cons. After the Civil War he went to France; settled in Buenos Aires, Argentina, in 1940. His music, delicate and coloristic, with an admixture of robust humor, is frequently performed. —— Works: two string quartets (1923; 1926); *Colores* for piano (1923); *Preludio* for orch. (1929); *Juerga,* ballet (Opéra-Comique, Paris, 1929); *Sonatina-Trio* for violin, viola, and cello (1930); *Suite all' antica* for orch. (1932); *Obertura para una opera grotesca* (International prize, 'Union Radio,' 1932); *Preludio y Danza* for guitar (1924); songs: *La flûte de jade* (Paris, 1931); *3 ciudades* (Barcelona, 1938), etc.

Bax, Sir Arnold (Edward Trevor), an outstanding English composer; b. London, Nov. 8, 1883; d. Cork, Ireland, Oct. 3, 1953. He studied at the Royal Academy of Music with Matthay and Corder. Although not ethnically Irish, Bax became interested in ancient Irish folklore; many of his works are inspired by Celtic legends. In 1910 he visited Russia, and wrote a series of piano pieces in a pseudo-Russian style: *May Night in the Ukraine; Gopak; In a Vodka Shop,* etc.; also wrote music to James M. Barrie's skit, *The Truth about the Russian Dancers.* He was an excellent pianist, but was reluctant to play in public; he also never appeared as conductor of his own works. His position was high in English music and he was knighted at the Coronation of George VI (1937); in 1941 he succeeded Sir Walford Davies as Master of the King's Musick. He was an extremely prolific composer; his style is rooted in neo-romanticism, but impressionistic elements are much in evidence in his instrumental works; his harmony is elaborate and rich in chromatic progressions; his contrapuntal fabric is free and emphasizes complete independence of component melodies. His works include: ballets *Between Dusk and Dawn* (1917); *The Truth About the Russian Dancers* (1920); 7 symphonies: I (London, Dec. 2, 1922); II (Boston, Dec. 13, 1929); III

(London, March 3, 1930); IV (San Francisco, March 16, 1932); V (dedicated to Sibelius; London, Jan. 15, 1934); VI (London, Nov. 21, 1935); VII (dedicated to the American people; New York, June 9, 1939); symph. poems: *In the Faery Hills* (1909); *Christmas Eve in the Mountains* (1912); *Nympholept* (1912); *The Garden of Fand* (1916); *November Woods* (1917); *Tintagel* (1917); *Summer Music* (1920); *Mediterranean* (1921); *The Happy Forest* (1922); other orchestral works: 4 orchestral pieces: *Dance in the Sun; Pensive Twilight; From the Mountains of Home;* and *Dance of Wild Irravel* (1912-13); *Scherzo sinfonico* (1913); *Romantic Overture* (1923); *Overture to a Picaresque Comedy* (1930); *The Tale the Pine Trees Knew* (1931); *2 Northern Ballads* (1933; 1937); *Overture to Adventure* (1935); *Rogues' Comedy Overture* (1936); *London Pageant* (1937); *Legend* (1944); *Coronation March* (1953). Instrumental works with orchestra: *Symphonic Variations* for piano and orch. (1917); *Phantasy* for viola and orch. (1920); cello concerto (1932); violin concerto (1937); piano concerto for left hand (1948). Vocal music: *Fatherland,* for tenor, chorus and orch. (1907); *Enchanted Summer* (from Shelley's *Prometheus Unbound*), for 2 sopranos, chorus and orch. (1909); *The Bard of the Dimbovitza,* 6 poems for voice and orch. (1915); *Mater Ora Filium,* motet (1920); *Of a Rose I Sing,* for small chorus, harp, cello and double bass (1921); *Now is the Time of Christymas,* for male voices, flute and piano (1921); *This Worlde's Joie,* motet (1922); *The Morning Watch* for chorus and orch. (1923); *To the Name above Every Name,* for soprano, chorus and orch. (1923); *The Boar's Head,* carol for male voices (1923); *St. Patrick's Breastplate,* for chorus and orch. (1923-24); *I sing of a Maiden* for 5 voices unaccompanied (1926); *Walsinghame* for tenor, chorus and orch. (1928); also many solo songs. Chamber music: 3 string quartets (1918; 1924; 1936); piano quintet (1915); quintet for strings and harp (1919); quintet for oboe and strings (1923); string quintet (1931); trio for flute, viola and harp (1916); *An Irish Elegy* for English horn, harp and strings (1917); *Nonet* for winds, strings and harp (1931); octet for horn, piano and strings (1934); concerto for flute, oboe, harp and strings (1934); concerto for bassoon, harp and strings (1936); 3 violin sonatas (1910-27); 2 viola sonatas (2nd with harp; 1921; 1928); cello sonata (1923); *Legend Sonata* for cello and piano (1943); clarinet sonata (1934); 4 piano sonatas; works for 2 pianos, etc. In his many settings of folksongs, Bax succeeded in adapting simple melodies to effective accompaniments in modern harmonies; in his adaptations of old English songs, he successfully recreated the archaic style of the epoch. In his candid autobiography *Farewell My Youth* (London, 1943), Bax gives a vivid account of his life and travels. Bibl.: Edwin Evans, *Arnold Bax* in the 'Mus. Quarterly' (April, 1923); R. H. Hull, *A Handbook on Arnold Bax's Symphonies* (London, 1932).

Bayer, Josef, Austrian composer and conductor; b. Vienna, March 6, 1852; d. there, March 12, 1913. He studied at the Vienna Cons. (1859-70) with Georg and Josef Hellmesberger (violin), Dachs (piano) and Bruckner (theory). He was then violinist in the Court Opera; from 1885 till his death was director of the ballet music. He wrote many operettas and ballets, which acquired considerable popularity in his time, thanks to his gift for facile melodic writing and piquant rhythms. He traveled a great deal; visited New York in 1881. Operettas: *Der Chevalier von San Marco* (1st perf. at the Thalia Theater, New York, Feb. 4, 1881, conducted by the composer); *Menelaus* (Vienna, 1892); *Fräulein Hexe* (Vienna, 1898); *Der Polizeichef* (Vienna, 1904); ballets produced at the Vienna Court Opera: *Wiener Waltzer* (1886); *Die Puppenfee* (1888); *Sonne und Erde* (1889); *Ein Tanzmärchen* (1890); *Rouge et Noir* (1892); *Die Donaunixe* (1892); *Eine Hochzeit in Bosnien* (1893, with Bosnian folk melodies); *Burschenliebe* (1894); *Rund um Wien* (1894); *Die Braut von Korea* (1896); *Die kleine Welt* (1904); ballets produced at Berlin: *Deutsche Märsche* (1887); *Die Welt in Bild und Tanz* (1892); *Die Engelsjäger* (1896); *Columbia* (1893). Bayer also wrote the music for numerous aristocratic festival productions (*Aschenbrödel, Paris in Wien, Jeunesse,* etc., and the ballet *Nippes* at the Schönbrunner Schlosstheater in April, 1911). Works in MS. are *Alien Fata* (a Bosnian opera) and *Der Goldasoka* (a Hindu opera).

Bazin (bah-zan'), **François-Emanuel-Joseph,** French composer; b. Marseilles, Sept. 4, 1816; d. Paris, July 2, 1878. He studied with Berton and Halévy at the Paris Cons.; was awarded the Prix de Rome in 1840; from 1844 taught at the Paris Cons.; in 1871 succeeded Ambroise Thomas as prof. of composition; in 1872 succeeded Carafa as member of the Académie. He wrote 7 operas which were produced at the Opéra-

Comique; also a *Cours d'harmonie théorique et pratique,* adopted at the Paris Conservatory.

Bazzini (bah-tsē'-nē), **Antonio,** Italian violinist and composer; b. Brescia, March 11, 1818; d. Milan, Feb. 10, 1897. He studied the violin; encouraged by Paganini, before whom he played in 1836, Bazzini embarked upon a series of successful tours through Italy, France, Spain, Belgium, Poland, England and Germany (1837-63); taught at the Milan Cons. from 1873, and in 1882 became its director. Works: *Turanda,* opera after Gozzi's *Turandot* (La Scala, Milan, Jan. 13, 1867); *Francesca da Rimini,* symph. poem (1890); symph. overtures to Alfieri's *Saul* (1877) and to Shakespeare's *King Lear* (1880); numerous violin pieces, of which *Ronde des Lutins* became extremely popular.

Beach, Mrs. H. H. A. (maiden-name Amy Marcy Cheney), American composer; b. Henniker, N. H., Sept. 5, 1867; d. New York, Dec. 27, 1944. She studied piano with E. Perabo and K. Baermann; theory with Junius W. Hill. In composition she was largely self-taught, guiding herself by a study of the masters. She made her debut as a pianist when she was 16. She married Dr. H. H. A. Beach of Boston on Dec. 2, 1885. Her first important work was a Mass in E flat, performed by the Handel and Haydn Society (Boston, Feb. 18, 1892). Her *Gaelic Symphony* (Boston Symph. Orch., Oct. 30, 1896), was the first symph. work by an American woman. She also appeared as soloist in her piano concerto (Boston Symph. Orch., April 6, 1900). Other works: cantatas, *The Minstrel and the King, The Rose of Avontown, Sylvania, The Sea Fairies* and *The Chambered Nautilus;* 2nd piano concerto; piano quintet; suite for 2 pianos; *Variations on Balkan Themes* for 2 pianos; violin sonata; numerous choral works, songs and piano pieces, most of them published by Arthur P. Schmidt. Her music, conservative in its idiom and academic in structure, retains its importance as the work of a pioneer woman composer in America. Bibl.: Percy Goetschius, *Mrs. H. H. A. Beach, Analytical Sketch* (Boston, 1906; contains contemporary reviews and a catalog).

Beach, John Parsons, American composer; b. Gloversville, N. Y., Oct. 11, 1877; d. Pasadena, Cal., Nov. 6, 1953. He studied piano at the New England Cons. in Boston; studied composition in Paris with Gédalge, in Venice with Malipiero, and in Boston with Loeffler; for four years taught piano and composition at the Minneapolis Univ., Minn.; then in New Orleans and Boston; lived at various times in New York and Paris; finally settled in Pasadena, Cal. Works: operas *Pippa's Holiday* (Théâtre Rejane, Paris, 1915); *Jornida and Jornidel;* the ballets *Mardi Gras* (New Orleans, Feb. 15, 1926); *Phantom Satyr* (Asolo, Italy, July 6, 1925, in ballet form; 1st concert perf., Rochester, N. Y., Dec. 28, 1926); the orchestral works *New Orleans Street Cries* (Philadelphia, April 22, 1927; Stokowski conducting); *Asolani* (Minneapolis, Nov. 12, 1926); *Angelo's Letter* for tenor and chamber orch. (Pro Musica Concert, New York, Feb. 27, 1929); *Naïve Landscapes* for piano, flute, oboe and clarinet (Rome, 1917); *Poem for string quartet* (Flonzaley, London, 1920); *Concert* for violin, viola, cello, flute, oboe and clarinet (1929); many songs.

Beale, Frederic Fleming, American organist and composer; b. Troy, Kansas, July 13, 1876; d. Caldwell, Idaho, Feb. 16, 1948. He studied in Chicago with Adolf Weidig and Wilhelm Middelschulte; was church organist in Chicago, and in St. Joseph, Mo. From 1908-11 he taught piano at the Univ. of Washington, Seattle; in 1939 was appointed director of music at the College of Idaho at Caldwell. He wrote 3 operettas: *The Magic Wheel, Fatima* and *Poor Richard; Dance-Caprice* for orch.; numerous songs.

Beale, William, English organist and composer; b. Landrake, Cornwall, Jan. 1, 1784; d. London, May 3, 1854. His early training was as chorister in Westminster Abbey; he then studied with Dr. Arnold and Robert Cooke. In 1813 his madrigal *Awake, sweet Muse* was awarded first prize by the Madrigal Society; collections of his glees and madrigals were published in 1815 and 1820. From 1816-20 Beale was one of the Gentlemen of the Chapel Royal; served as organist of Trinity College, Cambridge (1820), Wandsworth Parish Church (1821), and St. John's, Clapham Rise.

Beaton, Isabella, American pianist; b. Grinnell, Iowa, May 20, 1870; d. Mt. Pleasant, Henry Co., Iowa, Jan. 19, 1929. She studied in Berlin with Moszkowski (1894-99); received her M.A. and Ph.B. from Western Reserve Univ. (1902); taught many private pupils in Cleveland (1910-19); also gave recitals. She wrote an opera *Anacoana,* a symphony, a scherzo, and piano pieces.

Beaufils (boh-fēs'), **Marcel,** French musicologist; b. Beauvais, Dec. 30, 1899; studied in Paris and Vienna; author of a biography of Schumann (Paris, 1931) and of the essay *Wagner et le wagnerisme* (Paris, 1946).

Beaulieu (boh-lyö'), **Marie-Désiré,** French composer and author, whose real name was Martin-Beaulieu; b. Paris, April 11, 1791; d. Niort, Dec. 21, 1863. He studied with Méhul at the Paris Cons.; won the Prix de Rome in 1810; wrote operas *Anacréon* and *Philadelphie*; oratorios *L'Hymne du matin, L'Hymne de la nuit,* etc.; also other sacred music as well as secular songs. He published the essays: *Du rythme, des effets qu'il produit et de leurs causes* (1852); *Mémoire sur ce qui reste de la musique de l'ancienne Grèce dans les premiers chants de l'Église* (1852); *Mémoire sur le caractère que doit avoir la musique de l'Église* (1858); *Mémoire sur l'origine de la musique* (1859). His main contribution to French musical culture was his organizing of annual music festivals in provincial towns; founded the Association Musicale de l'Ouest, to which he bequeathed 100,000 francs.

Becher (běk'-er), **Alfred Julius,** composer and music critic; b. Manchester, England, April 27, 1803; d. Vienna, Nov. 23, 1848. He studied at Heidelberg, Berlin and Göttingen; traveled widely on the continent and in England, working as an advocate, editor and professor of composition; taught harmony at the Royal Academy of Music in London (1840); in 1841 he settled in Vienna, where, on the advice of Mendelssohn, he became a music critic; in 1848 became editor of the revolutionary paper, 'Der Radikale'; that same year he was court-martialed for his political activities, and shot. He was the author of *Jenny Lind: eine Skizze ihres Lebens* (Vienna, 1846; 2d augmented ed., 1847); *Das niederrheinische Musikfest, ästhetisch und historisch betrachtet* (1836); also wrote a symphony, chamber music and songs.

Becher, Joseph, German composer; b. Neukirchen, Bavaria, Aug. 1, 1821; d. Mintraching, Sept. 23, 1888. He was a pastor in Mintraching; wrote 60 masses and other sacred music.

Bechler, Johann Christian, composer; b. Island of Oesel, in the Baltic Sea, Jan. 7, 1784; d. Herrnhut, Saxony, April 15, 1857. He came to the U. S. in 1806 and became a professor of theology at the seminary in Nazareth, Pa.; served as deacon, principal and pastor in Philadelphia; returned to Europe in 1836 as a bishop, and was for some years active in Sarepta and Astrakhan, Russia. Bechler was one of the 'Moravians' active in Pennsylvania. His works, which include anthems, hymns and ariettas, are more interesting from a historic than a musical standpoint. —— Cf. A. G. Rau and H. T. David, *A Catalogue of Music by American Moravians, 1742-1842* (Bethlehem, Pa.; The Moravian Seminary, 1938).

Bechgaard, Julius, Danish composer; b. Copenhagen, Dec. 19, 1843; d. there, March 4, 1917. He studied at the Leipzig Cons. and with Gade in Copenhagen; lived in Germany, Italy and Paris; then settled in Copenhagen. He wrote 2 operas: *Frode* (Copenhagen, May 11, 1893) and *Frau Inge* (Prague, 1894); many piano pieces and songs.

Bechstein, (Friedrich Wilhelm) Karl, German piano manufacturer; b. Gotha, June 1, 1826; d. Berlin, March 6, 1900. He worked in German factories; also in London; in 1853 set up a modest shop in Berlin; constructed his first grand piano in 1856; established branches in France, Russia and England; after World War I, the London branch continued under the direction of C. Bechstein, grandson of the founder; following his death (1931), it became an independent British firm, Bechstein Piano Co., Ltd. The firm, one of the largest and best-known in Europe, built, in 1901, the London concert auditorium, Wigmore Hall. —— Cf. *Bechstein-Chronik* (Berlin, 1926); Count du Moulin-Eckart, *Neue Briefe Hans von Bülow* (containing correspondence with Bechstein; Munich, 1927).

Beck, Conrad, distinguished Swiss composer; b. Schaffhausen, June 16, 1901; studied at the Zürich Cons. with Andreae, and in Paris with Honegger and Ernst Lévy; lived in Paris and Berlin; in 1939 returned and was appointed radio conductor in Basel, Switzerland. A prolific composer, Beck excels in instrumental writing, in a neo-classical style, rich in contrapuntal texture. Several of his works have been featured at the Festivals of the International Society for Contemporary Music: overture *Innominata* (Vienna, June 16, 1932); chamber cantata (Warsaw, April 15, 1939), etc. He has written 6 symphonies (1925-53); *Lyric Cantata* (Munich, May 22, 1931); piano concerto (1933); *Konzertmusik* for oboe and string orch. (Basel, April 30, 1933); chamber concerto for cembalo and string orch. (Basel, Nov. 27, 1942); viola concerto (1949); oratorio *Der Tod zu Basel* (Basel, May 22, 1953); concertino for clarinet, bassoon and orch. (1954); Christmas motet, *Es kommt ein Schiff geladen;* 4 string quartets; 2 violin sonatas; 2 cello sonatas; 2 string trios;

piano music; choral works, etc. See Willi Schuh, *Schweizer Musiker der Gegenwart* (Zürich, 1948).

Beck, Franz, German violinist and composer; b. Mannheim, Feb. 15, 1723; d. Bordeaux, Dec. 31, 1809. He was a violinist and favorite of the Prince Palatine; after killing his opponent in a duel he fled to France and settled in Bordeaux (1761). In 1783 he went to Paris, where he became a successful teacher. His works include 24 symphonies; several stage works; violin quartets; piano sonatas; church music; the operas *La belle jardinière* (Bordeaux, Aug. 24, 1767); *Pandora* (Paris, July 2, 1789); *L'Ile déserte* (unperformed). Bibl.: R. Sondheimer, *Die Sinfonien F. Becks* (Basel, 1921).

Beck, Jean-Baptiste, Alsatian-American musicologist; b. Gebweiler, Aug. 14, 1881; d. Philadelphia, June 23, 1943. He studied organ; received his *Dr. phil.* at Strasbourg Univ. with the thesis *Die Melodien der Troubadours* (1908); later publ. a somewhat popularized edition of it in French, *La musique des Troubadours* (Paris, 1910). Beck came to the U. S. after World War I; settled in Philadelphia; taught at the Curtis Institute and at Univ. of Pennsylvania. In 1927 he initiated a project of publishing a *Corpus Cantilenarum Medii Aevi,* in 52 vols., but was able to bring out only 4 vols., under the subtitle *Les Chansonniers des Troubadours et des Trouvères* (all in French), containing phototype reproductions of medieval manuscripts, transcriptions in modern notation and commentary: *Le Chansonnier Cangé* (2 vols.; Philadelphia, 1927); *Le manuscrit du Roi* (2 vols.; Philadelphia, 1938). Among his other important writings is an essay *Der Takt in den Musikaufzeichnungen des XII. und XIII. Jahrhunderts* (in the 'Riemann Festschrift,' 1909). Beck was an outstanding scholar of medieval vocal music; his application of the modal rhythm of the polyphony of that time to the troubadour melodies was an important contribution to the problem of proper transcription into modern notation.

Beck, Johann Heinrich, American conductor and composer; b. Cleveland, Sept. 12, 1856; d. there May 26, 1924. He was a pupil of Reinecke and Jadassohn at the Leipzig Cons. (1879-82), subsequently returning to America. In 1895 he was appointed conductor of the Detroit Symph. Orch., and from 1901-12 conductor of the Cleveland Pops Orch. Works: *Moorish Serenade,* for orch. (1889); a cantata, *Deukalion;* string quartet; string sextet; overture to Bryon's *Lara; Aus meinem Leben,* symph. poem; miscellaneous pieces for various instruments.

Beck, Johann Nepomuk, Hungarian singer; b. Budapest, May 5, 1827; d. Pressburg, April 9, 1904. His dramatic baritone voice was 'discovered' in Budapest, where he made his professional debut; he then sang in Vienna, Frankfurt, and many other German cities; was a member of the Court Opera in Vienna from 1853; retired in 1885; died insane.

Beck, Karl, Austrian tenor; b. 1814; d. Vienna, March 3, 1879. He was the first to sing the role of Lohengrin (Weimar, Aug. 28, 1850).

Beck, Thomas Ludvigsen, Norwegian composer; b. Horten, Dec. 5, 1899. He studied at the Leipzig Cons. Since 1930, active in Oslo as church organist and choral conductor. He has written the cantatas *Arnljot Gelline* (1937) and *Hyfjellet* (1945); *Ballade* for orch. (1940); choruses.

Becker, Albert (Ernst Anton), German composer; b. Quedlinburg, June 13, 1834; d. Berlin, Jan. 10, 1899. He was a pupil of Dehn in Berlin (1853-6); was appointed teacher of composition at Scharwenka's conservatory (1881), and became the conductor of the Berlin Cathedral Choir (1891). His Symphony in G minor was awarded the prize of the Gesellschaft der Musikfreunde in Vienna (1861); also wrote an opera, *Loreley* (1898); cantatas; and a number of sacred works.

Becker, Constantin Julius, German composer and author; b. Freiberg, Saxony, Feb. 3, 1811; d. Oberlössnitz, Feb. 26, 1859. He studied singing with Anacker and composition with Karl Becker; from 1837-46 edited the 'Neue Zeitschrift für Musik,' in association with Schumann; in 1843 settled in Dresden; taught singing, composed and wrote novels on musical subjects; in 1846 he went to Oberlössnitz, where he spent the remainder of his life. He wrote an opera, *Die Erstürmung von Belgrad* (Leipzig, May 21, 1848); a symphony; various vocal works. However, he is best known for his manuals: *Männergesangschule* (1845), *Harmonielehre für Dilettanten* (1842), and *Kleine Harmonielehre* (1844). He also published the novel, *Die Neuromantiker* (1840); translated *Voyage musicale* by Berlioz into German (1843).

Becker, Georg, music editor; b. Frankenthal, Palatinate, June 24, 1834; d. Lancy, near Geneva, July 18, 1928. He was a pupil of Prudent; lived in Geneva most of his life; published *La Musique en Suisse* (Geneva, 1874; reprinted, 1923); *Aperçu sur la chanson française* (from the 11th to 17th centuries); *Pygmalion de Jean-Jacques Rousseau; Les projets de notation musicale du XIXe siècle; La Musique à Genève depuis 50 ans; Eustorg de Beaulieu; Guillaume de Guéroult; Notice sur Claude Goudimel; Jean Caulery et ses chansons spirituelles; H. Waelrant et ses psaumes* (1881); *De l'instrumentation du XVe au XVIIe siècle* (1844); edited the 'Questionnaire de l'Association Internationale des Musiciens-Écrivains'; contributed to the 'Monatshefte für Musikgeschichte.'

Becker, Gustave Louis, American pianist and teacher; b. Richmond, Texas, May 22, 1861. He made his public debut at the age of eleven; studied in New York with Constantin von Sternberg and at the Hochschule für Musik, Berlin (1888-91); took courses with Moritz Moszkowski and Scharwenka. Returning to New York, he became Rafael Joseffy's assistant at the National Cons. He continued his teaching activities privately. On May 23, 1952, the 80th anniversary of his public appearance as a child prodigy, he gave a piano recital in Steinway Hall; on his 94th birthday, May 22, 1955, played at a concert in N. Y., arranged by his friends. He wrote 2 suites for string quartet; *Herald of Freedom* for chorus (1925); many vocal and piano pieces, about 200 numbers in all. He published several pedagogic works: *Exercise for Accuracy; Superior Graded Course for the Piano; Musical Syllable System for Vocal Sight Reading;* and many magazine articles.

Becker, Hugo, famous German cellist, son of Jean; b. Strasbourg, Feb. 13, 1863; d. Geiselgasteig, July 30, 1941. He first studied with his father; later with Grützmacher; was cellist in the Frankfurt opera orch. (1884-86); was a member of the Heermann quartet (1890-1906); taught at the Königliche Hochschule in Berlin (1909-29). He was not only one of the finest soloists, but also a remarkable ensemble player; was for many years a member of the Marteau-Dohnányi-Becker trio; also played with Ysaÿe and Busoni. Among his compositions are a cello concerto and smaller cello pieces. He publ. *Mechanik und Ästhetik des Violoncellspiels* (Vienna, 1929).

Becker, Jean, German violinist; b. Mannheim, May 11, 1833; d. there, Oct. 10, 1884. He studied with Vincenz Lachner; was concertmaster of the Mannheim Orch. until 1858; later settled in Florence, and established the renowned 'Florentine Quartet' (dissolved in 1880). The remaining years of his life were spent touring with his children: **Jeanne,** pianist, pupil of Reinecke and Bargiel (b. Mannheim, June 9, 1859; d. there April 6, 1893); **Hans,** violist (b. Strasbourg, May 12, 1860; d. Leipzig, May 1, 1917); and the cellist, **Hugo** (q.v).

Becker, John J., American composer; b. Henderson, Ky., Jan. 22, 1886. He studied at the Wisconsin Cons., Milwaukee; was a pupil of Middelschulte and von Fielitz; has taught and conducted at Notre Dame Univ., College St. Scholastica, College St. Mary of the Springs, East Columbus, Ohio (Hon. B.A.), and the Univ. of St. Paul. In 1939 he was appointed director of the Federal Music Project in Minn.; from 1943, Director of Music and composer in residence at Barat College of the Sacred Heart, Lake Forest, Ill. Becker has written many articles for musical publications and was associate editor of the quarterly, 'New Music.' His compositions are characteristically bold, ultra-modern, employing highly complex harmonic and contrapuntal combinations; he wrote several works for various instrumental groups under the title *Soundpiece,* thus indicating the constructive character of the music, without references to programmatic connotations. Works: 3 symphonies (1912, 1920, 1929); *Rouge Bouquet,* for male chorus (1917); *Out of the cradle endlessly rocking,* for chorus, soli, narrator and orch. (1929); *Concerto arabesque,* for piano and orch. (1930); *Concertino pastorale,* for orch. (1933); horn concerto (1933); *Dance Figure,* ballet (1933); *Obongo* for orch. (1933); *A Marriage With Space,* subtitled 'a new stage form' (1933); *Missa Symphonica,* for male chorus (1933); *Prelude to Shakespeare,* for orch. (1935); viola concerto (1937); *Soundpiece* for string orch. (1937); incidental music to *Life of Man* (1937); stage music for *Antigone* (1938); 2nd piano concerto, *Satirico* (St. Paul, Minn., March 28, 1939); *Homage to Mozart,* for orch. (1942); *Out of Bondage,* for orch. (1943); *Deirdre of the Sorrows,* lyric drama in one act (1945); violin concerto (1948).

Becker, Karl Ferdinand, German organist and writer; b. Leipzig, July 17, 1804; d. there, Oct. 26, 1877. He was church organist at Leipzig and organ teacher at the Cons. (1843). Among his published writings are: *Systematisch-chronologische Darstellung der Musikliteratur* (1836; Supplement, 1839); *Die Hausmusik in Deutsch-*

land im 16., 17., und 18. Jahrhundert (1840); *Die Tonwerke des 16. und 17. Jahrhundert,* etc. He composed piano and organ pieces, and wrote a chorale book. He gave his library, containing valuable theoretical works, to the city of Leipzig.

Becker, Reinhold, German composer; b. Adorf, Aug. 11, 1842; d. Dresden, Dec. 7, 1924. He was originally a violinist, but because of a muscular disorder, was obliged in 1870 to give up his playing; then lived in Dresden as a composer; from 1884-94 was conductor of the 'Dresdener Liedertafel,' for which he wrote numerous choruses. Works: *Frauenlob,* opera (Dresden, 1892); *Ratbold,* opera (Mainz, 1896); *Der Prinz von Homburg,* symph. poem; 2 violin concertos; a string quartet; violin sonata; many works for male chorus.

Becker, René Louis, organist and composer; b. Bischheim, Alsace, Nov. 7, 1882; d. Detroit, Mich., Jan. 28, 1956. He studied in Strasbourg at the Municipal Cons.; settled in the U. S.; taught piano at St. Louis Univ. (1905-11); was organist at the Blessed Sacrament Cathedral, Detroit (1930-42); then at St. Alphonsus Church in Dearborn; retired in 1952. Works: 6 masses; 4 sonatas for organ; motets; numerous compositions for piano and organ.

Becker, Valentin Eduard, Austrian composer; b. Würzburg, Nov. 20, 1814; d. Vienna, Jan. 25, 1890. He wrote 2 operas: *Die Bergknappen* and *Der Deserteur;* masses; a quintet for clar. and strings; many popular male choruses.

Becking, Gustav, German musicologist; b. Bremen, March 4, 1894; lost his life in Prague May 8, 1945, during street fighting. He studied in Berlin with J. Wolf and in Leipzig where he was assistant to H. Riemann; received his degree of *Dr. phil.* (1920); taught at Erlangen Univ. (1922); succeeded Rietsch at the German Univ. in Prague (1929); was also president of the German Chamber Music Society. His writings included *Studien zu Beethovens Personalstil* (1921); *Zur musikalischen Romantik* in the 'Vierteljahrsschrift für Literatur' (1924); *Englische Musik* in the 'Handbuch für England-Kunde' (1929), etc. He edited the collected edition of the music of E. T. A. Hoffmann.

Beckwith, John Christmas, English organist; b. Norwich, Dec. 25, 1750; d. there, June 3, 1809. He studied at Oxford; became organist of St. Peter Mancroft (1794); was awarded the degrees Mus. Bac. and Mus. Doc., Oxon. (1803); became organist of Norwich Cathedral (1808). Beckwith's proficiency as an organist was coupled with fine musical scholarship. His collection of chants, 'The First Verse of Every Psalm of David, with an Ancient or Modern Chant in Score, adapted as much as possible to the Sentiment of each Psalm' (London, 1808), includes a valuable preface, 'A short history of chanting.' He also published numerous pieces for chorus and organ.

Beckmann, Gustav, German musicologist; b. Berlin, Feb. 28, 1883; d. there Nov. 14, 1948. He studied philology; served as a librarian at the Berlin State Library (1906-11); from 1934 to his death was councillor of the Univ. Library. He took courses with Kretzschmar and Johannes Wolf; conducted an amateur orch. from 1919. He wrote some instrumental and vocal music; publ. the valuable paper *Das Violinspiel in Deutschland vor 1700* (Leipzig, 1918) and an essay on Leopold Mozart (1937); edited various bibliographical publications.

Beckmann, Johann Friedrich Gottlieb, German composer and organist; b. 1737; d. Celle, April 25, 1792. He was one of the finest players and improvisers on the organ of his time; was for many years active in Celle. He wrote an opera, *Lukas und Hannchen* (Hamburg, 1782); 6 concertos; 12 piano sonatas; miscellaneous piano pieces.

Becquié (beck-yā'), **A.,** French flutist; b. Toulouse, 1800; d. Paris, Nov. 10, 1825. He was a pupil of Tulou and Guillou at the Paris Cons.; became first flutist at the Opéra-Comique; wrote many compositions for flute, including *Grande fantaisie et variations* (concerto); *Les Regrets* (sonata); rondos, airs, etc. His brilliant career was cut short by his untimely death at the age of 25.

Becquié ('de Peyreville'), Jean-Marie, brother of A. Becquié; French violinist; b. Toulouse, April 28, 1795; d. Paris, Jan., 1876. He studied with R. and A. Kreutzer at the Paris Cons.; wrote chamber music and many pieces for violin.

Bečvařovsky (betch-vah-rzhohv'-skē), **Anton Felix,** Bohemian organist; b. Jungbunzlau, April 9, 1754; d. Berlin, May 15, 1823. He was organist at Prague; then at Brunswick (1779-96); after 1800, lived in Berlin; wrote 3 piano concertos, 3 piano sonatas; many songs for voice and piano.

Bédard (bā-dahr'), **Jean-Baptiste,** French violinist and harpist; b. Rennes, c. 1765; d. Paris, c. 1815. He lived in Paris after 1796;

wrote 2 'Symphonies périodiques,' and numerous works for the harp.

Bedford, Herbert, English composer; b. London, Jan. 23, 1867; d. there, March 13, 1945. He studied at the Guildhall School of Music; at the same time was active as a painter. He wrote an opera, *Kit Marlowe; The Optimist* for orch.; *Nocturne,* for alto voice and orch.; *Sowing the Wind,* symph. poem; *Over the Hills and Far Away,* symph. interlude; *Queen Mab,* suite for orch.; *Ode to Music* and other songs; also an essay *On Modern Unaccompanied Song* (1923). He married Liza Lehmann in 1894.

Bedos de Celles (bŭ-doh' dŭ sell), **Dom François,** French organ theorist; b. Caux, near Béziers, Jan. 24, 1709; d. Saint-Denis, Nov. 25, 1779. He was a Benedictine monk at Toulouse; wrote an important treatise, *L'Art du facteur d'orgues* (3 vols.; Paris, 1766-78); a 4th volume, containing historical notes on the organ, appeared in German (1793); a modern edition was publ. in Kassel (1936). He also wrote an account of a new organ at St. Martin de Tours in the 'Mercure de France' (Jan. 1762; a German translation is included in Adlung's *Musica mechanica organoedi*). Bibl.: R. Raupel in the 'Bulletin de la Société française de Musicologie' (Vol. I, 1917).

Beecham, Sir **Thomas,** eminent English conductor; b. St. Helens, near Liverpool, April 29, 1879. He was educated at Rossall School and at Wadham College, Oxford Univ.; took lessons with Dr. Sweeting and Dr. V. Roberts. Of independent means, he was able to pursue his musical career without regard to economic necessities. In 1899 he founded, chiefly for his own pleasure, an amateur orch. at Huyton. In 1902 he became conductor of K. Truman's traveling opera company, gaining valuable practical experience; after the conclusion of the tour, he resumed further serious study of music. In 1905 he gave his first symph. concert in London with the Queen's Hall Orch.; in 1906 he established the New Symph. Orch., which he conducted until 1908, when he resigned and formed the Beecham Symph. Orch. By that time his reputation as a forceful and magnetic conductor was securely established. His precise yet dramatic interpretive style suits equally well the music of the classics and the moderns, thus closing the esthetic gap between the 18th and 20th centuries. In 1910 Beecham appeared in a new role, that of operatic impresario. With a company of excellent artists and his own well-trained orchestra, he gave a season of opera in London, conducting most of the performances himself; the variety of the repertory and the high level of production made this season a memorable one; he presented the first English performance of *Elektra* at Covent Garden (Feb. 19, 1910); also other Strauss operas *(Salome, Der Rosenkavalier* and *Ariadne auf Naxos); A Village Romeo and Juliet* by Delius, *The Wreckers* by Ethel Smyth, *Shamus O'Brien* by Stanford, *Tiefland* by Eugene d'Albert, and *Le Chemineau* by Leroux; in subsequent years he continued to champion English operas, producing *Dylan* by Holbrooke, *The Critic* by Stanford, and *Everyman* by Liza Lehmann. In 1929 he organized and conducted the Delius Festival in London, to which Delius himself, though paralyzed, was brought from his residence in France. Beecham's activities continued unabated for several decades. In 1928 he toured the U. S. for the first time, subsequently continued to appear in America, through 1956. He made a tour of Australia and Canada at the outbreak of World War II; was conductor of the Seattle Symph. from 1941-43; also conducted at the Metropolitan Opera House (1942-44). In 1943 he married the British pianist, Betty Humby, after divorcing Utica Welles, whom he had married in 1903. Beecham returned to London in 1945; organized the Royal Philh. Orch. in 1947, and toured in the U.S. and Canada (1949-51); conducted at the Edinburgh Festivals since 1947. On May 4, 1953, he gave in Oxford the first complete performance of the opera *Irmelin* by Delius. Beecham was knighted on Jan. 1, 1916. He published his autobiography, *A Mingled Chime,* in 1943. He arranged several orchestral suites from Handel's works, using material from Handel's operas and chamber music, and performed them as ballet scores; of these, *The Great Elopement* (1945) is particularly effective. See Ethel Smyth: *Beecham and Pharaoh* (London, 1935).

Beecher, Carl Milton, American composer; b. La Fayette, Ind., Oct. 22, 1883. He graduated in 1908 from Northwestern Univ.; then studied in Berlin with Paul Juon and Joseph Lhévinne. He was on the faculty of Northwestern Univ. from 1913 to 1936; then spent eleven years (1936-47) on the South Sea Island of Tahiti, where he devoted his time to composition. He returned to America in 1947 and settled in Portland, Oregon, where he became head of the theory dept. at the Portland School of Music. He has written mainly for piano: a set of 6 pieces, *Remembrances of Times Past;* a set of 9 pieces, *Musical Profiles;* 5 *Aquatints;* etc.

Beecke, Ignaz von, German clavierist and composer; b. Wimpfen, Oct. 28, 1733; d. Wallerstein, Jan. 2, 1803. He was a captain of dragoons; later became 'Musikintendant' to the prince of Öttingen-Wallerstein. A highly accomplished pianist, he was a friend of Jommelli, Gluck and Mozart. Among his compositions are 7 operas; an oratorio, *Die Auferstehung Jesu;* a cantata; symphonies; quartets; 4 harpsichord trios; 6 harpsichord sonatas; songs; etc. Bibl.: L. Schiedermair, *Die Blütezeit der Öttingen-Wallerstein'schen Hofkapelle* in the 'Sammelbände der Internationalen Musik-Gesellschaft' (Oct., 1907).

Beellaerts, Jean. See **Bellère.**

Beer (bār), **Jacob Liebmann.** Original name of **Giacomo Meyerbeer** (q.v.).

Beer, Josef, clarinetist, b. Grünwald, Bohemia, May 18, 1744; d. Potsdam, 1811. He was a Royal Prussian chamber-musician; introduced an improvement of a fifth key for the clarinet; wrote many compositions for his instrument, and influenced Heinrich Bärmann in the further extension of virtuoso technique on the clarinet.

Beer, Max Josef, Austrian pianist and composer; b. Vienna, Aug. 25, 1851; d. there, Nov. 25, 1908. He was a pupil of Dessoff; wrote the comic operas *Friedel mit der leeren Tasche* (Prague, 1892); *Der Streik der Schmiede* (Augsburg, 1897); *Das Stelldichein auf der Pfahlbrücke;* a cantata, *Der wilde Jäger;* many songs and piano pieces.

Beer-Walbrunn, Anton, German composer; b. Kohlberg, Bavaria, June 29, 1864; d. Munich, March 22, 1929. He was a pupil of Rheinberger, Bussmeyer and Abel at the Akademie der Tonkunst in Munich; from 1901 instructor there; made professor in 1908. He wrote the operas: *Shüne* (Lübeck, 1894); *Don Quixote* (Munich, 1908); *Das Ungeheuer* (Karlsruhe, 1914); *Der Sturm* (after Shakespeare); incidental music to *Hamlet*; a symphony; *Mahomet's Gesang* (for chorus and orch.); *Lustspielouvertüre*; violin concerto; piano quintet; church music; many compositions for various instruments. He also supervised new editions of works of Wilhelm Friedemann Bach. — Cf. monograph by O. G. Sonneck in his *Suum cuique: Essays in Music* (New York, 1916).

Beeth (bāt), **Lola,** dramatic soprano; b. Cracow, Nov. 23, 1862; d. Berlin, March 18, 1940. She studied with Mme. Viardot-Garcia and Désirée Artôt; made her debut as Elsa in *Lohengrin* at the Berlin Court Opera (1882); sang there from 1882 till 1888; and at the Vienna Court Theater (1888-95). After appearances in Paris and New York she settled in Berlin as a teacher.

Beethoven, Ludwig van, the great German composer who represents the fullest maturity (in emotional scope, in formal construction and in instrumental treatment) of the allied classic forms of the sonata, concerto, string quartet and the symphony; b. Bonn, probably Dec. 16 (baptized Dec. 17), 1770; d. Vienna, March 26, 1827. His grandfather, Ludwig van Beethoven, was born in Malines, Belgium, Jan. 5, 1712; moved to Louvain in 1731; went to Liège in 1732. In 1733 he became court musician in Bonn, where he married Marie Poll. The youngest of his three children was Johann, father of the composer; he was a tenor singer in the Electoral choir, and married a young widow, Marie Magdalena Laym (born Keverich), daughter of the court cook at Ehrenbreitstein. Ludwig's musical education was taken in hand by his father, a stern master, who was interested in exhibiting the boy in public for profit. Beethoven learned the violin as well as the piano. His instructors, besides his father, were Pfeiffer, a music director and oboist; Van den Eeden, the court organist; and the latter's successor, Christian Gottlob Neefe. He was already a notable improviser on the piano; he could play Bach's *Wohltemperiertes Clavier* with fluency; in 1781 he composed his first published pieces (3 piano sonatas); in 1782, during Neefe's absence, Beethoven, then not quite twelve, was formally installed as his deputy at the organ; in 1783 he was appointed cembalist for the rehearsals of the court theater orchestra, as yet without emolument. In 1784 the new Elector Max Franz appointed Beethoven assistant organist at a salary of 150 florins; he held this place till 1792; from 1788 he also played second viola in the theater orchestra under the direction of Reicha. In 1787 he made a visit to Vienna for a few months, and played for Mozart, eliciting from him the oft-quoted exclamation: "This young man will leave his mark on the world." Beethoven's mother died in July 1787 and his father gave way to intemperance, gradually losing his voice. Beethoven's home life became wretched. He found consolation in the family of Frau von Breuning, the widow of a court councillor, to whose daughter and youngest son Beethoven gave music lessons. In their refined society his taste for literature was quickened. About this time he made the acquaintance of the young Count Waldstein, his life-long friend, admirer and benefactor. In his leisure hours he gave other lessons, and occupied himself with composition. Despite his remarkable faculty for improvisation, the number of known works for the period up to the age of 21 is relatively small: half a dozen songs; a rondo; a minuet, and 3 preludes for piano; 3 piano quartets; a piano trio; a string trio; 4 sets of piano variations; a rondino for wind instruments; the *Ritter-Ballet* with orch.; most of the Bagatelles, op. 33; 2 piano rondos, op. 51; the *Serenade Trio,* op. 8. To these should be added the lost cantata praised by Haydn; a lost trio for piano, flute and bassoon, and an Allegro and Minuet for 2 flutes. When Beethoven arrived in Vienna in 1792, he brought with him a considerable number of compositions in MS; some of these early works, e.g., the piano rondos, op. 51, he revised and published later (which accounts for the high opus-number); others were lost. In 1910 Fritz Stein found, in Jena, the score and parts of a symphony in C, which antedates the one known as the First; but the authenticity of this 'Jena Symphony' was never definitely established. In 1911, it was published by Breitkopf & Härtel. In point of fact, Beethoven never possessed the fatal facility of invention which rejoices in rapidity rather than solidity of production. His way of working is exhibited in the 'sketch books' of this early period, which contain motives, themes, ideas; fragments jotted down in moods of inspiration, frequently reappearing in modified forms, and in many cases recognizable as the germs of later compositions. This method of tentative notation and careful working-over was typical of Beethoven through his whole life.

The year 1792 marks a turning point. Haydn, passing through Bonn, warmly praised a cantata by Beethoven; the Elector, probably influenced by the master's opinion and the representations of the friendly Waldstein, decided to send Beethoven to Vienna, then the musical center of Europe. Here, a member of the highest circles of artists and art lovers, to which his native genius and letters from the Elector procured speedy admission, Beethoven found himself in a most congenial atmosphere. Besides his salary from the Elector (discontinued in 1794), and an annual stipend of 600 florins from Prince Lichnowsky, one of his truest friends and warmest admirers, his income was derived from the increasing sale of his works. He applied to Haydn for further instruction; but, dissatisfied with his methods of teaching, and angered at his lack of appreciation of compositions submitted to him for approval, he surreptitiously took lessons with Schenk, carrying his exercises, after correction by Schenk, to Haydn. This peculiar arrangement continued for a little more than a year, terminating at Haydn's departure (Jan. 1794) for England. During 1794 he had quite regular lessons in counterpoint with Albrechtsberger, whose verdict, 'He has learned nothing, and will never do anything properly,' can hardly be called prophetic; Salieri gave him many valuable hints on vocal style; and Aloys Förster contributed good counsel on the art of quartet-writing. Beethoven's contrapuntal exercises under Albrechtsberger (publ. Paris, 1832; revised ed. by Nottebohm, in vol. I of his 'Beethoven-Studien,' in 1873) illustrate the irrepressible conflict between Beethoven's imagination and the dry course of prescribed study.

A frequent guest at the private musical soirées of the Vienna aristocracy, Beethoven did not play in public until March 29, 1795, when he performed one of his piano concertos (probably op. 19, in B-flat) at a concert in the Burgtheater. In 1796 he visited Nuremberg, Prague and Berlin, and played before King Friedrich Wilhelm II. The publication of the E-flat piano sonata (op. 7) in 1797, a work of strongly individual type, is noteworthy. Two public concerts given by Beethoven in Prague in 1798 are chronicled as making a profound impression. In the same year he met two famed piano virtuosi: Steibelt, whose challenge to Beethoven as an extemporizer and composer resulted in his own overwhelming discomfiture; and Wölffl, a worthier opponent, with whom Beethoven associated and made music on a friendly footing (Wölffl inscribed 3 sonatas to him). To 1798 and 1799 belong the 3 sonatas for piano and violin (op. 12), the *Grande sonate pathétique* (op. 13), the first piano concerto (in C) and several lesser publications. About 1800, Beethoven's so-called 'first period' of composition (after the generally accepted classification by W. von Lenz in his *Beethoven et ses trois styles,* St. Petersburg, 1852) ends; the 'second period' extends to 1815; the 'third,' to the end of his life in 1827. The works of his first period include op/p. 1-13 (4 piano trios, 4 string trios, the first 6 string quartets, 10 piano sonatas), several sets of variations, septet for winds and strings (op. 20), the solo cantata *Adelaide* (op. 46), etc. At that time (1800-1801) a dread malady, which later resulted in total deafness, began to make alarming progress, and caused Beethoven acute mental suffering. From his entrance into Viennese society he was known as an 'original'; his spirit of independence, his love of freedom, his refusal to be obsequious, were strange in a world in which even such great musicians as Haydn had to practice subservience. No doubt, he deliberately cultivated his eccentricity. (He remarked that 'it is good to mingle with aristocrats, but one must know how to impress them.') His genius as an artist, and his noble generosity, won the hearts of music lovers, and caused them to overlook his occasional outbursts of temper. With increasing deafness, however, his character altered; he gradually grew taciturn, morose and suspicious (traits aggravated by the sordid meanness of his brothers, Karl and Johann, who had also settled in Vienna), and treated his best friends outrageously. From about 1820, deafness was nearly total; as early as 1816 he had to use an ear-trumpet. When his brother Karl died in 1815, leaving a son to Beethoven's guardianship, Beethoven undertook the boy's education as a sacred trust; his mental anguish at the failure of this task forms one of the saddest chapters in the great man's life, and still further darkened his declining years.

Beethoven's freest and most joyous creative period was his second. It was the period of the fullest flow of ideas, not as yet overcast by the gloom of his anguish. Major works included in it are the six symphonies from the third to the eighth; his opera, *Fidelio;* the music to *Egmont;* the ballet *Prometheus;* the mass in C, op. 86; the oratorio *Christus am Oelberg* (1803); the *Coriolanus* overture; the piano concertos in G and E-flat; violin concerto; the quartets in F minor, E-flat, and those inscribed to Razumovsky; 3 piano trios (op. 70, Nos. 1 and 2; op. 97); and 14 piano sonatas (among them the Sonata *quasi una fantasia,* op. 27, No. 2, commonly known as the *Moonlight Sonata;* the *Pastorale,* op. 28; op. 31, No. 2, in D m.; the one dedicated to Waldstein, op. 53; the *Appassionata,* op. 57; and *Les Adieux, l'absence, et le retour,* op. 81); also the *Liederkreis,* etc.

The third period includes the five piano sonatas opp. 101, 106, 109, 110, 111; also op. 102, Nos. 1 and 2; the *Missa solemnis* in D, op. 123; the Ninth Symphony, op. 125; the orchestral overture op. 124; the grand fugue for string quartet, op. 133; and the great string quartets op. 127 (E-flat), op. 130 (B-flat), op. 131 (C# m.), op. 132 (A m.), and op. 135 (F).

The work on his only opera, *Fidelio,* cost Beethoven more pains and exasperation than any other of his compositions. As early as 1803 he arranged with Schikaneder, manager of the Theater-an-der-Wien, to write an opera; it was produced on Nov. 20, 1805, amid the commotion and gloom incident to the entrance, just a week before, of the French army into Vienna. Originally in three acts, it was withdrawn after three consecutive performances; then, after considerable revisions and cuts, was brought out again (March 29, 1806) with more success, but withdrawn by the composer after only two performances. Once more sweepingly revised, it was staged in 1814, very successfully. The opera was first named *Leonore,* after the heroine; its overture was rewritten twice; the present *Fidelio* overture is quite different. Beethoven's sketch-book for his opera contains 300 large pages of 16 staves each, crammed with heterogeneous notes.

The *Eroica* symphony (No. 3) has an interesting history. Schindler's report (based on a story told by Lichnowsky and Ries) that Beethoven tore off the title page of the MS of the *Eroica* with a dedication to Napoleon after learning of Napoleon's proclamation as emperor, seems apocryphal; while the original MS is lost, a copyist's score (in the library of the Gesellschaft der Musikfreunde in Vienna) shows that Beethoven inked out the title and renamed the symphony as 'Sinfonia eroica composta per festeggiare il sovvenire d'un grand' uomo' (heroic symphony, composed to celebrate the memory of a great man). However, in a letter to Breitkopf & Härtel dated Aug. 26, 1804 (long after Napoleon's proclamation) Beethoven still refers to the *Eroica* as "entitled Bonaparte."

With the Ninth Symphony Beethoven achieved a sublime greatness of expression in symphonic form; the choral finale where orchestral and vocal music blend in an outburst of ecstasy (the words are from Schiller's 'Hymn to Joy'), is a true apotheosis of musical art.

Up to 1814, Beethoven's material welfare had increased, though hardly in proportion to his artistic triumphs. An honored and frequent guest at the houses of the princes Carl Lichnowsky, Lobkowitz and Kinsky, the counts Moritz Lichnowsky, Rasumovsky and Franz von Brunswick, and Baron von Gleichenstein, Beethoven was treated as a social equal (the nobiliary particle "van" in his full name, Ludwig van Beethoven, made him technically a member of the aristocracy, and Beethoven regarded this sign of nobility with some seriousness); at the time of the Vienna Congress, as a guest of

Archduke Rudolf, he met the various reigning monarchs as their peers, and even (as he said himself) let them pay court to him. A curious incident was the invitation extended to Beethoven in 1809, by the *de facto* 'King of Westphalia,' Jerome Bonaparte, to assume the post of maître de chapelle at Kassel at a salary of 600 ducats (about $1,500). Beethoven never considered accepting this offer; he really wanted to become Imperial Kapellmeister at Vienna; but the bare possibility of losing the great composer so dismayed his Viennese admirers, that Archduke Rudolf and Princes Lobkowitz and Kinsky bestowed on Beethoven an annuity of 4,000 florins (nominally $2,000, but in depreciated paper of fluctuating value). In December, 1826, he caught a violent cold, which developed into pneumonia; dropsy then supervened, and after several unsuccessful operations he succumbed to the disease on March 26, 1827. Hundreds attended his funeral and titled personages vied with each other in their expression of homage and regret.

While Beethoven, in choosing the conventional sonata form as a vehicle for the expression of his thought (in 81 works, i.e., about one-third of all), still belongs to the 'classic' school, his methods of moulding this form were eminently unconventional; indeed, so much so, that even at the beginning of his 'second period' the progressive 'Allgemeine musikalische Zeitung' of Leipzig berated him for his 'daring harmonies and venturesome rhythms'. Even among musicians no genuine appreciation of his last string quartets and piano sonatas was found until half a century after his death. His innovations on the formal key scheme of his predecessors, his original elaboration of connecting links both in thematic development and between separate movements, his fertility in incidental modulation, and the inexhaustible freshness of his rhythms, render the structure of his compositions thoroughly individual. But his loftiest originality, and that whence the differences in formal construction naturally flowed, is the intensity and fervor of subjective emotion which pervades his music. It is this mood of profound subjectivity, of powerful soul-expression, that separates Beethoven's music from the classical works of Bach, Haydn and Mozart, opening the era of 'romantic' composition. Technically, Beethoven's art of orchestration reaches a perfection in detail and a grandeur of effect theretofore unknown; and his diversified development of the motives (melodic, harmonic, rhythmic) surpasses anything before Wagner. As specimens of what can be done in thematic treatment, his variations on given or original themes are a *ne plus ultra* of musical ingenuity. It is noteworthy that, according to contemporary accounts, his 'free improvisations' at the piano, which held his auditors spellbound, were developments of kindred nature; not mere rhapsodies, but the spontaneous elaborations of a teeming invention; in vocal music, his *Fidelio* and the *Missa solemnis* are creations of unique power.

Monuments were erected to Beethoven in 1845 at Bonn (by Hähnel), and in 1880 at Vienna (by Zumbusch).

Beethoven's works comprise 138 opus-numbers, and many unnumbered compositions. A list of his publ. works is given below. Certain works are in both instrumental and vocal categories (the 9th symphony, *Egmont, Ruins of Athens,* etc.). They have been listed in that group with which they are customarily associated.

INSTRUMENTAL WORKS

Nine Symphonies: No. 1, op. 21, in C; 2, op. 36, in D; 3, op. 55, in E♭ (*Eroica*); 4, op. 60, in B♭; 5, op. 67, in C m.; 6, op. 68, in F (*Pastoral*); 7, op. 92, in A; 8, op. 93, in F; 9, op. 125, in D m. (*Choral*).

The Battle of Vittoria (op. 91); Symphony in C (*Jena,* publ. 1911; of doubtful authenticity); music to the ballet *Prometheus* (op. 43), and to Goethe's *Egmont* (op. 84), both with overtures.

Nine further overtures: *Coriolanus* (op. 62); *Leonore* (No. 1, op. 138; Nos. 2 and 3, op. 72a); *Fidelio* (from op. 72b); *King Stephen* (from op. 117); *Ruins of Athens* (from op. 113); *Namensfeier* (op. 115); *Weihe des Hauses* (op. 124).

Other compositions for orch. or band: Allegretto in E♭; March from *Tarpeia,* in C; Military Marches in D and F; *Ritter-Ballet;* 12 Minuets; 12 *deutsche Tänze;* 12 *Contretänze;* 2 Marches in F; March in C; Polonaise in D; Ecossaise in D.

Violin concerto, op. 61, in D.

Two Romances for violin and orch. (op. 40, in G; op. 50, in F).

Two cadenzas to the violin concerto.

Five piano concertos: No. 1, op. 15, in C; 2, op. 19, in B♭; 3, op. 37, in C m.; 4, op. 58, in G; 5, op. 73, in E♭ (*Emperor*); also a piano concerto arranged from the violin concerto; a Rondo in B♭, for piano and orch. (left incomplete and finished by Czerny).

8 cadenzas to the first 4 piano concertos, and 2 cadenzas to Mozart's piano concerto in D m. (K. 466).

A triple concerto, op. 56, for piano, violin,

cello and orch.; a *Choral Fantasia,* op. 80, for piano, chorus and orch.

Two Octets for wind, both in E♭ (the first op. 103).

Septet for strings and wind, in E♭, op. 20.

Sextet for strings and 2 horns, in E♭, op. 81b.

Sextet for wind, in E♭, op. 71. Also, a March, in B♭, for 6 woodwinds.

Three Quintets for strings: Op. 4, in E♭; op. 29, in C; op. 104, in C m. Also a Fugue for string quintet, op. 137.

For four trombones: Three *Equale.*

Sixteen String Quartets: Op. 18, Nos. 1-6, in F, G, D, C m., A, and B♭ (first period). Op. 59, Nos. 1-3, in F, E m., and C; op. 74 in E♭ (*Harfenquartett*); op. 95, in F m. (second period). —Op. 127, in E♭; op. 130, in B♭; op. 131, in C♯ m.; op. 132, in A m.; op. 135, in F. Also a Grand Fugue for string quartet, op. 133, in B♭ (third period).

Five string trios: Op. 3, in E♭; op. 9, Nos. 1-3, in G, D, C m.; op. 8, in D (*Serenade*). Also 6 *Ländlerische Tänze.*

Trio for 2 oboes and Engl. horn, op. 87, in C. Also a Serenade for flute, violin and viola op. 25, in D.

Quintet for piano and wind, op. 16, in E♭.

Four Quartets for piano and strings: in E♭, D, C (juvenile); in E♭ (arrangement of the piano quintet).

Nine Trios for piano, violin and cello: Op. 1, Nos. 1-3, in E♭, G, C m.; op. 70, Nos. 1-2, in D, E♭; op. 97, in B♭; in E♭, B♭ (both posthumous, the latter in one movement); in D (incomplete). Also for piano, violin and cello: 14 variations, op. 44, in E♭; Variations, op. 121a, on 'Ich bin der Schneider Kakadu'; an arrangement of the 2nd symph., op. 36.

Two Trios for piano, clar. (or violin) and cello: Op. 11, B♭; op. 38, in E♭ (after the septet, op. 20). Also a Trio for piano, flute and bassoon.

Sonatina in C m., for piano and mandolin. Also an Adagio in E♭, for piano and mandolin.

Ten Sonatas for piano and violin: Op. 12, Nos. 1-3, in D, A, E♭; op. 23, in A m.; op. 24, in F; op. 30, Nos. 1-3, in A, C m., G; op. 47 in A (*Kreutzer*); op. 96, in G. Also for piano and violin: Rondo in G; 12 Variations, in F, on 'Se vuol ballare' from Mozart's *Marriage of Figaro;* 6 *Deutsche Tänze.*

Five Sonatas for piano and cello; Op. 5, 1-2, in F, G; op. 69, in A; op. 102, Nos. 1-2, in C, D. Also for piano and cello: 12 variations on 'Ein Mädchen oder Weibchen', op. 66, in F; 12 variations in G, on 'See, the Conquering Hero Comes'; 7 variations, in E♭, on 'Bei Männern, welche Liebe fühlen'.

Sonata for piano and horn, op. 17, in F.

Two sets of 'varied themes' for piano with obbligato flute (or violin); op. 105 with 6 themes; op. 107 with 10 themes.

For piano, 4 hands: Sonata, op. 6, in D; 3 Marches, op. 45, in C, E♭, D; Variations, in C, on a theme by Count Waldstein; Song with variations, in D ('Ich denke dein'); Grand Fugue, op. 134 (an arr. of op. 133); an Allegro in B♭; Gavotte in F; *Marzia lugubre* (incomplete).

Thirty-eight Sonatas for piano solo: Op. 2, Nos. 1-3, in F m., A, C (ded. to Haydn); op. 7, in E♭; op. 10, Nos. 1-3, in C m., F, D; op. 13, in C m. (*Pathétique;* ded. to Prince Lichnowsky); op. 14, Nos. 1-2, in E, G; op. 22, in B♭; op. 26, in A♭ (ded. to Prince Lichnowsky); op. 27, Nos. 1-2, in E♭, C♯ m.; (the latter known as *Moonlight Sonata*); op. 28, in D (*Pastoral*); op. 31, Nos. 1-3, in G, D m., E♭; op. 49, 2 easy sonatas in G m., G; op. 53, in C (ded. to Count Waldstein); op. 54, in F; op. 57, in F m. (*Appassionata*); op. 78, in F♯; op. 79, little sonata in G; op. 81a, in E♭ (*Les Adieux, l'absence, le retour;* ded. to Archduke Rudolph); op. 90, in E m. (ded. to Count Lichnowsky); op. 101, in A; op. 106, in B♭ (*Hammerklavier;* ded. to Archduke Rudolph); op. 109, in E; op. 110, in A♭; op. 111, in C m. Also three sonatas in E♭, F m., D; an easy sonata in C (incomplete); two sonatinas in G, F.

Also for piano solo: 21 sets of variations, including op. 34, in F; op. 35, in E♭ (*Eroica*); op. 76, in D; op. 120, in C (*Diabelli*). Bagatelles, op. 33, 119, 126. 5 Rondos, including op. 51, Nos. 1-2, and op. 129; Fantasia, op. 77, in G m.; 3 Preludes, including op. 39, Nos. 1-2 (for piano or organ); Polonaise, op. 89, in C; Andante in F; 7 Minuets; 13 Ländler; a *Kleines Stück* in B♭; a German dance in G; *Letzter Gedanke* in C; 6 easy variations, in F, for piano or harp; *Für Elise* (Bagatelle in A m.); Allegretto in C m.; Allemande in A; 2 Bagatelles in C m., C; 8 Ecossaisen; 2 *Kleine Clavierstücke* (*Lustig, Traurig*); 2 Waltzes in E♭, D.

For organ: A 2-part fugue.

Vocal Music

Opera, *Fidelio,* in 2 acts, op. 72b.

Two Masses, op. 86, in C, and op. 123, in D (*Missa Solemnis*).

Oratorio, *Christus am Oelberg,* op. 85.

Cantata, *Der glorreiche Augenblick,* op. 136 (also arr. as *Preis der Tonkunst*).

Meeresstille und glückliche Fahrt, op. 112 (poem by Goethe).

Ah, perfido!, scena and aria for soprano with orch., op. 65.

Tremate, empi, tremate, trio for soprano, tenor and bass, op. 116.

Opferlied, for soprano, chor. and orch., op. 121b.

Bundeslied, for 2 soli, 3-part chorus and wind, op. 122.

Elegischer Gesang, for 4 voices and strings, op. 118.

Cantate auf den Tod Kaiser Joseph des Zweiten; Cantate auf die Erhebung Leopold des Zweiten zur Kaiserwürde; Chor zum Festspiel: Die Weihe des Hauses; Chor auf die verbündeten Fürsten.

For bass and orch.: *Prüfung des Küssens*. Also *Mit Mädeln sich vertragen*.

Two arias for Ignaz Umlauf's Singspiel *Die schöne Schusterin (O welch ein Leben!; Soll ein Schuh nicht drücken)*.

For soprano and orch: *Primo amore piacer del ciel*.

Music to Friedrich Duncker's drama *Leonore Prohaska*.

Trauergesang for 4-part male chor. and 4 trombones; *Lobkowitz-Cantate* for 3 voices and piano; *Gesang der Mönche* for 3 voices; *Abschiedsgesang* for 3 male voices; *O care selve* (song from Metastasio's *Olimpiade*), for unison chorus and piano.

Seventy-five songs with piano accomp.; one duet; twenty-three vocal canons; seven books of English, Scotch, Irish, Welsh and Italian songs for voice, piano, violin and cello.

Breitkopf & Härtel were the first to publ. a 'complete edition' in 24 series comprising 40 volumes (1864-67, ed. by Rietz, Nottebohm, David, Hauptmann, Reinecke and others). An additional volume, containing 48 works subsequently found, appeared in 1887.

BIBLIOGRAPHY

A. Biographical: F. G. Wegeler and F. Ries, *Biographische Notizen über L. van B.* (Koblenz, 1838; new ed. by A. Kalischer, Leipzig, 1906); A. Schindler, *Biographie von L. van B.* (Münster, 1840; new ed. by A. Kalischer, Berlin, 1909; Eng. transl. by Moscheles, London, 1841); W. v. Lenz, *B.: eine Kunststudie* (2 vols., Kassel, 1855; I. *Das Leben des Meisters*, new ed. by A. Kalischer, Berlin, 1908; II. *Der Stil in B.; Die Mit- und Nachwelt B.'s; Der B. Status Quo in Russland*); A. B. Marx, *L. van B.'s Leben und Schaffen* (2 vols., Berlin, 1859; 6th ed. Leipzig, 1906); L. Nohl, *B.'s Leben* (3 vols., Vienna, 1864-77); id., *B. nach den Schilderungen seiner Zeitgenossen* (Stuttgart, 1877); G. v. Breuning, *Aus dem Schwarzspanierhause* (Vienna, 1874); J. W. v. Wasielewski, *L. van B.* (2 vols., Berlin, 1888); T. v. Frimmel, *Neue Beethoveniana* (Berlin, 1887; revised and augmented as *Beethovenstudien*, 2 vols., Munich, 1905-6); id., *B.* (in Riemann's *Berühmte Meister*, Berlin, 1901); R. Rolland, *B.* (Paris, 1903; in English, N. Y., 1917); F. Kerst, *B. im eigenen Wort* (Berlin, 1904; Engl. transl. by H. E. Krehbiel, N. Y. 1905); G. A. Fischer, *B., a Character Study* (N. Y., 1905); E. Walker, *B.* (2d ed. London, 1907); A. Kalischer, *B. und seine Zeitgenossen* (4 vols., Leipzig, 1910); P. Bekker, *B.* (Berlin, 1911; Engl. transl. and adaptation by M. M. Bozman, London, 1925); M. E. Belpaire, *B., een kunsten levensbeeld* (Antwerp, 1911); V. d'Indy, *B.: Biographie critique* (Paris, 1911; Engl. transl. by T. Baker, Boston, 1913); W. A. Thomas-San Galli, *L. van B.* (Berlin, 1913); A. Hensel, *B. Der Versuch einer musik-philosophischen Darstellung* (ib., 1918); J. G. Prod'homme, *La jeunesse de B.* (Paris, 1920; new ed., 1927); G. Bilancioni, *La sordità di B.* (Rome, 1921); T. v. Frimmel, *B. im zeitgenössischen Bildnis* (Vienna, 1923); W. Krug, *B.'s Vollendung* (Munich, 1924); S. Ley, *B.'s Leben in authentischen Bildern und Texten* (Berlin, 1925); L. Schiedermair, *Der junge B.* (Leipzig, 1925; 2nd ed., 1951); B. issue of the 'Mus. Quarterly' (1927); B. Bartels, *B.* (Hildesheim, 1927); L. Bertrán, *Anecdotario completo de B.* (Buenos Aires, 1927); E. Newman, *The Unconscious B.* (N. Y., 1927); A. Orel, *B.* (Vienna, 1927); J.-G. Prod'homme, *B. raconté par ceux qui l'ont vu* (Paris, 1927); A. Schmitz, *Das romantische Beethovenbild* (Berlin, 1927); O. G. Sonneck, *The Riddle of the Immortal Beloved*, a supplement to Thayer's 'Life of B.' (N. Y., 1927); W. J. Turner, *B., the Search for Reality* (London, 1927); R. J. J. van Aerde, *Les ancêtres flamands de B.* (Malines, 1928); E. Closson, *L'élément flamand dans B.* (Brussels, 1928; Engl. transl. London, 1934); W. Fischer, *B. als Mensch* (Regensburg, 1928); R. Rolland, *B.: les grandes époques créatrices* (Paris, 1928 ff.); id., *B. the Creator* (Engl. transl. by E. Newman, N. Y., 1929); R. H. Schauffler, *B., the Man who Freed Music* (N. Y., 1929); E. Herriot, *La vie de B.* (Paris, 1929; Engl. transl. N. Y., 1935); R. Rolland, *Goethe et B.* (Paris, 1930; Engl. transl. N. Y., 1931); A. Boschot, *B., la musique et la vie* (Paris, 1931); R. Specht, *Bildnis B.'s* (Hellerau, 1931; Engl. transl. London, 1933); E. Brümmer, *B. im Spiegel der zeitgenössischen rheinischen Presse* (Würzburg, 1932); F. S. Howes, *B.* (London, 1933); M. Scott, *B.* (ib., 1934); E. Bücken, *L. van B.* (Potsdam, 1935); C.

Carpenter, *French Factors in B.'s Life* (N. Y., 1935); E. Buenzod, *Pouvoirs de B.* (Paris, 1936); K. Kobald, *B.* (Leipzig, 1936); W. Riezler, *B.* (Berlin, 1936; Engl. transl. London, 1938); H. Schultz, *L. van B., sein Leben in Bildern* (Leipzig, 1936); *B. und die Gegenwart* (Berlin and Bonn, 1937); H. Kesser, *B. der Europäer* (Zürich, 1937); H. v. Hofmannsthal, *B.* (Vienna, 1938); R. Petzoldt, *L. van B., Leben und Werk* (Leipzig, 1938); R. van Aerde, *A la recherche des ascendants de B.* in the 'Revue belge archéologique' (1939, No. 2); C. Brandt, *B., su vida, su obra, y el sentido de su música* (Caracas, 1940); A. Orel, *Grillparzer und B.* (Vienna, 1941); L. Schrade, *B. in France* (New Haven, 1942); H. Volkmann, *B. in seinen Beziehungen zu Dresden* (Dresden, 1942); J. N. Burk, *The Life and Works of B.* (N. Y., 1943); E. C. C. Corti, *B.- Anekdoten* (Berlin, 1943); E. Ludwig, *B., Life of a Conqueror* (1943); A. Albertini, *B., l'uomo,* 4th ed. (Milan, 1944); *Les cahiers de conversation de B. (1819-1827),* trans. and ed. by J. G. Prod'homme (Paris, 1946); A. Pryce-Jones, *B.* (London, 1948); S. Axnelson, *B.'s ferne und unsterbliche Geliebte* (Zürich, 1953; purporting to prove that the "immortal beloved" was Josephine Deym-Stackelberg, sister of Therese Brunswick; that Beethoven was with her in Prague, July 3, 1812, and that Josephine's child Minona, born in Vienna on April 9, 1813, was in fact Beethoven's); Editha and Richard Sterba, *B. and his Nephew, a Psychoanalytical Study of their Relationship* (N. Y., 1954). The standard and most extensive biography is the monumental work of A. W. Thayer, *L. v. B.'s Leben* (5 vols., 1866-1908). The English original was never published. The first 3 volumes appeared in a German transl. by H. Deiters (Berlin, 1866, 1872, 1877). After the author's death Deiters completed vols. IV and V from Thayer's material, but died also before their publication. He had also revised and enlarged vol. I (Leipzig, 1901). Deiters' manuscript was revised and edited by H. Riemann (vol. IV, Leipzig, 1907; vol. V, ib., 1908). Vols. II and III were then revised and enlarged by Riemann along the lines followed by Deiters in the revision of vol. I (Leipzig, 1910-11). The 4th ed. of Thayer's work was revised by Riemann and published in 1919 (abridged English ed. by Krehbiel, in 3 vols., N. Y., 1921).

B. CORRESPONDENCE: The several partial collections of letters edited by Nohl, Köchel, etc., have been superseded by the following complete editions: A. C. Kalischer, *B.'s sämmtliche Briefe* (5 vols., Berlin, 1906-8; partial Engl. transl. by J. S. Shedlock, London, 1909); F. Prelinger, *L. van B.'s sämmtliche Briefe und Aufzeichnungen* (5 vols., Vienna, 1907-10); E. Kastner, *L. van B.'s sämmtliche Briefe* (Leipzig, 1910). Also A. Leitzmann, *B.'s Aufzeichnungen* (Leipzig, 1918); M. Unger, *B. und seiner Verleger Steiner-Haslinger-Schlesinger* (Berlin, 1921); id., *B.'s Handschrift* (Bonn, 1926); O. G. Sonneck, *B. Letters in America* (N. Y., 1927); G. Kinsky, *Die Handschriften zu B.'s Egmont Musik* (Vienna, 1933). Other letters have been edited by U. Steindorff (in Engl.; Los Angeles, 1933); *Briefe und das heiligenstädter Testament,* ed. by A. Klarer (Zürich, 1944); *L. v. B., ein Bekenntnis mit Briefen und Zeitdokumenten,* edited by H. Freiberger (Berlin, 1951).

C. CRITICISM, ANALYSIS.—General: L. v. Seyfried, *L. van B.'s Studien im Generalbass, Kontrapunkt, und in der Kompositionslehre* (Vienna, 1832; new ed. by Nottebohm, Leipzig, 1873; also by L. Köhler, ib., 1880); W. v. Lenz, *B. et ses trois styles* (St. Petersburg, 1852; new ed. by M. D. Calvocoressi, Paris, 1909); A. v. Oulibicheff, *B., ses critiques et ses glossateurs* (Paris, 1857; Ger. transl. by L. Bischoff, Leipzig, 1859); G. Nottebohm, *Ein Skizzenbuch von Beethoven* (Leipzig, 1865; 2d ed. ib., 1880; new rev. ed. by P. Mies, 1924); R. Wagner, *B.* (Leipzig, 1870; reprinted in vol. IX of 'Ges. Schriften und Dichtungen'; Engl. transl., 3rd ed., N. Y., 1883); G. Nottebohm, *Beethoveniana* (Leipzig, 1872); id., *Neue Beethoveniana* (orig. publ. in 'Musikal. Wochenblatt,' 1878; revised and enlarged E. Mandyczewski as *Zweite Beethoveniana* (Leipzig, 1887); T. de Wyzewa, *B. et Wagner* (Paris, 1898; 4th ed., 1914); D. G. Mason, *B. and His Forerunners* (N. Y., 1904); H. Berlioz, *A Critical Study of B.'s Nine Symphonies* (transl. by E. Evans; N. Y., 1913); R. Rolland, *B.* (transl. by B. Constance Hull, with a brief analysis of the sonatas, the symphonies and the quartets by A. Eaglefield Hull; N. Y., 1917); H. Mersmann, *B., die Synthese der Stile* (Berlin, 1922); id., *B.'s Skizzen* (Basel, 1924); F. Cassirer, *B. und die Gestalt* (Stuttgart, 1925); P. Mies, *Die Bedeutung der Skizzen B.'s zur Erkenntnis seines Stiles* (Leipzig, 1925; Engl. transl. London, 1929); T. v. Frimmel, *B.-Handbuch* (2 vols., Leipzig, 1926); J. W. N. Sullivan, *B., His Spiritual Development* (London, 1927); T. Veidl, *Der musikalische Humor bei B.* (Leipzig, 1929); H. Naumann, *Strukturkadenzen bei B.* (Meissen, 1931); W. Haas, *Systematische Ordnung Beethovenscher Melodien* (Leipzig, 1932); D. F. Tovey, *Essays in Musical Analysis* (5 vols., London, 1935-37); A. Schering, *B. und die Dichtung* (Berlin, 1936); W. Broel, *Die Durchführungsgestaltung in B.'s Sonatensätzen* (Brunswick, 1937); A. Schering, *Zur Erkenntnis B.'s; neue Beiträge zur Deutung seiner Werke* (Würzburg, 1938); J. Boyer, *Le 'romantisme' de B.* (Paris, 1939); Storck-Wieman, *Wege zu B.* (Regensburg, 1942); D. F. Tovey, *B.* (London, 1945); L. Misch, *B.-Studien* (Berlin, 1950; Engl. transl., Norman, Okla., 1954). —Symphonic: G. Erlanger et al., *B.'s Symphonien erläutert* (Frankfurt, 1896); G. Grove, *B. and His Nine Symphonies* (London, 1896); A. Colombani, *Le nove sinfonie di B.* (Turin, 1897); J. Hartog, *L. van B. en zijne negen symphonieën* (Amsterdam, 1904); J.-G. Prod'homme, *Les symphonies de B.* (Paris, 1906); F. Weingartner, *Ratschläge für Aufführungen der Symphonien B.'s* (Leipzig, 1906; 2d ed. 1916; Engl. transl. N. Y., n. d.); M. H. Barroso, *La IX sinfonía de B.* (Madrid, 1912); H. Schenker, *B.'s neunte Symphonie* (Vienna, 1912); *Eigenhändiges Skizzenbuch zur 9. Symphonie* (Leipzig, 1913; facsim. ed.); E. Evans, *B.'s Nine Symphonies . . .* (2 vols., London, 1923-24); E. de la Guardia, *Las sinfonías de B.* (Buenos Aires, 1927); D. E. Berg, *B. and the Romantic Symphony* (N. Y., 1927); J. Braunstein, *B.'s Leonore-Ouvertüren* (Leipzig, 1927); W. Hutschenruijter, *De symphonieën van B. geänalyseerd* (The Hague, 1928); K. Nef, *Die neun Sinfonien B.'s* (Leipzig, 1928); O. Baensch, *Aufbau und Sinn des Chorfinales in B.'s Neunter Symphonie* (Berlin, 1930); J. Chantavoine, *Les Symphonies de B.* (Paris, 1932); E. Magni Dufflocq, *Le sinfonie di B.* (Milan, 1935). —Chamber music: J. Matthews, *The Violin Music of B.* (London, 1902); H. Riemann, *B.'s Streichquartette* (in 'Musikführer,' Leipzig, 1901-7); T. Helm, *B.'s Streichquartette* (2nd ed. Leipzig, 1910); H. Riemann, *B.'s Streichquartette erläutert* (Berlin, 1910); S. Midgley, *Handbook to B.'s Sonatas for Violin and Pianoforte* (London, 1911); O. Rupertus, *Erläuterungen zu B.'s Violinsonaten* (Cologne, 1915); E. Albini, *B. e le sue cinque sonate per violoncello* (Turin, 1923); J. H. Wetzel, *B.'s Violinsonaten, nebst den Romanzen und dem Konzert* (Berlin, 1924); J. de Marliave, *Les quatuors de B.* (Paris, 1925; Engl. transl. by H. Andrews, London, 1928); M. Herwegh, *Technique d'interprétation sous forme d'essai d'analyse psychologique expérimentale appliqué aux sonates pour piano et violon* (Paris, 1926); W. H. Hadow, *B.'s Op. 18 Quartets* (London, 1926); W. Engelsmann, *B.'s Kompositionspläne dargestellt in den Sonaten für Klavier und Violine* (Augsburg, 1931); S. Grew, *B.'s 'Grosse Fuge'* (in the 'Mus. Quarterly,' 1931); R. Giraldi, *Analisi formale ed estetica dei primi tempi dei Quartetti Op. 18* (Rome, 1933); S. Kjellström, *B.'s strakkvartetter, en orientering* (Stockholm, 1936); G. Abraham, *B.'s Second-Period Quartets* (1942); D. G. Mason, *The Quartets of B.* (N.Y., 1947).—Piano Music: E. v. Elterlein, *B.'s Klaviersonaten* (Leipzig, 1856; 5th ed. 1895; Engl. transl. London, 1898); C. Reinecke, *Die Beethovenschen Klaviersonaten* (Leipzig, 1897; Engl. transl. London, 1898); A.B. Marx, *Anleitung zum Vortrag Beethovensche Klavierwerke* (Berlin, 1898); W. Nagel, *B. und seine Klaviersonaten* (2 vols., Langensalza, 1905); R. Nesieht, *Das goldene Zeitalter der Klaviersonate* (Cologne, 1910); H. Riemann, *L. van B.'s sämtliche Klavier-Solosonaten* (3 vols., Berlin, 1919-20); S. Leoni, *Le sonate per pf. di B.* (Turin, 1922); F. Volbach, *Erläuterungen zu den Klaviersonaten B.'s* (3d ed. Cologne, 1924); A. F. Milne, *B., the Pianoforte Sonatas* (London, 1925-28); I. Peters, *B.'s Klaviermusik* (Berlin, 1925); W. Behrend, *L. van B.'s Pianoforte Sonatas* (transl. from the Danish; London, 1927); J. A. Johnstone, *Notes on the Interpretation of 24 Famous Pianoforte Sonatas by B.* (London, 1927); H. Westerby, *B. and His Piano Works* (ib., 1931); A. Coviello, *Difficulties of B.'s Pianoforte Sonatas* (ib., 1935); D.F. Tovey, *A Companion to B.'s Pianoforte Sonatas* (ib., 1935); R. Kastner, *B.'s Pianoforte Sonatas; a Descriptive Commentary on the Sonatas in the Light of Schnabel's Interpretations* (ib., 1935); H. Leichtentritt, *The Complete Pianoforte Sonatas of B.* (N. Y., 1936); J.-G. Prod'homme, *Les sonates pour piano de B.* (Paris, 1937); E. Blom, *B.'s Pianoforte Sonatas Discussed* (London, 1938). —Vocal and choral music: M. Bouchor, *La messe en ré de B.* (Paris, 1886); M. Remy, *Missa solemnis* (Brussels, 1897); R. Sternfeld, *Zur Einführung in L. van B.'s Missa solemnis* (Berlin, 1900); H. de Curzon, *Les Lieder et airs détachés de B.* (Paris, 1905); W. Weber, *B.'s Missa solemnis* (Leipzig, 1908); M. Kufferath, *Fidelio de L. van B.* (Paris, 1913); M. Chop, *L. van B.: Missa solemnis geschichtlich und musikalisch analysiert* (Leipzig, 1921); H. Böttcher, *B.'s Lieder* (Berlin, 1927); id., *B. als Liederkomponist* (Augsburg, 1928); J. Schmidt, *Unbekannte Manuskripte zu B.'s weltlichen und geistlichen Gesangsmusik* (Leipzig, 1928); F. Lederer, *B.'s Bearbeitungen schottischer und anderer Volkslieder* (Bonn, 1934).

D. Catalogues, Year-Books, Etc.: The first catalogue, revised by Beethoven personally, and completed by A. Gräffer (Vienna, 1828), as well as several published subsequently, leave much to be desired. The first valuable thematic catalogue was issued by Breitkopf & Härtel (Leipzig, 1851). It was thoroughly revised and enlarged by G. Nottebohm and published as *Thematisches Verzeichnis der im Druck erschienenen Werke von L. van B.* (Leipzig, 1868); new edition, together with *Bibliotheca Beethoveniana,* by E. Kastner, giving a complete list of all books (and important articles written in periodicals) about Beethoven from 1829-1913 (Leipzig, 1913; 2d ed. by T. von Frimmel, 1925). As a precursor to his great biography, Thayer published a *Chronologisches Verzeichniss der Werke L. van B.'s* (Berlin, 1865), which includes unpublished works. In 1908 T. von Frimmel began the publication of a 'B.-Jahrbuch,' the name of which, in 1911, was changed to 'B.-Forschung' (Vienna). See also the yearly publications of the Beethovenhaus in Bonn (since 1920); especially J. Schmidt-Görg, *Katalog der Handschriften des B.-Hauses und B.-Archivs Bonn* (Bonn, 1935) and T. Lohmer, *Das B.-Haus in Bonn und seine Sammlungen* (Bonn, 1936; English transl., 1937); 'Neues B.-Jahrbuch' ed. by A. Sandberger (Augsburg, 1924 ff.); W. Korte, *L. van B., Darstellung seines Werkes* (Berlin, 1936); A. Bruers, *B., Catalogo ragionato delle opere principali* (Rome, 1937). Of value and interest also are G. Adler, *Verzeichnis der musikalischen Autographe von L. van B.* (Vienna, 1890), and A. C. Kalischer, *Die B.-Autographe der Kgl. Bibliothek zu Berlin,* in 'Monatshefte für Musikgeschichte' (Oct., 1895); report of the Beethoven Centenary (Vienna, 1927); G. Biamonti, *Catalogo cronologico di tutte le musiche di B.* (Rome, 1952). A thematic and bibliographic index of all Beethoven's works, prepared by Georg Kinsky and completed, after Kinsky's death, by Hans Halm, was published in Munich in 1955.

Beffara, Louis-François, French writer on music; b. Nonancourt, Eure, Aug. 23, 1751; d. Paris, Feb. 2, 1838. He was 'Commissaire de Police' in Paris from 1792-1816; left his rare collection of books and MSS. to the city of Paris. Practically all of these were burned during the Commune in 1871, but a few are preserved in the Opéra library and at the Bibliothèque Nationale. He wrote a *Dictionnaire de l'Académie royale de Musique* (7 vols.) and 7 vols. of rules and regulations of the 'Académie' (Grand Opéra) also a *Dictionnaire alphabétique des acteurs,* etc. (3 vols.); *Tableau chronologique des représentations journalières,* etc. (from 1671); *Dictionnaire alphabétique des tragédies lyriques . . . non représentées à l'Académie, etc.* (5 vols.); and *Dramaturgie lyrique étrangère* (17 vols.).

Behaim, Michel, singer; b. Sulzbach, near Weinsberg, 1416; d. there (murdered), 1474. He was active as a soldier and singer in the service of various German, Danish and Hungarian princes; was one of the earliest of the Meistersinger who still retained some of the characteristics of the Minnesinger; finally settled in Sulzbach as village major or magistrate. He composed many songs; eleven are preserved at Heidelberg and Munich. Cf. Alfred Kühn, *Rhythmik und Melodik Michel Behaims* (1907).

Behm (bām), **Eduard,** German composer; b. Stettin, April 8, 1862; d. Bad Harzburg, Feb. 6, 1946. He studied at the Leipzig Cons.; taught at the Erfurt Academy of Music; became director of the Scharwenka Cons. in Berlin (until 1901), and prof. in 1917. He was awarded the Mendelssohn prize for a symphony and the Bösendorfer prize for a piano concerto. He wrote the operas, *Der Schelm von Bergen* (Dresden, 1890), *Marienkind* (1902), *Das Gelöbnis* (1914); a string sextet, using the Stelzner violotta; a piano trio; a clarinet quintet; 3 violin sonatas; a violin concerto; *Frühlingsidylle* for violin and orch.; male choruses, songs, etc. Behm wrote a short autobiography in 'Musik in Pommern' (Vol. I, 1932).

Behnke (bān'-kĕh), **Emil,** vocal teacher; b. Stettin, 1836; d. Ostende, Sept. 17, 1892. He lived chiefly in London as an authority on voice-training, and teacher of voice production for singers and speakers; also lecturing on physiology of voice. He wrote *The Mechanism of the Human Voice* (London, 1880); *Voice, Song and Speech* (with Lennox Browne, 1883); *Voice-training Exercises* 1884); and *The Child's Voice* (1885), the last two in collaboration with Dr. C. W. Pearce.

Behr, Franz, German composer; b. Lübtheen, Mecklenburg, July 22, 1837; d. Dresden, Feb. 15, 1898. He published many salon pieces for the piano, some under the pseudonyms of William Cooper, Charles Morley and Francesco d'Orso.

Behrend, William, Danish musicologist; b. Copenhagen, May 16, 1861; d. there April 23, 1940. He studied law; held various government positions. At the same time he took courses in music theory; from 1917 taught music history at the Royal Danish Cons. He was one of the founders of the Wagner

Society of Denmark. Under the influence of Niels Gade he turned to music criticism, and became critic of 'Politiken.' Among his writings are biographies of J. P. E. Hartmann (1895) and of Gade (1917). He contributed to the Danish *Illustreret Musikhistorie* (1905; Vol. II, from Gluck to modern times); and to Salmonsen's *Konversationslexikon.*

Beilschmidt, Curt, German composer; b. Magdeburg, March 20, 1886. He studied in Magdeburg with Fritz Kauffmann; then in Leipzig (1905-09) with Stephan Krehl (theory), Adolf Ruthardt (piano) and Hans Sitt (violin). He served in the army in World War I; returned to Leipzig in 1923 and founded a choral-symphonic group which he continued to lead in 1954. His catalogue comprises 141 opus numbers, among them a dance opera *Das Abenteuer im Walde* (Leipzig, 1918); opera buffa *Meister Innocenz;* pastoral play *Der schlaue Amor* (Leipzig, 1921); musical divertimento *Der Tugendwächter* (Halle, 1927) and numerous works for orch. and chamber groups.

Beinum (bā'-noom), **Eduard van,** eminent Dutch conductor; b. Arnhem, Sept. 3, 1901. He studied violin with his brother, and composition with Sem Dresden; also proficient as pianist. In 1926 he became conductor of the Orkest Vereenigung in Haarlem; then was second conductor of the Concertgebouw, Amsterdam (1931-38); in 1938 an associate conductor with Mengelberg, and in 1945 succeeded him as its principal conductor, maintaining the high standard of performance. He also was guest conductor of other European orchestras, the Leningrad Philharmonic (1937); London Philharmonic (1946, 1949 and 1950), etc.; made his American debut with the Philadelphia Orch. on Jan. 8, 1954; toured the U. S. with the Concertgebouw Orchestra in the autumn of 1954. In 1956 he was appointed conductor of the Los Angeles Philh. Orch.

Beissel, Johann Conrad, German-American composer of religious music; founder of the sect of Solitary Brethren of the Community of Sabbatarians; b. Eberbach on the Neckar, Palatinate, April, 1690; d. Ephrata, Pa., July 6, 1768. He migrated to America in 1720 for religious reasons. His first attempt to build up a 'solitary' residence failed, but in 1735 he started the community at Ephrata which became a flourishing religious and artistic center. Beissel, who styled himself Bruder Friedsam (Brother Peaceful), was a prolific writer of hymns in fanciful German, published in various collections, some printed by Benjamin Franklin, some by the community at Ephrata. He composed tunes for his hymns and harmonized them according to his own rules. His compositions were collected in beautifully illuminated MSS., many of which are preserved at the Library of Congress and the Library of the Historical Society of Pennsylvania. Beissel was not a trained musician, but had original ideas; his religious fanaticism inspired him to write some startling music; in several of his hymns he made use of an antiphonal type of vocal composition with excellent effect. He left a tract explaining his harmonic theory and his method of singing. Beissel's hymns are collected chiefly in *Zionistischer Weyrauchs Hügel* (1739), *Das Gesang der einsamen und verlassenen Turtel Taube, das ist der christlichen Kirche* (1747) and *Paradisisches Wunder Spiel* (two independent publications, 1754 and 1766). Only texts were printed in these volumes, but the 1754 issue was arranged so that the music could be inserted by hand. Beissel's life was first described in the *Chronicon Ephratense,* compiled by the brethren Lamech and Agrippa, published at Ephrata in a German edition in 1786, and in an English translation by J. M. Hark at Lancaster in 1889. Cf. J. F. Sachse, *The German Sectarians of Pa.* (Philadelphia, 1899-1900); do., *The Music of the Ephrata Cloister* (Lancaster, 1903); *Church Music and Musical Life in Pa. in the 18th Century* (publ. by the Pennsylvania Society of the Colonial Dames of America, vol. II, pp. 26-84 and 242-253; Philadelphia, 1927); W. C. Klein, *J. C. Beissel: Mystic and Martinet* (1942).

Bekker, Paul, eminent writer on music; b. Berlin, Sept. 11, 1882; d. New York, March 7, 1937. He studied violin with Rehfeld, piano with Sormann, and theory with Horwitz; began his career as a violinist with the Philh. Orch. in Berlin; then conducted at Aschaffenburg and Görlitz; returned to Berlin (1906) as music critic for the 'Neueste Nachrichten'; also wrote program notes for the concerts of the Philharmonic Society; in 1909 was music critic for the 'Berliner Allgemeine Zeitung'; then settled temporarily in Frankfurt (1911) as critic for the 'Frankfurter Zeitung'; was Intendant of the Prussian State Theater in Kassel (1925); director of the State Theater at Wiesbaden (1927-32); owing to political developments he came to the U. S. in 1934, and settled in New York as music critic of the 'New Yorker Staatszeitung und Herold'; in 1936 was expatriated by the German National

Socialist Government. He published biographies of Oskar Fried (1907) and Jacques Offenbach (1909); also *Das Musikdrama der Gegenwart* (1909); *Beethoven* (1911; in English, 1926); *Das deutsche Musikleben, Versuch einer soziologischen Musikbetrachtung* (1916); *Die Sinfonie von Beethoven bis Mahler* (1918; in Russian, 1926); *Franz Schreker* (1919); *Kunst und Revolution* (1919); *Die Weltgeltung der deutschen Musik* (1920); *Die Sinfonien G. Mahlers* (1921); *Richard Wagner* (1924; in English, 1931); *Von den Naturreichen des Klanges* (1924); *Musikgeschichte als Geschichte der musikalischen Formwandlungen* (1926; in French, 1929); *Das Operntheater* (1930); *Briefe an zeitgenössische Musiker* (1932); *Wandlungen der Oper* (Zürich, 1934; English translation by Arthur Mendel as *The Changing Opera,* N. Y., 1935); *The Opera Walks New Paths,* in the 'Mus. Quarterly' (July, 1935); *Liszt and His Critics,* in the 'Mus. Quarterly' (July, 1936); *The Story of the Orchestra* (his last book; written in English; N. Y., 1936).

Belaiev (Belaieff) (bā-lah'-yev), **Mitrofan Petrovitch,** renowned Russian music publisher; b. St. Petersburg, Feb. 22, 1836; d. there, Jan. 10, 1904. His father, a rich lumber dealer, gave Belaiev an excellent education. After his father's death in 1888, Belaiev decided to use part of the income from the business for a music publishing enterprise devoted exclusively to the publication of works by Russian composers (the printing was done in Leipzig); he also established concerts of Russian music in St. Petersburg (ten symphony concerts and four concerts of chamber music each season) and provided funds for prizes awarded for the best compositions. Rimsky-Korsakov, Glazunov and Liadov were placed by Belaiev on the jury for these multifarious activities. The "Belaiev Editions" became a vital factor in the development of Russian national music. Although a conservative, Belaiev was generous towards representatives of the modern school, such as Scriabin, for whom he provided financial means to travel in Europe early in Scriabin's career. The catalogue of Belaiev's publications includes the greatest names in Russian music: Mussorgsky, Rimsky-Korsakov, Borodin, Balakirev, Cui, Scriabin; also Glière, Glazunov, Gretchaninov, Liadov, Liapunov, Taneyev, Nicolas Tcherepnin, as well as many lesser and even obscure composers, such as Akimenko, Alferaky, Amani, Antipov, Artzibushev, Blumenfeld, Kalafati, Kopylov, Sokolov, Steinberg, Wihtol, Zolotarev and others. The complete list of Belaiev's editions is available in the *Verzeichnis der in Deutschland seit 1868 erschienenen Werke russischer Komponisten* (Leipzig, 1950). See also M. Montague Nathan, *Belaiev, Maecenas of Russian Music,* in the 'Mus. Quarterly' (July, 1918).

Belaiev (bā-lah'-yev), **Victor Mikhailovitch,** Russian writer on music; b. Uralsk, Feb. 5, 1888. He studied at the St. Petersburg Cons. (1908-14) with Liadov, Wihtol and Glazunov; was secretary of the Conservatory Council (1917-22); moved to Moscow, where he was a member of the Russian State Publishing Department (1922-23), and a professor at the Moscow Cons. (1923-24); subsequently settled in Leningrad. In 1923 he founded the Society for Contemporary Music in Russia. He has written textbooks on counterpoint and musical forms; also 20 biographical pamphlets on living Russian and foreign composers. He is author of a monograph on Glazunov (1921); editor of the correspondence between Scriabin and M. P. Belaiev (1922); translator into Russian of Prout's *Fugal Analysis* (1923); also prepared many articles for foreign magazines, including several articles in the 'Mus. Quarterly': *Rachmaninov* (1927); *The Folk-Music of Georgia* and *The Longitudinal Open Flutes of Central Asia* (1933); and *Turkish Music* (1935).

Belcke, Friedrich August, German trombone player; b. Lucka, Altenburg, May 27, 1795; d. there, Dec. 10, 1874. He was a member of the Gewandhaus Orch. in Leipzig (1815); a chamber musician in Berlin (1816-58); was the first concert virtuoso on the trombone, for which he wrote concertos and études.

Beliczay (bā-lē-tsi), **Julius von,** Hungarian composer; b. Komorn, Aug. 10, 1835; d. Budapest, April 30, 1893. He was a pupil of Joachim, Hoffmann and Franz Krenn; in 1888 was appointed professor of theory at the National Academy in Budapest. Works: Mass in F; a symphony; *Ave Maria* for soprano, chorus and orch.; string quartet; *Andante* for orch.; serenade for strings; many vocal and piano pieces. In 1891 he published the first part of a 'Method of Composition' in Hungarian. Cf. A. Janitschek, *Julius von Beliczay* (Carlsbad, 1889).

Bell, William Henry, English composer; b. St. Albans, Aug. 20, 1873; d. Capetown, South Africa, April 13, 1946. He studied at St. Albans, and sang in the Cathedral choir; won the Goss scholarship at the Royal Academy of Music, London (1889); studied with Steggall (organ), Burnett (violin), Izard (piano), F. Corder (composition) and Stanford (counterpoint); was prof. of harmony there (1903-12); became director of the South African College of Music, Capetown in 1912; retired in 1936. As a composer, he was extremely self-critical and destroyed almost all of his early works. Most of his compositions were written in South Africa and performed by the Municipal Orch. of Capetown. Among his surviving works are the operas *Hippolytus* (after Euripides) and *Isabeau;* 3 symphonies, including a *Walt Whitman Symphony;* symph. prelude, *Song in the Morning* (1901); music for Ben Jonson's masque, *A Vision of Delight* (1908); *Arcadian Suite* for orch. (1909), symph. poems, *Love Among the Ruins* (1908), *The Shepherd* (1908), *La Fée des sources* (1912), and *Veldt Loneliness* (1921); *Song of Greeting* (written for the centenary of the Royal College of Music); viola concerto; violin sonata; *Maria Assumpta* for chorus (published); etc. Bibl.: M. van Someren Godfrey, *The Symphonic Works of W. H. Bell,* in 'The Mus. Times' (May and June, 1920).

Bella, Johann Leopold, Slovakian composer; b. Lipto-Szentmiklós, Upper Hungary, Sept. 4, 1843; d. Bratislava, May 25, 1936. He was a priest and canon at Neusohl; later cantor and music director at Hermannstadt; retired in 1922 and lived in Vienna. He wrote much church music in the strict style; an opera, *Wieland der Schmied* (Bratislava, April 28, 1926); a symph. poem, *Schicksal und Ideal* (Prague, March 19, 1876); chamber music; numerous songs and piano pieces. Cf. Dobroslav Orel, *J. L. Bella* (Bratislava, 1924); J. Jindrá, *J. L. Bella* (1933); K. Hudec, *J. L. Bella* (Prague, 1937); E. Zavarsky, *J. L. Bella* (Bratislava, 1955).

Bellaigue (bel-läg'), **Camille,** French music critic; b. Paris, May 24, 1858; d. there, Oct. 4, 1930. Originally a law student, he took music courses at the Paris Cons. with Paladilhe and Marmontel; from 1885 was music critic for 'La Revue des Deux Mondes'; also wrote for 'Le Temps.' He bitterly opposed modern music and was particularly violent in his denunciation of Debussy, his classmate at the Paris Cons. His selected essays are published under the following titles: *L'année musicale* (5 vols., 1886-91); *L'année musicale et dramatique* (1893); *Psychologie musicale* (1894); *Portraits et silhouettes de musiciens* (1896; English, 1897; German, 1903); *Études musicales et nouvelles silhouettes de musiciens* (1898; English, 1899); *Impressions musicales et littéraires* (1900); *Études musicales* (2 vols., 1903, 1907); *Mozart: biographie critique* (1906); *Mendelssohn* (1907); *Les Époques de la musique* (2 vols., 1909); *Gounod* (1910); *Paroles et musique* (1925), etc. —Cf. L. Gillel, *Camille Bellaigue* (Paris, 1931).

Bellamann, Henry, American author and pianist; b. Fulton, Mo., April 28, 1882; d. New York, June 16, 1945. He studied at Westminster College, Fulton, Mo. (1897-98); at the Univ. of Denver (1898-1900), also in London and Paris. He was dean of the School of Fine Arts, Chicora College for Women, Columbia, S. C. (1907-24); served as chairman of the Examining Board of the Juilliard School (1924-26) and of the Rockefeller Foundation (1927-28); was dean of the Curtis Institute (1931-32). He was a pianist and lecturer on modern French music; was made Officer of Public Instruction (France, 1924), Mus. Doc. (De Pauw Univ., 1926); Chevalier of the Légion d' Honneur (1931). Among his writings on music are: *A Music Teacher's Notebook* (1920); *Charles Ives, The Man and his Music,* in the 'Mus. Quarterly' (Jan., 1933); etc. He was the author of a successful novel, *King's Row.*

Bellasio, Paolo, Italian composer; b. Verona, May 20, 1554; d. Rome, July 10, 1594. He was church organist in Rome from 1587; published 5 books of madrigals, beginning with 1578; also *Villanelle alla Romana* (1595).

Bell'Avere. See **Bell'Haver.**

Bellazzi (bel-läht'-sē), **Francesco,** Venetian composer who flourished in the early 17th century. He was a pupil of Giovanni Gabrieli; later a follower of Monteverdi; published (1618-28) a mass, psalms, motets and other sacred music.

Bellère (bel-lär') (or **Bellerus,** properly **Beellaerts**), **Jean,** music publisher; d. Antwerp, 1595. He was a partner of Pierre Phalèse, *fils.* His son **Balthasar** transferred the business to Douai, and printed much music up to c. 1625. His catalogue of compositions, published from 1603-5, was found by Coussemaker in the Douai library.

Bellermann, Johann Friedrich, German music scholar; b. Erfurt, March 8, 1795; d. Berlin, Feb. 5, 1874. He dedicated himself mainly to the study of ancient Greek music; his chief work was *Die Tonleitern und Musiknoten der Griechen,* explanatory of the Greek system of notation (Berlin, 1847). He further wrote *Die Hymnen des Dionysios und Mesomedes* (Berlin, 1840) and edited essays by authors of classical antiquity: *Anonymi scriptio de musica, Bacchii* *senioris introductio* (1841). Bibl.: *Friedrich Bellermann; seine Wirksamkeit auf dem Gebiet der Musik,* reprint from the 'Allgemeine Musikzeitung' (Leipzig, 1874, No. 9).

Bellermann, (Johann Gottfried) Heinrich, German music teacher and theorist, son of the preceding; b. Berlin, March 10, 1832; d. Potsdam, April 10, 1903. He studied at the Royal Institute for Church music; also with Eduard Grell; from 1853 taught singing at 'Graues Kloster' and in 1861 was appointed Royal Musikdirektor; in 1866 succeeded Marx as professor of music at Berlin Univ. His book, *Die Mensuralnoten und Taktzeichen des 15. und 16. Jahrhunderts* (Berlin, 1858; 3d edition, 1930), gives an excellent exposition of the theory of mensural music; his treatise *Der Kontrapunkt* (1862; 4th ed., 1901) revives the theories of J. J. Fux's 'Gradus ad Parnassum.' Bellermann attempted to justify his adherence to Fux in a pamphlet *Die Grösse der musikalischen Intervalle als Grundlage der Harmonie* (1873). He also contributed valuable articles to the 'Allgemeine musikalische Zeitung' (1868-74) and published a biography of Eduard Grell (1899); also composed many vocal works.

Belleville-Oury, Caroline de. See **Oury.**

Bell'Haver, Vincenzo, Italian organist; b. Venice, about 1530; d. there, in Oct., 1587. He was a pupil of Andrea Gabrieli, and upon the latter's death, succeeded him as first organist of San Marco on Oct. 30, 1586; Bell'Haver died a year later, and his position was taken over by Gioseffo Guami. Bell'Haver published several books of madrigals (1567-75), of which only Book II, containing works for 5 voices, is extant; single works survive in various collections. See G. Benvenuti, *Andrea e Giovanni Gabrieli e la musica strumentale in San Marco,* vol. II of 'Istituzioni e Monumenti dell'arte musicale italiano' (Milan, 1932).

Belli, Domenico, Italian composer of the early 17th century. He lived most of his life in Florence. On Sept. 19, 1619 he and his wife entered the service of the Medici court. As a composer he was one of the earliest representatives of the new monodic style; Caccini praised his music. However, the claim that his short opera, *Il pianto d'Orfeo,* or *Orfeo Dolente* (Florence, 1616; reprinted Brussels, 1927, in Tirabassi's edition) was the earliest ever written is questionable. Among his instrumental works is *Arie . . . per sonarsi con il chitarrone* (Venice, 1616). Bibl.: E. Schmitz, *Geschichte der weltlichen Solokantate* (Leipzig, 1914); A. Tirabassi, *The Oldest Opera: Belli's 'Orfeo Dolente'* in the 'Mus. Quarterly' (Jan. 1929); see also M. Bukofzer, *Music in the Baroque Era* (N. Y., 1947).

Belli, Girolamo, composer of the Venetian school; b. Argenta (Ferrara), 1552; a pupil of L. Luzzaschi; chapel-singer to the Duke of Mantua. Publ. 3 books of madrigals *a* 6 (1583; 1584; 1593), 9 books of madrigals *a* 5 (1584; 1586; 9th ed., 1617); 2 books of canzonets *a* 4 (1584; 1593); *Sacrae cantiones a* 6 (1585), *a* 8 (1589), and *a* 10 (1594); 2 magnificats (1610); and *Salmi a* 5; some 5-part madrigals in the collection 'De' floridi virtuosi d'Italia' (1586).

Belli, Giulio, Italian composer, b. Longiano, c. 1560; d. c. 1621. He was a student of Cimelli and held numerous posts as maestro di cappella: at Imola (1582); at Capri (1590), where he joined the Franciscan order; at Ferrara (1592-3); at the church of Frari in Venice (1594 and 1606); at Montagnana (1596); at Forlì (1599); at the S. Antonio in Padua (1606-8); again at Imola (1613); and at San Marco, Venice (1615). He was a prolific composer; publications of his works appeared between 1584 and 1615; some being reissued several times, among them madrigals and canzonets (1584; 1593); psalms and vespers (1596; 1604); masses (1586; 1595; 1608); *sacrae cantiones* (1600); motets (1605); *falsi bordoni* (1605, 1607); *concerti ecclesiastici* (1613); etc. Many of these works are provided with *basso continuo.* —Cf. A. Brigidi, *Cenni sulla vita e sulle opere di Giulio Belli* (Modena, 1865).

Bellincioni (bel-lĭn-choh'-nē), **Gemma,** Italian dramatic soprano; b. Monza, Italy, Aug. 18, 1864; d. Naples, April 23, 1950. She studied with her father and with Roberto Stagno whom she later married (1881); made her debut in Naples in Pedrotti's *Tutti in maschera* (1881); appeared in the U.S. in 1899. She sang Santuzza at the première of *Cavalleria Rusticana* (Rome, May 17, 1890). Her repertoire included virtually all soprano roles; particularly successful in *La Traviata.* She publ. an autobiography, *Io e il palcoscenico* (1920). Bibl.: Bianca Stagno Bellincioni, *Roberto Stagno e Gemma Bellincioni* (Florence, 1943).

Bellini, Renato, Italian conductor and composer; b. Naples, March 7, 1895. He studied piano and theory at the Naples Cons.; then was active as opera coach. He was asst. conductor of the Chicago Opera Co. (1919-21). From 1921-34 he was in Europe; in 1934 he returned to the U. S. for a concert tour with Tito Schipa; settled in

New York in 1936 as voice teacher. He has written numerous songs, including the popular *Ninna Nanna a Liana.*

Bellini, Vincenzo, famous Italian opera composer; b. Catania, Sicily, Nov. 3, 1801 (birth registry); d. Puteaux, near Paris, Sept. 23, 1835. He was of a musical family; both his grandfather and his father were organists at the Catania Cathedral; he received his first musical education from them, and when still a child began to compose sacred and secular music. His talent was called to the attention of the Duchess of Sammartino, and she enabled him to enter the Cons. of San Sebastiano at Naples. He studied harmony with Giovanni Furno, counterpoint with Giacomo Tritto and piano with Carlo Conti; he continued his advanced studies with Nicola Zingarelli. At the same time he made a thorough study of the works of Jommelli, Paisiello and Pergolesi. Among his student compositions were a symphony, 2 masses, several psalms and a cantata *Ismene.* His first opera *Adelson e Salvini* was given at the Cons. (Jan. 12, 1825), and its success encouraged Bellini to continue to write for the stage. The well-known impresario Barbaja commissioned him to write an opera for the San Carlo Theater in Naples; this was *Bianca e Fernando,* staged (May 30, 1826) with considerable approval; this success was followed by a new opera *Il Pirata* presented at La Scala on Oct. 27, 1827, and *La Straniera* (La Scala, Feb. 14, 1829). The series of Bellini's successes was interrupted when he met with his first fiasco, the production of his opera *Zaira* in Parma (May 16, 1829). Undaunted by this reverse, he accepted an offer from La Fenice Theater at Venice for which he rapidly wrote *I Capuleti e i Montecchi* (March 11, 1830), which was acclaimed as a masterpiece. His inspiration seemed to receive a new impetus; he produced in succession two operas destined to become famous: *La Sonnambula* (Teatro Carcano, Milan, March 6, 1831) and *Norma* (La Scala, Milan, Dec. 26, 1831). The celebrated prima donna Giuditta Pasta created the title role in *Norma.* Bellini regarded *Norma* as his greatest achievement; the verdict of the musical public confirmed his judgment, for the popularity of the opera spread quickly throughout Europe. Strangely enough, this supreme achievement was followed by a distinct failure in his next production, *Beatrice di Tenda,* given at La Fenice (March 16, 1833). In 1833 Bellini visited London; then he went to Paris on Rossini's advice. There he wrote his last opera *I Puritani,* which was brilliantly produced at the Théâtre-Italien (Jan. 25, 1835), with such celebrated artists as Grisi, Rubini, Tamburini and Lablache in the cast. Bellini died in his 34th year, at full maturity of his lyric genius. His remains were removed to Catania 40 years after his death. Bellini's music represented the Italian operatic school at its best; together with Donizetti he gave the lyric stage its finest and most singable melodies; harmonic elaboration was not Bellini's aim; hence, the impression of monotony produced on some critics. However, the unassuming grace of Bellini's melodies continues to serve as an unfailing attraction to the musical public at large, and his best operas remain in the repertory of the opera houses in both hemispheres. Bibl.: F. Cicconetti, *Vita di V. B.* (Prato, 1859); A. Pougin, *B., sa vie, ses œuvres* (Paris, 1868); F. Clementi, *Il linguaggio dei suoni: Belliniani e Wagneristi* (Rome, 1881); M. Scherillo, *Belliniana* (Milan, 1885); L. Salvioli, *B., Lettere inedite* (Milan, 1885); A. Amore, *V. B.; arti, studi e ricerche* (Cantania, 1894); A. Cametti, *B. a Roma* (Rome, 1900); P. Voss, *V. B.* (Florence, 1901); W. A. Lloyd, *V. B.* (London, 1908); L. Parodi, *V. B.* (Sanpierdarena, 1913); Ild. Pizzetti, *La musica di V.B.* (Florence, 1918; reprinted in his *Intermezzi critici,* 1921); A. Cametti, *La musica teatrale a Roma 100 anni fa* (Rome, 1920); A. Damerini, *Norma di V. B.* (Milan, 1923); A. Rapisarda, *Vita di B.* (Turin, 1925); Cecil Gray, *V. B.* in 'Music and Letters' (1926); O. Andolfi, *Norma di V. B.* (Rome, 1928); O. Andolfi, *La Sonnambula di V. B.* (Rome, 1930); B. Miraglia, *V. B.,* in 'Rivista Musicale Italiana' (1931); V. Ricca, *V.B.* (Catania, 1932); Luisa Cambi, *B.* (Verona, 1934); G. Ammirata, *La vita amorosa di V.B.* (Milan, 1935); A. della Corte, *V.B., il carattere morale, i caratteri artistici* (Turin, 1935); A. Einstein, *V. B.,* in 'Music and Letters' (1935); G. G. Mezzatesta, *V.B. nella vita e nelle opere* (Palermo, 1935); G. Monaldi, *V.B.* (Milan, 1935); G. Policastro, *V.B.* (Catania, 1935); C. Reina, *Il cigno catanese: B., la vita e le opere* (Catania, 1935); Ild. Pizzetti (ed.), *V.B.: l'uomo, le sue opere, la sua fama* (Milan, 1936); O. Tiby, *V.B.* (Turin, 1938); A. Fraccaroli, *B.* (Verona, 1941); P. Cavazzuti, *B. a Londra* (Florence, 1945). A collection of Bellini's letters was issued in Catania on the occasion of the centenary of his death (1935); a facsimile reproduction of his opera *Norma* was published in Rome (1936).

Bellison, Simeon, Russian-American clarinetist; b. Moscow, Dec. 4, 1883; d. New

York, May 4, 1953. He studied at the Moscow Cons.; was first clarinetist at the Moscow Opera (1904-14); toured the Far East and the U. S. with a chamber music group (1917-20); in 1920 became first clarinetist of the N. Y. Philharmonic, retiring in 1948. He made transcriptions for clarinet of Hebrew melodies, and songs by Russian composers.

Bellman, Carl Mikael, Swedish poet and composer; b. Stockholm, Feb. 4, 1740; d. there Feb. 11, 1795. He publ. an important collection of songs to his own words, *Bacchanaliska ordenskapitlets handlingar* (1783); wrote lyric ballads expressive of folk life, *Fredmans epistlar* (1790) and *Fredmans sanger* (1791). Bibl.: Hendrik Van Loon, *The Last of the Troubadours, C. M. Bellman, His Life and His Music* (N. Y., 1939).

Bellmann, Karl Gottlieb, German organist; b. Muskau, Sept. 6, 1772; d. Schleswig, Dec. 26, 1861. He was organist in Schleswig from 1813; composed the German national song *Schleswig-Holstein meerumschlungen;* a Christmas cantata, motets, etc.

Belloc, Teresa Giorgi, dramatic mezzo-soprano; b. San Benigno, near Turin, July 2, 1784; d. San Giorgio Cavanese, May 13, 1855. She sang with La Scala, Milan (1804-24); toured through Italy and to Paris and London; retired in 1827. Her repertory comprised roles in 80 operas, Rossini's being her favorites. —Cf. *La cantante Teresa Belloc* by C. Boggio (Milan, 1895).

Bely, Victor, Soviet composer; b. Berdichev, Ukraine, Jan. 14, 1904. He studied with Conius (violin) and Miaskovsky (composition) at the Moscow Cons.; later became an instructor there. In his early period he was influenced by Scriabin; later his style changed towards a more vigorously national idiom. He has written a number of mass songs and choral suites on Chuvash and Bashkir themes.

Bemberg (băhn-bär'), **Herman,** French dramatic composer; b. Paris, March 29, 1859; d. Bern, Switzerland, July 21, 1931. He studied at the Paris Cons. with Dubois, Franck and Massenet; won the Rossini prize in 1885. Among his works are: cantata for soprano and orchestra, *La Mort de Jeanne d'Arc* (1886); short opera, *Le Baiser de Suzon* (Paris, 1888); grand opera *Elaine* (Covent Garden, London, July 5, 1892; N. Y., Dec. 17, 1894). He also published numerous songs, of which *Chant hindou* became extremely popular.

Bembo, Antonia, composer; b. presumably in Venice, c. 1670; death date unknown. Between 1690-95 she went to Paris; sang for Louis XIV, and received a pension from him enabling her to devote herself to composition. Extant works (in the Paris Bibliothèque Nationale): *Produzioni armoniche,* collection of 40 pieces (motets, duets, soli for soprano, etc., with figured bass or instrumental accompaniment, set to sacred Latin, French and Italian texts); *Te Deum* for 3 voices and string orch.; *Divertimento* for 5-voiced chorus with string orch.; *Te Deum,* with large orch.; *Exaudiat* for 3 voices, 2 'symphonie' parts and *basso continuo;* an opera, *L'Ercole Amante* (1707); and *Les sept Pseaumes de Dauid,* for various vocal combinations with instrumental accompaniment. Cf. Yvonne Rokseth, *A. Bembo, Composer to Louis XIV,* in the 'Mus. Quarterly' (April, 1937).

Bemetzrieder, Anton, music theorist; b. Alsace, 1743; d. London, 1817. Was at first a Benedictine monk; on leaving the order he became Diderot's pupil and protégé at Paris, and lived from 1782 till 1817 in London. He wrote *Leçons de clavecin et principes d'harmonie* (Paris, 1771; London, 1778), and other textbooks (of doubtful value); also polemical pamphlets.

Benatzky, Ralph, Czech composer of light opera; b. Moravské-Budejovice, June 5, 1884; studied in Prague (with Veit and Klinger) and in Munich (with Mottl). He lived in Vienna, Berlin and Switzerland; came to the U. S. in 1940; returned to Europe and settled in Zürich. He wrote 92 stage works, 250 film scores and some 5000 songs. Among his successful operettas are *Der lachende Dreibund* (Berlin, Oct. 31, 1913); *Yuschi tanzt* (Vienna, April 3, 1920); *Adieu Mimi* (Vienna, June 9, 1926); *Casanova* (Berlin, Sept. 1, 1928), etc.

Benda, Franz, famous violinist; b. Alt-Benatek, Bohemia, Nov. 24, 1709; d. Potsdam, March 7, 1786. He was a pupil of Löbel, Koniček, and of J. S. Graun at Ruppin (1733); was first violinist in the orch. of the Crown Prince (afterwards Frederick II) whom he accompanied in some 10,000 flute concerts during 40 years' service. Published works: 2 violin concertos; 6 trio-sonatas for 2 violins with basso continuo; 6 sonatas for violin with basso continuo; violin studies; several symphonies and concertos by him are in MS. His autobiography was printed in the 'Neue Berliner Musikzeitung' (vol. X; Nos. 32-35); in English, in Paul

Nettl's *Forgotten Musicians* (N. Y., 1950). See F. Berten, *Franz Benda* (Cologne, 1928).

Benda, Friedrich Ludwig, German composer, son of Georg Benda; b. Gotha, Sept. 4, 1746; d. Königsberg, March 20, 1792. He was director of the Hamburg opera (1780); court musician at Schwerin (1782); concert director in Königsberg (1789). He wrote incidental music for *The Barber of Seville* (Dresden, 1776); also operas, cantatas, and many works for various instruments. Cf. H. Güttler, *Königsberger Musikkultur im 18. Jahrhundert* (Kassel, 1925).

Benda, Friedrich (Wilhelm Heinrich), German violinist; son of Franz Benda; b. Potsdam, July 15, 1745; d. there, June 19, 1814. He studied music with his father; was a royal chamber musician at Potsdam (1765-1810); wrote the operas *Orpheus* (1785) and *Alceste* (1786); a comic opera, *Blumenmädchen* (Berlin, July 16, 1806); a cantata, *Pygmalion;* much chamber music.

Benda, Georg, brother of Franz; b. Alt-Benatek, Bohemia, June 30, 1722; d. Köstritz, Nov. 6, 1795. He was the third son, and pupil, of Hans Georg Benda; served as chamber musician at Berlin (1742-49); then at Gotha, where he became court Kapellmeister (1750); in 1764 went to Italy, returning in 1766. He remained in Gotha until 1788, producing 14 *Singspiele* and melodramas (his best works: *Ariadne auf Naxos, Medea, Almansor und Nadine*); then resigned, lived in Hamburg, Vienna and other towns; finally settled in Köstritz. Most of his other works (church music, symphonies, concertos, sonatas, etc.) are in MS. in the Berlin Library. He developed the novel idea of the music-drama with spoken words, the music being carried out by the orchestra only. Bibl.: biographies by Hodermann (Coburg, 1895); F. Brückner (Rostock, 1904); see also E. Istel, in *Die Entstehung des deutschen Melodrams* (Berlin, 1906); Vl. Helfert, *G. Benda und J. J. Rousseau* (Munich, 1908); also in his *Zum Problem der böhmischen Musiker-Emigration* (Brno, 1929); H. Martens, *Das Melodram* (Berlin, 1933); Jan van der Veen, *Le mélodrame musical de Rousseau* (The Hague, 1955).

Benda, Karl Hermann Heinrich (son of Georg Benda), German violinist; b. Potsdam, May 2, 1748; d. there, March 15, 1836. He was the concertmaster at the Royal Chapel and teacher of King Friedrich Wilhelm III; wrote much chamber music.

Bendel, Franz, German pianist; b. Schönlinde, Bohemia, March 23, 1833; d. Berlin, July 3, 1874. He was a pupil of Proksch (Prague) and Liszt (Weimar); from 1862 taught at Kullak's Academy in Berlin. Compositions: symphonies, 4 masses, piano concerto; piano trio; salon pieces for piano; violin sonata; nocturnes, romances, several books of songs, etc.

Bendeler, Johann Philipp, German organ theorist; b. Riethnordhausen (near Erfurt), Nov., 1654; d. Quedlinburg, Dec., 1709. He went to Quedlinburg in 1681 as an instructor at the Gymnasium there; in 1687 added the duties of cantor, which post he held for the rest of his life. As an organ theorist he belongs, with Werckmeister, to the middle German group whose ideas were realized in the organs of Arp Schnitger. His most important work is *Organopoeia* (c. 1690; reprinted in 1739 as *Orgelbaukunst*), a treatise on organ building. Other works are *Collegium Musicum de Compositione* (mentioned in Mattheson's *Ehrenpforte*); *Melopeia practica* (1686); and *Aerarium melopoeticum* (1688). In addition, he wrote two books on mathematics. Bibl.: Chr. Mahrenholz, *Die Berechnung der Orgelpfeifenmensuren* (Kassel, 1938).

Bender, Paul, German bass singer; b. Driedorf, July 28, 1875; d. Munich, Nov. 25, 1947. He sang at the Bayreuth Festivals (1902), and at Munich (from 1903). He made his American debut at the Metropolitan Opera House (Nov. 17, 1922). His repertoire there included several Wagnerian roles.

Bendix, Max, American conductor and composer; b. Detroit, March 28, 1866; d. Chicago, Dec. 6, 1945. He studied in Germany; was concertmaster of the Metropolitan Opera House (1885) and the Thomas Orch. in New York and Chicago (1886-96); later was opera conductor in New York. He wrote a violin concerto; *Pavlova,* valse-caprice for orch.; also ballet scores for special productions.

Bendix, Otto, pianist; b. Copenhagen, July 26, 1845; d. San Francisco, March 1, 1904. He was a pupil of Niels Gade; then studied with Kullak in Berlin and Liszt at Weimar; taught piano at the Copenhagen Cons., and was oboist in a theater orchestra; came to the U. S. in 1880; settled in Boston as a piano teacher at the New England Cons.; in 1895 moved to San Francisco, where he established his own music school; gave successful concerts in Europe and America; published some piano pieces, etc.

Bendix, Victor Emanuel, Danish composer, brother of Otto Bendix; b. Copenhagen, May 17, 1851; d. there, Jan. 5, 1926. He studied with Niels Gade; was active as a choral conductor; wrote 4 symphonies in a romantic vein; piano concerto; church music.

Bendl, Karl, Czech composer; b. Prague, April 16, 1838; d. there, Sept. 16, 1897. He studied with Blažek and Pietsch at Prague; was choirmaster of the German Opera in Amsterdam (1864); returned to Prague in 1865; after 1866 was conductor of the male choral society 'Hlahol'. Jointly with Smetana and Dvořák, he contributed to the general recognition of Czech music. Works: Czech national operas *Lejla* (Prague, Jan. 4, 1868), *Břetislav and Jitka* (1869), *Cernohorci* (1881), *Karel Skréta* (1883), *Dité Tábora (Child of the Camp,* 1892), *Mother Mila* (1895), *The Bagpiper* (1907); all produced at the National Theater, Prague, and in its standing repertory; also a ballet, *Bohemian Wedding;* 3 masses; several cantatas for soli, chorus and orch.; an overture, a *Dithyramb,* a *Concert Polonaise,* a *Slavonic Rhapsody,* etc., for orch.; a string quartet; 200 Czech songs and choruses; piano music.

Benedict, Sir **Julius,** composer; b. Stuttgart, Nov. 27, 1804; d. London, June 5, 1885. He was the son of a Jewish banker; from his early years he showed a decisive musical talent in various fields. He first studied with J. C. L. Abeille in his native city; then with Hummel at Weimar. Hummel introduced him to Weber, and he became Weber's pupil at the age of 17. In 1823, Benedict was appointed conductor of the Kärnthnerthor Theater in Vienna; in 1825 he received a similar post at the Teatro San Carlo in Naples, where he made his debut as composer with the opera *Giacinta ed Ernesto* (1829) without signal success. His second opera in Italian was *I Portoghesi in Goa,* produced in Stuttgart (1830). He went to Paris in 1834; the following year he settled in London, where he remained for the rest of his life. In 1836 he became music director of the Opera Buffa at the Lyceum Theater. His first opera in English, *The Gypsy's Warning,* was produced, April 19, 1838, at Drury Lane, where Benedict was engaged as conductor. He also conducted at Covent Garden; led the Monday Popular Concerts; was musical director of the Norwich Festivals from 1845-78, and the Liverpool Philharmonic Society from 1876-80. In recognition of his services, he was knighted in 1871. Benedict enjoyed a very great reputation as a musician in Europe and in America; he accompanied Jenny Lind on her American tour in 1850-52. Among his operas *The Lily of Killarney* (Covent Garden, Feb. 8, 1862) enjoyed considerable success, and was produced in the U. S. and Australia. Other operas are: *The Brides of Venice* (Drury Lane, April 22, 1844); *The Crusaders* (Drury Lane, Feb. 26, 1846); *The Lake of Glenaston* (1862); *The Bride of Song* (Covent Garden, Dec. 3, 1864); he also wrote the cantatas *Undine* (1860); *Richard Cœur-de-Lion* (1863); *St. Cecilia* (1866); *St. Peter* (1870); *Graziella* (1882); 2 symphonies; 2 piano concertos, etc.; wrote biographies of Mendelssohn (1850) and Weber (1881; 2nd ed., 1913).

Benedictus Appenzeller. See **Appenzeller.**

Benedito y Vives, Rafael, Spanish conductor, pedagogue, and editor; b. Valencia, Sept. 3, 1885. He studied at Madrid Cons.; in 1917 he organized an orchestra under his own name and a university chorus. In subsequent years he devoted himself to the organization of music festivals with folk singing. He has published several collections of songs of a popular nature; also pedagogical works: *El piano amigo del niño; Cómo se enseña el canto y la música;* etc.

Benelli, Alemanno. See **Bottrigari, Ercole.**

Benelli, Antonio Peregrino, singer and composer; b. Forlì, Romagna, Sept. 5, 1771; d. Börnichau, Saxony, Aug. 16, 1830. In 1790 he was first tenor at the Teatro San Carlo in Naples; held the same position in London (1798), and in Dresden from 1801-22, when his voice failed; then taught singing at the Royal Theater School in Berlin; was dismissed in 1829 on account of an unjust attack on his benefactor, Spontini. His most valuable work is a vocal method *Gesangslehre* (Dresden, 1819; originally published in Italian as *Regole per il canto figurato,* 1814); also wrote *Bemerkungen über die Stimme* in the 'Allgemeine musikalische Zeitung' (Leipzig, 1824); composed many vocal pieces and some piano pieces.

Benet, John, English composer who flourished in the 15th century. He wrote church music, of which the following works are extant: a Mass, 2 motets *(Lux fulget ex Anglia* and *Tellus purpureum),* an isorhythmic motet *Gaude pia Magdalena,* and several numbers from incomplete masses. Stylistically he belongs to the school of John Dunstable and Lionel Power. His *Sanctus* and *Agnus* are found in Wooldridge's *Early English Harmony* (1897); a *Gloria* is included in 'Denkmäler der Tonkunst in Österreich' (vol. XXXI).

Benevoli, Orazio, Italian composer; b. Rome, April 19, 1605; d. there June 17, 1672; son of a French baker who italianized his name. He studied with Vincenzo Ugolini and sang in the boys' choir at the school 'dei francesi' in Rome (1617-23). He held numerous posts as maestro di cappella: at Santa Maria in Trastevere (1624-30); at San Luigi dei francesi in Rome (1638-44); at the Vienna Court (1646); at Santa Maria Maggiore in Rome (1646); and thereafter in the Vatican. His work shows influences of the conservative Palestrina style combined with the polychoral technique of the Venetians; some of his sacred works call for twelve separate choirs. Benevoli's mass, commissioned for the consecration of the Salzburg Cathedral (1628), was in 52 parts with cembalo; this mass and a hymn in 56 voices are reprinted in the 'Denkmäler der Tonkunst in Österreich' (Vol. X, 1903). Another mass (performed at the Church of Santa Maria sopra Minerva, Rome, 1650) is for 12 choirs of 4 voices each. Bibl.: A. Cametti, *La Scuola dei pueri cantus di San Luigi dei francesi in Roma e suoi principali allievi* in the 'Rivista musicale italiana' (Oct., 1915); M. Bukofzer, *Music in the Baroque Era* (N. Y., 1947).

Bengtsson, Gustav Adolf Tiburt, Swedish conductor and composer; b. Vadstena, March 29, 1885. He studied music in Stockholm; then in Berlin with Juon and in Leipzig with Riemann; returned to Sweden and settled in Karlstad as composer and teacher; from 1942-46 was conductor of an orchestra in Linköping. He composed 3 symphonies: (I, 1908; II, 1910; III, 1921); string quartet (1907); piano trio (1916); violin sonata; various orchestral works; songs.

Ben-Haim, Paul (real name, Frankenburger), Israeli composer; b. Munich, July 5, 1897. He studied piano, conducting and composition in Munich; went to Palestine in 1933 and settled in Tel-Aviv, as a teacher and composer. He has written 2 symphonies (1941; 1948); piano concerto (Tel-Aviv, Feb. 1, 1950); chamber music; songs. He has also made arrangements of Israeli folk melodies.

Benincori, Angelo Maria, composer; b. Brescia, March 28, 1779; d. Paris, Dec. 30, 1821. He was a pupil of Cimarosa; lived in Spain, Italy and Vienna until 1803, when he went to Paris and brought out three unsuccessful operas; he completed Isouard's opera *Aladin;* published several string quartets and 3 piano trios.

Benjamin, Arthur, English composer and pianist; b. Sydney, Australia, Sept. 18, 1893. He studied at the Royal College of Music in London (1911-14) and, after war service (1914-18) became prof. at the Sydney Cons. (1919-21); returning to England, he was appointed prof. at the Royal College (from 1926). He was conductor of the Vancouver Symphony Orch. (1941-46), then returned again to London. He has written the operas: *The Devil Take Her* (London, Nov. 30, 1932); *Prima Donna* (1933; London, Feb. 23, 1949); *A Tale of Two Cities* (B.B.C., London, April 17, 1953; prize winner at the Festival of Britain); the ballet *Orlando's Silver Wedding* (London, Festival of Britain, May, 1951); instrumental works: *Pastoral Fantasia* (Carnegie Award, 1924); Sonatina for violin and piano (1925); Suite for piano (1927); Concertino for piano and orch. (1928); violin concerto (1932); *Light Music,* for orch. (1933); *Overture to an Italian Comedy* (London, March 2, 1937); *Romantic Fantasy,* for violin, viola and orch. (London, March 24, 1938); *Cotillon,* a suite of dance tunes for orch. (B.B.C., Feb. 3, 1939); *Prelude to a Holiday,* for orch. (Indianapolis Symphony Orch., Jan. 17, 1941); *Jamaican Rumba* (WOR Orch., Jan. 21, 1942; highly successful); Symphony No. 1 (Cheltenham Festival, June 30, 1948); piano concerto (Sydney Symphony Orch., Sept. 5, 1950, composer soloist); concerto for harmonica and orch. (London, Aug. 15, 1953, Larry Adler soloist); also numerous smaller works.

Bennet, John, English composer of the 16th-17th centuries, possibly born in Lancashire. In 1599 he published *Madrigalls to Foure Voyces,* containing 17 compositions. He contributed a well-known madrigal 'All creatures now are merry minded' to *The Triumph of Oriana* (1601), and composed 6 songs for Ravenscroft's 'Briefe Discourse' (1614). Bennet's works have been reprinted by Fellowes in 'The English Madrigal School.' Bibl.: E. H. Fellowes, *English Madrigal Composers* (Oxford, 1921).

Bennet, Théodore. See **Ritter, Théodore.**

Bennett, George John, English composer and organist; b. Andover, May 5, 1863; d. Lincoln, Aug. 20, 1930. He won the Balfe scholarship, and studied with G. A. Macfarren at the Royal Academy of Music (1878-84); took courses in Berlin (1885) and Munich (1886-87). After returning to London, he was appointed prof. of harmony and composition at the Royal Academy (1888). From 1890 to 1895 was organist in several London churches; from 1895 till his death, organist of the Lincoln Cathedral. Works: *Festival Evening Service* (for dedication of St. Paul's Cathedral, 1890); 2 overtures: *Jugendträume* (1887) and *Cymbeline* (1895); a piano trio (1893); piano pieces, songs, etc. He was the author of the manuals *Florid Counterpoint* and *Elements of Music for Choir-boys.*

Bennett, Joseph, English critic and writer on music; b. Berkeley, Gloucestershire, Nov. 29, 1831; d. Purton, June 12, 1911. After serving in various musical positions in London, he wrote music criticism for 'The Sunday Times,' 'Pall Mall Gazette,' and 'The Graphic'; was a contributor to the 'Daily Telegraph' and 'The Musical Times'; was editor of 'Concordia' (1875-6) and 'The Lute' (1883-6); annotator of the programs of the Philh. Soc. (1885-1903) and of the Saturday Popular Concerts; also wrote libretti for several English composers. —Publications: *Letters from Bayreuth* (1877); *The Musical Year* (1883); *History of the Leeds Musical Festivals, 1858-1889* (1892; with F. R. Spark); *Story of Ten Hundred Concerts* (1887; an account of the origin and rise of the Saturday Popular Concerts, 1857-87); *Forty Years of Music* (1908).

Bennett, Robert Russell, American composer and arranger; b. Kansas City, June 15, 1894. He studied in New York and in Paris with Nadia Boulanger; held Guggenheim Fellowships for two consecutive years (1927-28); first gained recognition with a symphonic work which won honorable mention in a contest sponsored by 'Musical America' (1927). In 1930 he worked in film studios in Hollywood; then settled in New York. His main activity has been that of expert orchestrator of musical comedies, a field in which he has attained a very high position, financially and artistically. His own works are distinguished by immediate effectiveness of instrumental writing and a facile flow of musical ideas; among them are the following: operas, *Maria Malibran* (N. Y., April 8, 1935) and *The Enchanted Kiss* (1944); operetta *Endymion* (1927); for orch.: *Charlestown Rhapsody* (1926); *Paysage* (1928); *Sights and Sounds* (Victor Contest Award, 1929); *March* for two pianos and orch. (Los Angeles, July 18, 1930); *Abraham Lincoln Symphony* (Philadelphia, Oct. 24, 1931); *Early American Ballade* on melodies of Stephen Foster (1932); *Adagio Eroico* (Philadelphia, April 25, 1935); *Concerto Grosso* for band (Rochester, Dec. 9, 1932); *Variations on a theme by Jerome Kern* (N. Y., Dec. 3, 1933); *Hollywood Scherzo* (N.B.C., Nov. 15, 1936); *Eight Etudes* for orch. (C.B.S., July 17, 1938); *Symphony in D* "for the Dodgers" (N. Y., Aug. 3, 1941); violin concerto (N.B.C., Dec. 26, 1941); *The Four Freedoms,* symph. sketch after 4 paintings by Norman Rockwell (Los Angeles, Dec. 16, 1943); *Classic Serenade* for string orchestra (1945); Symphony (1946); *Overture to an Imaginary Drama* (Toronto, 1946); *A Dry Weather Legend* (Knoxville, 1947); piano concerto (1948). He further wrote a violin sonata (1927); *Toy Symphony* for 5 woodwinds (1928); organ sonata (1929); *Water Music* for string quartet (1937); *Hexapoda* for violin and piano (1940); *Five Improvisations* for trio (1946); *Sonatine* for soprano and harp (1947); *Six Souvenirs* for 2 flutes and piano (1948); *Nietzsche Variations* for chorus; songs, etc.; 2 piano sonatinas (1941, 1944), etc. He also reorchestrated Bizet's *Carmen* for the all-Negro production *Carmen Jones* (N. Y., Dec. 2, 1943).

Bennett, Sir William Sterndale, English pianist, conductor and composer; b. Sheffield, April 13, 1816; d. London, Feb. 1, 1875. His father, an organist, died when Bennett was three years old, and he was educated by his grandfather, John Bennett. At eight he entered the choir of King's College Chapel, and at ten, the Royal Academy of Music, where he was a pupil of Charles Lucas, Dr. Crotch, Cipriani Potter and William Henry Holmes; performed (1833) his own piano concerto there, which was later published by the Academy. In 1837 the Broadwoods sent him to Leipzig for a year, a visit repeated in 1841-42; he was intimate with Schumann and Mendelssohn, and the influence of both, particularly the latter, is reflected in some of his compositions. From 1843-56 he gave a series of chamber concerts in England; married Mary Anne Wood in 1844; founded the Bach Society in 1849; conducted the concerts of the Philharmonic Society from 1856-66; also led the Leeds Music Festival in 1858; received the degree of Mus. Doc. from Cambridge (1856), after his election to the chair of Musical Professor. In 1866 he was chosen Principal of the Royal Academy of Music, and resigned the conductorship of the Philharmonic. The additional degree of M.A. was conferred on him by Cambridge in 1867; that of D.C.L. by Oxford in 1870; and in 1871 he was knighted. The subscription fund of the Bennett testimonial presented to him at St. James' Hall in 1872 was converted by the recipient into a scholarship at the Royal Academy of Music. He is buried in Westminster Abbey. Sterndale Bennett ranks high among English composers of genuine ability. His compositions are polished and carefully elaborated; a great many of his piano works display the versatility of the piano as a solo instruments.——Works: 4 piano concertos; a symphony; 5 overtures: *Parisina* (1834); *The Naiads* (1836; his best work, long in the active orchestral repertory); *The Wood Nymphs* (1841); *Paradise and the Peri* (1862); *Marie du Bois; Caprice* for piano and orch. (1844); *Ode for the Opening of the International Exhibition* (1862); *Cambridge Installation Ode* (1862); a pastoral, *The May Queen* for soli, chorus and orch. (Leeds, 1858); an oratorio, *The Woman of Samaria* (Birmingham, 1867; and performed for many years afterwards); music to Sophocles' *Ajax;* piano sextet; piano quintet; piano trio; sonata-duo for piano and cello; numerous piano pieces, among them a sonata surnamed *The Maid of Orleans;* pedagogical works for piano; anthems, songs. Bibl.: J. R. S. Bennett, *The Life of W. S. Bennett* (Cambridge, 1907); C. V. Stanford, *W. S. Bennett* in the 'Mus. Quarterly' (Oct. 1916). The 'Mus. Times' publ. a series of articles on Bennett in its issues of May-August, 1903; and an article by F. Corder (May, 1916).

Benoist (bŭ-nwăh'), **André,** French pianist; b. Paris, April 4, 1879; d. Monmouth Beach, N. J., June 19, 1953. He studied at the Paris Cons. with Pugno and Saint-Saëns; toured in Europe and America as accompanist to Casals, Heifetz, Albert Spalding, Tetrazzini and other celebrated artists.

Benoist (bŭ-nwăh'), **François,** French composer and organist; b. Nantes, Sept. 10, 1794; d. Paris, May 6, 1878. He studied at the Paris Cons. (1811-15) with Adam and Catel, and won the Prix de Rome in 1815 with the cantata *Enone;* returning from Italy in 1819, he was appointed prof. of organ at the Paris Cons.; in 1840, 'chef du chant' at the Opéra; pensioned in 1872. Works: 2 operas, *Léonore et Félix* (1821) and *L'Apparition* (1848); 4 Ballets, *La Gipsy* (1839), *Le Diable amoureux* (1840), *Nisida, ou les Amazons des Açores* (1848), and *Pâquerette* (1851); 'Bibliothèque de l'organiste' (12 books of organ pieces), etc.

Benoit-Berbiguier. See **Berbiguier.**

Benoit (bŭ-nwăh'), **Peter,** foremost Flemish composer; b. Harlebeke, Belgium, Aug. 17, 1834; d. Antwerp, March 8, 1901. He studied at the Brussels Cons. with Fétis (1851-55); while there he earned his living by conducting theater orchestras. He also wrote music for Flemish plays; at the age of 22 he produced his first opera in Flemish, *Het dorp in't gebergte (A Mountain Village),* staged in Brussels on Dec. 14, 1856. With his cantata *Le Meurtre d'Abel* Benoit obtained the Belgian Prix de Rome (1857); however, he did not go to Italy, but traveled instead in Germany. As part of his duties he submitted a short *Cantate de Noël* to Fétis, who praised Benoit's music; he also wrote an essay *L'école de musique flamande et son avenir* proclaiming his fervent faith in the future of a national Flemish school of composition, of which he was the most ardent supporter. His one-act opera *Roi des Aulnes* was presented in Brussels (Dec. 2, 1859); the Théâtre-Lyrique of Paris tentatively accepted it; Benoit spent many months in Paris awaiting its production, which never took place; in the meantime he acted as second conductor at the Bouffes-Parisiens. In 1863 he returned to Belgium, where he produced his second Flemish opera *Isa* (Brussels, Feb. 24, 1867). In 1867 he founded the Flemish Music School in Antwerp; he militated for many years to obtain an official status for it. In 1898 it was finally granted and the school became the Royal Flemish Cons.; Benoit remained its director to the end of his life. In Belgium Benoit is regarded as the originator of the Flemish musical traditions both in composition and in education; but although he cultivated the Flemish idiom in most of his works, his musical style owes much to French and German influences. Apart from his successful early operas, he wrote the opera *Pompeja* (1895) which was not produced; the Flemish oratorios *Lucifer* (Brussels, Sept. 30, 1866; highly successful; considered his masterpiece); *De Schelde* (1869); *De Oorlog* (*War;* 1873); a dramatic musical score *Charlotte Corday* (1876); historic music drama *De Pacificatie van Ghent* (1876); *Rubens Cantata* (1877; greatly acclaimed); children's oratorio *De Waereld in* (*In the World;* 1878); cantata *Hucbald* (1880); cantata *De Genius des Vaderlands* (1880); oratorio *De Rhijn* (1889), etc. Of his church music, the most important is his *Quadrilogie religieuse* (Antwerp, April 24, 1864), of which the component parts had been separately performed in 1860, 1862 and 1863; also *Drama Christi* (1871). Benoit wrote relatively little instrumental music; his symph. poems for piano with orch. and flute with orch. have been performed. He also composed many songs in French and in Flemish. In his propaganda for national Flemish music, Benoit contributed numerous papers and articles, among them *Considérations à propos d'un projet pour l'institution de festivals en Belgique* (1874); *Verhandeling over de nationale Toonkunde* (2 vols.; Antwerp, 1877-79); *De Vlaamsche Muziekschool van Antwerpen* (1889; a history of the Antwerp School of Music); *De Oorsprong van het Cosmopolitisme in de Muziek* (1876). In 1880 he was elected a corresponding member of the Belgian Royal Academy; in 1882, full member. Bibl.: M. E. Belpaire, *Een vlaamsche meester; Peter Benoit* (Belfort, 1901); C. Stoffels, *P. Benoit et le mouvement musical flamand* (Antwerp, 1901); Th. Radoux, *Paroles prononcées à l'annonce de la mort de P. Benoit* in 'Bulletins Lettres et Beaux-Arts' (Brussels, 1901); J. Sabbe, *P. Benoit; zijn leven, zijne werken, zijne beteekenis* (Ghent, 1902); L. Mortelmans, *P. Benoit* (Antwerp, 1911); H. Baggaert, *P. Benoit, een kampion der nacionale gedachte* (Antwerp, 1919); H. P. Morgan-Browne, *Peter Benoit, né Pierre Benoit* in 'Music and Letters' (1929); J. Horemans, *P. Benoit* (Antwerp, 1934); A. M. Pols, *Het leven van P. Benoit* (Antwerp, 1934); Ch. van den Borren, *Peter Benoit* (Brussels, 1942); R. R. Boschvogel, *P. Benoit* (Tiel, 1944); A. Corbet, *P. Benoit, leven, werk en beteekenis* (Antwerp, 1944); G.-M. Matthijs, *P. Benoit* (Brussels, 1944).

Bentinelli, Bruno, Italian composer; b. Milan, June 4, 1913. He studied at the Milan Cons. with Paribeni and R. Bossi. He has written *Invenzioni* for string orch. (1938); 3 symphonies (1939, 1944, 1947); Concerto for orch. (1940); *Fantasia e fuga su temi gregoriani* (1942); *Divertimento* for chamber orch. (1945); *Fantasia concertante* for string quartet and orch. (1949); *Psalm IV* for soprano and orch. (1950); songs.

Bentonelli, Joseph (real name Benton), American tenor; b. Sayre, Oklahoma, Sept. 10, 1900. He studied general musical subjects at the State Univ. of Oklahoma (B.A., 1920; Mus. Bac., 1921), voice with Jean de Reszke (Paris) and with Vanzo (Milan); made his debut in Nice (1925) with the de Reszke Ensemble; made guest operatic appearances in Europe and Egypt; in 1928 sang at the inauguration of the Teatro Miramare in Tripoli; returned to the U. S. (1934); sang with the Chicago Opera for four years; then with the Metropolitan Opera from 1936-38; made his debut there as Des Grieux in *Manon* (Jan. 10, 1936). He has made extensive tours throughout the U. S.; his repertoire includes the standard leading Italian tenor roles; sang leading parts in Vittadini's *Anima Allegra* (1931), Refice's *Cecilia* (Rome, 1930), etc.

Bentzon, Jörgen, Danish composer; cousin of Niels Viggo Bentzon; b. Copenhagen, Feb. 14, 1897; d. Hørsholm, July 9, 1951. He studied music with Carl Nielsen (1915-19), then took a course at the Leipzig Cons. (1920-21). Returning to Denmark, he was active in the field of musical education for the masses; was president of the People's Music Schools from 1937 till 1946. As a composer, he followed the romantic school, closely related to Nielsen's ideals. Bentzon wrote 2 symphonies (the 1st, subtitled *Dickens Symphony,* was performed on the Copenhagen radio in 1941); the opera *Saturnalia* (Copenhagen, Dec. 15, 1944); 5 string quartets and other chamber music.

Bentzon, Niels Viggo, eminent Danish composer; b. Copenhagen, Aug. 24, 1919. He is a descendant of Johan Ernst Hartmann (1726-93), an early Danish composer. The musical tradition of the family continued through many generations (his cousin was Jörgen Bentzon). He studied piano with his mother, and composition at the Copenhagen Cons. with Jeppesen. From his earliest works, Bentzon assimilated a neo-classical idiom, distinguished by compact contrapuntal writing and harmonic clarity without avoidance of justifiable dissonance. Between 1943 and 1953 he wrote 7 symphonies; No. 4 (subtitled *Metamorphoses*) was performed in Copenhagen on June 18, 1949; No. 7, on April 21, 1953. His ballet *Metaphor* was staged in Copenhagen on March 31, 1950. Among his other works are a piano concerto (1948); 2 string quartets (1941; 1946); quintet for flute, oboe, horn, bassoon and piano (1943); quartet for flute, violin, cello and piano (1949); 3 violin sonatas (1940, 1943, 1944); cello sonata (1946); horn sonata (1947); 4 piano sonatas (1946-49), etc.

Benvenuti, Giacomo, Italian musicologist, b. Tremosina, Lake Garda, March 16, 1885; d. Salò, Jan. 20, 1943. He studied at the Liceo Mus., Bologna, with M. E. Bossi; edited 2 volumes of selected works by Andrea and Giovanni Gabrieli for the 'Istituzioni e Monumenti dell' Arte Musicale Italiana' (with valuable documentary prefaces); 12 harpsichord sonatas by B. Galuppi; works by Cavazzoni (1919) and Paradies (with D. Cipollini; 1920); *35 Arie di vari autori del secolo XVII* (1922), etc. He also wrote an opera *Juan José* (not performed); songs and a string quartet.

Benvenuti, Tommaso, Italian opera composer; b. Cavarzere (Venice), Feb. 4, 1838; d. Rome, Feb. 26, 1906. When he was 18 years old, his opera *Valenzia Candiano* was announced for performance in Mantua, but was taken off after a rehearsal. The following year, he succeeded in having his second opera *Adriana Lecouvreur* produced in Milan (Nov. 26, 1857). Other productions followed: *Guglielmo Shakespeare* (Parma, Feb. 14, 1861); *La Stella di Toledo* (Milan, April 23, 1864); *Il Falconiere* (Venice, Feb. 16, 1878); *Beatrice di Suevia* (Venice, Feb. 20, 1890); opera buffa *Le baruffe Chiozzotte* (Florence, Jan. 30, 1895). Although Benvenuti's operas are workmanlike and effective, they failed to hold the stage after initial successes.

Berardi, Angelo, Italian theorist; b. S. Agata, Feltria, c. 1635; d. c. 1700. He was maestro di cappella at Spoleto in 1681, and at Viterbo in 1687. In 1693 he was at the Basilica of Santa Maria in Trastevere. He published several treatises on harmony and related subjects: *Ragionamenti musicali* (Bologna, 1681); *Documenti armonici* (Bologna, 1687); *Arcani musicale* (Bologna, 1690); *Il Perchè musicale ovvero Staffetta armonica* (Bologna, 1693); composed a *Missa pro defunctis* (1663); *Salmi concertati* (Bologna, 1668); *Concentus cum Missa* (Bologna, 1669); *Musiche diverse variemente concertate per camera* (Bologna, 1689); many canons; etc.

Berat (bā-răh'), **Frédéric,** French song composer; b. Rouen, 1800; d. Paris, Dec. 2, 1855. He was a friend of the poet Béranger, many of whose lyrics he set to music; wrote many popular romances and chansonettes: *A la frontière, Bibi, La Lisette de Béranger, Le Départ, Ma Normandie,* etc.

Berber, Felix, notable German violinist; b. Vienna, March 11, 1871; d. Munich, Nov. 2, 1930. He studied at the Dresden Cons.; then with Adolf Brodsky in Leipzig; was concertmaster at the Gewandhaus Orch. there (1897-1903); taught at the Royal Academy of Music in London (1904-7); at the Hoch Cons. in Frankfurt and at the Geneva Cons. (1908). In 1910 he made a highly successful tour of the U. S.; in 1912 he settled in Munich, teaching privately.

Berbiguier (băr-bē-g'yā'), **Benoit-Tranquille,** French flutist; b. Caderousse, Vaucluse, Dec. 21, 1782; d. Pont-Levoy, near Blois, Jan. 20, 1838. He was a pupil of Wunderlich at the Paris Cons.; wrote many important works for flute, including: 15 books of flute duos; 2 books of duos for flute and violin; 10 concertos; 7 books of sonatas, with cello or viola; 8 sets of variations with piano or orch.; 6 books of flute trios, etc.

Berchem (băr'-hem) (or **Berghem**), **Jachet** (de) (also **Jaquet, Jacquet**), Flemish composer; b. Berchem, near Antwerp, early in the 16th century; he was organist to the Duke of Ferrara in 1555. He has been confused with his contemporary Jachet de Mantua; also with Jachet Buus and Giaches de Wert. Berchem's 27 madrigals for 5 voices appeared in 1546, and 24 madrigals for 4 voices in 1555; three books containing settings of stanzas from *Orlando furioso* and dedicated to Duke Alfonso II of Ferrara were publ. in 1561. Modern reprints of Berchem's works are included in the following editions: R. van Maldeghem, *Trésor musical* (1865-93), volumes XI and XX (chansons); vols. XXVII and XXVIII (madrigals); R. Eitner, *Publikationen älterer praktischer und theoretischer Musikwerke* (1873-1905), vols. IX and XI (chansons). Bibl.: R. Eitner, *Jachet da Mantua und Jachet Berchem* in 'Monatshefte für Musikgeschichte' (1889); A. Einstein, *The Italian Madrigal* (Princeton, 1949); G. Reese, *Music in the Renaissance* (N. Y., 1954).

Berens, Hermann, noted pianist and pedagogue; b. Hamburg, April 7, 1826; d. Stockholm, May 9, 1880. He studied with his father, Karl Berens, in Hamburg; then studied with Reissiger in Dresden, and with Czerny. In 1847 he settled in Sweden; organized the Quartet Soirées in Stockholm; in 1849 became Royal Music Director in Örebro; taught at the Royal Academy in Stockholm. He wrote the opera *Violetta* (1855) and 3 light operas: *Ein Sommernachtstraum, Lully und Quinault,* and *Riccardo;* some chamber music. His book of piano studies, *Neueste Schule der Geläufigkeit,* has become a standard work for piano students, and has gone through numerous editions.

Beretta, Giovanni Battista, Italian music theorist; b. Verona, Feb. 24, 1819; d. Milan, April 28, 1876. He was director of the Bologna Cons.; then devoted himself to continuing the 'Dizionario artistico-scientifico-storico-technologico-musicale' begun by A. Barbieri (publ. Milan, 1869-72), but did not complete it; also wrote a treatise on harmony, and another on instrumentation and orchestration; composed instrumental and sacred music.

Berezovsky, Maximus Sozontovitch, Russian singer and composer; b. Glukhov, Russia, Oct. 27, 1745; d. St. Petersburg, April 2, 1777; he studied at the Kiev Ecclesiastic Academy; then was chorister at the Court Chapel in St. Petersburg. He attracted attention by his lyric voice, and in 1765 was sent by the Russian government to Bologna for further study. He became a pupil of Padre Martini, and wrote an opera *Demofoonte* (1773) which was produced in Bologna. Upon his return to Russia, he was unable to compete with Italian musicians who had acquired all the lucrative positions in the field of vocal teaching and opera; he became despondent and cut his throat. In addition to his opera, he left a *Credo* and 17 other sacred works; in these he made an attempt to follow the natural accents of the Russian text, which was an innovation at the time. Bibl.: N. Lebedev, *Berezovsky and Bortniansky as Church Music Composers* (St. Petersburg, 1882).

Berezowsky, Nicolai, talented composer; b. St. Petersburg, Russia, May 17, 1900; d. New York, Aug. 27, 1953. He studied singing, violin and piano; graduated from the Court Chapel of St. Petersburg in 1916; played the violin in the orch. of the Opera House in Saratov (1917-19); then in the orch. of the Bolshoy Theater in Moscow. He crossed the border to Poland in 1920 and reached New York in 1922. He found employment as a theater violinist; took a course in the Juilliard Graduate School of Music, where he was a pupil of Rubin Goldmark and Paul Kochanski; was a member of the violin section of the N. Y. Philh. (1923-29); a member of the Elizabeth Sprague Coolidge String Quartet (1935-40); was also active as a radio conductor; held a Guggenheim Fellowship (1948). His music was widely performed; its style, conditioned mainly by national Russian influences, is distinguished also by coloristic effects in sonorous modern harmonies. Works: Sinfonietta (N.B.C. Orch., May 8, 1932; won a prize); Symph. I (Boston Symph., March 16, 1931, composer cond.); Symph. II (Boston, Koussevitzky cond., Feb. 16, 1934); Symph. III (Rochester, Jan. 21, 1937); Symph. IV (Boston Symph., Oct. 22, 1943, composer cond.); *Christmas Festival Overture* (N. Y. Philh., Dec. 23, 1943); *Soldiers on the Town* (N. Y. Philh., Nov. 25, 1943); violin concerto (Dresden, April 29, 1930, composer cond., Carl Flesch, soloist); viola concerto (Chicago Symph. Orch., Jan. 29, 1942, Stock cond., Primrose soloist); *Concerto Lirico* for cello and orch. (Boston, Feb. 22, 1935, Koussevitzky cond., Piatigorsky soloist); harp concerto (Philadelphia Orch., Jan. 26, 1945); *Passacaglia* for the theremin and orch. (N. Y. Philh., Feb. 29, 1948). Chamber music: 2 string quartets, 2 woodwind quintets, string sextet, brass suite, etc. Cantata *Gilgamesh* (New York, May 16, 1947); *Babar the Elephant,* children's opera (New York, Feb. 21, 1953; very successful, numerous performances given in the U. S.). See *Duet with Nicky* (New York, 1943) by his first wife, Alice Berezowsky.

Berg, Adam, German music printer who was active at Munich between the years 1567 and 1599; he published the important collection *Patrocinium musices,* in 12 vols., printed between 1573 and 1598. Of these, 7 volumes are devoted to Orlandus Lassus.

Berg, Alban, outstanding Austrian composer; b. Vienna, Feb. 9, 1885; d. there, Dec. 24, 1935. He studied music by himself; as a young man he met Arnold Schoenberg, who became his teacher and intimate friend. Berg embraced the atonal method of his master, and later adopted the full-fledged 12-tone technique. With Schoenberg, he led the radical movement in Viennese music; was one of the founders of the Society for Private Performances in Vienna, which made propaganda for new music; was also a member of the Austrian section of the International Society for Contemporary Music (from 1925). He taught privately in Vienna; contributed to modern music magazines ('Anbruch,' '23'); also gave occasional lectures on modern music. The interest shown in his work by Hertzka, the president of Universal Edition, and the devotion of his friends and admirers enabled him to continue his work. He evolved a markedly individual style of composition, remarkable for its outspoken lyricism and dramatic tension, while using the 12-tone technique as thematic foundation. His early works stem from Wagner and Mahler; in later works tonality is abandoned in favor of a free melodic and harmonic discourse. His major work is the opera *Wozzeck,* after the romantic play by Büchner; the score contains several symphonic sections (a passacaglia with 29 variations; a dance suite; a rhapsody, etc.); the idiom is entirely atonal. *Wozzeck* was first produced at the State Opera in Berlin (Dec. 14, 1925) and aroused a storm of protests; the criticisms in the Berlin press, some of extreme violence, were collected and published in a special booklet by Berg's friends as a means of combating the injustice to the work. The production of the opera in Prague was accompanied by similar outbursts. However, the first American performance of *Wozzeck* (Philadelphia, March 19, 1931, Stokowski conducting) aroused tremendous interest; after World War II numerous performances were given in Europe and the U. S. with great acclaim, and *Wozzeck* became recognized as a modern operatic masterpiece. The original score of *Wozzeck* was acquired from the composer by the Library of Congress in Washington. Berg's second opera *Lulu* (derived from two plays by Wedekind) was left unfinished; 2 acts and two fragments of the 3d act were first performed in Zürich (June 2, 1937). Berg's last completed work was a violin concerto commissioned by the American violinist Louis Krasner, who gave its first performance at the Festival of the International Society for Contemporary Music in Barcelona (April 19, 1936); the score bears the inscription 'Dem Andenken eines Engels' as a memorial to Alma Mahler's young daughter. The concerto is written in the 12-tone technique, applied with great freedom without avoidance of passing tonality; it has since become part of the modern violinist's repertory. Other works are: *7 frühe Lieder* (1905-8); piano sonata (1908); 4 songs (1909); string quartet (1910); 5 Songs with orch. (1912); 4 pieces for clarinet and piano (1913); 3 pieces for orch. (1914); *Chamber Concerto* for piano, violin and 13 wind instruments (1925); *Lyrische Suite* for string quartet (1926; Kolisch Quartet, Vienna, Jan. 8, 1927; 3 movements arranged by Berg for string orch.; 1st perf., Berlin, Jan 21, 1929); *Der Wein* for soprano and orch., after Baudelaire (Königsberg, June 4, 1930). Berg made piano arrangements of Schoenberg's *Gurre Lieder* and F♯ minor quartet and compiled analyses of Schoenberg's *Kammersymphonie, Pelleas und Melisande,* as well as the *Gurre Lieder.* The basic biography of Alban Berg is by Willi Reich (Vienna, 1937; with contributions by Theodore Wiesengrund-Adorno and Ernst Krenek), which includes musical analyses; Reich also compiled a guide to *Wozzeck* (publ. in English, N. Y., 1931). See also the Alban Berg issue of 'Eine Wiener Musikzeitschrift' (Vienna, 1936); Hans Hollaender, *Alban Berg* in the 'Mus. Quarterly' (Oct. 1936); René Leibowitz, *Alban Berg's Five Orchestral Songs* in the 'Mus. Quarterly' (1948); René Leibowitz, *Schoenberg and his School* (N. Y., 1949); P. J. Jouvé and M. Fano, *Wozzeck, ou le nouvel opéra* (Paris, 1953). Alban Berg's talk on atonality is printed in English in N. Slonimsky, *Music Since 1900* (N. Y., 1937).

Berg, Johann von, Flemish music printer; b. Ghent; d. Nuremberg, 1563. He lived in Ghent; settled in Nuremberg in 1531 where he became Ulrich Neuber's partner.

Berg, Conrad Mathias, Alsatian pianist; b. Colmar, April 27, 1785; d. Strasbourg, Dec. 13, 1852. He studied at the Paris Cons. (1806-07); then settled in Strasbourg as a piano teacher (1808). He wrote 4 string quartets; 10 piano trios; 3 piano concertos; sonatas; many other pieces for his instrument; his essay *Ideen zu einer rationellen Lehrmethode der Musik mit Anwendung auf das Klavierspiel* appeared in 'Cäcilia' (vol. XVII, 1835); he also wrote an *Aperçu historique sur l'état de la musique à Strasbourg pendant les 50 dernières années* (1840).

Berg, Natanaël, Swedish composer; b. Stockholm, Feb. 9, 1879. He first studied surgery; then singing at the Stockholm Cons.; later composition in France, Austria and Germany; was president of the Association of Swedish Composers (1918-25). He has written 5 operas which were produced in Stockholm: *Lelia* (Feb. 29, 1912); *Engelbrekt* (Sept. 21, 1929); *Judith* (Feb. 22, 1936); *Birgitta* (Jan. 10, 1942); *Genoveva* (Oct. 25, 1947); the ballets *Alvorna* (1914), *Sensitiva* (1919), and *Hertiginnans friare* (*The Duchess' Suitors;* 1920); the symph. poems *Traumgewalten* (1911); *Alles endet, was entstehet* (1913); *Varde ljus!* (1914); *Arstiderna* (*The Tides;* 1916), and *Makter* (*Power;* 1917); *Pezzo sinfonico* (1918); *Sinfonia delle passioni* (1922); the oratorios *Mannen och kvinnan* (*Man and Woman;* 1911); *Israels lovsäng* (*Israel's Hymns;* 1915) and *Das Hohelied* (1925); violin concerto; *Serenade* for violin and orch.; chamber music (string quartet, piano quintet); songs.

Berger, Arthur, American composer and music critic; b. New York, May 15, 1912. He studied with Piston at Harvard Univ. (M.A., 1936); then in Paris with Milhaud and Nadia Boulanger, on a Paine Fellowship from Harvard (1937-39). Returning to America, he taught at Mills College, Brooklyn College, and the Juilliard School of Music in New York; was music critic of the 'N. Y. Sun' (1943-46), and of the 'N. Y. Herald Tribune' (1946-53). In 1953, appointed assoc. prof. of music at Brandeis Univ. Berger's early compositions reveal an atonal trend, which was later changed to a neo-classical style, largely influenced by Stravinsky. His works include a ballet, *Entertainment Piece* for 3 dancers and 'modern style piano' (1940); *Serenade Concertante,* for violin, woodwind quartet and small orch. (Rochester, N. Y., Oct. 24, 1945; revised, 1951); 3 pieces for string orch. (N. Y., Jan. 26, 1946); *Ideas of Order* for orch. (N. Y.

Philh., April 11, 1953); woodwind quartet (1941); 2 Duos for violin and piano (1948; 1950); Duo for cello and piano (1951); Duo for oboe and clarinet (1952); *Fantasy* for piano (1942); *Capriccio* for piano (1945); *Partita* for piano (1947); songs. He has published a monograph on Aaron Copland (N. Y., 1953); has contributed special articles to various publications; active in modern music organizations, etc.

Berger, Erna, German soprano, b. Dresden, Oct. 19, 1900. She began studying voice rather late but made rapid progress, and was engaged to sing at the Dresden Opera; she later joined the staff of the Berlin State Opera, where she distinguished herself in Mozart's works. She sang in various European opera houses; in 1949 made her American debut at the Metropolitan Opera.

Berger, Francesco, English pianist and composer; b. London, June 10, 1834; d. there (at the age of 98), April 25, 1933. He studied harmony with Luigi Ricci in Trieste, piano with Karl Lickl in Vienna; later studied with Hauptmann and Plaidy at Leipzig; returned to London, where he was professor of piano at the Royal Academy of Music and at the Guildhall School of Music; made frequent concert tours through Great Britain and Ireland; was for some years director, and from 1884-1911 honorary secretary of the Philharmonic. He composed an opera, *Il Lazzarone,* and a mass; overtures and incidental music to Wilkie Collins' *The Frozen Deep* and *The Lighthouse;* many songs and piano pieces. He published *First Steps at the Pianoforte; Reminiscences, Impressions and Anecdotes; Musical Expressions, Phrases and Sentences;* and a *Musical Vocabulary in 4 Languages* (1922); in 1931 he published his memoirs entitled (with reference to his age), *97.*

Berger, Jean, choral conductor and composer; b. Hamm, Sept. 27, 1901. He studied musicology under Besseler in Heidelberg (1927; Ph.D., 1931). From 1931-39 he was in Paris, where he took lessons in composition with Louis Aubert; was also conductor of 'Les Compagnons de la Marjolaine,' a mixed choral group specializing in his modern harmonizations of French folk-tunes. In 1935, Berger became a French citizen. In 1939-41 he was in Rio de Janeiro, where he coached French opera at the Municipal Theater. In 1941 he settled in New York. Among his choral compositions, *Le sang des autres* won first prize at the international contest in Zürich in 1937.

Berger, Ludwig, German pianist and composer; b. Berlin, April 18, 1777; d. there, Feb. 16, 1839. He studied harmony and counterpoint with Gürrlich in Berlin (1799); studied piano with Clementi at St. Petersburg, where he was also influenced by Field's technique; went to Stockholm in 1812, and then to London, rejoining Clementi and meeting Cramer; finally settled in Berlin (1815) as a piano teacher; among his pupils were Mendelssohn, Henselt, Taubert and Fanny Hensel. With Klein, Reichardt and Rellstab he founded the junior 'Liedertafel' (1819). He composed many effective piano studies; also an opera *Oreste* (never performed); cantatas; male quartets; songs, etc. A biography of him was published by L. Rellstab in the 'Berlinische Zeitung' of Feb. 12, 1839 (reprint, 1846).

Berger, Rudolf, opera singer; b. Brünn, Moravia, April 17, 1874; d. New York, Feb. 27, 1915. He began his vocal studies at the Brünn Cons. (1891); made his debut there, as a baritone (1896); subsequently successfully sang baritone roles at various German theaters; from 1904-07 was a member of the Royal Opera at Berlin. He then retired for a year; studied with Oscar Saenger in New York, changing to tenor; returned to Germany, where he appeared in Berlin (1909) as Lohengrin, and sang tenor roles (chiefly Wagner) thereafter; in 1913 married the soprano Marie Rappold; then settled in New York, where he was a member of the Metropolitan Opera (1914-15). He had a large repertory, consisting of 96 baritone and 18 tenor roles; sang Jokanaan, in *Salome,* 79 times.

Berger, Theodor, Austrian composer; b. Traismauer, Lower Austria, May 18, 1905. He studied in Vienna with Franz Schmidt. His music reflects Schmidt's influence; he takes particular interest in structural problems. Among his works are *Malinconia* for string orchestra in 25 parts (1938); *Ballade* for orchestra (1941); *Rondo ostinato* for wind instruments with percussion (1947); quintet for horns; 2 string quartets, etc.

Berger, Wilhelm, German composer; b. Boston, Mass. (of German parents), Aug. 9, 1861; d. Jena, Jan. 15, 1911. When an infant he was taken to Germany; studied at the Hochschule für Musik in Berlin (1878-81); taught at the Klindworth-Scharwenka Cons. (until 1903); then was court conductor at Meiningen. He was a very prolific composer; wrote 105 opus numbers; his music, though lacking in originality, commanded respect for its technical skill. He wrote 2 symphonies (no. 1 was perf. in Boston on Nov. 4, 1899); oratorio *Euphorion;* 3 Ballades for baritone with orch.; *Gesang der Geister über den Wassern* for chorus and orch.; piano quartet; many piano works; choral pieces; about 80 songs. A full catalogue of his works was publ. by W. Altmann (Leipzig, 1920); biography by A. Kohut in the 'Neue Musikzeitung' (Stuttgart, 1902, nos. 21-23); see also E. Krause, *W. Berger* in 'Monographien moderner Musiker' (Leipzig, 1907); G. Ernest, *W. Berger* (Berlin, 1931).

Berggreen (bärg-grān), **Andreas Peter,** Danish composer; b. Copenhagen, March 2, 1801; d. there, Nov. 8, 1880. He studied law, but turned to music later. He occupied various posts as church organist and teacher of singing in Denmark; in 1859 he became inspector of singing in Danish public schools. His first important work was a comic opera *Billedet og Busten (The Portrait and The Bust)*, produced in Copenhagen on April 9, 1832. He also wrote incidental music to various theatrical plays. His most important contribution is the compilation of 11 volumes of folksongs of various nations, published under the title *Folkesange og Melodier* (1842); and 14 volumes of songs for use in schools (1834-76); also edited church anthems. Among his students was Gade. His biographical sketch, by Skou, was published in 1895.

Bergh, Arthur, American composer and conductor; b. St. Paul, Minn., March 24, 1882. He studied violin; played in the orchestra of the Metropolitan Opera (1903-08); then conducted a series of municipal concerts in New York (1911-14); later became associated with various recording companies. Among his works are 2 melodramas with orch., *The Raven* and *The Pied Piper of Hamelin;* a romantic opera *Niorada;* a symphonic chorale *The Unnamed City;* 2 operettas, *In Arcady* and *The Goblin Fair;* about 100 songs; a number of violin pieces, etc. From 1941 Bergh lived in Hollywood as librarian for moving picture companies.

Bergh, Rudolph, composer and writer; b. Copenhagen, Sept. 22, 1859; d. Davos, Dec. 7, 1924. He studied biology and music in Copenhagen and Berlin; in 1922 was a member of the Board of the Copenhagen Cons. He composed the choral works *Requiem für Werther; Geister der Windstille;* and an oratorio, *The Mount of Holy Fire;* also about 150 songs; 50 piano pieces; chamber music, etc.

Berghem, Jachet de. See **Berchem.**

Bergman, Erik, Finnish composer; b. Nykarleby, Nov. 24, 1911. He studied at the Sibelius Academy in Helsinki; then in Berlin, Vienna and Paris. Works: *Majnätter* for soprano and orch. (1946); *Livete träd,* cantata (1947); piano pieces and songs.

Bergmann, Carl, German conductor; b. Ebersbach, Saxony, April 12, 1821; d. New York, Aug. 16, 1876. He was a pupil of Zimmermann in Zittau, and Hesse in Breslau; emigrated to the U. S. in 1850 and joined the traveling 'Germania' Orch.; later became its conductor until the group disbanded in 1854. Bergmann also conducted the Handel and Haydn Society (1852-54). In 1854 he was in Chicago; in 1855 became associate conductor (with Theodore Eisfeld) of the New York Philh. Orch; in 1862 became its sole conductor, retaining this post until his death. He also conducted the German male chorus 'Arion'. Bergmann played an important role in American music; an ardent admirer of Wagner and Liszt, he introduced their works to American audiences.

Bergmans, Paul Jean Étienne Charles, Belgian musicologist; b. Ghent, Feb. 23, 1868; d. there, Nov. 14, 1935. Studied at the Univ. of Ghent; *Dr. phil.,* 1887; 1892, assistant librarian; 1919, chief librarian and prof. there; member of the Royal Academy of Belgium. He published a number of very valuable studies and books, the most important of which are: *P. J. Leblan, carilloneur de la ville de Gand au XVIIIe siècle* (1884); *H. Waelput* (1886); *Variétés musicologiques* (3 vols., 1891, 1901, 1920); *La vie musicale gantoise au XVIIIe siècle* (1897); *Peter Philips* (1903); *Les Musiciens de Courtrai et du Courtraisis* (1912); *Notice sur Fl. van Duyse* (1919); *Corn. Verdonck* (1919); *Henri Vieuxtemps* (1920); *Le baron Limnander de Nieuwenhove* (1920); *Quatorze lettres inédites du comp. Philippe de Monte* (1921); *Tielman Susato* (1923); *Notice sur le chevalier X. van Elewyck* (1925); *De l'histoire de la musique* (1927); *Les origines belges de Beethoven* (1927); *Une Famille de musiciens belges du XVIIIe siècle: Les Loeillet* (Brussels, 1927; establishes for the first time accurate biographical data on members of the Loeillet family); *La typographie musicale en Belgique au XVIe siècle* (1930). He also wrote an introduction to vol. I (1932; piano music, ed. by J. Watelet) of 'Monumenta musicae Belgicae'.

Bergner, Wilhelm, organist; b. Riga, Nov. 4, 1837; d. there, June 9, 1907. He was organist of the English church at Riga (1861) and at the Riga Cathedral (1868-1906); exercised great influence on the development of musical culture in Latvia.

Bergonzi, Carlo, Italian violin maker; b. Cremona, c. 1683; d. there, 1747. He began manufacturing violins in 1716, modeling them after Stradivarius, with whose son he was associated. It is doubtful whether Bergonzi was trained by the master himself. His son, Michel Angelo Bergonzi (1722-1770), continued the trade, as did his grandsons, Carlo, Nicola and Zosimo (sons of Michel Angelo Bergonzi).

Bergson, Michael, composer; b. Warsaw, May 20, 1820; d. London, March 9, 1898. He studied with Schneider in Dessau and with Rungenhagen and Taubert in Berlin. He was in Paris in 1840 and in Italy in 1846; his opera *Luisa di Monfort* was produced in Florence in 1847. He then lived in Vienna, Berlin and Leipzig. On his second visit to Paris he brought out an operetta *Qui va à la chasse, perd sa place* (1859). In 1863 he was appointed professor of piano at the Geneva Cons.; later became its director. He eventually settled in London as piano teacher. He wrote numerous pieces of piano music, clearly in imitation of Chopin (*Polonaise héroïque, 12 Grandes Études caractéristiques,* etc.); also a manual *École du mécanisme,* etc.

Bergsma, William, American composer; b. Oakland, Calif., April 1, 1921. He studied at Stanford Univ., and with Hanson and Rogers at the Eastman School of Music in Rochester; received a Guggenheim Fellowship in 1946. His works include 2 ballets: *Paul Bunyan* (San Francisco, June 22, 1939) and *Señor Commandante* (Rochester, May 1, 1942); symphony for chamber orch. (Rochester, April 14, 1943); *Music on a Quiet Theme* for orch. (Rochester, April 22, 1943); *Suite from a Children's Film* (1945); Symphony No. 1 (1946-49; CBS, May 20, 1950); choral symph. poem *A Carol on Twelfth Night* (1953); 3-act opera *The Wife of Martin Guerre* (N. Y., Feb. 15, 1956); in smaller forms: a suite for brass quartet (1940); 2 string quartets (1942; 1944); *3 Fantasies* for piano (1943); *Showpiece* for violin and piano (1934); *Pieces for Renard* for recorder and 2 violas (1943); 2 choral pieces, *In a Glass of Water* (1945) and *On the Beach at Night* (1946). —Cf. A. Skulsky, *The Music of William Bergsma,* in 'The Juilliard Review' for Spring 1956 (with a list of works).

Bergt, Christian Gottlob August, noted German composer; b. Öderan, Saxony, June 17, 1772; d. Bautzen, Feb. 10, 1837. He was organist at Bautzen from 1802; also taught music at the Seminary and was conductor of the singing society. He wrote 6 operas; several symphonies; chamber music; songs, of which a set of Lieder, *Congé,* became very popular. His sacred works were for a time constantly performed throughout Germany; he wrote a Passion; the hymns *So weit der Sonne Strahlen* and *Christus ist erstanden* for 4 voices and orch.; the canticle *Herr Gott, dich loben wir,* etc. His book *Briefwechsel eines alten und jungen Schulmeisters* (1838) contains a biographical sketch.

Beringer, Oscar, pianist and pedagogue; b. Furtwangen, Baden, July 14, 1844; d. London, Feb. 21, 1922. His father was a political refugee in 1849, and settled in London; Oscar Beringer received his rudimentary education at home; then enrolled in the Leipzig Cons., where he studied with Plaidy, Moscheles, and Reinecke (1864-66); he further studied in Berlin with Tausig; in 1869 became prof. in Tausig's Schule des höheren Klavierspiels; returned to London in 1871, and in 1873 established an Academy for the Higher Development of Pianoforte Playing, organized on the model of Tausig's Berlin school. From 1885 he was also prof. at the Royal Academy of Music. He was a pianist of great perfection of method; his book of technical exercises is valuable for students. Among his published compositions are a piano concerto; 2 piano sonatinas; various minor piano pieces; songs. He also published *Fifty Years' Experience of Pianoforte Teaching and Playing* (1907).

Bériot (bā-rē-oh'), **Charles (-Auguste) de,** celebrated Belgian violinist; b. Louvain, Feb. 20, 1802; d. Brussels, April 8, 1870. He owed his technical foundation to the careful instruction of his guardian, Tiby, a provincial teacher; as a boy, he had lessons with Viotti, whose concerto he played in public at the age of nine. He made a triumphant debut in Paris (1821); became chamber violinist to the King of France; played successfully in many concerts in England; was solo violinist to the King of the Netherlands; from 1830-5 made concert tours through Europe, many with Mme. Garcia-Malibran, whom he married in 1836. From 1843-52 he was prof. of violin at Brussels Cons.; failure of eyesight and paralysis of the left arm necessitated his retirement. Among his compositions are: 7 violin concertos; *duos brillants* for violin and piano; 11 sets of variations for violin. His pedagogical works are still useful; he wrote *Premier guide des violonistes; Méthode de Violon* (3 parts; Paris, 1858; his best work); many studies for violin, etc. Bibl.: E. Heron-Allen, *A Contribution towards an Accurate Biography of de Bériot and Malibran,* in No. VI of 'De fidiculis opuscula' (1894); A. Bachmann, *Les grands violonistes du passé* (Paris, 1913).

Bériot, Charles-Wilfride de (son of Charles-Auguste de Bériot), French pianist; b. Paris, Feb. 21, 1883; d. Sceaux du Gâtinais, Oct. 22, 1914. He was a pupil of Thalberg (1855); later taught piano at the Paris Cons.; wrote a symph. poem, *Fernand Cortez;* overtures; 3 piano concertos; a collection for violin and piano entitled *Opéras sans paroles,* etc.; was co-author, with his father, of a *Méthode d'accompagnement.*

Berkeley, Lennox, English composer; b. Boar's Hill, near Oxford, May 12, 1903. He received his education at Merton College, Oxford (1922-26); studied in Paris with Nadia Boulanger (1926-32). He was attracted from the beginning by the spirit of neo-classical music, and his early works bear the imprint of the French style, with superimposed influences of Stravinsky. He succeeded, however, in creating an individual manner of writing in his more mature compositions. The list of his works includes: oratorio *Jonah* (1935); *Overture* (I.S.C.M. Festival, Barcelona, April 23, 1936); *Serenade* for strings (1939); symphony (London, Promenade Concerts, July 8, 1943, composer conducting); *Domini est terra,* for chorus and orch. (I.S.C.M. Festival, London, June 17, 1938); ballet, *The Judgment of Paris* (London, 1938); piano concerto (1947); opera in 3 acts, *Nelson* (1951; preview with piano accompaniment, London, Feb. 14, 1953; first complete performance, London, Sept. 22, 1954); *4 Sonnets of Ronsard,* for 2 tenors and piano (London, March 8, 1953); *3 Greek Poems,* for voice and piano (London, March 15, 1953); flute concerto (London, July 29, 1953); opera in 1 act, *A Dinner Engagement* (Aldeburgh Festival, June 17, 1954); also chamber music (suite for oboe and cello; 2 violin sonatas; viola sonata; string trio; 2 string quartets); *Polka* for 2 pianos, etc.

Berkenhead, John L., blind organist, who was active in the U.S. towards the end of the 18th century. He arrived in America in 1795; was organist at Trinity Church in Newport from 1796 to 1804. His piece for harpsichord, *Abolition of the Bastille,* was invariably featured at his concerts in Boston and other New England cities.

Berlijn (ber-lin'), **Anton** (real name, Aron Wolf), Dutch composer; b. Amsterdam, May 2, 1817; d. there, Jan. 16, 1870. He studied with L. Erk in Berlin and with G. W. Fink at Leipzig; returning to Amsterdam in 1846, he became conductor of the Royal Theater; wrote 9 operas, two of which (*Die Bergknappen* and *Proserpina*) became popular; 7 ballets; an oratorio, *Moses auf Nebo;* symphonies; chamber music; etc.

Berlin, Irving (real name Isidore Balin), American composer of popular music; b. Temun, Russia, May 11, 1888; brought to the U.S. in 1893. He received no formal musical training, and never learned to read or write music; nonetheless, he succeeded in producing lyrical songs (to his own words) that are remarkable for their innate feeling, for the melodic phrase and the perfect blend of words and melodies. His first published song was *Marie from Sunny Italy* (1907), for which he wrote only the lyrics; he made his mark with the celebrated song *Alexander's Ragtime Band* (1911); in the same style were *Everybody's Doing It* (1911); *International Rag* (1913); *Ragtime Violin* (1911); *When that midnight choo-choo leaves for Alabam* (1912); *I want to go back to Michigan* (1914); ballads, *When I lost you* (1912), *When I leave the world behind* (1915). His first musical show, for which he composed the entire score, words and music, was *Watch Your Step* (1916); 1917 brought out his war show, *Yip, Yip, Yaphank,* which included the famous song *O how I hate to get up in the morning.* He then wrote the first three of his *Ziegfeld Follies* (1918, 1919, 1920; including the songs, *A pretty girl is like a melody* and *Mandy*); the *Music Box Revues* (1921, 1922; 1923, 1925); built the Music Box Theater with Sam Harris in 1921. His other shows are: *Face the Music* (1932); *As Thousands Cheer* (1933, including the songs *Easter Parade* and *Heat Wave*); *Louisiana Purchase* (1939); *This is the Army* (1942); *Annie Get Your Gun* (1946); *Miss Liberty* (1949); *Call me Madam* (1950). Among his songs and ballads that have spread far and wide all over the world are: *What'll I do* (1924); *All Alone* (1924); *Remember* (1925); *Always* (1925); *The Song is Ended but the Melody Lingers On* (1927); *Russian Lullaby* (1927); *Blue Skies* (1927); and *White Christmas* (enormously popular during World War II). He has also composed musical scores for the moving pictures: *Top Hat* (1935); *Follow the Fleet* (1936); *On the Avenue* (1937); *Carefree* (1938); *Second Fiddle* (1939); *Holiday Inn* (1942); *Blue Skies* (1946); *Easter Parade* (1948);

etc. To promote the publication and distribution of his music, he founded in 1919 the firm of Irving Berlin, Inc. He was a charter member of ASCAP (1914). In July 1954 he received the Congressional Medal for his patriotic songs, particularly *God Bless America* (composed in 1918; revived in 1938 and made famous during and after World War II). See A. Woollcott, *The Story of Irving Berlin* (N. Y., 1925).

Berlinski, Jacques, Polish-French conductor and composer; b. Radom, Dec. 13, 1913. He went to France in 1931, and studied with Nadia Boulanger and Roger Ducasse; then conducted concerts in Paris, Brussels and in South Africa. He has written a symph. poem, *Kenaan,* a cantata *Habacouc,* a symphony and chamber music.

Berlioz, Gabriel Pierre; French composer (not related to Hector Berlioz); b. Paris, June 25, 1916. He studied in Paris with Roussel and d'Indy. He has written a viola concerto (1935); *Francezaïc,* comic opera (1939); *Symphonie parisienne* (1942); *Jardin hanté* ballet (1943); piano trio (1944); *Divertissement* for violin, cello, piano and string orch. (1945); Concerto for kettledrums and orch. (1951; Paris, Jan. 25, 1953); bassoon concerto (1952); Symphony No. 2 (1953); pieces for tuba and piano, saxophone and piano, flute and piano, etc.

Berlioz (bär-lē-ohz), **Hector (-Louis),** great French composer; b. Côte-Saint-André, Isère, Dec. 11, 1803; d. Paris, March 8, 1869. His father, a physician, sent him to Paris to study medicine. But Berlioz took little interest in medicine and became deeply engrossed in music, even though he was not proficient on any instrument except the guitar. Despite his lack of musical training, he entered the Paris Conservatory where he studied with Lesueur and Reicha. He soon became dissatisfied with the formal training given by his teachers and began to compose music in a romantic manner free from all restrictions of the rigorous classical school. From the very first Berlioz endeavored to transcend the limits of practical composition and performance; he dreamed of huge orchestras which could adequately embody his romantic ideas. His first work was an orchestral *Messe solennelle,* which he had produced at the church of St. Roch (July 10, 1825), employing 150 players. Still he was ambitious enough to covet academic honors. He submitted a cantata *La Mort d'Orphée* for the Prix de Rome in 1827; a performance was tentatively scheduled for July 22, 1828, but was cancelled when the music committee declared the score unplayable. The cantata was not performed until a century later, Oct. 16, 1932, when Cortot conducted it in Paris (the MS was regarded as lost, but was discovered by Boschot). Undaunted, Berlioz again applied for the Prix de Rome, and obtained second prize in 1828; he finally carried first prize in 1830 with a more conventional work, *Sardanapale.* In the meantime his overtures *Waverley* and *Les Francs-Juges* were performed at a Conservatory concert on May 26, 1828. He then embarked on his most individual work, the *Symphonie fantastique,* subtitled 'épisode de la vie d'un artiste.' The completion of this score at the age of 26 signalized the opening of a new era in program music; in it Berlioz abandons the classical method of thematic development, and instead establishes what he himself called an 'idée fixe,' a basic theme recurring throughout the music. Berlioz gives this description of the *Symphonie fantastique*: "A young musician of morbid sensibility and ardent imagination poisons himself with opium in a fit of amorous despair. The narcotic dose, too weak to result in death, plunges him into a heavy sleep accompanied by the strangest visions, during which his sensations, sentiments and recollections are translated in his sick brain into musical thoughts and images. The beloved woman herself has become for him a melody, like a fixed idea which he finds and hears everywhere." The titles of the 5 movements are: I. *Dreams, Passions;* II. *A Ball;* III. *Scene in the Fields;* IV. *March to the Scaffold;* V. *Walpurgisnight's Dream.* The genesis of the symphony is no less remarkable than its form; it was intended to be an offering of both adoration and condemnation to the Irish actress Harriet Smithson, whose performances of Shakespeare Berlioz had attended in Paris (even though he knew no English). The first performance of the *Symphonie fantastique* was given in Paris on Dec. 5, 1830; Berlioz hoped that Harriet Smithson would attend but she was professionally occupied on that day. Berlioz wrote a sequel to the *Symphonie fantastique* entitled *Lélio;* both parts were performed in Paris on Dec. 9, 1832, creating a sensation, particularly since by that time all Paris knew the story of Berlioz's infatuation. Harriet Smithson was present herself; they met, and over the opposition of both families, they were married on Oct. 3, 1833. The marriage proved unhappy; they separated; Harriet Smithson died in 1854; Berlioz remarried that same year; his second wife, Maria Recio, died in 1862.

Berlioz's next significant work was equally unconventional, *Harold en Italie* for solo viola and orch. (Paris, Nov. 23, 1834), inspired by Byron's *Childe Harold;* there followed the dramatic symphony *Roméo et Juliette* for solo voices, chorus and orch. (Paris, Nov. 24, 1839) and *Le Carnaval romain* (Paris, Feb. 3, 1844), the latter destined to become one of the most popular works in the orchestral repertory. Less successful was Berlioz's opera *Benvenuto Cellini,* to which *Le Carnaval romain* originally served as an orchestral introduction (in the 2nd act); it was performed at the Paris Opéra (Sept. 10, 1838) arousing little interest; however, its production by Liszt in Weimar (March 20, 1852) was received with great acclaim; Berlioz conducted it in London, on June 25, 1853. In the meantime Berlioz became a brilliant musical journalist; his articles in the 'Journal des Débats' and in the 'Gazette Musicale' exercised considerable influence and helped to arouse interest in new musical ideas. To eke out his earnings, Berlioz accepted the appointment as librarian of the Paris Conservatory (1852), and held it until his death. His Paris obligations did not interfere with his travels; he toured Germany and Italy; he also visited Austria, Hungary and Russia. German musicians, led by Liszt, were particularly sympathetic to his music; concerts of his music were organized by Liszt in Weimar (1855). On Aug. 9, 1862, Berlioz conducted in Baden-Baden the première of his opera *Béatrice et Bénédict.*

The creative life of Berlioz is not easily separable into distinct periods. Sometimes he dwelt on a favorite idea for many years before its ultimate embodiment. Still at the conservatory, he presented a cantata *8 scènes de Faust* (Nov. 29, 1829); much later he expanded the materials from this work in *La Damnation de Faust,* which Berlioz termed an 'opéra de concert.' He conducted it in concert form at the Opéra-Comique on Dec. 6, 1846; the complete work is seldom performed, but its symphonic interlude *Rákóczi March* has become famous; two other excerpts from the score, *Minuet of the Will-o'-the Wisps* and *Dance of the Sylphs,* are also widely known. A curious destiny was reserved for the opera *Les Troyens,* written in 1856-59, in 2 parts, *La Prise de Troie* and *Les Troyens à Carthage.* Only the 2nd part was performed in Berlioz's lifetime (Paris, Théâtre-Lyrique, Nov. 4, 1863); the 1st part was presented for the first time in Karlsruhe on Dec. 6, 1890; the whole work was produced in Cologne (in German) on two successive nights, March 30-31, 1898; in France, it was not performed in its entirety until 1920 when it was given in Rouen. Other works are: *Messe des Morts* (Paris, Dec. 5, 1837); a sacred trilogy *L'Enfance du Christ* (Paris, Dec. 10, 1854); symphonic overtures *King Lear* (1831), *Rob Roy* (1832) and *Le Corsaire* (1844); song cycles *Irlande* (1830) and *Nuits d'été* (1834-41; also with orch.); *Te Deum* for tenor, 3 choirs, orch., brass band and organ (1849). His *Traité d'instrumentation et d'orchestration modernes* (1844), a work of fundamental importance, has been translated into all European languages; supplemented editions were issued in German by Weingartner (1904) and Richard Strauss (1905). This treatise, no less than his orchestral music itself, led Weingartner to proclaim Berlioz the "creator of the modern orchestra." The extraordinary versatility of Berlioz's gifts is revealed in his literary writings. He publ. *Voyage musical en Allemagne et Italie* (1844; 2 vols.); *Les Soirées de l'orchestre* (1853; English translation by Ch. E. Roche, with introduction by Ernest Newman; London, 1929; a new translation by J. Barzun, N. Y., 1956); *Grotesques de la musique* (1859); *A travers chants* (1862); *Les Musiciens et la musique* (a series of articles collected from the 'Journal des Débats'; 1903, with introduction by André Hallays). His book of *Mémoires* (1870; 2nd ed., 2 vols., 1876; English translation, London, 1884; annotated and edited by Ernest Newman, N. Y., 1932) presents a vivid panorama of the musical life in Europe as reflected in his mind; factually it is not always trustworthy. A complete edition of Berlioz's works (with the exception of the operas *Benvenuto Cellini* and *Les Troyens*) has been publ. by Breitkopf & Härtel in 20 vols. under the editorship of Ch. Malherbe and F. Weingartner (but see Supplement 5 in Jacques Barzun's book *Berlioz and the Romantic Century* for the enumeration of musical and other errors). Breitkopf & Härtel also publ. (in German) the literary works of Berlioz in 10 vols., including his correspondence. Cf. C. Hopkinson, *A Bibliography of the Musical and Literary Works of Hector Berlioz* (Edinburgh, 1951).

BIBLIOGRAPHY. I. Biography: E. Hippeau, *Berlioz, l'homme et l'artiste* (3 vols., Paris, 1883-85); A. Jullien, *H.B.* (Paris, 1888); L. Pohl, *Hector Berlioz's Leben und Werke* (Leipzig, 1900); K. F. Boult, *Berlioz's Life as Written by Himself in His Letters and Memoirs* (London, 1903); R. Louis, *H.B.* (Leipzig, 1904); J.-G. Prod'homme, *H.B.* (Paris, 1905); A. Coquard, *Berlioz*

(Paris, 1908); B. Schrader, *Berlioz* (Leipzig, 1908); A. Boschot's monumental biography in 3 vols.: *La Jeunesse d'un romantique; H.B., 1803-31* (Paris, 1906); *Un Romantique sous Louis-Philippe; H.B., 1831-42* (Paris, 1908); and *Le Crépuscule d'un romantique: H.B., 1842-69* (Paris, 1913); A. Boschot, *Une vie romantique, H.B.* (Paris, 1919; 27th edition, 1951; complete biography in 1 vol.); P.-M. Masson, *B.* (Paris, 1923); J. Kapp, *H.B.* (Berlin, 1922); E. Rey, *La vie amoureuse de B.* (Paris, 1929); L. Constantin, *B.* (Paris, 1933); W. J. Turner, *B.; the Man and his Work* (London, 1934); Tom Wotton, *H. B.* (Oxford, 1935); J. H. Elliot, *B.* (London, 1938); G. de Pourtalès, *B. et l'Europe romantique* (Paris, 1939); J. Barzun, *Berlioz and the Romantic Century* (2 vols.; Boston, 1950; a most valuable investigation, correcting many accepted but erroneous data); A. W. Ganz, *B. in London* (London, 1950); H. Kuehner, *H.B., Charakter und Schöpfertum* (Berlin, 1952); Henry Barraud, *H.B.* (Paris, 1955).

II. Correspondence: D. Bernard, *Correspondance inédite de B.* (Paris, 1878); Ch. Gounod, *Lettres intimes* (Paris, 1882); La Mara, *Briefe von H.B. an die Fürstin Carolyne Wittgenstein* (Leipzig, 1903); J. Tiersot, *Les Années romantiques: Correspondance d'H.B.* (Paris, 1907). All the abovementioned letters are found in vols. III-V of the Breitkopf & Härtel edition; J. Tiersot, *Le musicien errant* (Paris, 1919); J. Tiersot, *Correspondance inédite de B.* (Paris, 1930); J.-G. Prod'homme, *Souvenirs de voyage* (Paris, 1932); G. Clarence, *Lettres inédites à Berlioz* in 'La Revue Musicale' (vol. XI, 1); S. Ginsburg, *Correspondance russe inédite de Berlioz* (ibidem); J. Barzun, ed., *New Letters of Berlioz, 1830-68* (N. Y., 1954).

III. Analysis and Criticism: F. Liszt, *Berlioz und seine Harold-symphonie* (1855; reprinted in vol. IV of Liszt's 'Gesammelte Schriften'); A. Ernst, *L'œuvre dramatique de H.B.* (Paris, 1884); R. Pohl, *H.B.: Studien und Erinnerungen* (Leipzig, 1884); E. Hippeau, *Berlioz et son temps* (Paris, 1892); J. Tiersot, *Berlioz et la société de son temps* (Paris, 1904); T. Mantovani, *La dannazione di Faust d'Ettore Berlioz* (Milan, 1923); J. Tiersot, *B. of the Fantastic Symphony* in the 'Mus. Quarterly' (1933); P. Schlitzer, *La messa da requiem di Ettore Berlioz* (Florence, 1940); N. Slonimsky, *Lexicon of Musical Invective* (N. Y., 1953).

Berlyn, Anton. See **Berlijn.**

Bermudo, Juan, Spanish music theorist; b. Ecija, Seville, c. 1510; d. after 1555. He first studied theology and devoted himself to preaching; later turned to music and studied at the Univ. of Alcalá de Henares. He spent 15 years as a Franciscan monk in Andalusia; in 1550 he entered the service of the Archbishop of Andalusia, where Cristóbal de Morales was choir director. The writings of Bermudo constitute an important source of information on Spanish instrumental music of the 16th century. His most comprehensive work is the *Declaración de Instrumentos Musicales* (Osuna, 1549 and 1555). It deals with theory, in which his authorities were Gafurius, Glareanus and Ornithoparchus; instruments, including problems of tuning, technique of performance, and repertoire; and critical evaluation of contemporary composers, showing familiarity with the works of Josquin, Willaert and Gombert. Bermudo also wrote *El Arte tripharia* (Osuna, 1550). 13 organ pieces by him are included in F. Pedrell, *Salterio Sacro-Hispano.* Bibl.: O. Kinkeldey, *Orgel und Clavier in der Musik des 16ten Jahrhundert* (1910); H. Collet, *Le Mysticisme musical espagnol au XVIe siècle* (Paris, 1913); R. Mitjana, *La Musique en Espagne,* in Lavignac's *Encyclopédie musicale;* H. Anglès and J. Subirá, *Catálogo Musical de la Biblioteca Nacional de Madrid* (vol. II). See also G. Reese, *Music in the Renaissance* (N. Y., 1954).

Bernabei, (Giuseppe) Ercole, Italian composer of vocal music; b. Caprarola, Papal States, c. 1620; d. Munich, Dec. (buried Dec. 6), 1687. He was a pupil of Orazio Benevoli, whom he succeeded in 1672 as chapel master at the Vatican; 1674, became court conductor at Munich. He wrote 5 operas (produced in Munich); published a book of madrigals, *Concerto madrigalesco* (1669), etc.; other works (masses, offertories, psalms) are MS. in various libraries. —Cf. R. Casimiri, *Ercole Bernabei, maestro di cappella musicale lateranense* (Rome, 1920); R. de Rensis, *E. Bernabei* (Rome, 1920).

Bernabei, Giuseppe Antonio, Italian composer, son of the preceding; b. Rome, 1649; d. Munich, March 9, 1732. He studied with his father and helped him as second chapel master in Munich from 1677; after his father's death, he assumed his post (1688). He composed 14 operas and much sacred music. See Karl Forster, *G.A. Bernabei als Kirchenkomponist* (Munich, 1933).

Bernac, Pierre (real name Pierre Bertin); French baritone; b. Paris, Jan. 12, 1899.

He studied with Reinhold von Wahrlich in Salzburg (1934). Assumed the pseudonym Bernac in order to avoid confusion with another Pierre Bertin, an actor. Bernac specializes in concert recitals of French and German songs; since 1936, has given numerous recitals in Europe and America with Francis Poulenc. He has also taught master classes at the American Cons. in Fontainebleau. Cf. R. Gelatt, *Music Makers* (N. Y., 1953).

Bernacchi (bär-nahk'-kē), **Antonio,** celebrated sopranist *(musico);* b. Bologna, June (baptized June 23d), 1685; d. there, March, 1756. He was a pupil of Pistocchi; sang in Venice and Bologna (1709-12); then appeared in London (1716); was again in Italy (1717-29), also sang in opera in Munich. In 1729 he was specially engaged by Handel as a substitute for Senesino for the Italian Opera in London; after initial successes, Bernacchi lost his following in London and returned to Italy, where he continued to sing until 1736. He settled in Bologna and opened a singing school. He revived the style of vocal embellishments which the French term 'roulades,' and was severely criticized for this practice. He left some compositions, among them *Grave et Fuga a 4; Kyrie a 5;* and *Justus ut palma a 5.* Bibl.: L. Frati, *Antonio Bernacchi e la sua scuola di canto* ('Rivista Musicale Italiana,' Sept. 1922).

Bernard (bär-nahr'), **Jean Emile Auguste,** French composer and organist; b. Marseilles, Nov. 28, 1843; d. Paris, Sept. 11, 1902. He studied at the Paris Cons. with Benoist (organ) and with Marmontel (piano); was organist at Notre Dame des Champs until 1895. He wrote 2 cantatas: *Guillaume le conquérant* and *La Captivité de Babylone;* an overture, *Béatrice;* piano quartet; piano trio; cello sonata; violin sonata; a *divertissement* for wind instruments; etc.

Bernard, Moritz (Matvey Ivanovitch), Russian music publisher and composer; b. Mitau, 1794; d. St. Petersburg, May 9, 1871. He studied with John Field in Moscow (1811); was music teacher in the household of Count Potocki (1816); then taught in St. Petersburg, where he opened a music store in 1829; his opera, *Olga,* was performed there in 1845. In 1840 he began issuing a musical monthly, 'Nouvelliste,' which continued publication until 1914, many years after his death. He also published collections of children's pieces 'L'enfant-pianiste'; arranged Russian folksongs for voice and piano (a collection posthumously published in 1886).

Bernard, Paul, French pianist and teacher; b. Poitiers, Oct. 4, 1827; d. Paris, Feb. 24, 1879. He studied at the Paris Cons. with Halévy and Thalberg; wrote criticisms for the 'Ménestrel' and the 'Revue et Gazette musicale'; composed many piano pieces.

Bernard, Robert, Swiss-born composer, editor and writer on music; b. Geneva, Oct. 10, 1900; he studied in Geneva with Templeton Strong, Barblan and Lauber. In 1926 he settled in Paris; in 1937 he became a lecturer at the Schola Cantorum and a music critic; for several years he was editor of 'La Revue Musicale.' He has published monographs on Franck, Aubert, Roussel and other French composers. He has written a piano concerto; a harp concerto; saxophone quartet; piano trio; trio for oboe, clarinet and trombone; and a number of piano pieces.

Bernardi, Bartolomeo, composer; b. Bologna, c. 1660; d. Copenhagen, May, 1732. He left Bologna about 1700 and settled in Denmark; two of his operas were performed in Copenhagen in 1703: *Il Gige fortunato* and *Diana e la Fortuna.* He also wrote an opera, *Libussa,* which was produced in Prague; his trio-sonatas were published in Bologna (1692; 1696).

Bernardi, Enrico, Italian conductor and composer; b. Milan, March 11, 1838; d. there, July 17, 1900. He toured in Italy with various opera companies as conductor; wrote several operas which he produced himself, and nearly 60 ballets, of which the first, *Illusioni d'un pittore* (Milan, 1854), was perhaps the most successful.

Bernardi, Francesco. See **Senesino.**

Bernardi, Steffano, Italian composer; b. Verona, c. 1576; d. 1636. He served as maestro di cappella at the church of the Santissima Madonna dei Monti in Rome; from 1611-22 was music director at the Cathedral of Verona; became Kapellmeister at the Salzburg Cathedral (1628); left Salzburg in 1634. Among his works are: 2 books of masses for 8 voices, and one for 4 and 5 voices; a book of madrigals for 3 voices (Rome, 1611) and 2 books for 5 voices (Venice, 1611; Rome, 1612); 2 books of *madrigaletti;* psalms and motets; also instrumental works (trio-sonatas, etc.). Reprints of some of his sacred works are to be found in the 'Denkmäler der Tonkunst in Österreich' (vol. XXXVI). Bernardi was also the author of the manual *Porta musicale per la quale il principiante con facile brevità all'acquisto delle perfette regole del contrap-*

punto vien introdotto (Verona, 1615; 7 subsequent editions). Bibl.: F. Posch, *Steffano Bernardis weltliche Vokal- und Instrumental-Werke* (Munich, 1928).

Bernasconi, Andrea, composer and conductor; b. Milan, 1706; d. Munich, Jan. 29, 1784. He was conductor at the court of Munich from 1755; wrote 18 operas, 14 of which were produced at Munich; also much sacred music. Bibl.: E. J. Weiss, *Andrea Bernasconi als Opernkomponist* (dissertation, Munich, 1923).

Berneker, Constanz, German composer; b. Darkehmen, East Prussia, Oct. 30, 1844; d. Königsberg, June 9, 1906. He studied at the Royal Academy in Berlin; then was organist at the Königsberg Cathedral; also taught at the conservatory. Works: cantatas, *Judith; Christi Himmelfahrt; Reformations-Kantate; Gott unsere Zuflucht; Christus ist mein Leben; Das Siegefest; Hero und Leander; Das hohe Lied; Mila, das Haidekind;* and many other cantatas. Bibl.: O. Laudien, *Constanz Berneker* (Berlin, 1909).

Berner, Friedrich Wilhelm, German organist and composer; b. Breslau, May 16, 1780; d. there, May 9, 1827. He taught at the Breslau Seminary; later became director of the Royal Academic Institute for Church Music; wrote church music and published theoretical essays on music. A biography of him was written by Hientsch (1829).

Berners, Lord (originally **Gerald Tyrwhitt**), English composer; b. Arley Park, Bridgenorth, Sept. 18, 1883; d. London, April 19, 1950. He served as a career diplomat in the British Embassies of Constantinople (1909-11) and Rome (1911-19); as a musician he was largely self-taught; Casella and Stravinsky gave him some advice on orchestration. His music is in a modern idiom, in which a humorous subject is depicted in dissonant harmonies; his set of piano pieces, *3 Funeral Marches (For a Statesman, For a Canary, For a Rich Aunt),* is a remarkable example of modernistic grotesque; his works for the theater are equally urbane and sophisticated. He wrote an opera *Le Carrosse du Saint-Sacrement* (Paris, April 24, 1921); the ballets, *The Triumph of Neptune* (London, Dec. 3, 1926, Diaghilev's Ballets Russes); *Luna Park* (London, 1930), *A Wedding Bouquet* (London, April 27, 1937), *Cupid and Psyche* (London, April 27, 1939); *Les Sirènes* (London, Nov. 12, 1946). In addition to his *Funeral Marches,* he wrote for piano *Fragments psychologiques (Hatred, Laughter, A Sigh); Valses bourgeoises,* etc. He published an autobiography in 2 consecutive volumes: *First Childhood* (1934) and *A Distant Prospect* (1945). Bibl.: J. Holbrooke, *Berners* in 'Contemporary British Composers' (1925).

Bernet Kempers, Karel Philippus, Dutch writer on music; b. Nijkerk, Holland, Sept. 20, 1897. He studied in Munich with Sandberger; received his Dr. Phil. in 1926; in 1929 was appointed teacher of music history at the Royal Cons. in The Hague and was secretary of the Federation of Dutch Composers. In 1946 he was appointed prof. at the Amsterdam Univ. Among his writings are: *Jacobus Clemens non Papa und seine Motetten* (1928); *Italian Opera, Peri to Puccini* (1929; English translation, 1947); *Muziekgeschiedenis* (Rotterdam, 1932; 4th ed., 1946); *Meesters der Muziek* (Rotterdam, 1939; 4th ed., 1948).

Bernhard, Christoph, German composer; b. Danzig, 1627; d. Dresden, Nov. 14, 1692. He studied with Paul Siefert in Danzig and with Schütz in Dresden. The Elector sent him to study singing in Italy (1649); in 1655 he became second Kapellmeister in Dresden, but was forced to resign through the disaffection of his Italian associates. He then went to Hamburg, where he served as a cantor (1664-74); was recalled by a new Elector to Dresden and was appointed first Kapellmeister, as successor to Schütz. He enjoyed a great respect as composer, particularly for his mastery of counterpoint. He published *Geistliche Harmonien* (Dresden, 1665) and *Prudentia prudentiana* (Hamburg, 1669); a treatise on composition and another on counterpoint are in MS. Some of his cantatas were published by M. Seiffert in vol. VI of 'Denkmäler Deutscher Tonkunst.' —Cf. J. M. Müller-Blattau, *Die Kompositionslehre Heinrich Schützens in der Fassung seines Schülers Christoph Bernhard* (Leipzig, 1926); H. Rauschning, *Musikgeschichte der Stadt Danzig* (1926).

Bernhard der Deutsche (known also as **Bernardo di Steffanino Murer**), celebrated organist and the reputed inventor of organ pedals; b. Germany, early in the 15th century; d. 1459; was organist of San Marco in Venice. —Cf. Michael Praetorius, *Syntagma musicum* (Vol. I, part I, chapter 14, p. 145; Vol. II, chapter 5, p. 96).

Bernier (bär-nyā'), **Nicolas,** French composer; b. Mantes (Seine-et-Oise), June 28, 1664; d. Paris, Sept. 5, 1734. He studied with Caldara in Rome; in 1692 returned to France; was organist at Chartres Cathedral

(1694-98). Bernier was one of the first French composers to cultivate the secular cantata; he published 8 books of such 'cantates profanes,' of which *Les nuits de Sceaux* is the most remarkable. His *Te Deum* was also much admired.

Bernier, René, Belgian composer; b. Saint-Gilles, March 10, 1905. He studied with Gilson. For a time taught at the Liège Cons.; then became supervisor of schools in Brussels. He was one of the original members of the Belgian group of composers called "Synthetistes" whose aim was to combine modern technique with classical forms. Works: *Melopées et rythmes* for orch. (1933); *Epitaphe symphonique* (1947); an oratorio *La Tour de Babel;* a lyrical fairy tale *La fête du vieux tilleul;* numerous pieces of chamber music and choruses.

Berno 'Augiensis', German theorist who flourished in the 11th century; was abbot of Reichenau monastery from 1008 until his death on June 7, 1048. He wrote learned treatises on music, to be found in J. P. Migne's *Patrologiae cursus completus* (vol. 142) and in Gerbert's *Scriptores* (vol. 2). A monograph on his system of music was published by W. Brambach (Leipzig, 1881).

Bernoulli (bär-nool'-lē), **Eduard,** Swiss music editor; b. Basel, Nov. 6, 1867; d. Zürich, April 17, 1927. In 1897 he took the degree of *Dr. phil.,* with the thesis *Die Choralnotenschrift bei Hymnen und Sequenzen im späteren Mittelalter* (Leipzig, 1898); then edited Heinrich Albert's *Arien* (vols. XII-XIII in 'Denkmäler deutscher Tonkunst'); also edited (with Holz and Saran) the *Jenaer Liederhandschrift* in modern notation (1901). His lecture, *Berlioz als Ästhetiker der Klangfarben,* given at Zürich Univ. in 1909, was published in that year; from 1921-27 Bernoulli was professor there. He wrote *Oratorientexte Händels* (1905); *Aus Liederbüchern der Humanistenzeit* (1910); many essays for various musical journals. He also revised editions of Prætorius' *Syntagma musicum III* (1916) and of Euler's *Tentamen novae theoriae musicae* (1926); issued facsimile editions of four of Attaignant's tablatures of dances from the years 1530-31 (5 vols., 1914; the 5th vol. contains a commentary by Bernoulli).

Bernstein, Leonard, American conductor and composer; b. Lawrence, Mass., Aug. 25, 1918. He studied music at Harvard Univ. with Walter Piston and E. B. Hill, graduating in 1939. In that year he went to the Curtis Institute of Music in Philadelphia, where he studied piano with Isabelle Vengerova, conducting with Fritz Reiner, and orchestration with Randall Thompson. He also entered Koussevitzky's summer master classes in conducting at the Berkshire Music Center at Tanglewood, and in 1942 became Koussevitzky's assistant. After Koussevitzky's death in 1951, he took over the conducting classes at Tanglewood. In 1943 he was appointed assistant conductor of the N. Y. Philh. Symph. Orch. On Nov. 14th of that year he was called upon at short notice to conduct a difficult program in substitution for Bruno Walter, who was ill. His debut was marked by instant acclaim, and it was followed by engagements as guest conductor with major symphony orchestras. For three seasons he was conductor of the N. Y. City Center Orch. (1945-47); he conducted at the International Music Festival in Prague in May, 1946; in April, 1947 he toured in Europe and in Palestine. As a composer, he writes both symphonic and popular music. His first important work was the *Jeremiah Symphony* (Pittsburgh Symph. Orch., Jan. 28, 1944, composer conducting; N. Y. Music Critics Circle Award, 1944). This work purports to represent the eternal aspirations of the Jewish people in modern terms. Still more remarkable is his 2nd symphony, *The Age of Anxiety,* after a poem by W. H. Auden, which traverses various styles and moods, from the religious to the ultra-modern, including a spectacular episode in the jazz idiom. Scored for piano and orch., it was first performed by Koussevitzky and the Boston Symph. Orch., with Bernstein as pianist, on April 8, 1949. He conducted his *Serenade for Violin Solo, Strings and Percussion* (after Plato's *Symposium*) at the Venice Festival, on Sept. 12, 1954, with Isaac Stern as soloist. Other works: clarinet sonata (1941); *5 Kid Songs* (1943); 2 song cycles, *I Hate Music* (1943) and *La Bonne Cuisine* (1947); 2 ballets, *Fancy Free* (1944) and *Facsimile* (1946). In a lighter vein, he wrote a 1-act opera to his own libretto, *Trouble in Tahiti,* which he conducted at the Festival of Creative Arts, Brandeis Univ., Waltham, Mass. (June 12, 1952). Bernstein is extremely adept at writing musical comedies in the popular style. His score, *On the Town* (1944), produced several song hits; even more successful was *Wonderful Town* (1952), which enjoyed a long run on Broadway. His versatility does not affect the excellence of his craftsmanship in any of his activities, but it is as a conductor that Bernstein is best known to the public. He was the first American conductor to lead a regular performance at La Scala (1953, in Cherubini's *Medea).* He married the actress Felicia Montealegre in Boston on Sept. 9, 1951.

Bernstein, Martin, American musicologist; b. New York, Dec. 14, 1904. He was educated at N. Y. Univ. (grad., 1925; Mus. Bac., 1927); played the double-bass in the New York Symph. Orch. (1925); the New York Philh. Orch. (1926-28) and the Chautauqua Symph. Orch. (1929-36); in 1924 joined the faculty at N. Y. Univ.; since 1955, head of Music Dept. in its Graduate School. He published *Score Reading* (1932; 2nd ed., 1949); *An Introduction to Music* (successful textbook; N. Y., 1937; 2nd ed., 1951); and contributed chapters on music to *An Intellectual and Cultural History of the Western World,* edited by Harry Elmer Barnes (N.Y., 1937).

Bernuth (bär-noot), **Julius von,** German conductor; b. Rees, Rhine Province, Aug. 8, 1830; d. Hamburg, Dec. 24, 1902. He was a practicing lawyer; studied music with Taubert and Dehn in Berlin, and at the Cons. of Leipzig, where he founded a chamber music society 'Aufschwung' (1857) and the 'Dilettanten-Orchester-Verein' (1859); later became conductor of the Hamburg Philh. Orch.; in 1873 founded a conservatory in Hamburg.

Berr, Friedrich, clarinetist and bassoonist; b. Mannheim, April 17, 1794; d. Paris, Sept. 24, 1838. He was bandmaster in various French regiments; settled in Paris (1823) as first clarinetist at the Théâtre des Italiens; from 1831 was prof. at the Paris Cons.; in 1836 was appointed Director of the new School of Military Music. He was the author of a *Traité complet de la clarinette à 14 clefs* (1836); also composed many works for clarinet and bassoon, and 500 pieces of military music.

Berré, Ferdinand, Belgian composer, b. Ganshoren, near Brussels, Feb. 5, 1843; d. Brussels, July 29, 1880. He wrote the operas, *L'Orage au moulin; Le Couteau de Castille;* published some 50 songs.

Bersa, Blagoje, Croatian composer; b. Ragusa, Dec. 21, 1873; d. Zagreb, Jan. 1, 1934. He studied music in Vienna, where he remained until 1919. He wrote 2 operas, *Fire,* and *The Cobbler of Delft;* the symph. poems *Sunny Fields, Ghosts* and *Hamlet;* a string quartet, a piano trio, and songs. Bersa was for many years professor of composition at the Zagreb Cons., and has influenced the development of the new generation of Croatian composers, several of whom were his pupils.

Bertali, Antonio, composer; b. Verona, March, 1605; d. Vienna, April 1, 1669. He was a Viennese court violinist from 1637; in 1649 succeeded Giovanni Valentini as court conductor. He produced in Vienna several cantatas (1641-46), 8 operas and 2 oratorios (1653-67).

Berté, Heinrich, Hungarian composer; b. Galgócz, May 8, 1858; d. Vienna, Aug. 25, 1924. He produced the ballets *Das Märchenbuch* (Prague, 1890); *Amor auf Reisen* (Vienna, 1895); *Der Karneval in Venedig* (Vienna, 1900); and *Automatenzauber* (Vienna, 1901); the operettas *Die Schneeflocke* (Prague, 1896); *Der neue Bürgermeister* (Vienna, 1904); *Die Millionenbraut* (Munich, 1905); *Der schöne Gardist* (Breslau, 1907; *Der kleine Chevalier* (Dresden, 1907); *Der Glücksnarr* (Vienna, 1909); *Kreolenblut* (Hamburg, 1911); *Der Märchenprinz* (Hanover, 1914); and *Das Dreimäderlhaus* (Vienna, Jan. 15, 1916), based on Schubert melodies; it was produced in English under the title *Blossom Time,* arranged by Romberg (N. Y., Sept. 21, 1921; very popular); also as *Lilac Time* (London, Dec. 22, 1922), arranged by Clutsam.

Bertheaume (bär-tohm'), **Isidore,** violinist; b. Paris, 1752; d. St. Petersburg, March 20, 1802. He was first violinist at the Grand Opéra in Paris (1774); conductor of the 'Concerts Spirituels' (from 1783); and first violinist at the Opéra-Comique (from 1788). The Revolution forced him to leave Paris in 1791; he settled in St. Petersburg as solo violinist in the Imperial Orch. He composed 2 symphonies concertantes for 2 violins; 3 sonatas for clavecin with violin; violin concerto; many other works for violin.

Berthold, (Karl Friedrich) Theodor, German organist; b. Dresden, Dec. 18, 1815; d. there, April 28, 1882. He was a pupil of Julius Otto and Johann Schneider; in 1864 succeeded Schneider as court organist at Dresden. He wrote an oratorio, *Petrus;* a symphony; much sacred music; was co-author with Fürstenau of the pamphlet *Die Fabrikation musikalischer Instrumente im Vogtlande* (1876).

Bertin (bär-tăn'), **Louise-Angélique,** French composer, singer and pianist; b. at Aux Roches, near Paris, Feb. 15, 1805; d. Paris, April 26, 1877. She was a pupil of Fétis; composed the operas *Guy Mannering; Le Loup-garou* (Paris, 1827); *Faust* (after Goethe, 1831); *La Esmeralda* (libretto adapted by Victor Hugo from his *Notre-Dame de Paris,* 1836); also many minor works, of which *Six Ballades* were published.

Bertini, Benoit-Auguste, French pianist; b. Lyons, June 5, 1780; d. London, after 1830. He was a pupil of Clementi in London (1793); later taught piano there; wrote the pamphlets *Stigmatographie, ou l'art d'écrire avec des points, suivie de la mélographie, nouvel art de noter la musique* (Paris, 1812), and *Phonological System for acquiring extraordinary facility on all musical instruments as well as in singing* (London, 1830).

Bertini, Domenico, Italian composer and music pedagogue; b. Lucca, June 26, 1829; d. Florence, Sept. 7, 1890. He studied at the Lucca Music School; later with Michele Puccini; in 1857 was director of the music institute and maestro di cappella at Massa Carrara; settled in Florence (1862) as singing teacher and music critic; and became director of the 'Cherubini Society.' He contributed to the 'Boccherini' of Florence, 'La Scena' of Venice, and other musical periodicals; also wrote a *Compendio de' principi di musica, secondo un nuovo sistema* (1866); composed 2 operas; masses; other sacred music; chamber music.

Bertini, Henri(-Jérôme), known as 'Bertini le jeune,' pianist and composer; b. London, Oct. 28, 1798; d. Meylau, near Grenoble, Oct. 1, 1876. When six months old, he was taken to Paris, where he was taught music by his father and his elder brother, Benoît-Auguste; at the age of twelve made a concert tour through the Netherlands and Germany; then studied further in Paris and Great Britain; lived in Paris as concert pianist from 1821 till 1859, when he retired to his estate at Meylau. He wrote valuable technical studies, some of which have been published in editions by G. Buonamici and by Riemann; also arranged Bach's '48 Preludes and Fugues' for 4 hands; composed much chamber music; many piano pieces.

Bertoldo, Sperindio (Sper'in Dio), Italian organist and composer; b. Modena, c. 1530; d. Padua, Aug. 13, 1570. He served as chief organist at the cathedral of Padua. His surviving compositions include two books of madrigals in 5 voices, published in Venice (book 1, 1561 and book 2, 1562). The first book includes an *Echo a 6 voci* and a *Dialogo a 8 voci;* several other madrigals are included in a collection by Cipriano and Annibale (Venice, 1561). Bertoldo's *Toccate, ricercari e canzoni francese . . . per sonar d'organo* (Venice, 1591) was published posthumously. Two ricercari for organ are included in L. Torchi, *L'Arte Musicale in Italia* (vol. III).

Berton, Henri-Montan, French composer, son of Pierre-Montan Berton; b. Paris, Sept. 17, 1767; d. there, April 22, 1844. He was a pupil of Rey and Sacchini; in 1782 was violinist at the Paris Opéra; in 1795 was appointed prof. of harmony at the Paris Cons.; and in 1818 succeeded Méhul as professor of composition; also conducted the Opera buffa (1807); was choirmaster at the Opéra (1809); in 1815 was made a member of the Academy. He composed 47 operas, of which the best are *Montano et Stéphanie* (1799); *Le Délire* (1799); and *Aline, reine de Golconde* (1803); he also wrote 5 oratorios; 5 cantatas; ballets; many *romances.* His theoretical works are curious rather than valuable. Bibl.: Raoul-Rochette, *Notice historique sur la vie et les ouvrages de M. Berton* (Paris, 1846); H. Blanchard, *Henri-Montan Berton* (Paris, 1839).

Berton, Pierre-Montan, French composer; b. Maubert-Fontaines (Ardennes), Jan. 7, 1727; d. Paris, May 14, 1780. He was conductor of the Royal Orch. and of the Grand Opéra at Paris; wrote additions to operas by Lully, Rameau and Gluck; had a significant influence upon the development of the French opera. He composed the operas *Érosine* (1765) and *Tyrtée* (1772); also *Silvie* (1765) and *Théonis* (1767) in collaboration with Trial; and *Adèle de Ponthieu* (with Laborde).

Bertoni, Ferdinando (Gioseffo), Italian organist and composer; b. Island of Salò, near Venice, Aug. 15, 1725; d. Desenzano, Dec. 1, 1813. He was a pupil of Padre Martini; in 1752 was appointed first organist of San Marco in Venice; made two trips to London, where many of his operas were produced; finally settled in Venice, where he succeeded Galuppi (1784) as maestro di cappella of San Marco; was choirmaster at the Cons. de' Mendicanti from 1757-97. He composed 34 operas, including *La vedova accorta* (Florence, 1745); *Quinto Fabio* (Milan, 1778); *Demofoonte* (London, Nov. 28, 1778); and *Nitteti* (Venice, 1786); also wrote 5 oratorios; much other sacred music; 6 harpsichord sonatas; chamber music; etc. See 'Musica d'oggi' (July, 1927).

Bertouille, Gérard, Belgian composer; b. Tournai, May 26, 1898. While studying law he took lessons in music with Francis de Bourguignon, Jean Absil, André Souris and Armand Marsick. He began to compose rather late in life; he wrote his first significant work, a violin sonata, in 1936. Since then he has developed energetic activity in composition; he has written a *Symphonie*

Picturale (1947); 2 piano concertos (1946; 1953); violin concerto (1942); trumpet concerto (1946); 6 string quartets (1939-54); 4 violin sonatas (1936-53); 2 string trios (1943-45); *Requiem des hommes d'aujourd'hui* (1950); 2 sets of songs to Baudelaire's poems, etc. In his music he occupies a moderate position, writing in a contemporary idiom while avoiding the extremes of modernism.

Bertrand, Aline, notable French harpist; b. Paris, 1798; d. there, March 13, 1835. She studied at the Paris Cons. with Naderman; then with Bochsa (1815); made her debut in 1820; then toured all of Europe, winning special acclaim upon her appearance in Vienna (1828). She published a *Fantaisie sur la Romance de Joseph* (on themes of Méhul's opera) for harp, and various other arrangements.

Bertrand, Antoine de, French composer; b. Fontanges (Cantal), c. 1545. He composed 7 books of 4-part chansons: *Les Amours de P. de Ronsard* (2 vols., 1576), *Sonets chrestiens* (2 vols., 1580) and *Chansons* (3 vols., 1578); his music shows harmonic daring in the use of chromatic progressions. Volumes 4-7 of H. Expert's *Monuments de la musique française au temps de la Renaissance* are devoted to Bertrand's works.

Bertrand, Jean-Gustave, French writer on music; b. Vaugirard, near Paris, Dec. 24, 1834; d. Paris, Feb. 9, 1880. He published the following books: *Histoire ecclésiastique de l'orgue* (1859); *Les origines de l'harmonie* (1866); *De la réforme des études du chant au Conservatoire* (1871); *Les nationalités musicales étudiées dans le drame lyrique* (1872).

Berutti, Arturo, Argentine opera composer; b. San Juan, March 27, 1862; d. Buenos Aires, Jan. 3, 1938. He studied with his father; then in Leipzig with Jadassohn. He lived for some time in Italy where he produced several operas: *La Vendetta* (Vercelli, May 21, 1892); *Evangelina* (Milan, Sept. 19, 1893); *Taras Bulba* (Turin, March 9, 1895). Returning to Argentina in 1896 he presented the following operas in various theaters of Buenos Aires: *Pampa* (July 27, 1897); *Yupanki* (July 25, 1899); *Khrise* (June 21, 1902); and *Los Heroes* (Aug. 23, 1919). He also wrote a *Sinfonia argentina* (1890), the first symphony on national themes by an Argentine composer.

Berwald, Franz, Swedish composer; cousin of Johann Friedrich Berwald; b. Stockholm, July 23, 1796; d. there, April 30, 1868. He was a member of a musical family of German extraction that settled in Sweden in the 18th century. He studied with his father, Christian Friedrich Berwald; was a violinist at the Royal Chapel in Stockholm; in 1819 he played in Finland with his brother Christian August Berwald. In 1829 he was in Berlin; after a brief return to Sweden, he lived in Vienna and Paris. In 1849 he received the post of musical director at the Univ. of Uppsala, succeeding his cousin Johann Friedrich Berwald. He taught at the Stockholm Academy from 1864-67, and at the Stockholm Cons. (from 1867 until his death). Berwald wrote the operas *Estrella di Soria* (1841; Stockholm, April 9, 1862; modern version by Moses Pergament, Göteborg, March 2, 1931) and *Drottningen av Golconda* (1864). His early operas *Gustaf Wasa* (1827), *Leonida* (1829) and *Der Verräter* remain unperformed. He wrote 6 symphonies, of which the most interesting are *Sinfonie sérieuse, Sinfonie capricieuse* and *Sinfonie singulière* (all written between 1842 and 1845). He also composed 5 cantatas; a violin concerto (1820); *Concertstück* for bassoon and orch. (1827); a piano concerto (1855); 5 piano trios and other chamber music. Berwald's music is romantic in derivation; his style was determined by the influences of Spohr and Weber, and later by Beethoven and Mendelssohn. A revival of interest in his music in Sweden led to the publication of several of his orchestral and chamber works. See A. Hillman, *Franz Berwald* (Stockholm, 1920).

Berwald, Johann Friedrich, Swedish violinist and composer; cousin of Franz Berwald; b. Stockholm, Dec. 4, 1787; d. there, Aug. 26, 1861. Of precocious talent, he appeared in public at the age of five; studied theory with Abbé Vogler; gave concerts in Finland, Germany and Austria; from 1808-12 was concertmaster at the Imperial Chapel in St. Petersburg; appointed chamber musician to the King of Sweden (1816), and conductor of the Royal Orch. in Stockholm (from 1819). Berwald wrote his first symphony when he was nine, but in his maturity he devoted himself chiefly to theater music. One of his operettas, *L'héroïne de l'amour,* was produced in St. Petersburg in 1811.

Berwald, William, German-American composer; b. Schwerin, Dec. 26, 1864; d. Loma Linda, Calif., May 8, 1948. He studied with Rheinberger at the Munich Cons. (1882-87), and with Faiszt in Stuttgart (1887-88). After a series of engagements as orchestral conductor in Germany and Russia, he settled in the U.S. (1892) as instructor of piano and theory at Syracuse Univ.; from 1921-24 he conducted the Syracuse Orchestra. Among his works are 3 cantatas, *Seven Last Words of Christ; Crucifixion and Resurrection; From Old Japan;* a music drama *Utopia* (1936); symph. poem *Eros and Psyche* (1943); numerous choruses and instrumental pieces, and about 250 anthems. He received many prizes for his works, and continued to compose to the end of his life.

Besard, Jean-Baptiste, French lutenist and composer; b. Besançon, 1567; d. probably in Augsburg. He studied philosophy at the Univ. of Dôle; after his marriage in 1602, he went to Rome and studied with the lutenist Lorenzini. Later lived in Germany, publishing at Cologne his *Thesaurus harmonicus* (1603), and at Augsburg his *Novus partus, sive Concertationes musicae duodena trium . . .* (1617) and *Isagoge in artem testudinariam* (1617). Some of the compositions in these works have been transcribed by O. Chilesotti in 'Biblioteca di rarità musicali'. See also O. Chilesotti, *Di G. B. Besardo e del suo Thesaurus harmonicus* (Milan, 1886).

Besekirsky. See **Bezekirsky.**

Besler, Samuel, composer; b. Brieg, Silesia, Dec. 15, 1574; d. Breslau, July 19, 1625. He was rector (from 1605) of the Gymnasium zum Heiligen Geist in Breslau; wrote a large number of sacred pieces, most of which are preserved at the library of St. Bernardinus in Breslau.

Besly, Maurice, English composer and conductor; b. Normanby, Yorkshire, Jan. 28, 1888; d. Horsham, March 20, 1945. He studied at the Leipzig Cons. with Teichmüller, Krehl and Schreck; then with Ernest Ansermet; taught music at the Tonbridge School (1912-14); was organist of Queen's College, Oxford (1919) and conducted the Oxford Orch. (1920); in 1922 made his debut as a conductor in London at Queen's Hall; after 1924 was conductor of the Glasgow Scottish Orch.; wrote the orchestral works *Mist in the Valley* and *Chelsea China;* incidental music to *The Merchant of Venice; A Tune with Disguises* and *Nocturne* for violin and piano; *Phaedra,* scene for soprano and orch.; *The Shepherds heard an Angel* for soprano, chorus and English horn; many anthems, songs and motets; publ. arrangements of some of J. S. Bach's music; also edited the 'Queen's College Hymn Book'.

Besozzi, Alessandro, celebrated Italian oboist; b. Parma, July 22, 1702; d. Turin, 1775. He was a musician at the ducal chapel, Parma (1728-31); made concert tours with his brother, Girolamo (see 3 below); appeared with him in Paris in 1735; then lived in Turin. He published numerous trio-sonatas for flute, violin and cello; 6 violin sonatas (with basso continuo), etc. Other members of the family who specialized in woodwinds were: (1) **Antonio,** oboist, nephew of Alessandro (b. Parma, 1714; d. Turin, 1781); (2) **Carlo,** oboist, son of Antonio (b. Naples, c. 1738); played in the Dresden orch. (1754); wrote several oboe concertos; (3) **Girolamo,** bassoonist, brother of Alessandro (b. Parma, April 17, 1704; d. Turin, 1778); (4) **Gaetano,** oboist, nephew of Alessandro (b. Parma, 1727; d. London, 1794); (5) **Girolamo,** oboist, son of Gaetano (b. Naples, c. 1750; d. Paris, 1785); (6) **Henri,** flutist, son of Girolamo; played at the Opéra-Comique; (7) **Louis-Désiré,** son of Henri (b. Versailles, April 3, 1814; d. Paris, Nov. 11, 1879), a student of Lesueur and Barbereau; he won the Prix de Rome in 1837, defeating Gounod.

Bessel, Vassili Vassilievitch, Russian music publisher; b. St. Petersburg, April 25, 1843; d. Zürich, March 4, 1907. He was the founder (1869) of the music publishing firm of Bessel & Co. at St. Petersburg, which has published works by many distinguished Russian composers (Anton Rubinstein, Rimsky-Korsakov, Tchaikovsky, Mussorgsky); also two short-lived periodicals: 'Musical Leaflet' (1872-77) and the 'Russian Musical Review' (1885-89). Bessel wrote *Reminiscences of Tchaikovsky,* who was his fellow student at the St. Petersburg Cons. In 1920 the firm was transferred to Paris, where it continued under the direction of Bessel's sons, Vassili and Alexander.

Besseler, Heinrich, German musicologist; b. Hörde, near Dortmund, April 2, 1900. He studied musicology in Freiburg, Vienna and Göttingen; was teacher at Freiburg (1922-25); prof. at the Univ. of Heidelberg (1928-45); from 1949 at the Univ. of Jena. Among his published writings are: *Studien zur Musik des Mittelalters,* in 'Archiv für Musikwissenschaft' (1925-27); *Grundfragen des musikalischen Hörens* and *Grundfragen der Musikästhetik* in 'Peters-Jahrbuch' (1925-26); *Die Musik des Mittelalters und der Renaissance* in 'Bücken's Handbuch' (1931); *Bourdon und Fauxbourdon* (Leipzig, 1950); also has contributed articles to 'Die Musik in Geschichte und Gegenwart.' He has edited works by Okeghem, Dufay, Gabrieli, etc.

Bessems (bes-săhn'), **Antoine,** Belgian violinist; b. Antwerp, April 6, 1809; d. there, Oct. 19, 1868. He was a pupil of Baillot at the Paris Cons. (1826); in 1829 was first violinist at the Théâtre-Italien, Paris; then made long concert tours; taught for a time in Paris; returned to Antwerp, and, from 1847-52, conducted the orchestra of the 'Société Royale d'Harmonie'. He composed a violin concerto; 12 *Grandes Études* for violin with piano; 12 *Grands Duos de concert* for violin with piano; many other violin pieces; also masses; motets; psalms, etc.

Best, William Thomas, eminent English organist; b. Carlisle, England, Aug. 13, 1826; d. Liverpool, May 10, 1897. He studied organ in Liverpool; held various posts as church organist in Liverpool and London. At his numerous concerts he introduced arrangements of symphonic works thus enabling his audiences to hear classical works in musicianly manner at a time when orchestral concerts were scarce. As a performer he aroused enthusiasm, and was greatly esteemed by his colleagues. His own works, popular in type, though classical in form, included sonatas, preludes, fugues, concert studies, etc. for organ. He published a *Handel Album* (20 vols.); *Arrangements from the Scores of the Great Masters* (5 vols.); *Modern School for the Organ* (1853); *The Art of Organ Playing* (1870), etc. Bibl.: H. H. Statham, *The Organ and its Position in Musical Art* (London, 1909); O. A. Mansfield, *W. T. Best* in the 'Mus. Quarterly' (April, 1918); J. Mewburn Levien, *Impressions of W. T. Best* (London, 1942).

Betti, Adolfo, Italian violinist; b. Bagni di Lucca, March 21, 1873; d. Lucca, Dec. 2, 1950. Of a musical family, he studied violin in Lucca; then with César Thomson in Liège (1892-96); later was in Vienna and Brussels. In 1903 he became the first violinist of the famous Flonzaley Quartet, and remained with it until it was disbanded in 1929; this group presented some 2500 concerts in America and about 500 concerts in Europe. In 1933 Betti was awarded the Coolidge Medal for eminent services to chamber music in America. He taught in New York before returning to Italy. He published *La vita e l'arte di Francesco Geminiani* (Lucca, 1933); also edited Schubert's string quartets, etc.

Bettinelli, Bruno, Italian pianist and composer; b. Milan, June 4, 1913. He studied with Paribeni and Bossi at the Milan Cons.; later taught harmony there. In his music, he has experienced influences of Stravinsky and Honegger; nonetheless, his style has remained Italian in its primary sources. He has also explored the resources of Gregorian Chant. Works: *Sinfonia da camera* (1939); *Concerto per orchestra* (1940; won the S. Cecilia prize); *Fantasia e Fuga su temi gregoriani* for string orch. (1942); *Sinfonia* for strings (1946); *Sinfonia drammatica* (1943); *Messa da requiem* for chorus a cappella (1945); *Fantasia concertante* for string quartet and orch. (1950); *Concerto da camera* (1952); piano concerto (1952); *Sinfonia breve* (1954); cello sonata; many songs; piano pieces, etc.

Betz, Franz, distinguished German baritone; b. Mainz, March 19, 1835; d. Berlin, Aug. 11, 1900. He sang from 1856-9 at Hanover, Altenburg, Gera, Cöthen and Rostock; after his debut as Don Carlos in *Ernani* at Berlin (1859), he was permanently engaged at the Royal Opera House until his retirement in 1897; was best known for his performances in Wagner's operas; created the roles of Hans Sachs at Munich (1868) and Wotan at Bayreuth (1876).

Beversdorf, Thomas, American composer and conductor; b. Yoakum, Texas, Aug. 8, 1924. He studied at the Univ. of Texas; served in the U.S. Air Force (1942-43); later studied with Bernard Rogers at the Eastman School, Rochester (1946); took a summer course with Copland and Honegger at the Berkshire Music Center (1947); in 1950, became a member of the faculty of the School of Music at the Univ. of Indiana. Beversdorf has written 2 symphonies (1946; 1950); *Symphony for Winds and Percussion* (Bloomington, Indiana, May 9, 1954, composer conducting); *Concerto Grosso* for chamber orch. with solo oboe (1950); Concerto for 2 pianos and orch. (1951); *Ode* for orch. (1952); *New Frontiers* for orch. (Houston, March 31, 1953); sonata for horn and piano (1945); *Suite on Baroque Themes* for clarinet, cello and piano (1947); *Cathedral Music* for brasses (1950); two string quartets (1952; 1955).

Bevignani (bā-vē-ñah'-nē), **Enrico (Modesto),** Italian conductor and composer; b. Naples, Sept. 29, 1841; d. there, Aug. 29, 1903. He studied composition with Albanese, Lillo and others; his first opera, *Caterina Bloom* (Naples, 1863), was very successful; but he gave up his career as a composer and settled, temporarily, in London as conductor at Her Majesty's Theatre (1864-70); conducted at Covent Garden

(1871) and at the Metropolitan Opera (1894).

Bevin, Elway, Welsh composer and organist; b. between 1560-70; d. c. 1640. He was a pupil of Tallis; was organist of Bristol Cathedral (1589) and Gentleman Extraordinary of the Chapel Royal (1605). His most valuable work is the theoretical pamphlet *A Briefe and Short Introduction to the Art of Musicke* (1631); also wrote a Short Service which is preserved in the collections of Barnard and Boyce; a song *Hark, Jolly Shepherds;* and an anthem, arranged in a canon of 20 voices.

Bewerunge (bā'-vär-ōng), **Henry,** music teacher and editor; b. Letmathe, Westphalia, Dec. 7, 1862; d. Maynooth, Ireland, Dec. 2, 1923. He studied music at the Würzburg Cons.; was ordained to the priesthood at Eichstatt (1885); then studied at the Institute for Church Music at Regensburg; subsequently settled in Ireland as prof. of church music at St. Patrick's College in Maynooth (1888-1914); then was prof. of music at Dublin College of the Irish National Univ. He published *Die vatikanische Choralausgabe* (2 parts, Düsseldorf, 1906-7; also in English and French); many valuable articles for 'Musica Sacra', Haberl's 'Kirchenmusikalisches Jahrbuch', 'The Irish Ecclesiastical Record', and 'The Catholic Encyclopedia'; also translated Riemann's *Katechismus der Musikästhetik* and *Vereinfachte Harmonielehre* into English. From 1891-3 he edited 'Lyra Ecclesiastica'.

Bexfield, William Richard, English organist; b. Norwich, April 27, 1824; d. London, Oct. 29, 1853. He was organist at Boston church in Lincolnshire; then at St. Helen's in London; took the degrees of Mus. Bac. at Oxford (1846) and Mus. Doc. at Cambridge (1849); wrote an oratorio, *Israel Restored* (1852); a cantata, *Hector's Death;* anthems; organ fugues; songs.

Beydts, Louis, French composer; b. Bordeaux, June 29, 1895; d. there, Sept. 16, 1953. He studied in his native city; became associated with the theater; wrote the operetta, *Canards Mandarins* (Monte Carlo, 1931); *Le Voyage de Tchong-Li,* Chinese legend in 3 scenes (1932); many songs in the popular manner; film music.

Beyer (bī-er), **Johann Samuel,** German choir director and composer; b. Gotha, 1669; d. Karlsbad, May 9, 1744. He was cantor at Freiburg, Saxony (1699) and at Weissenfels (1722); became Musikdirektor at Freiburg (1728). Among his publications are: *Primae lineae musicae vocalis* (1703); *Musikal. Vorrath neu variirter Festchoralgesänge* (1716); *Geistlich-musikalische Seelenfreude* (1724); 72 concert arias, etc.

Beyle, Marie-Henri. See **Stendhal.**

Beyschlag, Adolf, German conductor; b. Frankfurt, March 22, 1845; d. Mainz, March 22, 1914. He was a pupil of Vincenz Lachner in Mannheim; was theater conductor in Cologne, Frankfurt and Mainz (1868-80); then lived for a time in England; was deputy-conductor for Hallé in Manchester, and conductor of the Leeds Philh. Society; in 1902 returned to Germany. He publ. a valuable work *Die Ornamentik der Musik* (Leipzig, 1908); composed 4-hand dances for piano, in canon form; songs; arrangements.

Bezekirsky (bā-zā-kēr'-skē), **Vassili,** Russian violinist; b. Moscow, Jan. 26, 1835; d. there, Nov. 8, 1919. In 1858 he went to Brussels, where he studied violin with Hubert Léonard and composition with Damcke; then toured throughout Europe. He returned to Russia in 1871, and continued to give concerts. Tchaikovsky wrote about him: "He is not a star of the first magnitude, but brilliant enough on the dim horizon of contemporary virtuosity". Bezekirsky was one of the best violin teachers of his time; from 1882 he was professor at the Moscow Philharmonic School. He wrote a violin concerto (Moscow, Feb. 26, 1873) and published cadenzas to the concertos of Beethoven and Brahms. He edited the violin sonatas of Bach, with a preface *L'Art musical du violon du XVIIe jusqu'au XXe siècle* (Kiev, 1913). He also published a volume of reminiscences, *From the Notebook of an Artist* (St. Petersburg, 1910).

Bezekirsky, Vassili, Russian-American violinist, son and pupil of the preceding; b. Moscow, Jan. 15, 1880; made his debut in Moscow at the age of twelve. After several years in Europe, he came to the U.S. in 1914, and played in various orchestras. From 1916-28, he taught in Providence; from 1930-47, at the Univ. of Michigan, Ann Arbor. In 1955 he was living in retirement at East Windham, N.Y.

Biaggi (b'yăh'-jē), **Girolamo Alessandro,** Italian writer on music; b. Milan, Feb. 2, 1819; d. Florence, March 21, 1897. He studied violin and composition at the Milan Cons. (1829-39); after a short visit to France, he returned to Milan as maestro di cappella; wrote an opera, *Martino della*

Scala; was for some years editor of the 'Italia Musicale'; settled in Florence as prof. of music history and esthetics at the newly established Reale Istituto Musicale; wrote articles for the 'Gazetta d'Italia', under the pen-name Ippolito d'Albano. He published an essay *Della musica religiosa e delle questioni inerenti* (Milan; Ricordi, 1856); also *La riforma melodrammatica fiorentina; Su gli istrumenti a pizzico;* and *La Musica del Secolo XVII* (1894); a *Vita di Rossini* was left unfinished.

Bial (bē-ahl), **Rudolf,** violinist and conductor; b. Habelschwerdt, Silesia, Aug. 26, 1834; d. New York, Nov. 13, 1881. He was a member of the Breslau orch.; then toured Africa and Australia with his brother Karl; settled in Berlin as conductor of the Kroll Orch. and conductor of the Wallner Theater, where his numerous farces, operettas, etc. were performed; later conducted at the Italian opera in Berlin. In 1878 he settled in New York.

Bialosky, Marshall, American composer; b. Cleveland, Oct. 30, 1923. He studied at Syracuse Univ. (Bac. Mus., 1949); then took courses with Roy Harris, Ernst Bacon and Luigi Dallapiccola; held Fulbright Fellowship for study of composition in Italy (1954-56). He has composed works for various ensembles; some of his choral pieces have been published.

Bianchi (b'yăhn'-kē), **Bianca** (real name Bertha Schwarz), German soprano; b. Heidelberg, June 27, 1855; d. Salzburg, Feb., 1947. She studied in Heidelberg and Paris; made her debut as Barberina in *The Marriage of Figaro* at Karlsruhe (1873); sang in Vienna and London; in 1905 settled in Salzburg as a vocal teacher. She married her manager, Pollini, in 1897.

Bianchi (b'yăhn'-kē), **Francesco,** composer and conductor, b. Cremona, 1752; d. (by suicide) at Hammersmith, Nov. 27, 1810. He lived in Paris from 1775-8 as maestro al cembalo at the Comédie-Italienne, where his first opera, *La réduction de Paris,* was produced (Sept. 30, 1775); up to 1800 he wrote 47 operas of pleasing but ephemeral quality; went to Florence in 1780; then to Venice (1785) as organist at San Marco; also to London (1793) as conductor at the King's Theatre; from 1797-1801 was opera conductor in Dublin. His treatise *Dell' attrazione armonica* was never published. He was the teacher of Henry Bishop.

Bianchi (b'yăhn'-kē), **Valentine,** singer; b. Vilna, 1839; d. Candau, Kurland, Feb. 28, 1884. She studied at the Paris Cons.; made her debut as a soprano in Frankfurt (1855); sang at Schwerin (1855-61); St. Petersburg (1862-5); and Moscow (until 1867); retired in 1870. She married chief forester von Fabian in 1865. Her range was extraordinary, extending from low alto through high soprano notes.

Biber, Heinrich Ignaz Franz von, violinist and composer; b. Wartenberg, Bohemia, Aug. 12, 1644; d. Salzburg, May 3, 1704. He was successively in the service of the Emperor Leopold I (who ennobled him), the Bavarian court, and the Archbishop of Salzburg; was one of the founders of the German school of violin playing, and among the first to employ the 'scordatura', a system of artificial mistuning for purposes of virtuoso performance. He published a number of violin sonatas (reprints in David's 'Hohe Schule'; some others in 'Denkmäler der Tonkunst in Österreich,' V, 2; and XII, 2). There are also preserved in MS. the scores of 2 operas, *Chi la dura la vince* (Salzburg, 1681), and *L'ossequio di Salisburgo* (Salzburg, 1699); 2 requiems; offertories *a* 4; etc. Bibl.: A. Moser, *Geschichte der Violinspiels* (p. 127 ff.) and an article by Moser in 'Archiv für Musikwissenschaft', I; C. Schneider, *Biber als Opernkomponist* in 'Archiv für Musikwissenschaft', VIII; articles by P. Nettl in 'Zeitschrift für Musikwissenschaft', IV and in 'Studien zur Musikwissenschaft', VIII; also Thomas Russell, *The Violin 'Scordatura'* in the 'Mus. Quarterly' (Jan., 1938).

Bibl, Rudolf, Austrian organ virtuoso and composer for the organ; b. Vienna, Jan. 6, 1832; d. there, Aug. 2, 1902. He was a pupil of his father, **Andreas Bibl** (organist; b. Vienna, April 8, 1807; d. there, April 30, 1878), and of Simon Sechter; was organist at St. Peter's (1850) and at St. Stephen's Cathedral (1859); appointed court organist at Vienna in 1863, and from 1897 was court conductor. His works include: 4 masses with orch.; 1 mass a cappella; 2 requiems; a concerto for organ and orch.; preludes and fugues for organ solo; also a sonata for violin and piano, and many piano pieces. He was the author of an *Orgelschule.*

Bie (bē), **Oskar,** German teacher and writer on music; b. Breslau, Feb. 9, 1864; d. Berlin, April 21, 1938. He studied philology and art in Leipzig; then music with Philipp Scharwenka in Berlin, where he settled as teacher and musical journalist (1890); wrote many articles on the fine arts; published a number of brilliant books on music; in the spring of 1914, he accompanied Koussevitzky on a concert tour of the Volga, and reported his impressions in a book published in a limited edition in 1920. Other writings: *Das Klavier und seine Meister* (Munich, 1898; 2nd ed., 1900); *Intime Musik* (Berlin, 1904); *Tanzmusik* (Berlin, 1904); *Der Tanz* (Berlin, 1906; 2nd ed., 1925); *Die moderne Musik und Richard Strauss* (Berlin, 1906; 2nd ed., 1916); *Klavier, Orgel, und Harmonium* (Leipzig, 1910; 2nd ed., 1921); *Die Oper* (Berlin, 1913; 10th ed., 1923); *Das Klavier* (Berlin, 1921); *Das Rätsel der Musik* (Leipzig, 1922); *Franz Schubert* (Berlin, 1925); *Das deutsche Lied* (Berlin, 1926); *Richard Wagner und Bayreuth* (Zürich, 1931). His first book, *Das Klavier und seine Meister,* was publ. in English as *A History of the Pianoforte and Pianoforte Players* (London, 1899); his monograph on Schubert appeared in English under the title *Schubert the Man* (N. Y., 1928).

Biedermann (bē-der-mahn), **Edward Julius,** American organist and composer; b. Milwaukee, Wis., Nov. 8, 1849; d. Freeport, N. Y., Nov. 26, 1933. He was the son and pupil of A. Julius Biedermann; also studied piano, organ and theory in Germany from 1858-64; then lived in New York as teacher and organist at various churches; retired in 1918. He composed 6 grand masses for soli, chorus, organ and orch.; other sacred music; choruses for male voices; etc.

Biehle, Johannes, German organ theorist, b. Bautzen, June 18, 1870; d. there, Jan. 4, 1941. He studied at the Dresden Cons.; was appointed cantor at the Cathedral of Bautzen (1898), and music dir. (1908). He is best known for his *Theorie der pneumatischen Orgeltraktur und die Stellung des Spieltisches* (on organ building; Leipzig, 1911); and *Theorie des Kirchenbaues vom Standpunkte des Kirchenmusikers und des Redners . . . mit einer Glockenkunde* (on the acoustics of church construction; Wittenberg, 1913). His son, **Herbert Biehle** (b. Dresden, Feb. 16, 1901), is the author of several publications on vocal technique, among them, *Die Stimmkunst,* in 2 vols. (1931; 1933).

Bierey (bē'-rī), **Gottlob Benedikt,** German conductor and composer; b. Dresden, July 25, 1772; d. Breslau, May 5, 1840. He was a pupil of Christian E. Weinlig at Dresden; then was director of a traveling opera troupe. He was appointed Kapellmeister at Breslau (1808), succeeding Weber; retired in 1828. He composed 26 operas and operettas; 10 cantatas; masses; orchestral and chamber music; etc.

Biggs, Edward Power, organist; b. Westcliff-on-Sea, Essex, March 29, 1906. He studied at the Royal Academy of Music in London, graduating in 1929; came to the U.S. and became an American citizen (1938). He rapidly acquired a fine reputation as a scholar and performer; presented all of Bach's organ works in a series of consecutive recitals at Harvard Univ. He is known to the general public through his weekly broadcasts of organ music.

Bignami (bē-ñah'-mē), **Carlo,** renowned Italian violinist; b. Cremona, Dec. 6, 1808; d. Voghera, Aug. 2, 1848. He was in turn opera conductor at Cremona (1827), Milan, and Verona (1833); returned to Cremona (1837) as director and first violinist of the orchestra, and made it one of the best in Lombardy. Paganini called him 'il primo violinista d'Italia'. He composed many works for his instrument, including a concerto; a *Capriccio; Studi per violino; Grande Adagio; Polacca;* fantasias; variations, etc.

Bigot (bĭ-gŏh'), **Marie** (*née* Kiéné, pianist; b. Colmar, Alsace, March 3, 1786; d. Paris, Sept. 16, 1820. After her marriage in 1804, she lived in Vienna, where she was known and esteemed by Haydn and Beethoven; went to Paris in 1808, where she gave piano lessons from 1812 on; Mendelssohn was briefly her pupil in Paris at the age of 7.

Bilhon (or **Billon**) (bē-yohn'), **Jean de,** French composer who flourished c. 1530. He was the author of several masses, magnificats and motets, which are included in collections of church music published between 1534 and 1554.

Billings, William, pioneer American composer of hymns and anthems; popularizer of 'fuguing tunes'; b. Boston, Oct. 7, 1746; d. there, Sept. 26, 1800. A tanner apprentice, he acquired the rudiments of music from treatises by Tans'ur; he compensated for his lack of education by a wealth of original ideas and a determination to put them into practice. His first musical collection *The New England Psalm Singer* (Boston, 1770) contained what he described at a later date as "fuguing pieces . . . more than twenty times as powerful as the old slow tunes." The technique of these pieces was canonic with "each part striving for mastery and victory." His further published books were: *The Singing Master's Assistant* (1776); *Music in Miniature* (1779); *The Psalm Singer's Amusement* (1781); *The Suffolk*

Harmony (1786) and *The Continental Harmony* (1794). In one instance, he harmonized a tune, *Jargon,* entirely in dissonances; this was prefaced by a 'Manifesto' to the Goddess of Discord. There was further a choral work *Modern Music* in which the proclaimed aim was expressed in the opening lines: "We are met for a concert of modern invention—To tickle the ear is our present intention." Several of his hymns became popular, particularly *Chester* and *The Rose of Sharon;* an interesting historical work was his *Lamentation over Boston* written in Watertown while Boston was occupied by the British. However, he could not earn a living by his music; appeals made to provide him and his large family with funds bore little fruit, and Billings died in abject poverty. The combination of reverence and solemnity with humor makes the songs of Billings unique in the annals of American music, and aroused the curiosity of many modern American musicians; Henry Cowell has written a series of 'fuguing tunes' for orch. Bibl.: O. G. Sonneck, *Early Concert Life in America* (Leipzig, 1907; reprinted, 1949); E. H. Pierce, *The Rise and Fall of the Fugue tune in America,* in the 'Mus. Quarterly' (April, 1930); Frank J. Metcalf, *American Writers and Compilers of Sacred Music* (1925; pp. 54-55); I. Goldberg, *The First American Musician* in the 'American Mercury' (vol. 14); P. Scholes, *The Puritans and Music in England and New England* (Oxford, 1934); C. E. Lindstrom, *William Billings and his Times,* in the 'Mus. Quarterly' (Oct., 1939); J. T. Howard, *Our American Music* (N. Y., 1946, pp. 49-57).

Billington, Elizabeth (*née* Weichsel), English operatic soprano, b. London, c. 1765; d. near Venice, Aug. 25, 1818. Her mother, a singer, was a pupil of Johann Christian Bach. She received her early musical training from her father, a German oboist. She also studied with James Billington, a double-bass player by profession, whom she married on Oct. 13, 1783. Her operatic debut took place in Dublin (1784) as Eurydice in Gluck's opera; went to London, where she appeared as Rosetta in *Love in a Village* at Covent Garden on Feb. 13, 1786. Her success was immediate; she was reengaged at Covent Garden and also sang at the Concerts of Ancient Music in London. Her career was briefly disrupted by the publication, in 1792, of anonymous 'Memoirs' attacking her private life. This was immediately followed by an equally anonymous rebuttal 'written by a gentleman' defending her reputation. In 1794 she went to Italy where she sang for the King of Naples. He made arrangements for her appearances at the San Carlo, where she appeared in operas by Bianchi, Paisiello, Paer and Himmel, all written specially for her. Her husband died in 1794; she remained in Italy for two more years; then lived in France, where she married M. Felissent. Returning to London in 1801, she sang alternately at Drury Lane and Covent Garden, with great acclaim, at 4,000 guineas a season. This period was the peak of her success. She retired in 1809, except for occasional performances. After a temporary separation from Felissent, she returned to him in 1817, and they settled at their estate at St. Artien, near Venice.

Billroth (bil-roht), **Theodor,** eminent surgeon and amateur musician; b. Bergen, on the island of Rügen, April 26, 1829; d. Abazzia, Feb. 6, 1894. He received a thorough musical education; was an intimate friend of Hanslick and Brahms; the musical soirées at his home in Vienna were famous. Almost all the chamber music of Brahms was played there (with Billroth as violist), before a public performance. He wrote a treatise *Wer ist musikalisch?* (1896, edited by Hanslick). Bibl.: J. Fischer, *Theodor Billroth und seine Zeitgenossen* (1929); A. Fränkel, *Th. Billroth* (1931); Otto Gottlieb, *Billroth und Brahms* (1934). See also *Briefe Billroths* (1895).

Bilse, Benjamin, German conductor; b. Liegnitz, Aug. 17, 1816; d. there, July 13, 1902. He was 'Stadtmusikus' at Liegnitz (1843), and brought his orchestra to a remarkable degree of perfection; then lived in Berlin (1868-84) and conducted at the 'Concerthaus'; retired in 1894 with the title of 'Hofmusikus'. He composed salon music.

Bilstin, Youry (real name, Bildstein), Russian cellist; b. Odessa, Russia, Feb. 10, 1887; d. New York, Dec. 15, 1947. He studied at the Tiflis Cons.; then at St. Petersburg. After the Russian Revolution he lived in Paris; in 1932 settled in the U.S. as a teacher. He wrote several works for cello; also *Invocation to the light* for viola da gamba, flute, and piano (1932); *Variations diaboliques* for cello and piano; and a *Méthode Psycho-Physiologique d'Enseignement Musical.*

Bimboni, Alberto, Italian-American pianist and composer; b. Florence, Aug. 24, 1882. He studied in Florence; came to the U.S. in 1912 as opera conductor. In 1930 appointed to the faculty of the Curtis Institute in Philadelphia; taught opera classes at the Juilliard School of Music, N.Y., from 1933;

has appeared as a pianist in concerts with Ysaÿe, John McCormack and other celebrated artists. He has written the operas *Winona* (Portland, Oregon, 1926); *Karina* (Minneapolis, 1928); *In the Name of Culture* (Rochester, 1949); numerous songs (many of them published). See E. E. Hipsher, *American Opera and its Composers* (Philadelphia, 1927; pp. 72-76).

Binchois (băn-shwăh') **(de Binche), Gilles,** Burgundian composer; b. Mons in Hainaut, c. 1400; d. Soignies, near Mons, Sept. 20, 1460. His father was Jean de Binche, counsellor to two rulers of Hainaut. Binchois was in the service of William de la Pole, Earl of Suffolk in Paris (1424). From 1430 he was at the Burgundian court; advanced from fifth to second chaplain; probably visited Italy at some time. Tinctoris considered him the equal of Dunstable and Dufay. He is best known for his secular works; his chansons rank with the finest. Modern reprints of his works are contained in: J. Marix, *Les musiciens de la cour de Bourgogne au XVe siècle* (1937); L. Feininger (ed.), *Documenta polyphoniae liturgicae Sanctae Ecclesiae Romanae,* Ser. I (1947); W. Gurlitt (ed.), *Gilles Binchois, 16 weltliche Lieder zu 3 Stimmen* in 'Das Chorwerk' (vol. XXII); J. Stainer (ed.), *Dufay and his Contemporaries* (1898); 'Denkmäler der Tonkunst in Österreich' (vols. VII, XI, XXXI); A. W. Ambros, *Geschichte der Musik,* vol. II (1862-78, 1882); E. Droz and G. Thibault (eds.), *Poètes et musiciens du XVe siècle* (1924); A. Schering (ed.) *Geschichte der Musik in Beispielen* (Leipzig, 1931; reprinted, N.Y., 1950); E. Droz, G. Thibault and Y. Rokseth (eds.), *Trois chansonniers français du XVe siècle* (1927); H. Besseler, *Die Musik des Mittelalters und der Renaissance* in Bücken's 'Handbuch' series (1931); C. van den Borren (ed.), *Polyphonia Sacra: A Continental Miscellany of the Fifteenth Century* (1932); O. Dischner (ed.), *Kammermusik des Mittelalters. Chansons der 1. und 2. niederländischen Schule für drei bis vier Streichinstrumenten herausgegeben* (1927); A. Davison and W. Apel (eds.), *Historical Anthology of Music,* vol. I (Cambridge, Mass., 1950); H. E. Wooldridge, *Oxford History of Music,* vol. II (1932); C. Parrish and J. F. Ohl, *Masterpieces of Music before 1750* (N.Y., 1951); G. de Van, *A recently discovered Source of Early Fifteenth Century Polyphonic Music, the Aosta Manuscript,* in 'Musica Disciplina', vol. II (1948); J. Wolf, *Geschichte der Mensural-Notation von 1250-1460,* vol. III (1904); J. Wolf (ed.), *Music of Earlier Times* (1946). Bibl.: E. Closson, *L'Origine de Gilles Binchois* in 'Revue de Musicologie', vol. V (1924); A. Pirro, *Histoire de la musique de la fin du XIVe siècle à la fin du XVIe* (1940); Aurelio Gotti, *L'Ars Nova e il Madrigale* in 'Atti della Reale Accademia di Scienze, Lettere, e Arti di Palermo' (ser. IV, Vol. IV, Part II); W. Gurlitt in 'Basler Kongressbericht' (1924); H. Funk, in 'Acta musicologica' (vol. IV); H. Riemann, in 'Handbuch der Musikgeschichte' (Vol. III); G. Reese, *Music in the Renaissance* (N.Y., 1954).

Binder, Abraham Wolfe, American composer and conductor; b. New York, Jan. 13, 1895. He studied at Columbia Univ. (Mus. Bac., 1926); taught liturgical music at the Jewish Institute of Religion, N.Y.; conducted in Tel Aviv in 1931; has composed the symphonic works *Ha Chalutsim (The Pioneers,* 1931); *Holy Land Impressions* (1932), *The Valley of Dry Bones* (1935); violin pieces; songs on Jewish themes. He has compiled a *New Palestinian Song Book;* has written many articles on the history and development of Jewish music.

Binder, Christlieb Siegmund, German organist and composer; b. Dresden, July (baptized July 29), 1723; d. there, Jan. 1, 1789. He was organist at the court church in Dresden from 1753; wrote prolifically, in an 'elegant style' akin to that of K. Ph. E. Bach; published sonatas for harpsichord solo, and for harpsichord in various combinations with violin and cello; also 76 organ preludes, harpsichord concertos, quartets with harpsichord, and trio-sonatas for 2 violins with basso continuo, which have been preserved in MS.; some of his compositions have been reprinted by O. Schmid in 'Musik am sächsischen Hofe.' See H. Fleischer, *C. S. Binder* (Regensburg, 1941).

Binder, Karl, Austrian composer; b. Vienna, Nov. 29, 1816; d. there, Nov. 5, 1860. He was a theater conductor by profession; composed mostly for the stage: a melodrama *Der Wiener Schusterhut* (1840); an opera, *Die Drei Wittfrauen* (1841); a vaudeville comedy *Purzel* (1843); overture and choruses to the drama *Elmar;* a parody on *Tannhäuser* (1857); etc.

Binet, Jean, Swiss composer; b. Geneva, Oct. 17, 1893. He studied with Ernest Bloch and Otto Barblan in Geneva. From 1919-23 lived in the U.S.; from 1923-29 in Brussels. Returning to Switzerland he became active as a member of the Society of

Swiss Composers. Binet has written a number of works for the dance, drama and motion pictures: the 3 ballets *Die Strasse* (1934); *L'Ile enchantée* (1947) and *La Naissance du printemps* (1949); incidental music to *The Merry Wives of Windsor* (1940); radio operetta *La Chatte blanche* (1944); numerous choral works, including *Psaumes de délivrance* for baritone, chorus and orch. (1952); a number of songs with orchestral accompaniment, among them *L'or perdu* (1953); several orchestral suites of Swiss dances; *Divertissement* for violin and orch. (1934); string quartet (1929); *Dialogues* for flute and violin (1937); song cycles. Binet's musical idiom is largely determined by the practical considerations of performance, and does not transcend the limits of traditional harmonies; he makes effective use of national Swiss melodies.

Bing, Rudolph, international operatic impresario; b. Vienna, Jan. 9, 1902. He first studied singing, but soon entered the managerial field. He was successively with a Vienna concert agency (1923-27); Darmstadt State Theater (1928-30) and the Municipal Opera at Charlottenburg-Berlin (1930-33). In 1934 he went to England; managed the Glyndebourne Opera Co. from 1935-39 and 1946-49. He became a British subject in 1946. He was one of the most active organizers of the Edinburgh Festivals in 1947 and was musical director for three seasons. On May 25, 1949, he was appointed general manager of the Metropolitan Opera, N. Y.

Bingham, Seth, American organist and composer; b. Bloomfield, N. J., April 16, 1882. He studied with Horatio Parker; later in Paris with d'Indy, Widor (composition) and Guilmant (organ). Returning to America, he graduated from Yale University (B.A., 1904) where he won the organ and composition awards. He became (Presbyterian) church organist in New York and elsewhere; took his M.B. at Yale in 1908, and taught there until 1919; instructor and associate prof. at Columbia University (until 1954). His works include: *Wall Street Fantasy* (1912; performed as *Symphonic Fantasy* by the N. Y. Philharmonic, Feb. 6, 1916); *La Charelzenn,* opera (1917); *Tame Animal Tunes* for 18 instruments (1918); *Memories of France,* orchestral suite (1920); *Wilderness Stone* for narrator, soli, chorus and orchestra (1933); Concerto for organ and orchestra (Rochester, Oct. 24, 1946); *Connecticut Suite* for organ and strings (Hartford, March 26, 1954); Concerto for brass, snare drum and organ (Minneapolis, July 12, 1954). Among his compositions for organ the following have been frequently performed: *Suite* (1926); *Pioneer America* (1928); *Harmonies of Florence* (1929); *Carillon de Château-Thierry* (1936); *Pastoral Psalms* (1938); *12 Hymn-Preludes* (1942); *Variation Studies* (1950); *36 Hymn and Carol Canons* (1952).

Birchall, Robert, English music publisher; b. (?); d. London, 1819. He founded a music publishing firm in London; published several of Beethoven's works for the first time in England; letters from Beethoven to Birchall are contained in Nohl's collection. The firm, which later became Birchall, Lonsdale & Mills, had one of the first circulating music libraries ever established.

Birchard, Clarence C., American music-publisher; b. Cambridge Springs, Pa., July 13, 1866; d. Carlisle, Mass., Feb. 27, 1946. He established his firm in Boston in 1901 and specialized in educational books for public schools; of these, a ten-book series, *A Singing School,* introduced lavish profusion of color in design and illustration; the firm has also issued community song books, of which the most popular is *Twice 55 Community Songs* (several million copies sold). The catalogue includes orchestral scores by many American composers (Berezowsky, Bloch, Converse, Hadley, Ives, Janssen, Josten, Kelley, Loeffler, Mason, Morris, Shepherd and Sowerby); also cantatas by Cadman, Converse, Hanson, Rogers and Whithorne; and Copland's school opera *Second Hurricane.* After Birchard's death Thomas M. Moran succeeded to the presidency; after his death in 1949, Donald F. Malin became president. The firm publishes a house organ, 'The Birchard Broadsheet.'

Bird, Arthur, American composer; b. Belmont, Mass., July 23, 1856; d. Berlin, Dec. 22, 1923. He studied in Berlin with Loeschhorn; spent several months with Liszt at Weimar in 1885; returned to America briefly in 1886, and then lived in Berlin, identifying himself with conservative circles there. He was Berlin correspondent of American music magazines; in his articles he violently attacked Richard Strauss and other modern composers. Among his own works is a symphony; *2 Decimettes* for wind instruments (won Paderewski prize in 1901). He also wrote a comic opera *Daphne* (N.Y., 1897) and many piano pieces. Bibl.: W. L. Loring, *Arthur Bird, American Composer* in the 'Mus. Quarterly' (Jan., 1943).

Bird, Henry Richard, eminent English organist; b. Walthamstow, Nov. 14, 1842;

d. London, Nov. 21, 1915. He was a pupil of his father; then studied with James Turle; came to London in 1859, where he held various positions as organist, and conducted the Chelsea Choral and Orchestral Society; was appointed organist at St. Mary Abbott's in Kensington, and occupied this post until his death; was also prof. of piano at the Royal College of Music and at Trinity College from 1896. He was famous throughout England as an unexcelled accompanist, and was in constant demand by the foremost artists; in 1891 was appointed permanent accompanist of the 'Popular Concerts.'

Bird, William. See **Byrd.**

Biriukov, Youri Sergeyevitch, Russian composer; b. Moscow, April 14, 1908. He studied at the Moscow Cons. with Miaskovsky (composition) and Feinberg (piano), graduating in 1937. His first published work was a piano toccata (1936); in 1938 he published 24 Preludes for piano; has also written a piano concerto and several song cycles.

Birnbach (bērn-bah), **(Joseph Benjamin) Heinrich,** German pianist and music pedagogue, son of Karl Joseph Birnbach; b. Breslau, Jan. 8, 1793; d. Berlin, Aug. 24, 1879. He studied piano with his father; taught in Breslau from 1814-21; settled in Berlin as music teacher and founded a music institute. Among his pupils were Nicolai, Kücken and Dehn. He composed 2 symphonies; 2 overtures; concertos for oboe, clarinet and guitar; piano concertos; a piano quintet; piano sonatas; piano duos; etc.; also published a treatise, *Der vollkommene Kapellmeister* (1845).

Birnbach, Karl Joseph, German composer; b. Köpernick, Silesia, 1751; d. Warsaw, May 29, 1805. During the last years of his life he was conductor at the German Theater in Warsaw. A prolific composer, he wrote 2 operas; 10 symphonies; 16 piano concertos; 10 violin concertos; cantatas; masses; chamber music; piano pieces.

Bisaccia (bē-zăht'-chăh), **Giovanni,** Italian singer and composer; b. 1815; d. Naples, Dec. 20, 1897. He studied singing with Crescentini and composition with Raimondi and Donizetti; sang in the Nuovo and San Carlo theaters; later taught singing, and was maestro di cappella at the church of San Fernando, for which he wrote some music. In 1838 he brought out 2 musical farces, *I tre scioperati* and *Il figlio adottivo;* and in 1858 an opera buffa *Don Taddeo, ovvero lo Solachianiello di Cesoria.*

Bischoff, Georg Friedrich, German music director; b. Ellrich, Harz Mountains, Sept. 21, 1780; d. Hildesheim, Sept. 7, 1841. He was music director at Hildesheim from 1816; arranged the first Thuringian Festival at Frankenhausen (July 20 and 21, 1810), at which Spohr acted both as conductor and soloist.

Bischoff, Hans, German pianist and teacher; b. Berlin, Feb. 17, 1852; d. Niederschönhausen, near Berlin, June 12, 1889. He was a pupil of Theodor Kullak and Richard Wüerst; also studied at Berlin Univ. (*Dr. phil.,* 1873); taught piano and other subjects at Kullak's Academy from 1873; conducted Monday Concerts of the Berlin Singakademie. He edited the 2nd and 3rd editions of Adolf Kullak's *Ästhetik des Klavierspiels* (Berlin, 1876 and 1889; English translation, N.Y., 1895); also published an *Auswahl Händel'scher Klavierwerke; Kritische Ausgabe von J. S. Bach's Klavierwerken;* etc.

Bischoff, Hermann, German composer; b. Duisburg, Jan. 7, 1868; d. Berlin, Jan. 25, 1936. He was a pupil of Jadassohn at the Leipzig Cons.; lived for a time in Munich, where he was associated with Richard Strauss; then went to Berlin as director of the 'Musikschutzverband' and member of the board of directors of the 'Allgemein deutscher Musikverein'. He composed 2 symphonies; the first symph. had its world première in Essen, May 24, 1906; was given by the Boston Symph. under Karl Muck twice in one season (Jan. 4, 1908 and Feb. 29, 1908); attracted a great deal of attention at the time, but sank into oblivion later on. He also composed the symph. poems *Pan* and *Gewittersegen;* published an essay, *Das deutsche Lied* (1905).

Bischoff, Kaspar Jakob, German composer and teacher; b. Ansbach, April 7, 1823; d. Munich, Oct. 26, 1893. He was a pupil of Franz Lachner in Munich (1842); studied in Leipzig (1848); settled in Frankfurt, where he taught singing, and founded an 'Evangelical Sacred Choral Society' in 1850. He wrote an opera, *Maske und Mantilla* (Frankfurt, 1852); 3 symphonies; overture to *Hamlet;* chamber music; church music; also published a manual of harmony (1890).

Bischoff, Ludwig Friedrich Christian, German editor of music periodicals; b. Dessau, Nov. 27, 1794; d. Cologne, Feb. 24, 1867. He was teacher at Wesel (1823-49); then settled in Cologne, where he founded and edited the 'Rheinische Musikzeitung' (1850) and the 'Niederrheinische Musikzeitung' (1853); translated Oulibicheff's *Beethoven* into German.

Bishop, Anna, English soprano; b. London, Jan. 9, 1810; d. New York, March 18, 1884. She was of French descent (her maiden name was Rivière). She studied at the Royal Academy of Music in London; in 1831 married Henry Bishop. She made her London debut in 1834; in 1839 made an extensive concert tour with the harpist, Bochsa; soon afterwards abandoned her husband and went with Bochsa to France; however, she continued to use her married name, and appeared in concerts as Madame Bishop. She sang at Naples and in Ireland. In 1847 she went to America; in 1858 she married Martin Schultz of New York. In 1866 she toured China and Australia; the ship she was on became grounded on a coral reef in the Marianas for 21 days; but despite this experience she completed her tour, eventually returning to New York. She was extremely successful with the public, particularly in England and the U.S.

Bishop, Sir Henry Rowley, noted English composer; b. London, Nov. 18, 1786; d. there, April 30, 1855. He was a pupil of Francesco Bianchi; attracted attention with his first opera, *The Circassian Bride* (Drury Lane, Feb. 23, 1809); was engaged as composer and conductor at Covent Garden from 1810-11; in 1813 was alternate conductor of the Philharmonic; in 1819 oratorio conductor at Covent Garden; in 1825 conductor at the Drury Lane Theatre; in 1830 Musical Director at Vauxhall; took the degree of Mus. Bac. at Oxford (1839); from 1840 was music director at Covent Garden; then Prof. of Music at Edinburgh (1841-3); was knighted in 1842; engaged as conductor of the Ancient Concerts from 1840-8; then appointed Prof. of Music at Oxford (succeeding Dr. Crotch), where he received the degree of Mus. Doc. in 1853. He was a remarkably prolific dramatic composer, having produced about 130 operas, farces, ballets, adaptations, etc. His operas are generally in the style of English ballad-opera; some of the best are: *Cortez or The Conquest of Mexico* (1823); *The Fall of Algiers* (1825); *The Knight of Snowdoun* (after Walter Scott, 1811); *Native Land* (1824). His *Clari, or the Maid of Milan* (Covent Garden, May 8, 1823) contains the famous song *Home Sweet Home,* with text by the American, John Howard Payne; it appears repeatedly throughout the opera. The tune, previously published by Bishop to other words, was thought to have been of Sicilian origin, but after much litigation was accepted as Bishop's original composition (the MS. is owned by the Univ. of Rochester, N.Y.). A version of the melody was used by Donizetti in his opera *Anne Boleyn,* thereby causing the erroneous belief that Donizetti was its composer. Bishop also wrote *The Fallen Angel,* an oratorio (never performed); *The Seventh Day,* cantata (1834); many additions to revivals of older operas, etc.; his glees and other lyric vocal compositions are deservedly esteemed. (An article on the Glees, by G. A. Macfarren, is in the 'Mus. Times' of 1864, April *et seq.*) Bishop also published vol. I of *Melodies of Various Nations;* and 3 vols. of *National Melodies,* to which Moore wrote the poems. See F. Corder, *The Works of Sir Henry Bishop* in the 'Mus. Quarterly' (Jan., 1918); R. Northcott, *The Life of Sir Henry R. Bishop* (London, 1920).

Bispham (bisp'h'm), **David (Scull),** American baritone; b. Philadelphia, Jan. 5, 1857; d. New York, Oct. 2, 1921. He first sang as an amateur in the principal choruses of Philadelphia, in the choirs of Holy Trinity and St. Mark's churches, and in private theatricals; then went to Milan (1886) where he studied with Vannuccini, and Francesco Lamperti; later studied in London with Shakespeare and Randegger; made his professional operatic debut as Longueville in Messager's *Basoche* (Royal Opera, London, Nov. 3, 1891), in which his comic acting ability, as well as his singing, won praise; made his first appearance in serious opera as Kurwenal in *Tristan und Isolde* (Drury Lane, June 25, 1892). He was particularly effective in the Wagnerian baritone roles; made his American debut with the Metropolitan Opera as Beckmesser (Nov. 18, 1896). He also was very successful in recitation (*Enoch Arden,* with incidental music by Richard Strauss; *A Midsummer Night's Dream* with Mendelssohn's music, etc.). He also gave numerous recitals in London and New York, in programs of German Lieder sung in English. He was a strong advocate of opera in English; a Society of American Singers was organized under his guidance, presenting light operas in the English language. Bispham published an autobiography *A Quaker Singer's Recollections* (N.Y., 1920). A Bispham Memorial Medal Award was established by the Opera Society of America in 1921 for an opera in English by an American composer; among its winners were Walter Damrosch, Victor Herbert, Henry Hadley, Deems Taylor, Charles Cadman, Louis Gruenberg, Howard

Hanson, Otto Luening, Ernst Bacon, George Antheil and George Gershwin. Bispham left all the biographical and bibliographical material dealing with his career to the Music Division of the N. Y. Public Library.

Bitsch, Marcel, French composer; b. Paris, Dec. 29, 1921. He entered the Paris Cons. in 1939, studied composition with Busser, and won the second Prix de Rome, 1943; first Prix de Rome, 1945. He has written *Six Esquisses Symphoniques* (1949); *Sinfonietta* (1950); cantata *La Farce du Contrebandier* (1946); *Divertissement* for flute, clarinet, oboe and bassoon (1947); *3 Sonatinas* for flute and piano (1952); Concertino for piano and orch. (Paris, Nov. 28, 1954), etc.

Bitter, Karl Hermann, German writer on music; b. Schwedt-on-Oder, Feb. 27, 1813; d. Berlin, Sept. 12, 1885. He studied at the Berlin Univ.; then in Bonn; pursued a career in government; served in the finance dept.; in 1879 was appointed by Bismarck as Prussian Minister of Finance. He retired in 1882. He was the author of the following books on music: *J. S. Bach* (2 vols., Berlin, 1865; 2nd ed., 1881; abridged English ed., 1873); *Mozarts Don Juan und Glucks Iphigenie* (Berlin, 1866); *C. Ph. E. Bach und W. Fr. Bach und deren Brüder* (2 vols., Berlin, 1868); *Beiträge zur Geschichte der Oper* (1872); *Die Reform der Oper durch Gluck und Wagner* (1884); edited Karl Loewe's autobiography (1870).

Bittner, Julius, Austrian composer; b. Vienna, April 9, 1874; d. there, Jan. 10, 1939. He first studied law; then music with Bruno Walter and Josef Labor; was a magistrate in Vienna until 1920. At the same time he composed industriously. He devoted most of his energy to opera and also wrote his own librettos; composed 2 symphonies; sacred choruses; and numerous songs for his wife, Emilie Bittner, a contralto. During his last years, he suffered from a crippling illness, necessitating the amputation of both legs. Operas: *Die rote Gret* (Frankfurt, Oct. 26, 1907); *Der Musikant* (Vienna, April 12, 1910); *Der Bergsee* (Vienna, Nov. 9, 1911; revised, 1938); *Der Abenteurer* (Cologne, Oct. 30, 1913); *Das höllisch Gold* (Darmstadt, Oct. 15, 1916); *Das Rosengärtlein* (Mannheim, March 18, 1923); *Mondnacht* (Berlin, Nov. 13, 1928); *Das Veilchen* (Vienna, Dec. 8, 1934); also operettas, ballets and mimodramas. See R. Specht, *Julius Bittner* (Munich, 1921).

Bizet (bē-zā'), **Georges** (baptismal names **Alexandre-César-Léopold**), French opera composer; b. Paris, Oct. 25, 1838; d. Bougival, June 3, 1875. His parents were both professional musicians, his father a singing teacher and composer; his mother an excellent pianist. Bizet's talent developed early in childhood; at the age of nine he entered the Paris Cons., his teachers being Marmontel (piano), Benoist (organ), Zimmermann (harmony) and Halévy (composition), whose daughter, Geneviève, he married in 1869. In 1852 he won a first prize for piano, in 1855 for organ and for fugue, and in 1857 the Grand Prix de Rome. In the same year he shared (with Lecocq) a prize offered by Offenbach for a setting of a 1-act opera *Le Docteur Miracle;* Bizet's setting was produced at the Bouffes-Parisiens on April 9, 1857. Instead of the prescribed mass, he sent from Rome during his first year a 2-act Italian opera buffa, *Don Procopio* (not produced until March 10, 1906 when it was given in Monte Carlo in an incongruously edited version); later he sent 2 movements of a symphony, an overture (*La Chasse d'Ossian*); and a 1-act opera (*La Guzla de l'Emir;* accepted by Paris Opéra-Comique, but withdrawn by Bizet prior to production). Returning to Paris, he produced a grand opera, *Les Pêcheurs de perles* (Th.-Lyrique, Sept. 30, 1863); but this work, like *La jolie fille de Perth* (Dec. 26, 1867) failed to win popular approval. A 1-act opera, *Djamileh* (Opéra-Comique, May 22, 1872) fared no better. Bizet's incidental music for Daudet's play *L'Arlésienne* (Oct. 1 1872) was ignored by the audiences and literary critics; it was not fully appreciated until its revival in 1885. But an orchestral suite from *L'Arlésienne* brought out by Pasdeloup (Nov. 10, 1872) was acclaimed; a 2nd suite was made by Guiraud after Bizet's death. Bizet's next major work was his masterpiece *Carmen* (based on a tale by Mérimée, text by Halévy and Meilhac), produced after many difficulties with the management and the cast, at the Opéra-Comique (March 3, 1875). The reception of the public was not enthusiastic, and several critics attacked the opera for its lurid subject and the music for its supposed adoption of Wagner's methods. Bizet received a generous sum (25,000 francs) for the score from the publisher Choudens and won other honors (he was named chevalier of the Légion d'honneur on the eve of the première of *Carmen*); although the attendance was not high, the opera was maintained in the repertory. There were 37 perfs. before the end of the season; the original cast included Galli-Marie as Carmen, Lhérie as Don José and Bouhy as Escamillo. Bizet was chagrined by the controversial reception of the opera, but it is a melodramatic invention to state (as has been asserted by some biographers) that the alleged failure of *Carmen* precipitated the composer's death (he died on the night of the 31st perf. of *Carmen*). Soon the opera became a triumphant success all over the world; it was staged in London (in Italian at Her Majesty's Theatre, June 22, 1878); St. Petersburg, Vienna, Brussels, Naples, Florence, Mainz, New York (Academy of Music, Oct. 23, 1878), etc. The Metropolitan Opera produced *Carmen* first in Italian (Jan. 9, 1884), then in French, with Calvé as Carmen (Dec. 20, 1893). It should be pointed out that the famous *Habanera* is not Bizet's own, but a melody by the Spanish composer, Yradier, which Bizet inserted in *Carmen* (with slight alterations) mistaking it for a folk song. Bizet also wrote an operetta, *La Prêtresse* (1854); the operas *Numa* (1871) and *Ivan le Terrible,* in 4 acts (Bordeaux, Oct. 12, 1951; the score was believed to have been destroyed by Bizet, but was discovered among the manuscripts bequeathed to the Paris Cons. by the second husband of Bizet's widow); the cantatas *David* (1856) and *Clovis et Clothilde* (1857); *Vasco da Gama,* symph. ode with chorus (1859); *Souvenirs de Rome,* symph. suite in 3 movements (Paris, Feb. 28, 1869; publ. in 1880 as a 4-movement suite, *Roma*); orchestral overture *Patrie* (Paris, Feb. 15, 1874); *Jeux d'enfants* (suite for piano 4-hands); about 150 piano pieces of all kinds (Bizet was a brilliant pianist); etc. Bizet's first symphony, written at the age of 17, was published for the first time in 1935 from the MS preserved at the Paris Cons. and proved to be an astonishingly brilliant work. Bizet also completed Halévy's biblical opera *Noë* (1869). Bibl.: E. Galabert, *Georges Bizet* (Paris, 1877); Ch. Pigot, *Bizet et son Oeuvre* (1886; new ed. 1911); C. Bellaigue, *Bizet* (1891); P. Voss, *Bizet* (Leipzig, 1899); A. Weissmann, *Bizet* (Berlin, 1907); O. Séré, *Georges Bizet* in *Musiciens français d'aujourd'hui* (Paris, 1911); H. Gauthier-Villars, *Bizet; biographie critique* (Paris, 1911); R. Brancour, *La vie et l'œuvre de Bizet* (Paris, 1913); P. Landormy, *Bizet* in 'Les Maîtres de la Musique' (1924); Julius Rabe, *Bizet* (Stockholm, 1925); D. C. Parker, *Bizet, His Life and Works* (London, 1926); E. Istel, *Bizet und Carmen* (Stuttgart, 1927); J. Tiersot, *Bizet and Spanish Music,* in the 'Mus. Quarterly' (Oct., 1925); J. W. Klein, *Nietzsche and Bizet,* in the 'Mus. Quarterly' (Oct., 1925); M. Delmas, *Bizet* (1930); R. Laparra, *Bizet et l'Espagne* (Paris, 1934); Bizet issue of the 'Revue de musicologie' (Nov., 1938); M. Cooper, *Bizet* (London, 1938); W. Dean, *Bizet* (London, 1948); Mina Curtiss, *Unpublished Letters by Georges Bizet,* in the 'Mus. Quarterly' (July, 1950).

Bjelinski (byel-in'-skē), **Bruno,** Croatian composer; b. Trieste, Nov. 1, 1909. He studied law at the Univ. of Zagreb, and music at the Cons. with Bersa. In 1945, appointed prof. at the Zagreb Cons. He has written concertos for piano, violin, cello and bassoon; 2 string quartets; 3 violin sonatas; a piano trio and other chamber music.

Björkander, Nils (Frank Frederik), Swedish composer; b. Stockholm, June 28, 1893. He studied at the Stockholm Cons.; in 1917 he established a music school of his own. He is the author of many piano pieces that have achieved considerable popularity; he has also written a piano quintet; flute sonata; violin sonata, etc.

Björling (byör'-ling), **Jussi,** Swedish tenor; b. Stora Tuna, Feb. 2, 1907. He studied voice with John Forsell and Jullio Voghera at the Royal Opera School, Stockholm (grad. 1929); made his debut in Stockholm (1930) as Don Ottavio in *Don Giovanni;* since then has been principal tenor of the Stockholm opera; guest appearances in Vienna, Dresden and Prague; came to the U. S. first as a boy tenor in the Björling Quartet (with his father and two brothers); returned to the U. S. in 1937 when he sang at the Chicago Civic Opera; made his Metropolitan Opera debut in 1938. His repertory includes 54 operatic roles.

Blacher, Boris, outstanding modern composer; b. Newchwang, China (of Estonian-German parentage), Jan. 3, 1903. His family moved to Irkutsk, Siberia, remaining there from 1914-20; in 1922 he went to Berlin where he studied with F. E. Koch. He was subsequently active as a pedagogue in Berlin and in Dresden; after 1945 wrote incidental music for the Berlin Radio; in 1948 appointed prof. at the Hochschule für Musik in West Berlin; and in 1953, its director (succeeding W. Egk). His music is cast in a terse effective style; he has developed a system of 'variable meters' according to arithmetical progressions, with permutations contributory to variety. Works: Operas, *Fürstin Tarakanowa* (Wuppertal, Feb. 5, 1941); *Die Flut,* chamber opera (Dresden, March 4, 1947; first radio performance, Berlin, Dec. 20, 1946); *Die Nachtschwalbe,* 'a dramatic nocturne' (Leipzig, Feb. 29, 1948; aroused considerable protest on account of its bold subject); *Das preussisches Märchen,* opera-ballet (Berlin, Sept. 22, 1952); *Abstract*

Opera No. 1, for 3 soloists, 2 reciters, chorus and orch. (Frankfurt, June 28, 1953; produced a 'succès de scandale'). Blacher was also the author of the librettos for Einem's operas *Dantons Tod* and *Der Prozess.* Ballets: *Fest im Süden* (1936); *Chiarina* (Berlin, Jan. 22, 1950); *Hamlet* (Munich, Nov. 19, 1950); *Lysistrata* (Berlin, Sept. 30, 1951). For orch: concerto for 2 trumpets and 2 string orchs. (1931); *Kleine Marschmusik* (1932); *Capriccio* (1934); *Concertante Musik* (Berlin, Dec. 6, 1937); symph. (1939); concerto for string orch. (1942); *Partita* for string orch. and percussion (1945); *16 Orchestra Variations on a Theme by Paganini* (Leipzig, Nov. 27, 1947); 1st piano concerto (1948); violin concerto (1950); concerto for clarinet, bassoon, horn, trumpet, harp and strings (1950); 2nd piano concerto (Berlin, Sept. 15, 1952); *Ornaments,* based on 'variable meters' (Venice Fest., Sept. 15, 1953); viola concerto (Cologne, March 14, 1955). Chamber music: *Jazz-Koloraturen,* for saxophone and bassoon (1929); 3 string quartets (1941-49); violin sonata (1947); also songs and piano pieces. Cf. Karl H. Wörner, *Neue Musik in der Entscheidung* (Mainz, 1954; p. 237 *et seq.*).

Black, Andrew, British baritone singer, originally an organist; b. Glasgow, Jan. 15, 1859; d. Sydney, Australia, Sept. 15, 1920. He studied in Milan; won his first success in London at a Crystal Palace concert (July 30, 1887); then appeared at festivals in Leeds (1892), Gloucester (1895), Norwich (1896), Birmingham (1903), etc. He also gave concerts in the U. S. and Australia, where he settled in 1913.

Black, Frank, American conductor; b. Philadelphia, Nov. 28, 1894; he studied music and chemistry at Haverford College; later studied piano under Raphael Joseffy in New York, and wrote songs for vaudeville acts; from 1923-34 was conductor at the Fox Theater in Philadelphia; also served as music director of the Brunswick Record Corp. (1925-32); from 1925-38 was coach and accompanist for the Revellers' Quartet; in 1928 was appointed music director of NBC, conducting a string orchestra and organizing the entire music dept. Black holds an honorary Mus. Doc. from Missouri Valley College in Marshall. He is editor of the collection *Rhythmic Classics.*

Blackstone, Milton, American violinist and teacher; b. N. Y., Nov. 27, 1894. He toured the U. S. as a child violinist (1904); settled in Toronto (1912); graduated from the Canadian Academy of Music (1914); was a violin teacher at the Toronto Cons. (1920-23); joined the Hart House String Quartet as violist (1924) and toured the U. S. and Europe.

Blagrove, Henry Gamble, English violinist; b. Nottingham, Oct. 20, 1811; d. London, Dec. 15, 1872. He was a pupil of his father, and gave public performances as a very young child; was the first pupil of the Royal Academy of Music (opened 1823), where he won the silver medal in 1824; later studied with Spohr at Kassel (1833-34); then gave many concerts in London and at provincial festivals.

Bláha-Mikeš (blah'-hah-mē'-kesh), **Záboj,** Czechoslovakian composer; b. Prague, Nov. 22, 1887. He was a pupil of Vitězslav Novák; has composed the choral cycles *Man* for male chorus and *Song of Solomon* for female chorus and orch.; many other song cycles of popular or biblical content; Japanese songs; 2 orchestral suites; melodramas (*Tagore,* with orch.); *Nocturnes* and *Visions* for piano.

Blahetka, Marie Léopoldine, pianist and composer; b. Guntramsdorf, near Vienna, Nov. 15, 1811; d. Boulogne, Jan. 12, 1887. She studied piano with Josef Czerny, Kalkbrenner and Moscheles; also composition with Sechter. She made very successful tours on the continent; finally settled in Boulogne in 1840. She composed a romantic opera *Die Räuber und die Sänger* (Vienna, 1830); also many works for piano, including concertos, sonatas, polonaises, etc.; songs.

Blainville (blăn-vēl'), **Charles-Henri,** French cellist, music theorist and composer; b. in a village near Tours, 1711; d. Paris, 1769. He mistakenly supposed himself to have discovered a third 'mode hellénique' (actually the Phrygian mode) and composed a symphony (1751) in which he used it. The 'discovery' was much admired by Rousseau, but was flatly discredited by Serre. Blainville also composed about 5 other symphonies; 2 ballets; cantatas; a vol. of sonatas 'pour le dessus de viole avec la basse continue'; also arranged Tartini's sonatas as concerti grossi. He published *L'harmonie théorico-pratique* (1746); *Essai sur un troisième mode* (1751); *L'esprit de l'art musical* (1754; German transl. in Hiller's *Nachrichten*); and *Histoire générale, critique et philologique de la musique* (1767).

Blake, Dorothy Gaynor, American song composer and pedagogue; b. St. Joseph, Mo., Nov. 21, 1893. She studied piano with her mother Jessie S. Gaynor (q.v.); and theory with Thomas Tapper and Rudolph Ganz; in 1911, settled in Nashville, Tenn. She married R. E. Blake on July 24, 1912. She has written mostly for voice; her songs have been frequently performed in recitals. In 1948 she was living in Webster Groves, Mo. She has publ. 28 collections of simple exercises and tunes for schools.

Blamont (bla-mŏhn'), **François Colin de,** French composer; b. Versailles, Nov. 22, 1690; d. there, Feb. 14, 1760. He was a pupil of Lalande; became superintendent of the King's music; wrote many court ballets, 'fêtes,' operas; also cantatas and motets; published an *Essai sur les goûts anciens et modernes de la musique française* (1754).

Blanc (blahn), **Adolphe,** French composer; b. Manosque, Basses-Alpes, June 24, 1828; d. Paris, May 1885. He studied at the Paris Cons. and privately with Halévy; for a short time he was conductor at the Théâtre-Lyrique. In 1862 he was awarded the Prix Chartier for chamber music. He wrote a 1-act comic opera, *Une Aventure sous la Ligue* (1857); 2 operettas, *Les deux billets* (1868) and *Les Rêves de Marguerite;* a burlesque symphony; an overture; trios, quartets, quintets and septets for strings, with and without piano; piano pieces.

Blanc, Giuseppe, Italian composer; b. Bardonecchia, April 11, 1886. He was a pupil of Bolzoni (comp.); has written various operettas, including *La festa dei fiori* (Rome, Jan. 29, 1913), pantomimes, songs, etc. His song *Giovinezza* was adopted as a Fascist anthem during the Mussolini regime.

Blancafort, Manuel, Spanish composer; b. Barcelona, Aug. 12, 1897. He studied in Barcelona with Lamote de Grignon and Malats; has been awarded various composition prizes. Works: For orch., *Matin de Fête a Puig-Gracios* (Barcelona, 1929) and *El Rapto de las Sabines;* for chorus and orch., *Cami de Siena* (Barcelona, 1928); 2 piano concertos; piano sonata and descriptive pieces *(Le parc d'attractions, Chants intimes, Pastorale en Sol, Chemins,* etc.*)*; songs; etc.

Blanchard (blahn-shahr'), **Henri-Louis,** French musician; b. Bordeaux, Feb. 7, 1778; d. Paris, Dec. 18, 1858. He studied the violin; was conductor at the Théâtre des Variétés in Paris (1818-29); wrote music criticism; produced several operettas.

Blanchet (blahn-shā'), **Emile R.,** Swiss pianist and composer; b. Lausanne, July 17, 1877; d. Pully, March 27, 1943. He studied with his father Charles Blanchet (1833-1900); with Seiss, Franke and Strässer at the Cologne Cons.; and with Busoni in Weimar and Berlin. From 1904-17 he was teacher of piano at the Lausanne Cons. Among his works are *64 Preludes for Pianoforte in Contrapuntal Style,* a valuable pedagogic work; *Konzertstück* for piano and orch.; violin sonata; a Ballade for 2 pianos; many etudes and other piano works; songs; etc.

Blanck, Hubert de, conductor and educator; b. Utrecht, June 11, 1856; d. Havana, Nov. 28, 1932. He studied at the Liège Cons. with Ledent (piano) and Dupuy (comp.); subsequently served as theater conductor in Warsaw (1875); toured Europe as a pianist; with the violinist E. Dengremont, visited South America (1880). After teaching at the N. Y. College of Music, he settled in Havana (1883), and founded the first conservatory in Cuba, based upon European models (1885). He was exiled in 1896 for participation in the revolution; after the re-establishment of peace, he reopened his school in Havana and established branches in other towns. He composed piano pieces and songs; but it is as an enlightened educator that he is honored in the annals of Cuban music.

Blangini (blahn-jē'-nē), **Giuseppe Marco Maria Felice,** Italian composer; b. Turin, Nov. 18, 1781; d. Paris, Dec. 18, 1841. In 1789 he was choirboy at the Turin cathedral, and by the age of twelve played the organ, composed sacred music and was a skillful cellist. In 1799, his family moved to Paris, where Blangini gave concerts, wrote fashionable *romances,* and came into vogue as an opera composer when he completed Della-Maria's opera *La fausse duègne* (1802); he was also popular as a singing teacher. After producing an opera in Munich, he was appointed court Kapellmeister (1806); later was General Music Director at Kassel (1809); and upon his return to Paris in 1814, was made superintendent of the King's music, Court composer, and prof. of singing at the Cons., positions which he held until 1830. His works include 30 operas; 4 masses with orch; 170 nocturnes for 2 voices; 174 *romances* for one voice; etc. See his autobiography, *Souvenirs de F. Blangini,* ed. by M. de Villemarest (Paris, 1834).

Blankenburg, Quirin van, Dutch organist and writer; b. Gouda, 1654; d. The Hague, c. 1740. He was organist of the Reformed

Church in The Hague; wrote *Elementa musica* (1729), and *Clavicembel en Orgelboek der gereformeerde Psalmen en Kerkgezangen* (1732; 3rd edition, 1772); also a method for flute.

Blanter, Matvey Isaacovitch, Russian composer of popular songs; b. Potchep, Tchernigov district, Feb. 10, 1903. He studied in Moscow with G. Conius; then devoted himself exclusively to the composition of light music. He wrote an operetta *On the Banks of the Amur* (1939) and some incidental music. Among his songs the most popular is *Katyusha* (famous during World War II), which combines the melodic inflection of the typical urban ballad with the basic traits of a Russian folk song. Blanter is regarded in Russia as a creator of the new Soviet song style.

Blaramberg, Pavel Ivanovitch, Russian composer; b. Orenburg, Sept. 26, 1841; d. Nice, March 28, 1907. His father was a geographer, of French origin; his mother was Greek. At the age of fourteen he came to St. Petersburg; later became a functionary of the Central Statistical Committee there. He was largely self-taught in music, apart from occasional advice from Balakirev and Rimsky-Korsakov. In 1878 he settled in Moscow as instructor at the newly founded Philharmonic Institute. In 1898 he went to the Crimea, then to France. He was primarily an opera composer; wrote stage music for Ostrovsky's *Voyevoda* (1865) and for Lermontov's *Demon* (1869); the operas *The Mummers* (1881); *Russalka* (Moscow, April 15, 1888); *Maria Tudor,* after Hugo (produced as *Mary of Burgundy* on account of the censor's objection to the original libretto; Moscow, Oct. 29, 1888); *Tushintsy* (Moscow, Feb. 5, 1895; his most successful opera; had several revivals); and *The Waves* (1902). He also wrote a symphonic poem *The Dying Gladiator* (1882), a symphony (1886), and songs.

Blaserna, Pietro, Italian music theorist; b. Fiumicello, near Aquileja, Feb. 29, 1836: d. Rome, Feb. 26, 1918. He studied natural sciences in Vienna and Paris; later taught physics at the Univs. of Palermo (1863) and Rome (1872). An exponent of the acoustic purity of intervals, he made important scientific contributions in the field of acoustics. His principal work is *La teoria del suono nei suoi rapporti colla musica* (1875; German translation, 1876; French translation, 1877).

Blasius, Mathieu-Frédéric, composer; b. Lauterburg, Alsace, April 23, 1758; d. Versailles, 1829. He was a violinist, clarinetist, flutist and bassoonist; taught wind instruments at the Paris Cons. (1795-1802); conducted at the Opéra-Comique (1802-16). He wrote 3 operas; 3 violin concertos; many popular pieces for wind instruments in various combinations.

Blauvelt, Lillian Evans, American soprano; b. Brooklyn, N. Y., March 16, 1874; d. Chicago, Aug. 29, 1947. After studying violin for several years she took vocal lessons in N. Y. and Paris; gave concerts in France, Belgium and Russia; made her operatic debut at Brussels, in Gounod's *Mireille* (1893); sang before Queen Victoria (1899); sang the coronation ode and received the coronation medal from King Edward (1902); appeared for several seasons at Covent Garden. She married the composer, Alexander Savine, in 1914; created the title role in his opera *Xenia* (Zürich, 1919).

Blaze (blahz), (called **Castil-Blaze**), **François-Henri-Joseph,** French writer on music; b. Cavaillon, Vaucluse, Dec. 1, 1784; d. Paris, Dec. 11, 1857. He studied with his father, a lawyer and amateur musician; went to Paris in 1799 as a law student; held various administrative posts in provincial towns in France. At the same time he studied music and compiled information on the opera in France. The fruit of this work was the publication in 2 volumes of his book *De l'opéra en France* (Paris, 1820; 1826); this work dealt not only with the historical aspects of French opera, but also with the esthetic principles of composition and the libretti. He became music critic of the 'Journal des Débats' in 1822, signing his articles 'XXX', and exercised considerable influence on musical affairs in Paris. He resigned from this post in 1832, but continued to publish books on music, of factual and critical nature, including valuable compilations of musical lexicography: *Dictionnaire de musique moderne* (1821, 2 vols.; 2nd ed., 1825; 3rd ed., edited by J. H. Mees, with historical preface and a supplement on Netherlands musicians, 1828, in 1 vol.); *Chapelle-musique des Rois de France* (1832); *La Danse et les Ballets depuis Bacchus jusqu'à Mlle. Taglioni* (1832); *Mémorial du Grand Opéra* (from Cambert, 1669, down to the Restoration); *Le Piano; histoire de son invention* ('Revue de Paris,' 1839-40); *Molière musicien* (1852); *Théâtres lyriques de Paris* in 2 vols., on the Grand Opéra (1855), and on the Italian opera (1856); *Sur l'opéra français; vérités dures mais utiles* (1856); *L'art des jeux lyriques* (1858); translated into French many libretti of German and Italian operas. He himself wrote 3 operas; compiled a collection of *Chants de Provence;* some of his popular ballads attained considerable popularity.

Blaze, Henri, Baron de Bury (son of François Blaze), French music critic; b. Avignon, May 17, 1813; d. Paris, March 15, 1888. He wrote many essays for the 'Revue des Deux Mondes' and other periodicals; these essays were subsequently collected as *Musiciens contemporains* (1856); *Meyerbeer et son temps* (1865); *Musiciens du passé, du présent, etc.* (1880); *Goethe et Beethoven* (1882); his most valuable book is *La Vie de Rossini* (1854).

Blech, Leo, eminent German opera conductor and composer; b. Aachen, April 21, 1871. After leaving school he tried a mercantile career; then studied briefly at the Hochschule für Musik in Berlin; returned to Aachen to conduct at the Municipal Theater (1893-99); also took summer courses in composition with Humperdinck (1893-96). He was engaged as opera conductor in Prague (1899-1906); at the Berlin Opera from 1906 to 1923, and again from 1926 until 1936. He conducted in Riga (1938-41) and in Stockholm (1941-49). In 1949 he returned to Berlin, and soon retired. His works include the operas *Aglaja* (1893) and *Cherubina* (1894); 'opera-idyl' *Das war ich* (Dresden, Oct. 6, 1902; his most successful stage work); *Alpenkönig und Menschenfeind* (Dresden, Oct. 1, 1903; rewritten and produced as *Rappelkopf* at the Royal Opera, Berlin, in 1917); opera *Aschenbrödel* (Prague, 1905); short opera *Versiegelt* (Hamburg, 1908; N. Y., 1912); an operetta *Die Strohwitwe* (Hamburg, 1920); 3 symphonic poems, *Die Nonne, Waldwanderung, Trost in der Natur;* choruses, songs, piano pieces; *10 Kleinigkeiten* for piano 4 hands; music for children, etc. His music is in the Wagnerian tradition; his knowledge and understanding of instrumental and vocal resources enabled him to produce highly effective works. Bibl.: E. Rychnowsky, *Leo Blech* (Prague, 1905); id., *Leo Blech,* in vol. III of 'Monographien moderner Musiker' (Leipzig, 1909); W. Jacob, *Leo Blech* (1931).

Bledsoe, Jules, American Negro baritone singer and composer; b. Waco, Texas, Dec. 29, 1902; d. Hollywood, July 14, 1943. He studied at Chicago Mus. College (B. A., 1919); took singing lessons in Paris and Rome. He sang in the première of J. Kern's *Show Boat* (1927) and other musical plays; from 1932 appeared in grand opera as Rigoletto, Boris and the title role in Gruenberg's opera *Emperor Jones.* He wrote an *African Suite* for orch. and several songs in the style of Negro spirituals.

Bleichmann, Yuly Ivanovitch, Russian composer; b. St. Petersburg, Dec. 6, 1868; d. there, Dec. 5, 1909. He studied with Soloviev and Rimsky-Korsakov at the St. Petersburg Cons.; later with Jadassohn and Reinecke in Leipzig. Returning to St. Petersburg, he founded the Popular Symphony Concerts in 1893; also conducted the Philharmonic Symphony Concerts. He composed 2 operas, greatly influenced by Wagner: *St. Sebastian* and *The Dream-Princess* (Moscow, Oct. 23, 1900); also songs.

Blessinger, Karl, German musicologist; b. Ulm, Sept. 21, 1888. He studied in Heidelberg and Munich; was theater conductor in Bremen and Bonn; was on the staff of the Akademie der Tonkunst in Munich (1920-45); since 1945 teaching privately. Among his published writings are: *Ulmer Musikgeschichte im 17. Jahrhundert* (dissertation; Ulm, 1913); *Die musikalischen Probleme der Gegenwart* (1920); *Die Überwindung der musikalischen Impotenz* (1920); *Grundzüge der musikalischen Formenlehre* (1926); *Melodielehre als Einführung in die Musiktheorie* (1930); a pamphlet, *Mendelssohn, Meyerbeer, Mahler* (1938); *Judentum und Musik; Ein Beitrag zur Kultur- und Rassenpolitik* (Berlin, 1944; an exposition of the antisemitic policy of the Nazi regime).

Blewitt, Jonathan, English composer; b. London, July 19, 1782; d. there Sept. 4, 1853. He studied with his father, and with Battishill; was organist in several churches; served as conductor at the Theatre Royal in Dublin. Returning to London (1825), he was appointed music director at Sadler's Wells Theatre; produced several operas, stage pieces with incidental music, pantomimes, etc., at Drury Lane and elsewhere. He composed many popular ballads; was the author of a treatise on singing, *The Vocal Assistant.*

Bleyle, Karl, German composer, b. Feldkirch, Vorarlberg, May 7, 1880. He studied with Wehrle (violin) and S. de Lange (comp.) in Stuttgart and with Thuille (comp.) in Munich. He was active as teacher and theater conductor in Graz, Weimar and Munich; in 1923 returned to Stuttgart, where he was still living in 1954. Works: 2 operas, *Hannele und Sannele* (Stuttgart, 1923) and *Der Teufelssteg* (Rostock, 1924); many works for soli, chorus and orch. (*An den Mistral, Lernt Lachen, Mignons Beisetzung, Heilige Sendung, Die Höllenfahrt Christi, Ein Harfenklang, Prometheus, Trilogie der Leidenschaft, Requiem,* etc.); orchestral pieces *Flagellantenzug, Gnomentanz, Siegesouverture, Reinecke Fuchs, Legende;* a symphony; violin concerto; string quartet; violin sonata; songs; piano pieces; etc.

Bliss, Sir **Arthur (Edward Drummond),** eminent English composer, b. London, Aug. 2, 1891. He studied at Pembroke College, Cambridge; then at the Royal College of Music in London with Stanford, Vaughan Williams and Holst. He was an officer of the British Army during World War I; was wounded in 1916, and gassed in 1918. Returning to England after the war, he resumed his musical studies; his earliest works, *Madam Noy,* for soprano and 6 instruments (1918) and *Rout,* for soprano and chamber orch. (1919; Salzburg Festival, Aug. 7, 1922) were highly successful, and established Bliss as one of the most brilliant composers in the modern style. From 1923-25, Bliss was in the U. S.; on a later visit, lived in Hollywood, where he wrote the musical score for the motion picture *Things to Come,* after H. G. Wells (1935). He returned to London; during World War II he was Musical Director of the B.B.C. (1942-44); he was knighted in 1950; was named Master of the Queen's Musick in 1953 as successor to Sir Arnold Bax. His works include: opera, *The Olympians* (London, Sept. 29, 1949); ballets, *Checkmate* (Paris, June 15, 1937); *Miracle in the Gorbals* (London, Oct. 26, 1944); and *Adam Zero* (London, April 8, 1946); for orch.: *Mélée fantasque* (1920); *Colour Symphony* (the title refers to 4 heraldic colors: purple, red, blue and green; 1st perf., Gloucester, Sept. 7, 1922 under the composer's direction); concerto for 2 pianos and orch. (1933); *Hymn to Apollo* (1926); *Morning Heroes* (symphony in 6 movements for chorus, orator and orch., dedicated to his brother killed in action; 1st perf., Norwich, Oct. 6, 1930); *Music for Strings* (1935); piano concerto (commissioned by the British Council for the British Week at the N. Y. World's Fair, dedicated "to the people of the United States of America"; N. Y., June 10, 1939); violin concerto (London, May 11, 1955). His vocal music includes (besides *Madam Noy* and *Rout*): *Rhapsody* for soprano, tenor, flute, English horn, string quartet and double-bass (1919; Salzburg Festival, Aug. 5, 1923); *2 Nursery Rhymes* for soprano, clarinet and piano (1921); *The Women of Yueh,* song cycle for soprano and small orch. (1923); *Pastoral* for mezzo-soprano, chorus, strings, flute and drums (1928); *Serenade* for baritone and orch. (1929); *The Enchantress* for contralto and orch. (1951); *A Song of Welcome* for soprano, baritone, chorus and orch., composed for the return of Queen Elizabeth II from her Australian voyage (1st perf., London, July 29, 1954); several song cycles *(3 Romantic Songs; The Ballads of the Four Seasons; 7 American Poems).* Chamber music: *Conversations* for violin, viola, cello, flute and oboe, in 5 movements (1919; a humorous work); 3 string quartets (1924; 1941; 1950); quintet for oboe and strings (1927; Vienna Festival, June 21, 1932); quintet for clarinet and strings (1931); viola sonata (1932); piano pieces. Bibl.: Percy A. Scholes, *Notes on a Colour Symphony* (London, 1922); Alan Frank, *Arthur Bliss* in *Modern British Composers* (London, 1953).

Bliss, P. Paul, American organist and music editor; b. Chicago, Nov. 25, 1872; d. Oswego, N. Y., Feb. 2, 1933. He studied in Philadelphia; then went to Paris where he was a pupil of Guilmant (organ) and Massenet (comp.). Returning to America, he was active as organist in Oswego, N. Y.; served as music director with the John Church Co. (1904-10) and the Willis Music Co. (from 1911). He composed 3 operettas, *Feast of Little Lanterns, Feast of Red Corn, In India;* cantatas, *Pan on a Summer Day, Three Springs, The Mound-Builders;* piano suite, *In October;* many songs and choruses; also compiled a 'Graded Course for Piano' (4 vols.)

Blitzstein, Marc, American composer; b. Philadelphia, March 2, 1905. He studied piano and organ at the Univ. of Pennsylvania; also composition with Scalero at the Curtis Institute, and piano with Siloti in New York. He went to Europe in 1926, where he took courses with Nadia Boulanger in Paris and Schoenberg in Berlin. Returning to the U. S., he devoted himself to composition; also taught at the New School for Social Research. In 1940 he was awarded a Guggenheim Fellowship; during World War II he was stationed in England with the U. S. Army. Blitzstein is particularly successful in writing for the theater. Stage works: *Triple Sec,* opera-farce (Philadelphia, 1928); *Parabola and Circula,* 1-act opera-ballet (1929); *Cain,* ballet (1930); *The Harpies,* 1-act opera, commissioned by the League of Composers (1931; 1st production, Manhattan School of Music, N. Y., May 25, 1953); *The Cradle Will Rock,* 1-act opera of 'social significance' (N. Y., June 16, 1937, with the composer cond. from the piano); *No For An Answer,* short opera (N. Y., Jan. 5, 1941); also musical revues, one of which, *Regina,* to Lillian

Hellman's play *The Little Foxes,* he expanded into a full-fledged opera (Boston, Oct. 11, 1949). Vocal works: *Gods* for mezzo-soprano and string orch. (1926); oratorio *The Condemned* (1930); *Airborne,* cantata (N. Y., March 23, 1946); *Cantatina* for women's voices and percussion; songs to words by Whitman and Cummings, etc. Orchestral works: *Jig-Saw,* ballet-suite (1927); *Romantic Piece* (1930); piano concerto (1931); *Variations* (1934); *Freedom Morning,* symph. poem (London, Sept. 28, 1943). Chamber music: string quartet (1930); *Serenade* for string quartet (1932), etc.; also *Percussion Music* for piano (1929); piano sonata and minor pieces of various descriptions. His Americanized version of Kurt Weill's *Three-Penny Opera* (1954) has scored great success.—Cf. H. Brant, *Marc Blitzstein,* in 'Modern Music' (July, 1946).

Bloch, André, French composer; b. Wissembourg, Alsace, Jan. 18, 1873. He studied at the Paris Cons. with Guiraud and Massenet; received Premier Grand Prix de Rome in 1893. He was conductor of the orchestra of the American Cons. at Fontainebleau. His works include the operas *Maida* (1909); *Une Nuit de Noël* (1922); *Brocellande* (1925); *Guignol* (1949); the ballet *Feminaland* (1904); the symphonic poems *Kaa* (1933) and *L'isba nostalgique* (1945); *Les maisons de l'éternité* for cello and orch. (1945); *Concerto-Ballet* for piano and orch. (1946), etc.

Bloch, Ernest, eminent composer; b. Geneva, July 24, 1880. He studied solfeggio there with Jaques-Dalcroze and violin with L. Rey (1894-97); later (1897-99) at Brussels Cons. with Ysaÿe (violin) and Rasse (comp.); in 1900 took courses in composition with Iwan Knorr in Frankfurt and with Thuille in Munich. After a brief sojourn in Paris, he returned to Geneva in 1904 as lecturer at the Geneva Cons.; conducted symph. concerts at Lausanne and Neuchâtel (1909-10); then was prof. of comp. and esthetics at the Geneva Cons. (1911-15). In 1916 he made his first American tour as conductor for the dancer Maud Allan; in 1917 settled in New York where he taught at the Mannes School; conducted his own works with the leading orchestras in the U.S.; won the Coolidge prize for his viola suite (1919); from 1920-25 was director of the Institute of Music in Cleveland; from 1925-30, director of the San Francisco Cons. When the magazine 'Musical America' announced a contest for a symph. work (1927) Bloch won first prize for his 'epic rhapsody in three parts' with a choral ending, entitled *America;* however, the score did not measure up to Bloch's other music in artistic value. After 1930 Bloch lived mostly in Switzerland; returned to the U. S. in 1939; settled in Oregon in 1943; taught summer classes at the Univ. of Calif., Berkeley; then devoted himself entirely to composition. The sources of Bloch's inspiration are threefold: modern European, during his early period; racially Jewish, representing his most intense feelings and his greatest power of expression; structural, in a neo-classical manner, characteristic of his later period. Works: opera *Macbeth* (1904-09; Opéra-Comique, Paris, Nov. 30, 1910; Naples, March 1, 1938); an unfinished opera *Jézabel* (about 1918). For voice and orch.: *Poèmes d'Automne,* songs for mezzo soprano and orch. (1906); Prelude and 2 Psalms (Nos. 114 and 137) for soprano and orch. (1912-14); *Israel,* symphony with 2 sopranos, 2 contraltos and bass (1912-16; 1st perf. N. Y., May 3, 1917, composer conducting); Psalm 22 for baritone and orch. (1914). For orch.: *Vivre et Aimer,* symph. poem (1900); Symphony in C♯ m. (1901; perf. in part at Basel, June 1903; 1st complete perf. at Geneva, 1910; 1st American perf. by N. Y. Philh., May 8, 1918, composer conducting); *Hiver-Printemps,* symph. poem (1904-05; N. Y., Dec. 3, 1917); *Trois Poèmes Juifs* (1913; 1st perf., Boston with composer conducting, March 23, 1917; very successful); *Schelomo,* Hebrew rhapsody for cello and orch. (1916; 1st perf. N. Y., May 3, 1917, Kindler soloist, composer conducting); *Concerto Grosso* No. 1 for strings and piano (1924-25; 1st perf. Cleveland, June 1, 1925, composer conducting); *America,* symph. poem (1926; 1st perf. N. Y., Dec. 20, 1928; next day simultaneously in Chicago, Philadelphia, Boston and San Francisco); *Helvetia,* symph. poem (1928; Rome, Jan. 22, 1933); *Voice in the Wilderness,* with cello obbligato, in 6 movements (1936; 1st. perf. Los Angeles, Jan. 21, 1937); *Evocations,* symph. suite in 3 movements (1937; San Francisco, Feb. 11, 1938); violin concerto (1938; 1st perf. by Szigeti, Cleveland, Dec. 15, 1938); *Suite symphonique* (Philadelphia, Oct. 26, 1945); *Concerto symphonique* for piano and orch. (Edinburgh, Sept. 3, 1949); *Scherzo Fantasque* for piano and orch. (Chicago, Dec. 2, 1950); *In Memoriam* (1952); *Suite hebraïque* for viola and orch. (Chicago, Jan. 1, 1953); *Sinfonia breve* (B.B.C., London, April 11, 1953); *Concerto Grosso* No. 2 for string orch. (B.B.C., London, April 11, 1953); Symphony for trombone solo and orch. (1953-54; Houston, Texas, April 4, 1956); Symphony in E-flat (1954-55; London, Feb. 15, 1956); *Proclamation* for trumpet and orch. (1955). Chamber music: *4 Episodes* for chamber orch. (1926); Quintet for piano and strings, with use of quarter-tones (1923; N. Y. League of Composers, Nov. 11, 1923); 1st string quartet (N. Y., Dec. 29, 1916); 2 suites for string quartet (1925); *3 Nocturnes* for piano trio (1924); suite for viola and piano (Coolidge prize, 1919; perf. Pittsfield, Mass., 1919; also arranged for orch.); 1st violin sonata (1920); 2nd violin sonata, *Poème mystique,* in 1 movement (1924); *Baal Shem,* for violin and piano (1923; also arranged for orch., 1939); *Méditation hébraïque* and *From Jewish Life,* for cello and piano (1925); piano sonata (1935); 2nd string quartet (1946; received the N. Y. Music Critics Circle Award for chamber music, 1947); 3d string quartet (1951); 4th string quartet (1953); other compositions for violin and piano *(Melody, Exotic Night,* etc.); further piano works *(Poems of the Sea, In the Night,* both arranged for orch.; *Nirvana, Five Sketches in Sepia,* etc.); a modern Hebrew ritual *Sacred Service* (1930-33; world première at Turin, Jan. 12, 1934; N. Y., April 11, 1934); *Historiettes au crépuscule,* 4 songs for mezzo soprano and piano (1903). Bloch has also written *Man and Music,* in the 'Mus. Quarterly' (Oct., 1933); other articles in various musical journals. In order to develop a greater interest in the music of Bloch, the Ernest Bloch Society was founded in 1937. Cf. Paul Rosenfeld, in *Musical Portraits* (1920); G. M. Gatti, *Ernest Bloch,* in the 'Mus. Quarterly' (1921); Roger Sessions, *Ernest Bloch,* in 'Modern Music' (1927); R. Stackpole, *Ernest Bloch,* in 'Modern Music' (1927); Mary Tibaldi Chiesa, *Bibliografia delle opere musicali di Ernest Bloch* (Turin, 1931) and *Ernest Bloch* (Turin, 1933); D. Newlin, *The Later Works of Ernest Bloch,* in the 'Mus. Quarterly' (Oct., 1947).

Bloch, Suzanne, lutenist and harpsichordist, daughter of Ernest Bloch; b. Geneva, Aug. 7, 1907. She came to the U. S. with her father; studied with him and with Roger Sessions; then in Paris with Nadia Boulanger. She became interested in early polyphonic music and began to practice on old instruments so as to be able to perform the music on instruments for which it was written. She has appeared in numerous lecture recitals, at museums and colleges in America and Europe.

Blockx (blohx), **Jan,** Flemish composer; b. Antwerp, Jan. 25, 1851; d. there May 26, 1912. He studied piano at the Flemish Music School with Callaerts and composition with Benoit. In 1886, became teacher of harmony at the Antwerp Cons.; also was musical director of the 'Cercle artistique' and other societies. With Benoit, he is regarded as the strongest representative of the Flemish school in Belgium; however, in his music, he followed traditional European methods; his operas betray a Wagnerian influence. He wrote the operas *Jets vergeten* (Antwerp, 1877); *Maître Martin* (Brussels, Nov. 30, 1892); *Herbergprinses* (Antwerp, Oct. 10, 1896; perf. in French as *Princesse d'Auberge,* N. Y., March 10, 1909); *Thyl Uylenspiegel* (Brussels, Jan. 18, 1900); *De Bruid der Zee* (Antwerp, Nov. 30, 1901; his best work); *De Kapel* (Antwerp, Nov. 7, 1903); *Baldie* (Antwerp, Jan. 25, 1908; revised and perf. in Antwerp, Jan. 14, 1912, under the title *Chanson d'amour*); a ballet *Milenka* (1887); *Rubens,* overture for orch.; *Romance* for violin and orch.; many choral works with orch.: *Vredezang; Het droom vant paradies; De klokke Roelandt; Op den stroom; Scheldezang.* See L. Solvay, *Notice sur Jan Blockx* (1920); F. Blockx, *Jan Blockx* (1943).

Blodek, Wilhelm, Czech composer; b. Prague, Oct. 3, 1834; d. there, May 1, 1874. He studied with J. B. Kittl and A. Dreyschock; taught for three years in Poland; then returned to Prague, and became prof. of flute-playing of the Prague Cons. (1860-70). In 1870 he became insane and spent the rest of his life in an asylum. His opera in the Czech language *V Studni (In the Well)* was produced with excellent success in Prague (Nov. 17, 1867); it was also given in German under the title *Im Brunnen* (Leipzig, 1893). His second opera, *Zitek,* remained unfinished; it was completed by F. X. Vana, and prod. in Prague at Blodek's centennial (Oct. 3, 1934). Blodek also wrote a flute concerto (1862) and a symphony (1866).

Blodgett, Benjamin Colman, American organist; b. Boston, March 12, 1838; d. Seattle, Sept. 22, 1925. He studied in Boston; played the organ in churches there. In 1878 he was appointed prof. of music at Smith College, where he established and was director of the Department of Music; then organist at Stanford Univ. (1906-14); finally settled in Seattle.

Blom, Eric, eminent English writer on music; b. Bern, Switzerland, Aug. 20, 1888, of Danish and British extraction on his father's side; his mother was Swiss. He was educated in England; wrote program notes for the Queen's Hall Concerts in London

(1919-26) in collaboration with Rosa Newmarch. He was the London music correspondent of the 'Manchester Guardian' (1923-31); music critic of the 'Birmingham Post' (1931-46) and of 'The Observer' (from 1949); was editor of 'Music & Letters' from 1937-50, and again from 1954; also ed. the new series 'Master Musicians.' In 1946 he was elected member of the Music Committee of the British Council; in 1948 became member of the Royal Musical Association. In 1955 he received the order of Commander of the British Empire in recognition of his services to music, and the hon. D. Litt. from Birmingham Univ. In his writing he combines an enlightened penetration of musical esthetics with a capacity for presenting his subjects in a brilliant journalistic style. His books include: *Stepchildren of Music* (1923); *The Romance of the Piano* (1927); *A General Index to Modern Musical Literature in the English Language* (1927; indexes periodicals for the years 1915-26); *The Limitations of Music* (1928); *Mozart* (in 'Master Musicians,' 1935); *Beethoven's Pianoforte Sonatas Discussed* (1938); *A Musical Postbag* (collected essays; 1941); *Music in England* (1942; revised edition, 1947); *Some Great Composers* (1944); also contributed articles to the 'Sibelius Symposium' (1947), etc. In 1946 Blom published his first lexicographical work, *Everyman's Dictionary of Music* (2nd revised ed., 1954), comprising, in one compact volume, a great number of biographical and terminological entries. In 1946 he was entrusted with the preparation of a newly organized and greatly expanded edition of Grove's *Dictionary of Music and Musicians.* It was brought out under his editorship in 1954, in 9 volumes, to which Blom himself contributed hundreds of articles, and translated articles by foreign contributors. This monumental edition is by far the most comprehensive reference work on music in the English language.

Blomdahl, Karl-Birger, Swedish composer; b. Växjö, Oct. 19, 1916. He studied composition with Hilding Rosenberg in Stockholm; then studied in Paris and Rome. In his works he has adapted a progressive idiom of the neo-classical type. He has written 3 symphonies (1943; 1947; 1948); viola concerto (1941); violin concerto (1947); and several works for various chamber groups.

Bloomfield, Fannie. See **Zeisler, Fannie Bloomfield.**

Blondeau (blohn-doh'), **Pierre-Auguste-Louis,** French violinist and composer; b. Paris, Aug. 15, 1784; d. there, 1856. He studied at the Paris Cons. with Baillot, Gossec and Méhul; won the Prix de Rome in 1808 with his cantata, *Maria Stuart;* was viola player in the Grand Opéra Orch. until 1842. He wrote an opera, *Alla fontana;* a ballet; 3 overtures; church music; chamber music; piano pieces and songs; also a number of theoretical works.

Blow, (Dr.) **John,** great English composer and organist; b. Newark-on-Trent, Nottinghamshire, Feb. (baptized 23rd), 1648/9; d. Westminster (London), Oct. 1, 1708. In 1660-61 he was a chorister at the Chapel Royal, under Henry Cooke; he later studied organ with Christopher Gibbons. His progress was rapid, and on Dec. 3, 1668, he was appointed organist of Westminster Abbey. In 1679 he left this post and Purcell, who had been Blow's student, became his successor. After Purcell's untimely death in 1695, Blow was reappointed, and remained at Westminster Abbey until his death; he was buried there, in the north aisle. He married Elizabeth Bradcock in 1673; she died in 1683 in childbirth, leaving five children. Blow held the rank of Gentleman of the Chapel Royal from March 16, 1673/4; on July 13, 1674, he succeeded Humfrey as Master of the Children; was Master of the Choristers at St. Paul's (1687-1702/3). He held the honorary Lambeth degree of Mus. Doc., conferred on him in 1677 by the Dean of Canterbury. Still as a young chorister of the Chapel Royal, Blow began to compose church music; in collaboration with Humfrey and William Turner, he wrote the *Club Anthem* ('I will always give thanks'); at the behest of Charles II, he made a two-part setting of Herrick's 'Goe, perjur'd man.' He wrote many secular part-songs, among them an ode for New Year's day, 1681/82 ('Great sir, the joy of all our hearts'), an ode for St. Cecilia; 2 anthems for the coronation of James II; *Epicedium for Queen Mary* (1695) and *Ode on the Death of Purcell* (1696). Blow's collection of 50 songs, *Amphion Anglicus,* was published in 1700. His best known work is *Masque for the Entertainment of the King: Venus and Adonis,* written about 1685; this is his only complete score for the stage, but he contributed separate songs for numerous dramatic plays. Purcell regarded Blow as "one of the greatest masters in the world." 14 large works by Blow, anthems and harpsichord pieces, have been preserved; 11 anthems are printed in Boyce's *Cathedral Musick* (1760-78). The vocal score of his masque *Venus and Adonis* was published by G. E. P. Arkwright in the

Old English Edition (No. 25; 1902); the complete score was published by the 'Editions de l'Oiseau Lyre' as edited by Anthony Lewis (Paris, 1939). Bibl.: G. E. P. Arkwright's introduction to 'Six Songs by Dr. John Blow' in the Old English Edition (No. 23; 1900); H. W. Shaw's *John Blow, Doctor of Music,* in the 'Musical Times' (Oct.-Dec., 1937; also separately, London, 1943); id., *Blow's Use of the Ground Bass,* in 'Mus. Quarterly' (Jan., 1938); id., *John Blow's Anthems,* in 'Music & Letters' (Oct. 1938); H. L. Clarke, *John Blow; a Tercentenary Survey,* in the 'Mus. Quarterly' (July, 1949).

Blum, Robert, Swiss composer, b. Zürich, Nov. 27, 1900. He studied at the Zürich Cons. with Andreae, Jarnach and others; later went to Berlin where he studied with Busoni (1923). Upon his return to Switzerland, he devoted himself to choral conducting. In 1943 he was appointed prof. at the Music Academy in Zürich. As a composer, he cultivates polyphonic music in the old style, embanked within a modern harmonic framework. Works: operas *Amarapura, Resurrection* and *Susanna;* 4 symphonies; *Lamentatio Angelorum* for orch.; *Passionskonzert* for organ and string orch. (1943); viola concerto (1950); chamber music; many fine choral works.

Blume, Clemens, German music scholar; b. Billerbeck, Jan. 29, 1862; d. Königstein, April 8, 1932. He studied theology; then taught it at the Catholic Univ. in Frankfurt. He was regarded as an outstanding authority on texts of medieval Latin hymns. His books include *Cursus Sanctus Benedicti* (liturgic hymns of the 6th to 9th centuries; 1908); Guide to Chevalier's *Repertorium Hymnologicum* (1911); *Analecta hymnica medii aevi* (his standard work; 1896-1922; vols. 1-48, co-ed. with C. M. Dreves; some vols. with H. M. Bannister). A selection from this valuable source book of hymnological research was extracted as *Ein Jahrtausend lateinischer Hymnendichtung* (2 vols., 1909). Blume also published *Unsere liturgischen Lieder* (Pustet, 1932).

Blume, Friedrich, eminent German musicologist and editor; b. Schlüchtern, Jan. 5, 1893. He was the son of a Prussian government functionary; first studied medicine in Eisenach (1911); then philosophy in Munich, and music in Munich and Berlin. During World War I he was in the German army; was captured by the British and spent three years in a British prison camp. In 1919 he resumed his studies at the Univ. of Leipzig, where he presented his dissertation *Studien zur Vorgeschichte der Orchestersuite im 15. und 16. Jahrhundert* (1921). He was appointed lecturer (1923) and then privatdozent (1925) at the Univ. of Berlin; published the treatise *Das monodische Prinzip in der protestantischen Kirchenmusik* (1925). Further writings: *Die Kultur der Abtei Reichenau* (1925); *Die evangelische Kirchenmusik* in Bücken's 'Handbuch der Musikwissenschaft' (1931); *Hermann Abert und die Musikwissenschaft* in 'Abert-Festschrift' (1928) and Abert's *Gesammelte Schriften und Vorträge* (1929), both edited by Blume. He prepared a collected edition of works by M. Praetorius (20 vols. in 155 installments; 1928-40); also edited a Passion by Demantius, *Sacri concerti* by Schütz; piano sonatas of Wilhelm Friedemann Bach, and *Geistliche Musik am Hofe des Landgrafen Moritz;* published minor studies on Mozart's piano concertos, on the works of Josquin des Prez (1929), and on Haydn's string quartets (1931). He was general editor of the valuable collection of old polyphonic music *Das Chorwerk* (until 1939, 50 vols.; includes works of Pierre de la Rue, Demantius, Josquin des Prez, Purcell, etc.). In 1943 he was entrusted with the preparation of the encyclopedia *Die Musik in Geschichte und Gegenwart,* which began appearing in 1949. Under Blume's direction this work has assumed monumental proportions; 50 installments in 5 vols. were publ. before 1957, reaching the letter K.

Blumenfeld, Felix Michailovitch, Russian composer and conductor; b. Kovalevska, Govt. of Kherson, April 19, 1863; d. Moscow, Jan. 21, 1931. He studied at the St. Petersburg Cons. (1881-85); taught there until 1897. He was conductor of the Imperial Operas at St. Petersburg (1898-1912). In 1918 he became professor at the Moscow Cons. His works, from op. 1 to op. 46, are published by Belaiev. They include a symphony, *To the Memory of the Beloved Dead;* a string quartet, piano pieces and songs.

Blumenschein, William Leonard, composer and choral conductor; b. Brensbach, Germany, Dec. 16, 1849; d. Dayton, Ohio, March 27, 1916. He studied various instruments and theory at the Leipzig Cons. with Wenzel and Reinecke (1869-72); then came to the U. S. and settled in Dayton, Ohio as organist and director of several choral societies. He published 50 effective piano pieces in the salon style; 60 anthems and sacred songs; secular songs and choruses.

Blumenthal, Jacob (Jacques), pianist; b.

Hamburg, Oct. 4, 1829; d. London, May 17, 1908. He studied music in Hamburg and Vienna; then at the Paris Cons. (1846) with Herz and Halévy; settled in London (1848) as teacher; also held the post of pianist to the Queen. He composed many melodious piano pieces in the salon style.

Blumer, Theodor, German conductor; b. Dresden, March 24, 1882. He was a pupil of Draeseke; occupied various posts as radio conductor in Germany; has written several comic operas, among them *Der Fünf-Uhr-Tee (Five o'clock Tea)* and *Trau schau wem!;* also the orchestral pieces *Carnivals-Episode, Erlösung, Legende der Tänzerin Thaïs,* and *Heiteres Spiel.* After World War II he lived in Berlin.

Blumner, Martin, German choral conductor and composer; b. Fürstenberg, Mecklenburg, Nov. 21, 1827; d. Berlin, Nov. 16, 1901. He studied philosophy and mathematics at Berlin Univ.; then music with Siegfried Dehn. In 1847 he became a member of the Berlin Singakademie; appointed associate conductor (1853) and chief conductor (1876). He composed the oratorios *Abraham* (1860) and *Der Fall Jerusalems* (1874); the cantatas *Columbus* (1852), *In Zeit und Ewigkeit* (1885), and *Festival Cantata* (1891); a *Te Deum* in 8 parts; motets; psalms; etc. —Cf. E. Dryander, *Zum Gedächtnis Martin Blumner* (Berlin, 1901).

Blüthner, Julius (Ferdinand), celebrated German piano maker; b. Falkenhain, near Merseburg, March 11, 1824; d. Leipzig, April 13, 1910. In 1853 he founded his establishment at Leipzig with three workmen; by 1897 it had grown to a sizable company, producing some 3,000 pianos yearly. Blüthner's specialty was the 'Aliquotflügel,' a grand piano with a sympathetic octave-string stretched over and parallel with each unison struck by the hammers. He was awarded many medals for his contributions to the advancement of piano construction. He was co-author, with H. Gretschel, of *Der Pianofortebau* (1872; 3d ed. revised by R. Hannemann, Leipzig, 1909).

Boccherini (bok-kā-rē'-nē), **Luigi,** famous Italian composer; b. Lucca, Feb. 19, 1743; d. Madrid, May 28, 1805. He was a pupil of Abbate Vannucci, and later studied in Rome (1757); returned to Lucca for a time as cellist in the theater orchestra. He then undertook a concert tour with the violinist Filippo Manfredi; the high point of their success was in Paris, when they appeared at the Concerts Spirituel. So popular was Boccherini as a performer, that his compositions were solicited by the leading Paris publishers; his first publications were 6 string quartets and 2 books of string trios. In 1796 Boccherini received a flattering invitation to the Madrid court, and became chamber composer to the Infante Luis, and, after Luis' death (1785), to King Carlos III. From 1787 he was also court composer to Friedrich Wilhelm II of Prussia, an amateur cello player. In this capacity, Boccherini was in Germany for a time; after the King's death (1797), he returned to Madrid. In 1800 he enjoyed the patronage of Napoleon's brother, Lucien Bonaparte, French ambassador to Madrid. Boccherini's last years were spent in ill health and poverty. He was buried in Madrid; in 1927 his remains were transferred to Lucca, and reinterred with great solemnity. Boccherini was an exceptionally prolific composer of chamber music. The list includes 20 chamber symphonies; 2 octets; 16 sextets; 125 string quintets; 12 piano quintets; 18 quintets for strings and flute (or oboe); 102 string quartets; 60 string trios; 21 violin sonatas; 6 cello sonatas; also 4 cello concertos. He further wrote 2 operas; a Christmas cantata; a Mass; etc. A full catalogue was compiled by L. Picquot in his monograph on Boccherini (Paris, 1851). His music is marked by natural melody and fluency of instrumental writing, if not by originality of style. He had profound admiration for the music of Haydn; indeed, so close is Boccherini's style to Haydn's that the affinity gave rise to the saying "Boccherini is the wife of Haydn." Bibl.: D. M. Cerù, *Cenni intorno alla vita e le opere di Luigi Boccherini* (Lucca, 1864); H. M. Schletterer, *Boccherini* (Leipzig, 1882); G. Malfatti, *Luigi Boccherini nell' arte, nella vita e nelle opere* (Lucca, 1905); R. Sondheimer, *Boccherini e la sinfonia in do maggiore,* in 'Rivista Musicale Italiana' (1920); C. Bouvet, *Boccherini inconnu* in 'Revue de musicologie' (Nov., 1929); Georges de Saint-Foix, *La correspondance de Boccherini avec I. Pleyel* in 'Revue de musicologie' (Feb., 1930); L. Parodi, *Luigi Boccherini* (1930); A. Bonaventura, *Boccherini* (Milan, 1931).

Bochsa, Robert-Nicolas-Charles, celebrated harpist; son of Karl Bochsa, a Bohemian flute player (d. 1821); b. Montmédy, Meuse, Aug. 9, 1789; d. Sydney, Australia, Jan. 6, 1856. He first studied music with his father; played in public at the age of seven; wrote a symphony when he was nine, and an opera *Trajan* at fifteen. He then studied with Franz Beck in Bordeaux, and later at the Paris Cons. with Méhul and Catel (1806). His harp teachers were Nadermann and Marin. Of an inventive nature, Bochsa developed novel technical devices for harp playing, transforming the harp into a virtuoso instrument. He was the court harpist to Napoleon, and to Louis XVIII. He wrote 8 operas for the Opéra-Comique (1813-16); several ballets, an oratorio, and a great number of works for the harp; also a Method for harp. In 1817 he became involved in some forgeries, and fled to London to escape prison. He became very popular as a harp teacher in London Society; organized a series of oratorio productions with Sir George Smart (1822). He was also the first professor of harp playing at the Academy of Music in London, but lost his position when the story of his dishonest conduct became widely known. However, he obtained a position as conductor of the Italian Opera at the King's Theatre (1826-32). Another scandal marked Bochsa's crooked road to success and notoriety when he eloped with the soprano singer Ann Bishop, the wife of Sir Henry Bishop. He gave concerts with her in Europe, America, and Australia, where he died. See a series of articles on Bochsa by Arthur Pougin under the title *Un musicien voleur, faussaire et bigame* in 'Le Ménestrel' (Jan. 19 to March 9, 1907).

Bockelmann, Rudolph, German baritone; b. Bodenteich, April 2, 1892. He studied singing with Oscar Lassner in Leipzig; appeared as a baritone at the Neues Theater (1921-26); at the Stadttheater in Hamburg (1926-32), and at the Staatsoper in Berlin (1932-45). After World War I he settled in Hamburg as a singing teacher. He also sang with the Chicago Opera (1930-31); was particularly noted for his interpretation of Wagnerian baritone roles.

Böckh, August, German authority on Greek literature and music; b. Karlsruhe, Nov. 24, 1785; d. Berlin, Aug. 3, 1867. He studied philology at the Univ. of Halle; received his doctorate with the treatise *De harmonice veterum* (1807). In 1811 he became professor at the Univ. of Berlin, a position which he retained until his death, 56 years later. He edited the works of Pindar with an introduction *De metris Pindari* from which modern research on old Greek music received a new impetus. Bibl.: M. Hoffmann, *A. Böckh* (Leipzig, 1901); G. Lehmann, *Theorie und Geschichte der griechischen Harmonik in der Darstellung durch August Böckh* (Würzburg, 1935).

Bocquillon-Wilhem (boh-kē-yohn'), **G. L.** See **Wilhem.**

Bodanzky, Artur, famous Austrian conductor; b. Vienna, Dec. 16, 1877; d. New York, Nov. 23, 1939. He studied at the Vienna Cons., and later with Zemlinsky. He began his carer as a violinist at the Vienna Opera. In 1900 he received his first appointment as conductor, leading an operetta season in Budweis; in 1902 he became assistant to Mahler at the Vienna Opera; conducted in Berlin (1905) and in Prague (1906-9). In 1909 he was engaged as music director at Mannheim. In 1912 he arranged a memorial Mahler Festival, conducting a huge ensemble of 1,500 vocalists and instrumentalists. He conducted *Parsifal* at Covent Garden, London, in 1914; his success there led to an invitation to conduct the German repertory at the Metropolitan Opera House; he opened his series with *Götterdämmerung* (Nov. 17, 1915). From 1916 to 1931 he was director of the Society of Friends of Music in New York; in 1919 he also conducted the New Symph. Orch. He made several practical arrangements of celebrated operas *(Oberon, Don Giovanni, Fidelio,* etc.*)* which he used for his productions with the Metropolitan Opera. His style of conducting was in the Mahler tradition, with emphasis on climactic effects and contrasts of light and shade.

Bodenschatz, Erhard, German theologian and music editor; b. Lichtenberg, 1576; d. Gross-Osterhausen, near Querfurt, 1636. He was a pupil of Calvisius in Pforta; then studied theology in Leipzig. In 1600 he became cantor in Schulpforta; in 1603 was pastor in Rehausen, and in 1608, in Gross-Osterhausen, where he remained until his death. He publ. several valuable collections of motets and hymns; particularly important is *Florilegium Portense* in 2 parts, of which the first was publ. in Leipzig in 1603 (1st ed. with 89 motets; 2nd ed. in 1618 with 120 motets); 2nd part (Leipzig, 1621) contained 150 motets, all by contemporary composers. There have been several reprints. He also publ. *Florilegium selectissimorum hymnorum* in 4 vols. (Leipzig, 1606). Bodenschatz's own compositions are not distinctive. Bibl.: Otto Riemer, *Erhard Bodenschatz und sein Florilegium Portense* (Leipzig, 1928).

Bodky, Erwin, German-American harpsichordist and music scholar; b. Ragnit, March 7, 1896. He studied in Berlin with Busoni and Richard Strauss. From 1926-33 he was prof. at the Academy for Church

Music and School Music in Berlin; in 1933 went to Amsterdam; in 1938 came to America. He taught at the Longy School of Music, Cambridge, Mass. (until 1948); in 1949 was appointed prof. at Brandeis Univ. at Waltham. He is the founder of the Cambridge Society for Early Music; has appeared on television as lecturer and harpsichord player; made recordings for various phonograph companies. He publ. a valuable treatise, *Der Vortrag alter Klaviermusik* (Berlin, 1932), dealing with the use of the clavichord in Bach's works; has contributed to various music magazines.

Boeckh, August. See **Böckh.**

Boehe, Ernst, German composer and conductor; b. Munich, Dec. 27, 1880; d. Ludwigshafen, Nov. 16, 1938. He studied with Rudolf Louis and Thuille in Munich; in 1907 was associate conductor, with Courvoisier, of the Munich 'Volkssymphoniekonzerte'; from 1913-20 was court conductor at Oldenburg; then conducted concerts in Ludwigshafen. His works are of a programmatic type, the orchestration emphasizing special sonorities of divided strings, massive wind instruments, and various percussive effects; his tone-poems show a decisive Wagnerian influence, having a system of identification motifs. His most ambitious work was an orchestral tetralogy on Homer's *Odyssey,* under the general title *Odysseus' Fahrten,* comprising: *Odysseus' Ausfahrt und Schiffbruch* (Munich, Feb. 20, 1903; Philadelphia, Dec. 3, 1904), *Die Insel der Kirke, Die Klage der Nausikaa,* and *Odysseus' Heimkehr;* also the symph. poem *Taormina* (Essen, 1906; Boston Symph., Nov. 29, 1907); several songs with orch.; etc. —Cf. Edgar Istel, *Ernst Boehe* in 'Monographien moderner Musiker' (Leipzig, 1909).

Boehm. See **Böhm.**

Boehme. See **Böhme.**

Boekelman (boo'-kel-mahn), **Bernardus,** pianist; b. Utrecht, Holland, June 9, 1838; d. New York, Aug. 2, 1930. He studied with his father; and at the Leipzig Cons. with Moscheles, Richter, and Hauptmann. In 1864 he emigrated to Mexico; in 1866 settled in New York and then taught in various private schools. He published some piano pieces, edited the collection 'Century of Music.' His analytical edition of Bach's *Well-Tempered Clavichord* and 2-part *Inventions* in colors (to indicate part-writing) is unique.

Boëllmann, Léon, French composer; b. Ensisheim, Alsace, Sept. 25, 1862; d. Paris, Oct. 11, 1897. He studied organ with Gigout; later was organ teacher in Paris. He left 68 published works, of which his *Variations symphoniques* for cello and orch. became part of the repertory of cello players. He wrote a symphony, *Fantaisie dialoguée* for organ and orch.; *Suite gothique* for organ; piano quartet; piano trio; cello sonata; *Rapsodie carnavalesque* for piano 4 hands; published a collection of 100 pieces for organ under the title *Heures mystiques.* Bibl.: P. Locard, *L. Boëllmann* (Strasbourg, 1901).

Boëly, Alexandre Pierre François, French organist and composer; b. Versailles, April 19, 1785; d. Paris, Dec. 27, 1858. His father, a court musician, gave him his first instruction in music. Boëly studied piano and organ; occupied various positions as church organist in Paris. As a teacher he exercised a profound influence; Franck and Saint-Saëns owed much to him in the development of their style of organ writing. Bibl.: A. Gastoué, *A Great French Organist A. Boëly and His Works* in the 'Mus. Quarterly' (July, 1944); this article gives a list of works and a bibliography of the principal studies on Boëly.

Boelza, Igor, Russian composer and musicologist; b. Kielce, Poland, Feb. 8, 1904. He studied at the Kiev Cons.; taught there (1929-41). He was editor of the *Sovietskaya Musica* (1938-41); member of the board of the State Music Publishing House in Moscow (1941-48). He has written 5 symphonies, an overture, *Lyric Poem,* a piano concerto, an organ concerto, chamber music and songs. He published *Handbook of Soviet Musicians* (London, 1943); *Czech Opera Classics* (Moscow, 1951); *History of Polish Musical Culture* (Moscow, 1954).

Boepple, Paul, choral conductor and pedagogue; b. Basel, Switzerland, July 19, 1896. He studied at the Basel Univ.; then took courses at the Dalcroze Institute in Geneva, and adopted the Dalcroze system in his own teaching of music; was a member of the faculty of the Dalcroze Institute (1918-26). In 1926 he settled in the U. S.; was director of the Dalcroze School of Music in New York (1926-32); taught at the Chicago Musical College (1932-34) and at Westminster Choir School in Princeton (1935-38); in 1936 he assumed the direction of the Dessoff Choirs and the Motet Singers in New York. He conducted the world première of Honegger's *King David* in Switzerland (1921) and many other choral works of the modern school.

Boer (boor), **Coenrad Lodewijk Walther,** Dutch cellist; b. The Hague, Sept. 2, 1891. He studied at the Amsterdam Cons.; graduated with honors; in 1920 appointed instructor; has also conducted a military band; toured in Europe as a cellist. He has published several valuable papers on old music.

Boero, Felipe, Argentine opera composer; b. Buenos Aires, May 1, 1884. He studied with Pablo Berutti; received a government prize for further study in Europe and attended the classes of Vidal and Fauré at the Paris Cons. (1912-14). Returning to Buenos Aires he became active as a teacher. Among his operas the following were produced at the Teatro Colón: *Tucumán* (June 29, 1918); *Ariana y Dionisios* (Aug. 5, 1920); *Raquela* (June 25, 1923); *Las Bacantes* (Sept. 19, 1925); *El Matrero* (July 12, 1929) and *Siripo* (June 8, 1937).

Boers (boors), **Joseph Karel,** Dutch music scholar; b. Nimwegen, Aug. 4, 1812; d. Delft, Nov. 1, 1896. He was a pupil of Lübeck at The Hague Cons.; then was theater conductor in Holland and in France; in 1841 returned to Nimwegen as teacher and choral conductor; in 1853 settled in Delft as music director. He wrote an interesting *History of Musical Instruments in the Middle Ages;* also a complete bibliography of ancient and modern musical works produced in the Netherlands.

Boësset (bwĕhs-sā'), **Antoine, Sieur de Villedieu,** French composer; b. c. 1585; d. Paris, Dec. 8, 1643. He was court musician to Louis XIII; celebrated as the composer of many *Airs du cour* in 4 or 5 parts, published from 1617 to 1642; reprinted by H. Expert in 'Chants de France et d'Italie.'

Boetius (bō-ā'tĭ-us) (or **Boethius**), **Anicius Manlius Torquatus Severinus,** Roman philosopher and mathematician; b. Rome, c. 480 A.D.; executed in 524 on suspicion of treason, by the Emperor Theodoric, whose counsellor he had been for many years. Boetius wrote a treatise in 5 books, *De Institutione Musica,* which was the chief source book for the theorizing monks of the Middle Ages; this treatise was published at Venice (1491; 1499), at Basel (1570), at Leipzig (1867), and in a German translation by Oscar Paul (Leipzig, 1872); a French translation, by Fétis, remains in MS. Whether the notation commonly called 'Boetian" (using the letters A to P for the two octaves from our A to a') is properly attributable to him, has been questioned for about three centuries (cf. Meibom, *Antiquae musicae auctores septem;* page 7 of introduction on Alypius). For a defense of its authenticity, see F. Celentano, *La Musica presso i Romani* in 'Rivista musicale italiana' (1913). L. Schrade has written several essays on Boetius: *Das propädeutische Ethos in der Musikanschauung des Boetius* in 'Zeitschrift für Geschichte der Erziehung und des Unterrichts' (1930); *Die Stellung der Musik in der Philosophie des Boetius* in the 'Archiv für Geschichte der Philosophie' (1932); and *Music in the Philosophy of Boetius* in the 'Mus. Quarterly' (April, 1947).

Bogatyrev, Anatoly Vasilievitch, Russian composer; b. Vitebsk, Aug. 13, 1913. He studied at the Belorussian Cons. in Minsk with Zolotarev; became instructor there and finally was appointed director. Bogatyrev has written two patriotic operas, *In the Forests of Polesye* (Moscow, Aug. 28, 1939) and *Nadezhda Durova* (1947); two symphonies; the cantatas *White Russia* and *The Leningraders.* Many of his works are inspired by the folk music of Belorussia (White Russia).

Boghen, Felice, Italian music editor; b. Venice, Jan. 23, 1869; d. Florence, Jan. 25, 1945. He studied with Martucci, Sgambati and Wolf-Ferrari; conducted orchestral concerts and theatrical productions in many Italian cities; was director of the School of Music at Reggio Emilia, and later taught theory at the Royal Music Institute in Florence; was pianist of the 'Trio Fiorentino' (Boghen, Tignani, and Coen). He edited *Anciennes chansons de France; Fughe d'antichi Maestri italiani; Partite e Correnti;* and selected works of Nardini, Cimarosa, Frescobaldi, Porpora, Tartini, Pasquini, Alessandro Scarlatti, Bach, Clementi, Liszt, etc.; was co-author with Sgambati of *Appunti ed esempi per l'uso dei pedali del Pianoforte* (Milan, 1915); also published *L'Arte di Pasquini* (1931); numerous articles on piano playing and technique. He wrote an opera, *Alcestis,* which has never been performed; also composed some piano pieces.

Bohlmann, Theodor Heinrich Friedrich, pianist; b. Osterwieck, Germany, June 23, 1865; d. Memphis, Tenn., March 18, 1931. He was a pupil of Eugene d'Albert and Moszkowski; made his début in Berlin in 1890; in the same year he emigrated to America and settled in Cincinnati as a teacher.

Böhm, Georg, German organist; b. Hohenkirchen, Thuringia, Sept. 2, 1661; d. Lüneburg, May 18, 1733. He studied at the Univ. of Vienna (1684); was in Hamburg in 1693; became organist at the Johanneskirche in Lüneburg (1698). His organ preludes and harpsichord pieces rank high among keyboard works of the time; undoubtedly Bach was influenced by Böhm's style of writing. A complete edition of Böhm's works was begun by Johannes Wolgast; vol. I containing piano and organ works (Leipzig, 1927); vol. II, vocal works (Leipzig, 1932). Bibl.: J. Wolgast, *Georg Böhm* (Berlin, 1924); also R. Buchmayer, *Nachrichten über das Leben Georg Böhms* in 'Programm-Buch des 4. Bachfestes' (1908); W. Wolffheim, *Die Möllersche Handschrift* in 'Bach-Jahrbuch' (1912).

Böhm, Joseph, violinist; b. Budapest, March 4, 1795; d. Vienna, March 28, 1876. He was a pupil of his father; at eight years of age he made a concert tour to Poland and St. Petersburg, where he studied for some years under Pierre Rode. His first concert at Vienna (1815) was very successful; after a trip to Italy, he was appointed (1819) violin professor at the Vienna Cons.; retired in 1848. He formed many distinguished pupils, including Joachim, Ernst, Auer, Hellmesberger (Sr.), Rappoldi and others.

Bohm, Karl, German pianist; b. Berlin, Sept. 11, 1844; d. there, April 4, 1920. He studied with Löschhorn; lived most of his life in Berlin. He wrote a number of piano pieces in the salon genre; also songs, of which *Still wie die Nacht* became popular.

Böhm, Karl, German conductor and music director; b. Graz, Aug. 28, 1894. He was a pupil of Eusebius Mandyczewski in Vienna; also studied law. His successful career as a conductor has included engagements at Graz (1917), the Munich Staatsoper (1921), Darmstadt (1927), Hamburg (1931), the Dresden State Opera (1934-43), the Vienna State Opera (1943-45); from 1945-54 he was guest conductor at various European opera houses; in 1954 assumed the directorship of the Vienna State Opera, but the pressure of other engagements forced him to resign in March 1956. He made his first appearance in America with the Chicago Symph. Orch., Feb. 9, 1956.

Böhm, Theobald, German flutist and inventor of the 'Böhm flute'; b. Munich, April 9, 1794; d. there, Nov. 25, 1881. He was the son of a goldsmith and learned mechanics in his father's workshop; studied flute playing, achieving a degree of virtuosity that made him one of the greatest flute players of his time; he was appointed court musician in 1818; gave concerts in Paris and London. His system of construction marks a new departure in the making of woodwind intruments. To render the flute acoustically perfect, he fixed the position and size of the holes so as to obtain, not convenience in fingering, but purity and fullness of tone; all holes are covered by keys, whereby prompt and accurate 'speaking' is assured; and the bore is modified, rendering the tone much fuller and mellower. Böhm published *Über den Flötenbau und die neuesten Verbesserungen desselben* (Mainz, 1847; English transl. by W. S. Broadwood, London, 1882); *Die Flöte und das Flötenspiel* (Munich, 1871). Cf. Charles Welch, *History of the Boehm Flute* (London, 1883); V. Mahillon, *Etude sur le doigté de la flûte Boehm* (1885); R. Rockstro, *A Treatise on the Construction, the History and the Practice of the Flute* (London, 1890).

Böhme, Franz Magnus, German writer on music; b. Willerstedt, near Weimar, March 11, 1827; d. Dresden, Oct. 18, 1898. He was a pupil of Hauptmann and Rietz at Leipzig; taught at Dresden (1859-78) and at the Hoch Cons. in Frankfurt (1878-85); spent the remaining years of his life in Dresden. Writings: *Das Oratorium, eine historische Studie* (Leipzig, 1861; revised ed., Gütersloh, 1887, under the title *Geschichte des Oratoriums*); *Altdeutsches Liederbuch,* a collection of German folksongs of the 12th to 17th centuries (Leipzig, 1877; later eds. 1913 and 1925); *Aufgaben zum Studium der Harmonie* (Mainz, 1880); *Kursus in Harmonie* (Mainz, 1882); *Geschichte des Tanzes in Deutschland* (2 vols., Leipzig, 1886); *Volkstümliche Lieder der Deutschen im 18. und 19. Jahrhundert* (Leipzig, 1895); *Deutsches Kinderlied und Kinderspiel* (1897). He edited Erk's *Deutscher Liederhort* (3 vols., 1893-94; new ed., 1925); also published several books of sacred songs and male choruses.

Bohn, Emil, German music bibliographer; b. Bielau, near Neisse, Jan. 14, 1839; d. Breslau, July 5, 1909. He studied philology at Breslau, and then music; was organist of the Breslau Kreuzkirche and founder (1881) of the Bohn Choral Society; was professor at the Univ. of Breslau, and music critic of the 'Breslauer Zeitung' (from 1884). Publications: *Bibliographie der Musikdruckwerke bis 1700, welche auf der*

Stadtbibliothek . . . zu Breslau aufbewahrt werden (1883); *Die musikalischen Handschriften des 16. und 17. Jahrhunderts in der Stadtbibliothek zu Breslau* (1890); *Die Nationalhymnen der europäischen Völker* (1908); edited piano works of Mendelssohn and Chopin. He also published the annotated chronicle of his choral society: *Bohn'scher Gesangverein; 100 historische Konzerte in Breslau* (1905).

Bohn, Peter, German organist and teacher; b. Bausendorf, Nov. 22, 1833; d. Trier, June 11, 1925. He was organist and teacher at Trier from 1852-1905; prepared German translations of Franco's *Ars cantus mensurabilis* (1880); *Dialogus de musica* of Odo de Clugny (1880); Glareanus' *Dodecachordon* (2 vols., 1888-89); and *Der Einfluss des tonischen Akzents auf die melodische und rhythmische Struktur der gregorianischen Psalmodie* (from 'Paléographie musicale,' Solesmes, 1894); also published *Das liturgische Rezitativ und dessen Bezeichnung in den liturgischen Büchern des Mittelalters* (1887) and *Philipp von Vitry* (1890).

Bohnen, Michael, German bass singer; b. Keulen, Jan. 23, 1886. He studied at the Keulen Cons.; made his début at Düsseldorf (1910); sang at the Berlin State Opera (1912) and at the Bayreuth Festival (1914); made guest appearances in London, Vienna, Barcelona, Stockholm and Buenos Aires; made his American début at the Metropolitan Opera as Francesco in *Mona Lisa* (March 1, 1923); created the leading part in the American performance of Krenek's *Jonny spielt auf* (Jan. 19, 1929); remained with the Metropolitan Opera until 1933; from 1934-45 was with the Berlin Opera.

Böhner, Ludwig, German composer; b. Töttelstedt, Gotha, Jan. 8, 1787; d. there, March 28, 1860. He studied with his father and with Johann Christian Kittel, a pupil of Bach. Having achieved considerable fame as pianist and composer, he failed to establish himself socially and economically, owing to his personal eccentricities. He wandered through Germany, often on foot, and worked irregularly as theatrical conductor and concert pianist. The claim he advanced that other composers plagiarized him, is supported by the fact that Weber had unintentionally borrowed one of the themes in *Der Freischütz* from Böhner's piano concerto. Böhner's life and character are understood to have inspired the figure of the eccentric genius, Kreisler, in E. T. A. Hoffmann's *Capellmeister Kreisler,* and by the same token Schumann's *Kreisleriana.* —Cf. K. F. Bolt, *J. L. Böhner. Leben und Werk* (Hildburghausen, 1940).

Bohnke, Emil, viola player and composer; b. Zdunska Wola, Poland, Oct. 11, 1888; d. Pasewalk, Pomerania, May 11, 1928 (in an automobile accident, en route from Berlin to Swinemunde). He studied at the Leipzig Cons.; then was violist in various chamber music groups. He wrote a violin concerto, a piano trio, a string quartet, and several violin sonatas.

Boieldieu (bwăhl-dyö'), **François-Adrien,** celebrated French opera composer; b. Rouen, Dec. 16, 1775; d. Jarcy, near Grosbois, Oct. 8, 1834. His father was a functionary who at one time served as secretary to Archbishop Larochefoucauld; his mother had a millinery shop; the family was fairly prosperous until the Revolution; the parents were divorced in 1794. Young Boieldieu received excellent instruction from Charles Broche, organist and pupil of Padre Martini; stories of Broche's brutality and of Boieldieu's flight to Paris are fabrications not supported by any evidence. At the age of fifteen, Boieldieu became assistant organist to Broche at the church of St. André in Rouen. He began to compose piano pieces and songs; he was only 17 when his first opera *La fille coupable* (to his father's libretto) was successfully produced in Rouen (Nov. 2, 1793). The boy adapted himself to the revolutionary conditions, and composed patriotic works which were then in demand. His *Chant populaire pour la Fête de la Raison* for chorus and orch. was presented at the Temple of Reason (former cathedral) in Rouen on Nov. 30, 1793. His second opera, *Rosalie et Myrza* was produced in Rouen on Oct. 28, 1795. In August 1796 he set out for Paris where he was befriended by the composer Louis Jadin, and was accepted in the salon of the piano manufacturer Erard; he met Cherubini and Méhul; with the tenor Garat he made a tour of Normandy, revisiting Rouen. The material success of this tour was so satisfactory that Boieldieu was able to pay off all his debts. In Paris he found a publisher who printed some of his songs *(Le Ménestrel, S'il est vrai que d'être deux,* etc.), and piano sonatas (a complete edition of these sonatas was republished by G. Favre in 2 albums, 1944-1945). Boieldieu produced one opera after another at the Paris theaters: *La famille suisse* (Feb. 11, 1797); *La dôt de Suzette* (Sept. 5, 1797); *Zoraine et Zulnare* (May 10, 1798). As a sign of his growing recognition, Boieldieu was appointed prof. of piano at the Paris Cons. in 1798. His opera *Beniowski* was produced (June 8, 1800) with moderate success; but *Le Calife de Bagdad* (Sept. 16, 1801) received tremendous acclaim, and became one of Boieldieu's most enduring operas. On March 19, 1802, he married the dancer Clotilde Mafleurai, but her dissolute character made the marriage a failure. His opera *Ma tante Aurore* was produced on Jan. 13, 1803. In the meantime, Boieldieu received an invitation from Russia, and left in Oct., 1803 for St. Petersburg, his wife remaining in Paris. His contract guaranteed him a handsome salary of 4,000 rubles annually, his duties being to write operas for the Imperial theaters and supervise music at the court. The quality of his music written during his sojourn in Russia was not of the highest; the opera *La jeune femme colère* (St. Petersburg, April 18, 1805) was the most successful. A vaudeville, *Les Voitures versées* (St. Petersburg, Dec. 4, 1806) was revised and produced in Paris (April 29, 1820) as a comic opera with considerable success. Other operas staged in St. Petersburg were *Aline, reine de Golconde* (1804); *Un tour de soubrette; Abderkan* (1805); *Télémaque dans l'isle de Calypso* (Dec. 28, 1806); *La dame invisible* (1803); music to Racine's *Athalie* (1808) and *Rien de trop ou les deux paravents* (Dec. 25, 1810). In 1811, Boieldieu asked the Russian government to release him from further employment (despite his raise in salary to 5,000 rubles) and returned to Paris. His first act was to petition for a divorce, which was, however, rejected by the authorities. His estranged wife died in 1826, and a few weeks later Boieldieu married the singer Jenny Phillis, whom he had known in Russia. Once in Paris, Boieldieu arranged a revival of *Ma tante Aurore* and the first Paris production of *Rien de trop*. He regained the favor of the public with *Jean de Paris* (April 4, 1812) which achieved instant popularity. His next operas were *Le nouveau seigneur de village* 1813); *La fête du village voisin* (March 5, 1816), and *Le petit chaperon rouge* (June 30, 1818; highly successful). In 1817 he was appointed professor of composition at the Paris Conservatory; resigned in 1826. In 1821 he was created Chevalier of the Legion of Honor. The culmination of his highly successful career was reached with the production of his great masterpiece *La dame blanche* (Dec. 10, 1825), which was hailed by the public and the press as the French answer and challenge to Rossini's rising fame in the operatic field. *La dame blanche* had 1000 performances in Paris alone from 1825 to 1862, and nearly 1700 performances before 1914; it also had numerous productions all over the world. At the height of his success, Boieldieu developed the first signs of a lung disease; his health deteriorated; a trip to Italy (1832) brought no improvement. His pecuniary circumstances were affected. Although he was offered his old position at the Cons., he could not teach because of his loss of voice. In 1833 he received a grant of 6,000 francs from the government of Louis Philippe, and retired to his country house at Jarcy, where he died. During the last years of his life he became interested in painting; his pictures, showing his considerable talent as a landscape artist, are preserved in the municipal museum at Rouen. Among his pupils were Fétis, Adam and Zimmerman. The historical position of Boieldieu is of great importance; he was one of the creators of French comic opera; he possessed melodic inventiveness and harmonic grace; in addition to facility in composition, he largely succeeded in attaining perfection of form and fine dramatic balance. Adopting the best devices of Italian operatic art, he nevertheless cultivated the French style which laid the foundation for the brilliant progress of French opera in the 19th century. Boieldieu wrote 40 operas in all, of which 8 are lost; he also collaborated with Cherubini in *La Prisonnière* (1799); with Méhul, Kreutzer and others in *Le Baiser et la quittance* (1803); with Cherubini, Catel and Isouard in *Bayard à Mézières;* with Kreutzer in *Les Béarnais, ou Henry IV en voyage* (1814); with Mme. Gail, pupil of Fétis, in *Angéla, ou L'Atelier de Jean Cousin* (1814); with Hérold in *Charles de France, ou Amour et gloire* (1816); with Cherubini, Berton and others in *Blanche de Provence, ou La Cour des Fées* (1821); with Auber in *Les trois Genres* (1824); with Berton and others in *La Marquise de Brinvilliers* (1831). His natural son, **Adrien-Louis-Victor** (b. Paris, Nov. 3, 1815; d. there, July 9, 1883; his mother was Thérèse Regnault, a singer) was also a composer; he wrote 2 operas: *Marguerite* (which had been sketched out but left incomplete by his father) and *L'Aïeule*. —Bibl.: G. Héquet, *A. Boieldieu, sa vie et ses œuvres* (Paris, 1864); A. Pougin, *Boieldieu, sa vie es ses œuvres* (Paris, 1875); E. Neukomm, *Trois jours à Rouen, Souvenirs du centenaire de Boieldieu* (Paris, 1875); H. de Thannberg, *Le Centenaire de Boieldieu, anecdotes et souvenirs* (Paris, 1875); E. Duval, *Boieldieu, notes et fragments inédits* (1883); P. L. Robert, *Correspondance de Boieldieu,* in 'Rivista Musicale Italiana' (XIX and XXII; also separately,

Rouen, 1916); G. de Saint-Foix, *Les premiers pianistes parisiens: Boieldieu,* in 'La Revue musicale' (Paris, Feb., 1926); G. Favre, *La danseuse Clotilde Mafleurai, première femme d'Adrien Boieldieu,* in 'La Revue musicale' (Jan., 1940); G. Favre, *Boieldieu, sa vie, son œuvre* (part I, Paris, 1944; part II, Paris, 1945; an exhaustive work on the subject). See also F. Clément and Larousse, *Dictionnaire des opéras* (Paris, 1906); L. Augé de Lassus, *Boieldieu,* in the series 'Les Musiciens célèbres' (Paris, 1908; contains catalogue of works); and Alfred Loewenberg, *Annals of Opera* (Cambridge, 1943; 2nd ed., 1955).

Boisdeffre (bwăh-def'fr), **Charles-Henri-René de,** French composer; b. Vesoul (Haute-Savoie), April 3, 1838; d. at his estate, Vézelise, Nov. 25, 1906. He studied with Ch. Wagner and Barbereau in Paris where he lived most of his life. He excelled in chamber music, for which he received the Prix Chartier in 1883. Many of his works have been published; among them, 3 piano sextets; 2 piano quintets; piano quartet; 3 piano trios; 2 violin sonatas; clarinet sonata; several suites for violin and piano (*Suite poétique, Suite romantique, Suite orientale,* etc.); oratorios, a symphony, etc. His style reflects the facile school of French romantic composers.

Boise, Otis Bardwell, American organist; b. Oberlin, Ohio, Aug. 13, 1844; d. Baltimore, Dec. 2, 1912. He studied with Moscheles and Richter in Leipzig and with Kullak in Berlin. Returning to America in 1865, he occupied various posts as organist and teacher; eventually settled in Baltimore, where he taught at the Peabody Cons. Among his pupils were Ernest Hutcheson, Howard Brockway and Arthur Nevin. He publ. the textbooks *Harmony Made Practical* (N. Y., 1900) and *Music and its Masters* (N. Y., 1902).

Boito (bo'ē-toh), **Arrigo,** Italian poet and opera composer; b. Padua, Feb. 24, 1842; d. Milan, June 10, 1918. He studied at the Milan Cons. with Alberto Mazzucato and Ronchetti-Monteviti; his two cantatas, written in collaboration with Faccio, *Il 4 Giugno* (1860) and *Le Sorelle d'Italia* (1862) were performed at the Cons., and attracted a great deal of favorable attention; as a result, the Italian government granted the composers a gold medal and a stipend for foreign travel for two years. Boito spent most of his time in Paris, and also went to Poland to meet the family of his mother (who was Polish); he also visited Germany, Belgium, and England. He was strongly influenced by hearing new French and German music; upon his return to Milan he undertook the composition of his first and most significant large opera *Mefistofele,* which contains elements of conventional Italian opera, but also dramatic ideas stemming from Beethoven and Wagner. It was performed for the first time at La Scala (March 5, 1868). A controversy followed when a part of the audience objected to the unusual treatment of the subject and the music, and there were actual disorders at the conclusion of the performance. After the second production, the opera was taken off the boards, and Boito undertook a revision to effect a compromise. In this new version, the opera had a successful run in Italian cities; it was produced in Hamburg (1880); in London (in Italian) on July 6, 1880, and (in English) in Boston, on Nov. 16, 1880. It was retained in the repertory of the leading opera houses but its success never matched that of Gounod's *Faust.* Boito never completed his second opera *Nerone,* the composition of which took him more than half a century, from 1862 until 1916. The orchestral score was revised by Toscanini, and performed by him at La Scala on May 2, 1924. There are sketches for an earlier opera *Ero e Leandro,* but not enough material to attempt a completion. Boito's gift as a poet is fully equal to that as a composer. He publ. a book of verses (Turin, 1877) under the anagrammatic pen name of Tobia Gorrio; he wrote his own libretti for his operas and made admirable translations of Wagner's operas *(Tristan und Isolde, Rienzi);* wrote the libretti of *Otello* and *Falstaff* for Verdi (these libretti are regarded as his masterpieces); also for *Gioconda* by Ponchielli; *Amleto* by Faccio, etc. Boito also publ. novels. He held various honorary titles from the King of Italy; in 1892 he was appointed Inspector-General of Italian conservatories; was made honorary Mus. Doc. by Cambridge Univ. and Oxford Univ.; in 1912 he was made senator by the King of Italy. Bibl.: P. G. Molmenti, *Impressioni letterarie* (Milan, 1875); A. Boccardi, *Arrigo Boito* (Trieste, 1877); D. Mantovani, *Letteratura contemporanea* (Turin, 1893); R. Giani, *Il Nerone di A. Boito* (Turin, 1901); R. Barbiera, *A. Boito, inverso l'ideale* (Milan, 1905); M. Risolo, *Il primo Mefistofele di A. Boito* (Naples, 1916); C. Trevor, *Boito's Nero* ('Mus. Times,' June, 1916); A. Lualdi, *A. Boito, un' anima* ('Rivista Musicale Italiana,' 1919); A. Pompeati, *A. Boito* (Florence, 1919); C. Ricci, *A. Boito* (Milan, 1919); F. Torrefranca, *A. Boito* ('La Critica Musicale,' Nov.-Dec., 1919); F. Torrefranca, *A. Boito* in the 'Mus.

Quarterly' (Oct., 1920); G. M. Gatti, *Boito's Nero* in the 'Mus. Quarterly' (Oct., 1924); V. Gui, *Il Nerone di Arrigo Boito* (Milan, 1924); A. Bonaventura, *A. Boito; Mefistofele* (Milan, 1924); G. Cesari, *Note per una bibliografia delle opere di A. Boito,* in 'Rassegna di Coltura' (March, 1924); R. de Rensis, *Franco Faccio e Boito, documento* (Milan, 1934); F. Ballo, *A. Boito* (Turin, 1938); R. de Rensis, *A. Boito; aneddoti e bizzarrie poetiche e musicali* (Rome, 1942); P. Nardi, *Vita di Arrigo Boito* (Verona, 1942; 2nd ed., Milan, 1944; complete documented biography); Massimiliano Vajro, *Arrigo Boito* (Brescia, 1955). Boito's letters were edited by R. de Rensis (Rome, 1932), who also edited Boito's articles on music (Milan, 1931).

Bolck, Oskar, German composer; b. Hohenstein, March 4, 1837; d. Bremen, May 2, 1888. He studied at the Leipzig Cons. with Rietz and Moscheles; was active as theater conductor in various German towns and, as teacher, at Riga, where his opera *Pierre und Robin* was produced (1876). He wrote 2 other operas, *Gudrun* and *Der Schmied von Gretna Green,* both of which remain unperformed.

Bologna, Jacopo da. See **Jacopo.**

Bölsche, Franz, German music editor; b. Wegenstedt, near Magdeburg, Aug. 20, 1869; d. Bad Oeynhausen, Oct. 23, 1935. He studied with Bargiel and Spitta in Berlin; became teacher of theory at the Cologne Cons. (1896-1931). He was an editor for the 'Denkmäler deutscher Tonkunst', and wrote the successful manual *Übungen und Aufgaben zum Studium der Harmonielehre* (Leipzig, 1911; 18th ed., 1938). Also composed a symphony, 4 overtures (*Tragödie der Menschen, Judith, Hero und Leander, Othello*), etc.

Bolzoni, Giovanni, Italian composer; b. Parma, May 14, 1841; d. Turin, Feb. 21, 1919. He studied at the Parma Cons.; was active as conductor in Perugia; director of the Liceo Musicale and theater conductor in Turin (1887). He composed the operas *Il Matrimonio civile* (Parma, 1870), *La Stella delle Alpi* (Savona, 1876), *Jella* (Piacenza, 1881); etc. A melodious minuet from one of his string quartets became a perennial favorite in numerous arrangements.

Bomtempo, João Domingos, Portuguese pianist; b. Lisbon, Dec. 28, 1775; d. there, Aug. 18, 1842. He studied in Paris; lived there and in London until 1815 when he returned to Lisbon. He founded a Philharmonic Society in Lisbon; in 1833 became director of the Lisbon Cons. He wrote 6 symphonies, 4 piano concertos, 14 piano sextets, a piano quintet, and several piano sonatas; also an opera *Alessandro in Efesso.* He publ. a piano method (London, 1816). Bibl.: M.A. de Lima Cruz, *D. Bomtempo* (Lisbon, 1937).

Bona, Giovanni, cardinal; b. Mondovi, Oct. 12, 1609; d. Rome, Oct. 25, 1674. His tract *De divina psalmodia . . . tractatus historicus, symbolicus, asceticus* (Rome, 1653) contains valuable information on church music. A complete edition of his works was publ. in Rome in 1747.

Bona (or **Buona**), **Valerio,** Italian composer; b. Brescia, c. 1560; date of death unknown, but he was still living in 1619. He was a Franciscan monk; maestro di cappella at the cathedrals of Vercelli (1591) and Mondovi, and at the Church of San Francesco, Milan (1596); musician at St. Francesco, Brescia (1611) and prefect at St. Fermo Maggiore, Verona (1614). He was a prolific composer in polyphonic style of sacred and secular vocal music (masses, litanies, lamentations, motets, madrigals, etc.), for much of which he used two choirs. Also a theorist, he publ. *Regole del contrapunto, et compositione brevemente raccolte da diuersi auttori . . .* (Casale, 1595); *Esempii delli passagi delle Consonanze, et Dissonanze, . . .* (Milan 1596); etc.

Bonanni, Filippo, Italian writer on music; b. Rome, Jan. 16, 1638; d. there, March 30, 1725. He was the author of the renowned manual *Gabinetto armonico pieno d'instromenti sonori, indicati, spiegati e di nuovo corretti ed accresciuti* (Rome, 1723, with 151 plates; 2nd ed. Rome, 1776).

Bonaventura, Arnaldo, Italian musicologist; b. Leghorn, July 28, 1862; d. Florence, Oct. 7, 1952. He studied law, violin and theory, but made musicology his career. He was prof. of history of music and librarian at the Royal Institute of Music until 1932; then became director of the Cons. and prof. of Music History and Esthetics. Writings: *Manuale di storia della musica* (Leghorn, 1898; 10th ed., 1920); *Elementi di Estetica musicale* (Leghorn, 1905; 3rd ed. 1926 as *Manuale di Estetica musicale*); *Dante e la musica* (Leghorn, 1904); *Storia degli stromenti musicali* (Leghorn, 1908; many other eds.); *La vita musicale in Toscana* (Florence, 1910, in 'La Toscana al fine del Granducato'); *Niccolo Paganini* (1911; 3rd ed., 1925); *Saggio storico sul teatro musicale italiano* (Leghorn, 1913); *Storia e* *letteratura del pianoforte* (Leghorn, 1918); *I violinisti italiani moderni; Verdi* (Paris, 1923); *Bernardo Pasquini* (Rome, 1923); *Giacomo Puccini* (Leghorn, 1923); *Manuale di cultura musicale* (1924); *'Mefistofele' di Boito* (Milan, 1924); *Storia del violino, dei violinisti e della musica per violino* (Milan, 1925); *L'opera italiana* (1928); *Domenico del Mela* (1928); *Luigi Boccherini* (1931); *Musicisti livornesi* (1931); *Rossini* (1934); numerous essays in various journals. He was editor of works of J. Peri, B. Strozzi, Frescobaldi, da Firenze and others.

Bonavia, Ferruccio, critic and composer; b. Trieste, Feb. 20, 1877; d. London, Feb. 5, 1950. He studied music in Trieste and Milan; went to England as a violinist (1898); became music critic of the 'Manchester Guardian' and of the London 'Daily Telegraph'. His compositions include a one-act opera, violin concerto, string octet, string quartet, songs, etc. He wrote a monograph on Verdi (London, 1930; 2nd ed., 1947); miniature biographies of Mozart (1938) and Rossini (1941); also a fanciful book of imaginary conversations, *Musicians in Elysium* (1949).

Bonawitz (or **Bonewitz**), **Johann Heinrich,** German pianist and composer; b. Dürkheim-on-Rhine, Dec. 4, 1839; d. London, Aug. 15, 1917. He studied at the Liège Cons. until 1852, when his parents took him to America; from 1872-73, conducted the Popular Symphony Concerts in New York, an enterprise that failed owing to lack of popular appreciation; then produced 2 operas in Philadelphia, *The Bride of Messina* (1874) and *Ostrolenka* (1875). In 1876, he returned to Europe and lived in Vienna and London. He composed 2 other operas, *Irma* (1885) and *Napoleon;* a Requiem; a Stabat Mater a cappella; orchestral works; piano music; etc. He also edited 'Historische Klaviermusik' (including selections from Frescobaldi, Froberger, Couperin, Rameau, Marcello and others).

Bonci (bon'-tchē), **Alessandro,** Italian lyric tenor; b. Cesena (Romagna), Feb. 10, 1870; d. Viserba (near Rimini), Aug. 8, 1940. He studied with Carlo Pedrotti in Pesaro; made his début in 1896 at the Teatro Regio in Parma as Fenton in *Falstaff;* then sang at La Scala, and at St. Petersburg, Vienna, Berlin, Lisbon, Madrid, London, etc; later made appearances in South America and Australia. In Dec., 1906, he made his New York début at the new Manhattan Opera House, where he was engaged for three seasons; made his début at the Metropolitan Opera as the Duke in *Rigoletto* (Nov. 22, 1907); was on the staff for three seasons. Later he made guest appearances at many European opera houses, and after his retirement taught voice privately in Milan. His was a lyric tenor of great charm, and he was one of the few Italian artists to achieve distinction as a singer of German lieder.

Bond, Carrie Jacobs, American composer of sentimental songs; b. Janesville, Wis., Aug. 11, 1862; d. Hollywood, Dec. 28, 1946. From her childhood she was interested in music and painting, and improvised many songs to her own words. Because of the refusal of publishers to print her songs, she established her own printing press. Although deficient in musical training and technique, she succeeded in producing melodies with suitable accompaniment that became extremely popular; her first song *A Perfect Day* sold an enormous number of copies. Other songs are: *I Love You Truly, God Remembers When the World Forgets, Life's Garden,* etc. She published an autobiography *The Roads of Melody* (1927); also *The End of the Road* (an album of her poems, with philosophical comments).

Bondeville, Emmanuel de, French composer; b. Rouen, Oct. 29, 1898. He studied organ in Rouen, and composition in Paris with Jean Déré. He was music director of the Eiffel Tower Radio Station (1935-49); managing director of the Opéra-Comique from 1949 to 1952; then joined the administration of the Grand Opéra. His works include 2 operas, both produced at the Opéra-Comique: *L'École des Maris* (June 19, 1935) and *Madame Bovary* (June 1, 1951); a symph. triptych to poems from Rimbaud's *Illuminations: Le Bal des pendus* (Paris, Dec. 6, 1930), *Ophélie* (Paris, March 29, 1933; also many performances abroad) and *Marine* (Paris, March 11, 1934); choral works and songs.

Bonelli, Richard (real name Bunn), American baritone; b. Port Byron, N. Y., Feb. 6, 1894. He studied at Syracuse Univ., later with Jean de Reszke; made his operatic début as Valentine in *Faust* at the Brooklyn Academy of Music, N. Y., April 21, 1915; then sang in Europe at the Monte Carlo Opera, at La Scala, in Paris (with Mary Garden) and on tours throughout Germany. He was a member of the Chicago Opera (1925-31) and of the Metropolitan Opera (début as Germont in *Traviata,* Dec. 1, 1932); retired in 1945.

Bonis, Mélanie (Mme. Albert Domange), French composer; b. Paris, Jan. 21, 1858;

d. Sarcelles (Seine-et-Oise) March 18, 1937. She studied at the Paris Cons. with César Franck and Guiraud; wrote 22 chamber music works (of which a Trio is still performed); 150 piano pieces; 27 choruses; also a Fantasy for piano and string orch. About 200 of her works are published.

Bonnet (bohn-nā'), **Joseph**, eminent French organist; b. Bordeaux, March 17, 1884; d. Ste. Luce-sur-Mer, Quebec, Aug. 2, 1944. He studied with his father, organist at Ste. Eulalie; his progress was so rapid that at fourteen he was appointed regular organist at St. Nicholas, and soon after at St. Michel; entered the class of Guilmant at the Paris Cons. and graduated with the first prize. In 1906 he won the post of organist at St. Eustache over many competitors. After extensive tours on the continent and in England, he became organist of the Coscerts du Conservatoire as successor to Guilmant (1911). He made his American début in New York (Jan. 30, 1917), followed by successful tours of the United States. He was one of the outstanding organists of his time; was president of the Institut Grégorien. He wrote many pieces for his instrument, and edited for publication all the works played in his series of New York concerts as 'Historical Organ Recitals' (6 vols.; G. Schirmer); also publ. an anthology of early French organ music (N. Y., 1942). —Cf. H. B. Gaul, *Bonnet, Bossi, Karg-Elert. Three Aperçus,* in the 'Mus. Quarterly' (July, 1918).

Bononcini (bo-non-chē'-nē), **Antonio Maria** (not Marco Antonio as he is often listed), Italian opera composer, son of Giovanni Maria and brother of Giovanni; b. Modena, June 18, 1677; d. there, July 8, 1726. He studied with his father; his first success came with the production of his opera *Il trionfo di Camilla, regina dei Volsci* (Naples, Dec. 26, 1696). This opera was produced in many other theaters in Italy, sometimes under different titles, as *Amore per amore, La fede in cimento,* etc. It was presented in London (March 31, 1706) with great acclaim. In 1702 Bononcini was in Berlin; from 1704-1711 he was in Vienna where he produced the operas *Teraspo* (Nov. 15, 1704); *Arminio* (July 26, 1706); *La conquista delle Spagne di Scipione Africano* (Oct. 1, 1707); *La presa di Tebe* (Oct. 1, 1708); *Tigrane, re d'Armenia* (July 26, 1710). Returning to Italy, he produced the following operas in Milan: *Il tiranno eroe* (Dec. 26, 1715); *Sesostri, re di Egitto* (Feb. 2, 1716); and *Griselda* (Dec. 26, 1718). In his native town of Modena, he directed his operas *L'enigma disciolto* (Oct. 15, 1716); *Lucio Vero* (Nov. 5, 1716). Bononcini's last opera, *Rosiclea in Dania,* was staged in Naples (Oct. 1, 1721). He wrote 19 operas in all, and 3 oratorios. His most famous opera, *Il trionfo di Camilla,* has often been erroneously attributed to his brother; several songs from it were published in London by Walsh. See L. F. Valdrighi, *I Bononcini da Modena* (Modena, 1882); for details of his operatic productions see Loewenberg's *Annals of Opera* (1943; 2nd ed., 1955).

Bononcini, Giovanni (not Giovanni **Battista**, despite the fact that this name appears on some of his compositions), the most celebrated Italian composer of the Bononcini family; son of Giovanni Maria; b. Modena, July 18, 1670; d. Vienna, July 9, 1747 (buried July 11). His first teacher was his father; also studied with G. P. Colonna in Bologna, and took lessons from Giorgio in cello playing. In 1687 he was a cellist in the chapel of San Petronio, Bologna; in the same year he became maestro di cappella at San Giovanni, in Monte. He published his first work *Trattenimenti da camera* for string trio in Bologna at the age of fifteen, followed in quick succession by a set of chamber concertos, 'sinfonie' for small ensembles, Masses, and instrumental duos (1685-91). In 1691 he went to Rome, where he produced his first opera *Serse* (Jan. 25, 1694), and shortly afterwards, another opera *Tullo Ostilio* (Feb., 1694). In 1698 he went to Vienna as court composer; there he brought out his operas *La fede pubblica* (Jan. 6, 1699) and *Gli affetti più grandi vinti dal più giusto* (July 26, 1701). He spent two years (1702-04) at the court of Queen Sophie Charlotte in Berlin; at her palace in Charlottenburg he produced, in the summer of 1702, the opera *Polifemo;* here he also presented a new opera *Gli amori di Cefalo e Procri* (Oct. 16, 1704). After the Queen's death (Feb. 1, 1705), the opera company was disbanded, and Bononcini returned to Vienna, and staged the following operas: *Endimione* (July 10, 1706); *Turno Aricino* (July 26, 1707); *Mario fuggitivo* (1708); *Abdolonimo* (Feb. 3, 1709) and *Muzio Scevola* (July 10, 1710). In 1711 Bononcini returned to Italy with his brother (who was also in Vienna). In 1719 he was in Rome where he produced the opera *Erminia.* In 1720 he received an invitation to join the Royal Academy of Music in London, of which Handel was director, and the Italian Opera Company connected with it. A famous rivalry developed between the supporters of Handel, which included the King, and the group of noblemen (Marlborough, Queensberry, Rutland, and Sunderland) who favored Bononcini and other Italian composers. Indicative of the spirit of the time was the production at the King's Theater of the opera *Muzio Scevola* with the first act written by Amadei, the second by Bononcini (he may have used material from his earlier setting of the same subject), and the third by Handel (April 15, 1721). By general agreement Handel won the verdict of popular approval; this episode may have inspired the well known poem published at the time ("Some say, compar'd to Bononcini, That Mynheer Handel's but a ninny, etc."). Other operas brought out by Bononcini in London were: *Astarto* (Nov. 19, 1720); *Crispo* (Jan. 10, 1722); *Farnace* (Nov. 27, 1723); *Calpurnia* (April 18, 1724) and *Astianatte* (May 6, 1727). Bononcini soon suffered a series of setbacks, first with the death of his chief supporter, Marlborough (1722), and then with the revelation that a madrigal he had submitted to the Academy of Music was an arrangement of a work by Lotti, which put Bononcini's professional integrity in doubt. To this was added his strange association with one Count Ughi, a self-styled alchemist who claimed the invention of a philosopher's stone, and who induced Bononcini to invest his earnings in his scheme for making gold. After his London debacle, Bononcini went to Paris where he was engaged as a cellist at the court of Louis XV. He was referred to in 'Le Mercure de France' (Feb. 7, 1735) as the composer of 78 operas. In 1735 he was in Lisbon; in 1737, in Vienna where he produced the oratorio *Ezechia* (April 4, 1737) and a *Te Deum* (1740). Reduced to poverty, he petitioned the young Empress Maria Theresa for a pension, which was granted in Oct. 1742, giving him a monthly stipend of 50 florins, which he received regularly until his death on July 9, 1747 at the age of 77. This date, and the circumstances of his last years in Vienna, were first made known in the valuable paper by Kurt Hueber, *Gli ultimi anni di Giovanni Bononcini — Notizie e documenti inediti,* publ. by the Academy of Sciences, Letters and Arts of Modena (Dec., 1954). Among Bononcini's works, other than operas, are 7 oratorios (including *Ezechia;* all on various biblical subjects); and instrumental works published in London by Walsh: several suites for harpsichord; *Cantate e Duetti,* dedicated to George I (1721); Divertimenti for harpsichord (1722); *Funeral Anthem for John, Duke of Marlborough* (1722); *12 sonatas or chamber airs for 2 violins and a bass* (1732), etc. For further details regarding Bononcini's operas see Loewenberg's *Annals of Opera* (1943; 2nd ed., 1955).

Bononcini, Giovanni Maria, Italian composer; father of Giovanni and Antonio Maria Bononcini; b. Montecorone (Modena), Sept. 23, 1642; d. Modena, Oct. 19, 1678. He studied with Colonna in Bologna; as a very young man, he entered the service of Duke Francesco II, and was maestro di cappella at the churches of San Giovanni in Monte and San Petronio in Bologna. In 1668 he became a member of the celebrated Accademia Filarmonica there; then he returned to Modena; in 1671 he was a violinist in the court orchestra there; in 1674 was maestro di cappella at the Cathedral of Monte (Modena). He had 8 children, of whom the only two who survived infancy were Giovanni and Antonio Maria (q.v.). Bononcini published 11 sets of instrumental works: *I primi frutti del giardino musicale* (Venice, 1666); *Varii fiori* (Bologna, 1669); *Arie, correnti, sarabande, gighe e allemande* (Bologna, 1671); *Sinfonia, allemande, correnti e sarabande* (Bologna, 1671); *Sonate* (Venice, 1672); *Ariette, correnti, gighe, allemande e sarabande* (Bologna, 1673); *Trattenimenti musicali* (Bologna, 1675); *Arie e correnti* (Bologna, 1678); also vocal works: *Cantate da camara* for solo voice and 2 violins (Bologna, 1677); *Madrigali* for 5 voices (Bologna, 1678); and a treatise *Musico prattico* (Bologna, 1673; reprinted in 1688; a German translation was publ. in Stuttgart, 1701).

Bonporti, Francesco Antonio, Italian composer; b. Trento (baptized June 11), 1672; d. Padua, Dec. 19, 1749. He studied theology in Innsbruck and Rome; in 1695 returned to Trento; was ordained priest and served as a cleric at the Cathedral of Trento. He publ. 3 sets of 10 trio-sonatas each (Venice, 1696, 1698 and 1703); 10 sonatas for violin and bass (Venice, 1707); 10 'concerti a 4' and 5 'concertini' for violin and bass; 6 motets for soprano, violin and bass. He also wrote 2 sets of minuets (50 in each set) which are lost. Four of his 'Invenzioni' were mistaken for Bach's works and were included in the 'Bachgesellschaft' edition (XLV, part 1, p. 172). Henry Eccles publ. the fourth of these pieces as his own, incorporating it in his violin sonata No. 11. Bibl.: G. Barblan, *Un musicista trentino, F. A. Bonporti* (Florence, 1940); Ch. Bouvet, *Un groupe de compositions musicales de Bonporti publiées sous le nom de Bach,* in the bulletin of 'Union Musicologique' (The Hague, 1921).

Bontempi, Giovanni Andrea (real name Angelini), Italian composer and writer on music; b. Perugia, c. 1624; d. Castle of Bruso, Perugia, June 1, 1705. He was a choir boy at San Marco in Venice (1643); studied with Virgilio Mazzocchi; was maestro di cappella in Rome; then in Venice. He assumed the name Bontempi after his patron, Cesare Bontempi. In 1650 he entered the service of Johann Georg I of Saxony; in 1651 became head of the court chapel in Dresden; in 1680 he returned to Italy. His opera *Paride* (to his own libretto; Dresden, Nov. 3, 1662) was the first Italian opera produced in Dresden. Two later operas, both produced in Dresden, were *Apollo e Dafne* (in collaboration with Perandis; 1672) and *Giove e Io* (also with Perandis; 1673). He also composed an oratorio, *Martirio di San Emiliano;* published the treatises *Nova quatuor vocibus componendi methodus . . .* (Dresden, 1660); *Tractus in quo demonstrantur occultae convenientiae sonorum systematis participati* (Bologna, 1690); *Historia musica, nella quale si ha piena cognitione della teorica e della pratica antica della musica harmonica secondo la dottrina de' Greci . . .* (Perugia, 1695). Cf. G. B. Rossi Scotti, *Di Giovanni Andrea Bontempi di Perugia* (1878).

Bonvin (bŏhn-văn), **Ludwig,** choral conductor and scholar; b. Siders, Switzerland, Feb. 17, 1850; d. Buffalo, Feb. 18, 1939. His musical training in early youth was irregular; as a musician he was chiefly self-taught; studied medicine in Vienna; entered the Jesuit novitiate in Holland (1874), where he became organist and choirmaster; continued his musical studies, especially of early sacred works. He settled in Buffalo, N. Y., as a choral and orchestral director at Canisius College (1887-1907); then devoted himself exclusively to music scholarship; promulgated a theory of mensural rhythm in Gregorian chant. He published much sacred music, including 8 Masses; also a symphony; *Christmas Night's Dream* for string orch.; many pieces for organ, piano, violin, and voice; his works exceed 125 opus numbers. Writings: *Gregorian Accompaniment* in 'Musica sacra' (1931 and 1932); *Musical Accents in Gregorian Chant* (1932); *On Syrian Liturgical Chant* in the 'Mus. Quarterly' (Oct., 1918); *The 'Measure' in Gregorian Music* in the 'Mus. Quarterly' (Jan., 1929); etc. Cf. F. E. Bunse, *Ludwig Bonvin,* in 'Musica sacra' (Jan., 1933).

Boom, Jan (Johannes) van, Dutch pianist and composer; b. Utrecht, Oct. 15, 1807; d. Stockholm, March 19, 1872. He began his career as a concert pianist at the age of 18; after a tour in Scandinavia, he settled in Stockholm, where he taught at the Royal Academy (1849-65). He composed piano pieces of the salon type.

Boosey & Hawkes, British music publishers. Thomas Boosey was a London bookseller and a continental traveller since 1792. He was often asked to handle music, and in 1816 founded a music publishing house on Holles Street. On the continent he met eminent musicians of the time; he visited Vienna and negotiated about publication with Beethoven (who mentions Boosey's name in one of his letters to the Royal Philh. Society in London). Boosey's main stock consisted of Italian and French operas; he owned copyrights of Bellini, Donizetti and Verdi (until 1854); publ. inexpensive English editions of standard European works. In the 1820's he put his son, Thomas, in charge of musical publications. In 1846 the firm of Boosey & Sons began publishing band music; in 1855 (in conjunction with the flutist R. S. Pratten) the manufacture of improved flutes was begun; in 1868 the firm acquired Henry Distin's factory for musical instruments, and supplied band instruments for the British and Colonial armies. It was this development that eventually brought about the merger of Boosey and Hawkes. William Henry Hawkes was a trumpeter-in-ordinary to Queen Victoria. He established in 1865 a workshop of band instruments and an edition of concert music for orchestra and became a strong competitor of Boosey & Sons from 1885 on. Economic pressure forced the amalgamation of the two firms in 1930, combining valuable editions covering a whole century of music. A branch of Boosey & Sons had been established in New York (1892), discontinued in 1900 and re-established in 1906; after the merger, Boosey & Hawkes opened offices in New York, Chicago, and Los Angeles. In Canada, the business was inaugurated in 1913; the Editions Hawkes started a Paris branch in 1922; further affiliates were established in Australia (1933), India (1937), Argentine (1945), South Africa (1946), and Germany (1950). After World War II the factories for the manufacture of band instruments in London were greatly expanded; quantity production of wind instruments, harmonicas and drums enabled the firm to extend the market to all parts of the world. For a few years after World War II Boosey & Hawkes leased Covent Garden. In 1927 the firm acquired the American rights of Enoch & Sons; in 1943 the catalogue of Adolph Fürstner, containing all the operas of Richard Strauss, was bought for certain territories.

In 1947, the Koussevitzky catalogue (Edition Russe de Musique and Edition Gutheil) was purchased, including the major output of Stravinsky, Prokofiev and Rachmaninoff. Other acquisitions include the copyrights of publications of Winthrop Rogers and Rudall Carte.

Boott, Francis, American composer; b. Boston, Mass., June 24, 1813; d. there, March 2, 1904. He was educated at Harvard (grad., 1831); lived for a time in Florence, Italy, where he studied music; returned to the U. S. in 1874, settling in Cambridge, Mass. He bequeathed to Harvard Univ. the sum of $10,000, the interest to form an annual prize for the best 4-part vocal composition written by a Harvard man. He was a prolific composer of secular and sacred songs, anthems, and chorales, many of which were included in the service book of King's Chapel, Boston. His songs *Here's a health to King Charles, When Sylvia sings,* and *Lethe* were once very popular.

Bopp, Wilhelm, German conductor and pedagogue; b. Mannheim, Nov. 4, 1863; d. Baden-Baden, June 11, 1931. He studied at the Leipzig Cons.; also took courses in conducting with Emil Paur at Mannheim; was teacher at the Mannheim Cons.; in 1907 moved to Vienna, where he became director of the Conservatorium der Musikfreunde.

Borch, Gaston Louis Christopher, composer and conductor; b. Guines, France, March 8, 1871; d. Stockholm, Sweden, Feb. 14, 1926. He studied in Paris with Massenet (comp.) and Delsart (cello); then with Svendsen in Copenhagen; conducted various organizations in Norway (1896-99); came to the U. S. in 1899 as cellist with the Thomas Orch. in Chicago; then played in the Pittsburgh Orch. (1903-06); conducted various orchestras in Switzerland, France, Belgium, Holland, and Germany. He composed 3 symph. poems: *Geneviève de Paris, Quo Vadis,* and *Frithjof;* made popular arrangements of standard classics for piano, violin, and cello. His one-act opera, *Silvio* (written as a sequel to *Cavalleria Rusticana*) was produced in Oslo, 1897. He published a *Practical Manual of Instrumentation* (Boston, 1918).

Borchard (bohr-shahr'), **Adolphe,** French pianist and composer; b. Le Havre, June 30, 1882. He studied at the Paris Cons. with Diémer and Lenepveu, where he won prizes for piano (1903) and composition (1905; 1907); toured extensively as a pianist, making his American début in 1910; later settled in Paris as director of various musical activities sponsored by the French government. He composed *Es Kual Herria (The Basque Country)* for piano and orch. (Paris, 1922); *En Marge de Shakespeare* for orch. (1923); *L'Élan* for orch. (1923); *Sept estampes amoureuses* for orch. (1927); numerous songs.

Borchers, Gustav, German vocal teacher; b. at Woltwiesche (Brunswick), Aug. 18, 1865; d. Leipzig, Jan. 19, 1913. He studied at the Leipzig Cons. (1887-89); then conducted various choral societies; in 1898 he founded a seminary for singing teachers, which later employed the methods of Jaques-Dalcroze ('rhythmical gymnastics') and Eitz ('Tonwort'); Borchers published a monograph on the 'Tonwort' theory (1908).

Borck, Edmund von, talented German composer; b. Breslau, Feb. 22, 1906; killed in action near Nettuno, Italy, Feb. 16, 1944. He studied composition in Breslau (1920-26), and music history at the Univ. of Berlin; held several positions as opera conductor in Berlin and Frankfurt; then taught theory and composition in Berlin, until he was drafted into the Army in 1940. His progress as a composer was rapid; his early works indicated an original creative ability, and his death in combat was a great loss to German music. His style of composition is neo-classical, with strong contrapuntal structure; the rather austere and reticent mode of expression assumes in Borck's music a colorful aspect through a variety of melodic and rhythmic devices, often in a rhapsodically romantic vein. Works: concerto for alto saxophone and orch. (1932); violin sonata (1932); *Orchesterstücke* (1933); *Ländliche Kantate* (1934); concerto for orch. (1936); sextet for flute and strings (1936); *Kleine Suite* for unaccompanied flute (1938); *2 Fantasiestücke* for orch. (1940); piano concerto (1941); *Orphika,* 'an Apollonian transformation' for orch. (1941); an opera *Napoleon* (Gera, 1942). Bibl.: K. Laux, *Edmund von Borck* in *Musik und Musiker der Gegenwart* (Essen, 1949); S. Borris, *Beiträge zu einer Musikkunde* (Berlin, 1948); K. H. Wörner, *Musik der Gegenwart* (Mainz, 1949).

Borde, de la. See **Laborde.**

Bordes (bohrd), **Charles,** French choral conductor; b. Roche-Corbon, near Vouvray-sur-Loire, May 12, 1863; d. Toulon, Nov. 8, 1909. He studied piano with Marmontel; organ and composition with César Franck (1887-90). In 1890 he became maître de chapelle at St.-Gervais in Paris; in 1892 he established the 'Association des chanteurs de St.-Gervais' and presented with his church choir a series of regular concerts of French and Italian Renaissance music. In 1894, in association with Guilmant and d' Indy, he organized the Schola Cantorum, originally for the purpose of training singers in the Palestrina style; at the same time he founded the 'Tribune de St.-Gervais' as the official organ of the Schola Cantorum; the first issue appeared in Jan., 1895. In 1898 Bordes made a tour of France with his choir. In 1899 he founded a Schola Cantorum in Avignon; in 1905 he organized the 'Schola de Montpellier.' His influence on musical culture in France, particularly in the field of old choral music, was considerable; in his numerous articles in French newspapers and magazines, and particularly in 'La Grande Encyclopédie,' he disclosed profound scholarship. Bordes also took interest in folk music; in 1889 he was commissioned by the French government to make a study of Basque folksongs; he published 100 of these in 'Archives de la tradition basque.' Compositions: *Suite basque* for flute and string quartet (1888); *Danses béarnaises* (1888); *Rapsodie basque* for piano and orch. (1890); *Divertissement* for trumpet and orch. (1902); an opera *Les trois vagues* (unfinished; MS in the library of the Paris Opéra); numerous arrangements of Basque songs. He edited several anthologies of old French music, published by the Schola Cantorum. Bibl.: O. Séré, *Charles Bordes* in *Musiciens français d'aujourd'hui* (Paris, 1921); articles in the Aug. 1924 issue of 'La Revue musicale' (Paul Dukas, *Charles Bordes;* G. Samazeuilh, *Un Drame basque de Charles Bordes;* also a catalogue of works); F. P. Albert, *Charles Bordes à Maguelonne* (Paris, 1926); René de Castera, *La fondation de la Schola Cantorum* in 'La Schola cantorum en 1925.' See also *Charles Bordes, In memoriam* (Paris, Schola Cantorum, 1909).

Bordes-Pène, Léontine Marie, French pianist; b. Lorient, Nov. 25, 1858; d. Rouen, Jan. 24, 1924. She graduated with the first prize at the Paris Cons. in 1872; dedicated her concert career to propagandizing French music; she was the sister-in-law of Charles Bordes, and a friend of César Franck, Vincent d'Indy, etc. She suffered a paralytic stroke in 1890, and lived the rest of her life in Rouen. See G. Samazeuilh, *Madame Bordes-Pène* in 'La Revue musicale' (1924).

Bordier (bohr-d'yā'), **Jules,** French composer; b. Angers, Aug. 23, 1846; d. Paris, Jan. 29, 1896. He founded the concerts of the 'Association Artistique d'Angers' in 1875; went to Paris (1894) as partner in the music publishing house of Baudoux & Cie. He composed a *Danse macabre* for violin; the operas *Nadia* (Brussels, 1887) and *Le Fiancé de la Mer* (Rouen, 1895); choruses.

Bordogni, Giovanni Marco, distinguished Italian tenor and singing teacher; b. Gazzaniga, near Bergamo, Jan. 23, 1789; d. Paris, July 31, 1856. He was a pupil of Simone Mayr; made his début at La Scala, Milan, in 1813. From 1819-33 he was engaged at the Théâtre des Italiens, Paris; later devoted himself to teaching. From 1820 (with occasional interruptions) he was prof. at the Paris. Cons. His 36 vocalises, in 2 suites, have run through many editions; he also published several other sets.

Bordoni, Faustina. See **Hasse, Faustina.**

Borel-Clerc (real name, Clerc), **Charles,** French composer of popular music; b. Pau, Sept. 22, 1879. He studied music at first in Toulouse; at the age of 17 he went to Paris, where he studied the oboe at the Paris Cons. with Gillet, and composition with Lenepveu; then played oboe in various Paris orchestras. He wrote numerous operettas, music revues, and a great number of songs; his greatest success came with *La Matchiche* (1903), a song that became world-famous. His other celebrated songs are *C'est jeune et ça n'sait pas*; *Madelon de la Victoire* (1918; a sequel to the war song *Madelon* by Camille Robert); many chansonnettes for Maurice Chevalier and other artists.

Borgatti, Giuseppe, Italian tenor; b. Cento, March 19, 1871; d. Reno, Lago Maggiore, Oct. 18, 1950. He studied with Alessandro Busi in Bologna. He was engaged at La Scala in Milan and was particularly successful in Wagnerian roles. At the end of his career he became blind, but continued teaching activities.

Borgatti, Renata, Italian pianist, daughter of the tenor Giuseppe Borgatti; b. Bologna, March 2, 1894. She studied in Bologna and Munich; has appeared as soloist with major orchestras in Europe; has given programs of complete works of Debussy; also played all of Bach's *Well-tempered Clavichord* over the B.B.C. network in London. After World War II she taught in Switzerland and Italy.

Borge, Victor (real name, Borge Rosenbaum), Danish pianist; b. Copenhagen, Jan. 3, 1909. He studied with his father, Bernhard Rosenbaum (1847-1932); then with V. Schioler. He developed a type of humorous piano concerts *sui generis* and appeared in Danish musical revues. In 1940, he settled in the U.S. and became extremely successful in his specialty on the radio and in television; in the autumn of 1953 he opened a series of daily recitals on Broadway, billed as "comedy in music," which ran for two and a half seasons, unprecedented in New York theatrical annals for a one-man show. In 1956 he gave similar exhibitions in the largest auditoriums in other U. S. cities.

Borghi, Adelaide, Italian mezzo-soprano; b. Bologna, Aug. 9, 1829; d. there, Sept. 28, 1901. Acting on the advice of Pasta, she trained herself for the stage; made her début at Urbino (1846) in Mercadante's *Il Guiramento;* toured through Italy and to Vienna and Paris (1854-6); sang with the Grand Opéra in Paris (1856-9); appeared in London with great success (1860); then returned to Italy.

Borgioli, Dino, Italian stage-tenor, b. Florence, Feb. 15, 1891. He made his début at the Teatro dal Verme, Milan, in 1918; then sang leading parts in various Italian opera houses, at Covent Garden Opera, London, and in Spain; in 1924 he joined Mme. Melba on her farewell tour of Australia; was then a member of La Scala, Milan, for several years; appeared in the U. S. from 1928-30. Later he settled in London as a vocal teacher.

Borgström, Hjalmar, Norwegian critic and composer; b. Oslo, March 23, 1864; d. there, July 5, 1925. He studied with Ursin, Svendsen and Lindeman; also at Leipzig, Berlin, Paris and London. In 1901 he returned to Oslo; was music critic of the 'Aftenposten' from 1913. He wrote 2 operas, *Thora fra Rimol* and *Fiskeren;* 2 symphonies; symphonic poems *Hamlet, Jesus in Gethsemane, John Gabriel Borkman, Tanken; Reformation Cantata,* violin and piano concertos, chamber music, piano pieces, songs.

Bori, Lucrezia (real name, Lucrecia Borja y Gonzalez de Riancho), lyric soprano, b. Valencia, Dec. 24, 1887. She studied with Melchior Vidal; made her début in Rome on Oct. 31, 1908, as Micaëla; then sang in Milan, Naples, and in 1910 in Paris as Manon Lescaut, with the Metropolitan Opera Co., then on a European tour. In 1911 she sang at La Scala; in 1912, filled the first of numerous engagements with the Ravinia Opera Co., Chicago; made her début at the Metropolitan Opera House in New York as Manon Lescaut on Nov. 11, 1912, and sang there until the end of the season 1914-15. Her first outstanding success was as Fiora in the American première of Montemezzi's *L'Amore dei Tre Re* (Jan. 2, 1914). After a period of retirement, occasioned by a vocal affliction, she reappeared in 1919 at Monte Carlo as Mimi, returning to the Metropolitan in 1921 in the same role. Thereafter she appeared in New York with increasing success and popularity until the end of the 1935-36 season, when she retired permanently from opera. One of the greatest artistic triumphs of her career was her poetic delineation of the heroine of Debussy's *Pelléas et Mélisande,* which was given at the Metropolitan in 1925 (with Edward Johnson as Pelléas). She created the role of the Duchess of Towers in Deems Taylor's *Peter Ibbetson* (1931), and appeared in the American premières of Wolf-Ferrari's *L'Amore medico* (1914); Leoni's *L'Oracolo* (1915), etc. Besides her artistic contributions, she took an active part in raising funds to guarantee the continuance of the Metropolitan Opera after the financial collapse of 1929; in 1935, appointed member of the Board of Directors of the Metropolitan Opera Association.

Bořkovec, Pavel, Czech composer; b. Prague, June 10, 1894. He studied composition with J. Krička and J. B. Foerster, and later with J. Suk at the Prague Cons. (1925-27). In 1946 he became prof. at the new Academy of Musical Art in Prague. Among his works are the operas *The Satyr* (1937; Prague, Oct. 8, 1942) and *Tom Thumb* (1945-47); a pantomime, *The Rat-Catcher* (1939); a symphony (1926); a romantic tone poem *Twilight* (1920) and the modernistic symphonic allegro entitled *Start* (Liège Festival of the International Society for Contemporary Music, Sept. 6, 1930); *Sinfonietta* for chamber orch. (1944); 2 piano concertos, a violin concerto, a cello concerto, a nonet, 4 string quartets, violin sonata, piano pieces, songs, etc.

Borland, John Ernest, English organist and writer on music; b. London, March 6, 1866; d. there, May 15, 1937. He was educated at Queen's College, Oxford, and at the Royal College of Music, London, and subsequently held positions as organist and music director at numerous churches. He was editor of 'Musical News' (1895-1902) and musical advisor for the London County Council (1908-27); also prepared the music for the coronations of Edward VII, George V and George VI. His writings include *The Instruments of the Orchestra* and *Musical Foundations.*

Bornschein, Franz Carl, American composer; b. Baltimore, Feb. 10, 1879; d. there, June 8, 1948. He studied at the Peabody Cons. in Baltimore (1895-1902), and became teacher of violin and conductor of the student orchestra there in 1906. In subsequent years he was music critic of the Baltimore 'Evening Sun' (1910-13) and was active as choral conductor; also served as editor for several American publishing houses. His works include *The Phantom Canoe,* Indian suite for orch. (Baltimore, Nov. 24, 1916); *Onowa,* a cantata (1916); *The Sea God's Daughter,* symph. poem (Chicago, Feb. 10, 1924); *Old Louisiana,* symph. poem (1930); *The Willow Plate,* operetta (1932); *Leif Ericson,* symph. poem (Baltimore, Feb. 23, 1936); *Southern Nights,* symph. poem (Washington, March 1, 1936); *Moon over Taos* for flute, percussion, and string orch. (1939); some chamber music and vocal compositions.

Borodin (boh-roh-dēn'), **Alexander Porfirievitch,** celebrated Russian composer; b. St. Petersburg, Nov. 11, 1833; d. there, Feb. 27, 1887. He was the illegitimate son of a Georgian prince, Ghedeanov; his mother was the wife of an army doctor. In accordance with customary procedure in such cases, the child was registered as the lawful son of one of Ghedeanov's serfs, Porfiry Borodin; hence, the patronymic, Alexander Porfirievitch. He was given an excellent education; learned several foreign languages, and was taught to play the flute. He played four-hand arrangements of Haydn's and Beethoven's symphonies with his musical friend M. Shtchiglev. At the age of 14 he tried his hand at composition; wrote a piece for flute and piano and a string trio on themes from *Robert le Diable.* In 1850 he became a student of the Academy of Medicine in St. Petersburg, and developed a great interest in chemistry; he graduated in 1856 with honors, and joined the staff as assistant prof.; in 1858 received his doctorate in chemistry; contributed several important scientific papers to the bulletin of the Russian Academy of Sciences; traveled abroad on a scientific mission (1859-62). Although mainly preoccupied with his scientific pursuits, Borodin continued to compose. In 1863 he married Catherine Protopopova, who was an accomplished pianist; she remained his faithful companion and musical partner; together they attended concerts and operas in Russia and abroad; his letters to her from Germany (1877), describing his visit to Liszt in Weimar, are of great interest. Of a decisive influence on Borodin's progress as composer was his meeting with Balakirev in 1862; later he formed friendships with the critic Stassov, who named Borodin as one of the 'mighty Five' (actually, Stassov used the expression 'mighty heap'), with Mussorgsky, and other musicians of the Russian National School. He adopted a style of composition in conformity with their new ideas; he particularly excelled in a type of Russian orientalism which exercised a great attraction on Russian musicians at the time. He never became a consummate craftsman, like Rimsky-Korsakov; although quite proficient in counterpoint, he avoided purely contrapuntal writing; his feeling for rhythm and orchestral color was extraordinary; and his evocation of exotic scenes in his orchestral works and in his opera *Prince Igor* was superb. Composition was a very slow process for Borodin; several of his works remained incomplete, and were edited after his death by Rimsky-Korsakov and Glazunov. Works: *Prince Igor,* opera in 4 acts (begun in 1869, on the subject of the famous Russian medieval chronicle *Tale of Igor's Campaign;* completed posthumously by Rimsky-Korsakov and Glazunov; 1st perf. St. Petersburg, Nov. 4, 1890; London, June 8, 1914, in Russian; New York, Dec. 30, 1915, in Italian); an opera-farce *Bogatyry (The Valiant Knights,* anonymously produced in Moscow on Oct. 29, 1867; rediscovered in 1932, and produced in Moscow, Nov. 12, 1936, with a new libretto by Demian Biedny, to serve propaganda purposes in an anti-religious campaign, but two days later banned by the Soviet government for its mockery of Russian nationalism); sketches for the 4th act of an opera *Mlada,* each act of which was to be written by a different composer (never produced). Orchestral works: Symph. No. 1 in E (1862-67; St. Petersburg, Jan. 16, 1869); Symph. No. 2 in B minor (1869-76; St. Petersburg, March 10, 1877); Symph. No. 3 in A minor (1885-86; unfinished; two movements orchestrated by Glazunov); symph. sketch *In the Steppes of Central Asia* (1880); *Polovtzian Dances* from *Prince Igor* (perf. as an orchestral piece, St. Petersburg, March 11, 1879). Chamber music: String quartet No. 1 in A (1877-79); String quartet No. 2 in D (1881-87); *Serenata alla Spagnola,* 3rd movement of a quartet on the name B-la-f, by Borodin, Rimsky-Korsakov, Liadov, and Glazunov (1886); Scherzo for string quartet, in the collective set *Les Vendredis.* A string trio (dated 1860) and a piano quintet were discovered in 1915. For piano: *Polka, Requiem, Marche funèbre,* and *Mazurka* (posthumous) in the series of paraphrases on the theme of the *Chopsticks Waltz* (includes variations by Borodin, other members of the Russian school, and Liszt; 1880); *Petite Suite* comprising 7 pieces (*Au couvent, Intermezzo, Deux mazurkas, Rêverie, Sérénade, Nocturne;* 1885). Vocal works: *Sérénade de 4 galants à une dame* for a cappella male quartet (comical; no date); and the songs *Sleeping Princess* (1867), *The Princess of the Sea, The Song of the Dark Forest, The False Note, My Songs are full of venom* (1867-68), *The Sea* (1870), *From my tears* (1873), *For the shores of your distant country* (1881), *Conceit* (1884), *Arabian Melody* (1885), and *The Wondrous Garden* (1885). Bibl.: V. Stassov, *A. Borodin* (St. Petersburg, 1882; French transl. by A. Habets, in 2 vols., Paris, 1893); Rosa Newmarch, *Borodin and Liszt* (London, 1895); E. Braudo, *Borodin* (Moscow, 1922); W. Kahl, *Die russischen Novatoren und Borodin* in 'Die Musik' (1923); G. Abraham, *Borodin, the Composer and His Music* (London, 1927); 2 vols. of Borodin's letters, edited by S. Dianin (Moscow, 1928, 1936); G. Abraham, *Prince Igor: An Experiment in Lyrical Opera* in the 'Mus. Quarterly' (Jan., 1931); M. Rinaldi, *Borodin,* in 'Musica d'oggi' (1933); G. Khubov, *Borodin* (Moscow, 1933); N. Rimsky-Korsakov, *Memoirs of My Musical Life* (3rd to 5th eds., with preface and notes by A. Rimsky-Korsakov; Moscow, 1932-35); Y. Kremlev, *Borodin* (Leningrad, 1934); G. Abraham, *Studies in Russian Music* (London, 1935); M. D. Calvocoressi and G. Abraham, *Masters of Russian Music* (London and N. Y., 1936); D. Brook, *Six Great Russian Composers* (London, 1946); M. Ilyin and E. Segal, *Borodin* (Moscow, 1953); S. Dianin, *Borodin* (Moscow, 1955).

Borovsky, Alexander, Russian-American pianist; b. Mitau, March 18, 1889. He first studied with his mother (a pupil of Safonov), then with A. Essipova at the St. Petersburg Cons., winning the Rubinstein Prize in 1912. He taught master classes at the Moscow Cons. from 1915-20; then went to Turkey, Germany, France and England and gave a number of piano recitals; was soloist with virtually all major European orchestras; he also made several successful tours in South America. In 1941 he settled in the U. S. and became prof. of Boston Univ. (1956). Borovsky is distinguished by his objective intrepretation of classical and romantic works; his playing of Bach is notable for its architectural quality.

Borowski, Felix, composer and critic, b. Burton, England, March 10, 1872; d. Chicago, Sept. 6, 1956. He studied violin with his father, a Polish émigré; took lessons with various teachers in London, and at the Cologne Cons.; then taught in Aberdeen, Scotland. His early *Russian Sonata* was praised by Grieg; this provided impetus to his progress as a composer. In 1897 he accepted a teaching engagement at the Chicago Musical College; was its president from 1916-25. Subsequently he became active in musical journalism; in 1942 was appointed music editor of the 'Chicago Sun'; also served as program annotator for the Chicago Symph. Orch., beginning in 1908. For 5 years he taught musicology at Northwestern Univ. (1937-42). Among his many musical works, the violin piece entitled *Adoration* became widely popular. Other works: *Boudour,* ballet-pantomime (Chicago, Nov. 25, 1919); *Pierrot in Arcady,* ballet-pantomime (1920); *A Century of the Dance,* ballet (Chicago, 1934); *Fernando del Nonsensico,* satiric opera (1935); piano concerto (Chicago, 1914); *Allegro de Concert* for organ and orch. (Chicago, 1915); *Élégie symphonique* (Chicago, 1917); *Peintures* for orch. (Chicago, Jan. 25, 1918); *Le Printemps passionné,* symph. poem (Chicago North Shore Festival, Evanston, Ill., 1920); *Youth,* fantasy-overture (Chicago North Shore Festival, Evanston, Ill., May 30, 1923); *Ecce Homo,* symph. poem (New York, Jan. 2, 1924); *Semiramis,* symph. poem (Chicago, Nov. 13, 1925); *Overture to a Pantomime* for chamber orch. (Chicago, 1925); *Rhapsody* for organ and chamber orch. (Chicago, 1926); 3 symphonies (I, Chicago, 1933; II, Los Angeles, 1936; III, Chicago, 1939); *The Little Match Girl* (after Andersen), for narrator and orch. (1943); *Requiem for a Child* (1944); *The Mirror,* symph. poem (Chicago Symph. Orch., Jan. 5, 1956); 3 string quartets; many pieces for violin, organ, and piano; songs. Borowski revised G. P. Upton's *The Standard Operas* in 1928, and *The Standard Concert Guide* in 1930; in 1936 the two works were publ. in a single volume entitled *The Standard Opera and Concert Guide.*

Borras de Palau, Juan, Catalan writer on music; b. Barcelona, Sept. 24, 1868; d. there, Jan. 29, 1953. He was a lawyer by profession; published numerous songs, some of which became popular; was for more than 50 years music critic of the 'Correo Catalan.'

Borresen, Hakon, Danish composer; b. Copenhagen, June 2, 1876. He studied with

Svendsen; was awarded the Ancker scholarship for competition in 1901. He was president of the Danish Composers Society from 1924-49. Borresen's compositions include the operas *Den Kongelige Gaest* (Copenhagen, Nov. 15, 1919) and *Kaddara* (Copenhagen, March 16, 1921); a ballet *Tycho Brahes Dröm* (*Tycho Brahe's Dream,* Copenhagen, March 1, 1924); 3 symphonies; a violin concerto; chamber music; piano works; songs.

Borris, Siegfried, German composer; b. Berlin, Nov. 4, 1906. He studied composition with Hindemith; musicology with Schering; in 1945 was appointed instructor at the Musikhochschule in Berlin. He has composed the radio operas *Hans im Glück* (1947) and *Hirotas und Gerlinde* (1948); also orchestral suites, a wind quintet, a string quartet, and many piano pieces; published the book *Einführung in die moderne Musik* (Halle, 1950). He is married to the Dutch singer Condoo Kerdyk.

Bortkiewicz (bohrt-kye'-vēch), **Sergei Eduardovitch,** Russian pianist and composer; b. Kharkov, Feb. 28, 1877; d. Vienna, Oct. 25, 1952. He was a pupil of Liadov at the St. Petersburg Cons. (1896-9); later studied with Jadassohn in Leipzig. He made his début as a pianist in Munich, in 1902, and subsequently made concert tours of Germany, Australia, Hungary, France, and Russia. From 1904-14, he lived in Berlin, and taught at the Klindworth-Scharwenka Cons.; then went back to Russia; was in Vienna from 1920-29; in Berlin from 1929-34; and again in Vienna after 1934. His compositions include an opera, *Acrobats;* 2 symphonies; *Austrian Suite* and *Yugoslav Suite* for orch.; 4 piano concertos; violin concerto; cello concerto; piano pieces; songs. He was the author of the book *Die seltsame Liebe Peter Tschaikowskys und der Nadezhda von Meck* (1938).

Bortniansky, Dimitri Stepanovitch, Russian composer; b. Glukhov, Ukraine, 1751; d. St. Petersburg, Oct. 7, 1825. He was a choirboy in the court chapel, where he attracted the attention of Galuppi, who was at the time conductor there; was sent to Italy where he studied with Galuppi and with other Italian masters in Venice, Bologna, Rome, and Naples (1769-79). In Italy Bortniansky produced his operas *Creonte* (Venice, 1776) and *Quinto Fabio* (Modena, 1779). In 1779 he returned to St. Petersburg and became director of vocal music at the court chapel (1796); as a conductor of the chapel choir he introduced radical reforms for improvement of singing standards; composed for his choir a number of sacred works of high quality, among them a Mass according to the Greek Orthodox ritual; 35 sacred concerti in 4 parts; 10 psalms in 8 parts; 10 concerti for double choir, etc. He also continued to compose for the stage; produced the comic operas in French, *Le Faucon* (Gatchina, Oct. 22, 1786) and *Le Fils rival* (Pavlovsk, Oct. 22, 1787). His sacred choral works are published in 10 vols., edited by Tchaikovsky. Bibl.: N. Findeisen, *History of Russian Music* (1929; vol. 2, pp. 260-76).

Borwick, Leonard, English pianist; b. Walthamstow, Feb. 26, 1868; d. Le Mans, France, Sept. 15, 1925. He studied with Clara Schumann in Frankfurt; made his début there (1889); then in London (May 8, 1889); made a concert tour in America and Australia (1911); also played in Europe. His programs included classics and moderns; in the last years of his career he played much music of Debussy and Ravel; made a transcription for piano of Debussy's *L'après-midi d'un faune.* See H. Plunket Greene, *L. Borwick* in 'Music & Letters' (1926).

Bos, Coenraad Valentyn, Dutch pianist and noted accompanist; b. Leiden, Dec. 7, 1875; d. Chappaqua, N. Y., Aug. 5, 1955. He was a pupil of Julius Röntgen at the Amsterdam Cons. (1892-95); later studied in Berlin. With two other countrymen, Jan van Veen (violin) and Jan van Lier (cello), he formed a trio in Berlin which enjoyed an enviable reputation during its active perod (1896-1910). His masterly accompaniments on a tour with Ludwig Wüllner attracted more than ordinary attention, and made him one of the most celebrated accompanists both in Europe and the U. S., where he eventually settled. He was the accompanist of Julia Culp, Frieda Hempel, Helen Traubel, Fritz Kreisler, Ernestine Schumann-Heink, Pablo Casals, Elena Gerhard, Jacques Thibaud, Geraldine Farrar, and many others. He taught at the Juilliard School of Music from 1934-52; published (in collaboration with Ashley Pettis) a book *The Well-Tempered Accompanist* (1949).

Boschot (boh-shoh'), **Adolphe,** French author and critic; b. Fontenay-sous-Bois, near Paris, May 4, 1871; d. Paris, June 1, 1955. He was music critic of 'Echo de Paris' from 1910; of 'Revue Bleue' from 1919; founded, with Théodore de Wyzewa, the Paris Mozart Society; was elected to the Institut de France in 1926, succeeding Widor as permanent secretary of the Académie des Beaux-Arts. His greatest work is an exhaustive biography of Berlioz in 3 volumes: *La Jeunesse d'un romantique, Hector Berlioz, 1803-31* (Paris, 1906); *Un Romantique sous Louis-Philippe, Hector Berlioz, 1831-42* (Paris, 1908); and *Crépuscule d'un romantique, Hector Berlioz, 1842-69* (Paris, 1913). For this work Boschot received a prize of the Académie. Other books are: *Le Faust de Berlioz* (1910; new ed. 1945); *Carnet d'art* (1911); *Une vie romantique, Hector Berlioz* (an abridgement of his 3 vol. work, 1919; 27th ed., 1951; also in English); *Chez les musiciens* (3 vols., 1922-26); *Entretiens sur la beauté* (1927); *La lumière de Mozart* (1928); *Le mystère musical* (1929); *La musique et la vie* (2 vols., 1931-33); *Théophile Gautier* (1933); *Mozart* (1935); *La vie et les œuvres d'Alfred Bruneau* (1937); *Musiciens-Poètes* (1937); *Maîtres d'hier et de jadis* (1944); *Portraits de Musiciens* (3 vols., 1946-50); *Souvenirs d'un autre siècle* (1947). Boschot translated into French the libretti of several of Mozart's operas. He was also prominent as a poet; publ. the collections *Poèmes dialogués* (1901) and *Chez nos poètes* (1925).

Boscovich, Alexander Uriah, Israeli composer; b. Klausenburg, Transylvania, Aug. 16, 1907. He studied in Paris with Paul Dukas. In 1928 he settled in Palestine at the Israel Cons. in Tel-Aviv. He has written an orchestral suite *Chansons Populaires Juives* (Haifa, March 15, 1938); violin concerto (1942); oboe concerto (1943; revised 1951); *Semitic Suite* for orch. (1948) and piano pieces.

Bösendorfer. Firm of piano makers at Vienna, specializing in concert grands; it was established by Ignaz Bösendorfer (b. Vienna, July 28, 1796; d. there, April 14, 1859) in 1828; later managed by his son Ludwig (b. Vienna, April 10, 1835; d. there, May 9, 1919). The firm, retaining its original name, was subsequently taken over by G. Hutterstrasser. The Bösendorfer Saal (opened by Hans von Bülow in 1872, and used until 1913) was one of the finest chamber music concert halls in Europe.

Bosmans, Henrietta, Dutch pianist and composer; b. Amsterdam, Dec. 5, 1895; d. there, July 2, 1952. She studied piano with her mother at the Amsterdam Cons.; composition with Willem Pijper; gave frequent recitals throughout Europe and on the radio. Her own music was mainly influenced by Ravel and Stravinsky. Works: violin sonata (1918); cello sonata (1919); piano trio (1921); 2 cello concertos (1922; 1924); *Poem* for cello and orch. (1929); piano concerto (1929); *Concertstück* for violin and orch. (1934); chamber works; songs; also cadenzas for Mozart's violin concertos.

Bosquet, Emile, Belgian pianist; b. Brussels, Dec. 8, 1878. He studied with Tinel and Busoni; taught at the Cons. of Antwerp (1906-19) and in Brussels (from 1919); also made European tours. He published *La Musique de clavier* (Brussels, 1953).

Bosse, Gustave, music book publisher; b. Vienenburg (Harz), Feb. 6, 1884; d. Regensburg, Aug. 27, 1943. He founded his firm in 1912 at Regensburg; was the publisher of the 'Zeitschrift für Musik' (since 1929) and 'Deutsche Musikbücherei' (a collection of music books).

Bossi, (Marco) Enrico, Italian composer, b. Salò, Brescia, April 25, 1861; d. at sea (en route from America to Europe), Feb. 20, 1925. Son and pupil of the organist Pietro Bossi, of Morbegno (1834-1896), he studied (1871-73) at the Liceo Rossini in Bologna, and at Milan (1873-81) under Sangali (piano), Fumagalli (organ), Campanari (violin), Boniforti (counterpoint), and Ponchielli (composition). He subsequently was maestro di cappella and organist at Como Cathedral (1881-89); then, until 1896, prof. of organ and harmony in the Royal Cons. San Pietro at Naples; prof. of advanced composition and organ at the Liceo Benedetto Marcello, Venice (1896-1902); and director of the Liceo Musicale at Bologna (1902-12). After a brief period of retirement from teaching he was director of the Music School of the St. Cecilia Academy, Rome (1916-23); also conductor of the Benedetto Marcello Society Concerts in Venice. He was a member of the permanent government commission for musical art, and of many academies (Berlin, Stockholm, Amsterdam, Venice, Bologna); toured Europe, England and the U. S. as a pianist and organist. Works: operas *Paquita* (Milan, 1881), *Il Veggente* (Milan, 1890; rewritten and produced as *Il Viandante,* Mannheim, 1896), and *L'Angelo della notte; Intermezzi Goldoniani* for string orch.; *Concertstück* for organ and orch.; *Inno di Gloria,* for chorus and organ; *Tota pulchra,* for chorus and organ; *Missa pro Sponso et Sponsa* (Rome, 1896); *Il Cieco,* for solo, chorus and orch. (1897); *Canticum Canticorum,* biblical cantata; *Il Paradiso Perduto,* for chorus and orch. (Augsburg, 1903); *Surrexit pastor,* motet; *Giovanna d'Arco,* mystery play (Cologne, 1913); *Primavera classica,* for 5-part chorus a cappella; *Salve Regina,* for 2 voices and organ; etc. For organ: *Inno Trionfale; Res severa magnum gaudium;* 2 sonatas; *Marche héroïque; Etude symphonique; Pezzo da concerto;* and other pieces; *Santa Caterina di Siena,* for violin, string quartet, harp, celesta and organ; string trio; piano trio, etc. He also wrote *Metodo di Studio per l'organo moderno* (in collaboration with G. Tebaldini; Milan, 1893). Cf. H. B. Gaul, *Bonnet, Bossi, Karg-Elert, Three Aperçus,* in the 'Mus. Quarterly' (July, 1918); E. Dagnino, *M. E. Bossi, Cenni biografici* (Rome, 1925); L. Orsini, *Fascicolo commemorativo* (Milan, 1926); G. C. Paribeni, L. Orsini and E. Bontempelli, *Marco Enrico Bossi: il compositore, l'organista, l'uomo* (Milan, 1934); F. Mompellio, *M. E. Bossi* (Milan, 1952; contains a complete list of works).

Bossi, Renzo, Italian conductor and composer; son of Enrico Bossi; b. Como, April 9, 1883. He studied in Venice and in Leipzig; took a course in conducting with Nikisch; conducted at various cities in Italy; in 1916 was appointed instructor at the Verdi Cons. in Milan. Works: operas, *Passa la ronda* (Milan, March 3, 1919); *Volpino il calderaio* (Milan, Nov. 13, 1925); *Rossa Rossa* (1940); ballet *Il trillo del diavolo* (1948); a symphony in 5 movements; violin concerto; many minor pieces for various instruments. His biographical data and a complete list of works are appended to F. Mompellio's monograph on his father (Milan, 1952). See also S. Pintacuda, *Renzo Bossi* (Milan, 1955).

Bote & Bock, German music publishing firm established in Berlin in 1838 by Eduard Bote (retired 1847) and **Gustav Bock** (b. 1813; d. 1863); the directorship was assumed after Gustav Bock's death by his brother **Eduard Bock** (d. 1871), followed by his son **Hugo Bock** (b. Berlin, July 25, 1848; d. there, March 12, 1932) who handled the affairs of the firm for over sixty years. He acquired for the firm a great number of operas and operettas, and also a number of instrumental works by celebrated 19th-century composers. In 1904 Hugo Bock purchased the catalogue of Lauterbach & Kuhn of Leipzig, including the works of Max Reger (from op. 66 on). His successor was his son **Gustav Bock** (b. Berlin, July 17, 1882) who headed the firm until 1938, and again from 1947. The headquarters of the firm remained in Berlin; in 1948 a branch was formed in Wiesbaden. Apart from its musical publications, the firm publ. the 'Neue Berliner Musikzeitung' (1847-96). A centennial volume was issued in 1938 as 'Musikverlag Bote & Bock, Berlin, 1838-1938.'

Botstiber, Hugo, b. Vienna, April 21, 1875; d. Shrewsbury, England, Jan. 15, 1941. He was a pupil of R. Fuchs, Zemlinsky, H. Rietsch and Guido Adler; in 1896, assistant librarian of the Vienna Cons.; 1900, secretary of the 'Konzertverein' there; and in 1905 secretary of the 'Akademie für Musik'; was (until 1938) general secretary of the Vienna 'Konzerthaus-Gesellschaft'; Knight of the Order of Franz Josef. He went to England in 1939. He edited the 'Musikbuch aus Österreich' (1904-11); also organ compositions by Pachelbel, piano works of the Vienna masters, and waltzes of Johann Strauss for the 'Denkmäler der Tonkunst in Österreich'; author of *Joseph Haydn und das Verlagshaus Artaria* (with Franz Artaria; Vienna, 1911); *Geschichte der Ouvertüre* (Leipzig, 1913); *Beethoven im Alltag* (Vienna, 1927); completed Pohl's biography of Haydn (vol. III, 1927); publ. a new edition of Kretzschmar's *Führer durch den Konzertsaal* (1932). Of special interest to American musicians is his article *Musicalia in der New York Public Library* in the bulletin of the Société Internationale de Musique (Oct., 1903) calling international attention for the first time to the music collection of the New York Public Library.

Bott, Jean Joseph, German violinist and conductor; b. Kassel, March 9, 1826; d. New York, April 28, 1895. He studied with his father, the court musician A. Bott, and later with M. Hauptmann and L. Spohr; was court conductor at Meiningen (1852-57) and Hanover (1865); retired in 1878; settled in New York in 1885. He wrote 2 operas, a symphony, overtures, violin concertos, piano music, etc.

Botta, Luca, dramatic tenor; b. Amalfi, Italy, April 16, 1882; d. New York, Sept. 29, 1917. He was a pupil of G. Vergine; made his operatic début as Turiddu in *Cavalleria Rusticana* (Naples, 1911); then sang in Malta, Turin, Mantua, Verona, Barcelona, Buenos Aires, and Milan; came to the U. S. in 1912 and sang with the Pacific Coast Opera Company in San Francisco; made his Metropolitan Opera House début as Rodolfo in *La Bohème* (New York, Nov. 21, 1914).

Bottée de Toulmon, Auguste, French writer on music; b. Paris, May 15, 1797; d. there, March 22, 1850. A lawyer by profession, he turned his attention to music, becoming a good amateur cellist; was the librarian of the Paris Cons. from 1831-48. Writings: *L'Art musical depuis l'ère chrétienne jusqu'à nos jours* (Paris, 1836); *De la chanson en France au moyen-âge* ('L'Annuaire historique,' 1836); *Notice biographique sur les travaux de Guido d'Arezzo* ('Mémoires de la Société des Antiquaires de France,' 1837); *Des instruments de musique en usage au moyen-âge* ('L'Annuaire historique,' 1838); *Observations sur les moyens de restaurer la musique religieuse dans les églises de Paris* (Paris, 1841); *Notice des manuscrits autographes de Cherubini* (Paris, 1843).

Bottesini, Giovanni, Italian double-bass virtuoso, conductor and composer; b. Crema, Dec. 22, 1821; d. Parma, July 7, 1889. He studied double-bass with Rossi at the Milan Cons. (1835-39); theory with Basili and Vaccai. He made his début at a concert in his native town in 1840; in 1846 he went to Havana as a member of the orchestra there; he visited the U. S. in 1847; then was in England (1848) as a cello player in chamber music, producing a profound impression on the London music lovers. In 1853 he was again in America, where he conducted the New Orleans Opera; in 1856 was conductor at the Théâtre des Italiens in Paris; then toured in Russia and Scandinavia (1866-68). In 1871 he was invited by Verdi to conduct the world première of *Aida* in Cairo; in his last year of life he was appointed director of the Parma Cons. Bottesini was the first real virtuoso on the double-bass, and became a legendary paragon for the few artists who essayed this instrument after him; thus Koussevitzky was often described as the Russian Bottesini. Operas: *Cristoforo Colombo* (Havana, 1847); *L'Assedio di Firenze* (Paris, 1856); *Il Diavolo della notte* (Milan, 1858); *Marion Delorme* (Palermo, 1862); *Vinciguerra* (Paris, 1870); *Alì Babà* (London, Jan. 18, 1871); *Ero e Leandro* (Turin, Jan. 11, 1879); and *La Regina di Nepal* (Turin, 1880); the oratorio *The Garden of Olivet* (Norwich Festival, 1887); symphonies, overtures, quartets; effective pieces for double-bass (*Carnevale di Venezia, Tarantella,* etc.). He published an excellent *Metodo completo per contrabasso,* in 2 parts, treating the double-bass as an orchestral and as a solo instrument (an English adaptation of this method by F. Clayton was publ. in London, 1870). Bibl.: L. Escudier, *Mes souvenirs: les virtuoses* (Paris, 1868); C. Lisei, *G. Bottesini* (Milan, 1886); F. Warnecke, *Der Kontrabass* (Hamburg, 1909); A. Carniti, *In memoria di G. Bottesini* (Crema, 1922).

Bottrigari, Ercole, Italian music theorist; b. Bologna (baptized Aug. 24), 1531, d. San Alberto, near Bologna, Sept. 30, 1612. He was an illegitimate son of the nobleman Giovanni Battista Bottrigari; studied mathematics and music in the house of his father; learned to sing and play several instruments; his house teacher was Bartolomeo Spontone. In 1551 he married a rich lady. In his residence he met many celebrated poets of the day, including Tasso. Having acquired profound learning in several scientific and artistic disciplines, he devoted much of his energies to theoretical musical subjects; published numerous papers, many of them of a polemical nature. Writings on music: *Il Patricio ovvero de' tetracordi armonici di Aristosseno* (Bologna, 1593); *Il Desiderio ovvero de' concerti di vari stromenti musicali* (Venice, 1594, without Bottrigari's name, but under the pseudonym Alemanno Benelli, anagram of the name of his friend, Annibale Melone; 2nd ed. with Bottrigari's name, Bologna, 1599; modern reprint of this edition, in 1924, with introduction and annotations by Kathi Meyer; 3rd ed., Milan, 1601, under the name of Melone); *Il Melone, discorso armonico* (Ferrara, 1602). He left translations of Boetius and other writers in MS, preserved in the library of the Liceo Musicale in Bologna. Bibl.: *Notizie biografiche intorno agli studii ed alla vita del Cavaliere Bottrigari* (Bologna, 1842); G. Gaspari, *Dei Musicisti Bolognesi al XVI secolo* in 'Atti e Memorie . . .' (Bologna, 1876).

Boucher (boo-shā'), **Alexandre-Jean,** famous French violinist; b. Paris, April 11, 1778; d. there, Dec. 29, 1861. A brilliant violin virtuoso, he styled himself 'l'Alexandre des violons.' Boucher began his career at the age of 6, playing with the Concerts Spirituels in Paris; was soloist in the court of Charles IV of Spain (1787-1805); traveled extensively on the continent and in England. He wrote 2 violin concertos. Cf. *Boucher, son temps, etc.* in 'Etudes d'histoire, etc.' by G. Vallat (1890).

Boughton, Rutland, English composer; b. Aylesbury, Jan. 23, 1878. He studied at the Royal College of Music in London with Stanford and Walford Davies; without obtaining his diploma, he engaged in professional activity; was for a time a member of the orchestra at Haymarket Theatre, London; taught at Midland Institute, Birmingham (1904-11); also conducted a choral society there. He became a firm believer in the universality of arts on Wagnerian lines; formed a partnership with the poet Reginald

Buckley; their book of essays, *The Music Drama of the Future,* expounding the neo-Wagnerian idea, was published in 1908. To carry out these plans, he organized stage festivals at Glastonbury, helped by his wife Christina Walshe. Boughton's opera, *The Immortal Hour,* was performed there on Aug. 26, 1914; his choral music drama, *The Birth of Arthur,* had a performance in 1915; these productions were staged with piano instead of an orchestra. After an interruption during World War I, Boughton tried to revive the Glastonbury festivals, but was unsuccessful. In 1927 he settled in the country in Gloucestershire. He continued to compose, however, and produced a number of stage works, as well as instrumental pieces, few of which have been performed. His ideas of universal art have in the meantime been transformed into concepts of socialist realism, with an emphasis on the paramount importance of folk music as against formal constructions. Works for the stage: *The Birth of Arthur* (1909); *The Immortal Hour* (1913); *Snow White* (1914); *The Round Table* (1916); *The Moon Maiden,* choral ballet for girls (1919); *Alkestis,* music drama (1922; Glastonbury, Aug. 26, 1922; Covent Garden, London, Jan. 11, 1924); *The Queen of Cornwall,* music drama after Thomas Hardy (Glastonbury, Aug. 21, 1924); *May Day,* ballet (1926); *The Ever Young,* music drama (1928); *The Lily Maid,* opera (1934); *Galahad,* music drama (1944); *Avalon,* music drama (1946). Orchestral works: *The Skeleton in Armour,* symph. poem with chorus (1898); *The Invincible Armada,* symph. poem (1901); *A Summer Night* (1902); *Oliver Cromwell,* symph. (1904); *Love and Spring* (1906); *Midnight* (1907); *Song of Liberty* for chorus and orch. (1911); *Bethlehem,* choral drama (1915; his most successful work); *Pioneers,* after Walt Whitman, for tenor, chorus and orch. (1925); *Deirdre,* symph. (1927); Symphony in B minor (1937); trumpet concerto (1943). Chamber music: violin sonata (1921); quartet for oboe and strings (1930); string trio (1944); piano trio (1948); cello sonata (1948); numerous choral works. He published several pamphlets and essays: *The Death and Resurrection of the Music Festival* (1913); *The Glastonbury Festival Movement* (1922); *Bach, the Master* (1930); *Parsifal: a Study* (1920); *The Nature of Music* (1930); *The Reality of Music* (1934). Bibl.: *The Self-Advertisement of Rutland Boughton* (anonymous pamphlet without date, c. 1909); H. Antcliffe, *A British School of Music Drama: The Work of Rutland Boughton* in the 'Mus. Quarterly' (Jan., 1918).

Bouhy (boo-ē'), **Jacques-Joseph-André,** celebrated baritone; b. Pepinster, Belgium, June 18, 1848; d. Paris, Jan. 29, 1929. He studied at the Liège Cons.; then at the Paris Cons.; made his début as Mephistopheles in *Faust* at the Paris Grand Opera (1871); sang Escamillo in the first performance of *Carmen* (March 3, 1875); appeared at Covent Garden, London (April 22, 1882); in 1885 he went to New York as director of the N. Y. Cons. (until 1889); he was again in New York from 1904-7; then returned to Paris and settled there as a successful singing teacher.

Boulanger (boo-lahn-zhā), **Lili** (full name **Marie-Juliette**), talented composer, sister of Nadia; b. Paris, Aug. 21, 1893; d. Mézy, near Paris, March 15, 1918. She studied at the Paris Cons. with Vidal and Caussade; in 1913, she won the Grand Prix de Rome with her cantata *Faust et Hélène* (first woman to gain this distinction). Her early death at the age of 24 was a great loss to French music. Other choral works with orch.: *Soir sur la plaine; Hymne au Soleil; La Tempête; Les Sirènes; Sous Bois; La Source; Pour les funerailles d'un soldat; Trois Psaumes; Vieille prière bouddhique.* For orch.: symph. poems *D'un soir triste* and *D'un matin de printemps;* incidental music to Maeterlinck's *La princesse Maleine.* Songs: *Pie Jesu,* for voice, strings, harp and organ; etc. Also a string quartet, violin pieces, flute pieces, etc. Cf. C. Mauclair, *La vie et l'œuvre de Lili Boulanger,* in the 'Revue musicale' (Aug. 1921); P. Landormy, *Lili Boulanger,* in the 'Mus. Quarterly' (Oct., 1930).

Boulanger, Nadia, famous teacher; sister of Lili; b. Paris, Sept. 16, 1887; studied with Fauré (comp.) and Widor (organ) at the Paris Cons.; won 2nd Prix de Rome (1908); then became a lecturer at the Paris Cons.; taught harmony at the American Conservatory at Fontainebleau; in 1935 was appointed teacher of comp. at the Ecole Normale de Musique as successor to Paul Dukas. At the same time she formed a large group of private students; soon her fame as a teacher of composition spread through the musical world, and talented young musicians of many nations came to Paris to take courses with her; many of them have become celebrated composers in their own right: Igor Markevitch, Jean Françaix, Lennox Berkeley; among Americans, Aaron Copland, Roy Harris, Walter Piston and others. Nadia Boulanger has made frequent trips to the U. S.; she was guest conductor with the Boston Symph. Orch. (1938) and of the N. Y. Philh. (Feb. 11, 1939); in 1939 she gave courses at Wellesley College, at Radcliffe College, and also at the Juilliard School of Music, N. Y. She has particularly distinguished herself in conducting large choral works (Fauré's *Requiem,* etc.); has also appeared as an organist. As director of music for the principality of Monaco, she selected and conducted the program performed at the wedding ceremony of Prince Rainier and the American actress Grace Kelly (April, 1956).

Boulez (bŏŏ-lĕz'), **Pierre,** French composer of the advanced school; b. Montbrison, March 26, 1925. He studied with Messiaen at the Paris Cons., graduating in 1945 with a prize; later took lessons with René Leibowitz (1946). In 1948 he became a theater conductor in Paris; visited the U. S. with the French ballet in 1952. Boulez has developed an extremely complex idiom of composition, derived mainly from dodecaphonic principles, in which utmost freedom of rhythm and great variety in dynamics are combined with precision in design. He has written *Le visage nuptial,* for 2 solo voices, chorus and orch. (1946-50); *Symphonie concertante* for piano and orch. (1950); *Polyphonie X* for 17 instruments (first perf. at the Donaueschingen Music Festival, Oct. 6, 1951); flute sonata (1946); 2 piano sonatas (1946 and 1948), and a string quartet (1949). Owing to the extreme nature of his modernistic idiom, performances of Boulez's works have often led to disturbances in the audience.

Boulnois, Joseph, French composer; b. Paris, Jan. 28, 1884; killed in battle at Chalaines, Oct. 20, 1918. He studied piano and composition at the Paris Cons.; later became church organist, and from 1909 was choir leader at the Opéra-Comique. He wrote an opera *L'Anneau d'Isis,* a *Symphonie funèbre,* a cello sonata, and various pieces for organ, piano and voice. His works remain mostly in MS. There has been a revival of interest in his music, which has resulted in some performances of his songs and choruses.

Boult, Sir **Adrian Cedric,** eminent English conductor; b. Chester, April 8, 1889. He studied at the Westminster School and at Christ Church, Oxford; received the degree of D. Mus. from Oxford Univ.; then went to Leipzig, where he studied conducting with Nikisch (1912-13); also took a course with Max Reger. He held a subsidiary position at Covent Garden in 1914; made his début as orchestral conductor with the Royal Philh. Society (1918); gave 4 concerts with the London Symph. Orch., in which he included *The Planets* by Holst and *London Symphony* by Vaughan Williams. In 1919 he became instructor in conducting at the Royal College of Music. In 1923 he conducted the Birmingham Festival Choral Society; in 1924 was engaged as conductor of the City of Birmingham Orch.; in 1930 obtained the post of mus. dir. and conductor of the B.B.C. Symph. Orch. Under his direction this orchestra became one of the finest ensembles in England; in 1950 the age limit necessitated his retirement from the B.B.C.; the same year he was appointed conductor of the London Philharmonic Orch. While the center of his activities is London, Boult has conducted concerts with the major orchestras in Europe and America; he was guest conductor of the Boston Symph. and N. Y. Philh. in 1938-39. He was knighted in 1937. As conductor, Boult is objective in his emphasis upon primary musical values; he is equally proficient in the classical, romantic and modern repertories; he has given numerous performances of works by British composers. He is the author of *A Handbook on the Technique of Conducting* (Oxford, 1921). Bibl.: Donald Brook, *International Gallery of Conductors* (Bristol, 1951; pp. 52-60).

Bourgault-Ducoudray (boor-goh'dü-coo-drā'), **Louis-Albert,** French composer; b. Nantes, Feb. 2, 1840; d. Paris, July 4, 1910. At the age of 18 he composed his first opera, *L'Atelier de Prague* (Nantes, 1859); was a pupil of Ambroise Thomas at the Paris Cons., taking the Grand Prix de Rome in 1862 with a cantata, *Louise de Mézières.* He founded an amateur choral society in Paris (1868); spent some time in research in Greece, after which he publ. *Souvenirs d'une mission musicale en Grèce, 30 Mélodies popularies de Grèce et d'Orient,* and *Etudes sur la musique ecclésiastique grecque* (1877). He was appointed prof. of music history at the Paris Cons. in 1878. Works: 4 operas: *Thamara* (Paris Opéra, Dec. 28, 1891); *Michel Colomb* and *Bretagne* (not performed), *Myrdhin* (posth., Nantes, March 28, 1912); for orch.: *Le Carnaval d'Athènes* (from his *Danses grecques,* originally for piano 4 hands); *Rapsodie Cambodgienne;* vocal works: *François d'Amboise,* cantata (1866); *Stabat mater* (1868); *La conjuration des fleurs; Symphonie religieuse,* etc.; piano pieces; numerous songs, including *30 Mélodies populaires de la Basse-Bretagne,* with French translations (1885). Bibl.: M. Emmanuel, *Éloge funèbre* *de Louis-Albert Bourgault-Ducoudray* (Paris, 1911; with complete catalogue of works).

Bourgeois (boor-zhwăh), **Loys (Louis),** b. Paris, c. 1510; d. there, c. 1561; a follower of Calvin, with whom he lived (1545-57) in Geneva; then returned to Paris; was still living in 1561. He is renowned for having composed, or adapted, almost all the melodies the Calvinists sang to Marot's and Bèze's French versions of the Psalms. Clément Marot, poet in the service of Francis I as 'valet de chambre,' translated (1533-39) 30 psalms in metrical form, which found great favor with the court, who sang them to light melodies. However, the Sorbonne soon condemned them, and, in 1542, Marot had to flee to Geneva. The first edition of Calvin's Genevan Psalter, containing Marot's 30 psalms, his versifications of the Paternoster and Credo, 5 psalms of Calvin, and his versions of the Song of Simeon and Decalogue, was publ. at Geneva in 1542. 17 of the melodies, all but 3 of which were more or less altered, were adapted by Bourgeois from the earlier Strasbourg Psalter of Calvin (1539); 22 new ones were added. After arriving at Geneva, Marot added 19 other psalms and the Song of Simeon; these, together with the 30 previously publ., compose the so-called 'Cinquante Pseaumes,' which, with Marot's Décalogue, Ave and Graces (all with music), were added in the 1543 edition of the Psalter. By 1549, 17 of the melodies previously used were more or less altered by Bourgeois, and 8 others replaced; in 1551 he modified 4 and substituted 12 new tunes. Thus, several of the melodies are of later date than the psalms. On Marot's death, in 1544, Théodore de Bèze undertook completing the Psalter. In 1551 he added 34 psalms, in 1554 6 more, and in 1562 the remaining 60. Bourgeois composed, or adapted, the tunes to all except the last 40, they being set, supposedly, by Pierre Dubuisson, a singer. In 1557 Bourgeois left Geneva and severed his immediate contact with the work there, although he still continued his activity on the psalter. Claude Goudimel publ. harmonized editions of the Genevan Psalter after 1562, thereby creating the erroneous belief that he was the author of the melodies themselves. Bourgeois himself harmonized, and publ. in 1547, 2 sets of psalms in 4-6 parts, intended only for private use. His treatise, *Le droict chemin de musique,* etc. (Geneva, 1550), proposed a reform in the nomenclature of the tones to fit the solmisation-syllables, which was generally adopted in France (see Fétis, 'Biographie des Musiciens' vol. II, p. 42). Bibl.: Douen, *Clément Marot et le Psaultier Huguenot* (2 vols.; Paris, 1878-79); G. A. Crawford, *Clément Marot and the Huguenot Psalter,* in the 'Mus. Times' (June-Nov., 1881); G. R. Woodward, *The Genevan Psalter of 1562,* in the 'Proceedings of the Mus. Assoc.', session 44 (London, 1918); Sir Richard R. Terry, *Calvin's First Psalter,* ib., session 57 (lecture; ib., 1930); id., *Calvin's First Psalter* (book; London, 1932; contains a facsimile and transcription into modern notation of the 1539 Strasbourg Psalter); W. S. Pratt, *The Music of the French Psalter of 1562* (N. Y., 1939); P. A. Gaillard, *L. Bourgeois: sa vie, son œuvre comme pédagogue et compositeur* (Lausanne, 1948).

Bourguignon (boor-gē-nyon'), **Francis de,** Belgian composer; b. Brussels, May 28, 1890. He studied at the Brussels Cons. with Dubois and Tinel (comp.) and Arthur de Greef (piano), graduating with first prize at 18. He was in the Belgian Army and was wounded in 1915; was evacuated to England; then made a tour with Melba in Australia. He continued to travel as pianist on concert tours in Canada, South America, Asia and Africa, having circled the world six times. In 1925 he returned to Brussels, where he made additional studies in composition with Paul Gilson. In 1926 he became a member of a group of Belgian musicians who called themselves "Synthétistes," whose aim was to promote modern music. From then on he dedicated himself to composition and teaching. Among his works is a chamber opera *Le mauvais Pari* (1937); ballet *La Mort d'Orphée* (1928); a symphony (1924); symph. poem *Le Jazz vainqueur* (1929); symph. poem *Oiseaux de Nuit* (Paris, June 28, 1937); symph. suite *Puzzle* (1938); symph. suite *Juventus* (1941); concerto grosso (1944); violin concerto (1947); piano concerto (1949); *Récitatif et Ronde* for trumpet and orch. (1951); piano trio; string trio; 2 string quartets; oboe quintet; choral works, songs and several piano suites (*3 petites fantaisies polytonales; En Floride; Berceuse inutile,* etc.).

Bousquet (boos-kā'), **Georges,** French conductor and music critic; b. Perpignan, March 12, 1818; d. St. Cloud, near Paris, June 15, 1854. He studied at the Paris Cons.; won the Prix de Rome (1838); conducted at the Opéra (1847) and at the Théâtre Italien (1849-51); wrote music criticism for 'Le Commerce', 'l'Illustration', and the 'Gazette musicale'. He composed 3 operas, which were performed in Paris: *l'Hôtesse de Lyon* (Paris Cons., 1844); *Le Mousquetaire* (Opéra-Comique, 1844);

Tabarin (Théâtre-Lyrique, 1852); also a cantata; church music; chamber music.

Boutmy, Josse, Belgian organist and composer; b. Ghent, Feb. 1, 1697; d. Brussels, Nov. 27, 1779. He was a member of a musical family and received his training from his father, a church organist. In 1721 he went to Brussels where he became a teacher of the clavecin; also was organist at the Royal Chapel (from 1744). He published two books of clavecin pieces (Brussels, 1738; 1750); partial reprints are in volume V of 'Monumenta Musicae Belgicae' (Antwerp, 1943), edited by Suzanne Clercx, with a biographical essay in Flemish and French.

Bouvet (boo-vā'), **Charles,** French musicologist; b. Paris, Jan. 3, 1858; d. there May 22, 1935. He studied at the Paris Cons.; in 1903 founded a Bach Society; in 1919 was appointed archivist at the Paris Opéra; was general secretary of the French Musicological Society (1920-27). Writings: *Les Couperin* (Paris, 1919); *L'Opéra* (1924); *Massenet* (1929). He was the editor of works of Bonporti and Couperin; prepared for publication several collections of old French music.

Bouzignac (boo-zē-ñak'), **Guillaume,** French composer of early seventeenth century; biographical data are lacking but several specimens of his music are extant. It is known that he was choir boy at Narbonne; in 1609 was the 'maître des enfants' at the Grenoble Cathedral. His creative period comprises the years 1610-40; he wrote a number of effective motets in the popular French style, distinguished by dramatic expression, as well as religious works. H. Quittard publ. several of these pieces in his paper *Un musicien oublié du XVIIe siècle* in the 'Bulletin de la Société Internationale de Musique' (Paris, 1905).

Bovery (boh-vrē'), **Jules** (real name Antoine-Nicolas-Joseph Bovy), Belgian violinist and conductor; b. Liège, Oct. 21, 1808; d. Paris, July 17, 1868. He was employed in theater orchestras in France and Holland; eventually settled in Paris. He was the author of several operettas and semi-popular instrumental pieces in the salon style.

Bovy, Charles-Samuel, Swiss pianist and composer; b. Lysberg, March 1, 1821; d. Geneva, Feb. 25, 1873. He studied with Chopin, and with Delaire at the Paris Cons.; then returned to Switzerland, where he taught piano at the Geneva Cons. He wrote a comic opera, *La Fille du carillonneur* (Geneva, 1854); a piano sonata, *l'Absence;* is best known for his brilliant piano pieces in the salon style, some of which are publ. under a nom de plume, Lysberg, after his place of birth.

Bovy (boh-vē'), **Vina,** operatic soprano; b. Ghent, Belgium, May 22, 1900. She studied piano and voice at Ghent Cons. (1915-17); made her début at the Théâtre de la Monnaie in Brussels; also appeared at the Opéra-Comique, Paris. After a series of operatic performances in Italy she was engaged by Toscanini at La Scala; later sang in Buenos Aires. She made her American début with the Metropolitan Opera as Violetta (Dec. 24, 1936). In 1938 she returned to Europe; in 1948 became managing director of the Ghent Opera.

Bowen, Edwin York, English composer and pianist; b. London, Feb. 22, 1884. He studied at the Royal Academy of Music, where he won the Erard and Sterndale Bennett scholarships; his teachers were Matthay (piano) and F. Corder (comp.). Upon graduation he was appointed instructor in piano there. A prolific composer, Bowen has written 3 symphonies; 3 piano concertos; violin concerto; viola concerto; a rhapsody for cello and orch; several symph. poems (*The Lament of Tasso, Eventide,* etc.); orchestral suites; many practical piano pieces in miniature forms. Bowen is the author of a manual *Pedalling the Modern Pianoforte* (London, 1936).

Bowers, Robert Hood, American composer; b. Chambersburg, Pa., May 24, 1877; d. New York, Dec. 29, 1941. He studied in Chicago, Baltimore and Philadelphia; was active in radio and theatrical conducting; served for 16 years as recording director of the Columbia Phonograph Co. His compositions include *The Anniversary,* one-act opera; the operettas *The Red Rose* (N. Y., 1911), *Old English* (1924), *Oh Ernest* (1927), *Listen In* (1929), etc.

Bowles, Michael, Irish conductor and composer; b. Riverstown, Nov. 30, 1909. He studied at the Irish Army School of Music, and obtained the Mus. B. degree at University College in Dublin. From 1940 till 1948 he was in charge of the music for Radio Eire; he conducted symphony concerts in Ireland with the radio orch.; from 1948-50 he conducted in Italy, Belgium and Sweden. From 1950 to 1953 he was director of the New Zealand National Orch., and also conducted in Australia. In 1954 he was in Canada; in 1955 appeared as guest conductor with the Boston Pops and other American orchestras.

Bowles, Paul Frederic, American composer; b. New York, Dec. 30, 1910. He studied with Aaron Copland and Virgil Thomson; won a Guggenheim Fellowship in 1941, and traveled extensively in Spain, Northern Africa, the Sahara, the Antilles and South and Central America for the purpose of collecting folk music. Works: for the stage, the operas *Denmark Vesey* (1937) and *The Wind Remains* (1943); the ballets *Yankee Clipper* (1937), *The Ballroom Guide* (1937); *Sentimental Colloquy* (1944), and *Pastorela* (N. Y., 1947). For orch., *Suite* (1933) and *Danza Mexicana* (1941). Chamber music: *Anabase,* for voice, oboe and piano (1932); *Trio* (1936); *Melodia,* for 9 instruments (1937); *Prelude and Dance,* for wind instruments, percussion, double-bass, and piano (N. Y., 1947); *A Picnic Cantata,* for 4 women's voices, 2 pianos and percussion (N. Y., March 23, 1954). Bowles is the author of a novel, *The Sheltering Sky* (1949), which was acclaimed by the press as the revelation of an important literary talent, so that Bowles became known as primarily a writer.

Bowman, Edward Morris, American organist; b. Barnard, Vt., July 18, 1848; d. New York, Aug. 27, 1913. He studied with William Mason in New York, and with Weitzmann in Berlin; was the first American to pass the examinations of the Royal College of Organists in London (1881). After his return to America he was active as organist, choir conductor and teacher in St. Louis and New York; was director of the music department at Vassar College (1891-95). In 1884, with 15 others, he founded the American College of Musicians and was its first president. He publ. the Bowman-Weitzmann *Manual of Musical Theory* (1877; a compilation of notes, from oral communications, of Weitzmann's principles and rules of harmony; later translated into German).

Boyce, William, celebrated English musician; b. London, 1710; d. Kensington, Feb. 7, 1779. He was chorister in St. Paul's Cathedral under Charles King; then studied organ with Maurice Greene, the cathedral organist. After holding various positions as a tutor in private schools, he obtained an organist's post at St. Michael's, Cornhill; in 1758 he became on organist of the Chapel Royal. A victim of increasing deafness, he was compelled to abandon active musical duties after 1769. His main task consisted in composing sacred works; he also contributed incidental music to theatrical productions. He conducted the Festivals of the Three Choirs (Gloucester, Worcester, Hereford) in 1737, and was Master of the Royal Band in 1755. His magnum opus was the completion of the collection, 'Cathedral Music' (3 vols., 1760-78; 2nd ed. 1788; later editions, 1844 and 1849). This collection comprises morning and evening services, anthems and other church music by a number of British composers: Aldrich, Batten, Bevin, Blow, Bull, Byrd, Child, Clarke, Creyghton, Croft, Farrant, Gibbons, Goldwin, Henry VIII, Humfrey, Lawes, Locke, Morley, Mundy, Purcell, Rogers, Tallis, Turner, Tye, Weldon, Wise. Of his own music, there are remarkable instrumental works: 12 overtures (London, 1720); 12 sonatas for 2 violins and bass (London, 1745); 8 symphonies (London, 1750; modern edition by Constant Lambert); 10 voluntaries for organ (London, 1785). 2 overtures, edited by Lambert, and publ. under the titles *The Power of Music* and *Pan and Syrinx* are by John Stanley and not by Boyce. Stage works: *The Chaplet* (1749); *The Roman Father* (1750); *The Shepherd's Lottery* (1751); *Harlequin's Invasion* (with M. Arne, 1759); also incidental songs to Shakespeare's plays; an Ode in Commemoration of Shakespeare (1757). Vocal works: *Lyra Britannica* (several books of songs and duets; 1745-55); 15 anthems (1780); a collection of anthems (1790); these were republished in Novello's edition of Boyce's church music in 4 vols.; various songs originally published in the anthologies 'The British Orpheus,' 'The Vocal Musical Mask,' and others. A considerable number of Boyce's songs still in MS are in the British Museum.

Boyd, Charles N., American editor and writer on music; b. Pleasant Unity, Pa., Dec. 2, 1875; d. Pittsburgh, April 24, 1937. He was church organist and teacher of church music at the Western Theological Seminary (1903-37); director of the Pittsburgh Music Institute (1925-37); served as annotator for the Pittsburgh Symph. Orch. (1907-11), and was an associate editor of the American supplement to Grove's 'Dictionary' (1928); published *Lectures on Church Music* (1912).

Boyden, David D., American musicologist; b. Westport, Conn., Dec. 10, 1910; studied music at Harvard Univ. (A.B., 1932; M.A., 1938); in 1939 appointed to the staff of Univ. of California, Berkeley. He publ. *A Manual of Counterpoint* (1944); *The History and Literature of Music, 1750 to the Present* (1948); *An Introduction to Music* (1956).

Boyle, George F., pianist and composer; b. Sydney, Australia, June 29, 1886; d.

Philadelphia, Pa., June 20, 1948. He received his early musical training from his father and mother; then studied with Busoni in Berlin (1905). At the age of 16, Boyle toured Australia and New Zealand with Mark and Boris Hambourg; later toured Holland with Emma Nevada; lived for 2 years in London, where he married (April 23, 1908) Elise van den Heuvel, a noted Dutch singer; settled in the U. S. in 1910, and taught piano at the Peabody Cons., Baltimore (1910-22); Curtis Institute in Philadelphia (1924-26); and the Juilliard School of Music, N. Y. (1926); lived in Philadelphia after 1926, where he was director of the Boyle Piano Studios. He composed 2 cantatas: *The Pied Piper of Hamelin* (after Browning) and *Don Ramiro* (after Heine); *Aubade* for orch. (St. Louis, March 5, 1916); piano concerto (Worcester Festival, Sept. 28, 1911); cello concerto (Washington, Feb. 7, 1918); 3 piano trios; violin sonata, viola sonata, cello sonata; about 100 piano pieces and 50 songs.

Bozza, Eugène, French composer and conductor; b. Nice, April 4, 1905. He studied violin, conducting and composition (with Busser) at the Paris Cons.; won the Premier Prix as a violinist in 1924; as conductor in 1930; carried the Grand Prix de Rome in 1934. In 1939, Bozza became conductor at the Opéra-Comique. He wrote an opera *Léonidas* (1947); the ballets *Fête romaine* (1942) and *Jeux de plage* (1946); a symphony (1948); symphonic poem *Pax triomphans* (1948); violin concerto (1938); cello concerto (1947); concertino for trombone and orch. (1947), and several sacred choral works.

Bradbury, William Batchelder, American music editor; b. York, Maine, Oct. 6, 1816; d. Montclair, N. J., Jan. 7, 1868. He studied with Lowell Mason; then went to Germany where he took courses with Hauptmann and Moscheles in Leipzig. Returning to America, he became active in various musical enterprises; from 1854-67 he was in business as maker of pianos. He edited some 50 collections of songs and instrumental pieces; one of these collections, *Fresh Laurels for the Sabbath School* (1867) reached the circulation of 1,200,000 copies; other collections were *Bradbury's Golden Shower of Sunday School Melodies; Bright Jewels for the Sunday School; Musical Gems for School and Home.* He was the author of well-known hymn tunes: *He leadeth me; Saviour, like a shepherd lead me;* etc.

Bradsky, Wenzel Theodor, Bohemian composer; b. Rakovnik, Jan. 17, 1833; d. there Aug. 10, 1881. He studied in Prague; then was a choir singer in Berlin; in 1874 he was given the title of court composer by Prince Georg of Prussia, whose drama *Iolanthe* he set to music. He wrote the operas *Roswitha* (Dessau, 1860); *Das Krokodil* (1862); *Jarmila* (Prague, 1879); *Der Rattenfänger von Hameln* (Berlin, 1881); also many choruses and solo songs.

Braga, Francisco, Brazilian composer; b. Rio de Janeiro, April 15, 1868; d. there, March 14, 1945. He played clarinet in military bands in Rio de Janeiro; at the age of 18 he composed an overture, which was played at the inauguration of the Society of Popular Concerts in Rio de Janeiro. He then went to Paris where he studied with Massenet; also traveled in Germany and Italy. Influenced mainly by Massenet and Mascagni, Braga wrote the opera *Jupira,* which was staged at Rio de Janeiro (March 20, 1899). From 1908 till 1933, he conducted symphonic concerts in Rio. His symph. works include the programmatic pieces *Insomnia, Cauchemar, Paysage,* etc. Braga was the teacher of many Brazilian composers and contributed much to the musical culture of his country. A brief biography by T. Gomes was publ. in Rio de Janeiro in 1937.

Braga, Gaetano, Italian cellist and composer; b. Giulianova, Abruzzo, June 9, 1829; d. Milan, Nov. 20, 1907. He studied at Naples Cons. with C. Gaetano (1841-52); made tours as a cellist in Europe and America; lived mostly in Paris and London. His piece for cello *Leggenda valacca* (known as *Angels' Serenade*) attained tremendous popularity and was arranged for various instrumental combinations; also as a vocal solo. Braga wrote several operas: *Alina* or *La spregiata* (1853), *Estella di San Germano* (Vienna, 1857), *Il Ritratto* (Naples, 1858), *Margherita la mendicante* (Paris, 1859), *Mormile* (La Scala, Milan, 1862), *Ruy Blas* (1865), *Reginella* (Lecco, 1871), *Caligola* (Lisbon, 1873); sacred choruses, and a valuable *Metodo di Violoncello.* Bibl.: V. Bindi, *Gaetano Braga: da ricordi della sua vita* (Naples, 1927); A. de Angelis, *Gaetano Braga,* in 'Rivista Musicale Italiana' (June, 1929).

Bragard, Roger, Belgian musicologist; b. Huy, Nov. 21, 1903. He studied philology at the Univ. of Liège; received his Ph. D. with a dissertation, *Les sources du 'De Institutione Musica' de Boèce* (1926); then studied in Paris with Pirro (musicology) and Vincent d'Indy (composition). In 1931 he worked in various European libraries on problems of medieval music. In 1935 he became prof. of music history at the Cons. of Brussels. He publ. a number of valuable papers, among them, *Lambert de Sayve* (Liège, 1934); *Panorama de la musique belge du XIVe au XVIIIe siècle* (Brussels, 1938); *Boethiana* (Antwerp, 1945); *Histoire de la musique belge* (3 volumes, 1946; 1949; 1956), etc.

Braham (real name Abraham), **John,** renowned English tenor; b. London, March 20, 1774; d. there Feb. 17, 1856. He studied with Leoni in London, with Rauzzini in Bath, and with Isola in Genoa. He made his début at Covent Garden (April 21, 1787); then appeared at Drury Lane in 1796, in the opera *Mahmoud* by Storace. He was subsequently engaged to sing at the Italian Opera House in London. In 1798 he undertook an extensive tour in Italy; also appeared in Hamburg. Returning to England in 1801, he was increasingly successful. Endowed with a powerful voice of 3 octaves in compass, he knew no difficulties in operatic roles. He was the original Huon in Weber's *Oberon* (1826). As a ballad writer he was very popular; he wrote much of the music for the operatic roles which he sang; often he added portions to operas by other composers, as in *The Americans* (1811), with its famous song *The Death of Nelson;* contributed incidental music to 12 productions. In 1831 he entered upon a theatrical business venture; he acquired the Colosseum in Regent's Park; in 1836 he had built the St. James's Theatre, but failed to recoup his investment, and lost much of his considerable fortune. He made an American tour in 1840-42 despite the weakening of his voice with age; however, his dramatic appeal remained undiminished and he was able to impress the American public in concert appearances. He then returned to London; made his final appearance in 1852. Bibl.: J. Mewburn Levien, *The Singing of John Braham* (London, 1945).

Brahms, Johannes, one of the greatest masters of music; b. Hamburg, May 7, 1833; d. Vienna, April 3, 1897. His father, a double-bass player at the Hamburg Opera, was his first teacher; his subsequent instructor was one Otto Cossel; but the man who gave Brahms his first real appreciation of the art was Eduard Marxsen. He became proficient as a child pianist, and played at a public concert in Hamburg at the age of 14, including his own variations on a folk tune. He earned some money by playing in taverns; met the Hungarian violinist Reményi, and undertook a tour with him in Germany. Joseph Joachim heard Brahms and sent him to Liszt and Schumann. Liszt expressed his admiration for the Scherzo in E♭ minor and the piano sonatas which Brahms played for him, but their relationship never grew into a spiritual affinity. Much warmer was the reception by Schumann in Düsseldorf, and Brahms became a close friend of Robert and Clara Schumann. In a famous article 'Neue Bahnen' ('New Paths') in the 'Neue Zeitschrift für Musik' Schumann saluted the 20-year-old Brahms as the coming genius of German music, appearing 'fully equipped, as Minerva sprang from the brain of Jupiter'. Schumann also arranged for the publication of Brahms' 3 piano sonatas and 3 sets of songs. It was only natural that Brahms had become a convinced follower of Schumann's ideals in music; a curious episode in his biography is the issuance of a manifesto (1860, signed by Brahms and Joachim), attacking the 'Music of the Future' as promulgated by Liszt and Wagner. In 1862 Brahms went to Vienna, where he conducted the concerts of the Singakademie (1863-64). The next 5 years he spent in various towns (Hamburg, Baden-Baden, Zürich, etc.); in 1869 he was again in Vienna; conducted orchestral concerts of the Gesellschaft der Musikfreunde there from 1871-74. After some travel in Germany, Brahms made his home in Vienna in 1878. Meanwhile, his fame as composer grew. In 1877 Cambridge Univ. tendered him the degree of Mus. Doc., but Brahms was reluctant to make the journey, and declined the honor. He accepted, however, the degree of *Dr. phil.* given him by Breslau Univ., and acknowledged it by composing the *Akademische Festouvertüre,* with its rousing finale based on the German student song 'Gaudeamus igitur.' Other honors followed. In 1886 he was made a Knight of the Prussian 'Orde pour le mérite', and elected a member of the Berlin Academy of Arts. In 1889 he was presented with the freedom of his native city, Hamburg, an honor which he particularly cherished. Meanwhile, his work at composition continued unabated. His first years in Vienna were extremely productive; he wrote several works of chamber music, a genre that he had enriched more than any composer after Beethoven. He also composed several sacred works, culminating in the creation of *Ein deutsches Requiem,* which was performed for the first time in its entirety at the Bremen Cathedral on Good Friday, April 10, 1868 (1st U. S. performance by the N. Y. Oratorio Society, March 15, 1877). Brahms conducted the

Bremen performance himself; later added another movement in memory of his mother. This noble work marks the highest achievement in his vocal writing; the idea of writing an opera seemed natural, and it was not entirely alien to his mind (cf. Widmann's *Johannes Brahms in Erinnerungen*); but Brahms never made a practical beginning in composing for the theater. Some critics have suggested that he was committed to the role of a defender of 'absolute music' as an artistic ideal, and that the opposition of his friends and champions of Brahms to Wagner precluded his interest in writing for the stage. But Brahms himself was not hostile to Wagner; he studied his scores assiduously and expressed his admiration for some of Wagner's music. Brahms was not an innovator; but he was a master rather than a slave of established forms, and never hesitated to deviate from conventional lines when it suited his artistic purpose. Ever since Robert Schumann saluted the young Brahms as a coming genius of the age, a great responsibility to justify this prediction fell on Brahms. Many of his early admirers expected him to continue the tradition of romanticism as established by Schumann. However, Brahms chose to establish himself as the standard bearer of the glorious art of the past. His austerity of spirit was not broken by the blandishments of the Muse of Programs; his music proves that the classical forms were far from exhausted, even by the titanic Beethoven, and that further expansion was possible. It was in this mood that he approached the composition of his 1st symphony in C minor, the symphony that Hans von Bülow so pointedly described as 'The Tenth,' thus placing Brahms in the direct line from Beethoven. It was also von Bülow who coined the phrase 'Three B's of Music,' Brahms, being the third B after Bach and Beethoven. The themes for this work were present in the master's creative mind many years back; the famous horn solo of the last movement was inspired by a shepherd's horn call, and Brahms wrote it down in a letter to Clara Schumann dated Sept. 12, 1868. Brahms completed the score in 1876, when he was 43 years old; the 2nd symphony followed in 1877; the 3rd symphony was written in 1883; the fourth in 1885. Thus, after a late beginning as a symphonic composer, Brahms completed all of his 4 symphonies within less than a decade. The chamber music he produced during this period (piano quartet, op. 60; string quartet, op. 67; piano trio, op. 87; string quintet, op. 88), the great violin concerto, and the 2nd piano concerto, all are symphonic in design, grandeur of form, and fertility of thematic material. In his songs Brahms reveals himself as a master of the highest caliber, an equal of the great representatives of the art of the *Lied,* Schubert and Schumann. The gift of musical poetry is revealed in his handling of the words, in the perfection with which the mood of the poem is translated into melody. The piano accompaniment in the songs of Brahms is so closely knit with the melody that both seem to flow on together in one broad, deep current. His piano works, some of them of transcendent difficulty, add a new dimension to the technique of piano playing. Brahms himself was an unusual performer; despite his mastery of the keyboard he never became a popular virtuoso, and confined himself to the playing of his own music; those who heard him report the impression of solidity, sonority, and power. Brahms was doubtless one of the greatest contrapuntists of his time; the ingenuity and easy skill with which the separate thematic strains are combined without resulting in harmonic harshness, are truly astounding. Yet Brahms was not a musical scientist, a cerebral composer, as some of his critics described him. In Vienna, Brahms assimilated the poetic and sentimental expressiveness that marks the music of Schubert, Schumann, and such lesser Viennese composers as Johann Strauss. In his *Hungarian Dances* he shows his great feeling for folk rhythms; his settings of German folksongs are of the finest in the genre. Brahms was noted for his good nature, modesty and humor. He had no personal enemies, and in his mature years never participated in polemics, even when critical assaults from the Wagnerian camp transgressed the limits of the permissible (as in Hugo Wolf's violent criticisms). Brahms never married; he lived the simple life of a middle-class citizen, and enjoyed fairly good health until the last years of his life; he died of cancer of the liver. The appreciation of Brahms in the musical world at large grew after his death. In 1906 there was founded in Berlin the 'Deutsche Brahmsgesellschaft', with the aim of publishing books about the master. Numerous Brahms societies were also formed in other German and Austrian cities; in America the music of Brahms was received coldly at first, but soon was wholeheartedly accepted. The frequency of performances of his symphonies is not much below that of Beethoven's. The literature, biographical and analytical, dealing with Brahms, is increasing every year with new publications in many languages.

Compositions: For orch.: Serenade in D

(op. 11; 1857-58); 2 piano concertos (I, op. 15, in D m., 1854; II, op. 83, in B♭, 1878-81); Serenade in A for small orch. (op. 16; 1857-60; revised and republ., 1875); Variations on Theme by Haydn (op. 56a; 1873); 4 symphonies (I, op. 68, in C m., 1855-76; II, op. 73, in D, 1877; III, op. 90, in F, 1883; IV, op. 98, in E m., 1884-85); violin concerto in D (op. 77; 1878); *Akademische Festouvertüre* (op. 80; 1880); *Tragische Ouvertüre* (op. 81; 1880-81); Double concerto in A m. for violin and cello (op. 102; 1887); Hungarian Dances (arrangements without opus no.). Chamber music: 3 trios for violin, cello and piano (I, op. 8, in B, 1853-54; revised 1889; II, op. 87, in C, 1880-82; III, op. 101, in C m., 1886); 2 string sextets (I, op. 18 in B♭, 1860; II, op. 36, in G, 1864-65); 3 piano quartets (I, op. 25, in G m., 1861; II, op. 26, in A, 1861; III, op. 60, in C m., 1855-75); piano quintet in F m. (op. 34; 1864; after the Sonata for two pianos, 4 hands, op. 34a); 2 cello sonatas (I, op. 38, in E m., 1862-65; II, op. 99, in F, 1886); Trio in E♭ for horn (or cello or viola), violin and piano (op. 40; 1865); 3 string quartets (I, in C m., II, in A m.: both op. 51; 1859-73; III, op. 67, in B♭, 1875); 3 violin sonatas (I, op. 78, in G, 1878-79; II, op. 100, in A, 1886; III, op. 108, in D m., 1886-88); 2 string quintets (I, op. 88, in F, 1882; II, op. 111 in G, 1890); Trio in A m. for clarinet, cello and piano (op. 114; 1891); Quintet in B m. for clarinet and strings (op. 115; 1891); 2 clarinet sonatas (I, in F m., II, in E♭; both op. 120; 1894); Movement in C m. in a violin sonata by Brahms, Schumann and Dietrich (1853). Choral works: *Ave Maria,* for women's voices, organ and orch. (op. 12; 1858); *Funeral Hymn,* for chorus and wind orch. (op. 13; 1858); 4 Songs for women's voices, 2 horns and harp (op. 17; 1860); *Marienlieder,* for mixed chorus (7 songs; op. 22; 1859); 13th Psalm, for women's voices and organ (op. 27, 1859); 2 Motets for 5-part a capp. chorus (op. 29; 1860); *Lass dich nur nichts dauern,* for 4-part chorus with organ (op. 30; 1856); 3 Sacred Choruses for women's voices a capp. (op. 37; 1859-63); *5 Soldatenlieder,* for 4-part male chorus a capp. (op. 41; 1861-62); 3 Songs for 6-part mixed chorus a capp. (op. 42; 1859-61); 12 Songs and Romances for women's voices a capp. (op. 44; 1859-63); *Ein Deutsches Requiem* for soli, chorus and orch. (op. 45; 1857-68); *Rinaldo,* cantata for tenor, male chorus and orch. (after Goethe; op. 50; 1863-68); *Rhapsodie,* for alto, male chorus and orch. (after Goethe's *Harzreise;* op. 53; 1869); *Schicksalslied,* for chorus and orch. (op. 54; 1871); *Triumphlied,* for 8-part chorus and orch. (op. 55; 1870-71); 7 Songs for a capp. chorus (op. 62; 1874); 2 Motets for a capp. chorus (op. 74; 1863-77); *Nänie,* for chorus and orch. (after Schiller; op. 82; 1880-81); *Gesang der Parzen,* for 6-part chorus and orch. (after Goethe; op. 89; 1882); 6 Songs and Romances for 4-part a capp. chorus (op. 93a; 1883-84); *Tafellied,* for 6-part chorus with piano (op. 93b; 1884); 5 Songs for a capp. chorus (op. 104; 1888); *Deutsche Fest- und Gedenksprüche,* for a double a capp. chorus (op. 109; 1886-88); 3 Motets for 4- and 8-part a capp. chorus (op. 110; 1889); 13 canons for women's voices and piano (op. 113; 1863-90); 14 *Volkskinderlieder,* with piano (without op.-no.; 1858); 14 German Folk-songs (2 vols.; without op.-no.; 1864). Organ works: 11 *Choralvorspiele* (2 vols.; op. 122; 1896; posth.); Fugue in A♭ m. (1856); *O Traurigkeit,* Chorale, Prelude and Fugue in A m. (1856). Piano solos: 3 sonatas (I, op. 1, in C, 1852-53; II, op. 2, in F♯ m., 1852; III, op. 5, in F m., 1853); Scherzo in E♭ m. (op. 4; 1851); Variations on a Theme by Schumann (op. 9; 1854); 4 Ballades (op. 10; 1854); Variations in D: I, on Original Theme; II, on Hungarian Theme (op. 21; 1857); Variations and Fugue on a Theme by Handel (op. 24; 1861); 28 Variations (*Studien*) on a Theme by Paganini (2 vols.; op. 35; 1862-63); 8 Pieces (2 vols.; op. 76; 1871-78); 2 Rhapsodies (op. 79; 1879); 7 *Fantasien* (2 vols.; op. 116; 1892); 3 *Intermezzi* (op. 117; 1892); 6 Pieces (op. 118; 1892); 4 Pieces (op. 119; 1892); 2 cadenzas to Beethoven's piano concerto in G (posth.). For 2 Pianos: Sonata in F m. (op. 34b; 1864; original version of piano quintet, op. 34); Variations on a Theme by Haydn (op. 56b; 1873). Piano duets: Variations on a Theme by Schumann (op. 23; 1861); 16 Waltzes (op. 39; 1865); *Liebeslieder,* waltzes with 4 voices (op. 52; 1868-69); *Liebeslieder* without voice parts (op. 52a; arranged 1874); *Neue Liebeslieder,* waltzes with 4 voices (op. 65; 1874); Hungarian Dances (4 vols.; without op.-no.; 1852-69).

Brahms' vocal quartets are publ. in sets, varying in number, as op. 31, 64, 92, 103 (*Zigeunerlieder*), and 112; his vocal duets as op. 20, 28, 61, 66, and 75; and his songs for one voice with piano accomp. as op. 3, 6, 7, 14, 19, 32, 33 (from Tieck's 'Magelone'), 43, 46-9, 57-9, 63, 69-72, 84-6, 91, 94-7, 105-7 and 121.

WORKS WITHOUT OP.-NO.: The song *Mondnacht* is without op.-no., as are 7 vols. of German songs (I-VI: for solo voice;

VII: for soli and small chorus). Brahms also wrote 5 *Songs of Ophelia,* for the actress Olga Precheisen, fiancée of his friend, Lewinsky. They were performed in 1873 in Prague, but were not publ. until 1935 (N. Y.); they are not included in Breitkopf & Härtel's collection ed. of Brahm's works. *Studien* for piano (5 vols.: I. Chopin's F m. Étude aranged in sixths; II, Weber's *Moto perpetuo* in C; III and IV, 2 arrangements of Bach's *Presto*; V. Bach's *Chaconne* [for left hand alone]); 51 Exercises for piano (7 books; 1890); Gluck's Gavotte in A arranged for piano; Joachim's Overture to *Henry IV* arranged for piano 4 hands. He also ed. piano works of Couperin for Chrysander's 'Denkmäler der Tonkunst', Schumann's *Presto Appassionato* and *Scherzo,* 3 posth. works of Schubert, including a transcription of *Ellens zweiter Gesang* (for soprano, women's chorus and wind instruments); provided accompaniments for an edition of vocal duets by Handel; amplified the figured bass of 2 violin sonatas by C.P.E. Bach; edited Mozart's *Requiem* for the complete edition of Mozart's works; and collaborated in the preparation of the complete edition of Chopin's works.

In 1924 a copy from the original score of a trio in A, presumably written by Brahms when he was about 20 years old (see letter to R. Schumann, 1853), was discovered in Bonn; it was edited and published by E. Bücken and K. Hasse. See E. Bücken, *Ein neuaufgefundenes Jugendwerk von J. B.,* in 'Die Musik' (Oct., 1937); Fr. Brand, *Das neue B.-Trio* (ibid., Feb., 1939).

A Thematic Catalogue was publ. by N. Simrock (Berlin, 1897; new augmented ed., prepared by J. Braunstein, N. Y., 1956). In 1926-28 Breitkopf & Härtel publ. a collection of Brahms' entire works.

BIBLIOGRAPHY.—A. BIOGRAPHY: M. Kalbeck, *Johannes Brahms* (8 vols., Berlin, 1904-14; the standard work); H. Deiters, *J. B. Eine Charakteristik* (Leipzig, I [1880], II [1898]; both in Waldersee's 'Sammlung mus. Vorträge'); H. Reimann, *J. B.* (Berlin, 1897; 6th ed. 1922); A. Dietrich, *Erinnerungen an J. B. in Briefen, besonders aus seiner Jugendzeit* (Leipzig, 1898); J. Widmann, *J. B. in Erinnerungen* (Berlin, 1898; 3d ed. 1910). This and the preceding in Engl. translations by Hecht as *Recollections of J. B.* (London, 1899); F. May, *The Life of J. B.* (2 vols., London, 1905); J. Erb, *B.* (ib., 1905); H. Antcliffe, *B.* (ib., 1905); H. Imbert, *J. B.: sa vie et son œuvre* (Paris, 1906); G. Henschel, *Personal Recollections of J. B.* (Boston, 1907); W. Pauli, *J. B.* (Berlin, 1907); R. von Perger, *B.* (Leipzig, 1908); H. C. Colles, *B.* (London, 1908); R. von der Leyen, *J. B. als Mensch und Freund* (Berlin, 1908); J. Fuller Maitland, *B.* (London, 1911); W. Thomas San Galli, *J. B.* (Munich, 1912); E. M. Lee, *B., the Man and His Music* (London, 1915); W. Niemann, *J. B.* (1920; in Engl., N. Y., 1929); Heinrich Reimann, *B.* (1920); Paul Landormy, *B.* (1920); G. Ophüls, *Erinnerungen an J. B.* (1921); W. Nagel, *J. B.* (1923); Jeffrey Pulver, *J. B.* (London, 1926; new ed. 1933); R. Specht, *J. B.* (1928; in Engl., 1930); J. F. Cooke, *J. B.* (Phila., 1928); M. Komorn, *J. B. als Chordirigent in Wien* (1928); G. Ernest, *J. B.* (1930); J. Ch. v. Sell, *J. B.* (1931); R. H. Schauffler, *B., Poet and Peasant,* in the 'Mus. Quarterly' (1932); id., *The Unknown B., His Life, Character and Works* (N. Y., 1933); Brahms issue of the 'Mus. Quarterly' (April, 1933; includes G. Adler, *J. B., His Personality, etc.;* Karl Geiringer, *B. as a Reader and Collector,* and other articles); Karl Geiringer, *J. B.* (Vienna, 1933; new ed. 1935; in English, N. Y., 1936); G. Adler, *J. B.* (1933); A. von Ehrmann, *J. B.: Weg, Werk und Welt,* with a supplementary volume containing complete thematic catalogue and bibliography of first editions (Leipzig, 1933); Ralph Hill, *B.* (London, 1933); Wm. Murdock, *B.* (with an analytical study of the complete piano works; London and N. Y., 1933); J. Müller-Blattau, *B.* (Berlin, 1933); Ludwig Koch, *B. in Ungarn* (Budapest, 1933); R. Fellinger, *Klänge um B.* (Berlin, 1933); R. Hernried, *J. B.* (Leipzig, 1934); R. Lienau, *Erinnerungen an J. B.* (Berlin, 1935); Konrad Huschke, *Frauen um B.* (Karlsruhe, 1937); Alfred Orel, *J. B.'s Leben in Bildern* (Leipzig, 1937); L. Koch, *B.-Bibliografia* (Budapest, 1943); M. Goss and R. H. Schauffler, *B., the Master* (1943); K. Laux, *Der Einsame, J. B., Leben und Werk* (Graz, 1944); Walter und Paula Rehberg, *J. B., sein Leben und Werk* (Zürich, 1947); P. Latham, *B.* (London, 1948); A. Orel, *J. B., Ein Meister und sein Weg* (Vienna, 1950); F. Grasberger, *J. B., Variationen um sein Wesen* (Vienna, 1952; contains chronological and alphabetical list of works; also new photographs); Claude Rostand, *Brahms* (Paris, 1954). —For Brahms iconography see W. Müller, *Ein B.-Bilderbuch* (Vienna, 1905); and Maria Fellinger, *B.-Bilder* (Leipzig, 1911). Unclassifiable in Brahms literature is the book of mystic speculation, *Brahms Noblesse* by Frederic Horace Clark (Berlin, 1912; parallel German and English texts); see also Arthur M. Abell, *Talks With Great Composers* (N. Y., 1955).

B. CORRESPONDENCE: The 'complete' correspondence has been publ. by the 'Deutsche Brahmsgesellschaft' in 16 vols. (Berlin; begun in 1906) as follows: I, II. Ed. by M. Kalbeck, *J. B. im Briefwechsel mit Heinrich und Elisabet von Herzogenberg* (1906); III. Ed. by W. Altmann, *J. B. im Briefwechsel mit Reinthaler, Bruch, Deiters, Heimsoeth, Reinecke, Rudorff, Bernhard und Luise Scholz* (1907); IV. Ed. by R. Barth, *J. B. im Briefwechsel mit J. O. Grimm* (1907); V, VI. Ed. by A. Moser, *J. B. im Briefwechsel mit Joseph Joachim* (1908); VII. Ed. by L. Schmidt, *J. B. im Briefwechsel mit Levi, Gernsheim sowie den Familien Hecht und Fellinger* (1910); VIII. Ed. by M. Kalbeck, *J. B. im Briefwechsel mit Widmann, Vetter, Schubring* (1915); IX-XII. Ed. by M. Kalbeck, *J. B. im Briefwechsel mit Peter J. Simrock u. Fritz Simrock* (1917); XIII. Ed. by J. Röntgen, *J. B. im Briefwechsel mit Th. W. Engelmann* (1918); XIV. Ed. by W. Altmann, *J. B. im Briefwechsel mit Breitkopf & Härtel, Senff, Rieter-Biedermann, Peters, Fritzsch und Lienau* (1920); XV. Ed. by E. Wolff, *J. B. im Briefwechsel mit Franz Wüllner* (1922); XVI. Ed. by C. Krebs, *J. B. im Briefwechsel mit Ph. Spitta* (1922) and *J. B. im Briefwechsel mit Otto Dessoff* (1922). Of these, vols. I and II appeared in English translation by Hannah Bryant (N. Y., 1909). Interesting letters of Brahms are found in *Clara Schumann, J. B.: Briefe aus den Jahren 1853-96,* ed. by B. Litzmann (in German and English; 2 vols., 1927); K. Stephenson, *J. B.'s Heimatbekenntnis in Briefen an seine Hamburger Verwandten* (Hamburg, 1933); Otto Gottlieb-Billroth, *B. und Billroth im Briefwechsel* (Vienna, 1935); Karl Geiringer, *Wagner and B.* (unpublished letters), in the 'Mus. Quarterly' (April, 1936); R. Litterscheid, ed., *J. B. in seinen Schriften und Briefen* (Berlin, 1943); F. Callomon, *Some unpublished B. Correspondence,* in the 'Mus. Quarterly' (Jan., 1943).

C. CRITICISM, APPRECIATION: L. Köhler, *J. B. und seine Stellung in der Musikgeschichte* (Hanover, 1880); E. Krause, *J. B. in seinem Werken* (Hamburg, 1892); D. G. Mason, *From Grieg to Brahms* (New York, 1902); R. Barth, *J. B. und seine Musik* (Hamburg, 1904); G. Jenner, *J. B. als Mensch, Lehrer und Künstler* (Marburg, 1905); W. A. Thomas, *J. B. Eine musikpsychologische Studie* (Strassburg, 1905); J. Knorr and H. Riemann, *J. B. Symphonien und andere Orchesterwerke erläutert* (Berlin, 1908); M. Burkhardt, *J. B.; ein Führer durch seine Werke* (ib., 1912); W. Hammermann, *J. B. als Liederkomponist* (Leipzig, 1912); E. Evans, *Historical, Descriptive and Analytical Account of the Entire Works of J. B.* (London; I, vocal works, 1912; II and III, chamber and orchestral music, 1933-35; IV, piano works, 1936); W. Nagel, *Die Klaviersonaten von J. B.* (Stuttgart, 1915); M. Friedländer, *B.'s Lieder* (Berlin, 1922; in English, London, 1928); P. Mies, *Stilmomente und Ausdrucksstilformen im B.-schen Lied* (Leipzig, 1923); G. Ophüls, *B.-Texte* (3rd ed. Berlin, 1923); H. Meyer, *Linie und Form: Bach, Beethoven, Brahms* (ib., 1930); E. Markham Lee, *B.'s Orchestral Works,* in the 'Mus. Pilgrim' series (London, 1931); D. G. Mason, *B.'s 3rd Symphony,* in the 'Mus. Quarterly' (July, 1931); H. S. Drinker, *The Chamber Music of B.* (Philadelphia, 1932); A. Schering, *B. und seine Stellung in der Musikgeschichte des 19. Jahrhunderts,* in 'Jahrbuch Peters' (1932); H. C. Colles, *The Chamber Music of B.* (London, 1933); D. G. Mason, *The Chamber Music of B.* (N. Y., 1933); P. A. Browne, *B.: The Symphonies* ('Mus. Pilgrim' series, London, 1933); W. Blume, *B. in der Meininger Tradition* (Stuttgart, 1933); K. Huschke, *J. B. als Pianist, Dirigent und Lehrer* (Berlin, 1935); F. Brand, *Das Wesen der Kammermusik von B.* (Berlin, 1937); J. A. G. Harrison, *Brahms and his Four Symphonies* (London, 1939).

Brailowsky, Alexander, noted pianist; b. Kiev, Russia, Feb. 16, 1896. After study with his father, a professional pianist, he was taken to Vienna in 1911 and was accepted by Leschetizky as a pupil; made his début in Paris after World War I; presented a complete cycle of Chopin's works in Paris (1924), and repeated it there several times. He made a highly successful tour all over the world; made his American début at Aeolian Hall, N. Y., Nov. 19, 1924; made a coast to coast tour of the U. S. in 1936; first gave the Chopin cycle in America during the 1937-38 season, in 6 recitals in New York.

Brain, Aubrey, English horn player; b. London, July 12, 1893. His father was also a horn player; he studied at the Royal College of Music in London; joined the London Symphony Orch.; then played in the B.B.C. Symph. Orch.; retired in 1945. He was appointed prof. at the Royal Academy of Music in 1923, and held this position for 30 years. His brother, Alfred, is also a horn player, as is his son Dennis Brain.

Brain, Dennis, English horn player; b. London, May 17, 1921. He studied with his father; played in various Bach ensembles in London; was first horn player in the Royal Philharmonic; then joined the Philharmonia

Orch.; participated in the Festivals at Lucerne and Amsterdam (1948). He has rapidly acquired the reputation of a foremost performer on his instrument. Benjamin Britten's *Serenade* for tenor, horn and strings was written for Dennis Brain.

Braine, Robert, American composer; b. Springfield, Ohio, May 27, 1896; d. (suicide) New York, Aug. 22, 1940. He studied at the Cincinnati College of Music; acted as radio conductor in New York. He composed three operas: *The Eternal Light* (1924); *Virginia* (1926); *Diana* (1929); symph. pieces, *S.O.S.; The House of Usher, The Raven* for baritone and orch.; *Concerto in Jazz* for violin and orch.; *Barbaric Sonata* for piano; and many other piano pieces; also about 50 songs.

Braithwaite, Sam Hartley, English composer; b. Egremont, Cumberland, July 20, 1883; d. Arnside, Westmoreland, Jan. 13, 1947. He studied at the Royal Academy of Music; upon graduation joined its faculty as instructor. His compositions include *Military Overture* (London, 1911); the tone poem *A Night by Dalegarth Bridge* (Bournemouth Festival, 1921); etc.

Braithwaite, Warwick, British conductor; b. Dunedin, New Zealand, Jan. 9, 1898. He studied at the Royal Academy of Music in London. Was conductor of the Cardiff Musical Society (1924-32); and of the National Orchestra of Wales (1928-31). He then conducted opera at Sadler's Wells, London (1933-43); also directed the Scottish Orchestra, Glasgow; toured in New Zealand in 1947. From 1949 he has conducted ballet at Covent Garden, London. He published *The Conductor's Art* (London, 1952).

Brambach, Kaspar Joseph, German composer; b. Bonn, July 14, 1833; d. there, June 19, 1902. He studied composition at the Cologne Cons.; then taught there (1858-61); later was active as teacher and composer in Bonn (1861-69). He wrote many secular cantatas, among them *Trost in Tönen, Das Eleusische Fest, Die Macht des Gesanges, Prometheus,* and *Columbus* (awarded the $1,000 prize at the Milwaukee Festival; performed there July 23, 1886); also an opera *Ariadne;* concert overture *Tasso;* a piano concerto; piano sextet; string sextet; 2 piano quartets, and songs.

Brambach, Wilhelm, brother of Kaspar Joseph; b. Bonn, Dec. 17, 1841; d. Karlsruhe, Feb. 26, 1932. He studied classical languages and musical science at the Univ. of Bonn; taught philology at the Univ. of Freiburg (1866-72); then was for 32 years librarian of the district library at Karlsruhe (1872-1904). Writings on music: *Das Tonsystem und die Tonarten des christlichen Abendlandes im Mittelalter* (Leipzig, 1881); *Die Musikliteratur des Mittelalters bis zur Blüte der Reichenauer Sängerschule* (Karlsruhe, 1883); *Hermanni Contracti musica* (Leipzig, 1884); *Die Verloren geglaubte 'Historia de Sancta Afra Martyri' und das 'Salve regina' des Hermannus Contractus* (Karlsruhe, 1892); *Gregorianische-bibliographische Lösung der Streitfrage über die Ursprung des Gregorianischen Gesangs* (Leipzig, 1895; 2nd ed., 1901).

Brambilla, Marietta, Italian contralto, daughter of Paolo Brambilla; b. Cassano d'Adda, June 6, 1807; d. Milan, Nov. 6, 1875. She was a member of a musical family; her four sisters were singers. She made her début in London in 1827 as Arsace in Rossini's *Semiramide;* then sang in Italy, Vienna, and Paris. She eventually settled in Milan as a teacher; published collections of vocalises.

Brambilla, Paolo, Italian composer; b. Milan, July 9, 1787; d. there, 1838. He wrote 4 operas, produced in Milan and Turin, and 6 ballets for La Scala. He was the father of Marietta and Teresa Brambilla.

Brambilla, Teresa, Italian opera singer, sister of Marietta; b. Cassano d'Adda, Oct. 23, 1813; d. Milan, July 15, 1895. She studied singing at the Milan Cons.; made her début in 1831 and traveled through Europe, including Russia. Her appearances at La Scala were highly successful. After several seasons in Paris, she was engaged at the Teatro Fenice in Venice, where she created the role of Gilda in *Rigoletto* (March 11, 1851).

Brancaccio (brăhn-kăht'-chŏh), **Antonio,** Italian composer; b. Naples, 1813; d. there, Feb. 12, 1846. He studied at Naples, and produced his first opera, *I Panduri,* during the carnival of 1843; his other operas included *L'Assedio di Constantina* (Venice, 1844); *Il Puntiglione* (Naples, 1845); *L'Incognita* (Venice, 1846); *Le Sarte calabresi* (Naples, 1847; posthumous); *Lilla* (Venice, 1848; posthumous).

Brancour, René, French music critic; b. Paris, May 17, 1862; d. there, Nov. 16, 1948. Educated at the Paris Cons., he became curator of the collection of music instruments there; in 1906 began a course of lectures on esthetics at the Sorbonne; also wrote newspaper criticism. A brilliant writer, he poured invective on the works of composers of the advanced school; his tastes were conservative, but he accepted French music of the impressionist period. He wrote biographies of Félicien David (1911) and Méhul (1912) in the series of 'Musiciens célèbres;' of Massenet (1923) and Offenbach (1929) in 'Les Maîtres de la Musique.' Other books are *La vie et l'œuvre de Georges Bizet* (1913); *Histoire des instruments de musique* (1921); *La Marseillaise et le Chant du départ,* etc.

Brand, Max, outstanding composer; b. Lwow, April 26, 1896; studied with Franz Schreker at the State Academy of Music in Vienna. He made use of the 12-tone method of composition as early as 1927, but did not limit himself to it in his later works. His most spectacular work was the opera, *Maschinist Hopkins,* to his own libretto, chosen as the best operatic work of the year by the Congress of German Composers, and first produced at Duisburg on April 13, 1929; it was later staged in 37 opera houses in Europe, including Russia; it marked the climactic point of the 'machine era' in modern music between the two wars. Brand was also active in the field of experimental musical films in the triple capacity of author, composer, and director. From 1933-38 he remained in Vienna; then went to Brazil; in 1940 arrived in the U. S., becoming an American citizen in 1945. He settled in New York. —Works: *Nachtlied* (from Nietzsche's 'Also Sprach Zarathustra') for soprano and orch. (1922); 3 Songs to poems by Lao-Tse (Salzburg Festival, 1923); *Eine Nachtmusik* for chamber orch. (1923); string trio (1923); *Die Wippe,* ballet (1925); *Tragœdietta,* ballet (1926); 5 Ballads, a study in 12 tones (1927); *Maschinist Hopkins,* opera in 3 acts (1928); *The Chronicle,* scenic cantata for narrator, soli, chorus, and orch. (1938); *Piece for Flute and Piano,* in 12 tones (1940); *Kyrie Eleison,* study in 12 tones for chorus (1940; perf. by Villa-Lobos, Rio de Janeiro, 1940); *The Gate,* scenic oratorio, with narrator (N. Y., May 23, 1944); *The Wonderful One-Hoss Shay,* symph. rondo for orch., after Oliver Wendell Holmes (Philadelphia Orch., Ormandy cond., Jan. 20, 1950); *Night on the Bayous of Louisiana,* tone poem (1953); *Stormy Interlude,* opera in one act, libretto by the composer (1955).

Brandeis, Frederick, composer and pianist; b. Vienna, July 5, 1832; d. New York, May 14, 1899. He was a pupil of Carl Czerny; settled in the United States in 1849, where he was active as solo pianist, conductor, and organist. He wrote numerous pieces for military band; a *Romanza* for oboe and orch.; a ballade, *The Sunken Cloister* (1882); some chamber music and a variety of piano works and songs. His style of composition was entirely without distinction.

Brandl, Johann, German composer; b. Kloster Rohr, near Regensburg, Nov. 14, 1760; d. Karlsruhe, May 25, 1837. During the latter part of his life he was musical director to the Archduke of Baden in Karlsruhe. A prolific composer, he wrote 2 operas, *Germania* (1810) and *Hermann* (1814); a melodrama, *Hero;* a symphony; oratorios; masses; many instrumental pieces.

Brandt, Jobst vom (or **Jodocus de Brant**), German musician; b. Waltershofen, near Marktredwitz, Oct. 28, 1517; d. Brand, near Marktredwitz, Jan. 22, 1570. In 1530 he enrolled at Heidelberg Univ.; in 1548 had become Captain of Waldsassen and Administrator of Liebenstein. He was one of the most important composers of the Senfl school; his music is distinguished by deep feeling and a skillful use of counterpoint. Extant works: 45 *Psalmen und Kirchengesänge* (Eger, 1572-73; preserved in the library of K. Proske); 55 vocal pieces in G. Forster's collection 'Ein Auszug guter alter und neuer teutscher Liedlein' (III; Wittenberg, 1549, and IV-V, 1556). Reprints are in R. von Liliencron's 'Deutsches Leben im Volkslied 1530'; in Jöde's 'Chorbuch' III; in 'Kaiserliederbuch für gemischten Chor'; in 'Staatliches Jugendliederbuch'; in the 'Chorsammlung für gemischten Chor des Arbeitsängerbundes'; in 'Monatshefte für Musikgeschichte' (vol. 26; etc.

Brandt, Marianne (real name Marie Bischoff), Austrian contralto; b. Vienna, Sept. 12, 1842; d. there, July 9, 1921. She studied at the Vienna Cons. with Frau Marschner; then in Paris with Viardot-Garcia; made her operatic début as Rachel in *La Juive* (Graz, Jan. 4, 1867); sang in Hamburg and at the Berlin Opera; in 1872 she appeared in London; in 1882 sang the role of Kundry in the second performance of *Parsifal* at Bayreuth, alternating thereafter with Materna, who had created the role; made her American début as Leonore at the Metropolitan Opera (New York, Nov. 19, 1884), and reappeared there during subsequent seasons of German opera. In 1890 she settled in Vienna as a singing teacher. See La Mara, 'Musikalische Studienköpfe' (Leipzig, 1902).

Brandt, Noah, American composer; b. N. Y., April 8, 1858; d. San Francisco, Nov. 11, 1925. He studied at the Leipzig Cons. with Ferdinand David (violin) and Jadassohn (theory); toured in Europe and the U. S. as a violinist with a theater orch., finally settled in San Francisco. He was the author of a light opera *Captain Cook* (San Francisco, Sept. 2, 1895); his other operas *Wing Wong* and *Daniel* were not produced.

Brandts-Buys, Jan, composer; b. Zutphen, Sept. 12, 1868; d. Salzburg, Dec. 8, 1933. He was a pupil of M. Schwarz and A. Urspruch at the Raff Cons. in Frankfurt; lived for a time in Vienna; later settled in Salzburg. In 1897 his piano concerto in F won the Bösendorfer prize, and attracted favorable attention; thereafter the Fitzner Quartet produced some of his chamber music, and Lilli Lehmann sang a number of his songs. His first attempt at opera, *Das Veilchenfest* (Berlin, 1909), met with opposition; a second opera, *Das Glockenspiel* (Dresden, 1913), was received more kindly, while a third, *Die drei Schneider von Schönau* (Dresden, 1916), was quite successful; subsequent operas were: *Der Eroberer* (Dresden, 1918), *Micarême* (Vienna, 1919), *Der Mann im Mond* (Dresden, 1922), and *Traumland* (Dresden, 1927). He also wrote a ballet, *Machinalität* (Amsterdam, 1928), 2 piano concertos (in addition to the one in F, mentioned above); a *Konzertstück* for cello and orch.; chamber music; piano pieces and songs.

Brandukov, Anatol Andreyevitch, Russian cellist; b. Moscow, Jan. 6, 1859; d. there, Feb. 15, 1930. He was a pupil of Cossmann and Fitzenhagen at the Moscow Cons.; then went to France, where he made his début under Saint-Saëns at Angers in 1881; subsequently played in principal Paris and London concerts; founded a quartet with Marsick in 1886; lived in Paris until 1889; settled in Moscow. He composed some effective cello pieces.

Brandus, Defour et Cie. Paris firm of music publishers, founded by M. Schlesinger (1834), and taken over in 1846 by the brothers Louis and Gemmy Brandus.

Branscombe, Gena, composer; b. Picton, Ontario, Canada, Nov. 4, 1881. She studied at Chicago with Felix Borowski (comp.) and Rudolf Ganz (piano); in Berlin with Humperdinck and Alexander von Fielitz. She has held teaching positions at the Chicago Musical College and the Whitman Cons., Washington; has organized and conducted the Branscombe Choral Society; has appeared as guest conductor of her own compositions in Chicago, Toronto and elsewhere. Works: Symphonic suite, *Quebec* (Chicago, 1930); *Pilgrims of Destiny,* choral drama for soli, mixed chorus and orch. (Boston, 1929; awarded a prize by the National League of Pen Women); *The Phantom Caravan,* for men's chorus and orch. (1932); *Youth of the World,* for women's voices and orch. (N. Y., 1933; one of her most successful works); *Sun and the Warm Brown Earth,* for chorus (1935); *Procession* for orch. (1935); *Valse joyeuse,* for orch. (1946); *Coventry's Choir,* for soprano, women's voices, piano, organ and percussion (1944); *Procession* for trumpet, organ and piano (1948); many songs; piano pieces, violin compositions; other choral works; etc.

Branson, David, English pianist and composer; b. King's Lynn, July 13, 1909. He studied with Harold Samuel; composition with John Ireland; made his début at the age of eleven. He has written a number of piano miniatures and songs. Branson is also known as a painter.

Brant, Henry Dreyfus, composer of ultramodern music; b. Montreal, Sept. 15, 1913. He studied in Montreal, and at the Juilliard School, N. Y., with Friskin (piano) and Goldmark (comp.); later with George Antheil. In his music, he explores unusual sonorities; has experimented with directional sound, in which the location of the instruments is widely varied in performances; has also written scores for unspecified instruments. Works: 2 symphonies (1931 and 1937); 4 choral-preludes (1932); concerto for double bass and orch. (1932); *Gallopjig Colloquy,* ballad for orch. (1934); *Whoopee Overture* (1937); clarinet concerto (1939; $100 prize of Society of Professional Musicians); saxophone concerto (1940); *Music for an Imaginary Ballet* (N. Y., 1947); cantata *Spanish Underground* (N. Y., Jan. 14, 1947); *Millennium No. 2,* for 10 trumpets, 10 trombones, 8 horns, 2 tubas and 4 percussion instruments (N. Y., Jan. 11, 1954). Chamber works: *Variations* for 4 instruments (1930); sonatas for oboe (1932) and for viola or cello (1937); *Poem and Burlesque* for 11 flutes (1932); *Five and Ten Cent Store*

Music, for piano and 20 instruments (1932); *Lyric Piece,* for chamber orch. (1933); 2 sarabandes for piano (1930); and sonata for 2 pianos (1931); also film music; expanded his score for the Palestinian film *My Father's House* (1947) into a 'symphony of Palestine' *The Promised Land* (Cincinnati Symph. Orch., Nov. 26, 1948).

Brant, Jobst vom. See **Brandt.**

Branzell, Karin Maria, Swedish contralto; b. Stockholm, Sept. 24, 1891. She studied in Stockholm with Thekla Hofer, in Berlin with Bachner, and in New York with Rosati; made her début in Stockholm in 1911; from 1912-18 was a member of the Stockholm Royal Opera; from 1919-23 sang with the Berlin State Opera; made her American début as Fricka in *Die Walküre* at the Metropolitan Opera (N. Y., Feb. 6, 1924); appeared in concert in the U. S. and toured extensively throughout Europe. Possessing a voice of exceptional range, she occasionally sang soprano roles. In 1946 she was engaged as vocal instructor at the Juilliard School of Music in New York.

Braslau, Sophie, American contralto; b. New York City, Aug. 16, 1892; d. there, Dec. 22, 1935. She studied piano under Alexander Lambert; then voice with Buzzi-Peccia; made her début at the Metropolitan Opera in *Boris Godunov* (Nov. 28, 1914); was a member of the Metropolitan company until 1921; created the leading role in Cadman's opera, *Shanewis* (March 23, 1918); in 1931 toured Scandinavia and Holland. A large collection of her programs, reviews, and biographical materials was given by the family to the Music Division of the N. Y. Public Library (1938).

Brassin, Leopold, pianist; b. Strasbourg, May 28, 1843; d. Constantinople, May, 1890. He studied music with his brother, Louis (q. v.); was court pianist at Koburg; taught at the Bern Music School, and later in St. Petersburg and Constantinople; wrote concertos and many pieces for piano.

Brassin, Louis, French pianist; b. Aix-la-Chapelle, June 24, 1840; d. St. Petersburg, May 17, 1884. He was a pupil of Moscheles at the Leipzig Cons.; made concert tours with his brothers Leopold and Gerhard; taught at the Stern Cons., Berlin (1866); at the Brussels Cons. (1869-79); then at the St. Petersburg Cons. He composed an operetta, *Der Thronfolger* (Brussels, 1865); the valuable *École moderne du piano;* 12 *études de concert;* 2 piano concertos; salon pieces for piano, and songs. His effective piano transcription of the Magic Fire music from *Die Walküre* is well known.

Braudo, Eugen, Russian music scholar; b. Riga, Feb. 20, 1882; d. Moscow, Oct. 17, 1939. He studied natural science and musicology in Moscow, St. Petersburg and Germany; in 1914 became professor at St. Petersburg Univ.; from 1924 taught at the Moscow Pedagogical Institute and at the Institute for Drama and Opera. He wrote a music history (1921-27; 3 vols.); published the monographs, *E. T. A. Hoffmann* (1921); *A. Borodin* (1922); *Nietzsche, Philosopher and Musician* (1922); *Beethoven* (1927); translated numerous musical books into Russian (including a collection of Wagner's letters); publ. several other studies, especially on musical problems from a sociological viewpoint.

Braun, Karl, German bass singer; b. Meisenheim, Prussia, June 2, 1885. A pupil of H. Gausche and E. Robert-Weiss, he appeared frequently on the concert stage and in opera in Europe (1904-1913), and sang leading roles at the Metropolitan Opera (1913-1917) with great acclaim. Returning to Germany at the beginning of World War I, he sang principal parts at the Berlin State Opera and at Wagner Festivals in Bayreuth. He appeared again in the U. S. during the seasons of 1929-30 and 1930-31 as a member of the Gadski Opera Co.; retired as a singer in 1939, and founded a theatrical agency in Berlin, where he still lived in 1955.

Braun, Wilhelm. See **Brown, William.**

Braunfels, Walter, German composer; b. Frankfurt, Dec. 19, 1882; d. Cologne, March 19, 1954. He studied piano in Vienna with Leschetizky and composition in Munich with L. Thuille. He became active both as an educator and a composer. From 1913-25 he lived near Munich; in 1925 he became a co-director of the Hochschule für Musik in Cologne. With the advent of the Nazi regime, he was compelled to abandon teaching; from 1933-37 he was in Godesberg; from 1937-45 in Überlingen. At the end of the war he was reappointed director of the Cologne Hochschule; he held this post until he retired in 1950. He excelled mainly as an opera composer; the following operas are notable: *Prinzessin Brambilla* (Stuttgart, March 25, 1909; revised in 1931); *Ulenspiegel* (Stuttgart Nov. 9, 1913); *Die Vögel* (after Aristophanes; Munich, Dec. 4, 1920; his most successful opera; given also in Berlin and Vienna); *Don Gil* (Munich, Nov. 15, 1924); *Der gläserne Berg* (Cologne, Dec. 4, 1928); *Galathea* (Cologne, Jan. 26, 1930); *Der Traum, ein Leben* (1937); *Die heilige Johanna* (1942); also a mystery play, *Verkündigung,* after Paul Claudel (1936). He further wrote *Der Tod der Kleopatra* for voice and orch (1946); 2 piano concertos; organ concerto; *Revelation of St. John* for tenor, double chorus and orch.; *Die Ammen-Uhr,* for boys' voices and orch.; *Te Deum; Grand Mass;* orchestral fantasies on themes of Mozart, Beethoven and Berlioz; piano music and songs. His last work of importance was *Sinfonia brevis* (1949). In his style Braunfels was a disciple of the Germanic romantic school without adopting the radical devices of modern music. He believed in the artistic and practical value of Wagnerian leading motives; in his harmonies, he was close to Richard Strauss; but he also applied impressionistic devices related to Debussy. His admiration for Berlioz is reflected in the flamboyant brilliance of his orchestral writing.

Bravničar, Matija, Yugoslav composer; b. Tolmin, near Gorica, Feb. 24, 1897. He studied at Gorica; from 1915-18 was in the Austrian army; from 1919-45 was a violinist at the opera theater in Ljubljana; meanwhile he graduated from the Academy of Music in Ljubljana in 1933; since 1945, prof. of composition there. In 1949 he was elected president of the Slovenian Composers' Union; in 1953, president of the Yugoslav Composers' Union. In his works, Bravničar cultivates a neo-classical style, with thematic material strongly influenced by the melorhythmic inflections of Yugoslav folk music. He has written an opera-farce in 3 acts, *Pohujšanje v dolini Sentflorjanski (Scandal in St. Florian's Valley;* produced in Ljubljana, May 11, 1930); the opera in 8 scenes, *Hlapec Jernej i njegova pravica* (*Knight Jernej and his Right;* Ljubljana, Jan. 25, 1941); *Hymnus Slavicus* for orch. (Ljubljana, May 14, 1932); overture *King Mattias* (Ljubljana, Nov. 14, 1932); *Antithèse symphonique* (Ljubljana, Feb. 9, 1948; also at Salzburg Festival, June 29, 1952); 2 symphonies (performed in Ljubljana, Feb. 20, 1951 and Oct. 27, 1952); *Divertissements* for string orch. and piano, *Sonata in modo antico* for violin and piano; and several collections of piano pieces.

Brecher, Gustav, conductor and editor; b. Eichwald, near Teplitz, Bohemia, Feb. 5, 1879; d. Ostend, May, 1940. His family moved to Leipzig in 1889, and he studied there with Jadassohn. His first major work, the symph. poem *Rosmersholm,* was introduced by Richard Strauss at a Liszt-Verein concert in Leipzig (1896); made his début as a conductor there (1897); was vocal coach and occasional conductor of operas in Leipzig (1898); conducted in Vienna (1901); served as first Kapellmeister in Olmütz (1902), in Hamburg (1903), and Cologne (1911-16); then went to Frankfurt (1916-24) and Leipzig (1924-33). He committed suicide with his wife aboard a boat off the Belgian coast while attempting to flee from the advancing Nazi troops. His compositions include a symph. fantasia *Aus unserer Zeit.* He was the author of several essays: *Über die veristische Oper; Analysen zu Werken von Berlioz und Strauss; Richard Strauss;* and *Über Operntexte und Opernübersetzungen* (1911).

Brediceano, Tiberiu, Rumanian composer; b. Lugoj, Transylvania, Apri 12, 1877. He studied music in Rumania; was director of the National Opera in Cluj; later became President of the Astra Cons. in Brasov. Works: *Le poème musical ethnographique; La Sezatoare; La grande soirée,* lyric scene for Christmas Eve; dance music; vocal works; etc. The inspiration for his compositions is drawn chiefly from the folk material of Rumania.

Bree (brā), **Jean Bernard van,** Dutch violinist and composer; b. Amsterdam, Jan. 29, 1801; d. there, Feb. 14, 1857. He was a pupil of Bertelmann; in 1819 played the violin in the orchestra of the Théâtre Français (Amsterdam); in 1829 became director of the Felix Meritis Society, and in 1840 founded the Cecilia Society; later became director of the Music School of the Society for the Promotion of Music. Works: the operas *Sappho* (in Dutch; Amsterdam, March 22, 1834); *Nimm dich in Acht* (in German; 1845); and *Le Bandit* (in French; The Hague, 1840); also 2 melodramas; several Masses; cantatas, overtures; chamber music; etc. See H. Beijermann, *Jean Bernard van Bree* (1857).

Brehme, Hans, German composer; b. Potsdam, March 10, 1904. He studied in Berlin with Wilhelm Kempff (piano) and Robert Kahn (comp.). He taught at the Stuttgart Hochschule für Musik from 1928-44, and again from 1950. In 1945-49 he was a teacher at Trossingen. A highly industrious composer, he has written music in every form; his style is neoclassical, with a moderate admixture of advanced harmonies. He wrote the operas *Der Tor und der Tod* (1928); *Der Uhrmacher von Strassburg* (1940); and *Versiegelten Bürgermeister* (1944); Symphony No. 1 (1925); clarinet concerto (1928); *Concerto sinfonico* for 5 wind instruments, string orch. and percussion (1930); piano concerto (1936); *Triptychon* for orch. on a theme by Handel (1937; highly successful); Symphony No. 2 (1950); 2 string quartets; wind quintet; sextet for wind and string instruments; violin sonata; saxophone sonata; sacred choruses; songs; piano pieces. He also wrote several works for the accordion: suite for accordion solo (1945); ballet suite for an orchestra of accordions (1946), and a symphonic prelude for an orch. of accordions (1952). See Karl Laux, *Musik und Musiker der Gegenwart* (Essen, 1949).

Breil, Joseph Carl, American composer; b. Pittsburgh, June 29, 1870; d. Los Angeles, Jan. 23, 1926. He studied voice in Milan and Leipzig, and for a time sang in various opera companies. He composed the first score ever written to accompany a motion picture, *Queen Elizabeth* (Chicago, 1912); wrote words and music for the comic operas *Love Laughs at Locksmiths* (Portland, Maine, Oct. 27, 1910); *Prof. Tattle* (1913); and *The Seventh Chord* (1913). His serious opera *The Legend* was accepted by the Metropolitan Opera, and perf. on April 4, 1919. His opera *Asra* (after Heine) had a single perf. in Los Angeles (Nov. 24, 1925). See E. E. Hipsher, *American Opera and Its Composers* (Philadelphia, 1927; pp. 87-90).

Breithaupt, Rudolf (Maria), German pianist; b. Brunswick, Aug. 11, 1873; d. Ballenstedt, April 2, 1945. Studied at the Leipzig Cons.; in 1918 was appointed professor at Stern's Cons. in Berlin. His writings include *Die natürliche Klaviertechnik* in 3 parts (1905, 1909, 1919; part 2 was translated into French, Russian and English); essays published as *Musikalische Zeit- und Streitfragen* (1906); and *Praktische Übungen* (5 vols., 1916-21). He also composed piano pieces.

Breitkopf & Härtel, important German firm of book and music publishers. As an established printing firm in Leipzig, it was bought in 1745 by Bernhard Christoph Breitkopf (b. Klausthal Harz, March 2, 1695; d. Leipzig, March 23, 1777). His son, Johann Gottlob Immanuel (b. Nov. 23, 1719; d. Jan. 28, 1794) entered the business in 1745; it was his invention which made the basis for the firm's position in the publication of music. In 1756 he devised a font with much smaller division of the musical elements and thus greatly reduced the cost of printing chords (and hence piano music). The firm soon began to issue numerous piano reductions of popular operas for amateur consumption. The earliest music publications, such as the *Berlinische Oden und Lieder* (3 vols., 1756, 1759, 1763) were made by Johann Gottlob Immanuel Breitkopf himself, and bore the name *Leipzig, Druckts und Verlegts Johann Gottlob Immanuel Breitkopf;* from 1765 to 1777 the name appears as *Bernhard Christoph Breitkopf und Sohn;* from 1777-1787 (after Christoph's death) Gottlob Immanuel's name again appears alone; Immanuel's second son, Christoph Gottlob (b. Leipzig, Sept. 22, 1750; d. there April 4, 1800), joined the firm in 1787; from 1787 to 1795 publications were issued as 'im Breitkopfischen Verlage' (or Buchhandlung, or Musikhandlung); in 1795 (the year after Immanuel's death) Christoph Gottlob took as his partner his close friend, Gottfried Christoph Härtel (b. Schneeburg, Jan. 27, 1763; d. near Leipzig, July 25, 1827); since 1795 the firm has been known as Breitkopf und Härtel, although no Breikopf has been actively associated with the firm since Christoph Gottlob's death in 1800. Härtel's tremendous energy revitalized the firm. He added a piano factory; founded the important periodical 'Allgemeine musikalische Zeitung' (1798; editor, J. F. Rochlitz); introduced pewter in place of the harder copper for engraving music; used Senefelder's new lithographic process for either title pages or music where suitable; issued so-called 'complete' editions of the works of Mozart, Haydn, Clementi and Dusek. The firm also began the practice of issuing catalogues with thematic indexes and keeping stocks of scores. From 1827-1835 Florenz Härtel was head of the firm; Hermann Härtel (b. Leipzig, April 27, 1803; d. there, Aug. 4, 1875) and his brother, Raimund Härtel (b. Leipzig, June 9, 1810; d. there, Nov. 9, 1888) together dominated the book business of Leipzig (and thus all Germany) for many years; the sons of two sisters of Raimund and Hermann, Wilhelm Volkmann (b. Halle, June 12, 1837; d. Leipzig, Dec. 24, 1896) and Dr. Oskar von Hase (b. Jena, Sept. 15, 1846; d. Leipzig, Jan. 26, 1921) succeeded them. After Wilhelm Volkmann's death, his son, Dr. Ludwig Volkmann (1870-1947), headed the firm jointly with von Hase; von Hase's son, Hermann (1880-1945) entered the firm in 1904 and was a co-partner from 1910-14. Hermann von Hase published essays tracing the relation of J. Haydn, K. Ph. E. Bach, and J. A. Hiller to the firm; in 1915 he became a partner in the book business of K. F. Koehler. His brother, Dr. Hellmuth von Hase (b. Jan. 30, 1891) became director of the firm in 1919. The old house was destroyed during the air bombardment of Dec. 4, 1943; it was rebuilt after the war. In 1950 Dr. Hase moved to Wiesbaden where he established an independent business, reclaiming the rights for the firm in West Germany. Important enterprises of the firm throughout its existence are editions of Bach, Beethoven, Berlioz, Brahms, Chopin, Gluck, Grétry, Handel, Haydn, Lassus, Liszt, Mendelssohn, Mozart, Palestrina, Schein, Schubert, Schumann, Schütz, Victoria, and Wagner. The German government supported the publication by Breitkopf and Härtel of the two series of *Denkmäler deutscher Tonkunst* (1892-1931 and 1900-1931). Other publications of the firm are: *Der Bär,* yearbook (since 1924); *Katalog des Archivs von Breitkopf und Härtel,* edited by Dr. F. W. Hitzig (2 vols., 1925-26); *Allgemeine musikalische Zeitung* (weekly; 1798-1848 and 1863-65); *Monatshefte für Musikgeschichte* (1869-1905); *Mitteilungen des Hauses Breitkopf und Härtel* (1876-1940; resumed in 1950); *Vierteljahrsschrift für Musikwissenschaft* (1869-1906); *Zeitschrift der Internationlen Musikgesellschaft* (monthly; Oct., 1899-Sept., 1914); *Sammelbände der Internationalen Musikgesellschaft* (quarterly; 1899-1914); *Korrespondenzblatt des Evangelischen Kirchengesangvereins für Deutschland* (monthly; 1886-1922); *Zeitschrift für Musikwissenschaft* (monthly; 1919-35); *Archiv für Musikforschung* (1936-43).

Brema, Marie (real name, Minny Fehrman), English mezzo-soprano of German-American parentage, b. Liverpool, Feb. 28, 1856; d. Manchester, March 22, 1925. She began serious study (after her marriage to Arthur Braun of Liverpool in 1874) with Henschel, and made her début at the Popular Concert in London (Feb. 21, 1891) under the name of Bremer (her father being a native of Bremen); made her stage début at Oxford in 1891 in *Adrienne Lecouvreur.* She made several American tours (1894-97) appearing in Wagnerian roles with the Damrosch Co. (1894-95) and the Metropolitan Opera (1895-96). She was personally engaged by Cosima Wagner to take part at Bayreuth Festivals (1896-97). She appeared with success in numerous other standard operas, and also created Beatrice in Stanford's *Much Ado About Nothing* (May 30, 1901) and the Angel in Elgar's *Dream of Gerontius* (1900, Birmingham Fest.) Her later years were devoted to operatic teaching at the Royal College of Music in Manchester.

Brendel, Karl Franz, German writer on music; b. Stolberg, Nov. 26, 1811; d. Leipzig, Nov. 25, 1868. He studied piano with Wieck; entered the Schumann circle and became editor of the 'Neue Zeitschrift für Musik' (1845-56); then was co-editor (with R. Pohl) of the monthly 'Anregungen für Kunst, Leben und Wissenschaft' (1856-61). He was later appointed professor of music history at the Leipzig Cons.; was one of the founders (1861), and for years the president, of the 'Allgemeiner deutscher Musikverein.' In his articles, he championed Wagner and Liszt. Writings: *Grundzüge der Geschichte der Musik* (1848); *Geschichte der Musik in Italien, Deutschland und Frankreich von den ersten christlichen Zeiten bis auf die Gegenwart* (1852; 7th ed., edited by Kienzl, 1888; new augmented ed., edited by R. Hövker, 1902, and reissued in 1906); *Die Musik der Gegenwart und die Gesamtkunst der Zukunft* (1854); *Franz Liszt als Sinfoniker* (1859); *Die Organisation des Musikwesens durch den Staat* (1865); *Geist und Technik im Klavierunterricht* (1867); also many newspaper articles, published as *Gesammelte Aufsätze zur Geschichte und Kritik der neueren Musik* (1888).

Brenet, Michel (real name Marie Bobillier), French musicologist; b. Lunéville, April 12, 1858; d. Paris, Nov. 4, 1918. After living in Strasbourg and Metz, she made her home in Paris from 1871. Writings: *Historie de la symphonie à orchestre depuis ses origines jusqu'à Beethoven* (1882); *Grétry, sa vie et ses œuvres* (1884); *Deux pages de la vie de Berlioz* (1889); *Jean d'Okeghem* (1893); *La musique dans les processions* (1896); *Sébastien de Brossard* (1896); *La musique dans les couvents de femmes* (1898); *Claude Goudimel* (1898); *Notes sur l'histoire du luth en France* (1899); *Les concerts en France sous l'ancien régime* (1900); *Additions inédites de Dom Jumilhac à son traité* (1902); *La jeunesse de Rameau* (1903); *Palestrina* (1906, in 'Les Maîtres de la Musique'; 3rd ed. 1910); *La plus ancienne méthode française de musique* (1907); *Haydn* (1909, in 'Les Maîtres de la Musique'; in English, 1926); *Les Musiciens de la Sainte-Chapelle: documents inédits* (1910); *Musique et musiciens de la vieille France* (1911); *Handel* (1912, in 'Musiciens célèbres'); *La musique militaire*

(1917); *Dictionnaire pratique et historique de la musique* (posthumous; completed by A. Gastoué, Paris, 1926); valuable essays and articles in the 'Grande Encyclopédie', 'Correspondant,' 'Guide musical,' 'Journal musical,' 'Revue musicale,' 'Tribune de St.-Gervais,' 'Rivista Musicale Italiana,' and the 'Musical Quarterly.' See L. de la Laurencie, *Michel Brenet,* in the 'Bulletin de la Société française de Cologne' (1919, No. 4).

Brent-Smith, Alexander, English composer; b. Brookthorpe, Gloucestershire, Oct. 8, 1889; d. there, July 3, 1950. After the completion of his studies, he devoted himself to a pedagogical career. His works consist mainly of choral pieces and concertos for various instruments.

Brenta, Gaston, Belgian composer; b. Brussels, June 10, 1902. He studied with Paul Gilson; became a member of the Belgian "Groupe des Synthétistes"; from 1939, music director of the Brussels Radio. He wrote an opera, *Le Khâdi dupé* (1929); a ballet *Florilège de valses* (1947); a symphony (1946); a piano concerto (1949), and an oratorio *Passion* (1949); also several songs with orchestra.

Bresgen, Cesar, German organist and composer; b. Florence (of German parents), Oct. 16, 1913. He was brought up in Munich; studied with Haas at the Munich Akademie der Tonkunst; in 1931 was organist at St. Rupert, Munich. His works include a chamber concerto for 8 solo instruments (Munich, 1934); concerto for 2 pianos (Weimar, 1936); children's opera *Der Igel als Bräutigam* (Nuremberg, Nov. 13, 1951); concerto grosso (1936); also short operas, *Die Freier* (1936), *Dornröschen* (1939); *Das Urteil des Paris* (1943), and *Paracelsus* (1943); numerous cantatas, piano pieces, etc. See E. Valentin, *C. Bresgen* in 'Neue Zeitschrift für Musik' (Aug., 1938).

Breslaur, Emil, German music teacher and writer on music; b. Kottbus, May 29, 1836; d. Berlin, July 26, 1899. He studied at the Stern Cons. in Berlin (1863-7); taught at Kullak's Academy (1868-79); from 1863 was choirmaster at the Berlin Reformed Synagogue. A music teachers society founded by him in 1879 developed in 1886 into the 'Deutscher Musiklehrer-Verband.' He was also editor of the 'Klavierlehrer,' and the author of several important works on piano playing: *Die technischen Grundlagen des Klavierspiels* (1874); *Führer durch die Klavierunterrichts-Literatur* (1887); *Zur methodischen Übung des Klavierspiels; Der entwickelnde Unterricht in der Harmonielehre; Über die schädlichen Folgen des unrichtigen Übens.* He also edited the 11th ed. of Schuberth's 'Musikalisches Konversationslexikon' (1892); composed choral works, piano pieces, songs, etc.

Bressler-Gianoli, Clotilde, operatic contralto, b. Geneva (of Italian parents), June 3, 1875; d. there, May 12, 1912. She received her vocal training at the Milan Cons. with Sangiovanni, and made her operatic début at the age of 19 at Geneva in *Samson et Dalila.* She later appeared at La Scala, the Opéra-Comique in Paris, and at numerous other European opera houses. She sang in the U. S. with the San Carlo Co. at New Orleans and N. Y., the Manhattan Opera House (1906-08) and the Metropolitan Opera (1909-10). Her best roles were Carmen and Mignon.

Bretón y Hernández (är-năhn'-dāth), **Tomás,** Spanish opera composer; b. Salamanca, Dec. 29, 1850; d. Madrid, Dec. 2, 1923. As a youth he played in restaurants and theaters; was graduated from Madrid Cons. (1872); conducted at the Madrid Opera; in 1901 joined the faculty of the Madrid Cons. A fertile composer, he contributed greatly to the revival of the zarzuela. He was at his best in the 1-act comic type (*género chico*). Among his operas (all produced in Madrid) are: *Los Amantes de Teruel* (1899); *Juan Garín* (1892); *Dolores* (1895); *El Domingo de Ramos* (1896); *La Verbena de la Paloma* (1897); *Raquel* (to his own libretto; Jan. 20, 1900); *El Caballo del señorito* (1901); *Farinelli* (1903); *Tabaré* (1913). He also wrote an oratorio, *Apocalipsia* (Madrid, 1882) and works for orch.: *Escenas Andaluzas;* Funeral March for Alfonso XII; violin concerto, etc. Bibl.: Angel S. Salcedo, *Tomás Breton: su vida y sus obras* (1924).

Breuer (broi-er), **Hans** (real name Johann Peter Joseph), German tenor; b. Cologne, April 27, 1868; d. Vienna, Oct. 11, 1929. He was a pupil of Iffert and Stolzenberg at the Cologne Cons. (1890-92); then studied with Kniese at the Bayreuth 'Stilbildungsschule'; made his operatic début in 1896 as Mime at Bayreuth, and appeared regularly there until 1914. He made his Metropolitan Opera début in *The Flying Dutchman* (New York, Jan. 6, 1900); then become a member of the Vienna Opera; also appeared at the Mozartfest in Salzburg (1906).

Breuning (broi'-ning), **Moritz Gerhard von,** Austrian writer on music; b. Vienna,

Aug. 28, 1813; d. there, May 6, 1892. He was a son of Beethoven's friend Stephan von Breuning; wrote *Aus dem Schwarzspanierhause* (Vienna, 1874; new ed., with additions by Kalischer, Berlin, 1907).

Bréval, Lucienne (stage name of Bertha Schilling), opera singer; b. Männedorf, Switzerland, Nov. 4, 1869; d. Paris, Aug. 15, 1935. She studied piano in Lausanne and Geneva, and then voice at the Paris Cons.; made her début at the Paris Opéra as Selika in *L'Africaine* (Jan. 20, 1892) and was then engaged as principal dramatic soprano; made appearances in the U. S. (1900-02); then settled in Paris. See 'Le Monde Musical' (Sept., 1935).

Bréville, Pierre-Onfroy de, French composer; b. Bar-le-Duc, Feb. 21, 1861; d. Paris, Sept. 23, 1949. He studied at the Paris Cons. with Théodore Dubois (1880-82); later with César Franck; was professor of counterpoint at the Schola Cantorum; wrote music criticism for 'La France,' 'La Revue internationale de Musique,' and 'Mercure de France.' Works: an opera, *Eros Vainqueur* (Brussels, March 7, 1910); *Sainte Rose de Lima* for chorus, soli and orch.; 3-part Mass (with organ, string orch. and harp); overture to Maeterlinck's drama *La Princesse Maleine,* and incidental music to his *Sept Princesses;* the orchestral suites *Nuit de décembre* and *Stamboul;* an organ suite; cello sonata; rondels; motets; liturgical choral compositions; piano pieces; songs; etc. He completed (with d'Indy and others) Franck's unfinished opera *Ghiselle;* wrote a monograph *Sur les chansons populaires françaises* (1901).

Brewer, Sir **Alfred Herbert,** English organist and composer; b. Gloucester, June 21, 1865; d. there, March 1, 1928. He studied at the Royal College of Music with Parratt, Stanford and Bridge; became active as organist and choirmaster of several churches, and director of musical societies. His compositions include many sacred cantatas (*Emmaus, The Holy Innocents, A Song of Eden,* etc.), which were performed at festivals in Gloucester, Worcester, Hereford, Cardiff and Leeds; patriotic odes, such as *England, my England;* organ pieces, songs, etc. He was knighted in 1926. —Cf. H. Brewer, *Memories of Choirs and Cloisters* (London, 1931).

Brewer, John Hyatt, American organist and composer; b. Brooklyn, N. Y., Jan. 18, 1856; d. there, Nov. 30, 1931. He studied organ and composition with Dudley Buck; was active as organist and music director of numerous local churches and musical societies; taught at Adelphi College from 1899-1906. He was a prolific vocal composer; wrote the cantatas (for women's voices) *Hesperus, The Sea and the Moon, Herald of Spring,* etc.; and (for men's voices) *Birth of Love, The Dunderberg,* etc.; also quartets, anthems, glees, and choruses. His instrumental works include pieces for organ, piano and string instruments.

Brian, Havergal, English composer; b. Dresden, Staffordshire, Jan. 29, 1876. He studied organ; began to compose without formal education; served as a music critic in Manchester. He has written 6 symphonies; 4 English suites for orch.; 2 violin concertos; several piano pieces and numerous choral works. His source of inspiration is mainly romantic literature and English folksongs.

Briard (brē-ahr'), **Etienne,** type-founder at Avignon, active early in the 16th century. In his engraving he employed round note-heads instead of the ordinary angular ones, and separate notes instead of ligatures. Peignot holds that another printer, Granjon, used these methods prior to Briard (see his 'Dictionnaire de la bibliologie,' supp., p. 140); in any case, Briard's characters are much better formed and more easily read. Schmidt's *Ottaviano Petrucci* contains a facsimile of them. The *Liber primum missarum Carpentras* (works of Eleazar Genet, called 'Il Carpentrasso'), printed with them at Avignon in 1532, is in the library of the Paris Conservatory. See K. Meyer, *Music-printing, 1473-1934* in 'Dolphin' (N. Y., 1935).

Briccialdi (brēt-chahl'-dē), **Giulio,** Italian flutist; b. Terni, Papal States, March 2, 1818; d. Florence, Dec. 17, 1881. A precocious musician, he held an appointment with the St. Cecilia Academy at Rome at the age of 15; made concert tours in England and America; after 1842 lived chiefly in London. He wrote an opera, *Leonora de' Medici* (Milan, 1855); many compositions for flute; also a method for flute.

Bricken, Carl Ernest, American composer; b. Shelbyville, Kentucky, Dec. 28, 1898. He studied at Yale Univ., and in New York, at the Mannes School, with Rosario Scalero; went to Europe and completed his studies with Alfred Cortot in Paris and with Hans Weisse in Vienna; then taught piano at the Mannes School (1925-28); won a Pulitzer Prize in 1929, and was awarded a Guggenheim Fellowship in 1930-31. In 1931 he was appointed associate prof. and chairman of the Department of Music at the Univ. of Chicago; also taught at the Univ. of Wisconsin (1938-44). He was conductor of the Seattle Symph. Orch. from 1944-48. He gave many successful piano recitals. His compositions include a Suite for orch. (1931); a symphony (1935); a string quartet (1925); piano quintet (1930); cello sonata; violin sonata; variations on an old English theme for 2 pianos; children's songs; etc.

Brico, Antonia, American conductor; b. Oakland, California, June 26, 1902. She was educated at the Univ. of California (grad., 1923); then studied music with Karl Muck at the State Academy of Berlin; also with Sigismund Stojowski; appeared as a concert pianist early in her career; then devoted herself to conducting; made her début as a conductor with the Berlin Philh. Orch. (1920), and her American début with the Los Angeles Philh. (1930); subsequently attracted attention as guest conductor of European orchestras. She founded a women's orchestra in the U. S., which she conducted at special concerts organized by her; these concerts aroused a certain curiosity.

Bridge, Frank, distinguished English composer; b. Brighton, Feb. 26, 1879; d. Eastbourne, Jan. 10, 1941. He studied violin at the Royal College of Music; then composition with Stanford. He played the viola in the Joachim Quartet (1906) and later in the English String Quartet; won the gold medal of the Rajah of Tagore. His professional employment was as conductor of the Marie Brema Opera at the Savoy Theatre, London (1910-11); then conducted at Covent Garden during the seasons of Raymond Roze and Beecham; he also appeared as a symph. conductor at the Promenade Concerts. In 1923 he made a U. S. tour and conducted his own works in Rochester, Boston, Detroit, Cleveland and New York; he made two subsequent visits to the U. S., in 1934 and 1938. As a composer he received a belated recognition towards the end of his life, and posthumously; although he wrote a great deal of music, particularly for small instrumental combinations, his name never figured prominently in the constellation of modern English composers who came to the fore in the first decades of the century. His chamber music is eminently practical, designed for easy performance; however, there is no concession to popular taste in his works. As a teacher he enjoyed a great reputation among English musicians; among his pupils was Benjamin Britten. Works: *The Christmas Rose,* children's opera (1919-29); *Isabella,* symph. poem (1907); *Dance Rhapsody* (1908); *Dance Poem* (1909); incidental music to *The Hunchback* (1910); *The Sea,* orchestral suite (1910-11; Promenade Concerts, London, Sept. 24, 1912); *Summer,* symph. poem (1914); *2 Poems* (after Richard Jeffries, 1915); *Lament* for string orch. (in memory of the victims of the sinking of the Lusitania; 1915); *Rebus for orch.* (London, Feb. 23, 1941); *3 Novelettes* for string quartet (1904); Phantasie Quartet (1905); piano quintet (1906); *3 Idylls* for string quartet (1906); string quartet in E minor (1906; received a Bologna prize); *Miniatures* for piano trio (1906); Phantasie Trio for piano (1908); *An Irish Melody (Londonderry Air)* for string quartet (1908); Phantasie Quartet for piano, violin, viola and cello (1910); string sextet (1912); cello sonata (1913-17); string quartet in G minor (1915); *Sally in Our Alley* and *Cherry Ripe* for string quartet (1916); *Sir Roger de Coverly* for string quartet (1922; also arranged for orch.); Trio No. 2 for piano, violin and cello (1929); 4th string quartet (1937, dedicated to Mrs. E. S. Coolidge; performed at the Berkshire Festival, 1938); violin sonata (1904); cello sonata (1916-17); violin pieces; viola pieces; cello pieces; much piano music, including a sonata (1922-25); *4 Characteristic Pieces* (1915); *Arabesque* (1915); *3 Sketches* (1906); suite, *A Fairy Tale* (1917); 2 Capriccios (1903; 1916); organ pieces; vocal music including *A Prayer* for chorus and orch. (London, 1919); *Blow out, you Bugles* for tenor and orch. (1918); about 100 fine songs, which attained great popularity throughout the world. See the 'Musical Times' (Feb., 1919); 'Monthly Musical Record' (April, 1930), Herbert Howells, *Frank Bridge* in 'Music & Letters,' XXII (1941, p. 208).

Bridge, Sir **John Frederick,** English organist, conductor and composer; b. Oldbury, near Birmingham, Dec. 5, 1844; d. London, March 18, 1924. At the age of fourteen he was apprenticed to John Hopkins, organist of Rochester Cathedral; later studied under John Goss; was organist at churches in Windsor and Manchester; then principal organist at Westminster Abbey (1882-1918); took the degree of Mus. Doc. at Oxford in 1874 with his oratorio, *Mount Moriah;* then taught harmony and organ at various music schools, including the Royal College of Music (from 1883); was conductor of the Highbury Philh. Society (1878-86), the Madrigal

Society, and the Royal Choral Society (1896-1922); also served as chairman of Trinity College of Music. He was knighted in 1897. Works: the cantatas *Boadicea* (1880); *Rock of Ages* (1885); *Callirrhoë* (Birmingham, 1888); and *The Lobster's Garden Party* or *The Selfish Shellfish* (1904); a dramatic oratorio, *The Repentance of Nineveh* (Worcester, 1890); *The Lord's Prayer* (after Dante, 1892); *The Cradle of Christ* (1894); concert overture for orch., *Morte d'Arthur* (1896); the choral ballades *The Festival, The Inchcape Rock, The Flag of England* (after Rudyard Kipling), and *The Ballad of the Camperdown* (after Kipling); *The Forging of the Anchor* for baritone and chorus (1901). He published primers on counterpoint, canon, organ accompaniment and other subjects; also *A Course of Harmony* (with Sawyer; 1899); *Samuel Pepys, Lover of Music* (1903); an autobiography, *A Westminster Pilgrim* (1918); *12 Good Musicians from John Bull to Henry Purcell* (1920); *The Old Cryes of London* (1921); *Shakespearean Music in the Plays and Early Operas* (1923); edited selected motets of Orlando Gibbons (1907).

Bridge, Joseph Cox, English organist and composer, brother of John Frederick Bridge; b. Rochester, Aug. 16, 1853; d. St. Albans, March 29, 1929. He studied with his brother and with John Hopkins; from 1877-1925 was organist of Chester Cathedral; in 1879 he revived the Chester Triennial Music Festival and became its conductor until 1900; also founded (1883) and conducted for 20 years the Chester Musical Society; from 1908 was professor of music at Durham Univ. Works: an oratorio, *Daniel* (1885); the cantatas *Rudel* (1891) and *Resurgam* (1897); *Evening Service* with *orch.* (1879); *Requiem Mass* (1900); an operetta, *The Belle of the Area;* a symphony (1894); string quartet; cello sonata; anthems, organ music, piano pieces, songs, etc.

Brinsmead, John, English piano maker; b. Wear Giffard, Devon, Oct. 13, 1814; d. London, Feb. 17, 1908. He founded his celebrated piano factory in London in 1836. In 1863 his sons, Thomas and Edgar, were admitted to partnership; in 1900 the firm was incorporated and assumed its permanent title, John Brinsmead & Sons, Ltd. In 1868 they patented an improvement in piano construction, 'Perfect Check Repeater Action.' In 1908, upon the death of John Brinsmead, the controlling interest was purchased by W. Savile, a director of J. B. Cramer & Co. Edgar Brinsmead (d. Nov. 28, 1907) wrote a *History of the Pianoforte* (1868; revised and republished, 1879).

Bristow, George Frederick, American composer; b. Brooklyn, N. Y., Dec. 19, 1825; d. New York, Dec. 13, 1898. He was the son of William Richard Bristow (b. England, 1803; d. 1867), who was a well known conductor in New York. George Bristow was first active as a violinist; played in the orch. of the Olympic Theater in New York (1836); and in the N. Y. Philh. Society (from 1842); was organist at several churches; also conducted the Harmonic Society (1851-62) and later the Mendelssohn Union; from 1854 he was a teacher in the New York public schools. Bristow was one of the earliest American composers to write operatic and chamber music. He was a militant champion of music by Americans, and made frequent pronouncements urging musical organizations to perform American music.—Works: opera *Rip Van Winkle* (N. Y., Sept. 27, 1855); unfinished opera *Columbus* (overture performed by the N. Y. Philh., Nov. 17, 1866); oratorios: *Praise to God* (N. Y. Harmonic Society, March 2, 1861); *Daniel* (N. Y., Dec. 30, 1867); cantatas: *The Great Republic* (Brooklyn Philh. Society, May 10, 1879); *Niagara,* for soli, chorus, and orch. (Manuscript Society, Carnegie Hall, N. Y., April 11, 1898). Orchestral works: symphony in D minor, written for the French conductor Jullien (Jullien's concert, N. Y. Philh., March 1, 1856); symphony in F♯ minor (N. Y. Philh., March 26, 1859); *Arcadian Symphony* (N. Y. Philh., Feb. 14, 1874); overture *Jibbenainosay* (Harlem Philh., N. Y., March 6, 1889); 2 string quartets; organ pieces; piano pieces; violin pieces; choral pieces; songs; also publ. a *New and Improved Method for Reed or Cabinet Organ* (N. Y., 1888).—Cf. J. T. Howard, *Our American Music* (N. Y., 1939).

Britain, Radie, American composer; b. Amarillo, Texas, March 17, 1903. She studied piano at the American Cons. in Chicago, and theory with Noelte in Munich. Works: *Heroic Poem* (on Lindbergh's flight to Paris; won a prize in the Hollywood Bowl International Contest; 1st perf., Rochester, March 3, 1932); *Light* (dedicated to Edison; 1st prize, 1935, in the National Contest for Women Composers; Chicago, Nov. 29, 1938); *Southern Symphony* (Chicago, March 4, 1940); *Fantasy* for oboe and orch. (1941); *Cactus Rhapsody* for orch. (1945); 2 string quartets; and several choral works, among them *Drums of Africa* (1934); *Rain* (1937) and *Lasso of Time* (1940); also a music drama *Ubiquity* (1937).

Britt, Horace, cellist; b. Antwerp, June 18, 1881. He studied at the Paris Cons. with Jules Delsart (cello) and Albert Lavignac (harmony); was later a private pupil of André Caplet; was soloist with the Lamoureux Orch. (1897); made his American debut with the Chicago Symph. Orch. (1907); then toured extensively in the U. S. with Georges Barrère and Carlos Salzedo; was co-founder of the 'Barrère-Britt Concertino', a chamber music group organized in 1937.

Britten, Benjamin, remarkable English composer; b. Lowestoft, Suffolk, Nov. 22, 1913. He played piano and composed at a very early age; then took lessons with Frank Bridge; received a scholarship at the Royal College of Music (1930) where he studied composition with John Ireland, and piano with Arthur Benjamin and Harold Samuel; graduated in 1934. He became connected with the theater and the cinema; wrote documentary films, and incidental music. His *Fantasy Quartet* for oboe and strings was performed at the Festival of the I.S.C.M. in Florence (April 5, 1934) and obtained excellent success; other works were performed at the festivals in Barcelona (1936) and London (1938). He was in the U. S. at the outbreak of World War II; returned to England in the spring of 1942; was exempt from military service as a conscientious objector. He produced his first opera *Paul Bunyan* at Columbia Univ., N. Y. (May 5, 1941). His first great operatic success was with *Peter Grimes* (London, June 7, 1945) which was originally commissioned by the Koussevitzky Foundation; it was performed at the Berkshire Music Festival in 1946; numerous performances followed in Europe and America. Subsequent operas were: *The Rape of Lucretia* (Glyndebourne, July 12, 1946); *Albert Herring* (Glyndebourne, June 20, 1947); *The Beggar's Opera,* a 'new realization' (Cambridge, May 24, 1948); *The Little Sweep,* or *Let's Make an Opera,* 'an entertainment for young people' with optional audience participation (Aldeburgh, June 14, 1949); *Billy Budd,* after Melville (London, Dec. 1, 1951); *Gloriana* (on the subject of Elizabeth and Essex; 1st performance during Coronation Week, June 8, 1953, at Covent Garden, in the presence of Queen Elizabeth II); *The Turn of the Screw,* after Henry James (Venice, Sept. 14, 1954).—For orch.: *Sinfonietta* (1932); *Simple Symphony* for strings (1925; revised in 1934); *Variations on a Theme by Frank Bridge* for strings (1937); *Canadian Carnival* (1939); *Sinfonia da Requiem* (N. Y., Philharmonic, March 29, 1941); *Scottish Ballad* for 2 pianos and orch. (Cincinnati, Nov. 29, 1941); *Les Illuminations* for voice and strings (London, Jan. 30, 1940); *Diversions on a Theme* for piano (left hand alone) and orch. (Phila., Jan. 16, 1942, Paul Wittgenstein, soloist); *Serenade* for tenor, horn and string orch. (London, Oct. 15, 1943); *The Young Person's Guide to the Orchestra,* variations and fugue on a theme by Purcell (originally, music for film 'The Instruments of the Orchestra', 1945); *Divertimento,* for chamber orch. (Basel, Jan. 24, 1952).—For chorus: *Hymn to the Virgin* (1930); *A Boy Was Born* (1933); *Friday Afternoons* for children's voices (1934); *Ballad of Heroes* (1939); *A Ceremony of Carols,* for boys' chorus and harp (Aldeburgh, June 14, 1942); *Hymn to St. Cecilia* (BBC, Nov. 28, 1942); *Rejoice in the Lamb,* festival cantata (1943); *Festival Te Deum* (1945); *St. Nicolas,* cantata (Aldeburgh, July 24, 1948); *Spring Symphony,* for soloists, chorus and orch. (Amsterdam, July 14, 1949).—Chamber music: *Fantasy Quartet* for oboe, violin, viola and cello (1932); *Suite* for violin and piano (1935); 2 string quartets (1941; 1945); also *Six Metamorphoses,* after Ovid, for oboe solo (1951); 'new realizations' of some works by Purcell (*The Golden Sonata* for two violins, cello and piano, etc.). Arrangements: two orchestral suites from Rossini, *Soirées musicales* (1936) and *Matinées Musicales* (1941); also folksong transcriptions. Britten has appeared as conductor, and as pianist; made numerous tours with the tenor, Peter Pears, in programs of his own and other songs. A whole literature has arisen about him; a voluminous compendium, *Benjamin Britten: A Commentary on His Works from a Group of Specialists,* was published under the editorship of D. Mitchell and Hans Keller (London, 1953); see also E. W. White, *Benjamin Britten* (London, 1948; new enlarged edition, 1954); numerous magazine articles have been published dealing with Britten's individual works. It has been said that Britten is the first significant British composer of operas since Purcell. His success is explained, apart from a genuine gift for dramatic and lyric expression, by his ability to sustain melodic interest and a clear rhythmic line in a contemporary modern style, making free use of dissonant harmony, and his ability to obtain sonorous effects with small orchestras in his operatic scores, thus making it possible to perform them outside the great opera stages.

Brixi, Franz Xaver, Bohemian composer of church music; b. Prague, Jan. 2, 1732; d. there, Oct. 14, 1771. He was a pupil of

Segert in Prague; held several positions as church organist. He wrote a great number of sacred works: 105 masses, 263 offertories and anthems; 6 oratorios; 3 organ concertos, etc. See O. Kamper, *Franz Xaver Brixi* (Prague, 1926).

Brkanović (brkah'-no-vitch), **Ivan,** Croatian composer; b. Skaljari, Bocca of Kotor, Dec. 27, 1906. He studied music in Zagreb with Bersa and Lhotka. He has written 5 symphonies, 2 string quartets, and several choral cycles. His opera *Equinox* was performed in Zagreb in 1950. Since 1952, he has been musical adviser of the Zagreb Opera. In his works, Brkanović derives thematic materials from national folk music, but his harmonic idiom follows modern usage.

Broadwood & Sons, oldest keyboard instrument manufactory in existence; established in London in 1728 by the Swiss harpsichord maker **Burkhard Tschudi,** or **Shudi** (b. Schwanden, Switzerland, March 13, 1702; d. London, Aug. 19, 1773). **John Broadwood** (b. Cockburnspath, Scotland, 1732; d. London, 1812), a Scotch cabinet maker, was Shudi's son-in-law and successor; in 1773 he began to build square pianos modeled after Zumpe's instruments; in 1780 he marketed his own square pianos, which he patented in 1783; in these, he dispensed with the old clavichord arrangement of the wrest-plank and tuning-pins and transformed the harpsichord pedals into damper and piano pedals; another important invention came in 1788, when he divided the long bridge, which until then had been continuous. Broadwood's improvements were soon adopted by other manufacturers. In 1794 the range of the keyboard was extended to six octaves. John Broadwood's sons, **James Shudi Broadwood** (b. London, Dec. 20, 1772; d. there, Aug. 8, 1851) and **Thomas Broadwood,** were admitted to the firm in 1795 and 1807 respectively, and the business was then carried on under the name of John Broadwood & Sons. Beethoven received a Broadwood piano in 1817. **Henry John Tschudi Broadwood** (d. Feb. 8, 1911), great-grandson of the founder, patented the so-called 'barless' grand piano; he became a director of John Broadwood & Sons, Ltd., established in 1901, with W. H. Leslie as chairman. In 1925 the firm moved to new quarters in New Bond Street. Members of the Broadwood family are still active in its affairs.—Cf. W. Dale, *Tschudi, the Harpsichord Maker* (London, 1913).

Broche, Charles, French organist and composer; b. Rouen, Feb. 20, 1752; d. there, Sept. 30, 1803. He was a church organist at the age of fourteen. In 1771 he went to Paris; then to Italy and studied with Padre Martini in Bologna. In 1777 he returned to Rouen as organist of the cathedral. Among his pupils was Boieldieu. Broche publ. three piano sonatas (1782) and wrote some music for organ. Cf. G. Favre, *Un organiste de la Cathédrale de Rouen, Charles Broche* ('Revue de Musicologie', 1937).

Brockway, Howard A., American composer and pianist; b. Brooklyn, Nov. 22, 1870; d. New York, Feb. 20, 1951. He studied in Berlin (1890-95); returning to the U. S., he settled in N. Y. as a teacher and concert pianist; from 1903-10 taught at the Peabody Cons. in Baltimore; since 1910 again in N. Y. as teacher and concert pianist. Among his works are *Sylvan Suite* for orch. (Boston, April 6, 1901); Symphony in D (Berlin, Feb. 23, 1895; Boston, April 6, 1907, Karl Muck cond.); a cantata, *Herr Oluf; Des Sängers Fluch* for 8-part chorus a cappella; *Moment musical* for violin and piano; many character pieces for piano (*Moods, Dance of the Sylphs,* etc.). He wrote piano accompaniments for 2 albums of Kentucky songs (to words collected by Loraine Wyman), which were publ. as *Lonesome Tunes* (N. Y., 1916) and *20 Kentucky Mountain Songs* (Boston, 1920).

Brod, Max, writer and composer; b. Prague, May 27, 1884. Well known in Europe for his psychological novels, he was active in Prague as a music critic; translated the libretti of Janáček's *Jenufa* and Weinberger's *Schwanda* into German. In 1939 Brod settled in Palestine, where he has written several musical works, including *Requiem Hebraicum* for baritone and orch., *Two Rustic Dances* for orch. (Tel-Aviv, April 24, 1947), songs, etc.

Broder, Nathan, American musicologist and editor; b. New York, Dec. 1, 1905. He studied at the College of the City of New York. In 1945 he became associate editor of the 'Musical Quarterly'; was also manager of the publication department of G. Schirmer, Inc. (until 1954). From 1946-52 he was lecturer in music at Columbia Univ. Broder is the author of numerous articles and reviews; has contributed to the 5th edition of Grove's Dictionary and to 'Die Musik in Geschichte und Gegenwart'; published a monograph on Samuel Barber (N. Y., 1954); edited Mozart's piano sonatas and fantasies, according to the original MSS (Bryn Mawr, 1956). In 1956 he received a Guggenheim Fellowship to work on a project in music history.

Brodsky, Adolf, distinguished violinist; b. Taganrog, Russia, March 21, 1851; d. Manchester, England, Jan. 22, 1929. He was a pupil of Joseph Hellmesberger; then studied at the Vienna Cons. (1860-63); was a member of the Hellmesberger Quartet and of the Vienna Orch. (1868-70); took lessons with Laub in Moscow (1873-5) and succeeded him as professor at the Moscow Cons. Leaving Moscow in 1879, he conducted symphony concerts in Kiev; in 1881 he made a highly successful tour which included concerts in Paris, Vienna, and London. He gave the first public performance of Tchaikovsky's violin concerto with the Vienna Philh. Society in 1882, and won a sensational success, not in any way diminished by Hanslick's savage attack on the concerto. In 1883 Brodsky succeeded Henry Schradieck as professor at the Leipzig Cons., where he taught until 1891. In Leipzig he established the Brodsky Quartet (with Hugo Becker, Hans Sitt and Julius Klengel), which enjoyed an international reputation, appearing on frequent tours of Germany, Russia, Italy, Holland and Belgium. From 1891-4 Brodsky was in New York as concertmaster of the N. Y. Symph. Orch.; also toured the U. S. and Canada; then returned to Germany for further concerts in that country and Russia. In 1895 he settled in Manchester as concertmaster of the Hallé Orch. and professor of violin at the Royal College of Music. Three weeks after his arrival Sir Charles Hallé died, and Brodsky succeeded him as director of the Royal College of Music in Manchester, a position which he held until his death. There he also established another quartet (with Briggs, Spielman and Fuchs). In 1892 he was honored with the Norwegian Order of St. Olaf; in 1902 Victoria Univ. conferred upon him an honorary Mus. Doc. degree. He was on intimate terms with many celebrated musicians; Tchaikovsky met Brahms and Grieg for the first time at Brodsky's home in Leipzig.

Brodsky, Vera, American pianist; b. Norfolk, Virginia, July 1, 1909. She studied with Alexander Lambert for six years; then held a fellowship at the Juilliard Foundation, where she was a pupil of Josef and Rosina Lhevinne (1929-32); made concert appearances as soloist with orchestras in Europe (1930) and in the U. S. (1931); in 1932 she and Harold Triggs gave piano duo concerts in an extensive tour of the U. S.

Broekman, David, composer and conductor; b. Leyden, May 13, 1902. He studied at the Cons. of The Hague with Van Anrooy; as a young man conducted opera performances in Holland and Germany. He came to the U. S. in 1924 as music editor for M. Witmark & Sons; then went to Hollywood as composer of film scores. He eventually settled in New York, developing energetic activity as conductor of ultra-modern music. He has written 2 symphonies (Hollywood Bowl, 1934; Cincinnati Symph., March 7, 1947); motion picture scores (*All Quiet on the Western Front; The Phantom of the Opera,* etc.). Has published a book, *The Shoestring Symphony* (N. Y., 1948), describing the life of a composer in Hollywood.

Brogi, Renato, Italian composer; b. Sesto Fiorentino, Feb. 25, 1873; d. San Domenico di Fiesole, Florence, Aug. 24, 1924. He first studied music in Florence; then with Ferroni at the Milan Cons.; won the Steiner Prize in Vienna with his opera *La prima notte* (Florence, Nov. 25, 1898). He also composed the operas *L'Oblio* (Florence, Feb. 4, 1890) and *Isabella Orsini* (Florence, April 24, 1920); the operettas *Bacco in Toscana* and *Follie Veneziane* (both produced in Florence, 1923); a violin concerto; a string quartet; a piano trio; songs.

Broman, Natanael, Swedish pianist and composer; b. Kolsva, Dec. 11, 1887. He studied piano and composition at the Stockholm Cons.; then with Ignaz Friedman and Kempff in Berlin; returned to Stockholm, where he was active in radio and as a pianist. He has composed a symph. poem, *Fritiof och Ingeborg* (1912); a ballade, *Kung Lif och Drottning Död* (1913); a violin sonata; *Romance* for violin and piano; piano pieces; songs.

Bronsart von Schellendorf, Hans, German pianist and composer; b. Berlin, Feb. 11, 1830; d. Munich, Nov. 3, 1913. He studied at Berlin Univ. (1849-52); was also a pupil of Dehn (theory) and Kullak (piano); later studied with Liszt at Weimar; gave piano concerts in Germany, Paris, and St. Petersburg; from 1860 to 1895 was active as conductor and theater Intendant in Berlin, Hanover, and Weimar; retired in 1895 and devoted himself entirely to composition. Works: an opera, *Der Korsar;* a cantata, *Christnacht;* symph. with chorus, *In den Schicksalgewalten;* symph. poem, *Manfred* (1901); *Frühlingsfantasie* for orch.; a string sextet; piano concerto; piano trio; piano pieces.

Bronsart, Ingeborg von (*née* Starck), pianist and composer; b. (of Swedish parents) St. Petersburg, Aug. 24, 1840; d. Munich, June 17, 1913. She studied piano with Liszt at Weimar; in 1862 married Hans Bronsart von Schellendorf. She composed 3 operas: *König Hjarne* (Berlin, 1891); *Jery und Bätely* (Weimar, 1873); *Die Sühne* (Dessau, 1909); also piano concertos, piano sonatas, salon pieces, violin pieces, cello pieces and songs.

Broome, William Edward, Canadian conductor and composer; b. Manchester, England, 1868; d. Toronto, Canada, May 10, 1932. He studied piano and organ with Dr. Roland Rogers at Bangor Cathedral in Wales (1876-90), but was chiefly self-taught in theory and composition; was active as church organist in Bangor (1883-90) and as choral conductor; went to Canada and became organist in Montreal (1894-1905) and Toronto. He also taught at the Toronto Cons., specializing in voice-training and choral conducting; organized the Toronto Oratorio Society (1910); won prizes at Welsh National Festivals for his dramatic cantata *The Siege of Cardiff Castle* (1908) and other works; published much church music, including a *Hymn of Trust.*

Broqua, Alfonso, Uruguayan composer; b. Montevideo, Dec. 11, 1876; d. Paris, Nov. 24, 1946. He studied with Vincent d'Indy at the Schola Cantorum in Paris, where he settled. His works are characterized by a fine feeling for exotic material, which he presents in the brilliant manner of French modern music. Works: The 3-act opera *Cruz del Sur* (1918); *Thelen et Nagouëy,* Inca ballet (1934); *Isabelle,* romantic ballet (1936); *Tabaré,* poetic cycle for soli, women's chorus and piano or orch. (1908); *Poema de las Lomas,* triptych for piano (1912); piano quintet; *3 Cantos del Uruguay,* for voice, flute and 2 guitars (1925); *Cantos de Parana,* for voice and guitar (1929); *Evocaciones Criollas,* 7 pieces for guitar (1929); 3 *Préludes Pampéens,* for piano (1938; also in orchestral version).

Broschi (bros'-kē), **Carlo.** See **Farinelli.**

Brosig, Moritz, prolific church composer; b. Fuchswinkel, Upper Silesia, Oct. 15, 1815; d. Breslau, Jan. 24, 1887. He studied with Franz Wolf, the cathedral organist at Breslau, and succeeded him in 1842. He wrote 4 grand and 3 short instrumental masses; 7 books of graduals and offertories; 20 books of organ pieces; an *Orgelbuch,* a *Choralbuch,* a *Modulationstheorie* (1865), and a *Harmonielehre* (1874; 4th ed. 1899 as *Handbuch der Harmonielehre und Modulation,* ed. by Thiel); also *Über die alten Kirchenkompositionen und ihre Wiedereinführung* (1880). Leuckart publ. a selection of his works in 5 vols.

Brossard, Noël-Matthieu, French writer on music; b. Chalons-sur-Saône, Dec. 25, 1789; date of death unknown. He was a judge; became interested in music; published *Théorie des sons musicaux* (Paris, 1847), a treatise on the variability of tones according to modulation (he reckons 48 distinct tone-degrees within the octave).

Brossard, Sébastien de, French composer; b. Dompierre, Orne, 1655 (baptized Sept. 12); d. Meaux, France, Aug. 10, 1730. He studied theology at Caen (1670-76); was then in Paris (1678-87); in 1687 he went to Strasbourg; in 1689 became 'maître de chapelle' at the Strasbourg Cathedral; in 1698 received a similar post at the Cathedral of Meaux; in 1709 he became canon there. His fame rests upon the authorship of what was erroneously regarded as the earliest dictionary of musical terms; it was in fact preceded by many publications: the medieval compilation *De Musica antica et moderna* (c. 1100), the last section of which is a vocabulary of musical terms (to be found in Lafage's *Essais de dipthérographie musicale* vol. I, pp. 404-7), by Joannes Tinctoris' *Terminorum musicae diffinitorium* (c. 1475), and Janowka's *Clavis ad thesaurum magnae artis musicae* (1701), to none of which Brossard had access, however. The title of Brossard's own volume is *Dictionnaire de musique, contenant une explication des termes grecs, latins, italiens et français les plus usités dans la musique, etc.* (Paris, 1703; 2nd ed. 1705; there is also an Amsterdam reprint, marked 6th edition, but this designation is erroneous; English translation by Grassineau, 1740). Brossard also wrote *Lettre à M. Demotz sur sa nouvelle méthode d'écrire le plain-chant et la musique* (1729); a considerable variety of church music, including a *Canticum Eucharisticum* on the Peace of Ryswick (1697; new edition by F. X. Mathias); motets; etc. He brought out several volumes of *Airs sérieux et à boire.* His library of manuscripts was acquired by Louis XV in 1724, and formed the nucleus of the music collection of the Bibliothèque Nationale.—Cf. M. Brenet, *Sébastien de Brossard* (Paris, 1896); also E. Lebeau, *L'entrée de la collection musicale de Sébastien de Brossard à la Bibliothèque du Roi,* in the 'Revue de Musicologie' (Dec. 1950).

Brosses, Charles de, French magistrate and scholar; b. Dijon, Feb. 17, 1709; d. Paris, May 7, 1777. He first studied law, but later turned to science and literature, subjects on which he published several valuable dissertations; contributed the article *Musique* to the *Encyclopédie méthodique.* He was the first president of the parliament of Burgundy, and member of the Académie des Belles-Lettres (1758).—Cf. H. Mamet, *Le Président Charles de Brosses, sa vie et ses ouvrages* (Lille, 1874); Cunisset-Carnot, *La Querelle de Voltaire et du président Charles de Brosses,* in the 'Revue des Deux Mondes' (Feb. 15, 1888).

Brott, Alexander, Canadian composer; b. Montreal, March 14, 1915. He studied at McGill Cons. in Montreal; then at the Juilliard School of Music, N. Y. He was concertmaster of Les Concerts Symphoniques in Montreal; also active as conductor. His works include 3 symphonic poems: *Oracle* (1939); *War and Peace* (1944) and *Concordia* (1946); symphonic suite *From Sea to Sea* (1947); violin concerto (Montreal, March 7, 1950; N. Y., Oct. 16, 1953, under Stokowski); *Prelude to Oblivion* for chamber orch. (1951); septet for 4 recorders, violin, viola and cello (1948); *5 Miniatures* for 8 players (1950); quintet for strings and percussion (1950) and piano pieces.

Brouillon - Lacombe (broo - yohn' - lah - kohnb'). See **Lacombe.**

Brounoff, Platon G., composer and pianist; b. Elizavetgrad, Russia, May 10, 1863; d. New York, July 11, 1924. He studied at the St. Petersburg Cons. (1890) with Anton Rubinstein and Rimsky-Korsakov. In 1891 he went to the U. S., where he was conductor of 'The Modern Symph. Orch.', 'Russian Choral Society', and 'People's Male Chorus' in New York. Works: Opera *Ramona;* music dramas *Xilona* and *Titanic; Angel,* cantata for 2 solo voices, chorus and orch.; *The Glory of God,* oratorio; *Russia,* festival overture (N. Y., 1897); orchestral suites *Flower Garden* (1897), *Russian Village,* and *Palestine* (1908); piano pieces; collections of Russian and Jewish folk songs. He was the author of *Ten Commandments of Piano Practice* (publ. privately, 1910).

Brown, Eddy, American violinist; b. Chicago, July 15, 1895. He began his professional career as a child prodigy; in 1904 went to Europe and studied with Jenö Hubay at the Budapest Cons., and with Auer at the St. Petersburg Cons. He returned to the U. S. in 1915 and made several transcontinental tours, enjoying great success; in 1922 he founded the Eddy Brown String Quartet; then abandoned a concert career, and devoted himself mainly to educational work and the radio; was music director of the Mutual Broadcasting System (1930-37) and of station WQXR (1936-55). In 1956 he was appointed artistic coordinator of the Cincinnati College and Conservatory of Music.

Brown, James Duff, British music bibliographer; b. Edinburgh, Nov. 6, 1862; d. London, March 1, 1914. He was librarian of the Clerkenwell Library of London from 1888; co-author (with Stephen S. Stratton) of the valuable reference work *British Musical Biography: A Dictionary of Musical Artists, Authors and Composers born in Great Britain and its Colonies* (1897). He also published a *Biographical Dictionary of Musicians* (1886); *Guide to the Formation of a Music Library* (1893); *Characteristic Songs and Dances of All Nations* with historical notes and a bibliography (in collaboration with Moffat, 1901); and *Subject Classification* (1908). His *Manual of Library Economy* was publ. in several editions (3d ed., London, 1920).

Brown, (Dr.) **John,** English writer; b. Rothbury, Northumberland, Nov. 5, 1715; d. (suicide) Newcastle-on-Tyne, Sept. 23, 1766. He became vicar of Great Horkesley, Essex, in 1754, and of St. Nicholas', Newcastle, in 1758. He was the author of a *Dissertation on the Rise, Union, and Power, the Progressions, Separations and Corruptions of Poetry and Music, to which is prefixed The Cure of Saul, A Sacred Ode* (London, 1763). A revised edition was publ. in 1764 as *The History of the Rise and Progress of Poetry, through its Several Species* (in French, Paris, 1768; in German, Leipzig, 1769; in Italian, 1772).

Brown, William, flute player and composer, who settled in America in the middle of the 18th century. He gave a concert on the flute in Baltimore on Jan. 30, 1784; then went to Philadelphia, where he participated in numerous benefit concerts; in 1785 he established a series of Subscription Concerts in New York and Philadelphia (with Alexander Reinagle and Henri Capron). He composed *3 Rondos for the Pianoforte or Harpsichord* (dedicated to Francis Hopkinson). He was probably a German; may be identical with Wilhelm Braun of Kassel. (See J. D. Apell, *Galerie der vorzüglichsten Tonkünstler und merkwürdigen Musikdilettanten in Kassel,* 1806). See also J. T. Howard, *Our American Music* (N. Y., 1939); Carl Engel, *Introducing Mr. Brown* in the 'Mus. Quarterly' (Jan., 1944).

Browne, John Lewis, organist and composer; b. London, May 18, 1864; d. Chicago, Oct. 23, 1933. He was a pupil of his father, William Browne, a noted organist; later studied with S. P. Warren (1884) and F. Archer (1887); settling in America, he was active as organist in San Francisco, Atlanta, Philadelphia, and Chicago; during his career he gave more than 500 organ recitals. He designed an organ for Medinah Temple in Chicago, and inaugurated it with the first performance of Felix Borowski's *Allegro de Concert,* commissioned for the occasion. He wrote an opera, *La Corsicana,* which received an honorable mention in the Sonzogno Competition in 1902; it was first performed in Chicago on Jan. 4, 1923. Other works: an ode, *The Granite Walls Rise Fair* (1911); *Ecce Sacerdos Magnus* (Vatican, 1912); *Missa Solemnis* (1913); organ pieces; piano pieces; many songs. Browne received the David Bispham Memorial Medal in 1925. See E. E. Hipsher, *American Opera and its Composers* (Philadelphia, 1927; pp. 93-97).

Brownlee, John (full name, John Donald Mackensie Brownlee), baritone; b. Geelong, Australia, Jan. 7, 1900. He was educated at Geelong College, singing meanwhile as an amateur until he was heard by Melba who persuaded him to study seriously. He made his début at her farewell appearance in *La Bohème* at Covent Garden (June 26, 1926). In 1927 he joined the Paris Opéra. His first American appearance was at the Metropolitan Opera House, N. Y., in *Rigoletto* on Feb. 17, 1937. He remained in the U. S., and in 1956 was appointed director of the Manhattan School of Music, N. Y., while continuing on the staff of the Metropolitan Opera.

Bruch, Max, celebrated German composer; b. Cologne, Jan. 6, 1838; d. Friednau, near Berlin, Oct. 2, 1920. His mother, a professional singer, was his first teacher. He afterwards studied theory with Breidenstein in Bonn; in 1852 he won a scholarship of the Mozart Foundation in Frankfurt for four years, and became a pupil of Ferdinand Hiller, Reinecke, and Breuning. At the age of fourteen, he brought out a symphony at Cologne, and at 20 produced his first stage work, *Scherz, List und Rache,* adapted from Goethe's Singspiel (Cologne, Jan. 14, 1858). Between 1858 and 1861 he taught music in Cologne; also made prolonged visits to Berlin, Leipzig, Dresden and Munich; in 1863 he was in Mannheim, where he produced his first full-fledged opera, *Die Loreley* (April 14, 1863), to the libretto by Geibel, originally intended for Mendelssohn. About the same time he wrote an effective choral work *Frithjof,* which was presented with great success in various German towns, and in Vienna. In 1865 Bruch became a musical director of a concert organization in Koblenz; there he wrote his first violin concerto in G minor, which became a great favorite among violinists. In 1870 he went to Berlin; his last opera, *Hermione,* based on Shakespeare's *The Winter's Tale,* was produced at the Berlin Opera on March 21, 1872. In 1880 he accepted the post of conductor of the Liverpool Philharmonic, and remained in England for three years; in 1883 he visited the U. S., and conducted his choral work *Arminius* in Boston. From 1883-1890 he was music director of an orchestral society in Breslau; in 1891 he became professor of composition at the Musikhochschule in Berlin, retiring in 1910. Bruch was married to the singer Clara Tuczek (d. 1919). The Univ. of Cambridge conferred upon him the honorary degree of Mus. Doc. (1893); the French Academy elected him corresponding member; in 1918 the Univ. of Berlin gave him the honorary degree of *Dr. phil.* Bruch's music, although imitative in its essence and even in its melodic and harmonic procedures, has a great eclectic charm; he was a master of harmony, counterpoint and instrumentation; he was equally adept at handling vocal masses. He contributed a great deal to the development of the secular oratorio, using soloists, chorus and orchestra. In this genre he wrote *Odysseus, Arminius, Das Lied von der Glocke* and *Achilleus;* also *Frithjof* for baritone, female chorus and orch.; *Normannenzug* for baritone, male chorus and orch.; and several other works for various vocal ensembles. Among his instrumental works, the so-called *Scottish Fantasy* for violin and orch. (1880) was extremely successful when Sarasate (to whom the work was dedicated) performed it all over Europe; but the most popular of all works by Bruch is his *Kol Nidrei,* a Hebrew melody for cello and orch., composed for the Jewish community of Liverpool in 1880; its success led to the erroneous assumption that Bruch himself was Jewish (he was, in fact, of a clerical Protestant family.)—Cf. Fritz Gysi, *Max Bruch* (Zürich, 1922); Hans Pfitzner, *Meine Beziehungen zu Max Bruch: persönliche Erinnerungen* (Munich, 1938); see also A. Kleffel, *Max Bruch* in 'Musik' (1907); A. Ebel, in 'Allgemeine Musikalische Zeitung' (1913).

Bruck (or **Brouck**), **Arnold von** (known also as Arnold de Bruges and Arnoldo Flamengo), Flemish composer; b. Bruges, c. 1470; d. Linz, 1554. He studied with H. Finck in Salzburg; was in the service of the Hapsburgs in Vienna (1514); in 1529 was music director in the court of Kaiser Ferdinand I. Many of his motets, hymns and German part-songs are preserved in collections of the 16th century; reprints have been published by L. Nowak in 'Denkmäler der Tonkunst in Österreich' (vol. 37), R. Eitner in 'Publikationen älterer Musik' (vol. 2), A. Schering in *Geschichte der Musik in Beispielen* (No. 110), J. Wolf in 'Denkmäler deutscher Tonkunst' (vol. 34), Otto Kade in A. W. Ambros' *Geschichte der Musik* (vol. 5), and C. G. Winterfeld in *Der evangelische Kirchengesang*.

Brucken-Fock, Emil von, Dutch composer; brother of Gerard von Brucken-Fock; b. Koudekerke, Oct. 19, 1857; d. Aerdenhout, Jan. 6, 1944. He conducted a military band and wrote music criticism in Utrecht; influenced by Wagner he composed the music drama *Seleneia*. He also wrote many songs.

Brucken-Fock, Gerard von, Dutch pianist and composer; brother of Emil von Brucken-Fock; b. Koudekerke, Dec. 28, 1859; d. Heemstede, Aug. 15, 1935. He studied with Friedrich Kiel and W. Bargiel. He wrote two symphonies, an oratorio *De Wederkomst van Christus,* a violin sonata, etc. Some of his piano preludes and songs have acquired considerable popularity in Holland.

Brückler, Hugo, German song composer; b. Dresden, Feb. 18, 1845; d. there, Oct. 4, 1871. He studied at the Dresden Cons.; published 2 groups of songs, both based on Scheffel's poem, *Trompeter von Säckingen* (*Songs of Young Werner by the Rhine* and *Margaret's Songs*); also *Sieben Gesänge* (posthumous; selected and edited by Adolf Jensen); a ballad, *Der Vogt von Tenneberg* (posthumous, edited by Reinhold Becker); *Nordmännersang; Marsch der Bürgergarde.* See R. Musiol, *Hugo Brückler* (1896).

Bruckner, Anton, famous Austrian composer; b. Ansfelden, Sept. 4, 1824; d. Vienna, Oct. 11, 1896. A son of a village schoolmaster, he became an orphan early in life; chiefly by his own efforts he learned to play the organ, so that he was able to obtain an appointment as cathedral organist at Linz (1856) in competition with many rivals. As opportunity offered, he studied composition with Kitzler and Sechter. In 1867 he succeeded Sechter as court organist in Vienna, and also became instructor of organ and harmony at the Vienna Cons. In 1875 he received the post of lecturer on music at Vienna Univ.; in 1891 the Univ. gave him the title of *Dr. phil.* He traveled to France (1869) and to England (1871) and established himself as a great virtuoso on the organ. Recognition of the importance of Bruckner as a composer came slowly; in his symphonic works, he attempted to transplant the methods of Wagner to instrumental music. It was only many years after his death that his greatness as a symphonist was widely conceded. He discarded his two early symphonies: one in F minor (1863; discovered and perf. at Klosterneuburg, March 18, 1923); one in D minor (1864; revised 1869; perf. Klosterneuburg, Oct. 12, 1924; this symphony was marked by Bruckner as No. 0). The nine symphonies acknowledged by Bruckner and given in most catalogues are: No. 1 in C minor (1866; Linz, May 9, 1868, under Bruckner's direction; revised 1877-91); No. 2 in C minor (1872; Vienna, Oct. 26, 1873, under Bruckner; two revisions between 1875 and 1877); No. 3 in D minor (1873; dedicated to Wagner; Vienna, Dec. 16, 1877, under Bruckner; 2 revisions, 1877 and 1888); No. 4 in E flat major, surnamed 'Romantic' (1874; Scherzo and Finale revised, 1878-80; Vienna, Feb. 20, 1881, under Richter); No. 5 in B flat major (1875-77; revised 1878; Graz, April 8, 1894, under Schalk); No. 6 in A major (1879-81; Adagio and Scherzo perf. Vienna, Feb. 11, 1883, under W. Jahn; complete perf., posthumous, Feb. 26, 1899, under Mahler); No. 7 in E major (1881-83; Leipzig, Dec. 30, 1884, under Nikisch); No. 8 in C minor, surnamed 'Apocalyptic' (1884-87; revised 1890; Vienna, Dec. 18, 1892, under Richter); No. 9 in D minor (1895-96; the Finale remained unfinished; perf. posthumously by Löwe, Vienna, Feb. 11, 1903, with Bruckner's *Te Deum* substituted for the Finale). Other works are Overture in G minor (left in sketches; comp. 1861-63), publ. in an album in 1949, along with several military marches by Bruckner; *Requiem* in D minor (St. Florian, March 13, 1849); *Missa Solemnis* in B flat major (St. Florian, Sept. 14, 1854); the choral works: *Germanenzug* (1863); *Abendzauber* (1878); *Helgoland* (1893); 3 masses (1864; 1866; 1871); *Te Deum* (1881; revised 1884; perf. with orch., Vienna, Jan. 10, 1886); 105th Psalm (Vienna, Nov. 13, 1892); string quintet in F major, etc. For a complete list of works with dates of comp., see the exhaustive article by F. Blume in 'Die Musik in Geschichte und Gegenwart' (vol. II, pp. 342-382). A new monumental edition of Bruckner's symphonies in their original orchestration (without revisions made by Löwe and Schalk in the first prints) under the editorship of Robert Haas and Alfred Orel was publ. under the auspices of the National Library in Vienna and the International Bruckner Society; other works are included in the complete edition of 22 volumes. The International Bruckner Society in Vienna publ. 'Bruckner-Blaetter' (1929-37 and 1939). The Bruckner Society of America, founded in 1931, published a journal 'Chord and Discord'; it awarded Bruckner medals to Toscanini, Koussevitzky and others for performances of Bruckner's music.

BIBLIOGRAPHY: I. BIOGRAPHY. F. Brunner, *B.* (Linz, 1895); R. Louis, *A. B.* (Munich, 1905; new ed. 1917); Leon Funtek, *Bruckneriana* (Leipzig, 1910); F. Gräflinger, *A. B.; Bausteine zu seiner Lebensgeschichte* (Munich, 1911; new ed. 1927); M. Morold, *A. B.* (Leipzig, 1912; 2nd ed., 1920); Ernst Decsey, *A. B.* (1920); F. Gräflinger, *A. B.; Sein Leben und seine Werke* (1921); Erich Schwebsch, *A. B.* (Stuttgart, 1921; new ed. 1927); H. Tessmer, *A. B.* (Regensburg, 1922); K. Grunsky, *A. B.* (Stuttgart, 1922); Max Auer, *A. B.* (1923); Ernst Kurth, *A. B.* (2 vols., 1925); A. Orel, *A. B.; Das Werk; Der Künstler; Die Zeit* (1925); F. Klose, *Meine Lehrjahre bei Bruckner* (1927); F. Grüninger, *B.* (1930; new ed. 1950); G. Engel, *The Life of A. B.* (N. Y., 1931); Robert Haas, *A. B.* (Potsdam, 1934); A. Orel, *A. B. in Bildern* (Leipzig, 1936); August Göllerich and Max Auer, *A. B.* (4 vols., 1922-37; fundamental biogr. source); E. Schwanzara, *Bruckners Stamm- und Urheimat* (Berlin, 1937); K. Laux, *A. B. Leben und Werk* (Leipzig, 1940); W. Wolff, *A. B.; Rustic Genius* (N. Y., 1942); L. Van Vassenhove, *A. B.* (Brussels, 1942); P. Raabe, *Wege zu Bruckner* (Regensburg, 1944); A. Machabey, *La vie et l'œuvre d'A. Bruckner* (Paris, 1945); D. Newlin, *Bruckner, Mahler, Schoenberg* (N. Y., 1947); H. F. Redlich, *Bruckner and Mahler* (London, 1955).

II. ANALYSIS. A. Halm, *Die Symphonie A. B.'s* (1914); A. Orel, *Unbekannte Frühwerke Bruckners* (1921); Kurt Singer, *Bruckners Chormusik* (1924); M. Auer, *B. als Kirchenmusiker* (1927); Fr. Munch, *La musique religieuse de B.* (Paris, 1928); H. A. Grunsky, *Formenwelt und Sinngefüge in den B. Sinfonien* (2 vols., 1931); E. Wellesz, *A. B. and the Process of Musical Creation*, in the 'Mus. Quarterly' (1938); A. Maecklenburg, *Hugo Wolf and A. B.* (ibid., 1938); H. Unger, *A. B .und seine 7. Sinfonie* (Bonn, 1944); Ilmari Krohn, *Anton Bruckners Sinfonien: eine Untersuchung über Formenbau und Stimmungsgehalt* (Helsinki, 1955).

III. CORRESPONDENCE. Letters of Bruckner are contained in Gräflinger's monograph on Karl Waldeck, Bruckner's pupil and successor as Linz Cathedral organist (Linz, 1911); G. Bosse's 'Deutsche Musikbücherei' (vols. 49 and 55); and in A. Orel, *Bruckner-Brevier; Briefe, Dokumente, Berichte* (Vienna, 1953).

Brugnoli (brŏŏ-n'yoh'-lē), **Attilio**, Italian composer; b. Rome, Sept. 7, 1880; d. Bolzano, July 10, 1937. He studied piano and composition at the Naples Cons. with Paolo Serrao (grad., 1900); won the Rubinstein Prize in Paris (1905); taught at the conservatories of Parma (1907-21), and Florence (1921-37). His compositions include a piano concerto (1905); violin concerto (1908); piano suite, *Scene Napolitane* (1909); several songs; piano pieces; also a pedagogic work, *Dinamica pianistica* (Milan, 1926), for which he won a prize from the Italian government.

Brüll, Ignaz, Austrian pianist and composer; b. Prossnitz, Moravia, Nov. 7, 1846; d. Vienna, Sept. 17, 1907. He studied in Vienna with Epstein (piano) and Dessoff (composition); subsequenty made extended recital tours; eventually settled in Vienna, where he was professor of piano at the Horak Institute (1872-78). He was an intimate friend of Brahms, who greatly valued his advice. Works: the operas *Die Bettler von Samarkand* (1864); *Das goldene Kreuz* (Berlin, Dec. 22, 1875; his most successful opera); *Der Landfriede* (Vienna, Oct. 4, 1877); *Bianca* (Dresden, Nov. 25, 1879); *Königin Marietta* (Munich, 1883); *Gloria* (Hamburg, 1886); *Das steinerne Herz* (Vienna, 1888); *Gringoire* (Munich, March 19, 1892); *Schach dem Könige* (Munich, 1893); *Der Husar* (Vienna, 1898; very successful); *Rübezahl* (unfinished); a ballet, *Ein Märchen aus der Champagne* (1896); an overture, *Im Walde;* 3 serenades and a dance suite for orch.; two piano concertos, violin concerto; piano pieces; songs; etc. Bibl.: H. Schwarz, *Ignaz Brüll und sein Freundeskreis* (1922); also many references in the biographies of Brahms.

Brumel, Antoine, celebrated Flemish (or French) contrapuntist, contemporary of Josquin des Prez; b. 2nd half of the 15th century; d. in the 1st half of the 16th century. He was a chorister at the Cathedrals of Notre Dame, Chartres (1483), and Laon (1497); was a pupil of Okeghem; from

1498-1500 was choirmaster and canon at Notre Dame in Paris; then was in the service of Prince Sigismund Cantelmus of Sora at Lyons; in 1505 was engaged at the court of Alfonso I, Duke of Ferrara; nothing further is known of his life. The precise birth and death dates, 1475-1520, often given in music histories, are not supported by unimpeachable documentary evidence; nor is it known whether Brumel was Flemish or French. Five of his masses in 4 parts, and the *Missa super Dringhs* in 6 parts, were published by Petrucci (1503 and 1508), as well as many motets (1502-14); other masses can be found in the collections of A. Antiquus (1516), J. Ott (1539), and Petrejus (1539); portions of Brumel's masses are included in *Fragmenta missarum;* Henri Expert published his mass *De beata Virgine* in *Maîtres Musiciens* (vol. 9); other pieces are in Maldeghem's *Trésor*. A. Schering published the *Benedictus* from the *Missa super Dringhs* in his *Geschichte der Musik in Beispielen* (No. 64); further portions of masses are to be found in K. E. Roediger's *Die geistlichen Musikhandschriften der Universitäts-Bibliothek Jena* (Jena, 1935). A complete edition of his works was begun by A. Carapetyan in 1951 in Rome (the American Institute of Musicology). Some of Brumel's correspondence was published by E. Van der Straeten in *La Musique au Pays-Bas* (vol. 6). Masses, motets, magnificats, etc., in MS, are at Munich, Vienna, Bologna, Basel and Milan. —Cf. 'Monatshefte für Musikgeschichte' (XVI, 2); A. W. Ambros, *Geschichte der Musik* (III, p. 244); P. Wagner, *Geschichte der Messe* (I, p. 175); F. J. Fétis, *Biographie des Musiciens* (II, p. 95); A. Pirro, *Dokumente über Antoine Brumel, Louis van Pullaer und Crispin van Stappen* in 'Zeitschrift für Musikwissenschaft' XI, 6 (March, 1929); J. Delport, in 'Revue liturgique et musicale', XIV (Paris, 1930-31); Ch. van den Borren, *Études sur le XVe siècle musical* (Antwerp, 1941). See also Gustave Reese, *Music in the Renaissance* (N. Y., 1954).

Brun, Fritz, Swiss composer and conductor; b. Lucerne, Aug. 18, 1878. He studied in Lucerne and at the Cologne Cons.; lived first in Berlin, then in London and Dormund, where he taught at the Conservatory (1902-03); then settled in Bern as a teacher at the Bern Cons. and conductor of the symphony concerts; in 1920 he received an honorary *Dr. phil.* degree from Bern Univ. Between 1899 and 1950 he composed 9 symphonies; the first performance of the 9th was at Zürich, Dec. 12, 1950. Other compositions are: a symph. poem, *Aus dem Buche Hiob; Verheissung* for chorus; chamber music; violin sonatas; etc.—Cf. A. E. Cherbuliez, *Die Schweiz in der deutschen Musikgeschichte* (1932); a symposium, *Kleine Festgabe für Fritz Brun* (Bern, 1941).

Brune, Adolf Gerhard, composer; b. Bakkum, near Hanover, June 21, 1870; d. Chicago, April 21, 1935. He studied piano with his father; came to the U. S. in 1889 and was for five years organist in Peoria, Ill.; settled in Chicago in 1894; studied piano with Liebling and composition with Ziehn there, then taught piano and composition at Chicago Musical College (1898-1917). He wrote three symphonies and two symph. poems: *Lied des Singschwans* and *Evangeline*.

Bruneau (brü-noh'), (**Louis-Charles-Bonaventure-) Alfred**, French opera composer; b. Paris, March 3, 1857; d. there, June 15, 1934. In 1873 he entered the Paris Cons., where he was a pupil of Franchomme; won the first cello prize in 1876; later studied harmony with Savard and composition with Massenet; in 1881 he won the Prix de Rome with his cantata *Sainte-Geneviève*. He was music critic for 'Gil Blas' (1892-5); then for 'Le Figaro' and 'Le Matin'; from 1903-4 was first conductor at the Opéra-Comique; in 1900 he was made a member of the 'Conseil Supérieur' at the Cons. and in 1909 succeeded Reyer as Inspector of music instruction. He made extensive tours of Russia, England, Spain and the Netherlands, conducting his own works. He was made a knight of the 'Légion d'Honneur' in 1895; received the title 'Commandeur de St.-Charles' in 1907; became a member of the Académie des beaux Arts in 1925. His role in the evolution of French opera is of great importance; he introduced realistic drama on the French musical stage, working along parallel lines with Zola in literature. He used Zola's subjects for his most spectacular opera, *L'Ouragan,* and also for the operas *Messidor* and *L'Enfant-Roi*. In accordance with this naturalistic trend, Bruneau made free use of harsh dissonance when it was justified by the dramatic action of the plot. Operas (most of them produced in Paris at the Opéra-Comique): *Kérim* (June 9, 1887); *Le Rêve* (June 18, 1891); *L'Attaque du Moulin* (Nov. 23, 1893); *Messidor* (Feb. 19, 1897); *L'Ouragan* (April 29, 1901); *L'Enfant-Roi* (March 3, 1905), *Naïs Micoulin* (Monte Carlo, Feb. 2, 1907); *La Faute de l'Abbé Mouret* (March 1, 1907); *Les Quatre Journées* (Dec. 25, 1916); *Le Roi Candaule* (Dec. 1, 1920); *Angelo, tyran de Padoue* (Jan. 16, 1928); *Virginie* (Jan. 7,

1931); ballets: *L'Amoureuse leçon* (Feb. 6, 1913) and *Les Bacchantes* (after Euripides; Oct. 30, 1912); other works: the overtures *Ode héroïque* and *Léda;* symph. poem, *La Belle au Bois dormant;* symph. poem with chorus, *Penthésilée;* a requiem; *Lieds de France* and *Chansons à danser* (both to poems by C. Mendès); *Les Chants de la Vie* (to poems by H. Bataille, F. Gregh, etc.); *Le Navire* for voice and orch.; pieces for various combinations of string and wind instruments. He published *Musiques d'hier et de demain* (1900); *La musique française* (1901; German translation by M. Graf in 'Die Musik', Berlin, 1904); *Musiques de Russie et musiciens de France* (1903; German transl. by M. Graf in 'Die Musik', Berlin, 1904); *La vie et les œuvres de Gabriel Fauré* (1925); *Massenet* (1934).—Bibl.: A. Hervey, *Alfred Bruneau* in *Living Masters of Music* (London, 1907); O. Séré in *Musiciens d'aujourd'hui* (Paris, 1911); J. Tiersot, *Un Demi-siècle de musique française* (1918); A. Boschot, *La vie et les œuvres d'Alfred Bruneau* (Paris, 1937); L. Schiedermair in 'Die Musik' (II, 4); L. Laloy in 'Sammelbände der Internationalen Musik-Gesellschaft'; for detailed lists of performances see A. Loewenberg, *Annals of Opera* (1943; new ed., 1955).

Brunelli, Antonio, Italian theorist and contrapuntist of the late 16th and early 17th centuries; a native of Viterbo. He was a pupil of G. M. Nanini; served as maestro di cappella and organist at San Miniato, Tuscany, through 1606; then held the same posts at the Cathedral of Prato until 1610, and in Florence from 1614-16, where he was also maestro di cappella to the Grand Duke of Tuscany. Between 1605 and 1621 he published motets, canzonette, psalms, madrigals, requiems, etc.; also a ballet, which has been reprinted by Eitner. Some of his works also appeared in J. Donfried's *Promptuarium Musicum* (1623). He published the theoretical pamphlets *Regole utilissime per li scolari che desiderano imparare a cantare, . . . con la dichiarazione de tempi, proporzioni et altri accidenti che ordinariamente s'usono* (Florence, 1606; one of the first published methods for voice); *Esercizi ad 1 e 2 voci* (Florence, 1607); and *Regole et dichiarazioni di alcuni contrappunti doppii . . . con diversi canoni sopra un solo canto fermo* (Florence, 1610).

Brunetti, Domenico, Italian composer; b. Bologna, later part of 16th century. He was organist at the Church of S. Domenico about 1609; was maestro di cappella at the Bologna Cathedral (1620); founded (with F. Bertacchi) at Bologna the Accademia dei Filoschici (1633), which later was absorbed into the Accademia Filarmonica. Publ. *Euterpe* (Venice, 1606); *Varii Concentus unica voce, duabus, tribus, quatuor vel pluribus cum gravi et acuto ad Organum* (Venice, 1609); *Canticum Deiparae Virginis Octies iuxta singulos Rhytmorum Sacrorum . . .* (Venice, 1621). Several of his compositions (motets, madrigals, etc.) were publ. in contemporary collections (1611-26) of A. Schadeo, G. Donfried, A. N. di Treviso, F. Sammaruco, Z. Zanetti, and G. P. Biandrà.

Brunetti, Gaetano, Italian violinist and composer; b. Pisa, c. 1740; d. Madrid, 1808. He studied with Nardini in Florence; as a young man he went to Spain, where he was attached to the court as a protégé of Boccherini; he repaid him with ingratitude and intrigue. His instrumental works, many of which were publ. in Paris (sextets, quintets, duos for violin, etc.) show that he was an imitator of Boccherini, not without some skill in instrumental writing. He also wrote an opera, *Jason,* which was given at Madrid (Oct. 4, 1768).—Cf. J. Subirá, *La música en la casa de Alba* (Madrid, 1927).

Bruni, Antonio Bartolomeo, Italian violinist and composer; b. Cuneo, 1751; d. there, Aug. 6, 1821. He studied with Pugnani in Turin; in 1781 went to Paris as a theater orch. conductor. There he wrote 18 operas, of which the most successful were *Célestine* (1787), *Claudine* (1794), and *La Rencontre en voyage* (1798). He also wrote music for the violin; publ. a violin method and a viola method (the latter reprinted in 1928).—Cf. G. Cesari, H. Closson, L. de La Laurencie, A. Della Corte, and C. Zino, *Antonio Bartolomeo Bruni, musicista cunese* (Turin, 1931).

Brunner, Christian Traugott, German organist; b. Brünlos, Dec. 12, 1792; d. Chemnitz, April 14, 1874. He wrote instructive piano pieces, potpourris, etc.

Brunold, Paul, French organist and writer on music; b. Paris, Oct. 14, 1875; d. there, Sept. 14, 1948. He was a pupil of Marmontel (piano) and Lavignac (theory) at the Paris Cons.; later studied with Paderewski. Brunold made a specialty of playing early music; in 1915 he became organist at St. Gervais in Paris. With H. Expert, he edited the 'Anthologie des maîtres français du clavecin des XVIIe et XVIIIe siècles'; with A. Tessier he brought out a complete edition of Chambonnière's works; he also edited 2 volumes of works by Dieupart for the Lyre-Bird Press of Paris (*6 Suites pour clavecin* and *Airs et Chansons*). He published the book *Histoire du grand orgue de l'Église St. Gervais à Paris* (1934).

Brunswick, Mark, American composer; b. New York, Jan. 6, 1902. He studied with Victor Wittgenstein (piano), Rubin Goldmark, Ernest Bloch and Nadia Boulanger (theory and composition); lived for several years in Vienna, studying with A. von Webern; returned to New York in 1937, where he taught at the Studios of Music Education; appointed chairman of the music department at the College of the City of N. Y. in 1946. His works include Symphony in B flat (Minneapolis, March 7, 1947); the ballet *Lysistrata; Fragment of Sappho;* Fantasia for viola solo (1933); a string quartet (1936); 2 chorale preludes for organ; etc.

Brusilovsky, Evgenyi Grigorievitch, Russian composer; b. Rostov-on-the-Don, Nov. 12, 1905; studied with Steinberg at the Leningrad Cons. In 1933 he settled in Alma-Atu (Kazakistan) and devoted his energies to the writing of operatic and symphonic music based on native folksongs. His works include the operas *Kyz-Zhibek* (1934); *Zhalbyr* (1935) and *Aiman-Amangeldy* (1945); the ballet *Guland* (1939); three symphonies; a piano concerto (1947); two cantatas, *Soviet Kazakistan* (1947) and *Glory Be To Stalin* (1949); a string quartet (1946) and music for folk instruments.

Brustad, Bjarne, Norwegian composer; b. Oslo, March 4, 1895. He studied violin with Carl Flesch. From 1919-22, was violinist in the Oslo Philharmonic Orch.; 1928-43, first viola player in that orchestra. He wrote an opera *Atlantis* (1945); two violin concertos (1924; 1927); concertino for viola and chamber orch. (1933); *Serenade* for violin, clarinet and bassoon (1947); *Capricci* for violin and viola; and *Eventyrsuite* for unaccompanied violin. Brustad's music is inspired by Norwegian folksongs.

Bruyck (broik), **Karl Debrois van,** Austrian writer on music; b. Brünn, March 14, 1828; d. Waidhofen, Aug. 5, 1902. Originally a law student in Vienna, he turned to music in 1850. He published a *Technische und ästhetische Analyse des Wohltemperiertes Klaviers* (1867); and *Die Entwickelung der Klaviermusik von J. S. Bach bis R. Schumann* (1880).

Bryennius, Manuel, Byzantine writer on music, who flourished about 1320. His chief work, *Harmonicorum libri 3,* published in parallel Greek and Latin texts by Johannes Wallis in *Operum mathematicorum vol. 3* (Oxford, 1699), gives a comprehensive account of Greek music theories. Bibl.: R. Westphal, *Griechische Rhythmik und Harmonik* (Leipzig, 1867).

Bryson, (Robert) Ernest, English composer; b. Liverpool, March 31, 1867; d. St. Briavels, Gloucestershire, April 20, 1942. He was engaged in trade, and music was his avocation. He wrote 2 symphonies; several orchestral sketches, and an opera, *The Leper's Flute,* which was produced in Glasgow on Oct. 15, 1926.

Bucchi, Valentino, Italian composer; b. Florence, Nov. 29, 1916. He studied with Dallapiccola (composition) and Torrefranca (theory). He was music critic and radio consultant in Florence (1945-48). His works include a chamber opera *Le vergine dei Veleni* (1939); a one-act opera-grotesque *Il Contrabasso,* after Chekhov (Maggio Musicale, Florence, May 20, 1954); *Sinfonia* (1940); two cantatas, *La dolce pena* (1946) and *Pianto delle creature* (1948); Concertino for 8 instruments (1936); piano sonatina (1938); string quartet (1939); *Serenata* for 11 instruments (1940) and sonatina for harp (1940).—Cf. 'Rassegna Musicale' (April, 1950).

Bucharoff (real name Buchhalter), **Simon,** Russian-American pianist and composer; b. Berditchev, April 20, 1881; d. Chicago, Nov. 24, 1955. He settled in America as a youth; studied piano with Paolo Gallico in N. Y., and later with Julius Epstein and Emil Sauer in Vienna. He occupied various teaching posts; lived principally in Chicago and Hollywood. Works: operas, *A Lover's Knot* (Chicago Opera, Jan. 15, 1916); *Sakahra* (Frankfurt, Nov. 8, 1924; revised in 1953); *Jewel; Wastrel;* several symph. poems (*Reflections in the Water; Drunk; Doubt; Joy Sardonic,* etc.); published *The Modern Pianist's Textbook* (N. Y. 1931).—Cf. E. E. Hipsher, *American Opera and its Composers* (Philadelphia, 1927; pp. 93-97).

Bücher, Karl, German economist and writer on music; b. Kirchberg, near Wiesbaden, Feb. 16, 1847; d. Leipzig, Nov. 12, 1930. As professor of economics at the Leipzig Univ. (1892-1916), he became interested in the correlation between social conditions among primitive peoples and music; he published a book *Arbeit und Rhythmus* (1896), in which the origin of music is traced to natural rhythmic exertions during manual labor, with group singing in unison as a natural expedient for team-work. The book aroused a great deal of controversy, and went through several printings; 6th edition was published in 1924. Cf. Lotte (Bucheim) Stratil-Sauer, *Volksliedhaftes unter Büchers deutschen Arbeitsliedern* (Leipzig, 1931); also Bücher's memoirs, *Lebenserinnerungen* (1919).

Buchmayer, Richard, German pianist and music editor; b. Zittau, April 19, 1856; d. Tams (Salzburg), May 24, 1934. He studied at the Dresden Cons.; later taught piano there. In his recitals he presented many unknown works by old masters. In 1903 he discovered, in the municipal library of Lüneburg, some valuable manuscripts of 17th-century organ and piano works, throwing new light on the subject of organ tablatures. The results of these studies were publ. in 'Sammelbände der Internationalen Musik-Gesellschaft', 'Bach-Jahrbuch' (1908), 'Signale,' etc. He edited Ch. Ritter's cantata *O sanctissime sponse, Jesu* and G. Böhm's cantata *Mein Freund ist mein;* also 5 volumes of piano and organ works of the 17th century (1927).

Buchner, Hans, German organist; b. Ravensburg, Württemberg, Oct. 26, 1483; d. probably in Constance, 1538. His father was an organist in Ravensburg, and gave Buchner his first instruction. After a period of study in Vienna, he obtained the post of organist at the Cathedral of Constance (1512). His magnum opus is a *Fundamentum,* a manual for composition and improvisation on the organ (1551).

Buchner, Philipp Friedrich, German organist; b. Wertheim, Sept. 11, 1614; d. Würzburg, March 23, 1669. He was a chorister in Frankfurt; in 1634 became church organist there; from 1641 he traveled in Poland and Italy; in 1647 he was in Mainz. His *Concerti ecclesiastici* were published in 2 books (Venice, 1642; 1644); he also wrote instrumental music for violins, violas and cembalo.

Buck, Dudley, American organist, composer and teacher; b. Hartford, Conn., March 10, 1839; d. Orange, N. J., Oct. 6, 1909. He studied piano with W. J. Babcock; later at the Leipzig Cons. with Plaidy and Moscheles (piano), Hauptmann (comp.) and J. Rietz (instrumentation), and later in Paris. Returning to America in 1862 he held posts as church organist in Hartford, Chicago, Boston, Brooklyn and elsewhere. He was one of the first American composers to achieve general recognition for his church music and sacred and secular cantatas. Works: Comic opera *Deseret, or a Saint's Affliction* (N. Y., Oct. 11, 1880); grand opera *Serapis;* symph. overture *Marmion* (1880); a Canzonetta and Bolero for violin and orch.—Organ music: *Grand Sonata; Triumphal March; Impromptu and Pastorale; Rondo-Caprice; At Evening; Four Tone Pictures;* various transcriptions and sets of variations; also 18 *Pedal-phrasing Studies* (2 books). He wrote *Illustrations in Choir-accompaniment, with Hints on Registration,* a valuable handbook for organists and students.

Buck, Dudley (Jr.), American tenor, son of the preceding; b. Hartford, Conn., April 4, 1869; d. Fairfield, Conn., Jan. 13, 1941. He was a pupil of Vannucini in Florence, Stockhausen in Frankfurt, J. de Reszke in Paris, Shakespeare and Randegger in London; made his debut as Turidu in *Cavalleria Rusticana* in Sheffield, England, Sept. 8,1895. Until 1899 he appeared frequently throughout Great Britain in opera, oratorio and concert; then returned to the U. S. and was heard in concerts. He was active as a singing teacher in N. Y.; eventually settled in Chicago, where he was affiliated with the Columbia School of Music.

Buck, Sir Percy Carter, English organist; b. London, March 25, 1871; d. there, Oct. 3, 1947. He studied at the Guildhall School and Royal College of Music; subsequently served as organist of Worcester College, Oxford (1891-94), Wells Cathedral (1896-99), Bristol Cathedral (1899-1901). From 1901-27 he was music director at Harrow School; later taught at the Universities of Dublin, Glasgow, London and Sheffield. His works include an overture for orch., *Cœur de Lion;* string quartet; piano quintet; sonatas, piano pieces, etc. He was the author of *Ten Years of University Music in Oxford* (1894; with Mee and Woods); *Unfigured Harmony* (1911); *Organ Playing* (1912); *First Year at the Organ* (1912); *The Organ: A Complete Method for the Study of Technique and Style; Acoustics for Musicians* (1918); *The Scope of Music* (Oxford, 1924); *Psychology for Musicians* (London, 1944); and articles in various music journals. He also was editor of the introductory volume and volumes I and II of the 2nd edition of the 'Oxford History of Music'.

Bücken, Ernst, eminent German musicologist; b. Aachen, May 2, 1884; d. Overath, near Cologne, July 28, 1949. He studied with Sandberger in Munich; also with Courvoisier; *Dr. phil.,* 1912 with a thesis on Anton Reicha (published); in 1920 became *Privatdozent* at Cologne Univ.; in 1925, prof.; from 1945 lived in Overath. His writings include the following: *München als Musikstadt* (1923); *Der heroische Stil in der Oper* (1924); *Führer und Probleme der neuen Musik* (1924); *Musikalische Characterköpfe* (1925); *Frage des Stilverfalls,* in 'Kroyer Festschrift' (1933); *Deutsche Musikkunde* (1935); *Die Musik der Nationen* (1937); *Robert Schumann* (Cologne, 1940); *Kulturgeschichte der deutschen Musik* (1942). He was the editor of the monumental *Handbuch der Musikwissenschaft* in 10 vols., begun in 1927, to which he contributed 3 vols.: *Die Musik des 19. Jahrhunderts bis zur Moderne* (1928); *Musik des Rokokos und der Klassik* (1929); and *Geist und Form im musikalischen Kunstwerk* (1929); also compiled the collection *Musiker-Briefe* (1940).

Budashkin, Nicolai Pavlovitch, Russian composer; b. Lubakhovka, Kaluga, Aug. 6, 1910, of a peasant family. After working as a blacksmith, he went to Moscow and took a course with Miaskovsky at the Moscow Cons. He specializes in music for Russian popular instruments in symphonic combinations; he wrote 2 concertos for domra and orch. (1944; 1947); concert variations for balalaika with orch. on a Russian folksong (1946), and works for ensembles consisting entirely of such instruments. His early *Festive Overture* (1937) has achieved considerable success in Russia.

Buesst, Victor, Australian pianist and composer; b. Melbourne, Oct. 20, 1885. He received his musical education in Brussels (with Arthur de Greef) and Leipzig (with Teichmüller). He then settled in London as a piano teacher. Among his works is a violin concerto, a concerto for three pianos, and several piano solo pieces.

Bühler, Franz, German composer; b. Schneidheim, near Nördlingen, April 12, 1760; d. Augsburg, Feb. 4, 1824. He was a Benedictine monk at Donauwörth; choral conductor at Botzen (1794) and at Augsburg Cathedral (1801); wrote an opera *Die falschen Verdachte;* an oratorio, *Jesus, der göttliche Erlöser;* sonatas and preludes for organ; also several theoretical pamphlets.

Buhlig, Richard, American pianist; b. Chicago, Dec. 21, 1880; d. Los Angeles, Jan. 30, 1952. He studied in Chicago, and in Vienna with Leschetizky (1897-1900); made his début in recital in Berlin (1901); then toured Europe and the U. S. (American début with the Philadelphia Orchestra in N. Y., Nov. 5, 1907). In 1918 he was appointed teacher of piano at the Institute of Musical Art, N. Y.; later returned to Europe; eventually settled in Los Angeles as performer and teacher.

Buketoff, Igor, American conductor; b. Hartford, Conn., May 29, 1915. He studied first at the Univ. of Kansas; then at the Juilliard School of Music, N. Y.; subsequently taught conducting there (1935-45); was for several years conductor of young people's concerts of the N. Y. Philharmonic. In 1948 he was appointed conductor of the Fort Wayne Philharmonic Orchestra.

Bukofzer, Manfred F., eminent German-American musicologist; b. Oldenburg, March 27, 1910; d. Oakland, California, Dec. 7, 1955. He studied at the Hoch Cons. in Frankfurt, and at the Univs. of Heidelberg, Berlin and Basel (*Dr. phil.,* 1936); also took courses with Hindemith in Berlin. He lectured in Basel (1933-39); also at the Univs. of Oxford and Cambridge. In 1939 settled in the U. S.; became a naturalized citizen in 1945. He taught at Western Reserve Univ. in Cleveland (1940-41) then became assoc. prof., Univ. of California, Berkeley (1941); full prof. in 1946; was appointed chairman of the Music Dept. in 1954. His numerous publications are distinguished by originality of historical and musical ideas coupled with precision of factual exposition; having mastered the English language, he was able to write brilliantly in British and American publications; he was also greatly esteemed as teacher. His writings include: *Geschichte des englischen Diskants und des Fauxbourdons* (Strasbourg, 1936; very valuable); *Über Leben und Werke von John Dunstable* in 'Acta musicologica' (1936); *Hegels Musikästhetik,* in reports of 'Deuxième Congrès d'Esthétique et de Science de l'Art' (Paris, 1937); *Kann die 'Blasquintentheorie' zur Erklärung primitiver Tonsysteme beitragen?* in 'Anthropos' (1937); many other articles and important reviews in various magazines; also *Allegory in Baroque Music,* in the 'Journal' of the Warburg Institute (1939); *Sumer Is Icumen In: A Revision* (Berkeley, 1944), placing the date of this famous canon later than the generally accepted year 1240; *Music in the Baroque Era* (N. Y., 1947); *Studies in Medieval and Renaissance Music* (N. Y., 1950). He was also editor of the complete works of Dunstable (1954, as Vol. VIII of 'Musica Britannica').—Cf. David D. Boyden, *In Memoriam: Manfred F. Bukofzer,* in the 'Mus. Quarterly' (July, 1956), which contains a complete list of Bukofzer's writings.

Bull, John, famous English organist and contrapuntal composer; b. Somersetshire, England, c. 1562; d. Antwerp, March 12 or 13, 1628. He was a pupil of William Blitheman in the Chapel Royal; organist of Hereford Cathedral, 1582; later also Master of the Children; 1585, member of the Chapel Royal, becoming organist in 1591, on the death of his master; 1586, Mus. Bac.; 1592, Mus. Doc., Oxon. In 1596 he was appointed, on Queen Elizabeth's recommendation, prof. of music at Gresham College, a post resigned on his marriage, 1607. In 1611 he was in the service of Prince Henry, and left the country two years later, becoming one of the organists to the Archduke at Brussels. In 1617 he became organist of the cathedral of Notre Dame at Antwerp. He was acquainted with the great organist and composer Sweelinck and, with him, exerted a marked influence on the development of contrapuntal keyboard music. 200 compositions are attributed to John Bull; a list is given in Ward's 'Lives of the Gresham Professors' (1740); exercises and variations for the virginals, some canons, a sacred madrigal, and an anthem, were printed in the following collections: the 'Fitzwilliam Virginal Book' (45; modern ed. by J. A. Fuller Maitland and W. Barclay Squire, London, 1899), B. Cosyn's 'Virginal Book' (23), Forster's 'Virginal Book' (3), Leighton's *The Tears or Lamentacions of a Sorrowfull Soule;* in *Parthenia* (pieces for virginals by Bull, Byrd and Gibbons; new ed. by Margaret H. Glyn, London, 1927), and others. A reprint is to be found in A. Schering's *Geschichte der Musik in Beispielen* (no. 147); vol. I of Joseph Bonnet's 'Historical Organ Recitals' contains a Praeludium; various pieces were ed. by M. H. Glyn (London, 1922). The conjecture put forward by some writers, notably by Leigh Henry in his book, *Dr. John Bull* (London, 1937), that Bull was the author of *God Save the King,* does not have a scintilla of evidence.—Bibl.: Ch. Van den Borren, *Les Origines de la musique de Clavecin en Angleterre* (1913); Hugh Miller, *John Bull's Organ Works* in 'Music and Letters' (Jan., 1947); W. Mellers, *John Bull and English Keyboard Music* in the 'Mus. Quarterly' (July and Oct., 1954).

Bull, Ole Bornemann, famous Norwegian violinist; b. Bergen, Feb. 5, 1810; d. Lyso, near Bergen, Aug. 17, 1880. He received his first instruction in violin playing from a Danish teacher named Paulsen, but he soon struck out on a method of his own, ignoring academic study. In order to be able to play unbroken chords on all four strings, he used an almost level bridge and a flat fingerboard. At the age of nine he was admitted to a local orchestra. Later he was sent by his father to Christiania (Oslo) to study theology, but university training was not for him; for a time he conducted a musical society; in 1829 he went to Kassel, and applied to Spohr for instruction, but Spohr was highly critical of his playing, and he returned to Norway in considerable disillusion. There he gave a series of concerts; in 1831 he went to Paris, where he heard Paganini for the first time, and became determined to emulate the great Italian virtuoso. In this he succeeded only as far as eccentricity was concerned. In 1836-37 he played 274 concerts in England and Ireland; in 1840 he performed Beethoven's 'Kreutzer Sonata' with Liszt at the piano. He made five tours in the U. S., playing popular music and his own compositions on American themes (*Niagara, Solitude of the Prairies, To the Memory of Washington,* etc.) and a number of his arrangements of Norwegian folksongs. He had a strong conviction that Norway should form its own national art, but the practical applications of his patriotism were failures. In 1845 he started a theatrical enterprise in Bergen to promote national drama and music, but the project did not succeed, and was abandoned after a few seasons. In 1852 he purchased a large piece of land (125,000 acres) in Pennsylvania for a Norwegian settlement, but his lack of business acumen made him a victim of an easy swindle; subsequent lawsuits drained his last resources. The settlement was planned on socialist lines, and was given the name Oleana, thus establishing a personal connection with the name of its unlucky founder. Despite these reverses and eccentricities for which Ole Bull was notorious, he became a great national figure, revered in Norway for his passionate love of his native land. Some of his compositions have been published (*La Preghiera d'una madre, Variazioni di bravura, Polacca guerriera, Notturno,* etc.); their musical value is nil. Bibl.: J. Lie, *Ole Bulls breve i utdreg* (Copenhagen, 1881); *Ole Bull: A Memoir* (Boston, 1883) by Sara C. Bull, his second wife (German ed., Stuttgart, 1886); O. Vik, *Ole Bull* (Bergen, 1890); C. A. Aarvig, *Den unge Ole Bull* (Copenhagen, 1935); A. Björndal, *Ole Bull og Norsk folkemusik* (Bergen, 1940); M. B. Smith, *The Life of Ole Bull* (Princeton, 1943); Z. Hopp, *Eventyret om Ole Bull* (Bergen, 1945); Ola Linge, *Ole Bull* (Oslo, 1953).

Bullard, Frederick Field, American song composer; b. Boston, Sept. 21, 1864; d. there, June 24, 1904. He studied with Rheinberger at Munich; returned to Boston and became a music teacher; published about 40 songs, hymns and anthems.

Bülow, Hans Guido von, German pianist, conductor, and writer of great versatility and high attainments; b. Dresden, Jan. 8, 1830; d. Cairo, Egypt, Feb. 12, 1894. At the age of nine his teachers were Friedrich Wieck (piano) and Max Eberwein (theory). He studied law at the Univ. of Leipzig, and took a music course with Moritz Hauptmann. He then lived in Stuttgart, where he made his début as a pianist, playing Mendelssohn and Raff with the local orchestra. In 1850 he was in Berlin, where he joined the democratic groups and fell under the influence of Wagner's musical ideas. Shortly afterwards he went to Zürich, and became closely associated with Wagner, who was there in exile. After a year in Switzerland, where he was theater conductor, he went to Weimar to study with Liszt. In 1852 he published a collection of songs; wrote for the 'Neue Zeitschrift für Musik'; in 1853 he made a tour through Germany and Austria as pianist; in 1855 he succeeded Kullak as head of the piano department at the Stern Cons. in Berlin, retaining this post until 1864. In the meantime he married Liszt's daughter Cosima (1857); in 1863 he received the honorary degree of *Dr. phil.* from the Univ. of Jena. In 1864 he was called by Ludwig II of Bavaria to Munich as court pianist and conductor; the king, who was Wagner's great admirer and patron, summoned Wagner from exile to Munich; Hans von Bülow became Wagner's ardent champion and the best conductor of his music. He gave the first performances of *Tristan und Isolde* at the Court Opera in Munich on June 10, 1865 and the *Meistersinger* on June 21, 1868. A personal tragedy developed when Cosima abandoned him in 1869 for Wagner, whom she married the following year. Hans von Bülow went to live in Florence, where he remained until 1872. Despite his understandable bitterness towards Wagner, he continued to conduct Wagner's music; his growing admiration for Brahms cannot be construed as the result of his pique against Wagner. It was von Bülow who dubbed Brahms 'the third B of music'. He resumed his career in 1872 with worldwide piano tours; won triumphant successes in England and Russia; gave 139 concerts during his American tour in 1875-76; revisited America in 1889 and 1890. An important chapter in his career was his employment as conductor in Meiningen (1880-85). He married a Meiningen actress, Marie Schanzer, in 1882. After 1885 he conducted concerts in Hamburg and Berlin. He continued his untiring professional activities until 1893, when a lung ailment forced him to seek a cure in Egypt; he died shortly after his arrival in Cairo. Both as pianist and conductor, Hans von Bülow demonstrated his profound knowledge and understanding of the music he performed; as conductor he insisted on minute accuracy, but was able to project considerable emotional power. He was one of the first conductors to dispense with the use of the score. His memory was fabulous; it was said that he could memorize a piano concerto without the aid of an instrument, while on a journey. The mainstay of his repertoire was classical and romantic music, but he was hospitable towards composers of the new school; in Boston, he gave the world première of Tchaikovsky's first piano concerto; he encouraged the young Richard Strauss, and gave him his first position as conductor. He wrote a number of works, but they are entirely without enduring merit; on the other hand, as a writer and journalist, von Bülow was exceptionally brilliant; he was particularly apt at coining phrases, and his wit was legendary among musicians. Works: music to Shakespeare's *Julius Caesar;* a symphonic ballad, *Des Sängers Fluch;* a symphonic 'mood picture', *Nirwana; 4 Charakterstücke* for orch.; piano pieces; songs; also masterly transcriptions of the prelude to Wagner's *Meistersinger* and the whole of *Tristan und Isolde,* of Berlioz' overtures to *Le Corsaire* and *Benvenuto Cellini.* His critical editions of Beethoven's sonatas and of Cramer's études attest his excellent editorial ability. Bibl.: E. Zabel, *Hans von Bülow* (Hamburg, 1894); Th. Pfeiffer, *Studien bei Hans von Bülow* (Berlin, 1894; 6th ed., 1909); R. Sternfeld, *Hans von Bülow* (Leipzig, 1894); Vianna da Motta, *Nachtrag zu den Pfeiffer'schen 'Studien bei Hans von Bülow'* (Leipzig, 1895); W. Altmann, *Chronik des Berliner philharmonischen Orchesters, 1882-1901; zugleich ein Beitrag zur Beurteilung Hans von Bülows* (Berlin, 1902); G. Fischer, *Hans von Bülow in Hannover* (Hanover, 1902); H. Reimann, *Hans von Bülow; sein Leben und sein Wirken* (Berlin, 1909); C. Krebs, *Meister des Taktstocks* (1919); R. Du Moulin-Eckart, *Hans von Bülow* (1921); Marie von Bülow, *Hans von Bülow in Leben und Wort* (1925); Th. W. Werner, *Hans von Bülow* in *75 Jahre Opernhaus Hannover* (1927); Walter Damrosch, *Hans von Bülow and the 9th Symphony* in the 'Mus. Quarterly' (1927); Ludwig Schemann, *Hans von Bülow im Lichte der Wahrheit* (Regensburg, 1935). Hans von Bülow's writings were published by his widow, Marie von Bülow, under the title *Briefe und Schriften Hans von Bülows* (8 vols., Leipzig, 1895-1908; vol. III, republished separately in 1936, contains selected essays, while the other volumes contain letters); selected letters in English translation were published by C. Bache, *The Early Correspondence of Hans von Bülow* (London, 1896); F. Rösch, *Musikästhetische Streitfragen; Streitlichter zu den ausgewählten Schriften von Hans von Bülow* (Leipzig, 1897); La Mara, *Briefwechsel zwischen Franz Liszt und Hans von Bülow* (Leipzig, 1898); E. Förster-Nietzsche and P. Gast, *Friedrich Nietzsches gesammelte Briefe* (Berlin, 1905; vol. III contains the correspondence between Nietzsche and von Bülow); von Bülow's letters to Wagner, Cosima, Klindworth, Bechstein, and Daniela, edited by R. DuMoulin-Eckart (Munich, 1927; English transl., N. Y., 1931).

Bulthaupt, Heinrich, German dramatist and writer on music; b. Bremen, Oct. 26, 1849; d. there, Aug. 21, 1905. He studied jurisprudence at Göttingen, Leipzig and Berlin; spent some time in Kiev with private teachers, and then made an extensive trip in the Orient. In 1879 he was appointed librarian of the Municipal Library at Bremen. Besides his purely literary work, he wrote libretti for Rubinstein, Eugene d'Albert and others. His most important work dealing with music is *Dramaturgie der Oper* (2 vols.; Leipzig, 1887; 2nd ed., 1902). He also wrote a biography of Carl Loewe (1898) and *Richard Wagner als Klassiker* (1899).

Bunge, Sas (Ernest Alexander), Dutch composer and pianist; b. Amsterdam, July 9, 1924; studied at the Amsterdam Cons. (1942-46) winning the Prix d'Excellence as pianist; in composition was a pupil of Hendrik Andriessen. Works: *Serenade* for school orch. (1943); *Ballade des pendus* for chorus and orch. (1944); concertino for piano and orch. (1946); 2 string quartets (1948; 1952); Christmas cantata *Het Blijde Uur* (1952), etc.

Bungert, August, German composer; b. Mülheim, Ruhr, March 14, 1845; d. Leutesdorf, Oct. 26, 1915. He studied piano and composition at Cologne and Paris; lived mostly in Berlin. An ardent admirer of Wagner, Bungert devoted his life to the composition of a parallel work to Wagner's *Ring,* taking Homer's epics as the source of his libretti. The result of this effort was the creation of two operatic cycles: *The Iliad* comprising (1) *Achilleus,* (2) *Klytemnestra;* and *The Odyssey,* a tetralogy. The *Iliad* was never completed for performance, but all four parts of the *Odyssey* were performed in Dresden: *Kirke* (Jan. 29, 1898); *Nausikaa* (March 20, 1901); *Odysseus' Heimkehr* (Dec. 12, 1896, prior to premières of parts I and II); *Odysseus' Tod* (Oct. 30, 1903). There were also subsequent productions in other German cities, but everywhere Bungert's operas were received without enthusiasm, and the evident ambition to emulate Wagner without comparable talent proved his undoing. Among other works are the programmatic score *Zeppelins erste grosse Fahrt;* several symphonic overtures; *Symphonia Victrix;* a *German Requiem;* many songs. His most successful work was a comic opera, *Die Studenten von Salamanka* (Leipzig, 1884); he also wrote a mystery play, *Warum? woher? wohin?* (1908); incidental music to Goethe's *Faust,* etc. Bibl.: F. A. Geissler, *August Bungert,* in 'Musik' (Dec. 1907); M. Chop, *August Bungert, ein deutscher Dichterkomponist* (Leipzig, 1916).

Bunin, Vladimir Vasilievitch, Russian composer; b. Scopino, Riazan district, July 24, 1908. He studied at the Moscow Cons. with A. Alexandrov, graduating in 1938. In his music, Bunin follows the traditions of Russian classicism. He has written 2 symphonies, a violin concerto and numerous piano works. He received the 2nd Stalin Prize for his Second Symphony.

Bunnett, Edward, English organist and composer; b. Shipdham, Norfolk, June 26, 1834; d. Norwich, Jan. 5, 1923. He was a chorister at Norwich Cathedral; then occupied various posts as organist; served as conductor of the Norwich Musical Union. He produced several cantatas at Norwich Festivals: *Rhineland* (1872); *Lora* (1876); and *De Profundis* (1880); also wrote numerous organ pieces. His *Nunc Dimittis* (1867) was for many years performed in English churches.

Bunning, Herbert, English conductor and composer; b. London, May 2, 1863; d. Thundersley, Essex, Nov. 26, 1937. He studied music with John Farmer at Harrow. After graduating from Oxford, he entered the army and served with the Queen's Own Hussars (1884); continued his musical studies in Milan with Vincenzo Ferroni and others (1886-91); upon his return to London, was appointed conductor of the Lyric

Theatre (1892). Works: an opera, *Princess Osra* (Covent Garden, London, July 14, 1902); 2 overtures: *Mistral* (1897) and *Spring and Youth* (1897); an Italian scena, *Ludovico il Moro* (1892); also *Shepherd's Call,* intermezzo for horn and strings (1893); *Village Suite* for orch. (1896); *Sir Launcelot and Queen Guinevere* for tenor and orch. (1905); incidental music to *Robin Hood* (1906); songs.

Bunting, Edward, historiographer of Irish music; b. Armagh, Feb. 1773; d. Dublin, Dec. 21, 1843. He played organ at Belfast; then moved to Dublin. He published 3 collections of old Irish airs in 1796, 1809 and 1840; many of these were published for the first time; the first volume contained songs by O'Conolan and O'Carolan; the second included piano arrangements and a discussion of the Irish, British and Egyptian harps; the third contained a long dissertation on the history of Irish popular music. Bunting collected his material from old singers and harpers; his publications, therefore, have the value of authenticity.

Buonamente, Giovanni Battista, Italian composer who flourished in the first half of the 17th century; d. Assisi, 1643. He was maestro di cappella at the Austrian court in Vienna (1626); in Prague (1627); and at the Franciscan monastery in Assisi (1636). His importance in music history rests on his sonatas for violin, some of the earliest examples of this form; he published 7 books of such works in Venice between 1626 and 1637; also wrote trio-sonatas for 2 violins and bass. Bibl.: A. Moser, *Geschichte des Violin-Spiels* (Berlin, 1923); Paul Nettl, *G. B. Buonamente* in 'Zeitschrift für Musikwissenschaft' (1927).

Buonamici (bwoh-nah-mē'-tchē), **Giuseppe,** Italian pianist; b. Florence, Feb. 12, 1846; d. there, March 17, 1914. He first studied with his uncle, Giuseppe Ceccherini; then at the Munich Cons. with Hans von Bülow and Rheinberger (1868-70); in 1873 returned to Florence where he was active as a teacher and choral conductor. He published a compilation of the technical figures found in Beethoven's piano music, in the form of daily studies; edited the 'Biblioteca del Pianista' and the complete Beethoven sonatas; also published piano pieces of his own.

Buongiorno (bwon-johr'-noh), **Crescenzo,** Italian composer; b. Bonito, Province of Avellino, 1864; d. Dresden, Nov. 7, 1903. He studied with Serrao at the Naples Cons.; later settled in Dresden. He wrote 4 operas: *Etelka* (Naples, 1887; Prague, 1894); *Das Erntefest* (Leipzig, 1896); *Das Mädchenherz* (Kassel, 1901); and *Michel Angelo und Rolla* (Kassel, 1903); also 12 operettas, including *Abukadabar* (Naples, 1889); *Circe e Calipso* (Turin, 1892); and *La nuova Saltarella* (Trieste, 1894).

Buononcini. See **Bononcini.**

Buranello. See **Galuppi.**

Burbure (bür-bür') **de Wesembeek, Léon-Philippe-Marie,** Belgian music scholar; b. Termonde, Aug. 16, 1812; d. Antwerp, Dec. 8, 1889. A scion of an aristocratic family, he studied law at the Univ. of Ghent; he also received an excellent musical education at home with private teachers; In 1846 he settled at Antwerp, and became the keeper of Archives at the Cathedral. He made a profound study of materials on old music accessible to him, and published a number of valuable monographs dealing with the Renaissance music guilds of Antwerp, on lute-makers, etc. He also composed some 200 works, including an opera, 25 orchestral pieces, numerous choral works, etc. Writings: *Aperçu sur l'ancienne corporation des musiciens instrumentistes d'Anvers, dite de St. Job et de Ste. Marie-Madeleine* (Brussels, 1862); *Recherches sur les facteurs de clavecins et luthiers d'Anvers, depuis le XVIe jusqu'au XIXe siècle* (Brussels, 1869); *Notice sur Charles-Louis Hanssens* (Brussels, 1872); *Charles Luython (1550-1620), compositeur de musique de la Cour impériale* (Brussels, 1880); *Les œuvres des anciens musiciens belges* (Brussels, 1882). Bibl.: F. A. Gevaert, *Notice sur le Chevalier Léon de Burbure* (Brussels, 1893).

Burci. See **Burtius.**

Burck, Joachim, German church composer; b. Burg, near Magdeburg, 1546; d. Mühlhausen, Thuringia, May 24, 1610. His real name was Moller; he called himself Joachim à Burck. In 1563 he settled in Mühlhausen; became organist at the Protestant Church of St. Blasius in 1566. Works: *Harmoniae sacrae* (5 books of motets; Nuremberg, 1566); *Die deutsche Passion* (Wittenberg, 1568); *Crepundia sacra* (4 books; Mühlhausen, 1578); several books of motets, odes and German songs, reprinted in various collections. Bibl.: A. Prüfer, *Untersuchungen über den aussernkirchlichen Kunstgesang in den evangelischen Schulen des 16. Jahrhundert* (Leipzig, 1890); R. Jordan, *Aus der Geschichte der Musik in Mühlhausen* (Mühlhausen, 1905).

Burette (bü-ret'), **Pierre-Jean,** French writer on music; b. Paris, Nov. 21, 1665; d. there, May 19, 1747. A physician by profession, he had an interest in musical subjects; was the author of the valuable treatise, *La Musique et la danse des anciens,* dealing mainly with the problems of Greek music. It was publ. in the 'Mémoires de l'Académie des Inscriptions' (Nos. 1-17).

Burgin, Richard, Polish-American violinist and conductor; b. Warsaw, Oct. 11, 1892. He studied at the St. Petersburg Cons. with Auer; made his debut on Dec. 7, 1903 with the Warsaw Philharmonic. In 1907 he toured America; was concertmaster of the Helsinki Symphony Orch. (1912-15); and of the Oslo Symph. Orch. (1916-19). Since 1920, concertmaster of the Boston Symphony Orch. and since 1927, asst. conductor. On July 3, 1940, he married Ruth Posselt, the violinist. He was appointed conductor of the New England Cons. Orch. and of the Harvard Univ. Orch. in 1953.

Burgk, Joachim. See **Burck, Joachim.**

Burgmüller, Johann August Franz, German organist and conductor; b. Magdeburg, April 28, 1766; d. Düsseldorf, August 21, 1824. He was of a clerical family; having received a good education, he became a teacher and then a traveling theatrical conductor; he founded a musical society in Düsseldorf, and enjoyed a considerable reputation among musicians as a scholar. His two sons, Johann Friedrich Franz and Norbert, were both musicans.

Burgmüller, Johann Friedrich Franz, German composer of piano music; b. Regensburg, Dec. 4, 1806; d. Beaulieu, near Paris, Feb. 13, 1874. He was the son of Johann August Franz Burgmüller, and brother of Norbert; having settled in Paris, he adopted a light style to satisfy the demands of Parisian music lovers, and wrote numerous pieces of salon music for piano; he also published several albums of piano studies that have become standard works.

Burgmüller, Norbert, German composer; son of Johann August Franz and brother of Johann Friedrich Franz; b. Düsseldorf, Feb. 8, 1810; d. Aachen, May 7, 1836. He was extremely gifted, and composed music since his early childhood. After study at home, he took lessons with Spohr; wrote many songs and a symphony. His second symphony remained incomplete at the time of his death at the age of 26; Schumann, who thought highly of him, orchestrated the third movement, a scherzo; in this form, the symphony had many performances in Europe and America, and Burgmüller was mourned by musicians as another Schubert. The point of coincidence was that his unfinished symphony was in the same key as that of Schubert.—Cf. H. Eckert, *Norbert Burgmüller* (Augsburg, 1932).

Burgstaller, Alois, German tenor; b. Holzkirchen, Sept. 21, 1871; d. Gmund, April 19, 1945. He studied watch-making, until he met Cosima Wagner, who urged him to take up singing. After appearing in minor roles, he made his debut as Siegfried at Bayreuth in 1896. He was engaged at the Metropolitan Opera for the seasons 1903-08, making his American debut in *Die Walküre* (N. Y., Feb. 12, 1903); sang Parsifal at its first American performance (Dec. 24, 1903). In 1908 he returned to Germany.

Burian, Emil František, Czech composer; b. Pilsen, April 11, 1904. He grew up in a musical family; his father was an opera singer; his uncle, Karl Burian, was a famous tenor. He studied with J. B. Foerster; from his first steps in composition, he adopted an extreme modernistic method; was associated with the Dada theater in Prague. In 1927 he organized a 'voice band' which sang according to prescribed rhythm but without a definite pitch; his presentation of the voice band at the Siena Festival of the International Society for Contemporary Music (Sept. 12, 1928) aroused considerable controversy. During World War II Burian was put in a concentration camp, but survived, and in 1945 was appointed director of the National Theatre in Brno, a post which he abandoned after one season. His own works include 6 operas, a cantata *May* (1946); a symph. work *Siren* (1947); 6 string quartets; many songs. He has also written pamphlets *Polydynamika, Almanack of the Burian Brothers,* etc.

Burian, Karl, celebrated heroic tenor; b. Rusinov, near Rakovnik, Jan. 12, 1870; d. Senomaty, Sept. 25, 1924. He studied with F. Piwoda in Prague; made his debut in Brno (1891); then sang in Germany and Russia. In 1898 he was engaged to sing Parsifal at Bayreuth, and was extremely successful, becoming a favorite in Wagnerian roles. He sang the part of Herod in *Salome* at its world première in Dresden (Dec. 9, 1905). He made his American début as Tannhäuser on Nov. 30, 1906, at the Metropolitan Opera; remained on the staff until 1911; then became a member of the Vienna Opera. In America he used the name Karl Burrian.

Burk, John N., American writer on music; b. San José, Calif., Aug. 28, 1891. He graduated from Harvard Univ. (A. B., 1916). In 1934 he succeeded Philip Hale as program annotator of the Boston Symphony Orch. He edited Philip Hale's Boston Symphony program notes (1935); edited and annotated *Letters of Richard Wagner*, from the Burrell Collection (N. Y., 1950). He is the author of the books, *Clara Schumann, A Romantic Biography* (N. Y., 1940), and *The Life and Works of Beethoven* (N. Y., 1943).

Burkhard, Paul, Swiss conductor and composer; b. Zürich, Aug. 21, 1911. He was active as conductor in Bern; from 1944 engaged mainly in radio work. He has written several operettas, which enjoy excellent success in Switzerland: *Das Paradies der Frauen* (1938); *Der schwarze Hecht* (1939; revived under a new title, *Feuerwerk*); *Tic-Tac* (1945).

Burkhard, Willy, Swiss composer; b. Évillard sur Bienne, April 17, 1900; d. Zürich, June 18, 1955. He studied with Teichmüller and Karg-Elert in Leipzig, Courvoisier in Munich, and Max d'Ollone in Paris. Returning to Switzerland, he taught at the Bern Cons. (1928-33) and at the Zürich Cons. (1942). His style of composition presents an effective combination of old polyphonic procedures and highly advanced harmonic and rhythmic formulas; in all of his music, the sense of form (usually cyclic) is very strong. Works: opera *Die Schwarze Spinne* (Zürich, May 28, 1949); operetta *Tic-Tac* (Zürich, March 28, 1947); oratorios *Das Gesicht Jesajas* (his masterpiece; Basel, 1936) and *Das Jahr* (1941); cantatas *Till Ulenspiegel* (1929), *Vorfrühling* (1930), *Spruchkantate* (1933), *Cantique de notre terre* (1943); a symphony (1926-28); 2 violin concertos (1925; 1943); *Kleine Serenade* for strings; *Sonata da camera* for strings and percussion (1952); chamber music (2 string quartets, violin sonata, unaccompanied viola sonata, cello sonata, etc.); organ pieces; songs.

Burkhardt, Max, German music analyst and composer; b. Löbau, Sept. 28, 1871; d. Berlin, Nov. 12, 1934. He studied at the Leipzig Cons.; received his degree of *Dr. phil.* with the dissertation *Beiträge zum Studium des deutschen Liedes* (1897); then was a choral conductor in Cologne; in 1906 settled in Berlin as teacher and writer. He publ. several useful music guides: *Führer durch Richard Wagners Musikdramen* (Berlin, 1909; 3rd ed. 1913); *Führer durch die Konzertmusik* (Berlin, 1911; analyzes 1,500 works); *Johannes Brahms: Ein Führer durch seine Werke* (Berlin, 1912). He also wrote the operas *König Drosselbart* (Cologne, 1904) and *Das Moselgretchen* (Schwerin, 1912); choral works and a series of *Lautenlieder* with lute accompaniment.

Burleigh, Cecil, American composer and teacher; b. Wyoming, N. Y., April 17, 1885. He studied in Berlin with Witek (violin) and Leichtentritt (comp.); returning to the U. S., he taught at various American colleges; in 1921, settled as violin teacher at the Univ. of Wisconsin. He has composed more than 100 works, among them 3 violin concertos (1915, 1919, 1928); a 'trilogy of symphonies' (*Creation, Prophecy* and *Revelation*); and descriptive violin pieces (4 *Rocky Mountain Sketches*, 4 *Prairie Sketches*, 5 *Winter Evening Tales*, 6 *Nature Studies*, etc.; also a *Skeleton Dance*).

Burleigh, Henry Thacker, American baritone and song-writer; b. Erie, Pa., Dec. 2, 1866; d. Stamford, Conn., Sept. 12, 1949. He studied at the National Cons., New York. In 1892 he became baritone soloist at St. George's Church, N. Y.; retired in 1946 after 52 years of service. He gained wide popularity as a songwriter (*Love's Garden, Memory, A Prayer, Deep River, Saracen Songs, One Year, Little Mother of Mine*, etc.; also arrangements of Negro spirituals). On May 16, 1917, the National Association for the Advancement of Colored People awarded him the Spingarn Medal for highest achievement by an American citizen of African descent during the year 1916.

Burmeister, Joachim, German poet and musician; b. Lüneburg, 1564; d. Rostock, May 5, 1629. He settled in Rostock in 1586, and obtained a master's degree at Rostock Univ. He published in Rostock the following treatises: *Hypomnematum Musicae Poeticae* (1599); *Musicae Practicae sive artis canendi ratio* (1601); wrote several sacred songs, which were published in 1601. See Martin Ruhnke, *Joachim Burmeister*, (Kassel, 1955).

Burmeister, Richard, German composer and pianist; b. Hamburg, Dec. 7, 1860; d. Berlin, Feb. 19, 1944. He studied with Liszt at Weimar, Rome and Budapest, accompanying him on his travels; later taught at the Hamburg Cons., Peabody Institute in Baltimore, Dresden Cons. (1903-06), and Klindworth-Scharwenka Cons. in Berlin (1907-25). Burmeister also made extensive concert tours of Europe and the U. S. His works include the symph. fantasy *Die Jagd* *nach dem Glück*; a piano concerto; *The Sisters* (after Tennyson) for alto with orch.; a romanza for violin and orch.; songs; piano pieces. He also rescored Chopin's F minor concerto, Liszt's *Mephisto Waltz* and 5th Rhapsody (with new orchestral accompaniment), and Weber's *Konzertstück* for piano and orch.; arranged an orchestral accompaniment for Liszt's *Concerto pathétique*.

Burmester, Willy, German violinist; b. Hamburg, March 16, 1869; d. there, Jan. 16, 1933. He studied with his father, and with Joachim in Berlin; from 1886, made frequent concert tours throughout Europe and America. He composed a Serenade for string quartet and double-bass, and smaller virtuoso pieces; was the author of *Fünfzig Jahre Künstlerleben* (1926; in Danish, 1928).

Burney, Charles, celebrated English music historian; b. Shrewsbury, April 7, 1726; d. Chelsea, April 12, 1814. He was a pupil of Edmund Baker (organist of Chester Cathedral), of his eldest half-brother James Burney, and, from 1744-47, of Dr. Arne in London. In 1749 he became organist of St. Dionis-Backchurch, and harpsichord player at the subscription concerts in the King's Arms, Cornhill; resigned these posts in 1751, and, until 1760, was organist at King's Lynn, Norfolk, where he planned and began work on his *General History of Music*. He returned to London in 1760; received the degrees of Mus. Bac. and Mus. Doc. from Oxford Univ. in 1769. Having exhausted such material as was available in London for his *History of Music,* he visited France, Switzerland and Italy in 1770, and Germany, Holland and Austria in 1772, consulting the libraries, attending the best concerts of sacred and secular music, and forming contacts with the leading musicians and scholars of the period (Gluck, Hasse, Metastasio, Voltaire, etc.). The immediate result of these journeys was the publication of *The Present State of Music in France and Italy,* etc. (1771, in diary form) and *The Present State of Music in Germany, the Netherlands,* etc. (1773). His *General History of Music* appeared in 4 volumes (1776-89; new ed. by Frank Mercer in 2 vols. with 'Critical and Historical Notes', London and N. Y., 1935), the first volume concurrently with the complete work of his rival, Sir John Hawkins. From 1806 he received a government pension. Other publications: *La musica che si canta annualmente nelle funzioni della settimana santa nella Cappella Pontificia, composta da Palestrina, Allegri e Bai* (1771; a book of sacred works with Burney's preface); *An Account of the Musical Performances in Westminster Abbey . . . in Commemoration of Handel* (1785); *Memoirs of the Life and Writings of the Abate Metastasio* (3 vols., 1796); the articles on music for Rees' *Cyclopedia;* etc. He composed, for Drury Lane, music to the dramas *Alfred* (1745), *Robin Hood,* and *Queen Mab* (1750), and *The Cunning Man* (1765), text and music adapted from *Le Devin du village* by Rousseau; also sonatas for piano and for violin; violin and harpsichord concertos, cantatas, flute duets, etc. Bibl.: L. M. Isaacs, *A Friend of Dr. Johnson,* in the 'Mus. Quarterly' (Oct., 1915); C. Ricci, *Burney, Casanova e Farinelli in Bologna* (Milan, 1920); C. H. Glover, *Dr. Charles Burney's Continental Travels, 1770-72* (compiled from Burney's journals and other sources; London, 1927); P. A. Scholes, *The Great Dr. Burney* (a definitive biography; Oxford, 1948). Burney's daughter, **Frances Burney** (b. King's Lynn, Norfolk, June 13, 1752; d. London, Jan. 6, 1840), wrote the novel *Evelina,* and *Memoirs of Dr. Burney* (publ. in 3 vols., 1832). Cf. A. R. Ellis, *Early Diary of Frances Burney* (2 vols., 1889); C. Hill, *The House in St. Martin Street, being Chronicles of the Burney Family* (London, 1906).

Burr, Willard, American composer; b. Ravena, Ohio, Jan. 17, 1852; d. Boston, May 12, 1915. He studied with August Haupt in Berlin; then settled in Boston as teacher. He wrote numerous works for piano, such as a suite *From Shore to Shore*; also anthems and art songs.

Burrian, Karl. See **Burian, Karl.**

Burrowes, John Freckleton, English composer; b. London, April 23, 1787; d. there Mar. 31, 1852. He was a pupil of William Horsley; was organist of St. James' Church, Piccadilly, for many years. He wrote works for flute and other instruments, and made arrangements of operas. His 2 manuals *Thorough-Bass Primer* and *The Pianoforte Primer* were very successful and went through many editions before they became obsolete.

Burtius (also **Burci** or **Burzio**), **Nicolaus,** Italian theorist; b. Parma, c. 1450; d. there, after 1518. He was a cleric in Parma in 1472; then went to Bologna, where he publ. (1487) his *Musices opusculum,* which was one of the earliest printed books on music, containing mensural notes printed from wood-blocks.

Burton, Frederick Russell, American writer on music; b. Jonesville, Mich., Feb. 23, 1861; d. Lake Hopatcong, N. J., Sept. 30, 1909. He was a graduate of Harvard Univ. (1882); then went to New York where he was active as music teacher. He made a study of Indian music, and publ. *Songs of the Ojibway Indians* (1903; later expanded into *American Primitive Music*, publ. posthumously, 1909).

Busby, Thomas, English writer on music; b. Westminster, Dec., 1755; d. London, May 28, 1838. He was a chorister in London; then studied with Battishill (1769-74); served as church organist at St. Mary's, Newington, Surrey, St. Mary Woolnoth, and Lombard Street. He obtained the degree of Mus. Doc. from Cambridge Univ. in 1801. In collaboration with Arnold, he began publishing a *Musical Dictionary* (1786), but the project was not completed. He then published *A Grammar of Music* (1818) and *A History of Music* (London, 1819; 2 vols., compiled from Burney and Hawkins). In 1825 he brought out a set of 3 little volumes entitled *Concert Room and Orchestra Anecdotes of Music and Musicians, Ancient and Modern,* a compilation of some topical value, even though many of the stories are apocryphal. He also published *A Musical Manual, or Technical Directory* (1828). His anthology of sacred music *The Divine Harmonist* (1788) is valuable. His own compositions (oratorios and odes) are imitative of Handel. A melodrama, *Tale of Mystery,* with Busby's music was produced at Covent Garden, Nov. 13, 1807.—Cf. K. G. F. Spence, *The Learned Doctor Busby,* in 'Music & Letters' (April, 1956).

Busch, Adolf, distinguished violinist; b. Siegen, Westphalia, Aug. 8, 1891; d. Guilford, Vermont, June 9, 1952. He studied at the conservatories of Cologne and Bonn; was concert-master of the Vienna Konzertverein; then taught at the Musikhochschule in Berlin. In 1919 he organized the internationally known Busch Quartet (first American tour, 1939) and the Busch Trio (with his younger brother Hermann Busch, and his son-in-law Rudolf Serkin). He also appeared in frequent joint recitals with Serkin, specializing in the Beethoven violin sonatas.

Busch, Carl, Danish composer; b. Bjerre, Denmark, March 29, 1862; d. Kansas City, Mo., Dec. 19, 1943. He studied at the Royal Cons. in Copenhagen with Hartmann and Gade; then went to Paris: and in 1887 finally settled in Kansas City, where he was active as conductor and teacher. From 1912 to 1918 he was conductor of the Kansas City Symph.; also conducted his own works with various orchestras in the U. S., Denmark and Germany. Works: *The Passing of Arthur* (after Tennyson) and *Minnehaha's Vision,* for orch.; *Elegy,* for string orch.; cantatas (*The Four Winds, King Olaf, The League of the Alps, America,* etc.); many compositions for violin; songs. Cf. M. H. Barney, *Sir Carl Busch* (Kansas City, 1942).

Busch, Fritz, notable German conductor (brother of Adolph Busch); b. Siegen, Westphalia, March 13, 1890; d. London, Sept. 14, 1951. He studied at the Cologne Cons. with Steinbach, Boettcher, Uzielli and Klauwell; then was active as conductor at Riga, Russia (1909), Gotha (1911), Aachen (1912), at the Stuttgart Opera (1918), and at the Dresden Opera (1922). He left Germany in 1933, and made frequent appearances as symphonic conductor in Europe; conducted opera in South America (1942-45) and at the Metropolitan Opera, N. Y. (1945-50). He wrote an autobiography *Aus dem Leben eines Musikers* (Zürich, 1949; publ. in English under the title *Pages from a Musician's Life,* London, 1953).

Busch, William, English pianist and composer; b. London, June 25, 1901; d. Woolacombe, Devon, Jan. 30, 1945. Of German origin, he received his education in America and England; then studied in Germany with Leonid Kreutzer (piano) and Hugo Leichtentritt (theory). He made his debut in London (Oct. 20, 1927). His music shows competent craftsmanship; among his works are a piano concerto (1939); cello concerto (1941); piano quartet (1939); and pieces for piano solo.

Buschkötter, Wilhelm, German conductor; b. Höxter, Westphalia, Sept. 27, 1887. He studied cello and conducting in German provincial towns; from 1926-37 was conductor at the radio station in Cologne; then was in Stuttgart and Dortmund (1937-39) and in Berlin (1945-49). In 1950 he returned to his post at the Western German Broadcasting Corporation.

Bush, Alan Dudley, English composer; b. Dulwich, Dec. 22, 1900. He studied at the Royal Academy of Music, with F. Corder (composition) and Matthay (piano); also took private piano lessons with Artur Schnabel and composition with John Ireland. In 1929 he went to Berlin and took courses in philosophy and musicology at Berlin Univ. From 1925-55 he was on the staff of the Royal Academy of Music. He became interested in social theories of music; organized the Workers' Music Association (1936), and in subsequent years maintained close contact with musical development in Russia. His early works contain modernistic usages, in which every note acquires thematic value. In accordance with the general trend towards simplification in writing music for the masses, Bush gradually veered towards a more direct tonal language, and adopted programmatic subject matter. Works: *Wat Tyler,* historic opera (1950; awarded a prize at the Festival of Britain, 1951, but not performed in London; first complete performance on the Berlin radio, in German, April 3, 1952); *The Spell,* operetta (1953); for orch: Symphony No. 1 (London, Aug. 24, 1942, composer conducting); *Fantasia on Soviet Themes* (London, Aug. 27, 1945); *English Suite* for string orch. (London, Feb. 9, 1946); *Piers Plowman's Day* (Prague Radio, Oct. 16, 1947); Symphony No. 2, subtitled *Nottingham* (Nottingham, June 27, 1949); *Defender of the Peace* (Vienna Radio, May 24, 1952); piano concerto, with baritone solo and male chorus in the finale (1938); *The Winter Journey,* cantata (Alnwick, Dec. 12, 1946); violin concerto (B.B.C., July 16, 1948); *Song of Friendship* for bass, chorus and band (London, Workers' Music Assoc., Nov. 6, 1949); also a children's operetta, *The Press Gang* (Letchworth, March 7, 1947); *Dialectic* for string quartet (1929); a few piano pieces; many arrangements of English songs for various choral and instrumental combinations. A 'Tribute to Alan Bush' was published by the Workers' Music Assoc. on his 50th birthday (1950).

Bush, Geoffrey, English composer; b. London, March 23, 1920. He studied at Balliol College, Oxford; received his B.M. degree (1940) and D.M. (1946); he was active as organist; has also contributed articles to various music publications; he has written several choral works; an overture, *The Rehearsal* (1943); trumpet sonata (1944); violin sonata (1944); concerto for oboe and strings (1948); and a short opera, *The Spanish Rivals* (Brighton, 1948).

Busi, Alessandro, Italian composer; b. Bologna, Sept. 28, 1833; d. there, July 8, 1895. He was a conductor of the Communal Theater in Bologna and taught at the Bologna Liceo. His works include a choral symphony, *Excelsior; In alto mare* for chorus and orch.; many ballads for voice and piano; etc.—Cf. L. Torchi, *Commemorazione di Alessandro Busi* (Bologna, 1896).

Busnois (bü-nwah'), **Antoine** (properly **De Busne**), celebrated 15th-century contrapuntist; b. probably at or near Béthune, France; d. Bruges, Nov. 6, 1492. In 1467 he was chapel singer to Charles the Bold of Burgundy; in 1476 he was in Mons. Several of his works are still extant. They include 7 chansons in early publications of Petrucci's (1501-03), the MS Masses *L'homme armé, O crux lignum* and a *Regina coeli* in the Papal Chapel at Rome, and some magnificats, motets and chansons in other libraries. In his *In hydraulis quondam Pythagoras* ('Denkmäler der Tonkunst in Österreich', Vol. VII) he professed to be a pupil of Okeghem. Bibl.: Ch. van den Borren, *Études sur le XVe siècle musical* (Antwerp, 1941); full bibl. in 'Die Musik in Geschichte und Gegenwart'.

Busoni, Ferruccio Benvenuto, distinguished composer; b. Empoli, near Florence, April 1, 1866; d. Berlin, July 27, 1924. His father was a clarinet player; his mother, Anna Weiss, a good pianist; her father was a German. Busoni was musically brought up by his parents, and at eight gave a public piano recital in Trieste. At the age of ten he played in Vienna, in a program that included his own piano pieces. The following year the family moved to Graz, where he took lessons with W. A. Remy (Dr. W. Mayer). In Graz Busoni conducted his own *Stabat Mater*; he was then twelve years old. At 15 he was elected a member of the Reale Accademia Filarmonica; he performed his oratorio, *Il Sabato del Villaggio,* in Bologna (1883); went to Leipzig (1886); was for a season (1888-89) piano instructor at the Helsingfors Cons.; in 1890 he gave concerts and taught in Moscow, where he married Gerda Sjöstrand; received the Rubinstein Prize for his *Konzertstück* for piano and orch. In 1891 he accepted an offer to teach at the New England Cons. in Boston; appeared as pianist with the Boston Symph. Orch.; in 1893 he returned to Europe; made successful tours in Belgium, Denmark, and Italy; in 1894 he settled in Berlin. His fame as a pianist was now world-wide; he made triumphant tours of European countries, including Russia; in 1901-11 he gave concerts in the U. S. with great acclaim; he also conducted concerts of little known or seldom heard music (Berlin, 1905-07); taught at Vienna Cons.; in 1913 was director of the Liceo Musicale in Bologna; from 1915-20 he was in Zürich; returned to Berlin in 1920 and remained there until his death. In 1913 he received the order of Chevalier de la Légion d'Honneur, which had theretofore been bestowed on only two Italians: Rossini and Verdi. Busoni's virtuosity as pianist was distinguished by an element of tone color that gave it an orchestral quality; he particularly excelled in contrapuntal voice-leading, which he projected with extraordinary clarity and precision. His piano transcriptions of Bach's organ works are extremely effective and faithful to the spirit of the music. His edition of Bach's *Well-Tempered Clavichord,* with its penetrating annotations, is valuable to students, even though not all Bach scholars would accept Busoni's interpretation of the ornaments; he also edited the piano works of Liszt for Breitkopf & Härtel. Busoni was a believer in new ideas, in music and in general esthetics; his *Entwurf einer neuen Ästhetik der Tonkunst* (Trieste, 1907; English transl. by Th. Baker, N. Y., 1911) abounds in interesting suggestions; other writings are: *Versuch einer organischen Klaviernotenschrift* (Leipzig, 1910) and *Von der Einheit der Musik* (collected papers; Berlin, 1922). He applied his novel ideas in some of his works, particularly in the *Fantasia contrappuntistica,* where he used special scales and arpeggios. Works: the operas *Die Brautwahl* (Hamburg, April 12, 1912); *Arlecchino* and *Turandot* (Zürich, May 11, 1917); *Doktor Faust* (unfinished; completed by Philipp Jarnach; performed posthumously, Dresden, May 21, 1925); for orch.: 2 symph. suites (1888; 1895); *Lustspielouvertüre* (1897); *Turandot Suite* (1904); *Nocturne symphonique* (1912); *Tanzwalzer* (1920); piano concerto, with final chorus for male voices (1904); *Indianische Fantasie* for piano and orch. (1913); *Romanza e scherzoso* (1921); violin concerto (1897); clarinet concerto (1919); 2 string quartets (1880; 1889); 2 violin sonatas (1890; 1898); for piano: *Una festa di villaggio* (6 characteristic pieces, 1882); *Tre pezzi nello stilo antico* (1882); *Macchiette medioevali* (1883); *Zwei Tanzstücke* (1914); 6 sonatinas; 10 variations on Chopin's prelude in C minor (1922); *Fantasia contrappuntistica* (1910; also a version for 2 pianos, 1922); a number of liturgical songs; also songs to German, Italian and English words. Bibl.: H. Leichtentritt, *Ferruccio Busoni* (Leipzig, 1916); H. Leichtentritt, *Ferruccio Busoni as a Composer* in the 'Mus. Quarterly' (Jan., 1917); Gisella Selden-Goth, *Ferruccio Busoni* (Vienna, 1922); Jakob Wassermann, *In Memoriam Ferruccio Busoni* (1925); Paul Bekker, *Klang und Eros* (1931); S. Nadel, *Ferruccio Busoni* (1931); E. J. Dent, *Ferruccio Busoni, A Biography* (Oxford, 1933); G. M. Gatti, *The Stage Works of Ferruccio Busoni* in the 'Mus. Quarterly' (July, 1934); A. Santelli, *Busoni* (Rome, 1939); G. Guerrini, *Ferruccio Busoni, la vita, la figura, l'opera* (Florence, 1944); also an article on him in a special issue of 'Rassegna Musicale' (Jan., 1940). Collections of Busoni's letters are published by F. Schnapp, *Briefe an seine Frau* (Zürich, 1935; English transl. by R. Ley, London, 1938); Gisella Selden-Goth, *25 Busoni Briefe* (Vienna, 1937); see also P. Rosenfeld, *Busoni in His Letters* in the 'Mus. Quarterly' (April, 1939).

Busschop (bü-shohp'), **Jules-Auguste-Guillaume,** French composer; b. Paris, Sept. 10, 1810; d. Bruges, Belgium, Feb. 10, 1896. He was entirely self-taught, and became successful as a composer of motets, cantatas etc., including the prize-cantata *Le Drapeau belge* (1834) and a *Te Deum* (Brussels, 1860). He also wrote a symphony, several overtures, military music, etc.

Busser, Henri-Paul, French composer and organist; b. Toulouse, Jan. 16, 1872. He received his apprenticeship at the Toulouse Cathedral; then studied at the Paris Cons. with Guiraud, and privately with Widor, Gounod and César Franck; won 2nd Premier Prix de Rome in 1893 with his cantata *Antigone.* In 1892 he was appointed organist at St. Cloud; later was choirmaster at the Opéra-Comique; in 1902 appointed conductor of the Grand Opéra; resigned after 37 years in 1939; reappointed in 1947, when he was also named president of the Académie des Beaux Arts. He taught composition at the Paris Cons. from 1930-48. His debut as composer took place at the Opéra-Comique on Dec. 14, 1897, with a pastorale *Daphnis et Chloë.* Subsequent works include the operas, *Colomba* (Nice, Feb. 4, 1921), *Les Noces corinthiennes* (Paris, May 10, 1922) and *La Carosse du Saint Sacrement* (1936; Opéra-Comique, 1948); ballet, *La Ronde des Saisons* (1905); *Le Sommeil de l'Enfant Jésus* for violin and orch.; *A la Villa Medicis,* symph. suite for orch.; *Minerva,* concert overture for orch.; *Hercule au Jardin des Hespérides,* symph. poem; *Suite funambulesque* for small orch.; *A la Lumière* (*Poème lyrique*); *Suite brève* for small orch.; *Messe de Noël* for 4 voices with organ or orch.; *Pièce de Concert* for harp with orch.; *Appassionato* for alto with orch.; *Marche de Fête* for orch.; *Hymne à la France* for tenor with orch.; *Impromptu* for harp with orch.; several preludes and fugues for organ on themes by Gounod, Massenet, A. Thomas, etc. He publ. a *Précis de composition* (Paris, 1943) and a volume of memoirs *De Pelléas aux Indes Galantes* (1955).

Bussler, Ludwig, German music theorist and pedagogue; b. Berlin, Nov. 26, 1838; d. there, Jan. 18, 1900. His father was the painter, author, and privy councillor Robert Bussler; his maternal grandfather was the famous tenor singer, Karl Bader. He studied with Dehn, Grell and Wieprecht; then taught theory at the Ganz School of Music in Berlin (1865) and at the Stern Cons. (from 1879); was also active as a conductor at various Berlin theaters. In 1883 he became the music critic for the 'National-Zeitung'. His eminently practical writings are: *Musikalische Elementarlehre* (1867; 3rd ed., 1882; English transl. N. Y., 1895; also in Russian); *Der strenge Satz* (1877); *Harmonische Übungen am Klavier* (1877; in English, N. Y., 1890); *Kontrapunkt und Fuge im freien Tonsatz* (1878); *Musikalische Formenlehre* (1878; English edition, N. Y., 1883); *Praktische musikalische Kompositionslehre:* Part I, *Lehre vom Tonsatz* (1878); Part II, *Freie Komposition* (1879); also *Instrumentation und Orchestersatz* (1879); *Elementar-Melodik* (1879); *Geschichte der Musik* (1882, six lectures); *Modulationslehre* (1882); *Lexikon der musikalischen Harmonien* (1889).

Bustabo, Guila, American violinist; b. Manitowoc, Wisconsin, Feb. 25, 1919. A child prodigy, she played at a benefit concert in Chicago at the age of four; studied with Louis Persinger in New York; appeared with the N. Y. Philh., performing a Wieniawski concerto (Nov. 2, 1929). She then traveled in Europe; returned to the U. S. in 1937, and continued her concert career.

Buths (boots), **Julius,** German pianist; b. Wiesbaden, May 7, 1851; d. Düsseldorf, March 12, 1920. He was a pupil of his father; later of Hiller in Cologne and Kiel in Berlin; conducted the 'Cecilia' at Wiesbaden (1871-2); traveled to Milan and Paris (1873-4); conducted in Breslau (1875-9) and in Elberfeld (1879-90); from 1890-1908 was music director at Düsseldorf, and conducted several Rhine music festivals; in 1902 was appointed director of the Düsseldorf Cons. He wrote a piano concerto; a piano quintet; a string quartet; a piano suite; etc.

Butler, O'Brien (real name, Whitwell), Irish composer; b. Cahersiveen, Ireland, c. 1870; d. May 7, 1915 (lost on the Lusitania). He began his musical studies in Italy, then became a pupil of C. V. Stanford and W. Parratt at the Royal College of Music in London; later traveled extensively, and spent some time in India, where he wrote an opera *Muirgheis,* the first opera to be written to a libretto in the Gaelic language; it was produced in Dublin, Dec. 7, 1903. The work was also heard in concert-form in New York (1915) during the composer's visit to the U. S. Other compositions include a sonata for violin and piano (on Irish themes) and songs.

Butt, Clara, English contralto; b. Southwick, Sussex, Feb. 1, 1873; d. Worthsloke, Oxford, Jan. 23, 1936. She studied with J. H. Blower at the Royal College of Music, later with Bouhy in Paris and Etelka Gerster in Berlin; made her debut as Ursula in Sullivan's *Golden Legend* (London, Dec. 7, 1892); then appeared with great success at the festivals at Hanley and Bristol. She was heard twice in the U. S. (1899 and 1913); made a world tour with her husband, R. Kennerly Rumford, a noted baritone (1913-14). Several composers wrote works especially for her (Elgar, *Sea-Pictures*; F. Cliff, *Triumph of Alcestis;* H. Bedford, *Romeo and Juliet*; etc.). In 1920 she was made Dame of the British Empire. See W. Ponder, *Clara Butt* (London, 1928).

Butterworth, George Sainton Kaye, talented English composer; b. London, July 12, 1885; killed in the battle of Pozières, Aug. 5, 1916. He inherited his love for music from his mother, a singer, Julia Wigan; learned to play organ at school in Yorkshire; then studied piano at Eton. He later entered Trinity College, Oxford; then engaged in music teaching and writing music criticism; also became an ardent collector of folksongs, and prepared material for Vaughan Williams' *London Symphony.* He made several arrangements of folksongs and wrote an orchestral piece, *The Banks of Green Willows,* on folk themes (London, March 20, 1914). He enlisted in the British army at the outbreak of World War I. Published works: *Six Songs from 'A Shropshire Lad'* (1911); 11 folksongs from Sussex (1912); *On Christmas Night* for mixed chorus (1912); *Cherry Tree,* a prelude for orch. (1912); *Love Blows as the Wind Blows* for baritone and string quartet (1914).

Butting, Max, German composer; b. Berlin, Oct. 6, 1888. He studied in Berlin with the organist A. Dreyer, and in Munich with Prill, Klose and Courvoisier. He has since been active in Berlin as a teacher and writer, particularly interested in the movement for contemporary music. Works: 7 symphonies; *Trauermusik* for orch.; chamber symph. for 13 solo instruments; violin concerto; chamber music; piano and choral compositions; etc. He has also contributed many articles on modern subjects to 'Melos'. Cf. H. Strobel, in 'Melos', VI, 1.

Buttstädt. See **Buttstett.**

Buttstett, Franz Vollrath, German composer, grandson of Johann Heinrich Buttstett; b. Erfurt, April 2, 1735; d. Rotenburg, May 7, 1814. He was a member of a musical family; received his education at home; was active as organist in Weckersheim from 1756, and went to Rotenburg in 1767. He wrote cantatas and instrumental sonatas. See Hans Kern, *Franz Vollrath Buttstett: eine Studie zur Musik des Spätbarock* (Würzburg, 1939).

Buttstett, Johann Heinrich, German organist and composer; b. Bindersleben, near Erfurt, April 25, 1666; d. Erfurt, Dec. 1, 1727. He studied with Johann Pachelbel; occupied posts as organist in various churches in Erfurt. In 1713 he published an album of keyboard pieces, *Musikalische Klavier-Kunst*; also wrote 5 masses and 36 chorale preludes. His *Harmonia aeterna* is a polemical pamphlet directed against Mattheson. See E. Ziller, *Der Erfurter Organist, Johann Heinrich Buttstett* (Halle, 1934).

Buttykay, Akos, Hungarian pianist and composer; b. Halmi, July 22, 1871; d. Debrecen, Oct. 29, 1935. He studied at the Budapest Cons. and later in Weimar; became piano teacher at the Budapest Academy of Music in 1907. He wrote several operettas and musical fairy tales, most of which were produced in Budapest; for orchestra he wrote 2 symphonies, a Hungarian rhapsody and several symphonic poems; also a violin concerto; 2 violin sonatas, and piano pieces.

Buus, Jacques (Jachet de; van Paus; Jacobus Bohusius), Flemish contrapuntist; b. probably in Bruges; d. Vienna, late July, 1565. His first publications are 2 French songs, published in Lyons in 1538. In 1541 he went to Italy and was engaged as assistant organist at San Marco in Venice; he may have studied with Willaert there. He published in Venice 2 books of instrumental *Canzoni francese* (1543; 1550); 2 books of *Ricercari* (1547; 1549); and 1 book of *Motetti* (1549); his madrigals were published in various collections of the period; reprints are in Kinkeldey's *Orgel und Klavier in der Musik des 16. Jahrhunderts* (1910; p. 245 ff.) and Riemann's *Musikgeschichte in Beispielen* (No. 40). See G. Sutherland, *The Ricercari of Jacques Buus,* in the 'Mus. Quarterly' (Oct., 1945).

Buxtehude, Dietrich, famous organist and composer; b. Oldesloe (Holstein), c. 1637; d. Lübeck, May 9, 1707. His father Johann Buxtehude (1602-1674), an organist of German extraction, was active in Holstein, then under Danish rule. Despite diligent research, no documented information has been discovered to shed any light on Dietrich Buxtehude's early years. It is to be assumed that he studied with his father. He held a post as organist in Helsingborg, in 1657; was in Helsingör in 1660. On April 11, 1668, he was elected as successor to the famous organist Franz Tunder at the St. Mary Church in Lübeck; according to custom in such successions, he married Tunder's daughter (Aug. 3, 1668). In 1673 he established his celebrated musical services, the 'Abend Musiken', made up of organ music and concerted pieces for chorus and orch., held annually on the five Sundays before Christmas from 4 to 5. Handel journeyed to Lübeck (1703), with the apparent intention of securing Buxtehude's post after his retirement or death; but the notorious marriage clause which would have compelled him to marry one of Buxtehude's five daughters deterred him from further negotiations; in 1705 Bach traveled on foot 200 miles from Arnstadt to Lübeck to hear Buxtehude (see Ph. Spitta, *J. S. Bach,* vol. I, p. 258); it is to be presumed that Bach, too, declined the marriage as a means of obtaining the Lübeck post. There can be no doubt that Buxtehude exercised profound influence on Bach, both as organist and composer. A complete edition of his organ works was publ. by Spitta (2 vols., 1875-76) and by Josef Hedar (3 vols., 1952); a complete edition of his vocal music appeared in 7 vols. (1925-37). Carl Stiehl edited his instrumental works in the 'Denkmäler deutscher Tonkunst' (vol. XI); 19 newly discovered keyboard suites by Buxtehude were brought out by E. Bangert (Copenhagen, 1942). A complete edition of all of Buxtehude's works was begun by W. Gurlitt in 1925. Bibl.: H. Jimmerthal, *Buxtehude* (Lübeck, 1877); C. Stiehl, *Die Organisten an der Marienkirche und die Abendmusiken in Lübeck* (Leipzig, 1886); A. Pirro, *Buxtehude* (Paris, 1913); S. E. A. Hagen, *Diderik Buxtehude* (Copenhagen,

1920); W. Stahl, *Franz Tunder und Dietrich Buxtehude* (Leipzig, 1926); W. Stahl, *Buxtehude* (Kassel, 1937); W. Buszin, *Buxtehude,* in the 'Mus. Quarterly' (Oct., 1937); J. Hedar, *Buxtehude's Orgelwerke* (Stockholm, 1951). For a detailed list of editions and bibliographical minutiae, see 'Die Musik in Geschichte und Gegenwart'.

Buzzi-Peccia (boot-tsi-petch'-yah), **Arturo,** song composer and teacher; b. Milan, Oct. 13, 1854; d. New York, Aug. 29, 1943. He emigrated to America in 1898 and lived mostly in New York as a vocal teacher. He published numerous songs and choral works; also a book, *How to Succeed in Singing* (1925).

Buzzolla (bŏŏts'-sohl-lah), **Antonio,** Italian composer; b. Adria, March 2, 1815; d. Venice, March 20, 1871. He studied with his father, who was a conductor, and with Donizetti. After bringing out at Venice the operas *Ferramondo* (Dec. 3, 1836), *Mastino I della Scala* (1841), and *Gli Avventurieri* (May 14, 1842) he traveled, for the purpose of study, in Germany and France; returned to Venice in 1847, where he produced 2 later operas: *Amleto* (Feb. 24, 1847) and *Elisabetta di Valois* (Feb. 16, 1850). In 1855 he was appointed maestro di cappella at San Marco, for which he subsequently wrote much sacred music. An opera in Venetian dialect, *La Puta onorata,* remained unfinished.—Cf. A. Casellati, *Antonio Buzzolla,* in 'Musica d'oggi' (July, 1930).

Byrd (or **Byrde, Bird**), **William,** great English composer; b. probably in Lincolnshire, 1543; d. Stondon, Essex, July 4, 1623. Anthony Wood states that Byrd was 'bred up to musick under Tallis' and there are other indirect indications that Byrd was Tallis' pupil. He was appointed organist of Lincoln Cathedral on Feb. 27, 1563, was married to Juliana Birley in 1568; early in 1570 he was elected a member of the Chapel Royal, but retained his post at Lincoln Cathedral until the end of 1572; he then assumed his duties, together with Tallis, as organist of the Chapel Royal; in 1575 the two were granted a patent by Queen Elizabeth for the exclusive privilege of printing music and selling music paper for 21 years; however, the license proved unprofitable, and they petitioned the Queen in 1577 to give them an annuity in the form of a lease; this petition was granted. In 1585, after the death of Tallis, the license passed wholly into Byrd's hands. The first publication of the printing press of Byrd and Tallis was the first set of *Cantiones sacrae* in 5 and 6 voices (1575), printed for them by Vautrollier and dedicated to the Queen; the works issued by Byrd alone under his license were the following: *Psalmes, Sonets, and Songs of Sadness and Pietie* in 5 voices (1588; publ. by Thomas East; reprinted as vol. XIV by Fellowes, *English Madrigal School*); *Songs of Sundrie Natures* for 3-6 voices (1589; reprint in vol. XV of *English Madrigal School*); *Liber Primus Sacrarum Cantionum* for 5 voices (1589); *Liber Secundus Sacrarum Cantionum* (1591); also in 1591 appeared the famous collection of virginal music by Byrd 'My Ladye Nevells Booke' (42 pieces; modern edition publ. by Hilda Andrews, London, 1926). In 1593 Byrd moved to Stondon Place, near Ongar, Essex, and, owing to various litigations and disputes concerning the ownership of the property, did not publish anything until 1605, when he brought out the first book of *Gradualia*; 2 years later there followed the second book (both books republ. in 'Tudor Chirch Music', vol. 7). In 1611 the book of *Psalmes, Songs and Sonnets* was publ. (reprint in vol. XVI of Fellowes' *English Madrigal School*); in the same year Byrd contributed several pieces to 'Parthenia', a collection of virginal compositions by Byrd, Bull and Gibbons (newly ed. by Margaret H. Glyn; London, 1927); in 1614 he contributed 4 anthems to Leighton's 'Teares or Lamentacions of a Sorrowful Soule'; separate numbers were publ. in various other collections ('Musica Transalpina', 1588; Watson's 'Italian Madrigales', 1590; Barnard's 'Selected Church Music', 1641; Boyce's 'Cathedral Music'); other music for virginals and organ in 'Virginal Book of Queen Elizabeth', 'Fitzwilliam Virginal Book' (70 pieces), 'Forster Virginal Book' (33 pieces), and 'Cosyn's Virginal Book' (2 pieces). New editions (besides those mentioned above): 'Tudor Church Music' (vol. 2, English church music; vol. 9, masses, cantiones and motets); psalms, sonnets and madrigals, by E. H. Fellowes (1920); a collected edition of Byrd's vocal works, also by Fellowes (7 vols., 1937-38); 'Byrd Organ Book', a collection of 21 pieces edited for piano from the virginal MSS by Margaret H. Glyn (London, 1923); 14 pieces for keyboard instruments, by J. A. Fuller Maitland and W. Barclay Squire (London, 1923). A composer of great skill, Byrd was unsurpassed in versatility by any of his contemporaries; he excelled in all branches of composition, displaying his masterly technique equally well in ecclesiastical music, madrigal, solo song, chamber music and keyboard music. Bibl.: E. H. Fellowes,

English Madrigal Composers (1921); E. H. Fellowes, *William Byrd: a Short Account of His Life and Work* (Oxford, 1923; 3rd ed. London, 1936); Margaret H. Glyn, *About Elizabethan Virginal Music and Its Composers* (London, 1924; new revised ed., 1935); F. Howes, *William Byrd* (London, 1928); E. J. Dent, *William Byrd and the Madrigal,* in the 'Johannes Wolf Festschrift' (Berlin, 1929); J. A. Westrup, *William Byrd* in 'Music & Letters' (1943); W. Palmer, *Word-Painting and Suggestion in Byrd* in 'Music Review' (1952); W. Palmer, *Byrd and Amen* in 'Music & Letters' (1953). A list of Byrd's music that is obtainable in modern editions was publ. by the Byrd Tercentenary Committee (London, 1923).

C

Caballero. See **Fernandez-Caballero.**

Cabanilles, Juan Bautista José, Spanish organist, and composer; b. Algemesí, province of Valencia, Sept. 4, 1644; d. Valencia, April 29, 1712. He studied for the priesthood at Valencia and probably received his musical training at the Cathedral there; was appointed organist of Valencia Cathedral, May 15, 1665 (succeeding J. de la Torre) and retained that post until his death; was ordained a priest on Sept. 22, 1668. He was the greatest of the early Spanish composers for organ, and the most prolific. He composed chiefly 'tientos' (preludes), remarkable for the ingenious use of the variation form (on liturgical or popular themes). A complete edition of his works was begun by H. Anglès; 3 vols. have been publ. (Barcelona, 1927, 1933, 1936); 3 works by Cabanilles are included in J. Bonnet's 'Historical Organ Recitals' (N. Y., 1940); several others are in Muset's 'Early Spanish Organ Music' (N. Y., 1948). See H. Anglès, *Orgelmusik der Schola Hispanica vom XV.-XVI. Jahrhundert,* in 'P. Wagner-Festschrift' (Leipzig, 1926).

Cabezón (Cabeçon) (kah-bĕ-thôn'), **Antonio de,** great Spanish organist and composer; b. Matajudíos, near Burgos, in 1510 (the exact date is unknown: see S. Kastner's letter to the editor of 'Music & Letters' for April, 1955); d. Madrid, March 26, 1566. He became blind in infancy; went to Palencia about 1521 to study with the cathedral organist García de Baeza and with Tomás Gómez. He was appointed organist to the court of the Emperor Charles V and Empress Isabel (1526); after her death, Cabezón entered the service of Prince Philip and accompanied him to Italy, Germany, the Netherlands (1548-51) and England (1554); he returned to Spain (1556) and remained court organist until his death. His keyboard style greatly influenced the development of organ composition on the continent and the composers for the virginals in England; Pedrell called him "the Spanish Bach". The series 'Libro de cifra nueva' (1557) which contains the earliest editions of Cabezón's works, was reprinted by H. Anglès in *La música en la corte de Carlos V* (1944). His son and successor at the court of Philip II, **Hernando** (b. Madrid; baptized Sept. 7, 1541; d. Valladolid, Oct. 1, 1602) published his instrumental works as *Obras de música para tecla, arpa y vihuela* (Madrid, 1578). This volume contains exercises in 2 and 3 parts, arrangements of hymn-tunes, 4-part 'tientos' (preludes), arrangements of motets up to 6 parts by Josquin and other Netherlanders, and variations on tunes of the day (*El Caballero,* etc.). Copies are in the British Museum, in Sir Percy Wyndham's Collection, at Brussels, Berlin, Madrid and Washington, D.C. Pedrell has brought out a new edition in 'Hispaniae schola musica sacra' (4 volumes). Other examples can be found in A. Schering's *Musikgeschichte in Beispielen* (No. 113), Riemann's *Notenschrift und Notendruck* (1 'tiento'). G. A. Ritter's *Geschichte des Orgelspiels* (5 pieces), and J. Bonnet's *Historical Organ Recitals,* volumes 1 and 6 (5 pieces). A short MS work for 5 voices is in the Medinaceli Library, Madrid. Bibl.: Otto Kinkeldey, *Orgel und Klavier in der Musik des 16. Jahrhunderts* (1910); Willi Apel, *Early Spanish Music for Lute and Keyboard Instruments,* in the 'Mus. Quarterly' (July, 1934); S. Kastner, *Antonio de Cabezón* (Barcelona, 1952); T. Dart, *Cavazzoni and Cabezón,* in 'Music & Letters' (Jan. 1955; a rebuttal to Dart's conjecture concerning the relationship of Cavazzoni and Cabezón is found in Knud Jeppesen's article *Cavazzonì-Cabezón* in the summer 1955 issue of 'The Journal of the American Musicological Society'; also see Dart's postscript in the same issue).

Caccini, Francesca, daughter of Giulio Caccini, nicknamed 'La Cecchina'; b. Florence, Sept. 18, 1588; d. about 1640. She was probably the first woman composer of operas. Her opera-ballet *La liberazione di Ruggiero dall' isola d'Alcina* was produced at a palace, near Florence, on Feb. 2, 1625, and a book of songs from it was publ. in the same year. A modern reprint, edited by Doris Silbert, was publ. in Northampton, Mass. (1945). Francesca Caccini wrote further a *Ballo delle zingare* (Florence, Feb. 24, 1615) in which she acted as one of the gypsies. Her sacred opera *Il martirio di Sant' Agata* was produced in Florence, Feb. 10, 1622. See A. Bonaventura, *Il ritratto della 'Cecchina',* in 'La Cultura musicale' (1922); D. Silbert, *F. Caccini called 'La Cecchina',* in the 'Mus. Quarterly' (Jan., 1946).

Caccini (kahtch-chē'-nē), **Giulio,** Italian singer and composer, called **Romano** because he was born at Rome, c. 1546; d. Florence, Dec. 10, 1618. He was a pupil of Scipione della Palla in singing and lute playing. His first compositions were madrigals in the traditional polyphonic style; but the new ideas generated in the discussions of the artists and literati of the 'Camerata', in the houses of Bardi and Corsi at Florence, inspired him to write vocal soli in recitative form (then termed 'musica in stile rappresentativo'), which he sang with consummate skill to his own accompaniment on the theorbo. These first compositions in a dramatic idiom were followed by his settings of separate scenes written by Bardi, and finally by the opera *Il combattimento d'Apolline col serpente* (poem by Bardi); then appeared *Euridice* (1600; poem by Rinuccini); and *Il rapimento di Cefalo* (in collaboration with others; first performed on Oct. 9, 1600, at the Palazzo Vecchio in Florence). Then followed *Le nuove musiche,* a series of madrigals for solo voice, with bass (Florence, 1601; new editions, Venice, 1607 and 1615; modern reprints, Milan, 1919 and Rome, 1934). The song *Amarilli mia bella* from the first series became very popular. The foreword to *Le nuove musiche* is reproduced in English by O. Strunk in *Source Readings in Music History* (N. Y., 1950). Caccini also published *Fuggilotio musicale* (Venice, 2nd ed., 1613; including madrigals, sonnets, arias, etc.). From 1565 Caccini lived in Florence as a singer at the Tuscan court. He was called, by abbate Angelo Grillo, the 'father of a new style of music'; Bardi said of him that he had 'attained the goal of perfect music'. But his claim to priority in writing vocal music in the 'stile rappresentativo' is not supported by known chronology. Caccini's opera, *Il rapimento di Cefalo,* was performed three days after Peri's path-breaking *Euridice;* the closeness in time of operatic productions by both Caccini and Peri is further emphasized by the fact that when Peri produced *Euridice* in Florence (1600), he used some of Caccini's songs in the score. Caccini later made his own setting of *Euridice* (1600), but it was not produced until Dec. 5, 1602. On the other hand, Caccini was undoubtedly the first to publish an operatic work, for his score of *Euridice* was printed early in 1601, before the publication of Peri's work of the same title. Bibl.: A. Ehrichs, *Giulio Caccini* (Leipzig, 1908); R. Marchal, *Giulio Caccini,* in 'La Revue Musicale' (June, 1925); F. Ghisi, *Alle fonti della monodia* (Milan, 1940).

Cadman, Charles Wakefield, American composer; b. Johnstown, Pa., Dec. 24, 1881; d. Los Angeles, Dec. 30, 1946. His great grandfather was Samuel Wakefield, the inventor of the so-called "Buckwheat Notation". Cadman studied organ with Leo Oehmler in Pittsburgh, and comp. with Emil Paur; was music critic for 'Pittsburgh Dispatch' (1908-10). He was especially interested in American Indian music; gave lecture recitals with the Indian mezzo-soprano Tsianina Redfeather (1909-23); was one of the founders of the Hollywood Bowl Concerts, where he appeared seven times as soloist; received a Mus. Doc. from the Univ. of Southern California (1923); was a member of the National Institute of Arts and Letters. His most successful work, the opera *Shanewis* (*The Robin Woman*), was produced by the Metropolitan Opera, March 23, 1918; many subsequent performances were given elsewhere. Other theatrical works are: *The Sunset Trail,* operatic cantata (Denver, Dec. 5, 1922); *The Garden of Mystery* (N. Y., March 20, 1925); *A Witch of Salem* (Chicago, Dec. 8, 1926); a radio play, *The Willow Tree* (NBC, October 3, 1933); among his orchestral works are: *Thunderbird Suite* (Los Angeles, Jan. 9, 1917); *Oriental Rhapsody* (1917); *Dark Dancers of the Mardi Gras* (1933); *Suite on American Folktunes* (1937); cantatas, *Father of Waters* (1928); *House of Joy; Indian Love Charm* for children's choir; *The Vision of Sir Launfal* for male voices, written for the Pittsburgh Prize Competition (1909); symph. poem, *Pennsylvania* (Los Angeles, March 7, 1940); piano sonata; violin pieces; and about 180 songs, of which *At Dawning* acquired enormous popularity. Bibl.: E. E. Hipsher, *American Opera and its Composers* (Philadelphia, 1934; pp. 99-110).

Cady, Calvin Brainard, American music pedagogue; b. Barry, Illinois, June 21, 1851; d. Portland, Oregon, May 29, 1928. He studied at Oberlin College and at Leipzig with Richter, Papperitz and Paul (1872-4); taught harmony and piano at Oberlin, the Univ. of Michigan, and the Chicago College of Music (1888-94); then lived in Boston; from 1907 he lectured on music at Columbia Univ. His teaching emphasized the understanding of music as a gateway to all liberal education. He published 3 vols. of a manual, *Musical Education* (1902-07).

Cadzow, Dorothy, Canadian composer; b. Edmonton, Aug. 9, 1916. She studied at the Univ. of Washington, Seattle; from 1942-1945 took courses at Juilliard Graduate School with Frederick Jacobi and Bernard Wagenaar. In 1949 she joined the staff of the Univ. of Washington. She has written an orchestral suite *Northwestern Sketches* (1945); a string quartet and numerous song cycles of folksong inspiration.

Cafaro (Caffaro), Pasquale, Italian composer; b. San Pietro, in Galatina, Lecce, Feb. 8, 1706; d. Naples, Oct. 23, 1787. He became second master at the Naples Cons. della Pietà in 1759, and first master in 1771. He wrote the operas *Ipermestra* (Naples, Dec. 18, 1751); *La disfatta di Dario* (Naples, Jan. 20, 1756); *L'incendio di Troia* (Naples, Jan. 20, 1757); *L'Olimpiade* (Naples, Jan. 12, 1769); and *Antigono* (Naples, Aug. 13, 1770); also 6 oratorios; 4 cantatas and a *Stabat Mater* in 2 parts, with organ.

Caffarelli (real name Gaetano Majorano), artificial soprano (*musico*); b. Bitonto, April 12, 1710; d. Naples, Nov. 30, 1783. A poor peasant boy, endowed with a beautiful voice, he was discovered by a musician, Domenico Caffarelli, who taught him, and later sent him to Porpora at Naples. In gratitude to his patron he assumed the name of Caffarelli. He studied for five years with Porpora, who predicted a brilliant career for him. Caffarelli became a master of pathetic song, and excelled in coloratura as well; read the most difficult music at sight, and was an accomplished harpsichord player. His début at the Teatro Valle (Rome, 1724) in a female role (as was the custom for artificial soprani) was a triumph. In 1738 he sang in London; then in Paris and Vienna. His last public appearance took place on May 30, 1754 in Naples. He was in Lisbon during the earthquake of 1755; upon his return to Naples, he bought the dukedom of Santo-Durato with the fortune he had amassed during his career, and assumed the title of duke.

Caffi, Francesco, Italian music scholar; b. Venice, June 14, 1778; d. Padua, Jan. 24, 1874. After a period of study in Venice, he produced an allegorical drama, *L'armonia richiamata*, which was performed at the opening of the Istituto Filarmonico there (Aug. 20, 1811). In 1827 he moved to Milan; in 1840 to Rovigo. His most important work was a *Storia della musica sacra nella gia Cappella Ducale di San Marco in Venezia dal 1318 al 1797* (2 vols.; Venice, 1854-55; reprinted, 1931). This was the first part of an ambitious project dealing with music in Venice; the second part, *Storia della musica teatrale in Venezia durante la sua Repubblica* was completed by Caffi shortly before his death, but remained in MS. He further published monographs on Bonaventura Furlanetto (1820); Zarlino (1836); Lotti; Benedetto Marcello (in Cicognia's 'Venetiani Iscritioni'), and on Giammateo Asola (Padua, 1862). Caffi's grandson, F. A. Salvagnini, wrote his biography (Rome, 1905).

Cage, John, American composer of ultra-modern tendencies; b. Los Angeles, Sept. 5, 1912. He studied piano with Fannie Dillon in Los Angeles and with Lazare Lévy in Paris; composition with Adolph Weiss, Henry Cowell, Schoenberg and Varèse. He developed Cowell's ideas on piano technique, and initiated a type of performance on what he termed 'prepared piano'. The 'preparation' entailed placing on the piano strings various objects, such as screws, copper coins, rubber bands, and the like, which altered the tone color of individual keys and virtually transformed the piano into a multiplicity of varied sounds; the pitch was also altered upon occasion. As a performer on the 'prepared piano', John Cage attracted considerable attention at special concerts in America and Europe. His experiments in 'random composition' resulted in exhibitions such as *Imaginary Landscape*, led by the composer in New York on May 10, 1951; the work was scored for 12 radios, dialed according to prescribed wave lengths by the paticipants, resulting in assorted noises and also silences when no program happened to be broadcast over a particular dial number. In his desire to eliminate the subjective element in composition, Cage has adopted a method of composing with a set of Chinese dice, each throw indicating the pitch, note value, dynamics, instrumentation, etc., according to a prearranged system of indices. In his exploration of the ultimate negation of the creative principle, Cage submitted a piece entitled *4 Minutes and 33 Seconds* (1954), silent music for piano in 3 movements, during which period the pianist sits at the piano without playing.

Cagnoni (kah-ñoh'-nē), **Antonio,** Italian composer; b. Godiasco, near Voghera, Feb. 8, 1828; d. Bergamo, April 30, 1896. He studied with Ray and Frasi at the Milan Cons. (1842-7), where 3 of his operas were produced while he was an undergraduate: *Rosalia di San Miniato* (1845), *I due Savojardi* (1846), and his most successful work, *Don Bucefalo* (1847). From 1852-73 he was maestro di cappella in the cathedral of Vigevano; from 1873 in the cathedral of Novarra; from 1887 in Santa Maria Maggiore in Bergamo. From 1848-74 he brought out 15 operas in various Italian theaters; 3 additional operas remained in MS.

Cahier, Mme. Charles (*née* Sara Jane Layton-Walker), distinguished American contralto; b. Nashville, Tennessee, Jan. 8, 1870; d. Manhattan Beach, California, April 15, 1951. She studied with Ernestinoff in Indianapolis; later in Paris with Jean de Reszke and in Vienna with Gustav Walter. She made her operatic début in Nice (1904); married Charles Cahier on March 30, 1905. She was engaged at the Vienna Hofoper, and made guest appearances at the Metropolitan Opera; toured Europe and America for many years as a concert artist; later she taught at the Curtis Institute of Music in Philadelphia. Her repertory included Carmen and Wagnerian contralto roles.

Cahn-Speyer, Rudolf, Austrian conductor and musicologist; b. Vienna, Sept. 1, 1881; d. Florence, Dec. 25, 1940. He studied chemistry and music in Vienna; then in Leipzig and Munich; graduated from the Univ. of Munich in 1908 with the dissertation, *Franz Seydelmann als dramatischer Komponist* (Leipzig, 1909). He began conducting in Kiel (1908); subsequently conducted in Hamburg (1909-11); taught in Berlin; became conductor of the Budapest Volksoper (1913). In 1933 he left Germany to live in Italy. He published *Zur Opernfrage; das Wesen der Oper und ihre Entwickelung in der Gegenwart* (Leipzig, 1913); and *Handbuch des Dirigierens* (1919).

Caillet (kah-yā'), **Lucien,** orchestral arranger; b. Dijon, France, May 22, 1891. He studied at the Dijon Cons. (grad., 1913); and with Paul Fauchet, Georges Caussade and Gabriel Pares; settled in the U.S. in 1918, living first in Pennsylvania and later in California. He made a new orchestral setting of Mussorgsky's *Pictures at an Exhibition* for Eugene Ormandy and the Philadelphia Orch. (1937), and of numerous other pieces. His own orchestral compositions include *Memories of Stephen Foster* (1935); *Strains from Erin* (1936); variations on the theme *Pop! Goes the Weasel* (1938); many scores for Hollywood motion pictures.

Caix d'Hervelois, Louis de, French viola da gamba player; b. Paris, c. 1670; d. there, c. 1760. He studied with Sainte-Colombe; was active as a musician in the court of the Duc d'Orléans. His works include five volumes of *Pièces de Viole* (1725-52) and two volumes of *Pièces pour la Flûte* (1726; 1731). Some of these compositions have been edited by Karl Schroeder; various arrangements of his viola da gamba pieces have been made for contemporary instruments.

Caland, Elisabeth, piano teacher and music editor; b. Rotterdam, Jan. 13, 1862; d. Berlin, Jan. 26, 1929. She studied piano with Deppe in Berlin and theory with Rebiček; from 1915 taught piano in Berlin and Mecklenburg-Schwerin. Her piano manuals, most of which have gone through several editions, include the authoritative exposition of Deppe's method, *Die Deppesche Lehre des Klavierspiels* (Stuttgart, 1897; in English as *Artistic Piano-Playing,* 1903; also in French, Dutch and Russian); *Technische Ratschläge für Klavierspieler* (Magdeburg, 1897; also in English and Russian); *Die Ausnützung der Kraftquellen beim Klavierspiel* (Magdeburg, 1905); *Das künstlerische Klavierspiel in seinen physiologisch-physikalischen Vorgängen* (1910); *Praktische Lehrgänge für künstlerisches Klavierspiel* (Magdeburg, 1912); *Anhaltspunkte zur Kontrolle zweckmässiger Armbewegungen beim künstlerischen Klavierspiel* (1919). She also edited the pamphlets *Zehn Klavierstücke älterer Meister* (1916) and 'Philipp-Emanuel-Bach-Album' (1924).

Caldara, Antonio, Italian cellist and composer; b. Venice, 1670; d. Vienna, Dec. 28, 1736. He was a pupil of Legrenzi. His first opera was successfully produced in 1688; thereafter, he lived in Rome, Milan, Bologna, Mantua and Madrid; on Jan. 1, 1716, he was appointed assistant choirmaster to J. J. Fux in Vienna. Caldara composed 87 operas and sacred dramas, 32 oratorios, about 30 Masses, other church music, chamber music, etc. A selection of his church music was reprinted in the 'Denkmäler der Tonkunst in Österreich' (Vol. XIII, 1; ed. by Mandyczewski); other vocal works (cantatas, madrigals and canons) were also publ. in the 'Denkmäler der Tonkunst in Österreich' (Vol. XXXIX; ed. by Mandyczewski, with introduction and explanatory notes by Geiringer); further vocal works are reprinted in 'Musique d'Église des XVIIe et XVIIIe siècles', edited by Charles Pineau; a madrigal and 18 canons were edited by Geiringer in *Das Chorwerk* (1933); 28 three-part instrumental canons from Caldara's *Divertimenti musicali* are in *Spielkanons* (Wolfenbüttel, 1928); two trio-sonatas were edited by W. Upmeyer in 'Nagels Musik-Archiv' (No. 5, 1927; No. 12, 1928); a trio-sonata in B minor, attributed to Caldara but really by John Ravenscroft, is in Riemann's 'Collegium musicum' (No. 44). Bibl.: A. Schering on Caldara's 32 oratorios (in his *Geschichte des Oratoriums,* 1911); A. Gmeyner, dissertation on Caldara's 87 operas (Vienna, 1927); C. Gray, *Antonio Caldara (1670-1736),* in 'The Musical Times' (March, 1929).

Caldicott, Alfred James, English conductor and composer; b. Worcester, Nov. 26, 1842; d. near Gloucester, Oct. 24, 1897. He studied at the Leipzig Cons. under Moscheles, Hauptmann, etc.; became organist in Worcester (1864); received Mus. Bac. degree at Cambridge (1878); was appointed professor at the Royal College of Music, London (1883) and director of the College (1892); traveled in America as opera conductor (1890-91). His works include the cantatas *The Widow of Nain* (1881) and *A Rhine Legend* (for women's voices, 1883); 13 operettas; numerous glees, especially the popular *Humpty Dumpty* (1878).

Calegari, Antonio, Italian composer and music theorist; b. Padua, Feb. 17, 1757; d. there, July 22, 1828. He was active as a composer in Padua, Venice and Paris; spent the last years of his life as organist of the Church of San Antonio in Padua. He brought out three operas in Venice: *Le Sorelle rivali* (1784), *L'Amor soldato* (1786), and *Il Matrimonio scoperto* (1789). He published a curious treatise on composition, *Gioco pittagorico musicale* (Venice, 1801), which was republished in Paris, during his residence there, as *L'art de composer la musique sans en connaître les éléments* (1802). A *Sistema armonico* (1829) and a vocal method, *Modi generali del canto* (1836) were published posthumously.

Caletti-Bruni. See **Cavalli.**

Calkin, John Baptiste, English pianist, organist and composer; b. London, March 16, 1827; d. there, May 15, 1905. He was a pupil of his father, James Calkin; was organist, precentor and choirmaster at several London churches; was appointed professor at the Guildhall School of Music in 1899. Works: string quartet; piano trio; cello sonata; organ music; much sacred vocal music; piano pieces.

Callaerts (kahl-lahrts), **Joseph,** Belgian organist and composer; b. Antwerp, Aug. 22, 1838; d. there, March 3, 1901. He studied with Lemmens at the Brussels Cons.; was organist of the Jesuit College (1851-6) and later of the Antwerp Cathedral; from 1876 taught organ at the Music School in Antwerp. He composed a comic opera, *Le Retour imprévu* (Antwerp, 1889); a symphony (1879); a piano trio (1882); and sacred music, organ pieces and piano pieces.

Callas (real name Calogeropoulos), **Maria,** soprano of Greek descent; b. New York, Dec. 3, 1923. At the age of thirteen she went to Greece and studied at the Athens Cons.; returned to New York in 1945. Made her professional début at Verona in *Gioconda* (Aug. 3, 1947); on April 21, 1949 she married Giovanni Battista Meneghini, an Italian industrialist. She continued to sing in Italy, appearing in Wagnerian roles, as well as in the lyrical repertory. She later appeared in London and Paris. She sang Norma at her American début, which took place in Chicago (Nov. 1, 1954). She made a spectacular first appearance with the Metropolitan Opera in that role on Oct. 29, 1956, attended by an enormous flow of publicity and genuine enthusiasm, particularly for her dramatic ability. See R. Neville, *Voice of an Angel* in 'Life' (Oct. 31, 1955).

Callcott, John Wall, English organist and composer; b. Kensington (London), Nov. 20, 1766; d. Bristol, May 15, 1821. Although he received some instruction from his parish church organist, Callcott was mainly self-taught. Early in life he developed a particular talent for composing glees and catches. Dr. Arnold and Dr. Cooke became interested in him, and helped him in his musical pursuits. Callcott won three prize medals at a contest of the Catch Club of London (1785) for his catch *O Beauteous Fair;* a canon, *Blessed is He,* and a glee, *Dull Repining Sons of Care.* In 1789 he won all four medals of the Catch Club. He received his Mus. Bac. from Oxford (1785) and his Mus. Doc. (1800); was a co-founder of the Glee Club (1787); was joint-organist of St. Paul's Cathedral (1788). During Haydn's visit to London in 1791 he took a few lessons with him and wrote a symphony in imitation of his style. In 1806 he was appointed lecturer at the Royal Institute. Shortly thereafter, his mind gave way from overwork on a projected, but unrealized, music dictionary. He recovered, but not sufficiently to continue his work. In addition to numerous glees, catches and canons, he wrote *A Musical Grammar* (London, 1806), a standard elementary textbook that went through numerous editions in England and America. A 3-volume collection of glees, catches and canons was publ. posthumously by his son-in-law, William Horsley, with a biographical memoir (London, 1824).

Calleja (kah-yā'-hah), **Gómez Rafael,** Spanish composer; b. Burgos, Dec. 23, 1874; d. Madrid, Feb. 1938. He studied with Arrieta at the Madrid Cons.; subsequently conducted in Spain, Portugal and South America. He composed about 300 revues and musical comedies, including *El Principe Carnaval, El Mozo Crúo,* etc.; also a symph. poem, *Cantos de la Montaña;* collections of folksongs from Santander, Galicia and Asturias.

Callinet. See **Daublaine et Callinet.**

Calvé, Emma (real name Rosa Emma Calvet), famous French soprano; b. Décazeville (Aveyron), Aug. 15, 1858; d. Millau, Jan. 6, 1942. She was educated at the Convent of the Sacred Heart in Montpellier; then studied in Paris (1880-2) with Puget, the former stage tenor; made her operatic début as Marguerite at the Théâtre de la Monnaie (Brussels, Sept. 29, 1882); sang there for one year; studied for another year under Mme. Marchesi; created the role of Bianca in *Aben Hamet* by Dubois at the Théâtre des Italiens (Paris, Dec. 16, 1884); soon after, she entered the Opéra-Comique, and remained with it until 1887. Her successes received a temporary check at La Scala, Milan, in Jan., 1887, when she was hissed as Ophelia, but after 18 months' study with Laborde, she scored a triumph there in the same role. She was again with the Opéra-Comique from 1891-3; in 1892 appeared with great success at Covent Garden. She made her Metropolitan Opera House début as Santuzza (New York, Nov. 29, 1893); played Carmen on Dec. 20, 1893, and made an indescribable sensation. She returned to the Opéra-Comique for the season of 1894-5; then toured Europe (Madrid, Monte Carlo, St. Petersburg); created the part of Anita in Massenet's opera, *La Navarraise* (London, June 20, 1894); began her second American tour on Nov. 20, 1895; created the role of Sapho in Massenet's opera of that name at the Opéra-Comique (Nov. 27, 1897). Thereafter her career was an uninterrupted succession of triumphs. In the 1903-4 season she was engaged at the Opéra Municipal du Théâtre de la Gaité in Paris; in 1908 at the Manhattan Opera House in New York, where her Carmen aroused the same enthusiasm as before; after 1910 she practically retired from the stage, confining herself to concert appearances. The extraordinary success of her Carmen was undoubtedly responsible for the fact that she was heard only in a limited repertory. Her autobiography was published in English as *My Life* (London and N.Y., 1922). Towards the end of her life she published an additional volume of memoirs, *Sous tous les ciels j'ai chanté* (Paris, 1940). See A. Gallus, *Emma Calvé, Her Artistic Life* (N.Y., 1902).

Calvisius, Sethus (real name Seth Kallwitz), son of a poor peasant at Gorsleben, Thuringia; b. Feb. 21, 1556; d. Leipzig, Nov. 24, 1615. By his own efforts (at first as a street-singer for alms, afterwards as a teacher) he supported himself while studying in the Gymnasia of Frankenhausen and Magdeburg, and the Universities at Helmstadt and Leipzig. In Leipzig he became (1581) mus. director at the Paulinerkirche; from 1582-92 he was cantor at Schulpforta, then cantor of the Thomasschule at Leipzig, and (1594) musical dir. at the Thomaskirche and Nicolaikirche there. Calvisius was not only a musician, but a scholar of high and varied attainments. His writings are valuable sources: *Melopoeia seu melodiae condendae ratio* (1582; 2nd ed. 1592); *Compendium musicae practicae pro incipientibus* (1594; 3d ed. as *Musicae artis praecepta nova et facillima,* 1612); *Exercitationes musicae duae* (1600); *Exercitatio musicae tertia* (1611).—Publ. compositions: *Auserlesene teutsche Lieder* (1603); *Bicinorum libri duo* (1612); the 150th Psalm (12 parts); a coll., *Harmoniae cantionum ecclesiasticarum a M. Luthero et aliis viris piis Germaniae compositarum 4 voc.* (1596); 4-part arrangements of C. Becker's psalm-tunes (1602, 1616, 1618, 1621). MS motets, hymns, etc., in the Thomasschule Library, Leipzig. Reprints of his motets have been publ. by A. Schering in *Geschichte der Musik in Beispielen* (No. 160), G. Schreck in *Ausgewählte Gesänge des Thomanerchors,* and K. Straube in a 2nd series of the same name. Bibl.: K. Benndorf, *Sethus Calvisius als Musiktheoretiker,* in 'Vierteljahrsschrift für Musikwissenschaft' (1894); R. Wustmann, *Musikgeschichte von Leipzig,* vol. I (1909); G. Pietzsch, *Sethus Calvisius und Joh. Kepler,* in 'Die Musikpflege' (I, 8, 1930).

Calvocoressi, Michel D., eminent writer on music; b. (of Greek parents) Marseilles, Oct. 2, 1877; d. London, Feb. 1, 1944. In Paris he studied music with X. Leroux; was professor at the École des Hautes Etudes Sociales (1905-14), and correspondent for numerous French and foreign journals: 'Mercure de France', 'Musical Times' (London), 'Muzika' (Moscow), etc. An excellent lecturer, he was indefatigable in his propaganda for Russian music in France and England; was made an officer of the Russian order of St. Anna (1908). He translated many songs and operas into French, English and German; published *La Musique russe* (1907); monographs on Liszt (1905), Glinka (1911), and Schumann (1912); translated Rimsky-Korsakov's treatise on orchestration into French (1914); also published a biography of Mussorgsky (translated into English by A. E. Hull, London, 1919; German edition of C. Seelig, Leipzig, 1921); *The Principles and Methods of Musical Criticism* (1923; revised edition, 1931); *Musical Taste and How To Form It* (1925); *Mussorgsky's Musical Style,* in the 'Mus. Quarterly' (Oct., 1932); *Musicians' Gallery; Music and Ballet in Paris and London* (London, 1933); *Mussorgsky's Youth,* in the 'Mus. Quarterly' (Jan., 1934); *Mily Balakirev,* in the 'Mus. Quarterly' (Jan., 1937); *Masters of Russian Music* (with G. Abraham, 1936). See G. Abraham, *Michel D. Calvocoressi,* in the 'Musical Times' (March, 1944).

Calzabigi, Ranieri di, Italian poet and music theorist; b. Leghorn, Dec. 23, 1714; d. Naples, July, 1795. In 1750 he went to Paris, and soon engaged in polemics regarding the relative merits of French and Italian operas; he lent energetic support to Gluck in his ideas of operatic reform. He wrote for Gluck the libretti of *Orfeo, Alceste,* and *Paride ed Elena.* In 1780 he returned to Italy. He published *Dissertazione su le poesie drammatiche del Sig. Abate Pietro Metastasio* (1755), a controversial work concerning Metastasio and Hasse. Bibl.: Heinrich Welti, *Gluck und Calzabigi* in 'Vierteljahrsschrift für Musikwissenschaft' (1891); Ghino Lazzeri, *La vita e l'opera letteraria di Ranieri Calzabigi* (1907); J.-G. Prod'homme, *Deux Collaborateurs italiens de Gluck,* in the 'Rivista Musicale Italiana' (1916); R. Haas, *Gluck in Durazzo* (1924); *Gluck Yearbook* (vols. II and III, articles by A. Einstein; vol. IV, article by H. Michel).

Calzin, Alfred, pianist and teacher; b. Vigny, France, June 19, 1885. He studied with Alberto Jonas in Berlin; made his début with the Berlin Philh. Orch. (Feb. 27, 1907); subsequently toured Europe and America four times; taught in Chicago and at the Northwestern Cons. in Minneapolis. He composed piano works; edited and made transcriptions of the works of other composers.

Cambert (kăhn-bär'), **Robert,** the first French opera composer, preceding Lully; b. Paris c. 1628; d. London, 1677. Pupil of Chambonnières; organist at St. Honoré; intendant of music (1666) to the queen-dowager Anne of Austria. His first venture on the lyric stage was *La Pastorale,* written by Perrin and successfully produced at the Château d'Issy in 1659; it was followed by *Ariane, ou le Mariage de Bacchus* (rehearsed in 1661), and *Adonis* (1662; not performed; manuscript lost). Perrin having received, in 1669, letters patent for establishing the 'Académie royale de musique' (the national operatic theater, now the Grand Opéra), brought out, in collaboration with Cambert, the opera, *Pomone* (1671); another, *Les Peines et les plaisirs de l'amour,* was written, but never produced, Lully having meantime (1672) had the patent transferred to himself. These last two operas have been publ. in 'Chefs-d'œuvre classiques de l'opéra français' (Leipzig, Breitkopf & Härtel). Cambert's disappointment drove him to London; he became a bandmaster, and died as Master of the Music to Charles II. Bibl.: A. Pougin, *Les vrais créateurs de l'opéra français, Perrin et Cambert* (Paris, 1881); J. Ecorcheville, *La Musique des rois d'Angleterre,* in the 'Bulletin de la Société Internationale de Musique' (Nov., 1909).

Cambini, Giovanni Giuseppe, Italian composer; b. Leghorn, Feb. 13, 1746; d. Bicêtre, Dec. 29, 1825. A pupil of Padre Martini, and a prolific composer of instrumental works, writing over 60 symphonies within a few years; also 144 string quartets; ballets, operas and oratorios. He lived chiefly in Paris as a ballet-composer and conductor; he died in an almshouse.

Cameron, Basil, English conductor; b. Reading, Aug. 18, 1884; studied music with Tertius Noble (1900-1902) and in Berlin (1902-6), where he studied violin with

Joachim and composition with Max Bruch. Returning to England, he became conductor of the Torquay Municipal Orch. (1912-16), using the Germanized name Basil Hindenberg, but changing it back to his real name at the outbreak of World War I; served in the army and was wounded in Aug., 1918. He was conductor of the Hastings Municipal Orch. from 1923 to 1930, when he was appointed co-conductor (with Dobrowen) of the San Francisco Symph. Orch., producing such a favorable impression that he was subsequently selected to the post of conductor of the Seattle Symph. Orch., which he held from 1932 to 1938; during his tenure, he performed many modern works for the first time. Returning to England in 1938, he continued to be active as conductor of various orchestras in London; was also guest conductor with the Concertgebouw in Holland, Berlin Philh., Prague Philh., etc. He belongs to the category of 'objective' conductors, striving to project music rather than his own personality. This detached attitude, however, hampered his career in America, after initial success.

Cametti, Alberto, Italian musicologist; b. Rome, May 5, 1871; d. there, June 1, 1935. He studied at the Cons. della Accademia di S. Cecilia; maestro di cappella at St. Louis in Rome; was member of the commission appointed by Pope Pius X to investigate the condition of church music. Publ. many sacred and secular compositions, but was more important as a writer. In April, 1914, he publ. a full description and complete thematic catalogue in the 'Rivista Musicale Italiana' (XXI, 2) of 43 compositions for 1-3 voices with basso continuo (chiefly arias) by Orazio Michi which he had discovered in various Italian libraries, and which prove Michi to have been one of the earliest and most important Roman masters of the monodic style.—Principal works: *Cenni biografici di G. P. da Palestrina* (Milan, 1894); *Il testamento di Jacobella Pierluigi* (1903); *Cristina di Suezia, l'arte musicale e gli spettacoli in Roma* (1911); *Documenti inediti su Luigi Rossi* (Leipzig, 1912); *Chi era l'Ippolita del cardinale di Montalto?* (1913); *L'accademia Filarmonica Romana, 1821-60* (1924); *I musici di Campidoglio dal 1524 al 1818* (1925); *La musica teatrale a Roma cento anni fa (1816-26)* (1928); *Dove fu sepolto il Palestrina?* (1929); *Bibliogr. delle opere di Costanzo Festa* (1931); biographical studies of Felice Anerio (1915), Giacomo Carissimi (1917), G. B. Costanzi (1924), Leonardo Vinci (1924), Ruggiero Giovanelli (1925), Nicola Piccinni, etc.; several valuable essays in the 'Rivista Musicale Italiana': *Bellini a Roma* (1900); *Donizetti a Roma* (1904-7); *Mozart a Roma* (1907); *Frescobaldi a Roma* (1908), etc.

Camidge, Matthew, English organist; b. York, 1758; d. there Oct. 23, 1844; son of John, Sr., whom he succeeded at Belfry Church in York (Nov. 11, 1799); retired Oct. 8, 1842. He publ. *Cathedral Music; 24 Original Psalm- and Hymn-tunes;* piano sonatas and marches; a *Method of Instruction in Music by Questions and Answers,* etc.

Cammarano, Salvatore, Italian poet and librettist; b. Naples, March 19, 1801; d. there, July 17, 1852. He was a pupil of Gabriele Rossetti; first wrote prose dramas, which were produced in Florence: *Baldovino, Un Ritratto e due pittori,* etc.; after 1834 he devoted himself to writing opera libretti: Donizetti's *Lucia;* Pacini's *Reggente, Buondelmonte, Saffo, Merope,* etc.; Verdi's *Alzira, Battaglia di Legnano, Luisa Miller,* and *Il Trovatore;* also libretti for operas by Peri, Mercadante, Luigi Cammarano, etc. See T. Mantovani, *Salvatore Cammarano,* in 'Musica d'oggi' (1926).

Camp, John Spencer, American organist and composer; b. Middletown, Conn., Jan. 30, 1858; d. Hartford, Conn., Feb. 1, 1946. After receiving an M.A. from Wesleyan Univ. (1881), he studied in New York with Dudley Buck and with Dvořák; was organist and choirmaster at various churches in Connecticut; conducted the Hartford Philh. Orch. (1902-11); helped found the American Guild of Organists. He wrote numerous pieces for choir, organ, piano, and orch.; also anthems and songs.

Campagnoli (cahm-pah-ñoh'-lē), **Bartolommeo,** renowned Italian violinist; b. Cento, near Bologna, Sept. 10, 1751; d. Neustrelitz, Germany, Nov. 6, 1827. He studied in Bologna with Dall'Occa and in Florence with Nardini; for several years gave concerts in Italy; became music director to the Duke of Kurland in Dresden, and made several successful concert tours while in his service; from 1797-1818 was active as a violinist in Leipzig; then became maestro di cappella at the Neustrelitz court. He composed 41 *Capricci per l'alto viola* (revised by E. Kreuz and A. Consolini as *Caprices pour le viola,* 1922); also a violin concerto; études for violin; chamber music; etc. He was the author of several pedagogic manuals for the violin: *Nouvelle méthode de la mécanique progressive du jeu de violon* (1791; 2nd ed., 1803; in English, 1856), and *Metodo per violino* (1797; his chief work; publ., and reprinted in all European languages). Bibl.: G. Atti, *Biografia di B. Campagnoli* (Bologna, 1892).

Campana, Fabio, singing teacher and composer; b. Leghorn, Italy, Jan. 14, 1819; d. London, Feb. 2, 1882. He studied in Bologna; produced the operas *Caterina di Guisa* (Leghorn, 1838); *Giulio d'Este* (Venice, 1841); *Vannina d'Ornano* (Florence, 1842); *Luisa di Francia* (Rome, 1844); then went to London, where he settled as a singing teacher. His opera *Almina* was staged at Her Majesty's Theatre (April 26, 1860); another opera *Esmeralda* was produced in St. Petersburg (Dec. 20, 1869); Patti sang the title role in its productions in Western Europe. He also wrote hundreds of songs, which were popular in their day.

Campanari, Giuseppe, Italian dramatic baritone; b. Venice, Nov. 17, 1855; d. Milan, May 31, 1927. He began his career as a cellist; played in the orch. of La Scala, and started to study singing; went to the U. S. in 1884, and played cello in the Boston Symph. Orch. until 1893, when he joined Hinrich's Opera Company in N. Y. as a baritone; made his début (June 15, 1893) as Tonio in *Pagliacci;* after several years at the Metropolitan Opera he devoted himself to concert work and teaching.

Campanari, Leandro, Italian violinist and conductor; brother of Giuseppe Campanari; b. Rovigo, Italy, Oct. 20, 1857; d. San Francisco, Calif., April 22, 1939. He studied in Padua; appeared in Italy as a child prodigy; then attended the Milan Cons., where he studied with Bazzini and Faccio, graduating in 1877; after a tour of Europe, he came to the U. S. in 1881 and settled in Boston, where he organized the Campanari String Quartet. In 1887 he went back to Europe for three seasons, returning to America in 1890. He became a proficient conductor and was in charge of the Grand Orchestral Concerts at La Scala, Milan, from 1897 till 1905. In February 1907, he was engaged to complete the season of the Philadelphia Orchestra after the sudden illness of the regular conductor, Fritz Scheel. He failed to impress the orchestra or the audience, and was not reengaged. He continued his concerts as violinist in America; eventually settled in San Francisco as a teacher.

Campanini, Cleofonte, eminent Italian-American operatic conductor (brother of the famous tenor Italo Campanini); b. Parma, Sept. 1, 1860; d. Chicago, Dec. 19, 1919. He studied violin at the Parma Cons. and later at the Cons. of Milan; made his conducting début with *Carmen* at Parma (1883); the same year he assisted Vianesi, who conducted the first season of the new Metropolitan Opera House; conducted the first American performance of *Otello* (N.Y., April 16, 1888), while his brother Italo was impresario. Between 1888 and 1906, he conducted in Italy, at La Scala and San Carlo in Naples; in London at Covent Garden; and in South America. A larger field opened to him in 1906, when Hammerstein engaged him for the new Manhattan Opera House in New York. Campanini was not only the principal conductor but also the artistic director. His success was such that at the end of the first season the new company had become a dangerous rival of the older Metropolitan. Differences with Hammerstein led him to resign in 1909. In the following year he was engaged as principal conductor of the newly formed Chicago Opera Co.; in 1913 he was appointed general director, which post he held until his death. In Jan., 1918, he took the entire company to New York (four weeks), introducing Galli-Curci with sensational success. Among operatic conductors he occupied a place in the first rank; he seemed to be equally at home in all styles of music. After 1906 he introduced many new operas into the U.S., among them Massenet's *Thaïs, Sapho* and *Hérodiade;* Debussy's *Pelléas et Mélisande;* Charpentier's *Louise;* Wolf-Ferrari's *I Gioielli della Madonna* and *Il Segreto di Susanna;* Gnecchi's *Cassandra;* Nougès' *Quo Vadis;* Herbert's *Natoma;* Blockx's *Princesse d'Auberge;* etc. On May 15, 1887, he married, in Florence, Eva Tetrazzini (sister of Luisa Tetrazzini).

Campanini, Italo, brilliant Italian operatic tenor; b. Parma, June 30, 1845; d. Vigatto, near Parma, Nov. 14, 1896. In his early years he was an apprentice in his father's blacksmith shop; joined Garibaldi's army and was wounded in the Italian struggle for unification. Subsequently, he studied with Griffini and made his début in Odessa in *Il Trovatore* (1869), but sang for several years without marked success. Then, after a thorough study with Lamperti, he appeared at Bologna, in *Lohengrin* (Nov. 1, 1871), which started him on the road to fame. He made his London début as Gennaro in *Lucrezia Borgia* (May 4, 1872), and his American début, also as Gennaro, at the N. Y. Academy of Music (Oct. 1, 1873). He toured the U. S. again in 1878 and 1879-80; appeared in *Faust* at the opening of the Metropolitan Opera (Oct. 22, 1883); then lived several years in America; was briefly active as impresario; brought over his brother Cleofonte Campanini to conduct the American première of Verdi's *Otello* at the Metropolitan Opera (April 16, 1888).

Campbell-Tipton, Louis, American composer; b. Chicago, Nov. 21, 1877; d. Paris, May 1, 1921. He studied at Leipzig (1896-99) with Carl Reinecke and Gustav Schreck; returned to Chicago and was instructor of theory at the Chicago Musical College from 1900-05; then lived as private teacher in Paris. He wrote chiefly for piano (*Sonata Heroic, Sea Lyrics, The Four Seasons,* suite, serenade, etc.), *Suite pastorale* for piano and violin; also a number of very effective songs.

Campbell-Watson, Frank, American composer; b. New York, Jan. 22, 1898; studied at the Leipzig Cons. with Max Reger. Returning to the U. S., he held positions as editor with various publishing firms. He has written *Petite Suite* for strings (1933); *Symphonic Prologue* for band (1934); made transcriptions for string orch. of Bach, Reger, Mendelssohn and Albéniz. He was also the author of *University Course of Music Study* (1923); *Modern Elementary Harmony* (1930); edited *International Library of Music* (Piano, 14 vols., 1926; Vocal, 12 vols., 1927; Violin, 14 vols.); *La Mejor Música del Mundo* (in Spanish, also in Portuguese, for piano, 14 vols., 1929).

Campenhout, François van, Belgian composer, author of the Belgian national anthem; b. Brussels, Feb. 5, 1779; d. there April 24, 1848. Beginning as violinist in the Théâtre de la Monnaie, he studied singing under Plantade, and became a fine stage tenor, appearing in Belgium, Holland and France. He retired in 1827, and wrote 6 operas, 9 cantatas, etc. He is, however, chiefly remembered as the composer of *La Brabançonne,* which was written during the revolution of 1830, and eventually became the national anthem of Belgium.

Campion (Campian), Thomas, English physician; also poet, composer and dramatist; b. London, Feb. 12, 1567; d. there, March 1, 1620. He studied at Cambridge from 1581-85, residing at Peterhouse; nothing is recorded of his subsequent activities until 1602, when he first called himself Doctor of Physic, though no mention was made of any university or a degree; the only clue to his having studied medical science, is made in an oblique reference of Philip Rosseter in 1601, in which he speaks of Campion's poetry and music as the 'superfluous blossoms of his deeper studies.' Campion was primarily a lyric poet; his music was to enhance the beauty of the poetry by supplying unobtrusive and simple harmonies; in this he differed from such contemporaries as John Dowland who contrived elaborate lute accompaniments for his melodies. Works: 3 songs (1596); *A Booke of Ayres, Set Foorth to be sung to the Lute Orpherian, and Base Violl* (1601; consists of 2 separate books, one by Campion and one by Rosseter; Campion wrote both the words and music for his half of the work); First and Second Books of Airs (1613?); Third and Fourth Books of Airs (1617?); songs for masques at the marriages of Sir James Hay (1607), Princess Elizabeth (1613), and Robert, Earl of Somerset (1613); songs for a masque at Caversham House (1613); *Songs of Mourning* (for Prince Henry; 1613; words by Campion, music by John Coperario); *A New Way for Making Foure Parts in Counterpoint* (1618; also in Playford's 'Introduction to the Skill of Musick', with additions by Christopher Simpson, 1655 ff.). Campion also publ. *Poemata,* a volume of Latin epigrams and elegiacs (1595; reprinted 1619), *Observations on the Art of English Poesie* (1602; condemns 'the vulgar and unartificial custom of riming'), etc. The 5 books of Airs are reprinted in E. H. Fellowes' *English School of Lutenist Song-Writers.* Bibl.: A. H. Bullen, *Thomas Campion, Songs and Masques* (1903; includes comments on Campion's music by Janet Dodge); Percival Vivian's edition of the literary works of Thomas Campion (Oxford, 1909); Miles Kastendieck, *England's Musical Poet, Thomas Campion* (Oxford, 1938).

Campo y Zabaleta (thah-bah-lā'tah), **Conrado del,** Spanish violinist and composer in the romantic style; b. Madrid, Oct. 28, 1879; d. there, March 17, 1953. He studied at the Madrid Cons.; later became its director. He was well known as a chamber music player; was a member of the Cuarteto Frances and the Quinteto de Madrid. He composed the operas *El final de Don Alvaro* (1911), *La tragedia del beso* (1915), *El Avapiés* (Madrid, March 8, 1919), *La Dama desconocida, La Culpa, Leonor Teller, Romeo y Julieta, Dies Irae, La Malquerida, Fantochines* (one act), *La Flor del Agua,* most of which have been performed at the Madrid Opera House. Other works include the symph. poems *La Divina Comedia, Granada, Airinos; Kasida,* an oriental fantasy; *Evocación Medieval* for chorus and orch.; 8 string quartets, of which the *Caprichos Románticos* (1908) is very well known in Spain and France.

Campra (kahn-prah'), **André,** French opera composer; b. Aix (Provence) Dec. 4, 1660; d. Versailles, June 29, 1744. A pupil of Guillaume Poitevin, he was appointed maître de musique at the Toulon Cathedral at the age of 20; in 1681, maître de chapelle at Arles, and from 1683-94 at Toulouse Cathedral. He then went to Paris, where he was at first maître de chapelle at the Jesuit collegiate choir, and shortly after, at Notre Dame, an appointment which he held until the successful production of two operas (under his brother Joseph's name) induced him to choose a secular career. In 1722 he was made conductor of the Royal Orch. His operas had numerous performances in Paris, and he was regarded as a natural successor to Lully, until the advent of Rameau whose genius eclipsed his efforts. Operas: *L'Europe galante* (1697); *Le Carnaval de Venise* (1699); *Hésione* (1700); *Aréthuse, ou la vengeance de l'amour* (1701); *Tancrède* (1702); *Les Muses* (1703); *Iphigénie en Tauride* (1704); *Télémaque* (1704); *Alcine* (1705); *Le Triomphe de l'amour* (1705); *Hippodamie* (1708); *Les Fêtes vénitiennes* (1710); *Idoménée* (1712); *Les Amours de Mars et Venus* (1712); *Télèphe* (1713); *Camille* (1717); *Les Ages,* ballet-opera (1718); *Achille et Déidamie* (1735); and several divertissements, etc., for the Versailles court. He also wrote 3 books of *Cantates françoises* (1708; 1714; 1728); 5 books of motets (1695-1720); a Mass (1700); and 2 books of psalms (1737-38). Bibl.: A. Pougin, *André Campra* (Paris, 1861); L. de La Laurencie, *Notes sur la jeunesse d'André Campra,* in 'Sammelbände der Internationalen Musik-Gesellschaft' (X, 2, 1909); L. de La Laurencie, *André Campra, musicien profane,* in 'L'Année musicale' (1913); L. de La Laurencie, *L'Ecole française de violon de Lulli à Viotti* (1922-24).

Camussi, Ezio, Italian composer; b. Florence, Jan. 16, 1877; studied in Rome with Falchi and Sgambati; later with Massenet in Paris and at the Liceo Musicale, Bologna. He brought out the operas *La Dubarry* (Milan, Nov. 7, 1912); *I fuochi di San Giovanni* (Milan, 1920); *Il donzello; Scampolo* (Trieste, Feb. 22, 1925); *La principessa lontana; I Romanzeschi; Intermezzi giocosi* for puppet theater; for orch: *Baletto sinfonico, Pantomima romantica, Suita Romanesca, Intermezzi Goldoniani, Fantasticherie* for small orch., and *Festival Miniature Overture;* also *Scene medioevali* for violin and orch.; songs.

Canal, Marguerite, French composer; b. Toulouse, Jan. 29, 1890. She studied at the Paris Cons.; was professor there from 1919; in 1920 she won the Prix de Rome for her dramatic scene *Don Juan* (later arranged as a symphonic poem). Compositions: violin sonata; pieces for violin, for cello and for piano; about 100 songs, etc.

Cannabich, Christian, German composer; b. Mannheim, Dec. 28, 1731; d. Frankfurt, Jan. 20, 1798. He studied with Johann Stamitz in Mannheim; became a violinist in the Mannheim Orch. (1744); was sent by the Elector to Rome, where he studied with Jommelli (1753); returned to Mannheim, and after Stamitz' death (1757), became first violinist of the orch.; in 1774 was director of the instrumental music. Cannabich is usually credited with bringing the Mannheim Orch. to a degree of perfection theretofore never attained, particularly in the carefully graduated crescendo and diminuendo. He was also a prolific composer and wrote some 90 symphonies; 3 violin concertos; 45 various pieces of chamber music; also a Singspiel *Azakia* (Mannheim, 1778); a melodrama, *Elektra* (Mannheim, 1781); and 40 ballets. A symphony and an overture are publ. in vol. VIII of 'Denkmäler der Tonkunst in Bayern' (1907); a string quartet in vol. XV of the same collection (1914); H. T. David revised one of Cannabich's symphonies for an edition publ. by the N. Y. Public Library (1937). A thematic catalogue is publ. in vol. III of the 'Denkmäler der Tonkunst in Bayern'. Bibl.: H. Hofer, *C. Cannabich* (Munich, 1921); R. Kloiber, *Die dramatischen Ballette von C. Cannabich* (Munich, 1928); A. Sandberger, in the 'Propyläen' (Munich, 1932).

Cannon, Beekman Cox, American musicologist; b. Teaneck, N. J., Dec. 25, 1911. He studied at Yale Univ. (B. A., 1934; Ph. D., 1939). At first he taught general history at Yale, and then music history. He served in the U. S. Navy during World War II, returning to teaching at Yale in 1946; received a Guggenheim Fellowship in 1950. He published a valuable monograph, *Johann Mattheson, Spectator in Music* (Yale Univ., 1947).

Cantelli, Guido, Italian conductor; b. Novara, April 27, 1920; d. in an airplane crash at Orly, near Paris, Nov. 23, 1956. As a boy, he played in his father's military band; studied piano at the Cons. of Milan; composition with Ghedini. From 1943-45 he was held in a concentration camp in Stettin. After the war, he conducted the orch. of La Scala, and opera at other Italian theaters. By invitation of Toscanini, he was guest conductor of the NBC Orch. in N. Y., in 1948. In subsequent years he appeared with numerous orchestras in Europe and America, with outstanding success. Possessing an extraordinary memory, he conducted both rehearsals and performances without score. He lost his life flying to America to conduct a series of concerts with the N. Y. Philharmonic.

Canteloube de Malaret, Marie-Joseph, French pianist, composer and writer on music; b. Annonay, near Tournon, Oct. 21, 1879. He studied piano in Paris with Amélie Doetzer, a pupil of Chopin, and composition with d'Indy at the Schola Cantorum. He became an ardent collector of French folksongs and arranged and published many of them for voice with instrumental accompaniment. His *Chants d'Auvergne* (4 sets for voice with piano or orch., 1923-30) are frequently heard. Among his other albums *Anthologie des chants populaires français* (4 sets, 1939-44) is a comprehensive collection of regional folksongs. His original works include two operas, *Le Mas* (1911-13; Paris Opéra, April 3, 1929); *Vercingetorix* (Paris Opéra, June 26, 1933); a symph. poem *Vers la princesse lointaine* (1911); 3 symph. sketches *Lauriers* (Paris, Feb. 22, 1931); *Pièces françaises* for piano and orch. (1935); *Poème* for violin and orch. (1937); and *Rustiques* for oboe, clarinet and bassoon (1946). He also published a biography of Vincent d'Indy (Paris, 1949).

Capdevielle, Pierre, French composer and pianist; b. Paris, Feb. 1, 1906. He studied at the Paris Cons. with Gédalge and Vidal, and privately with d'Indy; has composed an opera, *Les Amants captifs* (1947-50); the orchestral works *Incantation pour la mort d'un jeune spartiate* (1931), *Ouverture pour le pédant joué* (1943), and *Cantate de la France retrouvée* (1946); *Sonatine pastorale* for flute and piano; a string quartet; etc.

Cape, Safford, American-Belgian choral conductor; b. Denver, June 28, 1906. He studied in Europe, principally in Brussels, with Charles van den Borren, whose daughter he married. In 1933 he established in Brussels a music society 'Pro Musica Antiqua' with which he gave numerous performances of choral and instrumental works by medieval and Renaissance composers.

Capell, Richard, English writer on music; b. Northampton, March 23, 1885; d. London, June 21, 1954. He was music critic for the London 'Daily Mail' (1911-31) and for the 'Daily Telegraph' (1928-33). From 1950 he edited 'Music & Letters'. During World War II he was war correspondent in the French, Greek and Italian campaigns. He published *Schubert's Songs* (London, 1928); a biography of Gustav Holst (London, 1928). He also made an English translation of Richard Strauss's opera *Der Friedenstag* (London, 1938).

Capellen, Georg, German music critic; b. Salzuflen, Lippe, April 1, 1869; d. Hanover, Jan. 19, 1934. Studied philosophy and law at Tübingen, Göttingen and Berlin; from 1914 lived in Hanover as music critic; notable writer on theory of music. Publ. *Harmonik und Melodik bei Richard Wagner,* in the 'Bayreuther Blätter' (1901); *Ist das Systems S. Sechters ein geeigneter Ausgangspunkt für die theoretische Wagnerforschung?* (1902); *Die musikalische Akustik als Grundlage der Harmonik und Melodik* (Leipzig, 1903); *Die Freiheit oder Unfreiheit der Töne und Intervalle als Kriterium der Stimmführung* (Leipzig, 1904; with appendix containing analyses of Grieg's works in proof of his theory); *Die Abhängigkeitsverhältnisse in der Musik* (ib., 1904; presenting a solution of the problems of figuration, sequence and inversion); *Die Zukunft der Musiktheorie* (ib., 1905; against dualism); *Ein neuer exotischer Musikstil* (Stuttgart, 1906); *Fortschrittliche Harmonie- und Melodielehre* (Leipzig, 1908); *Die Unmöglichkeit und Überflüssigkeit der dualistischen Molltheorie Riemanns* (in 'Neue Zeitschrift für Musik', 1901, Nos. 44-50).

Capet (kah-pā'), **Lucien,** distinguished French violinist and composer; b. Paris, Jan. 8, 1873; d. there, Dec. 18, 1928; studied at the Paris Cons.; 1896, concert master of the Lamoureux Orch.; 1899-1903, teacher at the Conservatory of St. Cécile, Bordeaux; 1907, conducted classes in chamber-music at the Paris Cons.; 1924, artistic dir. of the Institut de Violon, Paris; 1904-21, leader of the famous Capet Quartet, specializing particularly in the later Beethoven quartets, which he played for many years all over western Europe.—Works: *Le Rouet,* symph. poem; *Prélude religieux* for orch.; *Devant la mer* for voice and orch.; *23rd Psalm* for soloists, chorus and orch.;

Poème for violin and orch.; *Aria* for violin, viola and piano; 5 string quartets; 2 violin sonatas; 6 violin études.—Writings: *La technique supérieure de l'archet* (Paris, 1916); *Les 17 quatuors de Beethoven;* also a philosophical work, *Espérances.*

Caplet (kah-plā'), **André,** French composer; b. Le Havre, Nov. 23, 1878; d. Paris, April 22, 1925. He studied violin in Le Havre, and played in theater orchestras there and in Paris; entered the Paris Cons. (1896) where he studied with Leroux and Lenepveu; in 1901 received the Grand Prix de Rome for his cantata *Myrrha.* His *Marche solennelle* for the centennial of the Villa Medicis was performed by him in Rome (April 18, 1903). He was active in France as a choral and operatic conductor; was a close friend of Debussy and made piano transcriptions of several of his orchestral scores; conducted the first performance of Debussy's *Le Martyre de St. Sebastien* (Paris, May 22, 1911); also conducted opera in the U. S. with the Boston Opera Co. (1910-14) and in London at Covent Garden (1912). He served in the French army during World War I; later continued his musical activities; spent the summer of 1924 in Solesmes, studying Gregorian chant. Caplet's music is unequivocally impressionistic, with a lavish use of whole-tone scales and parallel chord formations; he combined this impressionism with neo-archaic usages and mystic programmatic ideas. Works: oratorio, *Miroir de Jésus* (Paris, May 1, 1924); *Prières* for voice and chamber orch.; *The Masque of the Red Death* (after Poe) for harp and orch. (Paris, March 7, 1909; later arranged for harp and string quartet and retitled *Conte fantastique;* perf. Paris, Dec. 18, 1923); *Epiphanie* for cello and orch. (Paris, Dec. 29, 1923); double wind quintet (Paris, March 9, 1901); *Messe des Petits de St. Eustache* (Paris, June 13, 1922); sonata for voice, cello and piano; septet for strings and 3 female voices; *Suite persane* for woodwind instruments; piano duets; piano pieces; minor choral works and songs. He left unfinished a *Sonata da chiesa* for violin and organ (1924), and *Hommage à Ste. Cathérine de Sienna* for orch. and organ. Bibl.: M. Brillant, *André Caplet, musicien mystique,* in 'La Revue Musicale' (July, 1925); R. Dumesnil, *Portraits de musiciens français* (Paris, 1938).

Capocci (kah-potch'-chi), **Gaetano,** Italian composer; b. Rome, Oct. 16, 1811; d. there, Jan. 11, 1898. Organ pupil of Sante Pascoli; studied later under Fioravanti and Cianciarelli, and in 1833 brought out his first oratorio, *Battista.* He became organist at the Church of S. Maria di Vallicella, and at S. Maria Maggiore (1839); elected (1855) maestro of the 'Cappella Pia' at the Lateran, succeeding Meluzzi; at that post, he was teacher of many distinguished musicians. He wrote and publ. a vast amount of sacred music: an oratorio, *Assalonne* (1842); Masses, motets, litanies, offertories, psalms, introits, etc.

Capoul (kah-pool'), **Joseph-Amédée-Victor,** brilliant French stage-tenor; b. Toulouse, Feb. 27, 1839; d. Pujaudran-du-Gers, Feb. 18, 1924. Pupil (1859) of Révial and Mocker at the Paris Cons.; début at Opéra-Comique, Aug. 26, 1861, as Daniel in Adam's *Le Chalet;* was at the Opéra-Comique 1861-72; then sang in London (with Nilsson), New York, and other cities; 1892, prof. of operatic singing in National Cons., New York; from 1897 stage-manager at the Grand-Opéra, Paris. He created the chief tenor parts in *La Colombe* (Gounod), *La Grand'tante* (Massenet), *Le Premier Jour de bonheur* (Auber), *Vert-Vert* (Offenbach), *Paul et Virginie* (Massé), etc. See A. de Lassus, in 'La Revue Musicale' (May, 1906).

Capron (kah-prŏhn'), **Henri,** prominent early American cellist and composer of French origin. Pupil of Gaviniés in Paris (1768); first appeared in Philadelphia in 1785; became active as manager (with Reinagle, William Brown, and Juhan) of subscription concerts in Philadelphia and N. Y.; played in the Old American Co. orchestra in N. Y., where he lived from 1788-92; 1794, settled permanently in Philadelphia and later was principal of a French boarding-school. Works: *New Contredances;* some songs.—Cf. O. G. Sonneck, *Early Concert Life in America* (N. Y., 1907); J. T. Howard, *Our American Music* (2nd ed. 1939).

Carabella, Ezio, Italian composer of light operas and orchestral works; b. Rome, March 3, 1891; pupil of Storti and Ferroni (Milan Cons.), Falchi (St. Cecilia, Rome), and of the Liceo Rossini in Pesaro.—Works: The operettas *Don Gil dalle calzi verdi* (Rome, 1922), *Bambù* (Florence, 1923), *La linea del cuore* (Rome, 1924), etc.; the comic opera *Il Landeliere* (Genoa, 1939); for orch.: *Impressione sinfonica* for small orch. (Rome, 1913); *Preludio* (ib., 1916); *Variazioni sinfoniche* (ib., 1921); incidental music to various comedies (perf. at the Teatro dei Piccoli, Rome).

Caracciolo (kah-răh-tchoh'loh), **Luigi,** Italian composer and singing teacher; b. Andria (Bari), Aug. 10, 1847; d. London,

July 22, 1887. Pupil of Cesi, Conti and Mercadante in Naples (1863-9). Called to Dublin (1878) as Director of the School of Singing in the Royal Irish Academy of Music; settled (1881) in London. Wrote a successful opera, *Maso il Montanaro* (Bari, 1874), and many popular songs (*Danza delle memorie, Un sogno fu!, Rime popolari,* etc.).

Carafa de Colobrano, Michele Enrico, prolific composer of operas; b. Naples, Nov. 17, 1787; d. Paris, July 26, 1872. He was a son of Prince Colobrano, Duke of Alvito; began to study music at an early age, and while very young wrote an opera, two cantatas, etc. Though he became an officer in the army of Naples, and fought in Napoleon's Russian campaign, he devoted his leisure time to music, and after Waterloo, adopted it as a profession. In 1827 he settled in Paris; succeeded Lesueur as a member of the Academy (1837); in 1840 was appointed professor of composition at the Paris Cons. Operas: *Gabriella di Vergy* (Naples, July 3, 1816); *Ifigenia in Tauride* (Naples, June 19, 1817); *Berenice in Siria* (Naples, July 29, 1818); *Elisabetta in Derbyshire* (Venice, Dec. 26, 1818); the following operas were produced at the Opéra-Comique, Paris: *Jeanne d'Arc* (March 10, 1821); *Le Solitaire* (Aug. 17, 1822); *Le Valet de chambre* (Sept. 16, 1823); *L'auberge supposée* (April 26, 1824); *Sangarido* (May 19, 1827); *Masaniello* (Dec. 27, 1827; on the same subject as Auber's *La Muette de Portici,* staged at the Paris Opéra two months later; yet Carafa's *Masaniello* held the stage in competition with Auber's famous opera for 136 nights); *La Violette* (Oct. 7, 1828); *Jenny* (Sept. 26, 1829); *Le livre de l'ermite* (Aug. 11, 1831); *La prison d'Edimbourg* (July 20, 1833); *Une journée de la Fronde* (Nov. 7, 1833); *La Grande Duchesse* (Nov. 16, 1835); *Thérèse* (Sept. 26, 1838). He also composed ballets, cantatas and much church music.

Cardus, Neville, English writer on music; b. Manchester, April 2, 1889. He was critic of 'The Manchester Guardian' from 1917-39; went to Australia in 1939, returning to England in 1947, when he again wrote for 'The Manchester Guardian'. In addition to musical journalism, Cardus wrote many newspaper articles on cricket. Books: *Music for Pleasure* (London, 1942); *Ten Composers* (London, 1945); *Autobiography* (London, 1947).

Carey, Bruce, choral conductor; b. Hamilton, Ontario, Canada, Nov. 16, 1876. He studied at the Guildhall School of Music, London, and with Karl Straube in Leipzig; returning from Europe, he taught at the Hamilton Cons. of Music, Ontario; then at Girard College, Philadelphia; retired in 1943. He founded and directed the Elgar Choir in Hamilton; conducted the 6,000 voice 'Sesquicentennial Choir' of Philadelphia (1926); directed the Bethlehem Bach Choir (1932-38), and other choral groups.

Carey, Francis Clive Savill, English baritone; b. Sible Hedingham, Essex, May 30, 1883. He studied with Stanford and Moszkowski at the Royal College of Music, London; from 1919-24 taught singing and opera there; from 1924-27 was professor of voice at Adelaide Univ. Cons. in Australia; then returned to London, and was active as opera producer at the Sadler's Wells Theatre (1931-39); from 1942-45 was again in Australia, teaching at the Melbourne Cons.; in the 1945-46 season, resumed the post of opera producer at Sadler's Wells. He made world-wide tours as a member of the English Singers; composed an operetta and numerous songs.

Carey, Henry, English writer for the theater; b. probably Yorkshire, c. 1687; d. by suicide, London, Oct. 4, 1743. He was a natural son of Henry Savile, Lord Eland; studied music with Linnert, Roseingrave and Geminiani; settled in London about 1710, where he was active as poet, librettist, playwright and composer; wrote nine ballad-operas, of which *The Contrivances* (London, Aug. 5, 1729) achieved the greatest success. He wrote the words of the popular song *Sally in Our Alley* and composed a musical setting for it, but his setting was replaced in 1790 by the tune *What though I am a Country Lass,* which has since been traditionally sung to Carey's original poem; also popular was his intermezzo with singing, *Nancy, or The Parting Lovers* (1739). In 1737 he published a collection of 100 ballads, *The Musical Century;* also pubished *Six Cantatas* (1732) and *Three Burlesque Cantatas* (1741). Carey's claim to authorship of *God Save The King* was put forth by his son George Savile Carey (1743-1807) more than 50 years after his father's death, without any supporting evidence; many anthologies still list Carey's name as the author of the British National Anthem. For a complete account of this misattribution of the tune see P.A. Scholes, *God Save The Queen!* (London, 1954; Appendix I; pp. 284-88). Further discussion of the authorship of the British National Anthem is to be found in W. H. Cummings, *'God Save the King', the Origin and History of the Music and Words* (London, 1902); O. G. Sonneck, *Report on the Star-Spangled Banner* (1909); F. S. Boas and J. E. Borland, *The National Anthem* (London, 1916); J. A. Fuller Maitland, *Facts and Fictions about 'God Save the King'*, in the 'Mus. Quarterly' (Oct., 1916); E. A. Maginty, *'America': The Origin of its Melody,* in the 'Mus. Quarterly' (July, 1934).

Carissimi, Giacomo, Italian composer of sacred music; b. Marino, near Rome, baptized April 18, 1605; d. Rome, Jan. 12, 1674. From 1624-7 he was organist at the Cathedral of Tivoli; from 1628 to his death maestro di cappella in the Church of S. Apollinare, Rome. A prolific and original composer, he broke with the Palestrina tradition, devoting himself to perfecting the monodic style, as is evidenced by his highly developed recitative and more pleasing and varied instrumental accompaniments. His music MSS were dispersed at the sale of the library of the German College, and many are lost; but a few printed works are still extant. There were publ. the 4 oratorios *Jephte* (his masterpiece), *Judicium Salomonis, Jonas, Balthazar;* 2 collections of motets *a* 2, 3 and 4 (Rome, 1664, 1667); Masses *a* 5 and 9 (Cologne, 1663, 1667); *Arie da camera* (1667); and detached pieces in several collections. The finest collection of his works is that made by Dr. Aldrich at Christ-Church College, Oxford. He also wrote a treatise, publ. only in German: *Ars cantandi, etc.* (Augsburg; 2d ed. 1692; 3d, 1696; another ed. 1718). F. Chrysander publ. 4 oratorios (*Jephte, Judicium Salomonis, Balthazar, Jonas*) in vol. II of 'Denkmäler der Tonkunst'; *Jonas, Judicium Salomonis* and *Jephte* were also publ. in 'I Classici della Musica Italiana', No. 5 (Milan, 1919); vocal duets are reprinted in L. Landshoff's *Alte Meister des Bel canto* (1927); a motet was publ. in 'Musique d'Eglise des XVIIe et XVIIIe siècles', ed. by Ch. Pineau. —Cf. M. Brenet, *Les Oratorios de Carissimi,* in 'Rivista Musicale Italiana' (1897); A. Schering, *Geschichte des Oratoriums* (Leipzig, 1911); A. Cametti, *Primo contributo per una biografia di Giacomo Carissimi,* in 'Rivista Musicale Italiana' XXIV, 3 (1917); F. B. Pratella, *G. Carissimi ed i suoi oratori,* in 'Rivista Musicale Italiana' XXIX, 1 (1920); J. Loschelder, *Nuovi contributi a una biografia di G. Carissimi* in the 'Archiv für Musikwissenschaft' (1940); G. Massenkeil, *Die Wiederholungsfiguren in den Oratorien Giacomo Carissimis,* in the 'Archiv für Musikwissenschaft' (Jan., 1956). Carissimi's collected works have been published in 3 vols. by the 'Istituto Italiano per la Storia della Musica' in Rome.

Carl, William Crane, American organist; b. Bloomfield, New Jersey, March 2, 1865; d. New York, Dec. 8, 1936. He first studied in New York; at the age of 17 was appointed organist of First Presbyterian Church in Newark, N. J.; in 1890 went to Paris where he studied for two years with Guilmant; returning to America, he was engaged as organist of the Old First Presbyterian Church in New York, a post which he held until his death. He made seven tours to the Pacific coast and one to Alaska; was also active as a choral conductor in N. Y. He founded (1899) and directed the Guilmant Organ School in N. Y.; was a founder and served on the Council of the American Guild of Organists. He published *Masterpieces for the Organ; 30 Postludes for the Organ;* 2 volumes of *Novelties for the Organ; Master Studies for the Organ.*

Carmichael, Mary Grant, English pianist and composer; b. Birkenhead, 1851; d. London, March 17, 1935. Pupil of O. Beringer, W. Bache and F. Hartvigson (piano), and E. Prout (comp.). She was an accomplished accompanist:—Works: an operetta, *The Frozen Heart, or The Snow Queen;* a suite for piano 4 hands, and minor piano pieces; and a song cycle, *The Stream.* She translated Ehrlich's *Celebrated Pianists of the Past and Present* (London, 1894).

Carner, Mosco, musicologist and conductor; b. Vienna, Nov. 15, 1904; studied musical subjects at the Vienna Cons., taking his Dr. Mus. in 1928, under Guido Adler. He conducted theater orchestras in Danzig and elsewhere until 1933 when he settled in London. He was guest conductor with various London orchestras; became active also as writer on music in English publications. —Books: *Dvořák,* miniature biography (London, 1941); *Study of 20th Century Harmony* (London, 1942); *Of Men and Music* (London, 1944); *The Waltz* (London, 1948).

Carneyro, Claudio, Portuguese composer; b. Oporto, Jan. 27, 1895. He studied violin, and then composition with Lucien Lambert at the Oporto Cons., and later in Paris with Widor; succeeded Lambert as prof. at the Oporto Cons. in 1930. He has written a number of choral works, both sacred and secular; orchestral suites on Portuguese themes (*Portugalezas, Raiana,* etc.); piano pieces; songs.

Carnicer (kahr-nē-thär'), **Ramón,** Spanish composer; b. Tárrega, near Lérida, Oct. 24, 1789; d. Madrid, March 17, 1855. From 1818-20, conductor of the Italian Opera, Barcelona; 1828-30, of the Royal Opera, Madrid; 1830-54, professor of composition at Madrid Cons. One of the creators of Spanish national opera (the *zarzuela*), he composed 9 operas, wrote much church music, many symphonies, Spanish songs, etc.; also *Dulce Patria,* the national hymn of Chile.

Carolan, Turlough, Irish song composer; b. near Nobber, County Meath, 1670; d. near Kilronan, March 25, 1738. He was an itinerant harper, and improvised Irish verses and tunes; these were published in various 18th-century collections of Irish music; the number of his original tunes is about 220. He is also known under the name O'Carolan.

Carol-Bérard, French composer and theorist; b. Marseilles, April 5, 1881; d. Paris, Dec. 13, 1942. He studied with Albéniz in Barcelona; then settled in Paris. His music, impressionistic with an oriental flavor, remains largely unpublished. He evolved a theory of 'chromophonie' (color in movement) and wrote several papers on the subject in 'La Revue Musicale' and other publications. He also wrote poetry under the pseudonym Olivier Realtor.—Works: *Symphonie dansée; Symphonie des forces mécaniques* (in 3 movements: *Navire perdu; Gare Nocturne; L'Aéroplane sur la ville,* utilizing phonograph records of noises); *L'Oiseau des îles,* lyric piece in 2 acts (to his own words); three piano suites, *Egypte, d'une existence antérieure,* and *Extrême-Asie;* humorous piano pieces, *Les heures civiles et militaires, L'Elégie à jouer dans une cave,* and a number of songs to poems of Verlaine and Mallarmé.

Caron (kah-rŏhn), **Philippe,** famous Netherlands contrapuntist of the 15th century, a pupil of Binchois or Dufay. O. J. Gombosi, in his monograph *Jacob Obrecht, eine stilkritische Studie* (Leipzig, 1925), groups Caron with composers of the Cambrai school interested in continuing Dufay's style; this work also contains a reprint of a 3-part chanson, *Vive Carloys,* MSS of which are in libraries at Rome and Florence. Other extant works include 4 Masses *a* 4 in the Papal Chapel, and a MS of 3 and 4 part chansons at Paris. Petrucci publ. a 5 part chanson, *Hélas que pourra deuenir,* in his *Odhecaton* (1501).

Caron, Rose (*née* Meuniez), French dramatic soprano; b. Monerville, Nov. 17, 1857; d. Paris, April 9, 1930. She entered the Paris Cons. in 1880, leaving in 1882 to study with Marie Sasse in Brussels, where her début was made as Alice in *Robert le Diable* (1884). Here she created Brunehilde in Reyer's *Sigurd* (1884); sang two years at the Opéra, Paris, and again in Brussels, creating Lorance (in *Jocelyn),* Richilde, and Salammbô (1890); in 1890 she returned to the Paris Grand Opéra, where she sang Sieglinde (1893) and Desdemona (1894) in the first performances of *Walküre* and *Otello* in France; in 1898 she sang Fidelio at the Opéra-Comique. From 1900 she appeared almost exclusively on the concert-stage; in 1902 appointed prof. of singing at the Paris Cons. See H. de Curzon, *Croquis d'artistes* (Paris, 1898).

Carpani, Giuseppe, Italian writer, b. Villalbese, Jan. 28, 1752; d. Vienna, Jan. 22, 1825. He studied and practiced law in Milan, later abandoning it for a literary career and writing on music. He was editor of the *Gazzetta di Milano* (1792-96); the French invasion forced him to go to Venice and then to Vienna. He wrote the libretto for Paer's opera *Camilla* and was the Italian translator of Haydn's *Creation.* A great admirer of Haydn, he published a monograph, *Le Haydine ovvero lettere su la vita e le opere del celebre Giuseppe Haydn* (Milan, 1812; enlarged ed., Padua, 1823). Stendhal printed a major part of this book as his own work, in French, under the pseudonym of Bombet (Paris, 1814); Carpani protested against this act of plagiarism in a pamphlet *Lettere dell'Autore delle Haydine* (Vienna, 1815), but Stendhal ignored the protest and republished his book in 1817, this time under the signature Stendhal. Carpani also wrote a monograph on Rossini, *Le Rossiniane* (Padua, 1824).

Carpenter, John Alden, American composer; b. Park Ridge, Chicago, Ill., Feb. 28, 1876; d. Chicago, April 26, 1951. He received his B.A. degree from Harvard Univ. in 1897; also studied music there with John K. Paine; entered his father's shipping supply business, and from 1909-36 was vice-president of the firm. During his earlier years in business he continued his musical studies with Edward Elgar in Rome (1906) and with Bernard Ziehn in Chicago (1908-12); was made a Knight of the French Legion of Honor (1921); received an honorary M.A. from Harvard Univ. (1922) and an honorary Mus. Doc. from Wisconsin Univ. (1933). After his retirement from business in 1936, he devoted himself entirely to composing; in 1947 was awarded the Gold Medal of the National Institute of Arts and Letters. From his musical contacts abroad he absorbed mildly modernistic and impressionistic techniques and applied them to his music based on American urban subjects, adding the resources of jazz rhythms. His first work in this American idiom was a 'jazz pantomime', *Krazy Kat,* after a well known cartoon series (1921); he then wrote a large-scale musical panorama, *Skyscrapers* (1926), performed as a ballet and an orchestral suite in America and abroad, attracting much critical comment as the first symphonic work descriptive of modern American civilization; as such, the score has historical significance. Works: the ballets *Birthday of the Infanta* (Chicago Opera, Dec. 23, 1919); *Krazy Kat* (Chicago, Dec. 23, 1921); and *Skyscrapers* (Metropolitan Opera, N. Y., Feb. 19, 1926; Munich, 1928); an orchestral suite, *Adventures in a Perambulator* (Chicago, March 19, 1915); concertino for piano and orch. (Chicago, 1916); a symphony (Litchfield County Choral Union Festival, Norfolk, Conn., 1917); *A Pilgrim Vision* for orch. (Philadelphia Orch., 1920; for the tercentenary Mayflower Celebration); *Patterns* for piano and orch. (Boston, Oct. 21, 1932); *Sea-Drift,* symph. poem after Whitman (Chicago, Nov. 30, 1933; revised version, 1944); *Danza* for orch. (Chicago, 1935); violin concerto (1936; Chicago Symph., Zlatko Baloković soloist, Nov. 18, 1937); Symphony in C (Chicago, Oct. 24, 1940); Symphony No. 2 (New York, Oct. 22, 1942); symph. poem, *The Anxious Bugler* (N. Y., Nov. 17, 1943); *The Seven Ages,* symphonic suite (New York, Nov. 29, 1945); *Carmel Concerto* for orch. (1948); *Song of Faith* for chorus and orch. (Washington Bicentennial Commission, 1932); *Song of Freedom* for chorus and orch. (1941); violin sonata (1912); string quartet (Elizabeth Coolidge Festival, Wash., D. C., 1928); piano quintet (1934); songs: *Improving Songs for Anxious Children* (1904); *Gitanjali,* song cycle to poems by Tagore (1913; also arranged for voice and orch.); *Water Colors,* four Chinese songs with chamber orch. (1918); many other songs and piano pieces. Bibl.: Olin Downes, *J. A. Carpenter, American Craftsman* and Felix Borowski, *J. A. Carpenter,* both in the 'Mus. Quarterly' (Oct., 1930); W. T. Upton, *Art-Song in America* (N. Y., 1930; pp. 197-213).

Carpentras (kahr-pǎhn-trah') (**Il Carpentrasso** in Italian; his real name was Elzéar Genet), composer and priest; b. Carpentras (Vaucluse), c. 1470; d. Avignon, June 14, 1548. In 1508, leading singer in, and 1513-21 maestro di cappella of the Pontifical chapel in Rome; in 1521 he was sent to Avignon on negotiations connected with the Holy See; in 1524, made his last visit to Rome. Four volumes of his works (Masses, 1532; Lamentations, 1532; Hymns, 1533; Magnificats, 1537), printed at Avignon by Jean de Channey, are of great interest for being the first works to introduce Briard's new types, with round instead of diamond-shaped and square notes, and without ligatures; a complete copy is in the Vienna Staatsbibliothek, an incomplete one in the Paris Cons. library. His works, though severe and dignified in style, were highly esteemed by his contemporaries. A few motets are printed in Petrucci's 'Motetti della Corona' (vol. I, 1514, and vol. III, 1519); other works in various contemporary collections. Bibl.: Quittard, *E. Genet de Carpentras,* in 'Tribune de St. Gervais,' Nos. 7-9 (1899); Ch. Requin. *Elzéar Genet, dit il Carpentrasso,* in the 'Mémoires de l'Académie de Vaucluse' (1918); J. Tiersot, *Elzéar Genet, dit Carpentras et la chanson 'a lombre d'ung buissonet',* in the 'Bulletin de la Société française de musicologie' (No. 3; 1918).

Carr, Benjamin, composer and publisher; b. London, Sept. 12, 1768; d. Philadelphia, May 24, 1831. He studied music with Samuel Arnold and Charles Wesley; established himself as a composer in London. He went to America with his father and brother in 1793; settled in Philadelphia and established 'Carr's Musical Repository', the first American music store. He was the first publisher of American compositions, and was co-founder in 1820 of the Musical Fund Society in Philadelphia. A versatile musician, he was proficient as singer, pianist and organist, and was an influential figure in early American musical life. Works: *Philander and Silvia,* a pastoral piece (London, Oct. 16, 1792); *The Archers, or Mountaineers of Switzerland,* a ballad opera, (N. Y., April 18, 1796); *Dead March for Washington* (1799); numerous songs and ballads.—Cf. O. G. Sonneck, *Early American Concert Life* in 'International Mus. Quarterly' (vol. VI); Wm. Henry Richards, *Carr Geneology* (1931); Virginia L. Redway, *The Carrs, American Music Publishers,* in the 'Mus. Quarterly' (Jan., 1932); John T. Howard, *Our American Music* (N. Y. 1948). The N. Y. Public Library owns the only known copy of Carr's *Federal Overture* (Philadelphia, 1794), a medley of popular airs, including the first printing of *Yankee Doodle.*

Carr, Frank Osmond, English composer; b. Yorkshire, Apr. 23, 1858; d. Uxbridge, Middlesex, Aug. 29, 1916. He received the Oxford degrees Mus. Bac. (1882) and Mus. Doc. (1891); composed the comic operas *The Rose of the Riviera* (1890), *Joan of Arc* (1891), *Blue-eyed Susan* (London, 1892), *In Town* (1892), *Morocco Bound* (1893), *Go Bang* (1894), *His Excellency* (1894, to a libretto by Gilbert), *Lord Tom Noddy* (1895), *The Clergyman's Daughter* (Birmingham 1896; subsequently performed in London under the title *My Girl*), etc.

Carr, Howard, English composer and conductor; b. Manchester, Dec. 26, 1880. He was a conductor of light operas in London (1903-06) and in Australia (1906-08); after further experience conducting in London, he again went to Australia in 1928; taught harmony and counterpoint at the Sydney Cons. until 1938, when he returned to London; then devoted himself to composing; also served as orchestrator for the B.B.C. Theatre Orch. He wrote the operettas *Under The Greenwood Tree* (for children) and *Master Wayfarer;* 2 symphonies; an orchestral suite, *The Jolly Roger; The Bush* for baritone solo, male chorus and orch.; etc.

Carraud, Michel-Gaston, French music critic and composer; b. Mée, near Paris, July 20, 1864; d. Paris, June 15, 1920. He studied with Massenet at the Paris Cons.; received the Premier Prix de Rome for his cantata *Cléopâtre*. He abandoned composition after 1905 and was mainly active as a music critic; published *La vie, l'œuvre et la mort d'Albéric Magnard* (Paris, 1921).

Carré, Albert, French opera impresario; nephew of the librettist Michael Carré; b. Strasbourg, June 22, 1852; d. Paris, Dec. 12, 1938. He assumed the directorship of the theater at Nancy in 1884; 1885-90, of the Cercle at Aix-les-Bains. From 1898-1912 he was director of the Opéra-Comique, succeeding Carvalho. He served in World War I, returning thereafter to the Opéra-Comique (with the Isola Brothers) and was made its honorary director in 1925. Later he directed the Municipal Theater in Strasbourg. He was the author of several libretti.

Carreño, Maria Teresa, famous pianist; b. Caracas, Venezuela, Dec. 22, 1853; d. New York, June 12, 1917. As a child she studied with her father, an excellent pianist; driven from home by a revolution, the family settled in New York in August, 1862. At the age of eight she gave a public recital in New York at Irving Hall (Nov. 25, 1862) and followed it with four more concerts in N. Y. in close succession. In January, 1863, she gave twelve concerts in Boston, creating a sensation; then engaged in serious study with Gottschalk. She sailed for Europe on April 7, 1866; was mainly in Paris from 1866-70, where she studied with George Mathias and then with Rubinstein; traveled in Spain late in 1866; from 1870-74 in England. She developed a singing voice and made an unexpected appearance in opera in Edinburgh as the Queen in *Les Huguenots* (May 24, 1872) in a cast that included Tietjens, Brignoli and Mario; was again in the U. S. early in 1876, when she studied singing in Boston; made occasional appearances as an opera singer; sang Zerlina in *Don Giovanni*. For the Bolivar centenary celebration in Caracas (Oct. 29, 1885), she appeared as singer, pianist and composer of the festival hymn, written at the request of the Venezuelan government; hence the frequent but erroneous attribution to Carreño of the national hymn of Venezuela, *Gloria al bravo pueblo* (the music of which was actually composed in 1811 by J. Landaeta, and officially adopted as the Venezuelan national anthem on May 25, 1881). In Caracas she once again demonstrated her versatility when for the last three weeks of the season she conducted the opera company managed by her husband, the baritone Giovanni Tagliapietra. After these musical experiments she resumed her career as a pianist; made her German début in Berlin, Nov. 18, 1889; in 1907 toured Australia; these appearances and many others in Europe and America securely established her reputation as one of the great pianists of her time. Her last appearance with an orchestra was with the N. Y. Philh. Society (Dec. 8, 1916); her last recital was in Havana (March 21, 1917). She impressed her audiences by the impetuous élan of her playing, and was described as 'the Valkyrie of the piano'. She was married four times: to the violinist Emile Sauret (June, 1873), to the baritone Giovanni Tagliapietra (1876), to Eugen d'Albert (1892-5), and to Arturo Tagliapietra, a younger brother of Giovanni (June 30, 1902). Early in her career, Teresa Carreño wrote a number of compositions, some of which were published: a string quartet; *Petite danse tsigane* arranged for orchestra; 39 concert pieces for piano; a waltz *Mi Teresita* which enjoyed considerable popularity, and other small pieces. She was one of the first pianists to play MacDowell's compositions in public; MacDowell took lessons from her in New York. Bibl.: M. Milinowski, *Teresa Carreño* (New Haven, 1940).

Carrillo (kahr-rē-yo), **Julián,** Mexican composer; b. Ahualulco, San Luis Potosí, Jan. 28, 1875. He was of Indian extraction; lived mostly in Mexico City, where he studied violin with Pedro Manzano and composition with Melesio Morales. He graduated from the National Cons. in 1899 and received a government stipend for study abroad as a winner of the President Diaz prize. He took courses at the Leipzig Cons. with Hans Becker (violin), Jadassohn (theory) and Hans Sitt (orchestration); played violin in the Gewandhaus Orch. under Nikisch. From 1902-4 he studied at the Ghent Cons., winning first prize as violinist. He returned to Mexico in 1905 and made numerous appearances as a violinist; also conducted concerts; was appointed general inspector of music and director of the National Cons. and held these posts until 1914; among his honorary positions were membership of the International Congress of Music in Paris (1900); presidency of it in Rome (1911). He visited the U. S. many times, and conducted his works in New York and elsewhere. During his years in Leipzig he wrote a symphony which he conducted there in 1902; at the same time he began experimenting with fractional tones; developed a theory which he named *Sonido 13,* symbolically indicating divisions beyond the 12 notes of the chromatic scale. He further devised a special number notation for quarter-tones, eighth-tones, and sixteenth-tones, and constructed special instruments for performance of his music in these intervals, such as a harp-zither with 97 strings to the octave; his Concertino for fractional tones was perf. by Leopold Stokowski with the Philadelphia Orch. on March 4, 1927. Carrillo also publ. several books dealing with music of fractional tones, and edited a monthly magazine, *El Sonido 13* in 1924-25. Works: operas *Ossian* (1903); *Matilda* (1909); *Zultil* (1922); for orch.: symphony No. 1 (1901); symphony No. 2 (1905); symphony No. 3 (1948); 3 symphonies for fractional tones (1926); triple concerto for violin, flute, cello and orch. (1918); Concertino for violin, guitar, cello, piccolo and harp in fractional tones, with orch. in normal tuning (1926); chamber music: string sextet (1902); piano quintet (1918); *Horizontes* for violin, cello and harp in fractional tones (1947); 4 'atonal quartets' (1928-48); *Preludio a Cristóbal Colón* for soprano with 5 instruments in fractional tones (1940); sonata in quarter-tones for guitar (1925); also sonatas for string instruments in quarter-tones with piano. Publications: an autobiography, *Julián Carrillo, su vida y su obra* (Mexico, 1945); *Leyes de metamórfosis musicales* (Mexico, 1949); several manuals of music theory.

Carrodus (real name, Carruthers), **John Tiplady,** eminent English violinist; b. Keighley, Yorkshire, Jan. 20, 1836; d. London, July 12, 1895. He studied with his father, a local musician of considerable attainments; played in public as a child; then commenced serious study with Molique in London and in Stuttgart, where he joined the court orchestra, of which Molique was first violinist. Upon his return to England, Carrodus occupied various positions in theatrical orchestras; was appointed violin instructor at the Royal College of Music (1876); also played. numerous concerts in England; toured in South Africa in 1880. He was an excellent teacher; published several pieces for the violin. See A. Carrodus, *J. T. Carrodus, Violinist: a Life-Story* (London, 1897).

Carroll, Walter, English music pedagogue; b. Manchester, July 4, 1869; studied piano and theory privately; then at the Univ. of Manchester, obtaining his Mus. Doc. in 1900. He was on the faculty of the Manchester College of Music from 1893-1920 and musical adviser to the City of Manchester Education Committee from 1918-34. He specialized in methods of education for children; published a manual, *The Training of Children's Voices,* and various collections of children's songs.

Carse, Adam von Ahn, English composer and writer on music; b. Newcastle-on-Tyne, May 10, 1878. He studied with F. Corder and Burnett at the Royal Academy of Music, London; from 1909-22 taught music at Winchester College; taught harmony and composition at the Royal Academy (1923-40). He assembled a collection of about 350 wind instruments, which he presented in 1947 to the Horniman Museum in London; published a catalogue of this collection in 1951. Works: the symph. poems *The Death of Tintagiles* (London, 1902) and *In a Balcony* (Promenade Concerts, Aug. 26, 1905); Symphony in C minor (London, July 3, 1906); Symphony in G minor (London, Nov. 19, 1908; revised for the Newcastle Festival, 1909); orchestral suites: *The Merry Milkmaids* (1922) and *The Nursery* (1928); *Judas Iscariot's Paradise,* ballade for baritone solo, chorus and orch. (1922); two sketches for string orch. (1923); *Barbara Allen* for string orch.; *Norwegian Fantasia* for violin and orch.; *The Lay of the Brown Rosary,* dramatic cantata; numerous choruses; chamber music; piano pieces; songs. Books: *Summary of the Elements of Music; Practical Hints on Orchestration; Harmony Exercises* (2 vols., 1923); *The History of Orchestration* (1925); *Orchestral Conducting* (1929); *Musical Wind Instruments* (London, 1939); *The Orchestra in the 18th Century* (Cambridge, 1940); *The Orchestra from Beethoven to Berlioz* (Cambridge, 1948); *The Orchestra* (London, 1948); *18th Century Symphonies* (London, 1951); *The Life of Jullien* (Cambridge, 1951).

Cartan, Jean, talented French composer; b. Nancy, Dec. 1, 1906; d. Bligny, March 26, 1932. He studied music with Marcel Samuel Rousseau; then with Paul Dukas at the Paris Cons. His works, composed within a brief period of six years, showed extraordinary promise, and his death at the age of 25 was mourned as a great loss to French music. He left a cantata *Pater Noster,* two string quartets, a sonatina for flute and clarinet (International Festival for Contemporary Music, Oxford, July 25, 1931); piano pieces and several cycles of songs. See A. Roussel, *Jean Cartan* in 'La Revue Musicale' (May, 1932).

Carte, Richard d'Oyly, English impresario; b. London, May 3, 1844; d. there, April 3, 1901. He studied at Univ. College, London; wrote an opera *Dr. Ambrosias* and songs; later turned to music management; he represented, among others, Gounod, Adelina Patti and the tenor Mario. He then became interested in light opera and introduced in England Lecocq's *Giroflé-Girofla,* Offenbach's *Périchole* and other popular French operettas. His greatest achievement was the launching of comic operas by Gilbert and Sullivan; he commissioned and produced at the Royalty Theatre their *Trial by Jury* (1875) and then formed a syndicate to stage other productions of works by Gilbert and Sullivan at the London Opéra Comique Theatre. Dissension within the syndicate induced him to build the Savoy Theatre (1881), which subsequently became celebrated as the home of Gilbert-and-Sullivan productions, with Carte himself as the leading 'Savoyard'. He successfully operated the Savoy Theatre until his death; the enterprise was continued by his wife (Helen Lenoir) until her death in 1913; and thereafter by his sons. In 1887 Carte attempted to establish serious English opera through the building of a special theater (now known as Palace Theatre), and the production in 1891 of Sullivan's grand opera *Ivanhoe* followed by commissions to other English composers (Hamish McGunn, F. H. Cowen, Goring Thomas) to write operas. However, the new works proved inferior in quality, and the venture collapsed. D'Oyly Carte introduced many improvements in theatrical management, including the replacement of gaslight by electric illumination. See F. Cellier and C. Bridgeman, *Gilbert, Sullivan and d'Oyly Carte* (London, 1927).

Carter, Elliott Cook, Jr., outstanding American composer; b. New York, Dec. 11, 1908. He studied music at Harvard Univ. with Walter Piston and E. B. Hill (M.A., 1932); then took courses with Nadia Boulanger in Paris. Returning to the U.S., he settled in New York, devoting most of his time to composing; also wrote music criticism in 'Modern Music' and other publications. He held a Guggenheim Fellowship in 1945 and again in 1950. In his music, Carter adopts a modern contrapuntal style, with a pronounced feeling for modal writing; his rhythms are vigorous and often asymmetrical; his treatment of the instruments and the voice is invariably idiomatic.—Works: *Tom and Lily,* comic opera in one act (1934); flute sonata (1934); ballet *The Ball Room Guide* (1937); ballet *Pocahontas* (N. Y., May 24, 1939); concerto for English horn (1937); *Tarantella* for male chorus and orch. (1936); *The Bridge,* oratorio (1937); *Madrigal Book* for mixed voices (1937); *Heart Not So Heavy As Mine* for a cappella chorus (1939); suite for quartet of alto saxophones (1939); *Pastoral* for viola and piano (1940); *The Defense of Corinth,* after Rabelais, for speaker, men's chorus, and piano 4 hands (Cambridge, Mass., March 12, 1942); Symphony No. 1 (Rochester, April 27, 1944); Adagio for viola and piano (1943); *Warble for Lilac Time,* after Walt Whitman, for soprano and instruments (Yaddo, Sept. 14, 1946); *Holiday Overture* for orch. (Baltimore, Jan. 7, 1948); *The Harmony of Morning* for female chorus and small orch. (N. Y., Feb. 25, 1945); piano sonata (1946); *The Minotaur,* ballet (N. Y., March 26, 1947); woodwind quintet (N. Y., Feb. 27, 1949); cello sonata (N. Y., Feb. 27, 1950); 8 études and a fantasy for flute, oboe, clarinet and bassoon (N. Y., Oct. 28, 1952); string quartet (1951); sonata for flute, oboe, cello and harpsichord (N. Y., Nov. 19, 1953); piece for 4 kettledrums (N. Y., May 6, 1952). See A. Skulsky, *E. Carter* in 'American Composers Alliance Bulletin' (Summer, 1953); Richard F. Goldman, *The Music of Elliott Carter,* in the 'Mus. Quarterly' (April, 1957).

Carter, Ernest Trow, American organist and composer; b. Orange, N. J., Sept. 3, 1866; d. Stamford, Conn., June 21, 1953.

He studied piano with Mary Bradshaw and William Mason (1874-84); then composition in Berlin with Wilhelm Freudenberg, Otis Boise and others; was organist and choirmaster of the American Church in Berlin (1897-8); returning to the U. S., he became organist and choirmaster at Princeton Univ. (1899-1901); settled in New York as arranger, conductor and composer. He received his B.A. from Princeton (1888); M.A., Columbia Univ. (1899); honorary Mus. Doc., Princeton (1932); won the David Bispham Medal in 1924 for his opera *The White Bird*.— Works: the operas *The Blonde Donna, or The Fiesta of Santa Barbara* (N. Y., Dec. 9, 1931) and *The White Bird* (Chicago, March 6, 1924; Osnabrück, Germany, Nov. 15, 1927); ballet pantomime, *Namba, or The Third Statue* (N. Y., April 22, 1933); *Symphonic Suite* for orch.; string quartet; anthems, including *The Lord's Prayer* and *Out of the Depths;* male quartets; piano pieces; songs. See E. E. Hipsher, *American Opera and its Composers* (Philadelphia, 1927; pp. 113-17).

Cartier (kăhr-t'yā), **Jean-Baptiste,** French violinist and composer; b. Avignon, May 28, 1765; d. Paris, 1841. He was a pupil of Viotti; violinist at Grand Opéra (1791-1821); 1804, member of the Imperial Orch. under Paisiello; then of the Royal Orch. (1815-30). He composed 2 operas; 2 symphonies; sonatas, variations, duets and études for violin; published a manual, *L'art du violon* (Paris, 1798, 1801), containing selections from eminent French, Italian and German masters of the 17th and 18th centuries.

Carulli, Ferdinando, Italian guitarist; b. Naples, Feb. 10, 1770; d. Paris, February, 1841. He was a brilliant performer, whose original method is the basis of modern guitar-playing. He lived in Paris, from 1808, as an eminently successful and popular concert-giver and teacher. His compositions number nearly 400 (concertos, quartets, trios and duos; fantasias, variations, and solos of all descriptions). He wrote a Method, and a treatise, *L'harmonie appliquée à la guitare* (Paris, 1825).

Caruso, Enrico, celebrated Italian tenor; b. Naples, Feb. 25, 1873; d. there, Aug. 2, 1921. He was the 18th child of a worker's family, his father being a machinist. All 17 children born before him died in infancy; two born after him survived. He sang Neapolitan ballads by ear; as a youth he applied for a part in *Mignon* at the Teatro Fondo in Naples, but was unable to follow the orchestra at the rehearsal, and had to be replaced by another singer. His first serious study was with Guglielmo Vergine (1891-94); he continued with Vincenzo Lombardi. His operatic debut took place at the Teatro Nuovo, Naples, on Nov. 16, 1894 in *L'Amico Francesco* by an amateur composer, Mario Morelli. In 1895 he appeared at the Teatro Fondo in *La Traviata, La Favorita* and *Rigoletto;* during the following few seasons he added *Aida, Faust, Carmen, La Bohème* and *Tosca* to his repertoire. The decisive turn in his career came when he was chosen to appear as leading tenor in the first performance of Giordano's *Fedora* (Teatro Lirico, Milan, Nov. 17, 1898), in which he made a great impression. Several important engagements followed. In 1899 and 1900 he sang in St. Petersburg and Moscow; between 1899 and 1903 he appeared in four summer seasons in Buenos Aires. The culmination of these successes was the coveted opportunity to sing at La Scala; he sang there in *La Bohème* (Dec. 26, 1900), and in the first performance of Mascagni's *Le Maschere* (Jan. 17, 1901). At the Teatro Lirico in Milan he took part in the first performances of Franchetti's *Germania* (March 11, 1902) and Cilea's *Adriana Lecouvreur* (Nov. 6, 1902). In the spring season of 1902, he appeared (with Melba) in Monte Carlo, and was reengaged there for three more seasons. He made his London début as the Duke in *Rigoletto* (Covent Garden, May 14, 1902) and was immediately successful with the British public and press. He gave 25 performances in London until July 28, 1902, appearing with Melba, Nordica and Calvé. Maurice Grau, the manager of the Metropolitan Opera House, who was in London at the time, offered him a five-year contract; the arrangements, however, were delayed owing to the retirement of Grau, and the contract was signed by his successor Conried. In the mid-winter season of 1902-03, Caruso sang in Rome and Lisbon; during the summer of 1903 he was in South America. Finally, on Nov. 23, 1903, he made his American début at the Metropolitan Opera, in *Rigoletto*. From that memorable occasion, Caruso was connected with the Metropolitan to the end of his life. He traveled with various American opera companies from coast to coast; he happened to be performing in San Francisco at the time the earthquake nearly destroyed the city. He achieved his most spectacular successes in America attended by enormous publicity. In 1907 Caruso sang in Germany (Leipzig, Hamburg, Berlin) and in Vienna; he was acclaimed there as enthusiastically as in the Anglo-Saxon and Latin countries.

A complete list of his appearances is given in the appendix of his biography by Pierre Key and Bruno Zirato (Boston, 1922). Caruso's fees soared from $2 as a boy in Italy in 1891 to the fabulous sum of $15,000 for a single performance in Mexico City in 1920. He made recordings in the U. S. as early as 1902; his annual income from this source alone netted him $115,000 at the peak of his career. He excelled in realistic Italian operas; his Cavaradossi in *Tosca* and Canio in *Pagliacci* became models which every singer emulated. He sang several French operas; the German repertory remained completely alien to him; his only appearances in Wagnerian roles were three performances of *Lohengrin* in Buenos Aires (1901). His voice possessed such natural warmth and great strength in the middle register that as a youth he was believed to be a baritone. The sustained quality of his bel canto was exceptional and enabled him to give superb interpretations of lyrical parts. For dramatic effect, he often resorted to the "coup de glotte" (which became known as the "Caruso sob"); here the singing gave way to intermittent vocalization without tonal precision. While Caruso was criticized for such usages from the musical standpoint, his characterizations on the stage were overwhelmingly impressive. Although of robust health, he abused it by unceasing activity. He was stricken with a throat hemorrhage during a performance at the Brooklyn Academy of Music (Dec. 11, 1920), but was able to sing in N. Y. for the last time, Dec. 24, 1920. Several surgical operations were performed in an effort to arrest a pleurisy; Caruso was taken to Italy, but succumbed to the illness after several months of remission. He was known as a convivial person and a lover of fine food (a brand of macaroni was named after him). He possessed a gift for caricature; a collection of his drawings was published in New York in 1922 (2nd ed., 1951). His private life was turbulent; his liaison (never legalized) with Ada Giachetti, by whom he had two sons, was painfully resolved by court proceedings in 1912, creating much disagreeable publicity; there were also suits brought against him by two American women. In 1906, the celebrated "monkey-house case" (in which Caruso was accused of improper behavior toward a lady while viewing the animals in Central Park) threatened for a while his continued success in America. On Aug. 20, 1918, he married Dorothy Park Benjamin of New York, over the strong opposition of her father, a rich industrialist. Caruso received numerous decorations from European governments, among them the Order of Commendatore of the Crown of Italy; Légion d'honneur; and Order of Crown Eagle of Prussia. A fictional film biography, *The Great Caruso,* was made of his life in 1950. Bibl.: E. Caruso, *How to Sing* (London, 1913; German translation by A. Spanuth, *Wie man singen soll,* Berlin, 1914); J. H. Wagenmann, *E. C. und das Problem der Stimmbildung* (Altenburg, 1911); M. H. Flint, *C. and His Art* (N. Y., 1917); Pierre Key and Bruno Zirato, *E. C.* (Boston, 1922); Emil Ledtner, *Erinnerungen an C.* (1922); S. Fucito and B. J. Beyer, *C. and the Art of Singing* (N. Y., 1922); P. M. Marafioti, *C.'s Method of Voice Production* (N. Y., 1922; new ed., 1933); Dorothy B. Caruso and Mrs. T. Goddard, *Wings of Song; The Story of Caruso* (1928); C. Armin, *E. C.'s Stimme und ihr Verhältnis zum Stauprinzip* (1929); Nicola Daspuro, *E. C.* (Milan, 1938); Eugenio Gara, *C., Storia di un Emigrante* (Milan, 1947); Dorothy Caruso, *E. C., His Life and Death* (N. Y., 1945); T. R. Ybarra, *C.: The Man of Naples and the Voice of Gold* (N. Y., 1953).

Carvalho (kahr-văhl'-yŭ), **Eleazar,** brilliant Brazilian conductor and composer; b. Iguatu, Brazil, July 28, 1912. His father was of Dutch extraction, and his mother Indian. He studied in Fortaleza at the Apprentice Seaman's School; later joined the National Naval Corps in Rio de Janeiro, and played tuba in the band. In 1941 he became assistant conductor of the Brazilian Symph. Orch. in Rio de Janeiro; went to the U. S. (1946) to study conducting with Koussevitzky at the Berkshire Music Center; was guest conductor of the Boston Symph. Orch. and the Chicago Symph. Orch. (1947-48), and subsequently of various European orchestras. Works: the operas *Descuberta do Brasil* (Rio, June 18, 1939) and *Tiradentes* (Rio, Sept. 7, 1941); *Sinfonia Branca* (1943); 3 symph. poems: *A Traicão* (1941), *Batalha Naval de Riachuelo* (1943), and *Guararapes* (1945); 3 overtures; 2 trios; 2 string quartets; violin sonata; songs.

Carvalho (kahr-văhl'-yŭ) (real name, Carvaille), **Léon,** distinguished French opera-manager; b. Port-Louis, near Paris, Jan. 18, 1825; d. Paris, Dec. 29, 1897. He began his career as a singer; in 1853 married the French soprano Marie Miolan; from 1872-4, was manager of the Théâtre du Vaudeville; then stage-manager at the Grand Opéra; from 1875, director of the Opéra-Comique, succeeding du Locle. After the fire of 1887, in which 131 persons perished, he was arrested and sentenced to six months' imprisonment, but was acquitted on appeal, and reinstated in 1891. He not only produced acknowledged masterworks, but encouraged many young artists by bringing out new operas.

Carvalho-Miolan (kăr-văhl'-yŭ-mē-yoh-lăhn'), **Caroline-Marie-Félix,** French dramatic soprano; b. Marseilles, Dec. 31, 1827; d. near Dieppe, July 10, 1895. She entered Paris Cons. at twelve; studied under Duprez; took first prize after four years; made her operatic debut Dec. 14, 1849, in *Lucia* at the Opéra-Comique, where she was engaged from 1849-55; 1856-67, sang at the Théâtre Lyrique, where she created the soprano parts in Gounod's *Faust, Roméo et Juliette, Mireille,* and Clapisson's *La Fanchonette;* 1868-1885, sang at the Opéra and at the Opéra-Comique; also appeared in London (1859-64, 1871-72), Berlin, Brussels, St. Petersburg, etc.; retired in 1885. In 1853 she married Léon Carvalho. See E. Accoyer-Spoll, *Mme Carvalho* (Paris, 1885); H. de Curzon, *Croquis d'artistes* (Paris, 1898).

Cary, Annie Louise, celebrated American contralto; b. Wayne, Kennebec County, Me., Oct. 22, 1841; d. Norwalk, Conn., Apr. 3, 1921. She studied in Boston and Milan; made her operatic debut in Copenhagen as Azucena; studied under Mme. Viardot-Garcia at Baden-Baden; engaged at Hamburg (1868), later at Stockholm; also appeared in Brussels, London and St. Petersburg. Returning to the U. S., she continued her operatic career in New York theaters; was the first American woman to sing a Wagnerian role in the U. S. (Ortrud in *Lohengrin,* 1877). She married C. M. Raymond in 1882, and retired at the height of her powers. She appeared in concert or oratorio in all leading cities of America. See G. T. Edwards, *Music and Musicians of Maine* (Portland, 1928; pp. 204-19).

Casadesus (kah-sah-dĕ-sü'), **François Louis,** French conductor and composer; b. Paris, Dec. 2, 1870; d. Suresnes, near Paris, June 27, 1954. He studied at the Paris Cons.; conducted the Opéra and the Opéra-Comique on tour in France (1890-92); in 1895 conducted the Opéra on a European tour; was the founder and director (1918-22) of the American Cons. at Fontainebleau; later was active as radio conductor; wrote music criticism for 'Quotidien', 'L'Oeuvre' and 'La Presse'. A collection of valedictory articles was published in honor of his 80th birthday (Paris, 1950). Works: the operas *Cachaprès* (Brussels, 1914), *La chanson de Paris* (1924), *Bertran de Born* (Monte Carlo, 1925), and *Messie d'Amour* (Monte Carlo, 1928); incidental music to *Le Moissonneur* (Tulle, 1909); *Symphonie scandinave; Au beau jardin de France* for orch. (Paris, 1918); symphony in E major; smaller compositions for orchestra; numerous songs.

Casadesus, Henri, French violinist, brother of the preceding; b. Paris, Sept. 30, 1879; d. Paris, May 31, 1947. He studied with Lavignac and Laforge in Paris; from 1910-17 was a member of the Capet Quartet; was a founder and director of the Société nouvelle des Instruments anciens, in which he played the viola d'amore; subsequently toured in the U. S., playing at the Elizabeth Sprague Coolidge Festivals, Library of Congress, Washington. Rare and ancient instruments, collected by Casadesus, are in the museum of the Boston Symphony Orchestra.

Casadesus, Jean, French pianist, son of Robert and Gaby Casadesus; b. Paris, July 7, 1927. He entered the Paris Cons. at the age of eleven; also studied piano with his parents; at the outbreak of World War II, he went to the U. S.; studied at Princeton Univ.; won the contest for young soloists held by the Philadelphia Orch. in 1946 and made his debut under Ormandy with Ravel's Piano Concerto in G; won a prize at the International Contest of Geneva (1947); appeared as soloist with the N. Y. Philh. and with major European orchestras; made tours of the U. S. and Canada. Like his father and other members of his family, he has been on the faculty of the American Cons. at Fontainebleau (from 1954).

Casadesus, Marius, French violinist, son of François Casadesus; b. Paris, Oct. 24, 1892. He studied at the Paris Cons., where he won the first prize in 1914; settled in Paris as a concert violinist and teacher; compositions include operas, chamber music, violin pieces, songs.

Casadesus, Robert, French pianist and composer; b. Paris, April 7, 1899. An offspring of a remarkable musical family, he absorbed music at home from his earliest childhood. His uncles were Henri and François Casadesus; another uncle, Marcel Louis Lucien (1882-1917), was a cellist, and his aunt, Rose, was a pianist. He received his formal musical education at the Paris Cons. with Diémer (piano) and Leroux (harmony); won prizes in 1913, 1919 and 1921. Beginning with 1922 he developed a wide-ranging career as a concert pianist; toured in Europe, South America and the U. S.

After the outbreak of World War II, he went to the U. S.; taught summer classes in Newport, Rhode Island (1940-41) and Great Barrington, Mass. (1942-47); lectured at Princeton Univ. (1945-46); appeared as soloist in his own piano concerto, op. 37 (Minneapolis, March 21, 1947) and in his concerto for two pianos, with his wife, Gaby Casadesus (N. Y. Philh., April 3, 1950); his second symphony was performed by the Cincinnati Orch. on Nov. 21, 1941. From 1934 he was professor at the American Cons. at Fontainebleau; was its director for some years after 1945. In addition to his two symphonies and piano concertos, he wrote 3 quintets; 6 sonatas for piano with various instruments; 28 preludes for piano; pieces for 2 pianos; miscellaneous compositions in small forms. As a pianist he is distinguished by the Gallic sense of balance and fine gradation of tonal dynamics. Avoiding virtuoso pieces, Casadesus has made his mark as a musicianly artist of great lyrical charm.

Casals (kăh-săhls'), **Pablo (Pau),** famous Spanish cellist; b. Vendrell, Catalonia, Dec. 29, 1876. His father, an organist and piano teacher, gave him his first instruction in music. Casals studied violin until he was twelve; then went to Barcelona, where he began taking cello lessons with José García; at the same time he studied harmony with José Rodoreda; his progress was amazingly rapid, and soon he was able to assist his teacher in his classes. In 1891 he graduated from the Municipal School of Music and began his concert career. In 1894 he went to Madrid where he attracted the attention of Count Morphy, secretary to the Queen, and was given a stipend; also played at the court. He continued his musical studies with Tomás Bretón and assisted in the chamber music class of Jesús de Monasterio; in 1895 he went to Paris as cellist at the Paris Opéra; in 1897 he taught at the Paris Cons.; also organized a string quartet. The real beginning of his career dates from his appearance, in Lalo's cello concerto, with Lamoureux on Nov. 12, 1899. During these years he also gave concerts in various countries of western Europe; appeared in London in 1898; made a successful tour through the U. S. in 1901-2, again in 1903-4, and in 1914-17; played concerts in South America in 1903. In 1906 he married his pupil, the Portuguese cellist Guilhermina Suggia (divorced in 1912); two years later he married the American singer Susan Metcalfe. In 1919 he established himself in Barcelona as the leader of the Orquestra Pau Casals; the first concert took place on Oct. 13, 1920. He was also a member of the celebrated Cortot-Thibaud-Casals Trio. During the Civil War in Spain (1936-39) Casals was an ardent supporter of the Loyalist Government, and after its defeat he settled in the village of Prades in France, on the Spanish frontier; in 1950 he inaugurated there a summer series of chamber music concerts which attracted international attention. His fame as a master musician and virtuoso is legendary; as a cellist he had no superior and few, if any, equals. Casals has composed several cello pieces, of which *La Sardana,* for an ensemble of cellos (Zürich, Oct. 14, 1951), presents a certain interest from the technical viewpoint. He also wrote a choral work, *La visión de Fray Martín.* Bibl.: L. Littlehales, *Pablo Casals* (N. Y., 1929); A. Conte, *La Légende de Pablo Casals* (Perpignan, 1950; in German as *Casals erzählt aus seinem Leben,* Bern, 1950); J. M. Corredor, *Conversations with Casals* (English translation by André Mangeot; London, 1956). A book of pictures, prepared by P. Moeschlin and A. Seiler, with German text, was publ. for his 80th birthday (1956).

Casamorata, Luigi Fernando, composer and music editor; b. Würzburg, of Italian parents, May 15, 1807; d. Florence, Sept. 24, 1881. He studied law and music in Florence; became co-editor of the Florentine 'Gazzetta Musicale' from its start (1842) and was the founder of Istituto Musicale in Florence (1860); was its director until 1881, and published its history, *Origine, storia e ordinamento dell' Istituto musicale fiorentino;* also published a *Manuale di armonia* (1876). His ballets and operas were unsuccessful, and he turned to instrumental and choral works, of which he wrote many.

Casanovas, Narciso, Spanish composer; b. Sabadell, near Barcelona, 1747; d. Montserrat, April 1, 1799. He was a member of the famous Catalan school of Montserrat; was ordained priest in 1763; served as organist at the Montserrat monastery. He wrote 5 motets, 13 psalms, several litanies, and many works for organ. His sonata in F (in Haydn's style) is reprinted in J. Nin's *17 Sonates et pièces anciennes d'auteurs espagnols* (Paris, 1929).

Casavola, Franco, Italian composer; b. Modugno, July 13, 1891; d. Bari, July 7, 1955. He studied in Rome with Respighi, but abandoning his academic pursuits, joined the futurist movement and composed music glorifying the mechanical age; also wrote futurist poetry. Among his works in this genre are a ballet, *Fantasia meccanica,* and

La danza dell' elica for flute, clarinet, violin, percussion, wind machine and blasting machine. At a later period he changed his ideas and veered toward musical realism with romantic overtones. His operas *Il gobbo del califfo* (1929), *Astuzie d'amore* (1936), and *Salammbô* (1948) have been produced with some success; he also wrote 2 ballets, *L'alba di Don Giovanni* (1932) and *Il castello nel bosco* (1931).

Cascia, Giovanni da. See **Giovanni.**

Casella, Alfredo, outstanding Italian composer; b. Turin, July 25, 1883; d. Rome, March 5, 1947. He began to play the piano at the age of four and received his early instruction from his mother; in 1896 he went to Paris, and studied with Diémer and Fauré at the Paris Cons.; won first prize in piano in 1899. He made concert tours as pianist in Europe, including Russia; appeared as guest conductor with European orchestras; in 1912 conducted the Concerts Populaires at the Trocadéro; taught piano classes at the Paris Cons. from 1912-15; returned to Rome and was appointed professor of piano at Santa Cecilia, as successor to Sgambati. In 1917 he founded the 'Società nazionale di musica' (later, the 'Società italiana di musica moderna'; since 1923 as the 'Corporazione delle Musiche Nuove', Italian section of the International Society for Contemporary Music). On Oct. 28, 1921 he made his American début with the Philadelphia Orch. in the triple capacity of composer, conductor and piano soloist; also appeared as guest conductor in Chicago, Detroit, Cincinnati, Cleveland and Los Angeles; was conductor of the Boston Pops in 1927-29, introducing a number of modern works, but failing to please the public. In 1928 he was awarded the first prize of $3,000 given by the Musical Fund Society in Philadelphia; in 1934 won the Coolidge Prize. In 1938 he returned to Italy, where he remained until his death. Apart from his activities as pianist, conductor and composer, he was a prolific writer on music, and contributed numerous articles to various publications in Italy, France, Russia, Germany and America; he possessed an enlightened cosmopolitan mind, which enabled him to penetrate the musical cultures of various nations; at the same time he steadfastly proclaimed his adherence to the ideals of Italian art. In his music he applied modernistic techniques to the old forms; his style may be termed neo-Classical, but in his early years he cultivated extreme modernism.—Works: the operas *La donna serpente* (Rome, March 17, 1932); *La favola di Orfeo* (Venice, Nov. 6, 1932); *Il deserto tentato,* mystery in one act (Florence, May 6, 1937); the ballets *Il convento veneziano* (1912); *La Giara,* 'choreographic comedy' after Pirandello (his most successful work; Paris, Nov. 19, 1924); *La Camera dei Disegni,* for children (Rome, 1940); *La Rosa del Sogno* (Rome, 1943); orchestral works: Symphony No. I in B minor (1905); Symphony No. II in C minor (1908-9); Symphony No. III, op. 63 (Chicago, March 27, 1941); Suite in C (1909); *Italia,* rhapsody based on folk themes (Paris, April 23, 1910); *Le Couvent sur l'eau,* suite (1911-12; Paris, 1914); *Notte di Maggio* for voice and orch. (Paris, March 29, 1914); *Elegia eroica* (Rome, Jan. 21, 1917); *Pagine di guerra* (1916); *Pupazzetti,* five pieces for puppets (1918); *Partita* for piano and orch. (N. Y., Oct. 29, 1925); *Scarlattiana* on themes by Scarlatti, for piano and orch. (N. Y., Jan. 22, 1927); *Concerto romano* for organ and orch. (N. Y., March 11, 1927); violin concerto in A minor (Moscow, Oct. 8, 1928); *Introduzione, Aria e Toccata* (Rome, April 5, 1933); concerto for trio and orch. (Berlin, Nov. 17, 1933); Concerto (1937; Amsterdam, 1937); *Paganiniana,* on themes by Paganini (Vienna, 1942); vocal works: *L'Adieu à la vie,* cycle of 4 Hindu lyrics after Tagore's *Gitanjali* (1915; also for voice and orch., 1926); *4 Favole romanesche* (1923); *Ninna nanna popolare genovese* (1934); *3 Canti Sacri* for baritone and orch. (1943); *Missa solemnis pro pace* (1944); instrumental music: *Barcarola e scherzo* for flute and piano (1904); 2 cello sonatas (1907; 1927); *Siciliana e burlesca* for flute and piano (1914; second version for piano trio, 1917); *5 Pezzi* for string quartet (1920); concerto for string quartet (1923-24; also arranged for string orch.); *Serenata* for clarinet, bassoon, trumpet, violin and cello (1927); *Sinfonia* for clarinet, trumpet, cello and piano (1932); piano trio (1933); many piano pieces, including the two series of stylistic imitations, *A la manière de . . .* : Wagner, Fauré, Brahms, Debussy, Strauss, Franck (1911); and (in collaboration with Ravel): Borodin, d'Indy, Chabrier, Ravel (1913); *Sonatina* (1916); *A notte alta* (1917; also for piano and orch., 1921); *11 Pezzi infantili* (1920); *Due ricercari sul nome Bach* (1932); *Three pieces for pianola* (1918). Casella orchestrated Balakirev's *Islamey;* edited Beethoven's sonatas and piano works of Albéniz; arranged Mahler's 7th symphony for piano 4 hands. Writings: *L'Evoluzione della musica . . .* (publ. in Italian, French and English in parallel columns; 1919); *Igor Stravinsky* (1926; new ed., Milan, 1951);

'21 + 26' (about Rossini, Tolstoy, Busoni, etc.; 1931); *Il Pianoforte* (1938); a manual of orchestration, *La tecnica dell' orchestra contemporanea* (completed by V. Mortari; Milan, 1950). In 1941 Casella published his memoirs, under the title *I Segreti della Giara;* translated into English as *Music in My Time: The Memoirs of Alfredo Casella* (Oklahoma Univ. Press, 1955). Bibl.: L. Cortese, *Alfredo Casella* (Genoa, 1935); G. M. Gatti, *Musicisti moderni d'Italia e di fuori* (Bologna, 1925); a special number of 'Rassegna musicale' in honor of Casella's 60th birthday (May-June, 1943); G. M. Gatti, *In Memory of A. Casella,* in the 'Mus. Quarterly' (July, 1947).

Casella, Pietro, Italian composer who flourished in the 13th century. He was a personal friend of Dante; long thought to be the earliest Italian madrigalist; however, this idea is now believed doubtful (see L. Ellinwood, *Origins of the Italian Ars Nova,* in the Papers of the American Musicological Society, 1937; p. 30).

Casimiri, Raffaele Casimiro, Italian writer on music; b. Gualdo Tadino, Nov. 3, 1880; d. Rome, April 15, 1943. He was a pupil of L. Bottazzo (Padua); 1899, teacher at the Schola cantorum of the Seminary in Nocera Umbra; 1901-3, editor of the 'Rassegna Gregoriana' (Rome); 1911 appointed conductor of San Giovanni di Laterano (Rome) after having been conductor at many provincial churches; founded the magazines 'Psalterium' (1907), 'Note d'Archivio' (1924), and 'Sacri Concentus' (yearbook in 8 vols.). In 1922 he founded the Basilica choir, 'Società polifonica romana', with which he later toured. Casimiri specialized in Palestrinian research; edited vols. 1-15 of the complete works of Palestrina (Rome, 1939-52); *Bibliotechina Ceciliana; Anthologia polyphonica auctorum saeculi XVI* (1932); *Laudi spirituali dei XVI e XVII secoli; Societatis polyphonicae romanae repertorium* (6 vols., 1925-34).—Writings: *Il 'codice 59' dell' Archivio musicale Lateranense, autografo di G. Pierl. da Palestrina* (Rome, 1919); *La rinascita della musica sacra nel secolo XVI* (Rome, 1924); articles (mostly in 'Psalterium'): *G. P. da Palestrina; nuovi documenti biografici* (1918); *Orlando di Lasso* (1920); *Ercole Barnabei* (1920); *F. Anerio* (1920); *Firmin Le Bel* (1922); *Nuove ricerche sul Palestrina* (1923); *Cantantibus organis!* (1924); *'Il Vittoria'; nuovi documenti per una biografia sincera di T. L. de Vittoria* (1934). He composed 2 oratorios, *San Pancrazio* and *Santo Stefano; Madrigali e Scherzi* for mixed chorus; many masses, motets, offertories, etc. —Cf. E. Dagnino, *R. Casimiri,* in 'Rassegna Musicale' (April, 1943).

Casini, Giovanni Maria, Italian organist and composer; b. Florence, c. 1670; d. there, 1715. He studied composition in Florence, and later in Rome with Matteo Simonelli and Bernardo Pasquini (organ). He became a priest and served as organist at the Cathedral of Florence from 1703-14. As a keyboard composer Casini represents the late Baroque style. As a theorist he was a follower of Nicolo Vicentino and Giovanni Battista Doni in their studies of the music of Greek antiquity. Existing publications of his works are: *Canzonette spirituali* (Florence, 1703); a collection of motets (in the style of Palestrina) in 4 voices, op. 1 (Rome, 1706); *Responsori per la Settimana Santa,* op. 2 (Florence, 1706); *Pensieri per l'organo,* op. 3 (Florence, 1714). There is also an oratorio by Casini (in manuscript), *Il viaggio di Tobia.* Modern reprints of 2 numbers from his op. 3 are found in L. Torchi's *L'Arte Musicale in Italia* (vol. III).

Cassadó, Gaspar, distinguished Spanish cellist, son of Joaquín Cassadó (q.v.); b. Barcelona, Sept. 30, 1897; pupil of March and Casals; has toured Europe and America (made his N. Y. début, Dec. 10, 1936) as recitalist and soloist with leading orchs.; made another U. S. tour in 1949. He composed a piano trio; cello sonatas (*nello stile antico spagnolo*); concerto for cello and orch.; Partita for cello; Serenade for cello; other pieces for his instrument (*Lamento de Boabdil, Requiebros,* etc.); *Catalonian Rhapsody* for orch. (N. Y. Philh., Nov. 8, 1928); also arranged for cello and orch. Weber's clarinet concerto, Mozart's horn concerto, and transcribed for cello various piano pieces.

Cassadó, Joaquín, Spanish organist and composer; b. Mataro, near Barcelona, Sept. 30, 1867; d. Madrid, May 25, 1926. He was choir director at Nuestra Señora de la Merced, Barcelona, then organist at San José; 1890, founded and conducted a choral society, Capilla Catalana, in Barcelona; the last years of his life were spent mostly in Paris.—Works: *El Monjo Negro,* comic opera (Barcelona, Jan. 24, 1920); symph. poems; *Sinfonía dramática; Hispania,* fantasy for piano and orch. (Paris, 1911); church music; cello pieces; etc.

Cassiodorus, **Magnus Aurelius,** historian, statesman and monk; b. Scyllacium (Squillace), Bruttii, c. 485; d. Vivarese, Calabria, c. 580. He was a contemporary of Boetius;

held various civil offices under Theodoric (d. 526) and Athalaric until c. 540, when he retired. He founded the monasteries of Castellum and Vivarium; at the latter he wrote his *De artibus ac disciplinis liberalium litterarum;* the section treating of music, *Institutiones musicae,* a valuable source, is printed in Gerbert's 'Scriptores', vol. I; a partial reproduction is to be found in Strunk's *Source Readings in Music History* (N. Y., 1950). Bibl.: A. Franz, *A. Cassiodorus* (1872); W. Brambach, *Die Musikliteratur des Mittelalters . . .* (1883); H. Abert, *Zu Cassiodor,* in 'Sammelbände der Internationalen Musik-Gesellschaft' (vol. III, 3, p. 439ff.); H. Abert, *Die Musikanschauung des Mittelalters . . .* (p. 132 ff.; 1905); G. Pietzsch, *Die Klassifikation der Musik . . .* (1929); G. Pietzsch, *Die Musik im Erziehungs- und Bildungsideal . . .* (p. 30 ff.; 1932).

Cassirer, Fritz, German conductor and writer on music; b. Breslau, March 29, 1871; d. Berlin, Nov. 26, 1926. He first studied philosophy (1889-92); then turned to music; was orchestral and operatic conductor in many German towns; also in London (1905-7). Writings: *Edgar,* a poem (1894); *Beethovens Briefe,* an essay in 'Die Musik' (1909); *Helldunkle Weltgeschichte* (1920; pseudonym: Friedrich Leopold); *Beethoven und die Gestalt* (1925).

Castagna (kah-stah'-n'yah), **Bruna,** Italian contralto; b. Bari, Oct. 15, 1908. She began to study music at the age of seven, and at fourteen appeared as a pianist; then studied voice for three months with Mme. Tina Scognamiglio of Milan; made her operatic debut as Marina in *Boris Godunov* (Mantua, 1927) with Ezio Pinza in the title role; then engaged at the Teatro Colón, Buenos Aires, for three seasons; toured in Australia, Chile, Brazil, Germany, France and Egypt; début at Metropolitan Opera House as Amneris in *Aida,* March 2, 1936.

Castagnone (kăh-stăh-n'yoh'-nē), **Riccardo,** Italian composer; b. Brunate, Como, Sept. 10, 1906. He studied with Frugatta (piano), Paribeni (composition), and Scherchen (conducting). Works: *Passacaglia* and *Preludio giocoso,* for orch.; *Suite d'Antiche Danze,* for small orch.; *Toccata,* for piano and orch.; *Tre canzoni,* for soprano and string orch.; etc.

Castel, Louis-Bertrand, French Jesuit; b. Montpellier, Nov. 11, 1688; d. Paris, Jan. 9, 1757. He became interested in Newton's observation on the correspondence, in proportionate breadth, of the 7 prismatic rays with the string-lengths required for the scale *re, mi, fa, sol, la, si, do;* acting upon this observation, he attempted the construction of a 'Clavecin oculaire,' to produce color-harmonies for the eye as the ordinary harpsichord produces tone-harmonies for the ear. These expensive experiments led to no practical result. His 'Clavecin' is explained in an essay, *Nouvelles expériences d'optique et d'acoustique* (1735; English transl., London, 1757; German transl., Hamburg, 1739). See the compendious article by A. Wellek in 'Die Musik in Geschichte und Gegenwart'.

Castelli, Ignaz Franz, Austrian librettist; b. Vienna, March 6, 1781; d. there, Feb. 5, 1862. He was 'Court Theater-Poet' at the Kärntnerthortheater; founder, and editor, of the 'Allgemeiner musikalischer Anzeiger' (1829-40). He wrote the libretto of Weigl's *Schweizerfamilie,* and other popular opera-books, and translated many foreign operas for the German stage. His *Memoirs* were publ. in 1861 in 4 vols.

Castelmary (kahs-tĕl-mah'-rē) (stage-name of Count Armand de Castan), French baritone; b. Toulouse, Aug. 16, 1834; d. New York, Feb. 10, 1897, on the stage of the Metropolitan Opera House, just after the first act of *Martha.* He made his début at the Paris Opéra (1864); remained there till 1870; then sang in London and New York; was particularly successful as Mephistopheles in *Faust* (Drury Lane, 1873).

Castelnuovo-Tedesco, Mario, Italian composer; b. Florence, April 3, 1895. He studied at the Cherubini Institute with del Valle (piano) and Pizzetti (composition); he began to compose at an early age; his first organized composition, *Cielo di Settembre* for piano, revealed impressionistic tendencies. He wrote a patriotic song, *Fuori i Barbari* during World War I. He attained considerable eminence in Italy between the two wars, and his music was often heard at European festivals. Political events forced him to leave Italy; in 1939 he settled in the U. S. He became active as a film composer in Hollywood, but continued to write large amounts of orchestral and chamber music. His style is remarkably fluent and adaptable to the various moods evoked in his music, often reaching rhapsodic eloquence. —Works: the operas *La mandragola* (libretto by the composer, after Machiavelli; Venice, May 4, 1926; won the National Prize); *The Princess and the Pea,* after Andersen, miniature opera with narrator (1943); *Bacco in Toscana,* dithyramb for voices and orch.

(La Scala, May 8, 1931); *Aucassin et Nicolette,* puppet show with voices and instruments (1938); 2 biblical oratorios: *Ruth* (1949) and *Jonah* (1951). For orch.: *Cipressi* (Boston Symph., Koussevitzky cond., Oct. 25, 1940; originally for piano, 1921); piano concerto No. 1 (Rome, Dec. 9, 1928); piano concerto No. 2 (N. Y. Philh., Nov. 2, 1939, composer soloist); 3 violin concertos: *Concerto italiano* (Rome, Jan. 31, 1926), *The Prophets* (Jascha Heifetz and N. Y. Philh., Toscanini conducting, April 12, 1933), 3d violin concerto (1939); cello concerto (N. Y. Philh., Jan. 31, 1935, Piatigorsky soloist, Toscanini conducting); *Variazioni sinfoniche* for violin and orch. (Rome, Dec. 19, 1930); overtures to Shakespeare's plays: *The Taming of the Shrew* (1930), *Twelfth Night* (1933), *The Merchant of Venice* (1933), *Julius Caesar* (1934), *A Midsummer Night's Dream* (1940), *Coriolanus* (1947), etc.; *Poem* for violin and orch. (1942); *The Birthday of the Infanta* (1942; New Orleans, Jan. 28, 1947); *Indian Songs and Dances,* suite (Los Angeles, Jan. 7, 1943); *An American Rhapsody* (1943); *Serenade* for guitar and orch. (1943); *Octoroon Ball,* ballet suite (1947); *Noah's Ark,* a movement for narrator and orch. from *Genesis,* a suite; other movements by Schoenberg, Stravinsky, Toch, Milhaud, Tansman, and N. Shilkret, who commissioned the work (Portland, Ore., Dec. 15, 1947). Chamber music: *Signorine: 2 Profili* for violin and piano (1918); *Ritmi* for violin and piano (1920); *Capitan Fracassa* for violin and piano (1920); *Notturno Adriatico* for violin and piano (1922); *I nottambuli* for cello and piano (1927); cello sonata (1928); 1st piano trio (1928); 1st string quartet (1929); *Sonata quasi una fantasia* for violin and piano (1929); *The Lark* for violin and piano (1930); 1st piano quintet (1932); 2nd piano trio (1932); toccata for cello and piano (1935); *Capriccio diabolico* for guitar (1935; later arranged as guitar concerto); concertino for harp and 7 instruments (1937); *Ballade* for violin and piano (1940); *Divertimento* for 2 flutes (1943); sonata for violin and viola (1945); clarinet sonata (1945); sonatina for bassoon and piano (1946); 2nd string quartet (1948); quintet for guitar and strings (1950); sonata for viola and cello (1950); *Fantasia* for guitar and piano (1950); *Concerto da camera* for oboe and strings (1950); sonata for violin and cello (1950); 2nd piano quintet (1951). For piano: *English Suite* (1909); *Questo fu il carro della morte* (1913); *Il raggio verde* (1916); *Alghe* (1919); *I naviganti* (1919); *La sirenetta e il pesce turchino* (1920); *Cantico* (1920); *Vitalba e Biancospino* (1921); *Epigrafe* (1922); *Alt-Wien* (Viennese rhapsody, 1923); *Piedigrotta* (1924); *Le Stagioni* (1924); *Le danze del Re David* (1925); *3 poemi campestri* (1926); *3 corali su melodie ebraiche* (1926); sonata (1928); *Crinoline* (1929); *Candide,* 6 pieces (1944); *6 canoni* (1950). Songs: *Le Roy Loys* (1914); *Ninna-Nanna* (1914; very popular); *Fuori i barbari,* a patriotic song (1915); *Stelle cadenti* (1915); *Coplas* (1915); *Briciole* (1916); *3 fioretti di Santo Francesco* (1919; also with orch.); *Girotondo de golosi* (1920); *Etoile filante* (1920); *L'Infinito* (1921); *Sera* (1921); *Due preghiere per i bimbi d'Italia* (1923); *1830,* after Alfred de Musset (1924); *Scherzi,* 2 series (1924-25); music to 33 Shakespeare songs (1921-25); *Indian Serenade* (1925); *Cadix* (1926); *3 Sonnets from the Portuguese,* after E. B. Browning (1926); *Laura di Nostra Donna* (1935); *Un sonetto di Dante* (1939); *Recuerdo* (1940); *Le Rossignol* (1942); *The Daffodils* (1944). For chorus: 2 madrigals a cappella (1915); *Lecho dodi,* synagogue chant for tenor, men's voices, and organ (1936); *Sacred Synagogue Service* (1943); *Liberty, Mother of Exiles* (1944).—Cf. G. M. Gatti, *Musicisti moderni d'Italia e di fuori* (Bologna, 1925); G. Rossi-Daria, *Mario Castelnuovo-Tedesco,* in the 'Chesterian' (Jan.-Feb., 1926); C. Valabrega, *Mario Castelnuovo-Tedesco,* in 'Il Pianoforte' (March, 1926); Roland von Weber, *Mario Castelnuovo-Tedesco,* in *The Book of Modern Composers,* ed. by David Ewen (N. Y., 1942). A list of works is found in 'Rassegna Musicale' (Jan., 1953).

Castéra, René de, French composer; b. Dax (Landes), April 3, 1873; d. Angoumi, near Dax, Oct. 9, 1955. He studied at the Schola Cantorum in Paris with Vincent d'Indy; wrote an opera *Berteretche;* a concerto for flute, clarinet, cello, and piano; a violin sonata; piano pieces. He founded a publishing enterprise, Édition Mutuelle, for publication of works by French composers.

Castil-Blaze. See **Blaze.**

Castillon (kah-stē-yohn'), **Alexis de,** Vicomte de Saint-Victor, French composer; b. Chartres, Dec. 13, 1838; d. Paris, March 5, 1873. He began composing under the guidance of Masse; later studied with César Franck. He was one of the first French composers of the 19th century to cultivate absolute music; was a founder (1871) of the Société Nationale de Musique.—Works: *Psalm 84* for soli, chorus and orch.; orchestral overture, *Torquato Tasso;* two orchestral suites; *Esquisses symphoniques;* piano concerto; piano quintet; piano quartet; 2 piano trios; string quartet; violin sonata; piano pieces; songs.

Caston, Saul, American conductor; b. New York, Aug. 22, 1901. He studied at the Curtis Institute, Philadelphia, with Chasins, Scalero and Reiner; played trumpet in the Philadelphia Orch. (1918-45); taught trumpet at the Curtis Institute (1924-42); was associate conductor of the Philadelphia Orch. (1936-45); conductor of the Reading Symph. Orch. (1941-44); in 1945 was appointed conductor of the Denver Symph. Orch.

Castro, Jean (Juan) de, composer who flourished in the 16th century; b. Liège (?); d. Cologne (?). From 1582-84 he was assistant choirmaster in Vienna; later, 1593-96, in Cleve, near Cologne.—Works: 3-part *Missae* (Cologne, 1599); *Sacrae cantiones,* 5-8 parts (1571), 3-part *Sacrae cantiones* (1593 and 1596); in 5-8 parts (1588); *Tricinia sacra* (1574); *Bicinia sacra* (1594); *Chansons, Odes et Sonnets par P. Ronsard à 4-8 voix* (1576); *Chansons, Stances, Sonnets et Epigrammes à 2 voix* (Antwerp, 1592); *Quintines, Sextines, Sonnets à 5 voix* (1594). Many of these works are very interesting because of the exact rhythmical arrangement of the verses.

Castro, José María, Argentine conductor and composer; brother of Juan José Castro; b. Buenos Aires, Nov. 17, 1892. He studied in Paris with Vincent d'Indy; in 1930 was appointed director of the Orquesta de Cámara de la Asociación del Profesorado Orquestal in Buenos Aires; in 1931 became director of the Orquesta Filarmónica there; 1933, director of the Banda Municipal de la Ciudad de Buenos Aires. —Works: The 3-act ballet, *Georgia* (Teatro Colón, Buenos Aires, June 2, 1939, composer conducting); *Obertura para una Opera Cómica,* for orch. (awarded prize of the Asociación del Profesorado Orquestal, 1935); *Concerto Grosso,* for orch. (Buenos Aires, June 11, 1933); piano concerto (Buenos Aires, Nov. 17, 1941); sonata for 2 cellos; piano pieces: 10 *Piezas Breves; Motivos Infantiles;* 5 *Piezas Poeticas;* 3 piano sonatas (awarded Beethoven Prize, 1926; and Municipal Prize, 1927); and *Sonata de Primavera* for piano (one of his best works; 1941).

Castro, Juan José, Argentine conductor and composer; brother of José María Castro; b. Buenos Aires, March 7, 1895; studied there, later in Paris with d'Indy; 1929, founded in Buenos Aires the Orquesta Renacimiento, which he conducted; from 1930 conducted at the Teatro Colón, and became the director of the Asociación del Profesorado Orquestal and Asociación Sinfónica; gave first performances in Argentina of Stravinsky's *Sacre du printemps,* Falla's *El Amor brujo,* etc.; in 1934 was in N. Y. as a fellow of the Guggenheim Foundation; from 1951-53 was conductor of the Victorian Symph. Orch., Melbourne, Australia; in 1955 returned to Argentina.—Works: the operas *Proserpina e Straniero* (received first prize at La Scala contest; Milan, March 17, 1952, composer conducting) and *Bodas de sangre* (Buenos Aires, Aug. 9, 1956); ballet, *Mekhano* (Buenos Aires, July 17, 1937). For orch.: *Dans le jardin des morts* (Buenos Aires, Oct. 5, 1924); *A una madre* (Buenos Aires, Oct. 27, 1925); *Sinfonía la Chellah,* based on an Arabian theme (Buenos Aires, Sept. 10, 1927). *Allegro, lento y vivace* (London, under Casella, at the Festival of the International Society for Contemporary Music, 1931); *Sinfonía Biblica,* a work in 3 movements for orch. and chorus: *Anunciación, Entrada a Jerusalem, Golgotha* (Buenos Aires, conducted by composer, Nov. 15, 1932); *Sinfonía Argentina* (Buenos Aires, Nov. 29, 1936); *Sinfonía de los Campos* (Buenos Aires, Oct. 29, 1939); *Corales Criollos,* symph. poem (1954; won the first prize of $10,000 at the Caracas Music Festival, 1954). For piano: *Suite infantil; Suite breve* (also orchestrated); sonatas; 9 Preludes. Other works: violin sonata; cello sonata; *Sarabande* for cello and piano; songs.

Castro, Ricardo, Mexican composer and pianist; b. Durango, Feb. 7, 1864; d. Mexico City, Nov. 28, 1907. He studied with Melesio Morales in Mexico; in 1883 he appeared as pianist at the New Orleans Cotton Exposition. In 1902 he went to Europe and presented concerts of his works in Paris; he was soloist in his own piano concerto in Antwerp (Dec. 28, 1904). Returning to Mexico, he produced an opera *La Leyenda de Rudel* (Nov. 8, 1906). He composed three more operas (*Atzimba, Satán vencido* and *La Rousalka*), 2 symphonies (1883; 1887) and a number of piano pieces.

Castrucci (kah-strŏŏ'-tchē), **Pietro,** Italian violinist; b. Rome, 1679; d. Dublin, Feb. 29, 1752. He was a pupil of Corelli; came to London (1715) as leader of Handel's opera orch. He was a fine player on the 'violetta marina', a stringed instrument invented by himself, and resembling the 'viola d'amore' in tone. In *Orlando,* Handel wrote an air accompanied on two 'violette marine' 'per gli Signori Castrucci' (Pietro, and Prospero, his brother). Castrucci published violin concertos, and 2 books of violin sonatas. **Prospero Castrucci,** who died in London, 1760, was a violinist in the Italian Opera-orch.; publ. 6 soli for violin and bass.

Catalani (kah-tah-lah'-nē), **Alfredo,** Italian dramatic composer; b. Lucca, June 19, 1854; d. Milan, Aug. 7, 1893. Taught by his father, a fine musician, and by F. Magi; wrote (1868) a Mass for 4 parts and orch., by which he gained admission without examination to the Paris Cons. Returned to Italy 1873; studied in Milan Cons. two years; then devoted himself to dramatic composition; he was the successor of Ponchielli as professor of composition in Milan Cons. (1886).—Operas: *Elda* (Turin, Jan. 31, 1880; revised and produced under the title *Loreley,* Turin, Feb. 16, 1890); *Dejanice* (Milan, March 17, 1883); *Edmea* (Milan, Feb. 27, 1886); *La Wally* (Milan, Jan. 20, 1892; Catalani's most successful opera). He also wrote a symph. poem, *Ero e Leandro* (1885) and a number of piano pieces and songs.—Cf. D. L. Pardini, *Alfredo Catalani* (Lucca, 1935); J. W. Klein, *Alfredo Catalani,* in the 'Mus. Quarterly' (July, 1937); A. Bonaccorsi, *Alfredo Catalani* (Turin, 1942); Carlo Gatti, *Alfredo Catalani* (Milan, 1953).

Catalani, Angelica, Italian soprano; b. Sinigaglia, May 10, 1780; d. Paris, June 12, 1849. She was taught at the convent of Santa Lucia di Gubbio in Rome; made her operatic début at the Teatro la Fenice, Venice (1795); then sang at La Pergola, Florence (1799) and at La Scala, Milan (1801). In 1801, while engaged at the Italian Opera in Lisbon, she married M. Valabrègue, an attaché of the French embassy; subsequently gave highly successful concerts in Paris and London. From 1814-17 she undertook, without signal success, the management of the Théâtre des Italiens in Paris; then resumed her singing career, appearing in major European cities and at provincial festivals until 1828, when she retired to her country home near Florence. She won great acclaim for her commanding stage presence, wide vocal range, and mastery of the *bravura* singing style.

Catel (kah-tel'), **Charles-Simon,** French music pedagogue; b. l'Aigle, Orne, June 10, 1773; d. Paris, Nov. 29, 1830. He studied in Paris with Gossec and Gobert at the École Royale du Chant (later merged with the Cons.); served as accompanist and teacher there (1787); in 1790 was accompanist at the Opéra and assistant conductor (to Gossec) of the band of the Garde Nationale. In 1795, on the establishment of the Conservatoire, he was appointed professor of harmony, and commissioned to write a *Traité d'Harmonie* (published in 1802; a standard work at the Conservatoire for twenty years thereafter). With Gossec, Méhul and Cherubini, he was made an inspector of the Cons., resigning in 1814; named a member of the Academy in 1815. As a composer, Catel was at his best in his operas, written in a conventional but attractive style of French stage music of the time; his most successful opera was *Les Bayadères* (Paris Opéra, Aug. 8, 1810); among his other operas (performed at the Paris Opéra and at the Opéra-Comique) are: *Sémiramis* (May 3, 1802); *L'Auberge de Bagnères* (April 16, 1807); *Les Artistes par occasion* (Feb. 24, 1807); *Les Aubergistes de qualité* (June 17, 1812); *Bayard à Mézières* (Feb. 12, 1814); *L'Officier enlevé* (May 4, 1819). He also wrote several symphonies and chamber music.—Cf. J. Carlez, *Catel; Étude biographique et critique* (Caen, 1895); F. Hellouin and J. Picard, *Un Musicien oublié: Catel* (Paris, 1910).

Catelani, Angelo, Italian music historian; b. Guastalla, March 30, 1811; d. San Martino di Mugnano, Sept. 5, 1866. He studied piano with Asioli and harmony with M. Fusco; also at the Naples Cons. (1831) and privately with Donizetti and Crescentini; conducted at the Messina opera (1834), at Correggio (1837); appointed maestro di cappella at the cathedral and court of Modena (1838); from 1859 served as assistant librarian of the Este Library. He composed three operas, of which one was successfully produced; then turned to writing on music. Works: *Notizie su padre Aaron e su Nicola Vicentino* in the 'Gazzetta musicale di Milano' (1851); *Epistolario di autori celebri in musica* (1852-4); *Bibliografia di due stampe ignote di Ottaviano Petrucci da Fossombrone* (1858); *Della vita e delle opere di Orazio Vecchi* (1858); *Della vita e delle opere di Claudio Merulo da Correggio* (1860); *Delle opere di Alessandro Stradella* (1866).

Catoire (kăh-twahr'), **Georgy Lvovitch,** Russian composer of French descent; b. Moscow, April 27, 1861; d. there, May 21, 1926. While a student of mathematics at the Univ. of Berlin, he took lessons in piano with Klindworth and in composition with Rüfer; later studied with Liadov in St. Petersburg; lived in Moscow and devoted himself to composing; also taught composition at the Moscow Cons. —Works: a symphony in C minor; symph. poem, *Mtsÿri;* piano concerto; cantata, *Russalka;* three poems of Tiutchev for female voices with piano; string trio; string quartet; string quintet; four preludes for piano; violin sonata, *Poème;* piano quartet; piano quintet; many songs. He also published a manual on harmony in 2 vols. (1924; 1925). See V. Belaiev, *G. Catoire* (in Russian and German; Moscow, 1926).

Catunda, Eunice, Brazilian composer; b. Rio de Janeiro, March 14, 1915. She studied with Koellreutter, and later with Scherchen in Europe; has composed a cantata, *Petit noir de la bergerie* (1946); *Chant du soldat mort,* for chorus and orch. (1947); *Hommage à Schoenberg,* for five instruments (1950).

Caturla, Alejandro García, Cuban composer; b. Remedios, March 7, 1906; assassinated at Remedios, Nov. 12, 1940. He studied with Pedro Sanjuán in Havana; then with Nadia Boulanger in Paris (1928); was founder (1932) and conductor of the Orquesta de Conciertos de Caibarién (chamber orchestra) in Cuba; served as district judge in Remedios. His works have been performed in Cuba, Europe and the U. S. In Caturla's music, primitive Afro-Cuban rhythms and themes are treated with modern techniques and a free utilization of dissonance. Major works: Suite of three Cuban dances: *Danza del Tambor, Motivos de Danzas, Danza Lucumí* (Havana, 1928; also performed in Barcelona, Seville and Bogotá); *Bembé* for fourteen instruments (Paris, 1929); *Dos Poemas Afro-Cubanos,* for voice and piano (Paris, 1929; also arranged for voice and orch.); *Yambo-O,* Negro liturgy for chorus and orch. (Havana, 1931); *Rumba,* for orch. (1931); *Primera Suite Cubana* for piano and eight wind instruments (1930). Bibl.: Alejo Carpentier, *Música en Cuba* (Havana, 1946); Otto Mayer-Serra, *Música y músicos de Latino-América* (Mexico, 1947); Adolfo Salazar, *La obra musical de Alejandro Caturla* in the 'Revista Cubana' (Jan., 1938); Nicolas Slonimsky, *Caturla of Cuba,* in 'Modern Music' (Jan., 1940).

Cauchie (koh-shē'), **Maurice,** French musicologist; b. Paris, Oct. 8, 1882. He was first a physicist and chemist; after 1917 devoted himself exclusively to music; specialized in the study of French music of the 16th and 17th centuries. He edited *Deux chansons à 5 voix de Clément Janequin* (1925); *Quinze chansons françaises du XVIe siècle à 4 et 5 voix* (1926); *Trente chansons de Clément Janequin* (1928); the collected works of Clément Janequin; wrote *La Pratique de la musique* (1948); numerous essays in French magazines on Okeghem, Attaingnant, Janequin, Cléreau, Costeley, Boesset, Couperin, Gluck, Beethoven, etc.; compiled a thematic index of the works of François Couperin (1949).

Caudella, Edoardo, Rumanian violinist and composer of Italian origin; b. Jassy, June 3, 1841; d. there, April 11, 1923. He studied in Berlin (1853-54) and Paris (1855-60); later took lessons with Vieuxtemps. He was director of the Jassy Cons. His opera *Petru Raresch* (Bucharest, Nov. 14, 1900) had considerable success.

Caurroy, Eustache du. See **Du Caurroy.**

Cavaccio (că̆h-vă̆ch'-yo), **Giovanni,** Italian composer; b. Bergamo, 1556; d. there, Aug. 11, 1626. He was maestro di cappella at the Cathedral of Bergamo (1581-1604) and at Santa Maria Maggiore in Bergamo from 1604 till his death. Among his published works are collections of madrigals (1585, 1597, etc.); Psalms (1585); a Requiem (Milan, 1611); and a collection of keyboard pieces, *Sudori Musicali* (Venice, 1626). Music by Cavaccio was included in a publication of Psalms dedicated to Palestrina (1592), and pieces by him were printed in Bonometti's *Parnassus Musicus.* A *Canzon francese per organo* and a toccata are reprinted in L. Torchi, *L'Arte Musicale in Italia* (vol. III).

Cavaillé-Coll (kăh-văh-yā'-kohl), **Aristide,** celebrated French organ builder; b. Montpellier, Feb. 2, 1811; d. Paris, Oct. 13, 1899. His father, Dominique Hyacinthe (1771-1862), was also an organ builder. Aristide went to Paris in 1833; built the organ at St.-Denis, and thereafter many famous organs in Paris (St.-Sulpice, Madeleine, etc.), the French provinces, Belgium, Holland and elsewhere. He invented the system of separate wind-chests with different pressures for the low, medium, and high tones; also the 'flûtes octaviantes.'—Writings: *Études expérimentales sur les tuyaux d'orgues* (report for the Académie des Sciences, 1849); *De l'orgue et de son architecture* ('Revue générale de l'architecture des Travaux Publics', 1856); and *Projet d'Orgue monumental pour la Basilique de Saint-Pierre de Rome* (1875). Bibl.: A. Peschard, *Notice biographique sur A. Cavaillé-Coll et les orgues électriques* (Paris, 1899); C. and E. Cavaillé-Coll, *A. Cavaillé-Coll; ses origines, sa vie, ses œuvres* (Paris, 1928).

Cavalieri (kăh-văh-l'yā'rē), **Emilio del,** Italian composer; b. c. 1550; d. Rome, March 11, 1602. He was a nobleman who served as 'Inspector-General of Art and Artists' at the Tuscan court in Florence. He was one of the 'inventors' and most ardent champions of the monodic style, or 'stile recitativo', which combines melody with accompanying harmonies. His chief work, *La Rappresentazione di anima e di corpo* (published by A. Guidotti, Rome, 1600, with explanatory preface; revived Munich, 1921), once regarded as the first oratorio, is really a morality play set to music; other dramatic works (*Il Satiro,* 1590; *Disperazione di Filene,* 1590; *Giuoco della cieca,* 1595) exemplify in similar manner the beginnings of modern opera form. In all of Cavalieri's music there is a 'basso continuato' with thorough-bass figuring; the melodies are also crudely figured. A facsimile edition of the libretto for *La Rappresentazione* was published by D. Alaleona (Rome, 1912); a facsimile edition of the orchestral score is to be found in Mantica's 'Collezione di prime fioriture del melodramma italiano' (Rome, 1912).—Bibl.: D. Alaleona, *Su E. Cavalieri,* etc. in 'Nuova Musica' (Florence, 1905); L. Guidiccioni-Nicastro, *La rappresentazione di anima e di corpo* (Leghorn, 1911); Henry Prunières, *Une lettre inédite d'Emilio de Cavalieri,* in the 'Revue Musicale' (1923); U. Rolandi, *Emilio de Cavalieri,* in the 'Rivista Musicale Italiana' (1929); B. Becherini, *La musica nelle Sacre Rappresentazioni fiorentini,* in the 'Rivista Musicale Italiana' (1951).

Cavalieri, Katharina, Austrian soprano of Italian descent; b. Währing, near Vienna, Feb. 19, 1760; d. Vienna, June 30, 1801. She studied with Salieri; sang with great success at the Italian Opera and then at the German Opera in Vienna. Although she never sang outside of Vienna, a passage in one of Mozart's letters, describing her as 'a singer of whom Germany might well be proud', procured for her deserved recognition. She retired in 1793. Mozart wrote for her the role of Constanze in *Die Entführung,* and the aria 'Mi tradi' in *Don Giovanni.*

Cavalieri, Lina, Italian dramatic soprano; b. Viterbo, Dec. 25, 1874; d. Florence, Feb. 8, 1944. She studied with Madame Mariani-Masi in Paris; made her debut at Lisbon (1900); sang several seasons in Naples, Rome, Florence, Palermo, Warsaw and St. Petersburg; made her American debut at the Metropolitan Opera as Fedora (Dec. 5, 1906) and sang there until 1908; from 1908-9 engaged at the Manhattan Opera, N. Y.; with the Chicago Opera (1915-16). On July 10, 1913 she married the tenor Lucien Muratore (divorced, 1927); in 1927 she married Giuseppe Campari. She returned to Europe and lived in retirement, first in Paris and later at her villa near Florence, where she was killed during an air raid.

Cavalli, Pier Francesco, celebrated Italian composer of operas; b. Crema, Feb. 14, 1602; d. Venice, Jan. 14, 1676. His father (whose real name was Gian Battista Caletti-Bruni) was maestro di cappella at Crema; his protector was a Venetian nobleman, Federigo Cavalli, and according to the prevailing fashion, he took the latter's name. Francesco Cavalli studied music in Venice; sang at San Marco under Monteverdi (1617); was appointed second organist there (1640); then first organist (1655) and finally maestro di cappella (1668). He composed prolifically; wrote forty-one operas, which show a marked advance, in formal balance and power of dramatic expression, over Monteverdi's early type of opera. Three of Cavalli's operas achieved outstanding success and were performed repeatedly in Italian theaters: *Giasone* (Venice, Jan. 5, 1649); *Serse* (Venice, Jan. 12, 1654; chosen to be presented at the marriage festivities of Louis XIV of France, in 1660); *Ercole Amante* (written for the inauguration of the hall of the Tuileries, and performed there Feb. 7, 1662). Cavalli also composed a requiem and much church music.—Bibl.: L. Galvani, *I teatri musicali di Venezia nel secolo XVII* (1878); H. Kretzschmar, *Die venezianische Oper und die Werke Cavallis und Cestis* in 'Vierteljahrsschrift für Musikwissenschaft' (Leipzig, 1892); Taddeo Wiel, *F. Cavalli* (Venice, 1914); Egon Wellesz, *Cavalli und der Stil der venezianischen Oper von 1640-1660* in 'Studien zur Musikwissenschaft' (1913); H. Prunières, *Cavalli et l'opéra vénitien au XVIIe siècle* (Paris, 1931). See also A. Loewenberg, *Annals of Opera* (1943; 2nd ed., 1955).

Cavan, Marie (stage name of Mary Edith Cawein), American soprano; b. New York, Feb. 6, 1889. She studied in New York with Rose Marie Heilig and Harriet Ware; she made her operatic debut as Irma in *Louise* (Chicago Opera, Nov. 9, 1910); was engaged there until 1912; then at the Hamburg Stadttheater (1912-15), where she sang Mimi with Enrico Caruso in 1913; and at the Neues Deutsches Theater of Prague (1915-33). In Prague she married the Czechoslovakian tenor Otakar Mařák. They returned to New York in 1935.

Cavazzoni, Girolamo, Italian organist and composer; b. Urbino, c. 1520; d. Venice, 1560. He was a son of Marco Antonio Cavazzoni and godson of Cardinal Pietro Bembo. His *Intavolatura cioè Ricercari, Canzoni, Hinni, Magnificati* (Venice, 1542) contains the first examples of the polyphonic ricercar of the 16th century. His organ ricercars, though related to the motet, differ from it in their extension of the individual sections by means of more numerous entries of the subject and more definite cadences between sections. The two canzonas from the same work mark the beginnings of an independent canzona literature for the keyboard. Reprints of Cavazzoni's works are found in L. Torchi, *L'Arte Musicale in Italia* (vol. III); Tagliapietra, *Antologia di Musica* (vol. I); Davison and Apel, *Historical Anthology of Music;* and Schering, *Geschichte der Musik in Beispielen.* Cf. C. Sartori, *Precisazioni bibliografiche sulle opere di Girolamo Cavazzoni,* in 'Rivista Musicale Italiana' (1940).

Cavazzoni, Marco Antonio (da Bologna; or d'Urbino), Italian composer and singer, father of Girolamo Cavazzoni; b. Bologna, c. 1490; d. c. 1570 (the date appearing on his will is April 3, 1569). He went to Urbino about 1510 and became acquainted with Cardinal Pietro Bembo; then became a musician in the private chapel of Pope Leo X (1515). In Venice (1517) he was employed by Francesco Cornaro, nephew of the Queen of Cyprus. Back in Rome (1520) he was again in the employ of Pope Leo X. From 1522-24 and from 1528-31 he was in Venice, and in 1536-37 was organist at Chioggia. From 1545-1559 he was a singer at San Marco (Venice) where Adriaen Willaert was maestro di cappella. As a youth, Cavazzoni wrote a mass *Domini Marci Antonii,* so named because he derived its theme from the solmization syllables of his Christian names. His most important work is a collection of keyboard pieces, *Recerchari, motetti, canzoni, Libro I* (Venice, 1523). The ricercars are toccata-like rather than contrapuntal, and the motets and canzonas are instrumental transcriptions of vocal pieces. Modern reprints (with biographical notes) are found in Benvenuti's *I Classici musicali italiani* (Milan, 1941) and in K. Jeppesen, *Die italienische Orgelmusik am Anfang des Cinquecento* (Copenhagen, 1943). See also T. Dart, *Cavazzoni and Cabezón* (suggesting a conjecture that Marco Antonio may have been a brother of Cabezón, the latter being a possible Spanish form of Cavazzoni's name) in 'Music & Letters' (Feb., 1955); a rebuttal to this by Jeppesen appeared in the Summer 1955 issue of the 'Journal of the American Musicological Society' together with a final postscript by Dart.

Cavos, Catterino, Italian-Russian composer; b. Venice, 1775; d. St. Petersburg, May 10, 1840. He studied with Francesco Bianchi; his first work was a patriotic hymn for the Republican Guard, performed at the Teatro Fenice (Sept. 13, 1797); he then produced a cantata *L'eroe* (1798). In 1799 he received an invitation to go to Russia as conductor at the Imperial Opera in St. Petersburg. He was already on his way to Russia when his ballet *Il sotterraneo* was presented in Venice (Nov. 16, 1799). He remained in St. Petersburg for the rest of his life. His Russian debut as a composer was in a collaborative opera *Russalka* (adapted from *Das Donauweibchen* by F. Kauer). This was followed by the operas *The Invisible Prince* (1805); *Three Hunchback Brothers* (1808) and several ballets. His most significant work was *Ivan Susanin,* which he conducted at the Imperial Theater on Oct. 30, 1815. The subject of this opera was used 20 years later by Glinka in his great opera *A Life for the Tsar;* the boldness of Cavos in selecting a libretto from Russian history provided the necessary stimulus for Glinka and other Russian composers. (Cavos conducted the première of Glinka's opera.) His subsequent operas were also based on Russian themes: *Dobrynia Nikitich* (1818) and *The Firebird* (1822). Cavos was a notable voice teacher; among his pupils were several Russian singers who later became famous (Ossip Petrov, Anna Vorobyova, etc.).

Cebotari, Maria, soprano; b. Kishinev, Bessarabia, Feb. 10, 1910; d. Vienna, June 9, 1949. She studied in Germany; made her debut in Dresden as Mimi; 1947-48, toured widely in Europe. During her brief career she was greatly admired. See A. Mingotti, *Maria Cebotari, Das Leben einer Sängerin* (Salzburg, 1950).

Čelanský (chĕh-lahn'-skē), **Ludvík Vitězslav,** Czech conductor and composer; b. Vienna, July 17, 1870; d. Prague, Oct. 27, 1931. He studied at the Prague Cons.; then conducted theater orchestras in Pilsen and Zagreb. Returning to Prague, he organized the Czech Philharmonic Orch. (1901) and led it for several seasons; also conducted opera and concerts abroad (Kiev, Lwow, Paris, etc.). He wrote an opera *Camille* (Prague, Oct. 23, 1897); a symph. trilogy, *Adam, Noë, Moïse* (1915-19); church music; songs. A valedictory brochure, ed. by V. Balthasar, was publ. in honor of his 50th birthday (Prague, 1920).

Celibidache, Sergiu, Rumanian conductor; b. Roman, June 28, 1912. He studied musicology and conducting in Berlin with Fritz Stein and Tiessen; conducted the Berlin Philh. (1945); then in London (1949), Mexico (1950), and again in Europe. He published (in German) several treatises on composing; also a monograph on Josquin des Prez; composed 4 symphonies and a piano concerto.

Cellier (sĕl-yā'), **Alfred,** English conductor and composer; b. (of French parents) London, Dec. 1, 1844; d. there, Dec. 28, 1891. He was a chorister at St. James' Chapel Royal; studied music with Thomas Helmore; in 1866 conductor at Belfast of the Ulster Hall concerts and the Philharmonic; from 1871-5 at the Prince's Theatre, Manchester; from 1877-9 at the London Opéra-Comique; and (with Sullivan) at the Promenade Concerts in Covent Garden. He then spent some years in America and Australia, returning to London in 1887. He wrote a number of light operas: *Charity Begins at Home* (London, 1870); *The Foster Brothers* (London, June 17, 1873); *The Sultan of Mocha* (Manchester, Nov. 16, 1874); *The Tower of London* (Manchester, Oct. 4, 1875); *Nell Gwynne* (Manchester, Oct. 16, 1876); *Dora's Dream* (London, Nov. 17, 1877); *The Spectre Knight* (London, Feb. 9, 1878); *Bella Donna or The Little Beauty and the Great Beast* (Manchester, April 27, 1878); *After All* (London, Dec. 16, 1878); *In the Sulks* (London, Feb. 21, 1880); *The Masque of Pandora,* after Longfellow (Boston, Mass., Jan. 10, 1881); *The Carp* (London, Feb. 11, 1886); *Dorothy* (London, Sept. 25, 1886); *Mrs. Jarramie's Genie* (London, Feb. 14, 1888); *Doris* (London, April 20, 1889); *The Mountebanks* (London, Jan. 4, 1892); also a setting of Gray's *Elegy,* written for the Leeds Festival (Oct. 10, 1883); a symphonic suite; many popular songs.

Černohorsky. See **Czernohorsky.**

Černušák (chĕr-noo-shăk), **Gracian,** Czech music lexicographer; b. Ptení, near Prostějov, Moravia, Dec. 19, 1882. He studied in Prague and Cracow; taught music in Brno (1918-38); in 1945 was appointed prof. at the music academy there. With Vladimir Helfert he undertook the publication of a music dictionary, but only the first volume (to the letter K) of the projected two was published (Brno, 1937). He also wrote a history of music for schools (2 vols.; Prague, 1910; 2nd ed., Brno, 1931); also a survey of music history (2 vols., Brno, 1947).

Cerone (chĕh-roh'-nĕ), **Domenico Pietro,** Italian tenor and music theorist; b. Bergamo, c. 1560; d. Naples, 1625. In 1592 he went to Spain, and became a singer in the court choir; later appointed teacher of plainsong to the clergy of the church of the Annunciation at Naples; from 1610 until his death sang in the Royal Chapel Choir there. He published the manual *Regole per il canto fermo* (Naples, 1609), and *El Melopeo y Maestro, tractado de música teórica y práctica* (Naples, 1613). This treatise, written in Spanish, numbers 1160 pages, containing a compendium of early music theory; it is divided into 22 books and 849 chapters; its pedantic exposition and inordinate length were the main target of Eximeno's satirical novel *Don Lazarillo Vizcardi;* Book XII was published in English in O. Strunk's *Source Readings in Music History* (N. Y., 1950); in the U. S., copies of the entire work are to be found in the Library of Congress, the N. Y. Public Library, the Hispanic Society of N. Y., and the Sibley Music Library, Rochester, N. Y.—Bibl.: F. Pedrell, *P. Antonio Eximeno* (includes chapters on Cerone; 1920); G. Pannain, *L'Oratorio dei Filippini* (1934); Ruth Hannas, *Cerone, Philosopher and Teacher,* in the 'Mus. Quarterly' (Oct., 1935) and *Cerone's Approach to the Teaching of Counterpoint* in the 'Papers of the American Musicological Society' (1937).

Cerreto (chăr-rā'-toh), **Scipione,** Italian composer, lutenist and theorist; b. Naples, 1551; d. there, c. 1632. He published two theoretical works containing valuable information on the music and musical instruments of his time: *Della prattica musica vocale e strumentale* (Naples, 1601), and *Arbore musicale* (Naples, 1608); a third work, *Dialogo harmonico,* remained unpublished (two forms, 1628 and 1631).

Certon (săr-tŏhn'), **Pierre,** French contrapuntist; b. c. 1510; d. Paris, Feb. 22, 1572. He was a pupil of Josquin des Prez; was choirmaster of the Sainte-Chapelle in Paris (about 1532); composed masses, motets, psalms, magnificats and 4-part chansons, which were printed in the collections of Ballard, Attaignant, Susato, Phalèse and others between 1527 and 1560. Reprints of his masses (*Sur le pont d'Avignon; Adjuva me; Regnum mundi*) are to be found in H. Expert's *Monuments de la musique française au temps de la Renaissance,* vol. 2 (1925). See M. Brenet, *Les Musiciens de la Sainte-Chapelle* (Paris, 1910).

Cervantes (Kawanag), Ignacio, Cuban pianist and composer; b. Havana, July 31, 1847; d. there, April 29, 1905. He studied with Gottschalk (1859-61) and at the Paris Cons. (1866-68), with Alkan and Marmontel; in 1870 returned to Cuba; in 1898 went to Mexico; also visited the U. S. He was one of the pioneers of native Cuban music; in his *Danzas Cubanas* for piano he employs Cuban rhythms in an effective salon manner; also wrote an opera, *Maledetto* (1895), and some orchestral pieces. Bibl.: E. Sánchez de Fuentes, *Ignacio Cervantes Kawanag* (Havana, 1936); Alejo Carpentier, *La música en Cuba* (Mexico, 1946).

Červený (chär'-vā-nē), **Wenzel Franz,** inventor of brass instruments; b. Dubeč, Bohemia, Sept. 27, 1819; d. Königgrätz, Jan. 19, 1896. He was a good performer on most brass instruments when he was only twelve years old; learned his trade with Bauer, a music instrument maker in Prague; worked at various times in Brünn, Bratislava, Vienna and Budapest; in 1842 established his own shop at Königgrätz. He invented the following instruments: Cornon (1844), Contrabass (1845), Phonikon (1848), Baroxiton (1853), Contrafagotto in metal (1856), Althorn obbligato (1859), Turnerhorn, Jägerhorn, army Trombones (1867), and Primhorn (1873). After the success of the Primhorn, he created the complete Waldhorn quartet, which he considered his greatest achievement. Then followed the Subcontrabass and the Subcontrafagotto; and finally an entire family of improved Cornets ('Kaiserkornette') and the 'Triumph' Cornet. His 'roller' cylinder-mechanism is an invention of the greatest importance. He also improved the Euphonion, the Russian Signal-horns, the Screw-drum and the church kettledrums. His instruments took first prizes at exhibitions in Europe and America. After 1876 the firm became known as 'W. F. Cerveny & Söhne'.

Cervetto (chär-vet'-toh), **Giacomo** (real name Bassevi), distinguished cellist; b. Italy, c. 1682; d. London, Jan. 14, 1783. He settled in London in 1728, where he was a player and then manager of the Drury Lane Theatre. He lived to be 100 years old. His son, **Giacomo** (b. London, 1747; d. there, Feb. 5, 1837), was a fine cellist and concert player; published soli for violin, and duets for violin and cello.

Cesana (chā-zăh'-năh), **Otto,** composer; b. Brescia, Italy, July 7, 1899. He came to the U. S. as a young boy; studied music with Julius Gold; was active as staff composer and arranger for various film studios in Hollywood; later settled in New York, where he was engaged as music arranger for the Radio City Music Hall and for several radio programs. Works: 6 symphonies; *Negro Heaven* for orch.; 6 concertos (for clarinet, trumpet, trombone, piano, 2 pianos, 3 pianos with orch.); a ballet, *Ali Baba and the 40 Thieves; Swing Septet* (Indianapolis, Jan. 23, 1942). He is the author of several theoretical books, including *Course in Modern Harmony* (1939); *Course in Counterpoint* (1940); *Voicing the Modern Dance Orchestra* (1946).

Cesari, Gaetano, Italian musicologist; b. Cremona, June 24, 1870; d. Sale Marasino, Oct. 21, 1934. First a double-bass player in an Italian opera orch.; later a pupil of Krug in Hamburg, Mottl at the Academy of Music in Munich, and Sandberger and Kroyer at the Univ. there; teacher of music history at the Istituto Manzoni in Milan; 1917-24, librarian at the Liceo Verdi; then critic of the 'Corriere della Sera,' and docent at the Univ. of Milan.—Publications: *Die Entstehung des Madrigals im 16. Jahrhundert* (in German, Cremona, 1908; in Italian, in 'Rivista Musicale Italiana', 1912); *Giorgio Giulini musicista* (Milan, 1916); the very valuable *Musica e musicisti alla Corte Sforzesca* in the 'Rivista Musicale Italiana' (1922); *Lezioni di storia della musica* (vol. I only published; Milan, 1931); *Amilcare Ponchielli nell' arte del suo tempo* (Cremona, 1934); also wrote the preface to vol. II (works of Giovanni Gabrieli) and edited vol. VI (works of Ingegneri and Monteverdi) of the 'Istituzioni e Monumenti dell' arte musicale italiana'; he was working on a complete edition of Monteverdi at the time of his death. In collaboration with A. Luzio, he publ. the important source book, *I copialettere di Verdi* (1913). His *Scritti inediti* were publ. posthumously (Milan, 1937).

Cesi (chĕh'-sē), **Beniamino,** Italian pianist and pedagogue; b. Naples, Nov. 6, 1845; d. there, Jan. 19, 1907. First a pupil of his father and Albanesi, then of Mercadante and Pappalardo at the Naples Cons., and finally of Thalberg; from the age of 18 he gave concerts throughout Italy, and in the principal cities of Europe and in Egypt; 1866-85, piano prof. at the Royal Collegio of Naples; 1885, at the invitation of Rubinstein, became instructor at the St. Petersburg Cons., resigned in 1891 because of ill health; 1894, taught at Palermo Cons.; 1895, returned to Naples Cons., where he taught a chamber music class until his death. Among his many pupils were his sons, Napoleone and Sigismondo (both pianists and composers), also G. Martucci, Cilea, A. Longo, and others. He publ. an important

Metodo per pianoforte (3 parts), chamber works for voice, piano pieces, and numerous transcriptions for piano; also wrote a lyric opera, *Vittor Pisani.* Cf. A. Longo, *B. Cesi,* in 'L'Arte pianistica' (Jan. 1914).

Cesti (cheh'-stē), **Marc' Antonio** (real baptismal name, Pietro), renowned dramatic composer; b. Arezzo, Aug. 5, 1623; d. Florence, Oct. 14, 1669. As a boy, he entered the Minorite monastic order; was probably a pupil of Carissimi at Rome in 1640-45; later was maestro di cappella to Ferdinand II de' Medici, at Florence; 1660, tenor singer in the Papal choir; 1666-68, assistant Kapellmeister to the Emperor Leopold I, at Vienna; then returned to Florence. His first opera, *Orontea* (Venice, Jan. 20, 1649), was much applauded; other dramatic ventures were also successful; *Cesare amante* (Venice, 1651); *Argia* (Innsbruck, 1655); *Dori* (Florence, 1661; selections printed in vol. XII of 'Publikationen der Gesellschaft für Musikforschung'); *Il Principe generoso* (Vienna, 1665; authorship disputed); *Tito* (Venice, Feb. 13, 1666); *Nettuno e Flora festeggianti* (Vienna, July 12, 1666); *Il Pomo d'oro* (Vienna, 1667; published in its entirety in 'Denkmäler der Tonkunst in Österreich', III, 2 and IV, 2); *Semiramide* (Vienna, June 9, 1667); *Le disgrazie d'Amore* (Vienna, 1667); *Argene* (Venice, 1668); *Genserico* (Venice, Jan. 31, 1669). Cesti wrote numerous cantatas which are preserved in various European libraries; his dramatic flair was reflected in the theatrical forms of his cantatas; he also wrote madrigals, songs, etc. A. Schering's *Geschichte der Musik in Beispielen* contains an aria from *Argia* (No. 203); H. Riemann's 'Kantaten-Frühling' (Leipzig, 1912; No. 9), F. Vatielli's 'Antiche cantate d'amore' (Bologna, 1920; No. 8), and G. Adler's 'Handbuch' (2nd ed. 1930; p. 439 ff.) each contain a solo-cantata by Cesti. Bibl.: H. Kretzschmar, *Die venezianische Oper und die Werke Cavallis und Cestis,* in 'Vierteljahrsschrift für Musikwissenschaft' (1892); E. Wellesz, *Ein Bühnenfestspiel aus dem 17. Jahrhundert,* in 'Sämmelbande der internationalen Musik-Gesellschaft,' XV (1913; p. 134 ff.); F. Coradini, *Padre A. Cesti, Nuove notizie biografiche,* in the 'Rivista Musicale Italiana' (July, 1923; very valuable for biographical documentation); A. Sandberger, in the bulletin of the 'Union Musicologique' (1925; pp. 121-73); P. Nettl, *Ein verschollenes Tournierballett von M. A. Cesti,* in the 'Zeitschrift für Musikwissenschaft' (April, 1926); A. Tessier, *L'Orontée de Lorenzani et l'Orontea du Padre Cesti,* in 'La Revue Musicale', IX, 8 (1928).

Chabrier (shah-br'yā'), **(Alexis-) Emmanuel,** famous French composer; b. Ambert, Puy de Dôme, Jan. 18, 1841; d. Paris, Sept. 13, 1894. He studied law in Paris; later harmony with Semet and Hignard, and piano with Édouard Wolff. He served in the government from 1862; at the same time cultivated his musical tastes; with Duparc, Vincent d'Indy and others he formed a private group of music lovers, and was an enthusiastic admirer of Wagner. He began to compose in earnest, and produced two light operas: *L'Étoile* (Paris, Nov. 28, 1877) and *Une Éducation manquée* (Paris, 1879). In 1879 he went to Germany with Duparc to hear Wagner's operas; returning to Paris he published some piano pieces; then traveled to Spain; the fruit of this journey was his most famous work, the rhapsody *España* (1883), which produced a sensation when performed by Lamoureux in 1884. Another work of Spanish inspiration was the *Habanera* for piano (1885). In the meantime he served as chorus master for Lamoureux; this experience developed his knowledge of vocal writing; he wrote a brief cantata for mezzo-soprano and women's chorus, *La sulamite* (1884), and his two operas *Gwendoline* (Brussels, April 10, 1886) and *Le roi malgré lui* (Opéra-Comique, Paris, May 18, 1887); another opera *Briséis* remained unfinished. In his operas Chabrier attempted a grand style; his idiom oscillated between passionate Wagnerianism and a more conventional type of French stage music; although these operas enjoyed a *succès d'estime,* they never became popular, and Chabrier's place in music history is secured exclusively by his *España,* and piano pieces such as *Bourrée fantasque* (1891; orchestrated by Felix Mottl); his *Joyeuse Marche* for orch. (originally entitled *Marche française,* 1888) is also popular. Other works are *Ode à la musique* for voices and orch. (1890); *Dix Pièces pittoresques* for piano (1880; four of them orchestrated and performed as *Suite pastorale*); *Trois Valses romantiques* for two pianos (1883); songs.—Bibl.: O. Séré, *E. Chabrier,* in *Musiciens français d'aujourd'hui* (Paris, 1911); René Martineau, *E. Chabrier* (Paris, 1911); G. Servières, *E. Chabrier* (Paris, 1912); A. Cortot, *L'œuvre pianistique de E. Chabrier,* in 'La Revue musicale' (Oct., 1926); Joseph Desaymard, *Chabrier d'après ses lettres* (Paris, 1934); J.-G. Prod'homme, *Chabrier in his Letters,* in the 'Mus. Quarterly' (Oct., 1935).

Chadwick, George Whitefield, eminent American composer; b. Lowell, Mass., Nov. 13, 1854; d. Boston, April 4, 1931. He first studied music with Eugene Thayer in Boston; then became head of the music department at Olivet College in Michigan (1876); from 1877-8 studied at the Leipzig Cons. with Reinecke and Jadassohn; his graduation piece was an overture to *Rip Van Winkle,* which he conducted with the Leipzig Cons. Orch. on June 20, 1879; then studied organ and composition at Munich under Rheinberger; in 1880 returned to Boston as organist of the South Congregational Church and teacher of harmony and composition at the New England Cons.; in 1897 succeeded Faelten as director. He received the honorary degree of M.A. from Yale, and an honorary LL.D. from Tufts College in 1905; received the Gold Medal of the Academy of Arts and Letters in 1928; for several seasons was conductor of the Worcester Music Festival; also head of music festivals in Springfield and Worcester, Mass.; was a member of the Boston Academy of Arts and Letters. Chadwick was one of the leading American composers; usually regarded as a pillar of the 'Boston Classicists', he was actually an ardent romanticist; his musical style was formed under the influence of the German programmatic school; his harmonies are Wagnerian, his orchestration full and lush. A list of his chief works follows: For the stage: the comic operas *The Quiet Lodging* (privately performed, Boston, 1892) and *Tabasco* (Boston, Jan. 29, 1894); *Judith,* lyric drama (Worcester Festival, Sept. 26, 1901); *The Padrone* (1915), opera; *Love's Sacrifice,* pastoral operetta (1916); incidental music to *Everywoman* (N. Y. and London, 1911). For orch.: three symphonies: I, in C; II, in B♭ (Boston Symph., Dec. 11, 1886); III, in F (Boston Symph., Oct. 20, 1894); the overtures *Rip Van Winkle, Thalia, The Miller's Daughter, Melpomene* (Boston, Dec. 24, 1887; also arranged for piano 4 hands), *Adonais* (Boston, Feb. 3, 1900), *Euterpe* (Boston Symph., April 23, 1904; composer cond.), and *Anniversary Overture* (Norfolk Festival, 1922); Serenade in F for string orch.; *A Pastoral Prelude* (Boston, 1894); Sinfonietta in D (Boston, Nov. 21, 1904); the symphonic poems *Cleopatra* (Worcester Festival, 1905) and *Angel of Death* (N. Y., 1919); *Symphonic Sketches,* suite (*Jubilee, Noël, Hobgoblin,* and *A Vagrom Ballad;* Boston Symph., Feb. 7, 1908); Theme, Variations and Fugue for organ and orch. (Boston, 1908; arranged by J. Wallace Goodrich for organ solo); *Suite symphonique* (Philadelphia, 1911; first prize of the National Federation of Music Clubs); *Aphrodite,* symph. fantasy (Norfolk Festival, 1912); *Tam O'Shanter,* symph. ballad (Norfolk Festival, 1915). Choral works: *Dedication Ode* (1886) for soli, chorus and orch.; *Lovely Rosabelle,* ballad for solo, chorus and orch. (Boston, 1889); *The Pilgrims* for chorus and orch. (Boston, 1891); *Ode for the Opening of the Chicago World's Fair,* for chorus with piano or orch. (1892); *Phoenix Expirans,* for soli, chorus and orch. (Springfield Festival, 1892); *The Lily Nymph,* cantata (1893); *Lochinvar,* for baritone and orch. (Springfield Festival, 1897); *Noël,* Christmas pastoral for soli, chorus and orch. (Norfolk Festival, 1908); *Aghadoe,* ballad for alto and orch.; numerous sacred works: *Ecce jam noctis* (Yale, 1897); *The Beatitudes; Jubilate;* etc.; many choruses for men's, women's, and mixed voices; also school choruses. Chamber music: 5 string quartets (I, in G minor; II, in C; III, in D; IV, in E minor; V, in D minor); piano quintet (1888); violin and cello pieces; etc. He composed about 100 songs with piano, organ or orch. (*Allah, Ballad of the Trees and Masters, The Danza, Before the Dawn,* etc.). Organ works: *10 Canonic Studies for Organ* (1885); *Progressive Pedal Studies for Organ* (1890); miscellaneous pieces (*Requiem, Suite in Variation Form,* etc.); also numerous piano pieces. He was the author of *Harmony, A Course of Study* (Boston, 1897; revised ed., 1922) and *Key to the Textbook on Harmony* (Boston, 1902); was co-editor of *A Book of Choruses for High Schools and Choral Societies* (N. Y., 1923). For a full list of works, dates of composition, performance and publication, see C. Engel, *G. W. Chadwick,* in the 'Mus. Quarterly' (July, 1924); also A. L. Langley, *Chadwick and the New England Conservatory,* in the 'Mus. Quarterly' (Jan., 1935).

Chaffin, Lucien Gates, American organist and composer; b. Worcester, Mass., March 23, 1846; d. New York, May 26, 1927. He studied at Brown Univ. (graduated, 1867); was active as a language teacher; studied music in Boston with Eugene Thayer; was organist in various churches in Boston, Buffalo and New York; was music editor of the Buffalo 'Express' (1879-83) and the N. Y. 'Commercial Advertiser' (1884-90); lectured on music and contributed articles to various musical publications. He composed a cantata, *Holy Night;* many pieces for organ and piano; songs; made numerous arrangements for church of works by Grieg, Cornelius, Poldini, etc.; published a manual, *Song-writing and Song-making* (N. Y., 1923).

Chaikovsky. See **Tchaikovsky.**

Chaix (shā), **Charles,** French teacher and composer; b. Paris, March 26, 1885. He studied at the École Niedermeyer, Paris; then at the Geneva Cons., where he later taught theory (1909-24), counterpoint (1927) and composition (1937). He has written 2 symphonies (1914; 1928); Scherzo for orch. (1910); *Poème funèbre* for soli, chorus and orch. (1922); piano quintet (1941); chorale for oboe and string orch. (1944); string quartet (1948); also works for unaccompanied chorus. He edited Rousseau's opera *Le Devin du Village* for the Édition Nationale Suisse (1924); published a treatise on harmony, *Éléments d'écriture musicale* (1935).

Chajes (chā'-hās), **Julius,** composer; b. Lwow, Poland, Dec. 21, 1910. He studied piano with Richard Robert and Hedwig Rosenthal in Vienna; composition with Hugo Kauder; in 1933 won a prize at the International Contest for pianists in Vienna; from 1934-36 taught piano at the Tel-Aviv Cons., Israel; in 1937 came to the U. S.; from 1939-40 taught at the N. Y. College of Music; then became director of music at the Jewish Community Center in Detroit (from 1940). Works: *Fantasy* for piano and orch. (Vienna Radio, Oct. 9, 1928, composer soloist); cello concerto (Karlsbad, Aug. 5, 1932); *142nd Psalm* for soli, chorus and strings (Jüdischer Kulturbund, Berlin, June, 1937; 1st American perf., N. Y., May 18, 1944); piano concerto (Vienna Radio, Nov. 25, 1953; Detroit Symph., Dec. 17, 1953, composer soloist); several cantatas on biblical subjects; string quartet; piano trio; piano pieces; arrangements of Israeli folksongs for choir (awarded the prize of the Jewish Cultural Association, Berlin, 1937).

Chaliapin, Feodor. See **Shaliapin.**

Challier (shăhl-yā'), **Ernst,** German music publisher; b. Berlin, July 9, 1843; d. Giessen, Sept. 19, 1914. His company, located in Berlin, published songs, duets, and trios.

Chalmers, Donald, American bass; b. in Pennsylvania, Aug. 4, 1879; d. Wannamassa, N. J., May 16, 1937. He toured the U. S. with E. Schumann-Heink in 1912, and sang at many music festivals with Nordica and Melba; organized the Criterion Quartet of New York; from 1917-37 was director of the Ocean Grove Auditorium.

Chamberlain, Houston Stewart, English writer on music; b. Portsmouth, Sept. 9, 1855; d. Bayreuth, Jan. 9, 1927. He received his earliest education at Versailles, and then studied at Cheltenham College, Gloucester. Because of ill health he was obliged to abandon his intention of following a military career (his father was a British admiral), and in 1870 he went to Stettin. His association with Prof. Kuntze there filled him with enthusiasm for Germanic culture and civilization, to the study of which he devoted many years. The results of these studies he published in a remarkable work, *Die Grundlagen des 19. Jahrhunderts* (Munich, 1899-1901; 10th ed. 1914; English translation by Lord Redesdale, London, 1910). The years 1879-81 he spent in Geneva, studying science at the Univ. (taking his degree with the dissertation *Recherches sur la sève ascendante*) and music with A. Ruthardt. During his residence at Dresden (1885-9) he began his activities as contributor to various German, French and English journals, writing with equal facility in three languages. From 1889-1908 he lived in Vienna. In the latter year he married Wagner's daughter, Eva, then lived in Bayreuth. Chamberlain was one of the most ardent and influential apostles of Wagner's art, a man of deep penetration and keen analytical power. His great Wagner biography is, in fact, rather a profound psychological study than a mere record of events. Besides books dealing with literature and philosophy Chamberlin published the following: *Das Drama Richard Wagners* (Leipzig, 1892; 6th ed., 1921; French translation 1894; English translation 1915); *Richard Wagner. Echte Briefe an F. Praeger* (Bayreuth, 1894; 2d ed. 1908); *Richard Wagner* (Munich, 1896; 9th ed. 1936; English translation 1897; French translation 1899); *Die ersten 20 Jahre der Bayreuther Bühnenfestspiele* (Bayreuth, 1896); *Parsifalmärchen* (Munich, 1900; 3rd ed. 1916); *Lebenswege meines Denkens,* autobiography (1919).—Cf. L. von Schroeder, *Houston Stewart Chamberlain* (1918); Anna Chamberlain (his first wife, married 1878, divorced 1908), *Meine Erinnerungen an Houston Stewart Chamberlain* (1923).

Chambonnières (shăhn-bŏhn-yär), **Jacques Champion** (called **Champion de Chambonnières**), French clavecinist and composer, b. c. 1602; d. Paris, 1672. He was first chamber musician to Louis XIV, and the teacher of the elder Couperins, d'Anglebert, Le Bègue, Hardelle and others. Considered the founder of the French clavecin school, he was famed throughout Europe, and his style strongly influenced that of contemporary German composers, among them Froberger. Two books of his clavecin pieces were printed (1670). H. Quittard publ. his complete works. A complete edition of his clavecin pieces was brought out by Brunold and Tessier in 1926.—Bibl.: H. Quittard, *Chambonnières,* in the 'Revue Internationale de Musique' (1898; no. 12); H. Quittard, *Un claveciniste français du XVII*[e] *siècle: Jacques Champion de Chambonnières,* in 'Tribune de St. Gervais' (1901).

Chaminade (shăh-mē-năhd'), **Cécile (-Louise-Stéphanie)**, French composer and pianist; b. Paris, Aug. 8, 1857; d. Monte Carlo, April 18, 1944. She was a pupil of Lecouppey, Savard and Marsick; later studied composition with Benjamin Godard. She became successful as a concert pianist; wrote a great number of agreeable piano pieces, in the salon style, which acquired enormous popularity in France, England and America; her more serious works were much less successful. She made her American debut playing the piano part of her *Concertstück* with the Philadelphia Orch. (Nov. 7, 1908); also wrote a lyric symphony, *Les Amazones* (Antwerp, 1888); two orchestral suites; 2 piano trios; more than 200 piano pieces in a romantic style, including *Étude symponique, Valse-Caprice, Les Sylvains, La Lisonjera, Arabesque, Impromptu, Six Airs de ballet,* etc.; numerous songs.

Chamlee, Mario (real name, Archer Cholmondeley), American lyric tenor; b. Los Angeles, May 29, 1892. He studied at the Univ. of Southern California (M. Mus., 1924); then voice with Achille Alberti in Los Angeles and with Riccardo Dellera in N. Y.; made his operatic debut as the Duke in *Rigoletto* (San Francisco Opera, 1917); from 1917-19 served with the U. S. Army in France; married the soprano Ruth Miller on Oct. 2, 1919; first appeared with the Metropolitan Opera as Cavaradossi in *Tosca* (Nov. 22, 1920); also sang at Ravinia Park, Chicago, and at various European opera houses (London, Paris, Prague, Vienna); made extensive concert tours of the U. S., and many radio broadcasts; in 1940 settled in Hollywood as a voice teacher.

Champagne, Claude, Canadian composer; b. Montreal, May 27, 1891. He studied violin, piano and composition in Montreal; in Paris (1920-28) with Gédalge and Laparra. His works comprise *Suite Canadienne* for chorus and orch. (Paris, Oct. 20, 1928); 2 symphonies (1945, 1951); piano concerto (1948) and numerous violin pieces. He has also published several manuals on solfeggio.

Champein (shăhn-păn'), **Stanislas,** French composer; b. Marseilles, Nov. 19, 1753; d. Paris, Sept. 19, 1830. He studied under Peccico and Chavet in Paris; at 13 he became maître de musique at the Collegiate Church at Pignon, for which he wrote a magnificat, a mass, and psalms; in 1770 he went to Paris, where some sacred works, and two operettas, made his name known. Up to 1792 he produced 22 operas, the best of which were *La Mélomanie* (1781); *Les Dettes* (1787); and *Le nouveau Don Quichotte* (1789). From 1793-1804 he filled a government position; continued to compose for the stage, but without success; spent the last years of his life in poverty; a pension, arranged for him through the efforts of Boieldieu and Scribe, came only 18 months before his death. Though one of the best known stage composers of his time, Champein's works are wholly forgotten.

Champion, Jacques. See **Chambonnières.**

Chanler, Theodore Ward, American composer; b. Newport, Rhode Island, April 29, 1902. He studied in Boston with Hans Ebell (piano) and with Arthur Shepherd (composition); then at the Cleveland Institute of Music with Ernest Bloch; later went to England where he took courses at Oxford Univ. (1923-25); also studied with Nadia Boulanger in Paris. He returned to America in 1933. His music, mostly in smaller forms, is distinguished by a lyrical quality; his songs are particularly expressive; he employed the modern idiom of polytonal texture without overloading the harmonic possibilities; the melody is free, but usually within tonal bounds. Works: Mass for two female voices and organ (1930); 2 song-cycles *Epitaphs* (1937); *Pas de Trois,* ballet; *Ann Gregory,* for chorus; *Joyful Mystery,* fugue for two pianos; *The Children,* song-cycle; violin sonata (1927); *Five Short Colloquies,* piano suite (1936); *The Pot of Fat,* chamber opera (Cambridge, Mass., May 8, 1955).

Chanot (shăh-noh'), **François,** French violin maker; b. Mirecourt, 1787; d. Brest, 1823. He was the son of an instrument-maker; became a naval engineer, was retired on half-pay, and during his forced inactivity invented a violin, made on the principle that the vibratory power would be increased by preserving the longitudinal wood-fibres intact as far as possible. Thus his violin had no bouts, but slight incurvations like a guitar; the sound-holes were almost straight, and the belly nearly flat; the strings were attached to the edge of the belly, instead of to a tail-piece. The violin was submitted to the Academy, whose report after testing it rated it equally with those of Stradivari and Guarneri; despite this evaluation, Chanot's violin never became popular. His brother, a *luthier* at Paris, manufactured a number of them, but gave it up when a few years had demonstrated their unpractical character.

Chantavoine (shăhn'-tăh-vwăhn'), **Jean,** French writer on music; b. Paris, May 17, 1877; d. Mussy-sur-Seine, July 16, 1952. He studied the history of music with Friedländer in Berlin (1898; 1901-2); from 1903-20 was music critic of 'Revue Hebdomadaire" and 'Excelsior' (1911-21); contributed music criticism to other journals, and was one of the editors (1911) of 'L'Année Musicale'; from 1921-23 lived in Wiesbaden as a member of the International Commission for the Rhine Province; in 1923 was appointed General Secretary of the Paris Cons. He edited the biographical series 'Les Maîtres de la Musique', to which he contributed the monographs on Beethoven (1906) and Liszt (1910; 3rd ed., 1913). Further writings: *Musiciens et Poètes* (Paris, 1912; contains an account of Liszt's early opera, *Don Sanche,* the score of which was found by Chantavoine); *De Couperin à Debussy* (1921); *Les symphonies de Beethoven* (1932); *Petit guide de l'auditeur de musique* (Paris, 1947); *Mozart dans Mozart* (1948). He published for the first time the scores and piano arrangements of Beethoven's twelve minuets for orch. (written, 1799; discovered by R. von Perger in 1872); also edited Beethoven's *Prometheus.*

Chapí y Lorente (chah-pē' ē loh-rĕn'-tĕh), **Ruperto;** Spanish composer of light opera; b. Villena, near Alicante, March 27, 1851; d. Madrid, March 25, 1909. He studied at the Cons. of Madrid; received a stipend from the Spanish Academy for further study in Rome (1874); wrote some operas (*La hija de Jefte, La hija de Garcilaso,* etc.), but discovered that his talent found more suitable expression in the lighter zarzuela, in which form his first success was won with *La Tempestad* (1882); his work is noted for elegance, grace and exquisite orchestration; of one of his last zarzuelas (*La Revoltosa*) Saint-Saëns remarked that Bizet would have been proud to sign his name to the score. His last zarzuela, *Margarita la Tornera* (Madrid, Feb. 24, 1909) was produced shortly before his death. Chapí y Lorente wrote 155 zarzuelas and 6 operas. In 1893 he founded the Sociedad de Autores, Compositores y Editores de Música.

Chapman, William Rogers, American choral conductor; b. Hanover, Mass., Aug. 4, 1855; d. Palm Beach, Florida, Mar. 27, 1935. He was a chorus-leader and conductor in New York; founder and conductor of the Apollo (male voices) and Rubinstein (female voices) Clubs, and from 1903 conductor of the annual Maine Festival at Bangor and Portland; wrote church music, choral works, piano pieces, songs, etc.

Chappell & Co., Ltd., London music publishers, concert agents, and piano manufacturers. Founded in 1810 by Samuel Chappell, J. B. Cramer (the pianist), and F. T. Latour. Cramer retired in 1819, Latour in 1826, and S. Chappell died in 1834, when his son **William** (1809-88) became the head of the firm. In 1840 he established the Musical Antiquarian Society, for which he edited Dowland's songs; he also edited and publ. *A Collection of National English Airs* (2 vols., 1838-9), later enlarged as *Popular Music of the Olden Time* (2 vols., 1855-9; revised by H. E. Wooldridge and publ. in 2 vols., 1893); he left an unfinished *History of Music* (vol. I, London, 1874). His brothers, **Thomas Patey** (1819-1902) and **S. Arthur** (1834-1904), were respectively the founder and manager of the Monday and Saturday Popular Concerts. In 1897 the partnership became a limited company, and Thomas was succeeded by his son, **T. Stanley** (d. 1933), as board chairman; later, William Boosey became managing director. In 1929 the firm was acquired by Louis Dreyfus.—The American branch, under the direction of Max Dreyfus, brother of Louis, has publ. the songs and musical comedies of Richard Rodgers, Jerome Kern, Cole Porter, Harold Arlen, and other popular composers.

Chapple, Stanley, English-American conductor; b. London, Oct. 29, 1900. He studied at the Royal Academy of Music; became accompanist with the British National Opera Co. (1918-21); musical director of the Vocalion Gramophone Co. (1924-29) and opera conductor at the Guildhall School of Music (1935-39). He also conducted at the BBC (1937-39). He had, meanwhile, been making annual summer appearances in the U. S. (1929-39) and was assistant conductor at the Berkshire Music Center (1939-47); also conductor of the St. Louis Civic Chorus (1946-48). In 1948 he became director of the School of Music at the Univ. of Washington in Seattle.

Chapuis (shăh-püē'), **Auguste-Paul-Jean-Baptiste,** French composer; b. Dampierre-sur-Salon (Haute-Saône), April 20, 1858; d. Paris, Dec. 6, 1933. He was a pupil of Dubois (harmony), Massenet (counterpoint), and César Franck (organ and composition) at Paris Cons., taking 1st prize in harmony (1877), 1st prize for organ (1880), and the Rossini prize in 1885. From 1882-7, he was organist at Notre-Dame-des-Champs; then at Saint-Roch. From 1894, prof. of harmony at the Cons.; from 1895, Inspector-General of music instruction in the Paris schools.—Works: The 4-act lyric drama *Enguerrande* (Opéra-Comique, 1892; fiasco); *Les Demoiselles de Saint-Cyr* (Monte Carlo, 1921); *Yannel,* opera; *Les Ancêtres,* dramatic legend for soli, chorus and orch.; *Les jardins d'Armide,* dramatic cantata; incidental music to *Elen* (1894); *Tancred,* 3-act lyric drama (Opéra-Comique, 1898); an oratorio, *Les Sept Paroles du Christ;* Solemn Mass, for soli, chorus and orch.; several short masses with organ; motets; Fantaisie for orch.; chamber music; organ music; numerous songs; choruses for children's, women's, men's and mixed voices. Also published a *Traité d'Harmonie théorique et pratique.*

Char (kahr), **Friedrich Ernst (Fritz),** German composer and conductor; b. Cleve, May 3, 1865; d. Velden, Sept. 21, 1932. He studied with Wüllner at Cologne (1883-86); then held various posts as opera conductor. He wrote the text and music of a successful romantic opera *Der Schelm von Bergen* (Zwickau, 1895); cantata *Spielmann;* piano concerto; numerous piano pieces; song cycles.

Charles, Ernest, American composer; b. Minneapolis, Minn., Nov. 21, 1895. He studied voice with Charles Wood; from 1943-45 lived in Hollywood; 1945-47, was producer of the radio program 'Great Moments in Music' in N. Y.; in 1953 returned to Hollywood. He composed many successful songs, including *Clouds, My Lady walks in loveliness, Sweet song of long ago,* etc.

Charpentier (shar-păhn-t'yā'), **Gustave,** French composer; b. Dieuze, Lorraine, June 25, 1860; d. Paris, Feb. 18, 1956. He studied at the Paris Cons. (1881-7) with Massart (violin), Pessard (harmony), Massenet (composition), and took the Grand Prix de Rome in 1887 with the cantata *Didon.* Succeeded Massenet in 1912 as member of the Institute. Always interested in the welfare of the working classes, he founded, in 1900, the society 'L'œuvre de Mimi Pinson,' which he reorganized during World War I as an auxiliary Red Cross Society. He owes his fame to one amazingly successful opera, *Louise* (Paris, Feb. 2, 1900; Metropolitan Opera, Jan. 15, 1921), which has become a standard work in opera houses all over the world. This opera was conceived in the spirit of naturalism, and included such realistic touches as the street cries of Paris vendors. Nostalgic and sentimental, it has preserved its poetic appeal even to later generations. Other works by Charpentier are: an orchestral suite, *Impressions d'Italie* (1892); the songs *Les fleurs du mal* and *Quinze poèmes* (some of the latter with chorus and orch.); *Fausses Impressions,* for chorus and orch.; *Chant d'Apothéose; Sérénade à Watteau,* for chorus and orch.; an opera, *Julien* (Paris, Jan. 3, 1913; N. Y., 1914); symphonic drama *La Vie du Poète* (Paris Opéra, 1892); symph. poem *Napoli* (1891). A catalogue of Charpentier's works is to be found in 'Bollettino bibliografico musicale' vol. 5 (1930). Bibl.: O. Séré, *Gustave Charpentier,* in *Musiciens français d'aujourd'hui* (2nd ed. Paris, 1911); André Himonet, *Louise* (Paris, 1922); Marc Delmas, *Gustave Charpentier et le Lyrisme français* (Paris, 1931); K. O'D. Hoover, *Gustave Charpentier,* in the 'Mus. Quarterly' (July, 1939).

Charpentier, Marc-Antoine, French composer; b. Paris, 1634; d. there, Feb. 24, 1704. While he studied painting in Italy, his admiration for Carissimi's music led him to take up serious musical study with him. He then returned to Paris and was appointed maître de chapelle to the Dauphin, but lost the post through Lully's opposition. This episode so embittered Charpentier against Lully, that he totally eschewed Lully's style, often to the detriment of his own compositions. He was appointed maître de chapelle and music teacher to Mlle. de Guise; then intendant to the Duke of Orleans; maître de chapelle of the Jesuit collegial church and monastery; and maître de chapelle of Sainte-Chapelle, a post which he held until his death. He composed 16 operas and lesser works for the stage; several 'tragédies spirituelles' for the Jesuits; masses, motets, pastorales, drinking-songs, etc. It has been claimed that Charpentier was Lully's superior in learning, if not in inventive power; his oratorio *Le Reniement de Saint-Pierre* was revived in Paris with considerable success, and his pastorale, *La Couronne de fleurs,* edited by H. Busser, was published there in 1907.—Bibl.: M. Brenet, Preface to the *Concerts Spirituels* (publ. by Schola Cantorum); M. Brenet, *Les musiciens de la Sainte-Chapelle* (1910); H. Quittard, *Notes sur un ouvrage inédit de Marc-Antoine Charpentier,* in 'Zeitschrift der Internationalen Musikgesellschaft' (May, 1905); L. de La Laurencie, *Un opéra inédit de Marc-Antoine Charpentier, La descente d'Orfée,* in

'La Revue de Musicologie' (No. 31); C. Crussard, *Un Musicien français oublié, Marc-Antoine Charpentier* (Paris, 1945); H. Wiley Hitchcock, *The Latin Oratorios of Marc-Antoine Charpentier,* in the 'Mus. Quarterly' (Jan., 1955). Some works by Charpentier are reprinted in *Musique d'Église des XVII*e *et XVIII*e *siècles,* edited by Pineau.

Chase, Gilbert, American critic and musicologist; b. Havana, Cuba (of American parents), Sept. 4, 1906; studied piano in N. Y. and theory with Max Wald in Paris; from 1929-35 was music critic of London 'Daily Mail' (Continental Edition) in Paris; also Paris correspondent for 'Musical America' and the 'Musical Times'; associate editor of the *International Cyclopedia of Music and Musicians* (1938); associate editor of the 4th edition of Baker's *Biographical Dictionary of Musicians* (1940); from 1940-43 was consultant on Spanish and Latin American music at the Library of Congress (Washington); 1947-48, music supervisor at the NBC 'Univ. of the Air' in New York; then manager of Education Department of RCA Victor (Camden, N. J.); instructor in 'Music for Radio' and American music, Columbia Univ. (1944-48); consultant to Library of Congress for 'Music Loan Libraries' in Latin America (1944-45; with travel to nine Latin American countries); from 1951-55 was in the Foreign Service of the U. S. (cultural attaché in Lima and Buenos Aires). In 1955, appointed Director of the School of Music at the Univ. of Oklahoma. He published a valuable source book *The Music of Spain* (1941; Spanish translation, Buenos Aires, 1943) and *America's Music* (historical survey of music in the U. S. A.; N. Y., 1955); handbooks, *Music of the New World* and *The Story of Music* (NBC series, 1943-46); music editor, *Handbook of Latin American Studies* (1940-42); *A Guide to Latin American Music* (1945); editor, *Music in Radio Broadcasting* (1946); contributor to *Harvard Dictionary of Music, Collier's Encyclopedia,* and other publications in the U. S. and in Latin America.

Chasins, Abram, brilliant American composer and pianist; b. New York, Aug. 17, 1903. He studied at the Juilliard School of Music, Columbia Univ., and Curtis Institute; his teachers included Ernest Hutcheson, Rubin Goldmark and Josef Hofmann; made his debut playing his own piano concerto with the Philadelphia Orch. (Jan. 18, 1929); subsequently made extensive tours of Europe and the U. S. as a concert pianist; was a member of the faculty of Curtis Institute from 1926-35; in 1943 was appointed music consultant of the radio station WQXR (director since 1947). Chasins was the first American composer to have his works performed by Toscanini. He has written over 100 compositions, mostly for piano. Major works: 1st piano concerto (see above); 2nd piano concerto (Philadelphia, March 3, 1933, composer soloist; revised version performed by the N. Y. Philh., April 7, 1938); *Three Chinese Pieces* (originally for piano, 1925; orch. version performed by Toscanini and N. Y. Philh., April 8, 1931). His piano music is ingratiatingly effective and excellently written for the instrument; his 24 Preludes (1928) are often used as teaching pieces; the *Three Chinese Pieces* have been included in the programs of many celebrated pianists, among them, Josef Lhévinne and Josef Hofmann.

Chaumet (shoh-mā'), **William,** French composer; b. Bordeaux, Apr. 26, 1842; d. Gajac, Gironde, Oct., 1903. He took the 'prix Cressent,' and the 'prix Rossini' for composition. Works: The comic opera *Le péché de M. Géronte* (1873), dramatic poem *Idéa* (Bordeaux, 1873), comic opera *Bathyle* (1877), dramatic poem *Hérode* (Paris Cons., 1885), *Mam'zelle Pioupiou* (1889); lyric drama *Mauprat* (MS); *La petite maison* (1903); orchestral pieces; piano music; songs, etc.

Chausson (shoh-sŏhn'), **Ernest,** distinguished French composer; b. Paris, Jan. 20, 1855; d. Limay, near Mantes, June 10, 1899 (in a bicycle accident). He studied with Massenet at the Paris Cons.; then took private lessons with César Franck, and began to compose. The influence of Wagner as well as that of Franck determined the harmonic and melodic elements in Chausson's music; but despite these derivations, he succeeded in establishing an individual style, tense in its chromaticism and somewhat flamboyant in its melodic expansion. The French character of his music is unmistakable in the elegance and clarity of its structural plan. He was active in musical society in Paris and was secretary of the Société Nationale de Musique. He composed relatively little music; possessing private means, he was not compelled to seek employment as a professional musician. Works: Operas: *Les Caprices de Marianne* (1880); *Hélène* (1885); *Le Roi Arthus* (perf. posthumously, Brussels, Nov. 30, 1903); incidental music to *La Légende de Sainte Cécile* (Paris, Jan. 25, 1892); for orch.: *Viviane,* symph. poem (1883); *Solitude dans les bois* (1886); Symphony in B♭ major (Paris, April 18, 1898; still in the repertoire); *Poème* for violin and orch. (Concerts Colonne, Paris, April 4, 1897; very popular among violinists); *Poème de l'amour et de la mer* for voice and orch. (1882-92); *Chanson perpetuelle* for voice and orch. (1898); for chorus: *Hymne védique* (1866; with orch.); *Chant nuptial* for women's voices and piano (1887); piano trio; piano quartet; string quartet (unfinished); songs: *Chansons de Miarka* to words by Jean Richepin; *Serres chaudes* to words by Maeterlinck; *Deux poèmes* to words by Verlaine; etc.—Bibl.: O. Séré, *Musicens français d'aujourd'hui* (Paris, 1911); Special issue of 'La Revue musicale' (Dec., 1925; includes a catalogue of his works); J. P. Barricelli and Leo Weinstein, *Ernest Chausson* (a centennial biography; Norman, Okla., 1955).

Chavanne (shăh-văhn'), **Irene von,** Austrian contralto; b. Graz, April 18, 1868; d. Dresden, Dec. 26, 1938. She studied at the Vienna Cons.; in 1885 joined the Dresden Court Opera; was appointed 'Kammersängerin' in 1894. She was praised for the volume and range of her voice.

Chavarri (shăh-văh'-rē), **Eduardo Lopez,** Spanish composer; b. Valencia, Jan. 31, 1875. He was a pupil of F. Pedrell; taught and conducted at the Valencia Cons.; founded a chamber orchestra there. His compositions include *Acuarelas valencianas* for string orch.; *Rapsodía valenciana* for piano and orch.; *Concerto español* for piano and string orch.; *Leyenda* for chorus and orch.; *Quarteto hispano;* quartets for four violins; *Andaluza* for cello and piano; *Leyenda del Castillo Moro* for piano; piano pieces; songs. He published a music history (2 vols.; 3rd ed., 1929); *Música popular española* (1927; 2nd ed., 1940); *Chopin* (Valencia, 1950); *Folklore musical español* (Madrid, 1955).

Chávez (chăh'vāz), **Carlos,** distinguished Mexican composer and conductor; b. Mexico City, June 13, 1899. He studied piano with Manuel Ponce; began to compose very early, and published some piano pieces written in a salon style. He traveled to France in 1922; lived in New York for several years, where he became associated with various modern music societies. Upon his return to Mexico, he organized the Orquesta Sinfónica, which he conducted from its foundation (1928); was director of the National Cons. of Mexico (1928-34) and of the National Institute of Fine Arts (until 1953). Periodically, he appeared as guest conductor with major orchestras in the U. S.; on May 16, 1940 he presented a program of Mexican music at the Museum of Modern Art in New York; at all his concerts he included works by Mexican composers; also gave many performances in Mexico of symphonic works by North American composers. Chávez embraced the cause of modern music early in his twenties, and formed a style of his own, rhythmically strong, but austere in its harmony and orchestration. An important aspect of his music is the pronounced national Mexican element, both the primitive Indian and the later Spanish-Mexican types; yet, he seldom, if ever, resorts to quotations of actual folk melodies in his music.—Works: Ballets: *El fuego nuevo* (1921; Mexico City, Nov. 4, 1928); *Los cuatro soles* (1926; Mexico City, July 22, 1930); *HP* (i.e., *Horsepower,* Philadelphia, March 31, 1932); *Hija de Colquide* (*Daughter of Colchis;* presented by Martha Graham under the title *Dark Meadow,* N. Y., Jan. 23, 1946); *Antígona* (Mexico City, Sept. 20, 1940; originally conceived as incidental music to Sophocles' *Antigone,* 1932); For orch.: Symphony (1919); *Cantos de Méjico* for Mexican orch. (1933); *Obertura Republicana* (Mexico, Oct. 18, 1935); *Sinfonía India* (1935; broadcast Jan. 23, 1936; also Boston Symph. Orch., April 10, 1936, composer conducting); concerto for 4 horns (Coolidge Festival, Washington, D. C., April 11, 1937; composer conducting); piano concerto (1938-40; world première, N. Y. Philh., Jan. 1, 1942); *Cuatro Nocturnos,* for voice and orch. (1939); *Xochipilli Macuilxochitl,* for ensemble of traditional Indian instruments (N. Y., May 16, 1940; composer conducting); *Toccata* for percussion instruments (Mexico City, Oct. 31, 1947); violin concerto (Mexico City, Feb. 29, 1952); Symphony No. 3 (1951; Caracas, Dec. 11, 1954, composer conducting; N. Y. Philh., Jan. 26, 1956); Symphony No. 4 (Louisville, Feb. 11, 1953; composer conducting); *Symphony for Strings* (Los Angeles, Dec. 1, 1953, composer conducting). Choral works: *Tierra Mojada,* for chorus, oboe, and English horn (Mexico, Sept. 6, 1932); *El Sol* for chorus and orch. (Mexico, July 17, 1934); *Sinfonía Proletaria (Llamadas)* for chorus and orch. (Mexico, Sept. 29, 1934); *La Paloma Azul,* for chorus and chamber orch. (1940); *Arból que te sequeste* for unaccompanied chorus (1942); *Canto a la Tierra* for chorus and piano (1946). Chamber music: string quartet, No. 1 (1921); Sonatina for violin and piano (1924); *Energía* for 9 instruments (1925; Paris, June 11, 1931); Sonata for horns (1930); string quartet, No. 2 (1932); *Soli* for oboe, clarinet, trumpet, and bassoon (1933); *Espiral* for violin and piano (1934); string quartet, No. 3 (1944). For piano:

Solo, Blues, and Fox (1928); Three études (1950). Vocal music: *Tres Poesías de Pellicer, Novo y Villaurrutia* (1938); *La casada infiel* (1941). Chávez also published, in English, a theoretical work *Toward a New Music* (N. Y., 1937). Bibl.: *Carlos Chávez: Catalog of His Works* (Washington, D. C., 1944); Henry Cowell, *Carlos Chávez* in Ewen's *The Book of Modern Composers* (N. Y., 1942); O Mayer-Serra, *Música y músicos de Latino-América* (Mexico, 1947); H. Weinstock, *Carlos Chávez* in the 'Mus. Quarterly' (Oct., 1936).

Chélard (shā-lähr'), **Hippolyte-André-Jean-Baptiste**, French composer; b. Paris, Feb. 1, 1789; d. Weimar, Feb. 12, 1861. He was the son of a clarinetist at the Grand Opéra; was a pupil of Fétis, then of Gossec and Dourlen (1803) at the Paris Cons., taking the Grand Prix de Rome in 1811. He continued his musical studies under Baini, Zingarelli and Paisiello; in 1815 his first opera, *La casa da vendere,* was brought out at Naples. Returning to Paris, he entered the Opéra orch. as a violinist, and gave music lessons. After a long wait, his opera *Macbeth* (text by Rouget de Lisle) was produced (June 29, 1827), but was a flat failure. Discouraged, he went to Munich, where *Macbeth,* rewritten in great part, was so successful as to earn him the position of court Kapellmeister (1828). He returned to Paris in 1829; had a second failure with *La Table et le logement;* opened a music shop, which was ruined in the revolution of 1830. Back in Munich, he produced a new opera *Mitternacht* (June 19, 1831) and a German version of *La Table et le logement,* under the title of *Der Student* (Feb. 19, 1832); conducted the German Opera in London (1832-3), which also failed; and again revisited Munich, where his best opera, *Die Hermannsschlacht,* appeared in 1835. From 1836, he was court Kapellmeister at Augsburg; from 1840, Hofkapellmeister at Weimar, where he brought out two comic operas, *Der Scheibentoni* (1842) and *Die Seekadetten* (1844). He lived in Paris from 1852-4. A posthumous opera, *Le Aquile romane,* was presented at Milan in 1864.

Chelius (kā'-lē-ŭs), **Oskar von** (pen-name Siegfried Berger), German composer; b. Mannheim, July 28, 1859; d. Munich, June 12, 1923. Pupil in Mannheim of E. Steinbach, in Kassel of Reiss, in Leipzig of Jadassohn; made his career in the army, rising to the rank of major-general in 1911. He wrote the operas *Haschisch* (Dresden, 1897) and *Die vernarrte Prinzess* (Wiesbaden, 1905); symph. poem, *Und Pippa tanzt; Requiem* for chorus and orch.; Psalm 121; violin sonata; piano pieces; songs; etc.

Chelleri (kel'-lĕ-rē), **Fortunato** (real family name, Keller), Italian composer and choral director; b. Parma, 1686; d. Kassel, Dec. 11, 1757. He studied music with his uncle, F. M. Bassani, who was maestro di cappella at Piacenza Cathedral. His first opera, *Griselda* (Piacenza, 1707), was followed by fifteen more, written for various Italian stages. He settled in Kassel in 1725 as court music director, and remained there until his death, except for brief journeys to London (1726) and Stockholm (1731). Besides his operas, he wrote an oratorio *Dio sul Sinai* (1731); overtures; church music, etc. He published a volume of cantatas and arias (London, 1726), and a collection of 'Lessons' for harpsichord (London, 1750), containing two piano sonatas (really suites).

Chemin-Petit (shŭ-măn' pŭ-tē), **Hans,** German composer; b. Potsdam, July 24, 1902. He studied with H. Becker and P. Juon at the Berlin Hochschule; 1929, theory teacher at the State Academy for Church and School Music; from 1939-44 was choral director in Magdeburg; from 1945-48 conducted the city choirs in Potsdam. Works: 2 chamber-operas, *Der gefangene Vogel* (1927) and *Lady Monika* (1930); incidental music to *König Nicolo* and *Komödie der Irrungen;* cello concerto (1932); Sinfonietta for orch. (1932); Second Symphony in C major (1949; Potsdam, July 9, 1950, composer cond.); chamber works: 2 string quartets, Lyric Suite for soprano and 6 instruments, etc.; vocal works: madrigals, 8-part motet and fugue, hymns for baritone and orch., etc.

Chennevière, Daniel. See **Rudhyar, Dane.**

Cherbuliez (shär-büh'-l'yā), **Antoine-Elisée,** Swiss musicologist; b. Mulhouse, Alsace, Aug. 22, 1888. He was a student of philosophy and the natural sciences at Strasbourg Univ. (1907-08); studied engineering at the Univ. of Zürich (1907-11); later taught engineering in Darmstadt. His musical studies began with A. Köckert in Geneva and with N. Salter at the Strasbourg Cons. While an engineering student he studied music at the Zürich Cons. with Hegar and de Boer (1907-11). After 1913 he abandoned his scientific career, and turned his energies exclusively to music; was a pupil of Max Reger in Meiningen (1913-16) and later in Jena; from 1917-24 was director of music and organist in St. Gall, Switzerland; then taught piano, cello and theory in Chur; in 1923 became an instructor of musicology at Zürich Univ., and in 1932 professor. He composed a string quartet; a string trio; *Hymnus auf die Kunst* for mixed chorus and orch.; songs. Writings: *Gedankliche Grundlagen der Musikbetrachtung* (Zürich, 1924); *Zum problem der religiösen Musik* (Basel, 1924); *Die Anwendung der Sievers'schen Theorien auf die musikalische Interpretation* (Zürich, 1925); *Peter Cornelius* (Zürich, 1925); *J. S. Bach* (Zürich, 1926); *Die Schweiz in der deutschen Musikgeschichte* (Zürich, 1926; a valuable and extensive account of Swiss music history); *Musikpflege in Graubünden,* in 'Schweizerisches Jahrbuch für Musikwissenschaft', V (1931); *Joseph Haydn* (Zürich, 1932); *Geschichte der Musikpädagogik in der Schweiz* (1944); *Bibliographie de la chanson et de la musique populaire en Suisse,* in 'Le Folklore' (1949); biographies of Handel, Chopin, Grieg, Verdi and Tchaikovsky; monographs on Mozart, Beethoven and Brahms; many articles for musical journals.

Cherepnin. See **Tcherepnin.**

Cherkassky, Shura, Russian pianist; b. Odessa, Oct. 7, 1911. He was a pupil of his mother and later of Josef Hofmann. As a child he toured the U. S., beginning in 1923, when he played in the White House for President Hoover; soloist with the N. Y. Philh. Orch., Philadelphia Orch., London Symph. Orch. (1929-30), and many leading European orchestras (1937-38); made concert tours of Australia and New Zealand (1928), South Africa (1929; 1931), U. S. (1933-36), the Orient (1935), Europe and Russia (1935-38), the U. S. (1939); in 1939 he settled in Paris.

Cherniavsky (chär-n'yahv'-skē), the name of three brothers, members of an active trio, all born at Odessa, Russia: **Leo,** violinist, b. Aug. 30, 1890, was exhibited as a prodigy while still studying with Auer; later he studied in Vienna, and in 1906 with Wilhelmj in London; last N. Y. recital at Carnegie Hall, Jan. 19, 1937; **Jan,** pianist, b. June 25, 1892, was taught by his father; began to play in public at the age of seven, and was heard by Mme. Essipov, who then became his teacher; later studied with Leschetizky in Vienna; **Michail,** cellist, b. Nov. 2, 1893, at first studied violin, but at the age of five took up the cello with Verzhbilovitch; then studied under D. Popper. In 1900 the brothers formed a trio, and for three years toured Russia with phenomenal success; in 1904 they toured Germany, Holland and France; in 1906, Vienna, London and the English provinces; 1908-9 and 1911, South Africa; 1912, London and then (until 1914) India, New Zealand and Australia; 1916, Canada and the western states of the U. S.; they appeared for the first time in New York on Jan. 16, 1917.

Cherubini (kā-roo-bē-nē), **(Maria) Luigi (Carlo Zenobio Salvatore),** famous Italian composer; b. Florence, Sept. 14, 1760; d. Paris, March 15, 1842. As a young child he studied music with his father, cembalist at the Pergola Theater; his subsequent teachers were Bartolomeo and Alessandro Felici; then Bizarri and Castrucci; in 1777 he was sent by Duke Leopold II of Tuscany (the future Emperor Leopold III) to Milan to perfect himself in counterpoint under Sarti. At thirteen he had already written a mass, and a stage-intermezzo for a society theater; at fifteen he composed another intermezzo, *Il Giuocatore;* during his years of study with Sarti he confined himself to contrapuntal work and church-music; in 1780, *Quinto Fabio* (perf. at Alessandria della Paglia) opened the series of his dramatic works; its cool reception spurred him to renewed study, and *Armida* (Florence, 1782), *Adriano in Siria* (Leghorn, 1782), *Messenzio* (Florence, 1782), *Quinto Fabio* (revised; Rome, 1783), *Lo sposo di tre e marito di nessuna* (Venice, 1783), *Idalide* (Florence, 1784), and *Alessandro nelle Indie* (Mantua, 1784) received public approbation. Invited to London in the autumn of 1784, he brought out 2 operas, *La finta principessa* (1785), an opera buffa which had fair success, and *Giulio Sabino* (1786), which was less fortunate; Cherubini held the position of Composer to the King for one year, and in July, 1786, went to Paris for a one-year visit; in 1788 he brought out *Ifigenia in Aulide* at Turin; then settled permanently in Paris. His first French opera, *Demofoonte* (Grand Opéra, 1788), was a failure owing to his attempt to adapt his style of flowing melody to the ill-turned verses of Marmontel, the librettist. Next year Léonard, the Queen's hairdresser, obtained a license to establish Italian opera in a little playhouse called the Théâtre de la Foire de St.-Germain; and here Cherubini conducted, until 1792, the best works of Anfossi, Paisiello and Cimarosa. During this period he developed, inspired by the text of his opera *Lodoiska* (Théâtre de Monsieur, 1791), a new dramatic style destined to work a revolution on the French stage; the increased breadth and force of the ensemble numbers, the novel and rich orchestral combinations, and the generally heightened dramatic effect were imitated or expanded by a host of composers of the French school: Méhul, Berton, Lesueur, Grétry. Cherubini's next operas, *Eliza ou le voyage au mont St.-Bernard* (1794), and *Médée* (1797), were hampered by poor libretti. In 1795 Cherubini was appointed one of the Inspectors of the new Conservatoire. Composing steadily, he brought out *L'Hôtellerie portugaise* (1798), *La Punition* (1799), *La Prisonnière* (1799; pasticcio, with Boieldieu), and in 1800, at the Théâtre Feydeau, *Les deux journées* (perf. in London, 1801, as *The Water-carrier;* in Germany as *Der Wasserträger*), his greatest operatic work. Cherubini had fallen into disfavor with Napoleon, whose opinion in musical matters he had slighted; but after the success of *Les deux journées,* he was able to produce at the Grand Opéra *Anacréon, ou l'amour fugitif* (1803), and the ballet *Achille à Scyros* (1804), neither of which, however, had good fortune. At this juncture Cherubini was invited to write an opera for Vienna; *Faniska,* brought out in 1807 at the Kärnthnerthor Theater, was an overwhelming success; so much so that a Vienna critic who ventured the prophecy that Beethoven's *Fidelio* would one day be equally esteemed, was laughed at. Returning to Paris after the French occupation of Vienna, Cherubini wrote *Pimmalione* for the Italian opera at the Tuileries (1808), but did not win the Emperor's favor, and retired for a time to the château of the Prince of Chimay, where he occupied his leisure with botanizing. The request to write a mass for the church of Chimay turned the current of his thoughts; he composed the celebrated 3-part Mass in F, the success of which was so marked that Cherubini thenceforward devoted more time to sacred than dramatic composition, though he did bring out *Le Crescendo* (1810), *Les Abencérages* (Opéra, 1813), *Bayard à Mézières* (1814), *Blanche de Provence* (1821) and *Ali Baba* (Opéra, July 22, 1833). On a visit to London, in 1815, he wrote for the Philharmonic Society a symphony, an overture, and a Hymn to Spring. In this year he lost his place in the Cons. during the troublous times of the Restoration, but was recompensed by his appointment as superintendent of the Royal Chapel, succeeding Martini. In 1816 he was made prof. of composition at the Cons., and its director in 1821; he retired in 1841. Cherubini was one of the great modern masters of counterpoint, and his scores, particularly in his admirable sacred music, bear witness on every page to his skill and erudition. As an opera composer, his main failing was the undue musical prolongation of scenes in which swifter dramatic action would have been preferable. His own catalogue of his works (publ. 1843) includes 15 Italian and 14 French operas; (an uncatalogued, newly discovered opera, *Don Pistucchio,* was performed at Dresden, Nov. 27, 1926); a ballet; 17 cantatas and 'occasional' vocal works with orch.; many detached airs, romances, nocturnes, duets, etc.; 14 choruses; 4 sets of solfeggi (over 160 numbers); 11 solemn masses, 2 Requiems, many detached Kyries, Glorias, Credos, etc.; a Credo in 8 parts with organ; an oratorio (Florence, 1777); motets, hymns, graduals, etc., with orch.; a Magnificat, a Miserere, a Te Deum (each with orch.); 4 litanies, 2 Lamentations, 20 antiphons; etc.; for orch.: a symphony, an overture, 11 marches, 11 dances, etc.; chamber music: 6 string quartets, a string quintet; a sonata for 2 organs; for piano: 6 sonatas, a grand fantasia, a minuet, a chaconne; etc. Cherubini's *Cours de Contrepoint et de Fugue* was prepared for publication by his pupil Halévy. It appeared in a German translation by Stöpel (1835-36), in English translation by J. Hamilton (1837) and C. Clarke (1854). Two new German editions were prepared by G. Jensen (1896) and R. Heuberger (1911).

Bibliography: A. Bottée de Toulmon, *Notice des manuscrits autographes de Cherubini* (Paris, 1843); E. Bellasis, *Cherubini. Memorials illustrative of his life* (London, 1874; new augmented ed., Birmingham, 1912); F. J. Crowest, *Cherubini* (London and N. Y., 1890); M. E. Wittmann, *Cherubini* (Leipzig, 1895); M. Q. L'Épine, *Cherubini* (Lille, 1913); R. Hohenemser, *L. Cherubini Sein Leben und seine Werke* (Leipzig, 1913); H. Kretzschmar, *Über die Bedeutung von Cherubini's Ouvertüren und Hauptopern für die Gegenwart* (in Peters' 'Jahrbuch,' 1906); L. Schemann, *Cherubini* (Berlin, 1925); O. A. Mansfield, *Cherubini's String Quartets,* in the 'Mus. Quarterly' (1929); H. Mersmann, *Kammermusikführer* (analysis; 1932); P. Espil, *Les voyages de Cherubini, ou l'enfance de Mozart* (Bayonne, 1946); G. Confalonieri, *Prigionia d'un artista: il romanzo di Luigi Cherubini* (2 vols., Milan, 1948).

Cheslock, Louis, American composer; b. London, England, Sept. 9, 1899. He was brought to the U. S. as an infant; studied music at the Peabody Cons. in Baltimore: violin with Van Hulsteyn and Gittelson, composition with Strube; became violin instructor there in 1916, composition instructor in 1922; in 1952 was appointed chairman of the department of theory. He was a violinist in the Baltimore Symph. Orch. (1916-37); also served as guest conductor. Cheslock writes in a neo-romantic style, rooted in traditional music, but not without excursions into modern techniques, including a modified application of dodecaphonic principles. Works: a one-act opera, *The Jewel Merchants* (Baltimore, Feb. 26, 1940); oratorio, *David* (1937; a symphonic suite from it was performed in Baltimore, Feb. 19, 1939); Symphony in D major (1932); three tone poems for orch.: *Cathedral at Sundown, 'Neath Washington Monument,* and *At the Railway Station* (Chicago, April 29, 1923); two Dances for orch. (1926); ballet, *Cinderella* (Baltimore, May 11, 1946); oratorio, *The Congo* (Akron, Ohio, Oct. 30, 1942); violin concerto (Baltimore, Feb. 25, 1926); string quartet; piano pieces; publ. *Introductory Study on Violin Vibrato* (Baltimore, 1931).

Chevé (shŭ-vā'), **Émile-Joseph-Maurice,** French music theorist; b. Douarnenez, Finistère, May 31, 1804; d. Fontenay-le-Comte, Aug. 26, 1864. A physician of great merit, he became a zealous advocate of Pierre Galin's method of musical instruction explained in Galin's *Exposition d'une nouvelle méthode pour l'enseignement de la musique* (1818; 3rd ed. 1831), which attained considerable popularity; married Nanine Paris (d. 1868) and collaborated with her in a *Méthode élémentaire de musique vocale* (Paris, 1844; later ed. 1863; German translation by F. T. Stahl, 1878), in the preface to which he 'exposes' and attacks the 'defective' methods of the Conservatoire. He and his wife also published a *Méthode élémentaire d'harmonie* (with Galin; Paris, 1846); and Mme. Chevé wrote a *Nouvelle théorie des accords, servant de base à l'harmonie* (Paris, 1844). He published a long series of essays and articles by which he vainly sought to draw out the professors of the Conservatoire. Acrimonious polemics raged for years, and numerous pamphlets were issued in Paris by adherents and foes of the Chevé method.—Cf. A. Pagès, *La Méthode musicale Galin-Paris-Chevé* (Paris, 1860); A. L. Montandon, *École Galin-Paris-Chevé, Problème musical, historique, pédagogique, prophétique* (Paris, 1861); O. Comettant, *Les musiciens, les philosophes et les gaités de la musique en chiffres* (Paris, 1870).

Chevillard (shŭ-vē-yăhr'), **Camille,** French composer and conductor; b. Paris, Oct. 14, 1859; d. Chatou (Seine-et-Oise), May 30, 1923. He studied piano with Georges Mathias; won second prize at the Paris Cons. in 1880; was chiefly self-taught in composition. From 1886-97, he was assistant conductor of the Lamoureux Concerts; in 1897 succeeded Lamoureux as conductor; from 1907, professor of instrumental ensemble classes at the Paris Cons., and from 1913 conductor at the Grand Opéra. In 1903 he won the Prix Chartier for chamber music; in 1916 became president of the 'Société française de musique de chambre'; was an 'officier de l'instruction publique', and a chevalier of the Légion d'Honneur. He wrote several symph. works which he conducted himself at the Concerts Lamoureux: *Ballade symphonique* (Feb. 23, 1890); *Le chêne et le roseau* (March 8, 1891); *Fantaisie symphonique* (Oct. 21, 1894); also an *Etude chromatique* for piano; a piano quintet, piano quartet, piano trio; a string quartet; violin sonata; cello sonata; incidental music to Schure's *La Roussalka* (1903); songs with orch., *L'Attente* and *Chemins d'Amour*.—Cf. R. Rolland, *Musiciens d'aujourd'hui* (1908); O. Séré, *Camille Chevillard,* in *Musiciens français d'aujourd'hui* (2nd ed. Paris, 1911); R. Dumesnil, *Portraits des musiciens français* (Paris, 1938).

Chevreuille (shev-röi'), **Raymond,** Belgian composer; b. Brussels, Nov. 17, 1901. He took courses at the Brussels Cons., but was mainly self-taught in composition. He has written works in every genre; his style is greatly advanced in the direction of modern harmony; his liberal eclecticism allows him to use means of expression ranging from neo-classicism to individual expressionism, applying the devices of atonality and polytonality. His large catalogue of works includes a chamber opera, *Atta Troll* (1952); 3 ballets: *Jean et les Argayons* (1934); *Cendrillon* (1946); *Le Bal chez la portière* (1954); 5 symphonies: No. 1 (1939); No. 2, *Symphonie des souvenirs* (Brussels, Nov. 23, 1945); No. 3 (Brussels, June 25, 1952); No. 4, *Short Symphony;* No. 5, *Symphonie printanière* (1954); 2 piano concertos (1937; 1952); 2 violin concertos (1941; 1953); cello concerto (1940); concerto for oboe, clarinet, bassoon and orch. (1943); double concerto for viola, piano and orch. (1946); horn concerto (Brussels, July 12, 1950); trumpet concerto (1954); 6 string quartets (1930-45); piano trio (1936); string trio (1937); piano quartet (1938); quartet for cellos (1942); *Musiques Lilliputiennes* for 4 flutes (Brussels, Aug. 13, 1942); several cantatas: *Le Fléau* (1930); *Le cantique du soleil* (1941); *L'Eléphant et le papillon* (1941); *La dispute des orgues* (Brussels, Jan. 10, 1942); *Evasions* (1942); *Saisons* (1943); *Prière pour les condamnés à mort* for narrator and orch. (Brussels, Oct.

14, 1945); radio plays, *D'un diable de briquet* (1950); *L'Elixir du Révérend Père Gaucher* (1951).

Chiaromonte (k'yah-roh-mohn'-tē), **Francesco,** tenor and composer; b. Castrogiovanni, Sicily, July 26, 1809; d. Brussels, Oct. 15, 1886. Pupil of Ragusa, of Raimondi at Palermo, and of Donizetti at Naples. While active as a stage singer, he found time to compose; the first of his operas to be produced was *Fenicia* (Naples, 1844); he then became prof. of singing at the Royal Cons.; was imprisoned 1848-50 as a revolutionist, and banished from Naples in 1850 during the successful production of a new opera, *Caterina di Cleves.* He was less successful at Genoa and Milan, and proceeded (1858) to Paris, where he was appointed chorus-master at the Théâtre-Italien. Later he held a similar position in London (Italian Opera); then (1862) settled in Brussels, and became prof. in the Cons. (1872). He wrote 5 other operas; an operetta; an oratorio, *Hiob* (1884); and a valuable *Méthode de Chant.*

Chickering, Jonas, American piano-maker; b. New Ipswich, N. H., April 5, 1798; d. Boston, Dec. 8, 1853. In 1818 he was apprenticed to John Osborn, a Boston piano-maker; 1823, founded (with James Stewart) the firm of Stewart & Chickering; from 1829, known as Chickering & Mackay (John Mackay, d. 1841); later, as Chickering & Sons. Jonas Chickering pioneered in the development of the upright piano, and the full metal plate for square and grand pianos. His son and successor, Col. Thomas E. Chickering (b. Boston, Oct. 22, 1824; d. there, Feb. 14, 1871) was named Chevalier of the Legion of Honor in addition to taking the first prize for pianofortes at the Paris Exposition of 1867. His three sons and their successors carried on the factory, which was famous for quality and high rate of production, until 1908, when it became part of the American Piano Co., and the factory was moved from Boston to East Rochester, N. Y. Later, the firm became a subsidiary of the Aeolian American Corp.—See R. G. Parker, *A Tribute to the Life and Character of Jonas Chickering* (Boston, 1854); *The Commemoration of the Founding of the House of Chickering* (Boston, 1904).

Chignell, Robert, English composer; b. Romsey, Hants, May 8, 1882; d. London, Feb. 27, 1939. He won a scholarship to the Royal College of Music, where his teachers were G. Garcia (voice) and Sir C. V. Stanford (composition); later continued vocal studies with C. W. Clark; was soloist with the Sheffield Choir on its world tour. Works: operas *Romeo and Juliet, Herode, Aucassin and Nicolette;* two symph. poems; *Serenade humoresque* for orch.; *The Jackdaw of Reims, Sunrise and Sunset,* and *The Monks of Bangor* for chorus and orch.; about 250 songs.

Child, William, English organist and composer of sacred music; b. Bristol, 1606; d. Windsor, March 23, 1697. He was a boy chorister at Bristol Cathedral under Elway Bevin; in 1632 was in Windsor as organist at St. George's Chapel (jointly with J. Mundy) and then in London at the Chapel Royal; from 1643-60 he apparently lived in retirement, devoting himself to composition; in 1660 he was appointed chanter at the Chapel Royal, and a member of the King's private band. He received his Mus. Bac. in 1631 or 1639; his Mus. Doc. from Oxford in 1663. Child published psalms (1639; later editions 1650 and 1656), services, anthems, compositions in 'Court Ayres', canons, catches, etc. (included in collections of Arnold Boyce, Hilton, Playford and others); also instrumental works. Numerous services, anthems (including *O Lord, grant the King a long life*), a motet (*O bone Jesu*), and chants exist in manuscript.

Chilesotti (kē-lā-zot'-tē), **Oscar,** distinguished Italian music historiographer; b. Bassano, July 12, 1848; d. there, June 20, 1916. He was a graduate in law of Padua Univ.; was also a good flutist and cellist; self-taught in harmony. He lived at Milan, where he wrote regularly for the 'Gazzetta Musicale,' and contributed to other periodicals; was especially interested in tablatures and the art of the 15th and 16th centuries, on which subjects he lectured extensively in Italy. Works: *Biblioteca di Rarità musicali* (Milan, 1883; 9 vols.), containing transcriptions from little known works of the early 17th century, and (vol. IV) *Arianna* by Benedetto Marcello; *I nostri Maestri del passato* (Milan, 1882), biographical notes on the greatest Italian musicians, from Palestrina to Bellini; *Di G. B. Besardo e del suo 'Thesaurus Harmonicus'* (Milan, 1886; French ed. 1901); *Sulla lettera critica di B. Marcello contra A. Lotti . . .* (Bassano, 1885; *Sulla melodia popolare del cinquecento* (Milan, 1889); *Lautenspieler des 16. Jahrhunderts* (Leipzig, 1891); *L'evoluzione nella musica, appunti sulla teoria di H. Spencer* (Turin, 1911); etc. For Lavignac's 'Encyclopédie de la musique' he wrote an elaborate essay on tablatures. He publ. in modern notation Roncalli's *Capricci armonici* on the Spanish guitar (Milan, 1881); and translated Schopenhauer's *Aphorismen* and *Die Welt als Wille und Vorstellung* into Italian. Bibl.: V. Fedeli, *Il Dr. O. Chilesotti,* in 'Rivista Musicale Italiana', XXIII, 3-4 (1916).

Chisholm, Erik, Scottish composer; b. Glasgow, Jan. 4, 1904. He first studied music in Glasgow; then in London and in Edinburgh with Donald Tovey (composition) and Puishnov (piano); received his Mus. Bac. in 1932, and his Mus. Doc. from Edinburgh Univ. in 1934; in 1927 he was in the U. S.; returned to Glasgow in 1929; in 1930 became conductor of the Glasgow Grand Opera Society; was instrumental in arranging performances of works by modern Scottish and foreign composers; founded the Professional Organists' Association (1935), the Scottish Ballet Society (1936), the Barony Opera Society; from 1938-39 was music director of the Celtic Ballet; in 1940 joined the Carl Rosa Opera Company as conductor; in 1943 toured with the Anglo-Polish Ballet; later went to the Far East; organized the Singapore Symph. Orch., and conducted 50 concerts in Malaya; in 1946 was appointed Professor of Music and Director of the South African College of Music at Cape Town Univ.; also conducted operas in South Africa. Works: the operas *The Feast of Samhain* (1941); *The Inland Woman* (1950; Cape Town, Oct. 21, 1953); *Dark Sonnet* (after O'Neill's drama *Before Breakfast;* Cape Town, Oct. 20, 1952); *Simoon* (after Strindberg; 1953). *Dark Sonnet* and *Simoon* were later combined with a third short opera, *Black Roses* (libretto by the composer), to form a trilogy entitled *Murder in Three Keys* (performed at the Cherry Lane Theater, Greenwich Village, N. Y., July 6, 1954). Ballets: *The Pied Piper of Hamelin* (1937); *The Forsaken Mermaid* (1940); *The Earth Shapers* (1941); *The Hoodie* (1947); for orch.: *Straloch Suite* (1933); Symphony No. 1 (1938; BBC, London, 1949); Symphony No. 2 (1939); *The Adventures of Babar* (with narrator, BBC, 1940); *Piobaireachd Concerto* for piano and orch. (1940; composer soloist); *Pictures from Dante* (1948); *Hindustani Concerto* for piano and orch. (Cape Town, Nov. 22, 1949); violin concerto (1950; Cape Town Festival, March 18, 1952; also given at the Edinburgh Festival, 1952); *Concerto for Orchestra* (Cape Town Festival, March 29, 1952); chamber music: Double trio for clarinet, bassoon, trumpet, violin, cello and double-bass (London, 1933); choral works, songs, piano pieces. Chisholm's style of composition reaches the utmost complexity of contrapuntal, harmonic and rhythmic development, in an idiom quite free of conventional tonality, preserving formal cohesion only through a discipline of thematic economy; some elements of oriental music are in evidence in his works written during his sojourn in the East Indies; the interplay of all these components creates an impression of exotic modernism, related to expressionistic usages.

Chladni (**h**lahd'-nē), **Ernest Florens Friedrich,** eminent acoustician; b. Wittenberg, Nov. 30, 1756; d. Breslau, April 3, 1827. At first a student and professor of law at Wittenberg and Leipzig, he turned to physics, and made highly important researches in the domain of acoustics. He discovered the 'Tonfiguren' (tone-figures; i.e., the regular patterns assumed by dry sand on a glass plate set in vibration by a bow); invented the Euphonium (glass-rod harmonica) and Clavicylinder (steel-rod keyboard harmonica). To introduce his ideas and inventions, he made long journeys and delivered many scientific lectures. His earlier publications, *Entdeckungen über die Theorie des Klanges* (1787), *Über die Longitudinalschwingungen der Saiten und Stäbe,* and a series of minor articles in various periodicals, were followed by the important works *Die Akustik* (1802; 2nd ed., 1830; French translation, 1809); *Neue Beiträge zur Akustik* (1817); *Beiträge zur praktischen Akustik* (1821); *Kurze Übersicht der Schall- und Klanglehre* (1827). Bibl.: W. Bernhardt, *Dr. E. Chladni, der Akustiker* (Wittenberg, 1856).

Chlubna (**h**loob'-năh), **Oswald,** Czech composer; b. Brno, July 22, 1893; pupil of Janáček there; then taught at the Brno Cons. His works include the operas *Catull's Vengeance* (1917), *Alladina and Palomid* (after Maeterlinck; 1922), *Nura* (1931), *The Day of Beginning* (1935); and *The Love Affairs of the Squire of Heslow* (1940); the symph. poems *Fairy Land* (1916), *Dreams* (1916), *Before I Grow Dumb* (1918), *Two Fairy Tales* (1920), and *Song of My Longing* (1922); *Symphony of Life and Love* (1927); 2 orchestral suites; chamber music: Chamber Sinfonietta (1924); 3 cello quartets (1925; 1928; 1933); Ballad for string quartet (1928); Andante and Scherzo for piano trio; cello and piano pieces; the cantatas *Lord's Prayer; Minstrel's Child* (1922); *Cyrillian - Methodian Cantata* (1935); *Czech Resurrection* (1942-44); choruses; songs.

Chop, Max (pen name, 'Monsieur Charles'), German writer; b. Greuzen, Thuringia, May 17, 1862; d. Berlin, Dec. 20, 1929. A law student turned musician, he published several books of songs and ballades, 3 piano concertos, a piano trio, and 2 orchestral suites; lived from 1885-8 in Berlin as a writer of musical feuilletons; then, until 1902, in Neu-Ruppin as music critic and editor of the 'Märkische Zeitung'; in 1902 he was again in Berlin; from 1920 until his death, was editor-in-chief of 'Die Signale'. An ardent admirer of August Bungert, he published his detailed biography (Berlin, 1915); also analyses of his music dramas, and was (from 1911) the editor of 'Der Bund', the official organ of the Bungert Association. He published *Zeitgenössische Tondichter* (2 vols., 1888-1890, each containing 12 sketches); analyses of Liszt's symphonic poems, Wagner's music dramas, etc.; a sketch of August Bungert in volume III of 'Monographien moderner Musiker' (1903); *Vademecum für den Konzertsaal* (1904, et seq.); biographies of Delius (1907) and Rezniček (1920); *Führer durch die Musikgeschichte* (Berlin, 1912).

Chopin (shŏ-păn'), **(François-) Frédéric,** an incomparable composer for piano; b. Zelazowa Wola, near Warsaw, Feb. 22, 1810; d. Paris, Oct. 17, 1849. His father, Nicolas Chopin, teacher in the Warsaw gymnasium, was a native of Marainville, Alsace, who went to Warsaw as a teacher of French; his mother, Justine Kryzanowska, was Polish. Frédéric was brought up in his father's private school, among sons of the Polish nobility. His musical education was entrusted to the Bohemian pianist, Albert Zwyny and the Director of the Warsaw School of Music, Joseph Elsner. At the age of seven he played in public a piano concerto by Gyrowetz, and improvisations. His first attempts in composition were dances (Polonaises, Mazurkas and Waltzes); but he publ. (1825) as op. 1 a Rondo, and as op. 2 Variations on *Là ci darem la mano,* with orch. While a youth, he traveled in Europe, visiting Danzig, Dresden, Leipzig and Prague. In 1829, already a composer of eminent individuality and a finished performer, he set out for Vienna, Munich and Paris. His concert in Vienna, on Sept. 11, 1829, elicited high praise (see the Leipzig 'Allgemeine Musikalische Zeitung', Nov. 18, 1829, pp. 757-8). His first concert in Paris was given at Pleyel's house, before an invited audience of musicians, in 1831. His reception was so cordial that he made Paris his home for life. He was destined never to revisit Poland. Despite Kalkbrenner's finding fault with his fingering, and despite the dictum of Field (of all men!) that Chopin's talent was 'of a sick chamber order,' Chopin made a deep and lasting impression, not merely on gay Parisian society, of which he soon became the declared favorite, but on men like Liszt, Berlioz, Meyerbeer, Bellini, Adolphe Nourrit, Balzac and Heine, to whose intimacy he was admitted as a cherished and equal companion. From the beginning he taught the piano; his instruction was eagerly sought, chiefly by members of the French and Polish aristocracy; von Lenz (see below) gives a charming glimpse of Chopin the teacher. Chopin also gave yearly concerts to the musical *élite,* and played frequently in Parisian salons; but had an unconquerable aversion to miscellaneous concert-giving. His compositions took precedence over all else in the pianistic world. In 1839, Schumann wrote, reviewing some of Chopin's Preludes (op. 28), Mazurkas (op. 33), and Waltzes (op. 34): 'Er ist und bleibt der kühnste und stolzeste Dichtergeist der Zeit' [He is indeed the boldest and proudest poetic spirit of the time]. ('Neue Zeitschrift für Musik,' 1839; Schumann's 'Collected Works,' 3d ed., 1875; vol. II, p. 95.) His position, both in society and the world of art, was assured; the devotion of his pupils and admirers bordered on fanaticism. The Paris critics found a Shakespearian epithet for him: 'the Ariel of the piano'.

In 1837 Liszt introduced Chopin to George Sand (Mme. Dudevant); their mutual attachment formed an episode eventually most painful for the refined and sensitive nature of the artist, dominated by the coarse-fibred woman of the world. A severe attack of bronchitis in the autumn of 1838 overturned his usually normal health, and led Chopin to spend the ensuing winter in Majorca with Mme. Dudevant, who appears to have nursed him quite tenderly; but the Chopin thinly disguised as 'Prince Karol' in her unamiable novel, 'Lucrezia Floriani' (published shortly afterward), was not at all an engaging personality, and after Chopin's malady had developed into consumption, they parted (1847). Disregarding his failing health, Chopin visited Great Britain in 1848, and remained there 7 months, giving concerts and accepting invitations which exhausted his remaining energies; and finally returned to Paris to die. He was buried at Père Lachaise, between Cherubini and Bellini.

Chopin represents the full liberation of the pianoforte from traditionary orchestral and choral influences—its authoritative assumption of a place as a solo instrument *per se.* Chopin's music, as none before, breathes the piano-spirit, incarnates the piano-soul, revels in the pure piano-tone, and illustrates the intrinsic piano-style, without seeking 'orchestral' effects, tonal or technical. Not requiring of the piano the sonority of an orchestra, he may have seemed 'effeminate' beside the titanic Liszt; yet his works, more especially the scherzos, ballades, preludes, nocturnes, and even the concertos (pianistically considered), mark a boundary in piano effect which has never been surpassed. In the small forms he chose, there lies a world of originality in constructive ingenuity, in melody and melodic ornament, in harmonic progressions and arpeggiated figuration, of national melancholy or proud reminiscence, of tender or voluptuous sentiment and poetic reverie.

His playing was notable for flawless accuracy and remarkable brilliancy of technique, sensuous charm in touch and tone, and a peculiar flexibility in the tempo (*rubato*) which was at times almost exaggerated. He was a most exquisite interpreter of his own works, but did not much care to play other piano music; all in all, a remarkably self-centered 'composer-pianist.' A complete edition of Chopin's works in 14 volumes, edited by Liszt, Brahms, Bargiel, Franchomme, Reinecke and Rudorff, was publ. by Breitkopf & Härtel. Other excellent editions are those of Chopin's personal pupil, C. Mikuli, of Ignaz Friedman, of E. Ganche, of R. Joseffy (with introductions by J. G. Huneker), of Paderewski and Cortot. Innumerable editions of Chopin's works by categories have been brought out by virtually every large music publishing firm. A definitive edition of collected works in 26 vols. was initiated by Paderewski in collaboration with Joseph Turczynski and Ludwik Bronarski in 1940, and completed in 1954.

WORKS WITH OPUS No.: For piano with orch.: Variations on *Là ci darem la mano* (op. 2); 2 concertos (E m., op. 11; F m., op. 21); Grand Fantasy on Polish airs (op. 13); *Krakowiak,* concert-rondo (op. 14); Grand Polonaise (op. 22). For piano with other instruments: *Introduction et Polonaise,* for piano and cello (op. 3); piano trio in G m. (op. 8); cello sonata (op. 65); Rondo in C for 2 pianos (op. 73). For piano solo: Rondos (op. 1, 5, 16); Sonatas (op. 4, 35, 58); Mazurkas (op. 6, 7, 17, 24, 30, 33, 41, 50, 56, 59, 63, 67, 68); Nocturnes (op. 9, 15, 27, 32, 37, 48, 55, 62, 72); Études (op. 10, 25); Valses (op. 18, 34, 42, 64, 69, 70); Scherzos (op. 20, 31, 39, 54); Ballades (op. 23, 38, 47, 52); Polonaises (op. 26, 40, 44, 53, 61, 71); Preludes (op. 28, 45); Impromptus (op. 29, 36, 51); Fantasies (op. 49, 61, 66); also Grand Variations on *Je vends des Scapulaires* (op. 12); *Boléro* (op. 19); *Tarentelle* (op. 43); *Concert-Allegro* (op. 46); *Berceuse* (op. 57); *Barcarolle* (op. 60); 3 *Écossaises* and *Marche funèbre* (op. 72). For voice and piano: 17 Polish Songs (op. 74; ed. with English text, N. Y.). WITHOUT OPUS No.: *Duo concertant* in E, on themes from *Robert le Diable,* for piano and cello (with Franchomme); 3 Études (F m., A♭, D♭); 3 Mazurkas (G, B♭, D); Mazurkas in C; in A m. (No. 2 in 'Notre Temps'); in A m. à Gaillard; in A and F; Fantasy in G♭ m.; Fantasy in B m.; Fantasy in G♭; Var. No. VI from the *Hexaméron* (variations on the march from Bellini's *I Puritani,* the other variations being by Liszt, Thalberg, Pixis, Herz and Czerny); Valse in E; Valse in E m.; Polonaise (for Countess Victoire Skarbek); Polonaise (for Adalbert Zywny); Variations on the air, *Der Schweizerbub;* Polonaise in G♯ m.; Polonaise in G♭ (authenticity doubtful); Polonaise in B♭ m. (*Farewell to Wilhelm Kolberg*); Nocturne in C♯ m. (publ. as Adagio in 1875); Valse in E♭ and Valse in A♭ (from MSS. found in possession of family of J. Elsner); Prelude in A♭; Mazurka in F♯ (authenticity doubtful).

BIBLIOGRAPHY—A. BIOGRAPHY: M. Karasowski, *F. Chopin Sein Leben, seine Werke u. Briefe* (2 vols., Dresden, 1877 [4th ed. 1914]; Engl. tr. by E. Hill, London, 1879 [3rd ed. 1938]); J. Schucht, *F. Chopin und seine Werke* (Leipzig, 1879); A. Niggli, *F. Chopin's Leben und Werke* (ib., 1879); A. Audley, *Chopin, sa vie et ses œuvres* (Paris, 1880; largely drawn from Karasowski); F. Niecks, *F. Chopin as a Man and Musician* (2 vols., London, 1888; German translation by W. Langhans, Leipzig, 1890; a standard work); Ch. Willeby, *F. F. Chopin* (London, 1892); J. G. Huneker, *Chopin, The Man and His Music* (N. Y., 1900; new ed. 1925; very sympathetic, excellent analyses of the works); J. C. Hadden, *Chopin* (London, 1903; rev. ed. 1934); F. Hoesick, *Chopin* (Warsaw, 1904; 2nd ed., augmented to 3 vols., as *Chopin's Life and Works,* Warsaw, 1910-11; 3rd ed., in 2 vols., 1927); H. Leichtentritt, *F. Chopin* (Berlin, 1905); E. Poirée, *Chopin* (Paris, 1906); E. Redenbacher, *Chopin* (Leipzig, 1911); A. Weissmann, *Chopin* (Berlin, 1912); Ed. Ganche, *F. Chopin. Sa vie et ses œuvres* (Paris, 1913); Bernard Scharlitt, *Chopin* (1919); V. M. Gibert, *Chopin, sus obras* (in Spanish, 1920); Ad. Hillman, *Chopin* (1920); Henri Bidou, *Chopin,* in 'Les Maîtres de la Musique' (1926); Z. Jachimecki, *Chopin* (Cracow, 1927; in French, 1930); G. de Pourtalès, *Chopin ou le poète* (French, German and English, 1927); Paul Landormy, *Chopin,* in the 'Mus. Quarterly' (1929); Martial Douël, *Chopin and Jenny Lind,* in the 'Mus. Quarterly' (1932); Maurice Princet, *Chopin* (Paris, 1932); Basil Maine, *Chopin* (London and N. Y., 1933); G. Mariotti, *Chopin* (Florence, 1933); Leopold Binental, *Chopin* (Paris, 1934); Wm. Murdoch, *Chopin and His Life* (London, 1934); Ed. Ganche, *Voyages avec F. Chopin . . . illustrations et documents inédits* (Paris, 1934); John F. Porte, *Chopin, the Composer and His Music* (N. Y., 1935); Paul Egert, *Chopin* (Potsdam, 1936); Angelo Geddo, *Chopin* (Brescia, 1936); R. Koczalski, *F. Chopin* (Cologne, 1936); L. Bronarski, *Etudes sur Chopin* (3 vols., Lausanne, 1944) and *Chopin et l'Italie* (Lausanne, 1947); A. Hedley, *Chopin* (London, 1947); P. Leclerq, *Chopin et son époque* (Liège, 1947); K. Stromenger, *F. Chopin* (Warsaw, 1947); André Gide, *Notes sur Chopin* (Paris, 1948; English translation, N. Y., 1949); A. E. Cherbulliez, *F. Chopin, Leben und Werk* (Zürich, 1948); A. Cortot, *Aspects de Chopin* (Paris, 1949; in English as *In Search of Chopin,* London, 1951); T. Mayzner, *F. Chopin* (Berlin, 1949); W. Rehberg, *Chopin, sein Leben und seine Werke* (Zürich, 1949); H. Weinstock, *Chopin, the Man and His Music* (N. Y., 1949; in German as *Chopin, Mensch und Werk,* Munich, 1950); C. Wierzynski, *The Life and Death of Chopin* (N. Y., 1949; contains lurid correspondence with Potocka, which has since been proved spurious); R. Bory, *La Vie de F. Chopin par image* (Geneva, 1951); A. Cœuroy, *Chopin* (Paris, 1951); *Portret Fryderyka Chopina* (45 plates and annotations to Chopin's portraits; edited by M. Idzikowski and B. Sydow; Cracow, 1952). See also N. Slonimsky, *Chopiniana, Some Materials for a Biography,* in the 'Mus. Quarterly' (Oct., 1948); B. E. Sydow, *O Date Urodzenia Fr. Chopina,* in 'Ruch Muzyczny' (No. 10, 1948), in which the author argues in favor of acceptance of Chopin's birth date as March 1, 1810, and publishes (for the first time) a facsimile of Chopin's letter to the Polish Literary Society of Paris, giving this date; M. Glinski, *Kiedy Urodzil Sie Chopin?* (in 'Ruch Muzyczny,' No. 19, 1948), in which the author attempts to prove that Chopin was born on March 1, 1809.

B. Correspondence: The earliest edition of selected letters is contained in Karasowski's biography; M. Karlowicz, *Souvenirs inédits de F. Chopin* (Paris, 1904); G. Petrucci, *Epistolario di F. Chopin* (Rocca San Casciano, 1907); B. Scharlitt, *F. Chopin's gesammelte Briefe* (Leipzig, 1911); F. Hoesick, *Chopiniana* (vol. I, Correspondence, in Polish, Warsaw, 1912); Perćswiet-Soltan ed. Chopin's letters to Jan Bialoblocki (Warsaw, 1926); H. Opienski, *Chopin; Collected Letters* (translated from the original Polish and French with a preface and editorial notes by E. L. Voynich; N. Y., 1931); complete edition of Chopin's letters (collected by H. Opienski) and documents, translated by S. Danysz, with index of works (Paris, 1933; preface by Paderewski); *Correspondance générale de F. Chopin* (3 vols.; translated into French and annotated by B. E. Sydow, Paris, 1953; vol. I appeared under the title *Correspondance; L'Aube, 1816-31*).

C. Criticism, Appreciation: F. Liszt, *F. Chopin* (Paris, 1845; English translation by W. Cooke, London, 1877; also by J. Broadhouse, London, 1901; German translation by La Mara, Leipzig, 1880; reprinted in vol. I of F. Liszt's 'Gesammelte Schriften,' Leipzig, 1910); W. von Lenz, in *Die grossen Pianoforte-Virtuosen* (Berlin, 1872; English translation, N. Y., 1899); J. Kleczinski, *F. Chopin De l'interprétation de ses œuvres* (Paris, 1880 [new ed. Paris, 1906]; English translation, augmented by N. Janotha, as *Chopin's Greater Works,* London, 1896; German translation as *Chopin's grössere Werke,* Leipzig, 1898); E. Gariel, *F. Chopin La tradición de su música* (Mexico, 1895); G. C. Johnson, *A Handbook to Chopin's Works* (New York, 1905); H. Opienski, *Chopin as Creator* (in Polish; Warsaw, 1912); Ed. Stillman Kelley, *Chopin the Composer* (New York, 1913; a scholarly analysis); Ed. Ganche, *Dans le souvenir de Fr. Chopin* (1925); Helena Windakiewiczowa, *Die Urtypen Chopin'scher Melodik in der polnischen Volksmusik* (Cracow, 1926); Seweryn Barbag, *Über die Lieder von Fr. Chopin* (Lwow, 1927); H. Leichtentritt, *Analyse von Chopin's Klavierwerken* (2 vols., 1921-22); J. P. Dunn, *Ornamentation in the Works of Chopin* (London, 1921; new ed. 1930); G. Abraham, *Chopin's Musical Style* (Oxford, 1939); E. Lopez Chavarri, *Chopin* (Valencia, 1950); Jan Holcman, *The Legacy of Chopin* (N.Y., 1954).

Breitkopf & Härtel published a *Thematisches Verzeichniss der im Druck erschienenen Kompositionen von Fr. Chopin* (Leipzig, 1870); a second, augmented edition (1888) contains also a complete list of books written about Chopin up to 1888. Another thematic catalogue was publ. by F. Ch. Listy and H. Opienski (Warsaw, 1937). A comprehensive Chopin bibliography was publ. by B. E. Sydow in Warsaw in 1949; a lavish folio volume of facsimiles (portraits, music, etc.), under the title *Chopin w Kraju,* was brought out in Warsaw in 1955.

Chorley, Henry Fothergill, English writer on music; b. Blackley Hurst, Lancashire, Dec. 15, 1808; d. London, Feb. 16, 1872. He was at various times active as a dramatist, translator, art-critic, poet, novelist and journalist; from 1831-68 was music critic of the London 'Athenaeum'. During his extensive travels, he heard all the best music of the day, and met many musical celebrities; a partisan of Mendelssohn and Spohr, he was intolerant towards new musical ideas, and attacked Chopin, Schumann and particularly Wagner, with extraordinary violence. Writings: *Music and Manners in France and Germany* (London, 1844; 3 vols.); *Modern German Music* (1854; 2 vols.); *Thirty Years' Musical Recollections* (1862, 2 vols.; abridged American edition, N. Y., 1926); an interesting *Autobiography, Memoir and Letters* (1873, 2 vols.; edited by H. G. Hewlett); *National Music of the World* (1880; edited by Hewlett; 3rd edition, 1912); *Handel Studies* (1859); and the novel *A Prodigy: a Tale of Music* (1866, 3 vols.); the libretti to Wallace's opera *Amber Witch* and Bennett's cantata *May Queen;* English translations of Gounod's *Faust,* Hérold's *Zampa,* and Mendelssohn's *Son and Stranger.*

Choron (koh-rŏhn), **Alexandre Étienne,** French music editor and theorist; b. Caen, Oct. 21, 1771; d. Paris, June 28, 1834. A student of languages, and passionately fond of music, he took interest in music theory and through it in mathematics, which he studied till the age of 25; then, by several years' serious application to the Italian and German theorists, he acquired a thorough knowledge of the theory and practice of music. Becoming (1805) a partner in a music publishing firm, he devoted his entire fortune to editing and publishing classic and theoretical works and compositions, meanwhile contributing new works of his own. In 1811 he became a corresponding member of the Academy; he was entrusted with the reorganization of the 'maîtrises' (training schools for church choirs), and was appointed conductor of religious festivals. In 1816, director of the Paris Opera; reopened the Conservatoire (closed in 1815) as the 'École royale de chant et de déclamation'. Losing his directorship (1817) because he favored new works by unknown authors, he established, at first with a very moderate subsidy, the famous 'Institution de musique classique et religieuse', for which he labored indefatigably until the July Revolution (1830), when his subsidy was so reduced that he could no longer hope to carry out his plans.—**Publications:** *Principes d'accompagnement des écoles d'Italie* (1804); *Principes de composition des écoles d'Italie* (1808; 3 vols.; 2nd edition, 1816, 6 vols.); *Dictionnaire historique des musiciens* (1810-11, 2 vols.; with Fayolle); *Méthode élémentaire de musique et de plainchant* (1811); Francœur's *Traité général des voix et des instruments d'orchestre* (1813); translations of Albrechtsberger's *Gründliche Anweisung zur Komposition* and *Generalbassschule* (1814, 1815; new edition, 1830; English translation by A. Merrick, 1835), and of Azopardi's *Musico prattico* (1816); *Méthode concertante de musique à plusieurs parties* (written for his Conservatory, 1818; new edition, 1833); *Méthode de plainchant* (1818); *Manuel complet de musique vocale et instrumentale, ou Encyclopédie musicale* (1836-9; 6 vols. letter press and 5 vols. plates; with Lafage).—Cf. L. E. Gautier, *Eloge de Choron* (Caen, 1845); H. Réty, *Notice historique sur Choron et son école* (Paris, 1873); J. Carlez, *Choron, sa vie et ses travaux* (Caen, 1880); G. Vauthier, *Choron sous l'empire* (Poitiers, 1909).

Chotzinoff, Samuel, music critic; b. Vitebsk, Russia, July 4, 1889. He came early to the U. S. where he studied piano with Oscar Shack and theory with D. G. Mason; graduated from Columbia Univ. in 1912; toured as accompanist for Zimbalist and Heifetz; from 1925-30 was music critic of the N. Y. 'World', 1934-41, of the N. Y. 'Post'; lectured on music for the Carnegie Foundation; taught at Curtis Institute; in 1938 was appointed director of Chatham Square Music School; then became music director of NBC. He wrote a novel, *Eroica* (on Beethoven's life); an autobiographical work, *A Lost Paradise, Early Reminiscences* (N. Y., 1955); and a monograph, *Toscanini, An Intimate Portrait* (N. Y., 1956).

Chou, Wen-chung, Chinese-American composer; b. Chefoo, July 28, 1923. He studied in Shanghai; left China in 1942; settled in the U. S. in 1946; studied composition at the New England Cons. and privately with N. Slonimsky in Boston (1947-49); then with Edgard Varèse in N. Y., and with Otto Luening at Columbia Univ.; awarded a Guggenheim Fellowship in 1957. In his music, he combines Chinese themes in atonal counterpoint. Works: *Landscapes,* for orch. (San Francisco, Nov. 19, 1953); *7 Poems of T'ang Dynasty,* for tenor, 7 wind instruments, piano, and percussion (N. Y., March 16, 1952); *And the Fallen Petals,* a triolet for orch. (Louisville, Feb. 9, 1955); *In the Mode of Shang,* for chamber orch. (N. Y., Feb. 2, 1957).

Chouquet (shoo-kā'), **Adolphe-Gustave,** French writer on music; b. Le Havre, April 16, 1819; d. Paris, Jan. 30, 1886. He lived in America as a music teacher from 1840-60; then in Paris. He twice won the 'Prix Bordin': in 1864 for a history of music from the 14th to 18th centuries, and in 1868 for *Histoire de la musique dramatique en France depuis ses origines jusqu'à nos jours* (published, 1873). From 1871, was custodian of the collection of instruments in the Conservatory; in 1875 he published a catalogue of them (2nd edition, 1884; supplemented by L. Pillaut, 1894; 1899; 1903).

Christiani, Adolf Friedrich, pianist; b. Kassel, March 8, 1836; d. Elizabeth, N. J., Feb. 10, 1885. He went to London in 1855; then to America, teaching in Poughkeepsie, Pittsburgh, Cincinnati and New York. He wrote a theoretical work, *The Principles of Musical Expression in Pianoforte-playing* (N. Y., 1886; German ed. Leipzig, *Das Verständnis im Klavierspiel*).

Christiansen, Christian, Danish pianist and composer; b. Hillerod, Dec. 20, 1884; studied at the Copenhagen Cons. and with Breithaupt in Berlin; then became professor of piano at the Royal Cons. of Copenhagen and in 1947 was appointed its director. He has written chamber music and songs.

Christiansen, F. Melius, composer and choral conductor; b. Eidsvold, Norway, April 1, 1871; d. Northfield, Minn., June 1, 1955. He came to the U. S. in 1888; studied first at the Northwestern Cons. of Music (grad. 1894), then in Germany at the Leipzig Cons. (1897-99); from 1903-41 was director of the School of Music, St. Olaf's College, Northfield, Minn.; founder and director of the St. Olaf's Lutheran Choir there. Upon his retirement in 1941, his son, **Olaf Christian** (b. Minneapolis, Aug. 12, 1901), formerly choirmaster at Oberlin Cons., Ohio, succeeded him as director of the Music School at St. Olaf's. F. Melius Christiansen received honorary Mus. Doc. degrees from Muhlenberg College, Allentown, Pa. (1922); Capitol Univ.; Oberlin College (1927). Major works: *Reformation Cantata* (1917); *The Prodigal Son,* cantata (1918); *St. Olaf Choir Series* (6 vols., 1920); *Young Men's Choral Assembly for Schools* (1936); associate editor of *Lutheran Hymnary* (1913), *50 Famous Hymns for Women's Voices* (1914); *School of Choir Singing* (1916); publ. *Practical Modulation* (1916). See L. N. Bergmann, *Music Master of the Middle West* (Minneapolis, 1944).

Christie, Winifred. See **Moór.**

Christoff, Boris, Bulgarian bass-baritone; b. Sofia, May 18, 1918. He studied law and at the same time took part in choral performances. A private stipend enabled him to go to Rome where he studied with Stracciari; in 1945, went to Salzburg. He made his début in Rome in 1946; sang at La Scala in 1947; at Covent Garden in 1949. He has since given many recitals in Europe. Christoff excels in the Russian repertory; his interpretation of Boris Godunov is particularly notable, recalling that of Shaliapin. He made his American début in that role at the San Francisco Opera, Sept. 25, 1956, with great acclaim.

Christopher, Cyril (Stanley), English organist and composer; b. Oldbury, Worcestershire, June 23, 1897. He studied organ with Alfred Hollins and theory with Bairstow. He has held numerous posts as music master and choir conductor. He has written mainly for chorus, but he has also composed a symphony and two short tone poems: *Midsummer Night* and *The Lone Shore;* other works are songs and piano teaching pieces.

Christov, Dobri, noted Bulgarian composer; b. Varna, Bulgaria, Dec. 14, 1875; d. Sofia, Jan. 23, 1941. He was first a school teacher; then pupil of Dvořák at Prague; spent the greater part of his career as director and teacher of composition of the Sofia Conservatory. He composed orchestral suites based on folk tunes; an overture, *Jvailo;* the ballad, *Zar Samuil;* 50 Bulgarian choral songs; also edited Bulgarian folksongs.

Chrysander, Karl Franz Friedrich, German music historian and critic; b. Lübtheen, Mecklenburg, July 8, 1826; d. Bergedorf, Sept. 3, 1901. He received his *Dr. Phil.* from Rostock Univ.; from 1868-71, and 1875-82, editor of the 'Allgemeine musikalische Zeitung,' contributing many articles (sketch of history of music-printing, 1879; papers on the Hamburg opera under Keiser, Kusser, et al., 1878-9); from 1885 he edited (with Spitta and Adler) the 'Vierteljahrsschrift für Musikwissenschaft.' He also edited two 'Jahrbücher für musikalische Wissenschaft' (1863; 1867), with important papers by various writers. He published two pamphlets, *Über die Molltonart in Volksgesängen* and *Über das Oratorium* (1853); *Händels biblische Oratorien in geschichtlicher Entwicklung* (1896; 4th ed. 1922); he also edited 'Bach's Klavierwerke' (1856), and shared in the editing of the 'Denkmäler der Tonkunst' (5 vols., 1869-71); and was co-editor of 'Allgemeine deutsche Biographien'. Together with G. Gervinus he founded, in 1856, the 'Deutsche Händelgesellschaft' for the purpose of publishing a complete edition of the master's works from the original MSS., but before long the other members lost interest, and Chrysander and Gervinus alone constituted the society. At their own expense they set up a little printing shop at Bergedorf, near Hamburg; in 1859 King George of Hanover granted Chrysander an annual subvention of 1000 thaler, which, after the annexation of Hanover by Prussia in 1866, was continued by the Prussian government. After the death of Gervinus in 1871, Chrysander, with the assistance of one printer and one engraver, continued work on the project until volume 100 (the last) was completed in 1894. During the preparation of this monumental edition he made several protracted visits to London to study Handel's autograph scores and others, in the possession of V. Schölcher, containing corrections and remarks in Handel's own hand. Of the latter he subsequently acquired 80 volumes for the music library at Hamburg. The enormous amount of biographical material Chrysander had collected led him to begin a life of Handel, of which he wrote two volumes and half of a third, bringing the life down to 1740 (Leipzig, 1858-67). Max Seiffert undertook the responsible task of completing Chrysander's work. This publication is regarded as the definitive edition of Handel's works; it is valuable both for its emphasis on word-tone relations, and for its faithful restoration of the original ornamentation of arias, and the original orchestration. Bibl.: J. Schaeffer, *F. Chrysander in seinen Klavierauszügen zur deutschen Händel-Ausgabe* (Leipzig, 1876); W. Weber, *Erläuterungen von Händels Oratorien in Chrysander's neuer Übersetzung und Bearbeitung* (3 vols.; Augsburg, 1898-1902); H. Kretzschmar, *Fr. Chrysander,* in 'Jahrbuch Peters' (1902); Ed. Bernoulli, *Oratorientexte Händels* (1905).

Chrysanthos of Madytos; writer on sacred music. He was a teacher of church singing in Constantinople (about 1815); then became Archbishop of Durazzo in Albania (1845). His writings, *Introduction to the Theory and Practice of Church-Music* (1821) and *Great Theory of Music* (1832) are valuable for their simplification of Byzantine liturgical notation.

Chueca (chwĕh'-kăh), **Federico,** Spanish composer of zarzuelas; b. Madrid, May 5, 1846; d. there, June 20, 1908. He was a medical student; organized a band at the Univ. of Madrid; also conducted theater orchestras. He began to compose for the stage in collaboration with Valverde who helped him to harmonize and orchestrate his melodies. Thanks to his prodigious facility, he wrote a great number of 'zarzuelas' of which *La Gran Via,* produced in Madrid (July 2, 1886), became his greatest success obtaining nearly 1000 performances in Madrid alone; it has also been performed many times in Latin America and the U.S. The march from his zarzuela *Cadiz* served for a time as the Spanish national anthem; dances from his *El año pasado por agua* and *Locuras madrileñas* also enjoyed great popularity. Chueca is regarded as one of the creators of the 'género chico' (light genre) of Spanish stage music. See M. Zurita, *Historia del género chico* (Madrid, 1920); J. Delito y Piñuela, *Origen y Apogeo del género chico* (Madrid, 1949).

Chvála, Emanuel, Czech critic and composer; b. Prague, Jan. 1, 1851; d. there, Oct. 28, 1924. He was mainly active as a critic; he published articles in Czech and in German dealing with native music, of which *Ein Vierteljahrhundert böhmischer Musik* (1887) was a pioneer work. He was also the composer of an opera, *Zaboj,* written in 1907, and produced in Prague on March 9, 1918.

Chwatal (hwăh'-tăhl), **Franz Xaver,** Bohemian pianist and pedagogue; b. Rumburg, June 19, 1808; d. Elmen, June 24, 1879. He settled in Magdeburg as piano teacher; published a great number of piano pieces; his two piano methods (op. 93 and op. 135) were much used.

Chybinski (hi-bin'skē), **Adolf,** eminent Polish musicologist; b. Cracow, March 29, 1880; d. Poznan, Oct. 31, 1952. He studied at the Univ. of Cracow; later in Munich with Sandberger and Kroyer; also with Thuille (1905-7); *Dr. phil.,* Munich, 1908; 1912, instructor at Lwow Univ.; 1921, professor there from 1916 also professor of theory at the Cons.; 1924, music counselor for the Polish State Art Dept. Books (mostly in Polish): *Wagner's Meistersinger* (1908): *The Organ Tablatures of Joh. v. Lublin* (2 vols., 1911-14); *J. S. Bach* (2 vols., 1913); *Music Instruments of the Tatra* (1924-27); *Cracovian Music in the 17th Century* (Tarnov, 1928); *Musical Relations between Poland and France in the 16th Century* (Poznan, 1929); *Dictionary of Ancient Polish Musicians Before 1800* (in Polish; Cracow, 1949). He also translated German music books into Polish (Hausegger's *Musik als Ausdruck*); edited *Publications de*

Musique Ancienne Polonaise (17th vol. published in Warsaw, 1938; contains Bartolomei Perkiel's *Missa Pulcherrima ad instar Praenestini*).

Ciaia, A. B. See **Della Ciaia.**

Ciccolini, Aldo, Italian pianist; b. Naples, Aug. 15, 1925. He studied with Paolo Denza at the Naples Cons.; made his début in 1942 in Naples, playing Chopin's F minor Concerto. In 1948 he won the Santa Cecilia Prize in Rome; in 1949 he was the winner of the Long-Thibaud prize in Paris. He toured in France, Spain and South America; on Nov. 2, 1950, he made his American debut in Tchaikovsky's Concerto No. 1 with the N. Y. Philharmonic. He has since appeared with several major orchestras in the U. S., and has also continued his concerts in Europe. Ciccolini possesses a virtuoso technique combined with a lyrical sense of phrasing.

Cicognini, Alessandro, Italian composer; b. Pescara, Jan. 25, 1907. He studied at the Milan Cons. and in Paris with Paul Dukas. He has written a sonatina for cello and piano (1928); *Donna lombarda,* one-act melodrama (1929); a cantata *Saul* (1932) and a *Mass* (1943). He later specialized in film music. Cf. 'Rassegna Musicale' (April, 1950).

Ciconia, Jean, Walloon theorist and composer; b. Liège, c. 1335; d. Padula, between Dec. 11 and Dec. 24, 1411. Little is known about his life; he was in Italy from 1358 to 1367; was in Liège from 1372 until 1401. In 1402 he went to Padua where he was a canon. A treatise by him entitled *De proportionibus musicae,* which he completed shortly before his death, is extant. Several of his musical compositions are preserved in Italian libraries; modern reprints are in the 'Denkmäler der Tonkunst in Österreich' (vol. VII and XXXI). Ciconia's significance lies in his early use of musical devices that did not become current until much later; he applies the technique of French isorhythmic style as well as canonic imitation. Bibl.: Suzanne Clercx, *Johannes Ciconia de Leodio* (Amsterdam, 1953); see also her addendum, *Question de Chronologie* in the 'Revue belge de musicologie' (1955).

Cifra (chē'-frah), **Antonio,** Italian composer; b. probably near Terracina, 1584; d. Loreto, Oct. 2, 1629. He was a choirboy in the church of San Luigi, Rome; 1594-96, pupil of B. Nanini; also studied with Palestrina; 1609, maestro di cappella at the Collegio Germanico, Rome; 1609-22 and from 1626, maestro at Santa Casa di Loreto; 1623-25, at San Giovanni in Laterano, Rome. A prolific composer, he is considered one of the best of the Roman school; he published (between 1600 and 1638) 5 books of motets; 3 of psalms; 5 of masses; 10 sets of *concerti ecclesiastici* (over 200 numbers); many more motets and psalms (in 2-12 parts); antiphons; litanies; madrigals; *ricercari; Scherzi ed arie a 1, 2, 3 e 4 voci, per cantar del clavicembalo, etc.* See the article on him by A. Cametti, in 'Rivista Musicale Italiana' XXI (1915).

Cigna (chē'-ñăh), **Gina,** French soprano; b. Paris, 1904. She studied at the Paris Cons.; made her operatic début at La Scala, Milan, in 1929; sang at the Metropolitan Opera, N. Y. in 1937 (début as Aida, Feb. 6, 1937). After a few more performances in N. Y., she returned to Europe, and settled in Milan as voice teacher.

Cilèa (chē-lā'-ăh), **Francesco,** Italian opera composer; b. Palmi, Calabria, July 26, 1866; d. Varazze, Nov. 20, 1950. He studied at the Naples Cons. (1879-89) with Cesi (piano) and Serrao (composition); taught piano there (1890-2); then harmony at the Istituto Musicale in Florence (1896-1904); was head of the Palermo Cons. (1913-16); in 1916 was appointed director of the Majella Cons. (Naples). He was a member of the 'Reale Accademia Musicale' in Florence (1898) and a knight of the Order of the Crown of Italy (1893). Operas: *Gina* (Naples, Feb. 9, 1889); *La Tilda* (Florence, April 7, 1892); *L'Arlesiana* (after Daudet; Milan, Nov. 27, 1897; later revised from 4 to 3 acts and produced in Milan, Oct. 22, 1898); *Adriana Lecouvreur,* after Scribe (his most famous opera; Milan, Nov. 6, 1902; Covent Garden, Nov. 8, 1904; Metropolitan Opera, Nov. 26, 1906); *Gloria* (La Scala, April 15, 1907); also *Poema Sinfonico* for solo, chorus and orch. (Genoa, July 12, 1913); piano trio (1886); cello sonata (1888); variations for violin and piano (1931); piano pieces; songs.—Bibl.: Ettore Moschino, *Sulle opere di Francesco Cilèa* (Milan, 1932); C. P. Gaianus, *Francesco Cilèa e la sua nuova ora* (Bologna, 1939).

Cima (chē'-măh), **Giovanni Paolo,** Italian organist and composer; b. Milan, c. 1570; d. during the first half of the 17th century. In 1609 he was organist at the cathedral of Milan. Publications of his works, including *Concerti ecclesiastici* and motets, appeared between 1598 and 1622. His *Partito de Ri-*

cercari e Canzoni alla francese (Milan, 1606) is a keyboard collection with an appendix containing rules for tuning keyboard instruments. The *Canzoni alla francese* of this collection are specially written for keyboard, and the *ricercari* are highly developed in their use of imitation. A modern reprint of a *Ricercare per organo* is contained in L. Torchi's *L'Arte Musicale in Italia* (vol. III).

Cimadoro (chē-mah-dŏhr'-ŏh), **Giovanni Battista,** Italian composer; b. Venice, 1761; d. Bath, England, Feb. 27, 1805. After early successes in Italy, where he produced an opera *Pimmaglione* (*Pygmalion;* Venice, Jan. 26, 1790), he settled in London; several arias from *Pygmalion* were published in London, and acquired considerable popularity. While in England, he used the shortened form of his name, Cimador.

Cimara (chē'-mah-rah), **Pietro,** conductor; b. Rome, Nov. 10, 1887. He was educated at the Accademia Santa Cecilia (grad., 1914); was a pupil of Respighi; won the special medal of the Ministry of Public Instruction; made his debut as conductor in 1916 at the Teatro Costanzi, Rome; in 1927 began conducting at the Metropolitan Opera; remained at this post for 30 years. He has composed numerous songs, published in Italy and America.

Cimarosa (chē-mah-rŏh'-sah), **Domenico,** eminent Italian composer; b. Aversa, near Naples, Dec. 17, 1749; d. Venice, Jan. 11, 1801. The son of a poor mason and early orphaned, he attended the charity-school of the Minorites; his first music teacher was Polcano, organist of the monastery. His talent was so marked that in 1761 he obtained a free scholarship to the Conservatorio di Santa Maria di Loreto, where he was taught singing by Manna and Sacchini, counterpoint by Fenaroli, and composition by Piccini. In 1770 his oratorio *Giuditta* was performed in Rome; in 1772, having graduated from the Conservatory, he produced his first opera, *Le Stravaganze del Conte,* at Naples, with moderate success. But with *La finta parigina,* given next season at the Teatro Nuovo, Naples, he was fairly launched on a dramatic career singularly free from artistic reverses. His ease and rapidity of composition were phenomenal; in 29 years he wrote nearly 80 operas. His fame grew steadily, eventually rivaling that of Paisiello. In 1778 Cimarosa brought out *L'Italiana in Londra* in Rome, and lived, until 1781, alternately in Rome and Naples; following the custom of the period, he wrote one opera after another specially for the city in which it was to be performed. His speed of composition was such that during the year 1781 he brought out two operas in Naples, one in Rome, and two in Turin. His works became known far beyond the bounds of Italy; they were performed not only by Italian opera troupes in all European capitals, but also by foreign opera companies, in translation. After Paisiello's return from St. Petersburg, where he had served from 1776-85 as court composer, his post was offered to Cimarosa. He accepted, and set out for St. Petersburg in the autumn of 1787. His journey there was like a triumphant procession; at the courts of Florence, Vienna and Warsaw, he was overwhelmed with attentions; and he arrived in St. Petersburg, Dec. 2, 1787, wayworn and suffering from the wintry weather, but confident of success. Here he produced three operas, and during the three years of his stay wrote various other compositions for the court and nobility, including a ballet, *La felicità inaspettata* (Feb. 24, 1788) and a dramatic cantata, *Atene edificata* (June 29, 1788). But as Catherine the Great did not care for his choral works, he was replaced by Sarti, and in 1791 he left Russia; in the autumn of that year he arrived in Vienna, where Emperor Leopold engaged him at a salary of 12,000 florins as Kapellmeister. At Vienna, at the age of 42, he brought out his masterpiece, *Il Matrimonio segreto* (Feb. 7, 1792), the success of which eclipsed not only that of his former works but that of the works of all rivals, not excepting Mozart. It is probably the sole survivor, on the present-day stage, of all Cimarosa's dramatic works. Cimarosa remained long enough in Vienna to write two more operas; 1793 found him once more at home in Naples, where his *Matrimonio segreto* aroused unexampled enthusiasm, having 67 consecutive performances, the illustrious composer himself playing the cembalo for the first seven representations. In 1794 he visited Venice to bring out *Gli Orazi e Curiazi;* in 1796 and 1798 he was in Rome, periodically returning to Naples, and all the time actively engaged in operatic composition. In 1798, he was seriously ill at Naples; the year after, having openly taken part in the Neapolitan revolutionary demonstration on the entrance of the French army into the city, he was imprisoned for a number of days. He then went to Venice, and was at work on a new opera, *Artemisia,* when death suddenly overtook him. It was rumored abroad that he had been poisoned by order of Queen Caroline of Naples, as a dangerous revolutionist; the rumor was so persistent, and popular embitterment so great, that the Pope's personal physician, Piccioli, was sent to make an examination; according to his sworn statement, Cimarosa died of a gangrenous abdominal tumor.

Comedy opera was Cimarosa's *forte:* in his happiest moments he rivals Mozart; even in 'opera seria' many of his efforts are worthy of a place in the repertory. The fluidity and fecundity of his melodic vein, his supreme command of form, and his masterly control of orchestral resources still excite astonishment and admiration. He was the peer of his great Italian contemporary, Paisiello. Of the 76 operas known as his, some of the finest are mentioned below: *La finta parigina* (Naples, 1773); *Il Fanatico per gli antichi Romani* (Naples, 1777); *L'Italiana in Londra* (Rome, Dec. 28, 1778); *L'Infedeltà fedele* (Naples, July 20, 1779); *Caio Mario* (Rome, Jan., 1780); *Il convito di pietra* (Venice, Dec. 27, 1781); *Giannina e Bernardone* (Venice, Nov., 1781); *La ballerina amante* (Naples, 1782); *Artaserse* (Turin, Dec. 26, 1784); *Le Trame deluse* (Naples, Sept., 1786); *L'Impressario in angustie* (Naples, Oct., 1786); *Le vergine del sole* (St. Petersburg, Nov. 6, 1789); *Il Matrimonio segreto* (Vienna, Feb. 7, 1792; given in English with great success at the Metropolitan Opera, in 1937); *Le astuzie femminili* (Naples, Aug. 16, 1794); *Orazi e Curiazi* (Venice, Dec. 26, 1796). He also produced three oratorios; several cantatas; masses in four parts, with instrumental accompaniment; psalms, motets, requiems, arias, cavatinas, solfeggi, and a great variety of other vocal works; 7 symphonies; cembalo sonatas (of which 32 were edited and published by F. Boghen, Paris, 1926). Bibl.: P. Cambiasi, *Notizie sulla vita e sulle opere di D. Cimarosa* (Milan, 1901); F. Polidoro, *La vita e le opere di D. Cimarosa,* in 'Atti del' Accademia Pontiniana' (1902); A. della Corte, in *L'opera comica italiana nel 1700* (1925); R. Vitale, *D. Cimarosa* (Aversa, 1929); G. Biamonti, *Il matrimonio segreto* (Rome, 1930); M. Tibaldi Chiesa, *Cimarosa e il suo tempo* (Milan, 1939); Carl Engel, *A Note on Cimarosa's 'Il matrimonio segreto',* in the 'Mus. Quarterly' (April, 1947); A. Mooser, *Annales de la musique et des musiciens en Russie au XVIIIe siècle* (Geneva, 1951; pp. 451-455).

Cipollini (chē-poh-lē'-nē), **Gaetano,** Italian composer; b. Tropea, Cantanzaro, Feb. 28, 1851; d. Milan, Oct. 1, 1935. He was a pupil of Francesco Coppa; composed the effective melodrama in 3 acts, *Gennariello* (Milan, June 1, 1891); *Il piccolo Haydn,* lyric comedy (Como, Jan. 24, 1893); *Ninon de Lenclos,* lyric comedy (Milan, Dec. 3, 1895); a large number of *romanze* for voice; piano pieces. A five-act opera, *Simeta,* remained in MS.

Cipra, Milo, Croatian composer; b. Vareš, Bosnia, Oct. 13, 1906. He studied at the Zagreb Cons. with Bersa, and in 1952 was appointed professor there. His orchestral works include 2 symphonies and a *Slavic Rhapsody.* In addition he has written 4 string quartets, a piano trio, a violin sonata, and a cello sonata. His music reflects the national trend; his style is neo-classical. Cipra is regarded as one of the most prominent composers of chamber music in Croatia.

Cisneros (this-nä'rōhs), **Eleanora de** (neé **Broadfoot),** American mezzo-soprano; b. New York, Nov. 1, 1878; d. there, Feb. 3, 1934. She studied in N. Y. with Mme. Murio-Celli, later with Jean de Reszke and Angelo Trabadello in Paris; she first appeared at the Metropolitan Opera in Jan., 1900, at a Sunday concert; operatic debut same season at the Philadelphia Academy of Music as Amneris in *Aïda;* 1901, married Count Francesco de Cisneros of Havana. From 1907-09 sang at the Manhattan Opera House; was engaged at the Chicago Opera (1910), and at the Havana Opera (1915-1916).

Citkowitz, Israel, American composer; b. in Russia, Feb. 6, 1909; brought to the U.S. as an infant; became a U.S. citizen. He studied with Sessions, Copland and Nadia Boulanger. In 1939 he became instructor at the Dalcroze School of Music in New York. He has written mainly in the smaller forms; his choral music is distinguished by considerable power of expression.

Ciurlionis (chör-lyoh'-nēs), **Mikalojus Konstantinas,** Lithuanian composer; b. Varena, near Vilna, Sept. 22, 1875; d. near Warsaw, March 28, 1911. He studied with Noskowski at the Warsaw Cons. (graduated in 1898) and at the Leipzig Cons. (graduated in 1902); was also a noted painter; arranged several exhibits of his pictures in St. Petersburg. He wrote two symph. poems: *In the Forest* (1901) and *The Ocean* (1904); published collections of Lithuanian folksongs.

Claassen, Arthur, conductor and composer; b. Stargard, Prussia, Feb. 19, 1859; d. San Francisco, March 16, 1920. He studied in Weimar with Müller-Hartung, A. W. Gottschalk and B. Sulze. As early as 1878 his compositions aroused Liszt's interest. From 1880-84 he was a theater conductor in Göttingen and Magdeburg. In 1884 Claassen was chosen, on Leopold Damrosch's recommendation, conductor of the Brooklyn 'Arion', which post he held for 25 years, establishing his reputation as an outstanding choral conductor. In 1910 he settled in San Antonio, Texas, and became a powerful factor in stimulating the appreciation of music in the South through the founding of the San Antonio Symphony Society, and the Mozart and Beethoven choral societies. He lived in San Francisco in the last years of his life. Works: *Festival Hymn* for soli, chorus and orch.; symph. poem *Hohenfriedberg; The Battle,* for soli, chorus and orch.; *Waltz-Idyll* for string orch.; many choruses, among which *Der Kamerad* took 1st composition prize at the N. Y. Singing Festival.

Clapp, Philip Greeley, American composer and teacher; b. Boston, Mass., Aug. 4, 1888; d. Iowa City, April 9, 1954. He was educated at Harvard (B.A. 1908; M.A., 1909; Ph.D., 1911); also studied composition and conducting with Max Schillings in Stuttgart. Teaching positions: Harvard (1911-12), Dartmouth College (1915-18). In 1919 he became professor and director of music at the Univ. of Iowa, Iowa City; was on the faculty of Juilliard School, N. Y. (1927-28). Clapp was guest conductor with major orchestras, conducting his own works. He wrote 10 symphonies (No. 2, Boston, 1914; No. 3, Boston, 1917; No. 7, Boston, 1931); the symph. poems *Norge* (Pierian Sodality Centennial, Harvard Univ., 1908), *Summer* (St. Louis, 1914), *Song of Youth;* string quartet in C (Chicago, 1925); Sonata for violin; Sonatina for piano; *An Academic Diversion on Seven Notes,* a small symph. for chamber orch. (Chicago, 1933); *A Chant of Darkness* for chorus and orch.; smaller instrumental compositions; piano concerto; numerous songs; anthems (*O Gladsome Light,* etc.).

Clari (klah'-rē), **Giovanni Carlo Maria,** Italian composer and choral director; b. Pisa, Sept. 27, 1667; d. there, May 16, 1754. He studied under Colonna at Bologna, where his opera *Il Savio delirante* was produced in 1695; from 1712-36 he was in Pistoia as maestro di cappella of the cathedral; then went to Pisa. His best known work is a collection of madrigals for 2 and 3 voices (1720; reprinted by Carli, Paris, in 1825); also wrote masses, psalms, a requiem, other sacred music.

Claribel. Pen name of Mrs. **Charles Barnard.**

Clark, Edward, English conductor; b. Newcastle-on-Tyne, May 10, 1888. He studied in Paris, Vienna, and in Berlin with Schoenberg. He led the orchestra for Diaghilev's London seasons (1924-26); was with the BBC (1927-36); in 1940 he founded the North Eastern Regional Orch. in Newcastle. In 1947 he was elected president of the International Society for Contemporary Music. He is married to the composer Elizabeth Lutyens.

Clark, Frederick Scotson, English clergyman, organist and composer; b. London, Nov. 16, 1840; d. there, July 5, 1883. He studied with Sergent in Paris and with E. J. Hopkins; also studied at the Royal Academy of Music in London with Bennett, Goss, Engel, Pettit and Pinsuti; received his religious education at Cambridge and Oxford; was organist of Exeter College, Oxford; took further music lessons in Leipzig and Stuttgart; returned to London in 1873, where he founded the London Organ School; was the representative English organist at the Paris Exposition of 1878. His organ compositions (15 marches, 48 voluntaries, 6 communions; offertories, improvisations, impromptus, etc.) are his best works; composed over 100 piano pieces; sacred vocal music, songs, etc. Clark also played and composed for the harmonium.

Clark, Melville, one of the pioneers of the player-piano industry; b. Oneida Co., N. Y., 1850; d. Chicago, Nov. 5, 1918. In 1875 he established himself as an organ builder in Oakland, Calif.; moved to Chicago in 1880; in 1894 he also opened a piano factory, after he had become interested in pneumatic actions; his experiments leading to practical results which convinced him of the possibilities of the player-piano, he sold his organ factory, and, in 1900, organized the Melville Clark Piano Co., of which he was President. In 1901 he patented and placed on the market the 88-note roll, utilizing the full compass of the piano, and thus gave the impetus to the phenomenal player piano industry which later developed. In 1911 he patented a recording mechanism, which aimed to reproduce the actual performance of great pianists. He also held many other important patents.

Clark, Melville Antone, nephew of the preceding, harpist and harp manufacturer; b. Syracuse, N. Y., Sept. 12, 1883; d. there, Dec. 11, 1953. He received his first instruction on the harp from his father; pupil of Van Veachton Rogers (1896-9) and of John Aptommas in London (1908). While on a tour of Great Britain in 1908 he acquired a small Irish harp, formerly the property of the poet Thomas Moore; by the application of acoustic principles he improved the model and succeeded in producing a small, portable harp (39 inches high) of considerable tone-volume; founded the 'Clark Harp Manufacturing Co.' at Syracuse, which turned out the first small Irish harps in 1913; on a tour of the U. S. with John McCormack (1913-4) the inventor demonstrated the possibilities of the new instrument; took out fourteen patents on improvements for the portable harp and developed a new method of pedaling the concert harp; played about 4,000 recitals in the U. S., Canada and England; was cofounder of the Syracuse Symph. Orch.; Treasurer of the National Association of Harpists; President of the Clark Music Co. (1910); author of *How to Play the Harp, Romance of the Harp, Singing Strings.*

Clarke, Eric T., music educator; b. Harrow-on-the-Hill, England, Sept. 13, 1890; first studied medicine at Univ. College, London (1908-10), then music at the Guildhall School of Music (French horn, 1907-10), and Hampstead Cons. (cello); 1923-28, director of the Eastman Theater, Univ. of Rochester, N. Y.; 1928-33, managing director of the National Music League; 1933-36, musical consultant of Carnegie Corp.; 1936-40, founder and director of the Arts Program Association of American Colleges; 1940-45, Secretary of the Metropolitan Opera Association; 1945-49, officer in the Arts Program for the Allied Military Government of Germany; in 1949 appointed officer, Motion Picture Division, U.S. State Dept. He publ. *Music in Everyday Life* (N. Y., 1935).

Clarke, Henry Leland, American musicologist and composer; b. Dover, N. H., March 9, 1907; studied piano, violin and organ; then entered Harvard University, receiving his M. A. in 1929, and Ph.D. in 1947 with a treatise on John Blow. He continued his studies in composition with Nadia Boulanger in Paris. Upon his return to America, he taught at various colleges; in 1950 was appointed assistant professor at the University of California, L.A. He has contributed numerous essays to music magazines; has written a chamber opera, *The Loafer and the Loaf* (1951; first perf., University of California, May 1, 1956); orchestral sketch, *Monograph* (1952); 2 string quartets; *Nocturne* for viola and piano (1955); *No Man is an Island,* for men's chorus and symph. band (1951); several other choral works. His thematic material is based on selective rows of notes, approximating a dodecaphonic technique.

Clarke, Hugh Archibald, organist; b. near Toronto, Canada, Aug. 15, 1839; d. Philadelphia, Dec. 16, 1927. Pupil of his father, James Peyton Clarke; was organist in several churches in Philadelphia; in 1875 was elected Professor of the Science of Music in the University of Pennsylvania; retired in 1925. Clarke composed music to Euripides' *Iphigenia in Tauris,* an oratorio, *Jerusalem* (1891), piano music and songs. He published a treatise on harmony and one on counterpoint, also textbooks for organ; a book of fiction *The Scratch Club* (1888); *Music and the Comrade Arts* (1900); *Highways and Byways of Music* (1901).

Clarke, James Hamilton Smee, English organist; b. Birmingham, Jan. 25, 1840; d. Banstead, July 9, 1912. He was apprenticed to a land surveyor 1855-61; then turned to music, and in 1866 became organist to Queen's College, Oxford. In 1872 he succeeded Sullivan as organist of St. Peter's, South Kensington; was conductor of the D'Oyly Carte company on tour (1878); and also at the Lyceum Theatre, writing music for dramas given by Henry Irving. In 1893, first conductor of the Carl Rosa company. He published about 400 works, including music to *Hamlet, Merchant of Venice* and *King Lear;* the sacred cantata *Praise;* 8-part anthem, *The Lord is my light;* 2 symphonies; 6 overtures; organ music.

Clarke, James Peyton, Scottish organist; b. 1808; d. Toronto, Aug. 27, 1877. In 1829, leader of psalmody in St. George's Church, Edinburgh; 1834, organist of St. Mary's Episcopal chapel, succeeding Thomas Macfarlane; emigrated to Canada, 1835, settling as a farmer in Ellora, but went to Toronto about 1841; about 1845 was elected prof. of music in Upper Canada University, and in 1846 took degree of Mus. Bac. at King's College with the 8-part anthem *Arise, O Lord God, forget not the poor.*

Clarke, Jeremiah, English composer and organist; b. London, c. 1673; d. there (suicide), Dec. 1, 1707. He was a chorister in the Chapel Royal; in 1693 succeeded Dr. John Blow as master of the choristers at St. Paul's; in 1695 was appointed organist; in 1700 was made Gentleman Extraordinary of the Chapel Royal; in 1704 was appointed joint organist (with Croft) there. A hopeless love affair caused Clarke to take his own life. He composed (with others) the operas

The World in the Moon (1697) and *The Island Princess* (1699); wrote incidental music to several plays; was the first composer to set Dryden's *Alexander's Feast* to music (for St. Cecilia's Day, Nov. 22, 1697); also wrote a cantata, an ode, anthems, songs, etc. He was the real author of the famous *Trumpet Voluntary,* erroneously ascribed to Purcell, and popularized by Sir Henry Wood's orchestral arrangement. See C. L. Cudworth, *Some New Facts about the Trumpet Voluntary* in 'The Musical Times' (Sept., 1953).

Clarke, John (Clarke-Whitfield), English organist and composer; b. Gloucester, Dec. 13, 1770; d. Holmer, near Hereford, Feb. 22, 1836. He studied organ at Oxford with Philip Hayes; received his B. Mus. degree in 1793; was church organist at Ludlow, Armagh and Dublin; in 1799 he became choirmaster of Trinity and St. John's College in Cambridge; from 1820 to 1832 he was organist at the Hereford Cathedral. He was stricken with paralysis; was forced to resign his post, and was an invalid for the rest of his life. He wrote an oratorio *The Crucifixion and the Resurrection* (Hereford, 1822); four volumes of cathedral services and anthems (1805); 12 glees (1805); 12 songs; a *Selection of Single and Double Chants;* etc. He also edited the *Vocal Works of Handel* (1809, 17 vols.) with piano accompaniment.

Clarke, Rebecca, English composer and viola player; b. Harrow, Aug. 27, 1886. She studied at the Royal College of Music with Sir Charles Stanford (composition); was originally a violinist, but specialized later as a viola player. In 1916 she went to the U.S.; in 1923 returned to England; in 1928, formed the English Ensemble, a piano quartet, and toured with it in Europe. She began to compose seriously after her arrival in the U.S. during World War I; won second prize in the Coolidge competition at the Berkshire Festival of 1919 with a viola sonata; other works include a piano trio (1921); *Chinese Puzzle* for violin and piano (1922); *Rhapsody* for cello and piano (1923); also three *Irish Country Songs* for violin and cello. Her music is quite advanced in modern technique, touching the fringes of atonality in melodic outline; impressionistic influences are felt in her early works. See the entry on her chamber music in Cobbett's *Cyclopedic Survey of Chamber Music* (1929).

Clarke, Robert Coningsby, English song composer; b. Old Charlton, Kent, March 17, 1879; d. Walmer, Kent, Jan. 2, 1934. He studied with Sir John Frederick Bridge at Westminster Abbey; then served as church organist at Oxford. He wrote a number of popular ballads and piano pieces.

Clarke, William Horatio, American organist; b. Newton, Mass., March 8, 1840; d. Reading, Mass., Dec. 11, 1913. He was church organist in Boston, Dedham and Waltham from 1856 till 1871, when he went to Dayton, Ohio; later was in Indianapolis. He returned to Boston in 1878, and was organist at Tremont Temple; retired in 1887 to his estate in Reading, Mass., where he built a chapel of music, Clarigold Hall, containing a large 4-manual organ with 100 stops.

Clarus (klah'-rŏŏs), **Max,** German composer; b. Mühlberg, March 31, 1852; d. Braunschweig, Dec. 6, 1916. He studied with his father, who was a municipal music director, and with Löschhorn in Berlin. He became a theatrical conductor, traveling in Germany, Austria and Hungary; composed mostly for the stage and for chorus. Works: the operas (all produced in Braunschweig) *Des Königs-Rekrut* (1889); *Ilse* (1895; quite successful at the time); fairy operas *Der Wunschpeter* (1910) and *Der Zwerg Nase* (1912); also several ballets (*Opium-Träume,* etc.) and a tone-picture, *Die Wacht vor Samoa* for baritone solo, male chorus and orch., also numerous a cappella choruses.

Claudin le Jeune. See **Le Jeune.**

Claussen (klow'-sen), **Julia** (*née* Ohlson), dramatic mezzo-soprano; b. Stockholm, June 11, 1879; d. there, May 1, 1941. She studied at the Royal Academy of Music in Stockholm (1897-1902); then in Berlin with Prof. Friedrich. She made her debut as Leonora in *La Favorita* at the Stockholm Opera (Jan. 19, 1903); was engaged there from 1903 until 1912; made her debut at Covent Garden, London, in 1914; was a member of the Chicago Opera Company during World War I. She made her first appearance at the Metropolitan Opera House as Dalila on Nov. 23, 1917, and remained in the company until 1932; in 1934 she returned to Stockholm as a teacher at the Royal Academy of Music. After her death a memorial fund for vocal scholarships was established in Stockholm.

Clavé (klăh-vā'), **José Anselmo,** Spanish choral leader; b. Barcelona, April 21, 1824; d. there, Feb. 24, 1874. He was inspired by the success of the 'orpheons' in France, and organized male singing societies in Spain on a similar scale. At the first singing festival in Barcelona in 1860 he conducted a chorus of 200 voices; in 1864 he augmented his ensemble to 2,000 singers, representing 57 organizations. Some of his songs and choruses, especially composed for his festivals, enjoyed great popularity. Bibl.: J. Subirá, *El Músico-poeta Clavé* (Madrid, 1924); T. Caballé y Clós, *J. A. Clavé y su tiempo* (Barcelona, 1949).

Clay, Frédéric, composer; b. (of English parents) Paris, Aug. 3, 1838; d. Great Marlow, near London, Nov. 24, 1889. He studied with Molique at Paris and with Hauptmann in Leipzig. His early operettas, *The Pirate's Isle* (1859) and *Out of Sight* (1860), were performed privately in London; his first operetta to be produced at Covent Garden was *Court and Cottage* (1862); other light dramatic works subsequently performed at Covent Garden included *Constance* (1865); *Ages Ago* (1869); *The Gentleman in Black* (1870); *Happy Arcadia* (1872); *Cattarina* (1874); *Princess Toto* (1876); *Don Quixote* (1876). He also composed two cantatas, *The Knights of the Cross* (1866) and *Lalla Rookh* (1877; including the well-known aria *I'll sing thee songs of Araby*).

Clemens, Charles Edwin, organist; b. Plymouth, England, March 12, 1858; d. Cleveland, Ohio, Dec. 26, 1923. He studied at the Royal College of Music in London; as a boy played organ in churches; served as organist of the English Church in Berlin (1889-1896); settled in Cleveland as choirmaster at St. Paul's Church (1896-1911); then was organist at the Presbyterian Church (Cleveland); also taught at Western Reserve Univ. He published two manuals: *Pedal Technique* (1894) and *Modern School for the Organ* (1903).

Clemens, Hans, lyric tenor; b. Bicken-Gelsenkirchen, Germany, July 27, 1890. After successful appearances in Germany and at Covent Garden, London, he came to the U.S.; made his New York debut at the Metropolitan Opera House in *The Flying Dutchman* (Nov. 1, 1930); appeared also in other Wagnerian roles; was particularly effective as David in *Die Meistersinger,* a role which he sang more than 100 times. In 1938 he settled in Los Angeles as a vocal teacher.

Clemens, Jacobus (real name Clement), called **'Clemens non Papa,'** eminent Netherlandish contrapuntist; b. Ypres, c. 1510; d. Dixmude, c. 1556 (death date is surmised from the fact that vol. 1 of 'Novum et insigne opus musicum', publ. in 1558, contains the motet *Nanie,* composed by Jacob Vaet on Clemens' death). The exact meaning of 'non Papa' is not clear; it was once thought to mean 'not the Pope', to distinguish the composer from Clement VII; but a more recent interpretation suggests that 'non Papa' was intended to differentiate Clemens from a poet also living in the town of Ypres, named Jacobus Papa. His teachers are not known; he was in France for a time; returned in 1540 to the Netherlands and settled in Bruges; in 1545 he went to Antwerp; later lived in Dixmude, where he was buried. Works: 15 masses, numerous motets, chansons, etc., publ. by Phalèse (Louvain, 1555-80); 4 books of *Souterliedekens a 3,* i. e., psalms set to popular Netherlandish tunes, publ. by T. Susato (Antwerp, 1556-57); and many miscellaneous pieces in collections of the period. Reprints are to be found in K. Proske's 'Musica divina' (vol. II); R. J. van Maldeghem's 'Trésor musical', and F. Commer's 'Collectio operum musicorum Batavorum'. El. Mincoff-Marriage republished the text of the *Souterliedekens* (The Hague, 1922); a selection of 15 of these pieces, with music, was edited by W. Blanke (Wolfenbüttel, 1929). Bibl.: J. Schmidt, *Die Messen des Clemens non Papa,* in the 'Zeitschrift für Musikwissenschaft' (1926); K. P. Bernet Kempers, *Zur Biographie des Clemens non Papa* (ibid., 1927); K. P. Bernet Kempers, *J. Clemens non Papa und seine Motetten* (Augsburg, 1928). A complete ed. of his works was begun in Amsterdam (1953) under the editorship of K. P. Bernet Kempers.

Clément, Edmond, French tenor; b. Paris, March 28, 1867; d. Nice, Feb. 24, 1928. Pupil of Warot at the Paris Cons. in 1887; first prize, 1889; debut at Opéra-Comique, Nov. 29, 1889, as Vincent in Gounod's *Mireille.* His success was instantaneous, and he remained there until 1910 with frequent leave for extended tours; sang in the principal theaters of France, Belgium, Spain, Portugal, England and Denmark; 1909-10 at the Metropolitan Opera House; 1911-13, with the Boston Opera Co.; in the spring of 1913 he made an extended and very successful concert tour of the U. S. and Canada. His voice was a light tenor of very agreeable quality, with a range of two octaves. He created the chief tenor parts in the following operas (all at the Opéra-Comique): Bruneau's *L'Attaque du Moulin* (1893), Saint-Saëns' *Phryne* (1893), Cui's *Le Flibustier* (1894), Godard's *La Vivandière* (1895), Dubois' *Xavière* (1895), Hahn's *L'Île du*

Rêve (1898), Erlanger's *Le Juif polonais* (1900), Saint-Saëns *Hélène* (1904), Dupont's *La Cabrera* (1905), Vidal's *La Reine Fiammette* (1908). Was famous for his Werther and for Des Grieux (*Manon*).

Clément, Félix, French writer on music; b. Paris, Jan. 13, 1822; d. there, Jan. 23, 1885. He devoted himself especially to historical studies; filled several positions as organist and teacher, and finally became organist and choirmaster at the Church of the Sorbonne. In 1849 the government chose him to direct music of the 13th century at the Sainte-Chapelle; published in score as 'Chants de la Sainte-Chapelle,' in the same year (3d ed. 1875). He was active in establishing the 'Institution for Church Music.' Writings: *Méthode complète du plain-chant* (1854; 1872); *Histoire générale de la musique religieuse* (1860); *Les Musiciens célèbres depuis le XVI*e *siècle* (1868; 4th ed. 1887); *Dictionnaire lyrique, ou histoire des opéras* (1869, 4 supplements up to 1881; new augm. ed. by A. Pougin, 1897 and 1904, under the title *Dictionnaire des opéras*); *Méthode d'orgue, d'harmonie et d'accompagnement* (1874; 2d ed. 1894); *Histoire de la musique depuis les temps anciens jusquà nos jours* (1885); etc.

Clement, Franz, Austrian violinist and composer; b. Vienna, Nov. 17, 1780; d. there, Nov. 3, 1842. He learned to play the violin as a child, and at the age of ten went to London where he appeared as a soloist at concerts directed by Salomon and Haydn. Returning to Vienna, he continued his successful career; was conductor at the Theater an-der-Wien (1802-11); made a tour in Germany and Russia (1813-18); participated in the concerts of the famous singer Angelica Catalani. He was greatly esteemed as violinist and musician by his contemporaries; Beethoven wrote his violin concerto for him, and Clement gave its first performance in Vienna (Dec. 23, 1806). He wrote 6 concertos and 25 concertinos for violin, as well as numerous technical studies. See Robert Haas, *The Viennese Violinist Franz Clement,* in the 'Mus. Quarterly' (Jan., 1948).

Clementi, Muzio, celebrated pianist and composer; b. Rome, Jan. 23, 1752; d. at his country-seat at Evesham, England, March 10, 1832. His father, a goldsmith ('orefice'), was a devoted amateur of music, and had his son taught carefully, from early years, by Antonio Buroni, maestro di cappella in a Roman church. From 1759 the organist Condiceli gave him lessons in organ playing and harmony. So rapid was their pupil's progress that when but nine he obtained a position as organist, in competition with other and maturer players. Until fourteen years of age he pursued his studies in Italy, G. Carpani (composition) and Sartarelli (voice) being his next instructors. At a piano concert which Clementi gave in 1766, an English gentleman named Beckford was so delighted with his talent that he obtained the father's permission to educate the boy in England. Clementi lived and studied till 1770 in his patron's house in Dorsetshire; then, a thoroughly equipped pianist and musician, he took London by storm. In 1773 his op. 2 (3 piano sonatas dedicated to Haydn, and warmly praised by K. Ph. E. Bach) was published; they may be considered as finally establishing the form of the piano sonata. From 1777-80 he conducted, as cembalist, the Italian Opera. In 1781 he began a pianistic tour, giving concerts at Paris, Strasbourg, Munich and Vienna; here, on Dec. 24, 1781, he met Mozart in 'friendly' rivalry (Mozart's letters make no pretence of concealing his dislike of the 'Italian' composer and player); though the palm of final victory was awarded to neither, yet Clementi tacitly admitted, by changing from a mechanically brilliant to a more suave and melodious piano-style, the musical superiority of Mozart. In Vienna his opp. 7, 9, and 10 were published by Artaria. Excepting a concert season at Paris, in 1785, Clementi now remained in London for 20 years (1782-1802). He not only made his mark, and incidentally amassed quite a fortune, as a teacher, pianist and composer, but also (after losses through the failure of Longman & Broderip, the instrument makers and music sellers) established, with John Longman, a highly successful piano factory and publishing house (now Collard & Collard). With his pupil Field, Clementi set out for St. Petersburg in 1802, passing through Paris and Vienna; their tour was attended by brilliant success, and Field was so well received in St. Petersburg that he accompanied his master no further. Clementi resided for several years alternately in Berlin, Dresden and St. Petersburg; then, after visiting Vienna, Milan, Rome and Naples, he again settled in London. The business-man in Clementi now gained the upper hand; he no longer played in public, but devoted himself to composition and the management of his prosperous mercantile ventures. He never again went far from London, except during the winter of 1820-21, which he spent in Leipzig. As a teacher Clementi trained many distinguished mussicians; Field, Cramer, Moscheles, Kalkbrenner, Alexander Klengel, Ludwig Berger,

Zeuner, even Meyerbeer, all owed much to his instruction. His compositions include symphonies (which failed in competition wth Haydn's), and overtures for orchestra; 106 piano sonatas (46 with violin, cello, or flute); 2 duos for 2 pianos; 6 4-hand duets; fugues, preludes and exercises in canon-form, toccatas, waltzes, variations, caprices, *Points d'orgue . . .* (op. 19); an *Introduction à l'art de toucher le piano, avec 50 leçons,* etc.; by far the greater part of which are wholly forgotten. But his great book of études, the *Gradus ad Parnassum* (publ. 1817), is a living reminder that he was one of the greatest of piano teachers. Bülow's excellent selection of 50 of these études has been outdone by several later complete eds. (German, Italian, English), including that of Vogrich, arranged progressively (N. Y., 1898).—The Library of Congress, Wash., D. C., acquired, largely through the efforts of Carl Engel, numerous MSS by Clementi, including 4 symphonies (almost complete); other fragments are in the British Museum. The first 2 of these symphonies were restored and edited for publication by Alfredo Casella, who performed them (using Clementi's original instrumentation) for the first time (No. 1, Turin, Dec. 13, 1935; No. 2, Rome, Jan. 5, 1936).

Biographies of Clementi have been written by Giov. Froio: *Muzio Clementi, la sua vita, le sue opere e sua influenza sul progresso dell' arte* (Milan, 1876); by O. Chilesotti in *I nostri maestri del passato* (Milan, 1882); F. Clément has a sketch in his *Les Musiciens célèbres depuis le XVI siècle* (Paris, 1878); J. S. Shedlock in *The Pianoforte Sonata* (London, 1895); M. Unger, *Muzio Clementi's Leben* (Leipzig, 1914); G. C. Paribeni, *Muzio Clementi nella vita e nell'arte* (1921); A. Longo, *Gradus ad Parnassum* (analysis), in *Arte pianistica* (1922); G. de Saint-Foix, *Muzio Clementi,* in the 'Mus. Quarterly' (July, 1923); id., *Les symphonies de Clementi* in the 'Revue de Musicologie' (1924); id., *Clementi, a Forerunner of Beethoven,* in the 'Mus. Quarterly' (Jan., 1931); A. Stauch, *Muzio Clementis Klaviersonaten im Verhältnis zu den Sonaten von Haydn, Mozart, Beethoven* (dissertation, Cologne, 1929); A. Casella, *Muzio Clementi et ses symphonies,* in the 'Revue musicale' (March, 1936); H. Simon, *The Clementi Manuscripts at the Library of Congress,* in the 'Mus. Quarterly' (Jan., 1942).

Clemm, John (Johann Gottlob), German-American organ builder; b. Dresden, 1690; d. Bethlehem, Pa., May 5, 1762. Clemm reputedly learned organ making from A. Silbermann, probably while serving the Moravian Church settlement at Herrnhut, Saxony. He came to America with a group of Schwenkfelders in 1735, became a Separatist, and settled in Philadelphia in 1736. His first known organ was installed in Trinity Church, New York, in 1741. Subsequently, he assisted the Swedish-American organ builder, Hesselius, in Philadelphia. He reunited with the Moravians and moved to Bethlehem, Pa. (1756-58). There he continued his work with his assistant, David Tannenberg (q.v.) until his death. His descendants were important music dealers and publishers in Philadelphia up to 1879. His son, **John Clemm, Jr.**, was the first organist at New York's Trinity Church.—Cf. A. H. Messiter, *History of the Choir and Music of Trinity Church* (N. Y., 1907); Donald M. McCorkle, *The Moravian Contribution to American Music,* in 'Music Library Association Notes' (Sept., 1956).

Cleonides, a Greek writer on music; lived in the first half of the 2nd century, A.D. His treatise *Eisagoge harmonike* (*Introductio harmonica*), based on the theories of Aristoxenus, was for a long time ascribed to the mathematician Euclid, because it had been published under Euclid's name by Pena (Paris, 1557) and Meibom (Amsterdam, 1652), although it had been printed with the real author's name by Valla (Venice, 1497). A new critical edition was published by K. von Jan in 'Musici Scriptores Graeci'. There is a French translation by Ruelle (1896). For an English translation of the *Introductio harmonica* see Strunk's *Source Readings in Music History* (N. Y., 1950).

Clérambault (klär-ahn-boh'), **Louis Nicolas**, French composer and organist; b. Paris, Dec. 19, 1676; d. there, Oct. 26, 1749. He studied with André Raison; was organist at various Paris churches. He was a successful composer of theatrical pieces for the court: *Le Soleil vainqueur* (Paris, Oct. 21, 1721); *Le Départ du roi* (1745), etc. He also wrote a number of solo cantatas, in which genre he excelled; composed much organ music; some of his organ works are republished in Guilmant's 'Archives des maîtres de l'orgue.' His son, **César François Nicolas Clérambault** (1700-1760) was also an organist and composer.

Clercx, Suzanne, Belgian musicologist; b. Houdeng-Aimeries, June 7, 1910. She studied at the Univ. of Liège, obtaining a doctorate in art history and archeology (1939); studied musicology with Charles van den Borren; was librarian at the Brussels Cons. (1941-49). She published a number of valuable treatises on Belgian music, among them

H. J. de Croes (Brussels, 1940); *Grétry* (1944); *La baroque et la musique* (1948); *Pierre van Maldere* (1948); edited Boutmy's clavecin works in vol. V of 'Monumenta Musicae Belgicae' (Antwerp, 1943); contributed historical articles to various musicological magazines.

Clèreau, Pierre, 16th-century French composer. Virtually nothing is known about his life, except that he was a chorister in Toul as a youth. However, many of his sacred works and 3-part chansons have been preserved. The following are extant: 4 Masses (Paris, 1554); *Missa pro mortuis* (Paris, 1554); 2 books of odes to Ronsard's words (Paris, 1566; several reprints).—Cf. G. Thibault and L. Perceau, *Bibliographie des chansons de Ronsard mises en musique au XVIe siècle* (Paris, 1941).

Clérice (klā-rēs), **Justin,** opera composer; b. Buenos Aires, Oct. 16, 1863; d. Toulouse, Sept. 9, 1908. He left Argentina as a young boy and spent most of his life in Paris, studying at the Paris Cons. with Delibes and Pessard (1882). He wrote many comic operas, most of which were performed in Paris: *Figarella* (June 3, 1889); *Le 3e Hussards* (March 14, 1894); *Pavie* (Jan. 28, 1897); *L'Ordre de l'empereur* (March 3, 1902), etc. His most succesful comic opera *Le Meunier d'Alcala* was first performed in Portuguese (Lisbon, April 11, 1887); he also wrote an operetta *Phrynette* (1895); a pantomime, *Léda* (1896); a ballet-opera *Au temps jadis* (Monte Carlo, 1905).

Cleve (klā'-vĕ), **Halfdan,** Norwegian composer and pianist; b. Kongsberg, Oct. 5, 1879. He studied with his father, an organist, and with Winter-Hjelms in Oslo; continued his studies in Berlin with O. Raif and with Scharwenka brothers (1899-1903). He made his debut as pianist in Berlin (1902); returned to Oslo in 1910, and settled as pianist and teacher. Among his works are 5 piano concertos (1902, 1904, 1906, 1910, 1916); piano quintet; violin sonata; ballade for cello and piano; many piano pieces and songs.

Clicquot, French family of organ builders, of whom the earliest was **Robert Clicquot,** builder of the organ in the Versailles Chapel for Louis XIV (1711), and organs in the cathedrals of Rouen (1689) and Saint-Quentin (1703). His sons **Jean-Baptiste** (b. Paris, Nov. 3, 1678; d. there, 1744) and **Louis-Alexandre** (b. c. 1680; d. Paris, Jan. 25, 1760) were his helpers. The most renowned of the family was **François-Henri Clicquot** (b. 1732; d. Paris, May 24, 1790), who constructed the great organ of Versailles Cathedral (installed Oct. 31, 1761) and the organ of St. Sulpice, with 5 manuals, 66 stops and a 32-ft. pedal (1781). See F. Raugel, *Les Grandes Orgues des églises de Paris* (Paris, 1927); N. Dufourcq, *Les Clicquot* (Paris, 1942).

Cliffe, Frederick, English organist and composer; b. Bradford, Yorkshire, May 2, 1857; d. London, Nov. 19, 1931. He studied with his father, and showed such a precocious musical talent that at the age of eleven he performed his duties as organist at Wyke Parish Church; then was organist of the Bradford Festival Choral Society (1873-76); at the same time he continued his studies with Arthur Sullivan, Prout, Stainer and Franklin Taylor, as a scholarship student. In 1883 he joined the staff of the Royal College of Music, a post which he kept until his death. Works: symphony No. 1 (London, April 20, 1889); symphony No. 2 (Leeds, 1892); tone poem, *Cloud and Sunshine* (1890); violin concerto (1896); *Ode to the North-East Wind* for chorus and orch. (1905); church music.

Clifton, Chalmers, American conductor; b. Jackson, Miss., April 30, 1889. He studied at the Cincinnati College of Music; then at Harvard with E. B. Hill, Walter Spalding and W. C. Heilman; further in Paris with Vincent d'Indy and Gédalge. Returning to America he conducted at the Mus. Art Society in Boston; was musical director of the first Peterborough Festival in 1910; conducted the Cecilia Society of Boston (1915-17); enlisted in the U. S. Army, and served in the Intelligence Service. In 1919 he gave a concert of American music at the Paris Cons.; in 1920 conducted opera with the San Carlo Opera Co.; made appearances with orchestras in Cincinnati, Baltimore, Minneapolis and Boston; was active in the Federal Music Project in New York (1935-39); served in advisory capacity with various musical organizations. He has written a violin sonata; a suite for trumpet and orch.; two piano sonatas; etc.

Clippinger, David Alva, American choral conductor; b. Ohio, Sept. 2, 1860; d. Chicago, Feb. 20, 1938. He studied voice in London with William Shakespeare; then settled in Chicago where he conducted the Madrigal Club; edited the 'Mus. Monitor' and 'Western Mus. Herald'; publ. numerous manuals on the voice: *Systematic Voice Training* (1910); *The Head Voice and Other Problems* (1917); *Collective Voice*

Training (1924); *Fundamentals of Voice Training* (1929); *Sight-Singing Based on Rhythmic-Melodic-Harmonic Ear Training* (1931), etc.

Clokey, Joseph Waddell, American organist; b. New Albany, Indiana, Aug. 28, 1890. He studied at Miami Univ. (B.A., 1912) and at the Cincinnati Cons. of Music (grad., 1915); from 1915-26 taught theory of music at Miami Univ.; from 1926-39 taught organ at Pomona College, Claremont, Calif.; from 1939-46 was dean of the School of Fine Arts at Miami Univ.; retired and lived in Claremont, Calif. He has written much music for schools; among his works are the short operas *The Pied Piper of Hamelin* (Miami Univ., May 14, 1920); *The Nightingale* (after Andersen; Miami Univ., Dec. 12, 1925); *Our American Cousin* (Claremont, Calif., March 2, 1931); the sacred cantatas *The Vision; When The Christ Child Came; For He is Risen; We Beheld His Glory; Adoramus Te; Christ is Born; The Ways of God,* a choral cycle (1955); organ pieces; songs. He published the manuals *Plainsong* (Boston, 1934) and *In Every Corner Sing: an Outline of Church Music for the Layman* (N. Y., 1945). See E. E. Hipsher, *American Opera and Its Composers* (Philadelphia, 1927; pp. 122-25).

Closson, Ernest, Belgian writer on music; b. St. Josse ten Noode, near Brussels, Dec. 12, 1870; d. Brussels, Dec. 21, 1950. He was self-taught in music; occupied various posts as archivist; was assistant curator for the collection of music instruments at the Cons. of Brussels (1896); then taught at Brussels Cons. (1912); at the Cons. of Mons (1917); retired in 1935. From 1920-40 he was music critic of 'L'Indépendance Belge'. In some of his writings he used the pen name Paul Antoine. Publications: *Siegfried de Wagner* (1891); *Edvard Grieg* (1892); *La Musique et les Arts plastiques* (1897); *Chansons populaires des provinces belges* (1905; anthology with introduction and notes); *20 Noëls français anciens* (1911); *Le Manuscrit dit des Basses-Danses de la Bibliothèque de Bourgogne* (1912); *Notes sur la chanson populaire en Belgique* (1913); *Esthétique musicale* (1921); *L'Élément flamand dans Beethoven* (1928; second ed., 1946; in English, London, 1936); *Grandfather Beethoven,* in the 'Mus. Quarterly' (1933). Of his essays in various publications, *L'Instrument de musique comme document ethnographique* ('Guide musical', 1902) and *Le dix-neuvième siècle et l'époque contemporaine, Le Folklore* and *La facture instrumentale* (in 'La Musique en Belgique du moyen-âge à nos jours', 1950) deserve special mention. A collection, *Mélanges Closson,* dedicated to him (1948) contains a complete list of his writings.

Clough-Leighter (kluf-li'-ter), **Henry,** American music editor and composer; b. Washington, D. C., May 13, 1874; d. Wollaston, Mass., Sept. 25, 1956. He began to play piano as a child; then studied organ with G. Walter; held various positions as church organist. In 1901 he settled in Boston; was associate editor with Oliver Ditson & Co. (1901-8) and with the Boston Music Co. (1908-21); from 1921-56, editor-in-chief with E. C. Schirmer, Inc., Boston. He composed several cantatas and a number of other choral works; edited numerous music collections.

Clotz. See **Klotz.**

Cluer, John, English publisher and engraver of music; d. London, 1728; he claimed to be the inventor of engraving on tin plates. He set up his shop in London about 1715. He engraved and published Handel's operas, *Giulio Cesare, Tamerlano, Scipione,* and others; also Handel's *Suites de pièces de clavecin* and an 8vo collection of operatic arias. See F. Kidson, *British Music Publishers, Printers and Engravers* (London, 1900).

Clutsam, George H., Australian pianist and composer; b. Sydney, Sept. 26, 1866; d. London, Nov. 17, 1951. As a young pianist, he made tours of Australia, India, China and Japan; settled in London in 1889 and became a professional accompanist; gave concerts with Melba (1893). From 1908 until 1918 he was a music critic of 'The Observer' in London; at the same time wrote music for the stage. He composed the operas *The Queen's Jester* (1905); *A Summer Night* (London, July 23, 1910); *After a Thousand Years* (1912); *König Harlekin* (Berlin, 1912); incidental music to *Young England* (in collaboration with Hubert Bath; Birmingham, 1916). He also produced several musical comedies: *Gabrielle, Lavender, The Little Duchess* (Glasgow, Dec. 15, 1922). His greatest popular success was the production of *Lilac Time,* an arrangement of Heinrich Berté's operetta *Das Dreimäderlhaus,* based on Schubert's melodies; Clutsam's version in English was first staged in London on Dec. 22, 1922, and had many revivals. Another theatrical medley, arranged from Chopin's melodies, was Clutsam's musical comedy *The Damask Rose* (London, June 17, 1929).

Cluytens, André, Belgian conductor; b. Antwerp, March 26, 1905. He studied piano at the Antwerp Cons.; and received first prize at graduation. His father, conductor at the Théâtre Royal in Antwerp, engaged him as a choral coach; afterwards André Cluytens conducted opera there (1927-32); was theater conductor in Toulouse from 1932-35; in 1935 appointed opera conductor in Lyon; in 1949 became conductor of the Société des Concerts du Conservatoire de Paris, also conducting at the Opéra-Comique. He was subsequently appointed musical director of the Paris Opéra as well. He made appearances with major European orchestras in 1950-55, with ever increasing prestige. On Nov. 4, 1956, he made his American début in Washington as guest conductor of the Vienna Philharmonic. — Cf. B. Gavoty, *André Cluytens* in the series 'Les grands interprètes' (Geneva, 1955).

Coates, Albert, eminent English conductor, b. St. Petersburg, Russia (of an English father and a mother of Russian descent), April 23, 1882; d. Milnerton, near Cape Town, Dec. 11, 1953. He went to England for his general education; enrolled in the science classes of Liverpool Univ., and studied organ with an elder brother who was living there at the time. In 1902 he entered the Leipzig Cons., studying cello with Klengel, piano with Robert Teichmüller, and conducting with Artur Nikisch; served his apprenticeship there and made his début as conductor in Offenbach's *Les Contes d'Hoffmann* at the Leipzig Opera. In 1906 he was appointed (on Nikisch's recommendation) as chief conductor of the opera house at Elberfeld; in 1910 he was a joint conductor at the Dresden Opera (with Schuch); then at Mannheim (with Bodanzky). In 1911 he received the appointment at the Imperial Opera of St. Petersburg, and conducted many Russian operas. From 1913 he conducted in England, specializing in Wagner and the Russian repertoire; was a proponent of Scriabin's music. In 1921 he made his American début as guest conductor of the N. Y. Symph. Orch.; from 1923-25 he led conducting classes at the Eastman School of Music in Rochester, N. Y.; also conducted the Rochester Symph. Orch. and appeared as guest conductor with other American orchestras. Subsequent engagements included a season at the Berlin State Opera (1931) and concerts with the Vienna Philharmonic (1935). In 1946 he settled in South Africa where he conducted the Johannesburg Symph. Orch. and taught at the Univ. of South Africa at Cape Town. Coates was a prolific composer, but his operas and other works had few performances (usually conducted by himself). He wrote a symph. poem *The Eagle* (Leeds, 1925; unsuccessful); the operas *Assurbanipal* (planned for performance in Moscow in 1915, but abandoned in view of wartime conditions); *Samuel Pepys* (produced in German, Munich, Dec. 21, 1929); *Pickwick* (London, Nov. 20, 1936); and *Tafelberg se Kleed* (English title, *Van Hunks and the Devil;* produced at the South African Music Festival in Cape Town, March 7, 1952).

Coates, Eric, English composer and viola player; b. Hucknall, Nottinghamshire, Aug. 27, 1886. He took instruction at the Royal Academy of Music with Tertis (viola) and Corder (composition). He was a member of the Hambourg String Quartet with which he made a tour of South Africa (1908); was first violist in Queen's Hall Orch. (1912-18). In 1946 he visited the U.S. conducting radio performances of his works; in 1948 toured in South America. He gives a detailed account of his career in his autobiography *Suite in Four Movements* (London, 1953). As a composer, Eric Coates specializes in semi-classical works for orch. His first piece of this nature, *Miniature Suite,* was performed at the Promenade Concerts in London in 1911. His Valse Serenade *Sleepy Lagoon* (1930) attained enormous popularity all over the world, and was published in numerous arrangements; his *London Suite* (1933) was equally successful; its *Knightsbridge* movement became one of the most frequently played marches in England and elsewhere. He further wrote an orch. suite *Four Centuries* (1941) tracing typical historical forms and styles in 4 sections (*Fugue, Pavane, Valse,* and *Jazz*); *Three Elizabeths* for orch.; a great number of songs and instrumental pieces.

Coates, John, English tenor; b. Girlington, Yorkshire, June 29, 1865; d. Northwood, Middlesex, Aug. 16, 1941. He studied with his uncle, J. G. Walton, at Bradford; sang as a small boy at a Bradford church; began serious study in 1893 and took lessons with William Shakespeare in London. He sang tenor parts in Gilbert & Sullivan operettas, making his debut at the Savoy Theatre in *Utopia Limited* (1894); toured in the U. S. with a Gilbert & Sullivan co. Despite his growing fame and financial rewards, he interrupted his career to study voice in Paris with J. Bouhy. He made his debut in grand opera as Faust at Covent Garden (1901); also sang Lohengrin in Cologne and other German cities with considerable success;

later sang nearly all the Wagner parts in English with the Moody-Manners Co., Carl Rosa Co., and with Beecham (1910); from 1911-13 he toured with Quinlan's opera company in Australia and South Africa. He served in the British Army during World War I; in 1919, returned to London, devoting himself chiefly to teaching; also gave recitals of songs by English composers.

Cobbett, Walter Wilson, English patron of music; b. London, July 11, 1847; died there, Jan. 22, 1937. He was a business man and amateur violinist. An ardent enthusiast, he traveled widely in Europe and met contemporary composers. He was particularly active in promoting the cause of British chamber music, and arranged a series of Cobbett Competitions; also commissioned special works and established a Cobbett Medal for services to chamber music; the recipients included Thomas Dunhill (1924), Mrs. E. S. Coolidge (1925), and A. J. Clements (1926). Among composers who received the Cobbett commissions and awards were Frank Bridge, York Bowen, John Ireland, Vaughan Williams, James Friskin, Waldo Warner and Herbert Howells. Cobbett edited the extremely valuable *Cyclopaedic Survey of Chamber Music* (2 volumes; Oxford, 1929).

Cocchi (kŏhk'-kē), **Gioacchino,** dramatic composer; b. Padua, c. 1715; d. Venice, 1804. He was teacher at the 'Conservatorio degli Incurabili' in Venice; lived in London, 1757-63, writing operas; returned to Venice in 1773. His first opera was *Adelaide* (Rome, 1743); others were *Elisa* (1744); *Baiazette* (1746); *La Maestra* (Naples, 1747); *Arminio* (1749); *La Gismonda* (1750); *Semiramide riconosciuta* (1753); *Demofoonte* (1754); *Demetrio, re di Siria* (London, Nov. 8, 1757); *Zenobia* (London, 1758); *Ciro riconosciuto* (London, 1759); *La clemenza di Tito* (London, 1760); and *Tito Manlio* (London, 1761). He excelled in opera buffa and was also proficient in secular cantatas.

Coccia, Carlo, Italian opera composer; b. Naples, April 14, 1782; d. Novara, April 13, 1873. He studied with Paisiello; in 1808 went to Rome; in 1820 to London, where he became conductor of the Italian Opera. While there he produced his own opera *Maria Stuarda* (London, 1827) which was fairly successful. He returned to Italy in 1828; revisited London in 1833 and finally settled in Novara. Coccia wrote 37 operas in all; two of them especially, *Clotilda* (Venice, June 8, 1815) and *Caterina di Guise* (Milan, Feb. 14, 1833), had some success at the time.

Cochlaeus (real name Dobnek), **Johannes,** German music theorist; b. Wendelstein, near Nuremberg, Jan. 10, 1479; d. Breslau, Jan. 10, 1552. He studied philosophy at the Univ. of Cologne (1504); in 1509 became prof. there. In 1510 he taught history and geography in Nuremberg. From 1515 he traveled in Italy; obtained the degree of doctor of theology in Ferrara (1517); then was ordained priest in Rome; subsequently held various ecclesiastical posts in Germany; during the last seven years of his life he was at the Breslau Cathedral. Cochlaeus opposed Luther at the councils of Worms and Augsburg. He published numerous theological papers; was also the author of the treatise *Musica* (Cologne, 1507; enlarged ed. under the title *Tetrachordum musices,* Nuremberg, 1511 and 6 later editions). Bibl.: M. Spahn, *J. Cochlaeus* (Berlin, 1898).

Cocks (Robert) & Co., London firm of music publishers, founded 1823 by Robert Cocks; his sons, Arthur Lincoln Cocks and Stroud Lincoln Cocks, became partners in 1868. Upon the death of the original founder (1887) Robert Macfarlane Cocks became the proprietor, and carried on the business until 1898, when he retired, and transferred the house to Augener and Co. The catalogue of publications comprised 16,000 numbers.

Coclico, Adrianus Petit, Flemish musician and theorist; b. in Flanders c. 1500; d. Copenhagen in 1563 (of plague). He was a disciple of Josquin; held a teaching post at the Univ. of Wittenberg (1545); then was in Frankfurt-on-the-Oder (1546), in Königsberg (1547) and in Nuremberg (1550). In 1555 he was in Wismar; was compelled to leave Germany when a charge of bigamy was made against him; he settled in Copenhagen in 1556 as organist of the court chapel. He was the author of the important tracts *Compendium musices* (1552; reproduced in facsimile, Kassel, 1955, in the series of 'Documenta Musicologica' and ed. by M. Bukofzer); and *Musica reservata* (1552). See M. Van Crevel, *Adrianus Petit Coclico* (The Hague, 1940); also G. Reese, *Music in the Renaissance* (N. Y., 1954).

Coelho, Rui, Portuguese composer; b. Alcacer do Sal, Portugal, March 3, 1891. He studied in Lisbon, and in Germany with Humperdinck, among others; then returned to Lisbon, where he settled permanently.

—Works: The operas *Serão da Infanta; Vagabundo; Crisfal; Auto do Berço; Rosas de todo o ano; Ignez de Castro; Soror Mariana; Belkiss* (Lisbon, June 9, 1928); *Cavaleiro das mãos irresistiveis; Entre Giestas; Don João IV* (Lisbon, Dec. 1, 1940). For orch.: *Sinfonia Camoneana* No. 1 and No. 2; *Nun' Alvares,* heroic poem; *Alcacer,* symph. poem; *Rainha Santa,* legend; *Suite Portuguesa,* Nos. 1, 2, 3; *A princesa dos sapatos de ferro,* dance for orch.; *Petite Symphonie* for small orch. Chamber music: piano trio; 2 violin sonatas; sonatina for piano; songs; etc. He has written various articles on musical subjects; participated in the educational music programs of the Lisbon Radio.

Coenen, Franz, Dutch violinist; b. Rotterdam, Dec. 26, 1826; d. Leyden, Jan. 24, 1904. A pupil of his father, an organist; then of Vieuxtemps and Molique. After tours as concert violinist with Henri Herz, and in South America with E. Lübeck, he settled in Amsterdam; until 1895 he was director in the Cons.

Coenen, Johannes Meinardus, Dutch bassoonist and conductor; b. The Hague, Jan. 28, 1824; d. Amsterdam, Jan. 9, 1899. Pupil at the Cons. there, of Lübeck; 1864, conductor at the Grand Dutch Theater, Amsterdam; then at the Palais d'Industrie. The Palais Orch., which he founded, became world famous. He retired in 1896.

Coenen, Willem, pianist, brother of Franz; b. Rotterdam, Nov. 17, 1837; d. Lugano, March 18, 1918. He traveled in South America and the West Indies; taught, gave concerts, and composed in London (1862-1909); then retired and lived near Lugano. He wrote an oratorio, *Lazarus* (1878); published piano music and songs; many cantatas, masses, etc., remain in MS.

Coerne, Louis Adolphe, American composer; b. Newark, N. J., Feb. 27, 1870; d. Boston, Sept. 11, 1922. He was a pupil of F. Kneisel (violin); while pursuing the regular academic course at Harvard Univ., he studied composition with J. K. Paine (1888-90); then went to Germany and took courses with Rheinberger at the Akademie der Tonkunst in Munich. Later he returned to Harvard for post-graduate work, taking the first degree of Ph. D. in music given by an American university, with the thesis, *The Evolution of Modern Orchestration* (1905; publ., N. Y., 1908). From 1894-97, he was a church organist in Buffalo; then at Columbus, Ohio (1897-99); after a sojourn of three years in Germany, he had charge of the musical courses in the summer session at Harvard (1903), and was professor of music at Smith College (1903-4); from 1905 till 1907 was again in Germany; then held teaching positions in the U. S.; at Olivet College, Mich. (1909-10), where he received his Mus. Doc. (1910); head of Mus. Dept. at Univ. of Wisconsin (1910-15); from 1915, prof. of music at Connecticut College for Women, New London.—Major works: the operas, *A Woman of Marblehead* (1894; not produced); *Zenobia* (1902; Bremen, Dec. 1, 1905; the first opera by a native American composer to be staged in Europe); *The Maiden Queen; The Bells of Beaujolais,* operetta; *Sakuntala,* melodrama (1904); *Evadne,* ballet (1892). For orch.: *Concert Overture* in D; Suite in D m. for strings (Stuttgart, 1892); Concerto in E for strings, organ, horns and harp (Munich, 1892); *Hiawatha,* symph. poem (1893); *Jubilee March* in E♭ for band (1893); Overture; *Romantic* violin concerto in G m.; *Dedication Ode* (1915); incidental music to Euripides' *The Trojan Women* (1917); *On Mountain Crests; Enchantment* and *Exaltation,* Nos. 1 and 2 (1921); *Excalibur* (1921).—Vocal works: *Beloved America,* patriotic hymn for men's chorus and orch.; Mass in D m.; anthems, part songs, songs. Chamber music: string quartet in C m.; *Swedish Sonata* for violin and piano (1904); 3 piano trios in canon. Numerous MSS. are in the Boston Public Library.

Cœuroy (köh-r'wăh), **André** (real name Jean Belime), distinguished French music critic; b. Dijon, Feb. 24, 1891; studied in Paris at the École Normale Supérieure, and with Max Reger in Germany. He was in the French army in World War I, and was taken prisoner. He continued his musical activities in the German prison camp, organizing instrumental bands and giving lectures on Wagner and other composers. After his release, he taught languages in Paris; lectured on French music in the U. S. (1930-31). He was a founder and associate editor of 'La Revue Musicale' (1920) and wrote music criticisms in various French newspapers; also contributed several articles to the 'Mus. Quarterly' and other magazines. His musical works include several pieces for clarinet; also a clarinet quintet. His writings are valuable for the originality of presentation as well as scholarship and accuracy. Books: *La musique française moderne* (Paris, 1921); *Essais de musique et littérature comparées* (1923); *Weber* (1924); *Le Jazz* (in collaboration with A. Schaeffner, 1926); *Le Phonographe* (1927); *Panorama de la musique contemporaine* (1928); *Panorama* *de la Radio* (in collaboration with J. Mercier, 1929); *Histoire de la musique avec l'aide du disque* (in collaboration with R. Jardillier, 1931); *La Musique et le Peuple* (1942); *Histoire générale du Jazz* (1943); *Les Lieder de Schubert* (1948); *R. Schumann* (1949); *La Musique et ses formes* (1950); *Chopin* (1951); *Dictionnaire critique de la musique ancienne et moderne* (Lausanne, 1956).

Cogan, Philip, Irish composer; b. Cork, 1748; d. Dublin, Feb. 3, 1833. He was a chorister at Cork; in 1772 went to Dublin where he occupied various posts as church organist. He acquired great renown as a teacher and performer; Michael Kelly and Thomas Moore were his pupils. Cogan wrote numerous pieces for the harpsichord and the piano; two piano concertos; and two comic operas: *The Ruling Passion* (Dublin, Feb. 24, 1778) and *The Contract* (Dublin, 1782; revived under the title, *The Double Stratagem,* 1784). In some of his piano works he incorporated Irish rhythms, and is therefore regarded as a pioneer composer of instrumental music in Ireland.

Cohan, George Michael, American composer of popular songs; b. Providence, July 3, 1878 (Cohan, himself, believed that he was born on July 4, but the discovery of his birth certificate proves July 3 to be correct); d. New York, Nov. 5, 1942. He was a vaudeville performer and had a natural talent for writing verses and simple melodies in the ballad style. His greatest song, *Over There,* became sweepingly popular during World War I. A congressional medal was given to him for this song. See W. Morehouse, *George Michael Cohan, Prince of the American Theater* (N. Y., 1943).

Cohen, Harriet, distinguished pianist; b. London, Dec. 2, 1895. She was educated at the Royal Academy of Music (Fellow); studied piano with her parents and T. Matthay, London; debut at age of thirteen in Queen's Hall; soloist in many concerts (Salzburg International Festival of Contemporary Music, 1924; Bach concerts, Queen's Hall, under Sir Henry Wood, 1926; Barcelona, under Casals, 1928; Elizabeth Coolidge Festival, London, 1929; etc.); U. S. debut at Coolidge Festival, Chicago (Oct., 1930); chamber music player (sonata recitals with Szigeti, Tertis, etc., and appearances with many quartets); made Dame by King George VI (1937); in 1938 was awarded the C. B. E. for services; now living in London. She has made a specialty of old keyboard music; has also given first performances of many contemporary works, including a number of compositions written especially for her (by Bax, Vaughan Williams, Goossens, etc.). Author of *Music's Handmaid,* a book on piano music and playing (London, 1936; 2nd ed., 1950).

Cohen, Jules-Emile-David, French composer; b. Marseilles, Nov. 2, 1835; d. Paris, Jan. 13, 1901. Studied in Paris Cons. under Zimmerman, Marmontel, Benoist and Halévy, taking first prize for piano, organ, and counterpoint and fugue. His parents being well to do, he did not compete for the Grand Prix de Rome. Assistant teacher of ensemble singing at the Cons.; regular teacher (1870); chef du chant and chorusmaster at the Grand Opéra, 1877. He produced four unsuccessful operas, including *Les Bleuets* (Paris, Oct. 23, 1867); *Dea* (Paris, April 30, 1870); also composed choruses for *Athalie, Esther,* and *Psyché* (given at the Comédie-Française); 3 cantatas, several masses, symphs., and oratorios; 2 aubades; 200 songs; 200 piano pieces.

Cohn, Arthur, American composer and conductor; b. Philadelphia, Nov. 6, 1910; studied at Combs Cons. of Music, and with W. F. Happich. In 1933 he was awarded a fellowship in composition at Juilliard Graduate School, where he studied with Rubin Goldmark. He became supervisor, then director of the Edwin A. Fleisher Collection at the Free Library of Philadelphia (1934-52); conductor of Germantown Symph. Orch. (1949-55); director of the Settlement School of Music in Philadelphia (1952-55). In 1956, appointed Director of Symphonic and Educational Music, Mills Music, Inc., N. Y. —Works: For orch.: *5 Nature Studies* (1932); *Retrospections,* for string orch. (Phila., April 3, 1935); suite for viola and orch. (1937); *4 Preludes* for string orch. (N. Y., May 26, 1937); *4 Symphonic Documents* (1939); *Quintuple Concerto* (1940); concerto for flute and orch. (1941); variations for clarinet, saxophone and string orch. (1945).—Chamber music: *Music for Ancient Instruments* (1938; awarded first prize in a contest of the American Society of Ancient Instruments); *Music for Bassoon,* unaccompanied (1947); 4 string quartets; violin sonata; *Producing Units* for 2 pianos, etc.

Colasse (koh-lahss'), **Pascal,** French opera composer, b. Rheims, Jan. 22, 1649; d. Versailles, July 17, 1709. He was a pupil of Lully, who entrusted him with writing out the parts of his operas from the figured bass and melody. Later Colasse was accused of appropriating scores thrown aside by his master as incomplete. In 1683 he was appointed Master of the Music; in 1696, royal chamber musician. He was a favorite of Louis XIV, and obtained the privilege of producing operas at Lille, but the theater was burned; his opera *Polyxène et Pyrrhus* (1706) failed, and his mind became disordered. Of 10 operas, *Les Noces de Thétys et Pélée* (1689) was his best. He also composed songs, sacred and secular.

Colburn, George, American composer and conductor; b. Colton, N. Y., June 25, 1878; d. Chicago, April 18, 1921. He studied violin and singing at the American Cons. of Music in Chicago; then taught there (1903-15); conducted at Ravinia Park in 1913; from 1915 was director of municipal music at Winona, Minnesota. He wrote several symph. poems and scores for theatrical plays: *Masque of Montezuma* (1912); *Masque of Demeter and Persephone* (1913); *Anthony and Cleopatra* (1914); etc.; also some chamber music (piano quartet, etc.).

Cole, Rossetter Gleason, American composer; b. Clyde, Mich., Feb. 5, 1866; d. Lake Bluff, Ill., May 18, 1952. He studied music with C. B. Cady; in 1890 went to Germany where he studied composition with Max Bruch in Berlin, and organ with Middleschulte. Returning to America in 1892 he occupied various posts as teacher and organist in Wisconsin, Iowa and Illinois; lived mostly in Chicago from 1909. He won the David Bispham medal for his opera *The Maypole Lovers* (composed in 1919-27; orchestration completed, 1931; a suite from this opera was performed by the Chicago Symph. Orch., Jan. 9, 1936). Other works: *Hiawatha's Wooing* for narrator and orch. (1904); *King Robert of Sicily* for narrator and orch. (1906); *Ballade* for cello and orch. (Minneapolis, 1909); *Symphonic Prelude* (Chicago, March 11, 1915); *Pioneer Overture* (composed for the Centenary of the state of Illinois; performed by the Chicago Symph. Orch., composer conducting, March 14, 1919); *Heroic Piece* for organ and orch. (Chicago, Feb. 11, 1924); cantatas, *The Passing of Summer* (1902); *The Broken Troth* (1917); *The Rock of Liberty* (1920); violin sonata; several organ pieces; piano pieces (*From a Lover's Notebook, In Springtime, Sunset in the Hills,* etc.); songs (*Lilacs, Love's Invocation,* etc.). He also compiled vol. 6 of *The Art of Music* (1917), on choral and church music. In 1896 he married the pianist Fannie Louise Gwinner.

Cole, Sidney Robert, English organist and music educator; b. London, Oct. 21, 1865; d. there, Nov. 28, 1937. He studied at the Royal College of Music; later was examiner there. In 1902 he went to Australia, settling as a teacher in Melbourne. He returned to England in 1932. His numerous compositions for organ, chorus, and piano, almost all in manuscript, are preserved in the library of the British Music Society in Melbourne.

Cole, Ulric, American composer and pianist; b. New York, Sept. 9, 1905. She studied with Goetschius and Rubin Goldmark (composition) and Josef Lhévinne (piano). She wrote two piano concertos; a piano quintet; two violin sonatas and many piano pieces. She was the soloist in the première of her *Divertimento* for piano and string orchestra with the Cincinnati Symph. (March 31, 1939).

Coleridge-Taylor, Samuel, British composer of African Negro descent (his father was a native of Sierra Leone; his mother English); b. London, Aug. 15, 1875; d. Croydon, Sept. 1, 1912. Studied violin at the Royal Academy of Music (1890); won composition scholarship (1893); studied under Stanford until 1896. In 1903 he founded at Croydon an amateur string orch. which was very successful; later he added professional woodwind and brass; appointed violin teacher at the Royal Academy of Music (1898); conductor of the London Handel Society (1904-12); later lived as composer and teacher in Croydon. Made three concert tours of the U. S. in 1904, 1906 and 1910, conducting his own works. From the very beginning his compositions showed an individuality that rapidly won them recognition, and his short career was watched with interest.—Works: A three-act opera, *Thelma;* the operettas *Dream Lovers* and *The Gitanos*. For soli, chorus and orch.: the successful trilogy *The Song of Hiawatha,* including *Hiawatha's Wedding Feast* (London, 1898); *The Death of Minnehaha* (North Staffordshire, 1899); *Hiawatha's Departure* (Albert Hall, 1900); the entire trilogy was first performed in Washington, D. C. (Nov. 16, 1904, composer conducting); *The Blind Girl of Castel Cuille* (Leeds, 1901); *Meg Blane* (Sheffield, 1902); *The Atonement* (Hereford, 1903); *Kubla Khan* (Handel Society, London, 1906); *Endymion's Dream,* one-act opera (Brighton, England, Feb. 3, 1910); *A Tale of Old Japan* (London Choral Society, 1911). For orch.: *Ballade* for violin and orch.; symphony in A minor (London, 1896); *Legend* for violin and orch.; *Ballade* in A minor

(Gloucester Festival, 1898); *African Suite; Romance* for violin and orch.; *Solemn Prelude* (Worcester, 1899); *Scenes from an Everyday Romance,* suite (London Philh. Society, 1900); *Idyll* (Gloucester Festival, 1901); *Toussaint l'Ouverture,* concert overture (Queen's Hall Symphony Concerts, London, Oct. 26, 1901); *Hemo Dance; Ethiopa Saluting the Colours,* concert march; *4 Novelletten* for string orch.; *Symphonic Variations on an African Air* (London, June 14, 1906, composer conducting); *Bamboula,* rhapsodic dance (Norfolk Festival, Conn., 1910); violin concerto in G minor (ibid., 1911); *Petite Suite de concert;* incidental music to Phillips' *Herod* (1900), *Ulysses* (1902), *Nero* (1906), *Faust* (1908); etc. Chamber music: piano quintet; nonet for piano, strings and woodwind (1894); *Fantasiestücke* for string quartet (1895); clarinet quintet; string quartet; violin sonata. Vocal works: *Zara's Earrings,* rhapsody for voice and orch.; *Land of the Sun,* part song; *In Memoriam,* 3 rhapsodies for voice and piano; *The Soul's Expression,* 4 songs for contralto and orch.; *Sea Drift,* rhapsody for chorus; services, anthems, solo songs. For piano: *Silhouettes; Cameos; Scènes de ballet;* etc. Also other compositions for violin, organ pieces and arrangements.—Cf. M. Byron, *A Day with Samuel Coleridge-Taylor* (1912); *Golden Hours with Samuel Coleridge-Taylor* (1913); W. C. B. Sayers, *Samuel Coleridge-Taylor, His Life and Letters* (1915); Mrs. Samuel Coleridge-Taylor, *Samuel Coleridge-Taylor, A Memory Sketch* (1942).

Colin, François de Blamont. See **Blamont, François Colin de.**

Collaer, Paul, Belgian pianist and writer on music; b. Boom, June 8, 1891. He studied science at the Univ. of Brussels; then became interested in music; organized concerts; became director of the Brussels Radio and promoted performances of modern music.—Books: *Stravinsky* (1930); *J. S. Bach* (1936); *Signification de la musique* (1943); *Darius Milhaud* (1947); *La Musique moderne* (1955).

Collard, a family of pianoforte makers in London. M. Clementi, in partnership with John Longman, bought out the music publishers Longman & Broderip in 1798. Longman left to establish his own enterprise and Clementi entered into a new partnership including himself, Banger, F. A. Hyde, F. W. Collard and Davis; after several changes, the firm was known as Clementi, Collard & Collard (1823); following Clementi's death in 1832, it has been known as Collard & Collard. While Clementi undoubtedly played an important part in the success of the business, it was Collard's patented inventions which gave the pianofortes their distinctive character, and established the firm's reputation in that field.

Colles, Henry Cope, eminent British music scholar; b. Bridgnorth, Shropshire, April 20, 1879; d. London, March 4, 1943; he studied at the Royal College of Music with Parry (music history), organ with Walter Alcock, and theory with Walford Davies. Subsequently he received a scholarship at Worcester College, Oxford, to study organ; then entered Oxford Univ., obtaining his B. A. (1902), Mus. Bac. (1903) and M. A. (1907); honorary Mus. Doc. (1932). In 1905 he became music critic of 'The Academy'; from 1906-1919 was music critic of 'The Times'; in 1919 was appointed teacher of music history and criticism at the Royal College of Music; was also music director of Cheltenham Ladies' College; in 1923, became member of the board of professors at the Royal College of Music; in 1924, member of the association board; in 1923 served temporarily as music critic of 'The New York Times.' He was the editor of the third and fourth editions of Grove's 'Dictionary of Music and Musicians' (1927-29 and 1939-40).—Writings: *Brahms* (1908; in German, 1913); *The Growth of Music, a Study in Music History for Schools* (3 vols., 1912-16; 3rd ed., prepared by Eric Blom, 1956); *Voice and Verse, a Study in English Song* (1928); *The Chamber Music of Brahms* (1933); *English Church Music* (1933); *The Royal College of Music; a Jubilee Record, 1883-1933* (1933); *On Learning Music* (1940); *Walford Davies* (London, 1942). His *Essays and Lectures* were published posthumously in 1945. Articles: *Some Music Instruction Books of the 17th Century,* in 'Proceedings' of the Music Academy (1928-29); *Wagner* in D. Ewen's *From Bach to Stravinsky* (1933); *Sibelius* in 'Great Contemporaries' (1933). Colles revised and added chapters to Sir Hubert Parry's *Evolution of the Art of Music* (new ed. 1930); edited vol. VII of 'Oxford History of Music' (1934).

Collet (koh-lā'), **Henri,** French music critic; b. Paris, Nov. 5, 1885; d. there, Nov. 27, 1951. He was a pupil of J. Thibaut and Barès in Paris; then studied Spanish literature with Menéndez Pidal in Madrid, continuing his music studies under Olmeda. He coined the title 'Les Six Français' for a group of young French composers comprising G. Auric, L. Durey, A. Honegger, D. Milhaud, F. Poulenc and G. Tailleferre.—Works (compositions mostly in Spanish style): *El Escorial,* symph. poem; *Danses castillanes,* for orch.; *Gitanerías,* for orch.; *La Cueva di Salamanca,* orchestral intermezzo; *Impressions (Vers Burgos),* for string quartet; *Rhapsodie castillane* for viola and orch.; *Romería castellana* for woodwinds; a piano quintet; a string quartet; *Trio castillan; Sonata castillane* for violin and piano; many songs (based on texts by F. James and on Spanish folk themes). Writings: *Un tratado de Canto de órgano (siglo XVI°) MS. en la Biblioteca Nacional de Paris* (Madrid, 1913); *Le Mysticisme musical espagnol au XVIe siècle* (Paris, 1913); a biography of Victoria, in 'Maîtres de la Musique' (Paris, 1914); *Albéniz et Granados* (1926); *Samson et Dalila* (guide to Saint-Saëns' opera; 1926); *La Renaissance musicale en Espagne au XIXe siècle,* in 'Encyclopédie du Conservatoire'; *L'essor de la musique espagnole au XXe siècle* (1929); also historical essays in 'Bulletin Hispanique' and 'L'Année Musicale'.

Collingwood, Lawrance Arthur, English composer; b. London, March 14, 1887. He studied at the Guildhall School and later at Exeter College. In 1912 he went to Russia where he entered the St. Petersburg Cons., studying with Glazunov, Wihtol, Steinberg and Tcherepnin; he remained there until the Revolution; returned to England (1918), where he became active as opera conductor. He conducted his own opera, *Macbeth,* at the Old Vic Theatre on April 12, 1934; his second opera *The Death of Tintagiles* was produced in concert form in London on April 16, 1950. His two piano sonatas were published in Russia. He has written many other instrumental works and has edited Breton folksongs.—Cf. C. H. Glover, *Lawrance Collingwood* in the 'Mus. Quarterly', (April, 1926).

Colonna, Giovanni Paolo, eminent composer of church music; b. Bologna, June 16, 1637; d. there, Nov. 28, 1695. He studied organ with Filipuzzi in Bologna; composition in Rome with Carissimi, Benevoli and Abbatini. In 1659 he became organist at San Petronio, Bologna; appointed maestro di cappella in 1674. He was several times elected President of the Accademia Filarmonica. He composed mostly church music, but also wrote several operas (*Amilcare di Cipro,* 1692; etc.) and thirteen oratorios (*La profezia d'Eliseo,* 1686; etc.). Church works: *Motetti* for 2 and 3 voices (1681); three books of *Salmi brevi* for eight voices and organ (1681, 1686, 1694); *Motetti sacri a voce sola con due violini e bassetto di viola* (1681); *Litanie con le quattro antifone della B. Vergine* for 8 voices (1682); *Messe piene* for 8 voices with organ (1684); *Messa, salmi e responsori per li defonti* for 8 voices (1685); *Compieta con le tre sequenze dell' anno* for 8 voices (1687); *Sacre lamentazioni della settimana santa* for solo voice (1689); *Messa e salmi concertati* for 3 and 5 voices with instruments (1691); *Psalmi ad vesperas* for 3-5 voices (1694); many other church works are also extant in MS.—Cf. L. Frati, *Per la storia della musica in Bologna nel secolo XVII,* in the 'Rivista Musicale Italiana' (1925).

Colonne, Edouard (real name, **Judas**), French conductor and violinist; b. Bordeaux, July 23, 1838; d. Paris, Mar. 28, 1910. He studied at the Paris Cons. under Girard and Sauzay (violin) and with Elwart and Ambroise Thomas (composition). In 1873 he founded the 'Concerts National' (which later became famous as 'Concerts du Châtelet'; then 'Concerts Colonne') at which he brought out the larger works of Berlioz, and many new orchestral scores by contemporary German and French composers. In 1878 he conducted the official Exposition concerts; was conductor at the Grand Opéra in 1892; appeared frequently as visiting conductor in London, also in Russia, Portugal and with the New York Philharmonic (1905).

Combarieu (kŏhn-bah-r'yö'), **Jules (-Léon-Jean)**, eminent French music historian; b. Cahors, Lot, Feb. 4, 1859; d. Paris, July 7, 1916. *Docteur ès lettres;* prof. of history of music at the Collège de France.—Works: *Les rapports de la poésie et de la musique considérées du point de vue de l'expression* (1893; dissertation); *L'influence de la musique allemande sur la musique française* (1895; 'Jahrbuch Peters'); *Études de philologie musicale:* 1. *Théorie du rythme dans la composition moderne d'après la doctrine antique* (1896; critique and simplification of Westphal); 2. *Essai sur l'archéologie musicale au XIXe siècle et le problème de l'origine des neumes* (1896; these two latter were awarded prizes by the Académie); 3. *Fragments de l'Enéide en musique d'après un manuscrit inédit* (1898); *Eléments de grammaire musicale historique* (1906); *La musique: ses lois, son évolution* (1907; numerous eds.; in English, 1910); *Histoire de la musique des origines au début du XXe siècle* (3 vols., Paris, 1913-19; an admirable and authoritative work; 8th ed. of vol. I, 1948; 6th ed. of vol. II, 1946; new ed. of vol. III, 1947).

Combs, Gilbert Raynolds, American organist; b. Philadelphia, Jan. 5, 1863; d. there, June 14, 1934. His father, a distinguished organist, was his first teacher. He originally studied medicine but made such progress in music, that he decided to become a professional musician. He studied violin and cello as well as organ; in 1885 founded his own conservatory in Philadelphia. He published a number of piano pieces; also wrote a *Dramatic Symphony;* compiled the manuals *The Science of Piano Playing* and *Introductory Steps to the Science of Piano Playing.*

Comes, Juan Bautista, Spanish composer; b. Valencia, Feb. 29, 1568; d. there, Jan. 5, 1643. He studied with Juan Peréz; became choirmaster at the Cathedral of Lérida; was at the Royal College in Valencia (1605-13); in 1619 was called by Philip III to Madrid; from 1629 again in Valencia. He left 216 works, sacred (masses, psalms, litanies, etc.) and secular (villancicos, tonadas), most of them in manuscript, preserved at the Escorial. 2 volumes of selected numbers were published in Madrid in 1888.—Cf. Manuel Palau, *La Obra del Músico Valenciano Juan Bautista Comes* (Valencia, 1943).

Comettant (koh-met-tahn'), **Jean-Pierre-Oscar,** French music critic and composer; b. Bordeaux, April 18, 1819; d. Montvilliers, near Le Havre, Jan. 24, 1898. He entered the Paris Cons. in 1839 and studied with Elwart and Carafa; developed considerable proficiency as composer of semi-popular songs and marches; also published piano transcriptions of famous operas, variations and fantasias. From 1852 till 1855 he lived in America, where he continued to write salon music. Returning to France, he became the musical *feuilletoniste* for 'Le Siècle', and a contributor to various musical journals; founded (with his wife, a singer) an 'Institut musical' (1871). Writings: *Histoire d'un inventeur au 19e siècle: Adolphe Sax, ses ouvrages et ses luttes* (Paris, 1860); *Portefeuille d'un musicien; Musique et musiciens* (1862); *La musique, les musiciens et les instruments de musique chez les différents peuples du monde* (1869); *Les musiciens, les philosophes et les gaîtés de la musique en chiffres* (1870); *François Planté* (1874); *Les compositeurs illustres de notre siècle* (1883); *La Norvège musicale à Paris* (1889); *Histoire de cent mille pianos et d'une salle de concert: Histoire de la Maison Pleyel, Wolff et Cie* (1890); *La musique de la Garde Républicaine en Amérique* (1894); etc.

Commer, Franz, German music historian; b. Cologne, Jan. 23, 1813; d. Berlin, Aug. 17, 1887. Pupil of Leibl and Josef Klein at Cologne; in 1828, organist of the Carmelite Church and chorister at the cathedral. In 1832 he went to Berlin to study with A. W. Bach (organ) and A. B. Marx and Rungenhagen (composition). Commissioned to arrange the library of the Royal Institute for Church Music, he pursued historical researches, and edited the following important collections of old music: *Collectio operum musicorum Batavorum saeculi XVI.* (12 volumes); *Musica sacra XVI., XVII. saeculorum* (28 volumes); *Collection de compositions pour l'orgue des XVIe, XVIIe, XVIIIe siècles* (in 6 parts); and *Cantica sacra* of the 16th-18th cent. (2 volumes). He was 'regens chori' at the Catholic Hedwigskirche; singing teacher at the Elisabeth School, at the Theater School, at the French Gymnasium, etc.; the founder (1844, with Küster and Kullak) of the Berlin 'Tonkünstlerverein'; Royal Musikdirektor, Prof., Member of the Berlin Academy, Senator of the Academy and President of the 'Gesellschaft für Musikforschung'; wrote incidental music to the *Frogs* (Aristophanes) and *Electra* (Sophocles); masses, cantatas and choruses.

Commette, Edouard, French organist; b. Lyon, April 12, 1883; had his first appointment as church organist at Lyon in 1900; in 1956 was still active in this capacity; from 1928 he made recordings of the music of Bach. He wrote 34 organ works, and made many transcriptions for organ; also composed an opera and a symphony.

Compère (kohn-pär'), **Louis** (diminutive **Loyset**); important composer of the Flemish School; b. c. 1455; d. St. Quentin, Aug. 16, 1518. He was a chorister in St. Quentin; then a singer in the chapel of the Duke of Milan (1474-75); in 1486 was singer in the service of Charles VIII of France; was subsequently canon of St. Quentin. He was greatly esteemed by his contemporaries. Not many of his works are extant; they include pieces in collections published by Petrucci (21 vocal works in 3, 4 and 5 parts, in *Odhecaton, Canti B,* and *Canti C*), Petrejus and Rhaw; masses, motets, a magnificat and chansons in MS. The motet *Omnium bonorum,* in which Compère mentions several Netherlands composers beginning with Dufay and concluding with himself, was published from the Trent Codex 91 in volume VII of the 'Denkmäler der Tonkunst in Österreich'. Other reprints are found in Ambros' *Geschichte der Musik,* Maldeghem's *Trésor musical,* Bordes' *Anthologie des Maîtres* *religieux primitifs,* Riemann's *Handbuch der Musikgeschichte II, 1,* and Blume's *Das Chorwerk.*—Cf. O. Gombosi, *Ghizeghem und Compère; Zur Stilgeschichte der burgundischen Chanson,* in 'Adler-Festschrift' (Vienna, 1930); J. Delporte, *L'École polyphonique franco-flamande; Louis Compère* in 'Revue liturgique et musicale' (July-Aug., 1932).

Compinsky, Alec, cellist; b. London, Aug. 26, 1906; educated at Trinity College and the Juilliard Graduate School, N. Y.; pupil of Ludwig Le Bell and Felix Salmond; made debut as cellist in London, 1918; toured Europe and U. S. as member of the Compinsky Trio; 1933-34, teacher at the Univ. of Southern California; since 1934 director of the Pacific Institute of Music and Fine Arts, Los Angeles.

Compinsky, Manuel, violinist (brother of Alec); b. Manchester, Sept. 7, 1901; educated at Trinity College; violin pupil of Auer, Ysaÿe and Emile Sauret; debut in London 1916; tours of Europe and U. S. as member of Compinsky Trio (with Alec and his sister, Sara); 1920-25, violin teacher at Trinity College; founded the Pacific Symphony Orch., Los Angeles; 1933-34, taught violin and chamber music at the Univ. of Southern California; 1934-37, taught conducting at the Pacific Institute of Music and Fine Arts, Los Angeles.

Concone, Giuseppe, Italian vocal specialist; b. Turin, Sept. 12, 1801; d. there, June 6, 1861. He lived in Paris as a singing teacher (1832-48).—Works: 2 operas, *Un episodio del San Michele* (Turin, 1836); *Graziella* (not produced); vocal scenes, duets, songs, etc.; and a collection of famous solfeggi in 5 volumes (*50 Lezioni, 30 Esercizi, 25 Lezioni, 15 Vocalizzi,* and *40 Lezioni per Basso*).

Cone, Edward T., American composer; b. Greensboro, N. C., May 4, 1917. He studied at Princeton Univ. (A.B., 1939) with Roger Sessions; was in the U. S. Army (1942-45); received a Guggenheim Fellowship in 1947; then appointed to the faculty of Princeton Univ. Among his works are a cantata *The Lotos Eaters* (1939-47); clarinet quintet (1941); 2 string quartets; Rhapsody for viola and piano; 2 violin sonatas; many piano pieces.

Confalonieri, Giulio, Italian pianist and writer on music; b. Milan, May 23, 1896. He studied at the Univ. of Milan and Cons. of Bologna; lived for some years in London; returned to Milan where he settled as teacher and music critic. He has written an opera *Rosaspina* (Bergamo, 1939); has edited works by Cimarosa and Cherubini; has published a comprehensive biography of Cherubini under the title: *Prigionia di un artista: il romanzo di Luigi Cherubini* (2 volumes; Milan, 1948).

Conforti (Conforto), Giovanni Luca, Italian theorist; b. Mileto (Calabria), c. 1560; date of death unknown. He entered the Papal Choir in 1580 and remained there until Oct. 31, 1585, when he returned to Mileto; was chorister at the Papal Chapel again from Nov. 1, 1591. According to Baini, he was the first of his period to restore the 'trillo'.—Publications: *Breve et facile maniera d'essercitarsi ad ogni scolaro . . . a far passaggi . . .* (Rome, 1593; facsimile ed., with translation, edited by Johannes Wolf, Berlin, 1922) and *Passaggi sopra tutti li salmi . . .* (Venice, 1607; contains a set of vocal ornamentations to be used in the singing of the Psalms employed on Sundays and holidays throughout the year).

Confrey, Zez (Edward E.), American composer of light music; b. Peru, Ill., April 3, 1895; studied at the Chicago Musical College and privately with Jessie Dunn and Frank Denhart.—Works: *Kitten on the Keys* (1921; his most popular piece); *Stumbling* (1922); *Dizzy Fingers, Valse Mirage,* and *Three Little Oddities* (1923); *Concert Etude* (1922); *Buffoon* (1930); *Grandfather's Clock* (1933); *Oriental Fantasy* (1935); *Ultra Ultra* (1935); *Rhythm Venture* (1936); *Della Robbia* (1938); *Champagne,* etc.

Conradi, August, German opera composer; b. Berlin, June 27, 1821; d. there, May 26, 1873. Pupil of Rungenhagen (composition). Organist of the 'Invalidenhaus' in 1843; went in 1846 to Vienna, and brought out a symphony with marked success; was for years an intimate friend of Liszt at Weimar; then conducted in Stettin, Berlin, Düsseldorf, Cologne, and (from 1856) again in Berlin.—Operas (all produced in Berlin): *Rübezahl* (1847); *Musa, der letzte Maurenfürst* (1855); *Die Braut des Flussgottes* (1850); *Die Sixtinische Madonna* (1864); *Knecht Ruprecht* (1865); *So sind die Frauen; Im Weinberge des Herrn* (1867); *Das schönste Mädchen im Städtchen* (1868); also vaudevilles, farces, 5 symphonies, overtures, string quartets, etc. He arranged many popular potpourris.

Conried, Heinrich (real name, Cohn), operatic impresario; b. Bielitz, Austria, Sept. 13, 1848; d. Meran, Tyrol, April 27, 1909. He started as an actor in Vienna; in 1877 he managed the Bremen Municipal Theater; came to the U. S. in 1878 and took over the management of the Germania Theater in New York; then was in charge of various theatrical enterprises; from 1892 was director of the Irving Place Theater, New York, which he brought to a high degree of efficiency. From 1903 till 1908 he was the manager of the Metropolitan Opera and was instrumental in engaging numerous celebrated artists, including Caruso. During his first season he gave the first American production of *Parsifal,* despite the heated controversy regarding the rights of Wagner's heirs; his decision to produce the opera *Salome* by Richard Strauss in 1907 also aroused a storm of protests. Conried resigned in 1908 because of dissension within the management of the Metropolitan Opera, and retired in Europe. He was decorated by several European governments; received an honorary M.A. from Harvard Univ.—Cf. M. J. Moses, *Heinrich Conried* (N. Y., 1916).

Constantinesco, Jean, Rumanian conductor and composer; born Frumusita-Covurlui, Oct. 25, 1908. He studied at the Bucharest Cons. and in Paris with Gaubert and Munch; in 1943 was engaged to teach at the École Supérieur de Musique; made appearances as guest conductor in Paris and in South America.

Constantinesco, Paul, Rumanian composer; b. in Ploesti, June 20, 1909. He studied at the Bucharest Cons. and in Vienna; then became active as a theater conductor, and on the radio. He has written an opera, *Une nuit orageuse* (1935); ballet *Les noces en Carpathes* (1938); a symphony (1945); concerto for strings (1948); and chamber music.

Conti, Francesco Bartolomeo, Italian composer; b. Florence, Jan. 20, 1681; d. Vienna, July 20, 1732. He was court theorbist (from 1701) and court composer (from 1713); wrote about 40 stage works to Italian and German texts, of which the finest were *Clotilda* (Vienna, 1706) and *Don Chisciotte in Sierra Morena* (after Cervantes; Vienna, 1719); also 9 oratorios, and songs.

Contilli, Gino, Italian composer; b. Rome, April 19, 1907. He studied at the S. Cecilia Academy in Rome with Respighi. Since 1942, was teaching composition at the Liceo Musicale in Messina. He has written a Toccata for piano (1933); 2 concertos for orch. (1936, 1942); *Sinfonia italiana* (1938); a violin sonata (1947); *La notte,* lyric suite for voice and small ensemble (1950).

Conus, Georgy Eduardovitch, Russian composer and theorist; b. Moscow, Sept. 30, 1862; d. there, Aug. 29, 1933. He studied at the Moscow Cons. with Taneiev and Arensky; from 1891-99 he taught there; from 1902, professor at the music-school of the Philharmonic Society. He developed an original theory of metric analysis and published a brief outline of it; also wrote several symph. works, piano pieces, and songs.

Conus, Julius, Russian violinist and composer; brother of Georgy Conus; b. Moscow, 1869; d. there, 1942. He studied at the Moscow Cons.; later taught violin there. He was a friend of Tchaikovsky and was greatly esteemed in Moscow musical circles. His violin concerto, first performed by him in Moscow in 1898, has retained its popularity in Russia.

Converse, Charles Crozat, American composer; b. Warren, Mass., Oct. 7, 1832; d. Englewood, N. J., Oct. 18, 1918. He studied at the Leipzig Cons. with Richter, Hauptmann and Plaidy (1855-59). Upon his return to America he was a practicing lawyer at Erie, Pa.; then lived in Highwood, N. J. He composed a number of patriotic overtures and cantatas, among them *American Concert Overture* on 'Hail, Columbia' (1869); *God for us,* an American hymn (1887), etc.; also vocal quartets, music for strings, 2 symphonies, 2 oratorios, etc. His hymn *What a Friend we have in Jesus* was widely sung. In his writings he used the pen name **Karl** Redan. A man of many interests, he wrote articles on philosophical and philological subjects; proposed the use of the genderless pronoun of the third person, "thon", which has been incorporated in several dictionaries.

Converse, Frederick Shepherd, distinguished American composer; b. Newton, Mass., Jan. 5, 1871; d. Westwood, Mass., June 8, 1940. He graduated from Harvard Univ. (1893); studied music in Boston with Carl Baermann and Chadwick (1894-96); then in Munich at the Royal Academy of Music with Rheinberger, graduating in 1898. Returning to Boston, he taught harmony at the New England Cons. (1899-1901); was instructor of composition at Harvard Univ. (1901-7). He was vice-president of the Boston Opera Co. (1911-14); served as Captain in the U. S. Army (1917-19); was dean of the New England Cons. (1930-38); Mus. Doc., Boston Univ. (1933); member of the American Academy of Arts and Letters (1937). His early works reflect the influence of academic German training; later he began to apply more advanced harmonies; in his *Flivver Ten Million,* written to glorify the ten millionth Ford car, he adopted a frankly modern idiom, modeled after Honegger's *Pacific 231*—Works: operas: *The Pipe of Desire* (Boston Opera, Jan. 31, 1906; first American opera to be produced by the Metropolitan Opera Company, March 18, 1909; won David Bispham medal); *The Sacrifice* (Boston, March 3, 1911); *Sinbad the Sailor* (1913; not performed); *The Immigrants* (1914; not performed); oratorios: *Job,* dramatic poem for soli, chorus and orch. (Worcester Festival, Oct. 2, 1907; also in Hamburg, Nov. 23, 1908; first American oratorio to be heard in Germany); *Hagar in the Desert,* dramatic narrative for low voice and orch. (written for Mme. Schumann-Heink; sung by her in Hamburg, 1908); cantatas: *The Peace Pipe* (1914); *The Answer of the Stars* (1919); *The Flight of the Eagle* (1930); other vocal works: *La belle dame sans merci,* ballade for baritone with orch. (1902); psalm, *I Will Praise Thee, O Lord* (1924). For orch.: 6 symphonies (one in D minor, not numbered, performed in Munich on July 14, 1898); No. 1 (Boston Symph., Jan. 30, 1920); No. 2 (Boston Symph., April 21, 1922); No. 3 (1936); No. 6 (posthumously performed by the Indianapolis Symph. Orch., Nov. 7, 1940); concert overture, *Youth* (MS); *Festival March* (MS); *Festival of Pan* (Boston Symph., Dec. 21, 1900; also for piano 4 hands); *Endymion's Narrative* (1901; Boston Symph., April 9, 1903); *Night* and *Day,* two poems for piano and orch. (Boston Symph., Jan. 21, 1905; also arranged for 2 pianos); overture, *Euphrosyne* (Boston Pops, 1903); orchestral fantasy, *The Mystic Trumpeter* (Philadelphia Orch., March 3, 1905; many subsequent performances); incidental music to Mackay's *Jeanne d'Arc* and *Sanctuary;* symph. poem, *Ormazd* (St. Louis Symph., Jan. 26, 1912); symph. poem, *Ave atque Vale* (St. Louis Symph., Jan. 26, 1917); *Fantasia* for piano and orch. (1922); *Song of the Sea* (Boston Symph., April 18, 1924); *Elegiac Poem* (Cleveland, Dec. 2, 1926); fantasy, *Flivver Ten Million* (Boston Symph., April 15, 1927, Koussevitzky conducting); *California,* festival scenes (Boston Symph., April 6, 1928); symph. suite, *American Sketches* (Boston Symph., Feb. 8, 1935). Chamber music: 3 string quartets; violin sonata; cello sonata; piano trio; also a violin concerto with piano accompaniment (1902); also *Valzer Poetici* for piano 4 hands; *Scarecrow Sketches* (excerpts from the Photo-Music-Drama *Puritan Passions,* commissioned by the Film Guild of New York, 1923; originally for piano; orchestrated and performed, Boston, Dec. 18, 1923); piano pieces and songs.

Coogan, Philip. See **Cogan.**

Cooke, Arnold, English composer; b. Gomersal, Yorkshire, Nov. 4, 1906. He studied in Berlin with Hindemith; then at the Royal School of Music in Manchester and at Trinity College, London.—Works: piano concerto (1943); concerto for string orchestra (1947); symph. (1949); 2 overtures; 2 string quartets; quintet for harp, flute, clarinet, violin, cello; quartet for flute, violin, viola, cello; piano quartet; oboe quartet; piano trio; violin sonata; cello sonata.

Cooke, Benjamin, English organist and composer; b. London, 1734; d. there, Sept. 14, 1793. He studied with Pepusch, whom he succeeded in 1752 as conductor at the Academy of Ancient Music; in 1757 he became choirmaster (after Gates), in 1758 lay vicar, and in 1762, organist of Westminster Abbey; Mus. Doc., Cambridge (1775) and Oxford (1782); organist of St. Martin-in-the-Fields, 1782; in 1789 he resigned the Academy conductorship in favor of Arnold. His best works are in the form of glees, canons and catches, for which he took several Catch Club prizes (*Collection of 20 Glees, Catches, and Canons for 3-6 voices in score,* London, 1775; *9 Glees and 2 Duets,* 1795). He also wrote odes, instrumental concertos, church music, pieces for organ and harpsichord, etc., and added choruses and accompaniments to Pergolesi's *Stabat Mater* (1759) and Galliard's *Morning Hymn* (1772) for the Academy of Ancient Music.—His son **Robert** (b. Westminster, 1768; d. Aug. 13, 1814) became organist of St. Martin-in-the-Fields after his father's death in 1793, and on the death of Dr. Arnold, in 1802, was appointed organist and choirmaster of Westminster Abbey; ended his life by drowning himself in the Thames. He published a collection of glees in 1805.

Cooke, James Francis, eminent American writer on music; b. Bay City, Mich., Nov. 14, 1875. He was educated in Brooklyn and studied music with R. H. Woodman and W. H. Hall; went to Germany in 1900, and continued his studies with Meyer-Obersleben and H. Ritter; also spent several months studying pedagogic methods in various conservatories; contributed to 'Musikalisches Wochenblatt' and 'Neue Zeitschrift für Musik'; held several positions as organist in Brooklyn, taught singing and piano, and was assistant to Prof. F. W. Hooper, director of the Brooklyn Institute of Arts and Sciences. As editor of 'The Etude' for forty years (1908-49), he brought it to a high degree of popularity by promoting special features (columns dealing with performance and technique; simple arrangements of classics, etc.); 1910-27, President of the Philadelphia Music Teachers Association; 1917-18, President of the Drama League, Philadelphia; Mus. Doc., Grand Cons. of Univ. of the State of N. Y. (1906); Ohio Northern Univ. (1919); Capital Univ. (1927); Cincinnati Cons. (1929); Univ. of Pennsylvania (1930); LL.D., Ohio Northern Univ. (1925); Ursinus College (1927); L. H. D., Bethany College (1931); holds Cross of Chevalier of the Légion d'Honneur; president of the Presser Foundation (since 1918) and of the following music publishing houses: Theodore Presser Co. (1925-36); John Church Co. (1930-36); Oliver Ditson Co. (1931-36); lectured on music esthetics and education, etc.; published a number of successful piano pieces (*White Orchids, Moon Mist, Ballet Mignon, Sea Gardens, Italian Lake Suite*), and also songs. He is the author of *A Standard History of Music* (Phila., 1910); *Great Pianists on Piano Playing* (4th ed. 1914); *Mastering the Scales and Arpeggios* (1913); *Musical Playlets for Children* (1917); *Great Singers on the Art of Singing* (1921); *Great Men and Famous Musicians* (1925); *Young Folks' Picture-History of Music* (1925); *Light, more Light* (1925); *Johannes Brahms* (1928); *Claude Debussy* (1928); *Musical Travelogues* (1934); *How to Memorize Music* (1947); and many non-musical works, including plays and poems.

Cooke, Thomas Simpson, composer and singing teacher; b. Dublin, 1782; d. London, Feb. 26, 1848. A pupil of his father and Giordani; conducted theater orchestras in Dublin; was then for years an opera singer (tenor) and assistant conductor at Drury Lane, London, assistant conductor of the Philharmonic, and (1846) leader of the Concerts of Ancient Music. His versatility as an instrumentalist was displayed when, at one of his benefit concerts at Drury Lane, he performed on the violin, flute, clarinet, bassoon, horn, cello, double bass and piano. Also taught at the Royal Academy of Music; an esteemed singing teacher (Sims Reeves was his pupil), and the author of two vocal treatises, *Singing exemplified in a series of Solfeggi* and *Singing in Parts* (London, 1842). He composed nearly 20 operas for Drury Lane.

Coolidge, Elizabeth Sprague (Mrs. Frederick Shurtleff Coolidge), American music patron and accomplished composer; b. Chicago, Oct. 30, 1864; d. Cambridge, Mass., Nov. 4, 1953. In 1918 she established at Pittsfield, Mass., the Berkshire Festivals of Chamber Music, held annually under her auspices, which were later transferred to Washington, D. C. She was the sponsor of the Elizabeth Sprague Coolidge Foundation in the Library of Congress, created in 1925 for the purpose of producing concerts, music festivals, awarding prizes, etc., under the administration of the Music Division of the Library. Numerous eminent modern composers, including Loeffler, Schoenberg, Malipiero, Bartók, Casella, Stravinsky, Prokofiev, Piston, and Hanson, have written works commissioned for it. The Auditorium of the Library, including its organ, is also a gift of Mrs. Coolidge. In 1932 she founded the Elizabeth Sprague Coolidge Medal 'for eminent services to chamber music', which is awarded annually to one or more persons; its recipients have included Adolfo Betti, Walter W. Cobbett, Carl Engel, and E. T. Rice. She also initiated performances of modern and classical chamber music throughout the U. S. and Europe. Her sponsorship of the appearances of artists in the U. S. and abroad (the Pro Arte, Coolidge, Roth Quartets, etc.) was an important factor in the musical life of the U. S. In recognition of her many cultural contributions she was made honorary M. A. (Yale Univ., Smith College, Mills College), L. D. (Mt. Holyoke College), Mus. Doc. (Pomona College), LL. D. (Univ. of California). She received the Cobbett Medal and various foreign decorations.

Cools, Eugène, French composer; b. Paris, March 27, 1877; d. there, Aug. 5, 1936. He studied at the Paris Cons. with Gédalge, Fauré and Widor; won the Prix Crescent for his symphony (1906); was assistant of Gédalge at the Cons. (1907-23); taught at the École Normale de Musique (1919); was music critic for 'Le Monde Musical'; in 1928 he was appointed editor-in-chief for Max Eschig, Paris music publisher. Besides the symphony he wrote a music drama *Spartacus;* two operas, *Le Jugement de Midas* (1922) and *Kymris;* opera buffa, *Beaumarchais* on themes by Rossini; operettas, *Magda; Les Violettes de la Malmaison;* and *Ravioli;* symph. poem *La mort de Chénier; Hamlet,* symph. suite; *Deux* *pièces russes* for orch. (most of these pieces are also available in piano arrangements); piano quintet; string quartet; violin sonata; flute sonata; about 80 songs; many piano pieces.

Coombs, Charles Whitney, American organist and composer; b. Bucksport, Maine, Dec. 25, 1859; d. Orange, N. J., Jan. 24, 1940. He studied piano and composition in Germany; was organist of American Church in Dresden (1887-91); returned to America, and took charge of the music in the Church of the Holy Communion, New York, holding the position till 1908; at St. Luke's, 1908-28; retired in 1928. He was made honorary Mus. Doc. by Syracuse Univ. (1922).—Published works: cantatas *The Vision of St. John; Hymn of Peace; The First Christmas; The Ancient of Days; The Sorrows of Death; Song of Judith,* motet for soprano and baritone soli and chorus; a number of sacred songs, anthems, etc.; and about 75 secular songs, some of which are very popular.

Cooper, Emil, Russian conductor; b. Kherson, Dec. 20, 1877. He studied at the Odessa Cons., then went to Vienna where he took lessons in violin with Joseph Hellmesberger; later studied in Moscow with Taneyev. At the age of 22 he began to conduct at the Kiev Opera. In 1909 he conducted the Russian Ballet and Opera with the Diaghilev troupe in Paris. He then conducted in Moscow; was in charge of the Petrograd Philharmonic after the Revolution of 1917. In 1923 he went abroad; in 1929 he conducted the Chicago Civic Opera; from 1944-50 was on the staff of the Metropolitan Opera Co.; then became musical director of the Montreal Opera Guild; subsequently lived in New York.

Cooper, George, English organist; b. London, July 7, 1820; d. there, Oct. 2, 1876. His father was an organist, and he served his apprenticeship at an early age; played organ when he was thirteen at St. Benet Church; five years later became assistant organist at St. Paul's; in 1856, appointed organist of the Chapel Royal. An able performer, he did much to elevate the public taste, especially by his playing of Bach's organ works. He published *The Organist's Assistant,* selections from classical authors; *The Organist's Manual; Organ Arrangements* (3 volumes); *Classical Extracts for the Organ; Introduction to the Organ;* also songs.

Cooper, Martin, English music critic; b. Winchester, Jan. 17, 1910. He studied at Oxford (B.A., 1931); then took courses with Egon Wellesz in Vienna (1932-34); was music critic for 'The London Mercury' (1935-38); and 'The Daily Herald' (1946-50); in 1954 he became music critic of 'The Daily Telegraph.' He was editor of 'The Musical Times' from 1953 till 1956. He is the author of several valuable monographs, on Gluck (1935), Bizet (1938) and on Opéra-Comique (1949).

Coopersmith, Jacob Maurice, American musicologist; b. New York, Nov. 20, 1903. He attended N. Y. Univ. (B. S., 1929), Columbia Univ. (M. A., 1930), Harvard Univ. (Ph. D., 1932), also studied organ with Samuel A. Baldwin and Dr. A. M. Richardson; won the Schepp Foundation Scholarship (Harvard, 1930-31), John K. Paine Traveling Fellowship (1932), Charles E. Ditson Traveling Fellowship (1933), Juilliard Foundation Grant (1934); was connected as a librarian with various radio stations. In 1949 he was appointed Senior Music Cataloger at the Library of Congress; has published many articles relating to Handel, and an edition of *Messiah* based on the original sources.

Coperario (John Cooper, an Englishman who Italianized his patronymic after study in Italy), famous lutenist and viola-da-gamba player; b. c. 1575; d. London, 1626. He went to Italy about 1600 and upon his return to England became an acknowledged authority in the field of instrumental and vocal music, patterned closely on the Italian model. He became teacher of music of the children of James I, and of Henry and William Lawes. His improvisations on the organ were greatly admired. He wrote a set of 'Fancies' for organ, and a set for viols; music for 2 masques; songs (*Funeral Teares,* 1606; *Songs of Mourning,* 1613, etc.). Two of his anthems are included in Leighton's *Teares of Lamentations;* numerous works for string instruments, with organ, are in the Christ Church library at Oxford; compositions for viols are preserved at the Royal College of Music, London, and other works in the British Museum. His treatise *Rules How to Compose* (c. 1610) was published in facsimile in Los Angeles, 1951, with an introduction by the editor, Manfred Bukofzer.—Cf. J. Pulver, in the 'Monthly Musical Record' (April, 1927); J. Pulver, in his 'Biographical Dictionary of Old English Music and Instruments' (2nd ed. 1927). See also Ernst Hermann Meyer, *Die mehrstimmige Spielmusik des 17. Jahrhunderts in Nord und Mitteleuropa* (Kassel, 1934).

Copland, Aaron, distinguished American composer; b. Brooklyn, Nov. 14, 1900. He was educated at Boys' High School in Brooklyn; began to study piano at the age of thirteen; his piano teachers were Victor Wittgenstein and Clarence Adler; in 1917 he took theory lessons with Rubin Goldmark and soon began to compose. His first published work, the piano piece, *The Cat and the Mouse* (1919), shows the influence of Debussy. In 1921 he went to Paris, and became a student of Nadia Boulanger, from whom he received a thorough training in harmony and counterpoint. He returned to America in 1924, and has since lived mainly in New York. His musical activities have been manifold: a member of the Board of Directors of the League of Composers, organizer of the Copland-Sessions Concerts (N. Y., 1928-31), and of the Yaddo Festivals (1932); a founder of the American Composers' Alliance (1937), a participant in various organizations, such as the Koussevitzky Music Foundation, the Composers Forum, the Cos Cob Press, the U. S. section of the International Society for Contemporary Music, etc. He has lectured extensively and has given courses at the New School for Social Research; also at Harvard Univ. (1935 and 1944); was the Charles Eliot Norton lecturer at Harvard in 1951-52; has appeared as pianist and conductor in many countries in Europe; also in Israel and Latin America. He is the recipient of many awards: Guggenheim Fellowship (1925-27); RCA Victor award of $5,000 for his *Dance Symphony;* Pulitzer Prize for *Appalachian Spring* (1945). In 1956, he received an honorary degree of Doctor of Music from Princeton Univ.—As a composer, Copland makes use of a broad variety of idioms and techniques; his early works (particularly the piano concerto of 1927) incorporate jazz rhythms; in his Piano Sonata and Piano Variations he adopts an austere method of musical constructivism; he uses a modified twelve-tone series in his piano quartet (1950). He has been most successful in recreating American scenes, in such works as *A Lincoln Portrait, Rodeo, Appalachian Spring;* has also used Latin American themes in *El Salón México* and *Danzón Cubano.* He has published three books: *What to Listen for in Music* (N. Y., 1939); *Our New Music* (N. Y., 1941); *Music and Imagination,* a collection of lectures delivered at Harvard in 1951-52 (Cambridge, Mass., 1952).—Works: for the theater: *Grohg,* ballet in one act (1923; not performed; material incorporated into *Dance Symphony*); *The Second Hurricane,* a play-opera for high school (N. Y., April 21, 1937); *Billy the Kid,* ballet (Ballet Caravan Co., Chicago, Oct. 16, 1938; N. Y., May 24, 1939); *Sorcery to Science,* music for a puppet show (1939); *Rodeo,* ballet in one act (Ballet Russe de Monte Carlo, N. Y., Oct. 16, 1942); *Appalachian Spring,* ballet (Martha Graham Ballet, Washington, D. C., Oct. 30, 1944); *The Tender Land,* opera (N. Y., April 1, 1954).—For orch.: *Music for the Theater* (N. Y., League of Composers, Nov. 28, 1925, Koussevitzky conducting); Symphony for organ and orch. (N. Y., Jan. 11, 1925, Damrosch conducting; revised version without organ designated as First Symphony, 1928); *A Dance Symphony* (1922-25; Victor Talking Machine Co. Competition Prize; perf. by Stokowski and Philadelphia Orch., April 15, 1931); Concerto for piano and orch. (Boston Symph., Jan. 28, 1927, composer soloist, Koussevitzky conducting); *Symphonic Ode* (written for the 50th anniversary of the Boston Symph. and performed by Koussevitzky and the Boston Symph., Feb. 19, 1932; revised for the 75th anniversary of the Boston Symph. and rededicated to the memory of Koussevitzky; Boston Symph. under Munch, Feb. 3, 1956); *Short Symphony* (Mexico, Nov. 23, 1934, Chávez conducting); *Statements* (1933-35; first complete perf., N. Y. Philh., Jan. 7, 1942); *El Salón México* (Mexico City, Aug. 27, 1937, Chávez conducting); *Music for Radio* (CBS Symph. Orch., July 25, 1937; later renamed *A Saga of the Prairie*); *An Outdoor Overture* (N. Y., Dec. 16, 1938); *John Henry,* railroad ballad (CBS, March 5, 1940); *Our Town,* orchestral suite from the film (CBS, June 9, 1940); *Quiet City,* suite from the film, for trumpet, English horn and strings (N. Y., Jan. 28, 1941); *Billy the Kid,* suite from the ballet (Boston Symph., Jan. 30, 1942); *A Lincoln Portrait* for speaker and orch. (commissioned by André Kostelanetz and perf. by him with the Cincinnati Orch., May 14, 1942; highly successful; numerous subsequent performances by many orchestras in America and Europe); *Music for Movies,* instrumental suite (N. Y., Feb. 17, 1943); *Fanfare for the Common Man* for brass and percussion (Cincinnati, March 14, 1943); *Letter from Home* (broadcast, Oct. 17, 1944); *Variations on a Theme by Eugene Goossens* (with 9 other composers; Cincinnati, March 23, 1945); *Appalachian Spring,* suite from the ballet (première, N. Y. Philh., Oct. 4, 1945; simultaneous performances next day by the Boston Symph. and Cleveland Orchestra; Copland's most popular orchestral work; received the Pulitzer Prize for 1945); *Danzón Cubano* (originally for 2 pianos, 1942; orchestral version, Baltimore Orch., Feb. 17, 1946; won the N. Y. Music Critics

Circle Award for 1947); Third Symphony (in memory of Mme. Natalie Koussevitzky; Boston Symph., Oct. 18, 1946); concerto for clarinet, string orch., harp and piano (Benny Goodman and NBC Symph., Fritz Reiner conducting, N. Y., Nov. 6, 1950); *The Red Pony,* suite from the film (Houston, Nov. 1, 1948).—Choral works: *What do We Plant?* for high-school chorus (1939); *Lark* for mixed chorus (1939); *Las Agachadas* for mixed chorus (1942); *In the Beginning* for mezzo-soprano and chorus (commissioned for Harvard Symposium; perf. at Harvard Univ., May 2, 1947).—Chamber music: *Nocturne* and *Ukelele Serenade* for violin and piano (1926); *Lento Molto and Rondino* for string quartet (1928; also for string orch.); *As it fell upon a day* for soprano, flute and clarinet (1928); *Vitebsk,* trio for piano, violin and cello, on a Jewish theme (League of Composers, N. Y., Feb. 16, 1929); Sextet, for clarinet, piano and string quartet, arranged from *Short Symphony* (1933; N. Y., Feb. 26, 1939); violin sonata (1943); quartet for piano and strings (Coolidge Festival, Washington, D. C., Oct. 29, 1950). — For piano: *The Cat and The Mouse* (1919); *Passacaglia* (1922); *Piano Variations* (1930); two pieces for children: *Sunday Afternoon Music* and *The Young Pioneers* (1936); *Piano Sonata* (first performed by the composer; Buenos Aires, Oct. 21, 1941). — For organ: *Episode* (1941). — For voice and piano: *Twelve Poems of Emily Dickinson* (1948-50). — Film music: *The Five Kings* (1939); *Quiet City* (1939); *Of Mice and Men* (1939); *Our Town* (1940); *North Star* (1943); *The Cummington Story* (1945); *The Red Pony* (1948). Bibl.: Paul Rosenfeld, *An Hour With American Music* (Philadelphia, 1929; pp. 126-143); Theodore Chanler, *Aaron Copland,* in *American Composers on American Music* (edited by Henry Cowell; Stanford, 1933); Arthur Berger, *The Music of Aaron Copland,* in the 'Mus. Quarterly' (Oct., 1945); Arthur Berger, *Aaron Copland* (first full-length biography, N. Y., 1953); Julia Smith, *Aaron Copland* (N. Y., 1955; a lengthy biographical study, written as a doctoral thesis).

Coppet, Edward J. de, American patron of art and founder of the Flonzaley Quartet; b. New York, May 28, 1855; d. there, April 30, 1916. A man of wealth and refined artistic tastes, he engaged various artists for private quartet performances at his residence. When he realized that constant practice was indispensable for the attainment of a perfect ensemble, he commissioned A. Pochon, in 1902, to find four men of the highest artistic standing who were willing to devote all their time to quartet playing. In the summer of the following year Adolfo Betti, Alfred Pochon, Ugo Ara, and Ivan d'Archambeau (1st violin, 2nd violin, viola and cello, respectively) began to practice at Flonzaley, de Coppet's summer residence near Lausanne, Switzerland; in the spring of 1904 they made their first European tour, arousing admiration by the perfection of their ensemble; on Dec. 5, 1905, they gave their first public concert in America (Carnegie Chamber Music Hall, N. Y.) with overwhelming success. They then appeared regularly in America and Europe. After de Coppet's death, his son, André, continued the original policy until 1929, when the quartet disbanded. — Cf. D. G. Mason, *Edward J. de Coppet,* in the 'Mus. Quarterly' (Oct., 1916); E. T. Rice, *The de Coppet Music Room in New York and Switzerland,* in the 'Mus. Quarterly' (Oct., 1937).

Coppola, Piero, Italian conductor and composer; b. Milan, Oct. 11, 1888; studied at the Cons. there, graduating in 1910; conducted at La Scala and in Brussels (1912-13); in 1914 was in London; from 1915-19, in Scandinavia; then settled in Paris. He wrote 2 operas, *Sirmione* and *Nikita* (1914); a symphony (Concerts Pasdeloup, Paris, Nov. 13, 1924, composer conducting); *La Ronde sous la Cloche* (1924); symphonic dances; vocal works.

Coppola, Pietro Antonio (Pierantonio), Italian composer; b. Castrogiovanni, Sicily, Dec. 11, 1793; d. Catania, Nov. 13, 1877. For a short time he studied at the Naples Cons.; then began to compose operas, which obtained sufficient success to enable his friends and admirers to present him as a rival to Rossini. From the time he was 19, he produced one opera after another, but without much success until he composed *La Pazza per amore* (Rome, Feb. 14, 1835). This was his fifth opera and became popular all over Europe (presented in Paris under the title *Eva*). From 1839-43, and again from 1850 till 1871, he was conductor of the Lisbon Royal Opera. His other operas were: *Gli Illinesi* (Turin, Dec. 26, 1835); *Enrichietta di Baienfeld* (Vienna, June 29, 1836); *La Bella Celeste degli Spadari* (Milan, June 14, 1937); *Giovanna prima di Napoli* (Lisbon, Oct. 11, 1840); *Il folletto* (Rome, June 18, 1843). He also wrote church music, notably a *Salve Regina* which was highly regarded. His son published his biography (1899).

Coquard (koh-kahr'), **Arthur,** French composer and music critic; b. Paris, May 26, 1846; d. Noirmoutier, Vendée, Aug. 20, 1910. He took private lessons with César Franck (1862-66); was professor of music at the National Institute of the 'Jeunes Aveugles'; music critic for 'Le Monde' and 'Écho de Paris'.—Compositions: 2-act opera, *L'Épée du roi* (Angers, 1884); 3-act comic opera, *Le Mari d'un jour* (Paris, 1886); 2-act lyric drama, *L'Oiseau bleu* (Paris, 1894); 4-act lyric drama, *La Jacquerie* (Monte Carlo and Paris, 1895); 4-act opera, *Jahel* (Lyons, 1900); 3-act opera, *La troupe Jolicœur* (Opéra-Comique, May 30, 1902); an oratorio, *Jeanne d'Arc;* several secular cantatas.—He published (Paris, 1892) *De la musique en France depuis Rameau,* which received a prize from the Académie des Beaux-Arts.—Cf. N. Dufourcq, *Autour de Coquard, Franck et d'Indy* (Paris, 1952).

Cordeiro, José, Portuguese composer; b. Borba, Portugal, Feb. 8, 1886. He studied piano, trumpet and composition at the Lisbon Cons.; 1915-19, director of music at Ponta Delgada; founded the Academy Acoriana de Amadores de Musica; also organized a symph. orch. in connection with the Academy and directed the choral society of Ponta Delgada; in 1919, he was again in Lisbon, where a concert of his works was given at the Teatro Nacional (Dec. 25, 1919); was conductor of a regimental band in Lisbon (1920-24); was elected Minister of Instruction (1925). Cordeiro was the founder and 2nd director of the 'Eco Musical'; also founder and director of the critical journal 'Musica'.—Main works: The operas *Alfageme de Santarem, Rosa do Adro* (1926), *Cavaleiro do Graal* (1927), and *Ressurreicão* (1928); for orch.: overtures; suites; *Rapsodias de Cantos Acoreanoas; Adamastor,* symph. poem with voices; a cantata, *Primavera;* piano sonata; songs.

Corder, Frederick, English composer and eminent teacher of composition; b. London, Jan. 26, 1852; d. there, Aug. 21, 1932. Pupil at Royal Academy of Music; in 1875 won the Mendelssohn Scholarship; studied with Ferdinand Hiller at Cologne (1875-8); became conductor of Brighton Aquarium Concerts in 1880, and greatly improved their quality; from 1886, professor of composition at the Royal Academy of Music and, from 1889, also curator. In 1905 he founded the Society of British Composers. He was remarkably successful as a teacher, many prominent British composers having been his pupils; a zealous apostle of Wagner, he and his wife made the first English translation of the *Ring of the Nibelung, Meistersinger* and *Parsifal* for the original scores published by Schott; was also contributor to Grove's 'Dictionary'.—Works: The operas *Morte d'Arthur* (1877); *Nordisa* (Liverpool, Jan. 26, 1887; Drury Lane, London, May 4, 1887); *Ossian* (1905); the operettas *Philomel* (an operatic satire, 1880); *A Storm in a Teacup* (1880); *The Nabob's Pickle* (1883); *The Noble Savage* (1885); the cantatas *The Cyclops* (1881); *The Bridal of Triermain* (Wolverhampton Festival, 1886); *The Blind Girl of Castel-Cuillé* (1888); *The Sword of Argantyr* (Leeds Festival, 1889). For orch.: *Evening on the Sea Shore* (idyll, 1876); *Im Schwarzwald* (suite, 1876); *Ossian* (overture, 1882); *Nocturne* (1882); *Prospero* (overture, 1885); *Roumanian Suite* (1887); *Pippa Passes* (orchestral poem, 1897); *A Fairy Tale* (1913); incidental music to *The Tempest* (1886), *The Termagant* (1898), *The Black Tulip* (1899); *Dreamland,* ode for chorus and orch. (1883); *Roumanian Dances* for violin and piano (1883); *The Minstrel's Curse,* ballad for declamation with orch. (1888); *True Thomas,* musical recitation (1895); *The Witch's Song* (1904); *Elegy* for 24 violins (1908); *Empire Pageant Masque* (1910); *The Angels,* biblical scene for 6 choirs (1911); *Sing unto God,* 50-part motet (1912); also published the manuals, *Exercises in Harmony and Musical Composition* (1891); *The Orchestra and How to Write for It* (1895; 2nd ed. 1902); *Modern Composition* (1909); *Musical Encyclopaedia* (1915); *History of the Royal Academy of Music* (1922).—Cf. 'Musical Times' (London, Nov. 1913).

Corder, Paul, English composer; son of Frederick Corder; b. London, Dec. 14, 1879; d. there, Aug. 6, 1942. He entered the Royal Academy of Music in 1895, studied piano with Oscar Beringer and Tobias Matthay, composition with his father; studied violin, viola, horn, clarinet, etc. Appointed professor of harmony and composition at Royal Academy of Music, 1907; elected Associate of Royal Academy of Music in 1905.—Works: Two operas, *Grettir the Strong* and *Rapunzel* (finished 1917); *The Moon Slave,* terpsichorean fantasy; *Cyrano de Bergerac,* overture; *Dross,* music drama without words; op. 8, *Morar,* a 'Gaelic fantasy'; *The Dryad,* ballet; *Prelude and Fugue; Sea-Songs; 2 Choral Songs; Heroic Elegy;* many piano works (*Transmutations, 9 Preludes, Passacaglia,* etc.); songs.

Cordero, Roque, Panamanian Negro composer; b. Panama, Aug. 16, 1917. He first studied in Panama; then came to the U. S. (1943); studied with Krenek in Minneapolis and with Stanley Chapple (conducting) at the Berkshire Music Center. He received a Guggenheim Fellowship in 1949. He has written *Capriccio Interiorano* for band (1939); Piano concerto (1944); Symphony No. 1 (1947); *Rapsodia Campesina* for orch. (1949); quintet for flute, clarinet, violin, cello and piano (1949); and *8 Miniatures* for orch. (Panama City, July 18, 1953).

Cordon, Norman, American baritone; b. Washington, N. C., Jan. 20, 1904. He attended the Fishburne Military School; later studied at the Univ. of N. C. and at the Nashville (Tenn.) Cons. of Music; voice student of Gaetano de Lucas and Hadley Outland; in 1933 made his debut at the Civic Opera, Chicago, of which he was a member until 1936; in 1936 became a member of the Metropolitan Opera; also appeared with the San Francisco Opera and Cincinnati Summer Opera.

Corelli, Arcangelo, admirable violinist and composer; b. Fusignano, near Imola, Feb. 17, 1653; d. Rome, Jan. 8, 1713. His violin teacher was G. Benvenuti in Bologna; he learned counterpoint with Matteo Simonelli. Little is known of his early life; about 1671 he went to Rome where he was a violinist at the French Church (1675); in the beginning of 1679, he played in the orch. of the Teatro Capranica; Rome remained his chief residence to the end of his life, except for visits to Modena (1689-90) and Naples (1702). There is no substance to the story that in 1672 he went to Paris and was driven out by the intrigues of Lully; biographers mention also his stay at the court of the Elector of Bavaria in Munich about 1680, but there is no documentary evidence for this stay. Equally unfounded is the story that while he was in Naples, a mediocre violinist, Giuseppe Valentini, won the favor of the Roman public so that Corelli returned to Rome a broken man and died shortly afterwards. Quite contrary to these fanciful legends, Corelli enjoyed respect, security, and fame. In Rome he had a powerful protector in Cardinal Benedetto Panfili; later he lived in the palace of Cardinal Pietro Ottoboni, conducting weekly concerts which were attended by the élite of Roman society. One of Corelli's admirers was Queen Christina of Sweden, who lived in Rome at the time. Among his pupils were Baptiste Anet, Geminiani, Locatelli, and Giovanni Somis. Corelli was famous as a virtuoso on the violin and may be regarded as the founder of modern violin technique; he systematized the art of proper bowing, and was one of the first to use double stops and chords on the violin. His role in music history is very great despite the fact that he wrote but few works; only six opus numbers can be definitely attributed to him. His greatest achievement was the creation of the concerto grosso. Handel, who as a young man met Corelli in Rome, was undoubtedly influenced by Corelli's instrumental writing. Corelli was buried in the Pantheon in Rome.—Works: 12 *Sonate a tre, due violini e violone o arcileuto col basso per l'organo,* Op. 1 (Rome, 1681; dedicated to Queen Christina of Sweden); 12 *Sonate da camera a tre, due violini e violone o cembalo,* op. 2 (Rome, 1685); 12 *Sonate a tre, due violini e violone o arcileuto, col basso per l'organo,* op. 3 (Rome, 1689); 12 *Sonate a tre,* op. 4 (Rome, 1694; in Amsterdam as *Balleti da camera*); 12 *Sonate a violino e violone o cembalo,* op. 5 (Rome, 1700; later arranged by Geminiani as *Concerti grossi*; the 12th sonata of op. 5 is *La Follia,* the celebrated set of variations for violin); *Concerti grossi con due violini e violoncello di concertino obbligati, e due altri violini, viola, e basso di concerto grosso ad arbitrio che si potranno raddoppiare,* op. 6 (Amsterdam, 1714). All these were variously reprinted at the time; there are editions by Pepusch (London, opp. 1-4 and op. 6); by Joachim and Chrysander (London; opp. 1-6); by Moffat (6 numbers from op. 2); by Schaffler (op. 2); by G. Jensen (nos. 1-6 from op. 4); by Sitt (nos. 7-12 from op. 4); by Alard, David, Leonard, Thomson, Seiffert, and others (some numbers from op. 5, including *La Follia*). A. Schering's *Geschichte der Musik in Beispielen* contains a sonata from op. 2 (No. 240).—Cf. C. Piancastelli, *In onore di Corelli* (Bologna, 1914); A. Einstein, in 'Sammelbände der Internationalen Musik-Gesellschaft' IX (p. 414 ff.); F. T. Arnold, *A Corelli Forgery* (about a forged Antwerp ed. of 1693), in 'Proceedings' of the Musical Association (London, 1921); A. Moser, in 'Archiv für Musikwissenschaft,' I (p. 358 ff.); A. Moser, in 'Zeitschrift für Musikwissenschaft,' I (p. 287 ff.) and III (p. 415 ff.); A. Cametti, *Corelli à Saint-Louis des Français à Rome,* in the 'Revue Musicale' (Jan., 1922); F. Vatielli, *Il Corelli e i maestri bolognesi del suo tempo,* in 'Arte e vita musicale a Bologna' (1927); A. Toni, *Arcangelo Corelli, cenni biografici,* in 'Bolletino bibliografico musicale' (1927); H. Engel, *Das Instr.-Konzert* (Leipzig, 1932); M. Pincherle, *Corelli* (Paris, 1933; completely revised ed., 1954; English transl., N. Y., 1956); C. Sartori, *Le*

44 edizioni italiane delle sei opere di Corelli (listing full titles of original editions and reprints), in the 'Rivista Musicale Italiana' (Jan.-March, 1953); M. Rinaldi, *Arcangelo Corelli* (Milan, 1953; a comprehensive biography, bibliography, and catalogue of works). See also Bernhard Paumgartner's detailed article in 'Die Musik in Geschichte und Gegenwart.'

Cornelis (cor-nā'-lis), **Evert,** Dutch conductor and pianist; b. Amsterdam, Dec. 5, 1884; d. Bilthoven, Nov. 23, 1931. Pupil of de Pauw at the Amsterdam Cons.; in 1904, won organ prize; conductor at the Amsterdam opera (1908); assistant conductor of the Concertgebouw Orch. (1910-19); from 1922 conductor of the orch. at Utrecht, later choral director at Rotterdam; conductor of the Netherlands Bach Society (1927); toured Europe, Dutch East Indies, Australia, etc., as guest conductor. He pioneered extensively for modern music.

Cornelius (cor-nā'-li-ōōs), **Peter,** remarkable composer and writer; b. Mainz, Dec. 24, 1824; d. there, Oct. 26, 1874. A nephew of the painter Peter von Cornelius, he at first embraced the profession of an actor; but after an unsuccessful debut he changed his mind, studied theory with Dehn at Berlin (1845-52), and then joined Liszt's following in Weimar, as a champion of Wagner, contributing frequent articles to the 'Neue Zeitschrift für Musik.' His masterpiece, the opera, *Der Barbier von Bagdad,* was produced at Weimar (Dec. 15, 1858) under the direction of Liszt, who resigned his position there because of hostile demonstrations while he was conducting the opera. In 1859 Cornelius went to Wagner at Vienna, and followed him to Munich (1865), where he was appointed reader to King Ludwig II, and professor of harmony and rhetoric at the Royal Music School. A second opera, *Der Cid,* was produced at Weimar on May 21, 1865; a third, *Gunlöd,* (from the Edda) remained unfinished (completed by Lassen and produced at Weimar, May 6, 1891). *Der Barbier von Bagdad* was revived at Karlsruhe on Feb. 1, 1884, in a drastically altered version by F. Mottl. Cornelius published *Lieder-Cyclus* (op. 3); duets for soprano and baritone (op. 6); *Weihnachtslieder* (op. 8); *Trauerchöre* for male chorus (op. 9). A volume of 'Lyrische Poesien' was issued in 1861. Cornelius wrote the libretti of his operas, and was a fine translator. A complete edition of his works was issued by Breitkopf & Härtel (1905-6): I, Songs; II, Choruses; III, *Der Barbier von Bagdad;* IV, *Der Cid;* V, *Gunlöd* (completed and orchestrated by W. von Baussnern); his literary works were published by the same firm (1904-5); I, II, Letters and pages from his diary, edited by his son, Carl; III, Essays on music and art, edited by E. Istel; IV, Complete poems, collected and edited by A. Stern.—Cf. A. Sandberger, *Leben und Werke des Dichtermusikers Peter Cornelius* (Leipzig, 1887); E. Istel, *Peter Cornelius* (Leipzig, 1904); Max Hasse, *Peter Cornelius und sein Barbier von Bagdad* (exposing Mottl's transcription, 1904); E. Sulger-Gebing, *Peter Cornelius als Mensch und Dichter* (Munich, 1908); Max Hasse, *Der Dichtermusiker Peter Cornelius* (2 volumes, Leipzig, 1923); Carl Maria Cornelius, *Peter Cornelius, der Wort- und Tondichter* (2 volumes, Regensburg, 1925); A. E. Cherbuliez, *Peter Cornelius* (Zürich, 1925); E. Istel, *Peter Cornelius,* in the 'Mus. Quarterly' (July 1934); Paul Egert, *Peter Cornelius* (Berlin, 1940).

Cornell, John Henry, American organist and writer on music; b. New York, May 8, 1828; d. there, March 1, 1894. He studied in New York, Germany and England; was organist in several N. Y. churches (1848, St. John's Chapel; 1868-77, St. Paul's Church; 1877-82, Old Brick Church). His sacred compositions were highly esteemed; the more important of his writings are: *Primer of Modern Musical Tonality; Practice of Sight-Singing; Theory and Practice of Musical Form* (after L. Bussler); *Easy Method of Modulation; Manual of Roman Chant; Congregational Tune Book; The Introit Psalms as prescribed by the First Prayer book of Edward VI, set to Original Chants* (N. Y., 1871).

Corona, Leonora (real name Lenore Cohrone), American dramatic soprano; b. Dallas, Texas, Oct. 14, 1900; educated at the Southwestern Cons. of Music, Dallas, and Univ. of Washington, Seattle; later studied voice with Lilli Lehmann (Berlin) and Salvatore Cottone (Milan); made her debut in 1922, as Elena in Boito's *Mefistofele,* in Castelamare, Italy; was a member of La Scala (1924-25), Monte Carlo Opera, Paris Opéra-Comique, and the Metropolitan Opera (1927-35), where she made her debut as Leonora in *Trovatore.*

Coronaro, Gaetano, Italian violinist and composer; b. Vicenza, Dec. 18, 1852; d. Milan, Apri 5, 1908. He studied with Faccio at the Milan Cons. and briefly in Germany; upon returning, producing a choral work, *Un Tramonto* (Milan, 1873); was for several years professor of harmony in the Milan

Cons. He wrote the operas *La Creola* (Bologna, 1878), *Malacarne* (Brescia, 1894), and *Un curioso accidente* (Turin, 1903); also some instrumental music.

Coronaro, Gellio Benvenuto, Italian pianist and composer; b. Vicenza, Nov. 30, 1863; d. Milan, July 26, 1916. He was eight years old when he made his debut as pianist; at thirteen, was theater conductor at Marosteca; and chorus master at fifteen; in 1882 he entered the Liceo Rossini at Bologna, where his teachers were Busi, Parisini and Mancinelli; graduated in 1883, winning the first prize with a 1-act opera, *Jolanda,* which was produced at the Cons. (Milan, 1883). Other works: 1-act dramatic sketch *Festa a Marina* (took 1st Sonzogno prize in 1892); operetta *Minestrone Napoletano* (Messina, 1893); 2-act opera *Claudia* (Milan, 1895); *Bertoldo* (Milan, 1910); also wrote 2 masses, string quartet, songs, piano pieces, etc.

Correa de Araujo, Francisco, the most important Spanish organist between Cabezón and Cabanilles; b. Seville, c. 1576; was organist at the Collegiate Church of San Salvador in Seville, also rector and professor. His *Facultad Orgánica* (originally published in Alcalá de Henares, 1626) contains 70 pieces for organ in tablature (most of them by Correa himself), and appeared in the series of *Monumentos de la Música Española* edited by S. Kastner (Madrid, 1950). He left MSS of various psalms, motets and 'villancicos'. As a composer, Correa was a bold innovator, making notable advances in technique and expression. A 'tiento' is in J. Bonnet's 'Historical Organ Recitals', vol. VI (N. Y., 1940).—Cf. H. Anglès, *Orgelmusik der Schola Hispánica vom XV.-XVI. Jahrhundert* in 'P. Wagner-Festschrift' (Leipzig, 1926).

Corri, Domenico, Italian composer; b. Rome, Oct. 4, 1746; d. London, May 22, 1825. He was a pupil of Porpora in Naples; in 1781 went to Edinburgh as opera conductor. His attempt to organize his own opera company and a publishing firm there was a failure, and he sought better fortune in London (1790). There he engaged in various enterprises as publisher, composer and impresario. His opera, *The Travelers, or Music's Fascination* was given at Drury Lane on Jan. 22, 1806 with little success. He published four music manuals in English: *A Complete Musical Grammer* (1787); *A Musical Dictionary* (1798); *The Art of Fingering* (1799); and *The Singer's Preceptor* (1810). His daughter **Sophia Giustina,** a talented pianist and singer, married Dussek; his sons, **Montague Corri** (1784-1849) and **Haydn Corri** (1785-1860) were also musicians.

Corsi (**Corso**), **Giuseppe** (called **Celano** after his birthplace); Italian composer; dates of birth and death unknown; maestro di cappella at Santa Maria Maggiore, Rome (1659-61); at the Lateran palace chapel (1661-65); at Santa Casa di Loreto (1668-75); then returned to Rome, but, because of his dissemination of books placed on the Church Index, was persecuted and forced to leave (1678); from 1681, at the court of the Duke of Parma. Among his pupils were Jacopo Perti (at Parma) and Petronio Franceschini. He published *Motetti a 2, 3 e 4 voci* (Rome, 1667), *Miserere a 5,* and *Motetti a 9;* various other vocal works, in MS., are preserved in the library of the Liceo Musicale and the Archivio musicale di S. Petronio at Bologna. Several of his works appeared in collections of the time. He is mentioned in Giuseppe Pitoni's *Guida armonica.*

Corsi, Jacopo, a Florentine nobleman and patron of art; b. c. 1560; d. Florence, 1604. In his palace, as in that of his friend Bardi, were held the memorable meetings of the 'Camerata' in which Peri, Caccini, Emilio del Cavaliere, Galilei, the poet Rinuccini and others took part, leading to the creation of the earliest operas. Corsi was a good musician, a skillful player on the harpsichord and a composer; he wrote the concluding two numbers of the first opera *Dafne* by Peri, which was performed at his home in 1597; these settings are preserved in the library of the Brussels Cons.; publ. in Solerti's *Albori del Melodramma* (Milan, 1905).

Corte, Andrea della. See **Della Corte, Andrea.**

Corteccia (cor-tĕh'-chăh), **Francesco Bernardo;** b. Arezzo, July, 1504; d. Florence, June 7, 1571. Organist, in 1531, of the Church of S. Lorenzo at Florence; 1539-71, maestro di cappella to Duke Cosimo the Great.—Published: wedding music (for the Duke), 9 pieces, *a* 4, 6, and 8 (Venice, 1539); 3 books of madrigals (1544, 1547, 1547); *Responsoria et lectiones* (1570); 32 hymns *a* 4; *Canticorum liber primus* (1571); many others have been destroyed. His musical intermezzi to stage works (e.g., to Francesco d'Ambra's *Il furto,* 1544) are noteworthy in the development of opera.—Cf. O. G. Sonneck's articles in the 'Mus. Antiquary' (1911) and in his *Miscellaneous Studies in the History of Music* (N. Y., 1921).

Cortese, Luigi, Italian pianist and composer; b. Genoa, Nov. 19, 1899; studied in Bologna, Genoa, Rome, and Paris; has written an opera *Prometeo* (Bergamo, Sept. 22, 1951); oratorio *David* (1938); publ. a monograph on Casella (Genoa, 1935), who was one of his teachers.

Cortesi, Francesco, Italian composer; b. Florence, Sept. 11, 1826; d. there, Jan. 3, 1904. He studied at Bologna under Rossini and others; became a conductor and a composer of many light stage-works; settled in Florence about 1880 as a singing master and was appointed head of the vocal department in the government music school. Many celebrated singers were his pupils.—Operas: *Il Trovatore* (Trieste, 1852; then at Florence, as *La Schiava*); *Almina* (Rome, 1859); *La Dama a servire* (Ancona, 1859); *La Colpa del cuore* (Florence, 1870); *Mariulizza* (Florence, 1874); *L'Amico di casa* (Florence, 1881); all fairly successful.

Cortolezis, Fritz, German composer and conductor; b. Passau, Feb. 21, 1878; d. Bad Aibling, Bavaria, March 13, 1934. Studied in Munich with H. Bussmeyer (piano) and with L. Thuille (composition) from 1899-1902; was repetiteur at the opera in Schwerin (1903); chorus master at the National Theater in Berlin (1904); first conductor in Regensburg (1905) and in Nuremberg (1906); upon Mottl's recommendation he was appointed conductor of the court opera in Munich, and at the same time conductor of the 'Lehrer-Gesangverein' and the 'Akademischer Gesangverein' (1907-11); was engaged by Beecham in 1911 for the Wagner and Strauss performances in London; in 1912 first conductor at the Kurfürstenoper in Berlin; then in Karlsruhe (1913-24) and at the Breslau Opera (1925-28). He wrote the operas *Rosemarie* (Bremen, 1919), *Das verfemte Lachen* (Rostock, 1924) and *Der verlorene Gulden* (Breslau, 1928).

Cortot (kŏhr-toh'), **Alfred (Denis),** famous Franch pianist, b. (of a French father and a Swiss mother) Nyon, Switzerland, Sept. 26, 1877. He was a pupil at the Paris Cons., and studied with Decambes, Rouquou and Diémer; he won the first prize for piano in 1896; the same year he made his debut in Paris, playing Beethoven's C minor concerto at one of the Colonne concerts, and won signal success; he went to Bayreuth (1898) and studied Wagner's works with J. Kniese, and acted as répétiteur at the festivals from 1898-1901. Returning to Paris, he began a most active propaganda for the works of Wagner; on May 17, 1902, he conducted the French première of *Götterdämmerung* at the Théâtre du Château d'Eau, and in the same year established the 'Association des Concerts A. Cortot,' which he directed for two years, educating the public to an appreciation of Wagner; in 1904 he became conductor of the orchestral concerts of the 'Société Nationale' and of the Concerts Populaires at Lille (till 1908) and also conducted the second performance of *Tristan und Isolde,* shortly after Lamoureux had directed the French première (Dec. 14, 1904). In 1905, together with Jacques Thibaud (violin) and Pablo Casals (cello), he formed a trio, which soon gained a great European reputation; was appointed professor of piano at the Paris Cons. (1907), retiring from this post later to devote his time to concert work; founded, with A. Mangeot, the École Normale de Musique (1919), and became its director, also giving a summer course in piano interpretation there annually. Cortot has given many lecture recitals and appeared as guest conductor with various orchestras. He is Commandeur de la Légion d'Honneur and Knight of the Order of Isabella la Católica. Cortot has written many articles on the piano works of Debussy, Fauré, Franck, Chabrier in the 'Revue musicale' (1920-26); published a new working edition of Chopin's Preludes and Études; also published *Principes rationnels de la technique pianistique* (French and English, Paris, 1928; American ed., Boston, 1930); *La musique française de piano* (vol. I, 1930; English translation, London, 1932; vol. II, 1932); *Cours d'interprétation* (vol. I, Paris, 1934; in English, London, 1937); *Aspects de Chopin* (Paris, 1949; English, *In Search of Chopin*, London, 1951). The publication of a classified catalogue of Cortot's library, entitled *Bibliothèque Alfred Cortot,* edited by F. Goldbeck and A. Fehr with preface by H. Prunières, was begun in 1936 (Part I, *Théorie de la musique; traités et autres ouvrages théoriques des XVe-XVIIIe siècles;* Argenteuil, 1936).

Cossmann, Bernhard, German cellist; b. Dessau, May 17, 1822; d. Frankfurt, May 7, 1910. He was a pupil of Espenhahn and Drechsler; also of Theodor Müller and Kummer (in Dresden); member of the Grand Opéra Orch., Paris (1840); London (1841); Opéra-Comique, Paris (till 1846); Gewandhaus, Leipzig (1847-8), as solo cellist, also studying composition under Hauptmann; at Weimar with Liszt (in 1850); professor at Moscow Cons. (1866); lived at Baden-Baden (1870-8); thereafter, professor of cello at Frankfurt Cons.

Costa, Sir Michael (properly Michele), eminent conductor and opera composer; b. Naples, Feb. 4, 1806; d. Hove, England, April 29, 1884. He studied with his maternal grandfather, Giacomo Tritto, and with his father, Pasquale Costa (a composer of church music, and pupil of L. Leo). He then studied at the Naples Cons. with Crescentini (singing) and Zingarelli (composition). His operas *Il Sospetto funesto* (Naples, 1826), *Il Delitto punito* (1827), *Il Carcere d'Ildegonda* (Naples, 1828), and *Malvina* (Naples, 1829) were well received; when Zingarelli was commissioned to write a psalm *Super Flumina Babilonis* for the Music Festival of Birmingham, England, he sent Costa to conduct it. When Costa arrived in Birmingham, the directors of the Festival refused to accept him as conductor owing to his extreme youth, but offered to pay him a similar fee for performance as tenor in Zingarelli's psalm and in other works. He was compelled to accept, but his début as a singer was disastrous. Despite this setback, he decided to remain in England, in which he was encouraged by Clementi who was impressed by Costa's scoring of a Bellini aria. In 1830 Costa was engaged as 'maestro al cembalo' at the King's Theatre in London; in 1832 he became musical director; and in 1833, director and conductor. During this time he produced three of his ballets, *Kenilworth* (1831), *Une heure à Naples* (1832), and *Sir Huon* (1833, for Taglioni). In 1846 he became conductor of the Philharmonic and of the new Italian Opera; in 1848, of the Sacred Harmonic Society. From 1849 he was the regular conductor of the Birmingham Festivals; from 1857, of the Handel Festivals. He was knighted in 1869; was appointed 'director of the music, composer, and conductor' at Her Majesty's Opera in 1871. He produced two operas in London: *Malek Adel* (May 18, 1837; a revision of *Malvina*) and *Don Carlos* (June 20, 1844; a failure).

Costeley, Guillaume, organist; b. probably at Pont-Audemer (Normandy), 1531; d. Évreux, Feb. 1, 1606. The theory that he was an Irishman named Costello who settled in France as well as the theory that he was of Scottish extraction have been discarded. He was court organist to Charles IX of France. In 1571 he became the first annually elected 'prince' or 'maître' of a society organized in honor of St. Cecilia, which, beginning in 1575, awarded a prize each year for a polyphonic composition. Costeley excelled as composer of polyphonic 'chansons'; his *Musique,* a book of such works for 4-6 voices, appeared in 1570. Modern editions of some of those for 4 voices are in H. Expert, 'Maîtres Musiciens de la Renaissance française' (volumes III, XVIII, XIX); an example for 5 voices in Cauchie's *Quinze chansons.*—Cf. M. Cauchie, *Documents pour servir à une biographie de Guillaume Costeley,* in the 'Revue de musicologie' (May, 1926).

Cottlow, Augusta, American concert pianist; b. Shelbyville, Ill., April 2, 1878; d. White Plains, N. Y., April 11, 1954. She received her first instruction from her mother; appeared in public as a child; went to Berlin in 1896 to study with Busoni; played concerts in Germany, England, and Russia. In 1912 she married Edgar E. Gerst of Berlin; returned to America in 1917. She publ. a memoir, *My Years with Busoni,* in 'The Musician' (1925).

Cotton (Cottonius), John, an early music theorist (11th to 12th century); probable author of the treatise *Epistola ad Fulgentium* (printed by Gerbert in 'Scriptores', vol. II), a valuable work on music describing the modal system of the time and a phase of the development of organum. Six MS copies are preserved: in Leipzig, Paris, Antwerp, the Vatican Library, and two in Vienna. Various theories have been advanced concerning its authorship. In the copies at Antwerp and Paris the author is referred to as Cotton or Cottonius, while two others give the author's name as 'Joannes Musica'. In an anonymous work, *De script. eccles.,* quoted by Gerbert, there is a reference to a certain Joannes, an erudite English musician; the dedication of this volume, 'Domino et patri sua venerabili Anglorum antistiti Fulgentio', adds further strength to the contention that the author of the *Epistola* was English. However, J. Smits van Waesberghe identifies him with the Flemish theorist Johannes of Afflighem, author of the treatise *De Musica cum tonario* (reprinted Rome, 1950). For further views on the controversy, see L. Ellinwood, *John Cotton or John of Afflighem?* in 'Notes' (Sept., 1951) and J. Smits van Waesberghe's reply in 'Musica Disciplina' (1952; pp. 139-53). See also J. Pulver, *John Cotton,* in the 'Mus. Times' (Oct., 1933).

Couperin (koo-pŭ-ran'), a renowned family of French musicians. Its musical prominence dates from the three sons of **Charles Couperin,** merchant and organist of Chaume, in the department of Brie (now part of the department of Seine et Marne), and his wife, Marie Andry. The eldest of these, **Louis,** established the family in Paris, where it remained until the extinction of the male line in 1826. He was also the first of his name to hold the post of organist at St.-Gervais, Paris. He was followed in this position by his youngest brother, **Charles; François le Grand**, son of Charles, and the family's most illustrious representative; **Nicolas**, son of **François** (called Sieur de Crouilly); **Armand-Louis**, son of Nicolas; and by the two sons of Armand-Louis, **Pierre-Louis**, and **Gervais-François**. The following articles, arranged alphabetically, give the individual histories of the members of the Couperin family.

Couperin, Armand-Louis (son of Nicolas), b. Paris, Feb. 25, 1725; d. there, Feb. 2, 1789. His virtuosity on the organ was extraordinary; in 1748, succeeded his father as organist at St.-Gervais; was also organist to the King (1770-89), and held appointments at St.-Barthélemy, Ste.-Marguerite, the Ste.-Chapelle, St.-Jean-en-Grève, etc. He was one of the four organists of Notre-Dame. He died a violent death, having been knocked down by a runaway horse. His compositions include sonatas, a trio, motets, and other church music—His wife, **Elisabeth-Antoinette** (*née* **Blanchet**; b. Paris, Jan. 14, 1729), was also a remarkable organist and clavecinist, still playing in public at the age of 81 (in 1810). She was the daughter of Blanchet, the famous clavecin maker, and sister-in-law to Pascal Joseph Taskin, the court instrument keeper under Louis XV.

Couperin, Charles, b. Chaumes, April (bapt. Apr. 9), 1638; d. Paris, 1679. He succeeded his brother Louis, as organist at St.-Gervais in 1665. He married Marie Guérin (Feb. 20, 1662), and is principally remembered as being the father of the celebrated François le Grand.—Cf. C. Bouvet, *Quelques précisions biographiques sur Charles Louis Couperin,* in 'Revue de musicologie' (Paris, 1930).

Couperin, François (Sieur de Crouilly), b. Chaumes, c. 1631; d. Paris, c. 1701. Pupil of Chambonnières in harmony and clavecin playing; active as music teacher and organist. His daughter, **Marguerite Louise** (b. Paris, 1676; d. Versailles, May 30, 1728), was a well known singer and harpsichordist. She was a fellow member of the 'Chambre du roi' with her cousin, François le Grand, who wrote for her the verset *Qui dat nivem,* and other pieces.

Couperin, François, surnamed **le Grand** on account of his superiority in organ playing, the most illustrious member of a distinguished family, and one of the greatest of early French composers; b. Paris, Nov. 10, 1668; d. there, Sept. 12, 1733. He was the son of Charles Couperin, who was his first teacher; later pupil of Jacques-Denis Thomelin, organist of the King's chapel; in 1685 he became organist of St. Gervais, which post he held until his death; on Dec. 26, 1693, after a successful competition, he succeeded Thomelin as organist of the Chapelle Royale, receiving the title of 'organiste du roi'; in 1701 he was appointed 'claveciniste de la chambre du roi, et organiste de sa chapelle', and in 1717 he received the title 'Ordinaire de la musique de la chambre du roi'; also made chevalier of the Order of Latran; he was music master to the Dauphin and other members of the royal family, and ranked high in the favor of Louis XIV, for whom he composed the *Concerts royaux,* which, during 1714-15, were played in Sunday concerts in the royal apartments. He married Marie-Anne Ansault (April 26, 1689) from whom he had two daughters: **Marie-Madeleine** (b. Paris, Mar. 11, 1690; d. Montbuisson, April 16, 1742), who became organist of the Abbey of Montbuisson, and **Marguerite-Antoinette** (b. Paris, Sept. 19, 1705; d. there, 1778), who became a talented clavecin player; from 1731-33, she substituted for her father as 'claveciniste' to the king, being the first woman to hold this position (cf. C. Bouvet, *Les deux d'Anglebert et Marguerite-Antoinette Couperin,* in 'Revue de musicologie' Paris, 1928); there were also two sons, **Nicolas-Louis** (b. July 24, 1707), who died young, and **François-Laurent**, born c. 1708.

Famed as an organist, Couperin also acquired a high reputation for his remarkable ability as a performer on the clavecin. His compositions may be conveniently divided into three categories: those written for the church, those for the king, and those for the general public. More than half of his creative life was taken up with the religious compositions of the first two periods. These include *Pièces d'orgue consistantes en deux Messes* (1690, a total of 42 pieces), formerly attributed to his uncle, François de Crouilly, and, indeed, published under the latter's name in vol. 5 of 'Archives des maîtres de l'orgue', ed. by Guilmant, but now established, through the researches of A. Tessier and P. Brunold, as the early work of Couperin le Grand; motets; *Elévations; Leçons de Ténèbres;* etc. Couperin's last and most prolific period was concerned exclusively with instrumental works, and in this field he achieved his greatest and most enduring distinction. In 1713, 1716, 1722 and 1730, he published the 4 volumes of his

Pièces de clavecin, consisting of about 230 pieces or 27 'Ordres' or Suites, each suite being a series of dance forms, programmatic in title and content (*La Majestueuse, La Nanette, Les Petits Moulins à Vent, Le Carillon de Cythère, Les Barricades Mystérieuses, Les Tic-Toc-Choc ou les Maillotins,* etc.). In 1716 he published an expository work pertaining to the execution of his clavecin pieces, *L'Art de toucher le clavecin,* which attained wide celebrity, and which influenced the keyboard style of Couperin's great contemporary, J. S. Bach. Couperin also, introduced the trio sonata to France, his first works in this form being an imitation of Corelli. Later, in 1726, he publ. 4 sonatas, *Les Nations,* described as 'Sonades' or 'Suites de symphonies en trio', three of which are partial reworkings of earlier pieces. They are composed alternately in the strict primitive form, *sonata da chiesa,* and the more flexible composite of dance forms, *sonata da camera.* The last of the series, *L'Impériale,* perhaps represents his most mature and inspired style. Living at a time during which the rivalry between French and Italian music reached its climax, Couperin sought to adapt the new Italian forms to his own personal, and essentially French, style. In his *Les Goûts Réunis* (1724), a series of concerted pieces with strings very similar in form and spirit to the *Pièces de Clavecin,* one finds titles such as *Sicilienne* and *Ritratto dell' Amore,* and finally, as a closing number, a grand sonata *Le Parnasse ou l'Apothéose de Corelli.* In the following year he published an *Apothéose de Lully,* in which the rivals, Lully and Corelli, are made to unite for the furtherance of art. Couperin's style of composition was based on the *basso continuo,* the most important voices usually being the uppermost, carrying the melody, and the bass. Nevertheless, his music sometimes attains considerable complexity (on occasion requiring as many as three harpsichordists for its proper execution). His melodic invention, particularly in his use of the rondeau, was virtually inexhaustible, his themes swift and expressive. An outstanding feature was his inventive mode of ornamentation, in the 'gallant style' of the period.

In 1933 the Lyrebird Press in Paris published a 'complete' ed. of Couperin's works, in 12 volumes, under the chief editorship of Maurice Cauchie, assisted by P. Brunold, A. Gastoué, A. Tessier and A. Schaeffner. The contents are as follows: Vol. I, Didactic works: *Règle pour l'accompagnement* and *L'Art de toucher le clavecin;* Vols. II-V, The 4 books of *Pièces de clavecin;* Vol. VI, *Pièces d'orgue consistantes en deux Messes;* Vols. VII-X, Chamber music, including *Concerts royaux, Les Goûts Réunis ou Nouveaux concerts à l'usage de toutes les sortes d'instruments de musique, Les Nations, Le Parnasse ou l'Apothéose de Corelli, Apothéose de Lully, Pièces de violes avec la basse chiffrée,* and *Sonades inédites;* Vols. XI-XII, Secular vocal music and Religious music I and II.—Cf. H. Quittard, *Les Couperins* (Paris, 1913); C. Bouvet, *Une Dynastie de musiciens français: Les Couperins . . .* (Paris, 1919); L. de La Laurencie, *L'École française de violon de Lully à Viotti* (1922-24): Joan Llongueras, *Couperin o la Gracia* (1925); A. Tessier, *Couperin* (Paris, 1926); J. Tiersot, *Les Couperins* (Paris, 1926); J. Tiersot, *Two Centuries of a French Musical Family—The Couperins,* in the 'Mus. Quarterly' (July, 1926); P. Brunold, *Le grande Orgue de St.-Gervais à Paris* (Paris, 1934); P. Brunold, *François Couperin* (English transl., Monaco, 1949); M. Cauchie, *Thematic Index of Couperin* (Monaco, 1949); W. Mellers, *François Couperin and the French Classical Tradition* (London, 1950); M. Antoine, *Autour de François Couperin* in the 'Revue de Musicologie' (Paris, Dec., 1952); P. Citron, *Couperin* (Paris, 1956).

Couperin, Gervais-François (2nd son of Armand-Louis), b. Paris, May 22, 1759; d. there, March 11, 1826. Succeeded his brother, Pierre-Louis, as organist at St.-Gervais in 1789, also taking over his other appointments. He composed sonatas, variations, etc. He was the last of the Couperins to serve as organist at St.-Gervais, although his daughter, Céleste (b. 1793; d. Belleville, Feb. 14, 1860) played there at the time of her father's death. She was a teacher of singing and piano at Beauvais for about ten years.—Cf. C. Bouvet, *La fin d'une dynastie d'artistes: Gervais-François Couperin et sa fille,* in 'Revue de Musicologie' (Paris, 1926).

Couperin, Louis, b. Chaumes, c. 1626; d. Paris, Aug. 29, 1661. Went to Paris with Chambonnières, whose pupil he was; c. 1650, became organist of St.-Gervais, a post in which he was succeeded, without interruption, by descendants and members of the Couperin family until 1826; from 1656, violinist and violist in the orchestras of the court ballets, and musician of the 'Chambre du roi'. Composed *Pièces de clavecin, Carillons* for organ, also violin pieces, etc. He was one of the earliest of French composers for the harpsichord in the new harmonic style employing the *basso continuo,* possibly being preceded only by his teacher, Chambonnières. The Lyrebird Press in Paris published a 'complete' edition of his works, ed. by P. Brunold.—Cf. A. Pirro, *Louis Couperin,* in 'Revue de musicologie' (Paris, 1930).

Couperin, Nicolas (son of François de Crouilly), b. Paris, Dec. 20, 1680; d. there, July 25, 1748. In 1733 he succeeded his cousin, François le Grand, as organist at St.-Gervais.

Couperin, Pierre-Louis (called 'M. Couperin l'aîné or 'Couperin fils'), son of Armand-Louis; b. Paris, Mar. 14, 1755; d. there, Oct. 10, 1789. He was organist to the King, later at Notre-Dame, St.-Jean, St.-Merry, and at St.-Gervais (succeeded his father early in 1789; he died eight months later). Some of his compositions were publ. in contemporary collections; others are in MS.

Couppey. See **Le Couppey.**

Courboin (koor-bwăhn'), **Charles Marie,** organist; b. Antwerp, April 2, 1886; studied at the Cons. of Brussels (prizes, 1901 and 1902), and at the Brussels Univ.; pupil of J. Blockx and A. Mailly (organ); toured France, England and Germany as organist; 1902, appointed organist of the Antwerp Cathedral; 1904, came to the U. S.; organist at Oswego, N. Y., then in Syracuse, N. Y.; municipal organist of Springfield, Mass.; 1919-28, organist at Wanamaker's in N. Y. and Phila.; has made seven transcontinental tours of the U. S. and Canada, and two European tours; 1919, played the organ in the first performance of Widor's 6th Symph. (dedicated to him) with the Phila. Orch. under Stokowski; has given organ master classes at the Univ. of Southern Calif., Los Angeles, and at the Chicago College of Music, etc.; designer of 144 important organs in the U. S. (Memphis Auditorium, Wanamaker's, etc.).

Courtois (koor-twăh'), **Jean,** French contrapuntist in the first half of the 16th century, was maître de chapelle at Cambrai cathedral in 1539, when a 4-part motet of his, *Venite populi terrae,* was performed before Charles V of Spain. Many of his motets, psalms and songs appeared in publications of the period (printed at Paris, Lyons, Antwerp, Nuremberg, etc.); H. Expert reprinted some of his songs in 'Les Maîtres musiciens de la Renaissance française'. Masses, motets and songs in MS. are in the Munich State Library and the library at Cambrai.

Courvoisier (koor-vwăh-z'yā'), **Karl,** violinist; b. Basel, Nov. 12, 1846; d. Liverpool, Jan. 31, 1908. He studied with David and Röntgen at Leipzig Cons. (1867-9), and Joachim in Berlin (1869-70). In 1885 he settled in Liverpool as a teacher. He published *Die Violintechnik* (1878; English translation *The Techniques of Violin Playing,* by H. E. Krehbiel; 2nd ed., New York, 1896); an *École de la velocité* for violin and a *Méthode de violon* (text in German, English and French; London, 1892).

Courvoisier (koor-vwăh-z'yā'), **Walter,** Swiss composer and conductor; b. Riehen, near Basel, Feb. 7, 1875; d. Locarno, Dec. 27, 1931. He first studied medicine (M. D., 1900), later music with Thuille in Munich (whose son-in-law he became); was associate conductor of People's Symph. Concerts (1907); teacher of composition at the Academy of Music, Munich (1910; professor from 1919-30). — Works: The operas *Lanzelot und Elaine* (Munich, 1917), *Die Krähen* (Munich, 1921); the oratorio *Totenfeier;* chamber music; piano pieces; about 150 songs.

Coussemaker (kooss-măh-kär'), **Charles-Edmond-Henri de,** French music scholar; b. Bailleul, Nord, April 19, 1805; d. Bourbourg, Jan. 10, 1876. He studied music as a child; his main profession was the law. While studying law at the Univ. of Paris, he took private lessons with Pellegrini in singing and Anton Reicha in harmony. He continued his studies with Lefebvre in Douai, after becoming a practicing lawyer. At this time (1831-35) he found leisure to compose music of the most varied description, all of which, with the exception of a few *romances* and two sets of songs, is unpublished, and apparently lost. His interest in history and archaeology led him to the study of the authentic documents of music; he was also influenced by the scholarly articles in 'La Gazette et Revue Musicale' (then edited by Fétis). During successive terms as judge in Hazebrouck, Dunkerque and Lille, he continued to accumulate knowledge of musical documentation; he assembled a vast library; 1075 items in his library are listed in the 'Catalogue des livres, manuscrits et instruments de musique du feu M. Charles Coussemaker' (Brussels, 1877; issued for an auction). He published a great number of valuable treatises and collections: *Mémoire sur Hucbald* (Paris, 1841); *Notice sur les collections musicales de la bibliothèque de Cambrai . . .* (1843); *Essai sur les instruments de musique au moyen-âge* (in Dindron's 'Annales archéologiques,' illustrated); *Histoire de l'harmonie au moyen-âge* (1852); *Trois chants historiques* (1854); *Chants populaires des Flamands de France* (1856);

Drames liturgiques du moyen âge (1860); *Les harmonistes des XIIe et XIIIe siècles* (1865); a great work, intended for a supplement to Gerbert, entitled 'Scriptorum de musica medii ævi nova series' (1864-76, 4 volumes; new ed. by U. Moser, Graz, 1908; anastatic reprint, 1931, by 'Bolletino bibliografico musicale'); *L'art harmonique aux XIIe et XIIIe siècles* (1865); *Oeuvres complètes d'Adam de la Halle* (1872); etc.—Cf. A. Desplanque, *Étude sur les travaux d'historie et d'archéologie de M. Edmond de Coussemaker* (Paris, 1870).

Coverly, Robert, Portuguese composer of light music; b. Oporto, Sept. 6, 1864; d. there, Sept. 19, 1944. He studied in London and New York; composed a great number of effective marches and songs, of which *The Passing Regiment,* a military march for band, achieved great popularity.

Coward, Sir **Henry,** English choral conductor; b. Liverpool, Nov. 26, 1849; d. Sheffield, June 10, 1944. He was apprenticed to be a cutler but attended classes of solfeggio. He organized a choral group at Sheffield and became its conductor. After a period of hard study, he obtained the B. Mus. degree at Oxford (1889), and later D. Mus. (1894). He organized spectacular choral festivals in Sheffield, in which thousands of choristers participated; gave concerts with his chorus in Germany (1906); in 1908 he presented 16 concerts in Canada with members of the Sheffield Choral Union, headed by him. A world tour followed in 1911, which included the U. S., Canada, Australia and South Africa. Coward was the leader of choral groups at Leeds and Glasgow; acted as a judge at Competition Festivals. He was knighted in 1926. He composed several cantatas and other choral works; edited a collection of Methodist hymns (1901); published *Choral Technique and Interpretation* (1914); *Reminiscences* (1919).—Cf. J. A. Rodgers, *Dr. Henry Coward, The Pioneer Chorus-master* (London, 1911).

Coward, Noel, British playwright and author of musical comedies; b. Teddington, Middlesex, Dec. 16, 1899. At the age of eleven, he appeared on the stage, and has been associated with the theater ever since, in the triple capacity of actor, playwright and producer. Having had no formal education in music, he dictates his songs to a musical amanuensis. Among the musical comedies for which he wrote both words and music are *This Year of Grace* (N. Y., Nov. 7, 1928); *Bitter Sweet* (London, July 18, 1929); *Conversation Piece* (London, Feb. 16, 1934); *Pacific 1860* (London, Dec. 19, 1946); *Ace of Clubs* (London, July 7, 1950); *After the Ball,* to Wilde's *Lady Windermere's Fan* (London, June 10, 1954). 51 songs from his musical plays are published in the *Noel Coward Song Book* (N. Y., 1953; with the author's introduction). He also published an autobiography, *Present Indicative* (London, 1937); 2nd vol. *Future Indefinite* (London, 1954).

Cowell, Henry Dixon, American composer; b. Menlo Park, Calif., March 11, 1897; studied at the N. Y. Institute of Applied Music, and at the Univ. of California (guest student); also took private courses with Erich von Hornbostel in Berlin and with R. Huntington Woodman; studied piano with Richard Buhlig. Cowell toured Europe five times playing his own piano works; the U. S., twelve times; appeared as a soloist in his piano concerto with the Conductorless Orchestra, N. Y., April 26, 1930, and with the Havana Philharmonic (Dec. 28, 1930). As a young man he devised and developed the technique of 'tone clusters' produced by striking the piano keys with forearm, elbow or fist, embodying these devices in his piano concerto and in many of his other works. In collaboration with Leon Theremin, he invented the Rhythmicon, an instrument allowing the accurate production of sixteen different rhythms, from one to sixteen beats to a given unit of measure, the component tones being parts of the overtone series. He has held teaching positions at Stanford Univ.; the New School for Social Research in New York; Univ. of California; Mills College; Peabody Conservatory of Music in Baltimore; Columbia Univ.; etc.; was recipient of the Guggenheim Fellowship (1930-31). Cowell is one of the most active of American modern composers; he has written more than one thousand works of various descriptions; has championed serious new music in the U. S. and abroad; founded the 'New Music Quarterly' (1927) for publication of ultra-modern music, and was its editor until 1936; was also an organizer of the Pan-American Association of Composers. In 1951 Cowell was elected member of the National Academy of Arts and Letters. In 1956 he undertook a world tour.—Works: opera, *O'Higgins of Chile* (1949); symph. No. 1 (1918); No. 2, *Anthropos* (1939); No. 3, *Gaelic Symphony* (1942); No. 4, *Short Symphony* (Boston, Oct. 24, 1947); No. 5 (Washington, Jan. 5, 1949); No. 6 (1951; not performed); No. 7, (Baltimore, Nov. 25, 1952); No. 8, for chorus and orch. (Wilmington, Ohio, March 1, 1953); No. 9

(1953); No. 10, for chamber orch. (1953); No. 11, subtitled *Seven Rites of Music* (Louisville, May 29, 1954); No. 12 (1954); No. 13 (1955); No. 14 (1956); further works for orch.: *Communication* (1920); *Vestiges* (1924); *Some Music* (1927); *Synchrony* (Paris, June 6, 1931); *Rhythmicana,* for rhythmicon and orch. (1931); *Reel* (Copenhagen, 1933); *Scherzo* (Vienna, 1933); *Shipshape Overture* (1939; also for band); *Old American Country Set* (Indianapolis, Feb. 28, 1940); *Ancient Desert Drone* (1940); *Shoonthree* (1940); *Pastoral and Fiddler's Delight* (N. Y., July 26, 1940, Stokowski conducting); *Tales of the Countryside,* for piano and orch. (his most successful work; Atlantic City, May 11, 1941, Cowell soloist, Stokowski conducting); *Concerto piccolo,* for piano and orch. (1942); *Celtic Set* (1943; also for band); *Hymn and Fuguing Tune,* Nos. 1-8 (1943-47; based on the fuguing tunes of Billings; very successful); *United Music* (1944); *Big Sing* (1945); *Festival Overture,* for double orch. (1946).—For band: *Animal Magic* (1944); *Grandma's Rumba* (1945); *Fantaisie* (U. S. Military Acad. Band, West Point, N. Y., May 30, 1952); etc.—Chamber orch.: *Symphonietta* (1928); *Irish Suite* (1929); *Polyphonica* for twelve instruments (1930); *Exultation* for ten string instruments (1930); *Competitive Sport* (1931); *Steel and Stone* (1931); *Heroic Dance* (1931); *4 Continuations* (1933); *6 Casual Developments* for five instruments (1935).—Chamber music: *Ensemble* for 2 violins, viola, 2 cellos and two thundersticks (1925); *Seven Paragraphs* for trio (1926); Quartet (1927); Suite for violin and piano (1927); *Movement* (1934); *Mosaic Quartet* (1935); and *United Quartet* (1936), for strings; *Chrysanthemums,* for soprano, 2 saxophones and 4 strings (1937); *Sarabande,* for oboe, clarinet and percussion (1937); *Trickster Coyote,* for flute and percussion (1942); *Action in Brass,* for five instruments (1943); *Two Bits,* for flute and piano (1944); *Tall Tale,* for brass sextet (1947).—Choral works: *The Thistle Flower,* for women's voices (1928); *The Coming of Light* (1939); *Fire and Ice,* for male voices and band (1942); *American Muse* (1943); *To America* (1946); *The Road to Tomorrow* (1947); *Afternoon, Evening, Night, Morning* (1947); numerous piano pieces with fanciful titles, mostly with the application of tone clusters (*Amiable Conversation; Fabric; Dynamic Motion; Advertisement;* etc.); songs: *Where She Lies, The Birthing of Manaunaun,* etc.; 2 ballets, *The Building of Banba* (Halcyon Festival, 1922); *Atlantis* (1926).—Books: *New Musical Resources* (1930); ed., *American Composers on American Music* (1933); *Charles Ives and His Music* (N. Y., 1955; in collaboration with his wife, Sidney Cowell). See N. Slonimsky, *Henry Cowell* in *American Composers on American Music* (1933); David Ewen, *American Composers Today* (N. Y., 1949).

Cowen, Sir Frederic Hymen, English composer; b. Kingston, Jamaica, Jan. 29, 1852; d. London, Oct. 6, 1935. His evident talent for music caused his parents to take him to England to study at the age of four. He was a pupil of Benedict and Goss in London; studied at Leipzig under Hauptmann, Moscheles, Reinecke, Richter, Plaidy (1865-6); in Berlin under Kiel (1867-8); conductor of the London Philharmonic (1888-92) succeeding Sullivan; again from 1900-7; musical director of the Melbourne Centennial Exhibition (1888-9); conductor of the Liverpool Philharmonic from 1896-1913; Sir Charles Hallé's successor as conductor of the Manchester Concerts (1896-9); conducted Handel Triennial Festival (Crystal Palace, 1903-12); Cardiff Festival (1902-10). He received the degree Mus. Doc. from Cambridge (hon. c., 1900) and Edinburgh (1910); knighted in 1911.—Works: 4 operas, *Pauline* (London, Nov. 22, 1876); *Thorgrim* (London, April 22, 1890); *Signa* (London, June 30, 1894); *Harold, or the Norman Conquest* (4 acts; London, June 8, 1895); oratorios: *The Deluge* (1878); *St. Ursula* (1881); *Ruth* (1887); *The Veil* (Cardiff Festival, Sept. 20, 1910; his most successful work); cantatas. For orch.: 6 symphonies: 1. in C minor (1869); 2. in F minor (1872); 3. *Scandinavian,* in C minor (1880); 4. *Welsh,* in B♭ minor (1884); 5. in F (1887); 6. *Idyllic,* in E (1897); 3 suites: *The Language of Flowers; In the Olden Time; In Fairyland; Sinfonietta;* piano concerto; 4 overtures; *Of Life and Love,* fantasy. Chamber music: 2 piano trios; 2 string quartets; piano pieces; over 250 songs; etc. He published his memoirs as *My Art and My Friends* (London, 1913), and an amusing glossary of musical terms, *Music as she is wrote* (London, 1915); also, for the 'Masterpieces of Music' series, books (with biography and music) on Haydn, Mozart, Mendelssohn and Rossini.—Cf. 'Musical Times' (Nov., 1898).

Cowles, Cecil Marion, American composer; b. San Francisco, California, Jan. 14, 1898; studied at the Von Ende School, N. Y., and the Von Meyernich School, California; also a private pupil of Sigismund Stojowski, Hugo Mansfeldt and Carl Deis; since 1939, living in N. Y. as composer. She has writen works for piano (e.g., *Shanghai*

Bund), and songs (*Persian Dawn, Le Charme*, etc.).

Cowles, Walter Ruel, American composer; b. New Haven, Conn., Sept. 4, 1881. He graduated from Yale Univ. (B. A. 1906; Mus. Bac. 1907); studied with Horatio Parker; then at the Schola Cantorum, Paris; was instructor of piano at Yale Music School (1911-19); professor of Theory of Music at Florida State College for Women (1930-1951); won the Steinert prize for composition at Yale. He composed a piano concerto; a piano trio; songs and piano pieces.

Crabbé, Armand, Belgian baritone; b. Brussels, April 23, 1884; d. there, Sept. 14, 1947. He studied with Désiré Demest at the Brussels Cons. (1902-4); was engaged at the Théâtre de la Monnaie in Brussels where he created the role of the Friar in Massenet's *Jongleur de Nôtre-Dame* (also sung by him for the first time at Covent Garden, New York, Boston, etc.). In 1908 he joined Hammerstein's Manhattan Opera, N. Y.; then was with the Chicago Grand Opera (1910-11); returning to Europe, he settled in Brussels as a voice teacher. He wrote an opera *Les Noces d'or* (in collaboration with Auguste Maurage), which was published.

Craft, Marcella, American lyric soprano; b. Indianapolis, Aug. 11, 1880. She studied with Charles Adams in Boston (1897-1900) and with F. Mottino in Milan (1901-5); made her debut in Italy; sang in Germany until the outbreak of World War I, when she returned to the U. S.; subsequently appeared with the San Carlo Opera Co.; settled at Riverside, California, as a singing teacher.

Craft, Robert, American conductor; b. Kingston, N. Y., Oct. 20, 1923. He studied at the Juilliard School of Music and the Berkshire Music Center; conducting with Monteux; was in the U. S. Army Medical Corps (1943-44); 1947, conductor of the N. Y. Brass and Woodwind Ensemble and the Chamber Art Society. In his programs he emphasizes modern works (Stravinsky, Schoenberg, etc.).

Cramer (krah'-mer), **Johann Baptist,** famous German pianist and pedagogue, eldest son of Wilhelm Cramer; b. Mannheim, Feb. 24, 1771; d. London, April 16, 1858. He was brought to London as an infant, and throughout his life regarded it as his home. He received a fine musical education, first from his father, then from Clementi (1779-81) and K. F. Abel (1785). He began to travel as a concert pianist in 1788; visited Vienna where he met Haydn and Beethoven; in later years (1832-45) spent considerable time as teacher in Munich and Paris, finally returning to London. His greatest work is his piano method *Grosse Praktische Pianoforte Schule* (1815) in 5 parts, the last of which, *84 Studies* (op. 50; later revised and publ. as op. 81, including *16 nouvelles études*) is famous in piano pedagogy. Hans von Bülow made a selection of fifty studies from this collection, later revised and annotated in collections of 52 and 60; Henselt issued a different selection with accompaniment of 2nd piano; other editions of Cramer's studies are by Coccius, Riemann, Pauer, Lack, and Lickl; *100 Progressive Etudes* are also well known. Apart from his pedagogic collections, Cramer wrote 7 piano concertos; 105 piano sonatas; piano quartet; piano quintet, and numerous piano pieces of the salon type, but all these are quite forgotten, while his piano studies, with those of Czerny, have maintained their value for more than a century. Cf. J. Pembaur, *Die 84 Etüden von J. B. Cramer; Anleitung zu gründlichem Studieren und Analysieren derselben* (Leipzig, 1901); Th. Schlesinger, *J. B. Cramer und seine Klavier-Sonaten* (Munich, 1928).—In 1824, together with R. Addison and T. F. Beale, Cramer established a music publishing house (now J. B. Cramer & Co., Ltd.), of which he was director until 1842; in 1845 Addison retired and was succeeded by W. Chappell, the firm then becoming Cramer, Beale & Chappell; after Cramer's death in 1858, and Chappell's retirement in 1861, G. Wood became Beale's partner; about 1862 the firm began to devote much attention to the manufacture of pianos; on Beale's death in 1863, Wood became sole director, continuing it successfully until his death in 1893, although devoting more consideration to piano manufacture than to music publishing. His two nephews succeeded him. In 1897 the firm became a limited company.

Cramer, Wilhelm, German violinist; b. Mannheim, 1745; d. London, Oct. 5, 1799. He received his musical training, from his father, Jacob Cramer (1705-77), a violinist in the Mannheim orch. Wilhelm Cramer joined the orch. in 1757; went to London in 1772 where he held various positions as violinist and conductor. He was greatly admired as a concert performer. Of his works, three violin concertos and one string trio are published.

Cranz, August, music publishing firm in Hamburg, founded 1813 by August Heinrich Cranz (1789-1870). His son **Alwin** (b. 1834; d. Vevey, Apr. 10, 1923), who succeeded him in 1857, bought the firm of C. A. Spina of Vienna in 1876, and in 1886 the firm of C. A. Böhme of Hamburg. Alwin's son, **Oskar** (pen-name Anton Toska; d. Boston, Aug. 24, 1929), entered as partner in 1896. In 1897 the firm removed to Leipzig. Branches were established in Vienna (1876), Brussels (1883), and London (1896).

Cras, Jean Emile Paul, French composer; b. Brest, May 22, 1879; d. there, Sept. 14, 1932. He was an officer in the French Navy, reaching the rank of Vice-Admiral; he grew up in a musical atmosphere and when still a child began to compose; took lessons with Henri Duparc. Under the influence of Duparc's style, Cras composed a number of miniatures in an impressionistic vein; he was at his best in lyrical songs and instrumental pieces. He wrote an opera *Polyphème* (Paris, Opéra-Comique, Dec. 28, 1922) which won the Prize of the City of Paris; *Journal de Bord,* a symphonic suite (1927); *Légende* for cello and orch. (1929); piano concerto (1931); the following works for voice and orch.: *L'offrande lyrique* (1920); *Fontaines* (1923); *Trois Noëls* (1929); many pieces of chamber music, a number of songs.—Cf. René Dumesnil, *Jean Cras* in 'Portraits de musiciens français' (Paris, 1938, pp. 153-60).

Crawford, Robert, Scottish composer; b. Edinburgh, April 18, 1925. He studied composition with Hans Gál in Edinburgh and with B. Frankel in London. His quartet was performed at the Frankfurt Festival of the International Society for Contemporary Music in 1951. He has written some theater music; quintet for clarinet, piano and strings; piano sonata; etc.

Crawford, Robert M., baritone and conductor; b. Dawson, Yukon Territory, Canada, July 27, 1899; studied at Princeton Univ., and also took courses at the Juilliard Graduate School and at the American Cons. at Fontainebleau, France. Returning to the U. S., he held various posts as choral teacher and conductor; was in charge of the Newark Symph. Orch. and Chautauqua Orch. (1933); composed several orchestral suites and songs, of which the most popular is *The U. S. Air Force.*

Crawford, Ruth Porter, American composer; b. East Liverpool, Ohio, July 3, 1901; d. Chevy Chase, Maryland, Nov. 18, 1953. She studied composition with Palmer, Weidig, and Charles Seeger, piano with Heniot Levy, Louise Robyn and D. L. Herz; 1918-21, taught at the School of Mus. Art, Jacksonville, Florida; 1925-29, the American Cons., Chicago; 1926-29, Elmhurst College of Music, Ill.; won a Juilliard Scholarship for the years 1927-29, and a Guggenheim Fellowship in 1930. She was married to Charles Seeger; lived mostly in Silver Spring, Maryland. Her musical works are couched in a bold modernistic idiom, with subject matter often reflecting political and sociological ideas.—Works: *Sacco-Vanzetti* and *Chinaman Laundryman* for chorus (Workers' Olympiad, 1933); *Rissolty Rossolty* for 10 wind instruments, drums, and strings (1941); *4 Diaphonic Suites* for 2 cellos, 2 clarinets, oboe and flute; string quartet; violin sonata, etc. Her *Three Songs* for contralto, oboe, piano and percussion, with orchestral ostinato, were performed at the Amsterdam Festival of the International Society for Contemporary Music (June 15, 1933). She was also interested in American folk music; published *American Folk Songs for Children* (1948); *Animal Folk Songs for Children* (1950); *American Folksongs for Christmas* (1953).—Cf. Charles Seeger, *Ruth Crawford,* in Cowell's symposium, *American Composers on American Music* (Stanford Univ., 1933).

Creatore, Giuseppe, band conductor; b. Naples, June 21, 1871; d. New York, Aug. 15, 1952. He studied at the Naples Cons. with Nicola d'Arienzo and Camillo de Nardis. In 1900 he came to the U. S., organized his own band and toured from coast to coast and in Canada. In 1906 he returned to Italy, where he established a band which he brought to America for a tour. He then settled in New York, and was active as impresario of various opera companies, which however were not successful; conducted band concerts during summer seasons in various U. S. cities.

Crécquillon (Créquillon) (krā-kē-yohn'), **Thomas,** French contrapuntist; b. probably in Ghent; d. Béthune, 1557. It is known that he was maître de chapelle at Béthune in 1540; was court musician to Charles V of Spain between 1544-47; later was canon at Namur, Termonde and Béthune. His works, which rank with the best of that period, consist of 16 masses in 4 and 5 parts, 116 motets, *cantiones,* and 192 French *chansons* in 4, 5 and 6 parts. Reprints appear in Commer's *Collectio operum musicorum Batavorum saeculi XVI* and Maldeghem's *Trésor musical.* For a complete list of his works (published mostly between 1545 and 1636) and a detailed bibliography, see the article on him in 'Die Musik in Geschichte und Gegenwart'.

Crescentini (kräs-chĕhn-tē'-nē), **Girolamo,** one of the last and finest of the Italian artificial mezzo-sopranos; b. Urbania, near Urbino, Feb. 2, 1762; d. Naples, April 24, 1846. He studied singing with Gibelli at Bologna, and made a highly successful debut at Rome in 1783; subsequent successes in other European capitals earned him the surname of 'Orfeo Italiano'. He sang at Leghorn, Padua, Venice, Turin, London (1786), Milan and Naples (1788-9). Napoleon, having heard him in 1805, decorated him with the Iron Crown, and engaged him from 1806-12; Crescentini then retired from the stage and left Paris, on account of vocal disorders induced by the climate; in 1816 he became professor of singing in the Royal Cons., Naples. Cimarosa wrote his *Orazi e Curiazi* for him. Crescentini published several collections of *Ariette* (Vienna, 1797), and a *Treatise on Vocalization in France and Italy,* with vocal exercises (Paris, 1811).

Creser, William, English organist and composer; b. York, Sept. 9, 1844; d. London, March 13, 1933. He was taught by his father, in whose choir (at St. John's Church) he sang; studied later with G. A. Macfarren (organ and composition); as early as 1856 he occasionally acted as Sir J. Barnby's substitute at Holgate Road Church; appointed organist at Holy Trinity, Micklegate, in 1859, and later succeeded Barnby; then filled various other positions; organist at the Chapel Royal, St. James' (1891-1902); from 1902 examiner of Trinity College of Music, in which capacity he made frequent visits to musical institutions throughout the British colonies; Mus. Bac., Oxonian, 1869; Mus. Doc., Oxonian, 1880. His wife (*née* Amelia Clarke) was a well known mezzo-soprano.—Works: An oratorio, *Micaiah;* the cantatas *Eudora* (Leeds, 1882); *The Sacrifice of Freia* (Leeds, 1889); *The Golden Legend; Tegner's Drapa;* a mass; 2 Psalms; *Old English Suite* for orch.; string quartet; piano trio; violin sonata; organ music.

Creston, Paul (real name Joseph Guttoveggio), talented American composer; b. New York, Oct. 10, 1906; studied piano with Randegger and Déthier, theory and organ with Pietro Yon. He adopted the name Creston as a young man, before he began to compose; his first work was a set of dances for piano (1932). He received a Guggenheim Fellowship (1938-39); in a few years he advanced to the front ranks of American composers. In 1956 he was elected president of the National Association for American Composers and Conductors. His music is characterized by spontaneity, with strong melodic lines and full-bodied harmony; his instrumental writing is highly advantageous for virtuoso performance. Works: symph. No. 1 (N. Y., Feb. 22, 1941; N. Y. Music Critics' Circle Award); symph. No. 2 (N. Y. Philh., Feb. 15, 1945; his most successful work; many subsequent performances); symph. No. 3 (Worcester Festival, Oct. 27, 1950); symph. No. 4 (Washington, Jan. 30, 1952); symph. No. 5 (Washington, April 4, 1956). Other works for orch.: *Partita* for flute, violin and strings (1937); *Threnody* for orch. (1938); *Two Choric Dances* for woodwinds, piano, percussion and strings (1938); concertino for marimba and orch. (1940); *A Rumor,* symph. sketch (N. Y., Dec. 13, 1941); *Dance Variations* for soprano and orch. (1942); *Frontiers* for orch. (Toronto, Oct. 14, 1943); saxophone concerto (N. Y. Philh., Jan. 27, 1944); *Poem* for harp and orch. (1945); *Fantasie* for trombone and orch. (Los Angeles, Feb. 12, 1948); piano concerto (1949); *Walt Whitman,* symph. poem (1951); *Invocation and Dance* for orch. (Louisville, May 15, 1954). Chamber music: suite for saxophone and piano (1935); string quartet (1936); suite for viola and piano (1937); suite for violin and piano (1939); sonata for saxophone and piano (1939); suite for flute, viola and piano (1953). Choral works: *Three Chorales from Tagore* (1936); *Missa Pro Defunctis* (1938); *Dirge* (1940); piano pieces (*5 Little Dances, 5 Inventions,* etc.).—Cf. Henry Cowell, *Paul Creston,* in the 'Mus. Quarterly' (Oct., 1948).

Crews, Lucile (Mrs. Lucile Marsh), American composer; b. Pueblo, Colorado, Aug. 23, 1888; studied at the New England Cons., Northwestern School of Music, Redlands Univ. and the American Cons., Chicago; later in Paris with Nadia Boulanger and in Berlin with Hugo Kaun and Arthur Anderson; Mus. Bac. (1920); won the Pulitzer Travelling Scholarship in 1926, the prize offered by the California Federation of Music Clubs for a one-act opera, and the prize for chamber music (*Suite* for strings and woodwinds) of the Festival of Allied Arts, Los Angeles.—Major works: tone poem, *To an Unknown Soldier* (Hollywood Bowl, 1926); opera miniature, *Ariadne and Dionysus* (NBC Music Guild, 1935); chamber music; piano pieces; songs.

Crist, Bainbridge, American composer; b. Lawrenceburg, Indiana, Feb. 13, 1883. He studied piano and flute; later law at the George Washington Univ. (LL.B.); was a lawyer in Boston for six years (until 1912), continuing his music as an avocation; went to Europe to complete musical training (theory with P. Juon in Berlin and C. Landi, London, and singing with William Shakespeare); taught singing in Boston (1915-21) and Washington, D. C. (1922-23); returned to Europe (1923) and spent four years in Florence, Paris, Lucerne and Berlin; then came back to the U. S. and settled in Washington.—Major compositions: For the stage: *Le Pied de la Momie,* choreographic drama in 2 scenes (1915; Bournemouth Festival, England, 1925); *Pregiwa's Marriage,* a Javanese ballet in 1 scene (1920); *The Sorceress,* choreographic drama (1926). For orch.: *Egyptian Impressions,* suite (Boston Pops, June 22, 1915); *Abisharika,* for violin and orch. (1921); *Intermezzo* (1921); *Chinese Dance* (1922); *Arabian Dance* (1922); *Nautch Dance* (1922); *Dreams* (1924); *Yearning* (1924); *Nocturne* (1924); *An Old Portrait* (1924); *La Nuit revécue* (1933; Radio City, N. Y., March 8, 1936); *Vienna 1913* (1933); *Frivolité* (1934); *Hymn to Nefertiti* (1936); *Fête espagnole* (1937); *American Epic 1620,* tone poem (Washington, D. C., Feb. 28, 1943). For voice and orch.: *A Bag of Whistles* (1915); *The Parting,* poem (1916); *Rhymes* (1917); *O Come Hither!* (1918); *Drolleries* (1920); *Colored Stars,* a suite of 4 songs (1921); *Remember* (1930); *The Way That Lovers Use* (1931); *Noontime* (1931); *Evening* (1931); *By a Silent Shore* (1932). Choral works for mixed, male and female voices; piano pieces; songs. He is author of *The Art of Setting Words to Music* (N. Y., 1944).—Cf. J. T. Howard, *Bainbridge Crist* (N. Y., 1929); W. T. Upton, *Art-Song in America* (N. Y., 1930; pp. 236-49).

Cristofori, Bartolommeo, Italian instrument maker; b. Padua, May 4, 1655; d. Florence, Jan. 27, 1731; famous as the inventor of the first practical piano as opposed to the clavichord (which also employs a type of hammer action), although two keyed instruments called Piano e Forte are known to have existed in Modena in 1598, and a four-octave keyboard instrument shaped like a dulcimer, with small hammers and no dampers, dating from 1610, is yet in existence. He was a leading maker of clavicembali in Padua; about 1690 went to Florence, where he was instrument maker to Ferdinando de' Medici; on the latter's death in 1713, he was made custodian of the court collection of instruments by Cosimo III. According to an article by Maffei (published 1711 in the 'Giornale dei Letterati d'Italia'), Cristofori had up to that year made three 'gravecembali col piano e forte', these having, instead of the usual jacks plucking the strings with quills, a row of little hammers striking the strings from below. The principle of this hammer action was adopted, in the main, by Gottfried Silbermann, the Streichers, and Broadwood (hence called the 'English action'). Following the designation by its inventor, the new instrument was named *Piano-forte.* A piano of Cristofori's make is in the possession of the N. Y. Metropolitan Museum of Art.—Cf. F. Casaglia, *Per le onoranze a Bartolommeo Cristofori* (1876).

Crivelli, Giovanni Battista, Italian composer of the Lombardy school; b. Scandiano, Modena; d. Modena, 1682. He was organist at Reggio Cathedral; then maestro di cappella to the court of Ferrara; at the electoral court at Munich (1629-34); at the court of Francesco I at Modena (1651); at the Church of Santa Maria Maggiore, Bergamo (1642-48, and again in 1654). He published *Motetti concertati* (1626; 3rd ed. 1635) and *Madrigali concertati* (1626; 2nd ed. 1633).

Croce (kroh'-chĕ), **Giovanni,** eminent Venetian composer; b. Chioggia (hence surnamed 'il Chiozzotto'), c. 1560; d. Venice, May 15, 1609. He was a pupil of Zarlino; chorister at San Marco, where he succeeded Donato as maestro di cappella in 1603.—Publ. works: Sonatas *a* 5 (1580); 2 volumes of motets *a* 8 (1589, 1590; volume II reprinted 1605 with organ bass; both volumes with organ bass in 1607); 2 volumes of madrigals *a* 5 (1585, 1588); *Triacca musicale* (caprices, or humorous songs in Venetian dialect, *a* 4-7; went through 4 editions—1596, 1601, 1607, 1609, and was his most popular and famous work; it includes the contest between the cuckoo and the nightingale, judged by the parrot); madrigals *a* 5-6 (1590-1607); *Cantiones sacrae a* 8, with basso continuo for organ (1622; a 2nd volume was published in 1623); *Canzonette a* 4 (1588; new editions, 1595, 1598); masses *a* 8 (1596); Lamentations *a* 4 (1603, 1605) and *a* 6 (1610); Magnificats *a* 6 (1605), Vesper psalms *a* 8 (1589), etc. Younge printed some of Croce's madrigals in his 'Musica Transalpina' (1588), and a selection of his church music was published with English words as *Musica sacra, Penetentials for 6 voyces,* in London in 1608. Modern reprints include 3 masses published at Regensburg in 1888, 1891 and 1899, and other works in Proske's 'Musica Divina', Haberl's 'Repertorium', Torchi's 'L'Arte musicale in Italia', Bäuerle's '12 Hymnen und Motetten alter Meister', and the publications of the Motet Society (London).—Cf. F. X. Haberl, *Giovanni Croce,* in 'Kirchenmusikalisches Jahrbuch' (1888); L. Torri, in 'Rivista Musicale Italiana' (1900); Denis Arnold, *Giovanni Croce and the Concertato Style,* in the 'Mus. Quarterly' (Jan., 1953).

Croes (kroos), **Henri-Jacques de,** Belgian composer; b. Antwerp, Sept. 19, 1705; d. Brussels, Aug. 16, 1786. Violinist and assistant conductor at St.-Jacques, Antwerp; in 1729, musical director to the Prince of Thurn and Taxis, at Regensburg. He went to Brussels in 1749, conducted the choir of the Royal Chapel until 1755, and was then appointed maître de chapelle to Charles of Lorraine.—Works: Masses, motets, anthems and other church music; also symphonies, sonatas, etc. Cf. S. Clercx, *Henri-Jacques de Croes, Compositeur et Maître de Musique* (Brussels, 1940).

Croft (or **Crofts**), **William,** English organist and composer; b. Nether Ettington, Warwickshire, (baptized) Dec. 30, 1678; d. Bath, Aug. 14, 1727 (buried in Westminster Abbey). A chorister in the Chapel Royal, under Dr. Blow; Gentleman of Chapel Royal, 1700, and (with J. Clarke) joint organist in 1707. Succeeded Blow as organist of Westminster Abbey, Master of the Children, and Composer of the Chapel Royal (1708).—Works: *Musica sacra,* 30 anthems *a* 2-8, and a burial service in score (1724; in 2 volumes; the first English work of church music engraved in score on plates); *Musicus apparatus academicus* (2 odes written for his degree of Mus. Doc., Oxon., 1713); overtures and act tunes for several plays; violin sonatas; flute sonatas, etc.—Cf. F. G. E., *Dr. William Crofts,* in the 'Musical Times' (Sept., 1900; p. 577).

Crooks, Richard (Alexander), American tenor; b. Trenton, N. J., June 26, 1900. He studied voice for five years with Sydney H. Bourne and also took lessons with Frank La Forge; boy soprano soloist in N. Y. churches, later tenor soloist; after war service made debut with the N. Y. Symph. Orch. under Damrosch in 1922; gave concerts in London, Vienna, Munich, Berlin and in the U. S. (1925-27); made his American debut as Cavaradossi with the Philadelphia Grand Opera Co. (Nov. 27, 1930); debut as Des Grieux at the Metropolitan Opera (Feb. 25, 1933); toured Australia (1936-39); gave concerts from coast to coast in the U. S. and Canada, appeared in recitals, as orchestral soloist, and in festivals.

Crossley, Ada (Jessica), Australian mezzo-soprano; b. Tarraville, Gippsland, March 3, 1874; d. London, Oct. 17, 1929. She was a pupil of Fanny Simonson (voice) in Melbourne; having sung in several churches, she made her concert debut with the Melbourne Philharmonic Society in 1892; came to London in 1894, studied with Santley, and later with Mme. Marchesi in Paris; made her London debut at Queen's Hall on May 18, 1895; her success was so emphatic that she sang by command five times before Queen Victoria within the next two years; appeared as soloist at all important English festivals; her tour of Australia in 1904 was a succession of triumphs; also made successful tours of the U. S. and South Africa.

Crotch, William, eminent English composer; b. Norwich, July 5, 1775; d. Taunton, Dec. 29, 1847. His extraordinary precocity may be measured by the well authenticated statement (Burney's paper, *Account of an Infant Musician,* in the 'Philosophical Transactions' of 1779), that when two and a half years old he played on a small organ built by his father, a master carpenter. In Oct. 1779, he was brought to London, and played in public. At the age of eleven he became assistant to Dr. Randall, organist of Trinity and King's Colleges at Cambridge; at fourteen, composed an oratorio, *The Captivity of Judah* (performed in 1789); he then studied for the ministry (1788-90); returned to music, he was organist of Christ Church, Oxford; graduated as Mus. Bac., Oxon., in 1794 (Mus. Doc., 1799); in 1797 succeeded Hayes as professor of music in the University, and organist of St. John's College. He lectured in the Music School (1800-4), and in the Royal Institution, London (1804, 1805, 1807; and again from 1820); was appointed Principal for the new Royal Academy of Music in 1822.—Works: 2 oratorios, *Palestine* (1812), and *The Captivity of Judah* (1834; a different work from his juvenile oratorio of the same name); 10 anthems; 3 organ concertos; piano sonatas; an ode, *Mona on Snowdown calls;* a glee, *Nymph, with thee;* a motet, *Methinks I hear the full celestial choir* (these last 3 were very popular); other odes; other glees, fugues; also wrote *Elements of Music Composition* (1812; 1833; 1856); *Practical Thorough bass;* etc. A complete list of his compositions appeared in 'Musical News' (April 17 and 24, 1897).

Crouch, Frederick Nicholls, English conductor and composer; b. London, July 31, 1808; d. Portland, Maine, Aug. 18, 1896. He studied with Bochsa (cello), and entered Royal Academy of Music in 1822 (teachers: Crotch, Attwood, Howes, Lindley and Crivelli). At the age of nine he was cellist in the Royal Coburg Theater; played in Queen Adelaide's private band till 1832; was a teacher and singer in Plymouth, and cellist in various theaters. He went to New York in 1849; was in Philadelphia in 1856 as conductor of Mrs. Rush's Saturday Concerts; served in the Confederate Army, and settled in Baltimore, as a singing teacher.—Works: 2 operas; many collections of songs, some being original (among these latter the well-known *Kathleen Mavourneen*). Cora Pearl, the famous Parisian courtesan of the second Empire, was his daughter.

Crowest, Frederick J., English writer on music; b. London, Nov. 30, 1850; d. Edgbaston, June 14, 1927. He joined the editorial staff of Cassell, Petter & Galpin in 1886; held various editorial positions; in 1901 was appointed general manager and editor of Walter Scott Publishing Co., Ltd.; retired in 1917.—Writings: *The Great Tone Poets* (1874); *Book of Musical Anecdote* (1878; 2 volumes; revised edition, 1902, as *Musicians' Wit, Humour and Anecdote*); *Phases of Musical England* (1881); *Musical History and Biography in the Form of Question and Answer* (1883); *Advice to Singers* (many editions); *Musical Groundwork; Cherubini* (in 'Great Musicians' Series); *Dictionary of British Musicians* (1895); *The Story of British Music* (vol. I, 1895); *Catechism of Musical History* (many editions); *Story of Music* (1902; in America as *Story of the Art of Music*); *Verdi: Man and Musician* (1897); *Beethoven* (1899).

Crüger, Johann, noted German composer of church music; b. Grossbreese, near Guben, April 9, 1598; d. Berlin, Feb. 23, 1662. A student of divinity at Wittenberg in 1620, he had received thorough musical training at Regensburg under Paulus Homberger. He then traveled in Austria and Hungary; spent some time in Bohemia and Saxony, before settling in Berlin. His fame rests on the composition of many fine chorales (*Jesu, meine Freude; Jesu, meine Zuversicht; Nun danket alle Gott,* etc.), which were originally published in the collection *Praxis pietatis melica* (Berlin, 1644; reprinted in 45 editions before 1736). In addition he published the following collections: *Neues vollkömmliches Gesangbuch Augspurgischer Konfession . . .* (1640); *Geistliche Kirchenmelodeyen . . .* (1649); *Dr. M. Luthers wie auch andrer gottseliger christlicher Leute Geistliche Lieder und Psalmen* (1657); *Psalmodia sacra . . .* (1658); the valuable theoretical works *Synopsis musica* (1630; enlarged 1634); *Praecepta musicae figuralis* (1625); and *Quaestiones musicae practicae* (1650). —Cf. E. Fischer-Krückeberg's articles: *Johann Crüger als Musiktheoretiker* ('Zeitschrift für Musikwissenschaft', XII); *Johann Crüger's Choralbearbeitungen* (ibid., XIV); *Johann Crüger und das Kirchenlied des 17. Jahrhundert* ('Monatsschrift für Gottesdienst und kirchliche Kunst', XXXIV, 2). See Otto Brodde, *Johann Crüger, sein Weg und sein Werk* (Leipzig, 1936); also E. C. G. Langbecker, *J. Crügers Choral-Melodien* (Berlin, 1835).

Cruz, Ivo, Portuguese conductor and composer; b. Corumba, Brazil, May 19, 1901; was taken to Lisbon as a child and studied there and later in Munich. Returning to Portugal in 1931, he organized a choral society, the first permanent group of this nature in Lisbon; in 1937 formed the Orquestra Filarmonica de Lisboa; in 1938 was director of the Lisbon Cons. In 1949, conducted in Zürich and Salzburg. Works: orchestral suite *Nocturnos da Lusitania* (1928), 2 'symbolic poems,' *Lisboa* and *Coimbra* for piano and orch., and numerous songs and piano pieces, inspired by native themes.

Ctesibius, inventor of the hydraulis. He flourished between 246 and 221 B. C., and is known in literature as Ctesibius of Alexandria. The weight of evidence collected by H. G. Farmer tends to demonstrate that the first hydraulis was indeed constructed by Ctesibius.—Cf. P. Tannery, *Athénée sur Ctesibius et l'hydraulis* in the 'Revue des études grêcques' (Paris, 1896); H. G. Farmer, *The Organ of the Ancients* (London, 1931).

Cubiles, José, Spanish pianist and conductor; b. Cadiz, May 15, 1894. He studied in Paris with Diémer; gave concerts in Europe; was appointed professor at the Madrid Cons.

Cuclin, Dimitri, Rumanian composer; b. Galatz, April 5, 1885. He studied in Bucharest and Paris; in 1922 came to New York where he taught; returned to Bucharest in 1930 and was appointed professor at the Cons.—Works: operas: *Sorla* (1911) *Trajan et Dokla* (1921); *Agamemnon* (1922); *Bellerophon* (1924); oratorio, *David and Goliath* (1928); 9 symphonies (1935-49); violin concerto 1930); piano concerto (1939); sacred choruses, chamber music and songs.

Cui (kwē), **César Antonovitch,** Russian composer, one of the group of the 'Five'; b. Vilna, Jan. 18, 1835; d. Petrograd, March 24, 1918. He was the son of a soldier in Napoleon's army who remained in Russia, married a Lithuanian noblewoman and settled as a teacher of French in Vilna. Cui learned musical notation by copying Chopin's mazurkas and various Italian operas; then tried his hand at composition on his own. In 1849 he took lessons with Moniuszko who was in Vilna at the time. In 1850 he went to St. Petersburg, where he entered the Engineering Academy in 1851. After graduation in 1857 he became a topographer and later an expert in fortification. He participated in the Russo-Turkish war of 1877; in 1880 he became prof. at the Engineering Academy and was tutor in military fortification to the Czar Nicholas II. In 1856 Cui met Balakirev, who helped him master the technique of composition. In 1858 he married Malvina Bamberg; for her he wrote a scherzo on the theme *BABEG* (for the letters in her name) and *CC* (his own initials). In 1864 he began writing music criticism in the St. Petersburg 'Vyedomosti' and later in other newspapers, continuing as music critic until 1900. Cui's musical tastes were conditioned by his early admiration for Schumann; he opposed Wagner, against whom he wrote vitriolic articles; he attacked Strauss and Reger with even greater violence. He was an ardent propagandist of Glinka and the Russian National School, but was somewhat critical towards Tchaikovsky. He published the first comprehensive book on Russian music, *Musique en Russie* (Paris, 1880). Cui was grouped with Rimsky-Korsakov, Mussorgsky, Borodin and Balakirev as one of the 'Mighty Five'; the adjective in his case, however, is not very appropriate, for his music lacks grandeur; he was at his best in delicate miniatures, e.g., *Orientale,* from the suite *Kaleidoscope,* op. 50.—Works: 6 operas produced in St. Petersburg: *The Mandarin's Son* (1859; Dec. 19, 1878); *The Prisoner of the Caucasus* (1859; rewritten 1881; prod. Feb. 16, 1883); *William Ratcliff* (Feb. 26, 1869); *Angelo* (Feb. 13, 1876); *The Saracen* (Nov. 14, 1899); *The Captain's Daughter* (1911). Other operas: *Le Flibustier* (Opéra-Comique, Paris, Jan. 22, 1894); *Mam'zelle Fifi* (Moscow, Nov. 16, 1903); *Matteo Falcone* (Moscow, 1908). *A Feast in Time of Plague,* written originally as a dramatic cantata, was produced as a 1-act opera (Moscow, Nov. 23, 1901). Children's operas: *The Snow Giant; Little Red Ridinghood; Puss in Boots; Little Ivan the Fool.* Orchestral works: *Tarantella,* op. 12 (1859); *Marche solennelle,* op. 18 (1881); *Suite miniature* (op. 20); *Suite concertante* for violin and orch., op. 25 (1883); 2 *Morceaux* for cello and orch. (op. 36); Suite No. 2, op. 38 (1887); Suite No. 4, *À Argenteau,* op. 40 (1887); Suite No. 3, *In Modo populari* (op. 43); 3 Scherzos (op. 82). Chamber music: 3 string quartets (op. 45, 1893; op. 68; op. 91, 1913); *5 Little Duets* for flute and violin (op. 56); violin pieces: *2 Miniatures* (op. 24); violin sonata (op. 84); *Petite Suite* (op. 14); *12 Miniatures* (op. 20); *Kaleidoscope,* 24 numbers (op. 50); *6 Bagatelles* (op. 51). Choruses: op. 4, 28, 46, 53, 58, 59. Piano works: op. 8, 20-22, 26, 29-31, 35, 39-41, 52, 60, 61, 64, 83. Songs: op. 3, 5, 7, 9-11, 13, 15-17, 19, 23, 27, 32, 33, 34, 37, 42, 44, 48, 49, 55, 57, 62, 86; also without opus numbers. Cui contributed a number to a set of Variations on 'Chopsticks' (with Borodin, Liadov and Rimsky-Korsakov). In 1914-16 Cui completed Mussorgsky's opera *The Fair at Sorotchinsk.* A volume of his *Selected Articles* (1864-1917) was published in Leningrad in 1953.—Bibl.: Louise Mercy-Argenteau, *César Cui, Esquisse critique* (Paris, 1888); N. Findeisen, *C. A. Cui* ('Russian Musical Gazette', 1894); A. Koptyayev, *César Cui as Composer for the Pianoforte* ('Russian Musical Gazette', 1895); P. Weimarn, *César Cui as Song-writer* (St. Petersburg, 1896); *Musical Festival in Honor of C. A. Cui,* a symposium (St. Petersburg, 1910); G. Abraham, *Studies in Russian Music* (N. Y. and London, 1935); M. D. Calvocoressi and G. Abraham, *Masters of Russian Music* (N. Y., 1936). See also the biographical note in the Appendix to Cui's *Musique en Russie* (1880).

Culbertson, Alexander (Sascha), violinist b. Bessarabia, Aug. 10, 1894; d. N. Y., April 16, 1944. He received his first instruction on the violin from Zuckovsky, and at the age of nine entered the Rostov Cons.; pupil of Sevčik in Prague (1905-8); made his debut at Vienna (1908); toured Europe with extraordinary success (1908-14); joined the American Army (1918); debut in the U. S. (1919); gave concerts throughout the U. S. (1919-27); returned to Europe, residing in Paris as performer and teacher (1927-37); finally settled in New York as a teacher.

Culp (kŏŏlp), **Julia,** Dutch contralto; b. Groningen, Oct. 6, 1880. She first studied violin as a child; then became voice pupil of Cornelia van Zanten at the Amsterdam Cons. (1897), and later of Etelka Gerster in Berlin; made formal debut in Magdeburg in 1901; her tours of Germany, Austria, the Netherlands, France, Spain and Russia were highly successful from an artistic standpoint, establishing her as one of the finest singers of German lieder. Her American debut took place at New York, Jan. 10, 1913; for many years, she visited the United States every season. In private life Mme. Culp was the wife of Erich Merten; in 1919 she married an Austrian industrialist, Willy Ginzkey; lived in Czechoslovakia; after his death (1934) she returned to Amsterdam.

Culwick, James C., English organist and composer; b. W. Bromwich, Staffordshire, April 28, 1845; d. Dublin, Oct. 5, 1907. He was a pupil of T. Bedsmore; assistant organist at Lichfield Cathedral and organist at various churches until 1881, when he was appointed to the Chapel Royal at Dublin, where he remained till his death; also professor of piano and theory at Alexandra College, and conductor of the Harmonic Society and Orpheus; Mus. Doc. (hon. c.) from Dublin Univ., 1893. He wrote a dramatic cantata, *The Legend of Stauffenberg* (1890); piano pieces (suite, ballade, sonatina, etc.); several anthems and church services; author of *Rudiments of Music* (1880; 2nd edition 1882); *The Study of Music and Its Place in General Education* (1882); *The Works of Sir R. Stewart* (1902).

Cumberland, Gerald (real name C. F. Kenyon), English critic and writer; b. Eccles, May 7, 1881; d. Southsea, June 14, 1926. He was music critic of the 'Manchester Courier' (1909-12), of the 'Daily Citizen' (1921-25), and of various American papers; publ. books and pamphlets: *How to Memorize Music; Set Down in Malice* (1918); *Written in Friendship* (1923); *Imaginary Conversations With Great Composers* (1924).

Cummings, William Hayman, English singer and music antiquarian; b. Sidbury, Devonshire, Aug. 22, 1831; d. London, June 6, 1915. He was a chorister in London at St. Paul's and at the Temple Church; organist of Waltham Abbey (1847); tenor singer in the Temple, Westminster Abbey and Chapel Royal; professor of singing at the Royal Academy of Music (1879-96); in 1882, appointed conductor of the Sacred Harmonic Society; precentor of St. Anne's, Soho (1886-98); principal of Guildhall School of Music (1896-1900); received an honorary degree of Mus. Doc. from the Univ. of Dublin (1900). He was a cultivated singer and a learned antiquarian; was instrumental in founding the Purcell Society, and edited its first publications; was the author of a biography of Purcell (in the 'Great Musicians' series; London, 1882); also published a *Primer of the Rudiments of Music* (1877), and a *Biographical Dictionary of Musicians* (1892); contributed to Grove's Dictionary. His library of 4,500 volumes contained many rare autographs. He composed a cantata, *The Fairy Ring* (1873), sacred music, glees, part songs, etc.

Cundell, Edric, b. London, Jan. 29, 1893; he was first a horn player; then a pianist; taught at Trinity College (1914); was conductor of the Westminster Orchestral Society (1920) and of the Stock Exchange Orch. (London, 1924). In 1935, he founded the Edric Cundell Chamber Orch.; in 1938, succeeded Sir Landon Ronald as director of the Guildhall School of Music; in 1949 received the order of Commander of the British Empire. Cundell won the Hammond Prize for composition (1920) and the 'Daily Telegraph' Prize for chamber music (1933).—Works: Symphony in C; the symph. poems, *Serbia* (1919) and *The Tragedy of Deirdre* (1922); *Sonnet, Our Dead* for tenor and orch. (1922); piano concerto; piano quartet, string sextet, string quartet, *Rhapsody* for viola and piano; miscellaneous piano pieces (*Valse Fantastique; The Water Babies,* etc.); songs.

Curci (koor'-chē), **Giuseppe,** Italian composer; b. Barletta, June 15, 1808; d. there, Aug. 5, 1877. He studied in Naples with Zingarelli and Crescentini; became a singing teacher; composed several operas: *Il Proscritto* (Turin, 1837); *Don Desiderio* (Venice, 1837); etc.; traveled in Germany and Austria; taught voice in Paris (1848-56), where his opera, *Il Baccelliere* was produced; then returned to his native town. He published a manual, *Il bel canto.*

Curran, Pearl Gildersleeve, American composer; b. Denver, Colorado, June 25, 1875; d. New Rochelle, N. Y., April 16, 1941. She studied music privately; published about 40 songs, many of them to her own texts. The most successful include *Dawn; Life; Rain; Nursery Rhymes; Nocturne.*

Curry, Arthur Mansfield, American composer and pedagogue; b. Chelsea, Mass., Jan. 27, 1866; d. Atlanta, Georgia, Dec. 30, 1953. He studied with Franz Kneisel (violin) and Edward MacDowell (composition); taught at the New England Cons. (1915-39). His works include the orchestral overture *Blomidon* (Worcester, 1902); the symph. poem *Atala* (after Chateaubriand; Boston Symph., April 21, 1911, composer conducting); *The Winning of Amarac,* Celtic legend for narrator, women's chorus and orch. (Boston, 1934); choruses for men's, women's and mixed voices; piano pieces and many songs (*Before Night, The Fiddler of Dooney,* etc.).

Curschmann (koorsh'-man), **Karl Friedrich,** German composer; b. Berlin, June 21, 1804; d. Langfuhr, near Danzig, Aug. 24, 1841. Originally a law student, he devoted himself to music, studying with Hauptmann and Spohr at Kassel, where his one-act opera *Abdul and Erinnieh* was produced (Oct. 29, 1828). His songs possess a fine poetic quality; a collection of 83 lieder and 9 duets and trios was published posthumously in 2 volumes (Berlin, 1871). He was also a noted singer, and gave concerts in Germany and Italy.—Cf. G Meissner, *Karl Friedrich Curschmann* (Bautzen, 1899).

Curti (koor'-tē), **Franz (Francesco),** German composer; b. Kassel, Nov. 16, 1854; d. Dresden, Feb. 6, 1898. He studied medicine; became a dentist by profession; at the same time took music courses in Dresden with Kretschmer and Schulz-Beuthen. He wrote several operas: *Hertha* (Altenburg, 1887); *Reinhardt von Ufenau* (Altenburg, 1889); *Erlöst* (Mannheim, 1894); melodrama, *Schneefried* (Mannheim, 1895); 1-act Japanese fairy opera *Lili-Tsee* (Mannheim, 1896; New York, 1898); *Das Rösli vom Säntis* (Zürich, 1898); also a cantata *Die Gletscherjungfrau;* music to *Die letzten Menschen,* by W. E. Kirchbach; songs. A catalogue of his works appeared in 1898.

Curtis, Natalie, American writer on folk music; b. New York, April 26, 1875; d. Paris, Oct. 23, 1921. She studied with Arthur Friedheim, with Busoni in Berlin, Alfred Giraudet in Paris, and Julius Kniese at the 'Wagner-Schule' in Bayreuth; returning to the U. S., she became an ardent investigator of songs, legends and customs of the North American Indians. She was married to Paul Burlin of New York (July 25, 1917). Publications: *Songs of Ancient America* (1905); *The Indian's Book* (1907; containing over 200 songs of 18 different tribes); songs from *A Child's Garden of Verse: Negro Folk Songs* (4 volumes, 1918-19, collected in the South and recorded for the Hampton Institute, Virginia); *Songs and Tales from the Dark Continent* (1920).

Curtiss, Mina (real name Kirstein), American musicologist; b. Boston, Oct. 13, 1896; educated at Smith College (M. A., 1918); was associate professor of English literature there (1920-34). Apart from her literary publications, she has contributed articles to the 'Mus. Quarterly'; a biography of Bizet, based partly on unpublished correspondence, is in preparation.

Curwen, Rev. **John;** b. Heckmondwike, Yorkshire, Nov. 14, 1816; d. Manchester, May 26, 1880. In 1844 he was pastor at Plaistow, Essex. Becoming interested in Miss S. A. Glover's 'Tonic Sol-fa' system of teaching, he labored to improve it; established the Tonic Sol-Fa Association and the 'Tonic Sol-Fa Reporter' in 1853, and the Tonic Sol-Fa College in 1875, having resigned his pastorate in 1867 to devote himself entirely to propagating the system. His numerous publications relate chiefly to Tonic Sol-fa (issued by Novello).—Cf. J. S. Curwen, *Memorials of John Curwen* (London, 1882). In 1863 Curwen founded the firm of John Curwen & Sons, publishers of works for school use, choral music, etc., also of the periodicals 'The Musical News and Herald' (weekly) and 'The Sackbut' (monthly; discontinued in 1934). In 1923 the business merged with F. & B. Goodwin.

Curwen, John Spencer, son of the Rev. John Curwen; b. Plaistow, Sept. 30, 1847; d. London, Aug. 6, 1916. Pupil of his father and G. Oakey; later of G. A. Macfarren, Sullivan and Prout at the Royal Academy of Music. Like his father, he became an active promoter of the Tonic Sol-fa system; President of the Tonic Sol-fa College in 1880; frequent contributor to the 'Tonic Sol-fa Reporter' and its continuation, the 'Musical Herald'. Published *Studies in Worship Music* (1880), and a 2nd series in 1885; *Memorials of John Curwen* (1882); *Musical Notes in Paris* (1882); etc.

Curzon, Clifford, English pianist, b. London, May 18, 1907. Studied at the Royal Academy of Music, and later with Tobias Matthay in London, Artur Schnabel in Berlin, and Wanda Landowska in Paris. He made his American debut in New York on Feb. 26, 1939. During the war, he was in England; returned to America in 1947.

Curzon (kür-zŏhn'), **Emanuel-Henri-Parent de,** French music critic and writer; b. Le Havre, July 6, 1861; d. Paris, Feb. 25, 1942; *Dr. Phil.;* keeper of the government archives at Paris until 1926; music critic on the 'Gazette de France' (1889-1918); contributor to the 'Guide musical', 'Bulletin de la Société de l'histoire du théâtre', etc.—Writings: *Les dernières années de Piccini à Paris* (1890); *La légende de Sigurd dans l'Edda; L'opéra d'E. Reyer* (1890); *Musiciens du temps passé* (1893); *Croquis d'artistes* (1898); *Les Lieder de Schubert* (1899); *Biographie critique de Franz Schubert* (in 'Revue des études historiques,' 1899); *État sommaire des pièces et documents concernant la musique* (1899); *Guide de l'amateur d'ouvrages sur la musique* (1901); *Felipe Pedrell et 'Les Pyrénées'* (1902); *Les Lieder de Beethoven* (1905); *Essai de bibliographie mozartienne* (1906); *Grétry, biographie critique* (1907); *L'évolution lyrique au théâtre* (1908); *Meyerbeer, biographie critique* (1910); *Documents inédits sur le 'Faust' de Gounod* (with A. Soubies; 1912); *La vie artistique aux XVIIe et XVIIIe siècles; La Musique* (in 'Bibliothèque française,' 1914); *Mozart, biographie critique* (1914); *Rossini, biographie* (in 'Les Maîtres de la Musique', 1920); *L'œuvre de R. Wagner à Paris et ses interprètes* (1920); *A. Thomas* (1921); *G. Fauré* (1923); *E. Reyer* (1924); *Jean Elleviou* (1930); *Cosima Wagner et Bayreuth* (1930); *Berlioz, l'homme et le musicien* (1932); *Les opéras-comiques de Boieldieu* (in 'Revue Musicale', Nov. 1933); *Les archives anciennes de l'Opéra-Comique, Paris* (in 'Le Ménestrel', 1934). Translations: *Lettres complètes de Mozart* (1888, 1898); *Écrites de Schumann sur la musique et les musiciens* (1894, 1898); *Hoffmann: Fantaisies dans la manière de Callot* (1891); also several German, Italian, and Spanish opera libretti.

Cushing, Charles C., American composer; b. Oakland, California, Dec. 8, 1905. He studied at the Univ. of California (M. A., 1929); was awarded a prize for study in France where he took lessons with Nadia Boulanger (1929-31); since 1931, teaching at the Univ. of California, Berkeley; conductor of Univ. of California Concert Band (1934-52), for which he transcribed numerous classical and modern works; 1948, appointed prof. there; received Legion of Honor from the French government (1952). He wrote *Psalm XCVII* for chorus and band (1939); *Wine from China,* six songs for men's voices and piano, 4-part (1945); *Angel Camp* for band (1952); *Divertimento* for string orch.; 2 string quartets; 2 violin sonatas; *3 Eclogues* for 2 clarinets and bassoon; *Fantasy* for flute, clarinet and bassoon; incidental music for *The Thesmaphoriazusae* (Aristophanes).

Cusins (kŭz'-inz), Sir **William George,** English organist, b. London, Oct. 14, 1833; d. Remonchamps (Ardennes), Aug. 31, 1893. He was a choirboy of the Chapel Royal (1843); pupil of Fétis, in Brussels Cons. (1944), and of Bennett, Potter Lucas and Sainton, at the Royal Academy of Music (1847). Took the King's Scholarship in 1847 and 1849; in the latter year he was appointed organist of the Queen's private chapel, and became violinist in the Italian Opera orch. In 1851 he was a professor at Royal Academy of Music; succeeded Bennett (1867-83) as conductor of the Philharmonic, and also became conductor of the Royal Band in 1870; succeeded Bennett as examining professor at Queen's College (1875); professor at Trinity College and professor of piano at Guildhall School of Music (1885); knighted in 1892.—Works: *Royal Wedding Serenata* (1863); 2 concert overtures, *Les Travailleurs de la mer* (1869) and *Love's Labour's Lost* (1875); an oratorio, *Gideon* (Gloucester Festival, 1871); piano concerto; septet for wind and double-bass; piano pieces; songs.

Cuvillier, Charles, French composer of light opera; b. Paris, April 24, 1877; d. there, Feb. 14, 1955. He studied with Massenet at the Paris Cons.; then became interested in the theater; his first operetta, *Avant-hier matin,* was produced at the Théâtre des Capucines in Paris (1905); at the same theatre, Cuvillier produced *Son petit frère* (1907); *Algar* (1909); *Les Muscadines* (1910) and *Sapho* (1912). His most successful operetta *La Reine s'amuse* was first staged in Marseilles (1912); was revised and produced in Paris as *La Reine joyeuse* (Nov. 8, 1918) and in London as *Naughty Princess* (1920). His other operettas were *La fausse ingénue* (Paris, 1918); *Bob et moi* (1924); *Boufard et ses filles* (Paris, 1929), etc. Cuvillier was also active in musical administration as director of music at the Odéon in Paris. The waltz from *La Reine joyeuse* has retained its popularity in numerous arrangements.

Cuzzoni (coot-tsōh'-nē), **Francesca,** celebrated Italian soprano; b. Parma, c. 1700; d. Bologna, 1770. She studied with Lanzi; sang in Venice; was engaged at the Italian opera in London, making her debut as Teofane in Handel's opera, *Ottone* (Jan. 12, 1723). She made a profound impression on London opera lovers, and was particularly distinguished in lyric roles; but later her notorious rivalry with Faustina Bordoni nearly ruined her career. Following some appearances in Venice, she returned to London (1734); after several seasons she went to Holland, where she became impoverished and was imprisoned for debt. Eventually, she returned to Bologna, where she subsisted by making buttons.

Czapek, pen-name of **John Liptrot Hatton.**

Czernohorsky (chär-noh-hor'-skē), **Bohuslav,** Bohemian composer; b. Nimburg, Feb. 16, 1684; d. Graz, July 1, 1742. A Minorite monk, he was choirmaster at San Antonio, Padua, and organist at Assisi (Tartini was one of his pupils). Returning to Bohemia, he was Kapellmeister at the Teinkirche, Prague and (1735) at St. Jacob's (Gluck was among his pupils). Many MSS. were lost at the burning of the Minorite monastery (1754). An offertory *a* 4 and several organ fugues and preludes were published by O. Schmid in 'Orgelwerke altböhmischer Meister'; 5 organ fugues have been edited by K. Pietsch; a *Regina Coeli* for soprano, organ and cello obbligato, and a motet, *Quem lapidaverunt,* are also extant. The contrapuntal skill of Czernohorsky's fugal writing is remarkable; Kretzschmar described him as 'the Bach of Bohemia'; Czech writers refer to him as 'father of Bohemian music' despite the fact that Czernohorsky never made thematic use of native rhythms or melodies. —Cf. O. Schmid, *Die böhmische Altmeisterschule Czernohorskys* (1900); A. Hnilička, *Porträte* (1922).

Czerny (chär'-nē), **Carl,** celebrated pianist and pedagogue; b. Vienna, Feb. 20, 1791; d. there, July 15, 1857. He received his early education from his father, Wenzel Czerny; in 1800 he was brought to Beethoven, who accepted him as a student and taught him for three years; he also received advice from Clementi and Hummel. He traveled to Leipzig (1836), to Paris and London (1837), and to Italy (1846); with the exception of these trips, he remained all his life in Vienna. At a very early age Czerny showed extraordinary aptitude as a teacher; he was 15 when Beethoven asked him to give lessons to his nephew; among Czerny's celebrated pupils were Liszt, Döhler, Thalberg, Kullak, Jaëll and Ninette von Belleville-Oury. He was an amazingly prolific composer; wrote concertos, symphonies, overtures, chamber music, 24 masses and other sacred works, etc., but he owes his everlasting fame to his collections of piano studies and exercises, used by generations of pianists all over the world. Of these the most famous are *Die Schule der Geläufigkeit* (op. 299) and *Die Schule der Fingerfertigkeit* (op. 740). Other publications are: *Die Schule des Legato und Staccato* (op. 335), *Tägliche Studien* (op. 337), *Schule der Verzierungen* (op. 355), *Die Schule des Virtuosen* (op. 365), *Die Schule der linken Hand* (op. 399), *Die Schule des Fugenspiels* (op. 400), etc. He wrote an *Umriss der ganzen Musikgeschichte* (Mainz, 1851), and an autobiography, published in English in the 'Mus. Quarterly' (July, 1956).

Czersky. See **Tschirch.**

Czerveny. See **Červený.**

Czibulka (tchē'-bool-kăh), **Alphons,** Hungarian bandmaster and composer; b. Szepes-Várallya, Hungary, May 14, 1842; d. Vienna, Oct. 27, 1894. Originally a pianist, he became Kapellmeister at the Karltheater, Vienna, in 1865; bandmaster of the 17th regiment, and later of the 25th regiment at Prague; finally settled in Vienna, where he brought out the operetta *Pfingsten in Florenz* (Dec. 20, 1884); other stage works are *Der Glücksritter* (1887); *Gil Blas* (Hamburg, 1889); *Der Bajazzo* (Vienna, 1892); *Signor Annibale* (1893).

D

Dachs (dahks), **Joseph,** pianist and pedagogue; b. Regensburg, Sept. 30, 1825; d. Vienna, June 6, 1896. He studied in Vienna with Czerny and Sechter; in 1861 was appointed professor of piano at the Vienna Cons.; he had numerous distinguished pupils, among them Vladimir de Pachmann, Laura Rappoldi, and Isabelle Vengerova. He also gave concerts which were well received in Vienna.

Daffner, Hugo, German composer and musicologist; b. Munich, June 2, 1882; d. 1944 (in an air raid on Berlin). He studied with Thuille (composition); with Sandberger and Kroyer (musicology) at the Royal Academy in Munich; received his degree of *Dr. phil.* in 1904; then took private lessons with Max Reger. He conducted at the Munich Opera House from 1904 till 1906; was music critic in Königsberg (1907-10); founded a Society for New Music there; in 1922 returned to Berlin. He wrote 3 operas: *Macbeth, Truffaldino, Der eingebildete Kranke* (none of them produced); 2 symphonies; 2 string quartets; 2 piano trios; 2 piano quintets; various pieces for violin, piano, etc.; also songs.—Writings: *Die Entwicklung des Klavierkonzerts bis Mozart* (Leipzig, 1908); *Salome, ihre Gestalt in Geschichte und Kunst* (1912); edited Nietzsche's *Randglossen zu Bizets Carmen* (1912) and Ph. E. Bach's *Versuch über die wahre Art, das Klavier zu spielen* (1914).

Dahl, Ingolf, composer; b. Hamburg, Germany (of Swedish parents), June 9, 1912. He studied composition at the Cons. of Cologne and musicology at the Univ. of Zürich. Came to the U. S. in 1935; settled in California (1938), where he became active as conductor and composer; appointed assistant professor at the Univ. of Southern California (1945); received Guggenheim Fellowship (1952). He taught at the Berkshire Music Center, Tanglewood, in the summers of 1952-55. As composer, he adheres to an advanced polyphonic style in free dissonant counterpoint.—Works: *Andante and Arioso* for flute, clarinet, oboe, horn and bassoon (1942); *Music for Brass Instruments* (1944); *Concerto a tre* for clarinet, violin, and cello (1946); Duo for cello and piano (1946); Divertimento for viola and piano (1948); Concerto for saxophone and wind orch. (1949); *Symphony Concertante* for 2 clarinets and orch. (1953); *Sonata Seria* for piano (1953); *The Tower of Saint Barbara,* symphonic legend (Louisville, Jan. 29, 1955). Also arranged for 2 pianos Stravinsky's *Danses Concertantes.*

Dahl, Viking, Swedish composer; b. Osby, Oct. 8, 1895; d. Stockholm, Jan. 1, 1945. He studied at the Malmö and Stockholm Conservatories; later in Paris and London with Vidal, Viñes and Ravel; studied dancing with Isadora Duncan.—Works: The ballets *Oriental Suite* (Stockholm, 1919) and *Maison des fous* (Paris, 1920); *Pastorale* for oboe and orch.; chamber music; many songs.

Dahms, Walter, German writer on musical subjects; b. Berlin, June 9, 1887. He studied with Adolf Schultze in Berlin (1907-10); was music critic 'Kleines Journal', 1912; after 1922 has lived mostly in Rome. He published biographies of *Schubert* (Berlin, 1912), *Schumann* (1916), and *Mendelssohn* (1919); also *Die Offenbarung der Musik; eine Apotheose Friedrich Nietzsches* (Munich, 1921); *Musik des Südens* (1923); etc.

Dalayrac, Nicolas, French composer; b. Muret (Haute-Garonne), June 8 (baptized June 13), 1753; d. Paris, Nov. 27, 1809. (He signed his name d'Alayrac, but dropped the nobiliary particle after the Revolution.) His early schooling was in Toulouse; returning to Muret in 1767 he studied law and played violin in a local band. He then entered the service of Count d'Artois as his Guard of Honor, and at the same time took lessons in harmony with François Langlé at Versailles; he also received some help from Grétry. In 1781 he wrote 6 string quartets; his first theater work was a one-act comedy, *L'Eclipse totale* (Paris, March 7, 1782). From then on, he devoted most of his energies to the theater. He wrote 56 operas; during the revolution he composed patriotic songs for special occasions. He also enjoyed Napoleon's favors later on. During his lifetime and for some three decades after his death, many of his operas were popular not only in France but also in Germany, Italy and Russia; then they gradually disappeared from the active repertoire, but there were several revivals even in the 20th century. Dalayrac's natural facility enabled him to write successfully in all operatic genres. The list of his operas produced in Paris (mostly at the Opéra-Comique) includes the following: *Nina* (May 15, 1786; one of his most successful operas); *Sargines* (May 14, 1788); *Les deux petits savoyards* (Jan. 14, 1789); *Raoul, Sire de Créqui* (Oct. 31, 1789); *La soirée orageuse* (May 29, 1790); *Camille* (March 19, 1791); *Philippe et Georgette* (Dec. 28, 1791); *Ambroise* (Jan. 12, 1793); *Adèle et Dorsan* (April 27, 1795); *Marianne* (July 7, 1796); *La maison isolée* (May 11, 1797); *Gulnare* (Jan. 9, 1798); *Alexis* (Jan. 24, 1798); *Adolphe et Clara* (Feb. 10, 1799); *Maison à vendre* (Oct. 23, 1800; many revivals); *Léhéman* (Dec. 12, 1801); *L'antichambre* (Feb. 26, 1802); *La jeune prude* (Jan. 14, 1804); *Une heure de mariage* (March 20, 1804); *Gulistan* (Sept. 30, 1805); *Deux mots* (June 9, 1806); *Koulouf* (Dec. 18, 1806); *Le poète et le musicien* (posthumous, Paris, May 30, 1811).—Bibl.: R. C. G. de Pixérécourt, *Vie de Dalayrac* (includes a complete list of his operas; Paris, 1810); A. Fourgaud, *Les violons de Dalayrac* (1856); G. Cucuel, *Les créateurs de l'opéra-comique français* (Paris, 1914).

Dalberg, Johann Friedrich Hugo, German pianist, composer and writer on music; b. Herrnsheim, near Worms, May 17, 1760; d. there, July 26, 1812. He studied theology; became a canon in Trier; was also counsellor to the Elector of Trier at Coblenz. He traveled in Italy (1775) and England (1798); gave private concerts as pianist. Although he was not a professional musician, his compositions and particularly his writings reveal considerable musical culture. He published many vocal works; set to music Schiller's *Ode an die Freude* (1799); also wrote songs to English and French texts.—Writings: *Blicke eines Tonkünstlers in die Musik der Geister* (Mannheim, 1787); *Vom Erfinden und Bilden* (Frankfurt, 1791); *Untersuchungen über den Ursprung der Harmonie* (Erfurt, 1800); *Die Äolsharfe, ein al-*

legorischer Traum (Erfurt, 1801); etc.; translated Jones' *The Musical Modes of the Hindus* (1802).

D'Albert, Eugen. See **Albert, d'.**

Dalcroze. See **Jaques-Dalcroze.**

Dale, Benjamin James, English composer; b. Crouch Hill, July 17, 1885; d. London, July 30, 1943. He studied at the Royal Academy of Music with F. Corder; was organist at St. Stephen's Ealing; then taught composition at the Royal Academy of Music. His works comprise an overture, *The Tempest* (1902); a piano sonata in D minor (1905; was frequently performed); suites for piano and viola (1907); *Before the Paling of the Stars,* for chorus and orch. (1912); *Songs of Praise,* for chorus and orch. (1923); *Rosa mystica* and *Cradle Song* for mixed chorus; 2 songs (after Shakespeare) for voice with viola obbligato; sextet for violas; violin sonata; piano pieces; songs; etc. His last work was *The Flowing Tide* for large orch., completed in 1943, from sketches made in 1924. For analysis of his chamber music, see Cobbett's *Cyclopedic Survey of Chamber Music* (London, 1929, I, 310-13).

D'Alembert, Jean le Rond. See **Alembert, Jean le Rond d'.**

D'Alheim, Marie. See **Olénine-d'Alheim, Marie.**

D'Alheim, Pierre, French journalist; b. Laroche (Yonne), Dec. 8, 1862; d. Paris, April 11, 1922. In 1893 he married the singer Marie Olénine (q. v.) and organized her concerts in Moscow and in Paris. He became a propagandist of Russian music; published a book on Mussorgsky (Paris, 1896), and translated into French the libretti of *Boris Godunov* and *Khovanstchina* and Mussorgsky's songs.

Dall'Abaco, Evaristo Felice. See **Abaco, Evaristo Felice dall'.**

Dall'Abaco, Joseph. See **Abaco, Joseph dall'.**

Dallapiccola, Luigi, distinguished Italian composer; b. Pisino, Istria, Feb. 3, 1904. He went to school in Trieste and later in Graz; in 1921 moved to Florence where he took courses at the Cherubini Cons., studying piano with Ernesto Consolo (graduated, 1924) and composition with Vito Frazzi (graduated, 1931). In 1934 he was appointed to the faculty of the Cherubini Cons. As a composer, Dallapiccola became interested from the very first in the melodic application of atonal writing; in 1939 he adopted the dodecaphonic method of Schoenberg, with considerable innovations of his own (e.g., the use of mutually exclusive triads in thematic structure and harmonic progressions). He particularly excels in his handling of vocal lines in a difficult modern idiom. He visited London in 1946, and traveled on the continent; was engaged as instructor at the Berkshire Music Center in Tanglewood, Mass., in the summers of 1951 and 1952; in 1956, he was appointed prof. of composition at Queens College, N. Y., as successor to Karol Rathaus.—Works: for the stage: *Volo di notte,* opera after St.-Exupéry (Florence, May 18, 1940); *Il prigioniero,* opera (1944-48; radio première, Dec. 4, 1949; stage première, Florence, May 20, 1950); *Marsia,* ballet in one act (Venice, Sept. 9, 1948).—Instrumental works: *Partita,* for orch. (Florence, Jan. 22, 1933); *Piccolo concerto,* for piano and chamber orch. (1939-41); *Sonatina Canonica,* for piano (1943); *Ciaconna, Intermezzo e adagio,* for solo violin (1945); *Tartiniana,* for violin and orch., on Tartini's themes (Bern, March 4, 1952); *Variations for Orch.* (Louisville, Oct. 2, 1954).—Vocal works: 2 songs from the *Kalevala* for two soloists, chamber chorus, and chamber orch. (1931); 3 studies for soprano and chamber orch. (Venice Festival, 1932); *Estate,* for male chorus a cappella (1932); *La Mort de Roland,* for voices and small orch. (1934); *Rhapsody,* for voice and chamber orch. (1934); *Cori di Michelangelo* in 3 sets (1933-36); *3 Laudi,* for soprano and chamber orch. (Venice Festival, 1937); transcription of Monteverdi's *Il Ritorno di Ulisse in Patria* (1942); *Liriche greche,* for soprano and instruments (3 sets; 1942-45); *3 poemi,* for voice and instruments (1949); *Job, sacra rappresentazione* (Rome, Oct. 31, 1950); *Goethe-Lieder,* for voice and three clarinets (1953).—Cf. G. M. Gatti, *Luigi Dallapiccola,* in 'Monthly Mus. Record' (Feb., 1937); Domenico de Paoli, *An Italian Musician: Luigi Dallapiccola,* in 'The Chesterian' (July, 1938); *Nota bio-bibliografica* in 'Rassegna Musicale' (1950); see also an autobiographical fragment, *The Genesis of the Canti di Prigionia and Il Prigioniero,* in the 'Mus. Quarterly' (July, 1953).

Dalley-Scarlett, Robert, Australian conductor and organist; b. Manchester, England, April 16, 1890; went to Australia as a child, and studied in Sydney; eventually settled in Brisbane. He is active as choral conductor; has composed choruses and chamber music.

Dal Monte, Toti. See **Monte.**

Dalmorès (dahl-moh-räs'), **Charles,** French dramatic tenor; b. Nancy, Jan. 1, 1871; d. Hollywood, Calif., Dec. 6, 1939. After taking first prizes at the local Cons. for solfeggio and French horn at 17, he received from the City of Nancy a stipend for study at the Paris Cons., where he took first prize for horn at 19; played in the Colonne Orch. (2 years) and the Lamoureux Orch. (2 years); at 23, professor of horn playing in Lyons Cons. His vocal teacher was Dauphin, the bass singer; his début as tenor took place on Oct. 6, 1899 at Rouen; later he sang at the Théâtre de la Monnaie, Brussels; 7 seasons at Covent Garden; at the Manhattan Opera House, N. Y. (1906-10; début as Faust, Dec. 7, 1906); then was with the Chicago Opera Co. (1910-18). His repertoire was large, and included Wagnerian as well as French operas; in Chicago he sang Tristan and the title role in the first performance of *Parsifal* to be presented there.

Dalvimare (real name d'Alvimare), **Martin-Pierre,** French harpist and composer for harp; b. Dreux (Eure-et-Loire), Sept. 18, 1772; d. Paris, June 13, 1839. In 1800 he was harpist at the Paris Opéra; harpist to Napoleon, 1806; harp-teacher to the Empress Josephine (1807); retired to his estate at Dreux in 1812. He wrote several sonatas for harp and violin; duets for two harps, for harp and piano, and for harp and horn; fantaisies, variations, etc.

Damase, Jean-Michel, French composer and pianist, b. Bordeaux, Jan. 27, 1928; studied with Delvincourt at the Paris Cons.; received the Grand Prix de Rome in 1947; made his U. S. début, April 20, 1954, in New York, as pianist-composer.—Works: Ballets: *Le Saut du Tremplin* (Paris, 1944); *La Croqueuse de Diamants* (Paris, 1950). For orch.: *Interludes* (Nice, 1948); *Rhapsody,* for oboe and string orch. (Paris Radio, 1948); piano concerto (Cannes, 1950); violin concerto (Paris, Dec. 22, 1956). Chamber music: quintet for violin, viola, cello, flute and harp (1947); trio for flute, harp and cello (1949); also piano pieces and songs.

Dambois (dahn-bwăh'), **Maurice,** Belgian cellist; b. Liège, March 30, 1889. He studied at the Cons. there (1899-1905) and won many prizes (piano, harmony, chamber music, fugue, cello); début at 12 with Saint-Saëns' A minor concerto; toured Germany (1905), England (1906-8), France, Portugal, and the Netherlands; appointed director of the Académie de Musique at Liège (1910), and professor of cello at the Brussels Cons. (1912). After the outbreak of the war he went to England (until 1916); came to the U. S. in 1917 with Ysaÿe; American début New York, April 21, 1917, followed by successful tours. In 1926 he settled in Brussels, and resumed his post as prof. of cello at the Cons., retaining it for 30 years.

Damcke, Berthold, German conductor; b. Hanover, Feb. 6, 1812; d. Paris, Feb. 15, 1875. He was a pupil of Alexander Schmitt and F. Ries at Frankfurt; 1837, conductor of Potsdam Philharmonic Society, and of the Choral Union for operatic music (grand concerts, 1839-40); active in St. Petersburg (1845), Brussels (1855), Paris (1859). He was a friend and devoted admirer of Berlioz. He revised and edited, with F. Pelletan (q. v.), Gluck's two *Iphigénies;* composed oratorios, part songs, piano pieces.—Cf. *Berthold Damcke, Etude biographique et musicale* (Paris, 1895, anonymous).

Damerini, Adelmo, Italian musicologist and composer; b. Carmignano, near Florence, Dec. 11, 1880. He studied with Edgardo Binelli and Giannotto Bastianelli. Among his compositions are a Mass (perf. at the Cathedral of Pistoia, 1909) and many other church works (motets, psalms, anthems, etc.). He held teaching positions at the American Methodist Institute in Rome, at the Palermo Cons. and at the Cons. Boito in Parma; in 1933 was appointed to the faculty at the Cons. of Florence, succeeding Bonaventura; was also director of the Library there (until 1950); then became director of the Scuola Comunale in Pistoia. Writings: *Origine e svolgimento della sinfonia* (Pistoia, 1919); *Classicismo e romanticismo nella musica* (Florence, 1942).

Damm, Gustave. See **Steingräber.**

Damoreau (dah-moh-roh'), **Laure-Cinthie** (*née* Montalant; first known as 'Mlle. Cinti'), noted French operatic soprano; b. Paris, Feb. 6, 1801; d. Chantilly, Feb. 25, 1863. She studied at the Paris Cons.; made her début in 1819 at the Théâtre Italien; later was engaged at the Opéra (1826-35). Rossini wrote leading roles for her in *Le siège de Corinthe* and *Mosè,* and Auber did the same during her engagement (1835-43) at the Opéra-Comique (*Domino noir, L'Ambassadrice,* etc.). Retiring from the stage, she made concert-tours to England, Holland, Russia, and (with Artôt, the violinist) to the U. S. and Havana (1843). She was professor of singing at the Paris Cons. from 1834-56; then retired to Chantilly. Her husband was an actor at Brussels. She published an *Album de romances,* and a *Méthode de chant.*

Da Motta, José Vianna, noted Portuguese pianist; b. on Isle St. Thomas, Portuguese Africa, April 22, 1868; d. Lisbon, May 31, 1948. His family returned to Lisbon when he was a year old; he studied with local teachers; gave his first concert at the age of 13; then studied piano in Berlin with Xaver Scharwenka and composition with Philipp Scharwenka. In 1885 he went to Weimar, where he became a pupil of Liszt; also took lessons with Hans von Bülow in Frankfurt (1887). He then undertook a series of concert tours throughout Europe (1887-88), the U. S. (1892-93; 1899) and South America (1902). He was in Berlin until 1915; then became director of the Geneva Cons. In 1919 he returned to Lisbon and was appointed director of the Lisbon Cons., retiring in 1938. At the height of his career he was greatly esteemed as a fine interpreter of Bach and Beethoven. He was also the author of many articles in German, French and Portuguese; wrote *Studien bei Bülow* (1896); *Betrachtungen über Franz Liszt* (1898); *Die Entwicklung des Klavierkonzerts* (as a program book to Busoni's concerts); essays on Alkan; critical articles in the 'Kunstwart,' 'Klavierlehrer,' 'Bayreuther Blätter,' etc. He was a prolific composer; among his works are *Die Lusiaden,* for orch. and chorus; string quartet; many piano pieces, in some of which (e.g., the *5 Portuguese Rhapsodies* and the Portuguese dance *Vito*) he employs folk themes with striking effect.—Cf. F. Lopes Graça, *Vianna da Motta; subsidios para una biographia* (Lisbon, 1949).

Damrosch, Frank, son of Leopold Damrosch; choral conductor; b. Breslau, June 22, 1859; d. New York, Oct. 22, 1937. He studied with Bruckner, Jean Vogt, and von Inten and composition with his father and Moszkowski. 1882-5, conductor of Denver (Col.) Chorus Club, and (1884-5) Supervisor of Music in public schools, also organist at different churches; 1885-91, chorusmaster and assistant conductor at Metropolitan Opera House; and till 1887 conductor of the Newark Harmonic Society; 1892, organized the People's Choral Union, an enterprise for the popularization of choral singing, for which he publ. in 1894 *Popular Method of Sight Singing* (G. Schirmer, N. Y.); 1897-1905, was Supervisor of Music in N. Y. City Public Schools; conductor of the choral group, 'Musurgia' (1891-1900), 'Orpheus' and 'Eurydice' clubs of Phila. (1897-1905), Oratorio Society (1898-1912), 'Mendelssohn Glee Club' (1904-9). In 1893 he founded the 'Musical Art Society,' a chorus of 60 trained voices for the performance of a cappella music, which he conducted till 1920; in 1898 the 'Symph. Concerts for Young People,' of which he was conductor for many years. In 1905 he established an exemplary organization, the splendidly equipped Institute of Musical Art, which, in 1926, became affiliated with the Juilliard School of Music; retained his position as dean until his retirement in 1933. He received the degree of Mus. Doc. (hon. c.) from Yale Univ. in 1904; publ. vocal numbers (songs, choruses); also wrote *Some Essentials in the Teaching of Music* (N. Y., 1916) and *Institute of Musical Art, 1905-26* (N. Y., 1936).—Cf. E. T. Rice, *A Tribute to Frank Damrosch,* in the 'Mus. Quarterly' (April, 1939); L. P. and R. P. Stebbins, *Frank Damrosch* (1945).

Damrosch, Leopold, German-American conductor and violinist; b. Posen, Oct. 22, 1832; d. New York, Feb. 15, 1885. He studied with Ries, Dehn, and Böhmer; took the degree of *Dr. med.* (M.D.) at Berlin University in 1854, but then, against his parents' wishes, embraced the career of a musician; he appeared at first as a solo violinist in several German cities, later as a conductor at minor theaters, and in 1885 procured, through Liszt, the position of solo violinist in the Grand Ducal Orch. at Weimar. While here he was intimate with Liszt and many of his most distinguished pupils, and won Wagner's lifelong friendship; in Weimar, too, he married the singer Helene von Heimburg (b. Oldenburg, 1835; d. N. Y., Nov. 21, 1904). In 1858-60, Damrosch was conductor of the Breslau Philh. Concerts; gave up the post to make tours with von Bülow and Tausig; organized the Breslau Orchestral Society in 1862. Besides this, he founded quartet *soirées,* and a choral society; conducted the Society for Classical Music, and the theater orch. (for 2 years); and frequently appeared as a solo violinist. In 1871 he was called to New York to conduct the 'Arion Society,' and made his début, on May 6, 1871, as conductor, composer, and violinist. In New York his remarkable capacity as an organizer (which had aroused active opposition in Breslau by his strong leaning towards the new German school) found free scope; besides bringing the

'Arion' to the highest pitch of efficiency and prosperity, he founded the 'Symphony Society' in 1878, the latter's concerts succeeding those of the Thomas Orch. at Steinway Hall. In 1880 Columbia College conferred on him the degree of Mus. Doc.; in 1881 he conducted the first great Music Festival held in N. Y., with an orch. of 250 and a chorus of 1,200; in 1883 he made a highly successful western tour with his orch.; in 1884-5 he organized a German Opera Co., and, together with Anton Seidl, conducted a season of German opera at the Metropolitan Opera House (giving *The Ring, Tristan,* and *Meistersinger* for the first time in this country), which will ever remain memorable in the musical annals of America. He was also the first to perform Brahms' First Symph. in the U. S.—Works: 7 cantatas; Symphony in A; music to Schiller's *Joan of Arc;* marches for orch.; 3 violin concertos (in D min., F♯ min., and G); several pieces for violin and orch., and for solo voice and orch.; choruses for mixed voices and male voices; duets; many songs.—Cf. E. T. Rice, *Personal Recollections of Leopold Damrosch,* in the 'Mus. Quarterly' (July, 1942).

Damrosch, Walter Johannes, famous American conductor, composer, educator; son of Leopold Damrosch; b. Breslau, Jan. 30, 1862; d. New York, Dec. 22, 1950. He studied harmony with his father, also with Rischbieter and Draeseke in Dresden; piano with von Inten, Boekelmann and Max Pinner in the U. S.; and conducting with his father and with Hans von Bülow. He was conductor of the N. Y. Oratorio Society (1885-98) and of the N. Y. Symphony Society (1885-1903); assistant conductor of German opera at the Metropolitan Opera House (1885-91); organized the 'Damrosch Opera Co.' (1894) which he directed for five seasons, giving German opera (chiefly Wagner) in the principal cities of the U. S.; among the artists whom he first brought to the U. S. were Mmes. Klafsky, Gadski and Ternina; in 1896 he presented *Parsifal* in concert form for the first time in America; from 1900-02 he conducted Wagner's operas at the Metropolitan Opera House; then was conductor of the N. Y. Philharmonic Society (1902-3); in 1903 the N. Y. Symphony Society was reorganized with Damrosch as its regular conductor, a post he held until 1927; again conducted the Oratorio Society (1917); organized at the request of General Pershing the American Expeditionary Force bands and founded schools for bandmasters in Chaumont, France (1918); conducted a concert by the N. Y. Symphony Society Orch. in the first chain broadcast over the network of the newly organized N.B.C. (Nov. 15, 1926); appointed musical adviser to the N.B.C. (1927, retired 1947); conductor of the N.B.C. Symph. Orch. in a weekly series of music appreciation hours for the schools and colleges of the U. S. and Canada (1928-42). He conducted many famous works for the first time in the U. S. (Brahms' 3rd and 4th symphonies; Tchaikovsky's 4th and 6th symphonies; world première of *Tapiola* by Sibelius, etc.); was U. S. delegate at the Paris International Music Congress (1937). Mus. Doc. (hon. c.), Columbia Univ. (1914), Princeton Univ. (1929), Brown Univ. (1932), Dartmouth College 1933), N. Y. Univ. (1935); awarded the David Bispham medal (1929) and the gold medal of the National Institute of Arts and Letters (1938).—Works: the operas *The Scarlet Letter* (Damrosch Opera Co., Boston, Feb. 10, 1896); *Cyrano de Bergerac* (Metropolitan Opera House, Feb. 27, 1913; revised in 1939); *The Man Without a Country* (Metropolitan Opera House, May 12, 1937); *The Opera Cloak,* one-act opera (N. Y. Opera Co., Nov. 3, 1942); comic opera, *The Dove of Peace* (N. Y., 1912). Other works: *Manila Te Deum* (N. Y., 1898); *An Abraham Lincoln Song* (N. Y., 1936); incidental music to Euripides' *Iphigenia in Aulis* and *Medea* (Berkeley, Calif., 1915), and to Sophocles' *Electra* (N. Y., 1917); violin sonata; *At Fox Meadow* (1899); *Dunkirk,* a setting of R. Nathan's poem, for baritone, solo, male chorus, and chamber orch. (NBC broadcast, May 2, 1943); many songs, including *Death and General Putnam* (1936), *Danny Deever,* etc. He published an autobiography, *My Musical Life* (N. Y., 1923; 2nd edition 1930); co-editor, with Gartlan and Gehrkens, of the 'Universal School Music Series.' Cf. W. J. Henderson, *Walter Damrosch,* in the 'Mus. Quarterly' (Jan., 1932); also Gretchen Damrosch Finletter, *From the Top of the Stairs* (reminiscences of Walter Damrosch's daughter; Boston, 1946).

Dan, Ikuma, Japanese composer; b. Tokyo, April 7, 1924. He studied at the Tokyo Music Academy with S. Moroi; won the Prize of Kosaku Yamada (1952). Among his works are Symphony in A (Tokyo, March 21, 1950); *Sinfonia burlesca* (Tokyo, Jan. 26, 1954); 2 operas: *Yuzuru* (Tokyo, Jan. 30, 1952), *Kikimimizukin* (Tokyo, March 18, 1955); a dance suite *Silk Road* (Tokyo, June 23, 1955); a string trio (1947) and a string quartet (1948).

Dana, William Henry, American music pedagogue; b. Warren, Ohio, June 10, 1846; d. there, Feb. 18, 1916. He studied at Kullak's Academy of Music in Berlin and at the Royal Academy of Music, London (1881). He was a founder of the American Music Teachers' National Association. He published several manuals: *Practical Thorough-bass* (1873), *Orchestration* (1875), *Instrumentation for Military Bands* (1876), *Practical Harmony* (1884); composed a *De profundis* for soli, chorus and orch.; motets, songs, piano pieces, etc.

Danbé (dahn-bā'), **Jules,** French violinist and composer; b. Caen, Nov. 16, 1840; d. Vichy, Nov. 10, 1905. He was a pupil at the Paris Cons.; 2nd director of the Cons. concerts till 1892; conductor at the Opéra-Comique (1877-98); from 1899 until his death, conductor at the Théâtre Lyrique, where he successfully revived Gluck's *Iphigénie en Tauride* after a long period of neglect.

Danckert, Werner, German musicologist; b. Erfurt, June 22, 1900. He studied natural science and mathematics at Jena, then musicology in Leipzig with Riemann; was assistant in musicology to G. Becking at Erlangen Univ. (1922); instructor at Jena Univ. (1926-29); in Weimar (1929-31); in Erfurt (1932-37); in Berlin (1937-39); in Graz (1943-45); in Krefeld (since 1950). Author of *Geschichte der Gigue* (Leipzig, 1924); *Ursymbole melodischer Gestaltung* (Kassel, 1932); *Das europäische Volkslied* (Berlin; 1939); *Claude Debussy* (Berlin, 1950); articles in various musical journals.

Danckerts, Ghiselin, skillful contrapuntist and theorist; b. Tholen, Zeeland; entered the Papal Chapel in Rome as chorister in 1538; pensioned in 1565. He published (1559) two books of motets for 4-6 voices; single motets are included in Augsburg collections of 1540 and 1545. His ingenuity in counterpoint is demonstrated in the so-called 'Chessboard Canon' for 4 voices with alternating black and white notes. His autograph MS, pronouncing judgment on the theoretical dispute between Vincentino and Lusitano on the nature of ancient modes, is in the Vatican Library in Rome.

Dancla, Arnaud, French cellist; brother of Jean-Baptiste-Charles Dancla; b. Bagnères-de-Bigorre, Jan. 1, 1820; d. there, Feb. 1862; author of a method for cello; composed études, duos, and melodies for his instrument.

Dancla, (Jean-Baptiste-) Charles, French violinist and composer; b. Bagnères-de-Bigorre, Dec. 19, 1817; d. Tunis, Nov. 9, 1907. He entered the Paris Cons. in 1828, his teachers being Baillot (violin), Halévy, and Berton. In 1834, he was a violinist in the Opéra-Comique orch.; became renowned by his playing in the 'Société des Concerts,' and was appointed professor of violin at the Paris Cons. in 1857. His quartet *soirées* were famous. Besides four symphonies, he composed some 130 works for violin; 14 string quartets; 4 piano trios; published *Méthode élémentaire et progressive pour le violon; École du mécanisme; L'École de la mélodie; École de l'expression;* and (with Panseron) *L'Art de moduler sur le violon;* also books of essays, *Les compositeurs chefs d'orchestre* (1873), and *Miscellanées musicales* (1876).—Cf. *Charles Dancla, Notes et souvenirs* (Paris, 1893; 2nd edition 1898; contains catalogue of works).

Dancla, Léopold, French violinist; brother of the preceding; b. Bagnères-de-Bigorre, June 1, 1823; d. Paris, April 10, 1895. He was a pupil of Baillot at the Paris Cons., taking first prize in violin in 1842. He wrote 3 string quartets, *airs variés,* fantasies and studies for the violin.

Danco, Suzanne, Belgian soprano; b. Brussels, Jan. 22, 1911. She studied at the Brussels Cons.; in 1936 won the International Bel Canto Prize at Venice; in 1948 was engaged as soloist at the Edinburgh Festival; also sang in Milan; in 1950 made her American début. She has gained a fine reputation in Europe and America for her musicianly performances in opera (ranging from Mozart to Alban Berg) and in concert recitals (notably in Debussy's songs).

Dandelot, Georges, French composer; son of the impresario Arthur Dandelot (1864-1943); b. Paris, Dec. 2, 1895. He studied with Widor at the Paris Cons.; later took lessons with Dukas and Roussel. He was in the French Army during World War I, and received the Croix de Guerre for valor. In 1919 he became an instructor at the École Normale de Musique in Paris; in 1942, appointed prof. at the Paris Cons. Dandelot has written an oratorio *Pax* (first prize at the International Exposition in Paris, 1937); 2 operas, *Midas* (1947) and *L'Ennemi* (1948); the ballets *Le souper de famine* (1943); *Le jardin merveilleux* (1944); and *Pierrot et la rose* (1948); a symphony (1941); a piano concerto (Paris, Jan. 7, 1934); *Concerto romantique* for violin and orch. (1944); chamber music; songs.

Dandrieu, Jean François, French composer; b. Paris, 1682; d. there, Jan. 16, 1738. He was organist at Saint-Merry, Paris, in 1704; published: *Livre de Sonates en Trio* (1705); *Livre de Sonates* for solo violin (1710); *Principes de l'accompagnement du Clavecin* (1718); *Pièces de clavecin* (3 albums, 1724); organ pieces, airs. His importance lies in his works for clavecin written in a style closely resembling Couperin's.—Cf. P. Brunold, *Les Dandrieu* (Paris, 1954).

Daneau, Nicolas, Belgian composer; b. Binche, June 17, 1866; d. Brussels, July 12, 1944. He studied at the Ghent Cons. with Adolphe Samuel, graduating in 1892; won the Second Prix de Rome in 1895. He was director of the Cons. of Tournai (1896-1919), and of Mons (1919-31).—Works: *Linario,* lyric drama (Tournai, 1906); *Myrtis,* opera-idyll (Tournai, 1910); *Le Sphynx,* opera; *La Brute,* lyric drama.—For orch.: *Villes d'Italie; Adima et Hevah; Arles; Mardi-Gras; Petite Suite.*—Chamber music: suite for violin and piano; string quartet; piano quintet. His daughter, Suzanne **Daneau** (b. Tournai, Aug. 17, 1901), was his pupil. She has written orchestral works, chamber music, and piano pieces, mostly based on native folk songs.—Cf. L. J. Beatrice, *Daneau; Histoire d'une famille d'artistes* (Brussels, 1944).

D'Angeli, Andrea. See **Angeli, Andrea d'.**

D'Angelo, Louis. See **Angelo, Louis d'.**

Danhauser, Adolphe-Léopold, French composer and teacher; b. Paris, Feb. 26, 1835; d. there, June 9, 1896. He studied at the Paris Cons. with Halévy and Reber; won 1st prize in harmony (1857); 1st prize in fugue (1859); second prix de Rome (1862); was Chief Inspector of Instruction in Singing, in the Communal Schools, Paris and professor of solfeggio at the Cons. He wrote *Théorie de la musique;* published *Soirées orphéoniques,* a collection of 3-part choruses for equal voices. He composed *Le Proscrit,* musical drama with choruses, which was produced (1866) in a religious institution at Auteuil; a 3-act opera, *Maures et Castillans* (not performed). His *Solfège des solfèges* (3 volumes; translated into English and Spanish) is still in use throughout the U. S. and South America.

Danican. See **Philidor.**

Daniel-Lesur. See **Lesur, Daniel.**

Daniel, Salvador, French writer on music; b. Bourges, 1830; director of Paris Cons. for a few days under the Commune in 1871; was killed in battle on May 23 of that year. He was for some years a teacher of music in an Arab school at Algiers; published a monograph on *La musique arabe,* with a supplement on the origin of musical instruments (1863; English translation, N. Y., 1915); also a book of Arabian, Moorish, and cabalistic songs, and a treatise on the French *chanson.*

Daniels, Mabel Wheeler, American composer; b. Swampscott, Mass., Nov. 27, 1878. She studied at Radcliffe College (B.A. *magna cum laude,* 1900) and with Chadwick in Boston; then with Thuille in Munich; director of the Radcliffe Glee Club (1911-13); musical director at Simmons College, Boston (1913-18); a member of the advisory committee on music for the Boston Public Schools. Hon. M.A., Tufts College, 1933; Hon. Mus. Doc., Boston Univ., 1939; Hon. Citation, Radcliffe, 1954. As a composer she excels in vocal writing; her instrumental pieces are cautiously modernistic.—Works: operetta, *The Court of Hearts* (Cambridge, Jan. 2, 1901; she sang the part of Jack of Hearts); operatic sketch, *Alice in Wonderland Continued* (Brookline, Mass., May 20, 1904). Vocal works with orch.: *The Desolate City* (1913); *Peace with a Sword* (Handel and Haydn Society, Boston, 1917); *Songs of Elfland* (St. Louis Symph. Orch., Feb. 2, 1924); *The Holy Star* (1928); *Exultate Deo* (for the 50th anniversary of Radcliffe College; Boston, May 31, 1929); *Song of Jael,* cantata for dramatic soprano, mixed voices and orch. (Worcester Festival, Oct. 5, 1940); *A Psalm of Praise* (composed for the 75th anniversary of the founding of Radcliffe College; Cambridge, Dec. 3, 1954; Boston Symph. Orch., April 27, 1956); also a choral cycle for women's voices, *In Springtime* (1910); 3-part women's choruses with piano and 2 violins: *Eastern Song* and *The Voice of My Beloved* (Prize of National Federation of Music Clubs, 1911); sacred choruses a cappella (*The Christ Child, Salve festa dies,* etc.); duets; part songs. For orch.: *Deep Forest,* prelude for small orch. (Barrère Little Symph., N. Y., June 3, 1931; rescored for full orch., 1934; Boston Symph., April 16, 1937, Koussevitzky conducting); *Pirates' Island* (Harrisburg Symph., Feb. 19, 1935). Chamber music: *Pastoral Ode* for flute and strings (1940); *Three Observations* for oboe, clarinet and bassoon (1943); *Digressions* for strings, a ballet (Boston, 1947). She is the author of a lively book, *An American Girl in Munich* (Boston, 1905).

Danjou (dăhn-zhoo'), **Jean-Louis-Félix,** French music teacher; b. Paris, June 21, 1812; d. Montpellier, March 4, 1866. He studied organ with François Benoist at the Paris Cons.; then played organ at various churches from 1830; was organist at Notre Dame from 1840 till 1847. With his essay *De l'état de l'avenir du chant ecclésiastique* (1844) he became the pioneer in the movement for reforming plain chant; and his journal 'Revue de la musique religieuse, populaire et classique' (1845-49) showed profound erudition gained by assiduous historical research. He was the discoverer (1847) of the celebrated 'Antiphonary of Montpellier.' He labored to promote organ building in France; made a special study of organ manufacture in Germany and Holland; entered into partnership with the organ-builders Daublaine & Callinet of Paris, but lost his entire capital, gave up music, and in 1849 became a political journalist in Marseilles and Montpellier.

Dankers, Ghiselin. See **Danckerts.**

Dankevitch (dahn-kä'-vitch), **Konstantin,** Ukrainian composer; b. Odessa, Dec. 24, 1905. He has written overtures and other orchestral music; attracted attention by his opera *Bogdan Khmelnitzky* (Moscow, June 15, 1951) on a subject from Ukrainian history; the opera was attacked for its libretto and its unsuitable music, and Dankevitch revised the score, after which it gained favorable notices in Russia.

Danks, Hart Pease, American song composer; b. New Haven, Conn., April 6, 1834; d. Philadelphia, Nov. 20, 1903. He studied at Saratoga Springs with Dr. L. E. Whiting; in 1851 moved to Chicago, where he became a photographer, and also sang bass in church. In 1864 he settled in New York and developed energetic activity as a prolific composer of sacred hymns and popular songs; published a total of about 1,300 separate numbers; also compiled books of church anthems; wrote two operettas: *Pauline, or the Belle of Saratoga* (1872) and *Conquered by Kindness* (1881). Among his sacred songs the most popular was *Not Ashamed of Christ* (1873), which sold many thousands of copies; in the light genre, his greatest successes were the songs *Don't be angry with me, darling* and *Silver threads among the gold.*—Cf. G. L. Howe, *A Hundred Years of Music in America* (Chicago, 1889, pp. 98-99).

Dannreuther (dann'-roi-ter), **Edward,** pianist; b. Strasbourg, Nov. 4, 1844; d. London, Feb. 12, 1905. He went with his parents in 1849 to Cincinnati, where he was taught by F. L. Ritter; then studied at the Leipzig Cons. with Richter, Moscheles, and Hauptmann (1859-63). On April 11, 1863, he made his début in London, playing Chopin's Concerto in F minor (which had not been heard before in England), and his success was such that he decided to settle there permanently. He introduced into England the piano concertos of Liszt (in A), Grieg, and Tchaikovsky (B♭ minor). In 1872 he founded the London Wagner Society, conducting its concerts (1873-4); was an active promoter of the Wagner Festival (1877); appointed professor at the Royal Academy of Music in 1895. An indefatigable champion of the new composers, he was equally active on behalf of the older masters; the chamber music concerts that he gave at his home (1874-93) were famous. Dannreuther visited the U. S. several times.—Writings: *Richard Wagner and the Reform of the Opera* (1872 in the 'Monthly Musical Record'; separately, London, 1904); *Richard Wagner, His Tendencies and Theories* (London, 1873); *Musical Ornamentation* (2 vols., London, 1893-5; a valuable work, despite some misapprehensions exposed by later investigations); *The Romantic Period* (vol. VI of the 'Oxford History of Music,' London, 1905; 3rd ed. 1931); contributions to Grove's 'Dictionary.' He transl. into English several of Wagner's literary works: *Wagner's Briefe an einen französischen Freund* (1873); *Das Kunstwerk der Zukunft* (1873); *Beethoven* (1880); *Über das Dirigieren* (1885; 4th ed., 1940); gave lectures on Beethoven, Mozart and Chopin; composed piano pieces and songs.

Dannreuther (dann'-roi-ter), **Gustav,** American violinist, brother of Edward; b. Cincinnati, July 21, 1853; d. New York, Dec. 19, 1923. He studied at the Hochschule für Musik, Berlin, under de Ahna and Joachim (violin), and Heitel (theory); then lived in London; in 1877 he joined the Mendelssohn Quintette Club of Boston, traveling through the U. S., Canada and Newfoundland. From 1882-84 he was director of the Buffalo Philh. Society (a chamber music organization), and, during this period gave 60 concerts. In 1884 he founded the 'Beethoven String Quartet' of N. Y. (renamed 'Dannreuther Quartet' in 1894); was for three years concertmaster of the N. Y. Symphony and Oratorio Societies under Walter Damrosch. From 1899 he devoted himself exclusively to chamber music and private teaching; from 1907 taught violin at Vassar College.

Danzi, Franz, German composer and teacher; b. Mannheim, May 15, 1763; d. Karlsruhe, April 13, 1826. He studied with his father, Innocenz Danzi, a cellist; then with Abbé Vogler. He joined the court orch. on its removal to Munich in 1778; became assistant Kapellmeister in 1798; Kapellmeister at Stuttgart (1807-12), where he was the teacher of Carl Maria von Weber; then at Karlsruhe.—Dramatic works: *Cleopatra* (1780); *Azakia* (1780); *Der Triumph der Treue* (Munich, 1781); *Die Sylphe* (1782); *Der Kuss* (1799); *Die Mitternachtsstunde* (1801); *Der Quasi-Mann; Iphigenia in Aulis* (1807); *Turandot* (Karlsruhe, 1817); oratorios, cantatas; Masses; the 128th Psalm for chorus and orch.; symphonies, quintets, quartets, concertos, sonatas. He was an excellent singing-teacher, and wrote vocal exercises of practical value.—Cf. E. Reipschläger, *Schubaur, Danzi und Poissl als Opernkomponisten* (Rostock, 1911); M. Herre, *Franz Danzi* (Munich, 1924).

Da Ponte, Lorenzo, famous librettist; b. Ceneda, near Venice, March 10, 1749; d. New York, Aug. 17, 1838. His real name was Emanuele Conegliano; he was of a Jewish family; was converted to Christianity at the age of 14, and assumed the name of his patron, Bishop of Ceneda, Lorenzo da Ponte. He then studied at the Ceneda Seminary; in 1774 obtained a post as prof. of rhetoric at Treviso, but was dismissed for insubordination two years later. He then went to Venice where he led an adventurous life, and was banished in 1779; subsequently lived in Austria and in Dresden; in 1782 he settled in Vienna and became official poet to the Imperial Theaters; met Mozart and became his friend and librettist of his most famous operas, *Le Nozze di Figaro, Don Giovanni* and *Così fan tutte.* From 1792 to 1798 he was in London; traveled in Europe; then went to New York in 1805. After disastrous business ventures, with intervals of teaching, he became interested in various operatic enterprises. In his last years he was teacher of Italian at Columbia College. He published *Memorie* (4 vols., N. Y., 1823-7; English transls., London, 1929; Philadelphia, 1929).—Cf. A. Marchesan, *Della vita e delle opere di Lorenzo da Ponte* (Treviso, 1900); J. L. Russo, *Lorenzo da Ponte, Poet and Adventurer* (N. Y., 1922); A. Fitzlyon, *The Libertine Librettist* (London, 1955).

Daquin (dah-kan'), **Louis-Claude,** French organist and composer; b. Paris, July 4, 1694; d. there, June 15, 1772. He was a pupil of Marchand; at 6 played on the clavecin before Louis XIV; at 12 became organist at St.-Antoine, where his playing attracted crowds of curious listeners. From 1727 until his death he was organist at St.-Paul, winning the position in competition with Rameau. He published a book of *Pièces de clavecin* (1735; contains the celebrated piece *Coucou*); selections reprinted in Expert's *Les Maîtres du clavecin;* also revised by Brunold in 1926; a collection of *Noëls pour l'orgue ou le clavecin* (reprinted by Guilmant in 'Archives des Maîtres de l'Orgue'), and a cantata, *La Rose.*

D'Aranyi. See **Aranyi.**

D'Archambeau. See **Archambeau.**

Dargomyzhsky (dar-goh-mÿzh'-skē), **Alexander Sergeyevitch,** outstanding Russian composer; b. in the government of Tula, Feb. 14, 1813; d. St. Petersburg, Jan. 17, 1869. From 1817 he lived in St. Petersburg; his teacher was Schoberlechner. At 20 he was a brilliant pianist; from 1831-5 he held a government position, but then devoted himself exclusively to music, studying assiduously for 8 years; visited Germany, Brussels, and Paris in 1845; at Moscow (Dec. 17, 1847) produced an opera, *Esmeralda* (after Victor Hugo's *Notre-Dame de Paris*) with great success (excerpts published in piano score, Moscow, 1948). From 1845-55 he published over 100 minor works (vocal romances, ballads, airs, and duos; waltzes, fantasies, etc.); on May 16, 1856 he brought out his best opera, *Russalka,* at St. Petersburg (vocal score, with indications of instruments, published at Moscow, 1937); in 1867, an opera-ballet, *The Triumph of Bacchus* (written in 1845; performed in Moscow, Jan. 23, 1867); a posthumous opera *Kamennyi Gost* (*The Stone Guest,* after Pushkin's poem of the same title) was scored by Rimsky-Korsakov and produced at St. Petersburg on Feb. 28, 1872; of *Rogdana,* a fantasy-opera, only a few scenes were sketched. At first a follower of Rossini and Auber, Dargomyzhsky gradually became convinced that dramatic realism with nationalistic connotations was the destiny of Russian music; he applied this realistic method in treating the recitative in his opera *The Stone Guest* and in his songs (several of these to satirical words). His orchestral works (*Finnish Fantasia, Cossack Dance, Baba-Yaga,* etc.) enjoyed wide popularity. In 1867 he was elected President of the Russian Music Society.—Cf. N. Findeisen, *A. S. Dargomyzhsky: His Life and Work* (Moscow, 1902); S. B. Fried, *A. S. Dargomyzhsky* (St. Petersburg, 1913); N. Findeisen, *Dargomyzhsky* (biography, letters, etc.; Leningrad, 1921); A. N. Drosdov, *A. S. Dargomyzhsky* (Moscow, 1929); M. Pekelis, *Dargomyzhsky and the Folk Song* (Moscow, 1951).

Darke, Harold Edwin, English composer; b. Highbury, London, Oct. 29, 1888. He studied at the Royal College of Music; for 10 years was assistant organist at Temple Church; organist of St. Michael's, Cornhill (1916); conductor of the St. Michael Singers and teacher of harmony, composition and vocal ensemble at the Royal College of Music; Mus. Doc., Oxford Univ. (1919); organist of King's College, Cambridge (1941-45); later taught at Cambridge Univ.; composed orchestral works, cantatas, chamber music, etc. On June 4, 1956, a jubilee concert was given at St. Michael's, Cornhill, to mark the 40th anniversary of his tenure as organist there; the program included his *Song of David* for chorus, strings, harp, and organ and specially composed works by Vaughan Williams and others.

Darnton, Charles, English composer and organist; b. Islington, Oct. 10, 1836; d. London, April 21, 1933. He was almost entirely self-taught; was organist of St. Jude's Church, Canonbury (1860-67), Park Chapel, Camden Town (1867-91), Gospel Oak, Hampstead (1892-1901); composed 90 anthems (prize anthem; *I will sing of the mercies of the Lord,* London, 1897); many other sacred works; operettas; piano pieces, etc.

Darnton, Christian, English composer; b. near Leeds, Oct. 30, 1905. He took piano lessons at 4, and began to compose at 9; studied with F. Corder, Sr., at the Brighton School of Music, then with H. Craxton (piano) at the Matthay School, London; pupil of Benjamin Dale in composition; studied (1923-26) with Charles Wood (composition) and G. Rootham (theory) at Cambridge; with G. Jacob at the Royal College of Music (1927); with M. Butting in Berlin (1928-29); gave a concert of his works at Grotrian Hall, London (1927).—Works: 3 symphonies; 2 piano concertos; *5 Orchestral Pieces* (Warsaw Festival, April 14, 1939); author of *You and Music* (1940).—Cf. A. Rawsthorne, *Christian Darnton,* in 'Monthly Musical Record' (Jan. 1939).

Darrell, Robert Donaldson, American writer on music; b. Newton, Mass., Dec. 13, 1903; studied at the New England Cons. of Music; contributed to the 'Phonograph Monthly Review' and became its editor and publisher in 1930; received a Guggenheim Fellowship in 1939. He published valuable compilations, *Gramophone Shop Encyclopedia of Recorded Music* (1936) and *Schirmer's Guide to Books on Music and Musicians* (annotated bibliography of books in English available in print; N. Y., 1951); also *Good Listening* (N. Y., 1953). In 1956 he became associate editor of 'High Fidelity' magazine and 'Audiocraft.'

Dart, Thurston, English musicologist; b. London, Sept. 3, 1921. He studied at the Royal College of Music (1938-39) and also took courses in mathematics at London Univ. In 1947 he was appointed lecturer on music at Cambridge Univ.; received his M. A. there (1948). His specialty is old English music; he edited works for the recorder; published a book, *The Interpretation of Music* (London, 1954). He is also a skillful performer on the harpsichord, virginals, and other old keyboard instruments.

Dasch, George, American violinist, conductor and teacher; b. Cincinnati, Ohio, May 14, 1877; d. Chicago, April 12, 1955; graduated in 1895 from the Cincinnati College of Music, where he studied with J. A. Brockhoeven (theory) and L. Campanari (violin); member of the Cincinnati Symph. Orch. (1895-98), Chicago Symph. Orch. (1898-1923); then organized his own string quartet. He conducted the Chicago Civic Orch. and the Joliet, Ill., Symph. Orch.; in 1943 was appointed conductor of the Evansville Philharmonic. — Works: Overture, *Youth Courageous; Scherzo; Andante; Colonial Dance; A Rhythmelodic Sketch;* many arrangements; editor (in collaboration with F. Stock) of a 'Series for School and Community Orch.'

Daser (Dasser, Dasserus), Ludwig, German composer; b. Munich, c. 1525; d. Stuttgart, March 27, 1589. He preceded Orlando di Lasso as Kapellmeister at Munich to Duke Albert V of Bavaria; held that post until 1559.—Publ. works: A Passion *a* 4 (1578), and a few motets in the *Orgeltabulaturbuch* of J. Paix.—MSS in Royal Library at Munich (11 masses, 4 motets, 3 *Nunc dimittis,* hymns, etc.), also in Vienna, Augsburg, Basel, and Breslau.—Cf. A. Sandberger, *Beiträge zur Geschichte der Beyerischen Hofkopelle I.* (1894); B. A. Wallner, *Musikalische Denkmäler der Steinätzkunst* (1912).

Daublaine et Callinet (doh-blān' ā kăhl-lē-nā'), firm of Paris organ-builders; founded 1838 as 'Daublaine et Cie.' Daublaine was the business partner, Callinet the practical mechanician, Danjou (q. v.) an intelligent and progressive theorist. After a quarrel in 1843, Callinet demolished the new work partly finished for the organ of St.-Sulpice, dissolved the partnership, and entered Cavaillé's workshops. The firm name became 'Ducroquet et Cie.' in 1845; in 1855 it was succeeded by a limited company, later by 'Merklin, Schütze et Cie.' from Brussels; subsequently Merklin continued the business alone until his death in 1905. As a manufacturer of instruments, the firm no longer exists.

Dauney, William, music historian; b. Aberdeen, Scotland, Oct. 27, 1800; d. Georgetown, British Guiana, July 28, 1843. In the Advocates' Library at Edinburgh he discovered what is now known as the 'Skene MS,' a collection of 114 English and Scottish dances, ballads and songs (written in tablature between 1614-20), containing the oldest known (and probably original) versions of *John Anderson my Jo, The Flowers of the Forest,* etc. Dauney transcribed these into modern notation, and publ. them, in 1838, as *Ancient Scottish Melodies from a MS. of the reign of King James VI,* together with *An Introductory Enquiry Illustrative of the History of Music of Scotland.*

Dauprat (doh-prăh'), **Louis-François,** celebrated French horn player, teacher, and composer for horn; b. Paris, May 24, 1781; d. there, July 16, 1868. Studied with Kenn at the Paris Cons.; joined the band of the 'Garde Nationale,' and in 1799 the band of the 'Garde des Consuls,' with which he passed through the Egyptian campaign. From 1801-5 he studied theory at the Cons. under Catel and Gossec, and studied again with Reicha from 1811-14; 1806-08 first horn at the Bordeaux Theater; succeeded Kenn in the Opéra orch., and Duvernoy (as *cor solo*), retiring in 1831. He was chamber musician to Napoleon (1811), and Louis XVIII (1816); in 1816 he was appointed prof. of horn in the Cons., resigning in 1842.

Dauriac (doh-r'yăhk'), **Lionel Alexandre,** French psychologist and writer on music; b. Brest, Finisterre, Nov. 19, 1847; d. Paris, May 26, 1923. He graduated from the École Normale Supérieure of Brest, 1867; *Docteur ès Lettres,* Paris, 1878 (with the dissertations *Des Notions de Matière et de Force dans les Sciences de la Nature* and *De Heraclito Ephesio*); held teaching positions in philosophy at Brest, Toulouse, and Montpellier; lecturer at the Sorbonne on musical psychology (1896-1903); Laureate of the Academy of Moral and Political Sciences (awarded Prix Gegner, 1916); 1st President of Paris section of International Music Society; from 1907, Honorary President. Besides many works dealing with philosophy, he publ. the following concerning music: *Introduction à la Psychologie du Musicien* (Paris, 1891), *La Psychologie dans l'opéra français* (Paris, 1897), *Essai sur l'esprit musical* (Paris, 1904), *Rossini, biographie critique* (Paris, 1905), *Le Musicien-poète Richard Wagner* (Paris, 1908), *Meyerbeer* (Paris, 1913).

Daussoigne-Méhul (doh-swăhñ'mā-ül'), **Louis-Joseph,** French composer; b. Givet, Ardennes, June 10, 1790; d. Liège, March 10, 1875. Nephew and foster-son of Méhul. Pupil of Catel and Méhul at the Cons.; took the Grand Prix de Rome in 1809; after writing 4 operas, which were rejected, he at length produced his 1-act *Aspasie* at the Grand Opéra (1820) with moderate success. He did still better with *Valentine de Milan,* a 3-act opera left unfinished by Méhul, which he completed; but his former ill success had discouraged him. In 1827 he accepted the directorship of Liège Cons., which he retained, with great benefit to the school, until 1862. Daussoigne-Méhul was an associate of the Royal Academy, Brussels. He brought out a cantata with full orch. in 1828, and a choral symphony (*Une journée de la Révolution*) in 1834.

Dauvergne (doh-värñ'), **Antoine,** French composer and conductor; b. Clermont-Ferrand, Oct. 3, 1713; d. Lyons, Feb. 11, 1797. He received his first instruction from his father, went for further study to Paris, in 1739, and was appointed violinist in the Royal orch. (1741); 1755 appointed composer to the Royal orch.; 1762 conductor of 'Concerts Spirituels'; after 1769 active as conductor and manager of various enterprises, until his retirement to Lyons in 1790. He introduced into France the forms of the Italian intermezzo, substituting spoken dialogue for the recitative, and thus was the originator of a style that soon became typical of French dramatic composition. He wrote 15 operas, the first of which was produced at Paris in 1753 (*Les Troqueurs*), and is regarded as the first 'opéra-comique'; wrote also 2 books of symphonies; 12 sonatas for violin and basso continuo, etc.

Davenport, Francis William, English composer; b. Wilderslowe near Derby, April 9, 1847; d. Scarborough, April 1, 1925. He studied law at Oxford, but preferred music, and became the pupil (later son-in-law) of Sir G. A. Macfarren. In 1879, prof. at the Royal Academy of Music, and at the Guildhall School of Music in 1882.—Works: 2 symphonies (1. in D minor, won 1st prize at Alexandria Palace, 1876; 2. in C major); overture for orch., *Twelfth Night;* 6 pieces for piano and cello; *Pictures on a Journey,* a series of piano pieces; part songs and songs; wrote *Elements of Music* (1884), *Elements of Harmony and Counterpoint* (1886), and *Guide for Pianoforte Students* (with Percy Baker, 1891).

Davenport, Marcia, American writer on music; b. New York, June 9, 1903. She studied at Wellesley College and at the Univ. of Grenoble, France (graduated 1925). She has written successful novels, including one on a musical subject (*Of Lena Geyer,* 1936), a biography of Mozart (1932), and numerous articles.

Davey, Henry, English musicologist; b. Brighton, Nov. 29, 1853; d. Hove, Sussex, Aug. 28, 1929. He entered Leipzig Cons. in 1874, devoting himself chiefly to theoretical studies; lived for several years in Brighton as teacher. Publ. *The Student's Musical History* (London, 1895; 2nd ed. 1921), a valuable work, the result of original research.

Davico, Vincenzo, Italian composer; b. Monaco, Jan. 14, 1889. He studied in Turin, and later in Leipzig with Max Reger; graduated from the Leipzig Cons. in 1911; then lived for many years in Paris; since 1940, mostly in Rome.—Works: the operas *La dogaressa* (Monte Carlo, Feb. 26, 1920) and *La Principessa prigioniera* (Bergamo, 1940); ballets *L'agonia della rosa* (Paris, May 2, 1927); *Narciso* (San Remo, Feb. 19, 1935); oratorio, *La Tentation de Saint Antoine* (Monte Carlo, Dec. 15, 1921); for orch.: *La Principessa lontana* (after Rostand's *Princesse lointaine;* won the Augusteo prize, 1911); *Poema erotico* (also won the Augusteo prize, 1913); *Polifemo,* symph. poem (Turin, 1920); *Impressioni dal mio diario di viaggio* (1949); piano pieces and numerous songs.—Cf. G. Franchi, *Vincenzo Davico* (1924); Raymond Petit, *Les mélodies de Vincenzo Davico* (Nice, 1925); Massimo Gaglione, *Vincenzo Davico* in his book, *I giovani;* G. M. Gatti, in *I giovani sinfonisti* (Orfeo, Rome).

David (dah-vēd'), **Félicien (-César),** French composer; b. Cadenet, Vaucluse, Apr. 13, 1810; d. St.-Germain-en-Laye, Aug. 29, 1876. Of precocious talent, he was taught in the maîtrise of St.-Sauveur at Aix from 1818-25. He had a fine voice, and composed hymns, motets, and other music. He then studied in the Jesuit college for 3 years; became assistant conductor in the theater at Aix, and in 1829 maître de chapelle at St.-Sauveur; but a longing to widen his musical horizon drew him to Paris (1830), where he submitted specimens of compositions to Cherubini, and was admitted to the Cons., studying harmony with Reber and Millot, and counterpoint and fugue with Fétis. In 1831, when the meagre allowance given him by a rich and avaricious uncle had been withdrawn, he joined the socialistic movement of the St.-Simonists at Ménilmontant; here he composed a series of 4-part *hymnes* for men's voices (later publ. with the words, as the *Ruche harmonieuse*). On the dispersion of the society in 1833, David went to Marseilles with a group of the brotherhood, giving concerts on the way; they proceeded to Constantinople, Smyrna, and Egypt, where they finally dispersed; and, with an imagination stimulated by his long sojourn in the East, David returned alone to Paris in 1835. He now publ. a collection of *Mélodies orientales;* they met with small success, and he retired to the country, giving himself up to study and composition (2 symphonies, 24 small string quintets, 2 nonets for wind, romances, etc.). In 1838 his first symphony was produced; and at last he reaped the fruit of many years' study, his symphonic ode *Le Désert* being received, at its first performance in the hall of the Cons. (Dec. 8, 1844), with 'delirious' applause, and a series of repetitions given at the Salle Ventadour for a month, to crowded houses. The oratorio *Moïse au Sinaï* followed in 1846, but, like a second symphonic ode *Christophe Colomb* (Paris, March 7, 1847) and *L'Éden* (a 'mystery' in 2 parts, Grand Opéra, Aug. 25, 1848), met with a cool reception. However, his opera *La Perle du Brésil* (Théâtre Lyrique, Nov. 22, 1851) was quite successful; a second, *Le dernier amour,* was rejected by the Grand Opéra, and by the Théâtre-Lyrique; but the Grand Opéra took it up in 1859 as *Herculanum,* and for this opera the great state prize of 20,000 francs was awarded to David in 1867. *Lalla Roukh* (May 12, 1862) and *Le Saphir* (1865) were given at the Opéra-*Comique* (the former with great success, the latter with scarcely a 'succès d'estime'). David now abandoned dramatic composition, withdrawing his last opera, *La Captive.* In 1869 he was elected Académicien, taking Berlioz's chair, and succeeding him also as librarian of the Cons.—Besides the above works, he wrote 12 melodies for cello; *Les Brises d'Orient,* piano pieces; *Les Minarets,* 3 piano pieces; *Les Perles d'Orient,* 6 melodies for voice and piano; etc.—Cf. A. Azevedo, *Félicien David, Sa vie et son œuvre* (Paris, 1863); C. Bellaigue, *Félicien David,* in *Études musicales et nouvelles silhouettes* (Paris, 1898); J.-G. Prod'homme, *Félicien David d'après sa correspondance inédite,* in 'Mercure Musical' II, III (1907); R. Brancour, *Félicien David* (Paris, 1911).

David, Ferdinand, German violinist and pedagogue; b. Hamburg, Jan. 19, 1810; d. near Klosters, Switzerland, July 14, 1873. From 1823-4 he studied with Spohr and Hauptmann at Kassel; played in the Gewandhaus, Leipzig, 1825; in 1827 became a member of the Königstadt Theater in Berlin. In 1829 he became the first violinist in the private string quartet of the wealthy amateur Baron von Liphardt of Dorpat, Russia, whose daughter he married. He remained in Russia until 1835, giving concerts in Riga, Moscow, and St. Petersburg with great acclaim. In 1836, at Mendelssohn's suggestion, he was appointed first violinist of the Gewandhaus Orch. in Leipzig, of which Mendelssohn was the conductor. They became warm friends; Mendelssohn had a great regard for him, and consulted him constantly while writing his violin concerto; and it was David who gave its first performance (Leipzig, March 13, 1845). When the Leipzig Cons. was established in 1843, David became one of its most important teachers; his class was regarded as the finishing school of the most talented violinists in Europe; among his pupils were Joachim and Wilhelmj. He published many valuable editions of violin works by classical composers, notably *Die Hohe Schule des Violinspiels,* containing French and Italian masterpieces of the 17th and 18th centuries. His numerous violin exercises are still used by students. His pedagogical activities did not interfere with his concert career; he played in England in 1839 and 1841 with excellent success and was compared with Spohr as a virtuoso; also made occasional appearances on the continent. He wrote 5 violin concertos; many other pieces for violin; an opera *Hans Wacht* (Leipzig, 1852); 2 symphonies; string quartets and other chamber music. His violin pieces *Bunte Reihe* were transcribed for piano by Liszt.—Cf. J. Eckhardt, *Ferdinand David und die Familie Mendelssohn-Bartholdy* (Leipzig, 1888); A. Bachmann, *Ferdinand David* in *Les grands violinistes du passé* (Paris, 1913).

David, Hans Theodore, musicologist; b. Speyer, Palatinate, July 8, 1902. He studied at various German universities; received the degree of *Dr. phil.* at Berlin (1928); came to the U. S. (1936); was music editor of the New York Public Library (1937); Research Fellow of the American Philosophical Society for a study of 'Moravian' music (1937-38); occupied the same position for a study of the music of C. Beissel and the Ephrata Cloister (1939-40); lecturer at New York Univ. (1939); 1944, head of the department of musicology, Southern Methodist Univ., Dallas, Texas; 1950, prof. at the University of Michigan.—Writings: *Johann Schobert* (1928); studies on works by J. S. Bach, in 'Johannes Wolf-Festschrift,' 'Bach-Jahrbuch,' 'Jahrbuch der Musikbibliothek Peters,' the 'Mus. Quarterly,' etc.; *J. S. Bach's Musical Offering, History, Interpretation, and Analysis* (N. Y., 1945); ed., with A. Mendel, *The Bach Reader* (N. Y., 1945); co-author, with A. G. Rau, of 'A Catalogue of Music of American Moravians' (Bethlehem, Pa., 1938); ed. Bach's *Art of Fugue, Musical Offering* and *Overture in the French Manner* (first version); Handel's *Sonata a 5* (violin concerto); *Canzone* by Frescobaldi; sonatas by Purcell; also 'English Instrumental Music of the 16th and 17th Centuries'; 'Music of the Moravians in America'; 'The Art of Polyphonic Song,' etc. He has made orchestral versions of Bach's *Art of Fugue,* works by G. Gabrieli, etc.

David, Johann Nepomuk, outstanding composer; b. Eferding, Upper Austria, Nov. 30, 1895. He studied with Joseph Marx at the Vienna Academy (1920-23); was organist in Wels, Upper Austria (1924-33); in 1934 was engaged as professor of composition at the Leipzig Cons., becoming its director in 1939. He was subsequently director at the Salzburg Mozarteum (1945-47). In 1947 he was appointed professor of composition at the Musikhochschule in Stuttgart. David's music is severely polyphonic in its structure; almost all of his instrumental works are cast in forms influenced by the late Baroque; his mastery of counterpoint is revealed in his many choral pieces.—Works: For orch.: 5 symphonies (1936-51); concerto grosso for chamber orch. (1923); *Partita* (1935); *Duo concertante* for violin and cello with orch. (1937); flute concerto (1949); violin concerto (1949; Stuttgart Radio, April 25, 1954); etc. Chamber music: clarinet quintet (1924); 3 string quartets; several solo sonatas (for flute, for violin, for viola, for cello). Choral works: *Stabat Mater* in 6 parts (1927); *Mensch, werde wesentlich,* for men's voices; oratorio, *Das Ezzolied,* for soli, chorus, and orch.; many motets. Numerous organ works (*Chaconne, Ricercare, Fantasia super L'homme armé,* etc.); songs, piano pieces, etc.—He is the author of a study of Mozart's *Jupiter Symphony* (2nd ed., 1956).—Cf. Karl H. Wörner, *J. N. David,* in his book 'Musik der Gegenwart'

(Mainz, 1949); also articles in 'Neue Zeitschrift für Musik' (Feb., 1932; Jan., 1937; Sept. 1938).

David, Karl Heinrich, Swiss composer; b. St. Gall, Dec. 30, 1884; d. Nervi, Italy, May 17, 1951. He studied in Cologne and Munich; taught at the Basel Cons. (1910-14); then at Cologne and Berlin (1914-17); in 1918 returned to Switzerland. He was the editor of the 'Schweizer Musikzeitung' in Zürich (1928-41).—Works: operas: *Aschenputtel* (Basel, Oct. 21, 1921); *Der Sizilianer* (Zürich, Oct. 22, 1924); *Jugendfestspiel* (Zürich, June 8, 1924); *Traumwandel* (Zürich, Jan. 29, 1928); *Weekend,* a comic opera (1933). Other works: piano concerto (1929); *Ballet* for orch. (1931); *Pezzo sinfonico* (1945); concerto for saxophone and string orch. (1947); *Symphonie de la côte d'argent* (1948); *Mascarade,* overture (1950); *Andante and Rondo* for violin and chamber orch.; two pieces for piano and 9 woodwinds; viola suite; piano trio; quartet for saxophone, violin, cello, piano (1946); duet for horn and piano (1951); *Das hohe Lied Salomonis* for soprano, tenor, female chorus and orch.; songs.

David, Samuel, French composer; b. Paris, Nov. 12, 1836; d. there, Oct. 3, 1895. He studied at the Cons. with Halévy; won the Grand Prix de Rome (1858) for his cantata *Jephté,* and another prize for a work for male chorus and orch., *Le Génie de la terre,* performed by chorus of 6,000 singers (1859); professor at Collège de Sainte-Barbe (1861); music director in Jewish synagogues of Paris (1872). He wrote several operas, 4 symphonies, choruses, and songs.

Davidenko, Alexander Alexandrovitch, Russian composer; b. Odessa, April 1, 1899; d. Moscow, May 1, 1934. He organized, with Belyi, the Procoll (Production Collective of Composers) in Russia in 1925; wrote workers' songs. His most important work is the opera *1905* (written in 1929-33, with Boris Schechter); another opera, *Down the Cliff,* was left incomplete.

Davidov, Karl Youlievitch, Russian cellist; b. Goldingen, Kurland, March 15, 1838; d. Moscow, Feb. 26, 1889. He studied in Moscow with H. Schmidt (cello) and at St. Petersburg with G. Schubert; later studied composition with Hauptmann at Leipzig. His début at the Gewandhaus concerts (1859) was so successful that he was engaged as first cellist and also succeeded Fr. Grützmacher as teacher in the Leipzig Cons. In 1862, he was appointed solo cellist of the Russian Music Society and of the St. Petersburg Cons.; was director of the St. Petersburg Cons. (1876-87).—Works: Concertos, a ballade, and a song without words, for cello; piano pieces; chamber music (piano quintet; string quartet); a symph. poem, *The Gifts of Terek,* songs, etc.—Cf. V. Hutor, *Karl Davidov und seine Art, das Violoncell zu behandeln* (1899); S. Ginsburg, *Karl Davidov* (Leningrad, 1936).

Davidson, Harold Gibson, American composer; b. Low Moor, Virginia, Feb. 20, 1893; studied at the Cincinnati Cons. He has given numerous piano recitals, and has taught at several schools; settled in California. His music is of an experimental nature, exemplified by such titles as *Auto Accident* and *Hell's Bells* (for percussion); *Two Minor Disturbances and One Major Calamity,* piano suite; *Legend of the Flying Saucers,* etc. He has also written numerous teaching pieces.

Davies, Benjamin Grey (known as Ben Davies), Welsh tenor; b. Pontardawe, near Swansea, S. Wales, Jan. 6, 1858; d. Bath, England, March 28, 1943. He studied at the Royal Academy of Music under Randegger, winning the bronze, silver, and gold medals, and the Evill prize for best declamatory English singing; début at Birmingham, Oct. 11, 1881, in *The Bohemian Girl;* the next three years, with the Carl Rosa Opera Co.; then with several other troupes, mostly in light operas. His success in oratorio at the Norwich Festivals of 1890 caused him to abandon the stage (he appeared only one more season, in Sullivan's *Ivanhoe* and Messager's *Basoche*), and to devote himself to concert work. He visited the U. S. in 1893 and made several subsequent tours there; received the degree of Hon. Mus. Doc., Wales; Fellow of the Royal Academy of Music. His repertory included most of the oratorios, cantatas, and concert works performed in Britain.

Davies, (David Thomas) Ffrangcon. See **Ffrangcon-Davies.**

Davies, Fanny, English pianist; b. Guernsey, June 27, 1861; d. London, Sept. 1, 1934. She studied at the Leipzig Cons. with Reinecke and Paul (piano) and Jadassohn (theory) from 1882-83, and at the Hoch Cons., Frankfurt, with Clara Schumann (1883-85); also was a pupil of Scholz in fugue and composition. Her London début took place at the Crystal Palace, Oct. 17, 1885; then she made successful tours in England, Germany, France, and Italy.

Davies, Sir **Henry Walford,** English composer, organist, educator; b. Oswestry, Sept. 6, 1869; d. Wrington, Somerset, March 11, 1941. At 12 he became a chorister in St. George's Chapel, Windsor; pupil and assistant of Sir Walter Parratt and organist of the Park Chapel, Windsor (1885-90). From 1890-94, he held a scholarship in composition at the Royal College of Music; organist and choirmaster at St. Anne's, Soho (1890-91); organist of Christ Church, Hampstead (1891-98). In 1894 he qualified as Associate of the Royal College of Music for composition; and in 1895 succeeded Rockstro as professor of counterpoint there (till 1903); also Fellow of the Royal College of Organists. In 1898, he succeeded E. J. Hopkins as organist of the Temple Church (remained there till 1923); conducted the Bach Choir (1903-7) and London Church Choir Association (1901-13); he was examiner for music degrees at Oxford and Cambridge (1910-13); professor at the Univ. of Wales, at Aberystwyth (1919-26); knighted in 1922; and succeeded Sir Walter Parratt as organist of St. George's Chapel, Windsor (1924; on duty there 1927-32). Sir Henry was appointed Master of the King's Musick in 1934; wrote the coronation service book for George VI (May, 1937); musical adviser for the B.B.C.; inaugurated a novel broadcasting series 'Music Lessons to Schools' (1924-34); he was a Mus. Bac. (1892); Mus. Doc., Cambridge (1898); LL. D. (hon. c.), Leeds (1904).—Works: For soli, chorus, and orch.: *Hervé Riel* (1894); *The Temple* (Worcester Festival, 1902); *Three Jovial Huntsmen* (Windsor and Worcester, 1902); *Everyman* (Leeds Festival, 1904); *Lift up Your Hearts* (Hereford Festival, 1906); *Ode on Time* (Milton Celebration, 1908); *Noble Numbers,* choral song cycle (Hereford Festival, 1909); *Five Sayings of Jesus* (Worcester Festival, 1911); *Song of St. Francis* (Birmingham Festival, 1912); *Dante Fantasy* (Worcester, 1920); *Heaven's Gate* (London, 1916); *Men and Angels* (Gloucester Festival, 1925); *High Heaven's King* (Worcester Festival, 1926); *Christ in the Universe* (Worcester Festival, 1929); children's operetta, *What Luck!* (1931); *The Pied Piper of Hamelin* (1939). For orch.: *Dedication Overture* (1893); Overture to *Everyman* (1904); *Holiday Tunes* (1907); *Solemn Melody* for strings (1908); *Festal Overture* (1910); *Parthenia Suite* (1911); Suite in C 'after Wordsworth' (1912); *Conversations* for piano and orch. (London, Oct. 14, 1914); *Memorial Suite* (1923); *A Children's Symphony* (1927); *London Calling the Schools,* for piano, orch., and announcer (1932); *Big Ben Looks On,* orchestral fantasy (1937); *Solemn Melody* for band (1939); etc. Chamber music: *Prospice* for baritone and string quartet (1894); 2 violin sonatas (in E minor, 1894; in D minor, 1896); *Psalm 23* for tenor, harp, and string quartet (1896); *Six Pastorals* for 4 voices, string quartet, and piano (1897); *Songs of Nature* for voices, strings, flute, horn, and piano (1908-9); *Peter Pan,* suite for string quartet (1909). Church music, numerous songs and part songs; also various compilations.—Author of *The Musical Outlook in Wales* (London, 1926); *The Pursuit of Music* (London, 1935); *Music and Worship* (with Harvey Grace, London, 1935).—Cf. H. C. Colles, *Walford Davies, a Biography* (London, 1942).

Davis, John David, English composer and music teacher; b. Birmingham, Oct. 22, 1867; d. Estoril, Portugal, Nov. 20, 1942. In spite of musical precocity he was destined for a commercial career, and sent to Frankfurt, in 1885, to perfect his German, but studied at the Raff Cons.; the next year for the purpose of mastering French he was sent to Brussels, but again entered the Cons.; settled in 1889 as a teacher in Birmingham; instructor at the Midland Institute (1893-1904); from 1905, professor of composition at the Guildhall School of Music. His opera, *The Zaporogues* (i. e., *The Cossacks*) was produced in Birmingham (May 7, 1895) and at Antwerp (1903). He further wrote a symph. poem, *The Maid of Astolat,* concert overture *Germania,* and a *Coronation March* (1902).

Davison, Arabella. See **Goddard.**

Davison, Archibald Thompson, eminent music educator; b. Boston, Mass., Oct. 11, 1883. He studied at Harvard Univ. (B. A., 1906; M.A., 1907; Ph.D., 1908) and in Paris with Widor; taught organ at Harvard (1909-38); also conducted the Harvard Glee Club (1912-34) and the Radcliffe Choral Society (1913-28); professor of music at Harvard until his retirement in 1954; Mus. Doc., Williams College, Oxford Univ., and Harvard; Fellow of the Royal College of Music, London. He wrote a musical comedy, *The Girl and the Chauffeur,* upon his graduation from Harvard (performed in Boston, April 16, 1906); 2 overtures, *Hero and Leander* (1908) and *Tragic Overture* (Boston, 1918); the books, *Music Education in America* (1926); *Protestant Church Music in America* (1920; enlarged ed. 1933); ed., with W. Apel, *Historical Anthology of Music* (Cambridge, Mass., 2 vols., 1947, 1950); *Bach and Handel: the Consummation of the Baroque in Music* (Cambridge,

Mass., 1951); *Church Music; Illusion and Reality* (Cambridge, Mass., 1952).

Davison, James William, renowned English music critic; b. London, Oct. 5, 1813; d. Margate, March 24, 1885. Editor of the 'Mus. Examiner' (1842-44) and the 'Musical World' (1844-85); contributor to the 'Saturday Review,' 'Pall Mall Gazette,' and 'Graphic'; was the influential critic of 'The Times' (1846-79). In 1860 he married his pupil, Arabella Goddard. He wrote the analytical 'programme-books' for the Popular Concerts and the Hallé recitals; composed a few songs, several piano pieces, and a dramatic overture (for piano duet) to *Fortunatus,* a fairy tale. His memoirs were published by H. Davison as *From Mendelssohn to Wagner* (1912).

Davy, John, English song composer and violinist; b. Upton-Helions, near Exeter, Dec. 23, 1763; d. London, Feb. 22, 1824. He studied at Exeter, and then settled in London, where he played the violin at Covent Garden. He wrote the music to a number of plays: *A Pennyworth of Wit* (London, April 18, 1796); *Alfred, the Great,* a 'grand historical ballet' (London, June 4, 1798); etc. 'The Bay of Biscay, O!', one of the songs from his incidental music to a play, *Spanish Dollars,* was extremely popular.

Dawe, Charles D., choral conductor and arranger; b. Port Talbot, Wales, March 16, 1887; studied in London at the Tonic Sol-Fa College with several Welsh teachers; later settled in America and became conductor of the Orpheus Male Choir in Cleveland, with which he toured in Europe, including Russia (1935). From 1933 till 1943 he was chorus master of the Cleveland Orchestra Chorus. In 1956 he was conductor of three choirs (including the Orpheus) in Cleveland and three in Akron, Ohio. He has arranged 24 choruses for male voices from works by Handel, issued by various publishers, and has composed many sacred choral works.

Dawson, William Levi, American composer; b. Anniston, Alabama, Sept. 26, 1898. At the age of 13, he ran away from home to enter Tuskegee Institute; later played trombone on the Redpath Chautauqua Circuit; graduated from Tuskegee Institute in 1921; later studied with Carl Busch in Kansas City and at the American Cons. in Chicago. He received his M. A. in 1927. He played first trombone in the Chicago Civic Orch. (1926-30); then conducted the Tuskegee Choir. Among his works is a Negro folk symphony in 3 movements (Philadelphia Orch., Stokowski conducting, Nov. 16, 1934).

Day, Major **Charles Russell,** English writer on music; b. Horstead, Norwich, in 1860; d. Paardeberg, South Africa, Feb. 18, 1900. He was a soldier in the British army from 1880; served in India, later in South Africa where he was killed in battle. His chief work was *Music and Musical Instruments of Southern India and the Deccan* (London, 1891); also published *A Descriptive Catalogue of the Musical Instruments Recently Exhibited at the Royal Military Exhibition, London, 1890* (London, 1891), and papers and pamphlets on national and military music.—Cf. A. J. Hipkins, in the 'Musical Times' (April, 1900).

Dayas (dās), **William Humphreys,** American organist and teacher; b. New York, Sept. 12, 1863; d. Manchester, England, May 3, 1903. He studied piano with Joseffy; became organist of the Fifth Ave. Presbyterian church and of St. Andrew's; then studied in Germany, and was one of Liszt's last pupils at Weimar; also studied there with Kullak, Haupt, Ehrlich, and Urban. He was piano teacher in Helsingfors Cons. (1890); taught in Düsseldorf (1894), Wiesbaden and Cologne; returned for a while to New York, and then settled in Manchester (1896), where he taught at the Music College.

De Ahna, Heinrich Karl Hermann, eminent violinist; b. Vienna, June 22, 1835; d. Berlin, Nov. 1, 1892. He studied in Vienna with Mayseder and at the Prague Cons. with Mildner; made his début as violinist at the age of 12, at Vienna, London, etc. He was appointed chamber virtuoso to the Duke of Saxe-Coburg-Gotha (1849); then resumed concert tours in Holland and Germany; settled in 1862 in Berlin as a member of the Royal Orch., becoming its concertmaster in 1868.

Déak, Stephen, cellist and teacher; b. Szombathely, Hungary, Nov. 17, 1897. He studied at the Royal Academy of Music, Budapest; came to the U. S. in 1921 and continued his studies with Felix Salmond at the Curtis Institute, Philadelphia; then taught cello at Peabody Cons., Baltimore (1930-37) and at the Univ. of Southern California, Los Angeles (from 1943). He wrote a *Modern Method* for cello (1929).

Deakin, Andrew, English publisher and bibliographer; b. Birmingham, April 13, 1822; d. there, Dec. 21, 1903. While serving his apprenticeship as a printer, he taught himself music; established a publishing house in Birmingham, and held several positions as organist; 1876-94 mus. crit. of 'The Daily Gazette'; composed several Masses and a Stabat Mater. His chief work is *Outlines of Musical Bibliography* (Birmingham, 1900; a catalogue of works on music printed in England from the 15th to the 18th century).

Dean, Winton, English musicologist; b. Birkenhead, March 18, 1916. He studied at King's College, Cambridge (B. A., 1938; M. A., 1941). Although he had no professional training in music, he became interested in musical biography; his monograph on Bizet in the 'Master Musicians' series (London, 1948) is a valuable and accurate account. He has also written on Handel, Franck, and Puccini.

Debain (dŭ-băn'), **Alexandre-François,** the inventor of the harmonium; b. Paris, 1809; d. there Dec. 3, 1877. He established a factory of pianos and organs in Paris (1834), and after long experimentation with free reeds patented his 'harmonium' in 1840. He also invented the 'antiphonel' and the 'harmonichorde' and improved the accordion.

Debussy (du-bü-sē), **(Achille-) Claude,** great French composer; b. St. Germain-en-Laye, Aug. 22, 1862; d. Paris, March 25, 1918 (during a German bombardment of the city). Mme. Mauté de Fleurville, a pupil of Chopin, prepared him for the Cons. at Paris, where he was admitted at the age of 11. Here he continued his study of piano with Marmontel, and won the second prize in 1877; in the solfeggio class of Lavignac he won the medal three years in succession (1874; 1875; 1876). Émile Durand was his teacher in the harmony class (1876-80); he received no awards there. After his graduation in 1880, Debussy was recommended to Mme. Nadezhda von Meck, Tchaikovsky's patroness, as a household pianist to teach piano to her children and play four hands with them. She summoned him to Switzerland, where she was traveling (he was not quite 18 at the time), and took him to Italy and Russia; he stayed with her family in Moscow and at her country estate in the summer of 1881, and again in 1882. There he had an opportunity to acquaint himself with the music of Borodin and Mussorgsky, which was to influence him greatly in the subsequent period of his creative activity. Although he played Tchaikovsky's scores for Mme. von Meck (including the manuscript of the 4th symphony, dedicated to her) Debussy did not evince great interest in Tchaikovsky's works. Another influence in his youth was Mme. Vasnier, an excellent singer, whom he met during the years he was preparing for the Grand Prix (1881-4); he spent much of his time at the Vasnier residence at Ville-d'Avray; the first of his *Fêtes galantes,* on poems of Verlaine, as well as some other works, is dedicated to her. In the composition class of Guiraud he won a prize for counterpoint and fugue in 1882; the next year he was the winner of the second Prix de Rome, and finally, in 1884, he won the much coveted Grand Prix with his cantata *L'Enfant prodigue.* From the Villa Medici in Rome he sent as the fruit of the first year a fragment of a choral work, *Zuleïma* (after Heine's *Almanzor*), which he later destroyed; he also worked on a composition for the stage, *Diane au bois,* which he had begun in Paris, but this was never finished. The second year he wrote *Printemps,* a symphonic suite, which found no favor with the jury at the Academy. This did not prevent Debussy from following the path on which he had struck out, and, returning to Paris, he composed another cantata, *La Damoiselle élue,* even more advanced; at this time (1887) he also visited London. The work of the last year in Rome (1888) was a *Fantaisie* for piano and orch. The customary performance of the 'envois de Rome' never took place, because the committee refused to put *Printemps* on the program, and Debussy insisted that either all or none be produced. At about that time Debussy became an intimate of a group of French poets of the symbolist school, and was particularly fascinated by Mallarmé; he also made a visit to Bayreuth (1888), where he heard *Parsifal;* he repeated this visit in 1889; in that year he also became greatly interested in Oriental music which was presented at the Paris Exposition, and acquired a taste for exotic musical colors. His early enthusiasm for Wagner soon frittered away, and he became actually antagonistic to Wagner's ideas. Contacts with the Impressionist movement, added to the influence of modern French poetry, contributed to Debussy's mature style, in which formal structure becomes less important, while mood, atmosphere, and color assume special significance. His *Ariettes oubliées* (1888) to Verlaine's words, and *Cinq poèmes* (1890) to Baudelaire's verses, are the first revelations of this new style. He wrote *Petite Suite* for piano 4 hands (1889; arranged for orch. by H. Busser); in 1890 he began *Suite bergamasque* for piano, which includes the most celebrated single piece by Debussy, *Clair de lune* (the title is from Verlaine's poem, which also contains the word 'bergamasque' adopted by Debussy); it is interesting to observe that in the framework of a classical suite, Debussy applies his novel methods of musical coloring. The year 1892 marked the beginning of the composition of his orchestral *Prélude à l'après-midi d'un faune* (after Mallarmé; Paris, Dec. 23, 1894) and his only opera *Pelléas et Mélisande.* Debussy continued his productive work; he wrote a string quartet (1893; designated as *Premier Quatuor,* although it was the only quartet he wrote); the song volumes *Proses lyriques* (1894), and *Chansons de Bilitis* to poems of Pierre Louÿs (1898), the latter being one of his most poetic invocations; another work, also entitled *Chansons de Bilitis,* for two flutes, two harps, and celesta was performed semi-privately (Paris, Feb. 7, 1901) in the form of a mimo-melodrama. Debussy's major composition at the turn of the century was *Trois Nocturnes* for orch. (the first two, *Nuages* and *Fêtes,* were performed in Paris, Dec. 9, 1900; the third, *Sirènes,* for orch. and wordless choir of women's voices, was performed with the others on Oct. 27, 1901). On Oct. 19, 1899, Debussy married Rosalie Texier. (The *Nocturnes* are dedicated to her under the affectionate nickname 'Lily-Lilo.') However, in 1904 he eloped with Mme. Emma Bardac, the wife of a banker; Rosalie shot herself in despair, but recovered; the divorce followed on Aug. 2, 1904, and Debussy finally married Mme. Bardac. A daughter born to this marriage ('Chouchou,' to whom Debussy dedicated his *Children's Corner*), died at the age of fourteen on July 14, 1919.—*Pelléas et Mélisande* was produced at the Opéra-Comique on April 30, 1902, after many difficulties, among them the open opposition of Maeterlinck, on whose play the opera was based. Mary Garden sang Mélisande, arousing admiration as well as wonderment as to the reason why an American singer with imperfect French enunciation should have been selected; Maeterlinck's own choice for the part was his mistress, Georgette Leblanc. The opera was attacked violently by some critics for its decadent character, and for many years was a center of musical controversy. Performances followed but slowly; it was produced at the Manhattan Opera House, N. Y., on Feb. 19, 1908; at Covent Garden, London, on May 21, 1909; at the Metropolitan Opera House, N. Y. on March 21, 1925. At various times it was reported that Debussy had completed other dramatic works; in fact, the Metropolitan Opera House even announced its acquisition of the rights for the production of *Le Diable dans le beffroi, La Chute de la maison Usher,* and *La Légende de Tristan;* two versions of Debussy's libretto for *La Chute de la maison Usher* are in existence, but nothing is known of any music for these works beyond mention of it in correspondence or conversations. *La Mer,* his next important composition, was completed at Eastbourne, England, in March 1905; it was first performed by Chevillard in Paris, Oct. 15, 1905. Then followed the orchestral suite *Images,* of which *Ibéria* (1908), descriptive of a Spanish fiesta, with guitar-like strumming on the violins, was the most successful. On Dec. 18, 1908, Harold Bauer played the first performance, at the Cercle Musical in Paris, of Debussy's *Children's Corner;* an orchestration by Caplet was performed in Paris on March 25, 1911. In 1908 Debussy conducted *La Mer* and *Prélude à l'après-midi d'un faune* in London; in 1909 he appeared there again to conduct the *Nocturnes;* following this he filled various engagements as conductor in Paris, Vienna, and Budapest (1910), Turin (1911), Moscow and St. Petersburg (1913), and The Hague, Amsterdam, and Rome (1914). Diaghilev produced his ballet, *Jeux,* in Paris, May 15, 1913. Debussy contemplated an American tour with the violinist Arthur Hartmann in 1914, but abandoned the idea because of illness; thereafter his health failed rapidly owing to cancer, and, after two operations, he finally succumbed. Debussy's last appearance in public was on May 5, 1917, when he played (with Gaston Poulet) the piano part of his violin sonata.

Debussy is regarded as the creator and chief protagonist of musical Impressionism, despite the fact that he deprecated the term and denied his role in the movement. This, however, cannot alter the essential truth that, like Monet in painting and Mallarmé in poetry, Debussy created a style peculiarly sensitive to musical mezzotint from a palette of half-lit delicate colors. To accomplish the desired effect, Debussy introduced many novel technical devices. He made use of the Oriental pentatonic scale for exotic evocations, and of the whole-tone scale (which he did not invent, however; samples of its use are found in Glinka and Liszt); he emancipated dissonance, so that unresolved discords freely followed one another; he also revived the archaic practice of consecutive perfect intervals (particularly fifths and fourths). In Debussy's formal constructions, traditional development is abandoned, and the themes themselves are shortened and rhythmically sharpened; in instrumentation, the role of individual instruments is greatly enhanced and the dynamic range subtilized.

These applications aroused intense criticism on the part of traditionalists; a book *Le Cas Debussy,* published in 1910, gave expression to this opposition; see also N. Slonimsky, *Lexicon of Musical Invective,* N. Y., 1953.

PUBLISHED WORKS: — For the stage: *Pelléas et Mélisande,* opera (1892-1902); *Le Martyre de Saint Sébastien,* music to the mystery play by d'Annunzio, for soli, chorus, and orch. (1911); *Jeux,* ballet (1912); *Khamma,* ballet (1912). Choral works: *Printemps,* for women's voices (1882); *Invocation,* for men's voices (1883); *L'Enfant prodigue,* cantata (1884); *La Damoiselle élue,* for soli, chorus and orch. (1887-8); *Trois Chansons de Charles d'Orléans,* for unaccompanied chorus (1908); *Ode à la France,* for solo, chorus, and orch. (1916-17). For orch.: *Printemps,* symph. suite (1886-7); *Fantaisie* for piano and orch. (1888-9); *Prélude à l'Après-midi d'un faune* (1892-4); *Nocturnes* (1893-9); *La Mer,* 3 symph. sketches: 1. *De l'aube à midi sur la mer,* 2. *Jeux de vagues,* 3. *Dialogue du vent et de la mer* (1903-5); incidental music to Shakespeare's *King Lear* (1904); *Danse sacrée* and *Danse profane,* for harp and strings (1904); *Images: Gigues, Ibéria, Rondes de Printemps* (1906-12). Chamber music: String quartet (1893); *Rapsodie* for saxophone and piano (1903-5; also with orchl. accomp.); *Première rapsodie* for clarinet and piano (1909-10); *Petite pièce* for do. (1910); *Syrinx,* for flute alone (1912); cello sonata (1915); Sonata for flute, viola and harp (1915); violin sonata (1916-17). For piano solo: *Danse bohémienne* (1880); *Deux Arabesques* (1888); *Rêverie, Ballade, Danse, Valse romantique, Nocturne* (1890); *Suite bergamasque* (1890-1905); *Mazurka* (1891); *Pour le Piano* (1896-1901); *Estampes* (1903); *D'un cahier d'esquisses* (1903); *Masques* (1904); *L'Isle joyeuse* (1904); *Images,* 1st series (1905); *Images,* 2nd series (1907); *Children's Corner* (1906-8); *Hommage à Haydn* (1909); *La plus que lente* (1910); *Douze Préludes* (1st book, 1910; 2nd book, 1910-13); *La Boîte à joujoux,* children's ballet (1913); *Berceuse héroïque pour rendre hommage à S.M. le Roi Albert Ier de Belgique et à ses soldats* (1914); 2 books of *Douze Études* (1915). For piano duet: one movement of a *Symphonie en si* (1880; intended for orch.); *Triomphe de Bacchus* (1881); *Petite suite* (1889); *Marche écossaise sur un thème populaire* (1891: also for orch.); *Six Épigraphes antiques* (1914). For 2 pfs.: *Lindaraja* (1901); *En blanc et noir* (1915). 60 songs to texts by Verlaine, Bourget, Villon, Baudelaire, Louÿs, Girod, Mallarmé, and others. Various arrangements and orchestrations. Also *Masques et Bergamasques,* scenario for a ballet written in 1910.

UNPUBLISHED WORKS:—For the stage: *Rodrigue et Chimène,* opera (unfinished; 1891-2); *F. E. A.* (*Frères en art*), 3 scenes of a play (1900; with René Peter); *Le Diable dans le beffroi* (orchestral sketch for scene 1; 1903); 2 versions of a libretto for *La Chute de la maison Usher* (after Poe; 1908-18). Choral works: *Daniel,* cantata (1880-4); *Le Gladiateur* (1883); *Printemps* (1884). For orch.: *Intermezzo* (after a passage from Heine's *Intermezzo;* 1882; also arranged for piano duet). Chamber music: Trio in G for piano, violin, and cello (1880); *Chansons de Bilitis,* incidental music for Louÿs' poems, for 2 flutes, 2 harps, and celesta (1900). Songs: *Caprice* (1880); *Chanson espagnole* for 2 voices, *Rondel chinois, Romance, Aimons-nous, La Fille aux cheveux de lin, Eclogue* (1880-4); *Berceuse* for the play *La Tragédie de la mort* (1908). An intermezzo for cello and piano was found by Gregor Piatigorsky in Paris, 1938.—Debussy also contributed numerous criticisms and essays to the 'Revue Blanche,' 'Gil Blas,' 'Musica,' 'Mercure de France,' 'La Revue S.I.M.,' etc. Collected essays and criticisms publ. in various journals were issued as *Monsieur Croche, anti-dilettante* (Paris, 1923; English transl. 1928, 1948).

BIBLIOGRAPHY:—L. Gilman, *D.'s 'Pelléas et Mélisande'* (N. Y., 1907); Mrs. F. Liebich, *C.-A. D.* (London, 1908); L. Laloy, *C. D.* (Paris, 1909); F. Santoliquido, *Il Dopo-Wagner, C. D. e R. Strauss* (Rome, 1909); C. Caillard and J. de Berys, *Le cas D.* (Paris, 1910); G. Setaccioli, *D. è un innovatore?* (Rome, 1910); M. Rivière, *Études* (Paris, 1911); O. Séré, *Musiciens français d'aujourd'hui* (Paris, 1911); R. Rolland, *Musiciens d'aujourd'hui* (Paris, 1912); D. Chennevière, *D. et son œuvre* (Paris, 1913); C. Paglia, *Strauss, Debussy, e compagnia bella* (Bologna, 1913); G. Jean-Aubry, *La Musique française d'aujourd'hui* (Paris, 1916); E. Newman, *The Development of D.,* in 'The Mus. Times' (May and Aug., 1918); G. Jean-Aubry, *Some Recollections of D.,* in the 'Mus. Times' (May, 1918; full list of comps. and writings); L. S. Liebich, *An Englishwoman's Memories of D.,* in 'The Mus. Times' (June, 1918); G. Jean-Aubry, *C. D.,* in the 'Mus. Quarterly' (Oct., 1918); J.-G. Prod'homme, *C.-A. D.,* in the 'Mus. Quarterly' (Oct., 1918); A. Lualdi, *C. D. La sua Arte e la sua Parabola,* in 'Rivista Musicale Italiana' (vol. XXV, 2; 1918); Guido M. Gatti, *The Piano Works of C. D.,* in the 'Mus. Quarterly' (July, 1921); A. Cortot, *The Piano Music of C. D.* (1922); L. Fabian, *D.* (Munich, 1923); André Suarès, *D.* (Paris, 1923; new ed.

1936); E. Gianturco, *C. D.* (Naples, 1923); J. G. Palache, *D. as Critic,* in the 'Mus. Quarterly' (July, 1924); L. Perrachio, *L'opera pianistica di Cl. D.* (Milan, 1924); F. H. Shera, *D. and Ravel* (London, 1925); M. Emmanuel, *Pelléas et Mélisande* (Paris, 1926); Rient van Sant, *D.* (Hague, 1926); F. Gysi, *D.* (*Zürich,* 1926); M. Arconada, *En torno a D.* (Madrid, 1926); J. Durand, *Lettres de C. D. à son editeur* (Paris, 1927); Léon Vallas, *Les idées de D., musicien français* (Paris, 1927; in Engl., 1929); Ch. Koechlin, *D.* (Paris, 1927); J. Fr. Cooke, *D.* (Philadelphia, 1928); A. Coeuroy, *D.* (1930); M. Boucher, *D.* (1930); J. Lépine, *La vie de C. D.* (1930); R. Peter, *D.* (1931; augmented ed., 1944); M. Dumesnil, *How to Play and Teach D.* (N. Y., 1932); Ernst Decsey, *D.* (1933; new ed. 1936); Léon Vallas, *C. D. et son temps* (Paris, 1932; in English, London, 1933); Andreas Liess, *C. D. Das Werk in Zeitbild,* 2 vols. (Strasbourg, 1936); Ed. Lockspeiser, *D.* (London, 1936; revised 1951); id., *Mussorgsky and D.,* in the 'Mus. Quarterly' (Oct., 1937); Oscar Thompson, *D., Man and Artist* (N. Y., 1937); H. F. Kölsch, *Der Impressionismus bei D.* (Düsseldorf, 1937); M. Dumesnil, *C.D., Master of Dreams* (N. Y., 1940); H. Strobel, *C. D.* (Zürich, 1940); R. Paoli, *D.* (Florence, 1941); D.: *Lettres à deux amis* (Paris, 1942); G. Schaeffner, *C.D. und das Poetische* (Bern, 1943); L. Laloy, *C.D.* (Paris, 1944); Léon Vallas, *C.D.* (Paris, 1944); D.: *Correspondence avec Pierre Louys* (Paris, 1945); D.: *Correspondance avec d'Annunzio* (Paris, 1948); Guy Ferchault, *C.D., musicien français* (Paris, 1948); Rollo H. Myers, *D.* (London, 1948); H. B. Harvey, *Claude of France; the Story of Debussy* (N. Y., 1948); W. Danckert, *C.D.* (Berlin, 1948); E. Robert Schmitz, *The Piano Works of C.D.* (N. Y., 1950); A. Gauthier, *D., documents iconographiques* (Geneva, 1952); A. Colea, *Pelléas et Mélisande, analyse poétique et musicale* (Paris, 1952); J. van Ackere, *Pelléas et Mélisande* (Brussels, 1952); Germaine and D.E. Inghelbrecht, *D.* (Paris, 1953); J. d'Almendre, *Les modes grégoriens dans l'œuvre de C.D.* (Paris, 1953); Victor Seroff, *Debussy, Musician of France* (N. Y., 1956).

Dechevrens (dŭ-shŭ-vrăhn'), **Antoine,** Swiss musicologist; b. Chêne, n. Geneva, Nov. 3, 1840; d. Geneva, Jan. 17, 1912. Entered Jesuit Order in 1861; prof. of theology and philosophy at Univ. of Angers; devoted himself to the study of the Gregorian Chant and of neume notation. Publ. *Du rythme dans l'hymnographie latine* (1895); *Études de science musicale* (3 vols., Paris, 1898); *Composition musicale et composition littéraire* (Paris, 1910); also publ. a study on Chinese music in 'Sammelbände der Internationalen Musik-Gesellschaft,' vol. II.

Decreus (dŭ-krös), **Camille,** French pianist; b. Paris, Sept. 23, 1876; d. Fontainebleau, Sept. 26, 1939. He entered the Paris Cons. in 1885, and studied piano with Pugno; winner of several medals; 1st prize for piano, 1895; 1898-1900 chorus-master at the Opéra; début as pianist in Paris, 1906 (in recital); 1907 soloist with Colonne orch.; appeared with Queen's Hall orch. in 1908, and made tour of England, France and Germany; first tour of U. S. with Calvé (1906); again, in 1908, with Calvé and the violinist Renée Chemet (whom he married in 1909); 1912-14 with Ysaÿe; 1915-16 with A. Tourret; from 1912 lived in Washington as private teacher in the family of Senator W. Clark; then returned to France, where he was appointed (1924) director of the American Cons. at Fontainebleau; also prof. of piano there; lived in Paris. Knight of the Légion d'Honneur. Wrote many piano compositions and songs, publ. in France and the U. S.

Decsey (dĕh'-tchē), **Ernst,** German music scholar; b. Hamburg, April 13, 1870; d. Vienna, March 12, 1941. Pupil at Vienna Cons. of Bruckner, Schenner, J. and R. Fuchs; 1899-1908 music critic of 'Tagespost' in Graz; then music critic in Vienna until 1938. Author of *Hugo Wolf* (4 vols., Berlin, 1903-6; the standard biography); *Anton Bruckner* (1919); *Johann Strauss* (1922); *Franz Lehár* (1924); *Maria Jeritza* (1931); *Die Spieldose* (1928); and *Claude Debussy* (1933; new ed. 1936).

Deering, Henri, American pianist; b. St. Louis, Mo., Nov. 1894; studied with Artur Schnabel and Isidor Philipp; début in N. Y. in 1925; since then soloist with the leading orchestras of the U. S. (N. Y., Cleveland, Cincinnati, Los Angeles, San Francisco, etc.), also frequent recital tours of the U. S. and Europe; broadcasts; appearances with leading quartets as chamber music player.

Deering (or **Dering**), **Richard,** English composer; b. Kent, c. 1580; d. London, 1629/30 (buried March 22). Educated in Italy; returned to England as a well known musician and practiced in London; 1610, took the degree of Mus. Bac. at Oxford; 1617, organist at the convent of English nuns at Brussels; 1625, appointed organist to Queen Henrietta Maria. Publ. *Cantiones sacrae sex vocum cum basso continuo ad* *organum* (Antwerp, 1597); *Cantiones sacrae quinque vocum* (1617); *Cantica sacra ad melodium madrigalium elaborato senis vocibus* (Antwerp, 1618); *Cantiones sacrae quinque vocum* (1619); 2 books of *Canzonette* for 3 and 4 voices respectively (1620; author's name given as 'Richardo Diringo Inglese'); *Cantica sacra ad duos et tres voces, composita cum basso continuo ad organum* (posthumous; London, 1662). Sir Frederick Bridge ed. and publ. an elaborate work of Deering's entitled *The Cryes of London.* Various other compositions (anthems, motets, viol music), in MS, are preserved in the libraries of the British Museum, Christ Church, Oxford, the Royal College of Music, Peterhouse, Cambridge, Durham Cathedral, etc.—Cf. Jeffrey Pulver, 'Biographical Dictionary of Old English Music' (1923; 2nd ed. 1927); E. H. Meyer, *Die mehrstimmige Spielmusik des 17. Jahrhunderts in Nord- und Mitteleuropa* (Kassel, 1934); P. Platt, *Deering's Life and Training,* in 'Music & Letters' (Jan., 1952); E. Brennecke, *The Country Cryes of Richard Deering,* in the 'Mus. Quarterly' (July, 1956).

de Falla. See **Falla.**

Defauw, Désiré, Belgian conductor and violinist; b. Ghent, Sept. 5, 1885. Pupil of Johan Smit (violin); from 1914-18, leader of his own quartet (with L. Tertis, C. Woodhouse, E. Doehard); was professor at the Antwerp Cons.; later conductor of the Defauw Concerts in Brussels; also conductor of the Royal Cons. Orch. there and director of the National Institute of Radio; guest conductor with the NBC Symph. Orch. in N. Y. (1938); in Sept., 1940, he returned to the U. S.; was conductor of the Chicago Symph. Orch. (1943-47).

Deffés (dŭ-fäss'), **Pierre-Louis,** French composer, b. Toulouse, July 25, 1819; d. there, June 10, 1900. Pupil of Halévy at the Paris Cons., taking Grand Prix de Rome in 1847 for the cantata *L'Ange et Tobie.*

Defossez, René, Belgian composer; b. Spa, Oct. 4, 1905; he studied with his father, then at the Liège Cons. with F. Rasse; received the Belgian Prix de Rome in 1935; was teacher at the Brussels Cons. (since 1937) and conductor at the Théâtre de la Monnaie. Works: opera, *Le subterfuge improvisé* (1939); ballets, *Floriante, Les mousquets,* etc.; oratorio *Le frise empourprée* (1938); *Symphonie wallonne* (1932); *Images sousmarines* for orch. (1939); piano concerto (was selected at the International Pianists' Competition in Brussels, 1956, as the examination piece); chamber music.

Degen, Helmut, German composer; b. Aglasterhausen, near Heidelberg, Jan. 14, 1911. He studied in Cologne with Jarnach; was church organist; appointed instructor of composition at Duisburg Cons. (1937); at the Hochschulinstitut at Trossingen (1947). He is a prolific composer who writes strongly contrapuntal music in a neo-Classical style.—Works: For orch.: serenade for strings (1938); *Capriccio* (1939); piano concerto (1940); organ concerto (1943); concertino for 2 clarinets and orch. (1944); symphony (1945); concerto for cello and chamber orch. (1945); concerto for harpsichord and 6 instruments (1945); chamber symphony (1947); *Concerto sinfonico* (1948); *Triptychon* (1952); 2 ballets: *Der flandrische Narr* (1947-52); *Die Konferenz der Tiere* (1950).—Choral music: 2 cantatas and an oratorio.—Chamber music: piano trio (1943); 2 string quartets (1941, 1950); trio for flute, viola, and clarinet (1950); nonet for winds and strings (1951).—Piano music: 4 sonatas (1938-48); 30 concert studies (1943).—Organ works; pedagogic manuals.—Cf. K. Laux, *Musik und Musiker der Gegenwart* (Essen, 1949), pp. 57-64.

Degeyter (dŭ-gā-tär'), **Pierre,** b. Oct. 8, 1849; d. St. Denis, near Paris, Sept. 27, 1932. Originally a wood-carver, he wrote the famous workers' song *Internationale* in 1888. The authorship was contested by his brother, **Adolphe,** a blacksmith (b. 1858; d. Lille, Feb. 15, 1917), but after 18 years of litigation the Paris Appellate Court decided in favor of Pierre.

Degner, Erich Wolf, German composer; b. Hohenstein-Ernstthal, April 8, 1858; d. Berka, near Weimar, Nov. 18, 1908. Studied at the Grand-ducal school of music at Weimar, and later at Würzburg; taught at Regensburg and Gotha; 1885, director of the music school at Pettau, Styria; 1888, instructor at the Grand-ducal music school at Weimar; 1891, director of the music school of the Styrian Music Society at Graz; in 1902 again in Weimar as director of the music school.—Works: Symphony for organ and orch.; *Maria und die Mutter,* for soli, chorus and orch.; pieces for piano; songs; publ. *Anleitung und Beispiele zum Bilden von Kadenzen* (1902). The greater part of his works have remained in MS.—Cf. R. Mojsisowicz, *Erich Wolf Degner* (1909).

Dehn, Siegfried Wilhelm, famous German music theorist; b. Altona, Feb. 25, 1799; d. Berlin, April 12, 1858. Law-student at Leipzig, 1819-25; also studied harmony and cello playing. Adopted music as his profession in 1829, after losing his fortune; studied theory assiduously with Bernhard Klein in Berlin; and at Meyerbeer's instance (1842) was appointed librarian of the music department of the Royal Library, for his labors in which he was made Royal Professor in 1849. From 1842-8 he was also editor of the 'Caecilia' (Gottfried Weber's paper), to which he contributed valuable articles. Dehn was a profound theorist, and very successful as a teacher of theory, numbering among his pupils Anton Rubinstein, Th. Kullak, Glinka, Kiel, Heinrich Hofmann, etc. He publ. a *Theoretisch-praktische Harmonielehre* (Berlin, 1840; 2nd ed. Leipzig, 1858; his most important work); an *Analyse dreier Fugen aus J. S. Bachs Wohltemperiertem Clavier und einer Vokaldoppelfuge G. M. Buononcinis* (Leipzig, 1858); *Eine Sammlung älterer Musik aus dem 16. und 17. Jahrhundert* (Berlin; 12 books of vocal compositions *a* 4-10); a translation of Delmotte's work on Orlandus Lassus, *Biogr. Notiz über Roland de Lattre* (Vienna, 1837). A posthumous *Lehre vom Kontrapunkt, dem Kanon und der Fuge* (Berlin, 1859; 2nd ed. 1883) was edited by B. Scholz.

Deis (dīs), **Carl,** American music editor; b. New York, March 7, 1883. He began studying piano at age of 4 under supervision of parents (his father was bass-trombone player in N. Y. Symph. Orch.); at the age of 8, studied at the National Cons. of Music; at the age of 10, at the N. Y. College of Music; 1906, conductor of Saenger Friday Morning Choral Club; voice teacher and choral director at Peddie Institute for Boys, N. Y., Collegiate School for Girls, and Veltin School; 1909-22, accompanist of MacDowell Chorus, Schola Cantorum; 1917-19, organist at Temple Emanu-El; 1919-33, organist at the Society for Ethical Culture. He was for over 30 years (1917-1953) music editor of G. Schirmer, Inc.; his own works include numerous songs (*New Year's Day, The Flight of the Moon, Come Down to Kew, The Drums, Were I a Star,* etc.); in MS, compositions for strings and piano pieces.

Deiters (dī'-ters), **Hermann,** German writer on music, b. Bonn, June 27, 1833; d. Koblenz, May 11, 1907. Studied jurisprudence in Bonn, where he took the degrees of *Dr. jur.* and *Dr. phil.* in 1858. Teacher in the gymnasia at Bonn (1858) and Düren (1869); director of gymnasia at Konitz (1874), Posen (1878), and Bonn (1883); 'Provincial-Schulrath' at Koblenz (1885); assistant in the Ministry of Public Worship, at Berlin (1890); retired in 1903, living thereafter in Koblenz. Deiters wrote many musical articles for the 'Deutsche Musikzeitung,' for the 'Allgemeine musikalische Zeitung,' and other journals. He contributed several music biographies to Meyer's 'Konversations-Lexikon' (3d ed.); wrote a biography of Brahms in Waldersee's 'Sammlung Mus. Vorträge' 1882, 1898). His greatest achievement was his masterly translation into German of Thayer's *Life of Beethoven,* with critical comments by Deiters (Berlin 1866-79, in 3 vols.; 2nd ed., with 2 additional vols., edited by Riemann, Berlin, 1910-11).

Dejdler, Rochus, Austrian composer; b. Oberammergau, Jan. 15, 1779; d. Vienna, Oct. 15, 1822. He wrote the music of the Passion play still in use at Oberammergau.

Dejoncker, Theodore, Belgian composer; b. Brussels, April 11, 1894. He studied with Gilson; is a member of the 'Groupe des Synthétistes' with Poot and others; has written an overture, *Brutus;* 3 symphonies; *Portrait of Bernard Shaw,* for orch.; string quartet; saxophone quartet; songs.

De Jong, Marinus, Belgian composer of Dutch birth; b. Osterhout, Holland, Aug. 14, 1891. He studied with Mortelmans at the Antwerp Cons. He developed a neo-Impressionistic style, with polytonal counterpoint as its mainstay. Among his works are a cantata, *Hiawatha,* quartet for 4 cellos, etc. He visited America in 1921, and gave a piano recital in New York on Feb. 7, 1921.

De Koven, Henry Louis Reginald, American composer; b. Middletown, Conn., April 3, 1859; d. Chicago, Jan. 16, 1920. He was educated in Europe from 1870, taking his degree at St. John's College, Oxford, in 1879. Before this he studied piano under W. Speidel at Stuttgart, and after graduation studied there another year under Lebert (piano) and Pruckner (harmony). After a six-months' course in Frankfurt under Dr. Hauff (composition), he studied singing with Vannucini at Florence, and operatic composition under Genée in Vienna and Delibes in Paris. In 1902 he organized the Philh. Orch. at Washington, D. C., which he conducted for three seasons. He was music critic for the Chicago 'Evening Post' (1889-90), 'Harper's Weekly' (1895-7), N. Y. 'World' (1898-1900 and 1907-12), and later for the N. Y. 'Herald.' As a composer of operettas he had great success.—Works: the operettas *The Begum* (Philadelphia, Nov. 7, 1887); *Don Quixote* (Boston, Nov. 18, 1889); *Robin Hood* (his best-known work; Chicago,

June 9, 1890; London, Jan. 5, 1891; the celebrated song, *O Promise Me,* was written for the London performances); *The Fencing Master* (Boston, 1892); *The Knickerbockers* (Boston, 1893); *The Algerian* (Philadelphia, 1893); *Rob Roy* (Detroit, 1894); *The Tzigane* (N. Y., 1895); *The Mandarin* (Cleveland, 1896); *The Paris Doll* (Hartford, Conn., 1897); *The Highwayman* (New Haven, 1897); the following all had their premières in N. Y.: *The Tree Dragoons* (1899); *Red Feather* (1903); *Happyland* (1905); *Student King* (1906); *The Golden Butterfly* (1907); *The Beauty Spot* (1909); *The Wedding Trip* (1911); *Her Little Highness* (1913). A grand opera, *The Canterbury Pilgrims,* was produced at the Metropolitan Opera House on March 8, 1917; another opera, *Rip van Winkle,* was performed by the Chicago Opera Co. (Jan. 2, 1920). Besides these, he wrote some 400 songs and incidental pieces, including an orchestral suite (MS) and a piano sonata. —Cf. Anna de Koven, *A Musician and his Wife* (N. Y., 1926).

Delage (dŭ-lahzh'), **Maurice**, French composer; b. Paris, Nov. 13, 1879. He was engaged as a clerk in a maritime agency in Paris and in a fishery in Boulogne; in 1900 was in the army; then became interested in music and took lessons with Ravel. Subsequently he made voyages to the Orient, and was greatly impressed with Japanese art. His music reveals Oriental traits in subject matter as well as in melodic progressions. An ardent follower of Debussy's principles, Delage writes music in a highly subtilized manner and distinctive instrumental colors. After 1920 he lived mostly in Paris.—Works: symph. poem, *Conte par la mer;* several songs with small orch.; *4 poèmes hindous* (1921); *Roses d'octobre* (1922); *Sept Haï-Kaï* (1923); *Trois chants de la Jungle* (1935); *Deux fables de La Fontaine* (1949); *In Morte* (1951); also a string quartet (1948).

De Lamarter, Eric, American composer; b. Lansing, Michigan, Feb. 18, 1880; d. Orlando, Florida, May 17, 1953. He studied organ with Fairclough in St. Paul, Middleschulte in Chicago, and Guilmant and Widor in Paris (1901-2); then was organist of various churches in Chicago till 1936; assistant conductor of the Chicago Symph. Orch. from 1918-36; also conducted the Chicago Civic Orch. He was music critic of the Chicago 'Record-Herald' (1908-9), 'Chicago Tribune' (1909-10), and 'Inter-Ocean' (from 1910); held many teaching positions (Chicago Musical College; Olivet College, Mich., etc.).—Works: ballet, *The Betrothal* (N. Y., Nov. 19, 1918); ballet suite, *The Black Orchid* (Chicago Symph. Orch., Feb. 27, 1931, composer conducting); 3 symphonies (1914; 1926; 1931); overture, *The Faun* (1914); *Serenade* for orch. (1915); overture, *Masquerade* (1916); *Fable of the Hapless Folktune,* for orch. (1917); 2 organ concertos (1920 and 1922); *Weaver of Tales,* for organ and chamber orch. (1926); ballet suite, *The Dance of Life* (1931); *The Giddy Puritan,* overture on two early New England tunes (1921; N.B.C., June 6, 1938; Chicago Symph., March 9, 1942); organ works; songs.

Delaney, Robert Mills, American composer; b. Baltimore, July 24, 1903; d. Santa Barbara, Cal., Sept. 21, 1956. He studied music in the U. S., later in Italy, then in Paris (1922-27) with Capet (violin) and Nadia Boulanger and Arthur Honegger (composition). He won the Guggenheim Fellowship in 1929; in 1933 he received a Pulitzer Prize for his music to Stephen Vincent Benét's *John Brown's Body.* He then occupied various teaching posts; settled in Santa Barbara, California. Works: *Don Quixote Symph.* (1927); *John Brown's Song,* choral symph. (1931); *Night* (after William Blake) for chorus, string orch., and piano (1934); *Work 22,* overture (1939); Symph. No. 1 (1942); *Western Star* for chorus and orch. (1944); 2 string quartets.

Delannoy (dŭ-lan-nwăh'), **Marcel,** French composer; b. La Ferté-Alais, July 9, 1898. He served in the French Army in World War I; then took lessons with Gédalge and Honegger. After a few years of instruction, he produced an effective stage work, *Poirier de Misère* (Paris, Feb. 21, 1927) which obtained excellent success. Other works are the ballet-cantata *Le Fou de la Dame* (Geneva, April 6, 1929); *Cinderella,* ballet (Chicago, Aug. 30, 1931; revised and performed as *La pantoufle de vair* at the Opéra-Comique, Paris, May 14, 1935); a symphony (Paris, March 15, 1934); *Ginevra,* comic opera in 3 acts (Paris, Opéra-Comique, July 25, 1942); *Arlequin radiophile,* chamber opera (Paris, April 1, 1946); *Puck,* fairy opera after Shakespeare (Strasbourg, Jan. 29, 1949); *Concerto de mai,* for piano and orch. (Paris, May 4, 1950); *Travesti,* ballet (Enghien-les-Bains, June 4, 1952); ballet, *Les Noces fantastiques* (Paris, Feb. 9, 1955).

De Lara, Isidore, (real name Cohen), English composer of operas; b. London, Aug. 9, 1858; d. Paris, Sept. 2, 1935. He began to study the piano at the age of 10 with

H. Aguilar; also studied singing with Lamperti and composition with Mazzucato at the Milan Cons. He then went to Paris to study with Lalo; returning to London, he produced an opera *The Light of Asia* (Covent Garden, 1892, originally written as a cantata). From then on wrote one opera after another, and easily secured performances. These were: *Amy Robsart* (London, July 20, 1893); *Moina* (Monte Carlo, March 14, 1897); *Messalina* (Monte Carlo, March 21, 1899; his most successful work); *Sanga* (Nice, Feb. 21, 1906); *Solea* (Cologne, Dec. 12, 1907); *Les Trois Masques* (Marseilles, Feb. 24, 1912); *Naïl* (Paris, April 22, 1912); and *Les Trois Mousquetaires* (Cannes, March 3, 1921).

Delcroix (del-crwăh'), **Léon Charles**, Belgian composer; b. Brussels, Sept. 15, 1880; d. there, Nov. 14, 1938. He studied piano with J. Wieniawski, organ with A. Mailly, and composition with Théo. Ysaÿe in Brussels and Vincent d'Indy in Paris. He conducted theater orchestras in Belgium (1909-27); then devoted his entire time to composition.—Works: For the stage: *Ce n'était qu'un rêve* (1 act); *La bacchante*, ballet (Ghent, 1912); *Le petit Poucet*, opera (Brussels, Oct. 9, 1913); for orch.: a symphony (won the award of the Belgian Academy); *Le roi Harald, Çunacépa, Soir d'été à Lerici, Le val harmonieux; Rapsodie languedocienne; Marche cortège; Sérénade* for clarinet, piano, and orch.; *Elégie et Poème* for violin and orch.; many chamber music works (quartets, quintets, sonatas, etc.); piano works; church music (*Pie Jesu, Resurrexi, Ecce panis*); songs. He wrote a biography of his teacher, J. Wieniawski (Brussels, 1908).

Deldevez (del-dŭ-vā'), **Édouard-Marie-Ernest**, French conductor and composer; b. Paris, May 31, 1817; d. there, Nov. 5, 1897. Pupil, in Paris Cons., of Habeneck (violin), Halévy, and Berton. Was appointed assistant conductor at the Grand Opéra and of the Conservatoire concerts in 1859; professor in Cons. of the orchestral class from 1874; retired from all duties in 1885. He composed the ballets *Lady Henriette* (1844, with Flotow and Burgmüller), *Eucharis* (1844), *Paquita* (1846), *Vert-Vert* (1851, with Tolbecque); *Mazarina, Yanko le bandit;* the 2-act opera *Samson*, and the 1-act opera *Le Violon enchanté;* 3 symphonies; chamber music, church music, songs, etc.; wrote the monographs, *Curiosités musicales* (1873, on difficult and doubtful passages in classical compositions) and *La Notation de la musique classique comparée à la notation de la musique moderne, et de l'exécution des petites notes en général;* also publ. *L'art du chef d'orchestre* (1878); *La Société des Concerts de 1860 à 1885* (1887); *De l'exécution d'ensemble* (1888); and *Le passé à propos du présent* (1892), a continuation of his personal recollections publ .in 1890 as *Mes Mémoires*.—Cf. Ch. Malherbe, *Notice sur Deldevez*, in 'La Revue Internationale de Musique' (1899).

De Leone, Francesco B., American composer; b. of Italian parents in Ravenna, Ohio, July 28, 1887; d. Akron, Ohio, Dec. 10, 1948. He studied at Dana's Musical Institute, Warren, Ohio (1901-03), and at the Royal Cons. of Naples (1903-10); returned to the U. S. and established his home in Akron, where he founded the De Leone School of Music, and organized and directed the Music Dept. of the Univ. of Akron; also conducted the Akron Symph. Orch. He wrote the operas *Alglala* (Akron, O., May 23, 1924); *A Millionaire Caprice* (in Italian; Naples, July 26, 1910); *Cave Man Stuff*, operetta; *Princess Ting-Ah-Ling*, operetta; the sacred musical dramas *Ruth, The Prodigal Son, The Golden Calf* and *David; The Triumph of Joseph*, oratorio; pieces for symph. orch.: *6 Italian Dances, Italian Rhapsody, Gibraltar Suite;* over 400 songs; piano pieces.

De Leva, Enrico. See **Leva, Enrico de.**

Delgadillo, Luis Abraham, Nicaraguan composer; b. Managua, Aug. 26, 1887. He studied at the Milan Cons.; returning to Nicaragua, he became a band conductor and opened a music school, which later became a conservatory. His music is permeated with native rhythm and melos; virtually all of his output is descriptive of some aspect of Latin American culture and history. —Works: for orch.: *Sinfonia indigena* (1921); *Sinfonia mexicana* (1924); *Teotihuacan* (1925); *Sinfonia incaica* (1926; conducted by the composer in Caracas, May 20, 1927); *Sinfonia serrana* (1928); 12 short symphonies, all composed in one year (1953) and couched in different styles, from classical to modernistic; overtures in the styles of Debussy and Schoenberg (*Obertura Debussyana; Obertura Schoenbergiana*, 1955); 7 string quartets; church music; piano pieces in various forms.

Delibes (dŭ-lēb'), **(Clément-Philbert-) Léo**, famous French composer; b. St.-Germain-du-Val, Sarthe, Feb. 21, 1836; d. Paris, Jan. 16, 1891. He entered the Paris Cons. in 1848, Le Couppey, Bazin, Adam, and Benoist being his chief teachers. In 1853 he became accompanist at the Théâtre-Lyrique, and organist at the Church of St.-Jean et St.-François. His first stage-work was the 1-act operetta *Deux sous de charbon* (1855), followed by 12 more of the same class up to 1865, when he was appointed 2d chorusmaster at the Grand Opéra. He then tried his hand at ballet writing, and brought out the ballet *La Source* (produced later in Vienna as *Naila, die Quellenfee*) at the Opéra (Nov. 12, 1866); the next ballet, *Coppélia, ou la fille aux yeux d'émail* (Opéra, May 25, 1870) was triumphantly successful, and has held the boards ever since. *Sylvia, ou la nymphe de Diane* (June 14, 1876) was also successful. After resigning his post as chorusmaster, he succeeded Reber (1881) as professor of composition at the Cons.; and, in 1884, was elected as Massé's successor in the Académie. Delibes' dramatic music is distinguished by melodiousness, vivacity, and elegance of instrumentation. His stage-works also include the operas *Le Roi l'a dit* (Opéra-Comique, May 24, 1873), *Jean de Nivelle* (March 8, 1880), *Lakmé* (April 14, 1883; his masterpiece); *Kassya* (1893; posthumous, completed by Massenet); he left some sketches for a 3-act opéra comique, *Le Roi des Montagnes*. Besides these, a cantata *Alger* (1856); choruses for men's and women's voices; and a collection of 15 Melodies with piano, in German Lied style.—Cf. E. Guiraud, *Notice sur la vie et les œuvres de Léo Delibes* (Paris, 1896); O. Séré, *Musicens français d'aujourd'hui* (2nd ed. Paris, 1911); H. de Curzon, *Léo Delibes* (Paris, 1927).

Delius, Frederick, English composer (of German parentage); b. Bradford, Jan. 29, 1862; d. Grez-sur-Loing, France, June 10, 1934. He showed musical abilities as a boy, and learned to play the piano and violin. His father, who was an export merchant, was eager to have his son take up a business career, but Delius preferred adventure; at the age of 22 he went to Florida, where he cultivated orange groves. In Florida he met the organist, Thomas F. Ward, who gave him a brief course of musical instruction. In 1886 he entered the Leipzig Cons. and studied there with Reinecke, Sitt, and Jadassohn. One of the great events of his life was his meeting with Grieg in Norway; Delius became his friend and admirer; the subsequent style of his music was largely molded by Grieg's influence. In 1888 he settled at Grez-sur-Loing, near Paris, where he remained for the rest of his life, except for a few short trips. In 1897 he married the painter Jelka Rosen; in 1922 an illness set in which gradually developed into paralysis; Delius became a complete invalid, and also went blind. During this period, Eric Fenby, the English composer, served as his amanuensis and wrote down music at the dictation of Delius, including complete orchestral scores. In 1929 Sir Thomas Beecham organized a festival of Delius' music in London and the composer was brought from France to hear it (6 concerts; Oct. 12 to Nov. 1, 1929). In the same year Delius was made Companion of Honour by George V and hon. Mus. Doc. by Oxford. In his music, Delius follows divergent lines of thought; basically a Romanticist, influenced by Grieg, he was at his best in evocative programmatic pieces in small forms (*On Hearing the First Cuckoo in Spring; North Country Sketches,* etc.); but he also could produce brilliant stylizations of folk rhythms of various strains (*Brigg Fair, Appalachia, A Song of the High Hills*); his *Mass of Life* is his only work drawn on a large scale, with philosophic implications; he was also fascinated by possibilities of tone painting (as in his orchestral nocturne, *Paris: the Song of a Great City*). In his harmonic idiom, Delius used tense chromatic progressions, often resulting in clashing dissonances; he also applied Impressionistic devices, particularly the whole-tone scale. His orchestral writing is always lucid, with emphasis on individual instrumental color.—Works: For the stage: the operas *Irmelin* (1890-92; first performance Oxford, May 4, 1953, Beecham conducting); *The Magic Fountain* (1893); *Margot la Rouge* (1902); *Koanga* (Elberfeld, March 30, 1904); *Romeo und Julia auf dem Dorfe* (Berlin, Feb. 21, 1907; London, as *A Village Romeo and Juliet,* Feb. 22, 1910; contains *The Walk to the Paradise Garden*); *Fennimore und Gerda* (after Niels Lhyne by Jacobsen; Frankfurt, Oct. 21, 1919). For orch.: *Florida,* suite (1886-7); *Hiawatha,* tone poem (1888); *Paa Vidderne,* for narrator and orch., after Ibsen (1888); *Marche Caprice* and *Schlittenfahrt* (1888); *Rhapsodic Variations* (unfinished, 1888); *Pastorale* for violin and orch. (1888); *Petite Suite* (1889); *Légendes,* for piano and orch. (unfinished, 1890); *Sur les Cimes,* tone poem after Ibsen (1892); *Legend,* for violin and orch. (1893); *Over the Hills and Far Away* (1895); *Norwegian Suite,* as entr'acte music to Heiberg's *Folkeraadet* (1897); piano concerto (1897; revised in one movement, 1906); *The Dance Goes On,* tone poem (1898); *Paris: the Song of a Great City* (1899); *Life's Dance,* tone poem (revision of *The Dance Goes On;* 1901; first performance, Berlin, Nov. 15, 1912); *Appal-*

achia, orchestral variations with final chorus (1902); *Brigg Fair,* English Rhapsody (Liverpool, Jan. 18, 1908); *In a Summer Garden,* symph. poem, dedicated to his wife (London Philh., Dec. 11, 1908); *A Dance Rhapsody* (Hereford Music Festival, Sept. 7, 1909); *Summer Night on the River* and *On Hearing the First Cuckoo in Spring* (Leipzig, Oct. 2, 1913; first English performance of both pieces, London Philh., Jan. 20, 1914, Mengelberg conducting); *North Country Sketches* (1913-14); *Short Piece for String Orch.* (1915); Concerto for violin and cello with orch. (1915-16); *A Dance Rhapsody,* No. 2 (1916); violin concerto (1916); *Eventyr,* symph. poem, subtitled *Once Upon A Time* (London Promenade Concerts, Jan. 11, 1919); incidental music to James Elroy Flecker's *Hassan* (1920); cello concerto (1921); *A Song of Summer* (dictated by Delius to Eric Fenby in France; London, Sept. 17, 1931); *Fantastic Dance* (London, 1934). Vocal works: *Sea Drift,* rhapsody for baritone solo, chorus, and orch. to poem by Walt Whitman (1903; first performance, Essen, May 24, 1906); *A Mass of Life,* for soloists, chorus, and large orch. (London, June 7, 1909, Beecham conducting); *Songs of Sunset* (1906-7); *On Craig Dhu,* for unaccompanied chorus (1907); *Midsummer Song,* for unaccompanied chorus (1908); *Wanderer's Song,* for unaccompanied men's chorus (1908); *A Song of the High Hills* (1911-12); *Requiem,* "to the memory of all young artists fallen in the war" (composed 1914-18; London, Royal Philh., March 23, 1922); *A Song Before Sunrise* (1918); *Cynara* and *Arabesk* (London, Delius Festival, Oct. 18, 1929); numerous songs (several with orch.). Chamber music: 2 string quartets (1893, 1916-17); 3 violin sonatas (1892, 1915, after 1928); Romance for violin and piano (1896); cello sonata (1917); etc.—Cf. M. Chop, *Frederick Delius,* in Vol. II of 'Monographien moderner Musiker' (Leipzig, 1907); 'Musical Times,' March, 1915; Ph. Heseltine, *Frederick Delius* (London, 1923; new ed., 1931); R. H. Hull, *Frederick Delius* (London, 1928); E. Blom, *Delius and America,* in the 'Mus. Quarterly' (July, 1929); Clare Delius, *Frederick Delius, Memories of My Brother* (London, 1935); E. Fenby, *Delius as I Knew Him* (London, 1936); A. Hutchings, *Delius, A Critical Biography* (London, 1948).

Della Ciaia (del-lăh tchăh'-yăh), **Azzolino Bernardino,** Italian organist and composer; b. Siena, March 21, 1671; d. Pisa, Jan., 1755. He was an organist and also an experienced organ builder; constructed a large organ with 4 manuals and 100 stops for the St. Stephen Church in Pisa. He publ. *Salmi concertati* for 4 voices with instruments (Bologna, 1700); *Cantate da camera* (Lucca, 1701); *Sonate per cembalo* (Rome, 1727); much of his church music is extant in MS. He is regarded by some as an Italian originator of sonata form; his instrumental music, however, is more interesting for its florid ornamentation than for a strict formal development.—Cf. Fausto Torrefranca, *L'impressionismo ritmico e le sonate del Della Ciaia,* in the 'Rivista dei Amici della Musica in Milano' (1913); F. Vatielli, *Una lettera biografica di A. Della Ciaia,* in 'Critica Musicale' (IV, 8/9). Béla Bartók made a piano transcription of a keyboard sonata by Della Ciaia, in 'XVIIth and XVIIIth century Italian Cembalo and Organ Music transcribed for piano' (N. Y., 1930); Luigi Silva arranged *Toccata e Canzona* for cello and piano (1952). Alessandro Esposito edited and arranged Della Ciaia's *12 soggetti, 6 ricercari, messa* and 12 cembalo pieces (Padua, 1956).

Della Corte, Andrea, eminent Italian musicologist; b. Naples, April 5, 1883; teacher of music history at the Univ. of Turin (since 1939) and at the Turin Cons. (since 1926); music critic of 'La Stampa' (from 1919).—Publications: *Paisiello* (Turin, 1922); *Saggi di Critica Musicale* (Turin, 1922); *L'Opera comica italiana del 1700* (2 vols., Bari, 1923); *Piccola Antologia settecentesca, XXIV pezzi inediti o rari* (Milan, 1925); *Disegno storico dell'Arte Musicale* (Turin, 5th ed., 1950); *Antologia della Storia della Musica* (2 vols., Turin, 1927-29; 4th ed., 1945); *Niccolò Piccinni* (Bari, 1928); *Scelta di Musiche per lo Studio della Storia* (Milan, 3rd ed., 1949); *La Vita musicale di Goethe* (Turin, 1932); *Vincenzo Bellini* (in collaboration with Guido Pannain; Turin, 3rd ed., 1952; 2nd *Franco Alfano* (Turin, 1936); *Pergolesi* (Turin, 1936); *Un Italiano all'Estero: Antonio Salieri* (Turin, 1937); *Tre secoli di Opera Italiana* (Turin, 1938); *Verdi* (Turin, 1939); *Toscanini* (Vicenza, 1946; in French, Lausanne, 1949); *Satire e Grotteschi di Musiche e di Musicisti d'ogni tempo* (Turin, 1947); *Le sei più belle opere di Verdi: Rigoletto, Il Trovatore, La Traviata, Aida, Otello, Falstaff* (Milan, 1947); *Gluck* (Florence, 1948); *Baldassare Galuppi* (Siena, 1949); *Arrigo Serato* (Siena, 1949); *Storia della Musica* (3 vols.; in collaboration with Guido Pannain; Turin, 3rd ed., 1952; 2nd ed. translated into Spanish, 1950); *L'interpretazione musicale e gli interpreti* (Turin, 1951); edited song textbooks for the Italian schools. With Guido M. Gatti, he compiled a valuable *Dizionario di musica* (1926; new ed., 1952).

Della Maria, Pierre-Antoine-Dominique, opera composer; b. Marseilles, June 14, 1769; d. Paris, March 9, 1800; son of an Italian mandolinist. He was remarkably precocious; played the mandolin and cello at an early age, and at 18 produced a grand opera at Marseilles. He then studied composition in Italy (for a time with Paisiello) and produced in Naples a successful opera, *Il Maestro di cappella* (1792). He went to Paris in 1796; obtaining a libretto (*Le Prisonnier*) from Duval, he set it to music in eight days, brought it out at the Opéra-Comique (Jan. 29, 1798), and was at once famous. Before his death he finished 6 more operas, 4 of which were produced during his lifetime; a posthumous opera, *La fausse duègne* (completed by Blangini), was produced at Paris in 1802; several church compositions are in MS.

Delle Sedie (sā'-dē-eh), **Enrico,** Italian baritone and singing teacher; b. Leghorn, June 17, 1822; d. Garennes-Colombes, near Paris, Nov. 28, 1907. His teachers were Galeffi, Persanola, and Domeniconi. After imprisonment as a revolutionist (1848), he resumed the study of singing, and made his début at Florence (1851) in Verdi's *Nabucco*. Until 1861 he sang in the principal Italian cities; was then engaged at the Théâtre des Italiens, Paris, and appointed professor of singing in the Cons.; was regarded as one of the best singing teachers in Paris. His basic manuals, *Arte e fisiologia del canto* (Milan, 1876; in French as *L'art lyrique*, Paris, 1876) and *L'estetica del canto e dell'arte melodrammatica* (Milan, 1886) were published in New York in English as *Vocal Art* (3 parts) and *Esthetics of the Art of Singing, and of the Melodrama* (4 vols.). An admirable fusion and condensation (by the author) of both manuals was published in one volume as *A Complete Method of Singing* (G. Schirmer, N. Y., 1894).

Dellinger (del'-ing-er), **Rudolf,** composer and conductor; b. Graslitz, Bohemia, July 8, 1857; d. Dresden, Sept. 24, 1910. Pupil of the Prague Cons.; played clarinet in the city orch. at Brünn, 2d conductor there in 1880; 1883 at the Carl Schulze Theater in Hamburg; from 1893 till death conductor at the Residenz-Theater in Dresden. He produced the operettas *Don Caesar* (Hamburg, March 28, 1885; highly popular), *Lorraine* (ibid., 1886), *Capitän Fracassa* (ibid., 1889), *Saint-Cyr* (ibid., 1891), *Die Chansonnette* (Dresden, 1894; Prague, 1895, as *Die Sängerin*), *Jadwiga* (Dresden, 1901), *Der letzte Jonas* (1910).

Dello Joio (properly Dello Ioio), **Norman,** American composer; b. New York, Jan. 24, 1913 (descended from a musical Italian family). He studied with his father, an organist in New York, and later with his godfather, Pietro Yon; then took lessons with Bernard Wagenaar and Hindemith. He won the Town Hall Composition Award for his *Magnificat* in 1942, and held a Guggenheim Fellowship in 1944-45 and again in 1945-46; taught at Sarah Lawrence College (1944-50). In 1947 he toured Poland as pianist-composer. — Works: operas: *The Triumph of St. Joan* (Sarah Lawrence College, Bronxville, May 9, 1950); *The Ruby* (Bloomington, Ind., May 13, 1955); *The Trial at Rouen* (NBC, April 8, 1956; a different work from *The Triumph of St. Joan*); ballets: *Prairie* (1942); *Duke of Sacramento* (1942); *On Stage!* (Cleveland, Nov. 23, 1945); *Wilderness Stair* (Martha Graham, New London, Conn., Aug. 13, 1948). For orch.: Concertinos: for piano and chamber orch. (1939); for flute and strings (1940); for harmonica and chamber orch. (1942); *Sinfonietta* (1941); *Magnificat* (1942); concerto for 2 pianos and orch. (1942); *To a Lone Sentry* (1943); *Concert Music* (1944); *Ricercari* for piano and orch. (N. Y., Dec. 19, 1945, composer as soloist); Harp concerto (N. Y., Oct. 20, 1947); *Three Symphonic Dances: Variations, Chaconne, and Finale* (Pittsburgh, Jan. 30, 1948); *Serenade* (1948); concertante for clarinet and orch. (1949); *New York Profiles* (1949); *Epigraph* (1951); symphonic suite in three movements from the opera *The Triumph of Saint Joan* (1951). Chamber music: sextet for 3 recorders and string trio (1943); trio for flute, cello, and piano (1944); *Duo Concertante* for cello and piano (1945); *Variations* and *Capriccio* for violin and piano (1949). Piano works: 3 piano sonatas (1942; 1943; 1947); *Duo Concertante* for 2 pianos (1943); *Prelude: To A Young Musician* (1945); *Prelude: To a Young Dancer* (1946); *Two Nocturnes* for piano (1949). For chorus: *Vigil Strange* (1942); *Mystic Trumpeter,* cantata (1943); *Western Star,* with orch., narrator, and soloists (1944); *A Jubilant Song* (1946); *A Fable; Madrigal* (1947); *Psalm of David,* for chorus, brass, strings, and percussion (1950); *Lamentation of Saul,* for baritone and orch. (1954).

Dell'Orefice (dell-oh-rā-fē'-tchĕh), **Giuseppe**, Italian composer b. Fara, Abruzzio Chietino, Italy, Aug. 22, 1848; d. Naples, Jan. 3, 1889. Pupil of Fenaroli and Miceli in Naples Cons.; from 1878, conductor in the San Carlo Theater, Naples; wrote the ballet, *I Fantasmi notturni* (Naples, 1872), and the operas *Romilda de' Bardi* (Naples, 1874), *Egmont* (Naples, 1878), *Il Segreto della Duchesa* (Naples, 1879) and *L'oasi* (Vicenza, 1886); also songs and piano pieces.

Del Mar, Norman, English conductor; b. London, July 31, 1919. He studied composition at the Royal College of Music, London, with R. O. Morris and Vaughan Williams, and also played the violin and the French horn in the student orch. He then studied conducting with Constant Lambert. During the war, he played in Royal Air Force bands, and visited the United States with the R. A. F. Symphony in 1944. After the war he organized the Chelsea Symphony Orch. in London; in 1948 he toured Germany with the Sadler's Wells Ballet Company.

Delmas (del-mahs'), **Jean-François**, famous French dramatic bass; b. Lyons, April 14, 1861; d. St. Alban de Monthel, France, Sept. 29, 1933. Pupil of the Paris Cons., where he won the 1st prize for singing in 1886; début at the Grand Opéra, 1886, as St.-Bris in *Les Huguenots;* then a regular member of the Opéra, idolized by the public, and unexcelled as an interpreter of Wagner, in whose works he created the principal bass parts at all the French premières; he created also the chief roles in Massenet's *Le Mage* (1891) and *Thaïs* (1894), Duvernoy's *Hellé* (1896), Leroux's *Astarté* (1901), Saint-Saëns' *Les Barbares* (1901), Erlanger's *Le Fils de l'Étoile* (1904), etc.; besides an enormous French repertory, he also sang the operas of Gluck, Mozart, and Weber.—Cf. H. Curzon, *Croquis d'artistes* (Paris, 1898).

Delmas (del-mahs'), **Marc-Jean-Baptiste**, talented French composer; b. St. Quentin, March 28, 1885; d. Paris, Nov. 30, 1931; pupil of Vidal and Leroux; won the Prix de Rossini (1911), the Grand Prix de Rome (1919), the Chartier Prix for chamber music, the Prix Cressent and other awards for various compositions.—Operas: *Jean de Calais* (1907), *Laïs* (1909), *Stéfano* (1910), *Cyrce* (1920; perf. 1927); *Iriam* (1921), *Anne-Marie* (1922), *Le Giaour* (1925). Symph. music: *Les deux routes* (1913); *Au pays wallon* (1914); *Le poète et la fée* (1920); *Le bateau ivre* (1923); *Penthésilée* (1922); *Rapsodie ariégeoise* for cello and orch.; chamber music; piano pieces. Author of the books *G. Bizet* (Paris, 1930) and *G. Charpentier et le lyrisme français* (1931).

Del Monaco, Mario, Italian tenor; b. Florence, May 27, 1915. His father was a government official; his mother, a singer. His family moved to Pesaro when he was a child; he studied at the Cons. there, and sang a part in an opera performance at the age of 13 in a theater at Mondalfo, near Pesaro. He began serious study at 19; made his professional début in Milan on Jan. 1, 1941 as Pinkerton in *Madama Butterfly.* During World War II he was in the army. After the armistice, he was engaged to sing at La Scala. He produced a highly favorable impression, and was engaged to appear at Covent Garden, London; also made a successful tour in South America; sang at the Colón in Buenos Aires, in Rio de Janeiro, Mexico City. He made his American début with the San Francisco Opera; was then engaged to sing at the Metropolitan Opera House, where he made his first appearance in *Manon Lescaut* (Nov. 27, 1950). He was a regular member of the Metropolitan Opera Company during subsequent seasons. His repertory in Italian and French roles is extensive.

Delna, Marie (real name Ledan), contralto; b. Meudon, n. Paris, April 3, 1875; d. Paris, July 23, 1932. Pupil of Mme. Laborde; début at Opéra-Comique, June 9, 1892, as Didon in Berlioz's *Les Troyens;* sang there for 6 years with great success; from 1898-1901 at the Opéra; then again at the Opéra-Comique; in 1903 married a Belgian, A. H. de Saone, and retired temporarily from the stage; her reappearance at the Opéra-Comique, in 1908, was acclaimed with great applause; after that she was a prime favorite; in 1910 she sang Orfeo (in Gluck's opera) and Françoise in Bruneau's *L'Attaque du Moulin,* at the Metropolitan Opera House, making a deep impression; then returned to Paris, where she continued to sing at the Opéra-Comique for many years.

De Los Angeles, Victoria (real name Victoria Gomez Cima), Spanish soprano; b. Barcelona, Nov. 1, 1923. She made her début in Madrid in 1944; won an international contest at Geneva (1947); in 1949 toured in Scandinavia, France, England, and South America; sang at the Salzburg Festival (1950); made her American début at Carnegie Hall (Oct. 24, 1950); joined the Metropolitan Opera Company (1950); toured U. S. (1951). She married Enrique Magrina Mir on Nov. 28, 1948.

Delune, Louis, Belgian composer and conductor; b. Charleroi, March 15, 1876; d. Paris, Jan. 5, 1940. He studied with Tinel at the Brussels Cons.; won the Belgian Prix de Rome with his cantata *La Mort du roi Reynaud* (1905); then traveled as accompanist for César Thomson. He lived many years in Paris, and wrote most of his works there; composed *Symphonie chevaleresque;* the opera *Tania;* a ballet, *Le fruit défendu,* piano concerto, violin pieces, etc.

Del Valle de Paz (vah'l 'yĕh dĕh păhth), **Edgardo,** b. Alexandria, Egypt, Oct. 18, 1861; d. Florence, Italy, April 5, 1920. Studied at Naples Cons. under B. Cesi (piano) and P. Serrao (composition); made pianistic tours in Italy and Egypt when but 16; in 1893 he established the 'Circolo Del Valle' at Florence, and from 1896-1914 was director of the journal 'La Nuova Musica' and prof. in the Florence Cons. (from 1890). He publ. a *Scuola pratica del pianoforte,* adopted by several Italian music schools. His opera, *Oriana,* was produced at Florence (1907).

Delvincourt, Claude, outstanding French composer; b. Paris, Jan. 12, 1888; d. in an automobile accident, Bivio di Albinia, Orbetello, province of Grosseto, Italy, April 5, 1954. He studied with Widor at the Paris Cons.; in 1913 received the Prix de Rome for his cantata, *Faust et Hélène* (sharing the prize with Lili Boulanger). He was in the French army in World War I and on Dec. 31, 1915 suffered a crippling wound. He recovered in a few years, and devoted himself energetically to musical education and composition. He was director of the Cons. of Versailles; in 1941 he was appointed director of the Paris Cons. His music is distinguished by strong dramatic and lyric quality; he was most successful in his stage works.—Works: *Offrande à Siva,* choreographic poem (Frankfurt, July 3, 1927); *La Femme à Barbe,* musical farce (Versailles, June 2, 1938); *Lucifer,* mystery play (Paris Opéra, Dec. 8, 1948); two orchestral suites from the film score *La Croisière jaune: Pamir* (Paris, Dec. 8, 1935) and *Films d'Asie* (Paris, Jan. 16, 1937). He also wrote *Ce monde de rosée,* for voice and orch. (Paris, March 25, 1935); some chamber music (trio for oboe, clarinet, and bassoon; violin sonata, etc.); piano pieces, etc.—Cf. W. L. Landowski, *L'Oeuvre de Claude Delvincourt* (Paris, 1948).

Demantius, Christoph, German composer; b. Reichenberg, Dec. 15, 1567; d. Freiberg, Saxony, April 20, 1643. Cantor at Zittau, about 1596; at Freiberg, 1604-43; prolific composer of sacred and secular music, he ranks with Hassler, M. and H. Prätorius, and Eccard. He wrote *Deutsche Passion nach Johannes* (1631; ed. and publ. by F. Blume, 1934); *Triades precum vespertinarum* (1602), etc. Reprints of his works may be found in 'Staatliches Jugendliederbuch' (Peters) and in A. Schering's *Geschichte der Musik in Beispielen* (No. 154); his *Vier deutsche Motetten zu 6 Stimmen* were ed. by Anna Abert and publ. in 1936. He was the author of an instruction book, *Isagoge artis musicae* (Nuremberg, 1605; 10th ed. 1671).

Demarest, Clifford, American composer; b. Tenafly, N. J., Aug. 12, 1874; d. there, May 13, 1946. He was a pupil of R. H. Woodman at Metropolitan College of Mus., New York; organist at Church of the Messiah, N. Y. City; wrote 2 cantatas, *The Shepherds of Bethlehem* and *The Cross Victorious;* a *Pastoral Suite* for organ; *Fantaisie* in C minor for organ and piano (1917); *Rip van Winkle,* for organ (1925); about 30 anthems; songs, etc.; also published *Hints on Organ Accompaniment.*

De Menasce, Jacques. See **Menasce, Jacques de.**

Demenyi, Desiderius, Hungarian composer; b. Budapest, Jan. 29, 1871; d. there, Nov. 9, 1937. He was a pupil of V. Herzfeld and S. von Bacho; ordained priest at Gran, 1893; court chaplain (1897); on 3 different occasions he won the Géza Zichy Prize (with *Ungarische Tanzsuite, Festouvertüre,* and *Rhapsodie*); in 1902 he founded 'Zeneközlöny,' an important Hungarian music journal.—Works: 8 masses; *Hungarian Suite* for mixed chorus; *Scherzo* for male chorus; 2 *Bilder aus Algier; Serenata sinfonica;* an operetta, *Der sieghafte Tod;* several melodramas; many other choral and vocal works, including about 100 songs (mostly to German texts).

Demessieux, Jeanne, French organist; b. Montpellier, Feb. 14, 1921. She studied at the Paris Cons. with Tagliafero and Dupré; played organ at the age of 12 at the Saint-Esprit Church in Paris; toured widely in Europe; in 1952 was appointed professor at the Cons. of Liège; made a highly successful début in the U. S. (1953). She is regarded as one of the best improvisers on the organ; has also composed organ pieces and a *Poème* for organ and orch.

De Mol, Pierre, Belgian composer; b. Brussels, Nov. 7, 1825; d. Alost, July 2, 1899. He was a pupil at Brussels Cons.; took Grand Prix de Rome (1855); was first cellist at Besançon Theater and teacher at the Cons.; later director of the Cons. at Alost. Works: 3 cantatas, *Les chrétiens martyrs, Le dernier jour d'Herculaneum, La fête de Belsazar;* the oratorio *St. Cecilia;* a Mass; 12 string quartets; an opera, *Quentin Metsys.*

Demuth, Norman, English composer and writer on music; b. London, July 15, 1898. He studied with Parratt and Dunhill at the Royal College of Music in London. As a youth he joined the British army in 1915. After the end of the war he played organ in London churches. Later he became a choral conductor; in 1930 became professor of composition at the Royal Academy of Music. His works are influenced mainly by French music; in later years he became better known as the author of many books and unorthodox essays on music.—Works: 5 symphonies (two of which are entitled *Symphonic Study*); *Threnody* for strings (1942); *Overture for a Joyful Occasion* (1946); violin concerto (1937); saxophone concerto (1938); piano concerto (1943); piano concerto for the left hand (1947); 3 violin sonatas; cello sonata; flute sonata; many piano pieces.—Books: *The Gramophone and How to Use It* (London, 1945); *Albert Roussel* (London, 1947); *Ravel* in the 'Master Musicians' series (London, 1947); *An Anthology of Musical Criticism* (London, 1948); *César Franck* (London, 1949); *Paul Dukas* (London, 1949); *The Symphony: its History and Development* (London, 1950); *Gounod* (London, 1951); *A Course in Musical Composition* (London, 1951); *Musical Trends in the 20th Century* (London, 1952); *Musical Forms and Textures* (London, 1953).

Dencke, Jeremiah, 'Moravian' minister, organist, and composer; b. Langenbilau, Silesia, Oct. 2, 1725; d. Bethlehem, Pa., May 28, 1795. In 1748 he became organist at Herrnhut, the center of the European Moravians; came to America (1761) and served the Moravian settlements in Pennsylvania in various capacities. During the Revolutionary War he was warden of the Bethlehem congregation. Dencke was apparently the first both to perform and to write concerted church music in the Moravian settlements in Pennsylvania, and possibly the first to write such music in Colonial America. He was an able composer. The earliest work he is known to have composed in America is a simple anthem for chorus, strings, and figured bass, written in 1766 for the opening of a Provincial Synod at Bethlehem. His finest works are 3 sets of sacred songs for soprano, strings, and organ, composed in 1767-8. The first, written for the annual festival of the 'choir' of small girls, is included in the first volume of the series 'Music of the Moravians in America,' issued by the N. Y. Public Library in 1938. The other sets of solos were written for Christmas services. Dencke's compositions are listed in A. G. Rau and H. T. David, *Background for Bethlehem; Moravian Music in Pa.,* in 'Magazine of Art' (April, 1939).

Denéréaz (dŭ-nā-rā-ahz'), **Alexandre,** Swiss composer and musicologist; b. Lausanne, July 31, 1875; d. there, July 25, 1947. He studied at Lausanne Cons. with Blanchet and at the Dresden Cons. with Draeseke and Döring; in 1896 was appointed professor at the Lausanne Cons.; also taught musicology at the Lausanne Univ.; publ. an original theory of harmony.—Works: 3 symphonies; many symph. poems, cantatas, concerto grosso for orch. and organ, string quartets, organ works, a male chorus, and music to René Morax's *La Dime.* Author, in collaboration with C. Bourguès, of *La Musique et la vie intérieure: histoire psychologique de l'art musical* (appendix entitled *L'Arbre généalogique de l'art musical;* 1919).

Dengremont (dahn-gru-mohn'), **Maurice,** Brazilian violinist; b. Rio de Janeiro, Brazil, Mar. 19, 1866, of French parents; d. Buenos Aires, Sept., 1893; as a child prodigy attracted general notice in Europe in 1877 and some years thereafter.

Dennée, Charles (Frederick), American pianist and pedagogue; b. Oswego, N. Y., Sept. 1, 1863; d. Boston, April 29, 1946. He studied at the New England Cons., Boston; piano with A. D. Turner, and composition with S. A. Emery; also studied repertory with Hans von Bülow during the latter's last visit to the U. S. (1889-90); in 1883 he was appointed teacher of piano at the New England Cons.; an accident to his right wrist caused his retirement in 1897, after he had played almost 1100 recitals; subsequent devotion to teaching was fruitful, for many of his pupils held prominent positions on the faculties of various conservatories and music colleges. He was among the first to give illustrated lecture-recitals in the U. S. A selection of his essays was published as *Musical Journeys* (Brookline, Mass., 1938). Some of his teaching pieces achieved steady popularity with piano students; he also published a manual, *Progressive Technique.*

Denny, William D., American composer; b. Seattle, July 2, 1910. He studied at the Univ. of California (A.B., 1931; M.A., 1933); then in Paris with Paul Dukas (1933-35); later held the Horatio Parker Fellowship at the American Academy in Rome (1939-41). From 1942-45 he was instructor of music at Harvard and asst. prof. at Vassar; from 1945 teaching at the Univ. of California. He has written *Concertino* for orch. (San Francisco, April 25, 1939; composer conducting); Symphony No. 1 (1939); *Sinfonietta* for strings (1940); *Overture* for strings (1945); *Praeludium* for orch. (San Francisco, Feb. 5, 1947); Symphony No. 2 (San Francisco, March 22, 1951, composer conducting); 3 string quartets; viola sonata; choral works.

Densmore, Frances, specialist in Indian music; b. Red Wing, Minnesota, May 21, 1867; studied at Oberlin, Ohio, Cons. (hon. M. A., 1924); then took courses with Leopold Godowsky (piano) and J. K. Paine (counterpoint); began study of Indian music in 1893 at the World's Fair in Chicago, continuing privately until 1907, when she began systematic research for the Bureau of American Ethnology (Smithsonian Institution), including an exhaustive study of the Cheyenne, Arapaho, Maidu, Santo Domingo Pueblo, and New Mexican Indian tribes. She lectured extensively on Indian music, and published a number of books and articles on the subject.—Writings: *Chippewa Music,* a collection of Indian songs in 2 vols. (1910-13); *Poems from Sioux and Chippewa Songs* (words only; 1917); *Tetom Sioux Music* (1918); *Indian Action Songs* (1921); *Northern Ute Music* (1922); *Mandan and Hidatfa Music* (1923); *The American Indians and Their Music* (1926; 2nd ed. 1936); *The Music of the Tule Indians of Panama* (1926); *Some Results of the Study of American Indian Music* (reprinted from the journal of the Washington Academy of Sciences, Vol. XVIII, 14; 1928); *Pawnee Music* (1929); *Papago Music* (1929); *What Intervals do Indians Sing?* (reprinted from the 'American Anthropologist' Vol. XXXI, 2; April-June, 1929); *Yaman and Yaqui Music* (U. S. Bureau of American Ethnology, Bulletin 110; 1932); *Menominee Music* (ibid., Bulletin 102; 1932); *Cheyenne and Arapaho Music* (Southwest Museum, 1936); *Alabama Music* (Texas Folk-Lore Society, 1937); *Music of Santo Domingo Pueblo, New Mexico* (Southwest Museum, 1938). The April 1956 issue of the magazine 'Ethno-Musicology' contains a complete bibliography of her writings up to 1955 (pp. 13-29).

Densmore, John H., American composer; b. Somerville, Mass., Aug. 7, 1880; d. Boston, Sept. 21, 1943. He was educated at Harvard Univ. (B. A., 1904); wrote operettas for the Hasty Pudding Club. His mature works (mostly for chorus) are distinguished by practical adaptability.

Dent, Edward Joseph, eminent English music scholar; b. Ribston, Yorkshire, July 16, 1876. He was a pupil at Eton College of C. H. Lloyd, and at Cambridge of Charles Wood and Stanford; appointed professor of music at Cambridge (1926); Mus. Bac. (1899); Fellow King's College, Cambridge (1902); M. A. (1905); hon. Mus. Doc., Oxford (1931), Harvard (1936); was Raske-Orsted lecturer, Copenhagen (1935); Messenger lecturer, Cornell Univ. (1937). The International Society for Contemporary Music came into being in 1922 largely through his efforts; he was its president from 1922-38 and again in 1945; was also active in organizing an English section known as the British Music Society; president of the Société Internationale de Musicologie since 1931. He helped to produce various old English stage works, particularly those of Purcell (*Dido and Aeneas,* with Kurt Jooss, at Münster, Westphalia, in 1928); contributed to the Encyclopaedia Britannica, Grove's Dictionary, 'Musical Antiquary' (*The Baroque Opera,* 1910; *Italian Chamber Cantatas,* 1911), 'Athenaeum' (1919-24), Tilley's *Modern France* (chapter on French music, 1922), 'Oxford History of Music' (*Social Aspects of Mediaeval Music*), Cobbett's 'Cyclopedia of Chamber Music' (*Italian Chamber Music of the 17th Century*), the 'Mus. Quarterly' (*The Relation of Music to Human Progress,* 1928; *The Historical Approach to Music,* 1937), 'Acta musicologica' (*Music and Music Research,* 1931), E. G. Gardner's *Italy; a Companion to Italian Studies* (*Italian Music;* London, 1934), etc. Also author of *A. Scarlatti, His Life and Works* (London, 1905); *A Jesuit at the Opera, 1680,* in 'Riemann-Festschrift' (1909); *Mozart's Operas, a Critical Study* (London, 1913; revised ed., 1947); *Terpander, or Music and the Future* (1926); *Foundations of English Opera* (1928); *F. Busoni: a Biography* (1933); *Music of the Renaissance in Italy* (1934); *Handel* (1934); translated many opera librettos into English (Mozart, Wagner, Berlioz, Verdi, etc.), published editions of old English music, and revised *The Opera* by R. A. Streatfeild (London, 1932).—Cf. L. Haward, *E. J. Dent: Bibliography* ('Music Review,' Nov. 1946).

Denza, Luigi, Italian song composer; b. Castellammare di Stabia, Feb. 24, 1846; d. London, Jan. 26, 1922. He studied with Serrao and Mercadante at the Naples Cons. Besides the opera *Wallenstein* (Naples, May 13, 1876), which was not especially successful, he wrote about 600 songs (some in Neapolitan dialect), many of which won great popularity. In 1879 he settled in London; appointed professor of singing at the Royal Academy of Music (1898); Chevalier of the order of the Crown of Italy. His most famous song is *Funiculi-Funicula,* which was used (under the mistaken impression that it was a folksong) by Richard Strauss in *Aus Italien.*

Denzler, Robert, Swiss conductor and composer; b. Zürich, March 19, 1892. He studied with Volkmar Andreae in Zürich; from 1912-15 was active as choral conductor in Lucerne; then held posts as conductor at the Municipal theater in Zürich (1915-27); Berlin Opera (1927-32), and again in Zürich (1934-47). He has written a choral symphony, piano concerto, several instrumental suites, and songs.

Deppe, Ludwig, famous German piano pedagogue, b. Alverdissen, Lippe, Nov. 7, 1828; d. Bad Pyrmont, Sept. 5, 1890. He was a pupil of Marxsen at Hamburg in 1849, later of Lobe at Leipzig. He settled in Hamburg in 1857 as a music teacher, and founded a singing society, of which he was the conductor till 1868. Went to Berlin in 1874, and from 1886-8 was court conductor; also conducted the Silesian Musical Festivals established by Count Hochberg in 1876. He wrote a symph.; 2 overtures, *Zriny* and *Don Carlos;* published *Zwei Jahre Kapellmeister and der Kgl. Oper in Berlin.*—Cf. Amy Fay, 'Deppe as Teacher,' in her book, *Music Study in Germany* (1897); H. Klose, *Deppesche Lehre des Klavierspiels* (Hamburg, 1886); Elisabeth Caland, *Die Deppesche Lehre des Klavierspiels* (Stuttgart, 1897; in English as *Artistic Piano Playing,* 1903).

Deprès. See Des Prez.

Déré, Jean, French composer; b. Niort, June 23, 1886; studied at the Paris Cons. with Caussade, Diémer, and Widor; won the 2nd Prix de Rome (1919); living in Paris. Has composed the symph. poem *Krischna,* incidental music for Marlowe's *Faustus, 3 Esquisses* for piano and orch., chamber music, piano pieces, songs. In 1936, he was appointed professor of solfège at the Paris Cons.

De Reszke (rěsh'-kěh), **Edouard,** famous bass singer, brother of the tenor, Jean de Reszke, and of the soprano, Josephine de Reszke; b. Warsaw, Dec. 22, 1853; d. Garnek, Poland, May 25, 1917. He studied with an Italian teacher, Ciaffei, in Warsaw; also was trained by his older brother, Jean. He then went to Italy where he continued his study with various teachers. His professional début was at the Théâtre des Italiens in Paris when he sang Amonasro in *Aida* under Verdi's direction (April 22, 1876). He continued to make appearances in Paris for two seasons, and later sang at La Scala, Milan. From 1880-84 he sang in London with extraordinary success. He made his American début in Chicago as the King in *Lohengrin* (Nov. 9, 1891); then as Frère Laurent in *Roméo et Juliette* at the Metropolitan Opera House, N. Y. (Dec. 14, 1891); his brother Jean made his N. Y. début as Roméo at the same performance. His greatest role was that of Méphistophélès in *Faust;* he sang this part at the 500th performance of the opera at the Paris Opéra (his brother, Jeán, sang the title role) on Nov. 4, 1887; and he selected this part also for his last appearance in America (March 21, 1903). He then retired and lived on his country estate near Warsaw.—Cf. H. Klein, *E. de Reszke: The Career of a Famous Basso,* in the 'Musical Times' (July, 1917).

De Reszke (rěsh'-kěh), **Jean** (properly Jan Mieczislaw), celebrated tenor, brother of Edouard; b. Warsaw, Jan. 14, 1850; d. Nice, April 3, 1925. His mother gave him his first singing lessons. He sang at the Warsaw Cathedral as a boy; then went to Paris, where he studied with Sbriglia. He was first trained as a baritone, and made his début in Venice (1874) as Alfonso in *La Favorita* under the name of Giovanni di Reschi. He continued singing in Italy and France in baritone parts; his first appearance as tenor took place in Madrid on Nov. 9, 1879, in *Robert le Diable.* He created the title role of Massenet's *Le Cid* at the Paris Opéra (Nov. 30, 1885) and became a favorite tenor there. He appeared at Drury Lane, London, as Radames on June 13, 1887 (having previously sung there as baritone in 1874). He then sang at Covent Garden (until 1900). On Nov. 9, 1891, he made his American début in Chicago with the Metropolitan Opera Co. as Lohengrin; he remained with the Metropolitan Opera for eleven seasons. In order to sing Wagnerian roles, he learned German and made a sensationally successful appearance as Tristan (New York, Nov. 27, 1895). His farewell appearance at the Metropolitan Opera House was in *Lohengrin* (March 29, 1901). The secret of his success rested not so much on the power of his voice (some baritone quality remained in his singing to the end) as on the controlled interpretation, musical culture, and fine dynamic balance. When he retired from the stage in 1902, settling in Paris as voice teacher, he was able to transmit his method to many of his students, several of whom later became famous on the opera stage.—Cf. Clara Leiser, *Jean de Reszke and the Great Days of Opera* (London, 1933).

De Reszke, Josephine, Polish soprano, sister of Jean and Edouard de Reszke; b. Warsaw, June 4, 1855; d. there, Feb. 22, 1891. She studied at the St. Petersburg Cons.; first appeared in public under the name of Giuseppina di Reschi at Venice in 1874; sang Marguerite in Gounod's *Faust* (Aug. 1, 1874) with her brother Jean as Valentin; then was engaged at the Paris Opéra, where she made her début as Ophelia in *Hamlet* by Ambroise Thomas (Paris, June 21, 1875); later sang in Madrid and Lisbon; appeared as Aida in Covent Garden, London, on April 18, 1881; her career was cut short by her death at 35.

Dering. See **Deering.**

Desderi, Ettore, Italian composer; b. Asti, Dec. 10, 1892. He studied with Luigi Perrachio at the Turin Cons. and then with Franco Alfano in Bologna. From 1933-41 he was a director of the Liceo Musicale in Alessandria; from 1941-51, teacher of composition at the Milan Cons. In 1951 he was appointed director of the Cons. of Bologna.—Works: *Intermezzi all' Antigone,* for orch. (1924); *Job,* biblical cantata (1927); *Sinfonia Davidica,* for soli, chorus, and orch. (1929); violin sonata, cello sonata; many choral works. He published *La Musica Contemporanea* (Turin, 1930) and numerous magazine articles in Italian and German publications.—Cf. A. Bonacorsi, *Ettore Desderi,* in 'Il Pianoforte' (July, 1926); Mario Rinaldi, *Ettore Desderi* (Tivoli, 1943).

De Segurola, Andrés, Spanish bass singer; b. Valencia, March 27, 1874; d. Barcelona, Jan. 22, 1953. He studied with Pietro Farvaro; sang at the Teatro Liceo in Barcelona; made his American début at the Metropolitan Opera as Alvise in *La Gioconda* (Nov. 15, 1909). For twenty years (1931-51) he lived in Hollywood as teacher; then returned to Spain.

Deshevov, Vladimir, Russian composer; b. St. Petersburg, Feb. 11, 1889; studied with Steinberg and Liadov at the Cons. there. Many of his themes are drawn from folk sources. Among his works are the revolutionary operas, *The Red Hurricane* (Leningrad, Oct. 29, 1924), *Ice and Steel,* based on the Kronstadt rebellion of 1921 (Leningrad, May 17, 1930), and *The Hungry Steppe,* which has to do with socialist distribution of land in Uzbekistan.

Deslandres (dä-lahn'-dr), **Adolphe-Édouard-Marie,** French composer; b. Batignolles, Monceaux, Jan. 22, 1840; d. Paris, July 30, 1911. He was a pupil of Leborne and Benoist at the Paris Cons.; 1862 appointed organist at Ste.-Marie. He wrote the operas *Dimanche et Lundi* (1872), *Le Chevalier Bijou* (1875), *Fridolin* (1876); *Ode à l'harmonie; La Banque brisée;* a patriotic dirge, *Les sept paroles;* many sacred choruses.

Desmarets (dä-mah-rä), **Henri,** important French composer; b. Paris, 1662; d. Lunéville, Sept. 7, 1741. He was regarded as one of the most skilful musicians during the reign of Louis XIV. His first stage work produced was the opera, *Didon* (Paris, Sept. 11, 1693); there followed (all at Paris) *Circé* (Oct. 1, 1694); *Les Amours de Momus,* ballet (May 25, 1695); *Venus et Adonis,* serious opera (March 7, 1697); *Les Fêtes galantes,* ballet (May 10, 1698); *Iphigénie en Tauride,* opera (May 6, 1704); etc. His personal life was stormy and included an abduction, for which he was sentenced to death in absentia and had to flee France. He was then musician to Philip V of Spain, and intendant of music to the Duke of Lorraine at Lunéville. He was able to return to France in 1722 after his marriage to the abducted woman was recognized as valid by the French courts.—Cf. M. Brenet, *Desmarets, un compositeur oublié du 17e siècle* in 'Le Ménestrel' (1883, Nos. 39-42).

Desormière, Roger, brilliant French conductor; b. Vichy, Sept. 13, 1898. He studied at the Paris Cons.; conducted the Swedish Ballet in Paris (1924-25) and the Ballets Russes (1925-29); and later at La Scala, Covent Garden, and in Monte Carlo; was at the Opéra-Comique (1936-44); at the Grand Opéra (1945); conducted the BBC in London (1946-47). In 1950 he was stricken with aphasia and other disorders, and was compelled to give up his career.

Des Prez (dŭ-prā'), **Josquin**, the greatest of the late 15th-century Netherlands contrapuntists; b. c. 1450 in Hainault or Henegouwen (Burgundy); d. Condé-sur-Escaut, as provost of the Cathedral Chapter, Aug. 27, 1521. His name was variously spelled: *Després, Desprez, Deprés, Depret, Deprez, Desprets, Dupré,* and by the Italians *Del Prato* (Latinized as *a Prato, a Pratis, Pratensis*), etc.; while Josquin (contracted from the Flemish Jossekin, 'little Joseph') appears as *Jossé, Jossien, Jusquin, Giosquin, Josquinus, Jacobo, Jodocus, Jodoculus,* etc. His epitaph reads *Jossé de Prés.* However, in the motet *Illibata Dei Virgo* (contained in vol. 9 of the Josquin edition), of which the text is quite likely of Josquin's authorship, his name appears as an acrostic, thus: *I, O, S, Q, V, I, N, D[es], P, R, E, Z;* this seems to leave little doubt as to its correct spelling. Few details of Josquin's early life are known. He was a boy-chorister of the Collegiate Church at St.-Quentin, later becoming canon and choirmaster there; possibly a pupil of Okeghem, whom he greatly admired (after Okeghem's death, in 1495, he wrote *La déploration de Johan Okeghem*); 1475, at the Court of Duke Galeazzo Maria Sforza, Milan, as chorister; 1486-94, singer in the Papal choir under the Popes Innocent VIII and Alexander VI; he was also active, for various periods, in Florence, where he met the famous theorist Pietro Aron, in Modena, and in Ferrara (where Isaak was also). Later Josquin returned to Burgundy, finally settling in Condé-sur-Escaut. As a composer he was considered by contemporary musicians and theorists to be the greatest of his period, and he had a strong influence on all those who came into contact with his music or with him, personally, as a teacher; Adriaan Petit Coclicus, one of Josquin's distinguished pupils (publ. a Method in 1552, entitled *Compendium musices,* based on Josquin's teaching), terms him 'princeps musicorum.' His works were sung everywhere, and universally admired; in them he achieves a complete union between word and tone, thereby fusing the intricate Netherlandish contrapuntal devices into expressive and beautiful art-forms. Two contrasting styles are present in his compositions. Some are intricately contrapuntal, displaying the technical ingenuity characteristic of the Netherlands style; others, probably as a result of Italian influence, are definitely homophonic. —Publ. works: MASSES (in Petrucci's Lib. I, Venice, 1502): *L'omme armé; La sol fa re mi; Gaudeamus; Fortunata desperata; L'omme armé, sexti toni;*—(id., II, 1505): *Ave Maris stella; Hercules, dux Ferrarae; Malheur me bat; Lami Baudichon; Una musque de Buscaya; Dung aultre amor;*—id., III, 1514): *Mater patris; Faysans regrets; Ad fugam; Di dadi; De Beata Virgine; Sine nomine* (these 3 books republished by Junta, Rome, 1526);—(in Graphäus' 'Missae III'): *Pange lingua; Da pacem; Sub tuum praesidium;* some of these are scattered in other collections, and fragments are found in still others; several more masses are in MS at Rome, Munich, and Cambrai.—MOTETS were publ. by Petrucci (8 in the 'Odhecaton,' 1501; others in his books of motets); by Peutinger (*Liber selectarum cantionum,* 1520), and others of the period. —FRENCH CHANSONS were published by T. Susato (1545), P. Attaignant (1549), and Du Chemin (1553).—In modern notation, fragments of his works are to be found in Commer's 'Collectio operum musicorum Batavorum,' Choron's 'Collection' (a Stabat Mater), Schering's 'Geschichte der Musik in Beispielen' (Nos. 59-62), Blume's 'Das Chorwerk' (1929-30, 1932-36), etc.—A complete edition of Josquin's works was begun in 1921 by the 'Vereeniging voor Nederlandsche Muziekgeschiedenis' under the general editorship of A. Smijers; 20 instalments have appeared up to 1957.—Cf. E. Van der Straeten, *La Musique aux Pays-Bas avant le XIXe siècle,* VI (Brussels, 1882); F. de Ménil, *Les grands musiciens du Nord: Josquin de Prés* (Paris, 1897); A. Schering, *Die niederländische Orgelmesse im Zeitalter des Josquin* (Leipzig, 1912); A. Gastoué, *J. des Prés, ses precurseurs et ses emules,* in 'La Tribune de St. Gervais' (1921; pp. 201-23); T. W. Werner, *Anmerkungen zur Kunst Josquins und zur Gesamt-Ausgabe seiner Werke,* in 'Zeitschrift für Musikwissenschaft,' VII, 33-41 (1924); O. Ursprung, *Josquin Des Prez; Eine Charakterzeichnung,* in Bulletin of the 'Union musicologique,' VI, 1 (1926); A. Smijers, in 'Proceedings' of the Musical Association, Session 53 (London, 1926-27; pp. 95-116); M. Antonowitsch, *Die Motette Benedicta Es von Josquin Des Prez* (Utrecht, 1951). See also Gustave Reese, *Music in the Renaissance* (N. Y., 1954).

Dessau, Bernhard, German violinist; b. Hamburg, March 1, 1861; d. Berlin, April 28, 1923. He studied violin with Joachim and Wieniawski; held various posts as concertmaster in Germany and Holland; in 1906 was appointed professor at the Berlin Cons. He was a prolific composer; his violin concerto 'im alten Stil' was widely known.

Dessau, Paul, German composer; b. Hamburg, Dec. 19, 1894. He studied at the Klindworth Cons. in Berlin and later in Hamburg; in 1913 became coach at the

Hamburg Opera; then conducted in Cologne (1919-23), Mainz (1924), and Berlin (1925-33). In 1933, with the advent of the Nazi régime, he was compelled to leave Germany, and traveled in various European cities; also in Palestine; in 1939 he arrived in New York, where he remained until the end of the war. In 1948, he returned to Berlin and resumed his active participation in German musical life, aligning himself with the developments in East Germany. He has written much music for the theater and motion pictures; *Lanzelot und Sanderein* (Hamburg, 1918); two operas for children, *Das Eisenbahnspiel* (1932) and *Tadel der Unzuverlässigkeit* (1932); string quartet; 2 string trios; sonatina for viola and harpsichord; also choral music, particularly songs for the masses. His opera, *Das Verhör des Lukullus,* was presented at the Berlin State Opera on March 17, 1951, as a propaganda performance against military dictatorship, but it was severely criticized in East German newspapers, and was taken out of the repertory.

Dessauer, Joseph, composer, b. Prague, May 28, 1798; d. Mödling, near Vienna, July 8, 1876. He studied piano with Tomaschek and composition with Dionys Weber in Prague. He wrote several operas: *Lidwina* (Prague, 1836); *Ein Besuch in Saint-Cyr* (Dresden, May 6, 1838; his best work); *Paquite* (Vienna, 1851); *Domingo* (1860); and *Oberon* (not performed); also wrote overtures, string quartets, piano pieces, etc.

Dessoff, Felix Otto, German conductor; b. Leipzig, Jan. 14, 1835; d. Frankfurt, Oct. 28, 1892. He studied at the Leipzig Cons. with Moscheles, Hauptmann, and Rietz; then was theater conductor in various German cities (1854-60). In 1860 he became a conductor of the Vienna Opera; also conducted the Vienna Philharmonic Orch., and taught at the Vienna Cons. From 1875-81 he occupied similar posts at Karlsruhe; in 1881 he became opera conductor in Frankfurt. He was greatly esteemed for his musicianship by his many celebrated friends; his correspondence with Brahms was published by the Brahms Society. He also wrote chamber music (piano quintet; piano quartet, etc.).

Dessoff, Margarethe, choral conductor; b. Vienna, June 11, 1874; d. Locarno, Switzerland, Nov. 27, 1944. She was educated at the Frankfurt Cons.; taught there from 1912-17. She organized a madrigal singing group, and traveled with it in Germany (1916-21). In 1922 she settled in America, where she presented interesting programs of choral music (gave the first complete performance in New York of Vecchi's *L'Amfiparnaso,* 1933). In 1936 she went to Switzerland, where she remained until her death. The leadership of the Dessoff Choir, which she established in New York, was taken over in 1936 by Paul Boepple.

Destinn, Emmy (real name Kittl), famous dramatic soprano; b. Prague, Feb. 26, 1878; d. Budějovice (Bohemia), Jan. 28, 1930. She first studied the violin; her vocal abilities were revealed later by Mme. Loewe-Destinn, whose second name she adopted as a token of appreciation. She made her début as Santuzza in Berlin (1898) and was engaged at the Berlin Opera as a regular member. She then specialized in Wagnerian operas and became a protegée of Cosima Wagner in Bayreuth; because of her ability to cope with difficult singing parts Richard Strauss selected her for the title role in the Berlin and Paris premières of his *Salome.* She made her London début at Covent Garden on May 2, 1904, as Donna Anna; her success in England was spontaneous and unmistakable and she continued to sing opera in England until the outbreak of World War I. She made her American début in *Aida* with the Metropolitan Opera Co., Toscanini conducting (Nov. 16, 1908) and remained with the company until 1914. She returned to America after World War I to sing *Aida* at the Metropolitan Opera House (Dec. 8, 1919); retired in 1921. For a few years, following World War I, she used her Czech name, Ema Destinnová, but dropped it later on. Her voice was a pure soprano of great power; she was a versatile singer; her repertory included some 80 parts.—Cf. L. Brieger-Wasservogel, *Emmy Destinn und Maria Laiba* (1908); A. Rektorys, *Ema Destinnová* (Prague, 1936); M. Martínová, *Zivot Emy Destinnová* (Pilzen, 1946).

Destouches (dä-toosh'), **André-Cardinal,** French operatic composer; b. Paris, April, 1672 (baptized April 6); d. there, Feb. 3, 1749. After attending a Jesuit school in Paris, he went as a boy to Siam with his teacher, the missionary Gui Tachard (1686). He returned to France in 1688; served in the Royal Musketeers (1692-96) and later took lessons from André Campra, contributing 3 airs to Campra's opera-ballet *L'Europe Galante* (1697). After this initiation, Destouches produced his first independent work, *Issé,* a "heroic pastorale" in 3 acts

(Fontainebleau, Oct. 7, 1697); its popularity was parodied in several productions of a similar pastoral nature (*Les Amours de Vincennes,* by P. F. Dominique, 1719; *Les Oracles* by J. A. Romagnesi, 1741). Among his other operas, the following were produced in Paris: *Amadis de Grèce* (March 25, 1699); *Omphale* (Nov. 10, 1700), and *Callirhoé* (Dec. 27, 1712). In 1713 Louis XIV appointed him superintendent of the Paris Opéra; in 1728, he became director of the Académie Royale de Musique, retiring in 1730. A revival of *Omphale* in 1752 evoked Baron Grimm's famous *Lettre sur Omphale* inaugurating the so-called "Guerre des Bouffons" between the proponents of the French school, as exemplified by Destouches, and Italian opera buffa.—Cf. K. Dulle, *A. C. Destouches* (Leipzig, 1908); A. Tessier, *Correspondance d'A. C. Destouches et du Prince Antoine 1er de Monaco,* in 'La Revue musicale' (Dec., 1926 - May, 1927).

Destouches, Franz (Seraph) von, German composer; b. Munich, Jan. 21, 1772; d. there, Dec. 9, 1844. He was a pupil of Haydn in Vienna in 1787; was appointed music director at Erlangen (1797); then was second concertmaster at the Weimar theater (1799), later becoming first concertmaster and director of music (1804-8); in 1810 was professor of theory at Landshut Univ.; then conductor at Homburg (1826-42); retired to Munich in 1842.—Works: *Die Thomasnacht,* an opera (Munich, Aug. 31, 1792); *Das Missverständniss,* an operetta (Weimar, April 27, 1805); a comic opera, *Der Teufel und der Schneider* (1843; not performed); incidental music to Schiller's version of Gozzi's *Turandot* (1802); Schiller's *Die Braut von Messina* (1803); *Die Jungfrau von Orleans* (1803); *Wilhelm Tell* (1804); Kotzebue's *Die Hussiten vor Naumburg* (1804); and Zacharias Werner's play, *Wanda, Königin der Sarmaten* (1808); also a piano concerto; piano sonatas; fantasias; variations for piano; piano trio; clarinet concerto; a Mass; an oratorio *Die Anbetung am Grabe Christi.*—Cf. Ernst von Destouches, *Franz von Destouches* (Munich, 1904).

Destranges (dä-trahnzh'), **Louis Augustin Etienne Rouillé,** French music critic, b. Nantes, March 29, 1863; d. there, May 31, 1915. From 1890, editor of 'L'Ouest-Artiste' (Nantes); author of the following publications: *Le Théâtre à Nantes depuis ses origines* (1888); *Dix jours à Bayreuth* (1888); *L'Oeuvre théatrale de Meyerbeer* (1893); *Samson et Dalila de Saint-Saëns* (1893); *Tannhaeuser de Richard Wagner* (1894); *L'Évolution musicale chez Verdi* (1895); *Une partition méconnue: Proserpine de Saint-Saëns* (1895); *Les Femmes dans l'œuvre de Richard Wagner* (1899); *Consonances et dissonances* (1906); *L'Oeuvre lyrique de C. Franck;* also wrote thematic guides to Bruneau's *Messidor* (1877), Vincent d'Indy's *Le Chant de la cloche* (1890) and *Fervaal,* Chabrier's *Briseïs,* Berlioz' *Les Troyens,* Bruneau's *Le Rêve* (1896), Jaques-Dalcroze's *Sancho* (1897), Humperdinck's *Hänsel und Gretel* (1899), etc.

Deswert (or **de Swert**), **Jules,** brilliant Belgian cellist; b. Louvain, Aug. 15, 1843; d. Ostend, Feb. 24, 1891. He played in public at 9, and was a pupil of Servais at Brussels Cons. (1856-8). He became Konzertmeister at Düsseldorf in 1865; first cellist at Weimar in 1868; royal Konzertmeister, solo cellist, and professor at the Hochschule, Berlin (1869-73). He was in Leipzig in 1881, and in 1888 was appointed director of the Ostend Music School and professor at the Ghent and Bruges Cons.—Works: two operas, *Die Albigenser* (Wiesbaden, Oct. 1, 1878); *Graf Hammerstein* (Mainz, 1884); a symphony, *Nordseefahrt;* 3 cello concertos; romances, fantasias, duos, and solo pieces for cello with piano or orch.

Déthier (dā-t'yā), **Édouard,** Belgian violinist; b. Liège, April 25, 1886. Pupil at Liège Cons. (1895-1901); then at Brussels Cons. (1901-2); subsequently taught there (1902-4). He settled in the U. S. in 1906, appearing in recitals with the principal orchestras; taught at the Institute of Musical Art, and at the Juilliard Graduate School.

Déthier, Gaston-Marie, Belgian organist, brother of the preceding; b. Liège, April 18, 1875. He studied at the Liège Cons. (gold medal for piano and organ), and later with Guilmant in Paris; came to the U. S. in 1894; was organist at St. Francis Xavier's, New York; taught at the Institute of Musical Art; in 1915, gave a series of successful sonata recitals as a pianist, with his brother, the violinist.

Dett, Robert Nathaniel, distinguished Negro composer and writer; b. Drummondville, Quebec, Canada, Oct. 11, 1882; d. Battle Creek, Michigan, Oct. 2, 1943, where he was directing musical activities of the United Service Organizations. He studied at the Oberlin Cons. (Mus. Bac., 1908; Mus. Doc., 1926), Columbia Univ., Harvard Univ., Eastman School of Music, Howard Univ. (Mus. Doc., 1924), Univ. of Pennsylvania; won the Harmon Medal (1927) and several literary prizes. Teaching positions: Lane College, Jackson, Tenn. (1908-11); Lincoln Institute, Jefferson City, Mo. (1911-13); Hampton Institute, Virginia (1913-31); Samuel Houston College, Austin, Tex. (1935); Bennett College, Greensboro, N. C. (1937). He toured Europe as director of the Hampton Choir in 1929.—Compositions: Two successful oratorios, *The Chariot Jubilee* (1921) and *The Ordering of Moses* (Cincinnati Festival, May 7, 1937); piano works: *Magnolia Suite* (1911); *In the Bottoms Suite* (contains the popular *Juba Dance;* 1913); *Enchantment Suite* (1922); *Cinnamon Grove Suite* (1927); *Tropic Winter Suite* (1938); choruses: *Listen to the Lambs; O Holy Lord; Music in the Mine; Ave Maria; As Children Walk Ye; As by the Streams; Don't You Weep; Sit Down, Servant; Weepin' Mary; I'm so Glad;* and many others. He also published *Religious Folk Songs of the Negro* (1926) and *The Dett Collection of Negro Spirituals,* in 4 vols. (1936).

Deutsch (doitch), **Otto Erich,** eminent musicologist, specialist in Schubertian research; b. Vienna, Sept. 5, 1883. He studied literature and history of art at the Univ. of Vienna and in Graz; was for a season the art critic of the Vienna periodical 'Zeit' (1908-9); then became a book publisher; was librarian of the important collection of Anthony van Hoboken in Vienna (1926-35). In 1939 he emigrated to England and settled in Cambridge; in 1947 he became a British subject, but returned to Vienna in 1951.—Publications: *Schubert-Brevier* (Berlin, 1905); *Beethovens Beziehungen zu Graz* (Graz, 1907); *Franz Schubert: Die Dokumente seines Lebens und Schaffens* (in collaboration, first with Ludwig Scheibler, then with Willi Kahl and Georg Kinsky), planned as a comprehensive work in 3 volumes containing all known documents, pictures, and other materials pertaining to Schubert, arranged in chronological order, with a thematic catalogue (Munich, 1913; vol. II, part I, publ. in English in a translation by Eric Blom, London, 1946, as *Schubert: A Documentary Biography;* American ed., N. Y., 1947, under the title *The Schubert Reader: A Life of Franz Schubert in Letters and Documents;* catalogue of Schubert's works, prepared by Deutsch for an English ed., in collaboration with Donald R. Wakeling, publ. as *Schubert: Thematic Catalogue of all his Works in Chronological Order,* London, 1951); *Franz Schuberts Briefe und Schriften* (Munich, 1919; 4th ed., enlarged and annotated, Vienna, 1954; English transl., London, 1928); *Schuberts Tagebuch,* a facsimile ed. (Vienna, 1928); *Handel: A Documentary Biography* (N. Y., 1954); edited the series *Musikalische Seltenheiten* (Vienna, 1921); contributed numerous articles of bibliographical and biographical nature on Mozart, Haydn, Beethoven, Schumann, etc. to German, English, and American music publications.

Devčić (děv'-chitz), **Natko,** Croatian composer; b. Glina, June 30, 1914. He studied in Vienna with Joseph Marx; upon his return to Zagreb, became prof. of harmony at the Cons. there. His *Istrian Suite* for orch. is his most successful work; he has further written an *Overture of Youth;* and numerous choral works of a popular nature.

Devienne, François, versatile French musician; b. Joinville, Haute-Marne, Jan. 31, 1759; d. in the insane asylum at Charenton, Sept. 5, 1803. A flutist and bassoonist, member of the band of the Gardes Suisses, bassoonist at the Théâtre de Monsieur (1788), and prof. at the Paris Cons., he was an extraordinarily prolific composer of peculiar importance from the impulse which he gave to perfecting the technique of wind instruments. Works: 12 operas; many concerted pieces for various wind instruments with orch.; overtures; concertos, quartets, trios, sonatas, etc., for flute, piano, and other instruments; *Douze suites d'harmonies à 8 et 12 parties;* numerous romances, chansons, etc.; also a valuable *Méthode de flûte* (Paris, 1795), which went through several editions.

De Vito, Gioconda, Italian violinist; b. in Martina Franca (Lecce), July 26, 1907. She studied at the Liceo Musicale in Pesara, graduating in 1921; then taught at the Bari Cons. In 1944 she was appointed prof. at St. Cecilia Academy in Rome. From 1946-53 she gave concerts in England. She married David Bicknell, English record company executive, in 1949.

Devrient (dŭ-vrē-yăhn'), **Eduard,** German writer on musical subjects; b. Berlin, Aug. 11, 1801; d. Karlsruhe, Oct. 4, 1877. Pupil of Zelter; began his career as a baritone at the Royal Opera in 1819, but after the loss of his voice went over to the spoken drama, without losing his interest in music; he was the author of the text to Marschner's *Hans Heiling,* and also created the title role (1833). His chief work is *Geschichte der deutschen Schauspielkunst* (5 vols., 1848-74); his works concerning music are *Briefe aus Paris* (1840, about Cherubini) and *Meine Erinnerungen an Felix Mendelssohn-Bartholdy und seine Briefe an mich* (Leipzig,

1869). Within weeks after its publication, Wagner issued a polemical pamphlet entitled *Herr Eduard Devrient und Sein Styl* (Munich, 1869) under the pseudonym Wilhelm Drach, violently attacking Devrient for his literary style. Devrient's book was publ. in English in the same year (London 1869; 3rd ed., 1891).

Devries (dĕh-vrēs'), **Herman**, American bass; b. New York, Dec. 25, 1858; d. Chicago, Aug. 24, 1949. He studied in Paris; 1879, début at the Paris Opéra as the Grand Inquisitor in *L'Africaine;* 1880-8, at the Opéra-Comique; then appeared in Brussels, Marseilles, Aix-les-Bains, and Vichy; début at the Metropolitan Opera House as Capulet in *Roméo et Juliette,* Dec. 2, 1898; appeared there until 1899; established his own studio in Chicago in 1900; was music critic of the 'Chicago American'; composed various songs and several pieces for piano and orch.

Devries, Maurice, baritone, brother of above; b. New York, 1854; d. Chicago, 1919. Début at Liège as De Nevers in *Les Huguenots,* 1874; then sang in Toulouse, Antwerp, and Brussels, where, at the Théâtre de la Monnaie, he created the role of Gunther in Reyer's *Sigurd* (Jan. 6, 1884); subsequently appeared in Marseilles and Bordeaux; début at the Metropolitan Opera House, Nov. 18, 1895, singing there for 2 seasons; taught in Chicago afterward.

Deyo (da'yoh), **Felix**, American composer and pianist; b. Poughkeepsie, N. Y., April 21, 1888. He studied piano with his mother Mary Forster Deyo (1857-1947); then at the Brooklyn Cons. of Music; after graduation, he taught there (1911-39). Since 1939, director of the Baldwin, L. I., Cons. of Music; also active as lecturer and music critic. He has written 3 symphonies: *A Lyric Symphony* (Babylon, L. I., Dec. 8, 1949); *An Ancient Symphony* and *A Primeval Symphony;* also 2 piano sonatas, a violin sonata, and numerous piano pieces of a programmatic nature (*Flight of the Dodo Bird,* etc.). His wife Asta Nygren Deyo (1898-1953) was a piano teacher.

Deyo, Ruth Lynda, American pianist (second cousin of Felix Deyo); b. Poughkeepsie, N. Y., April 20, 1884. She studied piano with William Mason and Teresa Carreño; comp. with MacDowell; made her début at the age of 9 at the World's Columbian Exposition in Chicago (1893); concert début in Berlin (March 23, 1904); subsequently played with major orchestras in the U.S. and in Europe; appeared in recitals with Kreisler and Casals. In 1925 she settled in Egypt and devoted herself mainly to composition. In 1930 she completed the full score of a large opera on Egyptian themes, *The Diadem of Stars* (libretto by her husband Charles Dalton; unperformed). The Prelude to this opera was perf. by Stokowski with the Philadelphia Orch. (April 4, 1931).

Dezède (dŭ-zăd') (**Deziades, De Zaides**), **Nicolas**, opera composer; b. Eastern Europe, c. 1740; d. Paris, Sept. 11, 1792. He was active in Paris, where over 15 of his stage works were produced, including *Julie* (1772), *Le Stratagème découvert* (1773), *Cécile* (1781), *Blaise et Babet* (1783), *Alexis et Justine* (1785), *Alcindor* (1787). The overture of his opera *Blaise et Babet* and a Finale, for piano, figured frequently on early American concert programs (see O. G. Sonneck, *Early Concert-Life in America,* Leipzig, 1907).—Cf. A. Pougin, *Dezède* (Paris, 1862).

Diabelli, Anton, Austrian composer and publisher; b. Mattsee, n. Salzburg, Sept. 5, 1781; d. Vienna, April 8, 1858. He was a choir boy in the monastery at Michaelbeurn, and in Salzburg cathedral; studied for the priesthood at the Munich Latin School, but continued his musical work, submitting his compositions to Michael Haydn, who encouraged him. On the secularization of the Bavarian monasteries, Diabelli, who had already entered that at Raichenhaslach, embraced the career of a musician, went to Vienna (where Joseph Haydn received him kindly), taught piano and guitar for a living, and in 1818 became a partner of Cappi, the music publisher, assuming control of the firm (Diabelli & Co.) in 1824. He published much of Schubert's music, but underpaid the composer, and complained that he wrote too much. In 1852 he sold his firm to C. A. Spina. A facile composer, Diabelli produced an opera, *Adam in der Klemme* (Vienna, 1809; one performance), Masses, cantatas, chamber music, etc., which are consigned to oblivion; his sonatinas are still used for beginners. His name was immortalized through Beethoven's set of 33 variations (op. 120) on a waltz theme by Diabelli.

Diack (dē-ăhk), **John Michael**, British vocal pedagogue; b. Glasgow, June 26, 1869; d. London, Feb. 2, 1946. He lived in London as head of the publishing house of Paterson Sons & Co.; published valuable pedagogic works: *Vocal Exercises on Tone-Placing and Enunciation* (1920); *Song Studies* (1920);

Five Minutes Daily Exercises on Vocal Technique (Glasgow, 1920); *Tone Color and Interpretation* (1926); edited *New Scottish Orpheus* (2 volumes; 200 songs); *The Burns Song Book* (50 songs); and choral works of Bach and Handel.

Diaghilev, Sergei Pavlovitch, creator and director of the famous Russian Ballet; b. Government of Novgorod, March 19, 1872; d. Venice, Aug. 19, 1929. He was associated with progressive artistic organizations in St. Petersburg, but his main field of activity was in western Europe. He established the Ballet Russe in Paris; he commissioned Stravinsky to write the ballets *The Firebird, Petrouchka,* and *Le Sacre du Printemps;* also commissioned Prokofiev, Henri Sauguet, Milhaud, Poulenc, Auric, and other composers of the younger generation. Ravel and Manuel de Falla also wrote works for Diaghilev. The great importance of Diaghilev's choreographic ideas lies in the complete abandonment of the classical tradition; in this respect Diaghilev was the true originator of the modern dance.—Bibl.: Diaghilev issue of 'La Revue Musicale' (Dec., 1930); *The Russian Ballet* (London, 1931); C. W. Beaumont, *Sergei Diaghilev* (London, 1933); A. L. Haskell, *Diaghilev, His Artistic and Private Life* (London, 1935); V. Kamenev, *Russian Ballet through Russian Eyes* (London, 1936); Serge Lifar, *Serge Diaghilev: his Life, his Work, his Legend* (London, 1940); C. W. Beaumont, *The Diaghilev Ballet in London, A Personal Record* (London, 1940); S. L. Grigoriev, *The Diaghilev Ballet* (London, 1953); Richard Buehle, *In Search of Diaghilev* (N. Y., 1956).

Diamond, David, talented American composer; b. Rochester, N. Y., July 9, 1915. He studied at the Cleveland Institute of Music (1928-29); then at the Eastman School in Rochester, with Bernard Rogers (1930-34); took additional courses in New York with Roger Sessions and in Paris with Nadia Boulanger. Returning to New York, he devoted his time exclusively to composition; various grants and awards enabled him to continue his work. He received the Juilliard Publication Award for his *Psalm* (1937); Guggenheim Fellowships (1938 and 1941); American Academy in Rome award (1942); Paderewski Prize (1943); a grant of $1,000 from the National Academy of Arts and Letters (1944). His early music is marked by a great complexity of harmonic writing and atonal melodic progressions; later, however, his idiom receded towards neo-Romantic usages, with clear melody supported by basically tonal harmony. The element of rhythm (often derived from natural folk-like patterns) is very strong in all of Diamond's music.—Works: For orch.: *Sinfonietta* (Philadelphia, June 23, 1936); Symphony No. 1 (N. Y. Philh., Dec. 21, 1941); No. 2 (Boston, Oct. 13, 1944); No. 3 (1945; Boston, Nov. 3, 1950); No. 4 (Boston, Jan. 23, 1948); No. 5 (1950-57); No. 6 (Boston, March 8, 1957); *Hommage à Satie* (1934); *Threnody* (1935); *Psalm,* for orch. (Rochester, Dec. 10, 1936); violin concerto No. 1 (N. Y., March 24, 1937; composer conducting, Nicolai Berezowsky, soloist); violin concerto No. 2 (Vancouver, Feb. 29, 1948); 1st suite from ballet *Tom* (1936); *Variations on an Original Theme* (1937; Rochester, April 23, 1940); *Elegy in Memory of Maurice Ravel* for brass, harp, and percussion (or strings and percussion; Rochester, April 28, 1938); *Heroic Piece* (Zürich, July 29, 1938); cello concerto (1938; Rochester, April 30, 1942); *Concert Piece* (N. Y., May 16, 1940); concerto for chamber orch. (Yaddo, N. Y., Sept. 7, 1940, composer conducting); *Rounds* for string orch. (Minneapolis, Nov. 24, 1944; his most successful work); *Romeo and Juliet* (N. Y., Oct. 20, 1947); *The Enormous Room,* after E. E. Cummings (Cincinnati, Nov. 19, 1949); *Timon of Athens,* symph. portrait after Shakespeare (Louisville, 1949); piano concerto (1949); *Ahavah* for narrator and orch. (Washington, Nov. 17, 1954); *Diaphony* for brass, 2 pianos, timpani, and organ (N. Y., Feb. 22, 1956); *Sinfonia concertante* (Rochester, March 7, 1957).—Chamber music: *Partita* for oboe, bassoon, and piano (1935); concerto for string quartet (1936); string trio (1937); quintet for flute, string trio, and piano (1937); piano quartet (1938); cello sonata (1938); 4 string quartets (1940, 1943, 1946, 1951); violin sonata (1945); *Canticle for Perpetual Motion* for violin and piano (1947); *Chaconne* for violin and piano (1947); quintet for clarinet, 2 violas, and 2 cellos (1951); piano trio (1951).—Vocal music: *This is the Garden,* chorus a cappella (1935); *3 Madrigals,* after James Joyce, for chorus a cappella (1937); *Young Joseph,* after Thomas Mann, for women's chorus and string orch. (1944); *L'âme de Claude Debussy,* extracts from Debussy's letters to Jacques Durand (1949); *The Midnight Meditation,* cycle of 4 songs (1950).—For piano: sonatina (1935); concerto for 2 pianos (1941); *Album for the Young* (1946); sonata (1947).

Dianov, Anton Michailovitch, Russian composer; b. Moscow, Feb. 19, 1882; pupil of the Moscow Cons. (graduated 1912);

since 1920 director of the Music School (founded in honor of Mussorgsky) in Moscow. He wrote effective piano pieces, music for violin and piano (*Lyrische Fragmente*), and many songs.

Diaz (dē'ähz) **(de la Peña), Eugène (-Émile)**, French composer, son of the celebrated painter; b. Paris, Feb. 27, 1837; d. Coleville, Sept. 12, 1901. He was a pupil of Paris Cons. (Halévy, Reber); produced the comic opera *Le roi Candaule* (Paris, 1865) and won the government prize for the opera *La Coupe du roi de Thulé* (Paris, Jan. 10, 1873), which, however, proved a complete failure.—Cf. A. Jullien, *Airs variés* (Paris, 1877; pp. 202-10).

Diaz, Rafaelo, American tenor; b. (of Spanish-American parents) San Antonio, Texas, 1884; d. New York, Dec. 12, 1943. He studied music in Berlin; voice in Italy; made his opera début with the Boston Opera Co., Dec. 6, 1911; was a member of the Metropolitan Opera Co. from 1918 to 1936; then sang mostly in concerts.

Dibdin, Charles, English composer; b. Dibdin, near Southampton (bapt. March 4), 1745; d. London, July 25, 1814. 1756-59, chorister at Winchester Cathedral; took lessons there from Kent and Fussell, but was chiefly self-taught in composition; at 15 went to London, was engaged at Covent Garden as a singing actor, and soon began to write for the stage. His first piece, *The Shepherd's Artifice,* was produced at his benefit performance, at Covent Garden, on May 21, 1764. He was engaged at Birmingham, 1763-5, and at Covent Garden again till 1768, when he went over to Drury Lane. Falling out with Garrick, he went to France in 1776, remaining there until 1778, when he was appointed composer to Covent Garden, having up to that time brought out 8 operas. 1782-4, manager of the newly erected Royal Circus (later the Surrey Theatre). After the failure of certain theatrical enterprises, and a projected journey to India, he commenced a series of monodramatic 'table-entertainments,' of which song was a principal feature, and which were extremely popular from 1789 to 1805; in these Dibdin appeared as author, composer, narrator, singer, and accompanist. He then built and managed a small theater of his own, opened in 1796; he retired in 1805 on a pension, which was withdrawn for a time, but subsequently restored. A complete list of some 70 stage-pieces, with or without music, and 30 'table-entertainments,' can be found in Grove's Dictionary. Dibdin also composed numerous sea songs which were very popular at the time (mostly written for his 'entertainments'). He publ. *The Musical Tour of Mr. Dibdin* (1788), *History of the Stage* (1795, 5 vols.), his *Professional Life* (1803, 4 vols.), and various novels—Cf. E. R. Dibdin, *A Charles Dibdin Bibliography* (Liverpool, 1937). His grandson, **Henry Edward Dibdin** (b. London, Sept. 8, 1813; d. Edinburgh, May 6, 1866), was an organist, harpist, and teacher; compiler of the great collection 'The Standard Psalm Tune Book' (1851).

Di Capua, Eduardo, Italian composer of Neapolitan ballads; b. Naples, 1864; d. there, 1917. He earned his living by playing in small theaters and cafés in and around Naples, and later in the cinemas; also gave piano lessons. His most famous song was *O Sole mio* (1898); its popularity was immense, and never abated. Other celebrated songs were *Maria Marì* (1899); *Torna maggio* (1900); *Canzona bella,* etc. Di Capua sold these songs to publishers outright, and so did not benefit by their popularity. He died in extreme poverty.

Dick, Marcel, violinist, violist, and composer; b. Miskolcz, Hungary, Aug. 28, 1898. The famous Hungarian violinist Eduard Reményi was his great-uncle. He entered the Royal Academy of Music in Budapest at 11; studied violin with Joseph Bloch; composition with Kodály; after graduation, joined the Budapest Philharmonic as violinist; in 1921 went to Vienna; was first violist of the Vienna Symph. Orch. (1924-27); a member of the Kolisch Quartet and of the Rosé Quartet. In 1934 he was engaged as first violist of the Detroit Symph.; after a season there, he played in the Stradivarius Quartet in Boston; from 1943-49, was first violist of the Cleveland Orch.; in 1948 became head of the dept. of theory at the Cleveland Institute of Music. His works include a symphony (Cleveland, Dec. 14, 1950); *Capriccio for Orchestra* (Cleveland, Feb. 21, 1957, composer conducting); 2 string quartets (1935, 1938); *4 Elegies and an Epilogue* for cello unaccompanied (1951); sonata for violin and cello (1952); *Essay* for violin and piano (1955); also songs and piano pieces.

Dickinson, Clarence, American composer; b. Lafayette, Ind., May 7, 1873. Pupil of Wild and Weidig in Chicago; of Singer and Riemann in Berlin; of Moszkowski (piano), Guilmant (organ) and Pierné (composition) in Paris; in 1909 he settled in New York as organist; 1912, appointed prof. of church music at Union Theological Seminary, N. Y. (retired as director of its School of Sacred Music, 1945). He presented numerous organ concerts, lectures, and historic concerts in the U. S., Canada, France, England, and Spain. Works: a comic opera, *The Medicine Man* (Chicago, 1895); an opera, *Priscilla; Storm King,* for orch. (1920); many organ pieces, and songs; edited 'Historical Recitals for Organ' (50 numbers), sacred choruses, a 'Book of 80 Amens,' and a 'Book of 40 Antiphons.'—Books: *Excursions in Musical History* (1917); *Troubadour Songs* (1920); *Technique and Art of Organ Playing* (1921).

Dickinson, Edward, American historian of music; b. W. Springfield, Mass., Oct. 10, 1853; d. Oberlin, Ohio, Jan. 25, 1946. He studied at New England Cons. (1871-2); organ with Eugene Thayer (1878-9); attended lecture courses of Ph. Spitta in Berlin. He was director of music, Elmira College (1883-92); prof. of history and criticism of music, Oberlin College, from 1893.—Books: *Music in the History of the Western Church* (1902); *The Study of the History of Music* (1905; 2nd augm. ed. 1908); *The Education of a Music Lover* (1911); *Music and the Higher Education* (1915); *The Spirit of Music* (1925); also various magazine articles.

Dickinson, George Sherman, American music educator; b. St. Paul, Minn., Feb. 9, 1888; studied at Oberlin College (B.A., 1909), Oberlin Cons. of Music (Mus. Bac., 1910) and Harvard Univ. (M.A., 1912); 1913-14, pupil of Kaun and Juon in Berlin; 1908-21, organist and choirmaster in various churches; and taught at the Oberlin Cons. (1910-22) and at Vassar College (1922-39). He wrote *Foretokens of the Tonal Principle,* in 'Vassar Mediaeval Studies' (1923); *The Growth and Use of Harmony* (vol. 4 of *Fundamentals of Musical Art;* 1927); *Classification of Musical Compositions* (1938); *The Pattern of Music* (1939); articles in the 'Mus. Quarterly' and other musical journals.

Dickinson, Helen Adell, Canadian-American author; b. Port Elmsley, Ont., Canada, Dec. 5, 1875. She studied at Queen's Univ., Kingston, Canada (M. A., 1895); Heidelberg Univ. (Ph. D., 1901); married Clarence Dickinson (q.v.; 1904).—Writings: *Metrical Translation of 150 Ancient Carols* (1930); *A Book of Antiphons* (1919); *The Coming of the Prince of Peace: A Nativity Play of Ancient Christmas Carols* (1919); *A Treasury of Worship* (1926); etc.

Diderot (dē-droh'), **Denis,** b. Langres, Oct. 5, 1713; d. Paris, July 30, 1784. Projector and editor-in-chief of the 'Encyclopédie.' In his work, *Mémoires sur différents sujets de mathématiques* (The Hague, 1748), are the essays *Des principes d'acoustique* and *Projet d'un nouvel orgue,* the latter being an impracticable idea for a new kind of barrel organ.

Didur, Adamo, Polish basso; b. Sanok, Galicia, Dec. 24, 1874; d. Katowice, Poland, Jan. 7, 1946. Studied with Wysocki and Emerich; 1894, made his operatic début in Rio de Janeiro, thereafter appearing at the La Scala Opera, Milan, at the Warsaw Opera, in Moscow, St. Petersburg, Barcelona, Madrid, London, and Buenos Aires; 1907-8, appeared with the Manhattan Opera Co.; 1908, début as Méphistophélès at the Metropolitan Opera House, of which he was a leading member until 1932.

Didymus, a grammarian of Alexandria; b. 63 B. C. The number of his works was estimated by Seneca at 4,000; he wrote a tract on music, now known only by an epitome of Porphyry's, and some quotations by Ptolemy. In his system the octave of the diatonic genus was formed by two precisely similar tetrachords; and in all 3 species of tetrachord (diatonic, chromatic, enharmonic) the ratio for the interval of the major third is 4:5. He also recognized the difference between the major and minor whole tone; this difference (9/8 : 10/9= 81 : 80) is, therefore, rightly termed the 'comma of Didymus.' Salinas and Doni have written on his musical system.

Diémer (d'yā-mā'), **Louis,** distinguished French pianist; b. Paris, Feb. 14, 1843; d. there, Dec. 21, 1919. Pupil of Marmontel at the Cons., taking 1st piano prize in 1856; also of Ambroise Thomas and Bazin for composition, taking 1st harmony prize, 2d organ prize, and 1st prize for fugue. Played with great success at the Alard, Pasdeloup, and Cons. concerts; succeeded Marmontel (1887) as piano prof. at Cons. The immense success of his series of historical recitals, in 1889, determined him to make a specialty of early music, and led to the establishing of the 'Société des anciens instruments.' Widor, Saint-Saëns, Lalo, and others wrote pieces for him which he played at the Colonne and Lamoureux Concerts. He edited a number of old French keyboard pieces; his collection, *Clavecinistes français,* was publ. posthumously in 1928.

Dienel, Otto, German organist; b. Tiefenfurth, Silesia, Jan. 11, 1839; d. Berlin, March 7, 1905; studied music in Berlin at the Royal Institute for Church music, and at the Royal Academy. Teacher of music; organist at the Marienkirche, Berlin. He wrote compositions for organ, and choruses; author of *Die moderne Orgel* (1889, 2nd ed., 1891).

Diepenbrock, Alfons, eminent Dutch composer; b. Amsterdam, Sept. 2, 1862; d. there, April 5, 1921. Entirely self-taught in music; 1888-95, teacher at the Gymnasium at s'Hertogenbosch; then private teacher in Amsterdam. Wrote a Mass for male chorus and organ; *Te Deum* for double chorus; *Stabat Mater Speciosa; Stabat Mater Dolorosa; Les Elfes* for female voices; *Hymne* for violin and piano; etc. A collection of his writings, *Verzamelde Geschriften,* was publ. in Utrecht (1950).—Cf. *Missa in die festo A. Diepenbrock's Hertogenbosch* (biography in Dutch, 1921); Eduard Reeser, *A. Diepenbrock* (Amsterdam, 1936).

Dieren (dē'-ren), **Bernard van,** important composer and writer; b. Rotterdam, Dec. 27, 1884; d. London, April 24, 1936. After studying in Germany and Holland, he settled in 1909 in London as music correspondent of the 'Nieuwe Rotterdamsche Courant'; later devoted his time exclusively to composing. His works show radical tendencies.—Compositions: 6 Sketches for piano (1911); 4 string quartets (1912; 1917, performed at the Donaueschingen Music Festival in 1920; 1919; 1923, performed at the Frankfurt International Music Festival in 1925); Symph. for soli, chorus, and orch. on Chinese texts (1914); *Diaphony* for baritone and chamber orch. on 3 Shakespearean sonnets; *Overture to an Ideal Comedy* (1916); *Les Propous des Beuveurs,* introit for orch. (after Rabelais; London, 1921); *Sonata Tyroica* for violin and piano (1927); many songs (also with string quartet and chamber orch). Author of a book on the modern sculptor, Jacob Epstein (1920); and a collection of essays, *Down Among the Dead Men* (London, 1935).—Cf. E. Davis, *B. van Dieren,* in the 'Mus. Quarterly' (April, 1938).

Diet (d'yā), **Edmond-Marie,** French dramatic composer; b. Paris, Sept. 25, 1854; d. there, October, 1924. Pupil of César Franck and Guiraud; produced the operas *Stratonice* (1887), *Le cousin Placide* (1887), *Fleur de Vertu* (1894), *La Revanche d'Iris* (1905); also ballets and pantomimes (*Scientia,* 1889; *La Grève; Masque rose; M. Ruy-Blas,* 1894; *La Belle et la Bête,* 1895; *L'Araignée d'or,* 1896; *Rêve de Noël,* 1896; *Watteau,* 1900 (with Pujet), and the 3-act operetta *Gentil Crampon* (Paris, 1897); besides songs, and church music.

Dietrich, Albert Hermann, German conductor; b. Forsthaus Golk, n. Meissen, Aug. 28, 1829; d. Berlin, Nov. 19, 1908. Pupil of J. Otto in Dresden and Moscheles and Rietz at Leipzig (1847-51); studied with Schumann at Düsseldorf (1851-54). From 1855-61, concert conductor, and from 1859 municipal music director, at Bonn; from 1861, at Oldenburg; retired in 1890 and lived in Berlin; made Royal Prof. in 1899. He was one of Schumann's best pupils. Wrote *Erinnerungen an Johannes Brahms in Briefen, besonders aus seiner Jugendzeit* (Leipzig, 1898; in English, 1899).

Dietrich (or **Dieterich**), **Sixtus,** composer; b. Augsburg, 1490-1495; d. St. Gall, Switzerland, Oct. 21, 1548. Boy chorister at Constance, 1504-06; 1508-09, studied in Freiburg; 1517, choirmaster in Constance, becoming chaplain in 1522; 1540 and 1544, in Wittenberg. He was one of the most important early Protestant composers of sacred music. A book of magnificats (1535), and 2 collections of antiphons *a* 4 (1541 and 1545), were published separately; motets, songs, etc., are scattered through various German collections printed 1536-68; 5 pieces are in Glareanus' *Dodecachordon* (1547).—Reprints have been publ. in the 'Denkmäler deutscher Tonkunst,' 34, and by H. Zenck (13 hymns).—Cf. H. Zenck, *S. Dietrich, Ein Beitrag zur Musik und Musikanschauung im Zeitalter der Reformation* (Leipzig, 1928).

Dietsch (dētsh), **Pierre-Louis-Philippe,** French conductor; b. Dijon, March 17, 1808; d. Paris, Feb. 20, 1865. Pupil of Choron and the Paris Cons.; 1830 maître de chapelle at St.-Eustache, and later at Ste.-Madeleine; 1860-3, conductor at the Opéra; composer of 25 Masses and other sacred music. He would have been forgotten long ago, were his name not connected with that of Wagner. In 1842 he brought out at the Opéra *Le Vaisseau Fantôme,* written on Wagner's original sketch of *Der fliegende Holländer,* and in 1861 he conducted (most incompetently) the notorious three Paris performances of *Tannhäuser.*—Cf. Wagner's *Mein Leben* (vols. I and III).

Dietz, Max, Austrian musicologist; b. Vienna, Apr. 9, 1857; d. there, Aug. 5, 1928. Having obtained his degree *(Dr. phil.)* from the Univ. of Vienna, he spent some time in France in research work, the result of which he publ. in his *Geschichte des musikalischen Dramas in Frankreich während der Revolution bis zum Direktorium* (1885), a most valuable contribution to the history of opera; in 1886 he established himself as docent of musicology at the Univ. of Vienna; edited several Masses, a *Stabat Mater* and *Requiem* by Emperor Leopold I (1891), and *Recitativo e Duetto fra l'anima e Gesù Cristo* by A. de Liguori (1895).

Dieupart (d'yö-pahr'), **Charles,** French violinist and harpsichordist; went to London in 1700; was maestro al cembalo, for several years, of Handel's operas, and d. in London c. 1740, almost destitute. Publ. 6 *Suites de clavecin . . . composées et mises en concert pour un violon et une flûte, avec basse de viole et un archiluth.* Bach copied two of Dieupart's clavecin suites, and used various themes in his own 'English Suites.'—The Lyrebird Press of Paris publ. 2 vols. of Dieupart's works, ed. by P. Brunold (vol. I, *6 Suites pour clavecin;* vol. II, *Airs et Chansons).*

Diller, Angela, American pianist and pedagogue; b. Brooklyn, N. Y., Aug. 1, 1877; attended the schools there; later studied music at Columbia Univ. with Edward MacDowell and Percy Goetschius; also studied with Johannes Schreyer in Dresden; won the Mosenthal Fellowship for composition (Columbia Univ.); 1899-1916, head of the theory department, Music School Settlement, N. Y.; 1916-21, in charge of the normal work, David Mannes School; since then director of the Diller-Quaile School of Music, N. Y.; on the faculty of the Univ. of Southern Calif. (1932), Mills College (1935), New England Cons. (1936 and 1937); co-founder, with Margarethe Dessoff, of the Adesdi Chorus and A Cappella Singers of New York; has edited and written, with E. Quaile, K. Stearns Page, and Harold Bauer, many educational music works. In 1953 she received a Guggenheim Fellowship award. She publ. *First Theory Book* (1921); *Keyboard Harmony Course* (4 books; 1936, 1937, 1943, 1949), and *The Splendor of Music* (1957).

Dilling, Mildred, American harpist; b. Marion, Ind., Feb. 23, 1894; studied with Louise Schellschmidt-Koehne, later in Paris with Henriette Renié. After her Paris début she played in N. Y. (1913) with the Madrigal Singers of the MacDowell Chorus; appeared in Europe with Yvette Guilbert and the de Reszkes, in the U. S. with Alma Gluck and Frances Alda; toured the U. S. and Great Britain many times. She publ.: *Old Tunes for New Harpists* (1934); *Thirty Little Classics for the Harp* (1938).

Dillon, Fannie Charles, American pianist; b. Denver, Colo., March 16, 1881; d. Altadena, Calif., Feb. 21, 1947. She studied at Claremont College, Pomona, Calif. and in Berlin (1900-08) with Godowsky and Hugo Kaun, later in N. Y. with Rubin Goldmark; début as pianist in 1908; taught at Pomona College (1910-13), and from 1918 in Los Angeles High Schools. She wrote several orchestral pieces: *Celebration of Victory* (Los Angeles, 1918); *The Cloud* (1918); *A Letter From the Southland; Mission Garden; The Alps* (1920); *Chinese Symph. Suite;* etc.; many piano pieces (*Birds at Dawn,* etc.); songs; anthems.

Dillon, Henri, French composer; b. Angers, Oct. 9, 1912; d. in Indo-China, in combat, July 9, 1954. He studied at the Military School in St.-Cyr; was in the army during World War II. He was largely self-taught in music, and adopted a classical style of composition, derived mainly from the melodic patterns of French folksongs. Among his works are a cello concerto (1949); violin concerto (1949); viola concerto (1952); concerto for 2 trumpets and orch. (1953); *Arlequin,* divertimento for string orch. (1949); *Cassation* for 12 wind instruments (1953); sonata for saxophone and piano (1949); violin sonata (1952); concerto for 2 pianos (Paris, Dec. 15, 1952); piano sonata (1953); various works for piano.

Dima, Gheorghe, Rumanian composer; b. Brasov, Oct. 10, 1847; d. Cluj, June 4, 1925. Pupil of Giehne in Karslruhe, Uffmann in Vienna, Thieriot in Graz, and at the Leipzig Cons. (Richter, Jadassohn, and Reinecke); directed musical societies and church choirs in Sibiu and Brasov; also taught music in those cities.—Works: *La Mère d'Etienne le Grand,* oratorio; *Voilà la hora qui tourne,* for mixed chorus and orch.; *Salvum fac regem,* for voices and orch., etc.

D'Indy. See **Indy, d'.**

Dippel, Andreas, dramatic tenor and impresario; b. Kassel, Germany, Nov. 30, 1866; d. Hollywood, May 12, 1932. From 1882-87 he was employed in a banking house at Kassel, meanwhile beginning vocal study with Frau Zottmayr, a well-known singer at the court theater; was engaged at the Bremen Stadttheater (1887-92); made his American début at the Metropolitan Opera, N. Y. (Nov. 26, 1890); then sang at Covent

Garden, London, in Munich, and at Bayreuth. His repertory included nearly 150 roles; he was particularly successful in Wagner's operas. In 1908 he became administrative manager of the Metropolitan Opera House; in 1910 he assumed control of the Chicago Opera Company; was its manager till 1913; then organized his own company, specializing in light opera.

Diruta, Girolamo, celebrated Italian organist; b. Deruta, province of Perugia, 1550; date of death unknown. He was a pupil, in Venice, of Zarlino, Costanzo Porta, and Claudio Merulo, the last of whom mentions the fact with pride in the preface of Diruta's *Il Transilvano.* In 1574, Diruta was in the Minorite monastery at Correggio; then church organist in Venice (1582-93); at the cathedral of Chioggia (1597); and at Agobbio (Gubbio) Cathedral (1609-12). His *Il Transilvano* is a valuable treatise on organ playing, the first work to treat the organ and its playing technique as distinct and separate from the clavier. It is in 2 parts, in dialogue form: *Dialogo sopra il vero modo di sonar organi e istromenti da penna* (Venice, 1593; further editions, 1597, 1609, 1612, 1625); *Dialogo diviso in quattro libri . . . il vero modo e la vera regola d'intavolare ciascun canto* (Venice, 1609; 2nd ed., 1622). Dannreuther, in his *Musical Ornamentation,* gives a thorough analysis of Diruta's system of ornamentation. Volume III of L. Torchi's 'L'Arte Musicale in Italia' contains a ricercare and 2 toccatas for organ by Diruta.—Cf. F. Briganti, *Il primo libro dei Contrappunti di Girolamo Diruta* (Perugia, 1951).

Distler, Hugo, German composer; b. Nuremberg, June 24, 1908; d. (suicide) Berlin, Nov. 1, 1942. He studied at the Leipzig Cons. with Grabner and Martienssen. In 1931 he became a church organist at Lübeck; then was teacher at an ecclesiastical school in Spandau (1933-37); taught at Stuttgart (1937-40); from 1940 he was in Berlin. His early training and his connection with church music determined his style as composer; his music is marked by a strong sense of polyphony. He wrote but few works, mostly chamber music and choral pieces: concerto for cembalo and string orch. (1938); the cantatas *An die Natur* (1933); *Das Lied von der Glocke* (1937); and *Lied am Herde* (1940). His oratorio *Die Weltalter* (1942) remained unfinished. Distler's works have been heard in frequent performances since his death.—Cf. Karl Laux, *Musik und Musiker der Gegenwart* (Essen, 1949).

Ditson, Oliver, American music publisher; founder of the firm of Oliver Ditson & Co.; b. Boston, Oct. 20, 1811; d. there, Dec. 21, 1888. He established himself as a music seller and publisher in Boston in 1835; became a partner of G. H. Parker, his employer, under the firm name of Parker & Ditson; carried on the business in his own name (1842-57), when J. C. Haynes joined the firm, then changed to O. Ditson & Co. His eldest son, Charles, took charge of the N. Y. branch (Ch. H. Ditson & Co.) in 1867, the business being continued until his death. A Philadelphia branch, opened in 1875 by J. Edward Ditson as J. E. D. & Co., was in existence until 1910. A branch for the importation and sale of instruments, etc., was established at Boston in 1860 as John C. Haynes & Co. On Oliver Ditson's death, the firm of O. Ditson & Co. was reorganized as a corporation, with J. C. Haynes as President (d. May 3, 1907); from 1907 until his death, on May 14, 1929, Charles H. Ditson managed the business; he was succeeded by H. H. Porter. In 1931 Theo. Presser Co., Phila., took over the management of the firm; its catalogue embraced about 52,000 titles. Publishers of 'The Musical Record' (a monthly periodical) from 1878-1903, 'The Musician' from 1896-1918, and several library series. The music house Lyon & Healy was founded by Oliver Ditson in Chicago, 1864, as a western branch.—Cf. W. A. Fisher, *Notes on Music in Old Boston* (Boston, 1918); W. A. Fisher, *One Hundred and Fifty Years of Music Publishing in the U. S.* (Boston, 1933).

Dittersdorf, Karl Ditters von, eminent both as a violinist and composer; b. Vienna, Nov. 2, 1739; d. at Castle Rothlhotta, near Neuhaus, Bohemia, Oct. 24, 1799. At first taught by König and Ziegler, he became a favorite of Prince Joseph of Hildburghausen, who had him thoroughly trained by Trani (violin) and Bono (composition). He played in the prince's orch. till its dissolution in 1759, and then in the court theater at Vienna; accompanied Gluck on his Italian journey (1761), winning great fame as a violinist, and, on his return to Vienna, defeating the renowned Lolli. As Kapellmeister (1764-9) to the Bishop of Gross-Wardein, Hungary (succeeding Michael Haydn), he composed industriously (his first opera, *Amore in musica,* 1767; various oratorios, and much orchestral and chamber music). After traveling for a short time, he was appointed Kapellmeister to the Prince-Bishop of Breslau, Count von Schaffgotsch, at Johannesburg in Silesia, where he had a small theater built, for which he wrote several pieces;

though his best operas (*Doktor und Apotheker, Betrug durch Aberglauben, Liebe im Narrenhaus, Hieronymus Knicker,* and *Rotkäppchen*) were composed during visits to Vienna. In 1770 the Pope bestowed on Dittersdorf the Order of the Golden Spur; in 1773 he was ennobled by the Emperor ('von Dittersdorf'). On the decease of the Prince-Bishop (1795), Dittersdorf, who had been very prodigal of his means while at the zenith of his popularity, lived on a small pension, in straitened circumstances, until a friend, Baron von Stillfried, took him into his castle, Rothlhotta. Of his 28 operas only one, *Doktor und Apotheker* (Vienna, July 11, 1786), still survives; despite the vein of jovial humor, bright and fluent melody, and easy and correct style, they were eclipsed by Mozart's genius. Yet Dittersdorf may well be regarded as a worthy precursor of Mozart in national dramatic composition. Besides, this prolific author wrote several oratorios and cantatas; 12 symphonies for orch. on Ovid's 'Metamorphoses' (Vienna, 1785). Of these 12, only 6 are now extant, and have been republished (1899) by Reinecke Bros., Leipzig; they are remarkable specimens of early program music. The same firm also republished 2 other symphonies; the overture to *Esther* (oratorio); a short ballet; and the Divertimento *Il combattimento dell' umane passioni.* 41 MS symphonies, a *Concerto grosso,* for 11 concerted instruments, with orch.; 12 violin concertos; numerous string quartets (the best were edited by the Müller brothers, and publ.); 12 divertissements for 2 violins and cello; 12 4-hand sonatas for piano; 72 preludes, for piano; etc. A selection of his instrl. works was publ. in the 'Denkmäler der Tonkunst in Österreich,' XLIII, 2 (1936). Among his writings are *Briefe über Behandlung italienischer Texte bei der Composition* (Leipzig, 'Allgemeine musikal. Zeitung,' 1799), and an autobiography (Leipzig, 1801; edited by Spazier; reprinted by E. Istel, Leipzig, 1909; English transl. by A. D. Coleridge, London, 1896; new edition as *Lebensbeschreibung, seinem Sohn in die Feder diktiert,* Leipzig, 1940).—Cf. C. Krebs, *Dittersdorfiana* (Berlin, 1900; with thematic catalogue); K. M. Klob, *3 musikalische Biedermänner* (Ulm, 1911); K. Holl, *Karl Ditters von Dittersdorfs Opern für das wiederhergestellte Johannisberger Theater* (dissertation, Heidelberg, 1913); L. Riedinger, *Dittersdorf als Opernkomponist,* in 'Studien zur Musikwissenschaft,' II, 213 ff. (1914); Gertrude Rigler, *Die Kammermusik Dittersdorfs,* ibid., XIV, 179 ff. (1927).

Divitis (de Ryche, le Riche), **Antonius (Antoine)**, celebrated French (or Flemish) contrapuntist of late 15th and early 16th centuries; b. Louvain, c. 1475; d. probably after 1526, in which year he is mentioned as very likely being at St. Peter's in Rome as Antonius Richardus. He was singer and choirmaster at St. Donatien in Bruges (Brugge) from 1501-4; from 1504-5, choirmaster at St. Rombaut in Malines; then was in the service of Philippe le Beau in Brussels; chapel singer to Louis XII (1506-15).—Works: motets and chansons are scattered in collections, e.g., *Motetti de la corona* (1514), and others printed by Rhaw, Attaignant, etc. At Cambrai is a MS Mass; at Munich, 2 Credos and a Salve Regina *a* 5; at Rome, *Quem dicunt homines* for 4 voices.—Cf. G. van Doorslaer, *Antonius Divitis,* in 'Tijdschrift der Vereeniging voor Nederlandsche Muziekgeschiedenis,' XIII, 1 (1929).

Dixon, (Charles) Dean, American Negro conductor; b. New York, Jan. 10, 1915. He studied conducting at the Juilliard Graduate School with Albert Stoessel; obtained the M. A. degree at Teachers' College, Columbia Univ. He then organized an orchestra under his own name; was the first Negro conductor to lead the New York Philh. (Lewisohn Stadium, Aug. 10, 1941). In 1949 he went to Europe, where he appeared with the Berlin Philh.; also in Scandinavia, obtaining genuine success. He gave first performances in Europe of many modern American works.

Dizi (dē-zē'), **François-Joseph,** famous French harpist; b. Namur, France, Jan. 14, 1780; d. Paris, Nov., 1847. He set out for London when only 16; lost his harp on the way; but went on without it, and introduced himself to Érard, who gave him a harp, and obtained pupils for him. Besides winning fame as a concert player, and as a harpist at the principal theaters, he invented the 'perpendicular harp' (which was unsuccessful), and composed sonatas, romances, variations, studies, etc., for harp; also publ. an *École de Harpe, being a Complete Treatise on the Harp* (London, 1827). In 1830 he went to Paris, and established a harp factory with Pleyel, which did not do well. There he was appointed harp teacher to the Royal princesses.

Dlabacz (dlah'-batsh), **Gottfried Johann,** Bohemian music scholar; b. Brod, July 17, 1758; d. Prague, Feb. 4, 1820. He was librarian and choirmaster of the Premonstratensian monastery in Prague; publ. a valuable reference work, *Allgemeines historisches*

Künstlerlexikon für Böhmen (3 vols., 1815-18), and contributed articles to Riegger's 'Statistik von Böhmen.'

Döbber (döb'-bär), **Johannes,** German composer; b. Berlin, March 28, 1866; d. there, Jan. 26, 1921. Pupil in Stern Cons. of R. Radecke, L. Bussler (composition), and C. Agghazy (piano). He taught the first piano class in Kullak's Cons.; became Kapellmeister at Darmstadt; then was at Coburg-Gotha as tutor in music to Princess Beatrice; teacher and music critic of the 'Volkszeitung' in Berlin (1908). He wrote the operas *Die Strassensängerin* (Gotha, 1890); *Der Schmied von Gretna-Green* (Berlin, 1893); *Dolcetta* (Brandenburg, 1894); *Die Rose von Genzano* (Gotha, 1895); *Die Grille* (Leipzig, 1897); *Die drei Rosen* (Coburg, 1902); *Der Zauberlehrling* (Brunswick, 1907); *Die Franzosenzeit* (Berlin, 1913); song-play, *Fahrende Musikanten* (Magdeburg, 1917); the operettas *Die Millionenbraut* (Magdeburg, 1913) and *Des Kaisers Rock* (Berlin, 1915); also a symphony, piano pieces; over 60 songs; quartets, duets, arrangements, etc.

Dobiáš, Václav, Czech composer; b. Radčice, near Semily, Sept. 22, 1909. He took an academic course in music with Foerster and Novák; became interested in quarter-tone composition, and worked with Alois Hába. After 1945 he became greatly interested in the political side of music education; in conformity with the new trends, he abandoned his experimental work, and began to write music for the masses, influenced by similar developments in Russia. Among his works are the cantatas *Stalingrad* (1945); *Order No. 386* (1946); a sinfonietta (1946), and many marching songs.

Dobronić (doh'-brŭ-nitz), **Antun,** Croatian composer; b. Jelsa, Island of Hvar, April 2, 1878; d. Zagreb, Dec. 12, 1955. He studied music with Novák in Prague; then returned to Yugoslavia; in 1921 was appointed professor at the Cons. of Zagreb. He wrote many stage works, among them the operas *Ragusean Diptych; The Man of God; Mara; Dubrovnički triptihon* (1925); *Udovica Rozlinka* (1934); *Rkac* (1938); *Goran* (1944); the ballet, *The Giant Horse;* 4 symphonies (1938-49); the symph. poems *Au long de l'Adriatique* (1948); *Les Noces* (1949); chamber music in the national style, including a piano quintet subtitled *Bosnian Rhapsody;* 5 string quartets; also choruses and songs. Dobronić is the author of *A Study of Yugoslav Music,* in the 'Mus. Quarterly' (Jan., 1926).

Dobrowen (doh'-broh-vehn), **Issay Alexandrovitch,** Russian conductor; b. Nizhny-Novgorod, Feb. 27, 1893; d. Oslo, Dec. 9, 1953. He studied with Igumnov (piano) and Taneyev (composition) at the Moscow Cons. (Great Gold Medal, 1911); then went to Vienna for additional study with Leopold Godowsky (piano). Returning to Moscow, he became conductor of the Moscow opera; in 1922 he led the Dresden State Opera in the German première of Mussorgsky's opera, *Boris Godunov;* in 1924 he conducted opera in Berlin; during the season 1927-28 he conducted opera in Sofia, Bulgaria. In 1931 he made his American début; conducted the San Francisco Symph. Orch. (two seasons); was guest conductor with the Minneapolis Symph. Orch., Philadelphia Orch., and the N. Y. Philh. However, he was received indifferently by American audiences, and returned to Europe. He was a regular conductor of the Budapest opera from 1936-39; at the outbreak of World War II he went to Sweden, where he won his greatest successes, as conductor of both opera and symphony, at the Stockholm Opera and the Philh. of Göteborg. In 1948 he conducted at La Scala, Milan. On frequent occasions Dobrowen acted as stage director as well as conductor in German, Italian, and Swedish opera houses. He was a prolific composer; wrote several piano concertos and pieces for piano solo, in a Romantic vein; also an orchestral fairy-tale, *1001 Nights* (Moscow, May 27, 1922).

Dobrzynski (dobr-zhin'-skē), **Ignacy Felix,** Polish pianist; b. Romanov, Volhynia, Feb. 25, 1807; d. Warsaw, Oct. 9, 1867. Son of a violinist, J. Dobrzynski (1777-1841); he was taught by his father, then by Elsner, being a fellow pupil and close friend of Chopin; on subsequent pianistic tours (1845-6) to Leipzig, Dresden, and Berlin, he had great success. For a time he conducted the opera in Warsaw, where he finally settled. He wrote an opera *Monbar or The Filibuster* (Warsaw, 1861); *Symphonie caractéristique;* string sextet, 2 string quintets, 2 string quartets; piano trio; violin sonata; a nocturne for violin and piano, *Les Larmes;* mazurkas for piano; songs. His son Bronislaw Dobrzynski publ. a monograph on him (Warsaw, 1893).

Doche, Joseph-Denis, French composer; b. Paris, Aug. 22, 1766; d. Soissons, July 20, 1825. He was a chorister at the cathedral of Meaux; then was organist at Coutances in Normandy. He played string instruments in a theater orchestra in Paris from 1794 till 1810; then became conductor, retiring in

1823. He wrote numerous successful vaudevilles; also operas: *Point du bruit* (Oct. 25, 1802); *Les deux sentinelles* (Sept. 27, 1803), and others.

Doe, Doris, American contralto; b. Bar Harbor, Maine, March 23, 1899; concert début in New York (Feb. 18, 1925); opera début as Erda at the Dresden Staatsoper (1930); Metropolitan Opera House début as Brangäne (Feb. 3, 1932).

Doebler, Kurt, German composer of sacred music; b. Kottbus, Jan. 15, 1896; studied organ with A. Dreyer. From 1919-32 he was organist and choral leader at the Catholic Church in Charlottenburg; after occupying various positions as organist and teacher elsewhere, he returned to Charlottenburg (1950). In his music Doebler attempts to establish a modern style based on Palestrina's polyphony. His numerous choruses a cappella enjoy considerable renown in Germany.

Doenhoff, Albert von, American pianist; b. Louisville, Ky., March 16, 1880; d. New York, Oct. 3, 1940. He studied at the Cincinnati College of Music and then in N. Y. with Rafael Joseffy; made his professional début in N. Y. on March 8, 1905; subsequently developed a successful career as a concert pianist. He published many pieces for piano (*Arabesque, Revery,* etc.); also pedagogical material (*Three Modern Etudes for the Virtuoso; Six Special Studies Adapted to Small Hands,* etc.); edited and revised numerous editions of classics for G. Schirmer, Inc.

Doflein, Erich, German musicologist; b. Munich, Aug. 7, 1900. He studied with Weismann, Auerbach, and Praetorius, and later with Kaminski; was music instructor in Freiburg-im-Breisgau (1924-41); taught in Breslau (1941-44); was prisoner of war in Russia (1944-46). Since 1946, he has conducted a seminar at the Staatliche Hochschule für Musik in Freiburg; edited works of Quantz, Mozart, and Bartók.

Döhler, Theodor, pianist and composer; b. Naples, April 20, 1814; d. Florence, Feb. 21, 1856. He was a pupil of Julius Benedict at Naples and of Czerny (piano) and Sechter (composition) at Vienna. In 1831 he became pianist to the Duke of Lucca, lived for a time in Naples, made brilliant pianistic tours from 1836-46 in Germany, Italy, France, Holland, and England; in 1843 went to Copenhagen, thence to Russia, and in 1846 to Paris; settled in Florence in 1848. In 1846 the Duke, his patron, ennobled him, and he married a Russian countess. Works: A posthumous opera *Tancreda* (Florence, 1880; quite successful); many piano pieces; nocturnes; tarantellas; *12 Études de concert; 50 Études de salon;* variations, fantasias, transcriptions, etc.

Dohnányi (dŏh'-nahn-yē), **Ernst von,** noted Hungarian pianist and composer; b. Pressburg (Bratislava), July 27, 1877. He studied with his father, Friedrich von Dohnányi, prof. of mathematics and amateur cellist, and Karl Forstner (till 1894); then at the Budapest Academy of Music, with Stefan Thomán (piano) and Hans Koessler (composition). After graduation in 1897, he studied during the summer with Eugen d'Albert. His first independent piano recital was at Berlin on Oct. 1, 1897, followed by a concert tour to Cologne, Dresden, Frankfurt, Vienna, etc. He appeared as pianist in London on Oct. 24, 1898; then made several successful tours in the U. S. He was prof. of piano at the Hochschule für Musik in Berlin from 1908 till 1915; then settled in Budapest, where he became director of the Cons. (1919) and conductor of the Budapest Philh. He was also guest conductor throughout Europe. He was director of the Hungarian Academy and President of the Budapest Philh. Orch. until 1945; then went to Austria, after losing both his sons in the war; toured in England and U. S. (1948-49); was briefly teaching in Tucumán, Argentina (1949); in the autumn of 1949, he went to the U. S. and became professor of piano and composition at Florida State College in Tallahassee. Dohnányi's music represents the last flowering of the Hungarian Romantic era. His chief inspiration came from Brahms (who praised Dohnányi's early works); the element of form is strong and the traditional harmonic structure remains unshaken, but this conservatism does not exclude flashes of musical wit.—Works: Symphony in F (not numbered; won the Hungarian Millennium Prize in 1896); op. 1, piano quintet in C minor; op. 2, Overture *Zrinyi* (shared the prize with the symph. in 1896); op. 3, *5 Klavierstücke;* op. 4, Variations for piano in G; op. 5, Concerto for piano and orch. in E minor (won Bösendorfer prize in Vienna, 1899); op. 6, Passacaglia, for piano; op. 7, string quartet in A major; op. 8, Sonata for cello and piano in B♭ minor; op. 9, Symphony No. 1 in D minor (Manchester, England, Jan. 30, 1902); op. 10, Serenade, in C, for violin, viola, and cello; op. 11, *4 Rhapsodien* for piano; op. 12, *Konzertstück* for cello and orch.; op. 13, *Winterreigen* (10 bagatelles for piano): op. 14, 6 songs; op. 15, String quartet in D♭; op. 16,

Im Lebenslenz (6 songs); op. 17, *Humoresken in Form einer Suite,* for piano; op. 18, *Der Schleier der Pierrette* (pantomime; Dresden, 1910); op. 19, *Suite,* in F♯ minor, for orch.; op. 20, *Tante Simona* (1-act opera; Dresden, Jan. 20, 1913); op. 21, Sonata in C♯ minor for violin and piano; op. 22, Concerto for piano and orch., in D♭; op. 23, *3 Stücke für Klavier;* op. 24, Suite for piano; op. 25, *Variations on a Nursery Song,* for piano and orch. (1913; Berlin, Feb. 17, 1916, composer soloist; his most popular work); op. 26, 2nd piano quintet; op. 27, violin concerto; op. 28, 6 Concert Studies; op. 29, Variations on a Hungarian folksong for piano; op. 30, an opera, *The Tower of the Voivod* (Budapest, March 19, 1922; in German, Düsseldorf, 1926); op. 31, Festival Overture; op. 32, *Ruralia Hungarica* for piano (also for orch.) in 7 movements (Budapest, Nov. 17, 1924, composer conducting); *Szegedin Mass* (1930); a comic opera, *Der Tenor* (Budapest, Feb. 9, 1929); Symphony No. 2 (1944; London, Nov. 23, 1948; radically revised, and perf. in the new version, Minneapolis, March 15, 1957); 6 piano pieces (1945); piano concerto No. 2 (1946); 12 etudes for piano (1950); violin concerto, No. 2, scored for orch. without violins (San Antonio, Jan. 26, 1952); concertino for harp and orch. (1952); *American Rhapsody* for orch. (Athens, Ohio, Feb. 21, 1954, composer conducting).—Cf. Victor Papp, *Ernst von Dohnányi* (Budapest, 1927).

Doles, Johann Friedrich, German composer; b. Steinbach, April 23, 1715; d. Leipzig, Feb. 8, 1797. He was a student of theology in Leipzig; then became a pupil of Bach (1740-44), who recommended him for the post of cantor at Freiberg, Saxony. In 1756 he became cantor at the St. Thomas School in Leipzig; was also director of the St. Thomas Church until 1789, when he resigned owing to old age. He wrote a great number of sacred works, a full list of which is given in 'Die Musik in Geschichte und Gegenwart.' See also H. Banning, *J. F. Doles: Leben und Werke* (Leipzig, 1939).

Doležálek (doh-lā-zhăh'-lek), **Jan Emanuel,** Czech musician; b. Chotěboř, May 22, 1780; d. Vienna, July 6, 1858. He studied music in Vienna with Beethoven's teacher, Albrechtsberger, and through him came to know Beethoven himself. It is owing chiefly to this association that Doležálek's name is known in music history. He arranged a number of Czech songs, and published a collection of them.

Dolmetsch, Arnold, English music antiquarian; b. Le Mans, Maine, France, Feb. 24, 1858; d. Haslemere, Surrey, Feb. 28, 1940. While apprenticed in his father's piano-factory he learned to play both piano and violin, making such marked progress on the latter instrument that his father sent him to Brussels, where he became a pupil of Vieuxtemps; after completing his studies he went to Dulwich, was appointed instructor of violin at the College, and soon won a reputation as teacher. From his earliest years he had shown a decided predilection for the music of Bach and the old masters; when by chance he became the possessor of a well preserved viola d'amore, he did not rest until he had mastered the instrument; gradually he acquired the same skill on all the members of the viol family. He then gave up his large class of violin pupils and devoted his entire time to lecturing and giving recitals on the old instruments. In his quest for old music he found in the British Museum MSS of almost forgotten English composers (Simon Ives, Matthew Locke, Thomas Tomkins, John Jenkins, etc.). To become an authoritative interpreter of all this music he found it necessary to extend his investigations to the virginal, spinet, harpsichord, and clavichord. He began by collecting old books, in which those instruments were described by contemporary authorities; the mechanical skill he had acquired in his father's shop he turned to account in repairing the instruments he collected, and before long he was acknowledged as an authority on old music and instruments; he was not only a connoisseur and skilled workman, but also a masterly performer on every instrument in his large collection; with his wife and a pupil, Kathleen Salmon, he established the Dolmetsch Trio, devoted exclusively to the performance of old music on the original instruments. A tour of the U.S. in 1902 attracted so much attention that Chickering & Sons, of Boston, placed their factory and a force of their best workmen at Dolmetsch's disposal. The beginning was made with the restoration of a virginal by Hans Ruckers (1620); then a number of stringed and keyed instruments were built after the best models extant. The interest excited by the revival of these instruments induced several other artists (Wanda Landowska, Fuller Maitland, the brothers Casadesus, etc.) to give recitals on them. From 1902-9 Dolmetsch lived in Boston, supervising the construction of his instruments and concertizing; after that, he resided in England. In 1925 he founded at Haslemere, Surrey, annual historical chamber music festivals, where the works were played (many by himself) on modern reconstructions of the original historic instruments (clavichord, harpsichord, viols, recorders, etc.). The Dolmetsch Foundation, a society for the purpose of cultivating old music and making his ideas more widely known, was founded by his friends in 1928. He published *Select English Songs and Dialogues of the 16th and 17th Centuries* (2 vols., 1912) and *The Interpretation of the Music of the 17th and 18th Centuries* (London, 1915; new ed., 1944).—Cf. R. Donington, *The Work and Ideas of Arnold Dolmetsch* (Haslemere, 1932); Percy Grainger, *Arnold Dolmetsch, Musical Confucius,* in the 'Mus. Quarterly' (April, 1933).

Domaniewski (doh-mah-n'yĕv'-skē), **Boleslaus,** Polish pianist; b. Gronówek, Russian Poland, July 16, 1857; d. Warsaw, Sept. 11, 1925. He studied at the St. Petersburg Cons.; from 1890 to 1900 taught at the Cons. of Cracow; in 1900 he became director of the Warsaw Cons. His piano method, *Vademecum pour le pianiste,* enjoyed considerable popularity.

Dom Bedos. See **Bedos de Celles.**

Dominiceti (doh-mē-nē-tchā'-tē), **Cesare,** Italian composer; b. Desenzano, July 12, 1821; d. Sesto di Monza, June 20, 1888. He studied in Milan, where all his operas were brought out; lived for a long time in Bolivia, made a fortune there, and, some years after his return to Italy, was appointed prof. of composition at Milan Cons.—Operas: *Due mogli in una* (Milan, June 30, 1853), *La maschera* (Milan, March 2, 1854), *Morovico* (Milan, Dec. 4, 1873), *Il lago delle fate* (Milan, May 18, 1878), and *L'ereditiera* (Milan, Feb. 14, 1881).

Dommer, Arrey von, writer and critic; b. Danzig, Feb. 9, 1828; d. Treysa, Thuringia, Feb. 18, 1905. A theological student, he turned to music, and in 1851 became the pupil of Richter and Lobe (composition), and Schallenberg (organ) at Leipzig. He taught music at Leipzig, and went to Hamburg in 1863. He publ. *Elemente der Musik* (1862); *Musikalisches Lexikon* (1865; a revised ed. of Koch's); *Handbuch der Musikgeschichte* (1867; 2d ed., 1878; 3d ed., entirely rewritten and brought up to date by A. Schering, 1914).

Donalda, Pauline (real name Lightstone, translated by her father from Lichtenstein when he became a British subject), dramatic soprano; b. Montreal, March 5, 1882. She received her first musical training at Royal Victoria College, Montreal, and then was a private pupil of E. Duvernoy in Paris; début as Manon (Massenet) at Nice, Dec. 30, 1904; the next year she appeared at La Monnaie, Brussels, and Covent Garden; 1906-7, at the Manhattan Opera House, N. Y.; then chiefly at Opéra-Comique. From 1923-37 she had a large singing-school in Paris; 1937, returned to Montreal. In 1938 she presented her valuable music library (manuscripts, autographs, and music) to McGill Univ. Her stage name was taken in honor of Sir Donald Smith (later Lord Strathcona), who endowed the Royal Victoria College and was her patron.

Donati (Donato), Baldassare, famous Italian composer of motets and madrigals; b. Venice, c. 1530; d. there, 1603. He was choirmaster of the so-called 'small choir' at San Marco, Venice, from 1562-5; this was disbanded by Zarlino when he was appointed maestro di cappella in 1565, and Donati became a simple chorister; appointed maestro di canto to the Seminario Gregoriano di San Marco (1580); in 1590, he succeeded Zarlino as maestro di cappella.—His compositions are distinguished by their well defined rhythm and originality. Extant works include *Canzoni Villanesche alla Napoletana* (1550-58), several books of madrigals for 4 parts (1550-68), a volume of madrigals for 5-6 parts (1553; new eds., 1557, 1560), a volume of motets for 5-8 parts (1597), etc.

Donati, Ignazio, Italian composer; b. Casalmaggiore, 1585; d. Milan, 1638. He was maestro di cappella at the Urbino Cathedral (1612-16), then at Ferrara (1616-18); at Casalmaggiore (1618-23); at Novara and Lodi (1626-30). In 1631 he became maestro di cappella at the cathedral of Milan. He publ. 8 books of *concerti ecclesiastici,* 7 books of motets, Masses, and psalms.

Donato, Anthony, American violinist and composer; b. Prague, Nebraska, March 8, 1909. He studied at the Eastman School of Music in Rochester, N. Y., with Hanson, Rogers, and Royce; obtained the degrees of M. Mus. (1937) and Ph. D. (1947). He was then violin teacher at Drake Univ. (1931-37); Iowa State Teachers College (1937-39); the Univ. of Texas (1939-46); since 1947, prof. of composition at Northwestern Univ.; in 1951-52, in England on a Fulbright grant. Donato has written 2 symphonies (1944 and 1945); an overture *Prairie Schooner* (1947); *March of the Hungry Mountains* for chorus and orch. (1949); *The Plains,* for orch. (1953); *Solitude in the City* for narrator and instruments (1954); 3 string quartets (1941, 1947, 1951;

the Andante from string quartet No. 1 is also arranged for string orch.); 2 violin sonatas (1938, 1949); *Pastorale and Dance* for 4 clarinets (1947); sonatina for 3 trumpets (1949); sonata for horn and piano (1950); many choral works and piano teaching pieces. He received the 1955 Mendelssohn Glee Club award for his male chorus *The Sycophantic Fox and the Gullible Raven.*

Donato, Baldassare. See **Donati.**

Donaudy (dŏh-noh-dē'), **Stefano,** composer; b. (of French father and Italian mother) Palermo, Feb. 21, 1879; d. Naples, May 30, 1925. Pupil at Cons. of Palermo of G. Zuelli, 1896-1900; wrote the operas *Folchetto* (Palermo, 1892); *Scampagnata* (Palermo, 1898); *Theodor Körner* (Hamburg, Nov. 27, 1902); *Sperduti nel buio* (Palermo, April 27, 1907); *Ramuntcho* (Milan, March 19, 1921); *La Fiamminga* (Naples, April 25, 1922); a symph. poem, *Le Rêve de Polysende; Douze airs de style ancien* for voice and piano; and numerous piano pieces.

Donfried, Johann, German editor of church music; b. Veringenstadt, 1585; d. Rottenburg, 1654. He was rector of a school, and cantor at St. Martin's Church in Rottenburg. His most important publication is the *Promptuarium musicum* (3 vols., Strasbourg, 1622-27), containing sacred works by various composers; a collection of songs *Viridarium Musico-Marianum* (Strasbourg, 1627) and *Corolla Musica,* including 37 Masses (Strasbourg, 1628).

Doni, Antonio Francesco, Italian writer; b. Florence, 1513 (?); d. Monselice, near Padua, in Sept., 1574. For several years he was a member of the Servite fraternity in Florence; after leaving it in 1539, he led a wandering life as a lay priest.—Publ., besides various non-musical treatises, a *Dialogo sulla musica* (1544; includes a list of 17 composers living in Venice at the time, with works of each), and a *Libraria* (Venice, 2 vols., 1550-51), containing a description of all published or MS musical books in Italian, known at the time, as well as a list of the music academies then in existence and details of their foundation, etc.

Doni, Giovanni Battista, a Florentine nobleman; b. 1594; d. Dec. 1, 1647. He studied literature and philosophy at Bologna and Rome; from 1613-18 he was a law student at Bourges, France, and took his degree at Pisa. In 1621 he accompanied Cardinal Corsini to Paris, where he zealously prosecuted his literary and antiquarian studies; went to Rome in 1622, at the invitation of Cardinal Barberini, who was passionately fond of music, and with whom he traveled. In the intervals of his profound study of ancient music, he found time to construct the 'Lira Barberina' or 'Amphichord,' a species of double lyre, which he dedicated to Pope Urban VIII. Recalled to Florence in 1640 by deaths in his family, he settled there, married next year, and accepted a professorship of elocution offered him by the Grand Duke. His criticism and discussions of the earliest operas are very valuable, and were publ. for the first time by A. Solerti in *Origini del melodramma. Testimonianze dei contemporanei* (Turin, 1903).—Writings: *Compendio del trattato de' generi e de' modi della musica* (Rome, 1635); *Annotazioni* on the above (Rome, 1640); *De praestantia musicae veteris libri tres* . . . (Florence, 1647); and several essays in MS (some still extant in the library of Sta. Cecilia, Rome).—Cf. A. M. Blandini, *Commentarium de vita et scriptis G. B. Doni* (Florence, 1755); F. Vatielli, *La Lira Barberina di G. B. Doni* (Pesaro, 1909).

Donington, Robert, English musicologist; b. Leeds, May 4, 1907. He studied at Queen's College, Oxford (B. A., 1930); later became associated with Arnold Dolmetsch in the latter's workshop in Haslemere. He studied the technique of old instruments and contributed to the revival of Elizabethan instruments as player in the English Consort of Viols. He also edited the music magazine, 'The Consort.' Later he studied with Wellesz, and adopted the 12-tone method of composition in his works (string quartet and small pieces). He published *The Work and Ideas of Arnold Dolmetsch* (Haslemere, 1932); *A Practical Method for the Recorder* (with Edgar Hunt; 2 vols.; Oxford, 1935); *The Instruments of Music* (London, 1949).

Donizetti (doh-nē-tset'-tē), **Alfredo** (real name Ciummei), b. Smyrna, Sept. 2, 1867; d. Rosario, Argentina, Feb. 4, 1921. He studied (1883-9) at Milan Cons. under Ponchielli and Dominiceti; then settled in Argentina. He wrote the operas *Nama* (Milan, 1890) and *Dopo l'Ave Maria* (Milan, 1896); also piano pieces, and songs.

Donizetti (doh-nē-tset'-tē), **Gaetano,** one of the brilliant triumvirate (Donizetti, Rossini, and Bellini) of Italian opera composers in the first half of the 19th century, was b. at Bergamo, Nov. 29, 1797; d. there,

April 8, 1848. His father, a weaver by trade, later obtained a position in the local pawnshop, and desired that his son should become a lawyer. But Donizetti's inclinations were towards art; besides being strongly attracted to music, he studied architecture, drawing, and literature. His father finally allowed him to enter the Bergamo school of music; his teachers were Salari (voice), Gonzales (piano), and J. S. Mayr (harmony). In 1815 he changed to the Bologna Liceo Filarmonico, here completing his contrapuntal studies under Pilotti and Padre Mattei, to whom Mayr had recommended him. His father now insisted on his becoming a teacher, while Donizetti himself felt an irresistible bent for dramatic composition. The success of his first opera, *Enrico di Borgogna* (Venice, 1818), encouraged further production. His next opera, *Il Falegname di Livonia* (Venice, 1819; given at first as *Pietro il Grande, Czar delle Russie*), was likewise well received; but *Le Nozze in villa* (Mantua, 1820) was a failure. After the success of *Zoraide di Granata* (Rome, Jan. 28, 1822) he was exempted from further military service. From 1822 to 1829 inclusive, 23 operas flowed from his facile pen; during this period Donizetti was mostly a rather poor imitator of Rossini. But now, piqued by Bellini's successes, he wrote his *Anna Bolena* (Milan, 1830), which begins his second and more original period. Written for Pasta and Rubini—after the Italian fashion of adapting roles to singers—its vogue was more than local; in it, as Henry VIII, Lablache scored his first London triumph at the old 'King's Theatre.' In its wake followed *L'Elisir d'amore* (Milan, 1832), the tragic *Lucrezia Borgia* (La Scala, Milan, 1833), and the immensely popular *Lucia di Lammermoor* (Naples, Teatro San Carlo, 1835). Like that of so many other Italian opera composers, Donizetti's life was spent in traveling from place to place, bringing out opera after opera. Now, enjoying European celebrity, he visted Paris in 1835, and produced *Marino Faliero* at the Théâtre des Italiens. In May, 1837, he succeeded Zingarelli as director *pro tem* of the Naples Cons.; in July of that year he lost his wife, Virginia (*née* Vasselli), after 14 years of happy marital life. The censor's veto on the production of *Poliuto* (written for Ad. Nourrit after Corneille's *Polyeucte*) so angered him, that he left Milan for Paris. Here *La Fille du régiment* (Opéra-Comique, Feb. 11, 1840), *Les Martyrs* (an amplification of the forbidden *Poliuto;* Opéra, April 10, 1840), and *La Favorite* (Opéra, Dec. 2, 1840), made a veritable sensation. Upon his return to Italy, *Adelasia* (Rome, 1841) and *Maria Padilla* (Milan, 1841) had good fortune. In Vienna (1842) *Linda di Chamounix* evoked such enthusiasm that the Emperor conferred on him the titles of Court Composer and Master of the Imperial Chapel (he had also written a Miserere and an Ave Maria for the 'Hofkapelle,' in a severe purity of style warmly commended by the local critics). *Don Pasquale* was produced in Paris, 1843. Donizetti had reached the height of his fame and prosperity; though still maintaining the unbroken flow of creative activity, terrible headaches and mental depression warned him to desist; *Caterina Cornaro* (Naples, 1844) was his last work; one morning in 1845 he was found insensible on the floor of his bedroom, stricken with paralysis. He never recovered his mental powers, and died in 1848 at Bergamo. A monument by Vincenzo Vela was erected to his memory in 1855. Besides operas, he wrote many songs, ariettas, duets, and canzonets; 7 Masses, one being a Requiem; cantatas; vespers, psalms, motets; 12 string quartets; and piano music. —*Lucia di Lammermoor* is generally held to be his finest work; in it the vein of melody—now sparkling, now sentimental, now tragic—which embodies Donizetti's best claim on originality and immortality, finds, perhaps, freest and broadest development.

A list of Donizetti's operas follows: *Enrico di Borgogna* (Venice, Nov. 14, 1818); *Una follia* (Venice, Dec. 15, 1818); *Pietro il Grande, Czar delle Russie* (Venice, Dec. 26, 1819); *Le nozze in villa* (Mantua, Jan. 23, 1821); *Zoraide di Granata* (Rome, Jan. 28, 1822); *La zingara* (Naples, May 12, 1822); *La lettera anonima* (Naples, June 29, 1822); *Chiara e Serafina* (Milan, Oct. 26, 1822); *Alfredo il Grande* (Naples, July 2, 1823); *Il fortunato inganno* (Naples, Sept. 3, 1823); *L'aio nell' imbarazzo* (Rome, Feb. 4, 1824); *Emilia di Liverpool* (Naples, July 28, 1824); *I voti dei Sudditi* (Naples, March 6, 1825); *Alahor in Granata* (Palermo, Jan. 7, 1826); *Il castello degli invalidi* (Palermo, Feb. 27, 1826); *Elvida* (Naples, July 6, 1826); *Olivo e Pasquale* (Rome, Jan. 7, 1827); *Gli esiliati in Siberia* (Naples, May 13, 1827); *Il borgomastro di Saardam* (Naples, Aug. 19, 1827); *Le convenienze ed inconvenienze teatrali* (Naples, Nov. 21, 1827); *L'esule di Roma* (Naples, Jan. 2, 1828); *La regina di Golconda* (Genoa, May 12, 1828); *Gianni di Calais* (Naples, Aug. 2, 1828); *Il paria* (Naples, Jan. 12, 1829); *Il castello di Kenilworth* (Naples, July 6, 1829); *I pazzi per progetto* (Naples, Feb. 7, 1830); *Il diluvio universale* (Naples, March 6, 1830); *Il ritorno desiderato,* cantata (Naples, July 31, 1830): *Imelda de' Lambertazzi* (Naples, Aug. 23, 1830); *Anna Bolena* (Milan, Dec.

26, 1830); *Francesca di Foix* (Naples, May 30, 1831); *La romanziera e l'uomo nero* (Naples, June 18, 1831); *Fausta* (Naples, Jan. 12, 1832); *Ugo, conte di Parigi* (Milan, March 13, 1832); *L'elisir d'amore* (Milan, May 12, 1832); *Sancia di Castiglia* (Naples, Nov. 4, 1832); *Il furioso all'isola di San Domingo* (Rome, Jan. 2, 1833); *Parisina* (Florence, March 17, 1833); *Torquato Tasso* (Rome, Sept. 9, 1833); *Lucrezia Borgia* (Milan, Dec. 26, 1833); *Rosmonda d'Inghilterra* (Florence, Feb. 26, 1834); *Maria Stuarda* (Naples, Oct. 19, 1834); *Gemma di Vergy* (Milan, Dec. 26, 1834); *Marino Faliero* (Paris, March 12, 1835); *Lucia di Lammermoor* (Naples, Sept. 26, 1835); *Belisario* (Venice, Feb. 4, 1836); *Il campanello di notte* (Naples, June 1, 1836); *Betly* (Naples, Aug. 24, 1836); *L'assedio di Calais* (Naples, Nov. 19, 1836); *Pia de' Tolomei* (Venice, Feb. 18, 1837); *Roberto d'Evereux, Conte d'Essex* (Naples, Oct. 29, 1837); *Maria di Rudenz* (Venice, Jan. 30, 1838); *Gianni di Parigi* (Milan, Sept. 10, 1839); *La Fille du régiment* (Paris, Feb. 11, 1840); *Les Martyrs* (Paris, April 10, 1840); *La Favorite* (Paris, Dec. 2, 1840); *Adelia* (Rome, Feb. 11, 1841); *Maria Padilla* (Milan, Dec. 26, 1841); *Linda di Chamounix* (Vienna, May 19, 1842); *Don Pasquale* (Paris, Jan. 3, 1843); *Maria di Rohan* (Vienna, June 5, 1843); *Dom Sébastien, roi de Portugal* (Paris, Nov. 13, 1843); *Catarina Cornaro* (Naples, Jan. 12, 1844); *Rita, ou Le Mari battu* (1840; Paris, May 7, 1860; posthumously produced); *Il Duca d'Alba* (1840; Rome, March 22, 1882; posthumously produced).

BIBLIOGRAPHY: F. Cicconetti, *Vita di Donizetti* (Rome, 1864); F. Alborghetti and Galli, *Donizetti e S. Mayr* (Bergamo, 1875); Ch. Malherbe, *Catalogue biographique de la Section française à l'exposition de Bergame* (Paris, 1897); E. C. Verzino, *Le opere di G. Donizetti, contributo alla loro storia* (Milan, 1897); Ippolito Valetti, *Donizetti* (Rome, 1897); Adolfo Calzado, *Donizetti e l'opera italiana in Spagna* (Paris, 1897); A. Gabrielli, *Gaetano Donizetti* (Turin, 1904); A. Cametti, *Donizetti a Roma, con lettere e documenti inediti* (Milan, 1907); C. Caversazzi, *Donizetti* (Bergamo, 1924); G. Donati-Petteni, *Donizetti* (Milan, 1930); G. Gavazzeni, *G. Donizetti* (Milan, 1935); Gino Monaldi, *G. Donizetti* (Turin, 1938); A. Fraccaroli, *Donizetti* (Milan, 1944); G. Barblan, *L' opera di Donizetti nell' età romantica* (Bergamo, 1948); G. Zavadini, *Donizetti: vita, musiche, epistolario* (Bergamo, 1948; a greatly detailed biography, 1019 pp.); Lea Bossi, *Donizetti* (Brescia, 1956). An extensive collection of Donizetti's letters was publ. by Zavadini in *G. Donizetti: vicende della sua vita e catalogo* (Bergamo, 1941).

Donizetti, Giuseppe, Italian bandmaster and composer; brother of Gaetano Donizetti; b. Bergamo, Nov. 9, 1788; d. Constantinople, Feb. 10, 1856. In 1832 he was summoned by the Sultan of Turkey to take charge of Turkish military bands. He accepted, and successfully accomplished the task of introducing Western instruments and modernizing the repertory. The sultan richly rewarded him with honors and money, and Donizetti remained in Constantinople to the end of his life.

Donostia, José Antonio de, Basque composer and student of folklore; b. San Sebastián, Jan. 10, 1886. Donostia is his Basque name, corresponding to Dominus Sebastianus, or San Sebastián, his religious name; full family name, José Antonio Zulaica y Arregui. He attended the Capuchin College in Lecaroz (Navarra); at the age of 16 entered the Franciscan Order; ordained priest. He studied organ and violin with various teachers; composition with Eugène Cools in Paris. He lived many years in France; also traveled in South America; was compelled to leave Spain during the civil war of 1936-39. He was one of the founders of the Instituto Español de Musicología; corresponding member of the Academia de Bellas Artes in Madrid. His chief accomplishment is the collection of more than 1,000 Basque folksongs which he wrote down and transcribed during his methodical journeys through the Basque countryside; 493 of these are publ. in his Basque Cancionero, *Euskel Eres-Sorta* (1912); also publ. *De la música popular vasca; Como canta el vasco,* etc. He wrote several cantatas (*La vie profonde de Saint François d'Assise; Les trois miracles de Sainte Cécile; La quête héroïque de Graal*); *Préludes basques* for piano; many motets and other sacred choruses; *Itinerarium mysticum* for organ (3 vols.; based on Gregorian themes); has compiled a bibliography of Basque folk music.

Donovan, Richard Frank, American organist and composer; b. New Haven, Conn., Nov. 29, 1891. He studied at the School of Music, Yale Univ. (received the Steinert Prize) and the Institute of Musical Art, N. Y. (Mus. Bac., 1922), also in Paris with Charles Widor. Returning to America, he served as organist in various New York churches; in 1923, he joined the faculty of Smith College; in 1928 was appointed at the School of Music, Yale Univ.; in 1947, he became prof. of music; also organist and choirmaster of Christ Church in New Haven. He conducted the New Haven Symph. Orch. (1936-51). He has been active as an organizer of music festivals and served on the executive board of the quarterly publication 'New Music'; also a member of the Board of Governors of the American Composers' Alliance. As composer, Donovan was at first influenced by French music; his early pieces are Impressionistic; at the same time he cultivated a modern polyphonic idiom in his madrigals and other choral works. After 1950 he developed an astringent style verging on integral atonality, with strong asymmetric rhythms.—Works: *Wood-Notes,* for flute, strings, and harp (Smith College, June 14, 1925, composer conducting); *How Far is it to Bethlehem?,* for women's voices and organ (1927); *Chanson of the Bells of Oseney,* for women's voices and piano (1930); suite No. 1, for piano (1932); sextet for wind instruments and piano (1932); *Smoke and Steel,* a symph. poem after Carl Sandburg, for large orch. (1932); *To All You Ladies Now at Land,* for men's voices with orch. (1932); four songs, for soprano and string quartet (1933); symph. for chamber orch. (Yaddo Festival, Saratoga Springs, N. Y., Sept. 18, 1937, composer conducting); trio, for violin, cello, and piano (1937); *Ricercare* for oboe and string orch. (Yaddo Festival, N. Y., Sept. 11, 1938); three choruses for women's voices a cappella (1938); *Serenade* for oboe and string trio (1939); *Fantasy on American Folk Ballads,* for men's voices and piano or orch. (1940); suite for string orch. and oboe (1944-45); *Design for Radio,* for orch. (1945); *Hymn to the Night,* for women's voices (1947); *Two Choral Preludes on American Folk Hymns,* for organ (1947); *Good Ale,* for men's voices and piano (1947); *How Should I Love?,* for women's voices and piano (1947); *New England Chronicle,* an orch. overture (NBC Symph. Orch., May 17, 1947); *Paignion,* for organ (1947); *A Fable,* for soprano and piano (1948); *Passacaglia on Vermont Folk Tunes,* for orch. (1949); *Four Songs on English Texts,* for voice and piano (1950); *Terzetto* for two violins and viola (1950); suite No. 2 for piano (1953); quartet for woodwinds (1953); *Soundings,* for trumpet, bassoon, and 16 percussion instruments (1953); *Four Songs of Nature,* for women's voices (1953); *Three Madrigals,* for chorus a cappella (1954); *I will Sing unto the Lord,* for men's voices with organ (1954); Mass for unison voices and organ (1955); *Antiphon and Chorale,* for organ (1955); *Adventure,* for piano (1956); Symphony in D (1956).—Cf. A. Frankenstein, *Richard Donovan,* in the 'Bulletin of American Composers Alliance' (No. 4, 1956).

Dont, Jakob, Austrian violinist, teacher, and composer; b. Vienna, March 2, 1815; d. there, Nov. 17, 1888; son of the cellist, **Joseph Valentin Dont** (b. Georgenthal Bohemia, April 15, 1776; d. Vienna, Dec. 14, 1833); pupil of Böhm and Hellmesberger (Sr.) at Vienna Cons.; joined the orch. of the 'Hofburgtheater' in 1831, and the court orch. in 1834. He taught in the 'Akademie der Tonkunst,' and the Seminary at St. Anna; Leopold Auer was his pupil. From 1873 he was professor at the Vienna Cons. His book of violin studies, *Gradus ad Parnassum,* is widely known; he published altogether some 50 works.

Door (dohr), **Anton,** Austrian pianist; b. Vienna, June 20, 1833; d. there, Nov. 7, 1919. He was a pupil of Czerny (piano) and Sechter (composition). He gave successful concerts in Germany; after a tour in Sweden (1856-57), he went to Russia, where he taught at the Moscow Cons. (1864). In 1869 he returned to Vienna and became professor of the advanced piano class at the Vienna Cons., a post that he held for 32 years (1869-1901).

Doorslaer, George van, Belgian music scholar; b. Malines, Sept. 27, 1864; d. there, Jan. 16, 1940. He studied medicine; music was his avocation. In association with Charles van den Borren he began a detailed study of old Belgian music; became particularly interested in the history of the carillon.—Writings: *Le carillon et les carilloneurs de la Tour Saint-Rombaut, à Malines* (1893); *Les Waghevens, fondeurs de cloches* (1908); *Le carillon, son origine et son développement* (1911); numerous papers on Philippe de Monte, whose works he edited. For a complete list of publications see Albert van der Linden's article in 'Die Musik in Geschichte und Gegenwart.'

Dopper, Cornelis, eminent Dutch composer and conductor; b. Stadskanaal, near Groningen, Feb. 7, 1870; d. Amsterdam, Sept. 18, 1939. He studied at the Leipzig Cons.; returning to Holland, he became assistant conductor of the Concertgebouw Orch. in Amsterdam (1908), and was associated with that orchestra until 1931. He also traveled as opera conductor in America (1906-8). He wrote four operas: *Het blinde meisje von Castel Cuille* (1892); *Het Eerekruis* (Amsterdam, 1894); *Fritjof* (1895); *Willem Ratcliff* (1901); the ballet,

Meidevorn, with soli and chorus; 8 symphonies: No. 1, *Diana,* ballet symph. (1896); No. 2 (1903; finished after the 3rd); No. 3, *Rembrandt* (1892; later rewritten); No. 4, *Symphonietta* (1906); No. 5, *Symphonia Epica* with chorus and soli (1914); No. 6, *Amsterdam* (1912); No. 7, *Zuiderzee;* No. 8; other orchestral works: a symphonic rhapsody, *Paris;* 5 suites; *Divertimento; Ciaconna gotica,* symph. variations (his best known work; Concertgebouw, Amsterdam, Oct. 24, 1920, composer conducting); Concertino for trumpet and 3 kettledrums; cello concerto; 2 overtures. Chamber music: string quartet; violin sonatas; cello sonata; a scherzo for woodwinds and piano. Many choral works; songs; piano pieces.—Cf. Sem Dresden, *Het Muziekleven in Nederland sinds 1880* (Amsterdam, 1923).

Doppler, Albert Franz, Austrian composer and conductor; b. Lwów, Oct. 16, 1821; d. Baden, near Vienna, July 27, 1883. He studied music with his father; played first flute in the Pest Opera Orch.; in 1858 settled in Vienna as ballet conductor at the Court Opera; taught flute at the Vienna Cons. from 1865. His first opera *Benjowsky* was well received in Budapest (Sept. 29, 1847) and had several revivals under the title *Afanasia;* the following operas were also produced in Budapest: *Ilka* (Dec. 29, 1849); *Wanda* (Dec. 16, 1856); *Two Hussars* (March 12, 1853); his last opera, *Judith,* was produced in Vienna (Dec. 30, 1870). He also wrote 15 ballets.

Doppler, Árpád, Hungarian pianist, son of Karl Doppler; b. Pest, June 5, 1857; d. Stuttgart, Aug. 13, 1927. He went to Stuttgart as a young man and studied there; was engaged to teach in New York and spent three years there (1880-83); later returned to Stuttgart and taught at the Cons. He publ. a number of salon pieces for piano; also wrote a comic opera, *Haligula* (Stuttgart, 1891).

Doppler, Karl, Austrian composer and conductor; brother of Albert Franz Doppler; b. Lwów, Sept. 12, 1825; d. Stuttgart, March 10, 1900. Like his father and his brother, he became an excellent flute player; gave concerts in all major cities of Europe. He was then appointed as court Kapellmeister in Stuttgart, and held this position for 33 years (1865-98). He wrote an opera and pieces for the flute.

Dorati, Antal, distinguished conductor; b. Budapest, April 9, 1906. He studied with Kodály and Bartók; conducted at the Budapest Opera at the age of 18; conducted opera in Dresden (1928) and in Münster (1929-32); was conductor of the 'Ballet Russe de Monte Carlo' (1934-40), and toured Australia with it. He made his American début with the National Symph. Orch. in Washington (1937); in 1945 was appointed conductor of the Dallas Symph. Orch.; in 1948 was chosen to succeed Mitropoulos as conductor of the Minneapolis Symph. Orch. He became an American citizen on April 21, 1947. He has composed a string quartet, oboe quintet, divertimento for orch., violin pieces, and songs; also a successful ballet *Graduation Ball* (1939) arranged from the waltzes of Johann Strauss. On April 19, 1957, he conducted the Minneapolis Symph. Orch. in the première of his dramatic cantata, *The Way of the Cross.*

Doret (doh-rā'), **Gustave,** Swiss composer; b. Aigle, Sept. 20, 1866; d. Lausanne, April 19, 1943. He received his first instruction at Lausanne; studied violin with Joachim in Berlin; then entered the Paris Cons. as pupil of Marsick (violin) and Dubois and Massenet (composition); conductor of the 'Concerts d'Harcourt' and of the 'Société Nationale de Musique' in Paris (1893-95); conductor of the concerts at the National Exposition at Geneva (1896); conductor of the Saint-Saëns Festival at Vevey (1913); at the Opéra-Comique (1907-9); also appeared as visiting conductor in Rome, London, and Amsterdam. Doret was a member of the commission for editing Rameau's collected works. In his music Doret cultivated the spirit of Swiss folksongs; his vocal writing is distinguished by its natural flow of melody.—Works: The operas *Les Armaillis* (Paris, Nov. 8, 1906; very successful; a revised and enlarged version, Paris, May 5, 1930); *Le Nain du Hasli* (Geneva, Feb. 6, 1908); dramatic legend, *Loÿs* (Vevey, 1912); *La Tisseuse d'Orties* (Paris, 1926); *Voix de la Patrie,* cantata (1891); an oratorio, *Les Sept Paroles du Christ* (1895); *La Fête des Vignerons* (1905); incidental music to Shakespeare's *Julius Caesar* and to plays by René Morax: *Henriette, Aliénor, La Nuit des quatre-temps, Wilhelm Tell, Davel* (all produced at Mézières); several pieces for orchestra; string quartet; piano quintet; about 150 songs.—Books: *Musique et musiciens* (1915); *Lettres à ma nièce sur la musique en Suisse* (1919); *Pour notre indépendance musicale* (1920); *Temps et Contretemps* (1942).—Cf. J. Dupérier, *Gustave Doret* (Paris, 1932).

Dörffel, Alfred, German music editor; b. Waldenburg, Jan. 24, 1821; d. Leipzig, Jan. 22, 1905. He went to Leipzig at the age of

14, and studied with G. W. Fink and K. G. Müller. Mendelssohn and Schumann became interested in his musical education; in 1845 Schumann recommended him as arranger to Breitkopf & Härtel. In 1861 he opened a circulating library in Leipzig; it was later purchased by C. F. Peters and became the nucleus of the 'Musikbibliothek Peters' at Leipzig. The fame of the 'Edition Peters' is in large measure due to Dörffel's careful editorship. As a music critic and editor he was highly esteemed in Leipzig; in 1885 he received the degree of *Dr. phil.* (hon. c.) from the Univ. He published a catalogue of his library (1861; with supplement, 1890); a German translation of Berlioz's *Traité d'Instrumentation* (1863, authorized by Berlioz himself; 4th ed., 1888); *Führer durch die musikalische Welt* (1868); *Geschichte der Gewandhauskonzerte 1781-1881* (Leipzig, 1884; a very valuable compilation, with commentary, of programs given by the Gewandhaus orch. for 100 seasons); a thematic catalogue of Bach's instrumental works and of Schumann's complete works (1871).

Dorfmann, Ania, Russian pianist; b. Odessa, July 9, 1899; studied with Isidor Philipp in Paris; toured in Europe (1920-26); settled in America in 1936; made her first American appearance in a Town Hall recital in New York (Nov. 27, 1936); played with the N. B. C. Symph. Orch. under Toscanini (Dec. 2, 1939); also appeared in recitals.

Doria, Clara. Stage name of **Clara Kathleen (Barnett) Rogers.**

Dorian, Frederick (real name, Friedrich Deutsch), eminent musicologist; b. Vienna, July 1, 1902. He studied at the Univ. of Vienna with Guido Adler (*Dr. phil.,* 1925); also a graduate of the State Academy of Music in Vienna and a pupil of the Schönberg Seminar in Vienna; conducted operatic, concert, and broadcast performances in Austria, Germany, Italy, and the U. S.; was music critic of the 'Berliner Morgenpost' (1930-33), the 'Frankfurter Zeitung' (in Paris, 1934) and the 'Neues Wiener Journal'; then came to the U.S.; in 1936 he was appointed prof. of music at the Carnegie Institute of Technology in Pittsburgh; he became an American citizen in 1941.—Publications: *Die Fugenarbeit in den Werken Beethovens,* in 'Studien zur Musikwissenschaft' (1927; under the name Friedrich Deutsch); *Hausmusik alter Meister,* in 3 vols. (Berlin, 1933); *The History of Music in Performance* (N. Y., 1942); *The Musical Workshop* (N. Y., 1947).

Doring, Ernest Nicholas, American specialist in violins; b. New York, May 29, 1877; d. Fort Worth, Texas, July 9, 1955. He studied violin in Chicago; in 1894 he joined the violin maker John Friedrich of New York and remained with the firm for 33 years (until 1927). In 1933 he moved back to Chicago; was manager of the rare-violin dept. of the Wurlitzer Co. In 1938 he began publishing the magazine 'Violins and Violinists.' Author of *How Many Strads?* (Chicago, 1945) and *The Guadagnini Family of Violin Makers* (Chicago, 1949).

Döring, (Carl) Heinrich, German piano pedagogue; b. Dresden, July 4, 1834; d. there, March 26, 1916. He was a pupil at the Leipzig Cons. (1852-55) of Hauptmann, Lobe, Plaidy, and Richter. In 1858, teacher at the Dresden Cons.; appointed prof. in 1875.—Works: Instructive piano collections: *Die Grundpfeiler des Klavierspiels* (3 parts); *Praktische Studien und Übungsstücke für das polyphone Klavierspiel; Technische Hülfs- und Bildungsmittel;* numerous sonatas, sonatinas, and studies. Besides these he wrote many male choruses; suites for string orch.; a Mass; motets; also published *Rückblicke auf die Geschichte der Erfindung des Hammerklaviers im 18. Jahrhundert* (Dresden, 1898).

Dorn, Alexander (Julius Paul), son of Heinrich Dorn; prolific composer; b. Riga, June 8, 1833; d. Berlin, Nov. 27, 1901. He studied with his father; traveled as pianist and choral conductor; spent 10 years in Egypt (1855-65); then settled in Berlin, where he taught piano at the Hochschule. He wrote more than 400 compositions, including Masses and operettas; also a number of salon pieces for piano.

Dorn, Heinrich (Ludwig Egmont), b. Königsberg, Nov. 14, 1804; d. Berlin, Jan. 10, 1892. He was a law student at Königsberg in 1823, but studied music diligently, continuing in Berlin under L. Berger (piano), Zelter, and B. Klein. After teaching in Frankfurt, he became Kapellmeister of the Königsberg Theater in 1828; in 1829, music director (and Schumann's teacher) at Leipzig, where he met young Wagner; music director at the Cathedral of St. Peter's in Riga (1831-42); Kapellmeister and city music director at Cologne (1843), where he founded (1845) the 'Rheinische Musikschule' (which became the Cologne Cons. in 1850); 1844-47, conducted the Lower Rhenish Music Festivals. From 1849-69 he was court Kapellmeister at the Royal Opera,

Berlin; was pensioned, with the title of 'Royal Professor,' and busied himself with teaching and musical criticism.—Works: The operas *Die Rolandsknappen* (Berlin, 1826); *Der Zauberer* (Berlin, 1827); *Die Bettlerin* (Königsberg, 1828); *Abu Kara* (Leipzig, 1831); *Das Schwärmermädchen* (Leipzig, 1832); *Der Schöffe von Paris* (Riga, 1841); *Die Musiker von Aix-la-Chapelle* (1848); *Artaxerxes* (Berlin, 1850); *Die Nibelungen* (Berlin, March 27, 1854; anticipating Wagner in the operatic treatment of the subject, but, despite initial successes, failing completely in the end); *Ein Tag in Russland* (Berlin, 1857; comic); *Der Botenläufer von Pirna* (Mannheim, March 15, 1865); an operetta, *Gewitter bei Sonnenschein* (Dresden, 1865); and the ballet *Amor's Macht* (Leipzig, 1830). Other works: *Missa pro defunctis* (Berlin, 1851); cantatas, symphonies, orchestral pieces (*Siegesfestklänge*, 1866); piano music; songs. He was musical editor of the 'Berliner Post,' and a contributor to the 'Neue Berliner Musikzeitung.' He published an autobiography, *Aus meinem Leben*, with a collection of various essays (7 vols., 1870-86).—Cf. W. Neumann, *Die Componisten der neueren Zeit*, IV (Kassel, 1854); Adam Rauh, *H. Dorn als Opernkomponist* (Munich, 1939).

Dostal, Nico, Austrian composer of light music; b. Korneuburg, Nov. 25, 1895. He was brought up in a musical family; his uncle, Hermann Dostal (1874-1930), was a composer of celebrated military marches. Dostal studied in Linz and Vienna; specialized in arrangements of popular music, and began to compose on his own much later in life; wrote waltzes and light orchestral music; produced numerous successful operettas: *Clivia* (Berlin, 1933); *Prinzessin Nofretete* (Cologne, 1935); *Monika* (Stuttgart, 1937); *Manina* (Berlin, 1942); *Dr. Eisenbart* (Nuremberg, 1952), etc.

Doty, William, American organist and music educator; b. Grand Ledge, Mich., April 29, 1907. He studied at the Univ. of Michigan (Ph. D., 1936); took organ lessons with Joseph Bonnet in Paris and Karl Straube in Leipzig; was on the faculty of the Univ. of Michigan (1933-38) and of the Univ. of Texas (1938-57); publ. a students' workbook, *The Analysis of Form in Music* (1947).

Dotzauer, (Justus Johann) Friedrich, famous German cellist; b. Hässelrieth, near Hildburghausen, June 20, 1783; d. Dresden, March 6, 1860. Pupil of Heuschkel (piano), Gleichmann (violin), and Rüttinger (composition) at Hildburghausen, and of Hessner for cello; he took further lessons of Kriegck at Meiningen, where he played in the court orch. (1801-5); then was a member of the Leipzig orch. (1806-11). He joined the Dresden orch. in 1811; became first cellist in 1821 and was pensioned in 1852. Among his pupils were Karl Schubert, Drechsler, Kummer, and his own son, K. L. Dotzauer. —Works: An opera, *Graziosa* (Dresden, 1841); symphonies, overtures, Masses, and, more especially, cello concertos; sonatas, variations, exercises for cello.

Dotzauer, Karl Ludwig (Louis), German cellist; b. Dresden, Dec. 7, 1811; d. Kassel, July 1, 1897. He studied with his father, Friedrich Dotzauer; from his youth to his death, for 67 years, he was cellist of the court orch. in Kassel (1830-1897).

Dounis, Demetrius Constantine, Greek-American violinist and teacher; b. Athens, Dec. 7, 1886; d. Los Angeles, Aug. 13, 1954. He studied violin with Ondriček in Vienna and simultaneously enrolled as a medical student at the Univ. of Vienna; made several tours as a violinist in Europe, including Russia; after World War I he was appointed professor at the Salonika Cons. He then taught in England and eventually settled in America, where he acquired a great number of devoted students. He established his New York studio in 1939; went to Los Angeles in 1954. He originated the technique of the "brush stroke" in which the bow is handled naturally and effortlessly; published numerous manuals, including: *The Artist's Technique of Violin Playing; The Absolute Independence of the Fingers; Advanced Studies for the Development of the Independence of the Fingers in Violin Playing on a Scientific Basis; The Development of Flexibility*, etc.—Cf. V. Leland, *Dounis Principles of Violin Playing* (London, 1949).

Douthitt, Wilfrid. See **Graveure.**

Dow, Dorothy, American soprano; b. Houston, Texas, Oct. 8, 1920; educated at the Juilliard School of Music, N. Y.; sang in churches; also conducted choral performances. She made her operatic début in Buffalo (1946); then appeared successfully in Italy, Switzerland, and England.

Dowland, John, eminent lutenist and composer; b. Ireland, possibly in County Dublin, Dec. 1562; d. London, Jan. 21, 1626. He went to England c. 1578; was in Paris in the service of Sir Henry Cobham (1580-83);

then returned to England and married; Mus. Bac. (Oxford, 1588); went to Germany, where he was patronized by the Duke of Brunswick (1594), and thence to Italy, where he seems to have studied with the renowned Italian madrigalist Luca Marenzio; he subsequently returned to England for a short stay, then going to Dublin, where, it appears, he took up residence in Trinity College; appointed lutenist to the King of Denmark Christian IV (1598); lived at Elsinore, except for a time in 1601, until 1609, returning then to England; in 1612 he was lutenist to Lord Walden; later became one of the 6 lutenists in the service of Charles I. As the peer of the English school of lutenist-composers, Dowland brought about many innovations, chiefly in the structure of the song; among other things, he indulged in elaborate chromatic developments, and treated the accompanying part or parts as separate entities, obtaining, in them, harmonic effects quite modern even to present-day hearers.—Works: *The First Booke of Songes or Ayres of foure partes, with Tableture for the Lute* (1597); *The Second Booke of Songes or Ayres of 2. 4. and 5. partes* (1600); *The Third Booke of Songes or Ayres* (1603); *Lachrymae, or, Seven Teares, figured in seaven passionate Pavans . . . set forth for the Lute, Viols, or Violins, in five partes* (1605); songs in 'A Musicall Banquet' (1610), ed. by his son Robert; *A Pilgrimes Solace . . . Musicall Harmonie of 3. 4. and 5. partes . . . with Lute and Viols* (1612); and a translation of Ornithoparcus' *Micrologus* (1609). The *First Booke* was republ. by the Mus. Antiquarian Society (1844), and all 3 books, together with *A Pilgrimes Solace* and the 3 songs in 'A Musicall Banquet,' have been publ. with the original lute tablature by E. H. Fellowes in his 'English School of Lutenist Songwriters' (begun in 1920). The *Lachrymae,* transcribed into modern notation, were publ. by Peter Warlock (Oxford Univ. Press, 1927).—Cf. O. Becker, *Die englischen Madrigalisten W. Bird, Th. Morley und J. Dowland* (Leipzig, 1901); E. H. Fellowes, *The English Madrigal Composers* (Oxford, 1921); Peter Warlock, *The English Ayre* (London, 1926).

Dowland, Robert, English composer and lute player; son of John Dowland; b. London, 1586; d. there, 1641. He remained in London after his father went to Denmark; in 1626, succeeded his father as lutenist to Charles I. He publ. *Varietie of Lute Lessons* (1610); edited *A Musicall Banquett,* a collection of English, French, Spanish, and Italian airs.

Downes, Olin, eminent American music critic; b. Evanston, Ill., Jan. 27, 1886; d. New York, Aug. 22, 1955. He began study of music at an early age, later student of Dr. L. Kelterborn (piano, music history, and analysis), Carl Baermann (piano), Homer Norris and Clifford Heilman (harmony), and J. P. Marshall (harmony and music appreciation); 1906-24, music critic of the 'Boston Post'; in 1924 appointed music critic of the 'New York Times'; held this post until his death; lecturer at Boston Univ. under the auspices of Mass. Extension and Lowell Institute, and at the Brooklyn Academy of Arts and Sciences (1932-34), etc.; awarded Order of the Commander of the White Rose, Finland (1937); hon. Mus. Doc., Cincinnati Cons. of Mus. (1939).—Books: *The Lure of Music* (1918); *Symphonic Broadcasts* (1931); *Symphonic Masterpieces* (1935). He edited *Select Songs of Russian Composers* (1922); contributed articles to the 'Mus. Quarterly,' 'Music Review', and many other music magazines; compiled and annotated *Ten Operatic Masterpieces, From Mozart to Prokofiev* (1952). A selection from his writings was publ. in 1957 under the title *Olin Downes on Music,* ed. by his widow, Irene Downes.

Doyen, Albert, French composer; b. Vendresse (Ardennes), April 3, 1882; d. Paris, Oct. 22, 1935. He studied composition with Widor at the Paris Cons. In 1917 he established the choral society Fêtes du Peuple, and subsequently conducted more than 200 concerts. Among his works are a symphony, an ode in memory of Zola, a string quartet, a piano trio, a violin sonata, and numerous choral compositions. For a complete list, see 'Die Musik in Geschichte und Gegenwart.'

Draeseke, Felix (August Bernhard), German composer; b. Coburg, Oct. 7, 1835; d. Dresden, Feb. 26, 1913. He studied privately with Julius Rietz in Leipzig; became a friend of Liszt and Wagner, and an ardent disciple of the nationalist German school. In 1864 he went to Switzerland; taught at the Cons. of Lausanne (1864-74) and later in Geneva. In 1876 he returned to Germany and became prof. at the Dresden Cons. A Wagnerian in his youth, he was regarded as a radical, but he never accepted the modern tendencies of the 20th century, which he attacked in his pamphlet *Die Konfusion in der Musik* (1906), directed chiefly against Richard Strauss. He was a prolific composer, but his works are virtually unknown outside Germany. A Draeseke society was formed in Germany in 1931, and issued sporadic bulletins. Draeseke wrote 6 operas: *König Si-*

gurd (1853-57; only a fragment perf., Meiningen, 1867); *Herrat* (1879; Dresden, March 10, 1892); *Gudrun* (Hanover, Jan. 11, 1884); *Bertrand de Born* (1894); *Fischer und Kalif* (Prague, April 15, 1905); *Merlin* (perf. posthumously, Gotha, May 10, 1913); choral trilogy *Christus* (his major work), consisting of a prelude, *Die Geburt des Herrn;* I. *Christi Weihe,* II. *Christus der Prophet,* III. *Tod und Sieg des Herrn* (produced in its entirety in Dresden and Berlin, 1912); Symph. in G (1872); Symph. in F (1876); *Symphonia Tragica* (1886); *Symphonia Comica* (1912); sacred and secular choruses; many songs; piano concerto; violin concerto; 3 string quartets; quintet for piano, violin, viola, cello, and horn; clarinet sonata, etc. A complete list of works, including MSS, is found in H. Stephani's article on Draeseke in 'Die Musik in Geschichte und Gegenwart'. Draeseke's theoretical publications include: *Anweisung zum kunstgerechten Modulieren* (1875); *Zur Beseitigung des Tritonus* (1876); a versified *Lehre von der Harmonia* (1885); *Der gebundene Stil: Lehrbuch für Kontrapunkt und Fugue* (Hanover, 1902).—Cf. H. Platzbecker, *Felix Draeseke,* in vol. III of 'Monographien moderner Musikèr' (Leipzig, 1909); E. Röder, *Felix Draeseke* (2 vols.; Dresden, 1930; Berlin, 1935).

Draghi (drah'gē), **Antonio,** Italian composer of operas and oratorios; b. Rimini, 1635; d. Vienna, Jan. 16, 1700. He was a singer in Venice; in 1658 he settled in Vienna, and was appointed 'Hoftheater-Intendant' to Leopold I in 1673, also Kapellmeister to the empress. From 1661-99 he produced 67 operas, 116 festival plays ('feste teatrali') and serenades, 32 oratorios, 11 cantatas, 2 Masses, etc.—Reprints are to be found in the 'Denkmäler der Tonkunst in Österreich,' XXIII, 1 (2 Masses, a Stabat Mater, and 2 hymns), and in A. Schering's 'Geschichte der Musik in Biespielen,' No. 226 (an opera scene).—Cf. M. Neuhaus, *A. Draghi,* in 'Studien zur Musikwissenschaft,' I (1913).

Draghi, Giovanni Battista, Italian harpsichordist; lived in London from 1667-1706, was organist to the queen in 1677; also music teacher to Queens Mary and Anne. He wrote the music to Dryden's ode *From Harmony,* and (with Locke) to Shadwell's *Psyche* and d'Urfey's *The Wonders in the Sun, or The Kingdom of Birds* (London, 1706); also many songs, and instructive harpsichord lessons.

Dragoi, Sabin, Rumanian composer; b. Seliste, June 6, 1894; studied with Novák in Prague. He was instructor at the Cluj Cons. (1942-46); director at the Timisoara Cons. (1946-48); since 1949 at the Institute of Art there.—Works: the operas *Napasta* (1928) and *Kir Janulea* (1939); *Le poème de la nation,* for orch. (1938); piano concerto (1943); chamber music; choral pieces and songs.

Dragonetti, Domenico, noted Italian double-bass player; b. Venice, April 7, 1763; d. London, April 16, 1846. This 'Paganini of the contra-basso' was self-taught, excepting a few lessons from Berini, player at San Marco, whom he succeeded in 1782; he had already played in the orchestras of the Opera buffa and Opera seria for 5 years, and composed concertos, etc., with double-bass parts impracticable for any one but himself. He appeared at London in 1794; with the cellist Lindley, his close friend for 52 years, he played at the Antient Concerts and the Philharmonic. As late as 1845, his virtuosity still unimpaired, he led the double-basses, at the unveiling of the Beethoven monument in Bonn, in the C minor symphony. To the British Museum he left a remarkable collection of scores, engravings, and old instruments; to San Marco, his favorite cello (a Gasparo da Salò).—Cf. F. Caffi: *Vita di D. Dragonetti* (Venice, 1846).

Drake, Earl R., American violinist and composer; b. Aurora, Ill., Nov. 26, 1865; d. Chicago, May 6, 1916. He studied violin in Chicago, and later with Joachim in Berlin. Head of violin department in Gottschalk Lyric School, Chicago (1893-7); organized his own school of music in Chicago in 1900.—Works: *The Blind Girl of Castel-Cuille,* 3-act opera and ballet (Chicago, Feb. 19, 1914); *The Mite and the Mighty,* 3-act light opera (Chicago, 1915); *Dramatic Prologue* for orch.; *Ballet* for orch.; *Gypsy Scenes* for violin and orch.; pieces for violin and piano (*Polish Dance, Mazurka, An Alpine Farewell,* etc.).—Cf. E. E. Hipsher, *American Opera and its Composers* (Philadelphia, 1934, pp. 162-64).

Drangosch, Ernesto, Argentinian pianist and composer; b. Buenos Aires, Jan. 22, 1882; d. there, June 26, 1925. He studied in Buenos Aires with Alberto Williams and Aguìrre, and in Berlin with Max Bruch, Humperdinck, and Ansorge; later toured Europe and America as pianist; returned to Buenos Aires (1905), and founded his own conservatory. His piano pieces have been published.

Dranishnikov, Vladimir, Russian conductor; b. St. Petersburg, May 29, 1893; d. Kiev, Feb. 6, 1939. He studied at the St. Petersburg Cons. with Mme. Essipoff (piano), Steinberg, Liadov, and Wihtol (composition); violinist at the St. Petersburg Opera (1914); conductor there (1918); chief conductor of the Kiev Opera from 1930 till his death. He wrote 2 symph. poems, choral works, songs, and piano music.

Drdla, Franz, composer and violinist; b. Saar, Moravia, Nov. 28, 1868; d. Gastein, Sept. 3, 1944. After 2 years at the Prague Cons. he studied at the Vienna Cons. under Hellmesberger (violin) and Krenn (composition), winning 1st prize for violin and the medal of the 'Gesellschaft der Musikfreunde'; for several years violinist in the orch. of the Hofoper; then made successful tours of Europe; 1923-25, lived in the U. S.; then in Vienna and Prague. As a composer he did not appear until 1904; since then his pieces for violin and piano have won enormous popularity, especially *Souvenir, Vision,* and the first Serenade in A (dedicated to, and played by, Jan Kubelik); also composed 2 operettas, *Das goldene Netz* (Leipzig, 1916) and *Die Ladenkomtesse* (Prague, 1917).

Drechsler (dreks'-lär), **Joseph,** composer; b. Wällisch-Birken (Vlachovo Březí), Bohemia, May 26, 1782; d. Vienna, Feb. 27, 1852. A pupil of the organist Grotius at Florenbach; chorusmaster and Kapellmeister (1812) at the Vienna court opera, then conductor in the theaters at Baden (near Vienna) and Pressburg; returning to Vienna, he became organist of the Servite church, in 1816 precentor at St. Ann's, in 1823 Kapellmeister at the University church and the Hofpfarrkirche; from 1822-30 he was also Kapellmeister at the Leopoldstadt Theater, and from 1844 Kapellmeister at St. Stephen's, succeeding Gänsbacher.—Works: 6 operas, and about 30 operettas, vaudevilles, and pantomimes; a Requiem, 10 other Masses, 3 cantatas, offertories, etc.; string quartets, organ fugues, piano sonatas, other piano music, songs, etc.; a method for organ, and a treatise on harmony. He reëdited Pleyel's Piano School, and publ. a theoretico-practical guide to Preluding.—Cf. C. Preiss, *Joseph Drechsler* (Graz, 1910).

Dregert (drā'gĕrt), **Alfred,** German conductor; b. Frankfurt-am-Oder, Sept. 26, 1836; d. Elberfeld, March 14, 1893. Pupil at the Stern Cons., Berlin, of Marx (theory) and von Bülow (piano). Opera conductor at Stettin, Rostock, Bamberg, and Trier; then conductor of male choral societies in Cologne and Elberfeld.

Dresden, Sem, notable Dutch composer; b. Amsterdam, April 20, 1881; pupil there of B. Zweers, and of Hans Pfitzner in Berlin; teacher of composition, harmony, and counterpoint at the Amsterdam Cons. (1919); director of the Royal Cons. at The Hague (1924-29); director of the Amsterdam Cons., succeeding Julius Röntgen (1929-37); now director of the Cons. at The Hague. In 1914 he founded the Haarlemsche Motet en Madrigaal Vereeniging in Amsterdam, which he conducted until 1926. Dresden is president of the Dutch Composers Society and of many other societies. The music of Dresden combines elements of Germanic Romanticism and Gallic Impressionism; at the same time, there is an underlying melo-rhythmic strain of distinctive Dutch folk music; the contrapuntal fabric is often of austere chorale-like quality.—Works: Theme and variations for orch. (1914); Sinfonietta for clarinet and orch. (1938); 2 violin concertos (1936, 1941); oboe concerto (1939); piano concerto (1946); 7 pieces for school orch. (1949); flute concerto (1950); *Dansflitsen,* for orch. (The Hague, Oct. 20, 1951); organ concerto (1953). Chamber music: piano trio No. 1 (1902); violin sonata (1905); 3 sextets for woodwinds and piano (1910, 1913, 1920); trio for 2 oboes and English horn (1912); cello sonata No. 1 (1916); sonata for flute and harp (1918); string quartet (1924); *Rameau Suite* for sextet (1916); cello sonata No. 2 (1942); sonata for solo violin (1942); piano trio No. 2 (1943); suite for solo cello (1947). Vocal works: *Chorus Tragicus,* for chorus, 5 trumpets, 2 cornets, and percussion (1928); Vocalises for mezzo-soprano and chamber orch. (1935); *Chorus Symphonicus* for solo voices and orch. (1944); also an operetta, *Toto,* in 3 acts (1945). He is the author of *Het Muziekleven in Nederland sinds 1880* (Amsterdam, 1923); co-editor of the new edition of van Milligen's *Music History,* and with Worp and Milligen of *Algemeene Muziekleer* (1931) and *Kleine Muziekleer.*—Cf. P. F. Sanders, *Moderne Nederlandsche Componisten* (The Hague, 1930); C. Backers, *Nederlandse Componisten van 1400 tot op onze Tijd* (The Hague, 1949).

Dresel (drā-zĕl), **Otto,** German composer; b. Geisenheim, Dec. 20, 1826; d. Beverly, Mass., July 26, 1890. He was a pupil of Hiller at Cologne, and Mendelssohn at Leipzig. He went to New York as concert pianist and teacher in 1848; revisited Germany, but settled in Boston in 1852, where for some 15 years he was very influential in introducing German music to the American public. He published only a few songs and piano pieces; several other works, though still in MS, have been produced, among them *In Memoriam,* ballad for soprano and orch., on Longfellow's poem on Agassiz' 50th birthday; a piano quartet; a piano trio.

Dressel, Erwin, German composer; b. Berlin, June 10, 1909. He was a pupil of Klatte and Juon; conductor at Hanover (1927-28); later lived in Berlin.—Works: satirical operas *Armer Columbus* (1928), *Der Kuchentanz* (1929), *Der Rosenbusch der Maria* (1930); *Die Zwillingsesel* (1932); also *Die Laune der Verliebten,* lyric opera in 1 act (Hamburg, 1949); saxophone sonata (1933); 4 symphonies; *Allegro brioso,* for piano and orch. (1950); 2 string quartets; piano pieces.

Dreves (drā'-vĕs), **Guido Maria,** German music historian; b. Hamburg, Oct. 27, 1854; d. Mitwitz, near Kronach, June 1, 1909. He entered the Jesuit Order; lived in Vienna and Würzburg. For distinguished service to the cause of hymnology and medieval music, the Univ. of Munich made him *Dr. phil.* (hon. c.). He was co-editor, with C. Blume and H. M. Bannister, of the great *Analecta hymnica medii aevi* (53 vols., 1886-1911); other works: *Cantiones Bohemicae* (1886); *Die Hymnen des Johannes von Jenstein* (1886); *Aurelius Ambrosius, der Vater des Kirchengesanges* (1893); *Psalteria rhythmica* (1901); *Die Kirche der Lateiner in ihren Liedern* (1908).

Drewett, Nora, English pianist; b. Sutton, Surrey, June 14, 1882. She studied piano at the Paris Cons. (Duvernoy) and in Munich (Stavenhagen); appeared in recitals and with symph. orchestras in Germany, Great Britain, France, etc. She married the violinist Géza von Kresz in 1918, and settled in Toronto.

Dreyer (dry'-er), **Johann Melchior,** German organist and composer; b. Röttingen, Württemberg, June 24, 1746; d. Ellwangen, March 22, 1824. He studied in Ellwangen, where he became church organist; wrote chiefly church music, adopting a modern homophonic style. Among his published works are *6 Missae breves et rurales ad modernum genium* (1790); *24 Hymni brevissimi ad vesperas* (1791); *Sehr kurze und leichte Landmessen* (1793); *Deutsche Messe* (1800), etc. He also wrote organ music.

Dreyschock (drī'-shŏhk), **Alexander,** brilliant pianist; b. Zack, Bohemia, Oct. 15, 1818; d. Venice, April 1, 1869. A student of Tomaschek, he acquired a virtuoso technique and was regarded as a worthy rival of Liszt in technical dexterity. At 8 he was able to play in public; toured North Germany (1838); spent two years in Russia (1840-42); visited Brussels, Paris, and London, then Holland and Austria. In 1862 he was called to St. Petersburg to act as professor in the newly-founded Cons. In 1868, he went to Italy, where he died. His astounding facility in playing octaves, sixths, and thirds, and performing solos with the left hand alone cast a glamour about his performance; he reached the zenith of his fame about 1850.—Works: an opera, *Florette, oder die erste Liebe Heinrichs des IV.;* an overture for orch.; a rondo for orch.; a string quartet, and 140 piano pieces of the salon type.

Dreyschock, Felix, German pianist, son of Raimund Dreyschock; b. Leipzig, Dec. 27, 1860; d. Berlin, Aug. 1, 1906. He studied under Grabau, Ehrlich, Taubert, and Kiel; gave successful concerts, and was professor at the Stern Cons., Berlin. His piano pieces are well-written and effective; he also published a violin sonata and songs.

Dreyschock, Raimund, violinist, brother of Alexander Dreyschock; b. Zack, Bohemia, Aug. 20, 1824; d. Leipzig, Feb. 6, 1869. Pupil of Pixis, Prague; concertmaster at the Gewandhaus concerts (1850-69) and violin teacher in the Cons. at Leipzig.—His wife **Elizabeth** (b. Cologne, 1832; d. there, July, 1911) was a contralto singer who founded and managed a vocal academy in Berlin.

Drieberg (drē'-berg), **Friedrich Johann von,** b. Charlottenburg, Dec. 10, 1780; d. there, May 21, 1856. He was Spontini's pupil in Paris, and produced 2 operas, *Don Cocagno* (Berlin, 1812) and *Der Sänger und der Schneider* (Berlin, Nov. 23, 1814); others left in MS. He was best known as a writer on Greek music whose theories and conclusions, however, have long been entirely discredited.—Writings: *Die mathematische Intervallenlehre der Griechen* (1818); *Aufschlüsse über die Musik der Griechen* (1819); *Die praktische Musik der Griechen* (1821); *Die pneumatischen Erfindungen der Griechen* (1822); *Wörterbuch der griech. Musik* (1835); *Die griechische Musik, auf ihre Grundgesetze zurückgeführt* (1841); *Die Kunst der musikalishen Composition . . . nach griechischen Grundsätzen bearbeitet* (1858).

Driessler, Johannes, German composer of choral music; b. Friedrichsthal, near Saarbrücken, Jan. 26, 1921. He studied with Karl Rahner; at the age of 13 filled a regular position as church organist. In 1946 he was engaged as instructor at the Music Academy in Detmold. As a composer of oratorios, cantatas, and other choral works, he has shown outstanding practical ability, with the result that his works entered the active repertory of church and secular institutions in Germany.—Works: oratorios: *Dein Reich komme* (Essen, 1950); *Gaudia Mundana* (Frankfurt, 1952); *De profundis* (Essen, 1953); a cappella choruses: *Sinfonia Sacra* (Detmold, 1948); *Cantica Nova* (Berlin, 1951); etc.; also works for chamber music combinations; numerous educational compositions.

Drigo (drē'-goh), **Riccardo,** Italian composer and conductor; b. Padua, June 30, 1846; d. there, Oct. 1, 1930. He conducted at the Imperial Theater of St. Petersburg for many years; after the World War (1914-18), he returned to his native city. Among his works (operas, ballets, vocal music, piano pieces, etc.) are the well-known ballet *I milioni d'Arlecchino* (*Harlequin's Millions*), which includes the famous *Serenade,* and the popular *Valse Bluette.*—Cf. S. Travaglia, *Riccardo Drigo, l'uomo e l'artista* (Padua, 1929).

Drinker, Henry S., Jr., American music scholar and translator; b. Philadelphia, Sept. 15, 1880; pupil of Emmy Emery; by profession a lawyer. He translated the texts of all the Bach cantatas and of the complete vocal works of Brahms and Schumann; author of *The Chamber Music of Johannes Brahms* (Philadelphia, 1932).

Drobisch, Moritz Wilhelm, German scholar; b. Leipzig, Aug. 16, 1802; d. there, Sept. 30, 1896. 1826 prof. extraordinary of mathematics, and 1842 prof. ordinary of philosophy, at Leipzig Univ. Besides various works on mathematics and philosophy, he wrote several valuable essays on musical subjects; among the latter are *Über die mathematische Bestimmung der mus. Intervalle* (1846), *Über mus. Tonbestimmung und Temperatur* (1852), *Nachträge zur Theorie der mus. Tonverhältnisse* (1855), *Über ein zwischen Altem und Neuem vermittelndes Tonsystem,* in 'Allegemeine Musikalische Zeitung' (1871), *Über reine Stimmung und Temperatur der Töne* (1877).

Drouet (droo-ā'), **Louis-François-Philippe,** a distinguished flutist and composer; b. Amsterdam, 1792; d. Bern, Sept. 30, 1873. He studied at the Paris Cons., played there and at the Opéra when but 7 years old. From 1807-10, teacher to King Louis of Holland; 1811, solo flutist to Napoleon, afterwards to Louis XVIII. In 1815 he went to London, played in the Philharmonic in 1816, and thereafter made long concert tours throughout Europe. In 1836 he was appointed Kapellmeister at Coburg; visited America for a few months in 1854; then lived in Gotha and Frankfurt. — His works for flute, over 150 in number, comprise 10 concertos, 2 fantasias for piano and flute (op. 36, 37), 3 trios for 3 flutes (op. 33), 3 waltz duets (op. 24); ensemble sonatas, duets, variations, etc. He is said to have written the French popular air *Partant pour la Syrie* from Queen Hortense's dictation.

Droz, Eugénie, musicologist; b. Chaux-de-Fonds, Switzerland, Mar. 21, 1893; studied in Neuchâtel and in Paris; received diploma from École pratique des hautes-études; treasurer of the Société des anciens textes français; editor of the Société française de musicologie. She has publ. *Poètes et musiciens du XVᵉ siècle* (in collaboration with G. Thibault); also many valuable studies in the 'Revue de musicologie.'

Drozdov, Anatol Nikolaievitch, Russian teacher and composer; b. Saratov, 1883; d. Moscow, 1950. He studied at the Cons. of St. Petersburg (Gold Medal, 1909); prof. of composition at the conservatories in Ekaterinodar (1911-16), Saratov (1918-20), and Moscow (1920-24). Publ. 2 piano sonatas, many piano pieces, a piano quintet, a trio for piano, flute, and clarinet, a cello sonata, etc.

Drozdowski, Jan, Polish pianist; b. Cracow, Feb. 2, 1857; d. there, Jan. 21, 1918. He studied mainly at the Vienna Cons. with Dachs and Epstein; also took lessons with Bruckner. In 1889 he was appointed prof. of piano at the Cracow Cons. and retained that post till his death. He publ. a piano method, *Systematic School of Pianoforte Technique* (1887; German ed., Munich, 1889, under the pseudonym Jan Jordan).

Dryden, John, the famous English poet; b. Aldwinkle, Northamptonshire, Aug. 9, 1631; d. London, May 1, 1700. He wrote the libretto of *King Arthur* for Purcell; also the 'Ode for St. Cecilia's Day,' which Purcell, Handel, and others have set to music.—Cf. *The Songs of John Dryden,* ed. by C. L. Day (Cambridge, Mass., 1932); also R. M. Myers, *Handel, Dryden, and Milton* (London, 1956).

Drysdale, Learmont, Scottish composer; b. Edinburgh, Oct. 3, 1866; d. there, June 18, 1909. Pupil of the Royal Academy of Music, and winner of the Lucas prize for composition (1890).—Works for orch.: *The Spirit of the Glen,* a ballad (1889); *Thomas the Rhymer,* prelude (1890); *Tam O'Shanter,* overture (1891; awarded prize by Glasgow Society of Musicians); *Herondean,* overture (1894); *The Kelpie,* a cantata (1894); an opera, *The Red Spider,* was produced at Dundee (1898).

Dubensky, Arcady, violinist and composer; b. Viatka, Russia, Oct. 15, 1890. He graduated from the Moscow Cons. in 1909 (violin with Hřimalý; theory with Ilyinsky, and conducting with Arends). He was a violinist at the Moscow Opera (1910-19); then left Russia; played in hotels and restaurants in Constantinople (1920); settled in the U. S. in 1921; was a member of the New York Symph. Orch., and then of the New York Philh. Orch., retiring in 1953. His music is conservative in its idiom, continuing the traditions of the Russian national school; an impression of originality is produced, however, by his adroit use of unusual combinations (such as a quartet for double-basses, a fugue for 18 violins, suite for 9 flutes, etc.).—Works: For the stage: *Romance with Double-Bass,* after Chekhov, comic opera (Moscow, Nov. 18, 1916, composer conducting); *Down Town,* opera (1930); *The Raven,* melodeclamation (1931); *On Highway,* 1-act opera (1936); *Two Yanks in Italy,* 1-act opera (1944); For orch.: Symph. in G minor (1916); *Suite Russe* (N. Y., March 7, 1926); *Intermezzo and Compliment* (1927); *Tartar Song and Dance* (1927); *Russian Bells,* symph. poem (N. Y. Symph., composer conducting, Dec. 29, 1927); *Caprice* for piccolo and orch. (1930; publ. 1936); *Prelude and Fugue* (1932; 1st performance, Boston Symph. Orch., Koussevitzky conducting, April 12, 1943); *Rajah* (1930); *Old Russian Soldier's Song* (1932); *Tom Sawyer,* overture (for Mark Twain's centennial, Philadelphia Orch., Nov. 29, 1935); *Political Suite (Russian Monarchy, Nazi and Fascist, Communist;* N. Y. radio broadcast, Sept. 17, 1936); *Fantasy on a Negro Theme* for tuba and orch. (Indianapolis, 1938); *Stephen Foster,* suite (Indianapolis Symph. Orch., Jan. 31, 1941); *Serenade* for orch. (Saratoga, Sept. 6, 1947); *Trumpet Overture,* for 18 toy trumpets and 2 bass drums (Children's Concert, N. Y. Philh., Dec. 10, 1949, Stokowski conducting); *Concerto Grosso,* for 3 trombones and tuba with orch. (1950); *Trombone Concerto* (1953). Chamber music; *Gossips* for strings (Philadelphia, Nov. 24, 1928); *Anno 1600,* suite for strings (N. Y. Philh., April 23, 1939); *Fugue* for 18 violins (his most successful work; Philadelphia Orch., April 1, 1932, Stokowski conducting); string quartet (1932); *Prelude and Fugue* for 4 bassoons (Brooklyn, Feb. 16, 1947); *Suite for 9 flutes,* including a piccolo and basset horn (N. Y. Flute Club, Jan. 26, 1936, composer conducting); other chamber works for various combinations of instruments.

Dubinsky, Vladimir, Russian cellist; b. Russia, Sept. 10, 1876; d. Syracuse, N. Y., Jan. 10, 1938; studied cello at the Cons. of Moscow; début with the Moscow Symph. (1897); U. S. début in New York (1905); concert tour with Schumann-Heink; later cellist with the Tollefsen Trio in New York, where he lived for many years as a teacher.

Dubois (dü-bwah'), **Léon,** Belgian conductor and composer; b. Brussels, Jan. 9, 1859; d. Boitsfort, Nov. 19, 1935. He won the Prix de Rome at the Brussels Cons. in 1885; second conductor at the Théâtre de la Monnaie (1892-97); director of the Louvain Music School (1899-1912); then director of the Brussels Cons. (1912-26).—Works: 4 operas, *Son Excellence ma femme* (1884), *La Revanche de Sganarelle* (1886), *Edénie* (Antwerp, 1912), and *Mazeppa* (not perf.); also the 1-act ballet *Smylis* (Brussels, 1891), the mimodrama *Le Mort* (Brussels, 1894), a symphonic poem, *Atala,* etc.

Dubois (dü-bwah'), **(Clément-François) Théodore,** eminent French organist and composer; b. Rosnay, Marne, Aug. 24, 1837; d. Paris, June 11, 1924. After preliminary study at Rheims, he entered the Paris Cons. in 1853, working under Marmontel (piano), Benoist (organ), Bazin and Ambroise Thomas (composition), graduating (1861) as recipient of the Grand Prix de Rome with the cantata *Atala,* after having taken first prizes in all departments. From Rome he sent a solemn Mass (perf. at the Madeleine in 1870). a dramatic work, *La prova di un opera seria,* and 2 overtures; returning to Paris, he settled there as a teacher; became maître de chapelle at Sainte-Clothilde and then succeeded Saint-Saëns, in 1877, as organist at the Madeleine. In 1871 he was made harmony prof. at the Paris Cons., succeeding Elwart; in 1891 became Léo Delibes' successor as professor of composition; in 1894 was elected to the chair in the Academy left vacant by Gounod's death; in 1896 he succeeded Ambroise Thomas as director of the Cons.; retired, 1905. Dubois' compositions are very numerous; among them the comic operas *La Guzla de l'émir* (Paris, April 30, 1873) and *Le pain bis, ou la Lilloise* (Opéra-Comique, Feb. 26, 1879); a 4-act grand opera *Aben Hamet* (produced in Italian, Théâtre du Châtelet, Dec. 16, 1884); a 3-act 'idylle dramatique,' *Xavière* (Opéra-Comique, Nov. 26, 1895); the 3-act opera *Circe* (not perf.); the ballet *La Farandole* (Paris Opéra, Dec. 14, 1883); 2 oratorios: *Les Sept Paroles du Christ* (1867), *Le Paradis perdu* (1878; won the City of Paris prize); several cantatas (*L'Enlèvement de Proserpine, Hylas, Bergerette, Les Vivants et les morts, Délivrance*); several Masses, and other church music; many orchestral works: Concert overture in D; 3 airs de ballet; 3 orchestral suites; *4 petites pièces; 3 petites pièces; Marche heroïque de Jeanne d'Arc; Fantasie triomphale,* for organ and orch.; *Hymne nuptiale; Méditation-Prière* for strings, oboe, harp, and organ; *Concerto-Capriccio,* for piano, and a 2nd piano concerto (1895); a violin concerto; symphonic overture in C; overture to *Frithioff;* 2 symphonic poems, *Notre Dame de la Mer* and *Adonis; Symphonie française* (1908); *Fantasietta* (1917); piano pieces (*Chœur et danse des lutins; 6 poèmes sylvestres);* pieces for organ and for harmonium; a cappella choruses; etc. Dubois published a practical manual, *Traité de contrepoint et de fugue* (1901), a standard work at the Paris Cons.—Cf. Ch. - M. Widor, *Notice sur la vie et les travaux de Théodore Dubois* (Paris, 1924).

Dubuc, Alexander Ivanovitch, Russian pianist, composer, and teacher; b. Moscow, March 3, 1812; d. there, Jan. 8, 1898. He was a pupil of John Field, about whom he published a volume of memoirs; professor at the Moscow Cons. (1866-72). He wrote piano pieces, songs, and a work on piano technique.

Du Cange, Charles Du Fresne, Sieur, French scholar; b. Amiens, Dec. 18, 1610; d. Paris, Oct. 23, 1688. He belonged to the famed group of 17th-century French writers who established the precepts of modern historical criticism; he is important to musicology because he included definitions of Latin musical terms in his lexicographies. The most valuable of his many works are the *Glossarium ad scriptores mediae et infimae latinitatis* (Paris, 1678, 3 vols.; 1733-36, 6 vols.; 1840-50, 7 vols. 1883-87, 10 vols.) and the *Glossarium ad scriptores mediae et infimae graecitatis* (Lyons, 1688; Breslau, 1889). Almost all his works, in MS, are preserved in the Bibliothèque Nationale in Paris.—Cf. H. Hardouin, *Essai sur la vie et sur les ouvrages de Du Cange* (Amiens, 1849); L. J. Feugère, in the 'Journal de l'instruction publique' (Paris, 1852).

Ducasse, Jean. See **Roger-Ducasse.**

Du Caurroy (koh-rwăh'), **François-Eustache,** Sieur de St.-Frémin; French composer; b. Beauvais, Feb. (baptized Feb. 4), 1549; d. Paris, Aug. 7, 1609. He was a member of the French nobility; his father was 'procureur du roi.' He entered the Royal Chapel as singer in 1569; in 1575 received a prize for a chanson, *Beaux yeux;* in 1578 he was 'sous-maître'; in 1599 became superintendent of 'la musique du roi.' Influenced by Le Jeune, he began to compose 'musique mesurée'; advanced in the favor of the court, receiving honors and awards; held the ecclesiastical titles of canon at the Ste. Chapelle of Dijon, Ste. Croix of Orleans, and other provincial posts. His greatest work was a collection *Meslanges de la musique,* containing psalms, 'chansons mesurées,' noëls, in 4, 5, and 6 voices (posthumously published, Paris, 1610; some specimens reprinted in Expert's 'Maîtres musiciens,' vol. XIII). Other works: *Missa pro defunctis;* 2 vols. of *Preces ecclesiasticae;* instrumental *Fantaisies* for 3, 4, 5, and 6 parts (Paris, 1610; several numbers published separately by Expert); 5 vols. of his works in score are in the Bibliothèque Sainte-Geneviève in Paris.—Cf. M. Th. Luillier, *Note sur quelques artistes-musiciens dans la Brie* (1870); N. Dufourcq, *À propos d'Eustache Du Caurroy* in the 'Revue de Musicologie' (Dec., 1950); F. Lesure, *La Carrière et les fonctions de Du Caurroy* in the 'Revue de Musicologie' (1952).

Ducis, Benedictus (Benedikt Hertogh), distinguished composer of the 16th century; b. probably near Constance, c. 1490; d. Schalckstetten, near Ulm, 1544. He may or may not be identical with Benedictus de Opitiis, who was organist at the Antwerp Cathedral (1514-16) and organist at the Chapel Royal in London (1516-22). It is known for a certainty that Benedictus Ducis was in Vienna c. 1515; probably studied there; in 1532 he applied for a pastorate at Ulm (under the name 'Benedict Duch'), but failed to obtain it. In 1533 he succeeded in receiving a pastorate at Stubersheim, near Geislingen; in 1535 he became pastor at Schalckstetten and remained there till his death. Benedictus Ducis has been confused by many writers with Benedictus Appenzeller; the long list of Ducis' works given by Fétis is spurious; Barclay Squire (in 'Sammelbände der Internationalen Musik-Gesellschaft,' Jan., 1912) brought conclusive evidence that a considerable number of these works must be attributed to Benedictus Appenzeller (q.v.). Two works by Ducis were published in facsimile by M. Nijhoff (The Hague, 1925); 10 sacred motets were reprinted in the 'Denkmäler deutscher Tonkunst,' vol. XXXIV (ed. by Joh. Wolf). —Cf. F. Spitta, *Benedictus Ducis,* in 'Monatsschrift für Gottesdienst und Kirchliche Kunst' (Jan.-March, 1913); also Charles Van den Borren, *Benedictus de Opitiis,* in 'Musica sacra' (Sept., 1927); D. Bartha, *Benedictus Ducis und Appenzeller* (Wolfenbüttel, 1930).

Ducloux, Walter, conductor; b. Kriens, Switzerland, April 17, 1913. He studied at the Univ. of Munich (1932-35) and at the Academy of Music in Vienna (1935-37); was assistant to Toscanini at the Lucerne Festivals (1938-39); came to America and conducted opera in New York (1940-42); became bandleader in the U. S. Army (1943-46). He returned to Europe as opera conductor in Prague and Brno (1946-48); then settled in New York (1949) as music director of 'Voice of America' broadcasts. In 1953 he was appointed head of the opera department of the School of Music at the Univ. of Southern California.

Ducroquet. See **Daublaine.**

Dufau (dü-foh'), **Jenny,** soprano, b. Rothau, Alsace, July 18, 1878; d. Pau, France, Aug. 29, 1924. Pupil of Etelka Gerster in Berlin (1901-5); studied subsequently with Mme. Marchesi, P. Vidal, A. Selva, and G. Benvenuti; sang at Berlin Opera (1910-11); from 1911, member of Chicago Opera Co., of which she was one of the most distinguished artists; later, appeared in vaudeville.

Dufay (dü-făh-ē; in 3 syllables), **Guillaume,** chief representative of the Burgundian school, and famed particularly for his 3-part chansons and his Masses; b. probably at Hainault, c. 1400; d. Cambrai, Nov. 27, 1474. He was a choir-boy at the Cathedral of Cambrai, where he received an excellent training; his teachers were Loqueville and Grenon. He was in Rimini and Pesaro (1419-26); then returned to Cambrai, where he was chapel master (1426-28); then member of the Papal Chapel in Rome (1428-33); in the service of the Duke of Savoy (1433); again in Cambrai (1434); entered again the Papal Chapel (1435-37; not in Rome, however, but in Florence and Bologna); was again in Savoy (1438-44); studied jurisprudence at the Univ. of Turin, obtaining the degree 'Baccalarius in decretis' (c. 1445). In 1445 he settled at Cambrai, holding the important position of canon at the cathedrals of Cambrai and Mons. Under these fortunate circumstances, which enabled him to live in comfort, he spent the rest of his life, greatly esteemed by both the Church authorities and musicians; he was described by Compère as "the moon of all music, and the light of all singers." Dufay wrote music in almost every form practiced in his time, and was successful in each. Haberl gives a list of 150 works by Dufay, found in the libraries of Rome, Bologna, and Trieste; these include Masses, motets, a Magnificat, other church music, and a number of French chansons, in which Dufay excelled. Other MSS are in the libraries at Paris, Brussels, Florence, Venice, Oxford, Modena, Cambrai, and Munich.—Reprints: 19 of the 50 pieces in J. Stainer's *Dufay and his Contemporaries* (London, 1898); a hymn, Kyrie, and chanson in Schering's *Geschichte der Musik in Beispielen* (nos. 38-40); 12 sacred and secular pieces, edited by H. Besseler, in Blume's *Das Chorwerk* (Heft 19); hymns in 3 and 4 parts, edited by R. Gerber, ib. (Heft 49); 4 selections in Davison and Apel, 'Harvard Anthology of Music,' vol. I; many pieces in the 'Denkmäler der Tonkunst in Österreich' (vols. VII, XI, 1, XIX, 1, XXVII, 1, XXXI, and XL).—Bibl.: F. X. Haberl, *Wilhelm du Fay,* in 'Bausteine für Musikgeschichte,' Vol. I (Leipzig, 1885); H. Besseler, *Studien zur Musik des Mittelalters,* in 'Archiv für Musikwissenschaft' (June, 1925); Charles Van den Borren, *Guillaume Dufay; son importance dans l'évolution de la musique au XVe siècle* (Brussels, 1926); K. Geiringer, *Dufay's 'Gloria ad modum tubae',* in 'Zeitschrift für Musikwissenschaft' (Jan., 1927); K. Dèzes, *Das Dufay zugeschriebene 'Salve Regina' eine deutsche Komposition,* in 'Zeitschrift für Musikwissenschaft' (Feb., 1928); H. Besseler, *Die Musik des Mittelalters und der Renaissance,* in Bücken's 'Handbuch der Musikwissenschaft' series (1931-34); Charles Van den Borren, *Guillaume Dufay, Light of the 15th Century,* in the 'Mus. Quarterly' (July, 1935); H. Besseler, *Neue Dokumente zum Leben und Schaffen Dufays,* in 'Archiv für Musikwissenschaft' (Sept. 1952); D. Plamenac, *An Unknown Composition by Dufay?,* in the 'Mus. Quarterly' (April, 1954); see also chap. 2 in Gustave Reese, *Music in the Renaissance* (N. Y., 1954). H. Besseler's article in 'Die Musik in Geschichte und Gegenwart' incorporates new documentary discoveries on Dufay's life (many of them made by Besseler himself). Publication of Dufay's collected works was begun in Rome in 1947, edited by G. de Van and, after his death, by H. Besseler; another ed. was begun in the same year by L. Feininger.

Dufourcq, Norbert, French organist and music historian; b. St. Jean-de-Braye (Loiret), Sept. 21, 1904; studied with Gastoué; in 1923 became organist at St. Merry in Paris; in 1941 appointed professor of music history at the Paris Cons. He has written numerous valuable books dealing with the organ in France: *Documents inédits relatifs à l'orgue français* (1934-35; 2 vols.); *Esquisse d'une histoire de l'orgue en France du XIII*e *au XVIII*e *siècle* (1935); *Les Clicquot, facteurs d'orgue* (1942); 2 books on Bach: *J. S. Bach, génie allemand? génie latin?* (1947); *J. S. Bach, le maître de l'orgue* (1948); also *César Franck* (1949); *Le Clavecin* (1949); *La musique française* (1949); *La musique d'orgue française de Jehan Titelouze à Jehan Alain* (1949); *Autour de Coquard, Franck et Vincent d'Indy* (1952); *Nicolas Lebègue* (1954); contributor to and editor of *La musique des origines à nos jours* (Paris, 1946; new ed., 1956).

Dufranne (dü-frăhn'), **Hector,** dramatic baritone; b. Mons, Belgium, Oct. 25, 1870; d. Paris, May 5, 1951. He made his début as Valentine in *Faust* at La Monnaie, Brussels, Sept. 9, 1896; at Opéra-Comique, Paris, on June 18, 1900; at Manhattan Opera House, N. Y. (1908); member of Chicago Opera Co. (1910-13).

Dugan, Franjo, Croatian composer and organist; b. Krapinica, Sept. 11, 1874; d. Zagreb, Dec. 12, 1948. He studied music with Max Bruch in Berlin, and also attended classes in mathematics. He settled in Zagreb as church organist; taught at the Zagreb Cons.; publ. manuals on orchestration and musical form; also many organ pieces.

Dugazon (dü-găh-zohn'), **Louise Rosalie,** famous opera singer; b. Berlin, June 18, 1755; d. Paris, Sept. 22, 1821. She was brought up in the atmosphere of the theater; her father, F. J. Lefebvre, was a French dancer at the Berlin Opera; she herself began her career as a ballet dancer; then she became a singer, encouraged mainly by Grétry, who thought highly of her talent. She made her début in Paris in Grétry's opera *Sylvain* (June 19, 1774); in 1775 she married an actor who used the professional name Dugazon; although they were soon separated, she adopted this name for her professional appearances. She sang mostly at the Opéra-Comique; created some 60 new roles; her last public appearance was at the Paris Opéra on Feb. 29, 1804. She was greatly admired by her contemporaries, and her name became a designation of certain types of operatic parts ('jeune Dugazon', i. e., an ingénue).—Cf. H. and A. Leroux, *La Dugazon* (Paris, 1926).

Duggan, Joseph Francis, Irish pianist and composer; b. Dublin, July 10, 1817; d. London, 1900. He was engaged at the Italian Opera, New York; taught in Philadelphia, Baltimore, and Washington; then lived in London; became professor of singing in the Guildhall School of Music. He wrote 2 successful operas, *Pierre* (London, 1853) and *Leonie* (London, 1854); 2 symphonies, 6 string quartets, numerous piano pieces; also published *The Singing Master's Assistant* and transls. of Albrechtsberger's *Science of Music* (Philadelphia, 1842) and Fétis' *Counterpoint and Fugue.*

Duhamel, Antoine, French composer; b. Paris, July 30, 1925, a son of the famous writer, Georges Duhamel. He studied with René Leibowitz and from the very first began to compose in the dodecaphonic technique; has written a quintet for piano and wind instruments; also published a book, *L'Opéra depuis Wagner* (Liège, 1950).

Duiffoprugcar (properly **Tieffenbrucker**), **Gaspar,** Bavarian viol maker; b. Tieffenbrugg, Bavaria, 1514 (date established by Dr. Coutagne of Lyons, in his work *Gaspar Duiffoproucart et les luthiers lyonnais du XVI*e *siècle,* Paris, 1893); d. Lyons, Dec. 16, 1571. Long reputed to be the first maker of violins; but Vidal, in his *Les Instruments à archet,* states that all the so-called Duiffoprugcar violins are spurious, having been made by Vuillaume, who in 1827 conceived the idea of making violins after the pattern of a viola da gamba by Duiffoprugcar. Apparently, the latter learned his trade in Italy, the usual spellings of his name showing it to be Italianized rather than Gallicized; he settled in Lyons in 1553, and was naturalized in 1559.

Dukas (dü-kăh'), **Paul,** famous French composer; b. Paris, Oct. 1, 1865; d. there, May 17, 1935. From 1882-8 pupil at the Cons. of G. Mathias (piano), Th. Dubois (harmony), and E. Guiraud (composition); won 1st prize for counterpoint and fugue in 1886, and second Prix de Rome with a cantata *Velléda* (1888); music critic of the 'Revue Hebdomadaire' and 'Gazette des Beaux-Arts'; also contributor to the 'Chronique des Arts', 'Revue musicale', etc.; 1906, Chevalier Légion d'Honneur; 1910-12, prof. of the orch. class at the Cons.; 1918, elected Debussy's successor as member of the 'Conseil de l'enseignement supérieur' there; Dec. 1, 1927, appointed prof. of composition at the Paris Cons.; also taught at the École Normale de Musique; assisted in the revising and editing of Rameau's complete works for Durand of Paris. He was a composer of solid attainments, whose talent showed to greatest advantage in the larger instrumental forms, which he handled with mastery. Although he was not a prolific composer, he wrote a masterpiece of modern music in his orchestral scherzo *L'Apprenti Sorcier;* his opera *Ariane et Barbe-Bleue* is one of the finest French operas in the impressionist style. Shortly before his death he destroyed several manuscripts of his unfinished compositions.—Works: 3 overtures: *King Lear* (1883), *Götz von Berlichingen* (1884), *Polyeucte* (1891); a symph. in C (Paris, Jan. 3, 1897); *L'Apprenti Sorcier* (May 18, 1897; his most famous work); opera, *Ariane et Barbe-Bleue* (Opéra-Comique, May 10, 1907); a ballet, *La Péri* (Paris, April 22, 1912); *Villanelle* for horn and piano (1906); for piano: Sonata in E♭ minor; *Variations, interlude et finale* on a theme by Rameau; *Prélude élégiaque.* Together with Saint-Saëns he completed Guiraud's opera *Frédégonde.*—Cf. O. Séré, *Musiciens français d'aujourd'hui* (1911; revised ed. Paris, 1921); G. Samazeuilh, *Paul Dukas* (Paris, 1913); G. Jean-Aubry, *La Musique fr. d'aujourd'hui* (1916). V. d'Indy, *E. Chabrier et Paul Dukas* (1920); A. Cœuroy, *La Musique française moderne* (1922); A. Cortot, *La Musique française de Piano;* I. Schwerke, *Paul Dukas,* in the 'Mus. Quarterly' (1928); G. Samazeuilh, *Paul Dukas Musicien français* (Paris, 1936); Dukas issue of the 'Revue Musicale' (May-June, 1936). See also *Les écrits de Paul Dukas sur la musique* (Paris, 1948).

Duke, John, American pianist and composer; b. Cumberland, Maryland, July 30, 1899. He studied at the Peabody Cons. in Baltimore with G. Strube (composition) and H. Randolph (piano); later studied in Europe with Schnabel and Nadia Boulanger. In 1923, he was appointed instructor at Smith College.—Works: string trio (1937); concerto for piano and strings (1938); *Carnival Overture* (1941); piano trio (1943); 1-act opera, *Captain Lovelock* (N. Y., Feb. 20, 1956); many songs.

Dukelsky, Vladimir (pen-name as composer of light music: **Vernon Duke**), versatile composer of both 'serious' and popular music; b. Oct. 10, 1903, in the railroad station of the village Parfianovka (during his mother's trip to Pskov); pupil at the Kiev Cons. of Glière and Dombrovsky; left Russia in 1920 and went to Turkey, coming to the U. S. shortly afterward; later lived in Paris and London; settled in N. Y. in 1929; lieutenant in Coast Guard (1939-44); went back to France (1947-48), but then returned to U. S. to live in N. Y and Hollywood. He began to compose at a very early age; was introduced to Diaghilev, who commissioned him to write a ballet *Zéphyr et Flore,* the production of which put Dukelsky among the successful group of ballet composers. Another important meeting was with Koussevitzky, who championed Dukelsky's music in Paris and in Boston. In the U. S. Dukelsky began writing popular music; many of his songs, such as *April in Paris,* have enjoyed great popularity. At George Gershwin's suggestion, he adopted the name Vernon Duke for popular music works; in 1955 he dropped his full name altogether, and signed both his serious and light compositions as Vernon Duke; published an amusing autobiography, *Passport to Paris* (Boston, 1955).—Works: for the stage: *Zéphyr et Flore* (Paris, Jan. 31, 1925); *Yvonne,* operetta (London, 1926); *Demoiselle Paysanne,* opera in 2 acts (1928); *Public Gardens,* ballet (1935); *Le bal des blanchisseuses,* ballet (Paris, Dec. 19, 1946); *Souvenir de Monte Carlo,* ballet (1949-56); for orch.: piano concerto (1924; not orchestrated); 3 symphonies (No. 1, Paris, June 14, 1928; No. 2, Boston, April 25, 1930; No. 3, Brussels Radio Orch., Oct. 10, 1947); *Ballade* for piano and small orch. (1931); *Dédicaces,* for soprano, piano, and orch. (Boston Symph., Dec. 16, 1938); violin concerto (Boston, March 19, 1943); cello concerto (Boston, Jan. 4, 1946); *Ode to the Milky Way* (N. Y., Nov. 18, 1946); choral music: *Dushenka,* duet for women's voices and chamber orch. (1927); *Epitaph* (on the death of Diaghilev), for soprano solo, chorus and orch. (Boston Symph., April 15, 1932); *The End of St. Petersburg,* oratorio (Schola Cantorum, N. Y., Jan. 12, 1938); *Moulin-Rouge,* for mixed chorus (1941); *A Song About Myself,* for mixed chorus (1944); *5 Victorian Street Ballads,* for women's voices (1944); *Ballad Made in the Hot Weather* (1945); *Paris, aller et retour,* cantata (1947); four choruses to Ogden Nash's words (1955); chamber music: trio (variations) for flute, bassoon and piano (1930); *Etude* for bassoon and piano (1932); *Capriccio Mexicano,* for violin and piano (1933); 3 pieces for woodwind (1939); violin sonata (1949);

string quartet (1956); songs: *Three Chinese Songs* (1937); *Park Avenue Lyrics* (1945); *The Musical Zoo* (20 songs to Ogden Nash's lyrics, 1946); *A Shropshire Lad,* song cycle (1949); for piano: Sonata (1927): *Barrel Organ Barcarolle* (1943); *Homage to Boston,* suite (1943); *Surrealist Suite* (1944); *Souvenir de Venise* (1948); *Serenade to San Francisco* (1956). He wrote songs in the following musical comedies: *The Show is On, Garrick Gaieties, Walk a Little Faster, Three's a Crowd, Americana, Ziegfeld Follies, Cabin in the Sky,* etc.; arranged Gershwin's *Rhapsody in Blue* for 2 pianos; added 2 ballets and several songs to *Goldwyn Follies,* unfinished film score by George Gershwin (1937).

Dulcken, Ferdinand Quentin, pianist and composer; b. London, June 1, 1837; d. Astoria, L. I., Dec. 10, 1901. He was the son of Luise Dulcken, and nephew of Ferdinand David; was a pupil of Moscheles and Gade at the Leipzig Cons.; also received encouragement from Mendelssohn. He subsequently taught at the Warsaw Cons., and also at Moscow and St. Petersburg; made many concert tours in Europe as pianist with Wieniawski, Vieuxtemps, and others. In 1876 he emigrated to America and gave concerts with Reményi; settled in New York as teacher and composer. He publ. nearly 400 piano pieces of the salon type and also some vocal works.

Dulcken, Luise, pianist (*née* David; a sister of Ferdinand David); b. Hamburg, March 29, 1811; d. London, April 12, 1850. She was taught by C. F. G. Schwencke and Wilhelm Grund; played in public (in Germany) when 11 years of age. She married in 1828, and went to London, where she met with brilliant success as a pianist and teacher. Queen Victoria was one of her many pupils.

Dulichius (Dulich, Deilich, Deulich), Philippus, German composer and music theorist; b. Chemnitz, Dec. 18 (baptized 19th), 1562; d. Stettin, March 24 (buried on March 25), 1631. He studied at the Univ. of Leipzig; there is no evidence that he went to Italy and studied with Gabrieli, although this assertion appears in his biographies. He was cantor in Stettin from 1587 until his death. Of his numerous works (exclusively vocal) the most important are: *Novum opus musicum duarum partium continens dicta insigniora ex evangeliis* (Stettin, 1599); *Centuriae octonum et septenum vocum harmonias sacras laudibus sanctissimae Triados consecratas continentes* (4 parts, Stettin, 1607). R. Schwartz published 7 choruses from the *Centuriae* (1896); the complete *Centuriae* are published in the 'Denkmäler deutscher Tonkunst' (XXXI, XLI).—Cf. R. Schwartz, *Philippus Dulichius,* in 'Monatsschrifte für Gottesdienst und kirchliche Kunst' (1896).

Du Locle, Camille Théophile Germain du Commun, French librettist; b. Orange, Vacluse, July 16, 1832; d. Capri, Oct. 9, 1903. He was secretary of the Opéra under Perrin's direction; later, director of the Opéra-Comique. The librettos of Verdi's *Don Carlos* (French) and Reyer's *Sigurd* and *Salammbô* were from his pen.

Dülon, Friedrich Ludwig, a blind German flutist; b. Oranienburg, near Potsdam, Aug. 14, 1769; d. Würzburg, July 7, 1826. He was taught by his father (flute) and Angerstein (theory); in 1783 his concert travels began, and extended all over Europe. In 1793-94 he was chamber musician at the St. Petersburg court (gave first concert in St. Petersburg on March 30, 1793); then settled (1823) in Würzburg. He wrote an autobiography: *Dülons des blinden Flötenspielers Leben und Meinungen, von ihm selbst bearbeitet* (Zürich, 2 vols., 1807-8, ed. by Wieland).—Works: a flute concerto; 9 duets and variations for flute and violin; flute duets; caprices for flute.

Dumesnil (dü-mä-nēl'), **Maurice,** French pianist and writer; b. Angoulême, Charente, April 20, 1886. He received his academic training at the Lycée de Caen, Calvados; studied music at the Paris Cons. (graduated 1905), and with Isidor Philipp (piano), Emanuel Moor and A. Bernardi (harmony, composition, orchestration, and conducting); he received personal coaching from Debussy in the interpretation of the composer's works. Dumesnil then went to South America; was guest conductor in Argentina, Chile, and Mexico (1916-20); toured the U. S. as pianist with the historic piano of Chopin (1926-27); numerous tours of South and Central America (1920-30); appearances as pianist and radio commentator in the U. S. (1936-38). Since 1944, he has been editor of 'The Teacher's Round Table' in 'Etude' magazine; professor at Michigan State College (1944-47); since 1947, professor at Chicago Musical College. Dumesnil is married to Evangeline Lehman, American composer and author, who studied at the American Cons. of Fontainebleau, France, and who has written a symphonic choral legend, *Thérèse de Lisieux* (1933); a cantata, *Noël* (Paris, Dec. 24, 1933); piano pieces, songs and vocal ensembles.—Publications: *An Amazing Journey* (1932); *How to Play and Teach Debussy* (1933); *Claude Debussy, Master of Dreams* (1940).

Dumesnil (dü-mä-nĕl'), **René**, French writer; b. Rouen, June 19, 1879; living in Paris as literary and music critic. Besides numerous works on literature (G. Flaubert), he has written the following books on music: *Le rythme musical* (1921; 2nd augmented ed., 1949); *Le monde des musiciens* (1924); *Le Don Juan de Mozart* (1927); *Musiciens romantiques* (1928); *Richard Wagner* (1929); *La musique contemporaine en France* (1930); *Le livre du disque* (with P. Hemardinquer; 1931); *Histoire illustrée de la musique* (1934); *Portraits de musiciens français* (1938); *La musique romantique française* (1944); *La musique en France entre les deux guerres* (Geneva, 1946); *L'Envers de la musique* (Paris, 1949); *Histoire illustrée du théâtre lyrique* (Paris, 1953; received the Grand Prix for musical literature); *Richard Wagner* (Paris, 1954; a much larger work than his first Wagner book of 1929). He has also written articles on Roussel, Ferroud, Delannoy, Paul Dukas, and others in the 'Revue musicale,' etc.; collaborated in the compiling of the *Collection des grandes œuvres musicales.*

Dumler, Martin G., American composer; b. Cincinnati, Dec. 22, 1868; studied at the Cincinnati College of Music (graduated 1901); was subsequently vice-president of the board of trustees; also president of the Bruckner Society. His compositions are chiefly settings of sacred texts.

Dumont (dü-mon'), **Henri**, Belgian composer, b. Villers l'Evèque, near Liège, 1610; d. Paris, May 8, 1684; was chorister at Maestricht, ordained priest at Liège, and organist at St. Paul's, Paris, from 1639 until his death.—Works: *5 Messes Royales en plain-chant* (Paris, 1699; 4th ed. 1701); 3 books of *Meslanges à 2, 3, 4, 5* (Paris, 1649, 1657, 1661); 5 books of motets *a 2-4* (1652-86); etc.—4 of his works have been reprinted in 'Musique d'église des XVIIe et XVIIIe siècles,' ed. by Ch. Pineau.—Cf. H. Quittard, *Un musicien en France au XVIIe siècle, Henri Dumont* (1906); A. Gastoué, *Les Messes Royales de Henri Dumont* (Paris, 1912).

Dunayevsky, Isaak, Soviet composer of popular songs; b. Lokhvita, near Poltava, Jan. 30, 1900; d. Moscow, July 25, 1955. He began to study piano as a child; then entered the Kharkov Cons. and studied violin with Joseph Achron. He graduated in 1919, and went to Leningrad. He devoted himself mainly to popular music; some songs from his operettas and film scores have become famous. At one time he experimented with jazz rhythms, introducing them into his music. He received many honors from the Soviet government; in 1941 he won the first Stalin Prize for his music to the films *The Circus* and *Volga.*—Cf. L. Danilevitch, *Isaak Dunayevsky* (Moscow, 1947).

Dunbar, Rudolph, Negro conductor and composer; b. British Guiana, April 5, 1907. He played as a child in a local military band. In 1919 came to the U. S. and entered the Juilliard School of Music, graduating in 1928. Later studied in Paris, Leipzig, and Vienna. He made his London début as conductor on April 26, 1942, and in Paris, Nov. 18, 1944. He has written a ballet, *Dance of the 21st Century* (1938).

Duncan, William Edmondstoune, English composer and writer on music; b. Sale, Cheshire, April 22, 1866; d. there, June 26, 1920. He studied at the Royal College of Music with Parry and Stanford; then acted as music critic and correspondent of British and American music magazines. He wrote an opera *Perseus* (1892); ode for chorus and orch. *Ye Mariners of England* (Glasgow, 1890); *Ode to Music* (after Swinburne, 1893); a setting of Milton's sonnet *To a Nightingale* for soprano and orch. (1895), etc.; also publ. several books on music: *Schubert* (1905; 2nd ed., 1934; in Spanish, Buenos Aires, 1942); *The Story of Minstrelsy* (1907); *A History of Music* (1908); *The Story of the Carol* (1911); *Encyclopedia of Musical Terms* (1914); and *Ultra-Modernism in Music* (1917).

Dunham, Henry Morton, American organist; b. Brockton, Mass., July 29, 1853; d. Brookline, Mass., May 4, 1929. He studied at the New England Cons.; was organist at the Porter Congregational Church in Brockton (1870-81); of Ruggles Street Baptist Church, Boston (1883-93); Shawmut Congregational Church (1893-1905); and Harvard Church, Brookline (1906-12); then retired. He taught at the New England Cons. for 52 years (1876-1929).—Publ. works: *Organ School* (in 4 books); 3 organ sonatas; marches, preludes, fugues, passacaglias, and other organ music; also numerous arrangements; *A System of Technique for Piano; The Choir Manual; Hymn Music* (3 books); etc.—Cf. H. M. Dunham, *The Life of a Musician, Woven into a Strand of History of the New England Conservatory of Music* (posthumous, N. Y., 1931).

Dunhill, Thomas Frederick, English composer; b. London, Feb. 1, 1877; d. Scunthorpe, Lincolnshire, March 13, 1946. He entered the Royal Academy of Music in 1893, and studied with Franklin Taylor (piano) and Stanford (theory); became assistant prof. of piano at Eton College (1899-1908); in 1905 appointed prof. at Royal Academy of Music; in 1907 he founded the 'Concerts of British Chamber-Music,' which he conducted until 1916. He served as adjudicator for numerous music festivals.—Works: The operas *The Enchanted Garden* (Carnegie award, 1925; performed at Royal Academy of Music, London, 1927); *Tantivy Towers* (London, Jan. 16, 1931); *Happy Families* (Guildford, Nov. 1, 1933); ballet, *Gallimaufry* (Hamburg, Dec. 11, 1937); for orch.: Symphony in A minor (Belgrade, 1922, composer conducting); *Elegiac Variations* (Gloucester Festival, 1922); *The Pixies,* suite; *Dick Whittington,* suite; *Valse-Fantasia* for flute and orch.; *Capricious Variations,* for cello and orch.; chamber music: *Phantasy* for string quartet; piano quintet; quintet for violin, cello, clarinet, horn, and piano; quintet for horn and string quartet; piano quartet; viola sonata; *Pleasantries* (trio); 2 violin sonatas; *Comrades,* for baritone and orch.; *The Wind among the Reeds,* song cycle for tenor and orch.; *John Gilpin,* cantata for treble voices; children's choruses, operettas, and cantatas; songs (*The Cloths of Heaven, The Fiddler of Dooney,* etc.); violin pieces; compositions for cello.—Books: *Chamber Music* (a treatise for students, 1912); *Mozart's String Quartets* (2 vols., 1927); *Sullivan's Comic Operas* (1928); *Sir Edward Elgar* (biography, 1938).

Duni, Egidio Romoaldo, Italian composer of opera; b. Matera, Feb. 9, 1709; d. Paris, June 11, 1775. He first studied in the Cons. 'della Madonna di Loreto,' under Durante; then in the Cons. 'della Pietà de' Turchini.' His first opera, *Nerone* (Rome, May 21, 1735), was a great popular success. He went to London (1737) and Holland (1738); in 1739 he returned to Italy; in 1745 he was maestro di cappella at S. Nicolo di Bari, in Naples; became tutor at the Court of Parma, where, encouraged by the Duke, he began composing French operettas, one of which, *Le caprice amoureux ou Ninette à la cour* (Parma, 1756) was so well received that Duni decided to try his fortune in Paris, where he brought out a swarm of light and frivolous stage pieces which suited the prevailing taste; he is regarded by some music historians as a founder of French opéra-bouffe. He wrote about 15 Italian operas, and 20 in French.

Dunkley, Ferdinand (Luis), organist and composer; b. London, July 16, 1869; d. Waldwick, N. J., Jan. 5, 1956. He was a pupil at the Royal Academy of Music of Parry, Bridge, Martin, Gladstone, Sharpe, and Barnet; organist of St. Jude's, London (1885-7) and of St. Aubyn's, London (1888-93). In 1893 he was engaged as Director of Music at St. Agnes' School, Albany, N. Y.; professor of theory at Woman's College, Montgomery, Alabama (1927-29); organist at Temple Sinai, New Orleans (1924-34); in 1934 appointed prof. at Loyola Univ., New Orleans. He made his last public appearance on his 82nd birthday when he gave an organ recital.—Works: *The Wreck of the Hesperus,* ballade for soli, chorus, and orch.; the choral works, *Praise the Lord* (1919), *Green Branches* (1919), *God is my strong salvation* (1921), *Street Cries* (1924), *Blessed is the man* (1937); etc.

Dunlop, Isobel (Violet Skelton), Scottish violinist and composer; b. Edinburgh, March 4, 1901. She studied with Tovey and Dyson; gave concerts presenting her own works. She has written mainly for chorus; has also composed a viola sonata.

Dunn, James Philip, American composer; b. New York, Jan. 10, 1884; d. Jersey City, N. J., July 24, 1936. He studied at the College of the City of N. Y. (B.A., 1903); then at Columbia Univ. with MacDowell, and subsequently with Cornelius Rybner. He was then active as teacher and church organist in New York and elsewhere. As a composer, he attracted attention by his symph. poem descriptive of Lindbergh's transatlantic flight *We* (N. Y., Aug. 27, 1927). He also wrote an *Overture on Negro Themes* (N. Y., July 22, 1922), some chamber music and organ pieces. See John Tasker Howard, *James Philip Dunn* (N. Y., 1925)

Dunn, John, English concert violinist; b. Hull, Feb. 16, 1866; d. Harrogate, Dec. 18, 1940. He received his first instruction from his brother, who was conductor of the Hull Theatre Orch.; then was a pupil at the Leipzig Cons. of Schradieck (violin) and Jadassohn (theory). He made his début at Promenade Concerts, London (1882); toured England and Germany with success. He wrote several pieces for violin (including *Soliloquy* for violin and piano; *Berceuse* for violin and piano), a cadenza to Beethoven's violin concerto; his own concerto for violin and orch., and a sonatina for piano.—Book: *Manual of Violin Playing* (London, 1898).

Dunn, John Petri, Scottish pianist and writer on music; b. Edinburgh, Oct. 26, 1878; d. there, Feb. 4, 1931. He studied in London with Matthay; toured Europe as accompanist of Jan Kubelik in 1904; later was professor at the Stuttgart and Kiel Conservatories; 1914, returned to Great Britain; was prof. of music at the Edinburgh Univ. from 1920 until death.—Books: *Ornamentation in the Works of Chopin* (London, 1921); *A Student's Guide for Orchestration* (London, 1928); *The Basis of Pianoforte Playing* (London, 1933).

Dunstable (Dunstaple), John, English composer; b. probably at Dunstable, Bedfordshire, c. 1370; d. Dec. 24, 1453; buried in St. Stephen's Walbrook, London. He was the most important English composer of the early 15th century, rivalling his contemporaries Binchois and Dufay; also astrologer and mathematician. From April 28, 1419, to May 1440 he was canon of Hereford Cathedral and prebendary of Putson Minor; for some time he was in the service of John, Duke of Bedford; the Duke, as Regent of France, represented King Henry V in Paris for a number of years, and probably took his musicians with him. Practically nothing further is known of Dunstable's life. Much of his music is contained in the six MSS discovered by F. X. Haberl in the library of the cathedral of Trent in 1884 ('Trent Codices'). Adler and Koller published six sacred and a number of secular pieces of Dunstable's from these Codices in vol. VII of the 'Denkmäler der Tonkunst in Österreich'; other specimens of Dunstable's music are in vols. XXVII, XXXI, and XL. A list of Dunstable's works known to exist (about 54) is contained in Cecie Stainer's *Dunstable and the Various Settings of O Rosa Bella* in the 'Sammelbände der Internationalen Musik-Gesellschaft' (II, 1); a supplementary list was published by Bukofzer in his article *Über Leben und Werke von Dunstable* in 'Acta musicologica' (VIII, p. 111 ff.). An examination of these compositions reveals not only the existence of a highly developed art in England early in the 15th century, antedating the full flowering of the Burgundian school (Binchois, Dufay), but also Dunstable's most important contributions to the music of the period in making use of the declamatory motet (in which the rhythm of the spoken word largely governs the musical rhythm) and, apparently, introducing the motet with double structure (which provided the predominant technique of Mass composition in the 15th century). Besides the abovementioned articles, see H. Riemann, *Handbuch der Musikgeschichte* (Leipzig, 1907, II, 1, p. 106 et seq.); R. von Ficker, in Adler's 'Studien zur Musikwissenschaft' (VII and XI; on the 'Trent Codices'); Ch. Van den Borren, *The Genius of Dunstable,* in the 'Proceedings' of the Musical Association (London, 1921); Dom Anselm Hughes, in 'Laudate' (1936); M. Bukofzer, *John Dunstable and the Music of His Time,* in the 'Proceedings' of the Musical Association (London, 1938). Bukofzer prepared a complete edition of the extant works by Dunstable as vol. VIII of 'Musica Britannica' (1954); see also his article *John Dunstable; a Quincentenary Report* ('Mus. Quarterly,' Jan., 1954); and R. L. Greene, *John Dunstable; a Quincentenary Supplement* ('Mus. Quarterly,' July, 1954).

Dunstan, Ralph, English composer and writer on music; b. Carnon Downs, Truro, Nov. 17, 1857; d. London, April 2, 1933; Mus. Doc. Cambridge, 1892. Editor of *A Manual of Music* (1918; many eds.); *A Cyclopedic Dictionary of Music* (1925); *Composer's Hand Book; The Cornish Song Book; Cornish Dialect and Folk-Songs;* and other popular pedagogic and musical works. Also composed church music (21 Masses, anthems), cantatas, and songs for schools.

Duparc (Fouques Duparc), (Marie-Eugéne-) Henri, French song composer; b. Paris, Jan. 21, 1848; d. Mont-de-Marsan, Landes, Feb. 12, 1933. Pupil of César Franck from 1872-5; one of the founders of the 'Société Nationale de Musique.' A nervous affliction compelled him to renounce all artistic activity in 1885, after which he lived in retirement in Switzerland. Franck considered him the most gifted of all his pupils; his songs written between 1868 and 1884 are of extraordinary originality, presaging the early Impressionism of Fauré and Debussy, and characterized by fluid harmony of unrelated tonalities governing melody of evocative beauty. Among several works destroyed by Duparc himself were a sonata for cello and piano, *Poème nocturne,* and a suite for orch. His extant works are a symphonic poem, *Lénore* (1875); *Aux Étoiles,* for orch. (early work, publ. 1910; Paris, April 11, 1874); *Feuilles volantes,* 6 pieces for piano; *La Fuite,* duet for soprano and tenor (1872); and the songs *Sérénade, Romance de Mignon, Galop, Chanson triste, Soupir, Invitation au Voyage, La Vague et la Cloche, Extase, Sérénade florentine, Le Manoir de Rosamonde, Testament, Phidylé, Lamento,*

Elégie, La Vie antérieure, Au Pays où se fait la guerre.—Cf. O. Séré, *Musiciens français d'aujourd'hui* (rev. ed. Paris, 1921); Guy Ferchault, *Henri Duparc* (Paris, 1944); S. Northcote, *The Songs of Henri Duparc* (London, 1949).

Dupin (dü-păn'), **Paul** (pseudonym **Louis Lothar**), French composer; b. Roubaix, Aug. 14, 1865; d. Paris, March 5, 1949; first head of a factory, then a bookkeeper in Paris, turning, after 1912, to music as a profession. Studied with E. Durand, but otherwise self-taught as a composer, displaying great originality in his very numerous works, about 220 of which have been publ.—Compositions: A 4-act opera, *Marçelle;* an oratorio; orchestral works; 500 canons for 3-12 voices; songs; chamber music (violin sonatas, trio for cello, flute, and harp, piano trio, string quartet, 40 poems for string quartet); violin pieces; piano works (sonata, sonatina, *Esquisses fuguées, Dentelles,* duets).—Cf. R. Rolland, *Paul Dupin,* in 'Bulletin Français de la S.I.M.' (Dec. 15, 1908); C. Koechlin, *Dupin,* in the 'Revue musicale' (Jan., 1923); A. Cœuroy, *La Musique française moderne;* P. Ladmirault, *Les chœurs en canon de Paul Dupin; notice biographique et analytique* (Paris, 1925).

Dupont (dü-pŏhn'), **Gabriel,** French composer; b. Caen, Mar. 1, 1878; d. Vésinet, Aug. 2, 1914. Pupil of his father, the organist at the Cathedral; later, of Gédalge; then of Massenet and Widor at the Paris Cons.; won the 2nd Prix de Rome in 1901. In a contest conducted in 1903 by Sonzogno, the publishing house in Milan, his opera *La Cabrera* was selected, along with 2 others, to be performed and judged by the public (237 works were submitted); it was produced at Milan on May 17, 1904, with great success, thereby winning for Dupont the prize of 50,000 lire; other operas: *La Glu,* libretto by Jean Richepin (Nice, Jan. 24, 1910); *La Farce du Cuvier* (Brussels, March 21, 1912); *Antar* (the outbreak of the World War [1914] caused the suspension of its rehearsals; it was not produced until 1921 [after Dupont's death], when it was very successfully given at the Opéra on March 14); also *Les Heures dolentes,* for orch. (4 pieces from a suite of 14 compositions for piano, 1903-05); *Poèmes d'automne,* for piano; the symph. poems *Hymne à Aphrodite* and *Le Chant de la destinée; Poème* for piano quintet; many other piano pieces; etc.—Cf. M. Léna, *Gabriel Dupont, Souvenirs,* and H. Collet, *Antar,* in 'Le Ménestrel' (March 18, 1921); E. Vuillermoz, *Antar de Gabriel Dupont à l'Opéra,* in the 'Revue Musicale' (April, 1921); M. Dumesnil, *Gabriel Dupont, Musician of Normandy,* in the 'Mus. Quarterly' (Oct., 1944).

Dupont, Pierre, French song writer; b. Rochetaillée, near Lyons, April 23, 1821; d. St. Etienne, July 25, 1870. The son of a laborer, and himself uneducated, he made a name by his political and rustic ditties, of which he wrote the words, and then sang the airs to Reyer, who put them into shape. His political songs (*Le Pain, Le Chant des ouvriers,* etc.) created such disturbances that he was banished in 1851, but pardoned in 1852, after the 'coup d'état.' His song for basso, *Les bœufs,* is well known.

Duport (dü-pohr'), **Jean-Louis,** famous French cellist; b. Paris, Oct. 4, 1749; d. there, Sept. 7, 1819. Made his public début at the 'Concert Spirituel' (1768); joined his brother, Jean Pierre, in Berlin at the outbreak of the Revolution; returning in 1806, he became musician to Charles IV, the ex-king of Spain, at Marseilles; returned to Paris in 1812, where he was soon regarded as the foremost French cellist, joined the imperial orch. (remaining a member when it became the royal orch.), and was appointed prof. in the Cons. (suppressed 1815).—Works: 6 cello concertos; sonatas, duos, airs variées, 9 nocturnes (for harp and cello), etc. His *Essai sur le doigté du violoncelle et la conduite de l'archet, avec une suite d'exercices,* is still a standard text-book, and practically laid the foundations of modern cello virtuosity.

Duprato (dü-prah-toh'), **Jules-Laurent,** composer; b. Nîmes, March 26, 1827; d. Paris, May 20, 1892. He studied with Leborne at the Paris Cons.; 1848, won the Prix de Rome; 1866 instructor, 1871 prof. of harmony, at the Cons. He composed operettas, cantatas, songs, etc.; also recitatives for Hérold's *L'Illusion* and Balfe's *The Bohemian Girl.*—Cf. F. Clauzel, *Jules Duprato* (1896).

Dupré (du-prã'), **Marcel,** French organist and composer; b. Rouen, May 3, 1886. He was a pupil of his father, Albert Dupré, also an organist; he then entered the Paris Cons. (1904) and studied with Guilmant, Diémer, and Widor, winning 1st prizes for organ (1907) and for fugue (1909); in 1914 he won the Grand Prix de Rome for the cantata *Psyché.* He was interim organist at Notre-Dame in 1916; in 1920 he gave at the Paris Cons. a cycle of 10 recitals of Bach's complete organ works, playing from memory. On Nov. 18, 1921, he made his

New York début, followed by a transcontinental tour of 94 recitals given in 85 American cities; a second U. S. tour in 1923 included 110 concerts; he made his tenth tour of the U. S. in 1948. In 1939 he gave 40 concerts in Australia on his world tour. He had, meanwhile, been appointed prof. of organ at the Paris Cons. in 1926; in 1934 he succeeded Widor as organist at St. Sulpice; he became general director of the American Cons. in Fontainebleau in 1947 and was appointed director of the Paris Cons., in succession to Delvincourt, in 1954. Dupré wrote his first work, the oratorio *La Vision de Jacob,* at the age of 14; it was performed on his 15th birthday, at his father's house in Rouen, in a domestic production assisted by a local choral society. Most of his organ works are products of original improvisations (in which he is unexcelled in modern times for spontaneity and perfection of contrapuntal, fugal, and formal development). Thus *Symphonie-Passion,* first improvised at the Wanamaker organ in Philadelphia (Dec. 8, 1921), was written down much later and performed in its final version at Westminster Cathedral, London (Oct. 9, 1924). Similarly, *Le Chemin de la Croix* was improvised in Brussels (Feb. 13, 1931) and performed in a definitive version in Paris the following year (March 18, 1932). Among pre-composed works there are symphonies for organ: No. 1 (Glasgow, Jan. 3, 1929) and No. 2 (1946); Concerto for organ and orch. (Groningen, Holland, April 27, 1938, with Dupré as soloist); *Psalm XVIII* (1949); 76 chorales and several a cappella choruses; also numerous 'verset-préludes.' He is the author of a *Traité d'improvisation à l'orgue* (1925) and *Méthode d'orgue.*—Cf. R. Delestre, *L'œuvre de Marcel Dupré* (Paris, 1952); B. Gavoty, *Marcel Dupré* (Monaco, 1955).

Duprez (dü-prā'), **Louis-Gilbert,** French tenor; b. Paris, Dec. 6, 1806; d. there, Sept. 23, 1896. His fine boy-voice gained him admission to Choron's Institute; after diligent vocal and theoretical study, he made his début as Count Almaviva at the Odéon, in 1825. Dissatisfied with the results, he subjected himself to a long course of training in Italy, and in 1836 succeeded Nourrit at the Opéra. He was appointed prof. of lyrical declamation at the Cons. in 1842, but resigned in 1850 to establish a vocal school of his own, which flourished. After his retirement (1855) from the stage, he produced several operas, an oratorio, a Mass, etc., without great success. But his vocal methods, *L'art du chant* (1845) and *La Mélodie, études complémentaires vocales et dramatiques de l'Art du chant* (1846), are justly celebrated; also wrote *Souvenirs d'un chanteur* (1880).— Cf. A. A. Elwart, *Duprez, sa vie artistique* (Paris, 1838).

Dupuis (dü-püē'), **Albert,** outstanding Belgian composer; b. Verviers, March 1, 1877. Pupil of d'Indy at the Schola Cantorum in Paris; winner of Belgian Prix de Rome with his cantata *La Chanson d'Halewyn* (Verviers, Nov. 25, 1903; performed as a 3-act opera Antwerp, Dec. 6, 1913); in 1938 he became director of the Cons. at Verviers.—Works: The operas, *L'Idylle* (Verviers, 1896), *Bilitis* (ibid., 1899), *Jean Michel* (Brussels, March 5, 1903), *Martylle* (ibid., March 3, 1905), *Fidelaine* (Liège, 1910), *Le Château de la Grande Bretèche* (Nice, 1913), *La Passion* (Monte Carlo, April 2, 1916), *La Captivité de Babylone* (biblical drama), *La Barrière* (Verviers, 1920), *La Délivrance* (Lille, 1921), *Le Sacrifice* (Antwerp, 1921), *La Victoire* (Brussels, 1923); *Hassan,* oriental fairy tale (Antwerp, 1931); *Un drame sous Philippe II* (Brussels, Jan. 18, 1938); the cantatas *Les Cloches nuptiales, Oedipe à Colonne* and *Cortège lyrique;* ballets: *Évocation d'Espagne* and *Rêve d'enfant;* for orch.: 2 symphonies (1904 and 1923); violin concerto; piano concerto; Caprice for flute and orch.; *Valse Joyeuse* for orch.; choruses, songs, etc. In 1955 he was awarded by the Société des auteurs lyriques de Paris a prize for his creative output.—Cf. J. Dor, *Albert Dupuis* (Liège, 1935).

Dupuis, Sylvain, Belgian conductor; b. Liège, Oct. 9, 1856; d. Bruges, Sept. 28, 1931. Pupil of the Liège Cons., winning the Prix de Rome in 1881; teacher of counterpoint there; conductor of the singing society *La Légia;* established in 1888 the 'Nouveaux Concerts Symphoniques'; appointed 1st cond. at Théâtre de la Monnaie in Brussels, 1900, and conductor of the 'Concerts Populaires'; from 1911 director of the Cons. at Liège; member of the Belgian Academy.—Works: 2 operas, *Cour d'Ognon* and *Moïna;* 3 cantatas, *La Cloche de Roland, Camoëns,* and *Chant de la Création;* a symphonic poem, *Macbeth;* a concertino for oboe and orch.; 2 suites for orch.; pieces for violin; choruses; etc.

Durand (dü-rähn'), **Émile,** French composer; b. St.-Brieuc, Feb. 16, 1830; d. Neuilly, May 6, 1903. While still a student at the Paris Cons., he was appointed (1850) teacher of an elementary singing class, and in 1871 prof. of harmony. He publ. *Traité d'Harmonie* and *Traité de Composition musicale;* also wrote several light operas.

Durand, Marie-Auguste, French organist and publisher; b. Paris, July 18, 1830; d. there, May 31, 1909. Organ pupil of Benoist; in 1849, organist at St. Ambroise, then at Ste.-Geneviève, St.-Roch, and (1862-74) St. Vincent de Paul. He also occupied himself with music criticism and composition (his *Chaconne* and *Valse* for piano are especially popular). In 1870 he entered into partnership with Schönewerk (acquiring Flaxland's music-publishing business), the firm then being known as 'Durand & Schönewerk'; when his son, **Jacques** (b. Paris, Feb. 22, 1865; d. Bel-Etat, Aug. 22, 1928), replaced Schönewerk in 1891, the title became 'Durand & Fils.' The house is now known as 'Durand & Cie.'; it has made a specialty of publishing works of the outstanding French composers (Joncières, Lalo, Massenet, Debussy, Saint-Saëns, César Franck, Chausson, Ravel, etc.), and has also brought out French editions of Wagner's *Tannhäuser, The Flying Dutchman,* and *Lohengrin,* as well as several editions of old masters, including a complete critical one of Rameau, ed. by Saint-Saëns.—Cf. J. Durand, *Cours professionel à l'usage des employés du commerce de musique* (2 vols., 1923); J. Durand, *Quelques souvenirs d'un éditeur de musique* (2 vols., 1924-5). Jacques Durand also publ. *Lettres de Cl. Debussy à son éditeur* (Paris, 1927).

Durante, Francesco, celebrated Italian church composer and noted teacher; b. Frattamaggiore, near Naples, March 31, 1684; d. Naples, Aug. 13, 1755. He studied in Rome with Pitoni and, under the guidance of his uncle, D. Angelo, at the Cons. di Sant' Onofrio, where he taught in 1710-11; then became maestro at the Cons. di Santa Maria di Loreto, and at the Cons. dei Poveri di Gesù Cristo from 1728-39, and again at Sant' Onofrio from 1745 until his death. After Alessandro Scarlatti, and with Leo, Durante ranks as one of the founders and a chief representative of the 'Neapolitan school' of composition. He devoted himself almost exclusively to sacred music, in which the breadth, vigor, and resourcefulness of his style are more in evidence than marked originality. He was a very great teacher; his pupils, Duni, Traetta, Vinci, Jommelli, Piccinni, Guglielmi, Pergolesi, Paisiello, and others, took almost complete possession of the European lyric stage during the latter half of the 18th century.—The library of the Paris Cons. contains a rich collection of his works in MS: 13 Masses, and fragments of Masses; 16 psalms, 19 motets, several antiphons and hymns; besides 12 madrigals, 6 harpsichord sonatas, etc. His *Lamentations of Jeremiah* and a *Pastoral Mass* are in the Vienna Library (in MS). The libraries of the Naples and Bologna Cons. also possess MSS of Durante. Karmrodt of Halle printed a grand Magnificat (with additional accompaniments by Robert Franz); Breitkopf & Härtel published 12 *duetti da Camera;* H. Schletterer ed. a selection of his keyboard pieces; other reprints of keyboard pieces are publ. by A. Diversi in 'Arte antica e moderna' (vol. I; 3 studies), F. Boghen in 'Antichi maestri italiani' (4 fugues, 3 toccatas), A. Longo in 'Biblioteca d'oro' (vol. II; *Aria danzante*), G. Tagliapietra in 'Antologia di musica antica e moderna' (vol. XI), M. Vitali in 'Composizioni scelte' (vol. II). A. Diversi publ. a 4 voiced *Christe eleison* in his 'Biblioteca mus. Sacra'.—Cf. R. Fiammano, *F. Durante* in 'Musica d'oggi' (Aug.-Sept., 1936); V. de Rubertis, *Dos Bajetes de Francesco Durante, erroneamente interpretados por Fétis y de Nardis* (Buenos Aires, 1947), which reproduces in facsimile Durante's birth registry (confirming the date as March 31, 1684).

Durey, Louis, French composer; b. Paris, May 27, 1888; pupil of Léon Saint-Requier; associated with that group of young French composers termed 'Les Six Français' by H. Collet [q.v.] (cf. Collet, *Les Six Français et Erik Satie,* in the Paris 'Comoedia,' Jan. 16, 1920). Since 1950, music critic for 'L'Humanité.' Has written a Pastoral for orch.; *Eloges* (after St. Léger) for soli, chorus, and orch.; *L'Occasion,* lyric drama in 1 act after Mérimée; chamber music (string trio, 3 string quartets, piano trio; etc.); *Fantaisie concertante,* for cello and orch.; 3 *chansons musicales* (to words by Lorca, 1948); 3 short cantatas: *La Guerre et la Paix,* for a cappella chorus (1949); *La Longue Marche,* to words by Mao-Tse-Tung (1949); *Paix aux hommes par Millions,* to words by Mayakovsky (1949); many piano pieces and songs.

Dürrner, Ruprecht Johannes Julius, German conductor and composer; b. Ansbach, Bavaria, July 15, 1810; d. Edinburgh, June 10, 1859. Pupil of Friedrich Schneider at Dessau; from 1831-42, cantor at Ansbach, then studied under Mendelssohn and Hauptmann at Leipzig, and settled in Edinburgh as a conductor and vocal teacher. His choruses and quartets for male voices won great favor.

Duruflé, Maurice, French organist and composer; b. Louviers, Eure, Jan. 11, 1902. He studied organ with Guilmant, Tournemire, and Louis Vierne; took a course in composition with Paul Dukas, graduating with first prizes in all subjects. In 1930 he became organist of the church of St. Etienne-du-Mont in Paris. He has written mainly for organ; among his larger works is a *Requiem* (1947).

Dushkin, Samuel, distinguished violinist; b. Suwalki, Poland, Dec. 13, 1897; studied violin with Auer, Kreisler, and Remy (Paris), composition with Ganaye in Paris; 1918, European début; 1924, American début; extensive tours as recitalist and soloist with symph. orchs. in Europe, U. S., Egypt, Palestine, etc.; has given 1st performances of compositions by Ravel, Pierné, Stravinsky (who composed his violin concerto for him and toured with him extensively), etc. Has written numerous virtuoso and pedagogic works for violin and edited many classic violin works.

Dussek (Dušek, Duschek) (dŏŏ'shek), **Franz,** Bohemian pianist; b. Chotěborky, Bohemia, Dec. 8, 1731; d. Prague, Feb. 12, 1799. He studied with Wagenseil at Vienna; settled in Prague, 1763, winning fame as a teacher and performer; was a close friend of Mozart.—Publ. several sonatas (1773, 1774, 1799) and a piano concerto (op. 1); in MS: symphonies, concertos, quartets, trios, sonatas.

Dussek (Dušek), Johann Ladislaus, outstanding composer; b. Cáslav (Tschaslau), Bohemia, Feb. 12, 1760; d. St.-Germain-en-Laye, March 20, 1812. At first a boy-soprano at the Minorite church, Iglau, he was taught music by Father Spenar, while attending the Jesuit college; was organist at the Jesuit church in Kuttenberg for 2 years, and while studying theology at Prague Univ. found time to get a thorough musical training, so that after graduation he obtained, through Count Männer, his patron, the post of organist at the church of St.-Rimbaut, Mechlin. Thence he went to Bergen-op-Zoom, and (1782) to Amsterdam; then spent a year at The Hague, and in 1783 studied under K. Ph. E. Bach at Hamburg; won renown as a pianist and as a performer on Hessel's 'harmonica' in Berlin (1784) and St. Petersburg, then accepting an appointment from Prince Radziwill, with whom he lived in Lithuania for over a year. He played before Marie Antoinette in 1786, at Paris; soon went to Italy, and returned to Paris in 1788, whence the Revolution drove him to London. Here he married Sofia Corri, a singer, in 1792, and undertook a music business with his father-in-law; but his careless habits, and love of luxury and ease, ill fitted him for commercial pursuits; the enterprise failed, and he fled to Hamburg in 1800 to escape his creditors. Here he appears to have stayed about 2 years, giving concerts and teaching. In 1802 he gave a concert at Prague, and paid a visit to his father at Čáslav; he then entered the service of Louis Ferdinand of Prussia, whose heroic death in battle (1806) inspired one of Dussek's finest pieces, *Elégie harmonique* for piano. Afterwards, he was briefly attached to the Prince of Isenburg (1806-8); then went to Paris as chapel master to Prince Talleyrand.—Dussek's significance in music history is unjustly obscured; he was a master craftsman; some canonic devices in his piano sonatas are remarkable for their skill; his piano writing had both brilliance and science; there are some idiomatic harmonies that presage Schumann and Brahms. He was a virtuoso at the keyboard; with Clementi he shares the honor of having introduced the 'singing touch.' A composer of amazing industry, Dussek wrote 12 piano concertos, 14 piano trios, 3 string quartets, a piano quartet; piano quintet; 53 violin sonatas (some interchangeable with flute); about 40 piano sonatas; 9 sonatas for piano four-hands; a number of sets of variations, dances, etc., for piano, as well as topical pieces on world events (*The Sufferings of the Queen of France; The Naval Battle and Total Defeat of the Dutch Fleet by Admiral Duncan,* etc.). He also wrote an opera, *The Captive* (London, 1798); incidental music to Sheridan's play *Pizarro* (London, 1799); publ. a piano method.—Cf. H. Truscott, *Dussek and the Concerto,* in 'Music *Review*' (Feb., 1955).

Dustmann (dŏŏst'-mahn), **Marie Luise** (*née* **Meyer**), dramatic soprano; b. Aix-la-Chapelle, Aug. 22, 1831; d. Charlottenburg (Berlin), March 2, 1899. Made her début in Breslau (1849); after this she was engaged at Kassel (under Spohr), at Dresden (1853), Prague (1854), and Vienna (1857). She sang as a 'star' in the larger German cities, Stóckholm, and London. Married Dustmann (a bookseller) in 1858; made 'Kammersängerin' at Vienna in 1860; taught for some time at the Vienna Cons.

Dutilleux (dü-tē-yö'), **Henri,** talented French composer; b. Angers, Jan. 22, 1916. He studied at the Paris Cons. with H. Busser and with Jean and Noël Gallon; won first Grand Prix de Rome in 1938; subsequently was active on the Paris radio. He has developed a modernistic style which incorporates many procedures of Impressionism. His instrumental works have had numerous performances in France, England, and America; his most impressive work is a symphony (Paris, June 7, 1951; also performances in Germany, England, and America). Other works: *Les Hauts de Hurle-Vent,* symph. suite; *Symphonie de danses; Salmacis,* ballet; *Sarabande,* for orch. (1941); sonatine for flute and piano (1943); *La Giole,* for voice and orch. (1944); *La Princesse d'Elide,* incidental music to Molière's play (1946); *Monsieur de Pourceaugnac,* incidental music to Molière's play (1948); *Le Loup* (Paris, March 18, 1953); chamber music; piano pieces; film music and songs.

Duvernoy (dü-vär-nwăh'), **Charles,** French clarinetist; b. Montbéliard, 1776; d. Paris, Feb. 28, 1845. He came to Paris in 1810, and was first clarinet at the Théâtre de Monsieur and the Feydeau, retiring in 1824. Till 1802 he was also prof. at the Cons. He wrote several clarinet sonatas and clarinet duets.

Duvernoy, Henri-Louis-Charles, French composer; son of Charles; b. Paris, Nov. 16, 1820; d. there, Jan., 1906. Pupil of Halévy and Zimmermann at Paris Cons., in 1848 appointed prof. there. Publ. (with Kuhn) *Nouveaux choix de psaumes et de cantiques* (1848); *Solfège des chanteurs* (1855); *Solfège à changements de clefs* (1857); and *Solfège artistique* (1860); also some 100 light piano pieces.

Duvernoy, Victor-Alphonse, French pianist and composer; b. Paris, Aug. 30, 1842; d. there, March 7, 1907. He was a pupil of Bazin and Marmontel at the Paris Cons., taking the first prize for piano (1855). In 1869 he founded, together with Léonard, Stiehle, Trombetta, and Jacquard, a series of chamber-music concerts; he devoted his time otherwise to composing and teaching, and held a professorship in the Cons. For some 11 years, musical critic of the 'République française'; Chevalier of the Legion of Honor, and an officer of public instruction. As a dramatic composer he produced the 3-act opera *Sardanapale* (Liège, 1892); the 'scène lyrique' *Cléopâtre* (at the Concerts Colonne), and the 4-act opera *Hellé* (Grand Opéra, 1896). His symph. poem *La tempête,* produced at the Concerts Colonne, won the City of Paris prize in 1880; he also wrote a ballet, *Bacchus* (1902); an overture, *Hernani;* much piano music.

Duvosel, Seraphien Lieven, Flemish composer; b. Ghent, Dec. 14, 1877; studied there, then in Antwerp and Paris; had first success as a composer at the Colonne concerts in Paris, 1908; lived for a time in Berlin (where Nikisch and R. Strauss performed his works), later in The Hague and in Haarlem. His most representative work is the symph. cycle in 5 parts, *Leie:* 1. *De Morgen;* 2. *De Leie;* 3. *De Liefde aan der Leie;* 4. *Kerstnacht* (*Christmas*); 5. *Het Leieland.* Other compositions: 3 symphonies; the symph. poem, *Den Avond* (*Evening*); *Wereldwee* (*World's Grief*); many cantatas; male and mixed chor.; songs; and the earlier works *Vers la Lumière, La Charité,* and *La Tristesse et la Consolation.*

Dux, Claire, soprano; b. Bydgoszcz, Poland, Aug. 2, 1885; studied voice with Teresa Arkel in Berlin; made operatic début in Cologne in 1906; 1911-18, member of the Berlin State Opera (début in *La Bohème* with Caruso); 1912-14, sang at Covent Garden, London; 1918-21, member of the Royal Opera, Stockholm; came to the U. S. in 1921 and joined the Chicago Civic Opera Co. in 1923; toured the U. S.; then retired. She is married to Ch. Swift of Chicago, where she settled.

Dvořák (dvŏhr'-zhahk), **Antonin,** famous Bohemian composer; b. Mühlhausen, Sept. 8, 1841; d. Prague, May 1, 1904. His father, an innkeeper, wished him to enter the butcher's trade; but he, having learned to play the violin from the village schoolmaster, left home at the age of 16, and entered the Prague Organ School, studying under Pitzsch, and earning a precarious livelihood as a violinist in a small orchestra. For about a decade (1861-71), he played the viola in the orchestra of the National Theater in Prague. It was not until 1873 that he brought out an important work, a *Hymnus* for mixed chorus and orch., which was performed on March 9 of that year and attracted wide notice; in 1875 he was awarded the Austrian State Prize for a symph. in E♭ (performed in Prague by Smetana in 1874), and he received that stipend repeatedly thereafter. He then devoted himself to composition with increasing success, becoming the most celebrated of Czech national composers. Liszt, Brahms, and Hans von Bülow, by securing performances and publication of his work, did much to obtain for his compositions the vogue they deservedly enjoy. In 1873 Dvořák gave up playing in orchestras, when he was appointed organist at St. Adalbert's Church in Prague. His fame as composer spread and numerous pupils flocked to him; finally, a professorship in composition at the Prague Cons. was offered him. In 1884 he was invited to conduct his *Stabat Mater* in London. It was received with such enthusiasm that in the fall of the same year Dvořák conducted it at the Worcester Festival, and was commissioned to write a new work for the Birmingham Festival of 1885 (*The Spectre's Bride*). The following year (1886) he visited England again to direct his oratorio *St. Ludmila* at the Leeds Festival; in 1891 he was made hon. Mus. Doc. by Cambridge and hon. *Dr. Phil.* by the Czech Univ. in Prague. From 1892-5 he was the artistic director of the National Cons., New York. It was in America that he wrote his most celebrated work, the symphony *From the New World* (first performed by the New York Philh., Dec. 15, 1893); the themes seemed to reflect Negro spirituals; however, Dvořák denied any conscious design in this approximation. Upon returning to Prague, he resumed his professorship at the Cons.; was appointed its artistic director in 1901. He was the first musician to be made a life member of the Austrian House of Lords. — A composer of singular versatility and fecundity, the most prominent characteristics of his music are an inexhaustible, spontaneous melodic invention, rhythmic variety, free employment of national folk tunes, and an intensity of harmony which, in his finest works, has an electrifying effect, though sometimes bordering on the crude. His musical style was eclectic; the conflicting influences of Brahms and Wagner occasionally effected an inner incompatibility; however, his very lack of startling originality, combined with an uninhibited emotionalism, contributed to the lasting success of his music. Works: Operas (all first performed at Prague): *The King and Collier* (op. 14, 1871; Nov. 24, 1874; revised 1874, 1887); *The Blockheads* or *The Pig-Headed Peasants* (op. 17; 1874; Oct. 2, 1881); *Vanda* (op. 25; April 17, 1876); *The Peasant a Rogue* (op. 37; Jan. 27, 1878); *Dimitrij* (op. 64; Oct. 8, 1882; revised 1883, 1894); *The Jacobin* (op. 84; Feb. 12, 1889; revised 1897); *The Devil and Kate* (op. 112; Nov. 23, 1899); *Rusalka* (op. 114; March 31, 1901; Dvořák's best opera; many revivals; very popular in Eastern Europe); *Armida* (op. 115; March 25, 1904). For orch.: 7 published symphs.: op. 60, in D (1880); op. 70, in D minor; op. 76, in F (originally op. 24; 1875, 1887); op. 88, in G (1889); op. 95, in E minor (*From the New World,* 1893); in E♭ (originally op. 10, 1873; posthumous); in D minor (originally op. 13, 1874; posthumously, 1912); 2 unnumbered symphs.: in C minor, *The Bells of Zlonice* (originally op. 31, 1865; discovered in Prague, 1936) and in B♭ (originally op. 41, 1865); the symph. poems *The Watersprite* (op. 107; 1896); *The Midday Witch* (op. 108; 1896); *The Golden Spinning-wheel* (op. 109; 1896); *The Wood Dove* (op. 110; 1896); *Heroic Song* (op. 111; 1897); various overtures: *Amid Nature,* op. 91 (1891); *Carnival,* op. 92 (1891); *Othello,* op. 93 (1891-2); etc.; *Slavonic Rhapsodies* (op. 45) and *Dances* (opp. 46, 72); *Romance* for violin and orch., op. 11 (1873); piano concerto in G minor, op. 33 (1876); violin concerto in A minor, op. 53 (1879-80); cello concerto in B minor, op. 104 (1895); other compositions. Choral works: *Stabat Mater,* op. 58 (1876-7); cantata, *The Spectre's Bride,* op. 69 (1884); oratorio, *St. Ludmila,* op. 71 (1885-6; amplified and performed as an opera, *Svatá Ludmila,* Prague, Nov. 30, 1901); Psalm 149, op. 79 (1879, 1887); Mass in D, op. 86 (1887, 1892); Requiem, op 89 (1890); cantata, *The American Flag,* op. 102 (1892); *Te Deum,* op. 103 (1892); numerous other works. Chamber music: string sextet, 3 string quintets, 2 piano quintets, piano quartet, 13 string quartets, 5 piano trios, etc. Songs, vocal duets, piano pieces, etc. —Bibl.: J. Zubatsky, *Antonin Dvořák, biographische Skizze* (Leipzig, 1886; in English by W. H. Hadow in 'Studies in Modern Music,' 2nd series, London, 1895; 2nd ed. 1904); D. G. Mason, *From Grieg to Brahms* (N. Y., 1902); V. Joss, *Antonin Dvořák* (1903); K. Hoffmeister, *Antonin Dvořák* (in English by R. Newmarch, London, 1928); O. Šourek, *Antonin Dvořák* (in Czech, 4 vols., Prague 1916-33; in German as *Dvořák, Leben und Werk,* 1 vol., abridged by Paul Stefan from the original work, Vienna, 1935; in English, N. Y., 1954); H. Sirp, *Antonin Dvořák* (Potsdam, 1939); P. Stefan, *Antonin Dvořák* (N. Y. 1941); A. Robertson, *Dvořák* (London, 1945); J. Van Straaten, *Slavonic Rhapsody, the Story of Antonin Dvořák* (N. Y., 1948); H. Boese, *Zwei Urmusikanten: Smetana, Dvořák* (Zürich, 1955; contains bibl.). A complete edition of Dvořák's works under the general editorship of O. Šourek was begun in Prague in 1955 and continued after Šourek's death (1956) by a committee of Czech scholars. For a complete list of works see O. Šourek, *Dvořák's Werke: Ein vollständiges Verzeichnis in chronologischer, thematischer und systematischer Anordnung* (Berlin, 1917).

Dwight, John Sullivan, American music critic, and editor of 'Dwight's Journal of Music'; b. Boston, Mass., May 13, 1813; d. there, Sept. 5, 1893. He graduated from Harvard in 1832, and was one of the founders and most active members of the Harvard Musical Assoc. After studying for the ministry, he, in 1840, took charge of the Unitarian Church at Northampton, Mass. His literary and socialistic proclivities, however, gained the mastery; he gave up his pastorate, and entered the ill-starred Brook Farm Community as a teacher of German music and the classics. Returning to Boston in 1848, after the failure of the socialistic experiment, he devoted himself to literature, founded the 'Journal' in 1852, and remained its editor-in-chief until its discontinuance in 1881. A prominent feature in this paper were the valuable historical essays of A. W. Thayer. Dwight also published excellent *Translations of Select Minor Poems from the German of Goethe and Schiller, with Notes.* —Cf. George Willis Cooke, *J. S. Dwight, Brook-Farmer, Editor, and Critic of Music* (Boston, 1898); Cooke's ed. of Dwight's correspondence with George William Curtis (Boston, 1898); Edward N. Waters, *J. S. Dwight, first American Critic of Music,* in the 'Mus. Quarterly' (Jan., 1935).

Dykema (dī'kĕh-măh), **Peter W.**, pedagogue; b. Grand Rapids, Mich., Nov. 25, 1873; d. Hastings-on-Hudson, N. Y., May 13, 1951. From 1892-96, he studied law at the Univ. of Michigan (B. L., 1895; M.L., 1896); then voice with Frank Arens, N. Y. (1903-4), theory with Frank Shephard, and at the Institute of Musical Art (1911-12), later also in Berlin. Teaching positions: 1896-98, Aurora, Ill., High School; 1898-1901, principal, Jr. High School, Indianapolis; 1901-13, music prof., Ethical Culture School, N. Y.; 1913-24, prof. of music, Univ. of Wisconsin, chairman of the Dept. of Public School Music and director of the Madison Choral Union; 1924-39, prof. of music education, Teachers' College, Columbia Univ.; lectured on *Music in Education, Music in Normal Living, Music Education in Europe,* etc.—Publ.: *Twice 55 Community Songs* (6 vols., 1919-27); *The Check Book* (1930); *Music for Public School Administrators* (1931); *School Music Handbook* (1931; revised ed., by Hannah M. Cundiff, Boston, 1955); *Modern Orch. Series* (with N. Church; 1933); *Singing Youth* (1935); *Sing* (with D. Stevens; 1937); *Fox Festival Choral Series* (3 vols., 1937); *Golden Key Orch. Series* (1937); *Modern Band Training Series* (with N. Church; 1938); with K. W. Gehrkens, *The Teaching and Administration of High School Music* (Boston, 1941); collaborated in editing many popular school song books.

Dykes, Rev. **John Bacchus**, b. Kingston-upon-Hull, England, March 10, 1823; d. in an asylum at Ticehurst, Sussex, Jan. 22, 1876. An English divine and composer, educated at Cambridge; minor canon and precentor at Durham cathedral, 1849, where he also conducted the Music Society. He took the degree of Mus. Doc. in 1861, and was vicar of St. Oswald, Durham, from 1862. Some of his hymns are well-known (*Jesus, Lover of My Soul; Nearer, My God, to Thee;* etc.); he likewise composed a service in F; the 23d Psalm (The Lord is my shepherd); anthems; and part-songs. —Cf. J. T. Fowler, *Life and Letters of John Bacchus Dykes* (London, 1897).

Dyson (dī'-son), Sir **George**, English composer; b. Halifax (Yorkshire), May 28, 1883. He was a pupil at the Royal Academy of Music; won the Mendelssohn prize; from 1908, was music master at Royal Naval College, Osborne, Marlborough College, Rugby School, Wellington College, and Winchester College (1924-38); Mus. Doc. (Oxford, 1918); professor of the Royal College of Music; in 1937, director of the Royal College of Music; has lectured on modern music and published essays on that subject. —Works: *Prelude, Fantasy and Chaconne,* for cello and orch. (Hereford, 1936); symph. (London, 1937); violin concerto (1943); oratorio, *Quo Vadis* (1949); suite for small orch.; *3 Rhapsodies* for string quartet; piano pieces; pedagogic pieces; songs; choral works (*The Canterbury Pilgrims, The Blacksmith, St. John's Voyage to Melita, Nebuchadnezzar*); church music (services). —Books: *The New Music* (1924); *The Progress of Music* (London, 1932); autobiography, *Fiddling While Rome Burns; A Musician's Apology* (London, 1954).

Dzegelenok (dzĕh-gĕh-lyoh'-nok), **Alexander Michailovitch**, Russian composer and theorist; b. Moscow, Aug. 24, 1891; studied at the Philh. Institute in Moscow with Koreshtchenko. He has composed an orchestral suite *Egypt*; *Hiawatha* for voice and instruments; piano pieces and songs (some of them published by the State Edition).

Dzerzhinsky (dzähr-zhin'-skē), **Ivan Ivanovitch**, Russian composer; b. Tambov, April 21, 1909. He received his musical education in Moscow, studying with Gnessin; in 1930 he moved to Leningrad, where he entered the Cons. In Leningrad he wrote a *Spring Suite* for piano and a piano concerto. He has written other instrumental pieces; but his significance in the development of Soviet music lies chiefly in his stage works. Adopting a characteristically Russian melodic style, he uses sparingly some modernistic devices, remaining strictly in the diatonic framework. His most successful opera, *Quiet Flows the Don* (Leningrad, Oct. 22, 1935), has maintained its popularity throughout Russia. A sequel to this opera, *Soil Upturned* (Moscow, Oct. 23, 1937), was less successful. Other operas are: *The Tempest* (after Ostrovsky, 1940); *The Blood of the People* (1941), and *The Blizzard* (after Pushkin, 1946).

E

Eames (āmz), **Emma,** famous soprano; b. of American parentage at Shanghai, China, Aug. 13, 1865; d. New York, June 13, 1952. At the age of five she went with her mother, a talented musician and her first teacher, to the latter's native town of Bath, Maine; from 1883 she studied under Miss Munger, in Boston, and from 1886-8 under Mme. Marchesi (voice) and M. Pluque (stage-deportment, etc.) in Paris; made her début at the Grand Opéra, March 13, 1889, as Juliette in Gounod's *Roméo et Juliette* with great success. She sang in the Paris Opéra for two years; then at Covent Garden, London (début, April 7, 1891, as Marguerite in *Faust*); appeared in New York with the de Reszkes, as Juliette (Dec. 14, 1891); continued to appear regularly in New York and London in their respective seasons (except the winters of 1892-3, at Madrid, and 1895-6, during temporary ill health). Her last performance was at the Metropolitan Opera House in *Tosca* on Feb. 15, 1909. On July 13, 1911, she married the baritone Emilio de Gogorza. From 1923 to 1936, she lived alternately in Paris and Bath, Maine; in 1936, settled in New York, where she remained until her death. She received from Queen Victoria the Jubilee Medal, and was decorated by the French Academy with the order of 'Les Palmes Académiques.' She publ. an autobiography, *Some Memories and Reflections* (N. Y., 1927).

Eames, Henry Purmort, American music educator; b. Chicago, Ill., Sept. 12, 1872; d. Claremont, Cal., Nov. 25, 1950. He studied at Cornell College, Iowa (Mus. Doc., 1906), with W. Smith and W. H. Sherwood, later in Europe with Clara Schumann and with Paderewski; toured the U. S. (with Reményi; 1894-95) and Europe (1895-97); was prof. of piano and esthetics at the Univ. of Nebraska (1898-1908); founded the Omaha School of Music and Allied Arts (1911); taught at the Cosmopolitan School, Chicago (1912-20); director of the music dept. of the Illinois Wesleyan Univ. (1913-19); teacher at the American Cons., Chicago (1923-28); after 1928, music director of Scripps College, Claremont, California. He wrote music for pageants, choral works, and many songs.

Earhart, Will, American music educator; b. Franklin, Ohio, April 1, 1871. 1900-12, school supervisor in various cities of Ohio and Indiana; 1912, became director of music in the public schools of Pittsburgh; 1913-18 lecturer in music, 1918-21 prof., in School of Education of Univ. of Pittsburgh; 1921, became lecturer at Carnegie Institute of Technology, Pittsburgh; Mus. Doc., Univ. of Pittsburgh, 1920. —Writings: *Music in the Public Schools* (1914), *Music in Secondary Schools* (with O. McConathy; 1917), *The Eloquent Baton* (1931), *Music to the Listening Ear* (1932), *The Meaning and Teaching of Music* (1935), *Music Appreciation* (American ed. of P. Scholes' book; 1935), *Choral Technics* (1937), *Elements of Music Theory* (with Ch. N. Boyd; 2 vols., 1938), etc. He has ed. *Art Songs for High Schools* (1910), *The Congdon Music Primer No. 1* and *The Congdon Music Reader No. 4* (with C. H. Congdon), *The School Credit Piano Course* (with others; 1918), etc.

Easdale, Brian, English composer; b. Manchester, Aug. 10, 1909; studied at the Royal College of Music in London (1925-33). He became interested in theatrical music; has written 3 operas, *Rapunzel* (1927), *The Corn King* (1935), and *The Sleeping Children* (1951); incidental music to Shakespeare's plays and several film scores, of which the most successful was the music for *The Red Shoes*. Other works include a piano concerto and several orchestral pieces of a descriptive nature (*Dead March*; *The Phoenix*; *Bengal River*, etc.).

East (Easte, Este), Thomas, English music printer and publisher of Elizabethan madrigals; b. London, c. 1540; d. there, Jan. 1609. He received his license as printer in 1565; his first musical publication was Byrd's collection *Psalmes, Sonets and Songs of Sadnes and Pietie* (1587); he was also the assignee of Byrd's patent for printing music paper and musical compositions. In 1592 he brought out *The Whole Booke of Psalmes, with their wonted tunes as they are sung in Churches, composed in four parts,* containing harmonizations by Allison, Blancks, Cavendish, Cobbold, Dowland, Farmer, Farnaby, Hooper, Johnson, and Kirbye; republished in 1594 and 1604; reprinted in score by the Musical Antiquarian Society (1844). This collection is of historical significance, for it was the first to be printed in score rather than in separate part-books; also for the first time, the tunes were designated by specific names, such as 'Kentish,' 'Cheshire,' etc. Other works printed by East are Yonge's *Musica Transalpina* (1588),

Byrd's *Songs of Sundrie Natures* (1589), Watson's *Madrigals* (1590), Byrd's *Cantiones Sacrae* (2 books, 1589, 1591), Morley's *Canzonets* (1593), Mundy's *Songs and Psalmes* (1594), Kirbye's *Madrigals* (1596), Wilbye's *Madrigals* (1598), Dowland's *Ayres* (1600), Bateson's *Madrigals* (1603), Michael East's *Madrigals* (1604), Pilkington's *Songs or Ayres* (1604), Byrd's *Gradualia* (1605), Youll's *Canzonets* (1607). East's presumed son **Michael East** (c. 1580-c. 1648) was a composer; his set of madrigals was publ. by Thomas East in 1604. He served as organist at Lichfield Cathedral; received the degree of B. Mus. at Cambridge (1606); he published six sets of vocal pieces (madrigals, anthems, etc.) and a set of instrumental works (1638).—Cf. F. Kidson, *British Music Publishers* (London, 1900); E. H. Fellowes, *The English Madrigal Composers* (London, 1921; 2nd ed., 1948).

Eastman, George, famous American industrialist; b. Waterville, N. Y., July 12, 1854; d. (suicide, when he learned he had cancer), Rochester, March 14, 1932. Eastman made important and far-reaching contributions to the cause of education; invested immense sums in scientific institutions, particularly the Univ. of Rochester, which includes the Eastman Theater and School of Music (one of the leading music schools of the U. S.). This alone he endowed with $3,500,000.—Cf. Carl W. Ackerman, *George Eastman* (1930).

Easton, Florence (Gertrude), operatic soprano; b. Middlesbrough-on-Tees, Yorkshire, Oct. 25, 1884; d. New York, Aug. 13, 1955. She was educated in Toronto, where her parents settled when she was five; appeared at eight as pianist there; studied singing at the Royal Academy of Music in London and one year with Elliott Haslam in Paris; début as Madama Butterfly with the Moody-Manners Co. at Covent Garden (1903); in 1904 she married the tenor Francis Maclennan (divorced in 1929); her second husband was Stanley Rogers. She was engaged by Savage for his productions in English of *Parsifal* (1904-5) and *Madama Butterfly* (1906-7), touring the U. S.; at the Berlin Opera in leading roles (1907-13); at Hamburg (1913-15); frequent leaves of absence enabled her to take part in the Wagner and Strauss performances at Covent Garden; with the Chicago Opera Co. (1915-17). She was a celebrated member of the Metropolitan Opera Company (1917-29; made her début there in *Cavalleria Rusticana,* Dec. 7, 1917). From 1930-36, she was mostly in England; on Feb. 29, 1936, returned to the Metropolitan Opera for a single appearance as Brünnhilde in *Die Walküre*; made many conert tours as German Lieder singer; lived in New York during the last years of her life. She created Beatrice in Naylor's *The Angelus* (Covent Garden, Jan. 27, 1909), Natoya in Nevin's *Poia* (Berlin, April 23, 1910), Elektra in the English première of Strauss' opera (Covent Garden, Dec. 19, 1910), Serpina in the American première of Pergolesi's *La Serva Padrona* (N. Y., May 8, 1917), Elisabeth in the American première (operatic version in English) of Liszt's *Legend of St. Elisabeth* (N. Y., Jan. 3, 1918).

Eaton, Louis, American violinist, b. Waltham, Mass., Feb. 24, 1872; d. Hartford, Conn., May 4, 1927. He studied violin with Loeffler and Bernard Listemann and piano with Jessie Downer (b. Middlebury, Vt., Nov. 17, 1872; d. Hartford, Conn., Nov. 22, 1936) whom he married in 1899. In 1915 they settled in Hartford as teachers. With the cellist Arthur Hadley, they formed the Downer-Eaton Trio, which presented first American performances of a number of chamber works.

Ebel, Arnold, German composer and choral conductor; b. Heide, Holstein, Aug. 15, 1883. He studied at Berlin Univ.; also took private lessons with Max Bruch; from 1909 was active in Berlin as organist, choral conductor, and teacher; was prof. of composition at the Akademie für Kirchen- und Schulmusik (1930-45); served as president of the German Composers' Association (1920-33 and again from 1949). He has written numerous piano pieces and songs (most of them published); also a *Sinfonietta giocosa* for orch.

Ebell, Hans, pianist; b. St. Petersburg, April 21, 1888; d. Salem, Conn., Aug. 18, 1934. He was a pupil at the Cons. in St. Petersburg (1900-5); then continued his pianistic studies with Rachmaninov, Josef Hofmann, and Godowsky (until 1911); début in Vienna (1912); tours of Germany, Austria, Russia, France, and England (1912-14); in 1915, settled in the U. S. as teacher; lived mostly in Boston.

Eberhardt, Siegfried, German violin pedagogue; b. Frankfurt, March 19, 1883; son of the violinist and pedagogue Goby Eberhardt (1852-1926). He studied violin with Dessau at the Stern Cons. in Berlin, and then with Serato; was teacher of violin at the Stern Cons. (1908-35); then lived in Halle and Lübeck; in 1953 was in Zwickau.

—Didactic works: *Der beseelte Violinton* (with Carl Flesch; Dresden, 1910; 4 eds.; also in English); *Treffsicherheit auf der Violine* (1911; 22 eds.; also in English, French, and Swedish); *Virtuose Violintechnik* (1920); *Paganinis Geigenhaltung* (1921); *Die Lehre der organischen Geigenhaltung* (1922); *Der Körper in Form und Hemmung* (Munich, 1926); *Wiederaufstieg oder Untergang der Kunst der Geigen* (1956).—Cf. K. Schröter, *Flesch-Eberhardt, Naturwidrige oder natürliche Violintechnik?* (1924).

Eberl, Anton Franz Josef, Austrian pianist and composer; b. Vienna, June 13, 1765; d. there, March 11, 1807. On Feb. 27, 1787, he produced the opera *La Marchande de modes*; this was followed by the opera *Die Zigeuner* (1793). His symphonies and piano music were praised by Mozart and Gluck. He made a concert tour with Mozart's widow in 1795; lived in St. Petersburg from 1796 to 1799; revisited Russia in 1801; gave concerts there on Dec. 8, 15, and 28, 1801, presenting the first performances in Russia of Haydn's *The Creation;* returned to Vienna early in 1802; traveled through Germany in 1806. Besides 3 more operas, he wrote a cantata, symphonies, piano concertos, much chamber music, many piano works (especially sonatas), songs, etc.—Cf. Fr. J. Ewens, *Anton Eberl* (Dresden, 1927; with thematic catalogue); R. Haas, *Anton Eberl* in 'Mozart-Jahrbuch 1951' (Salzburg, 1953).

Eberlin (Eberle), Johann Ernst, composer; b. Jettingen, Bavaria, March 27, 1702; d. Salzburg, June 19, 1762; from 1729, cathedral organist and choirmaster at Salzburg; from 1749, court Kapellmeister to the Prince-Archbishop there.—Published works: *Der Blutschwitzende Jesus,* in 'Denkmäler der Tonkunst in Österreich' (XXVIII, 1); *XI Toccate e Fughe per l'organo* (Augsburg, 1747; several reprints); fugues and toccatas in Commer's 'Musica sacra'; 2 motets (publ. by Schott); 2 sonatas (publ. by Haffner); 5 pieces in L. Mozart's 'Der Morgen und der Abend' (Augsburg, 1759).—In MS: 13 oratorios in Regensburg (Proske's Library); an offertory and Miserere (Berlin Library); a volume of organ pieces (Royal Institute for Church Music, Berlin); other works in the Vienna Library (a 4-voiced Mass with organ motets, cantatas, etc.), the Munich Library (18 Masses and other pieces), and in the libraries of Kremsmünster and Salzburg (37 Masses with orch., 75 oratorios, 43 psalms with orch., 3 Te Deums, etc.).—Cf. Robert Haas, *Eberlins Schuldramen und Oratorien,* in 'Studien zur Musikwissenschaft' (1921); C. Schneider, *Geschichte der Musik in Salzburg* (Salzburg, 1935); K. A. Rosenthal, *Mozart's Sacramental Litanies and Their Forerunners,* in the 'Mus. Quarterly' (Oct., 1941).

Eberwein, Karl, German composer; b. Weimar, Nov. 10, 1786; d. there, March 2, 1868. He was a member of a musical family; after a study of general subjects at the Weimar High School he received an appointment as a court musician at the age of 16. He then studied with Zelter in Berlin; returning to Weimar, he held the posts of chamber musician (1810-18); music director of the Weimar town church (1818-26); and conductor of Weimar opera (1826-49). He was a friend of Goethe, who often mentions him, and for whom he composed some songs. Among his works are the operas *Die Heerschau, Der Graf zu Gleichen,* and *Der Teppichhändler;* several cantatas written for various state occasions; some chamber music, and a great number of songs with piano accompaniment. — Cf. W. Bode, *Goethes Schauspieler und Musiker* (1912, with autobiographical sketch of Eberwein); H. J. Moser, *Goethe und die Musik* (Leipzig, 1949).

Eberwein, Traugott Maximilian, German composer, brother of Karl Eberwein; b. Weimar, Oct. 27, 1775; d. there, Dec. 2, 1831. He played the violin in the Weimar court orch. as a very young man; like his brother, he was a protégé of Goethe, and wrote two operas, *Claudine von Villa Bella* (1815) and *Der Jahrmarkt von Plundersweilen* (1818), to texts by Goethe; he further composed church music and instrumental concertos.

Eccard, Johannes, eminent German composer; b. Mühlhausen, 1553; d. Berlin, 1611. He was a pupil (1571-4) of Orlandus Lassus in Augsburg; director of J. Fugger's private orch. at Augsburg (1577); in 1578 he moved to Königsberg, as a member of the Prussian chapel; in 1580 became its assistant conductor, and in 1604, chief conductor. In 1608 he was called to Berlin to serve as court musician to the Elector. He was an important composer of sacred music. He published (with Burgk) *Odae sacrae* (1574) and *Crepundia sacra* (in 2 parts, 1578); his own works include *Neue deutsche Lieder mit 4 und 5 Stimmen,* dedicated to J. Fugger (1578); *Neue geistliche und weltliche Lieder mit 4 und 5 Stimmen* (1589; ed. in score by R. Eitner, in 'Publikationen älterer Musik,' vol. 25); *Geistliche Lieder auf den Choral* *mit 5 Stimmen,* 51 songs (2 parts, 1597; new ed. by Teschner and Fr. von Baussnern, 1928); *Preussische Festlieder auf das ganze Jahr für 5-8 Stimmen* (posthumous in 2 parts, 1642-4; new ed. by Teschner, 1858); also occasional songs (many in the Königsberg Library).—Cf. C. von Winterfeld, *Der evangelische Kirchengesang . . . ,* I and II; A. Mayer-Reinach, *Zur Geschichte der Königsberger Hofkapelle,* in 'Sammelbände der Internationalen Musik-Gesellschaft' (vol. VI); H. E. Brinckmann, *Neue Forschungen zum Leben der grossen Mühlhauser Musiker,* in the 'Armin Tille Festschrift' (Weimar, 1930).

Eccles, Henry, brother of John Eccles; b. London, c. 1652; d. Paris, c. 1742. He was a violinist; a member of the King's Band (1674-1710), and then of the French court orch. In 1720 he published under his own name 12 violin solos, adaptations of works by Giuseppe Valentini and others.

Eccles, John, English violinist and composer; b. London, c. 1650; d. Kingston, Surrey, Jan. 12, 1735. He was the son and pupil of the violist Solomon Eccles (1618-1683). He became a member of the Queen's Band in 1694, and Master of it in 1700. He was active as a composer for the theater from about 1681; in 1694 wrote music for *Don Quixote* (with Purcell); in 1700, for Congreve's *The Judgment of Paris* and *The Way of the World*; 1710, publ. a collection of his own songs (about 100), which enjoyed wide popularity. He also publ. 3 volumes of 'Theatre Music' (c. 1700). In all, he wrote music for 12 masques and 56 pieces of incidental music for the stage.—Cf. John Jeffreys, *The Eccles Family* (Enfield, 1951).

Eckard (Eckardt, Eckart), Johann Gottfried, German composer of keyboard music; b. Augsburg, Jan. 21, 1735; d. Paris, July 24, 1809. He was a copper engraver by profession and learned music in his spare time. In 1758 he was taken to Paris by the piano manufacturer J. A. Stein, and remained there. He acquired a great facility as pianist, and gave successful concerts in Paris. In the preface to his album of six sonatas he states that his task was to compose music suitable for any keyboard instrument, but the indications of dynamics in the manuscript show that he had mainly the then novel piano in view. Mozart admired Eckard's works, and there are traits in Mozart's keyboard music of the Paris period that may be traced to Eckard's usages. A complete edition of Eckard's works for piano, ed. by Eduard Reeser, was begun in Amsterdam in 1956.

Eckardt, Hans, German musicologist, authority on Japanese music; b. Magdeburg, Oct. 10, 1905. He studied philology in Leipzig, Berlin, Paris, and Heidelberg (1925-29); musicology with Sachs, Hornbostel, and Schünemann. From 1932 to 1945 he was in Kyoto, Japan, as director of the Japanese-German Research Institute of Cultural History. In 1948 he settled in Heidelberg. He contributed articles on Asiatic music to 'Die Musik in Geschichte und Gegenwart'; wrote several papers in Japanese for *Monumenta Nipponica.*

Eckelt, Johann Valentin, German organist; b. Werningshausen, near Erfurt, May (baptized 8th), 1673; d. Sondershausen, Dec. 18, 1732. From 1696 he was organist at Wernigerode; from 1703, at Sondershausen.—Publications: *Experimenta musicae geometrica* (1715); *Unterricht, eine Fuge zu formieren* (1722); *Unterricht, was ein Organist wissen soll.* His MS Passion, cantatas, and organ works are of interest. His valuable library was acquired by E. L. Gerber, and utilized by the latter in the compilation of his Dictionary.—Cf. E. Jacobs, *Der Orgelspieler und Musikgelehrte J. V. Eckelt,* in the 'Vierteljahrsschrift für Musik-Wissenschaft' (1893, p. 311-332).

Ecker, Wenzel. Pen-name of **Wilhelm Gericke.**

Eckerberg, Sixten, Swedish conductor, pianist, and composer; b. Hjältevad, Sept. 5, 1909. He studied at the Stockholm Cons. (1927-32); received a Jenny Lind stipend to study conducting with Weingartner in Basel; also was piano pupil of Emil Sauer in Vienna and of Isidor Philipp in Paris. Since 1937 he has been conductor of the radio orch. in Göteborg. He has written 2 symphonies (1941; 1944); 2 piano concertos (1942; 1949), songs, and piano pieces.

Eckert, Karl Anton Florian, German composer and conductor; b. Potsdam, Dec. 7, 1820; d. Berlin, Oct. 14, 1879. At the age of 6 he was considered a prodigy; the poet F. Förster became interested in him and sent him to the best teachers; he studied piano with Rechenberg and Greulich, violin with Botticher and Ries, and composition with Rungenhagen. At 10 he wrote an opera, *Das Fischermädchen*; at 13, an oratorio, *Ruth.* After study (for a time at Leipzig under Mendelssohn) he went to the U. S. with Henriette Sontag; was then conductor of the Italian opera in Paris (1852); in 1853 appointed conductor and mus. director of the Vienna Opera; from 1860-67 held a similar post in Stuttgart; he was in Baden-Baden from 1867-69; then was called to Berlin to succeed Heinrich Dorn as director of the Berlin Opera. He wrote four operas, several oratorios, and a cello concerto which had little success; his songs, however, proved more popular; of these the *Swiss Echo Song* is the best known.

Eckhard, Jacob, one of early German organists in America; b. Eschwege (Hesse), Nov. 24, 1757; d. Charleston, S.C., Nov. 10, 1833. He came to the U. S. in 1776 and settled in Richmond, Va. In 1786 he was organist of St. John's Lutheran Church in Charleston; in 1809 received the post of organist at St. Michael's Episcopal Church. He published a hymn book (printed in Boston, 1816); wrote two patriotic naval songs, *The Pillar of Glory* and *Rise, Columbia, Brave and Free.*—Cf. G. W. Williams, *Jacob Eckhard and His Choirmaster's Book* in the 'Journal of the American Musicological Society' (Spring, 1954).

Eckhardt-Gramatté, Sophie Carmen, violinist, pianist, and composer; b. Moscow, Jan. 6, 1902. She studied both piano and violin at the St. Petersburg Cons. and later in Paris; toured Europe and the U. S. as pianist; also appeared as violinist; eventually settled in Vienna, where she married an art critic. Her compositions include a symphony (1940); a piano concerto (1946; awarded 2nd prize of the Vienna Gesellschaft der Musikfreunde); 2 string quartets (1939, 1943); and several other chamber works.

Écorcheville, Jules, French writer on music; b. Paris, March 18, 1872; d. Feb. 19, 1915 (fell in battle at Perthesles-Hurlus). He was a pupil of César Franck, 1887-90; student of literature and art-history in Paris and (1904-5) Leipzig; *Docteur ès lettres* (Paris, 1906); editor of 'La Revue musicale S.I.M.' and writer on the history and esthetics of music.—Works: *De Lully à Rameau: 1690-1730, l'Esthétique musicale* (1906); *Corneille et la musique* (1906); *Actes d'état civil des musiciens insinués au Châtelet de Paris de 1539 à 1650* (1907); *Catalogue du fonds de musique ancienne de la Bibliothèque Nationale* (thematic list of 10,000 items, to be completed in 10 vols.; only 8 vols. were publ.); *Un livre inconnu sur la danse* (F. de Lauze's *Apologie de la danse,* 1623), in 'Riemann-Festschrift,' 1909; also edited *Vingt Suites d'orchestre du XVIIe siècle français* (1906; facsimile and transcription).—Cf. *Le Tombeau de Jules Écorcheville: suivi de lettres inédites* (Paris, 1916).

Eddy, Clarence, distinguished American organist; b. Greenfield, Mass., June 23, 1851; d. Chicago, Jan. 10, 1937. He first studied with Dudley Buck in New York; in 1871 he went to Berlin to study piano with Loeschhorn. He made frequent tours in America and Europe; gave a series of 100 organ recitals in Chicago (1879) with completely different programs; appeared at the Vienna Exposition of 1873; at the Philadelphia Centennial in 1876; at the Chicago Columbian Exposition in 1893, etc. He wrote many pieces for organ; publ. *The Church and Concert Organist* (2 vols., 1882-5); *The Organ in Church* (1887); *A Method for Pipe Organ* (1917); and translated K. A. Haupt's *Theory of Counterpoint and Fugue* (1876).

Eddy, Nelson, popular American baritone; b. Providence, R. I., June 29, 1901; studied voice with W. Vilonat in New York; then in Dresden and Paris; was for 4 years a member of the Philadelphia Opera Co.; then sang on the radio with sensational success; also acted in musical films. He settled in Beverly Hills, California.

Edel, Yizschak, composer; b. Warsaw, Jan. 1, 1896. He studied in Kiev and Moscow. In 1929 he settled in Palestine as a music teacher. He has written *Capriccio,* for orch. (1947); 2 string quartets, a wind quintet, and numerous choral works.

Edelmann, Johann Friedrich, Alsatian composer, b. Strasbourg, May 6, 1749; d. Paris, July 17, 1794 (guillotined). He studied law at the Univ. of Strasbourg; in 1773 he went to Paris, where he learned to play piano, gave concerts, and publ. 15 collections of various piano pieces, which became very popular and were reprinted in Germany and in London. He also wrote an opera, *Ariane dans l'isle de Naxos* (Paris, Sept. 24, 1782), which was retained in the repertory for half a century. He went back to Strasbourg during the Revolution, and joined the Jacobins, which proved his undoing. A selection of his works was published by Riemann in 'Mannheimer Kammermusik' ('Denkmäler der Tonkunst in Bayern,' XV). His piano works were in the Couperin tradition; he affected suggestive subtitles in his piano sonatas (*La Coquette, La Caressante,* etc.) in the prevalent style of 18th-century French music.—Cf. M. Vogeleis, *Bausteine und Quellen zu einer Geschichte der Musik im Elsass* (Strasbourg, 1911); G. de Saint-Foix, *Les premiers pianistes parisiens: J. F. Edelmann,* in the 'Revue Musicale' (June, 1924).

Eder, Helmut, Austrian composer; b. Linz, Dec. 26, 1916. He studied music at home; was a soldier in World War II; then resumed his musical studies, taking courses with Hindemith, Carl Orff, and Johann Nepomuk David. He has written a symphony (1950); concerto for piano, 15 wind instruments, double-basses, and percussion (1952); string quartet (1948); trio for flute, clarinet, and bassoon (1952); *Partita* for 2 guitars (1954), etc., in a neo-classical manner.

Edgcumbe. See **Mount-Edgcumbe.**

Edmunds, Christopher, English composer; b. Birmingham, Nov. 26, 1899. He studied with Bantock; was organist at Aston from 1922; since 1945, prof. at the Birmingham School of Music. He wrote an opera *The Blue Harlequin;* 2 symphonies and chamber music.

Edmunds, John, American composer and music scholar; b. San Francisco, June 10, 1913. He studied with Rosario Scalero at the Curtis Institute and with Walter Piston at Harvard Univ., where he received his M.A. He later worked with Roy Harris at Cornell Univ. and with Otto Luening at Columbia Univ.; won the Bearns Prize at Columbia for a group of 40 songs, and later a Seidl Traveling Fellowship; subsequently held a Fulbright Fellowship to England (1951) for editing 100 songs by Purcell, and a fellowship from the Italian Government for the study of solo cantatas by Alessandro Scarlatti and Benedetto Marcello (1954-56); from 1957, in charge of the Americana Collection in the Music Division of the N. Y. Public Library. His compositions are almost entirely songs (more than 500), many of which have been published; also numerous 'realizations' of songs by Purcell and settings of folksongs.

Edson, Lewis, American music teacher; b. Bridgewater, Mass., Jan. 22, 1748; d. Woodstock, N.Y., 1820. Originally a blacksmith by trade, he became very active as a music teacher. He went to New York in 1776; moved to Woodstock in 1817. He compiled (with Thomas Seymour) *The New York Collection of Sacred Music*; composed the hymn tunes *Bridgewater, Lenox, Greenfield,* and others.

Edwards, Clara, American composer; b. Mankato, Minn., April 18, 1887. She studied there at the State Normal School; later took courses in Vienna; returned to the U.S. in 1914, and became active as a singer and pianist. She has written many songs to her own words *(By the Bend of the River; Into the Night,* etc.) also some music for animated cartoons and for children's plays.

Edwards, Henry John, English composer; b. Barnstaple, Devon, Feb. 24, 1854; d. there, April 8, 1933. He received his first instruction from his father, organist of the Barnstaple Parish Church; from 1874-6 studied with H. C. Banister (harmony), G. Macfarren (composition), and S. Bennett (piano and orchestration); at Oxford he took degrees of Mus. Bac. (1876) and Mus. Doc. (1885); succeeded his father in 1886; also conducted Barnstaple Music Festival Society, and Exeter Oratorio Society (1896-1921): retired in 1926. He wrote 2 oratorios, *The Ascension* (Exeter Festival, 1888) and *The Risen Lord* (Exeter Festival, 1906); a cantata, *The Epiphany* (1891); motets, etc.

Edwards, Henry Sutherland, English writer on music; b. Hendon (London), Sept. 5, 1829; d. London, Jan. 21, 1906. For many years he was critic of the 'St. James Gazette'; among his numerous books the following are the most important: *The Russians at Home* (1861); *History of the Opera from its Origin in Italy to the Present Time* (1862; 2nd ed. published in same year as *History of the Opera, from Monteverdi to Donizetti*); *Life of Rossini* (1869; in condensed form in 'Great Musicians' series, 1881); *The Lyric Drama* (2 vols., 1881); *Famous First Representations* (1886); *The Prima Donna . . . from the 17th to the 19 Century* (2 vols., 1888).

Edwards, Julian, operetta composer; b. Manchester, England, Dec. 11, 1855; d. Yonkers, N. Y., Sept. 5, 1910. He was a pupil in Edinburgh of Sir H. Oakeley, and in London of Sir George Macfarren; conducted the Royal English Opera Co. (1877) and the English Opera at Covent Garden (1883); came to U. S. in 1888, settling in Yonkers and devoting himself entirely to composition. Some of his comic operas achieved more than average success; among them, *Victoria* (Sheffield, March 6, 1883); *Jupiter* (N. Y., April 14, 1892); *Friend Fritz* (N. Y., Jan. 26, 1893); *King Rene's Daughter,* lyric drama (N. Y., Nov. 22, 1893); *Madeleine* (N. Y., July 31, 1894); *The Goddess of Truth* (N. Y., Feb. 26, 1896); *Brian Boru,* romantic Irish opera (N. Y., Oct. 19, 1896); *The Wedding Day* (N. Y., April 8, 1897); etc.

Edwards, Richard, English composer; b. Somersetshire, near Yeovil, c. 1522; d. London, Oct. 31, 1566. He studied at Oxford (M. A. in 1547); was (from 1561) master of the children of the Chapel Royal. With these choir-boys he presented in 1565 his musical play *Damon and Pithias* (publ. in 1571). Edwards is best known for his madrigal 'In going to my naked bed,' written about 20 years before the period when the madrigal became popular in England (this piece is reprinted by Fellowes in 'The English Madrigal School,' XXXVI).

Eeden (ā'-den), **Jean-Baptiste van den,** Belgian composer; b. Ghent, Dec. 24, 1842; d. Mons, April 4, 1917. Pupil of the Cons. at Ghent and Brussels, winning at the latter the 1st prize for composition (1869) with the cantata *Faust's laatste nacht.* In 1878, appointed director of Mons Cons., succeeding Huberti.—Works: The operas *Numance* (Antwerp, 1897) and *Rhena* (Brussels, 1912); oratorios *Brutus, Jacqueline de Bavière, Jacob van Artevelde, Le Jugement dernier,* and the dramatic scene for 3 voices *Judith*; 2 cantatas, *Het Woud* and *De Wind*; a symph. poem, *La lutte au XVIe siècle*; a *Marche des esclaves,* etc.; also choruses and songs.—Cf. Paul Bergmans, *Notice sur Jean van den Eeden* in the annual publ. of the Académie Royale (Brussels, 1924; pp. 375-436; contains a complete catalogue of works); M. Delsaux, *Jean van den Eeden et son œuvre* (Mons, 1925).

Effinger, Cecil, American composer; b. Colorado Springs, Col., July 22, 1914. He studied violin at the age of seven in Colorado Springs; and oboe in Los Angeles; then studied composition with Nadia Boulanger in Fontainebleau, and with Bernard Wagenaar in Colorado Springs; was first oboist of the Denver Symph. Orch. in 1935-41; bandmaster in the U. S. Army in France (1942-45); also taught classes at the American Univ. in Biarritz (1945); taught at Colorado College from 1936-41 and 1945-48; then appointed head of the theory department at the Univ. of Colorado, the position that he still held in 1956.—Works: *Pastoral and Scherzo* for oboe and piano (1940); *Western Overture* (1942); *Prelude and Fugue* for organ (1942); 3 anthems for chorus and organ (1943); concertino for organ and wind instruments (1943); 4 string quartets (1943-48); *American Man* for chorus and orch. (1943); viola sonata (1944); *Fanfare on Chow Call* for male voices and brass (1944); *Variations on a Cowboy Tune,* for orch. (1945); suite for cello and piano (1945); *Little Symphony* (St. Louis, 1945); *Tennessee Variations,* for orch. (Nashville, 1946); 1st Symphony (Denver, March 11, 1947); *Pastoral* for oboe and strings (1948); concerto for piano with chamber orch. (Denver, March 21, 1948); 2nd Symphony (Cincinnati, Feb. 4, 1949); *Chorale and Fugue* for band (1949); *3 Concert Fanfares* for band (1951-53); choral symphony (Denver, Dec. 2, 1952); *Christmas Cantata* (1953); 3rd Symphony (1954); *Tone Poem on the Square Dance* for orch. (1955). He is the inventor of a practical music typewriter patented in 1954, and marketed, under the name Musicwriter, in 1955.

Egenolff, Christian, an early German music printer; b. July 22, 1502; d. Frankfurt, Feb. 9, 1555. He published 2 collections of 4-part songs, *Gassenhawerlin* and *Reuterliedlin* (1535; facsimile ed. publ. by Moser, Augsburg, 1927) which are of decided value. —Cf. H. Grotefend, *Christian Egenolff* (Frankfurt, 1881).

Egge, Klaus, Norwegian composer; b. Gransherad, July 19, 1906. He studied piano with N. Larsen; composition with F. Valen in Oslo and with W. Gmeindl in Berlin. He has been president of the Norwegian Composers Society since 1945; a member of Unesco from 1946-49; music critic of the 'Arbeiderbladet' since 1945. His works are cast in classical form, with thematic content of national coloring. He signs his compositions with the notes e-g-g-e of his name. Works: Symphony No. 1 (Oslo, Oct. 4, 1945); Symphony No. 2 (1949); 2 piano concertos (1938 and 1946); *Fjell-Norig* (*Mountainous Norway*) for soprano and orch. (Oslo, Oct. 1, 1945); *Draumar i stjernesno* (*Starsnow Dreams*) for voice and orch. (1946); string quartet (1934); viola sonata (1934); piano sonata (1934); wind quintet (1939); piano trio (1941); woodwind quintet (1949); choruses and songs.

Eggen, Arne, Norwegian composer; b. Trondheim, Aug. 28, 1881; d. Drammen, Oct. 26, 1955. He studied in Oslo and in Leipzig; was organist for many years; also conducted operas in Norway and Sweden.—Works: 2 operas: *Olav Liljekrans,* after Ibsen (1940), *Cymbeline* (1949); symphony (1920); 2 violin sonatas, cello sonata, numerous choral works.

Eggen, Erik, Norwegian composer and musicologist; brother of Arne Eggen; b. Trondheim, Nov. 17, 1877. He received his Ph. D. at Oslo Univ., 1925.—Writings: *Edvard Grieg* (1911); *Norsk musikksoge* (1923); composed *Norsk Rapsodi,* for orch., a cantata, and choral works.

Egghard, Julius (pen-name of Count Hardegen), Austrian pianist; b. Vienna, April 24, 1834; d. there, March 23, 1867. He was a pupil of Czerny and became a concert pianist; wrote a number of piano pieces in salon style, which were extremely popular.

Egidi (ā'-gē-dē), **Arthur,** German organist and composer; b. Berlin, Aug. 9, 1859; d. there, June 3, 1943. He studied in Berlin; taught at Hoch's Cons. in Frankfurt (1885-92); then was organist and choral conductor in Berlin. He composed mostly for the organ; publ. a collection of reprints of works by old German masters under the title *Musikschätze der Vergangenheit.*

Egk, Werner, German composer; b. Auchsesheim, Bavaria, May 17, 1901. He studied piano with Anna Hirzel-Langenhan and composition with Orff. Primarily interested in theater music, he had his first contact with the stage at a Munich puppet theater; then was active on the radio; he wrote his own librettos. From 1929, Egk held various posts as conductor in Bavaria; conducted at the Berlin State Opera from 1938 to 1941; was head of the Composers' Union (1941-45); director at the Berlin Hochschule für Musik (1950-53); then settled in Munich.—Works: Radio opera *Columbus* (Munich, July 13, 1933; 1st stage performance, Frankfurt, Jan. 13, 1942); *Die Zaubergeige,* opera in 3 acts (Frankfurt, May 20, 1935); *Olympische Festmusik,* for orch. (Berlin Olympiad, Aug. 1, 1936); cantatas *Natur-Liebe-Tod* and *Mein Vaterland* (both performed at Göttingen, June 27, 1937); *Peer Gynt,* opera (Berlin, Nov. 24, 1938, composer conducting; highly successful despite the inevitable comparisons with Grieg); *Joan von Zarissa,* ballet (Berlin, Jan. 20, 1940); *Abraxas,* ballet (Baden-Baden radio, Dec. 7, 1947; stage performance, June 6, 1948, in Munich); *Circe,* opera after Calderón (Berlin, Dec. 18, 1948, composer conducting); *Französische Suite,* after Rameau, for orch. (Munich, Jan. 28, 1950); *Ein Sommertag,* ballet (Berlin, June 11, 1950); *Allegria,* suite for orch. (Baden-Baden radio, April 25, 1952); *Die Chinesische Nachtigall,* ballet after Andersen (Munich, May 6, 1953); *Chanson et Romance,* for coloratura soprano and chamber orch. (Aix-en-Provence, July 19, 1953); *Irische Legende,* opera after Yeats (Salzburg, Aug. 17, 1955); *Der Revisor,* opera after Gogol (Schwetzingen, May 9, 1957).

Egli, Johann Heinrich, Swiss song composer; b. Seegraben, near Zürich, March 4, 1742; d. there, Dec. 19, 1810. He was a pupil of Pastor Schmiedli at Wetzikon. Lived in Zürich; composed much sacred music, also publ. *Schweizer Volkslieder* and other collections of arrangements of national songs.

Ehlers, Alice, pianist and harpsichordist; b. Vienna, April 16, 1890. She studied there and in Berlin, later with Wanda Landowska (1913-18); toured Europe successfully; lived in Berlin, Vienna, and later in London. In 1936, she settled in the U. S.; since 1942, teaching at the Univ. of Southern California.

Ehlert, Louis, German composer and writer; b. Königsberg, Jan. 13, 1825; d. Wiesbaden, Jan. 4, 1884. He was a pupil of Schumann and Mendelssohn in Leipzig Cons.; also studied at Vienna, and then at Berlin, where he lived from 1850-63 as a teacher and critic. He frequently visited Italy, and was conductor of the Florentine 'Società Cherubini'; taught at Tausig's Schule des höheren Klavierspiels in Berlin (1869-71); then became tutor to the Meiningen princes; finally settled in Wiesbaden. His collection of essays, *Aus der Tonwelt* (Berlin, 1877) was publ. in English as *From the Tone World* (N. Y., 1885); he also wrote an entertaining volume, *Briefe über Musik an eine Freundin* (Berlin, 1859); in English as *Letters on Music, to a Lady* (Boston, 1870). Among his compositions are *Frühlings-Symphonie;* overture *Hafis;* songs.

Ehmann, Wilhelm, German musicologist; b. Freistadt, Dec. 5, 1904. He studied at the Univ. of Freiburg and in Leipzig; became instructor at Freiburg Univ. (1938); then appointed prof. of musicology at the Univ. of Innsbruck (1940); served in the German Navy (1943-45). Since 1948, director of the Westphalian church music school.—Publications: *Das Schicksal der deutschen Reformationsmusik* (Göttingen, 1935); *Adam von Fulda* (Berlin, 1936); *Die Chorführung* (2 vols., Kassel, 1949; 2nd ed., 1950); *Erziehung zur Kirchenmusik* (Gütersloh, 1951); *Erbe und Auftrag musikalischer Erneuerung* (Kassel, 1951); *Das Chorwesen in der Kulturkrise* (Regensburg, 1952). For a detailed list of his other writings, see his autobiographical entry in 'Die Musik in Geschichte und Gegenwart.'

Ehrenberg (är'-ehn-berg), **Carl Emil Theodor,** German conductor and composer; b. Dresden, April 6, 1878. He studied there with Fr. Wieck; then with Draeseke at the Dresden Cons. (1894-98). From 1898 he was engaged as conductor in Germany; in 1909-14, conducted at Lausanne; in 1915-18, was opera conductor in Augsburg; symph. conductor at Bad Homburg (1918-

22); conductor of the Berlin State Opera (1922-24); prof. at the Cologne Hochschule für Musik (1925-35); prof. at the Akademie der Tonkunst in Munich (1935-49), where he continued to live in 1955.—Works: 2 operas, *Und selig sind* and *Anneliese* (Düsseldorf, 1922); 2 early symphonies (1897-98); tone poem *Jugend; Nachtlied* for violin and orch.; choral works (*Sonnenaufgang, Dein Vaterland,* etc.); several string quartets; 9 piano trios; violin sonata; songs; etc.

Ehrlich, (Alfred) Heinrich, Austrian pianist and writer on music; b. Vienna, Oct. 5, 1822; d. Berlin, Dec. 29, 1899. He was a pupil of Henselt and Thalberg (piano), and of Sechter (composition). For several years he lived at Hanover as court pianist; then at Wiesbaden (1855-7), London, Frankfurt, and Berlin. He was a piano teacher at the Stern Cons. from 1864 to 1872 and again from 1886 to 1898. He was also music critic of the 'Berliner Tageblatt'.—Writings: *Schlaglichter und Schlagschatten aus der Musikwelt* (1872), *Für den Ring des Nibelungen gegen Bayreuth* (1876), *Wie übt man am Klavier?* (1879; 2nd ed. 1884; English transl. by Cornell as *How to Practice on the Piano;* 2nd ed., by F. Baker, 1901); *Die Musikästhetik in ihrer Entwickelung von Kant bis auf die Gegenwart* (1881); *Lebenskunst und Kunstleben* (1884); *Wagnersche Kunst und wahres Christentum* (1888); *Aus allen Tonarten* (1888); *Musikstudium und Klavierspiel* (1891); *Dreissig Jahre Künstlerleben* (1893); *Berühmte Klavierspieler der Vergangenheit und Gegenwart* (1893; in English as *Celebrated Pianists of the Past and Present Time,* 1894); *Berühmte Geiger der Vergangenheit und Gegenwart* (1893; in English as *Celebrated Violinists, Past and Present,* 1897); *Die Ornamentik in Beethovens Sonaten* (1896); *Die Ornamentik in Beethovens Klavierwerken* (1896; in French and English, 1898); also the novels *Abenteuer eines Emporkömmlings* (1858), *Kunst und Handwerk* (1862), *Vier Noveletten aus dem Musikantenleben* (1881).

Ehrling, Sixten, Swedish pianist and conductor; b. Malmö, April 3, 1918. He studied piano and composition at the Stockholm Cons.; conducting with A. Wolff in Paris. He conducted in Göteborg (1942-43); also appeared as pianist with European orchestras. Since 1944, conductor of the Royal Opera in Stockholm.

Eibenschütz, José, German conductor; b. Frankfurt, Jan. 8, 1872; d. Sülzhayn, Harz, Nov. 27, 1952. He studied at Hoch's Music School in Frankfurt; in 1894 was appointed orchestral conductor in Abo, Finland; there he remained until 1905; subsequent positions as conductor: Görlitz (1905-8); Hamburg Philh. Orch. (1908-21); Oslo Philh. (1921-27); North German Radio (1928). From 1938-46 he conducted in Scandinavia and in Russia; returned to Germany in 1946.

Eichberg (ih'-berg), **Julius,** violinist and composer; b. Düsseldorf, June 13, 1824; d. Boston, Jan. 19, 1893. His first teachers were J. Fröhlich (at Würzburg) and J. Rietz (at Düsseldorf); he then (1843-45) attended the Brussels Cons. (Fétis, Meerts, and Bériot); in 1846 was appointed prof. of violin and composition at the Geneva Cons.; in 1856 came to New York; settled in Boston in 1859 as director of the Museum Concerts (till 1866). He also became director of the Boston Cons., superintendent of music in the public schools; founded the Eichberg School for Violin.—Works: operetta *The Doctor of Alcantara* (Boston, 1862); *The Rose of Tyrol* (1865); *The Two Cadis* (Boston, March 5, 1868); studies, duets, and characteristic pieces for violin; trios and quartets for strings; songs.

Eichborn, Hermann Ludwig, German composer, writer, and inventor; b. Breslau, Oct. 30, 1847; d. Gries, near Bozen, April 15, 1918. In early youth he learned to play piano, flute, trumpet, horn, etc.; studied law at Breslau Univ.; also took music lessons with Dr. E. Bohn. He invented (1882) the Oktav Waldhorn (soprano French horn) in F, adopted by many Silesian bands.—Writings: *Die Trompete in alter und neuer Zeit* (1881); *Zur Geschichte der Instrumentalmusic* (1885); *Das alte Clarinblasen auf Trompeten* (1895); *Die Dämpfung beim Horn* (1897); *Militarismus und Musik* (1909); and various articles.

Eichheim, Henry, American composer and violinist; b. Chicago, Jan. 3, 1870; d. Montecito, near Santa Barbara, Cal., Aug. 22, 1942. He received his elementary musical training from his father, Meinhard Eichheim, a cellist in the Theodore Thomas Orch.; then studied with C. Becker and L. Lichtenberg at the Chicago Musical College. After a season as violinist in the Thomas Orch. in Chicago, he was a member of the Boston Symph. Orch. (1890-1912); then devoted himself to concert work and composition. He made four trips to the Orient (1915, 1919, 1922, 1928) and collected indigenous instruments, which he subsequently used in his orchestral music. All of his works are on oriental subjects; these are: *Oriental Impressions,* or *The Story of the Bell* (Boston

Symph., March 24, 1922, composer cond.); *The Rivals,* ancient Chinese legend, ballet (Chicago, Jan. 1, 1925; as an orch. piece, under the title *Chinese Legend,* Boston Symph., April 3, 1925, composer cond.); *Malay Mosaic* (International Composers' Guild, N. Y., March 1, 1925); *Impressions of Peking* and *Korean Sketch* for chamber orchestra and a group of oriental instruments (Venice Festival of the International Society for Contemporary Music, Sept. 3, 1925); *Burma,* symph. poem (Neighborhood Playhouse Co., N. Y., March 16, 1926, as incidental music for a play; Chicago Symph. Orch., Feb. 18, 1927, composer cond.); *Java* (Philadelphia Orch., Nov. 8, 1929, composer cond.; contains a 'gamelan' section, with 45 instruments); *Bali* (Philadelphia Orch., Stokowski cond., April 20, 1933, at a Youth Concert); also a violin sonata (1934) and other chamber music. The harmonic idiom of these works is derived from Debussy and Scriabin.

Eichner, Ernst, German composer and bassoon virtuoso; b. Mannheim, Feb. 9, 1740; d. Potsdam, 1777; concertmaster at the court of Pfalz-Zweibrücken; went to Paris in 1770, and after a very successful season in London (1773) was appointed member of the orch. of Prince Frederick William of Prussia. He is one of the important composers of the Mannheim School. —Works: 31 symphonies (thematic catalogue in vol. VII, 2, of 'Denkmäler der Tonkunst in Bayern'); piano concertos; piano trios; piano sonatas; duets for violin and viola; quartets for flute, violin, viola, and cello; quintets for flute and string quartet. A symphony in D was published by Riemann in vol. VIII, 1, of 'Denkmäler der Tonkunst in Bayern'; some chamber music in volumes XV, XVI; a symph. in F (1772) was revised for violin and piano by R. Sondheimer in 1923.—Cf. A. Volk, *Ernst Eichner* (Cologne, 1943).

Eilers, Albert, German bass singer; b. Cöthen, Dec. 21, 1830; d. Darmstadt, Sept. 4, 1896. He studied at the Cons. of Milan; made his opera début in Dresden (1854); sang at the German Theater in Prague (1858-65). In 1876 Wagner selected him to sing the part of the giant Fasolt at Bayreuth. In 1882 he became a member of the Darmstadt Opera. He wrote a fairly successful comic opera *Die Johannisnacht* (Koblenz, 1889).

Eimert, Herbert, German writer and composer; b. Bad Kreuznach, April 8, 1897; studied at the Cons. and Univ. of Cologne (musicology and philosophy); became interested in new musical techniques.—Writings: *Atonale Musiklehre* (Leipzig, 1924); *Zur Phänomenologie der Musik,* in 'Melos' (V,7); *Bekenntnis und Methode,* in 'Zeitschrift für Musikwissenschaft' (Nov., 1926); *Über ein methodisches Problem der musikalischen Stilkunde,* in 'Zeitschrift für Ästhetik' (1928); *Lehrbuch der Zwölftontechnik* (Wiesbaden, 1950).

Einem, Gottfried von, talented Austrian composer; b. Bern, Switzerland (where his father was attached to the Austrian Embassy), Jan. 24, 1918. He went to Germany as a child; studied at Plön, Holstein; then was opera coach at the Berlin Staatsoper. In 1938 he was arrested by the German Gestapo, and spent 4 months in prison. After his release he studied composition with Boris Blacher in Berlin (1942); was later in Dresden (1944); eventually settled in Salzburg. In 1953 he visited the U. S. His main interests are in the field of modern opera. Having absorbed the variegated idioms of advanced technique, Einem has produced a number of succesful short operas and ballets; in his music he emphasizes the dramatic element by dynamic and rhythmic effects; his harmonic idiom is terse and strident; his vocal line often borders on atonality, but remains singable.—Works: operas: *Dantons Tod* (Salzburg, Aug. 6, 1947); *Der Prozess (The Trial;* after Kafka; Salzburg Festival, Aug. 17, 1953); ballets: *Prinzessin Turandot* (Dresden State Opera, Feb. 5, 1944); *Pas de cœur* (Munich, July 22, 1952); *Rondo vom goldenen Kalb* (Hamburg, Feb. 1, 1952); for orch.: *Capriccio; Meditations* (Louisville, Nov. 6, 1954).

Einstein, Alfred, eminent musicologist; b. Munich, Dec. 30, 1880; d. El Cerrito, Calif., Feb. 13, 1952. A member of a family of scholars (Albert Einstein was his cousin), he first studied law, then turned to music and took courses with Sandberger and Beer-Walbrunn at the Univ. of Munich; *Dr. phil.,* 1903 (thesis: *Zur deutschen Literatur für Viola da Gamba*; Leipzig, 1905); 1918-33, editor of the 'Zeitschrift für Musikwissenschaft'; lived in Munich until 1927 as music critic of the 'Münchner Post'; 1927-33, influential critic of the 'Berliner Tageblatt'; in 1933 he left Germany; lived in London and Italy (near Florence); in 1938 settled in the U. S.; taught at Smith College (retired, 1950); naturalized as American citizen, March 2, 1945.—Principal writings: Revised editions of Riemann's *Musiklexikon* (9th ed., 1919; 10th ed., 1922; 11th enlarged ed.,

1929); *Neues Musiklexikon* (German ed. of A. Eaglefield-Hull's *Dictionary of Modern Music and Musicians,* 1926); *Geschichte der Musik,* with *Beispielsammlung zur älteren Musikgeschichte* (1917-18; 4th ed., 1930); new edition (3rd) of Köchel's *Mozart Verzeichnis* (Leipzig, 1937; very valuable; reprint ed. with numerous corrections, Ann Arbor, 1947); *A Short History of Music* (London, 1936; N. Y., 1937; 2nd ed., 1938; 3d ed., 1947; translation of *Geschichte der Musik*); *Gluck* (London, 1936). He contributed the following studies to the periodicals of the International Music Society: *Claudio Merulo als Herausgeber der Madrigale des Verdelot, Italienische Musiker am Hofe der Neuburger Wittelsbacher* (IX), *Augenmusik im Madrigal, Ein Madrigaldialog von 1594, Ein unbekannter Druck aus der Frühzeit der deutschen Monodie* (Nauwach, *Arie passeggiate 1623;* XIII); other articles: *Die Aria di Ruggiero; Ancora sull' Aria di Ruggiero* in 'Rivista Musicale Italiana' (1937); *Die Parodie in der Villanella,* in the 'Zeitschrift für Musikwissenschaft' (II); *Dante im Madrigal,* in the 'Archiv für Musikwissenschaft' (III); *Das Madrigal,* in 'Ganymed' (1921); *Heinrich Schütz* in 'Ganymed' (1925); *Agostino Steffani* in the 'Kirchenmusikalisches Jahrbuch' (1910); *Angelo Grillos Briefe als musikgeschichtliche Quelle* in the 'Kirchenmusikalisches Jahrbuch' (1911); *Eine Caccia im Cinquecento,* in the 'Liliencron Festschrift' (1911); *Lebensläufe deutscher Musiker* (Hiller, Neefe, Gyrowetz), a series begun in 1914; *Alessandro Stradella,* in 'Sandberger Festschrift' (1918); *Anfänge des Vokalkonzerts,* in 'Acta musicologica' (III, 1); *Annibale Padoano,* in 'Adler Festschrift' (1930); articles in the 'Mus. Quarterly': *The Madrigal* (Oct., 1924), *Dante, on the Way to the Madrigal* (Jan., 1939; also *A Supplement,* Oct., 1939), etc.; contributed two chapters to Adler's *Handbuch der Musikgeschichte* (1924; 2nd ed., 1930); made German transl. of Marcello's *Teatro alla Moda* (1917); new eds. of A. Steffani's *Ausgewählte Kammerduette* (in collaboration with Sandberger and Bennat) in 'Denkmäler der Tonkunst in Bayern' (VI, 2); Gluck's *L'Innocenza giustificata,* in 'Denkmäler der Tonkunst in Bayern' (vol. 82); G. Benda's *Ariadne* (1920); discovered Mozart's *Rondo* in A for piano and orch. (Univ. Ed., 1936); revised 5 little-known Haydn symphonies (No. 80, in D minor, publ. 1937), all of which were performed by the orch. of the New Friends of Music, N. Y., in 1939. He also prepared a modern ed. of Andrea Antico's publication of 1517, *Canzoni, Sonetti, Strambotti, et Frottole* (Northampton, Mass., 1941); ed. a collection, *The Golden Age of the Madrigal* (N.Y., 1942). His writings in America (publ. in English transl. from his original German) include: *Greatness in Music* (N.Y., 1941; German ed., *Grösse in der Musik,* Zürich, 1951); *Mozart; His Character, His Work* (N. Y., 1945); *Music in the Romantic Era* (N. Y., 1947; German ed., *Die Romantik in der Musik,* Vienna, 1950); *The Italian Madrigal,* in 3 vols. (Princeton, 1949; of fundamental importance); *Schubert: A Musical Portrait* (N. Y., 1950); *Essays on Music* (N. Y., 1956; posthumous). A profound scholar, Einstein was also a brilliant journalist, with a vivid, richly metaphorical style, capable of conveying to the reader an intimate understanding of music pertaining to widely different epochs.

Eisenberg, Maurice, outstanding cellist; b. Königsberg, Feb. 24, 1900; brought to the U. S. as a child; studied violin; then, at the age of 12, took up the cello. He played as a youth in café orchestras, and studied at the Peabody Cons. in Baltimore; was a cellist of the Philadelphia Orch. (1917-19); then joined the N. Y. Symphony (under Walter Damrosch). He went to Europe in 1927 and studied in Berlin with Hugo Becker; in Leipzig with Julius Klengel; in Paris with Alexanian; and in Spain with Casals; then taught at the École Normale in Paris (1930-37); returning to the U. S., he gave a concert in N. Y. (Dec. 27, 1937) with excellent success; then appeared with major symph. orchestras; taught at various colleges; publ. a book *Cello Playing of Today* (1957).

Eisenberger, Severin, Polish pianist; b. Cracow, July 25, 1879; d. New York, Dec. 11, 1945. He studied with Leschetizky in Vienna; was prof. at the Cracow Cons. from 1914-21; lived several years in Vienna, and later came to the U. S. He played as soloist with the Cincinnati Symph. Orch. in 1935, and gave recitals in Cleveland and elsewhere in the U. S.

Eisfeld, Theodor, German conductor; b. Wolfenbüttel, April 11, 1816; d. Wiesbaden, Sept. 2, 1882. He conducted at the Wiesbaden court theater (1839-43); then at the 'Concerts Viviennes,' Paris. He occasionally visited Italy; took lessons with Rossini at Bologna; became an honorary member of the Academy of St. Cecilia. From 1848-66, he lived in New York; he conducted the N. Y. Philharmonic for several years, and the Harmonic Society from its foundation; established quartet *soirées* in 1851 with Noll,

Reyer, and Eichhorn, joined also by Otto Dresel as pianist. Till 1865 he alternated with Bergmann in conducting the Philharmonic Concerts at New York; retired to Wiesbaden in 1866.

Eisler, Hanns, German composer; b. Leipzig, July 6, 1898; studied at the Academy of Music, Vienna; pupil of Arnold Schoenberg in composition; won the Music Prize of the City of Vienna (1924); was in Berlin until 1932; came to the U. S. in 1933; lectured on music at the New School for Social Research, N. Y.; was musical assistant of Charlie Chaplin in Hollywood (1942-47); left the U. S. under the terms of "voluntary deportation" in 1948, on account of his radical political past; then lived in Vienna and in Berlin. Under Schoenberg's influence, he adopted the 12-tone method of composition; most of his symph. works are in this advanced style. However, he demonstrated his capacity for writing simple songs for use of choral ensembles; several of his choruses for workers and for the Red Army have become popular in Russia. His divided allegiance to both Western modern music and to proletarian needs in East Germany and Russia evoked sharp criticism in the Communist press; his opera *Johannes Faustus,* produced in East Berlin (March 11, 1953) was criticized for the mysticism of its libretto and the complexity of the musical idiom, and was not revived. He has written, besides, a *Deutsche Symphonie* (perf. at the Paris Festival of the International Society for Contemporary Music, June 25, 1937); 3 short cantatas: *News from Vienna, Cantata of Exile,* and *Prison House* (London Festival of Music for the People, April 3, 1939); chamber music. He published a book, *Composing for the Films* (N. Y., 1947).

Eisler, Paul, Austrian pianist and conductor; b. Vienna, Sept. 9, 1875; d. New York, Oct. 16, 1951. He was a pupil of Bruckner at the Vienna Cons.; conducted in Riga, Vienna, and at the Metropolitan Opera in New York; made numerous tours as accompanist for Caruso, Ysaÿe, and other celebrated artists; composed several operettas *(Spring Brides; The Sentinel; The Little Missus; In the Year 1814).*

Eisner, Bruno, pianist; b. Vienna, Dec. 6, 1884; studied there at the Academy with Fischhof and Fuchs; for many years prof. at the Stern Cons., Berlin, later teaching in Hamburg; 1933 came to the U. S. and settled in New York; has toured Europe many times.

Eitler, Esteban, Austrian-Chilean composer; b. Bolzano, Tyrol, June 25, 1913. He studied at the Univ. of Budapest; left Europe in 1936; went to Buenos Aires, where he was associated with modernist music groups; in 1945 he settled in Santiago, Chile. He has written *Microsinfonia Politonal* (1943) for full orch. and *Policromia* (1950) for string orch.; *Serie Boliviana* for flute and string orch. (1941); concertino for piano and 11 instruments (1947); concertino for horn and 11 instruments (1949); a wind quintet (1945); quartet for piccolo, flute, trumpet, and saxophone (1945); quartet for flute, violin, viola, and cello (1950); etc.

Eitner, Robert, German musicologist; b. Breslau, Oct. 22, 1832; d. Templin, Feb. 2, 1905. A pupil of M. Brosig; settled (1853) in Berlin as a teacher, and gave concerts (1857-9) of his own compositions. He established a piano school in 1863, and published a *Hilfsbuch beim Klavierunterricht* (1871). He devoted himself chiefly to musical literature, and especially to researches concerning works of the 16th and 17th centuries. The Amsterdam Society for the Promotion of Music awarded him a prize for a Dictionary of Dutch Composers (1871, MS); he also prepared an edition of Sweelinck's organ works for the Society. One of the founders of the Berlin 'Gesellschaft für Musikforschung,' he edited its 'Monatshefte für Musikgeschichte' from 1869 till his death; also the 'Publikationen älterer praktischer und theoretischer Musikwerke.' Other writings: *Verzeichnis neuer Ausgaben alter Musikwerke aus der frühesten Zeit bis zum Jahr 1800* ('Monatshefte,' 1871); *Bibliographie der Musiksammelwerke des 16. und 17. Jahrhunderts* (with Haberl, Lagerberg, and Pohl); *Verzeichnis der gedruckten Werke von Hans Leo Hassler und Orlandus de Lassus* ('Monatshefte,' 1873-4); *S. G. Staden's 'Seelewig'* ('Monatshefte,' 1881); *Die Oper von ihren ersten Anfängen bis 1750* (3 vols., 1881-5); *Quellen und Hilfswerke beim Studium der Musikgeschichte* (1891); *Buch- und Musikaliendrucker nebst Notenstecher* (1904; as supplement to 'Monatshefte'). His principal work is the great *Biographisch-bibliographisches Quellenlexikon der Musiker und Musikgelehrten der Christlichen Zeitrechnung bis zur Mitte des 19. Jahrhunderts* (10 vols., Leipzig, 1899-1904; additions and corrections published from 1913-16 in a quarterly, 'Miscellanea Musicae Bio-bibliographica,' ed. by H. Springer, M. Schneider, and W. Wolffheim; reprinted, N. Y., 1947). Among Eitner's compositions (several of which were published) are a biblical opera *Judith,* an overture, a piano fantasia on themes from *Tristan und Isolde,* and songs.

Eitz (īts), **Karl Andreas,** German singing teacher; b. Wehrstadt, near Halberstadt, June 25, 1848; d. Eisleben, April 18, 1924. He originated a new system of solmisation ('Tonwortmethode'), accepted in some German schools, somewhat similar to the English Tonic Sol-fa system. He is the author of *Das mathematisch-reine Tonsystem* (1891); *100 geistliche Liedweisen in Tonsilben gesetzt* (1893); *Deutsche Singfibel* (1899); *Tonwort-Wandtafel* (1907); *Bausteine zum Schulgesangunterricht im Sinne der Tonwortmethode* (Leipzig, 1911; 2nd ed., edited by F. Bennedik, 1928).—Cf. G. Borchers, *Karl Eitz* (1908); O. Messmer, *Die Tonwortmethode von Karl Eitz* (Würzburg, 1911); F. Bennedik, *Historische und psychologisch-musikalische Untersuchungen über die Tonwortmethode von Eitz* (Langensalza, 1914); M. Koch, *Kurzgefasste Einführung in das Eitzsche Tonwort* (1925); F. Bennedik and A. Strube, *Handbuch für den Tonwortunterricht* (1926); R. Junker and R. M. Breithaupt, *Tonwort-Klavierschule* (1933); W. Stolte, *Carl Eitz in seiner Bedeutung für Wissenschaft und Schule* (Detmold, 1951).

Ek, Gunnar, Swedish composer; b. Asarum, Blekinge, June 21, 1900. He studied organ, cello, and composition at the Stockholm Cons.; served as a cellist in a Stockholm orchestra (1928-37); from 1942 occupied an organist's post in Lund. He has written 3 symphonies (1926; 1930; 1934); *Swedish Fantasy* for orchestra (1935); *Doomsday Cantata* (1946); piano concerto (1949); smaller orch. works; songs; organ pieces.

Ekman, Karl, Finnish pianist and conductor; b. Kaarina, near Åbo, Dec. 18, 1869; d. Helsinki, Feb. 4, 1947. He studied in Helsinki (1889-92); 1892-95, pupil of H. Barth in Berlin and A. Grünfeld in Vienna; 1895, piano teacher at, 1907-11 director of, the Helsinki Cons.; 1912-20, conductor of the orch. at Åbo. He arranged Swedish and Finnish folksongs, and edited a piano-method; published a biography of Sibelius at Stockholm, 1935 (English transl., 1936). —His wife Ida (b. Helsinki, April 22, 1875; d. Helsinki, April 14, 1942), a concert singer, studied in Helsinki, Paris, and Vienna; she distinguished herself by her performances of Sibelius' songs.

El-Dabh, Halim, Egyptian composer; b. Cairo, March 4, 1921; studied agriculture, and graduated from Cairo Univ. as an agrarian engineer (1945); then became interested in Egyptian musical instruments and composition; in 1950 received a Fulbright Fellowship for music study in America; took courses at the New England Cons. in Boston and at the Berkshire Center, Tanglewood, Mass. (with Irving Fine and Copland). Most of his music is derived from authentic Egyptian melodies and rhythms, but the contrapuntal and harmonic accoutrements are of a Western modern type. He has written 3 symphonies (1952-56); a concerto for an Egyptian drum with string orch. (1955); a string quartet (1951); sextet for wind instruments and percussion (1952); songs, and music for drums (for which he devised his own system of notation).

Elewijck (eh-leh-vīk), **Xavier Victor van,** Belgian music scholar; b. Brussels, April 24, 1825; d. in the insane asylum at Zickemont, April 28, 1888. He was the author of several monographs: *Discours sur la musique religieuse en Belgique* (1861); *Mathias van den Gheyn* (1862); and *De l'état actuel de la musique en Italie* (1875).

El Farabi. See **Alfarabi.**

Elgar, Sir Edward (William), eminent English composer; b. Broadheath, near Worcester, June 2, 1857; d. Worcester, Feb. 23, 1934. He received his musical education from his father, who was organist at St. George's Roman Catholic Church in Worcester for 37 years. At an early age he assisted his father at the organ, and took part in the rehearsals and concerts at the Worcester Glee Club; in 1879 he took a few violin lessons in London from Adolf Pollitzer; in the same year, he accepted an appointment as bandmaster at the County Lunatic Asylum in Worcester; he also played in Stockley's orch. in Birmingham; in 1882, was appointed conductor of the Worcester Amateur Instrumental Society; in 1885 succeeded his father as organist at St. George's. After his marriage (1889) to a daughter of Sir Henry Roberts, he tried his fortune in London but found conditions unfavorable, and settled in Malvern (1891), where he remained for 13 years. He went to Hereford in 1904, and later to London, until 1920, when he returned to Worcester, following the death of his wife. The first composition of Elgar that had a public performance was an orchestral intermezzo (Birmingham, Dec. 13, 1883); his first signal success was with the concert overture *Froissart* (Worcester Festival, Sept. 9, 1890). His cantata *The Black Knight* was produced by the Festival

Choral Society in Worcester (April 18, 1893) and was also heard in London, at the Crystal Palace (Oct. 23, 1897); the production of his cantata *Scenes From the Saga of King Olaf* at the North Staffordshire Festival (Oct. 30, 1896) attracted considerable attention; from then on, Elgar's name became familiar to the musical public. There followed the cantata *Caractacus* (Leeds Festival, Oct. 5, 1898), and Elgar's masterpiece, the oratorio *The Dream of Gerontius* (Birmingham Festival, Oct. 3, 1900). In the meantime, Elgar gave more and more attention to orchestral music. On June 19, 1899, Hans Richter presented the first performance in London of Elgar's *Variations on an Original Theme* (generally known as *Enigma Variations*). This work consists of fourteen sections, each marked by initials of fancied names of Elgar's friends; in later years, Elgar issued cryptic hints as to the identities of these persons, which were finally revealed. Elgar also stated that the theme itself was a counterpoint to a familiar tune, but the concealed subject was never discovered; various guesses were advanced in the musical press from time to time; a contest for the most plausible answer to the riddle was launched in America by the 'Saturday Review' (1953) with dubious results. It is most probable that no such hidden theme existed, and that Elgar, who had a stately sense of humor, indulged in harmless mystification. The success of the *Enigma Variations* was followed by the production of Elgar's *Pomp and Circumstance* marches (1901-30), the first of which became Elgar's most famous piece, through a setting to words by Arthur Christopher Benson, used by Elgar in the *Coronation Ode* (1902), and then published separately as *Land of Hope and Glory;* another successful orchestral work was the *Cockaigne Overture* (London, June 20, 1901). Elgar's two symphonies, written in close succession in 1908 and 1910, received respectful attention in England, but never became popular elsewhere. His violin concerto, first performed by Fritz Kreisler (London, Nov. 10, 1910), was more successful; there was also a cello concerto (London, Oct. 26, 1919). The emergence of Elgar as a major composer about 1900 was all the more remarkable since he had no formal academic training. Yet he developed a masterly technique of instrumental and vocal writing. His style of composition may be described as functional romanticism; his harmonic procedures remain firmly within the 19th-century tradition; the formal element is always strong, and the thematic development logical and precise. Elgar had a melodic gift, which asserted itself in the earliest works such as the popular *Salut d'amour;* his oratorios, particularly *The Apostles,* were the product of Elgar's fervent religious faith (he was a Roman Catholic); however he avoided archaic usages of Gregorian chant; rather he presented the sacred subjects in a communicative style of secular drama. Elgar's stature in England is very great. During his lifetime he was a recipient of many honors. He was knighted in 1904. He received honorary degrees of Mus. Doc. from Cambridge (1900), Oxford (1905), Aberdeen (1906); also an LL. D., from Leeds (1904). During his first visit to the U. S. in 1905 he was made Doctor of Music of Yale Univ.; in 1907 he received the same degree from the Univ. of Pennsylvania. He received the Order of Merit in 1911; was made K. C. V. O. in 1928 and a baronet in 1931; was appointed Master of the King's Musick in 1924, succeeding Sir Walter Parratt. Although he was not a proficient conductor, he appeared on various occasions with orchestras in his own works; during his second visit to the U. S., he conducted his oratorio *The Apostles* (N. Y., 1907); also led the mass chorus at the opening of the British Empire Exhibition in 1914. —Works: the oratorios op. 29, *The Light of Life* (Worcester, 1890); op. 38, *The Dream of Gerontius* (Birmingham, 1900); op. 49, *The Apostles* (Birmingham, 1903); op. 51, *The Kingdom* (Birmingham, 1906). Cantatas: op. 25, *The Black Knight* (1893); op. 30, *Scenes From the Saga of King Olaf* (1896); op. 33, *The Banner of St. George* (1897); op. 35, *Caractacus* (1898); op. 44, *Coronation Ode* (Sheffield, 1902); op. 69, *The Music Makers* (Birmingham, 1912). Choral works with orch.: op. 23, *Star of the Summer Night* (1892); op. 27, *Scenes from the Bavarian Highlands* (1896); op. 80, *The Spirit of England* (1916). For orch.: op. 1a, *The Wand of Youth,* suite in 7 movements (subtitled *Music to a Child's Play,* written at the age of 12 and orchestrated 37 years later; London, Queen's Hall Orch., Dec. 14, 1907); op. 1b, 2nd suite, *The Wand of Youth* (1908); op. 7, *Sevillana;* op. 10, *Three Pieces (Mazurka, Sérénade mauresque, Contrasts);* op. 12, *Salut d'amour* (Crystal Palace, London, Nov. 11, 1889); op. 15, *Two Pieces (Chanson du Matin; Chanson du soir);* op. 19, *Froissart,* overture (1890); op. 20, *Serenade,* for string orch. (1892); op. 32, *Imperial March,* for Queen Victoria's Diamond Jubilee (1897); op. 36, *Enigma Variations* (1899); op. 39, *Pomp and Circumstance,* 4 military marches (1901-7; a 5th composed in 1930); op. 40, *Cockaigne,* overture (1901); op. 43, *Dream Children,* two pieces for small orch. (London Symph. Orch., March 8, 1905, composer conducting); op. 47, *Introduction and Allegro,* for strings (London, March 8, 1905); op. 50, *In the South,* overture (1904); op. 55, Symphony No. 1 (Manchester, Dec. 3, 1908); op. 58, *Elegy* for strings (1909); op. 61, violin concerto (London, Nov. 10, 1910); op. 63, Symphony No. 2 (London, May 24, 1911); op. 65, *Coronation March* (1911); op. 68, *Falstaff,* symph. study (1913); op. 70, *Sospiri,* for string orch., harp, and organ (1914); op. 75, *Carillon,* for recitation with orch. (1914); op. 76, *Polonia,* symph. prelude (1915); op. 77, *Une Voix dans le désert,* for recitation with orch. (1915); op. 79, *Le Drapeau belge,* for recitation with orch. (1917); op. 85, cello concerto (1919); op. 87, *Severn Suite* for brass band (1930); *Nursery Suite* for orch. (1931). Besides, Elgar wrote incidental music for *Grania and Diarmid* (op. 42); a masque, *The Crown of India* (op. 66, 1912); *The Starlight Express* (op. 78, 1915); and music for Laurence Binyon's and J. M. Harvey's play, *King Arthur* (London, 1923). Chamber music: op. 6, quintet for wind instruments; op. 8, string quartet (MS destroyed); op. 9, violin sonata; op. 82, violin sonata in E minor (MS destroyed); op. 83, string quartet in C minor (1918); op. 84, piano quintet (1919); organ works (op. 14, voluntaries; op. 28, Sonata in G; etc.); part-songs (opp. 18, 26, 45, 71, 72, 73); songs (opp. 5, 16, 31, 41, 48, 59, 60; the last 3 with orch.).—Bibl.: R. J. Buckley, *Sir Edward Elgar* (London, 1904; new ed., 1925); E. Newman, *Elgar* (London, 1906); D. G. Mason, *A Study of Elgar,* in the 'Mus. Quarterly' (April, 1917); J. F. Porte, *Sir Edward Elgar* (London, 1921); J. H. Shera, *Elgar's Instrumental Works* (London, 1931); J. F. Porte, *Elgar and His Music* (London, 1933); B. S. Maine, *Elgar, His Life and Works* (2 vols., London, 1933); A. J. Sheldon, *Edward Elgar* (London, 1933); William H. Reed, *Elgar as I Knew Him* (London, 1936); Mrs. Richard Powell, *Edward Elgar: Memories of a Variation* (London, 1937; 2nd ed., 1947); William H. Reed, *Elgar* (London and N. Y., 1939; contains a complete list of works); W. R. Anderson, *Introduction to the Music of Elgar* (London, 1949); Diana McVeagh, *Edward Elgar, His Life and Music* (London, 1955); Percy Young, *Elgar, O. M.* (London, 1955). The following articles on Elgar were published in 'Music & Letters': A. H. Fox-Strangways, *Elgar* (Jan., 1934); R. C. Powell, *Elgar's Enigma* (July, 1934); articles by D. E. Tovey, H. J. Foss, R. Vaughan Williams, A. E. Brent Smith, F. Howes, and W. H. Reed (special Elgar issue; Jan., 1935); C. Barber, *Enigma Variations* (April, 1935). Percy Young edited *Letters of Edward Elgar and Other Writings* (London, 1956).

Elias Salomon (Salomonis), French monk at Sainte-Astère, Périgord. He wrote in 1274 a treatise *Scientia artis musicae* (printed by Gerbert, 'Scriptores,' vol. III), of value as the first practical work giving rules for improvised counterpoint.—Cf. E. Th. Ferand, *Die Improvisation in der Musik* (Zürich, 1938); E. Th. Ferand, *The 'Howling in Seconds' of the Lombards,* in the 'Mus. Quarterly' (July, 1939).

Elizalde, Federico, Spanish composer; b. Manila, Philippine Islands (of Spanish parents), Dec. 12, 1907. He entered the Madrid Cons. as a child and received the first prize as a pianist at the age of 14. Later he went to California, and studied law at Stanford Univ. At the same time he took lessons with Ernest Bloch. He was subsequently active as conductor of hotel orchestras in England; also visited Germany. Returning to his native islands, he became conductor of the Manila Symphony Orch. (1930); then conducted in Paris and Spain. On April 23, 1936, he conducted his *Sinfonia Concertante* at the Festival of the International Society for Contemporary Music in Barcelona. He was in France during World War II; in 1948 he assumed the post of president of the Manila Broadcasting Co., but has continued his travels in both hemispheres. His music is influenced mainly by Manuel de Falla; beginning with dance-like works in the Spanish vein, Elizalde has gradually changed his style toward neo-classicism. He has written an opera *Paul Gauguin* for the centennial of Gauguin's birth (1948); a violin concerto (1943); a piano concerto (1947); and much chamber music.

Elkan, Henri, conductor and publisher; b. Antwerp, Nov. 23, 1897; studied viola and piano at the conservatories of Antwerp (1914) and Amsterdam (graduated 1917); in 1920 came to the U.S.; played the viola in the Philadelphia Orch. (1920-28); was conductor of the Philadelphia Grand Opera Co. (1928-36) and of the Philadelphia Ballet Co. (1926-39). In 1926 he founded the Henri Elkan Music Publ. Co. in Philadelphia; it became the Elkan-Vogel Music Publ. Co. in 1928, when Adolphe Vogel, a cellist in the Philadelphia Orch., joined Elkan; the partnership was dissolved in 1952; then Elkan was again engaged as theater conductor (in California and elsewhere); in 1956 he formed a publ. firm under his own name, specializing in works by American and Latin American composers.

Elkus, Albert (Israel), American composer and teacher; b. Sacramento, Calif., April 30, 1884. He studied at the Univ. of Calif. (M. Lit., 1907), took piano lessons with Harold Bauer and Josef Lhévinne; studied composition with Oscar Weil and later in Vienna and Berlin with Robert Fuchs, Georg Schumann, and Franz Schalk. Returning to the U. S., he became head of the Theory Dept. at the San Francisco Cons. of Music (1923-25 and 1930-34); taught at Mills College (1929-33). He was appointed prof. of music at the Univ. of Calif., Berkeley, in 1935; in 1937 became chairman of the Dept. of Music there, retiring in 1951. —Works: *Concertino on Lezione III of Ariosto* for cello and string orch. (1917); *Impressions from a Greek Tragedy* (San Francisco Symph., Feb. 27, 1920); a chorus for men's voices, *I Am the Reaper* (1921); ed. the letters and papers of his teacher, Oscar Weil.

Ella, John, English writer on music; b. Leicester, Dec. 19, 1802; d. London, Oct. 2, 1888. He studied violin in London; then enrolled as a harmony student at the Royal Academy of Music; in 1827 went to Paris to study with Fétis. Returning to London, he played in theater orchestras; in 1845 established 'The Musical Union,' presenting morning concerts of chamber music, and was its director until 1880; in 1850 opened a series of 'Music Winter Evenings' which continued until 1859. For these organizations he wrote analytical program notes, of excellent quality for the time. He was a contributor of reviews and music articles to 'The Morning Post,' 'The Musical World,' and 'The Athenaeum'. —Writings: *Lectures on Dramatic Music Abroad and at Home* (1872); *Musical Sketches Abroad and at Home* (3 eds.: 1861, 1869, 1878); *Record of the Musical Union* (1845-80); *Personal Memoir of Meyerbeer* (1868); and other publications.—Cf. John Ravell, *John Ella,* in 'Music & Letters' (Jan., 1953).

Ellberg, Ernst Henrik, Swedish composer and pedagogue; b. Söderhamn, Dec. 11, 1868; d. Stockholm, June 14, 1948. He studied violin and composition at the Stockholm Cons., and was teacher there from 1904 to 1933; among his pupils were Hilding Rosenberg, Dag Wiren, and Gunnar de Frumerie. He wrote an opera, *Rassa,* which received a prize; several ballets and concert overtures, and some chamber music.

Ellegaard, France, Danish pianist; b. Paris (of Danish parents), Oct. 10, 1913. She studied at the Paris Cons. (1922-33); then toured in Germany, France, and England. From 1943-48 she was in Sweden; in 1949 she married the Finnish painter Birger Calstedt.

Eller, Louis, Austrian violinist; b. Graz, June 9, 1820; d. Pau, July 12, 1862. He studied with Hysel; from 1836 made tours in central Europe; traveled to Spain and Portugal with Gottschalk. He wrote several effective pieces for the violin: *Valse diabolique, Menuet sentimental,* etc.

Ellert, Laurence B., American music editor; b. Louisville, Jan. 3, 1878; d. Washington, D. C., Oct. 25, 1940. He attended Georgetown Univ.; 1900-02, was director of the Mandolin Club there; studied piano and harmony privately; in 1902 entered the music business; 1919, associated with the sales dept. of G. Schirmer, Inc.; 1920, general manager of Willis Music Co., Cincinnati; 1923, again in N. Y. as director of publication for the Boston Music Co. and Willis Music Co., specializing in educational music.

Ellerton, John Lodge (real name John Lodge); English poet and prolific composer; b. Chester, Jan. 11, 1801; d. London, Jan. 3, 1873. An Oxford graduate, he studied counterpoint under Pietro Terziani at Rome, where he composed 7 Italian operas; lived for some time in Germany, where he wrote 2 German operas. Besides his operas, he wrote an oratorio, *Paradise Lost;* 6 symphonies, 4 concert overtures, 3 quintets, 44 string quartets, 3 string trios, 8 trios for various instruments, 13 sonatas, 61 glees, 83 vocal duets, songs.

Elleviou, Jean, French operatic tenor; b. Rennes, June 14, 1769; d. Paris, May 5, 1842. He made his début in Monsigny's *Déserteur* at the Comédie Italienne in Paris in 1790, and sang there until 1813. The revival of interest in the works of Grétry in 1801 was largely due to his influence and excellent interpretations; Méhul wrote his *Joseph* (1807) and Boieldieu his *Jean de Paris* (1812) for him.—Cf. E. H. P. de Curzon, *Jean Elleviou* (1930).

Ellicott, Rosalind Frances, English composer; b. Cambridge, Nov. 14, 1857; d. London, April 5, 1924. She studied at the Royal Academy of Music (1875-6), and later with Thomas Wingham (1885-92); she received several commissions to write works for the Gloucester and Cheltenham Festivals; among them were the cantatas *Radiant Sister of the Dawn* (Cheltenham, 1887) and *Ely-*

sium (Gloucester, 1889). She retired from active musical work in 1900.

Elling, Catherinus, Norwegian composer and folklorist; b. Oslo, Sept. 13, 1858; d. there, Jan. 8, 1942. He studied music with native teachers; then in Leipzig (1877-8) and Berlin (1886-96). In 1908 a subvention was granted him by the state for the pursuit of his studies of Norwegian folksongs, on which he published various essays; he also wrote biographies of Ole Bull, Grieg, Svendsen, and Kjerulf, and published a book, *Norsk folkemusik* (Oslo, 1922). He composed an opera, *Kosakkerne* (1897); an oratorio, *The Prodigal Son:* a symphony; incidental music to *A Midsummer Night's Dream;* chamber music, and many songs.

Ellington, Edward Kennedy ("Duke" Ellington), American jazz pianist and composer; b. Washington, D. C., April 29, 1899. He studied piano since the age of 7, and as a boy, played in ragtime bands; has achieved great fame as an instinctive musician in the modern jazz idiom and as composer of striking pieces of rhythmic music.—Cf. B. Ulanov, *Duke Ellington* (N. Y., 1946).

Ellinwood, Leonard Webster, American musicologist; b. Thomaston, Conn., Feb. 13, 1905; studied at Aurora College, Illinois (B.A.) and the Univ. of Rochester (Eastman School), where he received the degrees of M.M. and Ph.D.; 1927-33, instrumental supervisor at the Mount Hermon School, Mass.; 1934-36, held the teaching fellowship (history and appreciation) of the Univ. of Rochester; 1936-39, prof. of theory and musicology at Michigan State College. In 1939, became cataloguer, Library of Congress. Writings: *Musica Hermanni Contracti,* containing Hermannus' Latin text, ed. after both the Vienna MS and the MS owned by the Eastman School, together with an English translation and notes (Publ. of Eastman School, 1936); *Francesco Landini and His Music,* in the 'Mus. Quarterly' (April, 1936); *Origins of the Italian Ars Nova* in 'Proceedings' of Music Teachers National Association (1937); *The Works of Francesco Landini* (complete ed., 1939); *The Conductus,* in the 'Mus. Quarterly' (April, 1941); *The History of American Church Music* (N. Y., 1953); chief author of the Episcopal *The Hymnal Companion* (N. Y., 1951; revised ed., 1956).

Ellis (real name Sharpe), **Alexander John,** English writer on musical science; b. Hoxton (London), June 14, 1814; d. Kensington, Oct. 28, 1890. He studied at Trinity College, Cambridge, graduating in 1837; his subjects were mathematics and philology; he also studied music; was elected Fellow of the Royal Society (1864) and was President of the Philological Society; publ. valuable papers in the 'Proceedings' of the Royal Society: *On the Conditions . . . of a Perfect Musical Scale on Instruments with Fixed Tones* (1864), *On the Physical Constitutions and Relations of Musical Chords* (1864), *On the Temperament of Instruments with Fixed Tones* (1864), and *On Musical Duodenes; or, The Theory of Constructing Instruments with Fixed Tones in Just or Practically Just Intonation* (1874). Papers containing new theories, etc., for the Musical Association are as follows: *The Basis of Music* (1877), *Pronunciation for Singers* (1877), and *Speech in Song* (1878). He was awarded a silver medal for his writings on musical pitch for the 'Proceedings' of the Society of Arts (1877, 1880, and 1881; publ. separately, 1880-1; and in summary form in the Appendix to the 2nd ed. of his transl. of Helmholtz's *Lehre von den Tonempfindungen* under the title, *On the Sensations of Tone, as a Physiological Basis for the Theory of Music;* 1st ed., 1875; 6th ed., 1948); also wrote *Tonometrical Observations, or Some Existing Non-harmonic Scales* (Royal Society, 1884), and *On the Musical Scales of Various Nations* (Society of Arts, 1885). He likewise translated Ohm's *Geist der mathematischen Analyse* (1868) and Preyer's *Über die Grenzen der Tonwahrnehmung* (1876-7, 'Proceedings' of the Musical Association).

Elman, Mischa, remarkable violinist; b. Stalnoye, Russia, Jan. 20, 1891. At the age of 6 he was taken by his father to Odessa and placed under Fidelmann, a pupil of Brodsky. Both technically and mentally, his progress was so extraordinary that Leopold Auer, hearing him in 1902, immediately accepted him in his class at the St. Petersburg Cons. In 1904 Elman made his début at St. Petersburg with sensational success; his tour of Germany was a succession of triumphs, and, in spite of his youth, he was ranked among the foremost violinists of the day; in England he was received with equal warmth, and his annual tours of the U. S. (since 1908) have been but duplications of his European triumphs; in the first 3 seasons he had appeared with every important symph. orch. (with the Boston Symph. Orch. alone in 31 concerts); toured extensively throughout the world; he has received several decorations (Officer of the Belgian Crown, etc.). He has published many arrangements for violin and piano (pieces by Schubert, Rachmaninov, Beethoven, etc.); has also composed some violin pieces (*Romance, In a Gondola*, etc.), songs, and a light opera.—Cf. S. Elman, *Memoirs of Mischa Elman's Father* (N. Y., 1933).

Elmore, Robert Hall, organist and composer; b. Ramapatnam, India, Jan. 2, 1913 (of American parentage); studied organ with Pietro Yon, composition with Harl McDonald, and at the Univ. of Pennsylvania (graduated 1937; Mus. Bac.); from 1936, organ teacher at the Clarke Cons. of Music, Philadelphia; 1940, teacher of composition at the Univ. of Pennsylvania. He has written a tone poem, *Valley Forge* (Philadelphia Orch., April 9, 1937, Stokowski cond.), an organ concerto, string quartet, many sacred songs and cantatas; secular songs, etc.

Elsenheimer, Nicholas J., German music educator, b. Wiesbaden, June 17, 1866; d. Limburg a. d. Lahn, July 12, 1935. He was a pupil of his father; took degree of LL.D. at Heidelberg; studied under G. Jacobsthal in Strasbourg. In 1890 he went to America; taught at the Cincinnati College of Music (1890-1906); after 1907 taught in New York; then went back to Germany.

Elsner, Joseph Xaver, Polish composer and music teacher; b. Grottkau, June 29, 1768 (of Swedish descent); d. Warsaw, April 18, 1854. He studied violin, voice, and organ at Grottkau, Breslau, and Vienna. In 1791 he became concertmaster of the Brünn Opera Theater; then was Kapellmeister at Lemberg (from 1792). He was Chopin's teacher at Warsaw, and founded a school there for organists which later became the Cons.; director of the Cons. (1821-30). —Works: 32 operas, including *King Wladislaw* (Warsaw, April 3, 1818), duo-dramas, and musical plays, of which 2 were produced in German at Lemberg (*Die seltenen Brüder*, 1794; *Der verkleidete Sultan*, 1796) and the rest in Warsaw; 17 Masses; several ballets; sacred and secular choral works; 3 symphonies; 2 string quartets; 2 piano quartets; 3 violin sonatas (a number of these works were published by Breitkopf & Härtel and by French and Polish publishers). He also published 2 treatises on the vocal treatment of Polish texts (Warsaw, 1818). A medal was struck in his honor on his 80th birthday (1848).—Cf. F. Hoesick, *From Elsner's Memoirs* (Warsaw, 1901, in Polish); J. Reiss, *Joseph Xaver Elsner* (Katowice, 1936).

Elson, Arthur, American writer on music; son of Louis C. Elson; b. Boston, Nov. 18, 1873; d. New York, Feb. 24, 1940. He studied with J. K. Paine at Harvard Univ. and at the New England Cons. of Music; received fundamental training from his father. He was a graduate of Harvard and of the Mass. Institute of Technology.—Publications: *A Critical History of the Opera* (1901; new edition, 1926, as *A History of Opera*); *Orchestral Instruments and Their Use* (1902; new ed. Boston, 1930); *Woman's Work in Music* (1903; new ed., 1931); *Modern Composers of Europe* (1905; new ed., 1922); *Music Club Programs from All Nations* (1906; new ed., 1928); *The Musician's Guide* (1913); *The Book of Musical Knowledge* (1915; new ed. N. Y., 1934); *Pioneer School Music Course* (1917). He was editor of and contributor to 'The World's Best Music' and 'University Musical Encyclopedia.'

Elson, Louis Charles, American music scholar; b. Boston, Mass., April 17, 1848; d. there, Feb. 14, 1920. He was a pupil of Kreissmann at Boston (singing) and of Karl Gloggner-Castelli at Leipzig (theory). Returning to Boston, he assumed the editorship of the 'Vox Humana'; then joined the staff of the 'Mus. Herald'; was for many years musical editor of the 'Boston Advertiser'; in 1880 became lecturer on music history at the New England Cons.; was for 7 years 'City Lecturer on Music' at Boston (240 lectures), and twice lecturer at Lowell Institute (18 lectures); correspondent of musical journals in Berlin, Paris, and Buenos Aires; editor-in-chief of 'University Encyclopedia of Music' (10 vols., 1912).—Writings: *Curiosities of Music* (1880); *History of German Song* (1888); *The Theory of Music* (1890; many eds,; revised by F. Converse, 1935); *European Reminiscences* (Chicago, 1891; new ed., Philadelphia, 1914); *The Realm of Music* (1892); *Great Composers and Their Work* (1898); *The National Music of America and Its Sources* (1899; new ed., revised by Arthur Elson, 1924); *Famous Composers and Their Works* (with Philip Hale; new series, Boston, 1900); *Shakespeare in Music* (1901); *History of American Music* (N. Y., 1904; 2nd ed., 1915; revised ed. by A. Elson, 1925); *Music Dictionary* (1905); *Pocket Music Dictionary* (1909; many reprints); *Folk Songs of Many Nations* (1905); *Mistakes and Disputed Points in Music* (1910); *Woman in Music* (1918); *Children in Music* (1918). Elson also composed operettas, songs, instrumental works; made translations and arrangements of over 2,000 songs, operas, etc.

El-Tour, Anna, Russian soprano; b. Odessa, June 4, 1886; d. Amsterdam, May 30, 1954. She studied at the St. Petersburg Cons. (voice with Mme. von Hecke; piano with Essipova). From 1913-20, she taught in Moscow; then left Russia; from 1922-25 was in Berlin; 1925-48, taught at the Conservatoire International de Paris. After 1948, she was professor of singing at the Amsterdam Cons. She traveled widely in the Far East; gave recitals in Israel in 1953.

Elvey, Sir George (Job), English organist and composer; b. Canterbury, March 27, 1816; d. Windlesham, Surrey, Dec. 9, 1893. He was a chorister at Canterbury Cathedral; studied with Skeats, Potter, and Dr. Crotch at the Royal Academy of Music. From 1835 until 1882 he served as organist and master of the boys at St. George's Chapel, Windsor; Mus. Bac., Oxford (1838); Mus. Doc. (1840); knighted in 1871. He wrote 2 oratorios, which were moderately successful: *The Resurrection and Ascension* (London, Dec. 2, 1840) and *Mount Carmel* (London, June 30, 1886); also many pieces of church music; glees, part-songs; organ pieces. His widow publ. a memoir, *Life and Reminiscences of George J. Elvey* (London, 1894).

Elvey, Stephen, English organist and composer, brother of Sir George Elvey; b. Canterbury, June 27, 1805; d. Oxford, Oct. 6, 1860. He was a chorister of Canterbury Cathedral, and a pupil of Skeats there; in 1830 he became organist of New College, Oxford; Mus. Bac. (1831); Mus. Doc. (1838). He was Choragus at Oxford from 1848 until his death. He wrote mostly church music, and publ. a successful handbook, *The Psalter, or Canticles and Psalms, Pointed for Chanting, upon a New Principle* (London; 6 eds. to 1866).

Elwart (el-vahr'), **Antoine-Aimable-Élie,** French writer on music and composer; b. Paris, Nov. 18, 1808; d. there, Oct. 14, 1877. A chorister at St.-Eustache when 10 years old, he was apprenticed at 13 to a mechanic, but ran away, and joined a small theater orch. as violinist. From 1825-34 he studied at the Paris Cons. (Fétis, Lesueur), taking the Grand Prix de Rome in 1834; taught at the Paris Cons. from 1836 to 1871. Among his pupils were Gouvy, Grisar, and Weckerlin.—Works: an opera, *Les Catalans* (Rouen, 1840); an 'oratorio-symphonie' *Noé, ou le déluge universel* (Paris, 1845); oratorio, *La naissance d'Ève* (Paris, 1846); *Les noces de Cana,* a mystery; *Ruth et Booz,* a vocal symphony; Masses, cantatas, a Te Deum, a Miserere, and other church music; symphonies, overtures, chamber music, etc., in MS. He is better known by his musico-literary works: *Duprez, sa vie artistique, avec une biographie authentique de son maître A. Choron* (1838), *Théorie musicale (Solfège progressif,* etc., 1840), *Feuille harmonique* (1841), *Le Chanteur accompagnateur* (1844), *Traité de contrepoint et de la fugue, Essai sur la Transposition, Études élémentaires de musique* (1845), *L'Art de chanter en chœur, L'Art de jouer impromptu de l'alto-viola, Solfège de jeune âge, Le Contrepoint et la fugue appliqués au style idéal, Lutrin et Orphéon* (theoretical and practical vocal studies), *Histoire de la Société des Concerts du Conservatoire* (1860; 2d ed. 1863), *Manuel des aspirants aux grades de chef et de souschef de musique dans l'armée française* (1862), *Petit manuel d'instrumentation* (1864), *Histoire des concerts populaires* (1864). His projected complete ed. of his own compositions (1867-70) reached only vol. III.

Elwell, Herbert, American composer and critic; b. Minneapolis, May 10, 1898. He studied at the Univ. of Minnesota; then with Ernest Bloch in New York and Nadia Boulanger in Paris; held a fellowship at the American Academy in Rome (1926); in 1928 appointed head of the advanced theory and composition courses at the Cleveland Institute; editor of the program notes of the Cleveland Orch. (1930-36); since 1932, music critic for the 'Cleveland Plain Dealer.' —Works: ballet *The Happy Hypocrite,* after Max Beerbohm (orch. suite performed by the Augusteo Orch., Rome, May 21, 1927, composer cond.; his most successful work, many revivals in ballet form); *Introduction and Allegro* for orch. (N. Y., July 12, 1942); *I Was With Him,* cantata for male chorus, tenor solo, and 2 pianos (Cleveland, Nov. 30, 1942); *Blue Symphony,* for voice and string quartet (Cleveland, Feb. 2, 1945); *Lincoln: Requiem Aeternam,* for chorus and orch. (Oberlin, Feb. 16, 1947); *Pastorale,* for voice and orch. (Cleveland, March 25, 1948); *Ode* for orch. (1950); *The Forever Young,* for voice and orch. (Cleveland, Oct. 29, 1953); 2 string quartets; piano sonata, violin sonata, etc.

Elwes, Gervase, English tenor; b. Billing Hall, near Northampton, Nov. 15, 1866; d. Boston, Mass., Jan. 12, 1921 (killed by train in station). He began as a diplomat, and while serving at Vienna (1891-5) studied composition with Mandyczewski; he then studied singing in Paris with Bouhy; then at Brussels with Démest, and in London with H. Russel and V. Beigel; début at Westmoreland Festival, Kendal (May, 1903); made a very successful tour of Germany in 1907, and of the U. S. in 1909; died while on his 2nd tour of the U. S. His specialty was oratorio; sang Elgar's *Dream of Gerontius* almost 150 times; was also an excellent interpreter of Brahms.—Cf. Winifred and Richard Elwes, *Gervase Elwes, The Story of His Life* (London, 1935).

Emerson, Luther Orlando, American composer and conductor; b. Parsonsfield, Maine, Aug. 3, 1820; d. Hyde Park, Mass., Sept. 29, 1915. He was a competent composer of church music, a popular conductor of the early musical conventions, and a compiler of numerous successful collections of songs and hymn-tunes: *The Romberg Collection* (1853), *The Golden Wreath* (1857, Sunday-school music), *The Golden Harp* (1860), *The Sabbath Harmony* (1860), *The Harp of Judah* (1863), *Merry Chimes* (1865), *Jubilate* (1866), and *The Chorus Wreath.*

Emery, Stephen Albert, American music teacher, writer, and composer; b. Paris, Maine, Oct. 4, 1841; d. Boston, April 15, 1891. His first teacher was H. S. Edwards, of Portland; in 1862 he went to Leipzig, where he studied with Plaidy, Papperitz, Richter, and Hauptmann. He returned to Portland in 1864; went to Boston in 1866; taught at the New England Cons. there from 1867; on the foundation of the College of Music of Boston Univ., he was appointed prof. of harmony and counterpoint. He was also assistant editor of the 'Musical Herald.' He publ. 2 textbooks, *Foundation Studies in Piano Playing* and *Elements of Harmony* (1879; several later editions).

Emery, Walter, English organist and writer; b. Tilshead, Wiltshire, June 14, 1909. He studied organ at the Royal Academy of Music in London; then was engaged as church organist; in 1937 became an associate of Novello & Co. in the editorial dept.; publ. several valuable books and pamphlets: *The St. Matthew Passion: its Preparation and Performance* (with Sir Adrian Boult; London, 1949); *Bach's Ornaments* (London, 1953); commentaries on Bach's organ works, etc.

Emmanuel (ehm-mah-nüel'), **Maurice,** eminent French music scholar; b. Bar-sur-Aube, May 2, 1862; d. Paris, Dec. 14, 1938. He received primary education in Dijon; sang in the church choir in Beaune; then studied at the Paris Cons. (1880-87) with Savard, Dubois, Delibes, and Bourgault-Ducoudray; then specialized in the musical history of antiquity under Gevaert in Brussels; also studied ancient languages at the Sorbonne; Licencié ès Lettres (1887); Docteur ès Lettres (1895) with the theses *De saltationis disciplina apud Graecos* (publ. in Latin, Paris, 1895) and *La danse grecque antique d'après les monuments figurés* (Paris, 1896; in English as *The Antique Greek Dance after Sculptured and Painted Figures,* N. Y., 1916). He was prof. of art history at the Lycée Racine and Lycée Lamartine (1898-1905); maître de chapelle at Ste.-Clotilde (1904-7); in 1907 he succeeded Bourgault-Ducoudray as prof. of music history at the Paris Cons., and held this post for thirty years; edited vols. 17 and 18 of the complete works of Rameau; also Bach's works in Durand's edition of the classical masters. His chief scholarly work is *Histoire de la langue musicale* (2 vols.; Paris, 1911; new ed., 1928); he also contributed the article *La Musique grecque antique* to Lavignac's Encyclopédie; further publications are: *Traité de l'accompagnement modal des psaumes* (Lyons, 1912); *La Polyphonie sacrée* (with R. Moissenet; Dijon, 1923); *Pelléas et Mélisande de Claude Debussy* (Paris, 1926); *César Franck* (Paris, 1930); *Antonin Reicha* (Paris, 1937); valuable articles in 'Revue de Paris': *La Musique dans les universités allemandes* (June 1, 1898) and *Les Conservatoires de Musique en Allemagne* (March 1, 1900); *Le chant à l'école* in 'Grande Revue' (Dec. 25, 1910 and Jan. 10, 1911); also articles in the 'Revue Musicale,' 'Mus. Quarterly,' etc. Maurice Emmanuel was a prolific composer; he wrote an opera *Salamine* (Paris, June 28, 1929); opéra-bouffe, *Amphitryon* (Paris, Feb. 20, 1937); 2 symphonies (1919; 1931); 2 string quartets and other chamber music; 6 piano sonatinas; vocal music (much of it published). See special issue of the 'Revue Musicale' devoted to Maurice Emmanuel (1947).

Emmett, Daniel Decatur, American composer of *Dixie* and other popular songs; b. Mt. Vernon, Ohio, Oct. 29, 1815; d. there, June 28, 1904. He began his career as drummer in military bands; then joined the Virginia Minstrels, singing and playing the banjo; later was a member of Bryant's Minstrels. He wrote the lyrics and the music of *Dixie* in 1859, and it was performed for the first time in New York on April 4, 1859; upon publication, the popularity of the song spread, and it was adopted as a Southern fighting song during the Civil War (even though Emmett was a Northerner). His other songs, *Old Dan Tucker, The Road to Richmond, Walk Along,* etc. enjoyed great favor for some years, but were eclipsed by *Dixie.*—Cf. Ch. B. Galbreath, *Daniel Decatur Emmett* (Columbus, Ohio, 1904);

John Tasker Howard, *Our American Music* (N. Y., 1939); R. B. Harwell, *Confederate Music* (Chapel Hill, N. C., 1950); Hans Nathan, *Dixie,* in the 'Mus. Quarterly' (Jan., 1949); H. O. Wintermute, *Daniel Decatur Emmett* (Mount Vernon, Ohio, 1955).

Enacovici (eh-nah-koh-vē'-sē), **Georg,** Rumanian composer; b. Focsani, April 22, 1891; studied at the Bucharest Cons.; then with Vincent d'Indy at the Schola Cantorum in Paris; received the Enesco Prize in composition (1915); returned to Bucharest and became professor at the Cons. there. Among his compositions are *Rapsodie roumaine* for orch. (1935); 2 *Poèmes* for violin and orch. (1924 and 1941); some chamber music, and songs.

Encina (or **Enzina**) (en-thē'-nah), **Juan del,** Spanish poet and composer; b. Salamanca, July 12, 1468; d. León, late in 1529. He was the son of a shoemaker of Salamanca named Juan de Fermoselle; became chorister at Salamanca Cathedral; studied music under his elder brother, Diego de Fermoselle, and under Fernando de Torrijos; took his degree in law at Salamanca Univ., where he enjoyed the favor of the chancellor, Don Gutiérrez de Toledo. About 1492 he entered the household of the 2nd Duke of Alba, for whom he wrote a series of pastoral eclogues that form the foundation of the Spanish secular drama. These eclogues included 'villancicos' or rustic songs, for which Encina composed the music. He went to Rome in 1500; on May 12, 1500, was appointed canon at the Cathedral of Salamanca; from Feb. 2, 1510 until 1512, he was archdeacon and canon of Málaga; on May 2, 1512, he again went to Rome; his *Farsa de Plácida e Vittoriano* was performed there in the presence of Julius II on Jan. 11, 1513. In 1517, he was 'subcollector of revenues to the Apostolic Chamber'; in 1519, appointed prior of León, and that same year made a pilgrimage to Jerusalem, where he was ordained a priest. He described his sacred pilgrimage in *Tribagia o Via Sacra de Hierusalem* (Rome, 1521). After the death of Leo X in 1521, Encina returned to Spain and spent his last years as prior at León. Besides being the creator of the Spanish drama, Encina was the most important Spanish composer of the reign of Ferdinand and Isabella; he cultivated with notable artistry a type of part-song akin to the Italian 'frottola,' setting his own poems to music. Sixty-eight of these songs are preserved in the valuable 'Cancionero musical de los siglos XV y XVI,' ed. by F. A. Barbieri (Madrid, 1890; new ed., in 3 vols., by H. Anglès, 1947, 1951, 1953). No religious music by Encina is known to exist.—Cf. E. Diaz-Jiménez, *Juan del Encina en León* (Madrid, 1909); R. Mitjana, *Estudios sobre algunos músicos españoles del siglo XVI* (Madrid, 1918); R. Espinosa Maeso, *Nuevos Datos biográphicos de Juan del Encina* (Boletín de la Royal Academia Española, Madrid, 1921); J. Subirá, *La música en la Casa de Alba* (1927); F. Pedrell, *Cancionero musical popular español* (new ed., 2 vols., Barcelona, 1936); J. P. Wichersham Crawford, *Spanish Drama Before Lope de Vega* (revised ed., Philadelphia, 1937); G. Chase, *Origins of the Lyric Theater in Spain,* in the 'Mus. Quarterly' (July, 1939); G. Chase, *Juan del Encina, Poet and Musician,* in 'Music & Letters' (Oct., 1939).

Enckhausen, Heinrich Friedrich, German organist and composer; b. Celle, Aug. 28, 1799; d. Hanover, Jan. 15, 1885. He studied with Aloys Schmitt in Berlin, succeeding him as court organist. He wrote an opera *Der Savoyard* (Hanover, 1832) and sacred music; publ. a book of chorales.

Ende, Heinrich vom, German music publisher; b. Essen, Aug. 12, 1858; d. Cologne, Jan. 20, 1904. He published popular manuals on music, such as *Schatzkästlein;* also composed a considerable number of male choruses (*Das Kätzchen; Es ist ein Brünnlein geflossen,* etc.), songs, and piano pieces.

Enesco (Enescu), Georges, foremost Rumanian composer and violinist; b. Liveni, Rumania, Aug. 19, 1881; d. Paris, May 4, 1955. He began to play violin when only 4 years old, taking lessons with a Rumanian gypsy violinist, Nicolas Chioru; then studied with the violinist and composer, Caudella; from 1888-93 he was a pupil at the Vienna Cons. under Hellmesberger (violin) and R. Fuchs (theory), winning first prize in violin playing and harmony (1892); 1894-9 he studied at the Paris Cons. with Marsick (violin), Fauré and Massenet (composition); won second *accessit* for counterpoint and fugue (1897) and first prize for violin playing (1899); at the same time he studied cello, organ, and piano, attaining more than ordinary proficiency on all these instruments. His talent for composition manifested itself very early, his first efforts (not published) dating from his student days in Vienna; on June 11, 1897, when he was not quite sixteen, he presented in Paris a concert of his own works (a string quintet, piano suite, violin sonata, and songs), which attracted the attention of Colonne, who produced the following year the youthful composer's op. 1, *Poème roumain.* He toured as a violin virtuoso (1899-1900), and was appointed court violinist to the Queen of Rumania; then lived in Paris; gave master classes in violin interpretation at the École Normale de Musique; among his pupils was Yehudi Menuhin. In 1912 he offered an annual prize for Rumanian composers (won by Jora, Enacovici, Stan Golestan, Otescu, and others); then toured Europe; first visited the U. S. in 1923, making his début as conductor, composer, and violinist in a New York concert of the Philadelphia Orch. (Jan. 2, 1923); returned to the U. S. in 1937, and conducted the N. Y. Philh. on Jan. 28, 1937, and several subsequent concerts with remarkable success; reengaged in 1938 and conducted the N.Y. Philh. in 14 concerts; appeared twice as a violinist; also conducted two concerts of Rumanian music at the New York World Fair (May, 1939). The outbreak of World War II found Enesco in Rumania, where he lived on his farm in Sinaia, near Bucharest. He remained there through the war years; in 1946 he came again to the U. S. to teach in N. Y. On Jan. 21, 1950, on the 60th anniversary of his first public appearance at the age of 8, he played a farewell concert in New York in the multiple capacity of violinist, pianist, conductor, and composer, in a program comprising Bach's double concerto (with his pupil, Yehudi Menuhin); his violin sonata (playing the piano part with Menuhin); his *Rumanian Rhapsody* (conducting the orch.). He then returned to Paris; in July 1954 he suffered a stroke, and became an invalid for his remaining days. In homage to his accomplishment in Rumanian music, his native village was renamed Enescu and a street in Bucharest was also named after him. Enesco had an extraordinary range of musical interests. His compositions include artistic stylizations of Rumanian folk strains; his style was neo-romantic, but he made occasional use of experimental devices, such as quarter-tones in his opera, *Oedipe*. He possessed a fabulous memory and was able to play complete symphonic scores without the notes.—Works (all performed in Paris): opera *Oedipe* (1932; March 10, 1936; revived in 1955); for orch.: *Poème roumain*, op. 1 (Feb. 6, 1898); *Pastorale-Fantaisie* (Feb. 19, 1899); *Rapsodie roumaine* (No. 1, 1901; No. 2, 1902; both perf. Feb. 7, 1908); Suite No. 1 (Dec. 11, 1904); 3 symphonies (No. 1, Jan. 21, 1906; No. 2, 1913; No. 3, Feb. 26, 1921); *Symphonie concertante* for cello and orch. (March 14, 1909); Suite No. 2 (1915); violin concerto (Feb. 13, 1921); Suite No. 3, *Villageoise* (1938; N. Y. Philh., Feb. 2, 1939); *Poème symphonique* (1950); *Concert Overture on Motifs in the Rumanian Character* (1948; Washington, D. C., Jan. 23, 1949, Enesco conducting); *Symphonie de chambre* (1954; Paris, Jan. 23, 1955). Chamber music: 3 violin sonatas (No. 1, 1897; Paris, Feb. 17, 1898; No. 2, 1899; No. 3, *Dans le caractère populaire roumain,* 1926); Octet, for 4 violins, 2 violas, 2 cellos (1900); trio, *Aubade,* for violin, viola, and cello (1901); *Intermezzo* for strings (1903); *Dixtuor* for strings and wind instruments (1906); quartet for piano, violin, viola, and cello (1911); 2 string quartets (No. 1, 1921; No. 2, 1945; Washington, D. C., Oct. 31, 1948); *Impressions d'enfance* for violin and piano (1940). Vocal works: *3 Mélodies de Fernand Gregh,* for chorus and piano (1897); *7 Chansons de Clément Marot,* for piano and chorus (1907-8). Piano works: Variations on an original theme for 2 pianos (1899); 2 suites for piano solo (No. 1, *Dans le style ancien,* 1897; No. 2, 1903); *Pièces impromptues* (1915-16); 3 sonatas (1924; 1927; 1934).—Cf. B. Gavoty, *Les Souvenirs de Georges Enesco* (Paris, 1955).

Engel, A. Lehman, American composer and conductor; b. Jackson, Miss., Sept. 14, 1910. He studied at the Cincinnati College of Music and at the Juilliard Graduate School, N. Y., where he took courses with Rubin Goldmark and Roger Sessions. After graduation (1934) he devoted himself chiefly to theater conducting; has toured with musical comedy troupes; conducted many premières of modern operas; was founder and conductor of the Madrigal Singers (1936-39), with which he presented early American music and works of the polyphonic masters. As a composer, Engel is at his best in theater music; his choral writing is expert.—Works: *Pierrot of the Minute,* opera (Cincinnati, 1928); *Medea,* opera after Euripides (1935); *Scientific Creation,* ballet (N. Y., 1932); *Traditions,* ballet (1938); incidental music to the following plays produced in New York: *Within the Gates, Murder in the Cathedral, Emperor's New Clothes, Horse Play, The Birds, Hero is Born.* Other compositions: *Rain,* for chorus (1933); *Chansons Innocentes* (Moscow Festival, 1934); *Rest,* chorus; Symphony No. 1 (1939); Symphony No. 2 (1945); overture (1945); violin concerto (1945); *Creation,* for narrator and orch. (CBS, June 20, 1948, Engel conducting); *The Soldier,* short opera (perf. in concert version, N. Y., Nov. 25, 1956, composer cond.); also chamber music.

Engel, Carl, German musical historiographer; b. Thiedenwiese, near Hanover, July 6, 1818; d. by suicide at Kensington, London, Nov. 17, 1882. Pupil of Enckhausen at Hanover (organ), and of Hummel (piano) and Lobe at Weimar. After residing in Hamburg, Warsaw, and Berlin, he went to Manchester, England, in 1846, and in 1850 to London. There he became an influential writer, and an authority of the highest rank on musical history and musical instruments. Published *The Pianist's Handbook* (1853), *Piano School for Young Beginners* (1855), and *Reflections on Church Music* (1856); his life-work began with *The Music of the most Ancient Nations, particularly of the Assyrians, Egyptians, and Hebrews* (1864), followed by *An Introduction to the Study of National Music . . .* (1866); *Musical Instruments of all Countries* (1869); *Catalogue of the Special Exhibition of Ancient Musical Instruments* (2d ed., 1873); *Descriptive Catalogue of the Musical Instruments in the South Kensington Museum* (1874); *Musical Myths and Facts* (1876); *The Literature of National Music* (1879, reprinted from articles in the 'Times'); *Researches into the Early History of the Violin Family* (1883). Among his unpublished MSS is a large history of the musical instruments of the world (4 quarto vols. with over 800 illustrations).—Cf. Carl Engel, *Some Letters to a Namesake,* in the 'Mus. Quarterly' (July, 1942) and Gustave Reese, *More About the Namesake,* in *A Birthday Offering to Carl Engel* (N. Y., 1943).

Engel, Carl, distinguished musicologist and writer on music; b. Paris, July 21, 1883; d. New York, May 6, 1944. He was a great-grandson of Josef Kroll, founder of Kroll's Etablissement in Berlin, and grandson of J. C. Engel, who made the 'Kroll Opera' famous. Carl Engel was educated at the Universities of Strasbourg and Munich; studied composition in Munich with Thuille. He came to the U. S. in 1905, and established himself as editor, musicologist, librarian, and publisher. He was editor and musical adviser of the Boston Music Co. (1909-21); chief of the Music Division of the Library of Congress (1922-34); president of G. Schirmer, Inc. (1929-32); in 1929 became editor of the 'Mus. Quarterly,' remaining in that capacity until his death; from 1934 again president of G. Schirmer, Inc., and honorary consultant in musicology for the Library of Congress; U. S. delegate to the Beethoven Centenary, Vienna, 1927; U. S. representative of the International Society of Musicology; first chairman of the Committee on Musicology, American Council of Learned Societies; president of the American Musicological Society (1937-38); honorary member of the Harvard Musical Association; Fellow of the American Academy of Arts and Letters; honorary Mus. Doc., Oberlin College (1934); Chevalier of the Légion d'Honneur (1937); recipient of the Elizabeth Sprague Coolidge medal 'for eminent services rendered to chamber music' (1935). A writer with a brilliant style and of wide learning, Carl Engel contributed valuable essays to the 'Mus. Quarterly' (*Views and Reviews;* articles on Chadwick, Loeffler, etc.); publ. two collections of essays: *Alla Breve, from Bach to Debussy* (N. Y., 1921); *Discords Mingled* (N. Y., 1931). Carl Engel was also a composer; his music was in the French tradition, in an impressionistic vein; his songs, particularly his settings of poems by Amy Lowell, were often sung (the best known among them is *Sea-Shell*); other works include *Triptych* for violin and piano; *Perfumes,* for piano (an album of 5 pieces); *Presque Valse* for piano was publ. posthumously.—Cf. G. Reese, ed., *A Birthday Offering to Carl Engel* (N. Y., 1943; limited edition; not for sale); Harold Bauer, *Carl Engel* in the 'Mus. Quarterly' (July, 1944); G. Reese, *A Postscript* (ibid.); H. Putnam and E. S. Coolidge, *Tributes to Carl Engel* in the 'Mus. Quarterly' (April, 1945).

Engel, David Hermann, German organist and composer; b. Neuruppin, Jan. 22, 1816; d. Merseburg, May 3, 1877. He studied in Breslau; in 1848 became organist at Merseburg; wrote a comic opera *Prinz Carneval* (Berlin, 1862); publ. a *Beitrag zur Geschichte des Orgelbauwesens* (1855).

Engel, Gabriel, American writer, violinist, and composer; b. Beregszasz, Hungary, May 4, 1892; d. Vergennes, Vermont, Aug. 1, 1952. He was the author of *The Life of Anton Bruckner* (N. Y., 1931) and *Gustav Mahler—Song-Symphonist* (N. Y., 1932); also editor of 'Chord and Discord,' the magazine of the Bruckner Society of America. During the last 15 years of his life he was engaged in the rare books business.

Engel, Gustav Eduard, German music critic and singing teacher; b. Königsberg, Oct. 29, 1823; d. Berlin, July 19, 1895. He was music critic of the 'Vossische Zeitung' from 1861; taught singing at Kullak's Academy from 1862; among his pupils was Lola Beeth. He publ. *Sängerbrevier* (daily vocal exercises, 1860), *Ästhetik der Tonkunst* (1884), and other books and articles.

Engel, Hans, musicologist; b. Cairo, Egypt, Dec. 20, 1894; studied at the Munich Academy of Music under Klose, then with Röhr, and musicology with Sandberger at the

Univ. of Munich; *Dr. phil.*, 1925; lecturer at Greifswald Univ. (1926); prof. in 1932; from 1936, prof. of music history at Königsberg; taught at the Hochschule für Musik in Karlsruhe (1945-47); in 1957, instructor at the Univ. of Marburg.—Books: *Die Entwicklung des deutschen Klavierkonzertes von Mozart bis Liszt* (1927); *Musik und Musikleben in Greifswalds Vergangenheit* (1929); *Das Instrumentalkonzert* (new Kretzschmar *Führer*, part I, vol. III, 1932); *Carl Loewe* (1934); *Franz Liszt* (1936); *Deutschland und Italien in ihren musikgeschichtlichen Beziehungen* (1944); *J. S. Bach* (1950); *Musik der Völker und Zeiten* (Hanover, 1952). He is the editor of works by Marenzio, Joh. Fischer, Torelli, also of *Denkmäler der Musik in Pommern;* contributor to *Deutscher Kulturatlas,* Stammler's *Verfasserlexikon,* etc. See his autobiographical notice in 'Die Musik in Geschichte und Gegenwart.'

Engel, Joel, writer and composer; a pioneer in the movement towards a new Jewish national music; b. Berdiansk, April 16, 1868; d. Tel-Aviv, Palestine, Feb. 11, 1927. He studied at Kharkov; later with Taneyev and Ippolitov-Ivanov in Moscow, where he was music editor of the 'Russkiya Vedomosti' and editor of the Russian edition of Riemann's *Musiklexikon;* lectured for many years in Moscow on Jewish folksongs. In 1922 he went to Berlin, where he organized a publishing house for propaganda of Jewish music; issued a collection of Jewish folksongs in 3 vols.; also published 20 songs for children. His publications in the Russian language are: *Pocket Music Dictionary* (Moscow, 1913); *Essays on Music History* (lectures for the historic symph. concerts of the Imperial Russian Music Society, Moscow, 1911); *In the Opera* (1911).

Engel, Johann Jakob, German musician and writer; b. Parchim, Mecklenburg, Sept. 11, 1741; d. there, June 28, 1802. He was tutor to the Crown Prince (later Friedrich Wilhelm III); publ. an interesting essay, *Über die musikalische Malerei* (1780).

Engelke, Bernhard, German musicologist; b. Brunswick, Sept. 2, 1884; d. Kirchbarkau, near Kiel, May 16, 1950. He studied at Halle with H. Abert and at Leipzig Univ. with Riemann (*Dr. phil.* 1908 for his dissertation on J. F. Fasch). In 1912 he went to Magdeburg as teacher and choirmaster at the Cathedral; in 1925 he settled in Kiel; taught at Kiel Univ. He published numerous and valuable articles in music journals dealing mainly with German church music and musicians; contributed an article on Martin Agricola to 'Die Musik in Geschichte und Gegenwart.'

English, Granville, American composer; b. Louisville, Jan. 27, 1895. He was educated at the Chicago Musical College (Mus. Bac., 1915); pupil of Felix Borowski, Charles Haubiel, and Wallingford Riegger; teacher at the Gunn School of Music, Chicago (1923-25); living in New York and teaching privately. His main works are: *Ugly Duckling,* cantata for junior chorus and orch. (1924; Chicago North Shore Festival, 1926); *Ballet Fantasy* for orch. (1937); *Among the Hills,* orchestral scherzo (Oklahoma City, March 9, 1952); *Mood Tropicale,* for orch. (Baltimore, Feb. 5, 1955); *Evenings by the Sea,* symphonic poem (Port Washington, Long Island, N. Y., Jan. 20, 1956); *Song of the Caravan* for male chorus (1937); piano pieces; violin pieces; songs.

Englund, Einar, Finnish composer; b. Gotland, June 17, 1916. He studied in Helsinki with Palmgren; has composed 2 symphonies; *Epinikia,* symph. poem; piano quintet; etc.; is regarded as one of the most talented Finnish composers.

Enna, August, eminent Danish composer; b. Nakskov, May 13, 1860; d. Copenhagen, Aug. 3, 1939. He was partly of German and Italian blood; his grandfather, an Italian soldier in Napoleon's army, married a German girl, and settled in Denmark. Enna was brought to Copenhagen as a child, and went to school there. He learned to play piano and violin; had sporadic instruction in theory; later became a member of a traveling orch. and played with it in Finland (1880). Upon his return to Copenhagen, he taught piano and played for dancers; in 1883 he conducted a theater orch.; and wrote his first stage work *A Village Tale,* which he produced in 1883. After these practical experiences, he began to study seriously; took lessons with Schjorring (violin), Matthesson (organ), and Rasmussen (composition) and soon published a number of piano pieces, which attracted the attention of Niels Gade, who used his influence to obtain a traveling fellowship for Enna; this made it possible for Enna to study in Germany (1888-89) and acquire a complete mastery of instrumental and vocal writing. He followed the German Romantic School, being influenced mainly by Weber's type of opera, and by Grieg and Gade in the use of local color; the first product of this period was his most successful work, the opera *Hexen (The Witch)* produced in Copenhagen (Jan. 24, 1892), then in Germany.

Enna's other operas also enjoyed a modicum of success; these are *Cleopatra* (Copenhagen, Feb. 7, 1894); *Aucassin and Nicolette* (Copenhagen, Feb. 2, 1896); *The Match Girl,* after Andersen (Copenhagen, Nov. 13, 1897); *Lamia* (Antwerp, Oct. 3, 1899); *Ung Elskov* (first produced in Weimar, under the title, *Heisse Liebe,* Dec. 6, 1904); *Princess on the Pea,* after Andersen (Aarhus, Sept. 15, 1900); *The Nightingale,* also after Andersen (Copenhagen, Nov. 10, 1912); *Gloria Arsena* (Copenhagen, April 15, 1917); *Comedians,* after Victor Hugo's *L'homme qui rit* (Copenhagen, April 8, 1920); *Don Juan Mañara* (Copenhagen, April 17, 1925). He further wrote the ballets: *The Shepherdess and the Chimney-sweep* (Copenhagen, Oct. 6, 1901); *St. Cecilia's Golden Shoe* (Copenhagen, Dec. 26, 1904); *The Kiss* (Copenhagen, Oct. 19, 1927); also a violin concerto, two symphonies; an overture *Hans Christian Andersen;* choral pieces.

Enriquez de Valderrabano, Enrique, Spanish 16th-century lutenist; native of Peñaranda de Duero. He wrote the tablature book *Libro de música de vihuela, intitulado Silva de Sirenas* (Valladolid, 1547), containing transcriptions for vihuela (large 6-stringed guitar) of sacred and secular vocal works (some arranged for 2 vihuelas), also some original pieces.—Cf. G. Morphy, *Les luthistes espagnols du XVI*e *siècle* (1902); J. B. Trend, *Luis Milán and the Vihuelistas* (1925); W. Apel, *Early Spanish Music for Lute and Keyboard Instruments,* in the 'Mus. Quarterly' (July, 1934).

Enthoven, Henri Emile, Dutch composer; b. Amsterdam, Oct. 18, 1903; d. New York, Dec. 26, 1950. He studied composition with Johan Wagenaar at The Hague and with Schreker in Berlin; piano with Andriessen and Bruno Eisner; 1927-28, assistant conductor to Felix Weingartner at Basel; in 1939 he went to New York. In 1945 he was special adviser for the United Nations Information Office. As a composer, Enthoven followed the German Neo-Romantic School (Mahler, Richard Strauss, etc.). His works include 3 symphonies; 3 orchestral suites; a suite for violin; *Lyric Suite* for voice and small orch.; *Festival Prelude* on 'Gaudeamus igitur' for woodwind, brass, and organ; songs (with piano and orch.); violin sonata; piano pieces; incidental music to the Egyptian play *Ichnaton* (Utrecht, 1926).

Entremont, Philippe, French pianist; b. Rheims, June 6, 1934. Both his parents were professional musicians and teachers, and he received his first training from them. He subsequently studied piano with Marguerite Long; then entered the Paris Cons.; won 1st prize in solfège at 12; 1st prize in chamber music at 14, and 1st prize in piano at 15. In 1951 he was the winner of the Belgian State Competition in Brussels. He then toured in Europe; on Jan. 5, 1953 he made his American début with the National Orch. Association in N. Y.; appeared with the Philadelphia Orch. and other American organizations in 1956 and 1957 with exceptional success.

Eppert, Carl, American composer; b. Carbon, Ind., Nov. 5, 1882. He studied in Chicago and in Germany; founder and conductor of the Civic Symph. Orch. in Milwaukee (1923-26).—Works: 4 symphonies; *Escapade,* for orch. (Indianapolis, Jan. 3, 1941); symph. fantasy, *Traffic* (NBC orch., May 8, 1932); 2 symphonic poems: *City Shadows* and *Speed* (both performed at Rochester, Oct. 30, 1935); *Two Symphonic Impressions* (Chicago, Feb. 13, 1941; received 1st prize in the Chicago Symph. Orch. Golden Jubilee in 1940-41).

Epstein, Julius, pianist, b. Agram, Croatia, Aug. 7, 1832; d. Vienna, March 1, 1926. He was a pupil at Agram of Ignaz Lichtenegger, and at Vienna of Anton Halm (piano) and Johann Rufinatscha (composition). From 1867 to 1901 he was prof. of piano at the Vienna Cons.; one of the editors of Breitkopf & Härtel's monumental edition of Schubert's works. Among his pupils were Gustav Mahler and Ignaz Brüll.—Cf. H. Schuster, *J. Epstein; Ein tonkünstlerisches Charakterbild zu seinem 70. Geburts-Feste* (Vienna, 1902).

Epstein, Peter, German musicologist; b. Strasbourg, Nov. 12, 1901; d. Breslau, June 9, 1932. He studied in Frankfurt; later at the Akademie für Kirchen- und Schulmusik, Berlin, and at the Univ. of Breslau.—Publications: Catalogues of church music MSS of the Library of the City of Frankfurt (1926; in collaboration with C. Süss), of musical instruments at the Historic Museum of the City of Frankfurt (1927), and of musical instruments in the Breslau Museum (1932); *Die Frankfurter Kapellmusik zur Zeit des Johann Andreas Herbst,* in 'Archiv fur Musikwissenschaft' (VI); contributions on early Italian monody of the 17th century, in his Univ. dissertation at Breslau, 'Archiv für Musikwissenschaft' (VIII, 416); 'Zeitschrift für Musikwissenschaft' (X, 216); *Görlitzer Schulmusik um 1600* (1929); *Apelles von Löwenstern* (1929); etc.; edited Schultze's St. Luke Passion (Delitzsch, 1653) in 1930.—Cf. A. Schmitz, *Peter Epstein,* in 'Zeitschrift für Musikwissenschaft' (XIV, 450).

Epstein, Richard, Austrian pianist, son of Julius Epstein; b. Vienna, Jan. 26, 1869; d. New York, Aug. 1, 1919. He was a pupil at the Vienna Cons. of his father and R. Fuchs (composition); prof. of piano at the Vienna Cons.; lived in London (1904-14); then in New York. He excelled as an accompanist, in which capacity he was frequently heard with such artists as Sembrich, Fremstad, Culp, Gerhardt, Destinn, Elman, Kreisler, and as assisting artist with famous chamber music organizations (Joachim, Rosé, Bohemian Quartets, etc.).

Érard (ā-rahr'), **Sébastien,** famous maker of pianos and harps; b. Strasbourg, April 5, 1752; d. in his château, La Muette, near Paris, Aug. 5, 1831. His family name was originally Erhard; his father was a cabinet-maker by trade, and in his shop Sébastien worked until he was 16, when his father died. He was then engaged by a Paris harpsichord maker, who dismissed him "for wanting to know everything"; under a second employer his ingenuity made a stir in the musical world, and the invention of a 'clavecin mécanique' (described by Abbé Roussier, 1776) made him famous. The Duchess of Villeroy became his patroness, and fitted up in her home a workshop for Érard, in which (1777) he finished the first pianoforte made in France. In the meantime, his brother, Jean-Baptiste, joined him, and they founded an instrument factory in the Rue Bourbon. Their growing success led to a conflict with the fan-makers' guild (to which the brothers did not belong), which tried to prevent them from working. But the Érards obtained a special 'brevet' from Louis XVI for the manufacture of 'forté-pianos' and this enabled them to continue their trade unmolested. In the following years, Érard invented the 'piano organisé' with two keyboards, one for piano and the other for a small organ; he also became interested in the harp, and invented the ingenious double-action mechanism, perfected in 1811. From 1786-96 he was in London; returning to Paris, he made his first grand piano, and employed the English action until his invention, in 1809, of the repetition action, which is regarded as his supreme achievement. An 'orgue expressif,' built for the Tuileries, was his last important work.—Cf. F. Fétis, *Notice biographique sur Sébastien Érard* (Paris, 1831).—His nephew, **Pierre Érard** (1796-1855), succeeded him; he published *The Harp in its present improved state compared with the original Pedal Harp* (1821), and *Perfectionnements apportés dans le mécanisme du piano par les Érards depuis l'origine de cet instrument jusqu'à l'exposition de 1834* (1834). Pierre's successor was his wife's nephew, Pierre Schäffer (d. 1878); the firm is still the leading French manufacturer of pianos and harps.

Eratosthenes, Greek philosopher; b. Cyrene, c. 276 B.C.; d. Alexandria, Egypt, c. 194 B.C. He wrote on numerous subjects, chiefly mathematics, and was custodian of the Alexandria library. The *Catasterismi,* attributed to Eratosthenes, contain scattered notes on Greek music and instruments, especially the 'lyra' (German transl. by Schaubach, 1795; Bernhardy publ. in 1822 an ed. of the original text). His work on music is lost; Ptolemy quotes his division of the tetrachord.

Erb, John Lawrence, American organist, pedagogue, and author; b. Reading, Pa., Feb. 5, 1877; d. Eugene, Ore., March 17, 1950. He studied at Pottstown, Pa. (1892-4) and at the Metropolitan College of Music, N. Y. City (1894-9); then was director of the Wooster, Ohio, Cons. (1905-13); director School of Music, Univ. of Illinois (1914-21); secretary and later president of the Music Teachers' National Association; lecturer at American Institute of Applied Music, N. Y. (1921-4); from 1923, at Connecticut College for Women.—Books: *Brahms,* a biography (1895; 1905; revised ed., London, 1934); *Hymns and Church Music* (1911); *Elements of Harmony* (1911); *Elementary Theory* (1911); *Music Appreciation for the Student* (1926); two chapters in Balzell's *History of Music* (1931); *Select Songs for the Assembly* (1931). He also composed songs, piano pieces, organ music, anthems, music for pageants.

Erb, John Warren, American music educator and composer; b. Massillon, Ohio, April 17, 1887; d. Pittsburgh, July 2, 1948. He studied in Berlin with Xaver Scharwenka, Siegfried Ochs, and Felix Weingartner, and in the U. S. with Stillman Kelley; chairman and director of department of instrumental music in School of Music Education of New York Univ.; conductor of Lake Placid Club Choral Festival, Biennial Festival of National Federation of Music Clubs, Baltimore, in 1929; director of music, Lafayette College (1938). Among his works are *An Early Greek Christmas, The Unfoldment* for strings (Saratoga Spa, 1937), etc.

Erb (ärp), **Marie Joseph,** Alsatian composer and organist; b. Strasbourg, Oct. 23, 1858; d. Andlau, July 9, 1944. He studied at first in Strasbourg; then (1875-80) in Paris, under Saint-Saëns, Gigout, and Loret, at the 'École de musique classique'; from 1880 in Strasbourg as teacher of piano and organ, and organist in the Johanniskirche (Roman Catholic) and at the Synagogue.—Works: The operas (all first performed in Strasbourg, unless otherwise noted) *Der Letzte Ruf* (1895), *Der glückliche Taugenichts* (1897), *Abendglocken* (1900), *Eifersüchtig* (Leipzig, 1901), *Der Riese Schletto* (1901), *Der Zaubermantel* (1901), *Die Vogesentanne* (1904), *Der Heimweg* (ballet-opera, 1907), *Prinzessin Flunkerli* (fairy-opera, 1912); a symphony in G; 3 violin sonatas; cello sonata; 2 string quartets; string trio; *Octet* for wind and strings; *Sonata liturgica* (1919); *Suite liturgique; Danses et pièces alsaciennes* (1924 and 1925); 8 Masses; organ pieces; pieces for piano (2 and 4 hands); songs; also 2 vols. of Alsatian folksongs.—Cf. *Marie Joseph Erb, sa vie et son œuvre,* ed. by P. de Bréville (Strasbourg, 1948).

Erbach, Christian, German organist and composer; b. Hesse, 1573; d. Augsburg, 1635. He was the successor of Hassler as town organist in Augsburg (1602); in 1625 became organist of the cathedral there. He publ. 3 books of *Modi sacri . . .* (1600, 1604, 1611; under varying titles) for 4-10 voices; several works by him are included in contemporary collections; 12 motets are in A. B. Gottron, *Christian Erbach* (Mainz, 1943). See E. F. Schmid's article on Erbach in 'Die Musik in Geschichte und Gegenwart.'

Erbse, Heimo, German composer; b. Rudolstadt (Thuringia), Feb. 27, 1924. He studied in Weimar, and in Berlin with Boris Blacher; from 1947-50 was opera coach in Jena, Meiningen, Sondershausen, and other German towns. His works include *Musik für 9 Musikanten* (1951); Capriccio for piano, percussion, and string orch. (1952); etc.

Erdmann, Eduard, Latvian pianist and composer; b. Tsezis (Wenden), March 5, 1896. He studied in Riga; then went to Berlin, where he studied piano with Konrad Ansorge (1914-17) and composition with Heinz Tiessen (1915-18). From 1925-35 he was prof. at the Cologne Cons.; active as concert pianist (1935-50); in 1950, appointed prof. of piano at the Hochschule für Musik in Hamburg. He has written 4 symphonies (No. 1, 1919; No. 2, 1923; No. 3, 1946; No. 4, 1951); piano pieces; songs.

Erdmannsdörfer, Max von, German conductor; b. Nuremberg, June 14, 1848; d. Munich, Feb. 14, 1905. He studied at the Leipzig Cons. (1863-7), and in Dresden (1868-9). From 1871 to 1880 he was court conductor at Sondershausen; then was active in Vienna, Leipzig, and Nuremberg. In 1882 he was engaged as conductor of the Imperial Musical Society in Moscow; in 1885 became prof. at the Moscow Cons.; organized a students' orchestra there. His symphonic concerts in Moscow were of great importance to Russian music; he introduced many new works by Russian composers, and his influence was considerable in the Moscow musical circles, despite the mediocrity of his conducting. Returning to Germany, he became conductor of the Bremen Philharmonic Concerts (until 1895); in 1897 he settled in Munich.

Erede, Alberto, Italian conductor; b. Genoa, Nov. 8, 1908. He studied at the Milan Cons. (piano, cello, theory); then in Basel, with Weingartner (conducting). He conducted opera in England from 1934-39, and after 1946; made his U.S. début with the NBC Symph. Orch. in 1939; in 1954 joined the staff of the Metropolitan Opera (chiefly for the Italian repertory).

Erhardt, Otto, German opera director; b. Breslau, Nov. 18, 1888. He studied violin; took courses in music and art at Breslau, Munich, Oxford, and London. He played violin in various orchestras (1908-11); then became a stage director; acted in this capacity with the Stuttgart Opera (1920-27); at the Dresden Opera (1927-32); Zürich (1923); Bayreuth Festival (1924); Rome and Turin (1925); was also engaged at Covent Garden for several seasons; was with the Chicago Civic Opera (1930-32); directed the festivals at Salzburg (1933-36). In 1938 he went to Buenos Aires, where he was stage director at the Teatro Colón and prof. at the Opera Academy (until 1948); after two seasons in Europe, he became stage director of the City Opera Co. in New York (1950); subsequently divided his time between South America, Europe, and the U. S. He published a book, *Die Operndichtung der deutschen Romantik* (Breslau, 1911); also a biography of Richard Strauss (Buenos Aires, 1950, in Spanish; German ed., 1953).

Erk, Ludwig (Christian), German music scholar and educator; b. Wetzlar, Jan. 6, 1807; d. Berlin, Nov. 25, 1883. He received good training in music from his father, Adam Wilhelm Erk (1779-1820), who was organist at Wetzlar. His further studies were under André in Offenbach and Spiess in Frankfurt. In 1826 he became prof. at the seminary in Mörs, where he taught until 1835; from 1836 to 1840 he was instructor in liturgical singing at Berlin, and conducted a choir. In 1852, he founded the 'Erk Gesangverein' for mixed voices. During his years as conductor of choral societies, he became interested in folksongs, and accumulated a great collection of authentic materials on the subject; also published songbooks for schools, which attained considerable popularity; some of these were written jointly with his brother Friedrich Erk, and his brother-in-law, Greef. He also published *Die deutschen Volkslieder mit ihren Singweisen* (1838-45); *Volkslieder, alte und neue* (1845-6); *Deutscher Liederhort* (folksongs; vol. 1 publ. 1856; MS of the remainder was bought—with the rest of his valuable library—for the Royal Hochschule für Musik, Berlin; continued and ed. by Magnus Böhme, and publ. in 4 vols., 1894); *Mehrstimmige Gesänge* (1833-5); *Volksklänge* (1851-60); *Deutscher Liederschatz* (1859-72); *Vierstimmige Choralgesänge der vornehmsten Meister des 16. und 17. Jahrhunderts* (1845); *J. S. Bachs mehrstimmige Choralgesänge und geistliche Arien* (1850-65); *Vierstimmiges Choralbuch für evangelische Kirchen* (1863); *Choräle für Männerstimmen* (1866); *Methodischer Leitfaden für den Gesangunterricht in Volksschulen* (1834, Part I).—Cf. *Chronologisches Verzeichnis der musikalischen Werke und literarischen Arbeiten von Ludwig Erk* (compiled by a group of friends; Berlin, 1867); K. Schultze, *Ludwig Erk* (Berlin, 1876); H. Schmeel, *Ludwig Erk, ein Lebensbild* (Giessen, 1908).

Erkel, Franz (Ferenc), the creator of Hungarian national opera; b. Gyula, Hungary, Nov. 7, 1810; d. Pest, June 15, 1893. He was taught by his father; at 24 became director of the Kaschau opera troupe, and went with it to Pest, where he was appointed conductor at the National Theater on its opening in 1837. He was the founder and director of the Budapest Philharmonic Concerts (1853), and first prof. of piano and instrumentation at the National Musical Academy. His numerous songs, in the national vein, became very popular. He composed the Hungarian National Hymn (1845).—Works: operas (all first presented in Budapest): *Báthory Mária* (Aug. 8, 1840); *Hunyady László* (Jan. 27, 1844; first truly national Hungarian opera; given almost 300 performances in the first 50 years); *Erzsébet* (May 6, 1857); *Kúnok* (1858); *Bánk-Bán* (March 9, 1861; highly successful in Hungary); *Sarolta*, comic opera (June 26, 1862); *Dózsa György* (April 6, 1867); *Brankovics György* (May 20, 1874); *Névtelen hosök* (Nov. 30, 1880); *István király* (March 14, 1885); music for plays; *Festival Overture*, for orch. (1887); many songs and anthems. A symposium of essays on Erkel was published in 'Zenetudományi Tanulmányok' (Budapest, 1954, vol. II) under the editorship of B. Szabolcsi.—Cf. K. Abrányi, *Franz Erkel* (Budapest, 1895); F. Scherer, *Franz Erkel* (Gyula, 1944).

Erkin, Ulvi Cemal, Turkish composer; b. Istanbul, March 14, 1906. He studied in Paris with Isidor Philipp (piano) and Nadia Boulanger (composition) from 1925-30; graduated from the École Normale de Musique (1930), and returned to Turkey. He taught piano at the State Cons. in Ankara, and was its director from 1949 to 1951.—Works: *Bayram*, tone poem (Ankara, May 11, 1934); piano concerto (1942); symph. No. 1 (Ankara, April 20, 1946); symph. No. 2 (1948-51); violin concerto (Ankara, April 2, 1948); string quartet (1936); piano quintet (1943); piano sonata (1946); songs and piano pieces.

Erlanger, Camille, French composer; b. Paris, May 25, 1863; d. there, April 24, 1919. He was a pupil of the Paris Cons. under Delibes, Durand, Matthias; in 1888, took the Grand Prix de Rome for his cantata ***Velléda***. He earned fame with his opera *Le Juif polonais* (Paris, April 11, 1900), which has remained in active repertory; other operas are: *Kermaria* (Paris, Feb. 8, 1897); *Le Fils de l'étoile* (Paris, April 20, 1904); *Aphrodite* (Paris, March 27, 1906); *Bacchus triomphant* (Bordeaux, Sept. 11, 1909); *L'Aube rouge* (Rouen, Dec. 29, 1911); *La Sorcière* (Paris, Dec. 18, 1912); *Le Barbier de Deauville* (1917); *Forfaiture* (performed posthumously at the Opéra-Comique in 1921). He also wrote several symphonic poems (*Maître et serviteur*, after Tolstoy, etc.) and a French requiem.

d'Erlanger, (Baron) **Frédéric**, member of the family of bankers; composer and opera director; b. Paris, May 29, 1868; d. London, April 23, 1943. In 1897 he assumed the pseudonym Regnal, formed by reading backward the last six letters of his name. He lived in London, where, for many years, he was one of the directors of the Covent Garden Opera. He wrote the operas, *Jehan de Saintre* (Aix-les-Bains, Aug. 1, 1893); *Inez Mendo* (London, July 10, 1897, under the pseudonym Regnal); *Tess*, after Thomas Hardy (Naples, April 10, 1906); *Noël* (Paris, Dec. 28, 1910; Chicago, 1913); a piano quintet; a string quartet; a violin concerto (London, March 12, 1903, Kreisler soloist); a violin sonata; Andante for cello and orch.

Erlebach, Philipp Heinrich, important German composer; b. Esens, East Frisia, July 25, 1657; d. Rudolstadt, April 17, 1714. He was Hofkapellmeister at Rudolstadt from at least 1681. His style was strongly influenced by that of Lully. He wrote orchestral suites (6 overtures publ. 1693); suites for violin, viola da gamba and continuo (1694), one of which was reprinted by Einstein in 'Zur deutschen Literature für Viola da Gamba' (1905); cantatas; sacred and secular songs, including *Harmonische Freude* (2 parts: 1697, 1710; reprinted by Kinkeldey in vol. 46/47 of the 'Denkmäler deutscher Tonkunst'); organ works; etc. Examples from his *Gottgeheiligte Singstunde* (1704) are printed in M. Friedlaender's *Das deutsche Lied im 18. Jahrhundert* (1902).

Erlebach, Rupert, English composer; b. Islington, London, Nov. 16, 1894. He studied at the Royal Academy of Music with Stanford and Vaughan Williams. As a composer, he makes considerable use of English folk material. Principal works: *Before Dawn, Aubade, A Memory, High Noon, Lark's Song at Evening,* for orch.; *Rhapsody* for cello and orch.; *Folksong Poems* for string orch.; *Rhapsody* for flute, oboe, violin, viola, and cello; *Moods* for string quartet; *Legends* for violin and piano; sonata for violin and piano; 2 sonatas for cello and piano (one, *Folksong Sonata*); piano pieces; organ pieces; songs; choral works.

Ermatinger, Erhart, Swiss composer; b. Winterthur, Feb. 16, 1900. He studied at the Zürich Cons. with Jarnach, then at the Berlin Hochschule; 1922-23, chorus master at the Zürich Opera; later a private teacher there; 1925-26, teacher of theory at the Freiburg Univ.; lived in Berlin, then in Holland; in 1945 returned to Switzerland. He has written an opera, *Gijsbrecht van Amstel* (1947); 2 symphonies, 2 string quartets, songs; publ. a book *Bildhafte Musik: Entwurf einer Lehre von der musikalischen Darstellungskunst* (Tübingen, 1928).

Ernst, Alfred, French writer and critic; b. Périgueux, April 9, 1860; d. Paris, May 15, 1898. A pupil of the 'École polytechnique,' he abandoned science for art; was a passionate admirer and defender of Wagner. Besides many contributions to musical journals, he published *L'Oeuvre dramatique de Berlioz* (1884), *Richard Wagner et le drame contemporain* (1887), *L'Art de Richard Wagner, l'œuvre poétique* (1893; a projected 2nd vol. on *l'œuvre musicale* remained unfinished); *Étude sur 'Tannhäuser,'* analysis and thematic guide (1895; with E. Poirée). He translated *Die Meistersinger* and *Der Ring des Nibelungen* into French.

Ernst, Heinrich Wilhelm, violinist and composer; b. Brünn, May 6, 1814; d. Nice, Oct. 8, 1865. He was a pupil of Böhm (violin) and Seyfried (composition) in Vienna, with further study under Mayseder; 1832-38, lived in Paris. From 1838 to 1850 he was almost continually on concert tours; then settled in London (1855). His works for violin are brilliant and effective; the *Élégie,* the concerto in F♯ minor (new ed. by Marteau, 1913), and *Carnaval de Venise,* are a few of the most celebrated.—Cf. A. Heller, *Heinrich Wilhelm Ernst im Urteile seiner Zeitgenossen* (Brünn, 1904).

Erpf, Hermann, German musicologist; b. Pforzheim, April 23, 1891. He studied at Heidelberg and with Riemann at Leipzig; was in the army (1914-18); teaching at Pforzheim (1919-23); at the Univ. of Freiburg (1923-25); assistant director at the Academy of Speech and Music in Münster (1925-27); in charge of the Folkwangschule in Essen (1927-43). In 1943-45, and again since 1952, director of the Hochschule für Musik in Stuttgart. Books: *Entwicklungszüge in der zeitgenössischen Musik* (Karlsruhe, 1922); *Studien zur Harmonie- und Klangtechnik der neueren Musik* (Leipzig, 1927); *Harmonielehre in der Schule* (Leipzig, 1930); *Vom Wesen der neuen Musik* (Stuttgart, 1949); *Neue Wege der Musikerziehung* (Stuttgart, 1953); *Gegenwartskunde der Musik* (Stuttgart, 1954). He has composed a Mass, numerous cantatas, 3 string quartets, and piano music.

Erskine, John, American educator and writer on music; b. New York, Oct. 5, 1879; d. there, June 1, 1951. He studied piano with Carl Walter; composition with MacDowell; then took up an academic and literary career, becoming highly successful as a novelist and essayist. He was educated at Columbia Univ. (B. A., 1900; M. A., 1901; Ph. D., 1903; LL. D., 1929); prof. of English there (1909-37); then prof. emeritus. In 1923 he resumed piano study under Ernest Hutcheson; played as soloist with the N. Y. Symph. Orch., the Baltimore Civic Orch.; was president of the Juilliard School of Music, N. Y. (1928-37); president of the Juilliard Music Foundation from 1948 until his death. He was editor of 'A Musical Companion' (1935). He received the degree of Mus. Doc. from Rollins College, Florida (1931), Cornell College, Iowa

(1935); also Litt. D. from Amherst College (1923) and the Univ. of Bordeaux, France (1929). Erskine was an Officer of the French Legion of Honor. He was married twice: to Pauline Ives (1910; divorced, 1945) and to Helen Worden (July 3, 1945). He published a number of novels, among them *The Private Life of Helen of Troy* (1925); and the librettos for Gruenberg's opera, *Jack and the Beanstalk* (1931) and Antheil's opera *Helen Retires* (1934). He was also the author of books on music, including *Is there a Career in Music?* (N. Y., 1929); *Song Without Words; The Story of Felix Mendelssohn* (1941); *The Philharmonic-Symphony Society of N. Y., Its First Hundred Years* (N. Y., 1943); *What is Music?* (Philadelphia, 1944); *The Memory of Certain Persons* (Philadelphia, 1947); *My Life as a Teacher* (N. Y., 1948); *My Life in Music* (N. Y., 1950).

Ertel, (Jean) Paul, German pianist and composer; b. Posen, Jan. 22, 1865; d. Berlin, Feb. 11, 1933. He studied with L. Brassin (piano) and later took lessons with Liszt; also studied law; was music critic of the 'Berliner Lokal Anzeiger' and editor of 'Deutscher Musikerzeitung' (1897-1905). He wrote several symph. poems in a general Lisztian vein (*Der Mensch, Die nächtliche Heerschau,* etc.); many ballads for voice and instruments; violin sonata and other chamber music.

Escher, Rudolf, Dutch composer; b. Amsterdam, Jan. 8, 1912. He studied in Leiden and in Rotterdam; later took lessons from Pijper. His music is impressionistic in harmony but strict in form. He is also the author of monographs on Debussy and Ravel.—Works: Symphony, in memory of Maurice Ravel (1940); *Letter from Mexico,* for baritone and piano (1941); trio for oboe, flute, and clarinet (1941); sonata for 2 flutes (1944); piano sonata (1935); sonata for unaccompanied cello (1945).

Eschig, Max, French music publisher; b. Opava, now Czechoslovakia, May 27, 1872; d. Paris, Sept. 3, 1927. He settled in Paris and founded a publishing firm under his name in 1907, prospering continually and forming an impressive catalogue of modern works by Ravel, Manuel de Falla, and many other French, Spanish, and English composers.

Eschmann, Johann Karl, Swiss pianist and pedagogue; b. Winterthur, April 12, 1826; d. Zürich, Oct. 27, 1882. He studied in Leipzig with Moscheles, and also had some lessons with Mendelssohn. He then settled in Zürich as a piano teacher; publ. a valuable manual *Wegweiser durch die Klavierliteratur* (Zürich, 1879; 8th ed., 1914), and *100 Aphorismen aus dem Klavierunterricht* (2nd ed., 1899).

Escobar, Luis Antonio, Colombian composer; b. Villapinzón, near Bogotá, July 14, 1925. He studied music at the Bogotá Cons.; then took courses with Nicolas Nabokov at the Peabody Cons. in Baltimore and with Boris Blacher in Berlin. He returned to Bogotá in 1953, and received the post of prof. at the Cons. He has written a symphony, a piano concerto, a flute concerto; 2 string quartets; 2 violin sonatas; 2 sonatas and 3 sonatinas for piano, etc. His style is brisk and terse in the modern manner; but there is in his music also a melorhythmic pattern of Spanish-American dances.

Escobedo, Bartolomé, Spanish composer of the 16th century; b. Zamora, c. 1515; d. in 1563 as canon at Segovia; from 1536-41, and again from 1545-54, singer in the Papal Choir at Rome. A motet by Escobedo is in Eslava's 'Lira Sacro-Hispana'; another motet was reprinted by Ambros in his *Geschichte der Musik* (vol. 5). MS compositions are in the Sistine Chapel and in Toledo. He wrote a Mass for the accession to the Spanish throne of Philip II (1563); was a judge in the famous dispute between Nicola Vicentino and Vincento Lusitano (1551) over the qualities of Greek modes.

Escudier (es-kü-d'yā'), **Léon,** French music journalist; b. Castelnaudary, Aude, Sept. 17, 1821; d. Paris, June 22, 1881. He was a brother and partner of **Marie Escudier,** b. Castelnaudary, June 29, 1819; d. Paris, April 17, 1880. In 1838, the brothers began publishing the periodical 'La France musicale' and soon afterwards established a music shop. Industrious writers, they issued jointly the following works: *Études biographiques sur les chanteurs contemporains* (1840), *Dictionnaire de musique d'après les théoriciens, historiens et critiques les plus célèbres* (1844, 2 vols.; reprinted in 1854 as *Dictionnaire de musique, théorique et historique*); *Rossini, sa vie et ses œuvres* (1854); *Vie et aventures des cantatrices célèbres, précédées des musiciens de l'Empire, et suivies de la vie anecdotique de Paganini* (1856). Léon broke up partnership with his brother in 1862, retaining the music business; he established a new paper, 'L'art musical,' which continued to appear until Sept. 27, 1894. Marie retained the publishing and editorial rights to 'La France musicale,' which ceased publ. in 1870.

Eslava y Elizondo, Miguel Hilarión, Spanish composer and scholar; b. Burlada, Navarra, Oct. 21, 1807; d. Madrid, July 23, 1878. He was a choirboy at the Cathedral of Pamplona; studied organ and violin; in 1827 he went to Calahorra, where he studied with Francisco Secanilla; at the age of 21 he was appointed music director at the Cathedral of Burgo de Osma, where he was ordained a priest. In 1832 he became music director at Seville; in 1847 he obtained the appointment as chapel master to Queen Isabella in Madrid; in 1854 he became prof. at the Madrid Cons. He also edited a periodical, 'Gaceta musical de Madrid' (1855-56). He wrote 3 operas with Italian texts: *Il Solitario del Monte Selvaggio* (Cádiz, 1841), *La tregua di Ptolemaide* (1842), and *Pietro il crudele* (1843); his fame rests, however, not on his musical compositions, but on his great collection in 10 vols., 'Lira sacro-hispana' (Madrid, 1869), an anthology of Spanish sacred music from the 16th to the 19th centuries, including some of Eslava's own works (*Requiem, Te Deum,* etc.). He also publ. a *Método de solfeo* (1846) and *Escuela de Armonía y Composición* (1861).—Cf. G. Chase, *Miguel Hilarión Eslava* in the 'Mus. Quarterly' (Jan., 1938).

Espagne (es-pähñ), **Franz,** German music editor; b. Münster, April 21, 1828; d. Berlin, May 24, 1878. He studied with Dehn; after Dehn's death, he became head of the Music Dept. of the Royal Library in Berlin; edited new classical editions (works by Palestrina, Beethoven, and others).

Espinosa (ehs-pē-noh'-sah), **Guillermo,** Colombian conductor; b. Cartagena, Jan. 9, 1905. He was a pupil of the Instituto de Música there; then received a government stipend for further study in Milan under J. Paribeni and R. Bossi; completed his studies at the Berlin Hochschule für Musik with J. Prüwer and in Basel with F. Weingartner. In 1928 he founded and conducted (until 1932) an orch. made up of foreign musicians residing in Berlin. After appearing as guest conductor in Italy, Switzerland, Denmark, and France, he returned to Colombia in 1932, and in 1936 founded the National Symph. Orch. at Bogotá, which he led for ten years. In 1947 he settled in Washington, D. C., as an official of the Division of Music in the Pan American Union; in 1953, succeeded Charles Seeger as chief.—Cf. F. C. Lange, *Guillermo Espinosa y la Sinfónica Nacional,* in 'Boletín Latino-Americano de Música' (1938).

Esplá, Oscar, Spanish composer; b. Alicante, Aug. 5, 1886; at first studied engineering and philosophy; then turned to music, traveling and studying for some years in Germany. He was the first president of the Junta Nacional de Música under the Spanish Republic (1934) and in 1936 was director of the Madrid Cons.; then lived in Brussels and Paris; eventually returned to Spain.—Works: *La Bella durmiente,* opera (Vienna, 1909); *La Balteira,* opera (1939); the ballets *Ciclopes de Ifach* and *El contrabandista;* orchestral works: *Suite levantina* (awarded prize in Vienna, 1909); *El Sueño de Eros, Don Quixote, Ambito de la Danza, Las Cumbres;* scenic cantata, *Nochebuena del diablo; Sonata del Sur,* for piano and orch. (1936-43); string quartet (1947); piano pieces; songs. He publ. the books *El Arte y la Musicalidad* and *Las actividades del espíritu y su fundamento estético.*—Cf. G. Chase, *Oscar Esplá,* in the 'Monthly Musical Record' (Sept., 1939).

Esposito, Michele, Italian composer and conductor; b. Castellamare, near Naples, Sept. 29, 1855; d. Florence, Nov. 23, 1929. He studied at the Cons. San Pietro at Naples with Cesi (piano) and Serrao (theory); for a time he gave piano concerts in Italy; from 1878-82 was in Paris; in 1882 he was engaged as piano teacher at the Irish Academy of Music in Dublin; he organized the Dublin Orch. Society in 1899 and conducted it until 1914, and again in 1927. He held the honorary degree of Mus. Doc. of Trinity College, Dublin. He composed several works on Irish subjects: Irish operetta, *The Post Bag* (London, Jan. 27, 1902); incidental music for *The Tinker and the Fairy* (Dublin, 1910); *Suite of Irish Dances* for orch.; 2 Irish rhapsodies; several arrangements of Irish melodies. He received first prizes for his cantata *Deirdre* (Irish Festival, Dublin, 1897); *Irish Symphony* (Irish Festival, Dublin, 1902); also wrote 2 string quartets, 2 violin sonatas, cello sonatas, etc.

Esser, Heinrich, German composer; b. Mannheim, July 15, 1818; d. Salzburg, June 3, 1872. He studied in Vienna with Lachner and Sechter. In 1847 he became conductor of the Vienna Opera, succeeding Otto Nicolai; in 1869 retired and lived in Salzburg. He was a competent opera conductor; he also had a modicum of success as opera composer; 3 of his operas were performed: *Silas* (Mannheim, 1839); *Thomas Riquiqui* (Frankfurt, 1843); and *Die zwei Prinzen* (Munich, 1844); also numerous vocal works; 2 symphonies; arrangements of Bach's organ works; a string quartet. —Cf. E. Hanslick, *Suite* (Vienna, 1884). Letters of Esser are found in E. Istel's *Wagner im Lichte eines zeitgenössischen Briefwechsels* (1902).

Essipoff (Essipova), **Anna Nicolayevna,** famous Russian pianist and pedagogue; b. St. Petersburg, Feb. 13, 1851; d. there, Aug. 18, 1914. She was a pupil of Leschetizky, and married him in 1880 (divorced 1892). She made her début in St. Petersburg; subsequently made long concert tours throughout Europe and in America; her distinguishing artistic quality was a singing piano tone and 'pearly' passage-work. From 1870 to 1885 she gave 669 concerts. In 1893 she was engaged as prof. of piano at the St. Petersburg Cons., and continued to teach there until the last years of her life. Many famous pianists and composers (Prokofiev, Borovsky, etc.) were her pupils.

Este, Thomas. See **East, Thomas.**

Esteban, Julio, noted pianist and pedagogue; b. Shanghai (of Spanish parentage), March 18, 1906; in 1907 was taken to Spain; studied at the municipal music school in Barcelona, graduating in 1924. He gave concerts in Spain from 1919 to 1924; in 1925 went to Manila, where he taught at the Cons. of Music of the Univ. of the Philippines until 1947, when he was appointed director of the Cons. of Music at the Univ. of Sto. Tomás there. He traveled through the Orient; gave concerts in Hongkong and in Japan in 1952; also played for the U. N. troops in Korea. In 1955 he left Manila and was appointed member of the faculty of the Peabody Cons. in Baltimore.

Estes, Charles E., American organist; b. Somersworth, N. H., Aug. 28, 1882. He studied at Dartmouth College with Charles S. Morse (1901-5; B. A.), and at Teachers College, Columbia Univ. (M. A.), also a pupil of Widor in Paris (1917-18) and of Seth Bingham in New York (1924-25); was head of the music department of the Robert College, Istanbul (Turkey) from 1910-17; from 1917-19, in Paris; 1919-25 and 1926-47, again at Robert College; in 1935, toured the eastern U. S. in a campaign for the Near-East colleges; resigned his position at Robert College (1947) and returned to America. Since 1948, organist and choirmaster at the First Parish Church, Dover, New Hampshire.

Esteve (eh-stä'-veh), **Pablo,** Catalonian composer; date of birth unknown; d. Madrid, June 4, 1794. He went to Madrid about 1760; was maestro di cappella to the Duke of Osuna; in 1778 appointed official composer for the municipal theaters of Madrid. He composed over 300 'tonadillas,' and some zarzuelas. His song, *El jilguerito con pico de oro,* has been arranged for modern performance (soprano and orch.) by Joaquín Nin.—Cf. F. Pedrell, *Teatro lírico español anterior al siglo XIX;* R. Mitjana, *La musique en Espagne,* in 'Encyclopédie du Conservatoire' (I, 4); J. Nin, *Les classiques espagnols du Chant* (2 vols.; Paris, 1926); J. Subirá, *La tonadilla escénica* (3 vols.; Barcelona, 1928-30); J. Subirá, *Tonadillas teatrales inéditas* (Barcelona, 1932; contains score of Esteve's *Los signos del año).*

Estrada, Carlos, Uruguayan composer and conductor; b. Montevideo, Sept. 15, 1909. He studied in Paris with Roger-Ducasse and Henri Busser (composition); conducting with Philippe Gaubert. Returning to Montevideo, he organized a chamber orchestra (1936); also taught music history in schools. His works include many piano pieces, and *series antiguas* for strings.

Estrada, Juan Agustin. See **Garcia Estrada.**

Etler, Alvin Derald, American oboist and composer; b. Battle Creek, Iowa, Feb. 19, 1913; studied at the Univ. of Illinois, Western Reserve Univ., and Yale Univ. (Mus. B., 1944); was oboist in the Indianapolis Symph. Orch. (1938-40); taught at Yale (1942-46); at Cornell (1946-47); from 1947, on the staff of the Univ. of Illinois. He held two Guggenheim Fellowships (1941-42). His works include 2 sinfoniettas; a woodwind quintet; a suite for oboe, violin, viola, and cello; sonata for oboe, clarinet, and viola, etc.

Ett, Kaspar, German organist and composer; b. Eresing, Jan. 5, 1788; d. Munich, May 16, 1847, where from 1816, he was court organist at St. Michael's Church. He was active in reviving the church music of the 16th-17th centuries; his own sacred compositions (of which but a few graduals and *cantica sacra* were printed) follow these early works in style. He composed 273 separate works; a complete enumeration is given by F. Bierling, *Kaspar Ett* (1906). See also K. F. E. von Schafhäutl, *Erinnerungen an Kaspar Ett,* in 'Kirchenmusikalisches Jahrbuch' (1891).

Ettinger, Max, composer and conductor; b. Lwow, Dec. 27, 1874; d. Basel, July 19, 1951; studied in Berlin and Munich. He was active as conductor in Munich (1900-20), Leipzig (1920-29), and Berlin (1929-33). In 1938 he went to Switzerland, where he remained until his death.—Works: operas, *Judith* (Nuremberg, 1921), *Der eifersüchtige Trinker,* after Boccaccio (Nuremberg, 1925), *Juana* (Nuremberg, 1925), *Clavigo,* after Goethe (Leipzig, 1926), *Frühlings Erwachen* (Leipzig, 1928); oratorio, *Weisheit des*

Orients, after Omar Khayyam (Nuremberg, 1924); *Jewish Requiem* (1947); also chamber music and songs.

Euclid, the famous Greek geometer, lived at Alexandria about 300 B.C. He is the reputed author of a treatise on music, *Katatomè kanonos (Sectio canonis),* following the theories of Pythagoras (new critical ed. by K. von Jan in 'Musici scriptores graeci'). For another treatise long ascribed to Euclid, see the entry on Cleonides.

Eulenburg (oi-len-bŏŏrg), **Ernst,** German music publisher; b. Berlin, Nov. 30, 1847; d. Leipzig, Sept. 11, 1926. He studied at the Leipzig Cons.; established, in 1874, in Leipzig the publishing house bearing his name; after his acquisition of Payne's 'Kleine Partitur-Ausgabe' (1892) he enormously increased the scope of that publication so that large orchestral scores could be included. His son, **Kurt Eulenburg** (b. Berlin, Feb. 22, 1879), joined the firm in 1911; upon his father's death in 1926 he became the sole owner. He enlarged the number of editions in miniature score and included the original text ('Urtext') of some of Mozart's works, edited by Einstein, Blume, Kroyer, and others. In 1939 he went to Switzerland. On Sept. 28, 1939 he opened a new company in London with a branch in Zürich. He settled in London in Nov., 1945.

Euler, Leonhardt, famous scientist; b. Basel, April 15, 1707; d. St. Petersburg, Sept. 3, 1783. He was prof. of mathematics at St. Petersburg (1730) and Berlin (1741); published several important works on musical theory and acoustics, chief among them being the *Tentamen novae theoriae musicae* (1739). Euler was the first to employ logarithms to explain differences in pitch.—Cf. S. Schulz-Euler, *Leonhardt Euler* (Frankfurt, 1907); also Treubner's ed. of Euler's *Opera omnia,* series 3, vol. I (1926).

Euting (oi-tēng), **Ernst,** English musicologist; b. London, Feb. 7, 1874; d. Berlin, April 21, 1925. From 1892-6 he attended the Hochschule für Musik in Berlin, then devoted himself to musicology at the Univ. there, and became *Dr. phil.* with the thesis *Zur Geschichte der Blasinstrumente im 16. und 17. Jahrhundert* (1899); in the same year he founded the 'Deutsche Instrumentenbau-Zeitung,' of which he was the editor; also edited the 'Zeitschrift' of the 'Internationale Musik-Gesellschaft' (1902-3).

Evans, David Emlyn, Welsh music editor and composer; b. near Newcastle Emlyn, Wales, Sept. 21, 1843; d. London, April, 1913. He was established in business at Cheltenham, but devoted his leisure hours to music; took part in many Welsh music festivals (Eisteddfodau), his works invariably winning prizes; after the Eisteddfod at Wexham in 1876, where he carried off all four prizes, he voluntarily withdrew from further competitions, but frequently acted as judge; at the National Eisteddfod in London, 1887, he was awarded a prize for his *Biography of Welsh Musicians;* for many years he was editor of 'Y Cerddor' (The Musician). His chief work is *Alawon Fy Ngwlad* (2 vols., 1896), a collection of 500 Welsh airs in piano arrangements; his publ. comps. include 2 cantatas, *The Christian's Prayer* and *The Fairy-tribe,* many glees, anthems, and part-songs.

Evans, Edwin, Sr., English organist and writer; b. London, 1844; d. there, Dec. 21, 1923. An assiduous and thorough scholar, he publ. basic analytic volumes on Beethoven and Brahms: *Beethoven's 9 Symphonies, fully described and analyzed* (London, 1923-24), and the remarkable 4-vol. edition (1581 pages; over 1000 mus. examples), *Historical, Descriptive and Analytical Account of the Entire Works of Johannes Brahms:* vol I, vocal works (1912); vol. II, chamber and orchestral music up to op. 67 (1933; reprinted, 1950); vol. III, chamber and orchestral music from op. 68 to the end (1935; reprinted, 1949); vol. IV, piano works (1936; reprinted, 1950). Vols. II, III, and IV were publ. posthumously. He also wrote *Accompaniment of Plainchant* (1911); *Wagner's Teachings by Analogy* (1915); *How to Compose; How to Accompany at the Piano* (London, 1917); *Method of Instrumentation* (vol. I, *How to Write for Strings); Technics of the Organ* (London, 1938); transl. Wagner's *Oper und Drama;* made organ arrangements of operatic overtures.

Evans, Edwin, Jr., English writer on music; son of the preceding; b. London, Sept. 1, 1874; d. there, March 3, 1945. He studied in Lille and at Echternach for a business career; was engaged in telegraphy, railroads, and finance from 1889 to 1913; then devoted himself exclusively to musical pursuits. He was music critic of the 'Pall Mall Gazette' (1914-23); editor of 'Music News and Herald' (1921-22); editor of 'The Dominant' (1931) and music critic of the London 'Daily Mail' (1931). He was one of the founders of the International Society for Contemporary Music (1922); in 1938 was elected its president, retaining this post until his death.—Books: *Tchaikovsky* (in the 'Master Musicians' series; London, 1906; reprint, 1921;

revised ed., 1935; reprint, 1949); *The Margin of Music* (London, 1924); *Stravinsky's Firebird and Petrouchka,* an analysis (London, 1933); *Music and the Dance* (posthumous; London, 1948). See the editorial, *Edwin Evans,* in the 'Mus. Times' (April, 1945).

Evans, Nancy, English mezzo-soprano; b. Liverpool, March 19, 1915. She studied with Maggie Teyte; made her début in London; sang at Glyndebourne in 1938; has made tours in Europe and in the Middle East. In 1949 she married the writer Eric Crozier.

Evesham (ēvz'm), **Walter of.** See **Odington.**

Evseyev, Sergey Vassilievitch, Russian composer and pedagogue; b. Moscow, Jan. 24, 1893; d. there, June, 1956. He studied piano with L. Conus and theory with Medtner; then at the Moscow Cons. with Goldenweiser (piano) and Taneyev (composition). In 1922 he was appointed instructor (later prof.) at the Moscow Cons. He wrote a symphony; violin pieces (*Idylle,* etc.); songs.

Ewen (ū'-ĕhn), **David,** prolific writer on music; b. Lwow, Poland, Nov. 26, 1907; came to the U. S. in 1912; attended the College of the City of N. Y.; pupil of Max Persin in harmony and counterpoint; studied at the Music School Settlement and Columbia Univ.; was musical editor of 'Reflex Magazine' (1928-29), 'The American Hebrew' (1935) and 'Cue' (1937).—Books: *The Unfinished Symphony* (1931); *Hebrew Music* (1931); *Wine, Women, and Waltz* (1933); *Composers of Today* (1934); *The Man with the Baton* (1936); *Composers of Yesterday* (1937); *Men and Women Who Make Music* (1939); *Musical Vienna* (with Frederic Ewen; 1939); *Living Musicians* (1940); *Pioneers in Music* (1941); *Music Comes to America* (1942; revised, 1947); *Dictators of the Baton* (1943; revised, 1948); *Men of Popular Music* (1944; revised, 1952); *Music for the Millions* (1944; revised, 1946, 1949; published under title *Encyclopedia of Musical Masterpieces,* 1950); *American Composers Today* (revised ed., 1949); *The Story of Irving Berlin* (1950); *The Story of Arturo Toscanini* (1951; in Italian, Milan, 1952); *Fun with Musical Games and Quizzes* (with Slonimsky, 1952); *The Complete Book of 20th Century Music* (1952); *European Composers Today* (1953); *The Story of Jerome Kern* (1953); *The Milton Cross Encyclopedia of Great Composers and Their Music* (with Milton Cross, 1953); *Encyclopedia of the Opera* (1955); *A Journey to Greatness, George Gershwin* (1956); *Panorama of American Popular Music* (1957); edited *From Bach to Stravinsky* (1933) and *The Book of Modern Composers* (N. Y., 1943; rev., 1950).

Excestre, William, English singer and composer who flourished c. 1390-1410. He was clerk of the Chapel Royal in 1393, and received a prebend in St. Stephen's, Westminster, in 1394. He was one of the composers whose music is contained in the 'Old Hall Manuscript'; a Gloria, a Credo, and a Sanctus (all for 3 voices) are extant.

Eximeno (y Pujades), Antonio, one of the most important Spanish writers on music; b. Valencia, Sept. 26, 1729; d. Rome, June 9, 1808; entered the Company of Jesus at the age of 16; became prof. of rhetoric at the Univ. of Valencia; 1764, appointed prof. of mathematics at the military academy in Segovia. When the Jesuits were expelled from Spain in 1767 he went to Rome, and in 1768 began to study music. In 1774 he publ. *Dell' origine e delle regole della musica colla storia del suo progresso, decadenza e rinnovazione* (Rome; Spanish transl. by Gutierrez, 1776, 3 vols.), in which he protested against pedantic rules and argued that music should be based on the natural rules of prosody. His theories were strongly controverted, especially by Padre Martini; in answer to the latter, Eximeno publ. *Dubbio di Antonio Eximeno sopra il Saggio fondamentale, pratico di contrappunto del Maestro Giambattista Martini* (Rome, 1775). His dictum that the national song should serve as a basis for the art-music of each country was taken up by Pedrell and led to the nationalist movement in modern Spanish music. Eximeno also wrote a satirical musical novel, *Don Lazarillo Vizcardi,* directed against the theories of Pietro Cerone (publ. by Barbieri, 1872-3, 2 vols.).—Cf. F. Pedrell, *Padre Antonio Eximeno* (Barcelona, 1921).

Expert (ex-pär'), **Henry,** eminent French music editor; b. Bordeaux, May 12, 1863; d. Tourettes-sur-Loup (Alpes-Maritimes), Aug. 18, 1952. He attended a Jesuit school in Bordeaux; went to Paris in 1881 and studied with César Franck and Eugène Gigout; taught at the École Nationale de Musique Classique, and lectured at the École des Hautes Études Sociales; from 1909, deputy-librarian of the Paris Cons.; chief of the library in 1921; founder (1903, with Maury) of the 'Société d'études musicales et concerts historiques,' also of the choral society 'Chanterie de la Renaissance' (1924). In 1933 he retired. His life-work was the editing and publication of Franco-Flemish music of the 15th and 16th centuries, in ten parts: I. *Les Maîtres-*

Musiciens de la Renaissance française (works by Orlando di Lasso, Goudimel, Costeley, Janequin, Brumel, La Rue, Mouton, Fevin, Mauduit, Claude Le Jeune, Regnart, Du Caurroy, Gervaise, and Attaingnant's collection of chansons, all in modern notation, with facsimiles, etc.; 23 vols. publ., 1894-1908); II. *Bibliographie thématique* (2 vols., catalogue of publications of Attaingnant); III. *Les Théoriciens de la musique au temps de la Renaissance* (works of Michel de Menhou); IV. 2 vols. of music by Antoine de Bertrand; V. *Commentaires;* VI. *Extraits des Maîtres Musiciens* (selected single compositions, arranged for modern use; a large number have been publ., including works by some composers not found in Part I, viz.: Bertrand, Bonnet, Certon, De La Grotte, Gardanne, Josquin des Prez, Le Heurteur, Le Pelletier, Passereau, Thoinot-Arbeau); VII. Vol. 3 of music by Antoine de Bertrand; VIII. Works by Claude Le Jeune; IX. Works by Goudimel; X. Works by Paschal de l'Estocart. In 1924 Expert began the publication of a new series of French music of the 16th century entitled *Monuments de la musique française au temps de la Renaissance* (with scores in modern notation), of which 10 vols. were published; these contain works by Le Jeune, in 2 vols. *(Octonaires de la vanité et inconstance du monde)*, Certon (3 Masses), Le Blanc (*Airs de plusieurs musiciens)*, Bertrand, in 4 vols. *(Amours de P. de Ronsard)*, Goudimel *(Messes à 4 voix)*, L'Estocart *(Octonaires de la vanité du monde)*. Expert also edited *Chansons mondaines des XVIIe et XVIIIe siècles français* (30 songs), *Airs français des XVIe et XVIIe siècles* (Boesset, Guedron, Tessier, Lambert), *Florilège du concert vocal de la Renaissance* (1928-29), in 8 parts (Janequin, Lassus, Costeley, Bonnet, Le Jeune, Mauduit), *Les Maîtres du clavecin des XVIIe et XVIIIe siècles* (Dandrieu, Daquin, Corrette), *Amusements des Maîtres français du XVIIIe siècle* (Chédeville, J. Aubert, Baton), *Répertoire de musique religieuse et spirituelle* (Campra, Charpentier, Dumont, Lully, Bernier, Couperin le Grand, Clérambault, Lalande, Rameau, etc.), *La Fleur des musiciens de P. de Ronsard* (1923), instrumental *Fantaisies* by Le Jeune and Du Caurroy; and *Le Pseautier huguenot du XVIe siècle* (the Huguenot Psalter; 1902). He contributed the chapter on the music of France during the 16th century to Lavignac's 'Encyclopédie de la Musique.'

Eybler (ī'-bler), **Joseph** (later **Edler von Eybler**), Austrian composer; b. Schwechat, near Vienna, Feb. 8, 1764; d. Schönbrunn, July 24, 1846. He studied with Albrechtsberger in Vienna; was a friend of Haydn and Mozart; in 1792, became choirmaster at the Carmelite Church; was tutor to the princes in 1810, and first court Kapellmeister in 1824, on Salieri's retirement. He composed symphonies, concertos, quartets, sonatas, etc.; also 2 oratorios, 32 Masses, a Requiem, 7 Te Deums, and 30 offertories.

Eyken (Eijken), Jan Albert van, Dutch organist; b. Amersfoort, April 26, 1823; d. Elberfeld, Sept. 24, 1868. He studied at the Leipzig Cons., and afterwards at Dresden with Schneider. In 1848, he became organist of the Remonstrantenkerk, Amsterdam; in 1853, of the Zuyderkerk, and teacher at the music school in Rotterdam; in 1854, he became organist at Elberfeld. His organ pieces (150 chorales with introductions, 25 preludes, a toccata and fugue on B-A-C-H, 3 sonatas, variations, transcriptions, etc.) are well and favorably known.

Eymieu (ā-m'yö), **Henry,** French composer and writer on music; b. Saillans, Drôme, May 7, 1860; d. Paris, March 21, 1931. He studied law; then turned to music, taking lessons with Widor; settling in Paris, he wrote for 'Le Ménestrel' and other musical publications; publ. *Études et biographies musicales* (Paris, 1892); composed a great variety of piano pieces, songs, and duets for piano and violin (58 published opus numbers in all); also produced a stage piece, *Un Mariage sous Néron* (Paris, 1898), and an oratorio, *Marthe et Marie* (Asnières, 1898).

Eysler, Edmund S., Austrian operetta composer; b. Vienna, March 12, 1874; d. there, Oct. 4, 1949. He produced a great number of stage works; in 1915 he wrote no fewer than four operettas *(Leutnant Gustl, Der grosse Gabriel, Ein Tag im Paradies, Die oder Keine)*. His most successful operetta was *Bruder Straubinger* (Vienna, Feb. 20, 1903; over 100 performances in that year). Other successful operettas: *Pufferl* (Vienna, April 13, 1905); *Künstlerblut* (1906); *Das Glückschweinchen* (1908); *Der unsterbliche Lump* (1910); *Das Zirkuskind* (1911); and *Die goldene Meisterin* (Vienna, Sept. 13, 1927).—Cf. R. Prosl, *Edmund Eysler* (Vienna, 1947).

F

Faber, Heinrich (known as 'Magister Henricus Faber'), German theorist; b. Lichtenfels, c. 1520; d. Ölsnitz, Saxony, Feb. 26, 1552. He entered the Univ. of Wittenberg in 1542; received the degree of Master of Liberal Arts in 1545; was then rector of the school of St. George's Monastery near Naumburg; in 1551 was appointed lecturer at Wittenberg Univ.; then was rector at Ölsnitz. He publ. *Compendiolum musicae pro incipientibus* (1548; reprinted many times and also issued in German transl. as *Musica, Kurtzer Inhalt der Singkunst,* 1572; edited by Adam Gumpelzhaimer and publ. as *Compendium musicae pro illius artis tironibus,* 1591). Faber further publ. *Ad Musicam practicam introductio* (1550); a *Musica poetica* remains in manuscript.

Fabini, Eduardo, Uruguayan composer; b. Solís del Mataojo, May 18, 1883; d. Montevideo, May 17, 1950. He studied violin in Montevideo, and later in Europe with César Thomson at the Brussels Cons., winning first prize; then gave concerts as a violinist in South America, and in the U. S. (1926); eventually returned to Montevideo, and was active there as composer and educator.—Works (all first performed in Montevideo): the ballets *Mburucuyá* (April 15, 1933) and *Mañana de Reyes* (July 31, 1937); symph. poem *Campo* (April 29, 1922); overture, *La Isla de los Ceibos* (Sept. 14, 1926); *Melga sinfónica* (Oct. 11, 1931); *Fantasia* for violin and orch. (Aug. 22, 1929); choral works; piano pieces; songs. His music is inspired entirely by South American folklore; the idiom is mildly modernistic, with lavish use of whole-tone scales and other external devices of impressionism.

Fabricius (făh-brē'-tsē-ŏŏs), **Johann Albert,** eminent bibliographer; son of Werner Fabricius; b. Leipzig, Nov. 11, 1668; d. Hamburg, April 30, 1736. A learned man, he was professor of elocution; publ. important books of reference, valuable to musicology for the information they contain on musical topics: *Thesaurus antiquitatum hebraicarum* (1713, 7 vols.); *Bibliotheca latina mediae et infimae aetatis* (1712-22; 2nd ed., 1734; 6 vols.); *Bibliotheca graeca sive notitia scriptorum veterum graecorum* (1705-28, 14 vols.).

Fabricius, Werner, German composer; b. Itzehoe, April 10, 1633; d. Leipzig, Jan. 9, 1679. He studied with Thomas Selle and Heinrich Scheidemann in Hamburg; then took courses in law in Leipzig, where he also served as organist of the Nicolaikirche and Paulinerkirche. He publ. a collection of pavanes, allemandes, etc., for viols and other instruments, under the title *Deliciae harmonicae* (Leipzig, 1656); *Geistliche Lieder* (Jena, 1659); *Geistliche Arien, Dialogen, Concerten, etc.* (Leipzig, 1662); motets, etc.

Faccio (făh'-tchŏh), **Franco,** Italian composer and conductor; b. Verona, March 8, 1840; d. near Monza, July 21, 1891. His first teacher was G. Bernasconi; from 1855-64 he studied at Milan Cons.; Arrigo Boito was his fellow-pupil and friend; they wrote together a patriotic music drama, *Le Sorelle d'Italia,* which was produced by the students, and served together under Garibaldi in 1866. His first opera was *I profughi fiamminghi* (La Scala, Nov. 11, 1863); this was followed by the Shakespearian opera *Amleto,* for which Boito wrote the libretto (Genoa, May 30, 1865). In 1866-68 Faccio made a tour in Scandinavia as symphonic conductor; in 1868 he became prof. at Milan Cons., and in 1871 succeeded Terziani as conductor at La Scala; on April 25, 1886, he conducted for the 1000th time there. His performances of Verdi's operas were regarded as most authentic; he gave the world première of *Otello* at La Scala (1887).—Cf. R. de Rensis, *Franco Faccio e Verdi* (Milan, 1934).

Fachiri, Adila, Hungarian violinist; grandniece of Joachim; sister of Yelly d'Aranyi; b. Budapest, Feb. 26, 1888. She studied with Joachim, and received from him a Stradivarius violin. In 1909 she settled in London, where she married Alexander Fachiri, a lawyer. She has appeared many times with her sister in duets; on April 3, 1930, the sisters gave in London the first performance of Holst's Concerto for 2 violins, written especially for them.

Faelten, Carl, pianist and teacher; brother of Reinhold Faelten; b. Ilmenau, Thuringia, Dec. 21, 1846; d. Readfield, Maine, July 20, 1925. He studied with Montag (a pupil of Hummel) at Weimar as a school boy; violin with J. Schoch at Frankfurt, and profited by advice from Raff. From 1878-82 he taught at the Hoch Cons. in Frankfurt; then was engaged at the Peabody Inst., Baltimore (1882-5); at the New England Cons., Boston (1885-97); was its director from 1890 until 1897, when he founded the Faelten Pianoforte School in Boston. He publ. *The Conservatory Course for Pianoforte* (an original series, 1888); *Fundamental Training Course for Pianoforte* (in collaboration with his brother, Reinhold Faelten; 1895); also *Technische Übungen* for piano: *30 Characteristic Studies* (transcribed from the violin sonatas of Bach); *30 Instructive Pieces* by G. F. Handel; transcriptions of 6 songs by Schubert; etc.

Faelten, Reinhold, pianist and teacher; b. Ilmenau, Thuringia, Jan. 17, 1856; d. Worcester, Mass., July 17, 1949. A pupil of Klughard and Gottschalk at Weimar; taught in Frankfurt, Baltimore, and Boston; founded, in 1897, with his brother Carl Faelten, the Faelten Pianoforte School in Boston. Jointly with his brother, he wrote several books on the Faelten method: *100 Ear-training Exercises; Keyboard Harmony;* also a *Transposition System.*

Fagan, Gideon, South African conductor and composer; b. Somerset West, Cape Province, Nov. 3, 1904. He studied in Cape Town with W. H. Bell and later in London at the Royal College of Music, where his teachers were Vaughan Williams and Kitson. He began to conduct at the age of 18, mainly for the theater and the cinema. In 1949 he was appointed associate conductor of the Johannesburg Opera Co. He has written *Afrikaans Folktune Suite* for orch. and various pieces of a descriptive nature.

Fago, Nicola, Italian composer, called 'Il Tarantino'; b. Taranto, Feb. 26, 1677; d. Naples, Feb. 18, 1745. He studied (from 1693) with Provenzale at the Cons. 'della Pietà' in Naples, becoming Provenzale's assistant in 1697 and succeeding him in 1705. From 1704-8 he was maestro di cappella at the Cons. 'di Sant' Onofrio'; from 1709-31, maestro di cappella at the Tesoro di San Gennaro. He retired on a modest pension in 1740. He was the teacher of Leonardo Leo, Francesco Feo, Jommelli, and Sala. He composed four operas: *Radamisto* (1707), *Astarto* (1709), *La Cassandra indovina* (1711), and *Lo Masillo* (1712); two oratorios, *Faraone sommerso* and *Il monte fiorito;* a *Te Deum* and other sacred music, much of it still preserved in MS in Naples, Paris, and London. His son **Lorenzo Fago** (b. Naples, Aug. 13, 1704; d. there, April 30, 1793), an organist and composer, was his successor at the Tesoro di San Gennaro (1731-66 and 1771-80), and taught at the Cons. 'della Pietà dei Turchini' for 56 years (1737-93) until his death.—Cf. E. Faustini-Fasini, *Nicola Fago, il Tarantino e la sua famiglia* (Taranto, 1931).

Fahrbach, Philipp, Austrian conductor; b. Vienna, Oct. 25, 1815; d. there, March 31, 1885. He was a pupil of Lanner; conducted his own orch. for years, and then a military band. His dances (over 150 works) were very popular. His three brothers, his son, and his nephews were all active as band musicians.—Cf. Ph. Fahrbach, *Alt-Wiener Erinnerungen* (Vienna, 1935).

Faignient (fā-nahn), **Noë,** Flemish 16th-century contrapuntist; d. about 1595. His compositions, written in the style of Orlando di Lasso, consist of 2 sets of chansons, madrigals, and motets for 4, 5, and 6 voices (1568; 1569). Two of his madrigals are included in Maldeghem's *Trésor musical.*

Fairchild, Blair, American composer; b. Belmont, Mass., June 23, 1877; d. Paris, April 23, 1933. He studied with J. K. Paine and Walter Spalding at Harvard Univ.; then in Florence with Buonamici; employed for a number of years in the U. S. diplomatic service in Turkey and Persia, then turned again to music and completed his studies in Paris with Widor; lived mostly in Paris. He wrote the ballet *Dame Libellule* (Paris Opéra-Comique, 1921); *Le Songe d'Isfendiar,* ballet pantomime; and *Belebat,* a ballet which was completed after his death by Louis Aubert and performed in Paris in 1938.—Works for orch.: *East and West,* orchestral poem (1908); the symph. poems *Zal, Tamineh* (after a Persian legend), and *Shah Feridoun; Etude Symphonique* for violin and orch.; *Rhapsody* on old Hebrew melodies for violin and orch.; violin sonatas, piano trio, string quartet, piano quintet; 6 Psalms for soli and chorus; 2 Biblical Lyrics for soli, chorus, and orch.; Requiem for tenor and male chorus; *In Memoriam* for soli and chorus; 5 sets of *Stornelli Toscani* (very popular); many song cycles (*Persian Folk Songs, Five Sea Prayers,* etc.) and other songs showing oriental influences; 2 organ fugues; violin pieces; piano pieces (the suites *En Voyage, From a Balcony,* and *Chants Nègres; Indian Songs and Dances; Été à Fontainebleau; 2 Garden Sketches;* etc.).—Cf. W. T. Upton, *Art-Song in America* (N. Y., 1930; pp. 169-76). See also W. T. Upton, *Our Musical Expatriates,* in the 'Mus. Quarterly' (Jan., 1928).

Fairclough, George Herbert, organist and composer; b. Hamilton, Canada, Jan. 30, 1869; d. Saratoga, Calif., March 27, 1954. He studied at Toronto Cons. (1887-90) and at the Hochschule für Musik, Berlin, with Karl Heinrich Barth and with Bargiel. From 1900 until 1937 he was organist at St. John's Episcopal Church, St. Paul; concurrently taught organ at the Univ. of Minnesota (1917-37); then retired. He published a *Te Deum* (1912); *Jubilate; Eventide,* for organ (1919); *Song of Happiness,* for organ (1929); *Communion Service* (1932) and many other sacred works.

Fairlamb, James Remington, American composer; b. Philadelphia, Jan. 23, 1838; d. Ingleside, N. Y., April 16, 1908. As a youth he played organ in several Philadelphia churches; in 1858 went to Paris; studied piano there with Marmontel. While in Europe, he was appointed by Abraham

Lincoln as American Consul at Zürich (1861) and stayed in Zürich until 1865, when he returned to the U. S. He organized an amateur opera company in Washington with which he brought out his 4-act grand opera *Valérie*. From 1872-98 he was church organist in Philadelphia, Jersey City, and New York. Besides *Valérie,* he wrote another grand opera *Lionello* (which was never performed) and three light operas: *Love's Stratagem, The Interrupted Marriage,* and *Treasured Tokens;* some 50 of his choral works and nearly 150 songs and organ pieces are published. He was one of the founders of the American Guild of Organists.

Faisst (fīst), **Immanuel Gottlob Friedrich,** German composer; b. Esslingen, Württemberg, Oct. 13, 1823; d. Stuttgart, June 5, 1894. He studied theology at Tübingen, and also learned to play the organ. He was encouraged by Mendelssohn to undertake a serious study of music, and subsequently took lessons with Dehn in Berlin. He became active as choral conductor and organist; organized a society for classical church music (1847) in Stuttgart, where he settled. He was the founder of the 'Schwäbischer Sängerbund' (1849); with Lebert, Stark, Brachmann, and others he established the Stuttgart Cons. (1857); became its director in 1859. He received a *Dr. phil.* at Tübingen Univ. for his essay *Beiträge zur Geschichte der Klaviersonate* ('Cäcilia,' 1846; reprinted in the 'Neues Beethovenjahrbuch' 1924, 1). He was the editor (with Lebert) of the famous edition of classical piano works, *Instruktive ausgewählte classische Werke,* publ. by Cotta; also (with Stark) of *Elementar- und Chorgesangschule* (2 vols.; Stuttgart, 1880-82). Faisst was a prolific composer; a number of his songs, ballads, choral works, etc., were publ. during his lifetime, but then were completely forgotten. He also publ. several school manuals on harmony.

Falchi, Stanislao, Italian composer; b. Terni, Jan. 29, 1851; d. Rome, Nov. 14, 1922. He studied in Rome with C. Maggi and S. Meluzzi; in 1877 he became a teacher at Santa Cecilia; from 1902 till 1915 was its director. Among his pupils were A. Bonaventura, A. Bustini, V. Gui, B. Molinari, L. Refice, and F. Santoliquido. He wrote the operas *Lorhelia* (Rome, Dec. 4, 1877), *Giuditta* (Rome, March 12, 1887), and *Il Trillo del diavolo* (Rome, Jan. 29, 1899); also a *Requiem* for the funeral of Victor Emmanuel II (Jan. 17, 1883).

Falcon (fāhl-kohn'), **Marie-Cornélie,** remarkable French dramatic soprano; b. Paris, Jan. 28, 1814; d. there, Feb. 25, 1897. She was a pupil of Bordogni and A. Nourrit; made her début at the Paris Opéra on July 20, 1832, as Alice in *Robert le Diable*. She sang at the Paris Opéra with brilliant success until 1837, when, though still a very young woman, she unaccountably lost her voice. After many attempts to regain her vocal powers, including quack medicines and bogus treatment of all sorts, she was forced to abandon the stage, and retired to her villa near Paris; she lived another sixty years. Despite the brevity of her active career, her singing of such roles as Valentine in *Les Huguenots* and Rachel in *La Juive* became a legendary memory, so that the description "Falcon type" was applied to singers who excelled in her roles.

Falconieri, Andrea, Italian composer and lutenist; b. Naples, 1586; d. there, July 29, 1656. He was in the service of the house of Farnese at Parma; studied with Santino Garsi there until 1614; in 1615 was in Florence; 1616, in Rome; 1619, again in Florence; 1620-21, at the court of Modena; then traveled in Spain and France; 1629-35, again at Parma; from 1639, maestro di cappella at the royal court, Naples; 1642, in Genoa; 1650, in Naples. His *Libro Primo di Villanelle a 1, 2 e 3 voci* (with alphabetical tablature for Spanish guitar) was publ. at Rome, 1616 (reprinted by Gardano at Venice); various other books followed, the *Libro V delle Musiche* appearing in 1619; probably one of his last works was the valuable instrumental collection *Primo Libro di Canzone, Sinfonie, Fantasie, Capricci . . . per Violini e Viole, overo altri Strumenti à 1, 2 e 3 voci con il basso continuo* (Naples, 1650). Reprints: arias (2 books) in the 'Raccolta nazionale delle musiche italiane'; in A. Parisotti's 'Arie antiche' and 'Piccolo Album di Musica Antica'; in L. Torchi's 'Eleganti Canzoni ed Arie italiane del secolo XVII'; and 'L'Arte Musicale in Italia' (vol. VII); *17 Arie a una voce,* publ. by G. Benvenuti; *2 Villanelle a 3,* ed. by C. Sabatini; 4 songs in *La Flora,* ed. by Knud Jeppesen (Copenhagen, 1949).—Cf. L. Valdrighi, *Atti* (1883; p. 488); L. Torchi, in 'Rivista Musicale Italiana' (1898; p. 65).

Falk, Richard, opera conductor; b. Moringen, Germany, April 29, 1886; studied at the Leipzig Cons. with Jadassohn and Riemann; conducting with Nikisch. After graduation in 1908 he began to conduct theater orchestras in Berlin and other German cities; from 1933-38 he conducted the International Chamber Opera at the Palazzo Doria in Rome; in 1939 he settled in the U. S. He has adapted and produced a number of 18th-century Italian operas.

Falkner, Donald Keith, English bass singer; b. Sawston, Cambridge, March 1, 1900. He was a chorister at New College School in Cambridge; then served in the Royal Navy during World War I. It was only after the end of the war that he began to study singing seriously, taking lessons with Plunkett Greene in London, Lierhammer in Vienna, and also in Paris, with Dossert. He made his professional début in Portsmouth (1922); American début in New York (1930); has been particularly successful in modern English and Elizabethan songs.

Fall, Fritz, Austrian conductor, nephew of Leo Fall; b. Vienna, July 25, 1901; studied at the Vienna Academy; was opera conductor in Austria, Germany, and Czechoslovakia (1925-37); in 1937 he went to America; 1938-42, conducted and taught in Tyler, Texas; during World War II was with the Office of Strategic Services of the U. S.; 1945-48, with the Allied Military Government in Europe; from 1948, teaching and conducting (Dept. of Agriculture Symph. Orch.) in Washington, D. C. He changed his first name from Fritz to Frederick after becoming an American citizen.

Fall, Leo, Austrian composer of light opera; b. Olmütz, Feb. 2, 1873; d. Vienna, Sept. 15, 1925. His father was a military bandmaster, and it was from him that Leo Fall received his training in practical music making; then he took up academic courses at the Vienna Cons., with Johann Fuchs and others. For some years he was theater conductor in Berlin, Hamburg, and Cologne, but lived for most of his life in Vienna. His operettas are typical Viennese products, light-hearted, romantic, and melodious. Although they never reached the height of international success obtained by such masters of the genre as Lehár, at least one of them, *Die Dollarprinzessin* (Vienna, Nov. 2, 1907), was famous for many years. The list of his operettas includes also *Der fidele Bauer* (Mannheim, July 27, 1907), *Eternal Waltz* (London, Dec. 22, 1911), *Die Rose von Stambul* (Vienna, Dec. 2, 1916), and *Mme Pompadour* (Vienna, March 2, 1923). His operetta *Der Rebell,* a failure at its first production (Vienna, Nov. 29, 1905), was revised and staged under the new title *Der liebe Augustin* (Berlin, Feb. 3, 1912), scoring excellent success.

Falla (făh'-yăh), **Manuel de,** one of the greatest Spanish composers; b. Cádiz, Nov. 23, 1876; d. Alta Gracia, in the province of Córdoba, Argentina, Nov. 14, 1946. He studied with J. Tragó (piano) and F. Pedrell (composition) in Madrid; composed some zarzuelas, which he later discarded. His opera, *La Vida breve,* won the prize awarded by the Academia de Bellas Artes, Madrid, in 1905; in that year he also won the Ortiz y Cussó Prize for pianists. In 1907 he went to Paris, where he became friendly with Debussy, Dukas, and Ravel, who aided and encouraged him. Under their influence he adopted the principles of impressionism without, however, giving up his personal and national style; in 1914, returned to Spain and in 1921 made his home in Granada, frequently touring Europe as conductor of his own works. In May, 1938, he was made President of the Instituto de España. In 1939, at the end of the Spanish Civil War, he went to Argentina; after conducting a few concerts of his music in Buenos Aires, he withdrew to the small locality of Alta Gracia, where he lived the last years of his life in seclusion. His art is rooted both in the folksongs of Spain and in the purest historical traditions of Spanish music. Up to 1919 his works were cast chiefly in the Andalusian idiom, and his instrumental technique was often conditioned by effects peculiar to Spain's national instrument, the guitar. In *El Retablo de Maese Pedro* he turns to the classical tradition of Spanish (especially Castilian) music; the keyboard style of his harpsichord concerto shows, in the classical lucidity of its writing, a certain kinship with Domenico Scarlatti (who lived in Spain for many years). Falla taught composition privately, his most gifted pupils being Ernesto Halffter and Joaquín Nin-Culmell.—Works: The opera *La Vida breve* (Nice, April 1, 1913; Metropolitan Opera, N. Y., March 7, 1926); *El Retablo de Maese Pedro,* for marionettes and singers (performed in Seville, in concert form, 1919; Paris, privately, at home of Princesse de Polignac, 1923; first complete public performance, Madrid, March 23, 1923); the ballets *El Amor brujo* (Madrid, April 15, 1915; a tremendously effective work; numerous performances as an orchestral suite) and *El Sombrero de tres picos* (London, July 22, 1919; very successful); *Noches en los jardines de España* for piano and orch. (1909-15; Madrid, April 9, 1916); Concerto for harpsichord (or piano), flute, oboe, clarinet, violin, and cello, written at the suggestion of Wanda Landowska (Barcelona, Nov. 5, 1926; composer conducting; Wanda Landowska soloist); *Homenajes,* in 4 parts: 1. *Pour le Tombeau de Debussy* (originally for guitar, 1920); 2. *Fanfare pour Arbós* (1933); 3.

Pour le Tombeau de Paul Dukas (originally for piano, 1935); 4. *Pedrelliana* (1938; first performance of the entire suite, Buenos Aires, Nov. 18, 1939, composer conducting); for piano: *4 Pièces espagnoles: Aragonesa, Cubana, Montañesa, Andaluza; Fantasia Bética;* songs: *Trois mélodies* (1909); *Siete canciones populares españolas* (1914); very popular); *Psyché,* for voice, flute, harp, violin, viola, and cello (1924); *Soneto a Córdoba,* for voice and harp (1927). A large work for soli, chorus, and orch., based on M. J. Verdaguer's Catalan poem *La Atlantida,* begun in 1928, was never completed. — Cf. G. Jean-Aubry, *Manuel de Falla* in the 'Mus. Times' (April, 1917); M. Castelnuovo-Tedesco, in 'Il pianoforte' (Jan., 1923); E. Istel, *Manuel de Falla,* in the 'Mus. Quarterly' (Oct., 1926); Roland-Manuel, *Manuel de Falla* (Paris, 1930); J. B. Trend, *Manuel de Falla and Spanish Music* (N. Y., 1929; new ed., 1934); G. Chase, *Falla's Music for Piano Solo,* in the 'Chesterian' (1940); Jaime Pahissa, *Vida y obra de Manuel de Falla* (Buenos Aires, 1947; also publ. in English, London, 1954); J. M. Thomas, *Manuel de Falla en la Isla* (Palma, 1947); J. Jaenisch, *Manuel de Falla und die Spanische Musik* (Freiburg, 1952); Kurt Pahlen, *Manuel de Falla und die Musik in Spanien* (Olten, 1953). Falla's writings on music were collected and edited by F. Sopeña and publ. as *Escritos sobre música y músicos* (Buenos Aires, 1950).

Faller, Nikola, Croatian conductor and composer; b. Varaždin, April 22, 1862; d. Zagreb, Feb. 28, 1938. He studied with Bruckner in Vienna and with Massenet in Paris. He was active as opera conductor in Split and Zagreb; composed choral works and dances.

Famintsyn (fah-min-tsÿn), **Alexander Sergeyevitch,** Russian critic and composer; b. Kaluga, Nov. 5, 1841; d. Ligovo, near St. Petersburg, July 6, 1896; studied with Jean Vogt in St. Petersburg, and then with Hauptmann and Richter in Leipzig. He taught music history at the St. Petersburg Cons. (1865-72); translated into Russian the textbooks *Allgemeine Musiklehre* by Marx and *Harmonielehre* by Richter. However, he soon abandoned his teaching activities and devoted himself chiefly to music criticism, taking a very conservative attitude; he indulged in frequent polemics against the Russian composers of the National School; Mussorgsky caricatured Famintsyn in his satirical song *The Classicist* and in a section of his burlesque *Rayok.* Famintsyn's publications on Russian instruments are valuable; he publ. essays on the gusli (1890) and the domra (1891). He was also a composer; his opera *Sardanapal* was produced in St. Petersburg on Dec. 5, 1875, but without any success; his other opera, *Uriel Acosta* (1883), was not performed. He further wrote a piano quintet, a string quartet, and some songs.

Fanciulli (fan-chŏŏ'-lē), **Francesco,** Italian conductor and composer; b. Porto San Stefano, July 17, 1850; d. New York, July 17, 1915. He studied in Florence; after some years as opera conductor in Italy, he came to America (1876) and earned his living as organist and theatrical conductor; in 1893 he succeeded Sousa as conductor of the Marine Band in Washington; was then bandmaster of the 71st Regiment, N. Y. (1898-1904); after that conducted his own band. He wrote an opera *Priscilla,* which was produced in Norfolk, Va. (Nov. 1, 1901); also two comic operas.

Fanelli, Ernest, French composer, b. Paris, June 29, 1860; d. there, Nov. 24, 1917. He played drums in orchestras as a small boy; entered the Paris Cons. in 1876, in the class of Delibes. He worked as a copyist and music engraver for many years; in 1912 he applied to Gabriel Pierné for work, submitting the score of his own symph. poem *Thèbes* as a specimen of his handwriting. This score, composed by Fanelli as early as 1883, seemed to anticipate the instrumental and harmonic usages of Debussy and other composers of impressionist music, and Pierné decided to perform it as a curiosity; he conducted it at the Colonne concert in Paris (March 17, 1912), and the novelty created a mild sensation in French musical circles; other works by Fanelli (*Impressions pastorales; L'Effroi du Soleil; Suite rabelaisienne,* etc.), all written before 1893, were also found interesting. However, the sensation proved of brief duration, and the extravagant claims for Fanelli's talent collapsed.—Cf. M.-D. Calvocoressi, *An Unknown Composer of Today,* in the 'Mus. Times' (April, 1912).

Faning, Eaton, English conductor and composer; b. Helston, Cornwall, May 20, 1850; d. Brighton, Oct. 28, 1927. He studied at the Royal Academy of Music, London, with Sterndale Bennett and Arthur Sullivan, winning the Mendelssohn Scholarship (1873) and the Lucas medal (1876); received Mus. Bac., Cambridge (1894) and Mus. Doc. (1899). From 1878 he taught piano at the Royal Academy of Music; in 1885 became music director at Harrow School (until 1901); thereafter occupied various educational posts, and was a member of examination boards. He wrote a symphony, some chamber music, and several operettas. An account of his career is found in the 'Mus. Times' of Aug., 1901.

Fano, Guido Alberto, Italian composer and writer on music; b. Padua, May 18, 1875. He studied with Pollini in Padua and Martucci in Bologna; at the same time he took courses in law; became *Dr. juris* of Bologna Univ. in 1898. In 1900 he was appointed teacher of piano at the Liceo Musicale in Bologna; was director of the Cons. of Parma (1905-11); then taught piano at Naples (1912-17), Palermo (1917-21), and Milan (1921-38). He wrote an opera *Iuturna;* a symph. poem *La Tentazione di Gesù;* also publ. several books: *Pensieri sulla musica* (Bologna, 1903); *Nella vita del ritmo* (Naples, 1916); *Lo studio del pianoforte* (3 vols.; Milan, 1923-34).

Fara, Giulio, Italian writer on music and composer; b. Cagliari, Sardinia, Dec. 3, 1880; d. Pesaro, Oct. 9, 1949. He studied singing and composition; became instructor in public schools of Sardinia; collected Sardinian folksongs, and used some of them in his own compositions, notably in the opera *Elia.* He publ. a biography of Rossini (1915) and a collection of essays *L'anima musicale d'Italia* (1921); contributed to the 'Rivista Musicale Italiana' and other Italian publications. His collection of Sardinian songs was publ. by Ricordi (1924).

Farabi. See **Alfarabi.**

Farinelli (real name Carlo Broschi), celebrated Italian artificial soprano; b. Andria, Jan. 24, 1705; d. Bologna, July 15, 1782. He adopted the name Farinelli to honor his benefactor Farina. He was a student of Porpora; sang in Naples with great success, achieving fame as 'il ragazzo' (the boy). At the age of 16 he sang in Rome in Porpora's opera *Eomene;* his fame spread in Italy and abroad. In 1727 he met the famous castrato singer Bernacchi in Bologna; in a singing contest with him, Farinelli acknowledged defeat, and persuaded Bernacchi to give him lessons to achieve virtuosity in coloratura. He visited Vienna in 1724, 1728, and 1731. In 1734 he was sent by Porpora to London to join the Italian opera there. He made his London début on Oct. 27, 1734, in *Artaserse* by Hasse, appearing with Senesino and Cuzzoni; he remained in London for two years, amassing a fortune; he then went to Paris, and in 1737 to Madrid, where he attained unparalleled success as court singer to King Philip V; his duty was to sing several arias every night to cure the king's melancholy. His influence on the ailing monarch, and on the Queen, was such that he was able to command considerable funds to engage famous performers at the Madrid court. When his voice began to fail, he undertook to serve as impresario, decorator, and stage director. He continued to enjoy the court's favor under Philip's successor, Ferdinand VI, but at the accession to the Spanish throne of Carlos III in 1759, Farinelli was dismissed. He went back to Italy in possession of great wealth; he assembled his family in a palatial villa which he built near Bologna, and spent his last 20 years of life in contentment.—Bibl.: G. Sacchi, *Vita del Cavaliere Don Carlo Broschi, detto Farinelli* (Venice, 1784); J. Desastre, *G. Broschi* (Zürich, 1903); G. Monaldi, *Cantanti evirati celebri* (Rome, 1919); F. Haböck, *Die Gesangskunst der Kastraten* (Vienna, 1923); R. Bouvier, *Farinelli, le chanteur des rois* (Paris, 1943).

Farinelli, Giuseppe, prolific Italian composer; b. Este, May 7, 1769; d. Trieste, Dec. 12, 1836. In 1785 he entered the Cons. della Pietà dei Turchini at Naples, his teachers being Barbiello, Fago, Sala, and Tritto; his first opera, *Il Dottorato di Pulcinella,* produced in 1792, was followed by 50 or 60 others, not original, but in very happy imitation of Cimarosa's style and chiefly comic. From 1810-17 he lived at Turin; then went to Venice, and finally (1819) settled in Trieste as maestro and organist at the Cathedral of San Giusto. He also wrote several oratorios, cantatas, 5 masses, 2 Te Deums, and other church music.

Farjeon, Harry, English composer; b. Hohokus, N. J. (of English parents), May 6, 1878; d. London, Dec. 29, 1948. He was a son of the English novelist B. L. Farjeon, and grandson of the famous actor Joseph Jefferson. He was educated in England, taking music lessons with Landon Ronald and John Storer; then studied composition with Corder at the Royal Academy of Music; won the Lucas Medal and other prizes. In 1903 he became an instructor there.—Works: the opera *Floretta* (1899) and 2 operettas, *The Registry Office* (1900) and *A Gentleman of the Road* (1902), all performed in London; piano concerto (1903); *Hans Andersen Suite* for small orch. (London, 1905); 2 song cycles, *Vagrant Songs* and *The Lute of Jade.* The score of a symph. poem *Summer Vision* (regarded by the composer as his best work) was sent to Germany shortly before World War I and was lost.

Farkas (fahr'-kash), **Edmund,** Hungarian composer; b. Puszta-Monostor, 1851; d. Klausenburg, Sept. 1, 1912. He studied engineering at the Univ. of Budapest; then took courses at the Budapest Academy of Music with Erkel, Volkmann, and others. Upon graduation he was appointed director at the Klausenburg Cons. There he organized an orchestra, established a musical journal, and promoted national Hungarian music.—Works: the operas (first performed in Budapest) *Bayadere* (Aug. 23, 1876), *Valentin Balassa* (Jan. 16, 1896), *The Inquest* (Oct. 5, 1900), and *The World of Kurucz* (Oct. 26, 1906); several symph. poems in a romantic vein (*Dusk, Storm,* etc.); church music; 5 string quartets; several piano pieces in the Hungarian style; publ. (in Hungarian) several papers on school music.

Farkas (fahr'-kash), **Ferenc,** Hungarian composer; b. Nagykanizsa, Dec. 15, 1905. He began to study piano as a child; then took courses with Leo Weiner and Albert Siklos at the Academy of Music in Budapest. He then conducted theater orchestras in Hungary; a state scholarship enabled him to go to Rome, where he studied with Respighi. Returning to Hungary, he was music teacher in the municipal school in Budapest (1935-41); in 1941 was appointed prof. at the Cons. in Kolozsvár (Cluj); in 1948 became prof. at the Academy of Drama in Budapest. At the same time he was active as composer.—Works: incidental music to plays by Shakespeare; film music; *The Magic Cupboard,* comic opera (Budapest, April 22, 1942); *Musica dodecatonica* for orch. (1947); a concertino for harp (1937); 2 violin sonatas; viola sonata; many piano pieces; songs.

Farmer, Henry George, eminent musicologist; authority on Oriental music; b. Birr, Ireland, Jan. 17, 1882. He studied piano and violin, and as a boy joined the Royal Artillery Orch. in London, playing the French horn at its concerts. He then studied philosophy and languages at Glasgow Univ.; conducted theater concerts; edited the 'Musician's Journal.' An extremely prolific writer, he publ. a number of original works, dealing with such varied subjects as military music and Arabic musical theories; has contributed to Grove's Dictionary and 'Die Musik in Geschichte und Gegenwart.' He was the founder and conductor of the Glasgow Sym. Orch. (1919-43); has written several overtures and some chamber music.—Publications: *Memoirs of the Royal Artillery Band* (1904); *The Rise and Development of Military Music* (1912); *The Arabian Influence on Musical Theory* (1925); *Byzantine Musical Instruments in the 9th Century* (1925); *The Arabic Musical MSS. in the Bodleian Library* (1926); *A History of Arabian Music to the 13th Century* (1929); *Music in Medieval Scotland* (1930); *Historical Facts for the Arabian Musical Influence* (1930); *The Organ of the Ancients* (1931); *Studies in Oriental Musical Instruments* (1931); *An Old Moorish Lute Tutor* (1931); *Al-Farabi's Arabic-Latin Writings* (Glasgow, 1934); *Turkish Instruments of Music in the 17th Century* (1937); *New Mozartiana* (1938); *Sa'adyah Gaon on the Influence of Music* (1943); *A History of Music in Scotland* (London, 1947); *Music Making in the Olden Days* (1950); *Military Music* (1950); *Oriental Studies, Mainly Musical* (London, 1953); *The History of the Royal Artillery Band* (1954); other studies and articles.

Farmer, John, Elizabethan madrigal composer, active from 1591 to 1601. In 1595 he was organist at Christ Church Cathedral in Dublin; in 1599 he left Dublin and went to London. Among his madrigals the best known are *Fair Phyllis I saw sitting all alone, You pretty flowers,* and *A little pretty bonny lass,* included in his *First Set of English Madrigals to Foure Voices* (London, 1599; reprinted in vol. 8 of E. H. Fellowes' *English Madrigal School*). He contributed a 6-part madrigal *Fair Nymphs, I heard one telling* to *The Triumphes of Oriana,* and several canticles and hymns to Thomas East's *Whole Booke of Psalmes* (1592). Extant MSS are in the Christ Church Library and Music School at Oxford, and in the British Museum. Farmer was also the author of *Divers and sundry waies of two parts in one* (London, 1591).—Cf. E. H. Fellowes, *The English Madrigal Composers* (1921; 2nd ed., 1948).

Farmer, John, English composer; b. Nottingham, Aug. 16, 1836; d. Oxford, July 17, 1901. He studied at the Leipzig Cons. and later at Coburg; then lived in Switzerland, returning to England in 1862; taught at Harrow School (1862-85); became organist at Balliol College, Oxford; was active in educational work. He composed an oratorio *Christ and His Soldiers* (1878); a fairy opera *Cinderella* (1882); comic cantata *Froggy Would A-wooing Go* (1887); settings of nursery rhymes for chorus and orch.; church music; chamber music (2 septets; a piano quintet, etc.).

Farnaby, Giles, English composer; b. Truro, Cornwall, c. 1560; d. London, Nov.

(buried Nov. 25), 1640. He graduated from Oxford in 1592, receiving the degree of B. Mus.; later moved to London, where he remained until his death.—Works: *Canzonets to Fowre Voyces* (1598; includes an added madrigal for 8 voices, one of the few such works in the English school; reprint by E. H. Fellowes, in vol. 20 of the *English Madrigal School*); vocal religious works in various collections, and motets, psalms, etc., in MS; more than 50 virginal pieces in the Fitzwilliam Virginal Book (ed. by J. A. Fuller Maitland and W. Barclay Squire, London, 1899); a madrigal, *Come, Charon,* is in MS at the Royal College of Music; part of another is in the British Museum. Farnaby's son, **Richard Farnaby**, was also a gifted composer.—Cf. E. H. Fellowes, *The English Madrigal Composers* (1921; 2nd ed., 1948).

Farnam, W. Lynnwood, Canadian-American organist; b. Sutton, Quebec, Jan. 13, 1885; d. New York, Nov. 23, 1930. He studied with his mother and local teachers; in 1900 won the Montreal Scholarship to the Royal College of Music, London, where he studied organ with James Higgs. He came to America in 1904; was organist at several churches in N. Y. and Boston.

Farnon, Robert, Canadian composer; b. Toronto, July 24, 1917. He studied piano, violin, and trumpet; in 1944 moved to London. He has written an *Ottawa Symphony* (1941); a set of 4 *Fairy-Tale Symphonettes* (1943); many pieces for orch. in the popular vein; also music for films.

Farnsworth, Charles Hubert, music educator; b. Cesarea, Turkey, Nov. 29, 1859; d. Thetford, Vt., May 22, 1947. He studied organ in Worcester, Mass.; held various positions as organist; was head of the music dept. at Colorado Univ. (1888-1900); then was on the faculty at Teachers College, Columbia Univ. (1900-25); retired and lived in Vermont. He publ. several pamphlets on music education; among them, *The Why and How of Music Study* (1927); *Short Studies in Musical Psychology* (N. Y., 1930). An appreciation of his work was publ. in 'The Musician' (1933).

Farrant, John, English organist and composer, active in the 16th century; he served as organist at the Ely Cathedral (1567-72); then was lay clerk at Salisbury, and subsequently organist at the Salisbury Cathedral (1587-92); he was briefly organist at Hereford (1593). Contemporary records testify to his intractable temper, which resulted in physical clashes with the dean of the Salisbury Cathedral, and led to his expulsion there. As a composer Farrant is chiefly distinguished for his Service in D minor (misattributed in a 19th-century ed. to Richard Farrant). His son, also named **John Farrant** (baptized Salisbury, Sept. 28, 1575; d. there, 1618), was a chorister at the Salisbury Cathedral in 1585, and organist there from 1598 till 1616. Another John Farrant, possibly related to the preceding, was organist at Christ Church, Newgate, London; he was the author of a Magnificat; this work, sometimes referred to as 'Farrant in G minor' is often confused with Richard Farrant's Service in A minor.

Farrant, Richard, English composer; b. c. 1530; d. Windsor, 1581. He was a Gentleman of the Chapel Royal during the reign of Edward VI; then became master of the choristers (1564) at St. George's Chapel, Windsor; also served as a lay clerk and organist there. Beginning with 1567 Farrant presented a play annually before the Queen. In 1569 he returned to the Chapel Royal. His will is dated November 30, 1580; this date was formerly erroneously given for his death. Farrant wrote mainly church music; his Cathedral Service in A minor and 2 anthems, *Hide not Thou Thy Face* and *Call to Remembrance,* are regarded as the most beautiful examples of English sacred music of the 16th century. A Service in D minor was published as that by Richard Farrant, but this was a misattribution, the real author being John Farrant of Salisbury. Several of Richard Farrant's works are in the British Museum and at Durham Cathedral.

Farrar, Ernest Bristow, English organist and composer; b. London, July 7, 1885; d. in the battle of the Somme, France, Sept. 18, 1918. He studied at the Royal College of Music with Stanford and Parratt; served as organist of the English Church in Dresden (1909); then at various churches in England (1910-14). His orch. suite *English Pastoral Impression* won the Carnegie Award; he further wrote the orch. pieces *The Open Road, Lavengro, The Forsaken Merman,* and *Heroic Elegy;* also *3 Spiritual Studies* for strings; variations on an old English sea song, for piano and orch.; the cantatas *The Blessed Damozel* and *Out of Doors;* chamber music (*Celtic Suite* for violin and piano, etc.); songs; preludes for organ, etc.

Farrar (far-rahr'), **Geraldine,** celebrated American soprano; b. Melrose, Mass., Feb.

28, 1882. She studied music with Mrs. J. H. Long of Boston; at 17, she went to Europe; took lessons with Emma Thursby in N. Y., with Trabadello in Paris and Graziani in Berlin; made a successful début at the Berlin Opera on Oct. 15, 1901, as Marguerite, under the direction of Karl Muck; then studied with Lilli Lehmann. She sang at the Monte Carlo Opera for three seasons (1903-6). Her career in Europe was well established before her American début as Juliette at the Metropolitan Opera (Nov. 26, 1906); she remained on the staff for 16 years; made her farewell appearance in *Zaza* on April 22, 1922, but continued to sing in concert; gave her last public performance at Carnegie Hall in 1931; then retired to Ridgefield, Conn. Her greatest success was *Madama Butterfly,* which she sang with Caruso on its American première at the Metropolitan on Feb. 11, 1907; subsequently sang this part in America more than 100 times. Her interpretation of Carmen was no less remarkable. She also appeared in silent motion pictures between 1915 and 1919; her film version of Carmen aroused considerable interest. On Feb. 8, 1916, she married the actor Lou Tellegen, from whom she was subsequently divorced. She made adaptations of pieces by Kreisler, Rachmaninoff, and others, for which she published the lyrics. She wrote an autobiography, *Such Sweet Compulsion* (N.Y., 1938). —Cf. H. T. Finck, *Success in Music* (N. Y., 1909); Ed. Wagenknecht, *Geraldine Farrar: An Authorized Record of her Career* (Seattle, 1929); Oscar Thompson, *The American Singer* (N. Y., 1937).

Farrenc (fah-rahnk'), **Jacques-Hippolyte-Aristide**, French flutist and music editor; b Marseilles, April 9, 1794; d. Paris, Jan. 31, 1865. He studied flute; went to Paris in 1815, and studied at the Cons.; at the same time was engaged as second flutist at the Théâtre Italien. In 1821 he established a music shop and printing press; publ. French editions of Beethoven; also composed music for the flute. He married Louise Dumont, a talented musician in her own right. He diligently collected material for the rectification of existing biographies, but generously turned it over to Fétis for use in the 2nd edition of his great work, of which Farrenc also read proofs. Jointly with Fétis' son, Edouard, he began the publication of *Trésor des pianistes* (20 vols., 1861-72), a collection of piano music from the 16th century to Mendelssohn, with historical notes; it was continued after his death by his wife. From 1854 he contributed papers to 'La France musicale' and other journals.

Farwell, Arthur, American composer and music educator; b. St. Paul, Minn., April 23, 1872; d. New York, Jan. 20, 1952. He studied at the Mass. Inst. of Technology, graduating in 1893; then studied music with Homer Norris in Boston, Humperdinck in Berlin, and Guilmant in Paris. He was lecturer on music at Cornell Univ. (1899-1901); in 1909 was on the editorial staff of 'Musical America'; then directed municipal concerts in N. Y. City (1910-13); was director of the Music School Settlement in N. Y. (1915-18); in 1918 he went to California; lectured on music there; was acting head of music dept. at the Univ. of Calif., Berkeley (1918-19); in 1919 he founded the Santa Barbara Community Chorus, which he conducted until 1921; was first holder of composers' fellowship of the Music and Art Association of Pasadena (1921-25); taught music theory at Michigan State College in East Lansing (1927-39); eventually settled in New York. Farwell was a pioneer in new American music, and tirelessly promoted national ideas in art. He contributed to various ethnological publications. In 1901 he established the Wa-Wan Press at Newton, Mass. Disillusioned about commercial opportunities for American music, including his own, he established at East Lansing, Mich., in April 1936, his own lithographic handpress, with which he printed his music, handling the entire process of reproduction, including the cover designs, by himself. His works are mostly based on American subjects. He wrote for orch. the following: *Symbolistic Study No. 3,* after Walt Whitman (1905; revised, 1922; Philadelphia Orch., March 30, 1928); *Pageant Scene* (1913); *The Gods of the Mountain* (Minneapolis Symph. Orch., Dec. 13, 1929); music for pageants, including Percy MacKaye's *Caliban by the Yellow Sands* (N. Y., May, 1916; written for the Shakespeare tercentenary); *Pilgrimage Play* (Hollywood, 1921); *Symph. Song on 'Old Black Joe'* (Hollywood, 1923); *Symph. Hymn on 'March! March!';* also *The Hako* for string quartet (1922); violin sonata (1928); concerto for 2 pianos and string orch., a version of *Symbolistic Study No. 6* (1931; won first prize of the National Federation of Music Clubs Competition; broadcast by CBS, May 28, 1939); numerous school choruses, and vocal compositions; piano pieces (many of them arranged for various instrumental ensembles); several collections of American Indian melodies and folksongs of the South and West; arrangements of Indian melodies (*Dawn,* a fantasy on Indian themes, in various versions, dated between 1901 and 1926, is characteristic of these works).

Fasch, Johann Friedrich, German composer; b. Buttelstadt, near Weimar, April 15, 1688; d. Zerbst, Dec. 5, 1758. He studied with Kuhnau at Leipzig, and later (1713) with Graupner and Grunewald at Darmstadt; in 1721 he went to Lukaveč, Bohemia, as Kapellmeister to Count Morzin; after 1722, Kapellmeister at Zerbst. A catalogue of his works, compiled in 1743, enumerates 7 complete series of church cantatas, 12 masses, 69 overtures, 21 concertos (for violin, flute, oboe, etc.), some of which have been printed in modern editions. Many scores are preserved in MS in the libraries of Darmstadt, Dresden, Leipzig, and Brussels; in the archives of the Thomasschule at Leipzig are the parts of five orchestral suites of Fasch in the handwriting of J. S. Bach, who entertained a very high opinion of the works of his contemporary. Hugo Riemann published 5 trio-sonatas and a quartet in 'Collegium Musicum' and 2 orchestral suites in Breitkopf & Härtel's 'Orchesterbibliothek.' Fasch's autobiography appeared in vol. III of F. W. Marpurg's *Historisch-kritische Beyträge zur Aufnahme der Musik* (Berlin, 1754-78). Cf. also J. A. Hiller, *Lebensbeschreibungen berühmter Musikgelehrten und Tonkünstler neuerer Zeit* (Leipzig, 1784); B. Engelke, *Johann Friedrich Fasch, sein Leben und seine Tätigkeit als Vokalkomponist* (Leipzig, 1908); B. Engelke, *Johann Friedrich Fasch, Versuch einer Biographie* in 'Sammelbände der Internationalen Musik-Gesellschaft' (1909); C. A. Schneider, *J. Fr. Fasch als Sonatenkomponist* (Münster, 1936).

Fasch, Karl Friedrich Christian, German composer, son of Johann Friedrich Fasch; b. Zerbst, Nov. 18, 1736; d. Berlin, Aug. 3, 1800. He learned to play the violin and harpsichord as a child; studied all musical subjects with Hertel at Strelitz. At the age of 15, he joined the violinist Franz Benda as his accompanist and at the age of 20 he was recommended by Benda as harpsichordist to Frederick the Great, jointly with K. P. E. Bach. He also taught music and composed contrapuntal pieces of considerable ingenuity and complexity. He was conductor at the Berlin Opera (1774-76). In 1790 he organized a choral society, which led to the foundation of the famous Singakademie. Fasch was greatly admired by musicians for his contrapuntal skill; the renown of his name was still strong in the first part of the 19th century; in 1839, 6 vols. of his sacred works were publ. by the Singakademie.—Cf. C. F. Zelter, *Biographie von Karl Friedrich Christian Fasch* (Berlin, 1801); M. Blummer, *Geschichte der Berliner Singakademie* (Berlin, 1891); G. Schünemann, *Die Singakademie zu Berlin* (Regensburg, 1941).

Fattorini, Gabriele, Italian composer; b. Faenza in the latter part of the 16th century; date of death unknown. He was maestro di cappella at Faenza, and possibly in Venice. His compositions include *Sacri Concerti a due voci* (Venice, 1600; further editions, 1602, 1608); *Completorium Romanum* (Venice, 1602); motets, madrigals, etc. Several of his works appeared in contemporaneous collections between 1605 and 1622 (Bodenschatz, Donfried, Diruta, etc.). Two of his *Ricercare* for organ are in vol. III of Torchi's *L'Arte Musicale in Italia.* Banchieri mentions Fattorini in his *Conclusioni del suono dell'Organo* (Lucca, 1591; Bologna, 1609). For bibliographical details, see F. Ghisi's article on Fattorini in 'Die Musik in Geschichte und Gegenwart.'

Fauchey, Paul, French composer; b. Paris, March 18, 1858; d. there, Nov. 15, 1936. He was active in the theater as chorus master and then began to compose light operas, of which *La Carmagnole* (Paris, 1897) was quite popular for a time.

Faulkes, William, English organist and composer; b. Liverpool, Nov. 4, 1863; d. there, Jan. 25, 1933. He studied with W. Dawson and H. Dillon-Newman; from 1886 he was active in Liverpool as organist and teacher; composed mostly for organ; publ. several albums of organ pieces.

Fauré (fŏh-rĕh'), **Gabriel-Urbain,** outstanding French composer; b. Pamiers (Ariège), May 12, 1845; d. Paris, Nov. 4, 1924. His father was a provincial inspector of primary schools; noticing the musical instinct of his son, he took him to Paris to study with Louis Niedermeyer; after Niedermeyer's death in 1861, Fauré studied with Saint-Saëns, from whom he received a thorough training in composition. In 1866 he went to Rennes as organist at the church of Saint-Sauveur; returned to Paris on the eve of the Franco-Prussian war in 1870, and volunteered in the light infantry. He was organist at Notre-Dame de Clignancourt, Saint-Honoré d'Eylau, and Saint-Sulpice; in 1877 became second organist at the Madeleine; in 1896 he was appointed chief organist there, and prof. of composition at the Paris Cons. He was an illustrious teacher; among his students were Ravel, Enesco, Koechlin, Roger-Ducasse, Laparra, Florent Schmitt, Louis Aubert, and Nadia Boulanger. In 1905 he succeeded Théodore Dubois as director; resigned in 1920, when growing deafness and ill health made it impossible for him to continue to direct the Conservatory. From 1903 till 1921 Fauré wrote occasional music reviews in 'Le Figaro' (publ. as *Opinions Musicales;* posthumous, Paris, 1930); he was elected member of the Académie des Beaux Arts in 1909; Commander of the Légion d'honneur in 1910. Fauré's stature as composer is undiminished by the passage of time. He developed a musical idiom all his own; by subtle application of old modes he evoked the aura of eternally fresh art; by using unresolved mild discords and special coloristic effects in his instrumental music he anticipated the procedures of impressionism; in his piano works he shunned virtuosity in favor of the classical lucidity of the French masters of the clavecin; the precisely articulated melodic line of his songs is in the finest tradition of French vocal music. Several of his works (significantly, those of his early period) have entered the general repertory: the great Requiem, first violin sonata, *Elégie* for cello and piano; songs (*Ici-bas, Les roses d'Ispahan, Clair de lune, Au cimetière,* etc.). — Works: For the stage: *Caligula,* incidental music to a play by A. Dumas, Jr. (Paris, Nov. 8, 1888); *Shylock,* after Shakespeare (Paris, Dec. 17, 1889); *Pelléas et Mélisande,* after Maeterlinck (London, June 21, 1898; often performed as an orchestral suite); *Prométhée,* lyric tragedy (Béziers, Aug. 1, 1900); *Le Voile du bonheur,* incidental music for Clemenceau's play (Paris, Nov. 4, 1901); *Pénélope* (Monte Carlo, March 4, 1913); *Masques et bergamasques,* stage music (Monte Carlo, April 10, 1919). For orch.: Symphony in D minor (Paris, March 15, 1885); a suite (1875; only one movement, *Allegro symphonique,* was publ.); *Pavane* (1887); *Ballade* for piano and orch. (1881); *Romance* for violin and orch. (1882); *Fantaisie* for piano and orch. (1919). Choral works: *Cantique de Jean Racine* for mixed chorus, harmonium, and string quartet (1873); *Les Djinns* for chorus and orch. (1875); *La Naissance de Vénus* for soli, chorus, and orch. (1882); *Messe de Requiem* for soli, chorus, organ, and orch. (1887); *Tantum ergo* for solo voice and chorus (1890); offertories and other church music. Chamber music: 2 violin sonatas (1879; 1886); 2 piano quartets (1879; 1886); 2 piano quintets (1906; 1921); 2 cello sonatas (1918; 1922); piano trio (1923); string quartet (1924); *Elégie* for cello and piano (1883); *Sérénade* for cello and piano (1908); also *Fantaisie* for flute and piano (1898). Piano works: 13 nocturnes, 13 barcarolles, 5 impromptus, 4 waltzes, etc.—96 songs: 4 to words by Victor Hugo; 4 after Théophile Gautier; 3 after Baudelaire; 16 after Paul Verlaine (including the cycle *La Bonne Chanson*), etc.—Bibl.: O. Séré, *Musiciens français d'aujourd'hui* (Paris, 1911); L. Vuillemin, *Gabriel Fauré et son œuvre* (Paris, 1914); the special Fauré issue of 'La Revue musicale' (Oct., 1922); Aaron Copland, *Gabriel Fauré; a Neglected Master,* in the 'Mus. Quarterly' (Oct., 1924); Alfred Bruneau, *La vie et les œuvres de Gabriel Fauré* (Paris, 1925); Charles Koechlin, *Gabriel Fauré* (Paris, 1927; English transl., London, 1945); Ph. Fauré-Fremiet, *Gabriel Fauré* (Paris, 1929); G. Servières, *Gabriel Fauré* (Paris, 1930); Paul Landormy, *Gabriel Fauré,* in the 'Mus. Quarterly' (July, 1931); V. Jankélévitch, *Gabriel Fauré et ses mélodies* (Paris, 1938; enlarged ed., 1951); G. Faure, *Gabriel Fauré* (Paris, 1945); Claude Rostand, *L'Oeuvre de Gabriel Fauré* (Paris, 1945); Norman Suckling, *Fauré* (in the 'Master Musicians' series; London, 1946); G. Samazeuilh, *Musiciens de mon temps* (Paris, 1947); Max Favre, *Gabriel Faurés Kammermusik* (Zürich, 1948); Ph. Fauré-Fremiet, ed., *Fauré, Lettres intimes* (Paris, 1951); also Florent Schmitt's article on Fauré's chamber music in Cobbett's 'Cyclopedia of Chamber Music'; the article by Fauré's son, Philippe Fauré-Fremiet, in 'Die Musik in Geschichte und Gegenwart' contains a very extensive bibliography of newspaper and magazine articles about Fauré.

Faure (fŏhr), **Jean-Baptiste,** famous French baritone; b. Moulins, Allier, Jan. 15, 1830; d. Paris, Nov. 9, 1914. He was a choir-boy at the Madeleine and other Paris churches; entered the Paris Cons. at the age of 21; after a short period of study he made his début at the Opéra-Comique, in Massé's opera *Galathée* (Oct. 20, 1852), and continued there for eight years; from 1861-76 he was on the staff of the Paris Opéra; his farewell appearance was in *Hamlet* by Ambroise Thomas (May 13, 1876), the role that he created in 1868. Subsequently he sang in concerts, appearing with enormous success in Vienna and in London. He was particularly impressive in dramatic roles in Meyerbeer's operas and also in Gounod's *Faust,* as Mephistopheles. He also wrote a number of songs, of which several became fairly successful (*Crucifix, Les Rameaux,* etc.).— Cf. H. de Curzon, *Jean-Baptiste Faure,* in the 'Mus. Quarterly' (April, 1918); H. de Curzon, *Jean-Baptiste Faure* (Paris, 1923).

Favarger (făh-văhr-zhā'), **René,** French pianist; b. Dun-sur-Auron, Cher, Feb. 25, 1815; d. Etretat, Aug. 3, 1868. He was successful as a teacher in Paris and in London; composed a number of salon pieces for piano.

Favart, Charles-Simon, French librettist; b. Paris, Nov. 13, 1710; d. Belleville, near Paris, March 12, 1792. He published satirical plays as a youth; after a successful performance of one of his vaudevilles at the Opéra-Comique, he was appointed stage manager there; in 1758 he became its director. He wrote about 150 plays used for operas by Duni, Philidor, and Gluck; he was also the author of *Les Amours de Bastien et Bastienne* (1753), used by Mozart in a German version for his early opera (1768).

Fay, Amy, American pianist; b. Bayou Goula, Miss., May 21, 1844; d. Watertown, Mass., Feb. 28, 1928. She studied in Berlin with Tausig and Kullak; then became a pupil of Liszt in Weimar. She publ. a vivid book of impressions *Music-Study in Germany* (Chicago, 1881), which went through more than 20 printings, and was translated into French and German.

Fayolle (fah-yohl'), **François - Joseph - Marie,** French writer on music and literature; b. Paris, Aug. 15, 1774; d. there, Dec. 2, 1852. A man of brilliant faculties, he was equally proficient in mathematics and poetry; also studied harmony and cello; after 1814 he lived in London; returned to Paris in 1830; he died in an alms-house. He contributed a number of articles to Fétis' *Biographie Universelle;* together with Choron, he publ. a *Dictionnaire historique des musiciens* (Paris, 1810-11); his other writings on music include *Notices sur Corelli, Tartini, Gaviniès, Pugnani et Viotti* (Paris, 1810); *Sur les drames lyriques et leur exécution* (Paris, 1813) and *Paganini et Bériot* (Paris, 1830).

Fayrfax, Robert, English composer; b. Deeping Gate, Lincolnshire, April, 1464 (baptized April 23); d. St. Albans, Oct. 24, 1521. He was a Gentleman of the Chapel Royal in 1496, and organist at St. Alban's Abbey and at King's Chapel (1497-98); B. A., Cambridge (1501); Mus. Doc., Cambridge (1504); Mus. Doc., Oxford (1511; with his mass, *O quam glorifica*). In 1520 was the leader of the Royal Singers in France. 32 works of Fayrfax are extant: 6 masses (4 are in the Oxford Music School Collection); 2 Magnificats, 13 motets, 9 part songs, 2 instrumental pieces. Sacred and secular vocal works of Fayrfax appear in the *Fairfax Book* (British Museum MS Add. 5465) and in other British MSS; lute arrangements of several sacred compositions and an instrumental piece for 3 parts are in the British Museum. Reprints of some of his compositions are in J. Stafford Smith's *Musica Antiqua* (1912).—Cf. J. Pulver, *Robert Fayrfax,* in 'Musical News' (Feb. 10, 1917); Dom Anselm Hughes, *An Introduction to Fayrfax* in 'Musica Disciplina' (1952).

Fechner, Gustave Theodor, German music theorist; b. Gross-Särchen, Niederlausitz, April 19, 1801; d. Leipzig, Nov. 18, 1887. He was prof. of physics at Leipzig from 1834. He publ. *Repertorium der Experimentalphysik,* in which musical phenomena are treated; also *Elemente der Psychophysik* (1860, 2 vols.), and *Vorschule der Aesthetik* (1870, 2 vols.), valuable as establishing a basis of musical esthetics.

Fedeli (fā-dā-lē), **Vito,** Italian composer; b. Fogligno, June 19, 1866; d. Novara, June 23, 1933. He was a pupil of Terziani in Rome; was director of the Cons. at Novara from 1904.—Works: The operas *La Vergine della Montagna* (Reggio-Calabria, Sept. 6, 1897) and *Varsovia* (Rome, Dec. 15, 1900); several masses a cappella; also pieces for orch. He contributed valuable historical articles to the 'Rivista Musicale Italiana' and the 'Zeitschrift der Internationalen Musik-Gesellschaft'; also wrote a book, *Giacomo e Gaudenzio Battistini* (1932).—Cf. G. Bustico, *Bibliografia di un musico novarese, Vito Fedeli* (1925).

Federhofer, Helmut, Austrian musicologist; b. Graz, Aug. 6, 1911. He studied piano with Anatol Vietinghoff-Scheel in Graz; musicology with Alfred Orel and Robert Lach at the Univ. of Vienna; was a graduate of the Vienna Music Academy (1934); .studied composition with Alban Berg; in 1944 appointed instructor in musicology at the Univ. of Graz; 1951 became prof. there. He has contributed valuable papers on Austrian and Netherlandish musicians to various learned magazines; also wrote articles for 'Die Musik in Geschichte und Gegenwart.'

Federici (fā-dā-rē'-tchē), **Vincenzo,** Italian dramatic composer; b. Pesaro, 1764; d. Milan, Sept. 20, 1827. He became an orphan at 16; lived in Turin, where he produced his first opera *L'Olimpiade* (Dec. 26, 1789). He then made his way to London, where he became cembalist at the Italian

Opera; returned to Italy in 1802; in 1814 he became teacher of harmony at the Milan Cons.

Federlein (fä'-der-līn), **Gottfried H.,** American organist, son of Gottlieb Federlein; b. New York, Dec. 31, 1883; d. there, Feb. 26, 1952. He studied with his father; then with Goetschius; in 1915 became organist at Temple Emanu-El in New York. He published a number of anthems and organ pieces.

Federlein, Gottlieb (Heinrich), organist and vocal pedagogue; b. Neustadt-an-der-Aisch, near Nuremberg, Nov. 5, 1835; d. Philadelphia, April 29, 1922. He studied with Rheinberger in Munich; was active as organist and singing teacher in New York; published numerous songs and a manual, *Practical School of Voice Culture* (N. Y., 1880).

Fedorov, Vladimir, music librarian and historian; b. near Tchernigov, Aug. 5, 1901. He studied at the Univ. of Rostov; emigrated to Turkey in 1920; then settled in Paris, where he studied art, archeology, and music; took lessons with Gédalge and Vidal; later took additional courses in Germany. In 1933 he became librarian at the Sorbonne; later took a post in the music division of the Bibliothèque Nationale in Paris. He publ. *Moussorgsky, biographie critique* (Paris, 1935) and numerous articles on a variety of musical subjects in French magazines; also compiled catalogues of music libraries; composed several piano works. For further details see his autobiographical notice in 'Die Musik in Geschichte und Gegenwart.'

Fehr (får), **Max,** Swiss musicologist; b. Bülach, near Zürich, June 17, 1887. He studied at the Univ. of Zürich with Eduard Bernoulli; *Dr. phil.,* with his thesis: *Apostolo Zeno und seine Reform des Operntextes* (Zürich, 1912); in 1917 he became librarian, and in 1923, president, of the Allgemeine Musikgesellschaft of Zürich; taught Italian and French at the Zürich High School (1912-18) and in Winterthur (1918-52); then retired. He was president of the Neue Schweizer Musikgesellschaft (1919-32). Writings: *Spielleute im alten Zürich* (Zürich, 1916); *Die Meistersinger von Zürich,* a satirical novelette (Zürich, 1916); *Unter Wagners Taktstock* (Winterthur, 1922); *Geschichte des Musikkollegiums Winterthur, I. Teil: 1629-1830* (1929); *R. Wagners Schweizer Zeit,* in 2 vols. (Aarau, 1934 and 1953).; *Die Familie Mozart in Zürich* (Zürich, 1942).

Feicht (fīcht), **Hieronim,** Polish musicologist; b. Mogilno, near Poznan, Sept. 22, 1894; first a theological student and missionary; then studied composition with Wallek-Walewski in Cracow and with Soltys in Lwow, where he also studied with Chybinski (*Dr. phil.,* 1925; dissertation, *Bartholomäus Pekiel, ein polnischer Komponist des XVII. Jahrhunderts und seine Kirchenmusikwerke;* publ.); from 1946-52, he was an instructor at the State High School in Breslau; since 1952, prof. at the Univ. of Warsaw. He has publ. important essays on Polish music: *Musikhistorische Bemerkungen über die Lemberger Handschriften des Bogarodzica-Liedes* (Poznan, 1925); *Wojciech Debolecki, ein polnischer Kirchenkomponist aus der 1. Hälfte des 17. Jahrhunderts* (Lwow, 1926). He has also written a history of church music in Poland and a valuable work on the old Polish church composer, Martin Leopolita. Feicht is a notable composer of church music.

Feinberg, Samuel Evgenievitch, eminent Russian pianist and composer; b. Odessa, May 26, 1890; graduated in 1911 from the Moscow Cons.; since 1922 a prof. of piano and composition there. Feinberg quickly established himself as a pianist. As a composer he is a follower of Scriabin. He is at his best in his piano works, which include 10 sonatas (No. 7, 1924; No. 8, 1933; No. 9, 1939; No. 10, 1940); 3 concertos (1931, 1944, 1947; the second concerto was performed Moscow, March 11, 1945, composer at the piano, and it was awarded a Stalin Prize); 2 fantasies and many other pieces (more than 20 op. numbers); has also composed orchestral and chamber music, songs, etc.—Cf. V. Belaiev, *Samuel Feinberg* (1927; in Russian and German).

Fekete, Zóltan, Hungarian conductor; b. Budapest, July 25, 1909. He studied music with Siklós at the Budapest Academy of Music. In 1937 he went to the U. S. and organized the New York Midtown Symphony Orch.; after 1946 he traveled in Europe as conductor. He made numerous arrangements of classical works in the form of orchestral suites, among them 9 suites based on unfamiliar works by Handel; also a 'Schubert Snow White Suite'; assembled a ballet suite from manuscript works of Josef Suk and conducted it under the title *Mr. Scrooge* (after Dickens) in Munich, Dec. 23, 1955.

Felderhof, Jan, Dutch composer; b. Amsterdam, Sept. 25, 1907. He studied at the Amsterdam Cons. with Sem Dresden; in 1934 appointed instructor of harmony there; in 1944 became conductor of a chorus and orch. in Bussum. He has composed an opera *Serenade in Sint Jansnacht* (1932); a work for narrator and orch. *Uw dochters zullen profeteren* (1946); a humorous cantata *Let Us Go to Vienna;* 2 string quartets; piano trio; 2 violin sonatas; 3 sonatinas for piano.

Felix, Hugo, Austrian composer of operettas; b. Vienna, Nov. 19, 1866; d. Hollywood, Aug. 24, 1934. He produced several operettas in Vienna: *Husarenblut* (1894); *Das Kätzchen* (1892), etc.; and several in Berlin (*Madame Sherry,* 1902, etc.). After World War I he settled in America; wrote an operetta with an English text, *The Sweetheart Shop* (Chicago, 1920); a grand opera *Resurrection* (not produced); also incidental music to Otis Skinner's *Sancho Panza,* and other plays.

Fellerer, Karl Gustav, German musicologist; b. Freising, July 7, 1902; studied musicology in Munich with Sandberger, and in Berlin with Abert, Wolf, and Sachs; 1927, docent at the Univ. of Münster; 1929-31 editor of the 'Kirchenmusikalisches Jahrbuch'; 1931, prof. in Freiburg, Switzerland; 1939, succeeded Theodor Kroyer as prof. of music history at the Univ. of Cologne; 1943-45, in the Army, returning to Cologne after the war.—Writings: *Beiträge zur Musikgeschichte Freisings von den ältesten Zeiten bis zur Auflösung des Hofes 1803* (1926); *Der Palestrinastil und seine Bedeutung in der vokalen Kirchenmusik des 18. Jahrhunderts* (1928); *Die Deklamationsrhythmik in der vokalen Polyphonie des 16. Jahrhunderts* (1928); *Orgel und Orgelmusik* (1929); *Grundzüge der Geschichte der katholischen Kirchenmusik* (1930; 2d ed., 1949); *Palestrina* (1929); *Beiträge zur Choralbegleitung und Choralverarbeitung in der Orgelmusik des ausgehenden 18. und beginnenden 19. Jahrhunderts* (1932); *Das deutsche Kirchenlied im Ausland* (1935); *Puccini* (1937); *Grieg* (1942); *Deutsche Gregorianik im Frankenreich* (1941); *Die Musik im Wandel der Zeiten und Kulturen* (1948); *Die Messe* (1951); and many other essays, mostly on church music.

Fellowes, Rev. **Edmund Horace,** eminent English musicologist and editor; b. London, Nov. 11, 1870; d. Windsor, Dec. 20, 1951. He attended Winchester and Oriel Colleges, Oxford; studied music with P. C. Buck, Fletcher, and L. Straus; Mus. Bac., Oxford (1896); hon. Mus. Doc., Dublin Univ. (1917), Oxford (1938), and Cambridge (1950); 1897-1900, precentor at Bristol Cathedral. 1900 canon, 1923-27 conductor at St. George's Chapel, Windsor Castle; 1918, librarian at St. Michael's College, Tenbury; 1927-29, toured the U.S. and Canada with the Choir of St. George's Chapel and Choristers of Westminster Abbey; also lectured on old English music at various universities; 1932-33, lecturer on music, Liverpool Univ. He ed. the valuable collections *The English Madrigal School,* including the works of Thomas Morley, Orlando Gibbons, John Wilbye, John Farmer, Thomas Weelkes, William Byrd, Henry Lichfild, John Ward, Thomas Tomkins, Giles Farnaby, Thomas Bateson, John Bennet, George Kirbye, etc. (36 vols., 1913-36), and *The English School of Lutenist Songwriters,* containing the collected works of John Dowland, Thomas Campion, Thomas Ford, Francis Pilkington, Robert Jones, etc. (32 vols. 1920-32); co-editor of the Carnegie edition, *Tudor Church Music,* including works of White, Tallis, Taverner, Byrd, Gibbons (10 vols; 1919-47); editor of collected works of William Byrd (20 vols.; 1937-50); 11 Fantasies for strings by Orlando Gibbons (1925); songs of Fletcher and Beaumont; etc. Books: *English Madrigal Verse* (1920; 2nd ed., 1931); *The English Madrigal Composers* (1921; 2nd ed., 1948); *William Byrd, A Short Account of his Life and Work* (1923; 2nd ed., 1928); *Orlando Gibbons* (1925; 2nd ed., 1951); *The English Madrigal* (London, 1925); *Windsor Castle, St. George's Chapel and Choir* (1927); *Repertory of English Cathedral Music* (in collaboration with C. H. Stewart, 1930); *The Catalogue of the Manuscripts at St. Michael's College, Tenbury* (1934); *William Byrd* (1936; an entirely different book from the monograph of 1923, and much larger in scope; 2nd ed., 1948); *Westminster Abbey and Its Music; Organists and Masters of the Choristers of St. George's Chapel in Windsor Castle* (1939); *English Cathedral Music from Edward VI to Edward VII* (1941; rev., 1945). He wrote an autobiography *Memoirs of an Amateur Musician* (London, 1946). Fellowes was a composer of church music; in his early years he wrote many anthems, *Morning and Evening Service,* songs, and a string quartet.

Fels, Joachim. Pseudonym of **Theodor Hagen.**

Felsztyn (Felstin, Felstinensis, Felsztynski), Sebastian von, notable Polish theorist and composer; b. Felsztyn, Galicia, c. 1490; d. c. 1543. He studied (1507-9) at the Univ. of Cracow (bachelor's degree); chaplain at Felsztyn, later at Przemysl; then provost in Sanok. He wrote a compendium on Gregorian chant and mensural music, publ. in several editions (1515, 1519, 1522, 1534, 1539) as *Opusculum utriusque musicae tam choralis quam etiam mensuralis.* He further publ. a practical manual for church singing, *Directiones musicae ad cathedralis ecclesiae Premisliensis usum* (Cracow, 1543); edited St. Augustin's *Dialogus de musica* (with comments), and composed a volume of hymns, *Aliquot hymni ecclesiastici vario melodiarum genere editi* (Cracow, 1522; partly lost). His significance as composer lies in the fact that he was the first Polish musician to employ consistent 4-part writing; one selection for 4 voices is reprinted in Surzynski's *Monumenta musices sacrae in Polonia* (vol. II). —Cf. A. Chybinski, *The Relationship of Polish and West-European Music of the 15th and 16th Centuries* (1909; in Polish); A. Chybinski, *The Mensural Theory in Polish Musical Literature of the 1st Half of the 16th Century* (1911); S. Lobaczewska, *Sebastian Felsztyn as Composer* (1928). See also Zofia Lissa's article in 'Die Musik in Geschichte und Gegenwart.'

Felumb (feh-lŏŏm'), **Svend Christian,** Danish composer; b. Copenhagen, Dec. 25, 1898. He studied in Copenhagen with L. Nielsen and Bruce, and in Paris with Blenzel and Vidal; from 1924 till 1947 he was oboist in the Danish Royal Orch.; then conducted the Tivoli Orch. He is founder of the Society 'Ny Musik' in Copenhagen and a leader of the movement for modern national Danish music.

Fenaroli, Fedele, Italian theorist; b. Lanciano, April 25, 1730; d. Naples, Jan. 1, 1818. He studied with his father, who was a church organist; then went to Naples, where he became a pupil of Francesco Durante and Leonardo Leo at the Cons. of Santa Maria di Loreto; in 1762 became second master there, and in 1777 the first; also taught at the Cons. della Pietà. He trained many famous musicians (Cimarosa, Conti, Mercadante, Zingarelli, etc.); his theoretical manuals were highly regarded, not only in Italy, but in France; he publ. *Partimento ossia Basso numerato* (Rome, 1800); *Studio del contrappunto* (Rome, 1800); *Regale musicali per i principianti di cembalo* (Naples, 1775). He was a prolific composer of church music, which, however, did not sustain its initial renown; composed two oratorios, *Abigaille* (1760) and *L'arca nel Giordano.*—Cf. T. Consalvo, *La teoria musicale del Fenaroli* (1826); G. de Napoli, *F. Fenaroli nel secondo centenario della nascita,* in 'Musica d'oggi' (March, 1930).

Fenby, Eric, English composer; b. Scarborough, April 22, 1906. He studied piano and organ; after a few years as organist in London, he went (1928) to Grez-sur-Loing, France, as amanuensis for Frederick Delius, taking down his dictation note by note, until Delius' death in 1934. Two years later he publ. his experiences in a book entitled *Delius as I Knew Him.* Because of the beneficent work he undertook, his own composition has been very limited; however, he has written some small pieces and a work for string orch.

Fendler, Edvard, conductor, b. Leipzig, Jan. 22, 1902. He studied conducting with G. Brecher; composition with Leichtentritt; conducted in Germany, France, and Holland (1927-41); conductor of the National Symphony Orch., Ciudad Trujillo, Dominican Republic (1942-44); then was in the U. S. (1945-47); conductor of the National Symph. Orch. in San José, Costa Rica (1948-49); returned to the U.S.A. in 1949; in 1952 he was appointed conductor of the Mobile, Alabama, Symph. Orch.

Feo, Francesco, celebrated Italian composer; b. Naples, 1691; d. there, 1761. He was a pupil of Fago at the Cons. della Pietà from 1704; his first opera was *Amor tirannico* (Naples, Jan. 18, 1713); then followed *La forza della virtù* (Naples, Jan. 22, 1719), *Teuzzone* (Naples, Jan. 20, 1720), *Siface, re di Numidia* (Naples, Nov. 4, 1720), *Andromaca* (Rome, Feb. 5, 1730), and *Arsace* (Turin, Dec. 26, 1740). He also wrote pieces for special occasions, including a serenade for the marriage of Charles of Bourbon, King of the Two Sicilies, to Princess Maria Amalia of Poland (1737) and a piece for the Spanish King's birthday (1738). Feo spent most of his life in Naples; was first maestro di cappella at the Cons. of Sant' Onofrio (1723-39); then at the Cons. dei Poveri di Gesù Cristo (1739-43). Most of his works (150 in all) are extant in manuscript at Naples.

Ferand, Ernest T., musicologist and educator; b. Budapest, March 5, 1887. He studied composition with H. Koessler and V. von Herzfeld at the Royal Academy of Music, from which he graduated in 1911; then collaborated with Jaques-Dalcroze in Dresden-Hellerau, and Geneva; professor of theory and ear training at Fodor Cons. of Music, Budapest (1912-19); professor of music education, Dalcroze School, Hellerau (1920-25); director of Hellerau-Laxenburg College in Vienna (1925-38); Ph. D., Vienna Univ. (1937). In 1938 he emigrated to the U. S.; since 1939, teaching at the New School for Social Research, N. Y. He publ. a textbook on harmony in Hungarian (Budapest, 1914); *Die Improvisation in der Musik* (Zürich, 1939); an anthology of improvised music, *Die Improvisation in Beispielen aus neun Jahrhunderten abendländischer Musik* (Cologne, 1956); contributed valuable articles to music magazines, among them the following to the 'Mus. Quarterly': *The "Howling in Seconds" of the Lombards* (July, 1939); *Two Unknown Frottole* (July, 1941); *"Sodaine and Unexpected" Music in the Renaissance* (Jan., 1951), etc.

Ferchault, Guy, French musicologist; b. Mer (Loire-et-Cher), Aug. 16, 1904. He studied philosophy and music; held teaching positions in music education in Orléans (1941), Poitiers (1942-49), Tours (1948-51), and Roubaix (since 1952). He published a monograph on Henri Duparc (Paris, 1944); *Les créateurs du drame musical* (Paris, 1944); *Faust, une légende et ses musiciens* (Paris, 1948); *Claude Debussy, musicien français* (Paris, 1948); *Richard Wagner* (Paris, 1955).

Ferguson, Donald Nivison, American music educator; b. Waupun, Wis., June 30, 1882. Since 1913, teaching music at the Univ. of Minnesota. Author of *History of Musical Thought* (N. Y., 1935; rev. 1948); *A Short History of Music* (N. Y., 1943); *Piano Music of Six Great Composers* (N. Y., 1947); *On the Elements of Expression in Music* (mimeographed ed. Univ. of Minn., 1940); *Masterworks of the Orchestral Repertoire* (Minneapolis, 1954).

Ferguson, Howard, British composer; b. Belfast, Oct. 21, 1908. He studied composition with R. O. Morris at the Royal College of Music in London; piano with Harold Samuel. After several appearances as pianist, he devoted himself exclusively to composition. His music is neo-classical in essence; in some of his works he incorporates elements of Irish folksongs. He has written a ballet *Chauntecleer* (1948); several orchestral works: *Partita* (1936), *Four Diversions* (1939-42), *Coronation Overture* (1953), piano concerto (London Philharmonic, May 29, 1952, Myra Hess, soloist); octet for clarinet, bassoon, horn, string quartet, and double-bass (1933); 2 violin sonatas (1931; 1946); 3 *Medieval Carols* for mezzo-soprano and piano (1934); pieces for clarinet and piano; *Partita* for 2 pianos; several works for piano solo, etc. In 1953 Ferguson visited the U. S., and played concerts of his own works.—Cf. R. Hull, *British Music of Our Time* (London, 1946).

Fernández Arbós. See **Arbós, Enrique Fernández.**

Fernández Bordas (făr-nahn'-dăth bohr-dahs), **Antonio,** eminent Spanish violinist; b. Orense, Jan. 12, 1870; d. Madrid, Feb. 18, 1950. He studied at the Madrid Cons. with Jesús de Monasterio, and at the age of 11, won first prize for violin students; gave concerts in England, France, and other European countries; returning to Spain he became prof. of violin at the Madrid Cons.; in 1921 he was elected director.

Fernández Caballero (făr-năhn'-dăth kăh-băh-l'ya'-rŏh), **Manuel,** Spanish composer, b. Murcia, March 14, 1835; d. Madrid, Feb. 20, 1906. He was a precocious musician; learned to play violin, piano, and the piccolo as a child, and at the age of 7, played in a school band. He then studied violin with Soriano Fuertes in Murcia; in 1850 he entered the Madrid Cons., where his teachers were Eslava and Pedro Albéniz; in 1856 he received first prize in composition; then conducted various theater orchestras and became interested in theatrical composition. During his career as conductor and composer, he wrote more than 200 zarzuelas, several of which attained great popularity: *Los Dineros del Sacristan* and *Los Africanistas* (Barcelona, 1894); *El cabo primero* (Barcelona, 1895); *La Rueda de la Fortuna* (Madrid, 1896); *Los Estudiantes* (Madrid, 1900). He also wrote sacred music.

Fernandez, Oscar Lorenzo, Brazilian composer; b. Rio de Janeiro, Nov. 4, 1897; d. there, Aug. 26, 1948. He studied music at the Instituto Nacionale de Musica, and appeared as composer, conductor, and pianist in his own works in Brazil and other Latin American countries. He won several prizes. In 1925 he became prof. at the Instituto Nacionale, and organized a choral society there; in 1929 he was (with Villa-Lobos) a Brazilian representative at the International Exposition in Barcelona; in 1935 he became prof. at the Instituto de Arte of the University of Rio de Janeiro district; in 1936 he was elected director of the Brazilian Cons. in Rio de Janeiro; in 1938 he was the Brazilian representative at the Bogotá Festival, where he conducted a concert of Brazilian music; he was a member of numerous musical societies, and active in various educational fields. In his music he adopted a strongly national style, derived from Brazilian folksongs, without, however, actual quotation; his mastery of the technique of composition was indisputable.—Works: Opera, *Malazarte* (Rio de Janeiro, Sept. 30, 1941, composer conducting); ballet on Inca themes, *Amayá* (Rio de Janeiro, July 9, 1939); suite for orch. *Imbapará* (Rio de Janeiro, Sept. 2, 1929); suite for orch. *Reisado do pastoreio* (Rio de Janeiro, Aug. 22, 1930; the last movement of this suite, *Batuque,* a Brazilian dance, has become very popular); violin concerto (1942); a symphony (performed posthumously by the Boston Symph. Orch., Eleazar de Carvalho conducting, Feb. 25, 1949); also a number of chamber music compositions: *Trio Brasileiro* (1924; won the prize of the International Chamber Music competition); suite for flute, oboe, clarinet, bassoon, and horn (Rio de Janeiro, Sept. 20, 1927); several piano works; songs. —Cf. Otto Mayer-Serra, *Música y Músicos de Latinoamerica* (Mexico City, 1947). A complete bibliography of magazine articles on Fernandez is found in Vasco Mariz, *Dicionario Bio-Bibliografico Musical* (Rio de Janeiro, 1948).

Fernström, John (Axel), Swedish conductor and composer; b. in I-Chang, Hupei, China (the son of a Swedish missionary), Dec. 6, 1897. He studied violin in Copenhagen and Berlin; later took courses in conducting. He settled in Hälsingborg, where he founded an oratorio society. A very prolific composer, he has written 11 symphonies with programmatic titles, 2 operas, several concertos, and a great deal of chamber music. He published an autobiographical book *Confessions* (1946).

Ferrabosco, Alfonso, Italian composer; son of Domenico Ferrabosco; b. Bologna, Jan. (baptized Jan. 18), 1543; d. there, Aug. 12, 1588. He went to England as a youth; in 1562 he was in the service of Queen Elizabeth; went back to Italy in 1564; and was again in England from 1564 to 1569. He lived in France for some time, and married a woman from Antwerp; after another sojourn in England (1572-78) he was in Turin in the service of the Duke of Savoy, whom he accompanied to Spain (1585); eventually he returned to Bologna. The historical position of Alfonso Ferrabosco is important for the influence of Italian music that he brought to the court of Queen Elizabeth. Some of his madrigals are found in Young's 'Musica transalpina' (London, 1588, 1597), Morley's 'Madrigals to Five Voyces' (London, 1598), Pevernage's 'Harmonia celesta' (1593) and other collections up to 1664; further compositions appear in collections of P. Phalèse (1583, 1591, 1593), A. Morsolina (1588), G. B. Besardo (1603), etc. MSS are in the Bodleian Library and Music School at Oxford, British Museum, St. Michael's College, Tenbury, and Royal College of Music Library.—Cf. G. E. P. Arkwright, *Un compositore italiano alla corte di Elisabetta, Alfonso Ferrabosco di Bologna,* in the 'Rivista Musicale Italiana' (1897); S. Cordero di Pamparato, *Musici alla Corte di Carlo Emanuele I di Savoia* (Turin, 1930); A. Einstein, *The Italian Madrigal* (Princeton, 1949); see also J. Kerman, *Master Alfonso and the English Madrigal,* in the 'Mus. Quarterly' (April, 1952).

Ferrabosco, Alfonso, composer; natural son of the preceding; b. Greenwich, England, c. 1575; d. there, March (buried March 11), 1628. He was educated in England, and remained there after his father returned to Italy in 1578. He was supported from the funds of the English Court; was one of the King's Musicians for the Violins from about 1602 until his death. During the last year of his life he was made Composer of the King's Music; also Composer of Music in Ordinary to the King. He was highly regarded as composer of the music for masques of Ben Jonson, of whom he was a close friend: *The Masque of Blackness* (1604-05), *The Masque of Hymen* (1605-06), *The Masque of Beauty* (1607-08), *The Masque for Lord Haddington's Marriage* (1607-08), and *The Masque of Queens* (1608-09). In 1609 he publ. a vol. of *Ayres* (dedicated to Prince Henry) and a book of *Lessons for 1, 2 and 3 Viols;* also contributed 3 compositions to Leighton's *Teares or Lamentacions* (1614). MSS are in libraries of the British Museum, the Music School and Church, Oxford, and the Royal College of Music. His works for viols demonstrate extraordinary ability in contrapuntal writing, while preserving the rhythmic quality of the dance forms (pavans, etc.) and the free ornamental style of the fantasies.—Cf. G. E. P. Arkwright, *Notes on the Ferrabosco*

Family, in the 'Mus. Antiquary' (July, 1912); G. Livi, *The Ferrabosco Family,* ibid. (April, 1913).

Ferrabosco, Domenico Maria, Italian composer; b. Bologna, Feb. 14, 1513; d. there, Feb. 1574. He was maestro di cappella at San Petronio in Bologna; in 1546 he was at the Vatican, returning to Bologna in 1548; was again at the Vatican from 1550 until 1555. He is chiefly known as a composer of madrigals; his book of 45 madrigals, *Il Primo libro de' Madrigali a 4 voci,* was publ. by Gardano in 1542; Gardano also publ. motets (1554) and other madrigals (1557) by Ferrabosco; some madrigals and a 4-voiced canzona, the latter in lute tablature, appeared in 1584 (publ. by Scotto).

Ferrari, Benedetto, Italian opera composer, called 'Della Tiorba' from his proficiency on the theorbo; b. Reggio, 1597; d. Modena, Oct. 22, 1681. He studied music in Rome; in 1637 he proceeded to Venice; there he wrote the libretto of *Andromeda* (music by Francesco Manelli), which was the first opera that was publicly performed anywhere; it was produced at the Teatro Tron di San Cassiano, early in 1637; he then produced in Venice four operas to his own librettos: *Armida* (Feb. 1639); *Il pastor regio* (Jan. 23, 1640); *La ninfa avara* (1641); *Il principe giardiniero* (Dec. 30, 1643). In 1645 he went to Modena, where he remained until 1651, at the ducal court; from 1651-53 he was in Vienna; then returned to Modena, where he produced an opera *Erosilda* (1658); he also wrote two cantatas *Premo il giogo delle Alpi* and *Voglio di vita uscir* (reprinted in Riemann's *Kantatenfrühling,* 1912).

Ferrari, Carlotta, Italian composer of operas; b. Lodi, Jan. 27, 1837; d. Bologna, Nov. 23, 1907. She studied with Strepponi and Mazzucato at the Milan Cons.; then devoted herself to the composition of operas to her own librettos. The following operas were produced: *Ego* (Milan, 1857), *Sofia* (Lodi, 1866) and *Eleanora d'Armorea* (Cagliari, 1871).

Ferrari, Domenico, Italian composer and violinist; b. Piacenza, c. 1725; d. Paris, 1780. He studied with Tartini; traveled as a concert violinist, obtaining great success; in 1753 he joined the orch. of the Duke of Württemberg in Stuttgart; in 1754 he went to Paris, where he became extremely successful; he excelled as a virtuoso; his employment of passages in octaves, and particularly of harmonics, was an innovation at the time. He wrote several sets of violin sonatas and also trio sonatas, which were published.

Ferrari, Gabriella, French pianist and composer; b. Paris, Sept. 14, 1851; d. there, July 4, 1921. She studied at the Milan Cons. and later in Paris, where she had lessons with Gounod; apeared as a child prodigy at the age of twelve, and subsequently wrote a number of effective piano pieces *(Rapsodie espagnole, Le Ruisseau, Hirondelle,* etc.) and songs *(Larmes en Songe, Chant d'Exil, Chant d'Amour,* etc.); she also wrote for orch. and finally ventured to compose operas, producing *Le dernier amour* (Paris, June 11, 1895), *Sous le masque* (Vichy, 1898), *Le Tartare* (Paris, 1906), and *Le Cobzar,* which proved to be her most successful opera (Monte Carlo, Feb. 16, 1909; several subsequent revivals).

Ferrari, Giacomo Gotifredo, Italian composer; b. Rovereto, Tyrol (baptized April 2), 1763; d. London, Dec. 1842. He studied piano at Verona with Marcola and theory with Marianus Stecher at the Monastery of Mariaberg, Switzerland. He then went to Naples, where he studied with Latilla. There he met Chevalier Campan, household master for Marie Antoinette; he was then appointed as court musician at the Tuileries. He arrived in Paris in 1787; after the Revolution he went to London, where he settled as a singing teacher. He produced in London the operas *I due Svizzeri* (May 14, 1799), *Il Rinaldo d' Asti* (March 16, 1802), *L'eroina di Raab* (April 8, 1813), and *Lo sbaglio fortunato* (May 8, 1817); he also wrote two ballets and several instrumental works (4 septets; 2 piano concertos, etc.). He publ. a *Concise Treatise on Italian Singing* (1818); *Studio di musica pratica, teorica* (1830), and a book of reminiscences, *Anedotti piacevoli ed interresanti* (London, 1830, in Italian; contains some vivid recollections of Haydn and other celebrities; new ed., Palermo, 1920).—Cf. D. G. Fino, *Giacomo Gotifredo Ferrari, musicista roveretano* (Trent, 1928); G. de Saint-Foix, *A Musical Traveler,* in the 'Mus. Quarterly' (Oct., 1939).

Ferrari, Gustave, Swiss composer, conductor, and lecturer; b. Geneva, Sept. 28, 1872; d. there, July 29, 1948. He studied at the Geneva Cons., and later in Paris. In 1900 he went to London, where he remained for many years. From 1917 till 1925 he conducted operetta in America; then returned to Europe and toured with Yvette Guilbert, as her accompanist in a repertory of French folksongs; later on he gave song recitals himself, singing with his own accompaniment folksongs of France and French Canada; also lectured on the subject, and edited collections of French folk music. As a composer, he wrote mostly incidental music for the stage; composed a cantata for the Rousseau Festival (Geneva, 1912); *The Wilderness,* a Greek dance ballad (London, 1915); other choral works; a song cycle *Le Livre pour toi.*

Ferrari-Fontana, Edoardo, operatic tenor; b. Rome, July 8, 1878; d. Toronto, Canada, July 4, 1936. As a young man he was engaged in the Italian consular service in South America, and also studied singing. Returning to Italy in 1906, he made his début in Ganne's light opera *Hans il suonatore di flauto* (Milan, Dec. 5, 1907); his appearance as Tristan in Turin (Dec. 23, 1909) was so successful that he was engaged to sing in the principal theaters of Italy, and later at the Teatro Colón in Buenos Aires; during the 1913-14 season he was with the Boston Opera Co.; also sang at the Metropolitan Opera House (début Jan. 2, 1913). Apart from Wagnerian roles, he was also successful as Don José in *Carmen,* and as Canio in *Pagliacci.* He was married (June 26, 1912) to Margarete Matzenauer. In 1926 he settled in Toronto, where he was active as a singing teacher.

Ferrari-Trecate, Luigi, Italian composer; b. Alexandria, Piedmont, Aug. 25, 1884. He studied with Antonia Cicognani at the Cons. of Pesaro, and also with Mascagni. He was active as organist in various churches; from 1928-31 was prof. of organ at the Liceo Musicale in Bologna; in 1931, appointed director of the Parma Cons. He has written numerous operas and lyric fairy-tales, among them *Ciottolino* (a marionette play; Rome, Feb. 8, 1922); *Pierozzo* (Alexandria, Sept. 15, 1922); *Bellinda e il mostro* (Milan, 1926); *Le astuzie di Bertoldo* (Genoa, Jan. 10, 1934); *Ghirlino* (La Scala, Milan, Feb. 4, 1940); *Il re Orso* (Milan, 1949); *La capanna dello Zio Tom (Uncle Tom's Cabin;* Parma, Jan. 17, 1953).

Ferrata, Giuseppe, composer; b. Gradoli, Romagna, Jan. 1, 1865; d. New Orleans, March 28, 1928. At the age of 14 he won a scholarship to study at Santa Cecilia in Rome, where he took courses with Sgambati and Terziani, graduating in 1885; then had the good fortune of benefiting from the last lessons that Liszt gave; in 1892 came to the U.S.; taught in Pittsburgh and at Tulane Univ. in New Orleans. He wrote a symphony, a piano concerto, and a string quartet, which obtained a prize of the Pittsburgh Art Society (1908) and was publ.; also publ. are numerous songs, to Italian and English texts *(Night and the Curtains Drawn, A Song of Thanksgiving, On Music, Alla musa,* etc.); piano pieces *(Humoresque, A Wave, An Eagle, Leonard Serpent, Serenade triste);* compiled a book of scales and *Esthetic Exercises of Technique.*

Ferrer, Mateo, Catalan composer; b. Barcelona, Feb. 25, 1788; d. there, Jan. 4, 1864. A highly gifted musician, he was famous for his improvisations on the organ. He was organist at the Barcelona Cathedral for 52 years from 1812 until his death. His Sonata (1814), printed by Joaquín Nín in his collection, *16 Sonates anciennes d'auteurs espagnols* (Paris, 1925), shows a certain affinity with early Beethoven.

Ferrer, Rafael, Spanish composer and conductor; b. St.-Celoni, near Barcelona, May 22, 1911. He studied with Luis Millet and Enrique Morera (composition) and Eduardo Toldrá (violin). He played the violin in various orchestras in Spain; then devoted himself mainly to conducting. He specializes in Spanish music, and has revived many little-known works of Granados, Turina, and other Spanish composers; he has also conducted zarzuelas. Ferrer has written a violin concerto, and an orchestral suite on Catalan melodies; has arranged for orch. several piano works by Granados.

Ferrero, Willy, conductor; b. Portland, Maine, May 21, 1906; d. Rome, March 24, 1954. He was taken to Italy in his infancy; as a child of six he conducted a performance at the Teatro Costanzi in Rome; at the age of eight he conducted symphony concerts in European capitals with sensational success, and was the object of extravagant praise as a phenomenal musician. World War I interrupted his career; he continued to conduct operas and concerts in Italy, but failed to fulfill the extraordinary promise of his early youth. He received an excellent academic education; studied at the Vienna Academy (graduated in 1924); composed a symph. poem, *Il Mistero dell' aurora,* and some chamber music.—Cf. Alberto de Angelis, *Willy Ferrero* in 'Noi e il Mondo' (Rome, 1919).

Ferretti, Dom **Paolo,** eminent Italian musicologist, b. Subiaco, Dec. 3, 1866; d. Bologna, May 23, 1938. He studied theology at the Benedictine College of San Anselmo in Rome; then taught in Malta, Genoa, and Parma; was abbot of the Benedictine Monastery of San Giovanni in Parma; in 1922 was appointed by Pope Pius XI director of the Pontifical Institute of Sacred Music. During the summers of 1925, 1927, and 1928 he taught courses in Gregorian chant at the Pius X School of Liturgical Music in New York. The importance of his investigations lies in a scholarly analysis of the rhythmic treatment and especially the forms of Gregorian chant. He publ. *Principii teorici e practici del Canto Gregoriano* (Rome, 1905); *Il Cursus metrico e il Ritmo delle melodie del Canto Gregoriano* (Rome, 1913); *Estetica gregoriana* (Rome, 1934; French trans., Tournai, 1938); also numerous articles in various Italian and French publications.

Ferri, Baldassare, celebrated artificial soprano; b. Perugia, Dec. 9, 1610; d. there, Sept. 8, 1680. At the age of 11 he was choirboy to Cardinal Crescenzio in Orvieto, in whose service he remained until 1625, when he entered the service of Prince Ladislaus of Poland in Warsaw, remaining with him until 1655, with some interruptions for trips to Italy. From 1655 he was in Vienna at the court of Ferdinand III; appeared briefly in London (1671); then returned to Italy. His success at the various courts, and with the public in several countries, must have been great, for he accumulated a fortune. According to contemporary accounts (e. g., A. Bontempi, *Historia Musica,* 1695), he possessed a phenomenal voice.—Cf. G. Conestabile, *Notizie biografiche di Baldassare Ferri* (Perugia, 1846).

Ferrier, Kathleen, English contralto; b. Higher Walton, Lancashire, April 22, 1912; d. London, Oct. 8, 1953. She studied piano; for a time made her living as a telephone operator; began studying voice at the age of 25. Having appeared as a soloist in *Messiah* at Westminster Abbey in 1943, she rapidly advanced to the first rank among English singers. She sang the title role in the première of Britten's *Rape of Lucretia* (Glyndebourne, 1946); made two highly successful tours in the U. S. in 1947-48 and in 1950-51. Towards the end of her brief career she acquired in England an almost legendary reputation for vocal excellence and impeccable musical taste, so that her death (of cancer) was mourned by musicians as a national calamity. Numerous articles and monographs were publ. on her life and her art, among them a symposium edited by N. Cardus, *Kathleen Ferrier, a Memoir* (London, 1954), and an extensive biography by Charles Rigby, *Kathleen Ferrier* (London, 1955). Her sister, Winifred Ferrier, publ. a volume of personal reminiscences, *Kathleen Ferrier* (London, 1955).

Ferroni, Vincenzo Emidio Carmine, Italian composer and educator; b. Tramutola, Feb. 17, 1858; d. Milan, Jan. 10, 1934. He studied at the Paris Cons. (1876-83) with Savard and Massenet; in 1888 returned to Italy, where he became prof. of composition at the Milan Cons., succeeding Ponchielli; resigned in 1929. He wrote 3 operas: *Rudello* (Milan, 1892), *Ettore Fieramosca* (Como, 1896), and *Il Carbonaro* (Milan, 1900); 2 symphonies, a symph. poem, *Risorgimento,* and many works in smaller forms. He also publ. *Della forma musicale classica.*

Ferroud (fehr-rŏŏ'), **Pierre-Octave,** French composer; b. Chasselay, near Lyons, Jan. 6, 1900; d. near Debrecen, Hungary (killed in an automobile accident), Aug. 17, 1936. He attended the Univ. of Lyons, and studied there and in Strasbourg with Erb, Ropartz, Witkowski, and Florent Schmitt; in 1923 settled in Paris, where he developed varied activities as composer, music critic, and adviser for radio broadcasting; was also active in organizing concerts of modern music. He first attracted attention with the performance of a ballet *Le Porcher* (Ballets suédois, Paris, Nov. 15, 1924); there followed the symph. poem *Foules* (Paris, March 21, 1926); an operatic sketch, *Chirurgie,* after Chekhov (Monte Carlo, March 20, 1928); and a symphony in A major (Paris, March 8, 1931, Monteux conducting; also at the Prague Festival of the International Society for Contemporary Music, Sept. 6, 1935); other works are the ballets, *Jeunesse* (Paris, April 29, 1933) and *Vénus ou l'équipée planétaire* (1935); cello sonata (1933); *Andante cordial* for violin, cello, and piano; trio for oboe, clarinet, and bassoon (1934); also several song cycles and piano pieces. Ferroud's music is distinguished by an adroit application of contrapuntal methods to compositions of essentially popular style; his chief influence was Florent Schmitt, about whom he wrote a book, *Autour de Florent Schmitt* (Paris, 1927). See René Dumesnil, *Pierre-Octave Ferroud,* in the 'Revue Musicale' (Oct.-Nov., 1931).

Fesca, Alexander Ernst, German pianist and composer, son of Friedrich Ernst Fesca; b. Karlsruhe, May 22, 1820; d. Brunswick, Feb. 22, 1849. He studied with his father, and later with Taubert. He was extremely successful as a concert pianist in 1839; in 1841 he became chamber musician to Prince Fürstenberg; settled in Brunswick in 1842, where he brought out his operas *Der Troubadour* (July 25, 1847) and *Ulrich von Hutten* (1849); he wrote also a piano sextet, 2 piano trios, a violin sonata, and many songs, some of which became popular. His early death at the age of 28 was regretted by many admirers who believed that he was a composer of uncommon talent.

Fesca, Friedrich Ernst, German composer; b. Magdeburg, Feb. 15, 1789; d. Karlsruhe, May 24, 1826. He studied violin; in 1804 he went to Leipzig, where he studied with August Eberhardt Müller; made a début in his own violin concerto; in 1806 he joined the orch. of the Duke of Oldenburg; in 1808 he obtained a similar position at the Westphalian court at Kassel; in 1813 he was in Vienna; in 1814 became a member of the Karlsruhe Orch. He was a prolific composer of chamber music (20 quartets and 5 quintets); also wrote 2 operas, *Cantemire* (1819) and *Omar und Leila* (1823); 3 symphonies, 4 overtures, etc.

Fesch, Willem de, Flemish organist; b. Alkmaar, Aug. 25, 1687; d. London, Jan. 3, 1761. He was organist at Antwerp; in 1731 went to London, where he produced his oratorios *Judith* (1733) and *Joseph* 1745).—Cf. F. van den Bremt, *Willem de Fesch, Nederlands Componist en Virtuoos* (Louvain, 1949).

Festa, Costanzo, Italian composer; b. Rome, c. 1490; d. there, April 10, 1545. He was a singer in the Pontifical Chapel from about 1517. He was a composer of much importance, being regarded as a forerunner of Palestrina, whose works were strongly influenced by those of Festa; was the first important Italian musician who successfully fused the Flemish and Italian styles, melodically and harmonically. He may well be considered one of the first, if not the first, of the native Italian madrigalists. The earliest known publ. work of his appeared in 1519. Of his numerous compositions, many sacred works were publ. in various collections from 1513 till 1549; a *Te Deum a 4* (publ. in Rome, 1596) is still sung in the Vatican on solemn festivals. A complete list of Festa's works, together with reprints, is found in A. Cametti's *Per un precursore del Palestrina; il compositore piemontese Costanzo Festa,* in 'Bollettino bibliografico musicale' (April, 1931); publication of a complete edition of his works was begun in 1940 by the Istituto Italiano per la Storia della Musica Sacra (Rome).

Festing, Michael Christian, English violinist; b. London, c. 1680; d. there, July 24, 1752. He was a pupil of Richard Jones and Geminiani. In 1735 he joined the king's private band and became first violin in an amateur group called the Philh. Society; 1737, appointed director of the Italian Opera; 1742, conductor at Ranelagh Gardens. In 1738 he established, with Dr. Greene and others, the 'Society of Musicians,' for the maintenance of impoverished musicians and their families. — Works: numerous solos and concertos for violin; 18 sonatas for violins and bass; cantatas; songs.

Fétis, Édouard-Louis François, Belgian music editor; son of François-Joseph Fétis; b. Bouvigne, near Dinant, May 16, 1812; d. Brussels, Jan. 31, 1909. He edited his father's 'Revue musicale' (1833-35); was for years librarian of the Brussels Library. He publ. *Les Musiciens belges* (1848) and *Les Artistes belges à l'étranger* (1857-65), and compiled a catalogue of his father's library. His brother, **Adolphe-Louis-Eugène Fétis** (b. Paris, Aug. 20, 1820; d. there, March 20, 1873), was a pupil of his father, and of Herz (piano); lived in Brussels and Antwerp, and from 1856 in Paris as a music teacher. He composed music for piano and harmonium.

Fétis (fā-tēs'), **François-Joseph,** erudite Belgian musical theorist, historian, and critic; b. Mons, March 25, 1784; d. Brussels, March 26, 1871. He received primary instruction from his father, an organist at the Mons cathedral; learned to play the violin, piano, and organ when very young, and in his ninth year wrote a concerto for violin with orch.; as a youth was organist to the Noble Chapter of Sainte-Waudru. In 1800 he entered the Paris Cons., where he studied harmony with Rey and piano with Boieldieu and Pradher; in 1803 he visited Vienna, there studying counterpoint, fugue, and masterworks of German music. Several of his compositions (a symphony, an overture, sonatas and caprices for piano) were published at that time. In 1806 Fétis began the revision of the plainsong and entire ritual of the Roman Church, a vast undertaking completed, with many interruptions, after 30 years of patient research. A wealthy marriage in the same year enabled him to pursue his studies at ease for a time; but the fortune was lost in 1811, and he retired to the Ardennes, where he occupied himself with composition and philosophical researches into the theory of harmony; in 1813, he was appointed organist for the collegiate church of St.-Pierre at Douai. In 1818 he settled in Paris; in 1821 became prof. of composition at the Paris Cons.; in 1824 his *Traité du contrepoint et de la fugue* was publ. and accepted as a regular manual at the Cons. In 1827 he became librarian of the Cons., and in the same year founded his unique journal 'La Revue musicale,' which he edited alone until 1832; his son edited it from 1833 until 1835, when its publication ceased. Fétis also wrote articles on music for 'Le National' and 'Le Temps.' In 1828 he competed for the prize of the Netherlands Royal Institute with a treatise *Quels ont été les mérites des Néerlandais dans la musique, principalement aux XIVe-XVIe siècles . . .*; Kiesewetter's essay on the same subject won the prize, but Fétis' paper was also printed by the Institute. In 1832 he inaugurated his famous series of historical lectures and concerts. In 1833 he was called to Brussels as maître de chapelle to King Leopold I, and Director of the Cons.; during his long tenure of the latter position, for nearly 40 years, the Cons. flourished as never before. He also conducted the concerts of the Academy, which elected him a member in 1845. Fétis was a confirmed believer in the possibility of explaining music history and music theory scientifically; in his scholarly writings he attempted a thorough systematization of all fields of the art; he was opinionated and dogmatic, but it cannot be denied that he was a pioneer in musicology. He published the first book on music appreciation, *La Musique mise à la portée de tout le monde* (Paris, 1830; numerous reprints and transls. into English, German, Italian, Spanish, Russian); further pedagogical writings are: *Solfèges progressifs* (Paris, 1837); *Traité complet de la théorie et de la pratique de l'harmonie* (Brussels, 1844). As early as 1806 Fétis began collecting materials for his great *Biographie universelle des musiciens et bibliographie générale de la musique* in 8 vols. (Paris, 1833-44; 2nd. ed., 1860-65; supplement of 2 vols. 1878-80, edited by A. Pougin). This work of musical biography was unprecedented in its scope; entries on composers and performers whom Fétis knew personally still remain prime sources of information. On the negative side are the many fanciful accounts of composers' lives taken from unreliable sources; in this respect Fétis exercised a harmful influence on subsequent lexicographers for a whole century. His *Histoire générale de la musique,* in 5 vols., only goes as far as the 15th century (Paris, 1869-76); this work exhibits Fétis as a profound scholar, but also as a dogmatic philosopher of music propounding opinions without convincing evidence to support them. Of interest are his *Esquisse de l'histoire de l'harmonie considerée comme art et comme science systématique* (Paris, 1840); *Notice biographique de Nicolo Paganini* (Paris, 1851; with a short history of the violin); *Antoine Stradivari* (Paris, 1856; with a commentary on bowed instruments); reports on musical instruments at the Paris Expositions of 1855 and 1867, etc. Fétis was also a composer; between 1820 and 1832 he wrote 7 operas, serious and light, for the Opéra-Comique; he composed church music, 3 string quartets, 3 string quintets, 2 symphonies, and a flute concerto. His valuable library of 7,325 vols. was acquired after his death by the Bibliothèque Royale of Brussels; a catalogue was publ. in 1877.—Cf. K. Gollmick, *Fétis als Mensch, Kritiker, Theoretiker und Komponist* (Berlin, 1852); L. Alvin, *Notice sur François-Joseph Fétis* (Brussels, 1874); R. Wangermée, *F.-J. Fétis, musicologue et compositeur* (Brussels, 1951).

Feuermann (foi'-er-man), **Emanuel,** cello virtuoso; b. Kolomea, Galicia, Nov. 22, 1902; d. New York, May 25, 1942. He studied with Anton Walter in Vienna and with Julius Klengel in Leipzig; taught at the Cologne Cons. at the age of 16; then toured Europe and the U.S.; from 1930-33 he was prof. at the Berlin Hochschule für Musik; in 1934 went to Vienna. He made his American début with the N.Y. Philharmonic, Jan. 2, 1935; also gave chamber music concerts with Schnabel and Hubermann. He owned a rare Stradivarius cello.

Fevin (feu-van'), **Antoine de,** French composer; b. probably in Arras, 1474; d. Blois, Jan. 1512. He was a younger contemporary of Josquin des Prez, whose style he emulated. He composed 12 masses, 6 of which were printed in collections by Petrucci (1515) and Antico (1516); also 29 motets, 3 Magnificats, and Lamentations (publ. by Montanus in 1549). 3 works by Fevin (in MS) are in the archives of Toledo Cathedral (cf. F. Rubio Piqueras, *Música y músicos toledanos,* 1923). 6 motets were printed in Petrucci's *Motetti della corona* (1514), and some French chansons in various collections. Fevin's mass *Mente tota* is reprinted in Expert's *Maîtres musiciens* (vol. 5); a 6-voice motet and parts of masses are in Eslava's *Lira sacro-hispana;* a 4-voice *Kyrie* in Burney's *General History of Music* (Vol. 2); the mass *Ave Maria* and *Benedictus et Hosanna* in Delporte's *Collection de Polyphonie classique;* several motets reprinted by B. Kahmann (Amsterdam, 1951).—Cf. P. Wagner, in *Geschichte der Messe* (Vol. I); J. Delporte, in 'Revue liturgique et musicale' (Jan.-Feb., 1935).

Fevin, Robert, composer; a native of Cambrai, probably a relative of Antoine Fevin. He was maestro di cappella to the Duke of Savoy at the beginning of the 16th century. One mass, *Le vilain jaloux,* probably by Robert Fevin, was printed by Petrucci as by Antoine Fevin; another, on *La sol fa re mi,* is in MS in the Munich Library.

Février (fā-vr'yā'), **Henri,** French opera composer; b. Paris, Oct. 2, 1875. He studied at the Cons. with Fauré, Leroux, Messager, Pugno, and Massenet; composed the operas *Le roi aveugle* (Paris, May 8, 1906), *Monna Vanna* (Paris, Jan. 13, 1909), *Gismonda* (Chicago, Jan. 14, 1919; Paris, Oct. 15, 1919), *La Damnation de Blanche-Fleur* (Monte Carlo, March 13, 1920), *La Femme nue* (Monte Carlo, March 23, 1929); the operettas *Agnès, dame galante* (1912), *Carmosine* (1913), *Île désenchantée* (Paris, Nov. 21, 1925), etc. Février is the author of the book *André Messager; mon maître, mon ami* (Paris, 1948).

Ffrangcon-Davies (frank'-ohn-), **David Thomas** (real name, David Thomas Davis; the surname Ffrangcon was taken from the Nant-Ffrangcon mountain range near his birthplace), prominent British baritone; b. Bethesda, Caernarvon, Dec. 11, 1855; d. London, April 13, 1918. He was ordained a priest in 1884, but later left the church to take up a musical career; studied singing with Richard Latter, Shakespeare, and Randegger in London; made his concert début in Manchester (Jan. 6, 1890); stage début at Drury Lane Theatre (April 26, 1890). From 1896-8, he sang in festivals throughout the U. S. and Canada; then lived in Berlin (1898-1901); from 1903, professor of singing at the Royal College of Music, London. After a nervous breakdown in 1907 he gave up public singing. His book, *The Singing of the Future* (London, 1905; preface by Elgar), was republished by his daughter, Marjorie Ffrangcon-Davies, as Part II of *David Thomas Ffrangcon-Davies, His Life and Book* (London, 1938; introduction by Ernest Newman).

Fibich, Zdenko, Czech composer; b. Seboriče, Dec. 21, 1850; d. Prague, Oct. 15, 1900. He studied first in Prague, then at the Leipzig Cons. with Moscheles (piano) and Richter (theory). Upon his return to Prague, he occupied the posts of conductor of the National Theater (1875-78) and director of the Russian Church choir (1878-81). From then on, he continued to live in Prague, devoting himself mainly to composition. In his music, he was greatly influenced by Wagner, and applied quasi-Wagnerian methods even when treating national Bohemian subjects. His main distinction was a gift of facile melody, and he was at his best in his short pieces, such as *Poème,* op. 41, no. 6, for piano, which has become extremely popular through many arrangements for various instrumental combinations.—Works: Operas (produced at Prague): *Bukovin* (April 16, 1874); *Blaník* (Nov. 25, 1881); *Nevěsta Messinska* (*The Bride of Messina;* March 28, 1884; very popular); *Bouře* (*The Tempest;* March 1, 1895); *Hédy* after Byron's *Don Juan* (Feb. 12, 1896); *Sarka* (Dec. 28, 1897); *Pad Arkuna* (*The Fall of Arkun;* produced posthumously, Nov. 9, 1900; his most important work); music to the dramatic trilogy *Hippodamia* by Vrchlický: (1) *The Wooing of Pelops* (Feb. 21, 1890); (2) *The Atonement of Tantalus* (June 2, 1891); (3) *Hippodamia's Death* (Nov. 8, 1891). For orch.: 3 symphonies (No. 1, F, 1883; No. 2, E♭, 1893; No. 3, E minor, 1898); symphonic poems: *Othello* (1873); *Zaboj, Slavoj a Ludek* (1873); *Toman a lesni panna* (*Toman and the Wood Nymph*; 1875); *Bouře* (*The Tempest*; 1880); *Věsna* (*Spring*; 1881); *Vigiliae,* for small orch. (1883); *V Podvečer* (*At Twilight*; 1893); a choral ballad, *Die Windsbraut;* melodramas: *Štědry Den* (*Christmas Day*; 1875); *Vodnik* (*The Water Sprite;* 1883); *Hákon* (1888); *Věčnost* (*Eternity*; 1878); *Spring Romanza* for chorus and orch. (1880); 2 string quartets; piano quartet; *Romance* for violin and piano; piano pieces; songs; choruses. He also published a method for piano.—Cf. C. L. Richter, *Zdenko Fibich* (Prague, 1899); Zd. Nejedlý, *Fibich* (Prague, 1900); O. Hostinský, *Erinnerungen an Fibich* (1909); J. Bartoš, *Zdenko Fibich* (1913); A. Rektorys, *Zdenko Fibich* (2 vols., Prague, 1952).

Ficher (fē-chär'), **Jacobo,** composer; b. Odessa, Jan. 14, 1896. He studied violin with Korguev and composition with Kalafati and Steinberg at the St. Petersburg Cons., graduating in 1917. He then left Russia and settled in Buenos Aires, where he earned his living by playing in theater orchestras; in the meantime he began to compose; in 1937 he won an Elizabeth Sprague Coolidge Prize for his second string quartet. He was a founder, with several Argentine composers, of a society, 'Grupo Renovación,' for the advancement of modern music. He was also active as conductor in Buenos Aires. Much of his early music was inspired by Jewish melodies; the influence of the Russian school was also noticeable. His mature style is characterized by a rhapsodic fluency of development, harmonic fullness, and orchestral brilliance.—Works: chamber operas: *The Bear* (1952) and *Proposal in Marriage* (1955), both after Chekhov; the ballets: *Colombina de Hoy* (1933), *Los Invitados* (1933), *Melchor* (1938-39), *Golondrina* (1942); for orch.: two suites (No. 1, on Jewish themes, 1924; No. 2, 1926); 5 symphonies (No. 1, 1932; No. 2, 1933; No. 3, 1940; No. 4, 1946; No. 5, 1947); *Poema Heroico* (1927; Leningrad Philh. Prize, 1928); *Sulamita,* symph. poem (1927; Buenos Aires, July 20, 1929); 2 symphonic poems, after Tagore (1928); *Obertura Patetica* (Buenos Aires, May 17, 1930); *3 Bocetos sinfónicos sobre el Talmud* (1930; 1st prize of Buenos Aires Philh.); violin concerto (1942); 2 piano concertos (No. 1, 1945; No. 2, 1954); chamber music: 4 string quartets (No. 1, 1927; No. 2, 1936; No. 3, 1943; No. 4, 1952); 2 violin sonatas (No. 1, 1929; No. 2, 1945); *Suite en estilo antiguo,* for flute, oboe, clarinet, bassoon, and horn (1930); sonata for viola, flute, and piano (1931); sonatina for saxophone, trumpet, and piano (1932); piano trio (1935); flute sonata (1935); clarinet sonata (1937); oboe sonata (1940); cello sonata (1943); sonata for flute and clarinet (1949); sonata for flute, oboe, and bassoon (1950); viola sonata (1953); 2 piano sonatas; several albums of piano pieces (including 2 sets of 'Fables', descriptive of animals, in a humorous vein); also choral works.

Fickenscher, Arthur, American composer and pianist; b. Aurora, Ill., March 9, 1871; d. San Francisco, April 15, 1954. He studied at the Munich Cons.; appeared there as a pianist (1895); toured the U. S. as accompanist to famous singers, among them Bispham and Schumann-Heink; taught at the Von Meyerinck School of Music, San Francisco, and Jenkins School of Music, Oakland, Calif.; also privately in Berlin, San Francisco, and New York. From 1920 till 1941 he was head of the Music Dept. of the Univ. of Virginia, Charlottesville, and organist of the Christ Episcopal Church there. In 1947 he settled in San Francisco. A musician of an inquisitive mind, he elaborated a system of pure intonation; invented the 'Polytone,' an instrument designed to play music in which the octave is subdivided into 60 tones; publ. an article, *The Polytone and the Potentialities of a Purer Intonation,* in the 'Mus. Quarterly' (July, 1941). His major work was the *Evolutionary Quintet,* evolved from a violin sonata and an orchestral scherzo written in the 1890's; the manuscripts were burned in the San Francisco earthquake and fire of 1906; the musical material was then used from memory for a quintet for piano and strings, in 2 movements; the second movement, entitled *The Seventh Realm,* became a separate work. He also wrote *Willowwave and Wellowway* for orch. (1925); *The Day of Judgment,* for orch. (1927; Grand Rapids, Feb. 10, 1934); *Out of the Gay Nineties,* for orch. (Richmond, Va., Dec. 4, 1934, composer conducting); *Variations on a Theme in Medieval Style* for string orch. (1937); *Dies Irae,* for chamber orch. (1927); *The Chamber Blue,* a mimodrama for orch., soli, women's chorus, and dancers (Univ. of Virginia, April 5, 1938); a large choral work, with orch. *The Land East of the Sun and West of the Moon* (after William Morris).

Ficker, Rudolf von, distinguished German musicologist; b. Munich, June 11, 1886; d. Igls, near Innsbruck, Aug. 2, 1954. From 1905-1912 he studied at the Univ. of Vienna with Adler (musicology), and in Munich with Thuille and Courvoisier (composition); 1913, *Dr. phil.;* lecturer at the Univ. of Innsbruck (1920); associate prof. of musicology at the Univ. of Vienna, and co-director of the Musicological Seminary there; succeeded Sandberger as professor at the Univ. of Munich (1930). He was a specialist in early Gothic music.—Writings: *Beiträge zur Chromatik des 14. bis 16. Jahrhunderts,* in Adler's 'Studien zur Musikwissenschaft' (1914); *Formprobleme der mittelalterlichen Musik,* in 'Zeitschrift für Musikwissenschaft' (1925); *Die Musik des Mittelalters und ihre Beziehungen zum Geistesleben,* in 'Vierteljahrsschrift für Literaturwissenschaft und Geistesgeschichte' (1925); *Primäre Klangformen,* in 'Jahrbuch der Musikbibliothek Peters' (1929); *Polyphonic Music of the Gothic Period,* in the

'Mus. Quarterly' (Oct., 1929); *Agwillare, a Piece of Late Gothic Minstrelsy,* in the 'Mus. Quarterly' (April, 1936); *Wandlungen des Mozartbildes* (1941); *Probleme der modalen Notation,* in 'Acta Musicologica' (1946). He edited vol. XXVII, 1 (4th selection from the Trent Codices; in collaboration with A. Orel) and vol. XXXI (5th selection) in the 'Denkmäler der Tonkunst in Österreich'; likewise the *Sederunt principes* of Pérotin (1930).

Fiedler, Arthur, American conductor; b. Boston, Dec. 17, 1894. He studied with his father, Emanuel Fiedler, a violinist of the Boston Symphony Orch.; after graduating from high school in Boston, he went to Berlin, where he studied with Willy Hess. He returned to the U. S. in 1914, and soon joined the Boston Symph. as viola player; in 1929 he organized the Esplanade Concerts in Boston, playing light and classical music outdoors; in 1930 he was appointed conductor of the Boston Pops, a series of summer concerts. Adroitly combining music of popular appeal with movements from classical symphonies and occasional modern works, and employing soloists, Fiedler has built an eager audience in Boston; traveled with his especially assembled orchestra all over the U. S.; has also made guest appearances with the San Francisco Orch. and in Europe. At various times he conducted the Cecilia Choral Society of Boston, and several other organizations.

Fiedler, Max, German conductor; b. Zittau, Dec. 31, 1859; d. Stockholm, Dec. 1, 1939. He was a piano pupil of his father, and studied the organ and theory with G. Albrecht; attended the Leipzig Cons. (1877-80); won the Holstein scholarship. In 1882 appointed teacher at the Hamburg Cons.; in 1903 director; 1904, succeeded Barth as conductor of the Hamburg Philh. Society. Although he had won an enviable reputation as a concert pianist, he soon abandoned that career (appearing only occasionally in ensemble), and rapidly won distinction as a conductor. He was guest conductor of the N. Y. Philh. Orch. in the season of 1905-06; 1907, conducted the London Symph. Orch.; 1908-12, conductor of the Boston Symph. Orch.; then returned to Germany, taking up his residence in Berlin; from 1916 conductor of the Symph. Orch. at Essen; 1934, guest conductor in Stockholm; 1935, again in Berlin. He composed a symphony, a piano quintet and a string quartet, a *Lustspiel* overture, piano pieces, and songs.—Cf. G. Degmek, *Max Fiedler; Werden und Werken* (Essen, 1940).

Field, John, Irish pianist and composer; b. Dublin, July 26, 1782; d. Moscow, Russia, Jan. 23, 1837. His father was a violinist; his grandfather, an organist; it was from his grandfather that he received his first instruction in music. He then had lessons with Clementi, and was also employed in the salesrooms of Clementi's music establishment in London. In 1802 he followed Clementi to Paris, and in 1803 to St. Petersburg, where Field settled as a teacher and performer. After many concert tours in Russia, he returned to England temporarily, and performed his Concerto in E♭ with the London Philharmonic (Feb. 27, 1832); he continued a European tour in 1833, playing in Paris, in Switzerland, and in Italy. He was stricken with an ailment at Naples, and remained in a hospital for nine months; at the end of his resources, he was persuaded by a friendly Russian family to return to Moscow. On the way, he was able to give a concert in Vienna with extraordinary success; but the combination of alcoholism and general ill health led to his death two years after arrival in Moscow. Field's historical position is of importance, even though his music in itself does not reveal a great original talent. He was undoubtedly a precursor of Chopin in his treatment of piano technique; he was also the originator of keyboard nocturnes. He greatly developed the free fantasias and piano recitative, while following the basic precepts of classical music. Like Chopin after him, Field wrote mainly for the piano; he composed 7 piano concertos; 4 sonatas; 18 nocturnes; polonaises and other pieces, also a quintet for piano and strings and 2 divertimenti for piano, strings, and flute.—Bibl.: H. Dessauer, *John Field, sein Leben und seine Werke* (Langensalza, 1912); Wm. H. Grattan Flood, *John Field of Dublin* (Dublin, 1920); E. von Tideböhl, *Reminiscences of John Field* in the 'Monthly Musical Record' (1923); E. Blom, *John Field* in the 'Chesterian' (1930); F. Liszt, *Über John Field's Nocturnes* (Hamburg, 1859; also in vol. IV of Liszt's 'Gesammelte Schriften,' Leipzig, 1882).

Fielitz, Alexander von, German conductor and composer; b. Leipzig, Dec. 28, 1860; d. Bad Salzungen, July 29, 1930. He was of Slavic origin; his mother was Russian. He studied piano with Julius Schulhoff and composition with Kretschmer in Dresden; in conducting he profited by the advice of Nikisch. He conducted opera in various German towns; a nervous disorder caused him to take a prolonged rest in Italy (1887-97); then he settled in Berlin as a teacher. From 1905-08 he was in Chicago, where he organized an orch. and conducted it for a season; in 1908 he returned to Berlin as teacher and later director (1916) at Stern's Cons. He wrote a number of songs and piano pieces; his song cycle *Eliland* and his songs based on Tuscan folk music were quite popular; he also wrote 2 operas, *Vendetta* (Lübeck, 1891) and *Das stille Dorf* (Hamburg, March 13, 1900).

Figner, Nicolay Nicolayevitch, celebrated Russian tenor; b. St. Petersburg, 1857; d. Kiev, Dec. 13, 1919. He was a lieutenant in the Russian Navy before his voice was discovered; then he studied diligently in Milan; in 1887 he returned to Russia, and was engaged as a tenor at the Imperial Theater in St. Petersburg. He was the favorite tenor of Tchaikovsky, and was selected to sing the leading role in the première of *The Queen of Spades;* his interpretation of Lensky in *Eugene Onegin* was also famous. In 1889 he married the Italian soprano Medea Mei, who wrote a book of memoirs (St. Petersburg, 1912), in which she described their careers.

Figueroa, José, Puerto Rican violinist; b. San Sebastian, Puerto Rico, March 24, 1905. He studied with Fernández Bordas in Madrid and J. Thibaud in Paris. He settled in New York in 1941.

Figulus (real name Töpfer), **Wolfgang,** German writer on music; b. Naumburg, c. 1525; d. Meissen, c. 1591. He studied in Leipzig; 1549-51, cantor at the Thomasschule in Leipzig; 1551-58, at the Fürstenschule in Meissen. He wrote *Elementa musicae* (1555; many other editions); revised Martin Agricola's *Deutsche Musica* (1560); publ. a book of motets, *Precationes* (Leipzig, 1553); *Cantiones sacrae* (1575); and *Hymni sacri et scholastici* (revised by his son-in-law, Friedrich Birck, 1604); a collection of Christmas songs, containing works of his own, of Martin Agricola and others, was publ. posthumously in two books (1594 and 1605). For a detailed list of MS works and bibliographical references, see W. Brennecke's article on Figulus in 'Die Musik in Geschichte und Gegenwart.'

Figuš-Bystrý (fē'-gŏŏsh bē'-strē), **Villiam,** Slovak composer; b. Banská Bystrica, Feb. 28, 1875; d. there, May 11, 1937. He spent many years in collecting Slovak folk melodies, which he publ. in 5 vols. (1906-15) for voice and piano; also publ. a collection of 1000 arranged for piano only (1928). He further wrote an opera, *Detvan* (Bratislava, Aug. 1, 1928); a cantata *Slovenská Piesen* (1913); an orchestral suite *From My Youth;* piano quartet; piano trio; 3 sonatines for violin and piano; violin pieces; piano works; choruses and songs.

Filiasi, Lorenzo, Italian composer; b. Naples, March 25, 1878. He studied at the Cons. di S. Pietro a Majella with Nicola d'Arienzo. His first success came with the opera *Manuel Menendez,* which won the Sonzogno Competition Prize in 1902, and was produced in Milan (May 15, 1904); his other operas were *Fior di Neve* (La Scala, April 1, 1911), *Messidoro* (1912), etc. He also wrote a pantomime, *Pierrot e Bluette* (1895); a choral work with orch., *La preghiera del marinaio italiano; Visioni romantiche* for orch.; violin pieces and many songs.

Filippi, Filippo, Italian composer and critic; b. Vicenza, Jan. 13, 1830; d. Milan, June 25, 1887. He studied law at Padua, taking his degree in 1853. In 1852 he began his career as a music critic with a warm defense of Verdi's *Rigoletto;* from 1858 till 1862 was editor of the 'Gazzetta Musicale,' and in 1859 music critic of the newly founded 'Perseveranza.' He publ. a collection of essays on great musicians, *Musica e Musicisti* (Milan, 1876); as a zealous Wagnerite he wrote a pamphlet, *Riccardo Wagner* (in German, as *Richard Wagner: eine musikalische Reise in das Reich der Zukunft,* 1876); also publ. a monograph *Della vita e delle opere di Adolfo Fumagalli* (Milan, 1857); composed a string quintet, 9 string quartets, piano trio; piano pieces, songs.

Filke, Max, German composer; b. Steubendorf-Leobschütz, Silesia, Oct. 5, 1855; d. Breslau, Oct. 8, 1911. He studied with Brosig in Breslau and with Haberl at the Kirchenmusikschule in Regensburg (1877) then with Piutti at the Leipzig Cons. (1880) was engaged as choirmaster at Straubing (1881) and conductor of the 'Sängerkreis' at Cologne (1890); then became director at the Cathedral in Breslau and prof. at the institute for church music there. His numerous compositions for the church assign him a distinguished position among composers of sacred music.

Filleul (fē-lyöl'), **Henri,** French composer; b. Laval, May 11, 1877. He studied at the Paris Cons. with Lavignac and Casadesus; since 1908 director of the École nationale de musique at St. Omer, Belgium

Officier de l'Instruction Publique.—Works: *Le Jugement de Triboulet,* comic opera (1923); biblical drama, *Marie Madeleine,* with soli, chorus, and incidental music (1925); oratorios: *Le Christ vainqueur* (1925), *Le Miracle de Lourdes* (1927), *Les Doulces Joyes de Nostre Dame* (1928), *Jeanne d'Arc* (1929), *Eva* (1931); *Variations symphoniques sur un thème languedocien* (1939); *Fantaisie concertante* for piano with orch. (1950); cello concerto; violin pieces with organ; motets; male choruses; etc.—Cf. *Hommage à Henri Filleul* (St. Omer, 1952).

Fillmore, Henry, American bandleader and composer of band music; b. Cincinnati, Dec. 2, 1881; d. Miami, Dec. 7, 1956. He was educated at the Miami Military Institute; in 1916 was in Cincinnati, where he organized the Henry Fillmore Concert Band; in 1938 settled in Florida. Under the name Harold Bennett he publ. a collection, *Bennett Band Books* (4 vols.); also used the names Al Hayes and Harry Hartley as compiler of military band pieces. Among his many marches is the very popular *Military Escort March.*

Fillmore, John Comfort, American music educator; b. New London, Conn., Feb. 4, 1843; d. there, Aug. 15, 1898. He was a pupil of G. W. Steele at Oberlin College, Ohio; then at Leipzig Cons. (1865-67). He was director of the music department at Oberlin College (1867); at Ripon College, Wis. (1868-78); at Milwaukee College for Women (1878-84). He founded (1884) the 'Milwaukee School of Music,' of which he was the director until 1895, when he took charge of the School of Music of Pomona College, Claremont, Calif. He published: *Pianoforte Music: its History, with Biographical Sketches and Critical Estimates of its Greatest Masters* (Chicago, 1883); *New Lessons in Harmony* (1887); *Lessons in Music History* (1888); *On the Value of Certain Modern Theories* (i.e., von Oettingen's and Riemann's); *A Study of Omaha Indian Music* (with Alice C. Fletcher and F. La Flesche; Peabody Museum, 1893); transl. into English Riemann's *Klavierschule* and *Natur der Harmonik.*

Filtz (Filz), Anton, talented composer, b. probably in Bohemia, 1730; d. Mannheim, March (buried March 14), 1760. He was a pupil of J. Stamitz; from 1754, first cellist in the Mannheim Orch. He belongs to the school of Mannheim Symphonists, early practitioners of classic instrumental style. That his works must have enjoyed great popularity seems to be proved by the numerous reprints issued at London and Amsterdam, pirated from the original Paris editions; these works show a very fertile invention; but the technical workmanship cannot rival the masterly treatment of similar works by Stamitz. He was exceptionally prolific; in the brief span of his life, he completed 41 symphonies, many trio-sonatas, string trios, sonatas for violin, cello, flute, etc., and concertos for various instruments. Riemann publ. 4 symphonies by Filtz in 'Denkmäler der Tonkunst in Bayern' (III, 1, and VII, 2); 2 trios (ibid., XV); and one in 'Collegium Musicum.'

Finagin, Alexei Vassilievitch, Russian musicologist; b. St. Petersburg, March 17, 1890; studied there at the Univ. He publ. (in Russian): *Russian Folksongs* (Petrograd, 1923); *Fomin; His Life and Works* (in vol. 1 of *Music and Musical Life of Old Russia;* Leningrad, 1927); contributed to various periodicals.

Finck, Heinrich, German composer; b. Bamberg, 1445; d. in the Schottenkloster, Vienna, June 9, 1527. He was in the service of 3 Polish kings: Johann Albert (1492), Alexander (1501), and Sigismund (1506); was in Cracow from at least 1491; 1492, visited Budapest, Vienna, and Torgau, but returned to Poland; 1510-13, Kapellmeister to Duke Ulrich at Stuttgart; then at the court of Maximilian I, in Augsburg; 1520, appointed composer of the cathedral chapter at Salzburg; 1525-26, Hofkapellmeister to Ferdinand I at Vienna, where he was succeeded by his pupil Arnold von Bruck.—Extant works: *Schöne auserlesene Lieder des hochberühmten Heinrich Finckens* (Nuremberg, 1536; reprinted in R. Eitner's 'Publikationen,' vol. VIII); other songs publ. by Salblinger (1545) and by Rhaw (1542). Reprints are to be found in Blume's *Das Chorwerk* (hymns ed. by R. Gerber; the *Missa in summis*), in A. W. Ambros' *Geschichte der Musik* (vol. 5), in the 'Denkmäler der Tonkunst in Österreich' (XXXVII, 2), in H. J. Moser's 'Kantorei der Spätgotik.'—Cf. H. Riemann, in 'Kirchenmusikalisches Jahrbuch' (1897); P. Wagner, in *Geschichte der Messe* (I, 275).

Finck, Henry Theophilus, American music critic and editor; b. Bethel, Missouri, Sept. 22, 1854; d. Rumford Falls, Maine, Oct. 1, 1926. He was brought up in Oregon; then entered Harvard Univ., where he studied with J. K. Paine. After graduation in 1876 he went to Germany; attended the first Bayreuth Festival and became greatly absorbed in the study of Wagner's music; returning to America he studied anthropology at Harvard; received a fellowship for travel in Germany; studied comparative psychology in Berlin and Vienna, and published a book *Romantic Love and Personal Beauty* (1887), propounding a theory that romantic love was unknown to the ancient nations; also wrote travel books and short stories. He was music critic for the 'Nation' magazine from 1881 to 1924; also music editor of the N. Y. 'Evening Post'; from 1888, lectured on music history at the National Cons. Finck was a brilliant journalist; in his books on music he stressed the personal and psychological elements; although an ardent admirer of Wagner, he turned against the further expansion of Wagnerian ideas by R. Strauss.—Publications: *Chopin, and Other Musical Essays* (1889); *Wagner and His Works* (N. Y., 1893; German transl., Breslau, 1897); *Pictorial Wagner* (1899); *Songs and Song Writers* (1900); *Grieg and His Music* (1909); *Success in Music and How It Is Won* (1909); *Massenet and His Operas* (1910); *Richard Strauss* (1917); *My Adventures in the Golden Age of Music* (1926). He edited *Fifty Master Songs* (1902), *Fifty Schubert Songs* (1903), and *Fifty Grieg Songs* (1909).

Finck, Hermann, German composer, great-nephew of Heinrich Finck; b. Pirna, Saxony, March 21, 1527; d. Wittenberg, Dec. 28, 1558. He was educated at the court chapel of King Ferdinand of Bohemia; studied at Wittenberg Univ. (1545); then taught music there (1554); was appointed organist in 1557. His major work is the treatise *Practica Musica,* publ. by Rhaw (1556), and subdivided into 5 parts. Some of Hermann Finck's works are reprinted by Eitner in his 'Publikationen' (vol. VIII, 1879).

Findeisen, Nicolai Fedorovitch, Russian music historian and editor; b. St. Petersburg, July 24, 1868; d. there, Sept. 20, 1928. He studied with Nikolai Sokolov; in 1893 he founded the 'Russian Musical Gazette' and remained its editor until it ceased publication in 1917; it was one of the most influential music journals in Russia, and supplied ample information on the activities of foreign musicians in addition to a thorough coverage of Russian musical events and publication of new materials on old Russian music. In 1909 Findeisen established in St. Petersburg, jointly with Siloti, a Society of the Friends of Music. His writings include monographs on Verstovsky (1890), Serov (1900), Dargomyzhsky (1902), Anton Rubinstein (1905), and Rimsky-Korsakov (1908); he published a series of brochures and books on Glinka; the first volume of a projected large biography, *Glinka in Spain,* appeared in 1896; a catalogue of Glinka's manuscripts, letters, and portraits was publ. in 1898; a monograph, *Glinka and his opera Russlan and Ludmilla,* was publ. in German (Munich, 1899); he also edited Glinka's correspondence (1908). He was on the editorial staff of the Russian edition of Riemann's *Musiklexikon* (St. Petersburg, 1901). His major achievement and a culminating point of his career was the extensive history of Russian music up to the year 1800, publ. in two vols. (partly posthumously) in Leningrad (1928-29) under the title *Sketches of Music in Russia from the most Ancient Times Until the End of the 18th Century.* He also contributed articles to foreign publications; among them, *The Earliest Russian Operas* in the 'Mus. Quarterly' (July, 1933).

Findeisen, Otto, composer of operettas and theater conductor; b. Brünn, Dec. 23, 1862; d. Leipzig, Jan. 23, 1947. He conducted in Magdeburg from 1890, and produced two of his operettas there: *Der alte Dessauer* (1890) and *Hennigs von Treffenfeld* (1891). Other light operas were: *Frau Holle* (Berlin, 1904); *Kleopatra* (Hamburg, 1897); *Der Spottvogel* (Bremen, 1898); *Der Sühneprinz* (Leipzig, 1904); *Sonnenguckerl* (Vienna, 1908); *Meister Pinkebank* (Vienna, 1909), etc.

Fine, Irving, talented American composer; b. Boston, Dec. 3, 1914. He studied with Walter Piston at Harvard Univ. (B.A., 1937; M.A., 1938) and with Nadia Boulanger in Cambridge, Mass. (1938) and in France (1939); also took a course in choral conducting with A. T. Davison. He was assistant prof. of music at Harvard (1947-50); in 1950 appointed prof. at Brandeis Univ.; also a member of the faculty at the Berkshire Music Center in Tanglewood, Mass. He was at first influenced by Stravinsky and Hindemith, and adopted a cosmopolitan style of composition in which contrapuntal elaboration and energetic rhythm were his main concerns; later on, however, he developed a distinctive style of his own with a lyrical flow of cohesive melody supported by lucid polyphony, without abandoning the strong rhythmic design. In some works, he follows a serial thematic method approximating the 12-tone technique. — Works: incidental theater music to *Alice in Wonderland*

(1942); cantata, *The Choral New Yorker* (1944); violin sonata (1946); *Toccata Concertante* for orch. (Boston Symph., 1948); *Partita* for wind quintet (1948); *The Hour Glass,* choral cycle (1949); string quartet (1950); piano pieces and songs.

Fine, Vivian, American composer; b. Chicago, Sept. 28, 1913. She studied composition with Roger Sessions; settled in New York as a pianist and teacher; has been associated with various modern societies. Although her style of composition is hypermodern, in bold and sometimes acrid linear counterpoint, the writing for instruments remains practical for actual performance.—Works: Piano concerto (1944); suite for oboe and piano (1939); *Opus 51,* ballet for piano and percussion (1940); *A Guide to the Life Expectancy of a Rose,* stage work commissioned by the Rothschild Foundation for the Arts and Sciences (1956). Her four songs for contralto and strings and *The Great Wall of China* for voice and flute are published by 'New Music.'

Fink, Christian, German organist and composer; b. Dettingen, Aug. 9, 1822; d. Esslingen, near Stuttgart, Sept. 5, 1911. He studied at the Leipzig Cons.; became organist there (1856-60); in 1863 was appointed church organist at Esslingen; published numerous organ works. He was greatly esteemed in Germany; his choral works and organ pieces were often performed.

Fink, Gottfried Wilhelm, German writer on music and editor; b. Sulza, Thuringia, March 7, 1783; d. Leipzig, Aug. 27, 1846. He studied music and theology in Leipzig; wrote the criticism in the 'Allgemeine Musikalische Zeitung' from 1808; in 1827 he became editor of this influential publication (until 1841); also contributed articles on music and musicians to various German encyclopedias. His extensive music history remained in MS. Among his publications are the collections of German songs, *Musikalischer Hausschatz* (Leipzig, 1843) and *Die deutsche Liedertafel* (Leipzig, 1846). For a complete list of his writings, see the article by W. Boetticher in 'Die Musik in Geschichte und Gegenwart.'

Finke, Fidelio Fritz, outstanding composer; b. Josefsthal in Northern Bohemia, Oct. 22, 1891; studied with Vitězlav Novák at the Prague Cons.; then taught there; was state inspector of the German music schools in Czechoslovakia; 1920, teacher of composition at the German Musikakademie, Prague; 1927, director; has won many prizes (Brahms Prize, 1910; Choral Prize, Vienna, 1920; Czech State Prize, 1928). He was director of the State Music Academy in Dresden (1946-51); since 1951, prof. of composition in the Hochschule für Musik in Leipzig.—Works: the operas, *Die Jakobsfahrt* (Prague, 1937) and *Der schlagfertige Liebhaber* (1950-53); *Das Lied der Zeit,* choreographic poem (1946); *Pan,* symph. poem; concerto for piano and orch. (1930); piano quintet; piano trio; 2 string quartets; 2 string trios; 2 sonatas for violin and piano; *Chaconne* (after Vitali) for violin and piano; Variations and Fugue for 13 solo instruments; *Frühling,* for soprano, tenor, and orch.; *Abschied,* for soprano, tenor, and orch.; *Mein Trinklied* for tenor, male chorus, and orch.; *Der zerstörte Tasso,* 5 settings for voice and string quartet; *Weihnachtskantilene,* for mixed voices (1933); pieces for female chorus (3-9 voices); *Reiterburleske* for piano; *Toccata* for piano, left hand; many organ works; songs.

Finney, Ross Lee, American composer and teacher; b. Wells, Minn., Dec. 23, 1906. He studied at the Univ. of Minnesota with Ferguson, and in Europe with Nadia Boulanger and Alban Berg; then took additional instruction with Roger Sessions and E. B. Hill; won a Guggenheim Fellowship twice (1937 and 1947); also a Pulitzer scholarship. He taught at Smith College (1929-47) and concurrently at Mt. Holyoke College (1938-44); in 1948 joined the staff of the Univ. of Michigan.—Works: piano concerto (1934); *Overture for a Drama* (Rochester, N. Y., Oct. 28, 1941); *Barber Shop Ballad* for orch. (C.B.S., Feb. 6, 1940); *Communiqué* for orch. (1943); violin concerto (1944); *John Brown* (1929); *Trail to Mexico* (1941); *Pilgrim Psalms* (1945); 7 string quartets; 4 piano sonatas; viola sonata; cello sonata; piano trio; several song cycles, etc. He edited Geminiani's 12 sonatas for violin and piano (Northampton, Mass., 1935); publ. *The Game of Harmony* (N. Y., 1947).

Finney, Theodore Mitchell, American music educator and historian; brother of Ross Lee Finney; b. Fayette, Iowa, March 14, 1902. He studied at the Univ. of Minnesota; then at the American Cons. at Fontainebleau (1926) and in Berlin (1927-28). He was a member of the viola section in the Minneapolis Symph. Orch. (1923-25); then assistant prof. of music at Carleton College (1925-32) and lecturer at the Smith College Summer School (1930-38). In 1936 he was appointed head of the music department at Pittsburgh Univ. He has published a *History of Music* (N. Y., 1935; revised ed., 1946; successful college textbook); also *Hearing Music, A Guide to Music* (N. Y., 1941); *We Have Made Music* (essays; Pittsburgh, 1955).

Fino, Giocondo, Italian composer; b. Turin, May 2, 1867; d. there, April 19, 1950. He studied Oriental languages and theology; concurrently took music lessons with Giovanni Bolzoni; he remained in Turin practically all his life.—Works: the operas *La festa del grano* (Turin, 1910), *Debora* (not produced), and *Campana a gloria* (Turin, 1916); several stage works in the Piedmont dialect; biblical cantata, *Noemi e Ruth* (Bergamo, 1908); ballets, pantomimes, choral works; chamber music and piano pieces.

Finzi, Gerald, English composer; b. London, July 14, 1901; d. Oxford, Sept. 27, 1956. As a youth, he took a course in composition with R. O. Morris; otherwise, self-taught. His first important work was a *Severn Rhapsody* for chamber orch. (1924); its contemplative manner of writing and simplicity of harmonic expression remain characteristic of Finzi's music; its materials are often related to the songs of the English countryside. Other works: *Introit* for violin and orch. (1935); *Farewell to Arms* for tenor and chamber orch. (1945); concerto for clarinet and strings (1949); *Intimations of Immortality* for tenor, chorus, and orch. (1950); cello concerto (1955); several groups of choral pieces.

Fiocco (fē-ŏk'-koh), **Jean-Joseph,** composer, second son of Pietro Antonio Fiocco (of the first marriage); b. Brussels, Dec. 1686 (baptized Dec. 15); d. there, March 30, 1746. He succeeded his father as music master at the ducal chapel, and held this post for 30 years (1714-44); wrote 5 oratorios, 8 psalms, 9 Requiems, motets, etc. Two copies of his *Sacri concentus* for 4 voices and 3 instruments are known to exist; most of his other works are lost.—Cf. Christiane Stellfeld, *Les Fiocco* (Brussels, 1941).

Fiocco (fē-ŏk'-koh), **Joseph-Hector,** composer, seventh child of Pietro Antonio Fiocco (of his second marriage); b. Brussels, Jan. 1703; d. there, June 22, 1741. He was music master of the cathedral of Antwerp from 1731-37; then at Ste.-Gudule in Brussels until his death. He wrote numerous sacred works published in 'Monumenta Musicae Belgicae' (vol. III, Antwerp, 1936); also wrote *Pièces de Clavecin* (two suites of 12 pieces each).—Cf. Christiane Stellfeld, *Les Fiocco* (Brussels, 1941).

Fiocco (fē-ŏk'-koh), **Pietro Antonio,** Italian composer; b. Venice, c. 1650; d. Brussels, Sept. 3, 1714. He traveled to Germany, where he produced an opera *Alceste* (Hanover, 1681). He then settled in Brussels, marrying a Belgian lady in 1682; she died in 1691, and Fiocco remarried in 1692. He was music master of the ducal chapel in Brussels; in 1694 he established an opera enterprise; wrote special prologues for the operas of Lully; also wrote music for the court; his pastoral play *Le Retour du Printemps* was produced in 1699. A collection of his sacred concertos was published in Antwerp (1691). Among his instrumental works only a *Sonate à quatre* is extant. Two of his sons, Jean-Joseph and Joseph-Hector (q.v.), became professional musicians. See the exhaustive monograph, *Les Fiocco,* by Christiane Stellfeld (Brussels, 1941).

Fioravanti, Valentino, Italian composer; b. Rome, Sept. 11, 1764; d. Capua, June 16, 1837. He studied in Rome with Jannaconi and with Sala and Fenaroli in Naples. Returning to Rome in 1782, he began his career as a prolific composer of operas. He visited Naples quite often; was in Paris in 1807; succeeded his teacher, Jannaconi, as maestro di cappella at St. Peter's in Rome in 1816; during his last period he wrote much church music. His earliest work, an intermezzo, was *Le avventure di Bertoldino* (Rome, 1784); he produced a comic opera *Gl' inganni fortunati* in Naples (1786); there followed *Il furbo contro al furbo* (Venice, Dec. 29, 1796). His greatest success was achieved by his comic opera *Le Cantatrici Villane,* first produced in Naples (1799) and then in Venice in a new version under the title *Le Virtuose ridicole* (Dec. 28, 1801); there were performances all over Europe, including Russia; the opera was particularly in favor with German audiences (under the title *Die Dorfsängerinnen*); other operas were: *La capricciosa pentita* (Milan, Oct. 2, 1802) and *I virtuosi ambulanti* (Paris, Sept. 26, 1807; also very successful); Fioravanti produced 77 operas and other stage works during his most active period, between 1784 and 1824. His autobiographical sketch was reprinted by G. Roberti in 'La Gazzetta musicale' (1895).

Fioravanti, Vincenzo, Italian composer, son of Valentino Fioravanti; b. Rome, April 5, 1799; d. Naples, March 28, 1877. He studied with his father, and also with his father's teacher, Jannaconi; he also took lessons with Donizetti. He wrote a number of operas in the Neapolitan dialect; only a few of them (translated into conventional Italian) were produced outside Italy. He composed about 40 operas in all.

Fiorillo, Dante, American composer; b. New York, July 4, 1905. He studied the cello, and later began to compose without formal instruction. He held Guggenheim Fellowships in composition for four successive years (1935-39), and in 1939 received a Pulitzer Prize. Extraordinarily prolific, he has written 12 symphonies; 11 string quartets; piano quintets and trios; piano sonatas; choral music.

Fiorillo, Federigo, violinist and composer; b. Brunswick, Germany (baptized June 1), 1755; date and place of death unknown. He was taught by his father, Ignazio Fiorillo; he traveled as violinist and conductor; was in Riga (1782-84); in 1785 he went to Paris, where he participated in the Concert Spirituel; in 1788 he was in London, where he played the viola in Salomon's quartet. He probably remained in London until about 1815; then he was in Amsterdam and again in Paris. He was a prolific composer for violin and various combinations of string instruments; but he is known chiefly through his useful collection, *Études de Violon,* comprising 36 caprices, which were frequently reprinted.

Fiorillo, Ignazio, Italian composer, father of Federigo Fiorillo; b. Naples, May 11, 1715; d. Fritzlar, near Kassel, 1787. He studied with Durante and Leo in Naples; composed his first opera *Mandane* at the age of 20 (Venice, 1736). Other operas were: *Artimene* (Milan, 1738), *Partenope nell' Adria* (Venice, 1738), and *Il Vincitor di se stesso* (Venice, 1741). He traveled as a theater conductor; was appointed court conductor at Brunswick (1751); in 1762 he received a similar post at Kassel, retiring in 1780. He wrote a number of German operas in Brunswick, and 3 Italian operas in Kassel. An oratorio, *Isacco,* a requiem, and other church works are also noteworthy.

Fiqué, Karl, German organist; b. St. Magnus, near Bremen, April 17, 1867; d. Brooklyn, Dec. 7, 1930. After studying at the Leipzig Cons. with Carl Reinecke he emigrated to the U. S. (1887) and settled in Brooklyn, where he served as church organist and lectured at the Brooklyn Institute of Arts and Sciences (1897-1915). He married the soprano Katherine Noack (d. 1940). He wrote 2 comic operas in German: *Priesewitz* (Brooklyn, 1893) and *Der falsche Mufti* (N. Y., 1901); a string quartet, several choral works, and numerous piano pieces. Shortly before his death, he finished an operetta, *Merry Madrid.*

Firkušny, Rudolf, brilliant Czech pianist; b. Feb. 11, 1912 at Napajedlá, Moravia. He studied at the Cons. of Brno with Vilem Kurz (piano) and with Janáček (composition); later in Prague with Karel and Suk; also studied with Schnabel. He toured in Europe as pianist (1928-38); made his American début in Town Hall, N. Y., Jan. 13, 1938. Since 1942, he has appeared as soloist with major symph. orchestras in America; toured South America in 1943. He has composed a piano concerto (Prague, 1929, composer soloist) and numerous piano pieces.

Fischer, Carl, music publisher; b. Buttstädt, Thuringia, Dec. 7, 1849; d. New York, Feb. 14, 1923. He came to the U. S. in 1872 and established a musical instrument business in New York in that year. Later the firm undertook all branches of publishing, especially of instrumental music, and has become one of the most important of American music publishing organizations. In 1907, the firm began the publication of a monthly periodical, the 'Musical Observer,' under the editorship of Gustav Sänger; in 1923 the business was incorporated and Carl Fischer's son **Walter S. Fischer** (b. April 18, 1882; d. New York, April 26, 1946) became president. After his death Frank H. Conner was appointed president. The firm represents the Composers' Music Corp., the Paterson Publishers, the De Paul Univ. Press, Allan & Co., Eastman School of Music, G. Henle-Verlag, and Societas Universalis Sanctae Ceciliae; also acquired the catalogs of William S. Pond & Co. (Robin Ellis), and the Fillmore Music House. Beside its two buildings in New York, the firm maintains branch stores in Boston and Chicago, and branch offices in Chicago, Dallas, and Los Angeles.

Fischer, Edwin, pianist and conductor; b. Basel, Oct. 6, 1886; pupil of Hans Huber in Basel and of M. Krause in Berlin; 1905-14, teacher at the Stern Cons., Berlin; 1926-28, conductor of the Musikverein, Lübeck; 1928-30, of the Bachverein, Munich; later, of a chamber orch. in Berlin; has made many successful tours of Europe; since 1942 living near Lucerne. He publ. *J. S. Bach* (Potsdam, 1945); *Musikalische Betrachtungen* (Wiesbaden, 1950; in English as *Reflections on Music,* London, 1951); *Beethovens Klaviersonaten* (1957).—Cf. B. Gavoty, *Edwin Fischer* (Geneva, 1954).

Fischer, Emil, operatic bass singer; b. Brunswick, June 13, 1838; d. Hamburg, Aug. 11, 1914. He received his vocal training entirely from his parents, who were opera singers; made his début in Graz in 1857; then was with the Danzig Opera (1863-70); in Rotterdam (1875-80) and with the Dresden Opera (1880-85); then went to America; made his début with the Metropolitan Opera Co. on Nov. 25, 1885, and remained on the staff for more than 20 years. He sang in public for the last time at the age of 71; lived mostly in N. Y. as vocal teacher; returned to Germany shortly before his death. He was particularly famous for his Wagnerian roles; his greatest impersonation was Hans Sachs in *Die Meistersinger.*

Fischer, Erich, German music editor and composer; b. Kreuzlingen, April 8, 1887. He studied musicology in Berlin at the Univ. under Kretzschmar, Stumpf, and Friedländer; received his *Dr. phil.* in 1909 with the dissertation *Über die Musik der Chinesen* (publ. by the 'Internationale Musik Gesellschaft,' 1910); in 1914, he founded in Berlin the 'Musikalische Hauskomödien,' a society for the performance of little-known music by German composers, arranged as 'singspiele' with new words; for this venture he organized his own company of singers. He edited the songs of J. A. Sixt (Donaueschingen, 1932); composed musical comedies (*Das heilige Kapplein,* produced in Hanover, 1913, etc.).

Fischer, Frederick, conductor; b. Munich, May 25, 1868; d. St. Louis, April 17, 1931. He studied at the Royal Academy of Music in Munich; then came to the U.S., where he conducted the California Opera Co.; in 1904 he settled in St. Louis and was assistant conductor of the St. Louis Symph.; also guest conductor of the Boston People's Orch., choral societies, etc.; wrote music to the pageant *Missouri 100 Years Ago,* choral works, and songs.

Fischer, Johann Kaspar Ferdinand, German composer of keyboard music; b. c. 1665; d. Rastatt, March 27, 1746. He served as house musician to the Margrave of Baden (1696-1716). During his lifetime he publ. the following: *Le journal du printemps,* op. 1 (airs and ballet numbers in the style of Lully; 1696; reprinted in the 'Denkmäler deutscher Tonkunst,' X, 1); *Les pièces de clavecin,* op. 2 (1696; reprinted 1698, under the title *Musikalisches Blumen-Büschlein*); *Vesper Psalms,* op. 3 (1701); *Ariadne musica neo-organoedum,* op. 4 (1715; contains 20 preludes and fugues for organ in 20 different keys, thus foreshadowing Bach's *Well-tempered Clavier*); *Litaniae Lauretanae,* op. 5 (1711); also *Musikalischer Parnassus* (9 keyboard suites named after the 9 Muses); and *Blumenstrauss* (a series of 8 preludes and fugues in 8 church modes). For discussion of Fischer's influence on Bach, see Max Seiffert, *Geschichte der Klavier-Musik,* vol. 1 (Berlin, 1899); also R. Opel, *Fischers Einfluss auf Bach,* in the 'Bach-Jahrbuch' (1910).

Fischer, Joseph, music publisher; b. Silberhausen, Germany, April 9, 1841; d. Springfield, Ohio, Nov. 24, 1901. He emigrated to the U.S. as a youth, and established the firm of J. Fischer & Bro. in Dayton, Ohio (1864) with his brother Ignaz Fischer; in 1875 the firm moved to N. Y. Joseph Fischer was succeeded at his death by his sons George and Carl; the sons of George Fischer, Joseph and Eugene, became proprietors of the firm in 1920. During its early years, J. Fischer & Bro. specialized in music for the Roman Catholic Church, but later expanded their activities to include instrumental music by contemporary composers, organ works, and also light opera.

Fischer, Ludwig, German bass singer; b. Mainz, Aug. 18, 1745; d. Berlin, July 10, 1825. He sang in Mainz, Mannheim, and Vienna, and with great success in Paris (1783) and Italy; from 1788 till 1815 was in Berlin. Mozart wrote the part of Osmin, in *Die Entführung aus dem Serail,* for Fischer.

Fischer, Michael Gotthard, German organist and composer, b. Alach, near Erfurt, June 3, 1773; d. Erfurt, Jan. 12, 1829. He was a pupil of Kittel; also concert conductor and teacher in the seminary at Erfurt. —Works: about 50 organ pieces; symphonies, concertos, chamber music, piano pieces, motets, chorales, concertos, etc.; publ. an *Evangelisches Choral-Melodienbuch.*

Fischer, Wilhelm, Austrian musicologist; b. Vienna, April 19, 1886; studied there with G. Adler at the Univ.; *Dr. phil.,* 1912; 1915, docent at the Vienna Univ.; 1928, prof. at the Univ. of Innsbruck; 1939 to

1945, worked in Vienna in a metal factory; 1945-48, teaching in Vienna; 1948, prof. of musicology at the Univ. of Innsbruck.—Writings: *Zur Entwicklungsgeschichte des Wiener klassischen Stils,* in Adler's 'Studien zur Musikwissenschaft' III (1915); *Zur Chronologie der Klaviersuiten J. S. Bachs,* in 'Basler Kongress-Bericht' (1924); *Zur Geschichte des Fugenthemas* (Leipzig, 1925); *Die konzertierende Orgel im Orchester des 18. Jahrhunderts* (Freiburg, 1926); *Beethoven als Mensch* (Regensburg, 1928); *Die Instrumentalmusik 1430-1880,* in Adler's 'Handbuch der Musikgeschichte.' Ed. the works of G. M. Monn in the 'Denkmäler der Tonkunst in Österreich,' XIX, 2. A 'Festschrift' was publ. on his 70th birthday.

Fischer-Dieskau, Dietrich, German baritone; b. Berlin, May 28, 1925. He studied at the Hochschule für Musik in Berlin; at the age of 23 made his début at the State Opera in Berlin. His first American appearances, in the spring of 1955 (N. Y. début, May 2, 1955), met with exceptional success.

Fischhof, Joseph, pianist; b. Butschowitz, Moravia, April 4, 1804; d. Vienna, June 28, 1857. He studied piano with Anton Halm in Vienna; then became a private teacher there, with growing success, and in 1833 was appointed prof. in the Vienna Cons. He published many piano pieces (rondos, variations, fantasias, dances, marches, etc.) and a *Versuch einer Geschichte des Klavier-Baus* (Vienna, 1853). He gathered a remarkable collection of musical MSS, including one of Bach's *Wohltemperiertes Klavier* (known as the 'Fischhof Autograph') and authentic materials for a Beethoven biography collected by Hotschewar (the guardian of Beethoven's nephew); these MSS were given, after Fischhof's death, to the Berlin State Library.

Fisher, William Arms, American music editor and publisher; b. San Francisco, April 27, 1861; d. Boston, Dec. 18, 1948. He studied theory with Horatio Parker; singing with William Shakespeare in London. When Dvořák came to New York in 1892 Fisher became his pupil. In 1897 he settled in Boston as editor & director of music publication for O. Ditson & Co.; was its vice-president from 1926-37; then retired. He edited several vocal albums, among them *60 Irish Folksongs* (Boston, 1915) and *Ye Olde New England Psalm Tunes* (Boston, 1930). He wrote the words *Goin' Home* to the melody of the slow movement of Dvořák's *New World Symphony,* a setting that became enormously popular. He was the author of the following books: *Notes on Music in Old Boston* (1918); *The Music that Washington Knew* (1931); *One Hundred and Fifty Years of Music Publishing in the U. S.* (1933); *Music Festivals in the U. S.* (1934).

Fissot (fēs-sŏh'), **Alexis-Henri,** French pianist and composer; b. Airaines (Somme), Oct. 24, 1843; d. Paris, Jan. 28, 1896. He entered the Paris Cons. as a child of nine, and studied piano with Marmontel, organ with Benoist, and composition with Ambroise Thomas till 1860, taking successively all first prizes. He then taught piano at the Paris Cons. (from 1887). He wrote many effective piano pieces (*12 Préludes, 2 Ballades, 3 Feuillets d'Album, 12 Pièces de Genre,* etc.).

Fistoulari, Anatole, Russian conductor; b. Kiev, Aug. 20, 1907. He studied with his father, the opera conductor Gregory Fistoulari; as a child prodigy, he conducted Tchaikovsky's Sixth Symph. at the age of 8; in 1920 went to Rumania and Germany; was in Paris as ballet conductor in 1933; later toured with the Ballet-Russe de Monte Carlo in the U. S. (1937). He was in the French Army in 1939; in 1940 made his way to London, where he settled as orchestral and theatrical conductor.

Fitelberg (fē'-tel-berg), **Gregor,** Polish conductor and composer; b. Dvinsk, Latvia, Oct. 18, 1879; d. Katowice, June 10, 1953. He studied at the Warsaw Cons. with Barcewicz and Noskowski; then played the violin in the Warsaw Philharmonic; became concertmaster, and eventually (1908) conductor. After the outbreak of World War I he went to Russia, as conductor of symphony concerts; in 1921 he went to Paris; conducted performances of Diaghilev's Russian Ballet; in 1923 he returned to Poland; in 1940 he was in Buenos Aires, after fleeing Warsaw via Vienna, Italy, and Paris; from 1942-45 he was in the U.S.; in 1947 he went back to Poland, and became conductor at the Polish Radio. At his symphonic concerts he gave many performances of works by Polish composers; was one of the best interpreters of Szymanowski. In 1951 the Polish government awarded him a state prize. Fitelberg was also a composer; he wrote 2 symphonies (1903; 1906); a Polish rhapsody for orch. (1913); a symph. poem *In der Meerestiefe* (1913), and some chamber music; his violin sonata received the Paderewski prize in 1896.

Fitelberg, Jerzy, talented Polish composer; son of Gregor Fitelberg; b. Warsaw, May 20, 1903; d. New York, April 25, 1951. He received his musical education mainly from his father; then took courses in the Hochschule für Musik in Berlin. In 1933 he went to Paris; in May 1940 he came to the U.S., where he remained until his death. In 1936 he received an Elizabeth Sprague Coolidge award for his string quartet, which was performed at the Coolidge Festival of Chamber Music in Washington (1937); his orchestral and chamber music was often performed in Europe; much of it was published. His works are couched in the neo-Classical style, and are cosmopolitan in thematic substance; they are distinguished by energetic rhythm and strong contrapuntal texture; only a few of his compositions reflect Polish melos.—Works: 3 suites for orch. (1926-30); concerto for string orch. (1928; arrangement of the second string quartet); violin concerto No. 1 (Vienna Festival of the International Society for Contemporary Music, June 20, 1932); violin concerto No. 2 (Paris Festival, June 22, 1937); *The Golden Horn* for string orch. (1942); *Nocturne* for orch. (New York Philh., March 28, 1946, Rodzinski conducting); octet for wind instruments; 5 string quartets; sonata for 2 violins and 2 pianos; sonatina for 2 violins; *3 Polish Folksongs* for women's voices (1942).—Cf. Emilia Elsner, *Jerzy Fitelberg,* in the 'Chesterian' (Sept.-Oct., 1939).

Fitzwilliam, Viscount **Richard,** wealthy collector of paintings, engravings, books, and musical MSS; b. London, 1745; d. there, Feb. 4, 1816. He bequeathed his library to the Univ. of Cambridge. The musical MSS include especially valuable works: the immensely important Fitzwilliam Virginal Book (often wrongly termed 'Virginal Booke of Queen Elizabeth'), anthems in Purcell's hand, sketches by Handel, and many early Italian compositions. Vincent Novello edited and publ. 5 vols. of the Italian sacred music as 'The Fitzwilliam Music' (London, 1825); J. A. Fuller Maitland and A. H. Mann made a complete catalogue of it (1893). The entire contents of the Fitzwilliam Virginal Book were edited and published by J. A. Fuller Maitland and William Barclay Squire (Breitkopf & Härtel, 1894-99; reprint, N. Y., 1949).—Cf. E. W. Naylor, *An Elizabethan Virginal Book* (London, 1905).

Flackton, William, English organist and composer; b. Canterbury, March, 1709; d. there, Jan. 5, 1798. He was organist at Faversham from 1735-52; wrote church music; also 6 'overtures' for harpsichord; 6 sonatas for 2 violins and cello; 3 cello sonatas and 3 viola sonatas; a song *The Chase* (with a horn obbligato).

Flagg, Josiah, American conductor; b. Woburn, Mass., May 28, 1737; d. c. 1795. He organized and drilled the first regular militia band of Boston (most probably the first group of that nature in America); on June 29, 1769, presented its first concert and on Oct. 28, 1773, gave a 'final Grand Concert' at Faneuil Hall with about 50 players. Subsequently he settled in Providence and served there as lieutenant colonel during the Revolution; little is known of his other activities. He publ. *A Collection of the best Psalm Tunes in 2, 3 and 4 parts . . . To which is added some Hymns and Anthems, the Greater part of them never before printed in America* (introduced the anthem to the English colonies; 1764; engraved by Paul Revere) and *Sixteen Anthems . . . To which is added a few Psalm Tunes* (1766). Flagg was the first in America to establish a connection between sacred and secular music. That he was an educated practical musician and was acquainted with European music is evidenced by the type of programs he conducted.—Cf. O. G. Sonneck, *Early Concert Life in America* (Leipzig, 1907); 'Dictionary of American Biography,' vol. VI (N. Y., 1931).

Flagler, Isaac Van Vleck, American organist; born Albany, N. Y., May 15, 1844; d. Auburn, N. Y., March 16, 1909. He studied with H. W. A. Beale at Albany, Edouard Batiste in Paris, and others. He was organist and music director of various churches; at Chautauqua he was organist and musical lecturer for 20 years; was also organ teacher at Syracuse and Cornell Univs., and at Utica Cons.; co-founder of the American Guild of Organists. He published *The Organist's Treasury, Flagler's New Collection of Organ Music,* and *Flagler's New Collection for Choirs and Soloists.*

Flagstad, Kirsten, dramatic soprano; b. Hamar, Norway, July 12, 1895. She studied with her mother (coach at the Oslo Opera) and with Ellen Schytte-Jacobsen in Oslo; 1913, début there at the National Theater as Nuri in d'Albert's opera *Tiefland;* then sang (till 1927) in oratorio, operettas, and musical comedies in Oslo; 1928-30, engaged at the Storm Theater at Göteborg; 1931-32, again at the National Theater; in 1933 and 1934, appeared at the Bayreuth Festival. On Feb. 2, 1935, she made a very successful début at the Metropolitan Opera as Sieglinde in *Die Walküre,* and sang the roles of Isolde (her most celebrated impersonation), Brünnhilde, Elizabeth, Elsa, and Kundry in her first season there; appeared at Covent Garden, London, as Isolde, May 18, 1936. She also sang with the San Francisco Opera (1935-38), Chicago City Opera (1937), and in numerous guest appearances throughout the U. S. and Australia. In 1941 she returned to Norway; in March, 1947, came to the U. S. for a concert tour, and again in 1948; retired from the concert stage in Dec., 1953; since then, living in Kristiansand, Norway.—Cf. *The Flagstad Manuscript* (an autobiography narrated to Louis Biancolli; N. Y., 1952).

Flament (flăh-măhn'), **Édouard,** French composer, conductor, and bassoon virtuoso; b. Douai, Aug. 27, 1880. He studied at the Paris Cons. with Bourdeau (bassoon), Lavignac, Caussade, and Lenepveu (composition). After graduation (1898), he played the bassoon in the Lamoureux Orch. (1898-1907) and in the Société des Instruments à Vent (1898-1923); conducted opera and concerts in Paris (1907-12), Algiers (1912-14), Marseilles (1919-20), summer concerts at Fontainebleau (1920-22); then with the Diaghilev Ballet in Monte Carlo, Berlin, London, Spain (1923-29). In 1930 he became conductor at the Paris Radio; was still active there in 1957. An exceptionally prolific composer, he wrote between 1894 and 1957 some 175 opus numbers, including the operas *La Fontaine de Castalie, Le Coeur de la Rose, Lydéric et Rosèle;* 8 symphonies; *Oceano Nox,* symph. poem; *Variations radiophoniques;* 5 piano concertos; *Concertstück* for bassoon and orch.; *Divertimento* for 6 bassoons; quintet for 5 bassoons; quartet for 4 bassoons; 3 string quartets; violin sonata, viola sonata, 2 cello sonatas, etc.; about 180 film scores. Few of his works are publ.; most of the larger ones remain unperformed.

Flammer, Harold, American music publisher; b. New York, Sept. 19, 1889; d. Bronxville, N. Y., Oct. 23, 1939. He studied at Princeton Univ. (Litt. B., 1911). In 1913 he entered G. Schirmer, Inc.; 1917, established Harold Flammer, Inc.; 1929-34, Vice-President and Business Manager of G. Schirmer; 1934, re-established own firm. During the years 1932-36 he was at various times treasurer, president, and vice-president of Music Publ. Association of the U. S. He published piano compositions, songs, and many song texts and translations; was a contributor to 'Musical America' and the 'Mus. Quarterly.'

Flaxland, Gustav-Alexandre, music publisher; b. Strasbourg, Jan. 26, 1821; d. Paris, Nov. 11, 1895. He studied at the Paris Cons.; founded a music publishing business in 1847, and, by acquiring copyrights of compositions of Schumann and Wagner, made it prominent. He sold his firm to Durand et Schönewerk in 1870, and commenced making pianos.

Flecha, Mateo, Spanish composer; b. Prades, Tarragona, 1530; d. Solsona, Lérida, Feb. 20, 1604. He received his musical education from his uncle, also named Mateo Flecha (1481-1553); was chamber musician at the courts of Charles V and Philip II; from about 1575 he was in Prague; returned to Spain in 1599. He publ. a book of madrigals in Venice (1568), and a collection *Las Ensaladas* (Prague, 1581) containing 'ensaladas' (quodlibets, comic songs) by his uncle, and some by himself. This collection was brought out in a modern edition by Higinio Anglés, with an introductory essay on the Flechas (Barcelona, 1954).

Fleck, Henry T., American music educator; b. Buffalo, N. Y., April 28, 1863; d. Rockaway Beach, Long Island, N. Y., Sept. 6, 1937. He studied music with Wüllner at Cologne; upon returning to the U. S., he organized in New York the Euterpe Choral Society (1889) and the Harlem Philharmonic Society (1890), which he conducted till 1901; also established free concerts of chamber music in N. Y. From 1901 until his death he was prof. of music at Hunter College, N. Y.

Flégier (flā-zh'yā), **Ange,** French composer; b. Marseilles, Feb. 25, 1846; d. there, Oct. 8, 1927. He studied first at the Cons. of Marseilles and then at the Paris Cons. (1866-9), returning to Marseilles in 1870.—Works: *Fatima,* comic opera; *Ossian,* lyric poem for soli, chorus, and orch.; *Françoise de Rimini,* cantata; miscellaneous orch. pieces (*Valse du rêve, Badinage, Habanera, Menuet, Berceuse, Mignardise,* etc.); many songs, of which *Le Cor* is the best known.

Fleischer, Anton, Hungarian conductor and composer; b. Makó, May 30, 1891. He studied in Budapest with Kodály; 1913-15, first conducted at the Budapest Municipal Theater; conducted at the Budapest Opera (1915) and taught at the National Cons. from 1918; won the Hungarian State Prize with his symph. on Oscar Wilde's *The Nightingale and the Rose* (1915).

Fleischer, Editha, German soprano; b. Falkenstein, April 5, 1898. She studied at the Scharwenka Cons. in Berlin and with Lilli Lehmann; engaged at the Berlin Opera from 1919 to 1921; appeared also at Salzburg Festivals, and was a member of a Wagnerian Opera co. that toured America in 1922-24; made her début at the Metropolitan Opera, Nov. 5, 1926, and remained on the roster until 1935, when she returned to Europe.

Fleischer, Oskar, eminent German musicologist; b. Zörbig, Nov. 2, 1856; d. Berlin, Feb. 8, 1933. He studied philology at Halle (1878-83); then musicology in Berlin under Spitta (till 1885); after 3 years spent in research work in various libraries, he returned to Berlin and was appointed custodian of the royal collection of music instruments (1888). In 1892 he became privatdozent at the Univ. of Berlin; promoted to professorship in 1895. He was a founder and first president of the 'Internationale Musik-Gesellschaft' (1899); together with Johannes Wolf, edited its publications, the 'Zeitschrift' and 'Sammelbände,' until 1904. In 1892 he represented the Prussian government at the Vienna Exhibition, of which he publ. an exhaustive report, *Die Bedeutung der internationalen Musik- und Theaterausstellung in Wien für Kunst und Wissenschaft der Musik* (Leipzig, 1894).—Writings: *Führer durch die königliche Sammlung alter Musikinstrumente* (Berlin, 1892); *Musikinstrumente aus deutscher Urzeit* (1893); *W. A. Mozart* (1899); *Führer durch die Bachausstellung* (Berlin, 1901); *Neumen-Studien* (4 vols., 1895, 1897, 1904, 1923; the 3rd. vol. with facsimiles of late Byzantine notation; the 4th entitled *Die germanischen Neumen als Schlüssel zum altchristlichen und gregorianischen Gesang*). He also wrote short biographies of the masters of music in *Grosse Männer* (1922-23); contributed valuable articles to various German music journals.

Fleisher, Edwin A., American patron of music; b. Philadelphia, July 11, 1877. He studied at Harvard Univ. (B. A., 1899). He founded a Symphony Club in Philadelphia (1909) and engaged conductors to rehearse an amateur orch. there; at the same time he began collecting orchestral scores and complete sets of parts, which became the nucleus of the great Edwin A. Fleisher Collection presented by him to the Free Library of Philadelphia. A partial catalogue of the collection was publ. in 1935, 2nd vol. in 1945, supplement in 1956.

Fleisher, Leon, American pianist; b. San Francisco, July 23, 1928 (of Russian parents). He gave his first public concert at the age of seven; then studied with Schnabel at Lake Como, Italy (1938-39). At sixteen he was soloist with the New York Philharmonic (Nov. 4, 1944) under Pierre Monteux; subsequently played in Europe. In 1952 he won the first prize at the International competition for pianists in Brussels.

Flesch, Karl, celebrated violinist and pedagogue; b. Moson, Hungary, Oct. 9, 1873; d. Lucerne, Switzerland, Nov. 14, 1944. He was a violin pupil of Grün at the Vienna Cons. (1886-9), then of Souzay and Marsick at the Paris Cons. (1890-4); début in Vienna, 1895; from 1897 to 1902 he was prof. at the Cons. in Bucharest and chamber virtuoso to the Queen of Rumania; from 1903-8, prof. at the Cons. in Amsterdam. The success of a series of five historical recitals in Berlin, in 1909, induced him to settle there; as a teacher he was no less successful than as a virtuoso, especially since the publication of his famous *Urstudien* for violin (1910); he toured all European countries, and the U. S. in 1913-14, meeting everywhere with an enthusiastic reception; taught at the Hochschule für Musik, Berlin, in 1921-22; from 1924 till 1928 was head of the violin dept. of the Curtis Institute in Philadelphia; then divided his time between the U. S. and Germany; in 1933 he went to England; and then to Switzerland. Karl Flesch wrote a standard pedagogic work for violin *Die Kunst des Violinspiels,* transl. into 5 languages (vol. I, 1923; vol. II, 1928; publ. in English, N. Y., 1930); also publ. new editions of Kreutzer's *Études,* Mozart's violin sonatas (with Schnabel), 20 Études of Paganini, and the violin concertos of Beethoven, Mendelssohn, Paganini, Brahms, etc. He also wrote *Das Klangproblem im Geigenspiel* (1931; in English, N. Y., 1934).—Cf. W. Altmann, *Karl Flesch als Erzieher,* in 'Die Musik' (XXI, 7); W. Brederode, *Karl Flesch* (Haarlem, 1938).

Fleta (flā'-tah), **Miguel,** Spanish tenor; b. Albalate, Dec. 28, 1893; d. Burgos, May 30, 1938. He studied in Barcelona; made his début in Trieste Nov. 14, 1919. After a successful career in Europe, Mexico, and South America, he came to the U. S. in 1923 and sang with the Metropolitan Opera; returned to Spain in 1926.

Fleta, Pierre, French tenor, son of Miguel Fleta; b. Villefranche-sur-Mer, July 4, 1925. He studied with his mother, Louise Pierrick-Fleta, a member of La Scala; then sang as a boy soprano at Cannes; went to London, where he was engaged as a professional singer before making his opera début in Barcelona in 1949. He made a concert tour in the Middle East in 1951; then was engaged as first tenor at the Théâtre de la Monnaie in Brussels (1952). He has also developed a repertory of French, Italian, Spanish, and English folksongs.

Fletcher, Alice C., American ethnologist; b. Cuba (of American parents), March 16, 1838; d. Washington, D. C., April 6, 1923. From 1886 she was assistant in ethnology at the Peabody Museum of American Archaeology and Ethnology, where she held the Thaw Fellowship, created for her in 1891; devoted her life to the study of North American Indians, among whom she lived for a number of years; 1896, became vice-president of American Association for the Advancement of Science; president of American Anthropological Society (1903) and American Folk Lore Society (1905). She is the author of *Indian Story and Song from North America* (1900); *A Study of Omaha Indian Music* (1903); *Indian Games and Dances* (1915); numerous articles in the 'Journal of American Folk Lore,' etc. — Cf. W. Hough, in 'American Anthropologist' (April-June, 1923); 'Dictionary of American Biography,' vol. VI (N. Y., 1931).

Fletcher, Grant, American composer and conductor; b. Hartsburg, Ill., Oct. 25, 1913; he studied at the Univ. of Michigan; then in Toronto with Healey Willan; in Rochester with Bernard Rogers and Howard Hanson; in Cleveland with Herbert Elwell. From 1945 until 1948 he was conductor of the Akron, Ohio, Orch. — Works: *The Crisis,* after Thomas Paine, for chorus and orch. (1945); *An American Overture* (Duluth, April 23, 1948); *A Song for Warriors* (on Yugoslav themes, Rochester, Oct. 25, 1945); *Panels from a Theater Wall* (Rochester, April 27, 1949); Symphony No. 1 (Rochester, April 24, 1951); 2 books of nocturnes for piano (1935); 4 American dance pieces for piano (1944); 5 string quartets; several choral works; songs.

Fletcher, Percy E., English composer; b. Derby, Dec. 12, 1879; d. London, Sept. 10, 1932. He went to London in 1899 as conductor at various theaters there; he composed many works in a light, melodious style, including the orchestral pieces *Woodland Pictures, Sylvan Scenes, Parisian Sketches, Three Frivolities,* the overture *Vanity Fair;* also a short sacred cantata, *Passion of Christ.*

Fleury, André, French organist and composer; b. Neuilly-sur-Seine, July 25, 1903. He studied with his father; later with Gigout, Marcel Dupré, and Louis Vierne. In 1930 he became organist at St. Augustin, Paris; in 1943 he was appointed prof. of organ playing at the École Normale de Musique; after World War II he taught at the Cons. of Dijon. Fleury has published 2 symphonies for organ and numerous other works for his instrument.

Fleury, Louis, eminent French flutist; b. Lyons, May 24, 1878; d. Paris, June 11, 1925. He studied at the Paris Cons.; from 1905 until his death was head of the famous Société moderne d'instruments à vent, also (1906) of the Société des Concerts d'autrefois (historic concerts), with which he gave concerts in England; made appearances with Melba and Calvé. Debussy composed *Syrinx* for unaccompanied flute for him. He edited much old flute music, including sonatas and other pieces by Blavet, Naudet, Purcell, J. Stanley, etc., and contributed to French and English periodicals (*Souvenirs d'un flûtiste* in 'Le Monde musical,' etc.).

Flodin, Karl, Finnish composer and music critic; b. (of German parents) Wasa, July 10, 1858; d. Helsinki, Nov. 29, 1925. A pupil of R. Faltin in Helsinki, then of the Leipzig Cons.; in 1907 he went to Buenos Aires as music critic on a German paper there; returned to Finland in 1920. He publ. numerous essays on Finnish music (in Finnish and German); wrote a biography of Martin Wegelius (1922); also composed incidental music to various plays; publ. some 80 piano pieces. He was married to the singer Adée Leander (1873-1935).

Floersheim (flors'-hīm), **Otto,** editor and composer, b. Aix-la-Chapelle, March 2, 1853; d. Geneva, Switzerland, Nov. 30, 1917. He was a pupil of Ferdinand Hiller at Cologne; went to New York in 1875, became editor of the 'Musical Courier' in 1880, and from 1894-1904 was manager of its Berlin branch. As a music journalist and a man of musical affairs, he was very influential in America; he was also highly regarded as a composer of competently put together piano pieces and songs in a German romantic vein.

Flood, (William Henry) Grattan, Irish organist and music historian; b. Lismore, Nov. 1, 1859; d. Enniscorthy, Aug. 6, 1928. At the age of 19 he became organist at a church in Dublin; took a few lessons from Dr. Kerbusch and Sir R. Stewart; was organist at Belfast (1878); taught music at the Jesuit College in Tullabeg and at St. Wilfrid's College, Staffordshire; in 1895 became organist at the Cathedral of Enniscorthy; Mus. Doc., Dublin Univ., 1907 (hon. c.). He achieved recognition as an archeologist, historian, and collector of Irish folksongs.—Writings: *History of Irish Music* (1895; 4th ed., 1927); *Story of the Harp* (1905); *Story of the Bagpipe* (1911); *W. Vincent Wallace, a Memoir* (1912); *John Field of Dublin* (Dublin, 1920); *Introductory Sketch of Irish Musical History* (1921); *Early Tudor Composers* (1925); *Late Tudor Composers* (1929). He contributed to Grove's 'Dictionary', 'The Catholic Encyclopaedia,' 'Dictionary of National Biography'; was the editor of 'Songs and Airs of O'Carolan,' 'Moore's Irish Melodies,' 'Armagh Hymnal,' and 'The Spirit of the Nation.'

Floquet, Étienne Joseph, French composer; b. Aix-en-Provence, Nov. 23, 1748; d. Paris, May 10, 1785. After studying in his native town, he went to Paris; there he wrote the opera-ballet *L'Union de l'Amour et des arts,* produced with great success at the Académie Royale de Musique (Sept. 7, 1773); his second opera *Azolan, ou le serment indiscret* (Nov. 22, 1774, also at the Académie), was a fiasco. Floquet then went to Italy, where he perfected his knowledge by studying with Sala in Naples and with Martini in Bologna. Returning to Paris, he had two operas performed at the Académie: *Hellé* (Jan. 5, 1779) and *Le Seigneur bienfaisant* (Dec. 14, 1780). He also wrote a comic opera *La nouvelle Omphale* (Comédie-Italienne, Nov. 22, 1782). In an attempt to challenge Gluck's superiority, Floquet wrote the opera *Alceste* on the same subject as Gluck's famous work, but it was never produced.—Cf. A. Pougin, *Étienne-Joseph Floquet* (Paris, 1863); F. Huot, *Étude biographique sur Étienne - Joseph Floquet* (Aix, 1903).

Florence, Evangeline (real name, Houghton), American soprano; b. Cambridge, Mass., Dec. 12, 1873; d. London, Nov. 1, 1928. She studied with Henschel and Lilli Lehmann. She made her début in London, in 1892; and carried on her entire concert career in England, where she attained great popularity. She retired from the stage in 1904.

Floridia, Pietro, Italian composer; b. Modica, Sicily, May 5, 1860; d. New York, Aug. 16, 1932. He studied in Naples with Cesi (piano) and Lauro Rossi (composition); while at the Naples Cons. he published several piano pieces which became quite popular. On May 7, 1882, he brought out in Naples a comic opera *Carlotta Clepier,* but despite a fairly successful production he burned the MS and undertook serious study for another period of several years; in 1889 completed a symphony, which won a prize. From 1888 to 1892 he taught at the Cons. of Palermo; then lived in Milan. In 1904 he emigrated to the U.S.; taught at the Cincinnati College of Music (1906-8); in 1908 settled in New York; in 1913 organized and conducted an Italian Symph. Orch. there. His music (mostly for the stage) is written in a competent manner, in the style of Mascagni.—Works: operas *Maruzza* (Venice, Aug. 23, 1894); *La Colonia libera* (Rome, May 7, 1899); *Paoletta* (Cincinnati, Aug. 29, 1910); also *The Scarlet Letter* (1902; not produced) and *Malia* (completed in 1932; not produced); incidental music to Oscar Wilde's *A Florentine Tragedy* (N. Y., Nov. 27, 1917); piano pieces and songs. Floridia edited a valuable collection in 2 vols., 'Early Italian Songs and Airs' (Philadelphia, 1923).

Florimo, Francesco, Italian musician and historian; b. S. Giorgio Morgeto, Calabria, Oct. 12, 1800; d. Naples, Dec. 18, 1888. In 1817 he entered the Collegio di Musica at Naples; Furno, Elia, Zingarelli, and Tritto were his teachers; from 1826-51 he was librarian there. He was Bellini's closest friend; in 1876 he escorted the latter's remains from Paris to Catania, and publ. the pamphlet 'Trasporto delle ceneri di Bellini a Catania'; composed *Sinfonia Funebre per la morte di Bellini;* founded the 'Bellini Prize,' a competition open to Italian composers not over 30. His chief work is *Cenno storico sulla scuola musicale di Napoli* (Naples, 1869-71, 2 vols.; republ. 1880-84, in 4 vols., as *La scuola musicale di Napoli e i suoi Conservatori*), a complete musical history of Naples and its conservatories, their teachers and pupils, etc.; despite numerous errors, it remains an extremely valuable guide. Other writings: *Riccardo Wagner ed i Wagneristi* (Naples, 1876); *Bellini, memorie e lettere* (Florence, 1882); an *Album Bellini* (Naples, 1886), containing opinions by many eminent musicians on Bellini's works; and a *Metodo di canto,* adopted by the Paris Cons. and described as "magistrale" by Rossini. Florimo was also an excellent singing teacher. — Cf. G. Megali, *Francesco Florimo* (Naples, 1901).

Florio, Caryl (real name, William James Robjohn), organist; b. Tavistock, Devon, Nov. 3, 1843; d. Morgantown, S. C., Nov. 21, 1920. He left England at the age of 14 and settled in New York; was engaged as a singer and organist at various churches in New York, Baltimore, Indianapolis, etc.; conducted choral societies in New York; eventually settled in Asheville, N. C. He wrote two operas to his own texts: *Guilda* (1879); and *Uncle Tom* (Philadelphia, 1882); several operettas; the cantatas *Song of the Elements* (1872) and *Bridal of Bethlehem;* two symphonies; a quintet for piano and 4 saxophones (the first work written for such an ensemble); piano concerto; 4 violin sonatas, and 2 piano sonatas.

Flothuis (flot'-häus), **Marius,** eminent Dutch composer; b. Amsterdam, Oct. 30, 1914. He studied with Hans Brandts-Buys; developed an individual style, redolent of neo-romanticism, but marked by a severely disciplined contrapuntal technique. He has written a cello sonata (1938); concerto for chamber orch. (1940); flute concerto (Utrecht, Dec. 19, 1945); horn concerto (1945); piano concerto (1948); partita for violin and piano (1950); *Love and Strife,* for contralto, flute, oboe d'amore, viola, and cello (Hilversum Radio, Sept. 26, 1951); violin concerto (Utrecht, Jan. 14, 1952); *Sonata da camera* for flute and harp (1952); 6 *Canonic Inventions* for 2 recorders (1952); *Divertimento* for clarinet, bassoon, horn, violin, viola, and double bass (Amsterdam, June 9, 1952); *Fantasia* for harp and chamber orch. (Amsterdam, May 26, 1955); *Sinfonietta Concertante* for clarinet, saxophone, and chamber orch. (Amsterdam, June 2, 1955); *Rondo festoso* for orch. (Amsterdam, July 7, 1956); etc. He has also publ. several monographs, and edited works by Monteverdi and Mozart.

Flotow (flŏh-tŏh), **Friedrich von,** famous German opera composer; b. Teutendorf, April 26, 1812; d. Darmstadt, Jan. 24, 1883. He was a scion of an old family of nobility, tracing its ancestry to the 13th century; received his first music lessons from his mother; then was a chorister in Güstrow. At the age of 16 he went to Paris, where he studied piano with J. P. Pixis and composition with Reicha. After the revolution of 1830, he returned home; but went to Paris again the following year; there he met Auber, Rossini, and Meyerbeer, and resolved to devote himself to opera. He associated himself with the influential composer Grisar, and contributed several arias and other numbers to Grisar's productions; his first independent work in Paris was the opera *Le Naufrage de la Méduse* (1839); then followed *L'Esclave de Camoëns;* also a ballet *Lady Henriette* (1844). He achieved his decisive success with the romantic opera *Alessandro Stradella,* based on the life of the composer Stradella; it was staged first in Hamburg (1844), and was produced subsequently in Paris and elsewhere with excellent success. Three years later, the production of his opera *Martha* (Vienna, 1847) established him as a celebrity; in this opera, which still retains its popularity after a century, Flotow demonstrated his ability to combine the German romantic spirit with Parisian elegance; the libretto (and some of the music) was elaborated from his early ballet *Lady Henriette,* with a setting in Queen Anne's England; an authentic Irish tune, *The Last Rose of Summer,* is used in the score as a recurrent theme, lending a certain nostalgic charm to an otherwise incongruous story. Flotow's aristocratic sympathies made it psychologically difficult for him to remain in Paris after the revolution of 1848; he subsequently lived in Schwerin, where he held the post of intendant of court music (1855-63); traveled in Austria and Italy, and revisited Paris (then under the Second Empire); in 1880 he retired and lived near Darmstadt. The list of his compositions includes: Operas: *Pierre et Catherine* (Schwerin, 1835); *Serafine* (Royaumont, Oct. 30, 1836); *Le Comte de Saint-Mégrin* (Royaumont, June 10, 1838); *Le Naufrage de la Méduse* (with Grisar and Pilati; Paris, May 31, 1839; in German as *Die Matrosen,* Hamburg, Dec. 23, 1845); *L'Esclave de Camoëns* (Paris, Dec. 1, 1843); *Alessandro Stradella* (Hamburg, Dec. 30, 1844); *L'Âme en peine* (or *Leoline;* Paris, June 29, 1846); *Martha* (Vienna, Nov. 25, 1847; his greatest success); *Sophia Catharina,* or *Die Grossfürstin* (Berlin, Nov. 19, 1850); *Indra* (a revision of *L'Esclave de Camoëns,* with a German libretto; Vienna, Dec. 18, 1852); *Rübezahl* (Frankfurt, Nov. 26, 1853); *Albin,* or *Der Pflegsohn* (Vienna, 1856; revived under the title *Der Müller von Meran,* Königsberg, Jan. 15, 1860); *Pianella* (Schwerin, Dec. 27, 1857); *La Veuve Grapin* (Paris, Sept. 21, 1859); *Naida* (St. Petersburg, Dec. 11, 1865); *Zilda* (Paris, May 28, 1866); *Am Runenstein*

(Prague, April 13, 1868); *L'Ombre* (Paris, July 7, 1870); also separate numbers for Grisar's operas *Lady Melvil* (1838) and *L'Eau merveilleuse* (1839). Ballets: *Lady Henriette* (Paris, Feb. 22, 1844); *Die Libelle* (Schwerin, Aug. 8, 1856); *Die Gruppe der Thetis* (Schwerin, Aug. 18, 1858); *Tannkönig* (Schwerin, Dec. 22, 1861); *Der Königsschuss* (Schwerin, May 22, 1864). Instrumental music: *Trio de salon* for piano, violin, and cello (1850); violin sonata (1861); *Chants du soir* for cello and piano (1845); Études for piano 4-hands (1872); a piano concerto in MS. — Bibl.: G. von Flotow, *Beiträge zur Geschichte der Familie von Flotow* (Dresden, 1844); W. Neumann, *Friedrich von Flotow* (Kassel, 1855); F. von Flotow, *Erinnerungen aus meinem Leben* (in Lewinsky's *Vor den Coulissen,* Berlin, 1882); R. Swoboda, *Friedrich von Flotows Leben; von seiner Witwe* (Leipzig, 1892); B. Bardi-Poswiansky, *Flotow als Opernkomponist* (Königsberg, 1927).

Flower, Sir **Newman,** English publisher and writer on music; b. Fontmell Magna, Dorset, July 8, 1879. He joined the firm of Cassel & Co. in 1906; purchased it in 1927. As an avocation, he became deeply interested in music; publ. an extensive biography, *G. F. Handel* (1923; revised ed., 1947); *Sir Arthur Sullivan, His Life and Letters* (with Herbert Sullivan; 1927; revised ed., 1950); *Franz Schubert* (1928; revised ed., 1949); also publ. a volume of memoirs, *Just as it Happened* (1950). He was knighted in 1938.

Floyd, Carlisle, talented American composer; b. Latta, South Carolina, June 11, 1926; studied at Syracuse Univ. with Ernst Bacon; obtained a M. Mus. degree there; also took private lessons with Rudolf Firkušny. In 1947 he joined the staff of the School of Music, Florida State Univ., Tallahassee. His musical drama in 2 acts and 10 scenes, *Susannah,* was produced there (Feb. 24, 1955); it was later staged at the City Center, N. Y. (Sept. 27, 1956); received the Music Critics Circle of New York Award as the best opera of the year. Floyd's other works include *Slow Dusk,* a musical play in one act (1949); *Fugitives,* a musical drama in 3 acts (1951); *Lost Eden* for 2 pianos (ballet; 1952); *Pilgrimage,* a cycle of 5 songs (1955), and other vocal and instrumental pieces.

Flury, Richard, Swiss composer; b. Biberist, March 26, 1896. He studied musicology in Basel, Bern, and Geneva, then theory and composition with Kurth, Hubert, Lauber, and Marx; conducted many orchestras and choral societies in Switzerland (Zürich, Bern, and Solothurn); since 1931, teaching at the Solothurn Canton School.—Works: operas: *Eine florentinische Tragödie* (1926), *Die helle Nacht* (1932), *Casanova e l'Albertolli* (1937); ballet *Die alte Truhe;* several festival music scores; 8 symphonies: No. 1 (1923), *Fastnachts-Symphonie* (1928), *Tessiner Symphonie* (No. 2, 1936), *Waldsymphonie* (1942), *Bucheggbergische Symphonie* (No. 3, 1946), No. 4 (1950), No. 5 (1952), No. 6 (1953); 6 symph. overtures; 3 violin concertos (1933, 1940, 1944); 2 piano concertos (1927, 1943); chamber music: oboe sonata (1926), 2 cello sonatas (1937, 1941), 4 string quartets (1926, 1929, 1938, 1940), piano quintet (1948); 7 piano sonatas; *50 romantische Stücke* for piano; 24 preludes for piano; 15 military marches and other music for band; choruses; about 150 songs. He wrote an autobiography, *Lebenserinnerungen* (1950; with a list of works).

Foch (real name **Fock**), **Dirk,** composer and conductor; b. Batavia, Java (where his father was Governor General of the Dutch East Indies), June 18, 1886. He studied in Holland and Germany; began his career in Sweden; conducted the Göteborg Symph. Orch. (1913-15); was guest conductor of the Concertgebouw in Amsterdam and of the orch. at The Hague (1917-19). He made his American début as conductor with a specially assembled orch. at Carnegie Hall, N. Y., April 12, 1920; also conducted orchestral groups in the U. S., and the Konzertverein in Vienna. In 1928 he settled in N. Y. Among his compositions are *Ein hohes Lied* (5 fragments from the Bible), for recitation and orch. (Amsterdam, 1931); a musical pageant in the style of the medieval mystery plays, *From Aeon to Aeon;* 3 ballades for piano (1913); a cycle of songs from the Chinese (1921); *Java Sketches* for piano (1948), etc.

Foerster, Adolph Martin, American composer; b. Pittsburgh, Pa., Feb. 2, 1854; d. there, Aug. 10, 1927. He owed his first musical training to his mother; studied at the Leipzig Cons. with Richter; then settled in Pittsburgh, where he was active as a teacher of singing and piano. He composed *Dedication March* for the opening of Carnegie Music Hall in Pittsburgh (Nov. 7, 1895); symph. poem *Thusnelda;* violin concerto; 2 piano trios; 2 piano quartets; 2 string quartets; numerous piano works; songs.

Foerster, Josef Bohuslav, Czech composer; b. Prague, Dec. 30, 1859; d. Nový Vestec, near Stará Boleslav, May 29, 1951. He was the son of the Czech organist, Josef Förster (1833-1907). He studied organ and was for several years organist of St. Adelbert's Church in Prague; conducted choruses; wrote music criticism. He married the opera singer Berta Lauterer in 1888; when she was engaged to sing at the Municipal Theater of Hamburg in 1893, Foerster followed her, and became prof. of the Hamburg Cons. and also music critic of the 'Hamburger Nachrichten'. Subsequently his wife was engaged by Mahler for the Vienna Court Opera (1903), and Foerster obtained a position at the 'Neues Konservatorium' in Vienna. In 1918, he returned to Prague, where he held teaching positions; taught composition at the Prague Cons.; was president of the Czech Academy (1931-39); in 1945, he received the honorary title of National Artist of the Republic of Czechoslovakia. He continued to teach privately and to compose almost to the end of his very long life; many Czech composers of the 20th century were his students. Foerster wrote in every genre; his music is suffused with lyric melos, and reveals characteristic national traits in his treatment of melodic and rhythmic material. His harmonic idiom represents the general style of central European romanticism, stemming from Dvořák, and ultimately from Wagner and Brahms. — Works: operas (all first performed in Prague): *Deborah* (Jan. 27, 1893), *Eva* (Jan. 1, 1899), *Jessica* (April 16, 1905), *Nepremoženi (The Conquerers;* Dec. 19, 1918), *Srdce (The Heart;* Nov. 15, 1923), *Bloud (The Simpleton;* Feb. 28, 1936); incidental music for Shakespeare's plays *Love's Labour's Lost, Twelfth Night,* and *Julius Caesar,* and for Strindberg's *Journey of Fortunate Peter;* 4 masses; oratorio *St. Venceslas* (1928); cantata *May* (1936); a cantata on the subject of the Thirty Years' War (1940); cantata entitled *1945,* written to celebrate the liberation of Czechoslovakia; 5 symphonies (1888, 1893, 1895, 1905, 1929); symph. poems *My Youth* (1900) and *Enigma* (1909); symph. suite *Cyrano de Bergerac* (1903); *Solemn Overture* (1907); 2 violin concertos (1911, 1926); cello concerto (1931); *Capriccio* for flute and small orch. (1940); 4 string quartets (1882, 1893, 1907, 1944); 3 piano trios (1883, 1894, 1921); string quintet (1886); wind quintet (1909); nonet for string and wind instruments (1931); 2 violin sonatas (1889, 1892); *Sonata quasi una fantasia* for violin and piano (1943); suite for viola and piano (1940). He publ. a book of memoirs, *Poutník v Cizině* (Prague, 1947; in German as *Der Pilger,* 1955). A symposium, *J. B. Foerster,* by various Czech writers, was publ. for his 90th birthday (Prague, 1949). See also Z. Nejedlý, *J. B. Foerster* (Prague, 1910); J. Bartoš, *J. B. Foerster* (Prague, 1923).

Fogg, Eric, English composer; b. Manchester, Feb. 21, 1903; d. London, Dec. 19, 1939. He studied organ with his father; composition with Granville Bantock; 1917-19, organist in Manchester; 1924, pianist of the Manchester station of the BBC, later becoming assistant to the North Regional musical director; from 1934, Empire musical director of the BBC and one of its conductors. He wrote *Seasheen,* for small orch.; *The Hillside,* for soli, chorus, and orch.; overture to the *Comedy of Errors* (1922); *Poem* for cello and piano; *Phantasy* for cello and piano; Suite for violin, cello, and harp; songs (*Love and Life, The Little Folk, 3 Chinese Songs,* etc.); piano pieces; choral works; etc.

Foggia (foh'-jăh), **Francesco,** Italian composer; b. Rome, c. 1604; d. there, Jan. 8, 1688. He was a pupil of A. Cifra; served at several German courts; returning to Rome, he was maestro di cappella at the Lateran (1636-61); at San Lorenzo in Damaso (1661), and, from 1677, at Santa Maria Maggiore. A prolific and masterly composer, he continued the traditions of the Roman School. He wrote the oratorios *David fugiens a facie Saul* and *San Giovanni Battista* (1670); numerous masses a cappella *a 3-9* (also a few with organ); litanies, motets, etc.

Fogliani (foh-l'yah'-nē), **Ludovico,** Italian theorist; b. Modena, 2d half of 15th cent.; d. there, 1539. Famous for his book *Musica theorica . . .* (Venice, 1529), in which he preceded Zarlino in declaring the correct proportion of the major third to be 4:5, and in distinguishing between the major and minor (greater and lesser) semitones. In Petrucci's 'Frottole' (1504-8) are some specimens of his compositions.

Foldes, Andor, concert pianist; b. Budapest, Dec. 21, 1913; studied at the Budapest Music Academy with Dohnányi; gave concerts in Europe until 1939, when he came to the U. S.; naturalized in 1948. He won the International Liszt Prize in 1933 at a piano contest in Budapest. He is the author of a book *Two on a Continent* (in collaboration with his wife, Lili Foldes; N. Y., 1947); and of *Keys to the Keyboard* (N. Y., 1948; transl. into several languages).

Foley (Signor Foli), **Allan James,** bass singer; b. Cahir, Tipperary, Ireland, Aug. 7, 1835; d. Southport, England, Oct. 20, 1899. He was a pupil of Bisaccia in Naples; from 1862-4 he sang in opera at Catania, Turin, Milan, and Paris, as 'Signor Foli'. He then sang at Her Majesty's Theatre, London (1865), in Covent Garden and Drury Lane; also in America, Austria, Russia, Australia, and South Africa (1893).

Folville, Juliette Eugénie-Émilie, composer; b. Liège, Belgium, Jan. 5, 1870; d. Dourgne, France, Oct. 28, 1946. She studied piano with her father, then violin with César Thomson. When she was only 17, her *Chant de Noël* was performed at the Liège Cathedral. In 1898 she was appointed professor at the Liège Cons. After the outbreak of World War I in 1914, she settled in Bournemouth, England, where she remained several years as a teacher, later returning to the Continent. She wrote an opera, *Atala* (Lille, 1892); *Oceano Nox* (symphonic poem); *Eva* (dramatic scene); miscellaneous pieces for piano, violin, organ; choruses.

Fomin (foh-mēn), **Evstigney Ipatovitch,** one of the earliest Russian national composers; b. St. Petersburg, Aug. 16, 1761; d. April, 1800. He studied music at the St. Petersburg Academy of Arts and graduated in 1782; was sent to Bologna to study with Padre Martini; returned to St. Petersburg in 1785; then became singing teacher and operatic coach at the theatrical school there. He composed about 10 operas, including *Novgorod Hero Vassily Boyeslavitch* (St. Petersburg, Dec. 8, 1786); *Yamshtchiki* (*Coachmen;* St. Petersburg, Jan. 13, 1787); *Witch, Fortune-Teller, and Marriage-Broker* (1791); *Orpheus and Eurydice* (St. Petersburg, Jan. 13, 1792), and *The Americans* (St. Petersburg, Feb. 19, 1800; MS discovered in 1940, and the opera was revived in a performance at Moscow, Jan. 17, 1947). A number of other operas were erroneously attributed to Fomin, among them the popular *Miller, Wizard, Cheat, and Marriage-Broker,* produced in Moscow on Jan. 31, 1779, the music of which was actually written by an obscure violinist named Sokolovsky.—Cf. A. Finagin, *E. Fomin,* in the collection, *Music in Old Russia* (Leningrad, 1927); N. Findeisen, *The Earliest Russian Operas,* in the 'Mus. Quarterly' (July, 1933); A. Rabinovitch, *Russian Opera Before Glinka* (Moscow, 1948; pp. 50-57 and 85-105).

Fonseca, Julio, Costa Rican composer; b. San José, May 22, 1885; d. there, June 22, 1950. He studied at the Milan Cons. and upon his return to Costa Rica was active as church organist and teacher.—Works: *Suite Tropical* for band (San José, Dec. 4, 1934); *Cantata a la Música* (San José, Oct. 11, 1935); also a number of salon dances and arrangements of folksongs.

Fontanelli, Alfonso, Italian madrigal composer; b. Reggio Emilia, Feb. 15, 1557; d. Rome, Feb. 11, 1622. He was in the service of Duke Alfonso II of Este in Ferrara (1588-97) and of his successor, Cesare II, until 1601, when he left the court to save himself from prosecution for a suspected complicity in the assassination of his second wife's lover. However, he was again in the service of the Estes in 1605, when he was in Rome as emissary of the Duke of Modena; in 1608 he was in Modena; in 1612-13, at the Spanish court. He took holy orders in 1621. He was a friend of Gesualdo, Prince of Venosa, and may have been influenced by him in his madrigals. He published anonymously 2 books of madrigals in 5 voices: *Primo libro* (Ferrara, 1595; reprint, Venice, 1603); *Secondo libro* (Venice, 1604; reprints 1609 and 1619). He was greatly esteemed by his contemporaries; Orazio Vecchi contributed an introduction to the 1603 ed. of his *Primo libro,* praising him for the inventiveness and dignity of his music.—Cf. F. Vatielli, *Il Principe di Venosa e Leonora d'Este* (Milan, 1941); A. Einstein, *The Italian Madrigal* (Princeton, 1949; vol. 2, p. 703).

Foote, Arthur, eminent American composer; b. Salem, Mass., March 5, 1853; d. Boston, April 8, 1937. He studied piano with a local teacher in Salem; in 1870 he entered Harvard Univ., studying composition with J. K. Paine; he received the A.M. degree in 1875 (the first such degree in music given in America). From 1874 he also studied organ with B. J. Lang, through whose influence he obtained an organist's position at the Church of the Disciples. In 1876 he attended the Wagner Festival in Bayreuth. In 1878 he became organist in the Boston First Unitarian Church, a post that he held until 1910. In 1881 he organized in Boston a series of chamber music concerts which continued until the end of the century; he was frequently pianist with the Kneisel Quartet (1890-1910), performing several of his own works. For 50 years, from 1883, he was a successful teacher in Boston. He was a member of the Music Teachers National Association; a founding member of the American Guild of Organists, and its president from 1909-12; also member of the National Institute of Arts and Letters and Fellow of the American Academy of Arts and Sciences. His music is distinguished by a fine lyrical feeling, in a romantic tradition. Many of his orchestral works were presented for the first time by the Boston Symphony Orchestra: overture, *In the Mountains* (Feb. 5, 1887; also performed at the Paris Exposition, July 12, 1889); Suite for Strings, D major, op. 21 (Nov. 23, 1889); symphonic prologue, *Francesca da Rimini* (Jan. 24, 1891); Suite in D minor, op. 36 (March 7, 1896); Suite for strings in E major, op. 63 (April 16, 1909). Of these, the Suite for Strings in E major is particularly popular. Other works include: Serenade in E major for strings, op. 25; *4 Character Pieces* after Omar Khayyám, op. 48, for orch.; a cello concerto; *A Night Piece* for flute and strings; the cantatas (for chorus and piano or orchestra): *The Farewell of Hiawatha,* for men's voices, op. 11; *The Wreck of the Hesperus,* op. 17; *The Skeleton in Armor,* op. 28. Chamber music: 3 string quartets, 2 piano trios, violin sonata, piano quartet, piano quintet, cello sonata, various pieces for instruments with piano accompaniment; more than 100 songs, of which the following are the best known: *The Night has a Thousand Eyes; I Know a little Garden Path; Constancy; In Picardie; Ashes of Roses;* also vocal quartets; church music. He was the author of several manuals: *Modern Harmony* (jointly with W. R. Spalding, 1905); *Some Practical Things in Piano-Playing* (1909); *Modulation and Related Harmonic Questions* (1919); also transl. Richter's *Treatise on Fugue;* ed. vol. 9 of 'The American History and Encyclopedia of Music' (1908-10). His autobiography was privately printed by his daughter, Katharine Foote Raffy (Norwood, Mass., 1946). See also his article *A Bostonian Remembers* in the 'Mus. Quarterly' (Jan., 1937).

Foote, George, American composer; b. Cannes, France, of American parents, Feb. 19, 1886; d. Boston, March 25, 1956. He studied with E. B. Hill at Harvard Univ.; then in Berlin with Koch and Klatte. Upon his return to the U. S. he was a member of the staff in the Music Dept. of Harvard Univ. (1921-23) and president of the South End Music School in Boston (until 1943).—Works: *Variations on a Pious Theme* for orch. (Boston Symph., Feb. 11, 1935); *In Praise of Winter,* symph. suite (Boston Symph., Jan. 5, 1940); *98th Psalm,* for chorus and organ (1934); religious pantomime, *We Go Forward* (1943); trio for flute, harp, and violin; other chamber music.

Forbes, Henry, English composer; b. London, 1804; d. there, Nov. 24, 1859. He studied with Sir George Smart in London, and with Moscheles and Hummel in Germany; was engaged as church organist and publ. a collection of psalm tunes, *National Psalmody* (1843). His opera *The Fairy Oak* was produced in London (Oct. 18, 1845) with considerable success.

Ford, Ernest A. C., English conductor and composer, b. London, Feb. 17, 1858; d. there, June 2, 1919. He was a pupil of Arthur Sullivan in the Royal Academy of Music and of Lalo in Paris; for some years conductor at the Royal English Opera House (where he conducted the première of Sullivan's *Ivanhoe* in 1891), then at the Empire Theatre; 1897-1908, Royal Amateur Orch. Society; from 1916, prof. of singing at Guildhall School of Music; Fellow of the Royal Academy of Music from 1899.—Works: operas; operettas; motet, *Domine Deus* (for 250th anniversary of Harvard Univ.); songs, duets, etc.; author of a *Short History of Music in England* (1912).

Ford, Thomas, English composer and lutenist; b. c. 1580; d. Nov. (buried Nov. 17), 1648. He was appointed musician to Prince Henry in 1611, and to Charles I in 1626. He was especially successful in the 'ayre,' a type of composition developed by Dowland, in which melodic prominence is given to the upper voice. These 'ayres' appear in alternative settings, either as solo songs with lute accomp. or as 4-part a cappella songs. He wrote *Musicke of Sundrie Kindes* (1607; 1st part contains 11 ayres); 2 anthems in Leighton's *Teares;* canons in Hilton's *Catch that catch can;* and the famous madrigal, *Since first I saw your face.* MSS are at Christ Church, Oxford, and at the British Museum.

Forkel, Johann Nikolaus, famous German music historian; b. Meeder, near Coburg, Feb. 22, 1749; d. Göttingen, March 20, 1818. He was a chorister at Lüneburg (1762-66) and 'Chorpräfect' at Schwerin (1766). In 1769 he began the study of law in Göttingen, supporting himself by teaching music. To musical history, however, he soon devoted his chief attention; he was appointed Univ. organist, and (1778) Univ. musical director; in 1780 he was made *Dr. phil.*—Works: *Über die Theorie der Musik, sofern* *sie Liebhabern und Kennern derselben nothwendig und nützlich ist* (1774); *Musikalisch-kritische Bibliothek* (Gotha, 1778-9, 3 vols.); *Über die beste Einrichtung öffentlicher Concerte* (1779); *Genauere Bestimmung einiger musikalischer Begriffe* (1780); *Musikalischer Almanach für Deutschland* (1782, 1783, 1784, and 1789); *Allgemeine Geschichte der Musik* (Leipzig, 1788 and 1801, 2 vols., covering the period up to 1550; his materials for later times went to the publisher Schwickert); *Allgemeine Literatur der Musik, oder Anleitung zur Kenntniss musikalischer Bücher* (1792; important as the pioneer work of its class); *Über Johann Sebastian Bachs Leben, Kunst und Kunstwerke* (Leipzig, 1802; the first full biography of Bach, based on information supplied by Bach's sons; in English, London 1820; new transl., London, 1920, by Terry). Forkel's unique transcriptions, in modern notation, of Graphäus' 'Missae XIII' (1539), and of the 'Liber XV. missarum' of Petrejus (1538; masses by Ockeghem, Obrecht, Josquin, and others), were engraved, and a proof pulled; but the invading French army melted down the plates for cannonballs. The proofsheets, corrected by Forkel, are in the Berlin Library. His publ. compositions include piano sonatas and songs; in MS are the oratorio *Hiskias;* 2 cantatas *Die Macht des Gesangs* and *Die Hirten an der Krippe zu Bethlehem;* symphonies, trios, choruses, etc.—Cf. Heinrich Edelhoff, *J. N. Forkel* (Göttingen, 1935); W. Franck, *Musicology and its Founder, J. N. Forkel,* in the 'Mus. Quarterly' (Oct., 1949).

Formes, Karl Johann, German bass singer; b. Mülheim, Aug. 7, 1815; d. San Francisco, Dec. 15, 1889. He made his opera début at Cologne, 1841; from 1843-8 he was engaged at Mannheim; 1852-7 at the Royal Italian Opera, London; in 1857 he made his first American tour; then divided his time between Europe and America. He wrote an autobiography, *Aus meinem Kunst- und Bühnenleben* (1888; in English, San Francisco, 1891).

Formes, Theodor, German tenor, brother of Karl Formes; b. Mülheim, June 24, 1826; d. Endenich, near Bonn, Oct. 15, 1874. He made his début at Ofen (1846); then sang opera in Vienna (1848) and Berlin (1851-66); made a tour in America with his brother. He lost his voice temporarily; returned to the stage for a few years; then suffered a setback, became insane, and died in an asylum.

Fornia-Labey, Rita (*née* Newman), American soprano; b. San Francisco, July 17, 1878; d. Paris, Oct. 27, 1922. She adopted the name Fornia from her native state of California; married J. P. Labey in 1910. She studied in Paris with Jean de Reszke; began her career as a coloratura soprano; then changed to mezzo-soprano. She made her début in Germany; came to the U. S. in 1906 as a member of H. W. Savage's Opera Co.; from 1908-22 she was on the staff of the Metropolitan Opera; also made appearances at Covent Garden in London. She was particularly effective in Wagnerian roles.

Foroni, Jacopo, Italian conductor and composer; b. Verona, July 25, 1825; d. Stockholm, Sept. 8, 1858 (of cholera). He settled in Stockholm in 1849, and became court conductor there; was very successful at his public concerts, and also as a composer. He wrote several operas, among them *I Gladiatori* (Milan, Oct. 7, 1851). His opera *Advokaten Patelin,* performed posthumously in Stockholm (Dec. 4, 1858), was revived several times until 1926.

Forqueray, Antoine, French player on the viola da gamba; b. Paris, 1671; d. Nantes, June 28, 1745. He held an appointment as royal chamber musician to Louis XIV from 1690; publ. pieces for his instrument. His brother, **Michel Forqueray** (b. Paris, Feb. 15, 1681; d. Montfort l'Amaury, May 30, 1757), was a Paris organist; **Jean Baptiste Forqueray** (b. Paris, April 3, 1699; d. there, Aug. 15, 1782), son of Antoine Forqueray, was also a player on the viola da gamba; transcribed for the harpsichord some of his father's pieces; **Nicolas Gilles Forqueray** (b. Paris, Feb. 15, 1703; d. there, Oct. 23, 1761), another son of Antoine, was a church organist.

Forrest, Hamilton, American composer; b. Chicago, Jan. 8, 1901; he sang as a chorister in Chicago churches; studied with Adolf Weidig; has written mainly for the stage: operas *Yzdra* (1925; received the Bispham Memorial Medal of the American Opera Society of Chicago) and *Camille* (Chicago, Dec. 10, 1930, with Mary Garden in the title role); also ballet music and *Watercolors* for 14 wind instruments and harp.

Forsell, John, famous Swedish baritone; b. Stockholm, May 6, 1868; d. there, May 30, 1941. He was in the Swedish Army before embarking on his vocal studies. He made his début in 1896 at the Stockholm Opera; sang there from 1896 to 1901, and again in 1903-09. He was on the roster of the Metropolitan Opera during the season of 1909-10. In 1924 he was appointed director of the Stockholm Opera, a post that he held until 1939; also taught singing at the Stockholm Cons. from 1924. A jubilee collection of essays, *Boken om J. Forsell,* was publ. on his 70th birthday (Stockholm, 1938).

Förster, Adolph M. See **Foerster.**

Förster, Alban, German violinist; b. Reichenbach, Oct. 23, 1849; d. Neustrelitz, Jan. 18, 1916. He was a pupil at Reichenbach of R. Blume; later of Dresden Cons.; in 1871, court musician at Neustrelitz, also conducting the Singakademie; 1881, teacher in Dresden Cons., and cond. of the Liedertafel; 1882-1908, court Kapellmeister at Neustrelitz. He wrote a ballet *Träumerei in der Waldmühle* (Zwickau, 1896); orchestral and chamber music (string trios and quartets), violin music, instructive piano pieces, and songs.

Förster, August, German piano manufacturer; b. 1829; d. Löbau, Feb. 18, 1897. He founded a piano factory in Bohemia; also owned the Förster Saal in Berlin. His firm constructed the first quarter-tone piano with two manuals (1924).

Förster, Emanuel Aloys, German composer and theorist; b. Niederstein, Silesia, Jan. 26, 1748; d. Vienna, Nov. 12, 1823. After service in the Prussian Army, where he played the oboe in a band, he went to Vienna for a thorough course in music, eventually becoming a teacher himself, even though without a school position. He became friendly with Beethoven, who expressed esteem for him. Förster was a prolific composer; he wrote 48 string quartets, 5 oboe concertos, 10 violin sonatas, 21 piano sonatas, etc. His variations on arias from operas by Mozart, Sarti, and others enjoyed great popularity. He also publ. a manual, *Anleitung zum Generalbass* (1805; several later editions).

Forster, Georg, German composer and compiler of music; b. Amberg, c. 1510; d. Nuremberg, Nov. 12, 1568. He sang at the Heidelberg chapel in 1521, matriculating in classical studies in 1528. In 1531 he undertook medical studies at Ingolstadt; in 1534, studied humanities in Wittenberg with Melanchthon. In 1544 he received his degree of doctor of medicine at Tübingen Univ.; then was medical practitioner in Amberg, Würzburg, Heidelberg, and Nuremberg (1544). He edited the valuable collection *Ein Auszug guter alter und neuer teutscher Liedlein* (in 5 parts; Nuremberg, 1539-56). Reprints are found in the 'Kaiser-Liederbuch,' 'Staatliches Jugend-Liederbuch,' F. Jöde's 'Das Chorbuch,' and Schering's *Geschichte der Musik in Beispielen* (No. 88). Part II of the collection is published in R. Eitner's 'Publikationen,' vol. 29.—Cf. H. J. Moser in 'Jahrbuch Peters' (1928; p. 45 ff.).

Förster, Joseph, Czech organist and composer; b. Osojnitz, Bohemia, Feb. 22, 1833; d. Prague, Jan. 3, 1907. He was organist in several churches in Prague, and prof. of theory at the Prague Cons. He wrote organ pieces, church music, and a treatise on harmony. He was the father of the celebrated Czech composer Joseph Bohuslav Foerster.

Förster, Joseph Bohuslav. See **Foerster.**

Forsyth Brothers, British music publishers. The firm was established in Manchester in 1857 by Henry and James Forsyth, formerly of John Broadwood & Sons. They opened their business as piano dealers. In 1872 they began publishing music in Manchester and in London. In 1901 the firm was made a limited company with James Forsyth as president. Henry Forsyth died in 1885. The firm specializes in educational music.

Forsyth, Cecil, English composer and writer on music; b. Greenwich, Nov. 30, 1870; d. New York, Dec. 7, 1941. He received his general education at Edinburgh Univ.; then studied at the Royal College of Music with Stanford and Parry. He joined the viola section in the Queen's Hall Orch.; also was connected with the Savoy Theatre, where he produced two of his comic operas, *Westward Ho!* and *Cinderella.* After the outbreak of World War I he went to N. Y., where he remained for the rest of his life. He composed a viola concerto and *Chant celtique* for viola and orch.; also songs, sacred music, and instrumental pieces. He was the author of a comprehensive manual *Orchestration* (N. Y., 1914; second ed., 1935; reprinted, 1948); *Choral Orchestration* (London, 1920); also *Music and Nationalism* (London, 1911; a treatise on English opera); publ. (in collaboration with Stanford) *A History of Music* (London, 1916); and a collection of essays *Clashpans* (N. Y., 1933).

Forsyth, Josephine, American song composer; b. Cleveland, July 5, 1889; d. there,

May 24, 1940. She was married to P. A. Meyers on April 29, 1928, and wrote a setting of the *Lord's Prayer* for her wedding. This setting later attained considerable popularity, and was sung for many years at Easter sunrise ceremonies at the Hollywood Bowl.

Fortlage, Karl, German theorist; b. Osnabrück, June 12, 1806; d. Jena, Nov. 8, 1881. He studied theology and philosophy; was prof. at Jena Univ. from 1846. In connection with his study of Greek philosophy, he became interested in the Greek musical system; publ. one of the earliest comprehensive works on the subject, *Das musikalische System der Griechen in seiner Urgestalt* (Leipzig, 1847).

Fortner, Wolfgang, German composer; b. Leipzig, Oct. 12, 1907. He studied at the Leipzig Cons. with Grabner (1927-31). In 1931 he joined the faculty of the Evangelical Church Music Institute at Heidelberg. In 1954 became teacher of composition at the Northwestern Music Academy in Detmold. In 1957 he was appointed dozent at the Musikhochschule in Freiburg - im - Breisgau. His works are marked by exceptional contrapuntal skill, in the style of Max Reger; the tonal fabric is clearly outlined, despite the use of an individual system of 12-tone melodies.—Works: operas: *Die Witwe von Ephesus* (Berlin, Sept. 17, 1952); *Der Wald,* after Garcia Lorca (Frankfurt, June 25, 1953); *Die Bluthochzeit* (Cologne, May 25, 1957); ballet *Die weisse Rose,* after Oscar Wilde's *The Birthday of the Infanta* (Berlin, April 28, 1951); concerto for strings (1932); Sinfonia concertante (1937); a symphony (1947); organ concerto (1932; revised as harpsichord concerto, 1935); piano concerto (1943); violin concerto (1947); cello concerto (1951); many choral works for various festive occasions; a cantata *Die Nachgeborenen* (1948); three string quartets; suite for saxophone after Sweelinck (1930); *Serenade* for flute, oboe, and bassoon (1948); also *Phantasie über B-A-C-H* for two pianos, 9 instruments, and orch., based on a 12-tone row (1950).—Cf. Karl Laux, *Wolfgang Fortner,* in *Musik und Musiker der Gegenwart* (Essen, 1949).

Foss, Hubert James, English writer on music; b. Croydon, May 2, 1899; d. London, May 27, 1953. He attended Bradfield College; 1921, became a member of the educational department of the Oxford Univ. Press and in 1924 founded the music department, of which he was head till 1941; 1922-23, critic of the 'New Witness,' 1923, of the 'Daily Graphic.' He composed *Seven Poems by Thomas Hardy* for baritone, male chorus, and piano; instrumental pieces; songs. He is the author of *Music in My Time* (1933); *The Concertgoer's Handbook* (London, 1946); *Ralph Vaughan Williams* (London, 1950); ed. 2 vols. of 'The Heritage of Music' (1927, 1934); also a contributor to many musical journals ('Music & Letters,' 'Musical Times,' etc.). His book, *London Symphony; Portrait of an Orchestra,* remained unfinished at his death, and was completed by Noël Goodwin (London, 1954).

Foss (real name Fuchs), **Lukas,** brilliant pianist and composer; b. Berlin, Aug. 15, 1922. He studied in Berlin with Julius Goldstein (piano and theory) and, from 1933, in Paris with Lazare Lévy (piano) and Noël Gallon (composition); also pupil of Moyse (flute) and Felix Wolfes (orchestration); in 1937, came with his parents to the U. S.; studied at the Curtis Institute, Philadelphia, with Isabelle Vengerova (piano), Rosario Scalero (composition), Randall Thompson (composition), and Fritz Reiner (conducting); for several summers was in Koussevitzky's conducting class at the Berkshire Music Center; further took a course with Hindemith at Yale Univ. He was the youngest composer to be awarded a Guggenheim Fellowship (1945). In 1944 he became the pianist of the Boston Symph. Orch., resigning in 1950, when he received a Fulbright Fellowship and went to Rome, remaining there until Dec., 1952. In Feb., 1953 he became a professor of composition and conductor of the Univ. orch. at the Univ. of California, L. A. He has appeared as piano soloist in his own piano concertos and in classical concertos with many American orchestras (Boston Symph., N. Y. Philh., St. Louis Symph., Los Angeles Philh., etc.); and in Europe (at the Venice Festival, etc.); has conducted in the U. S.; taught classes at the Berkshire Music Center. He began to compose at a very early age, and had pieces published at 15. His technical equipment is thorough; he is equally at ease in writing music in a strict polyphonic style and in a complex harmonic idiom; his modernism is circumscribed, however, by a disciplined sense of tonal organization. He has successfully essayed music in an American style.—Works: incidental music to Shakespeare's *The Tempest* (N. Y., March 31, 1940); *The Prairie,* cantata for mixed chorus, solo voices, and orch., after Carl Sandburg's poem (Collegiate Chorale, Robert Shaw, conductor, N. Y., May 15, 1944; a suite from it was performed earlier by the Boston Symph. Orch., Oct. 15, 1943); 1st piano concerto (CBS., 1944); Symph. in G (Pittsburgh Symph. Orch., Feb. 4, 1945, composer conducting); *Ode* for orch. (N. Y. Philh., March 15, 1945); *Gift of the Magi,* ballet (Boston, Oct. 5, 1945); *Song of Anguish,* 1st biblical solo cantata (1945; Boston Symph. Orch., March 10, 1950; composer conducting); *Pantomime,* for orch. (Baltimore Symph., Nov. 13, 1946); *Song of Songs,* 2nd biblical solo cantata (Boston Symph. Orch., March 7, 1947, Koussevitzky conducting); string quartet (1947); Set of 3 Pieces for 2 pianos; *Recordare,* for orch. (Boston, Dec. 31, 1948); oboe concerto (radio broadcast première, Feb. 6, 1950); opera, *The Jumping Frog of Calaveras County* after Mark Twain (Univ. of Indiana, Bloomington, May 18, 1950); 2nd piano concerto (Venice, Oct. 7, 1951, composer soloist; revised, 1953; Music Critics' Award, 1954); *A Parable of Death,* cantata, after Rilke (Louisville, March 11, 1953; a commissioned work); opera, *Griffelkin* (NBC television, Nov. 6, 1955); *Psalms,* for voices and orch. (N. Y., May 9, 1957).

Foster, Fay, American composer; b. Leavenworth, Kansas, Nov. 8, 1886. She studied at the Munich Cons. with H. Schwartz (piano) and S. Jadassohn (composition); studied piano further with M. Rosenthal and Sophie Menter; won a prize of 2000 marks at the International Waltz Competition (Berlin, 1910); 1st prize in American Composers' Contest (N. Y., 1913); also won other composition prizes; made several tours as a pianist; eventually settled in N. Y. She wrote 3 operettas; over 100 songs (*The Americans Come!, My Journey's End,* etc.); piano studies, etc.

Foster, Muriel, English alto singer; b. Sunderland, Nov. 22, 1877; d. London, Dec. 23, 1937. In 1896 she entered the Royal College of Music, her teacher being Anna Williams; that same year she sang at Bradford in Parry's *King Saul;* won an Open Scholarship in 1897; in 1898 obtained the London Musical Society's prize; and in 1900 the Musicians' Company's medal for the best student in the College. She sang before Queen Victoria in 1900; in 1901 toured Canada with Mme. Albani; awarded the Beethoven Medal of the London Philh. Society. After her marriage to Ludwig Goetz, in 1906, she appeared infrequently; retired in 1919.

Foster, Myles Birket, English organist; b. London, Nov. 29, 1851; d. there, Dec. 18, 1922. He was a pupil of Hamilton Clarke; later of Arthur Sullivan, Prout, and Westlake at the Royal Academy of Music; served as organist at Haweis' church (1873-74) and at the Foundling Hospital (1880-92); from 1888, Examiner of Trinity College, London, in which capacity he spent many years in Australia and South Africa; Fellow of the Royal College of Organists and of the Royal Academy of Music. He publ. *Anthems and Anthem-Composers* (1901), *History of the London Philharmonic Society, 1813-1912* (1913), and pedagogic works.

Foster, Stephen Collins, American composer of famous songs; b. Lawrenceville (Pittsburgh), Pa., July 4, 1826; d. New York, Jan. 13, 1864. He learned to play the flute as a child; publ. a song *Open thy Lattice, Love* at the age of 18. His father was a government worker and business man, active in politics; his brothers were engaged in commerce. About 1846 he went to Cincinnati as accountant for his brother Dunning. The total number of Foster's songs is 189, for most of which he wrote both words and music. Of these, *Old Folks at Home,* sometimes referred to as *Swanee Ribber* (from its initial line "Way down upon de Swanee Ribber"), was published on Oct. 21, 1851, with the subtitle "Ethiopian Melody as sung by Christy's Minstrels." Christy's name was given as author, in consideration of a small sum of money received by Foster, whose name was not attached to the song until 1879, upon the expiration of the original copyright. About 40,000 copies of this song were sold during the year after publication. Foster was greatly encouraged, and, as he wrote to Christy, hoped to establish himself as "the best Ethiopian song writer." Of other songs, the most notable are *Oh, Susanna!* (1848; became popular in the gold-rush of 1849); *My Old Kentucky Home, Massa's in de Cold Ground, Jeanie with the Light Brown Hair, Old Black Joe, Nelly was a Lady, Laura Lee,* etc. His last song was *Beautiful Dreamer* (1864). On July 22, 1850, Foster married Jane McDowell in Pittsburgh; they had a daughter, but the marriage was not happy. In 1853 Foster went to New York and stayed there for a year alone; in 1854 he was living in Hoboken, N. J.; went to New York again in 1860, while his wife remained with relatives. Foster died penniless at Bellevue Hospital; yet his earnings were not small; from 1849-1860 he received about $15,000 in royalties. Apart from the songs, Foster wrote 12 instrumental pieces in salon music style, and made numerous arrangements for flute, guitar, violin, etc. for the collection *Foster's Social Orchestra.* He had some knowledge of instrumental writing; his harmonies, though simple, are adequate. The extant manuscripts are mostly in the Foster Hall Collection at the Univ. of Pittsburgh (dedicated on June 2, 1937); bibliographical bulletins are issued periodically by this organization. A one-penny stamp bearing Foster's picture was brought out by the U. S. post office in 1940. In 1915 W. R. Whittlesey and O. G. Sonneck publ. a *Catalogue of First Editions of S. Foster.*—Bibl.: M. Foster (brother), *Biography, Songs and Musical Compositions of Stephen Foster* (1896; not always accurate); H. V. Milligan, *S. C. Foster* (N. Y., 1920); J. T. Howard, *Stephen Foster, America's Troubadour* (N. Y., 1934; new ed., 1953); J. T. Howard, *Stephen Foster and His Publishers,* in the 'Mus. Quarterly' (Jan., 1934); J. T. Howard also edited *Newly Discovered Fosteriana* (N. Y., 1935); G. P. Jackson, *Stephen Foster's Debt to American Folk-Songs* (N. Y., 1936); R. Walters, *Stephen Foster, Youth's Golden Gleam* (Princeton, N. J., 1936); J. T. Howard, *The Literature on Stephen Foster* (Washington, D. C., 1944); Evelyn Foster Morneweck, *Chronicles of Stephen Foster's Family* (2 vols.; Pittsburgh, 1944); Otto Gombosi, *Stephen Foster and 'Gregory Walker'* in the 'Mus. Quarterly' (April, 1944); F. Hodges, Jr., *Stephen Foster, Democrat,* in the 'Lincoln Herald' (June, 1945; published separately, Pittsburgh, 1946).

Foulds, John Herbert, English composer; b. Manchester, Nov. 2, 1880; d. Calcutta, April 24, 1939. At the age of 14 he played in theater orchestras; 1900-10, member of the Hallé Orch.; then conducted stage music. In 1921 he became director of the Univ. of London Music Society. He experimented with quarter-tones, and as early as 1898 wrote a string quartet using them.—Principal works: dramatic music: *Wonderful Grandmamma, The Whispering Well, Julius Caesar, Sakuntala, The Trojan Women, Debureau, The Fires Divine, The Vision of Dante;* for orch.: *Epithalamium; Music Pictures* (London, Sept. 5, 1912); *Celtic Suite;* incidental music to Bernard Shaw's *Saint Joan;* cello concerto; vocal works: *A World Requiem* for chorus (London, 1923), *Mood Pictures* for 3 voices, *The Easter Lover,* for alto and orch.; piano works; violin and vocal pieces; songs. He publ. *Music To-day: its Heritage from the Past, and Legacy to the Future* (London, 1934).

Fourdrain (fŏŏr-drän'), **Félix,** French composer; b. Nice, Feb. 3, 1880; d. Paris, Oct. 23, 1923. He studied with Widor; wrote the operas *Echo* (Paris, 1906), *La Légende du point d'Argentan* (Paris, April 17, 1907), *La Glaneuse* (Lyons, 1909), *Vercingétorix* (Nice, 1912), *Madame Roland* (Rouen, 1913), *Les Contes de Perrault* (Paris, 1913), *Les Maris de Ginette, La Mare au diable, La Griffe;* the operettas *Dolly* (Paris, 1922), *L'Amour en Cage, Le Million de Colette, La Hussarde* (Paris, 1925); incidental music to Cain's *Le Secret de Polichinelle* (Cannes, 1922); *Anniversaire,* for orch.; many songs (*Le Papillon, Sérénades, Revanche d'amour, Pays des cours,* etc.).

Fourestier (foo-rĕs-t'yā), **Louis,** French composer and conductor; b. Montpellier, May 31, 1892. He studied at the Paris Cons. under Gédalge and Leroux; won the Rossini Prize in 1924 (for his cantata, *Patria*), the Grand Prix de Rome in 1925 (for the cantata, *La Mort d'Adonis*), and the Heugel Prize in 1927 (for the symph. poem *Polynice*); served as conductor at Marseilles and Bordeaux; 1938, appointed conductor at the Paris Opéra; 1947-48, was in the U. S. as guest conductor of the Metropolitan Opera.

Fournier (fŏŏr-n'yā), **Émile-Eugène-Alix,** French composer; b. Paris, Oct. 11, 1864; d. Joinville-le-Pont, Sept. 12, 1897. He was a pupil of Delibes and Dubois at the Paris Cons.; took 2nd Grand Prix de Rome in 1891 and the Prix Cressent in 1892 for the 1-act opera *Stratonice* (Paris, 1892); publ. a number of songs, and finished a 3-act opera, *Carloman* (not produced).

Fournier, Pierre, French cellist; b. Paris, June 24, 1906. He made his début in 1925; from 1936 to 1948, toured in Europe; since 1948, annual appearances in the U. S.; teaching at the Paris Cons. — Cf. B. Gavoty, *Pierre Fournier* (Geneva, 1957).

Fournier, Pierre-Simon, French cutter and founder of music type; b. Paris, Sept. 15, 1712; d. there, Oct. 8, 1768. Instead of the lozenge-shaped types in the style of Hautin's (1525), Fournier introduced round-headed notes, described in his *Essai d'un nouveau caractère de fonte . . .* (1756); he also publ. a *Traité historique sur l'origine et le progrès des caractères de fonte pour l'impression de la musique* (Paris, 1765).

Fox, Charles Warren, American musicologist; b. Gloversville, N. Y., July 24, 1904. He studied psychology at Cornell Univ.

(B. A., 1929; Ph. D., 1933); also took courses in musicology with Otto Kinkeldey there. In 1933 he was appointed instructor in psychology at the Eastman School of Music, Rochester; 1934, began teaching musicology as well. He was vice-president of the American Musicological Society (1952-54); since 1952, editor of the Society's 'Journal'; president of the Music Library Association (1954-56); has contributed a number of valuable articles to American music magazines ('Mus. Quarterly,' 'Journal of the American Musicological Society,' 'Music Library Association Notes,' etc.).

Fox, Charlotte (*née* Milligan), b. Omagh, Ireland, 1860; d. London, Mar. 26, 1916. She was an enthusiastic musical amateur, specially interested in Irish music; in 1904 she founded the 'Irish Folk Song Society'; in her will she left the Bunting MSS to Belfast Univ. She publ. *Annals of the Irish Harpers* (London, 1911); composed the well known song *The Foggy Dew*.

Fox, Felix, pianist and teacher; b. Breslau, May 25, 1876; d. Boston, March 24, 1947. He studied at the Leipzig Cons. with Reinecke (piano) and Jadassohn (theory); then with Isidor Philipp in Paris, where he gave several recitals introducing works by MacDowell. In 1897 he returned to the U. S. and settled in Boston as pianist and teacher; in 1898 he established, with C. Buonamici, a piano school which enjoyed an excellent reputation; after Buonamici's death in 1920 it became the Felix Fox School of Pianoforte Playing; it was discontinued in 1935. Fox wrote many piano pieces; songs; made transcriptions of MacDowell works; also edited numerous piano works.

Fox-Strangways, Arthur Henry, English writer on musical subjects; b. Norwich, Sept. 14, 1859; d. Dinton, near Salisbury, May 2, 1948. He graduated from Oxford; 1893-1901, music director at Wellington College, London; 1911 to 1925, music critic of the 'Times,' London, later of the 'Observer'; In 1920 he founded the quarterly magazine 'Music & Letters,' of which he remained editor until 1936 (succeeded by Eric Blom). He was a specialist on Indian music and wrote several books on the subject, including *The Music of Hindustan* (1914); also publ. a collection of essays, *Music Observed* (1936) and a biography of Cecil Sharp (1933). He contributed the article *Folk-Song* to the introductory vol. of the 'Oxford History of Music' (1929).—Cf. 'Music & Letters' for Oct. 1939 (articles by Blom, Colles, Dent, Dyson, Vaughan Williams, etc.) and for July, 1948.

Fracassi, Américo, composer; brother of Elmérico Fracassi; b. Lucito, Campobasso, Italy, Feb. 29, 1880; d. Goya, Argentina, Aug. 15, 1936. With his brother, he left his native Italy as a very young man and settled in Buenos Aires, where he taught various musical subjects at a music school. He composed some songs and piano pieces.

Fracassi, Elmérico, composer; brother of Américo Fracassi; b. Lucito, Campobasso, Italy, Dec. 19, 1874; d. Buenos Aires, Oct. 12, 1930. He was taken to Buenos Aires as a boy, but returned to Italy in 1890 for his musical training (Cons. of Naples, with Rossomandi and D'Arienzo); toured Europe twice as a concert pianist; 1904, appointed director (together with G. d'Andrea) of the Almagro Cons. in Buenos Aires. He composed 2 operas, *Finlandia* (Turin, 1914) and *Merletti di Burano;* a piano concerto; violin sonata; piano studies; songs; and 4 Argentinian anthems, one of which, *Himno al Centenario,* won a prize from the Argentine Government.

Frackenpohl, Arthur, American composer; b. Irvington, N. J., April 23, 1924. He studied at the Eastman School of Music, Rochester, with Bernard Rogers; also with Milhaud at the Berkshire Music Center, and with Nadia Boulanger at Fontainebleau. In 1949 was appointed member of the faculty at the State Univ. Teachers' College, Potsdam, N. Y.—Works: sonatina for clarinet and piano (1948); brass quartet (1949); trio for oboe, horn, and bassoon (1949); cantata, *A Child This Day Is Born* (1951); *Suite for Strings* (1953); *An Elegy on the Death of a Mad Dog* (1955); *Allegro Giocoso* for band (1955); *A Jubilant Overture* for orch. (1956); etc.

Fradkin, Frederick, American violinist; b. Troy, N. Y., April 2, 1892. At the age of five he became a pupil of Schradieck; later studied with Max Bendix and Sam Franko in N. Y.; then went to Paris; studied at the Cons. there with Lefort, graduating in 1909 with first prize. He was concertmaster of the Bordeaux Opera Co.; then took instruction with Ysaÿe in Brussels. Returning to America, he made his début as concert violinist in N. Y. on Jan. 10, 1911; then gave concerts in Europe; in 1918-19 he was concertmaster of the Boston Symph. Orch.; later settled in N. Y. as private teacher.

Fraemcke, August, German pianist and pedagogue; b. Hamburg, March 23, 1870; d. N. Y., Jan. 18, 1933. He studied at the Hamburg Cons.; then at the Vienna Cons., where he won the Beethoven Prize. In 1891 he emigrated to the U. S., and joined the staff of the N. Y. College of Music, in 1906 becoming its co-director. He was active in the Bohemian Club in N. Y. City.

Framery (frah-mä-rē'), **Nicolas Étienne,** French composer, writer on music, and poet; b. Rouen, March 25, 1745; d. Paris, Nov. 26, 1810. He composed the text and music for the comic opera *La Sorcière par hasard* (1768); its performance at Villeroy earned him the position of superintendent of music with the Count of Artois. The opera was played at the Comédie-Italienne (Paris, Sept. 3, 1783), but suffered a fiasco because of the antagonism against Italian opera generated by the adherents of Gluck. He also wrote librettos for Sacchini, Salieri, Paisiello, Anfossi, and other Italian composers; compiled together with Ginguène and Feytou, the musical part of vol. I of 'Encyclopédie méthodique' (1791; vol. II by Momigny, 1818); edited a 'Calendrier musical universel' (1788-89); also edited the 'Journal de musique' in Paris from 1770 till 1778; besides smaller studies, he wrote *De la nécessité du rythme et de la césure dans les hymnes ou odes destinées à la musique* (1796); transl. into French Azopardi's *Musico prattico (Le Musicien pratique;* 2 vols., 1786).—Cf. J. Carlez, *Framery, littérateur-musicien* (Caen, 1893).

Françaix (frăhn-sā'), **Jean,** talented French composer; b. Le Mans, May 23, 1912. He first studied at Le Mans Cons., of which his father was director; then at the Paris Cons. with Isidor Philipp (piano) and Nadia Boulanger (composition). In his music, Françaix associates himself with the neo-French school of composers, pursuing the twofold aim of practical application and national tradition; his instrumental works represent a stylization of classical French music; in this respect, he comes close to Ravel.—Works: operas: *La Main de Gloire* (Bordeaux, May 7, 1950) and *La Princesse de Clèves* (1953); ballets: *Scuola di Ballo* (1933), *Les Malheurs de Sophie* (1935), *Le Roi Nu,* after Andersen (Paris, June 15, 1936), *Le Jeu Sentimental* (1936), *La Lutherie Enchantée* (1936), *Verreries de Venise* (1938), *Le Jugement du Fou* (1938), *Les Demoiselles de la Nuit* (1948); *L'Apostrophe,* musical comedy in 1 act, after Balzac (Amsterdam, July 1, 1951); oratorio, *L'Apocalypse de St. Jean* (Paris, June 11, 1942); *Cantate de Méphisto* for bass solo and strings (Paris, Oct. 8, 1955); a symphony (Paris, Nov. 6, 1932); concertino for piano and orch. (1934); piano concerto (Paris Festival, June 25, 1937); *Musique de cour,* suite for flute, violin, and orch. (1937); *Le Diable boiteux,* musical dialogue for men's voices (1937); *Paris à nous deux,* lyric fantasy (Fontainebleau, Aug. 7, 1954); *Divertissement* for bassoon and string quartet (1944); *Invocation à la volupté* for baritone and orch. (1946); *Rapsodie* for viola and wind instruments (1946); *Cantate satirique,* after Juvenal, for 4 string instruments and piano -4 hands (1947); wind quintet (1948); *Variations sans thème* for cello and piano (1951); *Sonatine* for trumpet and piano (1952); *Ode à la gastronomie* for mixed chorus (1953).

Francescatti, Zino, brilliant violinist; b. Marseilles, Aug. 9, 1905. His father, a Frenchman of Italian birth, was a cellist. Francescatti made his first public appearance at the age of 5, and played the Beethoven violin concerto with an orch. at 10; settled in Paris as a concert violinist (1927); has since toured Europe, South America, and the U. S. with excellent success.

Francesco, Cieco, or **degli Organi.** See **Landino, Francesco.**

Franchetti (fran-kĕt'-tē), **Alberto,** Italian composer; b. Turin, Sept. 18, 1860; d. Viareggio, Aug. 4, 1942. He studied in Turin with Niccolò Coccon and Fortunato Magi; then with Rheinberger in Munich and with Draeseke in Dresden. He devoted his entire life to composition, with the exception of a brief tenure as director of the Cherubini Cons. in Florence (1926-28). He wrote the following operas: *Asrael* (Reggio Emilia, Feb. 11, 1888); *Cristoforo Colombo* (Genoa, Oct. 6, 1892); *Fior d'Alpe* (Milan, March 15, 1894); *Il Signor di Pourceaugnac* (Milan, April 10, 1897); *Germania* (his most successful opera; produced at La Scala, March 11, 1902; also had repeated performances in New York, London, Buenos Aires, etc.); *La figlia di Jorio* (Milan, March 29, 1906); *Notte di leggenda* (Milan, Jan. 14, 1915); *Giove a Pompei* (with Umberto Giordano; Rome, July 5, 1921); *Glauco* (Naples, April 8, 1922); also wrote a symphony (1886); a symph. poems *Loreley* and *Nella selva nera; Inno* for soli, chorus, and orch. (for the 800th anniversary of the Univ. of Bologna); several pieces of chamber music and songs.

Franchinus. See **Gaforio.**

Franchi-Verney (frahn'kē-vär-nā'), **Giuseppe Ippolito,** Conte della Valetta, Italian composer and writer; b. Turin, Feb. 17, 1848; d. Rome, May 15, 1911. He studied jurisprudence, but gave up his career as a lawyer for music. He was one of the founders of the Società del Quartetto (1875); under the pen-name of Ippolito Valetta he wrote for the 'Gazzetta del Popolo'; later for 'Il Risorgimento' and other papers. In 1889 he married the violinist Teresina Tua. Among his compositions (most of them in a Wagnerian vein) are a 'lyric sketch' *Il Valdese* (Turin, 1885) and a ballet, *Il Mulatto* (Naples, 1896).

Franchomme (frahnk-ŏhm'), **Auguste-Joseph,** famous French cellist; b. Lille, April 10, 1808; d. Paris, Jan. 21, 1884. He studied at the Paris Cons. with Levasseur; then played cello in various opera houses. In 1846 he was appointed prof. at the Paris Cons. He was an intimate friend of Chopin; established evenings of chamber music in Paris with Hallé and Alard. He wrote cello pieces, mostly in variation form, and operatic potpourris.

Franck (frahnk), **César (-Auguste),** great Belgian composer and organist; b. Liège, Dec. 10, 1822; d. Paris, Nov. 8, 1890. He studied first at the Royal Cons. of Liège with Daussoigne and others; at the age of 9 he won first prize for singing, and at 12 first prize for piano. As a child prodigy he gave concerts in Belgium. In 1835 his family moved to Paris, where he studied privately with Anton Reicha; in 1837 he entered the Paris Cons., studying with Zimmermann (piano), Benoist (organ), and Leborne (theory). A few months after his entrance examinations he received a special award of 'grand prix d'honneur' for playing a fugue a third lower at sight; in 1838 he received the 1st prize for piano; in 1839, a 2nd prize for counterpoint; in 1840 1st prize for fugue; and in 1841 2nd prize for organ. In 1842 he was back in Belgium; in 1843 he returned to Paris, and settled there for the rest of his life. On March 17, 1843, he presented there a concert of his chamber music; on Jan. 4, 1846, his first major work, the oratorio *Ruth,* was given at the Paris Cons. On Feb. 22, 1848, in the midst of the Paris revolution, he married; in 1851 he became organist of the church of St.-Jean-St.-François; in 1853, maître de chapelle and, in 1858, organist at Ste.-Clotilde, which position he held until his death. In 1872 he succeeded his former teacher Benoist as prof. of organ at the Paris Cons. Franck's organ classes became the training school for a whole generation of French composers; among his pupils were Vincent d'Indy, Chausson, Bréville, Bordes, Duparc, Ropartz, Pierné, Vidal, Chapuis, Vierne, and a host of others, who eventually formed a school of modern French instrumental music. Until the appearance of Franck in Paris, operatic art dominated the entire musical life of the nation, and the course of instruction at the Paris Cons. was influenced by this tendency. By his emphasis on organ music, based on the contrapuntal art of Bach, Franck swayed the new generation of French musicians towards the ideal of absolute music. The foundation of the famous 'Schola Cantorum' by Vincent d'Indy, Bordes, and others in 1894 realized Franck's teachings. After the death of d'Indy in 1931, several members withdrew from the 'Schola Cantorum' and organized the 'École César Franck' (1938).—César Franck was not a prolific composer; but his creative powers rose rather than diminished with advancing age; his only symphony was completed when he was 66; his remarkable violin sonata was written at 63; his string quartet was composed in the last year of his life. Lucidity of contrapuntal design and fulness of harmony are the distinguishing traits of Franck's music; in melodic writing he balanced the diatonic and chromatic elements in fine equilibrium. Although he did not pursue innovation for its own sake, he was not averse to using unorthodox procedures. The novelty of introducing an English horn into the score of his symphony aroused some criticism among academic musicians of the time. Franck was quite alien to the Wagner-Liszt school of composition, which attracted many of his own pupils; the chromatic procedures in Franck's music derive from Bach rather than from Wagner.—Works: Operas: *Le Valet de Ferme* (1852); *Hulda* (1882-85; Monte Carlo, March 8, 1894); *Ghisèle* (unfinished; orchestration completed by d'Indy, Chausson, Bréville, Rousseau, and Coquard; 1st performance, Monte Carlo, April 6, 1896). Oratorios: *Ruth* (1845); *La Tour de Babel* (1865); *Les Béatitudes* (1869-79); *Rédemption* (1871; 2nd version 1874); *Rébecca* (Paris, March 15, 1881; produced as a 1-act sacred opera at the Paris Opéra, May 25, 1918). Symph. poems: *Les Éolides* (Paris, May 13, 1877); *Le Chasseur maudit* (Paris, March 31, 1883); *Les Djinns* (Paris, March 15, 1885); *Psyché* (Paris, March 10, 1888). Other works for orch.: *Variations symphoniques* for piano and orch. (Paris,

May 1, 1885); symphony in D minor (Paris, Feb. 17, 1889). Chamber music: 4 piano trios (early works; 1841-42); *Andante quietoso* for piano and violin (1843); *Duo pour piano et violon concertants,* on themes from Dalayrac's *Gulistan* (1844); quintet in F minor for piano and strings (1879); violin sonata (1886); string quartet (1889).—Organ works: *6 pièces (Fantaisie; Grande pièce symphonique; Prélude, Fugue, and Variations; Pastorale; Prière; Finale)*; 3 *pièces (Fantaisie; Cantabile; Pièce héroique)*; *Andantino*; *3 Chorales*; an album of 44 *Petites pièces;* an album of 55 pieces, entitled *L'Organiste,* etc.—Sacred music; *Messe solennelle* (1858); *Messe à trois voix* (1860); *Panis angelicus* for tenor, organ, harp, cello, and double-bass; offertories, motets, etc.; 16 songs, among them *La Procession* (also arranged for voice and orch.); piano pieces (*4 fantaisies; Prélude, choral et fugue; Prélude, aria et final; Trois petits riens, Danse lente,* etc.).

Bibliography: A. Coquard, *C. Franck* (Paris, 1890; new ed., 1904); E. Destranges, *L'œuvre lyrique de C. Franck* (Paris, 1896); G. Servières, *La musique française moderne* (Paris, 1897); G. Derepas, *C. Franck; étude sur sa vie, son enseignement, son œuvre* (Paris, 1897); A. Meyer, *Les critiques de C. Franck* (Orléans, 1898); P. Locard, *Les maîtres modernes de l'orgue* (Paris, 1900); P. L. Garnier, *L'héroïsme de C. Franck; psychologie musicale* (Paris, 1900); F. Baldensperger, *C. Franck, l'artiste et son œuvre* (Paris, 1901); D. G. Mason, *From Grieg to Brahms* (N. Y., 1904); R. Canudo, *C. Franck e la giovane scuola musicale francesa* (Rome, 1905); Ch. Van den Borren, *L'œuvre dramatique de C. Franck* (Brussels, 1906); Vincent d'Indy, *C. Franck* (Paris, 1906; in English, London, 1910); Romain Rolland, *Le Renouveau,* in *Musiciens d'aujourd'hui* (Paris, 1908); O. Séré, *Musiciens français d'aujourd'hui* (Paris, 1911); J. Rivière, *Études* (Paris, 1911); J. W. Hinton, *C. Franck, Some Personal Reminiscences* (London, 1912); May de Rudder, *C. Franck* (Paris, 1920); E. Closson, *C. Franck* (Charleroi, 1923); R. Jardillier, *La musique de chambre de C. Franck* (Paris, 1929); M. Emmanuel, *C. Franck* (Paris, 1930); A. Cortot, *La musique française de piano* (Paris, 1930); Ch. Tournemire, *C. Franck* (Paris, 1931); Thelma Lynn, *C. Franck: a Bio-bibliography* (N. Y., 1934); H. Haag, *C. Franck als Orgelkomponist* (Kassel, 1936); P. Kreutzer, *Die sinfonische Form César Francks* (Düsseldorf, 1938); M. Kunel, *La vie de C. Franck* (Paris, 1947); John Horton, *César Franck* (London 1948); N. Demuth, *C. Franck* (London, 1949); N. Dufourcq, *C. Franck: le milieu, l'œuvre, l'art* (Paris, 1949); L. Vallas, *La véritable histoire de C. Franck* (Paris, 1950; in English, London, 1951); Charlotte Taube, *César Franck und wir; eine Biographie* (Berlin, 1951); Nancy van der Elst, *Organist van de Sinte Clotilde* (Tilburg, 1953).—Wilhelm Mohr, in his book, *Cäsar Franck; ein deutscher Musiker* (Stuttgart, 1942), purports to prove that Franck was ethnically German; the same contention is advanced by R. Zimmermann in his similarly titled book, *Cäsar Franck; ein deutscher Musiker in Paris* (Aachen, 1942). A rebuttal is found in M. Monnikendam's biography, *César Franck* (Amsterdam, 1949), which presents documentary evidence that Franck was of Flemish and Walloon extraction.—Franck's brother, **Joseph Franck** (b. Liège, Oct. 31, 1825; d. Issy, near Paris, Nov. 20, 1891), was also an accomplished musician. He studied organ with Benoist at the Paris Cons., obtaining the 1st prize (1852); then was organist at the church of St. Thomas d'Aquin in Paris. He composed sacred music, piano works, and publ. several manuals on harmony, piano technique, and other pedagogical subjects.

Franck, Eduard, German pianist, pedagogue, and composer; b. Breslau, Oct. 5, 1817; d. Berlin, Dec. 1, 1893. At the age of 17 he studied with Mendelssohn; later he met Schumann and became his friend. These associations were the formative factor in the development of his career; he wrote piano pieces and songs in a romantic vein, closely adhering to the style of Mendelssohn and, to some extent, of Schumann. As a piano teacher, he enjoyed great renown. He taught in Cologne (1851-58), then in Bern (1859-67) and in Berlin (1867-78). Among his works are 2 piano concertos, 2 violin concertos, much chamber music, and numerous collections of piano pieces. See R. Franck, *Musikalische und unmusikalische Erinnerungen* (Heidelberg, 1928).

Franck, Johann Wolfgang, German composer; b. Unterschwaningen, June (baptized June 17), 1644; d. c. 1710. He was brought up in Ansbach, and served there as court musician from 1665 till 1679; produced 3 operas at the Ansbach court: *Die unvergleichliche Andromeda* (1675), *Der verliebte Föbus* (1678), and *Die drei Töchter Cecrops* (1679). On Jan. 17, 1679, in a fit of jealousy, he killed the court musician Ulbrecht, and was forced to flee. He found refuge in Hamburg with his wife Anna Susanna Wilbel (whom he married in 1666), and gained a prominent position at the Hamburg Opera; between 1679 and 1686 he wrote and produced 17 operas, most important of which was *Diokletian* (1682). His private life continued to be stormy; he deserted his wife and their ten children, and went to London, where he remained from 1690 to about 1695. The exact place and date of his death are unknown. In London he organized (with Robert King) a series of 'Concerts of Vocal and Instrumental Music'; publ. 41 English songs. Other publications are: *Geistliche Lieder* (Hamburg, 1681, 1685, 1687, 1700; republished in 1856 by D. H. Engel, with new words by Osterwald; newly edited by W. Krabbe and J. Kromolicki in vol. 45 of the 'Denkmäler deutscher Tonkunst', series 1, 1911; 12 arrangements for 4 voices by A. von Dommer, publ. 1859; separate reprints by Riemann, Friedlaender, and others); *Remedium melancholiae* (25 secular solo songs with basso continuo; London, 1690); arias, etc.—Cf. F. Zelle, *J. W. Franck, ein Beitrag zur Geschichte der ältesten deutschen Oper* (Berlin, 1889); A. Werner, *J. W. Francks Flucht aus Ansbach,* in the 'Sammelbände der Internationalen Musik-Gesellschaft' (XIV, 2); W. Barclay Squire, *J. W. Franck in England,* in the 'Musical Antiquary' (July, 1912); R. Klages, *J. W. Franck, Untersuchungen zu seiner Lebensgeschichte und zu seinen geistlichen Kompositionen* (Hamburg, 1937); G. Schmidt, *Die Musik am Hofe der Markgrafen von Brandenburg-Ansbach* (Munich, 1953).

Franck, Melchior, German composer, b. Zittau, c. 1579; d. Coburg, June 1, 1639. He went to Nuremberg in 1601 and in 1602 obtained the post of Kapellmeister at Coburg, where he remained to the end of his life. He was an excellent contrapuntist; composed sacred and secular vocal music, and exerted considerable influence on his contemporaries. A selection from his instrumental works was publ. by F. Bölsche in vol. XVI of "Denkmäler deutscher Tonkunst"; vol. XVII of the 'Monatshefte für Musikgeschichte' contains a careful description of his printed works, also of MSS preserved in public libraries. Reprints of his sacred vocal works have been publ. by F. Commer, E. Mauersberger, F. Jöde; secular works in the 'Staatliches Liederbuch,' 'Kaiser-Liederbuch,' and other collections. — Cf. Aloys Obrist, *Melchior Franck* (Berlin, 1892).

Franck, Richard, German pianist, son of Eduard Franck; b. Cologne, Jan. 3, 1858; d. Heidelberg, Jan. 22, 1938. He studied with his father in Berlin and also attended the Leipzig Cons. (1878-80). He was in Basel from 1880-83 and again from 1887 till 1900, and was active there as pianist and teacher. He later lived in Kassel, and finally in Heidelberg. He was highly regarded as an interpreter of Beethoven's sonatas; published a book of memoirs, *Musikalische und unmusikalische Erinnerungen* (Heidelberg, 1928).

Franckenstein, Clemens von, German composer; b. Wiesentheid, July 14, 1875; d. Munich, Aug. 19, 1942. He spent his youth in Vienna; then went to Munich, where he studied with Thuille; later took courses with Knorr at the Hoch Cons. in Frankfurt. He traveled with an opera company in the U. S. in 1901; then was engaged as a theater conductor in London (1902-7). From 1912-18 and from 1924-34 was intendant at the Munich Opera. He wrote several operas, the most successful of which was *Des Kaisers Dichter* (on the life of the Chinese poet, Li-Tai Po), performed in Hamburg (Nov. 2, 1920) and elsewhere in Germany. Other operas are: *Griselda* (Troppau, 1898), *Fortunatus* (Budapest, 1909), and *Rahab* (Hamburg, 1911). He also wrote several orchestral works. — Cf. W. Zentner, *Clemens von Franckenstein,* in the 'Zeitschrift für Musik' (1929; pp. 769-75).

Franco of Cologne, medieval theorist and practical musician. His identity is conjectural; there was a learned man known as Magister Franco of Cologne who flourished as early as the 11th century; several reputable scholars regard him as identical with the musical theorist Franco; against this identification is the improbability of the emergence of theories and usages found in Franco's writings at such an early date. The generally accepted period for his activities is the middle of the 13th century (from 1250 to about 1280). The work on which the reputation of Franco of Cologne rests is the famous treatise *Ars cantus mensurabilis.* Its principal significance is not so much the establishment of a new method of mensural notation as the systematization of rules that had been inadequately or vaguely explained by Franco's predecessors. The treatise is valuable also for the explanation of usages governing the employment of concords and discords. It was reprinted, from different MSS, in Gerbert's 'Scriptores' (vol. III) and in Coussemaker's 'Scriptores' (vol. I). Gerbert attributes it to a Franco of Paris, a shadowy figure who may have been the author of a treatise and three summaries, all beginning with the words 'Gaudent brevi-tate moderni.' The *Ars cantus mensurabilis* is reproduced in English in O. Strunk's *Source Readings in Music History* (N.Y., 1950).—Cf. O. Koller, *Versuch einer Rekonstruktion der Notenbeispiele zum 11. Kapitel von Francos Ars cantus mensurabilis* in the 'Vierteljahrsschrift für Musikwissenschaft' (vol. VI, p. 242 ff.); J. F. R. Stainer, *The Notation of Mensurable Music,* in the 'Proceedings' of the Musical Association of London (vol. XXVI, p. 215 ff.; London, 1900); Hugo Riemann, *Geschichte der Musiktheorie* (p. 114 ff.; Leipzig, 1898); Johannes Wolf, *Handbuch der Notationskunde* (vol. I, Leipzig, 1913); G. Reese, *Music in the Middle Ages* (p. 288 ff.; N. Y., 1940); W. Apel, *The Notation of Polyphonic Music, 900-1600* (p. 310 ff.; Cambridge, Mass., 1942); Y. Rokseth, *Polyphonies du XIIIe siècle* (Paris, 1948); F. Gennrich, *Franco von Köln, Ars Cantus Mensurabilis* (Darmstadt, 1955). See also H. Besseler's article in 'Die Musik in Geschichte und Gegenwart.'

Franco of Paris. The reputed author (according to Gerbert's 'Scriptores') of the medieval treatise *Ars cantus mensurabilis,* generally ascribed to Franco of Cologne (q.v.).

Franco, Johan, composer; b. Zaandam, Holland, July 12, 1908. He studied with Willem Pijper in Amsterdam; in 1936 settled in the U. S.; served in the U. S. Army (1942-45).—Works: Symph. No. 1 (1933); a symph. poem *Péripétie* (1935); *Concertino Lirico* for violin and orch. (N. Y., 1938); violin concerto (Brussels, Dec. 6, 1939); Symph. No. 2 (1939); *Serenata concertante* for piano and chamber orch. (N. Y., March 11, 1940); *Symphonie concertante* for piano and orch. (N. Y., March 17, 1941); symph. poem *Baconiana* (1941); *Serenade* for flute, cello, and 2 harps (1944); *Divertimento* for flute and string quartet (1945); suite for violin and piano (1947); piano pieces and songs; has contributed articles to the 'Mus. Quarterly' and other journals.

Francœur (frahn-kör'), **François,** French violinist; b. Paris, Sept. 28, 1698; d. there, Aug. 7, 1787. He was a member of the orch. of the Paris Opéra, a chamber musician to the King, and one of the '24 violons du roi' (1730). Conjointly with his inseparable friend François Rebel, he was director of the Opéra (1751) and superintendent of the King's music (1760). He wrote 2 books of violin sonatas; produced 10 operas (in collaboration with Rebel).

Francœur, Louis-Joseph, French violinist, nephew of François Francœur; b. Paris, Oct. 8, 1738; d. there, March 10, 1804. He entered the orch. of the Paris Opéra at the age of 14; became its conductor at 27. During the Revolution he was imprisoned as a suspect, but released after the Thermidor coup d'état (1794) and was appointed director of the Paris Opéra. He wrote an act for the opera *Lindor et Ismène* (Paris, Aug. 29, 1766); publ. a treatise *Diapason général de tous les instruments à vent* (1772). The MS of his *Essai historique sur l'établissement de l'opéra en France* is preserved in the library of the Cons. in Paris.

Frank, Alan, English music scholar; b. London, Oct. 10, 1910. He studied the clarinet, conducting, and composition. At the age of 17 he joined the staff of the Oxford Univ. Press; during the war was in the Royal Air Force. In 1947 he was appointed music editor of the Oxford Univ. Press, and in 1954 became head of the Music Department. In 1935 he married Phyllis Tate, the composer. He has published *The Playing of Chamber Music* (with George Stratton; London, 1935; 2nd ed., 1951); *Modern British Composers* (London, 1953); he is also co-author (with Frederick Thurston) of *A Comprehensive Tutor for the Boehm Clarinet* (London, 1939).

Frank, Ernst, German conductor and composer; b. Munich, Feb. 7, 1847; d. Oberdobling, near Vienna, Aug. 17, 1889. He studied with M. de Fontaine (piano) and F. Lachner (composition); 1868, was conductor at Würzburg; 1869, chorus master at the Vienna Opera; 1872-77, conductor at Mannheim; 1877-79, at Frankfurt; 1879 at the Hanover court opera. He wrote the operas *Adam de la Halle* (Karlsruhe, 1880) *Hero* (Berlin, 1884), and *Der Sturm* (after Shakespeare; Hanover, 1887); completed H. Götz's opera *Francesca da Rimini* and produced it at Mannheim (1877). Frank was a friend of Brahms.—Cf. A. Einstein, *Briefe von Brahms an E. Frank,* in 'Zeitschrift für Musikwissenschaft' (April, 1922).

Frankel, Benjamin, English composer; b. London, Jan. 31, 1906. As a boy, he worked in the watchmakers' trade; studied in Germany, returning to London in 1923, where he played piano and violin in cafés. He then began to write music for films; since 1946 teaching at the Guildhall School of Music.—Works: *The Aftermath* for tenor, trumpet, harp, and strings (1947); violin concerto (1951); 4 string quartets; trio for clarinet cello, and piano; *Sonata ebraica* for cello and harp; *Elégie juive* for cello and piano; piano quartet (1953); songs.

Frankenstein, Alfred, American music critic; b. Chicago, Oct. 5, 1906. He studied at the Univ. of Chicago (graduated, 1932); played clarinet in the Civic Orch. of Chicago (1923-30); held a music school scholarship at Yale Univ. (1930-31); was assistant music critic of the 'Chicago American' (1931-34); lecturer in the history of music at the Univ. of Chicago (1932-34); since Dec., 1934, music and art critic of the 'San Francisco Chronicle'; program annotator of the San Francisco Symph. Orch. since 1935; visiting lecturer at the Univ. of California, Stanford, and Harvard (2 sessions, 1951, 1952). He published a collection of essays, *Syncopating Saxophones* (Chicago, 1925); became deeply interested in art; in 1947, held a Guggenheim Fellowship to prepare a book on the 19th-century American still-life; the resulting publication was *After the Hunt* (Univ. of California Press, 1953; deals with William Harnett). He was the first to discover and publish the sketches of Victor Hartmann that inspired Mussorgsky's *Pictures at an Exhibition* (in the 'Mus. Quarterly,' July, 1939); also brought out an illustrated edition of this score (1951).

Franklin, Benjamin, the great American statesman; b. Boston, Jan. 17, 1706; d. Philadelphia, April 17, 1790. An amateur musician, he invented (1762) the Harmonica, an instrument consisting of a row of glass discs of different sizes set in vibration by light pressure. A string quartet attributed to him came to light in Paris in 1945, and was publ. there (1946). The parts are arranged in an ingenious 'scordatura'; only open strings are used, so that the quartet can be played by rank amateurs. Franklin also wrote entertainingly on musical subjects; his letters on Scotch music are found in vol. VI of his collected works.—Cf. O. G. Sonneck, *Suum cuique: Essays in Music* (N. Y., 1916); Lionel de la Laurencie, *Benjamin Franklin and the claveciniste Brillon de Jouy,* in the 'Mus. Quarterly' (April, 1923); *L'harmonica de Benjamin Franklin* in 'Dissonances' (Geneva, July-Aug., 1944).

Franko, Nahan, American violinist and conductor; brother of Sam Franko; b. New Orleans, July 23, 1861; d. Amityville, N. Y., June 7, 1930. As a child prodigy he toured with Adelina Patti; then studied in Berlin with Joachim and Wilhelmj. Returning to America, he joined the orch. of the Metropolitan Opera; was its concertmaster from 1883-1905; was the first native-born American to be engaged as conductor there (1905-1907).

Franko, Sam, American violinist; b. New Orleans, Jan. 20, 1857; d. New York, May 6, 1937 (from skull fracture as a result of a fall). He was educated in Germany; studied in Berlin with Joachim, Heinrich de Ahna, and Eduard Rappoldi. Returning to the U. S. in 1880, he joined the Theodore Thomas Orch. in N. Y., and was its concertmaster from 1884-91; in 1883 he toured the U. S. and Canada as soloist with the Mendelssohn Quintette Club of Boston. In order to prove that the prejudice against native orchestral players was unfounded, he organized in 1894 the American Symphony Orchestra of 65 American-born performers; this orchestra he later used for his 'Concerts of Old Music' (1900-09); from 1893 to 1901 he gave chamber music concerts at the Aschenbrödel Club in N. Y. In 1910 he went to Berlin and taught at Stern's Cons.; he returned to N. Y. in 1915 and remained there for the rest of his life. At the celebration of his 79th birthday (1936), he gave his valuable collection of music MSS to the Music Division of the N. Y. Public Library. He publ. for piano *Album Leaf* (1889); *Viennese Silhouettes* (a set of 6 waltzes, 1928), etc.; several violin pieces; practical arrangements for violin and piano of works by Bach, Chopin, Mendelssohn, Rimsky-Korsakov, etc.; and string orch. transcriptions of works by Bach, Vivaldi, Pergolesi, etc.; also edited classical music albums. His memoirs were publ. posthumously under the title *Chords and Discords* (N. Y., 1938).

Franz, J. H. Pen-name of Count **Bolko von Hochberg** (q.v.).

Franz, Robert, famous German song composer; b. Halle, June 28, 1815; d. there, Oct. 24, 1892. His family name was Knauth; his father, Christoph Franz Knauth, legally adopted the name Franz in 1847. The parents did not favor music as a profession, but Franz learned to play the organ and participated as an accompanist in performances in his native city. In 1835, he went to Dessau, where he studied with Friedrich Schneider; in 1837, he returned to Halle. He published his first set of songs in 1843; they attracted immediate attention and were warmly praised by Schumann. Shortly afterwards he received an appointment as organist at the Ulrichskirche in Halle, and also as conductor of the Singakademie there; later he received the post of music director at Halle Univ., which conferred on him the title of Mus. Doc. in 1861. The successful development of his career as a musician was interrupted by a variety of nervous disorders and a growing deafness, which forced him to abandon his musical activities in 1868. Liszt, Joachim, and others organized a concert for his benefit, collecting a large sum of money (about $25,000); his admirers in America (Otto Dresel, S. B. Schlesinger, B. J. Lang) also contributed funds for his support. Franz was undoubtedly one of the finest masters of the German lied. He published about 350 songs; among those best known are *Schlummerlied, Die Lotosblume, Die Widmung,* and *Wonne der Wehmuth.* He also wrote: 117th Psalm for double chorus a cappella; Kyrie for chorus a cappella and solo voices; Liturgy; arranged works by Bach *(St. Matthew Passion, Christmas Oratorio,* 10 cantatas, etc.) and Handel *(Messiah; L'Allegro, Il Penseroso, ed Il Moderato,* etc.); published *Mitteilungen über J. S. Bachs Magnificat* (Leipzig, 1863); *Offener Brief an Ed. Hanslick über Bearbeitungen älterer Tonwerke, namentlich Bachscher und Händelscher Vokalwerke* (Leipzig, 1871). Both were reprinted by R. Bethge as *Gesammelte Schriften über die Wiederbelebung Bachscher und Händelscher Werke* (Leipzig, 1910).—Cf. F. Liszt, *R. Franz* (Leipzig, 1855; reprinted in 'Gesammelte Schriften,' vol. IV, Leipzig, 1882); H. M. Schuster, *R. Franz* (Leipzig, 1874); La Mara, *R. Franz,* in vol. III of 'Musikalische Studienköpfe' (Leipzig, 1868-82; publ. separately, 1911); W. Waldmann, *R. Franz; Gespräche aus zehn Jahren* (Leipzig, 1894); R. Procházka, *R. Franz* (Leipzig, 1894); W. Golther, *R. Franz und Arnold Freiherr Senfft von Pilsach; ein Briefwechsel 1861-89* (Berlin, 1907); R. Bethge, *R. Franz; ein Lebensbild* (Halle, 1908); H. Kleemann, *R. Franz,* in the 'Mus. Quarterly' (Oct., 1915); O. Lessmann, *Persönliche Erinnerungen an R. Franz,* in 'Allgemeine Musikalische Zeitung' (1915); S. E. Barbak, *Die Lieder von R. Franz* (Vienna, 1922); H. von der Pfordten, *R. Franz* (Leipzig, 1923).

Fränzl, Ferdinand, German violinist and composer, son of Ignaz Fränzl; b. Schwetzingen, May 24, 1770; d. Mannheim, Nov. 19, 1833. He studied with his father; later was a pupil in composition of F. X. Richter and Pleyel at Strasbourg, and of Mattei at Bologna. He entered the Mannheim court orchestra at the age of 12; in 1785 began to travel on concert tours with his father. He was appointed conductor of the Munich Opera in 1806, but continued his tours; retired in 1826; finally settled in Mannheim. As a master violinist he enjoyed great renown. He was a prolific composer: wrote 8 violin concertos; a double concerto for 2 violins; 6 operas; 9 string quartets; 6 string trios; symphonies, overtures, and songs.

Fränzl, Ignaz, German violinist and composer, father of Ferdinand Fränzl; b. Mannheim, June 3, 1736; d. there, 1811. He entered the Mannheim court orchestra as a boy of 11, and was its conductor from 1790 to 1803. He made several concert tours with his son; composed symphonies and music for the violin, and also wrote for the stage. His 'Singspiel,' *Die Luftbälle,* was produced in Mannheim with excellent success (April 15, 1787); he also wrote music for Shakespeare's plays.

Fraser, Norman, Chilean-English pianist and writer on music; b. of English parents, Valparaiso, Chile, Nov. 26, 1904. He pursued his musical studies in Chile and later in Lausanne; gave concerts in Europe (1924-30); then settled in London. He made several trips to South America as a representative of various organizations; contributed articles on Latin American composers to the 5th edition of Grove's Dictionary. He is married to **Janet Fraser,** British mezzo-soprano (b. Kirkcaldy, May 22, 1911), with whom he has given numerous joint recitals.

Frazzi, Vito, Italian composer; b. San Secondo Parmense, Aug. 1, 1888. He studied organ at the Parma Cons.; also took courses in piano and theory. In 1912 he joined the staff of the Florence Cons. He has written a music drama *Re Lear* after Shakespeare (Florence, 1939); an opera *Don Quixote* (Florence, April 27, 1952); several symph. poems; chamber music; has orchestrated Monteverdi's stage works.

Freccia, Massimo, Italian conductor; b. Florence, Sept. 19, 1906. He studied at the Florence Cons. and later in Vienna with Franz Schalk. In 1933-35 he conducted the Budapest Symph. Orch.; was guest conductor at the Lewisohn Stadium in N. Y. in 1938-40; then was conductor of the Havana Philh. Orch. (1939-43), and of the New Orleans Symph. Orch. (1944-52). In 1952, he was appointed conductor of the Baltimore Symph. Orch.

Frederick II (the Great), of Prussia; b. Berlin, Jan. 24, 1712; d. Potsdam, Aug. 17, 1786. He was an enlightened patron of music, a flute player of considerable skill, and an amateur composer. He studied flute with Quantz; in 1740, when he ascended the throne, he established a court orchestra and an opera house; Bach's son Karl Philipp Emanuel was his harpsichordist until 1767. In 1747 J. S. Bach himself was invited to Potsdam; the fruit of this visit was Bach's *Musical Offering,* written on a theme by Frederick II. A collection of 25 flute sonatas and 4 concertos by Frederick was publ. by Spitta (3 vols., Leipzig, 1889); other works were publ. in vol. XX of 'Die Musik am preussischen Hofe.' Selections from different compositions were edited by Barge, G. Lenzewski, E. Schwarz-Reiflingen, H. Osthoff, G. Müller, G. Thouret, and others. Besides instrumental works, Frederick contributed arias to several operas: *Demofoonte* by Graun (1746); *Il re pastore* (1747; with Quantz and others); *Galatea ed Acide* (1748; with Hasse, Graun, Quantz, and Nichelmann), and *Il trionfo della fedelità* (1753; with Hasse and others).—Cf. K. F. Müller, *Friedrich der Grosse als Kenner und Dilettant auf dem Gebiete der Tonkunst* (Potsdam, 1847); W. Kothe, *Friedrich der Grosse als Musiker* (Leipzig, 1869); G. Thouret, *Friedrichs des Grossen Verhältniss zur Musik* (Berlin, 1895); G. Thouret, *Friedrich der Grosse als Musikfreund und Musiker* (Leipzig, 1898); Karl von Forstner, *Friedrich der Grosse, Künstler und König* (Berlin, 1932); G. Müller, *Friedrich der Grosse, seine Flöten und sein Flötenspiel* (Berlin, 1932); G. M. Fitzgibbon, *Of Flutes and Soft Recorders,* in the 'Mus. Quarterly' (April, 1934); John Bourke, *Frederick the Great as Music Lover and Musician,* in 'Music & Letters' (Jan., 1947). Frederick's correspondence with Algarotti was publ. by F. Förster (Berlin, 1837); correspondence between him and the margravine of Bayreuth is contained in chapter IV of Mary Burrell's *Thoughts for Enthusiasts at Bayreuth* (London, 1891).

Freed, Arnold, American composer; b. New York, Sept. 29, 1926; studied with Mark Brunswick at the City College of N. Y. and with Philip James at N. Y. Univ.; also with Vittorio Giannini at the Juilliard School of Music. He won a Fulbright Scholarship for travel in Italy and studied with Luigi Dallapiccola there (1952-54). Among his works are a violin sonata, a piano sonata, and a number of choral works and songs.

Freed, Isadore, composer; b. Brest-Litovsk, Russia, March 26, 1900. He came to the U. S. at an early age; graduated from the Univ. of Pennsylvania in 1918 (Mus. Bac.); then studied with Ernest Bloch and with Vincent d'Indy in Paris; returned to the U. S. in 1934; held various teaching positions; in 1944 was appointed head of the music department at Hartt College of Music, Hartford, Conn.—Works: For the stage: *Vibrations,* ballet (Philadelphia, 1928); operas, *Homo Sum* (1930) and *The Princess and the Vagabond* (Hartford, May 13, 1948). For orch.: *Jeux de Timbres* (Paris, 1933); Symph. No. 1 (1941); *Appalachian Symphonic Sketches* (Chautauqua, July 31, 1946); *Festival Overture* (San Francisco, Nov. 14, 1946); *Rhapsody* for trombone and orch. (radio première, N. Y., Jan. 7, 1951); Symph. No. 2, for brass (San Francisco, Feb. 8, 1951, composer conducting); violin concerto (N. Y., Nov. 13, 1951); cello concerto (1952); concertino for English horn and orch. (1953). Chamber music: 3 string quartets (1931, 1932, 1937); trio for flute, viola, and harp (1940); *Triptych* for violin, viola, cello, and piano (1943); *Passacaglia,* for cello and piano (1947); quintet for woodwinds and horn (Hartford, Dec. 2, 1949); sonatina for oboe and piano (Boston, March 31, 1954); also choral works; piano and organ pieces; songs; co-editor of 'Masters of Our Day' (contemporary educational material for piano; N. Y., 1936-37).

Freeman, Harry Lawrence, American Negro composer; b. Cleveland, Ohio, Oct. 9, 1869; d. New York, March 24, 1954. He studied theory with J. H. Beck and piano with E. Schonert and Carlos Sobrino; taught at Wilberforce Univ. (1902-4) and Salem School of Music (1910-13); organized and directed the Freeman School of Music (1911-22) and the Freeman School of Grand Opera (from 1923); conducted various theater orchestras and opera companies. In 1920 he organized the Negro Opera Co.; in 1930 received the Harmon Gold Award; conducted a pageant *O Sing a New Song,* at the Chicago World's Fair in 1934. He was the first Negro composer to conduct a symphony orchestra in his own work (Minneapolis, 1907), and the first Negro to write large operatic compositions. All his music is written in folksong style; his settings are in simple harmonies; his operas are constructed of songs and choruses in simple concatenation of separate numbers. — Works: the grand operas (all on Negro, Oriental, and Indian themes): *The Martyr* (Denver, 1893); *Valdo* (Cleveland, May, 1906); *Zuluki* (1898); *African Kraal* (Wilberforce Univ., Chicago, June 30, 1903; with an all-Negro cast, composer conducting; revised

1934); *The Octoroon* (1904); *The Tryst* (N. Y., May, 1911); *The Prophecy* (N. Y., 1912); *The Plantation* (1914); *Athalia* (1916); *Vendetta* (N. Y., Nov. 12, 1923); *American Romance,* jazz opera (1927); *Voodoo* (N. Y., Sept. 10, 1928); *Leah Kleschna* (1930); *Uzziah* (1931); *Zululand,* a tetralogy of music dramas: *Nada, The Lily* (1941-44; vocal score contains 2150 pp.), *Allah* (1947), and *The Zulu King* (1934); *The Slave,* ballet for choral ensemble and orch. (Harlem, N. Y., Sept. 22, 1932); songs (*Whither, If thou did'st love,* etc.).—Cf. E. E. Hipsher, *American Opera and its Composers* (Philadelphia, 1934; pp. 189-95).

Freer, Eleanor (*née* Everest), American composer; b. Philadelphia, May 14, 1864; d. Chicago, Dec. 13, 1942. She studied singing in Paris (1883-86) with Mathilde Marchesi; then took a course in composition with Benjamin Godard. Upon her return to the U. S., she taught singing at the National Cons. of Music., N. Y. (1889-91). On April 25, 1891, she married Archibald Freer of Chicago; they lived in Leipzig from 1892-99; then settled in Chicago where she studied theory with Bernard Ziehn (1902-7). She publ. some light pieces under the name Everest still as a young girl, but most of her larger works were written after 1919; she composed 9 operas, of which the following were performed: *The Legend of the Piper* (South Bend, Ind., Feb. 28, 1924), *The Court Jester* (Lincoln, Nebr., 1926), *A Christmas Tale* (Houston, Dec. 27, 1929), *Frithiof* (1929), *The Masque of Pandora* (1930), and *A Legend of Spain* (1931); a song cycle (settings of Elizabeth Browning's entire *Sonnets from the Portuguese);* about 150 songs; piano pieces. Vocal scores of several of her operas, and many songs, have been published. She wrote an autobiography, *Recollections and Reflections of an American Composer* (Chicago, 1929). See also A. G. Foster, *Eleanor Freer and her Colleagues* (Chicago, 1927); E. E. Hipsher, *American Opera and its Composers* (Philadelphia, 1927; pp. 196-204).

Freitas Branco, Luiz de, Portuguese composer; b. Lisbon, Oct. 12, 1890; d. there, Nov. 26, 1955. He studied in Berlin with Humperdinck, later in Paris; wrote 3 symphonies, a cello concerto, ballade for piano and orch., an oratorio, organ works, chamber music, and songs.

Fremstad, Olive, famous dramatic soprano; b. Stockholm, March 14, 1871 (entered into the parish register as the daughter of an unmarried woman, Anna Peterson); d. Irvington-on-Hudson, N. Y., April 21, 1951. She was adopted by an American couple of Scandinavian origin, who took her to Minnesota; she studied piano in Minneapolis; came to New York in 1890 and took singing lessons with E. F. Bristol; then held several church positions; in 1892 she sang for the first time with an orch. (under C. Zerrahn) in Boston. In 1893 she went to Berlin to study with Lilli Lehmann; made her operatic début in Cologne as Azucena in *Il Trovatore* (1895); sang contralto parts in Wagner's operas at Bayreuth during the summer of 1896; in 1897 made her London début; also sang in Cologne, Vienna, Amsterdam, and Antwerp. From 1900 to 1903 she was at the Munich Opera. She made her American début as Sieglinde at the Metropolitan Opera on Nov. 23, 1903. Subsequently she sang soprano parts in Wagnerian operas; at first she was criticized in the press for her lack of true soprano tones; however, she soon triumphed over these difficulties, and became known as a soprano singer to the exclusion of contralto parts. She sang Carmen with great success at the Metropolitan (March 4, 1906), with Caruso; her performance of Isolde under Mahler (Jan. 1, 1908) produced a deep impression; until 1914, she was one of the brightest stars of the Metropolitan Opera, specializing in Wagnerian roles, but also was successful in *Tosca* and other Italian operas. She sang Salomé at the first American performance of the Strauss opera (N. Y., Jan. 27, 1907) and in Paris (May 8, 1907). After her retirement from the Metropolitan, she appeared with the Manhattan Opera, the Boston Opera, the Chicago Opera, and in concerts; presented her last song recital in N. Y. on Jan. 19, 1920. In 1906 she married Edson Sutphen of N. Y. (divorced in 1911); in 1916 she married her accompanist, Harry Lewis Brainard (divorced in 1925). In Willa Cather's novel, *The Song of the Lark,* the principal character was modeled after Olive Fremstad.

French, Jacob, American composer of psalm-tunes; b. 1754; d. ?. He publ. *New American Melody* (1789), *Psalmodist's Companion* (1793), and *Harmony of Harmony* (1802).—Cf. J. T. Howard, *Our American Music* (N. Y., revised ed., 1939).

Frere, Rudolph Walter Howard, English music scholar; b. Dungate, near Cambridge, Nov. 25, 1863; d. Mirfield, Yorkshire, April 2, 1938. He studied at Trinity College,

Cambridge; was ordained curate in 1887; from 1923 to 1934 he was bishop of Truro. He specialized in plainsong, and contributed valuable articles on this subject to Grove's Dictionary and to the 'Oxford History of Music.' Among his important publications are *Bibliotheca musica liturgica* (1901) and an introduction to *Hymns, Ancient and Modern* (1909). He edited the 'Graduale Sarisburiense' (1893), 'The Sarum Gradual and the Gregorian Antiphonale Missarum'; and, with John Stainer and H. B. Briggs, *A Manual of Plainsong* (1902); also 'Pars antiphonarii' (1923); 'Holy Week Services of the Church of England' (2nd ed., 1933).

Freschi (frĕs'-kē), **Giovanni Domenico,** Italian composer; b. Bassano, Vicenza, 1640; d. Vicenza, 1690. He was maestro di cappella at the Cathedral of Vicenza; publ. 2 masses and a number of psalms (1660; 1673). In 1677, he went to Venice, remaining there for eight years; wrote 10 operas, which were successfully produced there, and a series of short pieces for an opera house in Piazzola near Padua. He also wrote two oratorios, *Giuditta* and *Il Miracolo del mago.*—Cf. Paolo Camerini, *Piazzola* (Milan, 1925).

Frescobaldi, Girolamo, famous Italian organist and composer; b. Ferrara, 1583 (baptized Sept. 9); d. Rome, March 1, 1643. After studying under Luzzasco Luzzaschi at Ferrara, he traveled to Flanders and in 1607 took up residence in Brussels; in 1608 he publ. his first work, a collection of 5-part madrigals, at Antwerp (printed by Phalèse), and visited Milan and Ferrara; also in 1608 he was appointed organist of St. Peter's, at Rome, succeeding Ercole Pasquini; his fame was already such that 30,000 people are said to have attended his first performance. He held this post until his death, leaving Rome only once, from 1628-34, during which period he was court organist at Florence, and was represented in Rome by a deputy. From 1637-41, Froberger, court organist of Vienna, came to Rome especially to study with Frescobaldi. As a composer, Frescobaldi occupies a very prominent place; his works are distinguished by an effective use of chromatic devices.—Works: *Fantasie a 2, 3, e 4* (Milan, 1608, Book I); *Ricercari e canzoni francese* (Rome, 1615); *Toccate e partite d'intavolatura di cembalo* (Rome, 1615); *Il 2º libro di toccate, canzoni, versi d'inni, magnificat, gagliarde, correnti ed altre partite d'intavolatura di cembalo ed organo* (Rome, 1616); *Capricci sopra diversi soggetti* (Rome, 1624); *Arie musicale a più voci* (Florence, 1630); etc. The 3 fugues ascribed to Frescobaldi by Clementi in his *Selection of Practical Harmony* (London, 1811-15) are probably spurious (cf. G. Benvenuti in 'Rivista Musicale Italiana,' 1920, p. 133 ff.). Haberl publ. a selection of Frescobaldi's organ pieces, prefaced by a biographical sketch (Leipzig, 1888); smaller collections were publ. by B. Litzau, E. Pauer (12 toccatas), L. Torchi in vol. III of 'L'Arte musicale' (20 pieces), Casella in Nos. 43-47 of 'Raccolta nazionale delle musiche italiane,' II. David (*2 canzoni;* 1933), Opel (2 pieces), F. Boghen (*Arie musicali;* 1933), F. Germani (*Toccate e partite;* Rome, 1936), and in Davison and Apel, *Historical Anthology of Music,* vol. II (Cambridge, Mass., 1950).—Cf. A. Cametti, *Girolamo Frescobaldi in Roma,* in the 'Rivista Musicale Italiana' (1908, p. 701); A. Berenzi, *Per Girolamo Frescobaldi nel terzo centenario* (Cremona, 1908); N. Bennati, *Ferrara e Girolamo Frescobaldi* (Ferrara, 1908); A. Sostegni, *L'opera e il tempo di G. Frescobaldi* (1929); L. Ronga, *G. Frescobaldi* (Turin, 1930); G. Benvenuti, *Frescobaldiana,* in 'Bolletino bibliografico musicale' (Feb.-April, 1931); W. Apel, *Neapolitan Links between Cabezón and Frescobaldi,* in the 'Mus. Quarterly' (Oct., 1938); A. Machabey, *G. Frescobaldi, la vie, l'œuvre* (Paris, 1952).

Frešo, Tibor, Slovak conductor and composer; b. Stiavnik, Nov. 20, 1918. He studied with Alexander Moyzes, and later with Pizzetti in Rome. In 1951 he was appointed opera conductor at Košice. He has written choral music, and several suites for various instruments based on native folksongs.

Freudenberg, Wilhelm, German composer and conductor; b. Raubacher Hütte, near Neuwied, March 11, 1838; d. Schweidnitz, May 22, 1928. He studied in Leipzig; held various positions as theater conductor; founded a conservatory in Wiesbaden (1870); in 1886 went to Berlin, where he was active as choral conductor. He produced several comic operas: *Die Pfahlbauer* (Mainz, 1877), *Die Mühle im Wispertale* (Magdeburg, 1883), *Das Jahrmarktsfest zu Plundersweilen* (Bremen, 1908), etc.; a symph. poem *Ein Tag in Sorrent,* and numerous choral works.

Freund, John Christian, music journalist and editor; b. London, Nov. 22, 1848; d. Mt. Vernon, N. Y., June 3, 1924. He studied in London and in Oxford; in 1871 he settled in N. Y., where he became the editor of the 'Musical and Dramatic Times'; in 1890 he began publishing a magazine 'Music Trades.'

In 1898 founded 'Musical America,' and was its editor until his death. In his editorials and public lectures he urged American musicians to form a national movement in composition, performance, and musical scholarship.

Freund, Marya, soprano; b. Breslau, Dec. 12, 1876. She first studied violin, taking lessons with Sarasate; then began to study singing; made successful appearances in Europe and America with symphony orchestras and in recital. Her career as a singer is mainly significant, however, not for the excellence of her performances in standard repertory, but for her devotion to modern music. She sang the principal vocal works by Schoenberg, Stravinsky, Ravel, Bloch, Milhaud, and many others; eventually settled in Paris as singing teacher.

Freundt, Cornelius, German composer; b. Plauen, 1535; d. Zwickau, Aug. 26, 1591. He was a cantor at Borna; in 1565, became organist at Zwickau, where he remained until his death. His compositions were designed for use in church and school; most of his sacred works remain in MS. Georg Göhler wrote a dissertation on him (Leipzig, 1896).

Frey, Adolf, pianist; b. Landau, Germany, April 4, 1865; d. Syracuse, N. Y., Oct. 4, 1938. He was a pupil of Clara Schumann; served as court musician to Prince Alexander Friedrich of Hesse (1887-93); then emigrated to the U. S. and became prof. of music at Syracuse Univ.; was head of the piano dept. there for 20 years (1893-1913); in 1935, he founded the Frey School of Music in Watertown, N. Y.

Frey, Emil, Swiss pianist and composer; b. Baden, Switzerland, April 8, 1889; d. Zürich, May 20, 1946. He studied in Switzerland and in Paris; won the Rubinstein Composition Award with his piano trio in 1910; was prof. at the Moscow Cons. (1912-17); returned to Switzerland in 1918; toured South America as a pianist several times. He wrote a piano concerto, a violin concerto, a Swiss Festival Overture, many songs, and some chamber music; publ. a book, *Bewusst gewordenes Klavierspiel und seine technischen Grundlagen* (Zürich, 1933).

Frey, Walter, distinguished Swiss pianist, brother of Emil Frey; b. Basel, Jan. 26, 1898. He studied at the Zürich Cons. and taught there after 1930; won an international reputation as a performer of modern piano music; toured Europe several times.

Freytag, Werner, German musicologist; b. Stettin, Aug. 11, 1907; studied at the Univ. of Vienna (1929-35); from 1939, in Berlin, working in acoustic laboratories. After 1946 he devoted himself mainly to music history; publ. valuable papers on music in Pomerania; contributed articles to 'Die Musik in Geschichte und Gegenwart.'

Fricker, Herbert Austin, organist and composer; b. Canterbury, England, Feb. 12, 1868; d. Toronto, Nov. 11, 1943. He was a pupil of Dr. W. H. Longhurst (organist of Canterbury Cathedral), Sir Frederick Bridge, and Edwin Lemare; 1877-83, choirboy at Canterbury Cathedral; 1884-91, deputy organist there; 1891-98, organist and choirmaster at Holy Trinity Church, Folkstone; 1898-1917, organist to the Corporation of the City of Leeds; organist and chorusmaster of the Leeds Festival (1904-13) and conductor of the Leeds Philh. and Choral Societies; from 1917 lived in Toronto, Canada. His compositions include sacred and secular vocal works, organ works and arrangements.

Fricker, Peter Racine, English composer; b. London, Sept. 5, 1920. He studied at the Royal College of Music and later with Matyas Seiber. In 1952, appointed musical director at Morley College in London. Works: *Rondo scherzoso* for orch. (1948); 1st symph. (1949; awarded the Koussevitzky prize; Cheltenham Festival, July 5, 1950); 2nd symph. (1951; Liverpool Philh. Orch., July 26, 1951); *Canterbury Prologue,* ballet (London, 1951); concerto for viola and orch. (1952; commissioned and played by William Primrose, Edinburgh, Sept. 3, 1953); piano concerto (London, March 21, 1954); *Rapsodia Concertante* for violin and orch. (Cheltenham Festival, July 15, 1954); *Concertante* for 3 pianos, strings, and timpani (London, Aug. 10, 1956). Chamber music: wind quintet (1947); *3 sonnets of Cecco Angiolieri,* for tenor, wind quintet, cello, and double-bass (1947); string quartet in one movement (1948; Brussels Festival, 1950); *Prelude, Elegy,* and *Finale* for strings (1949); concerto for violin and chamber orch. (1950); violin sonata (1950); *Concertante* for English horn and strings (1950); 2nd string quartet (1953); also piano works and choruses.

Fricsay (frē'-chī), **Ferenc,** Hungarian conductor; b. Budapest, Aug. 9, 1914. He studied with Kodály and Bartók; conducted at Szeged in 1936. In 1945 he was conductor of the Budapest Opera; from 1945-49, in

Vienna, Salzburg, Holland, and in South America. In 1949 he became conductor of the RIAS Orch., in the American sector of Berlin. His American début, with the Boston Symph. Orch., was on Nov. 13, 1953. In the autumn of 1954 he was engaged as conductor of the Houston Symphony Orch., but owing to disagreements in matters of musical policy, he conducted only a few concerts there, later returning to Europe.

Frid, Géza, Hungarian pianist and composer; b. Mármarossziget, Jan. 25, 1904. He studied at the Budapest Cons.; settled in Amsterdam (1929); since 1946, teaching at the Rotterdam Cons.; made a tour of the East Indies as pianist (1948-49)—Works: *Paradou,* symph. fantasy (1949); cello concerto; *Serenade* for wind quintet; 3 string quartets; piano pieces; choruses.

Friderici, Daniel, German composer and theorist; b. Klein-Eichstedt, near Querfurt, 1584; d. Rostock, Sept. 23, 1638. He served as a choirboy; then studied music in Magdeburg; settled in Rostock, where he was cantor of St. Mary's Church from 1617 till his death. He died of pestilence. He publ. in Rostock a number of sacred and secular songs to German words, and a theoretical work, *Musica Figuralis oder neue Unterweisung des Singe Kunst* (1618; 6th ed., 1677).—Cf. W. Voll, *Daniel Friderici* (Kassel, 1936).

Fried (frēd), **Oskar,** German conductor and composer; b. Berlin, Aug. 10, 1871; d. Moscow, July, 1941. He studied with Humperdinck in Frankfurt and Ph. Scharwenka in Berlin; played the horn in various orchestras until the performance of his choral work with orch., *Das trunkene Lied,* given by Karl Muck in Berlin (April 15, 1904), attracted much favorable attention; he continued to compose prolifically; wrote *Verklärte Nacht* for solo voices and orch.; *Andante und Scherzo* for wind instruments, 2 harps, and kettledrums; *Präludium und Doppelfuge* for string orch., etc. At the same time he began his career as conductor, achieving considerable renown in Europe; he was conductor of the 'Gesellschaft der Musikfreunde' in Berlin (1907-10) and of the Berlin Symph. Orch. (1925-26); left Berlin in 1934 and went to Russia; became a Soviet citizen in 1940.. For several years before his death he was conductor of the Tiflis Opera, in the Caucasus.—Cf. Paul Bekker, *Oskar Fried* (Berlin, 1907); Paul Stefan, *Oskar Fried* (Berlin, 1911).

Friedberg, Carl, well-known pianist; b. Bingen, Germany, Sept. 18, 1872; d. Merano, Italy, Sept. 8, 1955. He studied at the Frankfurt Cons. with Kwast, Knorr, and Clara Schumann; also took a course in composition with Humperdinck; subsequently taught piano at the Frankfurt Cons. (1893-1904) and at the Cologne Cons. (1904-14). In 1914 he made his first American tour with excellent success; taught piano at the Institute of Musical Art in N. Y.; was a member of the faculty of the Juilliard School of Music, N. Y. Among his pupils were Percy Grainger, Ethel Leginska, Elly Ney, and other celebrated pianists.

Friedheim, Arthur, pianist; b. St. Petersburg (of German parents), Oct. 26, 1859; d. New York, Oct. 19, 1932. He was a pupil of Anton Rubinstein and Liszt, and became particularly known as an interpreter of Liszt's works. He made his first American tour in 1891; taught at the Chicago Musical College in 1897; then traveled; lived in London, Munich, and (after 1915) New York, as teacher and pianist; composed a piano concerto and many pieces for solo piano, as well as an opera, *Die Tänzerin* (Karlsruhe, 1897).

Friedlaender, Max, eminent German musicologist; b. Brieg, Silesia, Oct. 12, 1852; d. Berlin, May 2, 1934. He was first a bass singer; studied voice with Manuel Garcia in London; appeared at the London Monday Popular Concerts in 1880. He returned to Germany in 1881 and took a course at Berlin Univ. with Spitta; obtained the degree of *Dr. phil.* at Rostock with the thesis *Beiträge zur Biographie Franz Schuberts* (1887); then was 'Privatdozent' at Berlin Univ. in 1894, and prof. in 1903. He was Exchange Prof. at Harvard Univ. in 1911; lectured at many American universities and received the degree of LL.D. from the Univ. of Wisconsin; retired in 1932. He discovered the MSS of more than 100 lost songs by Schubert and publ. them in his complete edition (7 vols.) of Schubert's songs. Together with Johann Bolte and Johann Meier he searched for years in every corner of the German Empire in quest of folksongs still to be found among the people; some of these he publ. in a volume under the title *100 Deutsche Volkslieder* (1885); was a member of the commission that published the monumental 'Volksliederbuch fur Männerchor' (1906); was also editor of 'Volksliederbuch für gemischten Chor' (1912); ed. songs of Mozart, Schumann, and Mendelssohn, Beethoven's Scotch Songs, the first version of Brahms' *Deutsche*

Volkslieder (1926), *Volksliederbuch für die deutsche Jugend* (1928), etc. Besides numerous valuable essays (in 'Goethe Jahrbuch,' 'Vierteljahrsschrift für Musikwissenschaft', etc.), he publ. *Goethes Gedichte in der Musik* (1896); *Gedichte von Goethe in Kompositionen seiner Zeitgenossen* (1896 and 1916); *Das Deutsche Lied im 18. Jahrhundert* (2 vols., 1902); *Brahms' Lieder* (1922; in English, London, 1928); and *Franz Schubert, Skizze seines Lebens and Wirkens* (1928).—Cf. E. J. Dent, *Max Friedlaender* in the 'Monthly Musical Record' (June, 1934).

Friedman, Ignaz, famous pianist; b. Podgorze, near Cracow, Feb. 14, 1882; d. Sydney, Australia, Jan. 26, 1948. He was a pupil of Riemann (composition) in Leipzig, Adler (history) and Leschetizky (piano) in Vienna; from 1905 made successful tours in Europe, South America, and Australia. In 1920 he played concerts in America; in 1940 went to Sydney. He was especially notable as an interpreter of Chopin, of whose works he prepared a new ed. in 12 vols. (Breitkopf & Hartel); composed about 100 piano pieces (*Thème varié; Elle danse; Passacaglia; Fantasiestücke,* etc.); made many arrangements for piano; edited the piano works of Schumann and Liszt for Universal Edition.

Friedrich II (der Grosse). See **Frederick.**

Fries (frēs), **Wulf (Christian Julius),** cellist and teacher; b. Garbeck, Germany, Jan. 10, 1825; d. Roxbury, Mass., April 29, 1902. As a self-taught cellist he played in Norway, at the Bergen theater orch. (from 1842), and at Ole Bull's concerts. In 1847 he went to Boston, where he became a founder member of the Mendelssohn Quintette Club, with A. Fries (1st violin), Gerloff (2nd violin), Edward Lehmann (1st viola), Oscar Greiner (2nd viola), and himself as cellist. He belonged to it for 23 years; also figured in the Musical Fund Society and the Harvard Musical Association; played in trios with Anton Rubinstein, and until 1901 took part in concerts in New England.

Frijsh (frish), **Povla,** concert soprano; b. Marstal, Denmark; first studied piano and theory in Copenhagen with O. Christensen, later voice in Paris with Jean Périer; made her début in Paris at the age of 19; appeared in concert and recital in Paris and briefly in opera in Copenhagen; made her American début in 1915; gave many first performances of modern vocal music (Bloch's *Poèmes d'Automne,* Loeffler's *Canticle of the Sun,* songs by Griffes, etc.), and made a specialty of modern international song literature. She introduced Negro spirituals to Paris and Copenhagen.

Friml, Rudolf, operetta composer; b. Prague, Dec. 7, 1879. He was a pupil at Prague Cons. of Juranek (piano) and Foerster (theory and composition); toured Austria, England, Germany, and Russia as accompanist of Kubelik, the violinist, coming with him to the U. S. in 1900 and again in 1906; remained in the U. S. after the second tour; gave numerous recitals, appeared as soloist with several of the large symphony orchestras (played his piano concerto with the N. Y. Symph. Orch.), and composed assiduously; lived in New York and Hollywood, Calif., composing for motion pictures.—Works: The operettas *The Firefly* (Syracuse, Oct. 14, 1912), *High Jinks* (Syracuse, Nov. 3, 1913), *Katinka* (Morristown, N. Y., Dec. 2, 1915), *You're in Love* (musical comedy; Stamford, Conn., 1916), *Glorianna* (1918), *Tumble In* (1919), *Sometime* (1919), *Rose Marie* (N. Y., Sept. 2, 1924; very popular), *Vagabond King* (N. Y., Sept. 21, 1925; highly successful). In 1937 Metro-Goldwyn-Mayer made a film of *The Firefly,* the popular *Donkey Serenade* being added to the original score. He also wrote a great number of piano pieces in a light vein; paraphrases, potpourris, etc.

Frimmel, Theodor von, Austrian writer on music; b. Amstetten, Dec. 15, 1853; d. Vienna, Dec. 25, 1928. He first studied medicine in Vienna; then became interested in art and maintained an art gallery; taught history of art at the Athenäum in Vienna. In 1908 he became editor of the 'Beethoven-Jahrbuch.' His writings about music include valuable papers on Beethoven.—Publications: *Beethoven und Goethe* (1883); *Neue Beethoveniana* (1887, with 9 authentic portraits of Beethoven; 2nd enlarged ed., 1889); *Danhäuser und Beethoven* (1892); *Beethovens Wohnungen in Wien* (1894); *Ritratti e caricature di Beethoven,* in 'Rivista Musicale Italiana' (1897); *Beethoven,* in 'Berühmte Musiker' (1901; 5th ed., 1919); *Beethoven Studien:* I. *Beethoven's äussere Erscheinung* (1905), II, *Bausteine zu einer Lebensgeschichte des Meisters* (1906); *Beethoven im zeitgenössischen Bildnis* (Vienna, 1923); *Lose Blätter zur Beethoven-Forschung* (1911-28; 10 issues); *Beethoven-Handbuch* (2 vols., 1927).

Frischenschlager, Friedrich, Austrian composer and music scholar; b. Gross-Florian, Styria, Sept. 7, 1885. He studied at the Graz Cons. and later with Humperdinck in Berlin (1909-15). In 1918 he settled in Salzburg; from 1918 was librarian at the Mozarteum; also taught there. An industrious composer, he has written orchestral works (*Symphonische Aphorismen, Vaterländische Ouvertüre,* etc.), children's operas, instrumental music, and songs. His chamber opera, *The Princess and the Dwarf,* was performed in 1937 at Smith College, Northampton, Mass.

Friskin, James, pianist and composer; b. Glasgow, March 3, 1886. He entered the Royal College of Music in 1900 and studied with E. Dannreuther (piano) and Stanford (composition); then taught at the Royal Normal College for the Blind (1909-14). In 1914 he came to the U. S.; taught at the Juilliard Graduate School. In 1934 he gave 2 recitals in New York consisting of the complete *Wohltemperiertes Clavier* of Bach. In 1944 he married Rebecca Clarke (q.v.). Among his works are *Phantasy-Quintet* for piano and strings; violin sonata. He published *The Principles of Pianoforte Practice* (London, 1921; new ed., N. Y., 1937); also (with Irwin Freundlich) *Music for the Piano* (N. Y., 1954).

Fritzsch, Ernst Wilhelm, German music publisher; b. Lützen, Aug. 24, 1840; d. Leipzig, Aug. 14, 1902. He was a pupil (1857-62) at Leipzig Cons.; lived several years in Bern, and in 1866 took over the music publishing firm of Bromnitz in Leipzig, carried on under his own name until 1903, then acquired by C. F. W. Siegel. A warm advocate of progress in music, and of Wagner's tendencies in particular, he published the latter's *Gesammelte Schriften,* edited the radical 'Musikalisches Wochenblatt' (from 1870), and in 1875 started the 'Musikalische Hausblätter.' By publishing the works of rising composers (Rheinberger, Svendsen, Grieg, Cornelius), he very practically promoted modern musical development. He was an excellent musician and for many years a member of the Gewandhaus Orchestra in Leipzig.

Froberger, Johann Jakob, famous German organist; b. Stuttgart, May 18, 1616; d. Héricourt, Haute-Saône, France, May 7, 1667. Shortly after 1630 he went to Vienna, where he entered the Institute of 'Singer oder Canthoreyknaben'; there it was the custom to allow the choir-boys, when their voices had changed and when they had attained a certain degree of musical scholarship, to serve as apprentices to famous masters of the time on stipends given by Emperor Ferdinand II. Froberger, however, did not apply for the subvention until late 1636, when it was refused him; thereupon, he held the position of 3rd organist at the court from Jan. 1 to Sept. 30, 1637. He then again applied for leave of absence, with success, and was granted a stipend of 200 gulden; in Oct. of that year he left to study under Frescobaldi in Rome, remaining there for three and a half years. In March, 1641, he returned to Vienna, where he again was organist from 1641-45 and 1653-57; after this he made long concert tours (to Paris and London). Stories of his adventures in London, and of his appointment first as organ blower at Westminster Abbey and then as court organist to Charles II (first publ. by Mattheson, but not corroborated from any English sources) must be dismissed as apocryphal. He spent his last years in the service of the Duchess Sybille of Württemberg at her chateau near Héricourt. Although two collections of *toccate, canzoni,* and *partite* were publ. long after his death (1693 and 1696), there is internal evidence that the majority of these works were written before 1650. Thus Froberger must be regarded as the real creator of the keyboard suite as well as the master who definitely fixed the order of movements in the suite *(Allemande, Courante, Sarabande, Gigue).* —Organ works: Toccatas, fantasias, canzoni, fugues, etc., of which 3 MS vols. are in the Vienna Library; in Berlin are 2 printed vols., *Diverse ingegnosissime, rarissime, et non maj più viste curiose partite di toccate, canzoni, ricercari, capricci,* etc. (1693; reprinted at Mainz in 1695) and *Diverse curiose e rare partite musicali,* etc. (1696); also a vol. of suites de clavecin.—A complete ed. of Froberger's works was publ. by G. Adler in 'Denkmäler der Tonkunst in Österreich' (IV, 1; VI, 2; X, 2). A monograph on Froberger was publ. by Fr. Beier in Waldersee's 'Sammlung musikalischer Vorträge' (Nos. 59 and 60); and 2 letters from Duchess Sybille to Chr. Huygens concerning him were publ. by E. Schebek (Prague, 1874). A MS preface to Fuchs' thematic catalogue of Froberger's works (in the Berlin Library) also throws some light on his career.—Cf. A. W. Ambros, *Geschichte der Musik* (vol. IV, p. 463 ff.); E. Schebek, *Zwei Briefe über J. J. Froberger* (Prague, 1874); H. Riemann, *Handbuch der Musikgeschichte* (vol. II, 2; p. 364 ff.); A. Tessier, *Une pièce inédite de Froberger,* in the 'Adler-Festschrift' (1930); K. Seidler, *Untersuchungen über Biographie und Klavierstil Johann Jakob Frobergers* (1930).

Froidebise, Pierre, Belgian composer; b. Ohey, May 15, 1914. He studied at the Brussels Cons. with Moulaert and L. Jongen; became organist in Liège, and in 1949 founded a progressive society there under the name 'Variation.'—Works: *Antigona* for soli, chorus, and orch.; *Justorum Animae* for chorus and orch.; *5 Comptines* for voice and 11 instruments (Brussels International Festival, June 27, 1950), chamber music and songs.

Froment, Louis de, French conductor; b. Paris, Dec. 5, 1921. He studied at the Paris Cons.; won the Premier Prix de Direction d'Orchestre there (1948); conducted the orchestra of Radiodiffusion Française; was music director at the Casinos in Cannes, Deauville, and Vichy (1950-54); conducted at various festivals in France; toured in Germany, England, Sweden, Holland, and Spain.

Fromm, Andreas, German composer; b. Pänitz, near Wusterhausen, 1621; d. Strahow, 1683. A son of a Lutheran pastor, he studied theology; in 1649, he became cantor in Stettin; he was subsequently in Rostock (1651), Wittenberg (1668), and Prague, where he turned to the Roman Catholic Church. His principal musical work was an 'actus musicus' *Die Parabel von dem reichen Mann und dem armen Lazarus* (1649); the opinion that it was the first German oratorio (cf. R. Schwartz, *Das erste deutsche Oratorium,* in the 'Jahrbuch der Musikbibliothek Peters' 1899) is discounted by later analysts. See Hans Engel's article in 'Die Musik in Geschichte und Gegenwart.'

Fromm, Herbert, composer; b. Kitzingen, Germany, Feb. 23, 1905. He studied privately with A. Reuss in Munich. He was conductor at the Civic Theater in Bielefeld (1930) and at Würzburg (1931-33). Came to the U. S. in 1937; was organist at Temple Beth Zion, Buffalo (1937-41); since 1941, music director at Temple Israel in Boston. He has published 12 choral works for the Hebrew service; also a violin sonata. His cantata *The Stranger* was performed in N. Y., March 12, 1957.

Frontini, Francesco Paolo, Italian composer; b. Catania, Aug. 6, 1860; d. there, July 28, 1939. He was a pupil of his father, Martino Frontini, who was also an opera composer, and of Lauro Rossi at Naples; was director of the Catania Cons. until 1923. He wrote the following operas: *Nella* (Catania, March 30, 1881), *Malia* (Bologna, May 30, 1893), *Il Falconiere* (Catania, Sept. 15, 1899); the oratorio *Sansone e Dalila* (Catania, Aug. 23, 1882) and numerous choral pieces and songs. Ricordi published his collection of Sicilian songs *Eco di Sicilia* (1883) and of Sicilian dances *Antiche danze di Sicilia* (3 vols., 1936).—Cf. G. C. Balbo, *Note critico-biografiche su F. P. Frontini* (Catania, 1905).

Froschauer, Johann, an Augsburg printer (end of 15th century), once thought to have been the first to print music with movable type, in Michael Keinspeck's 'Lilium musicae planae' (1498); however, it is now known that wood blocks were employed for the music illustrations in that work; it also appears fairly certain that music printing with movable type preceded Froschauer's work.

Frost, Charles Joseph, English composer; b. Westbury-on-Trym, June 20, 1848; d. Brockley, Oct. 13, 1918. He was engaged as organist and choral leader in various provincial towns in England; was active also as a lecturer; he wrote a cantata *By the Waters of Babylon* (1876), much sacred music, and pieces for organ (55 hymn-tune voluntaries, 40 preludes, a sonata, etc.).

Frost, Henry Frederick, English organist and writer; b. London, March 15, 1848; d. there, May 3, 1901. He was a boy chorister at Windsor; was organist of the Chapel Royal (1865-91); then taught organ at the Guildhall School of Music (1880-88); also wrote for 'The Athenaeum' and 'The Standard.' He wrote a biography of Schubert for the 'Great Musicians' series; publ. *Savoy Hymn-tunes and Chants.*

Frotscher, Gotthold, German musicologist; b. Ossa, near Leipzig, Dec. 6, 1897. He studied in Bonn and Leipzig; was univ. instructor in Danzig (1924-32); professor at Berlin Univ. (1935-45). He wrote a valuable history of organ playing, *Geschichte des Orgelspiels und der Orgelkomposition* (2 vols., Berlin, 1935).

Frotzler, Carl, Austrian organist and composer; b. Stockerau, Lower Austria, April 10, 1873. Of very precocious talent, he wrote a grand mass at 14; then entered the Vienna Cons., where he studied with Franz Krenn. He later occupied various posts as organist: at the Pfarrkirche, Stockerau (1887-93); at Tosis, Hungary, as Kapellmeister to Count Nicolaus Esterhazy (1893-97); then lived in Linz; in 1938 was in Vienna; in 1953 lived in retirement in Stockerau.

Frugatta, Giuseppe, Italian pianist and composer; b. Bergamo, May 26, 1860; d. Milan, May 30, 1933. He studied with A. Bazzini (composition) and C. Andreoli (piano) at Milan Cons., where he became prof. He composed a number of effective piano pieces (*Polonaise de concert, Moments poétiques,* etc.); also a piano trio (prize of the Academy at Florence, 1893); a string quartet (prize of St. Cecilia Academy at Rome, 1898); and a piano quintet with clarinet (prize, London, 1899). He published *Preparazione al 'Gradus ad Parnassum' di Clementi* (1913).

Früh, Armin Leberecht, German musical inventor; b. Mühlhausen, Thuringia, Sept. 15, 1820; d. Nordhausen, Jan. 8, 1894. He invented, in 1857, the 'Semeiomelodicon' (an apparatus for facilitating musical instruction, consisting of a series of note-heads which, when pressed by the finger, produced tones of corresponding pitch); he traveled to introduce his invention to prominent musicians, and established a factory in Dresden in 1858, but soon failed.

Früh, Huldreich Georg, Swiss pianist and composer; b. Zürich, June 16, 1903; d. there, April 25, 1945. He studied at the Zürich Cons.; wrote ballets and chamber operas, designed mainly for community festivals; also wrote popular songs and music for films.

Frumerie, (Per) Gunnar (Fredrick) de, Swedish composer; b. Nacka, near Stockholm, July 20, 1908. He studied at Stockholm Cons. (1929); was a stipendiary of the Jenny Lind Foundation until 1931; later studied with Erwin Stein and Emil von Sauer (Vienna) and Leonid Sabaneyev and Alfred Cortot (Paris). His works include a suite for chamber orch. (1930); 2 piano concertos (1929; 1935); variations and fugue for piano and orch. (1933); concerto for violin and orch. (1936); partita for string orch. (1938); *En moder,* melodrama to text by Andersen; *Singoalla,* opera (Stockholm, March 16, 1940); *Fader var,* cantata (1946).

Fry, William Henry, American composer and journalist, one of the first to champion the cause of the American composer and of opera in English; b. Philadelphia, Aug. 10, 1813; d. Santa Cruz, West Indies, Sept. 21, 1864. He was a pupil of L. Meignen in harmony and counterpoint. On June 4, 1845, he brought out at Philadelphia his *Leonora,* the first publicly performed grand opera by a native American; shortly after which he went to Europe as a foreign correspondent for the N. Y. 'Tribune'; there he became acquainted with several important European musicians, including Berlioz. In 1852-53 he gave a comprehensive series of lectures on music in New York, in the last of which he attacked the complete indifference of American artists and audiences alike to their own native music and emphasized the importance of having American works produced and their composers encouraged. Fry's symph. picture, *Niagara,* was given in New York, May 4, 1854. His 4 symphonies, *Santa Claus, The Breaking Heart, Childe Harold,* and *A Day in the Country,* were perf. by Jullien in 1853. He wrote 3 more operas: *The Bridal of Dunure; Aurelia the Vestal;* and *Notre Dame de Paris,* the last of which was produced at the Philadelphia Festival, May 3, 1864; he also composed a *Stabat Mater,* several cantatas, many songs.—Otto Kinkeldey presented excerpts from *Leonora* in concert form at a concert of the 'Pro Musica' Society (N. Y., Feb. 27, 1929).—Cf. J. T. Howard, *Our American Music* (N. Y., rev. ed., 1939); W. T. Upton, *The Musical Works of William Henry Fry* (Philadelphia, 1946); W. T. Upton, *William Henry Fry, American Journalist and Composer-Critic* (N. Y., 1954).

Frye, Walter, English composer of the 15th century; nothing is known regarding his life, but from indirect indications, it appears that he was attached to the court of Burgundy. Of his 3 Masses (in MS at the Royal Library in Brussels) two are without a Kyrie, a lack characteristic of the English school; his *Ave Regina* is an early example of the 'song motet'.—Cf. M. Bukofzer, *An Unknown Chansonnier of the 15th Century,* in the 'Mus. Quarterly' (Jan., 1942; reproduces a chanson by Frye on p. 42 ff.); G. Reese, *Music in the Renaissance* (N. Y., 1954, pp. 92-95; contains Frye's *Ave Regina* on p. 94 f); D. Plamenac, *A Reconstruction of the French Chansonnier in the Bibl. Colombina, Seville,* in the 'Mus. Quarterly' (Oct., 1951).

Fryer, George Herbert, English pianist and pedagogue; b. London, May 21, 1877; d. there, Feb. 7, 1957. He studied at the Royal College of Music; then with Matthay in London and Busoni in Weimar. He made his début as a pianist in London (Nov. 17, 1898); then traveled in Europe; in 1914 he made a tour in the U. S.; in 1915 gave recitals for the British Army in France; in 1917 returned to London; taught at the Royal College of Music (1917-47). He wrote miscellaneous pieces for piano; also publ. a book, *Hints on Pianoforte Practice* (N. Y., 1914).

Fryklöf, (frēk'-löf), **Harald Leonard,** Swedish composer and teacher, b. Upsala, Sept. 14, 1882; d. Stockholm, March 11, 1919. He studied theory with J. Lindegren at the Stockholm Cons. and piano with Ph. Scharwenka in Berlin. In 1911 he became prof. of harmony at the Cons. of Stockholm. With G. Sandberg, A. Hellerström, and H. Palm, he edited the choral series *Musica sacra* (1915); also publ. *Koralharmonisering-Kyrkotonarterna* (Choral Harmonizations-Church Modes; 1915); wrote a concert overture, songs, piano pieces.

Fryklund (frēk'-lund), **Lars Axel Daniel,** Swedish musicologist and specialist on musical instruments; b. Västerås, May 4, 1879. He studied Romanic philology at the Univ. at Upsala; taught at the Univ. of Hölsingborg (1921-44).—Publications: *Swedish Instruments* (Upsala, 1910), *African Instruments* (1915), *Study on the Pocket Violin* (1917), *Tromba Marina* (1919), *Viola d'amore* (1921), etc.

Frysinger, J. Frank, American organist; b. Hanover, Pa., April 7, 1878; d. York, Pa., Dec. 4, 1954. He began to play the organ at the age of 8; then studied with F. W. Wolff in Baltimore (1887-95) and with E. S. Kelley (1898-1900); was organist at First Presbyterian Church at York, Pa., from 1909-11 and again from 1922-53; retired a year before his death. He publ. about 200 works for organ; also piano pieces and songs.

Fuchs (fōōks), **Albert,** composer and pedagogue; b. Basel, Aug. 6, 1858; d. Dresden, Feb. 15, 1910. He studied with Selmar Bagge in Basel, and later at the Leipzig Cons. with Reinecke and Jadassohn (1876-79). He conducted oratorios in Trier (1880-83); then lived in Dresden; was subsequently director of the Wiesbaden Cons. (1889-98). In 1898 he joined the staff of the Dresden Cons.; was also conductor at the Schumann Singakademie (from 1901); wrote music criticism for the 'Dresdener Zeitung.' He was a prolific composer, and publ. a number of choral works and songs; wrote 2 oratorios: *Selig sind, die in dem Herrn sterben* (1906) and *Das tausendjährige Reich* (1908); several instrumental concertos; publ. *Taxe der Streichinstrumente* (1907; many reprints); edited an album of Italian songs of the early 18th century, and a collection of Italian arias.—Cf. F. A. Seissler, *Albert Fuchs,* in vol. III of 'Monographien moderner Musiker' (Leipzig, 1909).

Fuchs, Johann Nepomuk, Austrian composer; b. Frauenthal, Styria, May 5, 1842; d. Vöslau, near Vienna, Oct. 5, 1899. He studied with Sechter at Vienna; appointed Kapellmeister of the Pressburg Opera in 1864; held similar positions at Cologne, Hamburg, Leipzig, and at the Vienna Opera. In 1894 he succeeded Hellmesberger as director of the Vienna Cons. He produced the opera *Zingara* (Brünn, 1892) and several others.

Fuchs, Karl Dorius Johann, distinguished German music scholar; b. Potsdam, Oct. 22, 1838; d. Danzig, Aug. 24, 1922. He studied piano with Hans von Bülow, Weitzmann, and Kiel; took the degree of *Dr. phil.* at Greifswald, with the dissertation *Präliminarien zu einer Kritik der Tonkunst.* In 1868 he became teacher at the Kullak Academy in Berlin; then gave piano concerts in Germany. In 1874 he went to Danzig, where he was organist at the Petrikirche and music critic of the 'Danziger Zeitung' (1887-1920); was also organist for many years at the Synagogue in Danzig, and wrote *Andachtslieder für Tempel und Haus.* Fuchs was a friend of Nietzsche, with whom he corresponded.—Writings: *Betrachtungen mit und gegen Arthur Schopenhauer* ('Neue Berliner Musikzeitung', 1868); *Ungleiche Verwandte unter den Neudeutschen* (1868); *Virtuos und Dilettant* (Leipzig, 1871); *Die Zukunft des musikalischen Vortrags* (Danzig, 1884); *Die Freiheit des musikalischen Vortrags* (Danzig, 1885); *Praktische Anleitung zum Phrasieren* (Berlin, 1886, with Hugo Riemann; English transl., N. Y., 1892); *Künstler und Kritiker* (1898); *Takt und Rhythmus im Choral* (Berlin, 1911); *Der taktgerechte Choral, Nachweisung seiner 6 Typen* (Berlin, 1923). His letters were publ. by his son, Hans Fuchs in 'Ostdeutsche Monatshefte' (Sept. 1923).

Fuchs, Robert, Austrian composer and pedagogue; brother of Johann Nepomuk Fuchs; b. Frauenthal, Feb. 15, 1847; d. Vienna, Feb. 19, 1927. He taught at the Vienna Cons. from 1875, and was reputed to be one of the best teachers of composition there; wrote several serenades for string orch., a piano concerto, and a symphony.—

Cf. Anton Mayr, *Erinnerungen an Robert Fuchs* (Graz, 1934).

Fučik (foo'-tchik), **Julius,** Czech composer of band music; b. Prague, July 18, 1872; d. Leitmeritz, Sept. 25, 1916. He was a bassoon player at the German Opera in Prague (1893) and later in Zagreb and Budapest; studied composition with Dvořák; was bandmaster of the 86th and 92nd Austrian regiments. He wrote a great number of dances and marches for band, including the immensely popular march, *Entrance of the Gladiators.*

Fuenllana (fŏŏen-l'yah'-nah), **Miguel de,** blind Spanish vihuela virtuoso and composer: b. Navalcarnero, Madrid, early in the 16th century; date of death unknown. He was chamber musician to the Marquesa de Tarifa, and later at the court of Philip II, to whom he dedicated (1554) his *Libro de música para vihuela, intitulado Orphenica Lyra.* From 1563, he was chamber musician to Queen Isabel de Valois, 3rd wife of Philip II. The *Libro* gives evidence of a high state of musical art in Spain during the 16th century; besides fantasias and other compositions for vihuela by Fuenllana and old Spanish ballads (such as the famous *Ay de mi, Alhama),* it contains arrangements for vihuela of works by Vásquez, Morales, P. and F. Guerrero, Flecha, Bernal, and several Flemish masters.—Cf. H. Riemann, in 'Monatshefte für Musikgeschichte' (1895); G. Morphy, *Les Luthistes espagnols* (Leipzig, 1902); A. Koczirz, *Die Gitarrekompositionen in Miguel de Fuenllana's Orphenica Lyra,* in 'Archiv für Musikwissenschaft' (1922); H. Anglès, *Dades desconegudes sobre Miguel de Fuenllana, vihuelista,* in 'Revista Musical Catalana' (April, 1936).

Fuentes (y Pelaez), Eduardo Sanchez de. See **Sanchez de Fuentes.**

Fuentes (fwehn'-täs), **Juan Bautista,** Mexican composer; b. Guadalajara, Jalisco, March 16, 1869; d. Leon, Guanajuato, Feb. 11, 1955. He studied in Mexico City; then taught music in various schools there. He published the manuals *Teoría de la Música* (1899); *Tratado de Intervalos y Trasposición* (1909); *Método de Armonía* (1920); composed a number of piano pieces in a salon style; also some orchestral works, among them *Sinfonia Mexicana.*

Fuerstner, Carl, composer and conductor; b. Strasbourg, June 16, 1912. At the age of 11 he made his first public appearance as pianist, in Jena; then studied in Cologne at the Hochschule für Musik with Abendroth, Braunfels, and Jarnach (1930-34); still as a student he conducted opera at Cologne; in 1939 he emigrated to the U. S.; was assistant conductor of the San Francisco Opera Company; was also active as accompanist. He has taught at Brigham Young University at Provo, Utah, and at the Eastman School of Music in Rochester. He began to compose early in life; as a youth wrote incidental music for the Cologne Opera. Among his works is a *Concerto Rapsodico* for cello and orch. (Rochester, May 11, 1947); *Metamorphoses on a Chorale Theme,* scored for 20 trombones, 2 tubas, and percussion (Rochester, April 5, 1949); *Divertimento* for string quartet (1949); quintet for clarinet and string quartet; *Berceuse* for 4 recorders; violin sonata, etc.

Fugère (füh-zhär'), **Lucien,** French baritone; b. Paris, July 22, 1848; d. there, Jan. 15, 1935. He began as a singer in cabarets; then sang in light opera; in 1877 joined the Opéra-Comique, and acquired a great following as a brilliant performer of the comic parts; his best roles were Figaro and Bartolo. He was also well known as a teacher; among his pupils was Mary Garden.

Führer, Robert (Johann Nepomuk), composer and organist; b. Prague, June 2, 1807; d. Vienna, Nov. 28, 1861. He studied with Johann Vitásek; was organist in provincial towns before succeeding his teacher as Kapellmeister at the Prague Cathedral in 1839. He became involved in fraudulent transactions and was dismissed from his post in 1845. He then held various positions as organist and choral conductor in Vienna, Salzburg, Munich, Augsburg, and Gmunden. A series of embezzlements and other criminal offenses perpetrated by him resulted in his dismissal from several of his positions, but he continued to compose and perform; in 1856 he was Bruckner's competitor for the organist's post in Linz, arousing great admiration for his skill, even though Bruckner was selected. He served a prison term in 1859, but was given full freedom to write music. He published numerous sacred works (32 masses, 14 Requiems, 4 litanies, etc.) and many organ pieces; also handbooks on harmony and organ playing. Despite his notoriously dishonest acts and professional untrustworthiness (he publ. one of Schubert's masses under his own name), he enjoyed a remarkably high reputation for his musicianship among his colleagues. See **F.**

Haberl's detailed article on him in 'Die Musik in Geschichte und Gegenwart.'

Fukai, Shiro, Japanese composer; b. in Akita-City, April 4, 1907. He studied composition in Tokyo with M. Sugawara; among his works are the orchestral suite *Paradise* (Tokyo, Jan. 29, 1937); *Tropical Scene* (Tokyo, Jan. 14, 1943); a large choral work, *Prayer for Peace* (Tokyo, Aug. 15, 1949); a cantata, *Heiankyo* (1939); and the ballets *A City* (Tokyo, June 18, 1936), *Ocean* (Tokyo, Jan. 30, 1938), and *Distorted Letters ABC* (1955).

Fuleihan (fŏŏ-lā-hahn'), **Anis** (ăh-nēs), American pianist, conductor, and composer; b. Kyrenia, Cyprus, April 2, 1900; studied there at the English School; came to the U. S. in 1915 and continued his study of the piano in New York with Alberto Jonás; toured the U. S., also the Near East, from 1919 to 1925; then lived in Cairo, returning to the U. S. in 1928; was on the staff of G. Schirmer, Inc. (1932-39); 1947, became prof. at Indiana Univ.; 1953, director of the Beirut Cons., Lebanon.—Works: for orch.: *Mediterranean Suite* (1922; Cincinnati, March 15, 1935); *Preface to a Child's Story Book* (1932); symphony No. 1 (N. Y. Philharmonic, Dec. 31, 1936); concerto No. 1 for piano and string orch. (Saratoga Springs, N. Y., Sept. 11, 1937, composer soloist); concerto No. 2 for piano and orch. (N. Y., 1938); Fantasy for viola and orch. (1938); violin concerto (1930); *Fiesta* (Indianapolis Symph. Orch., Dec. 1, 1939); *Symphonie Concertante,* for string quartet and orch. (N. Y. Philharmonic, April 25, 1940); concerto for 2 pianos and orch. (Hempstead, N. Y., Jan. 10, 1941); *Epithalamium* for piano and strings (Philadelphia, Feb. 7, 1941); concerto for theremin and orch. (N. Y., 1945); *Invocation to Isis* (Indianapolis Symph. Orch., Feb. 28, 1941); *Three Cyprus Serenades* for orch. (Philadelphia Orch., Dec. 13, 1946, Ormandy cond.); Rhapsody for cello and string orch. (Saratoga Springs, Sept. 12, 1946); *Overture for Five Winds* (N. Y., May 17, 1947); *The Pyramids of Giza,* symph. poem (1952); 2 string quartets; 4 piano sonatas; choral pieces; songs.

Fuller Maitland, John Alexander, eminent English music scholar, b. London, April 7, 1856; d. Carnforth Lane, March 30, 1936. He studied at Westminster School and Trinity College in Cambridge (M.A., 1882); then took piano lessons with Dannreuther and W. S. Rockstro. He was the music critic of the 'Pall Mall Gazette' (1882-84); of the 'Manchester Guardian' (1884-89); lectured extensively on the history of English music; appeared as pianist with the Bach Choir and as performer on the harpsichord in historical concerts; contributed to the first ed. of 'Grove's Dictionary' and edited the 'Appendix'; editor-in chief of the 2nd ed. (1904-10); ed. of 'English Carols of the 15th Century' (1887), 'English Country Songs' (1893; with L. E. Broadwood), 'Fitzwilliam Virginal Book' (1899; with W. Barclay Squire, his brother-in-law), 12 trio sonatas and *St. Cecilia Ode* of Purcell in the monumental edition of the Purcell Society, the piano works of Purcell's contemporaries (1921). Together with Clara Bell he translated Spitta's *Bach* (3 vols., 1884; 2nd ed., 1899); compiled the catalogue of the music division of the Fitzwilliam Museum (1893). He is the author of the following books: *Schumann* (1884); *Masters of German Music* (1894); *The Musician's Pilgrimage* (1899); *English Music in the 19th Century* (1902); *The Age of Bach and Handel* (vol. IV of 'The Oxford History of Music,' 1902; new ed., 1931); *Joseph Joachim* (1905); *Brahms* (1911; in German, 1912); *The Concert of Music* (1915); *The "48"—Bach's Wohltemperiertes Clavier* (2 vols., 1925); *The Keyboard Suites of J. S. Bach* (1925); *The Spell of Music* (1926); *A Door-Keeper of Music* (1929); *Bach's Brandenburg Concertos* (1929); *Schumann's Concerted Chamber Music* (1929); *The Music of Parry and Stanford* (Cambridge, 1934).

Fumagalli, four brothers, natives of Inzago, Italy: **Disma,** b. Sept. 8, 1826; d. Milan, March 9, 1893. He was a pupil at, and from 1857 prof. in, Milan Cons. Prolific composer of piano music (over 250 numbers). —**Adolfo,** b. Oct. 19, 1828; d. Florence, May 3, 1856, at the age of 27. Pianist, pupil of Gaetano Medaglia, and later of Angeleri and Ray at Milan Cons.; then undertook tours throughout Italy, France, and Belgium, earning the sobriquet of the 'Paganini of the pianoforte.' During his brief lifetime he publ. about 100 elegant and effective piano pieces, which obtained an extraordinary vogue. Filippo Filippi wrote a sketch, *Della vita e delle opere di Adolfo Fumagalli* (Milan, 1857).—**Polibio,** b. Oct. 26, 1830; d. Milan, June 21, 1891. Pianist; composer for piano and for organ.—**Luca,** b. May 29, 1837; d. Milan, June 5, 1908. He was a pupil of the Milan Cons.; played with great success in Paris (1860), and published salon-music for piano; also produced an opera, *Luigi XI* (Florence, 1875).

Fumet, Dynam-Victor, French organist and composer; b. Toulouse, May 4, 1867; d. Paris, Jan. 2, 1949. He studied with César Franck and with Guiraud at the Paris Cons. At an early age he became involved in the political activities of French anarchists and was forced to leave school. For a time he earned his living as piano player in Paris night clubs; in 1910 became organist of St. Anne's Church in Paris. His music follows the precepts of French Wagnerism; the influence of Franck is also noticeable. Fumet wrote several orchestral works on mystic themes, among them *Magnetisme céleste* for cello and orchestra (1903); *Trois âmes* (1915); *Transsubstantiation* (1930); *Notre mirage, notre douleur* (1930). During the German occupation he wrote *La Prison glorifiée* (1943).

Fumi, Vinceslao, Italian conductor; b. Montepulciano, Tuscany, Oct. 20, 1823; d. Florence, Nov. 20, 1880. He conducted opera in various Italian cities; also in Constantinople, Montevideo, and Buenos Aires; finally at Florence. His compositions include the opera, *Atala* (Buenos Aires, 1862), a symphony, and other orchestral works. A collection of folksongs of all times and nations, which he undertook, remained unfinished.

Fursch-Madi, Emma, operatic soprano; b. Bayonne, France, 1847; d. Warrenville, N. Y., Sept. 20, 1894. She studied at the Paris Cons.; her first opera engagement was in Paris as Marguerite. She visited America in 1874 with the New Orleans French Opera Co.; sang at Covent Garden (1879-81) and at the Metropolitan Opera, where her final appearance (Feb. 6, 1894) was as Ortrud in *Lohengrin*. She was married three times: to Madi Manjour, a violinist, to Henry Verié, and to M. Wurst.

Fürstenau, Moritz, German writer on music and flutist; b. Dresden, July 26, 1824; d. there, March 25, 1889. He was a member of the Dresden court orch. from 1842; librarian of the music section, Royal Library, from 1852; from 1858, flute teacher in the Cons. He published: *Beiträge zur Geschichte der königlich-sächs. musikalischen Kapelle* (1849); *Zur Geschichte der Musik und des Theaters am Hofe zu Dresden* (1861-2, 2 vols.; a supplement, by Dr. Hans van Brescius, entitled *Die königliche sachs. musikalische Kapelle von Reissiger bis Schuch, 1826-98,* was publ. at Dresden, 1898); *Die Fabrikation musikalischer Instrumente im königlich sächsischen Vogtland* (1876, with Th. Berthold); also essays and articles in musical journals, in 'Mittheilungen des königlich sächsischen Alterthumsvereins,' in Mendel's 'Musikal. Conversations-Lexikon,' etc.

Fürstner, Adolf, German publisher; b. Berlin, April 3, 1833; d. Bad Nauheim, June 6, 1908. He was a member of a family of merchants; although lacking in musical education he showed a keen understanding of commercial values of good music. He founded a music publishing firm under his own name in Berlin in 1868; in 1872 he acquired the catalogue of the Dresden firm of C. F. Meser, which owned several operas by Wagner and some works of Liszt; he subsequently purchased the rights of operas by Massenet, and later demonstrated his business acumen by securing *Pagliacci*. His firm distinguished itself as the earliest publisher of Richard Strauss. Fürstner was succeeded after his death by his son Otto (b. Berlin, Oct. 17, 1886); in 1933, Otto Fürstner was compelled to leave Germany; he went to England, where he resumed his business and gradually won back the German rights to the original editions of the firm.

Furtwängler (fŏŏhrt-väng-ler), **Wilhelm,** celebrated German conductor; b. Berlin, Jan. 25, 1886; d. Baden-Baden, Nov. 30, 1954. He grew up in Munich, where he studied music with Schillings, Rheinberger, and Beer-Waldbrunn; conducting with Mottl. His first appearances as conductor were in opera, at Zürich and Strasbourg; then in Lübeck (1911-15) and Mannheim (1915-19). From 1919-21, he conducted the Tonkünstler Orch. in Vienna; from 1920-22, the Staatskapelle, Berlin. In 1919 he became musical director of the Berlin State Opera. In 1922 he was appointed conductor of the Berlin Philharmonic as successor to Nikisch; he also conducted the Gewandhaus Orch. in Leipzig (until 1928) and at the Bayreuth Festivals (1931-32). He made a sensationally successful American début with the N. Y. Philharmonic on Jan. 3, 1925, and led the orch. again in February, 1926, and March, 1927. On April 17, 1932, he was awarded the Goethe Gold Medal. In 1933-34, he had several clashes with the Nazi Government on questions of policy, and on Dec. 4, 1934, resigned his posts at the Berlin Philharmonic, the State Opera, and the Reichsmusikkammer (of which he had been briefly deputy president). However, a few months later, he made an uneasy peace with the Nazi authorities and agreed to resume his post with the Berlin Philharmonic (April 25, 1935). In 1936 he was offered a contract as permanent conductor of the N. Y. Philharmonic, but declined when objections were raised in America against his collaboration with the Nazis. He continued conducting in Germany during World War II; in 1945 he went to Switzerland. Returning to Germany in 1946, he was absolved from the charges of pro-Nazi activities (Dec. 17, 1946). He was tentatively engaged to conduct the Chicago Symph. Orch. in 1949, but the contract was cancelled when public opinion proved hostile. In Western Europe, however, Furtwängler was received most enthusiastically, when he led the Berlin Philharmonic in guest appearances in England and France. He was to conduct the Berlin Philharmonic in its first American tour in 1955, but death intervened, and Herbert von Karajan was appointed his successor. Furtwängler was also a composer; he wrote 2 symphonies, a piano concerto, a *Te Deum,* and some chamber music; publ. a monograph, *Johannes Brahms und Anton Bruckner* (Leipzig, 1942); collections of essays, *Gespräche über Musik* (Zürich, 1948; in English as *Concerning Music,* London, 1953); *Ton und Wort* (Wiesbaden, 1954); and *Der Musiker und sein Publikum* (Zürich, 1954).—Cf.: R. Specht, *Wilhelm Furtwängler* (1922); A. Einstein, *Wilhelm Furtwängler,* in the 'Monthly Mus. Record' (Jan., 1934); O. Schrenck, *Wilhelm Furtwängler* (1940); F. Herzfeld, *Wilhelm Furtwängler, Weg und Wesen* (Leipzig, 1941); Berta Geissmar, *Two Worlds of Music* (N. Y., 1946); Willy Siebert, *Furtwängler, Mensch und Künstler* (Buenos Aires, 1950); Curt Riess, *Furtwängler; Musik und Politik* (Bern, 1953).

Furuhjelm (fŏŏ'-rŏŏ-yelm), **Erik Gustav,** Finnish composer, b. Helsinki, July 6, 1883. He studied violin; then took lessons in composition with Sibelius and Wegelius; continued his studies in Vienna with Robert Fuchs. In 1909 he was appointed prof. at the Helsinki Cons. He wrote two symphonies, a *Romantic Overture,* a *Konzertstück* for violin and orch., *Exotica-Suite* for orch., *Intermezzo* and *Pastorale* for orch., a *Konzertstück* for piano and orch., a piano quintet, and other orchestral and chamber works. He has also written a book on Sibelius (Helsinki, 1916; in Swedish and in Finnish).

Fussan, Werner, German composer; b. Plauen, Dec. 25, 1912. He studied at the Hochschule für Musik in Berlin; was in the army (1940-45); then taught at the Wiesbaden Cons. (1946-48). Among his works are a *Capriccio* for orch.; wind quintet; duo for flute and piano; 2 piano sonatinas; and songs.

Fux (fŏŏks), **Johann Joseph,** Austrian composer and learned theorist; b. Hirtenfeld, Styria, 1660; d. Vienna, Feb. 14, 1741. Nothing definite is known concerning his teachers or course of study. In 1696 he was appointed organist at the Schottenkirche, Vienna; in 1698 he was made court composer; in 1704 Kapellmeister at St. Stephen's, and assistant Kapellmeister to the court in 1713, succeeding Ziani as first Kapellmeister (the highest position attainable for a musician) in 1713. This office he held until his death, under 3 successive emperors, and received many tokens of imperial favor. Of his 405 extant works, comparatively few have been published. The greatest and the most enduring is his treatise on counterpoint, *Gradus ad Parnassum,* published originally in Latin (Vienna, 1725), since then in German, Italian, French, and English (1791; part of the *Gradus ad Parnassum* was published in English as *Steps to Parnassus,* N. Y., 1943); Mozart and Haydn studied it; Cherubini and Albrechtsberger adopted its method, which was sanctioned by Piccini and Padre Martini. Vogler, however, condemned it (see introduction to Vogler's *Choral-System,* p. 1; Fröhlich's biography of Vogler, p. 18). Fux was well aware of the weakness of contemporary music practice and, in trying to arrive at a satisfactory remedy, disregarded the modern idiom already established when he was writing and chose, as the basis of his theory, the style of Palestrina. Although his presentation of that style is not very strong or even authentic, for, among other things, he could not have been very well acquainted with the main body of Palestrina's works because they were not commonly available at the time, the method is still valuable for its organization and the discipline it affords (cf. K. Jeppesen's *Counterpoint,* 1931; in English, N. Y., 1939).—His compositions include 18 operas; 10 oratorios; 29 partitas (among them the *Concentus musico-instrumentalis*); much sacred music: 50 Masses (the *Missa canonica* is a contrapuntal masterpiece), 3 Requiems, 2 *Dies irae,* 57 vespers and psalms, etc., and 38 'sacred sonatas.' A selection from his works is publ. in 'Denkmäler der Tonkunst in Österreich' I, 1 (4 Masses), II, 1 (27 motets), IX, 2 (2 sacred sonatas, 2 overtures), XVII (the opera *Costanza e fortezza;* later ed. by G. P. Smith, Northampton, Mass., 1936), XXIII, 2 (the *Concentus musico-instrumentalist*), LXXXV, ed. by E. Schenk (Vienna, 1947).—Cf. L. von Köchel,

Johann Joseph Fux (Vienna, 1872; full biography and thematic catalogue of works); C. Schnabl, *Johann Joseph Fux, der österreichische Palestrina,* in the 'Jahrbuch der Leo Gesellschaft' (Vienna, 1895); H. Rietsch, *Der Concentus von Johann Joseph Fux* in 'Studien zur Musikwissenschaft' (IV; 1912); A. Liess, *Johann Joseph Fux* (Vienna, 1948).

G

Gabriel, Mary Ann Virginia, English composer; b. Banstead, Surrey, Feb. 7, 1825; d. London, Aug. 7, 1877. She studied with Pixis, Döhler, Thalberg, and Molique; married George E. March (1874), who wrote most of her libretti.—Works: 3 cantatas, *Evangeline* (Brighton Festival, Feb. 13, 1873), *Dreamland,* and *Graziella;* 6 operettas, *Widows Bewitched* (London, Nov. 13, 1867), *Grass Widows, Shepherd of Cornouailles, Who's the Heir?, Follies of a Night,* and *A Rainy Day;* piano pieces.

Gabrieli, Andrea, eminent Italian organist and composer; b. Venice, c. 1520; d. there, 1586. He was a pupil of Adrian Willaert at San Marco and chorister there (1536); then traveled in Germany and Bohemia; was in Bavaria in 1562 and went to Frankfurt, to the coronation of Maximilian II, as court organist of Duke Albert V of Bavaria. In 1566 he returned to Venice and was appointed 2nd organist at San Marco; became 1st organist on Jan. 1, 1585, succeeding Merulo. He enjoyed a great reputation as organist (his concerts with Merulo, on 2 organs, were featured attractions). Among his pupils were his famous nephew, Giovanni Gabrieli, and Hans Leo Hassler. A prolific composer, he wrote a large number of works of varied description, many of which were published posthumously, edited by his nephew. His versatility is attested by the fact that he was equally adept in sacred music of the loftiest spirit, and in instrumental music, as well as in madrigals, often of a comic nature.—Works: *Sacrae cantiones* (37 motets, 1565); *Libro I di madrigali a 5 voci* (30 madrigals, 1566); *Libro II di madrigali a 5 voci* (28 madrigals, 1570); *Greghesche e justiniane* (15 numbers, 1571); *Primus Liber Missarum 6 vocum* (4 Masses, 1572); *Libro I di madrigali a 6 voci* (30 madrigals, 1574); *Libro di madrigali a 3 voci* (30 madrigals, 1575); *Ecclesiasticae cantiones a 4 voci* (58 motets, 1576); *Libro II de madrigali a 6 voci* (22 madrigals, 1580); *Psalmi Davidici a 6 voci* (7 Psalms, 1583); *Sonate a 5 strumenti* (lost, 1586); *Concerti di Andrea et di Giovanni Gabrieli* (39 motets, 26 madrigals, 1587); *Edippo Tiranno* (choruses for Sophocles' *Oedipus,* performed in Vicenza in 1585, 1588); *Libro III di madrigali a 5 voci* (22 madrigals, 1589); *Madrigali et ricercari* (24 madrigals, 7 ricercars, 1589); *Intonazioni d'organo* (12 *intonazioni,* 1593); *Ricercari di Andrea Gabrieli* (13 ricercars, 1595); *Libro III de ricercari* (6 ricercars, 1 fantasia, 1 motet, 1 *canzon,* 2 madrigals, 1 capriccio on the *passamezzo antico,* 1596); *Mascherate di Andrea Gabrieli et altri* (3 *mascherate,* 3 madrigals, 1601); *Canzoni alla francese et ricercari* (4 *canzoni,* 7 ricercars, 1605); *Canzoni alla francese* (9 *canzoni,* one ricercar, 1605); and a large number of detached works in contemporary and later collections.—Modern editions: G. Benvenuti, 'Istituzioni e monumenti dell' arte musicale italiana' (vol. I; vocal and instrumental pieces); L. Torchi, 'L'arte musicale in Italia' (vols. II and III; 16 motets and pieces for organ); K. von Winterfeld, in *Joh. Gabrieli und sein Zeitalter* (1834; 2 vols. and a musical supplement); J. von Wasielewski, in *Geschichte der Instrumental-Musik im 16. Jahrhundert* (1878) and in the music supplement of *Die Violine im 17. Jahrhundert* (2nd ed., 1905); A. G. Ritter, *Geschichte des Orgelspiels im 14.-18. Jahrhundert* (1884; revised by Frotscher, 1933); G. d'Alessi, in 'Classici della musica italiana' (vol. VI); de la Moskowa, *Recueil des morceaux de musique ancienne* (1843); H. Riemann in *Alte Kammermusik* (8-voiced ricercar); O. Kinkeldey in *Orgel und Klavier in der Musik des 16. Jahrhunderts* (organ arrangements by Andrea Gabrieli of Orlando di Lasso's chanson, *Susanne un jour);* J. Wolf, in *Sing- und Spielmusik* (a *Canzona francese);* H. Bäuerle *(Missa Brevis,* 1932); W. Schöllgen (Easter Motet, 1932); A. Einstein, in 'Denkmäler der Tonkunst in Österreich,' vol. XLI (3 madrigals in 6, 7, 8 voices, 1934), in the musical supplement (No. 21) of *A Short History of Music* (N. Y., 1938), in *The Golden Age of Music* (N. Y., 1942), and in *The Italian Madrigal* (vol. III, Princeton, 1949); A. Schering, in *Geschichte der Musik in Beispielen* (No. 130); Davison and Apel, in *Historical Anthology of Music* (vol. I, Nos. 135, 136); Parish and Ohl, in *Masterpieces of Music before 1750* (No. 21).—Cf. G. Benvenuti, *Andrea e Giovanni Gabrieli e la musica strumentale in S. Marco,* in 'Istituzioni e monumenti dell' arte musicale italiana' (vol. II); Ilse Zerr-Becking, *Studien zu Andrea*

Gabrieli (Prague, 1933); G. Reese, *Music in the Renaissance* (N. Y., 1954); see also bibliography listed under Giovanni Gabrieli.

Gabrieli (Gabrielli), **Domenico** (called the 'Menghino dal violoncello,' Menghino being the diminutive of Domenico), Italian composer; b. Bologna, c. 1650; d. there, July 10, 1690. An excellent cellist, he played in the orchestra of San Petronio, Bologna (1680-87); was a member of the Bologna Philharmonic Academy (1676); then became its president (1683). He was one of the earliest composers for cello solo. He produced 12 operas in Bologna, Venice, Modena, and Turin; his last opera, *Tiberio in Bisanzio,* was performed posthumously in Lucca (Jan. 20, 1694). Other works: *Ricercari per violoncello solo* (1689; MS at the Liceo in Bologna); *Balletti, gighe, correnti e sarabande* for 2 violins, cello, and basso continuo (1684; 2nd ed., 1704); *Vexillum pacis* (motets for contralto with instrumental accompaniment; posthumous, 1695). L. Landshoff edited 3 *Arie* with instrumental obbligato (in *Alte Meister des Bel Canto,* 1912) and 2 cello sonatas (1930); A. Einstein printed a chamber cantata in the music supplement (No. 28) of his *A Short History of Music* (N. Y., 1938).—Cf. E. Albini, *Domenico Gabrieli, il Corelli del violoncello,* in 'Rivista Musicale Italiana' (1937).

Gabrieli, Giovanni, celebrated Venetian composer; nephew and pupil of Andrea Gabrieli; b. Venice, between 1554 and 1557; d. there, Aug. 12, 1612. He lived in Munich from 1575-79, taken to that court by Lassus. On Nov. 1, 1584 he was engaged to substitute for Merulo as 1st organist at San Marco in Venice; on Jan. 1, 1585, was permanently appointed as 2nd organist (his uncle meanwhile took charge of the 1st organ); retained this post until his death. As a composer, he stands at the head of the Venetian school; he was probably the first to write vocal works with parts for instrumental groups in various combinations, partly specified, partly left to the conductor, used as accompaniment as well as interspersed instrumental *sinfonie (Sacrae Symphoniae).* His role as a composer and teacher is epoch-making; through his innovations and his development of procedures and devices invented by others (free handling of several choirs in the many-voiced vocal works, 'concerted' solo parts and duets in the few-voiced vocal works, trio-sonata texture, novel dissonance treatment, speech-rhythm, root-progressions in fifths, use of tonal and range-levels for structural purposes, coloristic effects) and through his numerous German pupils (particularly Schütz) and other transalpine followers, he gave a new direction to the development of music. His instrumental music helped to spark the composition of German instrumental ensemble music, which reached its apex in the symphonic and chamber music works of the classical masters. Of interest also is the fact that one of his ricercars, a 4-part work in the 10th tone (1595), is an early example of the 'fugue with episodes' (reprinted in Riemann's *Musikgeschichte in Beispielen,* No. 52, Leipzig, 1913).—Publications (very few) contain both sacred and secular vocal, as well as instrumental, works: *Concerti di Andrea et di Giovanni Gabrieli* (5 motets, 5 madrigals; 1587); *Intonazioni d'organo di Andrea Gabrieli et di Giovanni suo nepote* (11 *intonazioni;* 1593); *Sacrae Symphoniae Joannis Gabrielii* (42 motets, Mass, 12 instrumental *canzoni,* 3 sonatas; 1597); *Sacrarum Symphoniarum Continuatio* (9 motets, of which 5 are reprints; 1600); *Canzoni per sonare* (6 *canzoni;* 1608); *Sacrae Symphoniae Diversorum Autorum* (26 motets; 1613); *Sacrae Symphoniae, Liber II* (26 motets, Mass, 3 Magnificats; 1615); *Canzoni et Sonate* (15 *canzoni,* 5 sonatas; 1615); *Reliquiae Sacrorum Concentum* (1 Magnificat, 19 motets, of which 10 are reprints; 1615). Detached pieces in collections up to 1625: 25 more madrigals, 1 canticle, Magnificats, motets, ricercars, toccatas, fantasias.—G. Benvenuti publ. 3 secular vocal pieces in vol. I (1931) and G. Cesari, 13 *canzoni* and 2 *sonate* (from *Sacrae Symphoniae,* 1597) in vol. II (1932) of the 'Istituzioni e monumenti dell'arte musicale italiana' *(Andrea e Giovanni Gabrieli e la musica strumentale in S. Marco).* Other reprints are by K. von Winterfeld in *Johannes Gabrieli und sein Zeitalter* (1834; 2 vols. and a vol. of music supplements); by Proske, Griesbacher, Commer, etc. (motets); by J. von Wasielewski in *Geschichte der Instrumental-Musik im 16. Jahrhundert* (1878) and in the music supplement of *Die Violine im 17. Jahrhundert* (2nd ed., 1905); by Riemann in *Alte Kammermusik (Sonata a 3 violini* and *Canzona a 8);* by Torchi in 'L'arte musicale in Italia' (vols. II, III); by H. Besseler in Blume's *Das Chorwerk* (3 motets); by A. Schering in *Geschichte der Musik in Beispielen* (Nos. 130, 148); by G. Tagliapietra in 'Antologia di musica antica e moderna per piano' (vol. II, 1931); by A. Einstein *(Canzoni a 4,* 1933, Schott Antiqua; motet in the music supplement of his *Short History of Music,* No. 19, 1938; madrigal in

The Golden Age of the Madrigal, 1942, No. 6); by W. Danckert *(Sonata a 3 violini,* 1934); by Davison and Apel in *Historical Anthology of Music* (vol. I, Nos. 157, 173), by F. Stein *(Sonata pian e forte,* 1931), by J. F. Williamson (motet, 1932); by G. W. Woodworth (3 motets, 1950-52); by Bongiovanni (5 motets, 1954). Hans David has adapted several of Gabrieli's *canzoni* for modern use. A complete edition of Gabrieli's works was begun in 1956 (vol. I, 25 Motets, ed. by Denis Arnold).—Cf. A. G. Ritter. *Geschichte des Orgelspiels im 14.-18. Jahrhundert* (1884: revised by Frotscher, 1933): H. Leichtentritt, *Geschichte der Motette* (1908); O. Kinkeldey, *Orgel und Klavier in der Musik des 16. Jahrhunderts* (1910); G. S. Bedbrook, *The Genius of Giovanni Gabrieli,* in 'Music Review' (Jan., 1947); G. Reese, *Music in the Renaissance* (N. Y., 1954); H. J. Moser, *Heinrich Schütz* (2nd ed., 1954).

Gabrielli, Caterina, famous soprano; b. Rome, Nov. 12, 1730; d. there, Feb. 16, 1796. She was known under the nickname 'La Coghetta' (that is, little cook, for her father was a cook in a Roman nobleman's palace). She made her début at Venice in 1754; then went to Vienna, where she was hailed as a 'new star on the musical firmament' and was coached by Gluck and Metastasio; she sang many parts in the Vienna productions of Gluck's operas, up to 1761; made triumphant appearances in Milan, Turin, and Naples; then went to Russia (with Traetta) and sang in St. Petersburg with unfailing acclaim (1772-74). In 1775 she made her first appearance in London, arousing admiration among the cognoscenti; but she was also the object of common gossip related to her notoriously loose morals. She returned to Italy after only one season in London, and eventually settled in Rome.

Gabrielli, Nicolò, Italian composer; b. Naples, Feb. 21, 1814; d. Paris, June 14, 1891. He was a pupil of Buonamici, Conti, Donizetti, and Zingarelli at Naples Cons.; from 1854 he lived in Paris. He wrote 22 operas and 60 ballets, produced at Naples, Paris, and Vienna.

Gabrilovitch (gah-brē-loh'-vitch), **Ossip Solomonovitch,** notable pianist and conductor; b. St. Petersburg, Feb. 7, 1878; d. Detroit, Sept. 14, 1936. From 1888-94 he was a pupil at the St. Petersburg Cons., studying piano with A. Rubinstein and composition with Navrátil, Liadov, and Glazunov; graduated as winner of the Rubinstein Prize, and then spent two years (1894-6) in Vienna studying with Leschetizky; then toured Germany, Austria, Russia, France, and England. His first American tour (début Carnegie Hall, N. Y., Nov. 12, 1900) was eminently successful, as were his subsequent visits (1901, 1906, 1909, 1914, 1915, 1916). During the season 1912-13 he gave in Europe a series of six historical concerts illustrating the development of the piano concerto from Bach to the present day; on his American tour in 1914-15 he repeated the entire series in several of the larger cities, meeting with an enthusiastic reception. On Oct. 6, 1909, he married the contralto Clara Clemens (daughter of Mark Twain), with whom he frequently appeared in joint recitals. He conducted orchestral concerts in New York in 1917, and was appointed conductor of the Detroit Symph. Orch. in 1918. In 1928 and the following years he also conducted the Philadelphia Orch., sharing the baton with Leopold Stokowski, but still retaining his Detroit position.—Cf. Clara Clemens, *My Husband Gabrilovitch* (N. Y., 1938).

Gabussi, Giulio Cesare, Italian composer; b. Bologna, 1555; d. Milan, Sept. 12, 1611. He was a pupil of Costanzo Porta; in 1582 he was called to Milan as singer and composer at the cathedral, and remained in that post until his death, with the exception of a brief stay in Poland in the service of Sigismund III (1604). He publ. 2 books of madrigals for 5 voices (Venice, 1580 and 1598); motets for 4 and 5 voices (Venice, 1586); *Te Deum* for 4 voices (Milan, 1598), etc. He was one of the first composers whose works in the Ambrosian ritual (litanies, etc.) appeared in print.

Gade, Axel Willy, Danish violinist, son of Niels Gade; b. Copenhagen, May 28, 1860; d. there, Nov. 9, 1921. He studied with his father and with Joachim; was active in Copenhagen as theater conductor and teacher. He wrote a violin concerto and an opera, *Venezias Nat* (Copenhagen, Jan. 18, 1919).

Gade, Jacob, Danish composer; b. Vejle, Nov. 29, 1879. He studied violin; was a member of the New York Symph. Orch. (1919-21); then returned to Copenhagen and was active there as conductor. Among his light compositions, *Jalousie* (1925) attained great popularity. He also wrote several symphonic poems (*Den sidste Viking, Leda and the Swan,* etc.).

Gade (gah'-dĕ), **Niels (Wilhelm)**, Danish composer and founder of the modern Scandinavian school of composition; b. Copenhagen, Feb. 22, 1817; d. there, Dec. 21, 1890. He was the only child of an instrument maker; studied violin with a member of the Danish court band, and gave a concert in Copenhagen at the age of 16. He then took composition lessons with A. P. Berggreen; soon he began writing songs to German texts. At the age of 23, he wrote his overture, *Nachklänge von Ossian,* for which he was awarded a prize by the Copenhagen Musical Society. The work was performed in Copenhagen on Nov. 19, 1841, and was soon published; this early overture remained the most popular work of Gade, and endured in the orchestral repertory for many years. His next important work was a symphony in C minor. Gade sent this to Mendelssohn in Leipzig, and Mendelssohn performed it at a Gewandhaus concert on March 2, 1843. Subsequently Gade received a government stipend for travel in Germany; he went to Leipzig, where Mendelssohn accepted him as a friend, and let him conduct some of the Gewandhaus concerts. Gade's talent flourished in the congenial atmosphere; an ardent admirer of Mendelssohn and Schumann, he adopted a Romantic style in the prevalent Germanic spirit. After Mendelssohn's death in 1847, Gade assumed the conductorship of the Gewandhaus concerts, but on the outbreak of the Schleswig-Holstein war in the spring of 1848, he returned to Copenhagen. In 1850, he became chief conductor of the Copenhagen Musical Society; also was a co-founder of the Copenhagen Cons. in 1866. He visited Birmingham in 1876 to conduct his cantata, *Zion,* at the festival there. In the same year, the Danish government granted him a life pension. In Denmark, his position as a prime musician was by then fully established; but he was accepted in Germany, too, as a master composer. Despite his adherence to the Germanic school, he infused elements of national Danish melodies into his works, and so led the way to further development of Scandinavian music. — Works: 8 symphonies (1841-71); overtures: *Nachklänge von Ossian* (1840), *Im Hochlande* (1844), *Hamlet* (1861), *Michelangelo* (1861); violin concerto (1880); cantatas: *Comala* (1846), *Elverskud* (1853), *The Holy Night* (1861), *At Sunset* (1865), *Kalanus* (1871), *Zion* (1873), *The Crusaders* (1873), *The Mountain Thrall* (1873), *Gefion* (1875), *Psyche* (1882), *Der Strom,* after Goethe's *Mahomet* (1889); chamber music: 2 string quintets, string octet, piano trio, string quartet, 3 violin sonatas, *Folk Dance* for violin and piano, *Pictures of the Orient* for violin and piano; for piano solo: *Spring Flowers, Aquarelles* (3 books), *Idylls,* 4 *Fantastic Pieces, Folk Dance,* Sonata in E minor; also 21 vocal works for various combinations, in the style of folksongs; incidental music for a play, *Mariotta;* ballet music, etc.—Cf. Gade's autobiographical *Aufzeichnungen und Briefe,* ed. by Dagmar Gade (German transl., Basel 1893); C. Rubner, *Niels Wilhelm Gade, in Remembrance of the Centenary of His Birth,* in the 'Mus. Quarterly' (Jan., 1917); C. Kjerulf, *Niels Wilhelm Gade* (Copenhagen, 1917); W. Behrend, *Gade* (Leipzig, 1917); W. Behrend, *Minder om Gade* (Copenhagen, 1930).

Gadsby, Henry Robert, English music teacher; b. Hackney, London, Dec. 15, 1842; d. Putney, Nov. 11, 1907. He was a chorister at St. Paul's from 1849 to 1858; organist at St. Peter's, Brockley; in 1884 succeeded Hullah as prof. of harmony at Queen's College, London; was prof. at the Guildhall School of Music from its foundation (1880) until his death. He wrote 3 symphonies, several overtures, songs, etc.

Gadski, Johanna (Emilia Agnes), German soprano; b. Anclam, June 15, 1872; d. Berlin, Feb. 22, 1932. She was trained from her eighth year by Frau Schroeder-Chaloupka at Stettin. She made her début at Kroll's Theater, Berlin, in May, 1889, as Undine in Lortzing's opera; sang during the summers of 1889-93 at Kroll's, winters in Mainz, Stettin, Bremen, and Berlin. She went on a concert tour of Holland in 1894. On March 1, 1895, she made her American début as Elsa with the Damrosch Opera Co., winning instant favor; during the next three seasons she continued there, singing Elisabeth, Eva, Sieglinde, and creating the role of Hester Prynne in Walter Damrosch's opera *The Scarlet Letter* (1896); from 1898-1904 she was a member of the Metropolitan Opera Company and became one of the prime favorites through her superb interpretation of Brünnhilde and Isolde. From 1899 to 1901 she was at Covent Garden and in 1899 sang Eva at Bayreuth. From 1904-6 she made two transcontinental tours of the U. S., establishing her reputation as a great lieder singer. In 1907 she returned to the Metropolitan, where she sang every season until 1917. She then sang 4 more seasons at Covent Garden; toured the U. S. again as concert singer; returned to the stage with the German Grand Opera Co. (1929-31). On Nov. 11, 1892, she was married to Lieutenant Hans

Tauscher. In addition to a voice of great volume and purity, she had a stately presence and histrionic ability.

Gadzhibekov, Uzeir, Azerbaidzhan composer; b. Agdzhabedy, near Shusha, Sept. 17, 1885; d. Baku, Nov. 23, 1948. He studied in Shusha; then lived in Baku, where he produced his first opera on a native subject, *Leyly and Medzhnun* (Jan. 25, 1908). His comic opera *Arshin Mal Alan* (Baku, Oct. 25, 1913) had numerous performances; another opera *Kyor-Oglu* (*A Blind Man's Son*) was produced at the Azerbaidzhan Festival in Moscow (Jan. 13, 1937).

Gaforio (or **Gafori, Gafuri, Gaffurio**), **Franchino** (Latinized **Franchinus Gafurius;** often simply **Franchinus**), celebrated Italian theorist; b. Lodi, Jan. 14, 1451; d. Milan, June 24, 1522. He studied theology and music; lived in Mantua, Verona, and Genoa (1477); he formed an intimacy with the Doge Prospero Adorno (then in exile) and fled with him to Naples. There he met various distinguished musicians, and held public disputation with Johannes Tinctoris, Guarnier, and Hycart. The plague and the Turkish invasion compelled him to return to Lodi; he was choirmaster at Monticello for 3 years, made a short visit to Bergamo in 1483, and in 1484 became singer and master of the boys in Milan cathedral, and first singer in the choir of Duke Lodovico Sforza. In 1485 he also founded a music school at Milan, which prospered.—Writings: *Theoricum opus harmonicae disciplinae* (Naples, 1480; 2nd ed., Milan, 1492, as *Theorica musicae;* facsimile reprint, Rome, 1934); *Practica musicae Franchino Gaforio Laudensis . . . in IV libris* (Milan 1496; his magnum opus, with examples of mensural notation in block-print; other editions, 1497, 1502, 1508, 1512, 1522); *Angelicum ac divinum opus musicae materna lingua scriptum* (Milan, 1496); *De harmonia musicorum instrumentorum* (Milan, 1518, with biography of Gaforio by P. Meleguli); *Apologia Franchini Gafurii musici adversus Ioannem Spatarium et complices musicos Bononienses* (Turin, 1520; concerning the controversy between the Milanese and Bolognese schools). A complete ed. of his compositions, ed. by Lutz Finscher, was begun in 1955. —Cf. E. Prätorius, *Die Mensuraltheorie des Franchino Gaforio und der folgenden Zeit bis zur Mitte des 16. Jahrhunderts* (Leipzig, 1905); G. Cesari, *Musica e Musicisti alla corte Sforzesca,* in 'Rivista Musicale Italiana' (1922; with reprints); P. Hirsch, *Bibliographie der musikalischen Drucke des Franchino Gaforio* in 'J. Wolf-Festschrift' (1929); G. Zampieri, *Franchino Gaforio* (Milan, 1925); A. Careta, *Franchino Gafurio* (Lodi, 1951).

Gagliano (gahl-yăh'-noh), the name of a family of famous violin makers at Naples. **Alessandro,** who worked from 1695 to 1725, was a pupil of Stradivari, and he, as well as his sons **Nicola** (1700-40) and **Gennaro** (1710-50), followed largely the Stradivari model. The instruments of **Ferdinando Gagliano** (1736-81), a son of Nicola, exhibit less skillful workmanship than those of the older members of the family.

Gagliano, Marco da, Italian opera composer; b. Gagliano, c. 1575; d. Florence, Feb. 24, 1642. He was a pupil of L. Bati; 1608, became maestro at S. Lorenzo in Florence; 1609 canon, and 1614 Apostolic Protonotary. In 1607 he founded the 'Accademia degli Elevati.' Gagliano was among the first composers to write in the 'stile rappresentativo,' which he developed further by ornamentation. His compositions include: *Dafne,* 'opera in musica' (his most important work; first played at Mantua, 1608; published in Florence, 1608, and reprinted in shortened form by R. Eitner in vol. 10 of the 'Publikationen älterer Musikwerke'); *La Flora,* opera (with Peri; Florence, 1628); *Due Messe, a 4, 5* (Florence, 1594); 6 vols. of madrigals *a 5* (1602-17); *Sacrae cantiones* (*I a 6,* with a Mass, 1614; *II a 1-6,* with basso continuo, 1622); *Musiche a 1, 2, e 3 voci* (Venice, 1615, with continuo); etc.—Reprints have been publ. by L. Torchi in vol. IV of 'L'Arte Musicale in Italia' (2 madrigals and a Benedictus) and in 'Eleganti canzoni ed arie italiane del secolo XVII' (aria from *La Flora*); by L. Landshoff in 'Alte Meister des Bel Canto' (vol. I; sacred duet, *Vergine chiara*); and by A. Schering in *Geschichte der Musik in Beispielen* (No. 175).—Cf. L. Piccianti, *Marco da Gagliano,* in the 'Gazzetta Musical di Milano' (1843-44); E. Vogel, *Marco da Gagliano Zur Geschichte des florentiner Musiklebens 1570-1650,* in 'Vierteljahrsschrift für Musikwissenschaft' (1899); A. Solerti, *Musica alla Corte Medicea* (1905).

Gagnebin (gah-n'yā-băn'), **Henri,** composer and pedagogue; b. Liège, March 13, 1886, of Swiss parents. He studied in Lausanne, Berlin, Geneva, and at the Schola Cantorum, Paris, with Vincent d'Indy and Vierne; was organist as the Église de la

Rédemption, Paris (1910-16) and at St. Jean, Lausanne (1916-25); prof. at the Cons. in Lausanne; since 1926 director of the Cons. of Geneva. He has written 2 symphonies, several string quartets, 2 oratorios; publ. a book, *Entretien sur la musique* (Geneva, 1943).

Gailhard (gah-yahr'), **Pierre,** French operatic singer; b. Toulouse, August 1, 1848; d. Paris, Oct. 12, 1918. He began his vocal studies in his native city, and entered the Paris Cons. in 1866. After one year of study under Révial he graduated in 1867, winning three first prizes. He made his début at Opéra-Comique (Dec. 4, 1867) as Falstaff in Thomas' *Songe d'une nuit d'été;* on Nov. 3, 1871, he made his début at the Opéra as Mephistopheles in Gounod's *Faust.* At the height of his powers and success he gave up the stage when, in 1884, he accepted, jointly with M. Ritt, the management of the famous institution; on the appointment of M. Bertrand as successor to Ritt, in 1892, he retired, but joined Bertrand the following year as co-director; after the latter's death, in 1899, he remained sole director till 1907. His administration was remarkably successful, considering both the novelties produced and the engagement of new singers (Melba, Eames, Bréval, Caron, Ackté, Alvarez, Saléza, Renaud, the two de Reszkes, etc.). Against violent opposition he introduced, and maintained in the repertory, *Lohengrin* (1895), *Walküre* (1893), *Tannhäuser* (1895; the first perf. after the notorious fiasco of 1861), *Meistersinger* (1897), *Siegfried* (1902).—His son, **André Gailhard** (b. Paris, June 29, 1885), composed the operas *Amaryllis* (Toulouse, 1906), *Le Sortilège* (Paris, 1913), and *La Bataille* (Paris, 1931), and the cantata *La Sirène.*

Gaillard, Marius-François, French composer and conductor; b. Paris, Oct. 13, 1900. He studied with Diémer and Leroux at the Paris Cons. He began his career as a pianist; then started a series of symphonic concerts in Paris, which he conducted from 1928 till 1949. He traveled all over the world, collecting materials of primitive music. His compositions follow a neo-Impressionist trend.—Works: for the stage: *La Danse pendant le Festin* (1924) and *Détresse,* ballet (1932); 3 symphonies; *Guyanes,* symph. suite (1925); *Images d'Epinal,* for piano and orch. (1929); violin sonata (1923); string trio (1935); *Sonate baroque* for violin and piano (1950); *Minutes du Monde,* suite for cello and piano (1952); string quartet (1954); many songs and piano pieces.

Gaines, Samuel Richards, American vocal teacher; b. Detroit, April 23, 1869; d. Boston, Oct. 8, 1945. He studied composition with Goetschius and Chadwick; was active as vocal teacher, organist, choir dir., and lecturer in various cities; lived in Boston and Wellesley, Mass., as teacher. He won several national and international prizes for his choral compositions.

Gaisser, Dom **Ugo Atanasio (Josef Anton),** German music scholar; b. Aitrach, Dec. 1, 1853; d. Monastery Ettal, March 26, 1919. He specialized in the study of Byzantine church-music, on which he wrote a number of important studies.—Principal writings: *Guido von Arezzo oder St. Mauro* (Aix-la-Chapelle, 1889); review of Jacobsthal's *Die chromatische Alteration im liturgischen Gesange der abendländischen Kirche,* in 'Revue Bénédictine de Maredsous' (1897-98); *Le Système musicale de l'Église grecque d'après la tradition,* in 'Rassegna Gregoriana' (Rome, 1901); *Les 'hirmoi' de pâques dans l'office grec* (Rome, 1905); *Die Antiphon 'Nativitas tua' und ihr griechisches Vorbild,* in the 'Riemann-Festschrift' (1909).

Gaito (gī'-toh), **Constantino,** Argentine composer; b. Buenos Aires, Aug. 3, 1878; d. there, Dec. 14, 1945. He studied in Naples with Platania; lived in Buenos Aires as a teacher; wrote the operas (all produced at Buenos Aires) *Caio Petronio* (Sept. 2, 1919), *Flor de Nieve* (Aug. 3, 1922), *Ollantay* (July 23, 1926), and *La Sangre de las Guitarras* (Aug. 17, 1932); the ballet, *La Flor de Irupé* (Buenos Aires, July 17, 1929); oratorios, songs, and piano pieces.

Gál, Hans, composer and music scholar; b. Brunn, near Vienna, Aug. 5, 1890. He studied at the Univ. of Vienna with Mandyczewski and Guido Adler; obtained his degree of *Dr. phil.* in 1913 with the thesis *Die Stileigentümlichkeiten des jungen Beethoven* (publ. in the 'Studien zur Musikwissenschaft,' 1916); awarded the Austrian state prize for composition in 1915; prize of the City of Vienna, 1926; Schubert Centennial Prize, 1928; from 1919-29 he lectured at the Vienna Univ.; then went to Germany; was director of the Cons. of Mainz from 1929-33; returned to Vienna in 1933; after the advent of the Nazi government was compelled to leave Vienna in 1938, and settled in Edinburgh, where he became lecturer on music at the Univ., while continuing to compose. He has written works in every genre: the operas *Der Arzt der Sobeide*

(Breslau, 1919), *Die heilige Ente* (Düsseldorf, April 29, 1923), *Das Lied der Nacht* (Breslau, April 24, 1926), *Der Zauberspiegel* (Breslau, 1930; also as an orchestral suite), *Die beiden Klaas* (1933); 2 symphonies (1928; 1949); *A Pickwickian Overture* (1939); violin concerto (1933); 2 string quartets (1916; 1929); string trio (1931); piano quartet (1915); piano trio (1948); violin sonata (1921); numerous choral works, sacred and secular. He publ. a manual, *Anleitung zum Partiturlesen* (Vienna, 1923; in English under the title *Directions for score-reading,* 1924).

Galajikian (gah-lah-jē'-kē-ahn), **Florence Grandland,** American pianist and composer; b. Maywood, Ill., July 29, 1900. She graduated from Northwestern Univ. School of Music (Mus. Bac., 1918) and Chicago Musical College (1920); was a pupil of Oldberg, Lutkin, Beecher, Goldmark, and Noelte; toured extensively as a concert pianist, wrote a *Symphonic Intermezzo* for orch. (NBC award, 4th prize, 1932; perf. by NBC Symph., May 8, 1932); *Tragic Overture* (Chicago, Jan. 24, 1937); *Transitions,* ballet (Chicago, 1937); choral works; etc.

Galamian, Ivan, eminent violinist and pedagogue; b. Tahrig, Persia, Feb. 5, 1906; studied at the Moscow Philh. Institute, graduating in 1922; then with Lucien Capet in Paris (1923-24); played in recitals in France and Germany; emigrated to the U. S. in 1930, and was appointed to the staff of the Curtis Institute of Music in Philadelphia and the Juilliard School in New York; also teaches privately.

Galandia. See **Garlandia.**

Galeotti, Cesare, Italian composer; b. Pietrasanta, June 5, 1872; d. Paris, Feb. 19, 1929. He studied piano with Sgambati and composition with Guiraud at the Paris Cons. Several of his symphonic works were performed in Paris; his opera *Anton* was staged at La Scala, Milan (Feb. 17, 1900). Another opera, *Dorisse,* was first given in Brussels (April 18, 1910).

Gales, Weston, American organist and conductor; b. Elizabeth, N. J., Nov. 5, 1877; d. Portsmouth, N. H., Oct. 21, 1939. He studied composition with Horatio Parker at Yale Univ. and organ with Gaston-Marie Déthier in N. Y.; held various posts as church organist in Boston; then took additional instruction with Widor and Vierne in Paris. Returning to America, he was active as choral conductor. In 1914, he organized the Detroit Symph. Orch., of which he was conductor until 1917; then conducted the Wagnerian Opera Co. and the State Symph. Orch. in N. Y. (1924); was guest conductor with various European operatic organizations; returned to the U. S. in 1933.

Galilei, Vincenzo, celebrated writer on music, father of Galileo Galilei, the astronomer; b. Florence, c. 1520; d. there, June (buried July 2), 1591. A skilful lutenist and violinist, and student of ancient Greek theory, he was a prominent member of the artistic circle meeting at Count Bardi's house; his compositions for solo voice with lute accompaniment may be regarded as the starting-point of the monody successfully cultivated by Peri, Caccini, etc., the founders of the 'opera in musica.' A zealous advocate of Grecian simplicity, in contrast with contrapuntal complexity, he publ. a *Dialogo . . . della musica antica et della moderna* (Florence, 1581; to the 2nd ed. [1602] is appended a polemical *Discorso . . . intorno all' opere di messer Gioseffo Zarlino da Chioggia,* which had appeared separately in 1589); and *Fronimo. Dialogo . . .* (in 2 parts: Venice, 1568 and 1569; new ed. 1584); all of considerable historical interest.—Vol. IV of 'Istituzioni e Monumenti dell' Arte Musicale Italiana' (Milan, 1934), ed. by F. Fano, is devoted entirely to Galilei; it contains a large selection of music reprints from his *Fronimo. Dialogo . . .* (lute transcriptions by Galilei and original compositions), *Libro d'intavolatura di Liuto* (1584), *Il Secondo Libro de Madrigali a 4 et a 5 voci* (1587), and a 4 part *Cantilena,* together with biographical details, list of works, notes about extant MSS, reprints, transcriptions, etc. His *Contrapunti a due voci* (1584) was edited by Louise Read (Northampton, Mass., Smith College Music Archives, vol. VIII, 1947).—Cf. Otto Fleissner, *Die Madrigale Vincenzo Galileis und sein Dialogo della musica antica e moderna* (Munich, 1922).

Galin (găh-lăn'), **Pierre,** French music pedagogue; b. Samatan, Gers, 1786; d. Bordeaux, Aug. 31, 1821. He was teacher of mathematics at the Lycée in Bordeaux, and conceived the idea of simplifying music instruction by a method which he termed the 'Méloplaste' and explained in his work *Exposition d'une nouvelle méthode pour l' enseignement de la musique* (1818; 2nd and 3rd eds., 1824 and 1831). The method attracted attention, and was energetically promoted by Chevé (q. v.).

Galindo, Blas, Mexican Indian composer; b. San Gabriel, Jalisco, Feb. 3, 1910. He studied music with Chávez, Rolón, and Huízar in Mexico, and later with Copland at the Berkshire Music Center. In his music Galindo stresses native elements, but has also written in neo-classical contrapuntal style.—Works: ballets, *La mulata de Córdoba* (1939), *La creación del hombre* (1939), *Feria* (1947), *La Manda* (1951); *Impresión campestre,* for orch. (1940); *Tres Preludios para ballet* (Mexico, Nov. 23, 1940); piano concerto (Mexico, May 15, 1942); *Obra para orquesta mexicana* (with native instruments, 1938); *Sones Mariachi* (1940); suite for violin and cello (1933); sextet for wind instruments (1941); violin sonata (1945); *Sinfonia* (1956; first prize, shared with Camargo Guarnieri, at the Caracas Festival, 1957); also choral works and piano music.—Cf. C. Chávez, *Blas Galindo* ('Nuestra Musica,' Mexico, March, 1946).

Galitzin (gah-lē'-tsēn), **Nicolas Borissovitch,** a Russian prince; b. 1794; d. (murdered) Kursk, Oct. 23, 1866. Beethoven dedicated an overture (op. 124) and 3 quartets (opp. 127, 130, 132) to him; he also corresponded with Beethoven until the latter's death. Galitzin was an amateur of fine attainments, and a skilful cellist; in 1820 he founded a Philharmonic Society at St. Petersburg.

Gallay, Jules, French cellist and music publisher; b. Saint-Quentin, 1822; d. Paris, Nov. 2, 1897. A wealthy amateur, he became a good cello-player and a zealous student of *lutherie* in all its forms; publ. the following valuable pamphlets: *Les Instruments à archet à l'Exposition universelle de 1867* (Paris, 1867); *Les Luthiers italiens aux XVIIe et XVIIIe siècles, nouvelle édition du 'Parfait Luthier' (la Chélonomie) de l'abbé Sibire, suivie de notes sur les maîtres des diverses écoles* (Paris, 1869); a reprint of du Manoir's *Le Mariage de la musique avec la danse,* with historical introduction (Paris, 1870); *Les Instruments des écoles italiennes, catalogue précédé d'une introduction et suivi de notes sur les principaux maîtres* (Paris, 1872). As a member of the jury at Vienna, 1873, he edited the *Rapport sur les Instruments de Musique à archet* (Paris, 1875).

Gallenberg, Wenzel Robert, Austrian composer; b. Vienna, Dec. 28, 1783; d. Rome, March 13, 1839. He studied under Albrechtsberger; in 1803 he married Countess Giulietta Guicciardi (to whom Beethoven dedicated his Sonata Op. 27, No. 2). In Naples, shortly thereafter, he made the acquaintance of the impresario Barbaja; wrote numerous successful ballets for him, and from 1821-3 was his partner when Barbaja was director of opera in Vienna. He attempted the management of the Kärntnerthor-Theater in 1829, but failed, and was obliged to return to Italy, rejoining Barbaja. He wrote about 50 ballets; a sonata, marches, fantasies, etc., for piano. On one of his themes Beethoven wrote a set of variations.

Gallès, José, Catalan organist and composer; b. Casteltersol, Catalonia, 1761; d. Vich, 1836. He was for many years organist of the Vich Cathedral; was ordained priest. J. Nin published his piano sonata (1800) in the collection *17 Sonates et pièces anciennes d'auteurs espagnols* (Paris, 1929).

Galli, Amintore, Italian composer; b. Talamello, near Rimini, Oct. 12, 1845; d. Rimini, Dec. 8, 1919. He was a pupil of Mazzucato at Milan Cons. (1862-7); was musical editor for the publisher Sonzogno, and critic of 'Il Secolo'; later edited 'Il Teatro Illustrato' and 'Musica Popolare.'—Works: the operas *Il Corno d'oro* (Turin, Aug. 30, 1876) and *David* (Milan, Nov. 12, 1904); oratorios *Espiazione* (after Moore's *Paradise and Peri*) and *Cristo al Golgota;* Goethe's *Totentanz* for baritone solo and orch.; string quintet, etc. He published *Musica e Musicisti dal secolo X sino ai nostri giorni* (1871); *Estetica della musica* (1900); *Storia e teoria del sistema musicale* (1901); *Piccolo lessico di musica* (1902).

Galliard, Johann Ernst, German oboist; b. Zell, Hanover, 1687; d. London, 1749. He was a pupil of A. Steffani at Hanover. A skilful oboist, he went to London, 1706, as chamber musician to Prince George of Denmark; succeeded Draghi as organist at Somerset House; and composed industriously; 1713, played in the Queen's Theatre orch.; 1717 till 1736, engaged in writing music for the stage productions at Covent Garden and Lincoln's Inn Fields. He last appeared as an oboist probably in 1722. Besides the music to numerous plays, masques, and pantomimes, he wrote cantatas, a Te Deum, a Jubilate, anthems, soli for flute and cello, etc.; set to music the *Morning Hymn of Adam and Eve,* from Milton's *Paradise Lost,* and Hughes' opera *Calypso and Telemachus* (1712). He also made some translations.—Cf. 'Dictionary of National Biography' (London, 1921-22).

Gallico, Paolo, composer and pianist; b. Trieste, May 13, 1868; d. New York, July 6, 1955. At the age of 15, he gave a recital at Trieste; then studied at the Vienna Cons. under Julius Epstein, graduating at 18 with highest honors. After successful concerts in Italy, Austria, Russia, Germany, etc., he settled in New York in 1892 as concert pianist and teacher; toured the U. S. frequently as pianist in recitals and as soloist with the principal orchestras. He won the $500 prize of the National Federation of Music Clubs in 1921 with his dramatic oratorio *The Apocalypse* (performed by the New York Oratorio Society, Nov. 22, 1922). His symphonic episode, *Euphorion,* was performed in Los Angeles (April 6, 1923), New York, and Detroit; his sextet was performed by the Society of the Friends of Music, N. Y. He also wrote an opera, *Harlekin,* piano pieces, and songs. His son, Paul Gallico, is a well known writer.

Galli-Curci, Amelita, brilliant coloratura-soprano; b. Milan, Nov. 18, 1882. She studied in Milan and intended to be a pianist; graduated in 1903 from the Milan Cons., winning the 1st prize. She never took regular voice lessons, but acquired an excellent vocal technique by devising a unique method of self-instruction, listening to recordings of her own voice. She received advice from Mascagni and William Thorner. She made her début in Rome as Gilda (1909), then sang in various opera houses in Italy and in South America (1910). She continued her successful career as an opera singer in Europe until 1915; after the entry of Italy into the war, she went to America; made a sensationally successful début with the Chicago Opera Co. as Gilda (Nov. 18, 1916); she appeared in N. Y. with the Chicago Opera as Dinorah (Jan. 28, 1918). She made her first appearance with the Metropolitan Opera as Violetta (Nov. 14, 1920); remained as a member of the Metropolitan until 1930; then gave concert recitals; eventually retired to California, living near Beverly Hills. She was married twice: to the painter, Luigi Curci (1910; divorced 1920), and to Homer Samuels, her accompanist.—Cf. E. LeMassena, *Galli-Curci's Life of Song* (N. Y., 1945).

Gallignani (găhl-lēn-yăh'-nē), **Giuseppe,** Italian composer and writer on music; b. Faenza, Jan. 9, 1851; d. (suicide) Milan, Dec. 14, 1923. He studied at the Milan Cons.; was then choir leader at the Milan Cathedral; edited the periodical 'Musica Sacra' (1886-94); was director of the Parma Cons. (1891-97); from 1897, director of the Milan Cons. He produced the operas *Il grillo del focolare* (Genoa, Jan. 27, 1873), *Atala* (Milan, March 30, 1876), and *Nestorio* (Milan, March 31, 1888), which were unsuccessful; but his church music was greatly appreciated (particularly his Requiem for King Umberto I).

Galli-Marié, Célestine (*née* Marié de l'Isle), French dramatic mezzo-soprano; b. Paris, Nov., 1840; d. Vence, near Nice, Sept. 22, 1905. Her father, an opera-singer, was her only teacher. She made her début at Strasbourg (1859); sang in Toulouse (1860); and in Lisbon (1861). She sang the *Bohemian Girl* at Rouen (1862) with such success that she was immediately engaged for the Paris Opéra-Comique; made her début there (1862) as Serpina in *La Serva padrona.* She created the roles of Mignon (1866) and Carmen (1875).

Gallo, Fortune, impresario; b. Torremaggiore, Italy, May 9, 1878. He studied the piano in Italy; migrated to the U.S. in 1895; first directed the tours of a number of famous bands (1901-9), then founded the San Carlo Opera Co. (1909); in 1920, brought Anna Pavlova and her Ballet Russe to America; 1923, organized an opera season in Havana, Cuba; 1925, was director of the tour of Eleanora Duse; 1926 built and operated the Gallo Theater; 1928, made a film version of *Pagliacci;* presented performances of operetta in New York and elsewhere.

Gallon, Jean, French composer and pedagogue; b. Paris, June 25, 1878. He studied piano with Diémer and theory with Lavignac and Lenepveu at the Paris Cons.; was chorus director of the Société des Concerts du Conservatoire (1906-14) and at the Paris Opéra (1909-14). From 1919 till 1949 he taught harmony at the Paris Cons. Among his pupils were Robert Casadesus, Marcel Delannoy, Henri Dutilleux, Olivier Messiaen, and Jean Rivier. He published harmony exercises for use at the Cons.; with his brother Noël Gallon, he composed several pieces of theater music, among them a ballet, *Hansli le Bossu* (1914); also some chamber music and songs.

Gallon, Noël, French composer; brother of Jean Gallon; b. Paris, Sept. 11, 1891; studied piano with I. Philipp and Risler, theory with Caussade and Lenepveu at the

Paris Cons., and also with Rabaud. In 1910 he received 1st Prix de Rome. From 1920, on the faculty of the Paris Cons. as instructor in solfège, counterpoint, and fugue. As a composer, he was influenced by his brother, who was his first tutor in music; with him he wrote a ballet, *Hansli le Bossu* (1914); his own works comprise a few symph. pieces; suite for flute and piano (1921); quintet for horn and strings (1953); teaching pieces.

Gallus, Jacobus, a native of Carniola, whose real name was **Jacob Händl** (or **Handl, Hähnel**), composer; b. Reifnitz, July 31, 1550; d. Prague, July 24, 1591. He was Kapellmeister to the Bishop of Olmütz, later imperial Kapellmeister at Prague. As a composer he was an eminent contemporary of Palestrina and Lassus. Besides detached pieces in Bodenschatz's *Florilegium Portense,* Proske's *Musica divina,* and collections of Schöberlein, Zahn, Becker, Rochlitz, and others, many printed works are extant. They include: *Missae* (8, 7, 6, 5, 4 voices; 1 vol. reprinted in the 'Denkmäler der Tonkunst in Österreich' 1934, ed. by P. Pisk); *Opus Musicum harmoniarum, 4, 5, 6, 8 et plurium vocum* (1st part, 1586; 2nd and 3rd, 1587; 4th, 1590; reprinted in its entirety in 'Denkmäler der Tonkunst in Österreich,' vols. XII, 1, XV, XX, 1, XXIV, and XXVI, ed. by J. Mantuani and E. Bezecny); *Moralia 5, 6 et 8 vocibus concinnata* (1586); a Latin Passion (1587); *Epicedion harmonicum* (1589); *Harmoniae variae 4 vocum* (1591); *Harmoniarum moralium* (1589-90). After Gallus' death the following were printed: *Sacrae cantiones de praecipuis festis 4-8 et plurium vocum* (1597); *Motettae quae praestant omnes* (1610). Handel borrowed Gallus' well known motet, *Ecce quomodo moritur justus,* for his *Funeral Anthem.*—Cf. Paul Pisk, *Das Parodieverfahren in den Messen von Gallus* in 'Studien zur Musikwissenschaft,' V; Peter Wagner, *Geschichte der Messe* (p. 330 ff.); Th. Kroyer, in 'Zeitschrift für Musikwissenschaft,' I (p. 146 ff.).

Gallus, Johannes (Jean le Cocq, Maître Jean, Mestre Jhan), a Flemish contrapuntist; d. c. 1543. He was maestro di cappella to Duke Ercole of Ferrara in 1534 and 1541. Many pieces were publ. in collections and in a vol. of motets printed by Scotto (1543). He was long confused with Jhan Gero.

Galpin, Rev. **Francis William,** English writer on music; b. Dorchester, Dorset, Dec. 25, 1858; d. Richmond, Surrey, Dec. 30, 1945. He graduated with classical honors from Trinity College, Cambridge, B. A. (1882), M. A. (1885); received his music education from Dr. Garrett and Sterndale Bennett; held various posts as vicar and canon (1891-1921); Hon. Freeman Worshipful Company of Musicians (1905); wrote many articles on the viola pomposa and other old instruments in 'Music & Letters' and 'Monthly Mus. Record' (1930-33). A Galpin Society was formed in London in 1946 with the object of bringing together all those interested in the history of European instruments and to commemorate the pioneer work of Galpin; it published (at irregular intervals) 'The Galpin Society Journal.'—Books: *Descriptive Catalogue of the European Instruments in the Metropolitan Museum of Art, N. Y.* (1902); *The Musical Instruments of the American Indians of the North West Coast* (1903); *Notes on the Roman Hydraulus* (1904); *The Evolution of the Sackbut* (1907); *Old English Instruments of Music* (1910; new ed., London, 1932); *A Textbook of European Musical Instruments* (London and N. Y., 1937); *The Music of the Sumerians, Babylonians and Assyrians* (1937); *The Music of Electricity* (1938). Galpin was the editor of the revised and augmented ed. of Stainer's *Music of the Bible* (1913).

Galston, Gottfried, pianist; b. Vienna, Aug. 31, 1879; d. St. Louis, April 2, 1950. He was a pupil of Leschetizky in Vienna, and of Jadassohn and Reinecke at the Leipzig Cons.; 1903-7, taught at Stern's Cons. in Berlin. On his extended concert tours he proved himself a player of keen analytical powers and intellectual grasp; 1902, toured Australia; then Germany, France, and Russia; 1912-13, America; toured Russia 11 times (last, in 1926); 1921-27, lived in Berlin; returned to the U.S. in 1927 and settled in St. Louis. He published a *Studienbuch* (1909; 3rd ed., Munich, 1920; analytical notes to a series of 5 historical recitals).

Galuppi, Baldassare, surnamed **Il Buranello** from the island of Burano, near Venice, on which he was born; Italian composer; b. Oct. 18, 1706; d. Venice, Jan. 3, 1785. He studied with his father, a barber and violin player; in 1722 he brought out at Vicenza an opera, *La fede nell' incostanza,* which attracted attention to his talent; he then studied under Lotti in Venice, and in 1729 produced his opera *Dorinda.* He cultivated comic opera with such success as to earn the title of 'padre dell' opera buffa.' He was also a distinguished player on the harpsichord. In 1740 he was appointed 'maestro del coro' at the Ospizio dei Mendicanti; 1741, visited London and in 1743, St. Petersburg; 1748, returned to Venice, where he was 2nd maestro at San Marco; 1762-4, principal maestro there. From 1766-8 he acted as maestro to the Russian court; taught many Russian singers and composers; Bortniansky, who later followed him to Venice, was one of his pupils. Galuppi wrote a prodigious amount of music, some 112 operas and 20 oratorios; also sacred music and 12 harpsichord sonatas.—Reprints: Selected arias from his opera *Il filosofo di campagna,* ed. by G. F. Malipiero in 'Raccolta nazionale delle musiche italiane' (Nos. 54-58; Milan, 1919); aria from his opera *Il mondo della luna* in A. della Corte's 'Piccola antologia settecentesca' ('Raccolta nazionale delle musiche italiane', Milan, 1925); Missa in C ed. by H. Bäuerle (Leipzig, 1927); 2 sonatas in vol. V. of E. Pauer's 'Alte Meister'; 2 sonatas ed. by J. Henius (N. Y., 1909, 1912); 2 sonatas (together with a free transcription of the latter), in G. Tagliapietra's 'Antologia di musica antica e moderna' (Milan, 1932).—Cf. A. Wotquenne, *Baldassare Galuppi* in 'Rivista Musicale Italiana' (1899); F. Piovano, *Baldassare Galuppi, Note bio-bibliografiche,* in 'Rivista Musicale Italiana' XIII, 4 (1906), XIV, 2 (1907), XV, 2 (1908); A. della Corte, *L'opera comica italiana nel 1700* (1923); F. Raabe, *Baldassare Galuppi als Instrumentalkomponist* (Munich, 1926); F. Torrefranca, in 'Rivista Musicale Italiana' XVIII; Ch. Van den Borren, in 'Rivista Musicale Italiana' XXX; W. Bollert, *Die Buffo-Opern Baldassare Galuppis* (Bottrop, 1935); A. della Corte, *Baldassare Galuppi; profilo critico* (Siena, 1948).

Gamba, Pierino, precocious Italian conductor; b. Rome, Sept. 16, 1937. He conducted in Italy at the age of 8; made a European tour; also appeared in South America and the U. S.

Gamucci, Baldassare, Italian music scholar; b. Florence, Dec. 14, 1822; d. there, Jan. 8, 1892. He was a pupil of C. Fortini (piano) and L. Picchianti (composition). In 1849 he founded the 'Società Corale del Carmine,' which later became the 'Scuola Corale' of the Music Institute at Florence. He publ. *Intorno alla vita ed alle opere di Luigi Cherubini* (Florence, 1869); *Rudimenti di lettura musicale* (several times reprinted); many essays for the reports of the Institute; also contributions to various music journals.

Ganche, Edouard, French writer on music, b. Baulon (Ille-et-Vilaine), Oct. 13, 1880; d. Lyon, May 31, 1945. He studied with Imbert, Henry Expert, and others in Paris. He devoted his life to the study of Chopin and published *La vie de Chopin dans son œuvre* (1909); *Frédéric Chopin, sa vie et ses œuvres* (1913). He was also the editor of the Oxford edition of Chopin's works (1932).

Gandolfi, Riccardo (Cristoforo Daniele Diomede), Italian composer; b. Voghera, Piedmont, Feb. 16, 1839; d. Florence, Feb. 5, 1920. He was a pupil of Carlo Conti at the Naples Cons., then of Mabellini in Florence; appointed inspector of studies at the 'Real Istituto di Musica' in Florence (1869); chief librarian in 1889; pensioned in 1912. He began as a dramatic composer, then turned to the larger instrumental and vocal forms, and finally abandoned composition altogether, devoting himself to historical studies, which won him distinction.—Compositions: operas *Aldina* (Milan, 1863), *Il Paggio* (Turin, 1865), *Il Conte di Monreale* (Genoa, 1872), *Caterina di Guisa* (Catania, 1872); *Messa da Requiem;* a cantata, *Il Battesimo di S. Cecilia;* several overtures; chamber music.—Writings: *Sulla relazione della poesia colla musica melodrammatica* (1868); *Una riparazione a proposito di Francesco Landino* (1888); *Commemorazioni di W. A. Mozart* (1891); *Illustrazioni di alcuni cimeli concernanti l'arte musicale in Firenze* (1892); *Appunti di storia musicale* (1893); *Onoranze Fiorentine a G. Rossini* (1902).

Gange, Fraser, distinguished baritone; b. Dundee, Scotland, June 17, 1886. He studied there with his father; later was a pupil of Amy Sherwin in London; made his début as a basso at the age of 16 in Queen's Hall, London; toured England, Scotland, Australia, and New Zealand twice; taught singing at the Royal Academy of Music, London; 1923, came to the U.S. and made his American début at Aeolian Hall, N. Y. (Jan. 18, 1924); from 1932-46 prof. of voice at the Juilliard Summer School, N.Y.; since 1934 at Peabody Cons., Baltimore. His repertory includes 40 oratorios and more than 2000 songs; he presented in Baltimore a concert of songs on his 70th birthday.

Ganne, Louis Gaston, French composer; b. Buxières-les-Mines, Allier, April 5, 1862; d. Paris, July 13, 1923. He was a pupil of Th. Dubois, Massenet, and C. Franck at the Paris Cons. He was conductor of the balls at the Opéra, and at the municipal Casino at Monte Carlo; wrote successful comic operas, ballets, and divertissements. —Operas: *Rabelais* (Paris, Oct. 25, 1892); *Les Colles des femmes* (Paris, 1893); *Les Saltimbanques* (Paris, Dec. 30, 1899); *Miss Bouton d'Or* (*Paris,* Oct. 14, 1902); *Hans le joueur de flûte* (his most successful operetta; Monte Carlo, April 14, 1906); *Les Ailes* (Paris, Sept. 1, 1910); the ballets *Phryné, Au Japon* (1903; very successful), *Kermesse flamande* (1917); many orchestral dances, of which *La Czarine* and *La Tsigane* became favorites, and patriotic tunes, *La Marche Lorraine* and *Le Père de la Victoire,* immensely popular in France; about 150 piano pieces.

Gänsbacher, Johann, Austrian composer; b. Sterzing, Tyrol, May 8, 1778; d. Vienna, July 13, 1844. He studied with Abbé Vogler and Albrechtsberger in Vienna (1801); visited Prague, and Dresden and Leipzig; then resumed study under Vogler, at Darmstadt (Weber and Meyerbeer were his fellow-pupils). With Weber, he went to Mannheim and Heidelberg, and rejoined him later in Prague. In Vienna Gänsbacher also met Beethoven. He served in the war of 1813, led a roving life for several years, and finally (1823) settled in Vienna as Kapellmeister of the cathedral. Of his 216 compositions (Masses, requiems, etc., orchestral works, piano pieces, songs, etc.), only a small part has been published.—Cf. C. Fischnaler, *Johann Gänsbacher* (Innsbruck, 1878).

Gantvoort, Arnold Johann, Dutch musician; b. Amsterdam, Dec. 6, 1857; d. Los Angeles, Calif., May 18, 1937. He came to America in 1876; gave private lessons, and taught in various colleges; in 1894, head of dept. for preparing public school music teachers, College of Music, Cincinnati. He published *Familiar Talks on the History of Music* (N. Y. 1913), and a series of public school music readers.

Ganz, Rudolph, distinguished pianist and conductor; b. Zürich, Switzerland, Feb. 24, 1877. He was a pupil of R. Freund (piano) and F. Hegar (cello) in Zürich (1893-6); of C. Eschmann-Dumur (piano) and Ch. Blanchet (composition) in Lausanne; 1897-98, of F. Blumer (piano) in Strasbourg; 1899 of F. Busoni (piano) and H. Urban (composition) in Berlin. Although he had played occasionally in public (chiefly as cellist) since his twelfth year, his début as a mature artist took place with the Berlin Philh. Orch., Dec. 1899 (Beethoven's E♭ and Chopin's E minor concertos); in May of the following year the same orch. perf. his first Symphony; from 1900-05 he was head of the piano department at the Chicago Musical College, succeeding A. Friedheim; 1905-8, made successful tours of the U. S. and Canada; 1908-11, tours of Europe, playing 16 different piano concertos; after 1912 he divided his time touring in Europe and America; 1921-27, conductor of the St. Louis Symphony; 1938-49 conductor of the N. Y. Philh. Young People's Concerts; guest conductor at the Lewisohn Stadium (N. Y.), Hollywood Bowl, etc.; 1929-54, director of Chicago Musical College. He played for the first time many important works by contemporary composers (Busoni, Ravel, Bartók, Debussy, Dohnányi, d'Indy, Loeffler, Korngold etc.), and revived older works that had fallen into undeserved neglect. In July, 1900, he married Mary Forrest, an American concert singer.—Works: Symphony in E; *Animal Pictures,* a suite of 20 pieces for orch. (Detroit, Jan. 19, 1933, composer conducting); *Konzertstück* for piano and orch. (Chicago Symph. Orch., Feb. 20, 1941, composer soloist); *Variations on a Theme by Brahms,* for piano; several choruses for male voices; about 200 songs.

Ganz, Wilhelm, German pianist; b. Mainz, Nov. 6, 1833; d. London, Sept. 12, 1914. He studied music with his father, Adolf Ganz (b. Mainz, Oct. 14, 1796; d. London, Jan. 11, 1870) and with Anschütz. He followed his father to London, where he appeared as pianist; in 1856 he became accompanist to Jenny Lind. In 1879 he organized the Ganz Orchestral Concerts in London, and gave 1st London performances of works by Liszt and Berlioz; many celebrated artists (Saint-Saëns, Pachmann, etc.) made their English débuts at his concerts. After the discontinuance of his enterprise, in 1883, he devoted himself mainly to teaching. He publ. *Memories of a Musician* (London, 1913).

Garaguly, Carl, Hungarian-Swedish violinist and conductor; b. Budapest, Dec. 28, 1900. He studied with Hubay and in Berlin with Marteau. From 1923-30, he was concertmaster of the Göteborg Orch.; then violinist in the Stockholm Orch. In 1941, he was appointed conductor of the Stockholm Orch.; also formed a string quartet there.

Garat (găh-răh'), **Pierre-Jean,** famous French concert-singer and teacher; b. Bor-

deaux, April 27, 1762; d. Paris, March 1, 1823. His remarkable talent was discovered early, and he studied theory and singing with Franz Beck in Bordeaux; his father wished him to become a lawyer, and sent him to the Univ. of Paris in 1782. However, Garat neglected his legal studies, and aided by the Count d'Artois, he was introduced to Marie Antoinette, whose special favor he enjoyed up to the Revolution. He earned his livelihood as a concert-singer; accompanied Rode, in 1792, to Rouen, where he gave numerous concerts before being arrested as a suspect during the Terror; subsequently he went to Hamburg; he returned to Paris in 1794, and sang (1795) at the Feydeau Concerts, where his triumphs speedily procured him a professorship of singing in the newly established Conservatory. For 20 years longer, his fine tenor-baritone voice, trained to perfection, made him the foremost singer on the French concert stage. Nourrit, Levasseur, and Ponchard were his pupils.—Cf. Paul Lafond, *Garat* (Paris, 1899); B. Miall, *Pierre Garat, Singer and Exquisite; his Life and his World* (London, 1913); Isidoro de Fagoaga, *Pedro Garat, el Orfeo de Francia* (Buenos Aires, 1948).

Garaudé (găh-roh-dā'), **Alexis de,** French singer and composer; b. Nancy, March 21, 1779; d. Paris, March 23, 1852. He studied theory under Cambini and Reicha, and singing under Crescentini and Garat; was a singer in the royal choir from 1808-30 and prof. of singing in the Cons. from 1816-41. He publ. 3 string quintets, many ensemble pieces for violin, flute, clarinet, and cello, sonatas and variations for piano, a solemn Mass, vocalises, arias, duets, and songs; also a *Méthode de chant* (1809, op. 25; 2nd revised ed. as *Méthode complète de chant,* op. 40); *Solfège, ou méthode de musique; Méthode complète de piano;* and *L'Harmonie rendue facile, ou théorie pratique de cette science* (1835). He also arranged the vocal scores of Meyerbeer's *Le prophète* and other operas.

Garay, Narciso, Panamanian violinist, composer, and diplomat; b. Panama, June 12, 1879; d. there, March 27, 1953. He studied at the Brussels Cons., graduating with a Premier Prix; later he attended courses at the Schola Cantorum in Paris. He published a violin sonata and a valuable treatise on Panamanian folk music, *Tradiciones y Cantares de Panama* (1930). He also occupied diplomatic posts and at one time was Minister of Foreign Affairs.

Garbousova, Raya, cellist; b. Tiflis, Russia, Sept. 25, 1906; studied at the Cons. there (graduated 1923), and later with Hugo Becker, Felix Salmond, and Pablo Casals. After many concerts in Europe, she settled in the U. S. (1927); appeared with major American orchestras.

Garbuzov, Nikolai Alexandrovitch, eminent Russian musicologist; b. Moscow, July 5, 1880; studied at the Moscow Cons. In 1921 he was appointed a director of the State Institute of Musicology; published numerous essays dealing with acoustics and musical theory.

Garcia, Eugénie (*née* Mayer), wife and pupil of Manuel; French soprano; b. Paris, 1818; d. there, Aug. 12, 1880. She sang for several years in Italian theaters, then (1840) at the Opéra-Comique, Paris; 1842 in London; finally, separated from her husband, she lived as a singing teacher in Paris.

García, Francisco Javier (Padre García, called in Rome 'lo Spagnoletto'), Spanish composer of church music; b. Nalda, 1731; d. Saragossa, Feb. 26, 1809. He lived for some years in Rome as a student and singing teacher; in 1756 he was appointed maestro at Saragossa cathedral. His works show a marked contrast to the fugal style prevailing before, being more natural and simple. Wrote an oratorio, *Tobia* (1773); the operas *La Finta Schiava* (Rome, 1754), *Pompeo Magno in Armenia* (Rome, 1755), *La Pupilla* (Rome, 1755), *Lo Scultore deluso* (Rome, 1756); Masses and motets, chiefly in 8 parts. His most noted pupil was Caterina Gabrielli.

Garcia, Manuel del Popolo Vicente, famous tenor, singing teacher, and dramatic composer; b. Seville, Jan. 22, 1775; d. Paris, June 9, 1832. A chorister in Seville cathedral at 6, he was taught by Ripa and Almarcha, and at 17 was already well known as a singer, composer, and conductor. After singing in Cadiz, Madrid, and Málaga, he proceeded (1806) to Paris, and sang to enthusiastic audiences at the Théâtre-Italien; in 1809, at his benefit, he sang his own monodrama *El poeta calculista* with extraordinary success. From 1811 to 1816 he was in Italy. On his return to Paris, his disgust at the machinations of Catalani, the manageress of the Théâtre-Italien, caused him to break his engagement and go to London (1817), where his triumphs were repeated. From 1819-24 he was again the idol of the Parisians at the Théâtre-Italien sang as first tenor at the Royal Opera, in London (1824) and in 1825 embarked for New York with his wife, his son Manuel, and his daughter, Maria (Malibran), and the distinguished artists Crivelli *fils*, Angrisani, Barbieri, and de Rosich; from Nov. 29, 1825, to Sept. 30, 1826, they gave 79 performances at the Park and Bowery Theaters in New York; the troupe then spent 18 months in Mexico. Garcia returned to Paris, and devoted himself to teaching and composition. His operas, all forgotten, comprise 17 in Spanish, 18 in Italian, and 8 in French, besides a number never performed, and numerous ballets. A preeminently successful teacher, his 2 daughters, Mmes. Malibran and Pauline Viardot-Garcia, Nourrit, Rimbault, and Favelli were a few of his best pupils.—See the 'Mus. Quarterly,' July, 1915 to Jan., 1916: *Pauline Viardot-Garcia to Julius Rietz* (letters).

Garcia, Manuel Patricio Rodriguez, distinguished Spanish vocal teacher, son of preceding; b. Madrid, March 17, 1805; d. London, July 1, 1906 (aged 101). He was intended for a stage singer; in 1825 went to New York with his father, but in 1829 adopted the vocation of a singing teacher (in Paris) with conspicuous success. An exponent of his father's method, he also carefully investigated the functions of the vocal organs; invented the laryngoscope, for which the Königsberg Univ. made him *Dr. phil.* In 1840 he sent to the Academy a *Mémoire sur la voix humaine,* a statement of the conclusions arrived at by various investigators, with his own comments. He was appointed prof. at the Paris Cons. in 1847, but resigned in 1848 to accept a similar position in the London Royal Academy of Music, where he taught uninterruptedly from Nov. 10, 1848 until 1895. Among Garcia's pupils were his wife, Eugénie, Jenny Lind, Henriette Nissen, and Stockhausen. His *Traité complet de l'art du chant* was publ. in 1847; English ed., 1870; revised ed. by Garcia's grandson Albert Garcia, as *Garcia's Treatise on the Art of Singing* (London, 1924). He also publ. (in English) a manual, *Hints on Singing* (London, 1894).—Cf. M. Sterling Mackinlay, *Garcia, the Centenarian, and His Time* (Edinburgh, 1908); J. M. Levien, *The Garcia Family* (London, 1932).

Garcia, Maria-Felicitá. See **Malibran.**

Garcia, Pauline Viardot-. See **Viardot-Garcia.**

García Estrada, Juan Agustín, Argentine composer; b. Buenos Aires, Nov. 8, 1895. He studied law; then went to Paris, where he took lessons in composition with Jacques Ibert. Returning to Argentina, he became a municipal judge. Among his works are *Tres aires argentinos* for orch. (Paris, Feb. 28, 1929); an opera, *La Cuarterona* (Buenos Aires, Aug. 10, 1951); a number of songs.

Gardano, Antonio, one of the earliest and most celebrated Italian music-printers; b. c. 1500; d. Venice, 1571. From 1537 he reprinted many current publications as well as important novelties, and compositions of his own, e.g., *Motetti del frutto* (1538) and *Canzoni franzese* (1539). His works also appeared in various collections of the time. After 1571 his sons Alessandro and Angelo carried on the business till 1575, when they separated; the former later set up for himself in Rome (1582-91), while the latter remained in Venice till his death (1610); his heirs continued publishing under his name till 1677.

Garden, Mary, celebrated operatic soprano; b. Aberdeen, Scotland, Feb. 20, 1877. She came to the United States as a child; lived in Hartford, Conn., and then in Chicago. She studied violin and piano; in 1893 she began the study of singing with Mrs. Robinson Duff in Chicago; in 1895 she went to Paris, where she studied with many teachers (Sbriglia, Bouhy, Trabadello, Mathilde Marchesi, and Lucien Fugère). Her funds, provided by a wealthy patron, were soon depleted, and Sybil Sanderson, the American soprano living in Paris, came to her aid and introduced her to Albert Carré, director of the Opéra-Comique. Her operatic début was made under dramatic circumstances on April 10, 1900, when the singer who performed the title role of Charpentier's *Louise* at the Opéra-Comique was taken ill during the performance, and Mary Garden took her place. She revealed herself not only as a singer of exceptional ability, but also as a skilful actress. She subsequently sang in several operas of the general repertory; also created the role of Diane in Pierné's opera *La Fille de Tabarin* (Opéra-Comique, Feb. 20, 1901). A historic turning point in her career was reached when she was selected to sing Mélisande in the world première of Debussy's opera (Opéra-Comique, April 30, 1902). She also became the center of a raging controversy, when Maurice Maeterlinck, the author of the drama, voiced his violent objection to her assignment (his choice for the role was

Georgette Leblanc, his common-law wife), and pointedly refused to have anything to do with the production. Mary Garden won warm praise from the critics for her musicianship, despite the handicap of her American-accented French. She remained a member of the Opéra-Comique; also sang at the Grand Opéra, and at Monte Carlo. She made her American début as Thaïs at the Manhattan Opera House, N. Y. (Nov. 25, 1907), and presented there the first American performance of *Pelléas et Mélisande* (Feb. 19, 1908). She also undertook the performance of *Salome* at its 2nd production in N. Y. (Jan. 27, 1909). In 1910 she joined the Chicago Opera Co.; she became its impresario in the season 1921-22, during which the losses mounted to about one million dollars. She sang in the first American performances of Honegger's *Judith* (Chicago, Jan. 27, 1927), Alfano's *Resurrection* (1930), and Hamilton Forrest's *Camille* (1930), an opera she specially commissioned. After 1930 she made sporadic appearances in opera and concerts; in 1935, she gave master classes in opera at the Chicago Musical College; acted as technical adviser for opera sequences in motion pictures in Hollywood; in 1939 she returned to Scotland; made a lecture tour in the U. S. in 1947. With Louis Biancolli she wrote a book of memoirs, *Mary Garden's Story* (N. Y., 1951).

Gardes, Roger, French tenor; b. Paris, March 4, 1922; he sang in the chorus of the Opéra-Comique in 1950; in 1954, won first Grand Prix at a contest of tenors in Cannes, and was engaged as soloist at the Opéra-Comique (début, Aug. 14, 1954, in *La Bohème);* subsequently sang tenor roles in *Lakmé, Eugene Onegin, Les Pêcheurs de Perles,* etc.

Gardiner, Henry Balfour, English composer; b. London, Nov. 7, 1877; d. Salisbury, England, June 28, 1950. He was a pupil of Iwan Knorr in Frankfurt; taught singing for a short time in Winchester, but then devoted his whole time to composition. Among his works are a *Phantasy* for orch.; *English Dance;* a symphony in D; a string quintet; *News from Wydah,* for soli, chorus, and orch.; piano pieces; songs. His most successful piece was *Shepherd Fennel's Dance* (Promenade Concert, London, 1911).

Gardiner, William, British writer on music; b. Leicester, March 15, 1770; d. there, Nov. 16, 1853. His father, a hosiery manufacturer, was an amateur musician from whom he acquired rudiments of music. During his travels on the continent on his father's business he gathered materials for a collection *Sacred Melodies* (1812-15) adapted to English words from works by Mozart, Haydn, and Beethoven. His book *The Music of Nature* (London, 1832) enjoyed a certain vogue; he also published memoirs, *Music and Friends, or Pleasant Recollections of a Dilettante* (3 vols.; I-II, London, 1838; III, 1853); *Sights in Italy, with some Account of the Present State of Music and the Sister Arts in that Country* (London, 1847).

Gardner, John Linton, English composer; b. Manchester, March 2, 1917. He studied organ at Exeter College, Oxford, with Sir Hugh Allen, Ernest Walker, R. O. Morris, and Thomas Armstrong (Mus. B., 1939). In 1940 he joined the Royal Air Force. From 1946-54 he was opera coach at Covent Garden; in 1955 appointed instructor at Morley College. He began to compose at the age of 16; progressed rapidly, and soon acquired a solid technique of composition; he is adept equally in theater music, instrumental writing, and vocal works. His style is characteristically fluent and devoid of attempts at experimentation; modernistic devices are used sparingly.—Works: for the stage: incidental music to *Masque of Satan* (1936), *The Stoker's Dream* (1937), Marlowe's *Tamburlaine* (1951), *King Lear* (1953), *Hamlet* (1953); opera *The Moon and Sixpence,* after Somerset Maugham (commissioned by Sadler's Wells Opera, and produced there, May 24, 1957); for orch.: *Concert Overture* (1934), *Suite for School Orchestra* (1935), *Serenade* for oboe, piano, and strings (1937), *Chorale Prelude* for string orch. (1944), 1st symphony (Cheltenham, July 5, 1951), *A Scots Overture* (London, Aug. 16, 1954); chamber music: *Comic March* for 2 cellos and piano (1935), *4 Miniatures* for clarinet and piano (1935), *Rhapsody* for oboe and string quartet (1935), string quartet (1938), *Theme and Variations* for 2 trumpets, horn, and trombone (1951), *Romanza* for trombone and piano (1951), sonata for oboe and piano (1953); sacred and secular choruses; 2 piano sonatas and other piano pieces; songs.

Gardner, Samuel, violinist and composer, b. Elizabethgrad, Russia, Aug. 25, 1891. He came early to the U. S. and studied violin with Felix Winternitz and Franz Kneisel, composition with Goetschius, and later with Loeffler in Boston. He was a member of the Kneisel String Quartet (1914), of the Chicago Symph. Orch. (1915-16), the Elshuco

Trio (1916-17), etc. He wrote *Country Moods,* for string orch. (Staten Island Civic Symph., Dec. 10, 1946); a tone poem, *Broadway* (Boston Symph., April 18, 1930, composer conducting); violin pieces (5 Preludes, *Slovak, Romance, Jazzetto, From the Rockies, Coquetterie, Old Virginia, From the Canebrake,* etc.); piano quintet (1925). His early string quartet was given the Pulitzer Prize (1918).

Gariel, Edoardo, Mexican music pedagogue; b. Monterey, Aug. 5, 1860; d. Mexico City, March 15, 1923. He studied with Marmontel in Paris; upon his return to Mexico he occupied various teaching jobs (1887-1908). In 1915 he visited the U. S. From 1916 to his death he was in charge of the School of Theater Arts in Mexico City. He published *Chopin, Consideraciones sobre algunas de sus obras y la manera de interpretarlas* (1895); *Nuevo Sistema de Armoniá basado en cuatro acordes fundamentales* (1916; also in English as *A New System of Harmony based on four fundamental chords*).

Garlandia, Johannes de (sometimes called Johannes de Garlandia the Elder to distinguish him from a hypothetical Joh. Garlandia the Younger, proposed by H. Riemann on rather suppositional grounds), 13th-century writer on mathematics, theology, and alchemy; b. England, c. 1195. He studied at Oxford, then went to Paris; joined the Crusade against the Albigenses; quently returned to Paris; was probably still living in 1272. He is the supposed author of several tracts on music, among them the *De Musica Mensurabili Positio,* a valuable treatise on mensural music, 2 versions of which were printed by Coussemaker in his 'Scriptores,' vol. I. There are altogether 4 works printed under his name in Gerbert and Coussemaker.—Cf. H. Riemann, *Geschichte der Musiktheorie im 9.-19. Jahrhundert* (1898); L. J. Paetow, *The Life and Works of John of Garland,* in 'Memoirs' of the Univ. of Calif., IV, 2 (1927); G. Reese, *Music in the Middle Ages,* chap. 10 (N. Y., 1940).

Garratt, Percival, English composer, b. Little Tew Grange, May 21, 1877; d. London, April 16, 1953. He studied in Vienna, Berlin, and at Marlborough College; toured Europe and South Africa; was accompanist of Clara Butt and Elman; composed many piano pieces (*Pageant Piece, Rondel, Night Piece, Arabesque, Helston Furry Dance, Mock Antiques,* and others); *Cherry-stones,* a children's musical play; *A Cartload of Villains,* 3-act pantomime.

Garreta, Juli, Catalan composer; b. San Feliu, March 12, 1875; d. there, Dec. 2, 1925. Entirely self-taught, he learned piano and composition. He wrote a great number of 'sardanas' (the Catalan national dance); a friendship with Casals stimulated several larger works; his *Impressions symphoniques* for string orch. were performed in Barcelona on Oct. 29, 1907. His *Suite Empordanesa* for orch. received first prize at the Catalan Festival in 1920. He also wrote a cello sonata, a piano sonata, and a piano quartet.

Garrett, George Mursell, English composer and organist; b. Winchester, June 8, 1834; d. Cambridge, April 8, 1897. A pupil of Elvey and Wesley, he was assistant organist at Winchester cathedral (1851-4); organist of Madras cathedral (1854-6); of St. John's College, Cambridge (1857); organist to the Univ., 1873, succeeding Hopkins. He took the degree of Mus. Bac. 1857, Mus. Doc. 1867; also received the degree of M.A. *propter merita* in 1878. From 1883, he was Univ. Lecturer on harmony and counterpoint; also Examiner in Music of Cambridge Univ. He wrote 5 cantatas, 4 services, and other church music.

Garrison, Mabel, American coloratura soprano; b. Baltimore, Md., April 24, 1886. She was a pupil of W. E. Heimendahl and P. Minetti at Peabody Cons. (1909-11); then of O. Saenger in New York (1912-14), and of H. Witherspoon (1916). She made her début as Filina (*Mignon*) in Boston, April 18, 1912; was a member of Metropolitan Opera from 1914-22; made a world tour; in 1933 she taught singing at Smith College; then retired.

Gaspari, Gaetano, Italian historiographer; b. Bologna, March 15, 1807; d. there, March 31, 1881. He entered the Liceo Musicale in 1820; took 1st prize in composition in 1827. He served as maestro di cappella at various churches; then devoted himself to historical research.—Writings: *Ricerche, documenti e memorie risguardanti la storia dell' arte musicale in Bologna* (1867); *Ragguagli sulla cappella musicale della Basilica di S. Petronio in Bologna* (1869); *Memorie dell'arte musicale in Bologna al XVI secolo* (1875), etc.—Cf. F. Parisini, *Elogio funebre del professore Gaetano Gaspari* (1882).

Gasparini, Francesco, Italian composer; b. Camaiore, n. Lucca, March 5, 1668; d. Rome, March 22, 1727. He was a pupil of Corelli and Pasquini in Rome, where he taught for a time; about 1700, became director of music at the Cons. della Pietà, Venice. In 1725 he was appointed maestro di cappella at the Lateran, Rome. Between 1702-23 he produced about 50 operas at Venice, Rome, and Vienna, with great success; he also wrote Masses, motets, cantatas, psalms, oratorios, etc. His chief work was a method of thorough-bass playing, *L'Armonico pratico al cimbalo* (Venice, 1708; 7th ed., 1802), used in Italy for nearly a hundred years. His most famous pupil was Benedetto Marcello.—Cf. E. Celani, *Il primo amore di P. Metastasio,* in 'Rivista Musicale Italiana' (1904; pp. 243-51).

Gasparo da Salò (family-name **Bertolotti**), Italian instrument maker; b. Salò, 1540 (baptized May 20); d. Brescia, April (buried 14th), 1609. He came to Brescia in 1562, and settled there as a maker of viols, viole da gamba, and contrabass viols, which gained much celebrity; his violins were less valued. His pupils were his eldest son, Francesco; Giovanni Paolo Maggini, and Giacomo Lafranchini. Dragonetti's favorite double-bass was an altered 'viola contrabassa' of Gasparo's.—Cf. V. M. Rhò-Guerriero, *Gasparo da Salò* (Rome, 1892); P. Bettoni, *Gasparo da Salò e l'invenzione del violino,* in 'Commentari del Ateneo di Brescia' (1901); M. Butturini, *Gasparo da Salò: Studio critico* (Salò, 1901); G. Bignami, *Gasparo da Salò,* in 'Musica d'oggi' (Feb., 1940); A. M. Mucchi, *Gasparo da Salò* (Milan, 1940).

Gasperini, Guido, Italian musicologist; b. Florence, June 7, 1865; d. Naples, Feb. 20, 1942. He was a pupil of Tacchinardi (composition) and Sbolci (cello); from 1902, librarian and teacher of music history at Parma Cons.; later, librarian at Naples Cons.; in 1908 he founded the 'Associazione dei Musicologi Italiani,' one of the main purposes of which was the examination and cataloguing of all books on music and musical MSS in the Italian libraries; in 1909 it was affiliated with the 'Internationale Musik-Gesellschaft' (as its Italian branch), and began the issue of a quarterly 'Catalogo delle opere musicali . . . esistenti . . . nelle biblioteche e negli archivi pubblici e privati d'Italia.' Gasperini's writings are *Storia della musica* (1899; a series of 10 lectures); *Dell' arte d'interpretare la scrittura della musica vocale del Cinquecento* (1902); *Storia della Semiografia musicale* (1905); *I caratteri peculiari del Melodramma italiano* (1913); *Musicisti alla Corte dei Farnesi; L'Art Italien avant Palestrina,* in 'Mercure musical' II, 6-8; *Noterelle su due liutiste al servizio di Casa Farnese* (1923).

Gassmann, Florian Leopold, composer; b. Brüx, Bohemia, May 3, 1729; d. Vienna, Jan. 20, 1774. His father insisted on his adopting a commercial career, but Gassmann ran away from home and made his way to Padre Martini in Bologna, who taught him music for two years. After living at Venice in the service of Count Leonardo Veneri, he was called by Emperor Francis I (1764) to Vienna as theater conductor; in 1772, he succeeded Reutter as court Kapellmeister and founded the 'Tonkünstler-Societät' for the relief of the widows and orphans of musicians. He wrote 7 serious operas, 14 comic operas, 3 stage cantatas, and a quantity of orchestral and chamber music (which was highly esteemed by Mozart). His symphony in B minor was edited by Karl Geiringer (Univ. Ed., 1933). A selection of his sacred music was publ. in the 'Denkmäler der Tonkunst in Österreich' XLV. His most famous pupil, Salieri, was the teacher of Gassmann's two daughters, Maria Anna and Maria Theresia (Rosenbaum), distinguished opera-singers in Vienna.—Cf. R. Haas and G. Donath, *F. L. Gassmann als Opernkomponist,* in 'Studien zur Musikwissenschaft' (1914); F. Kosch, *F. L. Gassmann als Kirchenkomponist,* ibid. (1927); E. Girach, *F. L. Gassmann* (Reichenberg, 1930).

Gassner, Ferdinand Simon, Austrian violinist; b. Vienna, Jan. 6, 1798; d. Karlsruhe, Feb. 25, 1851. In 1816, he was violinist at the National Theater in Mainz; 1818, he became music director at Giessen Univ., which in 1819 made him *Dr. phil.* and lecturer on music. In 1826 he joined the court orch. at Darmstadt, and afterwards became teacher of singing and chorusmaster at the theater. From 1822-35 he publ. the 'Musikalischer Hausfreund' at Mainz; he edited (1841-5) the 'Zeitschrift für Deutschlands Musikvereine und Dilettanten.' He wrote *Partiturkenntniss, ein Leitfaden zum Selbstunterricht* (1838; French ed. 1851, as *Traité de la partition*); and *Dirigent und Ripienist* (1846); contributed to the Supplement of Schilling's 'Universallexikon der Tonkunst' (1842) and edited an abridgment of the entire work (1849). He composed 2 operas, several ballets, a cantata, songs, etc.

Gast, Peter. See **Köselitz, Heinrich.**

Gastaldon, Stanislas, Italian composer; b. Turin, April 7, 1861; d. Florence, March 7, 1939. At the age of 17 he began publishing nocturnes, *ballabili,* and other pieces for piano; was, for a number of years, music critic for the 'Nuovo Giornale' in Florence. He wrote about 300 songs, some of which have had great vogue *(La musica proibita; Ti vorrei rapire; Frate Anselmo; Donna Clara);* he was fairly successful with his operas *Mala Pasqua* (Rome, 1890), *Il Pater* (Milan, 1894), *Stellina* (Florence, 1905), *Il Sonetto di Dante* (Genoa, 1909), *Il Reuccio di Caprilana* (Turin, 1913). He also wrote marches for military band; a piano fantasia, *La dansa delle scimmie;* etc.

Gastinel, Léon-Gustave-Cyprien, French composer; born Villers, near Auxonne, Aug. 13, 1823; d. Fresnes-les-Rurgis, Oct. 20, 1906. He was a pupil of Halévy at the Paris Cons., taking 1st Grand Prix de Rome for his cantata *Vélasquez* in 1846. A successful composer of operas, he produced *Le Miroir* (1853), *L'Opéra aux fenêtres* (1857), *Titus et Bérénice* (1860), *Le Buisson vert* (1861), *Le Barde* (Nice, 1896), and the ballet *Le Rêve* (Opéra, 1890) besides other stage works: *La Kermesse, Eutatès, Ourania,* and *La Tulipe bleue;* also 4 oratorios and 3 solemn Masses, orchestral compositions, chamber music, choruses, etc.—Cf. F. Boisson, *Léon Gastinel* (1893).

Gastoldi, Giovanni Giacomo, Italian composer; b. Caravaggio; d. 1622. In 1581 he was a singer at the court of Mantua; contributed part of the score of *Idropica,* produced in Mantua on June 2, 1608. In 1609 he was maestro di cappella in Milan. A number of his works were publ.: 4 books of madrigals (1588, 1589, 1592, 1602); 4 books of canzonette (1592, 1595, 1596, 1597); many individual pieces are reproduced in contemporary collections. His 'balletti' (dance songs) are remarkable for their rhythmic vigor in folksong style.—Cf. A. Einstein, *The Italian Madrigal,* vol. III (Princeton, 1949). See also Denis Arnold's article on Gastoldi in 'Die Musik in Geschichte und Gegenwart.'

Gastoué (găh-stwā'), **Amédée,** French music scholar; b. Paris, March 13, 1873; d. there, June 1, 1943. He studied piano and harmony with A. Deslandres (1890), harmony with Lavignac (1891), then organ with Guilmant and counterpoint and composition with Magnard. From 1896-1905 he was editor of 'Revue du Chant Grégorien'; in 1897 he began to contribute to the 'Tribune de St.-Gervais,' became editor in 1904, and, on the death of Ch. Bordes (1909), editor-in-chief and director; he was prof. of Gregorian Chant at the Schola Cantorum from its foundation (1896); also music critic of 'La Semaine Littéraire' in 1905; he was appointed advisory member of the Pontifical Commission of the Editio Vaticana in 1905. For many years he was organist and maître de chapelle at St.-Jean-Baptiste-de-Belleville, Paris, where he also gave concerts of works in the Palestrina style; lecturer at the Catholic Univ. and École des Hautes Etudes Sociales; Laureate of the Académie des Inscriptions et Belles-Lettres; commander of the Order of St. Gregory the Great; 1925, member of the Académie des Beaux Arts.—Writings: *Cours théorique et pratique de plain-chant romain grégorien* (1904); *Historie du chant liturgique à Paris* (vol. I: *Des Origines à la fin des temps carolingiens,* 1904); *Les Origines du chant romain, l'antiphonaire grégorien* (1907); *Catalogue des manuscrits de musique byzantine de la Bibliothèque Nationale de Paris et des bibliothèques publiques de France* (1907; with facsimiles); *Nouvelle méthode pratique de chant grégorien* (1908); *Traité d'harmonisation du chant grégorien* (1910); *L'Art grégorien* (1911); *La Musique de l'église* (1911); *Variations sur la musique d'église* (1912); *Musique et liturgie. Le Graduel et l'Antiphonaire romain* (Lyons, 1913); *L'Orgue en France de l'antiquité au début de la période classique* (1921); *Les primitifs de la musique française* (1922); *Le Cantique populaire en France: ses sources, son histoire* (Lyons, 1924); *La Vie musicale de l'église* (1929); *La Liturgie et la musique* (1931); *Le Manuscrit de musique polyphonique du trésor d'Apt, XIVe—XVe siècles* (1936); *L'Église et la musique* (Paris, 1936). Gastoué edited several volumes of ecclesiastical music, collected from old sources, and wrote various articles on the subject.

Gatti, Guido Maria, eminent Italian music critic and writer; b. Chieti, May 30, 1892. He was editor of 'La Riforma Musicale,' Turin (1913-15) and 'Il Pianoforte,' Turin (1920-27), which changed its name in 1927 to 'La Rassegna Musicale.'—Publications: *Guida musicale della Giovanna d'Arco di Enrico Bossi; Biografia critica di Bizet* (1914); *Figure di musicisti francesi,* in 'Biblioteca della Riforma musicale' (Turin, 1915); *Musicisti moderni d'Italia e di fuori* (Bologna, 1920; 2nd ed. 1925); *Le Barbier de Seville de Rossini* (Paris, 1925); *Debora* *e Jaele di I. Pizzetti* (1922); *Dizionario Musicale* (in collaboration with A. della Corte; 1925, 2nd ed. 1930; revised ed. 1952); *Ildebrando Pizzetti* (Turin, 1934; in English, London, 1951); contributed to Grove's Dictionary; wrote numerous articles for music magazines in Europe and America.

Gatti-Casazza (găt-ti-căh-zăht'-tsăh), **Giulio,** Italian impresario; b. Udine, Feb. 3, 1868; d. Ferrara, Sept. 2, 1940. He was educated at the universities of Ferrara and Bologna, and graduated from the Naval Engineering School at Genoa; when his father, who had been chairman of the Board of Directors of the Municipal Theater at Ferrara, accepted a position in Rome in 1893, Gatti-Casazza abandoned his career as engineer and became director of the theater. His ability attracted the attention of the Viscount di Modrone and A. Boito, who, in 1898, offered him the directorship of La Scala at Milan. During the ten years of his administration the institution came to occupy the first place among the opera houses of Italy. From 1908-35 he was general director of the Metropolitan Opera, and the period of his administration was, both artistically and financially, the most flourishing in the history of the house; he vastly improved the orch., chorus, and all mechanical departments; one of his first suggestions to the Board of Directors was to offer a $10,000 prize for the encouragement of native operatic composers (won by Horatio Parker with *Mona,* 1912); the doors were opened to American composers (starting with Converse, Damrosch, and Herbert), and eminent foreign composers gladly accepted invitations to have the world première of new works take place at the Metropolitan (Humperdinck's *Königskinder,* Puccini's *Girl of the Golden West,* Granados' *Goyescas,* Giordano's *Madame Sans-Gêne,* etc.); the list of novelties produced is a long one, numbering 110 works; besides, there were noteworthy revivals of older works, e.g., Gluck's *Iphigénie en Tauride* (revised by Richard Strauss), etc. During this period, Giulio Setti was chorus master and set a high standard for the opera chorus. Gatti-Casazza procured the services of the best conductors available, bringing with him from La Scala such a master as Arturo Toscanini, and such able conductors as Polacco and Panizza. He resigned in 1935, Giulio Setti leaving with him, and went to Italy, where he lived in retirement. On April 3, 1910, Gatti-Casazza married the soprano Frances Alda; divorced in 1929; in 1930 he married Rosina Galli (d. April 30, 1940), première danseuse and ballet-mistress.—Cf. I. Kolodin, *The Metropolitan Opera, 1883-1935* (N. Y., 1936); Pitts Sanborn, *Metropolitan Book of the Opera* (N. Y., 1937). Gatti-Casazza's *Memories of the Opera* was posthumously published in English in 1941.

Gatty, Nicholas Comyn, English composer; b. Bradfield, Sept. 13, 1874; d. London, Nov. 10, 1946. He was educated at Downing College, Cambridge (B.A., 1896; Mus. B., 1898); then studied with Stanford at the Royal College of Music; was organist to the Duke of York's Royal Military School at Chelsea; music critic of 'Pall Mall Gazette,' 1907-14; also acted as assistant conductor at Covent Garden.—Works: the 1-act operas (all produced in London) *Greysteel* (1906), *Duke or Devil* (1909), *The Tempest* (April 17, 1920), *Prince Ferelon* (1921; received the Carnegie Award for this opera); *Macbeth,* 4-act opera (MS); *King Alfred and the Cakes;* Milton's *Ode on Time,* for soli, chorus, and orch.; *3 Short Odes;* Variations for orch. on *Old King Cole;* Suite for string orch.; piano concerto; piano trio; string quartet; waltzes for piano; songs.

Gatz, Felix Maria, German conductor; b. Berlin, May 15, 1892; d. Scranton, Pennsylvania, June 20, 1942. He studied at the Univs. of Berlin, Heidelberg, and Erlangen (*Dr. phil.,* 1917), and conducting with Nikisch and Paul Scheinpflug; in 1922-23, he was conductor of the Lübeck Civic Opera; 1923-33, conductor of Bruckner Society series with Berlin Philh.; 1925-34, prof. of esthetics at State Academy of Music, Vienna. In 1934 he settled in the U.S.; 1934-36, prof. at Duquesne Univ., Pittsburgh; 1936-37, visiting prof. at N. Y. Univ.; from 1937 head of music and art dept. of the Univ. of Scranton, Pa.; he was also founder (1938) and conductor (1938-39) of Scranton Philh. Orch.; publ. *Musik-Aesthetik grosser Komponisten* (Stuttgart, 1929), etc.

Gaubert (goh-băr'), **Philippe,** French conductor and composer; b. Cahors, July 3, 1879; d. Paris, July 8, 1941. He studied flute with Taffanel at the Paris Cons.; 1905, won second Prix de Rome; from 1919-38, was conductor of the Paris Conservatory concerts; 1920, first conductor at the Opéra, Paris.—Works: the operas *Sonia* (Nantes, 1913) and *Naïla* (Paris, April 7, 1927); a ballet, *Philotis* (Paris, 1914); the oratorio *Josiane* (Paris, Dec. 17, 1921); symphonic works: *Rhapsodie sur des thèmes populaires* (1909), *Poème pastoral* (1911), *Le Cortège* *d'Amphitrite* (Paris, April 9, 1911); *Fresques,* symph. suite (Paris, Nov. 12, 1923); *Les Chants de la mer,* 3 symph. pictures (Paris, Oct. 12, 1929); violin concerto (Paris, Feb. 16, 1930); *Les Chants de la terre* (Paris, Dec. 20, 1931); *Poème romanesque,* for cello and orch. (Paris, Jan. 30, 1932); *Inscriptions sur les portes de la ville,* 4 symph. tableaux (Paris, Nov. 18, 1934); symphony in F (Paris, Nov. 8, 1936); *Poème des champs et des villages* (Paris, Feb. 4, 1939); chamber music: *Médailles antiques,* for flute, violin, and piano; *Divertissement grec,* for flute and harp; *Sur l'eau,* for flute and piano; *Intermède champêtre,* for oboe and piano; violin sonata; songs; *Méthode complète de flûte,* in 8 parts (1923); many transcriptions for flute of works by Mozart, Beethoven, Lully, Rameau, etc.

Gaul, Alfred Robert, English composer; b. Norwich, April 30, 1837; d. Worcestershire, Sept. 13, 1913. A chorister in the cathedral at 9, he was apprenticed to Dr. Buck; was organist at Fakenham, Birmingham, and Edgbaston; graduated (1863) as Mus. Bac., Cantab.; became conductor of the Walsall Philharmonic in 1887, then teacher and conductor at the Birmingham and Midland Institute, and teacher at King Edward's High School for Girls and at the Blind Asylum.—Works: An oratorio, *Hezekiah* (1861); several sacred cantatas, some of which (*Ruth* and *The Holy City*) are popular in the U.S.; Passion music; the 96th Psalm; an ode, *A Song of Life;* glees, vocal trios and duets, songs and part-songs, etc.

Gaul, Harvey Bartlett, American conductor and composer; b. New York, April 11, 1881; d. Pittsburgh, Dec. 1, 1945. He studied harmony, composition, and organ in New York with G. F. Le Jeune and Dudley Buck (1895); later (1906), in England, he studied composition with A. R. Gaul and Dr. Armes. In Paris he attended the Cons. and the Schola Cantorum; studied composition and orchestration with Vincent d'Indy, and organ with Widor, Guilmant, and Decaux (1910). He was conductor of the Pittsburgh Civic String Orch. and guest-conductor elsewhere; member of the faculty of Carnegie Institute, Pittsburgh; lectured on music in various cities. He was also well known as a critic ('Post,' 'Sun,' 'Pittsburgh Index') and a contributor to music magazines. He composed many choruses (*Appalachian Mountain Melodies, Prayer of Thanksgiving,* etc.), chamber music, songs, organ pieces, etc.; won prizes in various competitions with his songs.

Gaultier (goh-t'yā'), **Denis,** famous French lute player and composer; b. Marseilles, c. 1600; d. Paris, late Jan., 1672. He was active as a composer from about 1625 or 1630; lutenist in Paris in 1626.—Works: *La Rhétorique des Dieux,* a collection of 69 compositions compiled between 1664-72 (facsimile reprint, together with transcription into modern notation, ed. by A. Tessier in 'Publications de la Société française de musicologie,' vols. VI, 1932, and VII, 1932-33); *Pièces de luth* (1669, publ.); *Livre de tablature* (publ. by his widow and Jacques Gaultier, 1672); many other MSS in the Berlin, Vienna, and Paris libraries. Much of his work is in the form of dance suites, each selection in the various groups bearing a descriptive title. As a composer Gaultier developed a type of ornamentation which influenced the keyboard style of Froberger and Chambonnières. Among his pupils were Mouton, DuFaux, Gallot, and others.—Cf. O. Fleischer, *Denis Gaultier,* in 'Vierteljahrsschrift für Musikwissenschaft' II, 1 ff (with transcription of *La Rhétorique,* 1886; also publ. separately, Leipzig, 1886); L. de la Laurencie, *Le Luthiste Gaultier,* in the 'Revue Musicale' (1924).

Gauthier (goh-t'-yā'), **Eva,** soprano; b. Ottawa, Canada, Sept. 20, 1885; studied voice there and at the Paris Cons. with Frank Buels and Jacques Bouhy, later with Schoen-René in Berlin; in 1909, she made her operatic début as Micaela in Pavia, Italy; 1910, appeared at Covent Garden, London (Yniold in *Pelléas et Mélisande);* later devoted herself to a concert career; performed many works of contemporary composers; during her world tours she also made a study of Javanese and Malayan folksongs.

Gauthier-Villars (goh-t'yā' vē-yahr'), **Henri** (called **Willy**), French music critic; b. Villiers-sur-Orge, Aug. 10, 1859; d. Paris, Jan. 12, 1931. He was music critic for the 'Revue des Revues'; writer for the 'Revue Internationale de musique,' the 'Écho de Paris' (over the signature 'L'Ouvreuse du Cirque'), and other Paris papers. Several volumes of his numerous criticisms have been published: *Lettres de l'ouvreuse, Bains de sons, Rythmes et rires, La Mouche des croches, Entre deux airs, Notes sans portées, La colle aux quintes;* he also wrote a biography of Bizet (1912).

Gautier, Jean-François-Eugène, French composer; b. Vaugirard, near Paris, Feb. 27, 1822; d. Paris, April 3, 1878. He was a pupil of Habeneck (violin) and Halévy (composition) at the Paris Cons.; 1848, 3rd conductor at the Théâtre-Italien; also prof. of harmony at the Cons.; and in 1872 prof. of history. He composed 14 comic operas; an oratorio, *La Mort de Jesus;* a cantata, *Le 15 août;* an *Ave Maria;* etc.

Gavazzeni, Gianandrea, Italian composer and writer on music; b. Bergamo, July 25, 1909. He studied at the Milan Cons. with Pizzetti and Pilati; has written *Preludio Sinfonico* for orch. (1928); *La Morte di Dafne* for voice and orch. (1929); violin sonata (1930); cello sonata (1930); piano trio (1931); *Concerto Bergamasco* for orch. (1931); *Paolo e Virginia,* melodrama (1932); *Il furioso nell' Isola di San Domingo,* ballet (1933); etc. He is the author of *Musicisti d'Europa* (Milan, 1954).

Gaviniès (găh-vēn-ñäs'), **Pierre,** French violinist and composer; b. Bordeaux, May 11, 1728; d. Paris, Sept. 8, 1800. He learned to play the violin as a child in the workshop of his father, who was a lute maker. In 1734, the family moved to Paris. Gaviniès made his first public appearance in a Concert Spirituel at the age of 13; he reappeared at these concerts as a youth of 20; his success with the public was such that Viotti described him as 'the French Tartini.' From 1773 to 1777 he was director (with Gossec) of the Concerts Spirituels. When the Paris Cons. was organized in 1794, he was appointed professor of violin. His book of technical exercises *Les 24 Matinées* (violin studies in all the 24 keys) demonstrates by its transcendental difficulty that Gaviniès must have been a virtuoso; he attracted numerous pupils, and is regarded as the founder of the French school of violin pedagogy. His original works are of less importance; he wrote 3 sonatas for violin accompanied by cello (publ. posthumously; the one in F minor known as *Le Tombeau de Gaviniès*); his most celebrated piece is an air, *Romance de Gaviniès,* which has been publ. in numerous arrangements; he wrote further 6 sonatas for 2 violins and 6 violin concertos, and produced a comic opera, *Le Prétendu* (Paris, Nov. 6, 1760). —Cf. C. Pipelet, *Éloge historique de Pierre Gaviniès* (Paris, 1802); L. de la Laurencie, *L'école française du violon* (Paris, 1923).

Gavoty, Bernard, French writer on music; b. Paris, April 2, 1908; studied philosophy and literature at the Sorbonne; also music at the Paris Cons. Under the nom-de-plume Clarendon, he wrote music criticism in 'Le Figaro.' He publ. *Louis Vierne, le musicien de Notre-Dame* (Paris, 1943); *Jehan Alain, musicien français* (Paris, 1945); *Souvenirs de Georges Enesco* (Paris, 1955); also issued a series of de luxe publications, under the general title *Les Grands Interprètes* (Geneva, 1953, et seq.), containing biographies and photographs of Gieseking, Furtwängler, Menuhin, etc.

Gawronski, Adalbert, Polish pianist and composer; b. Seimony, near Vilna, April 27, 1868; d. Kowanónak near Poznan, Aug. 6, 1910. He studied with Noskowski at the Warsaw Music Institute and later, in Berlin and Vienna; then went to Russia, where he organized a music school in Orel, returning to Warsaw after a few years. He wrote 2 operas, *Marja* and *Pojata;* a symphony; 3 string quartets (the 1st won the Leipzig Paderewski prize, 1898; the 2nd won the Moscow prize, 1903); piano pieces, songs, etc.

Gay, John, English librettist of *The Beggar's Opera;* b. Barnstaple, Devon, Sept. (baptized 16th), 1685; d. London, Dec. 4, 1732. The opera was brought out in London Jan. 29, 1728, and was immensely popular for a century, chiefly because of its sharp satire and the English and Scots folk melodies it used. It has had a number of successful revivals. The government disliked *The Beggar's Opera,* and forbade the performance of its sequel, *Polly,* the score of which was printed in 1729. When *Polly* was finally performed in 1777, it was a fiasco, because the conditions satirized no longer prevailed.—Cf. 'Dictionary of National Biography' VII (reprinted Oxford, 1921-22); C. E. Pearce, *Polly Peachum: the Story of 'Polly' and 'The Beggar's Opera'* (London, 1923); W. E. Schultz, *Gay's Beggar's Opera* (New Haven, Conn., 1923); O. Sherwin, *Mr. Gay; being a Picture of the Life and Times of the Author of the Beggar's Opera* (N. Y., 1929); Cäcilie Tolksdorf, *John Gay's Beggar's Opera und Bert Brechts Dreigroschenoper* (Rheinberg, 1934); E. Gagey, *Ballad Opera* (N. Y., 1937).

Gay (găh-ē'), **Maria,** dramatic contralto; b. Barcelona, June 10, 1879; d. New York, July 29, 1943. She studied sculpture and the violin and became a singer almost by chance, when Pugno, traveling in Spain, heard her sing and was impressed by the natural beauty of her voice. She sang in some of his concerts; also with Ysaÿe in Brussels; made her début there as Carmen

(1902), a role that became her finest. She then studied in Paris with Ada Adiny, and when she returned to the operatic stage made an international reputation. After tours in Europe, she made her American début at the Metropolitan Opera as Carmen on Dec. 3, 1908, with Toscanini conducting. She sang with the Boston Opera Co. in 1910-12 and with the Chicago Opera Co. from 1913 to 1927, when she retired from the stage. She and her husband, the tenor, Giovanni Zenatello, whom she married in 1913, settled in N. Y.

Gaynor, Mrs. **Jessie Smith,** American composer of children's songs; b. St. Louis, Feb. 17, 1863; d. Webster Groves, Missouri, Feb. 20, 1921. After studying piano with L. Maas and theory with A. J. Goodrich and A. Weidlig, she taught in Chicago, St. Louis, and St. Joseph, Mo. Among her published works are: *Songs of the Child World* (2 books), *Playtime Songs,* etc. and a children's operetta, *The House That Jack Built.*

Gaztambide (găth-tăhm-bē'-dĕ), **Joaquín,** Spanish composer; b. Tudela, Navarre, Feb. 7, 1822; d. Madrid, March 18, 1870. He studied at Pamplona and at the Madrid Cons. with Pedro Albéniz (piano) and Ramón Carnicer (composition). After a stay in Paris, he returned to Madrid as manager of several theaters and as conductor of the Cons. concerts; he became director of the 'Concert Society' in 1868. He was best known, however, for his zarzuelas, the satiric musical productions which are identified with the Madrid stage. Gaztambide wrote 44 zarzuelas, many of which became popular; one, *El juramento,* first produced in 1858, was revived in Madrid in 1933. He took a zarzuela company to Mexico and Havana in 1868-69.

Gazzaniga, Giuseppe, Italian opera composer; b. Verona, Oct. 1743; d. Crema, Feb. 1, 1818. He was a pupil of Porpora in Naples; after the production of his early opera *Il barone di Trocchia* there (1768), he traveled to Venice and to Vienna; his opera *Don Giovanni Tenorio* (Venice, Feb. 5, 1787) anticipated Mozart's *Don Giovanni;* he wrote 50 operas in all, several of which became quite popular at the time (*La locanda, L'isola di Alcina, La vendemmia, La moglie capricciosa,* etc.). Mozart's librettist, Lorenzo da Ponte, wrote the libretto of Gazzaniga's opera *Il finto cieco* (Vienna, Feb. 20, 1770).

Gebel, Georg (Jr.), German composer; b. Brieg, Silesia, Oct. 25, 1709; d. Rudolstadt, Sept. 24, 1753. He studied with his father; was organist at St. Maria Magdalene, Breslau, and Kapellmeister to the Duke of Oels. In 1735 he joined Count Brühl's orch. at Dresden, where he met Hebenstreit, the inventor of the 'Pantaleon,' and learned to play that instrument. In 1747 he was appointed Kapellmeister to the Prince of Schwarzburg-Rudolstadt. He was a precocious composer, and wrote a number of light operas (to German rather than Italian librettos, thus upholding the national tradition), and more than 100 symphonies, partitas, and concertos. Many MSS of his instrumental works are still preserved in German libraries.

Gebhard, Heinrich, pianist, composer, and teacher; b. Sobernheim, July 25, 1878. As a boy of 8, he came with his parents to Boston where he studied with Clayton Johns; after a concert début in Boston (April 24, 1896), he went to Vienna to study with Leschetizky. A fine interpreter of the classics, he also showed a decided predilection for the moderns, particularly of the impressionist school. He gave first American performances of works by Vincent d'Indy; his most notable intepretation was Loeffler's work for piano and orch., *A Pagan Poem,* which he played nearly 100 times with U. S. orchestras. His own works are also in an impressionistic vein: *Fantasy* for piano and orch. (N. Y. Philh., Nov. 12, 1925, composer soloist); symph. poem, *Across the Hills* (1940); *Divertimento* for piano and chamber orch. (Boston, Dec. 20, 1927); a string quartet; a *Waltz Suite* for two pianos; a song cycle, *The Sun, Cloud and the Flower;* many piano pieces. He also arranged Loeffler's *A Pagan Poem* for two pianos.

Gedalge (zheu-dahlzh'), **André,** eminent French theorist, composer, and pedagogue; b. Paris, Dec. 27, 1856; d. Chessy, Feb. 5, 1926. He began to study music rather late in life, and entered the Paris Cons. at the age of 28. However, he made rapid progress, and obtained the 2nd Prix de Rome after a year of study (under Guiraud). He then elaborated a system of counterpoint, later published as a *Traité de la fugue* (Paris, 1901), which became a standard work. In 1905, Gedalge was engaged as prof. of counterpoint and fugue at the Paris Cons.; among his students were Ravel, Enesco, Koechlin, Roger-Ducasse, Milhaud, and Honegger. He also publ. *Les Gloires* *musicales du monde* (1898) and other pedagogic works. As a composer, Gedalge was less significant. Among his works are a pantomime, *Le petit Savoyard* (Paris, 1891); an opera, *Pris au piège* (Paris, 1895), and 3 operas that were not performed: *Sita, La Farce du Cadi, Hélène;* he also wrote 3 symphs., several concertos, some chamber music, and songs. See *Hommage à Gedalge* in the 'Revue musicale' (March 1, 1926), containing articles by Koechlin, F. Schmitt, Honegger, Milhaud, and others.

Geehl, Henry Ernest, English composer; b. London, Sept. 28, 1881. A pupil of R. O. Morgan, he was appointed professor at Trinity College of Music, London, in 1919, and was still holding this post in 1954. He has written a symphony; a violin concerto; a piano concerto; pieces for brass band, including *Cornwall* and *Cornish Rhapsody;* pedagogic piano pieces; songs.

Gehot (gā-hoh'), **Jean** (also **Joseph**), Belgian violinist and composer; b. Brussels, April 8, 1756; d. in the U. S., about 1820. He went to London after 1780; there he publ. *A Treatise on the Theory and Practice of Music* (1784), *Art of Bowing the Violin* (1790), and *Complete Instructions for Every Musical Instrument* (1790). In 1792, he went to America; gave concerts in New York, where he presented his work, *Overture in 12 movements, expressive of a voyage from England to America.* He then played violin at the City Concerts in Philadelphia, under the management of Reinagle and Capron. However, he failed to prosper in America; most of his works were publ. in London, among them 17 string quartets, 12 string trios, and 24 'military pieces' for 2 clarinets, 2 horns, and bassoon. Some information on Gehot's life is found in J. R. Parker's *Musical Reminiscences* in the 'Euterpiad' (Feb. 2, 1822). See also O. Sonneck, *Early Concert Life in America* (1907).

Gehrkens, Karl Wilson, American music educator; b. Kelleys Island, Ohio, April 19, 1882. After graduation from Oberlin College (B.A., 1905; M.A., 1912), and attending Columbia Univ., he became prof. of school music at the Oberlin Cons. of Music in 1907; retired in 1942. He has been mainly influential in the field of school music teaching; formulated a new plan, adopted by many institutions, for the training of music supervisors. He was editor of 'School Music' from 1925 to 1934; co-editor, with Walter Damrosch and George Gartlan, of the 'Universal School Music Series,' a series of songbooks and teachers' manuals for grade and high schools (1923-36), etc.—Writings: *Music Notation and Terminology* (1914); *Essentials in Conducting* (1919); *An Introduction to School Music Teaching* (1919); *Fundamentals of Music* (1924); *Handbook of Musical Terms* (1927); *Twenty Lessons in Conducting* (1930); *Music in the Grade Schools* (1934); *Music in the Junior High School* (1936); with P. W. Dykema, *The Teaching and Administration of High School Music* (1941).

Geiringer (gī'-rin-gĕr), **Karl,** eminent musicologist; b. Vienna, April 26, 1899. He studied in Vienna at the Cons. and Univ. with Guido Adler; later in Berlin with Curt Sachs; from 1923-38, he was custodian of the archives and instrument collection of the Gesellschaft der Musikfreunde in Vienna; then lived in London; appointed professor at Boston University in 1941. In 1955 he was elected president of the American Musicological Society. During the American period of his activities he wrote his books in English.—Writings: *Die Flankelwirbelinstrumente in der bildenden Kunst des 14.-16. und der 1. Hälfte des 17. Jahrhunderts* (dissertation, 1923); the section devoted to musical instruments in Adler's *Handbuch der Musikgeschichte* (1924); *Vorgeschichte und Geschichte der europäischen Laute* (1928); *Joseph Haydn* in Bücken's 'Grosse Meister' (1932); *Johannes Brahms, Leben und Schaffen eines deutschen Meisters* (Vienna, 1935; in English, London, 1936; 2nd ed., 1947); *Musical Instruments, Their History from the Stone Age to the Present Day* (London 1943; N.Y., 1945); *Haydn, a Creative Life in Music* (N.Y., 1946); *The Bach Family* (N.Y., 1954); *Music of the Bach Family* (Cambridge, Mass., 1955). He edited Pergolesi's *Serva Padrona* and several little known works by Haydn; arranged and publ. orch. works by Dittersdorf, Johann Christian Bach, Florian Gassmann, Michael Haydn, and others; also a collection of piano works, *Wiener Meister um Mozart und Beethoven* (Vienna, 1935).

Geiser, Walther, Swiss composer; b. Zofingen, May 16, 1897. He studied in Basel with Hermann Suter and in Berlin with Busoni. Since 1924, he has taught at the Basel Cons. He has written a symphony (1953); *3 Fantasies* for orch.; a violin concerto (1930); *Konzertstück* for organ and chamber orch. (1940); 2 string quartets; a string trio and pieces for solo wind instruments with piano; also choral works. His style, determined by Busoni's influence, is neo-Classical.

Geisler, Paul, German conductor and composer; b. Stolp, Aug. 10, 1856; d. Posen, April 3, 1919. He was a pupil of his grandfather, who was a conductor at Marienburg, and also of Constantine Decker. As a conductor, Geisler was associated with the Leipzig musical theater (1881), A. Neumann's traveling Wagner company (1882); for the following two years he was conductor at Bremen. He lived in Leipzig and Berlin for most of his career before going to Posen, where he became director of the Cons. He wrote much music for the stage; his other work, including two cyclic cantatas, symphonic poems, and incidental stage music, is mostly in manuscript.

Geistinger, Maria (Marie) Charlotte Cäcilia, Polish operetta singer; b. Graz, Styria, July 26, 1833; d. Rastenfeld, Sept. 29, 1903. She sang chiefly in Vienna, but also in Prague, Leipzig, Berlin, etc. In 1897 she made a successful appearance in New York.

Gelinek (properly Jelinek), **Joseph,** composer; b. Seltsch, near Beraun, Bohemia, Dec. 3, 1758; d. Vienna, April 13, 1825. He studied philosophy in Prague and at the same time took lessons in music with Segert; became a good pianist (Mozart praised him); ordained priest in 1786, but did not abandon music; went to Vienna and settled there as a piano teacher; in 1795, became music master to Prince Esterhazy. He was a prolific composer; 92 opus numbers are listed in a catalogue issued by André; his fantasias, variations, and dances for piano were quite successful.

Geminiani (jeh-mē-ñah'-nē), **Francesco,** Italian violinist and writer; b. Lucca (baptized Dec. 5), 1687; d. Dublin, Sept. 17, 1762. He studied with Corelli in Rome and Alessandro Scarlatti in Naples; in 1706 returned to Lucca and played violin in the town orch. In 1714 he went to London, where he won a reputation as a teacher and performer; in 1731 he presented a series of subscription concerts in London; in 1733 he went to Dublin, where he established a concert hall and gave concerts; in 1734 he returned to London; in 1740 he was briefly in Paris; he was again in Paris for a longer period between 1749 and 1755, when he went back once more to London; in 1759 he settled in Dublin, where he was music master to Count Bellamont. Both in London and Dublin he was financially successful; besides music, he was interested in art, and bought and sold pictures. As a virtuoso, Geminiani continued the tradition established by his teacher, Corelli, and made further advances in violin technique by the use of frequent shifts of position, and by a free application of double-stops. In his compositions, he adopted the facile method of the Italian school; he excelled particularly in brisk allegro movements. During his years in England and Ireland he made a determined effort to please English tastes; his works are often extremely effective, but his inherent talents fell far short of Corelli's, and in music history he remains but a secondary figure. He publ. the earliest known violin method, *The Art of Playing on the Violin,* which appeared anonymously in Prelleur's *The Modern Musick Master, or the Universal Musician* (London, 1730); it was later publ. under Geminiani's own name as *The Compleat Tutor for the Violin;* in 1751 a third ed. appeared under the original title; it was translated into French (Paris, 1752) and German (Vienna, 1785); a facsimile edition, prepared by D. D. Boyden, was publ. in 1952. This manual is extremely valuable because it sets forth the principles of violin playing as formulated by Corelli, with many of the rules still in common use. Other didactic publications by Geminiani comprise: *Rules for Playing in a true Taste on the Violin, German Flute, Violoncello and Harpsichord* (London, 1745); *A Treatise on good Taste, being the second Part of the Rules* (London, 1749); *Guida Armonica o Dizionario Armonico being a Sure Guide to Harmony and Modulation* (London, 1742; in French, 1756; in Dutch, 1756); *A Supplement to the Guida Harmonica* (London, 1745); *The Art of Accompaniament* [sic] *or a new and well digested method to learn to perform the Thorough Bass on the Harpsichord* (London, 1755); *The Art of Playing the Guitar or Cittra, Containing Several Compositions with a Bass for the Violoncello or Harpsichord* (London, 1760); also compiled *The Harmonical Miscellany* (London, 1758). His musical works (all instrumental) comprise: op. 1, 12 sonatas for violin and figured bass (1716); op. 2, 6 concerti grossi (1732); op. 3, 6 concerti grossi (1733); op. 4, 12 sonatas for violin and figured bass (1739); op. 5, 6 sonatas for cello and figured bass (1739); op. 6, 6 concerti grossi (1741); op. 7, 6 concerti grossi (1746); also 12 string trios and arrangements of Corelli's works for various instrumental combinations. The concerti grossi have been publ. in modern editions by P. Mies (op. 2, no. 2) in 'Musik im Haus' (1928); M. Esposito (op. 2, no. 2, arranged for string orch., London, 1927); H. J. Moser (op. 2, nos. 4, 5, 6, arranged for strings and piano) in 'Das Musik-Kränzlein' (Leipzig, 1937); R. Hernried (op. 3, nos. 1-6, Leipzig, 1935). Violin sonatas have been publ. by: R. L. Finney (op. 1, nos. 1-12, Northampton, Mass., 1935); A. Moffat (op. 4, no. 8, Mainz, 1910; op. 4, no. 11, Berlin, 1899).—Cf. W. H. Grattan Flood, *Geminiani in England and Ireland* in the 'Sammelbände der Internationalen Musik-Gesellschaft' (1910-11; pp. 108-12); A. Betti, *La Vita e l'arte di Francesco Geminiani* (Lucca, 1933); R. Hernried, *Geminiani's Concerti Grossi, op. 3,* in 'Acta musicologica' (1937; pp. 22-30).

Gemünder, August Martin Ludwig, violin maker; b. Ingelfingen, Württemberg, Germany, March 22, 1814; d. New York, Sept. 7, 1895. He established a shop at Springfield, Mass., in 1846; then moved to Boston, where he was joined by his brother Georg (b. April 13, 1816; d. Jan. 15, 1899), also a violin maker, a pupil of J. B. Vuillaume in Paris. In 1852, the brothers settled in New York, where they established themselves as the foremost manufacturers of musical instruments; between 1860 and 1890 they received numerous medals for excellence at expositions in Europe and America. After the death of August Gemünder, the business was continued by 3 of his sons, as August Gemünder & Sons. Georg Gemünder wrote an autobiographical sketch, with an account of his work, *Georg Gemünder's Progress in Violin Making* (1880, in German; 1881, in English).—Cf. 'Dictionary of American Biography' VII (N.Y., 1931).

Genée (zhŭ-nā'), **(Franz Friedrich) Richard,** German opera composer; b. Danzig, Feb. 7, 1823; d. Baden, near Vienna, June 15, 1895. At first a medical student, he took up music, and studied under Stahlknecht at Berlin; was theater conductor (1848-67) at Riga, Cologne, Düsseldorf, Danzig, Amsterdam, and Prague; from 1868-78, conductor at the Theater an der Wien, Vienna, then retiring to his villa at Pressbaum, near Vienna. He wrote (some with F. Zell) several of his own libretti; he also wrote libretti for Strauss, Suppé, and Millöcker.—Operettas: *Der Geiger aus Tirol* (1857), *Der Musikfeind* (1862), *Die Generalprobe* (1862), *Rosita* (1864), *Der schwarze Prinz* (1866), *Am Runenstein* (with Fr. von Flotow, 1868), *Der Seekadett* (1876), *Nanon* (1877), *Im Wunderlande der Pyramiden* (1877), *Die letzten Mohikaner* (1878), *Nisida* (1880), *Rosina* (1881), *Die Zwillinge* (1885), *Die Piraten* (1886), *Die Dreizehn* (1887).

Generali, Pietro (real name, Mercandetti), Italian opera composer; b. Masserano, Oct. 23, 1773; d. Novara, Nov. 3, 1832. He studied in Rome; began to compose sacred music at an early age, but soon turned to opera. He traveled all over Italy as producer of his operas and also went to Vienna and Barcelona. Returning to Italy, he became maestro di cappella at the Cathedral of Novara. He anticipated Rossini in the effective use of dynamics in the instrumental parts of his operas and was generally praised for his technical knowledge. He wrote about 50 stage works, both in the serious and comic genre, but none survived in the repertory after his death. The following were successful at their initial performances: *Pamela nubile* (Venice, April 12, 1804); *Le lagrime di una vedova* (Venice, Dec. 26, 1808); *Adelina* (Venice, Sept. 16, 1810); *L'impostore* (Milan, May 21, 1815); *I Baccanali di Roma* (Venice, Jan. 14, 1816; reputed to be his best work); *Il servo padrone* (Parma, Aug. 12, 1818); *Il divorzio persiano* (Trieste, Jan. 31, 1828).—Cf. C. Piccoli, *Elogio del maestro Pietro Generali* (1833).

Genet (called Il Carpentrasso or Carpentras, from his native place). See **Carpentras.**

Genetz, Emil, Finnish choral composer; b. Impilahti, Oct. 24, 1852; d. Helsinki, May 1, 1930. He studied at the Dresden Cons. (1875-77); returning to Finland, he devoted himself chiefly to vocal music; many of his male choruses are well known and frequently sung in Finland.

Gennrich, Friedrich, German musicologist; b. Colmar, March 27, 1883. He studied Roman philology at the Univ. of Strasbourg; took courses in musicology with F. Ludwig. In 1921 he went to Frankfurt where he was docent of the Univ. from 1929 (prof. in 1934), teaching musicology and Romance literature. He is regarded as a leading authority on music of the troubadours, trouvères, and Minnesinger.—Writings: *Musikwissenschaft und romanische Philologie* (Halle, 1918); *Der musikalische Vortrag der altfranzösischen Chansons de geste* (Halle, 1923); *Die altfranzösiche Rotrouenge* (Halle, 1925); *Das Formproblem des Minnesangs* (Halle, 1931); *Grundriss einer Formenlehre des mittelalterlichen Liedes* (Halle, 1932; a comprehensive work); *Die Strassburger Schule für Musikwissenschaft* (Würzburg, 1940); *Abriss der frankonischen Mensuralnotation* (Nieder-

Modau, 1946; 2nd ed., Darmstadt, 1956); *Abriss der Mensuralnotation des XIV. und der 1. Hälfte des XV. Jahrhunderts* (Nieder-Modau, 1948); *Melodien altdeutscher Lieder* (Darmstadt, 1954); *Franco von Köln, Ars Cantus Mensurabilis* (Darmstadt, 1955). He further contributed numerous papers to special publications on Romance literature; for a complete list of his publications see his autobiographical entry in 'Die Musik in Geschichte und Gegenwart.'

Genzmer, Harald, German composer; b. Blumental, near Bremen, Feb. 9, 1909. He studied with Stephani in Marburg, later with Hindemith in Berlin; music theory with Sachs and Schünemann. From 1934-37, he was in Breslau; 1937-46, in Berlin; 1946-57, prof. of composition at the Hochschule für Musik in Freiburg-im-Breisgau; 1957, appointed to the faculty of the Hochschule für Musik in Munich. He made a study of the electronic instrument, Trautonium; his concerto for Trautonium and orch. was performed for the first time in a radio broadcast Dec. 17, 1952. Other works include: *Bremen Symphony* (1943); flute concerto (1946); cello concerto (1950); *Racine,* cantata (1948); septet for harp, 3 string instruments, and 3 wind instruments (1949); 2 violin sonatas; string quartet; 2 flute sonatas; 2 suites for Trautonium and piano.

Georges, Alexandre, French composer; b. Arras, Feb. 25, 1850; d. Paris, Jan. 18, 1938. He studied at the Niedermeyer School in Paris, and later became a teacher of harmony there. He occupied various posts as organist in Paris churches, and was a successful organ teacher. As a composer, he was mainly interested in opera; the following operas were produced in Paris: *Le Printemps* (1888); *Poèmes d' Amour* (1892); *Charlotte Corday* (March 6, 1901); *Miarka* (Nov. 7, 1905; his most successful work; revived and shortened, 1925); *Myrrha* (1909); *Sangre y sol* (Nice, Feb. 23, 1912). He also wrote the oratorios *Notre Dame de Lourdes, Balthazar, Chemin de Croix;* the symph. poems *Léila, La Naissance de Vénus, Le Paradis Perdu.* He wrote some chamber music for unusual combinations: *A la Kasbah* for flute and clarinet; *Kosaks* for violin and clarinet, etc. He is best known, however, for his melodious *Chansons de Miarka* for voice and piano (also with orch.). His arrangement of *Chansons champenoises à la manière ancienne,* by G. Dévignes, is also well known.

Georgescu, Georges, Rumanian conductor; b. Sulina, Oct. 16, 1887. He studied at the Bucharest Cons., then took cello lessons with Hugo Becker in Berlin; conducted symphony concerts in Bucharest (1919-38); from 1926 to 1932, made guest appearances in Europe; also was a guest conductor with the N. Y. Philharmonic (1930).

Georgiades, Thrasybulos, Greek musicologist; b. Athens, Jan. 4, 1907. He studied piano in Athens; then went to Munich, where he took a course in musicology with Rudolf von Ficker (1930-35); also studied composition with Carl Orff. In 1936, he was appointed prof. at the Odeon College in Athens. In 1947, he went again to Germany; lectured at the Univ. of Munich; in 1949, appointed prof. of musicology at Heidelberg Univ.; in 1955, settled in Munich. He contributed valuable papers to German music magazines on ancient Greek, Byzantine, and medieval music; publ. *Englische Diskanttraktate aus der ersten Hälfte des 15. Jahrhunderts* (Würzburg, 1937); *Volkslied als Bekenntnis* (Regensburg, 1947); *Der griechische Rhythmus* (Hamburg, 1940). See his autobiographical notice in 'Die Musik in Geschichte und Gegenwart.'

Georgii, Walter, German pianist and musicologist; b. Stuttgart, Nov. 23, 1887. He studied piano in Stuttgart and musicology in Leipzig, Berlin, and Halle. In 1914, he became piano teacher at the Cologne Cons.; then taught at other schools there. In 1946, he was appointed piano teacher at the Munich Hochschule für Musik. Although Georgii appeared in recitals in Germany, he is mainly known as a pedagogue. He publ. several valuable books on piano playing: *Weber als Klavierkomponist* (Leipzig, 1914); *Geschichte der Musik für Klavier zu 2 Hände* (Zürich, 1941; revised ed., with added material on piano music for 1 hand, 3, 5, and 6 hands, 1950); *Klavierspielerbüchlein* (Zürich, 1953). He also edited piano works by Brahms, and publ. an anthology of piano music, *400 Jahre europäischer Klavier Musik* (Cologne, 1950).

Gérardy (zhā-răhr-dē'), **Jean,** Belgian cellist; b. Spa, Dec. 6, 1877; d. there, July 4, 1929. At the age of 5 he began to study the cello with R. Bellmann; he was a pupil of Massau at Liège Cons. from 1885-89, receiving the gold medal at graduation. In 1888 he played as a student in a trio with Ysaÿe and Paderewski; he made his début as soloist in London in 1890. He then toured Europe and America. He was noted as an ensemble player; with Ysaÿe and Godowsky, he formed a trio and toured the U.S. in 1913-14. Gérardy's instrument was a Stradivari, made in 1710.

Gerber, Ernst Ludwig, celebrated German lexicographer, son and pupil of Heinrich Nikolaus Gerber; b. Sondershausen, Sept. 29, 1746; d. there, June 30, 1819. He likewise studied law and music in Leipzig, becoming a skilful cellist and organist, in which latter capacity he became (1769) his father's assistant, and succeeded him in 1775. He was also a chamber musician. He was able to visit Weimar, Kassel, Leipzig, and other cities, and gradually gathered together a large collection of musicians' portraits; to these he appended brief biographical notices, and finally conceived the plan of writing a biographical dictionary of musicians. Though his resources, in a small town without a public library, and having to rely in great measure on material sent him by his publisher, Breitkopf, were hardly adequate to the task he undertook, his *Historisch-biographisches Lexikon der Tonkünstler* (Leipzig, 2 vols., 1790-92) was so well received, and brought in such a mass of corrections and fresh material from all quarters, that he prepared a supplementary edition, *Neues historisch-biographisches Lexikon der Tonkünstler* (4 vols., 1812-14). Though the former was intended only as a supplement to Walther's dictionary, and both are, of course, out of date, they contain much material still of value, and have been extensively drawn upon by more recent writers. He composed sonatas for piano, chorale-preludes for organ, and music for wind band. The Viennese 'Gesellschaft der Musikfreunde' purchased his large library.

Gerber, René, Swiss composer; b. Travers, June 29, 1908. He studied with Andreae in Zürich and with Nadia Boulanger and Paul Dukas in Paris. Upon his return to Switzerland he devoted himself to teaching; in 1947 was appointed director of the Cons. of Neuchâtel. He has written several orchestral suites, concertos, and songs.

Gerber, Rudolf, German musicologist; b. Flehingen, Baden, April 15, 1899; d. Göttingen, May 6, 1957. He attended the Universities of Halle and Leipzig, receiving his *Dr. Phil.* from the latter in 1925. He went as Abert's assistant to the Univ. of Berlin in 1926; in 1928, Gerber became professor at Giessen Univ.; he was head of the Music-Historical Institute there from 1937 to 1943, when he became a professor at Göttingen Univ. An authority on German music, he published the following: *Der Operntypus J. A. Hasses und seine textlichen Grundlagen* (Leipzig, 1925); *Das Passionsrezitativ bei H. Schütz* (Gütersloh, 1929); *Johannes Brahms* (Potsdam, 1938); *Christoph Willibald Gluck* (Potsdam, 1950); *Bachs Brandenburgische Konzerte* (Kassel, 1951). He was editor of the 'Mozart-Jahrbuch' III (1929); a collaborator in F. Blume's collected edition of Prätorius, and in 1943, began to edit the collected works of Gluck.

Gerbert, Martin, German scholar; b. Hornau, near Horb-on-Neckar, Aug. 12, 1720; d. St.-Blasien, May 13, 1793. A student in the Benedictine monastery at St.-Blasien, he joined the order in 1737, became a priest in 1744, then prof. of theology there; 1759-62, he made trips to Germany, France, and throughout Italy, collecting old MSS, particularly those on music history, of which he later made valuable use in his own works; also visited Padre Martini in Bologna, corresponding with him from 1761 until Martini's death in 1784; in 1764, he was elected Prince-Abbot of the monastery at St.-Blasien. His writings on music are *De cantu et musica sacra* (St.-Blasien, 1774, 2 vols.; from the beginnings of music to the 18th cent.), *Vetus liturgia alemannica* (1776, 2 vols.), *Monumenta veteris liturgiae alemannicae* (1777, 2 vols.), and *Scriptores ecclesiastici de musica sacra potissimum* (1784, 3 vols.; facsimile ed., Berlin, 1905; also reprinted in 'Bolletino bibliografico musicale,' Milan, 1931); the first and last are still among the most valued sources for the study of music history, the last being one of the two great collections of treatises by theorists of the Middle Ages (for the other see **Coussemaker**).—Cf. J. Bader, *Fürstabt Martin Gerbert* (Freiburg, 1875); Fr. Niecks, *Martin Gerbert: Priest, Prince, Scholar and Musician,* in the 'Mus. Times' (Nov.-Dec., 1882); A. Lamy, *Martin Gerbert* (Rheims, 1898); A. Brinzinger, *Zu Martin Gerbert's . . . 200jährigem Geburtsfest,* in 'Neue Musik-Zeitung' (Sept. 2, 1920); G. Pfeilschifter, *Die Korrespondenz des Fürstabtes Martin Gerbert von St. Blasien* (vol. I, 1752-73; 1931); Eliz. Hegar, *Die Anfänge der neueren Musikgeschichtsschreibung um 1770 bei Gerbert, Burney und Hawkins* (Strasbourg, 1932).

Gerhard, Roberto; b. Valls, near Tarragona (Spain), Sept. 25, 1896. Though of Swiss parentage and nationality, he has been prominently associated with the Catalonian musical movement. He studied with Pedrell in Barcelona (1916-21) and Schoenberg in Vienna. He went to England as a result of the Spanish civil war in 1936, and settled in Cambridge. He edited vol. I of the complete works of A. Soler (q.v.) for the Institude d'Estudis Catalans, and translated into Spanish J. Wolf's *History of Music* (1934).—Works: opera, *The Duenna,* after Sheridan (Frankfurt Festival, June 27, 1951); ballet, *Don Quixote* (London, Feb. 20, 1950); ballet, *Pandora* (Cambridge, Jan. 26, 1944, Kurt Jooss choreographer); cantata *L'alta naixença del Rei En Jaime* (1931); *6 cançons populars catalanes,* for soprano and orch. (Vienna, Festival of the International Society for Contemporary Music, June 16, 1932); *Ariel,* ballet suite (Barcelona Festival, April 19, 1936); *Albada, Interludi i Dansa,* for orch. (London Festival, June 24, 1938); *Alegrias,* ballet suite (London, BBC, April 4, 1944); violin concerto (Florence, Maggio Musicale, May, 1950); concerto for piano and strings (Aldeburg, June, 1951); symphony (Baden-Baden Festival, June 21, 1955); concerto for harpsichord, strings, and percussion (1956); quintet for flute, oboe, clarinet, bassoon, and horn (1928); *Capriccio* for solo flute (1949); viola sonata (1950); string quartet (1955); *Akond of Swat,* for voice and percussion (London, Feb. 7, 1956); incidental music to Shakespeare's plays *(Romeo and Juliet, Cymbeline, Taming of the Shrew, Midsummer Night's Dream, King Lear);* film music; harmonizations of Catalan melodies, etc. Gerhard's early style of composition followed the Catalan traditions of his teacher Felipe Pedrell; after his study with Schoenberg, he gradually veered towards the 12-tone method; in his later works he extended the dodecaphonic principle into the domain of rhythms (12 different time units in a theme, corresponding to the intervallic distances of the notes in the tone-row from the central note). See the Sept. 1956 issue of 'The Score,' publ. on the occasion of Gerhard's 60th birthday, with articles by Donald Mitchell, Norman Del Mar, John Gardner, Roman Vlad, David Drew, Laurence Picken, and Roberto Gerhard himself.

Gerhardt (gär-hahrdt), **Elena,** celebrated lieder singer (mezzo-soprano); b. Leipzig, Nov. 11, 1883. After studying at the Leipzig Cons. (1899-1903) with Marie Hedmont, she made her Leipzig début in 1903 in recital, with Nikisch as her accompanist. She toured Europe as a lieder singer with great success; made her English début at Queen's Hall, London, in 1906, and her American début in New York, Jan. 9, 1912. In 1928, she sang Schubert's complete *Winterreise* cycle in N. Y. From 1929 she taught in Leipzig and London; in 1933 she settled in London as a teacher. She compiled 'My Favorite German Songs' (1915), edited a selection of Hugo Wolf's songs (1932), and wrote her autobiography, *Recital* (London, 1953; preface by Dame Myra Hess).

Gericke (gā'rĭ-kĕh), **Wilhelm,** Austrian conductor; b. Schwanberg, Styria, April 18, 1845; d. Vienna, Oct. 27, 1925. He was a pupil of Dessoff in the Vienna Cons. 1862-5, and then became Kapellmeister of the theater at Linz; 1874, 2d Kapellmeister of the Vienna court opera (with Hans Richter); in 1880, succeeded Brahms as conductor of the 'Gesellschaftsconcerte,' and also conducted the Singverein. From 1884-9 he was conductor of the Boston Symphony Orch.; returning to Vienna, he resumed the direction of the 'Gesellschaftsconcerte' until 1895; from 1898-1906 he again conducted the Boston Symph. Orch., succeeding Emil Paur; after that he lived in retirement in Vienna. Gericke was a remarkably competent conductor and an efficient drill-master.—Cf. J. N. Burk, *Wilhelm Gericke: a Centennial Retrospect* in the 'Mus. Quarterly' (April, 1945).

Gerlach, Theodor, German conductor and composer; b. Dresden, June 25, 1861; d. Kiel, Dec. 11, 1940. A student of Fr. Wüllner, and also at Berlin Univ., Gerlach first attracted attention by an effective cantata, *Luthers Lob der Musica.* He went to Italy in 1884; in 1886, he became conductor of the German Opera in Posen. The success of his *Epic Symphony* resulted in his appointment as court conductor at Coburg in 1891. After several other posts as conductor, he settled in Karlsruhe as director of the 'Musikbildungsanstalt.' He wrote an opera *Matteo Falcone,* to his own libretto, which was produced with considerable success in Hanover (1898); of greater interest are his experiments with 'spoken opera' employing inflected speech; of these, *Liebeswogen* was produced in Bremen (1904) and *Das Seegespenst* in Altenburg (1914); he applied the same principle, using the spoken word over an instrumental accompaniment in his *Gesprochene Lieder.* He also wrote a number of other vocal works, and military marches.

Gerle, Hans, German lutenist; b. Nuremberg, c. 1500; d. there, 1570. He was well known in his time both as performer on the lute and manufacturer of viols and lutes. His works in tablature are of considerable historic value. They include *Musica Teusch auf die Instrument der grossen unnd kleinen Geygen, auch Lautten* (Nuremberg, 1532; 2nd ed., 1537; 3rd ed., under the title *Musica und Tabulatur,* 1546); *Tabulatur auff die Laudten* (Nuremberg, 1533); *Ein newes sehr künstlichs Lautenbuch* (Nuremberg, 1552; with pieces by Francesco da Milano, Ant. Rotta, Joan da Crema, Rosseto, and Gintzler). Reprints of his works have been ed. by W. Tappert in *Sang und Klang aus alter Zeit* (1906) and by H. D. Bruger in *Schule des Lautenspiels* I, 2, and *Alte Lautenkunst I.*—Cf. W. Tappert, *Die Lautenbücher des Hans Gerle* in 'Monatshefte für Musikgeschichte' (1886).

German, Sir Edward (real name Edward German Jones), English composer; b. Whitchurch, Feb. 17, 1862; d. London, Nov. 11, 1936. He began serious music-study in Jan., 1880, under W. C. Hay at Shrewsbury; in Sept. he entered the Royal Academy of Music, studying organ (Steggall), violin (Weist-Hill and Burnett), theory (Banister), and composition and orchestration (Prout), graduating with a symphony; he was elected Fellow of the Royal Academy of Music in 1895. In 1888-9 he conducted the orch. at the Globe Theatre; here his incidental music to Richard Mansfield's production of *King Richard III* was so successful that Sir Henry Irving commissioned him to write the music to *Henry VIII* (1892). German was then enabled to give up teaching and to devote himself entirely to composition. He was knighted in 1928; awarded the gold medal of the Royal Philh. Society in 1934. His works include: 2 symphonies; *Gypsy Suite* (1892); Suite in D minor (1895); English fantasia, *Commemoration* (1897); symph. poem, *Hamlet* (1897); symph. suite, *The Seasons* (1899); *Rhapsody on March-themes* (1902); *Funeral March* in D minor for orch.; *Welsh Rhapsody* (1904); *Coronation March and Hymn* (1911); Theme and 6 variations (1919); *The Willow Song* (1922); Serenade, for voice, piano, oboe, clarinet, bassoon, and horn; *The Guitar; Bolero* for violin and orch.; incidental music to *Richard III* (1889), *Henry VIII* (1892), *As You Like It* (1896), *Much Ado About Nothing* (1898), *Nell Gwyn* (1900), *The Conqueror* (1905).— Operas: The *Emerald Isle* (with Sullivan; 1901); *Merrie England* (1902); *A Princess of Kensington* (1903); *Tom Jones* (1907); *Fallen Fairies* (1909; the last libretto written by Sir W. S. Gilbert);—all at the Savoy Theatre; operetta *The Rival Poets* (1901);—many piano solos (incl. a suite) and duets; chamber music, organ pieces, etc.; Te Deum in F; Patriotic Hymn, *Canada;* Intercessory Hymn, *Father Omnipotent; Three Albums of Lyrics* (with Harold Boulton); *The Just So Song Book* (words by Rudyard Kipling); other songs; etc.—Cf. W. H. Scott, *Sir Edward German* (London, 1932).

Gernsheim, Friedrich, German composer and conductor; b. Worms, July 17, 1839; d. Berlin, Sept. 11, 1916. He studied piano with Rosenhain at Frankfurt, and as a young boy appeared in public there. He later studied at the Leipzig Cons. with Moscheles (piano) and Hauptmann (theory); then was in Paris (1855-61) for further studies. Returning to Germany, he became prof. at the Cologne Cons. (1865-74); then conducted choral concerts in Rotterdam (1874-80), subsequently taught at the Stern Cons. in Berlin (1890-97); also conducted various choral societies and continued to appear as a pianist. He was greatly appreciated as a composer in his lifetime. His works are marked by a characteristic Romantic quality, mostly as an epigone of Schumann; he was also influenced by Brahms, who was his friend. He wrote 4 symphonies, several overtures, a piano concerto, a violin concerto; 4 string quartets, 3 piano quartets, 2 piano trios, 1 string quintet, 3 violin sonatas, 2 cello sonatas, and numerous choral works, songs, and piano pieces, aggregating to 92 opus numbers.—Cf. K. Holl, *Friedrich Gernsheim, Leben, Erscheinung und Werk* (Leipzig, 1928).

Gérold (zhā-rōhl'), **Théodore,** eminent Alsatian music scholar; b. Strasbourg, Oct. 26, 1866; d. Allenwiller, Feb. 16, 1956. He studied theology at the Univ. of Strasbourg, and musicology with Gustaf Jacobsthal. In 1890 he went to Frankfurt to study singing with Jules Stockhausen; then took courses at the Paris Cons. He received his *Dr. phil.* from the German Univ. of Strasbourg with a dissertation, *Zur Geschichte der französischen Gesangskunst;* was a lecturer on music at the Univ. of Basel from 1916 to 1918; returned to Strasbourg in 1919 to lecture on music at the new French Univ., from which in 1921 he received the degree of *Dr. ès lettres,* and in 1927, the degree of *Dr. en théologie.* He retired from the Univ. in 1937; occupied an ecclesiastical lecturing position in Allenwiller in 1951. Among his writings are *Le Manuscrit de Bayeux, chansons du XVe siècle; Kleine Sängerfibel* (Mainz, 1908); *Chansons populaires des XVe et XVIe siècles* (Strasbourg, 1913);

Les Psaumes de Clément Marot et leurs mélodies (Strasbourg, 1919); *La musicologie médiévale* (Paris, 1921); *L'Art du chant en France au XVIIe siècle* (Strasbourg, 1921); *Schubert* (Paris, 1923); *J. S. Bach* (Paris, 1925); *Les Pères de l'église et la musique* (Paris, 1931); *La musique au moyen âge* (Paris, 1932); *Histoire de la musique des origines à la fin du XIVe siècle* (Paris, 1936). Gérold also made important contributions to Lavignac's 'Encyclopédie' and to the 'New Oxford History of Music.' He transcribed into modern notation (with critical notes) the melodies of the 14th-century 'drame provençal' *Le Jeu de Ste. Agnès,* ed. by A. Jeanroy (Paris, 1931).

Gerschefski, Edwin, American composer; b. Meriden, Conn., June 10, 1909. He studied composition at Yale Univ. with D. S. Smith and R. Donovan, graduating in 1931 (M.B.; Ph.D.). He was the first recipient of the C. Ditson Fellowship for study abroad; he went to London and entered the Matthay School as a piano pupil, winning the silver medal; he then took lessons with Schnabel in Italy; on his return to America he studied with Schillinger in New York. In 1940 he was appointed instructor in piano, theory, and composition at Converse College, Spartanburg, S. C.; since 1947, dean of the Converse College School of Music. As composer, Gerschefski often adopts experimental techniques. He is the author of a book, *Anyone Can Compose* (in MS). Works: *Classic Symphony;* violin concerto; piano concerto in one movement; Toccata and Fugue, for orch.; cantata *Half Moon Mountain,* after a story in 'Time' magazine (Spartanburg, April 30, 1948); *Discharge in E* and *Streamline* for band; septet for brass instruments; piano quintet; *Patterns* for string quartet; *Songs Without Words* for trumpet and piano; *Workout* for saxophone and piano; sonatina for clarinet and piano; 100 variations for unaccompanied violin; numerous choral and piano pieces.

Gershkovitch, Jacques, conductor; b. Irkutsk, Siberia, Jan. 4, 1884; d. Sandy, Oregon, Aug. 12, 1953. He studied at the St. Petersburg Cons. with Rimsky-Korsakov, Glazunov, and Nicolas Tcherepnin. He graduated with honors, and received a scholarship to study in Germany under Artur Nikisch. Upon his return to Russia, he became director of the Irkutsk Cons.; after the Revolution, he joined the orch. of Pavlova's ballet troupe as flutist, and traveled with it to the Orient. He settled in Tokyo, where he organized special concerts for young people; after the earthquake of 1923, he went to the U. S.; conducted guest engagements with the San Francisco Symph.; then settled in Portland, Oregon, where he founded the Portland Junior Symphony; he conducted it for 30 years until his death.

Gershwin, George, greatly talented American composer; b. Brooklyn, N. Y., Sept. 28, 1898; d. Beverly Hills, Calif., July 11, 1937. His real name was Jacob Gershvin, according to birth registry; his father was an immigrant from Russia whose original name was Gershovitz. Gershwin's extraordinary career began when he was 16, playing the piano in music stores to demonstrate new popular songs. His studies were desultory; he took piano lessons with Ernest Hutcheson and Charles Hambitzer in N. Y.; he studied harmony with Edward Kilenyi and with Rubin Goldmark; later on, when he was already a famous composer of popular music, he continued to take private lessons; he studied counterpoint with Henry Cowell and with Wallingford Riegger; during the last years of his life, he applied himself with great earnestness to studying with Joseph Schillinger in an attempt to organize his technique in a scientific manner; some of Schillinger's methods he applied in *Porgy and Bess* and in the piano preludes. But it was his melodic talent and a genius for rhythmic invention, rather than any studies, that made him a genuinely important American composer. As far as worldly success was concerned, there was no period of struggle in Gershwin's life; one of his earliest songs, *Swanee,* written at the age of 19, became enormously popular (more than a million copies sold; 2,250,000 phonograph records). Possessing phenomenal energy, he produced musical comedies in close succession, using the fashionable jazz formulas in original and ingenious ways. A milestone of his career was *Rhapsody in Blue,* for piano and jazz orchestra, in which he applied the jazz idiom to an essentially classical form. He played the solo part at a special concert conducted by Paul Whiteman at Aeolian Hall, N. Y., on Feb. 12, 1924. The orchestration was by Ferde Grofé, a circumstance that generated rumors of Gershwin's inability to score for instruments; this, however, was quickly refuted by his production of several orchestral works, scored by himself in a brilliant fashion. He played the solo part of his piano concerto in F, with Walter Damrosch and the N. Y. Symph. Orch. (Dec. 3, 1925); this work had a certain vogue, but its popularity never equalled that of the *Rhapsody in Blue.* Reverting again to a more popular idiom, Gershwin wrote a symphonic work, *An American in Paris* (N. Y. Philh., Dec. 13, 1928, Damrosch conducting). His *Rhapsody No. 2* was performed by Koussevitzky and the Boston Symph. on Jan. 29, 1932, but was unsuccessful; there followed a *Cuban Overture* (1934) and *3 Preludes* for piano (1936). In the meantime, Gershwin became engaged in his most ambitious undertaking: the composition of *Porgy and Bess,* an American opera in a folk manner, for Negro singers, after the book by Dubose Heyward. It was first staged in Boston on Sept. 30, 1935, and shortly afterwards in N. Y. Its reception by the press was not uniformly favorable, but its songs rapidly attained great popularity (*Summertime, I Got Plenty o' Nuttin', It Ain't Necessarily So, Bess, You Is My Woman Now*); the opera has been successfully revived in N. Y. and elsewhere; it received international recognition when an American company of Negro singers toured South America and Europe in 1955, reaching a climax of success with several performances in Russia (Leningrad, Dec. 26, 1955, and also Moscow); it was the first American opera company to visit Russia. Gershwin's death (of a brain tumor) at the age of 38 was mourned as a great loss to American art; memorial concerts have been held at Lewisohn Stadium, N. Y., on each anniversary of his death, with large attendance. His musical comedies include: numbers for *George White's Scandals* of 1920, 1921, 1922, 1923, and 1924; *Our Nell* (1922); *Sweet Little Devil* (1923); *Lady Be Good* (1924); *Primrose* (1924); *Tip Toes* (1925); *Song of the Flame* (1925); *135th Street* (one-act, 1923; produced in concert form Dec. 29, 1925, Paul Whiteman conducting); *Oh Kay!* (1926); *Strike Up the Band* (1927); *Funny Face* (1927); *Rosalie* (1928); *Treasure Girl* (1928); *Show Girl* (1929); *Girl Crazy* (1930); *Of Thee I Sing* (1931; a political satire which was the first musical to win a Pulitzer Prize); *Pardon My English* (1932); *Let 'Em Eat Cake* (1933); for motion pictures: *Shall We Dance, Damsel in Distress, Goldwyn Follies* (left unfinished at his death; completed by Vernon Duke). A collection of his songs and piano transcriptions, *George Gershwin's Song Book,* was publ.—Cf. S. N. Behrman, *Troubadour,* in 'The New Yorker' (May, 1929); I. Goldberg, *George Gershwin, A Study in American Music* (N. Y., 1931); C. Engel, *George Gershwin's Song Book* in Views and Reviews of the 'Mus. Quarterly' (Oct., 1932); V. Thomson, *George Gershwin,* in 'Modern Music' (Nov., 1935); F. Jacobi, *George Gershwin,* in 'Modern Music' (Nov.-Dec., 1937); D. Ewen, *Twentieth Century Composers* (N. Y., 1937); M. Armitage, editor, *George Gershwin,* a collection of articles (N Y., 1938); O. Levant, *A Smattering of Ignorance* (N. Y., 1938); J. T. Howard, *Our Contemporary Composers* (N. Y., 1941); D. Ewen, *The Book of Modern Composers* (N. Y., 1942); R. Chalupt, *George Gershwin, le musicien de la 'Rhapsody in Blue'* (Paris, 1949); M. V. Pugliaro, *Rapsodia in blu; l'arte e l'amore nella vita di George Gershwin* (Turin, 1951); D. Ewen, *A Journey to Greatness; George Gershwin* (N. Y., 1956).

Gerstberger, Karl, German music scholar and composer; b. Neisse, Feb. 12, 1892; d. Bremen, Oct. 30, 1955. He studied in Cologne with Othegraven and in Munich with Courvoisier. In 1926 he gave a concert of his works in Berlin. In his music he endeavored to revive the spirit of Lutheran polyphony. He wrote choral works, lieder, a string quartet, 2 string trios, etc.; published a collection of essays, *Zum Schicksal der Musik.*

Gerster, Etelka, Hungarian dramatic soprano; b. Kaschau, June 25, 1855; d. Pontecchio, near Bologna, Aug. 20, 1920. One of the renowned singers of her century, a 'prima donna assoluta,' she studied with Mathilde Marchesi in Vienna, then made her début in Venice as Gilda in *Rigoletto,* Jan. 8, 1876. Her great success resulted in engagements in Berlin and Budapest in Italian opera under the direction of Carlo Gardini. She married Gardini on April 16, 1877, and continued her successful career, making her London début on June 23, 1877 as Amina in *Sonnambula,* and her U. S. début in the same role on Nov. 18, 1878 at the N. Y. Academy of Music. She returned to London for three more seasons (1878-80), then sang again in N. Y. in 1880-83 and in 1887. After retiring, she taught singing in Berlin, and in N. Y. at the Institute of Musical Art (1907). She wrote *Stimmführer* (1906; 2nd. ed., 1908).

Gerster, Ottmar, German violist and composer; b. Braunfels, June 29, 1897. He studied in Frankfurt (1913-16); was in the Army during World War I; from 1927-39, teaching at the Folkwang-Schule in Essen; then again in the Army (1940); since 1946, prof. of composition at the Musik-Hochschule in Weimar; appointed director there (1948). He wrote the operas *Liselotte* (Essen, 1933), *Enoch Arden* (Düsseldorf, 1936;

very successful), *Die Hexe von Passau* (Düsseldorf, 1941), and *Das verzauberte Ich* (1949); a *Thuringian Symphony* (1953), and a great deal of instrumental music.—Cf. O. Goldhammer, *Professor Ottmar Gerster* (Berlin, 1953).

Gerstman, Blanche, South African composer; b. Cape Town, April 2, 1910. She studied at the South African College of Music with W. H. Bell; in 1950 she went to London and took additional courses at the Royal Academy of Music. Upon her return to South Africa she played double bass in the municipal orch. of Cape Town. She has written mainly for chorus, and has set a number of South African poems to music.

Gertler, André, Hungarian violinist; b. Budapest, July 26, 1907. He studied with Hubay and Kodály; in 1928 settled in Belgium; in 1931 he formed the 'Quatuor Gertler' in Brussels; since 1940 prof. at the Brussels Cons. Has made numerous tours in Europe, specializing in modern music.

Gervaise (zhär-vās'), **Claude,** French composer of the 16th century. He was a viol-player, chamber musician to François I and Henri II. He composed many dances and *chansons;* 6 vols. of his *Danceries à 4 et 5 parties* were published by Attaignant from about 1545 to 1556, but only 3 vols. remain; a selection of his dances is included in vol. 23 (*Danceries*) of 'Les Maîtres Musiciens' ed. by H. Expert (1908). Several *chansons* by Gervaise appear in 16th-century collections.

Gerville-Réache (zhär-vēl'-rā-ăhsh), **Jeanne,** French dramatic contralto; b. Orthez, March 26, 1882; d. New York, Jan. 5, 1915. She spent her childhood in Guadaloupe, French West Indies, where her father, from whom she received almost her entire education, was governor. In 1898 she was sent to Paris to study singing with Laborde; 1899-1900, pupil of Mme. Viardot-García, and in 1901 of Jean Criticos; début as Orfeo at the Opéra-Comique in 1900; engaged there for the season; 1902, at Théâtre de la Monnaie, Brussels; 1903, again at Opéra-Comique; 1904-6, tour of France; 1907-10, member of Manhattan Opera Co., New York; 1911-12, of Chicago Opera Co.; 1913-14, of National Grand Opera Co. of Canada. In 1908 she married Dr. G. Gibier-Rambeaud, director of the Pasteur Institute in New York. She created the rôles of Catherine (Erlanger's *Le Juif polonais,* 1900) and Geneviève *(Pelléas et Mélisande,* 1902).

Gesensway, Louis, American violinist and composer; b. Dvinsk, Latvia, Feb. 19, 1906. The family moved to Canada when he was a child; he studied violin and gave numerous recitals in Toronto and other Canadian cities. In 1926 he joined the Philadelphia Orch. as a violinist. Among his works are a *Suite for Strings and Percussion* (1935); flute concerto (Philadelphia, Nov. 1, 1946); *A Double Portrait* (N. Y. Philharmonic, Nov. 1, 1952); *The Four Squares of Philadelphia,* orchestral sketch (Philadelphia, Feb. 25, 1955); quartet for clarinet and strings (1950); quartet for oboe, bassoon, violin, and viola (1951); sonata for solo bassoon, etc. Gesensway has developed a system of 'color harmony' by expanding and contracting the diatonic scale into new intervallic progressions.

Gesualdo, Don **Carlo,** Prince of Venosa, lutenist and composer; b. Naples, c. 1560; d. there, Sept. 8, 1613. Probably studied with Pomponio Nenna; 1590, his unfaithful wife and 1st cousin, Maria d'Avalos, and her lover were murdered at Gesualdo's orders; 1594, he was at the court of the Estensi in Ferrara, where he married his 2nd wife, Leonora d'Este, in that year; some time after the death of the Duke of Ferrara, in 1597, Don Carlo returned to Naples, where he remained till death. Living at the epoch when the 'new music' (the homophonic style) made its appearance, he was one of the most original musicians of the time. Like Rore, Banchieri, and Vincentino, he was a so-called 'chromaticist'; his later madrigals reveal a distinctly individual style of expression and are characterized by strong contrasts, new (for their time) harmonic progressions, and a skilful use of dissonance; he was a master in producing tone-color through the use of different voice registers and in expressing the poetic contents of his texts.—Publ. 6 vols. of madrigals *a* 5 (Genoa, 1585, each part separately; an edition in score was publ. by G. Pavoni, Venice, 1613). Reprints of his works have been publ. by L. Torchi in 'L'Arte Musicale in Italia' IV, by A. Schering in *Musikgeschichte in Beispielen* (No. 167), by W. Weismann (a selection of 8 pieces; Peters Ed., 1931), etc. A group of 5-part madrigals, transcribed into modern notation by I. Pizzetti, is contained in Nos. 59-62 of the 'Raccolta nazionale delle musiche italiane' (Milan, 1919). The publ. of a complete ed. of his works was begun by the Istituto Italiano per la Storia della Musica (Rome); only one vol. (2 books of madrigals) appeared (1942).—Cf. Ferd.

Keiner, *Die Madrigale Gesualdos von Venosa* (diss., Leipzig, 1914); Cecil Gray and Philip Heseltine, *Carlo Gesualdo, Prince of Venosa, Musician and Murderer* (London, 1926); F. Vatielli, *Il Principe di Venosa e Leonora d'Este* (Milan, 1941).

Gevaert (gĕ-vahrt'), **François Auguste,** eminent Belgian composer and musicologist; b. Huysse, near Audenarde, July 31, 1828; d. Brussels, Dec. 24, 1908. He was a pupil of Sommère (piano) and Mengal (composition) at Ghent Cons. (1841-7), taking the Grand Prix de Rome for composition; from 1843 he was also organist at the Jesuit church. He produced 2 operas in 1848, with some success; lived in Paris for a year (1849-50), and was commissioned to write an opera for the Théâtre-Lyrique; then a year in Spain, his *Fantasía sobre motivos españoles* winning him the order of Isabella la Católica; he also wrote a *Rapport sur la situation de la musique en Espagne* (Brussels, 1851). After a short visit to Italy and Germany, he returned to Ghent in 1852, and up to 1861 brought out 9 operas in quick succession. In 1857 his festival cantata *De nationale verjaerdag* won him the order of Léopold. In 1867 he was appointed chorus master at the Opéra, Paris; in 1870, the German investment caused him to return home, and from 1871 he was director of the Brussels Cons., succeeding Fétis. In this position he gave evidence of remarkable talent for organization. As conductor of the 'Concerts du Cons.' he exerted a far-reaching influence through his historical concerts, producing the works of all nations and periods. In 1873 he was elected member of the Academy, succeeding Mercadante; in 1907 he was created a baron.—Works: 12 operas; 3 cantatas; a *Missa pro defunctis* and *Super flumina Babylonis* (both for male chorus and orch.); overture *Flandre au lion;* ballads *(Philipp van Artevelde,* etc.); songs (many in the collection 'Nederlandsche Zangstukken').—Even more important than Gevaert's compositions are his scholarly books: *Leerboek van den Gregoriaenschen Zang* (1856); *Traité d'Instrumentation* (1863; revised and enlarged as *Nouveau traité de l'Instrum.,* 1885; German translation by Riemann, 1887; Spanish by Neuparth, 1896; Russian by Rebikov, 1899); *Histoire et Théorie de la musique de l'antiquité* (2 vols., 1875, 1881); *Les Origines du chant liturgique de l'église latine* (1890; German translation by Riemann; threw new [for that time] light on the Gregorian tradition); *Cours méthodique d'Orchestration* (2 vols., 1890; complement of *Nouveau traité*); *La Mélopée antique dans l'église latine* (1895; a monumental work); *Les Problèmes musicaux d'Aristote* (3 vols., 1899-1902; adopts the theories of Westphal, certain of which were later proved untenable); *Traité d'Harmonie théorique et pratique* (2 vols., 1905, 1907). Edited 'Les gloires de l'Italie' (a collection of vocal numbers from operas, oratorios, cantatas, etc., of the 17th and 18th centuries); 'Recueil de chansons du XVe siècle' (transcribed in modern notation); 'Vademecum de l'organiste' (classic transcriptions).—Cf. F. Dufour, *Le Baron François Auguste Gevaert* (Brussels, 1909); E. Closson, *Gevaert* (Brussels, 1928).

Ghedini, Giorgio Federico, Italian composer; b. Cuneo, July 11, 1892. He studied piano and organ with Evasio Lovazzano in Turin, cello with S. Grossi, and composition with G. Cravero; then at the Liceo Musicale in Bologna with M. E. Bossi, graduating in 1911. In 1918 he became instructor at the Liceo Musicale in Turin; from 1938-41, taught composition at the Cons. of Parma; in 1941, held a similar post at the Cons. of Milan; in 1951, was appointed its director. —Works: operas: *Maria d'Alessandria* (Bergamo, Sept. 9, 1937); *Re Hassan* (Venice, Jan. 26, 1939); *La Pulce d'oro* (Genoa, Feb. 15, 1940); *Le Baccanti* (Milan, Feb. 22, 1948); *Billy Budd* (Venice, Sept. 7, 1949); *L'Ipocrita felice,* after Max Beerbohm's *The Happy Hypocrite* (Milan, March 10, 1956); for orch.: *Marinaresca e Baccanale* (Rome, Feb. 2, 1936); *Architecture* (Rome, Jan. 19, 1941); *Concerto dell'Albatro,* after Melville's *Moby Dick,* for narrator and small orch. (Rome, Dec. 11, 1945); piano concerto (1946); *Musica notturna* (1947); concerto for 2 pianos and chamber orch. (1947); concerto for violin and string orch., subtitled *Il Belprato* (1947); concerto for flute, violin, and chamber orch., subtitled *L'Alderina* (1951); concerto for 2 cellos and orch., subtitled *L'Olmeneta* (1951); *Concentus Basiliensis* for violin and orch. (1954); piano quartet; violin sonata; several sacred choral works; songs; several transcriptions for modern performance of works by Monteverdi, Andrea Gabrieli, Giovanni Gabrieli, etc.

Gheyn (gān), **Matthias van den,** Flemish organist and composer; b. Tirlemont, Brabant, April 7, 1721; d. Louvain, June 22, 1785. From 1741, organist at St. Peter's, Louvain, and, from 1745, town 'carillonneur'; he was celebrated in both capacities. —Publications: *Fondements de la basse continue* (lessons and sonatinas for organ and violin); 6 *Divertissements pour clavecin* (c. 1760); also pieces for organ and for carillon.—Cf. S. van Elewyck, *Matthias van den Gheyn* (Louvain, 1862).

Ghione (gē-ōh'-nā), **Franco,** Italian conductor; b. Acqui, Aug. 26, 1889. He studied violin with his father, organized a band which he later conducted. After study at the Parma Cons., he became assistant conductor to Toscanini at La Scala (1922-23). After guest appearances in Europe, he made his American début with the Detroit Civic Opera Co. (1937); from 1937 to 1940 he was associate conductor of the Detroit Symph. Orch. He is the composer of several orchestral works.

Ghis, Henri, French pianist and composer; b. Toulon, May 17, 1839; d. Paris, April 24, 1908. He studied at the Paris Cons. with Marmontel (piano); received 1st prize in 1854; also organ with Benoist (graduated in 1855). He became a fashionable piano teacher in Paris; many aristocratic ladies (to whom he dedicated his pieces) were his pupils. He was also the first teacher of Ravel. He publ. salon music for piano: waltzes, mazurkas, polonaises, polkas, gavottes, caprices, etc., often with superinduced titles, as *Séduction, Menuet de la petite princesse, La Marquisette,* etc.; but his name is mostly known through his extremely popular arrangement of an old aria, which he publ. for piano as *Air Louis XIII* (1868); the actual melody was definitely not by Louis XIII; its authorship is unknown; in all probability it is an old French folksong.

Ghisi, Federico, Italian musicologist; b. Shanghai, China (of Italian parents), Feb. 25, 1901. His father was a member of the diplomatic corps in China; the family returned to Italy in 1908, and settled in Milan. Ghisi studied music with Ghedini; graduated from the Turin Liceo Musicale; in 1932, settled in Florence; in 1937, became instructor at the Univ. of Florence; gave lectures on Italian music in France, England, and the U. S.—Publications: *I Canti Carnascialeschi* (Florence, 1937); *Le Feste musicali della Firenze Medicea* (Florence, 1939); *Alle Fonti della Monodia* (Milan, 1940); contributed to various musical journals. See his autobiographical entry in 'Die Musik in Geschichte und Gegenwart.'

Ghislanzoni, Antonio, Italian writer and dramatic poet; b. Lecco, Nov. 25, 1824; d. Caprino-Bergamasco, July 16, 1893. Intended for the church, his fine baritone voice led him to adopt the career of a stage singer (Lodi, 1846), which he speedily abandoned, however, for literary work. He became the manager of 'Italia Musicale,' and was for years the editor of the Milan 'Gazzetta Musicale,' to which he remained a faithful contributor till death. He wrote over 60 opera libretti, that of *Aida* being the most famous; publ. *Reminiscenze artistiche* (which contains an episode entitled *La casa di Verdi a Sant' Agata,* etc.).—Cf. T. Mantovani, *Librettisti Verdiani,* VI: *Antonio Ghislanzoni,* in 'Musica d'oggi' (March-April, 1929).

Ghys (gēs), **Joseph,** Belgian violinist; b. Ghent, 1801; d. St. Petersburg, Aug. 22, 1848. A pupil of Lafont at Brussels Cons., he later taught in Amiens and Nantes, and, beginning in 1832, made concert tours in France, Belgium, Germany, Austria, and northern Europe. He wrote *Le Mouvement perpétuel* for violin with string quartet, a violin concerto, and other music for the violin.

Giacche, Giacchetto. See **Berchem** and **Buus.**

Giacomelli (jah-cōh-mĕl'-lē), **Geminiano,** Italian composer; b. Piacenza, c. 1692; d. Parma, Jan. 24, 1740. He studied with Capelli at Parma, and wrote his first opera, *Ipermestra,* in 1724. It was the first of 19 operas which he wrote for Venice, Parma, Naples, and other Italian towns; the most popular was *Cesare in Egitto* (Milan, 1735). He was *maestro di cappella* for the church of San Giovanni in Piacenza from 1727 to 1732; he held a similar post at Santa Casa in Loreto from 1738. His many church compositions include an oratorio, *La conversione di Santa Margherita,* and a setting of Psalm VIII for two tenors and bass.—Cf. G. Tebaldini, *L'Archivio musicale della Cappella Lauretana* (Loreto, 1929); C. Anguissola, *Geminiano Giacomelli e Sebastiano Nasolini, musicisti piacentini* (Piacenza, 1935).

Gialdini (jăhl-dē'nē), **Gialdino,** Italian conductor and composer; b. Pescia, Nov. 10, 1843; d. there, March 6, 1919. He was a pupil of T. Mabellini at Florence. His first opera, *Rosamunda* (prize opera in a competition instituted by the Pergola Theater, Florence), given in 1868 was unsuccessful; after producing 2 'opere buffe,' *La Secchia rapita* (Florence, 1872) and *L'Idolo cinese* (1874), in collaboration with other musicians, he gave up opera writing, and devoted himself with success to conducting. Later he again turned to dramatic composition, producing the operas *I due soci* (Bologna, Feb. 24, 1892), *La Pupilla* (Trieste, Oct. 23, 1896), *La Bufera* (Pola, Nov. 26, 1910); these operas were successful. He also publ. 'Eco della Lombardia,' a collection of 50 folksongs.

Gianettini (jăh-nĕht-tē'-nē) (or Zanettini), **Antonio,** Italian composer; b. 1648; d. Munich, July 12, 1721. He was organist at San Marco, Venice (1676-86); produced 3 operas in Venice, winning a reputation that led to his appointment as maestro di cappella at the court of Modena; was organist at Modena from 1686 till 1721, except during 1695, when he brought out 3 operas in Hamburg. He moved to Munich with his family in May, 1721. He composed 6 operas; 6 oratorios; several cantatas; a Kyrie *a* 5; and Psalms *a* 4, with instruments (Venice, 1717). — Cf. E. J. Luin, *Antonio Gianettini e la musica a Modena alla fine del secolo 17* (Modena, 1931).

Gianneo, Luis, Argentinian composer; b. Buenos Aires, Jan. 9, 1897. He studied with Gaito and Drangosch; composed *Turay-Turay,* symph. poem (Buenos Aires, Sept. 21, 1929); *Overture for a Children's Comedy* (NBC Symph. Orch., Dec. 2, 1941); sinfonietta (Buenos Aires, Sept. 20, 1943); violin concerto (Buenos Aires, April 13, 1944); piano pieces and teaching material.

Giannetti, Giovanni, Italian composer; b. Naples, March 25, 1869; d. Rio de Janeiro, Dec. 10, 1934. He studied in Naples, Trieste, and Vienna; 1912-13, director of the Liceo Musicale, Siena; 1915, in Rome, where (from 1920) he was musical director of the Teatro dei Piccoli with which he toured Europe and South America.—Operas: *L'Erebo* (Naples, April 9, 1891), *Padron Maurizio* (Naples, Sept. 26, 1896), *Milena* (Naples, Nov. 15, 1897), *Il Violinaro di Cremona* (Milan, Nov. 23, 1898), *Don Marzio* (Venice, March 2, 1903), *Il Cristo alla festa di Purim* (Rio de Janeiro, Dec. 16, 1904), *Il Nazareno* (Buenos Aires, Jan. 20, 1911), *La Serenata di Pierrot,* pantomime (Rome, April 18, 1917), *Cuore e bautte* (Rome, June 5, 1918), and *Il Principe Re,* operetta (Rome, July 7, 1920).

Giannini, Dusolina, American soprano; b. Philadelphia, Dec. 19, 1902. She came of a musical family: her mother was a violinist; her father, Ferruccio Giannini (1869-1948), was a tenor who sang in Italy and made one of the earliest phonograph recordings (1896). She studied with Marcella Sembrich, made her concert début at Carnegie Hall in 1925. Her operatic début in Hamburg in 1927 was followed by appearances in London (1930-31), Berlin, Vienna, Oslo, and other European cities; she also sang at the Salzburg Festival (1934-36). She made her début with the Metropolitan Opera on Feb. 12, 1936 in the role of Aida. She continued to sing with the Metropolitan; created the part of Hester in *The Scarlet Letter,* by her brother, Vittorio Giannini, at Hamburg, June 2, 1938.

Giannini, Vittorio, American composer (brother of Dusolina Giannini); b. Philadelphia, Oct. 19, 1903. He won a scholarship at the Milan Cons. and studied there four years; returning to the U. S., he studied privately with Martini and Trucco in N.Y.; in 1925, entered the Juilliard Graduate School, where he was a pupil of Rubin Goldmark and Hans Letz. He graduated in 1931, and the next year won the Grand Prix de Rome of the American Academy and studied there for four years. He was appointed teacher of composition and orchestration at the Juilliard and Manhattan Schools of Music in 1939.—Works: operas: *Lucedia* (Munich, Oct. 20, 1934); *Flora* (1937); *The Scarlet Letter,* based on Hawthorne's novel (Hamburg, June 2, 1938); operas for radio: *Beauty and the Beast* (1938); *Blennerhasset* (1939); *The Taming of the Shrew* (in concert form, Cincinnati Symph. Orch., Jan. 31, 1953; in color telecast, NBC opera theater, March 13, 1954); for orch.: *Prelude and Fugue* for string orch. (1926); Suite, in 4 movements (1931); symph. (NBC orch., Jan. 19, 1936, composer conducting); piano concerto (N. Y., 1937); *Triptych* (1937); organ concerto (Vienna, 1937); symph. commissioned for N. Y. World's Fair (1939); concerto for 2 pianos (N. Y., 1940); vocal works: *Stabat Mater* (1920); *Madrigal* for vocal quartet (1930); cantata, *Primavera* (1933); *Requiem* (1937); cantata, *Lament for Adonis* (1940); *Canticle of the Martyrs* (commissioned for the 500th anniversary of the Moravian Church, 1957; Moravian Festival at Winston-Salem, N. C., June, 1957); piano quintet (1931); *Concerto grosso* for strings (1931); woodwind quintet (1933); piano trio (1933); 2 violin sonatas (1926, 1945); piano sonata; many songs.

Giarda (jahr'-dah), **Luigi Stefano,** Italian cellist and composer; b. Cassolnuovo, Pavia,

March 19, 1868; d. Viña del Mar, Chile, Jan. 3, 1953. He was a pupil at the Milan Cons.; teacher at the Padua music school (1893-7); instructor at the Royal Cons. in Naples (1897-1910); then went to Santiago, Chile, where he was vice-director of the Cons. of Santiago; also taught theory there.—Works: The operas *Reietto* (Naples, 1898) and *Giorgio Byron* (Santiago, Chile, 1910); symph. poems, *Loreley; La vida; Triptico* (*Civilization, War, Peace*) for 3 voices and orch.; concert pieces for cello and orch.; a string quartet; Adagio for 4 celli; 2 cello sonatas; Prelude and Scherzo for violin and cello; Suite for piano and violin; studies in the thumb position for cello; etc. He was also the author of a *Trattato di armonia* (1920).

Giardini (jahr-dē'-nē), **Felice de',** Italian violinist and composer; b. Turin, April 12, 1716, d. Moscow, June 8, 1796. He was a chorister at the cathedral of Milan; studied singing with Paladini and violin with Somis. As a young man, he played in various theater orchestras in Rome and Naples, and often improvised cadenzas at the end of operatic numbers. He acquired popularity in Italy, and made a tour in Germany (1748); then went to London (1750) where he made a series of successful appearances as a concert violinist. In 1752 he joined the Italian opera in London as concertmaster and conductor; he became its impresario in 1756, and was connected with the management, with interruptions, for several more seasons, returning to the career of virtuoso and teacher in 1766. He conducted the Three Choirs festival (1770-76), and was concertmaster at the Pantheon Concerts (1774-80), also conducted other theater orchestras. From 1784-89, he was in Italy, but returned to London in 1789 and led three seasons of Italian opera, without financial success. In 1796 he was engaged as violinist in Russia, and gave his initial concert in Moscow on March 24, 1796, but soon became ill, and died shortly afterwards. As a violinist he was eclipsed in London by Salomon and Cramer, but he left his mark on musical society there. He also wrote music for various pasticcios; among operas entirely by him were: *Rosmira* (April 30, 1757), *Siroe* (Dec. 13, 1763), *Enea e Lavinia* (May 5, 1764), and *Il re pastore* (March 7, 1765). He also wrote several overtures, concertos, string quartets, and violin sonatas.—Cf. R. A. Mooser, *Annales de la Musique et des Musiciens en Russie au XVIIIe siècle* (Lausanne, 1951; vol. 2, p. 657f.).

Giazotto, Remo, Italian musicologist; b. Rome, Sept. 4, 1910. He studied piano at the Milan Cons. and later took a course in literature at the Univ. of Genoa; undertook a detailed study of the musical history of Genoa, and publ. a work of fundamental value, *La musica a Genova nella vita pubblica e privata dal XIII al XVIII secolo* (1952). He is also the author of a definitive biography of Tomaso Albinoni (Milan, 1945), containing newly discovered materials as well as a thematic catalogue. He further publ. a monograph, *Ferruccio Busoni, la vita nell' opera* (Milan, 1948).

Gibbons, Christopher, English organist and composer; b. London (baptized Aug. 22), 1615; d. there, Oct. 20, 1676. He was the son of Orlando Gibbons; pupil at the Chapel Royal; in 1638, he became organist at Winchester Cathedral; in 1660, he was appointed organist of the Chapel Royal, private organist to Charles II, and organist at Westminster Abbey. He received the degree of Mus. D. from Oxford in 1663, at the special request of the king. He wrote anthems and many string fantasies, now in MS in the British Museum, Christ Church, Oxford, the Royal College of Music, Marsh's Library, Dublin, and Durham and Ely Cathedrals; some of his motets are in Playford's 'Cantica sacra' (1674). He also collaborated with Matthew Locke in the music for Shirley's masque, *Cupid and Death.*

Gibbons, Edward, English musician; b. Cambridge, 1568; d. probably Exeter, c. 1650. The eldest living son of William Gibbons, who founded this musical family, he was the brother of Ellis and Orlando. He received a B. Mus. degree from both Oxford and Cambridge; after serving as a lay clerk at King's College, Cambridge, he became master of choristers in 1593, and kept the post until 1598, when he went to Exeter Cathedral, where he served for many years, with the titles of "priest-vicar" and succentor, though he remained a layman. Little of his music is in existence; a few of his compositions, all for the church, are in the British Museum, at Christ Church, Oxford, and in the Bodleian Library.

Gibbons, Ellis, English composer and organist, brother of Edward and Orlando Gibbons; b. Cambridge, 1573; d. May, 1603. The only compositions of his which are known to exist are two madrigals included by Morley in his collection 'The Triumphes of Oriana' (*Long live fair Oriana* and *Round about her charret*).

Gibbons, Orlando, celebrated English composer and organist, brother of Edward and Ellis Gibbons; b. Oxford (baptized Dec. 25), 1583; d. Canterbury, June 5, 1625. He was taken to Cambridge as a small child; in 1596, he became chorister at King's College there; matriculated in 1598; composed music for various occasions for King's College (1602-3). On March 21, 1605, he was appointed organist of the Chapel Royal, retaining this position until his death. He received the degree of B. Mus. from Cambridge Univ. in 1606. In 1619 he became chamber musician to the King; in 1623, organist at Westminster Abbey. He conducted the music for the funeral of James I (1625); died of apoplexy 2 months later. His fame as a composer rests chiefly on his church music; he employed the novel technique of the 'verse anthem' (a work for chorus and solo voices, the solo passages having independent instrumental accompaniment, either for organ or strings); other works followed the traditional polyphonic style, of which Gibbons became a master. He was also one of the greatest English organists of the time. His works comprise: *Fantasies of 3 Parts . . . composed for viols* (1610; described on the title-page as 'Cut in copper, the like not heretofore extant in England'; ed. by E. F. Rimbault and reprinted 1843; new ed. by E. H. Fellowes, 1924); pieces for the virginal, in 'Parthenia' (1611, 21 pieces of Gibbons, Byrd, and John Bull; reprinted, 1834, by Musical Antiquarian Society; new ed. by Margaret H. Glyn, 1927); *The First Set of Madrigals and Mottets of 5 Parts* (London, 1612; reprinted, 1841, by Musical Antiquarian Society; new ed. by E. H. Fellowes in vol. V of 'The English Madrigal School,' 1921); 9 Fancies, appended to *20 konincklijche Fantasien op 3 Fiolen* by Th. Lupo, Coperario, and Wm. Daman (Amsterdam, 1648; reprinted by Rimbault, 1847); 2 anthems in Leighton's *Teares or Lamentacions of a Sorrowfull Soule* (the only sacred works by Gibbons publ. during his lifetime).—A 'complete' ed. of all extant sacred comps. is contained in vol. IV of 'Tudor Church Music' (Oxford, 1925); Gibbons' entire keyboard works were ed. by Margaret H. Glyn in 5 vols. (London, 1925). Further new eds. follow: The madrigal *God give you good morrow* (from 'The Cryes of London,' an early 17th cent. MS [in the Brit. Museum] containing 2 other sets of street-cries likewise polyphonically treated by T. Weelkes and R. Deering), ed. by Sir Fred. Bridge (London, 1920); 2 Fantazias for string quartet or small string orch. and a Pavan and Galliard for string sextet or small string orch., ed. by E. H. Fellowes (London, 1925); 10 pieces from the virginal book of B. Cosyn, arranged for modern organ by J. A. Fuller Maitland (London, 1925).—Cf. E. H. Fellowes, *The English Madrigal Composers* (1921); Margaret H. Glyn, *About Elizabethan Virginal Music and Its Composers* (1924); E. H. Fellowes, *Orlando Gibbons, a Short Account of His Life and Work* (1925); and *Orlando Gibbons and His Family* (1951).

Gibbs, Cecil Armstrong, English composer; b. Great Baddow near Chelmsford, Aug. 10, 1889. He studied at Trinity College, Cambridge, and at the Royal College of Music in London; later became an instructor there; in 1934 he received the Cobbett Gold Medal for his services to British chamber music. Among his works are the operas *The Blue Peter* (1924), *Twelfth Night* (1947), and *The Great Bell of Burley* (children's opera, 1949); 3 symphonies; *Spring Garland* for strings; oboe concerto; *Peacock Pie,* suite for piano and strings; rhapsody for violin and orch.; *Essex Suite* for strings; several string quartets; a lyric sonata for violin and piano; a piano trio; cantatas: *La Belle Dame sans Merci, The Lady of Shalott, Deborah and Barak, Before Daybreak, Odyssey;* also a *Pastoral Suite* for baritone, chorus, and orch. (1951). Gibbs has written more than 100 songs, many of them to poems of Walter de la Mare. His musical style adheres to the Romantic school; the influence of folk melodies and rhythms is also noticeable. See the entry on Gibbs in Cobbett's *Cyclopedic Survey of Chamber Music.*

Gibson, Archer, American organist; b. Baltimore, Dec. 5, 1875; d. Lake Mahopac, N. Y., July 15, 1952. He studied with his father, later with W. G. Owst (composition) and Harold Randolph (organ and piano); held various positions as church organist; wrote the cantatas *Emancipation* and *A Song to Music;* an opera, *Yzdra;* organ pieces; choral and orchestral arrangements.

Gideon, Miriam, American composer; b. Greeley, Col., Oct. 23, 1906. She studied in Boston with Felix Fox (piano); later in New York with Lazare Saminsky and Roger Sessions (composition); musicology at Columbia Univ. She subsequently taught music at Brooklyn College. — Works: *Three-cornered Pieces,* for flute, clarinet, and piano (1936); *Incantation on an Indian Theme,* for viola and piano (1940); *Epigrams,* for chamber orch. (1941); *Lyric Pieces,* for string orch. (1942); sonata for flute and piano (1943); *The Hound of Heaven,* for baritone, oboe, and string trio 1945); string quartet (1946); *Allegro* for woodwinds (1948); piano sonata; other piano pieces; songs.

Gieburowski, Waclaw, eminent Polish musicologist; b. Bydgoszcz, Feb. 6, 1876; d. Warsaw, Sept. 17, 1943. He was a student of theology in Regensburg, where he also took courses in church music with Haberl; then in Berlin with Wolf and Kretzschmar and in Breslau with Otto Kinkeldey; obtained a doctorate with his dissertation *Die Musica Magistri Szydlowitae, ein polnischer Choraltraktat des 15. Jahrhunderts* (1913; publ. Poznán, 1915). He settled in Poznán as prof. of church music at the Univ.; in 1916 was appointed choir conductor at the Poznán cathedral; wrote church music. In 1928 he began the publication of the valuable series 'Cantica Selecta Musices Sacrae in Polonia'; restored to use many sacred works by Polish composers of the Renaissance; published several treatises on this subject; also composed several sacred choral works.

Giegling, Franz, musicologist; b. Buchs, near Aarau, Feb. 27, 1921. He studied piano and theory at the Zürich Cons. with Cherbuliez; received his Ph.D. with the valuable dissertation, *Giuseppe Torelli, ein Beitrag zur Entwicklungsgeschichte des italianischen Konzerts* (1949); was music critic of the 'Neue Zürcher Zeitung' (1949-55); contributed articles to 'Die Musik in Geschichte und Gegenwart.'

Gieseking, Walter, distinguished pianist; b. Lyons, France, of German parents, Nov. 5, 1895; d. London, Oct. 26, 1956. He studied with Karl Leimer at the Hanover Cons., graduating in 1916; then served in the German army during World War I; began his concert career with extensive tours of Europe; made his American début at Aeolian Hall, N. Y., Feb. 22, 1926, and after that appeared regularly in the U. S. and Europe with orchestras and in solo recitals. He became one of the most brilliant and musicianly pianists of his generation, capable of profound and intimate interpretations of both classical and modern piano music. His dual German-French background enabled him to project with the utmost authenticity the piano masterpieces of both cultures. His playing of Debussy was remarkable; he was also an excellent performer of works by Profofiev and other modernists. He composed some chamber music and made piano transcriptions of songs by Richard Strauss. He became the center of a political controversy when he arrived in the U. S. early in 1949 for a concert tour; he was accused of cultural collaboration with Nazi régime, and public protests forced the cancellation of his scheduled performances at Carnegie Hall. However, he was later cleared by an Allied court in Germany, and was able to resume his career in America. He appeared again at a Carnegie Hall recital on April 22, 1953, and until his death continued to give numerous performances in both hemispheres. —Cf. B. Gavoty, *Gieseking,* in the series 'Les grands interprètes' (Geneva, 1955).

Gigli (jē'l-yē), **Beniamino,** famous Italian tenor; b. Recanati, March 20, 1890. He studied with Rosati in Rome; made his operatic début in Rovigno, near Venice, in 1914, as Enzo in *La Gioconda;* then sang in many Italian cities. His first American appearance was as Faust in Boito's *Mefistofele* with the Metropolitan Opera (Nov. 17, 1920); he remained on its staff until 1932, and returned there for one season in 1938. He then went back to Italy, where he remained during World War II. He revisited the U. S. in 1955 and gave a series of concerts with considerable success despite his age. At the height of his career, he ranked among the best tenors in opera; he was particularly impressive in the lyric roles of Verdi's and Puccini's operas; he also sang in the German and French repertory; his interpretation of Lohengrin was acclaimed. His voice possessed great strength and a variety of expressive powers. See R. Rosner, *Beniamino Gigli* (Vienna, 1929); R. de Rensis, *Il cantatore del popolo: Beniamino Gigli* (Rome, 1933; in German, Munich, 1936); D. Silvestrini, *Beniamino Gigli* (Bologna, 1937). Gigli's memoirs were publ. in English at London (1957).

Gigout (zhē-goo'), **Eugène,** French organvirtuoso and composer; b. Nancy, March 23, 1844; d. Paris, Dec. 9, 1925. He began music studies in the *maîtrise* of Nancy Cathedral; at 13 he entered the Niedermeyer School at Paris, in which he subsequently taught from 1863-85, and from 1900-5; for a time, pupil of Saint-Saëns. From 1863, Gigout was organist at the church of St.-Augustin; he won fame as a concert organist in France, England, Germany, Switzerland, Spain, and Italy; he was especially famous for his masterly improvisations. In 1885 he founded at Paris an organ school subsidized by the government, from which many excellent pupils graduated (Boëllmann, Fauré, Messager, A. Georges, A. Roussel, C. Terrasse, etc.); from 1911, prof. of organ and improvisation at the National Cons., Paris. He was also an esteemed writer on music and critic; Commander of the Order of Isabella la Católica; Officer of Public Instruction (from 1885); and Chevalier of the Legion of Honor (from 1895). As a composer he followed the severe style.—Works: For organ: *Cent pièces brèves* (Gregorian), *Album Grégorien* (3 vols., each containing 100 pieces exclusively in the church modes), *Rhapsodie sur des Noëls, Toccata, Scherzo, Prélude et Fugue* in B♭, *Marche de Fête, Rhapsodie sur des Airs Catalans, Rhapsodie sur des Airs Canadiens, Poèmes Mystiques,* piano sonata in F; other pieces for piano (2 and 4 hands); sacred choruses, songs.—Cf. *Hommage à Eugène Gigout* (Paris, 1923; contains a biographical sketch by Gabriel Fauré and catalogue of works).

Gilardi, Gilardo, Argentine opera composer; b. San Fernando, May 25, 1889. He studied with Pablo Berutti, then devoted himself to teaching and composing. Two of his operas were produced at the Teatro Colón in Buenos Aires: *Ilse* (July 13, 1923); *La Leyenda de Urutaú* (Oct. 25, 1934). He also wrote *Sonata Popular Argentina* for violin and piano (1939) and many dances and songs based on native melodies.

Gilbert, Henry Franklin Belknap, remarkable American composer; b. Somerville, Mass., Sept. 26, 1868; d. Cambridge, Mass., May 19, 1928. He studied at the New England Cons. and with E. Mollenhauer; 1889-92, pupil of MacDowell (composition) in Boston. Rather than do routine music work to earn his livelihood (he had previously been violinist in theaters, etc.), he took jobs of many descriptions, becoming, in turn, a real-estate agent, a factory foreman, a collector of butterflies in Florida, etc., and composed when opportunity afforded. In 1893, at the Chicago World's Fair, he met a Russian prince who knew Rimsky-Korsakov and gave him many details of contemporary Russian composers whose work, as well as that of Bohemian and Scandinavian composers which was based on folksong, influenced Gilbert greatly in his later composition. In 1895 he made his 1st trip abroad and stayed in Paris, subsequently returning to the U. S.; when he heard of the première of Charpentier's *Louise* he became intensely interested in the work because of its 'popular' character, and, in order to hear it, earned his passage to Paris, in 1901, by working on a cattle-boat; the opera impressed him so that he decided to devote his entire time thereafter to composition; 1902, associated with Arthur Farwell, whose Wa-Wan Press publ. Gilbert's early compositions. During this time (from 1903) he employed Negro tunes and rhythms extensively in his works. The compositions of his mature period (from 1915) reveal an original style, not founded on any particular native American material, but infused with elements from many sources, and are an attempt at 'un-European' music, expressing the spirit of America and its national characteristics. — Works: opera, *The Fantasy in Delft* (1915). For orch.: *Two Episodes* (Boston, Jan. 13, 1896); *Humoresque on Negro-Minstrel Tunes* (originally entitled *Americanesque,* 1903; Boston Pops, May 24, 1911); *Comedy Overture on Negro Themes* (1905; perf. at a N. Y. municipal concert, Aug. 17, 1910; Boston Symph., April 13, 1911; also perf. by Glière, in Feodosia, Crimea, July 22, 1914, and in Odessa, Aug. 1, 1914); symph. poem, *The Dance in Place Congo* (1906; perf. as ballet at the Metropolitan Opera, N. Y., March 23, 1918); *Strife* (1910); *Negro Rhapsody* (Norfolk, Conn., Festival, June 5, 1913, composer conducting); symph. prologue for Synge's *Riders to the Sea* (1904; MacDowell Festival, Peterboro, N. H., Aug. 20, 1914; rev. version, N. Y. Philharmonic, Nov. 11, 1917); *American Dances* (1915); *Indian Sketches* (Boston Symph., March 4, 1921); suite from *Music to Pilgrim Tercentenary Pageant* (Boston Symph., March 31, 1922); *Symphonic Piece* (Boston Symph., Feb. 26, 1926); *Nocturne,* a 'symphonic mood' after Walt Whitman (Philadelphia, March 16, 1928); *Suite for Chamber Orchestra* (commissioned by the E. S. Coolidge Foundation; first perf., Chamber Orch. of Boston, Slonimsky conducting, April 28, 1928); *To Thee, America,* a hymn for chorus and orch. (MacDowell Festival, Peterboro, N. H., Jan. 25, 1915); *Salammbô's Invocation to Tänith,* aria for soprano and orch. (N. Y., Elise Stevens, with the Russian Symph. Orch., March 10, 1906); an early string quartet. For piano: *Negro Episode, Mazurka, Scherzo, Two Verlaine Moods, The Island of the Fay* (also for orch.), *Indian Scenes, A Rag Bag, Negro Dances.* Songs: *Pirate Song,* after Stevenson; *Celtic Studies,* a cycle of 4 songs to poems by Irish poets; *The Lament of Deirdre; Faery Song; Two South American Gypsy Songs; Fish Wharf Rhapsody: Give me the Splendid Sun; The*

Owl; Orlamonde; Zephyrus; Homesick; Tell Me Where is Fancy Bred?; Croon of the Dew; Eight Simple Songs; Perdita; The Curl; School Songs; also edited *100 Folksongs* (Boston, 1910); contributed articles to the 'Mus. Quarterly' *(The American Composer,* April, 1915; *The Survival of Music,* July, 1916; *Originality,* Jan., 1919), and to other magazines. — Cf. Arthur Farwell, *Wanderjahre of a Revolutionist* in 'Mus. America' (April 10, 1909); *An American Composer's Triumph in Russia,* in 'Current Opinion' (May, 1916); E. C. Ranck, *The Mark Twain of American Music,* in 'Theatre Magazine' (Sept., 1917); Olin Downes, *An American Composer,* in the 'Mus. Quarterly' (Jan., 1918); *Gilbert, Henry,* in the 'Dictionary of American Biography' (vol. 7, N. Y., 1931); J. T. Howard, *Our American Music* (N. Y., 1939, and subsequent eds.); Olin Downes, *Henry Gilbert: Nonconformist,* in 'A Birthday Greeting to Carl Engel' (N. Y., 1943); E. Carter, *American Figure,* in 'Modern Music' (1943); H. G. Sear, *H. F. Gilbert,* in 'Music Review' (1944, p. 250); Gilbert Chase, *America's Music* (N. Y., 1955).

Gilbert (zhēl-bär'), **Jean** (pen-name of Max Winterfeld), German operetta composer; b. Hamburg, Feb. 11, 1879; d. Buenos Aires, Dec. 20, 1942. He studied with Scharwenka; was active as theater conductor in Hamburg and Berlin. In 1933 he left Germany, eventually settling in Buenos Aires. He wrote the operettas *Die keusche Susanne* (1910), *Polnische Wirtschaft* (1910), *Die Kino-Königin* (1911), *Puppchen* (1912), *Die Frau im Hermelin* (1918), *Die Braut des Lucullus* (1920), *Katja, die Tänzerin* (1922), *Das Weib im Purpur* (1923), *In der Johannisnacht* (1926), *Hotel Stadt Lemberg* (1929), *Das Mädel am Steuer* (1930). The song *Puppchen, du bist mein Augenstern,* from the operetta *Puppchen,* achieved immense popularity in Europe.

Gilbert, Timothy, piano maker in Boston. After 1820 made several innovations of his own invention to improve the action of the piano. Brought out the organ-piano in 1847.

Gilbert, Sir **William Schwenck,** British playwright, creator with Sir Arthur Sullivan of the famous series of comic operas; b. London, Nov. 18, 1836; d. Harrow Weald, Middlesex, May 29, 1911 (through accidental drowning). He was given an excellent education (at Boulogne and at King's College, London) by his father, who was a novelist. After a routine career as a clerk, Gilbert drifted into journalism, contributing drama criticism and humorous verse to London periodicals. His satirical wit was first revealed in a theater piece, *Dulcamara* (1886), in which he ridiculed grand opera. He met Sullivan in 1871, and together they initiated the productions of comic operas which suited them so perfectly. Some plots borrow ludicrous situations from actual Italian and French operas; Gilbert's libretti, in rhymed verse, were none the less unmistakably English. This insularity of wit may explain the enormous popularity of the Gilbert & Sullivan operas in English-speaking countries, while they are practically unknown on the Continent. Despite the fact that the targets of Gilbert's ridicule were usually the upper classes of Great Britain, the operas were often performed at court. He was knighted in 1907. After 20 years of fruitful cooperation with Sullivan, a conflict developed, and the two severed their relationship for a time. A reconciliation was effected, but the subsequent productions fell short of their greatest successes. The most popular of the Gilbert & Sullivan operettas are *H.M.S. Pinafore* (1878); *The Pirates of Penzance* (1880); *Iolanthe* (1884); *The Mikado* (1885), and *The Gondoliers* (1889). A special theater, the Savoy, was built for the Gilbert & Sullivan productions in London in 1881 by the impresario Richard D'Oyly Carte. For bibl., see entry under Sullivan.

Gilberté, Hallett, American song composer; b. Winthrop, Maine, March 14, 1872; d. New York, Jan. 5, 1946. He studied piano with J. Orth and C. Barmann and composition with E. Nevin in Boston. He wrote about 250 songs, some of which were quite successful (*Spanish Serenade, Mother's Cradle Song, In Reverie, Two Roses, Song of the Canoe, Ah, Love but a Day, Spring Serenade, Minuet La Phyllis, Moonlight and Starlight*).

Gilchrist, William Wallace, American composer; b. Jersey City, N. J., Jan. 8, 1846; d. Easton, Pa., Dec. 20, 1916. He studied organ with H. A. Clarke at the Univ. of Penna., which conferred on him the degree of Mus. Doc. in 1896. He was a choirmaster at various Philadelphia churches; from 1882, taught at the Philadelphia Music Academy. He formed the Mendelssohn Club and was its conductor later. He wrote cantatas, a Christmas oratorio, 2 symphonies, chamber music, church music, and songs.— Cf. Sumner Salter, *Early Encouragement to American Composers* in the 'Mus. Quarterly' (Jan., 1932).

Gilels, Emil, Russian pianist; b. Odessa, Oct. 19, 1916. He studied in Odessa with Yakov Tkatch and Berthe Ringold. He made his public début at the age of 13, in 1929, in Odessa; at 16, won first prize in the Soviet Pianists Contest; second prize in Vienna (1936); first prize in Brussels (1938). He was awarded the Stalin prize in 1946. He made his American début in Oct., 1955 with overwhelming success.

Giles, Nathaniel, English organist and composer of church music; b. Worcester, c. 1558; d. Windsor, Jan. 24, 1633. A son of Thomas Giles, organist of St. Paul's Cathedral, London, he studied at Oxford; was organist at Worcester Cathedral from 1581 to 1585, when he became clerk, organist, and choirmaster at St. George's Chapel, Windsor; in 1596, he took over the same duties at the Chapel Royal; in 1597, became Gentleman and Master of the Children there. He wrote four services for the Church; a great number of anthems; several motets and a 5-part madrigal (incomplete or in MS). Some of his compositions are included in Leighton's *Teares or Lamentacions of a Sorrowfull Soule* (1614); a service and an anthem are in Barnard's 'Church Music' (1641); Hawkins' 'History of Music' contains Giles' *Lesson of Descant of thirty-eighte Proportions of sundrie Kindes.*—Cf. J. Pulver, *Nathaniel Giles* in 'Monthly Musical Record' (Nov., 1933).

Gilibert (zhē-lē-bär'), **Charles,** dramatic baritone; b. Paris, Nov., 1866; d. New York, Oct. 11, 1910. He left the Paris Cons. as a prize-graduate, sang one season at the Opéra-Comique, and then went to the Théâtre de la Monnaie, Brussels, where he became a great favorite; 1900-3, member of the Metropolitan Opera; at his début on Dec. 18, 1900, and throughout the entire season, he failed to make a decided impression, but on his appearance in the second season took the public by storm; 1906-10, at the Manhattan Opera House, N. Y.; he was then reëngaged for the Metropolitan Opera, and was to have created Jack Rance in *The Girl of the Golden West,* but died just before the opening of the season. He was also a distinguished concert-singer and interpreter of old French songs.

Gillels, Emil. See **Gilels.**

Gillet, Ernest, French composer; b. Paris, Sept. 13, 1856; d. there, May 6, 1940. He studied cello at the Paris Cons., and was for many years a cellist in the orch. of the Paris Opéra. He publ. a number of melodious pieces, of which *Loin du bal* for piano became a perennial drawing-room favorite, available also in numerous arrangements.

Gillette, James Robert, American organist and composer; b. Roseboom, N. Y., May 30, 1886. He studied music at Syracuse Univ.; taught at Wesleyan College, Macon, Ga., and at Carleton College, Northfield, Minn.; then was organist of the First Presbyterian Church, Lake Forest, Ill. He composed a *Pagan Symphony* for band; *Cabins,* an American rhapsody for orch.; 3 cantatas: *On Calvary's Cross; The Shepherd and His Lamb; The Resurrection According to Nicodemus;* 42 anthems for church use; 7 overtures for symphonic band; 40 organ pieces *(Chanson de Matin, Toccatina, Pastorale,* etc.). He publ. *The Organist's Handbook* (1928) and *The Modern Band in Theory and Practice* (1936).

Gillis, Don, American composer; b. Cameron, Missouri, June 17, 1912. He played trumpet and trombone in school bands; graduated from the Christian Univ. at Fort Worth, Texas in 1936. In 1944 he was appointed program arranger by NBC in New York. He acquired a facility for effective orchestral writing; wrote 7 symphonies between 1939 and 1948, adding to these an intermediary work which he called Symphony No. 5½ or *Symphony for Fun* (it was performed by Toscanini); his other works for orchestra have whimsical titles *(The Panhandle; Thoughts Provoked on Becoming a Prospective Papa,* etc.), but he has also written in a serious vein, including a cantata *Crucifixion,* 6 string quartets, and some piano music.

Gilman, Lawrence, American music critic and author; b. Flushing, N. Y., July 5, 1878; d. Franconia, N. H., Sept. 8, 1939. He was self-taught in music; from 1901-13, music critic of 'Harper's Weekly'; 1915-23, musical, dramatic, and literary critic of 'North American Review'; from 1921, author of the program-notes of the N. Y. Philh. and Philadelphia Orch. concerts; from 1923, music critic of 'N. Y. Herald Tribune'; member of the National Institute of Arts and Letters. Author of *Phases of Modern Music* (1904); *Edward MacDowell* (1905, in 'Living Masters of Music'; rev. and enlarged as *Edward MacDowell: A Study,* 1909); *The Music of To-Morrow* (1906); *Guide to Strauss's 'Salome'* (1907); *Stories of Symphonic Music* (1907); *Guide to Debussy's 'Pelléas et Mélisande'* (1907); *As-*

pects of Modern Opera (1909); *Nature in Music* (1914); *A Christmas Meditation* (1916); *Taste in Music*, in the 'Mus. Quarterly' (Jan., 1917); *Music and the Cultivated Man* (1929); *Wagner's Operas* (1937); *Toscanini and Great Music* (1938). He set to music 3 poems of W. B. Yeats (*The Heart of the Woman, A Dream of Death,* and *The Curlew*).—Cf. Carl Engel, *Lawrence Gilman,* in the 'Mus. Quarterly' (Jan., 1940).

Gil-Marchex, Henri, French pianist; b. St. Georges d'Éspérance (Isère), Dec. 16, 1894; studied at the Paris Cons., then with L. Capet and A. Cortot; toured Europe, Russia, and Japan, and performed modern works at various festivals in Europe. In 1956, he was director of the Cons. at Poitiers. He publ. piano transcriptions of modern orchestral pieces.

Gilmore, Patrick Sarsfield, American bandmaster; b. County Galway, Ireland, Dec. 25, 1829; d. St. Louis, Mo., Sept 24, 1892. He went to Canada with an English band, but soon settled in Salem, Mass., where he conducted a military band. In 1859 in Boston he organized the famous 'Gilmore's Band.' As bandmaster in the Federal army at New Orleans (1864), he gave a grand music festival with several combined bands, introducing the novel reinforcement of strong accents by cannon-shots. He won wide renown by the 'National Peace Jubilee' (1869), and the 'World's Peace Jubilee' (1872), two monster musical festivals held in Boston; in the former, Gilmore led an orch. of 1000 and a chorus of 10,000; in the latter, an orch. of 2000 and a chorus of 20,000; the orch. was reinforced by a powerful organ, cannon fired by electricity, anvils, and chimes of bells. After the second Jubilee, Gilmore went to New York, and, as a popular bandmaster, traveled with his men throughout the U. S. and Canada, and also (1878) to Europe. He also led bands or orchestras in various resorts in and near New York.—Works: Military music, dance music, many arrangements for band. Some of his songs were popular. He claimed to be the composer of *When Johnny Comes Marching Home* (1863), a song that remained a favorite long after the Civil War. The song bears the name of Louis Lambert as composer; this may have been one of Gilmore's many aliases—at any rate, he introduced the song and started it on its way to popularity. — Cf. M. Darlington, *Irish Orpheus: the Life of Patrick Gilmore* (Philadelphia, 1950).

Gilse, Jan van, Dutch composer; b. Rotterdam, May 11, 1881; d. Leyden, Sept. 8, 1944. He was a pupil of Wüllner at the Cologne Cons., 1897-1902; then for a year of Humperdinck in Berlin; 1905-8, conductor of the Opera at Bremen; 1908-9, conductor of the Dutch Opera at Amsterdam; 1917-22, music-director of the City of Utrecht, Holland; 1922-33, lived in Berlin; 1933 director of the Utrecht Cons.—Works: 5 symphonies (1900, 1903, 1905-6, 1914, 1922-23; the 1st won the Beethoven-Haus prize in 1902, the 3rd the Michael Beer prize of the Berlin Academy in 1909); an overture; 2 Intermezzi for orch.; Variations on a Dutch song for orch.; 2 oratorios, *Lebensmesse* (1904) and *Der Kreis des Lebens* (1928); songs (several with orch., texts by Tagore); Nonet for strings and woodwinds, etc. He also wrote text and music of an opera, *Frau Helga von Stavern,* and 2 books: *The Problem of a National Dutch Opera; Holland and Correct Performances* (both in Dutch).

Gilson (zhil-sŏhn), **Paul,** Belgian composer, critic, and educator; b. Brussels, June 15, 1865; d. there, April 3, 1942. He studied with Auguste Cantillon and Charles Duyck, took lessons from Gevaert; in 1889, he won the Belgian Prix de Rome with his cantata, *Sinai,* performed at Brussels in 1890. His subsequent works, both choral and orchestral, won him a foremost place among modern Flemish composers. In addition to his composing, he wrote numerous books and articles on music, and taught, beginning in 1899 as prof. of harmony at Brussels Cons.; in 1904, also on the faculty of Antwerp Cons.; in 1909, he left both posts to become musical inspector in the Belgian schools. He was also an important music critic: for 'Soir' from 1906 to 1914, for 'Le Diapason' from 1910 to 1914, and later for 'Midi.' He was the founder of the 'Revue musicale belge' (1924). In 1942, he published his memoirs, *Notes de musique et souvenirs.* He also publ. *Les Intervalles, Le Tutti orchestral, Quintes et octaves, Traité d'harmonie, Traité d'orchestre militaire.*—Works: choral: *Inaugural Cantata* (for Brussels Exhibition, 1897); *Francesca da Rimini,* after Dante (Brussels, 1895); *Le Démon,* after Lermontov; *Que la lumière soit; Hymne à l'Art; Ludus pro Patria;* ballets: *La Captive* (Brussels, 1902), *Les Deux Bossus, Légende rhénane;* incidental music for E. Hiel's drama, *Alva;* operas: *Prinses Zonneschijn* (Antwerp, 1903), *Zeevolk* (Antwerp, 1904), *Rooversliefde* (*Les Aventuriers;* Antwerp, 1906), *Mater Dolorosa;* orch. works: 3 symph. poems: *La Mer*

(Brussels, 1892), *Italia, La Destinée;* 8 suites; *Danses écossaises; Rapsodie écossaise; Andante et presto sur un thème brabançon; Rapsodie canadienne;* 2 string quartets; a string trio; also pieces for military band; choruses; piano pieces; instrumental pieces; songs.

Giménez (Jiménez) (hē-mĕh'neth), **Jerónimo,** Spanish composer of zarzuelas; b. Seville, Oct. 10, 1854; d. Madrid, Feb. 19, 1923. He studied with Alard, Savard, and A. Thomas at the Paris Cons.; was conductor of Sociedad de Conciertos in Madrid. He wrote about 60 (for the most part) 1-act light operas *(género chico)* with very catchy melodies, some of which are still performed throughout the Spanish-speaking world *(El baile de Luis Alonso, La boda de Luis Alonso, La tempranica,* etc.); also a number of orchestral pieces.

Gimpel, Bronislaw, Polish violinist; b. Lwow, Jan. 29, 1911. He studied in Vienna with Flesch and Huberman. In 1929, he was concertmaster of the Radio Orch. in Königsberg; from 1931-36, in Göteborg; in 1937, became concertmaster of the Los Angeles Philharmonic; later organized a trio with Leopold Mannes and Luigi Silva; he has toured as soloist in Europe and America.

Ginastera, Alberto, talented Argentinian composer; b. Buenos Aires, April 11, 1916. He studied at the National Cons. of Music with Palma, Gil, and André, graduating in 1938. In 1946-47, he came to the U. S. on a Guggenheim Fellowship; in 1953, prof. at the National Cons. His music is in a national vein, in advanced harmonic texture.—Works: ballets, *Panambí* (Buenos Aires, July 12, 1940), *Estancia* (1941). For orch.: *Concierto Argentino* (Montevideo, July 18, 1941); *Sinfonia Porteña* (Buenos Aires, May 12, 1942); *Obertura para el 'Fausto' Criollo* (Santiago, Chile, May 12, 1944); *Variaciones Concertantes* (1953). Chamber music: *Impresiones de la Puna,* for flute and string quartet (1934); *Duo* for flute and oboe (1945); *Pampeana* No. 1 for violin and piano (1947); string quartet (1948); *Pampeana* No. 2 for cello and piano (1950); *Pampeana* No. 3 *(Pastoral Symphony;* 1953; Louisville Orch., Oct. 20, 1954). For piano: *Argentine Dances* (1937); *12 American Preludes* (1944); *Creole Dance Suite* (1946); sonata (1952); also songs.

Gingold, Josef, American violinist; b. Brest-Litovsk, Oct. 28, 1909. He came to the U. S. in 1920. He studied in New York, and later in Brussels with Eugène Ysaÿe. He gave 40 concerts in Belgium (1926-28); then returned to America. He was a member of the NBC Symphony Orch. under Toscanini (1937-44); concertmaster of the Detroit Symphony (1944-47). In 1947 he was appointed concertmaster of the Cleveland Orch.

Ginguené (zhăn-g'-nā), **Pierre Louis,** French historian of literature and writer on music; b. Rennes, April 25, 1748; d. Paris, Nov. 16, 1816. He studied at Rennes College; then went to Paris; was an original member of the Institute of France; served in government posts, then wrote extensively on the history of French and Italian literature. He was an ardent advocate of Piccini in the Gluck-Piccini controversy; his attacks on Gluck are contained in *Lettres et articles sur la musique, insérés dans les journaux sous le nom de Mélophile, pendant nos dernières querelles musicales, en 1780, 1781, 1782 et 1783* (Paris, 1783). He also wrote *Notice sur la vie et les ouvrages de Piccini* (Paris, 1800); contributed historical articles to the *Dictionnaire de musique* of the 'Encyclopédie méthodique.'—Cf. D. J. Garat, *Notice sur la vie et les ouvrages de P. L. Ginguené* (Paris, 1817).

Ginsburg, Semion Lvovitch, Russian musicologist; b. Kilb, May 23, 1901. He studied literature and musicology in Leningrad; publ. *Fundamentals of a Theory of the Musical Sciences,* in 'De musica' (Leningrad, 1923); *Russian Musical Theater, 1700-1835* (Moscow, 1941); *Paths of Development of Uzbek Music* (Leningrad, 1946).

Ginster, Ria, German soprano; b. Frankfurt, April 15, 1898. She studied there at Hoch's Cons., and later at the High School for Music in Berlin, graduating with distinction and winning the Mendelssohn Stipendium. As a concert singer, she appeared in recitals and with leading orchestras in Europe and the U. S. In 1938, she was appointed voice teacher at the Zürich Cons.

Giordani (jôr-dah'nē), **Giuseppe** (called **Giordanello**), Italian composer; b. Naples, c. 1753; d. Fermo, Jan. 4, 1798. He studied with Fenaroli at San Loreto Cons., Naples; Cimarosa and Zingarelli were fellow-students. His first opera, *Epponina,* was given in Florence in 1779. He continued to write operas for various Italian towns, but they were not outstanding and few of the 30-odd he wrote have survived. He also wrote several oratorios and church music. From 1791 until his death he was maestro di cappella at Fermo Cathedral. He is sometimes credited with *Il Bacio* and other operas and works produced in London by Tommaso Giordani; Giuseppe was not related to Tommaso, and never left Italy. The famous song, *Caro mio ben,* popularized in London by Pacchierotti, was probably written by Giuseppe.

Giordani, Tommaso, Italian composer; b. Naples, c. 1730; d. Dublin, late Feb., 1806. His family, which included his father, Giuseppe; his mother, Antonia; his brother, Francesco; and his sisters, Marina and Nicolina (known later as Spiletta from one of her opera roles), together formed a strolling opera company, with the father as impresario and singer and the rest of the family, except Tommaso, as singers. Tommaso was probably a member of the orch. and arranger of music. They left Naples about 1745 and moved northward, appearing in Italian towns, then in Graz (1748), Frankfurt (1750), and Amsterdam (1752). They made their London début at Covent Garden, Dec. 17, 1753, and returned in 1756, at which time Tommaso first appeared as a composer, with his comic opera, *La comediante fatta cantatrice* (Covent Garden, Jan. 12, 1756). The Giordani company next went to Dublin, appearing there in 1764; Tommaso continued active both in Dublin and in London; he was conductor and composer at the King's Theatre, London, in 1769 and many following seasons, and in Dublin, where he lived after 1783, was conductor and composer at the Smock Alley and Crow Street theaters; he also taught piano between operas. In 1794, he was elected president of the Irish music fund. He played an important part in Irish music circles, and wrote altogether more than 50 English and Italian operas, including pasticcios and adaptations; among his own works were *L'eroe cinese* (Dublin, 1766), *Il padre el il figlio rivali* (London, 1770), *Artaserse* (London, 1772), *Il re pastore* (London, 1778); *Il bacio* (London, 1782). He also wrote several cantatas, including *Aci e Galatea* (London, 1777); an oratorio, *Isaac* (Dublin, 1767); songs for the original production of Sheridan's *The Critic* (Drury Lane, London, Oct. 29, 1779); many Italian and English songs that were popular for a long time; concertos, string quartets, trios, many piano pieces.

Giordano (jôr-dah'-noh), **Umberto,** Italian opera composer; b. Foggia, Aug. 27, 1867; d. Milan, Nov. 12, 1948. He studied with Gaetano Briganti at Foggia, and then with Paolo Serrao at Naples Cons. (1881-86). His 1st composition performed in public was a symph. poem, *Delizia* (1886); he then wrote some instrumental music. In 1888 he submitted a short opera, *Marina,* for the competition established by the publisher Sonzogno; Mascagni's *Cavalleria Rusticana* received 1st prize, but *Marina* was cited for distinction. Giordano then wrote an opera in 3 acts, *Mala Vita,* which was performed in Rome Feb. 21, 1892; it was only partly successful; was revised and presented under the title *Il Voto* in Milan (1897). There followed a 2-act opera, *Regina Diaz* (Rome, Feb. 21, 1894), which obtained a moderate success. Then Giordano set to work on a grand opera, *Andrea Chénier,* to a libretto by Illica. The production of this opera at La Scala (March 28, 1896) was a spectacular success, which established Giordano as one of the best composers of modern Italian opera. The dramatic subject gave Giordano a fine opportunity to display his theatrical talent; but the opera also revealed his gift for lyric expression. *Andrea Chénier* was produced at the N. Y. Academy of Music shortly after its Milan première; a performance at the Metropolitan Opera House came considerably later (March 7, 1920). Almost as successful was his next opera, *Fedora* (Teatro Lirico, Milan, Nov. 17, 1898; Metropolitan Opera, Dec. 5, 1906), but it failed to hold a place in the world repertory after initial acclaim; there followed *Siberia,* in 3 acts (La Scala, Dec. 19, 1903). Two short operas, *Marcella* (Milan, Nov. 9, 1907) and *Mese Mariano* (Palermo, March 17, 1910), were hardly noticed and seemed to mark a decline in Giordano's dramatic gift; however, he recaptured the attention of the public with *Madame Sans-Gêne,* produced at a gala première at the Metropolitan Opera on Jan. 25, 1915, conducted by Toscanini, with Geraldine Farrar singing the title role. With Franchetti, he wrote *Giove a Pompei* (Rome, 1921); then he produced *La cena delle beffe* in 4 acts, which was his last signal accomplishment; it was staged at La Scala, Dec. 20, 1924, and at the Metropolitan, Jan. 2, 1926. He wrote one more opera, *Il Re* in 1 act (La Scala, Jan. 10, 1929). During his lifetime he received many honors, and was elected a member of the Accademia Luigi Cherubini in Florence and of several other institutions. Although not measuring up to Puccini in musical qualities or to Mascagni in dramatic skill, Giordano was a distinguished figure in the Italian opera field.—Cf. G. C. Parabeni, *Madame Sans-Gêne di Umberto Giordano* (Milan, 1923);

D. Cellamare, *Umberto Giordano: la vita e le opere* (Milan, 1949).

Giorni (jôr'nē), **Aurelio,** pianist and composer; b. Perugia, Italy, Sept. 15, 1895; d. Pittsfield, Mass., Sept. 23, 1938. He studied piano with Sgambati at the Cons. of Santa Cecilia in Rome (1909-11); composition with Humperdinck in Berlin (1911-13); in 1915 he came to the U. S. where he remained; taught at Smith College, Philadelphia Cons. of Music, Hartford School of Music, and other music schools; in his last years, was a teacher in N. Y. He wrote a symph. poem, *Orlando furioso* (1926); *Sinfonia concertante* (1931); symph. in D minor (1937); 3 trios; 2 string quartets; cello sonata; violin sonata; piano quartet; piano quintet; flute sonata; clarinet sonata; 24 concert études for piano; songs.

Giornovicchi (johr-noh-vēk'-kē), **Giovanni Mane,** Italian violinist, probably of Croatian extraction (his real name was Jarnowick); b. Raguso or Palermo, c. 1735; d. St. Petersburg, Russia, Nov. 23, 1804. He was a pupil of Antonio Lolli in Palermo; gave successful concerts in Europe; on the strength of his reputation, he was engaged as court musician to Catherine II, succeeding his teacher Lolli in that post. He was in Russia from 1789-91; then appeared in London (1791-94), Paris, Hamburg, and Berlin. He returned to Russia in 1803, and died there the following year. In his old age he abandoned the violin and devoted himself to playing billiards for money. Among his works are 20 violin concertos; 3 string quartets; *Fantasia e Rondo* for piano. He was probably the first to introduce the 'romance' into the violin concerto as a slow movement.—Cf. R. Aloys Mooser, *Annales de la musique et des musiciens en Russie au XVIIIe siècle* (Geneva, 1950; vol. II, pp. 379-81).

Giorza (jôr'-tsăh), **Paolo,** Italian composer; b. Milan, Nov. 11, 1832; d. Seattle, May 5, 1914. He was especially known for his ballet music; wrote more than 40 ballets. He lived in New York, in London, and in San Francisco; in 1906 settled in Seattle.

Giovannelli, Ruggiero, Italian composer; b. Velletri, 1560; d. Rome, Jan. 7, 1625. In 1587 he was maestro in the church of San Luigi de' Francesi at Rome, later in the Collegium Germanicum; in 1594 he succeeded Palestrina as maestro at St. Peter's, and in 1599 joined the Pontifical Chapel. One of the most famous masters of the Roman School; of his works there have been printed 3 books of madrigals *a* 5 (1586, 1587, 1589; completely reprinted 1600); 2 of *Madrigali sdruccioli a* 4 (1585 [7th ed. 1613], 1589 [5th ed. 1603]); 2 books of motets *a* 5-8 (1589, 1604); *Canzonette* and *Villanelle a* 3 (1592, 1593); also scattered works in collections publ. from 1583-1620 (Scotto, Phalèse, Schadaeus, etc.). K. Proske's 'Musica divina' contains a psalm (vol. III, 1859); L. Torchi's 'L'Arte Musicale in Italia' includes a motet and psalm *a* 8 and a madrigal *a* 5 (vol. II). In the Vatican Library are many sacred works in MS.—To Giovanelli was entrusted, by Pope Paul V, the preparation of a new ed. of the Gradual (1614, 1615, 2 vols.).—Cf. C. Winter, *Ruggiero Giovannelli (c. 1560-1625), Nachfolger Palestrinas zu St. Peter in Rom* (Munich, 1935).

Giovanni da Cascia (Johannes de Florentia (jŏh-vah'-nē dah kah'-shăh), Italian 14th-century composer. According to his younger contemporary, Filippo Villani, in *Liber de civitatis Florentiae famosis civibus,* he was the initiator of the stylistic reform which spread from Florence shortly after 1300. He was organist and probably chorus-master at Santa Maria del Fiore at Florence; lived at the court of Mastino II della Scala, Verona, from 1329-51. His compositions included madrigals, *ballate,* etc.; MSS may be found in libraries at Florence, Paris, and in the British Museum. In all, 28 works by Giovanni, in 2-3 parts, are known. The madrigal, *Agnel son bianco,* was edited and publ. by Johannes Wolf in 'Sammelbände der Internationalen Musik-Gesellschaft' (1902; Ex. 4); 2 other compositions were also edited and publ. by Wolf in his *Geschichte der Mensural-Notation* (pp. 61-64; Leipzig, 1904).—Cf. J. Wolf, *Florenz in der Musikgeschichte des 14. Jahrhunderts* in the 'Sammelbände der Internationalen Musik-Gesellschaft' (1902; pp. 609-10); H. Riemann, in *Handbuch der Musikgeschichte* (1922; p. 41); A. Morini, *Un celebre musico dimenticato, Giovanni da Cascia,* in 'Bollettino della regia deputazione di storia patria per l'Umbria' (Perugia, 1926; p. 305 ff).

Gipps, Ruth, English pianist and composer; b. Bexhill-on-Sea, Sussex, Feb. 20, 1921. She studied at the Royal College of Music in London with Vaughan Williams, piano with Matthay. She began to compose very early in life and at the age of eight won a prize for a piano piece. Her works include 2 symphonies (1942; 1946); clarinet concerto; oboe concerto; violin concerto; trio for oboe, clarinet, and piano; quintet for oboe, clarinet, violin, viola, and cello; also an oratorio, *The Cat* (1952); numerous solo pieces with picturesque titles; and songs.

Giraldoni, Eugenio, famous Italian baritone; b. Marseilles, France, May 20, 1871; d. Helsinki, Finland, June 23, 1924. Both his parents were professional singers; his father, Leone Giraldoni, was a renowned baritone and his mother, Carolina Ferni-Giraldoni, a famous soprano. He made his début in Barcelona as Don José in 1891; then sang in Buenos Aires and in Italy (at La Scala and other theaters); eventually settled in Russia, where he taught voice at the St. Petersburg Cons.

Giraudet (zhē-roh-dā'), **Alfred-Auguste,** dramatic basso and vocal pedagogue; b. Étampes, March 29, 1845; d. New York, Oct. 17, 1911. He studied with Delsarte; made his operatic début at the Théâtre-Lyrique in Paris as Mephistopheles (1868); then sang at the Théâtre-Italien, Opéra-Comique, and at the Opéra; in 1883 he retired from the stage and devoted himself to teaching; eventually settled in New York as a teacher. He wrote a book, *Mimique, Physionomie et Gestes* (1895).

Giuliani, Mauro, Italian guitar virtuoso; b. Barletta, 1781; d. Naples, May 8, 1828. He was entirely self-taught; at the age of 19 undertook a highly successful tour in Europe; settled in Vienna in 1807, where he became associated with Hummel, Moscheles, and Diabelli; Beethoven became interested in him, and wrote some guitar music expressly for his performances. In 1833 he visited London, where he won extraordinary acclaim; a special publication, named after him 'The Giulianiad' and devoted to reports about his activities, was initiated there, but only a few issues appeared in print. Giuliani publ. a number of guitar solos; he also perfected a new guitar with a shorter fingerboard ('la ghitarra di terza'). — See 'The Guitar Review' (N. Y., 1955, No. 18), containing a biographical sketch of Giuliani by Ph. J. Bone.

Giulini, Giorgio, Italian composer; b. Milan, 1716; d. there, 1780. He was the author of several instrumental works of considerable merit. — Cf. G. Cesari, *Giorgio Giulini, musicista,* in the 'Rivista Musicale Italiana' (1917).

Gladstone, Francis Edward, noted English organist; b. Summertown, near Oxford, March 2, 1845; d. Hereford, Sept. 6, 1928. He was a pupil of S. Wesley, 1859-64; filled positions as organist at Weston-super-Mare, Llandaff, Chichester, Brighton, London, and Norwich. After embracing the Catholic faith, he was choir-director at St. Mary of the Angels, Bayswater, until 1894. In 1876 he took the degree of Mus. Bac., Cambridge; in 1879, Mus. Doc.; prof. of harmony and counterpoint at Royal College of Music, 1883-1910.—Works: An oratorio, *Philippi* (1883), much church music, an overture, some chamber music (all in MS); publ. organ pieces, *The Organ-Student's Guide* and *A Treatise on Strict Counterpoint* (1906). He also wrote an a cappella chorus, *In Paradisium,* for his own funeral and trained four monks to sing it.

Glanville-Hicks, Peggy, Australian composer and critic; b. Melbourne, Dec. 29, 1912. She studied in London with Vaughan Williams, later in Vienna with E. Wellesz, and in Paris with Nadia Boulanger. Since 1939, she has been in the U. S.; 1957, awarded a Guggenheim Fellowship.—Works: operas: *Caedmon; The Transposed Heads,* after Thomas Mann (commissioned by the Louisville Orch.; perf. Louisville, March 27, 1954); 2 sinfoniettas; piano concerto; string quartet; choral suite for women's voices, oboe, and string orch.; *Concertino da Camera,* for flute, clarinet, bassoon, and piano (Amsterdam Festival, 1948); *Etruscan Concerto* for piano and chamber orch. (N. Y., Jan. 25, 1956).—Cf. 'Bulletin of American Composers' Alliance' (1954, I).

Glareanus, Henricus (real name, Heinrich Loris; Latinized: Henricus Loritus), Swiss musical theorist and writer; b. Mollis, in the canton of Glarus, June, 1488; d. Freiburg, Baden, March 28, 1563. He studied with Rubellus at Bern, and later with Cochläus at Cologne, where he was crowned poet laureate by Emperor Maximilian I in 1512, as the result of a poem he composed and sang to the emperor. He first taught mathematics at Basel (1515); went to Paris, where he taught philosophy; returned to Basel where he stayed till 1529, when he settled in Freiburg. His first important work, *Isagoge in musicen,* publ. at Basel in 1516, dealt with solmization, intervals, modes, and tones. A still more important volume, the *Dodecachordon,* was publ. in 1547; in it, Glareanus advanced the theory that there are 12 church modes, corresponding to the ancient Greek modes, instead of the commonly accepted 8 modes. The 3rd part of the *Dodecachordon* contains many works by 15th- and 16th-century musicians. A copy of the *Dodecachordon,* with corrections in Glareanus' own handwriting, is in the Library of Congress, Washington, D. C. A German transl., with the musical examples in modern notation, was publ. by P. Bohn in vol. 16 of 'Publikationen der Gesellschaft für Musikforschung' (Leipzig, 1888). A complete index of Glareanus' works is contained in P. Lichtenthal's 'Dizionario e bibliografia della musica' IV, pp. 274-76 (Milan, 1826). J. L. Wonegger publ. *Musicae epitome ex Glareani Dodekachordo* (1557; 2nd ed., 1559; in German: *Uss Glareani Musik ein Usszug,* 1557).—Biographies of Glareanus have been written by H. Schreiber (Freiburg, 1837) and O. F. Fritzsche (Frauenfeld, 1890). See also: P. Spitta in 'Vierteljahrsschrift für Musik-Wissenschaft' (vol. VII, p. 123 ff.); A. Schering, *Die Notenbeispiele in Glareanus Dodecachordon,* in 'Sammelbände der Internationalen Musik-Gesellschaft' (Leipzig, 1912); E. Refardt, *Musikerlexikon der Schweiz* (1928); E. Kirsch, *Studie zum Problem des Heinrich Loriti (Glarean),* in 'Festschrift A. Schering zum 60.sten Geburtstag' (Berlin, 1937).

Glasenapp, Carl Friedrich, b. Riga, Oct. 3, 1847; d. there, April 14, 1915. He studied philology at Dorpat; from 1875, headmaster at Riga. An ardent admirer of Wagner's art, he devoted his entire life to the study of the master's works, and was one of the principal contributors to the 'Bayreuther Blätter' from their foundation. His great work is the monumental biography of Wagner, *Richard Wagners Leben und Wirken,* of which the first two vols. were publ. at Kassel and Leipzig (1876, 1877); after the 2nd enlarged ed. (1882) these were rewritten, and the entire work was issued at Leipzig as *Das Leben Richard Wagners* (I, 1813-43 [1894]; II, 1843-53 [1896]; III, 1853-62 [1899]; IV, 1862-72 [1904]; V, 1872-77 [1907]; VI, 1877-83 [1911]). Vols. I, II, and III appeared in English transl. (with amplifications) by W. A. Ellis (London, 1900, 1901, 1903), but after that Ellis continued the biography as an independent work. Though Glasenapp's work was considered the definitive biography in its time, its value is diminished by the fact that he published only materials approved by Wagner's family; as a result, it was superseded by later biographies. His other works on Wagner include: *Wagner-Lexikon* with H. von Stein (1883); *Wagner-Encyklopädie* (2 vols., 1891); *Siegfried Wagner* (1906); *Siegfried Wagner und seine Kunst* (1911), with sequels, *Schwarzschwanenreich* (1913) and *Sonnenflammen* (1919); he also edited *Bayreuther Briefe, 1871-73* (1907) and *Familienbriefe an Richard Wagner, 1832-74* (1907).

Glass, Louis Christian August, Danish composer; b. Copenhagen, March 23, 1864; d. there, Jan. 22, 1936. He was a pupil of his father, Christian Hendrik (1821-93), then at Brussels Cons. of J. de Zarembski and J. Wieniawski (piano) and J. Servais (cello); appeared both as pianist and cellist, but was more important as composer.—Works: 6 symphonies (the fifth: *Sinfonia svastica,* in C, op. 59); 2 overtures, *Der Volksfeind* and *Dänemark; Sommerliv,* suite for orch.; a dance poem, *Artemis* (Copenhagen, Oct. 27, 1917; also as an orchestral suite); *Fantasie* for piano and orch.; concerto for oboe and orch.; string sextet; piano quintet; 4 string quartets; piano trio; 2 violin sonatas; numerous works for piano (3 sonatas, etc.).

Glaz, Herta, Austrian contralto; b. Vienna, Sept. 16, 1914. She studied at the Vienna Academy; made her début in Breslau; then sang at Prague; also with the Glyndebourne Opera. She made her début with the Metropolitan Opera Company as Amneris (Dec. 25, 1942); has also appeared in Wagnerian roles.

Glazunov (glăh-zoo-nŏhv'), **Alexander Konstantinovitch,** notable Russian composer; b. St. Petersburg, Aug. 10, 1865; d. Paris, March 21, 1936. Of a well-to-do family (his father was a book publisher), he studied at a technical high school in St. Petersburg, and also took lessons in music with a private tutor. As a boy of 15, he was introduced to Rimsky-Korsakov, who gave him weekly lessons in harmony, counterpoint, and orchestration. Glazunov made rapid progress and at the age of 16 completed his first symphony, which was performed by Balakirev on March 29, 1882 in St. Petersburg. So mature was this score that Glazunov was hailed by Stasov, Cui, and others as a rightful heir to the masters of the Russian National School. The music publisher Belaiev arranged for publication of Glazunov's works, and took him to Weimar, where he met Liszt. From that time Glazunov composed assiduously in all genres except opera. He was invited to conduct his symphonies in Paris (1889) and London (1896-7). Returning to St. Petersburg, he conducted many concerts of Russian music; however, he lacked interpretative powers, and his performances were merely correct renditions of the literal materials of the music. In 1899 he was engaged as instructor at the St. Petersburg Cons., and in 1905 he became its director, gradually building up a fine faculty and inspiring the students to higher achievements. He retained this post until 1928; then he left Russia and lived mostly in Paris. In 1929 he made several appearances as conductor in the U. S.; led his 6th symphony with the Detroit Symph. Orch. (Nov. 21, 1929) and also conducted the Boston Symph. He was the recipient of an honorary degree of Mus. D. from Cambridge and Oxford Universities (1907). Although he wrote no textbook on composition, his pedagogical methods left a lasting impression on Russian musicians through his many students who preserved his traditions. His music is often regarded as academic; yet there is a flow of rhapsodic eloquence that places Glazunov in the Romantic school. He was for a time greatly swayed by Wagnerian harmonies, but resisted this influence successfully; Lisztian characteristics are more pronounced in his works. Glazunov was one of the greatest masters of counterpoint among Russian composers, but he avoided extreme polyphonic complexity. The national spirit of his music is unmistakable; in many of his descriptive works, the programmatic design is explicitly Russian (*Stenka Razin, The Kremlin,* etc.). His most popular score is the ballet *Raymonda.* The major portion of his music was written before 1906, when he completed his 8th symph.; after that he wrote mostly for special occasions.—Works: incidental music to Grand Duke Konstantin Romanov's mystery play *The King of the Jews* (1914); ballets, *Raymonda* (1896; St. Petersburg, Jan. 7, 1898); *Ruses d'amour* (1898); *The Seasons* (1899). For orch.: Symph. No. 1 (1881); 2 *Overtures on Greek Themes* (1881-85); 2 Serenades (1883); *Stenka Razin,* symph. poem (1884); *A la mémoire d'un héros* (1885); *Suite caractéristique* (1885); *Idyll* and *Rêverie orientale* (1886); Symph. No. 2 (1886); *Une pensée à Franz Liszt* for string orch. (1886); *Mazurka* (1887); *The Forest,* symph. poem (1888); *Mélodie* and *Sérénade espagnole* for cello and orch. (1888); *Marche des Noces* for large orch. (1889); *Une Fête slave,* symph. sketch (1890; from *Quatuor slave*); *The Sea,* symph. fantasy (1890); *Oriental Rhapsody* (1890); *The Kremlin,* symph. picture (1890); Symph. No. 3 (1891); *Printemps,* musical picture (1892); *Triumphal March* on the occasion of the World's Columbian Exposition in Chicago (1893); overture *Carnaval* (1894); *Chopiniana,* suite on Chopin's themes (1894); 2 *Valses de concert* (1894); Symph. No. 4 (St. Petersburg, Feb. 3, 1894, composer conducting); *Cortège solennel* (1894); *Scènes de ballet* (1894); *Fantaisie* (1895); Symph. No. 5 (1895); suite from the ballet *Raymonda* (1897); Symph. No. 6 (1896); *Pas de caractère,* on Slavic and Hungarian themes (1900); *Intermezzo romantico* (1901); *Chant du Ménestrel* for cello and orch. (1901; also for cello and piano); *Ouverture solennelle* (1901); *Marche sur un thème russe* (1901); Symph. No. 7 (St. Petersburg, Nov. 15, 1902); *Ballade* (1902); *From the Middle Ages,* suite (1903); violin concerto (1904; London, Oct. 17, 1905, Mischa Elman, soloist); *Scène dansante* (1905); Symph. No. 8 (1906); *Le Chant du destin,* dramatic overture (1907); 2 Preludes: No. 1, *In Memory of V. Stasov* (1906); No. 2, *In Memory of Rimsky-Korsakov* (1908); *In Memory of Gogol* (1909); *Finnish Fantasy* (Helsingfors, Nov. 7, 1910, composer conducting); piano concerto No. 1 (1911); *Finnish Sketches* (1912); *Dance of Salomé,* after Oscar Wilde (1912); *Karelian Legend* (1914); 2nd piano concerto (1922); *Concerto-Ballata* for cello and orch. (Paris, Oct. 14, 1933, composer conducting, Maurice Eisenberg soloist); saxophone concerto (in collaboration with A. Petiot, 1934). Vocal works: *Coronation Cantata* (1894); *Hymn to Pushkin* for female chorus (1899); cantata for women's chorus with 2 pianos, 8 hands (1900); *Memorial Cantata* (1901); 21 songs. Chamber music: 7 string quartets: No. 1 in D (1882); No. 2 in F (1884); No. 3 in G (*Quatuor Slave,* 1889); No. 4 in A (1899); No. 5 in D (1900); No. 6 in B♭ (1930); No. 7 in C (1931); *5 Novelettes* for string quartet (1888); suite for string quartet (1894); string quintet (1895); suite for string quartet (1929); *Pensée à Liszt* for cello and piano; *Rêverie* for French horn and piano; *In modo religioso* for 4 brass instruments; *Elegy* for viola and piano; *Oberek* for violin and piano. Piano music: 2 sonatas (1898; 1899); *Barcarolle; Novelette; Prelude* and *2 Mazurkas; 3 Etudes; Petite Valse; Nocturne; Grande Valse de Concert; 3 Miniatures; Valse de Salon; 3 Morceaux; 2 Impromptus; Prelude and Fugue; Theme and Variations;* suite for 2 pianos (1920); 4 *Preludes and Fugues* (1922). Glazunov also completed and orchestrated the overture to Borodin's *Prince Igor* (from memory, having heard Borodin play it on the piano).—Cf. A. W. Ossovsky, *Glazunov: His Life and Work* (St. Petersburg, 1907); M. Montagu-Nathan, *Contemporary Russian Composers* (N. Y., 1917); V. Belaiev, *Glazunov* (Vol. 1, Petrograd, 1921); I. Glebov, *Glazunov* (Leningrad, 1924); M. D. Calvocoressi and G. Abraham, *Masters of Russian Music* (N. Y., 1936); Galina Fedorova, *Glazunov* (Moscow, 1947).

Gleason, Frederick Grant, American composer and critic; b. Middletown, Conn., Dec. 17, 1848; d. Chicago, Dec. 6, 1903. He studied in Hartford with Dudley Buck, later at the Leipzig Cons., in Berlin, and London. He returned to become organist at several churches in Connecticut; in 1884, taught at the Hershey School of Music in Chicago; from 1884-89, he was also music critic of the 'Chicago Tribune.' From 1900 to his death, he was director of the Chicago Auditorium Cons. He wrote 2 operas, *Otho Visconti* (posthumous production; Chicago, June 4, 1907) and *Montezuma;* 4 cantatas; symph. poem, *Edris;* 3 sketches for orch.; a piano concerto; 3 piano trios; organ and piano pieces; songs; 2 Episcopal church services. — Cf. E. E. Hipsher, *American Opera and its Composers* (Philadelphia, 1934; pp. 216-17).

Gleason, Harold, American organist and musicologist; b. Jefferson, Ohio, April 26, 1892; studied organ in California with Lemare, and in Paris with Bonnet; composition with Herbert Inch at the Eastman School, Rochester; occupied positions as church organist in Pasadena (1911-15), N. Y. (1918), Rochester (1919-49); was head of the organ department at the Eastman School from 1921-53; professor of musicology there from 1932-55. He designed organs for the Eastman School; was active in educational organizations. He publ. a *Method of Organ Playing* (1937); *Examples of Music before 1400* (1942; 2nd ed., 1945); *Music Literature Outlines* (5 issues; 1949-55); contributed papers to music magazines.

Glebov, Igor. Pen-name of **Boris Asafiev** (q.v.).

Glen, John, Scots collector of native music; b. Edinburgh, June 13, 1833; d. there, Nov. 29, 1904. His father **Thomas G.** (1804-73), the inventor of the 'Serpentcleide,' had established himself as a manufacturer of musical instruments, and the son succeeded to the business in 1866; he confined himself to the manufacture of bagpipes, of which he was soon recognized as the foremost manufacturer of Great Britain. He was equally noted for his research in Scottish music; compiled *The Glen Collection of Scottish Dance Music, Strathspeys, Reels and Jigs . . . containing an Introduction on Scottish Dance Music* (2 vols., 1891, 1895); vol. I contains 144, vol. II 148, tunes. His chief work is *Early Scottish Melodies: including examples from MSS. and early printed works, along with a number of comparative tunes, notes on former annotators, English and other claims, and Biographical Notices, etc.* (1900).—Cf. 'Musical Times,' Jan., 1905.

Glière, Reinhold Moritzovitch, eminent Russian composer; b. Kiev, Jan. 11, 1875; d. Moscow, June 23, 1956. He studied violin with Hrimaly; entered the Moscow Cons., where he took courses with Arensky, Taneyev, and Ippolitov-Ivanov (1894-1900), graduating with a gold medal. In 1905 he went to Berlin, where he remained for 2 years; returning to Russia, he became active as a teacher; was appointed prof. of composition at the Kiev Cons., and was its director from 1914-20; then was appointed to the faculty of the Moscow Cons., a post he retained to the end of his life. He traveled extensively in European and Asiatic Russia, collecting folk melodies; conducted many concerts of his own works; he made his last tour a month before his death, conducting in Odessa, Kishinev, and other cities. He was an extremely prolific composer, and was particularly distinguished in symphonic works, in which he revealed himself as a successor of the Russian National School. He never transgressed the natural borderline of traditional harmony, but he was able to achieve effective results. His most impressive work is his 3rd Symph., surnamed *Ilya Murometz,* an epic description of the exploits of a legendary Russian hero. In his numerous songs Glière showed a fine lyrical talent. He wrote relatively few works of chamber music, most of them early in his career. In his single opera, *Shah-Senem,* he made use of native Caucasian songs. Glière was the teacher of two generations of Russian composers; among his students were Prokofiev and Miaskovsky. — Works: opera, *Shah-Senem* (Baku, May 4, 1934); ballets: *Chrysis* (1912); *Cleopatra* (1925); *Comedians* (1922-30); *Red Poppy* (Moscow, June 14, 1927); *The Bronze Knight,* after Pushkin (1949). Incidental music to: *King Oedipus,* Sophocles (1921); *Lysistrata,* Aristophanes (1923); *Marriage of Figaro,* Beaumarchais (1927). For orch.: Symph. No. 1 (1899-1900); Symph. No. 2 (Berlin, Jan.

23, 1908, Koussevitzky conducting); *The Sirens,* symph. poem (1908); Symph. No. 3, *Ilya Murometz* (1909-11); *Two Poems* for soprano and orch. (1924); *Cossacks of Zaporozh,* symph. poem (1921); *Trizna,* symph. poem (1915); *For the Festival of the Comintern,* fantasy for wind orch. (1924); *March of the Red Army,* for wind orch. (1924); *Imitation of Jezekiel,* symph. poem for narrator and orch. (1919); concerto for harp and orch. (1938); *Friendship of Nations,* overture (1941); concerto for coloratura soprano and orch. (1942); *For the Happiness of the Fatherland,* overture (1942); *25 Years of the Red Army,* overture (1943); *Victory,* overture (Moscow, Oct. 30, 1945); cello concerto (1946); horn concerto (Moscow, Jan. 26, 1952, composer conducting); he left an unfinished violin concerto. Chamber music: 5 string quartets (No. 4 won the Stalin Prize, 1948; No. 5 left unfinished at his death); 3 string sextets; 1 string octet. Other music: 20 pieces for violin and piano; 12 duos for two violins; Ballad for cello and piano; 4 pieces for double bass and piano; 8 pieces for violin and cello; 12 pieces for cello and piano; 10 duos for 2 cellos; miscellaneous pieces for different instruments. He also wrote about 200 songs and 200 piano pieces. A biography of Glière by Igor Boelza was publ. in Moscow, 1955.

Glinka, Mikhail Ivanovitch, Russian composer; b. Novosspaskoye, Govt. of Smolensk, June 1, 1804; d. Berlin, Feb. 15, 1857. A scion of a fairly rich family of landowners, he was educated in an exclusive school at St. Petersburg (1818-22); he also took private lessons in music; his piano teacher was a resident German musician, Carl Meyer; he also studied violin; when the famous pianist, John Field, was in St. Petersburg, Glinka had an opportunity to study with him, but he had only three lessons owing to Field's departure. He began to compose even before acquiring adequate training in theory. As a boy he traveled in the Caucasus; then stayed for a while at his father's estate; at 20 entered the Ministry of Communications in St. Petersburg; he remained in government employ until 1828; at the same time, he constantly improved his general education by reading; he had friends among the best Russian writers of the time, including the poets Zhukovsky and Pushkin. He also took singing lessons with an Italian teacher, Belloli. In 1830 he went to Italy, where he continued irregular studies in Milan (where he spent most of his Italian years); he also visited Naples, Rome, and Bologna. He met Donizetti and Bellini. He became enamored of Italian music, and his early vocal and instrumental compositions are thoroughly Italian in melodic and harmonic structure. In 1833 he went to Berlin, where he took a course in counterpoint and general composition with the famous German theorist, Dehn; thus he was nearly 30 when he completed his theoretical education. In 1834, his father died, and Glinka went back to Russia to take care of the family affairs. In 1835 he was married; but the marriage was unhappy, and he soon became separated from his wife, finally divorcing her in 1846. The return to his native land led him to consider the composition of a truly national opera on a subject (suggested to him by Zhukovsky) depicting a historical episode in Russian history, the saving of the first Tsar of the Romanov dynasty by a simple peasant, Ivan Susanin. (The Italian composer, Cavos, wrote an opera on the same subject 20 years previously, and conducted it in St. Petersburg.) Glinka's opera was produced in St. Petersburg on Dec. 9, 1836, under the title, *A Life for the Tsar.* The event was hailed by the literary and artistic circles of Russia as a milestone of Russian culture, and indeed the entire development of Russian national music received its decisive creative impulse from Glinka's patriotic opera. It remained in the repertory of Russian theaters until the Russian Revolution made it unacceptable, but it was revived, under the original title, *Ivan Susanin,* on Feb. 27, 1939, in Moscow, without alterations in the music, but with the references to the Tsar eliminated from the libretto, the idea of saving the country being substituted for that of saving the Tsar. Glinka's next opera, *Ruslan and Ludmila,* after Pushkin's fairy tale, was produced on Dec. 9, 1842; this opera, too, became extremely popular in Russia. Glinka introduced into the score many elements of Oriental music; one episode contains the earliest use of the whole-tone scale in an opera. Both operas retain the traditional Italian form, with arias, choruses, and orchestral episodes clearly separated. In 1844, Glinka was in Paris, where he met Berlioz; he also traveled in Spain, where he collected folksongs; the fruits of his Spanish tour were two orchestral works, *Jota Aragonesa* and *Night in Madrid.* On his way back to Russia, he stayed in Warsaw for 3 years; the remaining years of his life he spent in St. Petersburg, Paris, and Berlin, where he died.—Works: operas: *A Life for the Tsar; Russlan and Ludmilla;* sketches for 3 unfinished operas; incidental music for Kukolnik's tragedy, *Prince Kholmsky;* incidental music for the play, *The Mol-*

davian Gypsy; for orch.: *Andante Cantabile and Rondo;* a larghetto; 2 overtures; a symphony in B♭ major; *Trumpet March* (1828); *Overture-Symphony on Russian Themes,* in D minor (1834; completed in 1938 by V. I. Shebalin); *Valse* in G major (1839); *Polonaise* (1839); *Valse-Fantaisie* (1839); *Valse* in B♭ major (1840); *Capriccio brillante* on the *Jota Aragonesa* (1845; afterwards renamed *Spanish Overture No. 1); Summer Night in Madrid: Spanish Overture No. 2* (1848); *Kamarinskaya* (1848); symph. poem on Gogol's *Taras Bulba* (unfinished, part of first movement only; 1852); *Festival Polonaise* on a bolero melody (1855); chamber music: septet in E♭ major (1824); 2 string quartets (1824, 1830); *Trio pathétique* (1827); 2 serenades (1832); sonata for piano and viola (1825-28); about 40 piano numbers (5 valses, 7 mazurkas, nocturnes, etc.); much vocal music, including choral works, quartets, duets, arias, and about 85 songs with piano accompaniment, many set to poems by Pushkin and Zhukovsky.—Cf. O. Comettant, *Musique et Musiciens* (Paris, 1862); A. N. Strugovschikov, *Memories of Glinka* in 'Russkaya Starina' (1874); C. Cui, *La Musique en Russie* (Paris, 1880); O. Fouque, *Glinka* (Paris, 1880); K. Albrecht, *Catalogue of Glinka's Vocal Works* (Moscow, 1891); P. Weimarn, *M. I. Glinka* (Moscow, 1892); L. Shestakova, *Glinka as He Was* (St. Petersburg, 1894); A. N. Serov, *Reminiscences of M. I. Glinka* in 'Critical Essays' (St. Petersburg, 1895); N. F. Findeisen, *M. I. Glinka* (St. Petersburg, 1896); N. F. Findeisen, *Glinka in Spain and the Spanish Folksongs Recorded by Him* (St. Petersburg, 1896); N. F. Findeisen, *Catalogue of the Musical Manuscripts, Letters, and Portraits of M. I. Glinka in the Manuscript Section of the Imperial Public Library in St. Petersburg* (St. Petersburg, 1898); V. Avenarius, *Glinka, the Creator of Russian Opera* (St. Petersburg, 1903); A. Pougin, *Essai historique sur la musique en Russie* (Paris, 1904); M. D. Calvocoressi, *Glinka* (Paris, 1913); M. Montagu-Nathan, *Glinka* (London, 1916); M. Montagu-Nathan, *Glinka Re-valued,* in the 'Mus. Times' (May, 1917); O. von Riesemann, *Monographien zur russischen Musik* (Munich, 1922); vols. II and III of 'Muzikalnaya Letopis,' articles by Rimsky-Korsakov, Glebov, etc. (Petrograd, 1923, and Leningrad, 1925); K. A. Kusnetzov, *Glinka and His Contemporaries* (1926); G. Abraham, *Glinka and his Achievement,* in 'Music and Letters' (1928); M. D. Calvocoressi and G. Abraham, *Glinka* in *Masters of Russian Music* (N. Y., 1936); G. Abraham, *The Foundation-Stone of Russian Music,* in 'Music and Letters' (Jan., 1937); M. S. Pekelis, *Glinka* in *History of Russian Music,* vol. I (Moscow, 1940); D. Brook, *Six Great Russian Composers* (London, 1946); I. I. Martinov, *M. I. Glinka* (Moscow, 1947); A. Altayev, *M. I. Glinka* (Moscow, 1947); B. Asafiev, *Glinka* (Moscow, 1947); Y. Keldish, *Glinka* in *History of Russian Music,* vol. I (Moscow, 1948); E. Kann-Novikova, *M. I. Glinka, New Materials and Documents* (Moscow, 1951); A. Orlova, *M. I. Glinka, Chronicle of Life and Work* (Moscow, 1952); P. G. Dippel, *Klingende Einkehr; Glinka und Berlin* (Berlin, 1953). Numerous articles on Glinka have appeared in 'Sovetskaya Musika' in 1934 (No. 3); 1937 (No. 3); 1938 (No. 3); 1939 (Nos. 2 and 3); 1944 (No. 2); 1946 (No. 6); 1947 (No. 1); 1949 (No. 5). Glinka's autobiographical sketch intended for inclusion in the *Biographie Universelle des musiciens* by Fétis was publ. for the first time in 'Muzikalnaya Letopis' in 1926; his collected letters, edited by N. Findeisen, were publ. in 1907; other letters in 'Muzikalny Sovremennik' (Petrograd, 1916).

Glinski, Mateusz (Matteo), Polish music scholar, conductor, and composer; b. Warsaw, April 6, 1892. He studied music at the Warsaw Cons. (1909-13) with Barcewicz (violin and conducting) and Statkowski (composition); then took courses in Leipzig with Riemann and Schering; also studied conducting with Nikisch. He went to St. Petersburg in 1914, and studied composition with Glazunov and Steinberg and conducting with Tcherepnin; gave several symphonic concerts there (1916-18). After World War I he returned to Poland, where he edited a monthly review, 'Muzyka' (1924-39). After the outbreak of World War II, he went to Rome and engaged in energetic activities as conductor, editor, historian, and lecturer. In 1946 he founded a music monthly in Italian, 'Musica'; in 1949 he established the 'Istituto Internazionale Federico Chopin,' of which he was elected president in 1954. He discovered documents on the Renaissance composer Asprilio Pacelli, ancestor of Pope Pius XII, and transcribed and edited his works; also transcribed and performed some of G. Francesco Anerio's oratorios (1619), which he demonstrated to be the forerunners of the classical oratorio. In 1956 he visited the U. S.; gave lectures on Chopin at the Univ. of Michigan, at Wayne Univ. and other colleges. Among his works are an opera, *L'Aiglon,* after Rostand (1918-1927); 2 symph. poems, *The Blind*

Singer and *Wagram; Purcelliana,* a suite for orch. (1934); *Tre Cantate d'Amore* (1940); *The Prayer of Polish Exiles* (1941); *Te decet Hymnus* (1944); *Couperiniana* (1950), and various transcriptions of old masters. He has publ. in Polish: *History of Conducting* (1917); *Fryderyk Chopin* (1928); *Scriabin* (1933); *Karol Szymanowski* (1937); and in Italian: *Asprilio Pacelli* (1941); *La prima stagione lirica all'estero* (1942); *La spiritualità dell'ottocento italiano* (1947); *Lorenzo Perosi* (1953).

Glock, William, English music critic; b. London, May 3, 1908. He studied at Caius College, Cambridge; then took piano lessons with Schnabel in Berlin. After a few appearances as pianist, he decided to become a music critic; he was in the Royal Air Force during World War II; in 1948 he founded a summer music school in Bryanston; he publishes a music magazine 'The Score'; also gives frequent lectures in England and Canada.

Glover, John William, Irish composer and conductor; b. Dublin, June 19, 1815; d. there, Dec. 18, 1899. He studied in Dublin, and was violinist in an orchestra there; in 1848, he became prof. of vocal music in the Normal Training School of the Irish National Education Board and also director of music in the Roman Catholic procathedral. He established the Choral Institute in 1851, and was noted for his promotion of choral music in Ireland. He edited Moore's 'Irish Melodies' (1859). — Works: opera, *The Deserted Village,* after Goldsmith (London, 1880); 2 Italian operas to librettos by Metastasio; cantata, *St. Patrick at Tara* (1870); *Erin's Matin Song* (1873); ode to Thomas Moore, *One hundred years ago* (1879); also concertos, piano pieces, songs, church music.

Glover, Sarah Ann, English piano pedagogue; b. Norwich, Nov. 13, 1786; d. Malvern, Oct. 20, 1867. She was the originator of the tonic sol-fa system of notation, a method later modified and developed by John Curwen (q.v.). She wrote: *Scheme for rendering Psalmody Congregational* (1835), *Manual of the Norwich Sol-fa System* (1845), and a *Manual containing a Development of the Tetrachordal System* (1850). She devised a pictorial chart called the 'Norwich Sol-fa Ladder.'

Glover, William Howard, English conductor and composer; b. London, June 6, 1819; d. New York, Oct. 28, 1875. At the age of 15, he became a violinist in the Lyceum Theater orch., studying with the conductor, William Wagstaff, and afterwards on the Continent. With Braham he toured Scotland; he formed an opera company at Manchester and Liverpool which he conducted, and later was a conductor in London, where he was music critic of the 'Morning Post' from about 1850 to 1865. In 1868 he came to New York, where he was conductor at Niblo's Garden until his death.—Works: opera, *Ruy Blas,* after Victor Hugo (Covent Garden, Oct. 21, 1861); operettas: *The Coquette; Aminta* (Haymarket, London, Jan. 26, 1852); *Once Too Often* (Drury Lane, Jan. 20, 1862); *Palomita, or The Veiled Songstress* (publ. in N. Y., 1875); cantata, *Tam o' Shanter,* after Burns (London, July 4, 1855, Berlioz conducting); overtures; piano music; songs.

Gluck, Alma (real name, Reba Fiersohn), American soprano; b. Bucharest, Rumania, May 11, 1884; d. New York, Oct. 27, 1938. Her parents brought her to New York as a small child; she was educated in the public schools, the Normal School (now Hunter College), and Union College, Schenectady, N. Y. After her marriage to Bernard Gluck, she studied singing with Buzzi-Peccia; she was engaged for the Metropolitan Opera in 1909, and made her début as Sophie in Massenet's *Werther* on Nov. 16, 1909. She became a favorite with the public, and sang more than 20 roles during her three years in opera. In 1912, she gave up opera for the concert stage; she also divorced Mr. Gluck; she studied for a year with Marcella Sembrich in Berlin; returned to the U. S. in 1913 for many years of successful concert work; she was noted also as a recording artist. She married the violinist Efrem Zimbalist in 1914. She returned from retirement to give a concert at the Manhattan Opera House in 1925. Glimpses of her career are shown in *Of Lena Geyer,* a novel publ. by her daughter, Marcia Davenport (q.v.).

Gluck, Christoph Willibald (Ritter von), renowned composer; b. Erasbach, near Weidenwang in the Upper Palatinate, July 2 1714; d. Vienna, Nov. 15, 1787. His father was a forester at Erasbach until his appointment as forester to Prince Lobkowitz of Eisenberg about 1729. Gluck received his elementary instruction in the village school at Kamnitz and Albersdorf near Komotau, where he also was taught singing and instrumental playing. Some biographers refer to his study at the Jesuit college at Komotau but there is no documentary evidence to support this contention. In 1732, Gluck went to Prague to complete his education, but it is doubtful that he took any courses at Prague Univ. He earned his living in Prague by playing violin and cello at rural dances in the area; also sang at various churches; there he had an opportunity to meet Bohuslav Černohorsky, who was chapelmaster at St. James' Church from 1735; it is probable that Gluck learned the methods of church music from him. He went to Vienna in 1736, and was chamber musician to young Prince Lobkowitz, son of the patron of Gluck's father. In 1737 he was taken to Milan by Prince Melzi; this Italian sojourn was of the greatest importance to Gluck's musical development. There he became a student of G. B. Sammartini and acquired a solid technique of composition in the Italian style. After 4 years of study, Gluck brought out his first opera *Artaserse,* to the text of the celebrated Metastasio; it was produced in Milan (Dec. 26, 1741) with such success that Gluck was immediately commissioned to write more operas. There followed *Demetrio* or *Cleonice* (Venice, May 2, 1742); *Demofoonte* (Milan, Dec. 26, 1742); *Il Tigrane* (Crema, Sept. 9, 1743); *La Sofonisba* or *Siface* (Milan, Jan. 13, 1744); *Ipermestra* (Venice, Nov. 21, 1744); *Poro* (Turin, Dec. 26, 1744); *Ippolito* or *Fedra* (Milan, Jan. 31, 1745). He also contributed separate numbers to several other operas produced in Italy. In 1745 Gluck received an invitation to go to London; on his way, he visited Paris and met Rameau. He was commissioned by the Italian Opera of London to write 2 operas for the Haymarket Theatre, as a competitive endeavor to Handel's enterprise. The first of these works was *La Caduta dei giganti,* a tribute to the Duke of Cumberland on the defeat of the Pretender; it was produced on Jan. 18, 1746; the second was a pasticcio, *Artamene,* in which Gluck used material from his previous operas; it was produced March 15, 1746. Ten days later, Gluck appeared with Handel at a public concert, despite the current report in London society that Handel had declared that Gluck knew no more counterpoint than his cook (it should be added that a professional musician, Gustavus Waltz, was Handel's cook and valet at the time). On April 23, 1746, Gluck gave a demonstration in London, playing on the 'glass harmonica.' He left London late in 1746 when he received an engagement as conductor with Pietro Mingotti's traveling Italian opera company. He conducted in Hamburg, Leipzig, and Dresden; on June 29, 1747, he produced a 'serenata,' *Le Nozze d'Ercole e d'Ebe,* to celebrate a royal wedding; it was performed at the Saxon court, in Pillnitz. Gluck then went to Vienna, where he staged his opera, *Semiramide riconosciuta,* after a poem of Metastasio (May 14, 1748). He then traveled to Copenhagen, where he produced a festive opera, *La Contesa dei Numi* (March 9, 1749), on the occasion of the birth of Prince Christian; his next productions (all to Metastasio's words) were *Ezio* (Prague, 1750); *Issipile* (Prague, 1752); *La Clemenza di Tito* (Naples, Nov. 4, 1752); *Le Cinesi* (Vienna, Sept. 24, 1754); *La Danza* (Vienna, May 5, 1755); *L'innocenza giustificata* (Vienna, Dec. 8, 1755); *Antigono* (Rome, Feb. 9, 1756); *Il re pastore* (Vienna, Dec. 8, 1756). In 1750 Gluck married Marianna Pergin, daughter of a Viennese merchant; for several years afterwards he conducted operatic performances in Vienna. As French influence increased there, Gluck wrote several entertainments to French texts, containing spoken dialogue, in the style of opéra-comique; of these, the most successful were *Le Cadi dupé* (December, 1761) and *La Rencontre imprévue* (Jan. 7, 1764; performed also under the title *Les pèlerins de la Mecque,* his most popular production in this genre). His greatest work of the Vienna period was *Orfeo ed Euridice* to a libretto by Calzabigi (in a version for male contralto; Oct. 5, 1762, with the part of Orfeo sung by the famous castrato, Gaetano Guadagni). Gluck revised it for a Paris performance, produced in French on Aug. 2, 1774, with Orfeo sung by a tenor. There followed another masterpiece, *Alceste* (Vienna, Dec. 16, 1767), also to Calzabigi's text. In the preface to *Alceste,* Gluck formulated his esthetic credo, which elevated the dramatic meaning of musical stage plays above the mere striving for vocal effects: "I sought to reduce music to its true function, that of seconding poetry in order to strengthen the emotional expression and the impact of the dramatic situations without interrupting the action and without weakening it by superfluous ornaments." Among other productions of the Viennese period were *Il Trionfo di Clelia* (Vienna, May 14, 1763); *Il Parnaso confuso* (Schönbrunn Palace, Jan. 24, 1765); *Il Telemacco* (Vienna, Jan. 30, 1765), and *Paride ed Elena* (Vienna, Nov. 30, 1770). The success of his French operas in Vienna led Gluck to the decision to try his fortunes in Paris, yielding to the persuasion of François du Roullet, an attaché at the French embassy in Vienna, who also supplied Gluck with his first libretto for a serious French opera, an adaptation of Racine's *Iphigénie en Aulide* (Paris, April 19, 1774). Gluck set out for Paris early in 1773, preceded by declarations in the Paris press by du Roullet and Gluck himself explaining in detail Gluck's ideas of dramatic music. These statements set off an intellectual battle in the Paris press and among musicians in general between the adherents of traditional Italian opera and Gluck's novel French opera. It reached an unprecedented degree of acrimony when the Italian composer Nicola Piccinni was engaged by the French court to write operas to French texts, in open competition to Gluck; intrigues multiplied, even though Marie Antoinette never wavered in her admiration for Gluck, who taught her singing and harpsichord playing. However, Gluck and Piccinni themselves never participated in the bitter polemics unleashed by their literary and musical partisans. The sensational successes of the French version of Gluck's *Orfeo* and of *Alceste* were followed by the production of *Armide* (Sept. 23, 1777), which aroused great admiration. Then followed Gluck's masterpiece, *Iphigénie en Tauride* (May 18, 1779), which established Gluck's superiority to Piccinni, who was commissioned to write an opera on the same subject, but failed to complete it in time. Gluck's last opera, *Echo et Narcisse* (Paris, Sept. 24, 1779), did not measure up to the excellence of his previous operas. By that time, Gluck's health had failed; he had several attacks of apoplexy, which resulted in a partial paralysis. In the autumn of 1779 he returned to Vienna, where he lived as an invalid for several more years. His last work was a *De profundis* for chorus and orchestra, written 5 years before his death. Besides his operas, he wrote several ballets, of which *Don Juan* (Vienna, Oct. 17, 1761) was the most successful; he further wrote a cycle of 7 songs to words by Klopstock, 7 trio-sonatas, several overtures, etc. Breitkopf & Härtel publ. excellent editions of Gluck's most important operas; other operas are included in 'Denkmäler der Tonkunst in Bayern' and 'Denkmäler der Tonkunst in Österreich'; H. Gál edited a Sinfonia in C, identical with the overture to *Ipermestra;* the trio-sonatas are found in Riemann's 'Collegium musicum'; songs in Delsarte's 'Archives du chant.' Wagner, while in Dresden (1842-49), made a complete revision of the score of *Iphigénie en Aulide;* this arrangement was so extensively used that a Wagnerized version of Gluck's music became the chief text for performances during the 19th century.—A complete ed. of Gluck's works was begun by the Bärenreiter Verlag in 1951.

BIBLIOGRAPHY: F. J. Riedel, *Über die Musik des Ritters Christoph von Gluck* (Vienna, 1775); C. P. Coqueau, *Entretiens sur l'état actuel de l'opéra de Paris* (Paris, 1779; dialogue on the Gluck-Piccinni controversy); G. M. Leblond, *Mémoires pour servir à l'histoire de la révolution opérée dans la musique par M. le Chevalier Gluck* (Paris, 1781; German transl., 1823; 2nd ed., 1837); J. G. Siegmeyer, *Über den Ritter Gluck und seine Werke* (Berlin, 1837); E. Miel, *Notice sur Gluck* (Paris, 1840); A. Schmid, *Christoph Willibald Ritter von Gluck* (Leipzig, 1854); W. Neumann, *Christoph Willibald Gluck* (Kassel, 1855); J. Baudoin, *L'Alceste de Gluck* (Paris, 1861); A. B. Marx, *Gluck und die Oper* (Berlin, 1863); L. Nohl, *Gluck und Wagner* (Munich, 1870); G. Desnoiresterres, *Gluck et Piccinni* (Paris, 1875); A. Jullien, *La Cour et l'Opéra sous Louis XVI* (Paris, 1878); E. Thoinan, *Notes bibliographiques sur la guerre musicale des Gluckistes et Piccinnistes* (Paris, 1878); H. Barbedette, *Gluck* (Paris, 1882); A. Reissmann, *Christoph Willibald von Gluck* (Berlin, 1882); K. H. Bitter, *Die Reform der Oper durch Gluck und Wagner* (Brunswick, 1884); H. Welti, *Gluck* (Leipzig, 1888); E. Newman, *Gluck and the Opera* (London, 1895); J. d'Udine, *Gluck* (Paris, 1906); J. Tiersot, *Gluck* (Paris, 1910); La Mara, *Gluck* (Leipzig, 1912; reprinted from 'Musik Studienköpfe'); Ernst Kurth, *Die Jugendopern Glucks* in 'Studien zur Musikwissenschaft' I (1913); H. Berlioz, *Gluck and His Operas* (transl. from the French by Edwin Evans, Sr.; London, 1915); S. Wortsmann, *Die deutsche Gluck-Literatur* (Nuremberg, 1914); W. B. Squire, *Gluck's London Operas,* in the 'Mus. Quarterly' (July, 1915); J.-G. Prod'homme, *Gluck's French Collaborators,* in the 'Mus. Quarterly' (April, 1917); J.-G. Prod'homme, *Les Portraits français de Gluck,* in 'Rivista Musicale Italiana' XXV, 1 (1918); M. Arend, *Gluck* (1921); W. Vetter, *Die Arie bei Gluck,* in 'Zeitschrift für Musikwissenschaft' III (1921); R. Haas, *Die Wiener Ballet-Pantomime im 18. Jahrhundert und Glucks 'Don Juan,'* in 'Studien zur Musikwissenschaft' X (1923); E. H. Müller, *Zwei unveröffentlichte Briefe Glucks an Carl August,* in 'Die Musik' (Stuttgart, 1923); G. Scuderi, *Christoph Gluck: Orfeo* (Milan, 1924); R. Haas, *Gluck und Durazzo im Burgtheater* (Vienna, 1925); Paul Brück, *Glucks Orpheus und Eurydike,* in 'Archiv für Musikwissenschaft' VII, 4 (1926); Georg Kinsky, *Glucks Reisen nach Paris,* in 'Zeitschrift für Musikwissenschaft' VIII; Georg Kinsky, *Glucks Briefe an Franz*

Kruthoffer (Vienna, 1929); M. Cauchie, *Gluck et ses éditeurs parisiens,* in 'Le Ménestrel' (1927); Th. Veidl, *Neues über Glucks Jugend,* in 'Auftakt' VIII, 3 (1928); Julien Tiersot, *Gluck and the Encyclopaedists,* in the 'Mus. Quarterly' (July, 1930); E. Istel, *Gluck's Dramaturgy,* in the 'Mus. Quarterly' (April, 1931); K. Huschke, *Gluck und seine deutsche Zeitgenossen,* in 'Zeitschrift für Musikwissenschaft' (March, 1933); L. de la Laurencie, *Gluck, Orphée: étude et analyse musicale* (Paris, 1934); D. F. Tovey, *Christoph Willibald Gluck and the Musical Revolution,* in H. Foss, *The Heritage of Music,* vol. 2 (London, 1934); M. Cooper, *Gluck* (London, 1935); A. Einstein, *Gluck* (London, 1936); R. Tenschert, *Christoph Willibald Gluck (1714-1787); sein Leben in Bildern* (Leipzig, 1938); P. Landormy, *Gluck* (Paris, 1941); A. Della Corte, *Gluck* (Turin, 1942); W. Brandl, *Christoph Willibald Ritter von Gluck* (Wiesbaden, 1948); A. Della Corte, *Gluck e i suoi tempi* (Florence, 1948); J.-G. Prod'homme, *Gluck* (Paris, 1948); R. Gerber, *C. W. Ritter von Gluck* (Potsdam, 1950); R. Tenschert, *Christoph Willibald Gluck: der grosse Reformator der Oper* (Freiburg, 1951). A thematic catalogue was publ. by A. Wotquenne (Leipzig, 1904; German transl. with supplement by J. Liebeskind). From 1914-18 there appeared a 'Gluck-Jahrbuch,' edited by H. Abert (Leipzig).

Glyn, Margaret Henrietta, English musicologist; b. Ewell, Surrey, Feb. 28, 1865; d. there, June 3, 1946. She studied in London under Henry Frost and Yorke Trotter; became an authority on keyboard music of the Tudor period. She edited organ and virginal music by Byrd, Orlando Gibbons, John Bull, and other composers, and wrote the following books: *The Rhythmic Conception of Music* (1907); *Analysis of the Evolution of Musical Form* (1909); *About Elizabethan Virginal Music and Its Composers* (1924; 2nd ed., 1934); *Theory of Musical Evolution* (1924). She also composed a number of works for organ.

Gnecchi (nĕk'-kē), **Vittorio,** Italian opera composer; b. Milan, July 17, 1876; d. there, Feb. 5, 1954. He studied at the Milan Cons. His opera, *Cassandra,* was performed at Bologna on Dec. 5, 1905; some years later, after the première of Richard Strauss' *Elektra,* there was considerable discussion when the Italian critic Giovanni Tebaldini pointed out the identity of some 50 themes in both *Cassandra* and *Elektra* (*Telepatia Musicale,* in 'Rivista Musicale Italiana,' May, 1908). Gnecchi also wrote the operas *Virtù d'Amore* (1896) and *La Rosiera,* after a comedy by Alfred de Musset (given at Gera, Germany, Feb. 12, 1927; in Italian, at Trieste, Jan. 24, 1931). — Cf. F. B. Pratella, *Luci ed ombre: per un musicista italiano ignorato in Italia* (Rome, 1933).

Gnessin (gnā'-sin), **Mikhail Fabianovitch,** Russian composer; b. Rostov-on-the-Don, Feb. 2, 1883; d. Moscow, May 6, 1957. He studied at the St. Petersburg Cons. with Rimsky-Korsakov and Liadov from 1901-08; went to Germany in 1911; in 1914, returned to Rostov, where he composed, taught music, and interested himself in various socialist activities. He made a trip to Palestine in 1921 to study Jewish music; some of his subsequent work reflected this visit. After 1923, he composed and taught alternately in Moscow and Leningrad. In addition to his Jewish music, he composed a number of works in the Romantic vein.—Works: dramatic music: *Balagan,* by Blok (1909); *The Rose and the Cross,* by Blok (1914); *Antigone,* by Sophocles (1909-15); *Phoenician Women,* by Euripides (1912-16); *Oedipus Rex,* by Sophocles (1914-15); *The Story of the Red-haired Motele,* by Utkin (1926-29); *The Inspector-General,* by Gogol (1926); operas: *Abraham's Youth* (1921-23) and *The Maccabees;* symph. movement for solo voices, chorus and orch., *1905-1917* (1925); for voice and orch.: *Ruth* (1909); *Vrubel* (1912); *The Conqueror Worm* (1913); for orch.: symph. fragment, *After Shelley* (1906-08); *Songs of Adonis* (1919); symph. fantasy, *Songs of the Old Country* (1919); suite, *Jewish Orchestra at the Town Bailiff's Ball* (1926); chamber music: *Requiem,* in memory of Rimsky-Korsakov, for string quartet and piano (1913-14); *Variations on a Jewish Theme,* for string quartet (1916); *Azerbaijan Folksongs,* for string quartet (1930); *Adygeya,* for violin, viola, cello, clarinet, horn, and piano (1933); *Sonata-Fantasia* for piano, violin, viola, and cello (1945); *Theme with Variations* for cello and piano (1955); several song cycles; piano pieces; arrangements of Jewish folksongs. He publ. *Reflections and Reminiscences of Rimsky-Korsakov* (Moscow, 1956).—Cf. L. Sabaneyev, *Modern Russian Composers* (N. Y., 1927); A. Drozdov, *Gnessin* (Moscow, 1927; in Russian and German).

Gobbaerts (gŏhb'-bahrts), **Jean-Louis,** Belgian pianist and composer; b. Antwerp, Sept. 28, 1835; d. Saint-Gilles, near Brussels, May 5, 1886. He studied at the Brussels Cons. He wrote more than a thousand light piano pieces, some quite popular, using the pseudonyms 'Streabbog' (Gobbaerts reversed), 'Ludovic,' and 'Lévi.'

Gobbi, Tito, Italian baritone; b. Bassano del Grappo, Oct. 24, 1915. He studied law at Padua Univ., then took vocal lessons in Milan; made his opera début at Rome in 1938; sang at La Scala in 1942; in 1947 began European tours; made his American début in San Francisco in 1948; appeared at the Metropolitan Opera as Scarpio in *Tosca* in 1956, obtaining a decisive success. His repertory contains some 100 roles; his musicianship was demonstrated by his expert performance of the difficult part of Wozzeck in Alban Berg's opera, at La Scala in 1952.

Godard (gŏh-dahr'), **Benjamin (Louis Paul)**, French composer; b. Paris, Aug. 18, 1849; d. Cannes, Jan. 10, 1895. He studied violin with Richard Hammer and later with Vieuxtemps, composition with Reber of the Paris Cons. He publ. his first work, a violin sonata, at the age of 16 and wrote several other chamber music pieces, obtaining the Prix Chartier. In 1878 he received a municipal prize for an orchestral work; in the same year he produced his first opera, *Les Bijoux de Jeannette.* His second opera was *Pedro de Zalamea* (Antwerp, Jan. 31, 1884), but it left little impact; then came his masterpiece, *Jocelyn,* after Lamartine's poem (Brussels, Feb. 25, 1888). The famous *Berceuse* from this opera became a perennial favorite, exhibiting Godard's lyric talent at its best. There followed the opera *Dante,* produced at the Opéra-Comique on Nov. 7, 1890. His opera, *La Vivandière,* was left unfinished at his death, and the orchestration was completed by Paul Vidal; it was staged posthumously in Paris on April 1, 1895; another posthumous opera, *Les Guelphes,* was produced in Rouen (Jan. 17, 1902). Godard wrote 3 programmatic symphonies: *Symphonie Gothique* (1883), *Symphonie Orientale* (1884), and *Symphonie Légendaire* (1886); and a *Concerto Romantique* for violin and orch. (1876); he also wrote 3 string quartets, 4 violin sonatas, a cello sonata, and 2 piano trios; piano pieces, and more than 100 songs. A 2-volume collection of Godard's piano works was publ. by G. Schirmer (N. Y., 1895); another collection of piano pieces was edited by Paolo Gallico (N. Y., 1909). —Cf. M. Clerjot, *Benjamin Godard* (Paris, 1902).

Goddard, Arabella, English pianist; b. St.-Servan, near Saint-Malo, France, Jan. 12, 1836; d. Boulogne, France, April 6, 1922. She began study with Kalkbrenner in Paris at the age of 6; made her first public appearance at the age of 14, in London at a Grand National Concert. After 3 years of study with the critic, J. W. Davison (whom she married in 1859), she made tours of Germany and Italy (1854-55); later toured the U. S., Australia, and India (1873-76). She wrote some piano pieces and a ballad.

Godebrye. See **Jacotin.**

Godfrey, Sir **Dan (Daniel Eyers),** English conductor; b. London, June 20, 1868; d. Bournemouth, July 20, 1939. He was the son of Daniel Godfrey, Sr.; studied at the Royal College of Music; was conductor of the London Military Band in 1890. In 1892, he settled in Bournemouth as conductor of the Winter Gardens orch.; founded the Symphony Concerts there in 1894, directed them until his retirement in 1934; he brought the concerts to a high level, and used all his efforts to promote the works of British composers. He was knighted in 1922 for his services to orchestral music. He wrote his memoirs, *Memories and Music* (1924).

Godfrey, Daniel, Sr., English bandmaster; b. Westminster, Sept. 4, 1831; d. Beeston, near Nottingham, June 30, 1903. Pupil and Fellow of the Royal Academy of Music, in which he was prof. of military music. Bandmaster of the Grenadier Guards, 1856; traveled with his band in the U. S., 1872; retired in 1896. He wrote popular waltzes (*Mabel, Guards, Hilda,* etc.), and made many arrangements for military band.

Godowsky (goh-dohf'-skē), **Leopold,** famous pianist; b. Soshly, near Vilna, Feb. 13, 1870; d. New York, Nov. 21, 1938. He played in public as a child in Russia; at 14, was sent to Berlin to study at the Hochschule für Musik, but after a few months there, proceeded to New York; gave his first American concert in Boston, Dec. 7, 1884; in 1885, played engagements at the N. Y. Casino; in 1886, toured Canada with the Belgian violinist Ovide Musin. He then went back to Europe; played in society salons in London and Paris, and became a protégé of Saint-Saëns. In 1890 he joined the faculty of the N. Y. College of Music; on May 1, 1891, married Frieda Saxe, and became an American citizen. He taught at the Broad Street Cons. in Philadelphia (1894-95); was head of the piano dept. of the Chicago Cons. (1895-1900); then embarked on a European tour; gave a highly successful concert in Berlin (Dec. 6, 1900), and remained there as a teacher; from 1909-14, conducted a master class at the Vienna Academy of Music; made tours in the U. S. from 1912-14, and settled permanently in the U. S. at the outbreak of World War I. After the end of the war, he traveled in Europe, South America, and Asia as a concert pianist; his career ended in 1930 when he suffered a stroke.—Godowsky was one of the outstanding masters of the piano; possessing a scientifically inclined mind, he developed a method of 'weight and relaxation'; applying it to his own playing, he became an outstanding technician of his instrument, extending the potentialities of piano technique to the utmost, with particular attention to the left hand. He wrote numerous piano compositions of transcendental difficulty, yet entirely pianistic in style; also arranged works by Weber, Brahms, and Johann Strauss. Particularly remarkable are his 53 studies on Chopin's Études, combining Chopin's themes in ingenious counterpoint; among his original works, the most interesting are *Triakontameron* (30 pieces; 1920; No. 11 is the well known *Alt Wien)*, and *Java Suite* (12 pieces). He also wrote simple pedagogical pieces, e.g., a set of 46 *Miniatures* for piano four-hands, in which the pupil is given a part within the compass of 5 notes only (1918); edited piano studies by Czerny, Heller, Köhler, etc.; composed music for the left hand alone *(6 Waltz Poems, Prelude and Fugue,* etc.), and publ. an essay, *Piano Music for the Left Hand,* in the 'Mus. Quarterly' (July, 1935). Maurice Aronson publ. a musical examination paper, providing an analysis of Godowsky's *Miniatures* (N. Y., 1935).—Cf. Leonard S. Saxe, *The Published Music of Leopold Godowsky,* in 'Notes' (March, 1957), containing an annotated list of original works, arrangements, and editions.

Godron, Hugo, Dutch composer; b. Amsterdam, Nov. 22, 1900. He studied with Sem Dresden there. He has written: *Divertimento, Musettes,* and *Cyclus* for chamber orch.; music for string orch.; a piano concerto; several string quartets; a piano sonatina and other piano pieces.

Goeb, Roger, American composer; b. Cherokee, Iowa, Oct. 9, 1914. He studied agriculture and chemistry, and also violin, viola, trumpet, and horn. After graduating in agriculture from the Univ. of Wisconsin (1936), played in jazz bands; then went to Paris, where he studied with Nadia Boulanger. Returning to America in 1939, he obtained his M. A. in Music at N. Y. Univ. and Ph. D at the State Univ. of Iowa. He subsequently taught music at the Juilliard School of Mus. and at Columbia Univ. He was awarded a Guggenheim Fellowship twice (1950 and 1952).—Works: for orch.: 1st symph. (1942-45); 2nd symph. (1946); 3rd symph. (N. Y., April 27, 1952, under Stokowski); *5 American Dances* (1952); violin concerto (N. Y., Feb. 12, 1954, WNYC American Music Festival). Chamber music: sonata for solo viola (1942); string quartet No. 1 (1942); string trio (1945); suite for 4 clarinets (1946); suite for woodwind trio (1946); *Lyric Piece,* for trumpet and piano (1947); *Prairie Song,* for woodwind quintet (1947); piano quintet (1948); string quartet No. 2 (1948); septet for brass (1949); quintet for trombone and string quartet (1950); 3 *concertantes* for various instruments (1951-52).

Goedicke (gö'-di-ke), **Alexander Fedorovitch,** Russian composer; b. Moscow, March 3, 1877. He came of a musical family of German extraction; studied piano and composition at the Moscow Cons.; won the Rubinstein Prize in Vienna in 1900 with his *Konzertstück.* He was appointed prof. of piano at the Moscow Cons. in 1903.—Works: For orch.: 1st symph. (1903); 2nd symph. (Moscow, Nov. 29, 1908, composer conducting); 3rd symph. (1921); operas: *At the Crossing* (1933) and *Jacquerie* (1937); cantatas: *Glory to Soviet Pilots* (1934) and *Fatherland of Joy* (1937); also a concerto for French horn and trumpet; a trio for violin, cello, and piano; a quintet for 2 violins, viola, cello, and piano; a string quartet; numerous piano pieces; songs, and arrangements of Russian folksongs; transcriptions from Scarlatti, Bach, and Beethoven. His 80th birthday was celebrated in Moscow at a gala banquet (1957).—Cf. V. Yakovlev, *A. F. Goedicke* (Moscow, 1927; in Russian and German).

Goehr, Walter, German conductor; b. Berlin, May 28, 1903. He studied theory with Schoenberg; then became conductor of the Berlin Radio (1925-31). In 1933 he went to England; from 1946-49, was conductor of the BBC Theatre Orch.

Goepfart, Karl Eduard, German pianist, conductor, and composer; b. Weimar, March 8, 1859; d. there, Feb. 8, 1942. He studied with his father, Christian Heinrich Goepfart (1835-1890); also had lessons with Liszt. He toured as theater conductor in the U. S. and in Germany; wrote several operas of which only one, *Der Müller von Sans Souci* was produced (Weimar, 1907). He further wrote 2 symphonies, church music, and many songs.

Goepp, Philip Henry, American organist and writer on music; b. New York, June 23, 1864; d. Philadelphia, Aug. 25, 1936. He studied in Germany (1872-77); graduated from Harvard with honors in music in 1884; while there, he studied composition with J. K. Paine; graduated from the Univ. of Pennsylvania Law School in 1888, and practiced law until 1892. He then devoted himself to music in Philadelphia, as organist, teacher, and writer; from 1900 to 1921, he wrote the program notes for the Philadelphia Orch.; publ. *Annals of Music in Philadelphia* (1896); *Symphonies and Their Meaning* (3 vols., 1898, 1902, 1913); and composed pieces for piano and organ, a *Christmas Cantata* and an operetta, *The Lost Prince.*

Goethe (gö'-tĕ), **Wolfgang von,** the illustrious German poet; b. Frankfurt-on-Main, Aug. 28, 1749; d. Weimar, March 22, 1832. Although he could not comprehend Beethoven, and even snubbed him, he had ideas of his own on music (see *Briefwechsel zwischen Goethe und Zelter,* Berlin, 1833); Ferd. Hiller also shows this in his *Goethes musicalisches Leben* (Cologne, 1883). In recent years Goethe's attitude toward music has been made the subject of investigation by several scholars.—Cf. K. Mendelssohn-Bartholdy, *Goethe und Felix Mendelssohn-Bartholdy* (Leipzig, 1871; in Engl., with additions, London, 2nd ed., 1874); A. Julien, *Goethe et la musique: ses jugements, son influence, les œuvres qu'il a inspirées* (Paris, 1880); J. W. von Wasielewski, *Goethe's Verhältnis zur Musik* (Leipzig, 1880; in Waldersee's 'Sammlung mus. Vorträge'); H. Blaze de Bury, *Goethe et Beethoven* (Paris, 1892); W. Nagel, *Goethe und Beethoven* (Langensalza, 1902); W. Nagel, *Goethe und Mozart* (Langensalza, 1904); J. Chantavoine, *Goethe musicien* (Paris, 1905); J. Simon, *Faust in der Musik* (Berlin, 1906); E. Segnitz, *Goethe und die Oper in Weimar* (Langensalza, 1908); W. Bode, *Die Tonkunst in Goethes Leben* (2 vols., Berlin, 1912); W. Bode, *Goethes Schauspieler und Musiker: Erinnerungen von Eberwein und Lobe* (1912); H. Abert, *Goethe und die Musik* (1922); P. Frenzel, *R. Schumann und Goethe* (1926); H. John, *Goethe, und die Musik* (1928); E. Ludwig, *Goethe, the History of a Man* (1928; in English); W. Nohl, *Goethe und Beethoven* (1929); R. Rolland, *Goethe et Beethoven* (Paris, 1930; in English, N. Y. and London, 1931); W. Engelsmann, *Goethe und Beethoven* (1931); *Goethe* issue of 'Revue musicale' (1932); Goethe issue of the 'Zeitschrift für Musikwissenschaft' (1932); A. della Corte, *La vita musicale di Goethe* (Turin, 1932); G. Kinsky, *Die Handschriften von Beethovens Egmont-Musik* (Vienna, 1933); F. Küchler, *Goethe's Musikverständnis* (Leipzig, 1935); F. W. Sternfeld, *Goethe and Music* (N. Y., 1954).

Goetschius, Percy, American teacher and writer on music; b. Paterson, N. J., Aug. 30, 1853; d. Manchester, N. H., Oct 29, 1943. He studied at Stuttgart Cons., and taught various classes there from 1876-85, when he received the title of Royal Württemberg Professor of Music, and taught music history and theory for 5 years; he was also concert critic for the 'Schwäbischer Merkur' and opera critic for the 'Neues Tageblatt.' He returned to the U. S. in 1890, as prof. of music history, theory, and piano at Syracuse Univ., from which he received the degree of Mus. Doc. (hon. c.). From 1892-96, he taught composition, harmony, and music history at the New England Cons., Boston, leaving in 1896 for private teaching; in 1905, he became head of the department of theory and composition at the N. Y. Institute of Musical Art, where he remained until his retirement in 1925. He publ. many books on the teaching of music and music history, among them: *The Material Used in Musical Composition* (Stuttgart, 1882; rev. ed., N. Y., 1889; 14th ed., rev. and augmented, 1913; a most valuable contribution to the science of harmony); *The Theory and Practice of Tone-relations* (Boston, 1892; 17th, revised ed 1917); *Models of the Principal Musical Forms* (Boston, 1895); *Syllabus of Mus. History* (1895); *The Homophonic Forms of Musical Composition* (N. Y., 1898; a masterly analysis of the Group-forms and Song-forms; 10th ed. 1921); *Exercises in Melody Writing* (N. Y., 1900; 9th, rev. ed. 1923); *Applied Counterpoint* (N. Y., 1902); *Lessons in Music Form* (Boston, 1904); *Exercises in Elementary Counterpoint* (N. Y., 1910; an original attempt to blend the disciplines of harmony and counterpoint); *Essentials in Music History* (N. Y., 1914; jointly with Thomas Tapper); *The Larger Forms of Musical Composition* (N. Y., 1915); *Masters of the Symphony* (Boston, 1929); *The Structure of Music*

(Philadelphia, 1934). He composed a number of pieces for piano; revised the complete piano works of Mendelssohn for the Cotta Ed. (Stuttgart, 1889); edited other music, and was joint editor of 'The School Credit Piano Course' (1918-22).—Cf. A. Shepherd, *Papa Goetschius in Retrospect* in the 'Mus. Quarterly' (July, 1944).

Goetz, Hermann, German composer; b. Königsberg, Prussia, Dec. 7, 1840; d. Hottingen, near Zürich, Dec. 3, 1876. He studied at the Stern Cons. in Berlin from 1860-63, with von Bülow in piano, and H. Ulrich in composition. In 1863, he took the post of organist at Winterthur, Switzerland; then lived in Zürich; gave private lessons; conducted a singing society. His most famous work is the opera, *The Taming of the Shrew (Der Widerspenstigen Zähmung)*, based on Shakespeare's play, which was given in Mannheim, Oct. 11, 1874; it was then given in Vienna, in Berlin, Leipzig, and other German cities, and produced in an English version in London (Drury Lane Theatre, Oct. 12, 1878). His other works include the opera, *Francesca da Rimini* (Mannheim, Sept. 30, 1877; unfinished; 3rd act completed by Ernst Frank); incidental music for Widmann's play, *Die heiligen drei Könige* (Winterthur, Jan. 6, 1866); symph. in F major; chamber music; several pieces for piano, and 24 songs.—Cf. A. Steiner, *Hermann Goetz* (Zürich, 1907); E. Kreuzhage, *Hermann Goetz: sein Leben und sein Werke* (Leipzig, 1916); G. R. Kruse, *Hermann Goetz* (1920).

Goetze, Walter W., German composer of light opera; b. Berlin, April 17, 1883. He began as a composer of popular ballads; then produced numerous operettas, among them *Der liebe Pepi* (1913); *Ihre Hoheit, die Tänzerin* (Stettin, May 8, 1919; highly popular; about 700 performances in Berlin alone); *Adrienne* (1926); *Der Page des Königs* (1933); *Akrobaten des Glücks* (1933); *Der goldene Pierrot* (Berlin, March 31, 1934; successful); *Sensation im Trocadero* (1936); *Liebe im Dreiklang* (1951).

Goetzl, Anselm, Bohemian composer; b. Karolinenthal, Aug. 20, 1878; d. Barcelona, Jan. 9, 1923 (while traveling). He studied with Winkler, Fibich, and Dvořák in Prague, and with Schalk and Adler in Vienna; came to the U. S. in 1913 as conductor of Dippel's Light Opera Co. He wrote 3 operettas, a piano quartet, 2 string quartets, a clarinet quintet, and songs.

Goeyvaerts, Karl, Belgian composer; b. Antwerp, June 8, 1923. He studied at the Antwerp Cons. (1943-47) and with Milhaud and Messiaen in Paris (1947-50); received the Lily Boulanger Award in 1949. In 1950 he was appointed instructor at the Antwerp Music Academy. In his music he has adopted a modified method of 12-tone technique; has written a violin concerto, pieces for 2 pianos, for 13 instruments, etc.; also *Music for Contralto, Violin, and Piano.* To emphasize the absolute character of his works, he avoids indication of form or content in the titles.

Gogorza, Emilio Edoardo de, American baritone; b. Brooklyn, N. Y., May 29, 1874; d. New York, May 10, 1949. After singing as a boy soprano in England, he returned to the U. S. and studied with C. Moderati and E. Agramonte in N. Y.; he made his début in 1897 with Marcella Sembrich in a concert; sang throughout the country in concerts and with leading orchestras. Beginning in 1925, was for several years instructor of voice at the Curtis Institute of Music, Phila. He married the American soprano, Emma Eames, in 1911.

Goh, Taijiro, Japanese composer, b. Manchuria, Feb. 17, 1907. He studied in Tokyo, has organized a Society of Japanese Composers. He has written a piano concerto; a symphonic suite, *Clouds.* His music follows the European academic type of harmonic and contrapuntal structure.

Göhler, (Karl) Georg, German conductor and composer; b. Zwickau, June 29, 1874; d. Lübeck, March 4, 1954. He was a pupil of Vollhardt at Zwickau; then studied at the Leipzig Univ. and Cons.; obtained his *Dr. phil.* with a dissertation on the 16th-century composer Cornelius Freundt; he then pursued the career of chorus conductor; from 1913-15, conducted opera at Hamburg; in 1915, succeeded Furtwängler as conductor of symph. concerts in Lübeck; in 1922, he became conductor of the State Theater in Altenburg; also conducted symph. concerts in Halle. He wrote 5 symphonies; a clarinet concerto; 2 violin concertos; a cello concerto; *Quartetto enimmatico* for piano and strings (1940); a string trio (1942); more than 200 songs, and numerous choral works; also 24 Bagatelles for piano. He edited works by Freundt, Hasse, Handel, Haydn, Schubert, Mozart, etc.; wrote numerous articles on various musical subjects. He was an admirer of Mahler and Bruckner and gave frequent performances of their symphonies.

Gold, Julius, American musicologist and teacher; b. St. Joseph, Missouri, Feb. 18, 1884. He studied at Chicago Musical College; then taught theory and composition at Drake Univ., Des Moines, Iowa (1910-14) and at Dominican College, San Rafael, Calif. (1930-34); since 1940, a teacher and lecturer in San Francisco.

Goldbach, Stanislaw, Czech composer; b. Strelce, near Brno, July 13, 1896. He studied with J. B. Foerster in Prague and Vincent d'Indy in Paris. He has written symph. poems: *Cyrano de Bergerac* (1924), *New Icarus* (1928), *May Festival* (1931); a symphony (1932); and *Anna Karenina,* opera after Tolstoy (1928-30).

Goldbeck, Fred, music critic; b. The Hague, Feb. 13, 1902. After study with various teachers in several European countries, he settled in Paris in 1925 as music critic; contributed numerous articles to the 'Revue Musicale' and many other publications; publ. a book, *The Perfect Conductor* (N. Y., 1951); edited the music magazine 'Contrepoints' (1946-52).

Goldbeck, Robert, pianist and conductor; b. Potsdam, April 19, 1839; d. St. Louis, May 16, 1908. He studied in Paris; made his concert début in London; came to New York in 1857, where he remained until 1867, when he founded a cons. in Boston. After a year in Boston, he went to Chicago, where he established a cons. and was its director until 1873; for the next 5 years he lived in St. Louis, where he conducted the Harmonic Society and was co-director of the Beethoven Cons. From 1880 to 1903 he lived variously in N. Y., Germany, St. Louis, Chicago, and London; in 1903 he returned to St. Louis. He publ. a textbook on harmony (1890) and a 3-volume *Encyclopedia of Music Education* (1903).

Goldberg, Johann Gottlieb, remarkable German organist and harpsichord player; b. Danzig, baptized March 14, 1727; d. Dresden, April 13, 1756. When a child, he was brought to Dresden by his patron, Count Hermann Carl von Kaiserling; he studied with Wilhelm Friedemann Bach, and later with J. S. Bach (1742-43); in 1751, he became musician to Count Heinrich Brühl, a post he held till his death. His name is immortalized through the set of 30 variations written for him by Bach, and generally known as *Goldberg Variations.* Goldberg's own compositions include 2 concertos; 24 *Polonaises;* a sonata with minuet and 12 variations for clavier; 6 trios for flute, violin, and bass; a motet; a cantata; and a Psalm.—Cf. E. A. Dadder, *Johann Gottlieb Goldberg: Leben und Werke* (Bonn, 1923).

Goldberg, Szymon, Polish violinist; b. Wloclawek, June 1, 1909. He studied with Flesch in Berlin; concertmaster of the Berlin Philharmonic from 1929-34; then forced to leave, despite Furtwängler's defense of the Jewish members of the orchestra, and went to London, and in 1938 to America. He has toured widely all over the world (South America, Australia, Palestine); on his tour in Asia, was interned in Java by the Japanese from 1941-45; then resumed his concerts in Europe and America.

Goldberg, Theo, German composer; b. Chemnitz, Sept. 29, 1921. He studied in Berlin. He has composed the chamber operas *Minotauros* and *Schwere Zeiten für Engel* (Berlin, Sept. 20, 1952); a ballet, *Nacht mit Kleopatra* (Karlsruhe, Jan. 20, 1952); several symphonic works.

Golde, Walter, American pianist; b. Brooklyn, N. Y., Jan. 4, 1887. After graduating from Dartmouth College in 1910, he studied at the Vienna Cons.; was accompanist for many noted artists; also guest conductor and vocal teacher; taught at Columbia Univ. from 1945-48. Composed songs and piano pieces.

Goldenweiser, Alexander Borissovitch, Russian piano pedagogue; b. Kishineff, March 10, 1875. He graduated from the Moscow Cons., winning the gold medal, in 1897; was prof. at the Moscow Philharmonic Institute from 1904-06; in 1906 he went to the Moscow Cons., of which he became director in 1922. He wrote pedagogic piano pieces, and edited classic piano works. A friend of Leo Tolstoy, he publ. a diary concerning his relations with him (1922).

Goldman, Edwin Franko, eminent American bandmaster; b. Louisville, Ky., Jan. 1, 1878; d. New York, Feb. 21, 1956. He was the nephew of Sam Franko and Nahan Franko, well-known conductors; was brought to N. Y. when he was 8; became a student at the National Cons., where he studied composition with A. Dvořák, and cornet with J. Levy and C. Sohst. He became solo cornetist of the Metropolitan Opera orch. when he was 17, remaining there for 10 years. For the next 13 years he taught cornet and trumpet; he formed his first band in 1911. In 1918, the Goldman Band outdoor concerts were inaugurated; the first concert series was on the Columbia Univ. green; later they were held on other campuses or in public parks; after 1934, they were given on the Mall at Central Park and in Prospect Park, Brooklyn. Goldman toured the U. S. with his band; during 1945, conducted concerts for service men in the Philippines and Japan. His band was noted not only for its skill and musicianship but for its unusual repertory, including modern works especially commissioned for the band. Its high standards influenced bands throughout the country. Goldman was a founder and 1st president of the American Bandmasters' Association; received honorary Doc. Mus. degrees from Philips Univ. and Boston Univ., and more than 100 medals and other honors from governments and associations throughout the world. He wrote more than 100 brilliant marches, of which the best known is *On the Mall;* also other band music; solos for various wind instruments; studies and methods for cornet and other brass instruments; several songs. He was the author of *Foundation to Cornet or Trumpet Playing* (1914); *Band Betterment* (1934); *The Goldman Band System* (1936).

Goldman, Richard Franko (son of Edwin Franko Goldman), American bandmaster and composer; b. New York, Dec. 7, 1910. He studied at Columbia Univ.; after graduation became an assistant of his father in conducting the Goldman Band; on his father's death, he succeeded him as conductor. He has written many works for various ensembles: *A Sentimental Journey* for band (1941); 3 duets for clarinets (1944); duo for tubas (1948); violin sonata (1952); many arrangements for band. A progressive musician, Goldman has experimented with modern techniques, and his music combines highly advanced harmony with simple procedures accessible to amateurs. He has published 2 reference books, *The Band's Music* (1938) and *The Concert Band* (1946), as well as articles and reviews. He has been editor of the 'Juilliard Review' since it was founded in 1953.

Goldmark, Karl, Austro-Hungarian composer; b. Keszthely, Hungary, May 18, 1830; d. Vienna, Jan. 2, 1915. The son of a poor cantor, he studied at the school of the Musical Society of Sopron (1842-44); while there, his talent as a violinist resulted in his being sent to Vienna, where he studied with L. Jansa (1844-45), later at the Vienna Cons., as a pupil of Preyer (harmony) and Böhm (violin). He spent most of his life in Vienna, where the first concert of his compositions was given March 20, 1857. He continued to compose; also taught the piano, and was a music critic for some time. Landmarks in his career were the first performance of his *Sakuntala* overture by the Vienna Philh. on Dec. 26, 1865, and the première of his 1st opera (on which he had worked 10 years), *Die Königin von Saba,* at the Vienna Court Opera on March 10, 1875; both were very successful.—Works: Operas (in addition to *Die Königin von Saba*): *Merlin* (Vienna, Nov. 19, 1886); *Das Heimchen am Herd,* based on Dickens' *The Cricket on the Hearth* (Vienna, March 21, 1896); *Die Kriegsgefangene* (Vienna, Jan. 17, 1899); *Götz von Berlichingen,* based on Goethe's play (Budapest, Dec. 16, 1902); *Ein Wintermärchen,* based on Shakespeare's *A Winter's Tale* (Vienna, Jan. 2, 1908). For orch.: 7 overtures: *Sakuntala, Penthesilea, Im Frühling, Der gefesselte Prometheus, Sappho, In Italien, Aus Jugendtagen;* symph., *Ländliche Hochzeit;* symph. in E♭ major; symph. poem, *Zrinyi;* several instrumental concertos. Chamber music: 2 piano trios, piano quintet, cello sonata, violin sonata; piano pieces; songs and choral works. He publ. an autobiography, *Erinnerungen aus meinem Leben* (Vienna, 1922; in English as *Notes from the Life of a Viennese Composer,* N. Y., 1927).—Cf. O. Keller, *Karl Goldmark* (1901); H. Schwarz, *Ignaz Brüll und sein Freundeskreis: Erinnerungen an Brüll, Goldmark und Brahms* (Vienna, 1922); L. Koch, ed., *Karl Goldmark* (Budapest, 1930; contains full bibliography); biographies in Hungarian by Kálmán (1930) and Klempá (1930); also *Ein Brief Carl Goldmarks über Beethoven* in the 'Neue Zeitschrift für Musik' (1930, pp. 454-56).

Goldmark, Rubin; American composer and teacher, nephew of Karl Goldmark; b. New York, Aug. 15, 1872; d. there, March 6, 1936. He studied at the Vienna Cons. from 1889-91 as a pupil of A. Door (piano) and J. N. Fuchs (composition); from 1891-93, he was a student at the National Cons. in New York, while at the same time teaching piano and harmony there; his own teachers were Joseffy (piano) and Dvořák (composition). He went to Colorado Springs for his health in 1894; taught at the College Cons. there (1895-1901). Returning to New York in 1902, for the next 20 years he gave private lessons in piano and theory; also made concert-lecture tours through the U. S.

and Canada; in 1909, he won the Paderewski chamber music prize. In 1924, he was appointed head of the composition department of the Juilliard School, N. Y., and remained there until his death; among his pupils were Aaron Copland, Abram Chasins, Frederick Jacobi, and other American composers.—Works: for orch.: overture, *Hiawatha* (Boston, Jan. 13, 1900); tone poem, *Samson* (Boston, March 14, 1914); *Requiem*, suggested by Lincoln's Gettysburg Address (N. Y., Jan. 30, 1919); *A Negro Rhapsody* (his most popular work; N. Y., Jan. 18, 1923); a piano quartet (Paderewski Prize, 1909; N. Y., Dec. 13, 1910); a piano trio; *The Call of the Plains,* for violin and piano (1915; also for orch., 1925); songs.

Goldovsky, Boris, Russian-American pianist and conductor; son of the violinist Lea Luboshutz; b. Moscow, June 7, 1908. He studied piano with his uncle Pierre Lubochutz; later in Berlin with Schnabel and Kreutzer, and in Budapest with Dohnányi. He appeared as soloist with the Berlin Philharmonic at the age of 13 in 1921; came to America in 1930; director of the Opera Workshop at the Berkshire Music Center, Tanglewood; founder of the New England Opera Co. in 1946. A versatile musician, he has given successful lecture-recitals; translated opera librettos into singable English; presented popular radio talks on music; acted as moderator for Metropolitan opera broadcasts. A collection of his comments was publ. as *Accents on Opera* (N. Y., 1953).

Goldsand, Robert, Austrian pianist; b. Vienna, March 17, 1911. He studied with A. Manhart, M. Rosenthal, Camillo Horn, and Joseph Marx. He played in public at the age of 10; then toured in Europe and South America; made his U. S. début at Carnegie Hall, March 21, 1927; then was again in Europe, but settled permanently in the U. S. in 1939.

Goldschmidt, Adalbert von, Austrian composer; b. Vienna, May 5, 1848; d. there, Dec. 21, 1906. He studied at the Vienna Cons.; from his earliest efforts in composition, he became an ardent follower of Wagner. At the age of 22, he wrote a cantata, *Die sieben Todsünden,* to a poem by Hamerling (Berlin, 1875) which gained him considerable notoriety, thanks to a very successful application of Wagnerian principles. This was followed by a music drama, *Helianthus* (Leipzig, 1884), for which he wrote both words and music. A dramatic trilogy, *Gaea* (1889), was his most ambitious work along Wagnerian lines. He also brought out a comic opera, *Die fromme Helene* (Hamburg, 1897); wrote about 100 songs and a number of piano pieces.—Cf. E. Friedegg, *Briefe an einen Komponisten: Musikalische Korrespondenz an Adalbert von Goldschmidt* (Berlin, 1909).

Goldschmidt, Berthold, composer; b. Hamburg, Jan. 18, 1903. He studied at Hamburg Univ. and the Berlin State Academy of Music; after serving as assistant conductor of the Berlin State Opera (1926-27), conductor of the Darmstadt Opera (1927-29), and guest conductor of the Leningrad Philh. Orch. (1931), he went to England in 1940; conducted the Glyndebourne Opera in 1947. He has written 2 operas: *Der gewaltige Hahnrei* (Mannheim, Feb. 14, 1932) and *Beatrice Cenci* (1951; won a prize at the Festival of Britain); a ballet, *Chronica;* a symphony and other orchestral works; chamber music; 2 piano sonatas.

Goldschmidt, Hugo, German writer on music; b. Breslau, Sept. 19, 1859; d. Wiesbaden, Dec. 26, 1920. He took the degree of *Dr. jur.* in 1884; studied singing under Stockhausen at Frankfurt (1887-90); was co-director of the Scharwenka-Klindworth Cons. in Berlin (1893-1905); then lived in Nice.—Writings: *Die italienische Gesangsmethode des 17. Jahrhunderts* (1890); *Der Vokalismus des neuhochdeutschen Kunstgesangs und der Bühnensprache* (1892); *Handbuch der deutschen Gegangspädagogik* (1896); *Studien zur Geschichte der italienischen Oper im 17. Jahrhundert* (2 vols., 1901, 1904; the 2nd vol. contains a reprint of Monteverdi's opera, *Incoronazione di Poppea); Die Lehre von der vokalen Ornamentik* (vol. I contains the 17th and 18th centuries to the time of Gluck; 1907); *Die Musikästhetik des 18. Jahrhunderts und ihre Beziehungen zu seinem Kunstschaffen* (Zürich, 1915); many articles in music journals. He edited excerpts from operas by Traetta in 'Denkmäler der Tonkunst in Bayern' (vols. 14 and 17).

Goldschmidt, Otto, German pianist; b. Hamburg, Aug. 21, 1829; d. London, Feb. 24, 1907. At first a pupil of Jakob Schmitt and F. W. Grund, then of Mendelssohn at the Leipzig Cons., and of Chopin at Paris (1848). In 1849 he played in London at a concert given by Jenny Lind; accompanied her on her American tour (1851), and married her at Boston, Feb. 5, 1852; from

1852-5 they lived in Dresden, from 1858 until her death (1887) in London. He was made an hon. member of the London Philh. Soc. in 1861, became vice-principal of the Royal Academy of Music; he founded the Bach Choir in 1875, and conducted it till 1885. He composed an oratorio, *Ruth* (Hereford, 1867); choral song, *Music,* for soprano and women's chorus (Leeds, 1898); piano music, including a concerto, piano studies, 2 duets for two pianos; was co-editor of *The Chorale Book for England,* a collection of hymns (1863).

Goleminov, Marin, Bulgarian composer; b. Kustendie, Sept. 28, 1908. He studied violin in Sofia; composition at the Schola Cantorum in Paris (1931-34); conducting with Ehrenberg in Munich (1938). He composed a choreographic drama, *Nestinarka* (Sofia, Jan. 4, 1942); symphonic poem, *Night* (1933); 2 wind quintets (1936, 1946); 3 string quartets (1934, 1937, 1945), the 3rd being on old Bulgarian modes. He also published a manual of orchestration (1947).

Golestan, Stan, Rumanian composer; b. Vaslui, May 26, 1872; d. Paris, April 22, 1956. He studied in Paris with Vincent d'Indy, Roussel, and Paul Dukas; lived there as composer and critic. He won the Rumanian National Prize and the Verley Prize (1920) for composition. — Major works: for orch.: *Rhapsodie roumaine, Hora, Ouverture symphonique; Rhapsodie concertante* for violin and orch.; piano concerto, subtitled *Sur les Cîmes Carpathiques* (Paris, 1946); *Concerto Moldave* for cello; *Rhapsodie* for cello, clarinet, and orch. Also string quartet; violin sonata; piano works (*Thème, variations et danses,* etc.); vocal pieces.

Göllerich, August, Austrian writer on music; b. Linz, July 2, 1859; d. there, March 16, 1923. He was a pupil of Liszt; studied composition with Bruckner; acquired Ramann's music school in Nuremberg in 1890, and established branches in Erlangen, Fürth, and Ansbach; from 1896, conductor of the Musikverein and director of the Cons. in Linz; his wife, Gisela Pászthory-Voigt (also a pupil of Liszt), supervised the other schools. He published *A. Reissmann als Schriftsteller und Komponist* (1884); *Liszt* (1887; being the continuation of Nohl's biography in Reclam's Ed.); *Beethoven* (1904); *Franz Liszt* (1908); guides to Liszt's *Graner Festmesse* and Wagner's *Ring des Nibelungen* (1897). His chief work, the biography of Bruckner (who himself selected him for this task), in 4 vols., was completed by Max Auer (1st vol., Regensburg, 1924; 2nd, 1928; remaining vols., 1932 and 1937).

Gollmick, Adolf, pianist and composer; son of Karl Gollmick; b. Frankfurt, Feb. 5, 1825; d. London, March 7, 1883. He studied with his father and other teachers in Frankfurt; in 1844, he settled in London as a pianist and teacher. He composed 3 comic operas: *Dona Constanza, The Oracle, Balthasar;* 2 'operatic cantatas' *The Blind Beggar's Daughter of Bethnal Green* and *The Heir of Lynne;* also several symphonic works, piano pieces, and songs.

Gollmick, Karl, German composer and music theorist; b. Dessau, March 19, 1796; d. Frankfurt, Oct. 3, 1866. He was of a musical family; his father, Friedrich Karl Gollmick (1774-1852), was an opera tenor. He studied theology in Strasbourg; in 1817, he settled in Frankfurt, where he taught French and served as chorusmaster. He wrote mostly for piano; publ. potpourris, etc. His writings include *Kritische Terminologie für Musiker und Musikfreunde* (1833; 2nd ed., 1839); *Fétis als Mensch, Kritiker, Theoretiker und Komponist* (1852); *Handlexikon der Tonkunst* (1858), etc. He also wrote an autobiography (1866).

Golovanov, Nikolai Semionovitch, Russian conductor and composer; b. Moscow, Jan. 21, 1891; d. there, Aug. 28, 1953. He was a pupil of Vassilenko at the Moscow Cons.; won the composition prize for his cantata *Princess Yurata;* toured as conductor of the Moscow synodal choir; from 1915, was choral leader at the Bolshoy Theater, Moscow; from 1925, teacher of opera and orchestral classes at the Moscow Cons. He received the Order of the Red Banner in 1935; 4 times recipient of the First Stalin Prize (1946, 1948, 1950, 1951) for his work at the Bolshoy Theater. He wrote 2 symph. poems (*Salome* and *From Verhaeren*), church music, songs (altogether more than 40 works).—Cf. N. Anosov, *Nikolai Semionovitch Golovanov* in 'Sovietskaya Musica' (May, 1951).

Golschmann, Vladimir, renowned conductor; b. Paris, Dec. 16, 1893. He studied violin and piano at the Schola Cantorum; as early as 1919 he organized the Concerts Golschmann in Paris, in programs featuring many first performances of modern works. In 1923 he conducted ballet in the U. S.; then returned to Paris; was conductor of the Scottish Orch., Glasgow, for 3 seasons (1928-30); in 1931 he was engaged as conductor of the St. Louis Symph. Orch., retaining this post for a quarter of a century; also appeared as guest conductor with other American orchestras. His brother, **Boris Golschmann** (b. Paris, June 25, 1906), is a pianist.

Goltermann, Georg (Eduard), German cellist and composer; b. Hanover, Aug. 19, 1824; d. Frankfurt, Dec. 29, 1898. He studied cello in Munich, where he was also a pupil of Lachner in composition. After concert tours in 1850-52, he became music director at Würzburg; in 1853, he was made 2nd Kapellmeister of the City Theater of Frankfurt; in 1874, he became 1st Kapellmeister. He composed a number of works for cello, including 6 concertos; sonatas with piano; *Morceaux caractéristiques; Danses allemandes; Elégie,* etc. He also wrote a symphony, 2 overtures, and songs.

Golther (gŏhl'-ter), **Wolfgang,** German writer; b. Stuttgart, May 25, 1863; d. Rostock, Dec. 14, 1945. He was prof. of Germanic philology at Rostock; beside works on this subject, he wrote several important books on the music of Richard Wagner: *Die Sage von Tristan und Isolde* (1887), *Die sagengeschichtlichen Grundlagen der Ringdichtung Richard Wagners* (1902), *Bayreuth* (1904), *Richard Wagner als Dichter* (1904; English transl. by Haynes, 1907), *Tristan und Isolde in den Dichtungen des Mittelalters und der neueren Zeit* (1907), *Zur deutschen Sage und Dichtung* (1911), *Parsifal und der Gral in deutscher Sage des Mittelalters und der Neuzeit* (1913; new ed., 1925); *Richard Wagner* (1926); *Cosima Wagner* (in 'Zeitschrift für Musik,' Nov., 1931; also in 'Die Musik,' 1933); *Der Schwanritter und der Gralsritter* (in 'Bayreuther Blätter,' 1936); edited 'R. Wagner an Mathilde Wesendonck' (1904; many editions), 'Briefe R. Wagners an Otto Wesendonck' (8th ed. 1905), 'Familienbriefe von R. Wagner' (1907), 'Robert Franz und Arnold Freiherr Senfft von Pilsach' (1907; correspondence), and *Richard Wagner, Zehn Lieder aus den Jahren 1838-58* (1921). He wrote an opera, *Hassan gewinnt* (Rostock, 1929).

Gombert, Nicolas, Flemish composer; b. southern Flanders, possibly between Lille and St. Omer, c. 1490; d. 1556. He was one of the most eminent pupils of Josquin des Prez, on whose death he composed a funeral dirge. The details of his early life are obscure and uncertain. He is first positively accounted for in 1526, when his name appears on the list of singers at the court chapel of Charles V that was issued at Granada in that year; the restless Emperor traveled continually throughout his extensive domain—Spain, Germany, and the Netherlands—and his retinue was obliged to follow him in his round of his courts at Vienna, Madrid, and Brussels; Gombert probably was taken into the service of the Emperor on one of the latter's visits to Brussels. He is first mentioned as 'maistre des enffans de la chapelle de nostre sr empereur' (master of the boys of the royal chapel) in a court document dated Jan. 1, 1529; he remained in the Emperor's employ until 1538-40, during which time he took an active part in the various functions of the court, composing assiduously. After his retirement from his post in the royal chapel, he seems to have returned to his native Netherlands (Tournai) and there continued to compose until his death. He held a canonship at Notre Dame, Courtrai, from June 23, 1537, without having to take up residence there, and was also a canon at the Cathedral of Tournai from June 19, 1534. Despite his many trips abroad and the natural influence of the music of other countries, Gombert remained, stylistically, a Netherlander. The chief feature of his sacred works is his use of imitation, a principle which he developed to a high state of perfection. The parts are always in motion, and pauses appear infrequently and, when they do occur, are very short. In his handling of the dissonance he may be regarded as a forerunner of Palestrina. His secular works, of which the earliest known printed examples (9 4-part chansons) are included in Attaignant's collection of 1529-49, are characterized by a refreshing simplicity and directness. Gombert's greatest contributions to the development of 16th-century music lay in his recognizing the peculiarities of the Netherlandish polyphony and his developing and spreading it abroad. He wrote 11 Masses and about 250 motets and chansons, many of which appeared in contemporary (mostly Spanish) lute and guitar arrangements, a fact which shows the great vogue they had. Reprints have been publ. by F. Commer in *Collectio operum musicorum Batavorum* (1839 ff.) VIII (1 motet) and XII (2 chansons); A. Reissmann in *Allgemeine Geschichte der Musik* (1863; 1 chanson); R. J. v. Maldeghem in 'Trésor musical' (1865 ff.) II (1 motet), XI (3 chansons), XII (1 motet), XIV (5 chansons), XVI (1 motet of doubtful authorship), XVII (1 chanson), XX (2 motets); R. Eitner in 'Publikationen älterer praktischer . . . Musikwerke' III

(1875; 2 chansons); A. W. Ambros in *Geschichte der Musik* V (3rd ed. 1911; 1 motet, revised by O. Kade); E. H. Wooldridge in *The Oxford History of Music* II (1905; 1 motet); Th. Kroyer in *Der vollkommene Partiturspieler* (1930; 10 Magnificat selections); A. Schering in *Geschichte der Musik in Beispielen* (1931; No. 102, portion of the Mass *Media vita);* a motet is in Attaignant's *Treize livres de motets* (Book I, pp. 167-75), reprinted by the Lyrebird Press (Paris, 1934). Gombert's *Opera omnia,* ed. by J. Schmidt-Görg, began publication in 1951 (American Institute of Musicology in Rome; vol. I, 1951; vol. II, 1954.—Cf. D. von Bartha, *Probleme der Chansongeschichte im 16. Jahrhundert* in 'Zeitschrift für Musikwissenschaft' XIII (Aug.-Sept., 1931); H. Eppstein, *Nicolas Gombert als Motettenkomponist* (Würzburg, 1935); J. Schmidt-Görg, *Die acht Magnifikat des Nicolas Gombert* in 'Gesammelte Aufsätze zur Kulturgeschichte Spaniens' V (1935; contains a *Magnificat secundi toni* and selections from other Magnificats); J. Schmidt-Görg, *Nicolas Gombert, Leben und Werk* (Bonn, 1938; contains bibliography of works, musical examples, etc.).

Gombosi, Otto, eminent musicologist; b. Budapest, Oct. 23, 1902; d. Natick, Mass., Feb. 17, 1955. He studied at the Academy of Music in Budapest; then at the Univ. of Berlin, where he received his Ph. D. for a dissertation on Jakob Obrecht. From 1926-28 he edited the progressive Hungarian music periodical, 'Crescendo.' In 1940 he came to the U. S.; was lecturer in music at the Univ. of Washington, Seattle; then taught at Michigan State College and at the Univ. of Chicago; in 1951, appointed prof. at Harvard Univ. He contributed numerous valuable papers to various periodicals, in Hungarian, German, Italian, and English; among his most important writings are *Jakob Obrecht* (Leipzig, 1925); *Tonarten und Stimmungen der antiken Musik* (Copenhagen, 1939); a treatise on V. Bakfark in 'Musicologia Hungarica' (Budapest, 1935; contains Bakfark's 10 fantasias); *Studien zur Tonartenlehre des frühen Mittelalters,* in 'Acta musicologica' (1938-39); several articles in the 'Mus. Quarterly': *The Melody of Pindar's Golden Lyre* (July, 1940); *About Dance and Dance Music in the Late Middle Ages* (July, 1941); *Stephen Foster and 'Gregory Walker'* (April, 1944); *Béla Bartók* (Jan., 1946); *Machaut's Messe Notre-Dame* (April, 1950). He contributed the chapter on Hungarian music to G. Reese's *Music in the Renaissance* (N. Y., 1954).

Gomes, Antonio Carlos, Brazilian composer; b. (of Portuguese parents) Campinas, Brazil, July 11, 1836; d. Pará (Belém), Sept. 16, 1896. He was a pupil of his father, then of the Cons. in Rio de Janeiro, where he prod. 2 operas, *Noite do Castello* (1861) and *Joanna de Flandres* (1863). The success of these works induced the Emperor Don Pedro II to grant him a stipend for further study under Rossi in Milan; there he soon made his mark with a little humorous piece entitled *Se sa minga* (a song from this work, *Del fucile ad ago,* became immensely popular), produced in 1867. After another piece in the same vein (*Nella Luna,* 1868), he made a more serious bid for fame with the opera *Il Guarany,* produced at La Scala on March 19, 1870, with brilliant success; this work, in which Amazon-Indian themes are used, quickly went the round of Italy, and was given in London (Covent Garden) on July 13, 1872. Returning to Rio de Janeiro, Gomes brought out a very popular operetta, *Telegrapho elettrico.* With the exception of *Fosca* (La Scala, Milan, Feb. 16, 1873), his other operas obtained considerable success; they comprise *Salvator Rosa* (Genoa, March 21, 1874), *Maria Tudor* (La Scala, Milan, March 27, 1879), *Lo Schiavo* (Rio de Janeiro, Sept. 27, 1889), and *Condor* (La Scala, Milan, Feb. 21, 1891). He wrote the hymn *Il saluto del Brasile,* for the centenary of American independence (1876); also the cantata *Colombo* for the Columbus Festival in 1892. In 1895 he was appointed director of the newly founded Cons. at Pará; illness delayed his departure for that city, and he died soon after arriving there. Besides his operas, he composed songs (3 books), choruses, and piano pieces.—Cf. S. Boccanera Júnior, *Um artista brasileiro: in memoriam* (Bahia, 1904); H. P. Vieira, *Carlos Gomes: sua arte e sua obra* (São Paulo, 1934); I. Gomes Vaz de Carvalho, *A vida de Carlos Gomes* (Rio de Janeiro, 1935; Italian transl., Milan, 1935); R. Seidl, *Carlos Gomes, brasileiro e patriota* (Rio de Janeiro, 1935); L. F. Vieira Souto, *Antonio Carlos Gomes* (Rio de Janeiro, 1936); centenary issue of 'Revista brasileira de musica' (1936); J. Prito, *Carlos Gomes* (São Paulo, 1936); R. Almeida, *Carlos Gomes* (Rio de Janeiro, 1937); M. de Andrade, *Carlos Gomes* (Rio de Janeiro, 1939); P. Cerquera, *Carlos Gomes* (São Paulo, 1944).

Gomes de Araújo (ah-răh-oo-zhoh), **João,** Brazilian composer; b. Pindamonhangaba, Aug. 5, 1846; d. São Paulo, Sept. 8, 1942. He studied at São Paulo and Milan; in

1905, became a teacher at São Paulo Cons., and remained there almost to the end of his long life. He wrote 4 operas: *Edmea; Carminosa* (Milan, 1888); *Maria Petrowna* (1904; São Paulo, 1929); *Helena* (São Paulo, 1910); also 6 symphonies, 6 Masses, vocal and instrumental works.

Gómez, Julio, Spanish composer and musicologist; b. Madrid, Dec. 20, 1886. He studied at the Madrid Cons., also at the Univ. there, where he received his *Dr. phil.* In 1911 he became director of the Archeological Museum in Toledo; later head of the music division of the National Library in Madrid, and librarian of the Cons. there; also editor of the review 'Harmonia.' His study of *Don Blas Laserna* was publ. in 'Revista de la Biblioteca, Archivo y Museo del Ayuntamiento de Madrid,' 1925-26. He wrote the comic operas *El Pelele* (1925) and *Himno al Amor;* also symphonies, piano pieces, songs, etc.

Gomezanda, Antonio, Mexican pianist and composer; b. Lagos, Jalisco, Sept. 3, 1894. He studied piano with Manuel M. Ponce; then went to Germany, where he took lessons in composition and conducting in Berlin. Returning to Mexico, he taught piano at the National Cons. (1921-29) and at the Univ. of Mexico (1929-32). Among his works are an 'Aztec ballet,' *Xiuhtzitzquilo,* which was produced in Berlin on Feb. 19, 1928; *Fantasia mexicana,* for piano and orch. (1923); piano pieces.

Gomolka, Michal, Polish musician, son of Mikolaj Gomolka; b. Sandomierz, 1564; d. Jazlowiec, March 9, 1609. He was active as a band conductor at various palaces of Polish noblemen; little is known of his life, except that he enjoyed the favor of Polish aristocratic society.

Gomolka, Mikolaj (Nicolas), Polish composer; b. Sandomierz, about 1535; date of death unknown. He was a chorister at Cracow (1545), and then played trumpet and flute in the court orchestra. In 1559 he returned to his native town, where he married and served as a judge. His chief work was *Melodiae na psalterz polski* (Cracow, 1580), containing 150 melodies to words from the Psalms translated by the poet Jan Kochanowski; new edition was publ. by J. W. Reiss in 1923; several pieces are included in the anthology by Jachimecki and Lissa, *Music of the Polish Renaissance* (Warsaw, 1954). — Cf. J. W. Reiss, *Melodye psalmowe M. Gomolki* (Cracow, 1912); A. Chybinski, *Slownik Muzykow Dawnej Polski* (Cracow, 1949).

Goodman, Benny, American clarinetist and jazz band leader; b. Chicago, May 30, 1909. He acquired a taste for syncopated music as a child by listening to phonographic recordings of ragtime and jazz. He also took lessons in clarinet playing. In 1928, he went to New York as a clarinetist in a jazz band. In 1934, formed his own band, which in 1935 was billed in Chicago as a swing band, the first use of the word 'swing' in relation to public performance. He also played clarinet parts in classical works in concert and for records, appearing as soloist in Mozart's Clarinet Concerto with the N. Y. Philharmonic (Dec. 12, 1940). His autobiography, *The Kingdom of Swing,* was published in 1939.

Goodrich, Alfred John, American music pedagogue; b. Chilo, Ohio, May 8, 1848; d. Paris, April 25, 1920. A self-taught musician, he became a teacher of theory at the Grand Cons., N. Y.; the Fort Wayne Cons., Ind.; director of the vocal department at the Beethoven Cons., St. Louis; member of music department, Martha Washington College, Abingdon, Va.; later lived in Chicago, Paris, and St. Louis as writer and teacher. He wrote: *Music as a Language* (1880); *The Art of Song* (1888); *Complete Musical Analysis* (1889); *Analytical Harmony* (1894); *Theory of Interpretation* (1898; publ. by subscription); *Guide to Memorizing Music* (1904; revised ed., 1906); *Synthetic Counterpoint* (in MS).

Goodrich, (John) Wallace, American organist, conductor, and writer on music; b. Newton, Mass., May 27, 1871; d. Boston, June 6, 1952. He studied at the New England Cons. in Boston (organ with Dunham, composition with Chadwick); then in Munich with Rheinberger (1894-95) and with Widor in Paris. In 1896-97, he was coach at the Leipzig Municipal Theater. In 1897 he returned to Boston and became an instructor at the New England Cons.; he was appointed dean in 1907, and director in 1931, a post he held until 1942, when he resigned, with the title of director emeritus. He was organist of Trinity Church from 1902-09, and for the Boston Symph. Orch., from 1897-1909. He founded the Choral Art Society in 1902 and was its conductor until 1907; he was also, at various periods, conductor of the Cecilia Society, the Boston Opera Co., and the Worcester County

Choral Association. He composed an *Ave Maria* for chorus and orch. (Munich, 1895) and other choral music; wrote *The Organ in France* (Boston, 1917) and translated A. Pirro's *J. S. Bach and his Works for the Organ* (1902) and d'Ortigue's *Méthode d'accompagnement du plain-chant* (1905).

Goodson, Katharine, English pianist; b. Watford, Hertfordshire, June 18, 1872. From 1886-92 she was a pupil of O. Beringer at the Royal Academy of Music, and from 1892-96 of Leschetizky in Vienna; début in London at a Saturday Pop. Concert, Jan. 16, 1897, with signal success; then followed tours of England, France, Austria, and Germany, which established her reputation; her American début, with the Boston Symph., took place Jan. 18, 1907; since then she made many tours of the U. S., also of Holland, Belgium, and Italy. In 1903 she married the English composer Arthur Hinton.

Goossens, Sir Eugene, outstanding English conductor and composer; b. London, May 26, 1893. A scion of a family of musicians of Belgian extraction, he was educated at the Bruges Cons., returning to England in 1906; he subsequently studied at the Liverpool College of Music (1906); then won a scholarship of the Royal College of Music in London (1907); studied violin with Rivarde, piano with Dykes, and composition with Charles Wood and Stanford; won the silver medal of the Worshipful Company of Musicians; then played the violin in the Queen's Hall Orch. He was associated with Sir Thomas Beecham's operatic enterprises (1915-20); conducted a season of concerts with his own orch. in London (1921). In 1923 he was engaged as conductor of the Rochester, N. Y., Philharmonic Orch.; in 1931 he was appointed conductor of the Cincinnati Symph. Orch., remaining at that post until 1946. From 1947 to 1956 he was director of the New South Wales Cons. of Music at Sydney and conductor of the Sydney Symph. Orch.; he was knighted in 1955. Goossens belongs to a group of English composers influenced by French impressionism, who cultivated exotic themes with modernistic harmonies stemming from Debussy. He conducted his first orchestral piece, *Variations on a Chinese Theme,* at the age of 19 at the Royal College of Music in London (June 20, 1912); continued to write prolifically in all genres (opera, ballet, symphony, chamber music); his mature style became a blend of impressionistic harmonies and neo-classical polyphony; while retaining a clear tonal outline, Goossens often resorts to expressive chromatic melos bordering on atonality. — Works: *Variations on a Chinese Theme* for orch. (1911); *Miniature Fantasy* for string orch. (1911); suite for flute, violin, and harp (1914); *Five Impressions of a Holiday* for flute, cello, and piano (1914); symph. poem *Perseus* (1914); symph. prelude *Ossian* (1915); *Phantasy Quartet* for strings (1915); string quartet No. 1 (1916); 2 sketches for string quartet: *By the Tarn* and *Jack o' Lantern* (1916); *Kaleidoscope,* suite of piano pieces in a humorous vein (1917-18); violin sonata No. 1 (1918); prelude to Verhaeren's *Philip II* (1918); *The Eternal Rhythm* for orch. (London, Oct. 19, 1920); *4 Conceits* for piano (1918); piano quintet (1919); *Lyric Poem* for violin and piano (1921; also arranged for violin and orch.); ballet *L'École en crinoline* (1921); *Silence* for chorus and piano (1922); incidental music to W. Somerset Maugham's *East of Suez* (1922); *Sinfonietta* (London, Feb. 19, 1923); string sextet (1923); *Pastoral and Harlequinade* for flute, oboe, and piano (1924) *Fantasy* for wind instruments (1924); opera, *Judith* (1925; Covent Garden, June 25, 1929); *Rhythmic Dance* for orch. (Rochester, March 12, 1927); *Concertino* for double string orch. (1928); oboe concerto (London, Oct. 2, 1930; Leon Goossens, soloist); violin sonata No. 2 (1930); opera *Don Juan de Mañara* (1934; Covent Garden, June 24, 1937); symph. No. 1 (Cincinnati, April 12, 1940); 2nd string quartet (1942); *Phantasy-Concerto* for piano and orch. (Cincinnati, Feb. 25, 1944, composer conducting; Iturbi, soloist); 2nd symph. (BBC, Nov. 10, 1946); oratorio *Apocalypse* (1951; Sydney, Nov. 22, 1954, composer conducting). Goossens is the author of *Overture and Beginners; a Musical Autobiography* (London, 1951).

Goossens, Leon, English oboist, brother of Eugene Goossens; b. Liverpool, June 12, 1897. He studied at the Royal College of Music; from 1913-24 was 1st oboist of the Queen's Hall Orch.; afterward played with the Royal Philharmonic Orch., the London Philharmonic Orch., and the Covent Garden Opera; held oboe professorships at the Royal College of Music and Royal Academy of Music; appeared in many countries, including the U. S., where he first performed with his brother, Eugene, in N. Y. in 1927.

Goovaerts (goh'-vahrts), **Alphonse Jean Marie André,** Belgian musicologist; b. Antwerp, May 25, 1847; d. Brussels, Dec. 25,

1922. He was a member of a literary family; as a youth he became greatly interested in Flemish literature and in church music. He arranged and publ. a collection of Flemish songs (1868-74); composed several pieces of church music, and performed them with a chorus which he established in Antwerp; also made transcriptions for chorus of works by Palestrina and Flemish contrapuntists. He publ. several papers propounding a reform in church music, which aroused opposition from conservative circles (*La Musique de l'eglise,* 1876; in Flemish as *De Kerkmuziek);* also publ. a valuable book, *Histoire et bibliographie de la typographie musicale dans le Pays-Bas* (1880; awarded the gold medal of the Belgian Academy); a monograph on the Belgian music printer, Pierre Phalèse, and other studies relating to Flemish music.

Gorczycki (gor-tchit'-skē), **Gregor Gervasius,** Polish composer; b. Cracow, c. 1664; d. there, April 30, 1734. He was a student of theology at Prague Univ.; was ordained priest in Cracow in 1692; became chapel master at the Cracow Cathedral in 1698, retaining this position until his death. He was the composer of many excellent motets, hymns, psalms, and Masses in a polyphonic style, a cappella and with instrumental accompaniment, to Latin texts; several of them were reprinted in the Polish collections edited by Cichocki, Surzynski, Sowinski, and Chybinski.—Cf. A. Chybinski, *G. G. Gorczycki* (Posen, 1927); also see Chybinski's *Slownik Muzykow Dawnej Polski* (Cracow, 1949) for a complete list of editions of Gorczycki's sacred works.

Gordigiani (gor-dē-jah'-nē), **Luigi,** Italian composer; b. Florence, June 12, 1806; d. there, April 30, 1860. He is chiefly known for his more than 300 songs for voice and piano; these *canzonette* and *canti popolari* were based on Italian folk tunes; Gordigiani wrote the words for many himself. He also publ. a collection of songs based on Tuscan folk poems. Ricordi has publ. 67 songs in 2 vols. in the series 'Canti popolari italiani.' Other works by Gordigiani include 10 operas, 3 cantatas, a ballet, and an oratorio.

Gordon, Gavin Muspratt, Scotch singer and composer; b. Ayr, Nov. 24, 1901. He studied at the Royal College of Music with Vaughan Williams; later was active as singer, film actor, and composer. He has written several ballets: *A Toothsome Morsel* (1930); *Regatta* (1931); *The Scorpions of Ysit* (1932); *The Rake's Progress* (London, Sadler's Wells, May 20, 1935).

Gordon, Jacques, violinist; b. Odessa, Russia, March 7, 1899; d. Hartford, Conn., Sept. 15, 1948. He graduated from the Imperial Cons. at Odessa in 1912; then studied at the Institute of Musical Art, N. Y., with Kneisel (violin) and Goetschius (theory); made his début as violinist in 1911 in Berlin; from 1918-21, was a member of the Berkshire String Quartet; in 1921 he founded the Gordon String Quartet. From 1921-30, he was concertmaster of the Chicago Symph. Orch., and violin teacher at the American Cons. in Chicago. In 1938, he was awarded the Elizabeth Sprague Coolidge medal for services to chamber music. He publ. some violin music and arrangements.

Gordon, James Carel Gerhard, flute maker; b. Cape Town, May 22, 1791; d. (insane) Lausanne, c. 1845. He was a son of a Dutch captain and a Swiss mother in South Africa. He joined the Swiss Guards of Charles X in Paris in 1814; at the same time, studied flute with Tulou; worked on improvements of its mechanism more or less at the same time as Böhm, so that the priority of the invention became a matter of insoluble controversy. He escaped with his life during the attack on the Swiss Guards in the Revolution of 1830; was pensioned and retired to Switzerland when his mind became deranged. — Cf. C. Welch, *History of the Boehm Flute* (London, 1896); Percival R. Kirby, *Captain Gordon, The Flute Maker,* in 'Music & Letters' (July, 1957).

Gorin, Igor, baritone; b. Grodek Jagiell, Ukraine, Oct. 26, 1908. He studied at the Vienna Cons., graduating in 1930; sang at the Vienna Opera and the Czech State Opera; also in recitals in many European cities; came to the U. S. in 1933; became a citizen in 1939; has sung with symph. orchestras and for radio. He is the composer of several songs, including *Lament, Caucasian Song, Lullaby, Within My Dreams, Remembered Mornings, The Jumping Jack,* etc.

Gorini, Gino, Italian composer and pianist; b. Venice, June 22, 1914. He studied there at the Cons. Benedetto Marcello; received diplomas in piano (1931) and composition (1933); later studied composition with Malipiero; in 1940 was appointed prof. of piano at the Venice Cons.; has made many tours in Italy and abroad, including two-piano team tours in Italy with Sergio Lorenzi. His major works include: *Maschere,* suite for small orch. (1932); *Tre omaggi,* for orch. (1933); suite for piano and orch. (1934); violin concerto (1934); a symph. (1935); *Introduction and Arioso* for orch. (1937); *Concertino* for 7 instruments (1933); *Contrasti* for 5 instruments (1933); 2 studies for piano and strings (1934); *Divertimento* for chamber orch. (1935); piano sonata (1936); string quartet (1936); cello sonata (1939); quintet for piano and strings (1939), etc.

Goritz, Otto, German dramatic baritone; b. Berlin, June 8, 1873; d. Hamburg, April 11, 1929. He received his entire musical education from his mother, Olga Nielitz; début, Oct. 1, 1895, as Matteo (*Fra Diavolo*) at the Hoftheater in Neustrelitz; his success led to an immediate engagement for 3 years; 1898-1900, at the Stadttheater in Breslau; 1900-3, at Stadttheater in Hamburg. On Dec. 24, 1903, he made his American début at the Metropolitan Opera House as Klingsor in the first production of *Parsifal* outside Bayreuth. In 1924, returned to Germany, where he sang in opera in Berlin and Hamburg.

Gorno, Albino, pianist and composer; b. Casalmorano (Cremona), March 10, 1859; d. Cincinnati, Ohio, Oct. 29, 1945. He studied at the Milan Cons., where he took 3 gold medals, and where his opera, *Cuore e Patria,* was produced. He was accompanist to Adelina Patti on her American tour (1881-82); stayed and became head of the piano department and dean of faculty at the Cincinnati College of Music. He wrote a cantata, many pieces for piano, and songs.

Gorno, Romeo, pianist and teacher; brother of Albino Gorno; b. Cremona, Italy, Jan. 1, 1870; d. Cincinnati, Nov. 28, 1931. He studied in Milan with his father, later a pupil of the Cons. there; made his American début in Cincinnati; was for many years prof. of piano at the Cincinnati College of Music.

Gorodnitzki, Sascha, pianist; b. Kiev, Russia, May 24, 1905; brought to the U. S. as an infant. He studied at the Institute of Musical Art and the Juilliard Graduate School in New York; appeared as a child prodigy at 9; toured the U. S. and Canada in recitals; in 1930, won the Schubert Memorial Prize, appointed prof. of piano at the Juilliard Graduate School in 1932.

Gorrio, Tobia. Pen name (anagram) of **Arrigo Boito.**

Gorter, Albert, German conductor and composer; b. Nuremberg, Nov. 23, 1862; d. Munich, March 14, 1936. He studied at the Royal Music School in Munich and in Italy; became assistant conductor of the Bayreuth festivals; then conducted in various German cities until 1925, when he settled in Munich. He wrote text and music of an opera, *Harold;* 3 comic operas, *Der Schatz des Rhampsinit* (Mannheim, 1894), *Das süsse Gift* (Cologne, 1906), and *Der Paria* (Strasbourg, March 31, 1908); 2 symph. poems; piano pieces, and songs.

Goss, Sir John, English organist and composer; b. Fareham, Hants, Dec. 27, 1800; d. London, May 10, 1880. A son of Joseph Goss, the Fareham organist, he became a child chorister of the Royal Chapel; then studied under Attwood. He was successively organist of Stockwell Chapel (1821), St. Luke's, Chelsea (1824), and St. Paul's Cathedral (1838-72). In 1856 he was appointed a composer to the Chapel Royal; he was knighted in 1872, and received the degree of Mus. Doc. from Cambridge Univ. in 1876. His music includes church services, anthems, chants, psalms, etc.; some orchestral pieces; songs and glees. He edited a collection of hymns, *Parochial Psalmody* (1827); *Chants, Ancient and Modern* (1841); *Church Psalter and Hymnbook* (1856; with Rev. W. Mercer). He publ. *The Organist's Companion,* 4 vols. of voluntaries and interludes, and *An Introduction to Harmony and Thorough-bass* (1833; many editions).

Goss, John, English baritone; b. London, May 10, 1894; d. Birmingham, Feb. 13, 1953. He began to study music relatively late in life, and was active as a singer and a music editor. He gave a number of successful recitals in England and America, in variegated programs of unusual old and new songs. He edited an *Anthology of Song* (London, 1928) and a collection, *Ballads of Britain* (London, 1937); also publ. a novel, *Cockroaches and Diamonds* (1937).

Gossec, François Joseph, Belgian composer; b. Vergnies, Jan. 17, 1734; d. Paris, Feb. 16, 1829. He showed musical inclinations at an early age, and was engaged as a chorister at the Cathedral of Antwerp; received some instruction in violin and organ playing there. In 1751 he went to Paris, and in 1754 joined a private musical ensemble of the rich amateur, La Pouplinière. There he wrote chamber music and little symphonies, in which he seems to have anticipated Haydn; these were publ.; several works for string quartet followed in 1759. After the death of La Pouplinière in 1762, Gossec became a member of the retinue of the Prince de Conti, and continued to compose for private performances. In 1760 he wrote a Requiem; then turned his attention to stage music; produced a one-act opera, *Le faux Lord* (Paris, June 27, 1765); obtained a decisive success with another short opera, *Les Pêcheurs* (June 7, 1766); there followed the operas (performed at the Comédie-Italienne and at the Paris Opéra) *Toinon et Toinette* (June 20, 1767); *Le double Déguisement* (Sept. 28, 1767); *Sabinus* (Feb. 22, 1774); *Alexis et Daphné* (Sept. 26, 1775); *La fête du village* (May 26, 1778); *Thésée* (March 1, 1782); *Rosine* (July 14, 1786); several other operas (*Nitocris, La Fédération,* etc.) were not performed. In 1770 he organized a performing society, Concerts des Amateurs; became a director of the Concert Spirituel (1773); was also an associate director of the Paris Opéra (1780-85) and manager of the École Royale de Chant (1784); when this school became the Conservatoire in 1795, Gossec became one of the inspectors, and also taught composition there; he publ. a manual, *Exposition des Principes de la Musique* for use of the Conservatoire. In 1795 he became a member of the newly founded Institut de France. Gossec welcomed the French Revolution with great enthusiasm, and wrote many festive works to celebrate Revolutionary events, among them *L'Offrande à la Liberté* (1792); *Le Triomphe de la République* (1793); *Le Cri de Vengeance* (1799), and numerous marches and hymns. During his long life, he saw many changes of régime, but retained his position in the musical world and in society throughout the political upheavals. He retired to Passy, then a suburb of Paris, at the age of 80. Gossec's historic role consists in his creation of a French type of symphonic composition, in which he expanded the resources of instrumentation so as to provide for dynamic contrasts; he experimented with new sonorities in instrumental and choral writing; his string quartets attained a coherence of style and symmetry of form that laid the foundation of French chamber music. In his choral works, Gossec was a bold innovator, presaging in some respects the usages of Berlioz; his *Te Deum,* written for a Revolutionary festival, is scored for 1200 singers and 300 wind instruments; in his oratorio, *La Nativité,* he introduced an invisible chorus of angels placed behind the stage; in other works, he separated choral groups in order to produce special antiphonal effects. Among reprints of Gossec's works are: Trio in E♭ in Riemann's 'Collegium musicum' (Leipzig, 1909); string quartet, op. 15, No. 2, in 'Veröffentlichungen der Musiksammlung W. Höckner' (facsimile reprint; Leipzig, 1932); string quartet, op. 14, No. 5, edited by S. Beck (N. Y., 1937); 2 symphonies, in E♭ and G, edited by S. Beck (N. Y., 1937); a symphony in C major is found in Sondheimer's collection *Werke aus dem 18. Jahrhundert* (Berlin, 1922-39); a symphony for 10 instruments, op. 5, No. 2, in G. Cucuël, *Études sur un orchestre de XVIIIme siècle* (Paris, 1913).—Cf. P. Hédouin, *Gossec, sa vie et ses ouvrages* (Paris, 1852); E. G. J. Gregoir, *Notice bibliographique sur M. Gossé, dit Gossec* (Paris, 1878); F. Hellouin, *Gossec et la musique française à la fin du XVIIIe siècle* (Paris, 1903); L. Dufrane, *Gossec* (Paris, 1927); F. Tonnard, *F. J. Gossec, musicien hennuyer de la Révolution française* (Brussels, 1938); J. G. Prod'homme, *F.-J. Gossec* (Paris, 1949).

Gotovac, Jakov, Yugoslav composer; b. Split, Oct. 11, 1895. He studied law in Zagreb, and music with Dobronić in Zagreb and Joseph Marx in Vienna. In 1923 he was appointed conductor of the Zagreb Opera. Gotovac is a prolific composer; his *Symphonic Kolo* (Zagreb, Feb. 6, 1927) is an effective national dance; his symph. poem *Guslar* (Zagreb, Oct. 7, 1940) is a musical portrait of a Croatian folk player. Gotovac has written several operas, of which the comic opera *Ero s onoga svijeta* (Zagreb, Nov. 2, 1935) has become very popular; under the title *Ero der Schelm* it was performed in German, in Karlsruhe (April 3, 1938). His other operas are: *Morana* (Brno, Nov. 29, 1930); *Kamenik* (Zagreb, Dec. 17, 1946); and the historic music drama *Mila Gojsalica* (Zagreb, May 18, 1952). He has also written incidental music for the theater.

Gotthelf, Felix, German composer; b. Gladbach, near Munich, Oct. 3, 1857; d. Dresden, April 21, 1930. He studied music while working for his M. D. degree; became coach at the Stadttheater in Cologne in 1892; in 1893 was conductor in Kolberg; from 1893-98, devoted himself to composition in Bonn; lived in Vienna from 1898 to 1920, when he settled in Dresden. He composed a mystery, *Mahadeva* (Stuttgart,

1909); orchestral works; chamber music; many songs.

Gottschalg (gŏt'-shăhlg), **Alexander Wilhelm,** German organist and editor; b. Mechelrode, Feb. 14, 1827; d. Weimar, May 31, 1908. He studied with G. Töpfer, and succeeded him as court organist at his death (1870); also publ. a biography of him. Gottschalg's most important publication is the *Repertorium für die Orgel* (issued serially, from 1860), to which Liszt contributed. His memoirs of Liszt were published posthumously (1910).

Gottschalk, Louis (Moreau), celebrated American pianist and composer; b. New Orleans, May 8, 1829; d. Rio de Janeiro, Dec. 18, 1869. He studied in Paris from 1841-46 (piano under Hallé and Stamaty; harmony under Maleden); began composing at 16. He made a successful tour through France, Switzerland, and Spain in 1852; returned to the U. S. in 1853 for a grand tour throughout the country, playing his own piano works and conducting his orchestral works at huge festivals; his popularity was phenomenal. The impresario Max Strakosch, who later introduced Patti, engaged Gottschalk for an even more extended tour throughout the U. S. Gottschalk died of yellow fever in Rio de Janeiro during his travels. His works, mostly with Spanish characteristics, include: 2 operas, *Charles X* and *Isaura de Salerno* (never performed); 2 symph. poems, *La Nuit des Tropiques* and *Montevideo; Grand Marcha solemne* for orch. (dedicated to the Emperor of Brazil); *Escenas campestres cubanas* for orch.; about 90 piano pieces, and about 12 songs. His *Notes of a Pianist* were translated from the French (Philadelphia, 1881).—Cf. O. Hensel, *Life and Letters of L. M. Gottschalk* (Boston, 1870; unreliable as to facts); L. R. Fors, *Gottschalk* (Havana, 1880); J. T. Howard, *L. M. Gottschalk* in the 'Mus. Quarterly' (Jan., 1932); C. F. Lange, *Vida y Muerte de Gottschalk,* in the 'Revista de Estudios Musicales' (Mendoza, Argentina, Aug., 1950; Dec., 1950; April, 1951; Aug., 1951).

Götz, Hermann. See **Goetz.**

Götze, Emil, celebrated German tenor; b. Leipzig, July 19, 1856; d. Charlottenburg, Sept. 28, 1901. He studied in Dresden; then was engaged at the Dresden Opera; afterwards sang with extraordinary success at other opera houses in Germany. Owing to an affection of the throat, he was forced to retire in 1885, but later resumed his career in Berlin.

Götze, Johann Nikolaus Konrad, German violinist; b. Weimar, Feb. 11, 1791; d. there, Feb. 5, 1861. He studied with Kreutzer in Paris; returning to Weimar, he became music director to the Grand Duke (1826-48). He played concerts in Germany and Austria; also wrote operas (some of which he produced in Weimar) and chamber music.

Götze, Karl, German composer; b. Weimar, 1836; d. Magdeburg, Jan. 14, 1887. A pupil of Töpfer and Gebhardi, later of Liszt; in 1855, chorusmaster at the Weimar opera; then theater conductor at Magdeburg, Berlin (1869), Breslau (1872), and Chemnitz (1875). — Works: the operas *Die Korsen* (Weimar, 1866); *Gustav Wasa, der Held des Nordens* (Weimar, 1868); *Judith* (Magdeburg, 1887); a symph. poem, *Eine Sommernacht;* piano pieces; songs.

Goudimel (goo-dē-mel'), **Claude** (his name was variously spelled in contemporary and later editions as **Gaudimel, Gaudiomel, Godimel, Gondimel, Goudmel, Gudmel,** etc.), celebrated French composer and theorist; b. Besançon, c. 1505; killed in the St. Bartholomew massacre at Lyons, Aug. 27, 1572. In 1549 Goudimel was in Paris, where he publ. a book of chansons as a joint publisher with Du Chemin. He lived in Metz between 1557 and 1568; there he became a Huguenot; in 1568 he returned to Besançon, and then lived in Lyons, where he perished. It was long supposed that he lived in Rome, where he founded a school of music, but this assertion is totally lacking in foundation. It seems certain that Goudimel never visited Italy, and it is significant that none of his numerous works appeared in Roman publications. Most of his music was publ. by Du Chemin in Paris; other contemporary publishers were Adrien Le Roy and Robert Ballard, who publ. his complete Huguenot psalter in 1564 under the title *Les CL pseaumes de David, nouvellement mis en musique à quatre parties;* it was publ. in Geneva in 1565 as *Les Pseaumes mis en rime françoise par Clément Marot et Th. de Bèze, mis en musique à quatre parties;* it was reprinted in a facsimile edition in Kassel, 1935; a 1580 edition, also issued in Geneva, was republished by H. Expert in vols. 2-4 of 'Les Maîtres Musiciens de la Renaissance' (1895-97). A German transl. of the psalms, with Goudimel's musical settings, first appeared in 1573;

many reprints followed. Goudimel also composed 5 Masses, publ. by Du Chemin (1, 1554) and Le Roy and Ballard (4, 1558), together with other sacred music. Two four-part motets were included in T. Susato's *Ecclesiasticarum cantionum* (Antwerp, 1553-55). Further reprints have been edited by R. J. v. Maldeghem in 'Trésor musical' III (1867; 12-part *Salve Regina* and 2 4-part motets) and XI (1875; 3 3-part chansons); C. Bordes in 'Anthologie des maîtres religieux primitifs' II (the Mass, *Le bien que j'ay*) and III (4-part motet); K. von Winterfeld, A. Ebrard, H. Bellermann, etc. (psalms). Three Masses are in H. Expert's 'Monuments de la musique française au temps de la renaissance' IX (1928); 9 psalms in P. Pidoux's 'Collection de musique protestante' (1935). — Cf. G. Becker, *Goudimel et son oeuvre* (1885); M. Brenet, *Claude Goudimel, Essai bio-bibliographique* (Besançon, 1898); H. Kling, *Les Compositeurs de la musique du Psautier Huguenot Genevois* in the 'Rivista Musicale Italiana' (1899); J. Tiersot, *Ronsard et la musique de son temps* (1901); G. R. Woodward, *The Genevan Psalter of 1562; set in 4-Part Harmony by Claude Goudimel in 1565* in 'Proceedings of the Musical Association' (London, 1918; pp. 167-89); E. H. Müller, *Claude Goudimel zum 350. Todestage* in the 'Neue Musikalische Zeitung' (1922; pp. 375-76); C. Schneider, *La Restauration du Psautier huguenot d'après les sources de 1562 et de 1565* (Neuchâtel, 1930); G. Thibault, *Bibliographie des éditions d'Adrien Le Roy et Robert Ballard* (Paris, 1955).

Goudoever, Henri Daniel van, Dutch cellist and composer; b. Utrecht, Nov. 12, 1898; pupil there of J. Wagenaar (theory) and E. Ferrée (cello); completed his studies under G. Hekking in Paris; 1922-24, solo cellist of the Concertgebouw, Amsterdam; 1924-27, conductor in Coburg, Germany; 1938, was conductor of the Utrecht Municipal Orch. He wrote for orch.: *Allegro* (1916); *Sphinx* (1919); *Impressions* (1920); etc.; also composed many cello pieces.

Gould, Glenn, Canadian pianist; b. Toronto, Sept. 25, 1932. He studied at the Royal Cons. of Music in Toronto with Alberto Guerrero (piano) and Leo Smith (composition); graduated at the age of 12, the youngest ever to do so. He made his début at the age of 14 as soloist with the Toronto Symph. Orch.; first U. S. concert in Washington (Jan. 2, 1955); N. Y. début one week later; first continental tour of the U. S. during the season 1956-57. European début in Berlin as soloist with Berlin Philh. under Herbert von Karajan (April 28, 1957). Apart from his highly successful career as a concert pianist, Gould cultivates the jazz style of piano playing; he has given numerous exhibitions in the U. S. as an improvisor with jazz groups; also composed jazz pieces.

Gould, Morton, brilliant American composer; b. New York, Dec. 10, 1913. He studied at the Institute of Musical Art; later was a radio pianist and leader of a program of light orch. music. He has appeared as guest conductor with major American orchestras. His music emphasizes American themes; he freely employs advanced harmonic usages. — Works: A musical comedy, *Billion Dollar Baby* (1945); *3 American Symphonettes* (1933, 1935, 1937); *Chorale and Fugue in Jazz,* for two pianos and orch. (Youth Orch., N. Y., Jan. 2, 1936, Stokowski conducting); piano concerto (1937); violin concerto (1938); *Foster Gallery* (Pittsburgh, Jan. 12, 1940); *Spirituals* for orch. (N. Y., Feb. 9, 1941, composer conducting); *Latin American Symphonette* (Brooklyn, Feb. 22, 1941); *Cowboy Rhapsody* (1942); *American Concertette* (broadcast Aug. 23, 1943); 1st symph. (Pittsburgh, March 5, 1943); *Symphony on Marching Tunes,* No. 2 (N. Y., June 4, 1944); viola concerto (1944); concerto for orch. (Cleveland, Feb. 1, 1945); *Harvest,* for harp, vibraphone, and strings (St. Louis, Oct. 27, 1945); *Minstrel Show* (Indianapolis, Dec. 21, 1946); 3rd symph. (Dallas, Feb. 16, 1947; composer conducting); *Fall River Legend,* ballet (N. Y., April 21, 1948); 4th symph. (for band; West Point, April 13, 1952, composer conducting); concerto for tap dancer and orch. (Rochester, Nov. 16, 1952, composer conducting); *Inventions* for 4 pianos and orch. (N. Y., Oct. 19, 1953); *Dance Variations* for 2 pianos and orch. (N. Y., Oct. 24, 1953); *Jekyll and Hyde Variations* for orch. (N. Y., Feb. 2, 1957); *Fiesta,* ballet (Cannes, France, March 17, 1957); 3 piano sonatas (1930, 1933, 1936), etc.

Gounod, Charles François, famous French composer; b. Paris, June 17, 1818; d. there, Oct. 18, 1893. His father, Jean François Gounod, was a painter, winner of the 2nd Grand Prix de Rome, who died when Gounod was a small child. His mother, a most accomplished woman, supervised his literary, artistic, and musical education, and taught him piano. He completed his academic studies at the Lycée St. Louis; in 1836, he entered the Paris Cons., studying with Halévy, Lesueur, and Paër. In 1837 he won the 2nd Prix de Rome with his cantata, *Marie Stuart et Rizzio;* in 1839 he obtained the Grand Prix with his cantata, *Fernand.* In Rome, he studied church music, particularly the works of Palestrina; composed there a Mass for 3 voices and orch., which was performed at the church of San Luigi dei Francesi. In 1842, during a visit to Vienna, he conducted a Requiem of his own; upon his return to Paris, he became precentor and organist of the Missions Etrangères; studied theology for two years, but decided against taking holy orders; yet he was often referred to as l'Abbé Gounod; some religious choruses were published in 1846 as composed by Abbé Charles Gounod. Soon Gounod tried his hand at stage music. On April 16, 1851, his first opera, *Sapho,* was produced at the Grand Opéra, with only moderate success; he revised it much later, extending it to four acts from the original three, and it was performed again on April 2, 1884; but even in this revised form it was unsuccessful. Gounod's second opera, *La Nonne sanglante,* in five acts, was staged at the Paris Opéra on Oct. 18, 1854; there followed a comic opera, *Le Médecin malgré lui,* after Molière (Jan. 15, 1858), which also failed to realize Gounod's expectations. In the meantime, he was active in other musical ways in Paris; he conducted the choral society Orphéon (1852-60) and composed for it several choruses. Gounod's great success came with the production of *Faust,* after Goethe (Théâtre-Lyrique, March 19, 1859; performed with additional recitatives and ballet at the Opéra, March 3, 1869); *Faust* remained Gounod's greatest masterpiece, and indeed the most successful French opera of the 19th century, triumphant all over the world without any sign of diminishing effect through a century of changes in musical tastes. However, it was widely criticized for the melodramatic treatment of Goethe's poem by the librettists, Barbier and Carré, and for the somewhat sentimental style of Gounod's music; in Germany, it is usually produced under the title *Margarete* or *Gretchen* to dissociate it from Goethe's work. The succeeding four operas, *Philémon et Baucis* (Paris, Feb. 18, 1860), *La Colombe* (Baden-Baden, Aug. 3, 1860), *La Reine de Saba* (Paris, Feb. 29, 1862), and *Mireille* (Paris, March 19, 1864), were only partially successful, but with *Roméo et Juliette* (Paris, April 27, 1867), Gounod recaptured universal acclaim. In 1870, during the Franco-Prussian War, Gounod went to London, where he organized Gounod's Choir, and presented concerts at the Philharmonic and the Crystal Palace; when Paris fell, he wrote an elegiac cantata, *Gallia,* to words from the Lamentations of Jeremiah, which he conducted in London on May 1, 1871; it was later performed in Paris. He wrote some incidental music for productions in Paris: *Les Deux Reines,* to a drama by Legouvé (Nov. 27, 1872) and *Jeanne d'Arc,* to Barbier's poem (Nov. 8, 1873). In 1875, he returned to Paris; there he produced his operas *Cinq-Mars* (April 5, 1877), *Polyeucte* (Oct. 7, 1878), and *Le Tribut de Zamora* (April 1, 1881) without signal success. The last years of his life were devoted mainly to sacred works, of which the most important was *La Rédemption,* a trilogy, first performed at the Birmingham Festival in 1882; another sacred trilogy, *Mors et Vita,* also written for the Birmingham Festival, followed in 1885. Gounod continued to write religious works in close succession, and produced (among many others) the following: *Te Deum* (1886); *La Communion des Saints* (1889); *Messe dite le Clovis* (1890); *La Contemplation de Saint François au pied de la croix* (1890); *Tantum Ergo* (1892). A Requiem (1893) was left unfinished, and was arranged by Henri Büsser after Gounod's death. One of Gounod's most popular settings to religious words is *Ave Maria,* adapted to the first prelude of Bach's *Well-tempered Clavichord* (1859); another *Ave Maria* was written to the second prelude of Bach (1892). Other works are: 2 symphonies (1855); *Marche funèbre d'une Marionette* for orch. (1873); *Petite Symphonie* for wind instruments (1888); 3 string quartets; a number of piano pieces, and songs. Among his literary works were *Ascanio de Saint-Saëns* (1889); *Le Don Juan de Mozart* (1890; in English, 1895), and an autobiography, *Mémoires d'un Artiste* (publ. posthumously, Paris, 1896; in English, N. Y., 1895).—Cf. A. Peña y Goñi, *Impressiones y recuerdos; Charles Gounod* (Madrid, 1879); M. A. de Bovet, *Charles Gounod* (Paris, 1890; in English, London, 1891); L. Pagnerre, *Charles Gounod, sa vie et ses œuvres* (Paris, 1890); C. Saint-Saëns, *Charles Gounod et le Don Juan de Mozart* (Paris, 1893); T. Dubois, *Notice sur Charles Gounod* (Paris, 1894); P. Voss, *Charles Gounod: Ein Lebensbild* (Leipzig, 1895); H. Tolhurst, *Gounod* (London, 1905); P. L. Hillemacher, *Charles Gounod* (Paris, 1906); C. Bellaigue, *Gounod* (Paris, 1910); J. G. Prod'homme and A. Dandelot, *Gounod: sa vie et ses œuvres,* in 2 vols., the standard biography (Paris, 1911); H. Soubiès and

H. de Curzon, *Documents inédits sur le Faust de Gounod* (Paris, 1912); J. Tiersot, *Charles Gounod, a Centennial Tribute* in the 'Mus. Quarterly' (July, 1918); J. G. Prod'homme, *Miscellaneous Letters by Gounod* in the 'Mus. Quarterly' (Oct., 1918); J. Tiersot, *Gounod's Letters* in the 'Mus. Quarterly' (Jan., 1919); C. Saint-Saëns, *Le Livret de 'Faust'* in 'Monde musical' (1914-19); R. d'Ollone, *Gounod et l'opéra comique* in the 'Revue musicale' (Nov., 1933); M. Cooper, *Charles Gounod and his Influence on French Music* in 'Music & Letters' (1940, p. 50); P. Landormy, *Gounod* (Paris, 1942); P. Landormy, *Faust de Gounod: étude et analyse* (Paris, 1944).

Gouvy (goo'-vē), **Louis Théodore,** prolific composer; b. Goffontaine, near Saarbrücken, July 2, 1819; d. Leipzig, April 21, 1898. The son of French parents, he graduated from the college at Metz; went to Paris to study law, but turned to music; presented a concert of his works in Paris in 1847; also made frequent trips to Germany, where his music was received with great favor. He wrote about 200 works, including an opera, *Der Cid;* 7 symphonies; a wind nonet; wind octet; sextet for flute and strings; piano quintet; string quintet; 5 string quartets; 5 piano trios; numerous piano pieces in an ingratiating salon manner; songs.—Cf. O. Klauwell, *L. T. Gouvy, Sein Leben und Seine Werke* (Berlin, 1902).

Gow, George Coleman, American music pedagogue; b. Ayer Junction, Mass., Nov. 27, 1860; d. Poughkeepsie, N. Y., Jan. 12, 1938. He studied music privately; graduated from Brown Univ. in 1884 and Newton Theological Seminary in 1889; then taught harmony and piano at Smith College for 6 years; from 1895 to 1932, he was professor of music at Vassar College. He wrote a textbook on notation and harmony, *The Structure of Music* (N. Y., 1895); composed organ pieces and songs.

Gow, Nathaniel, Scottish violinist, arranger, and music publisher; b. Inver, near Dunkeld, May 28, 1763; d. Edinburgh, Jan. 19, 1831. He played the trumpet in Scottish bands; then changed to violin. In 1788 he opened a music shop in Edinburgh; publ. numerous arrangements of Scotch tunes by his father and also his own arrangements of Scottish dances. He also led a band for various aristocratic assemblies. Among his original pieces there was an interesting instrumental composition, *Caller Herrin',* based on a street vendor's cry. — Cf. Henry G. Farmer, *History of Music in Scotland* (London, 1947; pp. 343-44).

Gow, Niel, Scottish violinist and composer; father of Nathaniel Gow; b. Strathbrand, Perthshire, March 22, 1727; d. Inver, near Dunkeld, March 1, 1807. He played Scottish reels on the violin, and as a young man earned his living by performing at social gatherings in Edinburgh and London. He publ. a number of 'Strathspey Reels'; however, many of them were not original compositions but arrangements of old dance tunes.—Cf. John Glen, *The Glen Collection of Scottish Dance Music* (Edinburgh, 1891).

Graben-Hoffmann, Gustav (properly **Gustav Hoffmann**), German composer; b. Bnin, near Posen, March 7, 1820; d. Potsdam, May 20, 1900. He studied with his father and with other teachers in Posen; then taught music in various localities in East Germany; in 1843, settled in Berlin; in 1850, he founded a Musikakademie für Damen; then went to Leipzig, where he studied composition with Moritz Hauptmann; in 1869, he returned to Berlin, where he taught singing. In the meantime, he composed industriously; wrote a number of songs, but was compelled to publ. them at his own expense, despite economic hardships; of these, *500,000 Teufel* had great vogue. He also publ. singing manuals, *Die Pflege der Singstimme* (1865); *Das Studium des Gesangs* (1872); *Praktische Methode als Grundlage für den Kunstgesang* (1874).

Grabert, Martin, German composer; b. Arnswalde (Neumark), May 15, 1868; d. Berlin, Jan. 23, 1951. He studied with Bellermann and Bargiel. In 1895 he settled in Berlin as church organist. He wrote some 80 op. numbers, mostly for chorus and for organ; a complete list of his works is given in Heinz Becker's article in 'Die Musik in Geschichte und Gegenwart.'

Grabner, Hermann, Austrian composer and theorist; b. Graz, May 12, 1886. He took his degree in law at Graz Univ. in 1909; then studied music with Reger and Hans Sitt at the Leipzig Cons.; he became a lecturer in theory at Strasbourg Cons. in 1913; served in the German army in World War I; after the armistice taught at the Mannheim Cons.; in 1924 was appointed prof. of composition at Leipzig Cons.; from 1938-46, taught at the Hochschule für Musik in Berlin; since 1950 at the Berlin Cons. His publications include: *Regers Harmonik* in Würz's symposium on Reger (Munich,

1920); *Die Funktionstheorie Hugo Riemanns und ihre Bedeutung für die praktische Analyse* (Munich, 1923); *Allgemeine Musiklehre* (Stuttgart, 1924; 5th ed., 1949); *Lehrbuch der musikalischen Analyse* (Leipzig, 1925); *Der lineare Satz; ein Lehrbuch des Kontrapunktes* (Stuttgart, 1930; new rev. ed., 1950); *Handbuch der Harmonielehre* (Berlin, 1944); several short books of exercises for theory students. He also wrote an opera, *Die Richterin* (Barmen, May 7, 1930); *Perkeo Suite* and *Burgmusik* for wind orch.; a concerto for 3 violins; organ pieces; songs, etc.

Grace, Harvey, English organist and writer on music; b. Romsey, Jan. 25, 1874; d. Bromley, Kent, Feb. 15, 1944. He studied with M. Richardson at Southwark Cathedral, London; was organist at various churches in London; directed the St. Cecilia Festivals; from 1918 to his death, he was editor of the 'Musical Times' and wrote editorial articles for it under the name 'Feste'; also edited *The New Musical Educator* (London, 1934). He wrote *French Organ Music, Past and Present* (N. Y., 1919); *The Complete Organist* (London, 1920; standard teaching manual; 4th ed., 1956); *The Organ Works of Bach* (London, 1922); *The Organ Works of Rheinberger* (London, 1925); *Ludwig van Beethoven* (London, 1927); *A Musician at Large* (collection of articles from the 'Mus. Times'; London, 1928); *A Handbook for Choralists* (London, 1928); also, with Sir Walford Davies, *Music and Worship* (London, 1935); composed 20 organ pieces; made 30 transcriptions from Bach, mostly for organ; edited Rheinberger's 20 sonatas for organ. — Cf. obituary article, *Harvey Grace,* in the 'Mus. Times' (March, 1944).

Grad, Gabriel, Lithuanian composer; b. Retovo, near Kovno, July 9, 1890. He studied in Ekaterinoslav and in Berlin; founded a Jewish music school in Kovno (1920-22); went to Palestine in 1924; since 1925, founder and director of the Benhetov Cons. in Tel-Aviv. He has written an opera, *Judith and Holofernes,* and about 250 other works, including chamber music, piano pieces, choruses, and songs, many of which are based on Jewish folk melodies.

Grädener, Hermann (Theodor Otto), German violinist and composer; son of Karl Grädener; b. Kiel, May 8, 1844; d. Vienna, Sept. 18, 1929. He studied at the Vienna Cons.; was violinist in the court orch. in Vienna; then taught theory at the Vienna Cons. (from 1874); in 1899 he became Bruckner's successor at Vienna Univ. He wrote 2 operas, *Der Richter von Zalamea* and *Die heilige Zita;* 2 symphonies; concertos for violin, for cello, and for piano; string octet; string quintet; piano quintet; 2 string quartets; *5 Impromptus* for piano and strings; *5 Intermezzi* for violin and piano; sonata for 2 pianos, etc.

Grädener, Karl Georg Peter, German cellist and composer; b. Rostock, Jan. 14, 1812; d. Hamburg, June 10, 1883. He was music director at Kiel Univ. for 10 years; in 1851, established an academy for vocal music in Hamburg; after 3 years at the Vienna Cons. (1862-65) he returned to Hamburg, and became teacher at the Cons. there; was also co-founder and a president of the Hamburger Tonkünstlerverein. He wrote *System der Harmonielehre* (Hamburg, 1877); his articles in music periodicals were publ. as *Gesammelte Aufsätze* (Hamburg, 1872).—Works: 2 operas, *König Harald* and *Der Müllerin Hochzeit;* an oratorio, *Johannes der Täufer;* 2 symphonies; *Fiesco,* an overture; a piano concerto; *Romance* for violin and orch.; a string octet; 5 piano quintets; 3 string quartets; string trio; 2 piano trios; 3 violin sonatas; a cello sonata; many piano pieces.

Gradenwitz, Peter, German-Israeli musicologist; b. Berlin, Jan. 24, 1910; studied literature and philosophy at Berlin Univ.; composition with Julius Weismann and Josef Rufer. In 1934 he went to Paris; in 1935, to London; in 1936, settled in Tel Aviv, where he became active as writer, lecturer, and organizer of concerts; established Israeli Music Publications; also active on the radio; publ. *Johann Stamitz* (Vienna, 1936); *The Music of Israel* (N. Y., 1949); books in Hebrew: *Music History* (Jerusalem, 1939); *The World of the Symphony* (Jerusalem, 1945; 7th ed., 1953); wrote a string quartet; *Palestinian Landscapes,* for oboe and piano; songs.

Gradstein, Alfred, Polish composer; b. Czenstochowa, Oct. 30, 1904; d. Warsaw, Sept. 9, 1954. He studied at the Warsaw Cons. (1922-25) and at the State Academy of Music in Vienna; from 1928-47 lived in Paris; then returned to Poland. He wrote mostly for piano; his piano concerto was publ. in 1932.

Graener, Paul, German composer; b. Berlin, Jan. 11, 1872; d. Salzburg, Nov. 13, 1944. He was a chorister at the Berlin cathedral; then studied piano with Veit and composition with Albert Becker. He then traveled in Germany as theater conductor. In 1896, he went to London where he taught at the Royal Academy of Music (1897-1902). He was then in Vienna as teacher at the Neues Konservatorium; subsequently directed the Mozarteum in Salzburg (1910-13); then lived in Munich; in 1920, he succeeded Max Reger as prof. of composition at the Leipzig Cons. (until 1924); was director of the Stern Cons. in Berlin (1930-34). He wrote music in all genres, and was fairly successful as an opera composer; in his style, he followed the Romantic movement, but also emphasized the folk element.—Works: Operas: *Don Juans letztes Abenteuer* (Leipzig, June 11, 1914); *Theophano* (Munich, June 5, 1918); *Schirin und Gertraude* (Dresden, April 28, 1920); *Hanneles Himmelfahrt* (Dresden, Feb. 17, 1927); *Friedemann Bach* (Schwerin, Nov. 13, 1931); *Der Prinz von Homburg* (Berlin, March 14, 1935); *Schwanhild* (Cologne, Jan. 4, 1941). For orch.: a symph.; *Romantische Phantasie; Waldmusik; Gothische Suite;* piano concerto; cello concerto. Chamber music: 6 string quartets; a piano quintet; 3 violin sonatas. In several of his chamber music works, Graener attempted to carry out a definite programmatic design, while maintaining traditional form, as in his *Kammermusik-Dichtung* for piano trio. — Cf. G. Graener, *Paul Graener* (Leipzig, 1922); P. Grümmer, *Verzeichnis der Werke Paul Graeners* (Berlin, 1937).

Graeser, Wolfgang, talented Swiss composer; b. Zürich, Sept. 7, 1906; d. (suicide) Nikolassee, June 13, 1928. He went to Berlin in 1921; studied violin with Karl Klingler, and quickly acquired erudition in general music theory; also made a serious study of various unrelated arts and sciences (mathematics, Oriental languages, painting). His signal achievement was an orchestration of Bach's *Kunst der Fuge* (performed at the Leipzig Thomaskirche by Karl Straube, June 26, 1927). He publ. a book, *Körpersinn* (Munich, 1927). A memorial symposium, *Wolfgang Graeser Gedächtnisheft,* was publ. in Munich shortly after his tragic death.—Cf. also H. Zurlinden, *Wolfgang Graeser* (Munich, 1935).

Graf, Herbert, Austrian opera stage director; son of Max Graf; b. Vienna, April 10, 1904. He studied at the Univ. of Vienna with Guido Adler; received his Ph. D. in 1925. He then was stage director at the opera houses in Münster, Breslau, Frankfurt, and Basel. In 1934 he came to the U. S.; was associated with the Philadelphia Opera in 1934-35; in 1936 he was appointed stage director of the Metropolitan Opera; in 1949, became head of the opera dept. at the Curtis Institute, Philadelphia. He is the author of two books, *The Opera and Its Future in America* (N. Y., 1941) and *Opera for the People* (Univ. of Minnesota, 1951).

Graf, Max, Austrian music critic, b. Vienna, Oct. 1, 1873. He studied at the Univ. of Vienna; taught music history and esthetics at the Staatsakademie für Musik; music critic of 'Wiener Allgemeine Zeitung' (from 1900-20); in 1939 came to the U. S.; after World War II, returned to Vienna. He is the author of: *Deutsche Musik im 19. Jahrhundert* (1898); *Wagner-Probleme und andere Studien* (1900); *Die Musik im Zeitalter der Renaissance* (1905); *Die innere Werkstatt des Musikers* (1910); *Legends of a Musical City* (1945); *Composer and Critic* (1946); *Modern Music* (1946; also appeared in German as *Geschichte und Geist der modernen Musik,* Frankfurt, 1954); *From Beethoven to Shostakovitch* (N. Y., 1947).

Graffigna (grahf-fē'-ña), **Achille,** Italian opera composer; b. S. Martino dall' Argine, near Mantua, May 5, 1816; d. Padua, July 19, 1896. He studied with Alessandro Rolla in Milan; wrote church music and theatrical cantatas; then devoted himself to opera; his *Ildegonda e Rizzardo* (La Scala, Milan, Nov. 3, 1841) was accepted with favor. In 1842 he went to Verona where he produced *Eleonora di San Bonifacio* (March 11, 1843); there followed *Maria di Brabante* (Trieste, Oct. 16, 1852); *L'assedio di Malta* (Padua, July 30, 1853); *Gli Studenti* (Milan, Feb. 7, 1857); *Veronica Cibo* (Mantua, Feb. 13, 1858; revised and produced at the Théâtre Italien, Paris, March 22, 1865, as *La Duchessa di San Giuliano*); *Il Barbiere di Siviglia* (Padua, May 17, 1879; intended as an homage to Rossini); *Il matrimonio segreto* (Florence, Sept. 8, 1883); *La buona figliuola* (Milan, May 6, 1886).

Graffman, Gary, talented American pianist; b. New York, Oct. 19, 1928. He studied with Isabelle Vengerova at the Curtis Institute of Music; made his 1st public appearance at the age of 10; won numerous prizes; was engaged as soloist with major American orchs. He made several European tours, beginning in 1950, and South American tours in 1955-56.

Gräflinger, Franz, Austrian writer on music; b. Linz, Nov. 26, 1876. He served as municipal accountant in Linz, and at the same time studied music; wrote criticism in local newspapers; then devoted his energies chiefly to Bruckner research; publ. two biographies of Bruckner (Munich, 1911; Regensburg, 1921) and *Liebes und Heiteres um Anton Bruckner* (Vienna, 1948); edited vol. I of Bruckner's *Gesammelte Briefe* (1924). In 1953 he was living in Ischl.

Grainger, Percy Aldridge, celebrated pianist and composer; b. Melbourne, Australia, July 8, 1882. He received his early musical training from his mother; at the age of 10, appeared as pianist at several public concerts; then had lessons with Louis Pabst; in 1894, went to Germany, where he studied with Kwast in Frankfurt; also took a few lessons with Busoni. In 1900 he began his concert career in England; then toured South Africa and Australia. In 1906 he met Grieg, who became enthusiastic about Grainger's talent; Grainger's performances of Grieg's piano concerto were famous. In 1914, Grainger settled in the U. S., made a sensational début in N. Y., Feb. 11, 1915; gave summer sessions at the Chicago Musical College from 1919 to 1931; was for one academic year chairman of the music dept. of N. Y. Univ. (1932-33). In 1935 he founded a museum in Melbourne, in which he housed all his manuscripts and his rich collection of musical souvenirs. After 1940 he lived mostly at White Plains, N. Y. He married Ella Viola Ström in 1928 in a spectacular ceremony staged at the Hollywood Bowl, at which he conducted his work, *To a Nordic Princess,* written for his bride. Grainger's philosophy of life and art calls for the widest communion of peoples and opinions; his profound study of folk music underlies the melodic and rhythmic structure of his own music; he made a determined effort to re-create in art music the free flow of instinctive songs of the people; he experimented with 'gliding' intervals within the traditional scales and polyrhythmic combinations with independent strong beats in the component parts. He has introduced individual forms of notation and orchestral scoring, rejecting the common Italian designations of tempi and dynamics in favor of colloquial English expressions.—Works: For orch.: *Mock Morris* (1911); *Irish Tunes from County Derry* (1911); *Molly on the Shore; Shepherd's Hey; Colonial Song* (1914); *In a Nutshell* (music to an imaginary ballet; 1916); *English Dance,* for orch. and organ (1925); *Ye Banks and Braes o' Bonnie Doon* (1932); *Harvest Hymn* (1933); *Danish Folk-song Suite* (1937). For chamber orch.: *The Nightingale and the 2 Sisters* (1931). For chorus and orch.: *Marching Song of Democracy* (1916); *The Merry Wedding* (1916); *Father and Daughter; Sir Eglamore; The Camp; The March of the Men of Harlech; The Hunter in His Career; The Bride's Tragedy; Love Verses from 'The Song of Solomon'; Tribute to Foster* (1931). For chorus and brass band: *I'm Seventeen come Sunday; We Have Fed our Seas for a Thousand Years* (1912); *Marching Tune.* For a cappella chorus: *Brigg Fair; The Innuit; Morning Song in the Jungle; A Song of Vermland; At Twilight; Tiger-Tiger!; The Immovable Do;* etc. All these are also issued in various arrangements. Chamber music: *Handel in the Strand* (1913); octet, *My Robin Is to the Greenwood Gone; Walking Tune,* for woodwind quintet; *Green Bushes* (1921); *Hill-Song No. 1* (1923); *Shallow Brown* (1924); *Hill-Song No. 2* (1929); *Spoon River* (1930); *Free Music for strings* (1935). For military band: *Children's March* (1918); march, *The Lads of Wamphrey; Lincolnshire Posy,* 6 folksongs from Lincolnshire, England; settings, in various combinations, of 20 of Kipling's poems (1911-38); 32 settings of British folksongs (1911-38); piano pieces, etc.—Cf. C. Scott, *Percy Grainger, the Music and the Man,* in the 'Mus. Quarterly' (July, 1916); D. C. Parker, *Percy A. Grainger, a Study* (N. Y., 1918); C. W. Hughes, *Percy Grainger, a Cosmopolitan Composer,* in the 'Mus. Quarterly' (April, 1937); R. L. Taylor, *The Running Pianist* (N. Y., 1950).

Gram, Hans, composer; he studied in Stockholm, and some time before 1790, settled in Boston, Mass., where he was organist of the Brattle Street Church. He composed *The Death Song of an Indian Chief* for voice, 2 clarinets, 2 horns, and strings, published in the 'Massachusetts Magazine' (March, 1791), apparently the first orchestral score publ. in the U. S.; *Sacred Lines for Thanksgiving Day* (1793), and other vocal works which appeared in the 'Massachusetts Magazine.' He was a co-editor of *The Massachusetts Compiler,* a progressive work on Psalmody; containing a music dictionary. See F. J. Metcalf, *American Writers and Compilers of Sacred Music* (1925); J. T. Howard, *Our American Music* (1939).

Gram, Peder, Danish conductor and composer; b. Copenhagen, Nov. 25, 1881; d. there, Feb. 4, 1956. After graduating from the Univ. there, he studied at the Leipzig Cons. with Sitt (theory) and Nikisch (conducting) from 1904-7; he received the Nikisch Prize at graduation for his string quartet. Returning to Copenhagen in 1908, he applied himself mainly to conducting; was chief conductor of the Danish Concert Society (1918-32); in 1937 became chief conductor of the Danish Radio Orch. His compositions include 2 symphonies; a violin concerto; a cello sonata; a wind quintet and other chamber music; publ. books (in Danish) on modern music (1934) and harmonic analysis (1948).

Grammann, Karl, German composer; b. Lübeck, June 3, 1844; d. Dresden, Jan. 30, 1897. He studied at the Leipzig Cons.; spent some years in Vienna; in 1885, settled in Dresden. As a youth, he wrote 2 operas, *Die Schatzgräber* and *Die Eisjungfrau,* which were not produced; the following operas were staged with some success: *Melusine* (Wiesbaden, 1875); *Thusnelda und der Triumphzug des Germanicus* (Dresden, 1881); *Das Andreasfest* (Dresden, 1882); 2 short operas, *Ingrid* and *Das Irrlicht* (Dresden, 1894). His last opera, *Auf neutralem Boden* was produced posthumously (Hamburg, 1901). He further wrote several cantatas, symphonies, string quartets, violin sonatas, and other chamber music works.— Cf. F. Pfohl, *Karl Grammann. Ein Künstlerleben* (Berlin, 1910).

Granados, Eduardo, Spanish composer, son of Enrique Granados; b. Barcelona, July 28, 1894; d. Madrid, Oct. 2, 1928. He studied in Barcelona with his father; then at the Madrid Cons. with Conrado del Campo; taught at the Granados Academy in Barcelona; was also active as conductor; presented many works by his father. He wrote several zarzuelas, of which the first, *Bufon y Hostelero,* was performed with some success in Barcelona (Dec. 7, 1917); other stage works are: *Los Fanfarrones,* comic opera; *La ciudad eterna,* mystery play; *Los Cigarrales,* operatic sketch; also musical comedies (*Cocktails del Nuevo,* etc.).

Granados, Enrique, outstanding Spanish composer; b. Lérida, July 27, 1867; d. at sea, March 24, 1916 (victim of the sinking by a German submarine of the S. S. Sussex in the English Channel). He studied piano at the Barcelona Cons. with Pujol, winning first prize (1883); then studied composition at the Madrid Cons., with Pedrell (1884-87). He first supported himself by playing piano in restaurants and giving private concerts. He first attracted attention as a composer with an opera, *Maria del Carmen* (Madrid, Nov. 12, 1898); in 1900 he conducted a series of concerts in Barcelona; also established a music school, Academia Granados. He then wrote 4 operas which were produced in Barcelona with little success: *Picarol* (Feb. 23, 1901), *Follet* (April 4, 1903), *Gaziel* (Oct. 27, 1906), and *Liliana* (1911). He then undertook the composition of a work that was to be his masterpiece, a series of piano pieces entitled *Goyescas,* inspired by the paintings and etchings of Goya; his fame rests securely on these imaginative and effective pieces, together with his brilliant *Danzas españolas.* Later, Fernando Periquet wrote a libretto based on the scenes from Goya's paintings, and Granados used the music of his piano suite for an opera, *Goyescas.* Its première took place, in the presence of the composer, at the Metropolitan Opera in New York, on Jan. 28, 1916, with excellent success; the score included an orchestral *Intermezzo,* one of his most popular compositions. It was during his return voyage to Europe that he lost his life. Other works by Granados include an intermezzo to *Miel de la Alcarría* (1893); symph. poems, *La Nit del Mort* and *Dante; Suite Arabe; Suite Gallega; Marcha de los Vencidos; Serenata;* orch. suites, *Elisenda* and *Navidad;* a piano trio; a string quartet; *Serenata* for 2 violins and piano; *Oriental* for oboe and strings; *Trova* for cello and piano; *Cant de les Estrelles* for chorus, organ, and piano. Piano works: *Danzas españolas* (4 vols.); *Goyescas:* (Part I) *Los Requiebros, Coloquio en la Reja, El Fandango del Candil, Quejas o la Maja y el Ruiseñor;* (Part II) *El Amor y la Muerte (Ballade), Epílogo (Serenade of the Spectre), El Pelele (Escena goyesca);* 6 Pieces on Spanish popular songs; *Valses poéticos; Cuentos para la Juventud; Marche Militaire* and *A la Cubana* (also arranged for orch.); *Deux danses caractéristiques: Danza gitana* and *Danza aragonesa;* songs: *Colección de Tonadillas, escritas en estilo antigua; Colección de Canciones amatorias.* Granados' music is essentially Romantic, with an admixture of specific Spanish rhythms and rather elaborate ornamentation. — Cf. special Granados number of 'Revista Musical Catalana' (June 15, 1916); G. Jean-Aubry, *Enrique Granados* in the 'Mus. Times' (Dec., 1916); E. Newman, *The Granados of the 'Goyescas'* in the 'Mus. Times' (Aug., 1917); G. Boladeres Ibern, *Enrique Granados, Recuerdos de su vida y estudio crítico de su obra* (Barcelona, 1921); H. Collet, *Albéniz et Granados*

(Paris, 1926); J. Subira, *Enrique Granados* (Madrid, 1926); E. L. Mason, *Enrique Granados* in 'Music & Letters' (XIV, 1933, p. 231); A. Livermore, *Granados and the Nineteenth Century in Spain* in 'Mus. Review' (VII, 1946, p. 80).

Grancino (gran-chē'-nŏh), a family of violin makers, active in the 17th and early 18th centuries. Andrea Grancino established a workshop in Milan in 1646; his son, Paolo, worked in Milan between 1665 and 1692; he belonged to the Amati school, and several violins attributed to Amati are apparently the work of Paolo Grancino. Paolo's son, Giovanni, began making violins in 1677; he is reputed to be the best of the family. His 2 sons, Giovanni Battista and Francesco, were active between 1715 and 1746; their labels are marked Fratelli Grancini.

Grancino (Grancini), Michel Angelo, Italian composer; b. Milan, 1605; d. there, 1669. He was organist at the Paradiso Church in Milan as a youth of 17; then appointed organist at San Sepolcro (1624) and later at San Ambrogio (1628). In 1630 he became a maestro di cappella of the Milan Cathedral, and retained this post until his death. During his lifetime, he publ. some 20 volumes of his works, which included madrigals, motets, and *concerti sacri,* only a few of which are extant. For a complete list, see Claudio Sartori's article on Grancino in 'Die Musik in Geschichte und Gegenwart.'

Grandi, Alessandro, Italian composer; place and date of birth uncertain; d. Bergamo, 1630. He was maestro di cappella at Ferrara, first at the Accademia della Morte (1597-1610), then at the Accademia dello Spirito (to c. 1616); 1617, was a singer at San Marco, Venice; 1620, 2nd maestro di cappella at San Marco; in 1627, he went to Bergamo as maestro di cappella at Santa Maria Maggiore; he and his family died there in 1630 of the plague. He was greatly admired by fellow-musicians; his works include 3 books of *Cantade et arie* (Venice, 1620-9); 2 books of *Madrigali concertati* (Venice, 1615-22); several books of motets (Venice, 1610-29); other music in MS is at the Fitzwilliam Museum, Cambridge; Christ Church, Oxford; in Berlin and Vienna.—Cf. Denis Arnold, *Alessandro Grandi, a Disciple of Monteverdi,* in the 'Mus. Quarterly' (April, 1957).

Grandjany (grăhn-zhăn-ne'), **Marcel,** French harpist; b. Paris, Sept. 3, 1891. He studied at the Paris Cons., winning 1st prize for harp (1905); made his Paris début on Jan. 24, 1909; his American début, N. Y., Feb. 7, 1924; taught at the Fontainebleau Cons. (1921-35); in 1936 settled in N. Y.; became an American citizen in 1945. In 1938 he joined the staff of the Juilliard School of Music; from 1943, also prof. at Montreal Cons. He has composed a *Poème symphonique* for harp, French horn, and orch., and several other works for harp; also songs to French texts.

Grandjean (grahn-zhan'), **Axel Karl William,** Danish composer; b. Copenhagen, March 9, 1847; d. there, Feb. 11, 1932. He began his career as an opera singer, but gave up the stage for teaching and composition; also conducted several choral societies in Copenhagen. He wrote the operas *Colomba* (Copenhagen, Oct. 15, 1882), *Oluf* (Copenhagen, April 7, 1894), and others; many choral works; also edited (for Holberg's bicentennial in 1884) a collection of incidental music written to Holberg's dramas.

Grandval, Marie Félicie Clémence de Reiset, French composer; b. Saint-Rémy-des-Monts (Sarthe), Jan. 21, 1830; d. Paris, Jan. 15, 1907. She studied composition with Flotow and Saint-Saëns; under various pen-names she wrote the operas *Le Sou de Lise* (Paris, 1859); *Les Fiancés de Rose* (Paris, May 1, 1863); *La Comtesse Eva* (Paris, Aug. 7, 1864); *La Pénitente* (Paris, May 13, 1868); *Piccolino* (Paris, Jan. 5, 1869); *Mazeppa* (Bordeaux, 1892); the oratorio *St. Agnès* (Paris, April 13, 1876); *La Forêt,* lyric poem, for soli, chorus, and orch. (Paris, March 30, 1875); songs.

Granichstaedten, Bruno, Austrian operetta composer; b. Vienna, Sept. 1, 1879. He began his career as a cabaret singer; in 1908 he turned to composing light opera; produced 16 stage works before 1930; of these, *Der Orlow* (Vienna, April 3, 1925) was the most successful; other operettas are *Bub oder Mädel, Auf Befehl der Kaiserin, Evelyne, Walzerliebe,* etc. In 1938 Granichstaedten left Austria and settled in the U. S.

Grant-Schaefer, George Alfred, composer and teacher; b. Williamstown, Ont., July 4, 1872; d. Chicago, May 11, 1939. He studied in Montreal, Chicago, and London; was organist and choirmaster in Chicago from 1896-1908; from 1908-20, head of vocal dept. of Northwestern Univ., Evanston, Ill.; he composed operettas for schools; pedagogic and other piano pieces; numerous songs, publ. a collection of French Canadian songs (Boston, 1925).

Grasse, Edwin, American violinist and composer; b. New York, Aug. 13, 1884; d. there, April 8, 1954. Blind from infancy, he dictated his compositions to an accompanist. He studied the violin with Carl Hauser in N. Y.; then went to Brussels for study with César Thomson; in 1899 entered the Brussels Cons., where he won 1st prize in 1900, and Diplôme de Capacité in 1901; toured Europe and America. His works include: an *American Fantasie* for violin and orch.; a violin sonata and other violin pieces; 3 piano trios; organ pieces.

Grassi, Eugène, composer; b. Bangkok, Siam, July 5, 1887; d. Paris, July, 1941. He was born of French parents in Siam; came to France as a youth and studied with Vincent d'Indy; he revisited Siam in 1910-13 to collect materials on indigenous music; his own works reflect this study, while his harmonic idiom is influenced by Debussy. Among his compositions, all with Oriental flavor, are *Le Revéil de Bouddha,* symph. poem (Paris, Feb. 20, 1920); *Poème de l'Univers* for orch. (Paris, April 9, 1922); *Les Sanctuaires* (Paris, March 25, 1926); also songs in the Impressionist manner.

Grassini, Josephina (Giuseppina), Italian contralto; b. Varese, April 8, 1773; d. Milan, Jan. 3, 1850. She made her début as an opera singer in Milan in 1794; soon attained popularity on all leading Italian stages; in 1800, she sang in Milan before Napoleon, who took her with him to Paris, where she sang at national celebrations. She was in London from 1804-6; then returned to Paris and sang at the French court; she was noted for her beauty and her acting as well as her voice.—Cf. P. Cambiasi, *Una famosa cantante varesina* in the 'Gazzetta Musicale di Milano' (Feb. 20, 1902); A. Pougin, *Une cantatrice 'amie' de Napoléon: Giuseppina Grassini* (Paris, 1920); A. Gavoty, *La Grassini* (Paris, 1947).

Grau, Maurice, operatic impresario; b. Brünn, Moravia, 1849; d. Paris, March 14, 1907. He was taken to the U. S. at the age of 5, and studied law at Columbia Univ. In 1872, he was a co-manager of the American tours of Anton Rubinstein; in 1873, he organized the Kellogg Opera Co.; was instrumental in bringing Offenbach to the U. S. In 1890, he presented a special season of 21 performances at the Metropolitan Opera House, with such famous artists as Adelina Patti, Emma Albani, Nordica, and Tamagno. From 1891 to 1897 the Metropolitan Opera was leased to the partnership of Abbey, Schoeffel and Grau, and upon Abbey's death, to the Maurice Grau Opera Co. (1898-1903). In 1903, Grau retired and went to Paris. The secret of Grau's success as an impresario was his perfect understanding of public taste in opera; he frankly subordinated the repertory to the favorite roles of the great European stars; he did not produce Wagner's operas until Wagnerian cycles presented by Damrosch had shown that American audiences were ripe for them. In fact, the growing popularity of Wagner contributed greatly towards the financial success of Grau's last seasons.

Graumann, Mathilde. See **Marchesi.**

Graun, August Friedrich, German composer, brother of Karl Heinrich Graun; b. Wahrenbrück, near Dresden, 1699; d. Merseburg, May 5, 1765. He was active as organist and cantor at Merseburg, where he settled in 1729. Only one of his works is preserved, *Kyrie et Gloria* for 4 voices with instruments.

Graun, Johann Gottlieb, German composer, brother of Karl Heinrich Graun; b. Wahrenbrück, near Dresden, 1703; d. Berlin, Oct. 27, 1771. He studied violin with Pisendel in Dresden and with Tartini in Padua. In 1726, he was appointed Kapellmeister in Merseburg, where he was the teacher of Wilhelm Friedemann Bach. In 1732 he became Konzertmeister for Crown Prince Frederick (later Frederick the Great) at Rheinsberg, and from 1741, held a similar position in the newly founded Royal Opera in Berlin, where his brother, Karl Heinrich, was Kapellmeister. His works include 100 symphonies, 20 violin concertos, 24 string quartets, and a number of sacred works. Only a few are published: 6 harpsichord concertos; 8 sonatas for 2 flutes and violin. Riemann reprinted 3 trio-sonatas in 'Collegium musicum' (1906). A complete list of works and editions is found in Werner Freytag's article on the Graun brothers in 'Die Musik in Geschichte und Gegenwart.'

Graun, Karl Heinrich, German composer; b. Wahrenbrück, near Dresden, May 7, 1704; d. Berlin, Aug. 8, 1759. He received his primary education at the Kreuzschule in Dresden (1713-20), where he studied with Grundig (voice) and Petzold (organ). He sang soprano in the town council choir; then began to study composition with Johann Christoph Schmidt. In 1725 he was engaged as operatic tenor at the Brunswick court; soon he began to compose operas for production at the court theater: *Sinilde* (Feb. 3, 1727), *Iphigenia in Aulis* (Aug. 16, 1728), *Polidorus* (1731), and *Scipio Africanus* (1732), all to German librettos. On June 14, 1733, he staged his first Italian opera, *Lo specchio della fedeltà* (also known under the title *Timareta)*. In 1735 Graun was invited by Frederick the Great (then Crown Prince of Prussia) to Rheinsberg, as musical director; Graun gladly accepted, and followed Frederick to Berlin when he became king (1740). In Rheinsberg, Graun wrote a great number of cantatas, in the Italian style; in Berlin, his chief duty was to establish an Italian opera troupe, for which purpose he traveled to Italy in search of good singers. Upon his return to Berlin, Graun produced his first opera for his company, *Rodelinda* (Dec. 13, 1741); there followed *Cleopatra e Cesare* (Dec. 7, 1742), staged for the inauguration of the new opera house. He continued to compose operas with unfailing regularity for each season, 28 in all, among them *Artaserse* (Dec. 2, 1743), *Catone in Utica* (1744), *Alessandro nell' Indie* (1744), *Adriano in Siria* (1746), *Mitridate* (1750), and *Semiramide* (1754). Frederick the Great himself wrote the librettos (in French) for Graun's operas *Montezuma* (Berlin, Jan. 6, 1755) and *Merope* (March 27, 1756). In those years Graun enjoyed very high renown and royal favor; only Hasse approached him in public esteem. In his operas, Graun adhered to the Italian tradition, and was preoccupied chiefly with the requirements of the singing voice. During the last years of his life he wrote some excellent church music; his *Te Deum* commemorating Frederick's victory at the battle of Prague (1756) is regarded as one of the finest sacred works in Germany; even more renowned is Graun's Passion oratorio, *Der Tod Jesu* (1755), which was performed annually for a century. Graun's instrumental music displays a high degree of contrapuntal craftsmanship, as well as a facile melodic gift, but despite these qualities, it failed to sustain interest as well as his sacred works did. He wrote a *Concerto Grosso* for flute, violin, viola da gamba, cello, and strings; about 30 concertos for harpsichord; 6 flute concertos; 3 quintets for harpsichord and strings; about 35 trio-sonatas; duets for various instruments, etc. — Cf. A. Mayer-Reinach, *Karl Heinrich Graun als Opernkomponist* (Berlin, 1899); K. Mennicke, *Zur Biographie der Brüder Graun*, in the 'Neue Zeitschrift für Musik' (1904); K. Mennicke, *Hasse und die Brüder Graun als Sinfoniker* (Leipzig, 1906; with biography and complete thematic catalogues); B. Hitzig, *Briefe Karl Heinrich Grauns* in the 'Zeitschrift für Musikwissenschaft' (1926, pp. 385-405).

Graupner, Christoph, German composer; b. Hartmannsdorf, near Kirchberg, Jan. 13, 1683; d. Darmstadt, May 10, 1760. He studied music at the Thomasschule, Leipzig, with Kuhnau and Heinichen; then was in Hamburg as opera accompanist under Keiser (1706-9). In 1710, he became vice-Kapellmeister and in 1712, Kapellmeister, at Darmstadt, where he remained all his life. He was offered the post of cantor at the Thomasschule in 1722, but decided against acceptance, and the position was given to Bach. Graupner was an industrious worker, and was active in Hamburg as composer, conductor, and teacher; he engraved for publication several of his keyboard pieces. He produced 6 operas in Hamburg of which only 3 are extant: *Dido* (1707); *Der angenehme Betrug* (1707, with Keiser; publ. in vol. 38 of 'Denkmäler deutscher Tonkunst'); *L'amore ammalato* or *Antiochus und Stratonice* (1708). He wrote 3 operas in Darmstadt, of which *La costanza vince l'inganno* is preserved. He publ. for harpsichord 8 *Partien* (2 vols., 1718 and 1726), the *Monatliche Klavier-Früchte* (1722), and the *Vier Jahreszeiten* (1733); also a *Hessen-Darmstädttisches Choralbuch* (1728). The Darmstadt library contains a great number of MSS by Graupner, among them 50 concertos, 80 overtures, and 116 symphonies; 6 harpsichord sonatas, trio-sonatas, and about 1300 sacred works. Selected examples from his cantatas are publ. in vols. 51-52 of 'Denkmäler deutscher Tonkunst.' — Cf. W. Nagel, *Christoph Graupner als Sinfoniker* (Langensalza, 1912); F. Noack, *Christoph Graupners Kirchenmusiken* (Leipzig, 1916).

Graupner, Johann Christian Gottlieb, composer; b. Verden, near Hanover, Oct. 6, 1767; d. Boston, April 16, 1836. He was the son of the oboist, Johann Georg Graupner, and became himself an oboist in military bands. In 1788, he was in London, and played in Haydn's orchestra in 1791. About 1795, he emigrated to America, settling in Charleston, S. C.; played his oboe concerto there on March 21, 1795; early in 1797, he went to Boston; in 1800, he opened a music store; also taught piano, and all orchestral instruments, on which he was fairly proficient; publ. works by himself and other composers; he became an American citizen in 1808. In 1810, he organized the Boston Philharmonic Society, which was the first semi-professional orchestra in Boston; it gave performances of Haydn's symphonies; it presented *Messiah* in 1818 and Haydn's *Creation* in 1819; the orchestra continued its activity until Nov., 1824. In 1815, Graupner was a co-founder of a musical organization which became the Handel and Haydn Society of Boston, and which greatly influenced the development of choral music in New England. In view of these accomplishments, Graupner is referred to by some writers as the 'father of American orchestral music.' In 1819, he publ. *Rudiments of the Art of Playing the Pianoforte, Containing the Elements of Music.* He was married to Catherine Hillier, a professional singer (1770-1821); on Dec. 30, 1799, she sang in Boston a Negro ballad; this fact led to erroneous reports that Graupner himself appeared as a blackface minstrel.—Cf. O. G. Sonneck, *Early Concert Life in America* (1907); J. T. Howard, *Our American Music* (N. Y., 1946; pp. 130-33); H. E. Johnson, *Musical Interludes in Boston* (N. Y., 1943), chap. VI. Typescript copies of a memoir on Graupner, compiled by his granddaughter, Catherine Graupner Stone (1906), are available in the Library of Congress, N. Y. Public Library, and Boston Public Library.

Graveure (grah-vürh'), **Louis** (real name Wilfred Douthitt), concert singer; b. London, March 18, 1888. He studied voice with Clara Novello-Davies; came to the U. S. and under his real name, Douthitt, sang the baritone part in the operetta, *The Lilac Domino,* in N. Y. on Oct. 28, 1914; in 1915 he reappeared in N. Y. as Louis Graveure (after his mother's maiden name) and became a popular concert artist, singing all types of music. On Feb. 5, 1928, he gave a concert in N. Y. as a tenor; from 1931-38, he was in Germany; 1938-40, in France; 1940-47, in England; in 1947, returned to the U. S.; taught in various music schools. —Cf. *The Case of a Beardless Baritone* in N. Slonimsky, *A Thing or Two About Music* (N. Y., 1948; pp. 220-21).

Gray, Alan, English organist and composer; b. York, Dec. 23, 1855; d. Cambridge, Sept. 27, 1935. He took degrees in law and music from Trinity College, Cambridge; was musical director of Wellington College (1883-92); 1892-1912, conductor of the Cambridge Univ. Musical Society; also organist at Trinity College (1892-1930). He wrote 5 cantatas, a *Coronation March;* chamber music; many organ works. He was also an editor for the Purcell Society.

Gray, Cecil, British writer on music; b. Edinburgh, May 19, 1895; d. Worthing, Sept. 9, 1951. He studied music with Healey Willan; in 1920, with Philip Heseltine (Peter Warlock), he edited a new magazine of music criticism, 'The Sackbut'; later was music critic for the 'Daily Telegraph' and the 'Manchester Guardian'; wrote 3 operas (to his own texts) and other music. His books include: *A Survey of Contemporary Music* (1924); *Carlo Gesualdo, Prince of Venosa; Musician and Murderer* (in collaboration with Philip Heseltine; 1926); *The History of Music* (1928); *Sibelius* (1931); *Peter Warlock* (1934); *Sibelius: the Symphonies* (1935); *Predicaments, or Music and the Future* (1936); *The 48 Preludes and Fugues of Bach* (1938); *Contingencies* (N. Y., 1947); memoirs, *Musical Chairs or Between Two Stools* (London, 1948).—Cf. R. Gorer, *The Music of Cecil Gray* in 'Mus. Review' (Aug., 1947).

Greatorex, Thomas, English organist, singer, and conductor; b. North Wingfield, Derby, Oct. 5, 1758; d. Hampton, near London, July 18, 1831. He was the son of an amateur organist; the family moved to Leicester in 1767. He studied with Dr. B. Cooke (1772); was befriended by Lord Sandwich and became musical director of his household for a time. He sang at the Concerts of Ancient Music in London (from 1776) and was organist at Carlisle Cathedral (1781-84). He then traveled in Holland, Italy, and France, and took lessons in Strasbourg with Pleyel. Settling in London, he became a highly popular singing teacher (in one week he gave 84 lessons at a guinea each). In 1793 he was appointed conductor of the Concerts of Ancient Music, a post which he held until his death, never missing a single concert. He assisted in the revival of the Vocal Concerts in 1801; from 1819 he was organist at Westminster Abbey; he conducted festivals throughout England, and was one of the founders of the Royal Academy of Music in London (1822). He published *A Selection of Tunes* (London, 1829); a collection *Parochial Psalmody* (1825); *12 Glees* (1832); anthems, psalms and chants, but it was as an organist that Greatorex was best known.

Greef, Arthur de, Belgian pianist and composer; b. Louvain, Oct. 10, 1862; d. Brussels, Aug. 29, 1940. He studied at the

Brussels Cons. with L. Brassin (piano) and Gevaert (composition); then traveled as pianist in Europe; in 1885 he was appointed prof. of piano at the Brussels Cons., retaining that post until 1930. He wrote an opera in Flemish, *De Marketenster* (Louvain, 1879); a symphony; a ballad for strings; 2 piano concertos; 2 violin sonatas; *Quatre vieilles chansons flamandes* for piano, and a number of piano études; also songs.—Cf. F. Rasse, *Notice sur Arthur de Greef* in the 'Annuaire de l'Académie Royale de Belgique' (1949).

Green, L. Dunton (Louis Grein), Dutch music critic; b. Amsterdam, Dec. 22, 1872; d. Ruysselede, Belgium, Dec. 30, 1933. He studied music in Germany and in Paris; lived for many years in London; contributed numerous articles on modern composers to English, Italian, French, and American magazines.

Green, Ray, American composer; b. Cavendish, Missouri, Sept. 13, 1909. He had his musical training in San Francisco with Albert Elkus; also took courses with Ernest Bloch: received a fellowship for study in Europe (1935-37); was on the staff of the Department of Music at the Univ. of California (1937-38); then was in charge of the Federal Music Project in California. He entered the armed forces in 1943; was chief of music for the Veterans Administration (1946-48); in 1948 became executive secretary of the American Music Center, N. Y. —Works: Symphony No. 1 (1945-53); *Sunday Sing Symphony* (1946); *Rhapsody* for harp and orch. (1950); violin concerto (1952); many pieces for band on American subjects (*Kentucky Mountain Running Set; Jig Theme and Six Changes,* etc.); several scores for ballet; *Duo Concertante* for violin and piano (1950); *Dance Sonata* for two pianos (1950); *5 Epigrammatic Portraits* for strings (1954); *Concertante* for viola and piano (1955); incidental music to plays, etc.

Greene, Harry Plunket, Irish singer; b. near Dublin, June 24, 1865; d. London, Aug. 19, 1936. He studied in Florence with Vannuccini, and in London under J. B. Welsh and A. Blume; made his début in *Messiah* at Stepney (Jan. 21, 1888) and soon became a popular concert artist. He made the first of several tours of the U. S. in 1893; also appeared in Canada. He was noted for his interpretations of Schumann and Brahms; publ. a valuable instruction book for singers, *Interpretation in Song* (London, 1912), a biography of Stanford (London, 1935), and a volume of musical reminiscences, *From Blue Danube to Shannon.*

Greene, Maurice, English organist and composer; b. London, 1695; d. there, Dec. 1, 1775. He served as a choirboy in St. Paul's Cathedral; became proficient as an organist; was appointed organist of St. Paul's in 1718. In 1727, he succeeded Croft as composer to the Chapel Royal; in 1730, he was Tudway's successor as prof. of music at the Univ. of Cambridge, receiving the title of Mus. Doc. In 1735, he became master of the King's Band of Music. Beginning in 1750, he accumulated and collated a great number of English sacred works; he willed this material to Boyce, who made use of it in his monumental collection, 'Cathedral Music.' Greene composed 2 oratorios, *Jephtha* (1737) and *The Force of Truth* (1744), and 3 dramatic pastorals: *Love's Revenge* (1734), *The Judgment of Hercules* (1740), and *Phoebe* (1748); other works are: *The Chaplet,* a collection of 12 English songs; *Spenser's Amoretti,* an album of 25 sonnets for voice with harpsichord and violin; also collected *40 Select Anthems in Score* (2 vols.; 1743); composed numerous catches and canons, organ voluntaries, harpsichord pieces, etc.—Cf. E. Walker, *The Bodleian MSS of Maurice Greene,* in the 'Mus. Antiquarian' (April-July, 1910).

Greff. See **Bacfart.**

Gregh (grăg), **Louis,** French composer and music publisher; b. Philippeville, Algeria, March 16, 1843; d. St. Mesme (Seine-et-Oise), Jan. 21, 1915. He began his musical career with the production of a light opera, *Un Lycée de jeunes filles* (Paris, 1881), which won a decided success; this was followed by several other operettas, *Le Présomtif* (1884), *Le capitaine Roland* (1895), and ballets. He then turned to publishing; the firm was continued by his son, Henri Gregh, who established it as Henri Gregh & Fils (1902); Henri Gregh's son, André, succeeded him as director in 1934.

Gregoir (grĕ-gwahr'), **Edouard** (**Georges Jacques**), Belgian composer and writer on music; b. Turnhout, near Antwerp, Nov. 7, 1822; d. Wyneghem, June 28, 1890. He studied piano, and was a professional accompanist; in 1851, he settled in Antwerp. He was a prolific composer; wrote 154 works in all. His Flemish opera, *Willem Beukels,* was produced in Brussels (July 21,

1856); he wrote incidental music to various patriotic plays: *De Belgen in 1848; La Dernière Nuite du Comte d'Egmont,* etc.; also composed a symphonic oratorio, *Le Déluge* (1849), and a historical symphony, *Les Croisades* (1846). Among his important writings are *Essai historique sur la musique et les musiciens dans les Pays-Bas* (1861); *Histoire de l'orgue* (1865, with biographical notes on Belgian and Dutch organists and organ builders); *Galerie biographique des artistes-musiciens belges du XVIIIe et du XIXe siècles* (1862; 2nd ed., 1885); *Notice sur l'origine du célèbre compositeur Louis van Beethoven* (1863); *Les Artistes-Musiciens néerlandais* (1864); *Du Chant choral et des festivals en Belgique* (1865); *Notice historique sur les sociétés de musique d'Anvers* (1869); *Recherches historiques concernant les journaux de musique depuis les temps les plus reculés jusqu'à nos jours* (1872); *Notice biographique d'Adrian Willaert; Réflexions sur la regénération de l'ancienne école de musique flamande et sur le théâtre flamand; Les Artistes-Musiciens belges au XIXe siècle; réponse à un critique de Paris* (1874); *Documents historiques relatifs à l'art musical et aux artistes-musiciens* (1872-76; 4 vols.); *Panthéon musical populaire* (1876-77; 6 vols.); *Notice biographique sur F.J. Gossé dit Gossec* (1878); *L'Art musical en Belgique sous les règnes de Léopold I et Léopold II* (1879); *Les Gloires de l'Opéra et la musique à Paris* (4 vols., 1880-3; vol. I embraces the period 1392-1750); *A.-E.-M. Grétry* (1883); *Souvenirs artistiques* (3 vols., 1888-9); etc.

Gregoir, Jacques Mathieu, Belgian pianist and composer, brother of Edouard Gregoir; b. Antwerp, Jan. 18, 1817; d. Brussels, Oct. 29, 1876. He studied with Henri Herz in Paris and with Rummel in Biebrich. He gave a number of successful piano recitals in Belgium, Germany, and Switzerland; wrote salon pieces for piano and several practical methods of piano playing; publ. duets for violin and piano in collaboration with Vieuxtemps; he also wrote an opera, *Le Gondolier de Venise* (1848).

Gregor, Christian Friedrich, composer and hymnologist; b. Dirsdorf, Silesia, Jan. 1, 1723; d. Zeist, Holland, Nov. 6, 1801. As organist, music director, composer, and hymnologist, Gregor was the most important musician of the international Moravian Church (Unitas Fratrum) of the 18th century. Joining the Moravian Brethren in 1742, he soon assumed leading positions in its management: financial agent of Zinzendorf, member of Unity Elders Conference (1764-1801), and bishop (1789-1801). He made numerous business trips to Germany, Holland, England, Russia, and North America (Pennsylvania, 1770-72); while in Pennsylvania, he gave instruction in composition to Johann Friedrich Peter (q.v.). During his stay at Herrnhut, Saxony, as organist, Gregor compiled the first hymnal published by the Moravians *(Choral-Buch, enthaltend alle zu dem Gesangbuche der Evangelischen Brüder-Gemeinen vom Jahre 1778 gehörige Melodien;* Leipzig, Breitkopf, 1784) and arranged the musical liturgies.—Works: 308 hymns *(Gesangbuch zum Gebrauch der evangelischen Brüder-Gemeinen;* Barby, 1778, et seq.), about 100 chorale tunes, and approximately 200 anthems and arias. The latter are preserved in MS in the Moravian Church Archives at Bethlehem, Pennsylvania, and Winston-Salem, North Carolina. Several of his anthems were republished frequently in 19th-century American tunebooks. —Cf. *Historische Nachricht vom Brüder-Gesangbuche des Jahres 1778, und von dessen Lieder-Verfassern* (Gnadau, 1835).

Gregori, Nininha, Brazilian composer; b. São Paulo, Jan. 20, 1925. She studied with Koellreutter. She writes in the 12-tone technique. Her compositions include 3 pieces for chamber orch.; trio for flute, violin, and viola; *4 Old Greek Poems* for soprano, 4 woodwind instruments, and celesta (Frankfurt Festival, 1951).

Gregorovitch, Charles, Russian violinist; b. St. Petersburg, Oct. 25, 1867; d. Gomel, 1920. He studied with Dont in Vienna and Joachim in Berlin. After a series of brilliant appearances in Europe, he made a successful American tour (1896-97); then was in St. Petersburg, where he played in various chamber music organizations; was regarded as one of the most musicianly performers of Classical and Romantic music.

Gregory I, 'the Great'; b. Rome, 540; d. there, March 12, 604. He was pope from 590-604; celebrated in music history as reputed reformer of the musical ritual of the Roman Catholic Church. It is traditionally believed that by his order, and under his supervision, a collection was made in 599 of the music employed in the different churches; that various offertories, antiphons, responses, etc., were revised, and regularly and suitably distributed over the entire year, in an arrangement which came to be known as Gregorian Chant. While for centuries the sole credit for the codification, which certainly took place, had been ascribed to Gregory, investigations by such scholars as Gevaert, Riemann, P. Wagner, Frere, Houdard, Gastoué, Mocquereau, and others have demonstrated that some of Gregory's predecessors had begun this reform, and even definitely fixed the order of certain portions of the liturgy; and that the work of reform was definitely completed under some of his immediate successors. Evidence in favor of Gregory's leading part in the reform is marshaled in E. G. P. Wyatt's *Saint Gregory and the Gregorian Music* (1904); evidence against his participation is given in Paul Henry Lang's *Music in Western Civilization* (N. Y., 1941). See also G. Morin, *Les véritables origines du Chant grégorien* (Maredsous, 1890); W. Brambach, *Gregorianisch* (Leipzig, 1895); F. H. Duddin, *Gregory the Great* (2 vols., London, 1905); F. Tarducci, *Storia di S. Gregorius e del suo tempo* (Rome, 1909); P. C. Vivell, *Der gregorianische Gesang: eine Studie über die Echtheit der Tradition* (Graz, 1904).

Greissle, Felix, composer and editor; b. Vienna, Nov. 15, 1899. He studied there at the Univ. with Guido Adler, and privately with Schoenberg and Alban Berg; from 1925-37, he conducted the Cantata Association of the Vienna State Opera. In 1938 he came to N. Y.; became associated with various music publishers. He has written numerous articles on music, including the first published explanation of Schoenberg's method of composition with 12 tones ('Anbruch,' 1925). In 1947 Greissle became director of publication for Edward B. Marks Music Corporation.

Greiter, Matthaeus, German poet and composer; b. Aichach, Bavaria, c. 1490; d. Strasbourg, Dec. 20, 1550. He wrote the texts and melodies of Psalm-Lieder for Lutheran services, and settings, for 4 voices, of German songs. He also wrote a tract, *Elementale Musicum Inventuti* (1544).—Cf. Th. Gérold, *Les plus anciennes melodies de l'Eglise protestante de Strasbourg et leurs auteurs* (Paris, 1928); E. E. Lowinsky, *Matthaeus Greiter's Fortuna; an Experiment in Chromaticism and in Musical Iconography* in the 'Mus. Quarterly' (Oct., 1956 and Jan., 1957).

Grell, Eduard August, German organist and composer; b. Berlin, Nov. 6, 1800; d. Steglitz, near Berlin, Aug. 10, 1886. He studied organ with his father and theory with Zelter; at the age of 17, he became a member of the Singakademie, and was connected with it for 59 years, until his death; he was director from 1853-76. Grell held the view that only vocal music was the true art; consequently, he wrote almost exclusively for voice. His works include a *Missa Solemnis* (in 16 parts a cappella); an oratorio, *Die Israelitin in der Wüste,* and other church music.—Cf. H. Bellermann, *Biographie Grells* (Berlin, 1899); Bellermann also edited Grell's essays, *Aufsätze und Gutachten* (posthumous; Berlin, 1887).

Gresnich, Antoine-Frédéric, Belgian composer; b. Liège, March (baptized March 2), 1755; d. Paris, Oct. 16, 1799. He was a chorister at the St. Lambert Church in Liège, and studied in Naples under Sala. He made several trips to London, where he produced his operas *Demetrio, Alessandro nell'Indie, Donna di Cattiva Umore,* and *Alceste* with considerable success. He was in Lyons in 1789-93; his opera *L'amour exilé de Cythère* was produced there in 1793. He then returned to Paris, where he died in poverty.

Gretchaninov (grĕtch-ah-nē'-nŏv), **Alexander Tikhonovitch,** Russian composer; b. Moscow, Oct. 25, 1864; d. New York, Jan. 3, 1956. He studied at the Moscow Cons. (1881-91) with Safonov (piano) and Arensky (composition); then entered the St. Petersburg Cons. as a pupil of Rimsky-Korsakov (1891-1903); prof. of composition at the Moscow Institute until 1922; then lived in Paris; visited the U. S., where he appeared with considerable success as guest conductor of his own works (1929-31); came to the U. S. again in 1939, settling in New York. He became an American citizen on July 25, 1946. He continued to compose until the end of his long life. A concert of his works was presented on his 90th birthday in Town Hall, New York (Oct. 25, 1954) in the presence of the composer. A complete catalogue of his works is appended to his autobiography, *My Life.* His music is rooted in the Russian national tradition; influences of both Tchaikovsky and Rimsky-Korsakov are in evidence in his eary works; towards 1910 he attempted to inject some Impressionistic elements into his vocal compositions, but without signal success. His masterly sacred works are of historical importance, for he introduced a reform into Russian church singing by using nationally colored melodic patterns; in several of his Masses he employed instrumental accompaniment contrary to the prescriptions of the Russian Orthodox faith, a circumstance that precluded the use of these works in Russian churches. His *Missa Oecumenica* represents a further expansion towards ecclesiastical universality; in this work he makes use of elements pertaining to other religious music, including non-Christian. His instrumental works are competently written, but show less originality than his vocal music. His early *Lullaby* (1887) and the song, *Over the Steppes* still retain their popularity, and have been published in numerous arrangements.—Works: the operas: *Dobrinya Nikititch* (Moscow, Oct. 17, 1903); *Sister Beatrice* (Moscow, Oct. 25, 1912; suppressed after 3 performances as being irreverent); *The Dream of a Little Christmas Tree,* children's opera (1911); *The Castle Mouse,* children's opera (1921); *The Cat, the Fox, and the Rooster,* children's opera (1919); *Marriage,* comic opera after Gogol (1945-6; Berkshire Music Festival, Aug. 1, 1948); *Idylle forestière,* ballet divertissement for orch. (N. Y., 1925); incidental music to Ostrovsky's *Sniegurotchka* (Moscow, Nov. 6, 1900), A. Tolstoy's *Tsar Feodor* (Moscow, Oct. 26, 1898), and *Death of Ivan the Terrible* (1899). For orch.: Concert Overture in D minor (1892; St. Petersburg, March, 1893); *Elegy in Memory of Tchaikovsky* (1893; St. Petersburg, Dec. 31, 1898, Rimsky-Korsakov conducting); 5 symphonies (No. 1, 1893, St. Petersburg, Jan. 26, 1895; No. 2, 1909, Moscow, March 14, 1909; No. 3, 1920-23, Kiev, May 29, 1924; No. 4, 1923-24, N. Y., April 9, 1942; No. 5, 1936; Philadelphia, April 5, 1939); *Poème elégiaque* (Boston, March 29, 1946); *Festival Overture* (Indianapolis, Nov. 15, 1946); *Poème lyrique* (1948). Vocal works: *Liturgy of St. John Chrysostom* (Moscow, Oct. 19, 1898); *Laudate Deum* (Moscow, Nov. 24, 1915); *Liturgia Domestica* (Moscow, March 30, 1918); *Missa Oecumenica,* for soli, chorus, and orch. (Boston, Feb. 25, 1944); 84 choruses; 14 vocal quartets; 8 duets; 258 songs (some with orch.). Chamber music: 4 string quartets, 2 trios, violin sonata, cello sonata, 2 clarinet sonatas, 2 *Miniatures* for saxophone and piano. For piano: 2 sonatas (2nd in 1944); *Petits tableaux musicaux* (1947), etc. In 1917 Gretchaninov wrote a new Russian national anthem, *Hymn of Free Russia* (sung in N. Y. at a concert for the benefit of Siberian exiles, N. Y., May 22, 1917). Gretchaninov wrote 201 op. numbers in all; op. 201 is a chorus a cappella, *Have Mercy O God.* He publ. a book of reminiscences, *My Life* (Paris, in Russian, 1934; in English, with additions and introduction by N. Slonimsky, N. Y., 1952; contains a complete catalogue of works). See also M. Montagu-Nathan, *Contemporary Russian Composers* (N. Y., 1917); J. Yasser, *Gretchaninov's 'Heterodox' Compositions,* in the 'Mus. Quarterly' (July, 1942).

Grétry, André Ernest Modeste, outstanding dramatic composer; b. Liège, Feb. 8, 1741; d. Montmorency, near Paris, Sept. 24, 1813. His father was a violinist at the church of St. Martin in Liège; at the age of 9, Grétry was entered as chorister at the St. Denis Church, but was dismissed 2 years later. At 12, he began to study violin and singing; he learned music under Leclerc and the organist Nicolas Rennekin. At that time, an Italian opera company gave a season in Liège, and young Grétry thus received his first impulse towards dramatic music. Still his early works were instrumental; in 1758, he wrote 6 small symphonies; his next work was a Mass, which interested the ecclesiastical authorities; as a result, he was enabled (through the Canon du Harlez) to go to Rome (1759), where he entered the College de Liège, a school founded for the education of natives of Liège. There he studied diligently, and composed several church works, 6 string quartets, a flute concerto, and a light opera, *Le Vendemmiatrici,* which was produced in Rome in 1765. In 1766, he was in Geneva as a music teacher. He met Voltaire, who advised him to go to Paris; before his departure, he produced in Geneva a stage work, *Isabelle et Gertrude,* to a libretto by Favart, after Voltaire. He arrived in Paris in the autumn of 1767; he sought the patronage of aristocrats and diplomats; the Swedish ambassador, Count de Creutz, gave him the first encouragement by obtaining for him Marmontel's comedy, *Le Huron;* it was performed with Grétry's music at the Comédie-Italienne (Aug. 20, 1768). From then on, Grétry produced operas, one after another, without interruption even during the years of the French Revolution. The list of his operas is long; they include: *Lucile* (Paris, Jan. 5, 1769); *Le Tableau parlant* (Paris, Sept. 20, 1769; very popular); *Les deux avares* (Fontainebleau, Oct. 27, 1770); *Sylvain* (Paris, Feb. 19, 1770); *L'Amitié à l'épreuve* (Fontainebleau, Nov. 13, 1770); *L'Ami de la maison* (Fontainebleau, Oct. 26, 1771); *Zémire et Azor* (Fontainebleau, Nov. 9, 1771); *Le Magnifique* (Paris, March 4, 1773); *La Rosière de Salency* (Fontainebleau, Oct. 23, 1773); *Céphale et Procris, ou L'Amour conjugal* (Versailles, Dec. 30, 1773); *La fausse magie* (Paris, Feb. 1, 1775): *Les Mariages samnites* (3 acts, from the 1-act opera of 1768; Paris, June 12, 1776); *Amour pour amour* (Versailles, March 10, 1777); *Mat-*

roco (Chantilly, Nov. 12, 1777); *Le Jugement de Midas* (Paris, March 28, 1778); *Les fausses apparences, ou L'Amant jaloux* (Versailles, Nov. 20, 1778); *Les Événements imprévus* (Versailles, Nov. 11, 1779); *Aucassin et Nicolette, ou Les Moeurs du bon vieux temps* (Versailles, Dec. 30, 1779); *Andromaque* (Paris, June 6, 1780); *Émilie* (Paris, Feb. 22, 1781); *La double épreuve, ou Colinette à la Cour* (Paris, Jan. 1, 1782); *Le Sage dans sa retraite* (The Hague, Sept. 19, 1782); *L'Embarras de richesses* (Nov. 26, 1782); *La Caravane du Caire* (Fontainebleau, Oct. 30, 1783); *Théodore et Paulin* (Versailles, March 5, 1784); *Richard Coeur de Lion* (his greatest masterpiece; Paris, Oct. 21, 1784); *Panurge dans l'isle des lanternes* (Paris, Jan. 25, 1785); *Amphitrion* (Versailles, March 15, 1786); *Les Méprises par ressemblance* (Fontainebleau, Nov. 7, 1786); *Le Comte d'Albert* (Fontainebleau, Nov. 13, 1786); *Le Prisonnier anglois* (Paris, Dec. 26, 1787; with alterations, in 1793 as *Clarice et Belton); Le Rival confident* (Paris, June 26, 1788); *Raoul Barbe-Bleue* (Paris, March 2, 1789); *Aspasie* (Paris, March 17, 1789); *Pierre le grand* (Paris, Jan. 13, 1790); *Guillaume Tell* (Paris, April 9, 1791); *Cécile et Ermancé, ou Les deux couvents* (Paris, Jan. 16, 1792); *A Trompeur, trompeur et demi* (Paris, Sept. 24, 1792); *Joseph Barra* (Paris, June 5, 1794); *Denys le tyran, maître d'école à Corinthe* (Paris, Aug. 23, 1794); *La Rosière républicaine, ou La Fête de la vertu* (Paris, Sept. 3, 1794); *Callias, ou Nature et patrie* (Paris, Sept. 18, 1794); *Lisbeth* (Paris, Jan. 10, 1797); *Anacréon chez Polycrate* (Paris, Jan. 17, 1797); *Le Barbier de village, ou Le Revenant* (Paris, May 6, 1797); *Élisca, ou l'-Amour maternel* (Paris, Jan. 1, 1799); *Le Casque et les colombes* (Paris, Nov. 7, 1801); *Delphis et Mopsa* (Paris, Feb. 15, 1803). The merit of Grétry's operas lies in their melodies and their dramatic expression. He was not deeply versed in the science of music; yet despite this lack of craftsmanship in harmony and counterpoint, he achieved fine effects of vocal and instrumental writing. His operas suffered temporary eclipse when Méhul and Cherubini entered the field, but public interest was revived by the magnificent tenor, Elleviou, in 1801. The changes in operatic music during the next 30 years caused the neglect of Grétry's works. Nevertheless, Grétry—'the Molière of music' as he was called—founded the school of French opéra-comique, of which Boieldieu, Auber, and Adam have been such distinguished alumni. During his lifetime, he was greatly honored: he was elected a member of many artistic and learned institutions in France and abroad; the Prince-Bishop of Liège made him a privy councillor in 1784; a street in Paris was named for him in 1785; he was admitted to the Institut de France in 1795, as one of the first three chosen to represent the department of musical composition; in 1795 he was also appointed Inspector of the Paris Cons., but resigned in a few months; his bust was placed in the Grand Opéra foyer, and a marble statue in the entrance hall of the Opéra-Comique; Napoleon made him a Chevalier of the Legion of Honor in 1802, and granted him a pension of 4,000 francs in compensation for losses during the Revolution. Grétry bought 'L'Ermitage,' Rousseau's former residence at Montmorency, and lived there in retirement. He was married, and had several children, but survived them all. His daughter, Lucille (real name, Angélique-Dorothée-Lucie; b. Paris, July 15, 1772; d. there, Aug. 25, 1790), was a gifted musician who died young; at the age of 13, with some assistance from her father, she composed an opera, *Le Mariage d'Antonio,* which was produced at the Opéra-Comique, July 29, 1786; her second opera, *Toinette et Louis,* was produced on March 23, 1787. Gretry's *Mémoires ou Essais sur la musique* were publ. in 1789 (reprinted in 1797 with 2 additional vols. edited by his friend, Legrand; in German, in 1800 at Leipzig, with critical and historical annotations by K. Spazier; in 3 vols. by Mass in 1829 and an enlarged edition by P. Magnette, Liège, 1914). In these essays, Grétry set forth his views on the paramount importance of the just declamation of every syllable set to music. He also wrote a *Méthode simple pour apprendre à préluder en peu de temps avec toutes les resources de l'harmonie* (1802); *De la Vérité,* an ardent avowal of Republican tenets, with remarks on the feelings and the best means of exciting and expressing them by music (1803), and *Réflexions sur l'art,* in 6 vols., were never published. During the last years of his life he wrote *Réflexions d'un Solitaire;* his friends did not think its publication was advisable; the MS was considered lost until C. Malherbe discovered it in 1908; it was publ. in 4 vols., ed. by L. Solvay and E. Closson, in Brussels and Paris, 1919-22. Besides his dramatic works, Grétry composed a *De Profundis, Confiteor,* a Requiem, an antiphon, motets, and a good deal of instrumental music. Under the auspices of the Belgian government, a complete ed. of his works was begun in 1883 (edited by Gevaert, Closson, Radoux, E. Fétis, Wotquenne, Wouters, Wilder, Mathieu, Solvay, duBois, Mestdagh, S. Dupuis, Wambach, Jongen). — Cf. Comte de Livry, *Recueil de lettres écrites à Grétry, ou à son sujet* (Paris, 1809); A. J. Grétry (the composer's nephew), *Grétry en famille* (Paris, 1815); Gerlache, *Essai sur Grétry* (Liège, 1821); F. van Hulst, *Grétry* (Liège, 1842); L. de Saegher, *Notice biographique sur André Grétry* (Brussels, 1869); E. Gregoir, *André E. M. Grétry* (1883); M. Brenet, *Grétry* (Paris, 1884); C. Gheude, *Grétry* (Liège, 1906); H. de Curzon, *Grétry* (Paris, 1907); E. Closson, *Grétry* (Turnhout, 1907); P. Long des Clavières, *La Jeunesse de Grétry et ses débuts à Paris* (Besançon, 1921); P. Long des Clavières, *Les Ancêtres de Grétry,* in 'Revue musicale' (IV, 3, 1923); O. G. Sonneck, *Grétry,* in the 'Scheurleer-Festschrift' (1925); H. Wichmann, *Grétry und das musikalische Theater in Frankreich* (Halle, 1929); Romain Rolland, *Grétry,* in *Musiciens d'autrefois* (Paris, 1908; 2nd ed., 1925; English transl., London, 1915); J. E. Bruyr, *Grétry* (Paris, 1931); P. Lasserre, *Essay en 'Philosophie du gout musical'* (Paris, 1931); J. Sauvenier, *André Grétry* (Brussels, 1934); J. de Froidcourt, *43 Lettres inédites de Grétry à A. Rousselin, 1806-12* (Liège, 1937); Gérard-Gailly, *Grétry à Honfleur* (Paris, 1938); S. Clercx, *Grétry* (Brussels, 1944); G. de Froidcourt, *Grétry, Rouget de Lisle et la Marseillaise* (Liège, 1945).

Grevillius (grĕh-vē'-lyus), **Nils,** Swedish conductor; b. Stockholm, March 7, 1893. He studied there at the Academy of Music (1905-11), receiving 1st prize for the violin and the Prix Marteau; from 1911-14 was leader of the Royal Opera orch.; conducted the Swedish ballet season in Paris in 1922-23; then returned to Stockholm to conduct the Radio Orchestra.

Grey, Madeleine, French soprano; b. Villaines-le-Juhel, Mayenne, June 11, 1897. She made her début in Paris in 1921 with the first performance of Fauré's *Mirages;* thereafter she was identified with modern French music; was chosen to present French art songs at 3 international festivals (Venice, 1930; Siena, 1932; Florence, 1934); also toured South America.

Grieg, Edvard Hagerup, celebrated Norwegian composer; b. Bergen, June 15, 1843; d. there, Sept. 4, 1907. The original form of the name was Greig. His great-grandfather, Alexander Greig of Scotland, emigrated to Norway about 1765, and changed his name to Grieg (see J. Russell Greig, *Grieg and his Scottish Ancestry,* in Hinrichsen's 'Music Year Book,' 1952). Grieg received his first instruction in music from his mother, an amateur pianist. At the suggestion of the Norwegian violinist, Ole Bull, young Grieg was sent to the Leipzig Cons. (1858), where he studied piano with Plaidy and Wenzel; later with Moscheles; theory with E. F. Richter, Moritz Hauptmann, and Reinecke. He became immersed in the atmosphere of German Romanticism, with the esthetic legacy of Mendelssohn and Schumann; Grieg's early works are permeated with lyric moods related to these influences. In 1863, he went to Copenhagen, where he took a brief course of study with Niels Gade. In Copenhagen, he also met the young Norwegian composer, Rikard Nordraak, with whom he organized the Euterpe Society for the promotion of national Scandinavian music, in opposition to the German influences dominating Scandinavian music. The premature death of Nordraak at the age of 23 (1866) left Grieg alone to carry on the project. After traveling in Italy, he returned to Norway, where he opened a Norwegian Academy of Music (1867), and gave concerts of Norwegian music; he was also engaged as conductor of the Harmonic Society in Christiania (Oslo). In 1867 he married his cousin, the singer, Nina Hagerup. At that time he had already composed his 2 violin sonatas and the first set of his *Lyric Pieces* for piano, which used Norwegian motifs. On April 3, 1869, Grieg played the solo part in the world première of his piano concerto, which took place in Copenhagen. Thus at the age of 25, he established himself as a major composer of his time. In 1874 he wrote incidental music to Ibsen's *Peer Gynt;* the two orchestral suites arranged from this music became extremely popular. The Norwegian government granted him an annuity of 1600 crowns, which enabled him to devote most of his time to composition. Performances of his works were given in Germany with increasing frequency; soon his fame spread all over Europe. On May 3, 1888, he gave a concert of his works in London; he also presented recitals of his songs with his wife. He revisited England frequently; he received the honorary degree of Mus. Doc. from Cambridge (1894) and Oxford (1906). Other honors were membership in the Swedish Academy (1872), the French Academy (1890), etc. Despite his successes, Grieg was of a retiring disposition, and spent most of his later years in his house at Troldhaugen, near Bergen, avoiding visitors and shunning public acclaim. However, he continued to compose at a steady rate. His death, of heart disease, was mourned by all Norway; he was given a state funeral and his remains were cremated, at his own request, and sealed in the side of a cliff projecting at the fjord at Troldhaugen. Grieg's importance as a composer lies in the strongly pronounced nationalism of his music; without resorting to literal quotation from Norwegian folksongs, he succeeded in recreating their melodic and rhythmic flavor. In his harmony, he remained well within the bounds of tradition; the lyric expressiveness of his best works and the contagious rhythm of his dance-like pieces imparted a charm and individuality which contributed to the lasting success of his art. His unassuming personality made friends for him among his colleages; he was admired by Brahms and Tchaikovsky. The combination of lyricism and nationalism in Grieg's music led some critics to describe him as 'the Chopin of the North.' He excelled in miniatures, in which the perfection of form and the clarity of musical line are remarkable; the unifying purpose of Grieg's entire creative life is exemplified by his lyric pieces for piano. He composed 10 sets of these pieces in 34 years, between 1867 and 1901. His songs, which he wrote for his wife, are distinguished by the same blend of romantic and characteristically national inflections. In orchestral composition, Grieg limited himself to symphonic suites, and arrangements of his piano pieces; in chamber music, his 3 violin sonatas, a cello sonata, and a string quartet are examples of fine instrumental writing.—Works: For orch.: *In Autumn,* concert overture (op. 11, 1865); *Two Elegiac Melodies* for string orch. (op. 34, based on songs from op. 33; *The Wounded One* and *The Last Spring);* Concerto in A minor for piano and orch. (op. 16, 1868); *Norwegian Dances* (op. 35, 1881); *Holberg* Suite for string orch. (op. 40, 1884-85); *Peer Gynt* Suite No. 1 (op. 46, 1876; includes *Morning, Aase's Death, Anitra's Dance, In the Hall of the Mountain King); Two Melodies* for string orch. (op. 53, 1891; based on songs from op. 21 and op. 23: *Norwegian* and *First Meeting*); *Peer Gynt* Suite No. 2 (op. 55, 1876; includes *The Abduction and Ingrid's Lament, Arab Dance, Peer Gynt's Homecoming, Solveig's Song*); *Sigurd Jorsalfar Suite* (op. 56, 1872); *Two Norwegian Melodies* for string orch. (op. 63, 1894-95; based on melodies from op. 17: *In the Style of a Folksong* and *Cowkeeper's Tune and Peasant Dance*); *Symphonic Dances* (1898); *Evening in the Mountains* for oboe, horn, and strings (arranged from op. 68, No. 4; 1898); *At the Cradle* for string orch. (arranged from op. 68, No. 5; 1898); *Funeral March in Memory of Rikard Nordraak* for military band (arranged from the piano solo written in 1866); *Lyric Suite* (arranged from piano solos op. 54, 1891; includes *Shepherd Boy, Norwegian March, Nocturne, March of the Dwarfs).* Chamber music; Sonata in F for piano and violin (op. 8, 1865); Sonata in G minor for piano and violin (op. 13, 1867); string quartet in G minor (op. 27, 1877-78); Sonata in A minor for cello and piano (op. 36, 1883); Sonata in C minor for violin and piano (op. 45, 1886-87); string quartet in F (2 movements only; 1892). Choral works: *At a Southern Convent's Gate* (op. 20, 1871); 2 songs from *Sigurd Jorsalfar* (op. 22, 1870); *Album for Male Voices* (op. 30; 1877); *Landsighting* (op. 31, 1872); *Scenes from 'Olav Trygvason'* (op. 50, 1873); *Ave Maris Stella* (no opus number); *Four Psalms* (op. 74, 1906); he also wrote *The Bewitched One* for baritone with strings and 2 horns (op. 32, 1878); and the ballad, *Bergliot* for declamation and orch. (op. 42, 1870-71). He wrote the incidental music for Björnson's *Sigurd Jorsalfar* (Christiania, April 10, 1872) and Ibsen's *Peer Gynt* (Christiania, Feb. 24, 1876), from which the suites so named were taken. For piano: piano solos: 4 pieces (op. 1, 1862); *Poetic Tone-Pictures* (op. 3, 1863); *Humoresker* (op. 6, 1865); Sonata in E minor (op. 7, 1865); *Funeral March in Memory of Rikard Nordraak* (1866); 10 sets of *Lyric Pieces* (Book 1, op. 12, 1867; Book 2, op. 38, 1883; Book 3, op. 43, 1884); Book 4, op. 47, 1888; Book 5, op. 54, 1891; Book 6, op. 57, 1893; Book 7, op. 62, 1895; Book 8, op. 65, 1896; Book 9, op. 68, 1898; Book 10, op. 71, 1901; among the most famous individual numbers of the *Lyric Pieces* are: *Butterfly, Erotik,* and *To Spring* in Book 3; *March of the Dwarfs* in Book 5); *Norwegian Dances and Songs* (op. 17, 1870); *Scenes fom Peasant Life* (op. 19, 1872); *Ballad in the Form of Variations on a Norwegian Folksong* (op. 24, 1875); *Album Leaves* (op. 28, 1864, 1874, 1876, 1878); *Improvisations on Norwegian Folksongs* (op. 29, 1878); *Holberg Suite* (op. 40, 1884); *Norwegian Folk Melodies* (op. 66, 1896); *Norwegian Peasant Dances* (op. 72, 1902); *Moods* (op. 73, 1906); *6 Norwegian Mountain Tunes* (no opus number); 3 piano pieces (no opus number; Nos. 2 and 3 written in 1898 and 1891); arrangements for piano solo of a number of his songs and orchestral works; original piano duets: *Norwegian Dances for 4 Hands* (op. 35, 1881); *Valses-Caprices* (op. 37, 1883); 2nd piano parts to 4 piano sonatas by Mozart (1877).—Songs: 25 sets of songs to German and Norwegian words; of these, *I Love Thee* attained enormous popularity.

BIBLIOGRAPHY: E. Closson, *Grieg et la musique scandinave* (Paris, 1892); D. G. Mason, *From Grieg to Brahms* (N. Y., 1902); G. Schjelderup, *Edvard Grieg og hans vaerker* (Copenhagen, 1903); H. T. Finck, *Edvard Grieg* (N. Y., 1905; considerably enlarged and publ. as *Grieg and His Music,* 1909; new ed., 1929); E. M. Lee, *Edvard Grieg* (London, 1908); G. Schjelderup and W. Niemann, *Edvard Grieg: Biographie und Würdigung seiner Werke* (Leipzig, 1908); R. H. Stein, *Grieg* (Berlin, 1921); M. Beyer, *Edvard Grieg: Breve til Frants Beyer 1872-1907* (Christiania, 1923); P. de Stoecklin, *Edvard Grieg* (Paris, 1926); J. Röntgen, *Grieg* (The Hague, 1930); E. von Zschinsky-Troxler, *Edvard Grieg: Briefe an die Verleger der Edition Peters 1866-1907* (Leipzig, 1932); Y. Rokseth, *Grieg* (Paris, 1933); D. Monrad Johansen, *Edvard Grieg* (Oslo, 1934; in English, Princeton, N. J., 1938); K. G. Fellerer, *Edvard Grieg* (Potsdam, 1942); G. Abraham, ed., *Grieg, a Symposium* (London, 1948); J. Horton, *Grieg* (London, 1950); K. Dale, *Grieg Discoveries,* in the 'Monthly Musical Record' (Dec., 1954).

Grieg, Nina Hagerup, Norwegian singer, wife of Edvard Grieg; b. near Bergen, Nov. 24, 1845; d. Copenhagen, Dec. 9, 1935. Her father, Herman Hagerup, was a brother of Grieg's mother. She studied singing with Helsted; she met Grieg in Copenhagen, and married him on June 11, 1867. Her interpretations of Grieg's songs elicited much praise from the critics.

Griend, Koos van de, Dutch composer; b. Kampen, near Zwolle, Dec. 11, 1905; d. Amsterdam, Jan. 12, 1950. He studied in Amsterdam and in Berlin. Returning to Amsterdam in 1933, he developed energetic activities as pianist, conductor, and music critic. He wrote 2 symphonies, a violin concerto, and 2 string quartets; also music for films.

Griepenkerl, Friedrich Konrad, German music editor; b. Peine, Dec. 10, 1782; d. Brunswick, April 6, 1849. He taught esthetics at Hofwyl, Switzerland, then settled in Brunswick as professor at the Carolinum there. He published a *Lehrbuch der Aesthetik* (1827); edited (ably) Bach's instrumental works.

Griepenkerl, Wolfgang Robert, playwright and music theorist, son of preceding; b. Hofwyl, May 4, 1810; d. Brunswick, Oct. 16, 1868. He studied philosophy and literature at Berlin Univ.; taught art history at the Carolinum, Brunswick (1839) and at the Brunswick Cadet School (1840-47). He wrote the tragedies *Robespierre* (which inspired Litolff's well-known overture) and *Girondistes.* He also published *Das Musikfest, oder die Beethovener* (a novel, 1838; 2nd ed., 1841); *Ritter Berlioz in Braunschweig* (1843); *Die Oper der Gegenwart* (1847); and papers in 'Neue Zeitschrift für Musik.'—Cf. O. Sievers, *Robert Griepenkerl* (Brunswick, 1879); Th. W. Werner, *Wolfgang Robert Griepenkerls Schriften über Musik,* in 'Zeitschrift für Musikwissenschaft' II (1920).

Griesbach, John Henry, English composer; b. Windsor, June 20, 1798; d. London, Jan. 9, 1875. He was of German descent; he studied cello with his father, and played in the court band. His major work was an oratorio, *Belshazzar's Feast* (1835; revised and performed as *Daniel,* London, June 30, 1854); also wrote a number of overtures and cantatas. He was an amateur scientist and wrote several papers dealing with acoustics which remained in manuscript.

Griesbacher, Peter, German theorist and church music composer; b. Egglham, March 25, 1864; d. Regensburg, Jan. 28, 1933. He studied theology; was ordained priest in 1886; was instructor at the Franciscan church in Regensburg (from 1894); edited various publications for Catholic church music; wrote 40 Masses, secular cantatas, and songs (about 250 op. numbers). He began as a composer in the strict style of contrapuntal writing; his later works, in which he applied modern harmonies to Gregorian melodies, aroused considerable opposition. He published several manuals: *Lehrbuch des Kontrapunkts* (1910); *Kirchenmusikalische Stilistik und Formenlehre* (3 vols., 1912-13); *Glockenmusik* (1926).—Cf. M. Tremmel, *Peter Griesbacher* (Passau, 1935).

Griffes, Charles Tomlinson, outstanding American composer; b. Elmira, N. Y., Sept. 17, 1884; d. New York, April 8, 1920. He studied piano with a local teacher, Mary S. Broughton; also took organ lessons. In

1903, he went to Berlin, where he was a pupil of Gottfried Galston (piano), Rüfer and Humperdinck (composition). To eke out his living, he gave private lessons; also played his own compositions in public recitals. In 1907, he returned to the U. S., and took a music teacher's job at the Hackley School for Boys at Tarrytown, N. Y.; at the same time he continued to study music by himself; he was fascinated by the exotic art of the French Impressionists, and investigated the potentialities of Oriental scales. He also was strongly influenced by the Russian School, particularly Mussorgsky and Scriabin. A combination of natural talent and determination to acquire a high degree of craftsmanship elevated Griffes to the position of a foremost American composer in the Impressionist genre; despite changes of taste, his works retain an enduring place in American music. The best of these is *The White Peacock* for piano (1917; also for orch., Philadelphia, Stokowski conducting, Dec. 19, 1919) and the tone poem, *The Pleasure Dome of Kubla Khan,* after Coleridge (Boston Symph. Orch., Nov. 28, 1919). His works include further: *The Kairn of Koridwen,* dance drama for 5 woodwinds, celesta, harp, and piano (N. Y., Feb. 10, 1917); *Shojo,* Japanese pantomimic drama for 4 woodwinds, 4 muted strings, harp, and percussion (1917); *Poem* for flute and orch. (N. Y., Nov. 16, 1919); *2 Sketches on Indian Themes* for string quartet (1922); for piano: *3 Tone Pictures* (*The Lake at Evening, The Vale of Dreams,* and *The Night Winds;* 1915); *Fantasy Pieces* (*Barcarolle, Notturno,* and *Scherzo;* 1915); *Roman Sketches* (*The White Peacock, Nightfall, The Fountain of Acqua Paola,* and *Clouds,* 1917); Sonata in F (1921); vocal works: *These Things Shall Be,* for unison chorus (1917); songs to German texts (*Auf geheimen Waldespfade, Auf dem Teich,* etc.); songs to English words: *The First Snowfall, The Half-ring Moon, Evening Song; Tone Images* (*La fuite de la lune, Symphony in Yellow,* and *We'll to the Woods, and Gather May;* 1915); *2 Rondels* (*Come, love, across the sunlit land* and *This book of hours;* 1915); *3 Poems* (*In a Myrtle Shade, Waikiki,* and *Phantoms;* 1916); *5 Poems of Ancient China and Japan* (*So-Fei gathering flowers, Landscape, The Old Temple, Tears,* and *A Feast of Lanterns;* 1917); *3 Poems* (*The Lament of Ian the Proud, Thy Dark Eyes to Mine,* and *The Rose of the Night;* 1918); *An Old Song Re-sung* (1920).—Cf. W. T. Upton, *The Songs of Charles T. Griffes,* in the 'Mus. Quarterly' (July, 1923); M. Bauer, *Charles T. Griffes as I Remember Him,* in the 'Mus. Quarterly' (July, 1943); E. M. Maisel, *Charles Tomlinson Griffes* (N. Y., 1943).

Griller, Sidney, English violinist; b. London, Jan. 10, 1911. He studied at the Royal Academy of Music, London; organized a string quartet in the ensemble class of Lionel Tertis (with Jack O'Brien, 2nd violin; Philip Burton, viola, and Colin Hampton, cello); then gave numerous concerts as Griller Quartet, in Europe and America, specializing in modern music.

Grimaud, Yvette, French composer and pianist; b. Algiers, Jan. 29, 1922. She studied piano there, and gave concerts as a child in Europe. She later entered the Paris Cons., graduating with a premier prix in 1941. She composes in a modern manner, employing the ondes Martenot and experimenting with quarter-tones.—Works: *4 Chants d'Espace* for voice, ondes Martenot, and percussion; *Chant de Courbes* for 2 ondes Martenot and timpani; etc.

Grimm, Carl Hugo, American organist and composer; b. Zanesville, Ohio, Oct. 31, 1890; studied with his father; held various positions as organist in Cincinnati, taught composition at the Cincinnati Cons. (1907-31). He composed *Erotic Poem* for orch. (1927; received a prize of the National Federation of Music Clubs); a trumpet concerto; *Byzantine Suite* for orch.; *Montana,* symphonic sketch (Cincinnati, March 26, 1943); *An American Overture* (Cincinnati, Feb. 15, 1946); also organ music.

Grimm, Friedrich Melchior (Baron von), German writer; b. Regensburg, Dec. 26, 1723; d. Gotha, Dec. 18, 1807. He went to Paris in 1750 and remained there till the Revolution, frequenting literary and musical circles and taking an active part in all controversies; his *Lettre sur Omphale* in the 'Mercure de France,' 1752, took the side of Italian opera in the 'guerre des bouffons' but some years later he upheld Gluck against the Italian faction supporting Piccinni. He edited the *Correspondance littéraire, philosophique et critique,* which offers important data on French opera (standard ed. in 16 vols., Paris, 1877-82). He befriended the Mozarts on their first visit to Paris (see the many references to him in E. Anderson, *Letters of Mozart and His Family,* London, 1938). He also wrote a satire on J. Stamitz, *Le Petit Prophète de Boeh-*

misch-Broda; it is reproduced in English in O. Strunk's *Source Readings in Music History* (N. Y., 1950).—Cf. Carlez, *Grimm et la musique de son temps* (1872); Jullien, *La Musique et les philosophes* (1873); E. Schérer, *Melchior Grimm* (1887); E. Hirschberg, *Die Encyklopädisten und die französische Oper im 18. Jahrhundert* (1903); H. Kretzschmar, *Die 'Correspondance littéraire' als musikgeschichtliche Quelle* in 'Jahrbuch Peters' (1903); P. Nettl, *Der kleine Prophète de Boehmisch-Broda* (Esslingen, 1951).

Grimm, Heinrich, German composer; b. Holzminden, c. 1593; d. Brunswick, July 10, 1637. He studied theology at the Univ. of Helmstedt; in 1619, became rector of the Magdeburg town school; in 1631, when the town was destroyed, he fled with his family to Brunswick, where he became a cantor at the church of St. Catherine; subsequently at St. Andrea's church (1632-37). He was an exponent of the concerted style, with thorough-bass, at that time still a novel technique in Germany. His extant works include Masses, psalms, Passions, and several pedagogical works; published *Unterricht, wie ein Knabe nach der alten Guidonischen Art zu solmisieren leicht angeführt werden kann* (Magdeburg, 1624) and *Instrumentum Instrumentorum* (1629); prepared a combined edition of *Melopoeia seu melodiae condendae ratio* by Calvisius and *Pleiades Musicae* by Baryphonus (Magdeburg, 1630).—Cf. B. Engelke, *Magdeburgische Musikgeschichte* (1914); H. Lorenzen, *Der Cantor Heinrich Grimm; sein Leben und seine Werke mit Beitrag zur Musikgeschichte Magdeburgs und Braunschweigs* (Hamburg, 1940).

Grimm, Julius Otto, composer; b. Pernau, Latvia, March 6, 1827; d. Münster, Dec. 7, 1903. He studied philosophy at the Univ. of Dorpat; then lived in St. Petersburg; in 1851, he went to Leipzig, where he studied with Moscheles and Hauptmann; there he formed a close friendship with Brahms and Joachim. In 1855, he went to Göttingen; in 1860, obtained a position as conductor in Münster. During 40 years of his life there, he presented some 1500 orchestral works, ranging from Bach to the modern Russian school. He wrote a symphony (1874); a suite for string orch. in canon form; several cycles of songs, and albums of piano pieces.—Cf. F. Ludwig, *Julius Otto Grimm* (Leipzig, 1925); see also *Brahms im Briefwechsel mit J. O. Grimm* (Berlin, 1912).

Grimm, Karl, German cellist; b. Hildburghausen, April 28, 1819; d. Freiburg, Jan. 9, 1888. He was for half a century the first cellist at the Wiesbaden Opera; composed many cello pieces, some of which attained considerable popularity.

Grimm, Karl Konstantin Ludwig, German harpist; b. Berlin, Feb. 17, 1820; d. there, May 23, 1882. He enjoyed a considerable reputation as a harp soloist; also wrote various pieces for his instrument.

Grisar, Albert, Belgian dramatic composer; b. Antwerp (of German-Belgian parentage), Dec. 26, 1808; d. Asnières, near Paris, June 15, 1869. Although intended for a mercantile career, he ran away from his Liverpool employer, and studied for a short time (1830) with Reicha in Paris. Returning to Antwerp, he brought out *Le Mariage impossible* (Brussels, March 4, 1833), and obtained a government subsidy for further study in Paris. On April 26, 1836 he produced *Sarah* at the Opéra-Comique; then *L'An mille* (June 23, 1837), *La Suisse à Trianon* (March 8, 1838), *Lady Melvil* (Nov. 15, 1838, with Flotow), *L'Eau merveilleuse* (Jan. 31, 1839, with Flotow), *Le Naufrage de la Méduse* (May 31, 1839, with Flotow and Pilati), *Les Travestissements* (Nov. 16, 1839), and *L'Opéra à la cour* (July 16, 1840, with Boieldieu, Jr.). In 1840 he went to Naples for further serious study under Mercadante; returning to Paris in 1848, he brought out *Gilles ravisseur* (Feb. 21, 1848), *Les Porcherons* (Jan. 12, 1850), *Bonsoir, M. Pantalon* (Feb. 19, 1851), *Le Carillonneur de Bruges* (Feb. 20, 1852), *Les Amours du Diable* (March 11, 1853), *Le Chien du jardinier* (Jan. 16, 1855), *Voyage autour de ma chambre* (Aug. 12, 1855); *Le Joaillier de St. James* (revision of *Lady Melvil;* Feb. 17, 1862); *La Chatte merveilleuse* (March 18, 1862), *Bégaiements d'amour* (Dec. 8, 1864), and *Douze innocentes* (Oct. 19, 1865). He left, besides, 12 finished and unfinished operas; also dramatic scenes, over 50 *romances,* etc. His statue (by Brackeleer) was placed in the vestibule of the Antwerp Theater in 1870.—Cf. A. Pougin, *Albert Grisar* (Paris, 1870).

Grisart (grē-zahr'), **Charles Jean Baptiste,** French composer; b. Paris, Sept. 29, 1837; d. Compiègne, March 11, 1904. He is known for his light operas, the most popular of which were: *La Quenouille de verre* (1873), *Les trois Margots* (1877), *Le Pont d'Avignon* (1878), *Les Poupées de* *l'Infante* (1881), *Le Bossu* (1888), *Le petit Bois* (1893), *Voilà le roi!* (1894). He also wrote many piano pieces, Masses, *mélodies*, etc., and a quantity of transcriptions.

Griselle, Thomas, American composer; b. Upper Sandusky, Ohio, Jan. 10, 1891; d. Hollywood, Dec. 27, 1955. He studied at the Cincinnati College of Music; later took courses in Europe with Nadia Boulanger and Arnold Schoenberg; toured as accompanist of Alice Nielsen and other singers; then became associated with radio and motion pictures; in 1928, won the $10,000 prize of the Victor contest for American composers with his *Two American Sketches.* In 1939, settled in Hollywood. He wrote a number of semi-popular pieces, often with humorous intent, such as *A Keyboard Symphony* for 6 pianos (Providence, March 27, 1928); *Tutti-Frutti* and *Czerny Pilots a Flying Saucer* for piano, etc.

Grisi, Giuditta, Italian mezzo-soprano; b. Milan, July 28, 1805; d. Robecco d'Oglio, near Cremona, May 2, 1840. She was a niece of the famous contralto, Josephina Grassini; a cousin of the dancer, Carlotta Grisi, and the elder sister of the celebrated soprano, Giulia Grisi. She studied at the Milan Cons.; made her 1st appearance in Vienna in 1823; afterward sang with success in Italy and in Paris at the Théâtre-Italien under Rossini's management; retired in 1834 on her marriage to Count Barni. Bellini wrote for her the part of Romeo in *I Capuleti ed i Montecchi* (Venice, March 11, 1830); her sister sang Juliet.

Grisi, Giulia, celebrated Italian soprano; b. Milan, July 28, 1811; d. Berlin, Nov. 29, 1869. She studied with her sister, Giuditta, and with Filippo Celli and Pietro Guglielmi, son of the composer; made her first appearance at 17 as Emma in Rossini's *Zelmira;* won the admiration of Bellini, who wrote for her the part of Juliet in *I Capuleti ed i Montecchi* (Venice, March 11, 1830); she sang in Milan until 1832; dissatisfied with her contract and unable to break it legally, she fled to Paris, where she joined her sister at the Théâtre-Italien; she made her Paris début in the title role of Rossini's *Semiramide* (Oct. 16, 1832); her success was phenomenal, and for the next 16 years she sang during the winter seasons at the Théâtre-Italien. She made her London début in Rossini's *La gazza ladra* (April 8, 1834), and continued to visit London annually for 27 years. With Rubini, Tamburini, and Lablache, she appeared in Bellini's *I Puritani* and other operas; when the tenor Mario replaced Rubini, Grisi sang with him and Tamburini; she married Mario (her second husband) in 1844; toured the U. S. with him in 1854; retired in 1861, and lived mostly in London, making occasional visits to the continent; on one such visit to Berlin, she died of pneumonia.

Griswold, Putnam, American bass; b. Minneapolis, Dec. 23, 1875; d. New York, Feb. 26, 1914. He studied with A. Randegger in London, with Bouhy in Paris, Stockhausen in Frankfurt, and Emerich in Berlin; sang at the Berlin Opera in 1904; in 1904-5 toured the U. S. with Savage's company, appearing in the English version of *Parsifal;* from 1906-11 was a popular singer at the Berlin Opera; made his Metropolitan Opera début on Nov. 23, 1911, in the role of Hagen in *Götterdämmerung.* He was identified with the bass parts in Wagner's works until his death; German critics pronounced him the greatest foreign interpreter of these roles, and he was twice decorated by the Kaiser.

Grocheo, Johannes de (active in Paris about 1280), author of the treatise *Theoria* (circa 1300), important as a source of information on secular music of the Middle Ages. It is printed in the original Latin with German transl. by J. Wolf in 'Sammelbände der internationalen Musik-Gesellschaft' (1899-1900; vol. I, pp. 69-130); emendations were provided by H. Müller (op. cit., vol. IV, pp. 361-8). See Ernst Rohloff, *Studien zum Musiktraktat des Johannes de Grocheo* (Leipzig, 1930); also J. A. Westrup, *Medieval Song,* in *New Oxford History of Music* (London, 1954; vol. II, pp. 223-9).

Grofé, Ferde (Ferdinand Rudolph von), American composer, pianist, and arranger; b. New York, March 27, 1892. He attended N. Y. and California public schools; studied music with Pietro Floridia; then was engaged as viola player in the Los Angeles Symphony Orch., at the same time working as popular pianist and conductor in theaters and cafés; joined Paul Whiteman's band in 1920 as pianist and arranger; it was his scoring of Gershwin's *Rhapsody in Blue* (1924) that won him fame. In his own works, Grofé successfully applied jazz rhythms, interwoven with simple ballad-like tunes; his *Grand Canyon Suite* (Chicago, Nov. 22, 1931, Paul Whiteman conducting) has become very popular. Other light pieces in modern vein include *Broadway at Night, Mississippi Suite, Three Shades of Blue, Tabloid Suite* (N. Y., Jan. 25, 1933), *Symphony in Steel* (N. Y., Jan. 19, 1937), *Hollywood Suite, Wheels Suite, New England Suite, Metropolis, Aviation Suite,* etc.

Gröndahl, Agathe (Ursula) Backer-. See **Backer-Gröndahl.**

Gröndahl, Launy, Danish conductor and composer; b. Ordrup, near Copenhagen, June 30, 1886. He studied violin with Anton Bloch and Axel Gade, and theory with Ludolf Nielsen; later took music courses in Paris, Italy, Vienna, and elsewhere. Returning to Denmark, he became president of the Society of Young Musicians; then was appointed conductor of the Danish State Radio Orch., giving his first concert on Oct. 28, 1925. Among his works are a symphony (1919); violin concerto (1917); trombone concerto (1924); bassoon concerto (1943); 2 string quartets; violin sonata, and numerous piano pieces and songs.

Groningen, Stefan van, Dutch pianist and pedagogue; b. Deventer, Holland, June 23, 1851; d. Laren, March 25, 1926. He studied with Kiel in Berlin; gave concerts as a pianist; taught in various music schools in The Hague, Utrecht, and Leiden. He wrote mostly piano music, also a piano quartet.

Groot, Cor de, Dutch pianist and composer; b. Amsterdam, July 7, 1914. He studied at the Cons. there; in 1936 won the international contest prize in Vienna; then gave concerts in Europe and made numerous recordings. He has written a ballet *Vernissage* (1941); 2 piano concertos and a piano concertino (1931, 1932, 1939); a concerto for 2 pianos and orch. (1939); also pieces for piano solo.

Grosbayne, Benjamin, American conductor; b. Boston, April 7, 1893; studied at Harvard Univ. (B. A., 1917) and at the New England Cons.; conducting with Monteux and Weingartner; was engaged as violinist and conductor with various opera companies in the U. S.; from 1931-38 was head of the Music Dept. of Brooklyn College; in 1955 made guest appearances as conductor in Europe. He publ. *Techniques of Modern Orchestral Conducting* (Cambridge, Mass., 1956).

Grosheim, Georg Christoph, German composer; b. Kassel, July 1, 1764; d. there, Nov. 18, 1841. He played viola in the court orch. at Kassel; edited a music magazine 'Euterpe' in 1797-98; wrote biographical articles on composers, and corresponded with Beethoven. He composed 2 operas, *Titania* (1792) and *Das heilige Kleeblatt* (1793); also set the Ten Commandments for voices. His autobiography was published by G. Heinrichs (1926).

Grosjean (groh-zhăhn'), **Ernest,** nephew of Jean Romary Grosjean; French organist and composer; b. Vagney, Dec. 18, 1844; d. Versailles, Dec. 28, 1936. He studied in Paris with Boëly and Stamaty; was organist at Verdun Cathedral from 1868-1916; then organist at St. Antoine, Versailles; from 1888-1914 was editor of the 'Journal des Organistes.' He wrote many works for organ and a *Théorie et pratique de l'accompagnement du plainchant.*

Grosjean, Jean Romary, French organist and composer; b. Epinal, Jan. 12, 1815; d. St. Dié, Feb. 13, 1888. He was organist at the St. Dié Cathedral from 1839; he publ. a 2-vol. collection of organ works, *Album d'un organiste catholique,* which included some of his own compositions; also edited a complete collection of noëls and folksongs of Lorraine.

Grosvenor, Ralph L., American organist and teacher; b. Grosvenor's Corners, N. Y., Dec. 5, 1893. He studied organ with Huntington Woodman in N. Y., composition with Ernest Bloch. He served in World War I, and remained in France after service, taking lessons in organ with Poillot and Moissenet. Upon his return to the U. S., he occupied various organ positions in and around New York; also took vocal lessons, and appeared as tenor in local opera companies. He wrote a number of sacred choruses and semi-popular songs (*My Desire, Wishing,* etc.).

Grosz, Wilhelm (Will), Austrian composer; b. Vienna, Aug. 11, 1894; d. New York, Dec. 9, 1939. He studied composition with Franz Schreker in Vienna; then lived in Berlin (1928-33). In 1933 he went to London; in 1938 came to New York. He wrote an opera, *Sganarell,* after Molière (Dessau, Nov. 21, 1925); *Der arme Reinhold,* a 'danced fable' (Berlin, Dec. 22, 1928); a modern musical comedy *Achtung, Aufnahme!* (Frankfurt, March 23, 1930); *Jazzband,* for violin and piano (1924); a violin sonata (1925); a song cycle, *Liebeslieder.* As Will Grosz, he wrote light songs, among them the popular *Isle of Capri* (1934).

Grout, Donald Jay, American musicologist; b. Rock Rapids, Iowa, Sept. 28, 1902. He studied at Syracuse Univ. (A.B., 1923); then at Harvard (A.M., 1932; Ph.D., 1939); was instructor in music there (1936-42); then taught at the Univ. of Texas (1942-45); in 1945, appointed prof. of music at Cornell Univ. He held a Guggenheim Fellowship in 1951; editor of the 'Journal of the American Musicological Society' from 1948-52. He is the author of *A Short History of Opera,* an extensive study of the subject from the inception of opera to modern times (2 vols., N. Y., 1947).

Grove, Sir **George,** eminent English musicographer; b. London, Aug. 13, 1820; d. there, May 28, 1900. He studied civil engineering; graduated in 1839 from the Institution of Civil Engineers, and worked in various shops in Glasgow, and then in Jamaica and Bermuda. He returned to England in 1846, and became interested in music; without abandoning his engineering profession, he entered the Society of Arts, of which he was appointed secretary in 1850; this position placed him in contact with the organizers of the 1851 Exhibition; in 1852 he became secretary of the Crystal Palace. He then turned to literary work; was an editor of the *Dictionary of the Bible;* traveled to Palestine in 1858 and 1861 in connection with his research; in 1865 he became director of the Palestine Exploration Fund. In the meantime, he accumulated a private music library; began writing analytical programs for Crystal Palace concerts; these analyses, contributed by Grove during the period 1856-96, established a new standard of excellence in musical exegesis. Grove's enthusiasm for music led to many important associations; with Arthur Sullivan he went to Vienna in 1867 in search of unknown music by Schubert, and discovered the score of Schubert's *Rosamunde.* In 1868, he became editor of Macmillan's Magazine; in 1878, he visited America; he received many honors for his literary and musical achievements, among them the D. C. L., Univ. of Durham (1875); LL.D., Univ. of Glasgow (1885). In 1883 he was knighted by Queen Victoria. When the Royal College of Music was formed in London (1882), Grove was appointed director, and retained this post until 1894. His chief work, which gave him enduring fame, was the monumental 'Dictionary of Music and Musicians,' which Macmillan began to publ. in 1879. It was first planned in 2 vols., but as the material grew, it was expanded to 4 vols., with an appendix, its publication being completed in 1889. Grove himself contributed voluminous articles on his favorite composers, Beethoven, Schubert, and Mendelssohn; he gathered a distinguished group of specialists to write the assorted entries. The 2nd ed. of Grove's 'Dictionary' (1904-10), in 5 vols., was edited by Fuller Maitland; 3rd ed. (1927-28), by H. C. Colles; an American supplement, first publ. in 1920, edited by W. S. Pratt and C. H. N. Boyd, was expanded and republished in 1928; 4th edition, also edited by H. C. Colles, was publ. in 5 vols., with a supplementary volume, in 1940. Eric Blom was entrusted with the preparation of an entirely revised and greatly enlarged 5th ed., which was publ. in 9 vols. in 1954; it became the largest music reference book in the English language; Grove's original articles on Beethoven, Schubert, and Mendelssohn were publ. separately in 1951, since their bulk was out of proportion even in this 9-vol. ed.; new articles on these composers were included instead. Grove further publ. *Beethoven and His Nine Symphonies* (1896; new ed., 1948); contributed prefaces to Otto Jahn's *Life of Mozart* and Novello's *Short History of Cheap Music;* also contributed numerous articles to the musical press.—Cf. C. L. Graves, *The Life and Letters of Sir George Grove* (London, 1904); C. L. Graves, *George Grove: a Centenary Study* in 'Music & Letters' (1920).

Grové, Stefans, South African composer; b. Bethlehem, Orange Free State, July 23, 1922. He studied piano with his mother and his uncle; later with Cameron Taylor at the South African College of Music; then took courses with W. H. Bell in Cape Town and with Piston at Harvard Univ. (1953-54). In 1956, he was appointed instructor at the Peabody Cons., Baltimore. Grové's music is distinguished by clarity of formal presentation and a free flow of melodic line; the contrapuntal structure is often complex, but it is invariably cast within clearly outlined harmonies.—Works: clarinet sonata (1947); string trio (1948); *Elegy* for string orch. (Cape Town, July 9, 1948); Duo for violin and cello (1950); ballet, *Die Dieper Reg* (1950); piano trio (1952); trio for oboe, clarinet, and bassoon (1952); quintet for flute, oboe, viola, bass clarinet, and harp (1952); trio for oboe, clarinet, and bassoon (1954); flute sonata (1955); *Sinfonia Concertante* (Johannesburg, Oct. 23, 1956); quartet for flute, oboe, clarinet, and bassoon (1956).

Groven, Eivind, Norwegian composer; b. Lardal, Telemark, Oct. 8, 1901. He studied at the Oslo Cons. and later in Berlin. He has composed *Mot Ballade* (1933) and 2 symphonies (1938, 1946). He has also arranged about 500 Norwegian folksongs. He publ. *Temperering og Renstemning,* dealing with a new system of piano tuning according to natural intervals (1948).

Grovlez, Gabriel (Marie), French conductor, writer, and composer; b. Lille, April 4, 1879; d. Paris, Oct. 20, 1944. He studied at the Paris Cons. under Diémer, Lavignac, Gedalge, and Fauré; won 1st prize in piano there (1899); then taught piano at the Schola Cantorum from 1908; after an engagement as conductor at the Opéra-Comique and at the Théâtre des Arts, he was appointed conductor at the Paris Opéra in 1914; also conducted the Chicago Opera Co. (1921-22 and 1925-26). His compositions include the operas *La Princesse au Jardin* (Monte Carlo, 1920), *Psyché,* and *Cœur de rubis* (Nice, 1922); an opéra-bouffe, *Le Marquis de Carabas* (1925; won the Ville de Paris composition prize in 1936); 2 ballets, *Maïmouna* (Paris Opéra, April 25, 1921) and *Le Vrai Arbre de Robinson* (Chicago, 1921); symph. poems, *Madrigal lyrique, La Vengeance des Fleurs, Le Reposoir des amants; Dans le jardin,* for soprano, women's chorus, and orch.; violin sonata; cello sonata; more than 50 songs, and many piano pieces, including *Recuerdos, Deux études, A Child's Garden, Nocturne, Le Royaume puéril, Deux Impressions,* and the sets, *Almanach aux images* and *London Voluntaries;* was an editor of Rameau's works; edited the collection, *Les plus beaux airs de l'opéra français* (in 8 vols., Paris, 1924); publ. a book, *L'Initiation a l'orchestration* (Paris, 1944).

Grua, Carlo Luigi Pietro, Italian composer; b. Florence, c. 1665; date of death unknown. He was in Dresden from 1691 to 1694, first as singer in the electoral chapel, then as assistant Kapellmeister; his opera, *Camillo generoso,* was produced in Dresden in 1693; he next went to the Palatine court at Düsseldorf as assistant Kapellmeister; his opera, *Telegono,* was given there during the 1697 Carnival; he remained in Düsseldorf for a number of years, then went to Venice, where he produced 2 operas: *Il pastor fido* (1721) and *Romolo e Tazio* (1722).

Grua, Carlo Pietro, Italian composer; place and date of birth uncertain; d. Mannheim, June, 1773. He may have been a son or relative of Carlo Luigi Pietro Grua. He was Kapellmeister at Mannheim from about 1734 until his death; during this time, wrote 2 operas, *Meride* (1742) and *La clemenza di Tito* (1748); also 5 oratorios and a *Miserere.*

Grua, Francesco de Paula, or **Paolo,** Italian composer, son of Carlo Pietro Grua; b. Mannheim, Feb. 2, 1754; d. Munich, July 5, 1833. He studied with Holzbauer at Mannheim, then went to Bologna, where he was a pupil of Padre Martini, and to Parma, where he studied with Traetta. Returning to Mannheim, he became a member of the electoral orch.; in 1778, accompanied the court to Munich; became court conductor there in 1784. He wrote one opera, *Telemaco,* given at the Munich Carnival in 1780; also much church music, including 31 orchestral Masses.

Gruber, Franz Xaver, Austrian composer and organist; b. Unterweizburg, Nov. 25, 1787; d. Hallein, near Salzburg, June 7, 1863. He acquired fame as the composer of the Christmas carol, *Stille Nacht, Heilige Nacht.* Of a poor family, Gruber had to do manual work as a youth, but managed to study organ; by dint of perseverance he obtained, at the age of 28, his first position as church organist and schoolmaster at Oberndorf. It was there, on Christmas Eve, 1818, that a young curate, Joseph Mohr, brought him a Christmas poem to be set to music, and Gruber wrote the celebrated song. — Cf. K. Weinmann, *Stille Nacht, Heilige Nacht* (Regensburg, 1918).

Gruber, Georg, Austrian conductor; b. Vienna, July 27, 1904. He studied music at the Vienna Univ.; received his Ph.D. in 1928. In 1930, he became conductor of the famous Vienna Choir Boys, and toured with them throughout Europe, South America, and the U. S. He also arranged for his choir folksongs and choral works of the Renaissance period.

Gruenberg, Eugene, Austrian violinist; b. Lwow, Oct. 30, 1854; d. Boston, Nov. 11, 1928. He studied at the Vienna Cons. with Heissler (violin), Hellmesberger (ensemble playing), Bruckner and Dessoff (composition); then went to Leipzig, where he played in the Gewandhaus Orch. In 1891 he emigrated to America and joined the Boston Symph. Orch. (resigned in 1898); subsequently taught at the New England Cons. He wrote a symphony, which he conducted in Leipzig; *Suite im antiken Stil;* violin sonata; studies for violin, etc.; also wrote a cadenza to Brahms' violin concerto; publ. *The Violinist's Manual* (N. Y., 1897; rev. ed., 1919 as *Violin Teaching and Violin Studies,* with a preface by Fritz Kreisler), etc. — Cf. his article, *Stagefright,* in the 'Mus. Quarterly' (April, 1919).

Gruenberg, Louis, eminent American composer; b. near Brest Litovsk, Poland, Aug. 3, 1884. He was brought to the U. S. as an infant; studied piano with Adele Margulies in N. Y.; then went to Berlin, where he studied with Busoni (piano and composition); in 1912 made his début as pianist with the Berlin Philh.; intermittently took courses at the Vienna Cons., where he also was a tutor. In 1919, he returned to the U. S., and devoted his entire energy to composing. He was one of the organizers and active members of the League of Composers (1923); became a champion of modern music, and one of the earliest American composers to incorporate jazz rhythms in works of symphonic dimensions (*Daniel Jazz, Jazzettes,* etc.); from 1933-36, he taught composition at the Chicago Mus. College; then settled in Santa Monica, Calif. His opera, *The Emperor Jones,* to O'Neill's play, produced at the Metropolitan Opera, N. Y., Jan. 7, 1933, attracted a great deal of attention by its dramatic effects and novel devices, particularly in the use of percussion; it received the David Bispham medal. Other stage works: *The Witch of Brocken* (1912); *The Bride of the Gods* (1913); *Dumb Wife* (1921); *Jack and the Beanstalk* (libretto by John Erskine; N. Y., Nov. 19, 1931); *Queen Helena* (1936); *Green Mansions,* radio opera (CBS, Sept. 7, 1937); *Volpone,* opera (1945); *The Miracle of Flanders,* mystery play (1950). For orch.: 5 symphonies (No. 1, 1919; rev. in 1929; won the $5,000 RCA Victor prize in 1930; performed by Koussevitzky and the Boston Symph., Feb. 10, 1934); Nos. 2, 3, 4, 5 (1942-48); *Vagabondia* (1920); *The Hill of Dreams,* symph. poem (won Flagler prize; N. Y., Oct. 23, 1921); *Jazz Suite* (Cincinnati, March 22, 1929); *The Enchanted Isle,* symph. poem (Worcester Festival, Oct. 3, 1929); *Nine Moods* (1929); *Music for an Imaginary Ballet,* 2 sets (1929; 1944); *Serenade to a Beauteous Lady* (Chicago, April 4, 1935); 2 piano concertos; violin concerto (Philadelphia Orch., Dec. 1, 1944, Heifetz soloist). Vocal works: *Daniel Jazz,* for tenor and 8 instruments (N. Y., Feb. 22, 1925); *Creation,* for baritone and 8 instruments (N. Y., Nov. 27, 1926); *Animals and Insects,* for voice and piano; *Four Contrasting Songs;* etc.; also published 4 vols. of Negro spirituals. Chamber music: suite for violin and piano (1914); 2 violin sonatas (1912; 1919); *Indiscretions* for string quartet (1922); *Diversions* for string quartet (1930); 2 string quartets (1937; 1938); *Jazzettes* for violin and piano (1926); 2 piano quintets (1929; 1937); *Poem in Form of a Sonatina* for cello and piano (1925); *4 Whimsicalities* for string quartet (1923). Piano works: *Jazzberries, Polychromatics, Jazz Masks, 6 Jazz Epigrams, 3 Jazz Dances,* etc.

Gruhn, Nora, English soprano; b. London, March 6, 1908. She studied at the Royal College of Music. She has sung with the Cologne Opera (1930-31), at Covent Garden (1931-34), and at Sadler's Wells (1946-48). She has appeared as Gretel in *Hänsel and Gretel* some 400 times in England.

Grumiaux, Arthur, Belgian violinist; b. Villers-Perwin, March 21, 1921. He studied at the Brussels Cons. and with Enesco; received the Vieuxtemps Prize in 1939. Since 1945, he has been giving concerts in Europe and teaching at the Brussels Cons.

Grümmer, Paul, German cellist; b. Gera, Feb. 26, 1879. He studied in Leipzig and Berlin; in 1899 went to London as cellist at Covent Garden and a member of the Jan Kubelik string quartet; in 1913, he joined the Adolf Busch quartet; from 1926-33 he taught at the Musikhochschule, Cologne; from 1933-40, prof. at the Musikhochschule in Berlin; from 1940-45, at the Vienna Music Academy; since 1945, living in retirement at Zürich. He has written pedagogic works for the cello and has edited Bach's unaccompanied cello suites.

Grün, Jakob, violinist and teacher; b. Budapest, March 13, 1837; d. Baden, near Vienna, Oct. 1, 1916. He was a pupil of J. Böhm in Vienna and M. Hauptmann in Leipzig; in 1858 he became a member of the Weimar court orch.; he was in Hanover from 1861-5, then traveled for 3 years, settling in Vienna in 1868, as concertmaster at the court opera; from 1877 till his retirement in 1909, he was prof. at the Vienna Cons.

Grund, Friedrich Wilhelm, German composer; b. Hamburg, Oct. 7, 1791; d. there, Nov. 24, 1874. He was brought up in a musical family, his father having been a theater conductor. As a youth he studied the cello, but a nervous affliction forced him to give up a career as performer. He then devoted himself mainly to conducting. In 1819, he founded in Hamburg the 'Gesellschaft der Freunde des religiösen Gesanges,' which later became the Hamburg Singakademie. In 1828, was engaged to lead the newly established Philharmonic Concerts, a post he held until 1862. In 1867 he organized (with Karl Grädener) the Hamburg Tonkünstlerverein. He wrote several operas, which were not performed; a cantata *Die Auferstehung und Himmelfahrt Christi;* some chamber music for unusual combinations (octet for wind instruments and piano; quintet for oboe, clarinet, horn, bassoon, and piano; *Trio de Salon,* for piano 4-hands and cello); many piano pieces, which enjoyed considerable success and were praised by Schumann.

Grünenwald, Jean-Jacques, French composer; b. Annecy, Feb. 2, 1911. He studied at the Paris Cons. with Dupré (organ; 1st prize, 1935) and Busser (composition; 1st prize, 1937); won 2nd Grand Prix de Rome (1939).—Works: *Bethzabée,* symph. poem (1946); *Concert d'été,* for piano and orch. (1946); *Le bateau ivre,* for voices and instruments; organ music; piano pieces *(Fantasmagorie, Cahier pour Gérard,* etc.).—Cf. A. Machabey, *Portraits de trente musiciens français* (Paris, 1949; pp. 93-96).

Grüner-Hegge, Odd, Norwegian conductor and composer; b. Oslo, Sept. 23, 1899. He studied piano and composition in Oslo; then studied conducting with Weingartner. He made his début in Oslo, 1927; since 1932, conducting at the Oslo Opera; guest conductor in Berlin, Paris, Stockholm, etc. He has written mostly chamber music.

Grünfeld, Alfred, pianist and composer; b. Prague, July 4, 1852; d. Vienna, Jan. 4, 1924. He studied in Prague, and later at Kullak's Academy in Berlin; settled in Vienna in 1873, and established himself there as a popular concert pianist and teacher; he also made tours in other European countries, including Russia. He composed an operetta, *Der Lebemann* (Vienna, Jan. 16, 1903) and the comic opera, *Die Schönen von Fogaras* (Dresden, 1907), which were unsuccessful; made brilliant arrangements for piano of waltzes by Johann Strauss; also publ. piano studies and various other pieces (*Spanish Serenade, Hungarian Fantasy, Barcarolle, Impromptu,* etc.).

Grünfeld, Heinrich, well known cellist, brother of Alfred Grünfeld; b. Prague, April 21, 1855; d. Berlin, Aug. 26, 1931. He studied at the Prague Cons.; went to Berlin in 1876, and taught cello at Kullak's Academy; also played chamber music with X. Scharwenka and G. Hollander. He publ. a book of memoirs, *In Dur und Moll* (Berlin, 1924).

Grunn, John Homer, American pianist and composer; b. West Salem, Wisconsin, May 5, 1880; d. Los Angeles, June 6, 1944. He studied piano with E. Liebling in Chicago and then at Stern's Cons. in Berlin; taught piano at the Chicago Mus. College (1903-7), then was in Phoenix, Arizona; in 1910, he settled in Los Angeles as piano teacher. He became especially interested in Indian music, and wrote a number of pieces based on Indian motives: ballets *Xochitl* and *The Flower Goddess* (both on Aztec subjects); *Hopi Indian Dance* for orch.; *Zuni Indian Suite* for orch.; many songs (*From Desert and Pueblo,* etc.).

Grunsky, Karl, German music critic; b. Schornbach, March 5, 1871; d. Vaihingen, near Stuttgart, Aug. 2, 1943. He studied political science at the Univ. of Stuttgart; obtained his Ph.D. in 1893, and began a career as political journalist; also studied music; wrote music criticisms in Stuttgart and Munich papers. He publ. *Musikgeschichte des 19. Jahrhunderts* (Leipzig, 1902; 4th ed., in 2 vols., 1923); *Musikgeschichte des 17. Jahrhunderts* (Leipzig, 1905; 3rd ed., 1925); *Musikgeschichte des 18. Jahrhunderts* (Leipzig, 1905; 2nd. ed., 1914); *Musikästhetik* (Leipzig, 1907; 4th ed., 1923); *Anton Bruckner* (Stuttgart, 1922); *Franz Liszt* (Leipzig, 1925); *Hugo Wolf* (Leipzig, 1928); *Der Kampf um deutsche Musik* (Stuttgart, 1933); *Richard Wagner* (Stuttgart, 1933); *Volkstum und Musik* (Esslingen, 1934). He publ. transcriptions for 2 piano, 8-hands, of all the Bruckner symphonies; wrote program notes for the Bayreuth Festivals (1924); commentaries to performances of Bruckner's works, etc.; also *Die Technik des Klavierauszuges, entwickelt am dritten Akt von Wagners Tristan* (Leipzig, 1911; valuable; contains technical discussion of arranging).

Grunwald, Hugo, German-American pianist and teacher; b. Stuttgart, March 17, 1869; d. New York, Oct. 3, 1956. He studied music at the Stuttgart Cons.; emigrated in 1893 to the U. S., where he taught at the N. Y. College of Music and at the Lambert

School of Music. He was one of the founders of the Bohemian Club of New York (1905).

Gruppe, Paulo Mesdag, American cellist; b. Rochester, N. Y., Sept. 1, 1891. He studied at The Hague Cons., then in Paris with J. Salomon; won a scholarship at the Paris Cons., where he studied with P. Casals; made his début at The Hague in 1907, then toured Europe; in 1909 made his 1st appearance in the U. S.; was a member of the Letz Quartet and the Tollefsen Trio; in 1953 lived in New Haven; then in Mexico City.

Grützmacher, Friedrich (Wilhelm Ludwig), renowned German cellist; b. Dessau, March 1, 1832; d. Dresden, Feb. 23, 1903. He received his musical training from his father, a chamber musician at Dessau; at the age of 16, he went to Leipzig and produced such a fine impression that Ferdinand David secured for him the post of first cellist of the Gewandhaus Orch. (1849). In 1860, he went to Dresden, where he remained for more than 40 years, until his death, acting as teacher and chamber music player. Among his pupils were Hugo Becker and several other well known cellists. He wrote a cello concerto; *Hohe Schule des Violoncellspiels* (Leipzig, 1891); several books of cello studies, and numerous arrangements for cello of works by classical composers; also edited cello works by Beethoven, Mendelssohn, Chopin, and Schumann. His brother, **Leopold Grützmacher** (b. Dessau, Sept. 4, 1835; d. Weimar, Feb. 26, 1900), was also a cellist; he studied in Dessau, and later joined the Gewandhaus Orch. in Leipzig; after occupying various posts in theater orchestras, he settled in Weimar as teacher at the court chapel. He wrote 2 cello concertos and a number of salon pieces for his instrument. Leopold's son, **Friedrich** (b. Meiningen, July 20, 1866; d. Cologne, July 25, 1919), carried on the family tradition of cello-playing; was a pupil of his father as well as of his uncle; was a member of various theater orchestras in Budapest and elsewhere; finally settled in Cologne as teacher at the Cons. there. He publ. a number of valuable cello collections and transcriptions.

Guadagni (gwăh-dăh'-ñē), **Gaetano,** famous male contralto; b. Lodi, c. 1725; d. Padua, Nov., 1792. He began his career in Parma (1747); in 1748, he went to London, where he attracted the attention of Handel, who gave him contralto parts in *Messiah* and *Samson;* after many successful appearances in London, he sang in Dublin (1751-52); then went to Paris (1754) and to Lisbon (1755), where he studied with Gizziello. He then returned to Italy; in 1762, Gluck secured an engagement for him in Vienna to sing Orfeo in Gluck's opera. In 1769, Guadagni was again in London. In 1770 he sang in Munich; in 1772, he appeared in Venice; in 1776, he was summoned by Frederick the Great to Potsdam, receiving great acclaim; in 1777, he settled in Padua, where he continued to sing at churches. He was not only a fine singer but an excellent actor; also wrote various arias, one of which, *Pensa a serbarmi,* is preserved in the Bologna library.

Guadagnini (gwah-dah-ñē'-nē), family of famous violin makers of Piacenza, Italy. **Lorenzo** (1695-1745) used the label 'Laurentius Guadagnini, alumnus Antonius Stradivarius,' and he may have studied with Stradivarius in Cremona shortly before the latter's death in 1737; certainly he followed Stradivarius' models in his violin-making. Lorenzo's son, **Giovanni Battista** (b. Cremona, 1711; d. Turin, Sept. 18, 1786), received his training presumably from his father, and may have been with him at the shop of Stradivarius; he followed his father from Cremona to Piacenza in 1737; worked in Milan (1749-58); was in Parma (1759-71); then settled in Turin. His violins are regarded as the finest of the Guadagninis. His two sons, **Giuseppe** (1736-1805) and **Gaetano** (1745-1817), continued the family tradition and manufactured some good instruments, but failed to approach the excellence of their father's creations. Violin-making remained the family's occupation through four more generations in Turin; the last representative, **Paolo Guadagnini,** perished in the torpedoing of an Italian ship, on Dec. 28, 1942.—Cf. W. L. von Lütgendorff, *Die Geigen- und Lautenmacher vom Mittelalter bis zur Gegenwart* (Frankfurt, 1904); E. N. Doring, *The Guadagnini Family of Violin Makers* (Chicago, 1949).

Gualdo, Giovanni (John), Italian musician and wine merchant. He arrived in Philadelphia from London in 1767 and opened a store there; among other things, he sold instruments, taught violin, flute, guitar, and other instruments; also arranged music; presented concerts; the first of these, given in Philadelphia on Nov. 16, 1769, was devoted largely to Gualdo's own compositions, and may well be regarded as the earliest 'composer's concert' in America. He planned a return to Italy for trade purposes, but never carried out his intention. He died insane at the Pennsylvania hospital, Philadelphia, Dec. 20, 1771. His *6 easy evening entertainments for 2 mandolins or 2 violins with a thorough bass for the harpsichord or violoncello* are in MS in the Library of Congress, Washington, D. C.; the printed op. 2, *6 Sonates for 2 German flutes with a thorough bass* (his name appears here as Giovanni Gualdo da Vandero) is in the British Museum. Copies of both sets are owned by the N. Y. Public Library.—Cf. O. G. Sonneck, *Early Concert-Life in America* (Leipzig, 1907; pp. 70-74).

Guami, Francesco, Italian musician, brother of Gioseffe Guami; b. Lucca, circa 1544; d. there, 1601. He was trombonist at the court chapel in Munich (1568-80), and maestro di cappella at Baden-Baden (1580-88), at Venice (1593), and at Lucca (1598-1601). He wrote madrigals on the Venetian model, and some church music.—Cf. L. Nerici, *Storia della Musica in Lucca* (1879).

Guami, Gioseffe (Giuseppe), Italian organist and composer; brother of Francesco Guami; b. Lucca, circa 1540; d. there, 1611. He was organist at the court in Munich (1568-79), maestro di cappella at the court in Genoa (1585). From 1588-91 he was first organist at San Marco in Venice (while Giovanni Gabrieli was second organist); in 1591 he returned to Lucca as church organist. His surviving compositions include madrigals, motets, and toccatas; in his madrigals, he followed the Venetian school. Some of his Masses are reprinted in F. Commer's *Musica Sacra* (vols. 17 and 18); a toccata is included in L. Torchi's *L'Arte Musicale in Italia* (vol. 3).—Cf. L. Nerici, *Storia della Musica in Lucca* (1879); G. Benvenuti (editor), 'Istituzioni e Monumenti dell'Arte Musicale Italiana' vol. 1 (1931).

Guarneri (gwahr-nā'-rē), famous family of violin makers in Cremona. The Italian form of the name was Guarnieri; Guarneri was derived from the Latin spelling, Guarnerius; the labels invariably used the Latin form. **Andrea,** head of the family (b. Cremona, c. 1625; d. there, Dec. 7, 1698), was a pupil of Nicolo Amati; he lived in Amati's house from 1641 on; in 1653, after his marriage, he moved to his own house in Cremona, and began making his own violins, labeling them as 'Alumnus' of Amati, and, after 1655, 'ex alumnis,' often with the additional words of 'sub titolo Sanctae Theresiae.' Andrea's son **Pietro Giovanni,** known as 'Peter of Mantua' (b. Cremona, Feb. 18, 1655; d. Mantua, March 26, 1720), worked first at Cremona; then went to Mantua, where he settled; he also used the device 'sub titolo Sanctae Theresiae.' Another son of Andrea, **Giuseppe** (b. Cremona, Nov. 25, 1666; d. there, c. 1740), worked in his father's shop, which he eventually inherited; in his own manufactures, he departed from his father's model, and followed the models of Stradivarius. Giuseppe's son, **Pietro** (b. Cremona, April 14, 1695; d. Venice, April 7, 1762), became known as 'Peter of Venice'; he settled in Venice in 1725, and adopted some features of the Venetian masters, Montagnana and Serafin. **Giuseppe Bartolomeo,** known as 'Giuseppe del Gesù,' from the initials I H S often appearing on his labels (b. Cremona, Aug. 21, 1698; d. there, Oct. 17, 1744), was a son of Giuseppe. He became the most celebrated member of the family; some of his instruments bear the label 'Joseph Guarnerius Andreae Nepos Cremonae' which establishes his lineage as a grandson of Andrea. His violins are greatly prized; only Stradivarius excelled him in the perfection of instrumental craftsmanship; he experimented with a variety of wood materials, and also made changes in the shapes of his instruments during different periods of his work. Paganini used one of his instruments.—Cf. G. de Piccolellis, *Liutai antichi e moderni, genealogia degli Amati et dei Guarnieri* (Florence, 1886); Lütgendorff, *Die Geigen- und Lautenmacher vom Mittelalter bis zur Gegenwart* (Frankfurt, 1904; 4th ed., 1922, in dictionary form); H. Petherick, *Joseph Guarnerius, His Work and His Master* (London, 1906); A. Pougin, *Une famille de grands luthiers italiens;* H. Wenstenberg, *Joseph Guarnerius del Gesù Abbildungen und Beschreibungen seiner Instrumente aus seinen drei Perioden* (Berlin, 1921); W. H. Hill, *Violin Makers of the Guarneri Family, 1626-1762: their Life and Work* (London, 1931).

Guarnieri, Camargo, Brazilian composer and conductor; b. Tiété, State of São Paulo, Feb. 1, 1907. He studied piano in São Paulo with E. Braga and A. de Sá Pereira, composition and conducting with Lamberto Baldi; went to Paris in 1938 and studied composition and orchestration with Ch. Koechlin, conducting with Fr. Rühlmann; also gave concerts of his own works there. In 1940, he was conductor of the Philharmonic Society of São Paulo and director of the Côral Paulistano; also teacher at the São Paulo Cons. In 1942, and 1946-47, he visited the U. S. as conductor of his own works. His compositions include: for orch.: *Curuçá* (São Paulo, July 28, 1930, Villa-Lobos conducting); 1st piano concerto (São Paulo, Dec. 30, 1936; composer conducting, S. Lima soloist); *Dansa Brasileira* (São Paulo, March 7, 1941, composer conducting); violin concerto (Rio de Janeiro, Sept. 20, 1942; 1st prize, Free Library of Philadelphia Contest); *Overture Concertante* (São Paulo, June 2, 1943, composer conducting); 1st symph. (Boston Symph. Orch., Nov. 29, 1946, composer conducting); 2nd symph. (1946); 2nd piano concerto (CBS, April 16, 1947; 1st national prize in Brazil, 1946); *Uiapuro,* symph. poem (2nd prize of the Reichhold Music Award, 1947); *Prologo e Fuga* (Boston, Dec. 26, 1947); *Brasiliana,* orchestral suite (Rio de Janeiro, May 1, 1951, composer conducting); also piano pieces and songs, mostly published in Brazil. His *Chôros,* for piano and orch., shared first prize at the Caracas Music Festival, 1957.

Guastavino, Carlos, Argentinian composer; b. Santa Fé, April 5, 1914. He studied in Buenos Aires with Athos Palma. He has written mostly in miniature forms, for piano or for voice, on native folk rhythms. Among his larger works are a ballet, *Once Upon a Time* (1942); piano sonata (1946); violin sonata (1952).

Gudehus, Heinrich, German tenor; b. Altenhagen, near Celle, March 30, 1845; d. Dresden, Oct. 9, 1909. He first studied organ, and also taught school; then took up singing; made his début in Berlin in Spohr's *Jessonda* (Jan. 7, 1871). After several engagements in various German towns, he sang Parsifal in Bayreuth (July 28, 1882) with excellent success; was with the Dresden Opera from 1880-90; appeared in London (1884) in Wagnerian roles; was with the German Opera in N. Y. (1890-91); then returned to Germany.

Gueden, Hilde, Austrian soprano; b. Vienna, Sept. 15, 1917. Both her parents were musicians. She made her début in operetta at the age of 16; in 1939 the family moved to Switzerland; in 1941 she sang Zerlina in Munich; in 1942, made her début in Rome. In 1947 Gueden became a member of the Vienna State Opera; also appeared at La Scala, Milan; in 1950 received the title of Kammersängerin of the Vienna Opera. In 1948 she appeared at the Edinburgh Festival; was engaged by Rudolf Bing for the Metropolitan Opera, where she made her American début on Nov. 15, 1951 as Gilda; she sang in the American première of Stravinsky's opera *The Rake's Progress* (Feb. 14, 1953). She married L. Lacey Herman in 1952.

Guédron, Pierre, French composer; b. Châteaudun, 1565; d. Paris, 1621. He was a choir boy in the chapel of Cardinal de Guise, and later sang in the royal chapel (1590). In 1601, he was appointed composer of the King's Music. He wrote ballets for the court, which included solo songs. Some of his airs are included in *Airs de Cour* (1615-18), and other contemporary collections. He is regarded as a precursor of Lully in the creation of French ballet music. —Cf. H. Quittard, *L'Air de cour: Pierre Guesdron* in the 'Revue Musicale' (1905); H. Prunières, *Le Ballet de cour en France avant Benserade et Lully* (Paris, 1914); L. de la Laurencie, *Un Musicien dramatique du XVIIe siècle français: Pierre Guédron* in 'Rivista Musicale Italiana' (1922).

Guénin, (Marie) Alexandre, French violinist and composer; b. Maubeuge, Feb. 20, 1744; d. Etampes, Jan. 22, 1835. He showed a precocious talent, and was sent to Paris for study with Gaviniès (violin) and Gossec (composition). In 1771 he joined the orchestra of the Paris Opéra; later was active as conductor in the Paris society called Concert Spirituel; taught at the Ecole Royale de Chant. Several works were publ. in his lifetime: 6 symphonies; 6 violin duos; 6 string trios.—Cf. L. de la Laurencie, *L'Ecole française du Violon* (Paris, 1922).

Guenther, Felix, pianist and writer on music; b. Trautenau, Austria, Dec. 5, 1886; d. New York, May 6, 1951. He studied at the Vienna Cons.; then at the Univ. of Berlin, obtaining his Ph.D. there in 1913; became accompanist for many outstanding singers and instrumentalists; in 1937, came to the U. S.; was connected with various music publishers in N. Y.; made arrangements and edited classical anthologies. He publ. *Weingartner* (Berlin, 1918), *Schuberts Lied* (Stuttgart, 1928), and *Mein Freund Schubert* (Hamburg, 1928).

Guéranger (gā-rähn-zhā'), Dom **Prosper Louis Pascal;** French ecclesiastic scholar; b. Sable-sur-Sarthe, April 4, 1805; d. Solesmes, Jan. 30, 1875. As abbot of the Benedictine monastery at Solesmes, his research and writings gave the impetus to and laid the foundations for scholarly investigations leading to the restoration of Gregorian melodies. Dom Guéranger and the Benedictines of

Solesmes played a role of prime importance in the accomplishment of this work. He wrote *Institutions liturgiques* (3 vols., 1840-53; 2nd ed., 4 vols., 1878-85); *L'Année liturgique* (15 parts, 1840-1901; continued by Fromage); *Ste. Cécile et la Société Romaine* (1873; 8th ed., 1898).—Cf. G. Guépin, *Prosper Guéranger* (Le Mans, 1876); *Bibliographie des Bénédictins de la Congrégation de France* (Solesmes, 1889); Chamard, *Guéranger et l'abbé Bernier* (Angers, 1901); P. Delatte, *Dom Guéranger, abbé de Solesmes* (2 vols., Paris, 1909).

Guerra-Peixe, César, Brazilian composer; b. Petropolis, March 18, 1914. He played the guitar as a child; then began to study seriously; played violin in motion picture theaters. In 1934 he settled in Rio de Janeiro and took lessons in composition with H. J. Koellreutter, from whom he learned the theory of 12-tone music; he wrote a string trio (1945), a symphony (1946), wind trio (1948), and a nonet. In 1949 he changed his orientation and adopted a folkloric style based on native rhythms; his overture (1950) is in this folk style. His works have been performed in Germany and Russia as well as in the U.S.A. and by the BBC in London.—Cf. Vasco Mariz, *César Guerra-Peixe* in the compendium *Musica Brasileña Contemporanea* (Rosario, Argentina, 1952; in Spanish).

Guerrero (gär-rā'-rōh), **Francisco,** Spanish composer; b. Seville, 1527; d. there, Nov. 8, 1599. He was a pupil of his brother, Pedro, and for a short time of Morales. In 1545, he became maestro di cappella of Jaén cathedral; in 1548, he went to Seville as cantor at the cathedral there. In 1554, he was offered a similar post at the cathedral of Malaga, but declined it. In 1556, he was in Lisbon; in 1567, in Cordova; in 1570, in Santander; in 1574 he went to Rome; in 1588, he was in Venice, whence he undertook a pilgrimage to Palestine. His account of his journey, *El viaje de Jerusalem que hizo Francisco Guerrero,* was publ. in 1611, and went through numerous editions. As a composer, he was greatly appreciated by his contemporaries; but the comparisons with Morales or Victoria overestimate his importance.—Works: *Sacrae cantiones vulgo moteta* (1555); *Psalmorum, Liber I, accedit Missa defunctorum* (1559; 2nd ed., with Italian title, 1584); *Canticum beatae Mariae quod Magnificat nuncupatur, per octo musicae modos variatum* (1563); *Liber I missarum* (1566; contains 9 Masses for 4-5 voices and 3 motets for 4-8 voices); *Motteta* (1570); *Missarum Liber II* (1582; contains 7 Masses and a *Missa pro defunctis); Liber vesperarum* (1584; includes 7 psalms, 24 hymns, 8 Magnificats, Te Deum, etc.); *Passio . . . secundum Matthaeum et Joannem more Hispano* (1585); *Canciones y villanescas espirituales* (1589); *Mottecta* (1589); *Missa Saeculorum Amen* (1597), etc. Reprints have been made by Eslava (2 *Passiones)* in 'Lira Sacro-Hispana' and by Pedrell in 'Hispaniae Schola musica sacra' (in vol. II: *Magnificat, Officium defunctorum,* Passions, antiphonals, etc.; in vol. VI: a *Falso bordone).* The *Libro de música para vihuela, intitulado Orphénica Lyra* of Miguel de Fuenllana contains some works by Guerrero arranged for vihuela. Publication in Barcelona of Guerrero's *Opera omnia* was begun in 1955; vol. I contains *Canciones y villanescas espirituales,* transcribed by Vicente García.—Cf. R. Mitjana, *Francisco Guerrero, estudio crítico-biográfico* (Madrid, 1922).

Guerrini, Guido, Italian composer; b. Faenza, Sept. 12, 1890. He was a pupil of Consolini (violin), and Torchi and Busoni (composition) at the Liceo musicale at Bologna; prof. of harmony there (1919-23); prof. of composition at Parma Cons. (1924-28); director of Cherubini Cons. in Florence (1928-44); director of Bologna Cons. (1944-50); in 1951 appointed director of the Santa Cecilia Cons. in Rome.—Works: operas: *Zalebi* (1915), *Nemici* (Bologna, Jan. 19, 1921), *La vigna* (Rome, March 7, 1935), *Enea,* after Virgil (Rome, March 7, 1953); for orch.: *La cetra d'Achille; La befana; Visioni dell' antico Egitto* (2 pieces); *L'ultimo viaggio; Missa pro defunctis,* in memory of Marconi, for solo voices, chorus, and orch. (1939); *La città perduta,* biblical cantata (1942); *Tre liriche* for voice and orch. (1947); chamber music: *La città beata,* chamber cantata (1942); *Arcadia,* for oboe and piano; piano quintet; 2 string quartets; 2 trios; violin and cello pieces; *Le Suore,* 3 pieces for harp; vocal works: *Le fiamme su l'altare,* for voice, double string quartet, and 2 harps; songs. He also wrote the books: *Trattato di armonia complementare* (1922); *Origine, evoluzione e caratteri degli strumenti musicali* (1926); *Prontuario de tempi e colori musicali* (1939); *F. Busoni, la vita, la figura, l'opera* (Florence, 1944); *Appunti d'orchestrazione* (1945).

Guerrini, Paolo, Italian music historian; b. Bagnolo Mella, near Brescia, Nov. 18, 1880. He specialized in Italian sacred music; founded the periodical 'Brixia Sacra' (1910-25); in 1930, he began publication of the historical studies 'Memorie storiche della Diocesi di Brescia'; served further as archivist and librarian in Brescia. He also founded the 'Società bresciana di storia ecclesiastica' (1946); in 1936, he was appointed canon of the Brescia cathedral. He revived and transl. into Italian the music books of Cardinal Katschthaler *(Storia della musica sacra);* publ. *Storia della Cappella musicale del Duomo di Brescia e del Duomo di Salò* and *Storia della Musica sacra in Italia nei sec. XIX e XX.*

Guglielmi (gŏŏl-yel'-mē), **Pietro Alessandro,** Italian composer; b. Massa di Carrara, Dec. 9, 1728; d. Rome, Nov. 18, 1804. He studied with his father, Jacob Guglielmi, and with Durante at the Cons. Santa Maria di Loreto at Naples. His 1st comic opera, *Lo solachianello 'mbroglione,* was performed at Naples in 1757; during the next 10 years, he wrote 24 operas, including *Il ratto della sposa* (Venice, 1765) and *La sposa fedele* (Venice, 1767), which were played all over Europe and became highly popular. He went to London in 1767; during his 5 years there, conducted and wrote several operas, among them *Ezio* (Jan. 13, 1770), in which his wife, Lelia Achiapati, sang. He returned to Italy in 1772; in 1793, was appointed maestro di cappella of San Pietro in Vaticano by Pope Pius VI, and turned to church music; composed several oratorios, of which *Debora e Sisara* (1794) was regarded as his masterpiece. A detailed list of Guglielmi's operas is found in F. Piovano's articles on him and on his son in the 'Rivista Musicale Italiana' (1905 and 1910). See also G. Bustico, *Pietro Guglielmi* (Massa, 1899); A. Della Corte, *L'Opera comica italiana nel settecento* (Bari, 1923).

Guglielmi (gŏŏl-yel'-mē), **Pietro Carlo,** Italian composer, son of Pietro Alessandro Guglielmi; b. Naples, c. 1763; d. there, Feb. 28, 1817. After study at the Cons. di Santa Maria di Loreto at Naples, he went to Spain; his first operas were performed at Madrid in 1793 and 1794; then lived in Italy, producing operas in Naples, Florence, and Rome. He went to London in 1809; presented several operas at the King's Theatre; returned to Italy in 1810, and was appointed maestro di cappella to the Duchess Beatrice at Massa di Carrara. A list of his works, including some 40 operas, oratorios, and cantatas, was publ. by Francesco Piovano in the 'Rivista Musicale Italiana' (1909-10).

Gui, Vittorio, Italian composer and conductor; b. Rome, Sept. 14, 1885. He studied with Falchi at the Liceo Musicale di Santa Cecilia in Rome; began his career as conductor there with Ponchielli's *Gioconda* (Dec. 7, 1907); then conducted in Parma, Naples, and at La Scala in Milan (1923); was in Turin from 1925-28; finally settled in Florence, where he organized a permanent orchestra, which he conducted until 1940; also was a founder of the 'Maggio Musicale Fiorentino' (1933); he then gave concerts in Stockholm (1940) and Vienna (1941); from 1947 appeared in England as opera conductor. He composed an opera, *Fata Malerba* (Turin, May 15, 1927); the symphonic works *Giulietta e Romeo* (1902), *Il tempo che fu* (1910), *Fantasia bianca* (1919; an orchestral experiment making use of films), *Giornata di Festa* (1921). He has written a volume of critical essays, *Battute d'aspetto* (Florence, 1944), and a monograph on Boito's *Nerone* (Milan, 1924).

Guidetti (gwē-det'-tē), **Giovanni Domenico,** Italian ecclesiastic scholar; b. Bologna, 1530 (baptized Jan. 1, 1531); d. Rome, Nov. 30, 1592. After taking holy orders, he went to Rome, where he became Palestrina's pupil, and in 1575 was appointed 'cappellano' (a clerical beneficiary) and chorister in the papal choir. From 1576 to 1581, he worked with Palestrina on a revised edition of the Gradual and Antiphonary; but this work being forestalled by the publication of Leichtenstein's edition (Venice, 1580), he obtained permission to publish the services for everyday use: *Directorium chori ad usum sacro-sanctae basilicae Vaticanae* (Rome, 1582, and several reprints); *Cantus ecclesiasticus passionis Domini Nostri Jesu Christi* (Rome, 1586); *Cantus ecclesiasticus officii majoris* (Rome, 1587; new ed., 1619); also publ. *Praefationes in cantu firmo* (Rome, 1588).

Guido d'Arezzo (gwē'-dŏh dah-ret'-sŏh), known also as **Guido Aretinus;** famous reformer of musical notation and vocal instruction; b. c. 990; d. Pomposa, May 17, 1050. He received his education at the Benedictine abbey at Pomposa, near Ferrara. He left the monastery in 1025, as a result of disagreements with his fellow-monks, who were envious of his superiority in vocal teaching; he was then summoned by Bishop Theobald of Arezzo to the cathedral school there; it was because of this association that he became known as Guido d'Arezzo. The assertions that he traveled in France and spent several years at the monastery of

Saint-Maur des Fossés, near Paris (see, e. g., Dom G. Morin in 'Revue de l'art chrétien,' 1888) are not borne out by documentary evidence. Still more uncertain are the claims of his travels in Germany, and even in England. However this may be, his fame spread and reached the ears of Pope John XIX, who called him to Rome to demonstrate his system of teaching (1028). In his last years, he was a prior of the Camaldolite fraternity at Avellano. Guido's fame rests on his system of solmization, by which he established the nomenclature of the major hexachord Ut, Re, Mi, Fa, Sol, La, from syllables in the initial lines of the Hymn of St. John:

Ut queant laxis *Re*sonare fibris
*Mi*ra gestorum *Fa*muli tuorum,
*Sol*ve polluti *La*bii reatum,
Sancte Joannes.

No less epoch-making was Guido's introduction of the music staff of 4 lines, retaining the red *f*-line and the yellow *c*-line of his predecessors, and drawing between them a black *a*-line, above them a black *e*-line, and writing the plainsong notes (which he did *not* invent) in regular order on these lines and in the spaces:

New black line e————
Old yellow line c————
New black line a————
Old red line f————

He also added new lines above or below these, as occasion required; thus, Guido's system did away with all uncertainty of pitch. Another invention credited to Guido is the so-called Guidonian hand, relating the degrees of the overlapping hexachords to various places on the palm of the left hand, a device helpful in directing a chorus by indicating manually the corresponding positions of the notes. Opinions differ widely as to the attribution to Guido of all these innovations; some scholars maintain that he merely popularized the already-established ideas, and that solmization, in particular, was introduced by a German abbot, Poncius Teutonicus, at the abbey of Saint-Maur des Fossés. Guido's treatises are *Micrologus de disciplina artis musicae* (publ. by A. Amelli, Rome, 1904; ed. by J. Smits van Waesberghe, 1955); *Regulae de ignoto cantu; Epistola de ignoto cantu* (publ. in English in Strunk's *Source Readings in Music History,* N. Y., 1950).—Bibliography: L. Angeloni, *Sopra la vita, le opere ed il sapere di Guido d'Arezzo* (Paris, 1811); R. G. Kiesewetter, *Guido von Arezzo* (1840); G. Ristori, *Biografia di Guido Monaco d'Arezzo* (2nd ed., 1868); M. Falchi, *Studi su Guido Monaco di San Benedetto* (1882); J. Wolf, *Handbuch der Notationskunde* (vol. I); H. Wolking, *Guidos Micrologus de disciplina artis musicae und seine Quellen* (Emsdetten, 1930); J. Smits van Waesberghe, *De musico-paedogogico et theoretico Guidone Aretino eiusque vita et moribus* (in Latin; Florence, 1953); H. Oesch, *Guido von Arezzo* (Bern, 1954).

Guignon, Jean-Pierre (Giovanni Pietro Ghignone), violinist and composer; b. Turin, Feb. 10, 1702; d. Versailles, Jan. 30, 1774. He came to Paris from Italy in his youth; was engaged as music tutor to the dauphin, and persuaded the king to revive and bestow on him the title of Roi des Violons et Ménétriers, which had last been used in 1695; every professional musician in France was required to join a guild and to pay a fee to Guignon as holder of the title; so much opposition was aroused by this requirement that parliament considered the case and deprived Guignon of this prerogative. He wrote several books of concertos, sonatas, and duos for violin.

Guilbert, Yvette, famous French *diseuse* and folksong singer; b. Paris, Jan. 20, 1867; d. Aix-en-Provence, Feb. 2, 1944. She made her début in Paris as an actress in 1885; in 1890 she began her career as a café singer; at first she sang popular songs in Paris; later, as she toured Europe and the U. S., where she first appeared in 1896, she became noted for her interpretations of French folksongs; she regarded herself as primarily an actress rather than a singer. She wrote her memoirs, *La chanson de ma vie* (Paris, 1927) and *Autres Temps, autres chants* (Paris, 1946).

Guillemain, Gabriel, French violinist and composer; b. Paris, Nov. 7, 1705; d. there (suicide), Oct. 1, 1770. He was a member of the king's orch. and gave concerts as a virtuoso. He was one of the first French composers to write violin sonatas with a developed clavichord accompaniment. He also wrote several ballets and instrumental music for various combinations.—Cf. L. de la Laurencie, *L'École française de violon,* vol. II.

Guilmant (gēl-măhn'), **Alexandre (Félix),** eminent French organist and composer; b. Boulogne, March 12, 1837; d. Meudon, near Paris, March 29, 1911. He studied organ with his father, Jean-Baptiste Guilmant (1793-1890); took harmony lessons with Gustave Carulli in Boulogne. In 1860, he took an advanced course in organ playing with Lemmens in Brussels. Still as a child, he substituted for his father at the church of St.-Nicolas in Boulogne; at 20, he taught at Boulogne Cons. and conducted choral concerts. He then played organ in various churches in Paris, including St.-Sulpice (1863) and Notre Dame (1868); in 1871, he was appointed organist of Ste. Trinité, remaining at this post for 30 years. He was one of the founders of the Schola Cantorum (1894); in 1896, he was appointed prof. of organ at the Paris Cons.; also appeared as organ soloist with Paris orchestras and subsequently all over Europe and in the U. S. (1893-97). He was not only a virtuoso of the first rank, but a master in the art of improvisation; he formed a great school of students, among whom were René Vierné, Joseph Bonnet, Nadia Boulanger, Marcel Dupré, and the American organist, William Carl. He was a prolific composer of works for organ, which include 8 sonatas, 2 symphonies for organ and orch., 25 books of organ pieces, 10 books of *L'Organiste liturgiste;* there are also 3 Masses, psalms, vespers, motets, etc. Of greater importance than these are Guilmant's monumental editions of old masters: 'Archives des Maîtres de l'Orgue' (Paris, 1898-1914; 10 vols.) and 'École classique de l'orgue' (1898-1903); he also edited selected works of French composers performed at his historical concerts (1902-6); made numerous arrangements for organ of various classical works.—Cf. *À la mémoire de Alexandre Guilmant,* by his friends of the Schola (Paris, 1911); A. Eaglefield-Hull, *The Organ Works of Guilmant* in the 'Monthly Mus. Record' (Oct.-Nov., 1914); N. Dufourcq, *La musique d'orgue française* (Paris, 1949).

Guion (gī'-on), **David (Wendell Fentress),** American composer; b. Ballinger, Texas, Dec. 15, 1895. He studied piano with Leopold Godowsky in Vienna; returning to the U. S. in 1915, he occupied various teaching posts in Texas colleges; then lived in New York; finally settled in Pennsylvania. Guion devoted many years to collecting and arranging American folksongs; of these, *Turkey in the Straw, Arkansas Traveler,* and *Home on the Range,* in various transcriptions, have become extremely popular. His works for orch. include an African ballet suite, *Shingandi; Southern Nights Suite; Sheep and Goat Walking to the Pasture; Alley Tunes; Mother Goose Suite; Suite for Orch.* He also made many choral arrangements of American folksongs.

Guiraud (gē-roh'), **Ernest,** composer; b. New Orleans, June 23, 1837; d. Paris, May 6, 1892. He studied with his father, Jean Baptiste Guiraud; produced his 1st opera *Le roi David,* in New Orleans at the age of 15. He then went to Paris, which was his home for the rest of his life; studied at the Paris Cons., with Marmontel (piano) and Halévy (composition); won the Grand Prix de Rome in 1859 with his cantata, *Bajazet et le joueur de flûte.* He stayed in Rome for 4 years; then returned to Paris, where his 1-act opera, *Sylvie,* was produced at the Opéra-Comique (May 11, 1864). He was appointed prof. at the Cons. in 1876; among his students were Debussy, Gedalge, Loeffler, and others. He wrote the recitatives to Bizet's *Carmen* and completed the orchestration of Offenbach's *Contes d'Hoffmann.* His operas (all first performed in Paris) include *En prison* (March 5, 1869); *Le Kobold* (July 2, 1870); *Madame Turlupin* (1872); *Piccolino* (April 11, 1876, his most popular stage work); *Galante aventure* (March 23, 1882); *Frédégonde* (completed by Saint-Saëns; Dec. 18, 1895). He also wrote a ballet, *Gretna Green* (1873); 2 suites for orch.; *Arteveld,* an overture; a Caprice for violin and orch.; and a treatise on instrumentation.

Gulak-Artemovsky, Semyon Stepanovitch, Ukrainian singer and composer; b. in the Ukraine, Feb. 16, 1813; d. Moscow, April 17, 1873. He studied voice in Italy; sang at the Imperial Opera of St. Petersburg (1842-64); then lived in Moscow. His opera *Zaporozhets za Dunayem (A Cossack Beyond the Danube)* was produced in St. Petersburg on April 26, 1863, and subsequently acquired great popularity.

Gulbins, Max, German organist and composer; b. Kammetschen, East Prussia, July 18, 1862; d. Breslau, Feb. 19, 1932. He studied at the Hochschule in Berlin; was organist at Elbing from 1900-8, then went to St. Elizabeth's in Breslau. He wrote, for men's chorus and orch., *Sturmlied, An das Vaterland,* and *Burggraf Friedrich von Nürnberg;* also organ pieces.

Gulbranson, Ellen *(née* Norgren), Swedish soprano; b. Stockholm, March 4, 1863; d. Oslo, Jan. 2, 1947. She studied at the Stockholm Cons., then with Mathilde Marchesi in Paris for two years; returning to Stockholm, she made her concert début in 1886, her opera début in 1889; thereafter she continued in opera; in 1896 she sang the part of Brünnhilde at Bayreuth, with great success; she appeared repeatedly in this role for many Festival seasons. She also sang in Berlin, Paris, Moscow, Amsterdam, and London.

Gulda, Friedrich, Austrian pianist; b. Vienna, May 16, 1930. He studied with Bruno Seidlhofer; won first prize at the International Pianists' Contest in Geneva (1946); then toured in Europe (1947-48), South America (1949); made his American début in Carnegie Hall, N. Y., Oct. 11, 1950; other concerts in the U. S. and Canada in the following seasons.—Cf. Erich Jantsch, *Friedrich Gulda. Die Verantwortung des Interpreten* (Vienna, 1953).

Gumbert, Ferdinand, German composer; b. Berlin, April 22, 1818; d. there, April 6, 1896. He was first trained by his father for book-selling, but he pursued his musical studies, developing a particular interest in opera. After a short study of singing, he appeared at the Cologne Opera (1840-42); in 1842 he settled in Berlin as a voice teacher and also began to compose. His songs, written in a facile, eclectic style, enjoyed a considerable vogue. He produced several operettas in Berlin: *Der kleine Ziegenhirt* (Jan. 21, 1854), *Bis der Rechte kommt* (Nov. 20, 1856), etc., which were not successful. He was also a translator of opera librettos from French and Italian; publ. *Musik, Gelesenes und Gesammeltes* (Berlin, 1860).—Cf. W. Neumann, *Ferdinand Gumbert* (Kassel, 1856).

Gumpeltzhaimer, Adam, German composer; b. Trostberg, c. 1559; d. Augsburg, Nov. 3, 1625. He studied music with Father Jodocus Enzmüller at the monastery of St. Ulric in Augsburg; then became musician to the Duke of Württemberg; from 1581 to 1621 he was cantor at St. Anna, Augsburg. Works: *Erster (zweiter) Teil des Lustgärtleins teutsch und lateinischer Lieder mit drei Stimmen* (1591 and 1611); *Erster (zweiter) Teil des Wirtzgärtleins 4 stimmiger geistlicher Lieder* (1594 and 1619); *Psalmus LI octo vocum* (1604); *Sacri concentus octonis vocibus modulandi cum duplici basso in organorum usum* (1601 and 1614; 2 parts); *10 geistliche Lieder mit 4 Stimmen* (1617); *2 geistliche Lieder mit 4 Stimmen; 5 geistliche Lieder mit 4 Stimmen von der Himmelfahrt Jesu Christi; Newe teutsche geistliche Lieder mit 3 und 4 Stimmen* (1591 and 1594); many other works in MS. A number of Gumpeltzhaimer's motets have been reprinted in Bodenschatz' *Florilegium Portense,* Schadaeus' *Promptuarium* and Vintzius' *Missae.* O. Mayr edited a selection of his works in the 'Denkmäler der Tonkunst in Bayern' (X, 2).—Cf. O. Mayr, *Adam Gumpeltzhaimer* (Munich, 1908).

Gumpert, Friedrich Adolf, German horn player; b. Lichtenau, April 27, 1841; d. Leipzig, Dec. 31, 1906. He studied with Hammann in Jena; from 1864, played 1st horn in the Gewandhaus Orch., Leipzig.—Works: *Praktische Hornschule;* a *Solobuch* for horn (difficult passages from operas, symphonies, etc.); *Hornquartette* (2 books); *Hornstudien;* and orchestral studies for clarinet, oboe, bassoon, trumpet, and cello.

Gumprecht, Armand J., American organist and composer; b. Boston, Mass., June 26, 1861; d. Washington, D. C., March 13, 1943. He studied violin with C. Eichler, organ with J. Singenberger and S. B. Whitney; from 1890 he was organist in various churches in Washington. From 1891 to 1918, was prof. of music and organist at Georgetown Univ.; from 1912-26, conductor of the Washington 'Sängerbund.' He wrote 4 Masses (with orch.), piano pieces, songs.

Gumprecht, Otto, German music critic; b. Erfurt, April 4, 1823; d. Meran, Feb. 6, 1900. He studied law in Halle and Berlin, but developed an interest in music, and began writing music criticism in 1849, continuing until 1889, when he suffered a stroke of paralysis. He publ. *Musikalische Charakterbilder* (1869); *Neue Charakterbilder* (1876); *Richard Wagner und der Ring des Nibelungen* (1873); *Unsere klassischen Meister* (2 vols., 1883-85) and *Neuere Meister* (2 vols., 1883); the last two are continuations of the *Charakterbilder;* he also edited 5 vols. of *Erlesene musikalische Meisterwerke.*

Gundry, Inglis, English composer; b. London, May 8, 1905. He studied at Oxford Univ.; then at the Royal College of Music in London with Vaughan Williams. — Works: operas: *Naaman* (1938), *The Return of Odysseus* (1941), *The Partisans* (1946), *Avon* (1949); a ballet, *Sleep* (1943); for orch.: *Comedy Overture* (1939), *Symphonic Fantasy* (1948); string quartet; duo for clarinet and viola, etc.

Gungl, Joseph, famous Hungarian bandmaster and popular composer; b. Zsámbék, Dec. 1, 1810; d. Weimar, Jan. 31, 1889. He played the oboe in an artillery regiment in the Austrian army, and later became that band's conductor; he wrote a number of marches and dances, which became extremely popular; traveled with his band all over Germany. In 1843, he established his own band in Berlin; made an American tour in 1849; then returned to Europe and lived mostly in Munich and Frankfurt.

Gunn, Glenn Dillard, American pianist and music critic; b. Topeka, Kans., Oct. 2, 1874. He studied at Leipzig Cons. with Carl Reinecke (piano); appeared as pianist in German cities; returning to the U. S. in 1900, he taught at the Chicago Mus. College (1901-5); was piano soloist with the Chicago Symph. Orch. In 1915 he founded 'The American Symph. Orch. of Chicago,' the object of which was the performance of American works and the engagement of American soloists. He was music critic for the Chicago 'Tribune' (1910-14) and the Chicago 'Herald and Examiner' (1922-36); in 1940, was appointed music critic of the Washington 'Times-Herald.' He publ. *A Course of Lessons on the History and Esthetics of Music* (1912) and *Music, Its History and Enjoyment* (1930).

Gunn, John, Scottish cellist and writer on music; b. Edinburgh, c. 1765; d. there, c. 1824. He went to London in 1790, where he taught cello and flute; returned to Edinburgh in 1795. He publ. *Forty Scotch Airs arranged as trios for flute, violin and violoncello; The Art of Playing the German Flute on New Principles; The Theory and Practice of Fingering the Violoncello* (London, 1793); *An Essay, Theoretical and Practical, on the Application of Harmony, Thorough-Bass, and Modulation to the Violoncello* (Edinburgh, 1801), and a valuable work, commissioned by the National Society of Scotland, *An Historical Inquiry respecting the Performance on the Harp in the Highlands of Scotland from the earliest Times until it was discontinued about the year 1734* (Edinburgh, 1807).

Gunsbourg, Raoul, Rumanian-French impresario; b. Bucharest, Dec. 25, 1859; d. Monte Carlo, May 31, 1955. After directing opera companies in Russia, he became the director of the Monte Carlo Opera; his first important production there was the stage version of *Damnation of Faust* by Berlioz (Feb. 18, 1893). Throughout the half-century of his active management in Monte Carlo, Gunsbourg produced a great number of new operas by important composers, among them Massenet (7), Saint-Saëns (3), Fauré (2), and one of each by Puccini, Ravel, and others. He produced at Monte Carlo and elsewhere several of his own operas (he wrote the piano scores, and the orchestration was done by L. Jehin); of these *Le vieil aigle,* after Maxim Gorky's fable (Monte Carlo, Feb. 13, 1909), had a modicum of success.

Gura, Eugen, operatic baritone; b. Pressern, near Saatz, Bohemia, Nov. 8, 1842; d. Aufkirchen, Bavaria, Aug. 26, 1906. He studied in Vienna and in Munich; he sang in Munich (1865-67), Breslau (1867-70), Leipzig (1870-6), obtaining extraordinary success; then was in Hamburg (1876-83) and Munich (1883-95), He was particularly impressive in Wagnerian roles; his performance of Hans Sachs was greatly praised. He publ. *Erinnerungen aus meinem Leben* (Leipzig, 1905). His son, **Hermann Gura** (b. Breslau, April 5, 1870), was also a baritone; like his father, he specialized in Wagnerian roles; after a successful career as an opera singer in Germany, he settled in Berlin as voice teacher.

Guridi, Jesús, Spanish composer; b. Vitoria, Basque province of Alava, Sept. 25, 1886. He studied in Madrid, at the Schola Cantorum in Paris, in Brussels (with Jongen), and in Cologne. He returned to Spain in 1909; became organist at Bilbao, where he remained until 1939; then moved to Madrid; appointed prof. of organ at the Madrid Cons. in 1944. During his 30 years in Bilbao, he promoted the cause of Basque folk music; publ. an album of 22 Basque songs. His zarzuelas make frequent use of Basque folk music; of these, *El caserio* (Madrid, 1926) attained enormous success in Spain; other stage works are *Amaya,* lyric drama in 3 acts (Bilbao, 1920), *La meiga* (Madrid, 1928), and *Mirentxu,* an idyll in 2 acts; he further wrote a symph. poem, *An Adventure of Don Quixote;* a *Sinfonia pirenáica; Basque Sketches* for chorus and orch.; an orch. suite, *10 Basque Melodies* (very popular in Spain); a number of choral works a cappella on Basque themes; 4 string quartets; pieces for piano; various songs.

Gurlitt, Cornelius, German composer; b. Altona, Feb. 10, 1820; d. there, June 17, 1901. He was a member of an artistic family; his brother, Louis Gurlitt, was a well-known landscape painter. He studied piano with Johann Peter Reinecke in Altona, and with Weyse in Copenhagen, where he went in 1840. In 1845, he made a journey through Europe; he met Schumann, Lortzing, Franz, and other eminent composers.

In 1864 he was appointed organist of the Altona cathedral, retaining this post until 1898; also taught at the Hamburg Cons. (1879-87). He wrote an opera, *Die römische Mauer* (Altona, 1860); another opera, *Scheik Hassan,* was not performed. He further composed 3 violin sonatas, 3 cello sonatas, several cycles of songs, etc. He is chiefly remembered, however, by his numerous piano miniatures, in Schumann's style; a collection of these was publ. by W. Rehberg, under the title, *Der neue Gurlitt* (2 vols.; Mainz, 1931).—Cf. Paul T. Hoffman, *Neues Altona* (Jena, 1929; vol. II).

Gurlitt, Manfred, German conductor and composer; b. Berlin, Sept. 6, 1890. He was of an artistic family; his grandfather was the well-known landscape painter Louis Gurlitt, whose brother was the composer Cornelius Gurlitt. He studied in Berlin with Humperdinck (composition) and Karl Muck (conducting); rapidly progressed as a professional conductor; was a coach at the Berlin Opera (1908) and at the Bayreuth Festival (1911); theater conductor in Essen and Augsburg; conductor and music director at the Bremen Opera (1914-27); then at the Berlin Opera and on the German radio. After 1933, he was deprived of his position by the Nazi régime; in 1939 he settled in Japan, as teacher and conductor; organized the Gurlitt Opera Company in Tokyo. Among his works are the operas *Die Heilige* (Bremen, Jan. 27, 1920), *Wozzeck* (Bremen, April 22, 1926; written almost at the same time as Alban Berg's *Wozzeck), Soldaten* (1929), *Nana* (1933), *Seguidilla Bolero* (1937), *Nordische Ballade,* and *Wir schreiten aus; Drei politische Reden* for baritone, men's chorus, and orch.; *Goya Symphony* (1950); *Shakespeare Symphony* (1954) for 5 solo voices and orch.; songs with orch.; concertos for piano, for violin, for cello; piano quartet, songs.

Gurlitt, Wilibald, German musicologist; b. Dresden, March 1, 1889. He is a grandnephew of the composer Cornelius Gurlitt, and a cousin of Manfred Gurlitt. He studied musicology at Heidelberg with P. Wolfrum and at the Leipzig Cons. with Hugo Riemann; received his Ph.D. in 1914 with a dissertation on Michael Praetorius; subsequently was assistant to Riemann. He served in World War I; was a war prisoner in France. After the Armistice he became a lecturer at the Univ. of Freiburg; was prof. of musicology there until 1937, when he was prevented by the Nazi régime from continuing his teaching; resumed his post in 1945. His investigations of the organ music of Praetorius led him to construct (in collaboration with Oscar Walcker) a 'Praetorius organ' which was to reproduce the tonal quality of the period. This created the impetus for a new movement in Germany, the aim of which was to give performances of historic works played on contemporaneous instruments. — Publications: *Burgundische Chanson und deutsche Liedkunst des 15. Jahrhunderts* (Basel, 1924); *François-Joseph Fétis* (Brussels, 1930); *Johannes Walter und die Musik der Reformationzeit* in 'Luther-Jahrbuch' (Munich, 1933); *Johann Sebastian Bach, der Meister und sein Werk* (Berlin, 1936; 3rd ed., Basel, 1949; English transl., St. Louis, 1954). Among his many editions are organ works of Michael Praetorius; vol. 17 of the collected works of Praetorius; facsimile reprint of Praetorius' *De Organographia* (Kassel, 1929); a reprint of Johann Walter's *Lob und Preis der löblichen Kunst Musica* (Kassel, 1938); also new editions of 16 chansons by Gilles Binchois and 12 *Liebesgesänge* by Paul Fleming (Kassel, 1948). In 1952 he became editor of the 'Archiv für Musikwissenschaft.' For a complete list of his writings, see his autobiographical article in 'Die Musik in Geschichte und Gegenwart.'

Gurney, Ivor, English song composer; b. Gloucester, Aug. 28, 1890; d. Dartford, Kent, Dec. 26, 1937. He was a chorister at Gloucester Cathedral; studied at the Royal College of Music in London with Stanford and Vaughan Williams; served in World War I, was wounded and gassed, and could never recover his physical and mental health; the 2 vols. of his war poems illustrate the turmoil of his inner life. After the Armistice, Gurney began to compose songs; 27 were publ. before his death, and several more were included in a 2-vol. edition of his melodies publ. posthumously. Gurney's gift was not for larger forms; he was at his best in his songs; he also wrote 5 *Western Watercolors* and 5 Preludes for piano and some violin pieces. A memorial Gurney issue of 'Music & Letters' with articles by Vaughan Williams, Walter de la Mare, and others, was publ. in 1938.

Gusikoff, Michel, American violinist and composer; b. New York, May 15, 1895. He studied violin with Franz Kneisel and composition with Percy Goetschius; made his début in 1920; was concertmaster of the Philadelphia Orch., N. Y. Symphony Orch., and NBC Orch.; also associate conductor of the Pittsburgh Symph. Orch. He made violin arrangements of songs by Gershwin; also wrote an *American Concerto* for violin and orch.

Gutheil-Schoder, Marie, German dramatic mezzo-soprano; b. Weimar, Feb. 10, 1874; d. there, Oct. 4, 1935. She studied in Weimar, made her début there in 1891; sang with the court opera until 1900, when she went to the Vienna Opera, becoming an outstanding singer-actress in such roles as Carmen, Elektra, Salome; in 1926 she was appointed stage director of the opera. She married the composer and conductor Gustav Gutheil. See L. Andro, *Marie Gutheil-Schoder* (1923).

Gutmann, Adolph, German pianist; b. Heidelberg, Jan. 12, 1819; d. Spezia, Oct. 27, 1882. He lived mostly in Paris, where he studied with Chopin, and became a close friend of his. He publ. an album of *Etudes caractéristiques* which were quite popular in the 19th century, and much salon music for piano. He was also a successful performer whose virtuoso technique made him popular with audiences.

Guyot, Jean, Flemish musician, also known under the names of Jean de Chatelet and Johannes Castileti; b. Chatelet (Hainaut) in 1512; d. Liège, March 11, 1588. He studied at the Univ. of Louvain, and received the degree of licencié-es-arts on March 22, 1537; in 1545 he was chaplain at St. Paul's in Liège; published his first motets in Antwerp in 1546; was later maître de chapelle at the Cathedral of St. Lambert in Liège; on Nov. 1, 1563, appointed music master at the Imperial Court in Vienna; he returned to Liège in Aug., 1564, and remained maître de chapelle at the Cathedral of St. Lambert to his death—Cf. C. Lyon, *Jean Guyot* (Charleroi, 1876).

Guy-Ropartz. See **Ropartz, Guy.**

Guzikov, Michal Jozef, famous performer on the xylophone; b. Szklow, Poland, Sept. 2, 1806; d. Aachen, Oct. 21, 1837. Of a Jewish musical family, he showed precocious talent; with four relatives he traveled all over Europe; his virtuosity on the xylophone was extraordinary, and elicited praise from the public as well as from celebrated musicians, among them Mendelssohn. Guzikov's programs consisted of arrangements of well-known works and also his own pieces; his most successful number was a transcription of Paganini's *La Campanella*.—Cf. S. Schlesinger, *Josef Guzikov* (Vienna, 1936).

Gyrowetz (gē'-roh-vets), **Adalbert,** prolific composer; b. Budweis, Bohemia, Feb. 19, 1763; d. Vienna, March 19, 1850. He studied organ with his father, a local choirmaster; then went to Prague, where he studied law; at the same time, began to compose band pieces and waltzes; he was befriended by Count Franz von Fünfkirchen, who was a music lover, and whose secretary he became. For the private orch. of Count von Fünfkirchen, Gyrowetz wrote 6 symphonies in Haydn's style; later, when he was in Vienna, he showed these works to Mozart, who encouraged him, and arranged for a performance of one of Gyrowetz's symphonies. From Vienna, he traveled through Italy; in Naples, he studied with Sala and Paisiello. In 1789, he went to Milan, Genoa, and finally to Paris, where several of his works were accepted by publishers. He then moved to London, where one of his pieces was performed at a Haydn concert (March 23, 1792). He was commissioned to write an opera, *Semiramide,* for the Pantheon Theatre, but before the announced performance, the opera building burned down, and with it perished the manuscript of *Semiramide.* After 3 years in London, he returned to the continent, eventually settling in Vienna (1793), where he became Kapellmeister at the Vienna Opera (1804-31). In Vienna, he enjoyed a great reputation as composer, and his name was often coupled with Beethoven's in public prints. He composed a number of operas, which were performed, one after another, at the Vienna Opera: *Selico* (Oct. 15, 1804); *Agnes Sorel* (Dec. 4, 1806); *Die Junggesellen-Wirtschaft* (June 18, 1807); *Die Pagen des Hertzogs von Vendome* (Aug. 5, 1808); *Der betrogene Betrüger* (Feb. 17, 1810); *Der Augenarzt* (his most successful opera; Oct. 1, 1811); *Das Winterquartier in Amerika* (Oct. 30, 1812); *Robert* (July 15, 1813); *Helene* (Feb. 16, 1816); *Aladin* (Feb. 7, 1819); *Der blinde Harfner* (Dec. 19, 1827); *Der Geburtstag* (Feb. 11, 1828); *Felix und Adele* (Aug. 10, 1831); also several operettas and *Singspiele.* In 1834, he produced in Dresden an opera, *Hans Sachs,* using essentially the same literary material as Wagner's *Meistersinger.* He further wrote a number of ballets; much church music; some 60 symphonies; about 60 string quartets; 30 trios; about 40 violin sonatas, as well as piano pieces and songs. The historical reasons for the rapid decline of Gyrowetz's repute as a composer after his death are not easy to explain; attempted revivals of his music proved futile. Gyrowetz publ. his autobiography (Vienna, 1848); it was brought out in an annotated edition by Alfred Einstein (Leipzig, 1915); numerous references to Gyrowetz are found in the Haydn literature; see also K. Mey, *A. Gyrowetz und seine neu aufgefundene Hans Sachs-Oper* in 'Die Musik' (Jan., 1903).

Gysi (gē'-sē), **Fritz,** Swiss musicologist; b. Zofingen, Feb. 18, 1888. He studied at the Basel Cons., at Zürich Univ., and at Berlin Univ.; in 1921 became lecturer in music at the Univ. of Zürich; in 1930, was made prof.; also music critic of the 'Tages-Anzeiger' in Zürich. — Books: *Mozart in seinen Briefen* (1921); *Max Bruch* (1922); *Claude Debussy* (1926); *Richard Wagner und die Schweiz* (1929); *Richard Strauss* (1934); *Hans Georg Nägeli* (1936).

H

Haapanen, Toivo, Finnish musicologist; b. Karvia, May 15, 1889; d. Asikkala, July 22, 1950. He studied music and philosophy at the Univ. of Helsinki; in 1925, appointed to its faculty. He specialized in bibliographical work and research in Finnish music of the Middle Ages.—Writings: Catalogue of manuscripts of the Middle Ages in the library of the Univ. of Helsinki (I. *Missalia,* 1922; II. *Gradualia, Lectionaria missae,* 1925; III. *Breviaria,* 1932; also *The Neume Fragments in the Univ. Library at Helsinki* 1924); *Die Finnen,* in Adler's 'Handbuch.'

Haarklou (hahr'-kloo), **Johannes,** Norwegian composer; b. Söndfjord, near Bergen, May 13, 1847; d. Oslo, Nov. 26, 1925. He studied at the Leipzig Cons.; then in Berlin with Haupt, Kiel, and Bungert; for 40 years (1880-1920) he was organist at the old Akers Church in Oslo; also conducted symphonic concerts there for 3 seasons. His 5 operas have not made their way beyond Norway, but among the works more generally known is an oratorio, *Skapelsen* (*The Creation,* 1891; Oslo, 1924). He further wrote 4 symphonies and *Olafs-Legende* for orch.; a violin sonata; piano pieces, choruses, and organ works.

Haas, Joseph, eminent German composer; b. Maihingen, March 19, 1879. He studied with Max Reger in Munich and with Karl Straube in Leipzig (organ). In 1911 he was appointed composition teacher at the Stuttgart Cons.; in 1921 became prof. at the Institute of Church Music in Munich; also taught at the Hochschule für Musik in Munich (retired in 1950). Through the long years of his pedagogical activities, Haas established himself as one of the most reputable teachers in Germany. At the time of his retirement, a Joseph Haas Society was organized in Munich, with the aim of issuing bulletins regarding his works. As a composer, Haas is equally estimable, but his music has failed to gain popularity outside his circle. He wrote more than 100 opus numbers. His principal works are: operas: *Tobias Wunderlich* (Kassel, Nov. 24, 1937) and *Die Hochzeit des Jobs* (Dresden, July 2, 1944); oratorios, *Die heilige Elisabeth* (1931), *Christnacht* (1932), *Das Lebensbuch Gottes* (1934), *Das Lied von der Mutter* (1939), *Das Jahr in Lied* (1952), *Die Seligen* (Kassel, April 12, 1957); *Variations on a Rococo Theme* for orch.; *Ouvertüre zu einem frohen Spiel* (1943); 2 string quartets (1908, 1919); trio for 2 violins and piano (1912); many song cycles. He publ. a biography of Max Reger (Bonn, 1949); contributed articles to various publications.—Cf. *Festgabe J. Haas* (a collection of articles by his students and colleagues on his 60th birthday, Mainz, 1939); a catalogue of works compiled by K. G. Fellerer (issued by the Haas Society, 1950; 2nd ed., 1953); K. Laux, *J. Haas* (Mainz, 1931; 2nd ed., 1954); special issue of the 'Zeitschrift für Musik' (on his 75th birthday, March, 1954).

Haas, Monique, French pianist; b. Paris, Oct. 20, 1906. She studied at the Paris Cons. with Lazare Lévy; became greatly interested in modern music, and gave numerous concerts all over Europe in programs of 20th-century composers; also appeared with orchestras in modern concertos. She is married to the composer Marcel Mihalovici.

Haas, Pavel, Czech composer; b. Brno, June 21, 1899; d. in the concentration camp at Auschwitz (Oswiecim), Oct. 17, 1944. He studied piano and composition in Brno; was a soldier in the Austrian army in World War I; after the Armistice, continued his study with Petřzelka and later with Janáček. He settled as a private teacher in Brno; tried to leave the country when Czechoslovakia was occupied by the Germans, but did not succeed; in 1941 he was placed in a concentration camp in Terezin; in Oct. 1944 he was sent to Auschwitz, and put to death there. Despite the tragic circumstances of the last years of his life, he continued to compose even in the concentration camp.—Works: opera, *Charlatan,* to his own libretto (Brno, April 2, 1938); incidental music to various plays produced in Czechoslovakia; symphony (1941; unfinished); 4 string quartets; wind quintet; several piano suites and other pieces; songs. His extant manuscripts are preserved in the Moravian Museum in Brno.

Haas, Robert Maria, distinguished musicologist; b. Prague, Aug. 15, 1886. He received his primary education in Prague; then studied music history in the universities of Prague, Berlin, and Vienna; received his Ph.D. at the Univ. of Prague for his dissertation *Das Wiener Singspiel* (1908). He then was assistant prof. at the Institute for Music History in Vienna (1908-09); from 1910-14 was engaged as theater conductor in various German cities; during World War I was in the Austrian army; in 1920 was appointed chief of the music division of the National State Library in Vienna; in 1923 became instructor at the Vienna Univ.; in 1929, appointed prof. there. Throughout this period he was active in various musical societies; contributed to many publications; was engaged in editorial work.—Writings: *Gluck und Durazzo im Burgtheater* (Vienna, 1925); *Die Wiener Oper* (Vienna, 1926); *Wiener Musiker vor und um Beethoven* (Vienna, 1927); *Die estensischen Musikalien* (Regensburg, 1927); *Die Musik des Barocks,* in Bücken's 'Handbuch der Musikwissenschaft' series (1928); *Aufführungspraxis der Musik* (ibid., 1931); *Mozart* (Potsdam, 1933; 2nd ed., 1950); *Bruckner* (Potsdam, 1934); *Bach und Mozart in Wien* (Vienna, 1951). He edited the symphonies of Bruckner, publ. by the International Bruckner Society (1935-45); for the 'Denkmäler der Tonkunst in Österreich' edited the works of Umlauf, Gassmann, Eberlin, Monteverdi, Gluck, and Schenk.

Haase, Hans, German musicologist; b. Neumünster (Schleswig-Holstein), May 12, 1929. He studied musicology at Kiel Univ. (1950-55) with Hans Albrecht, Friedrich Blume, Anna A. Abert, and Kurt Gudewill; also took courses at the Univ. of Innsbruck with Wilhelm Fischer and Karl Koch. In 1954 he joined the editorial staff of 'Die Musik in Geschichte und Gegenwart'; in 1957 became its editor; contributed a number of articles to it; also various papers to musical journals (mainly on German music of the Renaissance, but also on contemporary music).

Hába, Alois, notable composer of quarter-tone music; b. Vizovice, Moravia, June 21, 1893. He studied at the Prague Cons. with V. Novák and with Franz Schreker in Vienna and Berlin (1917-23). He became interested in the folk music of the Orient, which led him to consider writing in smaller intervals than the semitone; he was also influenced in this direction by Busoni's ideas. His first work in the quarter-tone system was a string quartet (1919); in another string quartet (No. 5, Op. 15, 1923) he applied an even smaller division, the sixth-tone. He notated these fractional intervals by modified or inverted sharps and flats. The piano manufacturing firm A. Förster constructed for him a quarter-tone piano. In 1923 Hába established a class of composition in fractional tones at the State Cons. in Prague, forming a large group of students from all parts of the world, among them his brother Karel Hába, Slavko Osterc of Yugoslavia, Necil Kazim Akses of Turkey, and others. He publ. an important manual of modern harmony, *Neue Harmonielehre des diatonischen, chromatischen, Viertel-, Drittel-, Sechstel-, und Zwölfteltonsystems* (Leipzig, 1927), accounting for new usages introduced by him in his classes; he further publ. *Die Harmonischen Grundlagen des Vierteltonsystems* (Prague, 1922) and *Von der Psychologie der musikalischen Gestaltung* (Prague, 1925). As a composer he has developed a 'non-thematic' method of writing (i.e., without repetition of patterns, or development). His most important work is the opera *Die Mutter,* in quarter-tones, produced in Munich on May 17, 1931; other operas with the application of quarter-tones are *Nová Země* (1935) and *Thy Kingdom Come* (1940); works in fractional tones include ten string quartets (1919-53); duo for 2 violins; fantasy for violin solo; fantasy for viola and piano; fantasy for cello and piano; symph. fantasy *The Path of Life* (Prague Festival, Sept. 6, 1935); 3 nonets for winds and strings (1931-53); violin concerto (1954); 10 fantasies for a quarter-tone piano; 2 suites for a quarter-tone guitar, etc. He has also written a considerable amount of music for ordinary instruments, in a diatonic style, and in the twelve-tone system. During the period of 1945-52, he wrote several choruses on social themes, in a traditional style; also a cantata *For The Peace* (1949).—See the article on Hába in Cobbett's Cyclopedic Survey of Chamber Music.

Hába, Karel, Czech composer, brother of Alois Hába; b. Vizovice, Moravia, May 21, 1898. He studied with Křička and Foerster at the Prague Cons.; was in his brother's class of quarter-tone music. For a time, he was a school teacher; then played viola in the Czech Philharmonic Orch. (1929-36). He publ. a manual on violin playing in quarter tones (Prague, 1927).—Works: opera: *Janošík* (Prague, Feb. 23, 1934); 2 symphonies (1949, 1954); violin concerto (Vienna Festival, June 16, 1932); cello concerto (Prague Festival, Sept. 1, 1935); septet for violin, clarinet, viola, horn, cello, bassoon, and piano (Liège Festival, Sept. 2, 1930); nonet (1948); 3 string quartets, etc. He does not employ quarter-tones as systematically as his brother, and frequently writes music in the traditional vein.

Habeneck, François-Antoine, French conductor and composer; b. Mézières, Jan. 22, 1781; d. Paris, Feb. 8, 1849. His father, a native of Mannheim and a member of a regimental band, taught him the violin. In 1800 Habeneck entered the Paris Cons., studying violin with Baillot. In 1806 Habeneck was appointed conductor of the student orchestra; in 1825, prof. of violin at the Cons., holding this post almost until his death. He was musical director of the Paris Opéra (1821-24); then its conductor (1824-46). In 1828 he founded the Société des Concerts du Conservatoire de Paris, comprising an orchestra of 80 musicians and a chorus of 80 singers. At his opening concert (March 9, 1828) he presented Beethoven's *Eroica;* subsequently gave concerts exclusively of Beethoven's works, culminating in the first Paris performance of the Ninth Symphony (March 27, 1831). Although Habeneck retained many characteristics of an amateur in conducting (for instance, he used the violin part, with other instruments cued in, instead of a full score), he became a major influence in French musical life because of the excellence of his programs; his championing of Beethoven exercised a profound influence on French composers, among them Berlioz. As a composer he was not significant. With Isouard and Benincori, he wrote an opera *Aladin ou la Lampe merveilleuse* (Paris Opéra, Feb. 6, 1822); composed 2 violin concertos and other violin music; publ. *Méthode théorique et pratique de violon* (Paris, 1835).

Haberbier, Ernst, German pianist; b. Königsberg, Oct. 5, 1813; d. Bergen, Norway, March 12, 1869. He studied with his father, an organist; left home in 1832; went to Russia and became a court pianist in St. Petersburg in 1847; gave concerts in London in 1850; in 1852 appeared in Paris, where he scored a sensational success; in 1866 he settled in Bergen. He perfected what he considered a novel system of piano technique, dividing difficult passages between the two hands (however, this had been done by Scarlatti and Bach long before). He wrote a number of effective piano pieces, of which *Etudes-Poésies* (op. 53) are the best known.

Haberl, Franz Xaver, eminent German theorist, music editor, and historiographer; b. Oberellenbach, Lower Bavaria, April 12, 1840; d. Regensburg, Sept. 5, 1910. He studied in the Boys' Seminary at Passau, and took holy orders in 1862; 1862-7, cathedral Kapellmeister and musical director at the Seminary; 1867-70, organist at Santa Maria dell' Anima, Rome; 1871-82, cathedral Kapellmeister at Regensburg, where he founded, in 1875, a world-renowned school for church music. He was an authority on Catholic church music, past and present. In 1872 he assumed the editorship (vacated by Schrems' death) of the collection 'Musica divina'; and edited the periodical 'Musica sacra' after Witt's death in 1888. In 1876 he began to publish the 'Cäcilienkalender,' the scope of which was greatly widened until, after 1885, it was issued under the more appropriate name of 'Kirchenmusikalisches Jahrbuch'; as such it has become one of the most important publications for historical studies concerning the church music of the 15th, 16th, and 17th centuries. Haberl continued as editor until 1907, when he resigned and was succeeded by Karl Weinmann. He founded a Palestrina Society in 1879, and (beginning with vol. X) was editor-in-chief of Breitkopf & Härtel's complete edition of Palestrina's works (33 vols. finished on the tercentenary of the master's death, 1894), which he aided not only by his experience and learning, but also by rare MSS from his private collection. In 1899 he was elected President of the 'Allgemeine Cäcilienverein,' and became editor of its official organ, 'Fliegende Blätter für katholische Kirchenmusik.' In 1889 he was made *Dr. theol.* (hon. c.) by the University of Würzburg; in 1908 'Monsignore.' Under his general supervision a new edition of the 'Editio Medicea' (1614) of the plainchant melodies was issued, with papal sanction, at Regensburg (1871-81). When modern scholarship had proved that the original edition had not been published with papal sanction and had not been revised by Palestrina; that, in fact, it contained the old melodies in badly distorted and mutilated form, the papal sanction was withdrawn, the edition suppressed and replaced by a new 'Editio Vaticana' in 1904. The result of this was that Haberl's books dealing with plainchant (which had been held in the highest esteem and had passed through many editions became practically worthless. The books thus affected are: *Praktische Anweisung zum harmonischen Kirchengesang* (1864), *Magister Choralis* (1865; 12th ed., 1899; transl. into English, French, Italian, Spanish

Polish, and Hungarian), *Officium hebdomadae sanctae* (1887, in German), *Psalterium vespertinum* (1888). His other writings, the value of which remains unimpaired, are *Bertalotti's Solfeggien* (1880), *Wilhelm Dufay* (1885), *Die römische 'Schola Cantorum' und die päpstlichen Kapellsänger bis zur Mitte des 16. Jahrhunderts* (1887), *Bibliographischer und thematischer Musikkatalog des päpstlichen Kapellarchivs im Vatikan zu Rom* (1888).

Habert, Johannes Evangelista, organist, composer, and writer; b. Oberplan, Bohemia, Oct. 18, 1833; d. Gmunden, Sept. 1, 1896. He was organist at Gmunden from 1861; wrote sacred music and organ pieces; a complete edition of his works was published by Breitkopf & Härtel. He was founder and editor of the 'Zeitschrift für katholische Kirchenmusik' (1868-83); publ. also *Beiträge zur Lehre von der musikalischen Komposition* (4 vols.; 1889 et seq.).—Cf.: A. Hartl, *Johannes Evangelista Habert, Organist in Gmunden* (Vienna, 1900).

Hackett, Charles, American tenor; b. Worcester, Mass., Nov. 4, 1889; d. New York, Jan. 1, 1942. He studied voice first in Boston, and then in Florence; made his opera début in Genoa; then sang at La Scala, Milan; subsequently appeared in South America, London, Paris, etc. On Jan. 31, 1919, he made his American début as the Count in *Il Barbiere di Siviglia* with the Metropolitan Opera Company; was a member of the Chicago Civic Opera (1923-33); in 1934 rejoined the Metropolitan Opera, and remained on its staff until his death.

Hackh, Otto (Christoph), music teacher and composer; b. Stuttgart, Sept. 30, 1852; d. Brooklyn, Sept. 21, 1917. He studied at the Stuttgart Cons.; traveled as a concert pianist in Europe; in 1880 settled in New York; was head of the Grand Cons. there (1880-89); then taught piano privately. He publ. some 200 pieces for piano, in a modern salon style, and also many songs, some of which became extremely popular.

Hadden, James Cuthbert, Scottish writer on music; b. Banchory-Ternan, near Aberdeen, Sept. 9, 1861; d. Edinburgh, May 1, 1914. He studied organ in London; was organist in Aberdeen and Edinburgh; edited the 'Scottish Musical Monthly' (1893-96); publ. several biographies: *Handel* (1888; new ed., 1905); *Mendelssohn* (1888; new ed., 1904); *George Thomson, the Friend of Burns* (1898); *Haydn* (1902); *Chopin* (1903); also *The Operas of Wagner; Their Plots, Music and History* (1908); *Master Musicians* (1909); *Favorite Operas* (1910); *Composers in Love and Marriage* (1912); *Modern Musicians* (1913); edited *The Lays of Caledonia,* a collection of Scottish airs (Glasgow, 1883).

Hadley, Henry (Kimball), eminent American composer and conductor; b. Somerville, Mass., Dec. 20, 1871; d. New York, Sept. 6, 1937. He studied piano and violin with his father and then with S. Emery and G. W. Chadwick at the New England Cons. in Boston; in 1894, studied theory with Mandyczewski in Vienna. Returning to America, he became director of music at St. Paul's School, Garden City (1895-1902); toured various cities in Germany conducting his own works (1905-09); conducted at the Stadttheater in Mainz (1908-09) and brought out there his one-act opera *Safie.* In 1909 he was engaged as conductor of the Seattle Symph. Orch.; from 1911-15 he was conductor of the San Francisco Symph. Orch., and from 1915-22, associate conductor of the N. Y. Philharmonic Orch. In 1924 he again toured Europe; conducted symphonic concerts in Buenos Aires in 1927; was conductor of the Manhattan Symph. Orch. (1929-32) producing many American works. He was conductor at the opening concert of the Berkshire Festival at Stockbridge, Mass., in 1933. He traveled extensively; conducted his own works in Japan and Argentina; spent his last years mostly in New York. He received a Mus. D. from Tufts College (1925); was a member of the National Institute of Arts and Letters and the American Academy of Arts and Letters; and received the Order of Merit from the French government. Hadley occupied a position of prominence among American composers. In his style, he frankly adhered to programmatic writing. Although he shunned the unresolved dissonances of the ultra-modern school, he was not averse to using fairly advanced harmonies in an impressionist vein; he often applied exotic colors when the subject matter demands it. He was an excellent craftsman, both as composer and conductor, and contributed much to the growth of American music culture.—Works: A comic opera *Nancy Brown;* the grand operas *Safie* (Mainz, April 4, 1909), *Azora, Daughter of Montezuma* (Chicago, Dec. 26, 1917), *Bianca* (N. Y., Oct. 18, 1918; composer conducting; won the $1000 William Hinshaw prize 1917), *Cleopatra's Night* (N. Y., Jan. 31, 1920), *A Night in Old Paris* (1925); a festival play, *The Atonement of Pan* (San Francisco, Aug. 10, 1912); 5 symphonies: No. 1, *Youth and Life* (N. Y. Philharmonic, Dec. 2, 1897), No. 2, *The Four Seasons* (N. Y. Philharmonic, Dec. 20, 1901; won the Paderewski prize and one offered by the New England Cons.), No. 3 (Berlin Philharmonic, Dec. 27, 1907; composer conducting), No. 4, *North, East, South, West* (Norfolk, Conn., Festival, Jan. 6, 1911; composer conducting), No. 5, *Connecticut* (Norfolk, Conn., Festival, 1934); the overtures *Hector and Andromache, In Bohemia* (Boston Symph., Dec. 16, 1901), *Herod, Othello* (Philadelphia Orch., Dec. 26, 1919), *Youth Triumphant, Aurora Borealis* (1931), *Academic Overture,* and *Alma Mater* (1932); the tone poems *Salomé* (composed in 1905, before the production of *Salome* by Richard Strauss; publ. in 1906; performed by Muck and the Boston Symph., April 12, 1907); *Lucifer* (Norfolk, Conn., Festival, June 2, 1914; composer conducting), *The Ocean* (N. Y. Philh., Nov. 17, 1921; composer conducting); an orchestral rhapsody, *The Culprit Fay* (Chicago Symph. at Grand Rapids, Mich., Oct. 30, 1909; composer conducting; won a $1000 prize of the National Federation of Music Clubs); the orchestral suites *Oriental* (1903), *Silhouettes, San Francisco* in 3 movements (Robin Hood Dell, July 17, 1932; composer conducting); *Streets of Pekin* (Tokyo, Sept. 24, 1930; composer conducting); *Scherzo Diabolique* for orch. 'to recall a harrowing personal experience during a terrifying automobile ride at night, exceeding all speed limits' (Century of Progress Exposition, Chicago, Aug. 1934; composer conducting); incidental music to *The Daughter of Hamilcar* and *Audrey;* a *Konzertstück* for cello and orch. (1937); a piano quintet (1920); 2 string quartets; 2 piano trios; a violin sonata; Elegy for cello and piano; choral works with orch.: *In Music's Praise* (1899; won the Oliver Ditson Prize), *Merlin and Vivien, The Fate of Princess Kiyo, The Nightingale and the Rose, The Golden Prince, The Fairy Thorn, Ode to Music* (1917), *The New Earth* (1919), *Resurgam* (Cincinnati Music Festival, May 1923), *Mirtil in Arcadia* (Harrisburg, Pa., Festival, May 17, 1928), *Belshazzar* (1932); 6 ballads (*The Fairies; In Arcady; Jabberwocky; Lelawala, a Legend of Niagara; The Princess of Ys; A Legend of Granada*); many anthems; piano pieces and over 150 songs to German and English words. A Henry Hadley Foundation for the Advancement of American Music was organized in 1938.—Cf. H. R. Boardman, *Henry Hadley, Ambassador of Harmony* (Emory Univ., Georgia, 1932); P. Berthoud, *The Musical Works of Dr. Henry Hadley* (N. Y., 1942).

Hadley, Patrick Arthur Sheldon, British composer; b. Cambridge, March 5, 1899. He studied with Rootham at Cambridge (M. A., 1925; D. Mus., 1938); also at the Royal College of Music in London with Vaughan Williams (1922-25); in 1938 became lecturer in music at Cambridge; in 1946, prof. of music. His works include *The Trees So High* for baritone, chorus, and orch. (1931); *La Belle Dame sans merci,* for tenor, chorus, and orch. (1935); *Travelers,* for soprano, chorus, and orch. (1940); *The Hills,* for soloists, chorus, and orch. (1946); *Fen and Flood,* cantata for soprano, baritone, chorus, and orch. (1956); a string quartet (1933), Fantasy for 2 violins and piano (1938); *One Morning in Spring,* rhapsody for string orch. (1942); *The Orphan's Song* for mezzo-soprano with orch. (1947); *Scene from The Cenci,* after Shelley, for soprano and orch. (1951); incidental music for the stage, etc.

Hadow, Sir William Henry, English music educator; b. Ebrington, Gloucestershire, Dec. 27, 1859; d. London, April 8, 1937. He studied at Malvern College (1871-78) and Worcester College, Oxford (1878-82); M. A., 1888; Mus. B., 1890. He studied piano in Darmstadt (1882); composition with C. H. Lloyd in Oxford (1884). He held various positions in English universities from 1885 till 1919; received numerous honorary degrees; was knighted in 1918. He wrote a cantata, *The Soul's Pilgrimage,* a string quartet, 2 violin sonatas, a viola sonata, and a number of anthems. These however are of little significance; Hadow's importance lies in his books, written in a lively journalistic style. His book on Haydn, *A Croatian Composer* (London, 1897), claiming that Haydn was of Slavonic origin, aroused considerable controversy; modern research proves the claim incorrect. Of more solid substance are his other writings: *Studies in Modern Music* (2 vols., 1892-95; 10th ed., 1921); *Sonata Form* (1896); *The Viennese Period* (vol. 5 of the 'Oxford History of Music,' 1904); *Beethoven* (1917); *William Byrd* (1923); *Music* (in the 'Home Univ. Library,' 1924; 3rd revised ed. by Sir George Dyson, 1949); *Church Music* (1926); *A Comparison of Poetry and Music* (1926); *Collected Essays* (1928); *English Music* (1931); *The Place of Music Among the Arts* (1933); *Richard Wagner* (1934). He edited songs of the British

Islands (1903); was editor-in-chief of the 'Oxford History of Music' from 1901-5 and in 1929; contributed articles to various British magazines and to the 'Mus. Quarterly' (Jan., 1915).

Hadrianus. See **Adriaensen.**

Haeffner, Johann Christian Friedrich, composer; b. Oberschönau, near Suhl, March 2, 1759; d. Upsala, Sweden, May 28, 1833. He was a pupil of Dierling at Schmalkalden; then studied at the Univ. of Leipzig, and served as proof-reader for Breitkopf; then became conductor of a traveling opera troupe; in 1780 he arrived in Stockholm, where he became an organist at a German church. He produced at Stockholm several operas in the style of Gluck: *Electra* (1787), *Alkides* (1795), *Renaud* (1801), which had a favorable reception; in 1793 he was appointed court conductor; in 1808 he went to Upsala, where he remained for the rest of his life, acting as organist of the cathedral and music director of the Univ. He took great interest in Swedish national music; publ. Swedish folksongs with accompaniment, and revised the melodies of the Geijer-Afzelius collection; edited a *Svenska Choralbok* (2 parts, 1819-21), in which he restored the choral melodies of the 17th century, and added preludes (1822); also arranged a collection of old Swedish songs in 4 parts (1832-33; he finished only 2 books).

Haesche, William Edwin, American music educator; b. New Haven, Conn., April 11, 1867; d. Roanoke, Va., Jan. 26, 1929. He studied violin with Bernhard Listemann and piano with Perabo; composition with Horatio Parker at Yale Univ. (Mus. Bac., 1897); taught orchestration at Yale Univ. (1903-22); in 1923 appointed violin teacher at Hollins College, Va., a post he held until his death. He was one of the organizers of the New Haven Symph. Orch., and was its concertmaster for 20 years. He wrote a symph. poem *Fridthjof and Ingeborg* (1897), *The Haunted Oak of Nannau,* for chorus and orch. (1902), a violin sonata, and other violin pieces.

Hagel, Richard, German conductor; b. Erfurt, July 7, 1872; d. Berlin, May 1, 1941. He studied with his father; was an orch. violinist in Abo, Finland (1889), Koburg (1890), Meiningen (1892), and Sondershausen (1893); later undertook serious study at the Leipzig Cons. (1898-1900); conducted at the Leipzig Stadttheater (1900-09) and at Brunswick (1911-14). From 1919 till 1925 he conducted the Berlin Philharmonic; subsequently taught at various schools. He publ. *Die Lehre vom Partiturspiel* (Berlin, 1937).

Hageman, Maurits Leonard, Dutch violinist and composer; b. Zutfen, Sept. 25, 1829; d. Nijmegen, April 16, 1906. He studied with Bériot and Fétis at the Brussels Cons., graduating in 1852. After playing violin in the Italian Opera orch. at Brussels, he became a conductor at Groningen; then was director of the Cons. of Batavia, Java (1865-75) and conductor of the orch. there. Returning to Holland, he founded a music school in Leeuwarden. He wrote an oratorio *Daniel;* several other choral works; piano pieces; songs.

Hageman, Richard, American composer; b. Leeuwarden, Holland, July 9, 1882. He studied piano with his father Maurice Hageman, who was director of the Amsterdam Cons.; then at the Brussels Cons. with Gevaert and Arthur de Greef; conductor at the Royal Opera in Amsterdam (1899-1903); accompanist for Mathilde Marchesi in Paris (1904-5); came to the U. S. as accompanist for Yvette Guilbert in 1906; appointed conductor at the Metropolitan Opera in 1908; was on the staff until 1926; conducted the summer opera at Ravinia Park, Chicago for 6 seasons; taught voice at Chicago Musical College; appeared as guest conductor with several American orchestras. In 1938 he settled in Hollywood; wrote several motion picture scores.—Works: the opera *Caponsacchi* (1931; produced in Freiburg, Germany, as *Tragoedie in Arezzo,* Feb. 18, 1932; at the Metropolitan, Feb. 4, 1937; received the David Bispham Memorial Medal); *The Crucible,* concert drama for solo voices, chorus, and orch. (Los Angeles, Feb. 4, 1943); numerous songs, some of which attained great popularity (*Do not go my love, At the well, Charity,* etc.).

Hagen, Francis Florentine, 'Moravian' minister and composer; b. Salem, N. C., Oct. 30, 1815; d. Lititz, Pa., July 7, 1907. Served as teacher and minister in various 'Moravian' congregations. He edited and compiled 'Church and Home Organist's Companion' (several vols.). Wrote a number of anthems, in which a definite sense for distinguished popular melody is noticeable; also a cantata and an overture. His *Morning Star,* a Christmas carol, which, in 'Moravian' communities, stood in continuous favor for almost a century, was reprinted in 1939. Another anthem is included in the series 'Music of the Moravians in America,' publ. by the N. Y. Public Library.—Cf. A. G. Rau and H. T. David, 'A Catalogue of Music by American Moravians' (Bethlehem, 1938).

Hagen, Friedrich Heinrich von der, German scholar; b. in the Ukraine, Feb. 19, 1780; d. Berlin, June 11, 1856, as prof. of German literature at the Univ. He publ. the valuable collection, *Minnesinger* (1838-56, in 5 vols.; in vol. III are 'Minnegesänge' in notation according to the Jena Codex and other sources, with a treatise on the music of the Minnesinger); *Melodien zu der Sammlung deutscher, vlämischer und französicher Volkslieder* (1807; with Büsching).

Hagen, Theodor, writer on music; b. Hamburg, April 15, 1823; d. New York, Dec. 21, 1871. He lived in New York from 1854 as a teacher and critic; edited the 'New York Weekly Review.' Publ. *Civilisation und Musik* (1845, under the pen-name 'Joachim Fels'); *Musikalische Novellen* (1848); also piano music and songs.

Hägg, Gustaf Wilhelm, eminent Swedish organist and composer; b. Wisby, Nov. 28, 1867; d. Stockholm, Feb. 7, 1925. After graduation from the Stockholm Cons., he studied in Germany (1897-1900) and France; returning to Stockholm, he was appointed teacher of theory and organ at the Cons. He enjoyed a distinguished reputation in Stockholm as organist, and gave numerous performances of works by Franck and Widor. He composed a symph., string sextet, string quartet, piano trio, etc.; also edited 87 Swedish folksongs.

Hägg, Jakob Adolf, Swedish composer; b. Oestergarn, June 29, 1850; d. Stockholm, March 1, 1928. He studied at the Stockholm Cons.; then went to Leipzig for additional study with Gade, whose influence proved decisive in Hägg's own works. He wrote a *Nordische Symphonie* (1870; revised 1890) and several other symphonies; a number of overtures; choral works; 3 string quartets; a piano trio, violin sonata, cello sonata; piano pieces.—Cf. G. Hetsch, *Ein schwedischer Komponist und sein Verhältnis zu N. W. Gade* (Leipzig, 1903).

Haggin, Bernard H., American music critic; b. New York, Dec. 29, 1900. He was music critic of the 'Brooklyn Daily Eagle' (1934-37); in 1936 became music critic of the 'Nation'; also lectured at various colleges. He publ. *A Book on the Symphony* (N. Y., 1937); *Music on Records* (N. Y., 1941; 4th revised ed., 1946); *Music for the Man Who Enjoys Hamlet* (N. Y., 1944); *Music in the Nation* (N. Y., 1949; collection of articles and reviews originally publ. in the 'Nation'). A 'critical' critic, Haggin devised in his writings an aggressive and personal manner of old-style journalism expressing his views candidly and without regard to conventional amenities. He resigned from the 'Nation' in 1957.

Hahn, Carl, American conductor; b. Indianapolis, Oct. 23, 1874; d. Cincinnati, May 13, 1929. A member of a musical family (his father was a flutist; his brother, a violinist), he studied several instruments (piano with Albino Gorno, cello with Lino Mattioli); played cello in the Theodore Thomas Orch., then was active as conductor in San Antonio (1900-11); then lived in New York and Cincinnati. He wrote a number of choruses and songs, publ. in America and Germany.

Hahn, Reynaldo, notable composer; b. Caracas, Venezuela, Aug. 9, 1875; d. Paris, Jan. 28, 1947. At the age of 3 he was brought to Paris and remained there during his whole life. He studied at the Paris Cons. with Dubois and Lavignac; also with Massenet, whose influence was considerable in Hahn's own development as composer. In 1934 he became music critic of 'Le Figaro'; in 1945, appointed musical director of the Paris Opéra. His music is distinguished by its facile melodic flow; some of his songs have become very popular in recitals. He publ. a book of essays, *Thèmes Variés* (Paris, 1946).—Works: operas: *L'ile du Rêve*, a 'Polynesian idyll' (Opéra-Comique, Paris, March 23, 1898); *La Carmelite* (Opéra-Comique, Dec. 16, 1902); *Nausicaa* (Monte Carlo, April 10, 1919); *Fête triomphale* Paris Opéra, July 14, 1919); *La Colombe de Buddha* (Cannes, 1921); *Ciboulette*, light opera (Paris, Théâtre des Variétés, April 7, 1923); *Le Marchand de Venise*, after Shakespeare (Paris Opéra, March 29 1935); *Malvina*, light opera (Gaité Lyrique 1935); incidental music to Daudet's *L'Obstacle* (1890), Croisset's *Deux Courtisanes* (1902), Racine's *Esther* (1905), Hugo's *Angelo* (1905), Hugo's *Lucrèce Borgia* (1911), Sascha Guitry's *Mozart* (1925) Wolff's and Duvernois' *Le Temps d'aimer* (1926); the pantomimes *Fin d'amour* (1892), *Le Bois sacré* (1912); the ballet *Béatrice d'Este* (1909), *La Fête chez Thérèse*

(1901), *Le Dieu bleu* (1912); 2 symph. poems, *Nuit d'amour bergamasque* (1897), *Prométhée triomphant* (1911); a Christmas mystery, *La Pastorale de Noël* (1908); violin concerto; violin sonata; *Concerto provençal* (1930; Paris, 1946); choruses; numerous songs; piano pieces.

Hahn, Ulrich. See **Han.**

Hähnel. See **Gallus, Jacobus.**

Haibel, Petrus Jakob, Austrian composer; b. Graz, July 20, 1762; d. Djakovar, March 24, 1826. He was engaged in Vienna as a tenor; in 1806 he settled in Djakovar; there he married Sophie Weber, sister of Mozart's widow. He produced several stage works in Vienna, among them the ballet *Le nozze disturbate* (May 18, 1795), and a singspiel *Der Tyroler Wastl* (May 14, 1796), which became very popular. Other productions were *Der Papagei und die Gans* (May 25, 1799); *Tsching, Tsching, Tsching* (Feb. 6, 1802); *Der kleine Cesar* (July 25, 1804), etc. Mozart's librettist, Schikaneder, wrote the texts for many of Haibel's operas.

Haiden. See **Heyden.**

Haieff, Alexei, Russian-American composer; b. Blagovestchensk, Siberia, Aug. 25, 1914. He received his primary education at Harbin, Manchuria; in 1931 came to the U. S.; studied with Rubin Goldmark and Frederick Jacobi at the Juilliard School of Music; also took private lessons with Alexander Siloti (piano); studied composition with Nadia Boulanger in Paris (1938-39). He held a Guggenheim Fellowship in 1946 and again in 1949. He also received a Fulbright Scholarship for study in Italy; was a Fellow at the American Academy in Rome 1947-48, composer in residence there 1952-53. His piano concerto received the N. Y. Music Critics' Award for 1952. In his music, Haieff follows Stravinsky's type of neo-Classicism, with broad melodies and rich tonal harmonies; in contrapuntal procedures, Haieff adheres to the principle of economy of means, achieving modernistic effects by a display of rhythmic agitation, often with jazz connotations.—Works: ballets, *Divertimento* (1944), *The Princess Zondilda and her Entourage* (1946), *Beauty and the Beast* (1947); for orch.: symphony (1942); violin concerto (1948); piano concerto (N. Y., April 27, 1952); chamber music: sonatina for string quartet (1937); 3 bagatelles for oboe and bassoon (1939-55); serenade for oboe, clarinet, bassoon, and piano (1942); *Eclogue* for cello and piano (1947); *La Nouvelle Héloïse* for harp and string quartet (1953); sonata for 2 pianos (1945); sonata for piano solo (1955); songs.

Haigh, Morris, American composer; b. San Diego, Calif., Jan. 26, 1932. He studied at Pomona College and at the Eastman School of Music with Bernard Rogers. He has composed *Serenade* for flute and piano (1954), violin concerto (1956), etc.

Haile, Eugen, composer; b. Ulm, Württemberg, Feb. 21, 1873; d. Woodstock, N. Y., Aug. 14, 1933. He was a pupil at the Stuttgart Cons. (1887-94); settled in New York in 1903; publ. about 200 songs, some of excellent quality (*Herbst, Der Todesengel singt, Teufelslied, Soldaten kommen,* etc.). His music to a spoken drama ('gesprochene Oper'), *The Happy Ending* (N. Y., Aug. 21, 1916), attempts to combine spoken word in the play with pitch inflections in the vocal parts; other operas, *Viola d'Amore* (1910) and *Harald's Dream* (1913), remained unperformed. His wife, Elise Haile, was a singer; together, they presented several concerts of his German songs in N. Y. When he suffered a paralytic stroke and became impoverished, a Eugen Haile Society was formed in N. Y. (1914) to provide funds for him and also to organize performances of his music.

Haines Bros., well known firm of piano makers founded in N. Y. by Napoleon J. (1824-1900) and Francis W. (1822-87) Haines. The brothers came to N. Y. from England as boys, worked in the piano workshops of A. H. Gale from 1839, and in 1851 established their own factory under the name of N. J. Haines & Co. They were the first to give up manufacturing 'square' pianos and were among the earliest makers of the modern 'overstrung' grand pianos. The business was taken over by the Aeolian American Corp., with factories at East Rochester, N. Y.

Hainl, François, French cellist and conductor; b. Issoire, Nov. 16, 1807; d. Paris, June 2, 1873. After graduating as a cellist from the Paris Cons. with a first prize (1830), he went to Lyons, where he conducted theater music (1841-63); then conducted at the Paris Opéra (1863-72). He wrote an orch. fantasy on Rossini's *William Tell;* publ. a valuable account *De la musique à Lyon depuis 1713 jusqu'à 1852.*

Haitzinger, Anton, tenor; b. Wilfersdorf, Liechtenstein, March 14, 1796; d. Vienna, Dec. 31, 1869. He studied in Vienna; made his opera début in 1821; then sang in Prague, Frankfurt, Paris, and London; retired in 1850, and returned to Vienna. In his prime he enjoyed an excellent reputation, and was equally successful in the Italian and German repertory. He publ. a song, *Vergiss mein nicht,* and a manual of singing.

Hakansson, Knut Algot, Swedish composer; b. Kinna, Nov. 4, 1887; d. Helsingborg, Dec. 13, 1929. He studied philosophy in Upsala; music in Stockholm; was then active as music critic and conductor in Göteborg and Helsingborg. He wrote a ballet *Mylitta* (Copenhagen, 1918); several suites for orch. on Swedish themes; a string quartet and a string trio; also songs.

Halász, László, Hungarian-American conductor; b. Debrecen, June 6, 1905. He studied at the Budapest Cons.; graduated in piano and conducting in 1929; was active as concert pianist in Europe (1928-31); conducted the Budapest Opera (1929-30), the Prague Opera (1930-32), the Vienna Opera and Volksoper (1933-36). In 1936, came to America; naturalized in 1943. He was conductor of the St. Louis Grand Opera (1939-42) and the New York City Opera Co. (1943-51), where he established a bold policy of producing operas of the modern repertory; personal differences with the management compelled him to resign; after 1951 he conducted opera performances in the U. S. and Europe.

Hale, Philip, eminent American music critic; b. Norwich, Vt., March 5, 1854; d. Boston, Nov. 30, 1934. He took music lessons from early youth and as a boy played the organ in the Unitarian Church, Northhampton, Mass. Graduate of Yale Univ., 1876; admitted to the Albany bar, 1880. First studied music in Europe, 1882-87 (organ with Haupt, Faiszt, Rheinberger, and Guilmant; composition with Urban, Bargiel, Rheinberger, and Guilmant; piano with Raif and Scholz). Was organist (1879-82) at St. Peter's, Albany; 1887-89, at St. John's, Troy; 1889-1905, of First Religious Society, Roxbury, Mass. From 1887-89, also conductor of the Schubert Club, a men's chorus, at Albany. Critic for the 'Boston Home Journal' (1889-91), 'Boston Post' (1890-91), 'Boston Journal' (1891-1903); then for 'Boston Herald'; 1897-1901, editor of the Boston 'Mus. Record'; and 1892-98, Boston correspondent of the 'Musical Courier,' N. Y. He also was drama editor of the 'Boston Herald.' From 1901 he edited the program books of the Boston Symph. Orch. Hale was one of the most forceful and brilliant writers for the American music press; his articles are valuable contributions to music literature, and often tinged with humor. He edited 2 vols. of *Modern French Songs* in 'The Musician's Library' (1904, Ditson); joint author with L. C. Elson of *Great Composers and Their Works* (1900). —Cf. *Philip Hale's Boston Symph. Programme Notes,* ed. by John N. Burk (N. Y., 1935; revised ed., 1939).

Hales, Hubert (James), English composer; b. Bradford, April 29, 1902. He studied at Eton College and at King's College in Cambridge; received a B. A. there and subsequently devoted himself to teaching; occupied various posts as director of music at schools and colleges. He has written music for dramatic productions, several works for orch., a string quartet, and a number of piano pieces.

Halévy, Jacques-François-Fromental-Élie, famous French opera composer; b. Paris, May 27, 1799; d. Nice, March 17, 1862. He was a child prodigy. At ten he entered the Paris Cons. as an elementary pupil of Cazot. In 1810 he studied piano with Lambert; in 1811, harmony with Berton; and counterpoint for five years with Cherubini. At seventeen he competed for the Prix de Rome, winning the 2nd prize with his cantata *Les derniers Moments du Tasse;* in 1817 he again won the 2nd prize with *La Mort d'Adonis;* in 1819 he gained the Grand Prix de Rome with his *Herminie.* He had previously composed an opera, *Les Bohémiennes* (never performed), published a piano-sonata for 4 hands, and set to music the 130th Psalm in Hebrew, the De Profundis. During his three years' stay in Italy he made great progress, writing another opera, etc. In 1822, on his return to Paris he made vain attempts to produce his grand opera *Pygmalion* and *Les deux Pavillons* (comedy-opera). It was not until 1827 that he brought out a one-act comedy-opera, *L'Artisan,* at the Théâtre Feydeau; though with little success. The same year he succeeded Daussoigne as prof. of harmony and accompaniment at the Cons.; following Fétis as prof. of counterpoint and fugue in 1833 and taking a class of advanced composition in 1840. In 1827 he was engaged as cembalist at the Italian Opera. In 1828, with Rifaut, he composed *Le Roi et le Bâtelier* in honor of Charles X. On Dec. 9 of the same year *Clari* (with Malibran as prima donna) was a success at the Théâtre Italien; *Le Dilettante d'Avignon* was produced on Nov. 7, 1829; and on May 3, 1830 the grand ballet *Manon Lescaut*. Halévy was now appointed 'chef du chant' at the Opéra, a post retained during 16 years. In 1831 *La Langue musicale* was produced at the Opéra-Comique; *La Tentation* (Paris, June 20, 1832; ballet-opera, with Gide), at the Opéra; *Les Souvenirs de Lafleur* (Opéra-Comique, March 4, 1833); and on May 16 of the same year a completion of Hérold's unfinished *Ludovic*, which proved very successful. On Feb. 23, 1835, the Paris Opéra produced Halévy's masterpiece, *La Juive*, which soon became one of the most spectacular successes of opera theaters throughout Europe and America. A few months later appeared *L'Éclair* (Dec. 16, 1835), a sparkling comedy-opera. To add to his growing reputation, Halévy was created Chevalier of the Legion of Honor. On the death of Reicha (1836) Halévy succeeded him as one of the three musical members of the Académie; and in 1854 was appointed Secretary for life. With *La Juive* Halévy attained not only the zenith of his powers, but also of his triumphs. In 1836 the blazing apparition of *Les Huguenots* paled the milder fires of the French composer, and Meyerbeer became the idol of the hour. *La Juive* was followed by *Guido et Ginevra* (March 5, 1838); *Les Treize* (April 15, 1839); *Le Shérif* (Sept. 2, 1839); *Le Drapier* (Jan. 6, 1840); *Le Guitarrero* (Jan. 21, 1841); *La Reine de Chypre* (Dec. 22, 1841); *Charles VI* (Feb. 3, 1843); *Le Lazzarone* (March 23, 1844); *Les Mousquetaires de la reine* (March 15, 1846). He collaborated with Adam, Auber, and Carafa in *Les premiers Pas* for the inauguration of the National Opera (1847). His next productions were: *Le Val d'Andorre* (Nov. 11, 1848); *La Fée aux roses* (Oct. 1, 1849); *La Dame de Pique* (Dec. 28, 1850). On June 8, 1850, Halévy conducted in London an Italian opera, *La Tempesta*. He then produced in Paris *Le Juif errant* (April 23, 1852); *Le Nabab* (Sept. 1, 1853); *Jaguarita* (May 14, 1855); *L'Inconsolable* (under the *nom-de-plume* 'Albert'; 1855); *Valentine d'Aubigny* (1856); *La Magicienne* (March 17, 1858).—Halévy was more inclined to aim at a high ideal than to please the popular taste. His music possesses true emotional and dramatic power, and is 'melodious, but combined with so many details and refinements of harmony and instrumentation' that it could not be appreciated by the general public; though he held a high rank among artists.—Besides his operas, Halévy wrote a piano sonata for 4 hands, *romances*, nocturnes, part-songs for men's voices; scenes from *Prometheus Unbound* (Paris, March 18, 1849); the cantatas *Italie* (1849) and *Les Plagues du Nil* (1859) and left the almost finished scores of two operas, *Vanina d'Ornano* (completed by Bizet) and *Le Déluge* (originally *Noé*, completed by Bizet; performed on April 5, 1885). In the Paris schools his *Leçons de lecture musicale* (Paris, 1857) was adopted as the textbook for singing. *Souvenirs et portraits* (1861) and *Derniers souvenirs et portraits* (1863) were collections of the funeral orations that, as Secretary of the Académie, he had delivered at the obsequies of deceased members. At the Paris Cons. he had many distinguished pupils, among them Gounod and Bizet (who married Halévy's daughter). — Short biographies of Halévy were published by his brother Léon (1862), E. Monnais (1863), A. Catelin (1863), and A. Pougin (1865); see also Mina Curtiss, *F. Halévy*, in the 'Mus. Quarterly' (April, 1953).

Halffter, Ernesto, talented Spanish composer; b. Madrid, Jan. 16, 1905. He studied composition with Manuel de Falla and Adolfo Salazar; as a young man he started a chamber orch. in Seville, with which he presented works by contemporary Spanish composers. He first attracted attention when his Sinfonietta, in a neo-Classical style, was presented at the Oxford Festival of the International Society for Contemporary Music (July 23, 1931). From 1934-36 he was director of the Seville Cons.; at the outbreak of the Spanish Civil War in 1936 he went to Lisbon, where he settled. His *Fantaisie portugaise*, for orch., was performed in Paris on March 23, 1941; his other works are an opera *La muerte de Carmen; Automne malade*, for voice and orch.; *Suite ancienne*, for wind instruments; chamber music, and a ballet, *Sonatina* (performed by La Argentina, Paris, 1928).—Cf. A. Salazar, *La música contemporanea en España* (Madrid, 1930).

Halffter, Rodolfo, Spanish composer, brother of Ernesto Halffter; b. Madrid, Oct. 30, 1900. He acquired a considerable technique of composition mainly by the study of classical works; received some instruction and advice from Manuel de Falla. As a young man, he was a member of a group of young Spanish composers promoting national music in a modern idiom. From 1934-36, he was music critic of 'La Voz.' During the Spanish Civil War he collaborated with the cultural sections of the Loyalist government; after its defeat, he fled to France, and then to Mexico, where he settled in 1939, as composer, teacher, and writer. He edited a journal 'Nuestra Musica' (1946-51). Among his works are the ballets *Don Lindo de Almería* (Mexico, Jan. 9, 1940); *La Madrugada del Panadero* (Mexico, Sept. 20, 1940); *Elena la Traicionera* (Mexico, Nov. 23, 1945); *Suite* for orch. (Madrid, Nov. 5, 1930); *Obertura Concertante* for piano and orch. (Valencia, May 23, 1937); violin concerto (Mexico, June 26, 1942); *Divertimento* for 9 instruments (Mexico, Nov. 18, 1943); *Obertura Festiva* (Mexico, May 25, 1953); *Pastorale* for violin and piano (1940); 2 piano sonatas; 11 bagatelles for piano; songs.

Halir (hah'-lir), **Karl,** distinguished violinist; b. Hohenelbe, Bohemia, Feb. 1, 1859; d. Berlin, Dec. 21, 1909. He was a pupil of Bennewitz at the Prague Cons., and of Joachim in Berlin. In 1884 he was appointed concertmaster of the court orch. at Weimar; in 1893 he obtained a similar post in Berlin; also appointed prof. at the Hochschule there; for a time he was a member of the Joachim Quartet, but later formed his own quartet (with Exner, Müller, and Dechert), which became famous. His tour of the United States (1896-97) was very successful. His pedagogic exercises for the violin, *Tonleiterstudien,* are still in use. In 1888 he married Theresa Zerbst, a fine soprano.

Hall, Charles King, English composer and writer; b. London, 1845; d. there Sept. 1, 1895. He was organist at various London churches; publ. *A School for Harmonium,* and produced a number of operettas, some of which were successful in their day (*Foster Brothers, Doubleday's Will, A Tremendous Mystery, The Artful Automaton, A Strange House, A Christmas Stocking,* etc.).

Hall, John, English song-writer; b. c. 1529; d. c. 1565. He was a surgeon by profession and a musician by avocation. A collection of 30 melodies and one song in 4 parts entitled *The Court of Vertu,* composed by him, is preserved.

Hall, Marie (Mary Paulina), English violinist; b. Newcastle-on-Tyne, April 8, 1884; d. Cheltenham, Nov. 11, 1956. As a small child, she gave performances with her father, an amateur harp player, her uncle (violin), her brother (violin), and her sister (harp), in the homes of music lovers in Newcastle, Malvern, and Bristol. Elgar heard her, and was impressed by her talent; he sent her to Wilhelmj in London for regular study; she also studied with Johann Kruse. At the age of 15 she won the first Wessely Exhibition at the Royal Academy of Music. She was recommended by Jan Kubelik to Ševčik in Prague (1901), from whom she received rigorous training; made her professional début in Prague (1902); then played in Vienna. After a highly successful London concert (Feb. 16, 1903), she made her American début as soloist with the New York Symphony, Walter Damrosch conducting (Nov. 8, 1905); toured Australia (1907) and India (1913). On Jan. 27, 1911 she married her manager Edward Baring, and settled in Cheltenham; continued to appear in concerts in England until 1955, with her daughter, Pauline Baring, as her accompanist. —Cf. J. Cuthbert Hadden, *Marie Hall,* in *Modern Musicians* (Edinburgh, 1913; pp. 176-83).

Hall, Pauline, Norwegian composer; b. Hamar, Aug. 2, 1890. She studied composition with Catharinus Elling in Oslo; later studied in Paris and in Dresden. She made her first appearance as composer in Oslo in 1915, playing her own piano concerto. In 1934 she became music critic of 'Dagbladet.' In her music, she follows the modern French tradition of classical clarity, enlivened by a constantly driving rhythm. Among her works are 3 orchestral suites: *Verlaine Suite* (1929), *Circus Sketches* (1933), *Julius Caesar* (1947); chamber music; piano pieces.

Hall, Reginald, American composer; b. Laurel, Md., Jan. 23, 1926; studied at the Peabody Cons. and at the Univ. of Michigan (with Ross Lee Finney); also with Halsey Stevens in California. He is a civil engineer by profession and music is only an avocation for him; yet he has developed a competent style in orchestral and chamber music. His *Elegy* for orch. won the George Gershwin Memorial Award in 1955, and was perf. by the N. Y. Philh., April 21, 1956.

Hall, Walter Henry, organist and choral conductor; b. London, April 25, 1862; d. New York, Dec. 11, 1935. He studied at the Royal Academy of Music; settled in America in 1883, was organist at various churches in Pennsylvania, before settling in New York; organist at St. James' (1896-1913). In 1893 he founded the Brooklyn Oratorio Society, which he led until his death; also conducted the Musurgia Society (1889-1906); in 1909 appointed lecturer of music at Columbia Univ.; prof. emeritus in 1930. He was a noted trainer of choirs; member of the committee of the Episcopal 'Hymnal' (1919); wrote services, anthems, etc.; publ. *Essentials of Choir Training.*

Halle. See **Adam de la Hale.**

Hallé, Sir **Charles** (real name Karl Hallé), renowned pianist and conductor; b. Hagen, Westphalia, April 11, 1819; d. Manchester, Oct. 25, 1895. Son of a local church organist, he revealed a musical talent as a child, and performed in public at the age of 4; at 15 he was sent to study music seriously with Rinck at Darmstadt; in 1836 he went to Paris, where he entered the friendly circle of Chopin, Liszt, and others. In 1846 he gave concerts of his own as a pianist in chamber music. After the Revolution of 1848, he went to England, settling in Manchester, where he conducted an orchestra, choruses, and opera. In 1857 he established subscription concerts with an orchestral ensemble of his own, which became famous as Charles Hallé's Orchestra, endured for a century, and eventually became an honored institution known as the Hallé Orchestra. Although his chief activities were connected with Manchester, he also conducted the London Popular Concerts; gave piano recitals; in 1861 he presented all of Beethoven's sonatas in 8 concerts, repeating this cycle in 2 successive seasons. From 1873 till 1893 he conducted the Bristol Festivals; in 1883 he became conductor of the Liverpool Philharmonic Society, as successor to Max Bruch. He was a champion of Berlioz in England, and gave several complete performances of Berlioz's *Damnation de Faust.* His first wife was Désirée Smith de Rilieu, his second wife the violinist Wilma Neruda. With her he made 2 Australian tours (1890 and 1891). He was knighted in 1888. He established a standard of excellence in orchestral performance which greatly influenced musical life in England. He publ. a *Pianoforte School* (1873) and edited a *Musical Library* (1876).—Cf: L. Engel, *From Handel to Hallé* (London, 1890); C. E. and M. Hallé, *Life and Letters of Sir Charles Hallé* (London, 1896); C. Rigby, *Sir Charles Hallé* (Manchester, 1952); C. B. Rees, *100 Years of the Hallé* (Manchester, 1957).

Hallén, Andreas, notable Swedish composer; b. Göteborg, Dec. 22, 1846; d. Stockholm, March 11, 1925. He studied with Reinecke in Leipzig, Rheinberger in Munich, and Rietz in Dresden; upon his return to Sweden, conducted in Göteborg (1872-78 and 1883-84); then was conductor of the Philharmonic Concerts in Stockholm (1884-92) and of the Royal Opera (1892-97). From 1908 till 1919 he was prof. of composition at the Stockholm Cons. His works include the operas *Harald Viking* (Leipzig, Oct. 16, 1881), *Häxfällan* (Stockholm, March 16, 1896), *The Treasure of Waldemar* (Stockholm, April 8, 1899), *Walpurgis Night* (Stockholm, 1902); choral works with orch. (*The Page and the King's Daughter, Dream-King and His Love, Goblin's Fate, Christmas Eve, Peace*); a *Missa solemnis* (Stockholm, 1923), which was very successful; symph. poems (*En Sommarsaga, Die Toteninsel, Sphärenklänge*); overtures, etc. — Cf. P. Vretblad, *Andreas Hallén* (Stockholm, 1918).

Haller, Michael, German church composer; b. Neusaat, Jan. 13, 1840; d. Regensburg, Jan. 4, 1915. He was educated at Matten monastery; took holy orders in 1864; appointed prefect of the Regensburg Cathedral Choristers' Institution. — Works: 14 Masses; psalms; litanies; a Te Deum; melodramas; string quartets, etc. He completed the third-choir parts of 6 compositions *a* 12 of Palestrina, which had been lost (vol. XXVI of the complete edition). Pedagogic writings: *Vademecum für den Gesangsunterricht* (1876; 12th ed., 1910); *Kompositionslehre für den polyphonen Kirchengesang* (1891); *Modulation in den Kirchentonarten; Exempla polyphoniae ecclesiasticae* (in modern notation, with explanatory notes); also contributed historical articles to Haberl's 'Kirchenmusikalisches Jahrbuch.'

Hallnäs, Hilding, Swedish composer, b. Halmstad, May 24, 1903. He studied at the Stockholm Cons. and later in Paris. He has composed Symphony No. 1 (1935); No. 2 (1942); *Sinfonia pastorale* (1944); *Sinfonia notturna* (1946); violin concerto (1945); *Ballata Concertante* for harp and small orch. (1939); chamber music, songs, etc.

Hallström, Ivar, Swedish composer; b. Stockholm, June 5, 1826; d. there, April 11, 1901. He studied law at the Univ. of Upsala; there he became a friend of Prince Gustaf, a music amateur; on April 9, 1847, jointly with Gustaf, he produced his first opera, *The White Lady of Drottningholm;* later he became librarian to Prince Oscar; in 1861 he became a member of the Academy of Music in Stockholm. His opera *Hertig Magnus* (Stockholm, 1867) contained 20 arias in minor keys, and this fact was held against him by some critics, so that the opera was not maintained in the repertory. He then produced another opera, *The En-*

chanted Cat (Stockholm, 1869), which had better success. With his next opera *Den bergtagna* (*The Bewitched One*), staged in Stockholm on May 24, 1874, he achieved the greatest success of his career; it had further performances in Germany and Denmark. In this work Hallström made use of Swedish popular motifs, a pioneer attempt in Scandinavian operatic art. His next opera, *Vikingarna* (Stockholm, June 6, 1877), was but moderately successful; there followed *Neaga* (Stockholm, Feb. 24, 1885) to a libretto by Carmen Sylva (Queen Elisabeth of Rumania). He also wrote several ballets, cantatas, and arrangements of Swedish folksongs for piano.

Halm, August, German composer and writer; b. Gross-Altdorf, Württemberg, Oct. 26, 1869; d. Saalfeld, Feb. 1, 1929. A member of a family of scholars, he received an excellent general education; then studied theology at Tübingen. In 1892 he went to Munich, where he took courses with Rheinberger. Subsequently he devoted himself mainly to musical pedagogy; taught in various schools in Thuringia; conducted choral societies and also wrote music criticism. An August Halm Society was organized after his death. He was a prolific composer, but his music failed to take hold. He wrote 2 symphonies, which were performed in Ulm and Stuttgart; a piano concerto; 2 string quartets; 2 suites for piano trio, and a number of piano studies. He publ. *Harmonielehre* (Berlin, 1905); *Von zwei Kulturen der Musik* (Munich, 1913; 3rd ed., 1947); *Die Symphonien A. Bruckners* (Munich, 1913; 2nd ed., 1923); *Von Grenzen und Ländern der Musik* (Munich, 1916); *Einführung in die Musik* (Berlin, 1926); *Beethoven* (Berlin, 1927).—Cf. H. Höckner, *Die Musik in der deutschen Jugendbewegung* (Wolfenbüttel, 1927).

Halvorsen, Johan, Norwegian violinist and composer; b. Drammen, March 15, 1864; d. Oslo, Dec. 4, 1935. He studied violin with Lindberg at the Stockholm Cons.; was concertmaster of the Bergen Orch.; then went to Leipzig to study with Brodsky; subsequently studied with César Thomson in Belgium; returning to Norway in 1892, he became conductor of a theater orch. in Bergen; in 1899 was appointed conductor at the National Theater in Oslo. He was married to a niece of Grieg; this association was symbolic of his devotion to Grieg's art; his music reflects Grieg's influence very strongly. He wrote incidental music to Björnson's *Vasantasena* and *The King,* to Drachmann's *Gurre,* Eldegard's *Fossegrimen, Dronning Tamara,* and others. He further wrote 3 symphonies, a violin concerto, 2 Norwegian rhapsodies, several orchestral suites on Norwegian themes. His most popular works are the march, *Triumphant Entry of the Boyars,* and an arrangement of Handel's Passacaglia for violin and viola (or cello).

Halvorsen, Leif, Norwegian composer and violinist; b. Oslo, July 26, 1887. He studied in Oslo, then in Paris and in St. Petersburg (with Leopold Auer); upon his return to Oslo, he was concertmaster in the National Theater Orch. (1915-17); then opera conductor (1918-21); leader of the Cecilia Society (1921-28); conductor of Fredrikstad Singing Society from 1925 till 1947. He has written music for theatrical plays and an orchestral suite, *Peasant's Legend;* also piano pieces and songs.

Ham, Albert, English organist; b. Bath, June 7, 1858; d. Brighton, Feb. 4, 1940. He studied at Dublin Univ.; in 1897 he went to Toronto, and became a cathedral organist there; also taught choral music at the Toronto Cons. He wrote a number of anthems and secular choruses. One of his choral songs, *Little Jack Horner,* became very popular.

Hamal, Henri-Guillaume, Belgian organist and composer; b. Liège, Dec. 3, 1685; d. there, Dec. 3, 1752. As a youth he excelled in the various capacities of harpsichord player, singer, and cellist; was also a versatile composer of songs to texts in many languages. However, none of his works is preserved, and his reputation was transmitted mainly by members of his family. His son, **Jean-Noël Hamal** (b. Liège, Dec. 23, 1709; d. there, Nov. 26, 1778), studied with his father and later served as chorus master at the Liège Cathedral; also traveled in Italy, where he acquired additional knowledge of composition. He wrote a great number of church works: 56 Masses, 32 cantatas, 5 oratorios, 179 motets, also operas, overtures, and numerous pieces for the harpsichord. **Henri Hamal** (b. Liège, July 20, 1744; d. there, Sept. 17, 1820), a nephew of Jean-Noël Hamal, studied with him, and later in Italy. He was a chorusmaster at the Liège Cathedral for some time. He wrote much church music, of which 3 volumes are preserved in the Royal Library of Brussels.—Cf. Louis de Lavalleye, *Les Hamal de Liège* (Liège, 1860).

Hambourg, a family of musicians of Russian extraction. **Michael Hambourg** (b. Yaroslav, 1856; d. Toronto, Canada, June 18, 1916), was a piano pedagogue; appointed prof. of piano at the Moscow Cons. in 1880. After the successful London début of his son and pupil, Mark Hambourg (1890), he settled in England as a teacher; in 1911 he went to Toronto where he established, with his sons Boris and Jan, the Hambourg Cons. **Boris Hambourg** (b. Voronezh, Jan. 8, 1884; d. Toronto, Nov. 24, 1954), son of Michael, was a cellist. He was taken to London in 1890; studied cello with Walenn; then with Hugo Becker in Frankfurt (1898-1903); made an Australian tour, and then gave a series of 5 historical recitals in London (May-June, 1906). He made his American début at Pittsburgh (Oct. 28, 1910); in 1911 he settled in Toronto where, with his father and brother Jan, he established the Hambourg Cons. He was an original member of the Hart House String Quartet (from 1924). **Jan Hambourg** (b. Voronezh, Aug. 27, 1882; d. Tours, France, Sept. 29, 1947), a violinist, studied with Sauret and Wilhelmj in London, with Heermann in Frankfurt, Ševčik in Prague, and Eugène Ysaÿe in Brussels. With his brothers Boris and Mark he made a successful tour of England in 1909; he was in New York from 1916-22; in Paris from 1922-36; in Sorrento, Italy, from 1936-39; then returned to London. He died during a concert tour in France. **Mark Hambourg** (b. Bogutchar, May 31, 1879), a pianist, studied with his father; made his début as a child prodigy in Moscow (1888); then went to Vienna to study with Leschetizky. He subsequently traveled all over the world as pianist; played his thousandth concert on June 16, 1906. After a tour in the U. S. with his brothers, in 1935, he returned to London. He publ. *How to Play the Piano* (Philadelphia, 1922); *From Piano to Forte; a Thousand and One Notes* (London, 1931); memoirs, *The Eighth Octave* (London, 1951). A daughter of Mark Hambourg, **Michal Hambourg** (b. London, June 9, 1919), is also a pianist; made her début in London in 1936.

Hamboys, John. See **Hanboys.**

Hamel, Fred, musicologist; b. Paris, Feb. 19, 1903. He studied chemistry and music in German univs.; graduated from the Univ. of Bonn (1926); Ph.D., 1930. He wrote music criticism; after 1945, taught church music in Hanover; became editor (1947) of the magazine 'Musica.' He publ. *J. S. Bach: Geistige Welt* (Göttingen, 1951).

Hamel (ah-mel'), **Marie-Pierre,** French organ builder; b. Auneuil, Oise, Feb. 24, 1786; d. Beauvais, July 25, 1879. He was from a family of jurists, and himself pursued a legal career; in 1817 he became a judge at Beauvais. Apart from his professional activities, he was from his childhood interested in music; he manufactured a small organ of 3 octaves at the age of 13, and successfully repaired an old organ in a neighboring village to the satisfaction of the church wardens. He later rebuilt the grand organ of the Cathedral of Beauvais (1826). He publ. several manuals and descriptions of organs in various French cities. Principal writings: *Rapport sur les travaux du grand orgue de l'Église de la Madeleine à Paris* (Paris, 1846); *Nouveau Manuel complet du facteur d'orgues* (Paris, 1849; 3 vols.; new ed. by Guédon, 1903; contains a history of organ building).

Hamelle (ah-mel'), **Jacques,** French music publisher; in 1877 he acquired the publishing firm established by J. Maho in 1855. After Hamelle's death in 1917, the business was taken over by his sons. Among the principal composers represented in the catalogue are Franck, Saint-Saëns, Fauré, and Vincent d'Indy.

Hamerik (real name Hammerich), **Asger,** Danish composer; b. Copenhagen, April 8, 1843; d. Frederiksborg, July 13, 1923. He was a son of a prof. of divinity, who discouraged his musical interests; despite this opposition, he studied with Gade in Copenhagen and with Hans von Bülow in Berlin. He met Berlioz at Paris in 1864, and accompanied him to Vienna in 1866, studying orchestration. Hamerik was probably the only pupil that Berlioz had. He received a gold medal for his work *Hymne de la Paix,* at the contest for the Paris Exposition. His opera *Tovelille* was performed in Paris in concert form (May 6, 1865); another opera, *Hjalmar and Ingeborg,* was not performed in its entirety. In 1870 he visited Italy and produced his opera in Italian *La Vendetta* (Milan, Dec. 23, 1870). He then received an invitation to become director of the newly organized Peabody Cons. in Baltimore. He accepted, and remained in Baltimore for 26 years, until 1898, when he returned to Copenhagen. In Baltimore he wrote a number of symphonic works, which he conducted with the cons. orch.: *5 Nordic Suites* (1872-78); *Symphonie poétique* (1879); *Symphonie tragique* (1881); *Symphonie lyrique* (1885); *Symphonie majestueuse* (1888); *Symphonie sérieuse* (1892); *Symphonie* *spirituelle,* for string orch. (1895); and a choral symph. (No. 7).

Hamerik, Ebbe, Danish composer, son of Asger Hamerik; b. Copenhagen, Sept. 5, 1898. He studied with his father; conducted opera in Copenhagen (1919-22) and symphony concerts (1927-31), also conducted in Germany. —Works: the operas *Stepan* (Mainz, Nov. 30, 1924), *Leonardo da Vinci* (Antwerp, 1939), *Marie Grubbe* (Copenhagen, May 17, 1940), and *Rejsekammeraten,* after Andersen (Copenhagen, Jan. 5, 1946); also 5 symphonies; 2 string quartets; piano pieces; songs.

Hamilton, Clarence Grant, American organist and music educator; b. Providence, June 9, 1865; d. Wellesley, Mass., Feb. 14, 1935. He studied piano with Arthur Foote in Boston and Matthay in London; composition with Chadwick. He occupied various positions as organist in and around Boston; taught at Wellesley College for many years (1904-34); wrote piano pieces and songs. He publ. *Outlines of Music History* (1908; new ed., 1924); *Piano Teaching* (1910); *Sound and Its Relation to Music* (1911); *Music Appreciation, based upon Methods of Literary Criticism* (1920); *Piano Music, Its Composers and Characteristics* (1925); *Epochs in Musical Progress* (1926); *Touch and Expression in Piano Playing* (1927); *What Every Piano Pupil Should Know* (1928); *Ornaments in Classical and Modern Music* (1929).

Hamilton, Iain, British composer; b. Glasgow, June 6, 1922. He studied engineering and turned to music at the age of 24, when he entered the Royal College of Music in London as a student of William Alwyn (composition) and Harold Craxton (piano). He made rapid progress and within 3 years wrote a clarinet quintet (1949); string quartet (1950); Nocturnes for clarinet and piano (1951); ballet, *Clerk Saunders* (1951); viola sonata (1951); clarinet concerto (1951); and 2 symphonies (No. 1, 1949; No. 2, 1951, first perf. at the Cheltenham Festival, June 9, 1953). His music is distinguished by an incisive rhythmic manner and terse melodic expression within a framework of broadly tonal harmony with strident dissonant contrapuntal lines adding to the impression of advanced modernity.

Hamilton, James Alexander, English musician; b. London, 1785; d. there, Aug. 2, 1845. He was a son of a bookseller; his voluminous reading gave him a fine literary education. He developed a knack of transmitting knowledge acquired from music books to the public in an easy and attractive form; his numerous manuals went through several editions, but because of his intemperate habits, he was always in penury. He publ. *Modern Instructions for the Piano; Catechism of Singing; Catechism of the Rudiments of Harmony and Thoroughbass; Catechism of Counterpoint, Melody and Composition; A New Theoretical and Practical Musical Grammar;* a dictionary of musical terms; transl. Cherubini's *Counterpoint and Fugue.*

Hamlin, George, American tenor; b. Elgin, Ill., Sept 20, 1868; d. New York, Jan. 20, 1923. He studied irregularly with various teachers; sang in oratorio; made his operatic début in Victor Herbert's *Natoma* (Philadelphia, Dec. 15, 1911); among his chief parts were Cavaradossi in *Tosca* and Don José in *Carmen.*

Hamm, Adolf, church organist and choral conductor; b. Strasbourg, March 9, 1882; d. Basel, Oct. 15, 1938. He studied with Straube in Leipzig; in 1906, settled in Basel, where he became chief organist at the cathedral; also organized the Bach Choir there; taught at the Basel Cons. Paul Sacher edited a memorial volume, *Adolf Hamm: Erinnerungsschrift* (Basel, 1942).

Hammer, Heinrich Albert Eduard, violinist, conductor, and composer; b. Erfurt, Germany, Oct. 27, 1862; d. Phoenix, Arizona, Oct. 28, 1954. He studied violin with A. Pott, theory with H. Ritter; also took singing lessons with Mme. Viardot-Garcia in Paris. He then lived in Holland (1893-96) and Bochum (1897-1901); conducted the Lausanne Symph. Orch. (1901-05); in 1905 he organized a symph. orch. in Göteborg, Sweden. In 1908 he settled in America; conducted his own orch. in Washington, until 1921, when he went to California; lived mostly in Pasadena; continued to compose until the end of his long life; at the age of 90, married his pupil Arlene Hammer, who helped him to edit his autobiography (MS). Among his works are a symphony; 3 American Indian Rhapsodies for orch.; symph. poem, *Sunset at Sea;* an orchestral ode, *Columbia Triumphant in Peace* (1915), and much church music.

Hammerich, Angul, Danish writer on music; brother of Asger Hamerik (whose real name was Hammerich); b. Copenhagen, Nov. 25, 1848; d. there, April 26, 1931. He studied cello; at the same time, occupied a post in the Dept. of Finance; wrote music criticism; taught musicology at the Univ. of Copenhagen. In 1898 he founded the Collection of Ancient Musical Instruments; was a founder of the Danish Musicological Society (1921).—Writings: *Studies in Old Icelandic Music* (1890; Danish and German); *The Conservatory of Music at Copenhagen* (1892; in Danish); *Essay on the Music at the Court of Christian IV* (1892; in German, 1893); *On the Old Norse Lurs* (1893; in German, 1894); *Descriptive Illustrated Catalogue of the Historical Musical Museum of Copenhagen* (1909; in Danish; German transl. by E. Bobé, 1911); *Medieval Musical Relics of Denmark* (1912; in Danish; English transl. by Margaret Williams-Hamerik, 1912); *J. P. E. Hartmann, Biographical Essays* (1916); a history of Danish music to c. 1700 (1921).

Hammerschlag, János, music critic and composer; b. Prague, Dec. 10, 1885; d. Budapest, May 21, 1954. He was taken to Budapest as a child and studied music and literature; as a young man, became a newspaper critic; also taught music history and conducted choral concerts at the Budapest Cons. (1919-47); led the Madrigal Society; publ. a book on Bach (Budapest, 1926); numerous other writings and musical compositions (in Hungarian and German) are listed in J. S. Weissmann's article on Hammerschlag in 'Die Musik in Geschichte und Gegenwart.'

Hammerschmidt, Andreas, important composer of sacred music; b. Brüx, Bohemia, 1612; d. Zittau, Nov. 8, 1675. In 1626, his father took him to Freiberg, Saxony, and it was there that he received his education; studied music with Stephen Otto; in 1634, appointed organist at Freiberg, and in 1639, at Zittau, retaining this post until his death. A statue was erected to his memory there. His works for the Lutheran services are of great significance. He was one of the earliest composers to adopt the new Italian style of writing elaborate instrumental accompaniments to polyphonic vocal works. His works comprise *Musikalische Andachten* (subtitled *Geistliche Concerten)* in 5 parts (1638; 1641; 1642; 1646; 1652); *Dialogi oder Gespräche zwischen Gott und einer gläubigen Seele,* in 2 parts (Dresden, 1645; first part reprinted in vol. VIII of the 'Denkmäler der Tonkunst in Österreich'); *Weltliche Oden oder Liebesgesänge,* in 2 parts (1642-43); *Musicalische Gespräche über die Sonntags- und Fest-Evangelia* (Dresden, 1655-56). Reprints by H. J. Moser in 'Alte Meister des deutschen Liedes' and A. Schering in 'Geschichte der Musik in Beispielen' (No. 194). Hugo Leichtentritt publ. a selection in vol. 40 of the 'Denkmäler deutscher Tonkunst'; other reprints by Commer in 'Musica sacra' (Nos. 25/26); Oppenheimer, Sulzbach, and others. —Cf. E. Steinhard, *Zum 300. Geburtstage Andreas Hammerschmidts* (Prague, 1914); G. Schünemann, *Beiträge zur Biographie Hammerschmidts,* in 'Sammelbände der Internationalen Musik-Gesellschaft' (XII); F. Blume, *Das monodische Prinzip in der protestantischen Kirchenmusik* (Leipzig, 1925).

Hammerstein, Oscar, celebrated impresario; b. Stettin, Germany, May 8, 1846; d. New York, Aug. 1, 1919. At the age of 16 he ran away from home; spent some time in England; then went to America, where he worked in a New York cigar factory. Possessing an inventive mind, he patented a machine for shaping the tobacco leaves by suction; later edited a tobacco trade journal. At the same time, he practiced the violin; learned to write music, and dabbled in playwriting; in 1868 he produced in New York a comedy in German; he also wrote the libretto and music of an operetta, *The Kohinoor* (N. Y., Oct. 24, 1893). His main activity, however, was in management. He built the Harlem Opera House (1888), Olympia Music Hall (1899), and the Republic Theater (1900), and presented brief seasons of plays and operas there. In 1906 he announced plans for the Manhattan Opera House in New York, his crowning achievement. The enterprise was originally planned as a theater for opera in English, but it opened with an Italian company in Bellini's *Puritani* (Dec. 3, 1906). Hammerstein entered into bold competition with the Metropolitan Opera, and engaged celebrated singers, among them Melba, Nordica, Tetrazzini, and Mary Garden; among spectacular events presented by him were the first American performances of 5 operas by Massenet, Charpentier's *Louise,* and Debussy's *Pelléas et Mélisande.* The new venture held its own for 4 seasons, but in the end Hammerstein was compelled to yield; in April, 1910, he sold the Manhattan Opera House to the management of the Metropolitan for $1,200,000, and agreed not to produce grand opera in New York for 10 years. He also sold to the Metropolitan (for $100,000) his interests in the Philadelphia Opera House built by him in 1908. (The texts of these agreements were published in full in the 'Musical Courier' of March 29, 1911.) Defeated in his main ambition in America, Hammerstein transferred his activities to England. There he built the London Opera House, which opened with a lavish production of *Quo Vadis* by Nougès (Nov. 17, 1911). However, he failed to establish himself in London, and after a season there, returned to New York. In contravention of his agreement with the Metropolitan Opera, he announced a season at the newly organized America Opera House in New York, but the Metropolitan secured an injunction against him, and he was forced to give up his operatic venture. The building then opened as the Lexington Theater, and its productions were limited to mixed theatrical entertainment.—See Vincent Sheean, *Oscar Hammerstein, I: The Life and Exploits of an Impresario* (with a preface by Oscar Hammerstein II; N. Y., 1956).

Hammerstein, Oscar, II, American lyricist; grandson of the preceding; b. New York, July 12, 1895. He studied law at Columbia Univ., graduating in 1917; then became interested in the theater. He collaborated in the librettos for Friml's *Rose Marie* (1924) and Romberg's *The Desert Song* (1926); his greatest success as a lyricist came with the production of Jerome Kern's *Show Boat* (1926), including the celebrated song *Ol' Man River.* In 1943 he joined hands with the composer Richard Rodgers, and together they produced several brilliant musical comedies, with spectacular success: *Oklahoma!* (1943; Pulitzer Prize); *Carousel* (1945); *Allegro* (1947); *South Pacific* (1949; Pulitzer Prize, 1950) *The King and I* (1951); *Me and Juliet* (1953); *Pipe Dream* (1955), etc. His lyrics are characterized by a combination of appealing sentiment and sophisticated nostalgia, making them particularly well suited to the modern theater. — See Deems Taylor, *Some Enchanted Evenings: The Story of Rodgers and Hammerstein* (N. Y., 1953); also David Ewen, *Richard Rodgers* (N. Y., 1957).

Hammond, John Hays, Jr., American inventor; b. San Francisco, April 13, 1888; studied at Sheffield Scientific School, Yale Univ. (B.S., 1910); received his Sc.D. at George Washington Univ. Besides inventions relating to radio, he made various improvements in pipe organ mechanisms, and invented a new type of reflecting modulator for pianos, a dynamic multiplicator for electric recording reproductions in phonographs, and the 'Pirafon,' a combination of radio, phonograph, and piano.

Hammond, Laurens, American inventor; b. Evanston, Ill., Jan. 11, 1895; studied at Cornell Univ. (1916). While employed as an engineer with a Detroit automobile concern, he experimented privately, developing a synchronous motor which he later used in his Hammond Organ, an instrument resembling a spinet piano in appearance, which reproduces through electrical impulses the sound of the pipe organ. He later developed the Novachord, an electrical device that can simulate the sound of nearly any instrument. It was first demonstrated in the Commerce Department auditorium, Washington, D. C., on Feb. 2, 1939. In 1940 he introduced Solovox, an attachment for piano which enables an amateur to project the melody in organ-like tones. In 1950 he brought out a 'chord organ' supplying basic harmonies by pressing a special button for each.

Hammond, Richard, composer; b. Kent, England, Aug. 26, 1896. He received his education in America; graduated from Yale; then took lessons with Nadia Boulanger; took active part in various modern music societies in New York City. In his own compositions he exploits exotic subjects; they include *Six Chinese Fairy Tales,* for orch. (1921); *Voyage to the East,* for voice and orch. (1926); *West Indian Dances,* for orch. (1930); 2 piano suites, *Gitanesques et Scènes Espagnoles* and *Valses Exotiques et Valses Conventionelles;* an oboe sonata; vocal works.

Han or **Hahn, Ulrich** (Udalricus Gallus), German music printer; b. Ingolstadt; d. Rome, 1478. He is believed to be the first to print music with movable type, in his *Missale secundum consuetudinem curie romane* (Rome, 1476). In this work the double-process method was employed, i.e., 2 impressions were made; first, the lines of the staff were printed, following which the note forms (mostly square black heads with a stem at the right side) were superimposed over them.—Cf. O. Kinkeldey, *Music and Music Printing in Incunabula,* in 'Papers' of Bibliographic Society of America (1932).

Hanboys (or **Hamboys**), **John**, English music theorist of the 15th century. He was one of the first Englishmen on whom the degree of Mus. D. was conferred. He also held an ecclesiastic rank. His Latin treatise, 'Summa super musicam continuam et discretam,' which describes the musical notation of his time, is printed by Coussemaker in his 'Scriptores' (vol. 1, p. 416).—Cf. J. Bale, *Illustrium Maioris Britanniae Scriptorum.*

Catalogus (1559; p. 617); J. Pulver, *Biographical Dictionary of Old English Music* (1923); J. Pulver, *The English Theorists, VI; John Hanboys,* in the 'Musical Times' (March, 1934).

Hanchett, Henry Granger, American music pedagogue and inventor; b. Syracuse, N. Y., Aug. 29, 1853; d. Siasconset, Mass., Aug. 19, 1918. He studied at the N. Y. Homoeopathic Medical College (M. D., 1884); at the same time he pursued pianistic studies with various teachers; from 1890, held teaching positions in music schools in N. Y. and elsewhere; also was organist at many churches (1884-1898). In 1874, he obtained a patent for the sustaining piano pedal, now in use on all grand pianofortes. He publ. *Teaching as a Science* (1882), *The Art of the Musician* (1905), and *An Introduction to the Theory of Music* (1918); also wrote several church services, anthems, etc.

Handel (written Händel in Germany, Haendel in France; also the forms Hendel, Hendeler, Händler, or Hendtler were used by various branches of the family), **Georg Friedrich** (at first spelled Hendel, in England; in his later period, he himself adopted the quasi-anglicized form of George Frideric Handel); b. Halle, Feb. 23, 1685; d. London, April 14, 1759. His father, a barber, afterwards surgeon and valet to the Prince of Saxe-Magdeburg, at the age of 63 married a second wife, Dorothea Taust, daughter of the pastor at Giebichenstein, near Halle. Handel was the second son of this marriage. At the age of 7, Handel was taken by his father on a visit to an elder stepbrother, valet at the court of Saxe-Weissenfels; here the boy gained access to the chapel and its organ. The Duke of Saxe-Weissenfels noticed the boy's eagerness in learning music and persuaded his father to give him a musical education. Although the father intended Handel to pursue a legal career, he made arrangements for music lessons with the organist of the cathedral of Halle, Friedrich Wilhelm Zachau. Under Zachau's efficient guidance, Handel practiced the oboe, harpsichord, and organ; also studied counterpoint and fugue. He was only 12 years old when he became assistant organist there; he composed 6 sonatas for 2 oboes and bass, and wrote a motet for every Sunday. That year (1697) his father died; in pious fulfillment of the parent's wishes, Handel entered the Univ. of Halle (1702) as a law student, but left school after a year and went to Hamburg. There he was engaged as 'violino di ripieno' by Reinhard Keiser, the director of the German Opera. In Hamburg he met Mattheson, and in his company made a journey to Lübeck (1703), seeking the position of organist, as successor to the aging Buxtehude. It was a custom for an incoming organist to marry the old organist's daughter, and this condition neither Mattheson nor Handel was willing to fulfill. Accordingly, they returned to Hamburg. Mattheson was apparently jealous of Handel's growing success, and annoyed by Handel's haughty manner. A violent quarrel occurred between the two in the course of a production of Mattheson's opera *Cleopatra.* Mattheson, who not only sang on the stage, but also directed from the harpsichord at the conclusion of his acting, asked Handel to take his place while he was on the stage. Handel refused to be a mere substitute, and would not give up his seat at the harpsichord. The story goes that a duel ensued, and shots exchanged; it was asserted even that Handel had a narrow escape, when a bullet hit his waistcoat button and was deflected. However, the conflict could not have been so vehement, since Mattheson remained Handel's friend and became his biographer. In the meantime, Handel made great progress as composer. He produced 2 operas at Hamburg, *Almira* (Jan. 8, 1705) and *Nero* (Feb. 25, 1705); he was also commissioned by Keiser's successor, Saurbrey, to write *Florindo und Daphne* (1708), an opera filling 2 evenings. In 1706, with 200 ducats saved from music teaching, Handel went to Italy, visiting Florence, Venice, Rome, and Naples. In Florence he brought out his first Italian opera, *Rodrigo* (1708); his next Italian opera, *Agrippina,* was produced in Venice (Dec. 26, 1709) with extraordinary success. In Rome he produced 2 oratorios, *La Resurrezione* (April 8, 1708) and *Il Trionfo del tempo e del disinganno* (1708), with the famous violin virtuoso Corelli as leader; and in Naples the serenata *Aci, Galatea e Polifemo* (July 19, 1708), remarkable for its bass solo for a voice of 2 octaves and a fifth in compass. He made the acquaintance of Domenico Scarlatti, with whom he vied at the harpsichord and organ; and he also met Alessandro Scarlatti. In 1710 Handel returned to Germany, and became Kapellmeister to the Elector of Hanover, replacing Steffani, who had especially recommended him as successor. Late in that year Handel visited England; he produced his opera *Rinaldo* at the Haymarket Theatre on Feb. 24, 1711, with excellent success, even though the score was compounded of arias and other material composed at an earlier date. He then returned to Hanover, but in 1712 obtained a leave of absence, and went again to London. The operas that he produced there, *Il Pastor fido* (Nov. 22, 1712) and *Teseo* (Jan. 10, 1713), were much superior to *Rinaldo,* but failed to win comparable acclaim; but an ode for Queen Anne's birthday, performed at Windsor on Feb. 6, 1713, and a *Te Deum* and *Jubilate* in celebration of the Peace of Utrecht (1713) won him royal favor, with an annuity of £ 200. Encouraged, Handel tarried in London for a longer time than the leave of absence from Hanover entitled him to. On Queen Anne's death, however, the Elector of Hanover became King George I of England. Handel, with his old patron on the English throne, decided to remain in England permanently; in 1727 he became a British subject. The story that George I was angry at Handel for his neglect of duty in Hanover, and that he was consequently cold to Handel in the first year of his reign, is to be regarded as a legend. All evidence points to continued favors bestowed on Handel by the King, who added another £ 200 to Handel's annuity. In 1716 Handel accompanied him on a visit to Hanover. On July 17, 1717, an aquatic fête on the Thames River was arranged by royal order. The King's boat was followed by a barge in which an orchestra of some fifty players was arrayed. It was Handel who was given the task of writing the music, and the King liked it so well that he ordered the playing to be repeated twice. Whether Handel's music played then was completely or even partly identical with the score later published as *Water Musick* is a moot question. In 1717 Handel succeeded Pepusch as chapel master to the Duke of Chandos, for whom he wrote his first English oratorio, *Esther,* the secular cantata *Acis and Galatea,* and the so-called Chandos Anthems. Handel also served as music master to the daughters of the Prince of Wales, and wrote for Princess Anne his first collection of *Suite de pièces* (1720) for harpsichord (*The Lessons*), which includes the air with variations later known (even though the nickname is gratuitous) as *The Harmonious Blacksmith.* He was then appointed director of the new Royal Academy of Music, established chiefly for the production of Italian opera, and on April 27, 1720, successfully brought out his opera *Radamisto.* It was about then that the strife arose between Handel and the Italian composer Bononcini, who had been invited to England by a rival enterprise and enjoyed the support of a powerful group of the English aristocracy. The feud was immortalized by the poet John Byrom in verse ('Some say, compar'd to Bononcini, that Mynheer Handel's but a ninny,' etc.). Handel won a Pyrrhic victory when Bononcini was caught in an act of plagiarism and was compelled to leave England in disgrace; Handel's own operas failed to gain public honor even with the elimination of his chief rival. During this period Handel staged, with varying success, the following operas at the King's Theatre: *Floridante* (Dec. 9, 1721), *Ottone* (Jan. 12, 1723), *Flavio* (May 14, 1723), *Giulio Cesare* (Feb. 20, 1724), *Tamerlano* (Oct. 31, 1724), *Rodelinda* (Feb. 13, 1725), *Scipione* (March 12, 1726), *Alessandro* (May 5, 1726), *Admeto* (Jan. 31, 1727), *Riccardo Primo* (Nov. 11, 1727), *Siroe* (Feb. 17, 1728), and *Tolemeo* (April 30, 1728). In 1727 he wrote 4 grand anthems for the coronation of George II and Queen Caroline. In 1729, after a visit to Germany and Italy, Handel associated himself with Heidegger, the owner of the King's Theatre, and inaugurated the season with his opera *Lotario* (Dec. 2, 1729), followed by *Partenope* (Feb. 24, 1730), *Poro* (Feb. 2, 1731), *Ezio* (Jan. 15, 1732), *Sosarme* (Feb. 15, 1732), and *Orlando* (Jan. 27, 1733), when the partnership ended. In 1732, Handel gave a special and successful production of his revised oratorio *Esther,* followed by *Acis and Galatea.* In 1733 he brought out the oratorios *Deborah* (March 17) and *Athalia* (July 10) at Oxford, where he publicly played the organ, and excited as much admiration by his performance as by his works; he was offered the degree of Mus. Doc. (hon. c.). The same year, Handel undertook the sole management of opera, but his manners and methods, a quarrel with his principal singer, Senesino, and a raising of prices, caused many of his chief subscribers to suspend their support and start a rival troupe, 'The Opera of the Nobility,' with Porpora and later Hasse as composer and conductor. They took possession of the King's Theatre, and Handel first went to Lincoln's Inn Fields, and then to Covent Garden, but in 1737 failed; the rival house also had to close. The operas of this period were a revision of *Il Pastor Fido* (preceded by a ballet, *Terpsicore,* 1734), *Ariodante* (Jan. 8, 1735), *Alcina* (April 16, 1735), *Atalanta* (May 12, 1736), *Arminio* (Jan. 12, 1737), *Giustino* (Feb. 16, 1737), and *Berenice* (May 18, 1737); the ode *Alexander's Feast* was also produced at Covent Garden (Feb. 19, 1736), and *Il Trionfo del tempo e della verità* (a revision of *Il Trionfo del tempo e del disinganno* of 1708) in 1737.

Handel's superhuman efforts to hold his own caused a failing of his strength; a stroke of paralysis incapacitated one of his hands, his brain was overtaxed, and, by the urgent advice of his friends, he went to Aix-la-Chapelle; he returned to London in November, 1737, with improved health. Heidegger had meantime formed a new company from the ruins of the two, and for this venture Handel wrote several operas: *Faramondo* (Jan. 3, 1738), *Serse* (April 15, 1738), *Jupiter in Argos* (May 1, 1739), *Imeneo* (Nov. 22, 1740), and *Deidamia* (Jan. 10, 1741). This last date marks a decisive turning point: he now abandoned stage composition for the work to which he owes enduring fame—oratorio. In close succession, Handel produced the oratorios *Saul* (Jan. 16, 1739) and *Israel in Egypt* (April 4, 1739). There followed the *Ode for St. Cecilia's Day* (Nov. 22, 1739), and *L'allegro, il pensieroso, ed il moderato,* after Milton (Feb. 27, 1740). In 1741, at the invitation of the viceroy of Ireland, Handel visited Dublin, and produced his immortal *Messiah* on April 13, 1742. His cordial reception in Ireland greatly compensated for previous disasters. On his return to London, he again became the popular favorite. *Messiah* was followed by *Samson* (Feb. 18, 1743), the *Dettingen Te Deum, Semele* (Feb. 10, 1744), *Joseph and his Brethren* (March 2, 1744), and *Belshazzar* (March 27, 1745). Once more, he became entangled in monetary troubles; however, his creative strength was not impaired thereby. Soon his two works, *Occasional Oratorio* (Feb. 14, 1746) and *Judas Maccabaeus* (April 1, 1747) were brought out; then appeared *Joshua* (March 9, 1748), *Susanna* (Feb. 10, 1749), *Solomon* (March 17, 1749), *Theodora* (March 16, 1750), *The Choice of Hercules* (March 1, 1751), and *Jephtha* (Feb. 26, 1752). In 1750, for the third time, Handel had retrieved his fortunes, and revisited his native country. In 1751, during the composition of *Jephtha,* he was afflicted with failing eyesight, and underwent three unsuccessful operations for cataract, total blindness being the result. He continued his musical performances under the direction of his pupil John Christopher Smith, and accompanied his oratorios, on the organ, up to his death. On April 6, 1759, *Messiah* was given as the final performance of the season, Handel presiding at the organ; on the 14th, the Saturday between Good Friday and Easter, he died. He was buried in Westminster Abbey, where a magnificent monument by Roubiliac marks his grave.

Handel had a commanding presence, and his features were animated and dignified. His health was robust. Of fearless independence, he was of a choleric temperament, and prone to forcible outbreaks, but he was easily restored to good humor, and possessed a fund of ready wit. His liberality and charitableness were renowned. He remained unmarried, and was never known to have associated romantically with a woman.

The grandeur and sustained power of Handel's oratorio style, the expressive simplicity of his melody, and the breadth and clarity of the harmonic structure form a wonderful artistic whole. He is unquestionably one of the 'great masters.' His *Messiah* took England, and after her the rest of the musical world, by storm. At the first London performance, when the grand 'Hallelujah Chorus' rang out, the entire audience rose like one man, carried away by lofty enthusiasm— thus originated the custom of standing during this chorus. Mozart, Mendelssohn, Brahms, and others have provided additional accompaniments to several of his works. Handel was peculiarly fortunate in coming to England just as the ebb of English national stage music after the death of Purcell (from whom Handel learned much) was turning toward the flood of Italian opera. His own dramatic works, strongly influenced by Keiser in Hamburg and the two Scarlattis in Italy, are of the finest of the period, and the best of them bear comparison with his oratorios. Precisely contemporary with J. S. Bach, he was quite outside the latter's sphere of influence and no communication existed between them. Of purely instrumental compositions Handel wrote a considerable number: For harpsichord: 3 sets of *Lessons;* 6 fugues; many minuets; a march; the *Forest Musick* (Dublin, 1742); short pieces. For orch.: *Water Musick* (1717); the *Fireworks Musick* (1749); 3 sets of 6 organ concertos each (1738, 1740, 1761); *Concertone* in 9 parts, for 2 violins, cello, oboe, and string orch. (1741); concerto for trumpets and horns; concerto for horns and sidedrums (MS). Chamber music: several trio sonatas for various instruments, a sonata for flute with bass, etc. — Many original MSS of his works he bequeathed to his amanuensis, John Christopher Smith; the latter's son, Handel's pupil, presented them to George III. They are now in the British Museum as a part of the King's Music Library, and comprise 32 vols. of operas, 21 of oratorios, 7 of odes and serenatas, 12 of sacred music, 11 of cantatas and sketches, and 5 of instrumental music. In the Fitzwilliam Collection at Cambridge are 7 vols. containing rough drafts, notes and sketches for various works; also a complete Chandos anthem, *O praise the Lord with one consent.*

An edition of Handel's works in 36 vols., by Arnold, was publ. by command of George III (1787-97), but it is incomplete and inaccurate. A monumental edition in 100 vols. was issued (1856-94) by the German Handel Society, under the editorship of Fr. Chrysander. J. M. Coopersmith has collected and edited 10 vols. of unpublished material to complete this edition, brought out an authentic version of *Messiah* in vocal score, and also completed a thematic index of the whole. In 1955 a new complete ed. was begun by Max Schneider and Rudolf Steglich for the Georg-Friedrich-Händel Gesellschaft in Halle. A series of yearbooks, 6 of which had been publ. from 1928-1933, was continued by the Halle group with vol. 7 in 1955.

BIBLIOGRAPHY—BIOGRAPHY: J. Mattheson, *Grundlage einer Ehrenpforte* (Hamburg, 1740; reprint, Berlin, 1910); J. Mainwaring, *Memoirs of the Late G. F. Handel* (London, 1760; German transl., with notes by Mattheson, 1761; French transl. by Arnauld and Suard, 1778); Ch. Burney, *An Account of the Musical Pantheon in Commemoration of Handel* (London, 1785); W. Coxe, *Anecdotes of G. F. Handel and J. C. Smith* (London, 1799); R. Clark, *Reminiscences of Handel* (London, 1836); K. E. Förstemann, *G. F. Händels Stammbaum* (Leipzig, 1844); W. H. Callcott, *A Few Facts in the Life of Handel* (London, 1850); H. Townsend, *An Account of Handel's Visit to Dublin* (Dublin, 1852); V. Schoelcher, *The Life of Handel* (London, 1857); A. E. Stothard, *Handel: His Life, Personal and Professional* (London, 1857); M. Delany, *Autobiography of Mary Granville* (London, 1862; contains a detailed account of Handel's death); F. J. van Kempen, *G. F. Handel: Een Leven* (Leyden, 1868); J. Marshall, *Handel* (London, 1881); W. S. Rockstro, *Life of Handel* (London, 1883); J. O. Opel, *Mitteilungen zur Geschichte der Familie des Tonkünstlers Händel* (Leipzig, 1885); F. Volbach, *Handel* (Berlin, 1897; augmented ed., 1906); F. C. A. Williams, *Handel* (London, 1904); J. C. Hadden, *Life of Handel* (London, 1905); R. A. Streatfeild, *Handel* (London, 1909); Romain Rolland, *Handel* (Paris, 1910; English transl., N. Y., 1923); H. Davey, *Handel* (London, 1912); G. Thormälius, *G. F. Händel* (Stuttgart, 1912); M. Brenet, *Haendel* (Paris, 1912); Newman Flower, *G. F. Handel, His Personality and His Times* (London, 1923; new ed., 1947); Hugo Leichtentritt, *Händel* (Stuttgart, 1924); J. Müller-Blattau, *Händel* (Potsdam, 1933); E. J. Dent, *Handel* (London, 1934); Ch. F. Williams, *Handel* (London, 1935); Lore Liebeman, *G. F. Händel und Halle* (Halle, 1935); H. Weinstock, *Handel* (N. Y., 1946); P. M. Young, *Handel* (London, 1946); W. C. Smith, *Concerning Handel, His Life and Works* (London, 1949); A. E. Cherbuliez, *G. F. Händel: Leben und Werk* (Olten, 1949); G. Abraham, ed., *Handel: a Symposium* (Oxford, 1954); Otto Erich Deutsch, *Handel, A Documentary Biography* (N. Y., 1954; most valuable; reproduces in chronological order all pertinent contemporary documents and notices in the press). The most elaborate biography is that by Fr. Chrysander, *G. F. Händel* (Leipzig, 1858-67); in 3 vols., bringing the life of Handel down to 1740; the work remained incomplete; an unchanged reprint was publ. in 1919. An extensive biography, *G. F. Händel; sein Leben, sein Werk,* by Walter Serauky, began publication in 1956, with vol. 3, covering the years 1736-1743. See also *Handel,* by J. Fuller Maitland and W. B. Squire in the 'Dictionary of National Biography.'

—CRITICISM. APPRECIATION: J. M. Weissebeck, *Der grosse Musikus Händel im Universalruhme* (Nuremberg, 1809); H. Chorley, *Handel-Studies* (2 vols., London, 1859); G. Gervinus, *Händel und Shakespeare* (Leipzig, 1868); R. Franz, *Über Bearbeitungen älterer Tonwerke, namentlich Bachscher und Händelscher Vokalmusik* (Leipzig, 1871; reprinted by R. Bethge as *Gesammelte Schriften über die Wiederbelebung Bachscher und Händelscher Werke* (Leipzig, 1910); E. Frommel, *Händel und Bach* (Berlin, 1878); Fr. Chrysander, *Händels biblische Oratorien in geschichtlicher Betrachtung* (Hamburg, 1897); F. J. Crowest, *Handel and English Music* (in vol. V. of Traill's 'Social England,' London, 1893-98); G. Vernier, *L'Oratorio biblique de Handel* (Cahors, 1901); J. A. Fuller Maitland, *The Age of Bach and Handel* (Vol. IV of 'The Oxford History of Music'; Oxford, 1902); J. Garat, *La Sonate de Handel* (Paris, 1905); S. Taylor, *The Indebtedness of Handel to Works by Other Composers* (Cambridge, 1906); J. R. Carreras, *El Oratorio musical desde su origen hasta nuestros días* (Barcelona, 1906); P. Robinson, *Handel and His Orbit* (London, 1908); A. Schering, *Geschichte des Oratoriums* (Leipzig, 1911); R. A. Streatfeild, *The Granville Collection of Handel MSS,* in the 'Mus. Antiquary' (July, 1911); W. J. Lawrence, *Handeliana; the Dublin Charitable Musical Society,* in the 'Mus. Antiquary'

(Jan., 1912); H. Abert, *Händel als Dramatiker* (Göttingen, 1921); R. Steglich, *Was weisst du von Händel?* (Leipzig, 1931); H. J. Moser, *Der junge Händel und seine Vorgänger in Halle* (Halle, 1929); E. Bairstow, *The Messiah* (London, 1928); F. Kahle, *Handels Cembalo-Suiten* (Berlin, 1928); J. M. Coopersmith, *A List of Portraits, Sculptures, etc., of Handel,* in 'Music & Letters' (1932); F. Ehrlinger, *Händels Orgelkonzerte* (Erlangen, 1934); Hugo Leichtentritt, *Handel's Harmonic Art,* in the 'Mus. Quarterly' (April, 1935); Virginia L. Redway, *Handel in Colonial and Post-Colonial America,* in the 'Mus. Quarterly' (April, 1935); J. M. Coopersmith, *Handelian Lacunae,* in the 'Mus. Quarterly' (April, 1935); Handel's letters, ed. by P. Rolli in 'Musica d'oggi' (Dec., 1932); *The Letters and Writings of G. F. Handel,* ed. by Erich Müller (London, 1935); R. M. Myers, *Handel's Messiah, A Touchstone of Taste* (N. Y., 1948); J. Herbage, *Messiah* (N. Y., 1948); J. P. Larsen, *Handel's Messiah* (N. Y., 1957). See also Loewenberg's *Annals of Opera* (Cambridge, 1943; new ed., 1955) for a list of revivals of Handel's operas.

Handrock, Julius, German piano pedagogue and composer; b. Naumburg, June 22, 1830; d. Halle, Jan. 5, 1894. He publ. several collections of piano studies which have retained their popularity among teachers and students for many years (*Moderne Schule der Geläufigkeit; 50 Melodisch-technische Klavier-Etuden,* etc.).

Handschin, Jacques, eminent musicologist; b. Moscow, April 4, 1886; d. Basel, Nov. 25, 1955. He studied organ in Munich (with Max Reger and Straube) and in Paris (with Widor); in 1909 he was appointed organ teacher at the St. Petersburg Cons.; in 1920, together with Prof. Kovalenkov, he founded a laboratory for the study of acoustics; went to Basel in 1921; became a teacher at the Univ. of Basel in 1924, then professor in 1930; also served as organist at St. Peter's Church in Zürich. From 1936 he was vice-president of the International Society for Musical Research. He publ.: *Mussorgsky* (1924), *Die Grundlagen des a cappella Stils* (Zürich, 1929), *Saint-Saëns* (1930), *Stravinsky* (1933); *Das Zeremonienwerk Kaiser Konstantins und die sangbare Dichtung* (Basel, 1942); *Der Toncharakter; eine Einführung in die Tonpsychologie* (Zürich, 1948); *Musikgeschichte im Überblick* (Lucerne, 1948); also many valuable articles.—A memorial volume, *Jacques Handschin, Aufsätze und Bibliographie,* containing reprints of some 50 articles by Handschin, was publ. in Basel in 1957, ed. by Dr. Hans Oesch.

Handy, William Christopher, American Negro composer, 'father of the blues'; b. Florence, Ala., Nov. 16, 1873. His father and grandfather were ministers. In 1892 he was graduated from the Teachers' Agricultural and Mechanical College, Huntsville, Alabama; became a school teacher and also worked in iron mills; learned to play the cornet and was soloist at Chicago World's Fair (1893); became bandmaster of Mahara's Minstrels. From 1900-02 he taught at Agricultural and Mechanical College; then from 1903-21, conducted his own orchestra and toured the South. He received the award of the National Association for Negro Music, St. Louis (1937). On Jan. 1, 1954, he married his secretary, Irma Louise Logan. His famous song, *Memphis Blues,* was originally written as a campaign song for the Mayor of Memphis, E. H. Crump (1911); even more celebrated was his *St. Louis Blues* (1914), which opened an era in popular music, turning the theretofore prevalent spirit of ragtime gayety to ballad-like nostalgia, with the 'blue' lowered seventh as a distinctive melodic peculiarity. He followed this with 3 more 'blues': *Yellow Dog, Beale Street, Joe Turner;* the march *Hail to the Spirit of Freedom* (1915); *Ole Miss,* for piano (1916); the songs, *Aunt Hagar's Children* (1920); *Loveless Love* (1921); *Aframerican Hymn;* etc. He publ. the anthologies *Negro Spirituals and Songs: a Treasury of the Blues* (N. Y., 1926; 2nd ed., 1949); *Book of Negro Spirituals* (N. Y., 1938); *Negro Music and Musicians* (N. Y., 1944); also *Negro Authors and Composers of the U. S.* (N. Y., 1936); wrote an autobiography, *Father of the Blues* (N. Y., 1941).

Hanff, Johann Nikolaus, German organist and composer; b. Wechmar, near Mühlhausen, 1630; d. Schleswig, 1711. He was organist in Eupin; later in Hamburg (1706-11). A few months before his death, he was appointed organist at the cathedral of Schleswig. He was a master of the chorale-prelude, and his works considerably influenced J. S. Bach's style in this form. Only six of his chorale-preludes are extant (publ. in 1907 by K. Straube in his 45 *Choralvorspiele alter Meister;* reprinted by E. White in *Masterpieces of Organ Music,* N. Y., 1949). —Cf. Hans Schillings, *Tobias Eniccelius, Friedrich Meister, Nikolaus Hanff: ein Beitrag zur Geschichte der evangelischen Frühkantate in Schleswig-Holstein* (Kiel, 1934);

H. J. Moser, *Die evangelische Kirchenmusik in Deutschland* (Berlin, 1954).

Hanfstängel, Marie, dramatic soprano; b. Breslau, April 30, 1846; d. Munich, Sept. 5, 1917. She studied at Baden-Baden with Mme. Viardot-Garcia; made her début as Agathe in *Der Freischütz* at the Théâtre Lyrique, Paris (Feb. 27, 1867). On the declaration of the Franco-Prussian war, she returned to Germany, and was engaged at the Stuttgart Opera. She sang at the Metropolitan Opera House in N. Y. (1884-86); then retired and lived mostly in Munich. She publ. *Meine Lehrweise der Gesangskunst* (1902).

Hanisch, Joseph, German organist and composer; b. Regensburg, March 24, 1812; d. there, Oct. 9, 1892. He studied with his father, and with Proske, with whom he went to Italy as an assistant (1834). In 1839 he became organist at the Regensburg cathedral. He wrote *Missa auxilium Christianorum; Quatuor hymni pro festo corporis Christi;* contributed organ accompaniments to the *Graduale* and *Vesperale Romanum* (with Haberl); also composed pieces for organ solo. He was a master of improvisation, and was regarded as one of the greatest in this field in his time.

Hanke, Karl, German composer; b. Rosswalde, Silesia, c. 1750; d. Flensburg, June 10, 1803. As a young man, he was sent to Vienna to pursue his music studies; there he briefly associated himself with Gluck, and profited by the master's advice. He then held the post of musical director in Brno (1778-81), Warsaw (1781-83), and Hamburg (1784-86). In 1791 he settled in Flensburg, where he remained until the end of his life. He composed several pieces for the stage; his Singspiel *Der Wunsch mancher Mädchen* (1781), dedicated to Gluck, was performed on various occasions with some success; 2 albums of his songs were publ. in 1796-97. — Cf. Alfred Einstein, *Ein Schüler Glucks,* in 'Acta Musicologica' (1938).

Hannikainen, Tauno, Finnish cellist and conductor; b. Jyväskylä, Feb. 26, 1896. He studied at the Helsinki Cons. (1914-17); then with Casals in Paris (1921); also took courses in Berlin, Vienna, and Milan. He was first cellist in the Helsinki Orch. (1916-19); was a member of the Hannikainen Trio with his brothers Arvo (violin) and Ilmari (piano). He was appointed conductor of the Symph. Orch. of Turku in 1927; came to the U. S. in 1939; made his début with the Boston Symph. Orch., Feb. 2, 1940. He was conductor of the Duluth Orch. (1942-46); assistant conductor of the Chicago Orch. (1947-50); then returned to Finland, and was appointed conductor of the Helsinki Symph. Orch. (1951). He married the Finnish soprano Anne Niskanen on June 21, 1933.

Hanon (ah-nohn'), **Charles-Louis,** French pianist and pedagogue; b. Rem-sur-l'Aire, 1820; d. Boulogne-sur-Mer, March 19, 1900. He wrote valuable studies for piano, *Méthode élémentaire de piano, Extraits de chefs-d'œuvre des grands maîtres,* and especially *Le Pianiste-Virtuose* (60 progressive studies), which became a standard piano method all over the world. Among musical curiosities must be counted his *Système nouveau pour apprendre à accompagner tout plainchant . . . sans savoir la musique.*

Hansen, (Emil) Robert, Danish cellist; b. Copenhagen, Feb. 25, 1860; d. Aarhus, July 18, 1926. He received his first instruction from his father, then studied with F. Neruda at the Copenhagen Cons., and with Fr. Grützmacher in Dresden; from 1877-89, member of the court orch. in Copenhagen. After a stay in London, he settled in 1891 in Leipzig, where he joined the Gewandhaus orch. and became prof. at the Cons. From 1918 he was conductor of the Symph. Orch. of Aarhus, Denmark. Hansen composed an opera, *Frauenlist* (Sondershausen, 1911), and an operetta, *Die wilde Komtesse* (Eisenach, 1913); a symphony; a symph. suite for strings and 2 horns; a piano concerto; a cello concerto; a piano quintet; a string quartet.

Hansen, Wilhelm, Danish music publishing firm founded in Copenhagen by Jens Wilhelm Hansen (1821-1904). His sons, Jonas W. Hansen (1850-1919) and Alfred W. Hansen (1854-1922), also played an active part in the business, which was eventually entrusted to the sons of Alfred, Asger (b. 1889) and Svend (b. 1890). A large proportion of published Scandinavian (Danish, Swedish, Norwegian) music is brought out by this firm; it has also bought other smaller firms, and publ. some of the works of Arnold Schoenberg. Branches have been established in Oslo, Stockholm, and Leipzig.

Hanslick, Eduard, influential music critic; b. Prague, Sept. 11, 1825; d. Baden, near Vienna, Aug. 6, 1904. He studied law at

Prague and Vienna; took degree of Dr. jur. in 1849, qualifying himself for an official position. But he had already studied music under Tomaschek at Prague; from 1848-49 was music critic for the 'Wiener Zeitung,' and soon adopted a literary career. His first work, *Vom Musikalisch-Schönen: ein Beitrag zur Revision der Aesthetik der Tonkunst* (Leipzig, 1854; in French, 1877; Spanish, 1879; Italian, 1883; English, 1891; Russian, 1895), brought him world-wide fame. Its leading idea is that the beauty of a musical composition lies wholly and specifically in the music itself; i.e., it is immanent in the relations of the tones, without any reference whatever to extraneous (non-musical) ideas, and can express no others. Such being his point of view through life, it follows logically that he could not entertain sympathy for Wagner's art; his violent opposition to the music-drama was a matter of profound conviction, not personal spite. On the other hand, he was one of the very first and most influential champions of Brahms. From 1855-64, Hanslick was music editor of the 'Presse'; thereafter of the 'Neue freie Presse'; he became lecturer on music history and esthetics at Vienna Univ., prof. extraordinary in 1861, and, in 1870, full professor, retiring in 1895 (succeeded by Guido Adler). At the Paris Expositions of 1867 and 1878, and the Vienna Exposition of 1873, Hanslick was a juror in the department of music. What gives his writings permanent value is the sound musicianship underlying their brilliant, masterly style. Yet, in music history, he is chiefly known as a captious and intemperate reviler of genius; Wagner caricatured him in the part of Beckmesser (originally, the name was to be Hans Lick). —Works: *Geschichte des Concertwesens in Wien* (1869); *Aus dem Concertsaal* (1870); a series begun with *Die moderne Oper* (1875) and followed by 8 more vols., giving a fairly comprehensive view of the development of opera from Gluck to 1900: II. *Musikalische Stationen* (1880); III. *Aus dem Opernleben der Gegenwart* (1884); IV. *Musikalisches Skizzenbuch* (1888); V. *Musikalisches und Litterarisches* (1889); VI. *Aus dem Tagebuch eines Musikers* (1892); VII. *Fünf Jahre Musik* (1896); VIII. *Am Ende des Jahrhunderts* (1899); IX. *Aus neuer und neuester Zeit* (1900); *Suite, Aufsätze über Musik und Musiker* (1885), *Konzerte, Komponisten und Virtuosen der letzten fünfzehn Jahre* (1886); *Aus meinem Leben* (2 vols., 1894). All these books passed through several editions. He also edited Th. Billroth's posthumous essay, *Wer ist musikalisch?* (1895; 4th ed., 1912); and wrote the commentary for the illustrated *Galerie deutscher Tondichter* (1873) and *Galerie französischer und italienischer Tondichter* (1874). A collection of Hanslick's articles in the 'Neue freie Presse' was published in English transl. under the title, *Vienna's Golden Years of Music, 1850-1900* (N. Y., 1950). —Cf. R. Schafke, *Eduard Hanslick und die Musikästhetik* (1922); S. Deas, *In Defense of Hanslick* (London, 1940).

Hanson, Howard, distinguished American composer; b. Wahoo, Nebraska, Oct. 28, 1896. His parents emigrated from Sweden to America in their youth; his Scandinavian ancestry played an important part in Hanson's spiritual outlook. He studied at the Luther College in Wahoo; then went to New York, where he studied with Percy Goetschius at the Institute of Musical Art; also at Northwestern Univ. in Evanston, Ill., with P. C. Lutkin and Arne Oldberg; after graduation in 1916, he became instructor at the College of the Pacific in San José, Calif.; was its dean in 1919-21. In 1921, he won the American Prix de Rome; spent 3 years at the American Academy in Rome and composed several important works there. In 1924, he was appointed by George Eastman as director of the Eastman School of Music, Rochester, N. Y.; in 1925, began there a series of orchestral concerts featuring works by American composers. During the more than 3 decades of his leadership of the Eastman School of Music and his conductorship of the American Music Festivals, Hanson has contributed greatly to the cause of American musical education, as well as to that of American music. In 1932, he conducted programs of American music in Europe; also was guest conductor with major American orchestras in programs of American music, including his own works. In 1935, he was elected a member of the National Institute of Arts and Letters; in 1938, a fellow of the Royal Academy of Music in Sweden. He has furthermore been, at various times, president of the National Association of Schools of Music; president of the Music Teachers' National Association; president of the National Music Council; also active in various capacities for numerous music organizations. He holds honorary D. Mus. degrees from Syracuse Univ., Univ. of Nebraska, Northwestern Univ.; awarded the Pulitzer Prize for his 4th Symph. (1944); Ditson Award (1945); George Foster Peabody Award (1946), etc. His music is permeated with outspoken Romanticism; he pointedly entitled one of his symphonies *Romantic Symphony;* his profound kinship for Scandinavia is expressed in his *Nordic Symphony* and other works. An influence of Sibelius is notable in Hanson's broad lyrical passages, and in the sombre coloring of his instrumentation. In his strong and often asymmetrical rhythms, Hanson follows the advanced modern schools of composition; in his harmonies, he reaches the border of polytonality; but he does not employ extreme effects of musical modernism. As a teacher, he has influenced a generation of American composers.—Works: For the stage: *California Forest Play of 1920,* for ballet and orch. (1920); *Merry Mount,* opera in 3 acts (1933; commissioned by the Metropolitan Opera; produced there, Feb. 10, 1934). For orch.: *Symph. Prelude* (1916); *Symph. Legend* (San Francisco, 1917); *Symph. Rhapsody* (Los Angeles, 1919); *Before the Dawn,* symph. poem (Los Angeles, 1920); *Exaltation,* a symph. poem for orch. with piano obbligato (San Francisco, 1920); Concerto for organ, strings, harp, and orch. (1921); Symph. No. 1 (*Nordic Symph.;* Rome, composer conducting, May 30, 1923; 1st American performance, Rochester, N. Y., March 19, 1924); *North and West,* symph. poem with choral obbligato (N. Y., 1923); *Lux Aeterna,* symph. poem with viola obbligato (Rome, 1923); *Pan and the Priest,* symph. poem with piano obbligato (London, 1926); Concerto for organ and orch. (Rochester, 1926); Symph. No. 2 (*Romantic Symph.;* commissioned for the 50th anniversary of the Boston Symph. Orch., Koussevitzky conducting, Nov. 28, 1930; very successful); Symph. No. 3 (NBC Symph., March 26, 1938, composer conducting); Symph. No. 4, subtitled *The Requiem* (Boston Symph., Dec. 3, 1943, composer conducting; won a Pulitzer Award, 1944); *Serenade,* for flute, strings, harp, and orch. (1945); piano concerto (Boston, Dec. 31, 1948); Symph. No. 5 (*Sinfonia Sacra;* Philadelphia, Feb. 18, 1955); *Elegy in Memory of Serge Koussevitzky* (Boston, 1956). Choral works: *The Lament of Beowulf* (Ann Arbor Festival, 1926); *Heroic Elegy,* for chorus and orch., without words (for the Beethoven centenary, 1927); *3 Songs from 'Drum Taps'* (Whitman), for voices and orch. (1935); *Hymn for the Pioneers,* for men's voices (1938); *The Cherubic Hymn* (1949); *How Excellent Thy Name* (1952); *The Song of Democracy,* for soli, chorus, and orch. (Philadelphia, April 9, 1957). Chamber music: piano quintet (1916); *Concerto da camera,* for piano and string quartet (1917); string quartet (1923; commissioned for the Coolidge Festival, Washington, D. C.); *Fantasia on a Theme of Youth,* for piano and strings (Northwestern Univ., Feb. 18, 1951). For piano: *Prelude and Double Fugue,* for 2 pianos (1915); *4 Poems* (1917-18); *Sonata* (1918); *3 Miniatures* (1918-19); *Scandinavian Suite* (1918-19); *3 Etudes* (1920); *2 Yuletide Pieces* (1920); etc.; songs; also an arrangement for mixed chorus and orch. of *Kyrie, Gloria and Credo* from Palestrina's *Missa Papae Marcelli* (1936). — Cf. E. Royce, *Howard Hanson,* in Cowell's symposium, *American Composers on American Music* (Stanford Univ., 1933); B. C. Tuthill, *Howard Hanson,* in the 'Mus. Quarterly' (April, 1936); M. Alter, *Howard Hanson,* in 'Modern Music' (Jan.-Feb., 1941).

Hanssens, Charles-Louis, Belgian cellist, conductor, and composer; b. Ghent, July 12, 1802; d. Brussels, April 8, 1871. As a child of 10, he played in the orch. of the National Theater, Amsterdam, and at 20 was appointed assistant conductor. In 1824, he became cellist and later assistant conductor of the orchestra in the Brussels Theater. In 1827, he was appointed professor of harmony at the Brussels Cons.; the political events of 1830 caused his retreat to Holland. He became solo cellist at the Théâtre Ventadour, Paris (1834), then composer and also conductor. He subsequently directed French opera at The Hague, again in Paris, then at Ghent. From 1848-69, he was conductor at the Théâtre de la Monnaie, Brussels. He wrote 8 operas, ballets, symphonies, overtures, orchestral fantasies; violin concerto, cello concerto, clarinet concerto, several piano concertos; string quartets; *Symphonie concertante* for clarinet and violin; Masses, cantatas, a cappella choruses. —Cf. L. de Burbure, *Notice sur Charles-Louis Hanssens* (Antwerp, 1872) and L. Bäwolf, *Charles-Louis Hanssens* (Brussels, 1895).

Harasiewicz (hăh-răh-sye'-vich), **Adam,** Polish pianist; b. Chodziez, Western Poland, July 1, 1932. He studied with Kazimierz Mirski until 1950; then at the State School of Music in Cracow. He entered the Chopin Contest in 1949, but failed to win a prize. In March, 1955, he competed again, at the 5th International Chopin Contest in Warsaw, in which pianists of 27 countries took part, and won the first prize of 30,000 zlotys.

Haraszti, Emile, eminent musicologist; b. Nagyvarad, Hungary (now Oradea Mare, Rumania), Nov. 1, 1885. He studied composition with E. Farkas and musicology in Vienna, Munich, Leipzig, Berlin, and Paris. He was awarded a Ph.D. in 1907 and then became music critic of the 'Budapesti Hirlap' (1908-30). He taught at the National Cons. in Budapest (1914); in 1917, appointed lecturer at the Univ. of Budapest; director of the National Cons. (1920-32). From 1940-45 was lecturer at the Budapest Univ.; in 1945, settled in Paris. His principal writings are: *Wagner et la Hongrie* (Budapest, 1916); *La Musique hongroise* (Paris, 1933); *Béla Bartók, His Life and Works* (Paris-Oxford, 1938, Lyre-Bird Press); *Un centenaire romantique: Berlioz et la Marche Hongroise d'après des documents inédits* (Paris, 1946); many valuable studies in various music magazines. For a complete list of his writings, see his autobiographical notice in 'Die Musik in Geschichte und Gegenwart.'

d'Harcourt (dahr-koor'), **Eugène, French** conductor and composer; b. Paris, May 2, 1859; d. Locarno, Switzerland, March 4, 1918. He studied at the Paris Cons. with Savard, Durand, and Massenet (1882-86), then in Berlin with A. Schulze and W. Bargiel (until 1890). In 1892 he built the 'Salle d'Harcourt' in Paris, and inaugurated the 'Concerts éclectiques populaires,' which, however, ended after the 3rd season; was commissioned by the French Government to study musical conditions in Italy, Germany, Austria, and Scandinavia (1906-09), and publ. reports on his findings. He wrote an opera, *Le Tasse* (Monte Carlo, 1903), 3 symphonies, chamber music, etc.

d'Harcourt, Marguerite, French composer, folksong collector and authority on Indian music; b. Paris, Feb. 24, 1884. She studied with Vincent d'Indy and Maurice Emmanuel; wrote 2 symphonies (2nd, *Les Saisons,* composed in 1952); *Concerto Grosso* for strings (1956); *Rapsodie péruvienne,* for oboe, clarinet, and bassoon (1945); other chamber music; many songs. With her husband, **Raoul d'Harcourt** (b. Oran, Algeria, March 30, 1879), prominent ethnologist, she publ. an important treatise, *Musique des Incas et ses survivances* (Paris, 1925; 2 vols.), based on materials gathered during journeys in Peru (1912-14 and 1919); also *Chansons populaires françaises du Canada* (240 songs, Paris, 1956); contributed (with her husband) the section on Indian music to Lavignac's 'Encyclopédie de la Musique' (vol. V).

d'Hardelot (dahr-d'loh'), **Guy** (Mrs. W. I. Rhodes, *née* Helen Guy), French song composer; b. 1858 at the Chateau d'Hardelot, Boulogne-sur-Mer; d. London, Jan. 7, 1936. She studied at the Paris Cons.; traveled with Emma Calvé in the U. S. in 1896; then married, and settled in London. She wrote many melodious songs: *Sans toi, Because* (very popular), *Tristesse,* etc., which were sung by Melba and Calvé.

Harker, F. Flaxington, organist and composer; b. Aberdeen, Scotland, Sept. 4, 1876; d. Richmond, Va., Oct. 23, 1936. While acting as assistant organist at the York Minster, he studied with T. Tertius Noble, who was organist there. In 1901 he came to the United States and served as organist in churches in Biltmore, N. C. and Richmond, Va. He wrote 2 cantatas, *The Star of Bethlehem* and *The Cross;* publ. Harker's Organ Collection (2 vols.; 27 works by modern masters of the organ).

Harline, Leigh, American composer; b. Salt Lake City, March 26, 1907. He studied music at the Univ. of Utah; went to Los Angeles in 1928, where he became arranger for Walt Disney (1931-42); then was engaged as composer of film music by various studios in Hollywood.

Harling, William Franke, American composer; b. London, Jan. 18, 1887. He was brought to the United States in his infancy; studied in Boston, London, and Brussels (with Théophile Ysaÿe). He was organist at the Church of the Resurrection, Brussels (1907-08) and at the U. S. Military Academy, West Point, N. Y., the following year; later settled in Hollywood. His works include a one-act opera, *A Light from St. Agnes* (Chicago, Dec. 26, 1925); a "native opera with jazz," *Deep River* (N. Y., Oct. 4, 1926); a symph. poem with narrator, *Monte Cassino* (1944); *3 Elegiac Poems* for cello and orch. (1946); more than 100 songs. He wrote the official march *West Point Forever.*—Cf. E. E. Hipsher, *American Opera and Its Composers* (Philadelphia, 1927; pp. 250-56).

Harman, Carter, American composer and music critic; b. Brooklyn, June 14, 1918. He studied with Sessions at Princeton Univ. (1936-40); was a pilot in the U. S. Army Air Corps in the Burma-Indo-China theater

(1942-45); then returned for further study at Columbia Univ. (1945-48). From 1947-52, he was a music critic of the 'N. Y. Times'; in 1952 became music editor of 'Time' magazine. He is the author of an opera, *Charms for the Savage*. He publ. *A Popular History of Music from Gregorian Chant to Jazz* (N. Y., 1956).

Harmat, Artur, Hungarian composer; b. Nyitrabajna (now Bojna, Czechoslovakia), June 27, 1885. He studied at the Budapest Academy of Music, and later took courses in Prague and Berlin. From 1920 till 1946 he was inspector of music in the Budapest schools; from 1924 till 1950 he was professor of religious music at the Budapest Academy. He has written several valuable manuals on counterpoint and has composed a great quantity of church music, based on the lines of Palestrina's polyphony.

Harmati, Sandor, violinist, conductor, and composer; b. Budapest, July 9, 1892; d. Flemington, N. J., April 4, 1936. He graduated from the Budapest Academy of Music (1909); was concertmaster of the State Orch. (1910-12) and People's Orch. (1912-14) there; came to the United States in 1914 and became a member of the Letz Quartet (1917-21), then of the Lenox Quartet (1922-25); conductor of the Omaha Symph. Orch. (1925-30) and of the Musicians' Symph. (1932-34); head of the music department of Bard College (1934-36). He was awarded the Pulitzer Prize (1923) for a symphonic poem, the Philadelphia Chamber Music Award (1925) for a string quartet, and the Juilliard Award for his *Prelude to a Melodrama*. He also composed incidental music to *Jeweled Tree* (1926); violin works; piano pieces; songs.

Harraden, Samuel, English music scholar; b. Cambridge, 1821; d. Hampstead, July 17, 1897. He studied with Walmisley; in 1841, became organist of St. Luke's, Manchester. In 1846, he went to India and settled in Calcutta, where he became organist at the Old Mission Church. He greatly influenced the musical life of Calcutta; founded the first glee club there; became an enthusiastic student of Hindu music; was on the staff of the Hindu College of Music. In appreciation of his contribution to native art, he was made Mus. D. by the Bengal Royal Academy of Music.

Harrell, Mack, American baritone; b. Celeste, Texas, Oct. 8, 1909; studied at Oklahoma City Univ. (1927-29); at the Settlement Music School in Philadelphia (1930-33), and at the Juilliard School of Music (1933-35); sang in recitals and with orchestras in the U. S. (1935-36); undertook European tours (1937, 1939, 1949, 1951, etc.); made his operatic début with the Metropolitan Opera Co., N. Y., in 1939; in 1945, became a member of the vocal faculty of the Juilliard School of Music; publ. *The Sacred Hour of Song* (N. Y., 1938).

Harris, Augustus, celebrated English impresario; b. Paris, 1852; d. Folkestone, England, June 22, 1896. An actor by profession, he was engaged at Manchester (1873) as stage manager. In 1879 he leased Drury Lane Theatre, where he won brilliant success with spectacular plays and pantomimes; in 1887, he took up Italian opera and secured control successively of Her Majesty's Theatre, Covent Garden, the Olympia, and various provincial stages. He also cultivated French, German, and English opera with almost uninterrupted success. He introduced to the English public many of the most famous singers of the day (Melba, Nordica, Hauk, Maurel, the de Reszkes). He was knighted in 1891.

Harris, Charles Kassell, American song composer; b. Poughkeepsie, N. Y., May 1, 1865; d. New York, Dec. 22, 1930. He was a director (1914-24) and then secretary (1924-30) of A.S.C.A.P.; established his own publishing firm in Milwaukee and New York. He wrote many popular songs, the most famous of which was *After the Ball* (1892); also the plays *A Limb of the Tree, The Luckiest Man in the World, The Barker, The Heart of a Man*. He publ. an autobiography, *After the Ball, 40 Years of Melody* (N. Y., 1926).

Harris, Roy (properly Leroy), outstanding American composer; b. Lincoln County, Okla., Feb. 12, 1898. His parents (of Irish and Scotch descent) were early settlers in Oklahoma; in 1903, the family moved to California. Roy Harris attended high school in Covina; entered the Univ. of California in 1919 as a special student in philosophy and economics; simultaneously studied music with the organist Charles Demarest and with Fannie Charles Dillon; his first serious study was with Henry Schoenfeld and Arthur Farwell; also took lessons in orchestration with Modest Altschuler and Arthur Bliss. His first performed work was a suite of pieces for string quartet, *Impressions of a Rainy Day* (1926). In 1926 he went to

New York, and received a private stipend which enabled him to go to Paris, where he studied with Nadia Boulanger. He received a Guggenheim Fellowship for 1927 and 1928; in 1929 he returned to the U. S. and lived in California; awarded the Creative Fellowship of the Pasadena Music and Arts Association in 1930 and 1931; returning again to the east, he held numerous teaching positions; head of the composition department of Westminster Choir School, Princeton, N. J. (1934-38); teacher at the Juilliard Summer School (1939); composer-in-residence at Cornell Univ. (1941-43), Colorado College, Colorado Springs (1943-48), Utah State Agricultural College at Logan (1948-49), Peabody College for Teachers, Nashville, Tenn. (1949-51); also at Sewanee, Tenn., where he established the Cumberland Summer Festivals (1951); Pennsylvania College for Women, Pittsburgh (1951-56), and the Univ. of Southern Illinois (1956-57); from 1957, at Indiana Univ., Bloomington. He received honorary Mus. Doc., Rutgers Univ., also from Univ. of Rochester; Elizabeth Sprague Coolidge Medal "For Eminent Services to Chamber Music" (1942). He was the organizer of the Pittsburgh International Contemporary Music Festival in 1952; has also conducted his works with major symphony orchestras in the U. S. His wife, Johana Harris (*née* Beula Duffey, b. Jan. 1, 1913 at Ottawa, Canada), is an accomplished pianist. Harris started on his composing career rather late in life; he has written prolifically in all genres except opera. He has developed a strikingly individual type of composing technique, broadly diatonic in essence, often derived from modal progressions; his harmony is polytonal; he has elaborated a special theory of kinship of major and minor chords. While not striving for orchestral opulence, Harris is not averse to using special effects (vibraphone, amplified piano, etc.).—Works: ballets: *Western Landscape* (1940); *From This Earth* (Colorado Springs, Aug. 7, 1941); *What So Proudly We Hail* (Colorado Springs, Aug. 7, 1942); for orch.: *Andante* (from an unfinished symph., *Our Heritage;* Rochester, N. Y., April 23, 1926); *American Portraits,* in 4 movements: *Initiative, Expectation, Speed, Collective Force* (1929); *Toccata* (1931); Symph. No. 1 (Boston Symph. Orch., Koussevitzky conducting, Jan. 26, 1934); *When Johnny Comes Marching Home,* symph. overture (Minneapolis, Jan. 13, 1935); *Prelude and Fugue* for string orch. (Philadelphia, Feb. 28, 1936); *Farewell to Pioneers,* symph. elegy (Philadelphia, March 27, 1936); Symph. No. 2 (Boston, Feb. 28, 1936); *Time Suite,* in 6 movements: *Broadway, Religion, Youth, Communication and Transportation, Philosophy, Labor* (Columbia radio network, Aug. 8, 1937); Symph. No. 3 (Boston Symph. Orch., Koussevitzky conducting, Feb. 24, 1939; his most successful work; many performances); Symph. No. 4 (*Folksong Symph.,* for chorus and orch.; Cleveland, Dec. 26, 1940); *Evening Piece* (N. Y., March 9, 1941); *Ode to Truth* (San Francisco Symph. Orch., March 9, 1941); *Cimarron,* symph. overture for band (Tri-State Festival, Enid, Okla., April 18, 1941, composer conducting); *Acceleration* (Washington, Nov. 2, 1941); Symph. No. 5 (Boston, Feb. 26, 1943); *Take the Sun and Keep the Stars,* for band (NBC broadcast from Denver, Jan. 30, 1944, composer conducting; originally scored for chorus and orch. under the title *Sammy's Fighting Sons*); Symph. No. 6 (*Gettysburg Address Symph.;* Boston, April 14, 1944); *Ode to Friendship* (Madison Square Garden, N. Y., Nov. 16, 1944); Concerto for accordion and orch. (N. Y., June 2, 1946); Concerto for 2 pianos (Denver, Jan. 21, 1947); *Quest* (Indianapolis, composer conducting, Jan. 29, 1948); *Elegy and Paean* for viola and orch. (Houston, Dec. 13, 1948); *Kentucky Spring* (Louisville, April 5, 1949); *Fruit of Gold* (Univ. of California Band, composer conducting; May 10, 1949); *Dark Devotion,* for band (Louisville, April 12, 1950); *Cumberland Concerto* (Cincinnati, Oct. 19, 1951); Symph. No. 7 (Chicago Symph. Orch., Nov. 20, 1952); piano concerto (Louisville, Dec. 9, 1953); *Ode to Consonance;* 1957). Chamber music: *Impressions of a Rainy Day,* for string quartet (Los Angeles, March 15, 1926); concerto for clarinet, piano, and string quartet (Paris, May 8, 1927); string quartet (N. Y., April 14, 1930); *Fantasy* for piano, flute, oboe, clarinet, bassoon, horn (Pasadena, April 10, 1932); *Chorale,* for strings (Los Angeles, Feb. 22, 1933; a movement from the string sextet composed in 1932); *Three Variations on a Theme* (2nd string quartet; Chicago, Oct. 22, 1933); *Four Minutes and Twenty Seconds,* for flute and string quartet (N. Y., April 15, 1934); piano trio (Berkshire Festival, Sept. 20, 1934); quintet, for piano and strings (N. Y., Feb. 12, 1937); 3d String Quartet (Washington; Sept. 11, 1939); *Soliloquy and Dance* for viola and piano (1939); string quintet (Washington, April 14, 1940); violin sonata (1941); *Four Charming Little Pieces* for violin and piano (1942). Vocal works: *Pueña Hueca,* for mixed chorus, violin, cello, and piano

(Pasadena, 1920); *Song Without Words,* for mixed chorus and 2 pianos (1922); *Whitman Triptych* for women's voices and piano (1927); *The Story of Noah* for mixed chorus a cappella (1933); *A Song for Occupations,* a cappella chorus after Whitman (Moscow, 1934; Westminster Choir); *Sanctus,* for mixed chorus (1935); *Symphony for Voices,* a cappella, after Walt Whitman (Princeton, May 20, 1936); *Railroad Man's Ballad* for chorus and orch. (Brooklyn, Feb. 21, 1941); *Challenge,* for chorus and orch. (N. Y., June 25, 1940); *American Creed,* for chorus and orch. (Chicago, Oct. 30, 1940); *A Red Bird in a Green Tree,* for chorus a cappella (Kentucky, Dec. 15, 1940); *Alleluia,* for mixed chorus, brasses, and organ (1945); *Fog,* after Carl Sandburg, for voice and piano (1946); *Blow the Man Down,* for chorus, band, and strings (Cleveland, May 12, 1946); *Service* (1946); *Madrigal,* for chorus (1947); *Easter Motet* for mixed chorus, organ, and brasses (1947); *Israel,* motet for tenor solo, mixed chorus, and organ (1947); *Mass,* for men's voices and organ (N. Y., May 13, 1948). Other works include: piano sonata (N. Y., March 3, 1929); *Variations on an Irish Theme,* for piano (1938); *Little Suite,* for piano (1938); *American Ballads,* for piano (*Laredo, Wayfaring Stranger, The Bird, Black is the Color of My True Love's Hair,* and *Cod Liver Ile;* 1942); *One Tenth of a Nation,* music for a film (N. Y., Jan. 12, 1941). In collaboration with Mrs. M. D. Herter Norton, Harris arranged Bach's *Kunst der Fuge* for string quartet (1934); edited and transcribed (with J. Evanson) the collection *Singing Through the Ages* (2 vols., 1940). He has also contributed as a writer to various magazines.—Cf. Paul Rosenfeld, *An Hour with American Music* (N. Y., 1929); A. Farwell, *Roy Harris,* in the 'Mus. Quarterly' (Jan., 1932); Henry Cowell, *Roy Harris,* in *American Composers on American Music* (Stanford Univ., 1933); W. Piston, *Roy Harris,* in 'Modern Music' (Jan.-Feb., 1934); A. Mendel, *The Quintet of Roy Harris,* in 'Modern Music' (Oct.-Nov., 1939); A. Copland, *Our New Music* (N. Y., 1941); Ch. Mills, *Roy Harris,* in *The Book of Modern Composers,* ed. by D. Ewen (N. Y., 1942); R. Evett, *The Harmonic Idiom of Roy Harris,* in 'Modern Music' (Spring, 1946); N. Slonimsky, *Roy Harris,* in the 'Mus. Quarterly' (Jan., 1947).

Harris, Victor, American song composer; b. New York, April 27, 1869; d. there, Feb. 15, 1943. He studied piano with Charles Blum, voice with William Courtney, theory with Fred K. Schilling, and conducting with Anton Seidl. He then served as organist at various churches in New York; was coach at the Metropolitan Opera, N. Y. (1892-95); conductor of St. Cecilia Club, N. Y., 1902-1936. He publ. about 150 songs, many of which enjoyed a considerable vogue; also a number of choruses.

Harrison, Beatrice, English cellist; b. Roorke, India, Dec. 9, 1892. She was brought to England in her infancy; studied with W. E. Whitehouse at the Royal College of Music, where at the age of 10 she won the first prize (gold medal) in competition with 4,000 aspirants (mostly adults). She made a most successful appearance with the Queen's Hall Orch. (May 29, 1907); then went to Berlin, where she studied with Hugo Becker, graduating as the winner of the coveted Mendelssohn Prize (for the first time awarded to a cellist). She made many European tours, mostly in company with her sister May, the violinist; she toured the United States in 1913 and 1932.

Harrison, Guy Fraser, conductor; b. Guildford, Surrey, England, Nov. 6, 1894. He studied at Oxford and at the Royal College of Music, where he won an organ scholarship; 1914-20, organist of Episcopal Cathedral, Manila, P. I.; then of St. Paul's Cathedral, Rochester, N. Y. (1920-24); 1924-29, conductor of Eastman Theater Orch., Rochester; 1929-51, of the Civic Orch.; 1930-51 associate conductor of Rochester Philh.; guest conductor with the Minneapolis Symph. Orch., Philadelphia Orch. (1936), etc. In 1951, he was appointed conductor of the Oklahoma City Symph. Orch.—Cf. Hope Stoddard, *Symphony Conductors of the U. S. A.* (N. Y., 1957).

Harrison, Julius Allen Greenway, English conductor and composer; b. Stourport, Worcestershire, March 26, 1885. He studied with Granville Bantock; was conductor of the Beecham Opera Co. and of the Scottish Symph. Orch.; in 1925, succeeded Goossens as leader of the Handel Society, London; since 1930, conductor of the Hastings Corp., Hastings. In his music, he makes skillful use of English folk material.—Works: opera, *The Canterbury Pilgrims; Down Among the Dead Men* (variations), for orch.; *Rapunzel* and *Worcestershire Pieces,* for orch. (1919, very successful); the cantatas *Cleopatra* and *Rosalys; Requiem of Archangels;* Mass in C (1947); 2 string quartets; a quintet for harp and strings; organ pieces; sacred music and numerous songs.

Harrison, Lou, American composer; b. Portland, Ore., May 14, 1917. He studied with Cowell and Schoenberg. From the first he adopted a completely free modern style of composition, particularly strong in rhythmic variety, polytonal harmonies, and atonal melodic lines. However, he has also written several works in a relatively conservative style. He lived in California from 1926-43; taught at Mills College (1937-40) and at the Univ. of California, Los Angeles (1942); in 1943 went to N. Y.; wrote music criticism for the 'N. Y. Herald Tribune' (1945-48); taught at Black Mt. College, N. C. (1951-52); in 1952 received a Guggenheim Foundation Award; also active as conductor and instrument maker; introduced two new principles for clavichord construction; built a Phrygian aulos; developed a process for direct composition for phonograph; invented theories of Interval Controls (1938) and Rhythm Controls (1942); also wrote plays and verse; constructed mobiles; engaged in various trades, including, for a time, that of a florist.—Works: opera *Rapunzel;* incidental music to *Peter Pan, Winter's Tale, The Only Jealousy of Emer, The Beautiful People,* etc.; ballets, *Perilous Chapel, Solstice, Johnny Appleseed, Almanac of the Seasons, Praises for Hummingbirds and Hawks;* many dances for orch.; a symph. in G; suite for violin, piano, and small orch. (N. Y., Oct. 28, 1952); 14 sinfonias for percussion orch.; songs for 8 baritones with orch.; piano pieces; etc.

Harrison, May, English violinist; b. Roorke, India, March, 1891. She studied at the Royal College of Music with E. Arbos and A. Rivarde; like her sister Beatrice, she won at the age of 10 the gold medal of the Associate Board of the Royal College of Music and Royal Academy of Music over 3,000 competitors; she then studied for some time under L. Auer in St. Petersburg; made her début in 1904 in London with marked success, and toured Europe, mostly in company with her sister.

Harriss, Charles Albert Edwin, composer and organist; b. London, Dec. 15, 1862; d. Ottawa, Ont., Aug. 1, 1929. At 8 he was chorister at St. Mark's, Wrexham, where his father was organist; assistant organist at St. Giles', Reading (1880); from 1883 he lived with his father in Montreal, Canada; organist at Christ Church Cathedral, then at the Church of St. James the Apostle, famous for its outstanding organ music. Harriss founded a glee and madrigal society.—Works: opera *Torquil* (Montreal, 1896); cantata *Daniel before the King* (1890); anthems; piano and organ music; songs.

Harsányi (hăhr'-shăh-nē), **Tibor,** composer; b. Magyarkanizsa, Hungary, June 27, 1898; d. Paris, Sept. 19, 1954. He studied at the Budapest Academy of Music, with Kodály; in 1923 he settled in Paris, where he devoted himself to composition. The melodic material of his music stems from Hungarian folk melos; his harmonic idiom is largely polytonal; the rhythms are sharp, often with jazz-like syncopation; the form remains classical.—Works: chamber opera *Les Invités* (Gera, Germany, 1930); radio opera *Illusion* (Paris, June 28, 1949); 4 ballets: *Le dernier songe* (Budapest, Jan. 27, 1920), *Pantins* (Paris, 1938), *Chota Roustaveli* (in collaboration with Honegger and A. Tcherepnin; Monte Carlo, 1945), and *L'Amour et la Vie* (1951); a puppet show, *L'Histoire du Petit Tailleur* for 7 instruments and percussion (1939). For orch.: *La Joie de vivre* (Paris, March 11, 1934, composer conducting); 2 divertissements (1940-41, 1943); violin concerto (Paris Radio, Jan. 16, 1947); *Figures et Rythmes* (Geneva, Nov. 19, 1947, composer conducting); *Danses variées* (Basel, Feb. 14, 1950, composer conducting); a symphony (Salzburg Festival, June 26, 1952). Chamber music: sonatina for violin and piano (1918); 3 pieces for flute and piano (1924); 2 string quartets (1918, 1935); cello sonata (1928); nonet for string and wind instruments (Vienna Festival, June 21, 1932); Rhapsody for cello and piano (1939); *Picnic* for 2 violins, cello, double-bass, and percussion (1951); several pieces for gypsy instruments (1953); many piano pieces, among which the most effective are: 5 *études rythmiques* (1934), 3 *pièces lyriques,* and albums for children. He also wrote several choral works, including *Cantate de Noël* for voices, flute, and strings (Paris, Dec. 24, 1945).—Cf. J. S. Weissmann, *Tibor Harsányi,* in the 'Chesterian' (1952).

Harshaw, Margaret, American opera singer; b. Narbeth, Pa., May 12, 1912. She won an audition with the Metropolitan Opera as contralto in 1942, and appeared in the roles of Amneris, Azucena, etc.; in 1950, changed to soprano, and specialized in Wagnerian roles; her interpretations (both as soprano and contralto) soon placed her among the most celebrated singers of Wagner's operas; she sang Isolde, Elisabeth, and all three Brünnhildes. She married Oskar Leopold Eichna (Sept. 7, 1935).

Hart & Sons, a firm of London violin makers, founded in 1825 by John Hart. His son, **John Thomas Hart** (b. Dec. 17, 1805; d. London, Jan. 1, 1874), a pupil of Gilkes, made a complete study of Cremonese and other violins of Italian make, establishing a reputation as an expert in his field. John Thomas' son, **George Hart** (b. London, March 23, 1839; d. near Newhaven, April 25, 1891), succeeded him. He was a good violinist himself; publ. valuable books, *The Violin: Its Famous Makers and Their Imitators* (London, 1875; French ed., Paris, 1886) and *The Violin and its Music* (London, 1881). His sons, George and Herbert Hart, inherited the business.

Hart, Frederic Patton, American composer; b. Aberdeen, Wash., Sept. 5, 1898. He studied at the American Cons. in Chicago (where he won the gold medal) and at the Art Institute there; later studied with Rubin Goldmark, Ernest Hutcheson, Nadia Boulanger, and at the Diller-Quaile School in N. Y. —Works: opera, *The Wheel of Fortune* (1934); ballet-opera, *The Romance of Robot* (N. Y., 1937); a trio (1926); Adagio and Scherzo for string quartet (1931); string quartet (1937); piano pieces and songs.

Hart, Fritz, English composer and conductor; b. Brockley, Kent, Feb. 11, 1874; d. Honolulu, July 9, 1949. He went to Australia in 1909 and settled there; director of the Melbourne Cons.; joint artistic director of the Melbourne Symph. Orch.; conducted both the Manila Symph. and the Honolulu Orch. (1931-36); settled in Honolulu in 1936 when appointed professor of music at the Univ. of Hawaii; retired in 1942.—Compositions: 16 operas, 2 operettas, a symph. and other orchestral works, chamber music; choral works, songs; etc.

Hart, James, English bass singer and composer; b. York, 1647; d. London, May 8, 1718. He was a singer in York Minster until 1670; then appointed Gentleman of the Chapel Royal and lay-vicar of Westminster Abbey; settled in London and composed songs publ. in 'Choice Ayres, Songs and Dialogues' (1676-84), 'The Theater of Musick' (1685-87), 'Banquet of Musick' (1688-92), and other collections. He wrote *Adieu to the pleasures and follies of love* for Shadwell's operatic adaptation of 'The Tempest' (1674), publ. as one of the 6 'Ariel's Songs.'

Hart, Lorenz, American lyricist; b. New York City, May 2, 1895; d. there, Nov. 22, 1943. He began as a student of journalism at Columbia Univ. (1914-17); then turned to highly successful theatrical writing. During his 18-year collaboration with Richard Rodgers, he wrote the lyrics for *Connecticut Yankee* (1927); *On Your Toes* (1936); *Babes in Arms* (1937); *The Boys from Syracuse* (1938); *I Married an Angel* (1938); *Too Many Girls* (1939); *Pal Joey* (1940); *By Jupiter* (1942). Some of their best songs (*Manhattan, Here in My Arms, My Heart Stood Still, Small Hotel, Blue Moon, Where or When, I Married an Angel*) are published in the album, *Rodgers & Hart Songs* (N. Y., 1951).

Hart, Philip, organist of various London churches; date and place of birth unknown; d. London, July 17, 1749; composed anthems, organ fugues, music for Hughes' *Ode in Praise of Musick* (1703), and for *The Morning Hymn* from Milton's 'Paradise Lost,' Book V (1729).

Hart, Weldon, American composer; b. Place-Bear Spring, Tenn., Sept. 19, 1911; d. East Lansing, Mich., Nov. 20, 1957. He studied music in Nashville, Univ. of Michigan, and Eastman School in Rochester with Howard Hanson and Bernard Rogers (Ph. D., 1946); head of the music dept. of Western Kentucky State College (1946-49); director of the School of Music of West Virginia Univ. (1949-57). In 1957 he was appointed head of the music dept. of Michigan State Univ., East Lansing, but died shortly after assuming his post. — Works: *Sinfonietta* (1934); symph. poem *The Dark Hills* (1939); a symphony (1945); *Pennyrile Overture* (1947); a violin concerto (1951); *3 West Virginia Folk Songs,* for chorus and orch. (1954); violin pieces; etc. He writes in a bold contemporary idiom, characterized by a strong rhythmic sense.

Härtel (music publisher). See **Breitkopf & Härtel.**

Hartmann, Arthur, violinist; b. Maté Szalka, Hungary, July 23, 1881; d. New York, March 30, 1956. He was brought to Philadelphia as a child and first studied with his father; then was a pupil of M. van Gelder, and later of C. M. Loeffler (violin) and Homer Norris (composition). He made his début in Philadelphia (1887) as a child prodigy; by the time he was 12, had played practically the entire modern violin repertory. He toured the United States, Canada,

Scandinavia; played in Paris in recitals with Debussy, and became his intimate friend. In 1939 he settled in New York; retired in 1954. He made numerous transcriptions and arrangements; discovered and edited 6 sonatas of Felice de' Giardini; wrote an essay on Bach's Chaconne which has been translated into 14 languages.

Hartmann, August Wilhelm, Danish organist and composer, son of J. E. Hartmann; b. Copenhagen, Nov. 6, 1775; d. there, Nov. 15, 1850. He studied with his father; he was first violinist in the Royal Chapel (1796-1817); then was appointed organist at the Garrison Church in Copenhagen. His organ works and other compositions are found in the Royal Library.

Hartmann, Carl, German tenor; b. Solingen, May 2, 1895. He studied at the Cologne Musikhochschule and with Senff in Düsseldorf; made his début (1928) as Tannhäuser in Elberfeld, followed by engagements in Cologne, Berlin, and Munich; then appeared in Dresden, Leipzig, Vienna, Paris, Barcelona, Prague, Stockholm; toured the United States (1930) with Gadski's German Opera Co., appearing in leading Wagnerian tenor roles; in 1937, appeared as Siegfried at the Metropolitan Opera (of which he is a member); sang Tristan at the Bayreuth Festival (1938); became member of the Chicago Opera the same year. He is also a lieder and oratorio singer.

Hartmann, Eduard von, German writer; b. Berlin, Feb. 23, 1842; d. Grosslichterfelde, near Berlin, June 5, 1906. He studied philosophy; at the same time he acquired, self taught, considerable knowledge of composition, wrote numerous songs, and began to compose an opera, *Der Stern von Sevilla* (unfinished). In his philosophical writings, he established some basic laws of musical esthetics; of chief importance are *Deutsche Ästhethik seit Kant* (Berlin, 1886) and *Philosophie des Schönen* (Berlin, 1887), which contains a chapter on *Idealismus und Formalismus in der Musikästhetik.*

Hartmann, Emil, Danish composer, son of Johann Peder Emilius Hartmann; b. Copenhagen, Feb. 21, 1836; d. there, July 18, 1898. He received his early education from his father and from Gade (who was his brother-in-law); was from 1861 till his death organist in various churches in Denmark. After Gade's death, he conducted a season of the Musical Society at Copenhagen (1891-92). He wrote the operas *Elverpigen* (Copenhagen, Nov. 5, 1867), *Korsikaneren* (Copenhagen, April 7, 1873), *Ragnhild* (1896), *Det store Lod* (1897); the ballet *Fjeldstuen* (Copenhagen, May 13, 1859); also some instrumental works.

Hartmann, Johan Peder Emilius, celebrated Danish dramatic composer; b. Copenhagen, May 14, 1805; d. there, March 10, 1900. He was the most famous of the Hartmann family in Denmark; grandson of Johann Ernst Hartmann, and son of August Wilhelm Hartmann. He studied law at the Univ. of Copenhagen, and for many years occupied a public position as a jurist (1828-70), but he was also profoundly interested in music; studied with his father, and became his assistant as organist at the Copenhagen Cathedral (1843), remaining in that capacity until his death. He also taught at the Cons. of Copenhagen (from 1827). In 1836 he was one of the organizers of the Danish Music Society; in 1868 was appointed its director. He was also co-director (with Gade) of the new Copenhagen Cons., established in 1867. He spent almost his entire life in Denmark; the only extensive traveling he undertook was in 1836, when he visited Germany and France. He was greatly esteemed in Denmark. A Hartmann Scholarship was founded on the occasion of his 50th jubilee, and he received the 'Daneborg' order. Gade was his son-in-law. He was a prolific composer; wrote the operas *The Raven* (Copenhagen, Oct. 29, 1832), *The Corsairs* (Copenhagen, April 23, 1835), *Little Christina* (Copenhagen, May 12, 1846); he also wrote the ballets, *Valkyrien* (Copenhagen, Sept. 13, 1861) and *Thrymskviden* (Copenhagen, Feb. 21, 1868); a melodrama, *The Golden Horns* (1834); overtures; a violin concerto; a flute sonata; a violin sonata; pieces for piano; songs. With Gade, he was a foremost representative of the Danish Romantic school of composition. —Cf. W. Behrend, *J. P. E. Hartmann* (Copenhagen, 1895); A. Hammerich, *J. P. E. Hartmann* (Copenhagen, 1916); R. Hove, *J. P. E. Hartmann* (Copenhagen, 1934).

Hartmann, Johann Ernst, composer and violinist, founder of the 'Hartmann dynasty' of musicians active in Denmark; b. Glogau, Silesia, Dec. 24, 1726; d. Copenhagen, Oct. 21, 1793. He studied violin in Silesia, and held various posts as band violinist. In 1766 he settled in Copenhagen; became conductor of the Royal Orch. in 1768. Most of his manuscripts were lost in a fire (1794), but his violin method and a few instrumental works are extant. His chief claim to fame is the fact that the melody of the present national anthem of Denmark, *Kong Christian stod ved højen Mast,* was used in the score he wrote for the melodrama *Fiskerne* (Copenhagen, Jan. 31, 1780), and was for a long time regarded as his own composition, although it may have been borrowed from some unknown source of folk origin. A study of this melody is included in Angul Hammerich's book, *J. P. E. Hartmann, Biographical Essays* (1916).

Hartmann, Karl Amadeus, outstanding German composer; b. Munich, Aug. 2, 1905. He studied with Josef Haas at the Music Academy in Munich (1923-27) and later with Scherchen. He began to compose rather late in life. His first important work was a trumpet concerto, which was performed at a Scherchen concert in Strasbourg (1933); his symphonic work *Miserae* was given at the Prague festival (Sept. 1, 1935), and his first string quartet at the London festival (June 18, 1938). However, he was dissatisfied with these early works, and destroyed the manuscripts. In 1941 he began to study advanced musical composition and analysis with Anton von Webern, and turned definitely towards the 12-tone method. After the end of World War II, he organized in Munich the society 'Musica viva.' He received a prize from the city of Munich in 1949; in 1952 was elected member of the German Academy of Fine Arts; in 1953 became president of the German section of the International Society for Contemporary Music. Despite his acceptance of the atonal idiom and his experimentation in the domain of rhythm, Hartmann retains the orthodox form and structural cohesion of basic Classicism.—Works: chamber opera, *Des Simplicius Simplicissimus Jugend* (Cologne, 1949); 6 symphonies (1940-51); concerto for piano, wind instruments, and percussion (Donaueschingen, Oct. 10, 1953); numerous works for various instrumental combinations; choruses; piano pieces; songs.

Hartmann, Pater (real name Paul Eugen Josef von An der Lan-Hochbrunn), German conductor and composer; b. Salurn, near Bozen, Dec. 21, 1863; d. Munich, Dec. 5, 1914. He entered the Franciscan order at the age of 16; studied theology and music in various monasteries; then completed his musical studies with Josef Pembaur in Innsbruck; ordained priest in 1886; appointed organist at the Church of the Redeemer in Jerusalem (1893) and at the Church of the Holy Sepulchre (1894); in 1895 he was transferred to Rome as organist of the monastery 'Ara Coeli' and director of the 'Scuola Musicale Cooperativa.' From 1906 till his death he lived in the Franciscan monastery of St. Anna at Munich. During the season of 1906-07 he visited the United States, conducting some of his oratorios. His sacred music retains its importance in Germany. He wrote the oratorios *Petrus* (1900), *Franziskus* (1902), *Das letzte Abendmahl* (1904), *Der Tod des Herrn* (1905), *Septem ultima verba Christi in Cruce* (1908); also a *Te Deum* (1913); Masses; organ works.

Hartmann, Thomas de, Russian composer; b. Khoruzhevka, Ukraine, Sept. 21, 1885; d. Princeton, N. J., March 26, 1956. He studied piano with Anna Essipova at the St. Petersburg Cons.; composition with Taneyev and Arensky. His first important work, the ballet *The Purple Flower,* was produced at the Imperial Theater in St. Petersburg in 1907 with Pavlova, Karsavina, Nijinsky, and Fokine. After the Revolution he went to the Caucasus; taught at the Tiflis Cons. (1919); then went to Paris, where he remained until 1951, when he settled in New York. His early music is in the Russian national style, influenced particularly by Mussorgsky; from about 1925, he made a radical change in his style of composition, adopting many devices of outspoken modernism (polytonality, etc.). — Works: *The Purple Flower,* ballet (St. Petersburg, Dec. 16, 1907); *Babette,* ballet (Nice, March 10, 1935); also an opera *Esther* (not performed); 3 symphonies (1915, 1944, 1953); 4th Symphony, unfinished (1955); cello concerto (1935; Boston, April 14, 1938); piano concerto (1940; Paris, Nov. 8, 1942); violin concerto (1943; Paris, March 6, 1947); double-bass concerto (1943; Paris, Jan. 26, 1945); harp concerto (1944); violin concerto (Paris, March 16, 1947); flute concerto (Paris, Sept. 27, 1950); *12 Russian Fairy Tales,* for orch. (Houston, April 4, 1955, Stokowski conducting); also violin sonata (1937); cello sonata (1942); trio for flute, violin, and piano (1946); 3 song cycles to words by Verlaine, Proust, and James Joyce; other songs; piano pieces.

Hartog, Edouard de, Dutch composer; b. Amsterdam, Aug. 15, 1829; d. The Hague, Nov. 8, 1909. He studied in Germany with Hoch and Mme. Dulcken, and in Paris with Elwart. He lived many years in Paris, where he produced the opera *Le Mariage de Don Lope* (1865); another opera by him, *L'Amour et son Hôte,* was produced in Brussels (1873). He also wrote several symph. works, chamber music, and piano pieces.

Hartog, Jacques, Dutch composer and writer; b. Zalt-Bommel, Oct. 24, 1837; d. Amsterdam, Oct. 3, 1917. He studied with Ferdinand Hiller at Cologne; upon his return to Holland, he was appointed prof. at the Amsterdam School of Music, and held this post for many years (1886-1913). He publ. monographs (in Dutch) on Beethoven (1904), Mozart (1904), Haydn (1905), Mendelssohn (1909), Schumann (1910), Bach (1911), and Wagner (1913); translated into Dutch several German theory books, also wrote some orchestral and chamber music.

Harty, Sir **Hamilton,** eminent conductor; b. Hillsborough, County Down, Ireland, Dec. 4, 1879; d. Brighton, Feb. 19, 1941. He received his entire musical education from his father, an organist, and substituted for him as a child. At the age of 12, he was able to fill a position as organist at Magheracoll Church, County Antrim; then was church organist in Belfast and Dublin. In 1900 he went to London, where he was active as an accompanist; on July 15, 1904 he married the singer Agnes Nicholls; also began to compose seriously; his piano quintet won a prize in 1904. It was much later in life that he devoted himself to conducting; he was appointed conductor of the Hallé Orch. in Manchester in 1920, remaining at this post for 13 seasons; his programs showed fine discrimination in balancing Classic and Romantic works; he gave many performances of Berlioz; also conducted several works by British composers. In appreciation of his work, he was knighted (1925). In 1931 he made his American début; in subsequent seasons he conducted in Boston, Chicago, Cleveland, and also at the Hollywood Bowl. In 1934 he conducted in Australia. Among his works, the most interesting is *Irish Symphony* (revised version, Manchester, Nov. 13, 1924); other works are *Comedy Overture* (1907); *Ode to a Nightingale,* after Keats, for soprano and orch. (1907); *With the Wild Geese,* a symph. poem (1910); violin concerto (1909); *The Mystic Trumpeter,* for baritone, chorus, and orch. (1913); *The Children of Lir,* poem for orch. (London, March 1, 1939); he made excellent arrangements of Handel's *Water Music* and *Fireworks Music* for modern orch.; also arranged *A John Field Suite,* from piano works by Field.

Harwood, Basil, English organist and composer; b. Woodhouse, Gloucestershire, April 11, 1859; d. London, April 3, 1949. He studied piano with J. L. Roeckel, organ with George Riseley; also with Reinecke and Jadassohn at the Leipzig Cons. Returning to England, he occupied various posts as organist: at St. Barnabus Church, Pimlico (1883-87), Ely Cathedral (1887-92), Christ Church Cathedral, Oxford (1892-1909); in 1900 he became choral director at Oxford Univ. (until 1909). He edited the 'Oxford Hymn Book' (1908), and wrote a number of sacred works for chorus, and organ pieces (2 sonatas, organ concerto, Christmastide, *Dithyramb,* etc.); a cantata, *Ode on May Morning,* after Milton (Leeds Festival, 1913).

Hase, Hermann von. See **Breitkopf & Härtel.**

Hase, Oskar von. See **Breitkopf & Härtel.**

Häser, August Ferdinand, German composer; b. Leipzig, Oct. 15, 1779; d. Weimar, Nov. 1, 1844. He was a member of a musical family; his 3 brothers and a sister were musicians. He was educated at the Thomasschule in Leipzig, and studied theology at the Leipzig Univ. In 1797 he went to Lemgo, Westphalia, where he taught mathematics in high school. He traveled in Italy, from 1806-13; then returned to Lemgo. In 1817 he was engaged in Weimar as music teacher to Princess Augusta (the future German empress); also conducted the chorus at the Court Opera there; was church organist and teacher of Italian. He wrote 3 operas, which were performed in Weimar; an oratorio, *Die Kraft des Glaubens* (perf. in Birmingham, 1837, as *The Triumph of Faith, or The First Crusade*), many sacred choruses, 4 overtures, several instrumental works in salon style. He publ. *Versuch einer systematischen Übersicht der Gesanglehre* (Leipzig, 1822); *Chorgesangschule für Schul- und Theaterchöre* (Mainz, 1831; in French as *Méthode pour apprendre à chanter en choeur à l'usage des écoles, des théâtres,* etc.).

Haskil, Clara, Rumanian pianist; b. Bucharest, Jan. 7, 1895. She made her début in Vienna at the age of 7; then entered the Paris Cons., where she studied with Cortot and Gabriel Fauré and won a first prize at the age of 14. Busoni heard her in Basel and invited her to study with him in Berlin. She played programs of Beethoven sonatas with Enesco, Ysaÿe, and Casals; appeared in recitals in leading European cities, played in England (with Beecham) and in the U. S. (with Stokowski, and, in 1956, with the Boston Symph. Orch., Munch conducting). She has maintained her technical ability to an extraordinary degree throughout her career; in America she was praised for exceptionally sympathetic interpretation of Mozart and Beethoven.

Hasler, Hans Leo. See **Hassler.**

Haslinger, Tobias, Austrian music publisher; b. Zell, March 1, 1787; d. Vienna, June 18, 1842. He went to Vienna in 1810 after studying music in Linz; was bookkeeper in Steiner's music establishment; later became partner, and after Steiner's retirement in 1826, sole proprietor. A gregarious and affable person, he made friends with many musicians, and was on excellent terms with Beethoven, who seemed to enjoy Haslinger's company; many letters to him from Beethoven are extant, among them the humorous canon *O Tobias Dominus Haslinger.* He was succeeded by his son **Karl Haslinger** (b. Vienna, June 11, 1816; d. there, Dec. 26, 1868). The latter studied with Czerny and became a brilliant pianist as well as an industrious composer; he publ. more than 100 works of various kinds. Continuing the tradition of his father, he publ. several symphonies, piano concertos, overtures, and other works by Beethoven, and later Liszt's piano concerto in E-flat; he was also the publisher of the Strauss waltzes. In 1875 the firm was bought from his widow by Schlesinger of Berlin (subsequently, R. & W. Lienau).

Hassard, John Rose Green, American journalist and music critic; b. New York, Sept. 4, 1836; d. there, April 18, 1888. He studied at St. John's College, Fordham; was a writer on the Chicago 'Republican' (1865); in 1866, joined the staff of the New York 'Tribune' as editorial writer and literary and music critic. In the latter capacity he was succeeded in 1884 by H. E. Krehbiel. His account of the Festival at Bayreuth in 1876 (later publ. as a pamphlet) was the fullest that appeared in any American newspaper.

Hasse, Faustina (*née* Bordoni), wife of Johann Adolf Hasse; famous mezzo soprano of noble birth; b. Venice, c. 1700; d. there, Nov. 4, 1781. She studied wih Gasparini and Benedetto Marcello. She made her début in 1716 in Pollarolo's opera *Ariodante,* and obtained such success that soon she was called the 'New Siren.' When she sang in Florence a few years later (1722), a special medal was issued in her honor; she was equally successful in Naples. She became a member of the court theater in Vienna in 1724, at a high salary. Handel heard her there, and engaged her for his opera enterprise in London, where she made her début on May 5, 1726, winning high praise. She remained in London for 2 seasons; her quarrel with Francesca Cuzzoni in a competition for public attention resulted in her departure from England. She went back to Venice; in 1730, she married Hasse, and devoted her life thenceforth to his success, without abandoning her own career. From 1731 till 1763 they lived in Dresden; then in Vienna (until 1775), finally settling in Venice. According to Burney, she could sustain a note longer than any other singer; her trills were strong and rapid; her intonation perfect. Burney also praised her physical qualities.—Cf. A. Niggli, *Faustina Bordoni-Hasse,* in Waldersee's 'Sammlung musikalischer Vorträge' (1880); G. M. Urbani de Gheltof, *'La Nuova Sirena' ed il 'Caro Sassone'* (Venice, 1890); Margarete Högg, *Die Gesangskunst der Faustina Hasse und das Sängerinnenwesen ihrer Zeit in Deutschland* (Berlin, 1931). An interesting novel rather than a biography is Elise Polko's *Faustina Hasse* (Leipzig, 1860; new ed., 1895).

Hasse, Johann Adolph, German dramatic composer; b. Bergedorf, near Hamburg, March 25, 1699; d. Venice, Dec. 16, 1783. He received his first instruction in music from his father, a schoolmaster and organist. At the age of 18, he went to Hamburg and, at the recommendation of Ulrich König, the poet, was engaged by Keiser, director of the Hamburg Opera, as tenor; he sang there 4 seasons, and later was tenor at the Brunswick theater; it was there that Hasse first appeared as composer, with his opera *Antioco* (Aug. 11, 1721). He then went to Naples to study the craft of composition more thoroughly; there he was a pupil of Porpora and later of Alessandro Scarlatti, and brought out his 2nd opera *Tigrane* (Nov. 4, 1723). In 1725 he wrote a serenade for 2 voices which was performed by Farinelli and Vittoria Tesi, and this further promoted Hasse's career in Italy; there followed a successful production of his new opera *Sesostrate* (Naples, May 13, 1726). In 1727 he was appointed to the staff of the Scuola degl' Incurabili in Venice; there he wrote his *Miserere,* which enjoyed excellent success throughout Italy for many years afterwards. His ability to ingratiate himself with society, his affable manners and handsome appearance, contributed to his artistic success; he was often referred to as 'il caro Sassone' (even though he was not a Saxon). In 1729 he met the famous singer Faustina Bordoni, and married her in Venice the following year. She sang the leading roles in many of his operas, and together they attained the highest positions in the operatic world. He wrote two operas for her: *Artaserse* and *Dalisa,* produced in Venice shortly after their marriage. In 1731 Hasse received an appointment as musical director of the Dresden Opera, with Faustina Hasse as prima donna; his first operatic production in Dresden was *Cleofide,* on Sept. 13, 1731, in which his wife scored a brilliant success. During frequent leaves of absence, they traveled in Italy, where Hasse produced the following operas: *Catone in Utica* (Turin, Dec. 26, 1731); *Caio Fabrizio* (Rome, Jan. 12, 1732); *Siroe, re di Persia* (Bologna, May 2, 1733); and *Tito Vespasiano* (Pesaro, Sept. 24, 1735). In Dresden, he produced *Senocrita* (Feb. 27, 1737), *Atalanta* (July 26, 1737), *Asteria* (Aug. 3, 1737), *Alfonso* (May 11, 1738), *Numa* (Oct. 7, 1741), *Arminio* (Oct. 7, 1745), *La Spartana generosa* (June 14, 1747), *Demofoonte* (Feb. 9, 1748); *Attilio Regolo* (Jan. 12, 1750), *Ciro riconosciuto* (Jan. 20, 1751), *Adriano in Siria* (Jan. 17, 1752), *Solimano* (Feb. 5, 1753), *Artemisia* (Feb. 6, 1754), *L' Olimpiade* (Feb. 16, 1756), etc. In 1734 Hasse visited London, where he was offered the management of the opera company established in opposition to Handel; although his opera *Artaserse,* which he presented there (Nov. 10, 1734), was very successful, he decided not to challenge Handel's superiority, and returned to Dresden. Among other capital cities he visited during this period was Warsaw, where he produced *Il sogno di Scipione* (Oct. 7, 1758) and *Zenobia* (Oct. 7, 1761). His productions in Vienna were *Ipermestra* (Jan. 8, 1744), *Alcide al Bivio* (Oct. 8, 1760), *Il trionfo di Clelia* (April 27, 1762), *Egeria* (April 24, 1764), *Partenope* (Sept. 9, 1767), and *Piramo e Tisbe* (Nov., 1768). His last opera was *Ruggerio,* produced in Milan on Oct. 16, 1771.—Although Hasse was fortunate in his artistic life and never lacked the support of the public, he had to face strong rivalry on the part of the famous Italian composer Porpora, who was engaged by the Dresden court in 1747. Furthermore, Porpora's pupil, a young singer named Regina Mingotti, became a formidable competitor to Faustina Hasse, no longer in her prime. Hasse succeeded in maintaining his firm position in Dresden, and Porpora departed for Vienna in 1752. In 1760, during the siege of Dresden in the course of the Seven Years' War, Hasse's house was set afire by bombing, and nearly all of his manuscripts perished. Hasse's vitality and determination overcame these challenges, and he never ceased to produce new works with astounding facility. His music did not break new paths in operatic art, but he was a master of singing melody in the Italian style, and a fine craftsman in harmony and instrumentation. *Pallido è il sole* and *Per questo dolce amplesso* from his opera *Artaserse* were the two airs that Farinelli sang every evening for 10 years to soothe the melancholy of the ailing Spanish King Philip. In addition to his operas, Hasse wrote 9 oratorios, 10 Masses, 3 Requiems, 10 psalms, 5 litanies, 22 motets, a Te Deum, and a Salve Regina (publ. in London in 1740, under the title *The Famous Salve Regina Composed by Signor Hasse*); also wrote instrumental concertos, string trios, sonatas, etc. An important collection of Hasse's MSS is in the Dresden Library. A selection of his works was publ. by A. Schering in the 'Denkmäler deutscher Tonkunst' (vols. 20, 29, 30) and by Otto Schmid in 'Musik am sächsischen Hofe' (vols. 1, 2, 6, 7, 8); G. Göhler edited *10 ausgewählte Orchesterstücke* (1904). Other reprints are by Christian I. Latrobe in his *Selection of Sacred Music* (6 vols., 1806-26), by B. Engländer (keyboard sonatas; Leipzig, 1930), etc. R. Gerber prepared Hasse's opera *Arminio* for publication in the 'Denkmäler deutscher Tonkunst.'—Cf. W. H. Riehl, *Musikalische Characterköpfe,* vol. 1 (6th ed., Stuttgart, 1879); K. Mennicke, *J. A. Hasse,* in 'Sammelbände der Internationalen Musik-Gesellschaft' (1904); K. Mennicke, *Hasse und die Brüder Graun als Symphoniker* (Leipzig, 1906; with a thematic catalogue); W. Müller, *J. A. Hasse als Kirchenkomponist* (Leipzig, 1911; with a thematic catalogue of Hasse's sacred works); L. Kamiensky, *Die Oratorien von J. A. Hasse* (Berlin, 1911); B. Zeller, *Das Recitativo accompagnato in den Opern Hasses* (Halle, 1911); Rudolf Gerber, *Der Operntypus J. A. Hasses und seine textlichen Grundlagen* (Leipzig, 1925).

Hasse, Karl, German composer and musicologist; b. Dohna, near Dresden, March 20, 1883. He studied with Kretzschmar and Riemann at the Univ. of Leipzig and with Straube and Nikisch at the Leipzig Cons.; later took courses at the Munich Academy with Reger and Mottl. He then held posts as choral conductor and organist in Heidelberg, Chemnitz, and Osnabrück. In 1919 he became prof. at the Univ. of Tübingen; founded a musicological seminar there; Ph.D., 1923. In 1935 he became director of the Hochschule für Musik in Cologne; after the end of World War II, he was pensioned and lived in Schluchtern; in 1955, returned to Cologne. He has written a number of works for orch., chamber groups, organ, and voice, aggregating 120 opus numbers; but he is mostly known for his writings; he publ. several books on Max Reger (Leipzig, 1921; Berlin, 1936; Leipzig, 1948; Dortmund, 1951); 3 books on Bach (Leipzig, 1925; Cologne, 1938; Leipzig, 1949); contributed numerous articles to various German music magazines.

Hasse, Max, German musicologist; b. Buttelstedt, near Weimar, Nov. 24, 1859; d. Magdeburg, Oct. 20, 1935. He was music critic of the 'Magdeburger Zeitung' from 1894 till 1927; publ. the basic works on Cornelius, *Peter Cornelius und sein Barbier von Bagdad* (1904) and *Der Dichter-Musiker Peter Cornelius* (2 vols., 1922-23); was also editor of the complete works of Cornelius, in 5 vols.

Hasselmans, Louis, French conductor; b. Paris, July 25, 1878. He was the son of a harpist-composer and grandson of a conductor. He studied the cello with Jules Delsart at the Paris Cons., winning first prize at the age of 15, and theory with Lavignac and B. Godard; member of the Capet Quartet, with which he toured (1893-1909); he made his début as conductor at the Lamoureux Concerts in Paris (1905); in 1907, founded and conducted the Hasselmans orchestral concerts in Paris; conductor at the Opéra-Comique, Paris (1909-11); conductor of the Montreal Opera in Canada (1911-13); conductor of the Marseilles Concerts Classiques (1911-13); conductor of the Chicago Opera (1918-20); then returned to France (1920) and again conducted at the Opéra-Comique; conductor of French works at the Metropolitan Opera House in New York from 1921 until 1936; from 1936, member of the music department at Louisiana State Univ., Baton Rouge; retired in 1948, then traveled widely in Europe and America; eventually settled in Aix-en-Provence.

Hassler, Hans Leo, celebrated German composer; b. Nuremberg, Oct. 25, 1564; d. Frankfurt, June 8, 1612. He studied with his father, Isaak Hassler (1530-91), and from his earliest years became extremely proficient on the organ. In 1584, he went to Venice to study with Andrea Gabrieli. Hassler was the first notable German composer who went to Italy for musical study; however, he did not remain long in Venice; after a year there, he was recalled to Germany, where he obtained the post of chamber musician to Count Octavianus Fugger in Augsburg; following the latter's death in 1600, he became a leader of the town band in Nuremberg and also organist at the Frauenkirche there. On Jan. 1, 1602, he received the post of chamber organist to the Court of Rudolf II at Prague; this was an honorary position rather than an actual occupation, and Hassler appeared but infrequently, if at all, at the imperial court in Prague. At the time he was busily engaged in the manufacture and installation of musical clocks; his commercial pursuits led to numerous litigations with business rivals. In 1604, he took a leave of absence from Nuremberg and went to Ulm; in 1609, he became organist to the Elector of Saxony in Dresden, and in 1612, accompanied him to Frankfurt; but he was weakened by tuberculosis and died shortly after arrival there. The style of Hassler's music is greatly influenced by his teacher Andrea Gabrieli, and the latter's nephew, Giovanni Gabrieli, with whom Hassler became friendly in Venice. Having absorbed the Italian techniques, Hassler applied his knowledge to the composition of strongly national German songs, and became one of the founders of national musical art in Germany.—Works: *Canzonette a* 4 (Nuremberg, 1590); *Cantiones sacrae a* 4-12 (Augsburg, 1591); *Neue teutsche Gesäng nach Art der welschen Madrigalien und Canzonetten a* 4-8 (Augsburg, 1596); *Madrigali a* 5-8 (Augsburg, 1596); 8 Masses *a* 4-8 (Nuremberg, 1599); *Sacri concentus a* 4-12 (Augsburg, 1601; 2nd ed., 1612); *Lustgarten neuer teutscher Gesäng, Balletti, Gailliarden und Intraden a* 4-8 (Nuremberg, 1601; later editions, 1605, 1610; reprints in Eitner's 'Publikationen älterer praktischer und theoretischer Musikwerke' vol. 15); *Psalmen und christliche Gesäng mit vier Stimmen auf die Melodien fugweis componirt* (Nuremberg, 1607); *Kirchengesänge, Psalmen und geistliche Lieder, auf die gemeinen Melodien mit vier Stimmen simpliciter gesetzt* (Nuremberg, 1608; 2nd enlarged ed., 1637); *Venusgarten oder neue lustige liebliche Tänz a* 4-6 (with V. Haussmann; Nuremberg, 1615); numerous motets, litanies, and organ works in various contemporary collections; 20 motets in Gruber's collection, *Reliquiae sacrorum concentuum G. Gabrielis, J.-H. Hasleri,* etc. (Nuremberg, 1615). Reprints are in the 'Denkmäler deutscher Tonkunst' (vols. 2, 7, 24, 25); 'Denkmäler der Tonkunst in Bayern' (vols. 4, 5, 11); in Riemann's *Illustrationen zur Musikgeschichte* and *Musikgeschichte in Beispielen;* Schering's *Geschichte der Musik in Beispielen;* Leichtentritt's *Meisterwerke deutscher Tonkunst,* etc. R. von Saalfeld edited the psalms and sacred songs (1925); H. Bäuerle edited 2 Masses. A chronological list of Hassler's printed works was publ. by Eitner in the 'Monatshefte für Musik-Geschichte' (1874).—Cf. R. Schwartz, *Hans Leo Hassler unter dem Einfluss der italienischen Madrigalisten,* in the 'Vierteljahrsschrift für Musikwissenschaft' (1893); A. Sandberger, *Bemerkungen zur Biographie Hans Leo Hasslers und seiner Brüder,* in the 'Denkmäler der Tonkunst in Bayern' (vol. V, 1; 1904); Hugo Leichtentritt, *Geschichte der Motette* (p. 293 et seq.; Leipzig, 1908); P. Wagner, *Geschichte der Messe* (p. 342 et seq.; 1914); M. Seiffert, *Geschichte der Klaviermusik* (p. 95 et seq.; 1899); H. J. Moser, *Geschichte der deutschen Musik* (vol. I, pp. 493-504; 5th ed., 1930).

Hassler, Jakob, German organist and composer; brother of Hans Leo Hassler; b. Nuremberg, Dec., 1569 (baptized Dec. 18); d. Eger, between April and Sept., 1622. Like his famous brother, he enjoyed the patronage of the Fugger family; was enabled to go to Italy in 1590 to improve his musical education; upon his return to Germany, on his brother's recommendation he received the honorary post of organist to Emperor Rudolf II in Prague. In 1611 he settled in Eger. He publ. a collection of Italian madrigals (Nuremberg, 1600) and a book of sacred works (Nuremberg, 1601). E von Werra publ. several keyboard pieces by Jakob Hassler in the 'Denkmäler der Tonkunst in Bayern' (1904).

Hässler, Johann Wilhelm, German composer and pianist; b. Erfurt, March 29, 1747; d. Moscow, March 29, 1822. His father was a maker of men's headwear; he followed his father's trade, while studying piano and organ with his uncle, Johann Christian Kittel. At the age of 14, he was able to earn his living as organist at an Erfurt church. After his father's death in 1769, he maintained for some years a manufacture of fur muffs. A meeting in Hamburg with Karl Philipp Emanuel Bach gave him a fresh impetus toward continuing his musical activities. He gave concerts as pianist, and publ. several piano sonatas. On Feb. 8, 1779, he married his pupil, Sophie Kiel. In 1780, he opened public winter concerts in Erfurt; his wife appeared there as a singer and choral director. In 1789, he played in Berlin and Potsdam; in Dresden he took part in a contest with Mozart, as organist and pianist, without producing much impression either on Mozart himself or on the listeners. In 1790, he went to London, where he performed piano concertos under the direction of Haydn. In 1792, he went to Russia, where he remained for 30 years, until his death. In Moscow, he became greatly renowned as pianist, composer, and particularly as teacher. Most of his works were published in Russia; these included sonatas, preludes, variations, fantasies, etc., and also pieces for piano, 4-hands. His style represents a transition between Bach and Beethoven, without attaining a degree of the imagination or craftsmanship of either. However, his piano pieces in the lighter vein have undeniable charm. His gigue in D minor was well known. His autobiography is included in Willi Kahl, *Selbstbiographien deutscher Musiker* (Cologne, 1948). See also W. Georgii, *Klavier-Musik* (Zürich, 1950).

Hassler, Kaspar, German composer; brother of Hans Leo Hassler; b. Nuremberg, Aug. (baptized, Aug. 17) 1562; d. there, Aug. 19, 1618. In 1586 he was appointed organist at the Lorenz-Kirche; also supervised the building of the organ in the Würzburg Cathedral. He wrote a number of organ pieces; edited several collections of sacred works by various authors.

Hastings, Thomas, American composer and hymn writer; b. Washington, Litchfield County, Conn., Oct. 15, 1784; d. New York, May 15, 1872. The family moved to Clinton, N. Y., when Hastings was 12; he became interested in practical music, and was a leader of a village chorus. He also collected hymns, which were later published in a collection, *Musica Sacra* (with S. Warriner, 1816). He moved to Utica in 1828 and was a member of a Handel and Haydn society there; he also edited a religious weekly publication, 'The Western Recorder.' In 1832 he settled in New York, where he was connected with the Normal Institute, in association with Lowell Mason. He received the honorary degree of Doctor of Music from N. Y. Univ. (1858). Among his many publications were *Musical Reader* (1817); *Dissertation on Musical Taste* (1822; 2nd enlarged ed., 1853); *The Union Minstrel* (1830); *Spiritual Songs for Social Worship* (with Lowell Mason, 1831); *Devo-*

tional Hymns and Religious Poems (1850); *History of Forty Choirs* (1854), and *Sacred Praise* (1856). His own hymn tunes have been estimated to number more than 1000, and, next to those of Lowell Mason, are regarded as the finest of his time in America. These include the celebrated tune, *Rock of Ages* (words by Augustus Toplady); other well-known hymn tunes are *Retreat, Zion,* and *Ortonville.* He publ. many of his melodies under foreign-looking names, and it is not always possible to ascertain their authorship.—Cf. F. J. Metcalf, *American Writers and Compilers of Sacred Music* (N. Y., 1925); J. T. Howard, *Our American Music* (N. Y., 1939, and subsequent eds.); M. B. Scanlon, *Thomas Hastings,* in the 'Mus. Quarterly' (April, 1946). See also the article on Hastings in the 'Dictionary of American Biography.'

Hastreiter, Helene, American dramatic contralto; b. Louisville, Ky., Nov. 14, 1858; d. Varese, Italy, Aug. 6, 1922. She sang as a child in a Chicago church; at the age of 22, went to Italy where she studied with the Lampertis (father and son) in Milan. She made her operatic début there, and after several successful appearances in Italy, was engaged by Col. Mapleson for his London season (1885). She then sang mostly in Italy; married Dr. Burgunzio there, and lived in Genoa. Some of her leading operatic parts were Orfeo, Euridice, Dalila, Senta, and Ortrud.

Hatton, John Liptrot, British composer of light music; b. Liverpool, Oct. 12, 1809; d. Margate, Sept. 20, 1886. He acquired facility as pianist and singer, and appeared on the vaudeville stage as a musical comedian. He publ. a great number of songs, among which *Anthea* and *Good-bye, sweetheart, good-bye* became extremely popular. In 1832 he went to London; produced his operetta, *The Queen of the Thames,* there (Feb. 25, 1843). He then went to Vienna, where he staged his opera *Pascal Bruno* (March 2, 1844). For some of his numbers he used the punning pseudonym Czapek (genitive plural of the Hungarian word for hat). In 1848-50 he made an extensive American tour. Returning to England, he was musical director at the Princess's Theatre (1853-59); wrote music for several Shakespeare plays there; wrote a cantata *Robin Hood* (Bradford Festival, Aug. 26, 1856); a grand opera *Rose, or Love's Ransom* (London, Nov. 26, 1864), and a sacred drama *Hezekiah* (Dec. 15, 1877); edited collections of old English songs.

Hattstaedt, John James, American pianist and pedagogue; b. Monroe, Mich., Dec. 29, 1851; d. Chicago, Nov. 30, 1931. He studied in Germany; then taught piano in Detroit (1870-72), St. Louis (1872-73), and Chicago (1875-86). In 1886 he founded the American Cons. of Music in Chicago. He publ. a *Manual of Musical History.*

Haubiel, Charles, American composer; b. Delta, Ohio, Jan. 30, 1892. He studied piano with Rudolph Ganz and Josef and Rosina Lhévinne; composition with Rosario Scalero; occupied various teaching posts, at Kingfisher College in Oklahoma, at the Institute of Musical Art, N. Y. (1921-29); at N. Y. Univ. (1922-47), etc.; was founder and president (1935) of the Composers' Press, Inc. He was the winner of the first prize in America at the Schubert Centennial contest (1928) for his set of symph. variations *Karma.* — Works: *Brigands Preferred,* musical satire (1925); *Karma,* symph. variations on a theme by Handel (1928; recorded by the Columbia Phonograph Co., 1929); *Mars Ascending,* for orch. (1923; honorable mention in the Paderewski symph. contest); *Rittrati* (*Portraits,* for orch.; Chicago, Dec. 12, 1935); *Pastoral* (for orch., 1935); *Suite Passacaglia* (Los Angeles, Jan. 31, 1936); *Symphony in Variation Form* (1937); *Vox Cathedralis,* for orch. (N. Y., May 6, 1938); *Miniatures,* for string orch. (N. Y., April 23, 1939); *Amphycromes,* for piano trio (1932); *Cryptics,* for bassoon and piano (1932); *Gay Dances,* for piano trio (1932); *Lodando la Danza,* for oboe, violin, cello, and piano (1932); *Pastorale,* for oboe and cello (1933); *Duoforms,* for trio (1934); *Echi Classici,* for string quartet (1936); trio for flute, cello, and piano (1942); *Gothic Variations,* for violin and piano (1943); string trio (1943); cello sonata (1944); *Nuances,* for flute and piano (1947); *Shadows,* for violin and piano (1947), etc.; many choral works: *Sea Songs* (1931), *L'Amore Spirituale* (1932), *Yeoman's Song* (1932), *Vision of Saint Joan* (1941), *Jungle Tale* (1943), *Father Abraham* (1944), *Both Grave and Gay* (1944), etc.

Haudebert, Lucien, French composer; b. Fougères, April 18, 1877. He studied organ; then went to Paris, where he took lessons in composition with Fauré. He followed in his music the traditions of César Franck, preferring large sonorities and clear tonal harmonies. He stood aloof from modern developments in France and had little recognition even among traditional musicians, despite praise from Romain Rolland. His most effective work is the oratorio, *Dieu Vainqueur* (1916-22); other significant works are: the oratorio *Moïse* (1928); *Symphonie bretonne* (1936); *Symphonie française* (1941); *Voyage en Bretagne,* for orch. (1953); *Chants de la Mer,* for voices and orch. (1950); also chamber music, including a quartet for saxophones.

Hauer, Josef Matthias, Austrian composer; b. Wiener-Neustadt, near Vienna, March 19, 1883. After attending a teachers' college, he became a public school instructor; at the same time he studied music. An experimenter by nature, with strong leanings towards mathematical constructions, he developed a system of composition according to 'tropes' or patterns, without repeated notes, and aggregating to thematic formations of 12 notes. As early as 1912 he publ. a piano piece entitled *Nomos* (Law), which embodies the germ of 12-tone music. The promulgation of his theory of tropes followed in 1921; other theoretical publications are *Vom Wesen des Musikalischen* (Berlin 1922); *Deutung des Melos* (Vienna, 1923); *Vom Melos zur Pauke* (Vienna, 1925); *Zwölftontechnik* (Vienna, 1926). Hauer asserted his priority in the establishment of the 12-tone method of composition with great vehemence; but while chronologically he may have anticipated Schoenberg in the bare statement that such a technique is esthetically self-consistent, the true development of the method, with full use of contrapuntal and canonic devices, did not appear until Schoenberg laid its foundations about 1924. From 1914, Hauer remained in Vienna, working as conductor, teacher, and composer. Despite the forbidding character of many of his works, most of them have been performed and published. He wrote an opera, *Salammbo* (1930); a musical play, *Die schwarze Spinne* (1931); 2 cantatas, *Wandlungen* (1928) and *Der Menschen Weg* (1953); 8 suites for orch.; some 30 instrumental pieces entitled *Zwölftonspiel;* a symph. for strings, harmonium, and piano; violin concerto (1928); piano concerto (1928); 6 string quartets; quintet for clarinet, violin, viola, cello, and piano; several sets of piano pieces entitled *Nomoi;* songs and choruses.—Cf. Willi Reich, *J. M. Hauer,* in 'Die Musik' (May, 1931); H. Picht, *J. M. Hauer, ein Vorkämpfer geistiger Musikauffassung* (Stuttgart, 1934).

Haufrecht, Herbert, American composer; b. New York City, Nov. 3, 1909. He studied with Roger Sessions, Quincy Porter, and Herbert Elwell at the Cleveland Institute of Music; later with Rubin Goldmark in New York. In 1936 he went to West Virginia, where he collected folk music; upon his return to N. Y. he became active as editor and arranger. Among his compositions are: *The Story of Ferdinand* for narrator and orch.; *Overture for an American Mural* (N. Y., Aug. 2, 1939); a pantomime-opera *Boney Quillan* (1951); a symphony for brass and timpani (1955); *Woodland Serenade* for woodwind quintet (1955); many pieces for school bands.

Haug, Hans, Swiss composer; b. Basel, July 27, 1900. He was a pupil of Ernst Lévy and Egon Petri at the Basel Cons. and later of Walter Courvoisier and Joseph Pembaur at the Academy of Music in Munich. He then was choral director in Solothurn (1926-28) and assistant conductor at the Municipal Theater of Basel (1928-34). From 1935 he was primarily active on the Swiss radio; also taught at the Lausanne Cons. (from 1947); conducted orchestral concerts on the Monte Carlo radio. As a composer, Haug is mainly interested in theatrical and choral music.—Works: operas: *Don Juan in der Fremde* (Basel, Dec. 5, 1930); *Madrisa* (Basel, Jan. 15, 1934); *Tartuffe* (Basel, May 24, 1937); *Le Malade imaginaire,* after Molière (Zürich, Feb. 8, 1947); *Der Spiegel der Agrippina* (1954); oratorio, *Michelangelo* (Solothurn, Feb. 28, 1943); a symphony (1948); violin concerto (1926); *Kurze Musik* for cello and orch. (1927); piano concerto (1938); flute concerto (1943); guitar concerto (1952); double concerto for oboe and viola (1953); 3 string quartets (1927-31); wind quartet (1925); wind quintet (1955).

Hauk, Minnie (real name Mignon Hauck), celebrated American soprano; b. New York, Nov. 16, 1851; d. Triebschen, near Lucerne, Switzerland, Feb. 6, 1929. Her father was a German carpenter who became involved in the political events of 1848, emigrated to America and married an American woman; he named his daughter Mignon after the character in Goethe's *Wilhelm Meister.* The family moved to Atchison, Kansas, when Minnie was very young; her mother maintained a boarding house at a steamboat landing on the Missouri. In 1860 they moved to New Orleans; there Minnie Hauk began to sing popular ballads for entertainment. She made her operatic début at the age of 14 in Brooklyn, in *La Sonnambula* (Oct. 13, 1866); then took lessons with Achille Errani of New

York. On Nov. 15, 1867, she sang Juliette at the American première of Gounod's opera in N. Y. She attracted the attention of the rich industrialist, Leonard Jerome, and Gustave Schirmer, the music publisher, who financed her trip to Europe. She sang in opera in Paris during the summer of 1868; made her London début at Covent Garden on Oct. 26, 1868; in 1870 she sang in Vienna. She sang the title roles in the first American performances of *Carmen* (N. Y. Academy of Music, Oct. 23, 1878) and Massenet's *Manon* (Dec. 23, 1885); appeared at the Metropolitan Opera during the season of 1890-91, but following a disagreement with the management, decided to organize her own opera group; with it, she gave the first Chicago performance of *Cavalleria Rusticana* (Sept. 28, 1891). She then settled in Switzerland with her husband Baron Ernst von Hesse-Wartegg, whom she had married in 1881; after his death, she lived mostly in Berlin; lost her fortune in the depreciation of her holdings in Germany. In 1919, Geraldine Farrar launched an appeal to raise funds for her in America. Her autobiography, collated by E. B. Hitchcock, was publ. as *Memories of a Singer* (London, 1925).—Cf. Oscar Thompson, *The American Singer* (N. Y., 1937; pp. 93-118).

Haupt, Karl August, German organist; b. Kuhnau, Silesia, Aug. 25, 1810; d. Berlin, July 4, 1891. He studied with Dehn and others in Berlin; played in various Berlin churches, and became famous for his masterly improvisations in the style of Bach. He was one of the experts consulted for the specifications in building the grand organ at the Crystal Palace in London. He had many distinguished pupils, including about 40 American organists. He publ. a valuable *Choralbuch* (1869); many other compositions for organ remain in manuscript.

Hauptmann, Moritz, eminent German theorist and composer; b. Dresden, Oct. 13, 1792; d. Leipzig, Jan. 3, 1868. His father was an architect, and hoped to bring up his son in that profession; however, there was no parental opposition to music studies; he took lessons with Scholz (violin) and Morlacchi (composition) in Dresden; in 1811 he went to Gotha to study violin and composition with Spohr and became his lifelong friend. In 1812, he joined the Dresden Court orch. as violinist; in 1815, he became music teacher in the family of the Russian military governor of Dresden, Prince Repnin, and went with them to Russia, where he remained for 5 years. In 1820, he returned to Dresden; in 1822, Spohr engaged him as violinist in the court orch. at Kassel. In 1842, at Mendelssohn's recommendation, he was appointed cantor at the Thomasschule and prof. of composition at the Leipzig Cons., retaining these posts until his death. He became greatly renowned as a teacher of violin and composition. Among his pupils were Ferdinand David, Joachim, Hans von Bülow, Jadassohn, and Arthur Sullivan. A master of classical form, he was a polished composer, in the tradition of Spohr and Mendelssohn; the architectonic symmetry of his instrumental works and the purity of part-writing in his vocal music aroused admiration among his contemporaries; yet his music failed to endure, and rapidly went into decline after his death. He publ. about 60 works, among them 3 violin sonatas, 4 violin sonatinas, 2 string quartets, piano pieces, sacred works, and a number of lieder, a genre in which he excelled. His theoretical work, *Die Natur der Harmonik und Metrik* (Leipzig, 1853; 2nd ed., 1873; English transl., London, 1888), is an attempt to apply Hegel's dialectical philosophy to the realm of music. It exercised considerable influence on the later development of German theory of harmony; among other German scholars, Riemann was influenced by it. Haptmann's other writings are: *Erläuterungen zu J. S. Bachs Kunst der Fuge* (Leipzig, 1841; 2nd ed., 1861); *Die Lehre von der Harmonik* (ed. by Oscar Paul; Leipzig, 1868); *Opuscula* (miscellaneous writings, edited by E. Hauptmann; Leipzig, 1874). His letters to Spohr and others were edited by F. Hiller (Leipzig, 1876). A. D. Coleridge publ. a selection, in English, of Hauptmann's correspondence as *Letters of a Leipzig Cantor* (1892).—Cf. O. Paul, *Moritz Hauptmann, Eine Denkschrift zur Feier seines Siebzigjährigen Geburtstages am 13. October 1862* (Leipzig, 1862); Stephan Krehl, *Moritz Hauptmann; ein Dank- und Gedenkwort* (Leipzig, 1918).

Hauschka, Vincenz, gifted cellist and composer; b. Mies, Bohemia, Jan. 21, 1766; d. Vienna, Sept. 13, 1840. He was a pupil of his father, a school teacher; became chorister in Prague cathedral; studied composition with Zöger, cello with Christ. He was appointed cellist to Count Joseph von Thun in Prague (1782); made successful concert tours through Germany performing not only on the cello, but also on the baryton (a popular instrument at the time; Haydn wrote numerous works for it). He publ. 9 sonatas for cello; a book of vocal canons; in MS are several pieces for the baryton.

Hausegger, Friedrich von, Austrian musicologist; b. St. Andrä, Carinthia, April 26, 1837; d. Graz, Feb. 23, 1899. He was a pupil of Salzmann and Otto Desoff; also studied law and became a barrister at Graz. In 1872 he became a teacher of history and theory of music at the Univ. of Graz. He contributed to music periodicals. His *Musik als Ausdruck* (Vienna, 1885) is a valuable addition to musical esthetics. He also wrote *Richard Wagner und Schopenhauer* (1890); *Vom Jenseits des Künstlers* (1893); *Die künstlerische Persönlichkeit* (1897). After his death, his book, *Unsere deutschen Meister,* was ed. by R. Louis (1901); his *Gesammelte Schriften* were brought out by his son in 1939.

Hausegger, Siegmund von, conductor and composer, son of the preceding; b. Graz, Aug. 16, 1872; d. Munich, Oct. 10, 1948. He was trained musically by his father; conducted at the Graz Theater (1895-96) and at Bayreuth (1897). From 1899 to 1902, he was conductor of the Kaim Orch. in Munich; then of the Museum Concerts at Frankfurt (1903-06), the Hamburg Philh. Concerts, and the Blüthner Orch. in Berlin; in 1922 he became president of the Academy of Musical Art in Munich, where he conducted concerts regularly; Mus. D. (1925), Kiel Univ. He married the daughter of Alexander Ritter, Hertha (d. Hamburg, Jan. 15, 1913). At the age of 16, he composed a grand Mass for soli, chorus, orch., and organ, which he himself conducted; in 1890 he brought out his first opera, *Helfrid,* in Graz; Richard Strauss produced his 3-act comic opera, *Zinnober,* at the Munich Court Theater (June 19, 1898); in 1899 he conducted his *Dionysische Fantasie* in Munich, and in 1900, his symphonic poem *Barbarossa* with the Berlin Philharmonic. He also wrote 2 songs for tenor with orch., 3 songs for baritone with orch., *7 Lieder der Liebe* (Lenau), *Hymnen an die Nacht;* the symph. poem *Wieland der Schmied;* the men's choruses with orch. *Schmied Schmerz, Neuweinlied, Schlachtgesang, Totenmarsch;* the mixed choruses with orch. *Stimme des Abends, Vor Sonnenaufgang, Schnitterlied, Weihe der Nacht;* a *Natursymphonie* (1911); symph. variations on a children's song, *Aufklänge* (1919). He also publ. *Alexander Ritter, ein Bild seines Charakters und Schaffens* (1907); edited *R. Wagners Briefe an Frau Julie Ritter* (1920) and letters of his father to Peter K. Rosegger (1924). Hausegger's collected essays have appeared under the title *Betrachtungen zur Kunst* (1921).

Hauser, Miska, violinist; b. Pressburg (Bratislava), 1822; d. Vienna, Dec. 8, 1887. He studied with Kreutzer and others in Vienna, and traveled as a child prodigy in Europe; he played in America and Australia (1853-58), achieving sensational success. However, he abandoned the public stage rather early in life; made his last appearance in Cologne in 1874. He wrote an operetta *Der blinde Leiermann;* numerous violin pieces, of which *Rapsodie hongroise* and *Lieder ohne Worte* enjoyed considerable popularity. He sent correspondence to the 'Ostdeutsche Post' during his American tour; these reports were collected and publ. in 2 vols., *Aus dem Wanderbuche eines österreichischen Virtuosen* (Leipzig, 1858-59). Vol. 3 of 'History of Music in San Francisco' (San Francisco, 1939; WPA publication) contains his letters of 1853.

Hausmann, Robert, cellist; b. Rottleberode, Harz, Aug. 13, 1852; d. Vienna, Jan. 18, 1909. He studied cello with Theodore Müller in Berlin and with Tiatti in London and Italy. He was the cellist of the Hochberg quartet in Dresden (1872-76); then joined the Joachim quartet (1879), with which he remained until its dissolution after Joachim's death (1907).

Hausmann, Valentin. Four musicians in direct lineal descent bore this name: **Valentin I,** the eldest, b. Nuremberg, 1484, composed chorales, and was a friend of Luther and of Kapellmeister Joh. Walter. His son, **II,** was organist and councillor at Gerbstädt, and an industrious composer of motets, canzonets, and dances (intrade, paduane, etc.). A selection of his secular songs and instrumental works was publ. by F. Bölsche in the 'Denkmäler deutscher Tonkunst' (vol. 16). **III,** son of the preceding, was organist at Löbejün, and an expert in organ construction. His son, **IV,** occupied the posts of chapel musician to the Köthen court and organist of Alsleben Chapel; author of a treatise on solmisation. The fifth musician in the Hausmann line, Bartholomäus, son of the preceding, b. Löbejün, 1678, became cathedral organist at Merseburg and Halle, and died as organist and burgomaster at Lauchstädt after 1740. He left in MS several theoretical works.

Haussermann, John, American composer; b. Manila, Philippines, Aug. 21, 1909. He studied in the U. S. at the Cincinnati Cons. and in Paris with Dupré (organ) and Le Flem (composition). — Works: Symphony No. 1 (Cincinnati, Feb 21, 1941); Symphony No. 2 (Cincinnati, March 31, 1944);

Symphony No. 3 (Cincinnati, April 1, 1949); quintet for flute, oboe, clarinet, bassoon, and harpsichord; 2 string quartets; *Suite Rustique* for cello, flute, and piano; piano works; organ solos; songs. A unique work is a *Concerto for voice and orch.* (Cincinnati, April 24, 1942), with the vocal part wordless.

Hausswald, Günter, German musicologist; b. Rochlitz, March 11, 1908. He studied piano with Max Pauer in Leipzig and composition with Karg-Elert; musicology with Theodor Kroyer and Grabner. He taught music in Leipzig and Dresden (1933-45); in 1950-53 was on the faculty of the Univ. of Jena. He publ. several valuable monographs: *Johann David Heinichens Instr.-Werke* (Dresden, 1937), *Heinrich Marschner* (Dresden, 1938), *Die deutsche Oper* (Cologne, 1941), *Mozarts Serenaden* (Leipzig, 1951), *Das neue Opernbuch* (Dresden, 1951; annual editions in 1953-56), *Richard Strauss* (Dresden, 1953); edited works by Gluck, Heinichen, Telemann, Weber, etc.

Havingha, Gerhardus, Dutch organist and theorist; b. Groningen, Nov. 15, 1696; d. Alkmaar, March 6, 1753. He studied with his father, a church organist at Groningen; then became an organist at various churches in Holland; publ. *Oorspronk en Voortgang der orgelen* (Alkmaar, 1727), an important source of organ history and practice in Holland. His suite for harpsichord (Amsterdam, 1725) was republ. by J. Watelet in 1951.

Hawes, William, English composer and conductor; b. London, June 21, 1785; d. there, Feb. 18, 1846. As a boy, he was a chorister at the Chapel Royal (1793-1801); then violinist at Covent Garden (1802); became Gentleman of the Chapel Royal in 1805; vicar-choral and master of choristers at St. Paul's Cathedral (1812); master of the children of the Chapel Royal (1817); and lay-vicar of Westminster Abbey (1817-20). He was director of English opera at the Lyceum; it was at his suggestion that Weber's *Der Freischütz* was given for the first time in England (July 22, 1824); he contributed some airs of his own composition to this production. Subsequently, he adapted and produced many Italian, French, and German operas for the English stage; he wrote and staged several light operas, among them, *Broken Promises* (1825), *The Quartette,* or *Interrupted Harmony* (1828), *The Sister of Charity* (1829), etc. Some of his glees were popular. He edited the publication (in score) of the *Triumphes of Oriana* (1818), various collections of glees, etc.

Hawkins, Sir **John,** English music historian; b. London, March 30, 1719; d. there, May 21, 1789. He studied law while serving as a clerk, and soon was able to act as an attorney. An ardent devotee of music, he entered the musical society of the time and was on friendly terms with Handel; he also participated in literary clubs, and knew Samuel Johnson, Goldsmith, and others. A wealthy marriage (1753) enabled him to devote his leisure to literature and music. In the meantime, he progressed on the ladder of success in the legal profession. In 1761, he became a magistrate; in 1763, chairman of the Quarter Sessions; he was knighted in 1772. His first publication dealing with music was brought out anonymously: *An Account of the Institution and Progress of the Academy of Ancient Music* (1770). The culmination of 16 years of labor was his monumental *General History of the Science and Practice of Music,* publ. in 1776 in 5 vols., 4to, containing 58 portraits of musicians; it was republ. in 1853 and 1875, by Novello, in 3 vols., 8vo. The first volume of Burney's *General History of Music* appeared at the same time as the 5 vols. of Hawkins; thus, Hawkins undoubtedly held priority for the first general history of music publ. in England; however, its reception was rather hostile; Burney himself derided Hawkins in an unpublished poem. Yet the Hawkins work contained reliable information, particularly dealing with musical life in London in the 18th century. Hawkins died of a paralytic stroke, and was buried in Westminster Abbey. Percy A. Scholes wrote a definitive biography, *The Life and Activities of Sir John Hawkins* (London, 1953). See also R. Stevenson, *'The Rivals'—Hawkins, Burney, and Boswell,* in the 'Mus. Quarterly' (Jan., 1950).

Hawley, Charles Beach, American organist; b. Brookfield, Mass., Feb. 14, 1858; d. Red Bank, N. J., Dec. 29, 1915. He studied organ at the Cheshire Military Academy; then took composition lessons in New York with Dudley Buck; then served as organist in various churches; publ. some songs, showing a facile melodic invention.

Hawthorne, Alice. See **Winner, Septimus.**

Hay, Edward Norman, Irish composer and organist; b. Faversham, April 19, 1889;

d. Belfast, Sept. 10, 1943. He studied organ with Koeller and Eaglefield-Hull; received Mus. Bac. (1911) and Mus. Doc. (1919), Oxford. He was organist of various churches in Ireland. He won the Feis Ceoil Prize in 1916 with his cello sonata on Irish folk tunes, the Cobbett Prize (1917) with his *Folksong Phantasy* for string quartet, and the Carnegie Award (1918) with his string quartet in A. He also wrote the orchestral compositions *The Gilly of Christ, Dunluce* (1921), etc.; organ works and songs.

Hay, Frederick Charles, Swiss composer; b. Basel, Sept. 18, 1888; d. Langau, July 18, 1945. He was a medical student; then studied with Huber in Basel, and Widor in Paris and F. Schalk in Vienna; conducted the Univ. of Bern orch. (1912) and oratorio concerts in Geneva (1920-25); taught musicology at the Univ. of Geneva. He wrote the orchestral works *Heaven and Earth, Der Dom;* concertos for oboe, violin, piano, and viola; *Notturno, Intermezzo e Capriccio,* for piano and woodwind orch.; choral works; hymns, and piano pieces.

Hayasaka, Fumio, Japanese composer; b. Sendai-City, Aug. 19, 1914. He studied in Tokyo with Alexander Tcherepnin; won the Weingartner Prize (1938). He has been particularly successful in writing for Japanese motion pictures; wrote the score for the film *Rashomon,* the recipient of first prize at the International Festival in Venice (1952). Among his works are Overture in D major (Tokyo, March 17, 1940); Piano Concerto No. 1 (Tokyo, June 22, 1948); *The Ancient Dance* (Tokyo, May 15, 1939); *Yukara,* suite (Tokyo, June 9, 1955); etc.

Haydn, (Franz) Joseph, renowned Austrian composer; b. Rohrau-on-the-Leitha, Lower Austria, March 31 (baptized April 1), 1732; d. Vienna, May 31, 1809. He was the second son of Matthias Haydn, a wheelwright, the sexton and organist of the village church and a fine tenor singer. His mother, Maria Koller, was a daughter of the market inspector, sang in the village choir, and had been cook in the household of Count Harrach, the lord of the village. Of their 12 children, 3 became musicians. On Sundays and holidays there was music at home, the father accompanying the voices on the harp, which he played by ear. At 5 years of age, Haydn's musical aptitude was noticed by a paternal cousin, Johann Matthias Frankh, a good musician and choral director at Hainburg. He took the boy home with him and gave him elementary instruction, taught him Latin, singing, the violin, and other instruments. Georg Reutter, musical director at St. Stephen's, Vienna, had his attention drawn to the boy's talent, and engaged him as chorister for St. Stephen's, undertaking his further education. Haydn was 8 years of age when he went to Vienna. Besides the daily service, and 2 hours' choir-practice, he studied religion, Latin, writing, and arithmetic. He also received instruction in singing, and on the violin and harpsichord, from Finsterbusch and Gegenbauer. Harmony and composition were supposed to be taught by Reutter, who did not trouble himself about the matter. Still, unaided, Haydn applied himself assiduously to composition; though ridiculed, instead of encouraged, by Reutter, he persisted, and spent a little money, begged from his father for the renewal of his clothing, in the purchase of Fux's *Gradus ad Parnassum* and Mattheson's *Vollkommener Kapellmeister,* the principles of which he labored to master. In 1748 his voice began to break, and he was supplanted by his brother Michael, who had joined him in 1745. Reutter made a practical joke which Haydn played on a fellow-student a pretext for punishment and dismissal. Some poor but kindhearted friends gave him shelter; he also obtained a few pupils, and a sympathetic Viennese tradesman lent him 150 florins; he was thus enabled to rent an attic room for himself, together with a rickety harpsichord. Here he could practice uninterruptedly; his chief sources of study were keyboard sonatas by K. P. E. Bach. He also diligently practiced the violin, but was (in his own words) 'no conjuror on any instrument, though able to play a concerto.' In the same house lived Metastasio, the poet, who taught him Italian, and recommended him as musical instructor to a Spanish family, the de Martinez, for their daughter Marianne. Through playing her accompaniments at the house of Porpora, her singing-teacher, he became acquainted with that surly old master, and in the performance of various menial services gained his good will sufficiently to receive valuable instruction in composition from him, and a recommendation to the Venetian ambassador for a stipend, which was granted, of 50 francs a month. Haydn went with Porpora to the baths of Mannersdorf, and made the acquaintance of Bonno, Wagenseil, Dittersdorf, and Gluck. Thus far he had composed sonatas, trios, and other instrumental music, a Mass and the Singspiel *Der krumme Teufel,* produced in 1752 at the Stadttheater (a satire on the lame Baron Affligio, official director of the court opera, and suppressed after the 3d representation but afterwards given in Prague, Berlin, and other cities). He received 25 ducats for this work, of which the libretto alone has been preserved. One of his sonatas earned the good graces of Countess Thun, who engaged him as harpsichordist and singing master. Haydn also met Baron Karl Josef Fürnberg, for whom he wrote his first string quartets. These two wealthy friends introduced him to Count Ferdinand Maximilian Morzin, who, in 1758, appointed Haydn 'Musikdirector' and 'Kammercompositeur' at Lukaveč, near Pilsen. In 1759 Prince Paul Anton Esterházy heard one of his symphonies, and asked the Count to release Haydn to him. In 1761 Haydn entered his service as 2nd Kapellmeister at the Prince's estate in Eisenstadt, becoming 1st Kapellmeister in 1766. On Nov. 26, 1760, Haydn married Maria Anna, the eldest daughter of an early benefactor, Keller, a wig-maker. He was in love with the second daughter, but she entered a convent, and Haydn was induced to marry the sister. Of an extravagant, vixenish, incompatible temperament, she made their married life miserable. In 1762 the 'great' Esterházy, Prince Nikolaus, succeeded his deceased brother, and under his *régime* the status of music and musicians was much improved. For the Prince's new palace at Esterház, besides the daily music, Haydn had to provide two weekly operatic performances and two formal concerts; while in his service, Haydn wrote some 80 symphonies, 43 quartets, numerous divertimenti, clavier works of all descriptions, and nearly all his operas, besides other instrumental and vocal comps. His music became known throughout Europe; in 1766 the official gazette alluded to him as 'our national favorite.' In 1780 he was elected member of the Modena Philharmonic Society; in 1784 Prince Henry of Prussia sent him a gold medal and his portrait; in 1785 he was commissioned to write a 'passione instrumentale,' *The Seven Last Words,* for the Cathedral of Cadiz; in 1787 King Friedrich Wilhelm II gave him a diamond ring; many other distinctions were conferred upon him. During his visits to Vienna, his friendship for Mozart developed. In 1790 Prince Nikolaus died, and his son Anton curtailed the chapel music, retaining Haydn, however, as Kapellmeister, and increasing his stipend of 1,000 florins by an additional 400. He was virtually independent; his time was his own, and he added to his income by the sale of his works. For some time he had received pressing invitations to visit London. He had settled in Vienna, when Salomon appeared with a tempting offer, and induced him to accompany him, although his friends, especially Mozart, tried to dissuade him. In 1791, he arrived in England, and remained there 18 months, fêted by royalty and the nobility. In July, Oxford Univ. conferred on him the honorary degree of Mus. D.; and his best orchestral works, the 'Salomon symphonies,' were written during this and the following visit. In 1792, Haydn returned via Bonn to Frankfurt, for the coronation of Emperor Franz II; went then to Vienna, also visiting his native place to witness the unveiling of a monument created in his honor by Count Harrach, his mother's former employer. In that year, he gave Beethoven the lessons with which the latter was so dissatisfied. In 1794, he revisited London; his former triumphs were repeated, and though pressed by the King to make England his home, he returned to his native land in affluence, at the invitation of a new Prince, to reorganize the Esterházy chapel. But his fame, though great, was not yet at its zenith. In 1797 he composed *Gott erhalte Franz den Kaiser,* which became the Austrian National Anthem; in 1798, he wrote his immortal oratorio *Die Schöpfung* (*The Creation*), and in 1801, *Die Jahreszeiten* (*The Seasons*). But his health began to fail, and thenceforward he lived in retirement. Only once did he again appear in public, on March 27, 1808, at a special performance of *The Creation;* but he had to be carried out before the finish, friends and pupils, among whom was Beethoven, surrounding him to take leave. He lingered until 1809, when his end was hastened by the shock of the bombardment of Vienna by the French. He was buried in the Hundsthurm churchyard. As a result of some fantastic events, his skull became separated from his body before his reinterment at Eisenstadt in 1820, and after many peregrinations, was exhibited in the hall of the Society of Friends of Music in Vienna. It was finally reburied in Eisenstadt with the body on June 5, 1954, attended by official ceremony.

Although of unprepossessing personal appearance, stern, dignified in aspect, and laconic in speech, Haydn was of a humorous, agreeable, and amiable temperament. The religious side of his character is shown in the inscriptions of all his scores, with the motto 'In Nomine Domini' and all ending with 'Laus Deo' or 'Soli Deo Gloria.'

Haydn was the first great master of the new instrumental style which reached its highest development in the works of Beethoven. Since the publication of instrumental works by his Viennese predecessors, by the composers of the 'Mannheim school,' and by other early symphonists, Haydn can no longer be regarded as the 'Father of the symphony' or the 'Father of the modern orchestra.' But he availed himself of the forms and achievements of his predecessors, and his greater genius soon caused the earlier efforts to fall into undeserved oblivion. That his music accomplished this is the most eloquent tribute to its inherent power and greatness; it is not the mere creation of a new form that counts, but the artistic content. Haydn's position as the first 'great master' of the new instrumental style remains unshaken. His melodic vein is inexhaustible; the gayety of 'Papa Haydn's' lighter music went straight to the hearts of the impressionable Viennese, and lent new vivacity to European concert halls; in his moods of tenderness or of passion, he is a worthy forerunner of Beethoven. And to all this must be added the marvelous fertility of his creative resources. The precise extent of Haydn's productivity will probably never be known. Many works are irretrievably lost; others, listed in various catalogues, may have never existed, or were duplications of extant works; some are of doubtful authenticity; several are definitely spurious. Thus, the celebrated *Toy Symphony* appears not to be a work by Haydn, but by Leopold Mozart. The authorship of the so-called Zittau Divertimenti, including the one in B-flat major with the *Chorale St. Antonii,* is also very doubtful. If Haydn was indeed not the author, then the *Variations on a Theme by Haydn* of Brahms, based on the *Chorale St. Antonii,* is a misnamed work. Two piano trios are now definitely known to be the works of Haydn's pupil Ignaz Pleyel, who was capable of imitating his master's style with amazing ingenuity. The generally accepted list of Haydn's authentic symphonies comprises 104 items; but see the monumental work *The Symphonies of Haydn* by H. C. Robbins Landon (1955) for particulars. Many of these symphonies bear descriptive titles, attached to them by publishers (only a few of them were authorized by Haydn himself, e.g., Nos. 6-8: *Le Matin, Le Midi,* and *Le Soir): the Abschiedssymphonie (Farewell Symphony;* performed by Haydn at Esterház in 1772 as a humorous and sad leave-taking when Prince Esterházy decided to disband the orchestra; this explanation of the origin of the Farewell Symphony, found in *Anedotti piacevoli ed interessanti* by G. G. Ferrari, 1830, is more plausible than the generally accepted one that the performance of the work was a hint that the orchestra needed a vacation); *La Chasse (The Hunt,* 1781); *L'Ours (The Bear,* 1786); *La Poule (The Hen,* 1786); *Oxford* (performed at Oxford in 1791, when Haydn was given an honorary degree); *Paukenschlag (Drumstroke,* 1791; known as *Surprise Symphony*); *Military Symphony* (1794); *Die Uhr (The Clock,* 1794); *Paukenwirbel (Drumroll,* 1795). The last of the 12 Salomon Symphonies (written for the London impresario Salomon) is known as the *London Symphony;* 6 symphonies written for performances in Paris are known as *Paris Symphonies.* Similarly distinctive titles are attached to some of Haydn's 82 string quartets: *Russian Quartets* (1781; known in Italian as *Gli scherzi;* the 2nd of the set, *The Joke;* 3d, *The Bird;* 5th, *How Do You Do?*); *Prussian Quartets* (1787; 5th of the set, *The Dream;* 6th, *The Frog,* or *The House on Fire,* or *The Row in Vienna*); *Razor Quartet* (1788; No. 2 of the set written for the Vienna merchant Johann Tost); *Lerchenquartett (Lark Quartet;* 1790; 5th of the Tost Quartets; also known as *Hornpipe Quartet); Quintenquartett (Quartet of the Fifths,* 1796-97; also known as *The Bell* or *The Donkey;* the minuet called *Hexenminuett*); *Kaiserquartett (Emperor Quartet,* 1796-97; contains variations on Haydn's hymn *Gott erhalte Franz den Kaiser); The Sunrise* (1796-97). Other instrumental works include about 15 piano concertos; 3 violin concertos; 2 cello concertos (the most celebrated one, in D major, has been ascribed, erroneously, to Anton Kraft); 2 horn concertos; trumpet concerto; flute concerto; 5 concertos for 2 liras with instruments; 8 *Notturni* for the King of Naples (1790); a *symphonie concertante* for oboe, violin, bassoon, cello, and orch. (1792); about 40 divertimenti; numerous string trios, and some 35 piano trios; 6 duets for violin and viola; a violin sonata; a great number of works for baryton, written for Prince Esterházy, who was a baryton player: 125 divertimenti for baryton with viola and cello, 6 duets for barytons, 6 sonatas for baryton and cello, 12 cassations for baryton with other instruments, 3 baryton concertos; about 60 piano sonatas (of which 8 are lost); various pieces for piano solo; 32 miscellaneous arrangements written for mechanical clocks. Vocal Works: Operas and Singspiele: *Der krumme Teufel* (1752) and *Der neue krumme Teufel* (1758); 4 Italian comedies, *La Marchesa Nespola, La vedova, Il dottore,* and *Il Sganarello* (all in 1762); *Acide,* opera seria (Eisenstadt, Jan. 11, 1763); *La cantarina,* opera buffa (Esterház, 1767); *Lo speziale,* opera buffa

(Esterház, 1768); *Le pescatrici,* opera buffa (Esterház, Sept. 16, 1770); *L' infedeltà delusa,* burletta (Esterház, July 26, 1773); *L' incontro improviso* (Esterház, Aug. 29, 1775); *Il mondo della luna* (Esterház, Aug. 3, 1777); *La vera costanza* (Esterház, 1779); *L' isola disabitata* (Esterház, Dec. 6, 1779); *La fedeltà premiata* (Esterház, Oct. 15, 1780); *Orlando Paladino* (Esterház, 1782); *Armida* (Esterház, Feb. 26, 1784); *Orfeo ed Euridice* (originally entitled *L' anima del filosofo;* 1791; revised form, 1805); incidental music to various plays; several marionette operas.—3 oratorios: *Il ritorno di Tobia* (Vienna, April 2, 1775), *The Creation* (Haydn's most famous choral work; written to an English text by Lidley; translated into German and first performed, April 29, 1798 at the Schwarzenberg Palace in Vienna), and *The Seasons* (German text by Gottfried van Swieten after James Thomson; Vienna, April 24, 1801); several cantatas, numerous arias, etc.; *The Seven Last Words* (*Die Sieben Worte des Erlösers am Kreuze;* 1785; originally written for the Cadiz Cathedral as a suite of 7 instrumental sonatas with a concluding movement *Il terremoto;* then a series of accompanied recitatives were added; also arranged by Haydn in 1796 for solo voices, chorus, and orch.); 14 Masses (only 13 extant; one of them, *Missa Rorate coeli desuper,* in G major, long regarded as lost, was discovered by H. C. Robbins Landon in 1957); 2 Te Deums; a Stabat Mater; offertories; about 45 songs with piano accompaniment; 2 vocal duets, 4 vocal trios, and 9 vocal quartets with piano accompaniment; about 50 canons and rounds for 3-8 voices; arrangements of 150 songs of Scotland, publ. by Napier as *Selections of Original Scots Songs in Three Parts, the Harmony by Haydn;* arrangements of Scotch, Irish, and Welsh melodies in Thomson's *Select Melodies of Scotland, Ireland and Wales;* the hymn *Gott erhalte Franz den Kaiser,* which was the Austrian national anthem (until 1918).

BIBLIOGRAPHY. — BIOGRAPHY: Simon Mayr, *Brevi notizie istoriche della vita e delle opere di H.* (Bergamo, 1809); G. A. Griesinger, *Biographische Notizen über H.* (Leipzig, 1810); A. K. Dies, *Biographische Nachrichten über H.* (Vienna, 1810); G. Carpani, *Le Haydine* (Milan, 1812; 2nd augmented ed., Padua, 1823); Th. von Karajan, *H. in London* (Vienna, 1861); A. Reissmann, *H.* (Berlin, 1879); L. Schmidt, *H.* (Berlin, 1898; new ed., 1914); La Mara, *H.*, in vol. IV of *Musikalische Charakterköpfe* (Leipzig, 1900; separate reprint, 1912); J. C. Hadden, *H.* (London, 1902; new ed., 1934); J. F. Runciman, *H.* (London, 1908); M. Brenet, *H.* (Paris, 1909; English trans., Oxford, 1926); A. Schnerich, *H. und seine Sendung* (Vienna, 1922); G. G. A. Fox, *H.* (London, 1929); Karl Geiringer, *H.* (Potsdam, 1932); K. Kobald, *H.* (Vienna, 1932); R. Tenschert, *H.* (Berlin, 1932); F. Amoroso, *H.* (Turin, 1933); E. F. Schmid, *H., Vorfahren und Heimat des Meisters* (Kassel, 1934); R. Tenschert, *H.: sein Leben in Bildern* (Leipzig, 1935); Karl Geiringer, *H., A Creative Life in Music* (N. Y., 1946); L. Nowak, *H.: Leben, Bedeutung und Werk* (Vienna, 1951); R. Sondheimer, *H., A Historical and Psychological Study Based on His Quartets* (London, 1951); Hans Rutz, *H.* (Munich, 1953). The most extensively planned biography, that of K. F. Pohl, *H.*, remained incomplete (2 vols., Leipzig, 1875, 1882; brings Haydn's life down to 1790; Hugo Botstiber completed the 3rd and final vol. in 1927). — CRITICISM, APPRECIATION: K. F. Pohl, *Mozart und H. in London* (Vienna, 1867); K. von Wurzbach, *H. und sein Bruder Michael* (Vienna, 1862); L. Wendschuh, *Über Haydns Opern* (Rostock, 1896); W. H. Hadow, *A Croatian Composer; Notes toward the Study of H.* (London, 1897; controversial; an attempt to prove Haydn's Slavic origin); H. E. Krehbiel, *Music and Manners in the Classical Period* (N. Y., 1898; contains Haydn's notes on his London visit); J. Hartog, *H., sijn broeder Michael en hunne werke* (Amsterdam, 1905); M. Puttmann, *H. als Vokalkomponist* (Langensalza, 1909); A. Schnerich, *Messe und Requiem seit H. und Mozart* (Vienna, 1909); H. Von Hase, *H. und Breitkopf & Härtel* (Leipzig, 1909); J. E. Engl, *Haydns handschriftlisches Tagebuch aus der Zeit seines zweiten Aufenthalts in London* (Leipzig, 1909); F. Artaria and Hugo Botstiber, *H. und das Verlagshaus Artaria* (Vienna, 1909); A. Sandberger, *Zur Geschichte des H.schen Streichquartetts* (Munich, 1921); A. Sandberger, *Zur Entwicklungsgeschichte von Haydns Sieben Worte* (Munich, 1921); F. Blume, *Haydns Persönlichkeit in seinen Streichquartetten,* in the 'Jahrbuch der Musikbibliothek Peters' (1931); Ludwig Koch, *H. Bibliography of the Budapest City Library* (in German and Hungarian; Budapest, 1932); A. Hindenberger, *Die Motivik in H. Streichquartetten* (Turbenthal, 1935); Haydn issue of the 'Mus. Quarterly' (April, 1932; contains articles by G. Adler, H. Botstiber, O. Strunk, G. de Saint-Foix, M. M. Scott, P. H. Lang, J. Muller, Karl Geiringer, and M. D. Herter Norton); Haydn issue of the 'Zeitschrift für Musik' (April, 1932); C. S. Smith, *Haydn's Chamber Music and the Flute,* in the 'Mus. Quarterly' (July and Oct., 1933); A. Sandberger, *Neue Haydniana,* in the 'Jahrbuch der Musikbibliothek Peters' (1933); O. Strunk, *Notes on a Haydn Autograph,* in the 'Mus. Quarterly' (April 1934; contains a chronological list of Haydn's late piano works); J. P. Larsen, *H. und das 'kleine Quartbuch'* in the 'Acta musicologica' (1935; reply by A. Sandberger in the 'Zeitschrift für Musik,' 1935); J. Frölich, *H., neu herausgegeben und eingeleitet von Adolf Sandberger* (Regensburg, 1936); J. P. Larsen, *Die H.-Überlieferung* (Copenhagen, 1939). The most comprehensive list of Haydn's works is found in J. P. Larsen's *Drei H. Kataloge in Faksimile* (Copenhagen, 1941); a descriptive catalogue of Haydn's symphonies, with exhaustive commentaries on their authenticity, chronology, and availability, is in H. C. Robbins Landon's *The Symphonies of H.* (London, 1955); see also his article *H. and Authenticity* in the 'Music Review' (May, 1955). A complete thematic catalogue, by Anthony van Hoboken, began to appear in 1957. A monumental edition of Haydn's works in about 80 volumes, prepared by G. Adler, H. Kretzschmar, E. Mandyczewski, M. Seiffert, and others, was begun in 1907 by Breitkopf & Härtel, but was interrupted twice by the two world wars; 4 vols. of symphonies (3 edited by E. Mandyczewski, the 4th by H. Schultz), 3 vols. of piano sonatas (ed. by Päsler); the oratorios *Die Schöpfung* and *Die Jahreszeiten* (Mandyczewski), and songs (Friedlaender) have appeared; an attempt to continue the publication was made by the Haydn Society of Boston in 1950, but it, too, failed.—CORRESPONDENCE: No complete edition of Haydn's letters is available. The largest collection is that translated by Lady Wallace in her book *Letters of Distinguished Musicians* (London, 1867); J. C. Hadden, *G. Thomson, His Life and Correspondence* (London, 1898), contains letters from Haydn. Haydn's correspondence with W. Forster is published in W. Sandys and S. A. Forster, *History of the Violin* (London, 1864).

Haydn, (Johann) Michael, Austrian composer, brother of Franz Joseph Haydn; b. Rohrau, Sept. 14, 1737; d. Salzburg, Aug. 10, 1806. He served as boy soprano at St. Stephen's Cathedral in Vienna (1745-55); his voice was remarkable for its wide range, reaching 3 octaves. He replaced his brother in solo parts, when a younger voice was required. He studied composition mainly by reading books on counterpoint, particularly *Gradus ad Parnassum* by Fux. In 1757 he became chapelmaster at Grosswardein; in 1762, musical director to Archbishop Sigismund at Salzburg. In 1768 he married the daughter of the organist Lipp, Maria Magdalena, an excellent soprano singer, who was praised by Mozart. The French occupation of Salzburg in 1800 deprived him of his property, but he was aided by his brother. The Empress Maria Theresia rewarded him handsomely for a Mass composed at her command; it was performed at Laxenburg Palace on Oct. 4, 1801, and Maria Theresia herself sang the soprano solo part. He opened a school of composition, and educated many distinguished pupils, including Reicha and Carl Maria von Weber. In 1833, Martin Bischofsreiter, a Benedictine monk, published *Partitur-Fundamente,* a collection of thoroughbass exercises written by Michael Haydn for his scholars. He composed a Mass and vespers for Prince Esterházy, who twice offered to make him assistant chapel master; but Haydn declined, hoping that the Salzburg chapel would be reorganized. A prolific composer, his best works were his sacred compositions, which his brother held in high esteem. Although he had advantageous offers for publication from Breitkopf & Härtel, he was reluctant to accept, so that most of his music remained in MS at the time of his death. He left some 400 sacred works, including oratorios, cantatas, Requiems, Masses, graduals, offertories, etc.; also several operas; 2 collections of 4-part songs; some 60 symphonies; serenades, marches, minuets; concertos for flute, violin, and harpsichord, and a double concerto for viola, organ, and strings; string quartets and quintets; also a sextet. A selection of his Masses was edited by A. M. Klafsky in the 'Denkmäler der Tonkunst in Österreich' (vols. XXII and XXXII), a selection of his instrumental works was edited and partly reorchestrated by L. H. Perger, in the 'Denkmäler der Tonkunst in Österreich' (vol. XIV, 2), including a symph. in E♭ major (1783), a symph. in C major (1788), a Turkish March, etc. —Cf. F. J. Schinn and G. Otter, *Biographische Skizze von J. M. Haydn* (Salzburg, 1808); C. Wurzbach, *Joseph Haydn und sein Bruder Michael* (Vienna, 1862); J. E. Engl, *Zum Gedenken J. M. Haydns* (Salzburg, 1906); O. Schmid, *J. M. Haydn: Sein Leben und Wirken* (Vienna, 1906); K. M. Klob, *Drei musikalische Biedermänner* (Ulm, 1911); F. Martin, *Kleine Beiträge zur Musikgeschichte Salzburgs* (Salzburg, 1913); A. M. Klafsky, *Michael Haydn als Kirchen-*

komponist, in Adler's 'Studien zur Musikwissenschaft' (1915); G. de Saint-Foix, *Histoire de deux trios de Michael Haydn,* in the 'Revue de musicologie' (No. 38); H. Jancik, *Michael Haydn, ein vergessener Meister* (Zürich, 1952).

Haydon, Claude M., Australian composer; b. South Yarra, Melbourne, Nov. 8, 1884. He settled in Wellington, New Zealand; wrote an opera *Paolo and Francesca,* produced at Melbourne in 1920; much incidental music; also chamber music.

Haydon, Glen, American musicologist; b. Inman, Kansas, Dec. 9, 1896. He studied at the Univ. of California, Berkeley (B.A., 1918; M.A., 1921); then in Paris (with Eugene Cools) and in Vienna; obtained his Ph.D. at Vienna Univ. in 1932. Concurrently, he held the post of music instructor at the Univ. of California; in 1934, appointed head of the Dept. of Music at the Univ. of North Carolina; lectured at the Univ. of Michigan (1947), Harvard Univ. (1956), etc.; was president of the American Musicological Society from 1942-44. Among his theoretical publications are the extensive study, *The Evolution of the Six-Four Chord* (Univ. of California Press, Berkeley, 1933) and *Introduction to Musicology* (N. Y., 1941); also publ. a *Graded Course of Clarinet Playing* (1927), and translated Jeppesen's *Counterpoint: The Polyphonic Vocal Style of the 16th Century* (N. Y., 1939).

Hayes, Gerald Ravenscourt, English writer; b. London, April 18, 1889; d. there, Sept. 13, 1955. He entered the Hydrographic Dept. of the Admiralty in 1911; became chief cartographer in 1934; then transferred to Secretary's Dept. (1946-53). Apart from his writings on cartography, he became interested in musical instruments; was one of the founders of the Dolmetsch Foundation; publ. *The Treatment of Instrumental Music* (1928); *The Viols and Other Bowed Instruments* (1930); *King's Musick,* an anthology (1937); *The Lute and Other Plucked Instruments* (1938); numerous articles on instruments in various publications.

Hayes, Philip, English organist and composer, son of William Hayes; b. Oxford, April, 1738; d. London, March 19, 1797. He studied mainly with his father; Mus. B., Oxford (May 18, 1763); became Gentleman of the Chapel Royal in 1767; organist of New College, Oxford (1776); succeeded his father as organist of Magdalen College and prof. of music in the Univ. (1777); also received his Mus. D. the same year; organist of St. John's College (1790).—Works: oratorio *Prophecy* (Oxford, 1781); a masque, *Telemachus;* odes, anthems, services, psalms, glees; 6 concertos for organ, harpsichord, or piano (1769); also some numbers in Dibdin's *The Two Misers* and Dr. Arnold's *Two to One.* He edited 'Harmonia Wiccamica' (London, 1780).

Hayes, Roland, distinguished Negro tenor; b. Curryville, Georgia, June 3, 1887. He studied with A. Calhoun at Chattanooga, and later at Fiske Univ. in Nashville; further in Boston with Arthur J. Hubbard and Henschel, and in Europe. Beginning in 1916, he gave concert tours in the U. S., and gradually won the respect of the musical world for his lyric rendition of classical lieder and for his incomparable interpretation of Negro spirituals. In 1921, he went to Europe for further study; in later years, gave successful concerts in major European cities. In 1925 he was awarded the Spingarn Medal for 'most outstanding achievement among colored people'; in 1939 he received the honorary degree of Mus. D. Wesleyan Univ., Delaware, Ohio. In his programs, he featured many songs by American composers; also modern French songs. His home is in Brookline, Mass. He has published arrangements of 30 Negro spirituals, *My Songs* (N. Y., 1948).—Cf. Mackinley Helm, *Angel Mo' and Her Son, Roland Hayes* (Boston, 1932).

Hayes, William, English organist and composer; b. Gloucester, Dec., 1705 (baptized on Jan. 6, 1706); d. Oxford, July 27, 1777. He was a chorister at Gloucester cathedral; organist of St. Mary's, Shrewsbury (1729-31); then of Worcester cathedral (1731-34). In 1734 he became organist of Magdalen College, Oxford; Mus. Bac. (Oxford, 1735); Univ. prof. of music (1742); Mus. D. (1749). He conducted the Gloucester music festival in 1757, 1760, and 1763. His canons *Allelujah* and *Miserere nobis,* and his glee *Melting airs soft joys inspire* won prizes offered by the Catch Club in 1763. His works include a masque, *Circe;* psalms, odes, glees, canons, ballads, and cantatas. He also wrote *Remarks on Mr. Avison's Essay on Musical Expression* (1762); *Anecdotes of the Five Music-Meetings* (1768); and was co-editor of Boyce's 'Cathedral Music.'

Haynes, John C., American music publisher; b. Brighton, Mass., Sept. 9, 1829; d. Boston, May 3, 1907. He entered the employ of Oliver Ditson in 1845; was given an interest in the business in 1851, and on Jan. 1, 1857, became a co-partner, the firm name being changed to O. Ditson & Co. In 1889, after the death of O. Ditson, Haynes became president on the firm's incorporation. —Cf. the 'Musician' (June, 1907).

Haynes, Walter Battison, English organist and composer; b. Kempsey, near Worcester, Nov. 21, 1859; d. London, Feb. 4, 1900. He studied first with his uncle, an organist, then with F. Taylor and E. Prout; also studied at the Leipzig Cons., with C. Reinecke and S. Jadassohn, where he won the Mozart scholarship. In 1884 he was appointed organist at St. Philip's Church, Sydenham; from 1890, also taught at the Royal Academy of Music. His works include a symphony; a concert overture; an *Idyll* for violin and orch.; a piano trio; organ pieces; 2 cantatas for women's voices, *Fairies' Isle* and *A Sea Dream.*

Hays, William Shakespeare, American song composer; b. Louisville, Ky., July 19, 1837; d. there, July 22, 1907. He wrote his first song at 16 years of age, and published nearly 300, which once had an enormous sale totaling several millions. The most widely known were *Evangeline, My Southern Sunny Home, Write Me a Letter from Home, Driven from Home,* and *Mollie Darling.*

Haywood, Charles, American musicologist; b. Grodno, Russia, Dec. 20, 1904; came to the U. S. in 1916; studied music at Columbia Univ. (M.A., 1940; Ph.D., 1949); also attended the Juilliard School of Music (1930-35). His first profession was that of a singer; he was a member of the Chautauqua Opera Company, Philadelphia Opera Company, etc.; also appeared as a singer on the radio; taught voice at the Juilliard School (1939-51). In 1939 he was appointed member of the faculty at Queens College, N. Y., as lecturer on opera, folk music, and American music. He publ. a valuable compendium, *A Bibliography of North American Folklore and Folksong* (N. Y., 1951); edited *Art Songs of Soviet Russia* (N. Y., 1947); has prepared for publication a large work on Shakespeare and music, and several bibliographical studies.

Hazlehurst, Cecil, English composer; b. Higher Runcorn, May 22, 1880. He studied at the Liverpool College of Music and the Univ. of Manchester. He composed a grand opera, *Cleopatra* (1918); comic opera, *The Prince Elect;* children's opera, *The Dream;* piano quintet; an organ fugue on a theme by Elgar; a choral ballad, *The Saga of Baldur;* songs and piano pieces.

Head, Michael, English singer, pianist, and composer; b. Eastbourne, Jan. 28, 1900. He studied at the Royal Academy of Music in London with Frederick Corder; in 1927, was appointed prof. of piano there. In 1947, he made a tour through Asia, Canada, and Australia as singer and pianist. He publ. several song cycles: *Over the Rim of the Moon* (1918); *Songs of the Countryside* (1929); *More Songs of the Countryside* (1932); *Snowbirds* (7 songs; 1954); etc.; also wrote choruses and chamber music.

Heap, Charles Swinnerton, English pianist and conductor; b. Birmingham, April 10, 1847; d. there, June 11, 1900. He won the Mendelssohn scholarship in 1865 and studied at the Leipzig Cons. for 2 years under Moscheles, Hauptmann, Richter, and Reinecke; Mus. Bac., Cambridge (1871); Mus. D. (1872). He was conductor of the Birmingham Philharmonic from 1870-86; also conducted the Wolverhampton Musical Festival, North Staffordshire Festivals (from their foundation in 1888 until 1899), the Birmingham Festival Choral Society (from 1895); became chorusmaster of the Birmingham Festival in 1897. He wrote an oratorio, *The Captivity;* cantatas, *The Voice of Spring* (1882), *The Maid of Astolat* (1886), and *Fair Rosamond* (1890); 2 overtures; a quintet for piano and wind instruments; a piano trio; violin sonata, clarinet sonata, piano sonata; anthems; songs and organ pieces.

Hebenstreit, Pantaleon, German musician; b. Eisleben, 1669; d. Dresden, Nov. 15, 1750. In his early years, he was engaged variously as a violinist and a dancing master in Leipzig, but fled from his creditors to Merseburg, where the idea of improving the dulcimer was suggested to him, and he invented the instrument with which he made long and brilliant concert tours, and which Louis XIV named the 'Pantaleon,' after its originator's Christian name. As a precursor of the piano, it has disappeared in the process of evolution. In 1706, Hebenstreit was appointed Kapellmeister and dancing master to the court at Eisenach; in 1714, 'pantaleon chamber musician' at the Dresden court.

Heckel, Emil, German music publisher and piano manufacturer; b. Mannheim, May 22, 1831; d. there, March 28, 1908. He was head (from 1857, co-partner) of the music house and piano manufactory founded by his father, K. Ferdinand Heckel. He was the first president of the 'Allgemeine Richard Wagner-Verein'; the bust of Wagner (by J. Hoffart) in his residence at Mannheim is the earliest Wagner monument. Heckel was instrumental in the organization of the Bayreuth Festivals; became one of the directors of Bayreuth. His son, Karl, edited *Briefe Richard Wagners an Emil Heckel* (1899; English transl., by W. A. Ellis, 1899).

Heckel, Johann Adam, German manufacturer of musical instruments; b. Adorf, July 14, 1812; d. Biebrich, April 13, 1877. From 1824-35, he worked with the bassoonist K. Almenräder on experiments for improving the clarinet and bassoon. His son and successor, **Wilhelm** (b. Biebrich, Jan. 25, 1856; d. there, Jan. 13, 1909), continued his experiments with success and constructed the 'Heckelphone' (a baritone oboe; used by R. Strauss in the score of *Salome*) in 1905; also made various changes in the construction of other woodwind instruments. He wrote *Der Fagott. Kurzgefasste Abhandlung über seine historische Entwicklung, seinen Bau und seine Spielweise* (1899; new ed., 1931).

Heckel, Wolf, German lutenist at Strasbourg in the 16th century. He publ. a *Lautenbuch* (Strasbourg, 1556, 1562), a valuable and interesting collection of old German, French, and Italian songs, dances, fantasias, ricercari, pavanes, and saltarelli, arranged for 2 lutes; a copy of it is in the Hamburg town library. Reprints from it have been publ. by J. Wolf and L. Nowak in 'Denkmäler der Tonkunst in Österreich,' XIV, 1 and XXXVII, 2 respectively, by H. D. Bruger in his 'Lautenschule' and W. Tappert in 'Sang und Klang aus alter Zeit.'

Heckscher, Céleste de Longpré (*née* Massey), American composer; b. Philadelphia, Feb. 23, 1860; d. there, Feb. 18, 1928. Of an artistic family (her grandfather was the artist Louis de Longpré), she studied piano and participated in the musical affairs of the city; was for many years president of the Philadelphia Operatic Society. She began to compose about 1890; wrote the operas *The Flight of Time* and *Rose of Destiny* (Philadelphia, May 2, 1918); *Dances of the Pyrenees,* an orch. suite (Philadelphia, Feb. 17, 1911); a fantasy *To the Forest* for violin and piano (1902); songs and piano pieces. Her style, melodious and without pretensions, is akin to Chaminade's.—Cf. E. E. Hipsher, *American Opera and Its Composers* (Philadelphia, 1927; pp. 256-58).

Hédouin (ā-d'wăn), **Pierre,** French lawyer and littérateur; b. Boulogne, July 28, 1789; d. Paris, Dec., 1868. He studied law in Paris from 1809; became an advocate, and for 30 years practiced in Boulogne. He settled in Paris in 1842 when he was appointed head of the Ministry of Public Works. His relationship with Monsigny fostered a predilection for music and the arts, and he occupied his leisure moments with literature, especially that of music, and in composition. He wrote novels, contributed to the 'Annales archéologiques,' 'Annales romantiques,' and to several musical periodicals; composed nocturnes, *romances,* and songs, also writing the words; furnished the libretti of several operas.—Musical writings: *Notice historique de Monsigny* (1821); *Gossec, sa vie et ses ouvrages* (1852); *De l'Abandon des anciens compositeurs; Ma première visite à Grétry; 'Richard Cœur de Lion' de Grétry; Lesueur; Meyerbeer à Boulogne-sur-Mer; Paganini; Joseph Dessauer* (publ. in 'Le Ménestrel'); *Trois anecdotes musicales* (on Lesueur, Mlle. Dugazon, and Gluck) in his 'Mosaïque' (1856; a published collection of his miscellaneous articles); *Gluck, son arrivée en France* (1859); etc.

Heermann (här'-man), **Hugo,** distinguished German violinist; b. Heilbronn, Württemberg, March 3, 1844; d. Merano, Nov. 6, 1935. As a boy he was taken to Rossini in Paris for advice; then was sent to the Brussels Cons., where he studied violin with L. J. Meerts; made his début playing his teacher's violin concerto (1860); graduated with 1st prize in 1861; then studied with Joachim. In 1864 he settled in Frankfurt, where he taught at Hoch's Cons.; was first violinist of the famous Frankfurt String Quartet. Frankfurt remained his permanent residence for 40 years; frequent leaves of absence enabled him to make extended tours in Europe, the U. S., and Australia. From 1906-09 he taught violin at the Chicago Mus. College; then taught at Stern's Cons. in Berlin (1911), and at the Geneva Cons. (1912). He retired in 1922, and lived mostly in Merano, Italy. He held the distinction of having been the first to play the Brahms violin concerto in Paris, New York, and Australia. He publ. a new ed. of Bériot's *École transcendentale du violon* (1896); publ. his memoirs, *Meine Lebenserinnerungen* (Leipzig, 1935).

Hegar, Friedrich, Swiss composer and conductor; b. Basel, Oct. 11, 1841; d. Zürich, June 2, 1927. He studied at the Leipzig Cons. with Hauptmann, Richter, Ferdinand David, Rietz, and Plaidy. In 1860, he played violin in a Warsaw orch.; then taught music in Gebweiler, Alsace. In 1863, he established himself in Zürich, where he was active as violinist, conductor, and pedagogue. He conducted the Choral Society of Zürich for 37 years (1864-1901), and the concerts of the Tonhalle Orch. for 41 years (1865-1906); also led various other choral organizations. He was a founder of the Zürich Music School (later, Zürich Cons.) in 1876, and its director until 1914. He received many honors, including membership in the Berlin Academy of Arts in 1917. As a composer, he contributed a great deal to Swiss choral music, particularly in the field of romantic ballads. His most successful work is *Manasse* for soli, mixed chorus, and orch. (Zürich, Oct. 25, 1885; revised version, Jan. 10, 1888); other works are *Hymne an die Musik,* for chorus and orch. (1870); *Das Herz von Douglas,* for soli, male chorus, and orch. (1905); *Festival Overture* (1895); cello concerto (1919); Ballade for violin and orch. (1922); a string quartet, a violin sonata; 16 songs, etc.—Cf. A. Steiner, *Friedrich Hegar, sein Leben und Wirken* (Zürich, 1928); W. Jerg, *Hegar, ein Meister des Männerchorliedes* (Lachen, 1946).

Hegedüs, Ferencz, celebrated Hungarian violinist; b. Fünfkirchen, Feb. 26, 1881; d. London, Dec. 12, 1944. His precocious talent was carefully fostered by his father, a professional cellist; his mother (of Spanish origin) was also a musician; he then studied at the Budapest Cons. with Hubay (1893-1916; his style of playing had the manner tours of Europe; played in the U. S. with excellent success in 1906-7 and again in 1916; his style of playing had the manner of the Hungarian school; but his performances of Beethoven and other classics were entirely traditional. He lived in Switzerland after 1930; then went to London.

Heger, Robert, conductor and composer; b. Strasbourg, Aug. 19, 1886. He studied composition with Max Schillings in Munich; then conducted opera in Strasbourg (1907), Nuremberg (1913-21), and at the State Opera in Vienna (1925-33); Berlin State Opera (1933-45); at the Berlin City Opera (1945-50), and (from 1950) at the Munich Opera. From 1950-54, he was president of the Munich Academy of Music. He wrote several operas, among them *Ein Fest auf Haderslev* (Nuremberg, Nov. 12, 1919), *Der Bettler Namenlos* (Munich, April 8, 1932), *Der verlorene Sohn* (Dresden, March 11, 1936), and *Lady Hamilton* (Nuremberg, Feb. 11, 1951); 2 symphonies; a symph. poem, *Hero und Leander;* many songs.

Hegner, Anton, cellist and composer; b. Copenhagen, March 2, 1861; d. New York, Dec. 4, 1915. He studied at the Copenhagen Cons.; played with great success in Copenhagen, Berlin, and New York, where he settled in 1899 as a teacher. He wrote *American Festival Overture,* for orch.; 4 quartets, a piano trio; many soli for cello, violin; about 60 songs; 2 concertos for cello.

Hegner, Otto, pianist; b. Basel, Nov. 18, 1876; d. Hamburg, Feb. 22, 1907. He studied with Huber in Basel and later with Eugene d'Albert. He appeared as a child prodigy in Germany; in 1888, at the age of 12, he made an American tour, and for several years, was regarded as one of the most phenomenal young pianists. His early death cut short the development of his brilliant career. His sister, **Anna Hegner** (b. Basel, March 1, 1881), was a fine violinist.

Hegyesi (hehg'ye-sē) (Magyarization of his real name, Spitzer), **Louis,** noted Hungarian cellist; b. Arpad, Nov. 3, 1853; d. Cologne, Feb. 27, 1894. He studied with Demis in Vienna and with Franchomme in Paris; then played in the orch. of the Vienna Opera; in 1887, he became prof. at the Cologne Cons. He publ. several brilliant cello pieces, and a valuable manual, *Neue rhythmische Tonleiter- und Akkordstudien.*

Heidingsfeld, Ludwig, German composer; b. Jauer, March 24, 1854; d. Danzig, Sept. 14, 1920. He studied at Stern's Cons. in Berlin, and later taught there. He subsequently settled in Danzig, and founded a conservatory there (1899). He wrote symph. poems, *King Lear* and *Der Totentanz;* piano pieces and songs.

Heifetz, Jascha, celebrated violinist; b. Vilna, Feb. 2, 1901. His father, Ruben Heifetz, an able musician, taught him the rudiments of violin playing at a very early age; he then studied with Elias Malkin at the Vilna Music School, and played in public before he was 5 years old; at the age of 6, he played Mendelssohn's concerto in Kovno. In 1910 he was taken by his father to St. Petersburg, and entered the Cons. there in the class of J. Nalbandian; after a few months, he was accepted as a pupil by Leopold Auer. He gave his first public concert in St. Petersburg on April 30, 1911. The following year, with a letter of recommendation from Auer, he went to Berlin; his first concert there (May 24, 1912), in the large hall of the Hochschule für Musik attracted great attention: Artur Nikisch engaged him to play the Tchaikovsky concerto with the Berlin Philharmonic (Oct. 28, 1912), and Heifetz obtained sensational success as a child prodigy of unexampled gifts. He then played in Austria and Scandinavia. After the Russian Revolution of 1917, he went to America, by way of Siberia and the Orient. His début at Carnegie Hall, N. Y. (Oct. 27, 1917) won for him the highest expression of enthusiasm from the public and in the press; veritable triumphs followed during his tour of the U. S., and soon his fame spread all over the world. He made his first London appearance on May 5, 1920; toured Australia (1921) and the Orient (1923), Palestine (1926), and South America. He revisited Russia in 1934, and was welcomed enthusiastically. He became a naturalized American citizen in 1925, and made his home at Beverly Hills, Calif.; in subsequent years he continued to travel as a concert violinist, visiting virtually every country in the world, and appearing with major symphony orchestras. The quality of his playing is unique in luminous transparency of texture, tonal perfection, and formal equilibrium of phrasing; he never allows his artistic temperament to superimpose extraneous elements on the music; this inspired tranquillity led some critics to characterize his interpretations as impersonal and detached. Heifetz made numerous arrangements for violin of works by Bach, Vivaldi, and pieces by contemporary composers (Poulenc, Aguirre, etc.); his most famous transcription is *Hora Staccato* by the Rumanian composer Gheorghe Dinicu (1865-1930), made into a virtuoso piece by adroit ornamentation and rhythmic elaboration. In his desire to promote modern music Heifetz commissioned a number of composers (Walton, Gruenberg, Castelnuovo-Tedesco, and others) to write violin concertos for him, and performed several of them.

Heiller, Anton, Austrian composer; b. Vienna, Sept. 15, 1923. He studied organ and composition privately, and later at the Vienna Cons. (1941-42). In 1945, he was appointed prof. of organ at the Vienna Academy of Music. In 1952, he received first prize for organ at the International Organ Contest in Haarlem, Holland. His music is distinguished by fine polyphonic writing. Among his works are: *Symphonie nordique* (1946); Toccata for two pianos (1943; his most successful work; performed at several music festivals); *Psalmen-Kantate* (Vienna, June 16, 1955); several Masses; organ pieces.

Heilman, William Clifford, American composer; b. Williamsport, Penn., Sept. 27, 1877; d. there, Dec. 20, 1946. He studied at Harvard Univ. (B.A., 1900) and in Europe with Rheinberger and Widor. He was a member of the music dept. of Harvard Univ. from 1905 till 1930. Among his works are a symph. poem, *By the Porta Catania* (1916), piano trio, Romance for cello and piano, a number of character pieces for piano, and choruses. He made arrangements of Negro spirituals.

Hein, Carl, conductor; b. Rendsburg, Germany, Feb. 2, 1864; d. New York, Feb. 27, 1945. He studied at the Hamburg Cons.; then played cello in the Hamburg Philh. Orch. In 1890, he emigrated to America, settling in New York, where he conducted various German choral societies ('Mozart-Verein,' 'Schubert-Chor,' etc.). In 1894 and 1907, he conducted the national choral festival at Madison Square Garden; then was active mainly as a vocal coach. He publ. several male choruses and vocal exercises.

Heinefetter. Six sisters, all well known as opera singers: **Sabina** (b. Mainz, Aug. 19, 1809; d. Illemau, Nov. 18, 1872) was an itinerant harpist as a child; at the age of 16, she went to Kassel to study with Spohr; then sang with brilliant success in Vienna, Berlin, and Milan. One of her outstanding roles was Donna Anna in *Don Giovanni*. She died insane. Her sister, **Maria** (Mme. Stöckel; b. Mainz, Feb. 16, 1816; d. Vienna, Feb. 23, 1857), achieved during her short career several notable successes; she also died insane. **Katinka** (1820-1858), **Fatima, Eva,** and **Nanette** were other sisters who appeared professionally on the opera stage.

Heinemeyer, Ernst Wilhelm, outstanding German flutist; b. Hanover, Feb. 25, 1827; d. Vienna, Feb. 12, 1869. He studied with his father, Christian Heinemeyer (1796-1872), who was the chamber flutist at Hanover. In 1847, he went to Russia, where he played the flute in the Imperial Orch. at St. Petersburg; in 1859, he returned to Hanover; in 1866, he went to Vienna. He wrote several concertos for the flute.

Heinichen, Johann David, notable German composer and theorist; b. Krössuln, near Weissenfels, April 17, 1683; d. Dresden, July 15, 1729. He was educated at the Thomasschule in Leipzig, studying with Schell and Kuhnau; at the same time, he studied law, and practiced as a lawyer in Weissenfels. His first opera, *Der angenehme Betrug,* was perf. in Leipzig in 1709; he then held a position as conductor at Zeitz. Councillor Buchta of Zeitz supplied the funds for Heinichen to accompany him to Italy (1713-18), where he produced several operas. In Venice, he joined the Elector of Saxony, Frederick Augustus, and followed him to Dresden as director of the Italian opera company there (1718). However, as a result of confusion brought about by a violent quarrel between Heinichen and the celebrated singer, Senesino, the Dresden opera was dissolved. Heinichen remained in Dresden as director of church and chamber music. He was a prolific composer; a thematic catalogue of his works is found in G. A. Seibel, *Das Leben des J. D. Heinichen* (Leipzig, 1913), listing, besides his operas, 2 oratorios, 16 Masses, 63 cantatas, more than 100 other sacred works, 4 symphonies, 2 overtures, 30 concertos, 17 sonatas, 7 pieces for flute, many separate airs, etc. Most of them are preserved in the Dresden library; few of his works have been published. Heinichen's importance lies not so much in his compositions as in his basic theoretical work, *Neu erfundene und gründliche Answeisung . . . zu vollkommener Erlernung des General-Basses* (Hamburg, 1711); new revised ed. as *Der General-Bass in der Composition* (Dresden, 1728).—Cf. R. Tanner, *J. D. Heinichen als dramatischer Komponist* (Leipzig, 1916); G. Hausswald, *J. D. Heinichens Instrumentalwerke* (Berlin, 1937).

Heinitz, Wilhelm, German musicologist; b. Altona, Dec. 9, 1883. He first studied the bassoon, and played in orchestras. In 1915 he became a member of the Phonetic Laboratory at the Univ. of Hamburg, where he studied primitive music as well as the languages of Africa and Polynesia; led a seminar in comparative musicology there until his retirement in 1949. He wrote a number of valuable articles on the problems of folk psychology, structural elements of speech, etc., printed in special publications; also the books, *Klangprobleme im Rundfunk* (Berlin, 1926), *Strukturprobleme in primitiver Musik* (Hamburg, 1931), *Neue Wege der Volksmusikforschung* (Hamburg, 1937); contributed the section *Instrumentenkunde* in Bücken's 'Handbuch der Musikwissenschaft' (Potsdam, 1929). A complete list of his writings is given in Hans Haase's article on Heinitz in 'Die Musik in Geschichte und Gegenwart.'

Heinrich, Anthony Philip (Anton Philipp), American violinist and composer of Bohemian birth; b. Schönbüchel, Bohemia, March 11, 1781; d. in extreme poverty in New York, May 3, 1861. As a boy he acquired proficiency on the piano and violin, but began life as a wholesale merchant and banker; having failed in business, he went to Bardstown, Ky., where, without any knowledge of harmony, he began to compose in 1818; these first songs and instrumental pieces he publ. later as Op. 1, *The Dawning of Music in Kentucky, or The Pleasures of Harmony in the Solitudes of Nature* (1820). He became director of music at Southwark Theater, Phila.; later, in Louisville, Ky. The year 1827 found him in London, playing violin in a small orch.; there he also studied theory, and about 1830 began to write for orch.; returned to the U. S. in 1832. In 1834 he again visited England, as well as Germany and Austria (1835), and had some of his works produced at Dresden, Prague, Budapest, and Graz (his symph., *The Combat of the Condor,* was perf. at Graz in 1836; also in France); in Vienna he entered a competition with a symphony, but the prize was awarded to Franz Lachner; disappointed, he returned to America and settled in New York, where he soon gained immense popularity, so that he was generally known as 'Father Heinrich'; during the '40's and '50's he was a commanding figure in the musical affairs of the U. S., publishing hundreds of piano pieces and songs, symphonies and oratorios, grand festivals of his works being arranged in N. Y., Philadelphia, and Boston, and the critics speaking of him as the 'Beethoven of America'; a tour of Germany in 1857-8 was a dismal failure. The quality of his works easily accounts for the speedy and complete oblivion of even his name; he wrote only for an enormous orch., *à la* Berlioz, and his musical ideas, out of all proportion to the means employed, recall the style of Haydn's imitators; nevertheless, he is historically important, being the first to employ Indian themes in works of large dimensions and to show decided nationalist aspirations. In 1917 O. G. Sonneck acquired for the Library of Congress Heinrich's 'Memoranda' (letters, programs, newspaper clippings, etc.), many publ. works and almost all the orchestral scores (in MS; many autographs) enumerated in a list made by Heinrich himself in 1857. A perusal of the titles is amusing and instructive: *Grand American Chivalrous Symphony; The Columbiad, or Migration of American Wild Passenger Pigeons; The Ornithological Combat of Kings, or The Condor of the Andes and the Eagle of the Cordilleras; Pocahontas, the Royal Indian Maid and the Heroine of Virginia, the Pride of the Wilderness; The Wild-wood Spirit's Chant or Scintillations of 'Yankee Doodle,' forming a Grand National Heroic Fantasia scored for a Powerful Orch. in 44 Parts;* etc.—Cf. F. A. Mussik, *Skizzen aus dem Leben des . . . A. Ph. Heinrich* (Leipzig, 1843); O. G. Sonneck, *Musical Landmarks in New York,* in the 'Mus. Quarterly' (April, 1920); 'Dictionary of American Biography' (1932); Wm. T. Upton, *A. Ph. Heinrich* (N. Y., 1939).

Heinrich, Max, baritone; b. Chemnitz, Germany, June 14, 1853; d. New York, Aug. 9, 1916. He studied at the Dresden Cons.; in 1873, came to America; taught at Marion, Alabama (1876-82), then moved to New York, where he appeared in oratorio with various orchestras. From 1888-93, he taught singing at the Royal Academy of Music in London; then lived in Chicago (1894-1903) and in Boston (1903-10). He gave numerous recitals of German lieder, the last of them shortly before his death.

Heinroth (hīn'-roht), **Charles,** American organist; b. New York, Jan. 2, 1874. He studied with M. Spicker and John White (organ) and Victor Herbert (composition); also took courses with Rheinberger in Munich (1896). He occupied various posts as church organist in New York and Brooklyn; from 1907 till 1932 was organist at the Carnegie Institute, Pittsburgh; from 1932-42, organist and head of the music dept. of The City College of N. Y.

Heinroth, Johann August Günther, German composer and writer; b. Nordhausen, June 19, 1780; d. Göttingen, June 2, 1846. He studied with his father, Christoph Gottlieb Heinroth, an able organist. He then attended the Univ. of Leipzig, and of Halle. In 1804, he became attached to the School of Jewish Studies organized by Israel Jacobson. This was the beginning of a lifelong study of the Jewish liturgy, which he reorganized, adding numerous original melodies that became part of the Jewish service. He also attempted the introduction of a simplified musical notation by figures. From 1818, he served as music director of the Univ. of Göttingen, in succession to Forkel.—Writings (all publ. at Göttingen): *Gesangunterrichts-Methode für höhere und niedere Schulen* (1821-23, 3 parts); *Volksnoten oder vereinfachte Tonschrift* (1828); *Kurze Anleitung, das Klavier oder Forte-Piano spielen zu lehren* (1828); *Musikalisches Hilfsbuch für Prediger, Kantoren und Organisten* (1833). Heinroth's ideas regarding musical education in schools exercised considerable influence. A monograph on him is included in W. Boetticher's book, *Die Musik an der Georgia Augusta-Univ. zu Göttingen* (1958).

Heinsheimer, Hans (Walter), publishing executive and writer on music; b. Karlsruhe, Sept. 25, 1900. He studied law in Heidelberg, Munich, and Freiburg (*Juris Dr.,* 1923); then joined Universal Edition in Vienna; was in charge of its opera dept. (1925-38). He came to the U.S.A. in 1938; was associated with Boosey & Hawkes; in 1947, became director of symphonic and operatic repertory at G. Schirmer, Inc. He contributed numerous articles to 'Anbruch,' 'Mus. Quarterly,' 'Holiday,' 'The Reader's Digest,' etc. He publ. two entertaining books, *Menagerie in F Sharp* (N. Y., 1947; transl. into German); *Fanfare for Two Pigeons* (N. Y., 1952).

Heintze, Gustaf Hjalmar, Swedish pianist and composer; b. Jönköping, July 22, 1879; d. Saltsjöbaden, March 4, 1946. He was of a musical family; his father Georg Wilhelm Heintze (1849-95) was a well-known organist, as was his grandfather, Gustaf Wilhelm Heintze (1825-1909). He studied at the Stockholm Cons.; in 1910 was appointed organist at a Stockholm church, a post that he held until his death. He wrote cantatas, 2 violin concertos, chamber music, and organ pieces.

Heinze, Sir **Bernard Thomas,** eminent Australian conductor; b. Shepparton, near Melbourne, July 1, 1894. He studied at the Univ. of Melbourne, Royal College of Music in London, and with Vincent d'Indy at the Schola Cantorum in Paris. After service in the Royal Artillery during World War I, he returned to Australia; in 1926, was appointed prof. of music at the Univ. of Melbourne. In 1938 he made a tour of Europe as conductor. He was conductor of the Melbourne Symph. Orch. from 1933 till 1949; was knighted in 1950. In 1956, he became director of the State Cons. in Sydney.

Heinze, Gustav Adolph, German composer and conductor; b. Leipzig, Oct. 1, 1820; d.

Muiderberg, near Amsterdam, Feb. 20, 1904. He received his early musical education from his father, a clarinet player in the Gewandhaus Orch. in Leipzig, and joined that orchestra as clarinetist at the age of 16. He then conducted opera in Breslau, and also produced 2 operas there. In 1850 he went to Amsterdam as conductor of the German opera, and remained in Holland till the end of his life. He composed, besides his operas, several oratorios and other choral works.

Heise, Peter Arnold, Danish composer; b. Copenhagen, Feb. 11, 1830; d. Stockkerup, Sept. 12, 1879. He studied music with Niels Gade and Berggreen in Copenhagen and with Hauptmann at the Leipzig Cons. Returning to Denmark, he became a music teacher and organist at Sorö, where he remained until 1865. He then settled in Copenhagen; produced 2 successful operas, *The Pasha's Daughter* (Sept. 30, 1869) and *King and Marshal* (Sept. 25, 1878). He also wrote a symphony, chamber music, etc., which remain mostly unpublished. It was in his many lieder to Danish texts that Heise achieved enduring fame. — Cf. G. Hetsch, *P. A. Heise* (Copenhagen, 1926).

Heiter, Amalie. Pen-name of **Marie Amalia Friederike,** Princess of Saxony. See **Amalia Friederike.**

Heiter, Ernst. Pseudonym of **Sechter.**

Hekking, André, French cellist; b. Bordeaux, July 30, 1866; d. Paris, Dec. 14, 1925. He was the son of the Dutch cellist, Robert Gérard Hekking (1820-75), who settled in France, and received his training from him. From 1909, he lived in Paris; in 1919, was appointed prof. at the Paris Cons.; also taught at the American Cons. in Fontainebleau. He publ. a practice book for cellists, *Violoncelle, exercices quotidiens* (Paris, 1927).

Hekking, Anton, notable cellist; brother of André Hekking; b. The Hague, Sept. 7, 1856; d. Berlin, Nov. 18, 1935. He studied at the Paris Cons. with Joseph Giese; then undertook an American tour with the pianist Mme. Essipova. Returning to Europe, he was first cellist of the Berlin Philh. (1884-88 and 1898-1902). After another American tour, he became first cellist of the Boston Symph. (1889-91) and later of the N. Y. Symph. (1895-98). He returned to Berlin in 1898; taught at Stern's Cons. there, and became a member of a trio with Schnabel and Wittenberg (1902).

Hekking, Gérard, French cellist; cousin of André and Anton Hekking, b. Nancy, Aug. 12, 1879; d. Paris, June 5, 1942. He studied at the Paris Cons., winning 1st prize (1899). He was first cellist of the Concertgebouw Orch. in Amsterdam (1903-14) and taught at the Amsterdam Cons.; also made tours in Russia, Spain, Germany, and France. He was in the French Army during World War I; from 1921-27, was again in Holland; in 1927, became prof. at the Paris Cons. He wrote several cello pieces; also revised *Principes de la technique du violoncelle* of François Gervais (Paris, 1930).

Helder, Bartholomäus, German composer; b. Gotha, 1585; d. Remstedt, near Gotha, Oct. 28, 1635. He studied theology in Leipzig; was school teacher at a village near Gotha (1607-16); then was for 20 years a pastor at Remstedt. He died of the plague. He publ. a collection of Christmas and New Year's songs, *Cymbalum genethliacum* (1614); a book of psalm tunes, *Cymbalum Davidicum;* many of his secular songs are included in contemporary anthologies. His New Year's song *Das alte Jahr vergangen ist* became very popular.

Helfer, Walter, American composer; b. Lawrence, Mass., Sept. 30, 1896. He studied at Harvard Univ.; then took courses with Caussade at the Paris Cons. and with Respighi in Rome (1925-28). Returning to the U. S., he joined the staff of Hunter College as prof. of composition; was chairman of the music dept. from 1938 till 1950. In 1939 he won the Paderewski Prize for his overture to *A Midsummer Night's Dream.* His other works are *Symphony on Canadian Airs* (1937); *Fantasy on Children's Tunes* for small orch. (1935); concertino for piano and chamber orch. (1947); string quartet; string trio; *Elegiac Sonata* for piano (1931); *Soliloquy* for cello and piano (1947); choral pieces.

Helfert, Vladimir, Czech musicologist; b. Plánice, Bohemia, March 24, 1886; d. Prague, May 18, 1945. He studied with Hostinsky in Prague and with Kretzschmar and Wolf at the Berlin Univ. (1908, Mus. D., with the dissertation *G. Benda und J. J. Rousseau*); 1921 instructor, 1926 prof. of musicology at the Univ. of Brno; director of the Czech Orchestral Society there; from 1924, editor of the paper 'Hudebni Rozhledy.' In 1940 he was arrested by the Nazis and held in Breslau; released in 1943; then rearrested in 1945 and taken to the Terezin concentration camp. He died a few days after his liberation.—Writings (mostly in Czech): *History of the Melodrama* (1908); *Jaroměřice and the Count J. A. Questenberg* (Prague, 1917); *The Music of the Jaroměřice Castle: A Critical Analysis of the Works of the Composer Franz Míča* (Prague, 1924); *Contribution to the Development of the History of the Marseillaise* (in Italian; Turin, 1922); *The Creative Development of Smetana* (Prague, 1924); *Zur Entwicklungsgeschichte der Sonatenform,* in the 'Archiv für Musikwissenschaft' (1925); *Histoire de la musique dans la république tchécoslovaque* (in collaboration with Erich Steinhardt; Prague, 1936); and other essays, mostly about Czech music in the 18th century; joint author of O. Pazdirek's 'Dictionary of Music' (in Czech; vol. I, 1929; vol. II, 1937).

Helfman, Max, conductor and composer; b. Radzin, Poland, May 25, 1901. He came early to the U. S. and studied at the David Mannes School, N. Y. (1919-23) and the Curtis Institute in Philadelphia (1929-32). He then settled in N. Y. as choral conductor of Jewish groups. He wrote *New Hagadah,* a dramatic cantata for narrator, chorus, and orch. (1949); Jewish liturgical music; edited a series of choral works for the Jewish Music Alliance ('Gesang und Kampf,' vols. 5 and 6; 1937-38) and an anthology of modern choral works.

Helfritz, Hans, composer; b. Hilbersdorf, July 25, 1902. He studied at the Hochschule für Musik in Berlin with Hindemith; in Vienna with Wellesz. In 1936 he emigrated to South America, and settled in Chile, where he became active in folklore research. Among his works are a concertino for piano and orch. (1940); saxophone concerto (1945); 2 string quartets; violin sonata; choral pieces. Most of his music is couched in austere polyphonic style, with dissonant counterpoint adding a modernistic touch; but he also utilizes South American melodic and rhythmic resources, and occasionally American jazz. In 1956 he undertook a journey along the west coast of Africa, and made recordings of native songs.

Hellendaal, Pieter, organist and composer; b. Rotterdam, March (baptized April 1), 1721; d. Cambridge, England, April 26, 1799. In 1760, he went to England and on June 12, 1760 was appointed successor to Charles Burney as organist at St. Margaret's, King's Lynn in Norfolk. He published 12 sonatas for violin (Amsterdam, 1744); 6 concertos for violin (London, 1760); 6 solos for violin with thorough-bass (London, 1761), and 8 solos for cello with thorough-bass (London, 1770); also a *Celebrated Rondo* for violin with instrumental accompaniment; *A Collection of Psalms for the Use of Parish Churches,* and 2 glees for 4 voices. —Cf. G. A. C. De Graaf, *Pieter Hellendaal, Musiquant (1721-1799),* in 'Mens en Melodie' (Aug., 1950).

Heller, Hans Ewald, composer; b. Vienna, April 17, 1894. He studied with J. B. Foerster and Camillo Horn; was engaged in Vienna as music critic and teacher. In 1938 he settled in the U. S. Among his compositions are the light operas *Satan* (Vienna, 1927), *Messalina* (Prague, 1928), and *Der Liebling von London* (Vienna, 1930); an overture *Carnival in New Orleans* (1940); a cantata, *Ode to Our Women* (1942); 2 string quartets; a suite for clarinet and piano; about 150 songs.

Heller, James G., American composer; b. New Orleans, Jan. 4, 1892. He studied at Tulane Univ., New Orleans (B. A., 1912), the Univ. of Cincinnati (M. A., 1914), the Hebrew Union College (Rabbi, 1916), and the Cincinnati Cons. of Music (Mus. D., 1934); for 12 years wrote the program notes for the Cincinnati Symph. Orch.; then taught musicology at the Cincinnati Cons. of Music. Among his works are *Elegy and Pastorale* for voice and string orch. (Cincinnati, Dec. 30, 1934); a string quartet; violin sonata; Jewish services (New Union Hymnal, 1930-32).

Heller, Stephen, celebrated pianist and composer; b. Budapest, May 15, 1813; d. Paris, Jan. 14, 1888. He was of a Jewish family, but was converted to Christianity as a youth. He studied piano with F. Brauer and showed such extraordinary ability that he was sent to Vienna to continue his studies; there he took lessons with Anton Halm. In 1828 he began a tour through Austria and Germany. However, the exertion of travel proved too much for him; in Augsburg, he became ill, and decided to remain there for a time; financial means were provided by a wealthy family. In 1838 he went to Paris, where he became friendly with Berlioz, Chopin, and Liszt. Soon he became very successful as a pianist; some critics even judged him as superior to Chopin. In Paris, Heller began to compose piano pieces in a Romantic vein, somewhat akin to Schumann's, and brilliant salon dances, studies, and characteristic pieces that became exceedingly popular. In 1849 he visited London, where his concerts charmed a large circle of music lovers. A nervous ailment forced him to curtail his appearances; in 1862, he revisited England and played with Hallé at the Crystal Palace. He then returned to Paris, where he remained for the rest of his life. He wrote in all several hundred piano pieces arranged in groups in 158 opus numbers; of these, the most effective are *Traumbilder; Promenades d'un solitaire; Nuits blanches; Dans les bois; Voyage autour de ma chambre; Tablettes d'un solitaire; Tarentelles;* admirable études; ballades (notably *La Chasse); 4* sonatas, 3 sonatinas, waltzes, mazurkas, caprices, nocturnes, variations, etc.—Cf. M. Hartmann, *Stephen Heller* in 'Monatshefte' (1859); H. Barbedette, *Stephen Heller* (Paris, 1876; English transl., London, 1877); R. Schütz, *Stephen Heller* (Leipzig, 1911; standard biography); see also Isidor Philipp, *Some Recollections of Stephen Heller,* in the 'Mus. Quarterly' (Oct., 1935).

Hellmesberger, Georg, Sr., renowned Austrian violinist; b. Vienna, April 24, 1800; d. Neuwaldegg, near Vienna, Aug. 16, 1873. His father, a country schoolmaster, gave him his first musical instruction; he succeeded Schubert as soprano chorister in the Imperial chapel; in 1820, became a pupil of the Vienna Cons. under Böhm (violin) and E. Förster (composition); in 1821, became assistant instructor there; in 1833, professor. In 1829 he succeeded Schuppanzigh as conductor of the Imperial Opera; 1830, member of the court chapel; pensioned in 1867. He had many distinguished pupils, including Ernst, Hauser, Auer, Joachim, and his own sons, Georg and Joseph.

Hellmesberger, Georg, Jr., Austrian violinist; son of preceding; b. Vienna, Jan. 27, 1830; d. Hanover, Nov. 12, 1852. He studied composition with Rotter; made a successful concert tour through Germany and England. At the age of 21, he was appointed concertmaster of the Hanover Royal orch., and produced there 2 operas, *Die Bürgschaft* and *Die beiden Königinnen* (1851), when his career, so brilliantly begun, was cut short by a lung ailment, to which he succumbed at the age of 22.

Hellmesberger, Joseph, Sr., distinguished Austrian violin virtuoso; another son of Georg Hellmesberger, Sr.; b. Vienna, Nov. 23, 1828; d. there, Oct. 24, 1893. In 1851, was appointed artistic conductor of the 'Gesellschaft der Musikfreunde' (till 1859, when he was succeeded by Herbeck), and director of the Vienna Cons. till 1893, where he was violin prof. (1851-77); concertmaster at the Imperial Opera (1860); solo violinist in the court orch. (1863); court conductor (1877). From 1849-87 he led the famous string quartet bearing his name (Hellmesberger, Durst, Heissler, Schlesinger), which opened a new era for chamber music in Vienna. —Cf. A. Barthlmé, *Vom alten Hellmesberger* (Vienna, 1908); R. M. Prosl, *Die Hellmesberger; hundert Jahre aus dem Leben einer Wiener Musikerfamilie* (Vienna, 1947).

Hellmesberger, Joseph, Jr., Austrian violinist and dramatic composer; son of the preceding; b. Vienna, April 9, 1855; d. there, April 26, 1907. He was solo violinist in the Imperial orch., and prof. at the Vienna Cons. (1878); then conducted opera and ballet; in 1887 he succeeded his father as leader of the Hellmesberger quartet. — Works: 10 operettas, produced (1880-1906) at Vienna, Munich, and Hamburg: *Kapitän Ahlström; Der Graf von Gleichen; Der schöne Kurfürst; Rikiki, oder Nelly, das Blumenmädchen; Das Orakel; Der bleiche Gast; Das Veilchenmädel; Die drei Engel; Mutzi;* and *Der Triumph des Weibes;* the ballets *Fata Morgana; Die verwandelte Katze; Das Licht; Die fünf Sinne;* etc.

Hellouin (ĕhl-wăn'), **Frédéric**, French writer on music; b. Paris, April 18, 1864; d. St. Germain-en-Laye, March 26, 1924. He was a pupil of Massenet at the Paris Cons.; from 1902, lecturer at the 'École des hautes études sociales.' He publ. *Feuillets d'histoire musicale française* (1902), *Gossec et la musique française à la fin du XVIII*e *siècle* (1903), *Essai de critique de la critique musicale* (1906), *Le Noël musical français* (1906), *Un musicien oublié: Catel* (1910).

Hellwig, Karl Friedrich Ludwig, German composer; b. Kunersdorf, near Wrietzen, July 23, 1773; d. Berlin, Nov. 24, 1838. He learned to play all the string instruments and piano; then studied theory with Zelter and others; at the same time, he was engaged in the manufacture of paint, which enabled him to pursue his musical studies as an avocation. In 1813 he became organist at the Berlin court. He wrote 2 operas, *Die Bergknappen* (Dresden, April 27, 1820) and *Don Sylvio di Rosalbo* (unperformed), much church music, and a number of German lieder, which show a certain poetic sensitivity and a ballad-like quality in the manner of Zelter and other early German Romanticists.

Helm, Everett, American composer and musicologist; b. Minneapolis, July 17, 1913. In 1935 he graduated from Harvard; received the John Knowles Paine traveling fellowship and studied in Europe with Malipiero and Vaughan Williams; head of the music department at Western College, Ohio (1943-44); toured South America (1944-46); theater and music officer under Military Government in Germany (1948-50).——Works: concerto for string orch. (1950); piano concerto (N. Y., April 24, 1954); *Adam and Eve,* an adaptation of a 12th-century mystery play (Wiesbaden, Oct. 28, 1951, composer conducting); concerto for 5 instruments, percussion, and string orch. (Donaueschingen, Oct. 10, 1953); *The Siege of Tottenburg,* opera in 3 acts commissioned by the Süddeutscher Rundfunk (1956); *Le Roy fait battre tambour,* ballet commissioned by the Frankfurt Opera (1956); *500 Dragon-Thalers,* a Singspiel (1956); 2nd piano concerto (Louisville, Feb. 25, 1956); woodwind quartet; string quartet; 2 piano sonatas; songs and choral pieces. He also edited the chansons (Northampton, Mass., 1942) and madrigals of Arcadelt.

Helm, Theodor, Austrian music critic; b. Vienna, April 9, 1843; d. there, Dec. 23, 1920. He was the son of a physician; studied jurisprudence in Vienna and became a government employee; in 1867, he began writing music criticism for various Viennese publications; in 1874 became music teacher at Horák's music school; from 1875 till 1901, he was editor of Fromme's 'Kalender für die Musikalische Welt'; published *Beethovens Streichquartette: Versuch einer technischen Analyse im Zusammenhang mit ihrem geistigen Gehalt* (Leipzig, 1885; 2nd ed., 1910); *50 Jahre Wiener Musikleben, 1866-1916,* in the 'Merker' (1917); many articles on Bruckner, and other essays.

Helman, Albert. See **Lichtveld.**

Helmholtz, Hermann (Ludwig Ferdinand) von, celebrated German scientist and acoustician; b. Potsdam, Aug. 31, 1821; d. Berlin, Sept. 8, 1894. His father was a school teacher in Potsdam, and Helmholtz received his education there. His mother, Caroline Penn, was of English extraction. He studied medicine at the Military Institute of Berlin; received his M.D., and became a member of the staff of the Charité Hospital there (1842); in 1843 he was appointed military surgeon at Potsdam; then recalled to Berlin as teacher of anatomy (for artists) at the Academy of Fine Arts (1848). In 1849, he obtained a position as prof. of physiology at Univ. of Königsberg; 1855, prof. at Bonn; 1858, at Heidelberg. In 1871, abandoning the teaching of physiology and anatomy, he accepted the position of prof. of physics at the Univ. of Berlin; publ. various scientific studies. The work of most interest to musicians, and indispensable for students of acoustics, is his *Lehre von den Tonempfindungen als physiologische Grundlage für die Theorie der Musik* (Brunswick, 1863); it was translated by Alexander John Ellis and publ. in London under the title, *On the Sensations of Tone as a Physiological Basis for the Theory of Music* (London, 1875; new ed., N. Y., 1948). By a long series of experiments, Helmholtz established a sure physical foundation for the phenomena manifested by musical tones, either single or combined. He supplemented and amplified the theories of Rameau, Tartini, Wheatstone, Corti, and others, furnishing impregnable formulae for all classes of consonant and dissonant tone-effects, and proving with scientific precision what Hauptmann and his school sought to establish by laborious dialectic processes. The laws governing the differences in quality of tone (tone-color) in different instruments and voices, covering the whole field of harmonic, differential, and summational tones; the nature and limits of musical perception by the human ear—these are the chief results of Helmholz's labors. — Cf. S. Epstein, *Hermann von Helmholtz als Mensch und Gelehrter* (Stuttgart, 1896); L. Königsberger, *Hermann von Helmholtz* (3 vols., Brunswick, 1902-03; 1 vol., 1911); E. Waetzman, *Zur Helmholtzschen Resonanztheorie* (Breslau, 1907); L. S. Lloyd, *Helmholtz and the Musical Ear,* in the 'Mus. Quarterly' (April, 1939): H. Ebert, *Hermann von Helmholtz* (Stuttgart, 1949).

Helsted, Gustaf, Danish composer; b. Copenhagen, Jan. 30, 1857; d. there, March 1, 1924. He was a pupil of Hartmann and Gade; from 1892, prof. of theory and from 1904 also of organ, at the Copenhagen Cons.; from 1915, organist of the Frauenkirche. He wrote 2 symphonies, a decimet for woodwinds and strings, a string sextet, 3 string quartets, a piano trio, 2 violin sonatas, and 2 cantatas: *Gurresånge* (Copenhagen, April 18, 1904) and *Vort Land* (Copenhagen, April 19, 1909).

Hempel, Frieda, brilliant German coloratura soprano; b. Leipzig, June 26, 1885; d. Berlin, Oct. 7, 1955. In 1900 she entered the Leipzig Cons. as a piano pupil; from 1902-05 she studied singing with Frau Nicklass-Kempner in Berlin; made her début at the Berlin Opera in Nicolai's *Merry Wives of Windsor* (Aug. 28, 1905); from 1905-07, at the Court Opera in Schwerin; 1907-12, member of the Royal Opera in Berlin; 1912-19, one of the foremost members of the Metropolitan Opera, where she made her début as the Queen in *Les Huguenots* on Dec. 27, 1912. In 1920 she impersonated Jenny Lind in the Lind centenary celebrations in New York and throughout the U. S. (70 concerts). She was married to William B. Kahn in 1918 (divorced in 1926). From 1940 till 1955 she lived in New York. A few months before her death, knowing that she was incurably ill, she returned to Berlin. Her memoirs, *Mein Leben dem Gesang,* were published posthumously (Berlin, 1955).

Hemsi, Alberto, composer; b. (of Italian-Jewish parents) Cassaba, Turkey, Dec. 23, 1896. He studied in Smyrna, and later at the Milan Cons. with Bossi; graduated in 1919. He was wounded while serving in the Italian Army in World War I. In 1928 he went (after a brief sojourn in Rhodes) to Alexandria, where he was appointed director of the Israelite Music School; from 1932-1940, taught at the Liceo Musicale Italiano there; later became instructor in harmony at the Alexandria Cons. In 1929 he founded the Edition Orientale de Musique.—Works: for orch.: *Danses bibliques; Croquis Egyptiens,* orchestral suite (Alexandria, March 19, 1951); for voice and orch.: *Five Hebrew Songs, Poème biblique, Mélodie religieuse; Tre arie antiche* for string quartet; string quintet; violin sonata; *Suite Séfardie* for violin and piano; *Trois danses égyptiennes* for violin and piano; *Six danses turques* for piano; *Coplas Séfardies* (six cycles of traditional Jewish chants) for voice and piano.

Henderson, William James, American music critic; b. Newark, N. J., Dec. 4, 1855; d. (suicide) New York, June 5, 1937. He was a graduate (1876) of Princeton (M. A., 1886); studied piano with Carl Langlotz (1868-73) and voice with Torriani (1876-77); chiefly self-taught in theory. He wrote many librettos of light operas, and also *Cyrano de Bergerac* for Walter Damrosch (1913). He was first a reporter (1883), then music critic of the 'New York Times' (1887-1902); and for 35 years, until his death, for the 'New York Sun' (1902-37); lectured on music history in N. Y. College of Music (1899-1902); from 1904, lectured on the development of vocal art at the Institute of Musical Art, N. Y.—Writings: *The Story of Music* (1889; 12th enlarged ed., 1912); *Preludes and Studies* (1891); *How Music Developed* (1898); *What is Good Music?* (1898); *The Orchestra and Orchestral Music* (1899); *Richard Wagner, His Life and His Dramas* (1901); *Modern Musical Drift* (1904); *The Art of the Singer* (1906); *Some Forerunners of Italian Opera* (1911); *Early History of Singing* (1921); also *The Function of Musical Criticism,* in the 'Mus. Quarterly' (Jan., 1915); *Beethoven After a Hundred Years,* in the 'Mus. Quarterly' (April, 1927); many other articles in various journals. In the series *Famous Composers and Their Works,* Henderson wrote the biographies of Goldmark, Tchaikovsky, and Wagner, as well as the chapter on Dutch composers. — Cf. O. Thompson, *An American School of Criticism: The Legacy Left by W. J. Henderson, R. Aldrich and Their Colleagues of the Old Guard,* in the 'Mus. Quarterly' (Oct., 1937). O. Thompson also edited excerpts from Henderson's scrapbook, published as *The Art of Singing* (N. Y., 1938).

Hendl, Walter, American conductor; b. West New York, New Jersey, Jan. 12, 1917. He studied regular musical subjects and conducting at the Curtis Institute of Music in Philadelphia (with Fritz Reiner); taught at Sarah Lawrence College (1939-41); joined the Berkshire Center at Tanglewood, as pianist and conductor, under the guidance of Koussevitzky (1941-42); in 1945 became associate conductor of the N. Y. Philharmonic; held this position until 1949; then conducted various performances in Europe and America. In 1949 he was appointed conductor of the Dallas Symph. Orch.; in 1955 conducted the Symphony of the Air during its tour in the Far East. He wrote incidental music for the play *Dark of the Moon* (1945); made orchestral transcriptions of various works.

Henkel, Heinrich, German pianist; son of Michael Henkel; b. Fulda, Feb. 14, 1822; d. Frankfurt, April 10, 1899. He was a pupil of his father; also studied with Aloys Schmitt He settled in Frankfurt in 1849, as a teacher. He publ. a piano method, *Vorschule des Klavierspiels,* an abridged ed. of A. André's *Lehrbuch der Tonsetzkunst* (1875), *Mitteilungen aus der musikalischen Vergangenheit Fuldas* (1882); piano pieces and songs.

Henkel, Michael, German composer of church music; b. Fulda, June 18, 1780; d. there, March 4, 1851. He studied with Vierling; then served as a local music teacher. He wrote a great number of sacred works, organ pieces, and instrumental works.

Henkemans, Hans, Dutch composer and pianist; b. The Hague, Dec. 23, 1913. He studied piano with Bernard van den Sigtenhorst-Meyer and composition with Pijper; made his début as composer-pianist in his piano concerto in Utrecht at the age of 19; also studied medicine at the Univ. of Utrecht, and obtained a doctor's diploma; was for a time a practicing psychiatrist. He received several state prizes, and decided to devote himself exclusively to music. In his style, he follows the early type of Impressionist music, with rich chromatic harmonies supporting melodic lines of a diatonic, often modal, character, and occasional bitonality. — Works: symphony (1934); 2 piano concertos (1932; 1936); flute concerto (1946); violin concerto (1948-50); viola concerto (1954); harp concerto (1955); 2 string quartets; quintet for flute, oboe, clarinet, horn, and bassoon; *Primavera,* for 9 instruments; cello sonata; violin sonata; sonata for 2 pianos; songs and choruses.

Henneberg, Albert, Swedish composer; son of Richard Henneberg; b. Stockholm, March 27, 1901. He studied in Stockholm, Vienna, and Paris. Returning to Stockholm in 1931, he became active as conductor, composer, and an organizer in the association of Swedish composers. He has written several operas (*Inka, Bolla och Badin, I Madonnas skugga*), 5 symphonies, piano concerto, cello concerto, trumpet concerto, trombone concerto, 2 string quartets, a quartet for flute, oboe, bassoon, and horn, violin sonata, etc.

Henneberg, Johann Baptist, Austrian composer of church music; b. Vienna, Dec. 6, 1768; d. there, Nov. 26, 1822. He conducted at Vienna theaters (1790-1803); then became a member of the orch. of Count Esterházy; in 1818, returned to Vienna. He wrote a great number of *Singspiele,* of which the most successful were *Die Waldmänner* (Hamburg, 1787) and *Liebe macht kurzen Prozess* (Leipzig, 1799).

Henneberg, Richard, conductor and composer; b. Berlin, Aug. 5, 1853; d. Malmö, Oct. 19, 1925. He studied piano with Liszt; then traveled as accompanist with various artists, including Wieniawski; held posts as operatic coach at the Italian Opera in London, at various theatres in Berlin and Stockholm; from 1885 until 1907 conducted at the Stockholm Opera; from 1914-20, was conductor of the Malmö Orchestra. Henneberg gave the first performance of *Tannhäuser* in Stockholm (1876) and the first complete production of the *Ring of the Nibelung* in Sweden (1907), and was an ardent propagandist of Wagner's music. He wrote a comic opera *Drottningens Vallfart* (Stockholm, 1882), incidental music to Ibsen's *Brand,* various Shakespearian pieces, a ballet *Undine,* some choral works and songs (all in a Wagnerian vein).

Hennerberg, Carl Fredrik, Swedish musicologist; b. Älgaras, Jan. 24, 1871; d. Stockholm, Sept. 17, 1932. As a young man, he was an organist at Varola; then went to Stockholm, where he studied at the Cons. (1899-1903) and remained on the faculty as harmony teacher. In 1909 he was appointed organist at the Royal Chapel; also served as librarian of the Music Academy. He specialized in the study of organ manufacture; traveled in European countries to collect information; publ. *Die schwedischen Orgeln des Mittelalters* (Vennna, 1909); *Orgelns byggnad och vard* (a treatise on organ building; Upsala, 1912; 2nd ed., 1928); contributed numerous bibliographical papers to musicological journals.

Hennes, Aloys, German pianist; b. Aachen, Sept. 8, 1827; d. Berlin, June 8, 1889. He studied with Hiller and Reinecke in Cologne; then taught piano in various provincial towns; in 1872, settled in Berlin. He publ. *Klavierunterrichtsbriefe,* containing ingenious teaching pieces. His daughter, Therese, was a child prodigy, who made an exceptionally successful tour in England in 1877.

Hennessy, Swan, composer; b. Rockford, Ill., Nov. 24, 1866; d. Paris, Oct. 26, 1929. He was the son of an American-Irish settler; studied general subjects in Oxford, and music in Germany; then traveled in Italy, France, and Ireland, eventually settling in Paris. He wrote about 70 compositions, several of which are derived from Irish folk melos; his technical equipment was thorough; his idiom, impressionistic. Among his Irish-inspired works are *Petit trio celtique* for violin, viola, and cello; *Rapsodie celtique* for violin and piano; *Rapsodie gaëlique* for cello and piano, and *Sonata in Irish Style* for violin and piano. Besides, he wrote several piano albums '*à* *la manière de . . .'* and characteristic piano pieces in a humorous vein, such as *Epigrammes d'un solitaire, Impressions humoristiques,* etc.; also 4 string quartets.

Hennig, Karl, German organist and composer; b. Berlin, April 23, 1819; d. there, April 18, 1873. A precocious musician, he brought out a psalm for soli, chorus, and orch. at the age of 14; began to conduct choral groups at an early age; then became a church organist at the Sophienkirche in Berlin; also was conductor of the Lyra Choral Society. He wrote a great number of miscellaneous pieces, sacred works, cantatas, as well as popular dances for piano.

Hennig, Karl Rafael, German music theorist and composer; son of Karl Hennig; b. Berlin, Jan. 4, 1845; d. Posen, Feb. 6, 1914. He studied music with his father; then with Richter in Leipzig and Kiel in Berlin; at the same time, studied law. After a brief period of teaching in Berlin, he went to Posen, where he founded the Hennig Vocal Society; also served as church organist. He composed several cantatas, choruses, songs, and instrumental pieces, but it is as a writer on theoretical subjects that he is mainly remembered. He publ. *Die Methodik des Schulgesang-Unterrichts* (Leipzig, 1885); *Die Unterscheidung der Gesangregister auf physiologischer Grundlage* (Leipzig, 1892); *Beitrag zur Wagner-Sache* (Leipzig, 1893); *Ästhetik der Tonkunst* (Leipzig, 1896); *Über die Entstehung der 'hohen Resonanz'* (Leipzig, 1902); *Musiktheoretisches Hilfsbuch* (Leipzig, 1903; 2nd ed., 1906); *Einführung in das Wesen der Musik* (Leipzig, 1906); and excellent analyses of Beethoven's 9th Symph. and *Missa Solemnis.*

Henriot, Nicole, French pianist; b. Paris, Nov. 23, 1925. She studied with Marguerite Long; entered the Paris Cons. at the age of 12, graduating with a 1st prize two years later. She toured Europe (1946-49), appearing with major orchestras; she made her American début on Jan. 29, 1948; toured Canada and South America (1949-50).

Henriques, Fini Valdemar, Danish composer; b. Copenhagen, Dec. 20, 1867; d. there, Oct. 27, 1940. He studied violin with Valdemar Tofte in Copenhagen, and with Joachim at the Hochschule für Musik in Berlin; composition with Svendsen; returning to Copenhagen, he was violinist in the court orch. (1892-96); also appeared as soloist. He organized his own string quartet, and traveled with it in Europe; also conducted orchestras. As a composer, he followed the Romantic school; he possessed a facile gift of melody; his *Danish Lullaby* became a celebrated song in Denmark. He also wrote an opera *Staerstikkeren* (Copenhagen, May 20, 1922); several ballets (*The Little Mermaid,* after Hans Andersen; *Tata,* etc.); *Hans Andersen Overture;* 2 symphonies; a string quartet; a quartet for flute, violin, cello, and piano; violin sonata; a number of piano pieces (several cycles, *Lyrik, Erotik,* etc.).—Cf. S. Berg, *F. V. Henriques* (Copenhagen, 1943).

Henriques, Robert, Danish cellist, conductor, and composer; b. Copenhagen, Dec. 14, 1858; d. there, Dec. 29, 1914. He studied cello with Popper, and composition with Kretschmer in Dresden. Upon his return to Copenhagen, he conducted the concerts of 'Symphonia' (1888-93); wrote music criticism; composed an overture *Olaf Trygvason;* symph. sketch, *Aquarellen;* a number of pieces for the cello.

Henry V, the English king; b. Monmouth, Aug. 1387; d. Bois de Vincennes, Aug. 31, 1422. During his reign (1413-22), he established a flourishing musical service at the Chapel Royal; was a musician himself; probably was the author of a Gloria and a Sanctus for 3 voices in the Old Hall MS (transcribed into modern notation, and publ. by the Plainsong and Medieval Music Society, 1933-38, vols. I and III; in that edition, these works are ascribed to Henry VI).

Henry VI, the English king; b. Windsor, Dec. 6, 1421; d. London, May 21, 1471. He reigned from 1422 till 1471. For a long time, he was regarded as the 'Roy Henry' who was the author of a Gloria and a Sanctus in the Old Hall MS; however, research by M. Bukofzer tends to indicate that the works may actually be by Henry V. —Cf. W. Barclay Squire, *Henry VI,* in the 'Sammelbände der Internationalen Musik-Gesellschaft' (1900-01, p. 342); G. R. Hayes, *King's Music,* an anthology (London, 1937).

Henry VIII, the English king; b. Greenwich, June 28, 1491; d. Windsor, Jan. 28, 1547. He reigned from 1509 to 1547. He received regular instruction in music. His compositions include 2 Masses (lost); a Latin motet for 3 voices (publ. in the 'Baldwin Collection,' 1591); the anthem *O Lord,* *the Maker of All Kings;* a secular ballad, *Passe tyme with good cumpanye,* for 3 voices (publ. in Chappell's 'Popular Music of the Olden Time'); five 4-part songs and twelve 3-part songs; also several pieces for 3 and 4 viols.—Cf. Lady Mary Trefusis, *Music Composed by Henry VIII* (Roxburghe Club, 1912; privately printed); G. R. Hayes, *King's Music* (London, 1937).

Henry, Harold, American pianist; b. Neodesha, Kansas, March 20, 1884. He studied with Karl Preyer at the Univ. of Kansas (1898-1902); then went to Berlin where he took lessons with Leopold Godowsky; also studied with Moszkowski in Paris. He made his American début in Chicago (Jan. 30, 1906); in his concerts he often included works by American composers, particularly MacDowell. He settled in New York as a teacher. He wrote a number of characteristic piano pieces (*Heroic Rhapsody, Fantasy Poem, Dancing Marionette, Night Sounds, Epilogue,* etc.); also songs (*In Autumn, Gather Ye Rosebuds,* etc.).

Henry, Hugh Thomas, American Roman Catholic priest, and writer on church music; b. Philadelphia, 1862; d. there, March 12, 1946. He taught church music at Overbrook Seminary from 1889 to 1917; was prof. of homiletics at Catholic Univ., Washington, from 1919-37. Besides his many religious and literary writings, he contributed the following articles to the 'Mus. Quarterly': *Music Reform in the Catholic Church* (Jan., 1915), *Choir-Boys in Catholic Churches* (July, 1917), and *Music in Lowell's Prose and Verse* (Oct., 1924).

Henry, Leigh Vaughan, English writer and conductor; b. Liverpool, Sept. 23, 1889; received his earliest training from his father, John Henry, a singer and composer; then studied with Granville Bantock in London, Ricardo Viñes in France, and Buonamici in Italy; taught music at Gordon Craig's Theatrical School in Florence (1912); then was in Germany, where he was interned during World War I. Returning to England, he edited a modern music journal 'Fanfare' (1921-22); also was active in various organizations promoting modern music; in 1930, he went to the U. S.; lectured at various colleges. He was music director of the Shakespeare Festival Week in London in 1938, 1945, and 1946; organized and conducted orchestral concerts of British music, and the National Welsh Festival Concerts; also at the B.B.C.; publ. the following: *Music: What it Means and How to Understand it* (London, 1920); *The Growth of Music in Form and Significance* (1921); *The Story of Music* (1935); *Dr. John Bull* (largely fictional; London, 1937); *My Surging World,* autobiography (with R. Hale; 1937). Among his compositions are *The Moon Robber,* an opera; *Llyn-y-Fan,* symph. poem; various pieces on Welsh themes.

Henry, Michel, a member of the 24 'violons du roi' under Henry IV and Louis XIII; b. Paris, Feb., 1555; date of death unknown. He wrote ballets for the court. His younger brother, known as Le Jeune, also in the 'violons du roi,' composed some very interesting instrumental music: a *Fantaisie* for 5 violins; another *Fantaisie* for 5 *cornetti; Pavane* for 6 oboes; some of this is reproduced by P. Mersenne in his *Harmonie universelle* (vol. 3, pp. 186-277). Dolmetsch made a modern arrangement of the *Fantaisie* for 5 violins.—Cf. F. Lesure, *Le Recueil de Ballets de Michel Henry* in 'Les Fêtes de la Renaissance' (Paris, 1956).

Henschel, Sir George (full name Isador Georg Henschel), conductor and singer; b. Breslau, Feb. 18, 1850; d. Aviemore, Scotland, Sept. 10, 1934. Both parents were of Polish-Jewish descent, but he was converted to Christianity when young. He studied with Julius Shäffer at Breslau, and with Moscheles (piano), Götze (singing), and Reinecke (theory) at the Leipzig Cons. (1867-70); then with Friedrich Kiel (composition) and Adolf Schulze (singing) in Berlin. He was a boy soprano; when his voice broke he gave concerts as a tenor; made his début in Leipzig (1868) as Hans Sachs (baritone) in a concert performance of *Die Meistersinger;* he then toured throughout Europe; later gave recitals as a bass, and in 1914 he appeared in London singing as a basso profundo. At the age of 78 he sang a group of Schubert lieder in London (Schubert centennial, 1928). An important turning point in his career came when he was selected by Higginson as the first conductor of the Boston Symphony, which he led for three seasons (1881-84); he also gave concerts in Boston and New York as a singer. Settling in England, he founded the London Symphony Concerts (inaugural concert. Nov. 17, 1886), and conducted them until the series was concluded in 1897. He was a vocal teacher at the Royal College of Music (1886-88) and conductor of the Scottish Symphony Orchestra (1893-95). From 1905-08 he was professor of singing at the Institute of Musical Art, New York. In 1931, at the age of 81, he was engaged to conduct a commemorative concert on the 50th anniversary of the Boston Symphony Orchestra, identical (except for one number) with his inaugural Boston concert of 1881. In 1881 Henschel married the American singer Lillian Bailey (see below), with whom he gave concerts; she died in 1901. In 1907 he was married, for a second time, to Amy Louis. He was knighted in 1914. His musical compositions (mostly vocal) are in the German Romantic tradition. They include the opera *Nubia* (Dresden, Dec. 9, 1899); *Stabat Mater* (Birmingham, Oct. 4, 1894); *Requiem,* in memory of his first wife (Boston, Dec. 2, 1902); Mass for 8 voices (London, June 1, 1916); a string quartet and about 200 songs (almost all published). He was the author of *Personal Recollections of Johannes Brahms* (Boston, 1907) and the autobiographical *Musings and Memories of a Musician* (1918). — Bibl.: Mark Antony de Wolfe Howe, *The Boston Symphony Orchestra, 1881-1931* (Boston, 1931); H. Earle Johnson, *Symphony Hall* (Boston, 1950).

Henschel, Lillian June (*née* Bailey), American soprano; b. Columbus, Ohio, Jan. 17, 1860; d. London, Nov. 4, 1901. She made her professional début in Boston at 16; then went to Paris to study with Mme. Viardot-García. On April 30, 1879, she appeared in London, at a Philh. concert, when she sang, besides her solo number, a duet with George Henschel. She then studied with him, and on March 9, 1881, was married to him. When Henschel was appointed first conductor of the Boston Symph. Orch., she came to Boston with him, and appeared as a soloist with him accompanying her at the piano, also in duets at Boston Symph. concerts. Until her untimely death, the Henschels were constantly associated in American artistic life. Her well-trained voice and fine musical feeling won her many admirers.—Cf. Helen Henschel, *When Soft Voices Die, a Musical Biography* (London, 1944).

Hensel, Fanny Cäcilia, pianist and composer; sister of Felix Mendelssohn; b. Hamburg, Nov. 14, 1805; d. Berlin, May 14, 1847. Brought up in the cultured atmosphere of the Mendelssohn family, she received an excellent musical education at home. She married the painter W. Hensel on Oct. 3, 1829, but remained very close to her brother, who constantly asked her advice in musical matters; her death, which occurred suddenly, was a great shock to Mendelssohn, who died a few months afterwards. She had a talent for composing; publ. 4 books of songs; a collection of part-songs, *Gartenlieder* (reprinted, London, 1878); also *Lieder ohne Worte* for piano.—Cf. Jack Werner, *Felix and Fanny Mendelssohn* in 'Music & Letters' (1947); S. Hensel, *Die Familie Mendelssohn* (Berlin, 1879).

Hensel, Heinrich, German dramatic tenor; b. Neustadt, Oct. 29, 1874; d. Hamburg, Feb. 23, 1935. He studied in Vienna and Milan; was a member of the Frankfurt Opera (1900-06), then at Wiesbaden (1906-10), where Siegfried Wagner heard him and engaged him to create the chief tenor part in his opera *Banadietrich* (Karlsruhe, 1910) and also to sing Parsifal at the Bayreuth Festival. He obtained excellent success; subsequently sang at Covent Garden, London (1911). He made his American début at the Metropolitan Opera House as Lohengrin (Dec. 22, 1911), and was hailed by the press as one of the finest Wagnerian tenors; he also appeared with the Chicago Opera.

Hensel, Octavia (real name Mary Alice Ives Seymour), American writer on music; b. 1837; d. near Louisville, May 12, 1897. She publ. *Life and Letters of Louis Moreau Gottschalk,* a regrettably unreliable volume (Boston, 1870); also *The Rheingold Trilogy* (Boston, 1884).

Hensel, Walther (real name Julius Janiczek), music educator; b. Moravska Trebova, Bohemia, Sept. 8, 1887; d. Munich, Sept. 5, 1956. He studied in Vienna, in Prague, and in Freiburg, Switzerland, where he obtained his *Dr. phil.* (1911); taught languages in Prague (1912-18). He traveled in Europe (1918-25) as organizer of folksong activities, with the aim of raising the standards of choral music for the young. From 1925-29, he was the head of the Jugendmusik School at the Dortmund Cons. In 1930, he went to Stuttgart, where he organized an educational program for the promotion of folk music. In 1938, he returned to Prague; taught at the German Univ. there. After 1945, he went to Munich. He edited a number of folksong collections (*Der singende Quell,* etc.); edited the periodicals 'Finkensteiner Blätter,' 'Lied und Volk,' etc.; publ. *Lied und Volk, eine Streitschrift wider das falsche deutsche Lied* (1921); *Über die gesamte Musikpflege in Schule und Haus,* in H. J. Moser's 'Grundfragen der Schulmusik' (1931); *Im Zeichen des Volksliedes* (1922; 2nd ed., 1936); *Auf* *den Spuren des Volksliedes* (1944); also publ. *Musikalische Grundlehre* (Kassel, 1937).

Henselt, Adolph von, distinguished German pianist and composer; b. Schwabach, May 9, 1814; d. Warmbrunn, Silesia, Oct. 10, 1889. The family moved to Munich when he was still an infant, and he studied piano there with Mme. von Fladt. In 1831, an allowance from King Ludwig I enabled him to continue piano study with Hummel at Weimar; then he took a course of theory under Sechter in Vienna. After a highly successful tour in Germany (1837), he went to St. Petersburg (1838), where he established himself as a piano teacher; was appointed chamber pianist to the Empress, and inspector of music at the Imperial Institutes for Girls in principal Russian cities. He remained in Russia for 40 years; a generation of Russian pianists studied under him. He was a virtuoso of the first rank; like Liszt (whose intimate friend he became), he developed an individual manner of playing, designed to express a personal feeling for the music. His technical specialty was the artful execution, in legato, of widely extended chords and arpeggios, for the achievement of which he composed extremely difficult extension studies. As a composer of piano pieces, he was praised by Schumann and Liszt. His principal works are a piano concerto, 2 sets of études, and a number of effective piano pieces *(Frühlingslied, La gondola,* etc.); all together, he publ. 54 works. A sympathetic character-sketch of Henselt is found in W. von Lenz, *Die grossen Pianoforte Virtuosen unserer Zeit* (Berlin, 1872; English ed., N. Y., 1899). See also La Mara, *Adolph Henselt,* in *Musikalische Studienköpfe* (vol. III, 1909; reprinted separately, 1911).

Hentschel, Ernst Julius, German music educator; b. Zudel, near Görlitz, July 26, 1804; d. Weissenfels, Aug. 14, 1875. He was taken to Langenwaldau as a child, where he was taught violin and piano; later he learned to play all the wind instruments also. He devoted himself mainly to musical education, and won the highest regard in this field. He compiled several collections of school songs; was co-founder and editor of the musical journal 'Euterpe.'

Hentschel, Franz, German conductor and composer; b. Berlin, Nov. 6, 1814; d. there, May 11, 1889. He studied with A. W. Bach; after conducting theater orchestras in provincial towns, he settled in Berlin as music teacher. He wrote an opera, *Die Hexenreise,* and numerous marches for military bands.

Hentschel, Theodor, German conductor and composer; b. Schirgiswalde, March 28, 1830; d. Hamburg, Dec. 19, 1892. He studied with Reissiger and Ciccarelli in Dresden; was active as theater conductor in Bremen (1860-90), and then at Hamburg. He wrote the operas *Matrose und Sänger* (Leipzig, 1857); *Der Königspage* (Bremen, 1874); *Die Braut von Lusignan, oder die schöne Melusine* (Bremen, 1875); *Lancelot* (Bremen, 1878); *Des Königs Schwerdt* (Hamburg, 1891); overtures and symphonic marches for orch.; piano music; songs; Mass for double chorus; etc.

Henze, Hans Werner, German composer; b. Güttersloh, July 1, 1926. He studied piano and percussion; was drafted into the German army in 1944; became a war prisoner of the British. Upon his release after the war, he studied with Wolfgang Fortner in Heidelberg and with René Leibowitz in Paris. From 1949-53, he lived mostly in Berlin and Munich; from 1953-56, in Ischia; in 1956, settled in Naples. In his music he adopts an uncompromising modern idiom, eventually tending towards an integrally dodecaphonic system. The performances of his theatrical works invariably aroused heated controversy, owing to the boldness of the librettos as well as the musical idiom. — Works: Operas: *Das Wundertheater,* operatic melodrama (Heidelberg, May 7, 1949); *Boulevard Solitude* (Hanover, Feb. 17, 1952); *König Hirsch* (Berlin, Sept. 23, 1956). Ballets: *Jack Pudding* (Wiesbaden, June 5, 1951); *Anrufung Apolls* (Wiesbaden, Oct. 28, 1951); choreographic fantasy, *Labyrinth* (Hamburg, April, 1952); *Der Idiot,* ballet pantomime, after Dostoyevsky (Berlin, Sept. 1, 1952); *Tancred und Canthylene* (Munich, 1952); *Pas d'action* (1952); *Die schlafende Prinzessin* (Essen, 1954); *Maratona di danza* (Berlin, Sept. 24, 1957). Orchestral works: Symph. No. 1 (Darmstadt, 1947); Symph. No. 2 (Stuttgart, Dec. 1, 1949); Symph. No. 3 (Donaueschingen Festival, Oct. 7, 1951); *Kranichsteiner Kammerkonzert* (Darmstadt, Sept. 27, 1946); *Ballet Variations* (Cologne, Oct. 3, 1949); violin concerto (Baden-Baden, Dec. 12, 1948); piano concerto (Düsseldorf, Sept. 11, 1952); *Ode an den Westwind,* for cello and orch. (Bielefeld, May 6, 1954); *Quattro Poemi,* symph. suite (Darmstadt, May 3, 1955); *Symphonische Etuden* (1956). Chamber music: sonatina for flute and piano (1947); violin sonata (1947);

string quartet (1952); serenade for cello solo (1953); wind quintet (1953); *Concerto per il Marigny,* for piano and instruments (Paris, March 9, 1956). Vocal music: *Ein Landarzt,* radio cantata, after Kafka (Hamburg, Nov. 29, 1951); *Das Ende einer Welt,* radio cantata (Hamburg, Dec. 4, 1953); 5 madrigals for chorus and chamber orch. (Frankfurt, April 25, 1950).

Herbart, Johann Friedrich, eminent German philosopher and musician; b. Oldenburg, May 4, 1776; d. Göttingen, Aug. 14, 1841. He studied at Jena with Fichte. In 1805, appointed prof. of philosophy at Göttingen; 1809-35, at Königsberg; 1835 (to his death) again at Göttingen. Of importance to music theory are his *Psychologische Bemerkungen zur Tonlehre* (1811), treating of intervals, and the chapter *Von den schönen Künsten,* in his *Kurze Enzyklopädie der Philosophie* (1931). He composed a piano sonata, which was published (Leipzig, 1808), and several other works. —Cf. W. Kahl, *Herbart als Musiker* (Langensalza, 1926).

Herbeck, Johann (Franz) von, Austrian conductor and composer; b. Vienna, Dec. 25, 1831; d. there, Oct. 28, 1877. He was a boy chorister at the Heiligenkreuz monastery, where he had instruction in organ; then studied composition with Ludwig Rotter in Vienna; also studied philosophy at Vienna Univ.; from 1859-66, and from 1875 to his death, he was conductor of the Gesellschaft der Musikfreunde; from 1866-71, court conductor; from 1871-75, director of the court opera. He was particularly successful as conductor and organizer of several choral societies in Vienna. Herbeck publ. numerous choral works of considerable worth, if not of any originality. His son, Ludwig Herbeck, publ. a biography, *Johann Herbeck, ein Lebensbild* (Vienna, 1885), which contains a complete catalogue of his works. See also the sketch on Herbeck in Hanslick's *Suite* (Vienna, 1885).

Herberigs, Robert, Belgian composer; b. Ghent, June 19, 1886. He studied at the Ghent Cons.; won first Belgian Prix de Rome with his cantata *De Legende van St. Hubertus* (1909). From 1951-53, he was director of the Flemish Opera in Antwerp; was also active in radio. Apart from his musical works, he publ. a number of novels. He wrote a comic opera, *Le Mariage de Rosine* (1925); 2 symphonies; *Cyrano de Bergerac,* symph. poem (1910); *Hiawatha's Song,* symph. suite (1921); 2 piano concertos (1932; 1952); 4 ballades for orch. (1954), *The Four Seasons* (after Breughel; Brussels, 1956); much chamber music; 22 sonatas and sonatinas for piano, etc.

Herbert, Victor, famous composer of light music; b. Dublin, Ireland, Feb. 1, 1859; d. New York, May 26, 1924. He was a grandson of Samuel Lover, the Irish novelist; his father died when he was an infant; soon his mother married a German physician, and settled in Stuttgart (1867) taking the boy with her. He entered the Stuttgart high school, but did not graduate; his musical ability was definitely pronounced by then, and he selected the cello as his instrument, taking lessons from the celebrated cellist Bernhard Cossmann in Baden-Baden. He soon acquired a degree of technical proficiency that enabled him to take a position as cellist in various orchestras in Germany, France, Italy, and Switzerland; in 1880, he became a cellist of the Eduard Strauss waltz band in Vienna; in 1881, returned to Stuttgart, where he joined the court orch., and studied composition with Max Seifritz at the Cons. His earliest works were for the cello with orch.; he performed his suite with the Stuttgart orch. on Oct. 23, 1883, and the first cello concerto on Dec. 8, 1885. On Aug. 14, 1886, he married the Viennese opera singer Therese Förster (1861-1927); in the same year she received an offer to join the Metropolitan Opera in New York, and Herbert was engaged as an orchestra cellist there, appearing in N. Y. also as soloist (played his own cello concerto with the N. Y. Philh., Dec. 10, 1887). In his early years in New York, Herbert was overshadowed by the celebrity of his wife, but soon he developed energetic activities on his own, forming an entertainment orchestra which he conducted in a repertory of light music; he also participated in chamber music concerts; was soloist with the Theodore Thomas and Seidl orchestras. He was the conductor of the Boston Festival Orch. in 1891; Tchaikovsky conducted this orchestra in Philadelphia in a miscellaneous program, and Herbert played a solo. He was associate conductor of the Worcester Festival (1889-91), for which he wrote a dramatic cantata, *The Captive* (Sept. 24, 1891). In 1893 he became bandmaster of the famous 22nd Regiment Band, succeeding P. S. Gilmore. On March 10, 1894, he was soloist with the N. Y. Philh. in his 2nd cello concerto. In the same year, at the suggestion of William MacDonald, the manager of the Boston Ideal Opera Company, Herbert wrote a light opera, *Prince Anan-*

ias, which was produced with encouraging success in New York (Nov. 20, 1894). From 1898 to 1904, Herbert was conductor of the Pittsburgh Symph. Orch., presenting some of his own compositions: *Episodes amoureuses* (Feb. 2, 1900); *Herc and Leander* (Jan. 18, 1901); *Woodland Fancies* (Dec. 6, 1901); *Columbus* (Jan. 2, 1903). In 1900 he directed at Madison Square Garden, New York, an orch. of 420 performers for the benefit of the sufferers in the Galveston flood. On April 29, 1906 he led a similar monster concert at the Hippodrome for the victims of the San Francisco earthquake. In 1904 he organized the Victor Herbert N. Y. Orch.; and gave concerts in New York and neighboring communities. But it is as a composer of light operas that Herbert became chiefly known. In the best of these he unites spontaneous melody, sparkling rhythm, and simple but tasteful harmony, while his experience as a symphonic composer and conductor imparted a solidity of texture to his writing that placed him far above the many gifted amateurs in this field. Furthermore, he possessed a natural communicative power in his music, which made his operettas spectacularly successful with the public. In the domain of grand opera, he was not so fortunate. When the production of his first grand opera, *Natoma,* took place at Philadelphia on Feb. 25, 1911, it aroused great expectations; but the opera failed to sustain lasting interest. Still less effective was his second opera, *Madeleine,* staged by the Metropolitan Opera Co. in New York on Jan. 24, 1914. Herbert was one of the founders of the American Society of Composers, Authors and Publishers (ASCAP) in 1914, and was vice-president from that date until his death. In 1916 he wrote a special score for the motion picture, *The Fall of a Nation,* in synchronization with the screen play. A list of his operettas follows: *Prince Ananias* (N. Y., Nov. 20, 1894); *The Wizard of the Nile* (Chicago, Sept. 26, 1895); *The Gold Bug* (N. Y., Sept. 21, 1896); *The Serenade* (Cleveland, Feb. 17, 1897); *The Idol's Eye* (Troy, N. Y., Sept. 20, 1897); *The Fortune Teller* (Toronto, Sept. 14, 1898); *Cyrano de Bergerac* (Montreal, Sept. 11, 1899); *The Singing Girl* (Montreal, Oct. 2, 1899); *The Ameer* (Scranton, Oct. 9, 1899); *The Viceroy* (San Francisco, Feb. 12, 1900); *Babes in Toyland* (Chicago, June 17, 1903); *Babette* (Washington, Nov. 9, 1903); *It Happened in Nordland* (Harrisburg, Nov. 21, 1904); *Miss Dolly Dollars* (Rochester, Aug. 31, 1905); *Wonderland* (Buffalo, Sept. 14, 1905); *Mlle. Modiste* (Trenton, Oct. 7, 1905; Herbert's most popular work); *The Red Mill* (Buffalo, Sept. 3, 1906); *Dream City* (N. Y., Dec. 25, 1906); *The Tattooed Man* (Baltimore, Feb. 11, 1907); *The Rose of Algeria* (Wilkes-Barre, Sept. 11, 1909); *Little Nemo* (Philadelphia, Sept. 28, 1908); *The Prima Donna* (Chicago, Oct. 5, 1908); *Old Dutch* (Wilkes-Barre, Nov. 6, 1909); *Naughty Marietta* (Syracuse, Oct. 24, 1910; highly successful); *When Sweet Sixteen* (Springfield, Mass., Dec. 5, 1910); *Mlle. Rosita* (later called *The Duchess,* Boston, March 27, 1911); *The Enchantress* (Washington, Oct. 9, 1911); *The Lady of the Slipper* (Philadelphia, Oct. 8, 1912); *The Madcap Duchess* (Rochester, N. Y., Oct. 13, 1913); *Sweethearts* (Baltimore, March 24, 1913); *The Débutante* (Atlantic City, Sept. 21, 1914); *The Only Girl* (Atlantic City, Oct. 1, 1914); *Princess Pat* (Atlantic City, Aug. 23, 1915); *Eileen* (Cleveland, Jan. 1, 1917, as *Hearts of Erin); Her Regiment* (Springfield, Mass., Oct. 22, 1917); *The Velvet Lady* (Philadelphia, Dec. 23, 1918); *My Golden Girl* (Stamford, Conn., Dec. 19, 1919); *The Girl in the Spotlight* (Stamford, Conn., July 7, 1920); *Oui, Madame* (Philadelphia, March 22, 1920); *Orange Blossoms* (Philadelphia, Sept. 4, 1922); *The Dream Girl* (New Haven, April 22, 1924). He also composed music for the following stage productions: *Cinderella Man* (1915), *The Century Girl* (1916), *Ziegfeld Follies* (1917, 1920-23), *The Willow Plate* (marionette play by Tony Sarg, 1924). Besides the above works he wrote *Serenade,* op. 12; a second concerto for cello, op. 30; *Suite romantique,* op. 31; *Pan-Americana;* a *Suite of Serenades* (composed for Paul Whiteman's orch.; perf. 1924); *Golden Days; Dramatic Overture;* orchestral arrangements; men's choruses; songs; many pieces for piano, violin and piano, and cello and piano.—Cf. J. Kaye, *Victor Herbert* (N. Y,. 1931); Edward N. Waters, *Victor Herbert* (exhaustive biography, with a full list of works; N. Y., 1955).

Herbst, Johannes, 'Moravian' minister and composer; b. Kempten, Swabia, July 23, 1735; d. Salem, North Carolina, Jan. 15, 1812. Herbst came to the United States in 1786 to serve as minister at Lancaster, Pa. and later at Lititz; brought with him an incredibly large collection of music manuscripts which he had copied in Europe. Included in the collection, which is preserved in its entirety in the Moravian Church Archives at Winston-Salem, N. C., are over 1000 anthems and sacred songs and about

50 important oratorios by principal contemporary European composers. In 1811 Herbst was elevated to the episcopate and transferred to the Southern Province of the Moravian Church at Salem, where he died the following year. He was the most prolific of all the American Moravian composers, having to his credit some 125 choral anthems and songs. Many of his works show him to have been a highly skilled musical craftsman. His music collection is particularly important as the principal source of music by American and European Moravian composers.—Cf. A. G. Rau and Hans T. David, *A Catalogue of Music by American Moravians* (Bethlehem, 1938); Hans T. David, *Musical Life in the Pennsylvania Settlements of the Unitas Fratrum,* in 'Transactions of the Moravian Historical Society' (Nazareth, Pa., 1942); H. T. David, *Background for Bethlehem: Moravian Music in Pennsylvania,* in 'Magazine of Art' (April, 1939); Donald M. McCorkle, *The Moravian Contribution to American Music,* in 'Notes' (Dec., 1956).

Hering, Karl (Friedrich August), German violinist; b. Berlin, Sept. 2, 1819; d. Burg, near Magdeburg, Feb. 2, 1889. He studied with Rungenhagen in Berlin and Tomaschek in Prague; established a music school in Berlin (1851); publ. *Methodischer Leitfaden für Violinlehrer* (1857) and an elementary violin method; also wrote a monograph on Kreutzer's studies (1858).

Hering, Karl Gottlieb, German music pedagogue; b. Bad Schandau, Oct. 25, 1765; d. Zittau, Jan. 4, 1853. He studied academic subjects at the Leipzig Univ.; music with J. G. Schicht. In 1811 he was appointed music teacher at the Zittau seminary, and remained there until 1836, when he retired. He publ. a number of manuals on practical music study: *Praktisches Handbuch zur leichten Erlernung des Klavier-Spielens* (Halberstadt, 1796); *Praktische Violin-Schule* (Leipzig, 1810), etc.; also compiled *Zittauer Choralbuch* (Leipzig, 1822), and other collections, including original compositions. Some of his pieces for children became celebrated in Germany and elsewhere, particularly *Steckenpferd* ('Hopp, hopp, hopp, Pferdchen lauf Galopp'); *Weihnachtsfreude* ('Morgen, Kinder, wirds was geben'), and (most famous of them all) *Grossvaterlied,* which was used by Schumann in his *Carnaval.* —Cf. Lucy Gelber, *Karl Gottlieb Hering,* in *Die Liederkomponisten . . .* (Berlin, 1936).

Héritte-Viardot, Louise - Pauline - Marie, vocal teacher; daughter of Pauline Viardot-García; b. Paris, Dec. 14, 1841; d. Heidelberg, Jan. 17, 1918. She was for many years a singing teacher at the St. Petersburg Cons.; then taught in Frankfurt, Berlin, and Heidelberg. She was married to a French consular official, Héritte. She was also a composer; her opera *Lindoro* was performed in Weimar (1879); she further wrote the cantatas *Das Bacchusfest* (Stockholm, 1880) and *Le Feu de ciel;* some chamber music, and vocal exercises. Her memoirs (translated from the original German MS) were publ. in English as *Memories and Adventures* (London, 1913), in French as *Mémoires de Louise Héritte-Viardot* (Paris, 1923).

Herman, Reinhold (Ludwig), conductor and composer; b. Prenzlau, Germany, Sept. 21, 1849; d. probably in New York, c. 1920. He studied at the Stern Cons. in Berlin; came to the U. S. in 1871 as singing teacher; from 1884, conducted the choral society 'Liederkranz'; from 1898-1900, conducted the Handel and Haydn Society in Boston; then lived in Italy; returned to New York in 1917. He publ. *An Open Door for Singers* (N. Y., 1912); wrote 3 operas, of which *Wulfrin* was perf. in Kassel (Oct. 11, 1898); also several choral works.

Herman, Woody (Woodrow Wilson), American clarinetist and band leader; b. Milwaukee, May 16, 1913. He studied there and at Marquette Univ. In 1931, joined a jazz band as a clarinet player, and in 1937 formed his own band, with which he made numerous successful appearances. On March 25, 1946, he presented in Carnegie Hall the first performance of Stravinsky's *Ebony Concerto,* written specially for him. He is also the composer of numerous popular songs.

Hermann, Hans, German composer; b. Leipzig, Aug. 17, 1870; d. Berlin, May 18, 1931. He studied with W. Rust in Leipzig, E. Kretschmer in Dresden, and H. von Herzogenberg in Berlin; from the age of 18, played the double bass in various European orchestras; then taught at the Klindworth-Scharwenka Cons. in Berlin (1901-07). From 1907 till 1927, he lived in Dresden; then returned to Berlin. He publ. some 100 songs, of which several became fairly well known (*Drei Wanderer, Alte Landsknechte,* etc.); he had a flair for imitating the simple style of the folk ballad; he further wrote a symphony subtitled *Lebensepisoden,* a stage work *Der rote Pimpernell;* pieces for clarinet with piano, etc.

Hermann, Matthias. See **Werrekoren.**

Hermann, Robert, Swiss composer; b. Bern, April 29, 1869; d. Ambach, Bavaria, Oct. 22, 1912. He studied in Frankfurt; as a youth, developed an original approach to composition; he met Grieg, who encouraged him; studied briefly with Humperdinck; his symph. was perf. by the Berlin Philh. Orch. (Nov. 7, 1895), and other works followed. —Cf. W. Niemann, *Robert Hermann,* in vol. III of 'Monographien moderner Musiker' (Leipzig, 1909).

Hermannus (surnamed **Contractus** on account of his paralyzed limbs), theoretician and composer; b. Saulgau, July 18, 1013; d. Altshausen, near Biberach, Sept. 24, 1054. He was the son of Hermann, Count of Vehringen. He was a student in Reichenau monastery; under the guidance of his tutor, Abbot Berno, he acquired wide learning. In 1043 he entered the Benedictine Order. His best known work (containing valuable historical notices on music) is a chronology from the time of Christ to 1054. It has been republ. several times, and is to be found in Peres' (Pertz's) Monumenta (vol. V). He was the author of *Opuscula Musica,* in which he gives a thorough discussion of the modes, and criticizes the Daseian notation used in the 10th-century tract, *Musica enchiriadis.* He proposed his own notation by Greek and Latin letters. In the indication of a change in pitch, it had an advantage over neume-notation. Hermannus' notation is written above the neume-notation in some MSS of the 11th and 12th centuries in the Munich Library. Hermannus was the composer of the Gregorian Marian antiphons, *Salve Regina* and *Alma Redemptoris Mater.* A transcription (into modern notation) of his *Versus ad discernendum cantum* is to be found in A. Schering's *Geschichte der Musik in Beispielen* (No. 7). —Cf. W. Brambach, *Hermanni Contracti Musica* (Leipzig, 1884); J. Wolf, *Handbuch der Notationskunde* (vol. I, pp. 126 and 143); Peter Wagner, *Einführung in die gregorianischen Melodien* (vol. III, pp. 316 and 496); Leonard Ellinwood, *Musica Hermanni Contracti* (Rochester, 1936), which gives the Latin text, ed. after both the Vienna MS and an 11th-century MS now at the Eastman School, Rochester, N. Y., an English translation, and commentary.

Hermesdorff, Michael, German musicologist; b. Trier (Trèves), March 4, 1833; d. there, Jan. 17, 1885. He entered the priesthood, and was appointed organist of Trier cathedral. He founded the Choral Society, chiefly for the exposition of Gregorian plain chant, on which he was an authority by virtue of his study of original sources. He edited the 'Graduale ad usum Romanum cantus S. Gregorii,' publ. (Leipzig, 1876-82, 10 numbers) in the monthly supplements of the 'Cäcilia' journal (Hermesdorff and Böckeler, Aix), but died before its completion. He revised the 2nd ed. of Lück's collection of sacred compositions (4 volumes); publ. German translation of the *Micrologus* and *Epistola* of Guido d'Arezzo; a *Kyriale,* and *Harmonica cantus choralis a* 4; a *Graduale,* several anthems, and *Praefatio* (prayers used in the Trier diocese); and 3 Masses of his own composition.

Hermstedt, Johann Simon, famous German clarinetist; b. Langensalza, Dec. 29, 1778; d. Sondershausen, Aug. 10, 1846. He was educated at the Annaberg school for soldiers' children; studied with Knoblauch and Baer; became clarinettist in the Langensalza regiment; then conducted a military band in Langensalza. He made improvements in his instrument; composed concertos, variations, and other pieces for clarinet. Spohr wrote a clarinet concerto for him.

Hernández (är-nahn'-dĕz), **Pablo,** Spanish composer; b. Saragossa, Jan. 25, 1834; d. Madrid, Dec. 15, 1910. He was first a church chorister; at 14, played organ at the San Gil church in Saragossa. At 22, he went to Madrid to study with Eslava at the Madrid Cons.; graduated with a gold medal (1861) and joined the faculty in 1863 as a singing teacher. He wrote 2 zarzuelas: *Gimnasio higienico* and *Un Sevillano en la Habana;* also many sacred works.

Hernández Moncada, Eduardo, Mexican composer; b. Jalapa, Sept. 24, 1899. He studied with Rafael Tello at the National Cons. in Mexico City. He conducted theater orchestras; in 1936 became assistant cond. of the Orquesta Sinfónica in Mexico. As a composer he made an impression with his symphony, first performed in Mexico City (July 31, 1942). His ballet *Ixtepec* (1945) employs Mexican rhythms.

Hernándo (är-nahn'-do), **Rafael José María,** Spanish composer; b. Madrid, May 31, 1822; d. there, July 10, 1888. He studied with Carnicer and Saldoni at the Madrid Cons. (1837-43); then went to Paris, where he took lessons with Auber. His *Stabat Mater* was performed there, and a grand opera, *Romilda,* was accepted for performance at the **Théâtre des Italiens,** but the revolutionary upheaval of 1848 prevented its production. Hernándo returned to Madrid, where he produced a number of zarzuelas, of which the most successful was *El duende* (June 6, 1849); others were *Palo de ciego* (1849), *Colegialas y soldados* (1849), *Bertoldo y Comparsa, Cosas de Juan, El tambor, Aurora,* etc.; also collaborated with Barbieri, Oudrid, and Gaztambide in *Escenas de Chamberi* and *Don Simplicio Bobadilla.* In 1852 he became secretary of the Madrid Cons.; later taught harmony there.

Hernried, Robert, writer on music and composer; b. Vienna, Sept. 22, 1883; d. Detroit, Sept. 3, 1951. He studied at the Univ. of Vienna; for some years conducted opera at provincial theaters (1908-14); taught theory at the Mannheim Academy of Music (1919-22), at the Cons. of Heidelberg (1923), in Erfurt, and in Berlin. In 1933 he left Germany and taught in New York, Davenport, Iowa, Dickinson, N. D., and at Fort Wayne, Ind. In 1946 he became prof. of music at the Detroit Institute of Musical Art. He wrote an opera, *Francesca da Rimini;* about 75 choral works; a Mass; some characteristic pieces for orch., etc.; publ. a monograph on Jaques-Dalcroze (Geneva, 1929), a biography of Brahms (Leipzig, 1934), and 2 theoretical works, *Allgemeine Musiklehre* (Berlin, 1932) and *Systematische Modulation* (Berlin, 1935; 2nd ed., 1948).

Hérold (ā-rŏhld'), **Louis - Joseph - Ferdinand,** celebrated French dramatic composer; b. Paris, Jan. 28, 1791; d. Thernes, near Paris, Jan. 19, 1833. His father, François-Joseph Hérold (pupil of Ph. E. Bach), a piano teacher and composer, did not desire his son to become a musician, and sent him to the Hix school, where his aptitude for music was noticed by Fétis, then assistant teacher there. After his father's death (1802), Hérold began to study music seriously; in 1806 he entered the Paris Cons., taking piano lessons with Louis Adam, and winning first prize for piano playing in 1810. He studied harmony under Catel, and (from 1811) composition under Méhul; in 1812 his cantata *Mlle. de la Vallière* won the Prix de Rome (the MS score is in the Cons. Library with works composed during his three years' study in Rome). From Rome he went to Naples, where he became pianist to Queen Caroline; here he produced his first opera, *La gioventù di Enrico Quinto* (Jan. 5, 1815), which was well received. From Naples he went to Vienna, and after a few months' stay returned to Paris, where he finished the score of Boieldieu's *Charles de France,* an 'opéra d'occasion' (Opéra-Comique, June 18, 1816), and where all the rest of his operas were produced. The flattering reception of *Charles de France* led to the successful production of *Les Rosières* (Jan. 27, 1817), *La Clochette* (Oct. 18, 1817), *Le premier venu* (Sept. 28, 1818), *Les Troqueurs* (Feb. 18, 1819), and *L'Auteur mort et vivant* (Dec. 18, 1820); the failure of the last-named opera caused him to distrust his natural talent, and to imitate, in several succeeding stage works, the style then in vogue—that of Rossini. With the comic opera *Marie* (Aug. 12, 1826) Hérold returned, however, to his true element, and won instant and brilliant success. Meantime he had obtained the post of chorusmaster at the Italian Opera (1824); during this period he brought out *Le Muletier* (May 12, 1823), *Lasthénie* (Sept. 8, 1823), *Vendôme en Espagne* (Dec. 5, 1823), *Le Roi René* (Aug. 24, 1824), and *Le Lapin blanc* (May 21, 1825). In 1827 he was appointed to the staff of the Grand Opéra, for which he wrote several melodious and elegant ballets: *Astolphe et Jaconde* (Jan. 29, 1827); *La Somnambule* (Sept. 19, 1827); *Lydie* (July 2, 1828); *La Fille mal gardée* (Nov. 17, 1828); *La Belle au bois dormant* (April 27, 1829); *La Noce de village* (Feb. 11, 1830). *La Somnambule* furnished Bellini with the subject of his popular opera. On July 18, 1829 Hérold produced *L'Illusion,* a one-act opera full of charming numbers. *Emmeline,* a grand opera (Nov. 28, 1829), was a failure, but his next opera *Zampa* (May 3, 1831) was sensationally successful and placed Hérold in the first rank of French composers. He then wrote *L'Auberge d'Aurey* (May 11, 1830) jointly with Carafa; *La Marquise de Brinvilliers* (Oct. 31, 1831) in collaboration with Auber, Batton, Berton, Blangini, Boieldieu, Carafa, Cherubini, and Paër; also produced *La Médecine sans médecin* (Oct. 15, 1832). His last work published in his lifetime, *Le Pré aux clercs* (Dec. 15, 1832), had a remarkable vogue. He died of consumption shortly before his 42nd birthday. His unfinished opera *Ludovic* was completed by Halévy and produced posthumously at the Opéra-Comique on May 16, 1833. Hérold's piano music, comprising 55 opus numbers, consists of sonatas, caprices, rondos, divertissements, fantasies, variations, and potpourris. —Cf. B. Jouvin, *Hérold, sa vie et ses œuvres* (Paris, 1868); Hector Berlioz, *Les Musiciens et la musique* (Paris, 1903); A. Pougin, *Hérold* (Paris, 1906).

Heron-Allen, Edward, English writer on the violin; b. London, Dec. 17, 1861; d. Selsey, Sussex, March 28, 1943. He is the author of a standard manual on the history of violin manufacture: *Violin-making, as It Was and Is* (London, 1884).

Herriot, Édouard, French statesman and writer on music; b. Troyes, July 5, 1872; d. Lyons, March 26, 1957. He entered politics as a member of the Radical Party; was premier of France 3 times between 1924 and 1932; then became president of the Chamber of Deputies. He was arrested in 1942 for refusing to cooperate with the Vichy Government, deported to Germany, and held in a castle near Potsdam until the end of the war. Returning to France, he resumed his activities; in 1946, he was elected to the French Academy. He was the author of a popular biography, *La vie de Beethoven* (Paris, 1929; many editions), publ. in English as *The Life and Times of Beethoven* (N. Y., 1935).

Herrmann, Bernard, American composer and conductor; b. New York, Jan. 29, 1911. He won a composition prize at the age of 13; then began to study music thoroughly, with Philip James at N. Y. Univ., and with Stoessel and Wagenaar at the Juilliard Graduate School of Music. He then became active as radio conductor; for several years conducted the C.B.S. summer series of the Columbia Broadcasting Symph. Orch., performing numerous works by American composers; then lived in Hollywood as film composer. His music is radical in its idiom, without losing contact with tonality and form; his scores for motion pictures are particularly effective.—Works: *Moby Dick,* dramatic cantata (N. Y. Philh., April 11, 1940); *Johnny Appleseed,* cantata (1940); *Wuthering Heights,* opera (1950). For orch.: *The City of Brass,* symph. poem (1934); *Sinfonietta for strings* (1935); *Currier and Ives,* suite (1935); *Fiddle Concerto* (1940); Symph. No. 1 (N. Y. Philh., Nov. 12, 1942); *For the Fallen* (N. Y., Dec. 16, 1943); also *Aubade* for 14 instruments (1933); string quartet and other chamber music. Film scores: *Citizen Kane* (1940); *The Devil and Daniel Webster* (1941); *Anna and the King of Siam* (1947), etc.

Herrmann, Eduard, conductor and composer; b. Oberrotweil, Germany, Dec. 18, 1850; d. Miami, Fla., April 24, 1937. He studied violin with Joachim in Berlin; played in various German orchestras; from 1878-81, he was concertmaster of the Imperial Orch. in St. Petersburg. In 1881, he settled in New York; formed a quartet with Schenck, Lilienthal, and Hauser, which enjoyed an excellent reputation; one of their features was the annual performance of all of Beethoven's quartets. He wrote a violin concerto, a string quintet, a string quartet, a sextet for oboe, clarinet, and strings, etc.

Herrmann, Georg. See **Armin, Georg.**

Herrmann, Hugo, German composer; b. Ravensburg, April 19, 1896. He learned to play the organ and acquired primary knowledge of music without systematic study; followed his father's profession as a school teacher in the provinces; then was drafted into the Germany army during World War I and severely wounded in 1918. After the Armistice, he turned to serious music study, and took courses with Schreker and Gmeindl in Berlin. In 1923 he went to the U. S., and was organist at the Church of the Holy Redeemer in Detroit and a member of the Detroit Symph. Orch. In 1925 he returned to Germany; in 1935 he obtained the post of director of a music school in Trossingen. Herrmann has written a great number of works in all genres; the operas *Gazellenhorn, Picknick, Vasantasena, Das Wunder, Paracelsus, Der Rekord, Der Überfall, Die Heinzelmännchen;* 5 symphonies; many symph. poems; violin concerto; 4 string quartets and other chamber music; choral works; lieder. Herrmann has been very active in organizing music festivals and school concerts. A believer in practical art, he has promoted various organizations for community music; took especial interest in the accordeon, and wrote works for it, with orchestra, and in other combinations; also wrote pieces for the mouth harmonica.—Cf. Armin Fett, ed., *Hugo Herrmann, Leben und Werk,* a 'Festschrift' on Herrmann's 60th birthday (Trossingen, 1956).

Herschel, Friedrich Wilhelm, eminent astronomer; b. Hanover, Nov. 15, 1738; d. Slough, near Windsor, Aug. 23, 1822. Son of a military musician, he was brought up as a musician like his three brothers. At 14 years of age he entered the band of the Hanoverian guards as oboist, and was stationed at Durham when that regiment came to England (1755). He later played organ at the Halifax parish church. In 1766 he was employed at the Octagon Chapel in Bath. He devoted his leisure to astronomy, constructed the great 'Herschel' telescope, discovered the planet Uranus, was appointed 'Astronomer Royal' (1781), and abandoned the musical profession. He received the honor of knighthood (1816) and an Oxford degree. He composed a symphony and 2 concertos for wind instruments.

Hertog, Johannes den, Dutch conductor and composer; b. Amsterdam, Jan. 20, 1904. He studied with his father, Herman Johannes den Hertog; then with Cornelis Dopper. He occupied various posts as operatic coach; was director and conductor of the Wagner Society in Amsterdam; from 1938-41, was assistant conductor of the Concertgebouw; also conducted at The Hague; in 1948, he was appointed conductor of the Flemish Opera in Antwerp. He has written a number of songs and some orchestral pieces.

Hertz, Alfred, eminent conductor; b. Frankfurt, July 15, 1872; d. San Francisco, April 17, 1942. After completing his academic studies, he entered the Raff Cons., where he studied with Anton Urspruch; then held positions as opera conductor in Altenburg (1892-95), Barmen-Elberfeld (1895-99), and Breslau (1899-1902). In 1902 he was engaged as conductor of the German repertory at the Metropolitan Opera; he conducted the first American performance of *Parsifal* (Dec. 24, 1903), which took place against the wishes of the Wagner family; consequently, Hertz could no longer obtain permission to conduct Wagner in Germany. In 1915 he was engaged to lead the San Francisco Symph. Orch.; he retained that post until 1930. He also organized the summer series of concerts at the Hollywood Bowl (1922), and conducted more than 100 concerts there; he was affectionately known as the 'Father of the Hollywood Bowl.'

Hertzka, Emil, music publisher; b. Budapest, Aug. 3, 1869; d. Vienna, May 9, 1932. He studied chemistry at the Univ. of Vienna; also took courses in music. He was engaged on the staff of the music publisher Weinberger in Vienna (1893); then joined the Universal Edition organized in 1901. In 1907 he became its director, and remained in that capacity until his death. He purchased the catalogues of several other music publishing firms: the Wiener Philharmonischer Verlag, Albert J. Gutmann Co. (which published Bruckner and Mahler), and acquired the rights of publication to works by many celebrated modern composers (Bartók, Schoenberg, Alban Berg, Kurt Weill, Krenek); also represented Soviet composers. An impassioned believer in the eventual worth of experimental music, he encouraged young composers, took active part in the organization of concerts of modern music, etc. An Emil Hertzka Foundation was established by his family after his death for the purpose of helping unknown composers to secure performances and publication of their works.

Hertzmann, Erich, musicologist; b. Krefeld, Germany, Dec. 14, 1902. He studied composition with Bernhard Sekles; then turned to musicology, studying under Moritz Bauer at the Univ. of Frankfurt and with J. Wolf, Abert, Schering, Sachs, Hornbostel, and Blume at the Univ. of Berlin. He then took an additional course with Pirro in Paris; received his Ph. D. at Berlin Univ. with a dissertation on Willaert (1931). From 1930 to 1933 he was musical correspondent in Berlin for several newspapers, including the London Times. In 1938 he left Germany and settled in the U. S.; in 1939 joined the faculty of Columbia Univ.; 1946, assistant prof.; 1949, associate prof.; 1956, full prof.; also lectured at Princeton Univ. (1946-49); in 1949 he held a Guggenheim Fellowship; in 1955 received a stipend from Columbia Univ. to study the creative processes of Beethoven.—Writings: *Adrian Willaert in der weltlichen Vokalmusik seiner Zeit* (Leipzig, 1931); *The Newly Discovered Autograph of Beethoven's Rondo à Capriccio,* in the 'Mus. Quarterly' (April, 1946); *Mozart's Creative Process,* in the 'Mus. Quarterly' (April, 1957); other articles in musical journals; edited *A. Willaert und andere Meister: Volkstümliche italienische Lieder* (Wolfenbüttel, 1930); Beethoven's *Rondo à Capriccio,* op. 129 (N. Y., 1947).

Hervé (properly **Florimond Ronger**), a French dramatic composer, the creator of French operetta; b. Houdain, near Arras, June 30, 1825; d. Paris, Nov. 4, 1892. He was a chorister and scholar of St.-Roch; he became organist at various churches in Paris. With his friend Kelm, in 1848, he sang in *Don Quichotte et Sancho Pansa,* an interlude of his own composition, at the Opéra National. In 1851 he conducted the orch. at the Palais Royal; in 1855 he opened the 'Folies-Concertantes,' a small theater for the production of pantomimes, *saynètes* (musical comediettas for two persons), etc., and, with phenomenal activity, developed the light French operetta from these diminutive and frivolous pieces, writing both librettos and music, conducting the orchestra, and often appearing as an actor on the stage. From 1856 to 1869 he led this feverish life in Paris, producing his works at various theaters, meeting failures by doubling his efforts. In 1870-71, when the Franco-Prussian War and the Commune stopped theatrical activities in Paris, he went to London, where he produced several of his light operas; he revisited London many times afterwards. In all, he wrote about 50 operettas, of which only one became a universal success, *Mam'zelle Nitouche* (Paris, Jan. 16, 1883, followed by numerous productions in European cities); other fairly successful works were *L'Oeil crevé* (Paris, Oct. 12, 1867) and *Le Petit Faust* (Paris, April 29, 1869). He also wrote a grand opera, *Les Chevaliers de la table ronde* (Paris, Nov. 17, 1866); the ballets, *Sport, La Rose d'Amour, Les Bagatelles,* etc.—Cf. L. Schneider, *Les Maîtres de l'opérette française, Hervé et Charles Lecocq* (Paris, 1924).

Hervey, Arthur, composer and writer; b. (of Irish parentage) Paris, Jan. 26, 1855; d. London, March 10, 1922. At first intended for the diplomatic service, he embraced a musical career in 1880; was critic for 'Vanity Fair' (1889-92); 1892-1908, on the staff of the London 'Morning Post.'—Author of *Masters of French Music* (London, 1894); *French Music in the XIXth Century* (1904); *Alfred Bruneau* (1907); *Franz Liszt and His Music* (1911); *Meyerbeer* (1913); *Rubinstein* (1913); *Saint-Saëns* (1921); etc.

Herz, Henri, brilliant Austrian pianist; b. Vienna, Jan. 6, 1803; d. Paris, Jan. 5, 1888. He was taught by his father, and by Hünten at Coblenz; later (1816) by Pradher, Reicha, and Dourlen at the Paris Cons., and won 1st piano prize; improved himself in Moscheles' style after that virtuoso's visit in 1821; was in high repute as a fashionable teacher and composer, his compositions realizing 3 and 4 times the price of those of his superior contemporaries. In 1831 he made a tour of Germany with the violinist Lafont; visited London in 1834, and at his first concert Moscheles and Cramer played duets with him. In 1842, was appointed piano prof. at the Paris Cons. He suffered financial losses through partnership with a piano manufacturer, Klepfer, and thereupon undertook a concert tour through the United States, Mexico, and the West Indies (1845-51). Returning, he established a successful piano factory, his instruments receiving 1st prize at the Paris Exhibition of 1855. He resigned his professorship at the Cons. in 1874. Herz acknowledged that he courted the popular taste; of his numerous works (over 200), at which Schumann frequently poked fun, only his Études and *Méthode complète de piano* (op. 100) survived him. They include piano concertos, variations, sonatas, rondos, violin sonatas, nocturnes, dances, marches, fantasias, etc. He publ. an interesting and vivid book, *Mes voyages en Amérique* (1866), a reprint of his letters to the 'Moniteur Universel,' describing his American tour.

Herzog (här'tsōhg), **Benedikt.** See **Ducis.**

Herzog, Emilie, brilliant German coloratura-singer and soubrette; b. Diessenhofen, Thurgau, 1859; d. Aarburg, Switzerland, Sept. 16, 1923. She was a pupil of the Zürich School of Music under Gloggner (1876-8); at Munich, under Schimon (1878-80); made her theatrical début as the Page in *Les Huguenots* (Munich, 1880). In 1889, she was engaged for the Berlin Court Opera, where she became especially famous as an interpreter of Mozart; extended tours of Germany established her reputation as one of the foremost lieder-singers; she taught at the Hochschule, Berlin (1903-10); at the Zürich Cons. (until 1922); then retired and lived in Aarburg. In 1890 she married the writer Dr. H. Welti.

Herzog, George, musicologist; b. Budapest, Dec. 11, 1901; studied musicology and anthropology at the Berlin Univ. and later at Columbia Univ., where he received his Ph.D. (1931); made a survey of Indian music in the southwestern U. S. for Columbia Univ.; collected folk melodies in Maine; in 1930-31, joined the Chicago Univ. expedition to Liberia, where he studied West African music, poetry, and signal drumming; made over 2000 records of primitive music in West Africa and North America; lectured on primitive music, African ethnology, phonetics, primitive languages, etc.; between 1929 and 1948, he occupied positions of research associate at Columbia Univ., Yale, and Chicago Univ. In 1948, he was appointed prof. of anthropology and folk music at the Univ. of Indiana.—Publications: *Die Musik der Karolinen-Inseln* (Hamburg, 1936); *Research in Primitive and Folk Music in the U. S.* (Washington, 1936); numerous articles in anthropological, folkloristic, and musical journals. For a complete list of his writings, see B. Krader, *Bibliography of George Herzog,* in 'Ethno-Musicology' (Middletown, Conn., Jan., 1956, pp. 11-20).

Herzog, Johann Georg, German organist and composer; b. Hummendorf, near Kronach, Aug. 5, 1822; d. Munich, Feb. 3, 1909. He studied at the music school in Schmölz, in Bavaria, and at the age of 11, began to earn a living playing the organ. In 1843, he went to Munich, where he was church organist, and later (1850) prof. at the Munich Cons.; among his pupils was Rheinberger. In 1854, he went to Erlangen; established a series of historical organ concerts there (1861-65); he then returned to Munich. He wrote a great number of organ works; also practical manuals.

Herzog, Sigmund, pianist; b. Budapest, June 13, 1868; d. New York, Aug. 28, 1932. He studied with Julius Epstein at the Vienna Cons., graduating in 1885; later with Rafael Joseffy in New York, where he then taught at the Institute of Musical Art. He publ. *The Art of Octave-Playing* and various piano pieces.

Herzogenberg, Heinrich von, pianist and composer; b. Graz, June 10, 1843; d. Wiesbaden, Oct. 9, 1900. He studied with Dessoff at the Vienna Cons.; then lived in Graz; went to Leipzig in 1872; with Spitta, Holstein, and Volkland, he founded the Bach-Verein there (1874); was its conductor from 1875-85; then was prof. of composition at the Hochschule für Musik in Berlin (1885-88); director of the 'Meisterschule' (1889-92 and 1897-1900). He was a very prolific composer; his chief influences were Brahms and Bruch; among his works are the oratorios *Die Geburt Christi, Die Passion, Erntefeier;* choral works with orch., *Der Stern des Liedes, Die Weihe der Nacht, Nannas Klage, Totenfeier,* and several psalms and motets; a cantata *Columbus;* a symph. poem *Odysseus;* 2 symphonies; piano quintet; string quintet; 5 string quartets; quartet for piano, horn, clarinet, and bassoon; 2 piano quartets; 2 piano trios; 2 string trios; trio for piano, oboe, and horn; 3 violin sonatas; 3 cello sonatas; several works for piano four-hands; fantasies for organ.—Herzogenberg's wife, Elisabet, *née* von Stockhausen (b. Paris, April 13, 1847; d. San Remo, Jan. 7, 1892), was an excellent pianist. They were great friends of Brahms, with whom they maintained a long correspondence (see M. Kalbeck, *Johannes Brahms im Briefwechsel mit Heinrich und Elisabet von Herzogenberg,* 1907). —Cf. J. H. Spengel, *Heinrich von Herzogenberg in seinen Vokalwerken* (Leipzig, 1893); W. Altmann, *Heinrich von Herzogenberg, Sein Leben und Schaffen* (Leipzig, 1903). J. Rieter-Biedermann publ. a complete catalogue of Herzogenberg's works (1900).

Heseltine, Philip (pen-name **Peter Warlock**), brilliant English composer and writer; b. London, Oct. 30, 1894; d. there, Dec. 17, 1930. He studied at Eton with Colin Taylor (1908-10); a meeting with Delius in France in 1910 influenced him profoundly in the direction of composition; he adopted a style that was intimately connected with English traditions of the Elizabethan period and yet revealed impressionistic undertones in harmonic writing. Another influence was that of Bernard van Dieren, from whom he absorbed an austerely contrapuntal technique. He publ. all his musical works under the name Peter Warlock. Psychological difficulties prevented him from utilizing his innate gifts to the full; most of his works are poetic miniatures, and yet their value appears incontestable. He was a conscientious objector during World War I; in 1917 was in Ireland; after the Armistice returned to London; in 1920 he founded the progressive journal of musical opinion, 'The Sackbut'; wrote criticism; made transcriptions of old English music; participated in organizing the Delius Festival in 1929. Suffering from depression, he committed suicide by gas in his London flat.—Books (under the name Philip Heseltine): *Frederick Delius* (London, 1923; revised ed. by Hubert Foss, London, 1952); *Carlo Gesualdo, Prince of Venosa, Musician and Murderer* (in collaboration with Cecil Gray; London, 1926); a pamphlet of 8 pages, *Thomas Whythorne: an Unknown Elizabethan Composer* (Oxford, 1927); as Peter Warlock, publ. a monograph, *The English Ayre* (London, 1926); ed. (with Ph. Wilson) 300 old songs (*English Ayres, Elizabethan and Jacobean; French Ayres);* co-editor, *Oxford Choral Songs* and the *Oxford Orchestral Series,* a collection of old English and Italian dances; transcribed for piano some lute music of John Dowland, *Forlorne Hope;* many other transcriptions. Musical compositions: song cycle *The Curlew* (with flute, English horn, and string quartet); *Saudades* (3 songs); *Lilligay* (5 songs); *Peterisms* (2 sets of 3 songs each); *Candlelight* (12 nursery songs), and many separate songs; *Capriol Suite* (on tunes from Arbeau's *Orchésographie,* in 2 versions: for string orch. and full orch.); *Corpus Christi* (2 versions, for chorus a cappella and for soprano and tenor soli with string quartet); numerous other vocal works.—Cf. Cecil Gray, *Peter Warlock: a Memoir of Philip Heseltine* (London, 1934); G.

Cockshott, *A Note on Warlock's Capriol Suite,* in the 'Monthly Musical Record' (1940); G. Cockshott, *Some Notes on the Songs of Peter Warlock,* in 'Music & Letters' (July, 1940); K. Avery, *The Chronology of Warlock's Songs,* in 'Music & Letters' (Oct., 1948).

Hess, Ludwig, German tenor; b. Marburg, March 23, 1877; d. Berlin, Feb. 5, 1944. He studied singing with Vidal in Milan; gave concerts of German lieder throughout Europe, specializing in the modern repertory (Richard Strauss, Max Reger, Hugo Wolf, etc.); made a successful tour of the U. S. and Canada in 1911; conducted a choral society in Königsberg (1917-20); then settled in Berlin. He was also a composer; wrote the operas *Abu und Nu* (Danzig, 1919) and *Vor Edens Pforte* (after Byron); *Kranion* (Erfurt, 1933); a symphony, and a symph. poem *Himmelskönig mit musizierenden Engeln* (after Hans Memling); *Ariadne,* a cantata; many choral works, and numerous songs. He publ. a book *Die Behandlung der Stimme vor, während und nach der Mutation* (Berlin, 1927).

Hess, Dame **Myra,** distinguished English pianist; b. London, Feb. 25, 1890. She studied at the Royal Academy of Music with Tobias Matthay. She made her début on Nov. 15, 1907, in London, playing Beethoven's G major concerto with Thomas Beecham, producing such an impression that her reputation was established almost immediately. She played in Germany and France; made a successful American tour in 1922, and repeated these tours at regular intervals. In 1941 she was created Dame of the British Empire. Her playing is marked by classical precision and poetic individuality; she avoids modernistic works, but occasionally performs piano music by contemporary British composers.

Hess, Willy, German violinist; b. Mannheim, July 14, 1859; d. Berlin, Feb. 17, 1939. His first teacher was his father, who was a pupil of Spohr. As a child, he was taken to the U. S.; at the age of 9, he played with the Thomas Orch. He then studied with Joachim in Berlin; later occupied posts as concertmaster in Frankfurt (1878-86), Rotterdam, where he taught at the Cons. (1886-88), and in Manchester, England, with the Hallé Orch. (1888-95). From 1895 to 1903, he was prof. of violin at the Cons. of Cologne; then taught at the Royal Academy of Music in London (1903-04); in 1904, he was engaged as concertmaster of the Boston Symph. Orch., and remained in that position until 1910; also organized the Hess Quartet in Boston. From 1910-28 he taught at the Hochschule für Musik in Berlin; there he remained until his death.—Cf. F. Bonavia, *Willy Hess,* in the 'Monthly Musical Record' (1931).

Hess, Willy, Swiss musicologist; b. Winterthur, Oct. 12, 1906. He studied with Volkmar Andreae and Paul Müller at the Zürich Cons.; in 1940, engaged as bassoon player in the city orch. at Winterthur; also active as teacher. He has contributed a great number of articles dealing with various obscure points of Beethoven's works; publ. an exhaustive volume, *Beethovens Oper Fidelio und ihre drei Fassungen* (Zürich, 1953); also a biography, *Beethoven* (Zürich, 1956).

Hesse, Adolph (Friedrich), German organist and composer; b. Breslau, Aug. 30, 1808; d. there, Aug 5, 1863. His father was an organ builder, and Hesse received his first instruction from him; he further profited by the advice of Hummel and Spohr. He was church organist at Breslau; visited Paris in 1844 for the inauguration of the new organ at St.-Eustache; his virtuoso handling of the pedal evoked praise. In 1851 he gave demonstrations of organ playing in London; then returned to Breslau; there he enjoyed a great reputation, not only as an organist, but also as conductor of the Breslau Symph. He publ. a collection, *Practical Organist;* his organ works were brought out by Steggall in a complete edition.

Hesse, Ernst Christian, German composer; b. Grossgottern, April 14, 1676; d. Darmstadt, May 16, 1762. He studied the viola da gamba, first at Darmstadt, then in Paris; gave successful demonstrations of his virtuosity in various European towns. In 1713, he married the opera singer, Johanna Döbricht. He wrote 2 operas and many works for viola da gamba.

Hesse, Julius, German pianist; b. Hamburg, March 2, 1823; d. Berlin, April 5, 1881. He originated and successfully introduced a new measurement for piano keys; publ. *System des Klavierspiels.*

Hesse, Max, German music publisher; b. Sondershausen, Feb. 18, 1858; d. Leipzig, Nov. 24, 1907. In 1880 he founded a publishing house at Leipzig and in 1883, the printing establishment Hesse & Becker, for music and books. Publications include 'Musikalische Handbücher' (series); Riemann's 'Musiklexikon'; 'Deutscher Musikerkalender'; the monthly 'Die Musik.'

Hesselberg, Edouard Gregory, pianist and teacher; b. Riga, May 3, 1870; d. Los Angeles, June 12, 1935. He studied at the Cons. of the Moscow Philh. Society (1888-92); later was a private pupil of Anton Rubinstein. In 1892 he came to the U. S.; taught at the Ithaca Cons. (1895-96), Music Academy in Denver (1896-1900), Cons. of Music at Wesleyan College (1900-05), Belmont College, Nashville (1905-12), and at the Toronto Cons. (1912-18). He wrote a *Russian Suite* and a *Russian Rhapsody,* for orch.; also piano pieces; made arrangements for 2 pianos of works by Bach, Chopin, and Schubert.

Hessen, Alexander Friedrich, Landgraf **von,** blind musician; b. Copenhagen, Jan. 25, 1863; d. Fronhausen, March 26, 1945. Although blind from birth, he began at a very early age to study piano and violin, as well as composition; for his teachers he had Herzogenberg, Joachim, Bruch, Weingartner, and Draeseke in Germany; also took lessons from Fauré in Paris (1899). His German lieder show a fine lyrical talent; he also composed chamber music (trio for clarinet, horn, and piano; 4 canons for 2 sopranos, 2 horns, and piano, etc.).—Cf. P. Hiller, *Der Liederzyklus von A. Fr. von Hessen* (1910).

Hessenberg, Kurt, German composer; b. Frankfurt, Aug. 17, 1908. He studied in Leipzig with G. Raphael (composition) and R. Teichmüller (piano). In 1933 he was appointed to the faculty of the Hoch Cons. in Frankfurt; in 1940 he received the National Prize for composition; in 1951, the Schumann Prize. Possessing great facility, Hessenberg evolved an effective idiom, basically classical, but containing Wagnerian elements in dramatic passages. One of his earliest works, *Struwwelpeter,* a suite for small orch. based on a well-known children's tale, became also his most successful composition (1933). He further wrote 3 symphonies (1936, 1943, 1954); concerto grosso (1938); *Konzertante Musik,* for 2 string orchestras (1947); *Spielmusik* for strings (1954); concerto for harpsichord and strings (1931); piano concerto (1940); concerto for 2 pianos and orch. (1950); 4 string quartets; quartet for violin, viola, cello, and piano; piano trio; string trio, etc.; many sacred choral works; several song cycles.—Cf. Karl Laux, *Kurt Hessenberg,* in *Musik und Musiker der Gegenwart* (Essen, 1949).

Hetsch, (Karl Friedrich) Ludwig, German conductor; b. Stuttgart, April 26, 1806; d. Mannheim, June 28, 1872. He studied with Abeille; was attached to the court of the King of Württemberg; then conducted in Heidelberg (1835-46) and in Munich (from 1846). He wrote an opera, *Ryno* (Stuttgart, 1833), orchestral works, and chamber music.

Heuberger (hoi'-bĕr-gĕr), **Richard (Franz Joseph),** conductor and composer; b. Graz, June 18, 1850; d. Vienna, Oct. 27, 1914. By profession a civil engineer, in 1876 he turned his full attention to music; became choral master of the Vienna 'Gesangverein,' and conductor of the Singakademie (1878); from 1902-09, conductor of the 'Männergesangverein'; appointed prof. at the Vienna Cons. (1902). In 1881 he became music critic of the 'Wiener Tageblatt,' then of 'Neue Freie Presse' (1896-1901), after 1904, of 'Neue Musikalische Presse,' and editor of 'Musikbuch aus Österreich' (1904-06).—Works: operas: *Abenteuer einer Neujahrsnacht* (Leipzig, 1886); *Manuel Venegas* (Leipzig, March 27, 1889), remodeled as the 3-act grand opera *Mirjam, oder Das Maifest* (Vienna, Jan. 20, 1894); *Barfüssele* (Dresden, 1905); the ballet *Struwwelpeter* (Dresden, 1897); cantata, *Geht es dir wohl, so denk' an mich,* from 'Des Knaben Wunderhorn'; overture to Byron's *Cain;* and songs. He also wrote the operettas (all first performed at Vienna) *Der Opernball* (Jan. 5, 1898; exceptionally successful; in N. Y., May 24, 1909); *Ihre Excellenz* (1899; new version as *Eine entzückende Frau*); *Der Sechsuhrzug* (1900); *Das Baby* (1902); *Der Fürst von Düsterstein* (1909); *Don Quixote* (1910). He publ. a selection of his critiques as *Musikalische Skizzen* (Leipzig, 1901); a biography, *Franz Schubert* (Berlin, 1902; 2nd ed., 1908); *Anleitung zum Modulieren* (Vienna, 1910); and a new ed. of G. Jensen's revision of Cherubini's *Counterpoint* (Leipzig, 1911).

Heubner (hoib'-ner), **Konrad,** German composer; b. Dresden, April 8, 1860; d. Coblenz, June 6, 1905. He studied with Riemann in Leipzig, with Nottebohm in Vienna, and with Nicodé in Dresden. In

1890 he was appointed director of the Coblenz Cons. He wrote a symphony, a cantata *Das Geheimnis der Sehnsucht,* several overtures, and a violin concerto.

Heugel, Henry, music theorist; b. Neuchâtel, Switzerland, Sept. 26, 1798; d. Nantes, France, May 2, 1841. He studied in Paris with Galin and Reicha; developed a 'méthode de méloplaste' along the lines of Galin's system; publ. *Nouvelle méthode pour l'enseignement de la musique inventée par H. Heugel et developpée par lui de manière à permettre d'apprendre sans maître* (1832).

Heugel (ö-zhĕl'), **Jacques-Léopold,** French music publisher; son of Henry Heugel; b. La Rochelle, March 1, 1811; d. Paris, Nov. 12, 1883. In 1839 he joined a music publishing establishment founded in Paris by J. A. Meissonnier (1812), and became its director; the name was changed to 'Heugel et Cie.' After his death, his nephew, Paul Chevalier Heugel (1861-1932) became its owner. The firm is now managed by Philippe and François Heugel, successors to their father, Jacques-Paul Heugel, who was the grandson of Jacques-Léopold Heugel. The list of publications includes the famous Paris Cons. methods, in all branches of music, and the works of celebrated composers (Bizet, Bruneau, Charpentier, Delibes, Fauré, Franck, Honegger, Ibert, d'Indy, Lalo, Massenet, Milhaud, Offenbach, Poulenc, Ravel, Roussel, Florent Schmitt, Widor, etc.). The firm also published the important weekly, 'Le Ménestrel' (founded in 1833; suspended publication during the Franco-Prussian War, 1870-71, and during World War I; ceased publishing in 1940).

Heuss (hois), **Alfred Valentin,** musicologist; b. Chur, Switzerland, Jan. 27, 1877; d. Gaschwitz, Germany, July 8, 1934. He studied at the Stuttgart Cons. (1896-98), then at the Akademie der Tonkunst in Munich, attending the Univ. of Munich simultaneously (1898-99); from 1900-03, he studied musicology with Kretzschmar at the Univ. of Leipzig (*Dr. phil.,* 1903, with his dissertation *Die Instrumentalstücke des 'Orfeo' und die venezianischen Opernsinfonien*). He was music critic of the 'Signale' (1902-05); of the 'Leipziger Volkszeitung' (1905-12); of the 'Leipziger Zeitung' (1912-18); editor of the 'Zeitschrift der Internationalen Musik-Gesellschaft' (1904-14), to which he contributed valuable articles; editor-in-chief of the 'Zeitschrift für Musik' (1921-29); wrote analyses of works by Bach, Beethoven, Liszt, Bruckner, etc., for Breitkopf & Härtel's 'Kleiner Konzertführer.' Of special value are his program books of the Bach Festivals at Leipzig (1904-27); he also publ. *Bachs Matthäuspassion* (1909). Other writings include *Über die Dynamik der Mannheimer Schule,* in the 'Riemann-Festschrift' (1909); *Kammermusikabende* (1919); *Beethoven: Eine Charakteristik* (1921); *Beethovens Orch.-Crescendo* (Basel, 1924); etc.

Heward, Leslie, English conductor and composer; b. Littletown, Liversedge, Yorkshire, Dec. 8, 1897; d. Birmingham, May 3, 1943. He was a pupil of his father, an organist; at the age of 17 he played organ in a church; later studied at the Royal College of Music in London. He then taught at various schools and conducted opera. From 1924-27 he was conductor of the Cape Town orch. in South Africa. Returning to England, he conducted the orch. of the city of Birmingham. Heward was also a composer; he wrote several orchestral suites, choruses, and songs. A memorial volume was published after his death under the editorship of Eric Blom (London, 1944).

Hewitt, Helen, American musicologist; b. Granville, N. Y., May 2, 1900; studied at Vassar College and at the Eastman School of Music; later, in Paris, with Nadia Boulanger (theory) and Widor (organ); returning to America, she took a course in musicology with Paul Lang at Columbia Univ. (M. A., 1933); also took a course with Besseler at Heidelberg; received her Ph.D. from Radcliffe College in 1938. She held a Guggenheim Fellowship in 1947; taught organ and theory at various American schools. In 1942 she joined the faculty of North Texas State College. She has contributed several valuable articles on the music of the Renaissance to various publications; edited Petrucci's anthology of secular choral music of the 15th century, *Harmonice Musices Odhecaton A* (Cambridge, Mass., 1942).

Hewitt, James, composer, publisher, organist, and violinist; b. Dartmoor, England, June 4, 1770; d. Boston, Aug. 1, 1827. He played in the court orch. in London as a youth. In 1792 he went to America and settled in New York, where he was described as one of the 'professors of music from the Opera House, Hanover Square, and Professional Concerts under the direction of Haydn, Pleyel, etc., London.' On Sept. 21, 1792 he gave a benefit concert with the violinists J. Gehot and B. Bergmann, the flutist W. Young, and a cellist named Phillips, which included Hewitt's *Overture in 9 Movements, expressive of a battle.* Subsequently, Young and Gehot went to Philadelphia, and in 1793 Hewitt, Bergmann, and Phillips gave a series of 6 subscription concerts; at their 5th concert (March 25, 1793) they presented for the first time in America, Haydn's *Passion of Our Saviour* (i.e., *The Seven Last Words*); in 1794 Henri Capron joined Hewitt in promoting his 'City Concerts'; meanwhile, Hewitt became the leader of the Old American Co. Orch., and in 1795 gave up his activities in connection with the subscription concerts. In 1798 he bought out the N. Y. branch of Carr's 'Musical Repository' and established a publishing business of his own. In 1812 he went to Boston, where he played organ at the Trinity Church and was in charge of the music presented at the Federal Street Theatre. In 1818 he returned to N. Y.; also traveled in the South. In N. Y. he was director of the Park Theatre.—Works: opera *Tammany* (produced in N. Y., 1794, under the auspices of the Tammany Society); ballad-operas, *The Patriot or Liberty Asserted* (1794); *The Mysterious Marriage* (1799); *Columbus* (1799); *Pizarro, or the Spaniards in Peru* (1800); *Robin Hood* (1800); *The Spanish Castle* (N. Y., Dec. 5, 1800); *The Wild Goose Chase* (1800); an overture *Demophon;* a set of 3 piano sonatas; *Battle of Trenton,* for piano (reprinted in the collection *Music from the Days of George Washington,* ed. by Carl Engel and Oliver Strunk); *The 4th of July — A Grand Military Sonata for the Pianoforte;* some other music, much of it extant in the Library of Congress, Washington; N. Y. Public Library; and the Boston Public Library. In 1816 Hewitt published a new setting of the *Star-Spangled Banner* to Key's poem, but it never took root. A *Nahant Waltz* is reprinted in J. T. Howard's *A Program of Early American Piano Music* (N. Y., 1931).—**John Hill Hewitt** (b. New York, July 11, 1801; d. Baltimore, Oct. 7, 1890), eldest son of James Hewitt, studied at West Point Academy; was a theatrical manager, a newspaper man, and drillmaster of Confederate recruits in the Civil War; wrote poems and plays; about 300 songs *(The Minstrel's Return from the War, All Quiet Along the Potomac, Our Native Land, The Mountain Bugle,* etc.); cantatas *(Flora's Festival, The Fairy Bridal, The Revelers,* and *The Musical Enthusiast);* ballad-operas *(Rip Van Winkle, The Vivandiere, The Prisoner of Monterey, The Artist's Wife).* His admirers dubbed him the 'father of the American ballad' but the form of a ballad existed in America long before him. He wrote a book of memoirs, *Shadows on the Wall* (1877).—**James Lang Hewitt,** another son of James (1807-1853) was associated with the publishing firm of J. A. Dickson in Boston (1825); after his father's death he returned to N. Y. and continued his father's publishing business. Cf. 'Sammelbände der Internationalen Musik-Gesellschaft' (vol. VI, p. 459); J. T. Howard, *The Hewitt Family in American Music,* in the 'Mus. Quarterly, (Jan., 1931); J. T. Howard, *Our American Music* (N. Y., 1939, and subsequent eds.).

Hewitt (eh-vit'), **Maurice,** French violinist; b. Asnières (Seine), Oct. 6, 1884. He studied at the Paris Cons.; was violinist in the Capet Quartet (1908-28); taught at the Cleveland Institute of Music (1930-34); from 1934, teacher at the American Cons. of Fontainebleau; at the Paris Cons. from 1938 (chamber music class); in 1928, organized in Paris the Quatuor Hewitt; in 1939, founded the Orchestre de Chambre Hewitt.

Hey (hī), **Julius,** German singing teacher; b. Irmelshausen, April 29, 1832; d. Munich, April 23, 1909. He first studied painting, but turned to music. He became an ardent Wagnerian after his introduction to the master by King Ludwig II, and worked under the direction of Hans von Bülow at the Munich School of Music (established by the King in accordance with Wagner's plans). After Bülow's departure (1869), he vainly tried to effect a reform from a German national standpoint in the cultivation of singing, but met with so many obstacles that he resigned when Wagner died (1883) and devoted himself to finishing his method of singing, *Deutscher Gesangsunterricht* (4 parts; 1886). It contains a complete and logical exposition of Wagner's views on vocal training. His book *Richard Wagner als Vortragsmeister* was publ. posthumously by his son Hans.

Heyden, Hans, German organist; son of Sebald Heyden; b. Nuremberg, Jan. 19, 1536; d. there, Oct. (buried Oct. 22), 1613. He was his father's successor as organist at St. Sebald Church, and was the inventor of the unique 'Geigen-Clavicymbel' ('Nürnbergisch Geigenwerk'), which he described in *Musicale instrumentum reformatum* (1605).—Cf. G. Kinsky, *Hans Heyden* in 'Zeitschrift für Musikwissenschaft' (1924).

Heyden (Heiden, Haiden), Sebald, German composer; b. Nuremberg, Dec. 8, 1499; d. there, July 9, 1561. In 1519, he was appointed cantor of the Hospital School in Nuremberg; in 1537, became rector at the Church of St. Sebald. He was the author of the important theoretical work *Musicae, i.e., artis canendi libri duo* (1537; 2nd ed., as *De arte canendi,* etc., 1540); composed the famous Passion song, *O Mensch, bewein dein Sünde gross.* —Cf. A. Kosel, *Sebald Heyden* (Würzburg, 1940).

Heyer (hī'ĕr), **Wilhelm,** German patron of music; b. Cologne, March 30, 1849; d. there, March 20, 1913. A wealthy co-owner of the wholesale paper manufacturing firm Poensgen & Heyer, he was an enthusiastic amateur, and was active in the musical affairs of Cologne in advisory capacities. In 1906 he established a historical musical museum in Cologne, in which he assembled more than 2600 instruments with accessories, about 20,000 autographs of musicians, 3500 portraits, and a library of books about music, containing many rare editions. Georg Kinsky, curator of the museum from 1909, publ. an illustrated catalogue of the Heyer collections. The museum was dissolved in 1927, and the instruments were acquired by the Musicological Institute of Leipzig Univ.; the books were dispersed by auction sales.

Heyman, Katherine Ruth Willoughby, American pianist; b. Sacramento, Calif., 1877; d. Sharon, Conn., Sept. 28, 1944. She made her début as soloist with the Boston Symph. Orch. in 1899; from 1905 till 1915, toured the U. S. and Europe with Schumann-Heink, Marcella Sembrich, and others. She became greatly interested in the works of Scriabin, and played recitals of his works in Europe and America; also publ. many articles on Scriabin's theosophic ideas. In 1928 she founded the Groupe Estival pour la musique moderne, Paris (reorganized in 1937); lived in New York and in Paris. She publ. *The Relation of Ultra-Modern to Archaic Music* (Boston, 1921); composed *Studies in Modern Idiom* for the piano, and songs.

Heymann, Werner Richard, composer; b. Königsberg, Germany, Feb. 14, 1896. He studied with Paul Juon in Berlin. He was first a composer of serious music (*Rhapsodische Sinfonie,* for orch. and baritone; *Frühlings-Notturno,* for orch.; a string quartet; songs with orch.); he then became a writer of successful songs; emigrated to the U.S. and settled in Hollywood as a composer for films.

Hickmann, Hans Robert Hermann, German musicologist; b. Rosslau, May 19, 1908; studied at Halle Univ. and in Berlin with C. Sachs, A. Schering, G. Schünemann, and J. Wolf. In 1933, settled in Egypt as organist and teacher in Cairo and Alexandria. He also was active on the radio in Switzerland, France, Germany, England, and Sweden (1949-52); has contributed numerous articles on ancient Egyptian music to various publications. Books: *Das Portativ* (Kassel, 1936); *La trompette dans l'Egypte ancienne* (Cairo, 1946); *Terminologie arabe des instruments de musique* (Cairo, 1947); a very valuable catalogue of musical instruments in the Cairo Museum (Cairo, 1949), etc. —See his autobiographical notice in 'Die Musik in Geschichte und Gegenwart.'

Hidalgo (ē-dahl'-gŏh), **Juan,** one of the earliest and most notable Spanish opera composers; b. c. 1600; d. Madrid, March 30, 1685. In 1631 he became a member of the Royal Chapel in Madrid as harpist and also as player of the 'clavi-harpa,' an instrument he is said to have invented. A document of 1677 attests that he was 'of superior skill, and had merited the highest honors from Their Majesties at all times.' So great was his reputation that the Duke of Infantado called him 'unique in the faculty of music.' He composed the opera *Celos aun del aire matan,* text by Calderón de la Barca (perf. Madrid, Dec. 5, 1660); the music of Act I (voices and basso continuo) was discovered by J. Subirá and publ. by him in 1933 (this is the longest extant specimen of Spanish operatic music from the 17th century). Hidalgo also wrote music for Calderón's comedies, *Ni amor se libra de amor* (1662) and *Hado y divisa de Leónido y de Marfisa* (1680), and for *Los celos hacen estrellas* by Juan Vélez (c. 1662). It is very probable that he also composed the opera *La púrpura de la rosa* (1660), text by Calderón. He was likewise known as a composer of sacred and secular songs (some preserved in the National Library, Madrid). Music by Hidalgo is reprinted in Pedrell's 'Cancionero' (IV) and

'Teatro lírico' (vols. III, IV, and V).—Cf. J. Subirá, *Celos aun del aire matan, Opera del siglo XVII* (Barcelona, 1933); J. Subirá, *El operista español Don Juan Hidalgo,* in 'Las Ciencias' I, 3 (Madrid, 1934); O. Ursprung, *Die älteste erhaltene spanische Oper,* in the 'Schering-Festschrift' (Berlin, 1937); G. Chase, *Origins of the Lyric Theater in Spain,* in the 'Mus. Quarterly' (July, 1939).

Hier, Ethel Glenn, American composer and pianist; b. Cincinnati, June 25, 1889. She graduated from the Cincinnati Cons. of Music (1911; hon. degree, 1922) and the Institute of Musical Art, N. Y. (1917). She studied composition with Rothwell, Stillman-Kelley, and Goetschius, then with Ernest Bloch (1918-21); was a private teacher in Cincinnati; then in N. Y. She has composed *Asolo Bells* for orch. (Rochester, Oct. 25, 1939); a cantata, *Mountain Preacher* for chorus and orch. (N. Y., Dec. 5, 1941); also for orch.: *Carolina Suite* and *Scherzo; Sextet Suite,* for flute, oboe, violin, viola, cello, and piano (1925); three quintets for flute, viola, cello, harp, and voice (1936); string quartet; *Rhapsody* for violin and piano (1940); also solo piano pieces.

Higginson, Henry Lee, founder of the Boston Symph. Orch.; b. New York, Nov. 18, 1834; d. Boston, Nov. 15, 1919. He studied singing and piano in Vienna (1856-60); in 1868 he established himself as a banker in Boston (Lee, Higginson & Co.). In 1881, in order to found the Boston Symph. Orch., he assumed the responsibility of providing for about $50,000 yearly of the annual budget of some $115,000, thus clearing the estimated deficit and assuring the organization's successful continuance; the orch., comprising 67 performers, gave its first concert at the old Music Hall on Oct. 22, 1881; in the summer of 1885, the series of concerts of lighter music, famous as the 'Pops,' were instituted; on Oct. 15, 1900, the Boston Symph. Orch. inaugurated its own permanent home, Symphony Hall; in 1903 the Pension Fund was established, for the benefit of which a special concert is given annually. A firm believer in the superiority of German musicians, Higginson engaged George Henschel as the first conductor of the orch. (1881-84); there followed a line of German conductors: Wilhelm Gericke (1884-89), Artur Nikisch (1889-93), Emil Paur (1893-98), Gericke again (1898-1906), Karl Muck (1906-08), Max Fiedler (1908-12), and again Karl Muck, from 1912 till 1918, when he was arrested as an enemy alien when the U. S. entered World War I. Higginson, distraught over Muck's arrest, resigned his position shortly after and selected a Board of Directors to control the orchestra. He died the following year.—Cf. M. A. de Wolfe Howe, *The Boston Symphony Orchestra* (Boston, 1914; new augmented ed., 1931); H. Earle Johnson, *Symphony Hall* (Boston, 1950).

Hignard (ēn-yahr'), **(Jean-Louis-) Aristide,** French composer; b. Nantes, May 20, 1822; d. Vernon, March 20, 1898; studied with Halévy at the Paris Cons., taking the 2nd Grand Prix de Rome. He was an earnest composer of lofty aims, but brought out operas and other works of secondary importance; his best opera, *Hamlet,* composed in 1868, was to be performed in Paris; unluckily for him, *Hamlet* by Ambroise Thomas was produced that same year, with such spectacular success that Hignard could not compete with it; accordingly, he had to be content with a provincial production in his native city (Nantes, April 21, 1888). His other operas that reached the stage include *Le Visionnaire* (Nantes, 1851), *Le Colin-Maillard* (Paris, 1853); *Les Compagnons de la Marjolaine* (Paris, 1855); *M. de Chimpanzé* (Paris, 1858); *Le nouveau Pourceaugnac* (Paris, 1860); *L'Auberge des Ardennes* (Paris, 1860); *Les Musiciens de l'orchestre* (Paris, 1861).

Hijman (hī-man), **Julius,** Dutch composer and pianist; b. Almelo, Jan. 25, 1901. He studied with Dirk Schaefer, and in Vienna; program annotator for the Concertgebouw Orch., Amsterdam (1934-1939); then came to the United States. He was instructor at the Houston Cons., Texas (1940-42), and Kansas City Cons. (1945-49); since 1949, teaching composition at the Philadelphia Musical Academy. He has composed mostly chamber music, including sonatas for violin, cello, saxophone, oboe, flute, with piano; 4 string quartets; a sonata for 2 violins and piano. He is the author of *New Austrian Music* (in Dutch; Amsterdam, 1938); has contributed to music journals.

Hildach, Eugen, German baritone; b. Wittenberge-on-the-Elbe, Nov. 20, 1849; d. Zehlendorf, near Berlin, July 29, 1924. He began to study voice at the age of 24; married Anna Schubert, a singer, and went to Dresden, where they both taught at the Cons.; also toured together in Germany. In 1904, they established their own singing school in Frankfurt. He publ. a number of songs, several of which became well known; particularly popular was *Der Lenz.*

Hiles, Henry, English composer and pedagogue; b. Shrewsbury, Dec. 31, 1826; d. Worthing, near London, Oct. 20, 1904. He filled various positions as organist and harmony teacher for nearly 60 years (1846-1904); was editor of the 'Quarterly Musical Review' (1885-88). He composed several oratorios, glees, and part-songs; publ. the manuals *Harmony of Sounds* (1871); *Grammar of Music* (2 vols., 1879); *First Lessons in Singing* (1881); *Part-Writing or Modern Counterpoint* (1884); *Harmony or Counterpoint?* (1889); *Harmony, Choral or Contrapuntal* (1894).

Hill, Alfred, Austrialian composer; b. Melbourne, Dec. 16, 1870. He studied at the Leipzig Cons.; played violin in the Gewandhaus Orch., including concerts under the direction of Brahms, Grieg, and Tchaikovsky. He then settled in New Zealand, where he became interested in aboriginal music. From 1916 to 1937 he taught at the Sydney Cons.; in 1947, was elected President of the Australian Composers' Society. Many of his works include melodic elements of primitive Maori music. He wrote a Maori opera, *The Weird Flute;* cantatas on Maori themes (*Hinemoa, Tawhaki,* etc.); a *Maori Symphony, Maori Rhapsody,* many lighter works for orch.; 17 string quartets (including the *Maori Quartet*); songs; publ. a manual, *Harmony and Melody* (Sydney, 1927).

Hill, Edward Burlingame, eminent American composer; b. Cambridge, Mass., Sept. 9, 1872. A member of a distinguished family of educators (his father was a professor of chemistry at Harvard, and his grandfather, president of Harvard), he pursued regular courses at Harvard Univ.; studied music with J. K. Paine; graduated in 1894 *summa cum laude;* took lessons in piano with B. J. Lang and A. Whiting, in composition with Chadwick and Bullard; also (for one summer) studied with Widor in Paris. He became greatly interested in the new tonal resources of the Impressionist school of composers; wrote articles (in the 'Boston Evening Transcript' and other publications) dealing with French music; publ. a book *Modern French Music* (Boston, 1924). In 1908 he joined the faculty of Harvard Univ. as instructor in music; became associate prof. in 1918; prof. from 1928-37; then James E. Ditson prof. (1937-40); retired in 1940, and lived mostly in New Hampshire; member of the National Institute of Arts and Letters, American Academy of Arts and Sciences; Chevalier of the Légion d'honneur; lectured at the universities of Strasbourg and Lyons (1921); was associate editor and contributor to the encyclopedia 'The Art of Music' (1915).—In his music, Hill reveals himself as a follower of the French school; clarity of design and elegance of expression are his chief characteristics. His best works are for orchestra; but he has also written chamber and choral music. — Orchestral works: symph. poem, *The Parting of Lancelot and Guinevere* (St. Louis, Dec. 31, 1915); *Stevensoniana Suite* No. 1 (N. Y., Jan. 27, 1918); symph. poem, *The Fall of the House of Usher,* after Poe (Boston, Oct. 29, 1920); *Stevensoniana Suite* No. 2 (N. Y., March 25, 1923). The following were perf. for the first time by the Boston Symph. Orch: *Waltzes* (Feb. 24, 1922); *Scherzo* for 2 pianos and orch. (Dec. 19, 1924); symph. poem, *Lilacs* (his best work in the Impressionist manner; Cambridge, March 31, 1927; many subsequent performances); Symphony in B♭, No. 1 (March 30, 1928); *An Ode* (for the 50th anniversary of the Boston Symph. Orch.; Oct. 17, 1930); Symphony in C, No. 2 (Feb. 27, 1931); Concertino for piano and orch. (Boston, April 25, 1932); Sinfonietta for string orch. (Brooklyn, April 3, 1936; also in Boston); Symphony in G, No. 3 (Dec. 3, 1937); violin concerto (Nov. 11, 1938); Concertino for string orch. (April 19, 1940); *Music for English Horn and Orch.* (March 2, 1945); *Prelude for Orchestra* (N. Y., March 29, 1953). *Diversion* for small ensemble was perf. at the Saratoga Festival (Sept. 6, 1947).—Chamber music: flute sonata (1926); clarinet sonata (1927); sextet for flute, oboe, clarinet, bassoon, horn, and piano (1934); string quartet (1935); piano quartet (1937); sonata for 2 clarinets (1938); quintet for clarinet and string quartet (1945); sonata for bassoon and piano (1948); sonatina for cello and piano (1949); sonatina for violin and piano (1951).—Vocal works: *Nuns of the Perpetual Adoration,* cantata for women's voices with orch. or piano (1908); *Autumn Twilight,* for soprano and orch.; *The Wilderness Shall Rejoice,* anthem for mixed chorus (1915); 2 pantomimes (with orchestral accompaniment): *Jack Frost in Midsummer* (1908); and *Pan and the Star* (1914); also *Poetical Sketches* for piano (1902); *Country Idyls,* a set of 6 piano pieces; *Jazz Study* for 2 pianos (1924).

Hill, Granville, English organist and music critic; b. Manchester, March 9, 1878; d. there, Dec. 26, 1953. As a youth, he was church organist in Manchester; later began to study piano; achieving a commendable degree of proficiency; in 1936 he was appointed piano prof. at the Leeds College of Music; also became music critic of the 'Manchester Guardian,' leaving that position shortly before his death.

Hill, Junius Welch, American organist and music editor; b. Hingham, Mass., Nov. 18, 1840; d. Hollywood, Sept. 7, 1916. After studying in Boston with J.C.D. Parker, he went to Germany, where he took courses in piano and composition with Moscheles, Plaidy, Richter, and Reinecke. Returning to Boston in 1863, he was organist at various churches; taught at Wellesley College (1884-97); then settled in California. He publ. a number of choral works for women's voices; edited several collections of music, among them 'Treasures of Lyric Art,' 'Arabesques,' 'Mozaïques,' 'Characteristic Piano Pieces,' etc.

Hill, Mabel Wood-. See **Wood-Hill.**

Hill, Ralph, English writer on music; b. Wattingford, Oct. 8, 1900; d. London, Oct. 20, 1950. He was first active in music publishing (1920-29); was music editor of the 'Radio Times' (1933-45); also wrote for the 'Daily Mail' (1933-39 and 1945-50); publ. *An Outline of Musical History* (1929); *Brahms: a Study in Musical Biography* (1933); *Liszt* (1936); *Challenges: a Series of Controversial Essays* (1943); *Music Without Fears* (1945).

Hill, Richard S., American music librarian; b. Chicago, Sept. 25, 1901. He was educated at Phillips Exeter Academy; studied at Cornell Univ. (B. A., 1924); postgraduate work at Oxford Univ., England (1924-26); held research fellowship in psychology under Kurt Koffka at Smith College (1927-29); returned to Cornell for further study and research in psychology and musicology, the latter under Otto Kinkeldey. In Sept., 1939, joined staff of Music Division, Library of Congress; made Head of Reference Section. 1950-51, vice president of the American Musicological Society. He was an associate editor of the quarterly journal of the Music Library Association, 'Notes,' during the last issues of its first series, and has served as editor since Dec., 1943. He was president of the International Association of Music Libraries (1951-55). He has contributed important articles to music magazines, one of the most notable being *Schoenberg's Tone Rows and the Tonal System of the Future* ('Mus. Quarterly,' Jan., 1936). In collaboration with Kurtz Myers, he edited a new type of discography publ. under the title *Record Ratings* (N. Y., 1956).

Hill, Ureli Corelli, American violinist and conductor; b. New York, c. 1802; d. Paterson, N. J., Sept. 2, 1875. His father, Uriah K. Hill, was a teacher of music in Boston and N. Y., and author of a manual, *Solfeggio Americano, a System of Singing* (N. Y., 1820). An admirer of Corelli, he named his son after him; the first name (Ureli) is a combination of the father's name Uriah and a friend's name, Eli. Ureli Corelli Hill played violin in various theaters in N. Y. as a boy; was violinist in the orch. of Garcia's opera company in 1825; then joined the N. Y. Sacred Musical Society, and conducted it in the first American performance, with orchestral accompaniment, of Handel's *Messiah* (1831). In 1836 he went to Germany, where he studied a year with Spohr. Returning to N. Y., he became a founder and first president of the N. Y. Philharmonic (1842-48); then went West in quest of fortune, which, however, failed to materialize. In N. Y. he exhibited a pianoforte of his own invention, in which he used small bell tuning-forks in place of strings, so as to secure perfect intonation; the attempt to promote this instrument met with failure. He played the violin in the N. Y. Philharmonic until 1873, when he retired because of age; continued to play engagements in various theater orchestras throughout his life; then moved to Paterson, N. J., where he engaged (unsuccessfully) in real estate schemes. Depressed on account of constant setbacks in his ventures of promotion in music and in business, he committed suicide by swallowing morphine.

Hill, W. E. & Sons, a firm of violin makers and music dealers in London. It is claimed that 'Mr. Hill, the instrument maker,' mentioned in Pepys' Diary (1660) was an ancestor of the present owners. The founder of the firm was Joseph Hill (1715-84); he served as an apprentice to Peter Wamsley; established his business about 1750. He had 5 sons, who were good violinists. **William Ebsworth Hill,** a grandson of the founder (b. London, 1817; d. Hanley, April 2, 1895), adopted the present name of the firm; his instruments took first prize at the expositions in London (1851) and Paris (1867). His sons, **William Henry, Arthur**

Frederick (b. 1860; d. London, Feb. 8, 1939), and **Alfred Ebsworth Hill** (d. London, April 21, 1940), collaborated in the writing of *Antonio Stradivari, His Life and Work* (London, 1902), a standard work. From material also gathered by them, Lady M. L. Huggins previously wrote *Giovanni Paolo Maggini. His Life and Work* (London, 1892). William Henry, Arthur F., and Alfred Ebsworth Hill are the joint authors of *The Violin-Makers of the Guarneri Family* (with introductory note by E. J. Dent; London, 1931). — The Ashmolean Museum at Oxford contains a valuable collection of stringed instruments, including a 1716 Stradivari violin with a bow dated 1694, presented by Arthur F. Hill.

Hill, Wilhelm, German pianist and composer; b. Fulda, March 28, 1838; d. Homburg, June 6, 1902. He studied in Frankfurt, and received a prize for his opera *Alona* in the competition for the opening of a new opera house. He was a prolific composer; publ. violin sonatas; piano quartet; piano pieces. His song *Es liegt eine Krone im tiefen Rhein* achieved immense popularity.—Cf. K. Schmidt, *Wilhelm Hill, Leben und Werke* (Leipzig, 1910).

Hille, Eduard, German composer and conductor; b. Wahlhausen, May 16, 1822; d. Göttingen, Dec. 18, 1891. He studied music with Heinroth. In 1855 he founded a 'Singakademie' in Göttingen, and gave many concerts of choral music. He wrote an opera, *Der neue Oberst* (Hanover, 1849), and a number of part-songs.

Hillemacher, two brothers, French composers; **Paul** (b. Paris, Nov. 29, 1852; d. Versailles, Aug. 13, 1933) and **Lucien** (b. Paris, June 10, 1860; d. there, June 2, 1909). They both studied at the Paris Cons.; Paul Hillemacher won the 2nd Prix de Rome in 1875, and the 1st in 1876, with the cantata *Judith;* Lucien Hillemacher obtained 2nd Prix de Rome in 1879, and the 1st in 1880. After graduation, they decided to write music in collaboration, and adopted a common signature—P. L. Hillemacher. Together they produced the following stage works: *Saint-Mégrin,* opera (Brussels, March 2, 1886); *Une Aventure d'Arlequin,* opéra-comique (Brussels, March 22, 1888); *Le Régiment qui passe* (Royan, Sept. 11, 1894); *Le Drac,* lyric drama (perf. at Karlsruhe in German as *Der Flutgeist,* Nov. 14, 1896); *Orsola,* lyric drama (Paris, May 21, 1902); *Circé,* lyric drama (Paris, April 17, 1907). Paul Hillemacher, who survived his brother by 24 years, wrote a short 'tableau musical' *Fra Angelico,* which was produced at the Paris Opéra-Comique on June 10, 1924. In addition to their operas, the brothers wrote a symph. legend *Loreley,* which won the prize of the City of Paris (1882); 2 orchestral suites, *La Cinquantaine* and *Les Solitudes;* an oratorio, *La Légende de Sainte Geneviève* (1886); songs. They also brought out a biography of Gounod (Paris, 1905).

Hiller, Ferdinand, German conductor and composer; b. Frankfurt, Oct. 24, 1811; d. Cologne, May 10, 1885. He was a member of a wealthy Jewish family; received a fine education; studied piano with Aloys Schmitt, and appeared in public at the age of 10. In 1825 he went to Weimar to study with Hummel, whom he accompanied to Vienna in 1827; visited Beethoven a few days before the latter's death. He lived in Paris from 1828-35, and became a friend of Chopin, Liszt, Berlioz, and many other celebrated musicians. When his father died in 1836, he went back to Frankfurt, where he conducted the concerts of the Cäcilien-Verein. He went then to Italy, where he produced an opera, *Romilda* (Milan, 1839). It was unsuccessful, but an oratorio, *Die Zerstörung Jerusalems,* which he wrote in the following year, aroused the interest of Mendelssohn, who invited Hiller to Leipzig, where it was performed by the Gewandhaus Orch. (April 2, 1840). In 1841 he went to Italy, where he studied church music. His subsequent activities consisted mainly of conducting in Germany; he led the Gewandhaus concerts in Leipzig during the 1843-44 season; then conducted in Dresden, where he staged his operas *Traum in der Christnacht* (1845) and *Konradin* (Oct. 13, 1847); was municipal conductor at Düsseldorf (1847-50), then at Cologne. He established the Cologne Cons., and was its 1st director until his death; also conducted the Lower Rhine Festival, which further enhanced his reputation. His other engagements were at the Italian Opera in Paris (1852-53) and in St. Petersburg, Russia, where he led a group of symph. concerts (1870); he also visited London several times between 1852 and 1872. He never ceased to compose works in large forms, despite their indifferent success; wrote 3 more operas, *Der Advokat* (Cologne, 1854), *Die Katakomben* (Wiesbaden, Feb. 15, 1862), and *Der Deserteur* (Cologne, Feb. 17, 1865); oratorio, *Saul;* cantatas, *Lorelei, Nal und Damajanti, Israels Siegesgesang, Prometheus, Rebecca, Prinz Papagei;* a ballad, *Richard Löwenherz,* for soli, chorus, and orch.; 3 symphonies, 3 overtures, 3 piano concertos, 5 string quartets, 5 piano quartets, 5 piano trios; many choral works; more than 100 songs; piano music. In his musical leanings, he was a conservative, and violently attacked Wagner. His classical training, and friendly association with Spohr and especially Mendelssohn, naturally influenced his style. Gifted in many fields of artistic endeavor, he was also a brilliant critic; his writings were publ. in collected form as *Die Musik und das Publikum* (1864); *Beethoven* (1871); *Aus dem Tonleben unserer Zeit* (2 vols.; 1868, 1871); *Musikalisches und Persönliches* (1876); *Briefe von M. Hauptmann an Spohr und andere Komponisten* (1876); *Felix Mendelssohn-Bartholdy, Briefe und Erinnerungen* (1874); *Briefe an eine Ungenannte* (1877); *Künstlerleben* (1880); *Wie hören wir Musik?* (1881); *Goethes musikalisches Leben* (1883); and *Erinnerungsblätter* (1884).—Cf. W. Neumann, *W. Taubert und Ferdinand Hiller* (Kassel, 1857); H. Hering, *Die Klavier Kompositionen F. Hillers* (Cologne, 1927).

Hiller, Friedrich Adam, German composer; son of Johann Adam Hiller; b. Leipzig, 1768; d. Königsberg, Nov. 23, 1812. He studied music with his father; was a conductor at various provincial theaters in Germany, and wrote a number of light operas: *Biondetta* (Schwerin, 1790); *Das Schmuckkästchen* (Königsberg, 1804); *Die drei Sultaninen* (Königsberg, 1809); etc.; also chamber music.

Hiller (Hüller), Johann Adam, German composer; b. Wendisch-Ossig, near Görlitz, Dec. 25, 1728; d. Leipzig, June 16, 1804. After completing his primary education in his native town, he went to Dresden, where he studied music with Homilius. In 1751 he entered the Univ. of Leipzig, where he studied law; at the same time he was forced to earn his living by performing at popular concerts as a singer and flute player. In 1754 he became tutor to a nephew of Count Brühl at Dresden, whom he accompanied in 1758 to Leipzig; there he finally settled, and devoted himself to a revival of the Subscription Concerts in 1763; these developed into the famous 'Gewandhaus' concerts, of which he was appointed conductor. In 1771 he founded a singing school, and from 1789-1801 was Cantor and music director of the Thomasschule as successor of Doles. Hiller was one of the originators of the 'Singspiel,' the precursor of German 'comedy-opera,' which had a distinct development contemporaneously with Italian opera buffa and French opéra-comique. In order to stress the disparity of characters in his operas, he assigned arias in a grand manner to the gentry, while persons of low degree were given simple songs. His 'Singspiele' were the following: *Lisuart und Dariolette, oder Die Frage und die Antwort* (Leipzig, Nov. 25, 1766), *Lottchen am Hofe* (Leipzig, April 24, 1767), *Die Liebe auf dem Lande* (Leipzig, May 18, 1768), *Die Jagd* (Weimar, Jan. 29, 1770; his best known work), *Der Krieg* (Berlin, Aug. 17, 1772), *Die Jubelhochzeit* (Berlin, April 5, 1773), *Das Grab des Mufti, oder Die zwey Geizigen* (Leipzig, Jan. 17, 1779). Several remained unperformed (*Das Orakel, Poltis, Die Friedensfeyer,* etc.). He further wrote many instrumental works, church music, and lieder, in which he excelled; particularly fine are his *Lieder für Kinder,* to words by C. F. Weisse (1769; new ed., 1865); also *Lieder mit Melodien an meinen Canarienvogel* (1759); *Letztes Opfer, in einigen Lieder-Melodien* (1790); setting of Horace's *Carmen ad Aelium Lamian;* 3 string quartets (1796); a symphony; keyboard compositions. He edited many Classical works, and also brought out numerous collections of contemporary pieces by German and Italian composers. He publ. *Allgemeines Choral-Melodienbuch für Kirchen und Schulen* (1793). He brought out a weekly publication on music 'Wöchentliche Nachrichten und Anmerkungen, die Musik betreffend' (1766-70), the first music periodical in Germany to report news regularly. His writings include *Lebensbeschreibungen berühmter Musikgelehrten und Tonkünstler* (1784); *Über Metastasio und seine Werke* (1786); *Anweisung zum musikalisch-richtigen Gesang* (1774); *Anweisung zum musikalisch-zierlichen Gesang* (1780); *Anweisung zum Violinspiel* (1792).—Cf. K. Peiser, *Johann Adam Hiller* (Leipzig, 1894); M. Friedländer, *Das deutsche Lied im 18. Jahrhundert* (1902); G. Calmus, *Die ersten deutschen Singspiele von Standfuss und Hiller* (Berlin, 1908); H. von Hase, *Johann Adam Hiller und Breitkopf,* in the 'Zeitschrift für Musikwissenschaft' (Oct., 1919); A. Schering, *Das Zeitalter J. S. Bachs und Johann Adam Hillers* (Leipzig, 1940). A. Einstein publ. a reprint of Hiller's autobiography in *Lebensläufe deutscher Musiker,* vol. I (Leipzig, 1914).

Hillis, Margaret, American choral conductor; b. Kokomo, Ind., Oct. 1, 1921. She studied piano, wind instruments, and double-bass. She received her B. M. degree in composition at Indiana Univ. (1947); then studied conducting with Robert Shaw in N. Y. and became assistant conductor of the Robert Shaw Chorale. From 1951 she presented numerous concerts in New York conducting various choral groups in programs ranging from early composers to modernists; she also conducted operas by Purcell, Gluck, etc. in concert form.

Hilsberg (real name Hillersberg), **Alexander**, violinist and conductor; b. Warsaw, April 24, 1900. He studied violin with Auer at the St. Petersburg Cons. In 1918 he went on a concert tour in Siberia, eventually reaching Harbin in Manchuria; there he played in a string quartet; in 1923 he went to the U. S. via Japan. In 1926 he joined the violin section of the Philadelphia Orch.; became its concertmaster in 1931, and associate conductor in 1945. He was also on the staff of the Curtis Institute of Music in the ensemble department (1927-51). The great success that Hilsberg achieved conducting the Philadelphia Orch. at a Carnegie Hall concert in 1950 led to his engagement as permanent conductor of the New Orleans Symph. Orch. (1952); in the spring of 1956 he took this orchestra on a tour of Latin America.—See Hope Stoddard, *Symphony Conductors of the U. S. A.* (N. Y., 1957; pp. 89-95).

Hilton, John (the Elder), English organist and composer; d. Cambridge, March, 1608. He was appointed organist at Trinity College, Cambridge on Jan. 26, 1594. He was probably the composer of the anthem *Lord, for Thy tender mercies' sake;* another anthem, *Call to Remembrance* (modern reprint by the Oxford Univ. Press), is also his. To distinguish him from a younger John Hilton, he is usually referred to as John Hilton, the Elder.

Hilton, John (the Younger), English composer; b. Oxford, 1599; d. London, March (buried March 21), 1657. He may have been the son of John Hilton, the Elder; obtained his degree of Mus. B. from Trinity College at Cambridge (1626); in 1628 he was appointed organist at St. Margaret's, Westminster.—Works: *Ayres, or Fa-las for 3 voyces* (1627; reprinted by the Musical Antiquarian Society); *Catch that catch can, or, a Choice collection of catches, rounds, and canons for 3 or 4 voyces* (1625); 2 services; *Elegy;* anthems. The British Museum has further MSS. Other compositions are to be found in F. Keel's collection *Elizabethan Love-Songs* (N. Y., 1913), C. K. Scott's *Euterpe* (vol. 12, London, 1910), and E. H. Meyer's *Spielmusik des Barock* (vol. 1, Kassel, 1934). Six pieces for string trio have been arranged by Peter Warlock (London, 1930).—Cf. W. H. G. Flood, *New Light on Late Tudor Composers: John Hilton,* in the 'Musical Times' (London, 1927).

Himmel, Friedrich Heinrich, German composer; b. Treuenbrietzen, Brandenburg, Nov. 20, 1765; d. Berlin, June 8, 1814. He studied theology at the Univ. of Halle; at the same time, he cultivated music. He received a stipend from Friedrich Wilhelm II to study with Naumann in Dresden; subsequently he went to Italy, where he acquired skill in stage music. His cantata *Il primo navigatore* was performed in Venice (March 1, 1794), and his opera *La Morte di Semiramide* in Naples (Jan. 12, 1795). He then returned to Berlin and was appointed court conductor. In 1798 he went to St. Petersburg, where he produced his opera *Alessandro.* In 1800 he returned from Russia by way of Sweden and Denmark; in Berlin he produced his Italian opera *Vasco di Gama* (Jan. 12, 1801). His subsequent operas, staged in Berlin, were in the nature of Singspiele, to German words: *Frohsinn und Schwärmerei* (March 9, 1801), *Fanchon das Leiermädchen* (May 15, 1804; his most successful work; many revivals), *Die Sylphen* (April 14, 1806), etc. His last opera, *Der Kobold,* was produced in Vienna (May 22, 1813). Many of his songs had great vogue (*An Alexis, Es kann ja nicht immer so bleiben,* etc.). He also composed an oratorio, *Isacco figura del Redentore* (Berlin, 1792); several works of sacred music; a piano concerto; piano sextet; piano quartet; pieces for piano solo.—Cf. L. O. Odendahl, *Fr. H. Himmel; Bemerkungen zur Geschichte der Berliner Oper um die Wende des 18. und 19. Jahrhunderts* (Bonn, 1917).

Hinckley, Allen (Carter), American bass singer; b. Gloucester, Mass., Oct. 11, 1877; d. Yonkers, N. Y., Jan. 28, 1954. He studied at Amherst College and the Univ. of Pennsylvania; then took singing lessons with Oscar Saenger in N. Y.; after singing in various churches, and also in light opera, he went to Germany, where he made his début in grand opera at Hamburg as the King in *Lohengrin* (1903); he remained a member of the Hamburg Opera until 1908; also sang at Bayreuth (1905, 1906). On Nov. 18, 1908, he sang the part of Hunding in *Die*

Walküre with the Metropolitan Opera Company in N. Y.; from 1917, taught voice in N. Y.

Hindemith, Paul, one of the leading composers of the 20th century; b. Hanau, near Frankfurt, Nov. 16, 1895. Very early in life he learned to play several musical instruments, and as a boy, played in dance bands. He then entered the Hoch Cons. in Frankfurt and studied with Bernhard Sekles and Arnold Mendelssohn. Having achieved considerable proficiency as a violinist, he became concertmaster of the Frankfurt Opera (1915-23); then made a specialty of the viola, and formed the Amar-Hindemith Quartet (Licco Amar, Kaspar, Hindemith, Maurice Frank), with which he traveled in Europe. He was associated with the 'Musikalische Jugendbewegung' (Musical Youth Movement); taught a master class in composition at the Berlin Hochschule für Musik (1927-35). In the meantime, his conflict with the ideology of the National Socialist Government in Germany became extremely sharp; he was attacked by propaganda agencies as a cultural Bolshevik, and was taken to task for his continued association with Jewish musicians. Although Furtwängler and other eminent German musicians sided with Hindemith, his works were banned for performance, and he finally decided to leave the country. In 1935 he was asked by the Turkish government to organize all branches of music study and research on occidental models; he made 3 visits to Ankara, and taught at the conservatory there. He made his first American appearance at the Coolidge Festival at the Library of Congress, Washington, playing his unaccompanied viola sonata (April 10, 1937); toured the U. S. again in 1938-39; taught at the Berkshire Music Center at Tanglewood, in 1940; then was appointed to the faculty of Yale Univ. (1940); in 1947, was named Battell Prof. of the Theory of Music at Yale, and elected member of the National Institute of Arts and Letters; was Charles Eliot Norton Lecturer at Harvard Univ. (1950-51); became an American citizen in 1946. He conducted in Holland, Italy, and England during the summer of 1947; in 1949, revisited Germany for the first time since the war; conducted the Berlin Philharmonic in a program of his works on Feb. 14, 1949; in 1953 he settled in Switzerland; taught at the Univ. of Zürich; conducted concerts in Germany and Austria. In 1954 he received the 'Sibelius Award' of $35,000, offered annually to great men of music and science by a Finnish ship owner, A. Wihuri.—Hindemith's early music reflects rebellious opposition to all tradition; this is noted in such works as the opera *Mörder, Hoffnung der Frauen* (op. 12, 1921) and *Suite 1922,* for piano (op. 26); at the same time he cultivated the techniques of constructivism, evident in such a work as his theatrical sketch, *Hin und Zurück* (op. 45a, 1927), in which 'Krebsgang' (retrograde movement) is applied to the action on the stage, so that events are reversed; in a work of a much later period, *Ludus Tonalis* (1943), the postlude is the upside-down version of the prelude. Along constructive lines is Hindemith's cultivation of so-called 'Gebrauchsmusik,' that is, music for use; he is also an ardent champion of 'Hausmusik,' to be played or sung by amateurs at home; the score of his *Frau Musica* (as revised in 1944) has an obbligato part for the audience to sing. A neo-Classical trend is shown in a series of works, entitled *Kammermusik,* for various instrumental combinations, polyphonically conceived, and Baroque in style. Although Hindemith has made free use of atonal melodies, he has never been tempted to adopt the 12-tone method, which he opposes on ideological grounds. Having made a thorough study of old music, he has written works of a neo-archaic nature, artfully assimilating the elements of old polyphonic music in a modern manner. His masterpiece of this period is his opera, *Mathis der Maler.* An exceptionally prolific composer, Hindemith has written works in all genres and for all instrumental combinations including a series of sonatas for each orchestral instrument with piano. Hindemith's style may be described as a synthesis of modern, Romantic, Classical, and archaic principles, a combination saved from the stigma of eclecticism only by Hindemith's superlative mastery of technical means. As a theorist and pedagogue, Hindemith has developed a self-consistent method of presentation derived from the acoustical nature of harmonic combinations.—Works: Operas: *Mörder, Hoffnung der Frauen,* one act, op. 12 (Stuttgart, June 4, 1921); *Das Nusch-Nuschi,* marionette opera, op. 20 (Stuttgart, June 4, 1921; revised version, Königsberg, Jan. 22, 1931); *Sancta Susanna,* one act, op. 21 (Frankfurt, March 26, 1922); *Cardillac* (Dresden, Nov. 9, 1926; revised version, Zürich, June 20, 1952); *Hin und Zurück,* op. 45a (Baden-Baden, July 15, 1927); *Neues vom Tage* (Berlin, June 8, 1929; revised version, Naples, April 7, 1954, composer conducting); *Wir bauen eine Stadt,* children's opera (Berlin, June 21, 1930);

Mathis der Maler (Zürich, May 28, 1938); *Die Harmonie der Welt* (Munich, Aug. 11, 1957; composer conducting). *Tuttifäntchen,* incidental music for a Christmas fairy-tale (1922). Ballets: *Der Dämon,* a pantomime (1922); *Triadisches Ballet* (1926-27); *Nobilissima Visione* (performed under the title *St. Francis* by the Ballet Russe de Monte Carlo in London, July 21, 1938); *Der Ploner Musiktag,* a pantomime (1932). Orchestral works: cello concerto op. 3; *Lustige Sinfonietta,* op. 4; piano concerto, op. 29 (1924); concerto for orch. with oboe, bassoon, and violin soli, op. 38 (Duisburg, July 25, 1925); *Konzertmusik,* for brass and strings (for 50th anniversary of the Boston Symph. Orch.; perf. there, April 3, 1931); *Philharmonisches Konzert* (Berlin Philh., April 15, 1932); *Der Schwanendreher,* for viola solo and orch. (Amsterdam, Nov. 14, 1935, Hindemith soloist); *Trauermusik,* for solo viola and string orch. (written for a memorial service for King George V; London, Jan. 22, 1936, Hindemith soloist); *Symphonic Dances* (London, Dec. 5, 1937); violin concerto (Amsterdam, March 14, 1940); cello concerto (Boston, Feb. 7, 1941, Piatigorsky soloist); *Symphony in E flat* (Minneapolis, Nov. 21, 1941); *Cupid and Psyche,* overture for a ballet (Philadelphia, Oct. 29, 1943); *Symphonic Metamorphosis on Themes by Weber* (N. Y., Jan. 20, 1944); *The Four Temperaments,* theme with 4 variations for piano and strings (Boston, Sept. 3, 1944); *Hérodiade,* for chamber orch. (1944); *Symphonia Serena* (Dallas, Feb. 1, 1947); piano concerto (Cleveland, Feb. 27, 1947); clarinet concerto (1947); concerto for trumpet, bassoon, and string orch. (1948; 2nd version, 1953); Sinfonietta (Louisville, March 1, 1950, composer conducting); concerto for horn and orch. (Baden-Baden, June 8, 1950); *Harmonie der Welt,* suite from the opera (Basel, Jan. 24, 1952). Chamber music: trio for clarinet, horn, and piano, op. 1; 1st string quartet, in C major, op. 2; piano quintet, op. 7; *3 Stücke,* for cello and piano, op. 8 (1917); 2nd string quartet, in F minor, op. 10 (1919); a set of 6 sonatas, op. 11, of which 2 are for violin and piano (1920), 1 for cello and piano (1922), 1 for viola and piano (1922), 1 for viola unaccompanied (1923), and 1 for violin unaccompanied (1923); 3d string quartet, in C major, op. 16 (1922); 4th string quartet, op. 22 (1922); *Kammermusik No. 1,* op. 24/1 (Donaueschingen Festival, July 31, 1922); *Kleine Kammermusik,* op. 24/2, for flute, oboe, clarinet, horn, and bassoon (1922); a set of 4 sonatas, op. 25: for viola alone (1923), for viola d'amore and piano (1929), for cello alone (1923), for viola and piano (1924); quintet for clarinet and string quartet, op. 30 (Salzburg Festival, Aug. 7, 1923); 2 sonatas for violin alone, op. 31/1 and 31/2 (1924); *Canonic Sonatina* for 2 flutes, op. 31/3 (1924); 5th string quartet, op. 32 (1924); 1st trio for violin, viola, and cello, op. 34 (1924); *3 Stücke,* for 5 instruments (1925); *Kammermusik No. 2,* op. 36/1, for piano and 12 instruments (Venice Festival, Sept. 3, 1925); *Kammermusik No. 3,* op. 36/2, for cello and 10 instruments (1925); *Kammermusik No. 4,* op. 36/3, for violin and small ensemble (1925); *Kammermusik No. 5,* op. 36/4, for solo viola and small ensemble (1927); *Konzertmusik* for wind instruments, op. 41 (1927; Liège Festival, Sept. 1, 1930); *Spielmusik, for* strings, flutes, and oboes, op. 43/1 (1927); *Kammermusik No. 6,* op. 46/1, for viola d'amore and chamber ensemble (1928); *Kammermusik No. 7,* op. 46/2, for organ and chamber ensemble (1928); trio for viola, heckelphone, and piano, op. 47 (1929); 14 easy duets for 2 violins (1932); 2 canonic duets for 2 violins (1932); 2nd trio for violin, viola, and cello (1934); *Meditation* for violin (or viola, or cello) and piano (1938); 3 violin sonatas (1935, 1938, 1939); flute sonata (1936); oboe sonata (1938); bassoon sonata (1938); viola sonata (1939); clarinet sonata (1939); horn sonata (1939); trumpet sonata (1939); harp sonata (1939); English horn sonata (1941); trombone sonata (1941); *Echo* for flute and piano (1942); 6th string quartet (1944); 7th string quartet (1945); *A Frog He Went A-Courting,* variations for cello and piano (1946); cello sonata (1948). Vocal works: *Melancholie,* for contralto and string quartet, op. 14 (1921); *Des Todes Tod,* op. 23/1, for soprano, 2 violas, and cello (1922); *Die junge Magd,* 6 poems, op. 23/2, for contralto, flute, clarinet, and string quartet (1922); *Die Serenaden,* little cantatas on romantic poems, op. 35, for soprano, oboe, viola, and cello (1925); *Frau Musica,* op. 45/1, for voices and instruments (1928; revised, 1944, under the title *In Praise of Music*); *8 Canons* for 2 voices and instruments, op. 45/2 (1928); *Martinslied,* op. 45/3, for voice and instruments (1931); *Das Unaufhörliche,* oratorio (Berlin, Nov. 21, 1931); *When Lilacs Last in the Dooryard Bloom'd,* an American requiem after Walt Whitman, for chorus and orch. (N. Y., May 14, 1946); *Apparebit Repentina Dies,* for chorus and brass (Harvard Symposium, Cambridge, Mass., May 2, 1947);

The Demon of the Gibbet, for chorus a cappella (1949); *Cantique de l'Espérance,* for mezzo soprano, chorus, and 2 orchestras (1952); *6 Chansons* for mixed voices (1939); 5 songs on old texts for mixed voices (1943). For voice and piano: *3 Hymnen,* after Walt Whitman, op. 13; 8 songs for soprano, op. 18 (1922); *Das Marienleben,* a cycle of songs after Rilke, op. 27 (Donaueschingen, June 17, 1923; revised radically, and perf., Hanover, Nov. 3, 1948); 9 English songs (1944); *Bal des pendus* (1946). For piano: 7 waltzes, op. 5, four hands; *In einer Nacht,* op. 15, a set of 15 piano pieces (1922); piano sonata, op. 17 (1917); *Tanzstücke,* op. 19 (1922); *1922 Suite,* op. 26 (1922); *Klaviermusik,* op. 37 (1927); *Übung in drei Stücken,* op. 37/1 (1925); *Reihe kleiner Stücke,* op. 37/2 (1927); 3 sonatas (1936); sonata for 2 pianos (1942); *Ludus Tonalis,* for piano solo (Chicago, Feb. 15, 1943).—Books: *Unterweisung im Tonsatz* (2 vols., 1937, 1939; in English as *The Craft of Musical Composition,* N. Y., 1941; revised, 1945); *A Concentrated Course in Traditional Harmony* (2 vols., N. Y., 1943, 1953); *Elementary Training for Musicians* (N. Y., 1946); *J. S. Bach: Heritage and Obligation* (New Haven, 1952; German ed., *J. S. Bach: ein verpflichtendes Erbe,* Wiesbaden, 1953); *A Composer's World: Horizons and Limitations* (Cambridge, Mass., 1952). — Bibliography: Franz Willms, *Paul Hindemith,* in 'Von neuer Musik' (Cologne, 1925); W. Altmann, *Paul Hindemith* (ibid.); Hans Kleemann, *Das Kompositionsprinzip Paul Hindemiths,* in the 'Gedenkschrift für Hermann Abert' (Halle, 1928); Edwin Evans, *Hindemith,* in Cobbett's 'Cyclopedic Survey of Chamber Music' (1929); A. Machabey, *Paul Hindemith, musicien allemand,* in 'Revue Musicale' (1930); Willi Reich, *Paul Hindemith,* in the 'Mus. Quarterly' (Oct., 1931); Paul Rosenfeld, *Neo-Classicism and Hindemith,* in *Discoveries of a Music Critic* (N. Y., 1936); H. H. Stuckenschmidt, *Hindemith Today,* in 'Modern Music' (1937); Frani B. Muser, *The Recent Works of Paul Hindemith,* in the 'Mus. Quarterly' (Jan., 1944); N. Cazden, *Hindemith and Nature,* in the 'Music Review' (Nov. 1954); R. Stephan, *Hindemith's Marienleben, an Assessment of its Two Versions,* in the 'Music Review' (Nov., 1954). The basic biography is that of Heinrich Strobel, *Paul Hindemith* (Mainz, 1928; 2nd enlarged ed., 1931; 3rd amplified ed., 1948). Kurt Stone compiled (for the Associated Music Publishers, N. Y., 1954) a catalogue of Hindemith's works, verified by the composer. A pictorial biography, *Paul Hindemith, Zeugnis in Bildern,* was brought out by Schott (Mainz, 1955).

Hindle, John, English composer; b. London, 1761; d. there, 1796. He was mainly known as a composer of glees, one of which, *Queen of the Silver Bow,* became extremely popular.

Hine, William, English composer and organist; b. Brightwell, 1687; d. Gloucester, Aug. 28, 1730. He studied with Jeremiah Clarke; then served as organist at Gloucester Cathedral. A collection of his anthems under the title *Harmonia sacra Glocestriensis* was published posthumously by his widow.

Hingston, John, English composer and organist; date of birth unknown; d. London, Dec. (buried Dec. 16), 1683. He studied with Orlando Gibbons; was in the service of Oliver Cromwell and taught music to his daughter. After the Restoration, he was engaged as Keeper of the Organs at the Court. Six vols. of his works are preserved in Oxford.

Hinrichs, Gustav, conductor; b. Ludwigslust, Germany, Dec. 10, 1850; d. Mountain Lake, N. J., March 26, 1942. He studied violin and piano with his father; composition with E. Marxsen in Hamburg. In 1870 he settled in America; was in San Francisco until 1885; then went to Philadelphia, where he organized his own opera company; gave the American premières of *Cavalleria Rusticana* (Philadelphia, Sept. 9, 1891) and *Pagliacci* (N. Y., June 15, 1893). From 1903-08, he conducted at the Metropolitan Opera House; then retired. He was the composer of an opera, *Onti-Ora* (Indian name of Catskill Mountains; first perf. Philadelphia, July 28, 1890).

Hinrichsen, Max, music publisher; b. Leipzig, July 6, 1901. He worked with his father, Heinrich Hinrichsen (1868-1942), in Peters Edition, Leipzig, until 1937, when he went to London, becoming a British subject in 1947. There he established the Hinrichsen Edition, Ltd.; since 1944, published 'Hinrichsen's Musical Year Book.' The catalogue of his London firm includes a number of orchestral and other works by modern European composers.

Hinrichsen, Walter, music publisher; brother of Max Hinrichsen; b. Leipzig, Sept. 23, 1907. He studied at the Univ. of Leipzig; then was connected with the Peters

Edition there, headed by his father Heinrich Hinrichsen (1868-1942; see **Peters, C. F.**). In 1936 Walter Hinrichsen came to America; was in the U. S. Army (1942-45); after the war he became a government employee in the U. S. Zone in Germany (1945-47). He then returned to America and in 1948 opened new offices of the C. F. Peters Corporation in New York.

Hinshaw, William Wade, American baritone; b. Union, Iowa, Nov. 3, 1867; d. Washington, D. C., Nov. 27, 1947. He studied voice with L. G. Gottschalk in Chicago; was choir director at various churches; made his operatic début as Méphistophélès in Gounod's *Faust* with the H. W. Savage Co. (St. Louis, Nov. 6, 1899); in 1903, opened the Hinshaw School of Opera in Chicago, which was later incorporated into the Chicago Cons.; Hinshaw became president of the combined institutions (1903-07). In 1909 he organized the International Grand Opera Co. of Chicago. He made his début at the Metropolitan Opera House, N. Y., on Nov. 16, 1910; in 1912 he sang in the Wagner festival at Graz, and in 1914, in the special *Ring* festival at Berlin; then returned to America. In 1916 he offered a prize of $1000 for the best 1-act opera by an American composer (awarded to Hadley for his opera *Bianca)*. From 1920-26 he produced Mozart's operas in English with his own company in the U. S., Canada, and Cuba (about 800 performances in all). He then settled in Washington.

Hinton, Arthur, English composer; b. Beckenham, Nov. 20, 1869; d. Rottingdean, Aug. 11, 1941. He studied at the Royal Academy of Music in London; then taught violin there; subsequently went to Munich for further study with Rheinberger. There he composed a symphony, which he conducted at one of the concerts of the Munich Cons.; traveled in Italy; returned to London in 1896. He continued to compose; his second symphony was performed in London in 1903. He married the pianist Katharine Goodson, who gave many performances of his piano works, including a concerto. He wrote the children's operettas, *The Disagreeable Princess* and *St. Elizabeth's Rose;* also a number of songs.

Hipkins, Alfred James, English authority on musical instruments; b. London, June 17, 1826; d. there, June 3, 1903. He was connected with the Broadwood piano manufacturers; acquired an excellent knowledge of the piano and was Chopin's favorite tuner on his last visit to England. He himself learned to play the piano well enough to give recitals. He contributed articles to Grove's 'Dictionary of Music and Musicians' and to the 'Encyclopedia Britannica'; publ. standard works on instruments, among them, *Musical Instruments, Historic, Rare, and Unique* (Edinburgh, 1888; contains numerous colored plates; reprinted, London, 1921) and *A Description and History of the Pianoforte, and of the Older Keyboard Stringed Instruments* (London, 1896).

Hirai, Kozaburo, Japanese composer; b. Kochi, Sept. 10, 1910; studied at the Academy of Music in Tokyo. He has written a ballet, *Festival of Insects* (Tokyo, Sept. 15, 1941), and a concerto for the Japanese national instrument *koto* with orchestra (Tokyo, Nov. 12, 1950).

Hirao, Kishio, Japanese composer, b. Tokyo, July 8, 1907. He studied literature in Tokyo; then went to Paris to study music at the Schola Cantorum. He has written several works for orch.; appointed professor at the Tokyo Music Academy.

Hirsch, Paul Adolf, bibliographer and collector; b. Frankfurt, Feb. 24, 1881; d. Cambridge, England, Nov. 25, 1951. He began collecting rare musical editions as a young man, and published successive catalogues of his rapidly growing library. In 1936 he left Germany and was able to transport his entire collection to England; it was purchased by the British Museum in 1946; the total of items was about 20,000. In 1922 he began the publication of new editions (several in facsimile, and with commentaries) of rare works; these are Francesco Caza, *Tractato vulgare de canto figurato* (Milan, 1492; ed. J. Wolf, 1922); Giovanni Luca Conforto, *Breve et facile maniera d'essercitarsi a far passaggi* (Rome, 1593; ed. J. Wolf, 1922); *Neujahrsgrüsse Seelen; eine Sammlung von Liedern mit Melodien und Bilderschmuck aus den Jahren 1770-1800* (ed. M. Friedlaender, 1922); Georg Philipp Telemann, *Fantaisies pour le clavessin: 3 douzaines* (ed. Max Seiffert, 1923); Hercole Bottrigari, *Il desiderio, overo de' concerti di varii strumenti musicali* (Venice, 1594; ed. Kathi Meyer, 1924); Karl Friedrich Zelter, *Fünfzehn ausgewählte Lieder* (ed. Moritz Bauer, 1924); Giovanni Spataro, *Dilucide et probatissime demonstratione* (Bologna, 1521; ed. J. Wolf, 1925); Nicolaus Listenius, *Musica, ab authore denuo recognita* (Nuremberg, 1549; ed. Georg Schünemann, 1927); Carl

Philipp Emanuel Bach, *Zwölf zwei- und dreistimmige kleine Stücke für die Flöte oder Violine und das Klavier* (1770; ed. Richard Hohenemser, 1928); Christoph Schultze, *Lukas-Passion* (Leipzig, 1653; ed. Peter Epstein, 1930); Martin Luther, *Deutsche Messe* (1526; ed. J. Wolf, 1934); Wolfgang Amadeus Mozart, *The ten celebrated String Quartets,* first authentic edition in score (ed. Alfred Einstein, 1945).—Cf. P. H. Muir, *The Hirsch Catalogue,* in the 'Music Review' (1948); a list of editions is found in the Jan. 1951 issue of 'Music Review.'

Hirschfeld, Robert, writer on music; b. Brünn, Moravia, Sept. 17, 1857; d. Salzburg, April 2, 1914. He studied at the Universities of Breslau and Vienna; in 1884, took his degree of *Dr. phil.* at the Vienna Univ. with a dissertation on Johannes de Muris; made arrangements of several stage works by Haydn, Mozart, etc., for modern performances.

Hirt, Franz Joseph, Swiss pianist; b. Lucerne, Feb. 7, 1899. He studied with Hans Huber and Ernst Lévy at the Cons. of Basel; later, with Egon Petri and Alfred Cortot; in 1919 he became a teacher at the Cons. of Bern; gave numerous recitals in Switzerland and elsewhere in Europe; publ. *Die Entwicklung der besaiteten Tasteninstrumente* in the 'Schweizerische Musikalische Zeitung' (Feb., 1948).

Hirt, Fritz, Swiss violinist; b. Lucerne, Aug. 10, 1888. He studied in Zürich and Prague; had an extended career as concert violinist in Europe; then settled in Basel as a teacher; was a member of the Basel String Quartet.

Hlobil, Emil, Czech composer; b. Mežimostí, Oct. 11, 1901. He studied with Křička and Novák in Prague; in 1941, was appointed instructor at the Prague Cons. He wrote several works for orch. in a Romantic style. His *Symphonic Elegy* in memory of the victims of the war (1945) is notable for its expressiveness; of his chamber music, the most interesting work is his nonet (1947).

Hoboken, Anthony van, Dutch music bibliographer; b. Rotterdam, March 23, 1887. He studied with Iwan Knorr at the Hoch Cons. in Frankfurt, and with Schenker in Vienna. In 1927 he founded the Archive for Photographs of Musical Manuscripts in the National Library at Vienna. He then began to collect first and other early editions of classical works; his Haydn collection is particularly rich. Received an honorary Ph. D., Kiel University (1957). In 1957 he publ. the first vol. of his thematic catalogue of Haydn's works.

Hobrecht. See **Obrecht.**

Hochberg, Bolko von (pseudonym, J. H. Franz), German composer; b. Fürstenstein Castle, Silesia, Jan. 23, 1843; d. near Salzbrunn, Dec. 1, 1926. He established and for several years maintained the Hochberg Quartet; also founded the Silesian music festivals (1876); was general intendant of the Berlin Royal Theaters (1886-1903). His works include the operas *Claudine von Villabella* (Schwerin, 1864) and *Die Falkensteiner* (Hanover, 1876; rewritten and produced as *Der Wärwolf,* Dresden, 1881); 3 symphonies, 3 string quartets; 2 piano trios; a concerto for piano; songs and choruses.

Hoddinott, Alun, Welsh composer; b. Bargoed, Aug. 11, 1929. He studied at the Univ. College of South Wales; since 1951 on the staff of the City of Cardiff College of Music and Drama. He has written a string trio (1949); clarinet concerto (1950); quartet for clarinet, violin, viola, and cello (1954); Symphony No. 1 (1955); oboe concerto (1955); harp concerto (1957); viola concertino (1957). His music, Romantic in essence, adopts chromatic procedures, tending towards 12-tone style; his asymmetric rhythmic system is essential in his thematic writing. —See A. F. Leighton Thomas, *Alun Hoddinott,* in the 'Mus. Times' (Oct., 1955).

Hodges, Edward, English organist and composer; b. Bristol, July 20, 1796; d. Clifton, Sept. 1, 1867. He was an organist at Bristol; received his Mus. Doc. at Cambridge (1825); in 1838, went to America, where he became an organist in Toronto and then in New York (1839). He publ. *An Essay on the Cultivation of Church Music* (N. Y., 1841). The Library of Congress acquired the bulk of his music library (743 vols.), including his own works in MS, in 1919.—Cf. A. H. Messiter, *History of the Choir and Music of Trinity Church* (N. Y., 1906). His daughter, **Faustina Hasse Hodges** (d. Philadelphia, Feb. 4, 1895), was also an organist in the U. S. She composed songs and instrumental pieces and publ. a biography of her father (N. Y., 1896). His son, Rev. **John Sebastian Bach Hodges** (d. Baltimore, May 1, 1915), an accomplished organist, composed many anthems and services.

Höeberg, Georg, Danish composer, conductor, and violinist; b. Copenhagen, Dec. 27, 1872; d. Vedboek, Aug. 3, 1950. He studied at the Cons. of Copenhagen, and later in Berlin; taught at the Copenhagen Cons. from 1900 till 1914; from 1914 till 1930, was conductor at the Royal Opera; from 1915 until 1949 he appeared as guest conductor in Scandinavia and Germany. He wrote the opera *Bryllup i Katakomberne* (*The Wedding in the Catacombs;* Copenhagen, March 6, 1909); the ballet *The Paris Cathedral* (Copenhagen, Oct. 25, 1912); several pieces for violin and orch.; a symphony; choral works and songs.

Hoérée (ö-rā), **Arthur (Charles Ernest);** critic and composer; b. Saint Gilles, near Brussels, April 16, 1897. He studied at the Brussels Cons., and later at the Paris Cons. with Paul Vidal and Vincent d'Indy; remained in Paris as a music critic. He publ. monographs on Stravinsky (1928), Albert Roussel (1938), and Honegger (1951). Among his works are the ballet *La Souris blanche et la Dame de Paris,* the oratorio *Ode au Soleil,* a *Symphonie chorégraphique,* and a septet for soprano, flute, piano, and strings (his most striking work; performed at the Zürich Festival of the International Society for Contemporary Music, June 23, 1926).

Hoesick, Ferdinand, Polish musicologist; b. Warsaw, Oct. 16, 1867; d. there, April 13, 1941. He received an excellent European education; studied at the Universities of Heidelberg, Cracow, and Paris, returning to Warsaw in 1891; was editor and writer on literature; his writings on music deal exclusively with Chopin; publ. (in Polish) the basic biography, *Chopin's Life and Works* (3 vols.; Warsaw, 1910-11; 2nd ed., in 2 vols., 1926); a brief preliminary biography, *Chopin* (Warsaw, 1898); *Selection from J. Elsner's Memoirs* (Warsaw, 1901); *Chopiniana* (letters, etc.; Warsaw, 1912); *Slowacki and Chopin, Historic-Literary Parallels and Sketches* (Warsaw, 1928).

Hoesslin, Franz von, German conductor; b. Munich, Dec. 31, 1885; d. (in a plane crash over southern France) Sept. 28, 1946. He studied general subjects at the Univ. of Munich; conducting with Felix Mottl, composition with Max Reger. He held the post of conductor at the Municipal Theater of St. Gall, Switzerland (1908-11); then conducted in Riga (1912-14); was in the German army during World War I; then in Lübeck (1919-20), Mannheim (1920-22), and at the Berlin Volksoper (1922-23); general music director in Dessau (1923-26); opera conductor in Barmen-Elberfeld (1926-27); later was engaged as conductor for the Bayreuth festival; conducted opera in France and Spain. He was also a composer; wrote some orchestral works, a clarinet quintet, and choruses.

Höffding, Finn, Danish composer; b. Copenhagen, March 10, 1899. He studied in Copenhagen with Knud Jeppesen and in Vienna with J. Marx. Since 1931, he has been professor at the Copenhagen Cons. —Works: opera, *Kejserens nye Klaeder* (*The Emperor's New Clothes*), after Hans Christian Andersen (Copenhagen, Dec. 29, 1928); opera, *Kilderejsen* (1931; Copenhagen, Jan. 13, 1942); school opera, *Pasteur* (1935; Copenhagen, March 9, 1938); cantatas, *Fem Svaner* (Copenhagen, Sept. 9, 1938); *Kristoffer Columbus* (Copenhagen, March 5, 1941); 4 symphonies: *Sinfonia impetuosa* (1923), *Il Canto liberato* for coloratura soprano, chorus, and orch. (1924), Symphony No. 3 for 2 pianos and orch. (1928), *Sinfonia concertante* for small orch. (1934); symph. fantasies: *Evolution* (Copenhagen, Tivoli Garden, Sept. 5, 1940) and *Det re ganske vist* (Copenhagen, March 6, 1944; as a pantomime, Tivoli Gardens, July 1, 1948); *Vår og Höst,* for baritone and orch. (Copenhagen Radio, Jan. 24, 1946); concerto for oboe and strings (1933); 2 string quartets (1920; 1925); wind quintet (1940); oboe sonata (1944); choruses and songs.—Cf. G. Carritt, *Finn Höffding,* in the 'Monthly Musical Record' (Sept., 1953).

Höffer, Paul, German composer; b. Barmen, Dec. 21, 1895; d. Berlin, Aug. 31, 1949. He studied piano with Walter Georgii in Cologne; music theory with Abendroth; then took courses in composition with Franz Schreker in Berlin. In 1923 he became piano teacher at the Hochschule für Musik in Berlin; in 1948, was appointed director. In his compositions he adopted a fairly radical idiom, making free use of the modern techniques of polytonality and atonality. However, most of his works preserve the formal unity of the Romantic school; the influence of his teacher Schreker is discernible. He wrote the operas *Borgia* (1931) and *Der Falsche Waldemar* (1934); the oratorios *Der reiche Tag* (1938), *Von edlen Leben* (1941), and *Mysterium der Liebe* (1942); *Sinfonie der grossen Stadt* (1937); piano concerto (1939); oboe concerto (1946); 3 string quartets; clarinet quintet;

wind sextet. —Cf. Karl Laux, *Musik und Musiker der Gegenwart* (pp. 127-35; Essen, 1949).

Hoffman, Richard, pianist and composer; b. Manchester, England, May 24, 1831; d. New York, Aug. 17, 1909. He received his first instruction from his father and then studied with Leopold de Meyer, Pleyel, Moscheles, Rubinstein, Döhler, and Liszt. He came to New York in 1847; traveled with Jenny Lind on her American tour (1850-52) as joint artist; appeared as soloist with Hans von Bülow in N. Y. (1875). He was a prolific composer, mainly of salon music for piano; wrote about 100 opus numbers; also about 100 songs; anthems, etc. He wrote *Some Musical Recollections of Fifty Years* (with biographical sketch by his wife; posthumous, 1910).

Hoffmann, Ernst Theodor Amadeus (his third Christian name was Wilhelm, but he replaced it by Amadeus from love of Mozart), famous German writer, who was also a composer; b. Königsberg, Jan. 24, 1776; d. Berlin, June 25, 1822. He was a student of law, and served as assessor at Poznan; also studied music with the organist Podbielski. He acquired considerable proficiency in music; served as music director at the theater in Bamberg; then conducted opera performances in Leipzig and Dresden (1813-14). In 1814 he settled in Berlin, where he remained. He used the pen-name of Kapellmeister Johannes Kreisler (subsequently made famous in Schumann's *Kreisleriana*); his series of articles in the 'Allgemeine Musikalische Zeitung' under that name were reprinted as *Phantasiestücke in Callot's Manier* (1814). As a writer of fantastic tales, he made a profound impression on his period, and influenced the entire Romantic school of literature; indirectly, he was also a formative factor in the evolution of the German school of composition. His own compositions are passable from the technical viewpoint, but strangely enough, for a man of his imaginative power, they lack the inventiveness that characterize his literary productions. If his music is occasionally performed, it is only as a curiosity. He wrote a number of operas: *Die Maske* (1799), *Scherz, List und Rache* (Poznan, 1808), *Der Renegat* (Plozk, 1803), *Faustine* (Plozk, 1804), *Die ungeladenen Gäste, oder der Canonicus von Mailand* (Warsaw, 1805), *Lustige Musikanten* (Warsaw, 1805), *Liebe aus Eifersucht* (Warsaw, 1807), *Der Trank der Unsterblichkeit* (Bamberg, 1808), *Das Gespenst* (Warsaw, 1809), *Aurora* (performance planned in Bamberg, 1811, when Hoffmann conducted the theater there, but production failed to materialize; the opera was revised by L. Böttcher, and produced in a new version in Bamberg, Nov. 5, 1933), *Undine* (Berlin, Aug. 3, 1816; his best work; vocal score edited by Hans Pfitzner, 1907), *Julius Sabinus* (unfinished); also a ballet, *Harlekin;* some sacred works; a symphony; a piano trio; 4 piano sonatas. Two vols. of Hoffmann's collected musical works were publ. in 1922-23, edited by Gustav Becking. His writings on music were publ. separately by Hans von Ende (Cologne, 1896). There is a large literature on Hoffmann as a writer; books and articles on Hoffmann as a musician include E. Istel, *E. T. A. Hoffmann als Musikschriftsteller,* in the 'Neue Zeitschrift für Musik' (1903); Hans von Müller, *Das Kreislerbuch* (Leipzig, 1903); Hans von Wolzogen, *E. T. A. Hoffmann und R. Wagner* (Berlin, 1906); E. Kroll, *E. T. A. Hoffmanns musikalische Anschauungen* (Königsberg, 1909); Hans Ehinger, *E. T. A. Hoffmann als Musiker und Musik-Schriftsteller* (Cologne, 1954).

Hoffmann, Hans, German musicologist; b. Neustadt, Silesia, Jan. 26, 1902. He studied at the Universities of Leipzig and Berlin; received his Ph. D. at Kiel; then taught at Kiel Univ. (1925-30); later at Halle (1930-33); also conducted concerts in Bielefeld (1933-36). He is the author of the books, *Heinrich Schütz und J. S. Bach* (Kassel, 1940) and *Zeitgenössische Kirchenmusik* (Neuwied, 1947).

Hoffmann, Heinrich August (called **Hoffmann von Fallersleben**), distinguished German writer; b. Fallersleben, Hanover, April 2, 1798; d. at Castle Korvei, Jan. 29, 1874. He received his education at the Univ. of Göttingen; in 1835 he was appointed prof. at Breslau Univ. For some years (1842-48) he was not allowed to teach or reside in Prussia, on account of his dissenting political views; after 1848 he was librarian to Prince Lippe at Korvei. He wrote several important books dealing with music, *Geschichte des deutschen Kirchenlieds* (1832; 2nd ed., 1854); *Schlesische Volkslieder mit Melodien* (1842); etc., but his chief claim to fame is the text of *Deutschland, Deutschland, über alles,* which he wrote to Haydn's *Emperor's Hymn.*

Hoffmeister, Franz Anton, German composer and publisher; b. Rottenburg, May 12, 1754; d. Vienna, Feb. 9, 1812. He went to Vienna as a law student, but became greatly interested in music, and in 1783, established his publishing firm, of historic significance owing to its publications of Mozart and Beethoven. In 1800 he went to Leipzig, where he organized (with Kühnel) a 'Bureau de Musique,' which eventually became incorporated into the celebrated firm of C. F. Peters. In 1805 he returned to Vienna, where he devoted himself mostly to composition. Amazingly prolific, he composed 9 operas, 66 symphonies and overtures, 42 string quartets, 5 piano quartets, 11 piano trios, 18 string trios, 12 piano sonatas; in addition to these he wrote a very great number of compositions for flute with various instruments. Hoffmeister's craftsmanship was of sufficient excellence to lead to confusion of his music with Haydn's. Regarding this, see E. F. Schmid, *F. A. Hoffmeister und die 'Göttweiger Sonaten'* in the 'Zeitschrift für Musik' (1937).

Hofhaimer (Hofheimer), Paul, celebrated organist and composer; b. Radstadt, Jan. 25, 1459; d. Salzburg, 1537. Cuspinianus and Luscinius both wrote of him as an unrivalled organist and lutenist. He was greatly appreciated at the various courts where he served. He was court organist to the Archduke Sigismund of Tyrol from 1480, residing at Innsbruck, and from 1490, at the court of the Emperor Maximilian I there. He was ennobled by the Emperor in 1515, when he played in St. Stephen's Cathedral in Vienna; he was also made Knight of the Golden Spur by King Ladislas of Hungary. Little of his organ music survives; some is preserved in the Berlin State Library. Extant works comprise *Harmoniae poeticae* (odes of Horace set for 4 voices; 35 by Hofhaimer and 9 by Senfl, Nuremberg, 1539; repub. by Achtleitner, 1868); 4-part German songs in contemporary collections (5 in Oeglin's *Liederbuch,* 1512; others in Forster's *Liederbuch,* 1539; etc. —Cf. H. J. Moser, *Paul Hofhaimer* (Stuttgart, 1929), containing transcriptions of Hofhaimer's surviving works.

Hofmann, Casimir, Polish pianist; father of Josef Hofmann; b. Cracow, 1842; d. Berlin, July 6, 1911. He studied at the Vienna Cons.; then conducted opera in Cracow. In 1878 he moved to Warsaw, where he taught and conducted. After the spectacular success of his young son, he followed him on his extended tours throughout Europe and America. From 1886, he lived mainly in Berlin. He wrote numerous works in various genres.

Hofmann, Heinrich (Karl Johann), German pianist and composer; b. Berlin, Jan. 13, 1842; d. Gross-Tabarz, Thuringia, July 16, 1902. He studied in Berlin with Grell, Dehn, and Wüerst. He became a concert pianist, then turned to composition. Exceptionally productive, he wrote a great deal of operatic, symphonic, and chamber music, choral works and solo piano pieces, all of which were published and frequently performed. His popularity declined precipitously towards the end of his life; his music vanished from concert programs after his death. His style reflected Wagnerian procedures, particularly in heroic moods; he possessed complete mastery of technique, but his music lacked originality or distinction. Hofmann wrote the following stage works: comic opera *Cartouche* (Berlin, 1869); heroic drama *Armin* (Dresden, Oct. 14, 1877); pastoral opera *Aennchen von Tharau* (Hamburg, Nov. 6, 1878); historic opera *Wilhelm von Oranien* (1882), and the comic opera *Donna Diana* (Berlin, Nov. 15, 1886). His *Frithjof Symphony* (1874) was enormously popular, having had 43 performances during the 1874-75 season in German cities alone; it was also performed in England and America. Similarly successful was his orchestral *Hungarian Suite* (1873). He also wrote a great number of choral works and songs; characteristic piano pieces; chamber music.

Hofmann, Josef, celebrated pianist; b. Podgorze, near Cracow, Jan. 20, 1876; d. Los Angeles, Feb. 16, 1957. He was the son of the pianist Casimir Hofmann; his mother was a professional opera singer. At the age of 4 he began to play the piano, tutored by an older sister and an aunt; at 5, his father began giving him regular lessons. He was barely 6 when he first appeared in public in Ciechocinek; at the age of 10 he played Beethoven's Concerto No. 1 with the Berlin Philharmonic, under Hans von Bülow. He also made a tour of Scandinavia; played in France and England; his concerts as a child prodigy became a European sensation; soon an American offer of a concert tour came from the impresarios Abbey, Schoeffel & Grau. On Nov. 29, 1887, Hofmann appeared at the Metropolitan Opera House, as a soloist in Beethoven's Concerto No. 1, with an orchestra conducted by Adolf Neuendorff, and played works by Chopin and some of his own little pieces. He electrified the audience, and hard-headed critics hailed his performance as a marvel. He appeared throughout the United States, giving 42 concerts in all; then agitation was started by the Society for the Prevention of Cruelty to Children against the exploitation of his talent. Alfred Corning Clark of N. Y. offered $50,000 to the family for his continued education. The offer was accepted, and young Hofmann began serious study with Moszkowski (piano) and Urban (composition) in Berlin. Then Anton Rubinstein accepted him as a pupil in Dresden, where Hofmann traveled twice a week for piano lessons. At the age of 18 he resumed his career, giving recitals in Dresden and elsewhere in Germany with enormous success; made his first tour of Russia in 1896, attaining huge popularity there; he reappeared in Russia frequently. In 1898 he again played in the U. S.; from then on, he appeared in American cities almost every year. At the peak of his career, he came to be regarded as one of the greatest pianists of the century. He possessed the secret of the singing tone, which enabled him to interpret Chopin with extraordinary delicacy and intimacy. He was also capable of summoning tremendous power playing Liszt and other works of the virtuoso school. His technique knew no difficulties; but in his interpretations, he subordinated technical effects to the larger design of the work. When the Curtis Institute of Music was founded in Philadelphia (1924), Hofmann was engaged to head the piano department; from 1926-38 he was director of the Curtis Institute. On Nov. 28, 1937, his golden jubilee in the U. S. was celebrated with a concert at the Metropolitan Opera House, where he had first played as a child 50 years before. He performed the D minor concerto of Anton Rubinstein, and his own *Chromaticon,* for piano and orch. From 1938 to his death he lived mostly in California. He became an American citizen in 1926. Hofmann was also a composer, under the pen-name Michel Dvorsky (literal translation into Polish of his German name, meaning 'courtyard man'). Among his works are several piano concertos; some symph. works; *Chromaticon,* for piano and orch. (first played by him with the Cincinnati Symph. Orch., Nov. 24, 1916); numerous piano pieces. He publ. a practical manual, *Piano-Playing with Piano-Questions Answered* (1915).

Hofmann, Ludwig, German baritone; b. Frankfurt, Jan. 14, 1895. He studied voice in Milan; was engaged at various German opera houses (1919-27); member of the Berlin State Opera (1928-32). He made his début with the Metropolitan Opera Co., N. Y., on Nov. 24, 1932, as Hagen, in *Die Götterdämmerung;* returned to Europe in 1939;. also appeared in South America. In 1949 he joined the staff of the Vienna Opera.

Hofmann, Richard, German violinist; b. Delitzsch, April 30, 1844; d. Leipzig, Nov. 13, 1918. He studied with Dreyschock and Jadassohn in Leipzig; later settled there as music teacher. He publ. instructive pieces for various instruments, and a valuable manual *Praktische Instrumentationsschule* (Leipzig, 1893; 3rd ed., 1907; in English, 1898); *Katechismus der Musikinstrumente* (many editions); *Neuer Führer durch die Violin- und Viola-Litteratur* (1909); *Die F-Trompete im 2. Brandenburgischen Konzert von J. S. Bach,* in the 'Bach-Jahrbuch' (1916).

Hofmeister, Friedrich, German music publisher; b. Strehlen, Jan. 24, 1782; d. Reudnitz, near Leipzig, Sept. 30, 1864. In 1807 he established in Leipzig the music firm that bears his name; beginning in 1829, he publ. a valuable monthly catalogue, the 'Musikalisch-litterarischer Monatsbericht.' His son and successor, **Adolf Hofmeister** (b. c. 1818; d. Leipzig, May 26, 1870), publ. a 3rd and enlarged ed. of Whistling's *Handbuch der musikalischen Litteratur* (1845), with supplementary vols. filled from issues of Hofmeister's 'Monatsbericht.' After 1852, the 12 'Monatsberichte' for each complete year were arranged in alphabetical order and issued as a 'Jahresbericht.' All these valuable editions were continued by the firm under the proprietorship of Albert Röthing (b. Leipzig, Jan. 4, 1845; d. there, Aug. 11, 1907). In 1905 Karl Günther became the head of the firm; he was succeeded by Karl Ganzenmüller. In 1935 the firm acquired the catalogue of Merseburger (Leipzig); after World War II the firm had offices both in Frankfurt and Leipzig.

Hogarth, George, Scottish writer on music; b. Carfrae Mill, near Oxton, Berwickshire, 1783; d. London, Feb. 12, 1870. He was a practicing lawyer in Edinburgh, and an amateur musician. He settled in London in 1830; contributed articles to the 'Harmonicon'; also wrote reviews for the 'Morning Chronicle.' His daughter married Charles Dickens in 1836; when Dickens became editor of the 'Daily News' (1846), Hogarth began writing music criticisms for it; also wrote for other papers. From 1850-64 he was secretary to the Philharmonic Society of London. He publ. the following books:

Musical History, Biography, and Criticism (1835); *Memoirs of the Musical Drama* (1838; 2nd ed., 1851, as *Memoirs of the Opera*); *The Birmingham Festival* (1855); *The Philharmonic Society of London* (1862), and *The Life of Beethoven.*

Hoiby, Lee, American composer; b. Madison, Wisconsin, Feb. 17, 1926. He received his B. M. in Madison in 1947; then studied piano with Egon Petri at Mills College, where he received his M. A. in 1952; studied with Menotti at the Curtis Institute (1948-52); in Rome and Salzburg (1952). —Works: Toccata for piano (1950); *Noctambulation,* for orch. (N. Y., Oct. 4, 1952); *Hearts, Meadows & Flags,* for orch. (Rochester, Nov. 6, 1952); *Pastoral Dances,* for flute and orch. (New Orleans, Nov. 6, 1956); *The Witch,* opera in one act (1956); incidental music to *The Duchess of Malfi* (N. Y., March 19, 1957); violin sonata (1952); 5 preludes for piano (1952); *Design for Strings* (1949-53); *Diversions,* 4 pieces for woodwind quintet (1954); *Songs of the Fool,* for mixed chorus (1956). In 1957 he received an award of $1,000 from the National Institute of Arts and Letters.

Hol, Richard, Dutch composer, conductor, pianist, and organist; b. Amsterdam, July 23, 1825; d. Utrecht, May 14, 1904. He studied organ with Martens and theory with Bertelmann. After traveling in Germany, he taught music in Amsterdam; in 1862, became city music director at Utrecht, succeeding Kufferath; then cathedral organist (1869) and director of the School of Music (1875); conducted concerts in The Hague and Amsterdam. A prolific composer, he wrote the operas *Floris V* (Amsterdam, April 9, 1892), *Uit de branding* (Amsterdam, 1894), and *De schoone schaapster;* the oratorio *David* (1880), 4 symphonies, choral and orchestral works, chamber music, and songs. From 1886-1900 he was editor of 'Het Orgel'; wrote a monograph on Sweelinck (1860). — Cf. H. Nolthenius, *Richard Hol, Levensschets* (Haarlem, 1904).

Holbrooke, Josef, English composer; b. Croydon, July 5, 1878. He received his primary education from his father; then studied at the Royal Academy of Music in London with F. Corder; received the Sterndale Bennett Scholarship. After graduation (1898), he went on a tour with A. Lloyd; conducted ballet and various summer orchestras. Although he composed prolifically, and had many ardent admirers of his music, he never succeeded in establishing himself as a representative British composer. Perhaps this was owing to the fact that he stood aloof from modernistic developments of European music, and preferred to write for a mass audience, which, however, failed to materialize at the infrequent performances of his music.—Works: Operas: *Pierrot and Pierrette* (London, Nov. 11, 1909); a trilogy (his main dramatic work: *The Cauldron of Anwyn:* I. *The Children of Don* (London, June 15, 1912), II. *Dylan, Son of the Wave* (London, July 4, 1913), III. *Bronwen, Daughter of Llyr* (Huddersfield, Feb. 1, 1929); *The Enchanter* (Chicago, 1915); *The Snob,* 1-act comic opera. Ballets: *The Red Masque, The Moth, The Enchanted Garden.* Orchestral works: symph. poems, *The Raven* (London, 1900); *The Viking; Ulalume* (1904); *Byron,* with chorus; *Queen Mab,* with chorus (Leeds Festival, 1904); *Homage to E. A. Poe,* with chorus; *The Bells,* with chorus (Birmingham, 1906); *The Skeleton in Armor; The Masque of the Red Death;* 5 symphonies; variations on *Three Blind Mice, The Girl I Left Behind Me,* and *Auld Lang Syne; Dreamland Suite; Les Hommages,* suite; *The Haunted Palace,* fantasy; *The New Renaissance,* overture. Chamber music: 5 string quartets; 4 string sextets; 3 violin sonatas; 2 piano quartets; 2 clarinet quintets; a piano quintet; a trio for violin, horn, and piano. He wrote many piano pieces, songs, and clarinet pieces; also, a book, *Contemporary British Composers* (1925). — Cf. George Lowe, *Josef Holbrooke and His Work* (1920); also a symposium, *Josef Holbrooke: Various Appreciations by many Authors* (London, 1937).

Holde, Artur, German music critic; b. Randzburg, Oct. 16, 1885. He studied at Berlin Univ. with Max Friedlaender and Hermann Kretzschmar. From 1910-36 he was conductor at the Frankfurt Synagogue, and at the same time was active as music critic for various Frankfurt publications. In 1937 he came to the U. S.; was choirmaster at the Hebrew Tabernacle in New York City (1937-43) and music critic of the German publication 'Aufbau' in New York; has contributed articles to the 'Mus. Quarterly' and other publications.

Holden, Oliver, American musician, carpenter, and minister; b. Shirley, Mass., Sept. 18, 1765; d. Charlestown, Mass., Sept. 4, 1844. After serving as a marine in the navy, he settled in Charlestown in 1787 and was active there as a justice of the peace and carpenter; then abandoned carpentry and established a music store (about 1790);

also offered music lessons; officiated as preacher of the Puritan Church; served as Charlestown Representative in the State House of Representatives (1818-33). He composed psalm tunes and odes; at least 21 hymns are known to be of his authorship, his best being *Coronation* (set to the words *All Hail the Power of Jesus' Name*), first published in vol. I of his *Union Harmony* (1793); it has retained its popularity until modern times. His *From Vernon's mount behold the hero rise,* one of the many works written in commemoration of George Washington's death, was sung at the Old South Meeting House, Boston, in Jan., 1800. Other publications are *The American Harmony* (1792), *The Massachusetts Compiler* (1795; with H. Gram and S. Holyoke), *The Worcester Collection* (1797; ed. and revised by Holden), *Sacred Dirges, Hymns and Anthems* (1800), *Modern Collection of Sacred Music* (1800), *Plain Psalmody* (1800), *Charlestown Collection of Sacred Songs* (1803), *Vocal Companion* (1807), and *Occasional Pieces.*—Cf. F. J. Metcalf, *American Psalmody* (1917); F. J. Metcalf, *American Writers and Compilers of Sacred Music* (1925); 'Dictionary of American Biography' IX (1932); J. T. Howard, *Our American Music* (N. Y., 1939).

Holguín, Guillermo. See **Uribe-Holguín.**

Hollaender, Alexis, German pianist; b. Ratibor, Silesia, Feb. 25, 1840; d. Berlin, Feb. 5, 1924. He studied at the Berlin Royal Academy with Grell and others; became instructor at Kullak's Academy (1861); conducted choral groups (1864) and the 'Cäcilienverein' (1870). He composed piano works, choruses, songs, etc.; publ. an instructive edition of Schumann's piano music and *Methodische Übungen fürs Halten einer tieferen Stimme.*

Hollaender, Gustav, German violinist; b. Leobschütz, Silesia, Feb. 15, 1855; d. Berlin, Dec. 4, 1915. He was taught the violin by his father, appeared in public at an early age; then studied at the Leipzig Cons. with Ferdinand David, and in Berlin with Joachim. At the age of 20 he embarked on a concert career; gave concerts of chamber music with Scharwenka and Grünfeld in Berlin (1878-81); in 1881 he was appointed teacher at the Cologne Cons.; in 1894 became director of the Stern Cons. in Berlin, which post he filled with distinction until his death. He wrote numerous pieces for violin, in an effective virtuoso style.

Hollaender, Viktor (pen-name, Arricha del Tolveno), German composer; brother of Gustav Hollaender; b. Leobschütz, April 20, 1866; d. Hollywood, Oct. 24, 1940. He studied with Kullak; was theater conductor in Berlin for a number of years; also theater conductor in London. He lived mostly in Berlin until 1933, when he went to America and settled in Los Angeles. His works include the light operas *San Lin, Trilby, The Bey of Morocco, Schwan von Siam, Die dumme Liebe, Der rote Kosak, Der Regimentspapa,* etc.; songs and piano pieces. His pantomime *Sumurun* was produced by Max Reinhardt.

Holland, Theodore, English composer; b. London, April 25, 1878; d. there, Oct. 29, 1947. He studied with Frederick Corder at the Royal Academy of Music and with Joachim at the Hochschule für Musik in Berlin. In 1927 he became prof. of composition at the Royal Academy of Music. Although his career was mainly that of a teacher, he was an estimable composer, particularly proficient in writing for the theater. Among his works is a children's operetta, *King Goldemar;* a musical play, *Santa Claus; Evening on a Lake,* for chamber orch. (1924); *Cortège* for an ensemble of cellos (1939); *Spring Sinfonietta* (1943); 2 string quartets; 2 piano trios; suite for viola and piano; and several song cycles.

Holle, Hugo, German writer on music; b. Mehlis, Thuringia, Jan. 25, 1890; d. Stuttgart, Dec. 12, 1942. He was a pupil of Max Reger; 1919-21, director of the Heilbronn Cons.; 1921-25, editor of the 'Neue Musikzeitung' in Stuttgart; since 1925 teacher of music theory at the Hochschule für Musik, Stuttgart; conductor of the famous 'Holle's Madrigal Choir,' with which he toured Central Europe; member of the Board of the Max Reger Society; co-editor of the 'Musikalische Volksbücher.' — Writings: *Goethes Lyrik in Weisen deutscher Tonsetzer bis zur Gegenwart* (1914); *Die Chorwerke Max Regers* (Munich, 1922); and numerous articles in music periodicals. He revised Storck's *Mozartbiographie* in 1923, and has edited old choral music for the Schott publ. firm (*Die hohen Feste, Motetten alter Meister,* etc.).

Höller, Karl, German composer; b, Bamberg, July 25, 1907. He received a good musical training as a chorister at the Cathedral of Bamberg; pursued his formal studies at the Cons. of Würzburg with Zilcher; later took courses in Munich with Joseph

Haas. He taught at Hoch's Cons. in Frankfurt (1937-45). After the end of the war he was appointed professor at the Musikhochschule in Munich.—Works: *Kammerkonzert* for harpsichord and chamber orch. (1935); 2 violin concertos (1938; 1952); 2 cello concertos (1941; 1950); a symphony (1952); 6 string quartets; piano trio; 8 violin sonatas; cello sonata; many works for organ; choral works; piano pieces.

Hollingsworth, John, English conductor; b. Enfield, Middlesex, March 20, 1916. He studied flute and violin at Bradfield College; then enrolled at the Guildhall School of Music in London. In 1940-41 he conducted a band of the Royal Air Force; after the war, director of a film studio orch.; from 1950, ballet conductor at Covent Garden.

Hollingsworth, Stanley, American composer; b. Berkeley, Calif., Aug. 27, 1924. He studied at the State College in San José, Cal.; then with Darius Milhaud at Mills College and with Gian Carlo Menotti at the Curtis Institute of Music in Philadelphia. He was then in Rome, at the American Academy (1955-56). As a composer, he follows the principles of practical modernism; in this respect he emulates Menotti. Among his works are *Dumbarton Oaks Mass* for chorus and string orch.; sonata for oboe and piano; opera *The Mother,* after Andersen (1954); quintet for harp and woodwind instruments; a television opera *La Grande Bretèche,* after Balzac (NBC production, Feb. 10, 1957); and *Stabat Mater* for chorus and orch. (San José, May 1, 1957). In some works, he has used the pseudonym Stanley Hollier.

Hollins, Alfred, blind English pianist; b. Hull, Sept. 11, 1865; d. Edinburgh, May 17, 1942. He studied piano at several schools for the blind; then studied with Hans von Bülow in Berlin. In 1886 he made a tour of the U. S. playing in an ensemble with other blind musicians; in 1888, appeared in America once more, as soloist with several orchestras. Returning to England, he became a church organist in Edinburgh (1897-1904). Then followed tours in Australia (1904), South Africa (1907, 1909, and 1916), and the U. S. (1925). He also composed some music. He publ. an autobiography, *A Blind Musician Looks Back* (London, 1936).

Hollmann, Joseph, cellist; b. Maestricht, Holland, Oct. 16, 1852; d. Paris, Jan. 1, 1927. He studied with Servais at the Brussels Cons., winning first prize (1870); then at the Paris Cons. with Jacquard; played many concerts in Europe and America; lived mostly in Paris. Saint-Saëns wrote his 2nd cello concerto for Hollmann.

Holmboe, Vagn, Danish composer; b. Horsens, Dec. 20, 1909. He was a pupil at the Copenhagen Cons. (1926-29), taking courses with Jeppesen; later studied in Berlin with Ernst Toch. A highly prolific composer, he has written 8 symphonies (1935-53); 12 chamber concertos for various instruments (1939-50); 2 violin sonatas; a wind quintet; a musical play, *Fanden og Borgmesteren* (1940); and a ballet, *Den galsindede Tyrk* (1944).

Holmes, Alfred, violinist; b. London, Nov. 9, 1837; d. Paris, March 4, 1876. His only teacher was his father, an amateur violinist; he sang at the Oratory in London as a soprano chorister; appeared as a violinist at the age of 9, playing a duet with his brother, Henry. The 2 brothers then went on a European tour, playing in Belgium, Germany, Sweden, Denmark, and Holland (1855-61). Alfred Holmes then lived in Paris (1861-64); visited Russia in 1867; then returned to Paris, making occasional visits to London. He composed several stage works; his opera *Inez de Castro* was not produced; he also wrote several programmatic symphonies, entitled *Robinhood, The Siege of Paris, Charles XII,* and *Romeo and Juliet;* also overtures, *The Cid* and *The Muses.* His brother, **Henry Holmes** (b. London, Nov. 7, 1839; d. San Francisco, Dec. 9, 1905), was also a precocious violinist; after 1865 he settled in London, where he taught at the Royal College of Music. In 1894, he went to San Francisco, where he remained until his death. He wrote 4 symphonies, 2 cantatas, and a violin concerto (London, Dec. 11, 1875); also some chamber music.

Holmès, Augusta (Mary Anne), French composer; b. Paris (of Irish parents), Dec. 16, 1847; d. there, Jan. 28, 1903. She progressed very rapidly as a child pianist, and gave public concerts; also composed songs under the pen-name Hermann Zenta. She studied harmony with H. Lambert, an organist; later became a pupil of César Franck. She then began to compose works in large forms, arousing considerable attention, mixed with curiosity, for she was undoubtedly one of the very few professional women composers of the time. Her music, impartially considered, lacks individuality or strength; at best, it represents a conventional by-product of French Romanticism, with an admixture of fashionable exotic elements. — Works: operas: *La Montagne noire* (Paris Opéra, Feb. 8, 1895), *Héro et Léandre, Astarte, Lancelot du lac;* for orch.: *Andante pastoral* (Paris, Jan. 14, 1877); *Lutèce* (Angers, Nov. 30, 1884); *Les Argonautes* (Paris, April 24, 1881); *Irlande* (Paris, March 2, 1882); *Ode triomphale* (Paris, March 4, 1888); *Pologne, Andromède, Hymne à Apollon,* etc.; cantatas, *La vision de la Reine; La chanson de la Caravane; La fleur de Neflier;* some piano pieces; 117 songs, some of which have remained in the active repertory of French singers. —Cf. P. Barillon-Bauché, *Augusta Holmès et la femme compositeur* (Paris, 1912); R. Pichard du Page, *Augusta Holmès; une musicienne versaillaise* (Paris, 1921).

Holmes, Edward, English pianist and author; b. London, 1797; d. there, Aug. 28, 1859. He received a fine education; was a friend of Keats at Enfield. He studied music with Vincent Novello. In 1826 he became a contributor to a literary journal, 'Atlas.' He publ. *A Ramble among the Musicians of Germany* (1828); *The Life of Mozart* (his most important work; 1845; 2nd ed., 1878); *Life of Purcell; Analytical and Thematic Index of Mozart's Piano Works;* also articles in the 'Musical Times' and other journals.

Holoubek, Ladislav, Slovak conductor and composer; b. Prague, Aug. 13, 1913. He studied with Alexander Moyzes at Bratislava and with Novák in Prague; became conductor of the Slovak National Theater at Bratislava, for which he wrote several operas: *Stella* (March 18, 1939); *Svitanie* (*Daybreak;* March 14, 1941); *Túžba* (*Desire;* Feb. 12, 1944); also composed symph. works.

Holst, Edvard; composer of light music; b. Copenhagen, 1843; d. New York, Feb. 4, 1899. He emigrated to America in 1874, and was active in New York as actor, dancing master, etc.; also wrote numerous pieces for military band (*Marine Band March, Battle of Manila,* etc.); a number of songs, and a comic opera, *Our Flats* (N. Y., 1897); in all, more than 2,000 numbers.

Holst, Gustav Theodore (real name, Gustavus Theodore von Holst; he removed the Germanic particle 'von' after 1914; before World War I, his works were published under the name Gustav von Holst), famous English composer; b. Cheltenham, Sept. 21, 1874; d. London, May 25, 1934. He was the son of a Swedish father, an able organist, and an English mother, an amateur pianist. Reared in a musical family, Holst performed on the organ and led a chorus in Wyck Rissington, Gloucestershire, at the age of 19. He then entered the Royal College of Music in London, where he studied composition with Stanford; also took up the trombone, and acquired such proficiency that he was able to earn his living as trombonist with the Carl Rosa Opera Co. and in various symphony orchestras. In 1905 he became music master at St. Paul's Girls' School; from 1907, he was music director at Morley College in London, retaining both positions until his death. From 1919 he also taught composition at the Royal College of Music. In 1923 he undertook a journey to the U. S.; lectured and performed his works at Harvard Univ. and at the Univ. of Michigan. His last years were devoted entirely to composition. In his music, he was inspired equally by exotic subjects and by English folklore; Oriental themes particularly fascinated him; he studied Hindu literature, and wrote several works reflecting Hindu legends. His most enduring work is the orchestral suite, *The Planets* (1914-16), depicted as astrological or mystical symbols. Also popular is his unassuming but effective work for string orch., *St. Paul's Suite* (1913). His daughter, Imogen Holst (b. Richmond, Surrey, April 12, 1907), compiled a detailed biography.— Works: Operas and other stage works: *Lansdown Castle,* operetta (Cheltenham, Feb. 7, 1893); *The Revoke,* op. 1 (one act; 1895); *The Youth's Choice,* op. 11 (1902); *Sita,* op. 23 (1899-1906); *Sāvitri,* chamber opera, op. 25 (after the Hindu epic *Mahabharata;* 1908; London, Dec. 5, 1916); *The Perfect Fool,* op. 39 (London, Covent Garden, May 14, 1923); *At the Boar's Head,* op. 42 (Manchester, April 3, 1925); *The Wandering Scholar,* op. 50 (1929); choral ballet, *The Morning of the Year,* op. 45a (1927); choral ballet, *The Golden Goose,* op. 45b (Liverpool, Jan. 11, 1929). Orchestral works: *Walt Whitman,* op. 7 (1899); *Cotswolds,* op. 8 (1900); symph. poem, *Indra,* op. 13 (1903); *Song of the Night,* for violin and orch., op. 19a (1905); *Marching Song* and *Country Song,* for small orch., op. 22 (1906); *Songs of the West,* op. 21a (1906), and *Somerset Rhapsody,* op. 21b (London, Queen's Hall, April 6, 1910); incidental music to *A Vision of Dame Christian,* op. 27a, and music for the Stepney Pageant, op. 27b (1909); Suite No.

1 for military band, op. 28a (1909); Oriental Suite, *Beni Mora,* op. 29a (1910; London, May 1, 1912); *Invocation,* for cello and orch., op. 19b (1911); Suite No. 2 for military band (1911); *Phantastic Suite* (1911); *St. Paul's Suite* for string orch. (1913); *The Planets,* suite for large orch. and voices, op. 32 (1914-16; London, Queen's Hall, Sept. 29, 1918); *Japanese Suite,* op. 33 (1915); *Fugal Overture,* op. 40, 1 (London, Queen's Hall, Oct. 11, 1923); *Fugal Concerto,* for flute, oboe, and strings, op. 40, 2 (London, 1923); *First Choral Symphony,* for soprano and mixed voices, op. 41 (Leeds Festival, Oct. 7, 1925); *Egdon Heath,* symph. poem (after Thomas Hardy; N. Y., Feb. 12, 1928); *Double Concerto,* for 2 violins, op. 49 (London, Queen's Hall, April 3, 1930); *Hammersmith,* prelude and scherzo, op. 52 (London, Queen's Hall, Nov. 25, 1931). Chamber music: *Fantasy Pieces* for oboe and strings, op. 2; piano quintet, op. 3 (1896); Suite in E♭, op. 10 (1900; London, April 6, 1904); woodwind quintet, op. 14 (1903). Choral and vocal works: *Clear and Cool,* for chorus and orch., op. 5 (1897); *Ornulf's Drapa,* scena for baritone and orch., op. 6 (1898); *Ave Maria,* for 8-part women's chorus, op. 9 (1900); *King Estmere,* ballade for chorus and orch., op. 17 (1903); *The Mystic Trumpeter,* for soprano and orch., op. 18 (1904); *The Cloud Messenger,* ode for chorus and orch., op. 30 (1910); *Christmas Day* (1910); 4-part songs for children; women's chorus, op. 20a (1905); 4 Carols for mixed chorus, op. 20b; *Two Eastern Pictures,* for women's chorus and harp (1911); *Hecuba's Lament,* for contralto, op. 31, No. 1 (1911); choral songs, op. 12; *Choral Hymns from the Rig-Veda,* op. 26 (1910); 2 Psalms for chorus, strings, and organ (1912); *Hymn to Dionysus,* op. 31, No. 2 (1913); *Dirge for Two Veterans,* for men's chorus and brass band (1914); part-songs for mixed chorus, op. 34 (1916); 3 Hymns for chorus and orch., op. 36a (1916); 6 Folksongs for chorus, op. 36b (1916); *Hymn of Jesus,* for 2 choruses, orch., piano, and organ, op. 37, 1 (1917); part-songs for children, op. 37, 2; *Ode to Death,* with orch., op. 38 (after Walt Whitman, 1919; Leeds Festival, 1922); choruses to *Alcestis,* for women's chorus, harp, and flutes (1920); motet, *The Evening Watch,* op. 43 (1924); *Choral Fantasia,* for soprano, chorus, organ, and orch., op. 51 (1930); 12 Welsh folksongs for mixed chorus (1930-31). Songs: op. 4, 15, 16, 35 (with violin); *The Heart Worships; Hymns from the Rig-Veda,* op. 24 (1908). For piano: Toccata on the Northumbrian pipe tune 'Newburn Lads' (1924); *Chrissemas Day in the Morning,* op. 46 (1926); *Nocturne* (1930); *Jig* (1932). — Bibliography: Louise B. M. Dyer, *Music by British Composers. No. 1: Gustav Holst* (London, 1931); E. Rubbra, *Gustav Holst* (Monaco, 1947); Imogen Holst, *Gustav Holst* (London, 1938); Imogen Holst, *The Music of Gustav Holst* (London, 1951); A. E. F. Dickinson, *Gustav Holst,* in 'The *Music Masters,'* vol. 4, ed. by A. L. Bacharach (London, 1954).

Holst, Henry, violinist; b. Copenhagen, July 25, 1899, of English parentage. He studied at the Copenhagen Cons., then with Willy Hess in Berlin; was concertmaster of the Berlin Philh. (1923-31); then taught at the Royal College of Music in Manchester (1931-45). From 1945 to 1954 he was prof. of violin at the Royal College of Music in London; then returned to Denmark.

Holstein, Franz (Friedrich) von, German composer; b. Brunswick, Feb. 16, 1826; d. Leipzig, May 22, 1878. His father was an army officer; at his behest, Holstein entered the Brunswick Cadet School; there he had an opportunity to study musical theory. While a lieutenant, he privately produced his operetta, *Zwei Nächte in Venedig* (1845). He fought in the Schleswig-Holstein campaign; returning to Brunswick, he wrote a grand opera, *Waverley,* after Walter Scott. He sent the MS to Hauptmann at the Leipzig Cons.; the latter expressed his willingness to accept Holstein as a student. Accordingly, he resigned from the army (1853) and studied with Hauptmann until 1856. He then undertook some travels in Italy, finally returning to Leipzig, where he settled. He was also a poet, and wrote his own librettos. The musical style of his operas was close to the French type, popularized by Auber. He was a man of means, and left a valuable legacy for the benefit of indigent music students. — Works: operas: *Der Haideschacht* (Dresden, Oct. 22, 1868), *Der Erbe von Morley* (Leipzig, Jan. 23, 1872), *Die Hochländer* (Mannheim, Jan. 16, 1876); another opera, *Marino Faliero,* remained unfinished; overture, *Frau Aventiure* (left in sketches only; orchestrated by Albert Dietrich; perf. posthumously, Leipzig, Nov. 13, 1879); *Beatrice,* scene for soprano solo with orch; a piano trio; other chamber music; part-songs for mixed and men's voices, etc.—Cf. G. Glaser, *Franz von Holstein: ein Dichterkomponist des 19. Jahrhunderts* (Leipzig, 1930).

Holter, Iver (Paul Fredrik), Norwegian composer; b. Gausdal, Dec. 13, 1850; d. Oslo, Jan. 25, 1941. He entered the Univ. of Christiania (Oslo) as a student of medicine, but devoted much more time to music, which he studied under Svendsen; then was a pupil of Jadassohn, Richter, and Reinecke at the Leipzig Cons. (1876-78); lived in Berlin (1879-81); became Grieg's successor as conductor of the 'Harmonie' in Bergen (1882); from 1886 to 1911 he was conductor of 'Musikföreningen' in Oslo, and from 1890-1905, also of 'Handvaerkersångföreningen'; in 1907, founded (and conducted until 1921) 'Holters Korförening,' a society devoted to the production of large choral works (sacred and secular); was conductor of several of the great Scandinavian festivals; in 1900 he conducted with Svendsen the 'Northern Concerts' in Paris. In 1919 the Norwegian Government granted him an artist's stipend. He was editor of 'Nordisk Musik Revue' (1900-06). His compositions include a symphony (1885), a violin concerto, and several cantatas: for the 300-year jubilee of Christiania (1924); for the 900-year Olavs-jubilee (1930); choruses, chamber music, songs.

Holtzner, Anton, German organist and composer of the early 17th century; d. 1635. He was educated in Italy. His keyboard canzonas make use of free rhythmic transformation of themes in the manner of Frescobaldi's 'variation canzonas'; one of them is reprinted in A. G. Ritter's *Geschichte des Orgelspiels im 14.-18. Jahrhundert* (1884).

Holy, Alfred, harpist; b. Oporto, Portugal, Aug. 5, 1866; d. Vienna, May 8, 1948. He studied violin and piano; then took harp lessons with Stanek at the Prague Cons. (1882-85). He subsequently was engaged as first harpist at the German Opera in Prague (1885-96); at the Berlin State Opera (1896-1903); at the Vienna Court Opera (1903-13). In 1913 he became first harpist of the Boston Symph. Orch.; retired in 1928 and returned to Vienna. He publ. studies for harp, arranged from the symphonic works of Richard Strauss, and various other harp transcriptions.

Holyoke, Samuel, American composer; b. Boxford, Mass., Oct. 15, 1762; d. East Concord, N. H., Feb. 7, 1820. His father was a clergyman, and Holyoke was naturally drawn to composing hymns. Although he received no formal training in music, he began to compose early, following his innate musical instinct. He wrote his most popular hymn tune, *Arnheim,* when he was only 16. He attended Harvard College, graduating in 1789; in 1793 he organized a school of higher education, known as the Groton Academy (later Lawrence Academy). In 1800 he went to Salem, where he was active as a teacher; was also a member of the Essex Musical Association in Salem. Holyoke was among those who did not favor the application of 'fuging' tunes in sacred music, as advocated by Billings, and generally omitted that style of composition from his collections; in the preface to his *Harmonia Americana* he states his reason for this as being because of 'the trifling effect produced by that sort of music; for the parts . . . confound the sense and render the performance a mere jargon of words.' His first collection was the *Harmonia Americana* (Boston, 1791); then followed *The Massachusetts Compiler* (co-ed. with Hans Gram and Oliver Holden; Boston, 1795); *The Columbian Repository of Sacred Harmony* (publ. Exeter, N. H., and dedicated to Essex Musical Association; copyright entry dated April 7, 1802; contains 734 tunes, many of his own composition); *The Christian Harmonist* (Salem, 1804); and *The Instrumental Assistant* (Exeter; 2 vols., 1800-07; includes instructions for violin, German flute, clarinet, bass viol, and hautboy). He also publ. the song *Washington* (1790), *Hark from the Tombs* (music for the funeral of Washington; 1800), etc. Cf. F. J. Metcalf, *American Psalmody* (N. Y., 1917); F. J. Metcalf, *American Writers and Compilers of Sacred Music* (Cincinnati, 1925).

Holzbauer, Ignaz, Austrian composer; b. Vienna, Sept. 17, 1711; d. Mannheim, April 7, 1783. While studying law, he taught himself music with the aid of *Gradus ad Parnassum* by Fux, whom he met later, and was encouraged towards further study. For a brief time, he was musical director to Count Rottach in Moravia; in 1741 he returned to Vienna, where he produced his first opera, *Ipermestra.* He traveled to Italy; on his journey in 1747, he was accompanied by his wife, an excellent singer. In 1750, he became court conductor at Stuttgart; in 1753 he was engaged as music director at Mannheim and remained there for most of his life. In 1756 he visited Rome; in 1757, Turin; in 1759, Milan; produced some of his operas there. He was greatly respected as a musician by his contemporaries; his church music was warmly praised by Mozart, who heard it in Mannheim in 1777. Historically, his most significant opera is *Günther* *von Schwarzburg,* in which Holzbauer presented a purely German story without concession to the prevalent Italian taste. It was produced in Mannheim in 1776, and the full score publ. at the time (reprint, in vols. 8 and 9 of the 'Denkmäler deutscher Tonkunst'). He also wrote 12 Italian operas: *Il figlio delle selve* (Schwetzingen, 1753), *L'isola disabitata* (Schwetzingen, 1754), *Issipile* (Mannheim, 1754), *Don Chisciotte* (Schwetzingen, 1755), *Le nozze d'Arianna* (Mannheim, 1756), *I cinesi* (Mannheim, 1756), *La clemenza di Tito* (Mannheim, 1757), *Nitteti* (Turin, 1757), *Ippolito ed Aricia* (Mannheim, 1759), *Alessandro nell' Indie* (Milan, 1759), *Adriano in Siria* (Mannheim, 1768), *Tancredi* (Munich, 1783). In addition, he wrote 4 oratorios (of which only one is extant), 21 Masses, 37 motets, and other church music. Most importantly, he was the composer of 69 symphonies, 17 divertimentos, string quartets, instrumental concertos, etc., in the innovating style of the Mannheim school; a thematic catalogue is in vols. 3 and 7 of the 'Denkmäler der Tonkunst in Bayern' and in vol. 16 of the 'Denkmäler deutscher Tonkunst.' His symphony in E-flat is reproduced in vol. 7 of the 'Denkmäler der Tonkunst in Bayern' (also reprinted by Carse in an English edition, 1939); a string quintet in E-flat is reprinted in the 'Denkmäler deutscher Tonkunst,' vol. 16.—Cf. K. M. Klob, *Drei musikalische Biedermänner* (Ulm, 1911).

Homer, Louise (*née* Louise Dilworth Beatty), American contralto; b. Pittsburgh, April 28, 1871; d. Winter Park, Fla., May 6, 1947. She studied in Philadelphia, and later in Boston, where her teacher in harmony was Sidney Homer, whom she married in 1895. With him she went to Paris, and there continued her study of voice with Fidèle Koenig; she also took lessons with Paul Lhérie in dramatic action. She made her début in opera as Leonora in *La Favorita* (Vichy, 1898). In 1899 she was engaged at the Théâtre de la Monnaie in Brussels, singing various parts of the French and Italian repertories. She subsequently sang Wagnerian contralto roles in German at Covent Garden, London. She made her American début in opera as Amneris with the Metropolitan Opera Co. (then on tour) at San Francisco (Nov. 14, 1900); sang the same part in N. Y. (Dec. 22, 1900); continued on the staff of the Metropolitan from 1900 to 1919; was then with the Chicago Opera Co. (1920-25); with the San Francisco and Los Angeles Opera companies (1926), and again with the Metropolitan, reappearing there on Dec. 13, 1927. Her classic interpretation of Orfeo at the Paris revival of Gluck's opera (1909) and subsequently in N. Y. (1910, under Toscanini) produced a great impression. One of her greatest operatic triumphs was her performance of Dalila, with Caruso singing Samson. After retiring from the opera stage, she gave recitals with her daughter, Louise Homer Stires, soprano. Her husband wrote a book of memoirs, *My Wife and I* (N. Y., 1939).

Homer, Sidney, American composer; b. Boston, Dec. 9, 1864; d. Winter Park, Fla., July 10, 1953. He studied in Boston, with Chadwick; then in Leipzig and in Munich. Returning to Boston, he taught theory of music. In 1895 he married Louise Dilworth Beatty, his pupil, and went with her to Paris. He retired in 1940 and settled in Winter Park. He publ. about 100 songs, many of which won great favor, particularly *A Banjo Song;* also *Dearest, Requiem, Prospice, Bandanna ballads, It was the time of roses, General William Booth enters into Heaven, The song of the shirt, Sheep and Lambs, Sing me a song of a lad that is gone, The pauper's drive;* also 17 lyrics from Christina Rossetti's *Sing-song.* Other works include a sonata for organ (1922), quintet for piano and strings (1932), violin sonata (1936), string quartet (1937), piano trio (1937). He publ. a book of memoirs, *My Wife and I* (N. Y., 1939).—Cf. H. C. Thorpe, *The Songs of Sidney Homer,* in the 'Mus. Quarterly' (Jan., 1931).

Homilius, Gottfried August, eminent German organist and composer; b. Rosenthal, Feb. 2, 1714; d. Dresden, June 5, 1785. He was a pupil of J. S. Bach; completed his education at the Univ. of Leipzig in 1735; became organist of the Frauenkirche in Dresden; then was appointed music director of 3 main churches there (1755). Published works are: Passion (1775); a Christmas oratorio, *Die Freude der Hirten über die Geburt Jesu* (1777); *6 deutsche Arien* (1786); in MS in the Berlin State Library and in the Dresden Kreuzchor archives: Passion according to St. Mark; church music for each Sunday and Feast-day in the year; motets, cantatas, fugued chorales, a thorough-bass method, 2 chorus books, etc. — Cf. R. Steglich, *Ph. Em. Bach und G. A. Homilius im Musikleben ihrer Zeit* ('Bach-Jahrbuch,' 1915). For a complete list of works, see Georg Feder's detailed article in 'Die Musik in Geschichte und Gegenwart.'

Honegger, Arthur (Oscar), a remarkable composer; b. Le Havre (of Swiss parents), March 10, 1892; d. Paris, Nov. 27, 1955. He studied violin with Lucien Capet in Paris; then took courses at the Zürich Cons. with L. Kempter and F. Hegar. Returning to France in 1912, he entered the Paris Cons. in the classes of Gedalge and Widor; further studied with Vincent d'Indy. His name first attracted attention when he took part in a concert of 'Nouveaux Jeunes' (Paris, Jan. 15, 1918). In 1920, the Paris critic Henri Collet published an article in 'Comoedia' in which he drew a parallel between the Russian Five and a group of young French composers whom he designated 'Les Six,' which comprised Honegger, Milhaud, Poulenc, Auric, Durey, and Germaine Tailleferre. The label persisted, even though the six composers went their separate ways and rarely gave concerts together. Honegger became famous with his 'symphonic movement' *Pacific 231,* a realistic tonal portrayal of a powerful American locomotive, depicting, in a series of rhythmic pulses, a gradual progress towards full speed, the slackening of pace, and the final stop. The piece, widely performed in 1924, became, in the mind of music critics and listeners, a perfect symbol of the 'machine age.' However, Honegger soon turned away from literal representation towards symphonic and choral music in quasi-Classical structures. Among his cantatas, *Le Roi David* and *Jeanne d'Arc au bûcher* are fine examples of modern vocal music; of his 5 symphonies, the 3rd (*Liturgique*) and the 5th (*Di tre re,* so designated by the composer to draw attention to the endings of each movement on a thrice repeated note D) are particularly impressive. Honegger makes free use of the devices of atonality in melodic writing, and polytonality in harmonic constructions, but only to enhance the basic sense of tonal unity. He lived most of his life in Paris; married the pianist Andrée Vaurabourg (who often played his works) in 1926. In 1929 he visited the U. S.; in 1947 was engaged to teach summer classes at the Berkshire Music Center in Tanglewood. — Works: For the stage: *Le Roi David,* dramatic Psalm (Mézières, June 11, 1921); *Antigone,* opera (Brussels, Dec. 28, 1927); *Judith,* biblical opera (Monte Carlo, Feb. 13, 1926); *Amphion,* melodrama (Paris, June 23, 1931); *Les Aventures du Roi Pausole,* operetta (Paris, Dec. 12, 1930); *Cris du monde,* stage oratorio (Paris, June 2, 1931); *La Belle de Moudon,* vaudeville (Mézières, 1933); *Jeanne d'Arc au bûcher,* stage oratorio (Basel, May 12, 1938); *L'Aiglon,* opera (Monte Carlo, March 11, 1937); *Les Mille et une Nuits,* spectacle (Paris Exhibition, 1937); *Les Petites Cardinal,* operetta (with J. Ibert; Paris, Feb. 20, 1938); *Nicolas de Flue,* dramatic legend (Neuchâtel, 1941); *Charles le Téméraire,* opera (Mézières, May, 1944). Ballets: *Vérité-Mensonge* (Paris, 1920); *Skating Rink* (Paris, Jan. 20, 1922); *Sous-marine* (Paris, June 27, 1925); *Sémiramis,* ballet-pantomime (Paris, May 11, 1934); *Le Cantique des cantiques* (Paris, Feb. 2, 1938); *L'appel de la montagne* (Paris, July 9, 1945); *Chota Roustaveli* (with Harsanyi and Tcherepnin; Monte Carlo, May 14, 1946). Incidental music: *Le Dit des jeux du monde* (Paris, Dec. 2, 1918); *La Mort de Sainte Alméenne* (1918); *La Danse macabre* (1919); *Saül* (Paris, June 16, 1922); *Fantasio* (1922); *L'Imperatrice aux rochers* (1925); *Phaedra* (1926). Film music: *Mlle. Doctor* (1937); *Pygmalion,* after Bernard Shaw's play (1938). For orch.: *Prélude d'Aglavaine et Sélysette* (Paris Cons., April 3, 1917, composer conducting); *Le Chant de Nigamon* (Paris, Jan. 3, 1920); *Pastorale d'Été* (Paris, Feb. 12, 1921); *Les Mariés de la tour Eiffel* (with Milhaud, Auric, Poulenc, and Tailleferre; Paris, June 19, 1921); *Horace Victorieux,* 'mimed symphony' (Lausanne, Oct. 30, 1921); *Prelude pour la Tempête* (Paris, May 1, 1923); *Chant de Joie* (Paris, May 3, 1923); *Pacific 231* (designated as *Mouvement symphonique No. 1;* Koussevitzky's concert, Paris, May 8, 1924); Concertino for piano and orch. (Paris, May 23, 1925, Andrée Vaurabourg soloist); *Rugby* (*Mouvement symphonique No. 2;* Stade Colombe, Paris, Dec. 31, 1928, during the intermission of the International Rugby Match between France and England); cello concerto (Boston, Feb. 17, 1930); Symphony No. 1 (Boston, Feb. 13, 1931); *Mouvement symphonique No. 3* (Berlin, March 27, 1933); Symphony No. 2, for string orch. (Basel, May 18, 1942); Suite, *Jour de fête suisse* (1943); Symphony No. 3, *Liturgique* (Zürich, Aug. 17, 1946); *Sérénade à Angélique,* for small orch. (Paris, Dec. 11, 1946); Symphony No. 4, *Deliciae Basilienses* (Basel, Jan. 21, 1947); *Concerto da camera,* for flute, English horn, and strings (1949); *Suite archaïque,* for orch. (Louisville, Feb. 28, 1951); Symphony No. 5, *Di tre re* (Boston, March 9, 1951); *Monopartita,* for orch. (Zürich, June 12, 1951). Radio music: *Radio Panoramique,* symphonic sketch (Radio-Geneva, March, 1935; in concert form, Paris, Oct. 19, 1935); *Christophe Colomb* (Radio, Lausanne, April 17, 1940); etc. Choral and vocal works: *Cantique de Pâques,* for soli, women's chorus, and orch. (1918); *Pâques à New York,* for voice and string quartet (1920); *La Danse des morts,* oratorio for soli, chorus, and orch. (Basel, March 2, 1940); *Chant de Libération,* for baritone, chorus, and orch. (Paris, Oct. 22, 1944); *Cantate de Noël* (Basel, Dec. 18, 1953). Chamber music: 1st string quartet (1916-17); Rhapsody for 2 flutes, clarinet (or 2 violins, viola), and piano (1917); 2 violin sonatas (1918; 1919); viola sonata (1920); sonatina for 2 violins (1920); cello sonata (1920); *Hymn,* for 10 strings (1920); sonatina for clarinet and piano (1922); *Trois Contrepoints,* for flute, English horn, violin, and cello (1922); sonatina for violin and cello (1932); 2nd string quartet (1934); 3rd string quartet (1936). For piano: *Trois pièces* (1910); *Hommage à Ravel* (1915); *Toccata et Variations* (1916); *Prélude et danse* (1919); *Le Cahier romand* (1923); *Hommage à Roussel* (1928); *Prélude, arioso et fughetta sur le nom de Bach* (1932); also a *Partita* for 2 pianos (arranged from *Trois Contrepoints;* 1928). Songs: *4 Poèmes* (1914-16); *6 Poésies de Jean Cocteau* (1920-23); *5 Mélodies-minute* (1941); publ. a book *Je suis compositeur* (Paris, 1951).—Cf. R. Chalupt, *Arthur Honegger,* in the 'Revue Musicale' (1922); E. B. Hill, *Modern French Composers* (N. Y., 1924); Roland-Manuel, *Arthur Honegger* (Paris, 1925); A. George, *Arthur Honegger* (Paris, 1926); Willy Tappolet, *Arthur Honegger* (Zürich, 1933, in German; French ed., Neuchâtel, 1938); Claude Gérard, *Arthur Honegger: catalogue succinct des œuvres* (Brussels, 1945); José Bruyr, *Honegger et son œuvre* (Paris, 1947); M. F. G. Delannoy, *Honegger* (Paris, 1953); Jean Matter, *Honegger* (Lausanne, 1956).

Honegger, Henri, Swiss cellist; b. Geneva, June 10, 1904. He studied with Casals in Paris; returning to Switzerland, he became 1st cellist in the Orchestre de la Suisse Romande; in 1950 he presented a series of concerts in New York, performing all of Bach's cello suites.

Hood, Helen, American song composer; b. Chelsea, Mass., June 28, 1863; d. Brookline, Mass., Jan. 22, 1949. She studied piano with B. J. Lang and composition with Chadwick; also took a piano course with Moszkowski in Berlin; lived most of her life in Boston. Among her published pieces are *The Robin* (part-song); 5 pieces for violin and piano; *Song Etchings* (a set of 6 songs); she also wrote some chamber music.

Hoogstraten, Willem van, Dutch conductor; b. Utrecht, March 18, 1884. He studied violin with Alexander Schmuller; then with Bram Eldering at the Cons. of Cologne and with Ševčik in Prague; played concerts with the pianist Elly Ney, whom he married in 1911 (divorced in 1927). From 1914-18 he conducted the municipal orch. in Krefeld; in 1922 he was engaged as conductor of the summer concerts of the N. Y. Philharmonic (until 1938); associate conductor of the N. Y. Philharmonic (1923-25). He was regular conductor of the Portland, Oregon, Symph. Orch. from 1925-37. During World War II he was in charge of the Mozarteum Orch. in Salzburg (1939-45). In 1949 he settled in Stuttgart; conducted the Stuttgart Philharmonic.

Hook, James, English organist and composer; b. Norwich, June 3, 1746; d. Boulogne, 1827. He exhibited a precocious talent as a boy; took lessons with Garland, organist of the Norwich cathedral. In 1764 he went to London, where he played organ at various entertainment places. In 1765 he won a prize for his *Parting Catch.* He was subsequently organist and music director at Marylebone Gardens, London (1769-73) and at Vauxhall Gardens (1774-1820); his last position was at St. John's, Horsleydown. He was a highly industrious composer of songs; he may have written as many as 2,000 numbers; of these, only a few escaped oblivion (*Within a mile of Edinboro' Town; Sweet Lass of Richmond Hill,* etc.); many oratorios and odes; concertos for harpsichord; 117 sonatas, sonatinas, and divertimentos for piano; about 30 theater scores, all produced in London: *Cupid's Revenge* (June 12, 1772), *The Lady of the Manor* (Nov. 23, 1778), *The Fair Peruvian* (March 8, 1786), *Jack of Newbury* (May 6, 1795), *Wilmore Castle* (Oct. 21, 1800), *The Soldier's Return* (April 23, 1805), *The Invisible Girl* (April, 28, 1806), *The Fortress* (July 16, 1807), *Safe and Sound* (August 28, 1809), etc. He publ. a manual, *Guida di musica,* in 2 parts (1785; 1794); some of the musical examples from it were reprinted by H. Wall in *Leaves from an Old Harpsichord Book.*

Hope-Jones, Robert, English organ manufacturer; b. Hooton Grange, Cheshire, Feb. 9, 1859; d. (by suicide) Rochester, N. Y., Sept. 13, 1914. As a boy, he entered the employ of Laird Bros., engineers at Birkenhead; then became chief electrician of the National Telephone Co.; at the same time, was engaged as church organist. In 1889 he set up his own business as organ builder. In 1903 he settled in America; was connected with the E. M. Skinner Co. of Boston; in 1907, founded the Hope-Jones Organ Co. at Tonawanda, N. Y., but sold the plant and his patents in 1910 to the Rudolph Wurlitzer Co. of N. Y. He introduced many innovations into the building of electrical organs; the development of the modern organ in the U. S. owes much to his inventive genius. One of the finest of his organs is in the Auditorium at Ocean Grove, N. J.—Cf. G. L. Miller, *The Recent Revolution in Organ Building* (N. Y., 1913).

Hopekirk, Helen, Scottish pianist; b. Edinburgh, May 20, 1856; d. Cambridge, Mass., Nov. 19, 1945. She studied with A. C. Mackenzie; then went to Germany; made her début with the Gewandhaus Orch., Leipzig (Nov. 28, 1878); also took lessons with Leschetizky in Vienna. She married William Wilson, a business-man, in 1882; lived in Vienna; in 1897, settled in Boston; taught at the New England Cons. In her recitals she featured many works of the modern French school (Debussy, Fauré, etc.). She wrote many piano pieces; played her piano concerto with the Boston Symph. Orch. (Dec. 27, 1900); publ. a collection of Scottish folksongs. —See Constance Hall, *Helen Hopekirk* (Cambridge, Mass., 1954).

Hopkins, Edward Jerome, American composer and musical journalist; b. Burlington, Vt., April 4, 1836; d. Athenia, N. J., Nov. 4, 1898. Self-taught in music (he took only 6 lessons in harmony), he learned to play piano sufficiently well to attain professional status. He studied chemistry at the N. Y. Medical College; played organ in N. Y. churches, and was active in various educational enterprises. In 1886 he organized several 'Free Singing and Opera Schools,' for which he claimed nearly 1,000 pupils. In 1889 he went to England on a lecture tour announcing himself as "the first American Operatic Oratorio composer and Pianist who has ever ventured to invade England with New World Musical theories and practices." He was the founder and editor of the N. Y. Philharmonic Journal (1868-85). Throughout his versatile career, he was a strong advocate of American music; his sensational methods and eccentric professional conduct brought him repeatedly into public controversy; in England he was sued for libel. As composer, Hopkins claimed a priority in writing the first "musicianly and scientific Kinder-Oper" *(Taffy and Old Munch,* a children's fairy tale, 1880). He further wrote an operatic oratorio, *Samuel,* and a great number of choruses and songs, few of which are published. He compiled two collections of church music and an *Orpheon Class-Book.* — Cf. N. Slonimsky, *The Flamboyant Pioneer,* in *A Thing or Two About Music* (N. Y., 1947, pp. 250-261).

Hopkins, Edward John, English organist and composer; b. London, June 30, 1818; d. there, Feb. 4, 1901. He was a chorister at the Chapel Royal (1826-33); then studied theory with T. F. Walmisley. In 1834 he became organist at Mitcham Church; from 1838, was at St. Peter's, Islington; from 1841, at St. Luke's, and from 1843 at the Temple Church, London. There he remained for 55 years, retiring in 1898; Walford Davies was his successor. Several of his many anthems have become established in the church repertory (*Out of the Deep, God is Gone Up, Thou Shalt Cause the Trumpet of the Jubilee to Sound,* etc.). His book, *The Organ: Its History and Construction* (in collaboration with Rimbault, London, 1855; 5th ed., 1887), is a standard work. He contributed articles to Grove's 'Dictionary of Music and Musicians' and to various musical publications. —Cf. Charles W. Pearce, *The Life and Works of Edward John Hopkins* (London, 1910).

Hopkinson, Francis, American statesman, writer, and composer; signer of the Declaration of Independence; b. Philadelphia, Sept. 21, 1737; d. there, May 9, 1791. By profession a laywer, he was deeply interested in music; learned to play the harpsichord; studied music theory with James Bremner; was a member of an amateur group in Philadelphia who met regularly in their homes to play music, and also gave public concerts by subscription. He was the composer of the first piece of music written by a native American, *Ode to Music,* which he wrote in 1754, and of the first original American song, *My days have been so wondrous free* (1759). At least, this is the claim he makes in the preface to his *7 Songs* (actually 8, the last having been added after the title page was engraved) *for the harpsichord or forte piano,* dated Philadelphia, Nov. 20, 1788, and dedicated to George Washington: "I cannot, I believe, be refused the Credit of being the first Native of the United States who has produced a Musical Composition." Other works: *Ode* *in Memory of James Bremner* (1780); a dramatic cantata, *The Temple of Minerva* (1781); there are also some songs. Hopkinson's music was couched in the conventional English style, modeled after pieces by T. A. Arne, but he undoubtedly possessed a genuine melodic gift. He also provided Benjamin Franklin's glass harmonica with a keyboard and introduced improvements in the quilling of the harpsichord, and invented the Bell-Harmonic, 'a contrivance for the perfect measurement of time.' He was probably, but not certainly, the compiler of *A Collection of Psalm Tunes with a Few Anthems,* etc. A MS book of songs in Hopkinson's handwriting is in the possession of the Library of Congress.—Cf. O. G. Sonneck, *Francis Hopkinson, the First American Poet Composer . . .* (Washington, 1905); H. V. Milligan, *The First American Composer: 6 Songs by Francis Hopkinson* (Boston, 1918); O. E. Albrecht, *Francis Hopkinson, Musician, Poet and Patriot* (Philadelphia, 1938); J. T. Howard, *Our American Music* (N. Y., 1939, and subsequent eds.). Hopkinson's son, Joseph Hopkinson, wrote the words to *Hail Columbia.*

Horák, Adolph, pianist and teacher; b. Jankovic, Bohemia, Feb. 15, 1850; d. Vienna, Jan. 14, 1921. With his brother Eduard he established the Horák Pianoforte School in Vienna; in collaboration, they publ. a valuable *Klavierschule;* Adolph alone wrote *Die technische Grundlage des Klavierspiels.*

Horák, Antonin, Czech composer; b. Prague, July 2, 1875; d. Belgrade, March 12, 1910. He was engaged as opera conductor in Prague and Belgrade; his own opera, *Babička* (*Grandmother*), was fairly successful at its first production, in Prague (March 3, 1900); he also wrote cantatas and other choral works.

Horák, Eduard, pianist and teacher; b. Holitz, Bohemia, April 22, 1838; d. Riva, Lake of Garda, Dec. 6, 1892. With his brother Adolph he founded in Vienna the Horák Pianoforte School, which soon acquired a European reputation. In collaboration with Fr. Spigl, who succeeded him as director of the Horák School, he published *Der Klavierunterricht in neue, natürliche Bahnen gelenkt* (Vienna, 1892; in 2 vols.), and with his brother, a practical manual, *Klavierschule.*

Horák, Wenzel Emanuel, church composer and organist; b. Mscheno-Lobes, Bohemia, Jan. 1, 1800; d. Prague, Sept. 15, 1871. He studied theory by himself, with the aid of the standard manuals of Vogler, Cherubini, etc.; also played organ, and was organist at various churches in Prague; wrote 10 Masses, motets, and a theoretical work, *Die Mehrdeutigkeit der Harmonien* (1846).

Horenstein, Jascha, conductor; b. Kiev, Russia, May 6, 1898. His family moved to Germany when he was a child, and he studied with Max Brode in Königsberg and with Adolf Busch in Vienna; also took advanced courses in composition with Franz Schreker in Berlin. After some concerts which he conducted in Vienna and in Berlin, he was appointed conductor of the Düsseldorf Opera; then appeared in France (1929) and in Russia (1931); made a tour in Australia (1936-37); conducted the Ballets Russes de Monte Carlo in Scandinavia (1937) and gave a series of concerts in Palestine (1938). After 1945 he conducted in the U. S. and South America as well as in Europe. In the spring of 1957 he conducted several programs at the Caracas (Venezuela) Festival.

Horký, Karel, Czech composer; b. Stemĕchy, near Třebič, Moravia, Sept. 4, 1909. He played in a military band as a boy; then in a theater orchestra in Brno; there he began to study composition with Pavel Haas; later went to Prague to study with J. Křička. In 1945 he became teacher of harmony at the Cons. of Brno. He has written several operas, including *Jan Hus* (Brno, May 27, 1950); the ballets *Lastura* (Brno, Oct. 23, 1945) and *Král Ječminek* (Brno, Sept. 8, 1951); also *Romantic Sinfonietta* and other orchestral works.

Horn, August, German composer and arranger; b. Freiberg, Sept. 1, 1825; d. Leipzig, March 25, 1893. He was a pupil of Mendelssohn at the Leipzig Cons.; wrote overtures and light music; but became principally known as arranger of symphonies, operas, etc. for piano, 2 and 4 hands. His comic opera *Die Nachbarn* was produced in Leipzig in 1875.

Horn, Camillo, composer; b. Reichenberg, Bohemia, Dec. 29, 1860; d. Vienna, Sept. 3, 1941. He was a pupil of Bruckner at the Vienna Cons.; conducted choruses there, and was also active as music critic. Many of his works have been published; he wrote a symphony; a cantata, *Bundeslied der Deutschen in Böhmen; Deutsches Lied* for chorus and orch.; many choruses a cappella; a number of piano pieces.

Horn, Charles Edward, composer and conductor; son of Karl Friedrich Horn; b. London, June 21, 1786; d. Boston, Oct. 21, 1849. He studied with his father, and practiced voice under the guidance of Rauzzini. Made his début as a singer in a light opera (June 26, 1809); sang Kaspar in the English production of *Der Freischütz.* In 1833 he emigrated to America; there he wrote several oratorios: *The Remission of Sin* (later named *Satan),* etc. In 1848 he became conductor of the Handel and Haydn Society in Boston. In the U.S., he was notable primarily as a singer and composer of ballads.

Horn, Karl Friedrich, German composer; b. Nordhausen, April 13, 1762; d. Windsor, England, Aug. 5, 1830. He settled in England at the age of 20 and with the patronage of Count Brühl, Saxon Ambassador in London, became a fashionable teacher. In 1823 he became organist of St. George's Chapel at Windsor. With Wesley he prepared an English edition of Bach's *Wohltemperiertes Klavier;* also wrote a treatise on thorough-bass; composed 12 sets of piano variations with flute obbligato; 6 piano sonatas; *Military Divertimentos.*

Hornbostel, Erich Moritz von, eminent musicologist; b. Vienna, Feb. 25, 1877; d. Cambridge, Nov. 28, 1935. He studied philosophy in Vienna and Heidelberg; 1900, *Dr. Phil.;* 1905-6 assistant of Stumpf in Berlin; 1906, came to the U. S. for the purpose of making a special study of Indian music (Pawnee), and made many records of it; 1906-33, director of the Phonogramm-Archiv in Berlin. In 1933 he left Germany and went to England. He was a specialist on tone-psychology.—Writings: *Studien über das Tonsystem und die Musik der Japaner* (in collaboration with Otto Abraham), in 'Sammelbände der Internationalen Musik-Gesellschaft' (1903); *Phonographierte türkische Melodien* (with O. Abraham), in 'Zeitschrift für Ethnologie' (1904); *Phonographierte indische Melodien* (with O. Abraham), in 'Sammelbände der Internationalen Musik-Gesellschaft' (1904); *Melodischer Tanz,* in 'Zeitschrift der Internationalen Musik-Gesellschaft' (1903-4); *Phonographierte Indianermelodien aus Britisch-Columbia* (with O. Abraham), in the 'Boas Memorial Volume' (1906); *Notiz über die Musik der Bewohner von Süd-Neu-Mecklenburg* in Stephan's and Gräbner's 'Neu Mecklenburg' (1907); *Phonographierte tunesische Melodien,* in 'Sammelbände der Internationalen Musik-Gesellschaft' (1907); *Vorschläge zur Transkription exotischer Melodien* (with O. Abraham), in 'Sammelbände der Internationalen Musik-Gesellschaft' (1909); *Phonographierte Melodien aus Madagaskar und Indonesien* (1909); *Wanyamwezi-Gesänge,* in 'Anthropos' (1909); *Über einige Panpfeifen aus Nordwest-Brasilien,* in Koch-Grümberge's 'Zwei Jahre unter den Indianern' (1910); *Notizen über kirgisische Musikinstrumente und Melodien,* in R. Karutz' 'Unter Kirgisen und Turkmenen' (1911); *Über ein akustisches Kriterium für Kulturzusammenhänge,* in 'Zeitschrift für Ethnologie' (1911); *Melodie und Skala,* in 'Jahrbuch Peters' (1913); *Systematik der Musikinstrumente* (in collaboration with C. Sachs), in 'Zeitschrift für Ethnologie' (1914); *Formanalysen an siamesischen Orchesterstücken,* in 'Archiv für Musikwissenschaft' (1920); *Die Entstehung des Jodelns,* in the 'Basler Kongressbericht' (1924); *Zur Psychologie der Tondistanz* (with O. Abraham), in 'Zeitschrift für Psychologie' (1925); *Musikalische Tonsysteme* (edited by Geiger and Scheel), in 'Handbuch der Physik' (1927); *Die Massnorm als kulturgeschichtliches Forschungsmittel,* in the 'P. W. Schmidt-Festschrift' (1928); *Tonart und Ethos,* in the 'J. Wolf-Festschrift' (1929); *African Negro-Music* (London, 1929); *Gestaltpsychologisches zur Stilkritik,* in the 'Adler-Festschrift' (1930); *Phonographierte isländische Zwiegesänge,* in 'Deutsche Islandforschung' (1930); other valuable essays. He edited a collection of records, *Musik des Orients* (Lindström, 1932); from 1922 until death was co-editor, with C. Stumpf, of the 'Sammelbände für vergleichende Musikwissenschaft.'

Horneman, Christian Emil, Danish composer; son of Johan Ole Horneman; b. Copenhagen, Dec. 17, 1841; d. there, June 8, 1906. He studied at the Leipzig Cons. (1858-60), where he became a friend of Grieg. He composed light music under various pseudonyms; returning to Copenhagen, he organized a concert society there; produced an opera, *Aladdin* (Nov. 18, 1888); also was active as choral conductor and teacher. He wrote, in addition, 2 string quartets and numerous songs.

Horneman, Johan Ole, Danish composer; b. Copenhagen, May 13, 1809; d. there, May 29, 1870. He composed music in a popular vein; in 1844 established a publishing firm with Emil Erslev. His collection of piano pieces, *Nordiske sange uden tekst (Nordic Songs Without Text),* enjoyed some popularity; he further published a piano manual, *Ny praktisk Pianoforteskole* (new ed. by L. Schytte).

Horner, Ralph Joseph, English conductor and composer; b. Newport, Monmouthshire, April 28, 1848; d. Winnipeg, Canada, April 7, 1926. He studied at the Leipzig Cons. (1864-67) with Moscheles, Reinecke, and Plaidy. On his return to England, he was active as choral conductor; also conducted light opera. From 1906-9 he was in New York; then settled in Winnipeg, where he became director of the Imperial Academy of Music and Arts and conductor of the Oratorio Society (1909-12). He wrote the operas *Confucius, Amy Rosbart,* and *The Belles of Barcelona;* the oratorios *St. Peter* and *David's First Victory;* a *Torch Dance* for orch. (won the Earl Grey Prize, 1911); many sacred cantatas, anthems, piano pieces, songs.

Hornstein, Robert von, German composer; b. Donaueschingen, Dec. 6, 1833; d. Munich, July 19, 1890. He studied at the Leipzig Cons.; then went to Munich where he became a teacher at the municipal school of music. He was a close friend of Wagner; composed operas in a Romantic vein; one of these, *Adam und Eva,* was produced in Munich in 1870; other works are a ballet, *Der Blumen Rache;* incidental music to Shakespeare's *As You Like It;* many songs.

Horowitz, Vladimir, remarkable pianist; b. Kiev, Oct. 1, 1904; studied there with Felix Blumenfeld; made his début in Kharkov at the age of 17; then went to Paris; his European tour in 1924 was sensationally successful. On Jan. 12, 1928, he made his American début with the N. Y. Philharmonic, in Tchaikovsky's 1st Concerto, Thomas Beecham conducting. He then appeared with many American orchestras, and also in recital, quickly earning the reputation of a virtuoso of the highest caliber. In 1933 he married Wanda Toscanini, daughter of Arturo Toscanini. In 1938-39 he lived mostly in Switzerland; in 1940 returned to America, and settled in N. Y. On Dec. 9, 1949, he played in Havana the first performance anywhere of Samuel Barber's piano sonata, op. 26. —Horowitz has made a virtuoso transcription for piano of Sousa's march *Stars and Stripes Forever,* a veritable tour de force of pianistic display, and has frequently performed it at his concerts.

Horsley, Charles Edward, English organist and composer; b. London, Dec. 16, 1822; d. New York, Feb. 28, 1876. He was a pupil of his father, William Horsley; then studied with Moscheles. In Leipzig he became friendly with Mendelssohn, who instructed him in composition. Upon his return to London, he obtained a post as organist of St. John's; wrote the oratorios *David, Joseph,* and *Gideon;* incidental music to Milton's *Comus.* In 1862 he went to Australia, and served as organist in Melbourne. There he wrote an ode, *Euterpe,* for the opening of the Town Hall (1870). He eventually settled in New York. His *Text Book of Harmony* was publ. posthumously (1876).

Horsley, William, English organist and composer; father of the preceding; b. London, Nov. 15, 1774; d. there, June 12, 1858. He had little formal study, but his friendly association with John Callcott, the composer of glees, led him to try his hand at the composition of light vocal pieces. He married Callcott's daughter in 1813. He was instrumental in the establishment of the choral society 'Concentores Sodales' (1798-1847) for which he wrote many anthems, catches, and glees; was also a founder of the Philharmonic Society of London (1813); occupied various posts as church organist. Many of his songs (*See the Chariot at Hand, O Nightingale,* etc.) were frequently sung. He further publ. 5 albums of glees (1801-7), hymn tunes (1820), canons, piano pieces, etc.; also *An Explanation of Musical Intervals and of the Major and Minor Scales* (1825); *Introduction to Harmony and Modulation* (1847); edited Callcott's glees, with a biography and analysis; brought out the 1st book of Byrd's *Cantiones Sacrae.*

Horst, Anthon van der, Dutch composer and organist; b. Amsterdam, June 20, 1899. He played organ at the Walloon Church in Amsterdam; in 1936, appointed prof. of organ and conducting at the Amsterdam Cons. In some of his works he has adopted the scale of alternating tones and semitones, which he calls 'modus conjunctus'; wrote a *Suite in modo conjuncto* for organ (1943). —Other works: *Psalm 90,* for voices and organ (1933); a symphony (1939); *Te Deum,* for double chorus, soli, organ, and orch. (1946); concerto for organ and orch. (1954); *Divertimento pittorale,* for orch. (1954); *Rembrandt Cantata,* for chorus, organ, and brass instruments (1956; for 350th anniversary of Rembrandt's birth).

Horszowski, Mieczyslaw, pianist; b. Lwow, June 23, 1892. He studied with M. Soltys at the Lwow Cons.; then went to Vienna to study with Leschetizky; made his first public appearance at the age of 9 in Warsaw. He began extensive concert tours in Europe a few years later; gave joint recitals with Casals; played with orchestras under Toscanini. In 1940 he settled in New York, and continued his career as soloist.

Horwitz, Karl, Austrian composer; b. Vienna, Jan. 1, 1884; d. Salzburg, Aug. 18, 1925. He studied with Arnold Schoenberg, and adopted an atonal idiom. He was active in organizing the Donaueschingen Festivals (from 1921) and in other societies devoted to modern music; among his works are a symphonic poem, *Vom Tode;* 2 string quartets, and several song cycles. In 1924 he suffered a loss of hearing, as a result of disease, and died shortly afterwards.

Hosmer, Elmer Samuel, American organist and composer; b. Clinton, Mass., March 21, 1862; d. Pawtucket, R. I., April 25, 1945. He studied music in Boston with George Whiting, Percy Goetschius, and others; occupied various positions as organist; composed cantatas (*Pilgrims of 1620, The Man Without a Country,* etc.) and many anthems.

Hosmer, Lucius, American composer; b. South Acton, Mass., Aug. 14, 1870; d. Jefferson, N. H., May 9, 1935. He studied with Chadwick at the New England Cons.; lived mostly in Boston; wrote a 'romantic comic opera' *The Rose of the Alhambra* (Rochester, 1905, N. Y., Feb. 4, 1907); a comic opera, *The Walking Delegate* (revised and produced under the title *The Koreans*); various light pieces for orch.: *On Tiptoe, Chinese Wedding Procession; Southern Rhapsody, Northern Rhapsody, Ethiopian Rhapsody,* etc.; also songs.

Hostinský, Otakar, Czech writer on music; b. Martinoves, Jan. 2, 1847; d. Prague, Jan. 19, 1910. He studied at the Univ. of Prague and later in Munich; became instructor of esthetics and history of music at Charles Univ. in Prague (1877); prof. in 1892. He publ. *Das Musikalisch-Schöne und das Gesammtkunstwerk vom Standpunkt der formalen Ästhetik* (1877), as a philosophical reply to Hanslick's famous book (in Czech as *Hostinského esthetika,* Prague, 1921); *Die Lehre von den musikalischen Klängen* (1879); *Über die Entwicklung und den jetzigen Stand der tschechischen Oper* (1880); *Über die Bedeutung der praktischen Ideen Herbarts für die allgemeine Ästhetik* (1883); his articles on Smetana were collected and publ. in 1901 (new ed., 1941); he wrote numerous articles on Czech folksongs, etc. A jubilee pamphlet was publ. in Prague on the occasion of his 60th birthday (1907).

Hothby, John, English music theorist; b. about 1415; d. probably in England, Nov. 6, 1487. He was a student at Oxford; was a member of the Carmelite order; lived in Florence, Italy, about 1440, and was known there under the Italianized name Ottobi; was then in Lucca (1468-86), where he taught in canonic schools. In 1486 he was recalled to England by Henry VII. He wrote about 12 treatises: *Ars musica; Regulae super proportionem; De cantu figurato; Regulae super contrapunctum; Regulae de monochordo manuali; Quid est proportio; Tractatus quarundam regularum artis musices;* etc. His *La Calliopea legale* was publ. by Coussemaker in *Histoire de l'harmonie au moyen-âge; Regulae super proportionem, De cantu figurato* and *Regulae super contrapunctum* in Coussemaker's *Scriptores de musica* (vol. 3).—Cf. U. Kornmüller, *Johann Hothby . . .* in 'Kirchenmusikalisches Jahrbuch' (1893); H. Schmidt, *Die 'Calliopea legale' des J. Hothby* (Leipzig, 1897).

Hotter, Hans, German baritone; b. Offenbach, Jan. 19, 1909. He was a choirboy in Munich, and also played the organ; took courses in music history at the Munich Academy. He then studied singing and rapidly progressed, so that at the age of 23 he became a member of the German Opera at Prague. In 1940 he joined the Munich Opera, and also made guest appearances with several other opera companies. As a Wagnerian singer, he obtained signal success at the Bayreuth Festivals.

Hotteterre (oht-tär'), a family of French musicians: **Nicolas Hotteterre** (b. 1637; d. Paris, May 10, 1694), a hurdy-gurdy player; his brother **Martin** (d. 1712), also a hurdy-gurdy player and a performer at at the court ballets; **Louis Hotteterre** (d. 1719), son of Nicolas, who played the flute at the French court for 50 years (1664-1714); his brother **Nicolas Hotteterre** (d. Paris, Dec. 4, 1727), who (like his brother) played flute and oboe in Lully's orchestra at the court of Louis XIV; **Jacques Hotteterre** (d. Paris, c. 1760), surnamed 'le Romain' evidently owing to his long sojourns in Rome, popularized the transverse (German) flute at the French court and published several manuals on that instrument and others: *Principes de la flûte traversière ou flûte d'Allemagne, de la flûte à bec ou flûte douce et du hautbois* (Paris, 1707; sometimes attributed to his cousin Louis; the 1728 ed. was reprinted in facsimile, Kassel, 1941); *Méthode pour la musette* (1738); *L'Art de préluder sur la flûte traversière, sur la flûte à bec, etc.* (Paris, 1712; 2nd ed. under the title, *Méthode pour apprendre . . .*, c. 1765); also wrote sonatas, duos, trios, suites, *rondes (chansons à danser)*, and minuets for flute. —Cf. J. A. Carlez, *Les Hotteterre* (Caen, 1877); E. Thoinan, *Les Hottetere et les Chédeville* (Paris, 1894); N. Mauger, *Les Hotteterre, nouvelles recherches* (Paris, 1912); H. M. Fitzgibbon, *Of Flutes and Soft Recorders,* in the 'Mus. Quarterly' (April, 1934).

Houdard (oo-dahr'), **Georges,** French authority on Gregorian chant; b. Neuilly-sur-Seine, March 30, 1860; d. Paris, Feb. 28, 1913. He studied with L. Hillemacher and with Massenet at the Paris Cons.; then devoted himself exclusively to old church music; publ. valuable treatises: *L'Art dit grégorien d'après la notation neumatique* (1897); *L'Evolution de l'art musical et l'art grégorien* (1902); *Aristoxène de Tarente* (1905); *La Rythmique intuitive* (1906); *Textes théoriques; Vademecum de la rythmique grégorienne des Xe et XIe siècles* (1912); also wrote some sacred music (a Requiem, offertories, elevations, etc.).

Houdoy, Jules. See **Hudoy.**

Houseley, Henry, organist and composer; b. Sutton-in-Ashfield, England, Sept. 20, 1852; d. Denver, Colo., March 13, 1925. He studied at the Royal College of Organists in London; then filled various posts as church organist. In 1888 he emigrated to the U. S., settling in Denver, where he was active in many musical and cultural fields; produced there several light operas: *The Juggler* (May 23, 1895); *Pygmalion* (Jan. 30, 1912); *Narcissus and Echo* (Jan. 30, 1912); also wrote a cantata, *Omar Khayyám,* which was performed in Denver on June 1, 1916.—Cf. E. E. Hipsher, *American Opera and Its Composers* (Philadelphia, 1934; pp. 268-69).

Housman, Rosalie, American composer; b. San Francisco, June 25, 1888; d. New York, Oct. 28, 1949. She studied with Arthur Foote in Boston; also took lessons in N. Y. with Ernest Bloch; composed *Color Sequence* for soprano and small orch.; women's choruses; children's pieces; songs.

Hovhaness (former spelling **Hovaness**), **Alan,** American composer of Armenian descent (father, Armenian; mother Scottish); b. Somerville, Mass., March 8, 1911. He studied piano with Heinrich Gebhard; composition with Frederick Converse; also took lessons with Bohuslav Martinu. While mastering the traditional technique of composition, he became fascinated by Indian and other Oriental musical systems; from his earliest works, he made use of Armenian melorythmic patterns. As a result, he gradually evolved an individual type of art, in which quasi-Oriental cantillation and a curiously monodic texture became the mainstay. By dint of ceaseless repetition of themes and relentless dynamic tension, a definite impression is created of originality; the atmospheric effects often suggest Impressionistic exoticism. He has written a great many works, of which he destroyed nearly a thousand in 1940. The list of his extant compositions written after 1940 is still very large. He has written 2 *Armenian Rhapsodies* for strings (1944-45); *Elibris,* for flute and strings (San Francisco, Jan. 26, 1950); *Lousadzak* (*Coming of Light*), for piano and strings (Boston, Feb. 4, 1945); concerto for trumpet and strings (N. Y., June 17, 1945); *Sosi* for violin, piano, percussion, and strings (N. Y., March 6, 1949); *Arekaval,* for orch. (N. Y., Feb. 18, 1952); *Janabar,* 5 hymns for violin, trumpet, piano, and strings (N. Y., March 11, 1951); *Concerto* for orch. (Louisville, Feb. 20, 1954); *Ad Lyram,* for orch. (Houston, March 12, 1957); a large number of works for chamber combinations; violin pieces; piano works; church melodies; etc. —Cf. Oliver Daniel, *Alan Hovhaness,* in 'Bulletin of American Composers Alliance' (Oct., 1952).

Howard, George Henry, American music pedagogue and song composer; b. Norton, Mass., Nov. 12, 1843; d. Boston, Feb. 27, 1917. He studied at the Boston Music School; then taught there (1864-69); subsequently went to Germany for further study at the Leipzig Cons. with Moscheles and Richter; also in Berlin with Haupt and Kullak. Returning to America, he devoted himself to pedagogy; taught at various schools. In 1891 he organized the Boston School for Teachers of Music. He publ. some songs; also wrote organ pieces.

Howard, John Tasker, American writer on music; b. Brooklyn, Nov. 30, 1890. He attended Williams College for 3 years (1910-13); honorary M. A., 1937; studied piano with P. Tidden, and composition with H. Brockway and Mortimer Wilson. He was managing editor of 'The Musician' (1918-22); educational director of the Ampico Corp. (1922-28); music editor of 'McCall's Magazine' (1928-30); music editor of U. S. George Washington Bicentennial Commission (1931-32; received the Commission's medal of award in 1932); music editor of 'Cue Magazine' (1936-38); music editor of the U. S. Constitutional Sesquicentennial Commission (1937); curator of the Americana Music Collection, New York Public Library (1940-56); librarian of the Henry Hadley Memorial Library (1940); member of the Board of Directors, American Society of Composers, Authors and Publishers (1945; secretary since 1953). He settled in Montclair, N. J. —Writings: *Our American Music* (1931; revised 1939, 1946, 1954); *The Music of George Washington's Time* (1931); *Stephen Foster, America's Troubadour* (1934; revised, 1953); *Ethelbert Nevin* (1935); *Our Contemporary Composers* (1941); *This Modern Music* (1942; revised ed., *Modern Music,* 1956); *The World's Great Operas* (1948); and (with G. K. Bellows) *A Short History of Music in America* (1957). Compiled and edited *A Program of Early American Piano Music; Early and Mid-19th Century American Songs; A Program of Stephen Foster Songs; A Treasury of Stephen Foster,* vol. 9 of *The Scribner Music Library.* —Compositions: *Foster Sonatina,* for violin and piano; *Fantasy on a Choral Theme,* for piano and orch. (New Jersey Orch., Orange, N. J., Feb. 20, 1929); piano pieces, and songs. —See G. K. Bellows, *John Tasker Howard,* in 'Notes' (Sept., 1957; with a complete list of published writings, musical and literary).

Howard, Kathleen, contralto; b. Clifton, Canada, July 17, 1884; d. Hollywood, Aug. 15, 1956. She studied in New York with Bouhy and in Paris with Jean de Reszke; sang at the Metz Opera (1907-9); then at Darmstadt (1909-12); at Covent Garden in London (1913); with the Century Opera Co. in N. Y. (1914-15). She made her first appearance with the Metropolitan Opera Co. in *The Magic Flute* (Nov. 20, 1916); remained on the staff until 1928. After her retirement from the stage, she was engaged in magazine work; was fashion editor of 'Harper's Bazaar' (1928-33); publ. an autobiography, *Confessions of an Opera Singer* (N. Y., 1918). She married Edward Kelley Baird on June 27, 1916.

Howe, Mary, American composer; b. Richmond, Va., April 4, 1882. She studied at the Peabody Cons. in Baltimore; was a pupil of Gustav Strube (composition) and Ernest Hutcheson (piano); in 1915, settled in Washington, where she played a prominent part in musical organizations. She was a vice-president of the Friends of Music of the Library of Congress; is a member of the Board of Directors of the National Symphony Orch. —Works: violin sonata (1922); Suite for string quartet and piano (1923); *Sand,* for orch. (1928); *Dirge,* for orch. (1931); *Castellana,* for 2 pianos and orch. (1935); *Spring Pastoral,* for solo violin and 13 instruments (1936); *Stars* and *Whimsy,* for 15 instruments (1937); *Potomac,* orchestral suite (1940); *Agreeable Overture* (1949); *Rock,* symphonic poem (Vienna Philh., Feb. 15, 1955). Choral works: *Chain Gang Song* (1925); *Prophecy, 1792* (1943). —Cf. M. Goss, *Mary Howe,* in 'Modern Music Makers' (N. Y., 1952).

Howell, Dorothy, English composer; b. Handsworth, Feb. 25, 1898. She studied at the Royal Academy of Music (piano and composition) from 1914 until 1919; since 1924 professor of piano there, also at the T. Matthay School, London.—Works: *Lamia,* symphonic poem (1919); *Koong Shee,* orchestral ballet (1921); piano concerto (1923); *The Rock,* overture (1928); *Phantasy,* for violin and piano; piano pieces; songs.

Howells, Herbert Norman, prominent English composer; b. Lydney, Gloucestershire, Oct. 17, 1892. He studied at the Royal College of Music in London with Stanford and Parry (1912-17); in 1920 appointed teacher there. He traveled in South Africa, Canada, and the U. S. in 1922-23; in 1936 succeeded Holst as music director at St. Paul's Girls' School; honorary Mus. Doc. in the Univ. of Oxford (1937); received the order of Commander of the British Empire in 1953.—Works: piano concerto in C minor (London, July 10, 1913); *The B's,* orchestral suite (1915); *Puck's Minuet* and *Merry-Eye,* for orch. (1920); *Procession,* for orch. (1922); *Sine nomine,* fantasy for 2 solo voices, chorus, organ, and orch. (his most representative work; Gloucester Festival, 1922); 2nd piano concerto (1924); *Paradise Rondel*, for orch. (1925); *A Kent Yeoman's Wooing Song*, for 2 solo voices, chorus, and orch. (1933); *King's Herald* (for the coronation of George VI, 1936); *Elegy*, for strings (1937); cello concerto (1937); *Music for a Prince*, suite for orch. (1949); *Lady Audrey's Suite* for string quartet; *Phantasy String Quartet; Rhapsodic Quintet* for clarinet, 2 violins, viola, and cello; suite for pipes (1951); *Hymnus Paradisi*, for soprano, tenor, chorus, and orch. (1951); organ sonatas and smaller pieces. Church music: *Mass in the Dorian Mode* (Westminster Cathedral, 1912); *Missa Sabrinensis* (Worcester Festival, Sept. 7, 1954); many motets, Magnificats, and anthems. —Cf. H. J. Foss, *Herbert Howells: A Brief Survey of his Music*, in the 'Mus. Times' (Feb., 1930); J. Reginald, *Howells' Hymnus Paradisi*, in 'Music & Letters' (1952).

Howes, Frank Stewart, English writer on music; b. Oxford, April 2, 1891. He studied at St. John College (1910-14); then at the Royal College of Music in London (1920-22). In 1925 he became second music critic of 'The Times'; succeeded H. C. Colles as chief critic in 1943. From 1927 to 1945 he edited the 'Journal of the English Folk Dance and Song Society.' He also interested himself in musical psychology. His publications include: *The Borderland of Music and Pyschology* (1926); *William Byrd* (1928); *Appreciation of Music* (1928); *A Key to the Art of Music* (1935); *A Key to Opera* (in collaboration with Ph. Hope-Wallace; 1939); *The Music of William Walton* (2 vols.; 1941); *Full Orchestra* (1942); *Man, Mind and Music* (1948); *Music: 1945-50* (1951); *The Music of Ralph Vaughan Williams* (1954); many shorter essays. In 1954 he was awarded the Order of Commander of the British Empire (C. B. E.). —See his autobiographical notice in 'Die Musik in Geschichte und Gegenwart.'

Howland, William Legrand, American composer; b. Asbury Park, N. J., 1873; d. at his cottage, Douglas Manor, Long Island, N. Y., July 26, 1915. He studied with Philip Scharwenka in Berlin, and lived most of his life in Europe. His one-act opera, *Sarrona*, to his own libretto, was produced in Italian in Bruges, Belgium (Aug. 3, 1903) and subsequently had a number of performances in Italy; it was staged in N. Y. (in English) on Feb. 8, 1910; in Philadelphia (in German) on March 23, 1911. He wrote another opera, *Nita;* 2 oratorios (*The Resurrection* and *Ecce Homo)*, and some choral works.

Hoyer, Karl, German organist and composer; b. Weissenfels, Saale, Jan. 9, 1891; d. Leipzig, June 12, 1936. He studied at the Leipzig Cons. with Reger, Straube, and Krehl; was organist in Reval (1911), Chemnitz (1912-26), and at the St. Nicholas Church in Leipzig (from 1926); also taught organ and theory at the Leipzig Cons. He wrote about 50 valuable organ works, also selections for organ and string orch.; chamber music; choral works; and songs.

Hřimalý (r'zhē-mah'-lē), **Adalbert (Vojtech)**, Czech violinist and composer; b. Pilsen, July 30, 1842; d. Vienna, June 15, 1908. A member of an exceptionally musical family, whose father was an organist, and whose 3 brothers were violinists, he received an early training at home; then studied with Mildner at the Prague Cons. (1855-61); was subsequently active as conductor, composer, and teacher in various towns in Holland, Sweden, and Rumania. He wrote a great number of various works, including an opera, *Zaklety princ* (*The Enchanted Prince;* Prague, May 13, 1872).

Hřimalý (r'zhē-mah'-lē), **Johann (Jan)**, celebrated violinist and teacher; b. Pilsen, April 13, 1844; d. Moscow, March 1, 1915. Like his older brother, Adalbert, he studied at the Prague Cons. At the age of 24 he went to Moscow, where he became prof. of violin at the Cons. (1874). He remained in Moscow for 40 years until his death, and was regarded there as a great teacher; 2 generations of Russian violonists studied under him. He also organized a string quartet in Moscow; publ. *Tonleiterstudien und Übungen in Doppelgriffen für die Violine* (Prague, 1895).

Hřimalý (r'zhē-mah'-lē), **Ottokar**, Czech violinist; son of Adalbert Hřimalý; b. Cernauti, Rumania, Dec. 20, 1883; d. Prague, July 10, 1945. He studied at the Vienna Cons. In 1909 he went to Moscow, upon recommendation of his uncle, Johann Hřimalý prof. at the Moscow Cons., and remained there until 1922; then lived in Rumania; in 1939, went to Prague. He was known not only as a violin teacher, but also as a composer; wrote an opera, 2 symphonies, the symphonic poems *Ganymed* and *Der goldene Topf;* also chamber music and violin pieces.

Hristić, Stevan, Serbian composer; b. Belgrade, June 19, 1885. He studied in Leipzig and Rome, and later in Moscow and

Paris. Returning to Belgrade, he became conductor at the Opera Theater. His stage works, colored by French Impressionism, are very effective; his most successful work is the ballet *Legend of Okhrid* (1947). He further wrote an opera *Sunset* (1925) and many choral works, of which *Jesen* (*Autumn*) is popular.

Hruby, Viktor, Austrian composer; b. Vienna, May 9, 1894. He studied at the Music Academy in Vienna with Camillo Horn, Franz Schmidt, and Robert Heger; then conducted theater orchestras and military bands. He has written a number of effective orchestral works; also paraphrases, transcriptions, and pot-pourris.

Hsien-Ming, Lee, Chinese pianist; b. Shanghai, Aug. 5, 1918. She studied there and later in Paris; gave concerts in Europe; married the composer, Alexandre Tcherepnin, and settled with him in Chicago (1949). She has also appeared as narrator in some of her husband's works.

Hubay, Jenö, celebrated Hungarian violinist; b. Budapest, Sept. 15, 1858; d. Vienna, March 12, 1937. He received his initial training from his father, Karl Hubay, prof. of violin at the Budapest Cons.; gave his first public concert at the age of 11; then studied with Joachim in Berlin (1873-76). His appearance in Paris, at a Pasdeloup concert, attracted the attention of Vieuxtemps, of whom he became a favorite pupil; in 1882 he succeeded Vieuxtemps as prof. at the Brussels Cons. In 1886 he became prof. at the Budapest Cons. (succeeding his father); from 1919 to 1934 he was its director. In Budapest he formed the celebrated Hubay String Quartet. In 1894 he married the Countess Rosa Cebrain. Among his pupils were Vecsey, Szigeti, Telmányi, Eddy Brown, and other renowned violinists. Hubay was a prolific composer. He wrote the following operas (all produced in Budapest): *Alienor* (Dec. 5, 1891), *Le Luthier de Crémone* (Nov. 10, 1894), *A Falu Rossza* (*The Village Vagabond;* March 20, 1896), *Moosröschen* (Feb. 21, 1903); *Anna Karenina* (Nov. 10, 1923), *Az Álarc* (*The Mask;* Feb. 26, 1931); 4 symphonies: No. 1 (1885); No. 2, *1914-15* (1915); No. 3, *Vita Nuova,* for soli, chorus, and organ; No. 4, *Petöfi-Sinfonie,* for soli, chorus, and orch.; also *Biedermeyer Suite,* for orch. (1913); 4 violin concertos; 14 pieces for violin and orch., in the Hungarian manner, *Scènes de la Csárda; Sonate romantique,* for violin and piano; also edited the violin études of Kreutzer (1908), Rode, Mayseder, and Saint Lubin (1910).

Hubeau, Jean, French composer and pianist; b. Paris, June 22, 1917; entered Paris Cons. at the age of 9; studied piano with Lazare Lévy; composition with Jean and Noël Gallon and Paul Dukas. He won first prize for piano at 13, and for composition at 16; in 1934 he received the 2nd Grand Prix de Rome with his cantata *La légende de Roukmani.* He then traveled in Europe as pianist; gave concerts in Germany, Switzerland, Holland, and England. In 1942 he was appointed director of the Cons. of Versailles. —Works: ballets: *Trois Fables de La Fontaine* (Paris, March 2, 1945), *La Fiancée du Diable* (Paris, Dec. 8, 1945), *Un cœur de diamant ou l'Infante* (Monte Carlo, April 7, 1949); for orch.: *Tableaux hindous* (Paris, Oct. 18, 1936), violin concerto (Paris, March 30, 1941), cello concerto (Paris, Nov. 28, 1942), *Concerto héroïque,* for piano and orch. (Paris, Dec. 22, 1946); chamber music: violin sonata (1941), *Sonatine-Humoresque,* for horn, flute, clarinet, and piano (1942), sonata for trumpet and piano (1943), *Sonate-Caprice* for 2 violins (1944); piano sonata, other piano pieces; songs and choral works.—Cf. A. Machabey, *Portraits de trente musiciens français* (Paris, 1949; pp. 97-100).

Huber, Hans, Swiss composer; b. Eppenberg, near Olten, June 28, 1852; d. Locarno, Dec. 25, 1921. He studied at the Leipzig Cons. with Richter, Reinecke, and Wenzel (1870-74); then taught music at Wesserling, at Thann (Alsace), and at Basel; received an honorary degree of *Dr. phil.* from Basel Univ. (1892). In 1896 he became director of the Basel Cons., a post that he held until his death. Huber composed prolifically in all genres; his style combined the rhapsodic form typical of Lisztian technique with simple ballad-like writing. He often used Swiss songs for thematic material. In Switzerland his renown is very great and his works are frequently performed, but they are virtually unknown elsewhere. —Works: the operas, *Weltfrühling* (Basel, March 28, 1894), *Kudrun* (Basel, Jan. 29, 1896), *Der Simplicius* (Basel, Nov. 22, 1912), *Die Schöne Bellinda* (Bern, April 2, 1916), and *Frutta di Mare* (Basel, Nov. 24, 1918); 8 symphonies (all except No. 2 performed first in Basel): No. 1, *William Tell* (April 26, 1881), No. 2, *Böcklinsinfonie* (Zürich, July 2, 1900), No. 3, *Heroische* (Nov. 9, 1917), No. 4, *Akademische* (May 23, 1909), No. 5, *Romantische* (Feb. 11, 1906), No. 6

(Nov. 19, 1911), No. 7, *Swiss* (June 9, 1917), No. 8 (Oct. 29, 1921); 4 piano concertos (Basel, 1878, 1891, 1899, 1910); violin concerto (1878); sextet for piano and wind instruments (1900); quintet for piano and wind instruments (1914); 2 string quintets (1890, 1907); string quartet; 2 piano quartets; 5 piano trios; 10 violin sonatas; 5 cello sonatas, and a number of piano works, among them 48 preludes and fugues for piano, 4 hands. —Cf. E. Refardt, *H. Huber* (Leipzig, 1906); E. Refardt, *H. Huber, Beiträge zu einer Biographie* (1922); E. Refardt, *H. Huber* (Zürich, 1944; supersedes his previous monographs; contains a complete list of works and full bibliography); see also Gian Bundi, *H. Huber, Die Persönlichkeit nach Briefen und Erinnerungen* (1925).

Huber, Kurt, musicologist; b. Chur, Switzerland, Oct. 24, 1893; executed by the Gestapo in Berlin, July 13, 1943, for participation in the student conspiracy against the Nazi government. He studied with Sandberger and Kroyer in Munich (*Dr. phil.,* 1917); from 1920, taught at the Munich Univ.; publ. *Ivo de Vento* (Munich, 1918); *Die Doppelmeister des 16. Jahrhunderts* (Munich, 1920); *Der Ausdruck musikalischer Elementarmotive* (1923). From 1925 he devoted himself to collecting and recording old Bavarian folksongs, and publ. them (with Paul Klem). —Cf. W. H. Rubsamen, *Kurt Huber of Munich,* in the 'Mus. Quarterly' (April, 1944); Clara Huber, *Kurt Huber zum Gedächtnis* (Regensburg, 1947). Huber's lectures on musical esthetics were reconstructed, ed. by Otto Ursprung, and publ. as *Musikästhetik* (1954).

Huberman (hoo'-ber-man), **Bronislaw,** famous violinist; b. Czenstochowa, near Warsaw, Dec. 19, 1882; d. Nant-sur-Corsier, Switzerland, June 15, 1947. At a very early age he began to study the violin with Michalowicz, a teacher at the Warsaw Cons.; he then studied with Isidor Lotto; in 1892 he was taken to Berlin, where he studied with Joachim. He made public appearances at the age of 11, in Amsterdam, Brussels, and Paris. Adelina Patti heard him in London and engaged him to appear with her at her farewell concert in Vienna (Jan. 12, 1895); on Jan. 29, 1896 he played Brahms' violin concerto in Vienna; Brahms, who was present, commended him warmly. Huberman toured the U. S. in 1896-97; many world tours followed; he gave a series of 14 concerts in Paris (1920), 10 in Vienna (1924), 8 in Berlin (1926); toured America again in 1937. At a concert arranged on May 16, 1909 by the city of Genoa for the sufferers by the Messina earthquake, Huberman was honored by an invitation to play upon Paganini's Guarneri violin (preserved in the Museum of Genoa). He was teacher of a master class at the Vienna State Academy (1934-36); in 1936 he organized a new Palestine Symph. Orch., consisting chiefly of Jewish musicians who had lost their positions in Europe. He came to the U. S. in 1940; returned to Europe after the war. He publ. *Aus der Werkstatt des Virtuosen* (Vienna, 1912); *Mein Weg zu Paneuropa* (1925).

Hubert (hü-bär'), **Marcel,** French cellist; b. Lille, Aug. 17, 1906. He studied with André Hekking; graduated with first prize from the Paris Cons. in 1919; made his début in Paris as soloist with the Colonne Orch.; appeared with many other French orchestras; made his American début in New York on April 2, 1934; subsequently settled in New York.

Hubert, Nicolay Albertovitch, Russian conductor and pedagogue; b. St. Petersburg, March 19, 1840; d. Moscow, Oct. 8, 1888. He studied with his father; then at the St. Petersburg Cons. (1863) with Zaremba and Rubinstein. In 1869 he was in Odessa as opera conductor; in 1870 engaged as prof. of music theory at the Moscow Cons.; he succeeded Nicholas Rubinstein as its director in 1881, resigning in 1883. Hubert also wrote music criticism in Moscow newspapers.

Huberti, Léon-Gustave, Belgian composer; b. Brussels, April 14, 1843; d. Schaerbeek, June 28, 1910. He studied at the Brussels Cons., where he won the Prix de Rome in 1865 for his cantata *La Fille de Jephté.* He was director of Mons Cons. (1874-78); then conductor in Antwerp and Brussels; in 1899, appointed prof. at the Brussels Cons.; director of the Music School of St.-Josse-ten-Noodle-Schaerbeek. In 1891 he was elected a member of the Belgian Academy. —Works: 3 oratorios, *Een Laatste Zonnestraal* (1874), *Bloemardinne,* and *Willem van Oranjes dood;* the dramatic poem *Verlichting* (*Fiat lux*), for soli, chorus, organ, and orch.; the symph. poem *Kinderlust en Leed,* for chorus and orch.; *Symphonie funèbre; Suite romantique; In den Garade; Triomffeest,* with organ; also various festival marches, etc.; vocal soli with orchestral accompaniment; numerous French, Flemish, and German songs with piano; an *Andante et intermezzo,* for 4 flutes and orch.; a piano concerto; compositions for the piano (*Étude, Conte d'enfant, Tarentelle, Impromptu, Historiette, Étude rythmique,* and *Valse lente*); a men's chorus, *Van Maerlantszang;* publ. a book, *Histoire de la musique religieuse des Italiens et des Néerlandais* (Brussels, 1873).

Huberty, Albert, Belgian operatic bass; b. Seraing-sur-Meuse, Feb. 2, 1879; d. Nieuport-les-Bains, March 10, 1955. He studied in Brussels; sang in Belgium, Holland, and England; then in Montreal (1909-13). He made his Paris début at the Opéra-Comique, on May 20, 1915, as Roméo; thereafter, sang 62 different roles there.

Hucbald (Hugbaldus, Ubaldus, Uchubaldus), Flemish monk and musical theorist; b. at or near Tournai, c. 840; d. Saint-Amand, near Tournai, June 20, 930. He was a pupil of his uncle Milo, director of the singing school at Saint-Amand; then director of a similar school at Nevers (860); subsequently returned to Saint-Amand and succeeded his uncle. The following works are printed under his name in Gerbert's 'Scriptores' (vol. I): *De Harmonica institutione; Musica enchiriadis* (gives the earliest detailed account of the beginnings of polyphonic music and of the Daseian notation, in which the Greek rough-breathing sign is used in various combinations and positions to produce 18 symbols indicating that many pitches); *Scholia enchiriadis;* fragments entitled *Alia musica;* and *Commemoratio brevis de tonis et psalmis modulandis.* However, it has been established (by W. Mühlmann, in *Die 'Alia Musica';* Leipzig, 1914) that Hucbald was not the author of *Musica enchiriadis.* —Cf. C. E. H. de Coussemaker, *Memoire sur Hucbald et sur ses traités de musique* (1841); J. F. Rowbotham, *History of Music* (vol. III, p. 366 et seq.); Ph. Spitta, *Die 'Musica enchiriadis' und ihr Zeitalter,* in 'Vierteljahrsschrift für Musikwissenschaft' (vol. 5, pp. 443-82 and vol. 6, pp. 293-309); R. Schlecht, German transl. of the *Musica enchiriadis* in 'Monatshefte für Musikgeschichte' (1874-76); H. Riemann, *Geschichte der Musiktheorie* (Leipzig, 1898); E. J. Grutchfield, *Hucbald, A Millenary Commemoration,* in the 'Mus. Times' (1930; 2 installments); A. H. Fox-Strangways, *A Tenth Century Manual,* in 'Music & Letters' (1932); J. Handschin, *Etwas Greifbares über Hucbald,* in 'Acta musicologica' (vol. VII, p. 158); R. Weakland, *Hucbald as Musician and Theorist,* in the 'Mus. Quarterly' (Jan., 1956).

Hudoy (Houdoy) (ü-dwah'), **Jules François Aristide,** French writer on music; b. Lille, Dec. 12, 1818; d. there, Jan. 28, 1883. He was President of the 'Société des Sciences et des Arts' at Lille; author of *Histoire artistique de la cathédrale de Cambrai* (Lille, 1880), a very valuable work as regards the music of the 15th century.

Hüe, Georges-Adolphe, French composer; b. Versailles, May 6, 1858; d. Paris, June 7, 1948. He was a pupil in the Paris Cons. of Reber and Paladilhe; took first Grand Prix de Rome in 1879, and the Prix Crescent in 1881; lived in Paris as teacher and composer; member (succeeding Saint-Saëns) of the Académie des Beaux-Arts (1922). —Works: the operas *Les Pantins* (Opéra-Comique, Dec. 28, 1881), *Le Roi de Paris* (Opéra, April 26, 1901), *Titania,* after Shakespeare (Opéra-Comique, Jan. 20, 1903), *Le Miracle* (Opéra, Dec. 30, 1910), *Dans l'ombre de la cathédrale,* after Blasco Ibañez (Opéra-Comique, Dec. 7, 1921), *Riquet à la houppe,* after Perrault (Opéra-Comique, Dec. 21, 1928); the ballet *Cœur brisé* (Paris, 1890); pantomime, *Siang Sin* (Opéra, March 19, 1924); *Rübezahl,* symphonic legend in 3 parts (Concerts Colonne, 1886); 'féerie dramatique' *La Belle au bois dormant* (Paris, 1894); *Résurrection,* 'épisode sacré' (1892); *Le Berger,* ballade and fantaisie for violin and orch. (1893); one symphony; *Rêverie* and *Sérénade* for small orch., *Romance* for violin and orch., choral works, and songs of more than average merit (6 songs from Heine's *Lyrisches Intermezzo; Croquis d'Orient; Chansons printanières; Berceuse pour les gueux, Deux Chansons,* etc.).

Hueffer, Francis, English author and music critic; b. Münster, May 22, 1843; d. London, Jan. 19, 1889. He studied modern philology and music in London, Paris, Berlin, and Leipzig; received a Dr. phil. degree from Göttingen Univ. for his first publication (1869), a critical edition of the works of Guillem de Cabestant, troubadour of the 12th century. In 1869 he settled in London as a writer on music, and from 1878 was music critic of the 'Times.' He wrote the librettos of Mackenzie's *Colomba* and *The Troubadour,* and of Cowen's *Sleeping Beauty;* translated the libretto of Verdi's *Otello* into English. He publ. *Richard Wagner and the Music of the Future* (1874), *The Troubadours: a History of Provençal Life and Literature in the Middle Ages* (1878), *Musical Studies* (1880; reprints of his articles from the 'Times' and 'Fortnightly

Review,' Italian transl., Milan, 1883), *Italian and Other Studies* (1883), *Half a Century of Music in England* (1889; 2nd ed., 1898); he also transl. the correspondence of Wagner and Liszt into English, and was editor of Novello's series of biographies 'The Great Musicians,' for which he wrote *Wagner* (1881).

Huehn, Julius, American baritone; b. Revere, Mass., Jan. 12, 1910. He studied at the Carnegie Institute of Technology; later studied voice with Anna Schoen-René at the Juilliard Graduate School, N. Y. He made his début with the Metropolitan Opera as the Herald in *Lohengrin* (Dec. 21, 1935); also appeared with the San Francisco, Chicago, and Los Angeles Operas.

Hughes, Dom **Anselm,** eminent English musicologist; b. London, April 15, 1889. He studied at Oxford (B.A., 1911; M.A., 1915); lectured on medieval church music in universities and colleges in the U. S. and Canada (1932, 1934, 1939, and 1940). He has contributed articles to 'Grove's Dictionary of Music and Musicians,' 'New Oxford History of Music,' and the 'History in Sound of European Music' (1948); edited *Missa O quam suavis* (1927) and (with others) the Old Hall Manuscript (1933-38); he is also a member of the editorial board of the New Oxford History of Music. His publications include *Early English Harmony* (vol. II; London, 1912); *Latin Hymnody* (London, 1923); *Worcester Mediaeval Harmony* (Burnham, 1928); *The House of My Pilgrimage* (London, 1929); *Anglo-French Sequelae* (London, 1934); *Index to the Facsimile Edition of MS Wolfenbüttel 677* (Oxford, 1939); *Liturgical Terms for Music Students* (Boston, 1940); *Medieval Polyphony in the Bodleian Library* (Oxford, 1951); *Catalogue of the Musical Manuscripts at Peterhouse, Cambridge* (Cambridge, 1953). He also contributed compositions to *The Tenor Tune Book* (London, 1917); composed *Missa Sancti Benedicti* (London, 1918); and various small pieces of church music.

Hughes, Edwin, American pianist; b. Washington, D. C., Aug. 15, 1884. He studied with S. M. Fabian in Washington, with Rafael Joseffy in New York (1906-07), and with T. Leschetizky in Vienna (1907-10); taught at the Ganapol School of Musical Art, Detroit (1910-12), Volpe Institute of Music, N. Y. (1916-17), and the Institute of Musical Art, N. Y. (1918-23); lectured at various schools. From 1920 to 1926 he was special editor of piano music for G. Schirmer, Inc.; edited Bach's *Well-tempered Clavichord* for Schirmer's Library of Musical Classics (with a preface in English and Spanish); publ. piano transcriptions of Strauss's Waltzes; wrote songs; etc.

Hughes, Herbert, Irish critic and composer; b. Belfast, March 16, 1882; d. Brighton, May 1, 1937. He studied at the Royal College of Music in London. He was one of the founders of the Irish Folksong Society and co-editor of its early journals; was music critic of the 'Daily Telegraph.' He collected and edited many folksongs, including the collections Boosey's *Modern Festival Series; Irish Country Songs* (in 4 vols.); *Old Irish Melodies* (3 vols.); *Historical Songs and Ballads of Ireland; Songs from Connacht; Songs of Uladh.* He composed incidental music to the comedy *And So To Bed,* the film *Irish Hearts; Nursery Rhymes,* studies in imitation (2 vols.); *Parodies,* for voice and orch. (2 vols.); *Brian Boru's March,* for piano; *3 Satirical Songs,* for violin, flute, clarinet, and bassoon; *Shockheaded Peter,* cycle for soprano, baritone, and piano; etc.

Hughes, Rupert, American writer on music; b. Lancaster, Mo., Jan. 31, 1872; d. Los Angeles, Sept. 9, 1956. He studied with W. G. Smith in Cleveland (1890-92), E. S. Kelley in New York (1899), and Ch. Pearce in London (1900-01). His publications include: *American Composers* (Boston, 1900; revised, 1914); *The Musical Guide* (2 vols., N. Y., 1903; republished as *Music Lovers' Encyclopedia,* in 1 vol., 1912; revised and newly edited by Deems Taylor and Russell Kerr as *Music Lover's Encyclopedia,* 1939; revised, 1954); edited 'Thirty Songs by American Composers' (1904). He composed a dramatic monologue for baritone and piano, *Cain* (1919); piano pieces, and songs. He was principally known, however, as a successful novelist.

Hugo, John Adam, American pianist and composer; b. Bridgeport, Conn., Jan. 5, 1873; d. there, Dec. 29, 1945. From 1888-97 he studied at the Stuttgart Cons. with Speidel, Faiszt, Doppler, and Zumpe; appeared as concert pianist in Germany, England, and Italy; returned to the U. S. in 1899. His one-act opera, *The Temple Dancer,* is one of the few operas by American composers presented in the Metropolitan Opera House, N. Y. (March 12, 1919); it was also produced in Honolulu (Feb. 19, 1925). His other works are the operas, *The Hero of Byzanz* (written while studying at the Stuttgart Cons.) and *The Sun God;* a symphony; 2 piano concertos; a piano trio; pieces for the violin; pieces for the cello; piano pieces, and songs.—Cf. E. E. Hipsher, *American Opera and Its Composers* (Philadelphia, 1927; pp. 270-74).

Hugon, Georges, French composer; b. Paris, July 23, 1904. He studied at the Paris Cons.; received the Prix Bizet (1926). He was director of the Cons. of Boulogne-sur-Mer (1934-41); in 1941, became prof. at the Cons. of Paris.—Works: oratorio, *Chants de deuil et d'espérance* (1947); 2 symphonies (1941, 1949); symph. poems, *Au nord* (1930) and *La reine de Saba* (1933); piano trio; string quartet; various pieces for piano; songs.—Cf. A. Machabey, *Portraits de trente musiciens français* (Paris, 1949; pp. 101-104).

Huhn, Bruno, song composer; b. London, Aug. 1, 1871; d. New York, May 13, 1950. He studied piano in London and New York; toured in Egypt, India, and Australia (1889-91). In 1891 he settled in New York, where he made a successful début as a pianist (April 17, 1896). Subsequently he held various positions as conductor of suburban choral groups and also as accompanist to singers. He wrote many sacred choruses and solo songs, of which his setting of Henley's *Invictus* (1910) attained great popularity.

Huízar, Candelario, Mexican composer; b. Jerez, Feb. 2, 1883. He studied violin and composition; in 1917 settled in Mexico City, where he continued his studies with Gustavo Campa. He was copyist in various music schools (1920-25), and in 1931 became librarian of the Conservatorio Nacional. His compositions reflect Mexican folklore, and often contain authentic Mexican themes.—Works: for orch. (all first performed in Mexico City): *Imágenes,* symph. poem (Dec. 13, 1929); Symphony No. 1 (Nov. 14, 1930); *Pueblerinas,* symph. poem (Nov. 6, 1931); *Surco,* symph. poem (Oct. 25, 1935); Symphony No. 2 (Sept. 4, 1936); Symphony No. 3 (July 29, 1938); Symphony No. 4 (Aug. 7, 1942); sonata for clarinet and bassoon (1931); string quartet (1938); choral works and songs.—Cf. J. C. Romero, *Candelario Huízar* in 'Nuestra Música' (Jan., 1952).

Hull, Arthur Eaglefield, English writer on music; b. Market Harborough, March 10, 1876; d. London, Nov. 4, 1928. He studied privately with Matthay and Charles Pearce in London; served as organist at Huddersfield Parish Church; was (from 1912) editor of the 'Monthly Musical Record.' In 1918 he founded the British Music Society; was its honorary director until 1921; Mus. Doc. (Queen's College, Oxford). In 1906 he married Constance Barratt, an accomplished violinist. A man of broad culture, he was an enthusiast for new music; was an early champion of Scriabin in England. In 1924 he brought out a *Dictionary of Modern Music and Musicians.* This was a pioneer volume, and despite an overabundance of egregious errors and misconceptions, is of service as a guide; a German transl. was made by Einstein, with numerous errors corrected (1926); another volume which still retains its value is *Modern Harmony: Its Explanation and Application* (London, 1914; 3rd ed., 1923; reprint, 1934). In 1927 he publ. a book, *Music, Classical, Romantic and Modern,* which proved to be a pasticcio of borrowings from various English and American writers; this was pointed out by many reviewers, and the book was withdrawn by the publishers in 1928; this episode led directly to Hull's suicide; he threw himself under a moving train at the Huddersfield Railway Station, suffered grave injuries and a loss of memory, and died a few weeks later. The list of his publications includes also *Organ Playing, Its Technique and Expression* (1911); *The Sonata in Music* (1916); *Scriabin* (1916); *Modern Musical Styles* (1916); *Design or Construction in Music* (1917); *Cyril Scott* (1918); he made English translations of Romain Rolland's *Handel* (1916) and *Vie de Beethoven;* edited the complete organ works of Bach and Mendelssohn (with annotations for students); was also editor of 'Music Lovers' Library' and 'Library of Music and Musicians' (in which his book on Scriabin appeared); other books by him in the same series were *Bach* and *Three English Composers.*

Hullah, John Pyke, English composer and organist; b. Worcester, June 27, 1812; d. London, Feb. 21, 1884. He was a pupil of William Horsley; in 1833 he studied singing with Crivelli at the Royal Academy of Music; as a composer he was entirely self-taught. At the age of 24 he produced an opera to a story by Charles Dickens, *The Village Coquette* (London, Dec. 6, 1836); 2 other operas followed: *The Barber of Bassora* (London, Nov. 11, 1837) and *The Outpost* (May 17, 1838). In the meantime, he obtained a post of church organist at Croydon. He made several trips to Paris, where he became interested in the new system of vocal teaching established by Wilhem; he modified it to suit English requirements, and, with the sanction of the National Education Committee, he opened his Singing School for Schoolmasters at Exeter Hall (1841). The school became the target of bitter criticism; nonetheless, it prospered; thousands of students enrolled; his wealthy supporters helped him build St. Martin's Hall for performances of vocal music by his students; the hall was inaugurated in 1850; it was destroyed by fire in 1860. From 1844-74 Hullah taught singing at King's College, and later at Queen's College and Bedford College in London. He conducted the student concerts of the Royal Academy of Music (1870-73); in 1872 he became Inspector of Training Schools. He held the honorary degree of LL. D. from Edinburgh Univ. (1876); was also a member of the Cecilia Society in Rome and of the Academy of Music in Florence. He edited Wilhem's *Method of Teaching Singing Adapted to English Use* (1841); publ. *A Grammar of Vocal Music* (1843); *A Grammar of Harmony* (1852); *A Grammar of Counterpoint* (1864); *The History of Modern Music* (1862); *The Third or Transition Period of Musical History* (1865); *The Cultivation of the Speaking Voice* (1870); *Music in the House* (1877); also brought out useful collections of vocal music: *The Psalter, The Book of Praise Hymnal,* the *Whole Book of Psalms with Chants.* He was the composer of the celebrated song *O that we two were Maying;* other popular songs are *The Storm* and *Three Fishers.* A *Life of John Hullah* was publ. by his wife (London, 1886).

Humbert (ön-bär'), **Georges,** Swiss organist and writer on music; b. St. Croix, Aug. 10, 1870; d. Neuchâtel, Jan. 1, 1936. He studied with Huberti at the Brussels Cons. and with Bargiel in Berlin. In 1892 he became prof. of music history at the Geneva Cons., retaining this post until 1912; from 1898 till 1918 he was organist at Morges. In 1918 he established the Neuchâtel Cons., and was its director until his death; also conducted various performing societies in Switzerland. He was editor of 'Gazette musical de la Suisse romande' (1894-96) and 'La Vie musicale' (1918-24); publ. *Notes pour servir a l'étude de l'histoire de la musique* (1904). He was the translator into French of Riemann's *Musiklexikon* (1899; 3rd ed., 1931).

Hume, Paul, American music critic; b. Chicago, Dec. 13, 1915; studied at the Univ. of Chicago; took private lessons in piano, organ, and voice; was organist, choirmaster, and a baritone soloist at various churches in Chicago and Washington; gave song recitals in Boston and in the Middle West; taught voice at Catholic Univ., Washington; in 1946, became music editor and critic of the 'Washington Post'; instructor in music history at Georgetown Univ. from 1949; contributor to 'Saturday Review' (N. Y.); active as lecturer and radio commentator on music; publ. *Catholic Church Music* (N. Y., 1956) and *Our Music, Our Schools, and Our Culture* (National Catholic Education Association, 1957). Paul Hume leaped to national fame in 1950 when President Truman, outraged by Hume's unenthusiastic review of Margaret Truman's song recital, wrote him a personal letter threatening him with bodily injury. Hume sold the letter to a Connecticut industrialist for an undisclosed sum of money.

Humfrey, Pelham, English composer; b. 1647; d. Windsor, July 14, 1674. He was among the first children appointed to the restored Chapel Royal in 1660, and (together with fellow-choristers John Blow and William Turner) he wrote the famous *Club Anthem.* In 1664 King Charles II sent him to study in France and Italy under the Secret Service Funds; that he worked under Lully remains unverified, nor can it be proved that he got to Italy. He returned to England in 1667 and was appointed Gentleman of the Chapel Royal on Oct. 26, 1667. An entry in Pepys' diary for Nov. 15, 1667 described him as being 'full of form, and confidence, and vanity' and disparaging 'everything, and everybody's skill but his own.' Humfrey's justification of his self-confidence lay in his undoubted mastery of the Italian declamatory style, greater than anyone had yet achieved in England. On July 15, 1672, he was appointed Master of the Children of the Chapel Royal. Two years later he died at the early age of 27. One of his wards was the young Henry Purcell, whose style clearly shows Humfrey's influence. Humfrey's works consist of 24 secular songs; 4 sacred songs; a dialogue, composed with John Blow; songs and vocal ensembles for Shadwell's version of Shakespeare's *The Tempest;* 3 odes, all to Charles II; 26 anthems, of which 19 are extant (one composed with John Blow and William Turner); *Have Mercy Upon Me, O God* in MS in the British Museum; *O Praise God in His Holyness* in MS at the Durham Cathedral Library; and *Hear My Prayer, O God* (in the Egerton MSS of the British Museum); etc.; one complete Service for the Anglican Church (Morning Prayer, Communion, and Evening Prayer); *The*

Grand Chant, a widely used Anglican chant. Seven anthems by Humfrey are included in Boyce's 'Cathedral Music'; 3 sacred songs in 'Harmonia Sacra' (1714); a number of secular songs in the following collections: Playford's *Choice Songs* (1673), *Choice Ayres, Songs and Dialogues* (1676-84); J. S. Smith's *Musica Antiqua* (1812).—Cf. W. Barclay Squire, *The Music of Shadwell's Tempest*, in the 'Mus. Quarterly' (Oct., 1921).

Humiston (hŏhm'-is-ton), **William Henry,** American organist; b. Marietta, Ohio, April 27, 1869; d. New York, Dec. 5, 1923. He studied organ with C. Eddy in Chicago (1885-94); at the same time, held various positions in and around Chicago as church organist. In 1896 he moved to New York, where he became a pupil of MacDowell (1896-99); served as organist at suburban churches until 1909; conducted traveling opera companies (1909-12). In 1912 he became the annotator of the programs of the N. Y. Philharmonic; also served as assistant conductor (1916). He wrote a *Southern Fantasy*, for orch. (1906); some overtures, and songs.

Hummel, Ferdinand, German composer and harpist; b. Berlin, Sept. 6, 1855; d. there, April 24, 1928. He gave concerts as a child harpist (1864-67); then studied music at Kullak's Academy in Berlin and later at the Hochschule für Musik there. He established himself as a teacher in Berlin, and also became a prolific composer. Much impressed by the realistic school of Italian opera (Mascagni), he wrote several short operas in the same genre: *Mara* (Berlin, 1893), *Angla* (Berlin, 1894), *Assarpai* (Gotha, 1898), *Sophie von Brabant* (Darmstadt, 1899), *Die Beichte* (Berlin, 1900), *Ein treuer Schelm*, and *Die Gefilde der Seligen* (Altenburg, 1917). He also wrote a symphony, a piano concerto, chamber music, choral works, aggregating to about 120 opus numbers.

Hummel, Johann Nepomuk, celebrated pianist and composer; b. Pressburg, Nov. 14, 1778; d. Weimar, Oct. 17, 1837. He studied with his father, Joseph Hummel, who was music master of the Imperial School for Military Music. In 1786 the father was appointed conductor at Schikaneder's Theater in Vienna, and there Mozart interested himself in young Hummel and took him into his house, and for 2 years instructed him. He made his début in 1787 at a concert given by Mozart in Dresden; 1788-93 he accompanied his father on professional concert tours as pianist, visiting Germany, Denmark, Scotland, England, and Holland. In London he studied briefly with Clementi; in Oxford he presented his string quartet. In 1793 he returned to Vienna, and began a course of studies with Albrechtsberger, and also profited by the counsel of Haydn and Salieri in composition. From 1804-11 he acted as deputy Kapellmeister for Haydn, in Prince Esterházy's service. In the meantime, he had his opera *Mathilde von Guise* produced in Vienna (March 26, 1810). He settled in Vienna in 1811 as a teacher; in 1816 was appointed court Kapellmeister at Stuttgart, and in 1819, at Weimar, a post he held until his death. His duties were not too rigorous, and he was allowed to make frequent professional tours. He traveled to St. Petersburg in 1822; in 1825 he was in Paris, where he was made Chevalier of the Legion of Honor; in 1826, visited Belgium and Holland; in 1827, was in Vienna, in 1828, in Warsaw, and in 1829, again in France. He conducted a season of German opera at the King's Theatre in London in 1833. The last years of his life were marred by ill health and much suffering. During the peak of his career as a pianist, he was regarded as one of the greatest virtuosos of his time; both as pianist and composer he was often declared to be the equal of Beethoven. His compositions were marked by excellent craftsmanship; his writing for instruments, particularly for piano, was impeccable; his melodic invention was rich, and his harmonic and contrapuntal skill was of the highest caliber. Yet, with his death, his music went into an immediate eclipse; performances of his works became increasingly rare, until the name of Hummel all but vanished from active musical programs. However, some of his compositions were revived by various musical societies in Europe and America, and as a result, at least his chamber music was saved from oblivion. He wrote 124 opus numbers; these include 9 operas, several ballets, cantatas; 3 Masses for 4 voices and organ; a Graduale and Offertorium, still in use in Austrian churches; 7 concertos and concertinos for piano and orch.; many works for piano solo; 6 piano trios; a piano quintet; quintet for violin, viola, cello, double bass, and piano; and septet in D minor (his most outstanding work), for flute, oboe, viola, horn, cello, double-bass, and piano. He also publ. *Anweisung zum Pianofortespiel* (1828), an elaborate instruction book and one of the first to give a sensible method of fingering. His wife, Elisabeth Hummel-Röckl (1793-

1883), was an opera singer.—Cf. G. Sporck, *L'Interprétation des sonates de J. N. Hummel* (Paris, 1933); K. Benyovszky, *J. N. Hummel, der Mensch und Künstler* (Bratislava, 1934).

Humperdinck, Engelbert, celebrated German composer; b. Siegburg, near Bonn, Sept. 1, 1854; d. Neustrelitz, Sept. 27, 1921. He first studied architecture in Cologne; there he met Ferdinand Hiller, who discovered his musical talent and took him as a student at the Cologne Cons.; his other teachers there were Gernsheim and Jensen (composition), Seiss and Mertke (piano), Rensberg and Ehlert (cello). In 1876 he won a Mozart scholarship of Frankfurt; studied in Munich with Franz Lachner and Rheinberger; there he published his first works, *Humoreske,* for orch. (1880) and *Die Wallfahrt nach Kevlaar,* for chorus (1897), which won the Mendelssohn prize (1897); previously he won the Meyerbeer prize of 7,600 marks (1881), which enabled him to visit Italy and France. In Italy he met Wagner, who invited him to be his guest at Bayreuth. Here Humperdinck assisted in preparing the score of *Parsifal* for publication; from then on, the relations between Humperdinck and the Wagner family were most cordial; Siegfried Wagner became Humperdinck's pupil and received his entire musical education from him. From 1885-87, Humperdinck was prof. in the Cons. in Barcelona; after his return to Germany, he taught for a short time in Cologne, and then went to Mainz in the employ of the Schott publishing firm; in 1890 he became prof. at Hoch's Cons. in Frankfurt, and music critic for the 'Frankfurter Zeitung.' On Dec. 23, 1893, in Weimar, he produced the fairy-opera *Hänsel und Gretel* (text by his sister, Adelheid Wette). The work, aside from its intrinsic merit, appeared at the right psychological moment. The German public, weary of the bombast of the Wagner-imitators, were almost willing to accept the blunt realism of the Italian 'verismo' as a relief from the labored dullness of its native composers. And now a new composer, drawing inspiration from native folk music, found musical expression for a thoroughly German subject, and the public was delighted. Before a year had passed, the work was in the repertory of every German opera house; also abroad its success was extraordinary and lasting (London, Dec. 26, 1894; N. Y., Oct. 8, 1895). A host of imitators ransacked German fairy-lore, but with ill success. Since Humperdinck's health had never been robust, he determined after this success to give up teaching, and in 1896 he retired to Boppard on the Rhine to devote himself entirely to composition. His next work was *Die sieben Geislein* (Berlin, Dec. 19, 1895), a fairy play for children, written for voice and piano; in 1898 he wrote incidental music to Rosmer's *Königskinder* (Munich, Jan. 23, 1897); in this music Humperdinck made a bold attempt to prescribe definite rhythmic and pitch inflections ('Sprechnoten') to the actors in the drama. He later recast the score into an opera, which was produced at the Metropolitan Opera House, N. Y. (Dec. 28, 1910). In 1900 he became director (with practically nominal duties) of the 'Akademische Meisterschule' in Berlin. His other operas are *Dornröschen* (Frankfurt, Nov. 12, 1902); *Die Heirat wider Willen* (Berlin, April 14, 1905); *Die Marketenderin* (Cologne, May 10, 1914), and *Gaudeamus* (Darmstadt, March 18, 1919); he wrote incidental music for Berlin productions of 5 plays of Shakespeare, *The Merchant of Venice* (Nov. 9, 1905), *The Winter's Tale* (Sept. 15, 1906), *Romeo and Juliet* (Jan. 29, 1907), *Twelfth Night* (Oct. 17, 1907), *The Tempest* (Oct. 8, 1915); to *Lysistrata,* by Aristophanes (Berlin, Feb. 27, 1908), and *The Blue Bird,* by Maeterlinck (Berlin, Dec. 23, 1912). He contributed music to Max Reinhardt's production of *The Miracle* (London, Dec. 23, 1911). He further wrote a choral ballade, *Das Glück von Edenhall* (1884), *Maurische Rhapsodie,* for orch. (1898), and a symphony. Among his songs, the cycle *Kinderlieder* is particularly fine. Humperdinck's lasting fame still rests, however, upon his one opera *Hänsel und Gretel,* which succeeded thanks to Humperdinck's ability to write melodies of ingenuous felicity, despite the almost incompatible Wagnerian instrumental and dramatic design. — Cf. G. Münzer, *E. Humperdinck,* in 'Monographien moderner Musiker' (Leipzig, 1906); E. Istel, *German Opera since Richard Wagner,* in the 'Mus. Quarterly' (April, 1915); O. Besch, *E. Humperdinck* (Leipzig, 1915); H. Kühlmann, *Stil und Form in Humperdincks 'Hänsel und Gretel'* (Marburg, 1930).

Humpert, Hans, German composer; b. Paderborn, April 19, 1901; killed in battle at Salerno, Sept. 15, 1943. He studied at the Frankfurt Cons. and in Berlin; then taught at Paderborn until he was called into the army. His music is marked by a neo-Romantic quality, with a strong contrapuntal structure. There was a considerable revival of his works after his death. He wrote 2 symphonies (1937, 1942); 3 string quartets; string trio; violin sonata; viola sonata; sonata for flute solo; 5 cantatas; 4 Masses; 3 motets; 7 psalms; many choral and organ works.—Cf. G. Hoffmann, *Hans Humpert,* in 'Musica' (Sept., 1953).

Huneker (hyu'-nĕh-kĕr), **James Gibbons,** brilliant American journalist and writer on music; b. Philadelphia, Jan. 31, 1860; d. Brooklyn, Feb. 9, 1921. He studied piano with Michael Cross in Philadelphia, and in 1878 in Paris with Th. Ritter; later with Joseffy at the National Cons. in N. Y.; then taught piano there (1888-98). He was music and drama critic of the N. Y. 'Recorder' (1891-95), the 'Morning Advertiser' (1895-97); music, drama, and art critic for the 'Sun' (1900-12). In 1917 he was music critic of the Philadelphia 'Press'; after one season (1918-19) with the 'N. Y. Times,' he became music critic for the 'N. Y. World,' a position he held until his death; also wrote for various journals in N. Y., London, Paris, Berlin, and Vienna. He published a novel dealing with artistic life in N. Y., *Painted Veils* (1921), but he devoted most of his uncommon gifts to musical journalism. He was capable of rising to true poetic style, when writing about Chopin and other composers whom he loved; but he also possessed a talent for caustic invective; his attacks on Debussy were particularly sharp. He had a fine sense of humor, and candidly described himself as an 'old fogy.' In addition to his literary publications, he furnished introductory essays for Joseffy's edition of Chopin's works. — Writings: *Mezzotints in Modern Music* (1899); *Chopin: The Man and His Music* (1900; in German, 1914); *Melomaniacs* (1902); *Overtones, a Book of Temperaments* (1904); *Iconoclasts: A Book for Dramatists* (1905); *Visionaries: Fantasies and Fiction* (1905); *Egoists: A Book of Supermen* (1909); *Promenades of an Impressionist: Studies in Art* (1910); *Franz Liszt: A Study* (1911; in German, 1922); *The Pathos of Distance* (1913); *Old Fogy, His Musical Opinions and Grotesques* (1913); *New Cosmopolis* (1915); *Ivory Apes and Peacocks* (1915); *Unicorns* (1917); *The Philharmonic Society of New York and Its 75th Anniversary* (1917); *Bedouins* (1920); *Steeplejack* (his memoirs; 1920); *Variations* (1921). A selection of his letters was publ. posthumously by Josephine Huneker (1922); a collection of essays, with an introduction by Mencken, in 1929.—Cf. B. De Casseres, *James Gibbons Huneker* (N. Y., 1925).

Hünten, Franz, German pianist and composer; b. Coblenz, Dec. 26, 1793; d. there, Feb. 22, 1878. He studied with his father, an organist; at the age of 26 he went to Paris, and took courses at the Cons. with Pradher (piano) and Cherubini (composition); composed salon music for piano (fantasies, variations on opera themes, waltzes, etc.), some 250 opus numbers in all, most of which he succeeded in publishing; also brought out a *Méthode nouvelle pour le piano,* and other didactic compilations which became popular among teachers and students; Hünten was very much in demand as a piano teacher in Paris. Having accumulated considerable capital from his enterprises, he returned to Coblenz in 1848, and remained there until his death.

Huré (üh-rā'), **Jean,** French composer and writer on music; b. Gien, Loiret, Sept. 17, 1877; d. Paris, Jan. 27, 1930. He received his musical education at a monastery in Angers; went to Paris in 1895; there he founded the École normale pour pianistes (1912) and the monthly magazine 'L'Orgue et les Organistes' (1923); in 1925 he became church organist at St. Augustin; in 1926 he won the Prix Chartier for composition. His opera, *Le Bois sacré,* was produced at the Opéra-Comique; he further wrote incidental music to Musset's *Fantasio,* 3 symphonies, a violin concerto, concerto for saxophone and orch., 2 string quartets, piano quintet, violin sonata, 3 cello sonatas, etc.; publ. the manuals *La Technique du piano* (1908), *La Technique de l'orgue* (1918); also *L'Esthétique de l'orgue* (1923) and *Saint Augustin, musicien* (1924).—Cf. G. Migot, *Jean Huré* (1926).

Hurley, Laurel, American coloratura soprano; b. Allentown, Pa., Feb. 14, 1927. Of a musical family, she studied with her mother, a church organist; at 16, appeared on Broadway (Aug. 21, 1943) as Kathie in Romberg's operetta *The Student Prince;* then toured with the company that produced it. She was the winner of the Walter W. Naumburg Foundation Award, which enabled her to give a song recital in N. Y. (Nov. 6, 1952). She made her début at the Metropolitan Opera on Feb. 8, 1955, in a minor role; on Jan. 11, 1957, she appeared in the title role of *La Périchole.* On May 6, 1949, she married John Peter Butz.

Hurlstone, William Yeates, English composer and pianist; b. London, Jan. 7, 1876; d. there, May 30, 1906. A precocious musician, he composed waltzes as a young child; studied at the Royal College of Music with Stanford (composition) and Edward Dannreuther (piano); performed his piano concerto in 1896. In 1905 he was appointed prof. at the Royal College of Music. Among his works are the fairy suite *The Magic Mirror,* for orch.; *Variations on a Hungarian Air* and *Variations on a Swedish Air,* for orch.; quartet for flute, oboe, horn, and bassoon; quintet for flute, oboe, horn, bassoon, and piano; piano trio; trio for clarinet, bassoon, and piano; clarinet sonata; bassoon sonata; several song cycles. — Cf. H. G. Newell, *W. Y. Hurlstone: Musician and Man* (London, 1936); Katharine Hurlstone, *William Hurlstone, Musician: Memories and Records by His Friends* (London, 1949).

Hurum, Alf, Norwegian composer; b. Oslo, Sept. 21, 1882. He studied in Oslo, Paris, and Berlin. In 1920 he went to Hawaii; conducted the Honolulu Symph. Orch. (1924-26); then returned to Norway, settling in Bergen. Among his works is an *Exotic Suite* (Oslo, Jan. 20, 1918); *Fairyland,* suite (1921); *Bendik and Aarolilja,* symph. poem (1923); chamber music; several piano suites (*Gothic Pictures, Nordic Suite,* etc.).

Husa, Karel, Czech composer; b. Prague, Aug. 7, 1921. He studied in Prague; in 1946, went to Paris where he took lessons with Honegger and Nadia Boulanger. In 1954 he was appointed a member of the music faculty at Cornell Univ. — Works: *Trois fresques,* for orch.; *Divertimento,* for string orch; *Concertino,* for piano and orch.; *Portarit,* for string orch. (Donaueschingen, Oct. 10, 1953); 2 string quartets; piano pieces.

Hus-Desforges, Pierre Louis, French cellist and composer; b. Toulon, March 14, 1773; d. Pont-le-Voy, near Blois, Jan. 20, 1838. He studied at the Paris Cons.; played the cello in various orchestras; held numerous posts as theatrical conductor and teacher. He was conductor at the Théâtre-Français in St. Petersburg early in the 19th century; returning to France, was cellist at the Théâtre Saint-Martin in Paris; from 1819 until 1822 taught at Metz; in 1823 was in Bordeaux; from 1824 again in Paris. His name as composer appears for the first time as Citoyen Desforges, on a song entitled *L'autel de sa patrie* (Paris, 1798); he was the author of a *Méthode de violoncelle à l'usage des commençants* (Paris, 1828); a string quartet, and a 'Sinfonia concertante' with violin and cello obbligato; he also published a historical novel, *Sapho à Leucade* (Paris, 1818).

Huss, Henry Holden, American composer and pianist; b. Newark, N. J., June 21, 1862; d. New York, Sept. 17, 1953. He was a descendant of Leonhard Huss, brother of the Bohemian martyr, John Huss. His mother, Sophia Ruckle Holden Huss, was a granddaughter of Levi Holden, a member of Washington's staff. Huss studied piano and theory with his father and with Otis B. Boise. In 1882 he went to Germany, and studied organ and composition with Rheinberger at the Munich Cons.; graduated with a *Rhapsody* for piano and orch. (1885), which he subsequently performed with several American orchestras; also played his piano concerto in B major with the N. Y. Philharmonic, Boston Symph., etc. In 1904 he married Hildegard Hoffmann, a concert singer; they appeared frequently in joint recitals. He continued to compose music almost to the very end of his long life. His works include the symph. poems *Life's Conflicts* (1921) and *La Nuit* (originally for piano solo, 1902; orchestrated, 1939; first perf., Washington, March 12, 1942); 4 string quartets; violin sonata; cello sonata; viola sonata; choral works: *The 23rd Psalm, Mankind's Own Song, Winged Messengers of Peace, The Flag, The Fool's Prayer, Captain, Oh My Captain, Lord, Make My Heart a Place Where Angels Sing,* etc.

Hutchens, Frank, pianist and composer; b. Christchurch, New Zealand, Jan. 15, 1892. He studied at the Royal Academy of Music in London with Matthay (piano) and Corder (composition); taught there from 1908-14; in 1914, was appointed prof. at the State Cons. at Sydney, N. S. Wales. His compositions include *Ballade* for orch. (1938); concerto for 2 pianos and orch. (1940); *Air Mail Palestine,* for voice and orch. (1942); also piano pieces.

Hutcheson, Ernest, pianist; b. Melbourne, July 20, 1871; d. New York, Feb. 9, 1951. He studied piano in Australia with Max Vogrich; played concerts as a very young child; then was sent to the Leipzig Cons. to study with Reinecke, graduating in 1890. In 1898 he performed his own piano concerto with the Berlin Philharmonic. In 1900 he arrived in the U. S.; was head of the piano dept. at the Peabody Cons. in Baltimore (1900-12). In 1915 he created a sensation in New York by playing 3 concertos (Tchaikovsky, Liszt, and MacDowell) in a single evening; in 1919 he repeated his feat, playing 3 Beethoven concertos in one evening; during 1924-37 he was dean of the Juilliard School; in 1937, appointed its president. Among his compositions are several symphonic works and numerous piano pieces. He publ. *Elements of Piano Technique* (N. Y., 1907); *Elektra by Richard Strauss: A Guide to the Opera* (N. Y., 1910); *A Musical Guide to the Richard Wagner Ring of the Nibelung* (N. Y., 1940); *The Literature of the Piano* (N. Y., 1948).

Hutschenruyter (hüts'-hen-röi-ter), **Wouter,** Dutch composer; b. Rotterdam, Dec. 28, 1796; d. there, Nov. 18, 1878. He was a pupil of Hummel; also studied trumpet, and became a famous trumpet player. An energetic promoter of music, he organized a music corps of the Civic Guard (1821), conducted the municipal band (1822), established a choral society called 'Eruditio musica'; also led various other music societies. He wrote an opera, *Le Roi de Bohème;* 4 symphonies; more than 150 works for military band; *Konzertstück* for 8 kettledrums with orch.; cantatas, songs.

Hutschenruyter, Wouter; grandson of the preceding; Dutch conductor and writer on music; b. Rotterdam, Aug. 15, 1859; d. The Hague, Nov. 24, 1943. After diligent study, he became a choral conductor; in 1890, was appointed assistant conductor of the Concertgebouw in Amsterdam; from 1894 to 1917 he conducted the municipal band in Utrecht, which he brought to a high degree of excellence; performed many works by Dutch composers. From 1917-25 he taught at Rotterdam; then lived in The Hague. He wrote a number of symphonic and chamber works; publ. many books and manuals: *Orkest en orkestspel na 1600* (1903); *Mozart* (1905; new ed., 1927); *De geschiedenis der toonkunst* (1919); *Geschiedenis van het orkest en van den instrumenten* (1926); *De symphonieën van Beethoven geanalyseerd en toegelicht* (1928); *Chopin* (1926); *Mahler* (1927); *Wagner* (1928); *Brahms* (1929); *Richard Strauss* (1929); *De sonates van Beethoven toegelicht* (1930); *De Antwikkeling der Symphonie door Haydn, Mozart en Beethoven* (1931); *De Programma-Muziek* (1933); also a volume of personal memoirs (1930).

Hüttenbrenner, Anselm, Austrian composer; b. Graz, Oct. 13, 1794; d. Ober-Andritz, near Graz, June 5, 1868. At the age of 7 he studied with the organist Gell; in 1815 he went to Vienna to study law; also took lessons with Salieri there. Schubert was his fellow student, and they became close friends. Hüttenbrenner also knew Beethoven intimately, and was present at his death. He was an excellent pianist and a prolific composer; Schubert praised his works. He wrote 4 operas, 6 symphonies, 10 overtures, 9 Masses, 3 Requiems, 3 funeral marches, 2 string quartets, a string quintet, piano sonatas, 24 fugues, and other piano pieces; some 300 male quartets and 200 songs. One of his songs, *Erlkönig,* was included in the collection *12 Lieder der deutschen Romantik,* ed. by H. H. Rosenwald (1929). His reminiscences of Schubert were publ. by Otto Deutsch in 1906. It was Hüttenbrenner who came into the possession of many Schubert MSS after Schubert's death; the MS of Schuberts *Unfinished Symphony* was held by him until 1865. It has been suggested that Hüttenbrenner had lost the 3rd and 4th movements of Schubert's work, and for that reason was reluctant to part with the incomplete MS, but the extant sketches for the Scherzo make that unlikely. —Cf. K. Kurth, *Anselm Hüttenbrenner als Liederkomponist* (Cologne, 1932); T. C. L. Pritchard, *The Unfinished Symphony,* in the 'Music Review' (Jan., 1942).

Huybrechts, Albert, Belgian composer; b. Dinant, Feb. 12, 1899; d. Woluwé, Feb. 21, 1938. He studied at the Brussels Cons. with Joseph Jongen; his first success was the winning of the Elizabeth Sprague Coolidge prize (1926) for his violin sonata; he also won first prize at the Ojai Valley Festival with his string quartet (1926). He wrote in a moderately advanced idiom, and his music won renewed appreciation after his death. —Works: 2 symph. poems: *David* (1923) and *Chant d'Angoisse* (1930; his most distinctive work); concertino for cello and orch. (1932); violin sonata (1925); trio for flute, viola, and piano (1926); sextet for wind (1927); suite for flute, oboe, clarinet, bassoon, and piano (1929); sonatina for flute and viola (1934); string trio (1935); wind quintet (1936); 2 string quartets; cello pieces; songs, of which the best known is *Horoscopes* (1926). A catalogue of his works was publ. by the Centre Belge de Documentation Musicale (1954).

Hyde, Walter, English tenor; b. Birmingham, Feb. 6, 1875; d. London, Nov. 11, 1951. He studied with Gustave Garcia; sang in light opera before he undertook Wagnerian roles, which became his specialty. He sang Siegmund at Covent Garden in 1908; his other roles included Walter in *Die Meistersinger* and also Parsifal. He was a frequent participant at many musical festivals in England.

Hyllested, August, pianist and composer; b. Stockholm, June 17, 1856; d. Blairmore, Scotland, April 5, 1946. He played in public as a child; then studied at the Copenhagen Cons. with Niels Gade, and subsequently with Th. Kullak (piano) and Fr. Kiel (composition) in Berlin; then had some lessons from Liszt. He gave concerts as pianist in England (1883) and in America (1885). From 1886-91 he was prof. and assistant director of the Chicago Musical College; from 1891-94, taught piano at the Gottschalk Lyric School, Chicago. After a concert tour in Europe, he returned to Chicago in 1897; he was in Glasgow from 1903-14; then again in the U. S. (1916-19); in Denmark and Sweden (1919-21); in 1923, retired to Blairmore, where he died shortly before his 90th birthday. He publ. numerous piano pieces in a Romantic style (*Album Leaf, Valse sentimentale, Suite romantique,* etc.), a suite of Scandinavian dances; also a fantasia on Scotch tunes; choral pieces; a symph. poem, *Elizabeth,* with double chorus (London, 1897, composer conducting).

I

Ibach (ē'bäh), **Johannes Adolf,** German piano maker; b. Barmen, Oct. 20, 1766; d. there, Sept. 14, 1848. In 1794, he founded a piano factory at Barmen; also manufactured organs from 1834, with his son **C. Rudolf Ibach;** then traded under the name of 'Adolf Ibach & Sohn'; from 1839, as 'Adolf Ibach & Söhne,' when his son **Richard** joined. From 1862 the firm was known as 'C. Rudolf & Richard Ibach,' to distinguish it from another business founded by a third son, **Gustav J.** The same year C. Rudolf died, and in 1869 his son **Rudolf** (d. Herrenalb, Black Forest, July 31, 1892) continued the piano factory alone as 'Rudolf Ibach Sohn,' establ. a branch at Cologne, gained medals for the excellence of his pianos, and became purveyor to the Prussian court. **Richard Ibach** continued the organ-factory.—Cf. *Das Haus Ibach 1794-1894* (1895).

Ibert (ē-bär'), **Jacques,** French composer; b. Paris, Aug. 15, 1890. He studied at the Paris Cons. with Gedalge and Fauré (1911-14); during World War I served in the French Navy; returned to the Paris Cons. after the Armistice and studied with Paul Vidal; received the Prix de Rome in 1919 for his cantata *Le Poète et la Fée;* while in Rome, he wrote his most successful work, the symph. suite *Escales (Ports of Call),* inspired by a Mediterranean cruise while serving in the Navy. In 1937 he was appointed director of the Academy of Rome, and held this post until 1955, when he became director of the united management of the Paris Opéra and Opéra-Comique (until 1957). In his music, Ibert combines the most felicitous moods and techniques of Impressionism and neo-Classicism; his harmonies are opulent; his instrumentation is coloristic; there is an element of humor in lighter works, such as his popular orchestral *Divertissement* and an even more popular piece, *Le petit âne blanc* from the piano suite *Histoires.* His craftsmanship is excellent; an experimenter in tested values, he never fails to produce the intended effect. —Works: Operas: *Angélique* (Paris, Jan. 28, 1927); *Persée et Andromède* (Paris, May 15, 1929); *Le Roi d'Yvetot* (Paris, Jan. 15, 1930); *Gonzague* (Monte Carlo, 1935); *L'Aiglon,* after Edmond Rostand, in collaboration with Honegger (Monte Carlo, March 11, 1937); *Les Petites Cardinal,* with Honegger (Paris, 1938); *Barbebleue,* radio opera (Lausanne Radio, Oct. 10, 1943). Ballets (all first performed in Paris): *Les Rencontres* (Nov. 21, 1925); *Diane de Poitiers* (April 30, 1934, produced by Ida Rubinstein); *Les Amours de Jupiter* (March 9, 1946); *Le Chevalier errant* (May 5, 1950). For orch.: symph. poem, *Noël en Picardie* (1914); *Ballade de la geôle de Reading,* after Oscar Wilde (Paris, Oct. 22, 1922); *Escales,* 3 symph. pictures (Paris, Jan. 6, 1924); *Féerique,* a symph. scherzo (Paris, Dec. 12, 1925); concerto for cello and wind instruments (Paris, Feb. 28, 1926); *Divertissement,* suite (Paris, Nov. 30, 1930; from incidental music to *Le Chapeau de paille d'Italie); Paris,* suite for chamber orch. (Venice, Sept. 15, 1932; from incidental music to *Donogoo,* play by Jules Romains); flute concerto (Paris, Feb. 25, 1934); *Concertino da Camera* for saxophone and chamber orch. (Paris, May 2, 1935); *Capriccio* (1938); *Ouverture de fête* (Paris, Jan. 18, 1942); *Suite élisabéthaine* (1944); *Symphonie Concertante,* for oboe and string orch. (Basel, Feb. 11, 1949); *Louisville Concerto* (Louisville, Feb. 17, 1954). Vocal works: *Le Poète et la Fée,* cantata (1919); *Chant de Folie* for solo voices, chorus, and orch. (Boston, April 23, 1926); *Trois chansons* for voice and orch. or piano; *La Verdure dorée,* for voice and piano; *Chanson du rien,* for voice and piano; *Quintette de la peur* for chorus and piano (1946). Chamber music: *2 mouvements,* for 2 flutes, clarinet, and bassoon (1923); *Jeux,* sonatina for flute and piano (1924); *3 pièces brèves,* for flute, oboe, clarinet, horn, and bassoon (1930); *Pastoral,* for 4 fifes (in *Pipeaux,* by various composers, 1934); *Entr'acte,* for flute and guitar (1935); string quartet (1944); trio for violin, cello, and harp (1944); *2 Interludes* for violin and harpsichord (1949); also 6 pieces for harp (1917); a piece for unaccompanied flute (1936). For piano: *Histoires* (10 pieces); *Les Rencontres,* arranged from the ballet (5 pieces); *Petite suite en 15 images* (1943).—Cf. A. Hoerée, *J. Ibert,* in 'Revue Musicale' (July, 1929); G. Samazeuilh, *Musiciens de mon temps* (Paris, 1947).

Idelsohn (ē'-dĕl-son), **Abraham Zevi,** eminent Jewish musicologist; b. Pfilsburg, near Libau (Latvia), July 13, 1882; d. Johannesburg, South Africa, Aug. 14, 1938. He studied in Königsberg, at the Stern Cons. in Berlin, and with Jadassohn and Kretzschmar at the Leipzig Cons. He possessed a powerful baritone voice and for a time was cantor of the Synagogue at Regensburg (1903); then went to Johannesburg and later (1905-21) to Jerusalem, where he founded an Institute for Jewish Music (1910) and a Jewish Music School (1919). In 1921, he returned to Germany; then lectured in England; from 1924-34, was prof. at the Hebrew Union College, Cincinnati. In 1934 he suffered a paralytic stroke; was taken to Miami, and in 1937 to Johannesburg, where he finally succumbed. Idelsohn was one of the greatest authorities on Jewish music and contributed much towards its establishment on a scientific basis. He publ. a quantity of studies in English, German, and Hebrew on Oriental and Hebrew music, of which the most important are; *History of Jewish Music* (in Hebrew, 1924; 2nd ed., 1928, also publ. in English); *The Ceremonies of Judaism* (1929-30); *Diwan of Hebrew and Arabic Poetry of the Yemenite Jews* (in Hebrew; 1930); *Jewish Liturgy and Its Development* (1932; reprint issued by the Hebrew Union College, N. Y., 1956); *Musical Characteristics of East European Jewish Folk-Songs,* in the 'Mus. Quarterly' (Oct., 1932). His most important contribution to the study of Jewish music is the monumental 'Thesaurus of Hebrew-Oriental Melodies' (10 vols.; 1914-32), in which are collected, with the aid of phonograph recordings, Jewish melodies of Northern Africa, Asia Minor, Palestine, and other parts of the world. He also composed and publ. 6 Synagogue Services, Hebrew songs (1929), a music drama *Jephtah* (1922), and a *Jewish Song Book for Synagogue, Home and School* (1929).

Ifukube, Akira, Japanese composer; b. Kushiro (Hokkaido), March 7, 1914. As a young man, he was trained in forestry; then turned to music, and took lessons from Alexander Tcherepnin, who was in Japan at the time. Ifukube has written several ballets based on Japanese melodies and employing Impressionistic harmonies: *Enchanted Citadel* (Tokyo, Dec. 20, 1949), *Drums of Japan* (Tokyo, Dec. 29, 1951), etc.; for orch.: *Japanese Rhapsody* (Boston, April 5, 1936); *Aboriginal Triptych* (1938); *Symphonie Concertante* for piano and orch. (Tokyo, March 3, 1942; music destroyed in an air raid); *Ballade Symphonique* (Tokyo, Nov. 20, 1943); *Arctic Forest* (Changchun, Manchuria, April 26, 1944); also a violin concerto (Tokyo, June 22, 1948).

Ikenouchi, Tomojiro, Japanese composer, b. Tokyo, Oct. 21, 1906. He received his musical education at the Paris Cons.; upon his return to Japan, was appointed professor of composition at Tokyo University. — Works: *Yuya,* music for a *Nō* drama (Tokyo, Feb. 1, 1943); 2 symph. movements (Tokyo, Nov. 4, 1951); 3 string quartets, etc.

Ikonen, Lauri, Finnish musicologist and composer; b. Mikkeli, Aug. 10, 1888. He studied at the Helsingfors Univ. and with Paul Juon in Berlin; editor of the Finnish music magazine 'Suomen Musikkilehti' (1923-29); in 1946, received the Sibelius stipend. He has written 5 symphonies (No. 3, 1942; No. 4, 1943; No. 5, 1945); violin concerto (1941); cello concerto (1942); piano concerto (1943); chamber music; choral works; piano pieces; songs.

Ikonomov (ē-koh-noh'-mohv), **Boyan,** Bulgarian composer; b. Nikopol, Dec. 14, 1900. He studied composition at the Schola Cantorum in Paris (1928-32) and conducting with Weingartner in Basel (1934), was music director of the Sofia Radio (1937-48); since 1948, music director of the Bulgarian film center.—Works: 2 symphonies (1937; 1947); violin concerto (1938); concertino for piano and string orch. (1939); 6 string quartets (1933-49).

Ilerici, Kemal, Turkish composer; b. Kastamonu, Oct. 15, 1910. He studied composition with Ferit Alnar. Among his works are a symphonic suite, *In My Village* (1945), *Pastoral Fantasy* for orch. (1951), a string quartet, a suite for oboe and piano, and choral works. He has also written a book on Turkish music, *Türk Musikisi Tonal Sistemi ve Armonisi* (1948).

Iliffe, Frederick, English composer; b. Smeeton-Westerby, Leicester, Feb. 21, 1847; d. Oxford, Feb. 2, 1928. He was organist at St. John's College in Oxford; wrote an oratorio, *The Visions of St. John the Divine* (1880); a cantata, *Lara* (1885); organ music; publ. *Critical Analysis of Bach's Well-tempered Clavichord* (London, 1896).

Ilitsch, Daniza, Serbian soprano; b. Belgrade, Feb. 21, 1919. She studied at the Stankovic Cons. there; made her début as Nedda in *Pagliacci* with the Berlin State Opera (Nov. 6, 1936); was on its staff for 2 seasons; then became a member of the Vienna State Opera (1938-41); the German army of occupation put her in a concentration camp in 1944, and she spent 4 months there until the liberation of Vienna. In 1947 she came to America; made her début with the Metropolitan Opera as Desdemona (March 12, 1947).

Illica (il'-lē-kah), **Luigi,** Italian librettist; b. Castell' Arguato, Piacenza, May 9, 1857; d. there, Dec. 16, 1919. He was engaged as a journalist in Milan; after 1892 devoted himself to writing librettos. He was the author (in collaboration with Giacosa) of librettos for Puccini's operas *La Bohème, Tosca,* and *Madama Butterfly;* and the sole writer of the text for Giordano's *Andrea Chenier* and *Siberia,* Mascagni's *Le maschere,* etc.

Ilyinsky, Alexander Alexandrovitch, Russian composer; b. Tsarskoye Selo, Jan. 24, 1859; d. Moscow, 1919. He studied in Berlin with Kullak (piano) and Bargiel (composition); upon returning to Moscow in 1885, was teacher at the Philharmonic Institute there. He wrote an opera, *The Fountain of Bakhtchissaray;* publ. *Trois valses brillantes* for piano, etc.

Imbert (an-bär'), **Hugues,** French music critic and essayist; b. Moulins-Engilbert, Nièvre, Jan. 11, 1842; d. Paris, Jan. 15, 1905. He studied violin in Paris with Faucheux; became editor of the Paris section of Kufferath's 'Guide musical'; in 1900, general editor. He publ. *Profils des Musiciens* (in 3 series: 1888, 1892, 1897); *Symphonie* (1891); *Portraits et Études* (1894); *Rembrandt et Wagner* (1897); *Charles Gounod, l'Autobiographie et les Mémoires* (1897); *Bizet* (1899); *La Symphonie après Beethoven* (1900); *Médaillons contemporains* (1902); *J. Brahms; Sa vie et son œuvre* (publ. posthumously, 1906).

Imbert, Maurice François, French composer; b. Sens, Yonne, April 25, 1893. He studied with Gedalge in Paris; from 1920, was active mainly as a music critic. He composed several symph. works: *Conquête de la Belle au Bois dormant, Journal de Vacances,* etc.; songs.

Imbrie, Andrew Welsh, American composer; b. New York, April 6, 1921. He studied piano with Leo Ornstein and Robert Casadesus; composition with Roger Sessions and Nadia Boulanger. He received his academic education at Princeton Univ. (A.B., 1942) and at the Univ. of California (M.A., 1947). During World War II he was in the U. S. Army Signal Corps. In 1947 he was awarded the American Prix de Rome. In 1953 he received a Guggenheim Fellowship. He was at the American Academy in Rome from 1947-51 and again in 1953-54; in the interim he taught at the Univ. of California. His style of composition is marked by formal clarity, lucidity of polyphonic texture, and sharp melodic line. His works include: *Ballad* for orch. (1947; performed in Florence, June 20, 1949); violin concerto (1953); string quartet No. 1 (N. Y. Music Critics' Award, 1944); piano trio (1946); piano sonata (1947); *Divertimento* for 6 instruments (1948); *On the Beach at Night* for mixed chorus and string orch. (1948); *Serenade* for flute, viola, and piano (1952); string quartet No. 2 (1953).

Inch, Herbert Reynolds, American composer; b. Missoula, Montana, Nov. 25, 1904. He studied at the State Univ. of Montana and then at the Eastman School of Music in Rochester, with Howard Hanson (Mus. Bac., 1925; M.M., 1928; B.A., 1931). After teaching for several years at the Eastman School, he became a member of the faculty at Hunter College, N. Y., in 1937. He was a fellow of the American Academy in Rome in 1931; traveled in India and Australia in 1934. — Works: *Variations on a Modal Theme* (Rochester, April 29, 1927); *Three Pieces,* for small orch. (Rochester, Oct. 24, 1930); Symphony No. 1 (Rochester, May 5, 1932); *Serenade,* for small orch. (Rochester, Oct. 24, 1939); piano concerto (1940); *Answers to a Questionnaire,* for orch. (1942); *Northwest Overture* (1943); violin concerto (Rochester, May 1, 1947); *Return to Zion,* for women's chorus (1945); piano quintet (1930); *Mediterranean Sketches,* for string quartet (1933); *Divertimento,* for brass (1934); string quartet (1936); cello sonata (1941); *Three Conversations,* for string quartet (1944).

d'Indy (dăn-dē'), **(Paul-Marie-Théodore-) Vincent**, eminent French composer; b. Paris, March 27, 1851; d. there, Dec. 2, 1931. Owing to the death of his mother at his birth, his education was directed entirely by his grandmother, a woman of culture and refinement who had known Grétry and Monsigny, and who had shown a remarkable appreciation of the works of Beethoven when that master was still living. From 1862-5 he studied piano with Diémer, and later harmony and theory with Marmontel and Lavignac. In 1869 he made the acquaintance of Henri Duparc, and with him spent much time studying the masterpieces of Bach, Beethoven, Berlioz, and Wagner; at that time, he wrote his op. 1 and 2, and contemplated an opera on Victor Hugo's *Les Burgraves* (1869-72; unfinished). During the Franco-Prussian war he served in the Garde Mobile, and wrote his experiences in *Histoire du 105ᵉ bataillon de la Garde nationale de Paris en l'année 1870-71* (1872). He then began to study composition with César Franck, continuing until 1880; when the latter was appointed prof. of organ at the Cons. (1873), he joined the class, winning a second accessit in 1874 and the first the following year. On his first visit to Germany in 1873 he met Liszt and Wagner, and was introduced to Brahms; in 1876, heard the first performances of the *Ring* dramas at Bayreuth, and for several years thereafter made regular trips to Munich to hear all the works of Wagner; also attended the première of *Parsifal* in 1882. From 1872-6, organist at St.-Leu; 1873-8, chorusmaster and timpanist with the Colonne Orch.; for the Paris première of *Lohengrin* in 1887 he drilled the chorus and was Lamoureux's assistant. In 1871 he joined the 'Société Nationale de Musique' as a junior member, and was its secretary from 1876 till 1890, when, after Franck's death, he became president. In 1894 he founded with Bordes and Guilmant the famous 'Schola Cantorum' (opened 1896), primarily as a school for plainchant and the Palestrina style. Gradually the scope of instruction was enlarged so as to include all musical disciplines, and the institution became one of the world's foremost music schools. From the beginning d'Indy not only was one of the directors, but also taught; after the death of Guilmant (1911) he became sole director. His fame as a composer began with the performance of *Le Chant de la cloche* at a Lamoureux concert in 1886; the work itself had won the City of Paris Prize in the competition of the preceding year. As early as 1874 Pasdeloup had played the overture *Piccolomini* (later embodied as the second part in the *Wallenstein* trilogy), and in 1882 the 1-act opera *Attendez-moi sous l'orme* had been produced at the Opéra-Comique; but the prize work attracted general attention, and d'Indy was recognized as one of the most important of modern French masters. Although he never held an official position as conductor, he frequently, and with marked success, appeared in that capacity (chiefly upon invitation to direct his own works); thus he visited Spain in 1897, Russia in 1903 and 1907, and the U. S. in 1905, when he conducted the regular subscription concerts of Dec. 1 and 2 of the Boston Symph. Orch. In 1892 he was a member of the commission appointed to revise the curriculum of the Conservatoire, and refused a proffered professorship of composition; but in 1912 accepted an appointment as prof. of the ensemble class. Besides other duties, he discharged, from 1899, those of inspector of musical instruction in Paris; last U. S. visit in 1921. He was made Chevalier of the Legion of Honor in 1892, Officer in 1912; was also member of many academies and artistic associations (in Belgium, Holland, Spain, Italy, Sweden, etc.).

Both as teacher and creative artist d'Indy continued the traditions of César Franck. Although he cultivated almost every form of composition, his special talent seemed to be in the field of the larger instrumental forms. Some French critics assign to him a position in French music analagous to that of Brahms in German music. His style rests on Bach and Beethoven; however, his deep study of Gregorian Chant and the early contrapuntal style added an element of severity, and not rarely of complexity, that renders approach somewhat difficult, and has prompted the charge that his music is lacking in emotional force.—For the edition of Rameau's complete works (ed. by Saint-Saëns and Malherbe) he revised *Dardanus, Hippolyte et Aricie,* and *Zaïs;* also ed. Monteverdi's *Orfeo* and *Incoronazione di Poppea;* he also made piano arrangements of orchestral works by Chausson, Duparc, and other composers. His numerous articles in various journals are remarkable for critical acumen and literary finish. He publ. an important manual, *Cours de Composition musicale* (Book I, 1903; Book II: Part 1, 1909, Part 2, 1933); *César Franck,* in 'Les Maîtres de la Musique' (1906); *Beethoven: Biographie critique* (1911; English transl. by Th. Baker, Boston, 1913); *La Schola Cantorum en 1925* (1927); *Wagner et son influence sur l'art musical français* (1930); *Introduction à l'étude de Parsifal* (1937; posthumous). — Works: for the stage: op. 14, *Attendez-moi sous l'orme,* 1-act comic opera (Opéra-Comique, Feb. 11, 1882); op. 18, *Le Chant de la cloche,* dramatic legend (Brussels, Théâtre de la Monnaie, Dec. 22, 1912); op. 40, *Fervaal,* lyric drama (Brussels, March 12, 1897); op. 53, *L'Étranger,* lyric drama (Brussels, Jan. 7, 1903); op. 67, *La Légende de Saint-Christophe,* lyric drama (Paris Opéra, June 9, 1920); op. 80, *Le Rêve de Cynias,* lyric comedy (Paris, June 10, 1927). For orch.: op. 5, *Jean Hunyade,* symph. (Paris, May 15, 1875); op. 6, *Antoine et Cléopâtre,* overture (Paris, Feb. 4, 1877); op. 8, *La Forêt enchantée,* symph. legend (Paris, March 24, 1878); op. 12, *Wallenstein,* symphonic trilogy: a) *Le Camp de Wallenstein* (April 12, 1880), b) *Max et Thécla* (Jan. 25, 1874; originally *Les Piccolomini*), c) *La Mort de Wallenstein* (April 11, 1884); op. 19, *Lied* for cello and orch. (Paris, April 18, 1885); op. 21, *Saugefleurie,* legend (Paris, Jan. 25, 1885); op. 25, *Symphonie Cévenole (sur un chant montagnard français)* for orch. and piano (Paris, March 20, 1887); op. 28, *Sérénade et Valse* (from op. 16 and 17), for small orch. (1887); op. 31, *Fantaisie* for oboe and orch. (Paris, Dec. 23, 1888); op. 34, incidental music to Alexandre's *Karadec* (Paris, May 2, 1891); op. 36, *Tableaux de Voyage* (Le Havre, Jan. 17, 1892); op. 42, *Istar,* symph. variations (Brussels, Jan. 10, 1897); op. 47, incidental music to Mendès' *Medée* (1898); op. 55, *Choral varié* for saxophone and orch. (Paris, May 17, 1904); op. 57, 2nd Symphony in B♭ (Paris, Feb. 28, 1904); op. 61, *Jour d'été à la montagne* (Paris, Feb. 18, 1905); op. 62, *Souvenirs,* tone poem (Paris, April 20, 1907); op. 67, *La Queste de Dieu,* descriptive symph. (from *La Légende de Saint-Christophe;* 1917); op. 70, 3rd symphony: *Sinfonia Brevis de Bello Gallico* (1916-18; Paris, Dec. 14, 1919); op. 77, *Le Poème des rivages* (N. Y., Dec. 1, 1921); op. 87, *Diptyque méditerranéen* (Paris, Dec. 5, 1926); op. 89, concerto for piano, flute, cello, and string orch. (Paris, April 2, 1927). Chamber music: op. 7, piano quartet in A minor (1878); op. 24, suite in D for trumpet, 2 flutes, and string quartet (Paris, March 5, 1887); op. 29, trio for piano, clarinet, and cello (1888); op. 35, string quartet No. 1 (1891); op. 45, string quartet No. 2 (1898); op. 50, *Chansons et Danses, divertissement* for 7 wind instruments (Paris, March 7, 1899); op. 59, violin sonata (1905); op. 81, piano quintet in G minor (1925); op. 84, cello sonata (1926); op. 91, *Suite en 4 parties* for flute, strings, and harp (Paris, May 17, 1930); op. 92, string sextet (1928); op. 96, string quartet No. 3 (1929); op. 98, trio No. 2, for piano, violin, cello (1929). Vocal works: op. 2, *Chanson des aventuriers de la mer,* for baritone solo and men's chorus (1870); op. 11, *La Chevauchée du Cid,* for baritone, chorus, and orch. (1879); op. 22, *Cantate Domino* (1885); op. 23, *Ste. Marie-Magdeleine,* cantata (1885); op. 32, *Sur la Mer,* for women's voices and piano (1888); op. 37, *Pour l'inauguration d'une statue,* cantata (1893); op. 39, *L'Art et le Peuple,* for men's chorus (1894); op. 41, *Deus Israël,* motet (1896); op. 44, *Ode à Valence* for soprano and chorus (1897); op. 46, *Les Noces d'or du Sacerdoce* (1898); op. 49, *Sancta Maria,* motet (1898); op. 90 and 100, *6 Chants populaires français,* for a cappella chorus (1928 and 1931); op. 93, *Le Bouquet de printemps,* for women's chorus (1929); songs (op. 3, 4, 10, 13, 20, 43, 48, 52, 56, 58, 64). For piano: op. 1, *Trois Romances sans paroles* (1870); op. 9, *Petite Sonate* (1880); op. 15, *Poème des Montagnes: Le Chant des Bruyères, Danses rythmiques, Plein-air* (1881); op. 16, *Quatre Pièces* (1882); op. 17, *Helvetia,* 3 waltzes (1882); op. 21, *Saugefleurie* (1884; also arranged for orch.); op. 26, *Nocturne* (1886); op. 27, *Promenade* (1887); op. 30, *Schumanniana,* 3 pieces (1887); op. 33, *Tableaux de Voyage,* 13 pieces (1889); op. 60, *Petite chanson grégorienne,* for piano 4 hands (1904); op. 63, sonata (1907); op. 65, *Menuet sur le nom de Haydn* (1909); op. 68, 13 short pieces; op. 69, *12 petites pièces faciles,* in old style; op. 73, *7 Chants de terroir* for piano 4 hands; op. 74, *Pour les enfants de tous les âges,* 24 pieces; op. 85, *Thème varié, fugue et chanson;* op. 86, *Conte de fées,* suite (1926); op. 95, 6 paraphrases on French children's songs; op. 99, *Fantaisie sur un vieil air de ronde française* (1931). For organ: op. 38, *Prélude et Petit Canon* (1893); op. 51, *Vêpres du Commun d'un Martyr* (1889); op. 66, *Prélude* (1913). Without opus number: *O gai Soleil,* canon *a* 2 (1909); incidental music to *Veronica* (1920); *3 Chansons anciennes du Vivarais* (1926); *La Vengeance du mari,* for 3 soli, chorus, and orch. (1931). — Bibliography: E. Deniau, *Vincent d'Indy* (Toulouse, 1903); A. Hervey, *French Music in the 19th Century* (London, 1903); F. Starczewski, *La Schola Cantorum de Paris; ou Vincent d'Indy considéré comme professeur* (Warsaw, 1905); O. Séré, *Musiciens français d'aujourd'hui* (2nd ed., Paris, 1911); L. Borgex, *Vincent d'Indy, Sa vie et son œuvre* (Paris, 1913); A. Sérieyx, *Vincent d'Indy* (Paris, 1913); Romain Rolland, *Musiciens d'aujourd'hui* (Paris, 1914); M. M. de Fraguier, *Vincent d'Indy* (Paris, 1933); J. Canteloube, *Vincent d'Indy* (Paris, 1949); E. B. Hill, *Vincent d'Indy, an Estimate,* in the 'Mus. Quarterly' (April, 1915); Paul Landormy, *Vincent d'Indy,* in the 'Mus. Quarterly' (July, 1932); L. Vallas, *The Discovery of Musical Germany by Vincent d'Indy in 1873* in the 'Mus. Quarterly' (April, 1939). The basic biography is by Léon Vallas, in 2 vols.: *Vincent d'Indy: I. La Jeunesse* (Paris, 1946); *II. La Maturité, La Vieillesse* (Paris, 1950); Norman Demuth, *Vincent d'Indy* (London, 1951); Guy-Ropartz, ed., *Le Centenaire de Vincent d'Indy, 1851-1951* (Paris, 1952).

Infantas, Fernando de las, Spanish musician and theologian; b. Córdoba, 1534; d. after 1607. He belonged to a noble family and enjoyed the protection of the Emperor Charles V and later of Philip II, who employed him on diplomatic missions in Italy. He went to Venice, and then to Rome, where he lived for 25 years (1572-97). He exerted a decisive influence upon the course of Catholic church music by opposing the plan for the reform of the Roman Gradual undertaken by Palestrina in 1578 at the request of Pope Gregory XIII. Backed by the authority of Philip II of Spain, he succeeded in having the project abandoned. He publ. *Sacrarum varii styli cantionum tituli Spiritus Sancti,* a collection of motets in 3 books: I for 4 voices, II for 5 voices (both publ. in Venice, 1578), III for 6-8 voices (Venice, 1579), and *Plura modulationum genera quae vulgo contrapuncta appellantur super excelso gregoriano cantu* (Venice, 1579; contains 100 contrapuntal exercises for 2-8 voices based on 1 plainsong theme; pointed the way to a new freedom and elasticity in polyphonic writing); separate compositions were also publ. in various collections of the time. A Sequence for 6 voices, *Victimae paschali,* was publ. by W. Dehn in *Sammlung älterer Musik aus dem 16. und 17. Jahrhundert,* vol. V, pp. 6-11 (Berlin, 1837-40).—Cf. R. F. Molitor, *Die nachtridentinische Choralreform* (vol. I); R. Mitjana, *Don Fernando de las Infantas, teólogo y músico* (Madrid, 1918).

Infante, Manuel, Spanish composer; b. Osuna, near Seville, July 29, 1883. He studied piano and composition with Enrique Morera; in 1909 he settled in Paris; gave concerts of Spanish music; wrote numerous pieces for piano, mostly on Spanish themes, in an Impressionistic idiom: *Gitanerias; Pochades Andalouses; Sevillana,* fantasy (1922); *El Vito* (variations on a popular theme); also an opera, *Almanza.*

Ingegneri (in-jeh-ñä'rē), **Marco Antonio,** Italian composer; b. Verona, 1545; d. Cremona, July 1, 1592. He was a pupil of Vincenzo Ruffo, organist of Verona Cathedral. He went to Cremona about 1568 and became maestro di cappella at the cathedral there (1576). Monteverdi was his pupil.—Works: a book of Masses *a* 5-8 (1573); a second, *a* 5 (1587); 4 of Madrigals *a* 4-5 (1578, 1579, 1580, 1584); *Sacrae cantiones a* 5 (1576); *Sacrae cantiones a* 7-16 (1589). The 27 celebrated Responses, formerly attributed to Palestrina, are by Ingegneri. They had been printed in Breitkopf & Härtel's edition of Palestrina's works (vol. 32) as of doubtful authenticity, but were eliminated when Haberl, in 1897, discovered a copy (printed in Venice, 1588) with the full name of Ingegneri. Many other motets and madrigals appeared in collections of the time. A reprint of one of his motets is in Johannes Wolf's *Sing- und Spielmusik aus älterer Zeit.*—Cf. F. Haberl, *M. A. Ingegneri,* in the 'Kirchenmusikalisches Jahrbuch' (1898); R. Casimiri, in 'Note d'Archivio' (1926); Ellinor Dohrn, *Marc Antonio Ingegneri als Madrigalkomponist* (Hanover, 1936); G. Cesari, *La musica in Cremona,* in 'Istituzioni e monumenti dell' arte musicale italiana' (vol. 6).

Ingenhoven, Jan, Dutch composer; b. Breda, May 29, 1876; d. Hoenderlo, May 20, 1951. He studied with L. Brandts-Buys in Rotterdam and Mottl in Munich; lived in Germany and Switzerland; conducted a madrigal choir in Munich (1909-12); then devoted himself mainly to composition. His works are influenced by Debussy, but he preserves an element of peculiarly native melos. Among his works are a symph. fantasy, *Brabant and Holland;* 3 symphonic poems (*Lyric; Dramatic; Romantic*); 4 string quartets; woodwind quintet; trio for violin, cello, and harp; trio for flute, clarinet, and harp; trio for piano, violin, and cello; several choral works in the classical tradition; songs.—Cf. D. Ruyneman, *De komponist Jan Ingenhoven* (Amsterdam, 1938).

Inghelbrecht, Désiré Émile, French conductor and composer; b. Paris, Sept. 17, 1880. He studied at the Paris Cons.; after graduation, conducted at various theaters in Paris; toured as conductor of the Ballets Suédois (1919-22); was director of the

Opéra-Comique (1924 and 1932-33). In 1945 he became conductor of the Paris Opéra; also conducted abroad. He publ. several books and pamphlets on conducting: *Comment on ne doit pas interpréter Carmen, Faust et Pelléas* (1932); *Diabolus in musica* (1933); *Mouvement contraire: souvenirs d'un musicien* (1947); and *Le chef d'orchestre et son équipe* (1948; English transl. as *The Conductor's World,* 1953). —Works: *La Nuit vénitienne,* opera in 3 acts after Musset (1908); the ballets, *La bonne Aventure* (1912), *El Greco* (Ballets Suédois, Paris, Nov. 18, 1920), *Le Diable dans le beffroi* (after Edgar Allan Poe; Paris Opéra, June 1, 1927), *Jeux de Couleurs* (Opéra-Comique, Feb. 21, 1933); for orch.: *Automne* (1905); *Pour le jour de la première neige au vieux Japon* (1908); *Rapsodie de printemps* (1910); *Trois poèmes dansés* (1925); *La Métamorphose d'Ève* (1925); *La Légende du grand St. Nicolas* (1925); chamber music: *Deux esquisses antiques,* for flute and harp (1902); *Poème sylvestre,* for woodwinds (1905); quintet for strings and harp (1918); pieces for cello and piano, and viola and piano; choral works: *Le Cantique des créatures de Saint François d'Assise,* for chorus and orch. (1919); *Requiem* (1940); *Quatre chansons populaires françaises,* for mixed chorus; piano works: *La Nursery,* four-hand pieces for children, 3 vols. (1905 and 1911); *Suite petite-russienne* (1908); *Paysages* (1918), etc.; also songs (*Mélodies sur des poésies russes,* 1905; *Au jardin de l'infante,* 1910; etc.).

Insanguine, Giacomo (Antonio Francesco Paolo Michele), called **Monopoli,** Italian composer; b. Monopoli, March 22, 1728; d. Naples, Feb. 1, 1795. He studied with Cotumacci at the Cons. of San Onofrio in Naples; then became his master's assistant (1767) and second teacher (1774); after Cotumacci's death (1785), first teacher. He concurrently was second organist at the Cappella del Tesoro di San Gennaro (1774), first organist (1776); and maestro di cappella there (1781). He wrote some 15 operas, among them: *Lo Fumaco revotato* (1756); *Didone abbandonata* (1772); *Arianna e Teseo* (1773); *Adriano in Siria* (1773); *Le astuzie per amore* (1777); *Medonte* (1779); *Calipso* (1782). His best work is the 71st Psalm for 3-part chorus and orch.; he also composed other psalms, hymns, Masses, etc.

Inten, Ferdinand von, pianist and teacher; b. Leipzig, Feb. 23, 1848; d. New York, Jan. 16, 1918. He studied at the Leipzig Cons. (1862-66) with Moscheles, Plaidy, Hauptmann, and Reinecke; in 1868, came to the U. S. and settled in New York; made his American début in N. Y. (Dec. 12, 1868). He organized concerts of chamber music, which became famous. As a teacher, he also achieved success; among his pupils were Frank and Walter Damrosch.

Inzenga (ēn-thěn'-gah), **José,** Spanish writer on music; b. Madrid, June 3, 1828; d. there, June 28, 1891. He first studied with his father, then at the Madrid Cons. and the Paris Cons.; prof. at the Madrid Cons. (1860). He was commissioned by the Minister of Public Instruction to make a collection of Spanish folksongs, which he publ. as *Cantos y bailes populares de España* (4 vols., 1888); also wrote a treatise on accompaniment, and *Impresiones de un artista en Italia.* He was very successful as a composer of zarzuelas: *Para seguir una mujer* (1851); *Don Simplicio Bobadilla* (1853); *Un día de reino* (1854); *El campamento* (1861); *Si yo fuera rey* (1862); etc.

Iparraguirre y Balerdí (ē-pah-rah-gēr'-reh ē bah-lär-dē'), **José María de,** Spanish-Basque composer and poet; b. Villarreal de Urrechu, Aug. 12, 1820; d. Zozobastro de Isacho, April 6, 1881. He led a wandering life; improvised songs, accompanying himself on the guitar; one of his songs, *Guernikako Arbola,* a hymn to the sacred tree of Guernica, became the national anthem of the Basques. As a result of the unrest in the Basque country, and his own participation in it, he was compelled to leave Spain; spent many years in South America; was enabled to return to Spain in 1877, and even obtained an official pension.

Ippolitov-Ivanov (real name Ivanov, but assumed his mother's name to distinguish himself from Michael Ivanov, the music critic), **Mikhail Mikhailovitch,** Russian composer; b. Gatchina, Nov. 19, 1859; d. Moscow, Jan. 28, 1935. He entered the St. Petersburg Cons. in 1875; studied composition with Rimsky-Korsakov, graduating in 1882. He then received the post of teacher and director of the Music School in Tiflis, in the Caucasus, where he remained until 1893; he became deeply interested in Caucasian folk music; many of his works were colored by the semi-Oriental melodic and rhythmic inflections of that region. Upon Tchaikovsky's recommendation, was appointed in 1893 prof. of composition at the Moscow Cons.; from 1906-22 he was its director.

Among his pupils were the composers Glière and Vasilenko. From 1899 on, he was conductor of the Mamontov Opera in Moscow; in 1925, became conductor of the Bolshoy Theater in Moscow. Outside Russia, he is known mainly by his effective symph. suite *Caucasian Sketches* (1895). — Works: Operas: *Ruth* (Tiflis, Feb. 8, 1887); *Azra* (Tiflis, Nov. 28, 1890); *Asya* (Moscow, Sept. 28, 1900); *Treason* (1909); *Ole from Nordland* (Moscow, Nov. 21, 1916); *The Last Barricade* (1934); also completed Mussorgsky's unfinished opera *Marriage* (1931). For orch.: *Symphonic Scherzo* (St. Petersburg, May 20, 1882); *Yar-Khmel,* spring overture (St. Petersburg, Jan. 23, 1883, composer conducting); *Caucasian Sketches* (Moscow, Feb. 5, 1895; composer conducting); *Iveria* (2nd series of *Caucasian Sketches;* Moscow, 1906); Symphony No. 1 (Moscow, 1908); *Armenian Rhapsody* (Moscow, 1909); *On the Volga* (Moscow, 1910); *Mtzyri,* symph. poem (Moscow, 1922); *Turkish March* (Baku, 1929); *From the Songs of Ossian,* 3 musical pictures (Moscow, 1927); *Episodes of the Life of Schubert* (1929); *In the Steppes of Turkmenistan; Voroshilov March; Musical Scenes of Uzbekistan;* symph. poem, *Year 1917; Catalan Suite* (1934); a suite on Finnish themes, *Karelia* (1935, last work; only the Finale was orchestrated). Chamber music: violin sonata; 2 string quartets; *An Evening in Georgia,* for harp, flute, oboe, clarinet, and bassoon. Vocal works: *Alsatian Ballad* for a cappella mixed chorus; *Five Characteristic Pieces* for chorus and orch. or piano; *The Legend of a White Swan,* for a cappella mixed chorus; *Cantata in Memory of Pushkin,* for children's chorus and piano; *Cantata in Memory of Zhukovsky,* for mixed chorus and piano; *Pythagorean Hymn to the Rising Sun,* for mixed chorus, 10 flutes, 2 harps, and tuba; *Cantata in Memory of Gogol,* for children's chorus and piano; *Hymn to Labor,* for mixed chorus and orch.; 116 songs. He publ. *The Science of the Formation and Resolution of Chords* (1897, in Russian) and *50 Years of Russian Music in My Memories* (Moscow, 1934; in English in 'Musical Mercury,' N. Y., 1937).—Cf. Sergei Boguslavsky, *Ippolitov-Ivanov* (Moscow, 1936).

Ireland, John, English composer; b. Inglewood, Bowden, Cheshire, Aug. 13, 1879. A member of a literary family (both his parents were writers), he received a fine general education. As his musical inclinations became evident, he entered the Royal College of Music in 1893, studying piano with Frederick Cliffe, and composition with Stanford. His parents died while he was still a student; he obtained positions as organist in various churches; the longest of these was at St. Luke's, Chelsea (1904-26). In 1905 he received the degree of Bac. Mus. at the Univ. of Durham; honorary Mus. Doc. there in 1932. He taught at the Royal College of Music for a number of years; Benjamin Britten, Alan Bush, E. J. Moeran, and other British composers were his pupils. He began to compose early in life; during his student years, he wrote a number of works for orch., chamber groups, and voices, but destroyed most of them. His creative catalogue, therefore, begins in 1903 (with the song cycle *Songs of a Wayfarer).* His early compositions were influenced by the German Romantic school; soon he felt the impact of modern musical ideas; he adopted many devices of the French Impressionist school; his rhythmic concepts were enlivened by the new Russian music presented by the Diaghilev ballet. At the same time, he never wavered in his dedication to the English spirit of simple melody; his writing is often modal or pentatonic, evocative of the basic outlines of insular folk music.—Works: For orch.: *The Forgotten Rite,* symph. prelude (1913); *Mai-Dun,* symph. rhapsody (1921); *A London Overture* (1936); *Concertino pastorale,* for strings (1939); *Epic March* (1942); *Satyricon* (1946); piano concerto (London, Oct. 2, 1930). Choral works: *Morning Service,* for voices with organ (1907-20); motet, *Greater love hath no man* (1912); *Communion Service* (1913); *Evening Service* (1915); *These things shall be,* for baritone solo, chorus, and orch. (1937); a number of four-part songs a cappella; two-part songs with piano accompaniment; unison choral songs with piano accompaniment. Chamber music: *Fantasy Trio* for piano, violin, and cello (1906); trio for violin, clarinet, and piano (1913; rewritten for violin, cello, and piano, 1915, and revised again in 1938); trio No. 2, for violin, cello, and piano (1917); violin sonata No. 1 (1909; revised twice, 1917, 1944); violin sonata No. 2 (1917); cello sonata (1923); *Fantasy Sonata,* for clarinet and piano (1943). For piano: *The Daydream,* and *Meridian* (1895; revised 1941); *Decorations* (1913); *The Almond Trees* (1913); *Rhapsody* (1915); *London Pieces* (1917-20); *Leaves from a Child's Sketchbook* (1918); *Summer Evening* (1919); sonata (1920); *On a Birthday Morning* (1922); *Soliloquy* (1922); sonatina (1927); *Ballade* (1929); *Indian Summer* (1932); *Green Ways* (1937); *Sarnia,* 'An Island

Sequence' (1941); *Three Pastels* (1941); organ works; about 100 songs, to words by D. G. Rossetti, Christina Rossetti, Thomas Hardy, A. E. Housman, Ernest Dowson, etc. A miniature essay on Ireland was publ. by J. & W. Chester, Ltd., in 1923; see also Edwin Evans' article on Ireland in Cobbett's 'Cyclopedic Survey of Chamber Music'; Josef Holbrooke, *Contemporary British Composers* (London, 1925); Nigel Townshend, *The Achievement of John Ireland,* in 'Music & Letters' (April, 1943).

Irino, Yoshiro, Japanese composer; b. Vladivostok (Siberia), Nov. 13, 1921. He studied economy at the Tokyo Imperial Univ.; studied music with S. Moroi; won the Mainichi Music Prize (1949; 1950); employed the 12-tone technique in his music. His works include: a symphony (1948); a concert overture (1948); *Sinfonietta* (Tokyo, Nov. 13, 1953); an operetta, *The Man in Fear of God* (Tokyo, May 25, 1954); a string quartet (1945); a piano trio (1948); a string sextet (1950); *Concerto da camera* for 7 instruments (1951); sonata for cello and piano (1945); etc.

Isaac (ē'zahk), **Heinrich** (or **Isaak, Izak, Yzac, Ysack;** in Italy, **Arrigo Tedesco** [Henry the German]; Low Latin **Arrighus**), Netherlandish polyphonist (the Italian term 'Tedesco' was used at the time for Netherlanders as well as Germans); b. Brabant, c. 1450; d. Florence, 1517. From 1480-92 he was in the service of Lorenzo de' Medici, in the capacities of organist, maestro di cappella, and teacher to Lorenzo's children. He afterwards spent several years in Rome, and finally was called to the court of Maximilian I, at Vienna, as 'Symphonista regis'; from 1514 until his death he lived in Florence. He was greatly influenced by the music of the countries in which he lived, writing with equal facility in the Netherlandish, Italian, and German styles as they flourished in his day.—Works: 23 Masses *a* 4-6 (of which 10 were publ. between 1506-39); those in MS are in the libraries at Vienna (8), Munich (4), and Brussels (1). Motets and psalms by Isaac were printed in some 40 collections from 1501-64 (see Eitner, 'Bibliographie der Musiksammelwerke'; Berlin, 1877). One of the most beautiful of German chorales, *Nun ruhen alle Wälder,* is sung to the melody by Isaac, *Inspruk, ich muss dich lassen.* A voluminous collection of motets, *Choralis Constantinus,* was ed. by his pupil Ludwig Senfl, in 1550 (3 parts). Parts I and II were republished in the 'Denkmäler der Tonkunst in Österreich' (vols. 5 and 16); Part III, by the Univ. of Michigan Press (1950; ed. by Louise Cuyler). Isaac's secular works were ed. by Joh. Wolf and also republished in the 'Denkmäler der Tonkunst in Österreich' (vol. 14). The *Missa carminum* was publ. in F. Blume's 'Das Chorwerk,' ed. by R. Heyden (1932). Other reprints are in Eitner's 'Publikation älterer Musikwerke' I (5 4-voiced vocal works) and A. Schering's *Geschichte der Musik in Beispielen* (a Kyrie and a canzona). 5 polyphonic Masses from Isaac's *Choralis Constantinus* were transcribed and ed. by Louise Cuyler (Univ. of Michigan, 1956). —Cf. H. Rietsch, *Heinrich Isaac und das Innsbrucklied,* in the 'Jahrbuch der Musikbibliothek Peters' (1917); Peter Wagner, *Geschichte der Messe* (pp. 281-317); P. Blaschke, *Heinrich Isaaks Choralis Constantinus,* in 'Kirchenmusikalisches Jahrbuch' (1931).

Ishii, Kan, Japanese composer; b. Tokyo, March 30, 1921. He studied at the Musashino Music School with T. Goh, T. Ikenouchi, and H. Odaka; later at the Hochschule für Musik in Munich, with Eichhorn and Orff. Among his works are a symph. poem, *Mountain* (Tokyo, Oct. 7, 1954); the ballets, *God and the Bayadere* (Tokyo, Nov. 6, 1950) and *Birth of a Human* (Tokyo, Nov. 27, 1954); a piano sonata (1948); etc.

Isidore of Seville, Spanish theologian; b. Cartagena; d. Seville, April 4, 636. He was brought to Seville as a child; in 599, became archbishop there. Between 622 and 633, compiled a treatise on the arts, *Etymologiarum sive originum libri XX;* he expressed the conviction that music can only be preserved through memory, for musical sounds could never be notated *(scribi non possunt).* The text was published in Oxford (1911); an English transl. of the pertinent parts is included in Strunk's *Source Readings in Music History* (N. Y., 1950). See also Karl Schmidt, *Quaestiones de musicis scriptoribus romanis imprimis Cassiodoro et Isidoro* (Leipzig, 1898).

Isler, Ernst, Swiss organist and music critic; b. Zürich, Sept. 30, 1879; d. there, Sept. 26, 1944. He studied in Zürich and Berlin; served as organist in Zürich, and taught organ there. He became music critic of the influential daily paper, 'Neue Zürcher Zeitung,' in 1902 and held this position until his death; he was editor of the 'Schweizerische Musikzeitung' from 1910-27. He publ. several monographs, on Hans Huber, Max Reger, etc., also a valuable compendium, *Das Zürcherische Konzertleben, 1895-1914* (Zürich, 1935), and its sequel, covering the years 1914-31 (Zürich, 1936).

Isolfsson, Pall, Icelandic organist and composer; b. Stokkseyri, Oct. 12, 1893. He studied in Leipzig with Reger and Straube; was assistant organist at the Thomaskirche (1917-19); then studied in Paris with Bonnet. Returning to Iceland, he was appointed director of the Reykjavik Cons. in 1937. He has written numerous choral and organ works.

Isouard (ē-zŏŏ-ahr'), **Nicolo,** opera composer; b. Malta, Dec. 6, 1775; d. Paris, March 23, 1818. A son of a prosperous merchant, he was sent to Paris to study engineering; afterwards, he served as a clerk in Malta, Palermo, and in Naples, where he took lessons with Sala and Guglielmi. In the spring of 1794 he produced his first opera, *L'avviso ai maritati,* in Florence; from that time on he abandoned business pursuits, dedicating himself to operatic composition. In order not to embarrass his family, and particularly his father, who was against his career as a musician, he adopted the name Nicolo de Malte, or simply Nicolo. He served as organist of St. John of Jerusalem at Malta (1795-98); in 1799, went to Paris, where he became increasingly successful as an opera composer; he was also popular as a pianist. In Paris he had to undergo strong competition with Boieldieu; but the lengthy list of productions of his operas up to 1816 shows that he had never relaxed his industry. The music of his operas demonstrates a facile melodic gift in the French manner, as well as sound craftsmanship; it is the lack of originality that led to the eventual disappearance of his works from active repertory. Besides operas, he also wrote church music. The best known of his operas are *Cendrillon, Joconde,* and *Jeannot et Colin.* A list of his operas, produced in Paris, includes: *Le Petit Page* (with R. Kreutzer; Feb. 14, 1800); *La Statue* (April 26, 1802); *L'Intrigue au Sérail* (April 25, 1809); *Cendrillon* (Feb. 22, 1810); *La Victime des arts* (Feb. 27, 1811); *La Fête du village* (March 31, 1811); *Le Billet de loterie* (Sept. 14, 1811); *Le Magicien sans magie* (Nov. 4, 1811); *Lully et Quinault* (Feb. 27, 1812); *Le Prince de Catane* (March 4, 1813); *Les Français à Venise* (June 14, 1813); *Joconde* (Feb. 28, 1814); *Michel-Ange* (Dec. 11, 1802); *Les Confidences* (March 31, 1803); *Le Baiser et la quittance* (June 18, 1803); *Le Médecin turc* (Nov. 19, 1803); *L'Intrigue aux fenêtres* (Feb. 26, 1805); *Le Déjeuner de garçons* (April 24, 1805); *La Ruse inutile* (May 30, 1805); *Léonce* (Nov. 18, 1805); *La Prise de Passaw* (Feb. 8, 1806); *Idala* (July 30, 1806); *Les Rendez-vous bourgeois* (May 9, 1807); *Les Créanciers* (Dec. 10, 1807); *Un Jour à Paris* (May 24, 1808); *Cimarosa* (June 28, 1808); *Jeannot et Colin* (Oct. 17, 1814); *Les Deux Maris* (March 18, 1816); *L'une pour l'autre* (May 11, 1816); *Aladin* (Feb. 6, 1822; posthumous work, completed by Benincori and Habeneck).—Cf. E. Wahl, *Nicolo Isouard* (Munich, 1906).

Isserlis, Julius, pianist; b. Kishinev, Nov. 7, 1888. He studied with Puchalski at the Kiev Cons.; then with Safonov and Taneyev at the Moscow Cons. (1906; gold medal); toured in Europe and America (1907-09); taught at the Moscow Philharmonic Institute of Music (1913-23); then in Vienna (1923-28); in 1928, settled in London. He has written a number of character pieces for piano.

Istel, Edgar, eminent musicologist; b. Mainz, Feb. 23, 1880; d. Miami, Fla., Dec. 17, 1948. He studied in Munich with Thuille and Sandberger; received his *Dr. phil.* with the dissertation *J. J. Rousseau als Komponist* (1900); then settled in Munich as a teacher; in 1919, taught in Berlin; in 1920 he moved to Madrid, where he remained until the outbreak of the civil war in 1936; then went to England, and eventually to the U. S. (1938). — Writings: *Das deutsche Weihnachtsspiel und seine Wiedergeburt aus dem Geiste der Musik* (Langensalza, 1901); *Richard Wagner im Lichte eines zeitgenössischen Briefwechsels* (1902); *Peter Cornelius* (1906); *Die Entstehung des deutschen Melodramas* (1906); *Die komische Oper* (1906); *Die Blütezeit der musikalischen Romantik in Deutschland* (1909); *Das Kunstwerk Richard Wagners* (1910); *Das Libretto* (1914; English ed. as *The Art of Writing Opera Librettos,* N. Y., 1922); *Die moderne Oper vom Tode Wagners bis zum Weltkrieg* (Leipzig, 1915); *Niccolo Paganini* (Leipzig, 1919); *Revolution und Oper* (1919); *Das Buch der Oper; die deutschen Meister von Gluck bis Wagner* (Berlin, 1919); *Bizet und Carmen* (Stuttgart, 1927). Between 1915 and 1934, he contributed a number of articles on various composers to the 'Mus. Quarterly'; edited the musical writings of E. T. A. Hoffmann, the collected essays of Cornelius, and Dittersdorf's autobiography; wrote analytical brochures on works of Mahler, Humperdinck, and others. Istel was also a composer: he wrote 6 operas; *Hymn to Zeus,* for chorus and orch.; songs.

Istomin, Eugene, American pianist; b. New York (of Russian parents), Nov. 26, 1925. He studied with Rudolf Serkin at the Curtis Institute in Philadelphia; in 1943 won the Leventritt Award for an appearance with the N. Y. Philharmonic, which he made on Nov. 21, 1943, playing the 2nd Concerto of Brahms. He has appeared with several other American orchestras, and has also played in recitals.

Ito, Ryuto, Japanese composer; b. Hiroshima, March 4, 1922. He studied at the Tokyo Univ.; then turned to music and studied composition with Ikenouchi, Moroi, and Takata. Subsequently he divided his interests between music and medicine. Several of his works received prizes awarded by the Tokyo newspaper 'Mainichi.'

Iturbi, José, celebrated pianist and conductor; b. Valencia, Spain, Nov. 28, 1895. He took lessons with Joaquin Malats in Barcelona as a small child; then played in cafés in Valencia to earn a living. A sum of 1400 pesetas was raised through a newspaper campaign to enable him to go to Paris for further study; he entered the Paris Cons., graduating with honors in 1912. He then went to Switzerland, where he again played in cafés and hotels. In 1919 he obtained the post of piano teacher at the Geneva Cons. From 1923 he turned to a virtuoso career; his playing of Spanish music was brilliantly successful; extensive tours in Europe and South America followed. In 1928 he made his American début, which at once established his reputation as a pianist of individual gifts; he gave 77 concerts in the U. S. during his second American tour in 1930; also appeared with leading symphony orchestras. In 1936 he began a career as conductor; conducted the Rochester Philharmonic Orch. for several seasons; also gave concerts in the dual role of pianist and conductor. He has written a number of pieces in the Spanish vein, of which *Pequeña danza española,* for piano, is particularly attractive. His sister, **Amparo Iturbi** (b. Valencia, March 12, 1899), is also a talented pianist; she appeared with Iturbi on numerous occasions in Europe and America as duo pianists.

Ivanov, Mikhail Mikhailovitch, Russian music critic and composer; b. Moscow, Sept. 23, 1849; d. Rome, Oct. 20, 1927. He studied at the Technological Institute in St. Petersburg, graduating in 1869; then went to Moscow, where he took private lessons with Tchaikovsky; from 1870-76 he lived in Rome, where he studied with Sgambati. In 1876 he returned to St. Petersburg, and became critic of the influential newspaper 'Novoye Vremya.' He assumed a hostile attitude towards composers of the National School; possessing a lively literary style, he used irony as well as direct attack against new musical developments; this earned him the enmity of most composers. In his own works, Ivanov imitated Tchaikovsky. He wrote a ballet, *Vestal Virgin* (St. Petersburg, Feb. 29, 1888); an opera, *Zabava Putiatishna* (Moscow, Jan. 15, 1899); another opera, *Potemkin Holiday,* written earlier, was produced in St. Petersburg on Dec. 16, 1902. He also wrote a symph. poem, *Grasshopper Musician,* and a number of songs; publ. *Pushkin in Music* (St. Petersburg, 1899); *The Historical Development of Music in Russia* (2 vols., St. Petersburg, 1910-12); translated into Russian Hanslick's *Vom Musikalisch-Schönen.*

Ivanov-Boretzky, Mikhail Vladimirovitch, Russian musicologist; b. Moscow, June 26, 1874; d. there, April 1, 1936. He studied law in Moscow; then went to Italy, where he studied music in Florence; returning to St. Petersburg, he took lessons with Rimsky-Korsakov. In 1921 he was appointed member of the Council of the State Institute of Musical Science; also was dean of the Moscow Cons. He edited a number of anthologies; translated several books by European music historians, and published little biographies of Palestrina, Mendelssohn, Schumann, and other composers.—Publications: *Materials and Documents of Music History* (with a synoptic table of 18th-century music; Moscow, 1934); preface to a transl. of Schweitzer's book on Bach (Moscow, 1934); articles on various composers in the Soviet Encyclopedia. He wrote 2 operas: *The Jewels of Aphrodite* and *The Witch;* also a pageant, *Festival of Electricity* (Omsk, 1925); some chamber music; choral works.

Ivanov - Radkevitch, Nicolay Pavlovitch, Russian composer; b. Krasnoyarsk, Siberia, Feb. 10, 1904. He studied at the Moscow Cons. with Glière, graduating in 1928. He has written 4 symphonies (1928, 1932, 1937, 1945); *Russian Overture* (1939); *Heroic Poem* (1942); *Rhapsody on Ukrainian Themes* (1946); *Sketches of the Russian Landscape;* violin sonata; cello sonata; clarinet sonata; piano pieces. His military marches, expertly orchestrated for band, are very popular in Russia. In 1943 he received a Stalin prize for his patriotic band pieces, *Our Own Moscow, The People's Avengers,* etc.

Ivanovici (ē-vah-noh'-vē-tchē), Rumanian composer; b. Banat, 1848; d. Bucharest, April 1, 1905. He was a military band leader; wrote a great number of effective pieces, of which the waltz, *The Waves of the Danube* (1880), achieved tremendous popularity.

Ives, Charles Edward, remarkable American composer; b. Danbury, Conn., Oct. 20, 1874; d. New York, May 19, 1954. His father, George Ives, was a band leader of the First Connecticut Heavy Artillery during the Civil War, and the early development of Charles Ives was determined by the village concerts organized by his father. At the age of 12 he played the drums in the band, and also received from his father rudimentary training in piano and cornet playing; at 13 he played organ at the Danbury church; soon he began to compose band music; his first piece was *Holiday Quick Step,* performed by the band in 1888. He attended the Danbury High School; then entered Yale Univ. (1894), where he took regular academic courses, and also studied composition with Horatio Parker and organ with Dudley Buck; graduated in 1898; was a clerk in an insurance company; also played organ at the Central Presbyterian Church in New York (1899-1902), and continued to compose. In 1907 he formed a partnership with Julian Myrick in an agency for insurance; the firm of Ives & Myrick prospered, and Ives was able to devote himself to music without thoughts of earning a living from it. In 1908, he married Harmony Twichell. He retired from business in 1930. About the same time he was compelled to stop writing music because of a diabetic condition which made it difficult for him to handle a pen. It is an extraordinary fact that his recognition as a composer came gradually only after that. His works, written early in the century, were performed for the first time decades later; in 1947 he received the Pulitzer Prize for his 3rd symphony, written in 1911. In 1919 Ives published, at his own expense, his *Concord Sonata,* for piano; and in 1922, a volume of 114 songs written between 1884 and 1921; copies were distributed free of charge; most of the songs were republished in 'New Music Quarterly'; 2 movements of his 4th symphony were publ. by 'New Music Quarterly' in 1929; an orchestral set, *Three Places in New England,* was publ. by Birchard (1935). As his fame grew, many of his works appeared in print. After his death, his manuscripts were given to Yale Univ. for study and eventual publication.— The role of Ives in American music is unique; he was a true pioneer of a strong national art, and at the same time he applied methods and techniques that anticipated by many years the advance of modern music elsewhere in the world. Virtually every work he wrote bears relation to American life, not only by literary association, but through actual quotation of American musical sources, from church anthems to popular dances and marches. He experimented with dissonant harmonies, simultaneous conflicting rhythms, and fractional intervals, such as quarter-tones, and combined simple diatonic tunes with chromatically embroidered counterpoints resulting in a highly complex polytonal and polyrhythmic texture. In some of his works he introduced an element of improvisation, in the manner of village musicians playing a constant refrain in a free style. In his orchestration, he often indicated interchangeable instruments and optional parts, so that the same work is available in several versions; thus in the last movement of the *Concord Sonata,* there is an optional part for flute obbligato. — Ives possessed an uncommon gift for literary expression; his annotations to his works are trenchant and humorous; he publ. *Essays Before a Sonata* (N. Y., 1920) as a literary companion volume to the *Concord Sonata;* contributed articles to the musical press. He was acutely conscious of his civic duties as an American, and once circulated a proposal to have federal laws enacted by direct popular referendum. — Works: For orch.: 5 symphonies: No. 1, in D minor (1896-98); No. 2 (1897-1902; N. Y., Feb. 22, 1951); No. 3 (1901-04; N. Y. May 5, 1947); No. 4 (1910-16; 2nd movement only perf. N. Y., Jan. 29, 1927); also incomplete fragments of a *Universe Symphony* (1911-16); *Three Places in New England* (1903-14; N. Y., Jan. 10, 1931; perf. by the Chamber Orch. of Boston, Slonimsky conducting); *Calcium Light Night,* for chamber orch. (1898-1907); *Central Park in the Dark* (1898-1907); *The Unanswered Question* (1908); *Theater Orchestra Set: In the Cage, In the Inn, In the Night* (1904-11); *Hallowe'en* for piano and strings (1911); *The Pond* (1906); *Browning Overture* (1911); *The Gong on the Hook and Ladder, or Firemen's Parade on Main Street,* for chamber orch. (1911); *Lincoln, the Great Commoner,* for chorus and orch. (1912); *A Symphony: Holi-*

days, in 4 parts, also performed separately: *Washington's Birthday* (1913), *Decoration Day* (1912), *Fourth of July* (1913), *Thanksgiving and/or Forefathers' Day* (1904); *Over the Pavements,* for chamber orch. (1913); Orchestral Set No. 2 (1915); *Tone Roads,* for chamber orch. (1911-15); Orchestral Set No. 3 (1919-27). Chamber music: string quartet No. 1, subtitled *A Revival Service* (1896); *Prelude,* from 'Pre-First Sonata,' for violin and piano (1900); trio for violin, clarinet, and piano (1902); 'Pre-Second String Quartet' (1905); *Space and Duration,* for string quartet and a mechanical piano (1907); *All the Way Around and Back,* for piano, violin, flute, bugle, bells (1907); *The Innate,* for string quartet and piano (1908); *Adagio Sostenuto,* for English horn, flute, strings, and piano (1910); violin sonata No. 1 (1908); violin sonata No. 2 (1910); trio, for violin, cello, and piano (1911); string quartet No. 2 (1913); violin sonata No. 3 (1914); *Set,* for string quartet and piano (1914); violin sonata No. 4, subtitled *Children's Day at the Camp Meeting* (1915). Choral works: *Psalm 67* (1898); *The Celestial Country,* cantata (1899); *Three Harvest Home Chorales,* for mixed chorus, brass, double bass, and organ (1898-1912); *General William Booth's Entrance into Heaven,* for chorus with brass band (1914). Piano pieces: *Three-Page Sonata* (1905); *Some Southpaw Pitching* (1908); *The Abolitionist Riots* (1908); sonata No. 1 (1909); *Twenty-Two* (1912); *Three Protests for Piano* (1914); sonata No. 2, for piano, subtitled *Concord, Mass., 1840-1860,* in 4 movements; *Emerson, Hawthorne, The Alcotts, Thoreau* (1909-15; 1st perf. in its entirety by John Kirkpatrick, N. Y., Jan. 20, 1939; the last movement requires the application of a strip of wood on the keys to produce pandiatonic or panpentatonic chords); *Three Quarter-tone Piano Pieces* (1903-24); 114 songs (1884-1921).—Bibliography: the basic biography is *Charles Ives and His Music,* by Henry and Sidney Cowell (N. Y., 1955). See also Henry Bellamann, *Charles Ives, The Man and His Music,* in the 'Mus. Quarterly' (Jan., 1933); Henry Cowell, *Charles Ives,* in *American Composers on American Music* (Stanford Univ., 1933); Paul Rosenfeld, *Discoveries of a Music Critic* (N. Y., 1936); Paul Rosenfeld, *Ives' Concord Sonata,* in 'Modern Music' (Jan.-Feb., 1939); Madeleine Goss, *Modern Music Makers* (N. Y., 1952); N. Slonimsky, *Charles Ives, America's Musical Prophet,* in 'Musical America' (Feb. 15, 1954); Gilbert Chase, *America's Music* (N. Y., 1955).

Ives (Ive), Simon, English composer; b. Ware, July (baptized July 20), 1600; d. London, July 1, 1662. He was organist in Newgate and a choral master at St. Paul's Cathedral in London; wrote music for masques at the court. His songs, catches, and rounds were published in several 17th-century collections: Playford's *Select Ayres and Dialogues* (1669) and *Musical Companion* (1672), Hilton's *Catch that Catch can* (1652), etc. He also wrote instrumental music, some of which was included in *Musick's Recreation* (1652 and 1661).

Ivogün, Maria (real name Inge von Gunther), Hungarian coloratura soprano; b. Budapest, Nov. 18, 1891. She studied with Irene Schlemmer-Ambros in Vienna; was a member of the Munich Opera (1913-25); Berlin State Opera (1925-45); taught at the Music Academy in Vienna (1948-50); in 1950, appointed prof. at the Musik Hochschule in Berlin. She was married to the Bavarian tenor, Karl Erb, in 1921 (divorced, 1932); then to her accompanist, Michael Raucheisen (1933).

Ivry, Richard d', French opera composer; b. Beaune, Feb. 4, 1829; d. Hyères, Dec. 18, 1903. He studied music as an avocation; wrote mostly for the stage; also songs and hymns; composed several grand operas: *Les Amants de Vérone,* after *Romeo and Juliet* (Paris, Oct. 12, 1878); *Fatma, Omphale et Pénélope,* etc. He used the anagram Yrvid as a *nom de plume.*

Iwamoto, Marito, Japanese violinist; b. Tokyo, Jan. 19, 1926. She studied at the Music Academy in Tokyo; played at 14 with the Tokyo Symph. Orch. She made her American début in N. Y. on June 14, 1950, with considerable success, and remained in the U. S.

J

Jacchia (yahk-kē'-ah), **Agide,** Italian conductor; b. Lugo, Jan. 5, 1875; d. Siena, Nov. 29, 1932. He studied at the Cons. of Parma (1886-91) and at the 'Liceo Musicale' at Pesaro (1891-98); won prizes for flute (1896), conducting (1897), and composition (1898). He made his début as conductor in Brescia (Dec. 26, 1898); then conducted in Ferrara (1899-1900) and at La Fenice in Venice (1901). In 1902 he accompanied Mascagni on his American tour; then filled various engagements in Italy (1903-06). He conducted the Milan Opera Co. on its American tour in 1907-09; was conductor of the Montreal Opera Co. (1910-13); of the Century Opera Co. (1914); and of the Boston National Opera (1915-16). In 1918 he became conductor of the Boston Pops concerts, and led them for 9 seasons (until 1926). In 1928 he returned to Italy.

Jachet of Mantua (Jaquet Collebaud de Vitré), composer; b. Vitré, France, c. 1495; d. Mantua, 1559. He served at the Cathedral of Mantua as maestro di cappella (1539-58). His published works include 4-part motets (Venice, 1539); 5-part motets (Venice, 1540); Mass in 4 parts (Paris, 1554); Masses in 5 parts (Venice, 1555); *Messe del Fiore* in 5 parts (Venice, 1561); Passions in 5 parts, and other church works (Venice, 1567). Many of his motets were included in contemporary anthologies. His Mass, *La Fede non debbe esser corrotta,* was reprinted by A. Reinbrecht in 1892.—Cf. G. Reese, *Music in the Renaissance* (N. Y., 1954; pp. 366-67).

Jachimecki (yah-ki-met'-skē), **Zdzislaw,** eminent Polish musicologist; b. Lwow, July 7, 1882; d. Cracow, Oct. 27, 1953. He studied in Lwow with S. Niewiadomski and H. Jarecki, and in Vienna with Adler (musicology) and Schoenberg (composition); *Dr. phil.* with a dissertation *150 Psalms by Mikolaj Gomolka* (1906). He then became a member of the faculty at the Univ. of Cracow. Jachimecki was one of the most renowned Polish musicologists; he was also a composer of choral works; was conductor of symphonic concerts in Cracow from 1908-24. Most of his writings are published in Polish, in Cracow. They include: *The Influence of Italian Music on Polish Music* (1911); *Organ Tablature of the Holy Ghost Cloister in Cracow, 1548* (1913); *Music of the Royal Court of King Wladyslaw Jagiello* (1915); *Outlines of Polish History of Music* (Warsaw, 1919); *Moniuszko* (Warsaw, 1921); *Chopin* (1926; in French as *F. Chopin et son œuvre,* Paris, 1930); monographs on Mozart, Haydn, Wagner, Szymanowski, etc.; contributed an article on Moniuszko to the 'Mus. Quarterly' (Jan., 1928); publ. *Muzyka Polska* (2 vols., 1948, 1951).

Jachino, Carlo, Italian composer; b. San Remo, Feb. 3, 1889. He studied with Luporini in Lucca and with Riemann in Leipzig; then taught at the Parma Cons. (until 1936), at Naples (1936-38), and at the Santa Cecilia in Rome (1938-50). He became director of the Cons. San Pietro in Naples in 1950. His opera *Giocondo e il suo re* was produced in Milan (June 24, 1924). He also wrote several works of chamber music; a treatise on the 12-tone method of composition, *Tecnica dodecafonica* (Milan, 1948); and *Gli strumenti d'orchestra* (Milan, 1950). In his early compositions he followed the Romantic Italian style; later he adopted a modified 12-tone method.

Jachmann-Wagner. See **Wagner, Johanna.**

Jackson, George K., English organist and theorist; b. Oxford, 1745; d. Boston, Mass., Nov. 18, 1822. He was a pupil of Dr. James Narer; became a surplice boy at the Chapel Royal, London; was among the tenor singers at the Handel Commemoration in 1784; 1791, Mus. Doc., St. Andrew's College. In 1796 he came to Norfolk, Va., then to Elizabeth, N. J., and N. Y. City (1804, music director at St. George's Chapel). By 1812 he was in Boston, where he remained as organist at various churches; also gave a series of oratorios with Graupner and Mallet. A collection of his music is in the library of the Harvard Music Association, Boston. He publ. *First Principles, or a Treatise on Practical Thorough Bass* (London, 1795); *David's Psalms* (1804); *A Choice Collection of Chants* (1816); *The Choral Companion* (1817); *Watt's Divine Hymns set to music.*—Cf. F. J. Metcalf, *American Writers and Compilers of Sacred Music* (1925); H. E. Johnson, *George K. Jackson, Doctor of Music (1745-1822)*, in the 'Mus. Quarterly' (Jan., 1943).

Jackson, George Pullen, American folklorist and writer; b. Monson, Maine, Aug. 20, 1874; d. Nashville, Jan. 19, 1953. He studied philology in Dresden and at the Univ. of Chicago (Ph. B., 1904; Ph. D., 1911); was teacher of German at Vanderbilt Univ. (1918-43); founder of the Tennessee State Sacred Harp Singing Association; elected president of the Tennessee Folklore Society (1942). He was the author of the following books: *The Rhythmic Form of the German Folk Songs* (1917); *White Spirituals in the Southern Uplands* (1933); *Spiritual Folksongs of Early America* (1937; 2nd ed., 1953); *White and Negro Spirituals* (1943); *Story of the Sacred Harp* (1944); *Another Sheaf of White Spirituals* (1952).

Jackson, Samuel P., organist; b. Manchester, England, Feb. 5, 1818; d. Brooklyn, N. Y., July 27, 1885. Son of the organbuilder James Jackson, he was taken to

America in 1825, and learned his father's trade; his music teachers were Moran (piano) and Thornton (harmony). From 1830-42 he played the organ at St. Clement's Church; at St. Bartholomew's from 1842-61; later at other churches. He taught organ and theory; was for many years music proof reader for G. Schirmer, Inc. Besides a variety of excellent vocal sacred music, he published *Gems for the Organ,* and 4 books of very popular *Organ-Voluntaries.*

Jackson, William (I), English organist and composer; b. Exeter, May 29, 1730; d. there, July 5, 1803. He was a pupil of Sylvester, organist of Exeter Cathedral, and of J. Travers in London. After teaching for years at Exeter, he became (1777) organist and choirmaster at the cathedral. Besides the operas *The Lord of the Manor* (London, Dec. 27, 1780) and *Metamorphoses* (London, Dec. 5, 1783), he composed odes (Warton's *Ode to Fancy;* Pope's *The Dying Christian to his Soul;* etc.) and a large number of songs, canzonets, madrigals, pastorals, hymns, anthems, church services, etc.; also sonatas for harpsichord.—Writings: *30 Letters on Various Subjects* (London, 1782); *Observations on the Present State of Music in London* (1791); and *The Four Ages, together with Essays on Various Subjects* (1798).

Jackson, William (II), English organist and composer; b. Masham, Yorkshire, Jan. 9, 1815; d. Bradford, April 15, 1866. A self-taught musician, he became organist at Masham in 1832; won first prize, offered by the Huddersfield Glee Club, in 1840; 1852, established a music business and became organist of St. John's Church at Bradford; later was conductor of Bradford Choral Union.

Jacob, Benjamin, English organist; b. London, May 15, 1778; d. there, Aug. 24, 1829. He was a pupil of Willoughby, Shrubsole, and Arnold (1796); served as organist at various churches, finally at Surrey Chapel (1794-1825). With Wesley and Crotch, he gave organ recitals (1808-14), which were attended by large crowds; conducted a series of oratorios in 1800, and the Lenten Oratorios at Covent Garden in 1818. Jacob was very active in spreading the Bach cult in London (see O. A. Mansfield, *J. S. Bach's First English Apostles* in the 'Mus. Quarterly,' April, 1935). He publ. *National Psalmody* (London, 1819) and other collections; also glees and catches.

Jacob, Gordon, English composer and pedagogue; b. London, July 5, 1895. He studied with Stanford at the Royal College of Music; from 1926, taught there; served as examiner of music schools; also was active as music editor (Penguin Scores, etc.). Among his works are 2 symphonies (1929 and 1944); 3 symph. suites; a *Sinfonietta* (1942); *Variations on an Air by Purcell,* for strings (1930); viola concerto (1925); concerto for piano and strings (1927); concerto for oboe and strings (1933); concerto for bassoon, strings, and percussion (1947); concerto for violin and string orch. (London, Aug. 21, 1953); *Rhapsody* for English horn and strings (1948); concerto for horn and strings (1951); quartet for oboe and strings (1938); quintet for clarinet and strings (1942); many arrangements for ballet performances (Schumann's *Carnaval, William Byrd Suite, Orlando Gibbons Suite,* also suites from works by Couperin, Liszt, Chopin, etc.); original ballets (*The Jew in the Bush, Uncle Remus,* etc.); film music. He publ. *Orchestral Technique: a Manual for Students* (Oxford, 1931) and *How to Read a Score* (Oxford, 1944).

Jacob, Maxime, French composer; b. Bordeaux, Jan. 13, 1906; studied in Paris with Gedalge, also with Koechlin and Milhaud; living in Paris. — Principal works: comic opera, *Blaise le Savetier;* incidental music to *Voulez vous jouer avec moi?* (Paris, 1921); a *Sérénade* for piano 4 hands (orchestrated, 1923); a number of songs to poems of Musset, Lamartine, Cocteau, and others; a cycle of 14 *Chansons d'amour* to 17th-century texts. In 1930 he joined the Benedictine Order, and devoted himself to sacred music.—Cf. Jean Roy, *Maxime Jacob,* in the 'Revue Musicale' (July, 1939).

Jacobi, Frederick, American composer; b. San Francisco, May 4, 1891; d. New York, Oct. 24, 1952. He studied with Paolo Gallico and Rafael Joseffy (piano) and Rubin Goldmark (composition); then went to Germany, where he studied with Paul Juon in Berlin. Returning to America, he took lessons with Ernest Bloch. From 1913-17, he was coach at the Metropolitan Opera; in 1917-18, played saxophone in army bands. In 1917 he married the pianist Irene Schwarz. He taught at the Master School of United Arts in N. Y. (1927) and at the Juilliard School of Music (1936-50). He was very active in modern music societies; was a member of the executive board of the League of Composers. In his compositions he often employed American Indian themes (he was a student of Indian music); another group of his works is based on Jewish motives; he also wrote music in a neo-Classical style. He received the David Bispham Memorial Award for his opera, *The Prodigal Son* (1944). His other works include: For orch.: *The Pied Piper,* symph. poem (1915); *A California Suite* (San Francisco, Dec. 6, 1917); *The Eve of St. Agnes* (1919); Symphony No. 1, 'Assyrian' (1922; San Francisco, Nov. 14, 1924); *Indian Dances* (Boston Symph., Cambridge, Nov. 8, 1928); *Three Psalms,* for cello and orch. (Paris, May 30, 1933); piano concerto (N. Y., May 7, 1936, Irene Schwarz-Jacobi soloist); violin concerto (Chicago, March 14, 1939); *Ave Rota,* 3 pieces for piano and small orch. (1939); *Night Piece,* for flute and small orch. (originally the 2nd movement from Symph. No. 1; later performed separately under the title *Nocturne,* Rochester, Dec. 30, 1926; revised and renamed *Night Piece;* first perf. San Diego, Cal., July 22, 1941); *Ode for Orchestra* (San Francisco, Feb. 12, 1943); *Concertino* for piano and string orch. (Saratoga Springs, Sept. 3, 1946); *2 Pieces in Sabbath Mood* (CBS Symph. Orch., N. Y., Feb. 5, 1947); Symphony No. 2 (San Francisco, April 1, 1948). Vocal works: *Three Songs* to poems by Sarojini Naidu (1916); *Three Songs* to poems by Chaucer (1922); *2 Assyrian Prayers,* for voice and orch. (1923); *The Poet in the Desert,* for baritone solo, chorus, and orch. (1925); *Sabbath Evening Service,* for baritone solo and mixed voices a cappella (1931); vocalises. Chamber music: *Nocturne,* for string quartet (San Francisco, Jan. 7, 1919); 3 preludes for violin and piano (1921); string quartet on Indian themes (1924); 2nd string quartet (1933); *Scherzo,* for flute, oboe, clarinet, bassoon, and horn (1936); *Swing Boy,* for violin and piano (1937); 3rd string quartet (1945); *Music for Monticello,* for flute, cello, and piano (1945); *Impressions from the Odyssey,* for violin and piano (N. Y., Jan. 11, 1947); *Meditation,* for trombone and piano (N. Y., April 13, 1947). For piano: cadenza to Mozart's Rondo K. 386 (1937); *Fantasy Sonata* (1945). — Cf. Lazare Saminsky, *Music of Our Day* (1932); Marion Bauer, *Twentieth Century Music* (1933); David Diamond, *Frederick Jacobi,* in 'Modern Music' (March-April, 1937); J. T. Howard, *Our American Music* (N. Y., 1939, and subsequent eds.).

Jacobi, George, violinist and composer; b. Berlin, Feb. 13, 1840; d. London, Sept. 13, 1906. He studied in Brussels with Bériot and in Paris with Massart and Gevaert; won first prize (violin) at the Paris Cons. in 1861; became first violinist at the Paris Opéra and also conducted concerts in Paris. In 1871 he became conductor at the Alhambra Theatre in London; from 1896, taught at the Royal College of Music. He wrote about 100 ballets and a comic opera, *The Black Crook,* which attained temporary popularity.

Jacobs-Bond. See **Bond, Carrie Jacobs.**

Jacobson, Maurice, English publisher and composer; b. London, Jan. 1, 1896. He studied with Stanford and Holst at the Royal College of Music; was active as a pianist; then joined the staff of J. Curwen & Sons; became director of the firm in 1933. He composed a ballet, *David* (1936), incidental music to Shakespeare's plays, the cantatas *The Lady of Shalott* (1942) and *The Hound of Heaven* (1953), many short instrumental pieces, songs, etc.

Jacobsthal (jah'-kŏhbs-tăhl), **Gustav,** German music theorist; b. Pyritz, Pomerania, March 14, 1845; d. Berlin, Nov. 9, 1912. He studied at the Univ. of Strasbourg (1863-70); from 1872, taught music there; publ. the valuable treatises, *Die Mensuralnotenschrift des 12. und 13. Jahrhunderts* (1871) and *Die chromatische Alteration im liturgischen Gesange der abendländischen Kirche* (1897). Friedrich Ludwig and Erich Schmidt publ. a memorial tribute, *Trauerfeier für Gustav Jacobsthal* (Berlin, 1912). See also Friedrich Gennrich, *Die Stassburger Schule für Musikwissenschaft* (1940).

Jacoby, Georg. See **Jacobi, George.**

Jacopo da Bologna (Jacobus de Bononia), 14th-century composer; one of the earliest representatives of the Florentine 'Ars nova'; he wrote madrigals, *ballate,* etc.; his MSS are in the libraries of Florence and Paris and at the British Museum in London. His complete works are publ. in W. T. Marrocco, *The Music of Jacopo da Bologna* (Berkeley and Los Angeles, 1954). Johannes Wolf publ. 3 madrigals in his *Geschichte der Mensuralnotation* (Nos. 40-42); one madrigal is in G. Reese's *Music in the Middle Ages* (N. Y., 1940; p. 363), and another in A. T. Davison and W. Apel, *Historical Anthology of Music* (Cambridge, Mass., 1947). A treatise by Jacopo da Bologna is described by Wolf in the 'Kroyer-Festschrift' (1933; *L'arte del biscanto misurato secondo el maestro Jacopo da Bologna*).

Jacotin (zhăh-kŏh-tan') (real name Jacques Godebrie), Flemish composer; b. Antwerp, c. 1445; d. there, March 23, 1529. He was for nearly half a century 'chapelain' in the choir of Notre Dame in Antwerp (1479-1528). His vocal works were publ. in collections by Attaignant (1529, 1530-35) and Rhaw (1545), in Le Roy's & Ballard's 'Chansons nouvellement composées' (1556), etc. He excelled especially in French chansons; of these *Trop dure m'est ta longue demeure* is reproduced in H. Expert's reprint of Attaignant's collection of 1529; and *Mon triste cœur,* in Eitner's 'Selection of 60 Chansons' (1899). Several motets attributed to Jacotin and publ. by Petrucci are of doubtful authenticity. His *Sancta Divinitas unus Deus* for 8 voices appeared in Uhlhardt's collection of 1546.

Jacques-Dalcroze. See **Jaques-Dalcroze.**

Jacques de Liège (Jacobus de Leodio), Belgian music theorist; b. Liège, about 1270; d. there, after 1330. He studied in Paris; then was a cleric in Liège. About 1330, already at an advanced age, he wrote the important compendium *Speculum musicae* in 7 parts, in 293 folios (586 pages; approximating some 2000 pages in modern typography); it was formerly attributed to Johannes de Muris, but the authorship of Jacques de Liège is proved by the specific indication in the manuscript (Paris, Bibliothèque Nationale) that the initial letters of the 7 chapters form the name of the author; these letters are I-A-C-O-B-U-S. W. Grossmann in his book, *Die einleitenden Kapitel des Speculum Musicae von J. Muris* (Leipzig, 1924), overlooks this indication. For detailed discussion of the problem, see R. Bragard, *Le Speculum Musicae du Compilateur Jacques de Liège* in 'Musica Disciplina' (1953-54; also printed separately); H. Besseler, *Studien zur Musik des Mittelalters* in the 'Archiv für Musikwissenschaft' (1925-27). Selections from the *Speculum musicae* are given in English transl. in O. Strunk's *Source Readings in Music History* (N. Y., 1950); the complete Latin text, ed. by R. Bragard, was publ. in the *Corpus Scriptorum de Musica* of the American Institute of Musicology (1956).

Jadassohn (yăh'-dăhs-son), **Salomon,** noted German pedagogue; b. Breslau, Aug. 13, 1831; d. Leipzig, Feb. 1, 1902. He studied piano and violin in Breslau; in 1848 he took courses at the Leipzig Cons.; in 1849 he was in Weimar, where Liszt accepted him as a student; then he returned to Leipzig, and studied privately with Hauptmann. He remained in Leipzig during his entire life; organized a choral society, Psalterion (1866); conducted the concerts of the Euterpe Society. In 1871 he was appointed instructor at the Leipzig Cons.; in 1887 he was made *Dr. phil. (honoris causa);* in 1893 he became Royal Professor. A scholar of the highest integrity and great industry, he codified the traditional views of harmony, counterpoint, and form in his celebrated manuals, which have been translated into many languages. He was a firm believer in the immutability of harmonic laws, and became the Rock of Gibraltar of conservatism in musical teaching; through his many students, who in turn became influential teachers in Germany and other European countries, the cause of orthodox music theory was propagated far and wide. He was also a composer; wrote 4 symphonies; a piano concerto; 3 piano quintets; a piano quartet; 4 piano trios; 2 string quartets; a serenade for flute and string orch.; a cavatina for cello with orch.; choral works; many piano pieces and songs. He was a master of contrapuntal forms, and wrote a number of vocal duets in canon; other contrapuntal devices are illustrated in many of his works. His music is totally forgotten; but his importance as a theorist cannot be doubted. His manuals, covering a wide range of musical subjects, are: *Harmonielehre* (Leipzig, 1883; 7th ed., 1903; English ed., N. Y., 1893, under the title, *A Manual of Harmony,* transl. by Th. Baker); *Kontrapunkt* (1884; 5th ed., 1909); *Kanon und Fuge* (1884; 3rd ed., 1909); *Die Formen in den Werken der Tonkunst* (1889; 4th ed., 1910); *Lehrbuch der Instrumentation* (1889; 2d ed., 1907); *Die Kunst zu Modulieren und Präludieren* (1890); *Allgemeine Musiklehre* (1892); *Elementar-Harmonielehre* (1895); *Methodik des musiktheoretischen Unterrichts* (1898); *Das Wesen der Melodie in der Tonkunst* (1899); *Das Tonbewusstsein; die Lehre vom musikalischen Hören* (1899); *Erläuterung der in Bachs 'Kunst der Fuge' enthaltenen Fugen und Kanons* (1899); *Der Generalbass* (1901).

Jadin (zhah-dan'), **Louis Emmanuel,** French composer and conductor; b. Versailles, Sept. 21, 1768; d. Paris, April 11, 1853. He was at first a page in the household of Louis XVI; after the Revolution, he was on the staff of the Théâtre de Monsieur; there he produced his comic opera, *Joconde* (Sept. 14, 1790). He then wrote all kinds of festive compositions to be performed on special occasions during the revolutionary years. In 1802 he became prof. of piano at the newly established Paris Cons., succeeding his brother, **Hyacinthe Jadin** (1769-1800). During the Napoleonic wars he continued to write patriotic pieces; his orchestral overture, *La Bataille d'Austerlitz,* enjoyed great popularity for a while. He also wrote pieces for piano, and piano duets. —Cf. G. de Saint-Foix, *Les Frères Jadin,* in the 'Revue Musicale' (1925).

Jadlowker (yăhd-lŏhv'-kĕr), **Hermann,** tenor; b. Riga, July 5, 1878; d. Tel Aviv, May 13, 1953. He left home as a boy to escape a commercial career and entered the Vienna Cons. He made his début as operatic tenor in Cologne (1889). In 1901 he was heard in Karlsruhe by Wilhelm II, who engaged him to sing in Berlin; after 5 years with the Berlin Opera, he went to Vienna. He made his American début at the Metropolitan Opera House in *Faust* (Jan. 22, 1910); in 1913, went again to Berlin; from 1929 until 1938 he was cantor at the synagogue of his native town, Riga; then went to Palestine, where he settled as a teacher.

Jaëll (yah'-el), **Alfred,** noted pianist; b. Trieste, March 5, 1832; d. Paris, Feb. 27, 1882. He studied with his father, Eduard Jaëll; appeared as a child prodigy in Venice in 1843; continual concert tours earned him the nickname of 'le pianiste voyageur.' He traveled in America in 1852-54; after this, he lived in Paris, Brussels, and Leipzig. In 1866 he married Marie Trautmann (see below); made piano transcriptions from Wagner, Schumann, and Mendelssohn.

Jaëll-Trautmann, Marie, pianist, wife of Alfred Jaëll; b. Steinseltz, Alsace, Aug. 17, 1846; d. Paris, Feb. 7, 1925. She studied with Henri Herz at the Paris Cons., where she won first prize. After her marriage, she accompanied her husband on his travels. She wrote many characteristic pieces for piano, and published pedagogical works: *La musique et la psycho-physiologie* (1895); *Le mécanisme du toucher* (1896); *Le toucher* (1899); *L'intelligence et le rythme dans les mouvements artistiques* (1905); *Le rythme du regard et la dissociation des doigts* (1906); *La coloration des sensations tactiles* (1910); *La résonance du toucher et la topographie des pulpes* (1912); *La main et la pensée musicale* (posthumous, 1925). —Cf. H. Kiener, *Marie Jaëll* (1952).

Jagel (yā'-gĕl), **Frederick,** American tenor; b. Brooklyn, June 10, 1897. His mother and father were pianists. He was a clerk for the Mutual Life Insurance Co.; studied in Milan (1923-27) and with William Brady in N. Y. (1932-42). He made his operatic début in 1924 in Leghorn as Rodolfo; then sang in Italy and Spain; début with the Metropolitan Opera Co. as Radames (Nov. 8, 1927). He was a member of the San Francisco Opera Co. (1931, 1939, 1942-44); at the Teatro Colón, Buenos Aires (1928, 1939-41). On June 12, 1928, he married Nancy Weir, an opera singer.

Jahn (yahn), **Otto,** learned German philologist and musicographer; b. Kiel, June 16, 1813; d. Göttingen, Sept. 9, 1869. He studied languages and antiquities at Kiel, Leipzig, and Berlin; then traveled in France and Italy; in 1839 he settled in Kiel as a lecturer on philology; in 1842 became prof. of archeology at Greifswald; was director of the Archeological Museum in Leipzig (1847); he lost this position in the wake of the political upheaval of 1848. In 1855 he was appointed prof. of archeology at Bonn Univ. He went to Göttingen shortly before his death. In the field of music, his magnum opus was the biography of Mozart (Leipzig, 1856-59, in 4 vols.; 2nd ed., 1867, in 2 vols.; 3rd ed., 1889-91, revised by H. Deiters; 4th ed., also revised by Deiters, 1905-07; 7th ed., revised by Hermann Abert, 2 vols., 1956). The English translation (by P. Townsend) appeared in 3 vols. in London (1882). Jahn's biography was the first musical life written according to the comparative critical method; it reviews the state of music during the period immediately preceding Mozart; this comprehensive exposition has become a model for subsequent musical biographies. Jahn intended to write a biography of Beethoven, according to a similar plan, but could not complete the task; Thayer utilized the data accumulated by Jahn in his own work on Beethoven; Pohl used Jahn's notes in his biography of Haydn. Numerous essays by Jahn were publ. in his *Gesammelte Aufsätze über Musik* (1866). He composed songs, of which 32 were publ. in 4 books; he also brought out a volume of songs for mixed voices; edited the vocal score of Beethoven's *Fidelio.* — Cf. J. Vahlen, *Otto Jahn* (1870); E. Petersen, *Otto Jahn in seinen Briefen* (Leipzig, 1912); J. Pulver, *Otto Jahn,* in the 'Musical Times' (April, 1913).

Jahn, Wilhelm, conductor; b. Hof, Moravia, Nov. 24, 1834; d. Vienna, April 21, 1900. At the age of 20 he became a theater conductor in Budapest; then occupied similar posts in Agram, Amsterdam, and Prague. He spent a number of years in Wiesbaden (1864-81); finally settled in Vienna, where he became musical director of the Vienna Opera. He retired in 1897, and was succeeded by Mahler.

Jähns (yäns), **Friedrich Wilhelm,** German vocal pedagogue and writer on music; b. Berlin, Jan. 2, 1809; d. there, Aug. 8, 1888. He studied singing with Grell; sang at the Berlin Opera as a boy soprano in the chorus. In 1845 he founded a singing society, which he conducted until 1870; in 1881 he became instructor of rhetoric at Scharwenka's Cons. He was very successful as a vocal teacher in Berlin; had some 1,000 pupils. His admiration for Weber impelled him to collect all materials pertaining to Weber's life and works; his unique library, containing 300 autograph letters and many other documents, pamphlets, essays, and first editions, was acquired in 1883 by the Berlin Royal Library. He publ. a treatise on Weber, with a thematic catalogue, *Carl Maria von Weber in seinen Werken* (Berlin, 1871). Apart from exhaustive bibliographical data, this book is historically interesting, because in the preface the author introduced, for the first time in print, the Wagnerian term 'Leitmotiv'; this was later popularized by Wolzogen and others. In 1873 Jähns publ. a biographical sketch of Weber. He was also a composer; his works include a *Grand Sonata* for violin and piano; a piano trio; a book of *Schottische Lieder,* and many other vocal pieces.

Jalas (yah'-lass), **Jussi** (real name, Blomstedt), Finnish conductor; b. Jyväskylä, June 23, 1908. He studied with Krohn in Helsinki, and later in Paris with Rhené-Baton and Monteux. Since 1945 he has conducted at the Helsinki Opera. He has appeared as guest conductor in Scandinavia, Germany, France, and England; also in the U. S. (1950 and 1955). Jalas is regarded as one of the most authentic interpreters of the music of Sibelius, whose son-in-law he was.

James, Dorothy, American composer; b. Chicago, Dec. 1, 1901. She studied with Gruenberg and Weidig at the Chicago Musical College and the American Cons. of Music (M.M.); in 1929, was appointed to the staff of the Michigan State Normal College. Among her works are *Three Symphonic Fragments* (Rochester, March 24, 1932); *3 Pastorales,* for clarinet, harp, and strings (1933); *Recitative and Air,* for viola, 2 violins, and 2 cellos (1943); also choral works: *The Little Jesus Came to Town* (1935), *Paul Bunyan* (1938), *Niobe* (1941), *Mary's Lullaby* (1942).

James, Philip, eminent American composer; b. Jersey City, N. J., May 17, 1890. He studied with Rubin Goldmark, Scalero, Norris, and Schenck. He was in the army during World War I; and after the Armistice was appointed bandmaster of the American Expeditionary Force General Headquarters Band. At various times, he conducted the Winthrop Ames Theatrical Productions (1915-16), Victor Herbert Opera Co. (1919-22), New Jersey Symph. Orch. (1922-29), Brooklyn Orchestral Society (1927-30), Bamberger Little Symphony (Station WOR; 1929-36); also was guest conductor with the Philadelphia Orch. and the N. Y. Philharmonic. In 1933 he was elected a member of the National Institute of Arts and Letters; won numerous prizes, among them one by the 'Homiletic Review' for a hymn (1927); $5000 1st prize offered by NBC, for his orch. suite, *Station WGZBX;* honorable mention in the American Composers' Conference, sponsored by the N. Y. Philharmonic, for his overture *Bret Harte;* 1st prize of $500 given by the Woman's Symph. Orch., N. Y. (1938), etc. Philip James had a distinguished career as teacher. In 1923 he joined the faculty of N. Y. Univ.; became chairman of the music dept. in 1933; retired in 1955.—Works: For the stage: *Judith,* dramatic reading with ballet and small orch. (1927); incidental music to the play *Arms for Venus* (1937). For orch.: suite for strings (N. Y. Univ., April 28, 1934); a *Sea Symph.* (1928); *Overture in Olden Style on French Noëls* (Montclair, N. J., Dec. 14, 1926, composer conducting); orchestral transcription of Bach's *Wir glauben all'* (1929; Brooklyn, Feb. 18, 1929, composer conducting); *Song of the Night,* symph poem (1931; N. Y., March 15, 1938); *Concertino* for piano and orch. (1931; after Mozart); *Station WGZBX,* satirical suite (NBC Symph. Orch., May 1, 1932); *Bret Harte,* overture (N. Y. Philh., Dec. 20, 1936); *Gwalia,* a Welsh rhapsody for orch. (N. Y., Feb. 18, 1940, composer conducting); Symph. No. 1 (1943; Vienna, 1952); *Sinfonietta* (1946; N. Y., 1950); 2nd suite (1943; Saratoga Springs, Sept. 5, 1946); for string orch. *Miniver Cheevy,* and *Richard Cory,* for narrator and orch. (Saratoga, N. Y., Sept. 9, 1947); *Brennan on the Moor* (CBS Symph. Orch. Nov. 28, 1939); symph. poem *Chaumont,* for small orch. (1948; N. Y., 1951); Symph. No. 2 (1949). Chamber music: string quartet

(1924); suite for flute, oboe, clarinet, bassoon, and horn (1936); piano quartet (1938). Choral works: *The Nightingale of Bethlehem,* for soloists, chorus, and orch. (1919); *The Nun,* for women's chorus and orch. (1922); *Song of the Future,* for mixed chorus a cappella (1922); *The Light of God,* for mixed chorus and organ (1919); *Missa Imaginum,* for mixed chorus and orch. (1929); *Stabat Mater Speciosa,* for mixed chorus and orch. (1921; rev. 1930); *General William Booth Enters Into Heaven,* for tenor, male voices, and small orch. (1932); *Psalm 150,* for mixed chorus and orch. (1940); *World of Tomorrow,* for mixed chorus and orch. (1938); *Psalm 117,* for mixed chorus (1944); *Shirat Ha-Yam,* for mixed chorus and orch. (1944); organ sonata (1930); organ suite; various minor works.—Cf. J. T. Howard, *Our American Music* (N. Y., 1939, and subsequent eds.); Gilbert Chase, *America's Music* (N. Y., 1955).

Jan (yahn), **Karl von,** German writer on music; b. Schweinfurt, May 22, 1836; d. Adelboden, Switzerland, Sept. 3, 1899. He took the degree of *Dr. phil.* at Berlin (1859) with the thesis *De fidibus Graecorum;* taught at the 'Graues Kloster' and at Landsberg until 1875, when he went to Saargemünd, and thence (1883) to the Lyceum at Strasbourg. He publ. several essays on ancient Greek music. An important work is his critical edition (superseding Meibom's) of the Greek writers on music: *Musici scriptores graeci; Aristoteles, Euclides, Bacchius, Cleonides, Nichomachus, Gaudentius, Alypius* (1895), with an appendix, *Melodiarum reliquiae,* containing all the vocal music known in his day to be extant (this also in a separate edition, augmented and revised, 1899).

Jan, Maistre. See **Gallus, Johannes.**

Janáček (yah'-năh-chěk), **Leoš,** renowned Czech composer; b. Hukvaldy, Moravia, July 3, 1854; d. Moravian-Ostrau, Aug. 12, 1928. At the age of ten he was placed at the Augustine monastery in Brno as a chorister; then studied in high school, and at the Cons. of Prague, where he took lessons in organ with Skuherský; later studied composition with L. Grill at the Leipzig Cons. (1879-80), and with Franz Krenn at the Vienna Cons. After a few months of study there, he returned to Brno, where he was active in many capacities throughout his life. He was appointed director of the Brno Organ School in 1881; was conductor of the Czech Philh. (1881-88); in 1919 became prof. of composition at the Brno Cons., attracting many young Czech composers whose creative efforts he greatly helped; was pensioned in 1925, and received an honorary *Dr. phil.* from the Univ. of Prague. Although he began to compose early in life, it was not until 1904, with the production of his opera, *Její Pastorkyna* (commonly known under its German title, *Jenufa),* that his importance as a national composer was established. Many performances followed in Vienna, throughout Germany and Russia, and in New York. He wrote several more operas, some of them on satirical subjects, which, however, had less impact on the outside world. In the field of religious music, he created a unique score, *Glagolitic Mass* (also known as *Festival Mass* or *Slavonic Mass),* to a text in old Slavonic, but not admissible to church performance because he made use of instrumental acompaniment contrary to the usage of the Eastern Church. Janáček took great interest in Russian literature and music; he visited Russia three times; his operas *Kata Kabanová* and *From the House of the Dead* and several other works are based on Russian literary works. There is an affinity between Janáček's method of dramatic prosody and Mussorgsky's ideas of realistic musical speech, but Janáček never consciously imitated the Russian models. He was a firm believer in the artistic importance of folksongs and collected a number of them in his native Moravia; contributed a paper on the musical structure of national songs to the Prague Academy (1901). During the last two decades of his life, Janáček was strongly influenced by the French school; the idiom of his instrumental works of that period clearly reflects Impressionist usages. — Works: operas: *Šarka* (1887; several revisions; perf. Brno, Nov. 11, 1925); *Počátek románu* (*Beginning of a Romance;* Brno, Feb. 10, 1894); *Její pastorkyna* (*Her Foster Daughter;* German title, *Jenufa;* 1894-1903; Brno, Jan. 21, 1904); *Osud* (*Fate;* 1904; Brno Radio, Sept. 18, 1934); modern comic operas, *Výlet pana Broučka do mesíce* (*Mr. Broucek's Excursion to the Moon*) and *Výlet pana Broučka do XV. stoleti (Mr. Broucek's Excursion into the 15th Century;* both in Prague, April 23, 1920); *Kata Kabanová* (after Ostrovsky's play, *The Storm;* Brno, Nov. 23, 1921); *Příhody Lišky Bystroušky (The Cunning Little Vixen;* Brno, Nov. 6, 1924); *Věc Makropulos (The Makropulos Affair;* 1923-25; Brno, Dec. 18, 1926); *Z mrtvého domu (From the House of the Dead;* 1928; after Dostoyevsky; posthumously produced, Brno,

April 12, 1930); a ballet, *Rákocz Rákoczy* (Prague, July 24, 1891); choral works: for chorus and orch.: *Amarus* (1898), *Na Soláni Carták* (1911), *Otče Náš (The Lord's Prayer), Glagolitic Mass (Slavonic Mass,* or *Festival Mass*), for soli, chorus, and orch. (Brno, Dec. 5, 1927); for chorus a cappella: *Potulný šilenec; Maryčka Magdónova;* orchestral works: *Valašské tanze* (Brno, May 23, 1889); symph. poem *Šumařovo dítě (The Musician's Child;* 1912; Prague, Nov. 14, 1917); *Taras Bulba,* rhapsody, after Gogol (Prague, Nov. 9, 1924); *Balada blanická (Ballad of Blanik,* symph. poem; Brno, March 21, 1920); Sinfonietta (Prague, June 29, 1926); concertino for piano and orch. (Brno, Feb. 16, 1926); *Capriccio* for piano, left hand and orch. (Prague, March 2, 1928); chamber music: piano trio, subtitled *From Tolstoy's Kreutzer Sonata* (1908); 3 violin sonatas (1879, 1913, 1921); 3 string quartets (1880, 1923, 1928); sextet for wind instruments (1924); piano pieces (a sonata, etc.); song cycles: *Ryhadly,* nursery songs; *Zápisník zmizelého (Diary of a Vanished Man);* also many excellent folksong arrangements. — Bibliography: Max Brod, *Leoš Janáček* (1924; in German, 1925); H. Hollander, *Leoš Janáček and His Operas,* in the 'Mus. Quarterly' (Jan., 1929); Daniel Muller, *Leoš Janáček* (Paris, 1930); J. Procházka, *Lašské Kořeny života i díla Leoše Janáčka* (Prague, 1948); J. Štědron, *Leoš Janáček: Letters and Reminiscences* (Prague, 1954; in English, 1955); H. Hollander, *The Music of Leoš Janáček—Its Origin in Folklore,* in the 'Mus. Quarterly' (April, 1955); J. Seda, *Leoš Janáček* (Prague, 1956, in Czech and English). A collection of documents and studies pertaining to Janáček's work was publ. in Prague under the title *O lidové písne a lidové hudbě* (1955). A complete list of works with exact dates of composition and performance is found in Gr. Černušák and Vlad. Helfert, *Pazdírkuv Hudebni Slovník Naučny,* vol. 2 (Prague, 1937).

Janeček, Karel, Czech composer; b. Czestochowa, Poland, Feb. 20, 1903. He studied at the Prague Cons. with Křicka and with Novák; in 1941 became instructor there. In his music Janeček has adopted a traditional national style.—Works: symphony (1940); 3 string quartets; string trio; trio for flute, clarinet, and bassoon; several choral works on national themes.

Janequin (zhăhn-kăn'), **Clément,** creator and chief representative of the new 16th-century French polyphonic chanson; b. Châtellerault, about 1485; d. c. 1560. He was a pupil of Josquin. In his youth he may have been in the service of Louis Ronsard, father of the poet Pierre Ronsard, and may have accompanied his master during the Italian campaigns, from 1507 to the battle of Marignano, 1515. About 1520 he was in Paris and later perhaps in Spain. There is evidence that in 1529 he was in Bordeaux, subsequently in the service of the Cardinal of Lorraine (d. 1550), then chaplain of the Duke de Guise, whose victories he celebrated by extended chansons. From 1545 to 1558 he was curate at Unverre. In a dedication in verse, of 1559, he bemoans his old age and poverty.—Besides many detached pieces in collections of the time (Attaignant's, Gardane's, etc.), and chansons in special editions, there were publ. 2 Masses (1532, 1554), *Sacræ cantiones seu motectæ 4 voc.* (1533), *Proverbs de Salomon mis en cantiques et ryme françoise* (1554), *Octante deux psaumes de David* (1559); etc. Among the most interesting 'Inventions' (chansons) in 4-5 parts are *La Bataille* (portraying the battle of Marignano; Verdelot added a fifth part to the original four), *La Prise de Boulogne, Le Chant des oiseaux,* etc. Some of Janequin's works are ambitious examples of program music. Reprints have been made by Henri Expert in his 'Maîtres Musiciens de la Renaissance française' (chansons; vol. 7) and by Maurice Cauchie in 'Les Concerts de la Renaissance,' Part 2 (a collection of 30 3- and 4-voiced chansons by Janequin; 1928). Cauchie also ed. 2 5-voiced chansons *(Le Caquet des femmes* and *La Jalouzie).* — Cf. M. Cauchie, *Clément Janequin: Recherches sur sa famille et sur lui-même,* in the 'Revue de musicologie' (Feb., 1923); M. Cauchie, *Clément Janequin, chapelain du duc de Guise,* in 'Le Ménestrel' (Jan. 21, 1927); M. Cauchie, *Les Psaumes de Janequin* (Liège, 1930); J. Levron, *Clément Janequin, musicien de la Renaissance* (Paris, 1948); F. Lesure, *Clément Janequin, Recherches sur sa vie et son œuvre,* in 'Musica Disciplina' (1951); G. Reese, *Music in the Renaissance* (N. Y., 1954; pp. 295-99 and 340).

Janigro, Antonio, Italian cellist; b. Milan, Jan. 21, 1918. He studied at the Milan Cons.; then with Alexanian in Paris; toured in Europe, South America, Africa, and Asia. In 1939 he was appointed prof. at the Zagreb Cons.

Janis, Byron (real name, Yanks), American pianist; b. Pittsburgh, March 24, 1928; appeared as soloist with the Pittsburgh

Symph. Orch. at the age of 15; then studied privately with Vladimir Horowitz. He has appeared with orchestras and in solo recitals in the U. S. and Europe. He made his American début with the Pittsburgh Symph. Orch. in Rachmaninoff's 2nd piano concerto (Feb. 20, 1944).

Jankélévitch, Vladimir, French music critic; b. Bourges, Aug. 31, 1903. He has publ. a number of biographical studies: *Gabriel Fauré et ses mélodies* (1938; new augmented ed., 1951); *Maurice Ravel* (1939); *Debussy et le mystère* (1949); also *La Rapsodie: verve et improvisation musicale* (1955); contributed a number of articles to music magazines.

Jankó, Paul von, Hungarian pianist and inventor; b. Totis, June 2, 1856; d. Constantinople, March 17, 1919. He studied at the Polytechnic, Vienna, and also at the Cons. (under Hans Schmitt, Krenn, and Bruckner); then (1881-2) at Berlin Univ. (mathematics), and with Ehrlich (piano); from 1892 lived in Istanbul (Constantinople). His keyboard, invented in 1882, is really a new departure in piano-mechanics, though standing in distant relationship to the older 'chromatic' keyboard advocated by the society 'Chroma.' It has six rows of keys in step-like succession; the arrangement of the two lowest rows (typical of the other two pairs) is as follows:

Second row: *c♯ d♯ F G A B*
Lowest row: *C D E f♯ g♯ a♯ C*

the capitals representing white keys, and the small letters black ones. The 3rd and 4th rows, and the 5th and 6th rows, are mere duplications of the 1st and 2nd; and corresponding keys in the 1st, 3rd, and 5th rows, and in the 2nd, 4th, and 6th rows, are on one and the same key-lever, so that any note can be struck in three different places. The fingering of all diatonic scales is alike; chromatic scales are played by striking alternative keys in any two adjoining rows. A full description of the keyboard was published in pamphlet form by its inventor (1886).—Cf. R. Hausmann, *Die Jankó-Klaviatur* (1892); K. W. Marschner, *Das Jankó-Klavier* (1899); H. Schmitt, *Zur Geschichte der Jankó-Klaviatur* (in 'Wiener Rundschau,' 1889); R. Hausmann, *Das Jankó-Klavier und seine technische Vervollkommnung* (in 'Zeitschrift der Internationalen Musik-Gesellschaft,' vol. V); G. Scrinzi, *The Jankó-Keyboard and Simplification* (ib.); H. F. Münnich, *Materialien für die Jankó-Klaviatur* (1905).

Jannaconi (yăhn-nah-coh'-nē), **Giuseppe,** one of the last composers in 'Palestrina-style'; b. Rome, 1741; d. there, March 16, 1816. A pupil of S. Rinaldini and G. Carpani, he succeeded Zingarelli in 1811 as maestro at St. Peter's. He is noted for his scoring of many of Palestrina's works, aided by his friend Pisari. His works remain in MS in the Santini College now at Münster; they include a Mass, a *Te Deum,* a *Magnificat,* a *Dixit Dominus,* and a *Tu es Petrus,* all *a* 16; 16 Masses in 4-8 parts, with organ; 14 other Masses; 32 psalms in 4-8 parts; 10 Masses with orch.; 16 motets in 2-6 parts; 57 offertories and anthems *a* 3-8; a canon *a* 64; 2 canons *a* 16; an *Ecce terrae motus* for 6 basses; an oratorio for 2 tenors and 1 bass, *L'Agonia di Gesù Christo;* etc.

Janowka, Thomas Balthasar, Bohemian organist; b. Kuttenberg, 1660; date of death unknown. He was the compiler of *Clavis ad thesaurum magnae artis musicae* (Prague, 1701), which was the second (after Tinctoris) music dictionary in print. Only a few copies are extant.

Jansa, Leopold, Bohemian violinist and composer; b. Wildenschwert, March 23, 1795; d. Vienna, Jan. 24, 1875. He studied in Vienna; then taught violin there; was dismissed in 1849 after he took part in a concert in London for the benefit of the Hungarian revolutionists. He remained in England as a teacher for several years until the amnesty of 1868, when he returned to Vienna and received a pension. He was greatly esteemed as a violinist; he composed much violin music, including 4 concertos and 36 violin duets; other works are 8 string quartets, 3 string trios, and some church music.

Janssen, Herbert, German baritone; b. Cologne, Sept. 22, 1895. He studied in Cologne and Berlin; gave recitals; then became a member of the Berlin State Opera. He made his American début with the Metropolitan Opera Co. (Philadelphia, Jan. 24, 1939) as Wotan in *Siegfried;* then sang in other Wagnerian roles.

Janssen, Werner, American composer and conductor; b. New York, June 1, 1899. He studied with Frederick Converse in Boston, and as a young man began to compose operettas; contributed musical numbers to Ziegfeld's Follies and other revues. After graduation from Dartmouth College, he won the Prix de Rome of the American Academy (1930), and made his début as conductor during his stay in Rome; he then conducted in Berlin and Budapest and in Scandinavia. He gave a concert of music by Sibelius in Helsinki (1934) and was highly praised by Sibelius himself; received the Finnish Order of the White Rose, First Class, for his services to Finnish music. After conducting various European orchestras as guest, he made his American début as conductor with the N. Y. Philharmonic (Nov. 8, 1934); then conducted other American orchestras. He was the regular conductor of the Baltimore Symph. from 1937-39; then went to Hollywood, where he organized the Janssen Symph., with the purpose of commissioning and performing new works (1940); toured South America in 1941. He was conductor of the Utah Symph. Orch., Salt Lake City (1946-47), of the Portland, Oregon, Orch. (1947-49), and of the San Diego Philharmonic (1952-54). In 1937 he married the famous motion picture actress Ann Harding. As a composer, Janssen tends towards illustrative representation of modern life. His most spectacular work of this nature is *New Year's Eve in New York* (Rochester, May 9, 1929), a symph. poem for large orchestra with jazz instruments; the orchestra men are instructed to shout at the end, 'Happy New Year.' Other works are *Obsequies of a Saxophone,* for 6 wind instruments and a snare drum (Washington, D. C., Oct. 17, 1929); *Louisiana Suite,* for orch. (1930); *Dixie Fugue* (extracted from the *Louisiana Suite;* Rome, Nov. 27, 1932); *Foster Suite,* for orch., on Stephen Foster's tunes (1937); 2 string quartets; *Kaleidoscope,* for string quartet; film music; also popular songs.

Janssens, Jean-François-Joseph, Belgian composer; b. Antwerp, Jan. 29, 1801; d. there, Feb. 3, 1835. He studied with his father and later with Lesueur in Paris. Returning to Antwerp, he became a lawyer; was a notary public until the siege of Antwerp (1832); composed in his leisure hours. Going to Cologne, he lost his manuscripts and other possessions in a fire on the night of his arrival; this misfortune so affected him that he became insane. He wrote 4 operas, 2 cantatas, 2 symphonies, 5 Masses; a number of motets, anthems, and hymns; also songs.—Cf. Hendricks, *Simple histoire. Boutades biographiques à l'occasion du 25me anniversaire de la mort de J.-F.-J. Janssens* (Antwerp, 1860); E. van der Straeten, *J.-F.-J. Janssens, compositeur de musique* (Brussels, 1866; contains a list of his works).

Jaques - Dalcroze (zhăhk dăhl - krohz'), **Émile,** composer and creator of 'Eurhythmics'; b. (of French parents) Vienna, July 6, 1865; d. Geneva, July 1, 1950. In 1873 his parents moved to Geneva; having completed his course at the Univ. and also at the Cons. there, he went to Vienna for further study under R. Fuchs and A. Bruckner, and then to Paris, where he studied orchestration at the Cons. with Delibes; in 1892 he returned to Geneva as instructor of theory at the Cons. Since he laid special stress on rhythm, he insisted on all his pupils' beating time with their hands, and this led him, step by step, to devise a series of movements affecting the entire body. Together with the French psychologist Édouard Claparide, he worked out a special terminology and reduced his practice to a regular system, which he called 'Eurhythmics.' When his application to have his method introduced as a regular course at the Cons. was refused, he resigned, and in 1910 established his own school at Hellerau, near Dresden. Even before that time the new system had attracted wide attention, and the school flourished from the beginning; within three years branches were opened in France, Russia, Germany, England, and the U. S. (Bryn Mawr College, New York, and Chicago). Conditions resulting from the war brought about the closing of the school at Hellerau in 1915. After that he founded another school at Geneva, the headquarters of which were later moved to Paris. In 1925 the Hellerau School was established in Laxenburg, near Vienna. Jaques-Dalcroze himself also taught in London; in his later years he lived in Geneva. Without question, the results obtained by Jaques-Dalcroze have contributed toward the recent development of the ballet. Aside from his rhythmical innovations, he also commanded respect as a composer of marked originality and fecundity of invention; many of his works show how thoroughly he was imbued with the spirit of Swiss folk music. — Works: the operas *Le Violon maudit* (Geneva, 1893), *Janie* (Geneva, March 13, 1894), *Sancho Panza* (Geneva, 1897), *Onkel Dazumal* (Cologne, 1905; as *Le bonhomme Jadis,* Paris, 1906), *Les Jumeaux de Bergame* (Brussels, 1908), *Fête de la jeunesse et de la joie* (Geneva, 1932); an operetta, *Respect pour nous* (Geneva, 1898); a pantomime, *Écho et Narcisse* (Hellerau, 1912); *Festival vaudois,* for soli, chorus, and orch.; *La Veillée,* for soli, chorus, and orch.; *Dance Suite in A* for orch.; *Suite de ballet;* 2 violin concertos; string quartet; suite for cello and piano; *Fantasia appassionata,* for violin and piano; *Images* (1928); *Dialogues* (1931); *Ariettes* (1931); *Rondeaux* for piano

(1933); several collections of songs (*Chansons romandes et enfantines, Chansons populaires et enfantines, Idylles et chansons, Volkskinderlieder, Tanzlieder für Kinder, Chansons religieuses, Chansons de la gosse,* etc.) He publ. *Le cœur chante; impressions d'un musicien* (Geneva, 1900); *L'Éducation par le rhythme,* a series of lectures (1907); a comprehensive *Méthode Jaques-Dalcroze* (5 parts, 1907-14); *Rhythm, Music and Education* (Basel, 1922; in German, French, and English); *Souvenirs* (Neuchâtel and Paris, 1942); *La musique et nous* (Geneva, 1945); also *The Child and the Pianoforte,* in the 'Mus. Quarterly' (April, 1928); *Eurhythmics and its Implications,* in the 'Mus. Quarterly' (July, 1930); *L'Improvisation au piano,* in 'Rhythm' (1932).—Cf. A. Seidl, *Die Hellerauer Schulfeste und die Bildungsanstalt Jaques-Dalcroze* (Regensburg, 1912); K. Storck, *Émile Jaques-Dalcroze: seine Stellung und Aufgabe in unserer Zeit* (Stuttgart, 1912); M. E. Sadler, *Eurhythmics* (London, 1912); 'Dalcroze Kongress-Bericht' (Geneva, 1926); H. Brunet-Lecomte, *Jaques-Dalcroze, sa vie, son œuvre* (Geneva, 1950).

Járdányi, Pál, Hungarian composer; b. Budapest, Jan. 30, 1920. He studied violin as a child; later took lessons with Kodály; in 1946 was appointed instructor at the Budapest Academy of Music; has also been active as music critic. His works follow the style of modern Hungarian music, based on national folksongs. Járdányi has written a symphonic poem, *Tisza* (1952); violin sonata (1944); string quartet (awarded the Bartók prize in 1948); several albums of dances for piano, and numerous arrangements of folksongs.

Jardillier, Robert, French statesman and writer on music; b. Caen, March 31, 1890. He studied in Paris and Lyons; was prof. at the universities of Rochefort (1913-18) and Dijon (1918-32); in 1936 was appointed postmaster general in Léon Blum's cabinet. He publ. several valuable books: *Smetana vu par les étrangers* (Paris, 1924); *Pelléas* (Paris, 1927); *La musique de chambre de César Franck* (Paris, 1929), etc.

Jarecki (yăh-rĕt'-skē), **Henryk,** Polish conductor and composer; b. Warsaw, Dec. 6, 1846; d. Lwow, Dec. 18, 1918. He studied with Moniuszko; from 1877 to 1900 he was conductor at the Lwow Opera; wrote 7 operas on subjects from Polish literature; also a *Polish Mass* and a number of songs.

Jarecki (yăh-ret'-skē), **Tadeusz,** Polish conductor and composer; b. Lwow, Dec. 31, 1888. He studied with his father, Henryk Jarecki, and with Niewiadomski; then with Taneyev in Moscow (1913), where he graduated from the Cons. In 1913 he came to the U. S.; won the Coolidge Prize in 1918 for his 2nd string quartet. He remained in New York until 1932; then went back to Poland; was guest conductor with the Warsaw Philharmonic and the Lwow Orch.; then led symph. concerts and opera in Stanislawow (1932-37); lived in Paris (1938) and subsequently in London. In 1948 he settled in New York. His works include the symph. poem *Chimère* (1926); symph. suite *La foule* (1928); *Sinfonia breve* (Lwow, Jan. 15, 1932); 3 string quartets; songs. On Feb. 23, 1921 he married the American lyric soprano **Louise Llewellyn Jarecka** (b. New York, Dec. 10, 1889; d. there, March 6, 1954).

Jarnach, Philipp, composer; b. Noisy, France, July 26, 1892. He was a son of the Catalonian sculptor E. Jarnach and a German mother. He studied at the Paris Cons. with Risler (piano) and Lavignac (theory). At the outbreak of World War I he went to Zürich, where he met Busoni; this meeting was a decisive influence in his musical development; he became an ardent disciple of Busoni; after Busoni's death, he completed Busoni's last opera, *Doktor Faust,* which was produced in Jarnach's version in Berlin on May 21, 1925. From 1922-27 Jarnach wrote music criticism in the 'Börsen-Courier' in Berlin. In 1927 he was appointed prof. of composition at the Cologne Cons., and remained at that post until 1949. In 1950 he became director of the Hamburg Cons. Jarnach's own music is determined by his devotion to Busoni's ideals; it is distinguished by impeccable craftsmanship, but it lacks individuality. He participated in the modern movement in Germany between the two world wars, and many of his works were performed at music festivals during that period. Among his works are a *Sinfonia Brevis* (1923); string quintet (1920); string quartet (1924); *Musik zum Gedächtnis des Einsamen,* for string quartet (1952); sonatina for flute and piano; cello sonatina, etc. —Cf. Hans Mersmann and E. G. Klussmann, *Philipp Jarnach zum 60. Geburtstag* (Hamburg, 1952); also references in E. J. Dent's *Ferruccio Busoni* (Oxford, 1933).

Järnefelt (yär'-neh-felt), **Armas,** Finnish conductor and composer; b. Viborg, Aug. 14, 1869. He studied with Wegelius at the

Helsinki Cons., and also with Busoni, who taught there at the time; he then went to Berlin (1890) and to Paris (1892), where he studied with Massenet. He began his career as an opera coach in Magdeburg (1896); then was at Düsseldorf (1897). Returning to Finland in 1898, he was conductor in his native town; in 1903 he received a government stipend for travel; was for 25 years conductor of the Stockholm Opera (1907-32); conductor of the Helsinki Opera (1932-36), and of the Helsinki Municipal Orch. (1942-43). He was married to the Finnish singer, Maikki Pakarinen (1893; divorced in 1908), then to another singer, Liva Edström. He wrote several works for orch., in a national Finnish style: *Korsholm, Suomen synty, Laulu Vuokselle, Abo slott,* etc.; his *Berceuse* and *Praeludium* for small orch. became extremely popular. See Väinö Pesola, *Armas Järnefelt* in *Suomen Säveltäjiä,* edited by Sulho Ranta (Helsinki, 1945; pp. 300-06).

Järnefelt, Maikki (*née* Pakarinen), Finnish soprano, wife of Armas Järnefelt; b. Joensuu, Aug. 26, 1871; d. Turku, July 4, 1929. She studied with Mme. Marchesi in Paris; became a well-known opera singer in Europe; also lived in America for several years. She was married to Järnefelt in 1893 and divorced in 1908; then was married to Palmgren (1910).

Jarno (yahr'-noh), **Georg,** composer; b. Budapest, June 3, 1868; d. Breslau, May 25, 1920. He conducted opera in Breslau; produced his own operas there: *Die schwarze Kaschka* (Breslau, May 12, 1895; his most successful opera), *Der Richter von Zalamea* (1899), and *Der Goldfisch* (1907); in Vienna he produced *Die Förster-Christel* (1907), *Das Musikantenmädel* (1910), and *Die Marine-Gustel* (1912). Another opera, *Das Farmermädchen,* was produced in Berlin (1913).

Jarnović, Giovanni. See **Giornovichi.**

Jarnowick, Pierre Louis Hus-Deforges. See **Hus-Desforges.**

Jarov (zhah'-rof), **Sergey,** Russian choral conductor; b. Moscow, March 20, 1896. He studied at the Academy for Church Singing at the Imperial Synod; then became an officer of the Cossacks. After the Revolution, and the defeat of the White Army, he left Russia and established a Don Cossack Chorus, with which he made successful tours in Europe; eventually settled in America. The repertory of his chorus includes popular Russian songs in artful arrangements, emphasizing dynamic contrasts, and also sacred works by Russian composers.

Jaubert, Maurice, French composer; b. Nice, Jan. 3, 1900; killed in action in France, June 19, 1940. He studied law and took lessons in piano and composition at the Cons. of Nice. He abandoned the legal profession in 1923, when he went to Paris. He obtained considerable success with the score for the French film, *Carnet de bal* (1938). His works include: *Suite française,* for orch. (St. Louis, Nov. 10, 1933); *Sonata a due,* for violin, cello, and string orch. (Boston, Dec. 27, 1946); *Jeanne d'Arc,* symph. poem (1937), etc.

Jausions (zhoh-z'yŏhn'), Dom **Paul,** French writer on church music; b. Rennes, Nov. 15, 1834; d. Vincennes, Indiana, Sept. 9, 1870. He entered the order of St. Benedict at Solesmes in 1856, and under the direction of Dom Guéranger began to study Gregorian Chant; continued his investigations in company with Dom Pothier, whose *Mélodies Grégoriennes* are the result of their joint labors. In 1869 he was sent to the U. S. to collect data for a biography of Bruté de Rémut, bishop of Vincennes (an uncle of Dom Guéranger), and died as he was about to return. His interpretation of the Gregorian melodies according to the tonic accent has become one of the guiding principles in the publications of the Benedictines of Solesmes. A complete list of his writings is found in the *Bibliographie des Bénédictins de la congrégation de France* (1907).

Jean-Aubry (zhŏn oh-brē'), **Georges,** French writer on music; b. Paris, Aug. 13, 1882; d. there, Nov. 14, 1949. He was a journalist; became interested in music; traveled in Europe and South America (1908-15); then lived in London, where he edited 'The Chesterian,' house organ of the publishing firm J. & W. Chester. He publ. *La Musique française d'aujourd'hui* (1915; in English, London, 1919) and *La Musique et les nations* (1922; in English, London, 1923).

Jean le Coq. See **Gallus, Johannes.**

Jeannin (zhăh-năn), Dom **Jules Cécilien,** French musicologist, specialist on Gregorian Chant; b. Marseilles, Feb. 6, 1866; d. Hautecombe, Feb. 15, 1933. He studied in Marseilles; later traveled extensively in

Syria and Mesopotamia, gathering material for his collection, *Mélodies liturgiques syriennes et chaldéennes* (in 3 vols.: I, 1925; II, 1928; III, not publ.). Other works: *Études sur le rythme grégorien* (Lyons, 1926); *Nuove osservazioni sulla ritmica gregoriana* (Turin, 1930); *La Question rythmique grégorienne* in 'Revue Musicale' (1930). As a scholar he was an opponent of Dom Mocquereau, and wrote a book, *Rythme grégorien: réponse à Dom Mocquereau* (Lyons, 1928), disputing his theories. He spent the last years of his life as organist in the Hautecombe monastery.—Cf. L. Bonvin, *Jules Cécilien Jeannin,* in the 'Kirchenmusikalisches Jahrbuch' (1930).

Jeanson (yahn'-son), **Bo Gunnar,** Swedish musicologist; b. Göteborg, Oct. 10, 1898; d. Stockholm, Jan. 20, 1939. He studied at the Stockholm Cons. with L. Lundberg (piano) and T. Norlind (musicology); then took courses in Vienna with Wellesz, and in Freiburg, Switzerland, with Peter Wagner. In 1926 he received the degree of *Dr. phil.* for a dissertation on August Söderman; in 1927 became editor of the musicological publication 'Svensk Tidskrift för Musikforskning.' He publ. a music history, *Musiken genom tiderna* (2 vols.; Stockholm, 1927 and 1931; revised by J. Rabe, 1945).

Jedliczka (yĕd'-lich-kah), **Ernst,** pianist; b. Poltava, Russia, June 5, 1855; d. Berlin, Aug. 3, 1904. He studied at the Moscow Cons. with Tchaikovsky and Nicholas Rubinstein; then taught there (1881-88). In 1888 he settled in Berlin; was first prof. of the Klindworth Institute (1888-97); then at the Stern Cons. (from 1897).

Jeep (yeh-ep), German composer, b. Dransfeld, 1581; d. Hanau, Nov. 19, 1644. He studied in Göttingen and Celle; traveled in Italy; was Kapellmeister in Weickersheim (1610-33); cathedral organist in Frankfurt (1633-40); from 1640, in Hanau. He publ. a book of songs for 3, 4, 5, and 6 voices, *Studentengärtlein* (2 vols., 1607 and 1609; many subsequent reprints; included in H. J. Moser, *Studentenlust,* 1930); sacred songs (1607); secular songs, *Tricinia* (1610).

Jeffries, George, English composer; date and place of birth unknown; d. 1685. He was a member of the Chapel Royal and organist to King Charles I; went to Oxford in 1643 as organist and composer. Many of his sacred works are extant in MS, preserved in the British Museum and at the Royal College of Music, among them about 190 motets and anthems and several services (in Latin); madrigals in the Italian manner; also masques, cantatas, dramatic dialogues, and other stage pieces.

Jehan. See **Gallus, Johannes.**

Jehin (zhŭ-ăn'), **François,** celebrated violinist; b. Spa, Belgium, April 18, 1839; d. Montreal, Canada, May 29, 1899. As a child he studied with Servais and with his uncle François Prume, whose name he added to his own, often performing as Jehin-Prume; then took lessons with Bériot at the Brussels Cons.; studied harmony with Fétis; won 1st prize in violin and in theory; at the age of 16, after completing advanced studies with Vieuxtemps and Wieniawski, he undertook a European tour; appeared with Anton and Nicholas Rubinstein, Jenny Lind, and other celebrities; formed a famous trio with Kontski and Monsigny. In 1863 he traveled through Mexico, Cuba, New York, to Montreal; met and married the singer Rosita del Vecchio. Thenceforth, his time was divided between Europe and America; he eventually settled in Montreal. Among his pupils was Eugène Ysaÿe. He wrote 2 violin concertos and many brilliant solo pieces for his instrument. He publ. in Montreal a book of memoirs, *Une vie d'artiste* (gives a list of his works from op. 1 to op. 88).

Jelich, Vincenz, Austrian composer; b. St. Veit, c. 1595; date and place of death unknown; during 1605-16 was in Graz as choirboy; in 1617, went to Zabern, Alsace, as court musician. He wrote *Parnassia militia* (1622); *Arion* (2 books of sacred songs, 1628); motets, etc.—Cf. H. Federhofer, *V. Jelich* in 'Archiv für Musikwissenschaft' (1955).

Jelinek, Hanns, Austrian composer; b. Vienna, Dec. 5, 1901. He studied with Schoenberg, and in the 1930's adopted the 12-tone method. He wrote for orch. *Sinfonia ritmica* (1932); *Divertimento No. 8,* for small clarinet, clarinet, basset horn, and bass clarinet (1952); string quartet; suite for strings; a series of piano pieces under the title of *Zwölftonwerk.* He is the author of the manual *Anleitung zur Zwölftonkomposition* (Vienna, 1952).

Jelinek, Joseph. See **Gelinek.**

Jelmoli (yehl-mŏh'-lē), **Hans,** Swiss pianist and composer; b. Zürich, Jan. 17, 1877; d. there, May 6, 1936. He studied with

Humperdinck and Iwan Knorr at Frankfurt; then conducted operatic productions in Mainz and Würzburg. Upon his return to Zürich, he was mainly active as teacher and writer; wrote music criticism for the 'Schweizerische Musikzeitung.' He composed the operas *Die Schweizer, Sein Vermächtnis,* and *Die Badener Fahrt;* incidental music to various plays; also 26 Swiss songs in the Zürich dialect. He publ. *Ferruccio Busonis Zürcher Jahre* (1928) and other pamphlets concerning musical life in Zürich.

Jemnitz (yem'-nitz), **Alexander,** Hungarian composer; b. Budapest, Aug. 9, 1890. He studied with Koessler in Budapest (1912-16); then with Straube in Leipzig (organ). From 1917-21 he occupied various posts as assistant conductor at opera theaters in Bremen and elsewhere; he was in Berlin from 1921 to 1924, and studied there with Schoenberg. In 1924 he returned to Budapest; was engaged as music critic, and continued to compose. His chosen idiom represents a cross between the contrapuntal style of Max Reger (with whom he took a few lessons in 1916) and the radical language of atonality, modelled after Schoenberg's early works. His works include a ballet, *Divertimento* (Budapest, April 23, 1947); *7 Miniatures* for orch. (1948); *Overture for a Peace Festival* (1951); trio for 2 oboes and English horn; trio for flute, oboe, and clarinet; 2 string trios; sonata for flute and cello; sonata for saxophone and banjo; trio for violin, viola, and guitar; string quartet; 3 violin sonatas; cello sonata; unaccompanied sonatas for various solo instruments (cello, harp, double-bass, trumpet, flute, etc.); 4 piano sonatas; several song cycles. His works were often performed at modern music festivals: Serenade for violin, viola, and cello, at the Geneva Festival (April 8, 1929); harp sonata, at the Prague Festival (Sept. 4, 1935); etc.

Jenkins, Cyril, Welsh composer; b. Dunvant, near Swansea, Oct. 9, 1885. He studied organ in his native town, and composition with Stanford in London. In 1911 his cantata *Young Lochinvar* was given at the Welsh National Festival; he wrote another cantata, *Llewelyn,* and *A Welsh Fantasy,* for string orch.; a symphony and a number of choral works on Welsh themes were presented at later Welsh festivals. In 1922 he went to Australia.

Jenkins, David, Welsh composer; b. Trecastle, Dec. 30, 1848; d. Aberystwyth, Dec. 10, 1915. He studied at the Univ. of Wales; then taught there; became widely known as choral conductor; wrote oratorios and other choral works for the Welsh festivals; his cantata, *The Ark of the Covenant,* was performed at the Caernarvon Festival in 1876. He was editor of the Welsh music periodical, 'Y Cerddor.'

Jenkins, John, English composer; b. Maidstone, 1592; d. Kimberley, Norfolk, Oct. 26, 1678. In his early years he was a domestic tutor and lute player to various aristocrats; also played at the courts of Charles I and Charles II. He wrote many *Fancies* for viols or organ, and light pieces which he called *Rants;* of these, *Mitter Rant* was included in Playford's *Musick's Handmaid* (1678); *The Fleece Tavern Rant* and *The Peterborough Rant,* both in Playford's *Apollo's Banquet* (1690); his popular air, *The Lady Katherine Audley's Bells* or *The Five Bell Consort,* appeared in Playford's *Courtly Masquing Ayres* (1662). He wrote some music for violin; an edition entitled *12 Sonatas for 2 Violins and a Base, with a Thorough Base for the Organ or Theorbo* attributed to Jenkins, and supposedly published in London in 1660, is not extant; the claim made by some historians that Jenkins was the first English composer of violin sonatas cannot be sustained inasmuch as William Young had anticipated him by publishing 11 violin sonatas in 1653. See *John Jenkins, Fancies and Ayres* (reprint), edited by Helen Joy Sleeper (Wellesley, 1950).

Jenner (yen'-ner), **Gustav,** German composer and writer; b. Keitum, Dec. 3, 1865; d. Marburg, Aug. 29, 1920. He studied with Mandyczewski, and also took some lessons with Brahms; in 1895, became music director at Marburg. He composed fine lieder, choral works, several violin sonatas, a trio for piano, clarinet, and horn; transcribed old German songs, etc.; publ. *Johannes Brahms als Mensch, Lehrer und Künstler* (1905; 2nd ed., 1930).—Cf. W. Kohleick, *Gustav Jenner* (1943).

Jensen (yĕn'-sen), **Adolf,** German composer; b. Königsberg, Jan. 12, 1837; d. Baden-Baden, Jan. 23, 1879. He stemmed from a family of musicians in Königsberg; studied with Ehlert and Köhler; began to compose as a boy; at 19, went to Russia as a music tutor; then was theater conductor in Posen (1857); was in Copenhagen (1858-60), where he studied with Gade; then returned to Königsberg. He subsequently taught at Tausig's school in Berlin (1866-

68); then lived in Dresden, Graz, and finally at Baden-Baden, where he died of consumption. A great admirer of Schumann, he closely imitated him in his songs, of which about 160 were published. He also wrote an opera, *Die Erbin von Montfort* (1864-65); it was revised by Kienzl, to a new libretto by Jensen's daughter, under the title *Turandot.* Other works are the cantatas, *Jephthas Tochter, Der Gang der Jünger nach Emmäus, Adonisfeier,* etc., and many characteristic piano pieces.—Cf. A. Niggli, *A. Jensen* (Zürich, 1895); another biography, also by Niggli, was publ. in Heinrich Reimann's *Berühmte Musiker* (Berlin, 1900); G. Schweizer, *Das Liedschaffen A. Jensens* (Frankfurt, 1933). Jensen's letters were publ. by P. Kuczynski (1879).

Jensen, Gustav, German violinist and composer; brother of Adolf Jensen; b. Königsberg, Dec. 25, 1843; d. Cologne, Nov. 26, 1895. He studied with his brother; then with Dehn in Berlin (theory) and with Joachim (violin). In 1872 he became prof. of composition at the Cologne Cons., and held that position until his death. He wrote a symphony; a string quartet; violin sonata; cello sonata; *Ländliche Serenade,* for string orch.; various violin pieces; publ. the series *Klassische Violinmusik;* translated into German Cherubini's *Manual of Counterpoint.*

Jensen (yĕn'-sen), **Ludvig Irgens,** Norwegian composer; b. Oslo, April 13, 1894. He studied philology, music theory, and piano in Oslo. He has written a cantata, *Der Gott und die Bajadere* (1921-32); an opera, *Heimferd* (Oslo, Aug. 27, 1947); for orch.: 2 symphonies (No. 1, 1930; No. 2, 1942); *Partita Sinfonica* (1948); *Variazioni* (1948); *Passacaglia* (1951). Also a violin sonata (1924), piano quintet (1927), and choral works.

Jensen, Niels Peter, Danish organist and composer; b. Copenhagen, July 23, 1802; d. there, Oct. 19, 1846. He was blind from childhood, but learned to play the flute and organ; was organist at St. Peter's Church in Copenhagen from 1828. He wrote 2 sonatas and other pieces for the flute.

Jeppesen (yep'-pe-sen), **Knud,** eminent Danish musicologist and composer; b. Copenhagen, Aug. 15, 1892. He studied at the Univ. there with Laub and Nielsen, and at the Univ. of Vienna with G. Adler and R. Lach (1922, *Dr. phil.* with the dissertation *Die Dissonanzbehandlung in den Werken Palestrinas;* English transl. by Margaret W. Hamerik, as *The Style of Palestrina and the Dissonance,* with introduction by E. J. Dent, Copenhagen, 1927; 2nd ed., 1946; very valuable); from 1920 to 1946, taught at the Cons. in Copenhagen; 1946-1957, prof of musicology at Univ. of Aarhus; from 1931 to 1954, editor of 'Acta musicologica'. He ed. *Der Kopenhagener Chansonnier* (1927). Other writings: *Kontrapunkt* (1930; English transl., with introduction by Glen Haydon, N. Y., 1939; 2nd German ed., Leipzig, 1956); *Die mehrstimmige italienische Laude um 1500* (1935); *Die italienische Orgelmusik am Anfang des Cinquecento* (Copenhagen, 1943); etc. — Compositions: opera, *Rosaura* (1946; Copenhagen, Sept. 20, 1950); symphony (1939); horn concerto (1941); *Little Summer Trio,* for flute, cello, and piano (1941); *Te Deum Danicum* (London, Oct. 27, 1948).

Jepson, Harry Benjamin, American organist; b. New Haven, Conn., Aug. 16, 1870; d. Noank, Conn., Aug. 23, 1952. He studied organ with Stoeckel, and composition with Horatio Parker; in 1895, was appointed instructor of organ at Yale Univ., and served in that capacity until 1950. He edited 'Yale University Hymns' and publ. a number of works for organ.

Jepson, Helen, American soprano; b. Titusville, Penna., Nov. 28, 1905. Of a musical family, she sang in church choirs at 13 in Akron, Ohio, where she went to school; worked as a corset fitter and sales girl; then was enabled to go to Philadelphia to study at the Curtis Institute (1923-28); in 1936, went to Paris to study with Mary Garden; also took lessons with Queena Mario; then became a member of the Philadelphia Grand Opera Co. She made her début with the Metropolitan Opera Co. on Jan. 24, 1935; also sang with the Chicago Civic Opera Co. She was married to George Rosco Possell (1931); divorced, and married Walter Dellera (1942).

Jeremiáš (yeh' - rĕh - mē - ahsh), **Jaroslav,** Czech composer; son of the organist and composer Bohuslav Jeremiáš (1859-1918); b. Pisek, Aug. 14, 1889; d. Budějovice, Jan. 16, 1919. He studied at the Prague Cons.; also took lessons with Novák. He was engaged as opera conductor at Ljubljana, Yugoslavia; then returned to Prague. Although he died at the age of 29, he left several significant works: the opera *Starý král (The Old King;* produced posthumously, Prague, April 13, 1919); oratorio *Jan Hus* (also posthumous; Prague, June 13, 1919); a viola sonata; songs.—Cf. B. Bělohlávek, *J. Jeremiáš* (Prague, 1935).

Jeremiáš, Otakar, Czech conductor and composer; brother of Jaroslav Jeremiáš; b. Pisek, Oct. 17, 1892. He studied, as did his brother, at the Prague Cons., and with Novák; directed a music school at Budějovice (1918-28); conducted the orch. of the Prague Radio (1929-45); in 1945 was appointed director of the Prague Opera. Among his many works are 2 operas, *The Brothers Karamazov* (Prague, Oct. 8, 1928) and *Till Eulenspiegel* (Prague, May 13, 1949); cantata, *Pisen rodné zemi (Song of the Native Land;* 1941); 2 symphonies (1911; 1914); chamber music; film music; songs.—Cf. J. Plavec, *Otakar Jeremiáš* (Prague, 1943; gives a list of works with dates of performance).

Jeritza (real name Jedlitzka), **Maria,** dramatic soprano; b. Brünn, Oct. 6, 1887. She studied voice and several instruments in Brünn; appeared first as a chorus singer at the Brünn Opera; made her début as a soloist as Elsa in *Lohengrin* at Olmütz (1910), followed by an engagement at the Vienna Volksoper (début as Elizabeth in *Tannhäuser);* guest appearances in Stuttgart (where she created the title role of Strauss' *Ariadne),* Zürich, Berlin, Munich, Basel, Bern, etc.; member of the Vienna State Opera (1912-35); member of the Metropolitan Opera Co. (1921-32; début as Marietta in Korngold's *Die tote Stadt,* Nov. 19, 1921), where she became especially celebrated for her interpretation of Tosca; appeared in Boston in Rudolf Friml's *Annina* (later changed to *Music Hath Charms),* with which she toured; has toured the U. S. many times in recital and as soloist with various orchestras. In 1935, she married the motion picture executive Winfield Sheehan, and settled in Hollywood; then was divorced; married Irving F. Seery on April 10, 1948. Her autobiography, *Sunlight and Song,* was published in London and New York (1924).

Jersild (yer'-sild), **Jørgen,** Danish composer; b. Copenhagen, Sept. 17, 1913. He studied in Paris with Roussel (1936); from 1943-49, teaching at the Copenhagen Cons.; also wrote music criticism in 'Berlingske Tildende.' His music is Impressionistic in harmony and color, and neo-Classical in form. Works: *Pastorale* for strings (1945); Serenade for 5 wind instruments, subtitled *At spille i Skoven (To be played in the woods,* 1947); *Trois pièces en concert* for piano; and some choral works.

Jervis - Read, Harold Vincent, English composer; b. Powyke, Worcestershire, March 14, 1883; d. Salisbury, Dec. 15, 1945. He studied at the Royal Academy of Music, and later taught there. He wrote for chorus *The Hound of Heaven, Dream Tryst, That Land, To the Daughter of Earth, High Tide,* etc.; a string sextet; 2 piano sonatas; *5 Caprices,* for piano; songs, etc.

Jirák (yē-rahk), **Karel Boleslav,** Czech composer and conductor; b. Prague, Jan. 28, 1891. He studied privately with Vitězlav Novák and with J. B. Foerster. In 1915 he was appointed conductor of the Hamburg City Opera; in 1918 went to Brno, where he was conductor at the National Theater for a season (1918-19). He then was choral conductor and prof. of composition at the Prague Cons. (1920-30); from 1930-45, music director of the Czechoslovak Radio. In 1947 he went to the U. S.; in 1948 became prof. of music at Roosevelt College in Chicago.—Works: opera, *Woman and the God* (1913; Brno, March 10, 1928); 5 symphonies: No. 1 (1916), No. 2 (1924), No. 3 (Prague, March 8, 1939), No. 4, surnamed *Episode from an Artist's Life* (1937), No. 5 (Edinburgh Festival, Aug. 26, 1951; winner of the Edinburgh International Festival prize); *Night Music* for violin and orch. (1918); *Overture to a Shakespeare Comedy* (Prague, Feb. 24, 1927); *Symphonic Variations* (Prague, March 26, 1941); *Psalm 23,* for chorus and orch.; numerous chamber works: string sextet; 3 string quartets (No. 1, 1915; No. 2, 1927; No. 3, 1940); *Divertimento* for string trio; sonata for cello, for violin, for viola, for piano, for flute; 2 piano suites and other pieces; the song cycles (with orch.) *Lyric Intermezzo* (1913), *Tragi-comedies* (1915), *Evening and Soul* (1921), *Awakening* (1925), *Fleeting Happiness* (1916), *3 Songs of Home* (1929), *Colors of the Rainbow* (1926), *Rok* (1941). He is also the author of a book on musical form (in Czech, 1924).—Cf. M. Očadlík, *Karel Boleslav Jirák* (Prague, 1941).

Jiránek (yē'-rah-nek), **Josef,** Bohemian pedagogue; b. Ledeč, March 24, 1855; d. Prague, Jan. 5, 1940. He studied with Smetana, who legally adopted him as a child; also studied violin with A. Hřímalý and harp with Stanek. He began his career as a harpist in Prague; in 1877 he went to Russia, where he taught piano in Kharkov; returned to Prague in 1891, and taught piano at the Prague Cons.; retired in 1923. He was very successful as a teacher and also as a player of chamber music; publ. a number of useful manuals (in German): *Schule des Akkordspiels und der Akkordzerlegungen; Theoretisch-praktische Schule der wesentlichen Verzierungen im Pianofortespiel; Anschlagübungen zur Erreichung gleichzeitig verschiedener Tongebung im mehrstimmigen Spiel; Tonleitern in Doppelgriffen; Technische Übungen in Verbindung mit praktischen Fingersatzstudien; Neue Schule der Technik und des musikalischen Vortags;* composed *Scherzo fantastique,* for orch.; piano quintet; 2 piano sonatas, and other pieces. While in Russia, he brought out a teaching guide, *Musical Grammar,* published in the Russian language.

Joachim, Amalie (*née* Weiss), concert singer; wife of Joseph Joachim; b. Marburg, May 10, 1839; d. Berlin, Feb. 3, 1899. Her real maiden name was Schneeweiss, but she abridged it to Weiss in 1854, when she appeared as a singer in Vienna. She began her career as a soprano; after her marriage to Joachim (1863), she abandoned the stage, but continued to give recitals as a lieder singer; her interpretations of Schumann's songs were particularly fine. —Cf. Olga Plaschke, *Amalie Joachim* (Berlin, 1899).

Joachim, Joseph, one of the greatest masters of the violin; b. Kittsee, near Pressburg, June 28, 1831; d. Berlin, Aug. 15, 1907. He began to study the violin at the age of 5; his first teacher was Szervaczinski, with whom he appeared in public, at the age of 7, playing a violin duet. At the age of 10 he was sent to the Vienna Cons., where he studied with Böhm; in 1843 he played in Leipzig at a concert presented by Pauline Viardot; Mendelssohn did him the honor of accompanying him on the piano. He appeared with the Gewandhaus Orch. (Nov. 16, 1843); then made his first tour in England (1844), arousing admiration for his mature musicianship and remarkable technique. Returning to Leipzig, he studied with Ferdinand David; also played as concertmaster of the Gewandhaus Orch. in David's absence. From 1849 till 1854 Joachim served as concertmaster of the court orch. in Weimar. Liszt, who reigned supreme in Weimar, did not favor young Joachim, and in 1854 Joachim went to Hanover as solo violinist at the court; in 1863 he married the singer Amalie Weiss. In 1868 he was appointed director of the 'Hochschule für ausübende Tonkunst' in Berlin. His fame as a teacher spread far and wide, and aspiring violinists from all over Europe flocked there to study with him. He did not, however, abandon his career as a virtuoso; he was particularly popular in England, which he visited annually after 1862; he received an honorary degree of Doc. Mus. from Cambridge Univ. (1877), and also from Oxford and Glasgow. His style of playing, nurtured on the best classical models, was remarkable for masterful repose, dignity, and flawless technique. It was his unswerving determination to interpret the music in accordance with the intentions of the composer; this noble objectivity made him an authentic exponent of the best of violin literature. As a player of chamber music, he was unexcelled in his day. The famous Joachim Quartet, organized in 1869, attained great and merited celebrity in Europe; the Joachim tradition of excellence and faithful interpretation of classical works influenced the subsequent generations of German violinists. His compositions for the violin are virtuoso pieces that have never ceased to attract performers; of these, the most famous is the concerto, op. 11, in D minor, known as the *Hungarian Concerto* (marked 'in ungarischer Weise'), which he wrote in Hanover in the summer of 1857, and first performed there on March 24, 1860; another concerto, in G major (Hanover, Nov. 5, 1864, composer soloist), was revised in 1889. Other works are: *Variations,* for violin and orch. (Berlin, Feb. 15, 1881, composer soloist); *Andantino* and *Allegro scherzoso,* for violin and orch.; *3 Stücke* (*Romanze, Fantasiestück, Frühlingsfantasie)* for violin and piano; *3 Stücke (Lindenrauschen, Abendglocken, Ballade*) for violin and piano; *Hebrew Melodies,* for viola and piano; *Variations on an Original Theme* for viola and piano; *Notturno,* for violin and orch.; several overtures; cadenzas for violin concertos by Beethoven and Brahms; songs. Bibliography: A. Moser, *J. Joachim, Ein Lebensbild* (Berlin, 1898; 2nd enlarged ed., 2 vols., 1908, 1910; English transl. from 2nd German ed., London, 1900); K. Storck, *J. Joachim, Eine Studie* (Leipzig, 1902); J. A. Fuller Maitland, *J. Joachim* (London, 1905); L. Brieger-Wasservogel, *Joachim-Gedenkbüchlein* (Dresden, 1907); H. J. Moser, *J. Joachim* (Zürich, 1908); G. Schünemann, *Aus Joachims Nachlass,* in 'Bericht der Hochschule' (vol. 53); S. Joachim-Chaigneau, *Trois épisodes de la vie de Joachim,* in the 'Revue Musicale' (Jan., 1940). Joachim's letters were publ. by A. Moser, *Johannes Brahms im Briefwechsel mit J. Joachim* (Berlin, 1908; vols. V and VI); Johannes Joachim and A. Moser,

Briefe an und von J. Joachim (3 vols., Berlin, 1911-13).

João IV, King of Portugal; b. Villa-Vicosa, March 19, 1604; d. Lisbon, Nov. 6, 1656. As a prince, he received a fine musical training at the court chapel. He began collecting church music, gradually accumulating a magnificent library, which was totally destroyed in the earthquake of 1755. However, its contents are known, for a catalogue of it was issued in Lisbon in 1649, and reprinted by Vasconcellos in 1873. João IV was a true music scholar, well acquainted with the flow of conflicting opinions regarding musical theory. He publ. (anonymously) the pamphlets *Defensa de la musica moderna contra la errada opinion del obispo Cyrillo Franco* (in Spanish; 1649); *Respuesta a las dudas que se pusieron a la missa 'Panis quem ego dabo' de Palestrina* (1654); Italian translations were made of both. He composed a considerable quantity of church music; his motets *Crux fidelis* and *Adjuva nos* are reprinted in S. Lück's *Sammlung ausgezeichneter Kompositionen für die Kirche* (1884-85).—Cf. J. Freitas Branco, *D. João IV, Músico* (Lisbon, 1956).

Jobert, Jean, French music publisher; b. Lyons, Oct. 11, 1883. He was an employee of the publishing firm of Fromont in Paris; he purchased the business in 1922, including the valuable catalogue of Debussy's early works *(L'Après-midi d'un faune, Clair de lune,* etc.). In 1945 he was elected president of the Syndicated Society of Music Publishers in France.

Jobst, Brant. See **Brandt.**

Jochum, Eugen, German conductor; brother of Georg Ludwig and Otto Jochum; b. Babenhausen, Bavaria, Nov. 1, 1902. He studied organ and piano at the Augsburg Cons. (1914-22); composition with Waltershausen at the Munich Academy of Music (1922-24); conducting with Sigmund von Hausegger (1924-25). He was opera coach at the Munich State Opera (1924-25); at Kiel (1926-27); then conductor there (1927-29); at the Mannheim National Theater (1929-30); at Duisburg (1930-32); at the Berlin Radio (1932-34); conductor and musical director of the Hamburg State Opera, succeeding Muck (1934-45); since 1949, conductor of the Radio Orchestra in Munich.

Jochum, Georg Ludwig, German conductor; brother of Eugen and Otto Jochum; b. Babenhausen, Dec. 10, 1909. He studied in Munich with Hausegger, Pembaur, and Haas; conductor of the City Orch. in Münster (1932-34); opera conductor in Frankfurt (1937-40); in Linz (1940-45); in 1946, appointed director of the Duisburg Cons.

Jochum, Otto, prolific German composer; brother of Eugen and Georg Ludwig Jochum; b. Babenhausen, March 18, 1898. He studied at the Augsburg Cons., and at the Munich Academy of Music, with Heinrich Kaspar Schmid, Gustav Geierhaas, and Joseph Haas (1922-31). In 1933 he was appointed director of the Municipal Singing School in Augsburg; 1949, director of the Augsburg Cons.; retired in 1952. He has composed about 150 opus numbers, among them 2 oratorios (*Der jüngste Tag* and *Ein Weihnachtssingen*); 12 Masses; a great number of works for chorus, accompanied and a cappella; arrangements of folk songs; a *Goethe-Sinfonie* (1941); *Florianer-Sinfonie* (1946); choral works with orchestra; songs.

Jöde (yö'-dŭh), **Fritz,** German music educator; b. Hamburg, Aug. 2, 1887. He began his career as a provincial school teacher; was in the German army during World War I; then undertook a serious study of music at the Univ. of Leipzig, with Abert (1920-21). In 1923 he was appointed prof. at the Academy for Church and School Music in Berlin. He organized numerous societies for the propagation of folk music, and was very active in various youth movements in Germany. In 1939 he became instructor at the Hochschule für Musik in Salzburg and leader of the seminar at the Mozarteum (1939-45); then instructor on school music in Hamburg (1947-52). After retirement, he continued to give private courses and lectures on folk music and related subjects in Germany. He publ. a number of books on music education and collected German folksongs. Among his anthologies are *Ringel-Rangel-Rosen* (children's songs; 1913; enlarged ed., 1927); *Der Rosengarten* (1917); *Der Musikant* (1923; new ed., 1942); *Der Kanon* (in 3 parts; 1925); *Chorbuch* (6 vols., 1927-31); *Die Singstunde* (1929); *Lasst uns singen* (1930); *Frau Musika* (songs for home; 1929); *Die Weihnachtsnachtigall* (1939); *Unser Mutterlied* (1940). He edited choral works by old masters (Haydn, Mozart, Beethoven, Brahms, etc.). Writings: *Musikalische Jugendkultur* (1918); *Musik und Erziehung* (1920); *Die Lebensfrage der* *neuen Schule* (1921); *Unser Musikleben Absage und Beginn* (1923); *Musikschulen für Jugend und Volk* (1924); *Die Kunst Bachs* (1926); *Elementarlehre der Musik* (1927); *Musikdienst am Volk* (1927); *Das schaffende Kind in der Musik* (1928); *Musik in der Volksschule* (1929); *Kind und Musik* (1930); *Deutsche Jugendmusik* (1934); *Vom Wesen und Werden der Jugendmusik* (1954). From 1940 to 1952 he was editor of the 'Zeitschrift für Spielmusik.'

Johannes Chrysorrhoas (John of Damascus), Christian Saint; b. Damascus, c. 700; d. at the monastery of St. Sabas, near Jerusalem, 754. He was canonized by both Greek and Roman churches; was the earliest dogmatist of the Greek church; wrote many examples of the kanon, a special type of Byzantine hymn that usually used a preexistent melody. John is credited, by what may be a legend, with having arranged the Byzantine Oktoechos and having improved Byzantine notation. —Cf. H. J. W. Tillyard, *Byzantine Music and Hymnography* (1923; p. 20 ff.); E. Wellesz, *Byzantinische Musik* (1927; p. 33 ff.); K. Wachsmann, *Untersuchungen zum vorgregorianischen Gesang* (1935; p. 78 ff.).

Johannes Cotton. See **Cotton.**

Johannes de Garlandia. See **Garlandia.**

Johannes de Grocheo. See **Grocheo.**

Johannes de Muris. See **Muris.**

Johannes Gallus. See **Gallus.**

Johannesen, Grant, American pianist; b. Salt Lake City, July 30, 1921. He studied with Robert Casadesus at Princeton (1941-46) and with Egon Petri at Cornell Univ. He made his début in New York in 1944; in 1947 and 1950, gave concerts in Europe; also toured in Alaska.

Johansen, David Monrad, Norwegian composer and music critic; b. Vefsen, Nov. 8, 1888. He studied with Elling and Holter in Oslo (1906-15); then took a course with Humperdinck in Berlin. Upon returning to Norway, he was engaged mainly in musical journalism; was music critic of 'Aftenposten' (1925-45); publ. a monograph on Grieg (1934; in English, Princeton, 1938; new ed., 1943). He composed mainly for chorus; for orch., *Pan* (1939); piano quartet (1947); several piano works.

Johner (yŏh'-nĕr), **Dominicus (Franz),** prior of the Beuron monastery; authority on ecclesiastical music; b. Waldsee, Dec. 1, 1874; d Beuron, Jan. 4, 1955. He studied theology and music in Prague and also in Portugal; entered the Benedictine Order in Beuron in 1894; was ordained priest at Lisbon in 1898; in 1900 he went back to Beuron; taught Gregorian Chant there, and at the Hochschule für Musik in Cologne (from 1925). He composed a cycle *Neue Marienlieder,* for chorus in unison with organ (2 books; 1916 and 1918) and *Neue Kommunionslieder* (1916). His writings, of great importance to students of Gregorian Chant, include *Neue Schule des gregorianischen Choralgesanges* (Regensburg, 1906; 6th ed., 1929); *Cantus ecclesiastici* (1909; 7th ed., 1925); *Die Psalmodie nach der Vaticana* (1911); *Litaniae Lauretanae octo modis accomodatae* (1921; 2nd ed., 1927); *Der gregorianische Choral* (1924; in Danish, Copenhagen, 1931); *Die Sonn- und Festtagslieder des vatikanischen Graduale* (1928); *Wie gelangen wir zu einem würdigen des gregorianischen Chorals?* (1928); *Erklärung des Kyriale* (1933); *Wort und Ton im gregorianischen Choral* (Leipzig, 1940). A collection of articles, *Der kultische Gesang der abendländischen Kirche,* ed. by F. Tack, was publ. in his honor on his 75th birthday (Cologne, 1950).

Johns, Clayton, American pianist and composer; b. New Castle, Del., Nov. 24, 1857; d. Boston, March 5, 1932. He studied architecture in Philadelphia (1875-79); then turned to music, studying at Boston with J. K. Paine (theory) and W. H. Sherwood (piano), and in Berlin (1882-82) with Kiel (composition), Raif, and Rummel (piano); settled in Boston. His works include a *Berceuse* and *Scherzino* for string orch.; several piano pieces; music for violin and piano; about 100 songs; also publ. *The Essentials of Pianoforte Playing* (1909); *From Bach to Chopin* (1911); and *Reminiscences of a Musician* (1929).

Johns, Emile, Austrian-American amateur; b. c. 1800; d. Paris, Aug. 10, 1860. He settled in New Orleans in 1822; music dealer and piano teacher; publ. *Album Louisiannais: Hommage aux Dames de la Nouvelle Orléans,* containing 8 piano pieces. His name is remembered in music annals because Chopin dedicated to him his 5 mazurkas, op. 7 —Cf. J. S. Kendall, *The Friend of Chopin and Some Other New Orleans Musical Celebrities,* in the 'Louisiana Historical Quarterly' (Oct., 1948).

Johnson, Edward, Canadian tenor and operatic impresario; b. Guelph, Ontario, Aug. 22, 1881. He studied at the Univ. of Toronto; in 1907, went to New York, where he sang in light opera; then went to Italy for further study; appeared there in opera under the name of Eduardo di Giovanni. In 1920 he returned to the U. S.; was a member of the Chicago Opera Co.; then joined the Metropolitan Opera Co. (début, Nov. 16, 1922); in 1935 he was appointed general manager of the Metropolitan Opera, succeeding Herbert Witherspoon. He resigned in 1950.

Johnson, Horace, American composer and journalist; b. Waltham, Mass., Oct. 5, 1893. He studied with Bainbridge Crist; from 1931-38, he was managing editor of the 'Musical Courier.' He has written several popular pieces for orch., among them *Imagery* (1925), *Astarte* (Richmond, Jan. 2, 1936), and *Streets of Florence* (Mexico, July 9, 1937). He has also composed songs that have frequently figured on concert programs *(The Pirate, When Pierrot Sings, The Three Cherry Trees,* and *Thy Dark Hair).*

Johnson, Hunter, American composer; b. Benson, N. C., 1906. He studied at the Univ. of North Carolina and at the Eastman School of Music (graduated in 1929); was head of the dept. of composition at the Univ. of Michigan (1929-33); received the Prix de Rome in 1933, and went to Italy for 2 years. He has written a symphony (1931); *Letter to the World,* ballet for Martha Graham (1940; suite therefrom for chamber orch., 1952); *Elegy* for clarinet and strings (1936); some chamber music.

Johnson, James Weldon, American Negro author and composer; b. Jacksonville, Fla., June 17, 1871; killed in an accident at Wiscasset, Maine, June 26, 1938. He taught literature at Fisk Univ. in Nashville; publ. 2 books of Negro spirituals, and wrote the 'Negro national anthem,' *Lift Every Voice and Sing* (in collaboration with his brother John Rosamond Johnson); he was the composer of a light opera, *The Czar of Zani,* and the songs *Congo Love Song, My Castle on the Nile, The Maid of Timbuctu,* etc.

Johnson, John Rosamond, American Negro composer and bass singer; brother of James Weldon Johnson; b. Jacksonville, Fla., Aug. 11, 1873; d. New York, Nov. 11, 1954. He studied at the Univ. of Atlanta (M.A., 1917) and at the New England Cons. in Boston; took voice lessons with David Bispham. He went to London, where he appeared as a music-hall artist; also sang in opera; subsequently toured America and Europe in programs of Negro spirituals (1930-32). He wrote a ballet, *African Drum Dance;* many vocal works *(I Told My Love to the Roses; Morning, Noon, and Night,* etc.). He also publ. *The Book of American Negro Spirituals* (1926) and *Rolling Along in Song* (a history of Negro music with 85 arrangements of Negro songs). In collaboration with his brother, he composed the 'Negro national anthem,' *Lift Every Voice and Sing.* He sang the role of Lawyer Frazier in the early performances of Gershwin's opera *Porgy and Bess.*

Johnson, Lockrem, American composer; b. Davenport, Iowa, March 15, 1924; was taken to Spokane, Wash., as a child; then lived mostly in Seattle, where he studied at the Cornish School of Music (1931-38) and Univ. of Washington (1939-42 and 1946-47); taught piano and theory in Seattle (1946-51); played piano in chamber music groups in Pacific Northwest and Alaska (1946-51); was on the faculty of the Univ. of Washington (1947-49) and pianist in the Seattle Symph. (1948-51). In 1951 he moved to New York; in 1954 appointed head of the orch. dept. of C. F. Peters Corporation in New York. He held a Guggenheim Fellowship in 1952-53. — Works: 6 piano sonatas; 3 violin sonatas (No. 2 subtitled *Sonata breve;* No. 3, *Sonata rinverdita);* 2 cello sonatas; 6 *Easy Pieces* for violin and piano; *Suite of Noëls* for mixed voices and organ: *A Letter to Emily,* chamber opera (N. Y., Jan. 25, 1955); *She,* a ballet.

Johnson, Thor, American conductor; b. Wisconsin Rapids, Wis., June 10, 1913 (of Norwegian parentage). He went to North Carolina as a boy, and at the age of 13 conducted a school orch. While a student at the Univ. of North Carolina, he was associate conductor of the North Carolina State Symph. He received the degree of M. A. in music at the Univ. of Mich. (1935). Still as a student, he organized a Univ. of Michigan Little Symphony, which he conducted from 1934 to 1936, and from 1938 to 1942, touring with it widely in the U. S. In 1936 he went to Europe on a Beebe Scholarship, and studied conducting in Salzburg and Prague, with Weingartner, Bruno Walter, and Malko, and at the Leipzig Cons. with Abendroth. In 1937 he returned to America, becoming assistant professor of music at the Univ. of Michigan. He studied conducting with Koussevitzky at the Berkshire Music Center (1940-41). He enlisted in the army in 1942, and organized the 1st army symph. orch. at Ft. Myer, Virginia. In June, 1946, he was discharged from the army. He conducted the Juilliard School Orch. in 1946-47. From 1947 to 1958 he conducted the Cincinnati Symph. Orch. He has been guest conductor of a number of leading orchestras. In 1955 he traveled with the Symphony of the Air in the Orient, conducting a number of concerts in Japan, Korea, etc. —Cf. Hope Stoddard, *Symphony Conductors of the U. S. A.*, chap. XII (N. Y., 1957).

Johnstone, Arthur Edward, composer and teacher; b. London, May 13, 1860; d. Wilkes-Barre, Penna., Jan. 23, 1944. He was brought to New York as a child and studied there with Leopold Damrosch (composition), William Scharfenberg and William Mason (piano), and S. P. Warren (organ); lecturer at Washington Univ. (summer sessions), St. Louis, for many years; from 1919, editor for the Art Publication Society, St. Louis (with Godowsky); composed an overture; piano works; songs; etc.; publ. a useful book, *Instruments of the Modern Symphony Orchestra and Band* (N. Y., 1917; revised ed., 1948).

Johnstone, John Alfred, Shakespearian scholar and writer on music; b. Cork, Ireland, July 6, 1861; d. Sidmouth, England, March 21, 1941. After studying literature and music in Dublin, he went to Australia in 1882; spent many years in Melbourne, where he was director of the music school of the Atheneum; returning to England, he continued to publish books and articles on the English theater and on music. In addition to his writings, he taught piano; publ. numerous manuals *(The Art of Expression in Piano Playing; The Royal Method for Scales and Arpeggios; The Simplicity Piano Tutor; Muscular Relaxation, Weight, Touch and Rotary Movement,* etc.).

Jokl (yohk'l), **Georg,** composer; brother of Otto Jokl; b. Vienna, July 31, 1896. He studied with Schreker; was active as accompanist and teacher in Vienna; in 1938, settled in New York. Among his works are a symph.; a symph. poem, *Heldensang* (Königsberg, 1923); *Burletta piccola,* for wind instruments (1952); music works.

Jokl (yohk'l), **Otto,** composer; brother of Georg Jokl; b. Vienna, Jan. 18, 1891. He studied with Hermann Brädener and Alban Berg (1926-30). His Suite for orch. (1934) won the Hertzka Prize in Vienna; other works are *Sinfonietta seria* (1935); 2 string quartets; piano sonatina (Oxford Festival, July 25, 1931); etc. He remained in Vienna until 1940; then settled in N. Y.

Jolivet (zhŏh-lē-vā'), **André,** French composer; b. Paris, Aug. 8, 1905. As a young man he experimented with novel ideas in literature, playwriting, and painting. He then took up serious study of music with Edgard Varèse and Paul Le Flem. He joined Olivier Messiaen, Daniel Lesur, and Yves Baudrier in a group called 'La Jeune France,' dedicated to the promotion of modern music with national leanings. Jolivet injected his empiric spirit into his music, making free use of polytonality and asymmetric rhythms, also experimenting with new sonorities produced by electronic instruments. Despite these esoteric preoccupations, Jolivet's music is primarily designed to please and impress. —Works: comic opera, *Dolores* (1942; Paris Radio, Jan. 4, 1947); 2 ballets, *Guignol et Pandore* (Paris, April 29, 1944) and *L'Inconnue* (Paris, April 19, 1950); cantata, *La Tentation dernière* (Paris, Oct. 28, 1942); 3 radiophonic legends: *La Queste de Lancelot* (Paris, Jan. 21, 1944, composer conducting); *Le Livre de Christophe Colomb,* to the poem of Paul Claudel (Paris, Feb. 21, 1947); *Hélène et Faust,* after Goethe (1949); for orch.: *Cosmogonie,* symph. prelude (1938; Paris, Nov. 17, 1947); *Cinq Danses Rituelles,* suite for orch. (Paris, June 15, 1942); *Symphonie de danses* (Paris, Nov. 24, 1943); *Suite delphique,* for wind instruments, harp, *ondes Martenot,* and percussion (1942; Vienna, Oct. 22, 1948); concerto for *ondes Martenot* (Vienna, April 23, 1948); concertino for trumpet, strings, and piano (1948); concerto for flute and strings (1949); concerto for piano, *Equatoriales* (Strasbourg Music Festival, June 19, 1951, composer soloist); harp concerto (1952); bassoon concerto (1954); *Suite transocéane,* for orch. (1955); chamber music; string quartet (1934); *Radiophonic Suite,* No. 1, for flute, viola, and harp (1941); *Serenade* for wind quartet (1945); *Radiophonic Suite,* No. 2, for flute, bassoon, and harp (1945); also *5 Incantations* for flute solo (1936); several albums of piano pieces; *Hopi Snake Dance* for two pianos (Tanglewood, Aug. 10, 1948).—Cf. *Un Musicien d'aujourd'hui, André Jolivet,* in 'Polyphonie' (1949; contains a catalogue of works).

Jommelli (yŏh-mĕl'-lē), **Niccolò,** eminent opera composer of the Neapolitan school, called 'the Italian Gluck'; b. Aversa, near Naples, Sept. 10, 1714; d. Naples, Aug. 25, 1774. He received elementary musical education from Mazillo, a Neapolitan ecclesiastic. It cannot be established whether he studied at any conservatory in Naples, but undoubtedly he had acquired sufficient knowledge of composition, for at the age of 23 he produced in Naples an opera, *L'errore amoroso* (1737); this was quite successful, and he brought out another opera, *Odoardo* (Naples, 1738). He went to Rome in 1740; there he staged his operas *Ricimero* (1740) and *Astianatte* (1741). Invited to Bologna, he became acquainted with Padre Martini, who gave him valuable advice on composition. In Bologna he produced the opera *Ezio* (1741). He then went to Venice, where he produced *Merope* (1741), with such success that he was appointed director of the important Conservatorio degli Incurabili (1743); in Venice he wrote several notable sacred works. He produced new operas almost every year in various towns in Italy: *Tito Manilio* (Turin, 1743); *Demofoonte* (Padua, 1743); *Alessandro nell' Indie* (Ferrara, 1744); *Sofonisba* (Venice, 1746); *Didone abbandonata* (Rome, 1747); *L'amore in maschera* (Naples, 1748); *Demetrio* (Parma, 1749). In 1749 he went to Vienna, where he formed a warm friendship with Metastasio. In Vienna he produced *Achille in Sciro* (1749) and contributed some numbers to *Andromeda* (1750) and *Euridice* (1750). Then he returned to Rome, where he produced *Ifigenia in Aulide* (1751), *Attilio Regolo* (1753), and some intermezzi. By the good offices of Cardinal Albani, he was appointed maestro at St. Peter's, as Bencini's assistant. He remained in that position until 1753, when he received the important appointment of Kapellmeister to the Duke of Württemberg in Stuttgart. His sojourn there was most productive; his operas staged in Stuttgart included *Fetonte* (1753); *Pelope* (1755); *L' asilo d' amore* (1758); *Nitteti* (1759); *Olimpiade* (1761); *La pastorella illustre* (1763), and several serenades and other occasional pieces; also sacred works. After 15 years in Stuttgart, he returned to Italy (1769), but his operas produced in Naples, *Armida abbandonata* (1770), *Ifigenia in Tauride* (1771), and *Cerere placata* (1772), did not succeed. However, he did not suffer privation, since he enjoyed a pension from the King of Portugal; 3 of his operas were produced in Lisbon: *Le avventure di Cleomede* (1772), *Il trionfo di Clelia* (1774), and *L' Accademia di musica* (1775). Shortly before his death he wrote a *Miserere* for 2 voices, which became one of his best-known works. The position of Jommelli in Italian music is largely determined by his partial adoption of the German style during his long stay in Stuttgart; the emphasis on instrumental accompaniment, and a more solid harmonic substance, characteristic of German opera of the time, did not suit the Italian taste. On the other hand, he played a progressive role in the development of Neapolitan music, by rejecting the conventional type of the *da capo* aria; he pursued a more dramatic and realistic form of expression than that of Alessandro Scarlatti, which explains the sobriquet 'the Italian Gluck.' That he possessed melodic invention and contrapuntal skill of a high order is proved by his handling of solo passages in his operas and sacred works. In addition to his famous *Miserere,* he wrote a number of other church works: *Laudate* for 4 soprani soli and double choir; *Dixit* for 8 voices; *In convertendo* for 6 solo voices and double choir; *Magnificat; Hymn to St. Peter* for double choir, etc. The opera *Fetonte* was published in vols. 22/23 of the 'Denkmäler deutscher Tonkunst'; *Salmo (Miserere),* for 2 and 4 voices with orch., by Breitkopf & Härtel; other works available in modern editions are: *Victimae paschali* for 5 voices; *Lux aeterna* for 4 voices; *Hosanna filio;* etc. —Cf. P. Alfieri, *Notizie biografiche di Niccolò Jommelli* (Rome, 1845); H. Abert, *Niccolò Jommelli als Opernkomponist* (Halle, 1908; includes a biography); A. della Corte, *L'opera comica italiana nel 1700* (1923).

Jonás (hŏh-năhss'), **Alberto,** pianist; b. Madrid, June 8, 1868; d. Philadelphia, Nov. 9, 1943. He studied in Madrid; then, at the age of 18, entered the Brussels Cons., where he studied with Gevaert and Arthur de Greef; won 1st prize for piano and 2 prizes in harmony. In 1890 he went to St. Petersburg, where he took lessons with Rubinstein. He made his pianistic début in Berlin (1891); then gave concerts in Europe; came to the U. S. in 1894, and taught piano at the Univ. of Michigan (1894-98) and at the Michigan Cons. of Music in Detroit (1898-1904). From 1904-14 he lived in Berlin; in 1914 settled in New York; also taught at the Broad St. Cons. of Music in Philadelphia. In the U. S. he established a fine reputation as a piano pedagogue. In collaboration with 16 pianists, he publ. *Master School of Modern Piano Playing and Virtuosity* (1922), which went through 5 editions; further publ. *Beginner's Master School of Combined Piano Playing, Solfeggio, Rhythm, Ear Training and Sight Reading; Pianoscript Books* (for beginners and for advanced students). As a composer, he wrote mostly for piano *(Northern Dances, Toccata, Scottish Dances, Evocation, Humoresque, Nocturne, Evening Song,* etc.).

Jonas (zhoh-nahs'), **Emile.** French composer; b. Paris, March 5, 1827; d. St.-Germain-en-Laye, May 21, 1905. He studied at the Paris Cons.; received the 2nd Grand Prix de Rome for his cantata *Antonio* (1849). After graduation he became instructor at the Paris Cons. (until 1865); also was music director at the Portuguese Synagogue, and a bandmaster. He wrote a number of light operas in the style of Offenbach, of which the first was *Le duel de Benjamin* (1855). Other operettas (most of them produced at the Bouffes-Parisiens): *La Parade* (Aug. 2, 1856); *Le Roi boit* (April, 1857); *Les petits prodiges* (Nov. 19, 1857); *Job et son chien* (Feb. 6, 1863); *Le manoir de La Renardière* (Sept. 29 1864); *Avant la noce* (March 24, 1865); *Les deux Arlequins* (Dec. 29, 1865); *Le Canard à trois becs* (Feb. 6, 1869); *Désiré, sire de Champigny* (April 11, 1869). He also wrote an operetta to an English libretto, *Cinderella the Younger* (London, Sept. 25, 1871; in French as *Javotte,* Paris, Dec. 22, 1871). He publ. a valuable *Receuil de chants hébraïques* (1854) for the Portuguese Synagogue.

Jonas, Maryla, Polish pianist; b. Warsaw, May 31, 1911; appeared as a child prodigy in Warsaw at the age of nine; studied with Paderewski, Sauer, and Turczynski; toured in Europe (1926-33); after the invasion of Poland by the Nazis in 1939, she escaped, and made her way to Rio de Janeiro; gave a series of concerts in South America and Mexico; then went to New York, where she made an exceptionally successful début in Carnegie Hall (Feb. 25, 1946); thereafter continued to appear in recitals, and as soloist with orchestras, in America and in Europe.

Jonas, Oswald, musicologist; b. Vienna, Jan. 10, 1897. He studied law at the Univ. of Vienna, and musical theory with Schenker. In 1938 he left Austria and settled in the U. S.; in 1940 was appointed member of the faculty at Roosevelt College, Chicago. He publ. *Das Wesen des musikalischen Kunstwerks* (Vienna, 1934) and a number of articles, and revised Schenker's *Harmonielehre* and *Der freie Satz.*

Joncières (zhohn-syär'), **Victorin de** (real name, Felix Ludger Rossignol), French composer; b. Paris, April 12, 1839; d. there, Oct. 26, 1903. He was first a student of painting; music was his avocation. At the age of 20 he produced a light opera for a student performance; encouraged by its success with the critics, he began to study music seriously, first with Elwart, then with Leborne at the Paris Cons. He was a great admirer of Wagner, and when Leborne expressed his opposition to Wagner, Joncières impulsively left his class. From 1871 he was the music critic of 'La Liberté.' Operas (all produced in Paris): *Sardanapale* (Feb. 8, 1867); *Le dernier jour de Pompei* (Sept. 21 1869); *Dimitri* (May 5, 1876; his most successful work); *La reine Berthe* (Dec. 27, 1878); *Le Chevalier Jean* (March 11, 1885; successful in Germany under the title *Johann von Lothringen); Lancelot du lac* (Feb. 7, 1900); he further wrote music to *Hamlet* (Nantes, Sept. 21, 1867); *Symphonie romantique* (Paris, March 9, 1873); a violin concerto (Paris, Dec. 12, 1869); a symph. ode, *La Mer;* etc.

Jones, Alton, American pianist; b. Fairfield, Nebr., Aug. 3, 1899. He studied at the Institute of Musical Art, N. Y., with Edwin Hughes and Buhlig; then taught there and later at the Juilliard Summer School; gave several recitals in N. Y. and elsewhere.

Jones, Arthur Barclay. See **Barclay, Arthur.**

Jones, Daniel, Welsh composer; b. Pembroke, Dec. 7, 1912. Both his parents were musicians. He attended the Univ. of Wales; then studied at the Royal Academy of Music, London, with Sir Henry Wood and Farjeon. He held the Mendelssohn Travelling Scholarship from 1935 until 1939; served in the Intelligence Corps (1940-46). An enormously prolific composer, he has written 4 symphonies (No. 1, 1944; No. 2, 1950; No. 3, 1951; No. 4, 1954, Liverpool, Aug. 6, 1954); symphonic poems *Cystuddiau Branwen* (1938) and *Cloud Messenger* (1943); a number of overtures; *Five Pieces for Orch.* (1939); 20 pieces for small ensemble (1947); 8 string quartets (1932-46); 5 string trios (1932-46); string quintet (1933); piano trio (1935); viola sonata (1934); unaccompanied cello sonata (1948); sonata for kettledrums (1947); *8 Pieces* for violin and viola (1948); suite for viola and cello (1949); wind septet (1949); wind nonet (1950). For piano solo:

6 sonatas (1930-39); 3 sonatinas (1933-43); 20 *Bagatelles* (1943-52); sacred and secular choruses. He is the author of *Music and Esthetic,* a book that expounds his general philosophy of music (1954).

Jones, Edward, Welsh musician and writer ('Bardy Brenin'); b. Llanderfel, Merionethshire, April 2, 1752; d. London, April 18, 1824. He was taught by his father, and the family organized a Welsh ensemble, consisting of harps and string instruments. In 1775 he went to London; in 1783, was appointed Welsh bard to the Prince of Wales. He publ. several anthologies of Welsh music: *Musical and Poetical Relicks of the Welsh Bards* (1784; 2nd ed., 1794; an additional vol. appeared under the title *The Bardic Museum,* 1802; 3rd vol., 1824; a supplementary vol. posthumously; the entire work contains 225 Welsh melodies); in addition to these, he publ. collections of melodies by other nations; also *Musical Trifles calculated for Beginners on the Harp.*

Jones, Robert (I), English composer; b. c. 1485; d. London, c. 1536. He served as a chorister in the Chapel Royal; traveled with Henry VIII in France (1513); held a royal patent in England (1514-19); in 1520 was in France again; then returned to England, remaining in London until his death. Some of his sacred works are preserved in MS.—Cf. W. H. Grattan Flood, *Early Tudor Composers* (London, 1925).

Jones, Robert (II), English lutenist and composer; flourished in the late 16th century and early 17th. He obtained a Mus. Bac. degree from Oxford in 1597; held grants to establish a school for children in London in 1610 and in 1615. He publ. *The First Book of Ayres* (1600), followed by 4 other books (1601, 1605, 1607, 1611); a book of madrigals, entitled *First Set of Madrigals of 3, 4, 5, 6, 7 and 8 Parts, for viols and voices or for voices alone; or as you please;* also a madrigal in 6 parts, *Oriana, seeming to wink at Folly,* in 'The Triumphes of Oriana' (1601), and 3 pieces in Leighton's *Teares or Lamentacions* (1614). The 5 books of Ayres were republished, with the original accompaniment of each song transcribed into modern notation, by E. H. Fellowes (London, 1925-27).—Cf. E. H. Fellowes, *The English Madrigal Composers* (Oxford, 1921; 2nd ed., 1948); Ph. Heseltine, *Robert Jones and His Prefaces,* in the 'Mus. Times' (1923; pp. 99-101 and 168-71); E. H. Fellowes, *The English Madrigal* (London, 1925); E. H. Fellowes, *The English Madrigal School* (London, 1926); Ph. Heseltine, *The English Ayre* (London, 1926); E. H. Fellowes, *The Text of the Songbooks of Robert Jones,* in 'Music & Letters' (1927).

Jones, Sidney, English composer of light music; b. London, June 17, 1861; d. there, Jan. 29, 1946. At an early age he became conductor of a military band; then toured the English provinces and Australia as conductor of various light opera companies; in 1905 he was appointed conductor at the London Empire Theatre. He owes his fame mainly to his enormously successful operetta, *Geisha* (London, April 25, 1896), which was for decades performed all over the world. His other operettas are: *The Gayety Girl* (London, 1893); *An Artist's Model* (London, 1895); *A Greek's Slave* (Vienna, 1899); *San Toy* (Vienna, 1899); *My Lady Molly* (London, 1903); *The Medal and the Maid* (London, 1903); *See See* (London, 1906); *The King of Cadonia* (London, 1908); *The Persian Princess* (London, 1909); *Spring Maid* (London, 1911); *The Girl from Utah* (London, 1913); *The Happy Day* (London, 1916).

Jones, William, known as Jones of Nayland, English minister and musician; b. Lowick, Northamptonshire, July 30, 1726; d. Nayland, Jan. 6, 1800. He studied at Oxford; was a vicar at Bethersden, Kent; then was a curate of Nayland. He published *A Treatise on the Art of Music* (1784; 2nd ed., 1827).

Jones, Sir **William,** English Orientalist; b. London, Sept. 28, 1746; d. Calcutta, April 27, 1794. He was a magistrate in India, where he lived from 1783; published *On the Musical Modes of the Hindus* (1784), which was included in vol. 6 of his collected works (1799). See 'Dictionary of National Biography' (vol. 10).

Jongen (yohn'-gen), **Joseph,** Belgian composer; b. Liège, Dec. 14, 1873; d. Sart-lez-Spa, July 12, 1953. He studied at the Liège Cons.; in 1897 won the Belgian Grand Prix de Rome with his cantata *Comala;* then traveled in Germany and France, returning to Belgium in 1902, settling in Brussels. During World War I he lived in England, where he formed a piano quartet with Defauw, Tertis, and Doehaerd, with which he gave numerous concerts; also played organ recitals. In 1919 he was again in Brussels; was appointed prof. at the Cons. there (1920); was its director from 1925-39. A prolific composer, he continued to write music to the end of his life; the total aggregates 137 op. numbers. His *Concert à cinq* for flute, violin, viola, cello, and harp, op. 71 (1923) has had many performances abroad; his piano pieces and songs are also well known. While not pursuing extreme modern effects, Jongen succeeded in imparting an original touch to his harmonic style. Works: opera, *Felyane* (1907); ballet, *S'Arka* (1910); symphony (1899); other orchestral works: *Fantaisie sur deux Noëls wallons* (1902); *Lalla-Rookh* (1904); *Deux Rondes wallonnes* (1912); *Impressions d'Ardennes* (1913;) *Tableaux pittoresques* (1917); *Passacaille et gigue* (1929); *Triptyque,* 3 suites (1935); *Ouverture-Fanfare* (1939); *Ouverture de fête* (1941); *Bourrée* (1944); *3 Mouvements symphoniques* (1951); violin concerto (1899); cello concerto (1900); harp concerto (1944); minor works for various instruments with orch.; 2 violin sonatas (1903; 1909); cello sonata (1912); flute sonata (1924); trio for piano, violin, and cello (1897); trio for piano, violin, and viola (1907); string trio (1948); piano quartet (1902); 3 string quartets (1894; 1916; 1921); quartet for saxophones (1942); 2 wind quintets (1933; 1942); a number of piano pieces, including 24 preludes in all keys (1941); solo pieces for various instruments with piano; many songs with instrumental accompaniment; choral works. A catalogue of his works is publ. by the Centre Belge de Documentation Musicale (Brussels, 1954).

Jongen (yohn'-gen), **Léon,** Belgian composer, brother of Joseph Jongen; b. Liège, March 2, 1885; studied organ and served as church organist. He received the Belgian Grand Prix de Rome for his cantata *Les Fiancés de Noël* (1913); was in the Belgian Army during World War I; after the end of the war traveled in the Far East. Returning to Belgium he became instructor at the Brussels Cons. (1934); from 1939-49 he was successor to his brother as its director. He wrote several stage works, of which *Thomas l'Agnelet* was perf. in Brussels (Feb. 14, 1924); also composed chamber music.

Jonsson (yohns'-son), **Josef Petrus,** Swedish composer; b. Enköping, June 21, 1887. He studied piano, but soon turned to musical journalism and composition; was also active in the Swedish Composers' Society. He wrote 3 symphonies (1922, 1931, 1947); symph. cantata *Korallrevet* (1916); piano quintet; suite for wind instruments and percussion (1950); etc.

Jora (yoh'-rah), **Mihail,** Rumanian composer; b. Jassy, Aug. 15, 1891; studied law; then went to Leipzig to study music; returning to Rumania, he was appointed prof. at the Bucharest Cons. He wrote several orchestral suites: *Conte hindou* (1920); *Paysages moldaves* (1923), etc.; *Marche juive* for piano and orch. (1925); piano album, *Joujoux pour Madame;* songs.

Jordá (hor-dah'), **Enrique,** Spanish conductor; b. San Sebastian, March 24, 1911. His father died when he was 5; his mother was a pianist and gave him his first lessons in music. He sang in the parochial school chorus; then played organ at his parish church; began to compose; in 1929 he went to Paris, where he studied medicine; but soon turned exclusively to music, studying with Marcel Dupré (organ), Paul Le Flem (composition), and Frans Rühlmann (conducting). He made his début as conductor with the Orchestre Symphonique de Paris in 1938. In 1940 he was engaged as the regular conductor of the Madrid Symph. Orch. On Jan. 21, 1944 he married Audrey Blaes. After 1945 he conducted in England; in 1947 he was appointed chief conductor of the Cape Town Symph. Orch. in South Africa; he remained in that post until 1951. During the 1952-53 season he was guest conductor of the San Francisco Symph., and was elected (by vote of the audience as well as by decision of the Board of Directors) regular conductor.

Jordan, Henry Bryce, American musicologist, flutist, and teacher; b. Clovis, N. M., Sept. 22, 1924. He was educated in the public school of Abilene, Texas; at the Univ. of Texas (B. Mus., 1948; M. Mus., 1949); and at the Univ. of North Carolina (Ph. D., 1956); studied flute with Donald Macdonald and musicology with Otto Kinkeldey and Glen Haydon; was flutist in various Army Air Force musical groups (1942-45); assistant prof. of music at Hardin-Simmons Univ. (1949-54); in 1954, was appointed assistant prof. at the Univ. of Maryland.

Jordan, Jules, American singer and composer; b. Willimantic, Conn., Nov. 10, 1850; d. Providence, March 5, 1927. He moved to Providence in 1870 and established himself as a singer, choral conductor, and teacher; for 40 years (1880-1920), conducted the Arion Club (250 voices). He was a successful composer of school operettas (*The Alphabet, Cloud and Sunshine,* etc.); wrote 6 light operas: *Star of the Sea*

An Eventful Holiday, The Buccaneers, Princess of the Blood, Her Crown of Glory, and *A Leap Year Furlough;* vaudeville sketches, *Cobbler or King, Managerial Tactics,* etc. His romantic comedy opera *Rip Van Winkle* was produced at the Providence Opera House (May 25, 1897); another opera, *Nisiea,* remained unperformed. He wrote his own librettos for his stage works as well as for his cantatas *The Night Service, Barbara Fritchie,* etc.—Cf. E. E. Hipsher, *American Opera and Its Composers* (Philadelphia, 1934, pp. 280-81).

Jordan, Mary, contralto; b. Cardiff, Wales, Nov. 27, 1879. She entered St. Cecilia's Convent, in Scranton, Pa.; then studied with various teachers in Seattle, San Francisco, and New York. She made her operatic début as Amneris with the Boston Opera Co. (March 28, 1911); also sang in churches in Brooklyn and New York; toured in the Orient, and was for some years prof. at the Manila Cons.; then settled in San Antonio, Texas, as vocal teacher.

Jordan (yohr'-dan), **Sverre,** Norwegian composer; b. Bergen, May 25, 1889. He studied in Berlin with Ansorge and Klatte (1907-14); in 1914, settled in Bergen; conducted the choral society 'Harmonien' there (1921-31). In his works he made liberal use of national folksongs; wrote more than 200 melodious songs, which acquired considerable popularity on the concert platform in Europe and America. Of his larger works, there are *Norwegiani,* for orch. (1921); a cantata *Norge i vare hjerter,* for the opening of the Bergen Exhibition (1928); cello concerto (Bergen, Jan. 15, 1948); incidental music to Björnson's play *Halte-Hulda.*

Jörn (yörn), **Karl,** tenor; b. Riga, Latvia, Jan. 5, 1876; d. Denver, Dec. 19, 1947. He studied in Riga and Berlin; then sang in provincial German towns; was on the staff of the Hamburg City Theater (1899-1902); then at the Berlin Opera; sang in London (1908); and in New York (1908-11); was particularly successful in Wagnerian roles; toured the U. S. with the German Grand Opera Co. (1931); then taught in Denver, where he remained until his death.

Joseffy, Rafael, distinguished pianist and teacher; b. Hunfalu, Hungary, July 3, 1852; d. New York, June 25, 1915. At the age of 8 he began to study piano with a local teacher at Miskolcz, and later at Budapest. In 1866 he entered the Leipzig Cons., where his principal teacher was E. F. Wenzel, though he had some lessons with Moscheles. From 1868 to 1870 he studied with Karl Tausig in Berlin, and the summers of 1870 and 1871 he spent with Liszt in Weimar; his association with Tausig and Liszt exercised a powerful and lasting influence on his pianistic style and interpretation. He made his début at Berlin in 1870; his excellent technique and tonal variety elicited much praise; his career was then securely launched. He made his American début in 1879 playing at a symph. concert of Leopold Damrosch in New York, where he settled permanently; taught at the National Cons. from 1888 till 1906. In America he gained appreciation both as a virtuoso and as a musician of fine interpretative qualities; his programs featured many works of Brahms at a time when Brahms was not yet recognized in America as a great master. As a pedagogue, Joseffy was eminently successful; many American concert pianists were his pupils. He brought out an authoritative edition of Chopin's works in 15 vols. (with critico-historical annotations by Huneker); also edited studies by Czerny, Henselt, Moscheles, Schumann, and others. His *School of Advanced Piano Playing* (1902; in German as *Meisterschule des Klavierspiels)* is a valuable practical method. Joseffy was also a composer; publ. a number of characteristic piano pieces *(Die Mühle, Romance sans paroles, Souvenir d'Amérique, Mazurka-Fantasie, Spinnlied,* etc.) and arrangements of works by Schumann, Bach, Boccherini, Gluck, Delibes.—Cf. E. Hughes, *Rafael Joseffy's Contribution to Piano Technique,* in the 'Mus. Quarterly' (July, 1916).

Josephson (yoh'-seff-son), **Jacob Axel,** Swedish composer and conductor; b. Stockholm, March 27, 1818; d. Upsala, March 29, 1880. He studied music in Upsala; then taught at the Cathedral School there (1841-43); in 1844 he went to Germany; studied with Hauptmann and Niels Gade in Leipzig. After further study in Rome (1845-46), he returned to Upsala, where he became conductor of the Philharmonic Society; became music director at Upsala Univ. in 1849; in 1864, was appointed organist at the cathedral there. He wrote mostly choral works (Psalms, cantatas); edited a series of articles on sacred songs, 'Zion' (1867-70).—Cf. K. Nyblom, *J. A. Josephson* (Stockholm, 1926).

Josquin. See **Des Prez.**

Josten, Werner, composer; b. Elberfeld, Germany, June 12, 1885. He entered upon a business career; later studied music in

Munich and in Paris; remained in Paris until 1914; at the outbreak of World War I, returned to Germany; was assistant conductor at the Munich Opera in 1918. In 1920 he visited the U. S. and appeared in concert as composer-accompanist with several singers. In 1923 he was appointed prof. of music at Smith College; also conducted the Smith College Orch., with which he presented performances of seldom-heard works by Monteverdi, Handel, and other composers. His early works are couched in a Romantic German style, with a strong flow of counterpoint underneath expansive harmonies. During his American period, he became interested in exotic art, and was considerably influenced by French modernism.—Works: For orch.: *Jungle,* a symph. movement, inspired by Henri Rousseau's painting 'Forêt Exotique' (Boston Symph., Oct. 25, 1929); *Batouala,* choreographic poem, also as an African ballet (1931); *Concerto Sacro I-II,* for string orch. and piano (1927); *Joseph and His Brethren,* concert suite from a ballet (1932); *Endymion,* concert suite from a ballet (1933); *Symphony for Strings* (Saratoga Springs, N. Y., Sept. 3, 1946); Symphony in F (Boston Symph., Nov. 13, 1936, composer conducting). Vocal works: *Crucifixion,* for bass solo and mixed chorus a cappella (1915); *Hymnus to the Quene of Paradys,* for women's voices, strings, and organ (1921); *Indian Serenade,* for tenor with orch. (1922); *Ode for St. Cecilia's Day,* for voices and orch. (1925); *A une Madone,* for solo tenor and orch., after Baudelaire (1929); about 50 songs. Chamber music: string quartet (1934); violin sonata (1936); cello sonata (1938); sonatina for violin and piano (1939); trio for flute, clarinet, and bassoon (1941); trio for violin, viola, and cello (1942); trio for flute, cello, and piano (1943); sonata for horn and piano (1944); *Canzona seria,* for flute, oboe, clarinet, bassoon, and piano (N. Y., Nov. 23, 1957).

Joteyko (yoh-tī'-kŏh), **Tadeusz,** Polish opera composer; b. Poczuiki, Ukraine, April 1, 1872; d. Teschen, Aug. 19, 1932. He studied in Brussels with Gevaert and in Warsaw with Noskowski; held positions as head of musical societies in Kalisz and Lodz; conducted the Warsaw Philharmonic from 1914 to 1918; taught at the Warsaw Cons. He wrote the operas *Grajek* (*The Player;* Warsaw, Nov. 23, 1919); *Zygmund August* (his most successful work; Warsaw, Aug. 29, 1925); *Królowa Jadwiga* (*Queen Jadwiga;* Warsaw, Sept. 7, 1928); chamber music; numerous songs and piano pieces.

Joubert, John, South African composer; b. Cape Town, March 20, 1927. He studied at the Royal Academy of Music in London with Howard Ferguson, on a scholarship of the Performing Rights Society (1946-50); in 1951 was appointed lecturer on music at Univ. College in Hull.—Works: *Legend of Princess Vlei,* ballet (Cape Town, Feb. 21, 1952); *Antigone,* radio opera (BBC, July 21, 1954); *Overture* (Cheltenham Festival, June 12, 1953); *Symphonic Prelude* (Durban Centenary Festival, May 15, 1954); violin concerto (York, June 17, 1954); sonata for viola and piano (1952); etc.

Jouret (zhoo-rā'), **Léon,** Belgian composer; b. Ath, Oct. 17, 1828; d. Brussels, June 6, 1905. He studied at the Brussels Cons.; in 1874, was appointed prof. of singing there. His 2 operas, *Quentin Metsys* and *Le Tricorne enchanté,* were produced semi-privately in Brussels (1865 and 1868); of more importance is his collection of folk melodies of his native region, *Chants populaires de pays d'Ath.*

Journet (zhoor-nā'), **Marcel,** French bass singer; b. Grasse, Alpes Maritimes, July 25, 1867; d. Vittel, Sept. 5, 1933. He made his operatic début at Montpellier (1893); performed at summer seasons at Covent Garden, London (1893-1900); sang at the Théâtre de la Monnaie in Brussels (1894-1900); made his American début at the Metropolitan Opera, N. Y. in 1908 and remained on the staff for 7 seasons; from 1908-14, was in Europe; at the outbreak of World War I in 1914, he joined the Chicago Opera Co., leaving it in 1916; later, returned to France. His repertory included 8 Wagner operas, 27 Italian and 65 French operas.

Jousse (zhooss), **Jean,** French music pedagogue; b. Orleans, 1760; d. London, Jan. 19, 1837. A scion of an aristocratic family, he was compelled to flee France during the Revolution, and settled in London, where he became a successful teacher of singing and piano. He publ. several textbooks, among them *Lectures on Thoroughbass* (1819; a new revised and augmented ed., N. Y., 1894, under the title, *A Catechism of Music).*

Juch (yooh), **Emma (Antonia Joanna),** operatic soprano; b. Vienna, July 4, 1863 (of American parents); d. New York, March 6, 1939. She was brought to the U. S. at the age of 4, and studied in N. Y. with Murio Celli; made her début in the old

Chickering Hall in 1881; stage début in London (1883); sang 3 seasons under Mapleson's management in England and in the U. S.; from 1886-88 she was principal soprano of the American Opera Co.; upon its failure in 1889, she organized the Emma Juch Grand Opera Co., which presented opera in the U. S. and Mexico (until 1891); after that, she confined herself chiefly to concert appearances. On June 26, 1894, she married District Attorney Francis L. Wellman, but was divorced in 1911.

Judge, Jack, English composer of popular songs; b. 1878; d. West Bromwich, July 28, 1938. His song *It's a long, long way to Tipperary,* written in 1912, attained enormous popularity in England and elsewhere as a wartime song during World War I.

Judson, Arthur, American concert manager; b. Dayton, Ohio, Feb. 17, 1881. He took violin lessons with Max Bendix; played in orchestras, and himself conducted summer resort orchestras. In 1900 he was appointed dean of the Cons. of Music of Denison Univ., Granville, Ohio. In 1907 he was in N. Y.; was connected with the editorial and advertising departments of 'Musical America.' From 1915 to 1935 he was manager of the Philadelphia Orch.; in 1922 he was appointed manager of the N. Y. Philharmonic Orch., and held this position for 34 years, resigning in 1956. In 1928 his concert management incorporated the Wolfsohn Musical Bureau; in 1930, these organizations merged into Columbia Concerts Corporation, with Judson as president.

Juhan, Alexander, violinist, conductor, and composer; probably son of James Juhan; b. Halifax, 1765; d. 1845. He was brought to Boston in 1768; was violinist and a manager in Philadelphia in 1783; later went to Charleston, S. C., where he was active from 1790 and 1792; returned to Philadelphia in 1792. He composed 6 piano sonatas, of which 3 are accompanied by a flute (or a violin); also a book of 12 songs, with instrumental accompaniment.

Juhan, James, French musician, who was active in Boston (1768-70) and in Charleston, S. C. (1771), and later in Philadelphia, where he exhibited the 'great North American Forte Piano' (1786).—Cf. O. G. Sonneck, *Early Concert Life in America* (1907).

Juilliard (zhŏŏ-l'yahr'), **Augustus D.,** American music patron; b. Canton, Ohio, April 19, 1836; d. New York, April 25, 1919. He was a prominent industrialist; left the residue of his estate for the creation of a Juilliard Musical Foundation (established in 1920). The objects of this Foundation are to aid worthy students of music in securing a complete musical education, to arrange and give concerts for the education of the general public in the musical arts. The Juilliard School of Music was founded and has been maintained by the Foundation. —Cf. 'Dictionary of American Biography,' vol. X (N. Y., 1933).

Jullien, Gilles, French organist; b. c. 1650; d. Chartres, Sept. 14, 1703. He became organist at the Chartres Cathedral in 1667, and held this post until his death. His *Premier Livre d'Orgue* was publ. by Lesclop in Chartres (1680); a modern reprint, with annotations and an introduction by Norbert Dufourcq, was issued in Paris (1952).

Jullien, Jean-Lucien-Adolphe, French writer on music; son of Marcel-Bernard Jullien; b. Paris, June 1, 1845; d. Chaintreauville, Seine-et-Marne, Aug. 30, 1932. He studied law in Paris and took private lessons with Bienaimé, a former prof. of the Paris Cons. He became a musical journalist; contributed to various magazines, and took a strong position in favor of the new music of Berlioz and Wagner.—Writings: *L'Opéra en 1788* (1873); *La Musique et les philosophes au XVIIIe siècle* (1873); *La Comédie à la cour de Louis XVI, le théâtre de la reine à Trianon* (1873); *Histoire du théâtre de Mme. Pompadour, dit Théâtre des petits cabinets* (1874); *Les Spectateurs sur le théâtre* (1875); *Le Théâtre des demoiselles Verrières* (1875); *Les grandes nuits de Sceaux, le théâtre de la duchesse du Maine* (1876); *Un Potentat musical* (1876); *L'Église et l'opéra en 1735; Mlle. Lemaure et l'évêque de Saint-Papoul* (1877); *Weber à Paris* (1877); *Airs variés; histoire, critique, biographie musicales et dramatiques* (1877); *La Cour et l'opéra sous Louis XVI; Marie-Antoinette et Sacchini; Salieri; Favart et Gluck* (1878); *La Comédie et la galanterie au XVIIIe siècle* (1879); *Histoire des costumes au théâtre* (1880); *Goethe et la musique* (1880); *L'Opéra secret au XVIIIe siècle* (1880); *La Ville et la Cour au XVIIIe siècle* (1881); *La Comédie de la cour . . . pendant le siècle dernier* (1883); *Paris dilettante au commencement du siècle* (1884); *Richard Wagner, sa vie et ses œuvres* (1886; also in English translation, Boston, 1892) and *Hector Berlioz* (1888); *Musiciens d'aujourd'hui* (1st series, 1891;

2nd series, 1894); *Musique* (1895); *Le Romantisme et l'éditeur Renduel* (1897); *Amours d'opéra au XVIIIe siècle* (1908); *Ernest Reyer* (1909). His masterpieces are the biographies of Wagner and Berlioz. — Cf. F. Delhasse, *A. Jullien* (Paris, 1884).

Jullien, Louis Antoine, French conductor; b. Sisteron, April 23, 1812; d. Paris, March 14, 1860. The son of a bandmaster, he went to Paris in 1833 and studied composition with Le Carpentier and Halévy, but could not maintain the discipline of learning music, and began to compose light dances instead; of these, the waltz *Rosita* attained enormous, though transitory, popularity in Paris. He left the conservatory in 1836 without taking a degree, and became engaged as conductor of dance music at the Jardin Turc. He also attempted to launch a musical journal, but an accumulation of carelessly contracted debts compelled him to leave France (1838). He went to London, where he conducted summer concerts at Drury Lane Theatre (1840) and winter concerts with an enlarged ensemble of instrumentalists and singers (1841). He then opened a series of 'society concerts' at which he presented large choral works, such as Rossini's *Stabat Mater,* as well as movements from Beethoven's symphonies. In 1847 he engaged Berlioz to conduct at the Drury Lane Theatre, which he had leased. He became insolvent in 1848, but attempted to recoup his fortune by organizing a 'concert monstre' with 400 players, 3 choruses, and 3 military bands. He succeeded in giving 3 such concerts in London in 1849. He then essayed the composition of an opera, *Pietro il Grande,* which he produced at his own expense at Covent Garden on Aug. 17, 1852. He used the pseudonym Roch Albert for his spectacular pieces, such as *Destruction of Pompeii.* He publ. some dance music under his own name *(Royal Irish Quadrille,* etc.). In 1853 he was engaged by Barnum for a series of concerts in the U. S. For his exhibition at the Crystal Palace in N. Y. (June 15, 1854), attended by a great crowd, he staged a simulated conflagration for his *Fireman's Quadrille.* Despite his eccentricities, however, Jullien possessed true interest in musical progress. At his American concerts he made a point of including several works by American composers: *Santa Claus Symphony* by William Henry Fry and some chamber music by George Frederick Bristow. In 1854 he returned to London; his managerial ventures resulted in another failure. In 1859 he went to Paris, but was promptly arrested for debt, and spent several weeks in prison. He died a few months later in an insane asylum to which he was confined.— Cf. J. W. Davison, *Memoirs* (London, 1912); J. T. Howard, *Our American Music* (N. Y., 1939; pp. 219-25); N. Slonimsky, *A Thing or Two About Music* (N. Y., 1948; pp. 226-35); A. Carse, *The Life of Jullien: Adventurer, Showman-Conductor and Establisher of the Promenade Concerts in England* (Cambridge, 1951).

Jullien, Marcel-Bernard, French scholar; b. Paris, Feb. 2, 1798; d. there, Oct. 15, 1881. He was secretary general to the 'Société des Méthodes d'enseignement' and a learned grammarian. — Writings: *De l'étude de la musique instrumentale dans les pensions des demoiselles* (1848); *De quelques points des sciences dans l'antiquité (Physique, métrique, musique)* (1854); and *Thèses supplémentaires de métrique et de musique ancienne* (1861).

Jumilhac (zhü-mēl-ăhk'), **Dom Pierre-Bênoit de.** Benedictine monk; specialist in Gregorian Chant; b. Château St. Jean-de-Ligourre, near Limoges, 1611; d. St. Germain-des-Prés, May 22, 1682. He wrote *La Science et la Pratique du plain-chant* (Paris, 1673; ed. by Nisard and Leclerq and republished in 1847), an erudite work containing many musical examples.

Junck, Benedetto, Italian composer; b. Turin, Aug. 21, 1852; d. San Vigilio, near Bergamo, Oct. 3, 1903. He was of Alsatian-Italian extraction; was trained for a commercial career, but practiced the piano in his free time; then entered the Milan Cons. for serious study, and developed a fine lyric talent for song writing; his youthful ballad *La Simona* became very popular; *Dolce sera,* from his album, *8 Romanze,* also was well known. In addition to songs, he wrote a string quartet and 2 violin sonatas.

Jüngst (yüngst), **Hugo,** German conductor; b. Dresden, Feb. 26, 1853; d. there, March 3, 1923. He studied at the Dresden Cons.; was conductor of the Dresden Male Choral Society, which he founded in 1876, and of numerous festivals; composed many men's choruses, including the well-known *Scissors Grinder.*

Juon (yü'-ŏhn), **Paul,** composer; b. Moscow, March 6, 1872; d. Vevey, Switzerland, Aug. 21, 1940. He was a pupil of Hřimaly (violin) and Taneyev and Arensky (composition) in Moscow; in Berlin, of Bargiel (1894-96); teacher of theory at the Baku

Cons. for one year; lived in Berlin; appointed professor of composition at the Hochschule für Musik in 1906; member of the Berlin Academy in 1919; won the state Beethoven prize in 1919. A notable composer, he cultivated the classical forms with success. — Works: for orch.: *Fünf Stücke* for string orch.; Symphony in A; *Vaegtevise,* fantasy on Danish folksongs; *Aus einem Tagebuch,* suite; *Serenade;* 3 violin concertos; *Episodes Concertantes,* triple concerto for violin, cello, and piano with orch.; chamber music: 4 string quartets; sextet for 2 violins, viola, 2 cellos, and piano; octet for piano, violin, viola, cello, oboe, clarinet, horn, and bassoon; 2 quintets for piano and strings; *Divertimento* for piano and woodwinds; *Rhapsodie* for piano quartet; other piano quartets; 3 piano trios; *Caprice, Legende* and *Litaniae* for trio; 6 *Silhouettes* for 2 violins and piano; sonatas for violin, viola, cello, flute, and clarinet (with piano); pieces for violin, cello, and piano *(Satyre und Nymphen, Intime Harmonien,* etc.); compositions for piano 4 hands; songs. He published *Praktische Harmonielehre* (1901); *Handbuch für Harmonielehre* (1920); *Anleitung zum Modulieren* (1929); *Der Kontrapunkt* (1932); translated into German Modest Tchaikovsky's *Life of Peter Tchaikovsky* (2 vols., 1904).

Jupin (zhü - pan'), **Charles - François,** French violinist and composer; b. Chambéry, Nov. 30, 1805; d. Paris, June 12, 1839. He studied with Baillot at the Paris Cons., taking 1st prize in 1823; wrote an opera, *La vengeance italienne* (1834); numerous pieces for violin.

Jürgens (yür'-gens), **Fritz,** German composer; b. Düsseldorf, April 22, 1888; killed in action in Champagne, Sept. 25, 1915. He studied music largely by himself; wrote some fine lieder; set to music 45 poems by Gustav Falke, and 35 by Martin Greif.

Jurgenson (yŏŏr-gen-son), **Pyotr Ivanovitch,** Russian music publisher; b. Reval, July 17, 1836; d. Moscow, Jan. 2, 1904. The youngest son of indigent parents, he learned the music trade with M. Bernard, owner of a music store in St. Petersburg; Jurgenson served in 3 other music-selling houses there, before opening a business of his own in 1861, in Moscow. With a small investment, he gradually expanded his firm until it became one of the largest in Russia. Through Nicholas Rubinstein he met the leading musicians of Russia, and had enough shrewdness of judgment to undertake the publication of works of Tchaikovsky, beginning with his op. 1. He became Tchaikovsky's close friend, and, while making handsome profit out of Tchaikovsky's music, he demonstrated a generous regard for Tchaikovsky's welfare; he publ. full scores of Tchaikovsky's symphonies and operas, as well as his songs and piano works. His voluminous correspondence with Tchaikovsky, from 1877 to Tchaikovsky's death, was publ. in 2 vols. in Moscow (1938 and 1952). Jurgenson publ. also many works by other Russian composers; issued vocal scores of Glinka's operas; also publ. the first Russian editions of the collected works of Chopin, Schumann, Mendelssohn, and Wagner's operas. His catalogue contained some 20,000 numbers. After his death, his son Boris Jurgenson succeeded to the business; it was nationalized after the Russian Revolution.

Jurjans (yur'-yahns), **Andrejs,** Latvian composer; b. Erlaa, Sept. 18, 1856; d. Riga, Sept. 28, 1922. He studied with Rimsky-Korsakov (1875-82) in St. Petersburg. In 1882 he was appointed prof. at the Cons. of Kharkov, where he taught for 34 years until 1916. In 1917 he went to Riga. He wrote a symph. poem, a cello concerto, some chamber music, and a number of orchestral arrangements of Latvian folk melodies, which he employed also in his original works.—Cf. Jahnis Straumes, *Our Musicians* (in Latvian; Riga, 1922).

Jurovský (yŏŏ-rov'-skē), **Simon,** Czechoslovak composer; b. Ulmanka, Slovakia, Feb. 8, 1912. He studied with Alexander Moyzes at the Academy of Music in Bratislava (1931-36) and with Josef Marx at the Academy of Music in Vienna (1943-44). In 1948 he was appointed head of the music division of the Bratislava Radio. He has written 2 orchestral suites (No. 1, 1939; No. 2, 1943); a symphonic scherzo (1941); symphonic poem, *The Beginning of a Journey* (1948); *Symphony for Peace* (1949); cello concerto (1953); a string quartet; a string trio; choral pieces; songs (including arrangements of folksongs). — Cf. Zdenka Bokesova, *Simon Jurovský* (Bratislava, 1955).

K

Kaan-Albest, Heinrich, pianist and composer; b. Tarnopol, Poland, May 29, 1852; d. Roudná, Bohemia, March 7, 1926. He studied in Prague with Blodek and Skuherský; went with Dvořák to London in 1884; from 1889, taught piano at the Prague Cons.;

was its director from 1907-18. He wrote two operas, *Escape* (1895) and *Germinal,* after Zola (1908); two ballets, *Bajaja* and *Olim;* symph. poem *Sakuntala; Frühlings-Eklogen* for orch.; many piano pieces and arrangements.

Kabalevsky (kah-bah-lev'-skē), **Dmitri Borisovitch,** noted Russian composer; b. St. Petersburg, Dec. 30, 1904. When he was 14, the family moved to Moscow; there he received his elementary education at the Scriabin Music School (1919-25); also studied privately with G. Catoire; in 1925 he entered the Moscow Cons. as a student of Miaskovsky (composition) and Goldenweiser (piano); graduated in 1929; appointed instructor at the Moscow Cons. in 1932. Kabalevsky began to compose in 1922, mostly for piano. After World War II Kabalevsky undertook several tours in Europe, playing his own music. The main influences in his early works emanated from Scriabin and Miaskovsky; later he developed an individual style, marked by clear tonality and energetic rhythms.—Works: 4 Preludes for piano (1928); piano sonata No. 1 (1928); string quartet No. 1 (1928); 1st piano concerto (1929); *The Poem of Struggle,* for orch. and chorus (1930); 2 sonatinas for piano (1930; 1933); Symph. No. 1 (1932); Symph. No. 2 (Moscow, Dec. 25, 1934); Symph. No. 3, subtitled *Requiem for Lenin,* for chorus and orch. (1933); 2nd piano concerto (1936); opera, *Colas Breugnon,* after Romain Rolland (Leningrad, Feb. 22, 1938); *The Comedians,* orchestral suite (1940); *Golden Blades of Grass,* ballet (1940); *My Great Fatherland,* cantata (1942); *People's Avengers,* suite for chorus and orch. (1942); opera, *Before Moscow* (1942); string quartet No. 2 (1945); piano sonata No. 2 (1945); piano sonata No. 3 (1946); opera, *The Family of Taras* (Moscow, Nov. 2, 1947; new version, Leningrad, Nov. 7, 1950); violin concerto (double première, Moscow and Leningrad, Oct. 29, 1948); cello concerto (Moscow, March 15, 1949); 3rd piano concerto (1952); opera, *Nikita Vershinin* (Moscow, 1955); Symph. No. 4 (1956); also 24 Preludes for piano (1943) and other piano pieces. —Cf. A. Poliakova, *Kabalevsky's Opera, The Family of Taras* (Moscow, 1953); L. Danilevitch, *Dmitri Kabalevsky* (Moscow, 1954).

Kabasta, Oswald, Austrian conductor; b. Mistelbach, Dec. 29, 1896; d. Kufstein, Austria, Feb. 6, 1946. He studied at the Vienna Academy of Music and in Klosterneuburg, was choir-director in Florisdorf, and teacher of singing in Viennese high schools. In 1924 he was appointed music director to the Municipal Theater of Baden near Vienna; in 1926, conductor of opera and concert in Graz and guest conductor of the Gesellschaft der Musikfreunde in Vienna; 1931-1937, music director of the Austrian Radio. In 1935 he was appointed director of the Gesellschaft der Musikfreunde. As conductor of the Vienna Radio Orchestra, he toured with it in London (1936), Berlin, Warsaw, Budapest, Amsterdam, etc. He was conductor of the Bruckner Festivals in Linz in 1936 and 1937; in 1938 he succeeded Von Hausegger as conductor of the Munich Philharmonic. Having compromised himself by a close association with the Austrian Nazis, he committed suicide a few months after the conclusion of World War II.

Kabeláč, Miloslav, Czech composer; b. Prague, Aug. 1, 1908. He studied composition with K. B. Jirák at the Prague Cons. (1928-31); then piano with Vilém Kurz at the Master School (1931-34). He has written 2 symphonies (1945 and 1947); 2 overtures; cantata, *Do Not Retreat* (1945); wind sextet; violin and piano pieces, and choral works.

Kade (kah'-deh), **Otto,** German musicologist; b. Dresden, May 6, 1819; d. Doberan, near Rostock, July 19, 1900. A stipend from King Friedrich August enabled him to study under J. Otto Schneider (composition) and J. G. Schneider (piano); in 1848 he established in Dresden the 'Cäcilia' singing society for ancient church music; in 1853 became conductor of the Neustadt Church choir. He was called to Schwerin in 1860 as conductor of the court choir; received the honorary degree of *Dr. Phil.* (Leipzig, 1884).—Writings: *M. Le Maistre* (1862); an *Offizielles Melodienbuch* and a *Choralbuch* for the Mecklenburg Landeskirche; a *Cantional* for the same, in 3 parts (1867-80; with the theologian Kliefoth); *Der neu aufgefundene Luthercodex vom Jahr 1530* (1872); *Die weltliche deutsche Liedweise* (lecture in pamphlet form; 1874); *Die ältere Passionkomposition bis zum Jahre 1631* (1892); *Thematischer Katalog der Musikalien der Schweriner Regierungsbibliothek* (1893, 2 vols.); many valuable historical papers for various periodicals; edited the musical supplements to vol. 1 of Ambros' *Geschichte der Musik* (1881, as a 5th vol.) and the revised edition of the 3rd vol. (1893). Some of his own compositions, in Gregorian style, are collected in the above *Cantional,*

Kadosa (kăh'-dŏ-shăh), **Paul,** Hungarian composer and pianist; b. Leva, Sept. 6, 1903. He studied at the Budapest Academy of Music with Kodály (composition) and Arnold Székely (piano); gave piano recitals in Hungary; taught at a music school in Budapest from 1927 till 1943. In 1928 he joined several young Hungarian musicians in organizing a modern musical society, eventually incorporated into the International Society for Contemporary Music. After the end of World War II, he became prof. of piano at the Academy of Music in Budapest; also was appointed vice-president of the Hungarian Arts Council. In his music he combines the elements of the cosmopolitan modern idiom with a strong feeling for Hungarian rhythms and folk-like melodies; in his treatment of these materials, he is closer to Bartók than to his teacher Kodály. The lyrical element is as distinctive in his works as the energetic rhythmic factor. — Works: opera, *Adventure at Hoszt* (1944-50); cantata, *De amore fatali* (1940); chamber symph. (1929); 2 divertimentos (1933); 2 symphonies (1942 and 1948); piano concerto (1931; Amsterdam Festival, June 9, 1933, composer soloist); 2 violin concertos (1932 and 1941); concerto for string quartet (1936); viola concerto (1936); concertino for piano and orch. (1939); 2 string quartets (1934-36); violin sonata (1925); partita for violin and piano (1931); sonata for 2 pianos (1946); 3 piano sonatas; 3 piano suites; several piano cycles: *7 Bagatelles* (1921), *8 Epigrams* (1921-24), *5 Esquisses* (1929-30), *6 Hungarian Folksongs* (1934-35), *6 Little Preludes* (1944); piano albums for children; songs.

Kaempfert, Max, German violinist and composer; b. Berlin, Jan. 3, 1871; d. Frankfurt, June 2, 1941. He studied violin in Paris and Munich; was concertmaster of the Kaim Orch. in Munich (1893-98); in 1899 went to Frankfurt, where he remained most of his life. He wrote an opera, *Der Schatz des Sultans,* in a folk style; a grand opera, *Der tote Gast;* 3 rhapsodies for orch.; chamber music and songs.

Kaffka, Johann Christoph (real name J. C. Engelmann), German composer and singer; b. Regensburg, 1754; d. Riga, Jan. 29, 1815. He studied with Riepel; appeared on the stage as a singer and actor in Berlin (1778), Breslau, and Dessau (1800); in 1803, settled in Riga as a bookseller. He wrote a dozen operas, several ballets, 2 oratorios, Masses, vespers, etc.

Kafka, Johann Nepomuk, Bohemian composer; b. Neustadt, May 17, 1819; d. Vienna, Oct. 23, 1886. He composed numerous popular salon pieces (many based on Austrian themes) for the piano.

Kahl, Willi, musicologist; b. Zabern, Alsace, July 18, 1893. He studied in Freiburg, Munich, and Bonn (*Dr. phil.,* 1919). He served in World War I; in 1923, became instructor and librarian at the Univ. of Cologne; in 1938, became prof. there; after 1945, remained in Cologne as instructor.— Writings: *Das lyrische Klavierstück zu Beginn des 19. Jahrhunderts* (Bonn, 1919); *Musik und Musikleben im Rheinland* (Cologne, 1923); *Herbart als Musiker* (Langensalza, 1936); *Verzeichnis des Schrifttums über Franz Schubert* (Regensburg, 1938); edited a collection, *Lyrische Klavierstücke der Romantik,* Norbert Burgmüller's *Ausgewählte Lieder,* J. A. P. Schulz's *Stücke für Klavier,* G. Benda's sonatinas; compiled the important documentary volume, *Selbstbiographien deutscher Musiker des 18. Jahrhunderts* (Cologne, 1947).

Kähler, Willibald, German conductor and composer; b. Berlin, Jan. 2, 1866; d. Klein-Machnow, Oct. 17, 1938. He was a pupil of Kiel and Herzogenberg at the Hochschule für Musik in Berlin; then occupied various posts as conductor; from 1891 in Mannheim, and from 1906, court conductor at Schwerin; after 1931 lived in retirement at Gauting near Munich. He wrote music for Goethe's *Faust;* symphonic prologue to Kleist's *Der Prinz von Homberg;* choral works; piano pieces, etc.; publ. a guide to Bruckner's 8th Symphony and *Te Deum;* revised the unfinished orchestral scores of some *Lieder* by Hugo Wolf and Weber's *Silvana* (1928).

Kahlert, August Karl Timotheus, German writer on music and composer; b. Breslau, March 5, 1807; d. there, March 29, 1864. He taught at Breslau Univ.; wrote *Blätter aus der Brieftasche eines Musikers* (1832); *Tonleben* (1838); contributed articles to the 'Allgemeine musikalischer Zeitung' and Dehn's 'Caecilia'; also composed songs.

Kahn, Erich Itor, pianist and composer; b. Rimbach, Germany, July 23, 1905; d. New York, March 5, 1956. He studied at the Hoch Cons. in Frankfurt; went to France in 1933; in 1938-39 toured as accompanist of Casals in France and North Africa; in 1941 emigrated to America, settling in New York as composer and pianist;

organized the Albeneri Trio (the name being derived from assorted syllables of the first names of the participants, Alexander Schneider, violin, Benar Heifetz, cello, and Erich Kahn, piano). In 1948 he was awarded the Coolidge Medal for eminent service to chamber music. He wrote several chamber works and piano pieces; adopted the 12-tone method of composition.—Works: Suite for violin and piano (1937); *Ciaccona dei tempi di guerra* for piano (40 variations on a 12-tone theme in the bass; 1943); string quartet (1953); 4 Nocturnes for voice and piano (1954); *Symphonies bretonnes* for orch. (1955); *Actus Tragicus* for 10 instruments (Baden-Baden Festival, June 18, 1955). —Cf. Dika Newlin, *In Memoriam: Erich Itor Kahn, Retrospect and Prospect,* in the 'American Composers' Alliance Bulletin' (No. 3, 1957).

Kahn, Otto Hermann, patron of music; b. Mannheim, Feb. 21, 1867; d. New York, March 29, 1934. He was engaged in the banking profession in London (1888-93); settled in N. Y. in 1893; member of the firm Kuhn, Loeb & Co.; became interested in the musical affairs of N. Y. City; from 1907 to his death was on the board of the Metropolitan Opera Co.; was vice president of the N. Y. Philharmonic. He was a brother of Robert Kahn, the composer.

Kahn, Robert, German pianist and composer; b. Mannheim, July 21, 1865; d. Biddenden, Kent, May 29, 1951. He was a pupil of Lachner (Mannheim), Kiel (Berlin), and Rheinberger (Munich). In 1885 he went to Berlin, where Joachim aided him; in 1890 he went to Leipzig, where he founded a Ladies' Choral Union in 1891, and gave concerts; in 1893 he was appointed teacher of piano at the Berlin Hochschule für Musik; 1917, member of the Academy of Arts, Berlin; retired in 1931 and lived in Feldberg (Mecklenburg). In 1937 he went to England, where he remained until his death. Works: *Mahomet's Gesang* (Goethe) for mixed chorus and orch.; a 'Singspiel,' *Sommerabend;* 2 cantatas, *Befreiung* and *Empor;* 3 violin sonatas; 2 string quartets; 4 piano trios; 3 piano quartets; 2 piano quintets; 2 cello sonatas; a trio for clarinet, cello, and piano; *Serenade* for piano, oboe, and horn; *Suite and Variations* for piano and violin (1925); *Konzertstück* for piano and orch.; *Sturmlied,* for chorus and orch.; *Festgesang,* for voice and orch.; *Feierliche Gesange,* for voice with piano, harmonium, or organ; a cappella choruses; trios and quartets for women's voices; piano pieces; numerous songs. He was a brother of the banker Otto Kahn. —Cf. E. Radecke, *Robert Kahn* (Leipzig, 1894).

Kahnt, Christian Friedrich, German music publisher; b. May 10, 1823; d. Leipzig, June 5, 1897. He was the founder, and, till 1886, head, of the music publishing firm of C. F. Kahnt at Leipzig and Zwickau; from 1857 publisher, and after 1868, titular editor, of Schumann's 'Neue Zeitschrift für Musik.' The firm and the magazine were acquired by Oscar Schwalm ('C. F. Kant Nachfolger') in 1886, by Dr. Paul Simon in 1888, and by Alfred Hoffmann in 1902. After Hoffmann's death in 1926, his wife, Paula, directed the business.

Kaim (kīm), **Franz,** German impresario; b. Kirchheim unter Tech, near Stuttgart, May 13, 1856; d. Munich, Nov. 17, 1935. Having built a concert hall and organized an orch. in Munich, he established there (1893) the celebrated series of concerts bearing his name, the 'Kaimkonzerte,' which presented classical works and also new compositions by German composers; the successive conductors were Hans Winderstein (1893), Zumpe (1895), Löwe (1897), Hausegger and Weingartner (1898), Raabe (1903), and Schneevoigt (1904, until the dissolution of the orch. in 1908). Besides the regular symph. concerts, a series of 'Volkssinfoniekonzerte' was given. Immediately after the dissolution of the orch., its members formed the 'Konzertverein' under the direction of Löwe (later under Pfitzner and Hausegger).

Kaiser, Alfred, composer; b. Brussels, March 1, 1872; d. London, Oct. 2, 1917. He was a pupil of Bruckner in Vienna and Foerster in Prague; lived in London. He wrote the operas *Le Billet de Joséphine* (Paris, 1902), *Die schwarze Nina* (Elberfeld, 1905), *Stella Maris* (Düsseldorf, 1910), a symphony, a piano concerto, 3 serenades for string orch.; 2 piano trios, etc.

Kajanus (kăh-yăh'-noos), **Robert,** outstanding Finnish conductor; b. Helsingfors, Dec. 2, 1856; d. there, July 6, 1933. He studied at the Helsingfors Cons., and later at the Leipzig Cons., with Reinecke, Richter, and Jadassohn (1877-79); he then went to Paris, where he studied with Svendsen (1879-80); then lived for some time in Dresden. In 1882 he returned to Helsingfors, where he devoted himself to composition and conducting. He established an orchestral and a choral school; trained these organizations with such competence that soon he was able to give regular orchestral and choral concerts in Helsingfors; in 1886 the orchestral society was reorganized as the Helsingfors Philharmonic Society, and in 1888 it gave the first performance of Beethoven's 9th Symph. in Finland. In 1897 he was appointed director of music at the Univ., a position he held until 1926, when he retired. Kajanus was the earliest champion of the music of Sibelius. In 1900 he was engaged by the French Government to present a concert of Finnish music with the Helsingfors Philharmonic at the World Exposition in Paris; he subsequently gave concerts in other European cities. He was also the composer of some orchestral and choral pieces in a Romantic vein (symph. poems *Kullervo* and *Aino;* orch. suite *Sommarminnen;* 2 Finnish rhapsodies; piano pieces and songs).—Cf. K. Flodin, *Finska musiker* (in Swedish; Helsingfors, 1900); Yrjö Suomalinen, *Robert Kajanus* (Helsinki, 1952).

Kalafati, Vassili Pavlovitch, Russian composer and pedagogue; b. Eupatoria, Crimea, Feb. 10, 1869; d. Leningrad, during the siege, 1942. He studied at the St. Petersburg Cons. with Rimsky-Korsakov, graduating in 1899. In 1900 he was appointed to the teaching staff; Prokofiev and Stravinsky were briefly his pupils. His music is entirely in the style of the Russian national school, coming closest to Glazunov. He wrote a symph., a piano quintet, 2 piano sonatas, a number of songs (all publ. by Belaiev).

Kalbeck, Max, German music historian; b. Breslau, Jan. 4, 1850; d. Vienna, May 4, 1921. He studied at Munich Univ.; in 1875 went to Breslau, where he wrote music criticism for the 'Schlesische Zeitung' and later the 'Breslauer Zeitung'; in 1880, Hanslick recommended him to the Vienna 'Allgemeine Zeitung'; he was also on the staff of the 'Wiener Montags-Revue' and the 'Neues Wiener Tageblatt.' He published studies on Wagner's *Nibelungen* (1876) and *Parsifal* (1880); his collected criticisms were publ. as *Wiener Opernabende* (1881), *Gereimtes und Ungereimtes* (1885), and *Opernabende* (2 vols., 1898); also *Humoresken und Phantasien* (1896). He made excellent German translations of many opera librettos. To Mozart's *Bastien et Bastienne* and *La finta giardiniera* he wrote entirely new texts; also wrote original librettos for various contemporary composers. His most important publication is the monumental biography *Johannes Brahms* (8 vols., 1904-14). He also edited Brahms' correspondence with Hanslick and E. von Herzogenberg (2 vols., 1906), with P. J. and Fritz Simrock, and with Jos. Widmann; and the correspondence of Keller-Heyse (1918).

Kalhauge (kăhl'-how-gĕ), **Sophus Viggo Harald,** Danish composer and teacher; b. Copenhagen, Aug. 12, 1840; d. there, Feb. 19, 1905. He studied with P. Heise, C. Rongsted, and J. C. Gebauer; also studied in Germany, Switzerland, and Italy; returned to Copenhagen as teacher of piano and singing. — Works: the operas *Zouavens Hjemkomst* (1868), *Paa Krigsfod* (1880), and *Mantillen* (1889); *An den Frühling,* for soli, chorus, and orch.; piano pieces and songs.

Kalinnikov, Vassili Sergeievitch, Russian composer; b. Voin, near Mtzensk, Jan. 13, 1866; d. Yalta, Crimea, Jan. 11, 1901. He studied in Orel, where he sang in a high school choir; as a young man, earned his living by tutoring and conducting choral groups. In 1884 he went to Moscow, where he entered the elementary classes of the Moscow Cons., but had to leave it a year later because of inability to pay; he then studied the bassoon at the Music School of the Moscow Philharmonic Society, which provided free tuition. He earned his living by playing bassoon in theater orchestras; he also studied composition with A. Ilyinsky and Blaramberg. Still as a student, he composed his first work, a symph. poem, *The Nymphs* (Moscow, Dec. 28, 1889); graduating in 1892, he continued to compose; he wrote another symph. poem, *The Cedar and the Palm;* the overture and entr'actes for *Tsar Boris,* and a prelude to the opera *In the Year 1812.* In 1895 he completed his most successful work, a symphony in G minor (Kiev, Feb. 20, 1897); a second symphony, in A major (Kiev, March 12, 1898), was not as successful; he also wrote a cantata, *John of Damascus;* a *Ballade* for women's chorus and orch.; 9 songs, and 4 piano pieces. Owing to his irregular habits and undernourishment, he contracted tuberculosis, and was sent to Yalta for treatment; there he died a few months later. Kalinnikov possessed a fine lyric talent; there is a definite trend in Russia towards greater recognition of his works. Several of his manuscript works (*Serenade* for strings; the overture *Bylina,* etc.) were published on the 50th anniversary of his death (1951). —Cf. V.

Paskhalov, *V. S. Kalinnikov, Life and Works* (Moscow, 1938; greatly enlarged ed., 1951); N. Slonimsky, *A Thing or Two About Music* (N. Y., 1948; pp. 155-56).

Kalisch, Paul, German dramatic tenor; b. Berlin, Nov. 6, 1855; d. St. Lorenz am Mondsee, Salzkammergut, Austria, Jan. 27, 1946. He had begun life as an architect, when Pollini discovered his voice and induced him to study in Milan with Leoni and Lamperti; he sang with considerable success in Italy (Milan, Rome, Florence); then at the Munich Opera; and from 1884-7 in Berlin; in 1887 he sang the Wagner roles at the Metropolitan Opera House with Lilli Lehmann, whom he married in New York the following year; then he appeared in various German cities. At the first Paris performance of *Tristan und Isolde* (1904) he and his wife sang the title roles; they were later separated (though not legally divorced); after Lilli Lehmann's death in 1929, he lived on her estate in Salzkammergut, remaining there until his death at the age of 90.

Kalischer, Alfred, German writer on music; b. Thorn, March 4, 1842; d. Berlin, Oct. 8, 1909. After taking the degree of *Dr. philol.* at Leipzig, he studied music with Burgel and Bohmer at Berlin, where he lived as a writer and teacher; edited the 'Neue Berliner Musikzeitung' (from 1873). Of special value are his writings about Beethoven; he also published philosophical works, poems, and dramas.—Works about music: *Lessing als Musikästhetiker* (1889); *Die 'Unsterbliche Geliebte' Beethovens* (1891); *Die Macht Beethovens* (1903); *Beethoven und seine Zeitgenossen* (4 vols., 1908: I., *Beethoven und Berlin;* II and III, *Beethoven's Frauenkreis;* IV, *Beethoven und Wien*). He also edited *Neue Beethovenbriefe* (1902); *Beethoven's sämtliche Briefe* (5 vols., 1906-8; in English, 1909); issued new eds. of Wegeler and Ries' *Notizen* (1905), Breuning's *Aus dem Schwarzspanierhaus* (1907), A. Schindler's *Beethoven* (1909).

Kalkbrenner, Christian, German composer and writer; father of Friedrich W. M. Kalkbrenner; b. Minden, Hanover, Sept. 22, 1755; d. Paris, Aug. 10, 1806. He studied piano with Becker and violin with Rodewald in Kassel; was choirmaster at the court of the Queen in Berlin (1788), then in the court of Prince Heinrich at Rheinsberg (1790-96); in 1797, went to Naples; in 1798 he became choirmaster at the Paris Opéra. At the Opéra he produced his opera *Olimpie* (Dec. 18, 1798); also some pasticcios from music by Mozart and Haydn; he further wrote 2 symphonies, a piano concerto, several piano sonatas, *Theorie der Tonkunst* (1789), and *Kurzer Abriss der Geschichte der Tonkunst* (1792).

Kalkbrenner, Friedrich Wilhelm Michael, celebrated pianist; b. near Kassel, between Nov. 2 and Nov. 8, 1785; d. Deuil, Seine-et-Oise, June 10, 1849. He was taught by his father, Christian Kalkbrenner. In 1798 he was enrolled at the Paris Cons., where he studied with Adam (piano) and Catel (harmony), taking first prizes in 1801. From 1803 he studied counterpoint with Albrechtsberger in Vienna; appeared as a concert pianist in Berlin, Munich (1805), and Stuttgart; also in Paris, with great success, in 1806. As a teacher, too, he was in great vogue. The years 1814-23 he spent in London; in 1818 he took up Logier's newly invented Chiroplast, simplified it, and applied it practically. After a German tour in 1823 with the harpist Dizi, Kalkbrenner settled (1824) in Paris as a partner in the Pleyel piano factory (the future Mme. Camille Pleyel was one of his pupils). He revisited Germany in 1833 and Belgium in 1836. Kalkbrenner was inordinately vain of the success of his method of teaching, which aimed at the independent development of the fingers and wrist; his practical method of octave playing became a standard of modern piano teaching. He likewise developed left-hand technique, and a proper management of the pedals. As a player, his technique was smooth and well rounded, his fingers supple and of equal strength, and his tone full and rich; his style, while fluent and graceful, lacked emotional power. His numerous études (among them several for left hand alone) are interesting and valuable. Chopin took some advice from him in Paris, but did not become his pupil despite Kalkbrenner's urging to do so.—Works: 4 piano concertos (the last, op. 125, for 2 pianos); piano septet with strings and two horns; quintet for piano, clarinet, horn, bassoon, and double bass; 2 piano sextets; piano quintets; 3 piano quartets; 7 piano trios; 15 sonatas; also rondos, fantasies, variations, caprices, etc., of a light character; a *Méthode pour apprendre le pianoforte à l'aide du guide-mains* (1830); a *Traité d' harmonie du pianiste* (1849).—Cf. *Memoir of Mr. Frederick Kalkbrenner,* in the 'Quarterly Mus. Magazine and Review' (1824); L. Boivin, *Kalkbrenner* (Paris, 1840).

Kallenberg, Siegfried Garibaldi, German composer; b. Schachen, near Lindau, Nov. 3, 1867; d. Munich, Feb. 9, 1944. He studied at the Cons. of Stuttgart with Faisst; from 1892, taught at Stettin, Königsberg, and Hanover. In 1910 he settled in Munich; a Kallenberg Society was established there in 1921 to promote his creative output. As a composer, Kallenberg was inspired by neo-Romanticism; in some of his works there are touches of Impressionism; his absorption in symbolic subjects brought him into a kinship with the Expressionist school in Germany. Apart from works on exotic subjects, he wrote a number of works in a traditional style; he was particularly strong in choral polyphony. — Works: operas: *Sun Liao, Das goldene Tor,* and *Die lustigen Musikanten;* choral works: *90th Psalm, Germania an ihre Kinder, Requiem, Den Gefallenen, Eine kleine Passionmusik, Eine Pfingstmusik;* 3 symphonies; *Impressionen,* for orch.; *Konzertante Fantasie,* for piano and orch.; about 10 chamber works; 3 piano sonatas, a set of *Miniaturen* for piano; and some 300 songs. He was the author of a monograph on Richard Strauss (1926).

Kalliwoda, Johann Wenzel, famous violinist and composer; b. Prague, Feb. 21, 1801; d. Karlsruhe, Dec. 3, 1866. He studied at the Prague Cons. with Pixis (1811-17); played in the Prague Orch. (1817-23). In 1823 he became conductor of Prince Fürstenberg's orch. in Donaueschingen; there he spent 30 years, eventually retiring to Karlsruhe. He enjoyed an enviable reputation; some of his music was highly praised by Schumann. — Works: 2 operas, *Blanda* (Prague, Nov. 29, 1827) and *Prinzessin Christine* (1827); 10 Masses; 7 symphonies; 14 overtures and 13 fantasias, for orch.; a violin concerto; concerto for 2 violins; 7 concertinos; 3 string quartets; 3 string trios, and a variety of solos for violin; also choruses, duets, and songs.—Cf. K. Strunz, *J. W. Kalliwoda* (Vienna, 1910).

Kalliwoda, Wilhelm, German pianist and composer; son of Johann Wenzel Kalliwoda; b. Donaueschingen, July 19, 1827; d. Karlsruhe, Sept. 8, 1893. He studied with Hauptmann in Leipzig; also took some lessons from Mendelssohn; wrote piano pieces and songs; was also a reputable conductor.

Kallstenius, Edvin, Swedish composer; b. Filipstad, Wärmland, Aug. 29, 1881. He first studied science at the Lund Univ., then music at the Leipzig Cons. (1904-1907); returning to Stockholm, he became music critic of the 'Svenska Dagbladet' and a composer.—Works: 3 symphonies (1922; 1935; 1948); 2 sinfoniettas (1923; 1946); *Sinfonia concertata,* for piano and orch. (1922); *Dalekarlia,* symph. rhapsody; *Cavatina,* for viola and orch. (1943); *Passacaglia enharmonica,* a set of orch. variations (1944); *Divertimento alla Serenata,* for strings (1925); clarinet quintet; *Divertimento,* for wind quintet (1943); 5 string quartets (1904-45); *Trio divertente,* for flute, violin, and viola (1950); also *When Mankind Perishes,* a requiem for mixed chorus and orch. (1919); piano pieces.

Kallwitz, or **Kalwitz.** See **Calvisius.**

Kálmán, Emmerich (Imre), Hungarian composer of light opera; b. Siófok, Oct. 24, 1882; d. Paris, Oct. 30, 1953. He studied with Kössler in Budapest; won the Imperial Composition Prize (1907). Settling in Vienna, he produced a great number of tuneful and successful operettas; in 1938 he left Vienna; was in Paris until 1940; then came to America; lived in New York and Hollywood; in 1949 went again to Europe. He made his début as composer with a symph. scherzo *Saturnalia,* performed by the Budapest Philharmonic Orch. (Feb. 29, 1904); later dedicated himself exclusively to the composition of operettas in the Viennese style. His first success was with *Ein Herbstmanöver* (Vienna, Jan. 21, 1909; performed in N. Y. in the same year as *The Gay Hussars);* his other popular operettas were *Gold gab ich für Eisen* (Vienna, Oct. 16, 1914; N. Y., Dec. 6, 1916 as *Her Soldier Boy), Fräulein Susi* (Budapest, Feb. 23, 1915; English and American productions as *Miss Springtime), Die Csardasfürstin* (Vienna, Nov. 17, 1915; in England as *Gypsy Princess;* in America as *The Riviera Girl*), *Gräfin Mariza* (Vienna, Feb. 28, 1924), and *Die Zirkusprinzessin* (*Circus Princess;* Vienna, March 26, 1926). The following were moderately successful: *Der gute Kamerad* (first version of *Gold gab ich für Eisen;* Vienna, Oct. 10, 1911); *Der kleine König* (Vienna, Nov. 27, 1912); *Die Faschingsfee* (Vienna, Jan. 31, 1917); *Die Bajadere* (Vienna, Dec. 23, 1921); *Golden Dawn* (N. Y., Nov. 30, 1927); *Die Herzogin von Chicago* (Vienna, April 6, 1928) *Ronny* (Berlin, Dec. 22, 1931); *Kaiserin Josephine* (Zürich, Jan. 18, 1936); *Marinka* (N. Y., July 18, 1945). His last work *Arizona Lady,* was performed posthumously in Berne in 1954.—See J. Bistron, *Emmerich Kálmán* (Vienna, 1932); R. Oesterreicher *Emmerich Kálmán* (Vienna, 1954).

Kalnins (kahl'-ninsh), **Alfreds,** Latvian composer; b. Zehsis, Aug. 23, 1879; d. Riga, Dec. 23, 1951; studied at the St. Petersburg Cons., with Homilius (organ) and Soloviev (composition); was organist at various Lutheran churches in Dorpat, Libau, and Riga; also played organ recitals in Russia. While in Riga, he was active as teacher and composer. From 1927 till 1933 he lived in New York; then returned to Latvia and settled in Riga. —Works: the operas *Banuta* (first national Latvian opera; Riga, May 29, 1920); *Salinieki* (*The Islanders;* Riga, 1925); *Dzimtenes Atmoda* (*The Nation's Awakening;* Riga, Sept. 9, 1933); symph. poem, *Latvia;* piano pieces; some 100 choruses; about 200 songs; arrangements of Latvian folksongs (publ. in Riga).

Kalnins, Janis, Latvian composer and conductor; son of Alfreds Kalnins; b. Riga, Nov. 3, 1904. He studied in Riga with Vitols and in Leipzig with H. Abendroth; was conductor at the Latvian National Theater in Riga (1924-33), and at the Riga Opera House (1933-44). In 1944 he settled in Canada; from 1952, conductor of the Fredericton Civic Orch. —Works: *Hamlet,* opera (Riga, Feb. 17, 1936); 2 ballets, *Autumn* and *The Nightingale and the Rose* (1938); *Symphony of the Beatitudes* (1951); a violin concerto (1948); a string quartet (1948); choruses; songs.

Kalomiris, Manolis, Greek composer; b. Smyrna, Dec. 26, 1883. He studied piano and composition at the Vienna Cons. (1901-06); from 1906-10, prof. at the Kharkov Cons.; in 1910 he settled permanently in Greece, where he became a prof. at the Athens Cons.; was director of the Hellenic Cons. of Athens (1919-26). He founded the national Cons. of Athens, and since 1926, has been director.—Works: Operas: *Protomastoras* (*Master-Builder*), the first opera by a Greek composer on a native subject (Athens, March 24, 1916); *L'Anneau de la mère* (1917); incidental music to Xenopoulos' *Stella Violanti.* For orch.: *Suite grecque; Symphonie de la Levendia; La Symphonie des braves gens;* piano concerto; *Rapsodie grecque,* for piano and orch. (orchestrated by Gabriel Pierné, who conducted it for the first time at the Concerts Colonne in Paris, April 3, 1926). Vocal works: *Iambes et Anapestes,* 2 suites for voice and orch.; *Le Colporteur,* symph. poem for voice and orch.; *L'Olivier,* for chorus; and songs. Chamber music: quartet for flute, viola, harp, and English horn; quintet with voice; piano trio; etc.

Kamburov, Ivan, Bulgarian writer on music; b. Leskovec, Oct. 22, 1883. He was a pupil of Reger and Krehl at the Leipzig Cons.; 1910-14, high school teacher at Plovdiv, Bulgaria; 1918-20, teacher at the State Music School in Sofia; 1922-24 and 1929-30, traveled for scientific research purposes; 1926-29, member of the Folksong Commission at the National Museum of Ethnography, Sofia; living there in 1953 as music critic and writer. Works (in Bulgarian): *Bulgarian Music* (1926); *Operatic Art* (1926); *Music and Nation* (1932); *Illustrated Music Dictionary; Music for All* (Sofia, 1934); *Polish Music* (Sofia, 1939); *Yugoslav Music* (Sofia, 1940); *Bulgarian Folksongs* (Sofia, 1941); *Dvořák* (Sofia, 1941).

Kamensky, Alexander, composer; b. Geneva, Dec. 12, 1900. He studied (1915-19) at the Cons. of St. Petersburg; 1921-23, piano professor at the Cons. in Rostov, then living in Leningrad as pianist and composer; published songs and piano pieces (also duets).

Kamienski (kah-myen'-skē), **Lucian,** Polish composer; b. Gniezno, Jan. 7, 1885. He studied composition with Max Bruch in Berlin; musicology with Kretzschmar and Johannes Wolf; *Dr. phil.* for his dissertation, *Die Oratorien von J. A. Hasse* (1910). He then was music critic at Königsberg (until 1919); in 1920 appointed instructor at the Music Academy in Poznan; taught musicology at the Univ. of Poznan. In 1939 he was forced to leave his post; returning to Poznan after 1945, he established himself as a private teacher. He has written 2 comic operas, *Tabu* (Königsberg, April 9, 1917) and *Dami i huzary* (Poznan, Oct. 2, 1938); a *Sinfonia paschalis* (1928); *Silesia sings,* a symph. sketch (1929); a violin sonata; several piano suites on Polish themes; an album of 60 workers' songs to his own words (Berlin, 1905-10), which he issued under the name Dolega-Kamienski; he also used this *nom de plume* for his operettas and other light music.

Kamienski (kah-myen'-skē), **Mathias,** the first composer of Polish opera; b. Ödenburg, Hungary, Oct. 13, 1734; d. Warsaw, Jan. 25, 1821. He studied composition in Vienna, and settled in Warsaw as a teacher. On May 11, 1778, his first opera, *Nedza uszczesliwiona* (*Comfort in Misfortune*), sung by Poles, was produced in Warsaw and enthusiastically received; he produced 4 more Polish operas, and wrote 2 German operas (not performed) and a ballad opera, *Zoska*

(Warsaw, Jan. 21, 1781); a cantata for the unveiling of the Sobieski statue, Masses, offertories, and polonaises.

Kaminski, Heinrich, eminent German composer; b. Tiengen, Baden, July 4, 1886; d. Ried, Bavaria, June 21, 1946. He studied at Heidelberg Univ. with Wolfrum and in Berlin with Kaun, Klatte, and Juon; taught a master class at the Berlin Academy of Music (1930-32); during the same period he conducted municipal concerts in Bielefeld. In 1933 he settled in Ried, where he remained to the end of his life. Kaminski's musical style developed along the lines of the new Baroque movement in Germany, although he never associated himself with any particular group of composers, preferring to work in creative solitude. His writing is strictly polyphonic, eminently tonal, and almost rigid in form; the religious and mystic character of his sacred music stems from his family origins (he was the son of a clergyman of Polish extraction); the chief influences in his work were Bach and Bruckner. Interest in his music was enhanced after his death by posthumous editions of his unpublished works. The list of his compositions includes: an opera, *Jürg Jenatsch* (Dresden, April 27, 1929); a music drama for narrator and orch., *Das Spiel vom König Aphelius* (his last work, completed in 1946; produced posthumously, Göttingen, Jan. 29, 1950); a Passion, after an old French mystery play (1920); many choral works: *69th Psalm* (1914), *Introitus und Hymnus* (1919), *Magnificat* (1925), *Der Mensch,* motet (1926), *Die Erde,* motet (1928), etc.; for orch.: *Concerto Grosso* for double orch. (1922), *Dorische Musik* (1933), piano concerto (Berlin, 1937), *In Memoriam Gabrielae,* for orch., contralto, and solo violin (1940), *Tanzdrama* (1942); chamber music: quartet for clarinet, viola, cello, and piano (1912), 2 string quartets (1913 and 1916), quintet for clarinet, horn, violin, viola, and cello (1924), music for 2 violins and harpsichord (1931), *Hauskonzert* (1941), *Ballade* for horn and piano (1943); organ works: *Toccata* (1923), *Chorale-Sonata* (1926), 3 chorale preludes (1928), *Toccata and Fugue* (1939); piano works: *Klavierbuch* (1934), *10 kleine Übungen für das polyphone Klavierspiel* (1935); songs: *Brautlied* for soprano and organ (1911), *Cantiques bretons* (1923), *3 geistliche Lieder* for soprano, violin, and clarinet (1924), *Triptychon* for alto and organ (1930), *Lied eines Gefangenen* (1936), *Weihnachtsspruch* (1938), *Hochzeitsspruch* for 2 altos and organ (1940), *Dem Gedächtnis eines verwundeten Soldaten* for 2 sopranos and piano (1941); folksong arrangements.—Cf. S. Günther, *Heinrich Kaminski* in 'Die Musik' (vol. XXII, No. 7); E. Krieger, *Heinrich Kaminski,* in 'Zeitschrift für Musik' (1933); K. Schleifer, *Heinrich Kaminski* (Kassel, 1945); K. Schleifer and R. Schwarz-Stilling, *Heinrich Kaminski: Werkverzeichnis* (Kassel, 1947).

Kaminski, Joseph, violinist and composer; b. Odessa, Russia, Nov. 17, 1903. He studied in Warsaw, Berlin, and Vienna; in 1935, went to Palestine and settled in Tel Aviv; was appointed concertmaster of the Israel Symph. Orch. there; traveled with this orch. on its tour in the U. S. in 1951.—Works: *Concertino* for trumpet and orch: (Tel Aviv, May 5, 1941); *Ballad,* for harp and chamber orch. (Tel Aviv, Feb. 2, 1946); violin concerto (1949).

Kämpf, Karl, German organist and composer; b. Berlin, Aug. 31, 1874; d. Munich, Nov. 14, 1950. He was a pupil of F. E. Koch; became a professional performer on the harmonium; in 1925, was appointed conductor of the choral society 'Liedertafel' in München-Gladbach. He wrote several symph. marches on literary subjects: *Hiawatha, Aus baltischen Landen, Andersens Märchen,* etc.; also a choral symph. in 6 movements, *Die Macht des Liedes;* piano works; various pieces for the harmonium, etc.—Cf. J. Hagemann-Bonn, *Karl Kämpf* (Leipzig, 1907).

Kandler, Franz Sales, Austrian writer on music; b. Klosterneuburg, Aug. 23, 1792; d. Baden, near Vienna, Sept. 26, 1831. As a boy he sang in the court choir in Vienna; studied with Albrechtsberger, Salieri, and Gyrowetz. He was an Imperial military draughtsman; when ordered to Italy (1815-26), he pursued the study of Italian music and its history as an avocation. He publ. *Cenni storico-critici intorno alla vita ed alle opere del celebre compositore Giovanni Adolfo Hasse, detto il Sassone* (1820); *Über das Leben und die Werke des G. Pierluigi da Palestrina, genannt der Fürst der Musik* (1834); and *Cenni storico-critici sulle vicende e lo stato attuale della musica in Italia* (1836). — Cf. L. Schiedermair, *Venezianer Briefe F. S. Kandlers,* in 'Riemann-Festschrift' (Leipzig, 1909).

Kanitz, Ernst, composer; b. Vienna, April 9, 1894. He studied with Richard Heuberger (1912-14) and with Franz Schreker (1914-20). From 1922 until 1938 he taught theory at the Neues Konservatorium in Vienna; also conducted a women's choir there (1930-38). In 1938 he emigrated to the U. S.; taught at Winthrop College, Rockhill, S. C. From 1941-44 was director of Music Dept. of Erskine College, S. C. In 1945 he was appointed prof. at the Univ. of Southern Calif. His works include an oratorio *Das Hohelied* (1921); a radio cantata *Zeitmusik* (1931); *Heitere Ouvertüre* (1918); concertino for Theremin and orch. (1938); *Intermezzo Concertante* for saxophone and orch. (1948); 2 string quartets; violin sonata; *Quintettino* for piano and wind instruments (1945). He is the author of *A Counterpoint Manual: Fundamental Techniques of Polyphonic Music Writing* (Boston, 1948).

Kann, Hans, Austrian pianist and composer; b. Vienna, Feb. 14, 1927. He studied piano with A. Göllner; composition with Pollnaur. At 18, after the end of World War II, he gave a series of piano recitals in Europe; won prizes at piano competitions in Geneva, Munich, and Vienna. He taught at the Academy of Music in Vienna (1950-52). In 1954 he was appointed prof. of piano at the Univ. of Tokyo (succeeding Leonid Kreutzer). He has written a number of piano works; also pieces for recorder and piano, and chamber music.

Kanner, Jerome Herbert, American violinist, composer, and arranger; b. New York, Nov. 17, 1903. He made his début as a violinist in N. Y. at the age of 8; studied violin with Kneisel, Stoeving, and Auer; conducting with Walter Damrosch and Albert Stoessel; composition with Edward Kilenyi; also took some lessons with Ravel in Paris. After 1925 he gave up the violin and devoted himself mainly to composing and conducting for radio and motion pictures. In 1949, at the request of Prince Pierre of Monaco, he composed a national song for Monaco.

Kanner-Rosenthal, Hedwig, piano pedagogue; b. Budapest, June 3, 1882. She studied with Leschetizky and Moriz Rosenthal, whom she married; appeared with him in duo recitals; taught in Vienna; in 1939 settled in New York as a teacher.

Kapell, William, American pianist; b. New York, Sept. 20, 1922, of Russian and Polish parents; d. in an airplane crash, at King's Mountain, near San Francisco, Oct. 29, 1953. He studied with Olga Samaroff at the Philadelphia Cons. of Music; made his N.Y. début on Oct. 28, 1941; subsequently appeared as soloist with all major American orchestras and also in Europe, specializing in modern music. He met his death returning from an Australian concert tour.

Kapp, Arthur, Estonian composer; b. Suure-Iani, Feb. 28, 1875; d. Tallinn (Reval), Jan. 14, 1952. He studied at the St. Petersburg Cons. with Rimsky-Korsakov. From 1904 to 1920 he was director of the Cons. of Astrakhan, on the Volga. From 1920 to 1943, director of the Reval (Tallinn) Cons. in Estonia. In that capacity he was the teacher of a generation of Estonian musicians. He wrote 4 symphonies, concertos (for piano, violin, cello, clarinet, and French horn), and a string sextet. His Symphony No. 4, subtitled *Youth Symphony* (1949), was awarded the State Prize in 1949, and the First Stalin Prize in 1950; he also wrote a cantata *For Peace* (1951).

Kapp, Eugen, Estonian composer, son of Arthur Kapp; b. Astrakhan, May 26, 1908. He studied with his father, who was director of the Astrakhan Cons.; followed him to Estonia in 1920, and was graduated from the Tallinn Cons. there in 1931. His operas, *Flames of Vengeance* (Tallinn, July 21, 1945) and *Freedom's Singer* (Tallinn, July 20, 1950), were awarded Stalin prizes. He has also written a ballet, *Kalebipoeg* (1949), a *Patriotic Symphony,* a cantata, *Power of the People,* 2 violin sonatas, piano pieces, and choral works. Kapp succeeded his father as prof. of composition at the Tallinn Cons. —Cf. G. A. Polyanovsky, *Eugen Kapp* (Moscow, 1951).

Kapp, Julius, German writer on music; b. Steinbach in Baden, Oct. 1, 1883. He studied in Marburg, Berlin, and Munich; *Dr. Phil.* in 1906; from 1904-7, editor of 'Literarischer Anzeiger,' which he founded in 1904; from 1923-45, was stage director of the Berlin State Opera and edited its bulletin, 'Blätter der Staatsoper'; from 1948-54 he held a similar post at the Berlin Municipal Opera. He publ. *Wagner und Liszt* (1908); *Franz Liszt* (1909; went through 20 printings before 1924); *Register zu Liszts Gesammelten Schriften* (1909); *Liszt-Brevier* (1910); *Liszt und die Frauen* (1911); *Wagner und die Frauen* (1912; 16th printing, 1929; completely rewritten and publ. in English transl. as *The Loves of Richard Wagner,* London, 1951); *Paganini* (1913; revised ed., 1928); *Berlioz* (1914); *Das Dreigestirn: Berlioz - Liszt - Wagner* (1920); *Meyerbeer* (1920; 8th printing,

1932); *Franz Schreker* (1921); *Das Opernbuch* (1922; 16th printing, 1928); *Die Oper der Gegenwart* (1922); *Weber* (1922; 5th rev. ed., 1931); *Die Staatsoper 1919 bis 1925* (1925); *Wagner und seine erste Elisabeth* (with H. Jachmann, 1926); *185 Jahre Staatsoper* (1928); *Wagner und die Berliner Staatsoper* (1933); *Wagner in Bildern* (1933); *Geschichte der Staatsoper Berlin* (1937); *200 Jahre Staatsoper in Bild* (1942). He edited Liszt's 'Gesammelte Schriften' (4 vols., 1910) and Wagner's 'Gesammelte Schriften und Briefe' (24 vols., 1914); made new translations of Meyerbeer's *Huguenots* (1932) and some Verdi operas.

Kappel, Gertrude, German dramatic soprano; b. Halle, Sept. 1, 1884; studied with Nikisch and Noe at the Leipzig Cons.; made her début in 1903 at the Hanover Opera, after which she was engaged in Munich, Berlin, and Vienna for the leading Wagner roles; appeared also in Amsterdam, Brussels, Madrid, London, and Paris; made her first American appearance as Isolde with the Metropolitan Opera on Jan. 16, 1928, and remained a member until 1936; 1932, sang the title part in *Elektra* at its first Metropolitan performance; in 1933 she joined the roster of the San Francisco Opera Co.; retired in 1937 and settled in Berlin.

Kapr, Jan, Czech composer; b. Prague, March 12, 1914. He studied first with his father, who was a professional musician; then took courses at the Prague Cons. with Ridky and with Křička. He was connected with the Czechoslovak Radio; in 1948 he began writing music criticism; also wrote music for films. Among his works are a symph. scherzo, *Marathon* (1939); 2 symphonies (1943 and 1946); piano concerto (1938); 2 string quartets (1937 and 1942); chamber music of various descriptions; also a cantata, *The Song of the Native Country* (1940).

Kaprál, Václav, Czech composer; b. Urcitz, March 26, 1889; d. Brno, April 4, 1947. He studied with Janáček in Brno; then with Novák in Prague; took a course in piano with Alfred Cortot in Paris. Returning to Brno in 1911, he established his own music school; was lecturer at the Univ. of Brno (1927-36); then taught at Brno Cons. He spent 3 years in a concentration camp during World War II; in 1946, became prof. at the Academy of Music in Brno. In his works he showed a fine eclectic talent; wrote mostly for piano (4 sonatas; fantasy, *Con duolo* for left hand alone; miniatures, etc.); also 2 string quartets, a *Ballade* for cello and piano (1946); choral pieces. His *5 Berceuses* for voice and chamber orch., inspired by the songs his mother sang for him and her 11 other children, were performed at the Festival of the International Society for Contemporary Music in Barcelona (April 20, 1936).

Kaprálová, Vitězslava, Czech composer; daughter of Václav Kaprál; b. Brno, Jan. 24, 1915; d. Montpellier, France, June 16, 1940. She received her early education from her father; then studied conducting and composition at the Brno Cons.; later at the Prague Cons. with Novák (composition) and Talich (conducting). In 1937 she went to Paris, where she continued to study conducting with Charles Munch, and composition with Martinu. Her early death cut short a promising talent. She wrote several orchestral works, among them a *Military Sinfonietta* (London Festival, June 17, 1938); *Suita Rustica* (1938); *Partita,* for strings and piano (1939); also a piano concerto (1935), a string quartet, and some songs.

Kapsberger, Johann Hieronymus von, 17th-century composer of a noble German family (known in Italy as Giovanni Geronimo Tedesco della Tiorba, because of his ability as a player); d. Rome, c. 1650. He was a noted virtuoso on the theorbo, chitarrone, lute, and trumpet. He lived in Venice about 1604, and then in Rome, enjoying the favor of Pope Urban VIII. His compositions are in the then 'modern' Florentine style; those for lute are written in a much simplified lute-tablature.—Works: *Intavolatura di chitarrone* (3 books: 1604, 1616, 1626); *Villanelle a 1, 2 e 3 voci* (4 books: 1610, 1619, 1619, 1623); *Arie passeggiate* (2 books: 1612, 1623); *Intavolatura di lauto* (2 books; 1611, 1623); *Motetti passeggiati* (1612); *Balli, gagliarde e correnti* (1615); *Sinfonie a 4 con il basso continuo* (1615); *Capricci a due stromenti, tiorba e tiorbino* (1617); *Missae Urbanae,* 4-8 voices (1631); *Apotheosis of St. Ignatius de Loyola;* a musical drama, *Fetonte* (1630); wedding cantatas, etc.—Cf. J. Wolf, *Handbuch der Notationskunde* (vol. 2, p. 194 ff.).

Karajan, Herbert von, Austrian conductor; b. Salzburg, April 5, 1908. He studied in Vienna; conducted the Berlin Opera from 1938 to 1945, and since then has toured widely in Europe and the U. S. He conducted the Berlin Philharmonic on its tour of the U. S. in the spring of 1954; became musical director of the Berlin Philharmonic after Furtwängler's death in 1954; in 1956, appointed head of the Vienna State Opera.—Cf. B. Gavoty, *Herbert von Karajan,* in the series 'Les grands interprètes' (Geneva, 1955).

Karajan, Theodor Georg von, Austrian writer on music; b. Vienna, Jan. 22, 1810; d. there, April 28, 1873. He studied history, philology, and law; after holding various minor posts, he became president of the Academy of Science (1859). His important monograph *J. Haydn in London, 1791 und 1792* (Vienna, 1861) contains Haydn's correspondence with Maria Anna von Genzinger; he also publ. *Aus Metastasios Hofleben* (Vienna, 1861).

Karasowski, Moritz, Polish writer on music; b. Warsaw, Sept. 22, 1823; d. Dresden, April 20, 1892. He was a cellist in the opera orch. in Warsaw from 1851, and later court cellist at Dresden. He publ. (in Polish) *History of Polish Opera* (Warsaw, 1859) and *Life of Mozart* (1868), but his most important contribution was his book *Chopin's Youth* (1862), and particularly the first comprehensive biography of Chopin, publ. in German as *F. Chopin, sein Leben, seine Werke und Briefe* (Dresden, 1877; in English, N. Y., 1878).

Karatygin (kah-rah-ty'-gin), **Vyatcheslav Gavrilovitch,** Russian writer on music; b. Pavlovsk, Sept. 17, 1875; d. Leningrad, Dec. 23, 1925. He taught music history at the Leningrad Cons.; was a specialist on Mussorgsky; edited fragments of Mussorgsky's opera *Salammbô* and the unfinished opera *The Fair at Sorochinsk;* publ. several monographs: *Scriabin* (1916); *Mussorgsky* (1922); *Shaliapin* (1922); also composed numerous songs. A memorial collection of articles, *V. G. Karatygin, His Life and Work,* was publ. by the Russian Institute for the History of Art (Leningrad, 1927).

Karel, Rudolf, Czech composer; b. Pilsen, Nov. 9, 1880; d. at the Teresin concentration camp, March 5, 1945. He was the last pupil of Dvořák, with whom he studied in Prague. In 1914 he went to Russia, and remained there during World War I; taught in Taganrog and in Rostov. After the Revolution, he made his way to Irkutsk, Siberia; became a member of the Czechoslovak Legion, and conducted an orchestra organized by the legionaries. He returned to Prague in 1920; from 1923-41, taught at the Prague Cons.; he was arrested in 1943; early in 1945 he was sent to Teresin, where he died of dysentery. His music reflects the Romantic concepts; he had a predilection for programmatic writing; the national element is revealed by his treatment of old modal progressions; his instrumental writing is rich in sonority; the polyphonic structure is equally strong. — Works: *Ilseino srdce (Ilsea's Heart),* lyric comedy (Prague, Oct. 11, 1924); *Smrt Kmotřička* (*Godmother's Death*), opera (Prague, Feb. 3, 1933); *Tři vlasy děda Vševěda* (*Three Hairs of Old Wise Man),* musical fairy tale (his last work, written in prison; orchestration completed by a pupil; Prague, Oct. 28, 1948); oratorio, *Vzkříšení* (*Resurrection;* Prague, April 9, 1928); 4 symphs.; symph. poem *Demon* (1920); *Revolutionary Overture* (1938-41); *Capriccio* for violin and orch. (1924); 3 string quartets; nonet for flute, oboe, clarinet, bassoon, horn, violin, viola, cello, and double-bass (1945); violin sonata (1912); piano sonata (1910); songs.—Cf. O. Šourek, *Rudolf Karel* (Prague, 1947).

Karg-Elert, Sigfrid, distinguished German organist and composer; b. Oberndorf, Württemberg, Nov. 21, 1877; d. Leipzig, April 9, 1933. He studied at the Leipzig Cons. with Reinecke and Jadassohn; in 1919 was appointed to its staff. Concurrently with his teaching activities, he began to give organ recitals, and soon became known as one of the greatest virtuosos on the instrument; he also played on the 'Kunstharmonium,' for which he wrote many original compositions. His real name, Karg, sounded unattractive to his audiences (it means 'coffin'), and he changed it to Karg-Elert. As a composer he developed a brilliant style, inspired by the music of the Baroque, but he embellished this austere and ornamental idiom with Impressionistic devices; the result was an ingratiating type of music with an aura of originality. In 1932 he undertook a concert tour in the U. S.—Works: for the Kunstharmonium: sets of pieces: *Skizzen* (1903), *Aquarellen* (1906), *Miniaturen* (1908), *Intarsien* (1911), *Impressions* (1914), *Idyllen* (1915), *Innere Stimmen* (1918); fundamental technical works: *Die Kunst des Registrierens; Die ersten grundlegenden Studien; Hohe Schule des Legatospiels; Die Harmoniumtechnik (Gradus ad Parnassum); Theoretische-praktische Elementarschule;* for organ: 66 Chorale Improvisations (1908-10); 20 Chorale Preludes and Postludes (1912); 10 *Poetic Tone Pictures; 3 Pastels, Cathedral Windows* (on Gregorian themes), etc. He further wrote a wind quintet; two clarinet sonatas; a sonata for flute unaccompanied; trio for oboe, English horn, and piano; *Trio bucolico* for violin, flute, and piano; a number of lieder; publ. *Akustische Ton-, Klang-, und Funktionsbestimmung* (1930) and *Polaristische Klang- und Tonalitätslehre* (1931). Hans Avril publ. a catalogue of Karg-Elert's works: *Kompositionsverzeichnis mit einer monographischen Skizze* (Berlin, 1908). See also A. Eaglefield Hull, *Karg-Elert,* in the 'Mus. Times' (Feb. and March, 1913); H. B. Gaul, *Bonnet, Bossi, Karg-Elert,* in the 'Mus. Quarterly' (July, 1918); Paul Schenk, *Sigfrid Karg-Elert* (Berlin, 1927); Godfrey Sceats, *The Organ Works of Karg-Elert* (Orpington, 1940; revised ed., London, 1950).

Karl, Tom, tenor; b. Dublin, Jan. 19, 1846; d. Rochester, N. Y., March 19, 1916. He studied in England with Henry Phillips, and in Italy with Sangiovanni. He sang in Italy for many years, then settled in N. Y. His remarkable success as Ralph in *Pinafore* (1879) determined him to abandon grand opera; some years later he organized (with H. C. Barnabee and W. H. MacDonald) the famous light opera company, 'The Bostonians.' He had a repertory of about 150 operas and operettas. He retired in 1896; had an operatic school in N. Y.; then went to Rochester, where he taught singing.

Karlowicz (kahr'-lo-vitch), **Jan,** Polish music scholar; father of Mieczyslaw; b. Subortowicze, near Troki, May 28, 1836; d. Warsaw, June 14, 1903. He studied music in Wilno, Moscow, Paris, Brussels, and Berlin. Settling in Warsaw, he publ. translations of several German textbooks on harmony; also publ. (in English, German, and French) a pamphlet, *Project of a New Way of Writing Musical Notes* (Warsaw, 1876); composed some songs.—Cf. F. Starczewski, *The Musical Activities of Jan Karlowicz* (Warsaw, 1904).

Karlowicz (kahr'-lo-vitch), **Mieczyslaw,** Polish composer; b. Wiszniewo, Dec. 11, 1876; d. Zakopane, Galicia, Feb. 8, 1909. He was the son of the theorist Jan Karlowicz; was sent to Germany to study violin as a child. In 1887 he began composition studies in Warsaw with Noskowski, Roguski, and Maszynski; violin with Barcewicz; later he continued his studies in Berlin with H. Urban (1895-1900). Returning to Warsaw, he devoted himself to composition and teaching; was director of the Warsaw Music Society (1904-6); after a sojourn in Germany (where he studied conducting with Nikisch in Leipzig), he settled in Zakopane; also traveled to France, Austria, and Germany. An enthusiastic mountain climber, he was killed in an accident, under an avalanche. Essentially a Romantic composer, he succeeded in blending the national elements of Polish folk music with the general European genre of mild modernism; there is an influence of Richard Strauss in his expansive tone painting. The appreciation of his music in Poland rose rather than declined after his death; some of his piano pieces and songs have been established in the concert repertory.—Works: *Serenade* for string orch. (1898); Symphony in E minor, subtitled *Renaissance* (1900); symph. poem, *Returning Waves* (1904); symph. trilogy, *Eternal Songs* (1908); *Lithuanian Rhapsody* for orch. (1906); *Stanislaw and Anna of Oswiecim,* symph. poem (1912); *Sad Story,* symph. poem (1908); *Episode at the Masquerade,* symph. poem (1908-9; unfinished; completed by G. Fitelberg). He publ. for the first time some theretofore unknown letters of Chopin (Warsaw, 1904; in French as *Souvenirs inédits de F. Chopin,* Paris, 1904).—Cf. F. Kecki, *Karlowicz* (Warsaw, 1934); A. Chybinski, *Karlowicz* (Cracow, 1947); Igor Boelza, *Karlowicz* (Moscow, 1951).

Karow, Karl, German composer; b. Alt-Stettin, Nov. 15, 1790; d. Bunzlau, Dec. 20, 1863. He taught music at Bunzlau; publ. a *Choralbuch,* a *Leitfaden für den Schulgesang-Unterricht,* motets, piano pieces, etc.

Karpath (kahr-paht), **Ludwig,** singer and music critic; b. Budapest, April 27, 1866; d. Vienna, Sept. 8, 1936. He was a pupil at the Cons. in Budapest; studied singing in Vienna; was a member of the National Opera Co. in the U. S. (singing minor bass roles) for 3 seasons (1886-88); returning to Vienna, he became an influential music critic; for many years (1894-1921) wrote for the 'Neues Wiener Tageblatt.' He publ. *Siegfried Wagner als Mensch und Künstler* (1902), *Zu den Briefen Wagners an eine Putzmacherin* (1906), *R. Wagner, der Schuldenmacher* (1914), *Wagners Briefe an Hans Richter* (1924).

Kartzev, Alexander Alexeyevitch, Russian composer; b. Moscow, July 19, 1883. He was a pupil of Juon in Berlin, and Taneyev and Glière in Moscow, where he settled. He has written an opera, *Undine;* a symphony; violin concerto; string quartet (1st prize at the Belaiev international competition, 1929); piano quintet; violin sonata, etc.

Karyotakis, Theodore, Greek composer; b. Argos, July 21, 1903. He studied in

Athens with Dimitri Mitropoulos and Varvoglis; has written an opera, *Moon's Flower* (1953); symph. study (1938); *Petite symphonie,* for strings (1949); violin sonata (1945); flute sonata (1946); etc.

Kasanli. See **Kazanly.**

Kasatchenko. See **Kazatchenko.**

Kashin, Daniil Nikititch, Russian composer; b. Moscow, 1769; d. there, Dec. 10, 1841. He was a serf, property of an aristocratic landowner, Gavril Bibikov. His master engaged Sarti, who was in Russia at the time, to teach Kashin; when Sarti accompanied Potemkin to southern Russia, Kashin went along. Returning to Moscow, he demonstrated his ability by presenting a piano concerto and an overture of his own composition (March 17, 1790). Bibikov sent him to Italy for further study; there Kashin spent 7 years; upon his return in 1798, he was given his liberty. On April 10, 1799, he gave in Moscow a monster concert with the participation of 200 executants, including an ensemble of Russian horns; at this concert he presented several of his Russian songs, which later became popular. He wrote 3 operas: *Natalia, the Boyard's Daughter* (Moscow, Oct. 21, 1801), *Fair Olga* (Moscow, Jan. 14, 1809), *The One-Day Reign of Nourmahal,* after Thomas Moore's *Lalla Rookh* (1817, not produced); also collections of 'patriotic songs' and an album of Russian folksongs. In 1806 he publ. 6 issues of a periodical, 'Musical Journal of Russia.' —Cf. R. A. Mooser, *Annales de la Musique et des Musiciens en Russie au XVIIIe Siècle* (vol. 2, Geneva, 1950, pp. 491-93).

Kashkin, Nikolai Dimitrievitch, Russian music critic; b. Voronezh, Dec. 9, 1839; d. Kazan, April 15, 1920. After receiving rudimentary instruction in music from his father, an amateur, Kashkin became a private tutor in elementary music in his native town. In 1860 he settled in Moscow, where he studied piano; in 1866 he joined the staff of the Moscow Cons., where he taught for 30 years. He became music critic of 2 Moscow papers, and his opinions exercised considerable influence in the musical life of Moscow in the last quarter of the 19th century. He was an intimate friend of Tchaikovsky; his little pamphlet *Reminiscences of Tchaikovsky* (Moscow, 1896) is valuable for authentic biographical and psychological data. A selection of his articles was publ. in Moscow (1953).

Kashperov, Vladimir Nikititch, Russian composer; b. Simbirsk, 1827; d. Romanzevo, near Mozhaisk, July 8, 1894. He studied with Voigt and Henselt in St. Petersburg and with Dehn in Berlin (1856); went to Italy to study singing (1858), and remained there until 1864; he wrote several operas in the Italian style which were produced in Italy: *Maria Tudor* (Milan, 1859), *Rienzi* (Florence, 1863), and *Consuelo* (Venice, 1864). In 1866 he returned to Russia and taught at the Moscow Cons. In Moscow he produced 2 operas with Russian librettos: *The Storm,* after Ostrovsky (1867) and *Taras Bulba,* after Gogol (1893). Even in his Russian works, Kashperov remained faithful to the Italian style of composition, taking Donizetti as a model.

Kaskel, Karl von, German composer; b. Dresden, Oct. 10, 1866; d. c. 1945. While a law student at Leipzig, he studied music in the Cons. under Reinecke and Jadassohn (1886-7) and later at Cologne under Wüllner and Jensen. He lived many years in Dresden; later in Munich. During his lifetime he was a fairly successful composer.—Works: operas, *Hochzeitsmorgen* (Hamburg, 1893), *Sjula* (Cologne, 1895), *Die Bettlerin vom Pont des Arts* (Kassel, 1899), *Der Dusle und das Babeli* (Munich, 1903), *Der Gefangene der Zarin* (Dresden, 1910), *Die Nachtigall* (Stuttgart, 1910), *Die Schmiedin von Kent* (Dresden, 1916); for orch., *Lustspielouvertüre; Humoresque; Ballade;* piano pieces; songs.—Cf. E. Schmitz, *Karl von Kaskel,* in 'Monographien moderner Musiker' (Leipzig, 1909).

Kassern, Tadeusz Zygfried, Polish composer; b. Lwow, March 19, 1904; d. New York, May 2, 1957. He studied with M. Soltys at the Lwow Cons. and with Opienski in Poznan. He also took a course in law; in 1931, went to Paris. In 1948 he was appointed cultural attaché at the Polish Consulate in N. Y. However, he broke with the Communist government in Poland, and remained in N. Y., petitioning for citizenship. This having been denied him, he attempted suicide. He died of cancer. Among Polish composers, he pursued a cosmopolitan trend; although many of his works are inspired by Polish folk music, the idiom and the method are of a general European modern character.—Works: 2 operas, *The Anointed* (1951) and *Sun-Up* (1952); *Dies irae,* symph. poem in memory of Marshal Pilsudski (1935); concerto for soprano (1928); concerto for double-bass and orch. (1937); concerto for string orch. (1944);

concertino for oboe and string orch. (1946); concertino for flute, string orch., xylophone, and celesta (1948); *Teen-Age Concerto,* for piano and orch. (N. Y., May 1956); choruses; chamber music; piano pieces; songs.

Kässmeyer, Moritz, Austrian violinist and composer; b. Vienna, 1831; d. there, Nov. 9, 1884. He studied with Sechter at the Vienna Cons.; then played violin in the orch. of the Vienna Opera; later became ballet conductor there. He wrote a comic opera, *Das Landhaus zu Meudon* (1869); symphonies; Masses and other church music; 5 string quartets; songs. His *Mesalliansen* for string quartet with piano 4 hands, and *Volksweisen und Lieder* for string quartet 'humoristisch und kontrapunktisch bearbeitet,' are amusing specimens of old-fashioned humor.

Kastalsky, Alexander Dmitrievitch, Russian choral conductor and composer; b. Moscow, Nov. 28, 1856; d. there, Dec. 17, 1926. He was a pupil of Tchaikovsky, Taneyev, and Hubert at the Moscow Cons. (1875-82). In 1887 he became instructor of piano at the Synodal School in Moscow; in 1891, assistant conductor of the Synodal Chorus; in 1910, appointed director of the school and principal conductor of the choir. In 1911 he took it on an extended European tour (Warsaw, Vienna, Dresden, Florence, Rome, etc.). In 1918 the Synodal School became a choral academy; in 1923 it merged with the Moscow Cons. Kastalsky was also teacher of conducting at the Moscow Philharmonic Institute (1912-22); in 1923, appointed prof. of choral singing at the Moscow Cons. He was a notable composer of Russian sacred music, into which he introduced modern elements, combining them with the ancient church modes. — Works: the opera *Clara Militch,* after Turgenev (Moscow, 1916); oratorio *The Furnace of Nabucho* (1909); *Requiem* (1916; in memory of Allied soldiers fallen in World War I; in 12 sections, based on the modes of Greek Orthodox, Roman Catholic, and Anglican Churches); *Rustic Symphony* (Moscow, Dec. 13, 1925); incidental music to *Stenka Rasin* (Moscow, 1918), to Shakespear's *King Lear* (Moscow, 1919), and to Hauptmann's *Hannele* (Moscow, 1920); a cantata, *1812;* symph. suite *Pictures of Russian Festivities* (1912); *A Market Place in Ancient Russia* (completed 1924); 5 choruses on patriotic texts; about 80 sacred choruses a cappella; *In Georgia,* suite for piano: *Ancient Times* (4 vols. of restorations of ancient music, for piano: I. China, India, Egypt; II. Greece, Judea, Islam; III. Early Christianity; IV. Ancient Russia). He publ. a valuable paper, *Peculiarities of the National Russian Musical System* (Moscow, 1923), greatly expanded by him during the last 3 years of his life, and publ. posthumously as *Foundations of National Polyphony,* ed. by Victor Belaiev (Moscow, 1948). His autobiographical sketch, *My Musical Career and My Thoughts on Church Music,* was publ. in the 'Mus. Quarterly' (April, 1925). See also W. S. Pring, *Kastalsky and Russian Folk Polyphony,* in 'Music & Letters' (1929).

Kastendieck, Miles Merwin, American music critic; b. Brooklyn, April 16, 1905. He studied at Yale Univ. with D. S. Smith. He became critic of the 'New Haven Journal-Courier' (1929-38), of the 'Brooklyn Eagle' (1938-46), the 'N. Y. Journal-American' since 1946, and N. Y. correspondent for 'The Christian Science Monitor' since 1945; was elected president of the Music Critics Association upon its founding in Oct., 1957. He wrote *England's Musical Poet, Thomas Campion* (N. Y., 1938).

Kastle, Leonard, American composer; b. New York, Feb. 11, 1929. He studied composition with George Szell and piano with Frank Sheridan and Paul Wittgenstein. In 1945 he entered the Curtis Institute and studied with Isabelle Vengerova (piano) and Rosario Scalero (composition); continued his studies with Gian-Carlo Menotti and Carl Bamberger (conducting); graduated in 1950. Among his works are a piano sonata (1950); a one-act opera for television, *The Swing* (N.B.C. television network, June 11, 1956); a choral work, *Whispers of Heavenly Death* (1956).

Kastner, Alfred, harpist; b. Vienna, March 10, 1870; d. Hollywood, May 24, 1948. He studied with Zamara at the Vienna Cons.; then played first harp in the orchestras of the Dresden Opera and Warsaw Opera; later taught harp in Budapest (1892-98); was in the U. S. (1898-1900); then in Switzerland. From 1904-19 he was harpist in the Queen's Hall Orch. in London; also taught at the Royal Academy of Music there. In 1919 he was engaged as first harpist of the Los Angeles Philharmonic. He publ. several concert pieces for the harp and various arrangements.

Kastner, Emmerich, Austrian writer on music; b. Vienna, March 29, 1847; d. there, Dec. 5, 1916. He published several valuable works dealing with Wagner: *Richard Wagner-Katalog* (1878); *Wagneriana* (1885); *Briefe R. Wagners an seine Zeitgenossen 1830-38* (1885); *Die dramatischen Werke R. Wagners* (1899). Other writings are *Bayreuth* (1884) and *Neuestes und vollständigstes Tonkünstler- und Opern-Lexikon* (1889; only A-Azzoni printed); edited *Beethovens sämmtliche Briefe* (Leipzig, 1911). He was editor of the 'Wiener musikalische Zeitung.'

Kastner, Georg Friedrich, Alsatian acoustician; son of Johann Georg Kastner; b. Strasbourg, Aug. 10, 1852; d. Bonn, April 6, 1882. He followed his father's ideas of music as a science; at the age of 20, read a paper before the Académie des Sciences in Paris, *Pyrophone: Flammes chantantes,* subsequently published; constructed the Pyrophone, an organ of 3 octaves on which the sound was produced by burning gas jets. Description and picture of the Pyrophone are in vol. 3 of H. Ludwig von Jan's biography of Kastner's father.

Kastner, Johann Georg; Alsatian composer and theorist; b. Strasbourg, March 9, 1810; d. Paris, Dec. 19, 1867. He studied organ as a child; later entered the Strasbourg Lutheran Seminary. He then gave up his theological studies and went to Paris. There he resumed his musical education, taking lessons with Berton and Reicha. An industrious scholar, Kastner acquired enormous erudition in various arts and sciences. He pursued the study of acoustics and formulated a theory of the cosmic unity of the arts. At the same time he took great interest in practical applications of music; he was active in organizing the contest of bands of 9 nations held at the Paris Exposition of 1867. He was a founder and vice-president of the 'Association des artistes-musiciens.' He was elected a member of the 'Institut' and an Officer of the Legion of Honor. Among the grandiose projects that he carried out were several volumes of 'Livres-Partitions,' that is, symphony-cantatas illustrating musico-historical subjects, preceded by essays upon them. Of these the following were published: *Les Danses des morts; dissertations et recherches historiques, philosophiques, littéraires et musicales sur les divers monuments de ce genre qui existent tant en France qu'à l'étranger;* and *Danse macabre, grande ronde vocale et instrumentale* (Paris, 1852; 310 pages); *La Harpe d'Éole, et la musique cosmique;* . . . and *Stéphen, ou la Harpe d'Éole, grand monologue avec chœurs* (1856); *Les Sirènes,* . . . and *Le Rêve d'Oswald ou les Sirènes, grande symphonie dramatique vocale et instrumentale* (1858); *Parémiologie musicale de la langue française,* . . . and *La Saint-Julien de ménétriers, symphonie-cantate à grand orchestre, avec solos et chœurs* (1862; 659 pages); *Les Voix de Paris* and *Les Cris de Paris, grande symphonie humoristique vocale et instrumentale,* making use of vendors' cries with orchestral accompaniment (1875). Kastner wrote several operas; 4 were produced in Strasbourg: *Gustav Wasa* (1832), *Oskars Tod* (1833), comic opera *Der Sarazene* (1834), and *Die Königin der Sarmaten* (1835). In Paris he produced 2 operas: *La Maschera* (June 17, 1841) and *Le dernier Roi de Juda* (1844). He also wrote 5 overtures, a sextet for saxophones, and 2 collections of men's choruses (*Les Chants de la vie,* 1854; *Chants de l'armée française,* 1855); publ. a useful and highly practical *Manuel général de musique militaire à l'usage des armées françaises* (Paris, 1848). His great project, *Encyclopédie de la musique,* was left uncompleted at his death. A monumental biography was publ. by H. Ludwig (real name, H. Ludwig von Jan), *J. G. Kastner, ein elsässischer Tondichter, Theoretiker und Musikforscher* (Leipzig, 1886; 3 vols.).

Kastner, Santiago, musicologist; b. London, Oct. 15, 1908. He studied at Amsterdam, Leipzig, Berlin, Barcelona; settled in Lisbon in 1933; has taught there and at Madrid; has lectured throughout Europe, and has made many appearances as concert pianist and harpsichordist. His writings include *Música hispanica* (Madrid, 1936); *Contribución al estudio de la música española y portuguesa* (Lisbon, 1941); *Federico Mompou* (Madrid, 1947); *Carlos de Seixas* (Coimbra, 1947); *Francisco Correa de Arauxo* (Barcelona, 1948).

Katchen, Julius, American pianist; b. Long Branch, N. J., Aug. 15, 1926. He studied in New York with David Saperton; made his début with the Philadelphia Orch. on Oct. 21, 1937. He studied academic subjects at Haverford College, graduating in 1945. In 1948 he toured Palestine; then settled in Paris; gave a series of successful concerts in Europe.

Kate, André ten, Dutch composer and cellist; b. Amsterdam, May 22, 1796; d. Haarlem, July 27, 1858. He studied cello with Bertelmann. He wrote the operas *Seid e Palmira* (1831) and *Constantia* (1835); also other operas; chamber music; part-songs, etc.

Katims, Milton, American conductor and violist; b. New York, June 24, 1909. He attended Columbia Univ.; studied viola and conducting with L. Barzin. From 1935-43 he was viola player and assistant conductor at WOR; in 1943, joined the N.B.C. Symph. Orch. as 1st violist and subsequently assistant conductor under Toscanini. In 1954 he was appointed conductor and musical director of the Seattle Symph. Orch.

Katwijk (kaht'-vik), **Paul van,** pianist and composer; b. Rotterdam, Dec. 7, 1885. He studied at the Cons. of The Hague; then in Berlin with Klatte and in Vienna with Godowsky; then devoted himself chiefly to conducting and teaching. In 1912 he settled in the U. S.; taught at Drake Univ., Des Moines, Iowa (1914-18) and also conducted the Des Moines Symph. Orch.; in 1919, appointed dean of music at Southern Methodist Univ., Dallas, Texas; resigned in 1949, but continued to teach piano there until 1955. He was conductor of the Dallas Municipal Opera (1922-25) and from 1925 till 1936 conductor of the Dallas Symph. Orch. He composed several symph. works; his orch. suite *Hollandia* was perf. by the Dallas Symph. Orch. on March 15, 1931.

Kauder, Hugo, composer; b. Tobitschau, Moravia, June 9, 1888; studied violin; was a member of the Konzertverein Orch. in Vienna. In 1938 he came to America and settled in New York. His music is contrapuntal, with canonic devices much used in free and often asymmetric rhythm, while the harmonies are conservative. He has written 2 symphs., a cello concerto, and a great number of works for chamber music combinations. He publ. *Entwurf einer neuen Melodie- und Harmonielehre* (Vienna, 1932).

Kauer, Ferdinand, Austrian composer; b. Klein-Tajax (Znaim), Moravia, Jan. 18, 1751; d. Vienna, April 13, 1831. As a boy he played organ in a Jesuit church at Znaim; in 1784 he played violin in a Vienna theater, and also supplied music for a number of plays performed there. He wrote some 100 operettas and other stage works; of these, *Das Donauweibchen* (Vienna, Jan. 11, 1798) was sensationally successful and was performed all over Europe for many years; other works (an oratorio *Die Sündflut,* a quantity of church music, symphonies, concertos, etc.) also enjoyed favor. Most of his MSS were lost in the flood of 1830; a list of extant works is given by Eitner in his *Quellen-Lexikon.* Kauer publ. a *Singschule nach dem neuesten System der Tonkunst* (1790), and a *Kurzgefasste Generalbass-Schule für Anfänger* (1800).—Cf. Th. Haas, *Ferdinand Kauer,* in the 'Neue Musik Zeitung' (1925); K. Manschinger, *Ferdinand Kauer* (Vienna, 1929).

Kauffmann, Emil, German composer and writer on music; son of Ernst Friedrich Kauffmann; b. Ludwigsburg, Nov. 23, 1836; d. Tübingen, June 18, 1909. He studied at the Stuttgart Cons. with Keller, Faiszt, Jung, and Singer; joined the court orch. in 1863 as violinist; teacher in the music school at Basel (1868-77); musical director at Tübingen Univ. (*Dr. phil.,* 1885). He wrote *Die Nacht;* over 60 lieder; male choruses; sonatas and other piano pieces; also the essays *Entwickelung der Tonkunst von der Mitte des 18. Jahrhunderts bis zur Gegenwart* (1884) and *Justinus Heinrich Knecht: ein schwäbischer Tonsetzer* (1892); contributed articles to the Leipzig 'Musikalisches Wochenblatt.'

Kauffmann, Ernst Friedrich, German composer; father of Emil Kauffmann; b. Ludwigsburg, Nov. 27, 1803; d. Stuttgart, Feb. 11, 1856. He was a self-taught pianist; studied at Tübingen Univ. (1825-27). He became principal of the Realschule at Ludwigsburg, but because of his connection with revolutionists he lost his position in 1835; was imprisoned in Asperg (1838-42), where he wrote 6 sets of songs, which became popular.

Kauffmann, Fritz, German composer; b. Berlin, June 17, 1855; d. Magdeburg, Sept. 29, 1934. He was an apothecary; began to study music seriously at 23, with Kiel in Berlin; 3 years later, won the Mendelssohn Prize for composition. After a sojourn in Vienna, he lived mostly in Berlin; in 1889 became choral conductor in Magdeburg; from 1897 till 1920 he conducted the 'Kirchengesangverein' there. He wrote a comic opera, *Die Herzkrankheit;* a symphony; 2 violin concertos; piano concerto; cello concerto; 2 piano sonatas; *Tanz-Improvisationen* for piano; choruses; songs.

Kauffmann, Leo Justinus, Alsatian composer; b. Dammerkirch, Sept. 20, 1901; killed in an air raid, Strasbourg, Sept. 25, 1944. He studied with Marie Joseph Erb in Strasbourg and with Jarnach and Abendroth in Cologne; from 1932-40, was active in radio work in Cologne; then taught at the Strasbourg Cons. (from 1940); appointed director there in 1942. He wrote the opera *Die Geschichte vom schönen Annerl* (Strasbourg, June 20, 1942); a Mass; a symph.; and a *Concertino* for double-bass with chamber orch.

Kaufman, Louis, American violinist; b. Portland, Ore., May 10, 1905. He studied with Kneisel; won the Loeb Prize in 1927, and the Naumburg Award in 1928. In 1950 and nearly annually thereafter, gave concerts in Europe.

Kaufmann, Armin, Rumanian composer; b. Itzkany, Bukovina, Oct. 30, 1902. In 1914 his family settled in Austria. He studied with Joseph Marx at the Vienna Academy; then became a member of the Rothschild String Quartet in Vienna; in 1938 entered the Vienna Symph. Orch. as the first viola player. Kaufmann has written a number of instrumental works, among them a horn concerto and a trumpet concerto; 5 string quartets; piano trio; and a quartet for mandolin, violin, viola, and cello.

Kaufmann, Friedrich, German inventor; b. Dresden, Feb. 5, 1785; d. there, Dec. 1, 1866. He invented a trumpet automaton (1808), the 'Belloneon,' the 'Klaviatur-Harmonichord,' the 'Chordaulodion,' and the 'Symphonion.' In 1851 his son, Friedrich Theodor Kaufmann (b. Dresden, April 9, 1823; d. there, Feb. 5, 1872), evolved the 'Orchestrion' from the 'Symphonion.'

Kaufmann, Harry, American pianist; b. New York, Sept. 6, 1894; studied at the Institute of Musical Art with Stojowski; later a pupil of Josef Hofmann; in 1924 he was appointed teacher of the art of accompanying at the Curtis Institute, Philadelphia. Though principally known as an excellent accompanist, he has also appeared as soloist with the N. Y. Philharmonic, the Philadelphia Orch., etc., and as a member of several chamber music groups.

Kaufmann, Helen, American writer on music; b. New York, Feb. 2, 1882. She studied at Barnard College; was active in various educational organizations. She wrote *From Jehovah to Jazz* (1937); *Home Book of Music Appreciation* (1942); *Story of One Hundred Great Composers* (1943); *Little Book of Music Anecdotes* (1948); *Little Guide to Music Appreciation* (1948); *The Story of Music Through the Ages* (1949); *The Story of Mozart* (1955); etc.

Kaufmann, Walter, conductor and composer; b. Karlsbad, April 1, 1907. He studied in Berlin with Schreker; musicology at the Univ. of Prague. In 1935 he went to India; was director of the Bombay Radio (1935-46); then taught piano at the Halifax Cons., Nova Scotia (1947-48); 1948-57, conductor of the Winnipeg Symph. Orch.; in 1957, joined the staff of Indiana Univ.—Works: the operas *Der Himmel bringt es an den Tag* (1934), *Anasuya,* radio opera (Bombay, Oct. 1, 1938), *Parfait for Irene* (1952), and *Bashmashkin* (after Gogol's *The Coat;* 1952); also 5 symphs. (1930, 1933, 1936, 1939, 1940); *Madras Express,* fantasy for orch. (Boston Pops, June 23, 1948); a piano concerto (1950); *Rubayyat,* for voice and orch. (1951-52); 7 string quartets; 2 piano trios; 2 string trios; piano pieces; songs.

Kaul (kowl), **Oskar,** German musicologist; b. Heufeld, Oct. 11, 1885. He studied music at the Cologne Cons.; then took courses in musicology with Sandberger in Munich; obtained his degree of *Dr. phil* at the Univ. of Munich in 1911. He was in the army during World War I; in 1922, became privat docent in Würzburg; in 1930, prof.; also director of the State Cons. there. He retired in 1945; lived in Unterwössen, Bavaria. He edited 5 symphonies and chamber music by Rosetti for the 'Denkmäler der Tonkunst in Bayern' (vols. 12 and 25) and publ. a dissertation, *Die Vokalwerke Anton Rosettis* (Cologne, 1911); other writings include *Geschichte der Würzburger Hofmusik im 18. Jahrhundert* (Würzburg, 1924); *Athanasius Kircher als Musikgelehrter* (Würzburg, 1932), and many valuable papers on the music history of Bavaria.

Kaun (kown), **Hugo,** German composer; b. Berlin, March 21, 1863; d. there, April 2, 1932. He studied piano with Oskar Raif and composition with Friedrich Kiel in Berlin; composed industriously as a very young man. In 1887 he went to live in America, settling in Milwaukee, where he remained for 14 years (1887-1901); was a successful teacher, and continued to compose. In 1902 he returned to Berlin to teach privately; in 1922, became prof. at the Klindworth-Scharwenka Cons.; publ. an autobiography, *Aus meinem Leben* (Berlin, 1932); also a manual for students, *Harmonielehre und Aufgabenbuch.* A cultured composer, thoroughly versed in the craft, he wrote a great number of works, and enjoyed recognition among large groups of friends; his musical style contained elements of both Brahmsian and Wagnerian idioms.—Works: operas:

Der Pietist (not produced), *Sappho* (Leipzig, Oct. 27, 1917), *Der Fremde* (Dresden, Feb. 23, 1920), and *Menandra* (staged in Kiel and several other German opera houses simultaneously, Oct. 29, 1925); for orch.: 3 symphonies; 2 piano concertos; *Der Sternenbanner,* a festival march on the *Star-Spangled Banner;* overture, *Der Maler von Antwerpen* (Chicago, Feb. 3, 1899); *Im Urwald,* 2 symph. poems, after Longfellow's *Minnehaha* and *Hiawatha* (Chicago, Feb. 7, 1903); etc.; *Auf dem Meere,* for baritone, chorus, and orch.; several settings of Psalms; a Requiem, and other church music; chamber music: octet for wind and string instruments; string quintet; 4 string quartets; piano trio; a violin sonata; numerous piano pieces. —Cf. W. Altmann, *Hugo Kaun* (Leipzig, 1906); G. R. Kruse, *Hugo Kaun,* in 'Die Musik' (1909-10); R. Schaal, *Hugo Kaun, Leben und Werk* (Regensburg, 1946).

Kay, Ulysses Simpson, American Negro composer; b. Tucson, Ariz., Jan. 7, 1917. He attended the Univ. of Arizona (B.M., 1938); then studied with Hanson and Bernard Rogers at the Eastman School of Music, Rochester; also with Hindemith at Yale Univ. He served in the U. S. Navy (1942-45); was at the American Academy in Rome (1949-52) as winner of the Rome Prize and a Fulbright Scholarship; also received a Gershwin Memorial Award (1947), a grant from the National Institute of Arts and Letters, etc. In 1953 he joined the staff of Broadcast Music, Inc., as editorial adviser. Of his works, only *Of New Horizons* (1944) has programmatic connotations; other music is in a terse neo-Classical vein: oboe concerto (Rochester, April 16, 1940); *5 Mosaics* for chamber orch. (Cleveland, Dec. 28, 1940); ballet, *Dance Calinda* (Rochester, April 23, 1941); *Of New Horizons,* overture (Lewisohn Stadium, N. Y., July 29, 1944); *A Short Overture* (N. Y., March 31, 1947); *Suite for Strings* (Baltimore, April 8, 1949); *Sinfonia in E* (Rochester, May 2, 1951); *6 Dances* for strings (1954); concerto for orch. (N. Y., Feb. 1954); *Song of Jeremiah,* cantata (Nashville, April 23, 1954); *Serenade* for orch. (Louisville, Sept. 18, 1954); *3 Pieces After Blake,* for soprano and orch. (N. Y., March 27, 1955); 2 string quartets (1953; 1956); quintet for flute and strings (1947); piano quintet (1949); piano sonata (1940); 2 one-act operas: *The Boor,* after Chekhov (1955) and *The Juggler of Our Lady* (1956); film score for *The Quiet One* (1948); choral works; songs.—Cf. N. Slonimsky, *Ulysses Kay,* in the 'Bulletin' of the American Composers Alliance (Fall, 1957).

Kayser, Heinrich Ernst, German violinist; b. Altona, April 16, 1815; d. Hamburg, Jan. 17, 1888. He was engaged as theater violinist in Hamburg (1840-57); then became a violin teacher there; wrote numerous violin studies that became standard exercises, and a violin method.

Kayser, Leif, Danish composer; b. Copenhagen, June 13, 1919. He studied at the Copenhagen Cons., and later with H. Rosenberg in Stockholm; was organist in Stockholm churches and studied theology. His works include 2 symphonies (1938, 1939); *Christmas Oratorio* (1943-47); organ and piano pieces; choruses.

Kayser, Philipp Christoph, German composer and pianist; b. Frankfurt, March 10, 1755; d. Zürich, Dec. 23, 1823. Both as pianist and composer he did not rise above mediocrity. In 1755 he settled in Zürich as a teacher. From Goethe's correspondence with him it appears that he wrote music to several of Goethe's singspiele, but only one, *Scherz, Liszt und Rache,* is preserved, in MS. He publ. a *Weihnachtskantate; Deux Sonates en symphonie,* for piano and 2 horns; and songs. —Cf. C. A. Burkhardt, *Goethe und der Komponist Philipp Christoph Kayser* (Leipzig, 1879); E. Refardt, 'Hist.-biogr. Mus.-Lexikon der Schweiz' (1928).

Kazanly, Nikolai Ivanovitch, Russian composer; b. Tiraspol, Dec. 17, 1869; d. St. Petersburg, Aug. 5, 1916. He was a pupil at the Odessa Music School (1879-83); then entered the St. Petersburg Cons. and studied with Rimsky-Korsakov (1891-94); also took some lessons from Balakirev. In 1897 he went to Germany; in 1899, conducted the German première of Glinka's opera, *Russlan and Ludmila,* in Munich; from 1897-1904 he conducted several concerts of Russian music with the Kaim Orch. there; contributed to Russian and German music journals; was a member of the commission for the improvement of Russian military music. —Works: opera, *Miranda* (St. Petersburg, 1910); a symphony: *Russalka,* for orch. and voices (Munich, 1897); *Leonore,* for orch. and voices; *The Villa by the Sea,* symph. fantasy, after Böcklin; *La Nuit du Carnaval,* for orch.; *Le Loup dans le chenil,* cantata for chorus and orch.; choruses and songs. Under the general title

'Philharmonica' he publ. over 100 classic pieces in arrangement for small orchestra.

Kazasoglou, George, Greek composer; b. Athens, Dec. 13, 1910. He studied with Kalomiris and Varvoglis; has written several ballets on subjects from Greek mythology, and incidental music for plays by Sophocles, Euripides, Shakespeare, and Ibsen. His wartime experience inspired a symphonic work *Upon Return from the Front* (1941); he has also written a symphony (1946) and many piano pieces.

Kazatchenko, Grigory Alexeyevitch, Russian composer; b. St. Petersburg, May 3, 1858; d. there, after 1924. He studied with Rimsky-Korsakov; appointed chorusmaster of the Imperial Opera; in 1898 was one of the conductors of the Russian concerts in Paris. In 1924 he became prof. of choral singing at the Leningrad Cons. He wrote 2 operas, *Prince Serebryanny* (St. Petersburg, 1892) and *Pan Sotnik* (St. Petersburg, Sept. 17, 1902); a symph.; 2 *Oriental Suites;* a fantasia on Russian themes for viola and orch.; a cantata, *Russalka;* a *Hymn to Pushkin;* etc.

Kazuro, Stanislaw, Polish composer; b. Teklinapol, near Wilno, Aug. 2, 1881. He studied in Warsaw, Paris, and Rome; after his return to Warsaw he was active mainly as a pedagogue and chorus conductor; he also published several school manuals. His compositions, in an academic style, were chiefly designed for pedagogic purposes; among them are 2 folk operas, several choral works, albums of pieces for piano, etc.

Kazynski, Wiktor, Polish composer; b. Wilno, Dec. 30, 1812; d. St. Petersburg, 1867. He studied in Warsaw with Chopin's teacher Elsner; produced an opera, *Fenella,* there (1840) to a Polish libretto, and another Polish opera, *Zyd tulacz* (*The Wandering Jew*) in Wilno (1840). About 1843 Kazynski moved to St. Petersburg; in 1845 he went to Germany with Lvov, the court composer, and published his *Notes on a Musical Journey in Germany.* In 1845 he became conductor at a theater in St. Petersburg; wrote an opera to a Russian text, *Man and Wife* (1848), which he produced; also wrote incidental music to numerous plays performed at the theater at which he was employed. He publ. a *History of Italian Opera* (St. Petersburg, 1851; in Russian); also songs, in 5 vols. (St. Petersburg, 1855). He was a good pianist, and one of the first performers of Chopin's music in Russia, although he rarely appeared professionally in concerts.

Kéfer, Paul, French cellist; b. Rouen, Dec. 30, 1875; d. Rochester, N. Y., May 22, 1941. He studied cello at the Paris Cons. with Delsart; won first prize in 1900. After coming to the U. S. in 1913, he formed, in N. Y., the 'Trio de Lutèce' with Barrère (flute) and Salzedo (harp); was also founder and a member of the Franco-American Quartet. In 1923 he became prof. of cello at the Eastman School of Music in Rochester; was first cellist of the Rochester Philharmonic Orch. (until 1935).

Keil, Alfredo, Portuguese composer; b. Lisbon, July 3, 1850; d. Hamburg, Oct. 4, 1907. He was of German extraction, and received his education in Germany. Returning to Portugal, he devoted his energies to the furtherance of national music, and was the first to produce an opera on a Portuguese subject in the Portuguese language. His song *A Portuguesa* (1890) was adopted as the national anthem of the Republic of Portugal in 1910.—Works: the operas, *Donna Bianca* (Lisbon, March 10, 1888), *Irene* (Turin, March 22, 1893), *Serrana* (the first grand opera in Portuguese; Lisbon, March 13, 1899); 2 symph. sketches, *India* and *Simao;* songs. —Cf. Lavignac's *Encyclopédie de la Musique* (vol. 4, p. 2453).

Keilberth, Joseph, German conductor; b. Karlsruhe, April 19, 1908. A member of a musical family, he was a conductor at the Karlsruhe State Opera (1935-40), of the Berlin Philharmonic Orch. (1940-45), at the Dresden Opera (1945-51); also guest conductor at the Berlin State Opera and in Hamburg. He founded the Philharmonic Orch. in Bamberg, and in 1951 toured with it in Switzerland, Holland, France, Spain, and Portugal. In 1953 he conducted the Wagner Festival in Bayreuth; in 1954, toured with the Bamberg Philharmonic Orch. in Cuba and Mexico; U. S. début at Carnegie Hall, April 4, 1954.

Keiser, Reinhard, notable German composer of opera; b. Teuchern, near Weissenfels, Jan. 9, 1674; d. Hamburg, Sept. 12, 1739. He studied with his father Gottfried Keiser, an organist; he was then sent to Leipzig, where he studied at the Thomasschule with Johann Schelle. In 1692 he was in Brunswick, where the success of his pastoral, *Ismene,* encouraged him to try his hand at a serious opera, *Basilius* (1693).

He went to Hamburg (1696), which then possessed the best operatic stage in Germany, and remained there. During his long years of unremitting labors in Hamburg, he wrote no fewer than 126 operas and other stage works. *Mahmuth II* (Hamburg, 1696) was the first, and *Circe* (Hamburg, March 1, 1734) was the last. He was the first German to employ popular subjects in opera; he also made use of his native language (instead of Italian) for his librettos; his productions frankly aimed to please, but at least they were original works, not mere copies of Italian models. Among his more popular operas in German were *Störtebecker und Goedje Michel* (Hamburg, 1701), *Die Leipziger Messe* (1710), *Der Hamburger Jahrmarkt* (Hamburg, 1725), and *Die Hamburger Schlachtzeit* (1725). In his grasp of dramatic expression, in the facility of his melodic invention, and in the mastery of his orchestration, he was easily the foremost composer of German opera of the day. Furthermore, he was proficient in administrative affairs; in 1703 he became director and manager of the Hamburg Opera, and brought it to a high degree of excellence. In 1709 he married into a wealthy family, which contributed further to the security of his social status in Hamburg. In 1717 he was in Copenhagen, which he revisited in 1722-24; produced several of his operas there; was given an honorary appointment as conductor to the King. Returning to Hamburg in 1724, he continued to write for the Hamburg Opera; in 1728 he was appointed canon and cantor at the Hamburg 'Katharinenkirche.' He also wrote many sacred works (oratorios, cantatas, motets, psalms, Passions, etc.) of which a number were publ.: *R. Keisers Gemüths-Ergötzung, bestehend in einigen Sing-Gedichten, mit einer Stimme und unterschiedlichen Instrumenten* (1698); *Divertimenti serenissimi* (duets and airs with harpsichord; 1713); *Musikalische Landlust* (cantatas with continuo for harpsichord; 1714); *Kaiserliche Friedenspost* (songs and duets with harpsichord; 1715); a *Weihnachts-Cantate*, etc. The opera *Jodelet* was ed. by F. Zelle in 'Publikationen der Gesellschaft für Musikforschung' (vols. 20-22); *Octavia* was ed. by F. Chrysander as a supplement to the Handel *Gesamtausgabe* (1902); the opera *Crösus* and selected numbers from *L'Inganno fedele* were publ. by Schneider in 'Denkmäler deutscher Tonkunst' (vols. 37 and 38). — Cf. E. O. Lindner, *Die erste stehende deutsche Oper* (Leipzig, 1855); F. A. Voigt, *Reinhard Keiser*, in 'Vierteljahrsschrift für Musikwissenschaft' (1890); Hugo Leichtentritt, *Reinhard Keiser in seinen Opern* (Berlin, 1901); R. Petzoldt, *Die Kirchenkompositionen und weltlichen Kantaten Reinhard Keisers* (Berlin, 1934). For details regarding the productions of Keiser's operas, see A. Loewenberg's *Annals of Opera* (1943; new ed., 1955).

Kelbe, Theodore, German conductor; b. Brunswick, Oct. 6, 1862; d. Milwaukee, Oct. 12, 1922. He studied violin in his native town; from 1879-82, was a member of the court orch. there; in 1882, joined the opera orch. in Cologne. In 1901 he came to America as concertmaster of the Milwaukee Symph. Orch.; in 1904, became conductor of the 'Sängerbund des Nordwestens' there; was in charge of its festivals in Milwaukee (1904), St. Paul (1906), Omaha (1910), St. Paul (1912), and Kansas City (1917).

Kelberine, Alexander, pianist; b. Kiev, Feb. 22, 1903; d. New York, Jan. 30, 1940. He studied at the Kiev Cons.; then at the Univ. of Vienna; took lessons from Busoni in Berlin; in 1923, came to America and studied at the Juilliard Graduate School, N. Y., with Siloti (piano) and Rubin Goldmark (composition); later also studied with Ernst Toch. He was head of the piano dept. of the Philadelphia Cons., of the Sternberg School of Music, and of the Zecker-Hahn Musical Academy in Philadelphia; appeared in recitals throughout the U. S.; publ. many piano compositions and arrangements.

Keldorfer, Robert, Austrian composer and conductor; son of Victor Keldorfer; b. Vienna, Aug. 10, 1901. He studied with his father; then at the Musical Academy in Vienna with Carl Prohaska and Max Springer. He occupied various posts as organist and choral conductor while studying; upon graduation in 1930 he went to Linz, where he became director of the Bruckner Cons.; in 1941, was appointed director of the District Cons. in Klagenfurt. He has written an opera, *Verena* (Klagenfurt, 1951), a great number of choral works, a cantata *Auferstehung*, church music, lieder, etc. His music is influenced by Richard Strauss.

Keldorfer, Victor, Austrian conductor and composer; father of Robert Keldorfer; b. Salzburg, April 14, 1873. He was a student at the Mozarteum in Salzburg; then conducted choruses in Vienna; in 1922, became director of the Vienna 'Schubertbund' and conductor of the 'Ostdeutscher Sängerbund,' which became a model for many Austrian male choruses. He publ. 150 opus numbers up to 1954: a *Missa solemnis,* 2 vols. of *Lieder für grosse und kleine Kinder,* many men's choruses, and arrangements of Strauss waltzes for men's chorus and orch. He also edited a complete collection of Schubert's men's choruses. After retiring from active work, he settled in Salzburg.

Kelemen, Milko, Croatian composer; b. Podravska Slatina, March 30, 1924. He studied composition at the Zagreb Cons. with Šulek. He has written a symphony, several orchestral works, and piano pieces. Kelemen represents the new school of Yugoslav composers, striving to establish a style ultimately derived from native folk music, but cast in classical forms.

Kéler-Béla (real name Albert von Keler), Hungarian violinist, band conductor, and composer of light music; b. Bartfeld, Feb. 13, 1820; d. Wiesbaden, Nov. 20, 1882. He was a law student; then became a farmer; finally took up music in 1845, studying under Sechter and Schlesinger in Vienna, and playing the violin at the Theater-an-der-Wien, where he developed his specialty, the composition of dance music. In 1854 he went to Berlin for a time to conduct the Gungl orch.; the following year he succeeded Lanner as the conductor of his band in Vienna. From 1856-63 he conducted an army band; then the Spa Orch. at Wiesbaden, resigning in 1873 owing to ill health. He wrote a great number of dances and other light pieces, some of which attained enormous popularity, such as the waltz *Hoffnungssterne,* the galop *Hurrah-Sturm,* and particularly his *Lustspiel Ouverture.* —Cf. Z. Sztehlo, *Kéler-Béla* (Budapest, 1930).

Kell, Reginald, English clarinet virtuoso; b. York, June 8, 1906. He studied with Haydn Draper at the Royal Academy of Music in London; in 1932, was engaged as 1st clarinetist in the London Philharmonic Orch.; also 1st clarinetist with the London Symph. Orch. (from 1937); from 1935-48 taught clarinet at the Royal Academy of Music, as successor to his teacher Draper. In 1948 he went to America; settled in New York. —Cf. R. Gelatt, *Music Makers* (N. Y., 1953; pp. 189-94).

Keller, Gottfried (called **Godfrey**), German harpsichord teacher in London, who was active late in the 17th century. He publ. *A Complete Method for Attaining to Play a Thorough-bass upon either Organ, Harpsichord, or Theorbo-lute* (1707; posthumous; reprinted in W. Holder's *Treatise on Harmony,* London, 1731); 6 suites for 2 violins, trumpet or oboe, viola, and continuo and 6 suites for 2 flutes with continuo.

Keller, Harrison, American music educator; b. Delphos, Kansas, Oct. 8, 1888. He studied violin at Bethany College, Lindsborg, Kansas (B. M., 1907; honorary D. M., 1954); then in Germany, at Stern's Cons., Berlin (1907-11); in Prague, with Anton Witek (1912), and in St. Petersburg, Russia, with Leopold Auer (1913-14). He served in the U. S. Army in World War I; received the French Legion of Honor. Returning to the U. S., he organized a string quartet in Boston; was head of the string dept. at the New England Cons. (1922-46); then became its director (1947-52) and president (1952-58).

Keller, Hermann, German organist and musicologist; b. Stuttgart, Nov. 20, 1885; studied with Max Reger (composition), Straube (organ), and Teichmüller (piano). He filled various posts as organist in Weimar, Stuttgart, etc.; from 1920 till 1950 taught at the Württemberg Hochschule für Musik. —Publications: *Reger und die Orgel* (1923); *Schule des Generalbassspiels* (1931); *Schule der Choralimprovisation* (1939); *Die Kunst des Orgelspiels* (1941); *Bachs Orgelwerke* (1948); *Bachs Klavierwerke* (1950); edited organ works by Bach, Frescobaldi, etc.

Keller, Karl, German composer and flutist; b. Dessau, Oct. 16, 1784; d. Schaffhausen, July 19, 1855. His father was a court organist and chamber musician. Keller was a flute virtuoso; he was court musician at Berlin (until 1806), Kassel (until 1814), Stuttgart (until 1816), and Donaueschingen (1817), where he later became chorusmaster. He married the opera singer Wilhelmine Meierhofer. In 1849 he received a pension and retired to Switzerland. He wrote 3 flute concertos; 4 polonaises with orch.; 2 divertissements with orch.; 6 part-songs for male chorus; duos and solos for flute; and songs.

Keller, Matthias, violinist and composer; b. Ulm, Germany, March 20, 1813; d. Boston, Oct. 12, 1875. He studied music in Stuttgart and Vienna; at 16 became first violinist of the Royal Chapel in Vienna (for 5 years); then bandmaster in the army (for 7 years); in 1846, came to

America and played in theater orchestras in Philadelphia; became interested in violin making and founded 'Keller's Patent Steam Violin Manufactory' (1857). He then went to New York and won a $500 prize for his *American Hymn* (*Speed our republic, O Father on high*), for which he wrote both words and music; composed over 100 songs, including some patriotic songs for the Civil War; also a *Ravel Polka* (1846); publ. *A Collection of Poems* (1874).—Cf. F. J. Metcalf, *American Writers and Compilers of Sacred Music* (1925); 'Dictionary of American Biography' (1933).

Keller, Max, Bavarian composer and organist; b. Trostberg, Oct. 7, 1770; d. Altötting, Dec. 16, 1855. He was organist at Altötting; publ. 6 Latin Masses; 6 German Masses; other sacred works and organ music.

Keller, Otto, Austrian writer on music; b. Vienna, June 5, 1861; d. Salzburg, Oct. 25, 1928. He was obliged to take up a career in the civil service, but at the same time studied music history with Hanslick and theory with Bruckner; 1906, retired and devoted himself to writing; publ. biographies of Beethoven (1885), Goldmark (1900), von Suppé (1905), Tchaikovsky (1914), and Mozart (2 vols., 1926-27); also an illustrated history of music (5th ed., 1926) and *Die Operette* (1926). From 1876 he compiled a valuable collection of contemporary source material relating to music and the theater.

Keller, Walter, American organist; b. Chicago, Feb. 23, 1873; d. there, July 7, 1940. He studied at the American Cons. of Music in Chicago (1891-94) and at the Leipzig Cons. (1894-96). Returning to America, he occupied various teaching posts; also was church organist in Chicago from 1903. He wrote a comic opera, *The Crumpled Isle;* a melodrama, *Alaric's Death;* and a *Synchronous Prelude and Fugue* for orch. (Chicago, 1924); also a number of works for organ; sacred choruses; songs.

Kellermann, Christian, Danish cellist; b. Randers, Jutland, Jan. 27, 1815; d. Copenhagen, Dec. 3, 1866. He studied with Merk in Vienna; made many concert tours; in 1847, was appointed soloist in the royal orch. at Copenhagen. He publ. solos for cello.

Kelley, Edgar Stillman, American composer and writer; b. Sparta, Wis., April 14, 1857; d. New York, Nov. 12, 1944. He studied first with F. W. Merriam (1870-74), then with Clarence Eddy and N. Ledochowsky in Chicago (1874-76). In 1876 he went to Germany, where he took courses at the Stuttgart Cons. (until 1880) with Seifritz (composition), Krüger and Speidel (piano), and Friedrich Finck (organ). Returning to the U. S., he served as organist in Oakland and San Francisco; conducted performances of light opera companies in New York; taught piano and theory in various schools and in the N. Y. College of Music (1891-92); was music critic for the San Francisco 'Examiner' (1893-95); lecturer on music for the University Extension of the Univ. of N. Y. (1896-97); then acting prof. at Yale Univ. (1901-02). In 1902 he went to Berlin, where he taught piano and theory (until 1910). In 1910 he was appointed dean of the dept. of composition at the Cincinnati Cons., retaining this post until his death, at the same time holding a fellowship in composition at Western College, Oxford, Ohio; honorary Litt. D., Miami Univ. (1916); honorary LL.D., Univ. of Cincinnati (1917). He contributed articles to various music journals; also publ. correspondence from Germany during his stay there. With his wife, Jessie Stillman Kelley (q.v.), he organized the Kelley Stillman Publishing Co., which publ. several of his scores. Although his stage works and his symphonic pieces were quite successful when first performed (some critics described him as a natural successor to MacDowell in American creative work), little of his music survived the test of time. —Works: *Theme and Variations* for string quartet (c. 1880); *Wedding Ode,* for tenor solo, men's chorus, and orch. (c. 1882); incidental music to *Macbeth,* for orch. and chorus (San Francisco, Feb. 12, 1885); comic opera *Puritania* (Boston, June 9, 1892; 100 consecutive performances; publ. in vocal score); *Aladdin,* Chinese suite for orch. (San Francisco, April, 1894); incidental music to *Ben Hur,* for soli, chorus, and orch. (N. Y., Oct. 1, 1900; highly successful, used for performances of that popular play some 6000 times up to 1918); music to Fernald's play, *The Cat and the Cherub* (N. Y., June 15, 1901); *Alice in Wonderland,* suite for orch. (Norfolk, Conn., Festival, June 5, 1919; composer conducting; also perf. as a pantomime, Chicago, 1921, and with children's chorus, 1925); 1st symph., *Gulliver* (begun c. 1900; completed in 1936; Cincinnati, April 9, 1937); 2nd symph., *New England* (Norfolk, Conn., Festival, June 3, 1913; composer conducting); *The Pilgrim's Pro-*

gress, a musical miracle play for soli, chorus, children's chorus, organ, and orch. (Cincinnati May Festival, May 10, 1918); *A California Idyll,* for orch. (N. Y., Nov. 14, 1918); *The Pit and the Pendulum,* symph. suite, after Poe (1925); *Israfel* and *Eldorado,* for voice and orch.; piano quintet; 2 piano quartets; many choral works, of which the best known are *My Captain,* after Whitman, and *The Sleeper,* after Poe; 3 pieces for piano: *The Flower Seekers, Confluentia* (also arranged for string orch., 1913), *The Headless Horseman;* a song, *The Lady Picking Mulberries* (1888); song cycle *Phases of Love* (1890). He also publ. *Chopin the Composer* (N. Y., 1913); *Musical Instruments* (Boston, 1925).

Kelley, Jessie Stillman (Mrs. Edgar S. Kelley), American piano pedagogue; b. Chippewa Falls, Wis., 1866; d. Dallas, April 3, 1949. She studied piano with William Mason and theory with Edgar Stillman Kelley (whom she later married); L.H.D., Western College, Oxford, Ohio; Litt. D., Miami Univ.; for many years, taught piano in San Francisco, New York, and Berlin; 1910-34, director of music, Western College; was active in music clubs.

Kellie, Lawrence, English tenor and song composer; b. London, April 3, 1862; d. there, Aug. 20, 1932. He was apprenticed to a solicitor; began to study music in 1884 at the Royal Academy of Music; appeared in a minor operatic role at Covent Garden in 1886; made his American début in a vocal recital in New York (May 23, 1887). His songs have had a great vogue; among them, the most popular were *Is it too late? Sleeping Tide, All for thee, This heart of mine,* and *Douglas Gordon.*

Kellner, Ernst August, English pianist and singer; b. Windsor, Jan. 26, 1792; d. London, July 18, 1839. He began to study piano at the age of 2; at 5 he played a Handel concerto before the court; also studied voice in England with W. Parsons, and in Italy with Nozzari, Casella, and Crescentini in Naples in 1815. Returning to England in 1820, he won acclaim as pianist and baritone; sang in Venice (1824); sang and played in St. Petersburg (1828) and Paris (1833); in 1834, became organist at the Bavarian Chapel in London. —Cf. a biographical sketch by Richard Cull, *Case of Precocious Musical Talent,* publ. in London (1839).

Kellogg, Clara Louise, American soprano; b. Sumterville, S. C., July 12, 1842; d. New Hartford, Conn., May 13, 1916. She received her vocal training in New York, from Manzocchi, Errani, and Muzio; made her professional début at the Academy of Music, N. Y. (Feb. 27, 1861); then sang in Boston. She sang Marguerite in the N. Y. première of *Faust* (Nov. 25, 1863); made her London début as Marguerite on Nov. 2, 1867. In 1872 she organized an opera company with Pauline Lucca, but the rivalry between them precluded its success. In 1873 she launched an opera enterprise of her own, known as the English Opera Co.; she extended her supervision to the translations of the librettos, the stage settings, and the training of the soloists and chorus. She herself sang 125 performances in the winter of 1874-75. After that, she divided her time between Europe and America. In 1887 she married her manager, Karl Strakosch, nephew of Maurice and Max Strakosch, and retired from the stage. She wrote *Memoirs of an American Prima Donna* (N. Y., 1913).

Kelly, Michael, Irish singer and composer; b. Dublin, Dec. 25, 1762; d. Margate, Oct. 9, 1826. He studied singing under Rauzzini, and in Naples (1779) under Fenaroli and Aprile. He then sang in Palermo, Leghorn, Florence, Bologna, and Venice. Visiting Vienna, he was engaged at the court opera for 4 years, becoming the friend of Mozart, and taking the role of Basilio in the production of *Figaro.* In 1787 he appeared for the first time at Drury Lane, and sang leading tenor roles there until his retirement. In 1789 his début as composer was made with *False Appearances* and *Fashionable Friends;* up to 1820 he wrote the music for 62 stage pieces, also many songs. He had a music shop from 1802-11; when it failed, he went into the wine trade; it was Sheridan who said, considering the quality of his music and wines, that he was "a composer of wines and an importer of music." His *Reminiscences,* publ. in the year of his death (1826), were written by Theodore Hook from material supplied by him; the volume is replete with amusing musical anecdotes.

Kelly, Robert, American composer; b. Clarksburg, West Va., Sept. 26, 1916. He studied composition with Scalero at the Curtis Institute, and violin with Samuel Gardner. After service in the U. S. Army (1942-43), he joined the faculty of the Univ. of Illinois at Urbana. He wrote *Adirondack Suite,* for orch. (1941); *A Miniature Symphony* (Austin, Texas, Oct. 15, 1950); *Chorale and Fugue for Antiphonal Brass Choirs and Timpani* (1951); *Passacag-*

lia and Fugue for woodwind quintet; sonata for 2 violins; sonata for trombone and piano; choruses; songs.

Kemmer, George, American organist; b. New York, Oct. 11, 1890. From 1923-45 he was organist at St. George's Episcopal Church in New York. He wrote several cantatas, other choral works, and organ pieces (many of them published).

Kemp, Barbara, German dramatic soprano; b. Kochem, 1886. She sang in opera in Rostock and Breslau before being engaged as a member of the Berlin State Opera in 1914. She married the composer Max von Schillings in 1923; in the same year (March 1) she sang the title role in his opera *Mona Lisa* at the Metropolitan Opera, N. Y. She returned to Germany; sang Wagnerian roles at Bayreuth; continued on the roster of the Berlin State Opera until 1932, when she retired. —Cf. Oscar Bie, *Barbara Kemp* (Berlin, 1921).

Kemp, Joseph, English composer and pedagogue; b. Exeter, 1778; d. London, May 22, 1824. He studied organ with W. Jackson; organist of Bristol cathedral (1802); Mus. Bac. from Cambridge (1808), Mus. Doc. (1809); then taught in London. As one of the earliest promoters of music instruction by classes, he publ. a pamphlet on a *New System of Musical Education* (1819). He composed *The Jubilee*, an 'occasional piece' (1809); *The Siege of Isca*, a melodrama (1810); *Musical Illustrations of the Beauties of Shakespeare; Musical Illustrations of The Lady of the Lake;* psalms; anthems, songs, etc.

Kemp, Robert, better known as 'Father Kemp,' the originator and conductor of the 'Old Folks' Concerts,' commencing in 1854; b. Wellfleet, Mass., June 6, 1820; d. Boston, May 14, 1897. His book, *Father Kemp and His Old Folks, etc.* (Boston, 1868) contains his autobiography. His regular business was that of a shoe dealer.

Kempe, Rudolf, German conductor; b. Niederpoyritz, near Dresden, June 14, 1910. He studied oboe, and became first oboist in the Gewandhaus Orch. at Leipzig in 1929. In 1936 he began to conduct various German orchestras; was musical director of the Dresden State Orch. (1949-52) and later of the Munich State Opera (1952-54). He then conducted opera in Berlin, Vienna, Salzburg, London, Barcelona, and at the Metropolitan Opera, N. Y.; made a tour in Australia and South America. —Cf. H. Jäckel and G. Schmiedel, *Bildnis des schaffenden Künstlers: ein Dirigent bei der Arbeit* (Leipzig, 1955).

Kempff, Wilhelm, German pianist and composer; b. Jüterbog, Nov. 25, 1895. He studied piano with his father, also named Wilhelm Kempff; composition with Robert Kahn in Berlin. He made several tours in Germany and Scandinavia as pianist, also featuring improvisation as part of his programs. From 1924-30 he taught at the Hochschule in Stuttgart; then lived in Potsdam; in 1944 he moved to Thurnau, near Kulmbach; in 1955, settled in Ammerland (Starnberger See). After the end of World War II, he toured all over the world; made many recordings of classical works, which assured him a wide following at his concerts; he is particularly appreciated as one of the best interpreters of Beethoven's sonatas. He has written several symphonies; a piano concerto; a violin concerto; *Arkadische Suite* for orch. (1939); *Deutsches Schicksal,* dramatic cantata (1937); the short operas *König Midas, Die Familie Gozzi, Die Fasnacht von Rottweil;* ballets; several string quartets; many pieces for piano and for organ. He publ. his autobiography, *Unter dem Zimbelstern* (1951). —Cf. B. Gavoty and Roger Hauert, *Wilhelm Kempff,* in the series 'Les grands interprètes' (Geneva, 1954).

Kempter, Karl, German organist and composer; b. Limbach, Jan. 17, 1819; d. Augsburg, March 11, 1871. He was choirmaster at Augsburg cathedral. He wrote 4 oratorios, numerous Masses and graduals; also publ. *Der Landchorregent,* a collection for use in small churches.

Kendall, Raymond, American musicologist; b. Pasadena, Calif., March 21, 1910. He studied at Occidental College (B.A., 1932), Stanford Univ. (M.A., 1937), Eastman School of Music (1937), Univ. of Basel, Switzerland (1938-39), and Cornell Univ. (Ph.D., 1940). He taught music at Stanford Univ. (1934-38) and at Dartmouth College (1940-43). In 1945 he joined the faculty of the Univ. of Michigan; director of the Graduate Division, School of Music there (1946-48); in 1948, appointed dean of the School of Music, Univ. of Southern California. In 1951 he was elected vice-president of the National Association of Schools of Music. He has contributed to the 'Mus. Quarterly' and other musical periodicals.

Kenessey, Jenö, Hungarian composer; b. Budapest, Sept. 23, 1906. He studied with Lajtha and Siklós in Budapest, and in Salzburg with Franz Schalk; was appointed conductor at the Budapest Opera in 1934. He conducted his opera *Gold and the Woman* there on May 8, 1943, and his ballet *Majalis* on Nov. 29, 1948; has written several other stage works and a number of orchestral overtures and suites inspired by Hungarian folk melodies; also chamber music and songs.

Kennan, Kent Wheeler, American composer; b. Milwaukee, Wis., April 18, 1913. He studied piano and organ before entering college; attended the Univ. of Michigan (1930-32); subsequently held a partial scholarship in composition at the Eastman School of Music in Rochester (Mus. B., 1934); went to Europe in 1935; taught at the Eastman School and received his M.M. there in 1936; won the Prix de Rome (1936); spent 3 years in Europe, studying for a time at the Royal Academy of St. Cecilia, Rome, with Pizzetti; in 1939, became a member of the faculty at Kent State Univ., Kent, Ohio; from 1942-46, served in the Pacific as band leader in the U. S. Army; 1957, teaching at the Univ. of Texas. — Works: a symphony (1939); *Nocturne,* for viola and orch.; *Il Campo di Fiori,* for trumpet and orch.; *Promenade,* for orch. (1938); *Night Soliloquy,* for flute and orch. (1938; N.B.C. Symph. Orch., Feb. 26, 1943; Toscanini conducting); *Andante* for oboe and small orch. (Philadelphia, March 7, 1947); *Concertino* for piano and orch. (1947); etc.

Kennedy-Fraser, Marjory, Scottish singer, pianist, and folksong collector; b. Perth, Oct. 1, 1857; d. Edinburgh, Nov. 21, 1930. She was the daughter of the famous Scottish singer David Kennedy (1825-1886) and traveled with him as his accompanist from the age of 12. She then studied with Mathilde Marchesi in Paris; also took courses in piano with Matthay and in music history with Niecks. Inspired by the example of her father, she became a dedicated collector of folksongs. In 1905 she went to the Outer Hebridean Isles, after which she made a specialty of research in Celtic music, including the adaptation and arranging of Gaelic folk material into art forms; publ. the famous collection *Songs of the Hebrides* with texts in Gaelic and English, in 3 vols. (1909, 1917, 1921); also wrote a *Hebridean Suite* for cello and piano; several collections of folk music for schools, piano pieces based on Hebridean folksongs, etc. She also publ. the important handbook *Hebridean Song and the Laws of Interpretation* (Glasgow, 1922); a similar volume for Lowland Scots songs; also an autobiography, *A Life of Song* (London, 1928); wrote the libretto for Bantock's opera *The Seal Woman.* She was married to A. J. Fraser, a school teacher in Glasgow.

Kent, James, English organist and composer; b. Winchester, March 13, 1700; d. there, May 6, 1776. He was chorister in Winchester cathedral and in the Chapel Royal; organist of Trinity College, Cambridge (1731-37), then of Winchester cathedral (1737-74). He wrote 2 services; also *Kent's Anthems* (2nd ed., 2 vols.; London, 1844).

Kentner, Louis, Hungarian pianist; b. Karvin, July 19, 1905. He studied piano with Arnold Szekely and composition with Kodály. As a youth he gave a series of concerts in Budapest, performing all of Beethoven's sonatas. In 1935 he settled in England; toured India with Yehudi Menuhin in 1954; made his American début in N. Y., Nov. 28, 1956.

Kenton, Egon F. (real name Kornstein), violist and musicologist; b. Nagyszalonta, Hungary, May 22, 1891. He studied with Hubay at the Budapest Academy of Music, graduating in 1911; joined the Hungarian String Quartet as violist; toured Europe with it, taking part in the first performances of the first and second quartets of Bartók and Kodály; appeared in sonata recitals with Ricardo Viñes in Budapest, Vienna, and Prague; studied musicology at the Univ. of Berlin; emigrated to the U. S. in 1923; played chamber music concerts at the Coolidge Festivals in Pittsfield and at the New School for Social Research; received his M.A. in musicology from N. Y. Univ. in 1947; then turned to teaching music history; was on the staff of Iowa Univ., Peabody College in Nashville, and (1957) at the Univ. of Connecticut. He has publ. articles and reviews in the 'Mus. Quarterly,' 'Notes,' 'Acta Musicologica,' etc.

Kepler, Johannes, the illustrious German astronomer; b. Weil, Württemberg, Dec. 27, 1571; d. Regensburg, Nov. 15, 1630; he elucidates the details of musical science, from a philosophical standpoint, in Books 3 and 5 of his *Harmonices mundi.*

Kerle, Jacobus de, Flemish organist and composer; b. Ypres, 1531/32; d. Prague, Jan. 7, 1591. In 1555 he was church organist at Orvieto, then at the court of Cardinal Otto Truchsess in Augsburg, Rome (1562), and Dillingen, Bavaria (1564); in 1565, returned to Ypres, then went to Rome again, and from 1568, was in Augsburg; from March 1579, was in Cambrai; 1582, in the service of the Elector Gebhard Truchsess of Waldburg in Cologne, and from Sept., 1582, chaplain at the Imperial Court in Prague under Rudolph II. He exerted a considerable influence on the musical culture of his time. —Works: *Preces speciales pro salubri generalis concilii sucessu,* for the Council of Trent (Venice, 1562); Masses (Venice, 1562; Munich, 1572, with the *Cantio de sacro foedere contra Turcas);* also hymns, psalms, madrigals, and various works in MS. The *Preces* were republ. by O. Ursprung in the 'Denkmäler der Tonkunst in Bayern,' vol. 26 (1926), together with a list of Kerle's publ. works, extant MSS, reprints, etc. —Cf. O. Ursprung, *Jacobus de Kerle* (Munich, 1913).

Kerll (or **Kerl, Kherl, Cherl**), **Johann Caspar,** German organist and composer; b. Adorf, Saxony, April 9, 1627; d. Munich, Feb. 13, 1693. He studied organ in Vienna under Valentini and in Rome under Carissimi. Returning to Germany, he was appointed Court Kapellmeister at Munich, and held this post from 1656 till 1674; it is said that he was forced to resign because of the intrigues of Italian singers at the Munich Court. He then went to Vienna, where he was organist at St. Stephen's cathedral from 1677-84, and also court organist. In 1684 he returned to Munich. He wrote preludes, interludes, and postludes for organ; toccatas and suites for harpsichord; a number of Masses; several Kyries and Glorias for voices and various instruments; a Requiem *a* 5; sacred concertos; etc. In Munich he produced several Italian operas: *Applausi festivi* (Aug. 28, 1658); *Antiopa giustificata* (Sept. 26, 1662); *Atalanta* (Jan. 30, 1667); *Le pretensioni del sole* (Nov. 6, 1667); *Amor tiranno* (Oct. 31, 1672); etc. Of importance is his organ work, *Modulatio organica super Magnificat octo tonis* (1689). Sandberger in the 'Denkmäler der Tonkunst in Bayern' (vol. 2, part 2) publ. a selection from his works; Adler publ., in the 'Denkmäler der Tonkunst in Österreich,' 2 Masses (vol. 49) and 3 Requiems (vol. 59).—Cf. K. Weitzmann-Seiffert, *Geschichte der Klaviermusik* (vol. 1, p. 185 ff.).

Kern, Jerome (David), famous American composer; b. New York, Jan. 27, 1885; d. there, Nov. 11, 1945. He was educated in N. Y. public schools; studied music with his mother; then with Paolo Gallico and Alexander Lambert (piano); with Austin Pearce and Albert von Doenhoff (theory). After a sojourn in London (1903), where he was connected with a theatrical production, he went to Germany, where he continued to study composition; returned to New York in 1907, became a pianist and salesman for a publishing firm, publ. his first song, *How'd You Like to Spoon With Me,* in 1905, and it became famous. In 1911 he obtained his first success as a composer for the stage with his musical comedy, *The Red Petticoat.* After that he continued to produce musical comedies in rapid succession; in 1917 alone he produced 7 shows on Broadway; altogether, he composed more than 60 works for the stage, including several motion picture scores. His most important productions include *Very Good, Eddie* (N. Y., Dec. 23, 1915), *Have a Heart* (N. Y., Jan. 11, 1917), *Head Over Heels* (N. Y., Aug. 29, 1918), *Sally* (N. Y., Dec. 21, 1920; extremely successful); *Stepping Stones* (N. Y., Nov. 6, 1923), *Sunny* (N. Y., Sept. 22, 1925), *Show Boat* (Washington, Nov. 15, 1927; N. Y., Dec. 27, 1927; his most remarkable score, one of the finest American works of its genre; includes the famous bass aria *Ol' Man River*); *The Cat and the Fiddle* (N. Y., Oct. 15, 15, 1931), *Music in the Air* (N. Y., Nov. 8, 1932), *Roberta* (N. Y., Nov. 18, 1933), *The Three Sisters* (London, 1934), *Gentlemen Unafraid* (1938), *Very Warm for May* (N. Y., Nov. 17, 1939). He also composed an orchestral work, *Portrait of Mark Twain* (Cincinnati, May 14, 1942). A motion picture on his life, *As the Clouds Roll By,* was produced posthumously (1946).—Cf. Robert Simon, *Jerome Kern,* in 'Modern Music' (Jan., 1929); David Ewen, *The Story of Jerome Kern* (N. Y., 1953). See also *The Jerome Kern Song Book,* with an introduction by Oscar Hammerstein II (N. Y., 1955).

Kerr, Harrison, American composer; b. Cleveland, Oct. 13, 1897. After completing his general studies in Cleveland, he went to France, where he took courses with Nadia Boulanger at the American Cons. in Fontainebleau. Upon his return to America, he taught music in Cleveland and in New York. He founded and edited a magazine of contemporary thought, 'Trend' (1932-35). In 1946 he was appointed chief of the Music,

Art & Exhibits Section of the Civil Affairs Division, Dept. of the Army, in which capacity he made several trips to the occupied areas in Europe and Asia (1947-49) and organized musical exchange agencies in Germany, Austria, Japan, and Korea. In 1949 he was appointed dean of the College of Fine Arts at the Univ. of Oklahoma. Works: Symphony No. 1 (Rochester, Oct. 24, 1945); Symphony No. 2 (1948); Symphony No. 3 (Oklahoma City, Feb. 23, 1951; composer conducting); Symphony No. 4 (1954); *Notations on a Sensitized Plate,* for voice and chamber ensemble (1935); *Wink of Eternity,* for chorus and orch. (1937); violin concerto (Norman, Okla., March 14, 1952); trio for clarinet, cello, and piano (1936); *Study* for cello unaccompanied (1937); 2 string quartets (1925 and 1937); 2 piano sonatas (1933 and 1947); sonata for unaccompanied violin (1954); sonata for violin and piano (1955). He also wrote a *Dance Sonata,* for dancers, 2 pianos, and percussion (1938).

Kes, Willem, violinist, composer, and conductor; b. Dordrecht, Holland, Feb. 16, 1856; d. Munich, Feb. 21, 1934. He studied with various teachers in Holland; in 1871 went to Germany, where he took lessons with Ferdinand David at the Leipzig Cons., and afterwards, with a stipend from the King of Holland, under Wieniawski (Brussels) and Joachim (Berlin). However, he did not attempt to pursue the career of a virtuoso, but turned to conducting. In 1876 he became conductor of the Park Orch. in Amsterdam, and in 1888 assumed the conductorship of the Concertgebouw. In 1895 he succeeded Henschel as conductor of the Scottish Orch. in Glasgow. In 1898 he went to Russia, where he conducted the Moscow Philharmonic Society, and also served as director of the Moscow Cons.; in these posts he exercised considerable influence on musical affairs in Russia. In 1904 he went to Germany; in 1905 he became director of the Cons. of Coblenz; retired in 1926, and settled in Munich. Among his works are a symph., several overtures, a violin concerto, a cello concerto, a choral work with orch. *Der Taucher;* a violin sonata; piano pieces; songs; also orchestrated Schumann's *Etudes Symphoniques.*

Kessler, Ferdinand, German composer, violinist, and teacher; b. Frankfurt, Jan., 1793; d. there, Oct. 28, 1856. He studied with his father and Vollweiler. One of his pupils was Franz Wüllner. He publ. sonatas, rondos, etc., for piano.

Kessler (real name Kötzler), **Joseph Christoph,** German pianist and pedagogue; b. Augsburg, Aug. 26, 1800; d. Vienna, Jan. 14, 1872. He studied with the organist Bilek in Feldsberg; then was tutor with the family of Count Potocki in Lemberg; there he spent 20 years; from 1855 lived in Vienna. He publ. a series of practical studies for piano; Moscheles used them in his teaching, and Liszt recommended them. Pyllemann publ. his reminiscences of Kessler in the 'Allgemeine musikalische Zeitung' (1872).

Kestenberg, Leo, eminent music educator and writer; b. Rosenberg, Hungary, Nov. 27, 1882; studied in Berlin, piano with Franz Kullak and Busoni, and composition with Draeseke; then taught at the Klindworth-Scharwenka Cons. and played piano recitals, distinguishing himself as a fine interpreter of Liszt's works. In 1918 he was appointed chairman of the music dept. of the Prussian Ministry of Art; in 1929, councilor in the ministry. In that capacity, he reorganized the system of musical education in Prussia, including the Berlin Hochschule and the Akademie für Kirchen- und Schulmusik, along the lines set forth in 3 pamphlets which he prepared in collaboration with W. Günther: *Prüfung, Ausbildung und Anstellung der Musiklehrer an der höheren Lehranstalten in Preussen* (1925); *Schulmusikunterricht in Preussen* (1925); *Privatunterricht in der Musik* (1929). He also was instrumental in organizing public school music festivals. After his sweeping reform, music was introduced into high schools in Germany, and music teachers received licenses to teach. In 1933 he was compelled to leave Germany; he settled temporarily in Prague, where he was active in music education. After the occupation of Czechoslovakia by the Nazis in 1939, Kestenberg went to Palestine; from 1939 to 1945 he was musical director of the Palestine Symph. Orch.; then lived in Tel Aviv as a teacher. In 1957 Kestenberg received from the West German government a large sum compensating him for his unlawful removal from his position in the Prussian Ministry of Art by the Nazi government.—Publications: *Musikerziehung und Musikpflege* (Berlin, 1921); editor of 'Jahrbuch der deutschen Musikorganisation' (with Beidler; 1929; 2nd ed., 1931) and of the magazines 'Die Musikpflege' (with E. Preussner) and 'Musik und Technik' (1930); general editor of a series of books, 'Musikpädagogische Bibliothek.'—Cf. P. Bekker, *Briefe an zeitgenössische Musiker* (Berlin, 1932; p. 44ff.).

Ketten, Henri, pianist; b. Baja, Hungary, March 25, 1848; d. Paris, April 1, 1883. He studied at the Paris Cons. with Halévy and Marmontel; wrote a number of ingratiating and successful piano pieces in the salon genre, also suitable as teaching material (*Chasse au papillon, Romance sans paroles, Tranquillité, Mélancolie,* etc.).

Kettenus (keht-nüs'), **Aloys,** Belgian violinist and composer; b. Verviers, Feb. 22, 1823; d. London, Oct. 3, 1896. He studied at the Liège Cons. and in Germany; 1845, leader of the Mannheim orch.; in 1855, became a member of the Hallé Orch. in London, and of the Royal Italian Orch. He wrote an opera, *Stella Monti* (1862); a violin concerto; a concertino for 4 violins and orch.; a duet for violin and piano; etc.

Ketterer, Eugene, French pianist and composer; b. Rouen, 1831; d. Paris, Dec. 18, 1870. He studied at the Paris Cons. He publ. 290 piano pieces in drawing-room style, many of which became popular (*Grand caprice hongrois, L'Argentine, La Châtelaine, Gaëtana, Rondo oriental,* etc.).

Ketting, Piet, Dutch composer; b. Haarlem, Nov. 29, 1905. He studied at the Utrecht Cons. and later with Willem Pijper, whose influence was decisive in shaping his compositions; he wrote music criticism; as a pianist he participated in many chamber concerts. In 1945 he was appointed director of the Music Lyceum in Amsterdam. — Works: symphony (1929); *De Havenstad,* cantata (1933); *Ballade du jeune marin* for vocal quartet (1934); *De verheerlijkte kokila,* cantata (1937); string trio (1925); 3 string quartets (1927-29); sonata for flute, bass clarinet, and piano (1928); sonata for flute, oboe, and piano (1936), and many other works for combinations of wind instruments; several preludes and fugues for piano; songs.

Keurvels (kör'-vels), **Edward H. J.,** Belgian conductor and composer; b. Antwerp, March 8, 1853; d. Eckeren (Hogblom), Jan. 19, 1916. He studied with Peter Benoit; was choirmaster and later conductor at the National Flemish Theater in Antwerp. In 1896 he established a series of symph. concerts at the Antwerp Zoological Gardens, which assumed considerable importance in Antwerp's musical life. He wrote an opera, *Parisina* (Antwerp, 1890); also numerous songs in the Flemish folksong style.

Keussler (kois'-lär), **Gerhard von,** composer and conductor; b. Schwanenburg, Latvia, July 5, 1874; d. Niederwartha, near Dresden, Aug. 21, 1949. He studied in St. Petersburg before taking a course in biology at the Univ. of Dortat. In 1900 he went to Leipzig, where he studied with Riemann and Kretzschmar at the Univ., and with Reinecke and Jadassohn at the Cons.; received the degree of *Dr. phil.* for his thesis *Die Grenzen der Ästhetik* (1902). He then became conductor of the 'Deutscher Singverein' in Prague (1906-18); in 1918 he went to Hamburg, where he led the 'Singakademie' and the Philharmonic concerts; later lived in Stuttgart and Dresden. In 1931 he went to Australia, conducting concerts in Melbourne and elsewhere. In 1934 he returned to Germany; lived in Berlin from 1934 till 1941; then settled in Niederwartha, near Dresden, where he remained until his death. He was an imaginative composer, writing in large forms and in a rhapsodic manner, rooted in German neo-Romanticism. —Works: the operas *Wandlungen* (1904), *Gefängnisse* (Prague, April 22, 1914), and *Die Geisselfahrt* (Hamburg, 1923); a melodrama, *An den Tod* (1922); several oratorios; 2 symphonies; symph. poem *Australia* (1936); numerous songs to his own texts; editions of choral works by Palestrina, Handel, Mozart, etc.; contributed articles on German music to various periodicals.

Kewitsch (kā'-vitch), **Theodor,** German composer and writer on music; b. Posilge, Feb. 3, 1834; d. Berlin, July 18, 1903. He studied organ with his father; was teacher and organist in various towns; received a pension in 1887 and went to Berlin; edited the 'Musikkorps' (1891-92), the 'Hanoverische Musikzeitung' (1893-97), and the 'Deutsche Militärmusiker - Zeitung'; also wrote articles for other music journals. He publ. a *Vade-mecum* for organists; much church music; 4-part songs for mixed and male chorus; piano pieces, etc.; also wrote *Vermächtnis an die deutschen Militärmusikmeister* (1901).

Key, Francis Scott, a Baltimore lawyer, author of the words of the American national anthem; b. Carroll County, Md., Aug. 1, 1779; d. Baltimore, Jan. 11, 1843. He wrote the text of the anthem aboard a British ship (where he was taken as a civilian emissary to intercede for release of a Maryland physician) on the night of Sept. 13, 1814, setting it to the tune of a drinking song *To Anacreon in Heaven,* popular at the time. The text and the tune did not become an official national anthem until March 3, 1931, when the bill establishing it as such was passed by Congress and signed by President Hoover.—Cf. O. G. Sonneck, *Report on the Star Spangled Banner, Hail Columbia, Yankee Doodle* (1909); O. G. Sonneck, *The Star Spangled Banner* (1914); J. Muller, *The Star Spangled Banner* (N. Y., 1935); J. A. Kouwenhoven and L. M. Patten, *New Light on 'The Star Spangled Banner,'* in the 'Mus. Quarterly' (April, 1937); J. T. Howard, *Our American Music* (N. Y., 1939; pp. 121-26).

Key, Pierre van Rensselaer, American music lexicographer; b. Grand Haven, Mich., Aug. 28, 1872; d. New York, Nov. 28, 1945. He was educated at the Chicago Musical College; then held positions as music critic of the 'Chicago Times-Herald,' 'Chicago American,' 'Chicago Examiner,' and the 'New York World' (1907-19). He was the editor of valuable compilations: *Pierre Key's Musical Who's Who* (1931); *Pierre Key's Music Year Book; Pierre Key's Radio Annual;* and the periodical 'Music Digest'; publ. *John McCormack: His Own Life Story* (1919); *Enrico Caruso,* with Bruno Zirato (1922); *This Business of Singing* (1936).

Khadzhiev, Parashkev, Bulgarian composer; b. Sofia, April 14, 1912. He studied with Vladigerov, and later with J. Marx in Vienna. In 1940 he joined the staff of the Music Academy in Sofia. His works include 2 violin sonatas (1942 and 1947); wind quintet (1943); concertino for flute and orch. (1945); 2 string quartets (1948 and 1949); arrangements of Bulgarian folksongs.

Khandoshkin, Ivan, Russian violinist and composer; b. 1747; d. St. Petersburg, March 16, 1804. He was the first Russian violin virtuoso, and the first to write instrumental music on Russian folk themes. He studied in St. Petersburg with an Italian musician, Tito Porta; then was sent to Italy, where he was a student at the Tartini school in Padua; it is probable that he took lessons from Tartini himself. Returning to Russia in 1765, he became a violinist in the Imperial Chapel; was concertmaster of the Court Orch. in 1773; also taught violin at the Academy of Arts in St. Petersburg, and later in Moscow and in Ekaterinoslav. These appointments were highly unusual honors to one of Khandoshkin's origin (he was a liberated serf). The following pieces were publ. during his lifetime: *6 Sonates pour deux violons* (Amsterdam, 1781); *Chansons russes variées pour violon et basse* (Amsterdam, 1781); *Nouvelles variations sur des chansons russes,* for violin (St. Petersburg, 1784). A set of Russian songs for unaccompanied violin was publ. in 1820; a number of works by Khandoshkin came to light in Russian archives in recent times; his concerto for viola and string orch. was publ. in 1947; a *Sentimental Aria* for unaccompanied violin was publ. in 1949.—Cf. G. Fesetchko, *Ivan Khandoshkin,* in 'Sovietskaya Musica' (Dec., 1950); R. Aloys Mooser, *Annales de la Musique et des Musiciens en Russie au XVIIIe siècle* (Geneva, 1950; vol. II, pp. 386-92); I. Yampolsky, *Russian Violin Art* (Moscow, 1951; vol. I, pp. 76-121; contains musical examples from Khandoshkin's works).

Khatchaturian (hah-tcha-tu-ryan'), **Aram,** brilliant Russian composer of Armenian extraction; b. Tiflis, June 6, 1903. His father was a bookbinder. He remained in Tiflis until the end of the civil war (1920), when he moved to Moscow, and entered the Gniessin School to study cello, and later, composition with Gniessin himself. In 1929 he became a student at the Moscow Cons., graduating in 1934 in the class of Miaskovsky. Although he started to compose very late, he developed rapidly, and soon progressed to the first rank of Soviet composers. His music is in the tradition of Russian Orientalism; he applies the characteristic scale progressions of Caucasian melos, without quoting actual folksongs. His piano concerto and the *Sabre Dance* from his ballet, *Gayane,* became part of the popular repertory all over the world. In 1948 Khatchaturian was severely criticized by the Central Committee of the Communist Party, along with Prokofiev, Shostakovitch, and others, for modernistic tendencies; although he admitted his deviations in this respect, he continued to compose essentially in his typical manner, not shunning highly advanced harmonic combinations and impressionistic devices. — Works: *Gayane,* ballet (Molotov, Dec. 9, 1942; received the Stalin Prize); *Spartak,* ballet (1953); Symph. No. 1 (1932); Symph. No. 2 (Moscow, Dec. 30, 1943); *Symphonie-Poème* (1947; criticized for its modernism); *Poem About Stalin,* for orch. (1938); violin concerto (Moscow, Nov. 16, 1940); cello concerto (Moscow, Oct. 30, 1946); *Masquerade,* symph. suite from incidental music to Lermontov's play (1944); string quartet (1932); trio for clarinet, violin, and piano (1932); violin sonata (1932); several piano pieces (*Poem, Toccata, Scherzo, Dance,* etc.). He conducted a concert of his works in London on Dec. 5, 1954, and also visited several other European capitals. He is married to Nina Markarova (q.v.).

Khodzha-Einatov, Leon, Russian composer; b. Tiflis, March 23, 1904; d. Leningrad, Nov. 1, 1954. He studied with Spendiarov; in 1927, went to Leningrad, where he wrote music for the stage. He wrote the opera *Rebellion* (Leningrad, May 16, 1938); 3 Armenian operas, *Arshak* (1945), *David Bek* (1951), and *Namus* (1952); also *Symphonic Dances* (16 numbers) and a symphony (1953).

Khrennikov, Tikhon, Russian composer; b. Elets, June 10, 1913. He studied at the Moscow Cons. with Litinsky and Shebalin. His idiom is tonal, strongly rhythmic, and based, melodically, on folk material. His works include: Symph. No. 1 (1933-35); Symph. No. 2, expressing 'the irresistible will to defeat the Fascist foe' (Moscow, Jan. 14, 1943); the operas *Brothers* (renamed *In the Storm;* Moscow, May 31, (1939), *Frol Skobeyev* (Moscow, Feb. 24, 1950), and *Mother* (Moscow, Oct. 26, 1957); a piano concerto (1933); many songs.

Kidson, Frank, English musical folklorist and bibliographer; b. Leeds, Nov. 15, 1855; d. there, Nov. 7, 1926. Originally a landscape painter, he became interested in historical studies and began to collect English, Scottish, and Irish folksongs and dance melodies; subsequently became one of the founders of the Folksong Society in England. He publ. *Old English Country Dances* (1890); *Traditional Tunes* (1891); *British Music Publishers, Printers and Engravers . . .* (1900); *English Folksong and Dance* (1915); *The Beggar's Opera, its Predecessors and Successors* (1922); contributed valuable articles to the 'Mus. Antiquary' and the 'Mus. Quarterly'; with A. Moffat, he ed. *The Minstrelsy of England; Songs of the Georgian Period; British Nursery Rhymes; Children's Songs of Long Ago; 80 Singing Games for Children;* etc.

Kiel, Friedrich, German pedagogue and composer; b. Puderbach, near Siegen, Oct. 7, 1821; d. Berlin, Sept. 13, 1885. He studied the rudiments of music with his father, a schoolmaster. One of his youthful works, a set of variations (1832-34), attracted the attention of Prince Karl von Wittgenstein, who gave him violin lessons in 1835, and took him into his orchestra. Kiel further studied with Kaspar Kummer at Coburg, becoming leader of the ducal orchestra there (1840): then moved to Berlin, and studied with Dehn (1842-44). He received a stipend from King Friedrich Wilhelm IV; in 1865 he was elected to the Prussian Academy of Fine Arts. From 1866-70 he taught composition at Stern's Cons., Berlin; then at the Hochschule für Musik. He wrote the oratorios *Christus* and *Der Stern von Bethlehem; Stabat Mater; Te Deum;* 4 piano sonatas. His most successful work was a Requiem (Berlin, 1862; numerous performances in Germany). He was a prolific composer, but it was as a pedagogue that he gained his greatest distinction. W. Altmann publ. a complete list of his works in 'Die Musik' (1901, No. 1).

Kielland, Olva, Norwegian conductor and composer; b. Trondheim, Aug. 16, 1901. He studied at the Leipzig Cons., and in Basel with Weingartner. He conducted in Göteborg (1925-31), Oslo (1931-45), Trondheim (1946-48), and in Bergen (since 1948). He has also appeared as guest conductor in Paris, London, and New York. He has written a symphony (1935), a violin concerto (1943), and many piano pieces.

Kienle (kēn'-leh), **Ambrosius,** an authority on Gregorian chant; b. Sigmaringen, May 8, 1852; d. in the monastery at Beuron, June 18, 1905. He entered the monastery in 1873, and devoted himself to the study of Gregorian chant. He publ. *Choralschule* (1884; 3d ed., 1899); *Kleines kirchenmusikalisches Handbuch* (1892); *Mass und Milde in kirchenmusikalischen Dingen* (1901), and essays in periodicals; also *Der gregorianische Choral* (1881: a transl. of Pothier's *Les Mélodies grégoriennes).*

Kienzl (kēn'-tsl), **Wilhelm,** Austrian composer; b. Waizenkirchen, Jan. 17, 1857; d. Vienna, Oct. 19, 1941. He studied music at Graz Gymnasium with Ignaz Uhl, and with W. A. Remy (composition); later with Josef Krejči at Prague, with Rheinberger in Munich, and with Liszt at Weimar, at length receiving his Ph.D. in Vienna in 1879 for the dissertation *Die musikalische Deklamation* (Leipzig, 1880). A second work, *Miscellen* (Leipzig, 1885), concerning impressions received in Bayreuth (1879), created a stir by its bold criticism. During 1880 he lectured on music in Munich; in 1881-82, made a pianistic tour in Hungary, Rumania, and Germany; in 1883, was appointed conductor of the German opera in Amsterdam. Shortly thereafter, he went to Crefeld to take up a similar position; in 1886 he married the concert singer Lili Hoke. From 1886-90 he was artistic director of the Styrian Musikverein at Graz, directed the symph. concerts and the programs of the provincial vocal and instrumental schools. From 1890-92 he held the position of 1st conductor at the Hamburg Opera; and from 1892-94, court conductor at Munich, before returning to Graz. In 1917, he received the honorary degree of Doc. Mus. from the Univ. of Graz; and, later, in Vienna, was music critic for various papers. His early operas include *Urvasi* (Dresden, Feb. 20, 1886; rewritten, 1909), *Heilmar, der Narr* (Munich, March 8, 1892; very successful), and *Der Evangelimann* (Berlin, May 4, 1895; his most famous work). Then followed *Don Quichote,* a 'musical tragi-comedy' (Berlin, Nov. 18, 1898); *In Knecht Rupprechts Werkstatt,* a 'Märchenspiel' (Graz, 1906); *Der Kuhreigen* (*Ranz des Vaches;* Vienna, Nov. 23, 1911); *Das Testament* (Vienna, Dec. 6, 1916); *Hassan der Schwarmer* (Chemnitz, 1925); *Sanctissimum* (Vienna, 1925); *Hans Kipfel,* a 'Singspiel' (Vienna, 1928). Kienzl finished Adolf Jensen's opera *Turandot,* and edited Mozart's *Titus.* His own published compositions comprise about 120 songs; much light piano music; incidental music to *Die Brautfahrt; Septuaginta* (1937); 3 *Phantasiestücke* for piano and violin; piano trio; 2 string quartets; choral music. He also composed the new Austrian national anthem, with a text by the future president of Austria, Karl Renner, to replace that written by Haydn in 1797; its adoption was announced by the Republican government on June 6, 1920, but on Dec. 13, 1929, the Haydn melody was once more adopted as a national anthem (with a different set of words). Kienzl edited Brendel's *Grundzüge der Geschichte der Musik* (Leipzig, 1886); Brendel's *Geschichte der Musik in Italien, Deutschland und Frankreich* (7th ed., Leipzig, 1889). In addition he wrote *Richard Wagner* (1904; 2nd ed., 1908); *Aus Kunst und Leben* (1904); *Im Konzert* (1908); *Betrachtungen und Erinnerungen* (1909); *Meine Lebenswanderung,* an autobiography (1926); *Hans Richter* (1930). — Cf. M. Morold, *Wilhelm Kienzl* (Leipzig, 1909); *Festschrift zum 60. Geburtstag von Wilhelm Kienzl* (1917); *Festschrift zum 80. Geburtstag* (Vienna, 1937); Hans Sittner, ed., Wilhelm Kienzl's *Lebenswanderung* (Vienna, 1953; includes his correspondence with Peter Rosegger).

Kiepura, Jan, Polish tenor; b. Sosnowiec, May 16, 1902. He studied in Warsaw, where he made his first public appearance in 1923; was then engaged as opera singer by a number of European opera houses (Vienna, Berlin, Milan, etc.). He made his American début at the Metropolitan Opera in N. Y. as Rodolfo in *La Bohème* (Feb. 10, 1938). He then settled in the U. S., making frequent tours in Europe as well. He is married to the Austrian singer Martha Eggerth.

Kiesewetter (kē - zeh - vet - ter), **Raphael Georg,** Edler von Wiesenbrunn, scholar and writer on musical subjects; b. Holleschau, Moravia, Aug. 29, 1773; d. Baden, near Vienna, Jan. 1, 1850. An excellent musician, he was educated for an official career as an Austrian functionary; was connected with the War Ministry; traveled in various European countries; in 1801 settled in Vienna. His musical interests impelled him to undertake serious study with Albrechtsberger, who instructed him in counterpoint. He was an indefatigable collector of old musical MSS, and archeological research became his specialty. He was a member of numerous musical and scientific societies; received the rank of nobility in 1845. A. W. Ambros was his nephew. —Writings: *Die Verdienste der Niederländer um die Tonkunst* (received the prize of the Netherlands Academy in 1826; Dutch transl., 1829); *Geschichte der europäisch-abendländischen, das ist unserer heutigen Musik* (Leipzig, 1834; English transl., 1846); *Über die Musik der neuern Griechen, nebst freien Gedanken über altägyptische und altgriechische Musik* (1838); *Guido von Arezzo, sein Leben und Wirken* (1840); *Schicksale und Beschaffenheit des weltlichen Gesangs vom frühen Mittelalter bis zur Erfindung des dramatischen Styles und den Anfangen der Oper* (1841); *Die Musik der Araber nach Originalquellen* (1842); *Der neuen Aristoxener; zerstreute Aufsätze* (1846); *Über die Oktave des Pythagoras* (1848); *Galerie der alten Kontrapunktisten* (1847; a catalogue of his old scores, bequeathed to the Vienna Library); several theoretical and historical works in MS; also essays on old music and on Gregorian notation in German periodicals; supervised Kandler's *Life of Palestrina* (1834).

Kiezewetter, Tomasz, Polish conductor and composer; b. Sosnowka, Sept. 9, 1911. He studied at the Warsaw Cons.; during the German occupation, was active in resistance groups. After 1945 he settled in Lodz as a teacher. He has written a symphony (1949), a viola concerto (1950), a string quartet, and choruses.

Kijima, Kiyohiko, Japanese composer; b. Tokyo, Feb. 19, 1917. He studied composition with Ikenouchi. He received 2 prizes given by the newspaper 'Mainichi' (1938; 1948).

Kiladze, Grigory Varfolomeyevitch, Russian composer; b. Batum, Dec. 6, 1903. He studied at the Tiflis Cons., and later at the Leningrad Cons. with V. Stcherbatchev. He has written operas on subjects from Caucasian revolutionary history: *Bakhtrioni* (1936), *Lado Ketzkhoveli* (1941); ballet, *Sinatle* (which received the 1st Stalin Prize in 1948); also *Poem About Stalin,* for chorus and orch. (1935); symph. poem, *The Hermit* (1936); *Heroic Symphony* (1944); oratorio, *Childhood and Adolescence of the Leader* (1951); film music.

Kilburn, Nicholas, English choral conductor and composer; b. Bishop Auckland, Durham, Feb. 7, 1843; d. there, Dec. 4, 1923. He studied in Cambridge, then conducted a musical society in his native town and the Philharmonic Society of Sunderland (from 1885); these posts he filled until his death. He publ. *Notes and Notions on Music; How to Manage a Choral Society; Wagner, a Sketch; Parsifal and Bayreuth; The Story of Chamber Music,* etc.; also wrote some choral works.

Kilenyi, Edward, Sr., composer, arranger, and pedagogue; b. Bekes, Hungary, Jan. 25, 1884. He studied in Budapest, at the Cons. of Cologne, and in Italy (with Mascagni). In 1908 he settled in the U. S.; took courses at Columbia Univ. with Rybner and Daniel Gregory Mason (M.A., 1915). In 1930 he went to Hollywood, where he remained as composer for the films and pedagogue. He was for 5 years the teacher of George Gershwin.

Kilenyi, Edward, Jr., American pianist; son of Edward Kilenyi, Sr.; b. Philadelphia, May 7, 1911. In 1927 he went to Budapest to study with Dohnányi at the Cons. there; after graduating (1930), he traveled in Europe, giving concerts; returning to America, he continued his career as concert pianist; American début, N. Y., Oct. 21, 1940, in recital. In 1942-46 he served in the U. S. Army.

Killmayer, Wilhelm, German composer; b. Munich, Aug. 21, 1927. He studied in Munich with H. W. von Waltershausen (1945-50); then at the Univ. of Munich (1950-52), and later with Carl Orff; was engaged as conductor of the Marionette Theater of Munich. He has written mostly for choral groups, in a modern madrigal manner, with rapidly altering rhythmic patterns and massive harmonies; the influence of Carl Orff is decidedly apparent. Among his works are a *Missa Brevis; Chansons* for tenor, flute, strings, and percussion; *Canti amorosi* for 6 voices a cappella; music for marionettes.

Kilpinen, Yriö, Finnish song composer; b. Helsingfors, Feb. 4, 1892. He had very little academic education in music; took a few courses at the Helsingfors Cons., in Berlin, and in Vienna. His chosen medium is that of lyric song; possessing an exceptional talent for expressing poetic lines in finely balanced melodies, he attained great renown in Finland, and has been called the Finnish Hugo Wolf. He has written about 800 lieder to words in German, Finnish, and Swedish, by classical and modern poets. In 1948 he was appointed member of the Academy of Finland. About 300 of his songs are publ.; other works are *Pastoral Suite* for orch. (1944); *Totentanz* for orch. (1945); 6 piano sonatas; a cello sonata; a suite for viola da gamba with piano; etc.

Kimball, Jacob, Jr., American composer; b. Topsfield, Mass., Feb. 22, 1761; d. in the almshouse there, Feb. 6, 1826. In 1775 he was a drummer in the Massachusetts militia; then entered Harvard University (graduated 1780); subsequently studied law and was admitted to the bar, but soon gave up that profession for music, teaching in various New England towns. He wrote hymns, psalm tunes, and 'fuguing pieces,' in the style of Billings; compiled *The Rural Harmony* (71 original compositions for 3 and 4 voices; Boston, 1793). Another collection, *The Essex Harmony* (44 tunes and 2 anthems) is also attributed to him; it was publ. in Exeter, N. H., 1800, and dedicated to the Essex, Mass., Music Association; the Boston Public Library possesses an imperfect copy. —Cf. F. J. Metcalf, *American Psalmody* (1917); F. J. Metcalf, *American Writers and Compilers of Sacred Music* (1925).

Kinder, Ralph, organist; b. Stalybridge, near Manchester, England, Jan. 27, 1876; d. Bala, suburb of Philadelphia, Nov. 14, 1952. He was taken to the U. S. at the age of 5; was a chorister in Bristol, R. I.; studied in America, and then in London with E. H. Lemare. He held various posts as church organist in Bristol (1890-98), Providence (1898), and in Philadelphia (from 1899). He wrote numerous organ pieces of considerable charm; of these the following are published: *Arietta, Berceuse, Caprice, Festival March, Jour de Printemps, Moonlight, Souvenir, In Springtime.*

Kindermann, Johann Erasmus, German organist and composer; b. Nuremberg, March 29, 1616; d. there, April 14, 1655. He was a student of J. Staden; in 1634, went to Venice, where he took lessons with Cavalli; returning to Nuremberg in 1636, he became a church organist. His works include *Cantiones pathetikai* (1639); *Friedensklag* (1640); *Opitianischer Orpheus* (1642); *Concentus Salomonis* (1642); *Musica catechetica* (1643); *Deliciae studiosorum* (1640-48, many reprints); *Intermedium musico-politicum* (a collection of quodlibets, 1643); *Harmonia organica* (in tablature; 1645; 2nd ed., 1665); *Göttliche Liebesflamme* (1640-75; 20 sacred songs), also various instrumental works. —Cf. H. J. Moser, *Corydon* (1933; vol. 1, pp. 31-42; vol. 2, pp. 77-88).

Kindler, Hans, cellist and conductor; b. Rotterdam, Jan. 8, 1892; d. Watch Hill, R. I., Aug. 30, 1949. He studied at the Rotterdam Cons., receiving first prize for piano and cello in 1906. In 1911 he was appointed prof. at the Scharwenka Cons. in Berlin, and first cellist at the Berlin Opera. In 1912-13 he made a successful tour of Europe; in 1914, came to the U. S. to become first cellist of the Philadelphia Orch., a post he held until 1920. In 1927 he made his début as a conductor in Philadelphia; in 1928 he conducted the world première of Stravinsky's ballet *Apollon Musagète* at the Library of Congress Festival in Washington, D. C.; in 1929, appeared as cellist in 110 concerts throughout the U. S. and Europe, also touring as far as Java and India. In 1931 he organized the National Symphony Orch. in Washington, D. C., of which he was permanent conductor until his resignation on Nov. 30, 1948.

King, Julie. See **Rivé-King.**

King, Matthew Peter, English composer; b. London, 1773; d. there, Jan., 1823. He composed 10 or 12 operas for the Lyceum Theatre; an oratorio, *The Intercession;* a quintet for piano, flute, and strings; piano sonatas; etc.; also publ. *A General Treatise on Music* (London, 1800) and an *Introduction to sight singing* (1806).

King, Oliver A., English pianist; b. London, 1855; d. there, Aug. 23, 1923. He was a pupil of J. Barnby; later studied piano with Reinecke at the Leipzig Cons. (1874-77). From 1880-83 he toured Canada, giving recitals, and visited New York. In 1893 he was appointed prof. of piano at the Royal Academy of Music in London. —Works: 3 cantatas, *The Romance of the Roses, Prosperina,* and *The Naiades; 137th Psalm* (Chester Festival, 1888); a symph. poem, *Night;* 2 overtures; piano concerto; violin concerto; pieces for piano solo and for organ.

Kinkel, Johanna (*née* Mockel), composer; b. Bonn, July 8, 1810; d. London, Nov. 15, 1858. She studied music in Berlin with Karl Böhmer, and married Gottfried Kinkel, the poet, in 1843. She wrote *Die Vogel-Cantate;* the operetta *Otto der Schutz,* and the well-known song, *The Soldier's Farewell;* also publ. *Acht Briefe an eine Freundin über Klavierunterricht* (1852).

Kinkeldey, Otto, eminent American musicologist; b. New York, Nov. 27, 1878. He graduated from the College of the City of N. Y. in 1898 (B. A.); then from N. Y. Univ. in 1900 (M. A.); then took lessons with MacDowell at Columbia Univ. (until 1902). After that he went to Germany, where he undertook a course of study with Radecke, Egidi, and Thiel at the 'Akademisches Institut für Kirchenmusik' in Berlin; studied musicology at the Univ. of Berlin with Fleischer, Friedlaender, Kretzschmar, and J. Wolf (1902-6). He received his Ph.D. from the Univ. of Berlin in 1909; Kinkeldey had been organist and choirmaster at the Chapel of the Incarnation, N. Y. (1898-1902); was organist and music director of the American Church in Berlin (1903-5); from 1909-14, instructor in organ and theory, lecturer on musicology, and music director at the Univ. of Breslau; named Royal Prussian Professor in 1910. Returning to the U. S. at the outbreak of World War I, he became organist and choirmaster at All-Souls Church, N. Y. (1915-17); was captain of infantry in the U. S. Army (1917-19); from 1915-23, and again from 1927-30, he was chief of the Music Division of the New York Public Library; from 1923-27, prof. of music at Cornell Univ.; from 1930-46, prof. of musicology and librarian there; Professor Emeritus, 1946. He was guest prof. at Harvard Univ. (1946-48); Univ. of Texas (1948-50); Princeton Univ. (1950-51); North Texas State College (1952-53); Univ. of Illinois (1953-54); Univ. of California, Berkeley (1954-55); Boston Univ. (1957); Univ. of Washington,

Seattle (1958). He was elected president of the American Musicological Society for 1934-36, and re-elected for 1940-42; has also been made an honorary member of the Musical Association, London. In 1947 he received a Litt. D. (*honoris causa*) from Princeton Univ. He published the valuable book (in German), *Orgel und Klavier in der Musik des 16. Jahrhunderts* (Leipzig, 1910); many articles in the 'Mus. Quarterly,' the 'Proceedings' of the Music Teachers' National Association, etc., and edited Erlebach's *Harmonische Freude musikalischer Freunde* for vols. 46 and 47 of the 'Denkmäler deutscher Tonkunst' (1914). Later publications include *A Jewish Dancing Master of the Renaissance, Guglielmo Ebreo* (reprinted in 1929 from A. S. Freidus Memorial Volume) and *Music and Music Printing in Incunabula* (reprinted in 1932 from the 'Papers' of the Bibliographical Society of America, vol. 26).—Cf. articles by E. J. Dent and G. S. Dickinson in the 'Mus. Quarterly' (Oct., 1938); Carleton Sprague Smith, *Otto Kinkeldey* in 'Notes' (Dec., 1948).

Kinsky, Georg, German musicologist; b. Marienwerder, Sept. 29, 1882; d. Berlin, April 7, 1951. He was self-taught in music; after working under Kopfermann for some months at the Royal Library in Berlin, he was appointed curator of the private museum of W. Heyer in Cologne (1909). The Heyer Library was dissolved in 1927. In 1921 Kinsky was appointed teacher at the Univ. of Cologne; in 1925, received his Ph. D. there. He publ. a very valuable illustrated catalogue of the Heyer collections: Vol. I, Keyed Instruments (1910); vol. II, Stringed Instruments (1912); vol. III, Wind and Percussion Instruments; vol. IV, MSS (1916). He also publ. a condensed *Handkatalog,* containing valuable historical notes (1913); *Briefe Glucks an Kruthoffer* (Vienna, 1927); *Geschichte der Musik in Bildern* (Leipzig and Paris, 1929; London, New York, and Milan, 1930; new ed. with introduction by Eric Blom, London, 1937); *Was Mendelssohn Indebted to Weber?,* in the 'Mus. Quarterly' (April, 1933); *Die Originalausgaben der Werke J. S. Bachs* (Vienna, 1937); *Manuscripte-Briefe-Dokumente von Scarlatti bis Stravinsky,* catalogue of autographs in the Louis Koch Collection (Stuttgart, 1953, posthumous); a thematic catalogue of Beethoven's works (completed by H. Halm and publ. 1955); etc.

Kipnis, Alexander, Russian bass singer; b. Zhitomir, Feb. 13, 1891. He first studied conducting at the Warsaw Cons., graduating in 1912 as military bandmaster; then voice at the Klindworth-Scharwenka Cons., Berlin, with Grenzbach. He made his professional début as a singer in Wiesbaden in 1917; in 1923 he settled in the U. S.; sang with the German Opera Co. in New York for one season, appearing first as Pogner in *Die Meistersinger* (Feb. 12, 1923); then was with the Chicago Civic Opera (1924); from 1925-35 he traveled widely in the U. S., South America, Australia, and Europe; was a member of the Berlin and Munich operas, and of the Vienna Opera; sang in Bayreuth (1924-33) and Salzburg (1937); on Jan. 6, 1940 he made his first appearance at the Metropolitan Opera House, as Gurnemanz in *Parsifal;* later sang the part of Boris Godunov (in which he excelled). Through the years, he appeared as soloist with Toscanini, Richard Strauss, Nikisch, Siegfried Wagner, and other celebrated conductors.

Kipper, Hermann, German composer; b. Koblenz, Aug. 27, 1826; d. Cologne, Oct. 25, 1910. He studied with Anschütz and H. Dorn. He was a music teacher and critic in Cologne. He wrote the comic operettas *Der Quacksalber, oder Doktor Sägebein und sein Famulus; Incognito, oder Der Fürst wider Willen; Kellner und Lord; Der Haifisch;* etc.

Kircher, Athanasius, famous Jesuit archeologist; b. Geisa, near Fulda, Germany, May 2, 1602; d. Rome, Nov. 28, 1680. He taught philosophy and mathematics at the Jesuit College in Würzburg (1630); in 1633 he went to Avignon, and in 1635 to Rome. His *Oedipus aegiptiacus* contains a curious chapter on hieroglyphic music; in his treatise *De arte magnetica* he gives examples of musical airs which were popularly regarded as a cure for tarantism; in fact, all his musical works exhibit a unique blending of real scientific insight with puerile credulity. His principal work is *Musurgia universalis sive ars magna consoni et dissoni* (Rome, 1650; in German, 1662). — Cf. Oskar Kaul, *Athanasius Kircher als Musikgelehrter,* in the 'Festschrift' of the Univ. of Würzburg (1932).

Kirchner, Fritz, German pianist and composer; b. Potsdam, Nov. 3, 1840; d. there, May 14, 1907. He studied piano with Theodor Kullak, and with Wüerst and Seyffert (theory) at Kullak's Academy; taught there (1864-89); then at the 'Mädchenheim' school in Berlin. He wrote educational pieces and other piano works (*Ball-Scenes;* 24 preludes), and songs.

Kirchner, Leon, American composer; b. Brooklyn, N. Y., Jan. 24, 1919. His family moved to Los Angeles when he was 9 years old; he studied piano as a child; theory with Albert Elkus and Edward Strickland at the Univ. of California, Berkeley; also took lessons with Ernest Bloch there. In 1942 he was in N. Y. studying with Roger Sessions; from 1943-46 he was in the U. S. Army; returning to the Univ. of California in 1946, he completed his graduate work, obtaining an M.A. degree. In 1947 he was appointed lecturer in music there. In 1948 he received a Guggenheim Fellowship; in 1950 he became associate prof. at the Univ. of Southern California, Los Angeles; in 1954, appointed prof. at Mills College, Oakland, Calif. —Works: *Letter* and *The Times are Nightfall,* for soprano and piano (1943); *Dawn,* for chorus and organ (1946); duo for violin and piano (1947); piano sonata (1948); string quartet (1949); *Of Obedience* and *The Runner,* after Walt Whitman, for soprano and piano (1950); *Sinfonia* (N. Y. Philharmonic, Jan. 31, 1952); *Sonata Concertante,* for violin and piano (1952); piano trio (1954); toccata for strings, wind instruments, and percussion (San Francisco, Feb. 16, 1956); piano concerto (N. Y. Philharmonic, Feb. 23, 1956; composer soloist). —Cf. A. L. Ringer, *Leon Kirchner,* in the 'Mus. Quarterly' (Jan., 1957).

Kirchner, Theodor, distinguished German composer; b. Neukirchen, near Chemnitz, Dec. 10, 1823; d. Hamburg, Sept. 18, 1903. On Mendelssohn's advice, he studied in Leipzig with K. F. Becker (theory) and J. Knorr (piano), and, in the summer of 1842, with Johann Schneider in Dresden. He was engaged as organist at Winterthur (1843-62) and then taught at the Zürich Music School (1862-72); later held the post of director of the Würzburg Cons. (1873-75). He then returned to Leipzig; finally went to Hamburg in 1890. As a youth, he enjoyed the friendship of Mendelssohn and Schumann, who encouraged and aided him with their advice. He wrote about 90 piano works, in the style of Schumann; some of his miniatures are of very high quality; also made numerous transcriptions for piano solo and piano duet (*Alte Bekannte in neuem Gewande*); *Kinder-Trios* for piano, violin, and cello; a piano quartet; a string quartet; 8 pieces for piano and cello; etc. —Cf. A. Niggli, *Theodor Kirchner* (Leipzig, 1880); Otto Klauwell, *Theodor Kirchner* (Langensalza, 1909); *Theodor Kirchner, Briefe aus den Jahren 1860-1868,* ed. by P. O. Schneider (Zürich, 1949).

Kiriac, Demetri, Rumanian musician; b. Bucharest, March 18, 1866; d. there, Jan. 8, 1928. As a young man he went to Paris and studied with Vincent d'Indy at the Schola Cantorum; returning to Rumania in 1900, he was appointed prof. at the Bucharest Cons. In 1901 founded the Choral Society Carmen in Bucharest. His chief work is a collection of sacred choruses in 5 vols. He was a noted folklorist, and also contributed to a resurgence of interest in the church music of the Orthodox faith.

Kirigin, Ivo, Croatian composer and music critic; b. Zadar, Feb. 2, 1914. He studied in Italy with Pizzetti; was active as theater conductor in Zagreb; among his works are a Concertino for piano and orch., and numerous songs.

Kirkby-Lunn, Louise, English dramatic contralto; b. Manchester, Nov. 8, 1873; d. London, Feb. 17, 1930. She studied at the Royal College of Music in London; while still a student there, she appeared as an opera singer at various London theaters; then toured with Sir Augustus Harris' company, and with the Carl Rosa Opera Co., until 1899, when she married W. J. Pearson, and retired from the stage for two years. In 1901 she reappeared as a member of the Royal Opera at Covent Garden, where she soon became one of the popular favorites. In 1902 she sang for the first time at the Metropolitan Opera, N. Y., where her interpretations of Wagnerian roles (Ortrud and Brangäne) made a deep impression; in 1904 she sang Kundry in Savage's production of *Parsifal* in English. From 1906-08 and 1912-14 she was again with the Metropolitan Opera; later toured in Australia. She was also prominent as a concert singer, appearing frequently at important music festivals in England.

Kirkman, Jacob (real name Kirchmann), founder of the firm of Kirkman and Sons, the harpsichord makers in London; b. Bischweiler, near Strasbourg, 1710; d. Greenwich, June (buried June 9), 1792. He settled in London about 1730; there he was associated with a Flemish harpsichord maker, Hermann Tabel. After Tabel's death, Kirkman married his widow, and acquired Tabel's tools. In 1755 he was naturalized as a British subject. In 1773 Kirkman, who was childless, formed a partnership with his nephew, Abraham Kirkman (1737-1794). The descendants of Abraham Kirkman continued the business until 1896, when the firm was merged with Collard; it was eventually absorbed by Chappell. For details and a list of surviving instruments, see the exhaustive article on Kirkman in Donald Boalch, *Makers of the Harpsichord and Clavichord* (London, 1956).

Kirkpatrick, John, American pianist; b. New York, March 18, 1905. He studied at Princeton Univ. (graduated in 1926); took summer courses in Paris with I. Philipp, C. Decreus, and Nadia Boulanger; returning to America in 1931, he appeared in recitals and in chamber music concerts. He became particularly interested in promoting American music. His most signal achievement was his performance, from memory, of the *Concord Sonata* by Charles Ives (N. Y., Jan. 20, 1939), which earned him a well-deserved success, not only for his musicianship, but for his perseverance as well (he spent 2 years studying this enormously difficult work); 1957, professor of music at Cornell University.

Kirkpatrick, Ralph, American harpsichord player and musicologist; b. Leominster, Mass., June 10, 1911. He studied piano at home; theory at Harvard Univ. (A.B., 1931) and with Nadia Boulanger in Paris; there he also took lessons in harpsichord playing with Wanda Landowska. He then worked with Arnold Dolmetsch at Haslemere in order to acquaint himself with old instruments; also with Heinz Tiessen in Berlin. He received a Guggenheim Fellowship in 1937 and undertook a journey throughout Europe, studying MSS and early editions of old chamber music; visited Spain, where he uncovered unknown materials on Domenico Scarlatti. In 1940 he was appointed to the staff of Yale Univ.; presented numerous harpsichord concerts and participated in festivals. He publ. valuable new eds. of Bach's *Goldberg Variations,* 60 keyboard sonatas of Domenico Scarlatti, etc. In 1953 he publ. his book, *Domenico Scarlatti,* an exhaustive biography coupled with scholarly analysis of the music, and containing a numbered list of the works that quickly became standard.

Kirnberger, Johann Philipp, noted German theorist; b. Saalfeld, April 24, 1721; d. Berlin, July 27, 1783. He first studied with P. Kellner at Gräfenroda, and with H. N. Gerber at Sondershausen. In 1739 he became a pupil of Bach in Leipzig, and spent 2 years with him. He then traveled in Poland (1741-50) as tutor in various noble Polish families; in 1751 he became violinist to Frederick the Great, and in 1758, Kapellmeister to Princess Amalie. He was greatly renowned as a teacher; among his pupils were Schulz, Fasch, and Zelter. As a theoretical writer, he was regarded as one of the greatest authorities of his time. In his own compositions he displayed an amazing contrapuntal technique, and seriously strove to establish a scientific method of writing music according to basic rules of combination and permutation; his *Der allzeit fertige Menuetten- und Polonaisen-Komponist* (1757) expounded the automatic method of composition. Other works are: *Die Kunst des reinen Satzes in der Musik aus sicheren Grundsätzen hergeleitet und mit deutlichen Beispielen versehen* (2 vols., 1774, 1779, his *magnum opus); Grundsätze des Generalbasses, als erste Linien zur Komposition* (1781; often republ.); *Gedanken über die verschiedenen Lehrarten in der Komposition, als Vorbereitung zur Fugenkenntniss* (1782); *Die Konstruction der gleichschwebenden Temperatur* (1760). *Die wahren Grundsätze zum Gebrauch der Harmonie* (1773) was claimed by a pupil of Kirnberger's, J. A. P. Schulz, as his work. —Cf. H. Riemann, *Geschichte der Musiktheorie* (Leipzig, 1898; p. 478 ff); A. Schering, *Kirnberger als Herausgeber Bachscher Choräle,* in the 'Bach Jahrbuch' (1918); S. Borris, *Kirnbergers Leben und Werk* (Berlin, 1933).

Kirsten, Dorothy, American soprano; b. Montclair, N. J., July 6, 1917. She studied singing at the Juilliard School of Music in N. Y.; Grace Moore took an interest in her and enabled her to go to Italy for further voice training. She studied in Rome with Astolfo Pescia; the outbreak of war in 1939 forced her to return to the U. S. She became a member of the Chicago Opera Co. (début, Nov. 9, 1940); made her first appearance in N. Y. as Mimi with the San Carlo Opera Co. (May 10, 1942); appeared with the Metropolitan Opera in the same role on Dec. 1, 1945. In 1947 she went to Paris, where she sang Louise in Charpentier's opera, coached by Charpentier himself. She was married 3 times; 3rd husband, Dr. John D. French (1955).

Kist, Florentius Cornelis, Dutch writer on music and teacher; b. Arnhem, Jan. 28, 1796; d. Utrecht, March 23, 1863. He was a physician, practicing in The Hague (1818-

25); as a youth, he played the flute and horn. In 1821 he gave up medicine and founded the 'Diligentia' music society; in 1841, settled in Utrecht, where he edited the 'Nederlandsch muzikaal. Tijdschrift' (1841-44). In Utrecht he also established amateur concerts and the singing society 'Duce Apolline.' He publ. *De toestand van het protestantsche kerkgezang in Nederland* (1840); *Levensgeschiedenis van Orlando de Lassus* (1841); translated Brendel's *Grundzüge der Geschichte der Musik* (1851); contributed articles to German musical journals; also wrote vocal music and pieces for the flute.

Kistler, Cyrill, German composer; b. Gross-Aitingen, near Augsburg, March 12, 1848; d. Kissingen, Jan. 1, 1907. He was a schoolteacher (1867-76); then studied music at Munich under Wüllner, Rheinberger, and Franz Lachner (1876-80). In 1883 he was called to the Sondershausen Cons.; from 1885 he lived in Bad Kissingen as principal of a music school and music publisher; he also edited the 'Musikalische Tagesfragen.' An enthusiastic admirer of Wagner, he unsuccessfully attempted to employ the master's forms and principles in his 10 operas, among them, *Kanhild* and *Eulenspiegel.* Besides these, he wrote 104 works (festive marches, funeral marches for orch., choruses, songs, pieces for organ and harmonium), a *Harmonielehre* (1879; based on Wagner's innovations; 2nd augmented ed., 1903); *Musikalische Elementarlehre* (1880); *Der Gesang- und Musikunterricht an den Volksschulen* (1881); *Volksschullehrer-Tonkünstlerlexikon* (3rd ed., 1887); *Jenseits des Musikdramas* (1888); *Franz Witt* (1888); *Über Originalität in der Tonkunst* (1894; 2nd ed., 1907); *Der einfache Kontrapunkt und die einfache Fuge* (1904); *Der drei- und mehrfache Kontrapunkt* (1908). —Cf. A. Eccarius-Sieber, *Cyrill Kistler* (Leipzig, 1906).

Kistner, Karl Friedrich, German music publisher; b. Leipzig, March 3, 1797; d. there, Dec. 21, 1844. In 1831 he took over Probst's music publishing business, which he carried on from 1836 under the firm name of 'Friedrich Kistner.' He acquired many works by Mendelssohn, Schumann, and Chopin for his catalogue. His son, Julius Kistner, succeeded him; in 1866 he sold his business to Karl Friedrich Ludwig Gurckhaus (1821-1884). In 1919 it was bought by Linnemann, and in 1923 merged with C. F. W. Siegel, and operated under the name 'Fr. Kistner & C. F. W. Siegel.'

Kitson, Charles Herbert, English theorist and music pedagogue; b. Leyburn, Yorks, Nov. 13, 1874; d. London, May 13, 1944. He studied for an ecclesiastical career, but also took a D. Mus. degree at Oxford (1902). He was organist of Christ Church Cathedral in Dublin (1913-20); also taught at the Royal Irish Academy of Music. In 1920 he was appointed prof. of music at the Univ. of Dublin, resigning in 1935. Returning to London, he was prof. of harmony and counterpoint at the Royal College of Music. He publ. a number of valuable manuals, distinguished by their clarity of presentation and didactic logic. The most important of these are: *The Art of Counterpoint* (1907); *Studies in Fugue* (1909); *Evolution of Harmony* (1914); *Applied Strict Counterpoint* (1916); *Elementary Harmony* (1920); *Invertible Counterpoint and Canon* (1927); *Rudiments of Music* (1927); *Elements of Fugal Construction* (1929); *Contrapuntal Harmony for Beginners* (1931); *The Elements of Musical Composition* (1936). He also wrote some church music.

Kittel, Bruno, German violinist and conductor; b. Entenbruch, near Posen, May 26, 1870; d. Wassenberg, near Cologne, March 10, 1948. He studied in Berlin; played in theater orchestras there. From 1901 till 1907 he was conductor of the Royal Theater Orch. in Brandenburg; also was director of the Brandenburg Cons. (until 1914). In 1902 he established the 'Kittelsche Chor,' which soon developed into one of the finest choral societies of Europe, and with which he made many tours. In 1935 he was appointed director of the Stern Cons. in Berlin.

Kittel, Johann Christian, German organist and composer; b. Erfurt, Feb. 18, 1732; d. there, May 18, 1809. He studied at the Thomasschule in Leipzig, and was one of Bach's last students there. After Bach's death, he became organist at Langensalza (1751); then at the Predigerkirche in Erfurt (from 1756). Despite the meager remuneration, he remained in Erfurt almost all his life; in search of betterment, he undertook several tours in nearby towns; even as an old man, in his late sixties, he traveled as organist giving concerts in Göttingen, Hanover, Hamburg, and Altona. He stayed in Altona for a few years; publ. a book of church melodies, *Neues Choralbuch,* there in 1803. In his last years he obtained a small stipend from Prince Primas of Dalberg. Among his other works are *Der* *angehende praktische Organist* (3 books; Erfurt, 1801-8; 3rd ed., 1831); 6 sonatas and a fantasia for clavichord; *Grosse Präludien, Hymne an das Jahrhundert* (1801); smaller organ pieces. The famous organist C. H. Rinck was one of his pupils.—Cf. A. Dreetz, *J. C. Kittel, der letzte Bach-Schüler* (Leipzig, 1932).

Kittl, Johann Friedrich, Bohemian composer; b. Castle Worlik, May 8, 1806; d. Lissa, in German Poland, July 20, 1868. He studied at a music school in Prague with Tomaschek; at the age of 19 brought out his opera *Daphnis' Grab* (1825). In 1837 he wrote a *Jagdsinfonie,* which was performed by the Gewandhaus Orch. in Leipzig on Jan. 9, 1840, at Mendelssohn's behest, and subsequently enjoyed considerable vogue in Germany. In 1843 Kittl was appointed director of the Prague Cons., resigning in 1864. He was a friend of Wagner, who wrote for him a libretto, *Bianca und Giuseppe,* which Kittl set to music and produced as *Die Franzosen vor Nizza* (Prague, Feb. 19, 1848). He further wrote the operas *Waldblume* (1852) and *Die Bilderstürmer* (1853); some symphonic and chamber music. —Cf. W. Neumann, *J. F. Kittl* (Kassel, 1857); E. Rychnovsky, *J. F. Kittl* (2 vols.; Prague, 1904-05); Jan Branberger, *Das Konservatorium für Musik in Prag* (Prague, 1911).

Kitzinger, Fritz, pianist and conductor; b. Munich, Jan. 27, 1904; d. New York, May 23, 1947. He studied at the Munich Cons. and the Univ. of Munich, graduating in 1924; conductor of the Dortmund Opera (1925-27), Berlin State Opera (1927-30), and Chemnitz Opera (1930); toured China and Japan as a symphonic conductor. In 1934 he came to the U. S. and subsequently settled in N. Y.

Kitzler, Otto, German conductor and cellist; b. Dresden, March 16, 1834; d. Graz, Sept. 6, 1915. He studied with Johann Schneider, J. Otto, and Kummer (cello); then at the Brussels Cons. with Servais and Fétis; was cellist in the opera orchestras at Strasbourg and Lyons; chorusmaster at theaters in Troyes, Linz, Königsberg, Temesvar, Hermannstadt, and Brünn. In 1868 he became director of the Brünn Music Society and of the Brünn Music School; also conductor of the Männergesangverein; retired in 1898. His reputation was very high. Bruckner, 10 years his senior, took orchestration lessons from him in 1861-63. He wrote orchestral music, piano pieces, songs, etc.; also *Musikalische Erinnerungen* (1904; containing letters from Wagner, Brahms, and Bruckner).

Kiyose, Yasuji, Japanese composer; b. Oita, Jan. 13, 1900. He studied with Yamada, Pringsheim, and Tcherepnin; has been active in the Tokyo Society for Contemporary Music. He has written several fine motion picture scores for Japanese films. Among his works are a piano concerto (Tokyo, March 10, 1955); *Scherzo* for 2 pianos (1937); trio for violin, viola, and cello (1949); Buddhist cantata, *Mountain Itaziki* (1955).

Kjellström, Sven, Swedish violinist; b. Lulea, March 30, 1875; d. Stockholm, Dec. 5, 1950. He studied in Stockholm and later in Paris. Returning to Sweden in 1909, he was active in chamber music societies; was director of the Stockholm Cons. (1929-40). He also formed a string quartet, with which he traveled to remote communities in Scandinavia, including Lapland; he publ. various articles on Swedish music and musicians; was an ardent collector of Swedish folk-songs. — Cf. O. Ottelin, *Sven Kjellström och folkets musikliv* (1945).

Kjerulf (yheh'-rŏŏlf), **Halfdan,** Norwegian song composer; b. Christiania, Sept. 15, 1815; d. Grefsen, near Christiania, Aug. 11, 1868. He was a member of a family of artists and scholars; at first he studied jurisprudence, but later became deeply interested in music; took lessons with a resident German musician, Carl Arnold; became a fairly successful piano teacher; already in his prime, he went to Leipzig to study counterpoint with Richter; returned to Norway in 1851. He limited himself to composition in small forms; although he followed the German model, he succeeded in communicating a lyric sentiment of individual charm; he injected melodic and rhythmic elements of a national Norwegian character into his songs; however, he never resorted to actual quotations from native melodies. Grieg was deeply influenced by his example and frequently expressed admiration for his music; many celebrated singers — Jenny Lind, Christine Nilsson, Henriette Sontag — included his songs in their programs, and thus made them known. He wrote 108 songs in all, among which the most popular are *Last Night, Tell Me, The Nightingale,* and *Synnöve's Song;* he also composed some 30 works for men's chorus, and 10 albums of piano pieces marked by a strong Scandinavian cast *(Elfin Dance, Shepherd's Song, Cradle*

Song, Spring Song, Album-leaf, Capriccio, Scherzo, Scherzino, etc.); also publ. an album, *25 Selected Norwegian Folk Dances* for piano (1861) and *Norwegian Folk Songs* for piano (1867); these are arrangements of Norwegian melodies from collections by Lindeman and others. In 1874 a monument was erected to him in Christiana.—Cf. A. Grønvold, *Halfdan Kjerulf,* in vol. I of 'Norske Musikere' (Christiania, 1883); K. Nyblom, *Halfdan Kjerulf* (1926); Dag Schjelderup-Erbe, *Modality in Halfdan Kjerulf's Music,* in 'Music & Letters' (July, 1957).

Klafsky, Anton Maria, Austrian musicologist and composer; nephew of Katharina Klafsky; b. Winden, Burgenland, July 8, 1877. He studied at the Univ. of Vienna; took lessons in composition with Hermann Grädener. He composed much church music, 3 symphonies, piano pieces, and songs; edited sacred choral works of Michael Haydn for the 'Denkmäler der Tonkunst in Österreich' (vol. 62).

Klafsky, Katharina, Hungarian soprano; born St. Johann, Sept. 19, 1855; d. Hamburg, Sept. 22, 1896. She sang in church at the age of 8; studied with Mme. Marchesi in Vienna at sixteen; sang in the chorus at various opera houses; then appeared as soloist in Salzburg, at 20. She married Hermann Liebermann, a merchant, in 1876; left the stage briefly, but then went to Leipzig, where she resumed her theatrical career in 1881 in leading roles; made a European tour as Sieglinde and Brünnhilde. In 1883 she sang at the Bremen Municipal Theater; in 1885, at Hamburg; then in German opera at London (1892, 1894). In 1886 she divorced her first husband and married Franz Greve, a baritone who died in 1892. On Jan. 31, 1895, she married Otto Lohse, the opera conductor at Hamburg; with him she made an American tour (1895-96). She was one of the most spectacular prima donnas of her day, and her death at the age of 41 was mourned by opera lovers as a great loss.—Cf. L. Ordemann, *Aus dem Leben und Wirken von Katharina Klafsky* (Hameln, 1903).

Klami, Uuno, Finnish composer; b. Virolahti, Sept. 20, 1900. He studied at the Helsinki Cons. (1920-24); in Paris with Ravel (1925), and in Vienna. The Finnish government granted him a life pension in 1938. Most of his music is nationalistic, although some of it reflects the influence of modern French and Russian composers.—Works: for orch.: *Habanera; Keinulaulu (Swing Song); Hispania* (1924; revised 1944); *Barcarola; Merikuvia (4 Pictures of the Sea;* 1929); *Maalaiskuvia (Rural Pictures;* 1930); *Kohtauksia Nukketeatterista (Episodes from a Puppet Theater); Karelian Rhapsody* (1927); *Wedding March; Symphonie enfantine* (1930); *Opernredoute* (1929); *Helsinki March* (1931); *Kalevala Suite* (1932; revised 1943); *Lemminkäinen* (1935); 2 symphonies (1937 and 1944); *Bicyclist* (1947); symph. poem, *Aurora borealis* (1949); incidental music for plays by Shakespeare and Eugene O'Neill; overtures; also 2 piano concertos (1924 and 1950); *Cheremissian Fantasy,* for cello (1930); *Hommage à Haendel,* for piano and strings (1931); violin concerto (1942); theme with variations for cello (1950); piano quartet (1921); piano quintet (1923); marches; songs.

Klatte, Wilhelm, German music critic and writer; b. Bremen, Feb. 13, 1870; d. Berlin, Sept. 12, 1930. He studied music in Leipzig, and took lessons with Richard Strauss in Weimar. For some time he held various positions as conductor and music critic; from 1904 he taught at Stern's Cons. in Berlin; in 1925 he was appointed prof. at the Academy for Church and School Music in Berlin. He publ. (in collaboration with A. Seidl) *Richard Strauss, eine Charakterskizze* (1895); *Zur Geschichte der Programm-Musik,* in the collection of monographs founded by Richard Strauss, 'Die Musik' (1905); *Franz Schubert* (1907); *Grundlagen des mehrstimmigen Satzes* (1922; 3rd ed., 1930).

Klauser, Julius, American writer on music; b. New York, July 5, 1854; d. Milwaukee, April 23, 1907. He studied with his father, Karl Klauser; also took courses at Leipzig Cons. (1871-74); returning to America he settled in Milwaukee as a music teacher. He wrote a book on harmony according to his own system, *The Septonate and the Centralization of the Tonal System* (1890); also *The Nature of Music* (1909).

Klauser, Karl, music editor and arranger; b. St. Petersburg, Russia, Aug. 24, 1823 (of Swiss parents); d. Farmington, Conn., Jan. 5, 1905. He studied music in Germany; went to New York in 1850, and settled in Farmington as a music teacher in 1856. He edited *Half-hours with the Best Composers* and also (with Theodore Thomas and J. K. Paine) *Famous Composers.*

Klauwell, Adolf, German pedagogue; b. Langensalza, Dec. 31, 1818; d. Leipzig, Nov. 21, 1879. He taught in the municipal schools at Leipzig. He publ. elementary class books, and instructive piano pieces *(Goldnes Melodien-Album)*.

Klauwell, Otto, German writer on music, b. Langensalza, April 7, 1851; d. Cologne, May 11, 1917. He served in the Franco-Prussian War; then entered Leipzig Univ., where he studied mathematics and music; obtained his degree of *Dr. phil.* with the dissertation *Die historische Entwicklung des musikalischen Kanons* (1874). In 1875 he was appointed prof. at Cologne Cons.; in 1905 became assistant director there. He publ. *Musikalische Gesichtspunkte* (1881; 2nd ed., 1892, as *Musikalische Bekenntnisse); Der Vortrag in der Musik* (1883; in English, N. Y., 1890); *Der Fingersatz des Klavierspiels* (1885); *Die Formen der Instrumentalmusik* (1894; 2nd ed., 1918); *Geschichte der Sonate* (1899); *Beethoven und die Variationenform* (1901); *Studien und Erinnerungen* (1904); *Geschichte der Programm-Musik* (1910). He was also a composer; wrote 2 romantic operas, *Das Mädchen vom See* (Cologne, 1899) and *Die heimlichen Richter* (Elberfeld, 1902); overtures; chamber music; piano pieces; songs.

Klebe, Giselher, German composer; b. Mannheim, June 28, 1925. He studied at the Berlin Cons. with Kurt von Wolfurt (1942-43), with Josef Rufer, and Boris Blacher (1946-51). He worked in the program division of the Berlin Radio (1946-49); was connected with various music organizations in Germany. An experimenter by nature, he has written music in widely ranging forms, from classically conceived instrumental pieces to highly modernistic works; his technique is basically dodecaphonic, the chief influences being Schoenberg and Anton von Webern; coloristic schemes play an important role in his music. —Works: Wind quintet (1948); *Geschichte vom lustigen Musikanten,* for tenor, chorus, and 5 instruments (1946-47); *Con Moto* for orch. (1948; Bremen, Feb. 23, 1953); Sonata for 2 pianos (1949); *Divertissement joyeux* for chamber orch. (Darmstadt, July 8, 1949); viola sonata (1950); *Zwitschermaschine* for orch. (Donaueschingen Festival, Sept. 10, 1950); sonata for unaccompanied violin (1950); string quartet (1951); *2 Nocturnes* for orch. (Darmstadt, July 20, 1952); *Pas de Trois,* ballet (1952); *Symphony for 42 string instruments* (Hamburg, Jan. 7, 1953); *5 Römische Elegien,* for speaking voice, piano, harpsichord, and double-bass (Donaueschingen, Oct. 10, 1953); *Overture* (Rome, April 12, 1954); concerto for violin, cello, and orch. (Frankfurt, June 19, 1954); a set of songs, *Lieder für Christinchen; Die Räuber,* opera after Schiller (Düsseldorf, June 3, 1957).

Kleber, Leonhard, German organist and composer; b. Göppingen, Württemberg, c. 1490; d. Pforzheim, March 4, 1556. He studied in Heidelberg; from 1521 was organist at Pforzheim. In 1524 he compiled a book of 112 pieces by Hofhaimer, Josquin, Obrecht, and others, arranged in keyboard tablature. Modern reprints are to be found in the following: A. G. Ritter, *Zur Geschichte des Orgelspiels* (1884); R. Eitner 'Monatshefte für Musikgeschichte' (1888); H. J. Moser, *Frühmeister der deutschen Orgelkunst* (1930); W. Apel, *Musik aus früher Zeit* (1934); W. Apel & A. T. Davison, *Historical Anthology of Music* (1946); W. Apel, *Early German Keyboard Music,* in the 'Mus. Quarterly' (April, 1937); 'Denkmäler der Tonkunst in Österreich' (XXXVII, 2; XIV, 1).—Cf. H. Löwenfeld, *Leonhard Kleber und sein Orgeltabulaturbuch* (Berlin, 1897).

Klee, Eugen, choral conductor; b. Kaiserslautern, Germany, Dec. 15, 1869; d. Philadelphia, Dec. 18, 1929. He studied with his father, Jacob Klee, and later with Thuille in Munich. In 1894 he emigrated to America and settled in Philadelphia, where he was active as leader of German choral societies; also trained similar societies in Brooklyn; in 1917 he was elected conductor of the 'Liederkranz' of N. Y.

Klee, Ludwig, German pianist and pedagogue; b. Schwerin, April 13, 1846; d. Berlin, April 14, 1920. He was a pupil at the Kullak Academy in Berlin, and then taught there, until he established a music school of his own. He publ. *Die Ornamentik der klassischen Klaviermusik,* treating ornamentation from Bach to Beethoven; also edited 2 vols. of *Klassische Vortragsstücke.*

Kleefeld, Wilhelm, German writer on music; b. Mainz, April 2, 1868; d. c. 1940. He was a pupil of Spitta in Berlin; took his degree of *Dr. phil.* at Berlin Univ. with the dissertation *Das Orchester der ersten deutschen Oper, Hamburg, 1678-1738* (publ., 1898); in 1898 he became teacher at the Klindworth-Scharwenka Cons.; from 1904 taught at Berlin Univ. He wrote numerous valuable articles on opera; under the title 'Opernrenaissance' he ed. a number of early operas; publ. a monograph on Clara Schumann (1910). He wrote many songs and piano pieces (for 2 and 4 hands).

Kleffel, Arno, German composer and conductor; b. Pössneck, Sept. 4, 1840; d. Nikolassee, near Berlin, July 15, 1913. He studied with Hauptmann in Leipzig; then conducted theater orchestras and opera in Riga, Cologne, Amsterdam, Berlin, Augsburg, Magdeburg, etc. In 1904 he became conductor of Stern's 'Gesangverein' in Berlin; in 1910, head of the operatic dept. at the Musikhochschule. He wrote an opera, *Des Meermanns Harfe* (Riga, 1865); music to Goethe's *Faust;* many characteristic piano pieces (*Ritornelles, Jungbrunnen,* etc.); teaching pieces; *Fête d'enfants; Nuits italiennes,* for 4 hands; also songs.

Kleiber, Erich, Austrian conductor; b. Vienna, Aug. 5, 1890; d. Zürich, Jan. 27, 1956. He studied at the Cons. and Univ. of Prague; in 1911, conductor at the Prague National Theater; then conducted opera in Darmstadt (1912-18), Barmen - Elberfeld (1919-21), and in Düsseldorf and Mannheim (1922-23). From 1923-35, he was general music director of the Berlin State Opera; in 1935, in protest against the German National Socialist government, he emigrated to South America, where he toured as guest conductor; also appeared in Mexico, Cuba, and the U.S.; from 1936-49, conducted German opera at the Teatro Colón in Buenos Aires. He conducted the Havana Philharmonic Orch. (1944-47); appeared as guest conductor of the N.B.C. Symph. Orch. (1945-46); was engaged as chief conductor of the Berlin Opera in 1954, but resigned in March, 1955, before the opening of the season, because of difficulties with the officials of the German Democratic Republic. He wrote a violin concerto, a piano concerto, orchestral variations, a *Capriccio* for orch., an overture, numerous chamber music works, piano pieces, and songs.

Klein, Bernhard, German composer; b. Cologne, March 6, 1793; d. Berlin, Sept. 9, 1832. He went to Paris in 1812 to study with Cherubini at the Paris Cons.; returning to Cologne, he was appointed music director of the Cathedral. In 1818 he settled in Berlin; from 1820 taught at the Royal Institute for Church Music. During his lifetime he was greatly praised for his contrapuntal craftsmanship in sacred works, and was even described by some as 'the Berlin Palestrina.' — Works: 2 operas: *Dido* (Berlin, Oct. 15, 1823) and *Ariadne* (1825; unperformed); another opera, *Irene,* remained unfinished; 3 oratorios: *Job* (Leipzig, 1820), *Jephtha* (Cologne, 1828), and *David* (Halle, 1830); the cantata *Worte des Glaubens* (1817); an 8-part *Pater noster,* a 6-part Magnificat, 6-part responses, 8 books of psalms, hymns, motets for men's voices, etc.; sonatas and variations for piano; songs. His younger brother, **Joseph Klein** (1801-1862), was also a composer; he lived mostly in Berlin. — Cf. C. Koch, *Bernhard Klein* (Rostock, 1902).

Klein, Bruno Oscar, composer, pianist, and pedagogue; b. Osnabrück, Germany, June 6, 1858; d. New York, June 22, 1911. He studied with his father, Karl Klein, organist of the Osnabrück Cathedral, and later at the Munich Cons. In 1878 he settled in America. From 1884 till his death in 1911 he was head of the piano dept. at the Convent of the Sacred Heart, N.Y.; also served as organist in various churches. His opera *Kenilworth* was performed in Hamburg (Feb. 13, 1895); he also wrote a piano concerto; a violin concerto; *American Dances* for orch.; choral music; chamber music; piano pieces.

Klein, Fritz Heinrich, composer and theorist; b. Budapest, Feb. 2, 1892. He went to a military school; then studied music; took lessons with Schoenberg and Alban Berg in Vienna; in 1932 he settled in Linz as prof. of music theory at the Bruckner Cons. there. In his music Klein espoused the ultra-modern methods of composition, strongly influenced by Schoenberg's theories; his work for chamber orch. *Die Maschine, eine extonale Selbstsatire* (1921), which he publ. under the pseudonym 'Heautontimorumenos' (i.e., self-tormentor), contains examples of 12-tone chords and intervallic combinations that were entirely new at the time. He also publ. an important theoretical treatise, *Die Grenze der Halbtonwelt* (Frontiers of the Semitone World), in 'Die Musik' (Jan., 1925); made the vocal score of Alban Berg's opera *Wozzeck.*

Klein, Herman, English music journalist; b. Norwich, July 23, 1856; d. London, March 10, 1934. He studied voice with Manuel Garcia; then taught singing; at the same time wrote music criticism; was critic of the 'Sunday Times' from 1881 to 1901; from 1902 till 1909 he was in America as critic of the 'N. Y. Herald.' He then returned to London as critic of the 'Saturday Review' (1917-21). —Books: *30 Years of Musical Life in London* (N. Y., 1903); *Unmusical New York* (London, 1910); *The Reign of Patti* (N. Y., 1920); *The Art of the Bel Canto* (London, 1923); *Musicians and Mummers* (London, 1925); *Great Women Singers of My Time* (London, 1931); *The Golden Age of Opera* (London, 1933). He was co-editor of Manuel Garcia's *Hints on Singing* (London, 1894); edited *Musical Notes 1886-89; Lieder in English* (a collection of about 60 translations of songs of Schubert, Schumann, Brahms, etc.). He also made a translation of *Carmen.*

Klein, Ivy Frances (born Salaman), English song composer; b. London, Dec. 23, 1895. She has written a number of songs to texts by English poets and has appeared in concerts singing and accompanying herself. In 1924 she married Daryl Klein. Among her songs are: *Ode on Solitude* (after Pope); *Music When Soft Voices Die* (Shelley). Her choral work *She Walked in Beauty* (Byron) was performed at Queen Elizabeth's coronation (1952).

Klein, John, American organist, conductor, and composer; b. Rahns, Penna., Feb. 21, 1915. He studied with Ornstein in Philadelphia; later, studied conducting with Bruno Walter and Felix Weingartner in Salzburg; composition with Nadia Boulanger in Paris and Hindemith at the Berkshire Music Center. After several years as church organist, he wrote music for films. His works include a violin concerto (1944), *Horace, the Bear,* for narrator and orch. (1946), and chamber music.

Klein, Manuel, conductor and composer; b. London, Dec. 6, 1876; d. New York, June 1, 1919. He studied in London; settled in N. Y. in 1904, where he was music director of the N. Y. Hippodrome and composer of the music for a great many of the productions there; in 1915 he returned to London.

Kleinheinz, Franz Xaver, German composer and conductor; b. Mindelheim, July 3, 1772; d. Budapest, Jan. 26, 1832. He played in the Munich Orch.; in 1803 he went to Vienna to study with Albrechtsberger; then was active in Brünn; subsequently in Budapest (1814-23). He made transcriptions of Beethoven's early piano sonatas for string quartet; wrote the operas *Harald* (Ofen, 1914) and *Der Käfig* (Budapest, 1816); much chamber music; sacred choral works; a piano concerto; etc. —Cf. Emil Haraszti, *Les compositions inconnues de F. X. Kleinheinz,* in the 'Revue Musicale' (March, 1930).

Kleinknecht, Jakob Friedrich, German flutist, conductor, and composer; b. Ulm, June 8, 1722; d. Ansbach, Aug. 14, 1794. In 1743 he appeared as flutist in the Margrave's orch. in Bayreuth; 1747, violinist; 1749, 2nd chorusmaster; then appointed court composer; 1761, 1st chorusmaster. He publ. a double concerto for flutes; trios for flute; sonatas for flute; also sonatas for violin, for cello, and for piano.

Kleinmichel, Richard, German pianist and composer; b. Posen, Dec. 31, 1846; d. Charlottenburg, Aug. 18, 1901. He studied with his father, Friedrich Kleinmichel (1827-1894), a bandmaster; subsequently took courses at the Leipzig Cons.; taught music in Hamburg for some years; returned to Leipzig in 1876, and in 1882 became music director of the Municipal Theater there; then was active in similar positions in Danzig and Magdeburg. He married Clara Monhaupt, a soprano. He wrote 2 operas, *Der Pfeiffer von Dusenbach* (Hamburg, 1881) and *Manon* (Hamburg, 1883); 2 symphs.; many characteristic pieces for piano; 4 books of piano études 'für kleine und grosse Leute' and other valuable pedagogical studies. He arranged for piano several of Wagner's scores, including the entire *Ring.*

Kleinsinger, George, American composer; b. San Bernardino, Cal., Feb. 13, 1914. He was taken to New York as a child; first studied dentistry; then entered N. Y. Univ. as a music student of Philip James; later studied at the Juilliard Graduate School with Jacobi and Wagenaar. Kleinsinger played piano in dance bands, served as music director in youth camps, and traveled through the country. He acquired a taste for simple American songs and rhythms; sophisticated pieces on native subjects, often with a satiric purpose, and with colorful instrumental effects, became his specialty; in this vein he wrote *Tubby the Tuba* for narrator and orch. (1942); *Pan the Piper* (1946), *Pee-Wee the Piccolo* (1946), *Street Corner Concerto* for harmonica and orch. (1947), *Brooklyn Baseball Cantata* (1948), and the chamber opera *Archy and Mehitabel* (1954), most of which enjoyed a considerable vogue. He has also written music of serious import: a symphony (1942); cello concerto (1946); violin concerto (1953); etc.

Klemetti, Heikki, Finnish composer and choral conductor; b. Kuortane, Feb. 14, 1876; d. Helsinki, Aug. 26, 1953. He studied philosophy, and then music at the Stern Cons. in Berlin. In 1900 he founded the famous men's choir, Suomen Laulu (became a mixed choir in 1907), with which he toured Scandinavia and Europe (1901-25); also the U. S. (1939). He publ. a history of music (in Finnish; several vols. since 1916), a textbook of choral singing (1917), and a textbook of voice production (1920); composed numerous choruses, Masses, and antiphons (collected and officially approved as the hymnal of the State Church of Finland in 1924); also arranged songs for school and home (3 vols., 1927-28) and some early church music.

Klemm, Johann Gottlob. See **Clemm.**

Klemperer, Otto, distinguished German conductor; b. Breslau, May 14, 1885. His family moved to Hamburg when he was a child; he received rudimentary musical training from his mother; he then studied at the Hoch Cons. in Frankfurt; then in Berlin with Ph. Scharwenka, James Kwast, and Pfitzner. In 1907, at the recommendation of Gustav Mahler, he was appointed conductor of the German National Theater in Prague; then conducted successively at the opera houses of Hamburg (1910), Barmen (1913), Strasbourg (1914), Cologne (1917), and Wiesbaden (1924). During the 1925-26 season, he conducted the N. Y. Symph. Orch.; also conducted in England, Russia, and South America. In 1927 he was appointed first conductor and music director of the Berlin State Opera. After the advent of the Nazi government in 1933 he settled in the U. S.; from 1933-39, was conductor of the Los Angeles Philharmonic; also appeared as guest conductor with several major American orchestras; in 1938, directed the reorganization of the Pittsburgh Symph. Orch.; during the summers he appeared at various European music festivals. His career suffered a serious setback in 1939 when he was operated upon for a brain tumor, but he recovered and resumed his activities. From 1947 to 1950 he conducted at the Budapest Opera; then conducted in Germany and England. In 1957 he led a complete cycle of Beethoven's symphonies in London. He composed some choral music; also a coloratura aria to be used in Rossini's *The Barber of Seville.*

Klenau, Paul (August) von, Danish conductor and composer; b. Copenhagen, Feb. 11, 1883; d. there, Aug. 31, 1946. He studied with Hilmer (violin) and Malling (composition) in Copenhagen; then in Berlin with Halir (violin) and Max Bruch (composition); in Munich with Thuille, and in Stuttgart with Max von Schillings. He began his conducting career in 1907 in Freiburg; from 1922 till 1930 he conducted the Philharmonic in Copenhagen; also led the 'Singakademie' in Vienna. —Works: operas, *Kjartan und Gudrun* (Mannheim, April 4, 1918; revised version as *Gudrun auf Island,* Hagen, Nov. 27, 1924); *Die Lästerschule,* after Sheridan's *School for Scandal* (Frankfurt, 1926); *Michael Kohlhaas* (Stuttgart, 1933); *Rembrandt van Rijn* (Berlin, Jan. 23, 1937); *Elisabeth von England* (Kassel, March 29, 1939; title changed to *Die Königin* after the outbreak of World War II); 3 symphonies; *Inferno* (3 fantasies for orch., after Dante); chamber music; piano pieces; songs. His most successful work was a ballet after Hans Christian Andersen, *Klein Ida's Blumen.*

Klengel, August Alexander, German composer; b. Dresden, Jan. 27, 1783; d. there, Nov. 22, 1852. He studied with Milchmayer, and from 1803, with Clementi, with whom he traveled through Germany, and in 1805, to St. Petersburg, where he remained as private tutor to aristocratic families until 1811. He then lived in Paris; visited London in 1815; returned to Dresden in 1816, and was appointed organist at the Roman Catholic Court Church. He was a fine organist and pianist, particularly distinguished by his *legato* piano style; as a composer, he was a master of contrapuntal forms; his canons were so ingenious that he was known under the sobriquet 'Kanon-Klengel.' His piano canons were publ. under the title *Les Avant-coureurs* (Dresden, 1841); he also wrote 48 canons and 48 fugues, taking Bach's 'Well-tempered Clavichord' as the model (publ. posthumously, 1854). His other published piano works include 2 concertos; a 4-hand fantasia; a rondo; *Promenade sur mer, interrompue par une tempête* and other salon music. —Cf. R. Jäger, *A. A. Klengel, und seine Kanons und Fugen* (Leipzig, 1928).

Klengel, Julius, German cellist; brother of Paul Klengel; b Leipzig, Sept. 24, 1859; d. there, Oct. 27, 1933. Brought up in a musical atmosphere (virtually all members of his family were professional or amateur musicians), he developed rapidly; studied cello with Emil Hegar and theory with Jadassohn. He joined the Gewandhaus Orch. in 1874, when he was 15; in 1881 he became 1st cellist, and remained in that post until his resignation in 1924. He also taught at the Leipzig Cons. He traveled widely in Europe as a soloist; composed a number of works for his instrument, among them 4 concertos; a *Konzertstück* for cello with piano; *Hymnus* for 12 cellos; a double concerto for violin and cello; and 2 string quartets and a piano trio; edited a number of cello works; publ. cello exercises.

Klengel, Paul, German conductor and composer; brother of Julius Klengel; b. Leipzig, May 13, 1854; d. there, April 24, 1935. He studied at the Leipzig Cons. and at Leipzig Univ.; took the degree of *Dr. phil.* with the dissertation *Zur Ästhetik der Tonkunst.* From 1881-86 he conducted the Leipzig Euterpe Concerts; 1888-93, 2nd court conductor at Stuttgart; then again in Leipzig; from 1898 to 1902 he conducted German choral societies in New York; then went back to Germany. He was a versatile musician, and was proficient as a violinist as well as a pianist, although he did not engage in a concert career. He wrote numerous works for violin, and also publ. many skilful arrangements for various combinations. —Cf. Eva Klengel, *Stammtafel der Familie Klengel* (Leipzig, 1929).

Klenovsky, Nikolay Semyonovitch, Russian composer; b. Odessa, 1857; d. St. Petersburg, July 6, 1915. He studied violin with Hřimalý and theory with Tchaikovsky at the Moscow Cons. He was then active as opera conductor (1883-93). In 1893 he was appointed director of the Cons. of Tiflis, in the Caucasus; in 1902, settled in St. Petersburg as conductor of the Court Chapel. He wrote 3 ballets, *Hashish* (Moscow, 1885), *Svetlana* (Moscow, 1886), and *Salanga* (St. Petersburg, 1900); incidental music to various plays; an orchestral suite *Fata Morgana; Georgian Songs,* for solo, chorus, and orch.; a *Georgian Liturgy* a cappella, etc.

Klenovsky, Paul. Pseudonym of **Sir Henry Wood.**

Klerk, Albert de, Dutch organist and composer; b. Haarlem, Oct. 4, 1917. He served as assistant organist in a Haarlem church as a boy; then studied at the Amsterdam Cons. In 1946 he was appointed teacher of organ playing in Utrecht; has also been active as choral conductor. He has written much music for the church; made arrangements of old Flemish songs; has composed a comic opera, *The Magic Violin.*

Kletzki, Paul, Polish conductor; b. Lodz, March 21, 1900. He studied violin with Emil Mlynarski, and later in Berlin; was a member of the Lodz Philharmonic (1914-19); from 1921-33 he lived in Berlin, then in Venice for a year; in 1935, settled temporarily in Milan as teacher of orchestration and composition at the Scuola Superiora di Musica. After 1945, he traveled widely in Europe; was conductor of the Liverpool Philharmonic (1954-55). In 1958 he was appointed conductor of the Dallas Symph. Orch. He is also a prolific composer; among his works are 2 symphonies; a violin concerto; 2 string quartets; piano trio; songs.

Kleven, Arvid, Norwegian composer and flutist; b. Drontheim, Nov. 29, 1899; d. Oslo, Nov. 23, 1929. He studied in Oslo, Paris, and Berlin; from 1919, played flute in the National Theater Orch. in Oslo, and in the Philharmonic Orch. there. He wrote a tone poem, *Lotusland* (Oslo, 1922), 2 *Aquarelles,* for orch. (1923); *Sinfonia libera* (1927); several works for violin; piano pieces; songs.

Klička (klitch'-kăh), **Josef,** Bohemian organist and composer; b. Klattau, Dec. 15, 1855; d. there, March 28, 1937. He studied with Skuherský in Prague; then conducted various choral societies there; from 1906-20 he was inspector of music in Bohemia. He was appointed prof. of organ at the Prague Cons. in 1885, and taught until his retirement in 1924. He wrote an opera, *The Miller's Beautiful Wife* (Prague, 1886); 9 Masses; 2 oratorios; many organ works, including a fantasia on the chorale melody *St. Wenzeslaus,* and *Legend* (both published in 'Les Maîtres contemporains d'orgue,' Paris); chamber music; also pieces for harp. —Cf. K. Hoffmeister, *Josef Klička* (Prague, 1944).

Klimov, Mikhail Georgievitch, Russian conductor and pedagogue; b. Moscow, Oct. 22, 1881; d. Leningrad, Feb. 20, 1937. He studied with Rimsky-Korsakov and Tcherepnin at the St. Petersburg Cons. (graduated 1908). In 1919 he was called upon to reorganize the former Imperial Church Choir into a secular society, and toured Europe with it in 1928.

Klindworth (klint'-vort), **Karl,** eminent German pianist, pedagogue, and editor; b. Hanover, Sept. 25, 1830; d. Stolpe, near Potsdam, July 27, 1916. He was a precocious musician, and learned to play violin and piano as a child; obliged to earn his own living, he obtained work as conductor of a traveling opera company when he was only 17. The enterprise failed in 1849, and he returned to his native city, where he gave piano lessons; later undertook a tour of Germany; then studied with Liszt in Weimar. He made rapid progress, and in 1854, armed with letters of introduction, went to London, where he remained until 1868, establishing himself as a popular piano teacher; also appeared as concert pianist. When Wagner was in London in 1855, they became friends; their mutual admiration led Klindworth to undertake the most important work of his life, the vocal scores of Wagner's tetralogy, *The Ring of the Nibelung.* In 1868, he was engaged as prof. at the newly-founded Moscow Cons., at the invitation of its director, Nicholas Rubinstein; after Rubinstein's death in 1881, Klindworth returned to Germany; was for a time conductor of the Berlin Philharmonic. In 1884 he established in Berlin his own 'Klavierschule'; in 1893 it was merged with the Scharwenka Cons. of Music in Berlin, as 'Konservatorium der Musik Klindworth-Scharwenka,' which became one of the most famous music schools in Germany. Klindworth remained on the faculty until 1897; then retired to Potsdam. Klindworth was an exceptionally competent arranger and music editor; apart from his masterly transcriptions of Wagner's operas, he made an arrangement for 2 pianos of Schubert's C major symphony; publ. a practical ed. of Beethoven's sonatas. He also wrote a number of virtuoso pieces for piano, of which the brilliant *Polonaise-Fantaisie* and 24 grand études in all keys enjoyed some vogue among pianists. —Cf. Hugo Leichtentritt, *Das Konservatorium der Musik Klindworth-Scharwenka, 1881-1931* (Berlin, 1931).

Klingenberg, Friedrich Wilhelm, German pedagogue; b. Sulau, June 6, 1809; d. Görlitz, April 2, 1888. He was director of the Music Academy at Breslau (1830-37); from 1840-85, cantor at the Peterskirche in Görlitz. He wrote a symphony, overtures, piano pieces, vocal church music, and songs.

Klitzsch, Karl Emanuel, German conductor and composer; b. Schönhaide, Oct. 30, 1812; d. Zwickau, March 5, 1889. He was a self-taught musician; taught in Zwickau; co-founder and conductor of the Music Society there; contributed articles to the 'Neue Zeitschrift für Musik.' Under the pen name of Emanuel Kronach, he publ. the opera *Juana, oder ein Tag auf St. Domingo;* the 96th Psalm, for soli, chorus, and orch.; also songs.

Klose, Friedrich, composer; b. Karlsruhe (of Swiss parents), Nov. 29, 1862; d. Ruvigliana, Lugano, Dec. 24, 1942. He studied in Karlsruhe and Geneva; in 1886 he went to Vienna, where he took a course with Bruckner. He traveled in Germany, Austria, and Switzerland, occupying teaching posts for a year or two in various places, until 1907, when he was appointed prof. of composition at the Akademie der Tonkunst in Munich. In 1920 he went to Switzerland. He left several large works that betray the influence of Bruckner and Wagner; of these, the most important is *Ilsebill,* described as a 'dramatic symphony' but in reality an opera (Munich, Oct. 29, 1905); another important work is an oratorio, *Der Sonne-Geist* (Basel, 1918); he further wrote a symph. poem, *Das Leben ein Traum;* organ works; a string quartet; songs. He publ. the books *Meine Lehrjahre bei Bruckner* (Regensburg, 1927), and *Bayreuth* (1929). —Cf. R. Louis, *Friedrich Klose* (Munich, 1905); H. Knappe, *Friedrich Klose* (1921). A symposium of articles, *Friedrich Klose, zum 80. Geburtstag,* was publ. at Lugano (1942).

Klosé, Hyacinthe-Éléonore, noted clarinetist and pedagogue; b. Isle of Corfu, Oct. 11, 1808; d. Paris, Aug. 29, 1880. He studied at the Paris Cons.; then taught there for nearly 30 years (1839-68). In 1843 he introduced an important innovation into Böhm's system of ring-keys, which was widely adopted; publ. a *Grande méthode pour la clarinette à anneaux mobiles* (1844) based on that system; also studies and exercises. He did much to promote the then novel saxophone, and wrote some music for it.

Kloss, Erich, German writer on music; b. Görlitz, Feb. 19, 1863; d. (in an automobile accident) Berlin, Nov. 1, 1910. He began his career as a teacher, but because of deafness he was obliged to give it up; directed his attention to writing. He publ. *20 Jahre Bayreuth* (1896); *Wagner, wie er war und ward* (1901); *Ein Wagner-Lesebuch* (1904); *Wagner-Anekdoten* (1908); *R. Wagner in seinen Briefen* (1908); *R. Wagner an seine Künstler* (1909); *R. Wag-*

ner im Liede (1910); *R. Wagner über die Meistersinger* (1910); *R. Wagner über den Ring des Nibelungen* (1913; publ. posthumously); also edited *Richard Wagner an Freunde und Zeitgenossen* (1909), and the 3rd augmented ed. of the Wagner-Liszt correspondence (1910).

Klotz, a family of Bavarian violin makers at Mittenwald. Their instruments were brought into repute by Matthias Klotz (b. Mittenwald, June 11, 1653; d. there, Aug. 16, 1743), the son of Egidius Klotz; he is believed to have learned the art of violin making from Nicola Amati, during his travels in Italy; he manufactured his best instruments between 1670 and 1696. His son Sebastian Klotz is regarded as even superior in making violins after Italian models; another son, Joseph Klotz, continued the tradition of the family. There followed, in the 18th century, several other violin makers named Klotz, but their relationship to the family cannot be established.

Klughardt, August (Friedrich Martin), German composer; b. Cöthen, Nov. 30, 1847; d. Dessau, Aug. 3, 1902. He was a pupil of Blassmann and Reichel at Dresden. In 1867 he was appointed theater conductor at Posen; had similar posts in Lübeck (1868) and Weimar (1869-73); he then was active in Neustrelitz (1873-82) and Dessau (from 1883). He wrote 4 operas: *Miriam* (Weimar, 1871), *Iwein* (Neustrelitz, 1879), *Gudrun* (Neustrelitz, 1882), and *Die Hochzeit Mönchs* (Dessau, Nov. 10, 1886; given in Prague as *Astorre*, 1888); 5 symphonies, chamber music, songs, and piano pieces. —Cf. L. Gerlach, *August Klughardt, Sein Leben und seine Werke* (Leipzig, 1902).

Knab, Armin, German composer; b. Neu-Schleichach, Feb. 19, 1881; d. Bad Wörishofen, June 23, 1951. He studied piano in Würzburg; from 1934-43, taught at the Hochschule für Musik-Erziehung, in Berlin. His works include the sacred cantatas *Mariae Geburt* (1928), *Vanitas mundi* (1946), *Engelsgruss* (1950), etc.; the musical fairy tales, *Sneewittchen* and *Rumpelstilzchen;* folksong cantatas *Singt und klingt* (1934), *Grüss Gott, du schöner Maien* (1935), and *Glück auf, ihr Bergleute* (1946); a great number of choral works; many instrumental pieces for school use. Knab was particularly esteemed in Germany as a composer of lieder. He followed the Romantic tradition, but tended towards a more severe modal style in his larger works. —Cf. O. Lang, *Armin Knab, ein Meister deutscher Liedkunst* (Munich, 1937).

Knabe, William (Valentine Wilhelm Ludwig), founder of the celebrated piano manufacturing firm of Baltimore; b. Kreuzberg, near Oppeln, Prussia, June 3, 1803; d. Baltimore, May 21, 1864. He opened his business in 1839 with Henry Gaehle; in 1854 the partnership was dissolved. His successors were his sons William Knabe (1841-89) and Ernest Knabe, joined later by Charles Keidel, and his grandsons Ernest J. Knabe and William Knabe (1872-1939). The firm was later amalgamated with the American Piano Corp.

Knappertsbusch, Hans, German conductor; b. Elberfeld, March 12, 1888. He studied with Steinbach and Lohse at the Cologne Cons. (1909-12); then occupied various positions as opera conductor at Elberfeld (1913-18), Leipzig (1918-19), and Dessau (1919-22). In 1922 he received the important appointment of conductor at the State Opera in Munich, which he held until 1938; in that year he became director of the Vienna State Opera. He also led numerous performances at the Salzburg festivals; specialized in Wagnerian repertory, in which he attained signal success.

Knecht, Justin Heinrich, German composer and organist; b. Biberach, Sept. 30, 1752; d. there, Dec. 1, 1817. He was organist and music director in Biberach from 1771 to the end of his life, traveling only briefly to Stuttgart, where he was court conductor from 1807 till 1809. Despite his provincial field of activity he attained considerable repute in Germany through his compositions and theoretical writings. He was a follower of the Vogler system of harmony; taught chord building by thirds up to chords of the eleventh on all degrees of the scale. His publications include: *Erklärung einiger missverstandenen Grundsätze aus der Vogler'schen Theorie* (Ulm, 1785); *Gemeinnützliches Elementarwerk der Harmonie und des Generalbasses* (4 parts, 1792-8); *Kleines alphabetisches Wörterbuch der vornehmsten und interessantesten Artikel aus der musikalischen Theorie* (1795); *Vollständige Orgelschule für Anfänger und Geübtere* (3 parts, 1795-8); *Theoretisch-praktische Generalbass-Schule; Kleine Klavierschule für die ersten Anfänger* (republ. as *Bewährtes Methodenbuch beim ersten Klavierunterricht); Allgemeiner musikalischer Katechismus* (Biberach, 1803); *Luther's Verdienst um Musik und Poesie* (1817). He wrote about 15 operas, several sacred works, and a piece for 15 instruments, *Tongemälde der Natur,* to which he supplied a programmatic description, seemingly anticipating Beethoven's 'Pastoral' Symphony. However, the resemblance is superficial, and there is no reason to believe that Beethoven was influenced by Knecht in this 'tone painting' of nature. —Cf. E. Kauffmann, *J. H. Knecht* (Tübingen, 1892); A. Bopp, *J. H. Knecht* (Kassel, 1930).

Kneisel, Franz, violin virtuoso; b. Bucharest (of German parentage), Jan. 26, 1865; d. New York, March 26, 1926. He studied at the Cons. of Bucharest, graduating at the age of 14; in 1879 went to Vienna, where he became a pupil of Grün and Hellmesberger at the Vienna Cons.; made his début on Dec. 31, 1882 in Vienna; in 1884 he went to Berlin, where he was concertmaster of the Bilse Orch. (1884-85). In 1885 he was engaged as concertmaster of the Boston Symph. Orch.; made his début as soloist in Boston on Oct. 31, 1885, playing the Beethoven Concerto. In 1886 he organized the celebrated Kneisel Quartet (Emmanuel Fiedler as 2nd violin; Louis Svecenski, viola; Fritz Giese, cello), which gave performances of high quality in Boston, New York, and other American cities, and also in Europe, obtaining world fame. The Kneisel Quartet was dissolved in 1917; it then consisted of Kneisel, Hans Letz, Louis Svecenski, and Willem Willeke. Kneisel was equally at home in Classic and Romantic violin literature, interpreting the concertos of Beethoven, Mendelssohn, and Brahms, or of Joachim and Goldmark, with masterly insight. He was admirable in ensemble playing; his service to the cause of chamber music in America was very great. He brought out before the American public the last Beethoven quartets, and (for the first time) Beethoven's *Grosse Fuge.* In recognition of his contribution to music in America he was made honorary Mus. Doc. by Yale Univ. (1911) and by Princeton Univ. (1915). A signal honor was conferred upon him in 1907, when he was invited to serve as a member of the jury of the violin competition of the Paris Cons. In 1893 he conducted the concerts of the Boston Symph. at the World's Fair in Chicago. In 1902 and 1903 he was assistant conductor of the Worcester (Mass.) Festival. In 1903 he resigned his post as concertmaster of the Boston Symph.; from 1905 he taught violin at the Institute of Musical Art in N.Y. He composed a *Grand Concert Etude* for violin; publ. *Advanced Exercises* for violin (1900); edited a collection of violin pieces (3 vols., 1900).

Kniese, Julius, German conductor; b. Roda, near Jena, Dec. 21, 1848; d. Dresden, April 22, 1905. He was a pianist and organist; studied with W. Stade in Altenburg; then in Leipzig with Brendel and C. Riedel (1868-70). From 1871-76 he was director of the Singing Academy at Glogau; then conducted the singing society at Rühl and the Wagnerverein at Frankfurt; music director at Aix (1884-89); from 1882 he was also chorusmaster for the festival operas at Bayreuth, where he settled in 1889; became director of the Preparatory School for Stage Singers (1890). He wrote an opera, *Jery und Bätely* (Weimar, 1937); publ. 4 albums of songs.

Knight, Joseph Philip, English song composer and clergyman; b. Bradford-on-Avon, July 26, 1812; d. Great Yarmouth, June 2, 1887. He studied organ with Corfe at Bristol. He began to compose songs at the age of 20, and from the very first, revealed an exceptional knack of contriving a melody with suitable harmony that was memorable and conveyed a sincere sentiment. While in the U.S. in 1839-41, he brought out his most celebrated song, *Rocked in the Cradle of the Deep,* which was sung by Braham and others with enormous success; another successful song was *Why Chime the Bells so Merrily?* After 2 years as vicar and organist at St. Agnes, Scilly Islands, he married, lived abroad for a time, and then returned to England. Among his songs written in England are: *Venice, Say What Shall My Song Be Tonight?, The Dream, All on the Summer Sea, She Wore a Wreath of Roses, Of What is the Old Man Thinking?,* etc.

Knipper, Lev Konstantinovitch, Russian composer; b. Tiflis, Dec. 16, 1898. He studied with Glière in Moscow; then went to Germany, where he took lessons with Jarnach in Berlin and Julius Weissmann in Freiburg. Returning to Russia, he continued to study; at that time, he had already written numerous pieces for piano and songs. His travels abroad influenced him in the direction of modern music; but this phase proved transitory, and he soon adopted a musical language derived from the traditions of the Russian nationalists. A prolific composer, he has written 13 symphonies; the choral finale from his 4th symphony was arranged as a song, which became very popular not only in Russia but in the U. S. (as *Meadowland, Cavalry of the Steppes,* etc.).

His opera *The North Wind* was produced in Moscow on March 30, 1930. In 1941 he was in Persia, where he collected native melodies; used Persian themes in a symph. suite, Mongol themes in the opera *On Baikal Lake* (1948), and Tadzhik themes in the ballet *The Source of Happiness* (1949).

Knittl, Karl, Bohemian conductor and composer; b. Polna, Oct. 4, 1853; d. Prague, March 17, 1907. He was a pupil of Skuherský at the Prague School for Organists; later studied singing with Pivoda and conducting with Smetana. From 1877-90, and again from 1897-1901, he conducted the choral society 'Hlahol' in Prague; in 1890 he was appointed prof. at the Prague Cons.; in 1904, succeeded Dvořák as its director. He wrote *Wintermärchen* and *Lied von der Glocke,* for orch.; cantatas; choruses; songs; piano pieces; also *Beispiele zur allgemeinen Musiklehre* and *Lehre vom homophonen Satze.*

Knoch, Ernst, conductor; b. Karlsruhe, Aug. 1, 1875. He studied at the Karlsruhe Cons., and later took a course in conducting with Felix Mottl, whose assistant he became at the Karlsruhe Opera (1898-1901). He made his professional début as conductor in Strasbourg (1901), where he remained till 1907; conducted at Bayreuth (1904-07), Essen (1907-09), and Cologne (1909-12). He then made a world tour in the Thomas Quinlan Co. as conductor of Wagner's operas; gave the first Australian performance of *Tristan und Isolde* (Melbourne, July 14, 1912). In 1913-14 he conducted 20 performances of *Parsifal* in Elberfeld. In 1914 he went to America; conducted opera in New York, Chicago, and Cleveland; settled in N.Y. as opera coach and teacher in 1938.

Knorr, Ernst Lothar von, German composer; b. Eitorf, near Cologne, Jan. 2, 1896. He studied at the Cologne Cons. with Fritz Steinbach, Bram Eldering, and Karl Körner. After serving in the German army during World War I, he played violin in various provincial orchestras; in 1926, settled in Berlin; 1937, became principal of the Hochschule für Musik there; in 1941, was vice-director of the Hochschule für Musik in Frankfurt; 1946, director of a similar school in Trossingen; in 1952, appointed director of the Music Academy in Hanover. From 1931-35 he was editor of the 'Pro Musica' series of modern music. During the bombing of Frankfurt in 1944, almost all of his manuscript works were destroyed. Among extant compositions are several cantatas (*Brüder, wir halten Totenwacht; Aus allem Eins; Lobe den Herrn; Vom Werden und Vergehen,* etc.); 2 school cantatas (*Strafe der Faulheit* and *Lohn des Fleisses*); concerto for 2 orchestras; chamber concerto for piano, saxophone, chorus, and small orch.; *Marienleben, Nacht,* and other choral works with orch.; some 80 choruses a cappella; 70 songs; school songs; pieces for recorder and for lute.

Knorr, Iwan, eminent German pedagogue and composer; b. Mewe, Jan. 3, 1853; d. Frankfurt, Jan. 22, 1916. His family went to Russia when he was 3 years old, returning to Germany in 1868; he then entered Leipzig Cons., where he studied piano with Moscheles and theory with Richter and Reinecke. In 1874 he went back to Russia, where he taught at the Kharkov Cons., and also at the Imperial Institute for Noble Ladies in St. Petersburg. He finally settled in Frankfurt in 1883 as teacher at the Hoch Cons.; in 1908, became its director. He had many distinguished pupils, among them Cyril Scott, Pfitzner, Braunfels, and Ernst Toch. He wrote music in a Romantic vein; several of his works are inspired by Ukrainian folksongs which he had heard in Russia. — Works: operas *Dunja* (Coblenz, March 23, 1904) and *Durchs Fenster* (Karlsruhe, Oct. 4, 1908); *Ukrainische Liebeslieder,* for vocal quartet and piano, op. 6 (1890); *Variationen* (on a Ukrainian folksong), op. 7 (1891); *Variations* for piano, violin, and cello, op. 1; piano quartet, op. 3; *Variations* for piano and cello, op. 4; etc. He wrote a biography of Tchaikovsky for the series 'Berühmte Musiker' (1900) and several pedagogic works: *Aufgaben für den Unterricht in der Harmonielehre* (1903), *Lehrbuch der Fugenkomposition* (1911), *Fugen des Wohltemperirten Klaviers in bildlicher Darstellung* (1912; 2nd ed., 1926); also a number of analyses for Schlesinger's 'Musikführer.' —Cf. Moritz Bauer, *Iwan Knorr* (Frankfurt, 1916; contains a complete list of works).

Knorr, Julius, eminent German pianist and pedagogue; b. Leipzig, Sept. 22, 1807; d. there, June 17, 1861. He made his début as pianist at the Gewandhaus, Leipzig, in 1831; was an intimate friend of Schumann, and an editor of the 'Neue Zeitschrift für Musik' during its first year. Knorr introduced the preparatory technical exercises that have become the groundwork of technical study on the piano. His publ. works are *Neue Pianoforteschule in 184 Übungen* (1835; 2nd ed., 1841, as *Die Pianoforteschule der neuesten Zeit; ein Supplement zu den Werken von Cramer, Czerny, Herz, Hummel, Hünten, Kalkbrenner, Moscheles . . . *); *Das Klavierspiel in 280 Übungen; Materialien für das mechanische Klavierspiel* (1844); *Methodischer Leitfaden für Klavierlehrer* (1849; often republ.); *Ausführliche Klaviermethode,* in 2 parts: *Methode* (1859) and *Schule der Mechanik* (1860); *Erklärendes Verzeichniss der hauptsächlichsten Musikkunstwörter* (1854).

Knote (knoh'te), **Heinrich,** German tenor; b. Munich, Nov. 26, 1870; d. Garmisch, Jan. 12, 1953. He studied with Kirchner; was a member of the court opera in Munich from 1892 till 1914, except for a short interval, when he sang in Hamburg. He frequently was granted leave of absence, and so was able to make guest appearances. He was first heard in America at the Metropolitan Opera in 1902, and sang for 3 more seasons; his voice was compared favorably with that of Caruso and Jean de Reszke; in Wagnerian roles, he was particularly distinguished. From 1915, he was the principal tenor at the Deutsches Opernhaus in Charlottenburg-Berlin; later in Würzburg; from 1924, until his retirement, again in Munich. —Cf. J. H. Wagenmann, *Der 60-jährige deutsche Meistersänger Heinrich Knote* (Munich, 1930).

Knyvett, Charles, Sr., English organist and tenor; father of Charles and William Knyvett; b. Norfolk, Feb. 22, 1752; d. London, Jan. 19, 1822. He was a chorister in London; in 1786, was appointed a Gentleman of the Chapel Royal, and in 1796, an organist there. From 1791-94 he led the Vocal Concerts (with S. Harrison).

Knyvett, Charles, Jr., English vocalist and organist; son of Charles Knyvett, Sr.; b. London, 1773; d. there, Nov. 2, 1859. He studied organ with Samuel Webbe; in 1801 he participated in the Vocal Concerts in London; in 1802 he became organist at St. George's; also was active as a teacher. He publ. a *Selection of Psalm Tunes* (1823).

Knyvett, William, English singer, conductor, and composer; son of Charles Knyvett; b. London, April 21, 1779; d. Ryde, Isle of Wight, Nov. 17, 1856. He sang alto at the Concerts of Ancient Music; in 1797, became a Gentleman of the Chapel Royal, and in 1802, a composer there. He participated in concerts in London as a singer for many years; also composed a number of glees, of which one, *When the Fair Rose,* won a prize of the Harmonic Society in 1800.

Kobald, Karl, writer on music; b. Brno, Aug. 28, 1876. He studied at Vienna Univ. with Guido Adler, Hellmesberger, and Hans Richter; also took lessons with Bruckner. In 1918 he became music adviser in the Austrian Ministry of Education; from 1932-38, and again in 1945-6, was president of the State Academy; then retired and lived in Rodaun, near Vienna. He publ. *Alt-Wiener Musikstätten* (1919; 2nd ed., 1923); *Schubert und Schwind* (1920); *Franz Schubert* (1922); *In Memoriam Anton Bruckner* (1924); *Johann Strauss* (1925); *Beethoven* (1927; new eds. 1936, 1946, and 1952); *Franz Schubert und seine Zeit* (1927); *Klassische Musikstätten* (1929); *Joseph Haydn* (1929); *Wo unsterbliche Musik entstand* (1950).

Kobbé, Gustav, American writer on music; b. New York, March 4, 1857; killed in his sailboat by a Navy seaplane maneuvering in the bay near Babylon, Long Island, July 27, 1918. He studied piano and composition with Adolf Hagen in Wiesbaden (1867-72), and with Joseph Mosenthal in New York. He attended Columbia College (School of Arts, 1877; School of Law, 1879). He was a frequent contributor, on musical and other subjects, to the daily press and to magazines. He publ. *Wagner's Life and Works* (N.Y., 1890; 2 vols., containing analyses, with the *Leitmotive* of the music dramas); *The Ring of the Nibelung* (1899; part of preceding, printed separately); *Opera Singers* (1901); the novel *Signora, A Child of the Opera House* (1902); *Loves of the Great Composers* (1905); *How to Appreciate Music* (1906); *Wagner and His Isolde* (1906); *Famous American Songs* (1906). Shortly before his accidental death, he finished his *Complete Opera Book,* which was publ. posthumously (N. Y., 1919) and proved so successful that 20 printings were issued before 1950; a revised and enlarged edition, *Kobbé's Complete Opera Book,* compiled by the Earl of Harewood (1246 pages; includes stories of many operas by modern composers), was publ. in 1954.

Koch, Caspar Petrus, organist and pedagogue; b. Carnap, Germany, Nov. 25, 1872. At the age of 10 he was taken to the U.S., where he studied at various colleges in

Illinois and Wisconsin. In 1892 he was appointed organist at Holy Trinity Church in Pittsburgh; took a leave of absence (1901-3) and went to Berlin, where he pursued additional studies with Heinrich Reimann (organ), Franz Kullak (piano), Heinrich Urban and Wilhelm Berger (composition); in 1903, returned to America and resumed his duties at Holy Trinity Church, keeping that post until 1925. He taught piano and organ at Duquesne Univ. (1909-14) and at Carnegie Institute of Technology in Pittsburgh (1914-41). He publ. a *Book of Scales for Organ; Bach's 15 Symphonies Arranged as Organ Trios; The Organ Student's Gradus ad Parnassum:* Book I, *The Elements of Interpretation* (1945), Book II, *Progressive Organ Studies* (1950); edited Bach's *8 Little Preludes and Fugues for Organ;* Bach's *Toccata and Fugue in D minor;* and other organ works. He made numerous organ transcriptions, and composed organ pieces, choral works, and songs.

Koch, Eduard Emil, German clergyman; b. Schloss Solitude, near Stuttgart, Jan. 20, 1809; d. Stuttgart, April 27, 1871. He was pastor at Gross-Anspach (1837), at Heilbronn (1847); then superintendent there (1853-64). He wrote the valuable work *Geschichte des Kirchenliedes und Kirchengesanges, insbesondere der deutschen evangelischen Kirche* (1847; 3rd ed. in 8 vols., 1866-77).

Koch, (Sigurd Christian) Erland von, son of Sigurd Koch, Swedish composer; b. Stockholm, April 26, 1910. He studied music with his father; then enrolled in the Stockholm Cons. He subsequently studied in Berlin, Paris, and London; took lessons in conducting with Clemens Krauss. A prolific composer, he has written 3 symphonies (1938; 1945; 1949); *Nordic Capriccio* for orch. (1943); piano concerto (1936); violin concerto (1937); viola concerto (1946); ballad opera *Lasse Lucidor* (1943); and a considerable amount of chamber music as well as songs and piano pieces.

Koch, Friedrich E., German composer and teacher; b. Berlin, July 3, 1862; d. there, Jan. 30, 1927. He studied cello with Hausmann and theory with Bargiel; played cello in the Court Orch. in Berlin (1883-91); then taught privately; in 1901, was elected a member of the Academy. As a composer, he cultivated almost exclusively the large forms; his style was somewhat severe in its elevation; his music followed the Romantic school of Mendelssohn. He wrote the opera *Die Halliger* (Cologne, 1897); another opera *Lea* was not produced; the oratorios *Von den Tageszeiten* and *Die Sündflut;* 2 symphonies; *Deutsche Rhapsodie,* for violin and orch.; a string trio; a piano trio; many choral works. — Cf. K. Kämpf, *F. E. Koch* (Leipzig, 1907).

Koch, Heinrich Christoph, German theorist; b. Rudolstadt, Oct. 10, 1749; d. there, March 12, 1816. He studied with Göpfert at Weimar; he was violinist in the orchestra at Rudolstadt (1768); then leader of chamber music there (1777). He publ. *Musikalisches Lexikon* (1802); *Versuch einer Anleitung zur Composition* (3 vols., 1782-93); *Handbuch bei dem Studium der Harmonie* (1811); a manual of enharmonic modulation (1812); contributed articles to periodicals. He also wrote a *Choralbuch* for wind band, and cantatas. He started a 'Journal der Tonkunst' in 1795, but it was unsuccessful.

Koch, (Richert) Sigurd (Valdemar) von, Swedish composer; b. Ägnö, near Stockholm, June 28, 1879; d. Stockholm, March 16, 1919. He studied piano in Germany; composed several symphonic works, instrumental concertos, and much chamber music; his violin sonata has been published.

Kochanski (koh-hahn'-skē), **Paul,** Polish violinist; b. Odessa, Sept. 14, 1887; d. New York, Jan. 12, 1934. He studied with Mlynarski in Warsaw; in 1901, became concertmaster of the Warsaw Philharmonic; in 1903, went to Brussels to study with César Thomson; in 1907, was appointed prof. at the Warsaw Cons. In 1913 he became prof. at the St. Petersburg Cons.; taught at the Kiev Cons. from 1917-19; then left Russia, reaching America in 1921; made his American début with the N.Y. Symph. Orch., Feb. 14, 1921. From 1924 he taught at the Juilliard School; gave concerts in the U.S. and Europe. He excelled in the performance of modern works; did a great service in promoting the violin music of Szymanowski; publ. several transcriptions for violin and piano, among them a *Spanish Popular Suite* (after *7 Spanish Popular Songs* of Manuel de Falla).

Köchel, Ludwig von, Austrian musicographer, compiler of the famous Mozart catalogue; b. Stein, near Krems, Jan. 14, 1800; d. Vienna, June 3, 1877. He studied natural sciences, and attained distinction in botany and mineralogy; music was his hobby; his love for Mozart's art moved him to compile a Mozart catalogue as methodically as he would a descriptive index of minerals; the result of this task of devotion was the great *Chronologisch-thematisches Verzeichnis sämmtlicher Tonwerke W. A. Mozarts* (Leipzig, 1862). The 'K numbers' used to identify Mozart's works have been supplemented by secondary numbers in Alfred Einstein's revision of the catalogue (1937; reprinted, with further alterations and corrections, in 1947). Köchel himself publ. some supplementary matter in the 'Allgemeine musikalische Zeitung' (1864); the 2nd ed. of the catalogue was prepared by Waldersee (1905). Köchel's writings on music include further *Über den Umfang der musikalischen Produktivität W. A. Mozarts* (1862), which preceded the publication of the catalogue; *Die kaiserliche Hofmusikkapelle in Wien von 1543 bis 1867* (1869); and *Johann Josef Fux* (1872); he also edited *83 neuaufgefundene Originalbriefe L. van Beethovens an den Erzherzog Rudolph* (1865).

Kocher, Conrad, German composer; b. Ditzingen, near Stuttgart, Dec. 16, 1786; d. Stuttgart, March 12, 1872. In 1803 he went to St. Petersburg, where he studied piano with Klengel and Berger, and composition with J. H. Müller; traveled in Italy (1819). Returning to Germany in 1820, he settled in Stuttgart and devoted himself to composition; received the honorary degree of Dr. phil. from Tübingen Univ. in 1827. He wrote 2 operas, an oratorio, etc.; also publ. a piano method; a manual of composition, *Die Tonkunst in der Kirche* (1823); and *Zionsharfe* (ancient and modern chorales).

Kocian, Jaroslav, Czech violinist; b. Usti nad Orlice, Feb. 22, 1883; d. Prague, March 8, 1950. He studied violin with Ševčik at the Prague Cons., and also took lessons in composition with Dvořák. After his graduation in 1901 he traveled widely as a concert violinist, almost rivaling the success of his famous compatriot Jan Kubelik. He made 4 American tours; also appeared in Asia and Africa. After 1920 he confined himself mainly to teaching; became prof. at the Master School of the Prague Cons. in 1924; retired in 1943. He composed several effective violin pieces (2 *Humoresques, Sérénade, Intermezzo pittoresque, Hymne au printemps, Dumka, Berceuse,* etc.). — A memorial vol., *Jaroslav Kocian: sborník statí a vzpomínek,* was published at Prague in 1953.

Koczalski (koh-tchahl'-skē), **Raoul (Armand Georg)**, Polish pianist; b. Warsaw, Jan. 3, 1884; d. Posnan, Nov. 24, 1948. He was trained by his mother; at the age of 4, he played at a charity concert in Warsaw, and was at once proclaimed an 'infant phenomenon'; his progress was watched by psychologists, and a detailed biography of him was publ. by B. Vogel when he was only 12. He gave concerts in Vienna (1892), Russia, Paris, and London (1893); made nearly 1000 public appearances before 1896. His sensational success diminished as he grew out of the prodigy age, but he was appreciated as a mature pianist for his sensitive playing of Chopin. He lived mostly in France, Germany, and Sweden; after World War II he returned to Poland and taught in Posnan; shortly before his death he was appointed to a state teaching post in Warsaw. He was precocious not only as a pianist but also as a composer; wrote some 50 opus numbers before he was 10. His opera *Rymond,* written at the age of 17, was produced at Elberfeld, Oct. 14, 1902; he wrote another opera, *Die Sühne* (Mühlhausen, 1909); many piano pieces.

Koczirz (kot'-shirsh), **Adolf**, Austrian music scholar; b. Wierowan, Moravia, April 2, 1870; d. Vienna, Feb. 22, 1941. He was a government functionary; studied musicology with Guido Adler in Vienna (*Dr. phil.,* 1903); ed. vols. XVIII and XXV of the 'Denkmäler der Tonkunst in Österreich' (lute music of the 16th and 17th centuries); contributed many essays on old instrumental music to various publications.

Kodalli, Nevit, Turkish composer; b. Mersin, 1924. He studied with Necil Kazim Akses at the Ankara Cons., graduated in 1948 and went to Paris, where he studied with Honegger. Among his works (all unpubl.) are a symphony (Ankara, May 20, 1950); an oratorio *Ataturk* (1952; Ankara, Nov. 9, 1953); *String Sinfonietta* (Ankara, May 3, 1952); piano pieces.

Kodály (koh'-dah-ē), **Zoltán**, outstanding Hungarian composer; b. Kecskemet, Dec. 16, 1882. He was brought up in a musical family; received general education at a high school in Magyszombat; at the same time, he took lessons in piano and violin; soon began to compose; wrote a Mass at the age of 16. He then enrolled at the Univ. of Budapest, and also studied composition with Hans Koessler at the Budapest Academy of Music. His early works were mostly sacred choral compositions and chamber music;

his doctor's thesis, *Strophic Structure in the Hungarian Folksong* (1906), indicates his growing interest in folk music. He became associated with Béla Bartók in collecting, organizing, and editing the vast wealth of national folksongs; he also made use of these melodies in his own works. He published his findings in the bulletins of the Hungarian Ethnographic Society. In 1906 he went to Paris, where he took some lessons with Widor; in 1907 he was appointed instructor at the Budapest Academy of Music; wrote music criticism for several newspapers in Budapest; also contributed correspondence to the 'Revue Musicale,' the 'Musical Courier,' and other journals. In 1913 he issued, with Bartók, a detailed paper dealing with the subject of collecting national songs. During World War I he continued to teach and compose, but his activity in collecting and publishing Hungarian folksongs was inevitably curtailed. In 1919 Kodály was appointed assistant director of the Academy of Music in Budapest; for political reasons he was relieved of this post; however, he resumed his teaching in 1922. In 1923 he was commissioned to write a commemorative work in celebration of the half-century of the union of Buda and Pest; for this occasion he wrote a *Psalmus Hungaricus,* which proved to be one of his most significant works. The initial performance in Budapest was followed by numerous productions all over Europe, and also in America. Another signal success was the presentation of Kodály's national opera, in a comic style, *Háry János* (1926); an orchestral suite from this work is widely played. Two suites of folk dances, arranged in a modern manner, *Marosszék Dances* and *Galanta Dances,* won for Kodály a world-wide popularity. His reputation as one of the most significant national composers was firmly established with the repeated performances of these works. During the turbulent events of 1939-45, Kodály remained in Budapest, working on his compilations of folksongs. In 1946-47 he visited the U.S. and conducted concerts of his works. — Kodály's musical style is not as radical as that of Bartók; he never departs from basic tonality, and his experiments in rhythm do not reach the primitivistic power of Bartók's percussive idiom. Kodály prefers a Romantic treatment of his melodic and harmonic materials; there is also a decided tinge of Impressionism in his orchestration. But there is no mistaking his ability to present nationally colored melorhythms in a pleasing and stimulating manner. — Works: Operas: *Háry János* (Budapest, Oct. 16, 1926); *Székelyfonó* (*The Spinning Room,* lyric scenes based on Hungarian folksongs and dances; Budapest, April 24, 1932); *Czinka Panna* (Budapest, March 15, 1948). For orch.: *Summer Evening,* tone poem (1906; revised 1930; N.Y. Philharmonic, April 3, 1930; Toscanini conducting); orch. suite from *Háry János* (N.Y., Dec. 15, 1927); *Ballet Music* (1925); *Theater Overture* (1927); *Marosszék Dances* (Dresden, Nov. 28, 1930); *Dances of Galanta* (for the 80th anniversary of the Budapest Philharmonic Society, 1934; Philadelphia, Dec. 11, 1936); *Variations on a Hungarian Folksong* (*Peacock Variations;* Amsterdam, Nov. 23, 1939); *Concerto for Orch.* (Chicago, Feb. 6, 1941); viola concerto (1947); concerto for string quartet (1947). For chorus: *Psalmus Hungaricus,* for tenor solo, chorus, and orch. (based on the 55th Psalm; his most important work; Budapest, Nov. 19, 1923; U.S. première, N.Y. Philharmonic, Dec. 19, 1927; Mengelberg conducting); *Te Deum,* hymn for soli, chorus, and orch. (for 250th anniversary of delivery of Budapest from the Turks; performed in the Budapest Cathedral, Sept. 11, 1936); *Missa Brevis,* for chorus and orch. (1945); *Kallo,* folk dances for mixed choir and small orch. (1951); numerous choruses (*Transylvanian Lament, Jesus and the Traders, Ode to Franz Liszt,* etc.). Chamber music: 1st string quartet (1908); cello sonata (1909-10); duo for violin and cello (1914); sonata for cello unaccompanied (1915); 2nd string quartet (1916-17); *Serenade* for 2 violins and viola (1919-20); an arrangement for cello and piano of 3 Chorale Preludes by Bach (1924). For piano: *Meditation* (1907); *9 Pièces pour piano* (1910); *Marosszek Dances* (1930); *24 Little Canons on the Black Keys* (1945); *Children's Dances* (1946). For voice and piano: *20 Hungarian Folksongs* (with Béla Bartók; 1906); *Magyar nepzene* (*Hungarian Folk Music;* 57 arrangements of folksongs; 1917-32); numerous songs and choruses for children and music students: *Bicinia Hungarica,* 1937-42; *333 Reading Exercises,* 1943; *441 Melodies,* collected in 4 books, subtitled *Pentatonic Music,* 1945-48; etc.; also song collections for general use; numerous articles in ethnographic and musical publications. — Cf. M. D. Calvocoressi, *Zoltán Kodály,* in the 'Monthly Musical Record' (April, 1922); A. Toth, *Zoltán Kodály,* in the 'Revue Musicale' (Sept.-Oct., 1929); Imre Waldbauer, *Kodály,* in Cobbett's 'Cyclopedic Survey of Chamber Music' (London, 1930; vol. 2); H. Mersmann, *Kodály,* in 'Kammermusik' (vol. IV, p. 186

et seq.); E. Haraszti, *Zoltán Kodály et la musique hongroise,* in the 'Revue Musicale' (Feb., 1947); *Emlékkönyv Kodály Zoltán* (on the occasion of his 70th birthday; 1953).

Koeberg, Frits Ehrhardt Adriaan, Dutch composer; b. The Hague, July 15, 1876. He studied with H. Viotta in Holland and with Xaver Scharwenka in Berlin; returned to The Hague in 1902; taught at the Cons. and conducted the orch. 'Musica' there. —Works: opera *Bloemenkind* (1917); 3 symphonies; symph. poems, *Zeelandia* (1920); *Chimères* (1941); *Suite de Lage Landen,* for orch. (1946); *Dances in the Village,* for orch. (1948); *Hollandia,* for band (1933); chamber music; songs.

Koechlin (keu-klan'), **Charles,** notable French composer; b. Paris, Nov. 27, 1867; d. Canaden, Var, Dec. 31, 1950. He studied at the Paris Cons. with Gedalge, Massenet, and Fauré, graduating in 1897. He lived mostly in Paris, where he was active as composer, teacher, and lecturer; made 3 visits to the U.S. (1918, 1928, 1937), lecturing on French music (in English); contributed to various journals ('Gazette des Beaux Arts,' 'Chronique des Arts,' etc.) and to Lavignac's 'Encyclopédie' (valuable and comprehensive essays on modern music). He also participated in modern-music societies, and worked in various social organizations for the promotion of world-wide music culture. In his own compositions he created a style that is unmistakably French in its clarity and subtlety of nuance and dynamics; although highly sympathetic to all innovation, he stopped short of crossing the borders of perceptible tonality and coherent rhythmic patterns; he was a master of orchestration. As a pedagogue he possessed a clear insight into the problems of musical technique; publ. several manuals of fundamental value: *Traité d'harmonie* (3 vols., 1927-30); *Étude sur les notes de passage* (1922); *Étude sur l'écriture de la fugue d'école* (1933); *Précis des règles du contrepoint* (1927; also in English as *A Summary of the Rules of Counterpoint*); *Traité d'orchestration* (4 vols.); *Théorie de la musique* (1935); also an advanced paper, *Essai sur la musique polytonale et atonale.* A *Traité de polyphonie modale* is in MS. He also publ. monographs on Gabriel Fauré (1927) and Debussy (1927). — Works: *Jacob chez Laban,* biblical pastoral (1896-1908; Paris, May 19, 1925); the ballets *La Forêt païenne* (Paris, June 17, 1925) and *L'Âme heureuse* (1947); for orch.: *La Forêt,* symph. poem (1896-1907); *En mer, la nuit,* symph. poem (1899-1904); *L'Automne,* symph. suite (1896-1909); *Nuit de Walpurgis classique,* symph. poem (1901-07); *Études antiques,* symph. suite (1908-14); symph. poems, *Le Printemps, L'Hiver, Nuit de juin, Midi en août* (1910-12); *Suite légendaire* (1915-20); *Rapsodie sur des chansons françaises* (1916); *La Course de printemps,* symph. poem after Kipling's *Jungle Book* (1925-27); *The 7 Stars Symphony,* symph. suite (1933); *Symphonie d'hymnes* (1936); *La Loi de la jungle,* after Kipling (1939); partita for chamber orch. (1945); also 2 symphonies, arranged mostly from earlier works; *Ballade* for piano and orch. (1919); *20 Chansons Bretonnes* for cello and chamber orch. (1934); *Offrande musicale sur le nom de B.A.C.H.* (15 pieces), for organ and orch. (1942): *Silhouettes comiques* (12 pieces), for bassoon and orch. (1943); 3 string quartets; several fugues for string quartet; *Suite en quatuor,* for flute, violin, viola, and piano; sonata for 2 flutes; piano quintet; *Divertissement,* for 2 flutes and bass flute; trio for flute, clarinet, and bassoon; modal sonatina for flute and clarinet; *Primavera,* for flute, violin, viola, cello, and harp; septet for flute, oboe, English horn, clarinet, bassoon, horn, and saxophone; also flute sonata, viola sonata, oboe sonata, violin sonata, cello sonata, horn sonata, bassoon sonata, and 2 clarinet sonatas; several suites of pieces for unaccompanied flute; several sets of piano pieces (*Paysages et marines, Les Heures persanes; Douze Pastorales, L'Ancienne Maison de campagne, Douze Petites Pièces très facile,* etc.); organ music; vocal duets, trios, and quartets; several cycles of songs. — Cf. M. D. Calvocoressi, *Charles Koechlin's Instrumental Works,* in 'Music & Letters' (1924); W. H. Mellers, *A Plea for Koechlin,* in 'Music Review' (1942); Pierre Renaudin, *Charles Koechlin* (Paris, 1952).

Koellreutter, Hans Joachim, composer; b. Freiburg, Germany, Sept. 2, 1915. He studied flute and composition in Berlin and Geneva. In 1938 he went to Brazil and settled in São Paolo as composer and teacher. He adopted the 12-tone technique in his music. His works include *American Psalm,* for chorus and orch. (1945); *Proletarian Psalm* (1946); *Konzertmusik,* for piano and chamber orch. (1946); etc.

Koemmenich, Louis, conductor; b. Elberfeld, Germany, Oct. 4, 1866; d. New York, Aug. 14, 1922. He studied at Kullak's Academy in Berlin; in 1890 emigrated to the U. S., settling in N. Y., where he became active as a choral conductor and a singing teacher; founded the Oratorio Society of Brooklyn for the production of new works (1898) and the New Choral Society of N. Y., which gave its 1st concert on April 4, 1918 (Verdi's *Requiem*). He wrote many choruses for men's voices, including *Lockung* and *Wer weiss wo,* which received prizes in 1894 and 1900.

Koenen, Friedrich, German composer; b. Rheinbach, near Bonn, April 30, 1829; d. Cologne, July 6, 1887. He studied piano and organ with his father, and cello with Biermann; in 1854, was ordained priest; from 1862-63, studied church music at Regensburg with Haberl, Schrems, and Witt. Went to Cologne, where he was appointed choirmaster of the cathedral; also taught music at the Seminary for Priests; in 1869, founded the 'Cäcilienverein.' Among his 58 compositions are 7 Masses, 2 church cantatas, a *Te Deum,* motets, psalms, organ preludes, and songs.

Koenen (koo-nen), **Tilly (Mathilde Caroline),** mezzo-soprano; b. Salatiga, Java, Dec. 25, 1873; d. The Hague, Jan. 4, 1941. She studied piano, on which she became a proficient performer; then took up voice with Cornelia van Zanten. She toured Germany and Austria from 1900 with excellent success; visited America in 1909-10 and in 1915-16. She was particularly impressive in her interpretations of German Romantic songs; also performed some songs by her compatriots.

Koennecke, Fritz, composer of German descent; b. New York, June 19, 1876. He studied with Thuille in Munich, where he lived from 1892-1929; then lived in Vomperberg, Tyrol. He wrote an opera *Cagliostro* (1907); a dramatic musical adaptation of Shakespeare's *The Tempest* (1909); *Der Fahrendt Schüler im Paradeis,* a carnival play after Hans Sachs (Karlsruhe, 1913); *Rokoko,* a 1-act pastoral play (1915); *Magdalena,* 3-act opera (Charlottenburg, 1919); the oratorio *Welten-Ende;* incidental music to Reinhardt's festival-play *Die Könige Saul und David* (1917); etc.; also songs and duets.

Koessler, Hans, German organist and composer; b. Waldeck, Jan. 1, 1853; d. Ansbach, May 23, 1926. He studied with Rheinberger in Munich; then taught at the Dresden Cons.; in 1882, went to Budapest to teach organ and, later, composition at the Academy of Music, remaining on the staff until 1908. In 1918 he retired to Ansbach. In his works, he follows the tradition of Brahms; although his technical achievements inspire respect, his works lack any durable quality that would distinguish them from the mass of other competent compositions by German composers of his generation. He wrote an opera *Der Münzenfranz* (Strasbourg, 1903); oratorio *Triumph der Liebe; Silvesterglocken,* for voices and orch.; *Hymne an die Schönheit,* for men's chorus and orch.; 2 symphonies; violin concerto; cello concerto; 2 string quartets; string quintet; string sextet; a violin sonata; a cello sonata; songs.

Koffler, Josef, Polish composer; b. Stryj, Nov. 28, 1896; d. Warsaw, 1943. He studied in Vienna wth Schoenberg and Guido Adler; graduated from the Univ. of Vienna; Mus. Doc., 1923; in 1924 he became prof. of composition at the Lwow Cons.; edited the Polish monthly reviews 'Orkiestra' (from 1929) and 'Echo' (from 1937). Koffler was in Warsaw during World War II, and perished during the revolt of the ghetto there. In some of his works, such as the *15 Variations for String Orch.* (Amsterdam Festival, June 9, 1933), he used the 12-tone system. He wrote 3 symphonies (3rd symph. performed at the London Festival, June 17, 1938); *Variations on a Waltz of Johann Strauss;* string trio (Oxford Festival, July 23, 1931); Divertimento for oboe, clarinet, and bassoon; a string quartet; *40 Polish Folksongs* for piano; *Quasi una sonata,* a cycle of pieces for piano; also *Love Cantata* (1932) and *4 Poems* for voice and piano.

Kofler, Leo, singing teacher and writer; b. Brixen, Austria, March 13, 1837; d. New Orleans, Nov. 29, 1908. He studied at Stern's Cons. in Berlin; in 1866, came to America, and held various positions as organist in St. Louis, Cincinnati, Brooklyn, and N. Y. He publ. *The Art of Breathing as the Basis of Tone Production* (7th ed., N. Y., 1897) and *Take Care of Your Voice, or, The Golden Rule of Health;* also ed. 'Selected Hymn-tunes and Hymn-anthems.'

Kogan, Leonid, outstanding Russian violinist; b. Dniepropetrovsk, Nov. 14, 1924; studied violin with his father, a photographer and amateur musician. At the age of 10 he was taken to Moscow; studied with Abram Yampolsky at the Moscow Cons., graduating in 1948; then appointed teacher there. In Moscow he organized a concert trio with the pianist Emil Gilels and the cellist Mstislav Rostropovitch; married a sister of Gilels, a violinist; appeared often with her in works for 2 violins. In 1951 he received the 1st prize at the International Competition in Brussels; then traveled widely; gave concerts in England, Italy, France, China, South America, etc. In Jan., 1958 he undertook his 1st American tour, playing with the Boston Symph., N. Y. Philharmonic, Philadelphia Orch., Los Angeles Philharmonic, etc.

Kogel, Gustav Friedrich, German conductor; b. Leipzig, Jan. 16, 1849; d. Frankfurt, Nov. 13, 1921. He studied at the Leipzig Cons.; was editor for C. F. Peters (1870-74); then was active as conductor in various provincial theaters; conducted the Berlin Philharmonic in 1888; was conductor of the Museum Concerts in Frankfurt from 1891 till 1903; also filled engagements as guest conductor in Russia, Spain, etc.; was guest conductor at the N. Y. Philharmonic in 1906. He edited full scores and piano scores of several operas; wrote piano pieces.

Köhler, Ernesto, flutist; b. Modena, Italy, Dec. 4, 1849; d. St. Petersburg, May 17, 1907. He studied flute with his father; became 1st flutist of the court orch. at Modena; then at the Karltheater in Vienna; in 1871, became 1st flutist of the Imperial Orch. in St. Petersburg. He wrote numerous compositions for the flute; also an opera, *Ben Achmed,* and several ballets.

Köhler, Ernst, German organist and pianist; b. Langenbielau, May 28, 1799; d. Breslau, May 26, 1847. He was 1st organist of the Elisabethkirche in Breslau from 1827 until his death. He wrote 2 symphonies, 9 overtures, 12 church cantatas, 12 large vocal works with orch., organ works, and piano pieces.

Kohler, Franz, American violinist and conductor; b. Clinton, Iowa, Feb. 20, 1877; d. Erie, Pa., Dec. 22, 1918. He studied with Karl Halir (violin) in Weimar and Berlin; returning to America in 1898, he joined the Pittsburgh Symph. Orch. as a violinist; was concertmaster briefly in 1910; in 1911-13 taught violin at Oberlin College; from 1913 till his death, conducted the Erie Symph. Orch.

Köhler, Louis, German composer of famous piano studies; b. Brunswick, Sept. 5, 1820; d. Königsberg, Feb. 16, 1886. He studied piano in Brunswick with Sonnemann; then took courses in composition in Vienna (1839-43) with Sechter and Seyfried; also studied piano there with Bocklet. After a season of theater conducting, he settled in Königsberg (1847) and established there a successful school for piano playing. In 1880 he received the title of 'Royal Professor.' He was one of the chief promoters of the Allgemeiner deutsche Tonkünstlerverein, founded in 1859 in Leipzig; also contributed music reviews to the weekly 'Signale.' He composed 3 operas, a ballet, a symphony, overtures, cantatas, and other works, but he is remembered exclusively for his albums of piano studies, which have been adopted in music schools all over the world; next to Czerny, he is the most popular purveyor of didactic piano literature; it must be observed that his studies are of great instructive value, and are also worthwhile from the purely musical standpoint. His chief work, in which he laid the foundation of methodical piano pedagogy, is *Systematische Lehrmethode für Klavierspiel und Musik,* in 2 vols.: I, *Die Mechanik als Grundlage der Technik* (1856; 3rd ed., revised by Riemann, 1888); II. *Tonschriftwesen, Harmonik, Metrik* (1858); other publications are *Führer durch den Klavierunterricht* (6th ed., 1879); *Der Klavierfingersatz* (1862); *Der Klavierunterricht, oder Studien, Erfahrungen und Ratschläge* (4th ed., 1877); *Die neue Richtung in der Musik* (1864); *Leichtfassliche Harmonie- und Generalbasslehre* (a valuable manual of harmony; 3rd ed., 1880); *Brahms und seine Stellung in der neueren Klavierliteratur* (1880); *Der Klavierpedalung* (1882); *Allgemeine Musiklehre* (1883).

Kohs, Ellis B., American composer; b. Chicago, May 12, 1916. He studied at the San Francisco Cons., at the Univ. of Chicago (with Carl Bricken), at the Juilliard School of Music, N. Y. (with Bernard Wagenaar), and at Harvard Univ. (with Walter Piston). He served in the army (1941-46); then occupied various teaching positions; taught at Wesleyan Univ. (1946-48), Cons. of Kansas City (1948-50), and (from 1950) at the Univ. of Southern California. In his music, he pursues the aim of classical clarity; uses established forms, and is particularly adept in variation structures; in some works he applies a modified dodecaphonic technique; employs asymmetrical rhythms in the manner of Béla Bartók; at all times he attempts to unify a given work by emphasizing the pervading melodic and rhythmic line, in accordance with Schenker's theories, which he follows.—Works: concerto for orch. (San Francisco, Aug. 9, 1942); *Legend* for oboe and string orch. (Columbus, Ohio, Feb. 27, 1947); cello concerto (1947); chamber concerto for viola and string nonet (1949); symph. No. 1 (1950); symph. No. 2, with chorus (1956); string quartet (1942); *Night Watch* for flute, horn, and kettledrums (1943); sonatina for bassoon and piano (1944); sonatina for violin and piano (1948); *Short Concert* for string quartet (1948); clarinet sonata (1951); variations for recorder (1956); *The Automatic Pistol,* for male voices a cappella (1943); 25th Psalm (1947); *Lord of the Ascendant,* for chorus, soloists, dancers, and orch. (1956); incidental music to Shakespeare's *Macbeth* (1947); *Passacaglia* for organ and string orch. (1946); *Capriccio* for organ (1948); *Etude in Memory of Bartók* for piano (1946); piano toccata (1948); *Fantasy on La, Sol, Fa, Re, Mi* (1949); 10 inventions (1950), etc. — See his autobiographical sketch *Thoughts from the Workbench,* in the 'Bulletin of American Composers Alliance' for Autumn, 1956.

Kohut, Adolf, writer on music; b. Mindszent, Hungary, Nov. 10, 1847; d. Berlin, Sept. 21, 1917. In 1912 the Univ. of Klausenburg conferred upon him the honorary degree of *Dr. phil.;* he publ. *Moses Mendelssohn und seine Familie* (1886); *Weber-Gedenkbuch* (1887); *Friedrich Wieck* (1888); *Das Dresdener Hoftheater in der Gegenwart* (1888); *Die grössten deutschen Soubretten im 19. Jahrhundert* (1890); *Joseph Joachim* (1891); *Bilder aus der Musikwelt* (1891); *Aus dem Zauberlande Polyhymnias* (1892); *Dur- und Mollakkorde* (1894); *Schiller in seinen Beziehungen zur Musik* (1905); *Die Gesangsköniginnen in den letzten drei Jahrhunderten* (1906); also wrote biographies of Auber, Meyerbeer, and Rossini for Reclam's 'Universalbibliothek.'

Kolar, Victor, conductor and composer, b. (of Bohemian parentage) Budapest, Feb. 12, 1888; d. Detroit, June 16, 1957. He was a pupil of Ševčik (violin) and Dvořák (composition) at the Prague Cons. In 1900 he came to America, and joined the Pittsburgh Orch. as violinist (1905-8); from 1908-20 was violinist in the N. Y. Symph. Orch.; in 1914 appointed assistant conductor under Walter Damrosch; in 1920 became associate conductor of the Detroit Symph. Orch., and later full-ranking conductor there; resigned in 1941. As assistant conductor of the N. Y. Symph. Orch., he brought out several of his own works: *A Fairy Tale,* symph. poem (Feb. 16, 1912); *Americana,* symph. suite (1914; won first prize of the Illinois State Teachers' Association Contest); symph. No. 1 (Jan. 28, 1916); with the Pittsburgh Orch. he presented his symph. poem *Hiawatha* (Jan. 31, 1908). Other works are: *Slovakian Rhapsody* for orch. (Norfolk, Conn., Festival, 1922); *3 Humoresques* for violin and piano (1915); numerous songs; 7 marches.

Kolbe, Oskar, German theorist; b. Berlin, Aug. 10, 1836; d. there, Jan. 2, 1878. He studied with Grell and Löschhorn in Berlin; taught theory at Stern's Cons. (1859-75). He publ. a *Kurzgefasstes Handbuch der Generalbasslehre* (1862) and a *Handbuch der Harmonielehre* (1873); also wrote an oratorio, *Johannes der Täufer;* an overture to *Wallenstein's Tod;* piano music; songs.

Kolberg, Oskar, Polish composer and song collector; b. Przysucha, near Radom, Feb. 22, 1814; d. Cracow, June 3, 1890. He studied at the Warsaw Cons. with Chopin's teacher Elsner; then in Berlin; returned to Warsaw in 1840. He devoted a major part of his life to traveling in the country in order to collect folksongs, while earning his living as an employee of the Warsaw-Vienna Railroad. He started a series of publications on Polish folklore, including folk music, in 1860; 23 vols. were issued before his death, and publication of the materials assembled by him was continued later by the Polish Academy. He also wrote a number of Polish dances for piano, and composed an opera, *Krol Pasterzy (The Shepherd's Inn;* Warsaw, March 2, 1859).

Kolff, J. van Santen, music essayist; b. Rotterdam, April 19, 1848; d. Berlin, Nov. 29, 1896. An erudite and cosmopolitan writer, he contributed hundreds of articles on music to the German, French, and Dutch press, among them *Geschichtliches und Ästhetisches über das Erinnerungsmotiv* (a history of the *Leitmotiv* before Wagner), in vols. VIII and IX of the 'Bayreuther Blätter,' and many other articles dealing with the esthetics and history of Wagner's operas, publ. in the 'Bayreuther Taschenbuch'; also contributed to the 'Revue Wagnérienne.'

Kolisch, Rudolph, violinist; b. Klamm, Austria, July 20, 1896. He studied at the Music Academy and the Univ. of Vienna (graduated 1913), also violin with Ševčik and composition with Schoenberg; in 1922 he founded the Kolisch Quartet; by 1927 it was constituted as follows: 1st violin, Kolisch; 2nd violin, Felix Khuner; viola, Jenö Lener; cello, Benar Heifetz. He successfully toured the U. S., Europe, Africa, and South America many times; American début at the Library of Congress Chamber Music Festival (1935). His is the first quartet to perform standard classic works from memory; it also made a specialty of contemporary works (Bartók's 3rd and 5th quartets; Schoenberg's 3rd and 4th quartets, Alban Berg's *Lyric Suite,* etc.). The Kolisch Quartet was briefly reorganized in 1939 with Jascha Veissi (viola) and Stefan Auber (cello); then disbanded; in 1942 Kolisch became the leader of the Pro Arte Quartet. He is one of the few professional left-handed violinists.

Kollmann, August Friedrich Christoph, composer; b. Engelbostel, Germany, 1756; d. London, March 21, 1829. He was organist in the German Chapel, St. James', London. Among his works are a symphony, *The Shipwreck;* 100 Psalms harmonized in 100 ways; Rondo for piano on the chord of the diminished 7th, etc.; also publ. *Essays on Practical Harmony* (1796), *First Beginning on the Pianoforte,* etc.

Kollo, Walter, German operetta composer; b. Neidenburg, March 28, 1878; d. Berlin, Sept. 30, 1940. He studied in Sondershausen and Königsberg. In 1901 he settled in Berlin and was active as theater conductor; wrote songs that became popular favorites. Among his most successful operettas are *Drei alte Schachteln* (Berlin, Oct. 6, 1917) and *Die Frau ohne Kuss* (Berlin, July 6, 1924); *Drei arme kleine Mädels* (1927), etc.

Kolneder, Walter, Austrian violinist and musicologist; b. Wels, July 1, 1910; studied composition with Johann Nepomuk David, conducting with Bernhard Paumgartner, and violin and viola with Max Strub. He was a violinist in the orch. of the Mozarteum in Salzburg (1929-35); teacher in Graz (1936-45); conductor at Wels (1945-47); viola player in the municipal orch. at Innsbruck (1947-53); in 1953 was appointed director of the Cons. of Luxembourg. He publ. the valuable treatises, *Die vokale Mehrstimmigkeit in der Volksmusik der österreichischen Alpenländer* (Innsbruck, 1949); *Aufführungspraxis bei Vivaldi* (Leipzig, 1955); edited violin music of Corelli, Stradella, Vivaldi, etc.

Kolodin, Irving, American music critic; b. New York, Feb. 22, 1908. He studied at the Institute of Musical Art, N. Y.; taught theory and harmony there for a year (1931); then was employed in the music dept. of the 'Brooklyn Eagle'; was music critic on the 'N. Y. Sun' from 1932-50. In 1947 he became ed. of the recordings section of the 'Saturday Review' of N. Y. (formerly 'Saturday Review of Literature'); greatly expanded his dept. in this publication by the monthly appendix, 'Saturday Review of Recordings'; from 1953 wrote program notes for the N. Y. Philharmonic; contributed articles on music to various magazines. He publ. *The Metropolitan Opera 1883-1935* (N. Y. 1936; 2nd ed., 1940; new revised ed., as *The Story of the Metropolitan Opera, 1883-1950,* N. Y., 1953); *The Kingdom of Swing* (with Benny Goodman; N. Y., 1939); *A Guide to Recorded Music* (N. Y., 1941; new ed., as *New Guide to Recorded Music,* Garden City, N. Y. 1947; 3rd revised ed., 1950); *Orchestral Music,* in the series 'The Guide to Long-Playing Records' (N. Y., 1955); *Musical Life* (N. Y., 1958); also edited *The Critical Composer* (N. Y., 1940) and *Composer as Listener: a Guide to Music* (N. Y., 1958).

Komorzynski, Egon, Austrian musicologist; b. Vienna, May 7, 1878; studied musicology with Guido Adler at the Univ. of Vienna and with Riemann at the Univ. of Leipzig. He devoted himself to the study of Mozart; publ. a fundamental work on Mozart's librettist Schikaneder (Vienna, 1901; revised ed., 1951); a monograph on Mozart (Berlin, 1941; 2nd ed., 1955); a novel about Schubert, *Genius zwischen 2 Welten* (Berlin, 1944).

Kondorssy, Leslie, composer; b. Pressburg (Czechoslovakia), June 25, 1915; studied at the Academy of Music in Budapest; came to America after World War II and settled in Cleveland. He has written several one-act operas: *Night in the Puszta; The Voice; The Pumpkin* (Cleveland, May 15, 1954); *Unexpected Visitor* and *The Two Imposters* (Cleveland, Oct. 21, 1956); also *Kossuth Cantata* (Cleveland, March 16, 1952).

Kondracki, Michal, composer; b. Poltava, Ukraine, Oct. 4, 1902; studied with Statkowski and Melcer at the Warsaw State Cons., graduating in 1926 with honors; then went to Paris, where he was a pupil of Paul Dukas; later also studied with Szymanowski; from 1928-33 lived in Paris; in 1933 returned to Warsaw as music critic of the daily newspaper 'ABC'; left Poland after the outbreak of war in 1939 and reached Brazil; stayed in Rio de Janeiro from 1940-48; then settled in N. Y. He has written an opera, *Popieliny* (Warsaw, May 3, 1934); a ballet, *Metropolis* (1929); *Cantata ecclesiastica* (1937); *Partita* for chamber orch. (1928); a symph. (1942); and a set of Brazilian dances for orch. (1944).

Könemann, Feodor Feodorovitch, Russian pianist and composer; b. Moscow, 1873; d. there, March 29, 1937. He graduated from the Moscow Cons. in 1897 with a gold medal for piano playing and composition; then toured Europe and the U. S. many times as accompanist of Shaliapin. He publ. choruses, piano pieces, and many songs; his dramatic ballad, *The King Goes Forth to War,* was one of Shaliapin's favorite numbers.

Königslöw, Johann Wilhelm Cornelius, German organist and composer; b. Hamburg, March 16, 1745; d. Lübeck, May 14, 1833. He was organist at the Marienkirche in Lübeck from 1773 until his death. He composed many 'Abendmusiken,' following Buxtehude's example.

Königslöw, Otto Friedrich von, German violinist and conductor; b. Hamburg, Nov. 13, 1824; d. Bonn, Oct. 6, 1898. He studied at the Leipzig Cons. with David (violin) and Hauptmann (theory); following 12 years of concert tours, he became conductor of the Gürzenich Orch. at Cologne (1858-81); also was a member of the staff of the Cologne Cons. In 1884 he settled in Bonn.

Koning, David, Dutch pianist and composer; b. Rotterdam, March 19, 1820; d. Amsterdam, Nov. 6, 1876. He studied with Aloys Schmitt in Frankfurt; from 1840, was conductor of the choral society 'Felix Meritis' in Amsterdam; was a member of various music organizations in Europe; was active mainly as a piano teacher. He wrote a comic opera, *The Fishermaiden;* an *Elegy on the Death of an Artist,* for soli, chorus, and orch.; much vocal music; many piano pieces and studies.

Konius, Georgy Eduardovitch. See **Conus.**

Konjović (kŏh-nyŏ'-vitch), **Petar,** Serbian composer; b. Sombor, May 6, 1882. He studied at the Prague Cons. with Novák; was choral director and teacher in Zemun and Belgrade (1906-14). In 1920 he toured Europe as pianist; from 1921-26 was music director of the Zagreb Opera. From 1927-33 he was director of national theaters in Osijek, Split, and Novi Sad; from 1933-39, intendant of the national theater in Zagreb. In 1939 he settled in Belgrade as rector and prof. of the Academy of Music. He wrote the operas *Vilin Vee* or *Zenidba Miloševa (The Wedding of Milos;* Zagreb, April 25, 1917), *Koštana* (Zagreb, April 16, 1931), *Knez od Zete (The Duke of Zeta;* Belgrade, May 25, 1939), and *Sel jaci (The Peasants;* Belgrade, March 3, 1952); Symphony in C (1908); *Capriccio Adriatico,* for violin and orch. (1920); *Makar Chudra,* symph. poem after Maxim Gorky (1944); 2 string quartets; solo pieces for violin, cello, and piano; 24 songs; 100 Yugoslav folksongs *Moja Zemlja* (of which 25 are arranged for voice and small orch.). He publ. a book of essays, *Ličnosti (Personalities;* Zagreb, 1920), and a monograph on Miloje Milojević (Belgrade, 1954).

Konoye, Hidemaro, composer and conductor; b. Tokyo, Nov. 18, 1898. A member of an aristocratic Japanese family, he received his education in Japan and in Europe; was head of the Imperial Music Academy in Tokyo; conducted in the U. S. in 1937, giving programs of Japanese works. He made another American visit in 1957. He is the composer of several orchestral pieces based on Japanese subjects; also orchestrated old Japanese court music for the modern Western orch.; arranged the music of *Madama Butterfly* for the films (inserting many Japanese folk melodies).

Kontski, Antoine, Polish pianist; brother of Apollinaire and Charles de Kontski; b. Cracow, Oct. 27, 1817; d. Ivanichi, near Okulova, Novgorod District, Russia, Dec. 7, 1899. He was the most famous member of the Kontski family of precocious musicians. He studied with John Field in Moscow (1830); went to Paris in 1851; then was in Berlin (1853); from 1854-67 he was in St. Petersburg; then he lived in London as piano teacher. He toured the U. S. in 1883 and again in 1885; lived for a time in Buffalo. At the age of nearly 80, he undertook a world tour (1896-98), giving concerts in Australia, Japan, and Siberia. He died at the estate of friends near St. Petersburg. He was a composer of effective salon music and virtuoso pieces for piano; his picturesque *Réveil du lion* was enormously successful for many years; it was an epitome of Romantic exuberance to the point of being ludicrous; he also wrote 2 piano concertos, the waltzes *La Victorieuse* and *Souvenir de Biarritz; Grande Polonaise;* a characteristic piece, *La Nuit sur la mer,* and several orchestral overtures; also 2 light operas, *Les deux distraits* (London, 1872), and *Le Sultan de Zanzibar* (N. Y., May 8, 1886).

Kontski, Apollinaire de, Polish violinist; brother of Antoine and Charles de Kontski; b. Warsaw, Oct. 23, 1825; d. there, June

29, 1879. He studied with his elder brother Charles; he appeared with his brothers as a small child in Russia and later in Germany, frankly exploited by his family for sensational publicity and gain. In 1837 he played for Paganini in Paris; in 1861 he became director of the Warsaw Cons., of which he was a founder, and remained in that post until his death. He publ. some violin music.

Kontski, Charles de, Polish pianist; brother of Antoine and Apollinaire de Kontski; b. Cracow, Sept. 6, 1815; d. Paris, Aug. 27, 1867. Like his brothers, he was a child prodigy, and made appearances with them at various public exhibitions and concerts. He studied in Warsaw and in Paris, eventually settling in Paris as a private piano teacher, enjoying considerable success in society.

Koole, Arend, Dutch musicologist, conductor, and composer; b. Amsterdam, April 22, 1908. He studied at the Amsterdam Cons., and later at Utrecht with Albert Smijers; his doctoral dissertation was a monograph on Locatelli (Amsterdam, 1949), a valuable piece of research. He also took lessons in conducting with Pierre Monteux; made appearances with several orchestras in Holland and Belgium. In 1949 he went to South Africa. He has written incidental music for several plays and a ballet, *The Snow Queen;* has published a biography of Mendelssohn (Haarlem, 1952).

Koons, Walter E., American writer on music; b. Evansville, Ind., May 12, 1892; studied privately; was active as an organist; contributed to various music magazines; was executive editor of the 'Musical Digest' (1924-28); was connected in various capacities with the National Broadcasting Co. (1933-40); then abandoned musical activities; became a partner, with his brother, of a steel import and export firm; in 1953, was living in Greenwich, Conn.

Koppel, Hermann, Danish composer; b. Copenhagen, Oct. 1, 1908. He studied in Copenhagen, Paris, and Berlin. His works include 4 symphonies; 3 piano concertos; *Capriccio,* for violin and orch.; concerto for violin, viola, and chamber orch.; 3 string quartets; sextet for wind instruments and piano; ballet; stage and film music; sacred choruses.

Kopylov (koh-pŷ-lohv'), **Alexander Alexandrovitch,** Russian composer; b. St. Petersburg, July 14, 1854; d. Strelna, near St. Petersburg, Feb. 20, 1911. He was a chorister at the Court Chapel; then became instructor there (1872-96). He wrote a symphony; a concert overture; 5 string quartets; *Souvenir de Peterhof* for violin and piano; 2 albums of *Tableaux musicaux de la vie enfantine,* for piano; and other piano pieces, most of them publ. by Belaieff. He was an epigone of the Romantic school of minor Russian composers, emulating Tchaikovsky. A complete list of his publ. works is found in the 'Verzeichnis russischer Komponisten' publ. by Fr. Hofmeister (Leipzig, 1949).

Korbay, Francis Alexander, Hungarian tenor and composer; b. Budapest, May 8, 1846; d. London, March 9, 1913. He was a pupil of Gustave Roger; sang at the Hungarian Opera in Budapest (1865-68); at the same time he pursued piano study, profiting by advice from Liszt, who was his godfather; made a rather successful tour as pianist in Europe (1869-71), and then went to the U. S., settling in N. Y. in 1871 as teacher of voice and piano. In 1894 he went to London; was prof. of singing at the Royal Academy of Music (1894-1903); remained in London until his death. He wrote an orchestral work, *Nuptiale;* a Hungarian overture; *Le Matin,* for solo voice and piano, which was arranged by Liszt for orch.; also numerous lieder and piano pieces.

Koreshtchenko (koh-rehsh'-chen-koh), **Arsenyi Nikolayevitch,** Russian composer; b. Moscow, Dec. 18, 1870; d. Kharkov, Jan. 3, 1921. He studied piano with Taneyev and composition with Arensky at the Moscow Cons., graduating in 1891 with the gold medal; then was appointed prof. of harmony there. After the Revolution he went to Kharkov, where he taught at the Cons. (1919-20); remained there until his death. Among his works are 3 operas, *Belshazzar's Feast* (Moscow, 1892), *The Angel of Death,* and *The House of Ice* (Moscow, Nov. 19, 1900). He further wrote a ballet, *The Magic Mirror* (Moscow, 1902); several orchestral pieces in a Romantic manner *(Barcarolle, Erzählung, Scène poétique,* etc.); an *Armenian Suite,* for orch., based on Armenian folksongs; a *Symphonie Lyrique* and other symphonic works; arranged Armenian and Georgian songs for chorus and orch.; also wrote piano pieces.

Korganov, Genari, Russian pianist; b. Kvarely, May 12, 1858; d. Rostov-on-the-Don, April 12, 1890. He studied with

Reinecke in Leipzig and L. Brassin in St. Petersburg. He publ. some 40 works, chiefly for the piano.

Korn, Clara Anna, composer and teacher; b. Berlin, Jan. 30, 1866; d. New York, July 14, 1940. She was brought to America at an early age; studied with Horatio Parker and Bruno Oscar Klein; taught at the National Cons. in N. Y. (1893-98); afterwards, settled in Brooklyn as a private teacher. She wrote an opera, *Their Last War;* a symphony; a symph. poem *Morpheus;* an orchestral suite, *Rural Snapshots;* a piano concerto; a violin concerto; piano pieces; songs.

Korn, Richard, American conductor; b. New York, Aug. 24, 1908. He studied at the Juilliard School of Music with Wagenaar; later played clarinet in the National Symph. Orch. In 1942 he joined the Coast Guard; 1945-47, conducted the N. Y. City Opera; 1948, appeared as guest conductor in Paris and Rome. In 1950 he was appointed conductor of the Memphis Symph. Orch.

Kornauth, Egon, Austrian composer; b. Olmütz (Olomouc), May 14, 1891. He studied in Vienna with Fuchs, Schreker, and Schmidt; took a course in musicology with Guido Adler at the Univ. (Ph. D., 1915). In 1912 he received the State Prize of 1000 Kronen for his viola sonata. He traveled widely. In 1910 he toured in the U. S. as pianist with the Vienna 'Gesangverein.' In 1926 he was engaged to organize an orchestra in Medan, Sumatra; despite the difficulties of such an undertaking he maintained this orchestra for 2 seasons; later he toured through Java, Celebes, and Ceylon with the Vienna Trio, which he had founded. Early in 1930 he returned to Europe. He played in Brazil with the Vienna Trio from 1933-35; appeared in Sweden in 1936; in 1937 he returned to Austria. Kornauth's music is marked by considerable contrapuntal skill; his instrumental pieces and songs are mostly in a Romantic vein. Among his works are 4 symph. suites (1913-39); symph. overture (1914; revised 1925); *Ballade* for orch., with cello obbligato (Vienna, Feb. 20, 1919); nonet for various instruments; string sextet; string quintet; piano quintet; clarinet quintet; string quartet; piano quartet; piano trio; violin sonata, viola sonata, cello sonata, clarinet sonata; various choral works and several song cycles. Cf. E. H. Müller von Asow, *Egon Kornauth* (Vienna, 1941; includes a complete list of works).

Körner, Christian Gottfried, German essayist and composer; b. Leipzig, July 2, 1756; d. Berlin, May 13, 1831. He was the father of Theodor Körner, the poet. He publ. an essay *Über den Charakter der Töne oder über Charakterdarstellung in der Musik,* in the 'Horen' (1775); also composed songs, etc.

Körner, Gotthilf Wilhelm, German music publisher; b. Teicha, near Halle, June 3, 1809; d. Erfurt, Jan. 3, 1865. He founded his music-publishing firm in 1838 and publ. many organ works; in 1886 the company merged with C. F. Peters. Körner also founded 'Urania' (1840), a periodical for organists.

Kornerup, Thorwald Otto, Danish writer on musical subjects; b. Copenhagen, March 11, 1864; d. there, Dec. 20, 1938. His publications, which deal mostly with the problems of acoustics and various special tone systems, include *The 19-Tone and 31-Tone Precursors of the Well-Tempered Systems; The Acoustical Theory of Atonality; From the Original Prototype of the 5-Tone Scales to the Golden Tones of Electrical Musical Instruments; The Indian Tone System with its 22 Srutis* (all in Danish).

Korngold, Erich Wolfgang, Austrian composer; b. Brno, May 29, 1897; d. Hollywood, California, Nov. 29, 1957. He received his earliest musical education from his father, Julius Korngold; he then studied with Fuchs, Zemlinsky, and Grädener in Vienna. His progress was astounding; at the age of 12 he composed a piano trio, which was soon published, revealing a competent technique and an ability to write in a modern style (strongly influenced by Richard Strauss). About the same time he wrote (in piano score) a pantomime, *Der Schneemann;* it was orchestrated by his teacher, Zemlinsky, and performed at the Vienna Court Opera (Oct. 4, 1910), creating a sensation. In 1911 Nikisch played his *Schauspiel-Ouvertüre* in a Gewandhaus concert at Leipzig; in the same year the youthful composer gave a concert of his works in Berlin, appearing also as a pianist; his *Sinfonietta* was given by Felix Weingartner and the Vienna Philharmonic in 1913. Korngold was not quite 19 when his two short operas, *Der Ring des Polykrates* and *Violanta,* were produced in Munich. His first lasting success came with the opera, *Die tote Stadt,* produced first in Hamburg (1920), and then on many opera stages all over the world. In 1929 he entered a fruitful collaboration with the famous director, Max Reinhardt; in 1934 he went to Hollywood to arrange Mendelssohn's music for the Reinhardt film production of *A Midsummer Night's Dream.* He was intermittently in Europe, taught at the music academy in Vienna (1930-34) before settling in Hollywood; composed a number of film scores; conducted light opera with the N. Y. Opera Co. in 1942 and 1944. He became an American citizen in 1943; after 1945 he divided his time between the U. S. and Europe; lived for some time in Vienna.—Works: operas: *Der Ring des Polykrates* and *Violanta* (Munich, March 28, 1916); *Die tote Stadt* (Hamburg, Dec. 4, 1920; Metropolitan Opera, N. Y., Nov. 19, 1921); *Die Wunder der Heliane* (Hamburg, Oct. 7, 1927); *Kathrin* (Stockholm, Oct. 7, 1939); *Die stumme Serenade* (Dortmund, Dec. 5, 1954); pantomime, *Der Schneemann* (Vienna, Oct. 4, 1910); for orch: *Schauspiel-Ouvertüre* (Leipzig, 1911); *Sinfonietta* (Vienna, Nov. 28, 1913); suite from the music to Shakespeare's *Much Ado About Nothing,* for chamber orch. (Vienna, 1919); *Sursum Corda,* symph. overture (1919); piano concerto for the left hand alone (written for Paul Wittgenstein); violin concerto (Jascha Heifetz with the St. Louis Symph. Orch., Feb. 15, 1947); *Symphonic Serenade* for string orch. (1949); Symph. in F♯ (1953); piano trio (1910); violin sonata; string sextet; piano quintet; 3 string quartets; 2 piano sonatas.—Cf. R. S. Hoffmann, *Erich Wolfgang Korngold* (Vienna, 1923).

Korngold, Julius, music critic; b. Brno, Dec. 24, 1860; d. Hollywood, Sept. 25, 1945. He was a law student; at the same time he studied music with Franz Krenn at the Vienna Cons. In 1902 he became music critic of the influential 'Neue Freie Presse.' He was much in the limelight when his son Erich began his spectacular career at the age of 13 as child composer, and an unfounded suspicion was voiced that Korngold was using his position to further his son's career. He published a book on contemporary German opera, *Deutsches Opernschaffen der Gegenwart* (1922). In 1938 he joined his son in the U. S., settling in Hollywood, where he remained until his death.

Kornmüller, Utto, German writer on church music; b. Straubing, Jan. 5, 1824; d. Metten, Feb. 15, 1907. He was ordained to the priesthood in 1847; became choirmaster of the Benedictine monastery at Metten (1858); also president of the Regensburg branch of the 'Cäcilienverein' until 1903. He publ. a *Lexikon der kirchlichen Tonkunst* (1870); *Der katholische Kirchenchor* (1868); *Die Musik beim liturgischen Hochamt* (1871); contributed articles to the 'Kirchenmusikalisches Jahrbuch' and 'Monatshefte für Musikgeschichte'; also wrote a number of Masses and motets.

Kortchmarev, Klimenty Arkadyevitch, Russian composer; b. Verkhnedneprovsk, July 3, 1899. He studied at the Odessa Cons. with Maliszewski; then went to Moscow. He is one of the first composers who began to write on revolutionary themes. In 1923 he wrote *March on the Left,* to words by Mayakovsky. In 1927 he produced an operatic fairy tale, *Ivan the Soldier,* and a ballet, *The Serf Ballerina* (Leningrad, Dec. 11, 1927). He further wrote 3 choral symphonies: *October* (1931), *Holland* (1933), *The Peoples of the Soviet Land* (1935); violin concerto (1937); several overtures; a violin sonata; sonata for viola and double-bass; etc. In 1939 he went to work in Turkistan, where he collected and publ. anthologies of native songs; also wrote works based on native subjects, among them the first Turkmenian ballet, *The Gay Deceiver.* In 1950 he wrote a cantata, *Free China,* for which he received a Stalin prize.

Korte, Werner, German musicologist; b. Münster, May 29, 1906; studied there, in Freiburg and Berlin (with Johannes Wolf); received his *Dr. phil.* degree with the dissertation, *Die Harmonik des frühen 15. Jahrhunderts in ihrem Zusammenhang mit der Formtechnik* (publ. 1929); was assistant in musicology at the Univ. of Heidelberg (1928-31); from 1932 at the Univ. of Münster. He publ. *Studie zur Geschichte der Musik in Italien im ersten Viertel des 15. Jahrhunderts* (1933); *J. S. Bach* (1934); *Beethoven* (1936); *Schumann* (1937); *Musik und Weltbild* (1940); *Händel und der deutsche Geist* (1942).

Kortschak, Hugo, violinist and conductor; b. Graz, Feb. 24, 1884; d. Honolulu, Hawaii, Sept. 20, 1957. He studied in Graz and with Ševčik at the Prague Cons., graduating in 1904. He played the violin in the Berlin Philharmonic; then emigrated to America, where he was 2nd concertmaster of the Chicago Symph. Orch.; in 1913, founded the Kortschak Quartet in Chicago; in 1915 it was reorganized as the Berkshire String Quartet. He was instrumental in building up the Coolidge Chamber Music Festivals at Pittsfield, Mass.; was conductor of the Stamford Symph. Orch. (1935) and associate conductor of the New Haven

Symph. Orch. (1936). In 1938 he received the Coolidge Medal for 'distinguished services to chamber music.'

Kósa, György, Hungarian composer and pianist; b. Budapest, April 24, 1897. He exhibited a talent for composition at an exceedingly early age. Béla Bartók gave him some lessons, and he also took courses with Albert Siklós and Victor Herzfeld; studied piano with Dohnányi. He then traveled as accompanist with violinists and other artists in Germany, Austria, and Italy. In 1927 he was appointed piano instructor at the Budapest Acedamy of Music; also performed at chamber music concerts. He remained in Budapest during World War II and was compelled to become a laborer in a war camp. After 1945 he resumed his teaching; in 1947 he was briefly in Paris, where he played his piano works. The primary influence in his music is that of Bartók; but he was also influenced by German Expressionists, particularly Schoenberg. He wrote music in all genres.—Works: operas: *The King's Robe* (1926-27), *Ye Two Knights* (Budapest, 1936), *Cenodoxus,* mystery opera (1941-42), *The Scholar Anselmus* (1944-45). *The Bees* (1946); incidental music to *Tartuffe;* ballets: *White Pierrot* (Budapest, 1920), *Laterna Magica,* pantomime with voices (Budapest, Feb. 23, 1927), *The Three Miracles of Joe the Orphan* (Budapest, Feb. 26, 1933), *King David,* biblical ballet (1936), *Burlesque,* a pantomime (1947); for orch.: 6 symphonies (1920, 1930, 1933, 1934, 1936, and 1947), *Fairy Tale Suite,* after Andersen (1931), *Fantasy on Hungarian Folksongs* (1948); 4 string quartets (1920-35); quintet for flute, clarinet, horn, bassoon, and harp (1937); trio for flute, viola, and cello (1941); string trio (1946); trio for soprano (wordless), violin, and clarinet (1947); violin sonata; piano pieces; many choral works, including 3 oratorios, *Joseph* (1939), *Elijah* (1940), and *Christus* (1943).

Koschat, Thomas, Austrian bass singer and composer; b. Viktring, near Klagenfurt, Aug. 8, 1845; d. Vienna, May 19, 1914. He sang in chorus at various churches; then turned to composition; publ. his first vocal quartets in the Carinthian dialect in 1871; they became so successful that he publ. some 100 more. In 1875 he organized the famous 'Kärnthner Quintett' with 4 other singers; their performances were exceedingly popular. His 'Liederspiel' *Am Wörthersee* (Vienna, March 22, 1880), containing many of his favorite vocal numbers, had great vogue; he also produced a 4-act 'Volksstück mit Gesang,' *Die Rosenthaler Nachtigall,* and the 'Singspiel' *Der Bürgermeister von St. Anna* (Vienna, May 1, 1884; given in Italian as *Un Colpo di fuoco*). —Cf. Karl Krobath, *Thomas Koschat, der Sänger Kärnthners* (Leipzig, 1912).

Köselitz, Heinrich (pen-name Peter Gast), German writer and composer; b. Annaberg, Jan. 10, 1854; d. there, Aug. 15, 1918. He studied with Richter at the Leipzig Cons. While in Basel, he formed an intimate friendship with Nietzsche, from whom he also took lessons in composition; after Nietzsche's death, he became his literary executor; edited Nietzsche's letters. As composer he elaborated the Wagnerian system of *Leitmotive;* he used the pen-name of Peter Gast for his musical productions, among them the operas *Wilbram und Siegeheer* (1879), *Scherz, List und Rache* (1881), *Die heimliche Ehe* (Danzig, 1891; publ. in 1901 as *Der Löwe von Venedig); König Wenzel* (not produced), and *Orpheus und Dionysos* (not produced); a festival play, *Walpurgisnacht* (1903); a symph. poem, *Helle Nächte;* choruses; songs.—Cf. L. Brieger-Wasservogel, *Peter Gast* (Leipzig, 1906); F. Götz, *Peter Gast* (Annaberg, 1934); F. Tutenberg, *Peters Gasts Löwe von Venedig,* in 'Zeitschrift für Musik' (Feb., 1940).

Koshetz, Nina, soprano; b. Kiev, Russia, Dec. 30, 1894. At the age of 11 she entered the Moscow Cons. to study piano; began to study singing at 16. She toured Russia under Koussevitzky; also toured with Rachmaninoff, of whose songs she was an eminent interpreter. She made her American début in 1921, and since that time appeared with many American orchestras as a soloist; also gave recitals in Europe. In 1941 she settled in Hollywood, and devoted herself to teaching.

Kosleck, Julius, German trumpet and cornet virtuoso; b. Neugard, Dec. 3, 1825; d. Berlin, Nov. 5, 1904. He was a trumpeter in the court orch. in Berlin; in 1871 he founded the 'Kaiser Cornett Quartett'; also a wind band, 'Patriotischer Bläserbund'; from 1873 taught at the Hochschule für Musik in Berlin. He was influential in reviving the historic art of the fanfare; publ. a method for the trumpet and cornet à pistons. In 1884 he introduced a trumpet with a broad, funnel-shaped mouthpiece, which was regarded as a 'Bach trumpet,' capable of playing high florid parts.

Kosma, Joseph, Hungarian-French composer; b. Budapest, Oct. 22, 1905; studied at the Music Academy there. In 1933 he went to Paris and settled there as a composer of ballet and film music.—Works: ballets, *Le rendez-vous* (Paris, June 15, 1945), *Baptiste* (1946), *Lecuyère* (1948); film scores to *La grande illusion* (1936); *Les enfants du paradis;* etc. He also wrote an oratorio, *Les ponts de Paris* (1947), a number of characteristic piano pieces *(Danse des automates,* etc.), and songs.

Kössler, Hans. See **Koessler.**

Kossmaly, Carl, German writer on music and conductor; b. Breslau, July 27, 1812; d. Stettin, Dec. 1, 1893. He studied in Berlin with Berger, Zelter, and Klein; then was chorusmaster at theaters in Wiesbaden, Mainz, Amsterdam, Bremen, Detmold, and Stettin, where he settled as teacher and concert conductor. He publ. *Schlesisches Tonkünstler-Lexikon* (1846-47); *Mozarts Opern* (1848); *Über die Anwendung des Programmes zur Erklärung musikalischer Compositionen* (1858); *Über Richard Wagner* (1873, anti-Wagnerian); contributed articles to music periodicals; also wrote symphonies, overtures, instrumental and vocal works, songs, etc.

Kostelanetz, André, Russian-American conductor; b. St. Petersburg, Dec. 22, 1901. He studied at the St. Petersburg Cons.; left Russia in 1922 and settled in America. He was employed as accompanist at the Metropolitan Opera; in 1930 became conductor with the Columbia Broadcasting System. He married the famous soprano Lily Pons (June 2, 1938); gave concerts with her for the armed forces during World War II, flying to Burma and India, as well as to European posts. He made numerous arrangements of light music; his technique of massive concentration of instrumental sonorities and of harmonic saturation (by filling in all chords with inner thirds and sixths) has greatly influenced the writing for films and the arranging for popular concerts. He commissioned works from Copland (*A Lincoln Portrait*), Schuman, and other American composers.

Köstlin, Heinrich Adolf, theologian and organizer of church festivals; b. Tübingen, Oct. 4, 1846; d. Cannstadt, June 4, 1907. He was the son of Josephine Lang-Köstlin, the song composer (1815-1880). In 1875 he united the choirs of 3 towns (Sulz, Kalw, Nagold) for church music performances, which became the nucleus of the Württemberg Evangelical 'Kirchengesangverein,' organized by him in 1877, the festivals of which he also conducted. In 1883, he organized, with L. Hallwachs, a similar society for all Germany, with annual meetings in different cities; this led to the establishment of more choral branches for sacred music (more than 2000 choirs in 1916). Köstlin publ. *Geschichte der Musik im Umriss* (1873; 6th ed., revised by W. Nagel, 1910); *Die Tonkunst: Einführung in die Ästhetik der Musik* (1878); *Luther als Vater des evangelischen Kirchenliedes* (1882); *Geschichte des christlichen Gottesdienstes* (1886); also a biographical sketch of his mother (Leipzig, 1881).

Köstlin, Karl Reinhold, German theorist; b. Urach, Sept. 28, 1819; d. Tübingen, April 12, 1894. He taught esthetics and art history at Tübingen Univ. He publ. *Ästhetik* (2 vols., 1863-69); an essay on musical esthetics in Vischer's *Ästhetik* (vol. 3); and a pamphlet on Wagner.

Kotek, Joseph, Russian violinist; b. Kamenetz-Podolsk, Oct. 25, 1855; d. Davos, Switzerland, Jan. 4, 1885. He studied violin with Ferdinand Laub and composition with Tchaikovsky at the Moscow Cons.; later took violin lessons with Joachim in Berlin. He was an intimate friend of Tchaikovsky, and often served as mediator in financial matters between him and Nadezhda von Meck; also worked over the solo part of Tchaikovsky's violin concerto, and played it with the composer at the piano, privately, at Clarens, Switzerland (April 3, 1878); however, he was reluctant to try it out in public performance despite Tchaikovsky's urgings. From 1878-82 he taught violin at the Hochschule für Musik in Berlin. He died of tuberculosis at the age of 29; Tchaikovsky made a special trip to Davos to see him before his death.

Kothe, Aloys, German music teacher; brother of Bernhard and Wilhelm Kothe; b. Gröbnig, Oct. 3, 1828; d. Breslau, Nov. 13, 1868. He studied with Grell in Berlin; taught at the Teachers' Seminary in Breslau. He publ. a Mass for men's voices; piano pieces, songs, etc.

Kothe, Bernard, German writer on music; brother of Aloys and Wilhelm Kothe; b. Gröbnig, May 12, 1821; d. Breslau, July 25, 1897. He studied in Berlin with A. B. Marx; in 1851, became church music director and teacher at Oppeln; then succeeded his brother Aloys Kothe as music teacher at the Teachers'

Seminary in Breslau, where he founded the Cäcilien-Verein for Catholic church music. He publ. *Musica Sacra;* 2 pamphlets, *Die Musik in der katholischen Kirche* (1862) and *Abriss der Musikgeschichte für Lehrerseminare und Dilettanten* (1874); also edited the 4th ed. of Seidel's *Die Orgel und ihr Bau* (1887); and, with Forchhammer, a *Führer durch die Orgellitteratur* (1890). He also publ. a book of organ preludes; other organ pieces; motets.

Kothe, Robert, German singer and folksong arranger; b. Straubing, Feb. 6, 1869; d. Gräfelfing, near Munich, May 24, 1944. He appeared as a singer, accompanying himself on the lute; established a school for lutenists in Gelsenkirchen; publ. 12 albums of folksong arrangements; also a method of lute playing (1929). —Cf. Fritz Jöde, *Robert Kothe* (1916).

Kothe, Wilhelm, German music teacher; brother of Aloys and Bernhard Kothe; b. Gröbnig, Jan. 8, 1831; d. Habelschwerdt, Dec. 31, 1897. He studied organ in Berlin; from 1871 until his death he was music teacher at the Teachers' Seminary in Habelschwerdt. He publ. a pamphlet on *Friedrich der Grosse als Musiker;* also methods for violin and voice, songs, and piano music.

Kothen (koh'-ten), **Karl Axel,** Finnish singer and composer; b. Frederikshamm, Aug. 15, 1871; d. Helsinki, July 7, 1927. He studied in Helsinki, Rome, St. Petersburg, Vienna, Paris, and Munich; returning to Helsinki in 1908, became prof. of singing at the Helsinki Cons. He wrote several choral works, among them *Vagorna sjunga* and *Finlands namm* (both for the Finland Jubilee of 1920); also a cantata for the festival of the tercentenary of Vasa; incidental music to *Kristina Vasa;* piano pieces and songs.

Kotilainen, Otto, Finnish composer; b. Heinävesi, Feb. 5, 1868; d. Helsinki, Aug. 9, 1936. He studied with Wegelius and Sibelius at the Helsingfors Cons., and in Berlin. He wrote a cantata, *Cygneus; Festsang* for chorus and horns; an orchestral suite; *Legend* for string orch.; incidental music for plays; pieces for violin and piano; choruses; songs.

Kotter, Hans, Alsatian organist and composer; b. Strasbourg, circa 1485; d. Berne, 1541. He was a disciple of Paul Hofhaimer; served as organist at Freiburg, Switzerland (1504-22) until he was banished for espousing the doctrines of the reformer Zwingli. In 1532 Kotter was able to return to Switzerland, and he took up residence in Berne as a schoolmaster. He compiled a collection of keyboard pieces in tablature (1513), including preambles, fantasies, dances, transcriptions of vocal music, and settings of plainchant. There is also in existence a setting of a *Nobis post hoc* by Kotter interpolated in a *Salve Regina* by Hofhaimer.—Cf. W. Merian, *Die Tabulaturen des Organisten Hans Kotter* (Leipzig, 1916); W. Apel, *Early German Keyboard Music* in the 'Mus. Quarterly' (April, 1937); G. Reese, *Music in the Renaissance* (N. Y., 1954).

Kottlitz, Adolf, violinist; b. Trier, Sept. 27, 1820; killed while hunting in Uralsk, Russia, Oct. 26, 1860. He began his career as a child prodigy; gave public concerts at the age of 10; spent 3 years in Paris, where he was a protégé of Liszt; then played violin in the orch. of the Königsberg Opera (1848-56). In 1856 he undertook a long tour in Russia, and finally settled in Uralsk as violin teacher. He publ. 2 string quartets. His wife Clothilde, *née* Ellendt (1822-67), was a singing teacher in Königsberg.

Kotzeluch. See **Kozeluch.**

Kotzolt, Heinrich, German vocal teacher; b. Schnellewalde, Aug. 26, 1814; d. Berlin, July 2, 1881. He first studied philology in Breslau, but turned to music, studying in Berlin with Dehn and Rungenhagen (1836-38); then sang at the Danzig Opera (1838-42). Returning to Berlin, he founded a singing society there in 1849. He publ. a method for a cappella singing; also the 54th Psalm, for double chorus a cappella; *Lobet den Herrn, alle Heiden,* for 8-part chorus; etc.

Kotzschmar, Hermann, organist; b. Finsterwalde, Germany, July 4, 1829; d. Portland, Maine, April 12, 1909. As a child, he learned how to play the organ and virtually all the orchestral instruments; then studied seriously in Dresden. In 1848 he came to America with the Saxonia Band and settled in Portland, Maine, as teacher; was for 47 years organist at the First Unitarian Church there. He publ. many vocal quartets, songs, and piano pieces. His *Te Deum* in F was often sung in American churches. He was also esteemed as a teacher; J. K. Paine was his pupil. —Cf. G. T. Edwards, *Music and Musicians of Maine* (Portland, 1928; pp. 167-69).

Kotzwara (*recte* Kocvara), **Franz,** Bohemian composer; b. Prague, 1730; d. London (by hanging himself), Sept. 2, 1791. He traveled in Europe; then settled in London towards the end of the 18th century. In 1790 he went to Dublin as violinist in the orchestra at the King's Theatre; returning to London the same year, he played in the orchestra at the Handel Commemoration in May. He is remembered solely for his piano piece, *The Battle of Prague,* which attained tremendous popularity in the 19th century.

Kountz (koontz), **Richard,** American composer; b. Pittsburgh, July 8, 1896; d. New York, Oct. 14, 1950. From 1927-39 he was manager of the Standard and Educational Publications dept. of M. Witmark & Sons in N. Y. He wrote *The Sleigh* and other songs; a *Pastorale* for organ, etc.; also made arrangements for various choral combinations.

Koussevitzky (koo-sĕh-vēts'-kē), **Sergey Alexandrovitch,** celebrated conductor; b. Vishny-Volotchok, Russia, July 26, 1874; d. Boston, June 4, 1951. At the age of 14 he went to Moscow and entered the music school of the Philharmonic Society there as a double-bass student in the class of Rambusek, selecting this instrument because it was taught without charge. He studied theory with Blaramberg and Kruglikov. In 1894 he joined the orchestra of the Bolshoy Opera Theater. In 1896 he made his first appearance as a soloist in Moscow; on March 27, 1903, he gave a double-bass recital in Berlin, attracting great attention. To supplement the meager repertory, he wrote several pieces for the double-bass and performed them at his concerts; with some aid from Glière, he composed a double-bass concerto, which he performed for the first time in Moscow on Feb. 25, 1905. On Sept. 8, 1905, he married Natalie Ushkov, of a wealthy tea-merchant family. He soon resigned from the orchestra of the Bolshoy Opera Theater and went to Germany, where he continued to give double-bass recitals; played the 1st cello concerto by Saint-Saëns on the double-bass. In 1907 he conducted a student orchestra at the Berlin Hochschule für Musik; his first public appearance as conductor took place on Jan. 23, 1908 with the Berlin Philharmonic. In 1909 he established a publishing house, Editions Russes de Musique; in 1915 he purchased the catalogue of the Gutheil Co.; among composers with whom he signed contracts were Scriabin, Stravinsky, Prokofiev, Medtner, and Rachmaninoff; the association with Scriabin was particularly fruitful, and in subsequent years Koussevitzky became the greatest champion of Scriabin's music. In 1909 he organized his own symph. orch. in Moscow, featuring works by Russian composers, but also including classical masterpieces; played many Russian works for the first time, among them Scriabin's *Prometheus.* In the summer of 1910 he took his orch. to the towns along the Volga River in a specially chartered steamboat. He repeated the Volga tour in 1912 and 1914. The outbreak of World War I made it necessary to curtail his activities; however, he continued to give his concerts in Moscow; in 1915 he presented a memorial Scriabin program. After the Revolution of 1917, Koussevitzky was offered the directorship of the State Symph. Orch. (former Court Orch.); in Petrograd he conducted it until 1920; also presented concerts in Moscow despite the hardships of the revolutionary times. In 1920 he left Russia; went first to Berlin, then to Rome, and finally to Paris, where he settled for several years. There he organized the Concerts Koussevitzky with a specially assembled orchestra; presented many new scores by French and Russian composers, among them Ravel's orchestration of Mussorgsky's *Pictures at an Exhibition,* Honegger's *Pacific 231,* and several works by Prokofiev and Stravinsky. In 1924 Koussevitzky was engaged as permanent conductor of the Boston Symph. Orch., a post that he was to hold for 25 years, the longest tenure of any conductor of that organization; until 1928 he continued his Paris series (during the summer months). Just as in Russia he championed Russian composers, in France the French, so in the U. S. he encouraged American composers to write works for the Boston Symph. Orch. Symphonic compositions by Aaron Copland, Roy Harris, Walter Piston, Samuel Barber, Howard Hanson, Edward Burlingame Hill, William Schuman, and others were performed by Koussevitzky for the first time. For the 50th anniversary of the Boston Symph. Orch. (1931) Koussevitzky commissioned works from Stravinsky *(Symphony of Psalms),* Hindemith, Honegger, Prokofiev, Albert Roussel, Ravel (piano concerto), Copland, Gershwin, etc. In 1950 he conducted in Rio de Janeiro, Israel, and in Europe; also was guest conductor at several concerts of the Boston Symph. after his successor, Charles Munch, became principal conductor. A highly important development in Koussevitzky's American career was the establishment of the Berkshire Music Center at Tanglewood, Mass. This was an outgrowth of the Berkshire Symph. Festival, organized in 1934 by Henry Hadley; Koussevitzky and the Boston Symph. Orch. presented summer concerts at the Berkshire Festival in 1935 for the first time; since then, the concerts have become an annual institution. The Berkshire Music Center was opened on July 8, 1940, with Koussevitzky as director, and Copland as assistant director; among the distinguished guest instructors were Hindemith, Honegger, and Messiaen; Koussevitzky himself taught conducting; he was succeeded after his death by his former student, Leonard Bernstein. Koussevitzky held many honorary degrees; Mus. Doc. from Brown Univ. (1926), Rutgers Univ. (1937), Yale Univ. (1938), Rochester Univ. (1940), Williams College (1943), and Boston Univ. (1945); an LL.D. degree from Harvard Univ. (1929) and from Princeton Univ. (1947); he was a member of the French Legion of Honor; held the Cross of Commander of the Finnish Order of the White Rose (1936). Besides his double-bass concerto, he wrote *Humoresque, Valse miniature, Chanson triste,* and other small pieces for his instrument; and an orchestral work, *Passacaglia on a Russian Theme* (Boston Symph., Oct. 12, 1934). Koussevitzky became an American citizen on April 16, 1941. In 1942 his wife died; he established the Koussevitzky Foundation as a memorial to her; the funds to be used for commissioning works by composers of all nationalities. He married Olga Naoumoff, a niece of Natalie Koussevitzky, on Aug. 15, 1947. As a conductor, Koussevitzky possessed an extraordinary emotional power; in Russian music, and particularly in Tchaikovsky's symphonies, he was unexcelled; he was capable of achieving the subtlest nuances in the works of the French school; his interpretations of Debussy were notable. As a champion of modern music, he introduced a great number of compositions for the first time anywhere; his ardor in projecting unfamiliar music before new audiences in different countries served to carry conviction among the listeners and the professional music critics. He was often criticized for the liberties he allowed himself in the treatment of classical masterpieces; undoubtedly his performances of Bach, Beethoven, Brahms, and Schubert were untraditional; but they were none the less musicianly in the sincere artistry that animated his interpretations.—Cf. A. Lourié, *S. A. Koussevitzky and His Epoch* (N. Y., 1931); Hugo Leichtentritt, *Serge Koussevitzky, The Boston Symph. Orch. and the New American Music* (Cambridge, Mass., 1946); M. A. DeWolfe Howe, *The Boston Symph. Orch. 1881-1931* (Boston, 1931); M. A. DeWolfe Howe, *The Tale of Tanglewood* (Boston, 1946); Moses Smith, *Koussevitzky* (N. Y., 1947, a controversial biography; Koussevitzky instituted suit against the author and publisher for invasion of his right of privacy, but lost his case in court).

Koutzen, Boris, violinist and composer; b. Uman, near Kiev, Russia, April 1, 1901. At the age of 11 he made his début playing a concerto at Kherson; at 17, became violinist in the orch. of the Moscow Opera House; from 1918-22 he also studied at the Moscow Cons. with Leo Zetlin (violin) and with Glière (composition). In 1922 he went to Germany; in 1923, settled in the U. S. and joined the Philadelphia Orch.; then he became head of the violin dept. of the Philadelphia Cons. — Works: for orch.: *Solitude,* poem-nocturne (Philadelphia, April 1, 1927, composer conducting); *Symphonic Movement* for violin and orch. (1929); *Valley Forge,* symph. poem (N. Y., Feb. 19, 1940); Symphony in C (1939); *Concerto* for 5 solo instruments and string orch. (Boston, Feb. 23, 1940); *From the American Folklore,* concert overture (1943); *Duo concertante,* for violin and piano (1943); violin concerto (Philadelphia, Feb. 22, 1952, Nadia Koutzen, composer's daughter, soloist); chamber music: 3 string quartets (1922); violin sonata (1928); *Legend* and *Nocturne,* for violin and piano (1928 and 1930); trio for flute, cello, and harp (1933); *Enigma,* for piano (1938); piano sonatina (1931); sonatina for 2 pianos.

Koval, Marian Victorovitch, Russian composer; b. Pristan Voznesenya, Olonetz district, Aug. 17, 1907. He began to study piano in St. Petersburg; in 1925 entered the Moscow Cons., and studied with Gnessin. At the Cons. he formed a group of students 'Procoll' ('Productive Collective') dedicated to the propaganda of music on sociological and revolutionary subjects. His major work is the opera *Emelian Pugatchev* (Moscow, Nov. 25, 1939), for which he won the 1st Stalin Prize. He also wrote the historic opera *Sevastopoltzy* (Molotov, Nov. 28, 1946); the cantatas *The People's Sacred War* (1941), *Valery Tchkalov* (1942), *The Kremlin Stars* (1947), and *Poem of Lenin* (1949); a children's opera, *The Wolf and Seven Little Goats* (1939); and a great number of choral works and song cycles.

Kovalev, Pavel Ivanovitch, Russian composer; b. Nikolayev, Jan. 7, 1890. He studied at the Cons. of Odessa, in Cracow, and in Leipzig (with Max Reger, Krehl, and Teichmüller); in 1919-22 was prof. at the Odessa Cons.; in 1922 moved to Moscow. He wrote an opera, *Ariadne and Bluebeard,* a string quartet; piano pieces; songs.

Kovařovic (koh'-vahr-zhoh-vits), **Karel,** Czech conductor and composer; b. Prague, Dec. 9, 1862; d. there, Dec. 6, 1920. He studied clarinet, harp, and piano at the Prague Cons., and composition with Fibich. In 1900 he was appointed opera conductor of the National Theater in Prague, and held this post until his death; he also led symph. concerts in Prague. As conductor, he demonstrated great craftsmanship and established a high standard of excellence in his operatic productions; his interpretations of Dvořák and Smetana were particularly notable; an ardent believer in the cause of Czech music, he promoted national compositions. In his own music, he also made use of national materials, but his treatment was mostly imitative of the French models; the influences of Gounod and Massenet are particularly noticeable. He publ. some of his lighter works under a series of humorously misspelled names of French opera composers (C. Biset, J. Héral, etc.).—Works: the operas (all produced in Prague): *Ženiohové* (*The Bridegrooms;* May 13, 1884), *Cesta Oknem* (*Through the Window;* Feb. 11, 1886), *Noc Šimona a Judy* (*The Night of Simon and Jude;* original title, *Frasquita;* Nov. 5, 1892), *Psohlavci* (*The Dog-Heads;* his most famous opera; April 24, 1898), *Na starém bělidle* (*At the Old Bleaching-House;* Nov. 22, 1901); ballets, *Hashish* (June 19, 1884), *Pohadka o nalezenem stesti* (*A Tale of Found Happiness;* Dec. 21, 1886), *Na zaletech* (*Flirtation;* Oct. 24, 1909); symph. works, a piano concerto; 2 string quartets; etc.

Koven, Reginald de. See **De Koven.**

Kowalski, Henri, pianist and composer; b. Paris, 1841; d. Bordeaux, July 8, 1916. He studied piano with Marmontel and composition with Reber; wrote characteristic piano pieces (*Marche hongroise, 12 Caprices en forme d'études, Barcarolle chinoise, Sérénade japonaise, etc.*). He described his American tour in a book, *À travers l'Amérique; impressions d'un musicien* (Paris, 1872; contains a list of his compositions).

Kowalski (koh-vahl'-skē), **Max,** German composer and pedagogue; b. Kowel, Poland, Aug. 10, 1882; d. London, June 4, 1956. He was taken to Frankfurt as an infant, and received his primary education there; studied law, obtaining his *Dr. juris* at Marburg Univ.; returning to Frankfurt, he studied music with Bernhard Sekles; in 1912 wrote a cycle of songs to Guiraud's *Pierrot Lunaire* (independently from Schoenberg's work of the same year) and during the following 20 years composed a number of lieder, which were widely performed in Germany. After 1933 he was put in the Buchenwald concentration camp, but was released in 1939, and went to England; settled in London as teacher and a synagogal cantor; eked out his existence also by tuning pianos.

Koželuch (koh-zhĕh-lŏŏh), **Johann Anton,** Bohemian composer, cousin of Leopold Koželuch; b. Welwarn, Dec. 14, 1738; d. Prague, Feb. 3, 1814. He studied in Prague and Vienna; served as choirmaster at the Prague Cathedral from 1784. He wrote 2 operas: *Alessandro nell'Indie* (Prague, 1769) and *Demofoonte* (Prague, 1772); 2 oratorios; a *Missa solennissima* and 44 other Masses; 4 Requiems; many other church works; also 5 symphonies, a piano concerto, bassoon concerto, oboe concerto, and a great number of other instrumental works; the bulk of these remain in manuscript.—Cf. R. Fikrle, *J. A. Koželuch* (Prague, 1944).

Koželuch (Kotzeluch), Leopold Anton, Bohemian composer; b. Welwarn, Dec. 9, 1752; d. Vienna, May 7, 1818. He was a law student at Prague; studied music with his cousin Johann Anton Koželuch. The success of a ballet of his own at the National Theater, Prague, in 1771 caused him to adopt the profession of music. Within six years he wrote 24 more ballets, 3 pantomimes, and incidental music; became music master to the Archduchess Elisabeth at Vienna in 1778, and followed Mozart as court composer in 1792. He was a brilliant pianist, and in high favor as a teacher among the aristocracy. His compositions include the operas *Le Mazet, Giudita, Deborah,* and *Didone abbandonata;* cantatas, symphonies, numerous piano compositions (about 50 concertos), chamber works, etc., but they are of scant interest. Beethoven referred to him contemptuously in a letter of 1812 as 'miserabilis.'

Kraft, Anton, cello virtuoso; b. Rokitzán, near Pilsen, Dec. 30, 1752; d. Vienna, Aug. 28, 1820. He began to study at an early age with his father, an amateur cellist; then went to Prague, and later to Vienna; there he enjoyed the friendship of Haydn, who recommended him for a post as cellist in the chapel of Prince Esterházy (1778); he was subsequently in the employ of Prince Grassalkowicz; in 1795 entered the service of Prince Lobkowitz in Vienna. Among Kraft's works are 3 sonatas, 3 'grand duos' for violin and cello, and several 'grand duos' for 2 cellos; a 'divertissement' for cello and double-bass; etc. For a time it was thought that Haydn's famous cello concerto in D major was actually written by Kraft, but it is now generally agreed by specialists that it is an authentic work by Haydn. Since it was written for Kraft, he may have made technical suggestions that were adopted by Haydn.

Kraft, Nicolaus, cellist and composer; son of Anton Kraft; b. Esterház, Hungary, Dec. 14, 1778; d. Stuttgart, May 18, 1853. He studied cello with his father, and went with him on concert tours while quite young; he and his father played chamber music with Mozart at the Dresden court (1789); when the Krafts went to Vienna in 1790, Nicolaus became a member of the famous 'Schuppanzigh Quartet.' He was subsequently chamber musician to Prince Lobkowitz, who sent him to Berlin in 1791 to study for a year with Duport. After concerts in Germany, he returned to Vienna, and joined the court orch. (1809); then entered the court orch. at Stuttgart in 1814. He retired after an accident to his hand, in 1834. He wrote 5 cello concertos; 6 duos and 3 'divertissements' for 2 cellos; a cello fantasia with string quartet; *Polonaise* and *Bolero* for cello with orch.; and other cello music. His son, **Friedrich Kraft** (b. Feb. 12, 1809; date of death unknown), was also a cellist, and played in the Stuttgart court orch. for many years.

Kramer, A. Walter, American music critic and composer; b. New York, Sept. 23, 1890. He studied music with his father, Maximilian Kramer; then took violin lessons with Carl Hauser and Richard Arnold; after graduation from the College of the City of N. Y. (1910), he joined the staff of 'Musical America' (1910-22); was its editor-in-chief from 1929-36; in 1936 he became managing director and vice-president of the Galaxy Music Corporation; resigned in 1956. He was one of the founders of the Society for Publication of American Music (1919); contributed the chapter, *The Modern Italians,* to 'The Art of Music' (1916). Among his works are *Symphonic Rhapsody* for violin and orch. (1912; Lewisohn Stadium, N. Y., Aug. 7, 1919); *The Lady of Ceret,* cantata; *In Normandy (A Rococo Romance),* choral cycle with orch. (1925); *Elizabethan Days,* suite for small orch.; *Eklog* for cello and piano; *Chant nègre* for violin and piano; a number of lyric songs *(Beauty of Earth, Swans, Green, Christmas Carol, The Faltering Dusk, The Last Hour,* etc.); piano pieces, etc.; also orch. arrangements of Bach and other classics.—Cf. J. T. Howard, *A. Walter Kramer* (N. Y., 1926); W. T. Upton, *Art-Song in America* (N. Y., 1930; pp. 225-35).

Kramm, Georg, German composer; b. Kassel, Dec. 21, 1856; d. Düsseldorf, Oct., 1910. He studied in Kassel; played violin in the court orch. there; then played in orchestras in Stettin and Hamburg; went to Düsseldorf, where he studied under Tausch; taught in the Düsseldorf Cons. He wrote the opera *Leonore* (Düsseldorf, 1903); cantata, *Der Felsenstrom;* for orch.: *Johannes; Fest bei Herodes: Salome tanzt; Polnische Festmusik; Andalusische Serenade;* also *Romanze* for cello and piano, piano pieces, and songs.

Kranich & Bach, well known firm of piano makers founded in New York, 1864, by Helmuth Kranich (b. Grossbreitenbach, Germany, Aug. 22, 1833; d. N. Y., Jan. 29, 1902) and Jacques Bach (b. Lorentzen, Alsace, June 22, 1833; d. N. Y., Oct. 29, 1894). The business, incorporated in 1890, has been continued by the founders' descendants: Frederick Kranich served as president from 1902-20, and was succeeded by Louis P. Bach from 1920-30; in 1930 Jacques Bach Schlosser (grandson of Jacques Bach) was elected president; Helmuth Kranich, son of Helmuth, Sr., was appointed a member of the Board of Directors in 1894; secretary of the firm in 1902, and president in 1946; retired in 1950. He died in N. Y. on Oct. 24, 1956. Other members of the Board of Directors included Philip Schlosser (grandson of Jacques Bach), Victor Kranich (son of Helmuth Kranich Sr.), Lucy Bach (daughter of Jacques Bach), and John J. Kuhn (grandnephew of Jacques Bach). Frederick Kranich invented the 'Isotonic' pedal, doing away with the shifting keyboard in grand pianos, and the 'Violyn' plate for upright pianos, and perfected various improvements in piano construction.—Cf. A. Dolge, *Pianos and Their Makers,* vol. II (Covina, California, 1913).

Krantz, Eugen, German pianist; b. Dresden, Sept. 13, 1844; d. Gohrisch, near Königstein, May 26, 1898. He studied at the Dresden Cons.; was chorusmaster at the court opera there (1869-84); taught at the Dresden Cons., becoming director in 1890, when he bought the institution. He was chiefly an accompanist; publ. some songs and a *Lehrgang im Klavierunterricht* (1882); was also critic for the Dresden 'Presse' and for the 'Nachrichten.'

Krasa, Hans, Czech composer; b. Prague, Nov. 30, 1899; d. Oswiecim, March 1, 1944. He studied with Zemlinsky and Keussler in Prague; in 1923 was in Paris; then returned to Prague and was active as teacher, conductor, and composer. In 1941 he was arrested by the German occupation authorities as a Jew and interned at the Theresienstadt concentration camp; early in 1944 he was taken to Oswiecim, Poland, and put to death in a gas chamber. He was a composer of some interesting works in a 'hedonistic' vein, aiming at entertainment in a sophisticated manner. His opera *Betrothal in a Dream* (1933) received a Czech State Prize; another opera, *Brundibar (The Organ Grinder)* was completed in 1940. His *Pastorale* and *March* (originally 1st and 2nd movements from a symphony) were performed in Paris (April 24, 1923) and also in America by the Boston Symph. (Nov. 19, 1926). His string trio was performed posthumously at the Aspen, Colorado, Festival (Oct. 22, 1951). He also wrote incidental music to *Lysistrata,* and the cantata *Die Erde ist des Herrn.*

Krasner, Louis, violinist; b. Cherkassy, Russia, June 21, 1903; was taken to the U. S. as a small child; studied at the New England Cons., Boston, graduating in 1923; then went abroad, where he studied violin with Karl Flesch, Lucien Capet, and Ševčik. He was concertmaster of the Minneapolis Symph. Orch. from 1944-49; then became prof. of violin and chamber music at Syracuse Univ. He commissioned Alban Berg in 1934 to write a violin concerto for him; gave its world première at the Barcelona Festival of the International Society for Contemporary Music (April 19, 1936); also gave the world première of Schoenberg's violin concerto (Philadelphia, Dec. 6, 1940, Stokowski conducting).

Kraus, Alessandro, German collector of musical instruments; b. Frankfurt, Aug. 6, 1820; d. Florence, Sept. 22, 1904. He was noted for his extensive and valuable collection of musical instruments; co-founder of the 'Tonkünstlerhilfsverein' in Frankfurt and of the Florentine 'Società del Quartetto.'

Kraus, Ernst, German tenor; b. Erlangen, June 8, 1863; d. Wörthsee, Sept. 6, 1941. He studied in Milan with Cesare Galliera and in Munich with Frau Schimon-Regan; made his début as a concert singer at a Kaim Concert in Munich (Jan. 18, 1893); opera début in Mannheim on March 26, 1893, as Tamino in *Die Zauberflöte;* then remained there as a member of the opera (1893-96); from 1896-1923, engaged at the Court Opera in Berlin; in 1924, returned to Munich as singing teacher.

Kraus, Felix von, bass singer; b. Vienna, Oct. 3, 1870; d. Munich, Oct. 30, 1937. He first studied musicology at the Univ. of Vienna *(Dr. phil.,* 1894); then singing with Stockhausen. In 1899, after a European tour as a concert singer, he appeared at the Wagner festival in Bayreuth as Hagen, and subsequently participated in the festivals every summer for many years; established himself as one of the finest interpreters of Wagnerian bass roles. He also taught dramatic singing in Munich. In 1899 he married the American singer, Adrienne Osborne (q.v.).

Kraus, Joseph Martin, important German-Swedish composer; b. Miltenberg, near Mainz, June 20, 1756; d. Stockholm, Dec. 15, 1792. He studied at the Jesuit School in Mannheim; later in Mainz (1773), Erfurt, and Göttingen (1776). In 1778 he went to Sweden and worked as a theater conductor in Stockholm; he became greatly interested in Swedish culture; wrote operas to Swedish texts; traveled with Gustaf III on the continent and in England (1782-87); was appointed court conductor in 1789. During his short life (he was almost an exact contemporary of Mozart) he wrote an enormous amount of operatic and instrumental music of high quality; he preserved the style of Gluck; his mastery of the craft established a high standard for Swedish music; Swedish historians give an increasingly appreciative account of his importance; editions of his unpublished manuscripts are beginning to be issued. His first Swedish opera was *Proserpine* (1781); there followed *Aeneas in Carthage* (1782; produced posthumously, Stockholm, Nov. 18, 1799) and *Soliman II* (his most successful opera; Stockholm, Sept. 22, 1789). When Gustaf III was assassinated in 1792, Krause wrote a memorial cantata for his funeral. His symphonies, overtures, and other instrumental works are preserved at the Upsala Library. He wrote an autobiography and publ. (anonymously) a pamphlet *Etwas von und über Musik* (1777); also some poetical works in German.—Cf. K. F. Schreiber, *Biographie über den Odenwälder Komponisten J. M. Kraus* (Baden, 1928); R. Engländer, *J. M. Kraus und die Gustavianische Oper* (Upsala and Leipzig, 1943).

Kraus, Lili, pianist; b. Budapest, April 3, 1905. She studied at the Budapest Academy of Music, graduating at 17; took courses with Bartók and Kodály (theory) and with Schnabel (piano). After teaching at the Vienna Cons. for several years, she embarked upon a tour of the world; in 1942 she was detained by the Japanese in the Dutch East Indies; after the end of the war she played in Australia (1946-47), in England, and in South Africa (1948); became a British subject in 1948. She also made several appearances in the U. S., playing with major symph. orchestras and in recital.

Krause, Anton, German pianist and conductor; b. Geithain, Nov. 9, 1834; d. Dresden, Jan. 31, 1907. He began to study piano at an early age; then studied at Dresden; from 1850 to 1853 studied at the Leipzig Cons. with Wenzel, Moscheles, Hauptmann, Richter, Rietz, and David; taught music and also conducted in Leipzig. In 1859 he succeeded Reinecke at Barmen as director of the Singverein and the Konzertgesellschaft, retiring in 1897. He wrote *Prinzessin Ilse,* for soli, female chorus, piano, and declamation; choral works; songs; also instructive piano pieces. He publ. a collection of classical sonatinas and a *Library for Two Pianofortes* (18 vols.).

Krause, Eduard, German teacher; b. Swinemünde, March 15, 1837; d. Berlin, March 28, 1892. He studied with Kroll in Berlin and Hauptmann in Leipzig; then went to Stettin as pianist and teacher. He publ. characteristic pieces for the piano (*Berceuse, Impromptu, Grosse Sonate, Ungarische Rhapsodie, Konzertfantasie über schwedische Volkslieder,* etc.).

Krause, Emil, German pedagogue and music critic; b. Hamburg, July 30, 1840; d. there, Sept. 5, 1916. He was a pupil of Hauptmann, Richter, Rietz, Moscheles, and Plaidy at the Leipzig Cons. In 1860 he went to Hamburg, where he taught piano and wrote music criticism for the 'Fremdenblatt' from 1864 until 1907. He publ. *Beiträge zur Technik des Klavierspiels,* with supplementary matter in *Ergänzungen; Aufgabenbuch für die Harmonielehre* (1869; 8th ed., 1908); *Praktische Klavierschule* (1892); *Neuer 'Gradus ad Parnassum'* (100 études); and *Anleitung zum Studium der Musikgeschichte* (1906); *Johannes Brahms in seinen Werken* (Hamburg, 1892; contains a catalogue of works); *Kurzgefasste Darstellung der Passion, des Oratoriums und modernen Konzertwerkes für chor, soli und orchester* (Langensalza, 1902). His compositions include an oratorio, *Den Heimgegangenen, Trio non difficile* for piano, violin, and cello (1863); songs; piano pieces.

Krause, Karl Christian Friedrich, German writer on music; b. Eisenberg, May 6, 1781; d. Munich, Sept. 27, 1832. He publ. many philosophical works; also *Darstellungen aus der Geschichte der Musik* (1827), *Vollständige Anweisung* (1808), and *Anfangsgründe der allgemeinen Theorie der Musik* (1838).

Krause, Martin, German pianist and pedagogue; b. Lobstadt, near Leipzig, June 17, 1853; d. Plattling, Bavaria, Aug. 2, 1918. He was a pupil of his father, a cantor, and of Wenzel and Reinecke at the Leipzig Cons. After successful tours in Holland and Germany (1878-1880), he was prostrated by nervous exhaustion for 2 years. He played before Liszt in 1883, and for 3 years, until Liszt's death, was in constant communication with the master and his pupils. In 1885 Krause, Siloti, Frau Moran-Olden, and others gave two grand concerts in Leipzig, which marked the establishment of the 'Lisztverein,' of which Krause was the chief promoter, chairman, and manager till 1900, when it was discontinued. After 1900 he taught in Leipzig, Dresden, and at Stern's Cons. in Berlin.

Krause, Theodor, German choir conductor and teacher; b. Halle, May 1, 1833; d. Berlin, Dec. 12, 1910. He was a theological student; studied music with Hentschel, Hauptmann, and Grell. He organized church choirs in Berlin; was conductor of the Seiffert a cappella society; taught singing at sight by using the 'Wandernote' (movable Do). He wrote church music, part-songs, and songs; was music critic for several Berlin papers; publ. *Die Wandernote* (1888) and *Deutsche Singeschule* (1888).

Kraushaar, Otto, German writer on music; b. Kassel, May 31, 1812; d. there, Nov. 23, 1866. He studied with Hauptmann, whose idea of the opposition of the major and minor modes he developed in a treatise on *Der accordliche Gegensatz und die Begründung der Scala* (1852), prior to Hauptmann's *Natur der Harmonik.* He also publ. *Die Construktion der gleichschwebenden Temperatur ohne Scheiblerische Stimmgabeln* (1838); contributed essays to periodicals; wrote songs.

Krauss, Clemens, Austrian conductor; b. Vienna, March 31, 1893; d. Mexico City,

May 16, 1954. He was a chorister at the Imperial Chapel; then studied at the Vienna Cons. with Reinhold (piano), Grädener, and Heuberger (theory), graduating in 1912. He was then choral director at the State Theater in Brno; subsequently acted as second conductor of opera in Riga (1913-14), in Nuremberg (1915-16), 1st conductor in Stettin (1916-21), opera and symph. conductor in Graz (1921-22), conductor at the Vienna State Opera and teacher of conducting at the Vienna Academy of Music (1922), and of the Tonkünstlerkonzerte (1923-27), conductor of the Frankfurt Opera and of the Museum Concerts in Frankfurt (1924-29), director of the Vienna State Opera and conductor of the Vienna Philharmonic (1929-34), 1st conductor at the Berlin State Opera (1934-36), musical director of the Munich Opera (1937-40), of the Mozarteum in Salzburg (1939-45). In 1929 he made guest appearances in the U. S. with the N. Y. Philharmonic and Philadelphia Orch. In 1945 he was appointed conductor of the Vienna Opera and the Vienna Philharmonic. He was married to the singer Viorica Ursuleac, whom he often accompanied at the piano at her recitals. Krauss was a close collaborator and friend of Richard Strauss; he wrote the libretto of Strauss's opera *Capriccio.* He was regarded as one of the finest operatic and symph. conductors in Austria and Germany. He died suddenly on a tour in Mexico.—Cf. A. Berger, *Clemens Krauss* (Graz, 1924; 3rd ed., 1929); J. Gregor, *Clemens Krauss, seine musikalische Sendung* (Vienna, 1953); Oscar von Pander, *Krauss in München* (Munich, 1955).

Krauss, Gabrielle, dramatic soprano; b. Vienna, March 24, 1842; d. Paris, Jan. 6, 1906. She studied general music subjects at the Vienna Cons.; voice with Mathilde Marchesi. She made her first important appearance at the Vienna Opera on July 20, 1860, in Rossini's *Wilhelm Tell;* remained on the roster until 1867; then went to Paris; sang Leonora in *Il Trovatore* at the Théâtre-Italien (Apr. 6, 1867) and became a favorite. The Franco-Prussian War of 1870 compelled her to leave Paris; she sang in Italy and in Russia. When the new building of the Paris Grand Opéra was opened in 1875, she sang *La Juive* (Jan. 5, 1875); remained with the opera until 1888, when she retired.

Krebs, Johann Ludwig, German organist and composer; b. Buttelstädt, Oct. 10, 1713; d. Altenburg, Jan. 2, 1780. He received methodical training in musical subjects from his father, an organist, and was sent to study at the Thomasschule in Leipzig, where he became a pupil of Bach for 9 years (1726-35); was Bach's assistant at the harpsichord in Bach's Collegium Musicum there. Later he was organist at Zeitz, Zwickau, and Altenburg. He publ.: *Klavierübungen* in 4 parts (Nuremberg, 1743-49); sonatas for clavier and flute; suites and preludes for clavier; string trios; organ pieces (including an organ fugue on the name B-A-C-H); these were reprinted in the series 'Masterpieces of Organ Music' (N. Y., 1944-45); Partita No. 2 is found in Pauer's 'Alte Meister'; a trio with continuo in Riemann's 'Collegium Musicum.' — Cf. Hans Löffler, *J. L. Krebs,* in the 'Bach-Jahrbuch' (1930).

Krebs, Karl, German music scholar and critic; b. Hanseberg, Feb. 5, 1857; d. Berlin, Feb. 9, 1937. He was a student of music in the Royal Hochschule, Berlin, and heard Spitta's lectures in the Univ. He took the degree of *Dr. phil.* at Rostock with the dissertation *Girolamo Dirutas 'Transilvano'* (Leipzig, 1893). He lived in Berlin as music critic for the 'Vossische Zeitung,' the 'Deutsche Rundschau,' and the 'Tag' (until 1931); was prof. of music history at the Hochschule für Musik (1896-1923); in 1911, became Secretary of the Berlin Academy. He publ. *Dittersdorfiana* (Berlin, 1900; with a biography and thematic catalogue); *Schaffen und Nachschaffen in der Musik* (Berlin, 1902); *Haydn, Mozart, Beethoven* (Leipzig, 1906; 3rd ed., 1920); *Meister des Taktstocks* (1919); valuable musico-historical essays in the 'Vierteljahrsschrift für Musikwissenschaft,' etc.; also edited K. P. E. Bach's *Sonatensammlung für Kenner und Liebhaber* (1895), Beethoven's sonatas (1898, in original form), etc.

Krebs, Karl August (real name Miedcke), German composer; b. Nuremberg, Jan. 16, 1804; d. Dresden, May 16, 1880. He studied with the opera singer J. B. Krebs, who adopted him; also at Vienna with Seyfried; gave successful concerts in Vienna in 1825; then became Kapellmeister at the Vienna court opera (1826), at the Hamburg court opera (1827), and at the Dresden opera (1850-72). He produced 2 operas, *Silva, oder die Macht des Gesangs* (Hamburg, 1830) and *Agnes, der Engel von Augsburg* (Hamburg, Oct. 8, 1833; revised version, *Agnes Bernauer,* Dresden, 1858); also wrote songs and piano pieces. Some numbers of his opera *Feodore* (composed when he was 7) were publ.; also his songs, many of which attained great popularity.

Krehbiel (krā'-bēl), **Henry Edward,** American writer on music and critic; b. Ann Arbor, Mich., March 10, 1854; d. New York, March 20, 1923. He was music critic of the Cincinnati 'Gazette' (1874-80); then editor of the N. Y. 'Musical Review' and critic for the 'N. Y. Tribune'; the latter post he held for some 40 years until his death; in 1909, received the honorary degree of M. A. from Yale Univ. He publ. *Notes on the Cultivation of Choral Music, and the Oratorio Society of New York* (1884); *Review of the N. Y. Musical Seasons 1885-90* (5 vols.); *Studies in the Wagnerian Drama* (1891); *The Philharmonic Society of New York: A Memorial* (1892); *How to Listen to Music* (1896); *Annotated Biography of Fine Art* (with R. Sturgis; 1897); *Music and Manners in the Classical Period* (1898); *Chapters of Opera* (1908; 2nd ed., 1911); *A Book of Operas* (1909); *The Pianoforte, and Its Music* (1911); *Afro-American Folksongs* (1914); *A Second Book of Operas* (1917); *More Chapters of Opera* (1919); transl. of Courvoisier's *Technic of Violin Playing* (N. Y., 1880; 2nd ed., 1896), Kerst's *Beethoven* (1905), and Kerst's *Mozart* (1905); also publ. and edited the English version of Thayer's *Beethoven* (3 vols., 1921); he was consulting editor of 'The Music of the Modern World' (1895-97) and American editor of the 2nd ed. of Grove's 'Dictionary of Music and Musicians' (1904-10); was also author, for many years, of the program notes of the N. Y. Philharmonic Society. He was a brilliant writer of music criticism, and was able to project his opinions (and his prejudices) in vivid prose in his newspaper reviews. He was an ardent champion of Wagner, and he also wrote with warm admiration for the late Romantic composers; but he deprecated the modern school, and particularly Stravinsky.

Krehl, Stephan, German theorist and composer; b. Leipzig, July 5, 1864; d. there, April 7, 1924. He studied at the Cons of Leipzig and Dresden. In 1889 he was appointed teacher of piano and theory at the Karlsruhe Cons.; from 1902, at the Leipzig Cons.; in 1911, director there. He publ. the manuals, *Praktische Formenlehre* (1902); *Allgemeine Musiklehre* (1904; 2nd ed., 1912; in Spanish, 1930); *Fuge: Erläuterung und Anleitung zur Komposition derselben* (1908); *Kompositionsunterricht und moderne Musik* (1909); *Musikerelend* (1912); *M. Hauptmann; ein Dank- und Gedenkwort* (1918); *Theorie der Tonkunst und Kompositionslehre* (vol. I: *Elementarmusiklehre,* 1921; vol. II: *Harmonielehre,* 1923; 2nd ed., 1928). He also composed a quintet for clarinet, 2 violins, viola, and cello; a cello sonata; *Slovenische Tänze* for piano 4-hands; a cantata, *Trostung,* and a prelude to Hauptmann's play *Hannele.*—Cf. F. Reuter, *Stephan Krehl* (1921).

Krein, Alexander Abramovitch, Russian composer; b. Nizhni-Novgorod, Oct. 20, 1883; d. Moscow, April 21, 1951. At the age of 13 he entered the Moscow Cons. and studied cello; also studied composition privately with Nikolayev and Yavorsky. Later he became instructor at the People's Cons. of Moscow (1912-17); after the revolution he worked in the Music Division of the Commissariat of Education and in the Ethnographic Department. From 1923 he was associated with the productions of the Jewish Drama Theater in Moscow, and wrote music for many Jewish plays. Together with Gnessin, he was a leader of the National Jewish movement in Russia. In general, his style was influenced by Scriabin and Debussy, but he made considerable use of old Hebrew material:—Works: operas, *Zagmuk,* on a revolutionary subject based on an ancient Babylonian tale (Moscow, May 29, 1930) and *Daughter of the People* (1946); a ballet after Lope de Vega, *Laurencie* (1938); incidental music to the Jewish plays *The Eternal One* (1923), *Sabbatai Zewi* (1924), *Ghetto* (1924), *The People* (1925), *The Doctor* (1925); for orch.: *Salome* (1913); *Elegy* for string orch. (1914); *La Rose and la Croix,* symph. fragments (1917-21); *Kaddisch,* symphonic cantata for tenor solo, mixed choir, and orch. (1921); a symphony (1922-25); *U.S.S.R., Shock Brigade of the World Proletariat,* symph. dithyramb for narrator, chorus, and orch. (1925); *Threnody in Memory of Lenin,* for chorus and orch. (1925); various symph. suites on Hebrew themes; chamber music: a string quartet, *Jewish Sketches* for clarinet and string quartet, *Elegiac Trio,* for violin, cello, and piano, *Jewish Capriccio* for violin and piano; piano sonata; *3 Poems* for piano; *Jewish Songs* (to Russian words); vocalises. — Cf. L. Sabaneyev, *Alexander Krein* (1928; in Russian and German).

Krein, Grigory Abramovitch, Russian composer, brother of Alexander Krein; b. Nizhni-Novgorod, April 15, 1880. He studied with Juon and Glière. His music underwent the influence of Jewish culture, and he wrote many works on Jewish themes; however, he also cultivated strict classical forms, adapting them to his needs. He wrote a descriptive symph. cycle on Lenin's life (1937); other works are a violin concerto, a string quartet, a *Hebrew Rhapsody* for clarinet and orch., and piano pieces.

Krein, Julian, Russian composer, son of Grigory Krein; b. Moscow, March 5, 1913. He studied with his father; wrote his first compositions at the age of 13. In 1927 he went to Paris; took some lessons with Paul Dukas. In 1933 he went back to Moscow and remained there. Besides composing, he also wrote music criticism. His music is marked by a lyric quality; in his harmonic procedures he adopts advanced methods bordering on polytonality. Among his works are *Five Preludes* for orch. (1927); a symph. prelude *Destruction* (1929); a cello concerto (Barcelona, Oct. 18, 1931, Eisenberg soloist); *Spring Symphony* (1938); piano pieces; songs.

Kreipl (krī-pl), **Joseph,** Austrian singer; b. 1805; d. Vienna, May, 1866. For years he was the favorite tenor in Linz; wrote some lyric songs, among which *Das Mailufterl* attained extraordinary vogue.

Kreisler, Fritz, celebrated violinist; b. Vienna, Feb. 2, 1875. His talent manifested itself at an early age and was carefully fostered by his father, under whose instruction the boy made such progress that at the age of 7 he was admitted to the Vienna Cons., where he studied under Auer and Hellmesberger, and, in 1885, carried off the gold medal. He then entered the Paris Cons., where he was a pupil of Massart (violin) and Delibes (composition); graduated in 1887 as winner of the Grand Prix (gold medal) over 40 competitors. He made his American début at Steinway Hall, N. Y., on Nov. 10, 1888. In the following year, he made a very successful tour of the U. S. with Moriz Rosenthal. On his return to Europe, he abandoned music for some years; studied medicine in Vienna, and art in Rome and Paris; then entered the Austrian army, serving as an officer in an Uhlan regiment. At his reappearance in Berlin (March, 1899) his playing created a sensation. Not only had he regained his outstanding virtuosity, but he had also developed into a great interpreter. On his second visit to the U. S. in 1900-01, when he appeared as soloist and in ensemble with Hofmann and Gerardy, he carried his audiences by storm; on his tour of England in the spring of 1901, he scored similar triumphs. In 1904 the London Philharmonic Society honored him by awarding him the Beethoven gold medal. At the outbreak of World War I in 1914, he joined his former regiment, was wounded at Lemberg (Sept. 6, 1914), and excused from further service. Fortunately his wound was slight (his hip and shoulder were injured in a Russian cavalry attack) so that at the end of 1914 he resumed his artistic career in the U. S. He remained in the U. S. throughout the rest of World War I despite the embarrassment of his status as an enemy alien; after the Armistice, went back to Europe, but continued to make frequent visits to America. He was made Commander of the Legion of Honor by the French government, and received many other honors from foreign governments. In 1938 he became a French citizen; in 1940 he returned to N. Y.; in 1943, became an American citizen. Kreisler's repertory contained almost everything of value written for the violin since the 17th century. He was the owner of a Stradivarius violin and of instruments by other masters; gathered a rich collection of invaluable manuscripts; in 1949 donated to the Library of Congress the original scores of Brahms' violin concerto and Chausson's *Poème* for violin and orch. He wrote some of the most popular violin pieces in the world, among them *Caprice Viennois, Tambourin Chinois, Schön Rosmarin, Liebesfreud,* etc. He also publ. a number of pieces in the classical vein, which he ascribed to various old composers (Vivaldi, Pugnani, Couperin, Padre Martini, Dittersdorf, Francoeur, Stamitz, and others). In 1935 he voluntarily admitted that these pieces were his own, with the exception of the first 8 bars from the 'Couperin' *Chanson Louis XIII,* taken from a traditional melody; he explained his motive in doing so by the necessity of building up well-rounded programs for his concerts that would contain virtuoso pieces by old composers, rather than a series of compositions under his own, as yet unknown, name. He also wrote the operettas *Apple Blossoms* (N. Y., Oct. 7, 1919) and *Sissy* (Vienna, Dec. 23, 1932); publ. numerous arrangements of early and modern music (Corelli's *La Folia,* Tartini's *The Devil's Trill,* Dvořák's *Slavonic Dances, Spanish Dance* by Granados, *Tango* by Albéniz, etc.). He publ. a book of reminiscences of World War I, *Four Weeks in the Trenches: The War Story of a Violinist* (Boston, 1915). —Cf. L. P. Lochner, *Fritz Kreisler* (N. Y., 1950; not fully reliable as to factual details). See also Olin Downes, *Kreisler's Delectable Musical Hoax,* in the N. Y. Times (March 3, 1935), reprinted in *Olin Downes on Music,* ed. by Irene Downes (N. Y., 1957; pp. 201-05).

Kreissle von Hellborn, Heinrich, Austrian writer; b. Vienna, 1812; d. there, April 6, 1869. He studied law; was *Dr. juris,* and secretary in the Ministry of Finance, Vienna. A passionate admirer of Schubert, he publ. *Franz Schubert, eine biographische Skizze* (1861), followed in 1865 by the exhaustive biography *Franz Schubert* (condensed English transl. by Wilberforce, 1866; full transl. by A. D. Coleridge, 1869, in 2 vols., with an appendix by Sir George Grove).

Krejčí (krā'-chē), **Iša,** Czech composer; b. Prague, July 10, 1904; studied with Novák and Jirák at the Cons. there. He was active in Bratislava as conductor (1928-32); then at the Prague National Theater (1933-34), and at the Prague Radio (1934-45). In 1945 he was appointed opera conductor at Olomouc. — Works: opera, *The Revolt at Ephesus* (Prague, Sept. 8, 1946); *Sinfonietta* (1929); concertino for piano and wind instruments (1935); concertino for violin and wind instruments (1936); *Divertimento* for flute, clarinet, trumpet, and bassoon (1925); string quartet (1928); clarinet sonata (Amsterdam Festival, June 15, 1933); trio for oboe, clarinet, and bassoon (1935); trio for clarinet, double-bass, and piano (1936); *Nachtklänge* (*Echoes from Czech Songs),* for voice and wind quintet (London Festival, June 22, 1938); nonet (1937). His music is distinguished by vivacious rhythm and freely flowing melody; the national Czech element is not ostentatious, but its presence is well marked.

Krejčí (krā'-chē), **Josef,** Bohemian organist; b. Milostin, Dec. 17, 1821; d. Prague, Oct. 19, 1881. He studied in Prague with Witasek and Josef Proksch; organist in various churches at Prague; in 1858, became director of the Organ School there; 1865, director of the Prague Cons. He wrote an oratorio, overtures, organ pieces, and songs.

Krejčí, Miroslav, Czech composer; b. Rychnov nad Kněžnou, Nov. 4, 1891. He studied science at Charles Univ. in Prague; then became a schoolmaster there, remaining in that employment for nearly 30 years (1914-43). In 1943 he became prof. at the Prague Univ. His own musical education was desultory; he studied 2 years with Novák as a youth, and acquired a thorough technique through actual composition. — Works: operas, *Léto* (*Summer;* Prague, Dec. 4, 1940) and *Poslední Hejtman (The Last Captain;* Prague, March 18, 1948); vocal symphony (1930); symph. in G minor (1946); viola concerto (1947); 5 string quartets; string quintet; quintet for clarinet and strings; violin sonata; viola sonata; cello sonata; several albums of piano pieces; songs.

Kremenliev, Boris, Bulgarian-American composer and musicologist; b. Razlog, May 23, 1911. He studied organ, cello, and flute; came to the U. S. in 1929; studied with La Violette in Chicago and with Hanson in Rochester, and conducting with Altschuler in Los Angeles. He was a member of the Psychological Warfare Branch of the U. S. Army in Europe; conducted concerts of the Frankfurt Radio (1945-46); in 1947, was appointed associate prof. of music theory at the Univ. of California, Los Angeles. His works include *Symphonic Variations* (1937); *Prelude and Poem* for orch., chorus, and soloists (1937); *Pravo Horo,* orchestral dance on Bulgarian folk themes (Rochester, April 18, 1940); *Song Symphony,* for contralto and orch. (1941); *Bulgarian Rhapsody,* for orch. (1952); *The Crucifixion,* orchestral suite from a film score (1952); 2 piano quintets; quartet for oboe, violin, viola, and cello; trio for flute, clarinet, and bassoon; saxophone quartet; suite for harpsichord; piano pieces. He publ. a valuable treatise, *Bulgarian-Macedonian Folk Music* (Los Angeles, 1952); has contributed articles to various journals.

Kremer, Isa, folk singer; b. Beltzi, Bessarabia, 1885; d. Cordoba, Argentina, July 7, 1956. She acquired early fame as a singer of Russian, Yiddish, Polish, and German ballads; made many tours in Russia and Eastern Europe before coming to the U. S. in 1923; in New York, she appeared in vaudeville; gave her final concert in America at Carnegie Hall on Dec. 3, 1950. She married Dr. Gregorio Bermann, an Argentinian psychiatrist, in 1940.

Krempelsetzer, Georg, Bavarian composer; b. Vilsbiburg, April 20, 1827; d. there, June 9, 1871. He was by trade a cloth weaver; studied music in Munich with Franz Lachner; became chorusmaster at theaters in Munich (1865), Görlitz (1868), and Königsberg (1870). He wrote the opera *Der Onkel aus der Lombardei* (1861), and the operettas *Die Franzosen in Gotha, Der Vetter auf Besuch* (1863), *Die Kreuzfahrer* (1865), *Das Orakel in Delphi* (1867), *Die Geister des Weins* (1867), *Aschenbrödel, Rotmantel* (1868), etc.

Kremser, Eduard, Austrian composer; b. Vienna, April 10, 1838; d. there, Nov. 27, 1914. He studied in Vienna; in 1869, became chorusmaster of the 'Männergesangverein' there; also conducted various other choral societies. He wrote the light operas *Der Botschafter* (Vienna, Feb. 25, 1886), *Der kritische Tag* (Vienna, Dec. 6, 1891), etc.; several symph. sketches with voices: *Balkanbilder, Prinz Eugen, Das Leben ein Tanz,* etc.; many part-songs (his settings of *6 altniederländische Volkslieder* are famed far and wide, especially the Dutch *Prayer of Thanksgiving); Das Herzklopfen, Erinnerungen,* and *Fröhliche Armuth,* for men's chorus and orch.; songs *(Jagdlied,* with accompaniment of 4 horns; 2 songs from *Der Trompeter von Säkkingen,* with solo cornet); piano music; also edited 'Wiener Lieder und Tänze' (2 vols., 1912, 1913).—Cf. H. von Paumgarten, *Eduard Kremser* (Vienna, 1915).

Krenek, Ernst, noted modern composer; b. Vienna, Aug. 23, 1900. He studied in Vienna, and in Berlin with Franz Schreker; lived in Zürich (1923-5); then was an opera coach in Kassel, under Paul Bekker (1925-27); in 1928 he returned to Vienna and became a correspondent of the 'Frankfurter Zeitung'; also traveled widely in Europe as lecturer and accompanist in programs of his own songs. In 1937 he came to the U. S.; was prof. of music at Vassar College (1939-42); then head of the music dept. at Hamline Univ., St. Paul, Minn. (1942-47); lived in Hollywood (1947-50). In the summer of 1950 and in following years he made successful tours of Germany as lecturer and conductor of his own works. He became an American citizen on Jan. 24, 1945. He was married to Anna Mahler (daughter of Gustav Mahler) in 1923; divorced in 1925, and married Berta Hermann, an actress. His evolution as a composer mirrors the development of modern music in general. The tradition of Mahler, strengthened by the domestic ties of his first marriage, was the dominant influence of his early life in music; he then became associated with the modern groups in Vienna, particularly Schoenberg, Berg, and Anton von Webern. In Germany he was associated with Hindemith as a creator of modern opera in a satiric manner. He achieved a masterly technique of composition in his earliest works, and developed his melodic and harmonic idiom in the direction of atonality and polytonality. His first international success came to him at the age of 26, with the production of his opera *Jonny spielt auf,* generally described as a 'jazz opera' (although no such title appears in the score). It deals with a jazz fiddler whose fame sweeps the world; in the apotheosis, Jonny sits atop a gigantic globe. The opera was first performed in Leipzig (Feb. 11, 1927), producing a sensation; it was subsequently translated into 18 languages and performed all over the world; a brand of Austrian cigarettes was named after it; it was staged at the Metropolitan Opera House, New York (Jan. 19, 1929) with the hero as a black-faced musician rather than a Negro as in the original. However, the opera fell into desuetude a few years later. Krenek produced several short operas, to which he wrote his own librettos, with transitory success. He also composed symphonic, choral, and chamber music; wrote books and articles on music history and modern methods of composition. In 1933 he adopted the 12-tone method of composition; his opera *Karl V* was written in this idiom; subsequent works use various ingenious applications of Schoenberg's basic method. In 1950 he completed a voluminous autobiography, the manuscript of which he deposited at the Library of Congress, not to be opened until 15 years after his death. Excerpts were publ. under the title *Self-Analysis.*—Works: operas and dramas with music: *Zwingburg* (Berlin, Oct. 16, 1924), *Der Sprung über den Schatten* (Frankfurt, June 9, 1924), *Orpheus und Eurydike* (Kassel, Nov. 27, 1926), *Jonny spielt auf* (Leipzig, Feb. 10, 1927), *Leben des Orest* (Leipzig, Jan. 19, 1930), *Karl V* (Prague, June 15, 1938), *Tarquin* (Vassar College, May 13, 1941), *What Price Confidence?* (1946), *Dark Waters* (1951), *Pallas Athene weint* (Hamburg, Oct. 17, 1955), *The Bell Tower* (Urbana, March 17, 1957), 3 short operas: *Der Diktator, Das geheime Königreich, Schwergewicht,* or *Die Ehre der Nation* (Wiesbaden, May 6, 1928).—For orch.: 5 symphonies (No. 1, 1921; No. 2, 1922; No. 3, 1922; No. 4, N. Y., Nov. 27, 1947; No. 5, Albuquerque, March 16, 1950), *2 Concerti grossi* (1921); *Symphonische Musik* for 9 solo instruments (Donaueschingen, July 30, 1922); piano concerto No. 1 (1923); concertino for flute, violin, harpsichord, and string orch. (1924); violin concerto (Dessau, Jan. 5, 1924); *Symphonie* for brass and percussion (1924-25); *3 Military Marches* (Donaueschingen, 1926); *Potpourri* (Cologne, Nov. 15, 1927); *Kleine Symphonie* (Berlin, Nov. 1, 1928); *Theme and Variations* (1931); *Music for Wind Orch.* (1931); piano concerto No. 2 (Amsterdam, March 17, 1938); *Symphonic Piece* for string orch. (Ann Arbor, Mich., Aug. 1,

1939); *Little Concerto,* for piano and organ, with chamber orch. (1940); *I Wonder as I Wander,* variations on a North Carolina folksong (1942); *Tricks and Trifles,* orchestral version of the *Hurricane Variations* (1945); *Symphonic Elegy* for strings, on the death of Anton von Webern (1946); piano concerto No. 3 (Minneapolis, Nov. 22, 1946, Mitropoulos pianist-conductor; the 12-tone system consistently used by Krenek after 1936 is not applied in this concerto); piano concerto No. 4 (1950); double concerto for violin, piano, and chamber orch. (Donaueschingen Festival, Oct. 6, 1951); concerto for harp and chamber orch. (Philadelphia, Dec. 12, 1952); concerto for 2 pianos and orch. (N. Y., Oct. 24, 1953); *Medea,* for contralto and orch. (Philadelphia, March 13, 1953); *Eleven Transparencies* (Louisville, Feb. 12, 1955).—Chamber music: violin sonata (1919); *Serenade* for quartet (1919); 8 string quartets (No. 1, 1921; No. 2, 1921; No. 3, 1923; No. 4, 1923-24; No. 5, 1930; No. 6, 1937; No. 7, 1943; No. 8, 1952); suite for clarinet and piano (1924); solo violin sonata (1924-25); suite for cello solo (1939); sonatina for flute and viola (1942); sonata for violin solo (1942); sonata for viola and piano (1948); string trio (1948); *Parvula Corona Musicalis ad honorem J. S. Bach,* for string trio (1950).—Piano works: *Double Fugue* for piano, 2 hands (1918); *Dance Studies,* in 'Grotesken-Album' (ed. by K. Seeling, 1922); piano sonata No. 1 (1919); 5 sonatinas (1920); *Toccata and Chaconne* on the chorale, *Ja, ich glaub' an Jesum Christum* (1922, also a suite of pieces on the chorale); 2 suites (1924); 5 pieces (1925); piano sonata No. 2 (1928); *12 Short Piano Pieces* (1938); piano sonata No. 3 (1943); *Hurricane Variations* (1944); *8 Piano Pieces* (1946); piano sonata No. 4 (1948); *George Washington Variations* (1950); piano sonata No. 5 (1950); piano sonata No. 6 (1951). For chorus: *Concert Aria,* text from Goethe's *Stella* (1928); *Von der Vergänglichkeit des Irdischen,* cantata (1932); *Reisebuch aus den Österreichischen Alpen* (1935); 2 a cappella choruses for women's voices on Elizabethan poems (1939); *Proprium Missae in Festo SS. Innocentium,* for women's voices (1940); *Lamentatio Jeremiae Prophetae, Secundum Brevarium Sacrosanctae Ecclesiae Romanae* (1941); *Cantata for Wartime* (1943); *5 Prayers,* for women's voices, from the *Litanie* by John Donne (1944); *The Santa Fe Time Table,* for chorus a cappella, to the text of names of railroad stops between Albuquerque and Los Angeles (1945); *In Paradisum,* motet for women's voices a cappella (1946). Krenek also composed an organ sonata (1941) and revised and orchestrated Monteverdi's *L'Incoronazione di Poppea* (1937); he is the author of the books *Über neue Musik* (collected lectures; Vienna, 1937; in English as *Music Here and Now,* N. Y., 1939); *Studies in Counterpoint* (N. Y., 1940; in German as *Zwölfton - Kontrapunkt Studien,* Mainz, 1952); *Selbstdarstellung,* autobiography (Zürich, 1948; in English as *Self-Analysis,* Albuquerque, 1953); *Musik im goldenen Westen; das Tonschaffen des U.S.A.* (Vienna, 1949); *Johannes Ockeghem* (N. Y., 1953); *De rebus prius factis* (Frankfurt, 1956).—Cf. A. Weissmann, *Ernst Krenek,* in 'Modern Music' (Dec., 1928); E. Evans, *Ernst Krenek,* in 'Cobbett's Cyclopedic Survey of Chamber Music' (London, 1930; vol. 2, pp. 76-79); J. M. Schneider, *Ernst Krenek,* in the 'Revue Musicale' (Aug., 1930); S. Günther, *Der Kurs in Ernst Kreneks jüngstem Schaffen,* in 'Die Musik' (May, 1931); R. Erickson, *Krenek's Later Music,* in 'Music Review' (Feb., 1948); H. Rosenwald, *Ernst Krenek,* in David Ewen, *The Book of Modern Composers* (2nd revised ed., N. Y., 1950; pp. 356-62).

Krenn, Franz, Austrian composer and pedagogue; b. Dross, Feb. 26, 1816; d. St. Andrä, June 18, 1897. He studied music with his father; occupied posts as church organist in Vienna; from 1869-93 was prof. of harmony and counterpoint at the Vienna Cons. Gustav Mahler was his pupil. Krenn left a large number of works, among them 29 Masses, a symphony, chamber music, and a manual, *Musik- und Harmonielehre* (1890).

Krentzlin, Richard, German piano pedagogue and composer; b. Magdeburg, Nov. 27, 1864; d. Oldendorf (Hesse), Nov. 27, 1956, on the morning of his 92nd birthday. He studied at the Kullak Academy; became a successful piano teacher; publ. numerous character pieces (*Bunte Bilder, Aus meiner Jugendzeit,* etc.) and 8 books of piano studies, *Der gute Pädagoge.*

Krenz, Jan, Polish composer; b. Wloclawek, July 14, 1926. He studied composition with Sikorski in Lodz; after 1945 he went to Katowice, where he conducted the Radio Orch. Among his works are a cantata entitled *A Conversation Between Two Towns* (1950); a symphony; 2 string quartets; etc.

Kresánek, Jozef, Slovak musicologist; b. Čičmany, Dec. 20, 1913. He studied in Prague with Karel and Novák; then taught at Bratislava Univ. His main field of endeavor is the collecting and codifying of Slovak folksongs; he publ. a paper on the subject in 1951; also wrote some chamber music and songs.

Kretschmer, Edmund, German composer; b. Ostritz, Aug. 31, 1830; d. Dresden, Sept. 13, 1908. He studied with Julius Otto (composition) and Johann Schneider (organ) in Dresden. In 1863 he became organist of the court, retiring in 1901. He was a successful composer; his choral work, *Geisterschlacht,* won a prize at the Dresden singing festival (1865); a 3-part Mass for men's chorus won the Brussels Academy's prize in 1868. He wrote several operas to his own librettos in a Wagnerian manner; at least 2 of them were successful: *Die Folkunger* (Dresden, March 21, 1874) and *Heinrich der Löwe* (Leipzig, Dec. 8, 1877); he also produced 2 light operas: *Der Flüchtling* (Ulm, 1881) and *Schön Rotraut* (Dresden, 1887); several choral works for festive occasions; church music; etc. — Cf. O. Schmid, *Edmund Kretschmer* (Dresden, 1890).

Kretzschmar, August Ferdinand Hermann, eminent German music scholar; b. Olbernhau, Jan. 19, 1848; d. Nikolassee, near Berlin, May 10, 1924. He was a chorister and a pupil of Julius Otto in Dresden; then studied with Richter, Reinecke, Oskar Paul, and Papperitz at the Leipzig Cons.; took his degree of *Dr. Phil.* at Leipzig with a thesis on ancient notation prior to Guido d'Arezzo, *De signis musicis* (1871). He then became teacher of organ and harmony at the Leipzig Cons.; also conducted choral societies there. In 1876 he was a theater conductor at Metz; 1877, music director at Rostock Univ.; 1880, municipal music director there. In 1887 he joined the faculty of the Leipzig Univ.; from 1888-97, Riedel's successor as conductor of the 'Riedelverein'; conducted the 'Akademische Orchesterkonzerte' initiated by himself (1890-95). In 1904 he went to Berlin as prof. at the Univ. there; from 1909-20, was also director of the Hochschule für Musik. He was a thoroughly educated musician, a good organist as well as choral conductor, and composer of some secular and sacred vocal music. But his importance in musicology lies in his establishment of certain historic and esthetic concepts that elucidate the historical process. He introduced a convenient term (taken from theology) 'Hermeneutik,' applying it to the explanation of musical melodies and intervallic progressions as expressive of human emotions. — Publications: *Peter Cornelius* (1880); *Führer durch den Konzertsaal,* in 3 vols.: I. Symphony and Suite (1887; 6th ed., 1921), II. Sacred Choral Works (1888; 2nd ed., 1932, supplemented by Noack and Botstiber), III. Oratorios and Secular Choral Works (1890; 4th ed., 1920; enlarged by Schnoor, 1932); *Geschichte des neuen deutschen Liedes* (1912; vol. 1 only, up to the songs of Zelter); *Geschichte der Oper* (1919); *Einführung in die Musikgeschichte* (1920); *Bach-Kolleg* (1922). His articles in various periodicals were publ. as *Gesammelte Aufsätze* (2 vols., 1911). He edited vols. 8, 9, and 42 of the 'Denkmäler deutscher Tonkunst,' of which he was general editor from 1911-19; brought out a new edition of Lobe's *Lehrbuch der musikalischen Komposition* (4 vols., 1884-87).—Cf. 'Festschrift zu Kretzschmars 70. Geburtstag' (Leipzig, 1918); H. Abert, *Kretzschmar,* in the 'Jahrbuch der Musikbibliothek Peters' (1924).

Kreubé (krö-bā'), **Charles Frédéric,** French conductor and composer; b. Luneville, Nov. 5, 1777; d. near Saint-Denis, 1846. He studied violin in Paris with R. Kreutzer (1800); joined the orch. of the Paris Opéra-Comique as violinist; from 1816-28, first conductor. He wrote 16 operas; also violin pieces.

Kreutz, Arthur, American composer; b. La Crosse, Wis., July 25, 1906. He studied violin and composition; in 1944-45 he received a Guggenheim Fellowship; in 1946, appointed instructor at Rhode Island State College. His works include a 'ballad' opera, *Acres of Sky* (Columbia Univ., N. Y., May 7, 1952); *Music for Symphony Orchestra* (N.B.C. Symph. Orch., June 16, 1940); *American Dances,* for chamber orch. (1941); *Winter of the Blue Snow,* symph. poem (1942); *Symphonic Sketch* on 3 American folk tunes (International Society for Contemporary Music Festival, Berkeley, Calif., Aug. 1, 1942); violin concerto (1942); *Triumphal Overture* (1944); *Symphonic Blues* (1945); 2 symphonies (1945 and 1946); *New England Folksing* for chorus and orch. (Brooklyn, Feb. 17, 1948); *Mosquito Serenade,* for orch. (N. Y. Philharmonic, Feb. 21, 1948); chamber works; piano pieces.

Kreutzer (kroi'-tser), **Auguste,** French violinist; brother of Rodolphe Kreutzer; b. Versailles, Sept. 3, 1778; d. Paris, Aug. 31, 1832. He studied with his brother at the Paris Cons.; played in the orch. of the Paris Opéra-Comique and Opéra; also in the court orchestras; taught at the Paris Cons. He wrote 2 violin concertos, 3 sonatas, etc.

Kreutzer, Konradin, German composer; b. Messkirch, Baden, Nov. 22, 1780; d. Riga, Dec. 14, 1849. He was a pupil of J. B. Rieger at Zwiefalten Abbey and of Ernst Weihrauch (1792-96). He then studied law at Freiburg for one year (1799-1800) before devoting himself to music. In 1800 he brought out his first operetta, *Die lächerliche Werbung,* in Freiburg. He lived for 5 years in Constance, and then in Vienna until 1811, studying counterpoint under Albrechtsberger. He produced, with considerable success, *Jerry und Bätely,* after Goethe (May 19, 1810); not being able to bring out 2 operas, *Konradin von Schwaben* and *Der Taucher,* in Vienna, he went, after a pianistic tour of a year, to Stuttgart, where, after the production of *Konradin von Schwaben* (March 30, 1812), he was appointed court conductor. In Stuttgart he produced 8 dramatic works, and then went to Donaueschingen in 1817 as conductor to Prince von Fürstenberg. There he produced *Adele von Budoy* in 1819, which was later successful in a revision entitled *Cordelia.* Returning to Vienna, he brought out *Libussa* (Dec. 4, 1822); was conductor at the Kärnthnerthor Theater (1825, 1829-32, and 1827-40) and at the Josephstadt Theater (1833-37); his most successful work, *Das Nachtlager von Granada* (Jan. 14, 1834), appeared, and was followed a month later by *Der Verschwender* (Feb. 20, 1834), incidental music for Ferdinand Raimund's play of that name. Together with *Jerry und Bätely,* these 2 works held the stage until the end of the century. From 1840-42 he was conductor at the Municipal Theater in Cologne; after 2 years in Vienna (1847-49), he accompanied his daughter Cäcilie, a singer, to Riga, where he died. Besides his many operas, he wrote an oratorio, *Die Sendung Mosis,* and a cantata, *Die Friedensfeier;* also church music, chamber music, and piano pieces; songs, and some noteworthy men's choruses *(Die Capelle, Sonntagsmorgen, Der Tag des Herrn,* etc.).—Cf. W. H. Riehl, *Musikalische Charakterköpfe* (vol. I, Stuttgart, 1879); R. Rossmayer, *Kreutzers Klaviermusik,* in 'Zeitschrift für Musikwissenschaft' (vol. XIII, p. 80 ff.); H. Burkard, *Konradin Kreutzers Ausgang* (Tübingen, 1920); A. Landau, *Das einstimmige Kunstlied Konradin Kreutzers* (Leipzig, 1930).

Kreutzer, Léon, French composer and music critic; son of Auguste Kreutzer; b. Paris, Sept. 23, 1817; d. Vichy, Oct. 6, 1868. He studied piano with Fleche and composition with Benoist. He wrote for the 'Revue et Gazette musicale,' 'Revue contemporaine,' 'La Quotidienne,' 'L'Union,' etc.; publ. an *Essai sur l'art lyrique au théâtre* (1845); also wrote an orchestral prelude to Shakespeare's *The Tempest;* string quartets, piano sonatas, etc.; and a treatise on modulation.

Kreutzer, Leonid, distinguished pianist; b. St. Petersburg, March 13, 1884; d. Tokyo, Oct. 30, 1953. He studied at the Cons. in St. Petersburg with Mme. Essipov (piano) and with Glazunov (composition); after two years in Leipzig, he went to Berlin in 1908; was prof. at the State Academy of Music there (from 1921-33). In 1926-28 he gave successful recitals in the U. S. In 1933 he went to Japan, where he conducted master classes at the Imperial Academy of Music in Tokyo. He wrote a ballet-pantomime, *Der Gott und die Bajadere* (Mannheim, 1921); also valuable pedagogic works for the piano, including *Das normale Klavierpedal* (1915) and *Das Wesen der Klaviertechnik* (1923); edited the works of Chopin.

Kreutzer, Rodolphe, famous violinist; b. Versailles, Nov. 16, 1766; d. Geneva, Jan. 6, 1831. His father, a German violinist in the Chapelle du Roi, and Anton Stamitz were his teachers. At the age of 13 he played a violin concerto of his own composition at a Concert Spirituel; in 1782 he was appointed 1st violin in the Chapelle du Roi, and in 1790 solo violin in the Théâtre-Italien, bringing out his first opera, *Jeanne d'Arc à Orleans* (May 10, 1790). It was followed by over 40 others, given at the Opéra, the Opéra-Comique, or the Théâtre-Italien; *Lodoiska* (Aug. 1, 1791) was perhaps his best. A year after his appointment as teacher of violin at the Cons., he made a triumphant concert tour through Italy, Germany, and Holland. In 1801 he succeeded Rode as solo violin at the Opéra, of which he became second conductor in 1816, and first conductor in 1817. From 1802 he was also chamber musician to Napoleon; from 1815, to Louis XVIII; retired in 1826, and so far lost influence that his last opera, *Mathilde,* was contemptuously rejected by the direction of the Opéra. Although his own music could not withstand the test of time, his name became immortal because it was to him that Beethoven dedicated the celebrated 'Kreutzer Sonata.' — Works: 43 operas; 19 violin concertos; 2 double concertos; *Symphonie concertante* for violin and cello, with orch.; 15 string quartets; 15 string trios; also duets, sonatas, variations, etc., for violin; but his masterwork, wherein his worthiness to rank with the great masters of the classic Parisian school of violin playing is convincingly proved, is the *40 Etudes ou Caprices* for violin solo, republished in countless editions, revised by Vieuxtemps and others. Kreutzer was joint author, with Rode and Baillot, of the great violin method used in the Paris Cons.—Cf. H. Kling, *R. Kreutzer* (Brussels, 1898); B. Cutter, *How to Study Kreutzer* (1907); J. Hardy, *R. Kreutzer; sa jeunesse à Versailles* (Paris, 1910); A. Moser, *Geschichte des Violinspiels* (p. 394 ff.).

Křička (kr'zhitch'-kah), **Jaroslav,** Czech composer; b. Kelč, Moravia, Aug. 27, 1882; studied at the Prague Cons. and in Berlin; 1906, taught music in Ekaterinoslav, Russia; 1909, returned to Prague and conducted (1911-20) the famous choral society 'Hlahol'; in 1919 he became prof. at the Cons., and in 1921 a member of the Czech Academy. His works include some 100 opus numbers; operas: *Hipolyta* (Prague, Oct. 10, 1917), *Ogaři (Country Lads;* Sept. 7, 1919), *Bílý Pan (White Ghost),* after Oscar Wilde (Brno, Nov. 27, 1929), *Tlustý Pradědeček (Fat Great-Grandfather;* Prague, Dec. 29, 1932), *Kral Lavra (King Lawrence,* Prague, June 7, 1940), *Jachym a Juliana (Joachim and Julia;* 1945-48); for orch.: Symph. No. 1, *Mladi (Youth,* 1905-6; revised 1942), *Nostalgie,* for string orch. and harp (1905), Symph. No. 2, *Summer Symph.* (1907), *Scherzo idyllique* (1908; Prague, Nov. 13, 1910), *Blue Bird,* overture after Maeterlinck (Prague, March 3, 1912, composer conducting), *Adventus,* symph. poem (Prague, Nov. 6, 1921), *Suite montagnarde* (Prague, Sept. 8, 1935), *Serenade* for strings (1941), violin concerto (1944); choral works, including the cantata *Pokušeni na poušti (Temptation in the Wilderness;* 1922); chamber music: 2 string quartets, piano trio, violin sonata; several albums of piano pieces, and a number of songs; also arrangements of folksongs.

Krieger, Adam, German composer; b. Driesen, Neumark, Jan. 7, 1634; d. Dresden, June 30, 1666. He studied with Samuel Scheidt in Halle; from 1655-57 he was organist at the Nikolaikirche in Leipzig; then went to Dresden as court organist. He was one of the most important of the early composers of German lieder; he called his 'Arien' and for most of them wrote the words as well as the music; they contain instrumental ritornels, for two violins and continuo in the early songs, for five strings and continuo in the later ones. Many of these 'Arien' have been preserved, although his original collection (1657) is lost; it was reconstructed by Osthoff (1929); the 2nd collection (1667) is reproduced in vol. 19 of the 'Denkmäler deutscher Tonkunst'; modern reprints of some were publ. by Seiffert and Hans Hoffmann. — Cf. H. Osthoff, *Adam Krieger* (Leipzig, 1929; with musical examples; a thematic catalogue of his arias, etc.).

Krieger (or **Krüger**), **Johann,** famous contrapuntist and organist, brother of Johann Philipp Krieger; b. Nuremberg, Dec. 28, 1651; d. Zittau, July 18, 1735. He studied with his brother, and became his successor as chamber organist at Bayreuth in 1672. He was subsequently a court musician at Greiz (1678-81); then went to Zittau, where he was active as municipal organist; he remained there for 54 years, until his death. His music was appreciated by Handel; some of his organ compositions are regarded as presaging the grand style of Bach. — Works: *Neue musikalische Ergetzligkeit,* arias for 5-9 voices (Frankfurt, 1684); *6 musikalische Partien,* dance music for clavichord (Nuremberg, 1697); *Anmuthige Clavier-Übung,* containing preludes, fugues, etc. (Nuremberg, 1699); also sacred music. Max Seiffert ed. (in the 'Denkmäler deutscher Tonkunst') 2 sacred choral works by Krieger (vol. 6, part 1) and complete keyboard works, with critical notes, lists of sacred and secular vocal music, dates of performance, notes on extant MSS, biographical details, etc. (vol. 18); an aria from the *Neue musikalische Ergetzligkeit* is reprinted in Schering's *Geschichte der Musik in Beispielen,* No. 235.

Krieger, Johann Philipp, German composer; b. Nuremberg, Feb. 25, 1649; d. Weissenfels, Feb. 7, 1725. He was a pupil of Johann Drechsel and Gabriel Schütz in Nuremberg; went to Copenhagen, where he became a pupil and later assistant of court organist Johann Schröder (1663-69). In 1670 he was appointed court organist and chamber composer at Bayreuth, with an interval of study in Italy (1673). He was subsequently court musician at Kassel, and at Halle (from 1677); on Dec. 23, 1680 he was appointed court conductor at Weissenfels and Halle, remaining in this capacity until his death. He received the rank of nobility from Emperor Leopold I during a visit to Vienna (1677). He produced some 20 stage works in Halle, Weissenfels, Hamburg, and other German towns; publ. 12 triosonatas for 2 violins with continuo (op. 1, 1688); 12 sonatas for violin with viola da gamba (op. 2, 1693); *Musikalischer Seelenfriede,* 20 sacred arias for violin with bass (1697); *Lustige Feldmusik,* 6 overtures for wind or other instruments (1704), etc. Modern reprints, ed. by Seiffert, are in vols. 53/54 of the 'Denkmäler deutscher Tonkunst' (contains a selection of 21 sacred compositions by Krieger with critical commentary, as well as a complete list of his sacred works perf. at Weissenfels, notes of extant MSS, biographical details, etc.), vol. 6 (2 sacred choral works with a practical transcription of one of them), and the appendix to vol. 18 (3 keyboard pieces). Other reprints are: instrumental suite from *Lustige Feldmusik,* in 'Perlen alter Kammermusik' (ed. by Schering, for strings; 1912); in 'Organum,' ed. by Seiffert (vol. 3, containing No. 3 of the *Feldmusik,* for chamber orch.); selected organ pieces are in vol. 4 of 'Organum,' etc.; 24 arias, in 'Haus- und Kammermusik aus dem XVI.-XVIII. Jahrhundert,' ed. by H. J. Moser (1930); 2 arias in Schering's *Geschichte der Musik in Beispielen;* Eitner ed. 2 partitas, 2 sonatas, and various vocal works in 'Monatshefte für Musikgeschichte' (supplement to vol. 30).

Kriens, Christian, pianist, violinist, and composer; b. Brussels, April 29, 1881; d. Hartford, Conn., Dec. 17, 1934. He was taken to Holland as a child; studied with his father, a clarinetist, and later at the Royal Cons. at The Hague. At 14 he made his début at Amsterdam, playing the *Emperor Concerto* and conducting his own 2nd symphony. From 1896-99 he toured Europe as a violinist; then taught at The Hague Cons. He came to America as conductor of the French Opera Co. (1906); settled in New York in 1907; was violinist in the N. Y. Symph., N. Y. Philh., and at the Metropolitan Opera. He then became director of the Traveller's Broadcasting Co., Station WTIC, Hartford, Conn. Despondent over his inability to find further work, he committed suicide.

Krigar, Hermann, German pianist; b. Berlin, April 3, 1819; d. there, Sept. 5, 1880. He studied at Leipzig with Schumann, Mendelssohn, and Hauptmann (1843-45); organized a singing society in Berlin; taught there. He wrote incidental music, motets, psalms, piano pieces, and songs.

Krips, Josef, Austrian conductor; b. Vienna, April 8, 1902. He studied with Mandyczewski and Weingartner in Vienna; was violinist at the Volksoper there (1918-21); then became operatic coach and choirmaster of the Volksoper (1921). In 1924 he conducted opera in Aussig; in 1925, at the Municipal Theater in Dortmund; from 1926-33, general music director at Karlsruhe. In 1933 he was appointed conductor at the Vienna State Opera; in 1935, became prof. at the Vienna Academy of Music. In 1938 he lost these positions, after the annexation of Austria to Germany; conducted a season of opera in Belgrade (1938-39). In 1945 he rejoined the staff of the Vienna State Opera; conducted in England, France, and Russia in 1947, producing an excellent impression. In 1950 he was appointed conductor of the London Symph. Orch.; in 1952 he became conductor of the Buffalo Symph. Orch.

Kriukov, Nikolai Nikolaievitch, Russian composer; brother of Vladimir Kriukov; b. Moscow, Feb. 14, 1908. He studied with Vassilenko; devoted himself chiefly to folksong arrangements and film music. He has written orchestral suites on folk themes gathered in various republics of the Soviet Union, sometimes including native instruments. He received 2 Stalin prizes for his film scores.

Kriukov, Vladimir Nikolaievitch, Russian composer; b. Moscow, July 22, 1902. He studied with Gretchaninov, Miaskovsky, and Catoire. He wrote the operas *Miserly Night* (composed at the age of 15), *The King at the Marketplace* (after Alexander Blok), and *The Station Master* (after Pushkin); also a dramatic prologue for orch. to Blok's drama *The Unknown Lady* as well as a considerable amount of chamber music.

Křížkovský, Karel (Pavel), Bohemian choral composer; b. Holasovice, Jan. 9, 1820; d. Brno, May 8, 1885. He was a chorister at Opava; then attended the Gymnasium there; became a school teacher; in 1845, joined the order of the Austin Friars, and assumed the name Pavel; was ordained priest in 1848. He was greatly interested in Moravian folksongs and collected many of them in the field. At the same time, he began to compose choruses in the national manner; one of his earliest works, *Utonulá (The Girl that Drowned),* became popular; other favorites are *Žaloba (The Plaint)* and particularly *Odvedeného prosba (The Recruit's Prayer).* He also wrote much sacred music (Roman Catholic) for the Olomouc Cathedral, where he was music director from 1873. Among his pupils was Janáček. Publication of his collected works was begun at Prague in 1949. —Cf. J. Geissler, *Křížkovský* (Prague, 1885); K. Eichler, *Křížkovský* (Brno, 1904); J. Racek, *Křížkovský* (Olomouc, 1946).

Kroeger, Ernest Richard, American organist and composer; b. St. Louis, Aug. 10, 1862; d. there, April 7, 1934. He studied piano in St. Louis; then was organist at various churches there; taught and lectured at a number of schools in the U. S. He composed orchestral works, including the overtures *Thanatopsis, Endymion, Sardanapalus, Hiawatha, Atala* and the symph. suites *Lalla Rookh* and *The Mississippi; A Masque of Dead Florentines,* for declamation or action with music; a piano trio; a piano quartet; a piano quintet; 4 string quartets; a violin sonata; pieces for organ; songs.

Krohn, Felix (Julius Theofil), Finnish conductor and composer; son of Ilmari Krohn; b. Tampere, May 20, 1898. He studied with his father; later at the Hochschule für Musik in Berlin. Returning to Finland in 1922, he was active as conductor. He wrote a folk opera, *Uskollinen sisar* (1945); also some chamber music.

Krohn, Ilmari (Henrik Reinhold), eminent Finnish music scholar; b. Helsingfors, Nov. 8, 1867. After studying with Richard Faltin in Helsingfors, he went to Germany, where he took courses at the Leipzig Cons. with Papperitz and Reinecke (1886-90); obtained his *Dr. phil.* with the thesis *Über die Art und Enstehung der geistlichen Volksmelodien in Finnland* (Helsingfors, 1899). Returning to Finland, he joined the staff of the Univ. of Helsingfors (1900); also taught at the Cons. there; lectured at musical congresses in London, Paris, Basel, Vienna, and Rome (1891-1914). In 1906 he founded the musical journal 'Säveletär'; was a member of the Songbook Commission (1918-23); proposed the construction of an 'Acoustic Harmonium' of his own invention, and publ. a paper on it, *System Krohn* (Vienna, 1906). —Publications: *Guide for Acoustic Intonation* (Helsingfors, 1911; in Swedish, 1912); a course of music theory, in 5 parts: I. Rhythm (1911-14); II. Melody (1917); III. Harmony (1923); IV. Polyphony (1929); V. Form (1937); *Der Formenbau in den Symphonien von Jean Sibelius* (Helsinki, 1942); *Der Stimmungsgehalt in den Symphonien von Jean Sibelius* (Helsinki, 1945-46; 2 vols.); *Sävelmuistoja elämäni varrelta* (memoirs; Helsinki, 1951). His most significant accomplishment is the compilation of some 7000 Finnish folksongs, *Suomen Kansan Sävelmiä,* which he began in 1886, and methodically arranged in 4 categories: I. sacred melodies; II. secular melodies; III. dance melodies; IV. runic melodies. The publication of these important materials stretched from 1898 till 1933. He also edited psalms (1903), introits (1908), antiphons (1915), Easter matins, New Year vigils, vespers, and the Order of the Mass for the church year (1925); *Iltakellot, Completorium I-IV* (1928); began a complete edition of the Finnish Psalter in 1952. He contributed valuable articles on Finnish music to various journals. Krohn was also a composer; wrote an opera, *Tuhotulva (Deluge,* Helsinki, Oct. 25, 1928); 2 oratorios, *Ikiaartehet (Eternal Treasures,* 1914) and *Viottajat (Victors,* 1937); many sacred choral works; a number of songs. On the occasion of his 60th birthday, his students publ. a collection of musical essays in his honor (Helsinki, 1927). — Cf. Sulho Ranta, *Ilmari Krohn* in *Suomen Säveltäjiä* (Helsinki, 1945; pp. 273-284).

Kroll, Erwin, German music critic and author; b. Deutsch-Eylau, Feb. 3, 1886. He studied at Königsberg and at the Munich Academy of Music and Munich Univ., with Pfitzner and Sandberger; was music critic in Königsberg until 1930, when he moved to Berlin; from 1945-53 he was musical director of the Northwest Radio. He publ. biographies of E. T. A. Hoffmann (1923), Pfitzner (1924), and Weber (1933); also wrote a number of songs and some chamber music.

Kroll, Franz, German pianist and music editor; b. Bromberg, June 22, 1820; d. Berlin, May 28, 1877. He was first a student of medicine; then took lessons from Liszt; settled in Berlin as a music teacher. He was the editor of Bach's *Well-Tempered Clavier* for the Bach Gesellschaft, to which he contributed an introduction, summarizing bibliographical data; also edited Mozart's piano works.

Kroll, William, American violinist; b. New York, Jan. 30, 1901. He studied in Berlin and at the Institute of Musical Art, N. Y. (graduated in 1922); then became 1st violinist of the Coolidge String Quartet, and appeared with it at numerous chamber music festivals in the U. S. and in Europe; subsequently organized a string quartet of his own, the Kroll Quartet.

Krommer, Franz, violinist and composer; b. Kamenitz, Moravia, Nov. 27, 1759; d. Vienna, Jan. 8, 1831. He first studied with his uncle, an organist; went to Vienna; joined the orch. of Count Styrum-Limburg at Simontornya as violinist, then conductor; became choirmaster at Fünfkirchen, Pecs; then bandmaster of the Karólyi regiment; went to Gödöllö as Kapellmeister of Count Grassalkovic's orch. He returned to Vienna, and in 1818, became Imperial Kapellmeister. He wrote a Mass; 5 symphonies; 5 violin concertos; a quantity of chamber music; quintets and quartets for wind instruments; etc. — Cf. W. H. Riehl, *Musikalische Charakterköpfe* (vol. 3, Stuttgart, 1879).

Kromolicki (kroh-moh-litz'-kē), **Joseph**, eminent musicologist; b. Posen, Jan. 16, 1882. He received a thorough education in music, studying with Haberl and Haller in Regensburg; and with Pfitzner, Kretzschmar, and Johannes Wolf in Berlin; received his *Dr. phil.* in 1909 with a thesis, *Die Practica artis musicae des Amerus.* He was active as choral conductor in Berlin churches; edited 'Musica sacra' from 1908 and vols. 45, 48, and 57 of the 'Denkmäler deutscher Tonkunst'; composed 5 Masses, a Te Deum, organ preludes, sacred songs, etc. He continued to live and work in Berlin in 1955.

Kronke, Emil, German pianist and composer; b. Danzig, Nov. 29, 1865; d. Dresden, Dec. 16, 1938. He was a pupil of Reinecke in Leipzig and of Nicodé and Kirchner in Dresden; won 1st prize for piano playing at the Dresden Cons. (1886). He was an ardent admirer of Liszt, and wrote several virtuoso pieces for piano; also publ. several manuals: *Das virtuose Arpeggiospiel; Chopin-Etüden; Die moderne Technik; Die hohe Schule des 4. und 5. Fingers.* Edited over 200 of Chopin's works.

Kronold, Hans, cellist; brother of Selma Kronold; b. Cracow, July 3, 1872; d. New York, Jan. 10, 1922. He studied in Leipzig and Berlin; came to America at the age of 14; joined the orch. of the Metropolitan Opera; then played in the N. Y. Symph. Orch.; taught at the N. Y. College of Music. He publ. cello pieces and songs.

Kronold, Selma, soprano; sister of Hans Kronold; b. Cracow, 1866; d. New York, Oct. 9, 1920. She made her début as Agatha in *Der Freischütz* at Leipzig, when she was 16; then was engaged to sing Wagnerian roles in various European cities. In 1888 she came to America; sang the leading roles in the American premières of *Cavalleria Rusticana* (Philadelphia, Sept. 9, 1891) and *I Pagliacci* (N. Y., June 15, 1893); in 1896, joined the Metropolitan Opera; retired in 1904 and founded the Catholic Oratorio Society. Her repertory included some 45 parts.

Kroyer, Theodor, eminent German musicologist; b. Munich, Sept. 9, 1873; d. Cologne, Jan. 12, 1945. He studied piano with Lang, counterpoint with Rheinberger, and musicology with Sandberger; took the degree of *Dr. phil.* in 1897; then became music critic of the 'Münchener Allgemeine Zeitung'; was on the staff of the Univs. of Munich (1902-20), Heidelberg (1920-23), and Leipzig (1923-33). In 1925 he purchased for the Univ. of Leipzig the rich collection of instruments, manuscripts, and portraits from the famous Heyer Museum in Cologne; also in 1925 he began issuing the valuable series 'Publikationen älterer Musik' (Deutsche Gesellschaft für Musikwissenschaft). In 1932 he became prof. at the Univ. of Cologne; retired in 1938. He edited vol. 1 of the complete works of Senfl in the 'Denkmäler der Tonkunst in Bayern' (1903); also edited a selection from the works of G. Aichinger for the same series (vol. 10). His writings include *Die Anfänge der Chromatik im italienischen Madrigal des XVI. Jahrhunderts; A cappella und conserto,* in the 'Kretzschmar-Festschrift' (1918); *Die Musica Speculativa des Magister Erasmus Heritius,* in the 'Sandberger-Festschrift' (1918); *Dialog und Echo in der alten Chormusik,* in the 'Jahrbuch Peters' (1909); *Die circumpolare Oper,* in the 'Jahrbuch Peters' (1919); *Zur Chiavettenfrage,* in the 'Adler-Festschrift' (1935); *Zwischen Renaissance und Barock,* in the 'Jahrbuch Peters' (1927); also biographies of Rheinberger, in Weinmann's 'Kirchenmusik' (1916), and of Walter Courvoisier (1929); also wrote 2 choral symphonies, several pieces of chamber music, and works for piano, as well as songs (all in MS). A 'Kroyer-Festschrift' was publ. in 1933.—Cf. O. Ursprung, *Theodor Kroyer,* in the 'Zeitschrift für Musikwissenschaft' (Nov., 1933).

Krstič (kris-tēch'), **Peter,** Serbian composer; b. Belgrade, March 2, 1877; studied at the Vienna Cons. with R. Fuchs. Returning to Belgrade, he conducted opera at the National Theater; in 1930, became inspector of several music schools. His works, based on Serbian national tunes, include the opera *Zalumcar* (1927); cantata *Jutro Slobode* (1919); several orchestral suites of national dances; choruses and songs. He edited a Serbian music dictionary.

Krückl, Franz, Moravian baritone; b. Edlspitz, Nov. 10, 1841; d. Strasbourg, Jan. 13, 1899. He studied with Dessoff; made his début in 1868 in Brünn; then sang in Kassel, Augsburg, Hamburg, and Cologne (1874-86); taught at the Hoch Cons. in Frankfurt; in 1892, became director of the Municipal Theater in Strasbourg. He publ. *Der Vertrag zwischen Direktor und Mitglied der deutschen Bühne* (1899).

Krueger, Felix Emil, music psychologist; b. Posen, Aug. 10, 1874; d. Basel, Feb. 24, 1948. He studied at the Univs. of Strasbourg, Berlin, and Munich (*Dr. phil.,* 1897), also at the Leipzig Psychological Institute and the

Kiel Psychological and Physiological Institute. After lecturing at the Univ. of Leipzig (1903-6), he went to Argentina and was prof. at the Univ. of Buenos Aires (1906-8); was prof. at Halle Univ. (1910-12); exchange prof. at Columbia Univ., N. Y. (1912-13); in 1918, was appointed prof. and director of the Psychological Institute of Leipzig Univ., succeeding Wilhelm Wundt; held an honorary LL.D. degree from Columbia Univ.; also honorary degrees from European institutions of learning. He retired in 1938; lived in Potsdam; then went to Switzerland, where he remained until his death.—Publications: *Beobachtungen an Zweiklängen,* in the 'Philosophische Studien' (1900); *Zur Theorie der Kombinationstöne* (ib., 1901); *Differenztöne und Konsonanz,* in the 'Archiv für die gesamte Psychologie' (vol. 1; in English as *Consonance and Dissonance,* in the 'Journal of Philosophy, Psychology and Scientific Methods,' 1913); *Beziehungen der experimentellen Phonetik zur Psychologie* (1907); *Die Theorie der Konsonanz,* in Wundt's 'Psychologie Studien' (1906-10); *Mitbewegungen beim Singen, Sprechen und Hören* (Leipzig, 1910); *Über Entwicklungspsychologie* (1915); *Über psychische Ganzheit* (1926). In 1934 his students and admirers publ. a Festschrift on his 60th birthday (2 vols.).

Krueger, Karl, conductor; b. Atchison, Kansas, Jan. 19, 1894. He first studied philosophy and law, then music, at the Univs. of Vienna and Heidelberg; received his M.A. from the Univ. of Kansas (1916); took courses with Chadwick and Goodrich in Boston, Widor in Paris, and R. Fuchs (composition) in Vienna; also conducting with Schalk, Nikisch, and Weingartner. From 1919-24 he was assistant conductor at the Vienna State Opera; he was conductor of the Seattle Orch. (1926-32), the Kansas City Philharmonic Orch. (1933-43), the Detroit Symph. Orch. (1943-49). In 1950 he organized a radio orch., but the broadcasts were discontinued after a season. He publ. a book, *Way of the Conductor* (N. Y., 1958).

Krug, Dietrich, German music teacher; b. Hamburg, May 25, 1821; d. there, April 7, 1880. He studied with Melchert and J. Schmitt. He wrote studies for the piano; also publ. a method.

Krug, Friedrich, German composer; b. Kassel, July 5, 1812; d. Karlsruhe, Nov. 3, 1892. He was a baritone singer; court musical director at Karlsruhe. He wrote the operas *Die Marquise* (Kassel, 1843), *Meister Martin der Kufer und seine Gesellen* (Karlsruhe, 1845), *Der Nachtwächter* (Mannheim, 1846).

Krug, (Wenzel) Joseph (called Krug-Waldsee), German composer and conductor; b. Waldsee, Nov. 8, 1858; d. Magdeburg, Oct. 8, 1915. He developed precociously; entered the Stuttgart Cons. at 14, studying violin, piano, singing, and theory; graduated in 1880, and went to Switzerland, where he was active as a teacher in Hofwyl; then conducted a choral society in Stuttgart (1882-89); was subsequently chorusmaster in Hamburg (1889-92), in Nuremberg and Augsburg (from 1894); then lived in Magdeburg. He wrote several cantatas in a grand manner; 4 operas; chamber music; songs.

Krüger, Eduard, German writer on music; b. Lüneburg, Dec. 9, 1807; d. Göttingen, Nov. 9, 1885. He studied philology in Berlin and Göttingen; also studied music; in 1861, became prof. of music at Göttingen Univ. He publ. *De musicis Graecorum organis circa Pindari tempora* (1830); a *Grundriss der Metrik* (1838); *Beiträge für Leben und Wissenschaft der Tonkunst* (1847); *System der Tonkunst* (1866); also contributed articles to various periodicals.

Krüger, Johann. See **Krieger.**

Krüger, Wilhelm, German pianist and composer; b. Stuttgart, Aug. 5, 1820; d. there, June 16, 1883. He studied piano with Ziegele and composition with Lindpaintner. In 1845 he settled in Paris, where he enjoyed an excellent reputation as pianist and teacher; in 1870, the outbreak of the Franco-Prussian war compelled him to return to Germany; he was then active as a pedagogue. He publ. a number of brilliant salon pieces for piano (168 opus numbers in all), which included caprices, nocturnes, genre pieces *(Harpe éolienne, Guitare),* a *Polonaise-Boléro,* études (*Les six jours de la semaine,* etc.), and transcriptions, fantasias, etc., of and on operatic airs. He edited a 2-vol. edition of Handel's clavier works.

Kruis (kroiss), **M. H. van't,** Dutch organist and composer; b. Oudewater, March 8, 1861; d. Lausanne, Feb. 14, 1919. He studied in The Hague; then filled various posts as organist and teacher; in 1886, founded a musical monthly 'Het Orgel.' He publ. a *Beknopt overzicht der muziekgeschiedenis* (1892); also wrote an opera, *De bloem van Island,* 3 symphonies, 8 overtures, organ music, piano pieces, etc.

Krumpholtz, Johann Baptist, Bohemian harpist and composer; b. Zlonice, near Prague, May 8, 1742; d. Paris, Feb. 19, 1790; received his first instruction from his father, a bandmaster in a Paris regiment; gave concerts in Vienna in 1772; studied composition with Haydn; from 1773-76, was a member of Prince Esterházy's orch. Following a long concert tour in Germany, he returned to France, and in Metz he married a Fräulein Meyer, a 16-year-old harpist, with whom he subsequently gave concerts in Paris and London. Krumpholtz added to his fame as harpist by inventing a harp with 2 pedals, loud and soft; he also stimulated Erard to make experiments that led to the invention of the modern pedal mechanism. His life ended tragically; he drowned himself in the Seine when his young wife eloped to England with another man. He wrote 6 concertos for harp and orch., a duo for 2 harps, 52 sonatas and other works entitled *Sonates pathétiques,* a symph. for harp with a small orch.; many short pieces.

Krumpholtz, Wenzel, violinist; brother of Johann Baptist Krumpholtz; b. Zlonice, 1750; d. Vienna, May 2, 1817. He was a member of the orch. at the Vienna Opera in 1796, and was friendly with Beethoven; when Krumpholtz died, Beethoven was moved to write a *Gesang der Mönche,* dedicated to his memory. Wenzel Krumpholtz wrote several pieces for unaccompanied violin, among them *Abendunterhaltung* and *Eine Viertelstunde für eine Violine.*

Kruse, Georg Richard, conductor and writer on music; b. Greiffenberg, Jan. 17, 1856; d. Berlin, Feb. 23, 1944. He studied at the Univ. of Bern and also in Leipzig; then was opera director and conductor in Germany. He came to America in 1891 and was music critic in Milwaukee until 1894; from 1894-96, toured the U. S. as conductor of a troupe presenting Humperdinck's *Hansel and Gretel;* returned to Europe and was municipal theater director in Bern, St. Gall, and Ulm (1896-1900); from 1900-09, editor of the 'Deutsche Bühnengenossenschaft.' In 1906 he founded and was director of the Lessing Museum in Berlin; in 1908, founded the Lessing Society and the Musik-Volksbibliothek des Tonkünstlerverein; also editor of dramatic and musical works for 'Reclams Universalbibliothek' and contributed articles to various journals. He publ. a comprehensive biography of A. Lortzing (1899); *Lortzings Briefe* (1901; enlarged 2nd ed., Regensburg, 1913); biographies of Otto Nicolai and Hermann Götz; essays; etc.

Kruseman, Jacob Philip, Dutch music publisher; b. Amsterdam, Nov. 17, 1887; d. The Hague, Jan. 31, 1955. He studied singing, and appeared in recitals and light opera in Holland until 1909, when he founded a publishing firm in The Hague, specializing in books on music and art; issued about 25 vols. of biographies of famous composers, and himself wrote a booklet, *Beethoven's Eigen Woorden* (The Hague, 1947). His most important publication is *Geïllustreerd Muzieklexicon,* ed. by himself with G. Keller (The Hague, 1932; supplement, ed. by Kruseman and Zagwijn, 1949); it is modelled after Riemann's *Musiklexikon,* but contains a great deal of information on Dutch musicians not available in other reference books. After his death, the management of his publishing firm was assumed by his widow.

Krygell (krü'-gel), **Johan Adam,** Danish organist; b. Naestved, Sept. 18, 1835; d. Copenhagen, July 27, 1915. He began his career as a painter, but turned his attention to music; entered the Copenhagen Cons. in 1867, studying organ under G. Matthison-Hansen; won the Ancker stipend, and spent 1874-75 studying in Germany; returning to Copenhagen in 1880, he became organist at St. Matthew's Church; also taught. He wrote an opera, *Saul* (not produced); an oratorio; a Mass; 24 string quartets; a septet; symphonies; overtures; organ works.

Krylov, Pavel Dimitrievitch, Russian composer; b. Tver, March 3, 1885; d. Moscow, April 21, 1935. He studied at the Philharmonic Institute in Moscow; graduated in 1910 with honors. In 1920 he joined the staff of the Moscow Cons. Among his works are an opera, *The Fountain of Bakhtchissaray;* a symphony; a symph. poem, *The Spring;* a symph. suite, *Volga;* concerto for clarinet and orch.; 3 piano sonatas; songs.

Kryzhanovsky, Ivan Ivanovitch, Russian theorist and composer; b. Kiev, March 8, 1867; d. Leningrad, Dec. 9, 1924. He studied medicine and music; took lessons with Rimsky-Korsakov at the St. Petersburg Cons.; worked in Dr. Pavlov's laboratory of conditioned reflexes; served in the medical corps in the Russian Army during World War I, and was taken prisoner. After his release, he lectured on the physiology of piano technique. He wrote several symphonic works, chamber music, and a piano concerto. His paper, *Biological Bases of the Evolution of Music,* was publ. in an English transl. from MS (London, 1928).

Kubelík, Jan, famous Czech violinist; b. Michle, near Prague, July 5, 1880; d. Prague, Dec. 5, 1940. He was taught by his father, who was a gardener; since he showed extraordinary talent, he was accepted by Ševčik as a student at the Prague Cons.; later he studied in Vienna, where he made his professional début on Nov. 26, 1898. In 1900 he began a series of triumphant concerts in Europe and America. He was regarded as a counterpart to Paderewski in virtuosity, dramatic appeal, and ability to communicate his art to audiences everywhere. In 1903 he married a Hungarian countess and became a naturalized Hungarian citizen. His career as a great virtuoso was stopped short with World War I; he appeared much less frequently than before; lived mostly in Prague. He composed 6 violin concertos in a brilliant style; also a symphony and some chamber music. —Cf. J. Čeleda, *Jan Kubelík* (Prague, 1930); K. Hoffmeister, *Jan Kubelík* (Prague, 1941); a symposium in his memory, ed. by J. Dostál, was publ. at Prague in 1942.

Kubelík, Rafael, conductor; son of Jan Kubelik; b. Býchory, near Kolín, June 29, 1914. He studied at the Prague Cons.; made his début with the Czech Philharmonic on Jan. 24, 1934; in 1938, conducted this orchestra in England. From 1939-41 he was conductor of the National Theater in Brno; from 1942-48, musical director of the Czech Philharmonic. From 1948-50 he was mainly in England. In 1950 he was appointed principal conductor of the Chicago Symph. Orch.; performed many modern works, including some by American composers. He resigned in 1953 and returned to Europe, where he served as musical director of the Covent Garden Opera in London, and also conducted frequent symph. concerts in France, Germany, Russia, etc. He wrote an opera, *Veronika* (Brno, April 19, 1947); a choral symph. (1945); a violin concerto (1940); a cello concerto (1944); chamber music.

Kubik, Gail, American composer; b. South Coffeyville, Okla., Sept. 5, 1914. He studied at the Eastman School of Music, Rochester, N. Y. During World War II he was in the Army Air Force. In 1946 he taught at the Univ. of Southern California; in 1948, received a Guggenheim Fellowship. His works include: for the stage: incidental music for *They Walk Alone* (1941); *Frankie and Johnnie,* ballet for dance band and folk singer (1946); *Mirror for the Sky,* folk opera on the life of Audubon (N. Y., May 12, 1947); for orch.: *American Caprice,* for piano and chamber orch. (Monmouth College Orch., Ill., May 1936); *Paratroops,* film music, suite for small orch. (1941); *Camptown Races* (Saratoga Springs, 1946); *Erie Canal* (Los Angeles, Feb. 22, 1947); *Symphonie-Concertante* (Little Orch. Society, N. Y., Jan. 7, 1952; received a Pulitzer Prize during that year); symph. No. 3 (N. Y. Philharmonic, Feb. 28, 1957); *Memphis Belle,* film score; violin concerto (1943); for band: *Stewball,* variations (1941); *Fanfare and March* (1946); overture (1946); for chorus: *A Wartime Litany* (1943); chamber music: *Trivialities,* for flute, horn, and string quartet (1934); piano trio (1934); *Puck, a Christmas Score,* for speaker, strings, and winds (1940); suite for 3 recorders (1941); sonatina for violin and piano (1944); toccata for organ and strings (1946); *Little Suite,* for flute and 2 clarinets (1947).

Kubín, Rudolf, Czech composer; b. Moravská Ostrava, Jan. 10, 1909. He studied cello at the Prague Cons. and also pursued special studies in modern music with Alois Hába. He has written music in disparate styles, some extremely modern, others designed for utilitarian purposes (mass songs, military marches, etc.). His opera *Naši furianti* (*Our Wild Ones*) was produced at Ostrava on Sept. 18, 1949. Other works are: clarinet concerto (1939); violin concerto (1943); symph. poem *Ostrava* (1951).

Kucharz (koo'-hahrtsh), **Johann Baptist,** Bohemian organist; b. Chotecz, March 5, 1751; d. Prague, Feb. 18, 1829. He studied at the Jesuit College in Königgrätz, at the Jesuit Seminary in Gitschin, then with Seegert in Prague; organist at the Heinrichskirche, then at Strahow Monastery; conductor of the Prague Opera (1791-1800). He made the first piano scores of Mozart's operas.

Kücken, Friedrich Wilhelm, German conductor and composer; b. Bleckede, Nov. 16, 1810; d. Schwerin, April 3, 1882. He studied with his brother-in-law Lührss, an organist, and Aron at Schwerin; then played in the duke's orch. there; in 1832, went to Berlin, where he studied counterpoint with Birnbach; in 1841, studied with Sechter in Vienna; conducted festivals of male choruses in Switzerland; was Kapellmeister in Stuttgart (1851-61). He wrote the operas *Die Flucht nach der Schweiz* (Berlin, Feb. 26, 1839) and *Der Prätendent* (Stuttgart, April 21, 1847); also sonatas for violin and for cello, etc. He is most noted for his songs (*Ach wie wär's möglich dann; Das Sternelein; O weine nicht; Trab, trab; The Maid of Judah; The Swallows,* etc.).

Kuczinski (koo-tchin'-skē), **Paul,** composer; b. Berlin, Nov. 10, 1846; d. there, Oct. 21, 1897. He was a banker by profession; also an excellent musician (studied with Bülow and Kiel). He was a friend of Adolf Jensen, whose letters he publ. in part as *Aus Briefen Adolf Jensens* (1879); also publ. *Erlebnisse und Gedanken, Dichtungen zu Musikwerken* 1898), showing his admiration for Wagner. He wrote the poems for his own numerous vocal scores.—Works: *Die Bergpredigt,* for baritone solo, chorus, and orch.; *Gesang des Turmwächters,* for tenor solo. and orch.; *Geschenke der Genien,* for female chorus and orch.; *Neujahrsgesang,* for tenor solo, chorus, and orch.; also piano pieces (*Humoreske, Intermezzo, Karnevalswalzer, Phantasiestücke*).

Kudelski, Karl Matthias, German violinist; b. Berlin, Nov. 17, 1805; d. Baden-Baden, Oct. 3, 1877. He studied with Lafont; played 1st violin in the orch. of the City Theater in Berlin; in a quartet in Dorpat (1830); Kapellmeister to a Russian prince (1839); from 1841-51, leader and director in the Imperial Theater, Moscow. He publ. a *Kurzgefasste Harmonielehre* (1865); also violin concertos; cello concertos; violin sonatas; piano trios; fantasies for violin and piano; etc.

Kufferath, Hubert Ferdinand, pianist and organist; brother of Johann Hermann and Louis Kufferath; b. Mülheim-on-Ruhr, June 11, 1818; d. Brussels, June 23, 1896. He studied first with his brothers; then with Hartmann (violin) in Cologne; with Ferdinand David and Mendelssohn in Leipzig. From 1841-44 he was conductor of the Männergesangverein of Cologne; then settled in Brussels, where he taught members of the royal family; in 1872, became prof. at the Brussels Cons. He wrote symphonies, piano concertos, piano pieces (*Capriccio, Etudes de concert, Charakterstücke,* etc.); also wrote a *Praktische Chorschule für 4 Vocal- oder Instrumentalstimmen zum Studium der Harmonie, des Kontrapunktes und der Orgel* (1896).

Kufferath, Johann Hermann, German violinist and composer; brother of Hubert Ferdinand and Louis Kufferath; b. Mülheim-on-Ruhr, May 12, 1797; d. Wiesbaden, July 28, 1864. He studied violin with Spohr and composition with Hauptmann; in 1823, became musical director at Bielefeld; in 1830, at Utrecht, where he also taught singing at the School of Music and conducted various societies; retired to Wiesbaden in 1862. He wrote cantatas (*Jubelkantate,* etc.), overtures, and motets; also a *Manuel de chant.*

Kufferath, Louis, pianist and teacher; brother of Hubert Ferdinand and Johann Hermann Kufferath; b. Mülheim-on-Ruhr, Nov. 10, 1811; d. near Brussels, March 2, 1882. He studied with his brother, Johann Hermann, and with Schneider at Dessau. From 1836-50 he was director of the Cons. at Leeuwarden, Holland; then in Ghent and Brussels. He publ. a Mass, 250 canons, a cantata, *Artevelde;* songs; etc.

Kufferath, Maurice, Belgian cellist and writer on music; son of Hubert Ferdinand Kufferath; b. Brussels, Jan. 8, 1852; d. there, Dec. 8, 1919. He studied cello with the Servais (*père* and *fils*); then at Brussels Univ.; from 1873-1900, wrote for 'L'Indépendence Belge'; editor of the 'Guide musical,' then proprietor; in 1900, became director of the Théâtre de la Monnaie, together with Guillaume Guidé; co-founder of the Ysaÿe concerts, with Ysaÿe and Guidé. He publ. essays on Wagner's operas, and a comprehensive work, *Le Théâtre de Wagner de Tannhäuser à Parsifal* (Brussels, 1891-98; 6 vols.; of these, *Parsifal* was publ. in English transl., N. Y., 1904); also a brochure, *L'Art de diriger l'orchestre* (Brussels, 1891; an account of Hans Richter's conducting in Brussels); a sketch of Henri Vieuxtemps (Brussels, 1883). He wrote the report on the musical instruments at the Brussels Exposition of 1880. Under the pen-name 'Maurice Reymont' he translated Wagner's librettos and texts of songs by Brahms into French. He was an ardent propagandist for Wagner's ideas in Belgium.—Cf. L. Solvay, *Notice sur Maurice Kufferath* (Brussels, 1923).

Küffner, Joseph, German composer; b. Würzburg, March 31, 1776; d. there, Sept. 8, 1856. He wrote 2 operas, *Sporn und Schärpe* and *Der Cornett;* 7 symphonies; 10 overtures; music for military band and wind instruments; a fantasy for violin with orch.; a quintet for flute and strings; string quartets; trios and duets for flutes; duets for clarinet; guitar music; violin sonatas; etc.

Kuhač (koo'-hahtch), **Franz Xaver,** theorist; b. Escheck, Croatia, Nov. 20, 1834; d. Agram, June 18, 1911. He studied at the Budapest Cons. and at the Leipzig Cons.; also with Hanslick in Vienna and Liszt in Weimar. He publ. several valuable studies on the music system, instruments, and notation of the South Slavic nations, and 4 vols. of Slavic folksongs. He claimed Haydn and Tartini as Croatian composers; publ. *Josip Haydn i hrvatske narodne popievke* (*Joseph Haydn and Croatian folk melodies;* Agram,

1880); *Das türkische Element in der Musik der Kroaten, Serben und Bulgaren* (1900); numerous minor essays.

Kuhe, Wilhelm, pianist; b. Prague, Dec. 10, 1823; d. London, Oct. 9, 1912. He studied with Proksch, Tomaschek, and Thalberg. He went to London with the singer Pischek in 1845 and settled there; from 1886-1904, prof. at the Royal Academy of Music. He wrote salon music (*Feu follet, Gondola, Rosée du soir, Étude de concert,* etc.); operatic fantasias for piano; also publ. *My Musical Recollections* (London, 1897).

Kuhlau, Friedrich, prolific composer; b. Ülzen, Germany, Sept. 11, 1786; d. Copenhagen, March 12, 1832. He lost an eye in a childhood accident; during his recovery studied piano; became a private tutor in Hamburg and studied composition there with E. F. G. Schwenke. He went to Copenhagen in 1810 in order to avoid conscription into Napoleon's army; there he prospered, and in 1813 was appointed court musician. He produced several stage works in Copenhagen: *Røverborgen* (*The Robber's Castle;* May 26, 1814); *Trylleharpen* (*The Magic Harp;* Jan. 30, 1817); *Elisa* (April 17, 1820); *Lulu* (Oct. 29, 1824); *William Shakespeare* (March 28, 1826); *Elverhøj* (*The Fairies' Mound;* Nov. 6, 1828; his most celebrated dramatic work); wrote 3 flute quartets; trios concertants, duets, etc., for flute; 8 violin sonatas; 2 piano concertos; instructive piano sonatas, and perennially popular sonatinas, much used for teaching purposes; also various pieces for 4 hands; songs and male quartets, once in great vogue.—Cf. C. Thrane, *Danske Komponister* (Copenhagen, 1875; with a list of works); C. Thrane, *Friedrich Kuhlau. Zur 100-jährigen Wiederkehr seines Geburtstages* (Leipzig, 1886).

Kühmstedt, Friedrich, notable German theorist; b. Oldisleben, Dec. 20, 1809; d. Eisenach, Jan. 10, 1858. He studied with Rinck at Darmstadt; then taught music there (1831-36); settled in Eisenach, where he taught at the seminary. He publ. a *Gradus ad Parnassum; Kunst des Vorspiels für Orgel; Theoretisch-praktische Harmonie- und Ausweichungslehre* (1838); composed valuable organ music (a double fugue, a *Fantasia eroica,* fugues, preludes, and postludes); also oratorios, a Mass, motets, piano concertos, etc.

Kuhnau, Johann, erudite German musician, organist, and theorist; b. Geising, Apr. 6, 1660; d. Leipzig, June 5, 1722. He studied at the Kreuzschule in Dresden with Hering and Albrici; then with Edelmann at Zittau, where he became cantor. He attended the Univ. of Leipzig from 1682-84; then succeeded Kühnel as organist at the Thomaskirche; in 1688 he organized a Collegium Musicum and also studied law. He became musical director of the Univ. of Leipzig in 1700; the following year he was appointed cantor at the Thomaskirche; was Bach's predecessor in the post. He publ. *Jura circa musicos ecclesiasticos* (Leipzig, 1688); *Der Musickalische Quacksalber . . . in einer kurtzweiligen und angenehmen Historie . . . beschrieben* (Dresden, 1700; a satire on Italian music); 3 treatises are in MS. Kuhnau was the first to publish a harpsichord sonata imitated from the instrumental sonata (properly a suite) in several movements. It is found in Part II of his *Neuer Clavier-Übung* (1692) and contains 3 movements, Allegro, Adagio, and Allegro (Rondo); there followed 7 sonatas in his *Frische Clavier-Früchte* (1696), which show a marked advance in treatment and melodic invention; 6 more harpsichord sonatas appeared under the title *Biblische Historien nebst Auslegung in sechs Sonaten,* in the highly original form of illustrations to biblical stories, thus presaging the development of program music; they set forth the fight between David and Goliath, David's cure of Saul, Jacob's Wedding, etc. (1700; new ed. of the first 2 by J. S. Shedlock, 1895; new ed. of the 1st by H. Bauer, 1927). Kuhnau's complete clavier works were publ. by Päsler in vol. 2 of the 'Denkmäler deutscher Tonkunst.' Schering publ. 4 church cantatas and a list of Kuhnau's sacred works in vol. 58/59 of the 'Denkmäler deutscher Tonkunst.'—Cf. H. Bischoff, *Über J. Kuhnaus Vorstellung einiger biblischen Historien* (1877); J. S. Shedlock, *The Pianoforte Sonata* (London, 1895; p. 38 ff.); R. Münnich, *Kuhnaus Leben,* in the 'Sammelbände der Internationalen Musik-Gesellschaft' (1902; p. 473 ff.); J. C. Martin, *Die Kirchenkantaten J. Kuhnaus* (Leipzig, 1928); H. F. Menck, *J. Kuhnaus 'Musickalische Quacksalber,'* in *Der Musiker im Roman* (Heidelberg, 1931; p. 61ff.).

Kühner, Basil, composer; b. Stuttgart, April 1, 1840; d. Vilna, Aug., 1911. He studied at the Stuttgart Cons. with Faiszt and Lebert; then studied violin with Massart in Paris, and piano with Henselt in St. Petersburg; then was director of the Tiflis Cons. (1870-76). In 1878 he settled in St. Petersburg, where he established his own music school (1892). He wrote the opera *Tarass Bulba* (after Gogol; St. Petersburg, Dec. 24, 1880; had only 3 performances); a symph. subtitled *Liberation of the Serfs in Russia*

(St. Petersburg, 1866); a string quintet; 2 string quartets; a suite for cello and piano; *Snowflakes*, suite for piano; other piano pieces.

Kühner, Konrad, German pianist and teacher; b. Markt-Streufdorf, Meiningen, March 2, 1851; d. Schmalkalden, Feb. 5, 1909. He studied at the Stuttgart Cons.; from 1889-99 he lived in Dresden as a piano teacher, then in Brunswick. He wrote the symph. poem *Maria Stuart;* piano music; a *Technik des Klavierspiels; Schule des 4-händigen Spiels* (12 vols.); a *Vortragsalbum* (5 vols.); *Etüdenschule des Klavierspielers* (12 vols.); also edited many works for the 'Edition Litolff.'

Kulenkampf, Gustav, German composer; b. Bremen, Aug. 11, 1849; d. Berlin, Feb. 10, 1921. He was at first a merchant; then studied music with Barth (piano) and Bargiel (composition). He organized in Berlin his own women's choir; taught musical subjects at various music schools; appeared as pianist. He wrote the operas *Der Page* (Bremen, 1890), *Der Mohrenfürst* (Magdeburg, 1892), *Die Braut von Cypern* (Schwerin, 1897), *König Drosselbart* (Berlin, 1899), *Ammarei* (1903), *Anneliese* (Kassel, 1904); women's choruses; a piano sonata; songs; etc.

Kullak, Adolf, German music theorist and critic, brother of Theodor Kullak; b. Meseritz, Feb. 23, 1823; d. Berlin, Dec. 25, 1862. He studied general subjects at the Univ. of Berlin, and also music with Bernhard Marx; then taught at his brother's Academy; contributed music criticism to various periodicals; publ. some piano pieces and songs. He wrote *Das Musikalisch-Schöne* (Leipzig, 1858) and *Ästhetik des Klavierspiels* (Berlin, 1861; 4th ed. rewritten by W. Niemann, 1906; 5th ed., 1916; in English, N. Y., 1892), a valuable and instructive summary of piano methods.

Kullak, Franz, German pianist and composer; son of Theodor Kullak; b. Berlin, April 12, 1844; d. there, Dec. 9, 1913. He studied with his father; also with Liszt for a brief while. In 1867 he became piano teacher in his father's Academy; assumed its directorship at his father's death in 1882, dissolving the institution in 1890. He wrote an opera, *Ines de Castro* (Berlin, 1877); piano pieces; songs; also an essay, *Der Vortrag in der Musik am Ende des 19. Jahrhunderts* (Leipzig, 1898).

Kullak, Theodor, famous German pianist and pedagogue; b. Krotoschin, Sept. 12, 1818; d. Berlin, March 1, 1882. He studied piano with local teachers; in 1837 he went to Berlin at his father's behest to study medicine; also studied music there with Dehn (theory); then in 1842 went to Vienna, where he took lessons with Czerny. Returning to Berlin in 1846, he became court pianist to the King of Prussia. In 1850 he founded a conservatory in Berlin in partnership with Julius Stern and Bernhard Marx; however, dissension soon arose among them and, in 1855, Kullak established his own school, the Neue Akademie der Tonkunst, which greatly prospered and became famous as 'Kullak's Academy.' He publ. valuable pedagogic works: *Materialien für den Elementar-Unterricht* (3 vols.); *Schule des Oktavenspiel;* various characteristic pieces for piano in a salon manner *(Ondine, Les Etincelles, Les Danaides, La Gazelle,* etc.); also *Kinderleben* (2 albums of piano pieces).—Cf. O. Reinsdorf, *Theodor Kullak und seine Neue Akademie der Tonkunst in Berlin* (1870); H. Bischoff, *Zur Erinnerung an Theodor Kullak* (1883).

Kullman, Charles, American tenor; b. New Haven, Jan. 13, 1903. He studied at Yale Univ. (graduated in 1924) and at the Juilliard Graduate School (graduated in 1927); then went to France, where he took lessons at the American Cons. at Fontainebleau. Returning to America in 1928, he sang with the American Opera Co.; then went to Germany, where he made a successful début at the Kroll Opera in Berlin as Pinkerton in *Madama Butterfly* (Feb. 24, 1931); then appeared at various European opera houses: at the Berlin State Opera (1932-36), Vienna State Opera, and Covent Garden in London (1934-36). On Dec. 20, 1935 he made his début with the Metropolitan Opera as Faust: remained on its roster until 1956, when he was engaged as resident tenor at the Indiana Univ. School of Music.

Kummer, Friedrich August, German cellist, oboist, and composer; b. Meiningen, Aug. 5, 1797; d. Dresden, May 22, 1879. His family moved to Dresden, where Kummer studied cello with Dotzauer; then he studied oboe in order to enter the court orch., which he did in Nov., 1814; in 1817 he again studied the cello and became a virtuoso of the first rank. He also taught at the Dresden Cons. He was a prolific composer; 163 of his compositions were printed; he wrote concertos, a concertino, divertissements, etc., for the cello; also concert pieces for oboe, clarinet, horn, trumpet; and a method for cello.

Kummer, Kaspar, German flutist and composer; b. Erlau, Dec. 10, 1795; d. Koburg, May 21, 1870. He was a member of the court orch. at Koburg; then musical director there. He wrote quintets and quartets for flute and strings; flute concertos, trios, duos, etc.; and a method for flute.

Kümmerle, Salomon, German collector of vocal music; b. Malmsheim, near Stuttgart, Feb. 8, 1838; d. Samaden, Aug. 28, 1896. He taught at a school in Samaden (1875-90); publ. several collections of vocal music, among them *Musica sacra; Grabgesänge; Zionsharfe; Choralbuch für evangelische Kirchenchöre; Encyklopädie der evangelischen Kirchenmusik* (3 vols., 1888-96).

Kunc (koonts), **Jan,** Czech composer; b. Doubravice, Moravia, March 27, 1883. He studied with Janáček in Brno and with Novák in Prague; was music critic in Brno (1909-18); in 1918-19 he toured as accompanist with his wife, a concert singer. In 1919 he became instructor at the Brno Cons.; from 1923-45 was its director; in 1947 became lecturer at the Masaryk Univ. in Brno.—Works: *Song of Youth,* symph. poem (awarded prize of Czech Academy, 1920); 2 string quartets; piano trio; violin sonata; 4 piano sonatas; numerous choral works: *Ostrava, The Garden, Sedmdesát tisíc (Seventy Thousand), Stála Kačenka u Dunaja (Catherine on the Danube);* and many folksong arrangements.

Kunits, Luigi von, violinist and conductor; b. Vienna, July 20, 1870; d. Toronto, Canada, Oct. 8, 1931. He studied composition with Anton Bruckner, history of music with Hanslick, and violin with Ševčik. In 1893 he came to America; from 1897-1910 was concertmaster of the Pittsburgh Symph.; taught at the Pittsburgh Cons.; later founded his own music school. After 2 years in Europe (1910-12), he went to Canada and settled in Toronto; taught at the Canadian Academy of Music; founded the 'Canadian Journal of Music' (1915-19); from 1923 till 1931 was conductor of the New Symph. Orch. of Toronto (renamed Toronto Symph. Orch. in 1927). He publ. a book, *The Hero as Musician: Beethoven* (1913); also contributed articles to various periodicals. His compositions include 2 violin concertos, a string quartet, a viola sonata, *Three Etudes* for violin and piano; *Romanza,* for violin and piano; songs.

Kunkel, Franz Joseph, German theorist and composer; b. Dieburg, Aug. 20, 1808; d. Frankfurt, Dec. 31, 1880. From 1828-54 he was rector and music teacher in the Bensheim Teachers' Seminary. He wrote a *Kleine Musiklehre; Die Verurteilung der Konservatorien zu Pflanzschulen des musikalischen Proletariats* (1855); *Kritische Beleuchtung des C. F. Weitzmannischen Harmonie-Systems; Die neue Harmonielehre im Streit mit der alten* (1863); etc.; also a cantata, psalms, motets, etc.

Künneke, Eduard, German operetta composer, b. Emmerich, Jan. 27, 1885; d. Berlin, Oct. 27, 1953. He studied with Max Bruch in Berlin; was subsequently engaged as a choirmaster in various theaters in Germany; produced two operas, *Robins Ende* (Mannheim, 1909) and *Coeur As* (Dresden, 1913), with little success; he then turned to light opera, and his first work in this genre, a Singspiel, *Das Dorf ohne Glocke* (Berlin, April 5, 1919) was received with great acclaim. His next light opera, *Der Vetter aus Dingsda* (Berlin, April 15, 1921), was no less successful; there followed *Lady Hamilton* (1926); *Glückliche Reise* (Berlin, Nov. 23, 1932); *Lockende Flamme* (1933); *Herz über Bord* (1935); *Der grosse Name* (1938); etc. His last operetta was *Hochzeit mit Erika* (1949). Besides his stage works, he wrote many film scores, an overture, a piano concerto, and other instrumental compositions.

Kunsemüller, Ernst, German conductor; b. Rehme, June 24, 1885; d. (as a result of war wounds) Düsseldorf, April 25, 1918. He studied at the Univs. of Berlin and Bonn *(Dr. phil.,* 1909); then at the Cologne Cons. with Friedberg, Wölsche, and Steinbach; from 1910-12, conducted an a cappella chorus at Neuss; in 1912, became conductor of the 'Verein der Musikfreunde' and 'Gesangverein' in Kiel; in 1914, appointed musical director at the Univ. of Kiel. He wrote a serenade for small orch., 2 piano sonatas, choruses, songs, etc.

Kuntze, Karl, German composer; b. Trier, May 17, 1817; d. Delitzsch, Sept. 7, 1883. He studied in Berlin with A. W. Bach, Marx, and Rungenhagen; cantor and organist at Pritzwalk; then organist at Aschersleben (1858); in 1873, settled in Delitzsch, where he taught at the seminary. He is best known for his humorous male choruses *(Adam und Eva, Der Hecht im Karpfenteich, Weingalopp, Der neue Bürgermeister, Die Schwiegermutter);* also wrote an operetta, *Im Gebirge* (Dessau, 1875); motets and songs for mixed chorus; organ pieces; etc. He edited the 3rd ed. of Seidel's *Die Orgel und ihr Bau* (1875).

Kuntzen. See **Kunzen.**

Kunwald, Ernst, Austrian conductor; b. Vienna, April 14, 1868; d. there, Dec. 12, 1939. He studied law at Vienna Univ. (*Dr. juris,* 1891); at the same time studied piano with Leschetizky and J. Epstein, and composition with H. Grädener; then at the Leipzig Cons. with Jadassohn. His first engagement as opera conductor was in Rostock (1895-97); then conducted opera in Sondershausen (1897-98), Essen (1898-1900), Halle (1900-01), Madrid (1901-02), Frankfurt (1902-05), and at Kroll's Theater in Berlin (1905-07); appointed conductor of the Berlin Philharmonic Orch. (1907-12). In 1906 he was guest conductor of the N. Y. Philharmonic Society; in 1912, became regular conductor of the Cincinnati Symph. Orch., and from 1914, also of the May Festival. He was arrested as an enemy alien on Dec. 8, 1917, but was released on bail and allowed to continue to conduct until his internment. In 1919 he went to Germany and conducted symph. concerts in Königsberg (1920-27); 1928-31, conductor of the Berlin Symph. Orch.; then returned to Vienna, where he remained until his death.

Kunz, Ernst, Swiss composer and conductor; b. Bern, June 2, 1891. He studied at the Univ. of Munich; then at the Academy of Music there; became a theater conductor in provincial towns, until he was called by Bruno Walter in 1917 to conduct at the Munich Opera. In 1919 he returned to Switzerland; from 1927, conducted various choral societies in Zürich and neighboring towns. His music is neo-Romantic in essence; the influences of Strauss and Pfitzner are particularly pronounced. He wrote the operas *Der Fächer* (1924; Zürich, 1929), *Vreneli ab em Guggisberg* (in Swiss dialect; 1935), *Die Bremer Stadtmusikanten* (1937); the oratorios *Vom irdischen Leben* (1931-49), *Christmas Oratorio* (1936), *Weisheit des Herzens* (1946), *Einkehr* (1951); 3 symphonies; several string quartets; organ works; piano pieces.

Kunz, Konrad Max, German composer; b. Schwandorf, Dec. 30, 1812; d. Munich, Aug. 3, 1875. He studied in Munich with Hartmann Stuntz; co-founder and conductor of the Munich Liedertafel. He wrote many popular male quartets (*Elstein; Odin, der Schlachtengott;* etc.); also *200 Canons for Piano;* publ. the satirical pamphlet, *Die Gründung der Moosgau-Brüderschaft Moosgrillia* (1866).

Kunzen, Adolf Karl, German pianist and organist; b. Wittenberg, Sept. 22, 1720; d. Lübeck, July, 1781. At the age of 8 he toured in Holland and England. Finally settled in Wittenberg as organist at the Marienkirche, He wrote an oratorio, a Passion, symphonies, 21 violin concertos, piano sonatas, etc. (many MSS are in the library of the Brussels Cons.).

Kunzen, Friedrich Ludwig Aemilius, composer; son of Adolf Karl Kunzen; b. Lübeck, Sept. 24, 1761; d. Copenhagen, Jan. 28, 1817. He studied music with his father, and jurisprudence at Kiel Univ. (1784-87); then settled in Copenhagen, where he taught music. He spent a few years in Berlin, and was Kapellmeister at Frankfurt and Prague; then became court conductor in Copenhagen (1795). He wrote the operas *Holger Danske* (Copenhagen, March 31, 1789); *Die Weinlese* (Frankfurt, May 3, 1793); *Hemmeligheden* (*The Secret;* Copenhagen, Nov. 22, 1796); *Dragedukken* (*The Good Fairy;* Copenhagen, March 14, 1797); *Erik Ejegod* (Copenhagen, Jan. 30, 1798); *Min Bedstemoder* (*My Grandmother;* Copenhagen, May 15, 1800); *Kærlighed paa Landet* (*Love in the Country;* Copenhagen, March 23, 1810); also wrote oratorios; overtures; sonatas; his musical style paralleled the models of Mozart and Haydn.

Kurpinski, Karol, Polish composer; b. Wloszakowice (Luschwitz), March 6, 1785; d. Warsaw, Sept. 18, 1857. He studied with his father, Marcian Kurpinski, an organist; in 1810, became a violinist at a Warsaw theater; then second conductor at the Warsaw Opera; also taught at the Warsaw Cons. He wrote the operas *Jadwiga* (Warsaw, Dec. 23, 1814), *The New Cracovians, The Castle of Czorsztyn* (Warsaw, May 11, 1819), and others; also many Polish dances. Wagner used one of his themes in his symph. overture *Polonia.* Kurpinski publ. a collection, *Historical Songs* (Warsaw, 1816).

Kurschmann. See **Curschmann.**

Kürsteiner, Jean Paul, American pianist and pedagogue; b. (of French-Swiss father and American mother) Catskill, N.Y., July 8, 1864; d. Los Angeles, March 19, 1943. He studied in Leipzig with Jadassohn and R. Hofmann; piano with Weidenbach and Teichmüller. Returning to America in 1893, he was appointed instructor of piano and theory at the Ogontz School in Philadelphia, holding this position until 1930. In 1938 he moved to Los Angeles. He wrote a number of piano pieces, of which *Invocation to Eros* became fairly well known. His works comprise 33 opus numbers. He publ. *Essays on Expert Aid to Artistic Piano Playing.*

Kurt (kŏŏrt), **Melanie,** Austrian soprano; b. Vienna, Jan. 8, 1880; d. New York, March 11, 1941. She studied piano at the Vienna Cons. (1887-94), winning the gold medal and Liszt prize; then with Leschetizky; made her début as concert pianist in Vienna in 1897; continued her pianistic career until 1900. In 1896 she had begun to take singing lessons from Fannie Mütter in Vienna, and made a successful operatic début as Elisabeth in *Tannhäuser* (Lübeck, 1902). From 1905-08 she sang in Brunswick; then (1908-12), at the Berlin Opera. She became an outstanding Wagner interpreter and appeared in London, Brussels, Milan, Budapest, etc. When the 'Deutsches Opernhaus' in Charlottenburg was opened in 1912, she was engaged as chief soprano for heroic roles. On Feb. 1, 1915, she made her début at the Metropolitan Opera House as Isolde. In 1917 she returned to Europe, living in Berlin and Vienna as singing teacher. In 1939 she settled in N. Y., where she remained until her death.

Kurth, Ernst, eminent musicologist; b. Vienna, June 1, 1886; d. Bern, Aug. 2, 1946. He studied at the Vienna Cons. with Guido Adler; received his *Dr. phil.* with the thesis *Der Stil der Opera seria von Chr. W. Gluck bis zum Orfeo* (1908), which was publ. in Adler's 'Studien zur Musikwissenschaft' (vol. 1); held various posts as teacher and conductor in Germany; then went to Bern in 1912, where he founded a Collegium Musicum; became prof. in 1927. His principal work, *Grundlagen des linearen Kontrapunkts: Bachs melodische Polyphonie* (Bern, 1917), is one of the most important and far-reaching theoretical investigations of modern times; the publication of this book exercised a profound influence on musicology, and on practical composition as well; the term 'linear counterpoint' became part of scientific nomenclature in music; a companion volume, *Romantische Harmonik und ihre Krise in Wagners Tristan* (Bern, 1920), introduced modern psychology into the analysis of Romantic music. His volume *Musikpsychologie* (Berlin, 1931) represents a synthesis of his theoretical ideas on musical perception. He also publ. a comprehensive biography of Bruckner (Berlin, 1925; 2 vols.) and several valuable studies: *Zur Ars cantus mensurabilis des Franko von Köln,* in 'Kirchenmusikalisches Jahrbuch' (1908); *Die Voraussetzungen der theoretischen Harmonik und der tonalen Darstellungssysteme* (Bern, 1913); *Zur Motivbildung Bachs,* in 'Bach Jahrbuch' (1917).—Cf. E. Bücken, *Kurth als Musiktheoretiker* in 'Melos' (vol. IV, 7/8); K. von Fischer, *In memoriam Ernst Kurth,* in the 'Musikalmanach' (Munich, 1948).

Kurtz, Edward Frampton, American violinist and composer; b. New Castle, Pa., July 31, 1881. He studied at the Univ. of Iowa (M.A.), Detroit Cons. (Mus. Bac.), and Cincinnati Cons. (M.M.); took lessons with Kunits and Ysaÿe (violin), and Clapp, Goetschius, and Kelley (composition). He occupied teaching positions at the Franklin Cons., Westminster College, Geneva College, and the Univ. of Kansas; in 1940, became head of the music dept. of Iowa State Teachers' College. He conducted the college orch. in performances of his 3 symphonies (No. 1, Waterloo, Iowa, Dec. 15, 1932; No. 2, Cedar Falls, Iowa, Feb. 12, 1939; No. 3, Cedar Falls, May 7, 1940) and his symph. poem, *The Daemon Lover* (Cedar Falls, Feb. 15, 1942). His other works include *La Charmante,* for orch. (1914); *Parthenope,* symph. poem for violin and orch. (1922); *From the West,* suite for string quartet (1928); string quartet; suite for organ; violin pieces; songs; etc.

Kurtz, Efrem, conductor; b. St. Petersburg, Nov. 7, 1900. He studied at the Univ. of Riga (1918-20); later in Berlin; graduated from the Stern Cons. in 1922. From 1921-33 he conducted ballet in Europe; 1933-42, toured with the Ballet Russe de Monte Carlo. He came to the U. S. and in 1943 was engaged as conductor of the Kansas City Philharmonic Orch., resigning in 1948 when he became conductor of the Houston Symph. Orch. (1948-54); in 1955 was appointed conductor of the Liverpool Symph. Orch.

Kurz, Selma, coloratura soprano; b. Bielitz, Silesia, Nov. 15, 1875; d. Vienna, May 10, 1933. She studied with Pless; made her first appearances at the Frankfurt Opera. In 1899 she was engaged by Mahler at the Vienna Court Opera, and remained on the roster until 1926. She made her London début at Covent Garden as Gilda (June 7, 1904), creating a profound impression; subsequently appeared in America, also with success. She was married to the famous Viennese gynecologist, Josef Halban.

Kusevitsky, Moshe, cantor; b. Smorgon, Poland, June 9, 1899. He studied in Wilna; became cantor at Warsaw in 1926, and also pursued a concert career; made his Paris début as a concert singer in 1930; then appeared several times in England; in 1934, gave concerts in Palestine; in 1938, sang in the U. S. He returned to Warsaw before the outbreak of World War II; escaped to Russia, where he remained from 1939 until 1946, and gave concerts in Leningrad, Moscow, Odessa, etc.; in 1946-47, toured in England; then settled in New York. Although his name is identical (in Russian characters) with that of Serge Koussevitzky, the two are not related.

Kusser (or **Cousser**), **Johann Sigismund,** composer; b. Pressburg, Feb. 13, 1660; d. Dublin, Nov. 1727. He received his early musical training from his father, Johann Kusser (1626-75), a minister and organist. He lived in Stuttgart as a boy; then spent 8 years in Paris (1674-82), where he became a pupil of Lully. He subsequently was in Ansbach (1682-83); then in Brunswick (1690). In 1694 he became co-director of the Hamburg Opera, but left 2 years later, and was active in Nuremberg and Augsburg as opera composer. He was again in Stuttgart from 1700-4. In 1705 he appeared in London, and after a year there, he proceeded to Dublin, where he held the posts of chapelmaster and instructor. He revisited Stuttgart briefly, but returned to Dublin, and remained there until his death. He was greatly esteemed as operatic conductor; Mattheson, in his *Volkommener Capellmeister,* holds him up as a model of efficiency. Kusser's historical significance lies in that he was the mediator between the French and the German styles of composition, and the first to use Lully's methods and forms in German instrumental music. Lully's influence is shown in Kusser's set of 6 suites for strings, *Composition de musique suivant la méthode française* (Stuttgart, 1682).—Works: operas: for Brunswick, *Julia* (1690), *Kleopatra* (1691), *Ariadne* (Feb. 15, 1692), *Andromeda* (Feb. 20, 1692), *Jason* (Sept. 1, 1692), *Narcissus* (Oct. 14, 1692), *Porus* (1693); for Hamburg, *Erindo* (1694) and *Der grossmüthige Scipio Africanus* (1694); for Stuttgart, *Der verliebte Wald* (1698) and *Erminia* (Oct. 11, 1698). 18 suites from the lost operas *Le Festin des Muses, La Cicala delle cetra d'Eunomio,* and *Apollon enjoué,* 6 operatic overtures, and several arias are extant. An aria from *Erindo* is publ. in Schering's *Geschichte der Musik in Beispielen* (No. 250). An overture was edited by Osthoff (1933).—Cf. F. Chrysander, *Die Hamburger Oper unter der Direktion von J. S. Kusser,* in the 'Allgemeine Musikalische Zeitung' (1879); Hans Scholz, *J. S. Kusser* (Munich, 1911).

Kussevitzky. See **Koussevitzky.**

Küster, Hermann, German writer on music; b. Templin, July 14, 1817; d. Herford, March 17, 1878. He studied in Berlin with A. W. Bach, Ludwig Berger, Marx, and Rungenhagen; from 1845-52, musical director at Saarbrücken; then settled in Berlin as music teacher; in 1857, became court and cathedral organist. He publ. *Über Händels Israel in Ägypten* (1854); *Populäre Vorträge über Bildung und Begründung eines musikalischen Urteils* (4 vols., 1870-77); *Methode für den Unterricht im Gesang auf höheren Schulanstalten* (1872); *Über die Formen in der Musik* (1872), etc.; also wrote 7 oratorios; orchestral music; church music; songs; etc.

Kutev, Filip, Bulgarian composer; b. Aytos, June 13, 1903. He studied in Sofia; from 1930-35 he conducted the Burgas Symph. Orch. Among his works are *Bulgarian Rhapsody* (1937); symph. poem, *Hermann* (1940); *Pastorale,* for flute and orch. (1941); cantata, *September the Ninth* (to honor the entry of the Red Army into Bulgaria in 1944); *Stalin Cantata* (1949); and a symphony (1949).

Kutzschbach, Hermann Ludwig, German conductor; b. Meissen, Aug. 30, 1875; d. Dresden, Feb. 9, 1938. He studied at the Dresden Cons. with Draeseke and others; was opera coach at various German theaters; from 1906-09, conductor of the court opera at Mannheim; then returned to Dresden, where he became conductor of the court opera (1914).

Kuula (koo'-lah), **Toivo,** Finnish composer; b. Vasa, July 7, 1883; d. Viborg, May 18, 1918. He studied at the Helsingfors Cons. with Wegelius, Järnefelt, and Sibelius (1900-8); then went to Italy, where he took courses with Bossi in Bologna; also in Paris with Labey; in 1910 he was appointed conductor of the orchestra at Uleaborg; from 1911-16, assistant conductor of the Helsingfors Orch.; then conductor of the orch. in Viborg. He was killed during a street fight, in the aftermath of the Finnish Civil War. His music is influenced by Finnish melos; his instrumental writing is expressive and colorful; to commemorate him and to cultivate his works, two societies were formed in Helsinki and Stockholm in 1948 and 1949.—Works: the cantata *Kuolemattomuuden toivo,* for baritone, chorus, and orch.; a *Stabat Mater,* for chorus, organ, and orch.; a symphony; 2 *South Ostrobothnian Suites* for orch.; *Naiads,* for soprano and orch.; *Impi and a Boyar's Son,* for soprano and orch.; incidental music to plays; a violin sonata; a piano trio; organ works; pieces for the piano; part-songs; etc. —Cf. T. Elmgreen-Heinonen and E. Roiha, *Toivo Kuula* (Helsinki, 1952).

Kuusisto, Taneli, Finnish composer; b. Helsinki, June 19, 1905. He studied at the Univ. of Helsinki, in Paris and in Leipzig; 1936-42 was assistant conductor at the Helsinki Radio; 1942-46, chorus director at the Opera there; from 1948, teaching at the Sibelius Academy. Among his works are *Jouluyö,* rhapsody for orch. (1941); *Laatokka,* a symph. ballad (1944); nocturne for cello and orch.; string quartet; violin sonata; many choruses. His music is Romantic in essence, with modal melodies and transparent harmonies; the undertone of Finnish folk music is clearly perceptible. — Cf. Sulho Ranta, *Taneli Kuusisto,* in *Suomen Säveltäjiä* (Helsinki, 1945; pp. 655-64).

Kuyper (koi'-per), **Elisabeth,** Dutch conductor and composer; b. Amsterdam, Sept. 13, 1877. She studied with Max Bruch in Berlin. From 1908-20 she taught theory at the Hochschule there; founder (1908) and conductor of the Berlin 'Tonkünstlerinnen Orch.'; in 1922 she led a few concerts of the London Women's Symph. Orch., and in 1923, conducted the New York Women's Symph. Orch.; later returned to Europe, and lived at Lago Maggiore in Brissago. She composed a symphony, a violin concerto, several violin sonatas, a ballade for cello and piano, a piano trio, songs.

Küzdö, Victor, violinist and teacher; b. Budapest, Sept. 18, 1869. He studied at the Budapest Cons. with Karl Huber; made his début there in 1882; toured in Europe, and visited the U. S. in 1884 and 1887. In 1894 he settled in New York; from 1918-31, taught at the summer school of Chicago Musical College; in 1932, settled in Glendale, Calif. He became totally blind in 1950. He publ. *Serenade* and *Witches' Dances* for violin.

Kuznetzov, Konstantin Alexeyevitch, Russian musicologist; b. Novotcherkassk, Sept. 21, 1883; d. Moscow, July, 1953. He studied at the Univ. of Heidelberg (*Dr. phil.,* 1906); was instructor at the Univ. of Moscow (1912-14); prof. at the Univ. of Odessa (1914-20); in 1921, returned to Moscow, where he remained until his death. An erudite musician, he wrote on music history from a broad sociological standpoint; publ. *Introduction to the History of Music* (Moscow, 1923); *Glinka and His Epoch* (Moscow, 1927); edited several publications for the Musicological Institute of Moscow.

Kvapil (kvah'-pēl), **Jaroslav,** Czech composer; b. Fryšták, April 21, 1892. He studied with Janáček in Brno and at the Leipzig Cons. with Teichmüller (piano) and Max Reger (composition). He was in the Austrian army during World War I; in 1919 he was appointed prof. of piano and theory at the Brno Cons.; also was musical director of the Philharmonic Society of Brno for 25 years (1920-45), performing many choral masterpieces. In 1946 he became prof. of composition at the Janáček Academy of Music in Brno. His works show the double influence of Janáček's national and rhapsodic style and Max Reger's strong polyphonic idiom. Among them are an opera, *Romance in May* (Prague, May 12, 1950); oratorio, *The Lion's Heart* (Brno, Dec. 7, 1931); 4 symphonies (1913; 1921; 1937; 1945); *Slavonic Overture* (1944); symph. poem, *Daybreak* (1949); violin concerto (Brno, March 6, 1928); *Burlesque,* for flute and orch. (1945); piano quintet (1915); quintet for brass (1925); quartet for flute, violin, viola, and cello (1948); 5 string quartets; 3 violin sonatas; cello sonata; 3 piano sonatas; several song cycles; many transcriptions of folksongs; a piano album of 100 folksongs from Moravian Slovakia (1914).—Cf. L. Kundera, *Jaroslav Kvapil* (Prague, 1944).

Kwalwasser, Helen, American violinist; daughter of Jacob Kwalwasser; b. Syracuse, Oct. 11, 1927. She showed a gift for violin playing at an early age; studied with Louis Persinger (1936-39), with Zimbalist at the Curtis Institute of Music in Philadelphia (1939-41), then with Galamian (1941-48); made her début in N. Y. on March 25, 1947; then toured Europe (1949); returning to N. Y., was active as violinist and teacher.

Kwalwasser, Jacob, music psychologist and educator; b. New York, Feb. 27, 1894; studied at the Univ. of Pittsburgh and the Univ. of Iowa, obtaining his Ph.D. in 1926; taught in the public schools in Pittsburgh (1918-23); head of public school music at the Univ. of Iowa (1923-26); in 1926, was appointed prof. and head of the dept. of music education at Syracuse Univ. He is the co-author of the well-known Kwalwasser-Dykema Music Tests; publ. a manual on the subject in 1913; also collaborated in establishing the Kwalwasser-Ruch Musical Accomplishment Test, and various other melodic, harmonic, and instrumental tests; publ. numerous magazine articles on music education—Publications: *Tests and*

Measurements in Music (1927; an influential code of rules, adopted in many educational institutions); *Problems in Public School Music* (1932; rev. ed., 1941; treats objectives of music education); *Exploring the Musical Mind* (N. Y., 1955).

Kwast, James, famous pianist and teacher; b. Nijkerk, Holland, Nov. 23, 1852; d. Berlin, Oct. 31, 1927. He studied with his father and Ferdinand Böhme; later with Reinecke and Richter at the Leipzig Cons.; also with Th. Kullak and Wüerst at Berlin, and with Brassin and Gevaert at Brussels. In 1874 he became instructor at the Cons. of Cologne; from 1883 till 1903 he taught at the Hoch Cons. in Frankfurt; from 1903-6, at the Klindworth-Scharwenka Cons. in Berlin; then at Stern's Cons. there. He was greatly esteemed by his colleagues and students as a piano pedagogue; many well-known pianists were his pupils at Frankfurt and Berlin. His first wife, Antonia (d. Stuttgart, Feb. 10, 1931), was a daughter of Ferdinand Hiller; his second wife, Frieda Hodapp-Kwast (b. Bargen, Aug. 13, 1880; d. Bad Wiessee, Sept. 14, 1949), was a concert pianist. He wrote a piano concerto and other piano music; edited works of Handel and Clementi for the 'Tonmeister' edition.

L

Labarre, Théodore, eminent French harpist; b. Paris, March 5, 1805; d. there, March 9, 1870. He studied privately with Cousineau, Boscha, and Naderman; then at the Paris Cons. with Dourlen, Eler, Fétis, and Boieldieu. From 1824-47 he lived alternately in London and Paris; became conductor of the Opéra-Comique; in 1851, was appointed conductor of Louis Napoleon's private orchestra; in 1867, prof. of harp at the Paris Cons. He wrote 4 operas, 5 ballets, numerous pieces for the harp, songs, etc.; also a *Méthode complète* for harp.

La Bassée, Adam de, medieval poet and composer; b. La Bassée; d. Lille, Feb. 25, 1286. He was an ecclesiastic at Lille; wrote religious songs, using sacred and secular melodies, adapting them to his own words; reprinted in facsimile by Abbé D. Charnel in the 'Messager des sciences historiques' (Ghent, 1858).

Labatt, Leonard, Swedish tenor; b. Stockholm, Dec. 4, 1838; d. there, March 7, 1897. He studied with J. Günther; then with Masset in Paris; made his début in Stockholm as Tamino in *Die Zauberflöte* (1866); in 1868-69 was at the Dresden Opera; from 1869 till 1883 at the Vienna Opera; sang in London in 1881; made an American tour in 1888-89. He was especially fine in Wagnerian roles.—Cf. F. Hedberg, *Svenska opera-sängare* (Stockholm, 1885).

L'Abbé, Joseph Barnabé Saint-Sevin (real name Saint-Sevin), French violinist and composer; b. Agen, June 11, 1727; d. Paris, July 20, 1803. A precocious musician, he began his study with his father, and became a member of the orchestra of the Comédie-Française at the age of 12; then studied with Leclair; was violinist at the Opéra (1742-62); also played at the Concert Spirituel (1741-55); devoted his later years to teaching and composition. He had an excellent violin technique, and was an innovator in that he wrote out cadenzas in full.—Works: 2 books of violin sonatas with continuo (1748-64), symphonies for 3 violins and continuo (c. 1754), 5 collections of airs arranged for 1 and 2 violins, and a manual, *Les Principes du violon* (1761).—Cf. L. de la Laurencie, *L'École française de violon de Lully à Viotti* (vol. 2, Paris, 1923).

Labey, Marcel, French conductor and composer; b. Le Vesinet, Seine-et-Oise, Aug. 6, 1875. He studied law in Paris, receiving his degree in 1898; then turned his attention to music, studying piano with Delaborde, harmony with Lenormand, and composition with Vincent d'Indy at the Schola Cantorum; taught piano there, and at d'Indy's death in 1931, became vice-principal of the school. His works include an opera, *Bérengère* (1912; Le Havre, April 12, 1929); 3 symphonies (1903; 1908; 1934); *Suite champêtre* for orch. (1923); *Ouverture pour un drame* (Paris, Jan. 22, 1921); a piano sonata; a viola sonata; 2 violin sonatas; a string quartet; a piano trio; a piano quartet; a piano quintet; songs; etc. He publ. piano arrangements of several orchestral works of d'Indy (Symph. in B♭, *Jour d'été à la montagne,* etc.).

Labia (lah'-byah), **Fausta,** Italian opera singer; sister of Maria Labia; b. Verona, April 3, 1870; d. Rome, Oct. 6, 1935. She became a great favorite in Sweden, but retired at the age of 25, after her marriage. She then lived many years in Rome and taught at the Santa Cecilia. Her method, *L'Arte del respiro nello recitazione e nel canto,* was publ. posthumously in 1936.

Labia, Maria, Italian soprano; sister of Fausta Labia; b. Verona, Feb. 14, 1880. She received her musical education from her mother, an excellent amateur singer; made her operatic début in Stockholm on May 19, 1905 as Mimi. From 1906-08 she was on the roster of the Komische Oper in Berlin. She was then engaged by the Manhattan Opera Co., where she first appeared on Nov. 9, 1908, as Tosca. After the demise of that company she joined the Vienna Opera; then taught voice at the Music Academy of Siena. She was an actress of great emotional power, and was particularly successful in such dramatic roles as Carmen, Santuzza, Nedda, and Violetta.

Labitzky, August, German violinist and conductor; son of Joseph Labitzky; b. Bečov (Petschau), Oct. 22, 1832; d. Reichenhall, Aug. 28, 1903. He studied at the Prague Cons., and with Ferdinand David and Hauptmann in Leipzig. He became conductor of the Karlsbad resort orch. in 1853; composed piano pieces, etc.

Labitzky, Joseph, German dance composer and violinist; father of August Labitzky; b. Schönfeld, Eger, July 4, 1802; d. Karlsbad, Aug. 18, 1881. He studied with Veit in Bečov (Petschau); in 1820, joined the orchestra in Marienbad as 1st violinist; then occupied a similar post in Karlsbad; organized his own orchestra and toured southern Germany. He studied with Winter in Munich, where he publ. his first dances (1827); returning to Karlsbad in 1835, he organized an orchestra and toured Europe. Many of his waltzes, galops, quadrilles, etc. (about 300 opus numbers) enjoyed a great vogue.

Lablache, Luigi, Italian bass singer of French and Irish descent; b. Naples, Dec. 6, 1794; d. there, Jan. 23, 1858. He studied voice with Valesi at the Naples Cons. della Pietà dei Turchini; at 18 he commenced his career there, as a *basso buffo*. In 1812 he married Teresa Pinotti, the daughter of an actor. In 1813 he went to Palermo as *primo basso cantante;* then appeared at La Scala in Milan; made his début in London as Geronimo in *Il Matrimonio Segreto* (March 30, 1830), with instantaneous success; in Paris, in the same role on Nov. 4, 1830. From 1836-37 Lablache lived in England as singing master to Queen Victoria. He also sang in Naples, Vienna, and St. Petersburg, always winning acclaim. He was greatly esteemed by his contemporaries; Schubert dedicated to him his 3 Italian songs (1827).—Cf. F. H. J. Castil-Blaze, *Biographie de Lablache* (Paris, 1850); G. Widén, *Luigi Lablache* (Göteborg, 1897).

Labor, Josef, Austrian pianist, organist, and composer; b. Horowitz, June 29, 1842; d. Vienna, April 26, 1924. He lost his sight as a youth; studied with Sechter at the Vienna Cons.; in 1863, was tutor to the princesses of Hanover, who were living then in exile with their family in Vienna. He played in London (1865), Paris, and in Russia; in 1868, returned to Vienna, where he settled as a teacher; among his students were Julius Bittner and Arnold Schoenberg. He wrote several sonatas; a piano quartet; pieces for organ and for piano; church music; songs, etc.; also edited Biber's violin sonatas for the 'Denkmäler der Tonkunst in Österreich.'

La Borde, Jean Benjamin de, French violinist and composer; b. Paris, Sept. 5, 1734; d. there (on the guillotine), July 22, 1794. He studied violin with Dauvergne and composition with Rameau; was chamberlain to Louis XV, and a member of the Compagnie des Fermiers-Généraux; then withdrew from the court and devoted himself to composition. He wrote 32 operas, and songs; also an *Essai sur la musique ancienne et moderne,* containing an early study of folksongs (1780); *Recueils de chansons avec un accompagnement de violon et la basse continue; Choix de chansons mises en musique* (4 vols., 1773); *Mémoires historiques sur Raoul de Coucy* (1781).—Cf. Jacques Devisme, *J. B. de La Borde, un favori des dieux* (Paris, 1936).

Labroca, Mario, Italian composer; b. Rome, Nov. 22, 1896. He was a composition pupil of Malipiero and Respighi and graduated from the Parma Cons. in 1921. From 1935-43 he was in charge of the important annual festival, Maggio Musicale Fiorentino. His compositions include the following: 2 operas, *La Principessa di Perepepè* (Rome, Dec. 11, 1927) and *Le tre figliuole di Pinco Pallino* (Rome, Jan. 27, 1928); a Stabat Mater for soprano, mixed chorus, and orch. (Rome, Dec. 15, 1935); symphony (1934); *Sinfonia* for string orch. (1927); 2 string quartets (1925 and 1934); a piano trio (1925); suite for viola and piano (1926); *Tre cantate dalla Passione secondo San Giovanni* (1950).

Labunski, Felix, composer and teacher; b. Ksawerynowo, Poland, Dec. 27, 1892. He studied at the Warsaw Cons. with Maliszewski and Marczewski, then in Paris with Nadia Boulanger and Paul Dukas. In 1927, in collaboration with Czapski, Perkowski, and Wiechowicz, he founded the 'Association of Young Polish Musicians in Paris.' In 1934-36 he was director of the classical music dept. of the Polish Radio in Warsaw; in 1936, came to America; was naturalized in 1941; in 1945 joined the staff of the College of Music of Cincinnati as teacher of composition, remaining in that post when the College merged with the Cons. of Music of Cincinnati in 1955. In 1948 he initiated the Mid-West Symposium for Student Composers there; in 1951, was given an honorary degree of Doctor of Music, Chicago Musical College. —Works: *Triptyque champêtre,* suite for orch. (Warsaw, 1931); *The Birds,* for soprano and orch. (Luxembourg, 1934); *Divertimento* for flute and piano (Paris, 1936); *Polish Cantata* (Warsaw, 1936); suite for string orch. (Festival of the International Society for Contemporary Music, Berkeley, Calif., Aug. 2, 1942); *Song Without Words,* for soprano and string quintet (Cincinnati, 1946); *There Is No Death,* cantata for mixed chorus and orch. (Cincinnati, 1950); *Variations for Orchestra* (Cincinnati, 1951); symph. in B minor (1954); *3 Bagatelles,* for flute, oboe, clarinet, and bassoon (1955); *Elegy* for orch. (Cincinnati, Dec. 11, 1955); *Images of Youth,* cantata for mezzo-soprano, baritone, and children's chorus (Cincinnati May Festival, May 11, 1956); *Xavieriana,* fantasy for 2 pianos and orch., for the 125th anniversary of Xavier Univ. (1956); a string quartet; 2 piano sonatas; many other piano pieces. He is a brother of Wiktor Labunski.

Labunski, Wiktor, pianist and composer; brother of Felix Labunski; b. St. Petersburg, April 14, 1895. He studied at the St. Petersburg Cons. with Nikolayev (piano), Kalafati and Vitols (composition); later, piano with Felix Blumenfeld and Safonov, and conducting with Emil Mlynarski. From 1919 till 1928 he was head of the piano dept. at the Cons. of Cracow; then came to the U. S.; made his début in 1928 as a pianist at Carnegie Hall, N. Y.; played recitals throughout the U. S.; was instructor at the Nashville Cons. (1928-31); prof. and director of the Memphis, Tenn., College of Music (1931-37); in 1937, appointed prof. and director of the Cons. of Music of Kansas City. In 1920 he married Wanda Mlynarska, daughter of his teacher Emil Mlynarski. —Works: symph. in G minor (1936; 2nd movement only, Kansas City, composer conducting, Aug. 18, 1940); concerto for piano and orch. in 3 movements: *Krakowiak, Nocturne, Mazurek* (Kansas City, Feb. 16, 1939, composer soloist); *Variations* for piano and orch. (Kansas City, 1945); concerto for 2 pianos and orch. (Kansas City, May 31, 1957); many piano pieces (*Impromptu, Minuet, 4 Variations on a Theme by Paganini, Reminiscence,* etc.).

Laccetti (lah-tcheht'-tē), **Guido,** Italian singer and composer; b. Naples, Oct. 1, 1879; d. Cava dei Tirreni, Oct. 9, 1945. He studied at the Cons. of Naples; from 1925 taught at the Palermo Cons. His works include the operas *La contessa di San Remo* (1904), *Hoffmann* (Naples, 1912), *Il miracolo* (Naples, 1915), *Carnasciali* (Rome, 1925), and *La favola dei gobbi* (1935).

Lacerda, Francisco de, Portuguese conductor and musicologist; b. Ribeira Seca, S. Jorge, Azores, May 11, 1869; d. Lisbon, July 18, 1934. He studied at the Lisbon Cons.; received a government stipend for study in Paris, where he took a course with Vincent d'Indy at the Schola Cantorum. In Paris he associated himself with Bourgault-Ducoudray and worked with him in the International Folklore Association; also conducted concerts. At the outbreak of World War I he returned to Portugal; in 1913 he organized the Orquestra Filarmonica in Lisbon. He compiled the important *Cancioneiro musical portugues,* containing some 500 folksongs; wrote a number of original compositions, among them the symph. works, *Adamastor, Almorol, Rapsodia insular,* etc.—Cf. A. Pinto, *Musica Moderna Portuguesa* (Lisbon, 1930; pp. 70-73).

Lach, Robert, Austrian musicologist and composer; b. Vienna, Jan. 29, 1874. He was a pupil of R. Fuchs at the Vienna Cons. (1893-99); also studied philosophy and musicology with Wallaschek, Rietsch, and Adler; *Dr. phil.,* Prague, 1902. After some years of research and study, he publ. *Studien zur Entwicklungsgeschichte der ornamentalen Melopöie* (Leipzig, 1913), viewing the entire field of musical history in the light of new discoveries of ethnographic investigation. From 1911-20 he was chief of the music division of the Vienna State Library; in 1915, joined the faculty of Vienna Univ. He recorded for the Phonogram Archives of Vienna the songs of Russian prisoners of World War I (with particular emphasis on Asian and Caucasian nationalities) and publ. numerous papers on these melodies. He was pensioned in 1939, and lived in Vienna in retirement, devoting his time to the compilation of oriental glossaries (Babylonian, Sumerian, Egyptian, etc.). The dedicatory brochure, *Robert Lach, Persönlichkeit und Werk, zum 80. Geburtstag* (Vienna, 1954), contains a complete list of his works and scientific writings. His publications include *Mozart als Theoretiker,* in 'Sitzungsberichte der Akademie' (1918); *Ge-*

sänge russischer Kriegsgefangener, ibid. (1926-52); *Zur Geschichte des musikalischen Zunftwesens,* ibid. (1923); *Die vergleichende Musikwissenschaft,* ibid. (1924); *Das Konstruktionsprinzip der Wiederholung in Musik, Sprache und Literatur,* ibid. (1925); *Vergleichende Kunst- und Musikwissenschaft,* ibid.; *Die Bruckner-Akten des Wiener Univs.-Archivs* (1926); *Gregorianische Choral und vergleichende Musikwissenschaft,* in 'Peter Wagner-Festschrift' (1926); *Geschichte der Wiener Staatsakademie für Musik* (1927); *Musik der Exoten,* in Adler's 'Handbuch'; *Das Ethos in der Musik Schuberts* (1928); *Die musikalische Konstruktionsprinzipien der altmexikanischen Tempelgesänge,* in 'Johannes Wolf-Festschrift' (1929); *Das Ethos in der Musik von J. Brahms,* in the 'Simrock-Jahrbuch' (1930); numerous other essays; also philosophical poems and mystery plays. His list of musical works attains 150 opus numbers, among them 10 symphonies; 25 string quartets; 14 string quintets; 7 string sextets; septet, octet, nonet, and decet; trios; sonatas; cantatas; 8 Masses; etc.

Lachmann, Robert, noted musicologist; b. Berlin, Nov. 28, 1892; d. Jerusalem, May 8, 1939. He studied languages in Berlin and London; served in the German army during World War I, when he began to collect folk melodies from the African and Indian war prisoners; later studied musicology with Stumpf and Johannes Wolf, and Arabic with Mittwoch at Berlin Univ.; received his Ph.D. (1922) with the thesis *Die Musik in den tunisischen Städten,* publ. in the 'Archiv für Musikwissenschaft' (1923). He was librarian of the music division of the Prussian State Library from 1927 until 1933, when he was ousted. In 1935 he went to Jerusalem, where he worked at the Hebrew Univ. His writings include the papers *Musik und Tonschrift des No,* in 'Kongress-Bericht' of the Deutsche Musik-Gesellschaft (1925); *Zur aussereuropäischen Mehrstimmigkeit,* in the 'Beethoven Centennial Report' (Vienna, 1927); a book, *Musik des Orients* (Breslau, 1929); *Die Musik der aussereuropäischen Natur- und Kulturvölker,* in Bücken's 'Handbuch' series (1929); *Jewish Cantillation and Song in the Isle of Djerba* (Jerusalem, 1940; publ. posthumously).

Lachmund, Carl Valentine, American pianist and teacher; b. Booneville, Mo., March 27, 1857; d. Yonkers, N. Y., Feb. 20, 1928. He studied at the Cologne Cons. with Hiller, and later with Liszt, of whom he was one of the last pupils (1881-84); taught at the Scharwenka Cons. in Berlin, and appeared as pianist, touring America with August Wilhelmj in 1880. Settling in New York in 1891, he established his own conservatory. He also founded the Women's String Orch., which he directed for 12 seasons.

Lachner, Franz, German composer and conductor; brother of Ignaz and Vincenz Lachner; b. Rain-on-Lech, April 2, 1803; d. Munich, Jan. 20, 1890. He studied with Sechter and Stadler in Vienna; became an intimate friend of Schubert; from 1827-34, conductor of the Kärnthnertor Theater in Vienna; in 1834, became conductor of the Mannheim Opera; in 1836, court conductor in Munich, then general music director (1852-65). A prolific composer, his works include 2 oratorios, *Moses* and *Die vier Menschenalter;* 4 operas, *Die Bürgschaft* (Pest, 1828), *Alidia* (Munich, 1839), *Catarina Cornaro* (Munich, Dec. 3, 1841), *Benvenuto Cellini* (Munich, 1849); 8 symphonies; a Requiem; Masses; choral works; much chamber music; piano pieces; songs; also an orchestration of Schubert's *Song of Miriam.*—Cf. O. Kronseder, *Franz Lachner,* in 'Altbayrische Monatsschrift' (vol. 4; contains a complete catalogue of works); M. von Schwind, *Die Lachner-Rolle* (Munich, 1904); A. Würz, *Franz Lachner als dramatischer Komponist* (Munich, 1927).

Lachner, Ignaz, German organist, conductor, and composer; brother of Franz and Vincenz Lachner; b. Rain-on-Lech, Sept. 11, 1807; d. Hanover, Feb. 24, 1895. He studied music with his father; in 1824, joined Franz in Vienna, where he became an assistant conductor at the Kärnthnertor Theater (1825). In 1831 he went to Stuttgart as court music director; in 1842, occupied a similar post in Munich; conductor at the theater in Hamburg (1853); in 1858, became court conductor in Stockholm; in 1861, settled in Frankfurt, as musical director.—Works: 3 operas: *Der Geisterturm* (Stuttgart, 1837), *Die Regenbrüder* (Stuttgart, May 20, 1939), *Loreley* (Munich, 1846); several 'Singspiele,' among them the popular *Letzte Fensterle;* ballets; melodramas; symphonies; chamber music; Masses; piano compositions; violin pieces; etc.

Lachner, Vincenz, German organist, conductor, and composer; brother of Franz and Ignaz Lachner; b. Rain-on-Lech, July 19, 1811; d. Karlsruhe, Jan. 22, 1893. He first studied with his father, and later in Vienna with his brothers, succeeding Ignaz as organist there in 1834, and Franz as court Kapellmeister at Mannheim in 1836. He conducted the German opera in London in 1842, and the municipal opera in Frankfurt in 1848. In 1873 he received a pension and settled in Karlsruhe, joining the faculty of the Cons. there in 1884. His 4-part male choruses are celebrated, particularly his settings of nearly all of Scheffel's songs, among the best being *Alt Heidelberg, du feine; Im schwarzen Wallfisch; Nun grüss' dich Gott;* also wrote symphonies, overtures, string quartets, a piano quartet, numerous songs, etc.

Lachnith, Ludwig Wenzel, Bohemian horn player and composer; b. Prague, July 7, 1746; d. Paris, Oct. 3, 1820. He was a member of the court orch. in Pfalz-Zweibrücken; in 1773, went to Paris and studied with Rudolph (horn) and Philidor (composition). He is known chiefly as a composer of pasticcios, using the music of several composers in one piece. His 'arrangement' of the music and libretto of Mozart's *Zauberflöte,* appearing under the title *Les Mystères d'Isis,* was justly parodied as *Les Misères d'ici.* In several of his ventures he had the older Kalkbrenner as his collaborator. Original compositions by Lachnith include the operas *L'Heureuse Réconciliation* (1785), *L'Antiquaire* (1789), and *Eugénie et Linval* (1798); 3 piano concertos; chamber music.

Lack, Théodore, French pianist and composer; b. Quimper, Finisterre, Sept. 3, 1846; d. Paris, Nov. 25, 1921. A precocious musician, Lack was appointed organist of his village church when he was only 10 years old. He entered the Paris Cons. at 14, where he studied piano with Marmontel, harmony with Bazin, and theory with Lefébure-Wély. Graduating from the Conservatory at 18, he became piano instructor there, and held this position for 57 years (1864-1921) until his death, without ever leaving Paris. He wrote a great many salon pieces for piano *(Tarentelle, Boléro, Études élégantes, Valse espagnole, Scènes enfantines, Souvenir d'Alsace, Polonaise de concert,* etc.).

Lacombe (lah-kŏhnb), **Louis (Brouillon),** French pianist and composer; b. Bourges, Nov. 26, 1818; d. Saint-Vaast-la-Hougue, Sept. 30, 1884. He studied at the Paris Cons. with Zimmermann, winning the 1st piano prize at the age of 13. After touring through France, Belgium, and Germany, he took courses with Czerny, Sechter, and Seyfried in Vienna. Following another concert tour, he settled in Paris (1839), concentrating on composition. —Works: a melodrama, *L'Amour* (Paris, Dec. 2, 1859); a one-act opera, *La Madone* (Paris, Jan. 16, 1861); a 2-act comic opera, *Le Tonnelier* (perf. as *Meister Martin und seine Gesellen* at Coblenz, March 7, 1897); a 4-act grand opera, *Winkelried* (Geneva, Feb. 17, 1892); the cantata *Sapho* (1878; won a prize at the Paris Exhibition); a grand *Épopée lyrique* for orch.; 2 dramatic symphonies with soli and chorus: *Manfred* (1847) and *Arva ou les Hongrois* (1850); *Lassan et Friss,* Hungarian fantasy for orch.; *Au tombeau d'un Héros,* elegy for violin and orch.; a quintet for piano, violin, cello, oboe, and bassoon; 2 piano trios; numerous piano pieces *(Études en octaves; Six romances sans paroles;* etc.); also choruses a cappella and with organ, etc. His essay on *Philosophie et musique* was publ. posthumously (Paris, 1895). —Cf. E. Bourdin, *Louis Lacombe* (Paris, 1882); H. Boyer, *Louis Lacombe et son œuvre* (Paris, 1888); L. Gallet, *Conférence sur Louis Lacombe et son œuvre* (Paris, 1891).

Lacombe, Paul, French composer; b. Carcassonne, Aude, July 11, 1837; d. there, June 5, 1927. He studied in Carcassonne with François Teysserre, an organist. He was a prolific composer; his works total more than 150, including an *Ouverture symphonique* (1876); 3 symphonies (Symph. No. 3 won the prize of the Société des Compositeurs de Musique, 1886); *Suite pastorale* for orch.; *Marche dernière,* for orch.; *Scène au camp* for orch.; *Dialogue sentimental,* for flute, bassoon, and piano (1917); 3 violin sonatas; a cello sonata; 3 trios; a string quartet; a Mass; a Requiem; songs; characteristic piano pieces (*Aubade aux mariés, Arabesques,* etc.).—Cf. Léon Moulin, *Paul Lacombe et son œuvre* (Paris, 1924).

Lacome (lah-kohm'), **Paul (Paul-Jean-Jacques Lacome de l'Estalenx),** French composer; b. Houga, Gers, March 4, 1838; d. there, Dec. 12, 1920. In 1860 he went to Paris; became known as a composer of operettas, including *Jeanne, Jeannette et Jeannot* (1876); *Le Beau Nicolas* (1880); *Madame Boniface* (1883); *Myrtille* (1885); *Ma mie Rosette* (1890); *Le Cadeau de noces* (1893); *La Bain de Monsieur* (1895); *Le Maréchal Chaudron* (1898); and *Les quatre filles Aymon* (1898); also the orchestral suites *Clair de lune, Suite ancienne, La Verbena;* quartets; trios; psalms; piano pieces *(Les Succès de famille,* etc.); over 200 songs *(L'Estudiantina,* etc.). He publ. *Introduction à la vie musicale* (1911).

Ladmirault (lahd-mē-roh'), **Paul-Émile,** French composer; b. Nantes, Dec. 8, 1877; d. Kerbili, near Penestin (Morbihan), Oct. 30,

1944. As a child, he studied piano, organ, and violin; entered the Nantes Cons. in 1892, winning 1st prize in 1893; he was only 15 when his 3-act opera *Gilles de Retz* was staged in Nantes (May 18, 1893); he entered the Paris Cons. in 1895, studying with Gedalge and Fauré; subsequently returned to Nantes, where he taught at the Cons. His *Suite bretonne* (1902-03) and symph. prelude *Brocéliande au matin* (Colonne concert, Nov. 28, 1909) were extracts from a second opera, *Myrdhin* (1902-09), which was never performed; the ballet *La Prêtresse de Koridwen* was produced at the Paris Opéra (Dec. 17, 1926). Other works include the operetta *Glycère* (Paris, 1928); a symphony (1910); *La Brière,* for orch. (Paris, Nov. 20, 1926); *La Jeunesse de Cervantes,* for orch.; *En forêt,* symph. poem (1932); incidental music to *Tristan et Iseult* (1929); *Printemps,* for women's voices and piano; *Dominical,* for soprano, alto, tenor, and bass with piano (1911); *Valse triste,* for piano and orch.; sacred music: *Offertoire* (1893), *Ave Maria* (1893), *Tota pulchra es* (1899), *Tantum ergo* (1904), *Messe brève* (1937); *Airs anciens,* for tenor, string quartet, and piano (1897); *Ballet bohémien,* for flute, oboe, double string quartet and piano (1898); *Fantaisie* for violin and piano (1899); *Chanson grecque* for flute and piano (1900); violin sonata (1901); *De l'ombre à la clarté,* for violin and piano (1936); clarinet sonata; piano pieces; songs; many arrangements of Breton folksongs, etc. He also contributed articles on music to various periodicals.—Cf. Claude Debussy, *Paul-Emile Ladmirault,* in 'Gil Blas' (March 9, 1903); Octave Séré, *Musiciens français d'aujourd'hui* (Paris, 1922).

Ladunka, Naum Ivanovitch, Russian composer; b. Dec. 13, 1730; d. St. Petersburg, Aug. 2, 1782. One of the few secular Russian composers of the 18th century, he is chiefly known for his arrangements of many Russian folksongs.

Ladurner, Ignaz Anton Franz Xaver, Austrian composer; b. Aldein, Tyrol, Aug. 1, 1766; d. Massy, Seine-et-Oise, March 4, 1839. He studied at the monastery of Benediktbeuren, succeeding his father as organist there (1782-84); studied in Munich under the patronage of Countess Heimhausen. In 1788 he settled in Paris, teaching at the Cons. there; Auber was one of his students. He wrote 2 operas, *Wenzel, ou Le Magistrat du peuple* (Paris, 1794) and *Les Vieux Fous* (Paris, 1796); 12 piano sonatas; 6 violin sonatas; a sonata for piano 4 hands; variations; divertissements; etc.

La Fage (lah-fahzh'), **Juste-Adrien-Lenoir de,** eminent French writer on music; b. Paris, March 30, 1801; d. Charenton, March 8, 1862. He studied in Paris with Perne and Choron, and in Rome with Baini. In 1829 he was maître de chapelle at St.-Étienne-du-Mont, Paris; then traveled again to Italy and also to Germany, Spain, and England. Returning to Paris, he became an important writer on ancient music. In 1859 he founded the periodical 'Le Plain-chant.' La Fage suffered from a nervous disorder in his later years, and ended his life at the Charenton Insane Asylum. —Writings: *Manuel complet de musique vocale et instrumentale* (6 vols.; 1836-38; elaborated from Choron's sketches and notes); *Séméiologie musicale,* elements of music after Choron's principles (1837; an epitome was also publ. in 1837, as *Principes élémentaires de musique); De la chanson considérée sous le rapport musical* (1840); *Histoire générale de la musique et de la danse* (2 vols.; 1844; incomplete); *Miscellanées musicales,* sketches of Bellini, Haydn, and others (1844); also sketches of Zingarelli, Mattei, Choron, Bocquillon-Wilhem, Baini, Donizetti; *Nicolai Capuani presbyteri compendium musicale* (1853); *De l'unité tonique et de la fixation d'un diapason universel* (1859); *Essais de diphthérographie musicale* (1864; a very valuable collection of source material); many works on plainsong: *De la réproduction des livres de plain-chant romain* (1853); *Lettre écrite à l'occasion d'un mémoire pour servir à la restauration du chant romain en France, par l'abbé Celeste Alix* (1853); *Cours complet de plain-chant* (2 vols.; 1855-56; an important manual); *Nouveau traité de plain-chant* (1859; a supplement to the former); *Routine pour accompagner le plain-chant; Extraits du catalogue critique et raisonné d'une petite bibliothèque musicale,* etc. La Fage was also a composer; wrote fantasias and variations for flute, and some sacred music. —Cf. R. D. Denne-Baron, *La Fage* (Paris, 1863).

L'Affilard, Michel, French 17th- and 18th-century composer. He was a singer at the Sainte-Chapelle in 1679, and at the royal chapel (1696-1709). His major work is a book on sight singing, *Principes très faciles, pour bien apprendre la musique* (Paris, 1691; Amsterdam, 1717), which is notable because the tempo of the airs is indicated according to a pendulum, thus anticipating the use of a metronome. Some of L'Affilard's airs may be found in Ballard's collections; some MSS are in the Versailles Library. —Cf. M. Brenet, *Les Musiciens de la Sainte-Chapelle du Palais* (Paris, 1910).

Lafont, Charles-Philippe, French violinist and composer; b. Paris, Dec. 1, 1781; d. Tarbes, Aug. 14, 1839. He received his first violin instruction from his mother; then studied in Paris with Kreutzer and Rode. From 1801-08 he toured Europe; then became Rode's successor at the Russian court in St. Petersburg (1808); returned to Paris in 1815 as solo violinist to Louis XVIII. He engaged in a violin-playing debate with Paganini in Milan (1816). During an extended tour with the pianist Henri Herz, beginning in 1831, Lafont was killed in a carriage accident in southern France. He wrote 7 violin concertos; fantasias, variations, etc., for violin with various instrumental groups; about 200 *romances* for voice; and 2 comic operas.

La Forge (lah-fohrzh'), **Frank,** American pianist, teacher, and composer; b. Rockford, Ill., Oct. 22, 1879; d. New York, May 5, 1953. He studied piano with Leschetizky in Vienna; toured Germany, France, Russia, and the U.S. as accompanist to Marcella Sembrich (1908-18), and to Schumann-Heink (1919). In 1920 he settled in New York as voice teacher; among his students were Lawrence Tibbett, Marian Anderson, Lucrezia Bori, and Richard Crooks. He died while playing the piano at a dinner given by the Musicians Club in N. Y. He wrote many effective songs *(To a violet, Retreat, Come unto these yellow sands, My love and I, To a messenger, I came with a song, Before the crucifix,* etc.) and piano pieces *(Gavotte and Musette, Valse de Concert, Improvisations,* etc.).

Lagoanère (lah-gwah-när'), **Oscar de,** French composer; b. Bordeaux, Aug. 25, 1853; d. Paris, May 23, 1918. He studied at the Paris Cons. with Marmontel, Duprato, and Savard. From 1876-1908 he conducted operettas at various theaters in Paris; from 1908-14, administrator and director of music at the Théâtre de la Gaité. He was a prolific composer of operettas, the most successful of which were *Le Cadeau d'Alain* (Paris, Sept. 14, 1902), *L'Habit de César* (Paris, May 14, 1906), *Amour et sport* (Paris, July 28, 1907). *Un Ménage au violon;* also piano pieces and songs.

La Guerre, Elisabeth Jacquet de, French composer, organist, and clavecinist; b. Paris, 1659; d. there, June 27, 1729. A member of a family of professional musicians, she evinced talent at an exceptionally early age; was favored by the court of Louis XIV, completing her education under the patronage of Mme. de Montespan. She married Marin de La Guerre, organist of several Paris churches. Her works include an opera, *Céphale et Procris* (Paris, March 15, 1694); a ballet (1691); keyboard suites; violin sonata; cantatas, mostly sacred; etc.

La Guerre, Michel, French organist and composer; b. Paris, c. 1605; d. there, Nov. 13, 1679. He was organist at Sainte-Chapelle from 1633 until his death. His historical importance rests upon his being the author of the first French opera, a 'comédie de chansons,' *Le Triomphe de l'amour sur bergers et bergères* (Paris, Louvre, Jan. 22, 1655), to a libretto by Charles de Beys, court poet. At least, this is the claim made for La Guerre by H. Quittard, in his article *La première comédie française en musique* ('Bulletin Français de la Société Internationale de Musique,' April and May, 1908). The claim is disputed by Romain Rolland and others.

Lahee, Henry, English pianist and composer; father of Henry Charles Lahee; b. Chelsea, April 11, 1826; d. London, April 29, 1912. He studied with Sterndale Bennett, C. Potter (piano), and J. Goss (composition). He was organist at Holy Trinity Church, Brompton (1847-74); also a concert pianist; member of the Philharmonic Society. He wrote madrigals and glees: *Hark, how the birds* (1869), *Hence, loathed melancholy* (1878), *Away to the hunt* (1879), *Love in my Bosom* (1880), etc.

Lahee, Henry Charles, writer on music; son of Henry Lahee; b. England, July 2, 1856; d. Hingham, Mass., April 11, 1953, as a result of injuries sustained in an automobile accident. He served in British mercantile marine (1871-79); in 1880, settled in Boston; was secretary of the New England Cons. (1891-99); then established a musical agency (1899); retired in 1951. —Books (all publ. in Boston): *Famous Singers of Today and Yesterday* (1898; new ed., 1936); *Famous Violinists of Today and Yesterday* (1899; 2nd ed., 1912); *Famous Pianists of Today and Yesterday* (1901); *Grand Opera in America* (1902); *The Organ and its Masters* (1903; new revised ed., 1927); *The Grand Opera Singers of Today* (1922); *Annals of Music in America* (1922; very valuable; contains a chronology of performances of major works); *The Orchestra: A Brief Outline of its Development in Europe and America* (1925).

La Hèle, George de, composer; b. Antwerp, 1547; d. Madrid, 1587. After early training as a chorister, he was sent to Madrid to join the royal chapel of Philip II in 1560, remaining in Spain for 10 years; in 1571, entered the Univ. of Louvain; 1572, choirmaster at the church of Saint-Rombaud in Malines, remaining there until 1574, when he accepted a similar post at the Tournai Cathedral; returned to Madrid in 1582 to take charge of music in the royal chapel. In 1576 he won prizes in the competition at Evreux for his motet *Nonne Deo subjecta* and his chanson *Mais voyez mon cher esmoy*. His 8 Masses (1577; printed by Plantin, Antwerp, 1578), dedicated to Philip II, are all parody Masses and are modeled on works by Josquin, Lassus, Rore, and Crecquillon; also wrote other sacred works. —Cf. G. van Doorslaer, *George de la Hèle, maître de chapelle-compositeur* (Antwerp, 1924).

Lahire (lah-ēr'), **Philippe de,** French writer; b. Paris, 1640; d. there, April 21, 1719. He was prof. of mathematics at Paris Univ.; wrote *Explications des différences des sons de la corde tendue sur la trompette marine,* and *Expériences sur le son.*

Lahmer, Ruel, Canadian-American composer; b. Maple, Ontario, March 27, 1912. He took courses at Columbia Univ.; later studied with Roy Harris; in 1948 he became a member of the staff of Colorado College. He has written several orchestral works, chamber music, and choral works derived from American melodic patterns.

Lahoussaye, Pierre, French violinist and composer; b. Paris, April 12, 1735; d. there, 1818. He studied with Pagin; later in Padua with Tartini. He played in the court orch. of Parma; in 1768, went to London with Guglielmi, becoming leader at the King's Theatre; returning to Paris, was appointed *chef d'orchestre* of the Concert Spirituel (1777-82); conductor of the Comédie-Italienne (1782-90); then conductor at the Théâtre de Monsieur (1790-1801); also taught at the Paris Cons. He wrote a comic opera, *Les Amours de Courcy* (Paris, Aug. 22, 1790); of his compositions, only 6 violin sonatas were publ.

Laidlaw, Anna Robena, English pianist; b. Bretton, Yorkshire, April 30, 1819; d. London, May 29, 1901. She studied in Edinburgh with Robert Müller, in Königsberg, and in London with Henry Herz. In 1837 she played with the Gewandhaus Orch. in Leipzig; continued her successful career as concert pianist until her marriage in 1855. She was an acquaintance of Schumann, whose *Fantasiestücke* are inscribed to her.

Lail, Lorri, Scandinavian mezzo-soprano; b. Oslo, Feb. 20, 1904. She settled in Stockholm, becoming a Swedish citizen in 1935. She sang at the Danzig Opera from 1938-40; then in Germany, Switzerland, and Scandinavia. In 1949 she went to England.

Lajarte (lah-zhart'), **Théodore-Edouard Dufaure de,** French writer on music and composer; b. Bordeaux, July 10, 1826; d. Paris, June 20, 1890. He studied at the Paris Cons. with Leborne; was archivist of the Grand Opéra (1873-90). He is best known for his writings on music: *Bibliothèque musicale du Théâtre de l'Opéra* (2 vols., 1876-78); *Instruments Sax et fanfares civiles* (1867); *Traité de composition musicale* (with Bisson; 1880); *Grammaire de la musique* (1880); *Petite Encyclopédie musicale* (1881-84); *Curiosités de l'Opéra* (1883); also publ. a collection of *Airs à danser de Lulli à Méhul;* and the series, *Chefs-d'œuvre classiques de l'opéra français.* Early in his career Lajarte wrote the operettas *Monsieur de Floridor* (Paris, Oct. 11, 1880), *Mamzelle Pénélope, Duel du Commandeur, Portrait, Roi de Carreau;* the ballet *Les Deux Jumeaux de Bergame* (Paris, Jan. 26, 1886); also marches and dances for military band.

Lajeunesse, Marie Louise Cecilia Emma. See **Albani.**

Lajtha, László, Hungarian composer; b. Budapest, June 30, 1891. He studied at the Academy of Music in Budapest; at the age of 19 he turned to the study of Hungarian folk music, which in the course of the years, became his specialty. In 1913 he became an associate of the Ethnographical Dept. of the Hungarian National Museum. In 1919 he became prof. of composition and also of musical ethnology at the Budapest Cons. He frequently lived in Paris; also visited London; but Budapest remained the center of his activities. He was awarded the Kossuth Prize for his work on Hungarian folk music in 1951; became prof. of musical folklore at the Budapest Academy of Music in 1952. As a composer, he follows disparate trends, with Hungarian national melos as focal strength; his formal influences were from German music, but prolonged contact with modern French developments left a trace in his harmonic idiom, which shows Impressionistic characteristics. —Works: *Chapeau bleu,* opera (1948-52); the ballets *Lysistrata* (Budapest, Feb. 25, 1937) and *Capriccio* (1944); 5 symphonies (1936, 1938, 1948, 1951, 1952); symph. poem *Evasion — Fruite — Liberté* (1942); Sinfonietta for strings (1946); 5

Transylvanian Dances (1952); violin concerto (1931); 8 string quartets (1923-51); 3 string trios (1927-45); piano trio (1928); 2 trios for flute, cello, and harp (1935; 1949); *Marionnettes,* suite for flute, violin, viola, cello, and harp (1937); trio for oboe, clarinet, and bassoon (1944); quintet for flute, violin, viola, cello, and harp (1948); violin sonata; cello sonata; piano sonata; several choral works including 2 Masses; songs; arrangements of folksongs. He publ. a valuable paper on Hungarian musical folklore in 'Musique et chansons populaires' (Paris, 1934); also many articles, in Hungarian and German, in various ethnographical publications.

Laks, Simon, Polish composer; b. Warsaw, Nov. 1, 1901. Concurrently with his mathematical pursuits at Warsaw Univ., he studied at the Warsaw Cons. with Melcer (conducting) and Statkowski (composition); went to Paris in 1925, continuing his musical studies under Rabaud and Vidal at the Paris Cons. In 1941 he was interned by the Germans at the Auschwitz concentration camp, but survived and returned to Paris in May, 1945. His compositions include a choral work, *Echos de Pologne* (1939); a symphony (1924); symph. poem *Farys* (1924); *Symphonic Blues,* jazz fantasy (1928); *Suite polonaise* (1936); a sinfonietta for strings (1936); a suite on Silesian tunes, for small orch. (1945); *Songs of the Polish Earth,* for orch. (1946); *From Roof to Roof,* fantasy on popular songs (1947); *3 Warsaw Polonaises,* for chamber orch. (1947); *Poem,* for violin and orch. (1947); a suite for string quartet; 3 string quartets; a quintet for flute, oboe, clarinet, bassoon, and horn; a trio for violin, cello, and piano; other chamber music and piano works; also songs, including several cycles on Polish and Jewish themes.

Lalande (Delalande), Michel-Richard de, French composer; b. Paris, Dec. 15, 1657; d. there, June 18, 1726. He was a pupil of Chaperon, and as a child sang in the choir of the church of Saint-Germain l'Auxerrois. He learned to play the violin; tried to become a member of Lully's orchestra, but failed. He then turned to study of the organ; was appointed superintendent of the royal chapel in Versailles in 1683, and was also teacher of the two daughters of Louis XIV. He became master of the royal chapel in 1704; in 1722 Campra, Bernier, and Gervais shared his duties at the chapel. Lalande wrote the following ballets (all performed at the Versailles Court): *Ballet de la jeunesse* (1686); *Le Palais de Flore* (1689); *Adonis* (1698); and *Ballet de la Paix* (1713). With Destouches he wrote the ballet *Les Éléments* (presented at the Tuileries Palace, Dec. 31, 1721); it was edited by Vincent d'Indy (Paris, 1883). Among Lalande's other works are 42 motets (publ. in 1729); incidental music to Molière's *Mélicerte;* a number of 'symphonies pour les soupers du roi' and 'symphonies de Noël' (instrumental interludes written for playing at Christmas time at the court). 22 'Noëls' (arranged in a series of 4 'symphonies') were edited by A. Cellier (Paris, 1937). See N. Dufourcq, ed., *Notes et Références pour servir à une histoire de Michel-Richard Delalande* (Paris, 1957; contains a thematic catalogue).

La Laurencie, Lionel de, French musicologist; b. Nantes, July 24, 1861; d. Paris, Nov. 21, 1933. After studying law and science, he became a pupil of Léon Reynier (violin) and Alphonse Weingartner (harmony), and Bourgault-Ducoudray at the Paris Cons. In 1898 he became lecturer at the École des Hautes Études Sociales; contributed regularly to several musical journals. — Writings: *La Légende de Parsifal et le drame musical de R. Wagner* (1888-94); *España* (1890); *Le Goût musical en France* (1905); *L'Académie de musique et le concert de Nantes* (1906); *Quelques Documents sur Jean Philippe Rameau et sa famille* (1907); *Rameau,* in 'Musiciens célèbres' (1908); *Lully,* in 'Les Maîtres de la Musique' (1911); *Contribution à l'histoire de la symphonie française vers 1750,* in 'L'Année musicale' (with G. de Saint-Foix; 1911); *Deux imitateurs français des bouffons: Blavet et Dauvergne,* in 'L'Année musicale' (1912); *André Campra, musicien profane,* in 'L'Année musicale' (1913); *Les Créateurs de l'opéra français* (1920; 2nd ed., 1930); *P. Guédron* (1922); *L'École française de violon, de Lully à Viotti* (3 vols.; 1922-24); *Les Luthistes,* in 'Musiciens célèbres' (1928); *La Chanson royale en France* (1928); *Inventaire critique du fonds Blancheton à la Bibliothèque du Conservatoire* (2 vols.; 1930-31); *Chansons au luth et airs du XVIe siècle* (with Thibault and Mairy; 1931); *Les Débuts de la musique de chambre en France,* in 'Revue de musicologie' (Feb., 1934); *Orfée de Gluck* (1934). In 1916 La Laurencie became editor of Lavignac's 'Encyclopédie de la Musique et Dictionnaire du Conservatoire,' to which he contributed on French music of the 17th and 18th centuries. A *Catalogue des livres de musiciens de la bibliothèque de l'Arsénal à Paris,* edited by La Laurencie and A. Gastoué, was publ. in 1936. —Cf. *Mélanges de musicologie offerts à M. Lionel de la Laurencie* (Paris, 1933).

Lalewicz, Georg, pianist; b. Suwalki, Poland, Aug. 21, 1875; d. Buenos Aires, Dec. 1, 1951. He studied piano with Annette Essipov and composition with Liadov and Rimsky-Korsakov in St. Petersburg. He was prof. of piano at Odessa Cons. (1902-05), Cracow Cons. (1905-12), and the Vienna Imperial Academy (1912-19). He toured Europe as concert pianist from 1905-14. In 1921 he went to Argentina, settling in Buenos Aires as prof. at the Conservatorio Nacional; changed his name to Jorge Lalewicz. An international prize for piano performance was established in his memory in 1952.

Laliberté, (Joseph François) Alfred, Canadian pianist and composer; b. St. Jean, Quebec, Feb. 10, 1882; d. Montreal, May 7, 1952. He studied in Berlin (1900-05) with Lutzenko (piano) and Klatte (theory); later took lessons with Teresa Carreño. In 1906 he formed a friendship with Scriabin and became an ardent propagandist of his music. Laliberté wrote an opera, *Sœur Béatrice* (after Maeterlinck), 2 string quartets, several piano pieces (some on Canadian themes); also made arrangements of some 800 Canadian songs. Most of his music remains in manuscript; a few original songs have been published.

Lalo, Charles, French writer on musical matters; b. Périgueux, Feb. 24, 1877. He studied philosophy in Bayonne and Paris; publ. *L'Esthétique expérimentelle contemporaine* (1908); *Esquisse d'une esthétique musicale scientifique* (1908; 2nd ed., 1939, as *Éléments d'une esthétique . . .*); *Les Sentiments esthétiques* (1909); *Introduction à l'esthétique* (1912); *L'Art et la vie sociale* (1921).

Lalo, (Victor-Antoine-) Édouard, distinguished French composer (of Spanish descent); b. Lille, Jan. 27, 1823; d. Paris, April 22, 1892. He studied with Baumann at the branch of the Paris Cons. in Lille; then at the Paris Cons. with Habeneck (violin) and Schulhoff and Crèvecœur (composition); played with equal skill on the violin and viola, and was violist of the Armingaud-Jacquard Quartet, a group organized in Paris for the purpose of spreading the works of the German masters. In 1848-49 he publ. his first songs (*L'Adieu au Désert, L'Ombre de Dieu, Le Novice, 6 Romances populaires de Béranger*) and subsequently some chamber music. All of this music met with indifference and Lalo was discouraged to. the point of abandoning composition for several years; his ambition, however, was stimulated again by his marriage (in 1865) to Mlle. Bernier de Maligny, a fine contralto singer who performed many of his songs. He wrote a 3-act opera, *Fiesque,* and sent the score to the competition established in 1867 by the Théâtre-Lyrique; it was ranked 3rd, and failed to reach production; the ballet music from it was performed under the title *Divertissement* at the Concert Populaire (Dec. 8, 1872) with excellent success. His next signal success was the performance of his violin concerto, played by Sarasate (Jan. 18, 1874) at a Châtelet concert; then came his most famous work, *Symphonie espagnole,* also performed by Sarasate (Feb. 7, 1875). This work, a true virtuoso piece with vibrant Spanish rhythms, became one of the greatest favorites in the violin repertory, and secured for Lalo international fame. His *Fantaisie norvégienne* for violin and orch. followed; it was subsequently re-arranged for orch. alone, and performed as *Rapsodie norvégienne* (Colonne Concerts, Oct. 26, 1879). He had not abandoned, however, his efforts at writing for the stage. As early as 1875 he began work on the opera *Le Roi d'Ys;* after several revisions, the work was produced at the Opéra-Comique (May 7, 1888), obtaining enormous success; repeated performances followed, in France and elsewhere in Europe; the American première took place at New Orleans, Jan. 23, 1890. In 1888 he was made officer of the Legion of Honor; also was awarded the Prix Monbinne by the Académie des Beaux-Arts. Besides the works already mentioned, there were the following: 1 act from an unfinished opera, *La Jacquerie* (completed by Artur Coquard; posthumously produced in Monte Carlo, March 9, 1895); the ballets *Namouna* (Paris, March 6, 1882) and *Néron* (Paris, March 28, 1891); 3 symphonies, 2 of them unpublished; cello concerto (Paris, Dec. 9, 1877); piano concerto (1889); 3 piano trios; a string quartet; violin sonata; 4 impromptus for violin and piano; *Soirées parisiennes,* for violin and piano; *Guitare,* for violin and piano; cello sonata; songs. —Cf. M. Dufour, *Édouard Lalo* (Lille, 1908); G. Servières, *Lalo* (Paris, 1925); centennial issue of the 'Revue musicale,' with articles by Paul Dukas, Adolphe Jullien, and Pierre Lalo (May, 1923); J. Tiersot, *Édouard Lalo,* in the 'Mus. Quarterly' (Jan., 1925).

Lalo, Pierre, French critic; son of Édouard Lalo; b. Puteaux, Seine, Sept. 6, 1866; d. Paris, June 9, 1943. He became music critic of 'Le Temps' in Oct., 1898; publ. *La Musique,* a selection of his articles (Paris, 1898-99); *De Rameau à Ravel: portraits et souvenirs* (Paris, 1947; posthumous).

Laloy (lah-lwah'), **Louis,** French musicologist and critic; b. Grey, Haute-Saône, Feb. 18, 1874; d. Dôle, March 3, 1944. He studied philosophy in Paris, receiving the degree of *Dr. ès Lettres* in 1904; from 1899-1905, was also a pupil of Bréville and d'Indy at the Schola Cantorum. He was co-founder (1901) of and contributor to the 'Revue d'histoire et de critique musicale'; in 1905 he founded, with J. Marnold, the 'Mercure musical'; contributed articles to 'Revue de Paris,' 'Grande Revue,' 'Mercure de France,' and 'Gazette des Beaux-Arts.' He publ. *Aristoxène de Tarente et la musique de l'antiquité* (1904); *Rameau* (1908); *Debussy* (1909; new ed., 1944); *Notes sur la musique cambodgienne* (in the 'Bericht über den zweiten Kongress' of the Internationale Musik-Gesellschaft at Basel, 1906; publ. Leipzig, 1907); *La Musique chinoise* (1910); *The Future of Music* (London, 1910); *L'Opéra,* in 'Cinquante ans de musique française, 1874-1923' (1924); *La Musique retrouvée, 1902-27* (1928); *Une Heure de musique avec Beethoven* (1930). He also provided the poem for Roussel's opera-ballet *Padmâvati* and for Debussy's *Ode à la France;* publ. a volume of transcriptions of Chinese compositions; and supplied the French versions of a number of Russian opera librettos.

La Mara. See **Lipsius, Marie.**

La Marre (Lamare), **Jacques-Michel-Hurel de,** French cellist; b. Paris, May 1, 1772; d. Caen, March 27, 1823. He toured Europe, including Russia, with great success; Clementi called him 'the Rode of the violoncello.' Four cello concertos and an *air varié* publ. under La Marre's name are actually by Auber.

Lambardi, Camillo, Italian tenor and composer; b. Naples, c. 1560; d. there, 1634. He sang at the Santa Casa dell' Annunziata at Naples; studied there with Gian Domenico da Nola, whom he succeeded as maestro di cappella in 1592. He publ. music for Holy Week for 2 choirs (1592), 2 books of madrigals, etc.

Lambardi, Francesco, Italian tenor, organist, and composer; son of Camillo Lambardi; b. Naples, 1587; d. there, July, 1642. As a youth he was a 'sopranello' in the Santa Casa dell' Annunziata at Naples; later tenor there; then organist of the royal chapel; first organist there (1615-36). He publ. 3 sets of *villanelle* for 3-5 voices (Naples, 1607; 1614; 1616). Some of Lambardi's songs are included in the collections of Scipione Lacorcia, Girolamo Montesardo, and Camillo Lambardi.

Lambelet, George, Greek composer and musicologist; b. Corfu, Dec. 24, 1875; d. Athens, Oct. 30, 1945. Both his father and older brother were composers; studied in Naples; returning to Greece in 1901, settled in Athens. He co-edited 'Critique' with Axiotis, and 'Musical Chronicles' with J. Papadopoulos; publ. a number of studies on Greek folk music, including *National Music,* in 'Panathenaea' (vol. 3, 1901); *Language and Music,* in 'Musical Chronicles' (April, 1928); *Greek Music and the Subdivisions of the Tone,* in 'Musical Chronicles' (1929); *The Spirit of Music in the Ancient Greek Tragedy,* in 'Nea Estia' (July-Aug., 1940); also publ. the pamphlets *Music and Poetry* (Athens, 1926) and *Nationalism in Art and Greek Folk Music* (Athens, 1928). He is noted for *La Musique populaire grecque* (Athens, 1934), a collection of 60 Greek folksongs and dances, together with harmonizations and a critical study. Lambelet's musical compositions have a strong national flavor. He wrote choral works: *The Hymn to Peace* (Athens, Oct., 1929), *Balkan Hymn, Prayer* for women's chorus and orch., *Hymn to Greece, In the Field,* etc.; *The Feast,* symph. poem; *Elegy,* for orch.; *Dirge,* for orch.; songs: *Lacrymae rerum, The Flower crowned,* etc.

Lambert, Alexander, pianist, composer, and teacher; b. Warsaw, Nov. 1, 1862; d. New York, Dec. 31, 1929. He studied piano with his father and then with Julius Epstein at the Vienna Cons.; also worked with Liszt at Weimar for a brief period. He went to New York in 1880; director of the N. Y. College of Music (1887-1905); continued to give concerts in Europe and America; also taught piano privately; had numerous distinguished pupils. He publ. a number of effective piano pieces (*Etude and Bourrée, Tarantella, Mazurka, Valse-Impromptu, Canzonetta,* etc.), and a valuable piano method, *A Systematic Course of Studies* (3 vols., 1907); also a brief *Piano Method for Beginners.*

Lambert, Constant, English composer, conductor, and writer on music; b. London, Aug. 23, 1905; d. there, Aug. 21, 1951. He was a member of an artistic family; studied at the Royal College of Music with R. O. Morris and Vaughan Williams. While he was still a student, Diaghilev commissioned a ballet from him (*Romeo and Juliet;* Monte Carlo, May 4, 1926). This early association with the dance proved decisive, for Lambert spent most of his life as a composer and conductor of ballets, being best known as the musical director of Sadler's Wells (1928-47). His compositions are notable for contrapuntal skill and for the assimilation of a jazz idiom, the latter found in his *Elegiac Blues* (1927), in his very successful *Rio Grande* (on a poem of Sacheverell Sitwell), for solo piano, chorus, and orch. (Manchester, Dec. 12, 1929), and in his piano sonata (1928-29) and piano concerto with small orch. (1931). He wrote the ballets *Pomona* (Buenos Aires, Sept. 9, 1927) and *Horoscope* (London, Jan. 27, 1938; also concert suite based on same material, 1938); *The Bird Actors,* overture for orch. (1925); *Music for Orchestra* (1927); *Summer's Last Will and Testament,* masque for chorus and orch. (after Thomas Nashe; London, Jan. 29, (1936); incidental music for Shakespeare's *Hamlet; Dirge* (Shakespeare), for male voices and strings (1940); *King Pest,* rondo burlesca for orch. (London, 1937); *Aubade héroïque,* for orch. (1942); *Prizefight,* for band (1923); *8 Chinese Songs* (on poems by Li-Po); also film music for *Merchant Seaman* (1943) and for *Anna Karenina* (1947). He transcribed and edited works by Boyce, Handel, Roseingrave, etc.; rescored Vaughan Williams' *Job* for theater orch. (1931), and arranged a ballet, *Apparitions,* to Liszt's music, which he also orchestrated. Lambert was music critic of the 'Sunday Referee,' wrote numerous articles, and also a book, *Music Ho!: A Study of Music in Decline* (London, 1934).

Lambert, Herbert, English clavichord and harpsichord maker; b. Bath, Dec. 22, 1881; d. there, March 7, 1936. Originally an excellent professional photographer, he turned his craftsmanship and research activity to the building of old keyboard instruments, especially clavichords. His experiments resulted in a successful, portable clavichord of good tone. His name is perpetuated in *Lambert's Clavichord* (1928), a small book of compositions for this instrument by Herbert Howells.

Lambert, Johann Heinrich, German music theorist; b. Mühlhausen, Aug. 29, 1728; d. Berlin, Sept. 25, 1777. A member of the Berlin Academy, he wrote *Sur quelques instruments acoustiques* (1763; German ed., 1796); *Sur la vitesse du son* (1768); *Remarques sur le tempérament en musique* (1774; German transl. in Marpurg's 'Historisch-kritische Beiträge,' vol. 5); and *Observations sur les sons des flûtes* (1775); all of the above are printed in the reports of the Berlin Academy.

Lambert, Juan Bautista, Catalan composer; b. Barcelona, 1884; d. there, May 4, 1945. He studied with Morera; was active in Barcelona as organist and conductor. He composed a successful light opera, *La Alborada;* also a symph. poem, *Vallencis;* also wrote numerous choral works, marches, and songs.

Lambert (lahn-bär'), **Lucien,** French composer and pianist; b. Paris, Jan. 5, 1858; d. Oporto, Portugal, Jan. 21, 1945. He studied first with his father; after a successful tour of America and Europe, returned to Paris to study at the Cons. there with Barbereau, Dubois, and Massenet, taking the Prix Rossini in 1885 with his cantata *Prométhée enchaîné.* He settled in Portugal in 1914; prof. of composition at the Oporto Cons. (1922-37). He wrote the operas *Brocéliande* (Rouen, Feb. 25, 1893), *Le Spahi* (Paris, Oct. 18, 1897), *La Marseillaise* (Paris, July 14, 1900), *La Flamenca* (Paris, Oct. 31, 1903); *Harald* (1937), *Penticosa,* and *La Sorcière;* the ballets *La Roussalka* (Paris, Dec. 8, 1911) and *Les Cloches de Porto* (1937); *Florette,* lyric comedy (1921); *Légende roumaine,* symph. poem; incidental music to *Sire Olaf* (Lille, 1887); *Fantaisie monothématique,* for orch., on an oriental theme (1932; Paris, March 19, 1933); *Tanger le soir,* Moorish rhapsody for orch.; *Esquisses créoles,* orchestral suite, on themes by Gottschalk; *Andante et fantaisie tzigane,* for piano and orch.; string quartet; string sextet; a Mass (1941); piano pieces; songs; etc.

Lambert, Michel, French lutenist and singer; b. Vivonne, Poitou, c. 1610; d. Paris, June 29, 1696. He was master of chamber music in the court of Louis XIV; also a celebrated singing teacher. His daughter married Lully. He publ. *Airs et brunettes* (1666; 2nd ed., 1689) and *Airs et dialogues* (1698; posthumous).

Lambeth, Henry Albert, British organist, conductor, and composer; b. Hardway, near Gosport, Jan. 16, 1822; d. Glasgow, June 27, 1895. He studied with Thomas Adams; went to Glasgow about 1853 as city organist; was conductor of the Glasgow Choral Union (1859-80); harmonized Scottish melodies; wrote several songs and piano pieces; and, with D. Baptie, edited the *Scottish Book of Praise* (1876).

Lambillotte (lahn-bē-yoht'), **Louis,** French writer and church composer; b. Charleroi, Hainault, March 27, 1796; d. Vaugirard, Feb. 22, 1855. He was organist at Charleroi, then at Dinant; in 1822, became maître de chapelle at the Jesuit Seminary at St.-Acheul, joining the order in 1825; subsequently settled in Vaugirard. —Works: 4 Masses, one in the Lydian mode; other sacred music; organ pieces; fugues, etc.; he publ. an *Antiphonaire de Saint-Grégoire, facsimile du manuscrit de Saint-Gall* (1851); *Clef des Mélodies grégoriennes* (1851); *Quelques mots sur la restauration du chant liturgique* (1855); *Esthétique, Théorie et Pratique du chant grégorien* (1855); other essays. —Cf. J. Dufour, *Mémoire sur les chants liturgiques restaurés par Lambillotte* (Paris, 1857); T. Nisard, *Le Père Lambillotte et Dom A. Schubiger* (Paris, 1857); M. de Monter, *Lambillotte et ses frères* (Paris, 1871).

Lambord, Benjamin, American composer; b. Portland, Maine, June 10, 1879; d. Lake Hopatcong, N. J., June 6, 1915. He studied in Boston with A. Whiting, at Columbia Univ. with MacDowell, with C. Rubner (composition), and in Paris with Vidal. He was organist and choirmaster in various churches in New York; also taught piano; organized the 'Lambord Choral Society' and the 'Modern Music Society.' He wrote *Introduction and Variations on an English Dance Theme,* for orch.; *Clytie,* for soprano and orch.; *Verses from Omar Khayyam,* for mixed chorus and orch.; *Ten Lyric Studies for Piano;* piano pieces; part-songs; songs; etc.

Lamm, Pavel Alexandrovitch, Russian musicologist; b. Moscow, July 27, 1882; d. there, May 5, 1951. He studied piano at the Moscow Cons.; toured Europe as accompanist of the singer Olenine d'Alheim; then was on the editorial board of the Russian State Publishing Dept. He edited the vocal score of Mussorgsky's original version of *Boris Godunov* (Moscow, 1928); was editor-in-chief for Mussorgsky's complete works.

Lammers, Julius, German composer; b. Leipzig, April 20, 1829; d. there, Sept. 20, 1888. He taught at the Leipzig Cons.; composed numerous songs and some piano pieces.

Lamond, Frederic Archibald, Scottish pianist; b. Glasgow, Jan. 28, 1868; d. Stirling, Feb. 21, 1948. He played organ as a boy in a local church; also studied oboe and violin; in 1882, entered the Raff Cons. in Frankfurt, studying with Heermann (violin), Max Schwarz (piano), and Urspruch (composition); then piano with Hans von Bülow, Clara Schumann, and Liszt. A brilliant concert pianist, Lamond appeared in Berlin, Vienna, London, Russia, and New York. He became renowned for his skilful interpretation of Beethoven; publ. an edition of Beethoven's sonatas (1923). He married Irene Triesch, a German actress, in 1904 and settled in Berlin, until the outbreak of World War II, when he moved to London. He was also a composer; wrote a symphony (Glasgow, Dec. 23, 1889), some chamber music, and numerous piano pieces. —Cf. F. Lamond, *Memoirs* (Glasgow, 1949).

Lamote de Grignon, Juan, Catalan conductor and composer; b. Barcelona, July 7, 1872; d. there, March 11, 1949. He studied at the Cons. of Barcelona, and upon graduation, taught piano there; made his début as conductor in Barcelona (April 26, 1902). In 1910 he founded the Orquesta Sinfónica of Barcelona, which carried on its activity until 1924; also led the municipal band (from 1914). He wrote a 1-act opera, *Hesperia* (Barcelona, Jan. 25, 1907); works for orch. (*Andalucía, Hispanicas, Scherzo, Cantos populares españoles, Poema romántico*); the oratorio *La Nit de Nadal;* numerous songs (*12 Chansons catalanes, Violetas, Tres motetes, Tres cantos espirituales, Passioneras,* etc.). He publ. *Musique et musiciens français à Barcelona, catalans à Paris* (Barcelona, 1935).

Lamote de Grignon, Ricard, Catalan cellist, conductor, and composer; son of Juan Lamote de Grignon; b. Barcelona, Sept. 23, 1899; studied cello and composition at the Barcelona Cons.; played cello in the Orquesta Sinfónica, conducted by his father; then conducted provincial orchestras; became assistant conductor of the municipal band of Barcelona. —Works: an opera, *La Caperucita verde,* and a children's opera, *La Flor;* a symph. poem, *Boires; Tríptico de Rabindranath Tagore,* for soprano and orch.; piano trio; songs. On April 19, 1936, he conducted, at the Barcelona Festival of the International Society for Contemporary Music, his symph. legend *Joan de Os;* his *Enigmas* for orch. received the municipal prize of Barcelona in 1951. He publ. a manual, *Síntesis de técnica musical* (Barcelona, 1948).

Lamothe (lah-moht'), **Georges,** French composer; b. 1837; d. Courbevoie, Oct. 15, 1894. He was a very prolific composer of dance music; more than 1,000 opus numbers.

Lamoureux (lah-moo-rö'), **Charles,** noted French conductor and violinist; b. Bordeaux, Sept. 28, 1834; d. Paris, Dec. 21, 1899. He studied at the Paris Cons. with Girard (violin), taking 1st prize in 1854; also studied with Tolbecque (harmony), Leborne (counterpoint), and Alexis Chauvet (theory). In 1850 he became solo violinist in the Théâtre du Gymnase orch.; then became a member of the Paris Opéra orch. In 1860 he and Colonne, Adam, and A. Pilet founded a society for chamber music; in 1873, organized the 'Société de l'Harmonie Sacrée'; became widely famed as a conductor; assistant conductor of the Conservatoire Concerts (1872-77); conductor of the Paris Opéra (1877-79). He founded the celebrated Concerts Lamoureux (Nouveaux Concerts) on Oct. 23, 1881. More than any other French musician, Lamoureux educated Parisians to appreciate Wagner; he was responsible not only for highly competent performances of classical masterpieces, but also for presentation of compositions of his contemporaries. —Cf. R. Rolland, *Musiciens d'aujourd'hui* (Paris, 1914; p. 234 ff.).

Lamperti, Francesco, Italian singing teacher; b. Savona, March 11, 1811; d. Como, May 1, 1892. He studied at the Milan Cons.; director at the Teatro Filodrammatico in Lodi; tutored many distinguished singers, including Albani, Mme. Artôt, both Cruvelis, Campanini, Collini, and Mme. Lagrange; taught at the Milan Cons. (1850-75). He publ. *Guida teorico-pratico-elementare per lo studio del canto; Studî di bravura per soprano; Esercizi giornalieri per soprano o mezzo-soprano; L'Arte del canto; Osservazioni e consigli sul trillo; Solfeggî;* etc. His methods and studies in voice production have also appeared in English transl.: *Studies in bravura singing for the soprano voice* (N. Y., 1875); *A Treatise on the Art of Singing* (London, 1877; revised ed., N. Y., 1890).

Lamperti, Giovanni Battista, Italian singing teacher; son of Francesco Lamperti; b. Milan, June 24, 1839; d. Berlin, March 18, 1910. At the age of 9 he was a choirboy at the Milan Cathedral; studied piano and voice at the Milan Cons.; served as accompanist in his father's class there. He taught first in Milan; in Dresden for 20 years; then in Berlin. Among his pupils were Sembrich, Schumann-Heink, Bulss, Stagno, etc. He publ. *Die Technik des Bel Canto* (1905; English transl. by Th. Baker; N. Y., 1905); *Scuola di Canto* (8 vols. of solfeggi and vocalises); other technical exercises. His pupil W. E. Brown publ. *Vocal Wisdom; Maxims of G. B. Lamperti* (N. Y., 1931).

Lampugnani (lam-pŏŏ-ñah'-nē), **Giovanni Battista,** Italian teacher and composer; b. Milan, 1706; d. there, 1781. In 1743 he became conductor of the Italian Opera in London; in 1799, maestro al cembalo at La Scala, Milan. Over the period 1732-69, he wrote 32 operas in the style of Hasse, presented in London, Venice, and Milan; publ. some trio sonatas; also wrote symphonies and concertos.

Land, Jan Pieter Nicholaas, Dutch orientalist and musicologist; b. Delft, April 23, 1834; d. Arnhem, April 30, 1897. In 1864 he was prof. of classical and oriental languages and of philosophy at the Amsterdam Academy; then was prof. of philosophy at Leyden Univ. (1872-94). He was an accomplished linguist, specializing in Semitic philology, and a doctor of theology; was deeply interested in musico-historical research, to which he made most valuable contributions: *Noord Nederlands muziekgeschiedenis* (1874-81); *De Koorboeken van de S'Pieterskerk te Leyden* (1880); *Over de toonladders der arabische muziek* (1880); *Musique et musiciens au XVIIe siècle. Correspondance et œuvres musicales de Constantijn Huygens* (with Jonckbloet; Leyden, 1882); *Recherches sur l'histoire de la gamme arabe* (Leyden, 1884); *Essai de notation musicale chez les Arabes et les Persans* (1885); *Tonschriftversuche und Melodieproben aus dem muhammedanischen Mittelalter,* in the 'Vierteljahrsschrift für Musikwissenschaft' (Sept., 1886); *Het Luitboek van Thysius* (Amsterdam, 1889); *Over onze kennis der javaansche muziek* (Amsterdam, 1891); *Remarks on the Earliest Development of Arabic Music,* in the 'Proceedings of the London Oriental Congress (Sept., 1892).

Landau, Siegfried, German-American conductor and composer; b. Berlin, Sept. 4, 1921. He studied at the Stern Cons. in Berlin and also at the Klindworth-Scharwenka Cons. He went to England early in 1939, where he continued his studies at Trinity College; in November 1940 he arrived in the U.S., where he studied conducting with Pierre Monteux. In 1955 he organized the Brooklyn Philharmonia, of which he is permanent conductor. He has written much music on Hebrew subjects: *Chassidic Suite* for viola and piano (1941); *Longing for Jerusalem,* for soprano and orchestra (1941); ballet, *The Golem* (1946); etc.

Landi, Stefano, Italian singer and composer; b. Rome, c. 1590; d. there, c. 1655. He was maestro di cappella to Bishop Cornaro of Padua; returned to Rome in 1620, and was appointed to a similar post at Santa Maria dei Monti (1624); in 1629, became contralto singer at the Cappella Giulia, St. Peter's. He was one of the most eminent contrapuntists of the Roman school; pupil of the 2 Naninis; one of the creators of the cantata, and one of the earliest operatic composers in Rome. He wrote *La morte d'Orfeo,* pastoral opera (Venice, 1619); *Il Sant' Alessio,* sacred opera (Rome, Feb. 23, 1632); also a *Missa in benedictione nuptiarum,* for 6 voices (1628); a book of Masses a cappella for 4-5 voices; madrigals for 4-5 voices (1619 and 1624); arias for 1-2 voices (5 vols., 1620-38); etc.

Landini, Benedetto, Italian organist and composer; b. Calenzano, Jan. 31, 1858; d. Florence, July 11, 1938. He studied at the Florence Cons., graduating in 1886; became teacher of organ there in 1888; also for many years, organist of the Church of Santissima Annunziata in Florence, and choirmaster at San Lorenzo and Santa Trinità; from 1891, active in church music reforms in Tuscany. He wrote a Mass, a Requiem, *De Profundis, Hymnus,* psalms and other sacred works; also a children's opera, *L'Arancia di Codino* (1913); edited works of Frescobaldi, Marco da Gagliano, and Corteccia, and numerous old Tuscan folksongs.

Landini (Landino), Francesco, Italian instrumentalist and composer; b. Fiesole, 1325; d. Florence, Sept. 2, 1397. Blinded as a youth, he turned early to music, becoming proficient in the art of playing the lute, guitar, flute, and organ. He was one of the most celebrated organ virtuosos of his time; was known as 'Francesco degli organi.' He studied with Giovanni da Cascia and Jacopo da Bologna; for many years, was organist at the Church of Lorenzo in Florence. Although not the first, he was probably the most famous master of the Florentine 'Ars nova' of the 14th century; his works, of which more than 150 are preserved in the libraries of Europe, represent over a third of extant Italian 14th-century music; he wrote madrigals, *cacce, ballate,* etc. —Cf. F. Ludwig, *Die mehrstimmige Musik des 14. Jahrhunderts,* in 'Sammelbände der Internationalen Musik-Gesellschaft' (1902); J. Wolf, *Geschichte der Mensuralnotation* (3 vols., 1904); J. Wolf, *Florenz in der Musikgeschichte des 14. Jahrhunderts,* in 'Sammelbände der Internationalen Musik-Gesellschaft' (vol. 3); F. Ludwig in Adler's 'Handbuch' (vol. 1); F. Ludwig in 'Zeitschrift für Musikwissenschaft' (vol. 5); G. Carducci in 'Opere' (vol. 8); H. Riemann in 'Handbuch der Musikgeschichte' (vol. 2); H. Riemann, *Das Kunstlied im 14.-15. Jahrhundert,* in 'Sammelbände der Internationalen Musik-Gesellschaft' (vol. 7); A. Schering, *Das Kolorierte Orgelmadrigal des Trecento,* in 'Sammelbände der Internationalen Musik-Gesellschaft' (vol. 13); A. Schering, *Studien zur Musikgeschichte der Frührenaissance* (1914); H. Besseler, *Die Musik des Mittelalters und der Renaissance* (1931); F. Villani, *Liber de civitatis Florentiae famosis civibus* (written c. 1400); edited by C. Galletti, 1874); L. Ellinwood, *Francesco Landini and His Music,* in the 'Mus. Quarterly' (April, 1936); M. Schneider, *Die Ars nova des 14. Jahrhunderts in Frankreich und Italien* (Wolfenbüttel, 1930); E. Li Gotti and N. Pirrotta, *Il Sacchetti e la tecnica del trecento italiano* (Florence, 1935); L. Ellinwood, *The Works of Francesco Landini* (Cambridge, Mass., 1939; contains all Landini's extant works in modern notation); Hélène Nolthenius, *Renaissance in Mei; Florentijns leven rond Francesco Landino* (Utrecht, 1956).

Landon, H. C. Robbins, American musicologist; b. Boston, March 6, 1926. He studied music history with Alfred J. Swan at Swarthmore College and composition with Harl McDonald there; then musicology with Karl Geiringer at Boston Univ. (B. Mus., 1947). In 1948 he went to Vienna, where he remained; there he was active in the field of Haydn research; married the harpsichordist Christa Fuhrmann. His monumental work *The Symphonies of Joseph Haydn* (London, 1955) not only settled numerous minor problems of authenticity, origin, and chronology of Haydn's symphonies, but it also established a large view of Haydn as a musician of his time; with Donald Mitchell, he ed. *The Mozart Companion* (London, 1956). In 1957 he discovered the Haydn Mass in G (No. 13), regarded as lost; and also the MS of the score of the so-called *Jena Symphony,* which he established as being by Friedrich Witt, not by Beethoven.

Landormy (lahn - dohr - mē'), **Paul (Charles-René),** French musicologist and critic; b. Issy, Jan. 3, 1869; d. Paris, Nov. 17, 1943. For a number of years he taught philosophy in the provinces; going to Paris in 1892, he studied singing with Sbriglia and Pol Plançon. Together with Romain Rolland, he organized a series of lectures on music history at the École des Hautes Études Sociales; established an acoustic laboratory there; music critic of 'La Victoire' (1918); also contributed articles to 'Le Temps' and various other journals. He publ. *Histoire de la musique* (Paris, 1910; augmented ed., 1923; English transl., N.Y., 1923); *Brahms*

(1920) and *Bizet* (1924), in 'Les Maîtres de la Musique'; *La Vie de Schubert* (Paris, 1928); *Gluck* (Paris, 1941); *Gounod* (Paris, 1942); *La Musique française de Franck à Debussy* (Paris, 1943); contributed articles to the 'Mus. Quarterly': *Chopin* (April, 1929), *Lili Boulanger* (Oct., 1930), *Gabriel Fauré* (July, 1931), *Vincent d'Indy* (Oct., 1932), *Déodat de Séverac* (April, 1934), *Albert Roussel* (Oct., 1938); co-author of *L'Initiation à la musique* (1935); editor of the series *Les Chefs-d'œuvre de la musique expliqués* (a guide to standard operas).

Landowska (lăn-dŏhv'-ska), **Wanda,** celebrated harpsichordist and authority on old music; b. Warsaw, July 5, 1877. She studied piano at the Warsaw Cons. with Michalowski and in Berlin with Moszkowski; also composition with Urban in Berlin. In 1900 she went to Paris, where she married Henry Lew, a writer. She traveled widely in Europe as pianist; in 1909 made a tour of Russia, and played for Tolstoy, who showed great interest in her ideas on classical music. Subsequently, she devoted her efforts principally to reviving the art of playing upon the harpsichord. In 1912 she commissioned the Pleyel firm of Paris to construct a harpsichord for her; this was the first of the many keyboard instruments built for her in subsequent years. In 1913 she was invited by Kretzschmar to give a special course in harpsichord playing at the Berlin Hochschule für Musik. The outbreak of World War I found her in Germany, and she was interned there until the Armistice; in 1918 her husband was killed in an automobile accident in Berlin. In 1919 she gave master classes of harpsichord playing at the Basel Cons.; then returned to Paris. In 1925 she bought a villa in St.-Leu-la-Forêt near Paris, and established a school of old music there. A concert hall was built there in 1927; she presented regular concerts of old music, and gave lessons on the subject; also assembled a large collection of harpsichords. Her school attracted students from all over the world; she also taught at the Cons. of Fontainebleau, and frequently appeared at concerts in Paris, both as pianist and harpsichordist. She commissioned Manuel de Falla to compose a chamber concerto for harpsichord, and played the solo part in its first performance in Barcelona (Nov. 5, 1926); another commission was Poulenc's *Concert champêtre* for harpsichord and instruments (Paris, May 3, 1929). She appeared for the first time in America on Nov. 20, 1923, as soloist with the Philadelphia Orch., under Stokowski; then returned to France. When the Germans invaded France in 1940, Landowska fled to Switzerland, abandoning her villa, her library, and her instruments. In 1941 she reached New York; presented a concert of harpsichord music in N. Y. on Feb. 21, 1942; then devoted herself mainly to teaching; also made recordings; settled in her new home at Lakeville, Conn. She is acknowledged as one of the greatest performers on the modern harpsichord; her interpretations of Baroque music are notable in their balance between classical precision and freedom from rigidity, particularly in the treatment of ornamentation. —Publications: *Bach et ses interprètes* (Paris, 1906); *Musique ancienne* (Paris, 1909; 7th ed., 1921; English transl. N. Y., 1924); many articles in various French and German magazines (on Bach, Chopin, harpsichord playing, etc.). She also wrote cadenzas for Mozart's concertos, etc. —Cf. A. Schaeffner, *Wanda Landowska et le retour aux 'humanités' de la musique,* in 'Revue Musicale' (June, 1927); R. Gelatt, *Music Makers* (N. Y., 1953; pp. 254-86); B. Gavoty, *Wanda Landowska* (Geneva, 1957).

Landowski, Marcel, French composer; b. Prêt L'Abbé (Finistère), Feb. 18, 1915. He studied with Büsser, Gaubert, and Munch; has been active as conductor. His works include the opera *Le Rire de Nils Halerius* (Mulhouse, Jan. 19, 1951); oratorio *Rythmes du Monde* (1941); *Clairs-Obscurs,* suite for orch. (Paris, 1938); *Edina,* symph. poem (1946); *Le Petit Poucet,* symph. suite (Paris, 1947); a symphony (Paris, 1949); piano concerto (Paris, March 1, 1942); cello concerto (Paris, 1946); also music for films.

Landowski, Mme. **W.-L. (Alice-Wanda),** French writer on music; b. Paris, Nov. 28, 1899. She studied piano in Paris at the Marguerite Long School; theory with Gustave Bret. She taught music history at the Cons. of Clermont; in 1945, became prof. at the Rouen Cons., a branch of the Paris Cons.; also was engaged as music critic of 'Le Parisien.' —Publications: *L'année musicale* (Paris, 1936-39; annual reports of musical events); *La musique à travers les âges* (1937); *Maurice Ravel* (1938); *Les Grands Musiciens* (1938); *Histoire universelle de la musique moderne* (1941); *Histoire générale de la musique* (1945); *L'œuvre de Claude Delvincourt* (1947); *Chopin et Fauré* (1946); *Le travail en musique* (1949); *La musique américaine* (1952); *Paul Paray* (1956). She adopted the initials W.-L. (L. for Ladislas, her father's name) to avoid confusion with Wanda Landowska, no relation.

Landré, Guillaume (Louis Frédéric), Dutch composer, son of Willem Landré; b. The Hague, Feb. 24, 1905. He studied law at the Univ. of Utrecht; received the degree of Master of Law in 1929; thereafter settled in Amsterdam. He studied music with Henri Zagwijn and Willem Pijper; became active in musical organizations; in 1948 appointed general secretary of the Council of Arts; also elected president of the Dutch Performing Rights Association (BUMA). His music is Romantic in essence, Impressionistic in harmonic and color devices; his idiom is definitely modern, with free application of polytonality; he strives for rhapsodic expression and opulent sonorities; the polyphonic fabric of his instrumental works remains translucent despite the occasional complexity of contrapuntal combinations. —Works: light opera *De Snoek (The Pike;* Amsterdam, March 24, 1938); 3 symphonies (No. 1, Amsterdam Festival of the International Society for Contemporary Music, June 9, 1933; No. 2, The Hague, March 6, 1946; No. 3, Amsterdam, June 16, 1951); *Sinfonia Sacra in Memoriam Patris* (Rotterdam, Nov. 7, 1948); *4 Mouvements Symphoniques* (The Hague, Jan. 17, 1950); a chamber symphony for 13 instruments (Amsterdam, Feb. 24, 1953); suite for string orch. and piano (1936); a cello concerto (1940); a violin concerto (1941); *Piae Memoriae pro patria mortuorum,* for chorus and orch. (1942); a cappella choruses; quintet for flute, oboe, clarinet, bassoon, and horn (1930); 3 string quartets (1927; 1943; 1949); piano trio (1929); violin sonata (1927); songs.

Landré, Willem, Dutch writer and composer; father of Guillaume Landré; b. Amsterdam, June 12, 1874; d. Eindhoven, Jan. 1, 1948. He was a pupil of Bernard Zweers. In 1901 he became music critic of the 'Oprechte Haarlemsche Courant' in Haarlem; music editor of the 'Nieuwe Courant' in The Hague (1901-05), then of the 'Nieuwe Rotterdamsche Courant' in Rotterdam (1905-37); taught theory, composition, and the history of music at the Rotterdam Cons.; editor of 'Caecilia, Het Muziekcollege.' —Works: the operas *De Roos van Dekama* (Haarlem, 1897) and *Beatrix* (The Hague, 1925); the orchestral works *In memoriam Matris, 3 Mood Pictures,* and *Le Jardin de Marguerite;* a *Requiem in memoriam uxoris; Fragments from the Book of Baruch,* for chorus; a piano concerto; a piano trio; numerous part-songs and songs.

Landshoff, Ludwig, German musicologist and conductor; b. Stettin, June 3, 1874; d. New York, Sept. 20, 1941. He studied music with Thuille, Urban, and Max Reger in Munich and Berlin; musicology with Sandberger, Max Friedlaender, and O. Fleischer; *Dr. phil.* (1901) from the Univ. of Munich with his treatise *Johann Rudolph Zumsteeg: ein Beitrag zur Geschichte des Liedes und der Ballade.* He established concerts at which old music was played on instruments of its time; conductor at Kiel, Würzburg, Breslau, and Hamburg; director of the Munich Bach Society (1919-28). He went to Paris in 1933, and to New York in 1939. —Writings: *Über das vielstimmige Accompagnement und andere Fragen des Generalbass-Spiels,* in the 'Festschrift zum 50. Geburtstage von Adolf Sandberger' (Munich, 1918); *Revisionsbericht zur Urtext-Ausgabe von Johann Sebastian Bachs Inventionen und Sinfonien* (1933); edited *Alte Meister des Belcanto* (5 vols., 1912-27; contains numerous 17th and 18th century unpubl. arias); Bach's *15 zweistimmige Inventionen und 15 dreistimmige Sinfonien, Trio-Sonaten; Musikalisches Opfer; 6 Suites avec leurs préludes.* —Cf. A. Einstein, *In Memoriam, Ludwig Landshoff,* in the 'Mus. Quarterly' (April, 1942).

Lane, Eastwood, American composer; b. Brewerton, N. Y., May 22, 1879. He attended Syracuse Univ.; then devoted himself to composition. His works are mostly in a light, descriptive vein, for piano; two of his piano sketches, *Sea Burial* and *Persimmon Pucker,* were orchestrated by Ferde Grofé for performance by Paul Whiteman; other works are piano suites, *Sleepy Hollow, Adirondack Sketches,* and *5 American Dances;* he also wrote 2 ballets, *Abelard and Heloise* and *A Caravan From China Comes.* —Cf. J. T. Howard, *Eastwood Lane* (N. Y., 1925).

Lang, Benjamin Johnson, American pianist and conductor; b. Salem, Mass., Dec. 28, 1837; d. Boston, April 3, 1909. He studied with his father and with Alfred Jaëll. In 1855 he went to Berlin for advanced studies; for a time took piano lessons with Liszt. Returning to America, he was engaged as church organist; was also organist of the Handel and Haydn Society in Boston for many years (1859-95); then was its conductor (1895-97); directed the Apollo Club and the Cecilia Society, from their foundation (1868 and 1874, respectively); gave numerous concerts of orchestral, choral, and chamber music on his own account. As a pianist, teacher, conductor, and organizer, he was in the first rank of Boston musicians for a third of a century, and brought out a long list of important works by European and American composers.

Among his pupils were Arthur Foote and Ethelbert Nevin. He was also a composer; wrote an oratorio, *David,* and a great many sacred works; songs and piano pieces.

Lang, Hans, Austrian operetta composer; b. Vienna, July 15, 1908; studied at the Vienna Cons.; wrote popular songs; composed the operettas *Lisa, benimm dich!* (Vienna, March 21, 1939; his most successful work); *Hofrat Geiger; Der alte Sünder; Mädel im Frack; X für ein U; Höchste Eisenbahn;* etc.

Lang, Henry Albert, pianist, teacher, and composer; b. (of German parents) New Orleans, Oct. 9, 1854; d. Philadelphia, May 27, 1930. He studied at the Stuttgart Cons. Following a concert tour of Germany, he taught piano at the Karlsruhe Cons.; then at Riga and Königsberg. He came to the U.S. in 1890; settled in Philadelphia, where he was instructor at several music schools. He wrote 2 symphonies; *Fantastic Dances* for orch.; violin concerto; cello sonata; piano quintet; 2 piano trios; 2 string quartets; songs.

Lang, Margaret Ruthven, American composer; daughter of Benjamin J. Lang; b. Boston, Nov. 27, 1867. She studied in Boston with her father and later in Munich; also with Chadwick and MacDowell. Her works include the overture *Witichis* (1893), *Dramatic Overture* (1893), the overture *Totila; Ballade* for orch. (1901); *Sappho's Prayer to Aphrodite,* aria for contralto with orch. (1895); *Phoebus,* aria for baritone and orch.; *In the Manger,* for mixed choir; *The Heavenly Noël,* for solo, women's chorus, piano, and string orch.; a *Christmas Cycle* for vocal quartet; piano pieces; some 200 songs. She stopped composing about 1930; was still living in Boston in 1957.

Lang, Paul Henry, eminent musicologist; b. Budapest, Aug. 28, 1901. He studied at the Royal Academy of Music, Budapest (composition with Kodály and Leo Weiner), Univ. of Budapest, Univ. of Heidelberg, the Sorbonne (Paris), and Cornell Univ. (Ph.D., 1934). He played bassoon in Budapest orchestras; also appeared as pianist in chamber music recitals; was assistant conductor of the Royal Opera in Budapest (1923-24). In 1928 he came to the U.S., and occupied various teaching posts: assistant prof. at Vassar College (1930-31); associate prof., Wells College (1931-33); visiting lecturer, Wellesley College (1934-35); associate prof. of musicology, Columbia Univ. (1933-39); full prof. there since 1939. He was treasurer of the American Musicological Society from its foundation to 1947; vice-president 1947-49; 1955-58, president of the International Musicological Society. In 1945 he became editor of the 'Mus. Quarterly'; from 1954, music critic of the 'N.Y. Herald Tribune.' He publ. a valuable book, *Music in Western Civilization* (N.Y., 1941); also articles in the 'Mus. Quarterly,' 'Revue Musicale,' 'American Scholar,' 'Columbia Quarterly,' and the 'Saturday Review of Literature.'

Lang, Walter, Swiss composer; b. Basel, Aug. 19, 1896. He was a pupil of Jaques-Dalcroze; taught at the Dalcroze School in Geneva; then studied in Munich with Klose, and in Zürich with Andreae and W. Frey; appeared as a concert pianist and as an accompanist; taught theory in Basel (1920-22); prof. of piano at Zürich Cons. (1922-41); music director of Monte Ceneri Radio (1942-48); in 1948, became instructor at the Basel Cons. He is married to the coloratura soprano Mimi Lang-Seiber. —Works: string quartet, op. 6; violin sonata, op. 8; cello sonata, op. 10; *Der Baumeister* (30 easy piano pieces); etc.

Langbecker, Emanuel Christian Gottlieb, German authority on Protestant chorales; b. Berlin, Aug. 31, 1792; d. there, Oct. 24, 1843. He was secretary to Prince Waldemar of Prussia; his researches on the origin of the Protestant chorale are embodied in *Das deutsch-evangelische Kirchenlied* (1830); *Johann Crügers Choral-Melodien* (1835); *Gesangblätter aus dem 16. Jahrhundert* (1838); and *Paul Gerhardts Leben und Lieder* (1841).

Langdon, Richard, English composer and organist; b. Exeter, c. 1729; d. there, Sept. 8, 1803. He studied at Oxford (Mus. Bac., 1761); was organist of Exeter Cathedral (1753-77), Bristol Cathedral (1778-82), Armagh Cathedral (1782-94); publ. *Divine Harmony,* a collection of psalms and anthems (1774); also *12 Glees* for 3-4 voices (1770); 2 cantatas; 12 songs.

Lange, Daniel de, Dutch cellist and composer; brother of Samuel de Lange; b. Rotterdam, July 11, 1841; d. Point Loma, Calif., Jan. 31, 1918. He studied cello with Servais and composition with Verhulst. As a young man he taught at the Lwow Cons. (1860-63); returning to Amsterdam, he occupied various teaching posts; in 1895 became director of the Amsterdam Cons., remaining in that post until 1913; gave numerous choral concerts of old Dutch music; also wrote music criticism. In 1913 he went to California, where he lived at the headquarters of the Universal Brotherhood and Theosophical Society at Point Loma. He wrote an opera, *De val van Kuilenburg;* 2 symphonies; a cello concerto; chamber music; sacred works; also publ. an *Exposé d'une théorie de la musique.* —Cf. Henry Viotta, *Onze hedendaagsche toonkunstenaars* (Amsterdam, 1894); A. Averkamp, *Levensbericht van Daniel de Lange* (Leyden, 1918). See also the 'Theosophical Field' (March, 1918).

Lange, Francisco Curt, musicologist; b. Eilenburg, Germany, Dec. 12, 1903. He studied philosophy and architecture; music with Nikisch, Abert, Bekker, Bücken, and Sandberger. In 1924 he emigrated to Uruguay and settled in Montevideo, where he developed energetic activity in the fields of phonograph recording and publishing; was prof. of music history and musicology at the Univ. of Montevideo (1932-40); in 1940, established the Instituto Interamericano de Música, and Editorial Cooperativo Interamericano de Compositores, which published a long series of works by Latin American composers. In 1934 he launched the slogan 'Americanismo Musical,' urging musicians of both North and South America to promote native music. In 1939 he visited the U.S. as a lecturer. After another lecture tour in the U. S. in 1948, he went to Argentina, and established the dept. of musicology at the Universidad Nacional de Cuyo, in Mendoza. In 1957, he settled again in Montevideo. Beginning in 1935, he edited the *Boletín Latino-Americano de Música,* a series of bulky volumes containing documentary data on Latin American music and composers; separate volumes appeared in Montevideo, Lima, Bogota, Caracas, Rio de Janeiro, etc. He also publ. *Fonografía pedagógica* (3 vols., 1934-38); numerous essays and pamphlets dealing with literature, philosophy, pedagogy, and sociology (all in Spanish); brought out an important anthology *Latin-American Art Music for the Piano* (G. Schirmer, Inc., N.Y., 1942) with biographical sketches of 12 composers; also published a collection of Brazilian church music of the 18th century.

Lange, Gustav, German pianist and composer; b. Schwerstedt, near Erfurt, Aug. 13, 1830; d. Wernigerode, July 19, 1889. He studied with A. W. Bach, Grell, and Löschhorn. For many years, he lived in Berlin; wrote more than 400 piano pieces, generally facile, elegant, and effective, and many of which gained great vogue.

Lange, Hans, violinist and conductor; b. Istanbul, Feb. 17, 1884 (of German parents). He studied the violin as a child, then at the Prague Cons. with Ševčik, graduating in 1902 with highest honors. In 1903 he made his début as solo violinist with the Berlin master of the Frankfurt Opera; settled in the U. S. in 1923; was assistant conductor of the N. Y. Philharmonic (1923-33) and later an associate conductor (1933-36); then associate conductor of the Chicago Symph. Orch. (1936-46). In 1951 he was appointed conductor of the Albuquerque Civic Symphony.

Lange, Konrad von, German esthetician; b. Göttingen, March 15, 1855; d. Tübingen, July 28, 1921. In his theories he introduced the basic concept of 'illusion' in the creation and appreciation of art and music. He publ. *Die Bewusste Selbsttäuschung* (1895); *Das Wesen der Kunst* (2 vols., 1907); *Das Wesen der künstlerischen Erziehung* (1902); *Der Zweck der Kunst* (1912).

Lange, Samuel de, organist and composer; brother of Daniel de Lange; b. Rotterdam, Feb. 22, 1840; d. Stuttgart, July 7, 1911. He studied with Verhulst in Holland and with Winterberger in Vienna. He was with his brother in Lwow (1859-63); then taught successively at the Rotterdam Music School (1863-74), the Basel Music School (1874-76), and the Cologne Cons. (1876-85); then was conductor of the Oratorio Society at The Hague (1885-93); finally was prof. of organ and composition at the Stuttgart Cons. (1894); became its director in 1900. He wrote a piano concerto; 3 symphonies; 4 string quartets; 2 piano trios; 4 violin sonatas; 2 cello sonatas; 8 sonatas for organ; an oratorio, *Moses;* 3 cantatas, *De Opstanding, Die Totenklage,* and *Eines Königs Tränen;* male choruses; songs.

Lange-Müller, Peter Erasmus, Danish composer; b. Frederiksborg, near Copenhagen, Dec. 1, 1850; d. Copenhagen, Feb. 25, 1926. He studied at the Copenhagen Cons. His early compositions show the influence of J. P. E. Hartmann; those of his later period exhibit distinct individuality. —Works: operas (all produced in Copenhagen), *Tove* (Jan. 19, 1878), *Spanske Studenter* (Oct. 21, 1883), *Fru Jeanna* (Feb. 4, 1891), *Vikingeblod* (April 29, 1900); incidental music for *Fulvia* and *Det var en gang; Niels Ebbeson,* for baritone, men's chorus, and orch.; 2 symphonies; the orchestral suites *Alhambra* and *Weyerburg;* trio for violin, cello, and piano; piano pieces, etc.; some 200 songs, many of which gained great popularity.

Langendorff, Frieda, German dramatic contralto; b. Breslau, March 24, 1868; d. New York, June 11, 1947. She studied with Mme. Leffler-Burckard; made her début in Strasbourg (1901); sang at the Metropolitan Opera, N. Y. in 1907-08 and 1910-11. She then made an extensive concert tour throughout the U.S. (1912-13). In 1914 she was engaged by the Dresden Royal Opera; also sang at Bayreuth, Berlin, Helsinki, Brussels, and Amsterdam. She returned to New York after World War II. Among 76 operatic roles (which included mezzo-soprano parts) in her repertory were Ortrud, Fricka, Amneris, Azucena, and Dalila.

Langenus, Gustave, clarinetist; b. Malines, Belgium, Aug. 6, 1883; d. New York, Jan. 30, 1957. He studied at Brussels Cons. As a youth of 18, he traveled with Sousa's band in Europe; then lived in England; in 1910, came to the U.S.; was clarinetist with the N.Y. Symphony (1910-20); was one of the founders of the Chamber Music Society in N.Y. (1914); member of the N.Y. Philharmonic from 1920-23; taught at the Juilliard School of Music, and the Dalcroze School of Music. He publ. *Fingered Scale Studies for the Boehm Clarinet* (N. Y., 1911); *Modern Clarinet Playing* (N.Y., 1913); *Virtuoso Studies and Duos for Clarinet* (N.Y., 1915); *Complete Method for the Boehm Clarinet* (8 vols., N.Y., 1916).

Langer, Eduard, Russian pianist and composer; b. Moscow, May 3, 1835; d. there, June 5, 1905. He was a pupil at the Leipzig Cons. of Moscheles, Richter, and Hauptmann; upon returning to Moscow, he taught at the Cons. there; publ. numerous arrangements for 2 pianos (4 and 8 hands) of operas and orchestral works by Russian composers; his own compositions include a string quartet, a string trio, 2 violin sonatas, and many piano pieces.

Langer, Ferdinand, German composer and cellist; b. Leimen, near Heidelberg, Jan. 21, 1839; d. Kirneck (Black Forest), Aug. 25, 1905. An excellent cellist, he joined the orchestra of the Mannheim court theater; later became 2nd Kapellmeister there. With Emil Heckel, he founded the first 'Wagnerverein' in Germany (1883). He produced several locally successful operas in Mannheim: *Die gefährliche Nachbarschaft* (1868), *Dornröschen* (1873), *Aschenbrödel* (1878), *Murillo* (1887), and the 'romantische Volksoper' *Der Pfeiffer von Haardt* (1894). He revised Weber's *Silvana* for its revival in 1885.

Langer, Hermann, German organist and theorist; b. Höckendorf, near Tharandt, July 6, 1819; d. Dresden, Sept. 8, 1889. He studied in Leipzig with K. F. Becker; in 1843, became organist of the Univ. of Leipzig church; 1845, teacher of liturgical song at Leipzig Univ.; 1857, musical director there; went to Dresden in 1887 as Inspector of Organ Building. He publ. a *Repertorium für Männergesang; Der erste Unterricht im Gesang* (3 courses; 1876-77); also edited the 'Musikalische Gartenlaube.'

Langer, Victor, Hungarian composer; b. Budapest, Oct. 14, 1842; d. there, March 19, 1902. He studied in Budapest with R. Volkmann, and later at the Leipzig Cons. Returning to Budapest, he was active as a teacher, theater conductor, and editor of a Hungarian music journal. His songs *Ögyek dalai,* Hungarian dances, arrangements, etc., publ. under the pen-name of 'Aladar Tisza,' are in the genuine national vein; they enjoyed great popularity.

Langert, Johann August Adolf, German composer; b. Coburg, Nov. 26, 1836; d. there, Dec. 21, 1920. He was theater conductor in Coburg, Mannheim, and Basel; in 1873, became court conductor at Gotha, retiring in 1897 to his native town. He composed several operas: *Die Jungfrau von Orleans* (Coburg, 1861), *Des Sängers Fluch* (Coburg, 1863), *Dona Maria* (Darmstadt, 1866), *Die Fabier* (Coburg, 1866), *Dornröschen* (Leipzig, 1871), and *Jean Cavallier* (Coburg, 1880; rewritten and produced as *Die Camisarden,* 1887).

Langey, Otto, cellist and composer; b. Leichholz, near Frankfurt on the Oder, Oct. 20, 1851; d. New York, March 16, 1922. He studied cello with Specht in Sorau, Ullrich in Halle, and Cabisius in Bremen; theory and composition with W. Fritze in Liegnitz. In 1877 he went to London, playing in the Hallé and Richter concerts; came to the U. S. in 1889, and made a tour as soloist with the Boston Symph. Club; settled in N. Y. as teacher; in 1909, became arranger of orchestral music for G. Schirmer, Inc. He publ. the *Langey Tutors* (methods for 28 different instruments) and numerous compositions for orch. (*Arabian Serenade, Liberty Overture, 3 Oriental Sketches,* etc.).

Langhans, Friedrich Wilhelm, German author, composer, and violinist; b. Hamburg, Sept. 21, 1832; d. Berlin, June 9, 1892. He studied at the Leipzig Cons. with David (violin) and Richter (composition); then in

Paris with Alard (violin); from 1852-56, 1st violinist in the Gewandhaus Orch. at Leipzig; 1857-60, concertmaster at Düsseldorf; then teacher and violinist in Hamburg, Paris, and Heidelberg; *Dr. phil.* from Heidelberg (1871). He taught music history at Kullak's Neue Akademie der Tonkunst in Berlin (1874-81); in 1881, joined the faculty of the Scharwenka Cons. In 1858 he married the concert pianist Louise Japha (divorced in 1874). He publ. *Das musikalische Urteil* (1872; 2nd ed., 1886); *Die königliche Hochschule für Musik in Berlin* (1873); *Musikgeschichte in 12 Vorträgen* (1878; Dutch transl., 1885); *Die Geschichte der Musik des 17., 18. und 19. Jahrhunderts* (2 vols.; 1882-86; a well-written continuation of Ambros' great work); transl. Niecks' biography of Chopin into German (1889). He composed a symphony, a string quartet, a violin sonata, studies for violin, etc.

Lang-Köstlin, Josephine, German song composer; mother of Heinrich Adolf Köstlin; b. Munich, March 14, 1815; d. Tübingen, Dec. 2, 1880. She studied with Frau Berlinghof-Wagner and Mendelssohn; publ. many lieder. See a biographical sketch of her life by her son (Leipzig, 1881).

Langlais, Jean, French organist and composer; b. La Fontenelle, Feb. 15, 1907. He was blind from infancy; studied organ with Dupré at the Paris Cons., winning 1st prize in 1930; studied composition with Paul Dukas. He became organist at Montrouge; from 1945, organist at Ste.-Clotilde in Paris; also taught organ at the School for the Blind. His works are mainly for organ *(Deux offertoires pour tous les temps, Trois paraphrases grégoriennes,* etc.); also wrote a symph. poem, *Cloches;* a suite for cello and orch.; numerous choral works; trio for flute, violin, and viola.—Cf. A. Machabey, *Portraits de trente musiciens français* (Paris, 1949; pp. 109-13).

Langlé (lahn-glā), **Honoré François Marie,** theorist and composer; b. Monaco, 1741; d. Villiers-le-Bel, near Paris, Sept. 20, 1807. He studied in Naples at the Conservatorio della Pietà dei Turchini, with Cafaro. In 1768 he went to Paris, becoming a singing teacher at the École Royale de Chant in 1784; then was prof. of harmony and librarian at the Paris Cons. He wrote an important *Traité d'harmonie et de modulation* (1793; 2nd ed., 1797; chord building by thirds); *Traité de la basse sous le chant* (1798); *Nouvelle méthode pour chiffrer les accords* (1801); *Traité de la fugue* (1805); also collaborated with Cherubini on the latter's *Méthode de chant;* edited Mengozzi's *Méthode de chant du Conservatoire* after Mengozzi's death. Langlé composed a number of operas, only one of which was presented: *Corisandre, ou Les Fous par enchantement* (Paris, March 8, 1791).

Langley, Allan Lincoln, American violinist, viola player, and writer; b. Newport, R. I., June 11, 1892; d. (of a heart attack) in a Hudson tube train between Jersey City and New York City, Nov. 12, 1949. He studied at Brown Univ., Providence (B. A., 1914), and at the New England Cons. with Shepherd, Chadwick, Winternitz, and Mason; played violin and viola in the Boston Symph. (1918), National Symph. (1920-21), N. Y. Philharmonic (1921-27), and Richmond Symph. Orch. (1932-33); also made guest appearances as conductor. He wrote *Justice for Gustav Mahler,* in the 'Mus. Quarterly' (April, 1926); *Chadwick and the New England Conservatory of Music,* in the 'Mus. Quarterly' (Jan., 1936), etc.; also articles for the 'American Mercury,' 'Nation,' 'Commonweal,' 'American Spectator,' etc.

Langlotz, Karl A., teacher and composer; b. Saxe-Meiningen, Germany, June 20, 1834; d. Trenton, N. J., Nov. 25, 1915. He was a member of the Liszt circle in Weimar; in 1853, came to America; lived in Philadelphia as music teacher; 1857-68, instructor of German at Princeton; 1868, entered the Theological Seminary, graduating in 1871; 1874, moved to Trenton, where he taught music. He is known for composing the famous Princeton song *Old Nassau* (1859), at the suggestion of the Princeton students and teachers who gathered regularly to sing college songs; the song was first publ. in the earliest Princeton song book, 'Songs of Old Nassau' (N. Y., 1859).—Cf. W. S. Conrow, *'Old Nassau'* (N. Y., 1905).

Langstroth, Ivan Shed, American pianist, teacher, and composer; b. Alameda, Calif., Oct. 16, 1887. He studied in San Francisco with T. Vogt, then in Berlin with Juon, Humperdinck, and Lhevinne. In 1915 he was coach at the Kiel Opera; 1916, organist at the American Church in Berlin; 1917-20, toured Scandinavia as concert pianist; 1921-28, teacher at the New Cons. in Vienna; then returned to America; from 1943-45 he was lecturer on music at Brooklyn College; then teaching privately in New York. He wrote orchestral and choral works, chamber music, piano and organ pieces, songs, etc.

Lanier, Sidney, American poet and musician; b. Macon, Ga., Feb. 3, 1842; d. Lynn, N. C., Sept. 7, 1881. Best known for his poetry, Lanier learned as a child to play the piano, flute, guitar, violin, and organ. After serving in the Civil War, he was organist and choirmaster for a short period at a church in Montgomery, Ala. In 1873 he became first flutist of the Peabody Symph. Orch. in Baltimore. He wrote a number of articles on music and composed songs and flute pieces. —Cf. H. C. Thorpe, *Sidney Lanier: A Poet for Musicians,* in the 'Mus. Quarterly' (July, 1925); A. H. Starke, *Sidney Lanier as a Musician* (ib., Oct., 1934).

Laniere, Nicholas, English composer, lutenist, and painter; b. Greenwich (baptized Sept. 10), 1588; d. London, Feb., 1666. He is important as having been probably the first to introduce the Italian recitative style into England, in his music to masques, of which the first was Ben Jonson's *Lovers made Men* (London, Feb. 22, 1617). He was Master of the King's Musick under Charles I and Charles II. He wrote a pastoral on the birth of Prince Charles, a funeral hymn for Charles I, a cantata *Hero and Leander,* and some New Year's songs; his songs are found in MS in the British Museum, Bodleian Music School, Christ Church, and Fitzwilliam Museum, also in the published collections 'Select Musicall Ayres and Dialogues' (1653, 1659), 'The Musical Companion' (1667), 'The Treasury of Musick' (1669), 'Choice Ayres and Songs' (1685), and J. S. Smith's 'Musica antiqua' (1812).—Cf. J. Pulver, 'A Biographical Dictionary of Old English Music' (1927); 'Dictionary of National Biography' (vol. II; reprinted Oxford, 1921-22).

Lankow, Anna, noted German singing teacher; b. Bonn, Jan. 13, 1850; d. there, March 19, 1908. She studied singing in Cologne, Leipzig, and Dresden; began her career as a concert singer; then was engaged as contralto in the Weimar Opera; however, because she had been lame since childhood, she was forced to abandon the stage. In 1883 she married the sculptor Paul Pietsch of Berlin; after his death in 1885, she came to America, settling in New York as a singing teacher; subsequently returned to Germany. She published a valuable treatise, *Die Wissenschaft des Kunstgesangs* (1899, in German and English).

Lanner, August (Joseph), Austrian violinist and composer; son of Joseph (Franz Karl) Lanner; b. Vienna, Jan. 23, 1834; d. there, Sept. 27, 1855. A talented violinist, dance composer, and conductor, he died in his 22nd year.

Lanner, Joseph (Franz Karl), Austrian violinist and dance composer; b. Vienna, April 12, 1801; d. Oberdöbling, near Vienna, April 14, 1843. A self-taught violinist and composer, he joined Pamer's dance orch. when he was 12. In 1818 he formed a trio which Johann Strauss, Sr., joined, making it a quartet. The group grew in size, and by 1824 it was a full sized classical orchestra which became famous and performed in coffee houses, taverns, at balls, etc. The orchestra was subsequently divided into two ensembles, with Lanner leading one, and Strauss the other. Lanner and Strauss are credited with the creation of the modern Viennese waltz. Lanner's output totals 207 popular pieces, including 112 waltzes, 25 Ländler, 10 quadrilles, 3 polkas, 28 galops, and 6 marches; he also wrote an overture to *Der Preis einer Lebensstunde; Banquet-Polonaise; Tarantella;* and a *Bolero.* His complete works in 8 vols., ed. by E. Kremser, were publ. by Breitkopf & Härtel in 1889; selections were brought out by Oscar Bie (Munich, 1920) and Alfred Orel, in the 'Denkmäler der Tonkunst in Österreich' (vol. 33).—Cf. H. Sachs, *J. Lanner* (Vienna, 1889); F. Rebay and O. Keller, *J. Lanner* (Vienna, 1901); F. Lange, *J. Lanner und Johann Strauss, Ihre Zeit, ihr Leben und ihre Werke* (Vienna, 1904; 2nd ed., 1919).

Lannoy (lăhn-nwăh'), **Eduard,** composer; b. Brussels, Dec. 4, 1787; d. Vienna, March 28, 1853. His family moved to Graz when he was a child; he studied there and in Paris. In 1813 he went to Vienna, where he became an active promoter of the 'Gesellschaft der Musikfreunde'; from 1830-35 he was a member of the executive board of the Vienna Cons. He wrote several operas and 'Singspiele,' a symphony, overtures, chamber music, piano pieces, songs, etc.

Lans, Michael J. A., Dutch composer and authority on Gregorian chant; b. Haarlem, July 18, 1845; d. Amsterdam, Feb. 3, 1908. A Roman Catholic priest, he started publication of an ecclesiastical periodical 'Gregoriusblad' (1876); composed several Masses; publ. *Palestrina* (1882), and a manual of strict counterpoint (1889).

Lantins, Arnold de, Netherlands composer; b. probably at Lantin, near Liège, c. 1400; date of death unknown. He traveled in Italy about 1427; was a singer in the Papal Chapel in Rome between Nov., 1431 and July, 1432. His employment of carefully connected chords suggesting purely harmonic procedures is of historical interest. Two motets, *Tota pulchra es* and *O pulcherrima mulierum* (from the *Song of Solomon)*, are reproduced in Charles Van den Borren's *Polyphonia Sacra: A Continental Miscellany of the 15th Century* (1932). Other works are found in J. Stainer, *Dufay and His Contemporaries* (London, 1898), in J. Wolf, *Geschichte der Mensural-Notation,* and in vol. 31 of 'Denkmäler der Tonkunst in Österreich.' —Cf. Charles Van den Borren, *Hugo et Arnold de Lantins* (Liège, 1935). See also G. Reese, *Music in the Renaissance* (N. Y., 1954; pp. 39-40).

Lantins, Hugo de, Netherlands singer and composer; possibly related to Arnold de Lantins; b. probably at Lantin, near Liège, shortly before 1400; death date unknown. As a young man, he was in Italy, where he wrote an ode *Tra quante regione* for the marriage of Theodore Palaiologos (1421); several motets and other ecclesiastical pieces are extant. —Cf. Charles Van den Borren, *Arnold et Hugo de Lantins* (Liège, 1935). See also G. Reese, *Music in the Renaissance* (N. Y., 1954; p. 41).

Lanza, Mario (real name, Alfredo Arnold Cocozza), American singer of Italian descent; b. Philadelphia, Jan. 31, 1921. He studied singing with Enrico Rosati; appeared in recitals and opera. In 1951 he was starred in the title role of a highly successful film, *The Great Caruso.*

Lanzetti (lahn-tseht'-tē), **Salvatore,** Italian cellist; b. Naples, c. 1710; d. Turin, c. 1780. He was one of the earliest virtuosos on the cello; during his residence in London (about 1739-56), he succeeded in establishing the cello there as a favorite solo instrument; returned to Italy as a member of the royal chapel at Turin. He publ. 2 books of cello sonatas (1736), 6 solos, and 6 sonatas for 2 cellos with continuo; also a method, *Principes de doigter pour le violoncelle dans tous les tons.*

Laparra, Raoul, French composer; b. Bordeaux, May 13, 1876; killed during an air raid near Paris, April 4, 1943. He studied at the Paris Cons. with Gedalge, Massenet, and Fauré; won the Grand Prix de Rome with his cantata *Ulysse* (June 27, 1903). He was music critic of 'Le Matin,' resigning in 1937 to dedicate himself entirely to composition. He was at his best in music inspired by Spanish subjects. —Works: the operas *Peau d'âne* (Bordeaux, 1899), *La Habanera* (Paris, Feb. 26, 1908; his best known work), *La Jota* (Paris, April 26, 1911), *Le Joueur de viole* (Paris, Dec. 24, 1925), *Las Toreras* (Lille, Feb., 1929), *L'Illustre Fregona* (Paris, Feb. 16, 1931); incidental music to *El Conquistador; Un Dimanche basque,* suite for orch. and piano, etc. He also wrote *La Musique et la Danse populaire en Espagne* for Lavignac's 'Encyclopédie,' and *Bizet et l'Espagne* (Paris, 1934).

Laporte, Joseph de, French writer; b. Belfort, 1713; d. Paris, Dec. 19, 1779. He was a Jesuit abbé; wrote *Anecdotes dramatiques* (3 vols., 1775; contains all varieties of theatrical works); *Dictionnaire dramatique* (3 vols., 1776); *Almanach des spectacles de Paris, ou Calendrier historique des théâtres de l'Opéra, des Comédies française et italienne et des foires* (48 vols. in all; those from 1750-79 by Laporte; the rest by Duchesne and others).

La Pouplinière (lah-pŏŏ-plē-ñär'), **Alexandre-Jean-Joseph Le Riche de,** French musical amateur; b. Chinon, July 26, 1693; d. Paris, Dec. 5, 1762. A wealthy member of the nobility and a statesman, he was a patron of music; pupil of Rameau. The musical soirées he gave in his private theater were famous; he engaged Gossec as mus. director (1751); introduced Johann Stamitz to the Parisian public; upon Stamitz's advice, he added horns, clarinets, and a harp to his orchestra, instruments seldom heard in a concert orchestra before that time. La Pouplinière wrote a number of arias, some of which Rameau incorporated into his own works. —Cf. Ancelet, *Observations sur la musique et les instruments* (Amsterdam, 1757); P. Hédouin, *Gossec* (Paris, 1852); P. Hédouin, *Mosaïque* (Paris, 1856); G. Cucuel, *La Pouplinière et la musique de chambre au XVIIIe siècle* (Paris, 1913).

La Prade, Ernest, American composer and writer; b. Memphis, Tenn., Dec. 20, 1889. He studied violin at the Cincinnati College of Music; at the Royal Cons. in Brussels with César Thomson, and in London with J. Jongen (composition). He subsequently taught at the Cincinnati College of Music; member of the Cincinnati Symph. Orch. (1909-12), of the Belgian and Holbrook Quartets in London (1914-17), of the N. Y. Symph. Orch. (1919-28); in 1929, joined the staff of N. B. C.; in 1950, supervisor of music research there. He wrote a comic opera, *Xantha* (London, 1917), and songs; publ. *Alice in Orchestralia* (1925); *Marching Notes* (1929); *Broadcasting Music* (1947); and many magazine articles.

La Presle, Jacques de, French composer; b. Versailles, July 5, 1888. He studied at the Paris Cons.; received the Grand Prix de Rome in 1921; in 1937, appointed prof. of harmony at the Paris Cons. His works include *Apocalypse de St.-Jean* (1928); *Album d'images,* a suite for orch. (1935); piano concerto (1949); chamber music; songs.

Laquai, Reinhold, Swiss composer; b. Zürich, May 1, 1894. He studied at the Zürich Cons.; later with Busoni in Berlin. In 1920 he became a teacher at the Zürich Cons.; works include the operas *Der Schleier der Tanit* and *Die Revisionsreise;* many orchestral works (3 symphonies, 5 overtures, 2 serenades, a concert piece for piano and orch., etc.); chamber music (trios, sonatas for violin, flute, cello, bassoon and horn, clarinet, etc., piano quintet); piano pieces and more than 200 songs.

Lara, Isidore de. See **De Lara.**

Laroche (lah-rohsh'), **Hermann Augustovitch,** Russian writer and critic; b. St. Petersburg, May 25, 1845; d. there, Oct. 18, 1904. He studied with Rubinstein and Zaremba at the St. Petersburg Cons., and with Tchaikovsky in Moscow. He became prof. at the Moscow Cons. (1867-70); then at the St. Petersburg Cons. (1872-79); contributed numerous articles to Russian journals; collected his essays and criticisms and published them in 1894. His most important work is *M. I. Glinka and His Place in Russian Music* (1868; new ed., 1953); with N. Kashkin he wrote *Reminiscences of Tchaikovsky* (1894); translated into Russian Hanslick's *Vom Musikalisch-Schönen.* He composed an overture to *Karmosina,* a symphonic *Allegro,* and songs. Most of his criticisms were publ. in 1913; his articles on Tchaikovsky (3 vols.) in 1913-24.

L'Arronge (lahr-rohnzh), **Adolf,** composer and conductor; b. Hamburg, March 8, 1838; d. Berlin, May 25, 1908. He studied at the Leipzig Cons. with R. Genée; theater conductor in Cologne, Danzig, Königsberg, Würzburg, Stuttgart, Budapest, etc.; in 1866, became director of the Kroll Opera, Berlin; then of the Lobetheater in Breslau (1874-78). Returning to Berlin, he bought the Friedrich - Wilhelmstädtisches Theater in 1881, and managed it until 1894 as 'Deutsches Theater.' He brought out many musical farces, 'Singspiele,' etc. at the Wallnertheater, including his comic operas *Das Gespenst* and *Der zweite Jakob,* the 'Volksstücke' *Das Grosse Los* (1868) and *Mein Leopold,* etc.; also wrote many songs.

Larsen, Jens Peter, Danish musicologist; b. Frederiksberg, June 14, 1902. He studied at the Univ. of Copenhagen with Th. Laub, taking an M.A. in 1928 and a Ph.D. in 1939; church organist (1930-45); lecturer in music at the Univ. of Copenhagen (1945); 1949, head of the Institute of Musicology. He has published valuable works on Haydn: *Die Haydn-Überlieferung* (Copenhagen, 1939); *Drei Haydn Kataloge in Faksimile* (Copenhagen, 1941); also *Handel's Messiah* (N. Y., 1957); was general editor of a proposed collected edition of Haydn's works, of which 4 vols. appeared in 1950.

Larsen, Nils, Norwegian pianist; b. Oslo, June 7, 1888; d. there, Nov. 7, 1937. He studied in Oslo with M. Knutzen and in Berlin with Ganz and da Motta. He wrote a number of piano pieces; edited the works of Christoph Graupner.

Larsén-Todsen, Nanny, Swedish soprano; b. Hagby, Kalmar län, Aug. 2, 1884. She studied at the Stockholm Cons. and in Germany and Italy. In 1906 she made her début at the Royal Theater in Stockholm as Agatha in *Der Freischütz;* was a member of the Royal Theater (1907-22), specializing in Wagnerian roles; sang at La Scala in Milan (1923-24), the Metropolitan Opera House in N. Y. (1925-27; début Jan. 31, 1925 as Brünnhilde in *Götterdämmerung),* at Bayreuth (1927-31), and made guest appearances at most of the European opera houses. Her principal roles were the 3 Brünnhildes, Isolde, Fricka, and Leonore. She married H. Todsen in 1916; following her retirement from the stage, she became a teacher in Stockholm.

Larsson, Lars-Erik, Swedish composer; b. Akarp, near Lund, May 15, 1908. He studied at the Royal Academy of Music in Stockholm, then with A. Berg in Vienna; also in Leipzig. In 1931 he was choirmaster of the Stockholm Opera; in 1932, returned to Akarp, devoting himself to composition. —Works: the opera *Prinsessan av Cypern* (Stockholm, April 29, 1937); incidental music to plays by Shakespeare, Schiller, and Strindberg; 3 symphonies (1928; 1936; 1945); saxophone concerto (1934); cello concerto (1948); *Ostinato,* for orch. (Stockholm, Nov. 24, 1937); 2 *Divertimenti* for chamber orch.; string quartet (1944); other chamber music; choral works; songs; piano pieces, etc. Several of his compositions were performed at the festivals of the International Society for Contemporary Music: *Sinfonietta* (Florence, April 5, 1934); overture (Barcelona, April 23, 1936); etc.

La Rue, Pierre de (Petrus Platensis, Pierchon, Pierson, Pierzon, Perisone, Pierazon de la Ruellien), eminent Netherlands contrapuntist and composer; b. probably in Tournai, where his family is known to have resided; d. Courtrai, Nov. 20, 1518. He was at the court of Burgundy (1477); attached to the chapel of Archduke Maximilian of Austria (April, 1485), and the chapel of Notre-Dame in Bois-leDuc (1490-91); chapel singer at the court of Burgundy (1492-1510); at the court of Margaret of Austria; canon at the court of Philippe le Beau in Malines (1501); prebend at Courtrai, Namur, and Termonde (from 1501); *cantor principis* at Courtrai (1502). He wrote about 40 Masses, of which many were publ.; others are in MS in libraries in Brussels, Malines, Rome, Vienna, Berlin, etc. Motets and madrigals were printed in collections of the time. A motet was scored by Dreher in his 'Cantiones sacrae' (1872). A Mass *Ave Maria* was publ. by H. Expert in *Les Maîtres-Musiciens de la Renaissance française* (1890), a Kyrie by A. Schering in *Geschichte der Musik in Beispielen* (No. 65), some motets, by R. J. van Maldeghem in *Trésor musical* (1865-93), motets and a Requiem by F. Blume in *Das Chorwerk* (vols. 3 and 11). —Cf. A. W. Ambros, *Geschichte der Musik* (vol. 3, p. 234 ff.); P. Wagner, *Geschichte der Messe* (p. 166 ff.); K. E. Roediger, *Die geistlichen Musikhandschriften der Universitäts-Bibliothek Jena* (1935); H. Riemann, *Handbuch der Musikgeschichte* (vol. 2, p. 286 ff.); Josef Robyns, *Pierre de la Rue* (Brussels, 1954; in Flemish); G. Reese, *Music in the Renaissance* (N. Y., 1954).

La Salette, Joubert de, French theorist; b. Grenoble, 1762; d. there, 1832. He wrote *Sténographie musicale* (1805; an unsuccessful invention on the lines of German tablature); *Considérations sur les divers systèmes de la musique ancienne et moderne* (1810; his best work); *De la notation musicale en général, et en particulier de celle du système grec* (1817); *De la fixité et de l'invariabilité des sons musicaux* (1824); and other essays.

Lasalle, Jean-Louis. See **Lassalle.**

Laserna, Blas, Spanish composer; b. Corella, Navarre, Feb. 4, 1751; d. Madrid, Aug. 8, 1816. He was official composer for several theaters; composed the music for Ramón de la Cruz's comedy *El café de Barcelona* (Barcelona, Nov. 4, 1788); also the operas *La gitanilla por amor* (Madrid, 1791; successful) and *Idomeneo* (Madrid, Dec. 9, 1792); incidental music to plays of Calderón, Lope de Vega, Moreto, etc.; composed many *tonadillas, sainetes,* etc.

Las Infantas. See **Infantas.**

Láska, Gustav, Bohemian composer and double-bass player; b. Prague, Aug. 23, 1847; d. Schwerin, Oct. 16, 1928. He studied at the Prague Cons. with Hrabe, Kittl, and Krejči. Following a year of giving double-bass concerts, he joined the court orch. in Kassel (1868-72); then in Sondershausen (1872-75); was theater conductor in Göttingen, Eisleben, and Halberstadt; played double-bass in Berlin; in 1878, became double-bass player in the court orch. in Schwerin. He wrote an opera, *Der Kaisersoldat;* a cantata, *Deutsches Aufgebot;* 2 symphonies; 2 overtures; double-bass concerto; 3 Masses; several works for double-bass and piano *(3 Romanzen, Rhapsodie, Erotik, Ballade und Polonaise, Schlummerlied, Karneval von Venedig,* etc.); piano pieces; songs.

Lasner, Ignaz, cellist; b. Drosau, Bohemia, Aug. 8, 1815; d. Vienna, Aug. 18, 1883. He studied with Goltermann in Prague, and Merk and Servais in Vienna. He was an orchestra player in Vienna; composed cello pieces.

Lassalle, Jean-Louis, French baritone; b. Lyons, Dec. 14, 1847; d. Paris, Sept. 7, 1909. After training in industrial designing and painting, he entered the Paris Cons. to study voice; also studied privately with Novelli. In 1869 he sang in Liège, Lille, Toulouse, and Brussels; début at the Paris Opéra, June 7, 1872; remained there for more than 20 years, with extended leaves of absence during which he toured throughout Europe, Russia, and the U.S. (début, Metropolitan Opera House, N. Y., Jan. 15, 1892, as Nelusco in *L'Africaine);* remained at the Metropolitan until 1897, and was one of the brightest stars in a company that included the de Reszkes, Plançon, Nordica, Melba, Calvé, and Eames. He returned to Paris in 1901 and settled there as à singing teacher; in 1903, became prof. at the Paris Cons. His repertory comprised about 60 operas, ranging from Donizetti to Wagner.

Lassen, Eduard, eminent conductor and composer; b. Copenhagen, April 13, 1830; d. Weimar, Jan. 15, 1904. His family moved to Brussels when he was a child; he entered the Brussels Cons., taking the Belgian Prix de Rome (1851). Following a tour through Germany and Italy, he went to Weimar, where Liszt fostered the presentation of his 5-act opera *Landgraf Ludwigs Brautfahrt* (1857). He became court music director in Weimar (1858); then conductor of the Weimar Opera (1860-95); led the world première of Saint-

Saëns' opera *Samson et Dalila* (Weimar, Dec. 2, 1877). He also wrote the operas *Frauenlob* (Weimar, 1860) and *Le Captif* (Brussels, 1865); a ballet, *Diana;* 2 symphonies; a *Fest-Cantate;* 2 overtures; a *Te Deum;* a set of *Biblische Bilder,* for chorus and orch.; songs, etc.; also incidental music to *Oedipus* (1874), Hebbel's *Nibelungen,* Goethe's *Faust* (parts 1 and 2; 1876), Scheffel's *Die Linde am Ettersberg* (1878), *Circe* (1881), Goethe's *Pandora* (1886).

Lassus, Ferdinand de, eldest son of Roland de Lassus; d. Aug. 27, 1609; musician at Munich court (1583-85); court conductor at Sigmaringen; tenor singer in Munich (1590); went with the court to Landshut (1595) and later became court conductor there. He publ. *Cantiones sacrae suavissimae* (1587; motets); edited, with his brother Rudolph, his father's *Magnum opus musicum.* —Cf. H. Delmotte, *Notice biographique sur Roland Delattre* (Valenciennes, 1836; includes biography and list of works of Ferdinand de Lassus).

Lassus, Ferdinand de, son of Ferdinand and grandson of Roland de Lassus; d. c. 1635; studied in Rome (1609); court conductor (1616) and official (1629) under the Duke of Bavaria. Of his works, written for 8-16-voiced double chorus in the style made popular by the Venetian school, few remain. He publ. *Apparatus musicus* (motets, Mass, Magnificat, Litany, etc.; 8 voices; 1622).

Lassus, Roland de (Latin, Orlandus Lassus; Italian, Orlando di Lasso), the greatest of the Netherlands composers and one of the foremost contrapuntists of the Renaissance; b. Mons, 1532; d. Munich, June 14, 1594. He was a chorister in the church of St. Nicolas, Mons; his voice was exceptionally beautiful, so that he was kidnapped three times to secure him for other choruses. His parents finally allowed him to enter the service of Ferdinando Gonzaga, viceroy of Sicily (1544); he followed Gonzaga to Palermo and to Milan; at the age of 18, he was placed in the service of Marchese della Terza (1550). From April, 1553 to Dec., 1554 he was chorusmaster at San Giovanni in Laterano. His parents died in 1554; Lassus subsequently joined Cesare Brancaccio, a music lover from Naples; with him he supposedly visited England and France; this visit was of brief duration, if it took place at all. In 1555 he settled in Antwerp. Both socially and artistically, he enjoyed a fine reputation in Antwerp, despite his youth; he had his first works printed in Venice (1555), containing 22 madrigals to poems of Petrarch; and in the same year, he publ. in Antwerp a collection of madrigals and motets to words in Italian, French, and Latin. In 1556 he was offered a highly desirable post at the court of Albert V of Bavaria, and settled in Munich; in 1558 he married an aristocratic lady, Regina Wechinger. He remained in Munich for 38 years, until his death, with the exception of a trip to Italy (1567-68), which he undertook to engage musicians and singers for the Bavarian court, and a further visit to Paris in 1571. He brought Giovanni Gabrieli to Munich in 1575. On Dec. 7, 1570 he received from the Emperor Maximilian a hereditary rank of nobility. His last journey was to Regensburg a year before his death. —Lassus represents the culmination of the great era of Netherlandish polyphony; his superlative mastery in sacred as well as secular music renders him one of the most versatile composers of his time; he was equally capable of writing in the most elevated style and in the popular idiom; his art was supranational; he wrote Italian madrigals, German lieder, French chansons, and Latin motets. Musicians of his time described him variously as the 'Belgian Orpheus' and the 'Prince of Music.' The sheer scope of his production is amazing; he left more than 2000 works in various genres. The publication of his collected works was begun by Breitkopf & Härtel of Leipzig in 1894, under the editorship of Haberl and Sandberger, and continued until 1919; 21 vols. were issued; a new series was begun in 1955 by the Bärenreiter Verlag under the editorship of W. Boetticher, who also publ. a complete catalogue of works (Berlin, 1956). The *Patrocinium musices* (1573-98), a 12-volume series published in Munich by Adam Berg, under ducal patronage, contained 7 vols. of Lassus' works: vol. I, 21 motets; vol. II, 5 Masses; vol. III, Offices; vol. IV, a Passion, vigils, etc.; vol. V, 10 Magnificats; vol. VII, 13 Magnificats; vol. VIII, 6 Masses. Lassus' sons publ. 516 of his motets under the title *Magnum opus musicum* (1604). Eitner publ. *Chronologisches Verzeichnis der Druckwerke des Orlando di Lassus* (Berlin, 1874). Lassus' most celebrated work, *Psalmi Davidis poenitentiales,* was publ. in modern notation by Dehn (1838) and Bäuerle (1906); collections of Proske, Rochlitz, Commer, and others contain several more detached pieces. A few selections are to be found in Schering's *Geschichte der Musik in Beispielen* (Nos. 125-127). Many pieces have been publ. by H. J. Therstappen in vols. 34, 37, 41, and 48 of *Das Chorwerk* (1935-37), and there are a considerable number in the catalogues of leading publishers. —Bibliography: H. Delmotte,

Notice biographique sur Roland Delattre connu sous le nom d'Orland de Lassus (Valenciennes, 1836); A. Mathieu, *Biographie de Roland de Lattre* (Mons, 1851); *Register für die Geschichte der Musik in Bayern,* ed. by D. Mettenleiter (Brixen, 1868); W. Bäumker, *Orlandus de Lassus, der letzte grosse Meister der niederländischen Tonschule* (Freiburg, 1878); J. Declève, *Roland de Lassus: sa vie et ses œuvres* (Mons, 1894); F. X. Haberl, *Synchronistische Tabelle über den Lebensgang von Giovanni Pierluigi da Palestrina und Orlando di Lasso,* in 'Kirchenmusikalisches Jahrbuch' (vol. IX, 1894); A. Sandberger, *Beiträge zur Geschichte der bayrischen Hofkapelle* (vols. I and III; Leipzig, 1894); E. Destouches, *Orlando di Lasso: ein Lebensbild* (Munich, 1894); E. Schmitz, *Orlando di Lasso* (Leipzig, 1915); E. Closson, *Roland de Lassus* (1919); R. Casimiri, *Orlando di Lasso, maestro di cappella al Laterano nel 1553* (Rome, 1920); Charles Van den Borren, *Orlande de Lassus* (Paris, 1920); A. Sandberger, *Ausgewählte Aufsätze* (Munich, 1921); A. Sandberger, *Orlando di Lasso und die geistigen Strömungen seiner Zeit* (Munich, 1926); Charles Van den Borren, *En quelle année Roland de Lassus est-il né?* (The Hague, 1926); E. Lowinsky, *Der Motettenstil Orlando di Lassos* (Heidelberg, 1933); L. Behr, *Die deutschen Gesänge Orlando di Lassos* (Erlangen, 1935); E. Lowinsky, *Das Antwerpener Motettenbuch Orlando di Lassos und seine Beziehungen zum Motettenschaffen der niederländischen Zeitgenossen* (The Hague, 1937); Lucie Balmer, *Orlando di Lassos Motetten* (Berne, 1938); J. Huschke, *Orlando di Lassos Messen* (Leipzig, 1941); F. Blume, *Lasso und Palestrina,* in 'Deutsche Musikkultur' (vol. IX, 1944); C. Van den Borren, *Roland de Lassus* (1944); A. Einstein, *The Italian Madrigal* (Princeton, 1949); G. Reese, *Music in the Renaissance* (N. Y., 1954); W. Boetticher, *Orlando di Lasso* (2 vols., Berlin, 1956; contains complete list of works).

Lassus, Rudolph de, organist and composer; son of Roland de Lassus; d. Munich, 1625. He was a musician in the court orch. at Munich from 1585 until his death; was an organist and composer of merit and repute; various works were publ.; 3 Masses and 3 Magnificats are in MS in Munich. Two motets are included in Proske's *Musica divina* (vol. I). With his brother Ferdinand, he edited his father's *Magnum opus musicum.* —Cf. H. Delmotte, *Notice biographique sur Roland Delattre connu sous le nom d'Orland de Lassus* (Valenciennes, 1836; includes biography and list of works).

László, Alexander, Hungarian composer; b. Budapest, Nov. 22, 1895; studied at the Budapest Academy with A. Szendy (piano) and Herzfeld (composition); in 1915 he went to Berlin; was active as a pianist; also worked on the radio and in film enterprises. In 1938 he emigrated to the U.S.; in 1945, settled in Hollywood. He cultivated the idea of music expressed through colors; introduced a specially constructed 'color pianoforte' *(Farblichtklavier)* at the Kiel music festival (June 14, 1925); for the projection of the colors corresponding to music in proportional wave lengths he invented the Sonchromatoscope and a new system of notation called Sonchromography. His book *Die Farblichtmusik* (1925) discusses this new technique. His works include, besides special compositions for color lights, the pantomimes *Marionetten* (Budapest, 1916), *Die schöne O-sang* (Hamburg, 1919), *Panoptikum,* etc.; *News of the Day, Hungarian Dance Suite,* and *Fantasy of Colors,* for piano; *Mechanized Forces,* for orch.; *Hollywood Concerto* and *The Ghost Train of Marshall Pass,* for piano and orch.; arrangements for piano of various works by classical composers; film music.

Latham, William Peters, American composer; b. Shreveport, La., Jan. 4, 1917. He studied at the Cincinnati Cons. of Music, and at the Eastman School of Music, with Eugene Goossens, Herbert Elwell, and Howard Hanson. He was appointed to the faculty of Iowa State Teachers College in 1946. His works include Symphony No. 1 (Rochester, April 25, 1950); Symphony No. 2 (1953); symph. poem *The Lady of Shalott* (Cincinnati, March 7, 1941); *River to the Sea,* ballad for baritone and orch. (1942); *Fantasy* for violin and orch. (1946); suite for trumpet and string orch. (1951); cantata *The Ascension of Jesus* (1952); *Psalm 130; Psalm 148;* chamber music; flute sonatina (1937); 3 string quartets (1938-40); 3 string trios (1938-39); violin sonata (1949); etc.

Latilla, Gaetano, Italian composer; b. Bari, Jan. 12, 1711; d. Naples, 1791. As a child, he sang in the choir of the cathedral in Bari; then studied at the Conservatorio di Sant' Onofrio in Naples. He was 2nd maestro di cappella at Santa Maria Maggiore in Rome from 1738-41, when illness forced him to return to Naples; in 1756 he became chorus-master at the Conservatorio della Pietà in Venice; 1762, 2nd maestro di cappella at St. Mark's in Venice. In 1772 Latilla again returned to Naples, where he remained until his death. He wrote about 50 operas, including *Li mariti a forza* (Naples, 1732); *An-*

gelica ed Orlando (Naples, 1735); *Gismondo* (Naples, 1737; also known as *La finta giardiniera;* perf. as *Don Colascione* in London, 1749); *Madama Ciana* (Rome, 1738; perf. as *Gli artigiani arrichiti* in London, 1750, and in Paris, 1753); *I sposi incogniti* (Naples, 1779); also the oratorio *L'onnipotenza e la misericordia divina;* 6 string quartets; church music; etc.

La Tombelle (lah-tohn-bel'), **Fernand de,** French organist and composer; b. Paris, Aug. 3, 1854; d. Château de Fayrac, Dordogne, Aug. 13, 1928. He first studied with his mother; then at the Paris Cons. with Guilmant (organ) and Dubois (composition); also with Saint-Saëns. From 1885-98 he was assistant organist at the Madeleine; 1896-1904, prof. of theory at the Schola Cantorum. —Works: the oratorios *Crux, L'Abbaye,* and *Jeanne d'Arc;* operettas *Un bon numéro* and *Un Rêve au pays du bleu* (1892); ballets *La Muse fleurie* and *La Roche aux Fées;* orchestral suites *Impressions matinales, Livres d'images, Tableaux musicaux, Suite féodale;* symph. poem *Antar;* cantatas *Ste.-Cécile* and *Ste.-Anne;* incidental music to *La Magdaléenne, Yannic, Conte bleu;* chamber music (quartets, trios, sonatas for violin and piano); a Mass; numerous sacred choruses; works for organ; songs. He also wrote a method for the harmonium.

Lattuada, Felice, Italian composer; b. Caselle di Morimondo, Milan, Feb. 5, 1882. He studied at the Milan Cons. with Ferroni, graduating in 1911. His works include the operas *La tempestà* (Milan, Nov. 23, 1922), *Sandha* (Genoa, Feb. 21, 1924), *Le preziose ridicole* (Milan, Feb. 9, 1929), *Don Giovanni* (Naples, May 18, 1929), *La caverna di Salamanca* (Genoa, March 1, 1938); *Canto augurale per la Nazione Eletta,* for tenor, chorus, and orch.; orchestral works: *Sinfonia romantica* (1911); *Cimitero di guerra; Il mistero della Passione di Cristo; Incanti della notte; Divertimento rustico; Prelude and Fugue;* other choral, orchestral, and chamber works; also music for films.

Laub, Ferdinand, violinist and composer; b. Prague, Jan. 19, 1832; d. Gries, near Bozen, Tyrol, March 17, 1875. A precocious violinist, he entered the Prague Cons. as a child; under the patronage of the Grand Duke Stephen, he went to Vienna for further study (1847); then made a German tour, visited Paris, and played in London; 1853, concertmaster at Weimar; in 1855, leader of the court orch. in Berlin; 1855-57, taught at the Stern Cons. After spending some time in Vienna (1862-65), he went on a Russian tour, following which he became prof. of violin at the Moscow Cons. (1866). He spent his last years in Karlsbad and Tyrol. He wrote an opera, *Die Griesbäcker;* brought out 2 collections of Czech melodies; publ. violin pieces. — Cf. B. Šich, *Ferdinand Laub* (Prague, 1951).

Lauber, Joseph, Swiss composer; b. Ruswil, Canton Lucerne, Dec. 25, 1864; d. Geneva, May 27, 1952. He studied in Zürich with Hegar, in Munich with Rheinberger, and in Paris with Massenet and Diémer. Returning to Switzerland, he taught at the Zürich Cons.; then conducted a theater orch. in Geneva (1905-07). He wrote more than 200 compositions, including the opera *Die Hexe;* oratorio *Ad gloriam Dei;* 5 symphonies, and other orchestral works; 5 concertos (including one for double-bass with orch.); chamber works; choral music; piano pieces; songs; etc.

Launis (low'-nis), **Armas Emanuel** (real name, Lindberg), Finnish musicologist and composer; b. Hämeenlinna (Tavastehus), April 22, 1884. He studied with Sibelius in Helsingfors; then at the Stern Cons. in Berlin with W. Klatte; in Weimar with W. von Baussnern; musical history at the Univ. of Helsingfors with Ilmari Krohn; *Dr. phil.* with the thesis *Über Art, Entstehung und Verbreitung der Estnisch-Finnischen Runenmelodien* (Helsingfors, 1913). In 1930 he settled in Nice. —Works: operas *Seitsemän veljestä (The 7 Brothers;* Helsingfors, April 11, 1913), *Kullervo* (Helsingfors, Feb. 28, 1917), *Le chant de la sorcière* (1934), *Aslak Hetta* (Nice, 1938), *Le Foulard enchanté* (1938), *Jehudith* (1940); 2 cantatas (1906 and 1910); chamber music; piano pieces; songs; etc.; also film music. He edited several collections of Finnish folksongs, including *Lappische Juoigos-Melodien* (1908), vol. 4 of I. Krohn's 'Suomen Kansan Sävelmiä' (I, 1910; II, 1930), etc.; also various essays on Norse runes (folk melodies).

Laurence, Frederick, English composer; b. London, May 25, 1884. After beginning his career in business, he studied music privately with Josef Holbrooke; also in Germany, France, and Austria. Returning to London, he was for a while active in music publishing and organization. His compositions include the orchestral works *The Spirit's Wayfaring* (London, Oct. 2, 1918), *The Dance of the Witch Girl* (London, Oct. 12, 1920), *A Miracle, Enchantment, Fire Earth, Milandor, Night, The Dream of Harlequin, The Passionate Quest, The Gate of Vision; Tristis,* for string orch.; the dance poem *The Revellers;* sextet for strings; trio for violin, cello, and piano; violin sonata; piano pieces; etc.

Laurencie, Lionel de la. See La Laurencie.

Laurencin, Ferdinand Peter, writer on music; b. Kremsier, Moravia, Oct. 15, 1819; d. Vienna, Feb. 5, 1890. He studied in Prague with Tomaschek and Pitsch; subsequently settled in Vienna as a writer; publ. the essays *Zur Geschichte der Kirchenmusik bei den Italienern und Deutschen* (1856), *Das Paradies und die Peri von R. Schumann* (1859), *Dr. Hanslicks Lehre vom Musikalisch-Schönen: Eine Abwehr* (1859), and *Die Harmonik der Neuzeit* (1861); also contributed articles to the 'Neue Zeitschrift für Musik,' which printed a biographical sketch of him by J. Schucht after his death (1890).

Laurens (loh-rahn'), **Edmond,** French composer and pedagogue; b. Bergerac, Sept. 2, 1851; d. Paris, Nov. 27, 1925. He studied with Guiraud at the Paris Cons.; later became teacher of harmony and composition there. Works: *La Harpe et le glaive,* grand opera; *Les Amours d'un soldat de plomb,* pantomime; *La Neuvaine,* lyric play; other works for the stage *(Irlande, Conte d'amour, Roses d'automne); Suite Japonaise* for orch.; *Silhouettes* for piano and orch.; piano pieces; numerous songs. He also was the author of the manuals, *Cours d'enseignement musical pianistique* and *L'Art du Correcteur.*

Laurenti, Bartolomeo Girolamo, Italian violinist and composer; b. Bologna, c. 1644; d. there, Jan. 18, 1726. He played violin at the Basilica San Petronio; was one of the earliest members of the Accademia Filarmonica in Bologna. He wrote *Sonate per camera a violino e violoncello* (1691); *Sei concerti a 3, cioè violino, violoncello ed organo* (1720); a sonata for violin and continuo; etc.

Laurischkus (low-rish'-kōōs), **Max,** German composer; b. Insterburg, Feb. 18, 1876; d. Berlin, Nov. 17, 1929. He studied with Bargiel and Herzogenberg at the Hochschule für Musik in Berlin. He wrote *Zug des Todes,* for chorus and orch.; cello concerto; *Konzertstück* for violin and orch.; *Pastorale* for 'Mustel' harmonium and celesta; choruses for women's voices; etc.

Lauri-Volpi, Giacomo, Italian tenor; b. Lanuvio, near Rome, Dec. 11, 1892. He studied at Santa Cecilia in Rome; then privately with Rosati. In 1920 he made his début in Rome; first American appearance, Metropolitan Opera House, N. Y., Jan. 26, 1923, as the Duke in *Rigoletto;* remained a member of the company until 1934; then returned to Italy. He publ. several books: *L'Equivoco* (Milan, 1939; autobiographical); *Cristali viventi* (Rome, 1948); *A Viso aperto* (Milan, 1953); *Voci parallele* (Milan, 1955). —Cf. A. Gustarelli, *Chi è Giacomo Lauri-Volpi?* (Milan, 1932).

Lauska, Franz (Seraphinus Ignatius), pianist and composer; b. Brünn, Jan. 13, 1764; d. Berlin, April 18, 1825. He studied in Vienna with Albrechtsberger; was chamber musician in Munich; 1794-98, taught in Copenhagen; settled in Berlin in 1798; became a teacher at the court; among his pupils was Meyerbeer. He wrote 24 sonatas *(Grande sonate, Sonate pathétique,* etc.); cello sonata; 4-hand pieces *(6 Easy and Agreeable Pieces, Polonaise,* etc.); rondos, variations for 2 hands, etc.

Lauterbach, Johann Christoph, German violinist and composer; b. Culmbach, July 24, 1832; d. Dresden, March 28, 1918. He studied in Würzburg with Bratsch and Fröhlich; then at the Brussels Cons. with Bériot and Fétis, receiving a gold medal in 1851; taught violin there; 1853, prof. of violin and concertmaster at the Munich Cons.; 1861, at the court orch. in Dresden; also head of the violin dept. of the Dresden Cons. (1861-77). He wrote a *Cavatine* for violin and orch.; *Capriccio* for violin and orch.; works for violin and piano *(Zwei Konzertetüden, Legende, Allegro scherzoso, Polonaise, Tarentelle,* etc.).

Lavagne, André, French composer; b. Paris, July 12, 1913. He studied at the Paris Cons.; won 1st prize in piano (1933), Premier Second Grand Prix de Rome (1938); in 1941, appointed inspector of music in Paris schools. His works include *Comme ils s'aiment* (Grand Prix de Théâtre Lyrique, 1942); *Concert dans un parc,* for piano and orch., inspired by Watteau's painting (1941); *Concerto romantique,* for cello and orch. (1941); *Nox,* symph. poem for voice and orch.; *Spectacle rassurant,* for voice and orch.; several ballets *(Le pauvre jongleur, Kermesse,* etc.). —Cf. A. Machabey, *Portraits de trente musiciens français* (Paris, 1949; pp. 115-19).

Lavagnino, Angelo Francesco, Italian composer; b. Genoa, Feb. 22, 1909. He studied with Renzo Rossi and Vito Frazzi at the Milan Cons., graduating in 1933; in 1941 joined the staff of the Accademia Musicale in Siena. Among his works are 2 symph. poems, *Volo d'api* (1932) and *Tempo alto* (1938); a violin concerto (1941); piano quintet (1942); violin sonata (1943); a *Pocket Symphony* (title in English; 1949).

Lavallée, Calixa, Canadian pianist and composer; b. Verchères, Quebec, Dec. 28, 1842; d. Boston, Jan. 21, 1891. He first studied with his father; then at the Paris Cons. with Marmontel (piano), and Bazin and Boieldieu *fils* (composition). Returning to Canada, he made tours of his native country and the U.S.; took part in the Civil War; in 1881, soloist in the company of Mme. Gerster, the German singer. He wrote the music to the Canadian national song *O Canada* (first perf. in Montreal, June 24, 1880; poem by Judge Routhier). He subsequently settled in Boston, where he became instructor at the Petersilea Academy; wrote a comic opera, *The Widow* (Springfield, Ill., March 25, 1882). —Cf. S. Salter, *Early Encouragement to American Composers,* in the 'Mus. Quarterly' (Jan., 1932); E. Lapierre, *C. Lavallée, Musicien National du Canada* (Montreal, 1937).

Lavigna (lah-vē'-ñah), **Vincenzo,** Italian composer; b. Altamura, Feb. 21, 1776; d. Milan, Sept. 14, 1836. He studied at the Cons. di Santa Maria di Loreto in Naples; subsequently went to Milan, where he was 'maestro al cembalo' at La Scala until 1832; also prof. of solfeggio at the Milan Cons.; he was the teacher of Verdi. He wrote 10 operas, of which his first, *La muta per amore, ossia Il medico per forza* (Milan, 1803), was his best; also 2 ballets. —Cf. G. De Napoli, *La Triade Melodrammatica Altamurana: G. Tritto, V. Lavigna, S. Mercadante* (Milan, 1931; pp. 47-66).

Lavignac (lah-vi-ñahk'), **(Alexandre Jean) Albert,** eminent French musicologist and pedagogue; b. Paris, Jan. 21, 1846; d. there, May 28, 1916. He studied at the Paris Cons. with Marmontel (piano), Bazin and Benoist (harmony), and A. Thomas (composition), winning 1st prize for *solfège* in 1857, 1st for piano in 1861, 1st for harmony and accompaniment in 1863, 1st for counterpoint and fugue in 1864, 2nd for organ in 1865; appointed assistant prof. of *solfège* there (1871); prof. of *solfège* (1875); prof. of harmony (1891). His *Cours complet théorique de dictée musicale* (6 vols., 1882) attracted considerable attention and led to the introduction of musical dictation as a regular subject in all important European conservatories; followed (1900) by *Dictées musicales* (additional exercises). His *magnum opus* was the famous *Encyclopédie de la musique et Dictionnaire du Conservatoire,* which he edited from 1913 until his death. —Other works: *Solfèges manuscrits* (6 vols.); *50 Leçons d'harmonie; École de la Pédale du piano* (1889); *La Musique et les musiciens* (1895; 8th ed., 1910; entirely revised, 1950; English transl. with additions on American music by **H. E.** Krehbiel, 1899); *Le Voyage artistique à Bayreuth* (1897; English transl. as *The Music Dramas of Richard Wagner,* 1898); *Les Gaîtés du Conservatoire* (1900); *L'Éducation musicale* (1902; English transl., 1903); *Notions scolaires de musique* (1905; Spanish transl., 1906); *Théorie complète des principes fondamentaux de la musique moderne* (1909). Lavignac's compositions (chiefly for the piano) are of little importance; together with T. Lack, he publ. arrangements for 2 pianos of Beethoven's symphonies No. 1 and 2.

Lavigne (lah-veñ'), **Antoine-Joseph,** oboist; b. Besançon, France, March 23, 1816; d. Manchester, Aug. 1, 1886. He studied at the Paris Cons.; settled in England in 1841; played in the Drury Lane Promenade Concerts; then in Hallé's Manchester orch. He applied Böhm's ring-key system to the oboe. In his later years he became destitute and died in the poorhouse at Manchester.

La Violette, Wesley, American composer; b. St. James, Minn., Jan. 4, 1894. He studied at Northwestern Univ. and at Chicago Musical College (M. M.; Mus. Doc., 1925); taught at Chicago Musical College (1923-33); in 1933, became head of the theory dept. of De Paul Univ.; went to Los Angeles in 1940; since 1946, teaching at the Los Angeles Cons. His works include the opera *Shylock* (1927; awarded the David Bispham Memorial Medal, 1930; excerpts performed, Chicago, Feb. 9, 1930); an opera on the life of Buddha, *The Enlightened One* (1955); Symph. No. 1 (Rochester, Oct. 19, 1938); Symph. No. 2, subtitled *Miniature,* or *Tom Thumb Symphony* (Chicago, May 25, 1942); *The Song of the Angels,* choral symph. (1952); cantata, *The Road to Calvary* (1952); 2 violin concertos (1929; 1938); *Penetrella,* for divided strings, 18 parts (Chicago, Nov. 30, 1928); *Osiris,* an Egyptian tone poem (1929); *Chorale* for large orch. (Chicago, July 31, 1936); *Music from the High Sierras,* or *San Francisco Overture* (San Francisco, March 4, 1941); *Concertino* for flute and orch. (1943); 3 string quartets; piano quintet (1927); octet (1937), sextet for piano, flute, oboe, clarinet, bassoon, and horn (1940); flute quintet (1943); flute sonata, 2 violin sonatas, viola sonata, piano sonata, etc. He is the author of *Music and Its Makers,* in 'University of Knowledge' (Chicago, 1937), and of several publications on philosophy and religion: *The Creative Light* (N. Y., 1947), *The Wayfarer* (a revision of The Dhammapuda; Los Angeles, 1956), etc.

Lavoix (lăh-vwăh'), **Henri-Marie-François,** French writer on music; b. Paris, April 26, 1846; d. there, Dec. 27, 1897. He was graduated from the Sorbonne; then studied harmony and counterpoint with H. Cohen; in 1865, became librarian of the Bibliothèque Nationale; contributed articles to the 'Revue et Gazette musicale.'—Writings: *Les Traducteurs de Shakespeare en musique* (1869); *La Musique dans l'imagerie du moyen-âge* (1875); *La Musique dans la nature* (1877); *Histoire de l'instrumentation* (1878; his chief work); *Le Chant, ses principes et son histoire,* in collaboration with T. Lemaire; *La Musique du siècle de Saint-Louis* (1884); *La Musique française* (1891).

Lavrangas, Denis, Greek conductor and composer; b. Argostoli, Cephalonia, Oct. 17, 1864; d. Razata, Cephalonia, July 30, 1941. He studied first in Argostoli with N. Serao (violin) and N. Tzanis (theory); then at the Cons. of San Pietro a Maiella in Naples; and at the Paris Cons. with Delibes, Massenet, and Dubois; conducted an opera company touring through France; went to Italy and conducted theater orchestras in Turin, Venice, etc. Returning to Greece in 1894, he became artistic director of the Philharmonic Society of Athens.—Compositions: the operas *Elda di Vorn* (Naples, 1890), *The Two Brothers* (Athens, July 22, 1900), *The Sorceress* (Athens, 1901), *Dido* (Athens, April 19, 1909; his best work), *Black Butterfly* (Athens, 1928), *Redeemer* (Corfu, 1935), *Facanapas* (1935; performed posthumously, Athens, Dec. 2, 1950); the operettas *White Hair* (Athens, 1915), *Sporting Club* (Athens, 1919); *Ouverture grecque, Suites grecques,* and other works for orch.; 2 Masses; choruses; piano pieces; songs. He also publ. teaching manuals.

Lavry, Marc, Israeli composer and conductor; b. Riga, Dec. 22, 1903. He studied with Teichmüller at the Leipzig Cons. He conducted in Saarbrücken (1927-28), in Munich (1929), in Berlin (1930); 1932-34, in Riga and Stockholm. In 1935 he settled in Palestine; 1951, appointed head of the music section of Kol Zion Lagolah, the Jerusalem broadcasting service. In 1952 he visited the U. S. His works include the opera *Dan Hashomer (Dan the Guard;* first Palestinian opera in Hebrew to receive a stage performance; Tel Aviv, Feb. 17, 1945, composer conducting); oratorio *Song of Songs; Israeli Country Dances,* for orch. (Nazareth, May 9, 1953); the symph. poems *Stalingrad* and *Emek (The Valley);* 2 piano concertos; choral works; many smaller works.

Law, Andrew, American singing teacher and composer; b. Milford, Conn., March, 1749; d. Cheshire, Conn., July 13, 1821. He was graduated from Rhode Island College; M.A., 1778; then studied theology and was ordained in Hartford (1787); subsequently was active as preacher in Philadelphia and Baltimore; later as pioneer singing teacher in New England. He invented a new system of notation, patented in 1802, which employed 4 (later increased to 7) different shapes of notes without the staff; it was not successful and was used in only a few of his own books. A second innovation (at least as far as American usages were concerned) was his setting of the melody in the soprano instead of in the tenor. In 1786 he received an honorary M.A. degree, Yale; 1821, LL.D. from Allegheny College, Meadville, Penna. He compiled *A Select Number of Plain Tunes Adapted to Congregational Worship* (1775); *Select Harmony* (Cheshire, Conn., 1778); *A Collection of Hymns for Social Worship* (Cheshire, 1782); *The Rudiments of Music* (Cheshire, 1783); *The Art of Singing,* in 3 parts, each separately paged: I. *The Musical Primer;* II. *The Christian Harmony;* III. *The Musical Magazine* (Cheshire, 1792-93; 4th ed., Windsor, Vt., 1803; part III contains 6 books of tunes); *Harmonic Companion, and Guide to Social Worship: Being a Choice Selection of Tunes Adapted to the Various Psalms and Hymns* (Philadelphia, 1807); *The Art of Playing the Organ and Pianoforte* (Philadelphia, 1809); *Essays on Music* (Philadelphia, 1814). Only one of his hymn tunes, *Archdale,* acquired some popularity; but his teaching books, quaintly but clearly written, contributed considerably to early music education in America. —Cf. F. J. Metcalf, *American Psalmody* (N. Y., 1917); F. J. Metcalf, *American Writers and Compilers of Sacred Music* (N. Y., 1925); 'Dictionary of American Biography' (vol. 11); J. T. Howard, *Our American Music* (N. Y., 1939 and subsequent editions).

Lawes, Henry, English composer; brother of William Lawes; b. Dinton, Wilts, Jan. 5, 1596; d. London, Oct. 21, 1662. He studied in London with Coperario; in 1626, became Epistler and Gentleman of the Chapel Royal, then clerk; member of the King's private band; also music master to the Earl of Bridgewater; lost appointments during the Protectorate, but was reinstated in 1660. He is interred in the cloisters of Westminster Abbey. He is historically important because his infinite care in setting texts with proper note and accent marked a step in the development of vocal composition which culminated in Purcell. —Works: *Coelum Britannicum,* masque (London, Feb. 17, 1634); *Comus,* masque (Sept. 29, 1634); *The Triumphs of Peace,* masque; *A Paraphrase upon the Psalmes of David* (1637); *Choice Psalmes put into Musick for 3 Voices* (1648; includes many compositions by his brother William Lawes); *Ayres and Dialogues for 1, 2 and 3 Voices* (3 vols., 1653, 1655, 1658); music to poems by Milton, Herrick, W. Cartwright, Davenant, etc.; songs and anthems in contemporary collections: 'The Treasury of Musick' (1669); Clifford's 'Divine Services and Anthems' (1664); manuscripts are in the libraries of the British Museum and Christ Church, Oxford. —Cf. 'Dictionary of National Biography' (vol. 11; Oxford, 1921-22); Willa McClung Evans, *Henry Lawes, Musician and Friend of Poets* (N. Y., 1941); E. F. Hart, *Introduction to Henry Lawes,* in 'Music & Letters' (1951; p. 217 ff.).

Lawes, William, English composer; brother of Henry Lawes; b. Salisbury (baptized May 1), 1602; d. Chester, 1645. He studied with Coperario, London; Musician in Ordinary to Charles I. He was killed in the service of the Royalist Army during the Civil War. He is best known for his part-song *Gather ye rosebuds while ye may;* other works include music to Shirley's *The Triumph of Peace* (with Simon Ives; 1633); *The Triumph of Prince d'Amour* (1635); one of his anthems appears in Boyce's 'Cathedral Music'; songs and vocal works in 'Select Musicall Ayres and Dialogues' (1653 and 1659); 'Catch that catch can' (1652), 'The Treasury of Musick' (1669), 'Choice Psalms' (1648); instrumental music in 'Courtly Masquing Ayres' (1662); *The Royal Consort* (66 short pieces for viols, lutes, etc.), and some *Airs* for violin and bass can be found in the British Museum; his *Great Consort* (6 suites for 2 treble viols, 2 theorbos, and 2 bass viols) is in the library of Christ Church, Oxford; other MSS of his anthems and canons are in the British Museum and the library of Christ Church, Oxford. —Cf. 'Dictionary of National Biography' (vol. 11); J. Pulver, *A Biographical Dictionary of Old English Music* (1927); R. Erlebach, *William Lawes,* in 'Proceedings' of the Musical Association (London, 1933).

Lawrence, Marjorie, Australian soprano; b. Dean's March, near Melbourne, Feb. 17, 1909. She studied in Melbourne with Ivor Boustead; then in Paris with Cécile Gilly. In 1932 she made her début at the Monte Carlo Opera as Elisabeth in *Tannhäuser;* 1932-36, member of the Paris Opéra. She came to the U.S. and made her début at the Metropolitan Opera House on Dec. 18, 1935 as Brünnhilde in *Walküre;* then joined the company; made guest appearances with the Chicago, San Francisco, St. Louis, and Cincinnati Operas, and in Buenos Aires. An attack of infantile paralysis while she was in Mexico (1941) interrupted her career. However, she staged a remarkable return at a concert in N. Y. on Nov. 9, 1942, when she sang reclining upon a couch. She appeared as Venus in *Tannhäuser,* Jan. 22, 1943, sitting in a chair. From Sept. to Dec., 1946, she made a tour of England, France, and Germany. In 1952 she retired to her ranch in Arkansas. Her autobiography, *Interrupted Melody, The Story of My Life* (N. Y., 1949), was made into a motion picture in 1955.

Lawrence, William John, writer on music; b. Belfast, Ireland, Oct. 29, 1862; d. Dulwich, Aug. 8, 1940. He was first in the wholesale wine business; then became interested in drama; lectured at Harvard Univ. on the Elizabethan theater (1925-26). He publ. *The Physical Conditions of the Elizabethan Public Playhouse* (Cambridge, Mass., 1927) and *Pre-Restoration Stage Studies* (1927); also a valuable study on the stage jig of the Elizabethan era, an early form of the ballad opera; contributed articles to the 'Mus. Quarterly,' the 'Shakespeare Year Book,' 'Music & Letters,' etc.

Lawton, Dorothy, music librarian; b. Sheffield, England, July 31, 1874. She came to the U.S. as a child; studied in N.Y. with Stojowski (piano), lectured on and taught piano, theory, and history of music until 1920, when she organized and became director of the Music Branch (Circulation Dept.) of the N. Y. Public Library; established a similar department in the American Library in Paris in 1930. She returned to England in 1945, and settled in London.

Lazar, Filip, Rumanian composer; b. Craiova, May 18, 1894; d. Paris, Nov. 4, 1936. He studied in Bucharest and Leipzig; settled in Paris. He received great encouragement from Koussevitzky, who performed several of his works with the Boston Symph.: *Tziganes* (Oct. 29, 1926), *Music for Orchestra* (March 23, 1928), and *Concerto*

Grosso (Feb. 21, 1930). He further wrote a concerto for 12 instruments and percussion (1935), *Bagatelles* and 3 suites for piano, and violin pieces.

Lazare (lăh-zăhr'), **Martin,** Belgian pianist and composer; b. Brussels, Oct. 27, 1829; d. there, Aug. 6, 1897. He studied in The Hague with van der Does, and at the Paris Cons. with Zimmerman; traveled to London, Germany, the U.S., and Canada. —Works: opera *Le roi de Bohème* (The Hague, 1852); operetta *Les deux Mandarins* (Brussels, 1878); chamber music; piano works *(Sicilienne, Valses de salon, 6 études de concert, 6 études de genre)*; etc.

Lazarus, Daniel, French composer; b. Paris, Dec. 13, 1898. He studied at the Paris Cons., taking 1st prize in composition (1915). His works include the ballet *Le Roseau* (Paris, Nov. 15, 1924); *Symphonie avec Hymne,* a large work in 5 parts for chorus and orch. portraying the destiny of the Jewish people; an 'épopée lyrique,' *Trumpeldor* (Paris, April 30, 1946; perf. in concert form); *Fantaisie* for cello and orch.; violin sonata; piano pieces; etc.

Lazarus, Gustav, German pianist and composer; b. Cologne, July 19, 1861; d. Berlin, May 24, 1920. He studied with I. Seiss, G. Jensen, and F. Wüllner; prof. of piano at the Scharwenka Cons. in Berlin (1887-99); 1899, became director of Breslaur's Cons. and Seminary in Berlin; appeared with success as a pianist in Germany, France, and England. He wrote 170 opus numbers, including the operas *Mandanika* (Elberfeld, 1899) and *Das Nest der Zaunkönige;* choral works with orch.; orchestral suite; chamber music; choruses; piano works; songs.

Lazzari (laht'-zah-rē), **Sylvio,** composer; b. Bozen, Dec. 31, 1857; d. Paris, June 18, 1944. Renouncing the study of law for music, he entered the Paris Cons. in 1883, studying with César Franck and Guiraud; became a naturalized French citizen, settling in Paris. Up to 1894 he was an active propagandist for the works of Wagner, contributing essays to various journals; then he devoted himself entirely to composition, adopting the principles of Impressionism. He visited the U.S. to conduct the world première of his opera *Le Sautériot* (Chicago, Jan. 19, 1918). He also wrote the operas *Armor* (Prague, Nov. 7, 1898), *La Lépreuse* (Paris, Feb. 7, 1912), *Melaenis* (Mulhouse, 1927), *La Tour de feu* (Paris, Jan. 16, 1928); a pantomime, *Lulu* (1887); orchestral works: a symphony; *Rapsodie espagnole; Ophélie,* symph. poem; *Impressions d'Adriatique; Effet de nuit,* symph. poem (1904); *Marche pour une fête joyeuse; Tableau symphonique d'après Verlaine; Chanson de Moulin; Au bois de Misène; Cortège nocturne; Fête bretonne; Et la jeune fille parla; Perdu en mer; Rapsodie* for violin and orch.; *Le Nouveau Christ,* for baritone and orch.; *Des choses . . . des choses,* for soprano and orch.; *Apparitions* for soprano and orch.; incidental music to *Faust;* piano trio; string quartet; octet for wind instruments; violin sonata; piano works; songs; etc.

Leach, Rowland, American violinist and composer; b. Haverhill, Mass., April 26, 1885. He studied violin and composition at the New England Cons., and Yale Univ. (Mus. Bac., 1910); then taught privately in Rockford, Ill. (1910-13); in Calgary, Canada (1913-14); Chicago (1914-28); De Pauw Univ., Indiana (1928-33), and at the Univ. of Redlands, Calif. (1933-47). In 1947 he went to live in Tucson, Arizona. He wrote a number of pieces for violin; also some orchestral works.

Le Bé (lŭ-bā'), **Guillaume,** early French type-founder. His 1540 types printed notes and lines simultaneously; those of 1555, printing notes and staff lines separately, necessitated two impressions, like Petrucci's. He also made tablature type. Ballard acquired his punches.

Lebègue (lŭ-băg'), **Nicolas-Antoine,** French organist; b. Laon, 1631; d. Paris, July 6, 1702, as court organist. He publ. 3 books of organ music (I, 1676; II and III, after 1678), a vol. of *Pièces de clavessin* (1677), and *Airs* for 2-3 voices with continuo. His complete organ works are to be found in Guilmant's *Archives* (vol. 9; 1909); selections from his clavecin music in Farrenc's *Trésor Musical.* A *Méthode pour l'orgue,* in MS, is in Tours. —Cf. N. Dufourcq, *Nicolas-Antoine Lebègue* (Paris, 1954).

Lebert (real name Levy), **Siegmund,** German pianist and pedagogue; b. Ludwigsburg, near Stuttgart, Dec. 12, 1822; d. Stuttgart, Dec. 8, 1884. He was a pupil of Tomaschek in Prague. In 1856 he founded, with Faiszt, Stark, Brachmann, and Speidel, the Stuttgart Cons. His *Grosse Klavierschule* (which included numerous studies of his own composition), publ. in cooperation with Stark, ran through many editions (revised by Max Pauer, 1904), and appeared also in English, French, Italian, and Russian translations. He also publ. an *Instructive Edition* of classical piano works and edited Clementi's *Gradus ad Parnassum.*

Lebeuf (lŭ-böf'), Abbé **Jean,** French music scholar; b. Auxerre, March 6, 1687; d. there, April 10, 1760, as canon and sub-cantor at the cathedral. In 1740 he succeeded to Lancelot's chair in the Académie. He wrote about 180 essays on all manner of subjects, including a series publ. in the 'Mercure de France' (1725-28) dealing with plainchant, in strong opposition to Motz's newly invented style of notation; other musical essays by him are: a *Lettre sur les orgues,* in the 'Mercure de France' (1737); a *Traité historique et pratique sur le chant ecclésiastique . . . précédé d'une nouvelle méthode pour l'enseigner et l'apprendre facilement* (1741); etc.

Leborne, Aimé-Ambroise-Simon, composer; b. Brussels, Dec. 29, 1797; d. Paris, April 1, 1866. He went to France as a child; studied at the Paris Cons. with Berton and Cherubini; 2nd Prix de Rome (1818); 1st Prix de Rome (1820); joined the faculty of the Paris Cons., first as prof. of counterpoint, then of fugue, and finally of composition; retained this post until his death; was also librarian of the Paris Opéra and of the Royal Chapel. He wrote the operas *Le Camp du drap d'or* (Paris, Feb. 28, 1828), *Cinq Ans d'entr'acte,* and *Lequel* (Paris, March 21, 1838); adapted Carafa's *Les Deux Figaros;* also edited a new edition of Catel's *Traité d'harmonie,* making numerous additions to the practical part (1848).

Leborne, Fernand, critic and composer; b. Charleroi, March 10, 1862; d. Paris, Jan. 15, 1929. He was a pupil at the Paris Cons. of Massenet, Saint-Saëns, and César Franck. He lived mostly in Paris; was music critic for 'Le Monde artiste,' later for the 'Petit Parisien'; as a composer, he won the Prix Chartier in 1901. —Works: operas *Daphnis et Chloé* (Brussels, May 10, 1885), *Hedda* (Milan, 1898), *Mudarra* (Berlin, April 19, 1899), *Les Girondins* (Lyons, March 25, 1905), *La Catalane* (Paris, May 24, 1907), *Cléopâtre* (Rouen, 1914), *Néréa* (Marseilles, Jan. 12, 1926); the orchestral works *Suite intime, Symphonie dramatique, Aquarelles, Temps de guerre, Fête bretonne, Marche solennelle, Ouverture guerrière, Ouverture symphonique, Symphonie-Concerto* for violin and piano with orch.; incidental music to *L'Absent* (Paris, 1903); string quartet, piano trio; violin sonata; a Mass, motets; piano pieces; songs; etc.

Lebouc (lŭ-bōōk'), **Charles-Joseph,** French cellist and composer; b. Besançon, Dec. 22, 1822; d. Hyères, March 6, 1893; studied at the Paris Cons. with Franchomme, Halévy, and Colet (composition), winning 1st prize for cello (1842) and 1st prize for harmony (1844). He played in the Paris Opéra orch. (1844-48); was a member of the Société des Concerts from 1842; founder of the 'Soirées de musique classique.' He wrote a *Trio de concert,* for piano, violin, and cello; *Ave verum,* for voice with piano and cello; duos for cello with piano; cello pieces; also a method for cello.

Lebrun (lŭ-brön'), **Franziska** (*neé* Danzi), renowned German soprano; wife of Ludwig August Lebrun; b. Mannheim, 1756; d. Berlin, May 14, 1791. She made her début in Schwetzingen on Aug. 9, 1772 as Sandrina in Sacchini's *La contadina in corte;* London début on Nov. 8, 1777 as Ariene in Sacchini's *Creso;* sang in Paris at the Concert Spirituel, and in Milan during the first season of the Teatro alla Scala; also appeared in Naples and Berlin. She was also a composer; publ. 36 sonatas for violin and piano.

Lebrun, Jean, French horn player; b. Lyons, April 6, 1759; d. Paris, c. 1809. He studied in Paris with Punto. His playing was remarkable for its purity of tone and for the ease with which he took the high notes. He played 1st horn in the Paris Opéra orch. (1786-92); after a visit to England, he entered the court orch. at Berlin; following extended tours, returned to Paris in 1806, but found no employment, and in despair, committed suicide. The mute for the horn is his innovation.

Lebrun, Louis-Sébastien, French tenor and composer; b. Paris, Dec. 10, 1764; d. there, June 27, 1829. Unsuccessful as a singer in the Paris Opéra and Opéra-Comique, he became one of the 4 'maîtres de chant' at the Opéra; in 1807, tenor in Napoleon's chapelle, and in 1810, 'chef du chant' there. He wrote 16 operas, the most successful being *Marcelin* (Paris, March 22, 1800) and *Le Rossignol* (Paris, April 23, 1816); also a *Te Deum* (1809); a Solemn Mass (1815); and a collection of *romances.*

Lebrun, Ludwig August, one of the greatest oboists of the 18th century; husband of Franziska Lebrun; b. Mannheim, 1746; d. Berlin, Dec. 16, 1790. He studied with his father; played in the court orch. at Mannheim (1764-78); then toured with his wife in Germany, Italy, Austria, France, and England, appearing in concerts, both solo and with his wife, creating a sensation in London (1781) and Paris (1784). He wrote ballet music, of which *Armida* and *Agus, ballet champêtre,* were publ.; also 7 oboe concertos; 12 trios for oboe, violin, and cello; easy duos for flutes.

Lebrun, Paul Henri Joseph, Belgian conductor and composer; b. Ghent, April 21, 1861; d. Louvain, Nov. 4, 1920. He was a pupil at the Cons. in Ghent; won the Belgian Prix de Rome in 1891 with his cantata *Andromeda,* and 1st prize of the Belgian Académie for a symph.; 1890, prof. of theory at the Ghent Cons. and conductor of the 'Orpheon' at Cambrai; 1895, also conductor of the 'Cercle artistique' at Ghent; from 1913 until his death, director of the music school in Louvain. He wrote an opera, *La Fiancée d'Abydos* (Ghent, 1897); orchestral and choral works; chamber music; etc.

Leça, Armando, Portuguese composer and folksong specialist; b. Leça da Palmeira, Aug. 9, 1893. He studied with Oscar da Silva; was active as choral conductor and collector of native folksongs; publ. an authoritative edition of popular Portuguese music (1922; expanded ed. in 2 vols., 1947). He wrote several dance suites for orch., of which the *Dansa de Don Pedro* attained considerable popularity; 2 operettas, *Maio florido* (1918) and *Bruxa* (1919); many piano pieces of pictorial character, and songs.

Le Carpentier (kăhr-pahn-t'yā'), **Adolphe-Clair,** French pianist and composer; b. Paris, Feb. 17, 1809; d. there, July 14, 1869. He was a pupil of Lesueur and Fétis at the Cons. (1818), winning several prizes. He publ. an excellent *Méthode de piano pour les enfants,* also 25 *Études élémentaires* (op. 59), and a collection of 24 études, *Le Progrès;* also nearly 300 fantasias on operatic and national airs, well arranged and of moderate difficulty.

Lechner, Leonhard (**Leonardus Lechner Athesinus**), composer; b. in the valley of Adige (Athesinus; hence his surname) in the Austrian Tyrol, c. 1550; d. Stuttgart, Sept. 9, 1606. He was a boy-chorister under Roland de Lassus in Munich and Ivo de Vento in Landshut; then teacher in Nuremberg (1570); Kapellmeister in Hechingen (1584); from 1585, in Tübingen; finally, Kapellmeister in Stuttgart (from 1587). His later works, as illustrated by his *Johannispassion, Hohelied Salomonis,* and *Deutsche Sprüche vom Leben und Tod,* show him to be one of the most gifted of the German composers in the period immediately preceding Heinrich Schütz. He publ. *Motettae sacrae* (in 4-6 voices; 2 vols., 1575 and 1581; the latter vol. bearing the title *Sacrae Cantiones,* partly reprinted by Commer); *Newe teutsche Lieder* (3-voiced villanellas; 2 vols., 1576 and 1577; collected ed., 1586 and 1590); *Newe teutsche Lieder* (in 4-5 voices; 1577); *Newe teutsche Lieder* (in 4-5 voices; 1582; reprinted by E. Fritz Schmid, 1926); 8 Magnificats (in 4 voices; 1578); 3 Masses (in 5-6 voices; 1584); 10 introits (in 5-6 voices; 1584); *Newe lustige teutsche Lieder, nach Art der welschen Canzonen* (in 4 voices; 1586 and 1588); *7 Psalmi Poenitentiales* (in 6 voices; 1587); *Harmoniae miscellae,* collection (1583); *Johannispassion* (1594; reprinted by Ameln, 1926); *Hohelied Salomonis* (in 4 voices; 1606; ed. by Ameln and Lipphardt, 1927); *Deutsche Sprüche vom Leben und Tod* (in 4 voices; 1606; ed. by Ameln and Lipphardt, 1927); other psalms and motets for 4-18 voices (1575-1604). He also made arrangements for 5 voices of 3-part villanellas by Regnart (1579; partly reprinted in 'Monatshefte für Musikgeschichte,' vol. 19, ed. by Eitner); publ. works of Lassus. —Cf. O. Kade, *Leonhard Lechner und sein Streit mit dem Grafen Eitel Friedrich von Hohenzollern im Jahre 1585,* in 'Monatshefte für Musikgeschichte' (vol. 1, 1869, with musical supplement); J. Sittard, in *Zur Geschichte der Musik und des Theaters am Württembergischen Hofe* (1890; p. 27 *et seq.*); O. Koller, *Leonhard Lechner,* in 'Musikbuch aus Österreich' (1904); A. Sandberger, in 'Denkmäler der Tonkunst in Bayern' (vol. 5); M. Schreiber, *Leonhard Lechner* (Munich, 1932); M. Schreiber, *Die Kirchenmusik des Kapellmeisters Leonhard Lechner Athesinus* (Regensburg, 1935). A complete edition of his works was begun in 1952 under the editorship of K. Ameln.

Lechthaler, Josef, Austrian church composer and musicologist; b. Rattenberg, Dec. 31, 1891; d. Vienna, Aug. 21, 1948. He studied philology in Innsbruck, and musicology with Guido Adler in Vienna; obtained his degree of *Dr. phil.* in 1919; from 1925, taught theory at the Vienna Academy of Music, and was director of the church music school there from 1933-38 and again from 1945 to his death. He wrote *Der katholische Organist als Baumeister des Gesamtkunstwerks,* in 'Kongress-Bericht für Kirchenmusik' (Berlin, 1927); composed the cantatas *Der lichte Tag* and *Lieder der Wanderschaft;* a cappella choruses; 2 string quartets; trio for violin, viola da gamba, and harpsichord; a song cycle *Conjunx conjugi,* etc.

Leclair, Jean Marie, celebrated French violinist; b. Lyons, May 10, 1697; d. Paris, Oct. 22, 1764. At first he was a dancer; was ballet master at Turin, where the violinist Somis was attracted by dance music he wrote, and gave him further instruction. From 1729-31, he played the violin in the orch. of the Paris Opéra; was a frequent performer at the Concert Spirituel (1728-34). Thenceforth he lived in Paris as composer and teacher; made brief visits to Holland and Spain in 1743-44. He was assassinated in his own house; the circumstances that no robbery was attempted and that he was stabbed 3 times, in the front part of his body, suggest that the murderer was known to him; it may have been his estranged wife, who was also his publisher and engraver of his music. (See *The Murder of Leclair* in N. Slonimsky's *A Thing or Two About Music;* N. Y., 1948; pp. 86-90.) Leclair was one of the best composers for the violin in the 18th century; although he followed the Italian school in his early works, he developed a distinct style in his later music; he used technical devices in the virtuoso category. —Works: opera *Glaucus et Scylla* (Paris, Oct. 4, 1746); opera ballet *Apollon et Climène* (1750); *Concerti grossi* for 3 violins, viola, cello, and organ; 6 trios, and 2 easy trios, for 2 violins with bass; duos for violins; and (his finest compositions) 48 sonatas for violin with continuo. New editions have been publ. by F. David (in his *Hohe Schule des Violinspiels* and *Vorschule),* Eitner (in 'Publikationen der Gesellschaft für Musikforschung,' vol. 31), D. Alard, M. Herwegh, Bouillard, Moffat, L. Lichtenberg, etc. A complete edition of his works in 16 vols. was begun in Paris in 1953, under the direction of M. Pincherle. —Cf. L. de la Laurencie, *Le Rôle de Leclair dans la musique instrumentale,* in the 'Revue Musicale' (April, 1923); A. Moser, *Geschichte des Violinspiels* (1923; p. 372 *et seq.*); H. Engel, *Das Instrumentalkonzert* (Part I, vol. 3, of Kretzschmar's 'Führer'; p. 172 *et seq.*); M. Pincherle, *Jean-Marie Leclair l'aîné* (Paris, 1952).

Leclair, Jean Marie (le cadet), younger brother of the preceding; b. Lyons, Sept. 23, 1703; d. there, Nov. 30, 1777. Like his brother, he was a violinist; he spent most of his life in his native town; publ. a book of violin sonatas; wrote several divertissements. —Cf. Léon Vallas, *Une famille de violinistes lyonnais, les Leclair,* in the 'Bulletin de la Société française de musicologie' (July, 1921).

Lecocq (lŭ-kŏhk'), **Charles,** French composer of light opera; b. Paris, June 3, 1832; d. there, Oct. 24, 1918. He studied at the Paris Cons. under Bazin (harmony), Halévy (composition), and Benoist (organ); obtained 1st prize for harmony (1850) and 2nd prize for fugue (1852). In 1857 he shared with Bizet a prize offered by Offenbach for the best opera buffa, with his *Le Docteur Miracle* (Paris, April 8, 1857). From that time on, he composed industriously for the stage; after several transient successes, he produced an operetta, *Fleur de thé* (1868), which had a run of a hundred nights in Paris, and was also well received in England and Germany. He produced 9 more operettas before *La Fille de Mme. Angot* (Brussels, Dec. 4, 1872; Paris, Feb. 21, 1873), which brought him fame. In Paris alone it enjoyed an uninterrupted series of performances for over a year. It was closely followed by its rival in popularity, *Giroflé-Girofla* (Brussels, March 21, 1874). Altogether, he produced some 40 operettas and comic operas, distinguished by melodic grace, instrumental finish, and dramatic acumen, not inferior to the productions of Offenbach and Hervé. His serious opera *Plutus* (Opéra-Comique, March 31, 1886) was unsuccessful. He publ., for piano, a ballet pantomime, *Les Fantoccini;* 24 'morceaux de genre,' *Les Miettes;* and a gavotte; also an *Aubade; mélodies* and *chansons* for voice with piano; sacred songs for women's voices *(La Chapelle au couvent);* etc. —Cf. L. Schneider, *Les Maîtres de l'operette, Hervé et Charles Lecocq* (Paris, 1924).

Le Couppey (lu-koo-pā'), **Félix,** French pianist; b. Paris, April 14, 1811; d. there, July 5, 1887. He was a pupil at the Paris Cons.; from 1843, taught piano and harmony there. He publ. several successful piano methods: *École du mécanisme du piano, 24 études primaires; Cours de piano élémentaire et progressif; L'Art du piano* (50 études with annotations); and a pamphlet, *De l'enseignement du piano: conseils aux femmes professeurs* (1865); also piano character pieces and songs.

Lecuona, Ernesto, Cuban composer of popular music; b. Havana, Aug. 7, 1896. He played piano as a child, and wrote his first song when he was 11 years old. He graduated from the National Cons. of Havana (1911); toured South America and Europe as leader of a Cuban dance band. Among his melodies, the most successful are *Malagueña, Andalucía,* and *Siboney.*

Ledebur (lā'dĕ-bōōr), **Karl,** German writer on music; b. Schildesche, near Bielefeld, April 20, 1806; d. Stolp, Oct. 25, 1872. He was a Prussian cavalry officer; publ. a *Tonkünstlerlexikon Berlins von den ältesten Zeiten bis auf die Gegenwart* (1860-61) and essays on Berlin court music.

Ledent (lŭ-dahn'), **Félix-Étienne,** Belgian pianist and composer; b. Liège, Nov. 20, 1816; d. there, Aug. 23, 1886. He studied at the Liège Cons. with J. Jalheau, and in Paris with Daussoigne-Méhul, taking the 2nd Prix de Rome (1843); in 1844, became prof. of piano at the Liège Cons. He publ. an *Adagio et Rondo* for piano and orch.; piano pieces and songs.

Lederer, Felix, conductor; b. Prague, Feb. 25, 1877; d. Berlin, March 27, 1957. He studied at the Prague Cons.; then at the Vienna Cons.; was conductor at the Municipal Theater in Nuremberg (1899-1903), at Augsburg (1903-05), Barmen (1905-08), Bremen (1908-10), and Mannheim (1910-22); in 1922, appointed opera conductor at Saarbrücken; from 1945 until his death, in Berlin as prof. at the Hochschule für Musik.

Leduc (lŭ-dük'), **Alphonse,** French publisher; b. Nantes, March 9, 1804; d. Paris, June 17, 1868. He studied with Reicha at the Paris Cons.; played piano and bassoon. In 1841 he founded a music business in Paris; after his death, his son Alphonse II (1844-1892) inherited the business; at the death of the latter, his widow directed the firm until 1904, when their son Emile Alphonse III (b. Nov. 14, 1878; d. Paris, May 24, 1951) became the next owner; his sons Claude and Gilbert Leduc (partners of their father from 1938) continued the business. From 1860-95 the firm publ. 'L'Art Musical,' which was then assimilated with the 'Guide Musical.' — Cf. Cecil Hopkinson, *Parisian Music Publishers, 1700-1950* (London, 1954).

Lee, Dai-Keong, Hawaiian composer of Chinese parentage; b. Honolulu, Sept. 2, 1915. He studied in the U. S. with Roger Sessions, Frederick Jacobi, and Aaron Copland. His works include the one-act opera *The Poet's Dilemma* (1940); the orchestral works *Hawaiian Festival Overture* (1942), *Golden Gate Overture* (1942), symph. in one movement (1942), *Pacific Prayer* (1942), violin concerto (1946), 2nd symph. (San Francisco, March 14, 1952), *Prelude and Hula, Renascence, Tropical Overture, Introduction and Allegro;* a string quartet (1944); works for chorus: *The Return, North Labrador, East and West;* etc.

Lee, Ernest Markham, English organist and writer on music; b. Cambridge, June 8, 1874; d. Eastbourne, Nov. 13, 1956. While a student at Emanuel Coll., he acted as organist at All Saints', Woodford Green, where he also established a regular series of chamber music concerts; in 1917 he was appointed prof. of organ at the Guildhall School of Music and examiner at the Univs. of London, Oxford, and Cambridge; visited Canada and New Zealand (1929-30), Jamaica and Canada (1933), and India (1934); then lived in London. He wrote services, anthems, sacred and secular songs, piano pieces *(Hesperis, Serapis, Modern Suite),* etc.; publ. the books, *Tchaikovsky* (1904); *Edvard Grieg* (1908); *The Story of Opera* (1909); *Brahms: The Man and His Music* (1915); *The Story of Symphony* (1916); *On Listening to Music* (1918); *Musical Theory and Knowledge* (1923); *Brahms' Orchestral Works* (1931); etc.

Lee, Louis, German cellist and composer; brother of Maurice and Sebastian Lee; b. Hamburg, Oct. 19, 1819; d. Lübeck, Aug. 26, 1896. He studied cello with J. N. Prell; gave concerts at the age of 12 in German cities and in Copenhagen. He organized chamber music soirées (with Hafner, then with Boie) in Hamburg; taught at the Hamburg Cons. until 1884; also was 1st cellist of the Philharmonic Society. He publ. a piano quartet; a piano trio; a cello sonata; a cello sonatina; pieces for piano and cello; piano pieces; also wrote music to Schiller's *Jungfrau von Orleans* and *Wilhelm Tell;* etc.

Lee, Maurice, German piano teacher; brother of Louis and Sebastian Lee; b. Hamburg, Feb., 1821; d. London, June 23, 1895, where he had long resided as a piano teacher and composer of popular salon music.

Lee, Sebastian, German cellist and composer; brother of Louis and Maurice Lee; b. Hamburg, Dec. 24, 1805; d. there, Jan. 4, 1887. He studied with J. N. Prell; from 1837-68, was solo cellist at the Opéra in Paris; returned to Hamburg in 1868, remaining there until his death. He publ. an excellent method for cello; also variations, divertissements, and fantasies for cello with orch.; variations for cello with string quartet; cello duos.

Lefébure (lŭ-fā-bür'), **Louis-François Henri,** French musician; b. Paris, Feb. 18, 1754; d. there, Nov. 1840. He was a government official until his retirement in 1814; publ. several instructive books on singing: *Nouveau Solfège,* a 23-page pamphlet (1780), containing ideas put into practice by Gossec in the *École royale de chant;* a polemical brochure, *Bévues, erreurs et méprises de différents auteurs célèbres en matières musicales* (1789); etc. He also composed 2 oratorios and other choral works.

Lefébure-Wély, Louis James Alfred, French organist and composer; b. Paris, Nov. 13, 1817; d. there, Dec. 31, 1869. A pupil of his father's from his fourth year, he took, at the age of 8, the latter's place as organist of the Church of Saint-Roch, becoming regular organist at 14. Entering the Paris Cons. in 1832, he was taught by Benoist (organ) and Laurent and Zimmerman (piano), taking first prizes for both instruments in 1835; studied composition with Berton and Halévy. From 1847-58 he was organist at the Madeleine; then at St. Sulpice. He was a thorough musician, a skillful performer on the organ, piano, and harmonium, and a versatile composer.—Works: a 3-act opera, *Les Recruteurs* (1861); a cantata, *Après la victoire* (1863); 3 Masses; 3 symphonies; a string quintet and a string quartet; much elegant salon music for piano (his most celebrated piece is *The Monastery Bells);* 50 piano études; harmonium music; etc.

Lefebvre, Charles Édouard, French composer; b. Paris, June 19, 1843; d. Aix-les-Bains, Sept. 8, 1917. He studied at the Paris Cons.; won the Premier Grand Prix de Rome in 1870 for his cantata *Le Jugement de Dieu;* following his study in Rome, and tours to Greece and the Orient, he returned to Paris in 1873; won the Prix Chartier for chamber music in 1884 and 1891; joined the faculty of the Paris Cons. in 1895. —Works: the operas *Lucrèce, Le Trésor* (Angers, 1883), *Zaïre* (Lille, 1887), *Djelma* (Paris, May 25, 1894), *Singoalla; Judith,* biblical drama (Paris, 1879); *Ouverture dramatique; Dalila,* symph. poem; *Éloa,* a 'poème lyrique'; the legend *Melka; Sainte Cécile,* for solo voice, chorus, and orch. (Paris, 1896); a Serenade for orch.; *Toggenburg,* overture (Paris, 1904); *La Messe du fantôme,* for voice and orch.; chamber music (sonatas, trios, quartets, suites, etc.).

Lefèvre (lŭ-fĕvr'), **Jean Xavier,** clarinetist; b. Lausanne, March 6, 1763; d. Paris, Nov. 9, 1829. He studied with Michel Yost in Paris; from 1787, played in concerts; from 1791-1817, was at the Paris Opéra; from 1795-1825, prof. at the Cons. He wrote the clarinet method (1802) adopted at the Cons., also 6 concertos for clarinet, trios, duos, sonatas, etc., for his instrument. He popularized the sixth key of the clarinet, but did not invent it, as often stated. —Cf. F. G. Rendall, *The Clarinet* (London, 1954; p. 74).

Leffler-Burckard, Martha, German soprano; b. Berlin, June 16, 1865; d. Wiesbaden, May 14, 1954. She made her début as coloratura soprano in Strasbourg (1890); then sang at Breslau, Cologne, and Bremen; from 1898-1900, was at the court theater in Weimar; 1900-02, at Wiesbaden; after that, at the principal German opera houses; in 1906, at Bayreuth; in 1908, at the Metropolitan Opera House in Wagner roles; from 1912-19, member of the Berlin Opera. Her best roles were Fidelio, Isolde, and the 3 Brünnhildes.

Le Flem, Paul, French composer; b. Lézardieux, Côtes-du-Nord, March 18, 1881. He was a pupil of Lavignac at the Paris Cons., and of Vincent d'Indy and Albert Roussel at the Schola Cantorum; also studied philosophy and literature; then taught at the Schola Cantorum. He became music critic for 'Comoedia,' taking a strong stand in favor of modern music; was instrumental in organizing a modern music society called 'La Spirale' (1935). His own music is influenced by Debussy and Roussel; in several of his stage works, he employs the melodic idioms of his native Brittany.—Works: *Aucassin et Nicolette,* fairy tale with voices (Paris, July 20, 1923); operas, *Le Rossignol de Saint Malo* (Opéra-Comique, May 5, 1942), *La Clairière des fées* (1943), and *La Magicienne de la mer* (Paris, Oct. 29, 1954); symphony (1907); *Fantaisie* for piano and orch. (1912); *Évocation* for voice and orch. (1920); *Hymne au vin* (1925); *La Fête du printemps,* for orch. (1937); *Le Village,* symph. sketch (1942); violin sonata (1905); piano quintet (1909); several choral works.

Le Fleming, Christopher (Kaye), English composer; b. Wimborne, Feb. 26, 1908. He studied piano, and has been active in teaching at primary schools. He has written

The Singing Friar, for tenor solo, chorus, and orch.; 5 Psalms; *Peter Rabbit Music Books* for piano; an orch. suite, *London River* (1956); incidental music for plays.

Leginska, Ethel (real name Liggins), pianist, teacher, and composer; b. Hull, England, April 13, 1886. She showed a natural talent for music at an early age; the pseudonym Leginska was given to her as a child by Lady Maud Warrender, under the illusion that a Polish-looking name might help her artistic career. She studied piano at the Hoch Cons. in Frankfurt, and later in Vienna with Leschetizky. She made her début as a pianist in London; also toured Europe; on Jan. 20, 1913, she appeared for the first time in America, at a recital in New York. Her playing was described as having masculine vigor, dashing brilliance, and great variety of tonal color; however, criticism was also voiced against an individualistic treatment of classical works. She gave concerts in the U. S. for many years, attracting considerable attention; her all-Chopin recitals were highly praised. In the midst of her career as a pianist, she developed a great interest in conducting; she organized the Boston Philharmonic Orch. (100 players), later the Women's Symph. Orch. of Boston; engaged also as conductor of the Chicago Women's Symph. Orch.; also appeared as guest conductor with various orchestras in America and in Europe. In this field of activity she also elicited interest, leading to a discussion in the press of a woman's capability of conducting an orchestra. While in the U. S., she took courses in composition with Rubin Goldmark and Ernest Bloch; wrote music in various genres, distinguished by rhythmic display and a certain measure of modernism. She was married to the composer Emerson Whithorne in 1907, was separated from him in 1912, and divorced in 1916. In 1939 she settled in Los Angeles as a piano teacher; formed a large class of pupils who presented periodic concerts in California and elsewhere. — Works: operas: *Gale* (Chicago Civic Opera Co., Nov. 23, 1935, composer conducting), *The Rose and the Ring* (1932; perf. for the first time, Los Angeles, Feb. 23, 1957, composer conducting); *From a Life,* for 13 instruments (N. Y., Jan. 9, 1922); *Beyond the Fields We Know,* symph. poem (N. Y., Feb. 12, 1922); *2 Short Pieces* for orch. (Boston Symph., Feb. 29, 1924, Monteux conducting); *Quatre Sujets Barbares,* inspired by Gauguin, suite for orch. (Munich, Dec. 13, 1924, composer conducting); *Fantasy* for orch. and piano (N. Y., Jan. 3, 1926); *Triptych,* for 11 instruments (Chicago, April 29, 1928); also a string quartet, after 4 poems of Tagore (Boston, April 25, 1921); *6 Nursery Rhymes* for soprano and chamber orch.; piano pieces; songs.

Legley, Victor, Belgian composer; b. Hazebrouck, French Flanders, June 18, 1915. He received his musical education at Ypres; then studied violin at the Royal Cons. in Brussels. In 1941 he took courses with Jean Absil, who became influential in shaping Legley's style. Later Legley adopted some devices of atonal music, without adhering to integral dodecaphonism. In 1947 Legley began work on the Flemish radio; in 1949 he was appointed to the staff of the Brussels Cons. Works: 3 symphonies (1942; 1947; 1953); *Symphonie Miniature* (1946; Palermo Festival, 1949); violin concerto (1947); *The Golden River,* symph. sketch (1948); piano concerto (1952); 2 string quartets (1941; 1947); trio for oboe, clarinet, and bassoon (1942); quartet for 4 flutes (1943); sextet for flute, oboe, clarinet, bassoon, horn, and piano (1945); *Musique de midi* for 9 instruments (1948); 5 sonatas for various instruments with piano (1943-53); also songs and radio music. A catalogue of his works was publ. by the Centre Belge de Documentation Musicale (1954).

Legrenzi, Giovanni, celebrated Italian composer; b. Clusone, near Bergamo, Aug. 12, 1626; d. Venice, May 26, 1690. He was a pupil of Pallavicino; organist at Bergamo; maestro di cappella to the Duke of Ferrara, and produced his first opera, *Achille in Sciro,* at Ferrara in 1663; from 1664 in Venice, becoming director of the Cons. de' Mendicanti in 1672, and in 1685 succeeding Natale Monferrato as maestro at San Marco, where he enlarged the orch. to 34 pieces (8 violins, 11 'violette,' 2 tenor viols, 3 viole da gamba and bass viols, 4 theorbos, 2 cornetti, 1 bassoon, and 3 trombones). His 18 operas show a noteworthy advance over those of his predecessors in the orchestral support of the vocal parts, and he treats the recitative and the melodic phrase with greater freedom. He was one of the most important composers of trio sonatas, for 2 violins and continuo, and one of the most important composers of chamber music before Corelli. He was a noted teacher; among his pupils were Gasparini, Lotti, and Caldara.—Works: *Concerto di messe e salmi a 3-4 con violini* (1654); *Motetti a 2-4 voci* (1655); *Motetti a 5 voci* (1660); *Sacri e festivi concerti, messe e salmi a due cori*

(1657); *Sentimenti devoti a 2 e 3 voci* (1660; 2 vols.); *Compiete con litanie ed antifona della Beata Vergine (a* 5; 1662); *Cantata e canzonette a voce sola* (1674); *Idee armoniche (a* 2 and 3; 1678); *Echi di riverenza* (14 cantatas for solo voice; 1679); *Motetti sacri con voce sola con 3 strumenti* (1692); *Suonate per chiesa* (1655); *Suonate da chiesa e da camera a tre* (1656); *Una muta di suonate* (1664); *Suonate a 2 violini e violone* (with organ continuo; 1667); *La Cetra* (sonatas for 2-4 instruments; 1673); *Suonate a 2 violini e violoncello* (1677); *Suonate da chiesa e da camera* (1693).—Cf. G. Tebaldini, *Giovanni Legrenzi,* in 'Musica d'oggi' (April, 1937); P. Fogaccia, *Giovanni Legrenzi* (Bergamo, 1954).

Leguerney, Jacques, French composer; b. Le Havre, Nov. 19, 1906. He studied with Nadia Boulanger; has devoted himself mainly to the composition of song cycles to poems by modern French writers; he has also written a ballet, *Endymion* (1949).

Lehár (lä'-hahr), **Franz,** famous operetta composer; b. Komorn, Hungary, April 30, 1870; d. Bad Ischl, Oct. 24, 1948. He was first instructed in music by his father, Franz Lehár (1840-1898), a military bandmaster; entered the Prague Cons. at 12 and studied violin with A. Bennewitz and theory with J. Foerster. In 1885 he was brought to the attention of Fibich, who gave him lessons in composition independently from his studies at the Cons. In 1887 Lehár submitted 2 piano sonatas to Dvořák, who encouraged him in his musical career. In 1888 he became a violinist in a theater orchestra in Elberfeld; in 1889, entered his father's band (50th Infantry) in Vienna, and assisted him as conductor; after 1890 he led various military bands in Pola, Trieste, Budapest, and Vienna. His first success as stage composer came with the production of his operetta *Kukuschka* (Leipzig, Nov. 28, 1896); most of his subsequent productions took place in Vienna. His most celebrated operetta is *Die lustige Witwe (The Merry Widow),* produced at Vienna in 1905; this was followed by innumerable performances throughout the world; in Buenos Aires it was played simultaneously in 5 theaters and 5 languages (1907); other operettas that achieved tremendous success were *Der Graf von Luxemburg* (1909) and *Zigeunerliebe* (1910). Lehár's music exemplified the spirit of gaiety and frivolity that was the mark of Vienna early in the century; his superlative gift of facile melody and infectious rhythms is combined with genuine wit and irony; a blend of nostalgia and sophisticated humor made a lasting appeal to audiences, and was not diminished through the upheavals of wars and revolutions.—Works: the opera *Kukuschka* (Leipzig, Nov. 28, 1896; rewritten as *Tatjana,* Brünn, Feb. 24, 1905); the operettas *Wiener Frauen* (Vienna, Nov. 25, 1902; in Berlin as *Der Klavierstimmer;* rewritten as *Der Schlüssel zum Paradiese,* Leipzig, 1906); *Der Rastelbinder* (Vienna, Dec. 20, 1902); *Der Göttergatte* (Vienna, Jan. 20, 1904); *Die Juxheirat* (Vienna, Dec. 22, 1904); *Die lustige Witwe* (Vienna, Dec. 28, 1905); *Mitislaw der Moderne* (Vienna, Jan. 5, 1907); *Der Mann mit den drei Frauen* (Vienna, Jan. 21, 1908); *Das Fürstenkind* (Vienna, Oct. 7, 1909); *Der Graf von Luxemburg* (Vienna, Nov. 12, 1909); *Zigeunerliebe (Gypsy Love;* Vienna, Jan. 8, 1910); *Eva* (Vienna, Nov. 24, 1911); *Endlich allein* (Vienna, Feb. 10, 1914; revised and produced as *Schön ist die Welt,* Vienna, Dec. 21, 1934); *Der Sterngucker* (Vienna, Jan. 14, 1916; revised and produced in Milan as *La Danza delle libellule,* Sept. 27, 1922); *Wo die Lerche singt* (Budapest, Feb. 1, 1918); *Die blaue Mazur* (Vienna, May 28, 1920); *Die Tangokönigin* (Vienna, Sept. 9, 1921); *Frasquita* (Vienna, May 12, 1922); *Die gelbe Jacke* (Vienna, Feb. 9, 1923; revised and produced as *Das Land des Lächelns,* Berlin, Oct. 10, 1929); *Clo-Clo* (Vienna, March 8, 1924); *Paganini* (Vienna, Oct. 30, 1925); *Der Zarewitsch* (Vienna, Feb. 21, 1927); *Friederike* (Berlin, Oct. 4, 1928); *Giuditta* (Vienna, Jan. 20, 1934). Besides his operettas, Lehár wrote an *Ungarische Fantasie* for violin and small orch.; *Huldigungsouvertüre; Ein Märchen aus 1001 Nacht; Il Guado,* symph. poem for orch. and piano; *Eine Vision,* overture; a symph. poem, *Fieber;* a song cycle, *Musikalischer Roman* (1936); numerous marches and dances for orch.—Cf. E. Decsey, *Franz Lehár* (Vienna, 1924; 2nd ed., Munich, 1930); A. von Lehár, *Unsere Mutter* (1930); A. Rivoire, *Une Heure de musique avec Franz Lehár* (Paris, 1930); S. Czech, *Franz Lehár, Weg und Werk* (Berlin, 1942); M. von Peteani, *Franz Lehár* (Vienna, 1949); W. Macqueen-Pope and D. L. Murray, *Fortune's Favorite: The Life and Times of Franz Lehár* (London, 1953). The plots of Lehár's most famous operettas are found in 'Reclams Opern- und Operettenführer' ed. by W. Zentner and A. Würz (Stuttgart, 1955).

Lehmann (lā'-mahn), **Friedrich J.,** American music pedagogue; b. Cleveland, Sept. 17, 1866; d. Oberlin, Ohio, April 23, 1950.

He began to study the piano at the age of 7; entered the Oberlin Cons., where he continued with piano and also studied voice and theory; later was a pupil of Fritz von Bose and Gustav Schreck in Leipzig. He taught at the Oberlin Cons. for 30 years (1902-32). He publ. *A Treatise on Simple Counterpoint in 40 Lessons* (N. Y., 1907); *Harmonic Analysis* (Oberlin, 1910); *The Analysis of Form in Music* (Oberlin, 1919); also co-edited, with A. E. Heacox, *Lessons in Harmony* (Oberlin, 1906; revised ed., 1931; a *Guide Through the Lessons in Harmony* was publ. in 1912).

Lehmann, George, American violinist; b. New York, July 31, 1865; d. Yonkers, N. Y., Oct. 14, 1941. He was a pupil at the Leipzig Cons., studying with Schradieck (violin), Lammers (harmony), and Jadassohn (counterpoint and fugue); then took some violin lessons with Joachim in Berlin. In 1886 he returned to the U. S.; was concertmaster of the Cleveland Symph. Orch. (1886-89); then was in Europe (1889-92). In 1893 he settled in N. Y.; from 1907-14, lived in Berlin; after 1914, again in N. Y. He publ. *True Principles of the Art of Violin Playing* (N. Y., 1899) and *The Violinist's Lexicon* (N. Y., 1918), also *Four Melodious Sketches* for violin and piano; etc.

Lehmann, Lilli, famous German soprano; b. Würzburg, Nov. 24, 1848; d. Berlin, May 16, 1929. Her mother, Marie Loew (1807-1883), who had sung leading soprano roles and had also appeared as a harpist at the Kassel Opera under Spohr, became harpist at the National Theater in Prague in 1853, and there Lilli Lehmann spent her girlhood. At the age of 6 she began to study piano with Cölestin Müller, and at 12 progressed so far that she was able to act as accompanist to her mother, who was the only singing teacher she ever had. She made her professional début in Prague on Oct. 20, 1865, as the First Page in *Die Zauberflöte;* then sang in Danzig (1868) and Leipzig (1869-70). In 1870 she became a member of the Berlin Opera, and soon established a reputation as a brilliant coloratura singer. During the summer of 1875 she was in Bayreuth, and was coached by Wagner himself in the parts of Wöglinde (*Rheingold* and *Götterdämmerung*), Helmwige, and the Forest Bird; these roles she created at the Bayreuth Festival the following summer. She then returned to Berlin under a life contract with the Berlin Opera; she was given limited leaves of absence, which enabled her to appear in the principal German cities, in Stockholm (1878), and in London (début as Violetta, June 3, 1880; as Isolde, July 2, 1884; as Fidelio in 1887). She made her American début at the Metropolitan Opera, N.Y., on Nov. 25, 1885, as Carmen; 5 days later she sang Brünnhilde in *Die Walküre,* then sang virtually all Wagner roles through subsequent seasons until 1889; also appeared as Norma, Aida, Donna Anna, Fidelio, etc. She sang Isolde at the American première of *Tristan* (Dec. 1, 1886), and appeared in Italian opera with the De Reszkes and Lassalle during the season of 1891-92. In the meantime her contract with the Berlin Opera was cancelled (1889) owing to her protracted absence, and it required the intervention of Wilhelm II to reinstate her (1891). In 1896 she sang the three Brünnhildes at the Bayreuth Festival. Her great admiration for Mozart caused her to take an active part in the annual Mozart Festivals held at Salzburg, and from 1905 she was practically the chief organizer of these festivals. In 1909 she still sang Isolde (in Vienna). Her operatic repertory comprised 170 roles in 114 operas (German, Italian, and French). She possessed in the highest degree all the requisite qualities of a great interpreter; she had a boundless capacity for work, a glorious voice, and impeccable technique; she knew how to subordinate her fiery temperament to artistic taste; on the stage she had plasticity of pose, grace of movement, queenly presence; her ability to project her interpretation to her audiences in different countries with conviction was not the least factor of her universal success. Although she was celebrated chiefly as an opera singer, she was equally fine as interpreter of German lieder; she gave recitals concurrently with her operatic appearances, and continued them long after she had abandoned the stage; her repertory of songs exceeded 600. She was also a successful teacher; among her pupils were Geraldine Farrar and Olive Fremstad. — On Feb. 24, 1888, she married the tenor Paul Kalisch in New York; they appeared together as Tristan and Isolde; some years later, they were legally separated (but not actually divorced). After Lilli Lehmann's death, Paul Kalisch inherited her manor at Salzkammergut, and remained there until his death in 1946, at the age of 90. —Lilli Lehmann was the author of the books *Meine Gesangskunst* (1902; English transl. by Richard Aldrich, under the title *How to Sing,* N. Y., 1902; 3rd revised and supplemented ed., transl. by Clara Willenbücher, N.Y., 1924; reprint, 1949); *Studie zu Fidelio* (1904); *Mein Weg,* an autobiography (1913; 2nd ed., 1920; in English as *My Path Through Life,* 1914). She also edited arias of Mozart and many classical songs for the

Peters Edition. —Cf. J. H. Wagenmann, *Lilli Lehmanns Geheimniss der Stimmbänder* (Berlin, 1905; 2nd ed., 1926); L. Andro, *Lilli Lehmann* (Berlin, 1907).

Lehmann, Liza (Elizabetha Nina Mary Frederica), English soprano and composer; b. London, July 11, 1862; d. Pinner, Middlesex, Sept. 19, 1918. She was of German-Scotch parentage; she grew up in an intellectual and artistic atmosphere; her grandfather was a publisher, her father a painter, her mother a singer. From her childhood she lived in Germany, France, and Italy; among guests at her house in Rome was Liszt. She studied voice with Alberto Randegger in London, and composition with Wilhelm Freudenberg in Wiesbaden. She made her professional début as a singer at a Monday Popular Concert in London (Nov. 23, 1885), and subsequently appeared at various festivals in England. On Oct. 10, 1894, she married the English painter and composer Herbert Bedford, and retired from the stage; instead, she applied herself with great earnestness to composition, with remarkable results, for she was able to produce a number of works (mostly vocal) of undeniable merit, and was the first English woman composer to enjoy success with a large public, in England and in America. Her best known work, which has become a perennial favorite, is *In a Persian Garden,* to words from Omar Khayyám's *Rubaiyát,* in Fitzgerald's version; it is a song cycle, with recitatives, scored for 4 voices with piano accompaniment; while the music itself is entirely conventional, the vocal parts are eminently effective, both in dramatic and in lyrical passages. In 1910 Liza Lehmann made a tour in the U.S., presenting concerts of her songs, with herself at the piano. —Works: *Sergeant Brue,* a musical farce (London, June 14, 1904); *The Vicar of Wakefield,* a 'Romantic light opera' (Manchester, Nov. 12, 1906); *Everyman,* one-act opera (London, Dec. 28, 1915); *Once Upon a Time,* a 'fairy cantata' (London, Feb. 22, 1903); *Young Lochinvar,* for baritone solo, chorus, and orch.; *Endymion,* for soprano and orch.; *Romantic Suite,* for violin and piano; *In A Persian Garden,* for vocal quartet and piano (London, Jan. 10, 1897, 1st American performance, Boston, Jan. 5, 1910); song cycles (several of a humorous nature): *The Daisy Chain* (12 songs of childhood), *More Daisies, Prairie Pictures, In Memoriam* (after Tennyson), *Nonsense Songs* (from *Alice in Wonderland), The Cautionary Tales and a Moral* (after Hilaire Belloc); piano pieces *(Cobweb Castles,* etc.). Her memoirs, *The Life of Liza Lehmann, by Herself,* were publ. shortly after her death (London, 1919).

Lehmann, Lotte, celebrated German soprano; b. Perleberg, Feb. 27, 1888. She studied in Berlin with Erna Tiedke, Eva Reinhold, and Mathilde Mallinger. She made her début in a minor role at the Hamburg Opera, but soon was given important parts in Wagner's operas, establishing herself as one of the finest Wagnerian singers. In 1914 she was engaged at the Vienna Opera. Richard Strauss selected her to sing the Young Composer in *Ariadne auf Naxos* when it was first performed in Vienna; then she appeared as Octavian in *Der Rosenkavalier,* and later as the Marschallin, which became one of her most famous roles. In 1922 she sang in South America; in 1930, made her U.S. début as Sieglinde with the Chicago Civic Opera; she sang the same part with the Metropolitan Opera, N.Y., on Jan. 11, 1934; became a member of the company, appearing chiefly in Wagnerian roles, and also as the Marschallin. In 1937 she toured Australia; in 1938 she settled in the U.S.; lived mostly in California, but also traveled abroad; in Sept., 1957 she gave in London a master course for the study of operatic roles and lieder. She publ. a novel, *Orplid Mein Land* (1937; in English as *Eternal Flight,* 1938), and an autobiography, *Anfang und Aufsteig* (Vienna, 1937; London, as *Wings of Song,* and N.Y. as *Midway in My Song,* 1938); also *More than Singing* (N.Y., 1945); *My Many Lives* (N.Y., 1948; a sequel to the previous volume).

Lehmann, Marie, dramatic soprano; sister of Lilli Lehmann; b. Hamburg, May 15, 1851; d. Berlin, Dec. 9, 1931. She was a pupil of her mother, and later of her sister; made her début in Leipzig (May 1, 1867); in 1876 she created the parts of Wellgunde (*Rheingold* and *Götterdämmerung*) and Ortlinde *(Walküre)* at Bayreuth; from 1881 until her retirement in 1902 she was a member of the Vienna court opera; then lived in Berlin as a teacher.

Lehmann, Robert, German cellist; b. Schweidnitz, Silesia, Nov. 26, 1841; d. Stettin, June 12, 1912. He studied organ and cello; settled in Stettin in 1875 as church organist and conductor. He publ. a series of waltzes for orch. under the title *Briefe aus Wien,* melodious pieces for cello, and some church music; also wrote an autobiography, *Erinnerungen eines Künstlers* (1895).

Leibowitz, René, composer and conductor; b. Warsaw, Feb. 17, 1913. His family settled in Paris in 1926; from 1930 till 1933 he studied in Berlin with Schoenberg and in Vienna with Anton von Webern; under their influence he adopted the 12-tone method of composition; upon his return to France he became the foremost representative of the French school of 12-tone music. He published several important treatises: *Schoenberg et son école* (Paris, 1947; in English, N.Y. 1949); *Introduction à la musique de douze sons* (Paris, 1949); also a manual of orchestration, *Thinking for Orchestra* (with Jan Maguire; N. Y., 1958). After World War II he became active as conductor, particularly of modern music. —Works: piano sonata (1939); 10 canons for oboe, clarinet, and bassoon (1939); string quartet (1940); symphony (1941); chamber concerto for violin, piano, and 17 instruments (1942); 3 songs to poems by Picasso (1942); *Tourist Death* for soprano and chamber orch. (1943); chamber concerto for 9 instruments (1944); wind quintet (1944); violin sonata (1944); *Variations* for orch. (1945); *L'Explication des métaphores* for narrator, 2 pianos, harp, and percussion (1947); chamber symphony for 12 instruments (1948); *La Nuit close,* music drama (1949).

Leibrock, Joseph Adolf, German cellist and harpist; b. Brunswick, Jan. 8, 1808; d. Berlin, Aug. 8, 1886. He studied in Berlin; *Dr. phil.;* cellist and harpist in the court orch. at Brunswick. He wrote music to Schiller's *Räuber;* part-songs; songs; arrangements for piano and cello; a *Musikalische Akkordenlehre;* etc.

Leichtentritt (liyh'-ten-tritt), **Hugo,** eminent music scholar; b. Pleschen, Posen, Jan. 1, 1874; d. Cambridge, Mass., Nov. 13, 1951. While pursuing a liberal arts course at Harvard Univ. (1891-94), he also studied music under Prof. J. K. Paine; went to Berlin in 1895, and completed his musical studies at the Hochschule für Musik; also attended classes in musicology at Berlin Univ.; obtained the degree of *Dr. phil.* (Berlin, 1901) with the dissertation *Reinhard Keiser in seinen Opern;* he then taught at the Klindworth-Scharwenka Cons.; wrote music criticism for the 'Vossische Zeitung,' 'Allgemeine Musik-Zeitung,' 'Die Musik,' 'Die Signale,' etc.; also was German correspondent of the 'Musical Courier' and the 'Musical Times.' In 1934 he left Germany, and became lecturer on music at Harvard Univ.; also gave lectures at N.Y. Univ. Although chiefly known as a scholar, he was also a composer; wrote a symph. in A; symph. variations on a Siamese dance tune; violin concerto; cello concerto; piano concerto; *Ein Sommertag,* cycle of 10 songs for women's chorus and chamber orch.; cycle of 8 Goethe songs for baritone and chamber orch.; cantata from the *Song of Solomon,* for contralto and orch.; chamber music (2 quintets, 3 string quartets, piano trio, sonatas); 33 variations for piano; 10 piano études, etc.; also a comic opera, *Der Sizilianer* (Freiburg, May 28, 1920), and a music drama, *Esther* (not performed). —Books: *Chopin* (1905; 2nd ed., 1913, in Heinrich Reimann's series 'Berühmte Musiker'); *Geschichte der Musik* (1905; in Hillger's 'Illustrierte Volksbücher'); *Geschichte der Motette* (1908; his most important book); *Musikalische Formenlehre* (1911; 3rd ed., 1927); *Erwin Lendvai* (1912); *Ferruccio Busoni* (1916); *Analyse der Chopinschen Klavierwerke* (2 vols.; 1920, 1922); *Händel* (1924; very valuable); *The Complete Piano Sonatas of Beethoven* (analytical notes; N.Y., 1936); *Everybody's Little History of Music* (1938); *Music, History, and Ideas* (Cambridge, Mass., 1938); *Serge Koussevitzky, the Boston Symph. Orch. and the New American Music* (Cambridge, Mass., 1946); *Musical Form* (Cambridge, 1951); *Music of the Western Nations* (posthumous; ed. and amplified by N. Slonimsky; Cambridge, Mass., 1956); also publ. numerous essays on historical topics, mainly in the publications of the International Music Society (1905-14), the 'Mus. Quarterly,' etc.; brought out new editions of Bussler's *Harmonielehre, Kontrapunkt,* and *Formenlehre;* completed vol. 4 of Ambros's *Geschichte der Musik,* incorporating what at the time were the latest researches on the monodic style (1909); and publ. a selection of Beethoven's letters (1912). Of early music, he ed., in the 'Denkmäler deutscher Tonkunst,' selected works of H. Prätorius (vol. 23) and A. Hammerschmidt (vol. 40); in 'Meisterwerke deutscher Tonkunst,' 36 part-songs of the 16th century; in 'Ed. Peters,' 12 madrigals of Monteverdi; for the publications of 'Vereeniging voor Nederlandsche Muziekgeschiedenis,' *Scherzi musicali* by J. Schenk (vol. 28); for G. Schirmer, Inc., Hasse's *Miserere* for women's chorus and string orch.; also ed. a collection, *Deutsche Hausmusik aus 4 Jahrhunderten* (1906), and Vecchi's *Amfiparnasso* (1933; with English words).

Leider, Frida, German opera soprano; b. Berlin, April 18, 1888. After several years of study in Milan, she became a member of the Berlin Opera; made her American début with the Chicago Opera as Brünnhilde in *Die Walküre* in 1928; appeared with the Metropolitan Opera for the first time on Jan. 16, 1933 as Isolde; then returned to Germany. In 1956 she was teaching in Berlin.

Leifs, Jón, foremost Icelandic composer and writer; b. Sólheimar, May 1, 1899. After completing his primary education at Reykjavik, he went to Germany, where he studied at the Leipzig Cons. with Teichmüller, Szendrei, Scherchen, Lohse, and Graener; then conducted concerts in various German towns; in 1926, led the Hamburg Philharmonic when it visited Iceland; from 1934-37, musical director of the Icelandic Radio; also president of the Council of Northern Composers (1951) and other musical societies in Iceland and Scandinavia. His music is technically derived from the German Romantic tradition; but in several of his works he makes use of Icelandic melodies and rhythms; often he abandons opulent harmonic accoutrements to portray Arctic nature in bleak, organum-like diaphony. —Works: wordless music dramas, *Loftr* (Copenhagen, Sept. 3, 1938) and *Baldr* (1950); *Hljomkvida,* symph. trilogy (Karlsbad, 1925); *Icelandic Overture* (Oslo, 1926; his most successful work); Kyrie on Icelandic themes for a cappella chorus; *Island-Kantate* (Greifswald, 1930); *Saga-symfoni* (Helsinki, Sept. 18, 1950); 2 string quartets; several piano cycles based on Icelandic dance tunes; songs. He publ. (in Icelandic) a manual on musical forms; in German, *Islands künstlerische Anregung* (Reykjavik, 1951); contributed articles on Icelandic music to 'Die Musik' (Oct. 1923), 'Volk und Rasse' (Munich, 1932), and other publications.

Leigh, Walter, English composer; b. June 22, 1905; killed in action near Tobruk, Libya, June 12, 1942. He studied at Univ. Coll. School and at Christ's Coll., Cambridge, with Edward Dent; also was a pupil of Harold Darke, and later of Paul Hindemith at the Hochschule für Musik in Berlin (1927-29); from 1931 was music director of the Cambridge Festival Theater. He wrote the operas *The Pride of the Regiment* (London, 1932) and *The Jolly Roger* (London, 1933); the revue *Nine Sharp* (London, 1938); incidental music to plays; musical scores for films and radio adaptations. Other compositions include *Interlude* for theater orch.; 3 Pieces for amateur orch. (Baden Festival, 1929); *Suite for Amateur Orch.* (1931); *Jubilee Overture (Agincourt)* for George V, for amateur orch. (1935); string quartet; *Movements* for string quartet; sonatina for viola and piano (International Society for Contemporary Music Festival, Vienna, June 17, 1932); trio for 3 pianos (1934); trio for flute, oboe, and piano (1935); concertino for harpsichord or piano and strings (1936); an orch. suite from incidental music to Shakespeare's *Midsummer Night's Dream* (1937); piano pieces; songs.

Leighton, Sir **William,** English musician, 'gentleman pensioner'; d. before 1617. He publ. *The Teares or Lamentacions of a Sorrowfull Soule Composed with Musicall Ayres and Songs both for Voyces and Divers Instruments* (1614), containing 54 metrical psalms and hymns, 17 being for 4 voices with accompaniments in tablature for the lute, bandora, and cittern, and 13 for 4 voices and 24 for 5 voices without accompaniment. The first 8 are by Leighton himself; the others are by Bull, Byrd, Dowland, Gibbons, Coperario, Weelkes, Wilbye, etc. Excerpts have been transcribed into modern notation and scored by S. Beck (New York Public Library, 1934). —Cf. M. Seiffert, in the 'Bulletin de la Société Musicologique' (1922); J. Pulver, 'A Biographical Dictionary of Old English Music' (1927).

Leinsdorf, Erich, conductor; b. Vienna, Feb. 4, 1912. He studied with Paul Emerich and Hedwig Kammer-Rosenthal at the Vienna *Gymnasium;* in 1934 he became assistant of Bruno Walter and Toscanini at the Salzburg Festival; subsequently appeared in Italy, France, and Belgium as symph. conductor. In 1938 he was engaged as assistant conductor of the Metropolitan Opera, and made his American début conducting *Die Walküre* (Jan. 21, 1938) with excellent success; he then conducted other Wagner operas with the Metropolitan; also gave performances at the San Francisco Opera Co. After the death of Bodanzky in 1939, Leinsdorf became his successor as conductor at the Metropolitan Opera; he was conductor of the Cleveland Orch. in 1943; in the U.S. Army in 1944; conducted in Europe in 1946-47; in 1947 he was appointed conductor of the Rochester Philharmonic Orch.

Leisinger, Elisabeth, German coloratura soprano; b. Stuttgart, May 17, 1864; d. there, Dec. 15, 1933. She was a daughter of the singer Bertha Leisinger (1825-1913), and received her training from her; subsequently studied with Pauline Viardot-Garcia in Paris. In 1884 she was engaged at the Berlin Opera; sang there for 10 seasons; she married in 1894, and retired from the stage.

Leite (lā'-itĕ), **Antonio da Silva,** Portuguese composer; b. Oporto, May 23, 1759; d. there, Jan. 10, 1833. He was conductor at the Oporto Cathedral from 1787 to 1826. He wrote 2 operas; publ. *Rezumo de todas as regras e preceitos de cantoria assim da musica metrica como da cantochão* (Oporto, 1787) and a guitar method, *Estudo de guitarra* (Oporto, 1796).

Leitert, Johann Georg, German pianist and composer; b. Dresden, Sept. 29, 1852; d. Hubertusburg, near Dresden, Sept. 6, 1901. He studied with Kragen and Reichel (piano) and Rischbieter (harmony). In 1865 he made his concert début in Dresden; then played in Leipzig, Berlin, Prague, etc.; toured successfully in England in 1867; also gave concerts in Austria and Russia. From 1879-81 he taught at the Horák Music School in Vienna; wrote many characteristic pieces for piano: *Esquisses, Chants du crépuscule, Herbstblätter, Strahlen und Schatten, Aus schönern Stunden, Feuilles d'amour, Lose Blätter, Valse Caprice,* etc.; also transcriptions for piano (chiefly from Wagner's works).

Leitzmann (līts'-măhn), **Albert,** German theorist and musicologist; b. Magdeburg, Aug. 3, 1867; d. Jena, April 16, 1950. He studied chiefly literature and esthetics; established himself as Privatdozent for German language and literature at the Univ. of Jena. Besides numerous books dealing with literature and philology, he publ. *Beethovens Briefe* (1909; 3d ed. 1933); *Mozarts Briefe* (1910); *Mozarts Persönlichkeit* (1914); *Beethovens Persönlichkeit* (2 vols., 1914); *Beethovens persönliche Aufzeichnungen* (1918); *Ludwig van Beethoven. Berichte der Zeitgenossen* (2 vols., 1921); *W. A. Mozart. Berichte der Zeitgenossen* (1926).

Le Jeune (lŭ zhön'), **Claude** (or **Claudin**), French composer; b. Valenciennes, 1528; d. Paris, Sept. 25, 1600. He was active chiefly in Paris, where he appears to have been for some time associated with the poet Antoine de Baïf in the Académie de Musique, founded to encourage the growth of a new style of musical composition known as 'musique mesurée,' in which the music is made to follow the metrical rhythm of the text in conformity with the rules of classical prosody. The type of poetry set to music in this manner was called 'vers mesurez,' and 33 examples of such settings by Le Jeune are to be found in the work entitled *Le Printemps,* publ. posthumously at Paris in 1603 by his sister Cécile Le Jeune. The metrical scanning is given at the head of each song. In the preface to this work Le Jeune is given credit for having been the first to achieve the 'mating of ancient rhythm and modern harmony'; if not the first, he was at least, together with his contemporary and friend, Jacques Mauduit, one of the earliest and most notable cultivators of this new style, which was of great importance in the development of music. Le Jeune also cultivated every other variety of vocal music known in his time, such as French chansons in 'vers rimez,' Italian madrigals, Latin motets, etc. Special mention must be made of his settings of the Psalms, of which several collections appeared from 1564-1606. So great was his renown even during his lifetime that a wood engraving dated 1598 bore the legend: 'Le Phénix des Musiciens.' His best-known work is his setting of the Genevan Psalter *a* 4 and 5, publ. by Cécile Le Jeune in 1613. This simple contrapuntal setting of the Psalms was widely used in the Reformed churches of France and Holland, and it was also publ. in a German transl. Some of these harmonizations even found their way into early New England psalm books, such as 'The Ainsworth Psalter' (cf. *Early Psalmody in America,* ed. by C. S. Smith for the New York Public Library, 1939). A more elaborate setting of some psalms, *Douze Psaumes de David,* in motet style for 2 to 7 voices, was contained in the work entitled *Dodecacorde,* publ. at La Rochelle in 1598. On the title page of this work, Le Jeune is described as 'compositeur de la musique de la chambre du roy,' showing that he was then attached to the court of Henri IV. It is known that he had espoused the Huguenot cause during the wars of the Catholic League, and it is said that his MSS narrowly escaped destruction during the siege of Paris in 1588, having only been saved by the intervention of his Catholic colleague Mauduit. In 1612 a nephew of Le Jeune publ. a *Second livre de meslanges à 4-10,* containing miscellaneous vocal pieces and two instrumental fantasias. The most important works of Le Jeune have been reprinted by H. Expert in his 'Maîtres Musiciens de la Renaissance française,' as follows: *Dodecacorde* (vol. 11), *Le Printemps* (vols. 12-14), one part of the *Livre de meslanges* (vol. 16), *Psaumes en vers mesurez* (vols. 20-22); also, in 'Monuments de la musique française,' the first part of the *Octonaires de la vanité et inconstance du monde* (vol. 1). —Cf. E. Bouton, *Esquisse biographique et bibliographique sur Claude Le Jeune* (Valenciennes, 1845); M. Cauchie, *La Mort de Claude Le Jeune* in 'Revue de musicologie' (Aug., 1927); D. P. Walker and F. Lesure, *Claude Le Jeune and Musique Mesurée,* in 'Musica Disciplina' (1949).

Lekeu (lŭ-kö'), **Guillaume,** talented Belgian composer; b. Heusy, near Verviers, Jan. 20, 1870; d. Angers, Jan. 21, 1894 (of typhoid fever). He went to school in Poitiers; in 1888, followed his family to Paris; there he studied with Gaston Vallin; he also received some advice from César

Franck; then took a course with Vincent d'Indy. He went to Brussels to compete for the Belgian Prix de Rome; won 2nd prize with his cantata *Andromède* (1891). Returning to Paris, he undertook the composition of several works of chamber music, but death intervened when he was barely 24 years old. —Works: *Barberine* (fragments for an opera); *Chanson de mai,* for chorus and orch.; *Chant lyrique* for chorus and orch.; 2 symph. studies: *Chant de triomphale délivrance* and *Hamlet; Fantaisie sur un cramignon liégeois;* Adagio for string quartet (also for string orch.); *Épithalame* for strings, trombones, and organ; *Fantaisie sur deux airs angevins;* 2 piano trios; string quartet; *Meditation* and *Minuet* for string quartet; *Noël* for soprano, string quartet, and piano; cello sonata (unfinished; completed by Vincent d'Indy); violin sonata (his best known work, frequently performed); piano quartet (unfinished; completed by Vincent d'Indy); piano sonata; *Tempo di mazurka* for piano; several songs. —Cf. A. Tissier, *Guillaume Lekeu* (Verviers, 1906); O. G. Sonneck, *Miscellaneous Studies in the History of Music* (N. Y., 1921); R. Vandelle, *Guillaume Lekeu,* in the 'Revue Musicale' (1921); M. Lorrain, *Guillaume Lekeu, Sa correspondance, sa vie et son œuvre* (Liège, 1923); R. Stengel, *Lekeu* (Brussels, 1944); P. Prist, *Guillaume Lekeu* (Brussels, 1946).

Lemacher, Heinrich, German composer; b. Solingen, June 26, 1891. He studied at the Cons. of Cologne; 1928, he became a teacher at the Cologne Hochschule für Musik. A disciple of the German Romantic school, he elaborated its principles in a number of choral and instrumental works; the chief influences are Bruckner and Reger; he wrote several symph. suites; chamber music; piano pieces. More important than these are his compositions for the Catholic service: several Masses, offertories, motets, cantatas with organ accompaniment, etc., in which he succeeded in establishing a practical style of modern polyphony. —Cf. Karl Laux, *Heinrich Lemacher,* in *Musik und Musiker der Gegenwart* (Essen, 1949; pp. 153-62).

Lemaire (or **Le Maire**), a French musician of the 16th-17th centuries. He is said to have urged the adoption of a 7th solmisation syllable *(si,* according to Rousseau; *za,* according to Mersenne); an invention tantamount to the abandonment of the old system of mutation. —Cf. H. Riemann, *Geschichte der Musiktheorie* (Leipzig, 1898).

Lemaire (lŭ-mär'), **Jean Eugène Gaston,** French composer; b. Château d'Amblainvilliers, Seine-et-Oise, Sept. 9, 1854; d. (suicide; body found in the Seine) Paris, Jan. 9, 1928. He studied at the École Niedermeyer; was a prolific composer of light music (operettas, piano pieces, and characteristic pieces for orch.). His works include *Perrette et le pot au lait,* pantomime (Paris, Feb. 11, 1891); *Conte de printemps,* pantomime (Paris, May 18, 1892); *La belle Tunisienne,* opera in 1 act (Paris, Aug. 26, 1892); the operettas *Les Maris de Juanita, Le Supplice de Jeannot, Le Rêve de Manette; Rose,* lyric fairy tale (Paris, March 14, 1895); the ballets *Feminissima* (1902) and *Pierrot venge son Rival* (1917). He also wrote a number of fox-trots, one of which, *La Grenouille,* became popular; and songs, of which *Vous dansez, marquise,* was a great favorite.

Le Maistre (or **Le Maître**) (lŭ-mā'tr), **Mattheus,** Flemish composer; b. near Liège, c. 1505; d. Dresden, 1577. In 1554 he succeeded J. Walter as Kapellmeister at the court in Dresden; retired on a pension Feb. 12, 1568. Fétis and Otto Kade wrongly identified him with Hermann Matthias Werrekoren, choirmaster in Milan. —Published works: *Magnificat octo tonorum* (1577); *Catechesis numeris musicis inclusa* (1563; for the choirboys of the Dresden Chapel); *Geistliche und weltliche teutsche Gesänge,* for 4-5 voices (1566); motets for 5 voices (1570); *Officia de nativitate et Ascensione Christi,* for 5 voices (1574); *Schöne und auserlesene teutsche und lateinische geistliche Lieder* (1577). In MS at the Munich Library: 3 Masses, 24 Offices and 4 versicles. A motet, *Estote prudentes* (4 voices) is in Commer's 'Collectio' (vol. 8); 2 lieder for 4 voices are in Ambros' *Geschichte der Musik* (vol. 5, 'Beispielband,' ed. by O. Kade, 1882); 5 sacred and 5 secular songs (including 2 quodlibets) are in O. Kade's monograph on Le Maistre (Mainz, 1862). —Cf. René Vannes, *Dictionnaire des Musiciens* (Brussels, 1947; pp. 242-44).

Leman, Albert Semyonovitch, Russian pianist and composer; b. Volsk, near Saratov, July 7, 1917. He studied at the Leningrad Cons.; has written a symph. (1940); 2 piano concertos, of which the 2nd is based on Tartar folk themes (1944); a violin concerto on the 30th anniversary of the Tartar Soviet Republic (1952); several symph. suites on Tartar themes; a string quartet; piano pieces. He is on the staff of the Kazan Cons.

Lemare, Edwin Henry, distinguished organist; b. Ventnor, Isle of Wight, Sept. 9, 1865; d. Los Angeles, Sept. 24, 1934. He received his first instruction from his father, and when only 8 years old began to act occasionally as substitute at the services; in 1876 he won the John Goss scholarship at the Royal Academy of Music, where he studied for 6 years under G. A. and W. C. Macfarren, Steggall, and Turpin; in 1882 appointed organist at St. John's, Finsbury Park, London; made his début as a recitalist at the Inventions Exhibition in London (1884); 1886, Fellow of the Royal College of Organists and organist at the Parish Church and Albert Hall, Sheffield, where he remained 6 years; in that time he gave some 300 recitals in the North of England. In 1892 he was called to Holy Trinity, London, where his weekly recitals made him famous, so that he was elected honorary Fellow of the Royal Academy of Music. From 1897 to 1902 he was organist at St. Margaret's Westminster. His reputation then was such that after the death of Best (1897) he was generally regarded as England's greatest living organist. He visited America for the first time in 1900, and in the following year played about 100 recitals in the U.S. and Canada. In 1902 he became organist of the Carnegie Institute in Pittsburgh; resigned in 1905; then traveled around the world as a concert organist. In 1915 he gave a number of recitals at the Panama Exposition. From 1917-21 he was municipal organist at San Francisco; 1921-23, municipal organist at Portland, Maine; 1924 until his retirement in 1929, municipal organist at Chattanooga, Tenn. He publ. over 200 original works (mainly church music) and many arrangements; some of his pieces have become part of the standard organ repertory. His well-known *Andantino in D-flat* received an additional fillip of popularity when its melody was used for the song *Moonlight and Roses*. Lemare left a booklet of reminiscences, *Organs I Have Met,* which was publ. posthumously by his widow (1957).

Lemmens, Nicolas Jacques, remarkable Belgian organist; b. Zoerle-Parwys, Jan. 3, 1823; d. at Castle Linterport, near Malines, Jan. 30, 1881. He was a pupil of his father, and of Van der Broeck at Diest; of Godineau at the Brussels Cons.; after playing the organ at Diest for some months, he took further lessons (1841) with Michelot (piano), Girschner (organ), and Fétis (counterpoint). In 1846 he went to Breslau, with a government stipend, to study under Hesse; in 1849 he was appointed prof. of organ playing at the Brussels Cons.; married the singer Helen Sherrington in 1857, and thenceforth spent much time in England. In 1879 he opened a seminary for Catholic organists and choirmasters at Malines. — Organ works: sonatas, improvisations, studies, etc. (over 60 in all); an *École d'orgue,* adopted in the Paris and Brussels Conservatories; 2 symphonies, a *Te Deum,* motets, songs, etc. Four large volumes of posthumous works, *Oeuvres inédites* (Masses, motets, organ works) were publ. by Breitkopf & Härtel. His book, *Du chant grégorien, sa mélodie, son rythme, son harmonisation,* was publ. posthumously in Ghent (1886).

Lemnitz, Tiana, soprano; b. Metz, Oct. 26, 1897. She studied with A. Kohmann at Hoch's Cons. in Frankfurt; 1922, made her operatic début, followed by engagements in Aachen, Hanover, Dresden, and Berlin and guest appearances in Holland, Belgium, Poland, England, and South America.

Lemoine, Antoine-Marcel, French music publisher, violist, and guitar player; father of Henry Lemoine; b. Paris, Nov. 3, 1763; d. there, April, 1817. A self-taught musician, he played viola at the Théâtre de Monsieur, conducted at minor Parisian theaters, and finally founded a music-publishing firm.

Lemoine, Henry, French music publisher, son of Antoine-Marcel Lemoine; b. Paris, Oct. 21, 1786; d. there, May 18, 1854. He studied at the Paris Cons. (1798-1809); in 1821 he also had harmony lessons from Reicha; taught the piano; at his father's death, in 1817, succeeded to the latter's music publishing business. He publ. methods for harmony, piano, and solfeggio; *Tablettes du pianiste: memento du professeur de piano;* sonatas, variations, dances, etc., for piano.

Lemont, Cedric Wilmot, organist; b. Fredericton, New Brunswick, Canada, Dec. 15, 1879; d. New York, April 27, 1954. He studied with Carl Faelten (piano) and Dunham (organ) in Boston; filled various positions as organist and choirmaster in Canada; in 1907, settled in the U. S.; taught in Chicago and Brooklyn. He publ. over 600 compositions, including piano pieces, anthems, etc.; brought out 3 vols. of *American History and Encyclopedia of Music.*

Lemoyne (lŭ-mwăhn), **Jean Baptiste,** French conductor and composer; b. Eymet, Périgord, April 3, 1751; d. Paris, Dec. 30, 1796. He was a conductor in provincial

French theaters before studying composition with Graun and Kirnberger at Berlin, where he became 2nd Kapellmeister to Frederick the Great. Returning to Paris, he brought out an opera, *Électre* (1782), pretending to be a pupil of Gluck, an imposture that Gluck did not see fit to expose until the failure of Lemoyne's piece. In his next operas, Lemoyne abandoned Gluck's ideas, copied the style of Piccinni and Sacchini, and produced nearly a score of quite successful works, including *Phèdre* (Fontainebleau, Oct. 26, 1786) and *Nephté* (Paris, Dec. 15, 1789).

Lenaerts (lĕ-nahrts'), **Constant,** Belgian conductor and composer; b. Antwerp, March 9, 1852; d. there, March 20, 1931. He studied with Peter Benoît; began to conduct at the Flemish National Theater at the age of 18; in 1914, was appointed teacher at the Antwerp Cons. He wrote a cantata, *De triomf van't licht* (1890), songs, and some instrumental music.

Lendvai (lend'-vī), **Erwin,** Hungarian conductor and composer; b. Budapest, June 4, 1882; d. London, March 31, 1949. He studied with Koessler; later went to Milan, where he had some lessons with Puccini; taught at Jaques-Dalcroze's School of Eurhythmics for a season (1913-14); then was instructor of dramatic composition at Hoch's Cons. in Frankfurt; later at the Klindworth-Scharwenka Cons. in Berlin (1919-22); teacher at the Hamburg Volksmusikschule (1923-25); choral conductor in Coblenz (1926-27); then in Munich and in Erfurt; in 1938 he went to Switzerland, and later to London, where he remained until his death. He composed a symphony (1909); *Archaische Tänze* for small orch.; *Masken,* an orchestral scherzo; *Nippon,* choral suite for women's voices; string quartet; several piano trios and other chamber music; also an opera, *Elga* (Mannheim, Dec. 6, 1916); he publ. a valuable method, *Chorschule.* —Cf. H. Leichtentritt, *Erwin Lendvai* (Berlin, 1912).

Lenepveu (lŭ-nep-vö'), **Charles (Ferdinand),** French composer and pedagogue; b. Rouen, Oct. 4, 1840; d. Paris, Aug. 16, 1910. As a law student he took music lessons from Servais; won 1st prize at Caen in 1861 for a cantata; entered Ambroise Thomas' class at the Paris Cons. in 1863, and in 1865 took the Grand Prix de Rome with the cantata *Renaud dans les jardins d'Armide* (Paris, Jan. 3, 1866). His comic opera *Le Florentin* also won a prize, offered by the ministry of Fine Arts (1867), and was performed at the Opéra-Comique (Feb. 26, 1874). The grand opera *Velléda* was produced at Covent Garden, London (July 4, 1882), with Adelina Patti in the title role. In 1891 Lenepveu succeeded Guiraud as harmony prof. at the Cons., and in 1893 again succeeded him as prof. of composition, taking an advanced class in 1894. In 1896 he was elected to Ambroise Thomas' chair in the Académie des Beaux-Arts; was Chevalier of the Legion of Honor, and Officer of Public Instruction. —Cf. R. de Saint-Arroman, *Charles Lenepveu* (Paris, 1898).

Léner, Jenö, violinist; b. Szabadka, Hungary, June 24, 1894; d. New York, Nov. 4, 1948. He studied with Hubay at the Budapest Academy of Music; was concertmaster of the Budapest Philharmonic Orch. until 1918, when he founded the Léner String Quartet (with Joseph Smilovits, Sandor Roth, and Imre Hartmann). The quartet then appeared in Vienna (1920), Paris (1921), and London (1922), enjoying an excellent reception from critics and public alike. In 1929 the Léner Quartet came to the U.S., establishing itself as one of the finest chamber music organizations in America.

Leng, Alfonso, Chilean composer; b. Santiago, Feb. 11, 1884. He was of mixed German and English descent; studied dentistry, and became a professional dentist in Santiago; also took music lessons with Enrique Soro. In his leisure time, he composed short symphonic sketches in a Romantic vein, songs, and evocative piano pieces. —Works: *La Muerte de Alsina,* symph. poem (Santiago, May 30, 1931); *Canto de Invierno,* for orch. (Santiago, May 19, 1933); *Fantasia* for piano and orch. (Santiago, Aug. 28, 1936); 9 preludes for piano; piano sonata (1950); songs. In 1957 he received the 'Premio Nacional de Arte.' A special issue of the 'Revista Musical Chilena' was publ. in his honor (Aug.-Sept., 1957) with articles by Domingo Santa Cruz, Alfonso Letelier, and others.

Lenormand (lŭ-nor-mahn'), **René,** French composer; b. Elbeuf, Aug. 5, 1846; d. Paris, Dec. 3, 1932. He received his musical training from his mother, who was an excellent pianist. His desire to follow a musical career was thwarted at first by his father's insistence on a more profitable course of life; to effect a compromise, Lenormand took a position in a commercial house as a youth; at the same time, he tried his hand at composition; in 1868, went to Paris, where he studied with Damcke, a good musician and a friend of Berlioz. Lenormand's main interest was in the creation of an international type of the German lied, and for that purpose he organized in Paris a society which he called 'Le Lied en tous pays.' In his own creative efforts, he was at his best in his melodious songs, of which he wrote about 150; they are distinguished by a poetic imagination, a fine melodic line, and a harmonic accompaniment that follows the usages of early Impressionism. Besides his songs, Lenormand wrote an opera, *Le Cachet rouge* (Le Havre, 1925); a piano concerto; *Le Lahn de Mabed* (on an old Arabian theme), for violin and orch.; *Le Voyage imaginaire,* symph. tableaux after Loti; *Deux Esquisses sur des thèmes malais,* for orch.; piano pieces *(Une journée à la campagne, Le Nuage vivant, Valses sérieuses, Pièces exotiques,* etc.; for 4 hands: *Divertissement américain, La Nouba Medjenneba,* etc.); also publ. a valuable manual on harmony, *Étude sur l'harmonie moderne* (Paris, 1912; English transl. as *A Study of Modern Harmony,* London, 1915). —Cf. H. Woollett, *Un mélodiste français: René Lenormand* (Paris, 1930).

Lent, Ernest, cellist and composer; b. Brandenburg, Germany, Sept. 18, 1856; d. Washington, D. C., Dec. 22, 1922. He studied at the Leipzig Cons. (1878-81); toured in Europe as a concert cellist; in 1884, settled in Washington as a teacher. He publ. numerous pieces for cello and piano, and some songs; also a manual, *Elementary Technics for the Violin* (4 books).

Lenz, Wilhelm von, writer on music; b. Riga, June 1, 1809; d. St. Petersburg, Jan. 31, 1883. He traveled in Europe; was a piano pupil, in Paris, of Liszt and also of Chopin (1842); returning to Russia, he became a government councillor in St. Petersburg. His writings are historically valuable because of the intimate personal experience that they reflect. His most notable book is *Beethoven et ses trois styles* (2 vols.; St. Petersburg, 1852; new ed., by Calvocoressi, Paris, 1909), in which he proposed for the first time the division of Beethoven's works into 3 chronological periods, the first (op. 1-21) being entirely classical, the second (op. 22-95) and to Lenz the best, truly Beethovenian in its nobility and individuality, and the third (from op. 96) as marking partly a decline, partly an attempt to scale unattainable heights. He further publ. *Beethoven: eine Kunststudie* (6 vols., 1855-60); vols. 4-6 separately publ. as *Kritischer Katalog der sämmtlichen Werke nebst Analysen derselben* (Hamburg, 1860), and vol. 1 as *Beethoven: eine Biographie* (2nd ed., 1879; reprinted, with additions by A. Kalischer, 1908); and *Die grossen Pianoforte-Virtuosen unserer Zeit* (brief character sketches of Liszt, Chopin, Tausig, and Henselt; 1872; English transl., N.Y., 1899).

Leo (lā'-ŏh), **Leonardo (Lionardo Oronzo Salvatore de Leo),** one of the founders, and an eminent teacher, of the 'Neapolitan' school of composition; b. San Vito degli Schiavi, near Brindisi, Aug. 5, 1694; d. Naples, Oct. 31, 1744. He studied with N. Fago at the Cons. della Pietà de' Turchini in Naples (1703-15); in 1716, 2nd maestro there, and maestro at the cathedral; 1717, maestro at Santa Maria della Solitaria and organist of the Royal Chapel, of which he was appointed 3rd maestro di cappella in 1731; vice maestro (1738); 1st maestro (1741); in 1725, succeeded A. Scarlatti as instructor in the Cons. di Sant' Onofrio, where he remained until his death, training many illustrious pupils, including Pergolesi, Jommelli, Piccinni, Sacchini, Traetta; simultaneously taught at the Cons. della Pietà. In 1713 he brought out a dramatic oratorio, *Il trionfo della castità di Sant' Alessio,* at the Cons. His first opera was *Pisistrato* (Naples, May 13, 1714); it was followed by nearly 60 others, *La Contesa dell' Amore colla Virtù* being the last; a list of the most important operas includes: *Sofonisba* (Naples, 1718); *Lucio Papirio* (Naples, 1720); *Caio Gracco* (Naples, 1720); *Arianna e Teseo* (Naples, 1721); *Timocrate* (Venice, 1723); *L'amore fedele* (Naples, 1724); *Lo pazzo apposto* (Naples, 1724); *Zenobia in Palmira* (Naples, 1725); *Il trionfo di Camilla* (Rome, 1726); *La semmeglianza di chi l'ha fatta* (Naples, 1726); *Dalli sdegni d'amore, ovvero L'Orismene* (Naples, 1726); *Il Cid* (Rome, 1727); *Lo matrimonio annascuso* (Naples, 1727); *Argeno* (Venice, 1728); *La pastorella commattuta* (Naples, 1728); *Catone in Utica* (Venice, 1729); *La schiava per amore* (Naples, 1729); *Rosmene* (Naples, 1730); *Evergete* (Rome, 1731); *Componimento drammatico pastorale* (Rome, Nov. 19, 1733); *Il castello d'Atlante* (Naples, 1734); *La clemenza di Tito* (Venice, 1735); *Demetrio* (Torre Maggiore, 1735); *Demofoonte* (Naples, 1735); *Emira* (Naples, 1735); *Onore vince amore* (Naples, 1736); *Farnace* (Naples, 1736); *Siface* (Bologna, 1737); *Ciro riconosciuto* (Naples,

1737) ;*L'amico traditore* (Naples, 1737); *La simpatia del sangue* (Naples, 1737); *L'Olimpiade* (Naples, 1737); *Il conte* (Naples, 1738); *Le nozze di Amore e di Psiche* (Naples, 1738); *Temistocle* (Florence, 1739); *Amor vuol sofferenze* (Naples, 1739); *Achille in Sciro* (Turin, 1739); *Ezio* (Modena, Dec. 26, 1739); *Carlo in Alemagnia* (Milan, 1740); *Viriati* (Pistoia, 1740); *Il verbo eterno e la religione* (Florence, 1741); *L'Andromaca* (Naples, 1742); *L'ambizione delusa* (Naples, 1742); *Il fantastico od Il nuovo Don Chisciotte* (Naples, 1743); *La fedeltà odiata* (Naples, 1744); *Vologeso* (Turin, 1744). Besides operas, he wrote 5 more oratorios, 5 Masses, Magnificats, Misereres, Credos, Dixits, motets, hymns, responses, etc.; most celebrated of all is his grand *Miserere* for double (8-part) chorus a cappella, ranking with Pergolesi's famous *Stabat Mater;* also 6 cello concertos with string quartet; 2 books of organ fugues; several harpsichord toccatas; etc. Most are in MS at Naples, Rome, Berlin, and Paris. A few have been publ. in modern editions: a duet from *Demofoonte* and an aria from *La clemenza di Tito* in Gevaert's 'Gloires d'Italie'; the above mentioned *Miserere* in Commer's 'Musica sacra' (vol. 8), also separately by Choron (Paris) and Schlesinger (Berlin); one *Dixit dominus a 8* by Stanford (London) and another *a 5* by Kummel in his 'Sammlung, etc.'; a *Credidi propter,* a *Tu es sacerdos,* a *Miserere a 4* in Braune's 'Cäcilia'; a *Di quanta pena* and an *Et incarnatus est,* in Rochlitz's 'Sammlung vorzüglicher Gesangstücke'; many solfeggi with bass, in Levesque's and Bêche's 'Solfèges d'Italie.' —Cf. C. V. Leo, *Leonardo Leo e sua epoca musicale* (Brindisi, 1894); G. Leo, *Leonardo Leo, musicista del secolo XVIII e le sue opere musicali* (Naples, 1905); F. Schlitzer, *T. Traetta, L. Leo, V. Bellini* (Siena, 1952); F. Piovano, *À propos d'une récente biographie de Leonardo Leo,* in 'Sammelbände der Internationalen Musik - Gesellschaft' (1906-07; pp. 70-95); E. J. Dent, *Leonardo Leo,* in 'Sammelbände der Internationalen Musik-Gesellschaft' (vol. 8, pp. 550-66); Karl Geiringer, *Eine Geburtstagskantate von P. Metastasio und Leonardo Leo,* in the 'Zeitschrift für Musikwissenschaft' (1927); F. Walker, *Cav. Giacomo Leo and His Famous 'Ancestor,'* in the 'Music Review' (Nov., 1948).

Léonard (lā-oh-nahr'), **Hubert,** Belgian violinist and pedagogue; b. Bellaire, near Liège, April 7, 1819; d. Paris, May 6, 1890. His first violin teacher was Rouma, at Liège; he then became a pupil of Habeneck at the Paris Cons.; in 1844 he embarked on an extended European tour; then succeeded Bériot as violin prof. at the Brussels Cons. In 1867 he went to Paris, where he remained until his death. He publ. *Petite gymnastique du jeune violoniste; 24 Études classiques; Études harmoniques;* a method for violin, *École Léonard; L'ancienne école italienne,* a collection of special studies in double stopping, including examples from Corelli, Tartini, Geminiani, and Nardini; *Le Violon au point de vue de l'orchestration;* also 5 violin concertos; 6 concert pieces with piano; a serenade for 3 violins; a concert duo for 2 violins; fantasias and character pieces.

Leoncavallo, Ruggiero, Italian dramatic composer; b. Naples, March 8, 1858; d. Montecatini, Aug. 9, 1919. He attended Naples Cons., where his teachers were B. Cesi (piano), and M. Ruta and L. Rossi (composition), and at 16 made a pianistic tour. His first opera, *Tommaso Chatterton,* was about to be produced in Bologna (1878), but the manager disappeared, and the production was called off. Leoncavallo earned his living as a young man by playing piano in cafés; this life he continued for many years, traveling through Egypt, Greece, Turkey, Germany, Belgium, and Holland before settling in Paris. There he found congenial company; became a friend of the famous baritone Victor Maurel; composed chansonettes and other popular songs; wrote an opera *Songe d'une nuit d'été (Midsummer Night's Dream,* after Shakespeare), which was privately sung in a salon. He began to study Wagner's scores, and became an ardent Wagnerian; he resolved to emulate the master by producing a trilogy *Crepusculum,* depicting in epical traits the Italian Renaissance; the separate parts were to be *I Medici, Girolamo Savonarola,* and *Cesare Borgia.* He spent 6 years on the basic historical research; having completed the first part, and with the scenario of the entire trilogy sketched, he returned to Italy in 1887. There, the publisher Ricordi became interested in the project, but kept delaying the publication and production of the work. Annoyed, Leoncavallo turned to Sonzogno, the publisher of Mascagni, whose opera *Cavalleria Rusticana* had just obtained tremendous vogue. Leoncavallo submitted a short opera in a similarly realistic vein; he wrote his own libretto based on a factual story of passion and murder in a Calabrian village, and named it *I Pagliacci.* The opera was given with sensational success at the Teatro dal Verme in Milan under the direction of

Toscanini (May 21, 1892), with Victor Maurel as Tonio, and rapidly took possession of the operatic stages throughout the world; it is often played on the same evening with Mascagni's opera, both works being of brief duration. Historically, these 2 operas signalized the important development of Italian operatic 'verismo,' which influenced composers of other countries also. The holograph score of *Pagliacci* is in the Library of Congress. —The enormous success of *Pagliacci* did not deter Leoncavallo from carrying on his more ambitious projects. The first part of his unfinished trilogy, *I Medici,* was finally brought out at La Scala, Milan, on Nov. 9, 1893, but the reception was so indifferent that Leoncavallo turned to other subjects; the same fate befell his youthful opera *Tommaso Chatterton* at its production in Rome (March 10, 1896). His next opera, *La Bohème* (Venice, May 6, 1897), won considerable success, but had the ill fortune of coming a year after Puccini's masterpiece on the same story, and was dwarfed by comparison. There followed a light opera, *Zazà* (Milan, Nov. 10, 1900), which was fairly successful, and was produced repeatedly on world stages. In 1904 Leoncavallo was commissioned by the German Emperor Wilhelm II to write an opera for Berlin; this was *Der Roland von Berlin,* on a German historic theme; it was produced in Berlin on Dec. 13, 1904, but despite the high patronage, it proved a fiasco. In 1906 Leoncavallo made a tour of the U.S. and Canada, conducting his *Pagliacci* and a new opera, *La Jeunesse de Figaro,* specially written for his American tour; it was so unsuccessful that Leoncavallo never attempted to stage it in Europe. Back in Italy he resumed his industrious production; 2 new operas, *Maia* (Rome, Jan. 15, 1910) and *Malbruk* (Rome, Jan. 19, 1910), were produced within the same week; another opera, *La Reginetta delle Rose,* was staged simultaneously in Rome and in Naples (June 24, 1912). In the autumn of that year, Leoncavallo visited London, where he presented the première of his *Gli Zingari* (Sept. 16, 1912); a year later, he revisited the U.S., conducting in San Francisco. He wrote several more operas, but they made no impression: 3 of them were produced during his lifetime: *La Candidata* (Rome, Feb. 6, 1915), *Goffredo Mameli* (Genoa, April 27, 1916), and *Prestami tua moglie* (Montecatini, Sept. 2, 1916); the following were produced posthumously: *A chi la giarettiera?* (Rome, Oct. 16, 1919), *Edipo re* (Chicago, Dec. 13, 1920), and *Il primo bacio* (Montecatini, April 29, 1923). Still another opera, *Tormenta,* remained unfinished. Salvatore Allegra collected various sketches by Leoncavallo and arranged from them a 3-act operetta, *La maschera nuda,* which was produced in Naples on June 26, 1925.

Leonhard, Julius Emil, German composer; b. Lauban, June 13, 1810; d. Dresden, June 23, 1883. He became prof. of piano at the Munich Cons. in 1852; at the Dresden Cons. in 1859. He wrote an oratorio, *Johannes der Täufer;* 3 cantatas for soli, chorus, and orch.; a symphony; overture to Oehlenschläger's *Axel und Walpurg;* a piano sonata; 2 violin sonatas; 3 string trios; a piano quartet; etc.

Leoni, Franco, Italian composer; b. Milan, Oct. 24, 1864; d. London, Feb. 8, 1949. He studied at the Milan Cons. with Dominiceti and Ponchielli; in 1892, went to London, where he remained for 25 years, until 1917; then lived in France and Italy, eventually returning to England.—Operas: *Raggio di Luna* (Milan, June 5, 1890); *Rip van Winkle* (London, Sept. 4, 1897); *Ib and Little Christina,* subtitled 'a picture in 3 panels' (London, Nov. 14, 1901); *The Oracle* (London, June 28, 1905; Metropolitan Opera, N. Y., Feb. 4, 1915; his most successful opera); *Tzigana* (Genoa, Feb. 3, 1910); *Le Baruffe chiozzotte* (Milan, Jan. 2, 1920); *La Terra del sogno* (Milan, Jan. 10, 1920); the cantatas *Sardanapalus* (1896), *Golgotha* (1911); oratorio, *The Gate of Life* (London, March 16, 1898); songs.

Leoni, Leone, Italian composer; flourished between 1580 and 1620; was maestro di cappella in Vicenza (1588). He was a disciple of the Venetian school; his works are characteristic for their application of chromatic devices in harmony, and antiphonal choral usages. He publ. 5 books of madrigals for 5 voices (Venice, 1588-1602); 4 books of motets with organ, under the title *Sacri fiori* (1606-22); *Aurea corona* for 4 voices accompanied by 6 instruments (1618). His motets are particularly fine.

Leonin (lĕh-oh-năn) **(Leoninus),** great master of the 'Notre Dame School' and of the 'Ars Antiqua'; probably flourished before the cornerstone of Notre Dame de Paris was laid in 1163; was theretofore active at the earlier church, Beatae Mariae Virginis; according to the treatise of Anonymus IV (Coussemaker, 'Scriptores,' I, 342), he compiled the *Magnus Liber organi de graduali et antiphonario pro servitio divino multiplicando,* a cycle of 2-part liturgical settings for the whole church year, a work later revised by Leonin's successor, Perotin (q. v.). The original of this collection has not been preserved, but there are 4 extant MSS containing music from it; of these, MS Wolfenbüttel 677 (formerly Helmstedt 628), dating from the 14th century (facsimile reprint in J. H. Baxter, *An Old St. Andrews Music Book,* 1931), though not the oldest, appears to preserve music from the *Magnus Liber* in purest form; the other 3 MSS are Pluteus 29.1 in the Biblioteca Medicea-Laurenziana of Florence, Wolfenbüttel 1206, and Madrid Biblioteca Nacional 20486. Leonin was the chief figure of his period, standing midway between the St. Martial school and Perotin; his technique is characterized by the juxtaposition in individual pieces of the note-against-note style, and the style in which, over a lower part characterized by long sustained notes, an upper part moves in freely flowing rhythm. (Both styles had already been used at St. Martial.) —Cf. Fr. Ludwig, *Die liturgische Organa Leonins und Perotins,* in 'Riemann-Festschrift' (1909); Fr. Ludwig, *Repertorium organorum recentioris et motetorum vetustissimi stili:* vol. I, *Catalogue raisonné der Quellen* (1910); J. Handschin, *Zur Notre Dame Rhythmik,* in 'Zeitschrift für Musikwissenschaft' (1925); H. Schmidt, *Zur Melodiebildung Leonins und Perotins,* in the 'Zeitschrift für Musikwissenschaft' (1931); M. Schneider, *Zur Satztechnik der Notre Dame-Schule,* in 'Zeitschrift für Musikwissenschaft' (1932); G. Reese, *Music in the Middle Ages,* chap. 11 (N. Y., 1940); W. G. Waite, *The Rhythm of Twelfth Century Polyphony* (New Haven, 1954).

Leonova (lĕh-ŏh'-nŏh-văh), **Darya Mikhailovna,** celebrated Russian contralto; b. Tver, 1829; d. St. Petersburg, Feb. 6, 1896. She studied singing in St. Petersburg; in 1852 sang the part of Vania in Glinka's *A Life for the Tsar,* and was greatly praised by Glinka himself; 1858, was engaged by the Imperial Theater in St. Petersburg, enjoying tremendous success with the public. She resigned in 1873; in 1875 she went on a concert tour around the world, through Siberia, China, Japan, and America. In 1879 she traveled in Southern Russia and the Crimea with Mussorgsky as accompanist; sang arias from Mussorgsky's operas and his songs; in 1880 opened a singing school in St. Petersburg, with Mussorgsky acting as coach. Mussorgsky lived in her house at the time of his final collapse.

Leopold I, Austrian Emperor from 1658-1705; b. Vienna, June 9, 1640; d. there, May 5, 1705. During his reign Vienna became the center of the world's operatic activity, no fewer than 400 new operas having been produced in that time; he was not only an enthusiastic patron but also a practically trained musician and diligent composer. His complete works are in MS in the State Library at Vienna: 15 oratorios, 7 operas, 17 ballet suites, 155 arias, 79 sacred compositions (2 Masses, 5 Offices for the Dead, 4-part *Miserere* with instruments, etc.). Guido Adler publ. a selection from his works (2 vols., 1892-3; contains also selected works of Emperors Ferdinand III and Josef I).—Cf. H. V. F. Somerset, *The Habsburg Emperors as Musicians,* in 'Music & Letters' (1949; p. 204).

Leps, Wassili, conductor and composer; b. St. Petersburg, May 12, 1870; d. Toronto, Dec. 22, 1943. He studied piano with Adolf Henselt; at the age of 9 he was taken to Germany, where he studied at the Dresden Cons. with Draeseke, Wüllner, and Theodor Kirchner. He subsequently became chorusmaster at the Dresden Opera. In 1894 he settled in America; taught at the Philadelphia Music Academy; then became conductor of the Philadelphia Operatic Society, which he led until 1923, producing 47 operas. In 1932 he organized the Providence Symph. Orch.; was its conductor until 1941, when he retired and went to Toronto to reside with a daughter. He wrote an opera on a Japanese subject, *Hoshi-San,* which he conducted with the Philadelphia Operatic Society on May 21, 1909; a cantata, *Yo-Nennen,* and some symphonic music.—Cf. E. E. Hipsher, *American Opera and Its Composers* (Philadelphia, 1934; pp. 290-94).

Leroux (lŭ-roo'), **Xavier,** French composer; b. Velletri, Papal States, Oct. 11, 1863; d. Paris, Feb. 2, 1919. He was a pupil of Dubois and Massenet at the Paris Cons.; 1st Grand Prix de Rome, 1885; appointed prof. at the Cons. in 1896.—Works: The operas *Cléopâtre* (Paris, Oct. 23, 1890), *Évangeline* (Brussels, 1895), *Astarté* (Paris, Feb. 15, 1901), *La Reine Fiammette* (Paris, Dec. 23, 1903; Metropolitan Opera, N. Y., Jan. 24, 1919), *Vénus et Adonis* (Nîmes, 1905), *William Ratcliff* (Nice, Jan. 26, 1906), *Théodora* (Monte Carlo, March 19, 1907), *Le Chemineau* (Paris, Nov. 6, 1907; Metropolitan Opera, N. Y., Jan. 31, 1919), *Le Carillonneur* (Paris, March 20, 1913); *La Fille de Figaro* (Paris, March 11, 1914);

Les Cadeaux de Noël (Paris, Dec. 25, 1915), *1814* (Monte Carlo, April 6, 1918), *Nausithoé* (posthumous; Nice, April 9, 1920), *La plus forte* (posthumous; Paris, Jan. 11, 1924), *L'Ingénu* (Bordeaux, Feb. 13, 1931); songs; piano pieces.

Le Roy, Adrien. Partner of Ballard. See **Ballard.**

Le Roy, René, distinguished flutist; b. Maisons-Laffitte, near Paris, March 4, 1898. He studied at the Paris Cons. with Hennebains, Lafleurance, and Gaubert; 1918, won the Cons. 1st prize and succeeded Gaubert as director of the Société des Instruments à Vent; 1922, founded the Quintette Instrumentale de Paris, with which he toured the world.

Lert, Ernst Josef Maria, opera intendant and writer; b. Vienna, May 12, 1883; d. Baltimore, Jan. 30, 1955. He studied at the Univ. of Vienna with G. Adler; 1908, *Dr. phil.;* then was dramatic coach at the Municipal Theater in Breslau from 1909 and in Leipzig from 1912; 1920-23, opera director of the Municipal Theater and teacher at the Hoch Cons., Frankfurt; 1923-29, stage director at La Scala, Milan (with Toscanini); 1929-31, stage director at the Metropolitan Opera House, N. Y.; 1936-38, head of the opera department of Curtis Inst. of Music; after 1938, head of the opera department of the Peabody Cons., Baltimore. He publ. *Mozart auf dem Theater* (Berlin, 1918; 4th ed., 1922); *Otto Lohse,* a biography (Leipzig, 1918).

Lert, Richard Johannes, conductor; brother of Ernst Lert; b. Vienna, Sept. 19, 1885. He studied at the Vienna Academy of Music; held posts as conductor in Düsseldorf, Darmstadt, Frankfurt, and Hanover; conducted in Paris. He emigrated to the U. S. in 1938; settled in Pasadena, Calif., as conductor and teacher. He married the novelist Vicki Baum (July 17, 1916).

Leschetizky (leh - shĕ - tit'- skē), **Theodor,** pianist and famous pedagogue; b. Lancut, Austrian Poland, June 22, 1830; d. Dresden, Nov. 14, 1915. He first studied with his father, who took him to Vienna, where he became a pupil of Czerny. He acquired a mastery of the piano in an amazingly short time, and he was only 15 when he himself began to teach. He also attended Vienna Univ. as a student of philosophy, until its closure in the wake of the 1848 revolution. In 1852 he went to Russia; his initial concerts in St. Petersburg were extremely successful, and gradually he attracted many pupils. He was also active as music director to the Grand Duchess Helen. In 1862 Anton Rubinstein, director of the newly opened St. Petersburg Cons., engaged him as teacher. After 16 years in Russia, Leschetizky returned to Vienna; there he married his former pupil Anna Essipova (she was his second wife); they were divorced in 1892; Leschetizky contracted 2 more marriages after that. He continued to make occasional concert tours, but he concentrated mainly on teaching; his fame grew, and pupils flocked from all over the world to his studio in Vienna. His most celebrated pupil was Paderewski; other pupils were Gabrilovitch, Schnabel, Isabelle Vengerova, etc., as well as his third and fourth wives, Dominirska Benislavska and Marie Rozborska. His method of playing with the 'Kugelhand' (arched hand) was to secure fullness of tone and finger dexterity, with the flexible wrist reserved for octave playing and chord passages. A Leschetizky Society, composed of his pupils, was organized after his death; a branch was established in the U. S. — Leschetizky was also a composer; he wrote an opera, *Die erste Falte* (Prague, Oct. 9, 1867), and some chamber music; but it is his piano pieces that still remain of interest and value; of these, the following are the most effective: *Les deux Alouettes; Grande Polka de Caprice; La Cascade; Perpetuum mobile; Valse chromatique; Souvenirs d'Italie; À la Campagne,* and *Trois Études caractéristiques.* —Cf. Malwine Brée, *Die Grundlage der Methode Leschetizky* (Vienna, 1902; also in English and French transls.); Countess Angèle Potocka, *Theodor Leschetizky* (London, 1903); Annette Hullah, *Theodor Leschetizky* (London, 1906); Ethel Newcomb, *Leschetizky as I Knew Him* (London, 1921).

Leslie, Henry David, conductor and composer; b. London, June 18, 1822; d. Llansaintfraid, near Oswestry, Feb. 4, 1896. He was a pupil of Charles Lucas; cellist in the Sacred Harmonic Society, and its conductor from 1853-61. In 1855 he organized (with Heming) an a cappella singing society, which won 1st prize at Paris in 1878; it was disbanded in 1880, but reorganized in 1882 with Randegger as conductor, and Leslie as president; Leslie resumed the conductorship in 1885. —Works: the operas *Romance, or Bold Dick Turpin* (1857); *Ida* (1864); the oratorios *Immanuel* (1853) and *Judith* (1858); the cantatas *Holyrood* (1860), *Daughter of the Isles* (1861), and a 'biblical pastoral,' *The First Christian Morn* (1880); a symphony; an overture, *The Templar*.

Lessard, John Ayres, American composer; b. San Francisco, July 3, 1920. He studied with Nadia Boulanger in Paris; served in the U. S. Army (1943-45); received a Guggenheim Fellowship in 1946 and a grant from the National Institute of Arts and Letters in 1952. —Works: a violin concerto (1941); a quintet for violin, viola, cello, flute, and clarinet (1943); 2 piano sonatas (1944-45); *Box Hill Overture* (N. Y., Sept. 18, 1946); *Cantilena,* for oboe and strings (N. Y., Nov. 12, 1947); concerto for wind instruments (N. Y., Jan. 29, 1951); Three Movements, for violin and piano (1952); concerto for flute, clarinet, bassoon, and strings (N. Y., Jan. 5, 1953); *Mother Goose* (6 songs; 1953); octet, for winds (1954); toccata, for harpsichord (1955).

Lessel, Franz, Polish pianist and composer; b. Pulawy, c. 1780; d. Petrikow, Dec. 26, 1838. He went to Vienna in 1797 to study medicine, but became a pupil of Haydn and one of his few intimate friends. He returned to Poland upon Haydn's death, continuing to compose; he left in MS a great number of instrumental works; his published compositions show a fine talent; he wrote a piano concerto, 2 fantasias for piano, 3 piano sonatas, a piano trio, and several symphonies; his songs (to Polish words) were often performed.

Lessmann, Otto, German pianist and critic; b. Rüdersdorf, near Berlin, Jan. 30, 1844; d. Jena, April 27, 1918. He studied with Hans von Bülow (piano), Kiel (theory), and Teschner (voice); taught piano at Stern's Cons.; was owner and editor of the 'Allgemeine Musik-Zeitung' (1882-1907).

Lester, Thomas William, organist and composer; b. Leicester, England, Sept. 17, 1889; d. Berrien Springs, Mich., Dec. 4, 1956. He came to the U. S. in 1902; studied with Wilhelm Middelschulte in Chicago; wrote music criticism for the Chicago 'Record-Herald'; also served as organist in various Chicago churches. He wrote 8 cantatas (sacred and secular); several suites for piano; organ pieces; numerous choruses; songs.

Le Sueur (or **Lesueur**) (lŭ-sü-ör'), **Jean François,** French composer; b. Drucat-Plessiel, near Abbeville, Feb. 15, 1760; d. Paris, Oct. 6, 1837. At 7 he was a choirboy at Abbeville; at 14, in Amiens, where he took a course of studies; interrupting his academic education, he became maître de musique at the cathedral of Séez; then an assistant at the Church of the Innocents in Paris. Abbé Roze gave him some instruction in harmony; this comprised practically all of his musical training; he developed his musical talent without teachers. His subsequent positions were as maître de musique in the cathedral of Dijon (1781), at Le Mans (1783), and at Tours (1784). He then returned to Paris, now serving (upon the recommendation of Grétry) as maître de chapelle at the Innocents. When the competition for the post of maître de chapelle at Notre Dame was announced in 1786, Le Sueur entered it, and won. He organized an orch. for the chief festive days, and brought out Masses, motets, services, etc., using a full orch., thus completely transforming the character of the services; he was greatly successful with the congregation, but the conservative clergy strongly objected to his innovations; other critics called his type of musical productions 'opéra des gueux' (beggars' opera). He expounded his ideas of effective and descriptive music in a pamphlet, *Essai de musique sacrée ou musique motivée et méthodique, pour la fête de Noël, à la messe du jour* (1787); this evoked an anonymous attack, to which he replied with another publication, *Exposé d'une musique unie, imitative, et particulière à chaque solennité* (1787), reasserting his aim of making church music dramatic and descriptive. He retired temporarily in 1788, and spent 4 years in the country. Upon his return to Paris, he brought out at the Théâtre Feydeau 3 operas: *La Caverne* (Feb. 16, 1793), which had a popular success, *Paul et Virginie* (Jan. 13, 1794), and *Télémaque* (May 11, 1796). When the Paris Conservatoire was organized in 1795, Le Sueur was appointed inspector, and a member of the Committee on Instruction; with Méhul, Langlé, Gossec, and Catel, he wrote the *Principes élémentaires de la musique* and the *Solfèges du Conservatoire.* Le Sueur was dismissed in 1802 on account of an altercation ensuing after the rejection, by the Opéra, of 2 of his operas in favor of *Sémiramis,* written by Catel. For 2 years he lived in poverty and suffering, until Napoleon, in 1804, raised him to the highest position attainable by a musician in Paris, by appointing him his maître de chapelle, succeeding Paisiello. His rejected opera, *Les Bardes,* was then produced (Paris, July 10, 1804) with great applause, and *La Mort d'Adam,* the other rejected work, was also staged (Paris, March 21, 1809). After the restoration of the monarchy, and despite Le Sueur's avowed veneration for Napoleon, the government of Louis XVIII appointed him superintendent and composer to the Chapelle du Roi; from 1818 he was also prof. of composition at the Paris Cons.; he had several celebrated pupils, among them Berlioz, Gounod, and Ambroise Thomas. He taught at the Cons. until his death; was a member of the Institut (1813), and held several other honorary positions. His last 3 operas were accepted for performance, but were not produced; these were *Tyrtée* (1794), *Artaxerse* (1797), and *Alexandre à Babylone;* other works were 2 secular cantatas, *L'Inauguration du temple de la Victoire* (Paris, Jan. 2, 1807) and *Le Triomphe de Trajan* (Paris, Oct. 23, 1807); several sacred oratorios *(Debora, Rachel, Ruth et Noémi, Ruth et Booz);* a solemn Mass for 4 voices, chorus, and orch.; a cantata, *L'Ombre de Sacchini; 3 Te Deums;* 2 Passions; a *Stabat Mater;* these, and some other works, were publ.; he left many more (over 30 Masses, etc.) in MS. He publ. a *Notice sur la mélopée, la rythmopée, et les grands caractères de la musique ancienne* (Paris, 1793); a sketch of Paisiello (1816); and some pamphlets.—Cf. C. P. Ducanel, *Mémoire pour J. F. Lesueur* (Paris, 1802); Raoul-Rochette, *Notice historique sur la vie et les œuvres de Jean-François Le Sueur* (Paris, 1837); Stéphen de la Madeleine, *Biographie de Jean-François Le Sueur* (Paris, 1841); P. O. Fouque, *Le Sueur comme prédecesseur de Berlioz,* in *Les Révolutionnaires de la musique* (Paris, 1882); H. Berlioz, *Les Musiciens et la musique* (Paris, 1903; on Le Sueur's oratorios); C. Pierre, *Hymnes et chants de la Révolution* (Paris, 1904); W. Buschkötter, *Jean François Le Sueur* (Halle, 1912); F. Lamy, *Jean François Le Sueur* (Paris, 1912); G. Servières, *Les Oratoires de Jean-François Le Sueur,* in *Episodes d'histoire musicale* (Paris, 1912).

Lesur, Daniel, French composer, pianist, and organist; b. Paris, Nov. 19, 1908. He studied at the Paris Cons. with Tournemire, Caussade, and Ferté; assistant organist at Ste.-Clothilde (1927-37); prof. of counterpoint at the Schola Cantorum (1935-39). In 1936 he and Yves Baudrier, O. Messiaen, and Jolivet organized 'La Jeune France.' His works include the ballet *L'Infante et le monstre* (with A. Jolivet, 1938); *Ave Maria sur un Noël,* for soprano, contralto, women's chorus, and organ (1938); *Andrea del Sarto,* symph. poem (Paris, June 21, 1949); *Hommage à J. S. Bach,* for string orch. (1933); *Suite française,* for orch. (1935); *Pastorale* for chamber orch. (1938); *Ricercare,* for orch. (1939); *Passacaille* for piano and orch. (1937); *L'Étoile de Séville,* suite for chamber orch. (1941); *Chansons cambodgiennes,* for voice and chamber orch. (1947); suite for piano and string trio (1943); *Suite médiévale,* for flute, violin, viola, cello, and harp (1946); *Le Village imaginaire,* for 2 pianos (1947); piano pieces *(Soirs, Les Carillons, Bagatelle, Pavane, Deux Noëls, Pastorale variée, Ballade,* etc.); organ music; songs *(Les Harmonies intimes, La Mort des voiles, 3 Poèmes de Cécile Sauvage, L'Enfance de l'art, Clair comme le jour,* etc.).

Letelier, Alfonso, Chilean composer and teacher; b. Santiago, Oct. 4, 1912. He studied with Allende at the Cons. Nacional in Santiago, where he became prof. of harmony (1947); aided in establishing the Escuela Moderna de Música. His compositions include a symph. poem, *La vida del campo,* for piano and orch.; *Aculeo,* suite for orch. (Louisville, Jan. 30, 1957); *Los sonetos de la muerte,* for female voice and orch.; a string quartet; *Variations* for piano; a Mass for chorus, string orch., and organ; songs. In 1956 he was appointed dean of the Faculty of Fine Arts of the Univ. of Chile.

Letorey, Omer, French composer; b. Châlon-sur-Saône, May 4, 1873; d. Paris, March 21, 1938. He studied at the École Niedermeyer, and with Pessard at the Paris Cons.; in 1895, won the Prix de Rome with his scena *Clarisse Harlowe.* Other works include the operas *Cléopâtre* (1918); *L'Oeillet blanc* (1930), and *Le Sicilien ou l'Amour Peintre* (Paris, Opéra-Comique, March 19, 1930).

Letz, Hans, violinist; b. Ittenheim, Alsace, March 18, 1887. He studied violin with H. Schuster at the Strasbourg Cons., and later with Joachim at the Hochschule für Musik in Berlin. In 1908 he emigrated to the U. S.; made his début in New York (Nov. 3, 1908); subsequently was concertmaster of the Chicago Symph. Orch. (1909-12), and 2nd violinist of the Kneisel Quartet (1912-17). In 1917 he settled in N. Y. as teacher at the Institute of Musical Art; also formed his own string quartet. He publ. a guide, *Music for the Violin and Viola* (N. Y., 1949).

Leuckart (loi'-cart), **F. Ernst Christoph,** German music publisher; b. Halberstadt, March 21, 1748; d. Breslau, Feb. 2, 1817. He established a music business at Breslau in 1782; it was acquired by Constantin

Sander in 1856, who removed it to Leipzig in 1870, and added to it by buying out the firms of Weinhold & Förster (Breslau), Damköhler (Berlin), and Witzendorf (Vienna). The new firm, 'Constantin Sander, vormals F. E. C. Leuckart,' publ. many learned works (e. g., by Ambros, Lussy, Westphal, Niecks, Molitor, etc.) and compositions of R. Franz, Rheinberger, Draeseke, Bossi, Hausegger, Huber, Klose, Duparc, Richard Strauss, Max Reger, Atterberg, Bantock, Ernest Bloch, Johan Wagenaar, Schjelderup, and others. Constantin Sander's son, Martin (b. Breslau, Nov. 11, 1859; d. Leipzig, March 14, 1930) was head of the firm until his death.

Lev, Ray, pianist; b. Rostov, Russia, May 8, 1912. Her father was a synagogue cantor; her mother, a singer. The family came to the U. S. in 1913; she sang in choruses conducted by her father in various synagogues in New York and Philadelphia. She studied piano with Walter Ruel Cowles in New Haven; then with Gaston Déthier. She won a scholarship in 1930 to study with Tobias Matthay in London, where she remained until 1933; made her American début with the National Orchestral Association in 1933, playing Tchaikovsky's 1st piano concerto.

Leva, Enrico de, Italian composer of popular music; b. Naples, Jan. 19, 1867; d. there, July 28, 1955. He studied with d'Arienzo; early in life, began writing popular ballads that proved of wide appeal *(Non mi guarda, E spingole frangese, Triste aprile, Ultima serenata,* etc.) and earned him great financial returns. He also wrote an opera, *La Camargo* (Turin, March 2, 1898).

Levadé (lŭ-vah-dā'), **Charles (Gaston),** French composer; b. Paris, Jan. 3, 1869; d. there, Oct. 27, 1948. He was a pupil of Massenet at the Paris Cons.; won the Grand Prix de Rome in 1899.—Works: the opera *Les Hérétiques* (Béziers, Aug. 27, 1905); the lyric comedies *La Rôtisserie de la reine Pédauque* (after Anatole France; Paris, Jan. 12, 1920) and *La Peau de chagrin* (after Balzac; Paris, April 24, 1929); orchestral suites; chamber music; piano pieces; songs.

Levant, Oscar, American pianist and composer; b. Pittsburgh, Dec. 27, 1906. He studied piano with Stojowski; also took a few composition lessons with Schoenberg and Schillinger. As a pianist, he established himself by his authentic performances of Gershwin's music *(Rhapsody in Blue, Concerto in F);* also emerged as a professional wit on the radio; publ. a brilliant book, *A Smattering of Ignorance* (N. Y., 1940). He has written music of considerable complexity, in the modern vein; was soloist in his piano concerto (N.B.C. Symph. Orch., Feb. 17, 1942); other works are *Nocturne* for orch. (Los Angeles, April 14, 1937); a string quartet (1937); piano pieces; film scores.

Levasseur (lŭ - vahs - sör'), **Jean - Henri,** French cellist and composer; b. Paris, c. 1765; d. there, 1823. He studied with Cupis and Duport; a member of the Paris Opéra orch. (1789-1823); professor of cello at the Paris Cons., and belonged to the Imperial 'chapelle.' He publ. sonatas, études, and duets for cello; was co-editor of the cello method used at the Paris Cons.

Levasseur (lŭ-vahs-sör'), **Nicolas-Prosper,** French bass; b. Bresles, March 9, 1791; d. Paris, Dec. 7, 1871. He was admitted to the Paris Cons. in 1807, and he entered Garat's singing class in 1811; made his début at the Paris Opéra (Oct. 14, 1813); sang subordinate roles until 1820, when his success at Milan in Meyerbeer's *Marguerite d'Anjou* (Nov. 14, 1820) attracted attention, and he was engaged for 5 years at the Théâtre Italien, Paris; later took leading bass roles at the Opéra. He was also prof. at the Paris Cons. (1841-69).

Levasseur (lŭ-vahs-sör'), **Rosalie** (real Christian names, Marie Claude Josèphe), French soprano; b. Valenciennes, Oct. 8, 1749; d. Neuwied-on-Rhine, May 6, 1826. She was the daughter of Jean-Baptiste Levasseur and Marie-Catherine Tournay, born out of wedlock; but the parents were married when she was 11. She was described by contemporaries as being not at all attractive; still, she must have possessed a fine voice and musical ability, for she was a formidable rival of Sophie Arnould. She first appeared on the stage under the name of Mlle. Rosalie; in 1775 she assumed the name Levasseur. The Austrian ambassador in Paris used his influence to promote her career; they lived as husband and wife.—Cf. J.-G. Prod'homme, *Rosalie Levasseur: Ambassadress of Opera,* in the 'Mus. Quarterly' (April, 1916).

Levens (lŭ-vahn'), maître de musique in a Bordeaux church; publ. (1743) an *Abrégé des règles de l'Harmonie, pour apprendre la composition, avec un nouveau* *projet sur un système de musique sans tempérament ni cordes mobiles,* in which he ingeniously (but futilely) contrasts the ascending harmonic progression (overtones) with the descending arithmetical progression (undertones), thereby obtaining a dual harmonic basis.

Levenson, Boris, composer and conductor; b. Ackerman, Bessarabia, March 10, 1884; d. New York, March 11, 1947. He studied at the St. Petersburg Cons. with Glazunov and Rimsky-Korsakov, graduating in 1907; from 1907-12, was conductor in St. Petersburg and Moscow; in 1920, emigrated to America; lived mostly in New York. He wrote a symphony (St. Petersburg, 1903); an orch. suite, *Palestine* (N. Y., 1927); *Night in Bagdad,* oriental tone poem (N. Y. Philharmonic, Aug. 17, 1938); *Volga,* tone poem; *Hebrew Suite,* for 8 instruments; 2 string quartets; songs.

Leveridge, Richard, English singer and composer; b. London, c. 1670; d. there, March 22, 1758. According to contemporary reports, he possessed a powerful bass voice, and was a successful singer in Italian operas; sang at Covent Garden and Drury Lane. He publ. a collection of songs (1727) in a popular style; of these. *The Roast Beef of Old England* became a favorite. He wrote incidental music for *Macbeth,* a number of masques, etc. He was also the owner of a coffee house in London.

Levey, Richard Michael, Irish composer and conductor; b. Dublin, Oct. 25, 1811; d. there, June 28, 1899. He received a practical musical education playing in various orchestras in Dublin and writing incidental music for productions of plays. About 1835 he became a theater conductor; wrote some 50 overtures and a number of ballet scores. He publ. a collection of old Irish airs.

Levey, William Charles, Irish conductor and composer; son of Richard Michael Levey; b. Dublin, April 25, 1837; d. London, Aug. 18, 1894. He studied with Auber, Thalberg, and Prudent in Paris; then became conductor at Drury Lane, London (1868-74), at Covent Garden, and other theaters. He wrote the operettas *Fanchette* (London, Jan. 4, 1864), *Punchinello* (London, Dec. 28, 1864), and *The Girls of the Period* (London, Feb. 25, 1869); incidental music to *Anthony and Cleopatra, King o' Scots, Amy Robsart, Lady of the Lake, Rebecca, Esmeralda;* various pantomimes; 3 cantatas; many songs; piano pieces; etc.

Lévi. See **Gobbaerts, Jean-Louis.**

Levi (lā'-vē), **Hermann,** eminent German conductor; b. Giessen, Nov. 7, 1839; d. Munich, May 13, 1900. He was a pupil of Vincenz Lachner in Mannheim (1852-55) and at the Leipzig Cons. (1855-58). He conducted at Saarbrücken (1859-61) and at the German Opera in Rotterdam (1861-64). He became court conductor at Karlsruhe in 1864, and in 1872 he received his most important appointment, at the court theater in Munich, retaining this position until 1896. He enjoyed great respect among German musicians, and was influential in spreading the Wagnerian gospel. He conducted the first performance of *Parsifal* at Bayreuth (July 28, 1882), and his interpretation received complete approval from Wagner himself, who, for the nonce, repressed his opposition to Jews. Levi conducted the musical program at Wagner's funeral. He was also a friend of Brahms; his correspondence with Brahms was publ. in vol. 7 of *Brahms Briefwechsel* (Berlin, 1912). Levi brought out new editions with revised texts of Mozart's *Così fan tutte, Don Giovanni,* and *Le Nozze di Figaro;* translated into German the librettos of Berlioz' *Les Troyens* and Chabrier's *Gwendoline,* and wrote *Gedanken aus Goethes Werken* (1901; 3rd ed., 1911). —Cf. E. Possart, *Erinnerungen an Hermann Levi* (Munich, 1901); A. Ettlinger, *Hermann Levi,* necrology in Bettelheim's 'Biographisches Jahrbuch' (1903).

Levi (or **Levy, Lewy**), **Jacob.** See **Lebert.**

Levidis, Dimitri, Greek composer; b. Athens, April 8, 1886; d. there, May 30, 1951. He studied at the Athens Cons., then with A. Denéréaz in Switzerland; in 1910, settled in Paris; from 1939 till his death, was again in Greece. He was the first to write works for the Martenot 'Ondes Musicales' (a radio-wave instrument), including *Poème Symphonique pour solo d'Ondes Musicales et Orchestre* (Paris, Dec. 23, 1928) and *De Profundis* for voice and 2 soli of Ondes Musicales (Paris, Jan. 5, 1930). Other works include a ballet, *Le Pâtre et la Nymphe* (Paris, April 24, 1924); *Divertissement* for English horn, harps, strings, celesta, and percussion (Paris, April 9, 1927); an oratorio, *The Iliad;* poem for violin and orch. (1927); *Chant payen* for oboe and strings; compositions for the 'Dixtuor æolien d'orchestre'; pieces for chamber ensembles; song cycles with piano and with orch. accompaniment; piano pieces.

Levine, Henry, American pianist, arranger, and editor; b. Boston, Jan. 2, 1892; He studied piano with Heinrich Gebhard in Boston; then entered Harvard Univ. (A.B., 1913). After a brief period of concert appearances, he devoted himself to teaching and editing. He was music editor for the Theodore Presser Co. (1942-50); then in a similar capacity with the Boston Music Co.; brought out a successful series for beginners, *Magic at the Piano* (extremely simplified, and *ne plus ultra* abridged piano reductions of classical and other pieces).

Levis, John Hazedel, music scholar; b. Shanghai (of British-Jewish parents), 1904. He studied piano in Shanghai, also mastering various native Chinese instruments; specialized in the study of Chinese music, on which he has written a comprehensive and authoritative work, *Foundations of Chinese Musical Art* (Peiping, 1936). He arranged Chinese melodies for piano and has given lecture recitals in the U. S. (1932, 1934). —Cf. Isaac Goldberg, *John Hazedel Levis and the Music of China,* in the 'Musical Record' (Philadelphia, April, 1934).

Levitin, Yuri Abramovitch, Russian composer; b. Poltava, Dec. 28, 1912. He studied at the Leningrad Cons. with Savshinsky (piano) and Shostakovitch (composition). He has written a number of patriotic works, among them the oratorios *The Sacred War* (1943), *Our Native Land* (1947), and *Fires Over the Volga* (1952); the threnody *In Memory of the Fallen Heroes* (1946); piano trio (1948); 6 string quartets; 24 piano preludes; many songs.

Levitzki, Mischa, pianist; b. Krementchug, Russia, May 25, 1898; d. Avon-by-the-Sea, New Jersey, Jan. 2, 1941. He studied at the Warsaw Cons.; when he was 8 years old, his parents, who were naturalized American citizens, returned to the U.S. He studied at the Institute of Musical Art, N.Y., with Stojowski (1906-11); at the same time, received an academic education in the public schools of N.Y. and Brooklyn. In 1911 he went to Germany, where he studied with Dohnányi at the Hochschule für Musik in Berlin; won the Mendelssohn Prize. In 1915 he returned to America; appeared in a N.Y. recital on Oct. 17, 1916; subsequently made numerous (more than 20) tours in the U.S.; also in the Orient (1925); was soloist with many orchestras in the U.S. and Europe. He publ. a number of attractive piano pieces (*Valse in A, Arabesque valsante, Valse tzigane, Gavotte, The Enchanted Nymph,* etc.).

Lévy, Alexandre, Brazilian composer; b. São Paulo, Nov. 10, 1864; d. there, Jan. 17, 1892. He studied with Emile Durand in Paris. His compositions include a symph. which received a Columbus Celebration prize in 1892; *Comala,* symph. poem; *Suite Brasileira* for orch.; chamber music and piano works (*Schumanniana,* suite; *Allegro appassionato,* etc.). Although his music is steeped in the European Romantic tradition, and his technique is limited, he appears as an important figure in Brazilian music because of his contribution to the nationalist musical movement; he was one of the earliest Brazilian composers to use native folk material in instrumental works. —Cf. Renato Almeida, *Compendio de Historia da musica brasileira* (Rio de Janeiro, 1947).

Lévy, Ernst, distinguished pianist and composer; b. Basel, Nov. 18, 1895. He studied in Basel with Huber and Petri, and in Paris with Pugno; 1916-20, teacher at the Basel Cons.; lived in Paris; came to the U.S. in 1941; taught at the New England Cons. in Boston (1941-45); member of the music faculty at Bennington College, Vermont (1946-51); at Chicago Univ. (1951-54): in 1954, became prof. of piano at Massachusetts Institute of Technology. He wrote 13 symphonies; works for chorus and orch.; chamber music; organ pieces; songs. Some of the more recent works are: *Psaume* (Paris, Dec. 17, 1933); *Fantaisie symphonique,* for harpsichord (1939); *Carillon,* for 27 bells and 8 players (1946); cello concerto (1947); *Fanfares,* for 3 trumpets (1947); 11th symphony (Basel, 1950); 12th symphony, with choral ending (Chicago, March 7, 1952, composer conducting); 13th symphony (1955).

Lévy, Heniot, pianist and composer; b. Warsaw, July 19, 1879; d. Chicago, June 16, 1946. He was a pupil at the Hochschule für Musik in Berlin, and of Max Bruch (composition); made his début as pianist with the Berlin Philharmonic Orch. (1899), followed by tours in Germany and Scandinavia. In 1900 he emigrated to America, and became piano teacher at the American Cons. in Chicago. Among his works are *24 Variations on an Original Theme* for orch. (Chicago, April 9, 1942); piano concerto; string sextet; string quintet; 2 piano quintets; 4 string quartets; 2 piano trios; cello sonata; numerous piano pieces; songs.

Lévy, Lazare, distinguished pianist and pedagogue; b. (of French parents) Brussels, Jan. 18, 1882. He studied with Diémer at the Paris Cons. (1894-98), where he was awarded the 1st prize for piano; also studied harmony with Lavignac and composition with Gedalge; gave concerts with the principal orchs. of Europe; in 1920 succeeded Alfred Cortot as prof. at the Paris Cons. He publ. numerous piano pieces.

Lévy, Michel-Maurice, French composer; b. Ville-d'Avray, June 28, 1883. He studied at the Paris Cons. with Lavignac and Leroux. From 1920-32, he was popular as a musical parodist in vaudeville under the name of Bétove (i.e., Beethoven); wrote operettas under that name: *Pom-Pom* (1928), *Les Exploits galants du Baron de Crac* (1932), *D'Artagnan* (1945). Under his own name he wrote the operas *Le Cloître* (Lyons, 1932), *Dolorés* (Paris, 1952); operettas *Lydia* (Brussels, 1936), *La Demoiselle de Carentan* (Paris, 1951); *Les Trois Pantins de Bois,* ballet suite for orch.; *Le Chant de la Terre,* symph. poem (1945); *Moïse,* a 'fresque lyrique' (Mulhouse, 1955); film music; choral works; songs.

Lewandowski (lā-vahn-dov'-skē), **Louis,** eminent Jewish scholar; b. Wreschen, near Posen, April 3, 1821; d. Berlin, Feb. 4, 1904. He studied at the Academy of Music in Berlin; became music director of the Berlin Synagogue from 1840; established himself as a voice teacher. His greatest accomplishment is the compilation of the Jewish service music for use by Berlin's Jewish community; in his arrangements of the traditional tunes, Lewandowski applied the technique of German Romantic music, and often reduced the exotic and asymmetrical pattern of the Jewish cantilena to simple song meters; his compositions for organ also employed ordinary 19th-century harmonies. This treatment contributed to the popularity of Lewandowski's service music, but at the same time, it traduced the true spirit of Jewish cantillation, so that the more nationalistic Jewish scholars refused to accept it.

Lewinger, Max, violinist and composer; b. Sulkow, near Cracow, March 17, 1870; d. Dresden, Aug. 31, 1908. He studied at the Conservatories of Cracow, Lwow, and Vienna; in 1893 became teacher of violin at the Bucharest Cons.; then played in the Gewandhaus orch. in Leipzig (1897) and in Dresden (from 1898). He publ. *Legende* for violin and orch., and a number of pieces for violin and piano *(Tarantella, Polonaise, Capriccio, Dumka, Serenade,* etc.).

Lewis, Leo Rich, American writer on music; b. South Woodstock, Vt., Feb. 11, 1865; d. Cambridge, Mass., Sept. 8, 1945. He was graduated from Tufts College (A.B., 1887); attended Harvard Univ. (M.A., 1889); then studied composition with Rheinberger at the Akademie der Tonkunst in Munich. From 1895 until his death he headed the music department and taught theory and music history at Tufts College; Litt. D. there in 1922. He originated a card system of thematic cataloguing of music. —Publications: *The Ambitious Listener* (1928); *Masterpieces of Music* (1928); *The Gist of Sight Singing* (1929); *Experiencing Music* (1929); edited the *National School Library of Song* (2 vols., 1894); *Church Harmonies, New and Old* (1895); *Tufts Song Book* (2 series, 1906, 1915); *Book of Tufts Music* (1922), etc.; composed the patriotic song *We Stand;* and an orch. set, *Intercollegiate Inklings.* He also composed a *Symph. Prelude* to Browning's tragedy *A Blot on the 'Scutcheon* (Boston, March 8, 1925). —Cf. H. A. Hersey, *A History of Music in Tufts College* (Manchester, N. H., 1947; pp. 302-16).

Lewisohn, Adolph, musical philanthropist; b. Hamburg, May 27, 1849; d. Saranac Lake, N.Y., Aug. 17, 1938. A prominent industrialist, his principal service to music and education was the erection of the Lewisohn Stadium in 1914, which he donated to the College of the City of N.Y., and the inauguration of summer concerts by the N.Y. Philharmonic there. He also founded the Lewisohn chamber music education courses at Hunter College, N.Y.

Lewkowitch, Bernhard, Danish composer; b. Copenhagen, May 28, 1927 (of Russian parents). He studied in Copenhagen and in Paris; from 1947, organist at the St. Angsar Church in Copenhagen. In his music (mostly choral) he adopts Russian modality in the framework of contrapuntal neo-Classicism. He has written a *Communion Mass* (1947), 3 piano sonatas, and an orchestral *Bolero* (1948).

Ley, Henry George, English organist and composer; b. Chagford, Dec. 30, 1887. He studied at the Royal College of Music in London with Parratt; won an organ scholarship at Keble College, Oxford; in 1909, became organist of Christ Church Cathedral there; also choral conductor at Oxford

Univ.; Mus. Doc. there (1914). In 1926 he became musical director at Eton College, Windsor, retiring in 1945; also teacher of organ at the Royal College of Music. His compositions include *Variations on a Theme by Handel* for orch.; a string quartet; a violin sonata; many organ works; church music; songs.

Ley, Salvador, Guatemalan pianist and composer; b. Guatemala City, Jan. 2, 1907. At the age of 15 he went to Berlin, where he studied piano with Georg Bertram and theory with Hugo Leichtentritt. He appeared as a pianist in Berlin in 1927; returned to Guatemala in 1934; in 1938 he gave a recital in New York; then became teacher of piano at the Cons. of Guatemala, and its director (1944). He has written a number of piano pieces, songs with orchestral accompaniment; some chamber music.

Leybach, Ignace, Alsatian pianist and composer; b. Gambsheim, July 17, 1817; d. Toulouse, May 23, 1891. He studied in Paris with Pixis, Kalkbrenner, and Chopin; in 1844, became organist at the cathedral of Toulouse. He publ. some 225 piano pieces, in a facile and pleasing manner; his 5th Nocturne, op. 52, became famous, and its popularity continued among succeeding generations of piano students; reprinted in countless anthologies of piano music; other piano compositions are: *Boléro brillant; Ballade; Valse poétique; Les Batelières de Naples,* etc.; he also publ. an extensive organ method (3 vols.; 350 pieces).

Leygraf, Hans, Swedish pianist; b. Stockholm, Sept. 7, 1920. He appeared as soloist with the Stockholm orch. at the age of 10; then studied at the Stockholm Cons., and in Munich and Vienna; performed as pianist and conductor in Switzerland, Holland, and Italy; particularly noted as a Mozart interpreter. He has written a concertino for piano and orch. and some chamber music (in a neo-Classical vein). In 1944 he married the Viennese pianist Margarete Stehle (b. Vienna, April 26, 1921).

Lhévinne, Josef, celebrated pianist; b. Orel, Russia, Dec. 13, 1874; d. New York, Dec. 2, 1944. After some preliminary study in his native town, he was taken to Moscow, and entered Safonov's piano class at the Moscow Cons.; at the age of 15 he played the *Emperor Concerto* with Anton Rubinstein conducting; he graduated in 1891; won the Rubinstein Prize in 1895. In 1899 he married; from 1900-2, he taught piano at the Cons. of Tiflis; 1902-6, at the Moscow Cons. In 1906 he went to the U.S.; made his American début in N.Y. with the Russian Symph. Orch., conducted by Safonov (Jan. 27, 1906); afterwards he made numerous concert tours in America. He lived mostly in Berlin from 1907 till 1919; was interned during World War I, but despite some limitations of his freedom there (as a Russian citizen), he was able to continue his professional activities. In 1919 he returned to the U.S.; appeared in recitals, and with major American orchestras; also in duo recitals with his wife. They established a music studio where they taught numerous pupils; also taught at the Juilliard Graduate School. Lhévinne's playing was distinguished not only by its virtuoso quality, but by an intimate understanding of the music, impeccable phrasing, and fine gradations of singing tone. He was at his best in the works of the Romantic school; his performances of the concertos of Chopin and Tchaikovsky were particularly notable.

Lhévinne, Rosina, pianist; wife of Josef Lhévinne; b. Kiev, Russia, March 28, 1880. She graduated from the Kiev Cons. in 1898, winning the gold medal; in 1899 she married Josef Lhévinne in Moscow; appeared as soloist in Vienna (1910), St. Petersburg (1911), Berlin (1912); remained in Berlin with her husband through World War I; in 1919, came to the U. S.; after her husband's death, many of his pupils continued to study with her; she taught at the Juilliard Graduate School; also privately in N.Y., establishing a reputation as a fine pedagogue.

Lhotka, Fran, composer and teacher; b. Wožice, Czechoslovakia, Dec. 25, 1883. He took lessons with Dvořák in Prague, and with Janáček and Klička (1899-1905). After a season of teaching in Ekaterinoslav, Russia (1908-9), he settled in Zagreb; in 1919, was appointed instructor at the Cons. of Zagreb, and conductor of the 'Lisinski Chorus,' with which he toured Central Europe; from 1923 to 1940 and again from 1948 to 1952 he was rector of the State Music Academy in Zagreb. —Works: the operas *Minka* (Zagreb, 1918) and *The Sea* (Zagreb, 1920); the ballets *The Devil of the Village* (Zürich, 1935; also performed in Vienna, Prague, etc.), *Ballad of Medieval Love* (Zürich, 1937; also at the Edinburgh Festival, 1951), *Luk* (Munich, 1938); a symphony; *Yugoslav Capriccio* for orch.; violin concerto; suite for 4 flutes; choral works; songs; a manual of harmony (Zagreb, 1948).

Lhotka-Kalinski, Ivo, Croatian composer, son of Fran Lhotka; b. Zagreb, July 30, 1913. He studied with Pizzetti in Rome; returning to Zagreb, he taught at the Cons. there. Among his works are the operas *Pomet* (1944) and *Matija Gubec* (1948); a symph. suite, *Impressions of Rome;* also pieces for piano and songs.

Liadov (lyah'-dov), **Anatol Konstantinovitch,** Russian composer, son of Konstantin Liadov; b. St. Petersburg, May 10, 1855; d. Novgorod, Aug. 28, 1914. He was a member of an exceptionally gifted musical family. His father was an outstanding opera conductor; his grandfather was conductor of the St. Petersburg Philharmonic Society; Liadov's uncles were also professional musicians. After his primary education at home, Liadov entered the St. Petersburg Cons. (1870); studied piano with G. G. Kross, theory with J. Johannsen, composition with Rimsky-Korsakov; he was expelled from the school for failing to attend classes (1876), but was allowed to compete for a diploma in 1878, and passed the final examination brilliantly. He was immediately engaged as instructor of theory and harmony at the Cons., and held this post until his death. Among his students were Prokofiev, Miaskovsky, Asafiev, and other notable Russian composers. —From his first attempts at composition, Liadov was fascinated by Russian folklore, and most of his works possess the imaginative quality of Russian fairy tales. He was not a prolific composer; he was at his best in miniatures, which he worked out with a fine artistic sense; of these, the piano cycle *Birulki* (1876) and *Tabatière à musique (Music Box,* 1893) are particularly popular; for orchestra he wrote the symph. tableaux, *Baba Yaga, Enchanted Lake,* and *Kikimora,* which are still in the permanent repertory of Russian orchestras; his arrangements of Russian songs are valuable for their authentic harmonization. —Works: for orch.: *Scherzo* (1887); *Mazurka* (1888); *Polonaise* (1900); *Baba Yaga* (St. Petersburg, March 18, 1904); *8 Russian Folksongs* (1906); *Enchanted Lake* (St. Petersburg, Feb. 21, 1909); *Kikimora* (St. Petersburg, Dec. 12, 1909); *Fragments from Apocalypse* (St. Petersburg, Dec. 8, 1912); *Nenie,* threnody (1914); for piano: *Birulki* (1876); *4 Arabesques (*1879); *4 Intermezzos* (1882-83); *2 Mazurkas* (1887); *Novellette* (1889); *Ballade* (1890); *Marionnettes* (1892); *Bagatelle* (1892); *Tabatière à musique* (1893; also for small orch.); *Variations on a Polish Theme* (1901); 4 pieces: *Grimaces, Twilight, Temptation, Recollection* (1910); several sets of preludes and études, etc.; vocal works: 120 Russian folksongs for voice and piano (1903); other Russian song arrangements and harmonizations. Liadov contributed a movement to the string quartet on the theme B-La-F, in honor of the publisher Belaiev (1895); and a polka to the collection *Fridays* (1899), for string orch. —Cf. M. D. Calvocoressi and Gerald Abraham, *Masters of Russian Music* (London, 1936; pp. 424-30); N. Zaporozhetz, *A. K. Liadov, Life and Work* (Moscow, 1954).

Liadov, Konstantin Nikolayevitch, Russian conductor; b. St. Petersburg, May 10, 1820; d. there, Dec. 19, 1868. He studied at the Theatrical School; in 1850 became conductor of the Imperial Opera; resigned shortly before his death, and was succeeded by Napravnik. He was an efficient drillmaster, and did much to raise the standard of performance; produced several Russian operas for the first time, and was instrumental in encouraging Russian music; he was greatly appreciated by his co-workers; Glinka often sought his advice on details of production of his operas.

Liapunov (lya-pōō-nov'), **Sergey Mikhailovitch,** Russian pianist and composer; b. Yaroslavl, Nov. 30, 1859; d. Paris, Nov. 8, 1924. He studied at the Moscow Cons. with Klindworth and Pabst (piano); Hubert, Tchaikovsky, and Taneyev (composition). From 1884-1902 he was sub-director of the Imperial Choir at St. Petersburg; 1902-10, inspector of music at St. Helen's Institute; in 1910, became prof. at the St. Petersburg Cons.; following the Russian Revolution, he lived in Paris. He was a member of the Imperial Geographic Society, which commissioned him in 1893 to collect the folksongs in the Governments of Vologda, Viatka, and Kostroma (publ. with piano accompaniment in 1897). He appeared as guest conductor in Berlin and Leipzig (1907), and as pianist in Germany and Austria (1910-11). Liapunov was a minor composer, but he possessed a thorough technique, and his writing for piano was extremely effective; his first piano concerto is still performed by Russian pianists; his style adheres closely to the principles of the Russian national school. —Works: a cantata, *Evening Song;* a symphony (1901; Berlin, Jan. 28, 1907); *Ouverture solennelle,* on Russian themes (St. Petersburg, May 6, 1896); *Zelazova Vola* (Chopin's birthplace; symph. poem written for Chopin's centennial, 1910); *Haschisch,* an oriental symph. poem (1914); *Polonaise* for orch.; *Ballade,* for orch.; *Rhapsody* on Ukrainian themes for piano and orch. (1908); 2 piano concertos (1890 and 1909); a violin concerto; for piano: *Trois morceaux, Sept préludes, Douze études d'exécution transcendante,* a piano sextet, etc.; arrangements of 35 Russian songs. He edited the correspondence between Tchaikovsky and Balakirev (1912, in Russian). —Cf. G. Abraham and M. D. Calvocoressi, *Masters of Russian Music* (1936).

Liatoshinsky, Boris Nikolayevitch, Russian composer; b. Zhitomir, Jan. 15, 1895. He studied law at the Univ. of Kiev and music at the Kiev Cons. with Glière, graduating in 1919; was then appointed teacher there; from 1935, prof. of composition and orchestration. —Works: the operas *The Golden Hoop* (1931), *Shchors* (Kiev, Sept. 1, 1938); 3 symphonies (1919, 1936, 1951); 4 string quartets (1915, 1922, 1928, 1943); 2 piano trios (1925, 1942); a Ukrainian quintet for piano and string quartet (1946); film music; more than 100 arrangements of Ukrainian folksongs for chorus or for solo voice. —Cf. Igor Boelza, *B. N. Liatoshinsky* (Moscow, 1947).

Libert (lē-behr'), **Henri,** French organist; b. Paris, Dec. 15, 1869; d. there, Jan. 14, 1937. He studied at the Paris Cons. with Marmontel and Diémer (piano), César Franck and Widor (organ), and Massenet and Godard (composition); took 1st organ prize (1894); was titular organist at the Basilica of St. Denis in Paris, and prof. of organ at the American Cons. in Fontainebleau. He wrote many organ works, including *Variations symphoniques, Chorals, Préludes et fugues;* piano pieces; motets; songs; also publ. didactic works.

Libon (lē-bohn'), **Philippe,** violinist and composer; b. (of French parents) Cadiz, Aug. 17, 1775; d. Paris, Feb. 5, 1838. He studied in London with Viotti; in 1796, became chamber violinist in Lisbon; in 1798, was a member of the court orch. in Madrid. In 1800 he settled in Paris as a member of the court orch. He publ. 6 violin concertos; 6 string trios; duets; 2 vols. of *Airs variés; Trente caprices* for violin solo.

Lichard, Milan, Slovak authority on folksongs; b. Uhorská Skalica, Feb. 24, 1853; d. Užhorod, April 21, 1935. He studied music in Budapest; also worked for the railway administration. He devoted his entire life to collecting and editing Slovak songs; contributed numerous articles on the subject to various scholarly magazines. From 1921 he lived in Užhorod, where he was also active as choral conductor.

Lichey (lē'-yhī), **Reinhold,** German organist and composer; b. Pohlsdorf, near Liegnitz, March 26, 1879. He studied with Baumert and Rurnick in Breslau, then at the Hochschule für Musik in Berlin; also took lessons with Max Bruch. He held the following positions: church organist at Aachen (1904-7); cantor and organist at the Trinitatiskirche in Königsberg (1907-19); choral conductor at Naumburg (1919-21); instructor in music at various schools in Pforta; from 1945, music director at Plaue near Arnstadt (Thuringia). His catalogue of works comprises about 75 opus numbers, including many pieces for organ; cantatas, motets, and other sacred works; also chamber music.

Lichnowsky, Prince **Carl,** a nobleman of Polish origin; a friend of Mozart and Beethoven; b. at the family castle, near Troppau, Silesia, 1756; d. Vienna, April 15, 1814. He received the title of nobility from the Russian government in 1773, but spent most of his life in Vienna. He was a pupil of Mozart, who accompanied him on a visit to the Prussian court in 1789. His relationship with Beethoven was disrupted by a domestic quarrel, but they were reconciled, and Beethoven visited Lichnowsky often before the latter's death. Beethoven's op. 1, 13, 26, and 36 are dedicated to Lichnowsky. In his home, Lichnowsky presented regular chamber music concerts with a quartet composed of Schuppanzigh, Sina, Weiss, and Kraft. Lichnowsky's younger brother, Count Moritz (1771-1837), was also a friend of Beethoven, who dedicated his op. 35, 51, and 90 to the Count and his wife.

Lichtenberg, Leopold, American violinist; b. San Francisco, Nov. 22, 1861; d. Brooklyn, N.Y., May 16, 1935. As a child, he began to study with Wieniawski; traveled as a concert violinist in Belgium and Holland; then returned to America; was a member of Theodore Thomas's Orch. in N.Y., and also of the Boston Symph.; in 1899, was appointed head of the violin dept. in the National Cons. in N.Y.; gave chamber music concerts.

Lichtenberger, Henri, French writer on music; b. Mulhouse, March 12, 1864; d. Biarritz, Nov. 4, 1941. In 1887 he became prof. of literature at the Univ. of Nancy; from 1905, prof. of German language and literature at the Univ. of Paris. He made a special study of Wagner's art and ideas, and publ. *Richard Wagner poète et penseur* (1890; 3rd ed., 1902; also transl. into German) and *Wagner,* a biography (1909; revised ed., 1925).

Lichtenstein, Karl August von, German theater manager and composer; b. Lahm, Franconia, Sept. 8, 1767; d. Berlin, Sept. 16, 1845. He studied music in Göttingen with Forkel; then was intendant of court theaters at Dessau (1798), Vienna (1800), Bamberg (1811), and Berlin (1823); in 1825, became director of the Berlin Opera; composed 11 operas and numerous vaudevilles.

Lichtenthal, Peter, Austrian composer and writer on music; b. Pressburg, May 10, 1780; d. Milan, Aug. 18, 1853. He was a doctor by profession, and composed music as an avocation; settled in Milan in 1810; produced 3 operas and 5 ballets at La Scala; publ. a string quartet, 2 piano trios, and piano pieces. His chief writings are: *Cenni biografici intorno al celebre maestro Wolfgang Amadeus Mozart* (1814); *Dizionario e bibliografia della musica* (1826; 4 vols., the last 2 containing bibliography); *Estetica, ossia dottrina del bello e delle belle arti* (1831); *Mozart e le sue creazioni* (1842).

Lichtenwanger, William, American librarian; b. Asheville, N.C., Feb. 28, 1915. He studied at the Univ. of Michigan (M.M., 1940); he was in the U.S. Army during World War II; in 1946 he became associate editor of 'Notes' of the Music Library Association; chief compiler of the list 'A Bibliography of Asiatic Musics,' publ. in 'Notes' (1947-51); also contributed articles to magazines and encyclopedias. Since 1945 he has been assistant reference librarian in the Music Division of the Library of Congress.

Lichtveld, Lou (Lodewijk Alphonsus Maria), Dutch composer; b. Paramaribo (Surinam), Nov. 7, 1903. He went to Amsterdam in 1922 as a journalist; in 1949, returned to Surinam; was for a time Minister of Education there. His works include a piano concertino; a piano sonata; the oratorio *Canciones;* a flute sonata, etc.; also experimental pieces employing oriental intervals smaller than a semitone. In his writings, he used the pen name Albert Helman.

Lickl, Johann Georg, Austrian composer and conductor; b. Korneuburg, April 11, 1769; d. Pécs, May 12, 1843. He was associated with Schikaneder in Vienna, where he wrote the music for various light operas. His large opera *Slawina von Pommern* was produced in Vienna in 1812. He settled in Pécs as a church choir leader. Among his published works are several string quartets. He also publ. a periodic edition, *Wiener Salon-Musik* (arrangements for piano and harmonium from popular classics).

Lidholm, Ingvar, Swedish composer; b. Jönköping, Feb. 24, 1921. He studied at the Stockholm Cons. with Charles Barkel, Hilding Rosenberg, and Tor Mann; later in Switzerland, Italy, and France. In 1947 he became conductor of the municipal orch. in Örebro. His compositions include a concerto for string orch. (1945); *Toccata e canto* for chamber orch. (1944); a string quartet; a flute sonata; a piano sonata; *Laudi* for chorus a cappella; etc.

Lidón, José, Spanish organist and composer; b. Béjar, 1752; d. Madrid, Feb. 11, 1827. He first served as organist in Málaga; in 1787, obtained the post of organist at the Chapel Royal in Madrid. He wrote an opera, *Glauca y Coriolano,* which was performed in Madrid (1792); music for organ and keyboard pieces. A keyboard sonata is printed in S. Kastner's collection, *Silva iberica* (Mainz, 1954). Lidón also publ. *Reglas muy útiles para los organistas y aficionados al piano.*

Lie (l'yā) **(Lie-Nissen), Erika,** Norwegian pianist; b. Kongsvinger, Jan. 17, 1845; d. Christiania, Oct. 27, 1903. She studied with Kjerulf in Christiania and with Th. Kullak in Berlin; later taught at Kullak's Academy there. She made concert tours throughout Europe; was particularly noted for her interpretation of Chopin. In 1870 she joined the faculty of the Copenhagen Cons. Returning to Norway, she married Dr. Oscar Nissen in 1874 and settled in Christiania.

Lie, Harald, Norwegian composer; b. Oslo, Nov. 21, 1902; d. there, May 23, 1942. At the age of 21 he went to America, where he earned his living as a piano tuner; then studied piano manufacturing in Leipzig. Returning to Norway in 1929, he took lessons in composition with Fartein Valen. During 12 years of composing he produced 2 symphonies (1934; 1937); a *Symphonic Dance* (1942); some choral works; only 12 op. numbers in all. He died of tuberculosis.

Lie, Sigurd, Norwegian composer; b. Drammen, May 23, 1871; d. there, Sept. 29, 1904. He was a pupil of Lindeman and Holter; then studied at the Leipzig Cons. (1891-93); spent several years in Berlin; then returned to Norway, where he was appointed conductor of the 'Handelsstand Sangforening' in Christiania (1902). —Works: Symphony in A minor (Christiania, Feb. 28, 1903); *Oriental Suite* for orch. (Christiania, Oct. 28, 1899); a violin concerto (Bergen, Feb. 13, 1896); *Erling Skjalgson* for baritone solo, men's chorus, and orch. (Christiania, Oct. 28, 1899); *Norske Dans* for violin and piano; men's choruses; a song cycle *Wartburg,* and many separate songs, of which *Schnee* became famous.

Liebe, Eduard Ludwig, German composer; b. Magdeburg, Nov. 19, 1819; d. Chur, Feb. 4, 1900. He studied in Kassel with Spohr and Baldewein; then was music director at Coblenz, Mainz, and Worms; went to Strasbourg as teacher; later in London. He wrote an opera, *Die Braut von Azola* (Karlsruhe, 1868); also publ. popular songs and piano pieces.

Liebermann, Rolf, Swiss composer; b. Zürich, Sept. 14, 1910. He studied with Wladimir Vogel; became an adherent to the 12-tone method of composition, although without following the strict technique of the Schoenberg school. His interest lies chiefly in the modern musical theater and radio; his dramatic works often bear an allegorical significance. —Works: the operas *Leonore 40/45* (Basel, March 25, 1952), *The School for Wives* (Louisville, Dec. 3, 1955), *Penelope* (Salzburg, Aug. 17, 1954); *Furioso* for orch. (1947; perf. in the U.S. by Stokowski with the Dallas Symph. Orch., Dec. 9, 1950); *Concerto for Jazzband and Orchestra* (Donaueschingen Festival, Oct. 17, 1954); cantatas *Streitlied zwischen Leben und Tod* and *Une des fins du monde;* piano sonata (1951); festival plays; film music; etc.

Lieberson, Goddard, composer and writer; b. Hanley, Staffordshire, England, April 5, 1911. He was brought to the U.S. as a child; studied at the Eastman School of Music, Rochester, with Bernard Rogers; settled in New York in 1936. In 1939 he became a member of the staff of Columbia Records, Inc.; then director of the Masterworks and Educational Depts.; later, appointed executive vice-president; and finally, president. He has written articles for N.Y. newspapers; also contributed to music magazines and encyclopedias. He is married to Vera Zorina. —Works: orch. suites, *Five Modern Painters* (1929), *Two Chasing Dances* (1929); *Three Chinese Poems* for chorus (1936); *Sonata for Quintet,* for oboe, bassoon, viola, cello, and piano (1934); incidental music for *Alice in Wonderland* (1936); songs to poems of Ezra Pound, James Joyce, etc.; ed. *Columbia Book of Musical Masterpieces* (N.Y., 1950).

Liebeskind (lē'-bĕs-kĭnd), **Joseph,** German music editor; b. Leipzig, April 22, 1866; d. there, Aug. 10, 1916. He studied at the Leipzig Cons. with Sitt, Reinecke, and Jadassohn; lived most of his life in Leipzig; edited and arranged a number of works by Gluck, Mozart, Dittersdorf. He was a notable music collector; owned a large library rich in Gluck items, including some manuscripts.

Liebich, Ernst (Johann Gottlob), eminent German violin maker; b. Breslau, April 13, 1830; d. there, Sept. 23, 1884. His father and grandfather were violin makers, and he was trained in their workshop; also worked with Vuillaume in Paris, Hart in London, and Bausch in Leipzig. His instruments were awarded several prizes at international exhibitions.

Liebig, Karl, German conductor; b. Schwedt, July 25, 1808; d. Berlin, Oct. 6, 1872. He was engaged as an oboist in the Alexander Grenadier Regiment in Berlin; in 1843 he organized the Berlin 'Symphoniekapelle,' which under his leadership attained a very high standard of performance; in 1867 the orchestra elected another conductor; Liebig's attempts to form a rival organization proved futile.

Liebling, Emil, pianist; brother of Georg Liebling; b. Pless, Silesia, April 12, 1851; d. Chicago, Jan. 20, 1914. He studied piano with Th. Kullak in Berlin, Dachs in Vienna, and Liszt in Weimar; composition with Dorn in Berlin. In 1867 he came to America, and lived in Chicago from 1872, actively engaged as a concert pianist and teacher. He wrote a number of effective piano pieces in a light vein *(Florence Valse, Feu follet, Albumblatt, Two Romances, Cradle Song, Canzonetta, Menuetto scherzoso, Mazurka de concert, Spring Song).* He edited 'The American History and Encyclopedia of Music.'

Liebling, Estelle, American singer and vocal pedagogue; sister of Leonard Liebling;

niece of Emil and Georg Liebling; b. New York, April 21, 1884. She studied with Mathilde Marchesi in Paris and S. Nicklass-Kempner in Berlin; made her début as Lucia at the Dresden Royal Opera; also appeared at the Stuttgart Opera, the Opéra-Comique, Paris, and the Metropolitan Opera House, N.Y. (1903-4); was soloist with leading symph. orchestras in the U. S., France, Germany; also with Sousa; from 1936-38 was prof. at the Curtis Institute of Music; then settled in N.Y. as vocal teacher. She publ. *The Estelle Liebling Coloratura Digest* (N.Y., 1943).

Liebling, Georg, pianist and composer; brother of Emil Liebling; b. Berlin, Jan. 22, 1865; d. New York, Feb. 7, 1946. He studied piano with Theodor and Franz Kullak, and Liszt; composition with Urban and Dorn; toured through Europe (1885-89); was court pianist to the Duke of Coburg (1890). From 1894-97 he directed his own music school in Berlin; 1898-1908, in London as prof. at the Guildhall School of Music; in 1908, lived in Munich as director of his own Cons. He came to the U.S. in 1924; N.Y. concert début, Nov. 19, 1924; then lived in California; honorary Mus. Doc., Univ. of Southern California (1931). He used the pseudonym André Myrot. —Works: *Great Mass,* for soli, chorus, orch., and organ (Los Angeles, 1931); 2 violin concertos; *Concerto Eroico,* for piano and orch. (1925); 2 violin sonatas, 3 Preludes for violin and piano, *Aria e Tarantella* for cello and piano, *Légende* for violin and piano, etc.; piano pieces; songs. —Cf. G. Braun, *Hofpianist Georg Liebling* (Berlin, 1896).

Liebling, Leonard, American music critic and editor; nephew of Georg and Emil Liebling; brother of Estelle Liebling; b. New York, Feb. 7, 1874; d. there, Oct. 28, 1945. He studied at the College of the City of New York, and privately with Leopold Godowsky (piano); then in Berlin with Kullak and Barth (piano) and Urban (composition); toured Europe and America as pianist. In 1902 he joined the staff of the 'Musical Courier,' N.Y., and in 1911 became its editor-in-chief; his weekly columns on topical subjects were both entertaining and instructive. He also served as music critic of the 'N. Y. American' (1923-34; 1936-37). He wrote some chamber music, piano pieces, and songs, as well as librettos of several light operas, including Sousa's *The American Maid.*

Liège, Jacques de. See **Jacques de Liège.**

Lienau (lē'-now), **Robert,** German music publisher; b. Neustadt, Holstein, Dec. 28, 1838; d. there, July 22, 1920. In 1864 he purchased Schlesinger's business in Berlin, and in 1875, Haslinger's in Vienna; with the latter, he acquired the most important works of Weber, Meyerbeer, Liszt, Spohr, and others. In 1910 the management of the business was taken over by his sons Robert and Wilhelm Lienau.

Liepe (lē'-peh), **Emil,** German singer and composer; b. Potsdam, Jan. 16, 1860; d. Berlin, Feb. 18, 1940. He studied in Leipzig and Vienna; from 1884-90, sang in various German opera theaters; in 1891-92 he appeared at the Bayreuth Festival; then retired from the stage, and taught voice at the Cons. of Sondershausen (1903-7) and, after 1907, in Berlin. He wrote an opera, *Colomba* (Danzig, 1894); symph. poems *Fatum* and *Rückblick;* a symphony; also a number of songs.

Lier, Bertus van. See **Van Lier.**

Lier, Jacques van. See **Van Lier.**

Lierhammer, Theodor, baritone and teacher; b. Lwow, Nov. 18, 1866; d. Vienna, Jan. 6, 1937. He was a practicing physician when he began to study singing with Ress in Vienna, Carafa in Milan, and Stockhausen in Frankfurt; made his début at Vienna in 1894 in a concert with Fritz Kreisler; toured Austria and Hungary (1896), Germany (1898), Russia (1899), France and England (1900), and the U. S. (1904). From 1904-14 he was prof. of singing at the Royal Academy of Music in London; served as army physician during World War I; 1922-24, in London as singer and teacher; 1924, named prof. of singing at the State Academy of Music in Vienna; 1932-35, taught at the Austro-American Summer Cons., Mondsee (Salzburg). One of his American pupils was Roland Hayes.

Lieurance, Thurlow, American composer; b. Oskaloosa, Iowa, March 21, 1878. He studied at the Cincinnati College of Music; served as army bandmaster during the Spanish-American War. He became interested in American Indian music, and lived on various reservations, studying the culture of Indian tribes; this research resulted in the composition of music showing the influence of Indian melodies; one of his songs, *By the Waters of Minnetonka,* achieved tremendous popularity; he publ. further *9 Indian Songs* (1919), *Songs of the North*

American Indian (1921), *8 Songs From the Green Timber* (1922), *Forgotten Trails* (1923); wrote several symph. pieces: *Medicine Dance, Colonial Exposition Sketches, Scenes Southwest, Prairie Sketches, Water Moon Maiden,* etc. In 1940 he was appointed dean of the music dept., Municipal Univ. of Wichita, Kansas; 1957, Dean Emeritus.

Lilburn, Douglas, New Zealand composer; b. Wanganui, Nov. 2, 1915. He studied at the Royal College of Music, London, with Vaughan Williams; then returned to New Zealand. — Works: *Forest,* symphonic poem (1937; Percy Grainger prize); *Aotearoa,* overture (London, April 16, 1940); *Song of the Antipodes,* for orch. (Wellington, Aug. 20, 1947); *Diversions,* for string orch. (London, June 28, 1947); Symphony No. 1 (first symphony by any New Zealand composer; Wellington, May 12, 1951); 2 string quartets (1939, 1946); 3 violin sonatas (1943-1950); string trio (1945); clarinet sonata (1948); piano sonata (1949); film music.

Liliencron, Rochus von, eminent German music scholar; b. Plön, Dec. 8, 1820; d. Coblenz, March 5, 1912. He studied law and theology in Kiel and Berlin; took a course of Nordic philology in Copenhagen; in 1850, became prof. of Norse literature at Kiel Univ.; in 1852, prof. of German literature at Jena Univ.; then privy-councillor at Saxe-Meiningen (1855-68); in 1869, went to Munich; there he edited the 'Allgemeine deutsche Biographie' (1875-1900); collected and annotated German folksongs of the Middle Ages, publ. as *Historische Volkslieder der Deutschen vom 13.-16. Jahrhundert* (4 vols. and an appendix; Leipzig, 1865-69); from 1876 he lived in Schleswig as provost of St. John's Monastery; in 1894, appointed editor of the 'Denkmäler deutscher Tonkunst.' —Publications: *Lieder und Sprüche aus der letzten Zeit des Minnesangs* (1854; contains 20 melodies with texts from the Jena Minnesänger Codex, c. 1320); *Über den Chorgesang in der evangelischen Kirche* (1881); *Deutsches Leben im Volkslied um 1530,* containing 147 polyphonic German folksongs of the 16th century (1885; 2nd ed., 1925); *Chorordnung für die Sonn- und Festtage des evangelischen Kirchenjahres* (1900; 2nd ed., by H. J. Moser, 1929); *Die Horazischen Metren in deutschen Kompositionen des 16. Jahrhunderts,* in 'Vierteljahrsschrift für Musikwissenschaft' (vols. 3 and 10); etc. He wrote an autobiography, *Frohe Jugendtage* (1902). In 1910, in honor of his 90th birthday, a 'Festschrift' was publ., to which many of the foremost German musicologists contributed (Riemann, Adler, Friedlaender, Kretzschmar, Sandberger, Seiffert, and others). — Cf. A. Bettelheim, *Leben und Wirken des Freiherrn Rochus von Liliencron* (1917).

Lilienthal, Abraham W., American composer and teacher; b. New York, Feb. 13, 1859; d. there, March 15, 1928. He received his entire musical training in New York; from 1886-91, was a violinist in the Thomas Orch.; for many years, played the viola in the N. Y. String Quartet; then lived in N. Y. as teacher and composer. He wrote a string quartet; a string quintet; a string sextet; a piano trio; a cello sonata; and a series of orchestral dances.

Liljeblad, Ingeborg, Finnish soprano; b. Helsinki, Oct. 17, 1887; d. there, Feb. 28, 1942. She studied in Berlin with Etelka Gerster, and in Paris with Félia Litvinne; was engaged at the Mannheim Opera (1911-13) and in Hamburg for the season of 1913-14. Returning to Helsinki in 1927, she taught at the Sibelius Academy. She was married to the conductor Leo Funtek.

Liljefors, Ingemar, Swedish composer; b. Göteborg, Dec. 13, 1906. He studied at the Stockholm Cons.; in 1938 was appointed to the faculty there.—Works: opera, *Hyrkusken* (1951); Rhapsody for piano and orch. (1936); piano concerto (1940); a symphony (1943); chamber music; piano pieces. He published a manual on harmony from the functional point of view (1937) and a book of harmonic analysis along the same lines (1951).

Liljefors, Ruben, Swedish composer and conductor; b. Upsala, Sept. 30, 1871; d. there, March 4, 1936. He studied in Upsala; then with Jadassohn at the Leipzig Cons.; later in Dresden with Draeseke; and with Max Reger in Leipzig. Returning to Sweden, he was active as choral conductor in Upsala (1902) and in Göteborg (1903-11); in 1912 he went to Gävle as conductor of the Orchestral Society.—Works: the cantata *Blomsterfursten (The Flower-Prince);* a symphony (1906); *Sommer-Suite* (1920); 3 Bagatelles for string orch.; Romance for violin and orch.; a piano concerto (1899; rewritten, 1922); incidental music to *Fritjof och Ingeborg;* a violin sonata; men's choruses; piano pieces; songs; etc.

Lillo, Giuseppe, Italian composer; b. Galatina, Lecce, Feb. 26, 1814; d. Naples, Feb. 4, 1863. He studied at the Naples Cons. with

Furno, Lanza, and Zingarelli; in 1846, became teacher of harmony at the Naples Cons.; later (1859), teacher of counterpoint and composition there. He had to retire from active life in 1861 because of mental illness. —Works: the operas *Una moglie per 24 ore* (Naples, 1834), *L'osteria d'Andujar* (Naples, 1840; his most successful work), etc.; symphonies; a piano quartet; much good piano music; also church music.

Limantour, José Yves, Mexican conductor; b. Paris (of Mexican parents), Aug. 9, 1919. He was educated at Trinity College, Cambridge; settled in Mexico in 1939; studied there at the Conservatorio Nacional; in 1940-41 he was in the U. S., where he took courses with Hindemith; from 1942-43 he was conductor of the orch. of the Ballet Russe de Monte Carlo in Mexico; from 1944-51 he was conductor of the Jalapa Symph. Orch.

Limbert, Frank, conductor and composer; b. New York (of German parents), Nov. 15, 1866; d. Hanau, Nov. 19, 1938. He was taken to Germany at the age of 8, and remained there; studied at the Hoch Cons. in Frankfurt; *Dr. phil.* at the Univ. of Strasbourg (1894), with the dissertation *Beitrag zur Kenntnis der volkstümlichen Musik, insbesondere der Balladen-Komposition in England;* from 1895 lived mostly in Hanau, where he conducted an oratorio society. He publ. a *Konzertstück* for piano and orch.; violin sonata; viola sonata; *Ein Zyklus von Sonetten* for chorus a cappella; other choruses; songs; piano pieces.

Limnander de Nieuwenhove (n'yö'-venhoh-vĕ), **Armand Marie Ghislain,** Belgian composer; b. Ghent, May 22, 1814; d. Moignanville, near Paris, Aug. 15, 1892. He studied in Freiburg with Lambillotte and in Brussels with Fétis; in 1835, became choral director in Malines; in 1845, settled in Paris. —Works: the grand opera *Le Maître-chanteur* (Paris 1853); the comic operas *Les Monténégrins* (Paris, 1849), *Le Château de la Barbe-Bleue* (1851), and *Yvonne* (1859); the symphony *La Fin des Moissons; Scènes druidiques,* for orch.; a string quartet; a cello sonata; church music; songs; etc.

Lincke, Joseph, cellist; b. Trachenberg, Silesia, June 8, 1783; d. Vienna, March 26, 1837. He was cellist in Schuppanzigh's famous quartet (1808-16) in Vienna; was 1st cellist at the Theater an der Wien (1818); finally at the Vienna Court Opera (1831). He composed some cello pieces.

Lincke, Paul, German composer of light music; b. Berlin, Nov. 7, 1866; d. Klausthal-Zellernfeld, near Göttingen, Sept. 3, 1946. He was active in many fields; was an orchestral musician, playing violin and bassoon, conductor of theater orchestras, and a music publisher in Berlin; from 1918-20, conducted at the Folies-Bergère in Paris. About 1900 he began to write operettas, all of which were produced in Berlin; was instrumental in establishing a special type of 'Berlin operettas' as distinguished from the Vienna school. Among his productions, the best known are *Venus auf Erden* (1897), *Im Reiche des Indra* (1899), *Frau Luna* (Dec. 31, 1899), *Fräulein Loreley* (1900), *Nakiris Hochzeit* (1902), *Lysistrata* (1902; contains the song *Glühwürmchen* [*Glow-worm*] which attained enormous popularity all over the world), *Prinzessin Rosine* (1905), *Grigri* (1911), and *Casanova* (1914). His last operetta was *Ein Liebestraum,* which was produced at Hamburg in 1940. A postage stamp in his honor, with a musical example showing a melody from *Glow-worm,* was issued by the West German Government in 1957. —Cf. Edmund Nick, *Paul Lincke* (Berlin, 1953).

Lind, Jenny, famous soprano, called 'the Swedish Nightingale'; b. Stockholm, Oct. 6, 1820; d. at her villa, Wynd's Point, Malvern Wells, England, Nov. 2, 1887. She studied singing at a school connected with the court theater; her early teachers there were C. M. Craelius and I. Berg; she later studied with A. F. Lindblad and J. A. Josephson. She made her professional début as Agathe in *Der Freischütz* at the Stockholm Opera on March 7, 1838; she then sang Euryanthe in Weber's opera, and several parts in French operas. In 1840 she was appointed a regular member of the Royal Swedish Academy of Music, and was also given the rank of court singer. However, she felt the necessity of improving her voice, and went to Paris, where she studied for about a year with Manuel Garcia, who gave her a thorough training according to his well-known 'scientific' method. In Paris Meyerbeer heard her, and was so impressed that he wrote for her the part of Vielka in his opera *Ein Feldlager in Schlesien.* Jenny Lind returned to Stockholm in 1842; in 1844 she went to Berlin; sang there, and also in Hanover, Hamburg, Cologne, and Coblenz; then appeared in Frankfurt, Darmstadt, Copenhagen, and again in Berlin; her other important engagements were at the Gewandhaus, Leipzig (Dec. 6, 1845), and at the Vienna Opera (April 18, 1846). By this time, her fame became legendary in Europe; she was engaged to sing in London, and her appearance there was preceded by an extraordinary publicity campaign. She made her London début as Alice in *Robert le Diable* on March 4, 1847, with sensational success; as Chorley reported, the town "went mad about the Swedish nightingale." If her success in England was great, her American tour exceeded all expectations in public agitation and monetary reward. She arrived in America in 1850, under the sponsorship of P. T. Barnum, the circus manager, who presented Jenny Lind as a natural phenomenon rather than an artist; nonetheless, she produced a fine impression on the musical public as well; she sang recitals in New York, Boston, St. Louis, and other cities; a 4-page broadside in folio format with golden type was issued in anticipation of her Boston appearance by the F. Gleason Publishing Co. (1850); poems were written in her honor, and accounts of her concerts were published in hundreds of newspapers. She earned about $130,000; of this sum she distributed $100,000 to various charitable institutions in Sweden. On Feb. 5, 1852 she married, in Boston, her accompanist Otto Goldschmidt; with him she returned to Europe; remained for some time in Dresden; in 1856 she went to London, and remained in England for the rest of her life, with the exception of a few appearances in Europe. She had left the operatic stage in 1849, before her American tour; in England she sang with her husband's 'Bach Choir'; her final public appearance was at the Rhenish Music Festival, in 1870, when she sang the principal part in her husband's oratorio *Ruth*. —Unlike many other celebrated singers of her era, Jenny Lind was a paragon of domestic virtue, and was distinguished by her lack of vanity; even her most ardent worshippers did not claim that she was beautiful, but there was no disagreement as to the quality of her voice and her musicianship. She possessed a fine coloratura, with a compass reaching high G; never striving for dramatic effect, she was able to maintain a perfect phrase. Among her best operatic parts were La Sonnambula and Lucia. A bust of Jenny Lind was unveiled in Westminster Abbey on April 20, 1894. A Jenny Lind Association was formed in N.Y. in 1922, and a Jenny Lind society was organized in Stockholm in 1943. —Bibliography: J. B. Lyser, *G. Meyerbeer und Jenny Lind* (Vienna, 1847); C. G. Rosenberg, *Jenny Lind in America* (N.Y., 1851); H. S. Holland and W. S. Rockstro, *Memoir of Mme. Jenny Lind-Goldschmidt* (2 vols., London, 1891; condensed edition, 1 vol., 1893); W. S. Rockstro and O. Goldschmidt, *Jenny Lind-Goldschmidt: A Record and Analysis of the Method of the Late Jenny Lind-Goldschmidt* (London, 1894); C. A. Wilkens, *Jenny Lind: Ein Cäcilienbild aus der evangelischen Kirche* (Gütersloh, 1854; 5th ed., 1926); *Jenny Lind's Singing Method* (a letter written by her), in the 'Mus. Quarterly' (July, 1917); T. Norlind, *Jenny Lind* (Stockholm, 1919); M. R. Werner, *Barnum* (N.Y., 1923); Mrs. Raymond Maude, *The Life of Jenny Lind* (London, 1926); Grace Humphrey, *Jenny Lind* (Philadelphia, 1928); E. C. Wagenknecht, *Jenny Lind-Goldschmidt* (Boston, 1931); Laura Benet, *Enchanting Jenny Lind* (N. Y., 1939); H. Headland, *The Swedish Nightingale, a Biography of Jenny Lind* (Rock Island, Ill., 1940); M. Pergament, *Jenny Lind* (Stockholm, 1945); K. Rotzen and T. Meyer, *Jenny Lind* (Stockholm, 1945); Joan Bulman, *Jenny Lind* (London, 1956).

Lindberg, Oskar Fredrik, Swedish composer and organist; b. Gagnef, Feb. 23, 1887; d. Stockholm, April 10, 1955. He studied at the Stockholm Cons. with Andreas Hallén and Ernst Ellberg; was organist at Trinity Church, Stockholm (1906-14); in 1919, appointed teacher of harmony at the Stockholm Cons. His compositions include the opera *Fredlös* (after Selma Lagerlöf's story *The Outlaw;* Stockholm, Nov. 25, 1943); *Det ljusa Landet,* for chorus and orch. (1935); *Skansen Cantata; Bergslags Cantata* (1947); a symphony (1912); *Dalmålningar* (*Pictures from Dalarna;* 1908); the symph. poems *Florez och Blanzeflor, Från de stora skogarna, Hemifrån, Vildmark, Gesunda;* overtures; orchestral suites; a piano quartet; a piano quintet; a Requiem; piano pieces; songs.

Lindblad, Adolf Fredrik, Swedish composer; b. Skänninge, near Stockholm, Feb. 1, 1801; d. Linköping, Aug. 23, 1878. He studied in Berlin with Zelter. His numerous songs, tinged with national color, won deserved popularity, especially after Jenny Lind, his pupil, sang them in public; he was called the 'Schubert of the North.' —Works: an opera, *Frondörerna (The Frondists;* Stockholm, May 11, 1835); 2 symphonies; 7 string quartets; a piano trio; a duo for piano and violin; songs *(The Song of the Dalecarlian Maiden, Lament, The Wood by the Åren Lake, A Day in Spring, A Summer's Day, Autumn Evening,* etc.). —Cf. M. Grandinson, *Brev till A. F. Lindblad från Mendelssohn* (Stockholm, 1913).

Lindblad, Otto (Jonas), Swedish composer; b. Karlstorp, March 31, 1809; d. Mellby, Jan. 24, 1864. He is chiefly known for his vocal ensemble music; formed a vocal and instrumental trio; also was opera and choral conductor. He wrote 66 vocal quartets; 5 choruses with solos; 14 vocal trios; 3 duets; 36 solo songs. —Cf. Ture Nerman, *Otto Lindblad* (Upsala, 1930).

Lindegren, Johan, Swedish teacher and authority on church music; b. Ullared, Jan. 7, 1842; d. Stockholm, June 8, 1908. He studied at the Stockholm Cons., where he became teacher of counterpoint in 1881; 1884, organist and cantor of St. Nicholas' Church. Among his pupils were Alfvén, Melchers, Bäck, Håkanson, and Wiklund. An authority on church music, he edited 'Tidning för kyrkomusik' (1881-82); also publ. a *Koralbok* (1905). Of his numerous compositions, only a few were published: *Hösttankar (Autumn Thoughts)*, an elegy; *Till Vegas jhältar (For Vega's Heroes)*, festival march; a string quartet; a piano sonata and fugue.

Lindeman, Ludvig Mathias, Norwegian organist and folksong collector; b. Trondhjem, Nov. 28, 1812; d. Christiania, May 23, 1887. He turned from theology to the study of music; in 1839, became organist at Our Saviour's Church in Christiania; in 1849, teacher of church singing at the Theological Seminary of Christiania Univ.; in 1883 he and his son Peter Lindeman (1858-1930) founded a music school which later developed into the Christiania Cons. He was one of the earliest and most active collectors of Norwegian folksongs; publ. nearly 600 folk melodies in the collection *Older and Newer Norwegian Mountain Melodies* (3 vols., 1853-67); also *68 Norwegian Mountain Melodies* (1841); *50 Norwegian Melodies* (1862); and *30 Norwegian Ballads* (1863). His *Chorale Book for the Norwegian Church* (1877) remains a standard work; it contains some melodies by Lindeman, including *Kirken den er et gammelt hus*, one of the best-known Norwegian hymn tunes; also composed *Draumkvoedet (Dream chant)* for chorus; organ fugues; etc. —Cf. O. M. Sandvik, *Ludvig Mathias Lindeman og folkemelodien* (Oslo, 1950).

Linden. See **Van der Linden.**

Lindley, Robert, English cellist; b. Rotherham, Yorkshire, March 4, 1776; d. London, June 13, 1855. He studied cello with Cervetto; from 1794-1851, was 1st cellist at the Royal Opera in London; in 1822, became prof. of cello at the Royal Academy of Music. He wrote pieces for the cello.

Lindner, August, German cellist; b. Dessau, Oct. 29, 1820; d. Hanover, June 15, 1878. He studied with Drechsler; in 1837 he became 1st cellist in the court orch. at Hanover. He composed a cello concerto and numerous vocal pieces.

Lindner, Ernst Otto Timotheus, German music scholar; b. Breslau, Nov. 28, 1820; d. Berlin, Aug. 7, 1867. He was editor of the 'Vossische Zeitung'; also conducted the Berlin Bach-Verein. —Publications: *Meyerbeers 'Prophet' als Kuntswerk beurteilt* (1850); *Die erste stehende deutsche Oper* (1855); *Geschichte des deutschen Liedes im 18. Jahrhundert* (1871; edited by Erk).

Lindpaintner, Peter Joseph von, German conductor and composer; b. Coblenz, Dec. 9, 1791; d. Nonnenhorn, Lake Constance, Aug. 21, 1856. He studied violin and piano in Augsburg; theory in Munich with Winter and Joseph Grätz; in 1812, became musical director of the Isarthor Theater in Munich; from 1819 until his death, conductor of the court orch. at Stuttgart, where his ability made the orchestra famous. He wrote 28 operas, including *Der Bergkönig* (Stuttgart, Jan. 30, 1825), *Der Vampyr* (Stuttgart, Nov. 21, 1828), *Die Genueserin* (Vienna, Feb. 8, 1839), *Lichtenstein* (Stuttgart, Aug. 26, 1846); 3 ballets *(Joko*, etc.); 5 melodramas; 5 oratorios; symphonies; overture to *Faust;* incidental music to *Lied von der Glocke;* 6 Masses; a *Stabat Mater;* songs *(Die Fahnenwacht, Roland*, etc.). —Cf. R. Hänsler, *Lindpaintner als Opernkomponist* (Munich, 1928).

Lineva (lē-nyo'-vah), **Evgenia Eduardovna** (*née* Papritz), Russian folksong collector; b. Brest-Litovsk, Jan. 9, 1854; d. Moscow, Jan. 24, 1919. She studied voice with her mother, who was a pupil of Glinka; then took lessons with Mathilde Marchesi in Vienna; later sang opera in Paris, London, and Moscow. In 1889 she married the engineer A. L. Linev (1840-1916); because of his revolutionary activities, he served a prison term, and was then forced to emigrate. Lineva was with him in London (1890-92) and in America; she gave concerts with a Russian choir (which she organized) at Carnegie Hall, New York (Dec. 10, 1892) and at the Chicago Exposition (1893). In America they experimented with phonograph recording. Upon their return to Russia

(1894), Lineva undertook a series of trips in the Volga region, using a phonograph constructed by her husband to record folk-songs. She published her findings in 2 vols. (with photographs and musical examples) in Russian and in English under the title *The Peasant Songs of Great Russia* (St. Petersburg, 1904); she further publ. *Songs of the Novgorod Region* (1909). —Cf. E. Kann-Novikova, *Evgenia Lineva* (Moscow, 1952).

Linley, George, English composer and author; b. Leeds, 1798; d. London, Sept. 10, 1865. He settled in London, where he wrote words and music of songs, many of which acquired great vogue *(Ever of thee; I cannot mind my wheel, mother; Thou art gone from my gaze,* etc.); he also wrote the cantata *The Jolly Beggars;* the operas *Francesca Doria* (1849), *La Poupée de Nuremberg* (London, 1861), *The Toy-Makers* (1861), *Law versus Love* (1862); part-songs, trios, duets, hymns; edited the collections *Scottish Melodies, Songs of the Camp, Original Hymn Tunes,* etc.; publ. *The Musical Cynics of London* (1862), a satirical poem aimed at the critic Chorley, and *Modern Hudibras* (1864).

Linley, Thomas, Sr., English composer; b. Badminton, Jan. 17, 1733; d. London, Nov. 19, 1795. He first studied with a church organist in Bath; then with Paradisi. He organized performances of oratorios in Bath; in 1774 he went to London, where he produced several oratorios, and various stage works, to which he contributed an occasional song; also arranged and orchestrated ballets, comic operas, etc., by other composers. He publ. *6 Elegies* for 3 voices (his finest work) and *12 Ballads;* 2 vols. of miscellaneous vocal pieces by him were publ. posthumously. The writer Sheridan was his son-in-law; Linley wrote 7 numbers for the production of *The Duenna* of Sheridan, and arranged the rest of the work from music by others; it was produced at Covent Garden, London, on Nov. 21, 1775, and became one of the most successful comic operas in England in the 18th century (about 75 performances during the first season). Linley's 3 sons and 3 daughters were also professional musicians. —Cf. C. Black, *The Linleys of Bath* (London, 1926).

Linley, Thomas, Jr., English violinist and composer; eldest son of the preceding; b. Bath, May 5, 1756; d. Grimsthorpe, Aug. 5, 1778. He was extremely gifted as a child, and played a violin concerto in public at the age of 8. He studied music in London with his father and with Boyce; was then sent to Florence, where he studied violin with Nardini, and while there, met Mozart, with whom he subsequently formed a close friendship. Returning to England, he played at his father's concerts at Bath and in London. He wrote incidental music for various plays in London. He lost his life by drowning at the early age of 22. Some of his vocal pieces were included in the posthumous collection of his father's music.

Linstead, George Frederick, Scottish pianist and composer; b. Melrose, Jan. 24, 1908. He wrote an oratorio at the age of 13, and an opera, *Agamemnon,* at 16; was church organist at Sheffield; in 1947, was appointed prof. at Sheffield Univ. Besides his youthful compositions, he has written an opera, *Eastward of Eden* (1937); a *Moto perpetuo* for orch. (1947); a violin sonata (1934); a string quartet (1941); piano pieces.

Lintermans, François-Joseph, Belgian singing teacher; b. Brussels, Aug. 18, 1808; d. Ixelles, May 14, 1895. He was director of the Brussels choral society 'Les Artisans réunis'; publ. male choruses *(Cri de guerre, Réveil, Chœur des buveurs,* etc.).

Lioncourt (l'yohn-koor'), **Guy de,** French composer; b. Caen, Dec. 1, 1885. He studied at the Schola Cantorum with Vincent d'Indy, who was his uncle by marriage; 1918, he won the Grand Prix Lasserre with his fairy opera *La Belle au bois dormant* (1912). In 1935 he was co-founder, with L. de Serres, of the École César Franck in Paris. —Dramatic works: *Le petit faune aux yeux bleus* (1911), *Les dix lépreux* (1920), *Jean de la lune* (1921), *Le mystère de l'Emmanuel* (Liège, 1924), *Le mystère de l'Alléluia* (1927), *Le reniement de St.-Pierre* (1928), *Le dict de Mme. Sante-Barbe* (1937), *Le navrement de Notre Dame* (1944), *Le mystère de l'Esprit* (1946). He also wrote a string quartet; piano quartet; 3 *Mélodies grégoriennes,* for organ; *Élevations liturgiques* for organ; 3 Masses; motets. He publ. *Un Témoignage sur la musique et sur la vie au XXe siècle* (Reims, 1956).

Lipatti, Dinu, Rumanian pianist and composer; b. Bucharest, March 17, 1917; d. Geneva, Dec. 2, 1950. His father was a violinist (pupil of Sarasate), and his mother a pianist. He received his early training from his parents; then studied with Floria Musicescu. He received a 2nd prize at the

International Competition at Vienna in 1934; Alfred Cortot, who was one of the judges, resigned from the jury in protest that the first prize was not awarded to Lipatti. Shortly afterwards, Lipatti went to Paris, where he studied piano with Cortot, conducting with Charles Munch, composition with Dukas and with Nadia Boulanger. He gave concerts in Germany and Italy, returning to Rumania at the outbreak of World War II. In 1943 he made his way to Stockholm, and then to Geneva. He visited England 4 times between 1946 and 1950; projected tours in America and Australia had to be cancelled owing to his illness (rheumatoid arthritis), which led to his early death. To preserve his piano playing for posterity, recordings were made in Geneva during a temporary improvement. Lipatti was married to Madeleine Cantacuzene, herself a concert pianist. He wrote a concertino for piano and orch., *Rumanian Dances* for orch. (Geneva, Oct. 11, 1945), a piano sonatina for left hand alone, etc. —Cf. W. Legge, *Dinu Lipatti,* in the 'Gramophone' (Feb., 1951); *Hommage à Dinu Lipatti* (Geneva, 1952); A. Lipatti, *La Vie du pianiste Dinu Lipatti, écrite par sa mère* (1954).

Lipawsky, Joseph, composer; b. Hohenmauth, Bohemia, Feb. 22, 1769; d. Vienna, Jan. 7, 1810. He studied philosophy in Prague; then settled in Vienna, where he enjoyed the friendship of Mozart, who gave him some instruction; was house musician for Count Adam Teleky; also gave public piano concerts. He wrote a symphony; *Grande sonate pathétique* for piano; songs. His music was highly regarded by his contemporaries.

Lipinsky, Carl, Polish violinist and composer; b. Radzyn, Oct. 30, 1790; d. near Lwow, Dec. 16, 1861. His father was a professional musician and gave him his primary education. He met Paganini, who agreed to teach him the violin; in 1835 he visited Leipzig; Schumann was greatly impressed by his playing and dedicated *Carnaval* to him. Lipinsky appeared in London on April 25, 1836, as soloist in his *Military Concerto* for violin and orch.; in 1839 he settled in Dresden as concertmaster of the Dresden Orch.; Liszt once played at the same concert with him. Lipinsky wrote a comic opera, *Klótnia przez zaklad* (Lwow, May 27, 1814), and other stage pieces; polonaises and *Rondos alla polacca* for violin and piano, and numerous technical violin studies.

Lipkovska, Lydia Yakovlevna, Russian soprano; b. Babino, Khotin District, Bessarabia, May 10, 1884; d. Beirut, Lebanon, Jan. 22, 1955. She studied voice with Madame Iretzkaya in St. Petersburg, and made her professional début there in the spring of 1909. She sang in Paris with great success, and received a contract for an American tour. Her American début took place with the Boston Opera Co. on Nov. 12, 1909, when she sang *Lakmé;* on Nov. 18, 1909, she appeared at the Metropolitan Opera House in *La Traviata* with Caruso. She was reengaged for the following season in the U.S.; also appeared in London (July 11, 1911). During World War I she was in Russia; after the Revolution she went to France; in 1919 she married Pierre Bodin, lieutenant in the French Army; toured the U.S. again in 1920. She then lived in France and her native Bessarabia; during the Rumanian occupation of Odessa (1941-44) she appeared at the Odessa Opera in her favorite role of Violetta; also acted in drama. In 1944 she went to Paris; then accepted a teaching position in Beirut (Lebanon); during her last years of life she was supported by the Tolstoy Foundation of N.Y.

Lipowsky, Felix Joseph, son of Thad Ferdinand Lipowsky; German music lexicographer; b. Wiesensteig, Jan. 25, 1764; d. Munich, March 21, 1844. In 1819 he was appointed archive keeper of Bavaria; composed some piano pieces; published a valuable *Baierisches Musik-Lexikon* (Munich, 1811).

Lipowsky, Thad Ferdinand, German composer; b. St. Martin, Bavaria, Dec. 28, 1738; d. Wiesensteig, March 18, 1767. He studied with Leopold Mozart in Salzburg; obtained a law degree in Wiesensteig (1763); composed many violin pieces. A lengthy account of his career is found in the *Baierisches Musik-Lexikon* compiled by his son, Felix Joseph Lipowsky.

Lipps, Theodor, German psychologist and writer on esthetics; b. Wallhalben, July 28, 1851; d. Munich, Oct. 17, 1914. He occupied the chair of philosophy at the universities of Bonn (1889), Breslau (1890-94), and Munich (from 1894). Besides the musical sections of his *Ästhetik* (2 vols., 1903-6), his writings on music comprise *Zur Theorie der Melodie* (1901); *Psychologische Studien* (vol. 2: *Das Wesen der musikalischen Harmonie und Disharmonie;* 1885; 2nd ed., 1905); *Tonverwandtschaft* *und Tonverschmelzung,* in the 'Zeitschrift für Psychologie und Physiologie' (1899). —Cf. P. Moos, *Theodor Lipps als Musikästhetiker* (1907); F. Liuzzi, *Essenza dell' arte e valore estetico nel pensiero di Theodor Lipps* (Bologna, 1924).

Lipsius, Marie (pen-name La Mara), writer on music; b. Leipzig, Dec. 30, 1837; d. Schmölen, near Wurzen, March 2, 1927. She received her entire education from her father, Dr. Adalbert Lipsius, rector of the Thomasschule in Leipzig; through R. Pohl, she was introduced to Liszt; in Liszt's circle at Weimar she had the happy fortune of meeting the foremost musicians of the time. Her writings on Liszt and Wagner, as well as on German composers of the Romantic school, possess a stamp of authority and intimate understanding. —Writings: *Beethoven* (1870; 2nd ed. 1873); *Musikalische Studienköpfe* (1868-82; 5 vols., often republished); *Musikalische Gedanken-Polyphonie: eine Sammlung von Aussprüchen berühmter Musiker über ihre Kunst* (1873); *Das Bühnenfestspiel in Bayreuth* (1877); *Musikerbriefe aus fünf Jahrhunderten* (1886; 2 vols.); *Klassisches und Romantisches aus der Tonwelt* (1892); *Briefe an August Roeckel, von Richard Wagner* (Leipzig, 1895); *Briefe von H. Berlioz an die Fürstin Carolyne zu Sayn-Wittgenstein* (1903); *Aus der Glanzzeit der Weimarer Altenburg, Bilder und Briefe aus dem Leben der Fürstin C. Sayn-Wittgenstein* (1906); *Marie von Muchanov-Kalergis in Briefen an ihre Tochter* (1907; 2nd ed., 1911); *Gräfin Therese Brunswik, die 'Unsterbliche Geliebte' Beethovens,* in the 'Neue Deutsche Rundschau' (1908); *Beethovens 'Unsterbliche Geliebte.' Das Geheimnis der Gräfin Brunswik und ihre Memoiren* (1909); *Liszt und die Frauen* (1911); *Durch Musik und Leben im Dienste des Ideals* (autobiography; 2 vols., 1917; 2nd ed., 1926); *Beethoven und die Brunsviks* (1920); *An der Schwelle des Jenseits: Letzte Erinnerungen an die Fürstin Carolyne Sayn-Wittgenstein* (1925). She also publ. popular biographies of many composers (Wagner, Berlioz, Rubinstein, Schumann, etc.).

Lirou (lē-roo'), **Jean François Espic,** Chevalier **de,** French composer and theorist; b. Paris, 1740; d. there, 1806. He was an officer in the 'Mousquetaires du roi,' for whom he wrote a *Marche des Mousquetaires,* which was performed until the Revolution. He publ. an *Explication du système de l'harmonie* (1785); this was the first French theory of harmony that opposed Rameau's system, and sought to establish the laws of chord progressions from the inherent affinities of tonality.

Lishin (lē-shin), **Grigory Andreyevitch,** Russian composer; b. St. Petersburg, May 5, 1854; d. there, June 27, 1888. He studied piano with his mother; became a proficient accompanist; also wrote music criticism. He composed 2 operas, *Don Caesar* (Kiev, 1888) and *Count Nulin* (after Pushkin), to his own librettos. His sentimental ballad, *She laughed,* was extremely popular with Russian singers.

Lisinski, Vatroslav, important Croatian composer; b. Zagreb, July 8, 1819; d. there, May 31, 1854. He was a student of Sojka and Wiesner von Morgenstern in Zagreb; as late as 1847, he went to Prague to study with Pitsch and Kittl. Although he never acquired a solid technique of composition, he was notable in that he tried to establish a national style in dramatic writing. He was the composer of the first Croatian opera, *Ljubav i zloba (Love and Malice),* for which he wrote only the vocal score; it was orchestrated by his teacher Wiesner von Morgenstern, and performed in Zagreb on March 28, 1846. His second opera, *Porin,* also in Croatian, was given many years after his death, in Zagreb, on Oct. 2, 1897. He further wrote 7 overtures and a number of choruses and songs. —Cf. F. Kuhač, *Vatroslav Lisinski* (Zagreb, 1887).

Lissa, Zofia, Polish musicologist; b. Lwow, Oct. 19, 1908. She studied with Chybinski, and after obtaining her degree of Ph.D. became prof. of music theory at the Lwow Cons. After World War II she served at the Polish Embassy in Moscow; then was appointed prof. of musicology at the Univ. of Warsaw. She wrote a number of books and smaller treatises on music history, education, broadcasting, film music, psychology of music, and social implications of music; among her publications are *The Outlines of Musical Science* (Lwow, 1934; new ed., 1948); *Remarks on the Marxist Method in Musicology* (Cracow, 1951); *The History of Russian and Soviet Music* (Warsaw, 1951). She has contributed articles on Polish music to 'Die Musik in Geschichte und Gegenwart.'

Lissenko, Nikolai Vitalievitch, Ukrainian composer; b. Grilki, near Krementchug, March 22, 1842; d. Kiev, Nov. 6, 1912. He was the son of a landowner; grew up in a musical atmosphere; the singing of Ukrainian songs by local peasants produced a lasting impression on him, and determined his future as a national composer. He studied natural sciences at the Univ. of Kiev, graduating in 1864; was a justice of the peace in the Kiev district (1864-66); then abandoned his non-musical pursuits and went to Leipzig, where he entered the Cons., and took courses with Richter (theory), Reinecke (piano), and Papperitz (organ). Returning to Russia in 1868, he taught piano at the Kiev Institute of the Daughters of Nobility; from 1874-76 studied orchestration with Rimsky-Korsakov in St. Petersburg. As early as 1868 he published his first collection of Ukrainian songs (printed in Leipzig); subsequent issues comprised 240 songs in 5 books, arranged according to their categories (Spring Songs, Midsummer Night Songs, Christmas Songs, etc.); he set to music a great number of poems from *Kobzar* by the Ukrainian poet Shevchenko (5 albums for 2, 3, and 4 voices; publ. in Kiev, 1870-97). In 1903, on the occasion of the 35th anniversary of the publication of his first collection of Ukrainian songs, Lissenko received a gift of 5,000 rubles from his admirers. —In his pamphlet *The Characteristics of the Ukrainian Dumki* (1874), Lissenko presents a theory that Ukrainian modes are derived from Greek music, and that antiphonal construction is one of the main features of Ukrainian songs, while the persistence of symmetrical rhythms distinguishes them from Russian songs. In his original compositions, Lissenko asserted himself as an ardent Ukrainian nationalist; he wrote several operas to Ukrainian librettos: *Chernomortsy* (1870); *Rizdviana Nitch,* after Gogol's *Christmas Eve Night* (1870); *Winter and Spring* (1880); *Utoplena,* after Gogol's *May Night* (1885); *Taras Bulba,* after Gogol's novel of the same name (1890; Kiev, Dec. 20, 1903; revised by Liatoshinsky and produced in Kiev in 1937); and his most popular stage work, after Kotlarevsky's play, *Natalka-Poltavka (Natalie from Poltava),* originally in the form of incidental music, then expanded into a 3-act opera (1890). He further wrote an opera, *Sappho,* with a Ukrainian text, which was unsuccessful; and 2 children's operas, *Pan Kotsky (Puss-in-Boots,* 1891) and *Koza-Dereza* (Kiev, April 20, 1901). Other works include 2 cantatas: *The Torrents Roar* (1877) and *Rejoice, Field Unplowed* (1883); also a *Cossack Scherzo,* for orch. (1872); *Capriccio elegiaco,* for violin and orch. (1894); 2 rhapsodies on Ukrainian themes, for piano; vocal pieces.

List, Emanuel, bass singer; b. Vienna, March 22, 1891. He was a chorister at the Theater-an-der-Wien; studied voice in Vienna, and made his début at the Volksoper there in 1922 as Méphistophélès in *Faust;* in 1923, was engaged at the Berlin State Opera, remaining there until 1933; specialized in Wagnerian roles. On Dec. 27, 1933 he made his first American appearance at the Metropolitan Opera, N.Y., as the Landgraf in *Tannhäuser;* in subsequent seasons, sang almost all Wagnerian bass roles; also appeared as singer of German lieder.

List, Eugene, American pianist; b. Philadelphia, July 6, 1918; was taken to Los Angeles when a year old; studied there at the Sutro-Seyler Studios and made his début with the Los Angeles Philharmonic at the age of 12; later studied in Philadelphia with Olga Samaroff, and at the Juilliard Graduate School in N.Y.; made his New York début playing the solo part in the American première of Shostakovitch's piano concerto with the N.Y. Philharmonic (Dec. 19, 1935). As a sergeant in the U.S. Army, he was called upon to play the piano at the Potsdam Conference in July, 1945, in the presence of Truman, Churchill, and Stalin. He married the violinist Carroll Glenn (Aug. 16, 1943).

Listemann, Bernhard, violinist and conductor; b. Schlotheim, Germany, Aug. 28, 1841; d. Chicago, Feb. 11, 1917. He studied with Ferdinand David in Leipzig, with Vieuxtemps in Brussels, and with Joachim in Hanover; became concertmaster of the court orch. in Rudolstadt (1859-67); then went with his brother Fritz Listemann to America; from 1871-74, was concertmaster in the Thomas Orch., N.Y.; in 1874 he went to Boston, where he founded the 'Philharmonic Club,' and later the 'Philharmonic Orch.,' which he conducted until 1881, when he became concertmaster of the newly-established Boston Symph. Orch. (for 4 years); meanwhile, he started the 'Listemann Quartet'; also was director of the 'Listemann Concert Co.' (1885-93). In 1893 he went to Chicago, where he taught violin at the Chicago College of Music (until 1907); with the exception of another sojourn in Boston (1907-9), he remained in Chicago until his death. He publ. a violin method.

Listemann, Franz, cellist; son of Bernhard Listemann; b. New York, Dec. 17, 1873; d. Chicago, March 11, 1930. He studied with Fries in Boston, with Julius Klengel in Leipzig, and with Haussmann in Berlin. After a year as 1st cellist in the Pittsburgh

Orch., he settled in N.Y.; he was soloist at the American première of Dvořák's cello concerto (1896).

Listemann, Fritz, violinist; brother of Bernhard Listemann; b. Schlotheim, Germany, March 25, 1839; d. Boston, Dec. 28, 1909. Like his brother, he studied with Ferdinand David at the Leipzig Cons.; was a member of the court orch. at Rudolstadt (1858-67); together with his brother he went to America; played violin in the Thomas Orch. in N.Y. (1871-74); then was in Boston, where he played in various chamber music organizations, and (from 1878) in his brother's 'Philharmonic Orch.'; from 1881-85, was a violinist in the Boston Symph. Orch.; then played in the 'Listemann Concert Co.' directed by his brother. He wrote 2 violin concertos; violin pieces.

Listemann, Paul, violinist; son of Bernhard Listemann; b. Boston, Oct. 24, 1871; d. Chicago, Sept. 20, 1950. He was taught by his uncle Fritz Listemann, and also by his father; as a boy participated in the various organizations directed by his father; then went to Germany, where he studied in Leipzig with Brodsky and in Berlin with Joachim; he was subsequently engaged as orchestral violinist in Pittsburgh, New York, etc.; was a member of the Metropolitan Opera Orch. from 1903 to 1920. In 1930 he moved to Chicago.

Listov, Konstantin, Russian composer; b. Odessa, Aug. 19, 1900. He learned music by ear; then studied piano in Tsaritsin (Stalingrad) and in Saratov. In 1923 he went to Moscow and began to write music for the theater. His Red Army song *Tachanka* became immensely popular.

Liszt, Franz (Ferencz), greatly celebrated pianist and composer; creator of the symphonic poem; b. Raiding, near Ödenburg, Hungary, Oct. 22, 1811; d. Bayreuth, July 31, 1886. His father, an excellent amateur, began his instruction on the piano at the age of 6; progress was so rapid that at 9 Franz played, at a public concert in Ödenburg, Ries' difficult E♭ Concerto with so great artistic success that his father decided on further concerts at Pressburg. After the second, several Hungarian aristocrats offered to provide 600 florins annually, for 6 years, for the boy's musical education. The offer was joyfully accepted, and the family moved in 1821 to Vienna. Here Liszt took piano lessons from Czerny for 18 months, and studied theory with Salieri, composing under the latter's supervision a considerable number of short church pieces. Beethoven asked to see him; at their memorable meeting the delighted master embraced Liszt after the latter's execution (without notes and accompaniment) of his trio, op. 97. Liszt's first public concerts in Vienna were given in 1823, with such flattering results that the father determined to take his son to the Paris Cons. On the way, concerts were given at Munich and Stuttgart. Young Liszt passed his examinations admirably; but Cherubini, then director of the Conservatoire, was opposed to infant prodigies and refused to admit him, using as an excuse a rule forbidding the entrance of foreigners. As a consequence, Liszt took no more piano lessons, developing his genius in his own way; he still studied composition, for a short time under Paër, but chiefly under Reicha, eagerly absorbing the latter's teachings, and bringing out a one-act operetta, *Don Sanche, ou le Château d'Amour,* which was played 5 times at the Académie Royale de Musique in 1825. (The score was believed to have been lost until Jean Chantavoine found it in 1903; the overture and an air from it were publ. in the May 1904 issue of 'Die Musik,' in a piano arrangement by Chantavoine.) Already a well-known pianist, Liszt now spent 2 years in concert tours; his father died in 1827, and he settled in Paris to support his mother and himself. He moved in the highest circles of letters and art; his spirit was strongly moved by the influences of the period: the Romanticism of Chopin, the socialistic ideas of St. Simon, the revolutionary rumblings of 1830; he even dreamt of entering the priesthood, but in the end a love of art conquered. Paganini's advent in 1831 inspired him to heretofore unheard-of feats in piano technique and expression; the music of Berlioz ripened his conviction about the poetic possibilities of his art; he became one of the most ardent champions and potent promoters of realism in music. His career was interrupted for a time by his *liaison* with the Countess d'Agoult (known as an authoress under the nom de plume of 'Daniel Stern'); with her he retired to Geneva (1835-39). Three children were born to them; Cosima, the younger of 2 daughters, eventually became the wife of Richard Wagner. During these 4 years, Liszt twice emerged from retirement to vanquish his only serious pianistic rival, Thalberg. Finally, in 1839, he set out on a triumphal progress through Europe, signalizing this step by generously assuming the responsibility for the completion of the Beethoven monument at Bonn, for which a large sum was still required. In 1848 he accepted the position of court Kapellmeister at Weimar, with the understanding that he was to further, by all means at his command, the progress of modern musical art. At all times he extended generous aid to struggling fellow artists. When the exiled Wagner, in despair over the non-production of his *Lohengrin,* sent the score to Liszt, the answer came back that the work was being prepared for its first performance (Weimar, Aug. 28, 1850). Here *Der fliegende Holländer* and *Tannhäuser* were also revived, and music by Berlioz was performed for the first time in Germany. Weimar became a center of attraction for artists of progressive tendency, reinforced by a multitude of Liszt's pupils. His relations with the Princess Carolyne Sayn-Wittgenstein, who left her husband and took up her residence with Liszt in Weimar, brought about momentous changes in his artistic life. She confirmed him in his resolution to abandon the career of a virtuoso and devote himself to composition in the larger forms. Up to that time he had confined himself mainly to composition for piano, the influence and importance of which upon the development of the modern pianoforte style can scarcely be overestimated. From this period on, Liszt appeared as a pianist only at rare intervals, but he sent into the world a new orchestral conception—the symphonic poem, an orchestral creation in one movement, and in a free form, expressive of some literary or philosophic idea. In 1859 he left Weimar, and until 1870 lived for the most part in Rome; in 1866 the Pope, Pius IX, conferred on him the dignity of Abbé. In 1870 he was invited to conduct the centennial Beethoven Festival at Weimar, which again became his residence; he spent there some months of each summer. In 1875 he was made president of the New Hungarian Academy of Music at Budapest; and between Weimar, Budapest, and Rome the last years of his life were divided, a throng of pupils and admirers following him from place to place. His death at Bayreuth, in 1886, occurred in the midst of the Wagner Festival. —According to a will made in 1860, Liszt's belongings, including all his MSS, passed into the possession of the Princess Carolyne Sayn-Wittgenstein. After the latter's death (March 7, 1887), everything was left to her daughter, Princess Marie Hohenlohe-Schillingsfürst. Immediately after Liszt's death, Grand Duke Karl Alexander of Weimar had suggested the idea of a foundation to honor the memory of the master. He himself donated the rooms that Liszt had occupied in the 'Hofgärtnerei.' Princess Hohenlohe turned over all treasures and MSS, and thus the 'Liszt Museum' was founded; she also founded the 'Liszt-Stiftung' by establishing a trust of 70,000 marks, the interest of which was awarded to talented composers and pianists. In 1905 the committee conceived the plan of publishing through Breitkopf & Härtel the master's complete works. The editors included E. d'Albert, F. Busoni, B. Kellermann, A. Stradal, Otto Taubmann, Dr. P. Wolfrum, B. Stavenhagen, and J. Vianna da Motta. The first vol. appeared in Dec., 1907; 33 vols. have so far been published. A Liszt Society was established in London in 1950, with E. J. Dent as president, to promote the republication of some of Liszt's less known works; vol. I contained late piano music.

Liszt, the creator of the transcendental style of piano playing, was without question the greatest piano virtuoso of the 19th century—even Anton Rubinstein could not match Liszt's supreme gifts. Liszt was called the 'Paganini of the piano' for his fabulous technique. But this virtuosity was but a means of recreating great music; Liszt held that the interpreter's duty was the revelation of the composer's innermost intention. The spiritual affinity that he felt for Beethoven moved him to superlative interpretation of Beethoven's piano sonatas; but he was also capable of rendering the intimate art of Chopin, whose close friend he was. Still, Liszt was a man of the world, a practical musician who was willing to give to his public what was expected of him; on the stage he was often an actor; he did not disdain the spectacular accoutrements of his calling. He wore white gloves, as was the custom of the day, and took them off with a grand gesture in front of the public; at some concerts he had 2 pianos on the stage, and played a group of pieces on each one in alternation, so that his hands could be seen from every side of the audience. He included in some of his programs free improvisations on themes offered by musical amateurs present in the audience; his flamboyant arrangements of popular operas were also concessions to prevalent musical tastes. It was Liszt who popularized the term 'recital,' which suited his programs so well the word was used for the first time in an advertisement for Liszt's concert in London in 1840.

Liszt's achievement as a composer is of revolutionary significance. Apart from the creation of the symphonic poem, he introduced a new conception of harmony and melody that presaged the development of modern music in the 20th century. He was allied with Wagner in the movement that was called, both in derision and admiration, 'Zukunftsmusik,' the music of the future. The term applied mainly to a mystical synthesis of the arts, which for Liszt meant the adoption of a programmatic design in the music, and liberation from the rules of prescribed musical form. In the last years of his life, Liszt experimented with new melodic progressions (including the whole-tone scale) and with harmonic combinations in which the dissonant notes, produced by suspensions, with long-delayed resolutions created an impression of atonality (in the melodic line) and polytonality (in harmony). Liszt defied tradition when he boldly opened his *Faust Symphony* with a theme consisting of 4 arpeggiated, chromatically descending, augmented triads, aggregating to 12 different notes. In his orchestration, he summoned huge sonorities by using a large orchestra; but in this he followed the precedent established by Berlioz. It was this overwhelming volume of sound that outraged the music critics of Liszt's day and moved them to denounce Liszt as a purveyor of infernal noise. But Liszt was also capable of writing lyric music of the utmost Romantic subtlety; his songs are on a par with the best 19th-century lieder; his piano pieces, such as the eternal favorite *Liebestraum,* distill the poetic quality suggested by the literary program, to the finest gradation of sentiment. His B-minor piano sonata alters the conception of the form; in place of an orderly succession of themes, Liszt adopts here an association of motifs, transforming the work into a musical poem. His 3 albums of *Années de Pèlerinage* for piano are tone paintings, approaching an Impressionistic style of evocation. For the virtuoso pianist, Liszt wrote his *Études d'exécution transcendante,* the *Mephisto-Waltz,* the 2 piano concertos, the brilliant *Hungarian Rhapsodies,* and the many transcriptions of lieder by Schubert and Schumann, Polish songs by Chopin, and numerous paraphrases of portions of operas by Auber, Donizetti, Gounod, Meyerbeer, Rossini, Verdi, and Wagner.

WORKS: For orch.: the symphonic poems (all conducted for the first time by Liszt himself, except when otherwise noted): *Ce qu'on entend sur la montagne,* after Victor Hugo (Weimar, Jan. 7, 1857), *Tasso, Lamento e Trionfo* (Weimar, Aug. 28, 1849; revised version, Weimar, April 19, 1854), *Les Préludes,* after Lamartine's 'Méditations poétiques' (Weimar, Feb. 23, 1854), *Orpheus* (Weimar, Feb. 16, 1854), *Prometheus* (Weimar, Aug. 24, 1850), *Mazeppa,* after Victor Hugo (Weimar, April 16, 1854), *Festklänge* (Weimar, Nov. 9, 1854), *Héroïde funèbre* (sketched in 1830 as *Symphonie révolutionnaire;* revised and orchestrated in 1850; first performance, Breslau, Nov. 10, 1857; Moritz Schön conducting), *Hungaria* (sketched in 1848; revised in 1856; first performance, Budapest, Sept. 8, 1856), *Hamlet* (1858; Sondershausen, July 2, 1876; Max Erdmannsdörfer conducting), *Hunnenschlacht,* after Kaulbach's painting (Weimar, Dec. 29, 1857), and *Die Ideale,* after Schiller (Weimar, Sept. 5, 1857); *Eine Faust-Symphonie,* in 3 characteristic pictures, after Goethe, with a choral finale (Weimar, Sept. 5, 1857); a *Symphony* to Dante's 'Divina Commedia,' with a female chorus (Dresden, Nov. 7, 1867); *2 Episodes* from Lenau's 'Faust' (1860-61); 2 *Mephisto Waltzes* (1860; 1880); *Trois Odes funèbres,* with male chorus (1860-66); *Salve Polonia* (1863); *Festival March* for Goethe's jubilee (1849); for piano and orch.: Concerto No. 1, in E♭ major (the 'Triangle Concerto'; so nicknamed because of the prominent use of a triangle solo; 1849; revised 1853; Weimar, Feb. 16, 1855; Berlioz conducting, Liszt at the piano), Concerto No. 2, in A major (1848; revised 1856-61; Weimar, Jan. 7, 1857, Hans von Bronsart at the piano), *Fantasie* on motifs from Beethoven's *Ruins of Athens* (Budapest, June 1, 1853), *Totentanz,* paraphrase on 'Dies irae' (1849; revised 1853-59; first performance, The Hague, April 15, 1865, Hans von Bülow soloist). For piano solo: *Album d'un Voyageur* (3 books); *3 Apparitions; Rondo sur un thème espagnol (El Contrabandista); Napolitana; Rhapsodie espagnole* (arranged for piano and orch. by Busoni); *3 Études de concert; 2 Études de concert (Waldesrauschen, Gnomenreigen); Harmonies poétiques et religeuses* (10 pieces); *Liebesträume* (3 nocturnes; originally they were songs); *3 Sonetti del Petrarca; Valse Impromptu; Mazurka brillante; 2 Polonaises; Scherzo and March; Grand Solo de concert* (also for 2 pianos); *Grand Galop chromatique; 12 Grandes Études* (originally publ. as *Études en forme de douze exercises pour piano*); *Ab irato, étude de perfectionnement;* Sonata in B minor (1854); *Berceuse; 2 Ballades; 3 Valses-Caprices; 6 Consolations; 20 Hungarian Rhapsodies* (No. 3 is the *Héroïde funèbre;* No. 9, the *Carnaval de Pest;* No. 15 the *Rákoczy March;* No. 20 is unpubl.; MS in the Liszt Museum at Weimar); *3 Airs Suisses; Années de pèlerinage* (3 series; contains such famous pieces as *Au bord d'une source, Venezia e Napoli,* and *Les Jeux d'eau à la Villa d'Este;* Book I is a revised version of Book I of the *Album d'un Voyageur); Ave Maria; 3 Élégies; 12 Études d'exécution transcendante;* 6 *Consolations; Mephisto-Waltz* (originally for orch.; 3 versions for piano solo; MS of No. 3 in the Liszt Museum at Weimar); *Via Crucis; Epithalamium; Bülow March; 3 Valses oubliées; Valse élégiaque; Weinachtsbaum* (12 pieces); *Mosonyi's Grabgeleit; Mephisto-Polka; Impromptu* in F♯; *2 Légendes: St. François d'Assise prédicant aux oiseaux, St. François de Paule marchant sur les flots; La lugubre gondole; Heroischer Marsch im ungarischen Stil; 2 Arabesques; Czardas obstiné; Czardas macabre; Hymne du Pape; 7 Ungarische Bildnisse; Rhapsody, nach Siebenbürgischen und Walachischen Motiven; Phantasy and Fugue on B-A-C-H;* Variations on a theme from Bach's B minor Mass; Variations on Bach's prelude, *Weinen, Klagen; Technische Studien* (12 books); transcriptions of Beethoven's symphonies, of Berlioz's *Symphonie fantastique, Harold en Italie,* and overtures to *Les Francs-juges* and *King Lear,* of Wagner's overture to *Tannhäuser,* of 6 of Chopin's *Chants polonais,* of 10 songs by Robert Franz, 7 songs by Mendelssohn, songs from several cycles by Schubert *(Schwanengesang, Winterreise, Geistliche Lieder, Müllerlieder,* also *Die Forelle,* etc.), Schumann's *Liebeslied,* and other songs, etc. Vocal works: *Missa solemnis* (the *Gran* Festival Mass); Hungarian Coronation Mass; Mass in C minor with organ; *Missa choralis* in A minor with organ; Requiem; 3 oratorios: *Die Legende von der Heiligen Elisabeth, Christus,* and *Stanislaus* (unfinished); 9 choruses with organ; *Die Seligkeiten,* for baritone solo, chorus, and organ; *Pater noster,* for mixed chorus and organ; *Pater noster* and *Ave Maria,* for men's voices and organ; *Psalm 13,* for tenor solo, chorus, orch.; *Psalm 18,* for men's chorus, orch., and organ; *Psalm 23,* for tenor (or soprano) solo, with harp (or piano) and organ (or harmonium); *Psalm 116,* for soli, men's (or mixed) chorus, organ, and orch.; *Psalm 137,* for solo, women's chorus, violin, harp, piano, and organ; *Christus ist geboren,* for chorus with organ; *An den heiligen Franziskus,* for men's voices, organ, trombones, and drums; *Les Morts,* for men's chorus and orch.; numerous minor sacred compositions; the cantatas *Die Glocken des Strassburger Münsters, Die heilige Cäcile, An die Künstler* (for soli, men's chorus, and orch.), *Hungaria* (for soli, mixed chorus, and orch.; has nothing in common with the symph. poem bearing the same title; score lost for many years, discovered by P. Raabe in 1912); *Zur Säcular-Feier Beethovens; Festalbum* (for Goethe's 100th birthday); *Festchor* (for the unveiling of the Herder monument, Weimar, 1850); numerous 4-part men's choruses *(Das Lied der Begeisterung; Weimars Volkslied; Was ist das Deutsche Vaterland?* with piano; *Festgesang,* with organ); about 60 songs with piano, many strikingly beautiful *(Du bist wie eine Blume, Es muss ein wunderbares sein, Die Macht der Musik, Jeanne d'Arc au bûcher).*—Publications: *De la fondation Goethe* ('Goethe-stiftung') *à Weimar* (1851); *Lohengrin et Tannhäuser de Richard Wagner* (1851; also in German); *Frédéric Chopin* (1852; 2nd ed., in French, Leipzig, 1879; in English, 1901); *Über Fields Notturnos* (1859); *Des Bohémiens et de leur musique en Hongrie* (French, 1859; also Hungarian, German; in English as *The Gypsy in Music); Robert Franz* (1872); *Keine Zwischenaktmusik mehr* (1879). His 'Gesammelte Schriften' were ed. by Lina Ramann and publ. in 6 vols. (Leipzig, 1880-83); also a selection as 'Volksausgabe' (4 vols., Leipzig, 1910); J. Kapp publ. an *Allgemeine Inhaltsübersicht* with full indices (1910). —BIBLIOGRAPHY: BIOGRAPHY: J. W. Christern, *Franz Liszt* (Hamburg, 1841); Lina Ramann, *Franz Liszt als Künstler und Mensch* (3 vols., Leipzig, 1880-94; English transl. of vol. 1, London, 1882); R. Pohl, *Franz Liszt: Studien und Erinnerungen* (Leipzig 1883); L. Nohl, *Liszt* (Leipzig, 1884; Part 2 by A. Göllerich, 1887; English transl., Chicago, 1887); T. C. Martin, *Franz Liszt* (London, 1886); E. Reuss, *Franz Liszt* (Dresden, 1898); R. Louis, *Franz Liszt* (Berlin, 1900); M.-D. Calvocoressi, *Franz Liszt* (Paris, 1905; English transl., in the 'Musical Observer,' N. Y., 1910-11); A. Göllerich, *Franz Liszt* (Berlin, 1908); J. Kapp, *Franz Liszt, Eine Biographie* (Berlin, 1909; 20th ed., 1924; a standard biography); A. W. Gottschalg, *Franz Liszt in Weimar und seine letzten Lebensjahre* (publ. posthumously, 1910); J. Chantavoine, *Liszt* (Paris, 1910; 5th ed., 1928); R. Ledos de Beaufort, *Franz Liszt: The Story of His Life* (Boston, 1910; with a list of works and pupils); A. Hervey, *Franz Liszt and His Music* (London, 1911); J. G. Huneker, *Franz Liszt* (N. Y., 1911; in German, Munich, 1922); Sir. A. Mackenzie, *Liszt* (London, 1913); B. Schrader, *Franz Liszt* (Leipzig, 1914); K. Grunsky, *Franz Liszt* (Leipzig, 1924); R. Wetz, *Franz Liszt* (Leipzig, 1925); F. Corder, *Liszt* (London, 1925; new ed., 1933); Guy de Pourtalès, *La vie de Franz Liszt* (Paris, 1926; also in English, N. Y., 1926); C. van Wessem, *Franz Liszt* (The Hague, 1927); P. Raabe, *Franz*

Liszt (2 vols., Stuttgart and Berlin, 1931); Sacheverell Sitwell, *Liszt* (London, 1934; revised, 1955); R. Bory, *Liszt et ses enfants: Blandine, Cosima et Daniel* (Paris, 1936); R. Bory, *La Vie de Franz Liszt par l'image* (Geneva, 1936); A. de Hevésy, *Liszt, ou de roi Lear de la musique* (Paris, 1936); R. Hill, *Liszt* (London, 1936); H. Engel, *Liszt* (Potsdam, 1936); Blandine Ollivier, *Liszt, le musicien passionné* (Paris, 1936); Z. Harsányi, *Magyar Rapszódia: Franz Liszt* (Budapest, 1936; in English, publ. in London, 1936, as *Hungarian Melody,* and in N. Y., 1937, as *Immortal Franz);* E. von Liszt, *Franz Liszt* (Vienna, 1937; family documents, etc.); M. Tibaldi Chiesa, *Vita romantica di Liszt* (Milan, 1937); C. Aragonnès, *Marie d'Agoult: une destinée romantique* (Paris, 1938); P. Raabe, *Wege zu Liszt* (Regensburg, 1943); Y. Milstein, *Liszt* (Moscow, 1956); see also the Liszt issue of the 'Mus. Quarterly' (July, 1936). —APPRECIATION, CRITICISM: W. Lenz, *Die grossen Pianoforte Virtuosen unserer Zeit* (Berlin, 1872; English transl., N. Y., 1899); L. Nohl, *Beethoven, Liszt, Wagner* (Vienna, 1874); R. Wagner, *Über Franz Liszts Symphonische Dichtungen,* in 'Gesammelte Schriften und Dichtungen' (vol. 5; Leipzig, 1883); Otto Lessmann, *Franz Liszt: eine Huldigung* (in German and English; N. Y., 1883); B. Vogel, *Franz Liszt als Lyriker* (Leipzig, 1887); A. Habets, *A. Borodin et Franz Liszt* (Paris, 1893; English transl., London, 1895); O. Bie, *Das Klavier und seine Meister* (Munich, 1898); A. O. von Pozsony, *Liszt und Hans von Bülow* (Munich, 1900); E. Segnitz, *Franz Liszt und Rom* (Leipzig, 1901); H. Gerstenberg, *Aus Weimars nachklassischer Zeit* (Hamburg, 1901); E. O. Nodnagel, *Jenseits von Wagner und Liszt* (Königsberg, 1902); La Mara, *Aus der Glanzzeit der Weimarer Altenburg* (Leipzig, 1906); F. H. Clark, *Liszts Offenbarung: Schlüssel zur Freiheit des Individuums* (Berlin, 1907); J. Kapp, *Richard Wagner und Franz Liszt: Eine Freundschaft* (Berlin, 1908); J. Kapp, *Liszt Brevier* (Berlin, 1910); J. Kapp, *Franz Liszt und die Frauen* (Berlin, 1911); La Mara, *Liszt und die Frauen* (Leipzig, 1911); A. de Angelis, *Franz Liszt a Roma* (Turin, 1911); A. Kohut, *Franz Liszt in seinen Wirken als Mensch und als Tonkünstler* (Leipzig, 1911); E. Reuss, *Franz Liszt in seinen Briefen* (Stuttgart, 1911); A. von Schorn, *Das nachklassische Weimar unter der Regierungszeit Karl Friedrichs und Maria Paulownas* (Weimar, 1911); E. Segnitz, *Liszts Kirchenmusik* (Langensalza, 1911); Cosima Wagner, *Franz Liszt: Ein Gedenkblatt von seiner Tochter* (Munich, 1911); F. Barberio, *Liszt e la principessa de Sayn-Wittgenstein* (Rome, 1912); A. von Schorn, *Zwei Menschenalter, Erinnerungen und Briefe aus Weimar und Rom* (Stuttgart, 1913); E. Hughes, *Liszt as a Lieder Composer,* in the 'Mus. Quarterly' (April, 1917); O. G. Sonneck, *Liszt's 'Huldigungsmarsch' and Weimar's Volkslied,* in the 'Mus. Quarterly' (Jan., 1918); Marie d'Agoult, *Erinnerungen an Franz Liszt* (ed. by Siegfried Wagner; 2 vols., 1928); C. Boissier, *Liszt pédagogue* (Paris, 1928); J. Heinrichs, *Über den Sinn der Lisztschen Programmmusik* (Kempen, 1929); H. Arminski, *Die ungarischen Fantasien von Franz Liszt* (Vienna, 1929); T. Weber, *Die symphonischen Dichtungen Liszts* (Vienna, 1929); E. Major, *Liszt's Hungarian Rhapsodies* (in Hungarian; Budapest, 1929); A. Stradal, *Erinnerungen an Franz Liszt* (Bern, 1929); M. Herwegh, *Au banquet des dieux: Franz Liszt, Richard Wagner et leurs amis* (Paris, 1931); J. Bergfeld, *Die formale Struktur der symphonischen Dichtungen Franz Liszts* (Eisenach, 1931); Z. Gárdonyi, *Die ungarischen Stileigentümlichkeiten in den musikalischen Werken Franz Liszts* (Berlin, 1931); K. Isóz, *Liszt and Budapest* (in Hungarian; Budapest, 1931); H. Dobiey, *Die Klaviertechnik des jungen Liszt* (Berlin, 1931); I. Philipp, *La Technique de Liszt* (2 vols.; Paris, 1932); B. Kellermann, *Erinnerungen an Franz Liszt* (1932); R. Kokai, *Franz Liszt in seinen frühen Klavierwerken* (Leipzig, 1933); E. Newman, *The Man Liszt: A Study of the Tragi-Comedy of a Soul Divided against Itself* (London, 1934); H. Westerby, *Liszt the Composer and His Piano Works* (London, 1936); G. Falk, *Liszt Breviarium* (in Hungarian; Budapest, 1936); E. Haraszti, *Franz Liszt — Author Despite Himself,* in the 'Mus. Quarterly' (Oct., 1947); H. Searle, *The Music of Liszt* (London, 1954); E. N. Waters, *Liszt and Longfellow,* in the 'Mus. Quarterly' (Jan., 1955). —CORRESPONDENCE: *Briefwechsel zwischen Wagner und Liszt* (2 vols.; Leipzig, 1887, 2nd ed., 1900; English transl., London, 1888; 2nd ed., 1897, with index; these 2 eds. contain only the letters from 1841-61, and many passages referring to persons still living at the time of publication were omitted; in the 3rd ed., prepared by Erich Kloss in 1910, all letters up to Wagner's death are included, and the omitted portions restored); La Mara, *Franz Liszts Briefe* (8 vols.; Leipzig, 1893-1905; about 2,500 letters in the original French or German; those to Carolyne Sayn-Wittgenstein, in vols. 4-7, all in French); C. Bache, *Letters of Franz Liszt* (2 vols.; London, 1894; in English transl.);

La Mara, *Briefwechsel zwischen Franz Liszt und Hans von Bülow* (Leipzig, 1898); R. von Seydlitz, *Ungedruckte Originalbriefe des Meisters an G. Freiherrn von Seydlitz* (Dresden, 1902); A. Stern, *Franz Liszts Briefe an Karl Gille* (Leipzig, 1903); La Mara, *Franz Liszt et Charles-Alexandre, grand-duc de Saxe: Correspondance* (Leipzig, 1909); C. A. René, 48 letters to A. W. Gottschalg, in *Franz Liszt in Weimar und seine letzten Lebensjahre* (1910); W. von Csapó, *Franz Liszts Briefe an Baron Anton Augusz, 1846-1878* (Budapest, 1911); N. de Gutmannsthal, *Souvenirs de Franz Liszt: Lettres inédites* (Leipzig, 1913); K. von Schlözer, *Römische Briefe, 1864-69* (Stuttgart, 1913); P. Raabe, *Briefwechsel zwischen Franz Liszt und dem Grossherzog Karl Alexander von Sachsen* (1918); A. Orel, *Briefe Liszts* (Vienna, 1930); correspondence with Mme. d'Agoult (in French), publ. by Daniel Ollivier, 1st series, 1833-40 (1933), 2nd series, 1840-64 (1934); correspondence with Liszt's daughter, Blandine, publ. by Ollivier, in 'Revue des Deux Mondes' (Dec. 15, 1935; Jan. 1, 1936); *The Letters of Franz Liszt to Marie Sayn-Wittgenstein,* ed. by H. E. Hugo (N.Y., 1953). See also La Mara, *Briefe hervorragender Zeitgenossen an Franz Liszt* (3 vols.; Leipzig, 1895-1904). —GUIDES, CATALOGUES, etc.: Separate analyses of all the larger works, including the oratorios, Masses, and psalms, are found in H. Kretzschmar's *Führer durch den Konzertsaal* (3 vols.; Leipzig, 1887; 4th ed., 1913); in Breitkopf & Härtel's 'Kleiner Konzertführer' (Leipzig), Schlesinger's 'Der Musikführer' and 'Meisterführer' (Berlin). Vol. 2 of Peter Raabe's biography (1931) includes a complete catalogue of works — Thematic catalogues of Liszt's works were publ. by Breitkopf & Härtel in 1855 and 1876; a complete catalogue of the publ. works by A. Göllerich appeared in the 'Neue Zeitschrift für Musik' (1887-88); a *Chronologisch-systematisches Verzeichnis* by L. Friwitzer was publ. in the 'Wiener musikalische Chronik' (Nov., 1887-March, 1888); see also H. Engel, *Das Klavierkonzert* (1932; p. 336 *et seq.);* W. Rüsch, *Liszts Années de Pèlerinage* (Zürich, 1932); L. Koch, *Liszt Bibliography* (Budapest, 1936; in Hungarian and German); A. Mirus, *Das Liszt-Museum zu Weimar und seine Erinnerungen* (Leipzig, 1887; 3rd ed., 1902). —A pictorial biography of Liszt was publ. by W. Füssmann and Béla Mátéka, as *Franz Liszt. Ein Künstlerleben in Wort und Bild* (Berlin, 1936).

Litaize, Gaston, French composer and organist; b. Ménil-sur-Belvitte, Aug. 11, 1909. He was blind from infancy; studied at the National Institute of the Blind; also at the Paris Cons.; won 2nd Prix de Rome (unprecedented for a blind person); was appointed organist at the church of St.-François Xavier, Paris; also on the staff of the National Institute of the Blind. In the autumn of 1957 he made his 1st American tour as concert organist. His works include the cantata *Fra Angelico* (1936); several Masses; other church music; many organ pieces.

Literes (lē-tā'-rēs) **Carrión, Antonio,** Spanish composer; b. Arta, Majorca, c. 1670; d. Madrid, Jan. 18, 1747. He was a composer and cello player under Charles II, Philip V, and Ferdinand VI. In 1693 he was appointed to the royal chapel as violinist. After the fire at the old Alcazar in Madrid on Christmas Eve, 1734, Literes and Nebra were charged with the reconstruction of musical MSS that were damaged or completely burned. They also wrote new music for church services to replace the material destroyed. Literes composed excellent church music (14 Psalms, 8 Magnificats, etc.); some of his sacred works are reprinted in Eslava's 'Lira Sacro-Hispana'; also wrote an opera, *Los Elementos,* and a zarzuela, *Accis y Galatea* (1709). His son **Antonio Literes Montalbo** (d. Madrid, Dec. 2, 1768), was a composer and organist under Ferdinand VI. —Cf. N. A. Solar Quintes, *Antonio Literes Carrión y sus hijos,* in vol. 5 of 'Anuario Musical' (Barcelona, 1950); also F. Pedrell, *Teatro Lírico Español* (vols. 2 and 4); J. Nin, *Classiques espagnols du chant* (Paris, 1926).

Litolff, Henry Charles, pianist, composer, and publisher; b. London (of an Alsatian father and English mother), Feb. 6, 1818; d. Bois-le-Combes, near Paris, Aug. 6, 1891. A precocious pianist, he studied with Moscheles; made his professional début in London on July 24, 1832, at the age of 14. An early marriage (at 17) forced him to seek a livelihood in Paris, where he attracted attention by his brilliant concerts; then he became an itinerant musician, traveling in Poland, Germany, and Holland; was in Vienna during the Revolution of 1848, and became involved, so that he was compelled to flee. He then settled in Brunswick; after the termination of his first marriage, he married the widow of the music publisher Meyer, acquiring the business. Litolff was one of the pioneers in the publication of cheap editions of classical music (Collections

Litolff). In 1860 he turned over the firm to his adopted son Theodor Litolff (1839-1912). Then he went to Paris, marrying for a third time (Comtesse de Larochefoucauld); after her death (1870) he married once more. Besides his business pursuits, he was a prolific composer; 115 of his works were publ.; of these, the most famous is the overture *Robespierre* (Paris, Feb. 2, 1870), which carries the idea of programmatic music to its utmost limit, with a vivid description of Robespierre's execution (drum beats, etc.). —Other works: the operas *Die Braut von Kynast* (Brunswick, 1847), *Les Templiers* (Brussels, Jan. 25, 1886); *Héloïse et Abélard* (Paris, Oct. 17, 1872); oratorio *Ruth et Booz* (1869); *Szenen aus Goethes Faust,* for soli, chorus, and orch.; 4 *Concertos-symphonies* for piano and orch.; the *Eroica* violin concerto; a funeral march for Meyerbeer; 3 piano trios; 6 *Études de concert* for piano; many character pieces for piano, of which *Chant de la Fileuse* became popular. —Cf. H. Berlioz, *Les Musiciens et la Musique* (Paris, 1878); P. Magnette, *Litolff* (Paris, 1914).

Litta, Giulio, Italian composer; b. Milan, 1822; d. Vedano, near Monza, May 29, 1891. A composer of precocious talent and excellent training, he produced an opera at 20, *Bianca di Santafiora* (Milan, Jan. 2, 1843), followed by 6 more operas: *Sardanapalo* (Milan, Sept. 2, 1844); *Maria Giovanna* (Turin, Oct. 28, 1851); *Edita di Lorno* (Genoa, June 1, 1853); *Il Viandante* (Milan, April 17, 1873); *Raggio d'amore* (Milan, April 6, 1879), and *Il Violino di Cremona* (Milan, April 18, 1882). He also wrote an oratorio, *La Passione;* church music; songs.

Litvinne, Félia (real name Françoise-Jeanne Schütz), Russian soprano; b. St. Petersburg, 1861; d. Paris, Oct. 12, 1936. She studied in Paris with Mme. Barth-Banderoli and Victor Maurel; made her début there in 1885 at the Théâtre des Italiens; then sang at the Academy of Music, N.Y., with Mapleson's company; made successful appearances in St. Petersburg, Moscow, and in Italy; returned to Paris, where she became a favorite in Wagnerian roles, at first in concert excerpts that Lamoureux was then introducing, later at the Wagner performances given by Cortot at the Château d'Eau (1902); then sang at the Opéra-Comique and the Théâtre Lyrique de la Gaîté, at Monte Carlo, at La Scala, Covent Garden, the Metropolitan Opera House; made a tour of South America. In 1927 she was appointed prof. of singing at the American Cons. of Fontainebleau. She publ. her memoirs, *Ma vie et mon art* (Paris, 1933).

Litzau, Johannes Barend, Dutch organist and composer; b. Rotterdam, Sept. 9, 1822; d. there, July 18, 1893. He studied with J. B. Bremer and B. Tours; in 1855, succeeded Bremer as organist of the Lutheran church in Rotterdam. He founded an organ school and wrote a number of organ works in the Classical style: 3 organ sonatas; *Konzertsatz im strengen Stil mit 4 Subjekten,* etc.; also a cantata, *Sneeuw-vermaak.*

Litzmann, Berthold, German writer on music; b. Kiel, April 18, 1857; d. Munich, Oct. 13, 1926. He wrote an exhaustive biography, *Klara Schumann, ein Künstlerleben, nach Tagebüchern und Briefen* (3 vols., Leipzig, 1902-10; English transl., 1913); also prepared for publication the correspondence between Brahms and Clara Schumann (2 vols., Leipzig, 1927; English transl., N.Y., 1927).

Liuzzi, Fernando, Italian composer and musicologist; b. Senigallia, Dec. 19, 1884; d. Florence, Oct. 6, 1940. He studied in Bologna with Fano, and at the Liceo di S. Cecilia in Rome; then went to Munich, where he studied with Mottl and Reger; also at the Cons. of Parma, winning the composition prize (1908); Dr. phil., Univ. of Bologna (1909); taught at the Cons. of Parma (1910-17), the Royal Cons. of San Pietro a Majella, Naples (1912-14), the Cons. 'Luigi Cherubini,' Florence (1917-23), Univ. of Florence, Royal Italian Univ. of Perugia, Royal Univ. in Rome (1926-38). —Works: the operetta *L'Augellin bel verde* (Rome, 1917); *Le Vergini Savie e le Vergini Folli (The Wise and the Foolish Virgins),* a liturgical drama transcribed and rearranged for soli, chorus, and orch. from a French MS of the 12th century (Florence, 1930); *La Passione,* for soli, chorus, and orch., based on religious melodies of the 13th century (1930); scenic rearrangement with orchestral intermezzi of Vecchi's *L'Amfiparnaso* (Florence, 1930); orchestral transcription and completion of A. Gabrieli's 'cori' for Sophocles' *Oedipus Rex; Hyla,* symph. poem; *Gaiola e Marechiaro,* Neapolitan rhapsody for orch.; violin sonata; *Sonata-fantasia* for violin and organ; songs; etc. —Writings: *Estetica della musica* (Florence, 1924); *Essenza dell' arte e valore estetico nel pensiero di T. Lipps* (Bologna, 1924); *La Lauda e i primordi della melodia Italiana* (2 vols. of facsimiles and transcriptions of medieval Italian music; Rome, 1935); *Musicisti Italiani in Francia; Classicità del Palestrina e romanticismo fiammingo,* in 'Nuova antologia' (Rome, 1926); etc. —Cf. E. T. Ferand, *In Memoriam: Fernando Liuzzi,* in the 'Mus. Quarterly' (Oct., 1942).

Liverati, Giovanni, Italian composer; b. Bologna, March 27, 1772; date and place of death unknown. He studied voice, and was engaged as a tenor in Spain; in 1796 he traveled with an Italian opera company in Germany; then turned to composition, and wrote various operas for traveling troupes. He was in Stockholm in 1803, in Paris in 1808, in Vienna in 1811, in London in 1815; he remained in London until about 1845, but probably traveled again on the Continent before that. —Operas: *La prova mancata* (1801), *Enea in Cartagine* (1809), *I selvaggi* (London, June 27, 1815), *Gastone e Bajardo* (London, Feb. 26, 1820); he also wrote an oratorio, *David* (1811), and contributed a setting of *In questa tomba oscura* to Mollo's collection (1808), which includes also the famous Beethoven setting of these words.

Liviabella, Lino, Italian composer; b. Macerata, April 7, 1902. He studied with Respighi at the Santa Cecilia Academy in Rome; then settled in Bologna, where he taught at the Martini Cons. —Works: *L'Usignola e la Rosa,* for chamber orch. (1926); *I canti dell' amore,* triptych for string orch. (1929); *Suite per una fiaba,* for orch. (1933); *Il Vincitore,* written for the Berlin Olympiad (1936); *Il poeta e sua moglia,* for orch. (1938); *La mia terra,* for orch. (1942); the oratorios, *Sorella Chiara* (1947), *Caterina da Siena* (1949), *O Crux Ave* (1953); *Conchiglia,* dramatic musical play (1955); 3 violin sonatas; a string quartet; songs.

Ljungberg (lyoong'-berg), **Göta (Albertina),** Swedish soprano; b. Sundsval, Oct. 4, 1893; d. Lidingö, near Stockholm, June 28, 1955. She studied at the Royal Academy of Music and the Royal Opera School in Stockholm; also privately in Berlin; in 1920, made her début (as Elsa) at the Royal Stockholm Opera; appeared in London, in the title role of *Judith* by Goossens (1925); then sang at the Strauss Festival in Mannheim, etc.; American début at the Metropolitan Opera, N.Y., on Jan. 20, 1932; remained on the roster until 1935; created the role of Lady Marigold Sandys in Hanson's *Merry Mount.* After World War II, she lived in N.Y. as voice teacher; then returned to Sweden.

Llobet (lyoh'-bĕt), **Miguel,** famous Catalan guitar virtuoso; b. Barcelona, Oct. 18, 1875; d. there, Feb. 22, 1938. He began his career as a painter; then turned to music and studied with Tarrega; lived in Paris (1904-14); toured in Argentina (1910), Chile (1912), the U.S. (1915-17), and throughout Europe. Manuel de Falla composed his *Homenaje* (for the *Tombeau de Debussy)* for him, and Llobet himself made many arrangements for the guitar.

Llongueras (lyon-gā'-rahs) **y Badía, Juan,** Catalan composer; b. Barcelona, June 6, 1880; d. there, Oct. 13, 1953. He studied in Barcelona with Morera, Millet, and Granados, and with Jaques-Dalcroze in Dresden and Geneva; founded the Institut Catala de Rítmica i Plástica in Barcelona for the exposition in Spain of the Dalcroze methods; was also music critic, writer, and prof. of music education in Barcelona. His compositions include piano pieces (*La vida sencilla, L'estiu efimer,* etc.), a quantity of *Canciones y juegos infantiles* and other songs; also wrote *Les cançons de Nadal* (Catalan Christmas songs); publ. the essays, *Couperin o la gracia; Bach o el fervor; Beethoven o la Passió;* etc., also a book of reminiscences, *Evocaciones y recuerdos de mi primera vida musical en Barcelona* (Barcelona, 1944).

Lloyd, Charles Harford, English organist and composer; b. Thornbury, Gloucestershire, Oct. 16, 1849; d. Slough, Oct. 16, 1919. He attended Magdalen Hall, Oxford (Mus. Bac., 1871; B.A., 1872; M.A., 1875; Mus. Doc., 1892); 1887-92, teacher of organ and composition at the Royal College of Music; 1892, instructor at Eton College; from 1914 until his death, organist at the Chapel Royal, St. James'. —Works: cantatas *Hero and Leander* (Worcester, 1884), *The Song of Balder* (Hereford, 1885), *Andromeda* (Gloucester, 1886), *A Song of Judgment* (Hereford, 1891), *Sir Ogie and Lady Elsie* (Hereford, 1894); church music, including the anthems *Art thou weary?, Blessed is he, Fear not, O land, Give the Lord the honor,* and *A Hymn of Thanksgiving;* organ works; etc.

Lloyd, George, English composer; b. St. Ives, June 28, 1913. He was instructed by his mother in piano playing; also learned the violin; then studied composition with Harry Farjeon. He was in the Royal Marines during World War II; served in the Arctic on convoys to Russia; nearly lost his life when his ship was sunk, but was saved; in 1942 he was relieved from active duty; lived in Switzerland in 1945-46; then returned to England. —Works: the operas *Iernin* (Penzance, Nov. 6, 1934), *The Serf* (London, Oct. 20, 1938), *John Socman* (1951); 5 symphonies; etc. —Cf. H. Farjeon, *George Lloyd,* in the 'Monthly Musical Record' (June, 1939).

Lobe, Johann Christian, German flutist, writer on music, and composer; b. Weimar, May 30, 1797; d. Leipzig, July 27, 1881. He studied with A. E. Müller; played a flute solo with the Gewandhaus Orch. in Leipzig (1811); then flutist, later viola player, in the Weimar court orch. until 1842; founded a music school; 1846-48, in Leipzig as editor of the 'Allgemeine Musikzeitung'; 1853, published the periodical 'Fliegende Blätter für Musik'; music editor of 'Illustrierte Zeitung'; also contributed articles to various journals. —Works: the operas (all produced in Weimar) *Wittekind, Die Flibustier, Die Fürstin von Granada* (Sept. 28, 1833), *Der rote Domino, König und Pächter;* 2 symphonies; overtures; concertos; piano quartets; variations and solos for flute. — Writings: *Die Lehre von der thematischen Arbeit* (1846); *Lehrbuch der musikalischen Komposition* (vol. I, *Harmony,* 1850; revised by Kretzschmar, 5th ed., 1884; vol. II, *Instrumentation,* 3rd ed., 1879; vol. III, *Canon, Fugue, etc.,* 1860; vol. IV, *Opera,* 1867; revised by Kretzschmar, 1884-87); *Katechismus der Musik* (1851; 28th ed., 1904; revised by Leichtentritt, 1926; English transl., N. Y., 1896); *Musikalische Briefe eines Wohlbekannten* (1852; 2nd ed., 1860); *Fliegende Blätter für Musik* (1853-57, 3 vols.); *Aus dem Leben eines Musikers* (1859); *Vereinfachte Harmonielehre* (1861); *Katechismus der Kompositionslehre* (1872; 7th ed., 1902; English transl., N. Y., 1891); *Consonanzen und Dissonanzen* (1869). See also *Goethes Schauspieler und Musiker, Erinnerungen von Eberwein und Lobe,* edited by W. Bode (1912); and *A New Catechism of Music on the Plan of Johann Christian Lobe,* edited by O. Coon (N. Y., 1905).

Lobkowitz, Prince **Franz Joseph (Maximilian Ferdinand) von,** Austrian art patron; b. Vienna, Dec. 7, 1772; d. Wittingau, Bohemia, Dec. 15, 1816. Beethoven dedicated to him the quartets op. 18; the 3rd, 5th, and 6th symphonies; the triple concerto; the quartet op. 74; and the song-cycle *An die ferne Geliebte.*

Lobo, Duarte (also Latinized as Eduardus Lupus), Portuguese composer; b. Alcáçovas, Sept. (baptized Sept. 19), 1565; d. Lisbon, Sept. 24, 1646. He was a pupil of Manuel Mendes at Evora; served as choirmaster there before moving to Lisbon; in 1594, became master of the chapel at the Cathedral. As a composer of church music, he enjoyed considerable renown; his mastery of polyphony inspired respect, but comparisons with Victoria, Benevoli, and other great composers of his time, are exaggerations. The following works were printed in his lifetime: *Natalitiae noctis responsoria, a* 4-8; *Antiphonae, a* 8; *Salve, a* 3-11 (Antwerp, 1602); *Officium defunctorum* (Lisbon, 1603); Magnificat, *a* 4 (Antwerp, 1605); 2 books of Masses, *a* 4-8 (Antwerp, 1621 and 1639); MSS in the British Museum, the Fitzwilliam Collection in Cambridge, at the Cathedrals of Granada and Toledo. An antiphon and 2 Masses are reprinted in J. E. dos Santos, *A polifonia clássica portuguêsa* (Lisbon, 1937); 16 Magnificats for 4 voices, transcribed by M. Joaquim (Lisbon, 1945).

Locatelli, Pietro, Italian violinist and composer; b. Bergamo, Sept. 3, 1695; d. Amsterdam, March 30, 1764. He studied in Rome with Corelli; after long professional tours, he settled in Amsterdam, establishing regular public concerts, and enjoying great fame there. His technical feats, particularly in double stops, were considered marvelous at the time; by changing the tuning of his violin, he produced apparently impossible effects; Paganini is said to have profited by Locatelli's innovations.—Works: 12 *Concerti grossi* (Amsterdam, 1721); flute sonatas with bass (Amsterdam, 1732); *L'arte del violino,* containing 12 concertos and 24 caprices for 2 violins, viola, cello, and continuo (1733); 6 *Introduzioni teatrali* and 6 concertos (1735); 6 *Sonates en trio* (1737); 6 sonatas for solo violin (1737); 6 *Concerti a quattro* (1741); trios for 2 violins and bass (1741); *L'arte di nuova modulazione: caprices énigmatiques; Contrasto armonico: concerto a quattro.* Some of Locatelli's works appeared in modern editions: 6 sonatas for solo violin; a few pieces in Alard's and David's methods; a theme with variations in Schering's 'Alt-Meister des Violinspiels'; a 'Tragic Symphony,' also publ. by Schering; 2 trio sonatas, publ. by Moffat, etc. —Cf. J. W. von Wasielewski, *Die Violine und ihre Meister* (1920); C. Vanbianchi, *Un celebre violinista bergamasco percursore di Nicolo Paganini,* in 'Bolletino della Civica Biblioteca di Bergamo' (May, 1920); A.

Schering, *Geschichte des Instrumental-Konzerts* (1927); A. Moser, *Geschichte des Violinspiels* (1923; pp. 224 ff.); M. Pincherle, *Les Violinistes* (Paris, 1924); A. Koole, *Leven en Werken van Pietro Locatelli* (Amsterdam, 1949).

Locke, Matthew, English composer; b. Exeter, c. 1630; d. London, Aug., 1677. He was a chorister in Exeter Cathedral, studying under Edward Gibbons and William Wake; then was composer to Charles II (1661); became a Roman Catholic, and was appointed organist to Queen Catherine. Prominent among English composers of his era, he wrote music to *The Tempest* and *Macbeth,* and to Shadwell's *Psyche* (London, March 9, 1675); to Shirley's masque *Cupid and Death* and Stapleton's comedy *The Stepmother;* also 6 suites, anthems, etc.; the first English work on thorough-bass, *Melothesia, or Certain General Rules for Playing Upon A Continued Bass* (1673); and pamphlets versus Salmon's attempt at reducing music notation to one universal character. P. Warlock and A. Mangeot published 6 *Consorts a 4* (London, 1932). The music for *The Tempest* and *Psyche* were publ. in 1675 as *The English Opera.* —Cf. J. Pulver, *A Biographical Dictionary of Old English Music* (1927).

Lockspeiser, Edward, English writer on music; b. London, May 21, 1905. He was a student of Alexandre Tansman and Nadia Boulanger in Paris; then attended the classes of C. H. Kitson and Malcolm Sargent at the Royal College of Music in London. From 1936-38 he contributed music criticism to the 'Yorkshire Post' and from 1938 to 'Musical America.' He publ. several valuable monographs: *Debussy* (London, 1936; revised ed., 1951); *Berlioz* (1940); *Bizet* (1947); translated into English *A New History of Music* by Prunières (London, 1943) with many emendations and additions.

Lockwood, Normand, American composer; b. New York, March 19, 1906. He studied at the Univ. of Michigan School of Music; then with Respighi in Rome (1925-26) and Nadia Boulanger in Paris (1926-28); 1930, was awarded a fellowship of the American Academy in Rome; 1932-43, instructor at Oberlin, Ohio, Cons.; 1943-45, holder of a Guggenheim Fellowship; 1945-53, lecturer at Columbia Univ.; then at Trinity Univ., San Antonio, Texas (1953-55); in 1955 he joined the faculty of the Univ. of Wyoming, at Laramie. In 1938 he won a $500 prize offered by G. Schirmer, Inc., with his choral work *Out of the Cradle Endlessly Rocking* (after Walt Whitman), for mixed high-school voices. —Works: opera *Scarecrow* (Columbia Univ., N.Y., May 19, 1945); a symphony (1941); *Mary Who Stood in Sorrow,* for soprano and orch. (1946); *Moby Dick,* for small orch. (1946); sonata for 3 cellos (1934); *Dichromatic Variation* for piano solo (1935); 6 string quartets (1937); piano quintet (1940); trio for flute, viola, and harp (1940); *3 Numbers for Woodwind Quartet* (1940); piano sonata (1944); *Serenades* for string quartet (1945); many choral works: *The Birth of Moses,* for women's chorus, flute, and piano; *How Far Is It to Bethlehem; Psalm 114,* for mixed chorus and orch.; *Two Sea Shanties,* etc.; also 4 songs from James Joyce's 'Chamber Music' for medium voice and string quartet (N. Y., March 28, 1948); oratorio, *Children of God* (Cincinnati, Feb. 1, 1957). —Cf. American Composers Alliance 'Bulletin' (No. 4, 1957).

Loeffler, Charles Martin (Tornow), outstanding American composer; b. Mulhouse, Alsace, Jan. 30, 1861; d. Medfield, Mass., May 19, 1935. His father was a writer, who sometimes used the nom de plume Tornow, which Loeffler later added to his name. When he was a child, the family moved to Russia, where his father was engaged in government work in the Kiev district; later they lived in Debreczin in Hungary, and in Switzerland. In 1875 Loeffler began taking violin lessons in Berlin with Rappoldi, who prepared him for study with Joachim; he studied harmony with Kiel; also took lessons with Bargiel. He then went to Paris, where he continued his musical education with Massart (violin) and Guiraud (composition). He was engaged briefly as violinist in the Pasdeloup Orch.; then was a member of the private orch. of the Russian Baron Paul von Derwies, at his sumptuous residences near Lugano and in Nice (1879-81). When Derwies died in 1881, Loeffler went to America, with letters of recommendation from Joachim. He played in the orch. of Leopold Damrosch in N.Y. In 1882 he became 2nd concertmaster of the newly organized Boston Symph. Orch., but was able to accept other engagements during late spring and summer months; in the spring of 1883, he traveled with the Thomas Orch. on a transcontinental tour; the summers of 1883 and 1884 he spent in Paris, where he took violin lessons with Hubert Léonard. He resigned from the Boston Symph. in 1903, and devoted himself to teaching and composition, living in Boston and suburban Medfield. He was married to Elise Burnett Fay (1910). After his death, she donated to the Library of Congress all of his MSS, correspondence, etc.; by his will, he left the material assets of his not inconsiderable estate to the French Academy and the Paris Cons. He was officer of the French Academy (1906); Chevalier in the French Legion of Honor (1919); member of the American Academy of Arts and Letters; Mus. Doc. *(honoris causa),* Yale Univ. (1926). —Loeffler's position in American music is unique: he was brought up under many different national influences, Alsatian, French, German, Russian, and Ukrainian. One of his most vivid scores, *Memories of My Childhood,* written as late as 1924, reflects the modal feeling of Russian and Ukrainian folksongs. But his esthetic code was entirely French, with definite leanings toward Impressionism; the archaic constructions that he sometimes affected, and the stylized evocations of 'ars antiqua,' are also in keeping with the French manner. His most enduring work, *A Pagan Poem,* is cast in such a neo-archaic vein. He was a master of colorful orchestration; his harmonies are opulent without saturation; his rhapsodic forms are peculiarly suited to the evocative moods of his music. His only excursion into the American idiom was the employment of jazz rhythms in a few of his lesser pieces. —Works: *The Nights in the Ukraine* (after Gogol, suite for violin and orch. (Boston, Nov. 20, 1891); *Fantastic Concerto* for cello and orch. (Boston, Feb. 2, 1894); *Divertimento* for violin and orch. (Boston, Jan. 4, 1895); *La Mort de Tintagiles* (after Maeterlinck), dramatic poem for 2 viole d'amore and orch. (revised for orch. and viola d'amore, 1900; 1st perf., Boston, Feb. 16, 1901); *Divertissement espagnol* for orch. and saxophone (1901); *La Villanelle du Diable,* symph. fantasy for orch. and organ (Boston, April 2, 1902); *Poem* for orch., inspired by Verlaine's *La bonne chanson* (Boston, April 11, 1902; reorchestrated, and perf. by the Boston Symph., Nov. 1, 1918); *A Pagan Poem* (after Virgil), for orch. with piano, English horn, and 3 trumpets obbligati (originally as chamber music, 1901; revised for orch. and piano, 1906; 1st perf., Boston Symph., Nov. 22, 1907, Karl Muck conducting); *Hora Mystica* for orch. and men's chorus (Boston Symph., March 2, 1917, Karl Muck conducting); *5 Irish Fantasies,* for voice and orch. (3 numbers perf., Boston, March 10, 1922); *Memories of My Childhood (Life in a Russian Village),* for orch. (awarded the Chicago North Shore Festival Association prize, 1924; Chicago Symph., Evanston, Illinois, May 30, 1924); *Canticum Fratris Solis (The Canticle of the Sun),* for solo voice and chamber orch. (commissioned by the E. S. Coolidge Foundation; 1st perf. at the Library of Congress Festival of Chamber Music, Oct. 28, 1925); *Evocation* for women's voices and orch. (on lines from the 'Select Epigrams of Greek Anthology' by J. W. Machail; commissioned for the opening of Severance Hall, Cleveland; perf. there, Feb. 5, 1931); Psalm 137, *By the Rivers of Babylon,* for 4-part women's chorus with organ, harp, 2 flutes, and cello obbligato (1907); *For one who fell in battle,* for 8-part mixed chorus a cappella (1911); *Beat! Beat! Drums!* (after Whitman), for men's chorus in unison, 6 piccolos, 3 saxophones, brass, drums, and 2 pianos (1917; Cleveland, Nov. 17, 1932); 2 Rhapsodies for oboe, viola, and piano *(L'Étang* and *La Cornemuse;* after poems by Maurice Rollinat; 1905); octet for 2 clarinets, 2 violins, viola, cello, double-bass, and harp; string sextet; *Music for Four Stringed Instruments* (in memory of the American aviator Victor Chapman; 1917); quintet for 3 violins, viola, and cello; *4 Melodies* for voice and piano (poems by G. Kahn; 1903); *4 Poems* for voice, viola, and piano (1904); *4 Poems* for voice and piano (1906); *The wind among the reeds,* for voice and piano (poems by W. B. Yeats; 1908); *The Reveller,* for solo voice, violin, and piano (1925); Partita for violin and piano (1930); in MS, a 4-act Chinese opera, *Life is but a Dream,* and an opera based on a short play by Cecil Sharp. Also wrote *Violin Studies for the Development of the Left Hand* (publ. 1936).—Bibliography: Carl Engel contributed an extensive essay on Loeffler to the 'International Cyclopedia of Music and Musicians,' ed. by Oscar Thompson (N. Y., 1938); Engel also wrote articles on Loeffler in the 'Chesterian' (March, 1920), in the 'Mus. Quarterly' (July, 1925), in 'Views and Reviews' of the 'Mus. Quarterly' (July, 1935), and in Cobbett's 'Cyclopedic Survey of Chamber Music.' See also Lawrence Gilman, in *Nature in Music and Studies in Tone Poetry of Today* (1914); Paul Rosenfeld in *Musical Portraits* (1923) and in his *An Hour With American Music* (N.Y., 1929; pp. 52-9); J. T. Howard in *Our American Music* (N. Y., 1939, and subsequent eds.); Gilbert Chase in *America's Music* (N.Y., 1955).

Loeillet (lö-yā'), **Jacques,** oboe player, brother of Jean-Baptiste Loeillet; b. Ghent, July 7, 1685; d. Versailles, Nov. 28, 1746. He played in court orchestras in Brussels and Munich. In 1727 he went to France;

demonstrated his virtuosity, performing on several wind instruments and on the violin, at the Versailles court, and was appointed chamber musician to Louis XV. He publ. 6 sonatas for 2 flutes and 6 sonatas for solo flute with continuo.

Loeillet (lö-yā'), **Jean-Baptiste** (known in England as John Loeillet), notable harpsichordist and flutist; brother of Jacques Loeillet; b. Ghent, Nov. 18, 1680; d. London, July 19, 1730. The family name has been variously spelled L'Oeillet, Luly, Lulli, Lullie, and even Lully, which latter form led to a great deal of confusion, so that Loeillet's Minuet in A has been misattributed in some editions to the great Lully. Loeillet studied in Ghent and in Paris. In 1705 he went to London, where he played the oboe and the flute at the Queen's Theatre (until 1710). He became extremely successful as teacher, player on the harpsichord, and collector of musical instruments. He popularized the German transverse flute in England. In his music, he followed the Italian tradition; his writing for the flute shows a thorough understanding of the virtuoso possibilities of the instrument. He publ. in London, under the name of John Loeillet, the following works: 6 suites of lessons for the harpsichord; 6 sonatas for various instruments; 12 sonatas for violins, German flutes, and common flutes; 12 solos for a German flute, common flute, and violin; the following were publ. under the name of Jean-Baptiste Loeillet de Gand: 4 books of solos for a flute and a bass; 6 sonatas for 2 flutes; and 6 sonatas for 2 German flutes. There are 2 different sets of opus numbers, which suggests that there was another Loeillet, possibly identifiable with John Loeillet's cousin, also named Jean-Baptiste, and active in Lyons. —Reprints of authentic and putative works by John Loeillet include a set of sonatas, ed. by Béon (Paris, 1911); a sonata ed. by Moffat; harpsichord pieces ed. by J. Watelet (Antwerp, 1932); 2 sonatas for flute and piano, ed. by J. van Etsen (Antwerp, 1938); etc. —Bibliography: Paul Bergmans, *Une Famille de musiciens belges du XVIII*[e] *siècle: Les Loeillet* (Brussels, 1927), prime source book, providing documentary information on members of the family; but see B. Priestman, *Catalogue thématique des œuvres de Jean-Baptiste, John et Jacques Loeillet,* in the 'Revue belge de musicologie' (Oct.-Dec., 1952; pp. 219-74), separating John Loeillet's works from those purported to be by his cousin; see also Priestman's article, *The Keyboard Works of John Loeillet,* in 'Music Review' (May, 1955).

Loeillet, John. See **Jean-Baptiste Loeillet.**

Loeschhorn, Albert. See **Löschhorn.**

Loesser (les'-ser), **Arthur,** American pianist and writer on music; b. New York, Aug. 26, 1894. He studied with Stojowski and Goetschius at the Institute of Musical Art, N.Y.; 1911, won the Loeb Memorial Prize; made his professional début as pianist in Berlin (1913); returning to America in 1915, he appeared in concerts in New York; then toured almost continuously in Australia (1920), Japan, China, the Philippine Islands, Singapore, Java; was assisting artist to Mischa Elman in Japan (1921). In 1926 he became teacher of piano at the Cleveland Institute of Music; head of piano dept. since 1953; was editor and annotator of programs of the Cleveland Orch. from 1937-42; music editor and critic of the 'Cleveland Press' from 1938-56. He appeared as soloist with the N.Y. Philharmonic (1937) and Cleveland Orch. (1938, and several times later). In 1943 he was commissioned in the U.S. Army as a Japanese-language officer; mastered Japanese, and lectured in that language in Tokyo; after cessation of hostilities, became the first American musician in uniform to play for a Japanese audience since World War II, appearing as soloist with the Nippon Philharmonic at its regular concerts in Tokyo in Feb., 1946. He published *Humor in American Song* (N.Y., 1943), and an entertaining volume, *Men, Women and Pianos: A Social History* (N.Y., 1954); also many magazine articles.

Loesser, Frank, American composer; brother of Arthur Loesser; b. New York, June 29, 1910. He was educated at the College of the City of N.Y., where he began writing songs for college activities; he subsequently was active as a reporter, singer, and vaudeville performer. In 1931 he settled in Hollywood and devoted himself mainly to writing musical comedies. During World War II he was in the U.S. Army, and wrote several Army songs *(What Do You Do in the Infantry?, Salute to the Army Service Forces, Praise the Lord and Pass the Ammunition, They're Either Too Young or Too Old,* etc.); continued to produce popular songs after the war *(On A Slow Boat to China; Small Fry; The Moon of Manakoora; Dolores; How Sweet You Are; Now That I Need You; Roger Young; Just Another Polka; Two Sleepy People; Spring Will Be a Little Late This Year; A Touch of Texas; Jingle Jangle Jingle; I Wish I Didn't Love You So; My Darling, My Darling; Baby, It's*

Cold Outside, etc.); also wrote music for several highly successful Broadway plays: *Where's Charley?, Guys and Dolls, The Most Happy Fella,* etc. —See Arthur Loesser's article, *My Brother Frank,* in Music Library Association 'Notes' (March, 1950).

Loevensohn, Marix, cellist; b. Courtrai, Belgium, March 31, 1880; d. Montauban, France, April 24, 1943. He studied at the Brussels Cons.; made his public début in London at the age of 14; then toured England as a joint artist with celebrated musicians, among them Paderewski and Adelina Patti; then was, successively, member of the string quartets of Wilhelmj, Ysaÿe, and Thomson. In 1906 he became teacher at both the Klindworth-Scharwenka and the Stern Conservatories in Berlin; in 1912 he taught at the Hochschule für Musik; in 1916 he became 1st cellist of the Concertgebouw Orch. in Amsterdam; in 1920 he joined the faculty of the Cons. of Brussels; from 1927, was at the Netherlands Academy in Rotterdam. He publ. some cello pieces and songs.

Loewe, Ferdinand. See **Löwe.**

Loewe, Frederick, composer; b. Vienna, June 10, 1904. He studied piano in Berlin with Busoni and Eugène d'Albert; composition with Rezniček. In 1924 he emigrated to the U.S.; was active as concert pianist; then devoted himself chiefly to production of popular music. Adapting himself adroitly to the American idiom, he became one of the most successful writers of musical comedies; among them are *Salute to Spring; Great Lady; The Life of the Party; What's Up?; The Day Before Spring; Brigadoon; Paint Your Wagon;* and (the most spectacularly successful of them all) *My Fair Lady,* after Shaw's *Pygmalion* (1956).

Loewe (lö'-vĕh), **Karl (Gottfried)**, outstanding German composer of lieder; b. Löbejün, near Halle, Nov. 30, 1796; d. Kiel, April 20, 1869. His father, a schoolmaster and cantor, taught him the rudiments of music; when he was 12, he was sent to the Francke Institute in Halle, where his attractive manner, excellent high voice, and early ability to improvise, brought him to the attention of Jerome Bonaparte, who granted him a stipend of 300 Thaler annually until 1813. His teacher was Türk, the head of the Francke Institute; after Türk's death in 1813, Loewe joined the Singakademie founded by Naue. He also studied theology at the Univ. of Halle, but soon devoted himself entirely to music. He began to compose as a boy; under the influence of Zelter, he wrote German ballades, and developed an individual style of great dramatic force and lyrical inspiration; he perfected the genre, and was regarded by many musicians as the greatest song composer after Schubert and before Brahms. His setting of Goethe's poem *Erlkönig* (1818), which came before the publication of Schubert's great song to the same poem, is one of Loewe's finest creations; other songs that rank among his best are *Edward, Der Wirthin Töchterlein, Der Nöck, Archibald Douglas, Tom der Reimer, Heinrich der Vogler, Oluf, Die verfallene Mühle,* etc. Loewe was personally acquainted with Goethe, and also met Weber. In 1820 he became schoolmaster at Stettin, and organist at St. Jacobus there. He lived in Stettin, except for frequent travels, until 1866, when he settled in Kiel. He visited Vienna (1844), London (1847), Sweden and Norway (1851), and Paris (1857), among other places. Loewe was an excellent vocalist, and was able to perform his ballades in public. His works include 5 operas, only one of which, *Die drei Wünsche,* was performed (Berlin, Feb. 18, 1834); 17 oratorios; cantata, *Die Hochzeit der Thetis;* a ballade for soli, chorus, and orch., *Die erste Walpurgisnacht* (after Goethe); 368 ballades for voice and piano, publ. in his collected edition and in numerous anthologies (Peters and Schlesinger publ. 'Loewe-Albums' containing 20 and 16 numbers respectively). Loewe's instrumental works (symphonies, overtures, 3 string quartets, a piano trio, several piano sonatas, etc.) are mostly in MS. He publ. several pedagogic works: *Gesanglehre für Gymnasien, Seminarien und Bürgerschulen* (Stettin, 1826; 5th ed., 1854); *Musikalischer Gottesdienst; methodische Anweisung zum Kirchengesang und Orgelspiel* (1851, and subsequent eds.); *Klavier- und General-bass-Schule* (2nd ed., 1851). A 'Gesamtausgabe der Balladen, Legenden, Lieder und Gesänge,' in 17 vols., ed. by Max Runze, was publ. by Breitkopf & Härtel (1899-1903). A Loewe-Verein was founded in Berlin in 1882. —Bibliography: *Selbstbiographie,* ed. by K. H. Bitter (Berlin, 1870); A. Wellmer, *Karl Loewe: Ein deutscher Tonmeister* (Leipzig, 1886); M. Runze, *Loewe redivivus* (Berlin, 1888); A. B. Bach, *The Art-Ballad: Loewe and Schubert* (London, 1890; 3rd ed., 1891); M. Runze, *Ludwig Giesebrecht und Karl Loewe* (Berlin, 1894); W. Wossidlo, *Karl Loewe als Balladenkomponist* (Berlin, 1894); A. Niggli, *Karl Loewe* (Zürich, 1897); H. Bulthaupt, *Karl Loewe, Deutschlands Balladenkomponist* (Berlin, 1898); M. Runze, *Goethe und Loewe* (as introduction to vols. 11 and 12 of the 'Gesamtausgabe' of Loewe's works; Leipzig, 1901); M. Runze, *Die musikalische Legende* (introduction to vols. 13 and 14 of the same; Leipzig, 1902); H. Draheim, *Goethes Balladen in Loewes Komposition* (Langensalza, 1905); K. Anton, *Beiträge zur Biographie Karl Loewes* (Halle, 1912); K. Anton, *Karl Loewe als Lehrer Walter von Goethes,* in the 'Goethe Jahrbuch' (vol. 23, 1913); H. Kleemann, *Beiträge zur Ästhetik und Geschichte der Loeweschen Ballade* (Halle, 1913); L. Hirschberg, *Loewe als Instrumentalkomponist* (Langensalza, 1919); O. Altenburg, *Karl Loewe* (Stettin, 1924); Hans Engel, *Karl Loewe: Überblick und Würdigung* (Greiswald, 1934); W. Serauky, *Zu Karl Loewes Biographie und musikalischen Schaffen,* in the 'Festschrift A. Schering' (Berlin, 1937); R. Sietz, *Karl Loewe: ein Gedenkbuch zum 150. Geburtstag* (Cologne, 1948).

Loewenberg, Alfred, musicologist; b. Berlin, May 14, 1902; d. London, Jan. 3, 1950. He studied at Jena Univ. (Ph.D., 1925); settled in London in 1934. His unique achievement is the compilation of *Annals of Opera: 1597-1940* (Cambridge, 1943; new ed., Geneva, 1955), tabulating in chronological order the exact dates of first performances and important revivals of some 4,000 operas, with illuminating comments of a bibliographical nature. Also publ. *Early Dutch Librettos and Plays with Music in the British Museum* (London, 1947), and a number of articles.

Loewengard, Max Julius, German writer on music and pedagogue; b. Frankfurt, Oct. 2, 1860; d. Hamburg, Nov. 19, 1915. He was a pupil of Raff in Frankfurt; from 1891 to 1904 he was on the faculty of the Scharwenka Cons. in Berlin, and wrote music criticism for the 'Börsen-Zeitung'; from 1904-8, taught at the Hamburg Cons.; founded the 'Institut für Musikwissenschaft' there. His compositions include an opera, *Die vierzehn Nothelfer* (Berlin, 1896), a serenade for orch., and many songs. He publ. several highly successful manuals: *Lehrbuch der Harmonie* (1892; 6th ed., 1906; English transl. by H. M. Peacock, 1905; F. Liebing, 1907; Th. Baker, 1910); *Lehrbuch des Kontrapunkts* (1902; English transl. by F. Liebing, 1907); *Aufgabenbuch zur Harmonielehre* (1903); *Lehrbuch des Kanons und der Fuge* (1903); *Lehrbuch der musikalischen Formen* (1904); *Praktische Anleitung zum Generalbassspiel, Harmonisieren, Transponieren und Modulieren* (1913).

Logier (loh-zhyā'), **Johann Bernhard,** German pianist, teacher, and composer; b. Kassel, Feb. 9, 1777; d. Dublin, July 27, 1846. Finding piano practice distasteful, he fled from home at the age of 10, and was taken to England by an Englishman who admired his flute playing (Logier had studied the flute under Weidner). In 1805 he joined a regimental band as flutist and accompanied it to Ireland, where he became organist at Westport some years later, and where he perfected the invention of the 'chiroplast,' an apparatus for holding the hands in correct position during piano practice. It was patented in 1814, and Logier traveled through the United Kingdom to introduce it. It obtained great vogue, and brought him fame and wealth. Stöpel was sent by the Prussian government to examine and report on the chiroplast, and Logier was invited to Berlin to introduce his system. He remained there 3 years, and then returned to Dublin (1826). This system, which soon spread over Great Britain and Germany, and was even adopted in the Paris Cons., was reinforced by Logier's original idea of the simultaneous practice of several pupils on different pianos, which became the most important part of this method of instruction. The system was not received without protest. In rebuttal, Logier published in 1816 *An Explanation and Description of the Royal Patent Chiroplast, or Hand-Director for Pianoforte,* etc.; bitter attacks were met by *An Authentic Account of the Examination of Pupils Instructed on the New System of Musical Education, by J. B. Logier* (1818). In *The First Companion to the Royal Patent Chiroplast,* Logier explains his method of simultaneous teaching; he also publ. *Logier's Practical Thorough-Bass,* and (in German) a *System der Musikwissenschaft und der musikalischen Komposition* (Berlin, 1827). His own works include a piano concerto; sonatas, etc., for piano; piano trios with flute and cello; and a method for bugle, titled 'A Complete Introduction to the Keyed Bugle.'

Logroscino (lŏ-grŏ-shē'-nŏ), **Nicola,** Italian composer; b. Bitonto (baptized Oct. 22), 1698; d. Palermo, after 1765. He was a pupil of Veneziano and Perugino (1714-27) at the Cons. di Santa Maria di Loreto in Naples; 1728-31, was organist at Conza (Avellino); in 1731, again in Naples. In 1747 he became first prof. of counterpoint at the Cons. dei Figliuoli Dispersi in Palermo, but spent his last years in Naples, where he produced a number of operas, chiefly in *buffo* style, in which he surpassed his precedessors Leo, Pergolesi, and Hasse, and introduced the novel effect of the finale in ensemble. His operas held the stage till Piccini attained fame; among them were *Inganno per Inganno* (1738), *Violante* (1741), *Ricciardo* (1743), *Leandro* (1744), *Don Paduano* (1745), *Il Governatore* (1747), and his two productions of 'opera seria,' *Giunio Bruto* (1748) and *Olimpiade* (1753). —Cf. H. Kretzschmar, *Zwei Opern Nicola Logroscinos,* in the 'Jahrbuch Peters' (1908); U. Prota-Giurleo, *Nicola Logroscino, il dio dell' opera buffa* (Naples, 1927); E. P. Morello, *A. Scarlatti e Nicolo Logroscino* (1927); A. della Corte, *L'opera comica italiana nel 1700* (Bari, 1923; vol. 1; p. 172 *et seq*).

Löhlein, Georg Simon, German composer; b. Neustadt, near Coburg, July (baptized July 16), 1725; d. Danzig, Dec. 16, 1781. On account of his tall stature (6 ft. 2 inches), he was seized on a journey and forced into the Prussian Guard; he was stationed at Potsdam and served at the palace of Frederick the Great. He was severely wounded at the battle of Collin during the Seven Years' War, but recovered and went to Jena, where he completed his interrupted musical education; at the age of 38 he enrolled at the Univ. of Leipzig; there he was active as both violinist and pianist. In 1781 he received a post as organist at the St. Mary Church in Danzig, but suffered from the rigors of the climate, and died a few months after arrival there. Löhlein wrote a singspiel, *Zemire und Azor* (Leipzig, 1775), several instrumental concertos, chamber music, etc., but he became known mainly through his pedagogical work, *Clavier-Schule* in 2 vols. (1765 and 1781), which passed through many editions and was revised by Czerny; he also publ. a *Violinschule* (1774). —Cf. F. von Glasenapp, *G. S. Löhlein* (Halle, 1937).

Lohmann, Peter, German poet and writer on music; b. Schwelm, April 24, 1833; d. Leipzig, Jan. 10, 1907. From 1856 he lived in Leipzig, and wrote (1858-61) for the 'Neue Zeitschrift für Musik.' He publ. *Über R. Schumanns Faustmusik* (1860) and *Über die dramatische Dichtung mit Musik* (1861; 2nd ed., 1864; 3rd ed. as *Das Ideal der Oper*, 1886).

Lohse, Otto, German conductor and composer; b. Dresden, Sept. 21, 1858; d. Baden-Baden, May 5, 1925. He was a pupil at the Dresden Cons. of Richter (piano), Grützmacher (cello), Draeseke and Wüllner (composition); 1880-82, teacher of piano at the Imperial Music School at Vilna; 1882-89, conductor of the Wagner Society and the Imperial Russian Music Society in Riga, and 1889-93, conductor of the Municipal Theater there; 1893-95, at the Stadttheater in Hamburg. There he married the famous singer Katharina Klafsky, and in the spring of 1896 both artists were members of the Damrosch Opera Co. in N. Y. (Lohse as conductor). From 1897 to 1904, Lohse conducted opera in Strasbourg; 1904-11, in Cologne; 1911-12, at the Théâtre de la Monnaie, Brussels; 1912-23, at the Leipzig Stadttheater. He composed an opera, *Der Prinz wider Willen* (Riga, 1890), and songs. —Cf. Ernst Lert, *Otto Lohse* (Leipzig, 1918).

Lolli, Antonio, Italian violinist and composer; b. Bergamo, c. 1730; d. Palermo, Aug. 10, 1802. Little is known of his early life; he was in Stuttgart at the court of the Duke of Württemberg from 1762 till 1772; asked for a leave of absence, but did not return to Stuttgart; however, he drew his salary until 1774. He gave violin concerts in Hamburg, Lübeck, and Stettin in 1773-74; then proceeded to St. Petersburg, where he became a special favorite of Catherine II, and also ingratiated himself with Potemkin. He received 4,000 rubles annually as violinist to the Empress and chapel master of the court. In Dec., 1777, he visited Stockholm, and then went to Germany. An incorrigible gambler, he dissipated the fortune of 10,000 florins he had accumulated from the Russian emoluments, and in 1780, after protracted journeys through Europe, went back to St. Petersburg; there he was able to regain his social and artistic position; gave concerts at Potemkin's palace in St. Petersburg, and also played in Moscow. Despite his frequent derelictions of duty, he was retained at the court until 1783, when his contract was cancelled and he was succeeded as chapel master by Paisiello. However, he continued to give some public concerts, and also lessons, before leaving Russia in 1784. In 1785 he appeared in London, then was in Paris and in Naples, finally settling in Palermo. Contemporary accounts indicate that Lolli was a violinist of great ability, but also addicted to eccentricities in playing technical passages. He composed and publ. several sets of violin works, among them *5 Sonates et Divertissement* for violin with continuo (1776; dedicated to Potemkin); other violin pieces (concertos, sonatas, etc.); also an *École du violon en Quatuor* (Berlin, 1776; many reprints by various German and French publishers). —Cf. A. Moser, *Arcangelo Corelli und Antonio Lolli; zwei künstlerische Ehrenrettungen,* in the 'Zeitschrift für Musikwissenschaft' (April, 1921); R.-Aloys Mooser, *Annales de la Musique et des Musiciens en Russie* (Geneva, 1950; vol. II, pp. 161-68).

Lomakin, Gavriil Joachimovitch, Russian singer and composer; b. St. Petersburg, April 6, 1812; d. Gatchina, May 21, 1885. While a chorister in the church choir of Count Scheremetiev, he studied theory with Sapienza; in 1830, became choirmaster, and singing master at several institutions in St. Petersburg, and later conductor of the court chapel (1848-59). Together with Balakirev, he established in 1862 the Free School for Music, and had charge of the singing classes until 1870. Ill health forced him to retire from musical activities in 1874. He wrote 10 *Cherubim Songs;* 14 *Penitential Songs;* a Liturgy, etc.; publ. a *Treatise on Choral Singing;* arrangements for chorus of old Russian hymns.

London, George (real name Burnstein), American bass baritone; b. Montreal, May 30, 1920, of Russian-Jewish parents. The family moved to Los Angeles in 1935; there he took lessons with Richard Lert (opera); made his début in the opera *Gainsborough* by Albert Coates, produced at the Hollywood Bowl in 1941. He then went to New York, where he studied singing with Paola Novikova; in 1947 he toured in the U. S. as a member of the Bel Canto Trio (Frances Yeend, soprano; Mario Lanza, tenor). In 1949 he was engaged to sing at the Vienna State Opera; in 1954, received the title of Kammersänger from the government of Austria. He appeared for the 1st time with the Metropolitan Opera Co. as Amonasro (Nov. 13, 1951); his other roles include Boris Godunov (in Russian), Eugene Onegin (also in Russian), Don Giovanni, Amfortas, Méphistophélès. —Cf. J. Wechsberg, *The Vocal Mission,* a 'profile' of George London, in the 'New Yorker' (Oct. 26 and Nov. 2, 1957).

Long, Marguerite, eminent French pianist and pedagogue; b. Nimes, Nov. 13, 1878. She studied with Marmontel in Paris; appointed instructor at the Paris Cons. in 1906; succeeded Diémer as prof. in 1920. She was notable for early performances of the music of Debussy and Ravel. She was married to Joseph de Marliave.

Longas, Federico, Spanish pianist and composer; b. Barcelona, Aug. 18, 1895. He was a pupil of Granados and Malats; toured widely in the U. S., South America, and Europe as accompanist of Tito Schipa and as soloist. He founded a piano school, the Acad. Longas, in Barcelona; later he went to Paris; then to the U.S., settling in N.Y. His works include effective piano pieces *(Jota, Aragon,* etc.); over 100 songs *(Castilian Moonlight, La Guinda, Muñequita,* etc.).

Longhurst, William Henry, English organist and composer; b. London, Oct. 6, 1819; d. Canterbury, June 17, 1904. He was a chorister in Canterbury Cathedral (1828-36); then assistant organist (1836-73); in 1873, became first organist, retiring in 1898 after 70 years of uninterrupted service in the Cathedral. He received the degree of Mus. Doc. in 1875; was music lecturer at St. Augustine's College, Canterbury. —Works: oratorio, *David and Absalom* (1872); a cathedral service; other church music; etc.

Longo, Achille, Italian composer, son of Alessandro Longo; b. Naples, March 28, 1900; d. there, May 28, 1954. He studied at the Naples Cons.; taught harmony there (1926-30); then at the Cons. of Parma (1930-34); in 1934, returned to Naples and taught composition at the Cons. until his death. His works include a suite for flute, oboe, clarinet, bassoon, and piano (1926; won the Bellini Prize); a piano concerto (Venice, 1932); a piano quintet (1934); a violin concerto (1937); *Notturno* and *Corteo* for orch. (1942); a Requiem (1947); and *Serenata in do,* for orch. (1950).

Longo, Alessandro, Italian pianist and music editor; b. Amantea, Dec. 30, 1864; d. Naples, Nov. 3, 1945. He studied with Cesi (piano) and Serrao (composition); in 1887, was appointed prof. of piano at the Naples Cons. In 1892 he founded the 'Circolo Scarlatti' to promote the works of Domenico Scarlatti; from 1914, edited the periodical 'L'arte pianistica.' His most important achievement is the complete edition of Domenico Scarlatti's harpsichord works (10 vols. and a supplement; the order of sonatas was partly superseded by Kirkpatrick's catalogue). He was also a prolific composer; publ. numerous pieces for piano solo and piano 4-hands; piano quintet; *Tema con variazioni* for harp; a suite for clarinet and piano; songs.

Longy (lohn-zhē'), **Georges,** French oboe virtuoso; b. Abbeville, Aug. 29, 1868; d. Mareuil (Dordogne), March 29, 1930. He studied at the Paris Cons. (1st prize, 1886); was a member of the Lamoureux Orch. (1886-88) and of the Colonne Orch. (1888-98). In 1898 he was engaged as first oboe player of the Boston Symph. Orch., and remained there until 1925. From 1899 to 1913 he conducted the Boston Orchestral Club. In 1900 he founded the Longy Club for woodwind chamber music. In 1916 he established his own music school in Boston (later Longy School of Music, Cambridge, Mass.).

Loomis, Clarence, American composer and pianist; b. Sioux Falls, S. D., Dec. 13, 1889. He studied at the Dakota Wesleyan Univ.; then at the American Cons. of Chicago, with Heniot Levy (piano) and Adolph Weidig (composition); won the gold medal as pianist, and was appointed piano teacher there in 1914, after a season of study with Leopold Godowsky in Vienna; from 1930-36 he taught theory at Arthur Jordan Cons. of Music in Indianapolis; in 1945, became instructor at Highlands Univ., Las Vegas, N. M. —Works: operas: *A Night in Avignon, Castle of Gold, Yolanda of Cyprus* (London, Ontario, Sept. 25, 1929; also given in Chicago, Washington, and New York), *David, The Fall of the House of Usher;* ballets *The Flapper and the Quarterback* (1st performed in Kyoto, Japan, at the coronation of Emperor Hirohito, Nov. 10, 1928), *Oak Street Beach; Erin,* choral cycle; incidental music to *King Lear;* numerous choruses a cappella. — Cf. E. E. Hipsher, *American Opera and Its Composers* (Philadelphia, 1934; pp. 298-301).

Loomis, Harvey Worthington, American composer; b. Brooklyn, Feb. 5, 1865; d. Boston, Dec. 25, 1930. He was a pupil in composition of Dvořák at the National Cons., N. Y. (1891-93), when Dvořák was director there; later lived mostly in Boston; became interested in Indian music, and published many arrangements of Indian melodies; also original works in that style *(Lyrics of the Red Man,* etc.).—Works: a grand opera, *The Traitor Mandolin;* 2 melodramas, *The Song of the Pear* and *The Story of a Faithful Soul;* 4 comic operas, *The Maid of Athens, The Burglar's Bride, Going Up?, The Bey of Baba;* the musical pantomimes *Put to the Test, Her Revenge, In Old New Amsterdam, The Enchanted Fountain, Love and Witchcraft, Blanc et Noir;* incidental music to *The Tragedy of Death* and *The Coming of the Prince; Fairy Hill,* cantata for children; piano pieces. His songs written for children deserve special mention: *Song Flowers for Children to Gather* (2 books), *Toy Tunes,* etc. He also wrote songs to words by Shakespeare, Browning, Heine, etc. Many of his MSS are in the Music Division of the Library of Congress. —Cf. Rupert Hughes, *Contemporary American Composers* (Boston, 1900; pp. 77-92).

Looser, Rolf, Swiss composer; b. Niederscherli, near Bern, May 3, 1920. He studied at the Bern Cons. with Richard Sturzenegger (cello), Moeschinger (theory), and Frank Martin (composition); later in Zürich with Willy Burkhardt (theory), and in Paris with Pierre Fournier (cello). He taught cello at Bern Cons.; then played in the Utrecht Symph. Orch., Holland (1947-49); returned to Bern in 1950.—Works: *3 Polyphonic Fantasies,* for string orch. (1946); suite for orch. (1949); *Introduction and Dialogues,* for cello and chamber orch. (1950); *Concertante Music,* for trombone, strings, harp, and timpani (1953).

Lopatnikov, Nikolai, outstanding composer; b. Reval, Estonia, March 16, 1903. He studied at the St. Petersburg Cons.; after the Revolution, continued his studies at the Cons. of Helsinki; then went to Karlsruhe, and Berlin, where he studied with Ernst Toch and with Grabner. In 1934 he went to London; in 1939, settled in New York; became an American citizen in 1944. In 1945 he was appointed prof. of composition at Carnegie Institute of Technology, Pittsburgh. His music is generally in the neo-Classical style, distinguished by a strong feeling of form, tonal harmony, a clear melodic outline, and vigorous rhythmic pulse.—Works: the opera *Danton; Introduction and Scherzo* for orch. (Boston, April 27, 1928); Symphony No. 1 (Königsberg, 1930); Symphony No. 2 (Boston, Dec. 22, 1939); *Sinfonietta* (Festival of International Society for Contemporary Music, Berkeley, Calif., Aug. 2, 1942); *Opus Sinfonicum* (1933-41; 1st prize of the Cleveland Orch.; perf. Cleveland, Dec. 9, 1943); *Concertino* for orch. (Boston, March 2, 1945); piano concerto No. 1 (Vienna Festival of the International Society for Contemporary Music, June 16, 1932); piano concerto No. 2 (N.Y., C.B.S. Symph., Nov. 27, 1946, composer soloist); violin concerto (Boston, April 17, 1942); 2 string quartets (2nd received the Belaiev Prize, 1929); Duo for violin and cello (1926); sonata for piano, violin, and snare drum (1926); cello sonata (1928); piano trio

(1938); *Variations and Epilogue,* for cello and piano (1946); piano sonata; a number of piano pieces *(2 Ironic Dances, 5 Contrasts, 5 Dialogues,* etc.); also pieces for mechanical piano (Baden-Baden, 1928).

Lopes Graça, Fernando, Portuguese composer; b. Tomar, Dec. 17, 1906. He studied at the Cons. of Lisbon; in 1932 became instructor at Coimbra; was compelled to leave Portugal in 1937 for political reasons, and went to Paris; there he studied composition with Charles Koechlin. After the outbreak of World War II he returned to Lisbon, where he became active in the modern musical movement. Among his works are a symphony (1944); *Suite rustica* for orch.; 2 piano concertos (1940; 1942); *Historia tragico-maritima,* for voice and orch. (1942); 2 piano sonatas and other piano pieces; also a great number of songs to Portuguese texts; arrangements of folksongs. He also publ. a number of books: *Música e músicos modernos* (Oporto, 1943); biographies of Mozart, Chopin, Bartók; essays on Portuguese music. —Cf. M. V. Henriques, *Fernando Lopes Graça na música portuguesa contemporanea* (Sacavém, 1956).

López-Buchardo, Carlos, Argentine composer; b. Buenos Aires, Oct. 12, 1881; d. there, April 21, 1948. He studied piano and harmony in Buenos Aires; composition with Albert Roussel in Paris; became director of the National Cons. in Buenos Aires. His music is set in a vivid style, rooted in national folksong; particularly successful in this respect is his symph. suite, *Escenas Argentinas* (Buenos Aires, Aug. 12, 1922, under Felix Weingartner). Other works are: the opera *El Sueño de Alma* (Buenos Aires, Aug. 4, 1914; won the Municipal Prize); lyric comedies, *Madame Lynch* (1932), *La Perichona* (1933), *Amalia* (1935); several piano pieces in Argentine folk manner; songs.

Lorentz, Alfred, composer and conductor; b. Strasbourg, March 7, 1872; d. Karlsruhe, April 23, 1931. He studied with Rheinberger in Munich (composition), and with Mottl at Karlsruhe (conducting). He was chorusmaster, and later conductor, at the Municipal Theater in Strasbourg; from 1899 to 1925, was court conductor in Karlsruhe. He wrote the operas *Der Mönch von Sendomir* (Karlsruhe, 1907), *Die beiden Automaten* (Karlsruhe, 1913), *Liebesmacht* (Karlsruhe, 1922), *Schneider Fips* (Coburg, 1928), and an operetta, *Die Mondscheindame* (Karlsruhe, 1919); also some orchestral works.

Lorenz, Alfred Ottokar, musicologist, composer, and conductor; b. Vienna, July 11, 1868; d. Munich, Nov. 20, 1939. He studied at the Univ. of Vienna with Spitta; conducted opera at Königsberg and Elberfeld (1894-97), and at Coburg-Gotha (1898-1916); from 1920, lived in Munich; lectured at Munich Univ. from 1923. He made a specialty of Wagnerian research; publ. the comprehensive work *Das Geheimnis der Form bei Richard Wagner,* in 4 vols.: *Die musikalische Formgebung in Richard Wagners Ring des Nibelungen* (1924), *Der musikalische Aufbau von Tristan und Isolde* (1926), *Die Meistersinger* (1930), *Parsifal* (1933); the musical architecture and form of the operas are here analyzed in minute detail. He further publ. *Alessandro Scarlattis Jugendoper* (1927); *Abendländische Musikgeschichte im Rhythmus der Generationen* (1928), and numerous smaller essays in various music magazines, on Bach, Mozart, Beethoven, Weber, Wagner, Richard Strauss, etc. He edited the early operas of Weber *(Waldmädchen, Peter Schmoll),* and (in collaboration with Max Meyer-Olbersleben) wrote out the continuo to the complete works of E. Kindermann, for the 'Denkmäler der Tonkunst in Bayern' (vols. 21-24). He composed an opera, *Helges Erwachen* (Schwerin, 1896); incidental music to various plays; the symph. poems *Bergfahrt* and *Columbus;* some chamber music; and songs.

Lorenz, Franz, Austrian writer on music; b. Stein, April 4, 1805; d. Vienna, April 8, 1883. He was a physician by profession; took great interest in music, and publ. valuable pamphlets on Mozart: *In Sachen Mozarts* (Vienna, 1851), *Mozart als Klavier-Komponist* (Breslau, 1866); numerous articles in Vienna newspapers and magazines.

Lorenz, Julius, German composer; b. Hanover, Oct. 1, 1862; d. Glogau, Oct. 1, 1924. He was a pupil of Reinecke and Jadassohn at the Leipzig Cons.; from 1884-95, he conducted the singing academy at Glogau; in 1895 he settled in New York as choral conductor; led the singing society 'Arion'; in 1911, returned to Glogau. He wrote an opera, *Die Rekruten;* many choral works, both sacred and secular; and some chamber music.

Lorenz, Karl Adolf, German composer; b. Köslin, Aug. 13, 1837; d. Stettin, March 3, 1923. He began to compose music as a schoolboy; studied music in Berlin with

Dehn, Kiel, and Gehrig; also at Berlin Univ. (*Dr. phil.,* 1861). He settled in Stettin, becoming conductor of the symph. concerts of the 'Lehrer-Gesangverein'; succeeded Loewe as municipal director of music; founded the 'Stettiner Musikverein' (for oratorio). — Works: the secular oratorios *Otto der Grosse, Winfried, Krösus, Die Jungfrau von Orleans, Das Licht;* a passion cantata, *Golgotha;* 2 operas, *Die Komödie der Irrungen* and *Harald und Theano;* a symphony; a piano trio; etc. —Cf. K. König, *Karl Adolph Lorenz* (Stettin, 1937).

Lorenz, Max, German tenor; b. Düsseldorf, May 17, 1901. He studied with Grenzebach; was the leading tenor of the Dresden Opera; from 1931-34, was a member of the Metropolitan Opera Co. (début as Walther in *Die Meistersinger,* Nov. 12, 1931); from 1934-39, was with the State Opera in Berlin and the Vienna Opera; then with the Chicago Opera (1939-40); also appeared in Buenos Aires, London, and at La Scala, Milan; sang at the Paris Opéra in 1949-50; sang Tristan and Siegfried at the Bayreuth Festival (1933, 1942, 1952).

Lorenzani, Paolo, Italian composer; b. Rome, 1640; d. there, Oct. 28, 1713. He was a pupil of Orazio Benevoli at the Vatican; having failed to obtain Benevoli's position after the latter's death in 1672, he was given the post of maestro di cappella at the Jesuit College in Rome; then held a similar position at the Cathedral of Messina; when Sicily was captured by the French, the Duc de Vivonne, who was the French viceroy, induced Lorenzani to go to Paris (1678); he found favor with Louis XIV, and became court musician; in 1679 he was sent to Italy to recruit singers for the French court; he produced his Italian pastoral, *Nicandro e Fileno,* at Fontainebleau (1681); from 1679-83 he was sur-intendant of music to the Queen; when the Queen died (1683) he became choirmaster at the Italian religious order of Théatins in Paris. For several years Lorenzani was supported by the Paris faction opposed to Lully; after Lully's death, Lorenzani produced an opera with a French libretto, *Orontée* (Paris, Aug. 23, 1687). This having failed, Lorenzani turned to the composition of motets, which proved his best works; the famous Paris publisher Ballard brought them out in an impressively printed edition; Ballard also publ. a book of Italian airs by Lorenzani. In 1694 he returned to Italy, and was appointed maestro of the Cappella Giulia at St. Peter's, the post that he had tried unsuccessfully to secure in 1672; there he remained until his death. His printed works include 25 motets for 1-5 voices (Paris, 1693); 6 Italian airs (Paris, 1690), and several separate vocal numbers; Henry Prunières reproduced a scene from Lorenzani's opera *Nicandro e Fileno* in the 'Revue Musicale' (Aug., 1922).—Cf. M. Brenet, *Les Concerts en France sous l'ancien régime* (Paris, 1900); Henry Prunières, *L'Opéra italien en France avant Lulli* (Paris, 1913); Henry Prunières, *Paolo Lorenzani à la cour de France* in the 'Revue Musicale' (Aug., 1922).

Lorenzi-Fabris, Ausonio de, Italian composer; b. Montebelluna, Jan. 18, 1861; d. Venice, July 30, 1935. He studied at the Liceo Benedetto Marcello in Venice. He composed the operas *Gli Adorati del fuoco* (Venice, Jan. 27, 1891), *Maometto II* (Venice, July 9, 1892; revised, Florence, May 9, 1903), *Il re si annoia* (Trieste, Dec. 19, 1904); and a religious play *Refugium Peccatorum* (Venice, March 24, 1897).

Lorenzo, Leonardo De, flutist; b. Viggiano, Italy, Aug. 29, 1875. He studied at the Naples Cons.; from 1897 to 1907, was flutist in various traveling orchestras. In 1910 he emigrated to the U. S.; was 1st flutist of the N. Y. Philharmonic (1910-12); later with the Minneapolis Symph. Orch., the Los Angeles Philharmonic, and the Rochester Philharmonic (1923-35); also taught flute at the Eastman School of Music in Rochester; in 1935, settled in Beverly Hills, Calif. He publ. several books of flute studies and some solo pieces, and an informative book on flute playing and flute players, *My Complete Story of the Flute* (N. Y., 1951).

Loriod, Yvonne, French pianist; b. Houilles, Jan. 20, 1924. She studied at the Paris Cons. with Messiaen; toured Europe as pianist; made her American début in 1949 as soloist in Messiaen's symphony *Turangalila.* She has written *Mélopées africaines,* for Ondes Martenot, piano, flute, and timpani.

Loris, Loritus. See **Glareanus.**

Lortzing, (Gustav) Albert, German opera composer; b. Berlin, Oct. 23, 1801; d. there, Jan. 21, 1851. His parents were actors, and the wandering life led by the family did not allow him to pursue a methodical course of study. He learned acting from his father, and music from his mother at an early age. After some lessons with Rungenhagen in

Berlin, he continued his own study, and soon began to compose songs. At the age of 21 he married the actress Rosina Regina Ahles in Cologne; they had 11 children. In 1824 he wrote his first opera (to his own libretto), *Ali Pascha von Janina,* which, however, was not produced until 4 years later (Münster, Feb. 1, 1828). In 1832 he brought out 2 vaudevilles, *Der Pole und sein Kind* and *Scenen aus Mozarts Leben,* which were well received on several German stages. From 1833 to 1844 he was engaged at the Municipal Theater of Leipzig as a tenor; there he launched a light opera, *Die beiden Schützen* (Feb. 20, 1837), which became instantly popular; on the same stage he produced on Dec. 22, 1837, his undoubted masterpiece, *Czaar und Zimmermann* (later spelling, *Zar und Zimmermann),* to his own libretto derived from various French plays, and based on the true history of Peter the Great of Russia, who worked as a carpenter in Holland. The opera was produced in Berlin in 1839, and from then on its success was assured; after a few years it became a favorite on most European stages. Lortzing's next opera, *Caramo, oder Das Fischerstechen* (Leipzig, Sept. 20, 1839), was a failure; there followed *Hans Sachs* (Leipzig, June 23, 1840) and *Casanova* (Leipzig, Dec. 31, 1841), which passed without much notice; subsequent comparisons showed some similarities between *Hans Sachs* and *Die Meistersinger,* not only in subject matter, which was derived from the same source, but also in some melodic patterns; however, no one seriously suggested that Wagner was influenced by Lortzing's inferior work. There followed a romantic opera, *Der Wildschütz* (Leipzig, Dec. 31, 1842), which was in many respects the best that Lortzing wrote, but its success, although impressive, never equalled that of *Zar und Zimmermann.* At about the same time, Lortzing attempted still another career, that of opera impresario, but it was short-lived; his brief conductorship at the Leipzig Opera was similarly ephemeral. Composing remained his chief occupation; he produced *Undine* in Magdeburg (April 21, 1845) and *Der Waffenschmied* in Vienna (May 31, 1846). In Vienna he also acted as conductor; after a season or two at the Theater an der Wien, he returned to Leipzig, where he produced the light opera *Zum Grossadmiral* (Dec. 13, 1847), which was only moderately successful. The revolutionary events of 1848 seriously affected his positions both in Leipzig and Vienna; after the political situation became settled, he produced in Leipzig an opera of a romantic nature, *Rolands Knappen* (May 25, 1849). Although at least 4 of his operas were played at various German theaters, Lortzing received no honorarium, owing to a flaw in the regulations protecting the rights of composers. He was compelled to travel again as an actor, but could not earn enough money to support his large family left behind in Vienna. In the spring of 1850 he was engaged as musical director at a small theater in Berlin; on Jan. 20, 1851 his last opera, *Die Opernprobe,* was produced in Frankfurt, while he was on his deathbed in Berlin; he died the next day. His opera *Regina, oder die Marodeure,* written in 1848, was edited by Richard Kleinmichel, with the composer's libretto revised by Adolf L'Arronge, and performed in Berlin on March 21, 1899; another opera, *Der Weihnachtsabend,* was not produced. Lortzing also wrote an oratorio, *Die Himmelfahrt Christi;* some incidental music to various plays, and songs. But it is as composer of characteristically Germanic romantic operas that Lortzing holds a distinguished, if minor, place in the history of dramatic music. He was a follower of Weber, without Weber's imaginative projection; in his lighter works, he approached the type of French operetta; in his best creations he exhibited a fine sense of facile melody, and infectious rhythm; his harmonies, though unassuming, were always proper and pleasing; his orchestration, competent and effective. —Bibliography: P. J. Düringer, *Albert Lortzing, sein Leben und Wirken* (Leipzig, 1851); G. R. Kruse, *Albert Lortzing* (Berlin, 1899; standard biography); R. Bürner, *Albert Lortzing in Detmold* (Detmold, 1900); G. R. Kruse, *Lortzings Briefe* (Leipzig, 1902; augmented ed., 1913; 3rd ed., 1947); H. Wittmann, *Lortzing* (Leipzig, 1902); H. Laue, *Die Operndichtung Lortzings* (Bonn, 1932; a valuable analysis); H. Killer, *Albert Lortzing* (Potsdam, 1938); O. Schumann, *Albert Lortzing, sein Leben in Bildern* (Berlin, 1941); E. W. Böhme, *Albert Lortzing in Lüneburg* (1951); J. Knodt, *Albert Lortzing* (1955).

Los Angeles, Victoria de. See **De Los Angeles.**

Löschhorn, Albert, German composer and pedagogue; b. Berlin, June 27, 1819; d. there, June 4, 1905. He studied at the Royal Institute for Church Music with L. Berger, Killitschgy, Grell, and A. W. Bach; became piano teacher there in 1851. He publ. a series of excellent piano studies, including *Melodious Studies, La Vélocité, Universal Studies, Le Trille, School of Octaves,* which became standard pedagogical works; also wrote attractive piano solos, *La belle Amazone, 4 Pièces élégantes, Tarentelle, Deux Valses,* the barcarolle *À Venise,* and *Trois Mazurkas;* suites, sonatas, sonatinas, etc. With J. Weiss he publ. a *Wegweiser in die Pianoforte-Literatur* (1862; 2nd ed., 1885 as *Führer durch die Klavierliteratur).*

Loth, Louis Leslie, American composer; b. Richmond, Va., Oct. 28, 1888. He studied piano with Herman Epstein in New York and Alberto Jonás in Berlin; composition with Paul Ertel there. He gave concerts in Germany; then settled in N. Y. as teacher and composer. He wrote more than 500 works, including 2 symphonies, several symph. poems *(Paean, Granada, Tarentelle,* etc.), 2 piano concertos, many piano pieces of an imaginative nature *(Valsette, The Bobolink, Teasing, March, Butterfly Waltz, Con Amore, Firelight Fancies, Valse Brillante,* etc.); also teaching pieces.

Lotti, Antonio, Italian organist and composer; b. Venice, c. 1667; d. there, Jan. 5, 1740. He was a pupil of Legrenzi in Venice; produced an opera, *Giustino,* at the age of 16; in 1687 he became chorister at San Marco; in 1690, assistant organist there, and in 1692, 2nd organist. On Aug. 17, 1704 he was appointed 1st organist; in 1736 he was elected maestro di cappella. While at San Marco, he industriously composed church music, Masses, anthems, etc.; he also wrote dramatic music. As a teacher, he was highly renowned; among his pupils were Alberti, Gasparini, Galuppi, and Marcello. He absented himself from Venice but once (1717-19), when he went to Dresden at the Crown Prince's invitation. — Works: 21 operas, including *Alessandro Severo* (Venice, Dec. 26, 1716), *Giove in Argo* (Dresden, Oct. 25, 1717), *Teofane* (Dresden, Nov. 13, 1719), *Costantino* (Vienna, Nov. 19, 1716; in collaboration with Fux and Caldara); 4 oratorios: *Il voto crudele, L'umiltà coronata, Gioa re di Giuda,* and *Giuditta;* many Masses, motets, etc., none of which were publ. by him. Lück's 'Sammlung ausgezeichneter Compositionen' contains 4 Masses and other numbers; Rochlitz, Proske, Trautwein, Commer, Schlesinger, and others have printed Misereres and other sacred music by Lotti; 8 Masses were edited by H. Müller in the 'Denkmäler deutscher Tonkunst' (vol. 60). Lotti himself publ. only *Duetti, terzetti e madrigali* (1705, dedicated to Joseph I; includes the madrigal, *In una siepe ombrosa,* the appropriation of which caused Bononcini's downfall). —Cf. Charlotte Spitz, *Antonio Lotti in seiner Bedeutung als Opernkomponist* (Leipzig, 1918); Charlotte Spitz, *'Ottone' von Händel und 'Teofane' von Lotti,* in the 'Sandberger-Festschrift' (p. 265 et seq.); A. Moser, *Arcangelo Corelli und Antonio Lotti: Zwei künsterlische Ehrenrettungen,* in the 'Zeitschrift für Musik' (April, 1921); A. Schering, *Geschichte des Oratoriums* (p. 202 et seq.). —The correspondence regarding the controversy with Bononcini was reproduced in *Letters from the Academy of Ancient Music at London to Signor Antonio Lotti of Venice with his Answers and Testimonials* (London, 1732); the case was described in the article *The Fall of Bononcini,* in the 'Mus. Times' (Jan., 1892).

Lotze, Rudolf Hermann, German writer on music; b. Bautzen, May 21, 1817; d. Berlin, July 1, 1881. He became prof. of philosophy at Leipzig Univ. in 1842; in 1844, prof. in ordinary, and court councillor, at Göttingen; settled in Berlin shortly before his death. He publ. *Geschichte der Ästhetik in Deutschland* (1868), which contains criticism of Helmholtz, Hauptmann, and others; also interesting ideas on musical esthetics.

Louel, Jean, Belgian conductor and composer; b. Ostend, Jan. 3, 1914. He studied with Joseph Jongen (theory) and Désiré Defauw (conducting). After graduation from the Brussels Cons., he obtained the Belgian Prix de Rome with his cantata *De Vaart van Ulysses* (1943). In 1948 he became teacher of harmony at the Brussels Cons. His works include 2 piano concertos, a flute concerto, a clarinet sonata, a flute sonata, and several choral works.

Louis XIII, King of France from 1610 to 1643. He was an amateur musician, and wrote madrigals. The well known *Amaryllis,* arranged by Henri Ghis, and widely published as 'Air of Louis XIII,' is a misattribution; the melody first appears in print as 'La Clochette' in the *Ballet-Comique de la Reine* by Balthazar de Beaujoyeux, produced in 1582, long before Louis XIII was born. A gavotte, also entitled *Amaryllis,* with a melody totally different from the apocryphal 'Air of Louis XIII' and dated 1620, may be an authentic composition of Louis XIII.

Louis Ferdinand, Prince of Prussia, nephew of Frederick the Great; b. Friedrichsfelde, near Berlin, Nov. 18, 1772; fell at Saalfeld, Oct. 10, 1806. He was an excellent amateur musician. While traveling in 1804, he met Beethoven, and showed great interest in the master's music. Beethoven's 3rd piano concerto in C minor is dedicated to Louis Ferdinand, which testifies to their mutual esteem. However, the statement sometimes made that Louis Ferdinand imitated Beethoven in his own works is untenable inasmuch as the Prince fell in battle two years after his first acquaintance with Beethoven's music. The following compositions by Louis Ferdinand are published: 2 piano quintets; 2 piano quartets; 4 piano trios; octet for clarinet, 2 horns, 2 violins, 2 cellos, and piano; a *Notturno* for flute, violin, cello, and piano; *Andante and Variations* for viola, cello, and piano; a *Rondo* for piano and orch., and a *Rondo* for piano solo.—Cf. Elisabeth Wintzer, *Louis Ferdinand, als Mensch und Musiker* (1916); H. Wahl, *Prinz Louis Ferdinand von Preussen* (1917); F. Lewald, *Prinz Louis Ferdinand* (1929); A. Semrau, *Prinz Louis Ferdinand* (1930); R. Hahn, *Louis Ferdinand* (Breslau, 1934); E. Poseck, *Prinz Louis Ferdinand* (Berlin, 1938; 2nd ed., 1943).

Louis, Rudolf, German writer on music; b. Schwetzingen, Jan. 30, 1870; d. Munich, Nov. 15, 1914. He studied philosophy at the Universities of Geneva and Vienna *(Dr. phil.,* 1894); music with Klose and Mottl; was conductor at the State Theater in Landshut (1895-96), and in Lübeck (1896-97); in 1897, settled in Munich, where he became critic for the influential periodical, 'Neueste Nachrichten' (from 1900).—Publications: *Der Widerspruch in der Musik* (1893); *Richard Wagner als Musikästhetiker* (1897); *Die Weltanschauung Richard Wagners* (1898); *Franz Liszt* (1900); *Hector Berlioz* (1904); *Anton Bruckner* (1905); *Die deutsche Musik der Gegenwart* (1909; 3rd ed., 1912); *Aufgaben für den Unterricht in der Harmonielehre* (1911); with L. Thuille he wrote *Harmonielehre* (1907; 8th ed., 1924; abridged as *Grundriss der Harmonielehre,* 1908). He was also a composer; publ. a symph. fantasy, *Proteus* (1903); *Zum Hochzeitstage* and *Albumblatt* for piano, 4-hands; songs.

Loulié (loo-l'yā'), **Étienne,** 17th-century French writer on music; inventor of the 'chronomètre,' the precursor of the metronome. He studied with Gehenault and Ouvrard under the patronage of Mlle. de Guise; was at the Saint-Chapelle in Paris from 1663-73. He publ. *Éléments ou principes de musique dans un nouvel ordre . . . avec l'estampe et l'usage du chronomètre* (Paris, 1696), which describes and illustrates his invention, an unwieldy device 6 feet tall; and a *Nouveau système de musique* (1698), describing the 'sonomètre' (a monochord to aid in tuning), which he also invented.

Lourié, Arthur (Vincent), composer; b. St. Petersburg, May 14, 1892. He studied at the St. Petersburg Cons.; participated in various modernistic groups, and wrote piano music, much influenced by Scriabin *(Préludes fragiles, Synthèses,* etc.); also experimented in futuristic composition (e.g., *Formes en l'air,* dedicated to Picasso, and graphically imitating a cubist design by omitting the staves instead of using rests); also composed religious music *(Lamentations de la Vierge,* etc.). After the Soviet Revolution, he was appointed chief of the music dept. of the Commissariat for Public Instruction; in 1921 he left Russia, and lived in Paris for many years; in 1941, emigrated to the U. S., and became an American citizen. In his music written after 1920, he followed mainly Stravinsky's practice of stylizing old forms, secular and sacred. — Works: *Nash Marsh (Our March,* poem by Mayakovsky), for declamation with piano (1918); *La naissance de la beauté,* cantata for a chorus of 6 sopranos, soprano solo, and piano (1922); *Dithyrambes* for flute solo (1923); *Liturgical Sonata,* for orch., piano, and chorus (1928); *Concerto Spirituale,* for piano, chorus, and double-basses (N. Y., March 26, 1930); *Sinfonia Dialectica* (Symph. No. 1; Philadelphia, April 17, 1931); *Kormtschaya* (Symph. No. 2; Boston, Nov. 7, 1941); *The Feast During the Plague,* opera-ballet after Pushkin (1935; arranged for soprano solo, mixed chorus, and orch.; Boston, Jan. 5, 1945); *De ordinatione angelorum,* for chorus (1948); *Piano Gosse* (1917; republished in N. Y., 1944 under the title *8 Scenes of Russian Childhood);* 2 pieces for piano: *Berceuse de la chevrette* (1936) and *A Phoenix Park Nocturne* (1938). He published a biography of Koussevitzky (N. Y., 1931).

Løveberg, Aase (*née* Nordmo), brilliant Norwegian soprano; b. Målselv, June 10, 1923, in a peasant family; spent her childhood on a farm near the Arctic Circle. When she was 19 she went to Oslo, where she studied voice with Haldis Ingebjart; made her opera début in Oslo on Dec. 3, 1948; then sang in Stockholm, Vienna, Paris, and London, with excellent success; her performances of Wagnerian roles were particularly praised, and she was described as a natural successor to Kirsten Flagstad. She made her 1st American appearance as soloist with the

Philadelphia Orch. (Dec. 6, 1957); was engaged by the Metropolitan Opera Co. for Jan.-May, 1959.

Løvenskjold (lö'-vens-yhohlt), **Herman Severin,** Norwegian organist and composer; b. Holdensjärnbruk, July 30, 1815; d. Copenhagen, Dec. 5, 1870. At the age of 13 his parents took him to Copenhagen, where he studied music; in 1836, brought out his ballet *Sylphiden* there with much success. After the production of his second ballet, *Sara,* in 1839, he went to Vienna, where he took some lessons with Seyfried; returned to Denmark in 1851; was appointed organist at the Slottskyrka in Christiansborg. He wrote an opera, *Turandot* (Copenhagen, Dec. 3, 1854); *Festouvertüre* (for the coronation of Christian VIII); *Ouverture de concert idyllique;* the overture *Fra Skoven ved Furesø;* a piano trio; a piano quartet; piano pieces for 2 and 4 hands.

Lover, Samuel, Irish novelist, poet, painter, and composer; b. Dublin, Feb. 24, 1797; d. St. Heliers, Jersey, July 6, 1868. He wrote music to several Irish plays, and to many songs; publ. *Songs and Ballads* (London, 1859). Among his most popular songs (some of which are set to old Irish tunes) are *The Angel's Whisper, Molly Bawn,* and *The Low-Backed Car.* He wrote an opera, *Grana Uile, or the Island Queen* (Dublin, Feb. 9, 1832). He devised a very successful musical entertainment, *Irish Evenings* (1844), with which he toured the British Isles, also the U. S. (1846). He was Victor Herbert's grandfather.

Löw, Joseph, Bohemian pianist and composer; b. Prague, Jan. 23, 1834; d. there, Oct. 5, 1886. In 1854 he toured through Moravia, Silesia, Galicia, and the Bukovina; returning to Prague in 1856, he was active as a concert pianist and composer. He publ. over 450 numbers of light piano music, including *Jugend-Album; Deux Impromptus romantiques; Allegro brillant* for 2 pianos; *Soir de printemps; Maiengruss,* etc.

Löwe (lö'-veh), **Ferdinand,** Austrian conductor; b. Vienna, Feb. 19, 1865; d. there, Jan. 6, 1925. He studied with Dachs, Krenn, and Bruckner at the Vienna Cons.; then taught piano and choral singing there (1883-96). In 1897 he became conductor of the Kaim Orch. in Munich; then of the court opera in Vienna (1898-1900); of the 'Gesellschaftskonzerte' (1900-4); in 1904, of the newly organized Vienna Konzertverein Orch., which he made one of the finest instrumental bodies in Europe; returned to Munich as conductor of the Konzertverein (1908-14), which comprised members of the former Kaim Orch.; also conducted in Budapest and Berlin; from 1919-22, was head of the Vienna Staatsakademie für Musik. He was a friend and trusted disciple of Bruckner; edited (somewhat liberally) several of Bruckner's works still during the master's lifetime; conducted the 3 finished movements of Bruckner's posthumous 9th Symphony (Vienna, Feb. 11, 1903), with considerable cuts and alterations, adding Bruckner's *Te Deum* in lieu of the unfinished finale. Löwe's editions of Bruckner were challenged by A. Orel and R. Haas, who brought out a more authentic edition (1934).

Löwe, Karl. See **Loewe.**

Lowinsky, Edward, musicologist; b. Stuttgart, Jan. 12, 1908. He studied at the Hochschule für Musik in Stuttgart and at the Univ. of Heidelberg *(Dr. phil.,* 1933); emigrated to the U. S. and taught at Black Mountain College, N. C. (1942-47); received a Guggenheim Fellowship (1947) and went to Italy; returning to America, he became prof. of music first at the Univ. of Chicago (1949), then at Queens College, N. Y., and finally at the Univ. of California, Berkeley; was a member of the Institute for Advanced Study at Princeton (1952-53). — Publications: *Orlando di Lassos Antwerpener Motettenbuch* (The Hague, 1937); *Secret Chromatic Art in the Netherlands Motet* (N. Y., 1946); contributed essays on 16th-century and other music to the 'Mus. Quarterly' and other periodicals.

Lualdi, Adriano, Italian composer, conductor, and critic; b. Larino, Campobasso, March 22, 1885. He studied with Falchi in Rome and Wolf-Ferrari in Venice. From 1908-13 he was an opera conductor; in 1918 he went to Milan, where, from 1923-27, he was music critic of the 'Secolo'; in 1928, was appointed head of the music dept. of the Italian government; director of music festivals in Venice and Florence; toured South America as conductor and lecturer in 1932; in 1936, became director of the Cons. of San Pietro a Maiella in Naples (until 1943), and also music critic for the 'Giornale d'Italia' in Rome; then in 1949, became director of the Florence Cons. — Works: operas: *Guerrin meschino* (Rome, 1920), *Le nozze di Haura* (not produced), *La figlia del re,* after the *Antigone* of Sophocles (Turin, March 18, 1922), *Le Furie* *d'Arlecchino* (Buenos Aires, June 19, 1924), *Il diavolo nel campanile* (La Scala, Milan, April 22, 1925), *La Granceola* (Venice, Sept. 10, 1932), *Lumavig e la Saetta* (Rome, Jan. 23, 1937); the cantata *Attollite portas; La morte di Renaldo,* dramatic scene (Milan, 1916); the symph. poems *La Leggenda del vecchio marinaio* (1910) and *L'interludio del sogno* (1917); *Il cantico,* intermezzo for soloists with orch. (1915); *Sire Halewijn,* for soprano and orch.; *La rosa di Saron,* for soprano, tenor, and orch. (1927); *Suite adriatica,* for orch. (1932); *Africa,* rhapsody for orch. (1936); *Samnium,* 3 folk melodies for orch. (1938); *Divertimento* for orch. (1941); chamber music; choruses; songs. — Publications: *Viaggio sentimentale nella Liborina* (1921); *Viaggio musicale italiano* (1931); *Viaggio musicale in Europa* (1928); *Serate musicali* (1928); *Arte e Regime* (1929); *Il Rinnovamento musicale italiano* (1931); *Viaggio musicale nel Sud-America* (Milan, 1934); *Confessione* (self-portrait), in the 'Rivista nazionale di musica' (Feb. 15, 1932); *L'Arte di dirigere l'orchestra* (1940); *Viaggio musicale nel l'U.R.S.S.* (1941); *Tutti vivi* (Milan, 1955; essays). —Cf. G. Confalonieri, *L'opera di Adriano Lualdi* (Milan, 1932); R. Mariani, *Adriano Lualdi,* in 'Augustea' (Nov. 15, 1934).

Luban, Isaac Isaacovitch, Russian composer; b. Cherikov, near Moghilev, March 23, 1906. He studied composition in the Byelorussian Cons.; has written a number of popular choruses and songs; also music for the theater and for films; became conductor and musical director of the Byelorussian National Ensemble of Song and Dance.

Lübeck, Ernst, Dutch pianist and composer; son of Johann Heinrich Lübeck; b. The Hague, Aug. 24, 1829; d. in France, Sept. 17, 1876. A precocious pianist, he gave his first public concert when he was 12; from 1849-54, toured in the U. S., Mexico, and Peru; returning to The Hague, he became court pianist there; in 1855, settled in Paris, where he participated in chamber music concerts with Lalo, Armingaud, and Jacquard; in 1860 he appeared with the London Philharmonic. He fled from Paris during the Commune in 1871; died insane. Lübeck's compositions are solely for the piano; they include *Berceuse; Tarentelle; Polonaise; Trilby the Sprite: rêverie caractéristique;* etc. He enjoyed a great reputation in Paris as a virtuoso; Berlioz wrote enthusiastically about his playing.

Lübeck, Johann Heinrich, Dutch violinist and composer; b. Alphen, Feb. 11, 1799; d. The Hague, Feb. 7, 1865. He was a Prussian regimental musician (1813-15); studied music in Potsdam; then was a player in theater orchestras in Riga and Stettin; in 1823, settled in Holland, giving violin concerts. From 1827 until his death he was director of the Cons. of The Hague; was also conductor of the 'Diligentia' concerts there, and in 1829, became court conductor.

Lübeck, Louis, Dutch cellist; son of Johann Heinrich Lübeck; b. The Hague, Feb. 14, 1838; d. Berlin, March 8, 1904. He studied with Jacquard in Paris; from 1863-68, taught cello at the Leipzig Cons.; toured Germany, Holland, England, and the U. S. (1875-81); in 1881 he settled in Berlin as cellist in the court orch. He wrote 2 concertos for cello, and solo pieces.

Lübeck, Vincentius (Vincenz), German organist and composer; b. Padingbüttel, Sept., 1654; d. Hamburg, Feb. 9, 1740. He was organist at Stade for almost 30 years; in 1702, became organist at the Nicolaikirche in Hamburg, remaining in that post until his death. Lübeck's works, including 3 cantatas, chorale preludes for organ, etc., were publ. by Gottlieb Harms (Klecken, 1921).

Lubin (lü-ban'), **Germaine,** French soprano; b. Paris, Feb. 1, 1890. She studied at the Paris Cons. with Martini and Isnardon, winning 3 first prizes in 1912 (for singing, light opera, and grand opera). She made her début at the Opéra-Comique in 1912, remaining there until 1914, when she joined the Paris Opéra, becoming the leading dramatic soprano in 1939.

Lubin, Napoleone Antonio Eugenio, Italian violinist and composer; b. Turin, July 8, 1805; d. Berlin, Feb. 13, 1850. He began his career as a child violinist; gave concerts at the age of 10; then studied with Spohr at Kassel; from 1830 lived in Berlin. He publ. 5 violin concertos; *6 Capricci* (edited by Hubay in 1910); many violin solos; 19 string quartets; also stage music.

Luboshutz (real name, Luboshits), **Léa,** violinist; b. Odessa, Feb. 22, 1887; studied violin with her father; played in public at the age of 7; after study at the Odessa Music School, she went to the Moscow Cons., graduating with a gold medal (1903); gave concerts in Germany and France, and also took additional lessons from Eugène

Ysaÿe in Belgium; returned to Russia, and organized a trio with her brother Pierre (piano) and sister Anna (cello); left Russia after the Revolution and lived in Berlin and Paris (1921-25). In 1925 she settled in New York; played the American première of Prokofiev's 1st violin concerto (Nov. 14, 1925); made several appearances in joint recitals with her son, Boris Goldovsky, pianist. From 1927, she was on the faculty of the Curtis Institute of Music.

Luboshutz, Pierre, pianist; brother of Léa Luboshutz; b. Odessa, June 17, 1894; first studied violin with his father; then turned to the piano, and entered the Moscow Cons. as a pupil of Igumnov, graduating in 1912; also studied in Paris with Edouard Risler; returning to Russia, he played in a trio with his two sisters, Léa (violin) and Anna (cello); in 1926 went to America as accompanist to Zimbalist, Piatigorsky, and others; appeared as a soloist under Toscanini, in the Brahms D-minor concerto (1935). In 1931 he married Genia Nemenoff (b. Paris, Oct. 23, 1908); with her he formed a piano duo (N. Y. début, Jan. 18, 1937); as Luboshutz-Nemenoff, they gave annual concerts with considerable success.

Lubrich, Fritz, German organist and writer on music; b. Bärsdorf, July 29, 1862; d. Eberswalde, March 29, 1952. He studied in Breslau with A. Fischer. In 1890 he became cantor at Peilau, Silesia; then in Neisse, Kyritz, and Sagan; from 1928 he was in Sprottau; after World War II he lived in Eberswalde. He was editor of 'Die Orgel' (1889-97 and again from 1909); in 1896, of 'Fliegende Blätter des evangelischen Kirchen-Musikvereins für Schlesien' and of 'Kirchenmusikalisches Archiv.' He publ. a number of important essays on church music, among them *Liturgischer Altargesang; Die Kirchentonarten; Das geistliche Volkslied; Der Bachchoralist; Der Kirchenchor;* etc. His son, **Fritz Lubrich,** Jr. (b. Neustädtel, Jan. 26, 1888), a student of Max Reger and Straube, was active in Breslau as organist; after 1945, in Hamburg. He wrote church music, chamber music, and songs.

Luca, Giuseppe de, Italian baritone; b. Rome, Dec. 25, 1876; d. New York, Aug. 26, 1950. He studied music at Santa Cecilia in Rome; made his first professional appearance in Piacenza (1897) as Valentine in *Faust;* then sang in various cities of Italy; from 1902, chiefly in Milan at the Teatro Lirico and La Scala; he created the principal baritone role in the world première of Cilea's *Adriana Lecouvreur* and in *Madama Butterfly.* He made his American début at the Metropolitan Opera, as Figaro in *Il Barbiere di Siviglia,* on Nov. 25, 1915, with excellent success, immediately establishing himself as a favorite; on Jan. 28, 1916 he sang the part of Paquiro in the world première of *Goyescas* by Granados, at the Metropolitan Opera, of which he became a member until 1935; after a sojourn in Italy, he returned to the U.S. in 1940, and made a few more appearances at the Metropolitan, his vocal powers undiminished by age. He sang almost exclusively the Italian repertory; his interpretations were distinguished by fidelity to the dramatic import of his roles; he was praised by the critics for his finely graduated dynamic range and his mastery of bel canto.

Lucantoni, Giovanni, Italian composer and singing teacher; b. Rieti, Jan. 18, 1825; d. Paris, May 30, 1902. He studied with his parents, who were both good amateur musicians; then with Giovanni Pacini in Lucca and Nicola Vaccaj in Milan. In 1857 he settled in Paris as a singing teacher; also lived in London. His vocal compositions were very popular for a time; particularly well known was the vocal duet *Una notte a Venezia;* he also wrote an opera, *Elisa* (Milan, June 20, 1850); a 4-part Mass; a cantata; a symphony; and various 'ballabili' for piano.

Lucas, Leighton, English conductor and composer; b. London, Jan. 5, 1903. He was trained to be a dancer and for 3 years was a member of the Diaghilev Russian Ballet (1918-21). Then he learned conducting, and traveled with various ballet companies. He also began to compose, mainly for the dance. He wrote the music for the ballets, *The Wolf's Ride* (1935), *The Horses* (1946); and made arrangements of classical compositions (Scarlatti and others) for dance presentations. He has also written chamber music.

Lucas, Mary Anderson, English composer; b. London, May 24, 1882; d. there, Jan. 14, 1952. She studied piano at the Dresden Cons.; later took lessons in composition with R. O. Morris and Herbert Howells. She adopted an advanced harmonic style of composition; her works comprise a ballet, *Sawdust* (1941), which had considerable success; 6 string quartets; trio for clarinet, viola, and piano; *Rhapsody* for flute, cello, and piano; and many songs.

Lucca, Pauline, Austrian soprano; b. Vienna, April 25, 1841; d. there, Feb. 28, 1908. The daughter of a Venetian father and a German mother, she acquired cosmopolitan culture as a young girl; also showed musical ability; at 15 she sang in the choir of the Karlskirche in Vienna; then took regular lessons with Uschmann and Lewy, after which she joined the chorus of the Vienna Opera. Her professional début took place at Olmütz as Elvira in *Ernani* (Sept. 4, 1859). Her appearance in Prague as Norma attracted the attention of the musical world; Meyerbeer, who heard her, arranged her engagements in Berlin. She sang in London in 1863 with extraordinary success, and was re-engaged there for a number of seasons. In 1872 she made her first appearance in the U. S.; 1874, returned to Europe. In 1869 she married Baron von Rhaden; divorced him in 1871; while in America, she married Herr von Wallhofen, who died in 1899. She was a member of the Vienna Opera from 1874 till 1889, allowing for her tours elsewhere; then retired. In her prime she was an exceptionally successful and musicianly singer; she was rated as 'prima donna assoluta,' and her private life was a constant subject of sensational stories; a curious pamphlet entitled *Bellicose Adventures of a Peaceable Prima Donna* was published for her American tour (N.Y., 1872), relating her experiences during the Franco-Prussian war. —Cf. Anna Mara-Jansen and D. Weisse-Zehrer, *Die Wiener Nachtigall; der Lebensweg der Pauline Lucca* (Berlin, 1935).

Luciani, Sebastiano Arturo, Italian musicologist; b. Acquaviva delle Fonti, June 9, 1884; d. there, Dec. 7, 1950. He studied in Naples and Rome; devoted his energies mainly to documentation of biographies of Italian composers. He published a monograph on Domenico Scarlatti (Turin, 1942); edited *Antonio Vivaldi: note e documenti sulla vita e sulla opere* (1939) and *La Scuola veneziana* (1940).

Lučić (lōō'-chich), **Franjo,** Croatian composer; b. Kuče, in Turopolje, March 31, 1889; prof. of theory and organ at the Zagreb Cons. His works include 2 symphonies, sacred choral compositions, and organ pieces. He is the author of a manual on harmony and counterpoint (2 vols.).

Luckstone, Isidore, American pianist and singing teacher; b. Baltimore, Jan. 29, 1861; d. New York, March 12, 1941. He studied piano with Ph. Scharwenka in Berlin; made a world tour as accompanist to Reményi (1884-91); in 1897 settled in New York as singing teacher and accompanist; from 1925 till 1939 was on the faculty of the School of Education, N.Y. Univ. He composed numerous songs.

Lucký (loots'-kē), **Stěpán,** Czech composer; b. Žilina, Jan. 20, 1919. He studied piano and composition at the Prague Cons.; was arrested by the Germans during World War II, and was in several concentration camps before the liberation in 1945, when he resumed his studies in Prague; wrote music criticism; in 1949 was appointed head of the music dept. at the Central Council of Artistic Activities in Prague. Among his works are: *Divertimento* for 2 trombones and string orch. (1946); a cello concerto (1946); piano concerto (1947); quintet for wind instruments (Amsterdam Festival of the International Society for Contemporary Music, June 10, 1948); quartet for 2 trumpets, horn, and trombone (1948); *Sonata brevis,* for violin and piano (1948); also studies for quarter-tone piano.

Ludford, Nicholas, English composer; b. c. 1485; d. c. 1557. He was one of the musicians at St. Stephen's Westminster; in 1521 was admitted to the Fraternity of St. Nicholas, a guild of musicians. His surviving works (all in MS) include Masses, motets, and a Magnificat. —Cf. H. Baillie, *Nicholas Ludford,* in the 'Mus. Quarterly' (April, 1958).

Ludikar, Pavel, bass singer; b. Prague, March 3, 1882. He studied law and philosophy (with Masaryk) in Prague; then turned to music, and took piano lessons, progressing so rapidly that at the age of 19 he was able to appear as pianist in the U.S.; soon afterwards he began to study voice; made his professional début at the National Opera in Prague in 1904; then sang in Vienna, Dresden, Milan, and Buenos Aires. He first sang in the U. S. as a member of the Boston Civic Opera (1913-14); from 1926 to 1935, was a member of the Metropolitan Opera Co.; was eminently successful as Figaro in *Il Barbiere di Siviglia,* and sang this role more than 100 times in the U.S.; he also performed the leading bass parts in Russian operas; created the title role of Krenek's opera *Karl V* in Prague (June 22, 1938). His repertory included about 80 parts in 4 languages.

Ludkewycz, Stanislaus, composer; b. Jaroslav, Austrian Galicia, Dec. 24, 1879. He studied music in Lwow, and later in Vienna with Grädener and Zemlinsky; received his *Dr. phil.* in 1908. From 1910-14 he was in Lwow as director of the Lissenko Society and Institute of Music; was recruited in the Austrian Army, and was taken prisoner by the Russians (1915). After the Revolution he was evacuated to Tashkent; liberated in 1918, he returned to Lwow, where he was still living in 1953. He received the order of the Red Banner from the Soviet Government in 1949. —Works: the operas *Bar Kochba* and *Dovbush* (1952); the symph. poems *Valse mélancolique* (1916), *Stone Carvers* (1926), *Dnieper* (1947), etc.; 2 piano concertos (1919; 1950); *Carpathian Symphony* (1951); *Caucasus,* a symph. ode for chorus and orch. (1911); *Salute to Lwow,* for chorus (1944); *Song About Stalin,* for chorus (1949); chamber music; a collection of Ukrainian songs for chorus (1906-14). He publ. a handbook of choral singing; 1500 Ukrainian melodies of Austria, in the ethnographic studies of the Musicological Society of Lwow (1900-2); a manual of music history and other pedagogical works. —Cf. A. Kos-Anatolsky, *S. Ludkewycz, Oldest Composer of the Ukraine,* in 'Sovietskaya Musica' (June, 1951).

Ludwig, August, German composer and musical journalist; b. Waldheim, Jan. 15, 1865; d. Dresden, April 9, 1946. He studied at the Cons. of Cologne, and later in Munich; brought out a number of orchestral compositions, notably the overtures *Ad Astra* and *Luther-Ouvertüre;* also a comic opera, *Kunst und Schein* (1906). From 1894 till 1903 he was editor of the 'Neue Berliner Musikzeitung.' He publ. *Geharnischte Aufsätze über Musik* (a collection of essays); *Der Konzertagent* (1894); *Stachel und Lorbeer* (1897); *Zur Wertschätzung der Musik* (1898); *Tannhäuser redivivus* (1908). He attracted unfavorable attention by his abortive attempt to 'complete' Schubert's Unfinished Symphony, adding 2 movements, a *Philosophen-Scherzo* and a *Schicksalsmarsch.*

Ludwig, Franz, Bohemian composer and musicologist; b. Graslitz, July 7, 1889; d. Münster, June 15, 1955. He studied first with his father, director of the Graslitz Music School; then with Pembaur, Reger, and Krehl at the Leipzig Cons., and with Riemann (musicology) at Leipzig Univ. He publ. a *Kurzgefasste Musikgeschichte des Erzgebirges* (1924); biographies of Franz Wüllner, etc. He composed an opera, *Schlag zwölf* (Münster, 1928); a scenic oratorio, *Das Lambertusspiel* (Bremerhaven, 1933); *Lustspielouvertüre* for orch.; a piano concerto; a horn concerto; *Serenade* for 8 wind instruments; sonatas and other pieces for piano; men's choruses; songs.

Ludwig, Friedrich, German musicologist; b. Potsdam, May 8, 1872; d. Göttingen, Oct. 3, 1930. He studied history and musicology at the Univs. of Marburg and Strasbourg. After traveling in France, England, and Italy (1899-1905), he joined the faculty of the Univ. of Strasbourg as teacher of musicology; wrote the dissertation *Die Aufgaben der Forschung auf dem Gebiete der mittelalterlichen Musikgeschichte,* publ. in the 'Münchener Allgemeine Zeitung' (1906); in 1911, became associate prof. at the Univ. of Strasbourg, then at the Univ. of Göttingen (1920); later, rector there. He was an authority on the music of the 11th to 14th centuries. —Writings: *Die mehrstimmige Musik des 14. Jahrhunderts,* in 'Sammelbände der Internationalen Musik-Gesellschaft' (vol. 4); *Die 50 Beispiele Coussemakers aus dem Codex Montpellier,* ibid. (vol. 5); *Entstehung und erste Entwicklung der lateinischen und französischen Motette,* ibid. (vol. 7); *Das Jacobsofficium des 12. Jahrhunderts,* in 'Kirchenmusikalisches Jahrbuch' (1905); *Die mehrstimmigen Werke der Handschrift Engelberg 314,* ibid. (1908); *Die liturgischen Organa Leonins und Perotins,* in the 'Riemann-Festschrift' (1909); *Mehrstimmige Musik des 11. und 12. Jahrhunderts,* in the Vienna 'Kongress-Bericht' (1909); *Repertorium organorum recentioris et motetorum vetustissimi stili* (vol. 1, 1910); *Perotinus Magnus,* in 'Archiv für Musikwissenschaft' (vol. 3, 1921); *Die Quellen der Motetten ältesten Stils,* ibid. (vols. 5 and 6, 1923-24); *Die mehrstimmigen Messen des 14. Jahrhunderts,* ibid. (vol. 7, 1925); *Mittelalterliche Musik bis Anfang des 15. Jahrhunderts,* in Adler's 'Handbuch der Musikgeschichte' (1924); *Über den Entstehungsort der grossen Notredame-Handschriften,* in the 'Adler-Festschrift' (1930); etc. He edited the musical works of Guillaume de Machaut (3 vols. of T. Kroyer's 'Publikationen älterer Musik'; 1926-34). —Cf. J. Müller-Blattau, *Dem Andenken Friedrich Ludwigs* (Kassel, 1931); K. Ameln, in 'Die Singgemeinde' (Oct.-Nov., 1930); C. Mahrenholz, in 'Musik und Kirche' (Nov.-Dec., 1930).

Luening, Otto, American composer; b. Milwaukee, June 15, 1900. He studied flute and composition; took courses at the Royal Academy of Music in Munich, and at the Zürich Cons. (with Jarnach and Andreae); also studied privately with Busoni. From

1915-20 he remained in Europe, conducting concerts in Switzerland; toured also as flutist and as piano accompanist in Europe, Canada, and the U.S.; was a co-founder of the American Grand Opera Co. in Chicago (1920); was executive director of the opera dept. of the Eastman School of Music (1925-28); in 1930 won a Guggenheim Fellowship; 1933, won the David Bispham Medal for American opera with his *Evangeline;* was associate prof. at the Univ. of Arizona (1932-34); prof. at Bennington College (1934-44); then at Barnard College (from 1944); in 1946, received the annual award of the National Institute of Arts and Letters. —Works: opera, *Evangeline* (1932; produced at the Columbia Univ. Festival, May 5, 1948, composer conducting); 2 symph. poems (1921; 1924); *Symphonietta* (1933); *Concertino,* for flute, harp, celesta, and strings (Philadelphia, Jan. 30, 1935); *Americana,* for orch. (1936); *2 Symphonic Interludes* (N.Y., April 11, 1936); *Prelude to a Hymn Tune* (after William Billings), for piano and small orch. (N.Y., Feb. 1, 1937); *Suite* for string orch. (Saratoga Springs, Sept. 12, 1937); *Fantasia Brevis,* for strings (1939); *Fuguing Tune,* for flute, oboe, clarinet, bassoon, and horn (1941); *Louisville Concerto,* for orch. (1951); *Legend,* for oboe and strings (1951); 3 violin sonatas; 3 string quartets; a sonata for cello solo; 2 flute sonatas; choral works; songs; etc. He also wrote several experimental works for tape recorder, e. g., *Low Speed,* in 2 sections: *Invention* and *Fantasy in Space* (Museum of Modern Art, N.Y., Oct. 28, 1952); with Vladimir Ussachevsky, he prepared a *Poem in Cycles and Bells* for tape recorder and orch. (Los Angeles, Nov. 18, 1954) and a *Suite from 'King Lear'* for tape recorder alone. —Cf. J. Beeson, *Otto Luening,* in 'Bulletin' of American Composers Alliance (Autumn, 1953).

Lugert, Josef, Bohemian composer and theorist; b. Frohnau, Oct. 30, 1841; d. Prague, July 24, 1936. He studied at the Prague School for Organists with Krejčí; violinist at the German Theater; instructor of piano and history of music at the Prague Cons. (1868); made inspector of all music schools under state control in 1876. He organized special orchestral schools at Petschkau and Pressnitz and technical schools for the manufacture of musical instruments at Graslitz and Schönbach. —Works: a symphony; orchestral suite; *Serenade* for orch.; *In Memoriam,* elegy for English horn and orch.; *Serenade* for string orch.; a piano quartet; string quartets; a piano trio; a violin sonata; piano pieces. —Writings: *Musikalische Formenlehre, Anleitung zur Partiturenkenntnis, Praktischer Lehrgang der Instrumentation, Leitfaden der Musikgeschichte, Stufengang beim Klavierunterricht.*

Luigini (lŏŏ-ē-jē'-nē), **Alexandre (-Clément-Léon-Joseph),** French composer; b. Lyons, March 9, 1850; d. Paris, July 29, 1906. He was the son of the Italian musician Giuseppe Luigini (1820-1898), who conducted at the Théâtre-Italien in Paris; studied at the Paris Cons. with Massart (violin) and Massenet (composition); then entered his father's orch. at Lyons (1869) as violinist, and began his very successful career as ballet composer with the production of his first stage work *Le Rêve de Nicette* (Lyons, 1870); in 1877 he became conductor at the Grand Théâtre at Lyons and prof. of harmony at the Lyons Cons.; after 20 years there, went to Paris as conductor at the Opéra-Comique, where he remained till his death, except during 1903, when he conducted the orch. at the Théâtre-Lyrique. His greatest success as composer came with the production of *Ballet égyptien* (Lyons, Jan. 13, 1875), still one of the most popular ballet scores; it was inserted, with Verdi's permission, in the 2nd act of *Aida* at its performance in Lyons in 1886. —Other works: comic operas: *Les Caprices de Margot* (Lyons, 1877), *La Reine des fleurs* (Lyons, 1878), *Faublas* (Paris, 1881); ballets: *Ballet égyptien* (Lyons, 1875), *Anges et Démons* (1876), *Les Noces d'Ivanovna* (1883), *Le Bivouac* (1889), *Les Écharpes* (1891), *Rayon d'Or* (1891), *Rose et Papillon* (1891), *Le Meunier* (1892), *Arlequin écolier* (1894), *Dauritha* (1894); also *Romance symphonique* for orch.; 3 string quartets (all won prizes); marches for orch.; numerous piano pieces.

Lukačić (lŏŏ'-kah-chich), **Ivan,** Croatian organist and composer; b. Šibenik, c. 1574; d. Split, Sept. 20, 1648. He studied music in Italy; spent most of his life in Split as a Franciscan cleric. His book *Sacrae Cantiones* (Venice, 1620) includes 27 motets; they reflect the influence of the early Baroque style and employ instrumental accompaniment. Of these motets, eleven were reprinted by Plamenac in his collection of 1935, publ. in Zagreb.

Lukin, Philip Mironovitch, Russian composer; b. Syaval-Sirmy, near Kazan, June 3, 1913, in a peasant family. He studied choral conducting and composition at the Moscow Cons.; became conductor of the Chuvash

Ensemble of Song and Dance; president of the Union of Chuvash composers. He has written a number of choruses and mass songs on Chuvash themes.

Lully (or Lulli), Jean-Baptiste, celebrated composer; b. Florence, Nov. 28, 1632; d. Paris, March 22, 1687. Son of a poor Florentine miller, he was taught the elements of music by a Franciscan monk, and also learned to play the guitar, and later the violin. Attracted by his vivacious temperament and a talent for singing, the Chevalier de Guise took him to Paris in 1646 as a page to Mademoiselle d'Orléans, a young cousin of Louis XIV. He soon adapted himself to the ways and manners of the French court, and quickly mastered the language, although he could never rid himself of a pronounced Italian accent. The story that he was ever a scullery boy is apocryphal, but he kept company with the domestic servants, and his talent as a violin player was first revealed by his improvisations in the royal kitchen; Count de Nogent heard him, and secured for him a position in the private band of Mademoiselle d'Orléans. When he set to music a satirical poem reflecting on his patroness, he lost favor with her, but entered the service of young Louis XIV (1652), winning his first success as a ballet dancer. He contrived to obtain instruction on the harpsichord, and in composition from Nicolas Métru, organist of St. Nicolas-des-Champs, and François Roberday, organist at the Église des Petits-Pères. He attended opera and concerts at the court, led by his compatriot Luigi Rossi, and conceived a passion for the theater, which became the determining factor in his entire career. After a brief association with the King's private orchestra, 'les 24 violons du roi,' he organized his own band of 17 instruments (later 21), 'les petits violons,' which he developed into a fine ensemble. He rose fast in royal favor; became a favorite composer of court ballets for various occasions; in several of these productions Louis XIV himself took part next to Lully, who danced and acted as 'M. Baptiste.' In 1661 he received the lucrative post of composer to the king, and in 1662, a further appointment as maître de musique of the royal family. In 1662 he married Madeleine Lambert, daughter of the court musician Michel Lambert. From 1663 to 1671 he wrote music for several comic ballets by Molière, including *Le Mariage forcé, L'Amour médecin,* and *Le Bourgeois gentilhomme,* which foreshadowed the development of opéra-comique. In 1672 he obtained letters patent for the establishment of an 'Académie royale de musique' (which eventually became the Grand Opéra), taking the privilege from Perrin and Cambert, who originally launched the enterprise in 1668. With the formation of a national opera house, Lully found his true calling, that of creating French operatic art, setting French texts to music with sensitivity to the genius of the language, and abandoning the conventional Italian type of opera, with its repetitive extensions of arias, endless fiorituras, etc. In this respect, Lully is the first of a line of reformers — one in each century (Gluck, Wagner) — that elevated dramatic action above superficial musical effects. In the theater, Lully did not confine himself to the composer's functions, but also acted as director, stage manager, conductor, and even, upon occasion, machinist. From 1672 he worked in close cooperation with a congenial librettist, Quinault, who followed Lully's ideas with rare understanding. Lully developed a type of overture which became known as the 'Lully Overture' or 'French Overture' and of which the earliest example occurs in his ballet *Alcidiane* (1658); this type of overture opens with a broad, sharply rhythmed section, in homophonic style, followed by a fast movement with some elements of canonic imitation; the concluding part is an extended coda in a much slower tempo. In vocal writing, Lully demonstrated his mastery of both dramatic recitative and songful arias; he imparted dramatic interest to his choral ensembles; the instrumental parts were also given more prominence than in early Italian opera. That an Italian-born musician should have become the founder of French opera is one of the many paradoxes of music history. — As a man, Lully was far from ideal; haughty, arrogant, and irascible, he brooked no opposition; his ambition was his prime counsellor; considerations of morality played a small part in his actions. With those in power, he knew how to be submissive; a shrewd courtier, he often gained his aims by flattery and obsequiousness; the manner in which he secured for himself the directorship of the Académie royale de musique through the royal favorite Mme. de Montespan moved some of his critics to berate him savagely. Yet, thanks to his volcanic energy and his disregard of all obstacles, he was able to accomplish an epoch-making task. His death resulted from a symbolic accident: while conducting, he vehemently struck his foot with a sharp-pointed cane used as a baton; gangrene set in, and he died of blood poisoning.

WORKS: Ballets (produced at court in Paris, Versailles, Saint-Germain, and Fontainebleau): *La Nuit* (Feb. 23, 1653); *Alcidiane* (Feb. 14, 1658); *La Raillerie* (Feb. 19, 1659); *L'Impatience* (Feb. 19, 1661); *Les Saisons* (July 30, 1661); *Hercule amoureux* (ballet music for Cavalli's opera *Ercole amante;* Feb. 7, 1662); *Les Arts* (Jan. 8, 1663); *Les Noces de village* (Oct. 3, 1663); *Le Mariage forcé* (Jan. 29, 1664); *Les Amours déguisés* (Feb. 15, 1664); *Les Plaisirs de l'isle enchantée* (May 8, 1664); *La Naissance de Vénus* (Jan. 26, 1665); *L'Amour médecin* (Sept. 15, 1665); *Les Muses* (Dec. 2, 1666); *Le Sicilien, ou l'Amour peintre* (Feb. 10, 1667); *Le Carnaval* (Jan. 18, 1668); *Georges Dandin* (July 18, 1668); *Flore* (Feb. 13, 1669); *Monsieur de Pourceaugnac* (Oct. 6, 1669); *Les Amants magnifiques* (Feb. 4, 1670); *Le Bourgeois gentilhomme* (Oct. 14, 1670); *Psyché* (Jan. 17, 1671). —Operas: *Cadmus et Hermione* (April 27, 1673); *Alceste, ou Le Triomphe d'Alcide* (Jan. 19, 1674); *Thésée* (Jan. 12, 1675); *Atys* (Jan. 10, 1676); *Isis* (Jan. 5, 1677); *Psyché* (a different work from the similarly named ballet; April 19, 1678); *Bellérophon* (Jan. 31, 1679); *Proserpine* (Feb. 3, 1680); *Le Triomphe de l'Amour* (Jan. 21, 1681); *Persée* (April 18, 1682); *Phaéton* (Jan. 9, 1683); *Amadis de Gaule* (Jan. 18, 1684); *Roland* (Jan. 8, 1685); *Idylle sur la paix* (July 16, 1685); *Le Temple de la paix* (Oct. 20, 1685); *Armide et Renaud* (Feb. 15, 1686); *Acis et Galatée* (Sept. 17, 1686); *Achille et Polyxène* (Nov. 7, 1687). For further details about productions and revivals of Lully's operas, see A. Loewenberg, *Annals of Opera* (1943; new ed., 1955). Ten stage works produced at the French court between 1653 and 1657 had several numbers contributed by Lully. Most of Lully's operas have been publ. by Breitkopf & Härtel, in 'Chefs-d'œuvre classiques de l'opéra français'; *Armide et Renaud* in Eitner's 'Publikationen älterer Musikwerke' (vol. 14; full score, and a piano score). Besides his stage works, Lully wrote a *Te Deum,* a Miserere, a 4-part Mass a cappella, many motets; instrumental works (string trios, airs for violin, etc.). In 1930, Henry Prunières undertook a complete ed. of Lully's works (9 vols. publ. from 1930-38). —Bibliography: Le Prevost d'Exmes, *Lully Musicien* (Paris, 1779); Th. Lajarte, *Lully* (Paris, 1878); E. Radet, *Lully, Homme d'affaires, propriétaire et musicien* (Paris, 1891); R. Gandolfi, *Accademia dedicata a G. B. Lulli e Luigi Cherubini* (Florence, 1902); Romain Rolland, *Musiciens d'autrefois* (Paris, 1908; in English, 1915); Henry Prunières, *Lully* (Paris, 1909); L. de La Laurencie, *Lully* (Paris, 1911); Henry Prunières, *L'Opéra italien en France avant Lully* (Paris, 1913); Henry Prunières, *Le Ballet de cour en France avant Lully* (Paris, 1914); special issue of the 'Revue Musicale' (Jan. 1925); Henry Prunières, *Lully and the Académie de Musique et de Danse,* in the 'Mus. Quarterly' (Oct., 1925); Henry Prunières, *La Vie illustre et libertine de J. B. Lully* (Paris, 1929; a somewhat romanticized biography, based on factual data); F. Böttger, *Die Comédie-Ballets von Molière und Lully* (Berlin, 1931); E. Borrel, *J.-B. Lully: le cadre, la vie, la personnalité, le rayonnement, les œuvres* (Paris, 1949); Th. Valensi, *Louis XIV et Lully* (Nice, 1951); see also N. Slonimsky's article in the 'Guide du Concert' (Feb. 1, 1952), which reproduces the text of Lully's birth certificate, establishing the date as Nov. 28, 1632.

Lumbye (lŏŏm-bü), **Hans Christian,** Danish composer of light music; b. Copenhagen, May 2, 1810; d. there, March 20, 1874. He played in military bands as a youth; in 1839 formed his own orch., soon achieving fame as a conductor and composer of dance music, especially with his concerts in the Tivoli amusement park in Copenhagen. He composed about 400 pieces of dance music (waltzes, galops, polkas, marches, etc), which earned him the sobriquet of 'the Johann Strauss of the North.' His two sons were also musicians; the elder, **Carl Lumbye** (b. Copenhagen, July 9, 1841; d. there, Aug. 10, 1911), was a violinist, conductor, and composer of dance music. The younger son, **Georg Lumbye** (b. Copenhagen, Aug. 26, 1843; d. there, Oct. 30, 1922), studied at the Paris Cons., and conducted dance music in Copenhagen; wrote the operetta *Heksefløtjen* (*The Witch's Flute;* 1869) and numerous vaudevilles. —Cf. G. Skjerne, *H. C. Lumbye og hans Samtid* (Copenhagen, 1912; 2nd ed., 1946).

Lund, Signe, Norwegian composer; b. Christiania, April 15, 1868. She studied in Berlin with Berger; then in Copenhagen and Paris; spent several years in America. Her style of composition was much influenced by Grieg. —Works: cantatas (including one to celebrate the centenary of the Norwegian constitution; 1914); music for the Björnson centenary in Chicago (1910); *The Road to France,* composed on the occasion of America's entering World War I (1917); also various pieces for small orch., piano, violin, and songs. In 1941 she received a state pension for her compositions. She published an autobiography, *Sol gjennem skyer* (Oslo, 1944).

Lunn, Charles, English tenor; b. Birmingham, Jan. 5, 1838; d. London, Feb. 28, 1906. He studied in Italy with Sangiovanni, Cattaneo, and Vizione; then sang in concert and oratorio (1864-67); settled as a teacher in Birmingham, where his pupils' concerts, given in the Town Hall, became important local events; in 1895 he moved to London. He wrote *The Philosophy of Voice,* a valuable work (1874; 10th ed., 1906), followed by a sequel, *Vox Populi* (1880); also *Vocal Expression, Empirical or Scientific* (1878).

Lunn, Louise. See **Kirkby-Lunn.**

Lunssens, Martin, Belgian conductor and composer; b. Molenbeek-Saint-Jean, April 16, 1871; d. Etterbeek, Feb. 1, 1944. He studied with Gevaert, Jehin, and Kufferath at the Brussels Cons., gaining the 1st Belgian Prix de Rome in 1895 with the cantata *Callirhoé;* then became prof. at the Cons. of Brussels; subsequently was director of the Music Academy at Courtrai (1905-16); at Charleroi (1916-21); at the Cons. of Louvain (1921-24); and finally at Ghent (from 1924). He was also known as an excellent conductor; was in charge of the Flemish Opera in Antwerp, where he conducted many Wagner operas. He wrote 4 symphonies, the first 3 with the programmatic titles *Symphonie romaine, Symphonie florentine,* and *Symphonie française;* several symph. poems *(Roméo et Juliette; Phèdre; Le Cid; Timon d'Athènes)*; 3 violin concertos; a viola concerto; a cello concerto; much chamber music; songs.

Lupi, Roberto, Italian composer and music scholar; b. Milan, Nov. 28, 1908. He studied at the Cons. of Milan (graduated in 1934); then became prof. of harmony and counterpoint at the Cherubini Cons. in Florence. Among his works are the cantata, *Orfeo* (Venice, 1951); *Sacra Sinfonia;* cello sonata; songs. He publ. a treatise, *Armonia di gravitazione* (Rome, 1946), emphasizing the importance of the focal tone in composition rather than key. He has edited several works by Galuppi, Caldara, Stradella, and other Italian composers.

Luporini, Gaetano, Italian opera composer; b. Lucca, Dec. 12, 1865; d. there, May 12, 1948. He was a pupil of Primo Quilici, and a protégé of Ricordi, the publisher. After graduating from the Pacini Music Institute in Lucca, he studied at the Milan Cons. with Carlo Angeloni and Catalani; returning to Lucca in 1902, he became director of the Pacini Music Institute; also choirmaster of the Lucca cathedral. — Works: operas: *I dispetti amorosi* (Turin, Feb. 27, 1894); *La Collana di Pasqua* (Naples, Nov. 1, 1896; renamed *Nora,* and performed under that title in Lucca, Sept. 7, 1908); *L'aquila e le colombe* (Rome, Feb. 17, 1914); *Chiaro di luna* (Bologna, Nov. 20, 1925); also orchestral pieces and songs.

Lupus, Eduardus. See **Lobo, Duarte.**

Lupus (Latinized name of De Wolf), **Michael,** Flemish composer; b. c. 1500; d. Lierre, July 15, 1567. Biographical data are scant, and identity uncertain. He had a prebend at Soignies in 1535; in the same year was named chaplain to the court of Charles V at Naples. Upon his return to the Netherlands, he received a new prebend at Lierre. He traveled with Charles V in Germany (1547-48); when the Emperor abdicated in 1555, Lupus lost his positions. 4 motets by Lupus are found in Fuenllana's collection of 1554, and in Petrucci's *Motetti de la Corona* (1526). —Cf. René Vannes, *Dictionnaire des Musiciens* (Brussels, 1947).

Lussan, Zélie de, soprano; b. Brooklyn, Dec. 21, 1862; d. London, Dec. 18, 1949. She received voice instruction from her mother, an opera singer; made her concert début at the age of 16 at the Academy of Music, Brooklyn; opera début with the Boston Ideal Opera Co. (1885), remaining with it for several seasons; went to London, where she was engaged by the Carl Rosa Co. (1889); in 1894 joined the staff of the Metropolitan Opera, but had the misfortune of singing Carmen there after Emma Calvé had created a sensation in that role during the preceding season, so that her real worth was not properly appreciated; she sang again at the Metropolitan in 1900-1901, this time with considerable acclaim; also appeared in Paris and Madrid. On Sept. 11, 1907, she married the pianist Angelo Fronani in London; he died in 1918; she remained in London until her death. She made her last professional appearance in 1910 with the Beecham Opera Co. in London.

Lussy (lü-sē'), **Mathis,** Swiss writer on music and piano teacher; b. Stans, April 8, 1828; d. Montreux, Jan. 21, 1910. He studied with Businger and Nägeli; went to Paris in 1847 as a piano teacher.—Works: *Exercices de mécanisme* (1863); *Traité de l'expression musicale* (1873; partial reprint as *Le Rythme musical,* 1883); *Histoire de la notation musicale* (1882; written with E.

David); *L'Anacrouse dans la musique moderne* (1903); *De la diction musicale et grammaticale,* in the 'Riemann-Festschrift' (1909); *La 'Sonate pathétique' de Beethoven* (publ. posthumously, 1912; edited by A. Dechevrens). — Cf. E. Monod, *Mathis Lussy et le Rythme Musical* (Neuchâtel, 1912).

Lütgendorff, Willibald Leo, German theorist; b. Augsburg, July 8, 1856; d. Weimar, Dec. 31, 1937. He studied at the Kunstakademie in Munich; in 1889, became director of the Kunstschule and curator of the Art Gallery in Lübeck. Besides writings on the plastic arts, he publ. *Die Geigen- und Lautenmacher vom Mittelalter bis zur Gegenwart* (1904; enlarged ed., 1913; in 2 vols., 1922), which is regarded as a standard authority.

Luther, Martin, the great religious reformer; b. Eisleben, Nov. 10, 1483; d. there, Feb. 18, 1546. His reform of the church extended to the musical services, in which he took the deepest interest. After leaving the Wartburg, near Eisenach (March 22, 1522), he gave his ideas practical shape; his *Formula missae* (1523) and *Deutsche Messe* (German Mass; 1526; facsimile ed. by J. Wolf, Kassel, 1934) established the new service. He changed the order of the Mass; a German psalm took the place of the introit; the German Creed was substituted for the Latin Credo. The German Mass was sung for the first time in the Parish Church at Wittenberg on Christmas Day, 1524. Kapellmeister Conrad Rupsch and cantor Johann Walter aided Luther in organizing the musical part of the Mass. Walter states that Luther invented chorale melodies on the flute (he was an excellent flutist), and that these were noted down by Walter and Rupsch. It is impossible to establish with certainty which hymn tunes ascribed to Luther are really his; *Jesaia dem Propheten das geschah* is definitely Luther's; and the celebrated hymn tune, *Ein' feste Burg ist unser Gott,* is most probably authentic. Most importantly, the words of many chorales were written, arranged, or translated from Latin by Luther. Koch in *Geschichte des Kirchenlieds* gives a list of 36. —Bibliography: A. J. Rambach, *Über Luthers Verdienst um den Kirchengesang* (Hamburg, 1813); K. von Winterfeld, *Luthers deutsche geistliche Lieder* (Leipzig, 1840); Karl Loewe, *Lutherstudien* (1846; publ. Wittenberg, 1918); H. von Stephen, *Luther als Musiker* (Bielefeld, 1899); M. Rade, *Martin Luthers Leben, Taten und Meinungen* (3 vols.; Tübingen, 1883; 2nd ed., 1901); F. Zelle, *Das älteste lutherische Haus-Gesangbuch* (Göttingen, 1903; with commentary); J. W. Lyra, *Luthers Deutsche Messe* (1904); F. Spitta, *Die Lieder Luthers in ihrer Bedeutung für das evangelische Kirchenlied* (Göttingen, 1905); F. Spitta, *Studien zu Luthers Liedern* (Göttingen, 1907); H. Lehmann, *Luther im deutschen Lied* (Halle, 1910); H. Kretzschmar, *Luther und die Musik,* in the 'Jahrbuch Peters' (1917); K. Anton, *Luther und die Musik* (1918); H. Preuss, *Luther der Künstler* (1931); H. J. Moser, *Die Melodien der Lutherlieder* (Leipzig, 1935); G. Wolfram, *'Ein' feste Burg ist unser Gott'* (Berlin, 1936); C. Mahrenholz, *Luther und die Kirchenmusik* (Kassel, 1937); Charles Schneider, *Luther poète et musicien et les Enchiridiens de 1524* (Geneva, 1942); Walter E. Buszin, *Luther on Music,* in the 'Mus. Quarterly' (Jan., 1946); F. Smend, *Luther und Bach* (Berlin, 1947); Paul Nettl, *Luther and Music* (Philadelphia, 1948); W. Stapel, *Luthers Lieder und Gedichte* (Stuttgart, 1950).

Lutkin, Peter Christian, American organist and hymnologist; b. Thompsonville, Wis., March 27, 1858; d. Evanston, Ill., Dec. 27, 1931. He studied music in Chicago; then went to Europe, and took lessons with A. Haupt (organ) and W. Bargiel (composition) in Berlin; and had further instruction in piano from Moszkowski in Paris and Leschetizky in Vienna. Returning to America, he filled various posts as organist in Chicago; taught theory at the American Cons. of Music in Chicago; for 20 seasons conducted the Chicago North Shore Festival Association (1909-30); publ. church music and pedagogical works for piano; edited the *Methodist Sunday School Hymnal;* was co-editor of the *Episcopal Church Hymnal.*

Lutoslawski, Witold, Polish composer; b. Warsaw, Jan. 25, 1913. He studied at the Warsaw Cons. with Maliszewski. His compositions include a symphony (1947); *Triptyque Silésien,* for soprano and orch. (1951); *Concerto* for orch. (Warsaw, Nov. 26, 1954); trio for oboe, clarinet, and bassoon (1945); *5 Dance Preludes* for clarinet, strings, harp, piano, and percussion (1955); piano sonata (1934); 12 Folk Melodies for piano (1945); *Bucolica* for piano (1952); choral pieces; several albums of children's songs. He received the 1st Government Prize in 1955. His *Little Suite* for small orch. was performed at the 1st Polish Festival of Contemporary Music (Warsaw, Oct., 1956); also in the U. S. (Hartford, Conn., March 26, 1958).

Lütschg, Karl, renowned piano pedagogue; b. St. Petersburg, Oct. 15, 1839; d. Blankenburg, Germany, June 6, 1899. He studied piano with Henselt in Russia, and with Moscheles in Germany; composition with Richter and Kiel. Returning to St. Petersburg, he became prof. at the Cons. there; publ. a number of valuable piano studies and instructive editions of classical works: *École d'études* (12 books), *Bibliothèque des œuvres classiques et modernes* (420 numbers); etc. His son, **Waldemar Lütschg** (b. St. Petersburg, May 16, 1877; d. Berlin, Aug. 29, 1948), was also a pianist; after his father's death in 1899 he settled in Berlin; taught piano at the Chicago Musical College in 1905-6.

Lutyens, Elizabeth, English composer; b. London, July 9, 1906. She studied at the Royal College of Music, and later at the Paris Cons. As a composer, she progressed from an early Romantic style to an intense Expressionist idiom, with the application of a *sui generis* dodecaphonic technique; with this consummation, she discarded her music written before 1935. Among her works are 6 chamber concertos for various ensembles (1939-48); 6 string quartets (1938-52); a viola concerto (1947); many choral works; piano pieces. The following were performed at festivals of the International Society for Contemporary Music: *3 Symphonic Preludes* (London, July 7, 1946); horn concerto (Amsterdam, June 12, 1948); 2nd string quartet (Warsaw, April 17, 1939); *The Pit,* a dramatic scene, for tenor, bass, women's chorus, and orch. (Palermo, April 24, 1949). She is the wife of the English conductor Edward Clark (q.v.).

Lutz, Wilhelm Meyer, operetta composer and conductor; b. Männerstadt, near Kissingen, 1822; d. London, Jan. 31, 1903. He studied music with his father, an organist, and later at Würzburg. In 1848 he settled in England; played organ in various churches in Birmingham, Leeds, and London; conducted theater music in London from 1851; in 1869 was appointed musical director at the Gaiety Theatre, for which he wrote numerous light operas; the following were successful: *Faust and Marguerite* (1855), *Blonde and Brunette* (1862), *Zaida* (1868), *Miller of Milburg* (1872), and *Legend of the Lys* (1873). He also wrote the popular dance *Pas de quatre.*

Lux, Friedrich, German composer; b. Ruhla, Nov. 24, 1820; d. Mainz, July 9, 1895. He studied with his father, a cantor at Ruhla; at 12 he gave an organ concert at Gotha; then studied with F. Schneider at Dessau, where he remained for 10 years as music director at the court theater. From 1851 to 1877 he was conductor at the City Theater in Mainz; from 1867 also conducted the Oratorio Society there. —Works: the operas *Das Käthchen von Heilbronn* (Dessau, March 23, 1846), *Der Schmied von Ruhla* (Mainz, March 28, 1882), and *Die Fürstin von Athen* (Frankfurt, 1890); 4 symphonies (No. 3 subtitled *Die vier Menschenalter;* No. 4, *Durch Nacht zum Licht,* with chorus); 3 string quartets; piano trio; many choral works and songs. He publ. transcriptions of Beethoven's symphonies (except the Ninth) for piano, 4-hands. —Cf. A. Reissmann, *F. Lux: Sein Leben und seine Werke* (Leipzig, 1888).

Luython, Charles, Flemish composer; b. Antwerp, c. 1556; d. Prague, 1620. After receiving elementary training as a chorister in his native land, he was sent, at the age of 10, to the Imperial Chapel in Vienna, where he remained until he was 15. He wrote 2 Masses for Emperor Maximilian II; in 1582 was appointed court organist by Rudolph II, for whom he wrote a book of madrigals (publ. by Gardano in Venice). He remained with Rudolph II at his residence in Prague; in 1603 became successor to Philippe de Monte as court composer, while continuing to hold his post as court organist. He retired from the service in 1611. Apart from his book of madrigals (Venice, 1582), he publ. *Sacrae Cantiones* for 6 voices (Prague, 1603); *Lamentationes* for 6 voices (Prague, 1604); 9 Masses for 3-7 voices (Prague, 1609). Among his extant works for instruments, there is a *Fuga suavissima* (publ. in Woltz's *Tabulatur-Buch,* 1617). Luython was a composer of considerable ingenuity; Michael Praetorius recounts in his *Syntagma musicum* that Luython owned a keyboard instrument with 3 manuals representing the diatonic, chromatic, and enharmonic intervals (18 notes to the octave), thus securing theoretically correct modulations through sharps or flats. —Cf. L. de Burbure, *Charles Luython* (Brussels, 1880); A. A. Smijers, *Luython als Motettenkomponist* (Vienna, 1917). See also A. G. Ritter, *Zur Geschichte des Orgelspiels* (1884; pp. 51-52).

Luzzaschi (lŏŏts-säh'skē), **Luzzasco,** Italian composer; b. Ferrara, 1545; d. there, Sept. 11, 1607. He studied with Cypriano de Rore as a child (until 1558); became organist at the ducal court, and attained great renown as a teacher; Frescobaldi was one of his many pupils. —Works: 7 books of madrigals for 5 voices, of which 5 are extant (1575-1604); *Sacrae cantiones,* also for 5 voices (1598); madrigals for 1-3 sopranos, with keyboard accompaniment (1601). Diruta's collection *Il Transilvano* contains an organ toccata and 2 ricercari by Luzzaschi; the toccata is reprinted in Ritter's *Zur Geschichte des Orgelspiels;* a 4-part *Canzon da sonar* is given in Rauerij's collection (1608); the accompanied madrigal *Ch'io non t'ami,* in Otto Kinkeldey's *Orgel und Klavier in der Musik des 16. Jahrhunderts* (Leipzig, 1910; p. 291). Other reprints are found in L. Torchi's 'L'Arte Musicale in Italia' (vol. 4), in Riemann's *Musikgeschichte in Beispielen* (No. 73), and in Schering's *Geschichte der Musik in Beispielen* (No. 166). —Cf. Otto Kinkeldey, *Luzzasco Luzzaschi's Solo Madrigale mit Klavierbegleitung,* in the 'Sammelbände der Internationalen Musik-Gesellschaft' (1908). See also G. Reese, *Music in the Renaissance* (N.Y., 1954, pp. 411-13).

Luzzi (lŏŏ'-tsē), **Luigi,** Italian composer; b. Olevano di Lomellina, March 28, 1828; d. Stradella, Feb. 23, 1876. He studied medicine at Turin, but later entered the musical profession; wrote successful songs *(Mia madre,* etc.); an opera, *Tripilla* (Novara, Feb. 7, 1874); a symphony; hymns for chorus and orch.; piano pieces.

Lvov, Alexey Feodorovitch, Russian violinist and composer; author of the Russian national anthem under the Tsars; b. Reval, June 5, 1798; d. Romano, near Kovno, Dec. 28, 1870. He was the son of the director of the Imperial Court Chapel in St. Petersburg; received his primary education at home; attended the Institute of Road Engineering (graduated in 1818); at the same time studied violin. In 1827 he was sent to the Turkish front in Bulgaria; then was attached to the Court. He wrote the national anthem 'God save the Tsar' in 1833, and it was first performed in Moscow on the name day of Tsar Nicholas I, on Dec. 6 (18), 1833; it remained the official anthem until the Revolution of 1917. In 1837 he succeeded his father as director of the Imperial Chapel (until 1861); in 1839 he organized instrumental classes there; edited a collection of services for the entire ecclesiastical year of the Greek Orthodox Church. In 1840 he traveled in Europe; played his violin concerto with the Gewandhaus Orchestra in Leipzig (Nov. 8, 1840); Schumann greatly praised his playing. Returning to Russia, he established a series of orchestral concerts in St. Petersburg, presenting classical programs. Growing deafness forced him to abandon his activities in 1867. As a composer, he followed slavishly the Italian school; wrote 3 operas: *Bianca* (Dresden, Oct. 13, 1844), *Ondine* (in Russian; St. Petersburg, Sept. 20, 1847), and *Starosta Boris, or Russian Muzhik and the French Marauders* (on the subject of the 1812 war; St. Petersburg, May 1, 1854); several violin works, including a concerto; publ. an essay, *On Free or Non-Symmetrical Rhythm* (St. Petersburg, 1858). —Cf. I. Yampolsky, *Russian Violin Art* (Moscow, 1951; vol. 1, pp. 205-27).

Lyford, Ralph, American composer; b. Worcester, Mass., Feb. 22, 1882; d. Cincinnati, Sept. 3, 1927. He began to study piano and violin as a child; entered the New England Cons. in Boston at 12, studying piano with Helen Hopekirk, organ with Goodrich, and composition with Chadwick; then went to Leipzig to study conducting with Artur Nikisch (1906). Returning to America, he became assistant conductor of the San Carlo Opera Co. (1907-8); then was with the Boston Opera Co. (1908-14). In 1916 he settled in Cincinnati, where he taught at the Cons., and also conducted the summer seasons of opera at the Zoölogical Gardens there; in 1925 he became associate conductor of the Cincinnati Symph. Orch. —Works: opera *Castle Agrazant* (Cincinnati, April 29, 1926; won the David Bispham Medal); piano concerto (1917); chamber music; songs. —Cf. E. E. Hipsher, *American Opera and Its Composers* (Philadelphia, 1934; pp. 304-8).

Lyman, Howard Wilder, American voice teacher; b. Lancaster, Mass., Feb. 2, 1879. He studied at the New England Cons. (graduated, 1909); was for many years on the music faculty at the Univ. of Syracuse (1912-45); also director of music at the Methodist Church there (1926-53); then taught privately.

Lyne, Felice, American soprano; b. Slater, Mo., March 28, 1887; d. Allentown, Pa., Sept. 1, 1935. Her family moved to Allentown when she was a child; studied there with F. S. Hardman; then in Paris with Mme. Marchesi, J. de Reszke, and L. d'Aubigne. She made a successful début as Gilda in *Rigoletto* at Hammerstein's London Opera (Nov. 25, 1911), and appeared there 36 times that season, creating the principal soprano parts in the English premières of Massenet's *Don Quichotte* and *Jongleur de Notre-Dame,* and Holbrooke's *Children of Don;* toured with the Quinlan Opera Co. Returning to the U.S., she became a member of the Boston Opera Co.; also appeared in concerts.

Lynes, Frank, American composer and organist; b. Cambridge, Mass., May 16, 1858; d. Bristol, N. H., June 24, 1913. He was a student at the New England Cons.; later studied piano and organ with B. J. Lang and harmony with J. K. Paine. He then went to Germany and enrolled in the Leipzig Cons. (1883-85), where his teachers were Reinecke (piano) and Jadassohn (theory). Returning to America, he settled in Boston. He held various positions as church organist; for some years conducted the 'Cantabrigia Ladies' Chorus.' He wrote mainly for piano; publ. *Analytical Sonatinas* (a set of 4, so named to emphasize the formal element), *10 Bagatelles, 12 Recreations, 8 Fairy Tales for Musical Children, Woodland Notes* (6 pieces), *Scenes from Alice in Wonderland* (10 pieces), *Independence* (16 studies); also pedagogical works: *Key Circle Exercises; 10 Special Studies;* pieces for piano 4-hands and 6-hands; pieces for 2 pianos, 8-hands; many songs; anthems. —Cf. Olin Downes, *Frank Lynes* (Boston, 1914; contains a complete list of works).

Lyon, James, an early American composer; b. Newark, N.J., July 1, 1735; d. Machias, Maine, Oct. 12, 1794. He graduated from Princeton in 1759; in 1765, accepted a pastorate in Nova Scotia; then in Machias, Maine (1771 until his death). The 'N.Y. Mercury' of Oct. 1, 1759 speaks of an ode composed by Lyon, a member of the graduating class of Princeton, and mentions its performance at the graduation exercises on Sept. 26; but the music of this work, written in the same year that Hopkinson wrote his first songs, is lost. The first known compositions of Lyon are 6 psalm tunes publ. by him in a collection, *Urania* (Philadelphia, 1762); also wrote settings of 2 poems by Watts, *A Marriage Hymn* and *Friendship,* and of Psalms 8, 17, 19, 23, 95, 104, and 150. —Bibliography: O. G. Sonneck, *Francis Hopkinson and James Lyon: Two Studies in Early American Music* (Washington, 1905); G. T. Edwards, *Music and Musicians of Maine* (Portland, 1928); 'Dictionary of American Biography' (vol. 11, N.Y., 1933); J. T. Howard, *Our American Music* (1939 and subsequent eds.).

Lyon & Healy, American manufacturers of musical instruments. The firm was founded in Chicago in 1864 by George Washburn Lyon (b. 1820) and Patrick Joseph Healy (b. March 17, 1840; d. Chicago, April 3, 1905). They began originally as dealers in sheet music, books, and the smaller musical instruments; in 1871 they took over the piano business of Smith & Dixon and gradually began also to manufacture other instruments. After the retirement of Lyon in 1889, Healy became the sole head and general manager; he expanded the manufacturing dept. and erected larger factories. Among the firm's instruments, the Lyon & Healy harp, put on the market in 1899, has become universally known; its collection of old violins once rivaled those of the world's most famous dealers. Besides the parent store in Chicago, there are several branches in other cities.

Lyra, Justus Wilhelm, German cleric and song composer; b. Osnabrück, March 23, 1822; d. Gehrden, Dec. 30, 1882. He studied philosophy and theology in Berlin; filled various church offices in Germany; eventually became 'pastor primarius' at Gehrden and Hanover. As a student, he wrote many scholastic songs, which became very popular in German universities (e.g., *Der Mai ist gekommen, Durch Feld und Buchenhallen, Zwischen Frankreich und dem Böhmerwald, Meine Mus' ist gegangen);* he also wrote church music (Christmas cantata, 1872); publ. 5 books of songs ranging from one voice to mixed chorus; *Die liturgischen Altarweisen des lutherischen Hauptgottesdienstes* (1873); *Andreas Ornithoparchus und dessen Lehre von den Kirchenakzenten* (Gütersloh, 1877); *Luthers Deutsche Messe* (posthumously publ., 1904). —Cf. Bär and Ziller, *J. W. Lyra* (Leipzig, 1901).

Lysberg, Charles-Samuel (real name Bovy-Lysberg), Swiss pianist and composer; b. Lysberg, near Geneva, March 1, 1821; d. Geneva, Feb. 25, 1873. He studied in Paris with Chopin (piano) and Belaire (composition); returned to Switzerland as prof. at the Geneva Cons. He wrote an opera, *La Fille du carillonneur* (Geneva, 1854); the romantic sonata *L'Absence;* he is chiefly known as a composer of piano pieces (over 130), which include *La Napolitaine, Deux Nocturnes, Le Réveil des oiseaux, Le Chant du rouet, Idylle, Les Ondines, Sur l'onde,* etc. —Cf. Pauline Long, *Charles-Samuel Bovy-Lysberg,* in the 'Schweizerisches Jahrbuch für Musikwissenschaft' (III, pp. 140-57).

M

Maas, Louis (Philipp Otto), composer and pianist; b. Wiesbaden, Germany, June 21, 1852; d. Boston, Sept. 17, 1889. He studied with Reinecke and Papperitz at Leipzig Cons. (1867-71), and for 3 summers with Liszt. From 1875-80 he taught at the Leipzig Cons.; in 1880 he emigrated to the U. S., settling in Boston; conducted the Boston Philharmonic Concerts (1881-82). As a token of gratitude to his adoptive country, he wrote an 'American Symphony,' *On the Prairies,* dedicated to President Chester A. Arthur, which he conducted in Boston, Dec. 14, 1882. This symphony, Germanic in form and harmonic language, contained some Indian themes. Maas further wrote overtures, suites, marches, fantasias, etc., for orch.; a string quartet; a piano concerto; 3 sonatas, 3 impromptus and 12 *Phantasiestücke* for piano; violin sonatas; and songs.

Maazel, Lorin, American conductor; b. Neuilly, France, March 5, 1930 (of American parents). He was brought to the U. S. as a child, and early developed an amazing musical memory and assimilative ability. He studied conducting with Vladimir Bakaleinikoff in Pittsburgh; at the age of 9 he led orchestras at the New York World's Fair (Aug., 1939) and at the Hollywood Bowl; 2 years later he conducted the NBC Symph. Orchestra, and subsequently led the N. Y. Philharmonic in several summer concerts at the Lewisohn Stadium. While still a child, he also conducted the Cleveland, Pittsburgh, and Chicago orchestras. In 1952 he married Mimi Sandbank, a Brazilian pianist; in the same year he received a Fulbright Scholarship to travel in Italy. There he gave a number of successful concerts; subsequently conducted in Germany; in 1956, in South America and Mexico; in 1957-58, again in Italy.

Mabellini, Teodulo, Italian composer; b. Pistoia, April 2, 1817; d. Florence, March 10, 1897. He studied with Pillotti in his native town, and then in the Istituto Reale Musicale at Florence; at the age of 19, he produced there an opera, *Matilda a Toledo* (Aug. 27, 1836), which made so favorable an impression that Grand Duke Leopold II gave him a stipend to study with Mercadante at Novara. His second opera, *Rolla* (Turin, Nov. 12, 1840), was no less successful; thereupon he wrote many more operas, among them *Ginevra degli Almieri* (Turin, Nov. 13, 1841), *Il conte di Lavagna* (Florence, June 4, 1843), *I Veneziani a Costantinopoli* (Rome, 1844), *Maria di Francia* (Florence, March 14, 1846), and *Fiammetta* (Florence, Feb. 12, 1857). He also wrote several effective oratorios and cantatas: *Eudossia e Paolo* (Florence, 1845), *Etruria* (Florence, August 5, 1849), *Lo spirito di Dante* (Florence, May 15, 1865), and a patriotic hymn *Italia risorta* (Florence, Sept. 12, 1847); *Grande Fantasia* for flute, clarinet, horn, trumpet, and trombone; sacred works for chorus and orch. He lived in Florence from 1843 until his death; conducted the concerts of the Società filarmonica (1843-59); taught composition at the Istituto Reale Musicale (1859-87). —Cf. M. Giannini, *Mabellini e la musica* (Pistoia, 1899); A. Simonatti, *Teodulo Mabellini* (Pistoia, 1923).

MacArdle, Donald Wales, American musicologist; b. Quincy, Mass., July 3, 1897. He studied science at the Massachusetts Institute of Technology (M.S. in chemical engineering); studied music at the Juilliard School in N. Y.; wrote program notes for radio broadcasts; then devoted his research mainly to Beethoven; publ. valuable papers on obscure points of Beethoven's life and works; articles in the 'Mus. Quarterly' include: *Beethoven, Artaria, and the C major Quintet* (Oct., 1948); *The Family van Beethoven* (Oct., 1949); *Five Unfamiliar Beethoven Letters* (with Katherine Schultze; Oct., 1951); *Minor Beethoveniana* (with Ludwig Misch; Oct., 1955). Translated and annotated (with Ludwig Misch) *New Beethoven Letters* (Norman, Okla., 1957).

Macbeth, Allan, Scottish organist and composer; b. Greenock, March 13, 1856; d. Glasgow, Aug. 25, 1910. He studied at the Leipzig Cons. with Richter, Reinecke, and Jadassohn (1875-76). His subsequent musical activities were largely confined to playing the organ in Glasgow churches and directing choral groups; from 1890 he was principal of the School of Music at the Glasgow Athenaeum. He wrote an operetta, *The Duke's Doctor;* 2 cantatas, *The Land of Glory* (1890) and *Silver Bells;* a *Jubilee Chorus* (1896); an *Intermezzo* for strings; *Danze pizzicate,* for orch.; also chamber music and songs.

Macbeth, Florence, American coloratura soprano; b. Mankato, Minn., Jan. 12, 1891. She studied in Europe; made her début in Paris; then sang in Germany. She made her American début, as Rosina, with the Chicago Opera Co. on Jan. 14, 1914, and remained with the company until 1935; for a season she had her own opera company, with which she toured in the U. S. At the height of her career she was dubbed the 'Minnesota Nightingale.' She married the novelist James M. Cain in 1947; settled in Maryland.

MacCunn, Hamish, Scottish composer and conductor; b. Greenock, March 22, 1868; d. London, Aug. 2, 1916. He studied at the Royal College of Music (1883-86) with Parry; then taught at the Royal Academy of Music (1888-94); in 1898, became conductor of the Carl Rosa Opera Co.; from 1900-5, of the Savoy Theatre; later he toured with various troupes, conducting light opera. In 1910 he was engaged by Beecham as assistant conductor at Covent Garden. —Works: operas: *Jeanie Deans,* after Scott's *The Heart of Midlothian* (Edinburgh, Nov. 15, 1894), *Diarmid* (London, Oct. 23, 1897), *The Masque of War and Peace* (London, Feb. 13, 1900); *The Golden Girl,* musical comedy (Birmingham, Aug. 5, 1905); the cantatas, *Lord Ullin's Daughter,* after Walter Scott (London, Feb. 18, 1888), *Bonny Kilmeny* (Edinburgh, Dec. 15, 1888), *The Lay of the Last Minstrel* (Glasgow, Dec. 18, 1888), *The Cameronian's Dream* (Edinburgh, Jan. 27, 1890), *Queen Hynde of Caledon* (Glasgow, Jan. 28, 1892), *The Wreck of the Hesperus,* after Longfellow (London, Aug. 28, 1905); the overtures *Cior Mhor* (London, Oct. 27, 1885), *The Land of the Mountain and the Flood,* after Scott (London, Nov. 5, 1887), *The Ship o' the Fiend* (London, Feb. 21, 1888), *The Dowie Dens o' Yarrow* (London, Oct. 13, 1888); *Highland Memories,* orchestral sketch (London, March 13, 1897); *Scotch Dances* for piano; songs; etc.

MacDermid, James G., pianist, vocalist, and composer; b. Utica, Ontario, June 10, 1875. He studied in London, Ontario; in 1893 went to Chicago for further studies, and remained in the U. S.; became an American citizen in 1906; for several seasons toured as accompanist to his wife, **Sibyl Sammis MacDermid,** soprano (b. Foreston, Ill., May 15, 1876; d. New York, Nov. 2, 1940). He publ. about 75 sacred and secular songs.

MacDowell, Edward Alexander, outstanding American composer; b. New York, Dec. 18, 1861; d. there, Jan. 23, 1908. His early teachers were J. Buitrago, P. Desvernine, and Teresa Carreño. Later he studied at the Paris Cons. (1876-78) with Marmontel (piano) and Savard (theory). In 1878 he went to Germany, where he studied for a few months with Louis Ehlert in Wiesbaden, and then entered the Frankfurt Cons. in 1879. There he was a piano student of Karl Heymann and, in composition, of Joachim Raff. Both Heymann and Raff quickly recognized their pupil's unusual talent and took a special interest in him. When Heymann resigned in 1881, he recommended MacDowell as his successor, but for some reason the authorities disregarded the suggestion, and MacDowell accepted a position at the Darmstadt Cons. In 1882 Raff introduced him to Liszt, who arranged for him to play his own *Modern Suite* at the annual concert of the Allgemeiner Musikverein (July 11, 1882). The favorable reception induced him to remain in Germany; he settled in Wiesbaden. In 1884 he returned briefly to America, and married a former pupil, Miss Marian Nevins (1857-1956). In 1888, he returned permanently, taking up residence in Boston. There his piano works attracted the attention of Gericke, then the conductor of the Boston Symph. Orch., under whose direction he played his new piano concerto in D minor (April 12, 1889). Under Gericke's immediate successors, Nikisch and Paur, all of MacDowell's orchestral works received their first hearing almost as soon as they were completed, and his fame spread rapidly. When Columbia Univ. created a chair of music in 1896, the trustees unanimously chose MacDowell as the first incumbent, citing him as 'the greatest musical genius America has produced.' His teaching duties absorbed most of his time, and virtually ended his career as a pianist, but he continued to compose. For 2 seasons (1897-99) he was also conductor of the Mendelssohn Glee Club. Soon a serious controversy arose between MacDowell and the trustees of Columbia Univ., and in 1904 MacDowell presented his resignation; he was outspoken in his dissatisfaction with the organization of the Division of Fine Arts; the whole affair was aired in the press; the trustees then published a statement in which MacDowell was accused of a lack of propriety in making public an intramural academic disagreement. Whether the shock of these events affected MacDowell's mental state directly is a moot point, but his health began to fail; the physicians diagnosed his illness as a gradual disintegration of the brain tissues, which eventually ended in insanity (1905); MacDowell spent the last years of his life in a child-like state, unconscious of his identity and his environment. In 1906 an appeal was launched for funds to maintain MacDowell in comfort for the rest of his life; signers included Horatio Parker, Victor Herbert, Arthur Foote, George Chadwick, Frederick Converse, Andrew Carnegie, J. Pierpont Morgan, and former President Grover Cleveland. —Unlike other men of genius, cut off in their prime, MacDowell lived to enjoy in a large measure the recognition of his talent; for this timely appreciation no small credit belongs to Teresa Carreño, who frequently placed her former pupil's works on her programs; she gave the first European performance of MacDowell's 2nd piano concerto at a Gewandhaus concert in Leipzig (1891). Shortly after MacDowell's death, a group of his admirers raised $50,000 and organized the MacDowell Memorial Association; Mrs. MacDowell deeded to the Association her husband's summer residence at Peterborough, N. H. This became a retreat where American composers and writers could live during the summer at very moderate rates and work in quiet and in inspiring surroundings. Soon the number of applicants could no longer be accommodated, and several cottages were built. During the summer of 1910 Mrs. MacDowell arranged an elaborate pageant with appropriate music from MacDowell's works, arranged and conducted by Chalmers Clifton. The success of this project led her to establish an annual 4-day festival in August, known as the Peterborough Festival. —Among American composers MacDowell occupies a very high place. He is pre-eminently a poet whose exquisite fancies find their happiest expression in the smaller forms. His most pronounced gift is a fertile invention, and his themes are generally short, always clearly defined, wonderfully expressive, and logically developed. His sense of proportion, symmetry, and artistic unity is well-nigh perfect; with unerring instinct he strikes and maintains a fundamental mood, carefully avoiding irrelevant or disturbing elements. His harmonic scheme is bold within the limits of the beautiful, his rhythm varied and incisive, his melody invariably noble, his climaxes powerful and stirring. Directness, freshness, and vitality constitute the perennial charm of MacDowell's music. Finally, MacDowell was the first American composer of stature who incorporated native elements in his music and depicted, in Romantic colors, the landscape of America. —Works: (op. 1-7 were publ. under the pseudonym of Edgar Thorn): For orch.: *Hamlet and Ophelia,* symph. poem, op. 22 (1885; Boston Symph., Jan. 27, 1893); *Lancelot and Elaine,* symph. poem, op. 25 (1888; Boston Symph., Jan. 10, 1890); *Lamia,* symph. poem, op. 29 (1889; Boston Symph., Oct. 23, 1908); *The Saracens* and *The Lovely Alda,* 2 symph. poems, op. 30 (Boston Philharmonic, Nov. 5, 1891); Suite no. 1 for orch., op. 42 (Worcester Festival, Sept. 24, 1891); Suite No. 2 *(Indian Suite)* (Boston Symph., Jan. 31, 1895); piano concerto No. 1, in A minor, op. 15 (1882; Zürich, July 11, 1882, composer soloist); piano concerto No. 2, in D minor, op. 23 (N. Y., March 5, 1889, composer soloist); *Romance* for cello and orch., op. 35 (1888). For chorus: 2 choruses for men's voices, op. 3, *Love and Time* and *The Rose and the Gardener* (1897); *The Witch,* for men's chorus, op. 5 (1898); *War Song,* for men's chorus, op. 6 (1898); 3 songs for men's chorus, op. 27 (1887); 2 songs for men's chorus, op. 41 (1890); *Two Northern Songs,* for mixed voices, op. 43 (1891); 3 choruses for men's voices, op. 52 (1897); *Two Songs from the 13th Century,* for men's chorus (1897); 2 choruses for men's voices, op. 53 (1898); 2 choruses for men's voices, op. 54 (1898); *College Songs,* for men's voices (1901); *Summer Wind,* for women's chorus (1902). For voice and piano: *Two Old Songs,* op. 9 (1894); 3 Songs, op. 11 (1883); 2 Songs, op. 12 (1883); *From an Old Garden* (6 songs), op. 26 (1887); 3 Songs, op. 33 (1888; revised 1894); 2 Songs, op. 34 (1888); *6 Love Songs,* op. 40 (1890); 8 Songs, op. 47 (1893); 4 Songs, op. 56 (1898); 3 Songs, op. 58 (1899); 3 Songs, op. 60 (1902). For piano: *Amourette,* op. 1 (1896); *In Lilting Rhythm,* op. 2 (1897); *Forgotten Fairy Tales (Sung Outside the Prince's Door, Of a Tailor and a Bear, Beauty in the Rose Garden, From Dwarfland),* op. 4 (1898); *6 Fancies (A Tin Soldier's Love, To a Humming Bird, Summer Song, Across Fields, Bluette, An Elfin Round),* op. 7 (1898); *Waltz,* op. 8 (1895); *First Modern Suite,* op. 10 (1880); *Prelude and Fugue,* op. 13 (1883); *Second Modern Suite,* op. 14 (1881); *Serenata,* op. 16 (1883); *2 Fantastic Pieces (Legend, Witches' Dance),* op. 17 (1884); 2 Pieces *(Barcarolle, Humoresque),* op. 18 (1884); *Forest Idyls (Forest Stillness, Play of the Nymphs, Revery, Dance of the Dryads),* op. 19 (1884); 4 Pieces *(Humoresque, March, Cradle Song, Czardas),* op. 24 (1887); 6 Idyls after Goethe *(In the Woods, Siesta, To the Moonlight, Silver Clouds, Flute Idyl, The Bluebell),* op. 28 (1887); 6 Poems after Heine *(From a Fisherman's Hut, Scotch Poem, From Long Ago,*

The Post Wagon, The Shepherd Boy, Monologue), op. 31 (1887); *4 Little Poems (The Eagle, The Brook, Moonshine, Winter),* op. 32 (1888); *Etude de Concert* in F-sharp, op. 36 (1889); *Les Orientales,* after Victor Hugo *(Clair de Lune, Danse le Hamac, Danse Andalouse),* op. 37 (1889); *Marionettes,* 8 Little Pieces *(Prologue, Soubrette, Lover, Witch, Clown, Villain, Sweetheart, Epilogue),* op. 38 (1888; originally only six pieces; *Prologue* and *Epilogue* were added in 1901); 12 Studies, Book I *(Hunting Song, Alla Tarantella, Romance, Arabesque, In the Forest, Dance of the Gnomes);* Book II *(Idyl, Shadow Dance, Intermezzo, Melody, Scherzino, Hungarian),* op. 39 (1890); Sonata No. 1, *Tragica,* op. 45 (1893); 12 Virtuoso Studies *(Novelette, Moto Perpetuo, Wild Chase, Improvisation, Elfin Dance, Valse Triste, Burleske, Bluette, Träumerei, March Wind, Impromptu, Polonaise),* op. 46 (1894); *Air* and *Rigaudon,* op. 49 (1894); Sonata No. 2, *Eroica,* op. 50 (1895); *Woodland Sketches,* 10 pieces *(To a Wild Rose, Will o' the Wisp, At an Old Trysting Place, In Autumn, From an Indian Lodge, To a Water Lily, From Uncle Remus, A Deserted Farm, By a Meadow Brook, Told at Sunset),* op. 51 (1896); *Sea Pieces (To the Sea, From a Wandering Iceberg, A.D. 1620, Star-light, Song, From the Depths, Nautilus, In Mid-Ocean),* op. 55 (1898); Sonata No. 3, *Norse,* op. 57 (1900); Sonata No. 4, *Keltic,* op. 59 (1901); *Fireside Tales (An Old Love Story, Of Br'er Rabbit, From a German Forest, Of Salamanders, A Haunted House, By Smouldering Embers),* op. 61 (1902); *New England Idyls,* 10 pieces *(An Old Garden, Midsummer, Midwinter, With Sweet Lavender, In Deep Woods, Indian Idyl, To an Old White Pine, From Puritan Days, From a Log Cabin, The Joy of Autumn),* op. 62 (1902); 6 Little Pieces on Sketches by J. S. Bach (1890); Technical Exercises, 2 Books (1893; 1895). —Bibliography: L. Gilman, *Edward MacDowell: A Study* (N. Y., 1909); E. F. Page, *Edward MacDowell: His Works and Ideals* (N.Y., 1910); J. Adams, *What the Piano Writings of MacDowell Mean to the Piano Student* (Chicago, 1913); T. P. Currier, *MacDowell as I Knew Him,* in the 'Mus. Quarterly' (Jan., 1915); O. G. Sonneck, *Suum cuique: Essays in Music* (N.Y., 1916); O. G. Sonneck, *Catalogue of First Editions of Edward MacDowell* (Washington, D.C., 1917); W. H. Humiston, *MacDowell* (N.Y., 1921); J. F. Porte, *A Great American Tone Poet: Edward MacDowell* (London, 1922); J. B. Matthews, *Commemorative Tributes to MacDowell* (N. Y., 1922); Abbie F. Brown, *The Boyhood of Edward MacDowell* (N.Y., 1924); Upton Sinclair, *MacDowell,* in the 'American Mercury' (1926); J. F. Cooke, *Edward MacDowell, A Short Biography* (Philadelphia, 1928); R. W. Brown, *A Listener to the Winds, Edward MacDowell,* in *Lonely Americans* (N. Y., 1929); Paul Rosenfeld, *An Hour with American Music* (Philadelphia, 1929, pp. 31-51); Anita Brown, *A Mosaic of Muses of the MacDowell Club of New York* (N.Y., 1930); *Catalogue of an Exhibition Illustrating the Life and Work of Edward MacDowell* (N.Y., 1938); J. T. Howard, *Our American Music* (N.Y., 1939; pp. 323-44); Marian MacDowell, *MacDowell's 'Peterborough Idea'* in the 'Mus. Quarterly' (Jan., 1932); Marian MacDowell, *Random Notes on Edward MacDowell and his Music* (Boston, 1950).

Macfarlane, William Charles, organist and composer; b. London, Oct. 2, 1870; d. North Conway, N. H., May 12, 1945. In 1874 he was taken to N.Y.; was taught by his father, Duncan Macfarlane (1836-1916), and by S. P. Warren. He made his début as organist in N. Y. on March 22, 1886; from 1898 to 1919 held various positions as organist and choral conductor; in 1941, retired to North Conway. He wrote *America First, a Boy Scout Operetta* (1917); the light operas, *Little Almond Eyes* (Portland, 1916) and *Sword and Scissors* (1918); cantata *The Message from the Cross* (1907); *The Church Service Book* (N.Y., 1912); numerous anthems and other sacred music; organ pieces *(Lullaby, Serenade, Scherzo, Romanza,* etc.).

Macfarren, Sir George Alexander, English composer and pedagogue; b. London, March 2 1813; d. there, Oct. 31, 1887. He studied with his father, George Macfarren, the dramatist, and with Charles Lucas and C. Porter (1829) at the Royal Academy of Music, where he became a professor in 1834. After many years of teaching there, he was appointed in 1875 successor to Sterndale Bennett as prof. of music at Cambridge Univ.; in 1876 he became principal of the Royal Academy of Music. He was knighted in 1883. In the last years of his life he became blind. —Works: the operas (all performed in London) *Don Quixote* (Feb. 3, 1846), *Charles II* (Oct. 27, 1849), *Robin Hood* (Oct. 11, 1860), *Helvellyn* (Nov. 3, 1864); the oratorios *St. John the Baptist* (Bristol, Oct. 23, 1873), *The Resur-*

rection (Birmingham, 1876), *Joseph* (Leeds, 1877), *King David* (Leeds, 1883); cantata, *The Lady of the Lake* (Glasgow, Nov. 15, 1877); many sacred works; songs, including the well-known *Pack, clouds, away;* chamber music. He publ. *Rudiments of Harmony* (1860; .14 eds.) and *Six lectures on Harmony* (1867; 3rd ed., 1880); also *Addresses and Lectures* (London, 1888). He edited 'Old English Ditties' (2 vols.), 'Old Scottish Ditties,' 'Moore's Irish Melodies,' 'Songs of England,' 'British Vocal Album'; also Purcell's *Dido and Aeneas,* Handel's *Belshazzar, Judas Maccabaeus, Jephtha,* and *Messiah,* etc. His wife, **Natalia Macfarren** (*née* Clarina Thalia Andrae; b. Lübeck, 1827; d. Bakewell, April 9, 1916), received her early education in New York; later studied singing in London; also took a course in composition with Macfarren, whom she married in 1844. She appeared as an opera singer (contralto) in New York, and in her husband's operas in England. She was a successful singing teacher; publ. a *Vocal Method* and an *Elementary Course of Vocalising and Pronouncing the English Language.* —Cf. H. C. Banister, *George Alexander Macfarren: His Life, Works, and Influence* (London, 1891).

Macfarren, Walter Cecil, English pianist and composer; brother of George Alexander Macfarren; b. London, Aug. 28, 1826; d. there, Sept. 2, 1905. He was a chorister at Westminster Abbey; then studied at the Royal Academy of Music, with Holmes (piano) and with his brother (composition). From 1846 until 1903 he was professor of piano at the Royal Academy of Music; conducted its concerts from 1873-80. He composed a number of overtures on Shakespearian subjects; a piano concerto; many piano pieces; edited Beethoven's sonatas, and several albums of piano pieces under the title *Popular Classics.* He publ. *Memories; an Autobiography* (London, 1905).

Mach, Ernst, eminent acoustician; b. Turas, Moravia, Feb. 18, 1838; d. Haar, near Munich, Feb. 22, 1916. He was a professor of physics in Prague (1864) and in Vienna (1895). Besides his scientific works of far-reaching importance, he published a number of books and studies dealing with musical acoustics: *Zwei populäre Vorträge über musikalische Akustik* (1865); *Einleitung in die Helmholtz'sche Musiktheorie* (1866); *Zur Theorie des Gehörorgans* (1872); *Beitrag zur Geschichte der Musik* (1892); *Die Analyse der Empfindungen und das Verhältnis des Physischen zum Psychischen* (5th ed., 1906); *Zur Geschichte der Theorie der Konsonanz,* in 'Populärwissenschaftliche Vorträge' (3rd ed., 1903). The unit of velocity of sound 'Mach' is named after him.

Machabey, Armand, French musicologist; b. Pont-de-Roide, Doubs, May 7, 1886. He studied at the Univ. of Paris; *docteur ès lettres,* 1928; subsequently active as a music historian and essayist. —Publications: *Histoire et évolution des formules musicales* (dissertation, 1928; revised, and publ. in 1955 as *Genèse de la tonalité musicale classique, des origines au XVe siècle); Précis-manuel d'histoire de la musique* (1942); *Anton Bruckner* (1946); *Maurice Ravel* (1947); *Traité de la critique musicale* (1947); *Le Bel canto* (1948); *Portraits de trente musiciens français* (1949); *La Notation musicale* (1952); *Frescobaldi* (1952); *Guillaume de Machaut: la vie et l'œuvre musicale* (2 vols., 1955). He contributed numerous valuable articles to various magazines; also wrote several orchestral suites and songs. He is married to **Emilienne Ganeval,** pianist and composer.

Machado (măh-shah'-dŏŏ), **Augusto,** Portuguese composer; b. Lisbon, Dec. 27, 1845; d. there, March 24, 1924. He was a pupil of Junior, Lami, and D'Almeide in Lisbon, and of Lavignac and Danhauser in Paris; 1892-1908, director of the San Carlos Theater in Lisbon; 1894-1910, director of the Cons. there. Besides numerous operettas, he wrote the operas *A Cruz de oiro* (Lisbon, 1873), *A Maria da Fonte* (Lisbon, 1879), *Lauriane* (Marseilles, Jan. 9, 1883; his most successful work), *Os Dorias* (Lisbon, 1887), *Mario Wetter* (Lisbon, 1898), *Venere* (Lisbon, 1905), and *La Borghesina* (Lisbon, 1909). For the third centenary of the death of Camoens he wrote the symph. ode *Camões e os Luziadas* (1880); also organ and piano pieces.

Machaut (măh-shŏh') (or **Machault, Machaud**), **Guillaume de (Guillelmus de Mascaudio)**, important French composer and poet; probably a native of Machaut in the Champagne; b. c. 1300; d. Rheims, 1377. He studied theology; took holy orders; from 1323-40 was in the service of King John of Bohemia (Duke of Luxembourg) as almoner (1330), notary (1332), and secretary (1335), traveling widely with that prince (their visits extended to Russia). Later he was at the court of Charles V of France. He held various ecclesiastical benefices (Houdain, Arras, Verdun), and from 1337 was canon of Rheims, where he resided from 1340 until his death (he visited Paris in 1363). His works include ballades, rondeaux, virelais, and motets. He wrote the earliest polyphonic setting of the Mass (4 voices) by a single composer. A complete ed. of Machaut's musical works was prepared by Friedrich Ludwig for the 'Publikationen älterer Musik' (vols. I, 1; III, 1; IV, 2; 1926-34, containing about two-thirds of his *opera omnia* and a commentary); the Mass, lais and hocket, not included in Ludwig's collection, were brought out for the 'Publikationen' by H. Besseler in 1943, but the printed copies were destroyed in an air raid. After the war, several editions of the Mass were publ. (by Chailley, Paris, 1948; by Machabey, Liège, 1948; by de Van, Rome, 1949; by Hübsch, Heidelberg, 1953; and Besseler's again, Leipzig, 1954). The complete works are publ. in L. Schrade, ed., 'Polyphonic Music of the 14th Century' (vols. 2 and 3; Monaco, 1956). 14 works (including parts of the Mass) are found in J. Wolf's *Geschichte der Mensuralnotation von 1250-1450* (Leipzig, 1904); 2 pieces in Schering's *Geschichte der Musik in Beispielen;* other pieces in Davison and Apel, *Historical Anthology of Music* (Cambridge, Mass., 1946). —Cf. H. Quittard, *Notes sur Guillaume de Machaut et son œuvre,* in the 'Bulletin de la Société française de musicologie' (1918); H. Besseler, in the 'Freiburger-Orgelbericht' (1926; p. 146 ff.); A. Machabey, *Guillaume de Machaut, la vie et l'homme,* in the 'Revue Musicale' (May, 1930; April and May, 1931); G. Reese, *Music in the Middle Ages,* chapter 12 (N. Y., 1940); A. Douce, *Guillaume de Machaut, Musicien et poète rémois* (Rheims, 1948); George Perle, *Integrative Devices in the Music of Machaut,* in the 'Mus. Quarterly' (April, 1948); Otto Gombosi, *Machaut's Messe Notre-Dame,* in the 'Mus. Quarterly' (April, 1950); S. Levarie, *Guillaume de Machaut* (N. Y., 1954); A. Machabey, *Guillaume de Machaut: la vie et l'œuvre musicale* (2 vols.; Paris, 1955). Machaut's poems were publ. by V. Chichmaref, as *Poésies lyriques de Guillaume Machaut* (2 vols., Paris, 1909).

Mackenzie, Sir **Alexander Campbell,** distinguished British composer and educator; b. Edinburgh, Aug. 22, 1847; d. London, April 28, 1935. A scion of a musical family (there were 4 generations of musicians in his paternal line), he showed musical aptitude as a child; was sent to Germany, where he studied violin with K. W. Uhlrich and theory with Eduard Stein, at the Sondershausen Cons. (1857-62); returning to England, he received the King's Scholarship at the Royal Academy of Music in London, where he studied with Sainton (violin) and Charles Lucas (theory). Subsequently, he was active in Edinburgh as violinist, conductor, composer, and teacher (1865-79). From 1879-88 he lived the greater part of each year in Florence, but from 1885-87 he spent considerable time in London as conductor of Novello's Oratorio Concerts. In 1888 he was elected principal of the Royal Academy of Music, and held this post until 1924, when he resigned. From 1892 to 1899 he was conductor of the Philharmonic Society of London. He held numerous honorary degrees from English universities; was knighted in 1895. As a composer, he was a staunch believer in programmatic music; he introduced national Scottish elements in many of his works; his *Pibroch Suite* for violin and orch., first introduced by Sarasate at the Leeds Festival (1889), acquired considerable popularity; Paderewski gave the first performance of his *Scottish Concerto* with the London Philharmonic (1897). —Works: operas (all first performed in London): *Colomba* (April 9, 1883), *The Troubadour* (June 8, 1886), *His Majesty* (Feb. 20, 1897), *The Cricket on the Hearth* (composed 1900; perf. June 6, 1914), *The Knight of the Road* (Feb. 27, 1905); cantatas: *Jason* (1882), *The Rose of Sharon* (Norwich Festival, Oct. 16, 1884), *The Story of Sayid* (1886), *The Witches' Daughter* (1904), *The Sun-God's Return* (1910); several odes for various occasions; a number of part-songs, anthems, and hymns; for orch.: *Cervantes,* overture (1877), *Scottish Rhapsody* No. 1 (1880), *Burns (Scottish Rhapsody* No. 2, 1881), *La Belle Dame sans merci,* after Keats (1883), *Twelfth Night,* after Shakespeare (1888), *Coriolanus,* suite (1901), *London Day by Day,* suite (1902), *Canadian Rhapsody* (1905), *Tam o'Shanter (Scottish Rhapsody* No. 3, 1911), *Youth, Sport and Loyalty,* overture (1922), violin concerto (1885), *Pibroch Suite* for violin and orch. (Leeds, Oct. 10, 1889), *Suite* (No. 2) for violin and orch. (London, Feb. 18, 1897), *Scottish Concerto* for piano and orch. (London, March 24, 1897); chamber music: piano trio (1874), string quartet (1875), piano quartet (1875), *From the North,* 9 pieces for violin and piano (1895), *4 Dance Measures,* for violin and piano (1915); several characteristic piano suites *(Rustic Suite, In the Scottish Highlands, Odds and Ends, Jottings, In Varying Moods);* a number of songs; arrangements of Scottish songs, etc. He publ. an autobiography, *A Musician's Narrative* (London, 1927).

Mackerras, Charles, oboist and conductor; b. Schenectady, N. Y., Nov. 17, 1925, of Australian parentage; was taken to Sydney at the age of 2; studied oboe at the Sydney Cons.; was first oboist of the Sydney Symph. Orch.; then began to conduct opera in Sydney. In 1946 he went to England; in 1947-48 he studied conducting with Vaclav Talich in Prague; returned to England and was engaged as conductor at the Sadler's Wells Opera; in 1954 was conductor of the BBC Concert Orch.; then conducted in Austria; established a fine reputation as opera and ballet conductor.

Mackinlay, Malcolm Sterling, English bass and singing teacher; son of the famous contralto, Antoinette Sterling; b. London, Aug. 7, 1876; d. there, Jan. 10, 1952. He studied at Trinity College, Oxford (M. A., 1901); studied singing with Manuel Garcia; then traveled as joint artist with his mother; in 1904 he gave up his concert career and established himself in London as a singing teacher; organized the Sterling Mackinlay Operatic Society. He publ. the following books: *Antoinette Sterling and Other Celebrities* (1906); *Garcia, the Centenarian, and His Times* (1908); *The Singing Voice and Its Training* (1910); *Light Opera* (technique and theatercraft; 1926); *Origin and Development of Light Opera* (1927); also 2 novels.

Maclean, Alexander Morvaren (Alick), English composer and conductor; son of Charles Donald Maclean; b. Eton, near Windsor, July 20, 1872; d. London, May 18, 1936. He studied with Sir Joseph Barnby; later conducted the Spa Orchestra at Scarborough (from 1911) and the New Queen's Hall Light Orchestra (1915-23). He wrote several operas; of these, 2 were produced in German, in Mainz: *Die Liebesgeige* (April 15, 1906) and *Waldidyll* (March 23, 1913); and 3 in London: *Petruccio* (June 29, 1895), *The King's Price* (April 29, 1904), and *Maître Seiler* (Aug. 20, 1909). His most successful opera, *Quentin Durward* (after Walter Scott), written in 1892, was not produced until many years later, at Newcastle-on-Tyne (Jan. 13, 1920). He also wrote an oratorio, *The Annunciation* (London, 1910); *Rapsodie monégasque* for orch. (1935); choral works.

Maclean, Charles Donald, English organist; b. Cambridge, March 27, 1843; d. London, June 23, 1916. He studied theory with Ferdinand Hiller in Cologne; later at Oxford Univ. (D. Mus., 1865). He was musical director at Eton College (1871-75); then entered the Indian Civil Service, returning to London in 1898. He was the English editor of the International Musical Society.

Maclean, Quentin Stuart Morvaren, English organist and composer; son of Alexander Maclean; b. London, May 14, 1896. He studied in Leipzig with Karl Straube (organ) and Max Reger (composition); was interned there during World War I. Upon his return to London, he served as assistant organist to Sir Richard Terry at Westminster Cathedral (1919-20). In 1939 he settled in Toronto as composer for the radio and church organist. His compositions, some in a humorous vein, include *Variations on the Carman's Whistle,* for orch. (1943); *Concerto for Electric Organ* (1945); *The Well-Tempered Orchestra* (1953); and a piano concerto (1953).

Maclennan, Francis, American tenor; b. Bay City, Mich., Jan. 7, 1879; d. Port Westminster, Long Island, July 17, 1935. He studied voice in N. Y., and later with Henschel in London and Franz Emerich in Berlin; made his début as Faust at Covent Garden (1902); in 1904 he sang Parsifal in Savage's Opera Co. on a tour of the U.S.; from 1907 till 1913 he sang at the Berlin Opera, where he had the distinction of being the first foreigner to sing Tristan in Germany; also performed Wagnerian roles in England; from 1915-17 he was a member of the Chicago Opera Co., appearing chiefly as a Wagnerian singer. In 1904 he married Florence Easton, with whom he appeared in duo recitals.

MacMillan, Sir **Ernest Campbell,** Canadian conductor and composer; b. Mimico, Ontario, Aug. 18, 1893. He studied music in Toronto; then at Edinburgh Univ. with Alfred Hollins and Frederick Niecks. He visited Bayreuth to attend the Wagner Festival in the summer of 1914, and was interned when the war broke out; after the Armistice he returned to Canada, and settled in Toronto; was director of the Toronto Cons. (1926-52) and conductor of the Toronto Symph. Orch. (1931-56); also conducted in the U.S., in England, Australia, etc. He was knighted in 1935. His works include: *England,* after Swinburne, for soli, chorus, and orch. (1917); *Two Sketches* for string orch., *Six Bergerettes du Bas Canada,* for voices, oboe, viola, cello, and harp; *4 Chansons* of French Canada, for male chorus; *3 Indian Songs of the West Coast;* collections of Canadian songs; etc. He publ. several educational works: *On the Preparation of Ear Tests; Graded Piano Sight Reading Exercises* (with H. Willan); *The Modern Piano Student* (with Boris Berlin); etc. He edited *Music in Canada* (Toronto, 1955).

Macmillen, Francis, American violinist; b. Marietta, Ohio, Oct. 14, 1885. He studied at the Chicago College of Music as a child; at the age of 10 was sent to Germany, where Joachim accepted him as a pupil; then studied with César Thomson at the Cons. of Brussels, winning the 1st prize in 1901; continued his studies with Karl Flesch in Berlin and Leopold Auer in St. Petersburg. He made his professional début at 17, in Brussels (March 30, 1903); then appeared in England; American début with the N. Y. Symph. Orch., on Dec. 7, 1906, followed by an extended tour of the U. S. From 1911 till 1914 he played all over Europe; at the outbreak of World War I returned to the U. S.; was teacher at the Ithaca, N. Y., Cons. of Music until 1929; then again gave concerts in Europe (1929-35); finally returned to America in 1935.

Maconchy, Elizabeth, English composer; b. Broxbourne, Herts., March 19, 1907. She studied with Vaughan Williams at the Royal College of Music in London (1923-29); won a traveling scholarship which enabled her to go to Prague; there her piano concerto was performed in 1930. Under the influence of Central European modernism, she developed an Expressionistic style of composition; her instrumental music is tense and concentrated. —Works: ballets: *Great Agrippa* (1933), *The Little Red Shoes* (1935), *Puck Fair* (1940); for orch.: *The Land,* suite (1929), *Theme and Variations* for strings (1942), symphony (1945-48), viola concerto (1937), *Dialogue,* for piano and orch. (1940), *Concertino,* for clarinet and strings (Copenhagen Festival of the International Society for Contemporary Music, June 2, 1947); 5 string quartets (1933-48); quintet for oboe and strings (1932); *Prelude, Interlude, and Fugue* for 2 violins (Prague Festival of the International Society for Contemporary Music, Sept. 4, 1935); viola sonata (1938); violin sonata (1944); several piano suites; a number of songs. —Cf. F. Howes, *Elizabeth Maconchy,* in the 'Monthly Mus. Record' (July-Aug., 1938).

Macpherson, Charles, Scottish organist and composer; b. Edinburgh, March 10, 1870; d. London, May 28, 1927. He was a chorister at St. Paul's Cathedral; studied organ with George Martin; then took courses at the Royal Academy of Music; held various positions as organist; succeeded his teacher George Martin as organist of St. Paul's in 1916; conducted the London Church Choirs Association from 1914 until his death. He wrote several overtures on Scottish themes; a number of choral works; edited 144 Scottish songs in 8 vols.; publ. *A Short History of Harmony* (London, 1917).

Macpherson, Stewart, English organist and educator; b. Liverpool, March 29, 1865; d. London, March 27, 1941. He studied with W. C. Macfarren at the Royal Academy of Music (piano) and with G. A. Macfarren (composition); then taught harmony there; conducted the Westminster Orchestral Society (1885-1902); in 1898 was appointed examiner to the Associated Board, in which capacity he visited Canada, Australia, and New Zealand (1900). He wrote a symphony, several overtures, and a Mass; edited the 'Music Student's Library' and the Joseph Williams 'Handbooks on Music' series; publ. *Practical Harmony* (1894); *Practical Counterpoint* (1900); *Rudiments of Music* (1907); *350 Exercises in Harmony* (1907); *Evolution of Musical Design; Form in Music* (1908); *Music and Its Appreciation* (1910); *Aural Culture Based upon Musical Appreciation* (with Ernest Read; in 3 parts: 1912, 1914, and 1918); *Studies in Phrasing and Form* (1911); *Musical Education of the Child* (1915); *Studies in the Art of Counterpoint* (1928); *A Simple Introduction to the Principles of Tonality* (1929); *Cameos of Musical History* (1937).

Macque, Giovanni (Jean de), Flemish composer; b. Valenciennes, c. 1550; d. Naples, Sept., 1614. In his marriage certificate (1592) he is named 'Fiammingo della città de Valencena'; a book of motets (Rome, 1596) describes him as a Belgian from Valenciennes. He studied with Philippe de Monte; then went to Rome (about 1570), where he became a member of the Compagnia dei Musici di Roma (organized in 1584); among its members were Palestrina and Marenzio. In 1586 Macque went to Naples and entered the service of Don Fabrizio Gesualdo da Venosa, father of the composer Carlo Gesualdo. On May 20, 1590, Macque was appointed 2nd organist of the Church of the Annunciation in Naples. In

1594 he was appointed organist of the viceregal chapel, and in Dec. 1599 became its choir director. Among his pupils in Naples were Ascanio Mayone, Giovanni Maria Trabaci, Luigi Rossi, and Falconieri. Several of Macque's madrigals are found in Younge's *Musica Transalpina* (1588) and in Morley's collection of Italian works (1598); extant keyboard pieces are reproduced in the 'Monumenta Musicae Belgicae' (Antwerp, 1938; with a list of sources and a biographical sketch). Macque was one of the first to employ rhythmic transformations of a single theme (in canzonas), which were later used extensively by Frescobaldi; Macque also applied the keyboard technique of Cabezón's 'diferencias' (variations). —Cf. U. Prota-Giurleo, *Notizie storico-biografiche sul musicista belga Jean Macque,* in the 'Report of the First Congress of the International Society for Musical Research' (1930); A. Davison and W. Apel, *Historical Anthology of Music* (Cambridge, Mass., 1946); G. Reese, *Music in the Renaissance* (N.Y., 1954; p. 543).

Maddy, Joseph Edgar, eminent American educator and conductor; b. Wellington, Kansas, Oct. 14, 1891; studied at Bethany College, Wichita College, and at the Columbia School of Music, Chicago; played the viola and clarinet; was a member of the Minneapolis Symph. Orch. (1909-14) and St. Paul Symph. (1914-18); supervisor of instrumental music in the public schools of Rochester, N.Y. (1918-20) and Richmond, Ind. (1920-24); instructor of public school methods at Earlham College (1922-24); in 1924, appointed to the faculty of the Univ. of Michigan as prof. of music education; founder and conductor of the National High School Orch., for which he established, with T.P. Giddings, the National Music Camp at Interlochen, Mich.; 1936-38, president, and from 1938-40, 1st vice-president of the Music Educators National Conference; in 1940, elected member of Music Education Research Council.

Maderna, Bruno, Italian conductor and composer of modern tendencies; b. Venice, 1920. He studied conducting with Scherchen, and conducted all over Europe; composition with Malipiero. Among his works are *Introduzione e passacaglia* for orch. (1947); piano concerto (1948); *Serenata* for 11 instruments (1946); *Studi per 'Il Processo' di Kafka,* for recitation, soprano, and small orch. (1950); *Musica per due dimensioni* (1952); and *Sintaxis* for 4 different but unspecified timbres produced electronically.

Madetoja, Leevi, outstanding Finnish composer; b. Uleaborg, Feb. 17, 1887; d. Helsinki, Oct. 6, 1947. He studied with Järnefelt and Sibelius; later in Paris with Vincent d'Indy (1910-11) and in Vienna with Robert Fuchs (1911-12). He conducted the Helsinki Philharmonic (1912-14) and the Viborg Orch. (1914-16); became a teacher at the Helsinki Cons. in 1916. Madetoja's music is inspired by Finnish melos; in his treatment, he follows the precepts established by Sibelius; his works are greatly appreciated in Finland. He wrote 2 operas, *Pohjalaisia* (Helsinki, Oct. 25, 1924) and *Juha* (Helsinki, Feb. 17, 1935); a ballet, *Okon Fuoko* (Helsinki, Dec. 2, 1930); 3 symphonies (1915; 1918; 1926); symph. poem *Kullervo* (1913); piano trio; violin pieces; several piano suites; a number of songs; cantatas to subjects from *Kalevala;* also recitations with piano accompaniment. —Cf. K. Tuukkanen, *Leevi Madetoja* (Helsinki, 1947).

Maegaard, Jan, Danish composer; b. Copenhagen, April 14, 1926. He studied with Knud Jeppesen; also played the double-bass. In 1954 he was appointed instructor at the Copenhagen Cons. — Works: a viola sonata; bassoon sonata; wind quintet; piano quartet; trio for oboe, clarinet, and bassoon (Baden-Baden Festival, June 19, 1955); *The Golden Harp,* for voice, oboe, cello, and piano.

Maelzel, Johannes Nepomuk, German inventor of the metronome; b. Regensburg, Aug. 15, 1772; d. on board a ship in the West Indies, July 31, 1838. He studied music with his father, an organ manufacturer. He went to Vienna in 1792, where he began constructing mechanical instruments, which attracted great attention in Vienna and subsequently in other European cities; of these the Panharmonicon was particularly effective; in 1812 he inaugurated an Art Cabinet, where he exhibited his inventions, including an automatic trumpeter. In 1816 he constructed the Metronome, the idea for which he obtained from Winkel, of Amsterdam (who had exhibited similar instruments, but without the scale divisions indicating the number of beats per minute). Maelzel put the Metronome on the market, despite a lawsuit brought by Winkel, and the initial of his last name was thenceforth added to the indication of tempo in musical compositions (M. M. —i. e. Maelzel's Metronome). Beethoven wrote a piece for Maelzel's Panharmonicon, which he subsequently orchestrated and published as *Wellington's Victory.* Among Maelzel's other inventions was an automatic chess player, an ingenious machine with collapsible gears, behind which a midget chess player was hidden. Maelzel was found dead in his cabin on board the brig Otis, bound for America.

Maganini, Quinto, American flutist, conductor, arranger, and composer; b. Fairfield, Calif., Nov. 30, 1897. He played the flute in the San Francisco Symph. Orch. (1917) and in the N.Y. Symph. (1919-28); studied flute playing with Barrère in N.Y., composition with Nadia Boulanger in France, at the American Cons. in Fontainebleau; 1927, won the Pulitzer Prize; 1928-29, awarded a Guggenheim Fellowship; 1930, conductor of the N.Y. Sinfonietta; in 1932 he organized his own orch., the Maganini Chamber Symph., with which he toured widely. In 1939 he was appointed conductor of the Norwalk, Conn., Symph.; in 1953 was elected president of American Schools of Music and Art, at Fontainebleau, France. —Works: *Tuolumne,* a Californian Rhapsody, for orch., with trumpet obbligato (N. Y., Aug. 9, 1924); *South Wind,* orchestral fantasy (N.Y., April 7, 1931); *Sylvan Symphony* (N.Y., Nov. 30, 1932); *A Suite of Music by Royalty,* orchestral transcriptions of works by Frederick the Great, Henry VIII, and others (N.Y., March 1, 1933); *Concerto for Strings* (N.Y., Jan. 6, 1935); *Napoleon,* an orchestral portrait (N.Y., Nov. 10, 1935); *The Royal Ladies,* orchestral suite on airs ascribed to Marie Antoinette, etc. (Greenwich, Conn., Feb. 3, 1940); an opera, *Tennessee's Partner* (American Opera Festival, Radio Station WOR, N. Y., May 28, 1942); numerous arrangements for small orch. of classical and modern works.

Maggini, Giovanni Paolo, Italian violin maker; b. Brescia, Aug. 25, 1580; d. there, c. 1630. He worked in the shop of Gasparo da Salò; after his marriage in 1615, he set up his own workshop and became prosperous thanks to the excellence of his manufacture; about 50 violins and 20 violas and cellos are extant; his instruments are prized particularly because of the softness of their tone in the deep register. His label reads: Gio. Paolo Maggini, Brescia. —Cf. M. L. Huggins, *Giovanni Paolo Maggini, His Life and Work* (London, 1892); A. Berenzi, *Gli artefici liutai bresciani* (Brescia, 1890); A. Berenzi, *Di Giovanni Paolo Maggini* (Cremona, 1907).

Magnard (mah - ñahr'), **(Lucien - Denis - Gabriel-) Albéric,** French composer; b. Paris, June 9, 1865; d. Baron, Oise, Sept. 3, 1914 (killed by German soldiers in his house). He was brought up in an intellectual family; his father was editor of 'Le Figaro.' He studied at the Paris Cons. with Dubois and Massenet, and later with Vincent d'Indy. He fell under the influence of Wagner, but succeeded in generating an element of national French music in his works; his mastery of instrumentation is incontestable, and the rhapsodic sweep of his symphonies is impressive. Despite these qualities, Magnard's symphonic music never gained a stable place in the orchestral repertory; his operas were even less successful. —Works: operas: *Yolande* (Brussels, 1892), *Guercœur* (1904; revised by Guy-Ropartz, and produced at the Paris Opéra, April 24, 1931), and *Bérénice* (Paris, Opéra-Comique, Dec. 15, 1911); 4 symphonies (1894; 1899; 1902; 1913); *Suite dans le style ancien,* for orch. (1892); *Hymne à la Justice* (1903); *Hymne à Vénus* (1906); quintet for wind instruments and piano (1904); string quartet (1904); piano trio (1906); violin sonata; cello sonata; songs. —Cf. M. Boucher, *Albéric Magnard* (Lyons, 1919); G. Carraud, *La Vie, l'œuvre et la mort d'Albéric Magnard* (Paris, 1921); C. Laforêt, *L'Esthétique d'Albéric Magnard,* in the 'Revue Musicale' (1920).

Magne, Michel, French composer; b. Lisieux, March 20, 1930. He began to compose as a very young man, adopting at once an ultra-modern method; his film score *Le Pain Vivant* (1955) received critical acclaim; he has also experimented with electronic music; on May 26, 1955, he conducted in Paris his *Symphonie Humaine* for 150 performers, making use of inaudible 'infrasounds' to produce a physiological reaction by powerful low frequencies. He wrote the musical score for Françoise Sagan's ballet, *Le Rendez-vous manqué* (1957).

Magomayev (măh-gŏh-măh'-yev), **Muslim,** Azerbaidzhan composer; b. Shusha, Sept. 18, 1885; d. Baku, July 28, 1937. He began his musical career as an improviser, and his first opera, *Shah Ismail* (Baku, 1916), was a series of songs and interludes on native themes. His second opera, *Nergiz* (Baku, Jan. 1, 1936), is based on the events of the Russian revolution.

Mahillon (măh-ē-yŏhn'), **Victor,** Belgian manufacturer of musical instruments, and a writer on acoustics; b. Brussels, March 10, 1841; d. Saint-Jean, Cap-Ferrat, June 17, 1924. He was the son of Charles Mahillon (1813-87), founder of the manufacturing firm of that name; he worked in his father's shop as a youth; applied himself to a study of acoustics; in 1869 he began publishing a periodical, 'L'Écho musical,' which he abandoned shortly before his father's death; then assumed the management of the factory; made excellent reproductions of rare instruments, among them a complete collection of all the wind instruments in use during the 16th and 17th centuries. In 1876 he became custodian of the instrumental museum of the Cons. of Brussels (founded by Fétis) and greatly enlarged the collection (more than 3500 specimens). —Publications: *Tableau synoptique des voix et de tous les instruments de musique; Tableau synoptique de la science de l'harmonie; Éléments d'acoustique musicale et instrumentale* (1874); *Catalogue descriptif et analytique du Musée instrumental du Conservatoire Royal de Musique de Bruxelles* (1880; 2nd ed., 5 vols., 1893-1922); *Le Matériel sonore des orchestres de symphonie, d'harmonie, et de fanfares* (1897); *Les Instruments à vent: I. Le Trombone, son histoire, sa théorie, sa construction;* II. *Le Cor;* III. *La Trompette* (1907).

Mahler, Fritz, conductor; nephew of Gustav Mahler; b. Vienna, July 16, 1901; studied composition in Vienna with Schoenberg, Anton von Webern, and Alban Berg; musicology with Guido Adler at the Univ. of Vienna (1920-24); conducting with Leopold Reichwein. He conducted summer orchestras in Bad Hall (1924-26); light opera at the Volksoper in Vienna; from 1930-35, conductor of the radio orch. in Copenhagen; in 1936 emigrated to America, where he taught at the Juilliard Summer School; conductor of the Erie, Penn., Philharmonic Orch. (1947-53); in 1953 appointed conductor of the Hartford, Conn., Symph. Orch. In the fall of 1957 he conducted guest engagements in Poland (Cracow, Katowice, Lodz, etc.).

Mahler, Gustav, great Austrian composer and conductor; b. Kalischt, Bohemia, July 7, 1860; d. Vienna, May 18, 1911. He attended the Iglau Gymnasium; then entered the Vienna Cons., where he studied with Julius Epstein (piano), Robert Fuchs (harmony), and Franz Krenn (composition). He also took courses in history and philosophy at the Univ. of Vienna (1877-79). In the summer of 1880 he received his first appointment as conductor, in the town of Hall; from then on, he held posts as theater conductor at Ljubljana (1881), Olmütz (1882), Vienna (1883), and Kassel (1883-85). In 1885 he succeeded Anton Seidl at the Prague Opera, where he directed performances of Wagner's music dramas. From 1886-88, he was assistant to Arthur Nikisch in Leipzig; in 1888 he received the important engagement of music director of the Royal Opera in Budapest; he thoroughly reorganized the management and repertory there; after three seasons, he was summoned to Hamburg, where he reasserted his growing competence as opera conductor (1891-97). In 1897 he was offered the directorship of the Vienna Court Opera; he held this position for ten years; under his guidance, the Vienna Opera reached a very high standard of artistic excellence; Mahler displayed an extraordinary talent as an organizer and an inspired conductor. His performances were admired for the perfection of ensemble, fidelity to the composer's intentions, and superlative theatrical effectiveness. He was also known as a relentless taskmaster who refused to sacrifice his artistic ideals to managerial expediency, or defer to the fame of the prima donnas. In 1907, he accepted the post of principal conductor of the Metropolitan Opera, where he made his début on Jan. 1, 1908, with a superb performance of *Tristan und Isolde;* also noteworthy were his revivals of *Fidelio* and *Don Giovanni.* In 1909, he was elected conductor of the N. Y. Philharmonic Soc., and endowed with autocratic powers, so that he could carry out his plans for the improvement of performing standards and the enlargement of the repertory. His uncompromising zeal aroused opposition among the conservative elements in the administration of the New York Philharmonic, and he was constantly engaged in a struggle with the board of trustees; when he left New York at the conclusion of the season of 1910-11, he was spiritually a broken man. He was also imprudent enough to conduct his last New York concert (Feb. 21, 1911) while he was in a high fever. He returned to Vienna in May 1911, and died shortly afterwards of pneumonia, at the age of 50. —Mahler was the last great composer of the Romantic School of Vienna. His symphonies and other works were drawn on the grandest scale, and the technical means employed for the realization of his ideas correspondingly elaborate. The sources of his inspiration were twofold: the lofty concepts of universal art, akin to those of Bruckner, and ultimately stemming from Wagner; and the simple folk melos of the Austrian countryside, in pastoral moods recalling the intimate episodes in Beethoven's symphonies. Mahler's symphonies are often assigned programmatic titles, although he explicitly denied such connotations. Mahler was not an innovator in his harmonic writing; he never departed entirely from the traditions of 19th-century music, but he brought the Romantic era to a culmination by virtue of the expansiveness of his emotional expression and the grandiose design of his musical structures. Morbid by nature, Mahler brooded upon the idea of death; one of his most poignant compositions is the cycle for voice and orch., *Kindertotenlieder;* the marginal remarks in the manuscript of his unfinished 10th symph., invoking death and annihilation, point to serious mental trouble. There was conflict in Mahler's religious persuasion: born in the Jewish faith, he became a Catholic in 1897; but his true philosophy was pantheistic. On March 10, 1902, he married Alma Maria Schindler; of their two daughters, one died in infancy; the other, Anna Justina (b. 1904), was married to Ernst Krenek. —Mahler's importance in the development of modern music in Austria was very great; the early works of Arnold Schoenberg and Alban Berg show the influence of his concepts. Festivals of Mahler's music were given in various countries; a society was formed in the U. S. in 1931 'to develop in the public an appreciation of the music of Bruckner, Mahler, and other moderns.' An International Gustav Mahler Society was formed in Vienna in 1955, with Bruno Walter as honorary president. —Works: 9 symphonies: No. 1, in D major, *Titan* (1883-88; Budapest, Nov. 20, 1889, Mahler conducting); No. 2, in C minor, *Resurrection,* with soprano, contralto, and chorus (1887-94; Berlin, Dec. 13, 1895, Mahler conducting); No. 3, in D minor, *Die fröhliche Wissenschaft* (1893-96; Krefeld, June 12, 1902, Mahler conducting); No. 4 in G major (1899-1901; Munich, Nov. 25, 1901, Mahler conducting); No. 5, in C# minor, *The Giant* (1901-02; Cologne, Oct. 18, 1904, Mahler conducting); No. 6, in A minor (1903-05; Essen, May 27, 1906, Mahler conducting); No. 7, in E minor (1904-06; Prague, Sept. 19, 1908 Mahler conducting); No. 8 in E♭ major, *Symphony of a Thousand,* with 8 solo voices and choruses (1906-07; Munich, Sept. 12, 1910, Mahler conducting); No. 9, in D major (1908-10; posthumous; Vienna, June 26, 1912, Bruno Walter conducting); No. 10 (unfinished; 1909; 2 movements, *Adagio* and *Purgatorio,* performed Vienna, Oct. 12, 1924, Franz Schalk conducting; publ. in facsimile by Alma Mahler, 1924). Vocal works: *Lieder und Gesänge aus der Jugendzeit,* 14 songs for voice and piano (1880-92); *Das klagende Lied,* for soprano, contralto, tenor, chorus, and orch. (1880-99); *Lieder eines fahrenden Gesellen,* 4 songs with orch. (1883-85); *Des Knaben Wunderhorn,* 10 songs, with piano or orch. (1888); 5 songs, to poems by Rückert (1902); *Kindertotenlieder,* 5 songs with piano or orch. (1901-04); *Das Lied von der Erde,* for contralto, tenor, and orch. (1907-10; posthumous; Munich, Nov. 20, 1911, Bruno Walter conducting); an unfinished opera, *Herzog Ernst von Schwaben;* arrangements of Weber's *Die drei Pintos* and *Oberon;* a suite of pieces culled from Bach's orch. works; fragments from early compositions. —Bibliography: L. Schiedermair, *Gustav Mahler* (Leipzig, 1901); Paul Stefan, *Gustav Mahlers Erbe* (Munich, 1908; a polemic against Felix Weingartner, Mahler's successor in Vienna); *Gustav Mahler. Ein Bild seiner Persönlichkeit in Widmungen* (Munich, 1910); Paul Stefan, *Gustav Mahler. Eine Studie über Persönlichkeit und Werk* (Munich 1910; 4th augm. ed., 1921; English transl., N.Y., 1913); R. Specht, *Gustav Mahler* (Berlin, 1913); Guido Adler, *Gustav Mahler* (Vienna, 1916); A. Neisser, *Gustav Mahler,* in 'Reclams Universal-Bibliothek' (Berlin, 1918); H. F. Redlich, *Gustav Mahler: eine Erkenntnis* (Nuremberg, 1919); Paul Bekker, *Mahlers Sinfonien* (Berlin, 1921); A. Roller, *Die Bildnisse Gustav Mahlers* (Leipzig, 1922); R. Mengelberg, *Gustav Mahler* (1923); Natalie Bauer-Lechner, *Erinnerungen an Gustav Mahler* (Vienna, 1923); Alma Maria Mahler, *Briefe Gustav Mahlers* (Berlin, 1924); W. Hutschenruyter, *Gustav Mahler* (The Hague, 1927); H. Holländer, *Gustav Mahler,* in the 'Mus. Quarterly' (Oct., 1931); G. Engel, *Gustav Mahler: Song-Symphonist* (N.Y., 1932); Bruno Walter, *Gustav Mahler* (Vienna, 1936; also in English transl., N. Y., 1957); Alma Maria Mahler, *Gustav Mahler: Erinnerungen und Briefe* (Amsterdam, 1940; in English, as *Memories and Letters,* London, 1946); Egon Wellesz, *The Symphonies of Gustav Mahler,* in the 'Music Review' (Jan.-April, 1940); Bruno Walter (with Ernst Krenek), *Gustav Mahler* (N.Y., 1941); Dika Newlin, *Bruckner-Mahler-Schoenberg* (N.Y., 1947); Arnold Schoenberg, *Gustav Mahler,* in *Style and Idea* (N. Y., 1950); N. Loeser, *Gustav Mahler* (Haarlem, 1950); Hans Tischler, *Mahler's Impact on the Crisis of Tonality,* in 'Music Review' (April, 1951); Theodore Reik, *The Haunting Melody* (N.Y., 1953); Erwin Stein, *Orpheus in New Guises* (London, 1953); H. F. Redlich, *Bruckner and Mahler,* in 'The Master Musicians' (London, 1955). Detailed analyses of Mahler's symphonies, by Istel, Schiedermair, Teibler, Weigl, and Gräner, are found in vol. 10 of 'Meisterführer'; 3rd symph., by L.

Schiedermair, in the series 'Der Musikführer' (Leipzig, 1902); another analysis of the 3rd symph., by E. O. Nodnagel (Darmstadt, 1904), attacking Schiedermair's interpretation; see also Donald Mitchell, *Some Notes on Mahler's Tenth Symphony,* in the 'Musical Times' (Dec., 1955). Vol. I of Donald Mitchell's monumental biography was publ. in London, 1958, under the title, *Gustav Mahler: The Early Years.*

Mahrenholz, Christhard, German musicologist; b. Adelebsen, near Göttingen, Aug. 11, 1900; studied organ; took courses at Leipzig Cons. with Schering; devoted himself mainly to church music. In 1933 he was elected president of the Association of Evangelical German Church Choirs; was co-editor of the magazine 'Musik und Kirche.' He publ. *Luther und die Kirchenmusik* (Kassel, 1937); ed. Adlung's *Musica mechanica organoedi* (Kassel, 1931) and works by Samuel Scheidt; co-editor of *Handbuch der deutschen evangelischen Kirchenmusik* (Göttingen, several vols., beginning 1932).

Maichelbeck, Franz Anton, German composer of keyboard music; b. Reichenau, July 6, 1702; d. Freiburg-im-Breisgau, June 14, 1750. He publ. *Die auf dem Clavier spielende Caecilia* (1736; contains 8 sonatas) and *Die auf dem Clavier lehrende Caecilia* (1738; a book of studies).

Maier (mā'-er), **Guy,** American pianist; b. Buffalo, Aug. 15, 1892; d. Santa Monica, Calif., Sept. 24, 1956. He studied at the New England Cons. in Boston, and privately with Schnabel. After a series of solo appearances in the U.S., he formed a partnership with Lee Pattison as duo pianist, and gave numerous concerts with him (until 1931). From 1933 till 1946 he taught at the Juilliard School of Music, N.Y.; in 1946 he went to California and taught at the Univ. of California, Los Angeles. He contributed, for many years, a monthly column on piano technique to 'Etude'; made numerous transcriptions of various classical works for piano.

Maier (mī'-er), **Julius Joseph,** German music scholar; b. Freiburg, Baden, Dec. 29, 1821; d. Munich, Nov. 21, 1889. He studied for a government career, but in 1849 took up music under Haussmann in Leipzig; taught for a time at the Munich School of Music; in 1857 was appointed custodian of the music dept. of the Munich Library. He publ.: *Klassische Kirchenwerke alter Meister* (1845; arranged for men's chorus); an *Auswahl englischer Madrigale* (1863); and the valuable catalogue, *Die musikalischen Handschriften der Königlichen Hof- und Staatsbibliothek in München* (1879; only Part I, *Die Handschriften bis zum Ende des 17. Jahrhunderts).*

Maikapar, Samuel. See **Maykapar.**

Maillart, Louis (called **Aimé**), French composer; b. Montpellier, March 24, 1817; d. Moulins, May 26, 1871. He studied at the Paris Cons. with Halévy and Leborne (composition) and with Guérin (violin); won the Grand Prix de Rome in 1841. He wrote 6 operas, all first performed at Paris: *Gastibelza* (Nov. 15, 1847); *Le Moulin des tilleuls* (1849), *La Croix de Marie* (1852), *Les Dragons de Villars* (Sept. 19, 1856; his most successful opera, performed also in Germany under the title *Das Glöckchen des Eremiten), Les Pêcheurs de Catane* (Dec. 19, 1860), and *Lara* (March 21, 1864); also several cantatas and other sacred works.

Maillart, Pierre, Belgian theorist; b. Valenciennes, 1550; d. Tournai, July 16, 1622. He was chorister at the Flemish chapel in Madrid; returning to his native land, he entered the Univ. of Louvain; was later in Antwerp (1574) and Tournai, where he was cantor (1606). He publ. *Les Tons, ou Discours sur les modes de musique* (Tournai, 1610).

Mailly (mah-yē'), **Alphonse-Jean-Ernest,** Belgian organist and composer; b. Brussels, Nov. 27, 1833; d. there, Jan. 10, 1918. He studied at the Cons. of Brussels; taught piano and organ there; gave numerous and successful organ concerts in France and England; wrote various pieces for piano and for organ.

Mainardi, Enrico, Italian cellist and composer; b. Milan, May 19, 1897; studied there, and later with Hugo Becker in Berlin; appeared in chamber music concerts with Dohnányi; in 1933 appointed prof. at the Academy of Santa Cecilia in Rome. — Works: suite for cello and piano (1940); cello concerto (Rome, May 13, 1947, composer soloist); several pieces of chamber music; an edition of Bach's cello suites.

Maine, Basil Stephen, English writer on music; b. Norwich, March 4, 1894; studied with Stanford at Queen's College, Cambridge; taught music and also mathematics at various schools; played organ in churches;

acted on the stage for a time; in 1921 became music critic of the 'Daily Telegraph'; in 1926 was on the staff of the 'Morning Post'; in 1931 traveled in the U.S. as lecturer on English music. —Publications: *Receive It So* (1926); *Behold These Daniels,* a volume of studies of contemporary critics (1928); *Reflected Music* (1930); a comprehensive biography of Elgar (2 vols., 1933); *Chopin* (1933); *The Glory of English Music* (1937); *The Best of Me* (autobiographical; 1937); *People Are Much Alike* (London, 1938, autobiographical); *On Music* (1945); *Twang with Our Music; Being a Set of Variants to Mark the Completion of Thirty Years' Practice in the Uncertain Science of Music Criticism* (London, 1957). He also composed some choral settings of religious texts, and songs.

Mainwaring, John, English writer; b. 1735; d. Cambridge, April, 1807. In 1760 he publ. *Memoirs of the Life of the late G. F. Handel,* which was the first biography of Handel, and the first biography in book form of any composer; it was translated into German by J. Mattheson (1761).

Mainzer (mīn' - tser), **Joseph,** singing teacher and musical journalist; b. Trier, March 7, 1801; d. Salford, Lancashire, Nov. 10, 1851. He was a chorister at the Trier Cathedral; then studied music in Darmstadt, Munich, and Vienna; returning to his native town, he was ordained priest; taught at the seminary there, and publ. a sight-singing method, *Singschule* (1831). He then abandoned priesthood; moved to Brussels (1833), and then to Paris (1834), where he started the short-lived 'Chronique musicale de Paris' (1838). In 1841 he went to England; lived for a time in London, and finally established himself in Manchester as a singing teacher. In 1844 he began publication of the monthly 'Mainzer's Musical Times and Singing Circular,' which in 1846 became the 'Musical Times' (publ. without interruption through more than a century). Mainzer mastered the English language to such an extent that he was able to engage in aggressive musical journalism. His methods of self-advertising were quite uninhibited; he arranged singing courses in open-air gatherings, and had pamphlets printed with flamboyant accounts of receptions tendered him. —Publications: *Singschule* (Trier, 1831); *Méthode de chant pour les enfants* (Paris, 1835); *Méthode de chant pour voix d'hommes* (Paris, 1836); *Bibliothèque élémentaire de chant* (Paris, 1836); *Méthode pratique de piano pour enfants* (Paris, 1837); *Abécédaire de chant* (Paris, 1837); *École chorale* (Paris, 1838); *Esquisses musicales, ou souvenirs de voyage* (Paris, 1838-39); *Cent mélodies enfantines* (Paris, 1840); *Singing for the Million* (London, 1841). —See Percy A. Scholes, *The Mainzer Movement,* in *The Mirror of Music* (London, 1947; vol. 1, pp. 3-10).

Maio, Giovanni. See **Majo.**

Mair, Franz, composer; b. Weikersdorf, in the Marchfeld, March 15, 1821; d. Vienna, Nov. 14, 1893. He was founder (1883) and conductor of the Vienna Schubertbund; composed music to *Die Jungfrau von Orleans* and other theatrical productions; wrote a number of male choruses, and a cycle of 15 folksongs of various nations arranged for men's chorus and orch., as *Die Völker und ihre Lieder.* His reminiscences were publ. by the Schubertbund under the title *Aus meinem Leben* (Vienna, 1897).

Maison (mā-zohn'), **René,** Belgian tenor; b. Frameries, Nov. 24, 1895. He studied at the Cons. of Brussels, and later went to the Paris Cons.; was on the roster of the Monte Carlo Opera (1922), then at the Opéra-Comique in Paris, and at Covent Garden, London. He was a member of the Chicago Civic Opera Co. (1927-32), at the Teatro Colón, Buenos Aires (1934-37); then joined the Metropolitan Opera, N.Y. (début as Walther in *Die Meistersinger,* Feb. 3, 1936).

Maitland, John Alexander Fuller. See **Fuller Maitland.**

Maitland, Rollo F., American organist; b. Williamsport, Penna., Dec. 10, 1884; d. Philadelphia, April 7, 1953. He was taught the rudiments of music by his father; then studied violin, piano, and organ with various teachers in Philadelphia; was active as a church organist there; taught theory and other subjects at the Zeckwer-Hahn Music Academy in Philadelphia. He publ. a number of compositions for organ; also contributed articles to the 'Diapason' and other publications.

Maître, Jehan, See **Gallus, Johannes.**

Majo (mah'-yŏh), **Giovanni** (called **Ciccio di Majo**), Italian composer; son of Giuseppe Majo; b. Naples, March 24, 1732; d. there, Nov., 1770. He received his primary education from his father; was church organist; then began to compose for the stage; wrote some 20 operas, of which the first was *Ricimero, re dei Goti* (Rome, Feb. 7, 1759); also wrote separate arias for various pasticcios.

Majo, Giuseppe, Italian composer; father of the preceding; b. Naples, Dec. 5, 1697; d. there, Nov. 18, 1771. He studied with Nicola Fago at the Conservatorio della Pietà dei Turchini in Naples; in 1744 became master of the royal chapel in Naples, retaining this post until his death. He wrote a considerable amount of church music; also several comic operas, and 2 serious operas.

Majone (Mayone), Ascanio, Neapolitan organist and composer; lived in the late 16th to early 17th centuries. He was a pupil of Giovanni Macque, and his assistant at the viceregal chapel at Naples, c. 1600. Existing musical publications by Majone are: *Primo libro di diversi capricci per sonare* (Naples, 1603); *Il primo libro di madrigali a 5 voci* (Naples, 1604); *Secondo libro di diversi capricci per sonare* (Naples, 1609). Two of his madrigals are included in the collection *Teatro di Madrigali a 5 v. de div. excell. musici Napolitani, posti in luce da Scipione Ricci, Libraro* (Naples, 1609). Majone is mentioned in Scipione Cerreto's *Della Prattica Musica vocale e strumentale* (Naples, 1601) as an outstanding performer on the organ and harp. Majone's keyboard toccatas are among the earliest examples of the affective Baroque style found later in Frescobaldi. —Cf. W. Apel, *Neapolitan Links between Cabezón and Frescobaldi,* in the 'Mus. Quarterly' (Oct., 1938); also M. Bukofzer, *Music in the Baroque Era* (N.Y., 1947).

Major (măh'-yŏhr), **Ervin,** Hungarian music scholar and composer; b. Budapest, Jan. 26, 1901. He studied with his father, Jakab Gyula Major; then took lessons with Kodály (1917-21); received his Ph. D. at the Univ. of Szeged (1930). From 1928 he was engaged as instructor at the Budapest Cons. He made a profound study of Hungarian folk music as it relates to the works of classical composers; publ. numerous papers on the subject; composed mostly in small forms, using as thematic material authentic Hungarian melodies. —Works: *Trio-Serenade,* for 2 violins and viola (1921); cello sonata (1932); *Elegy,* for clarinet and piano (1937); bassoon sonata (1938); sonata for double-bass and piano (1943); piano pieces; choruses.

Major (real name Mayer), **Jakab Gyula,** Hungarian pianist, conductor, and composer; b. Kosice, Dec. 13, 1858; d. Budapest, Jan. 30, 1925. He studied with Robert Volkmann; graduating from the Budapest Cons. in 1882, he became a teacher in Hungarian schools. He toured in Europe as a pianist; then returned to Budapest. His music follows the Romantic tradition of the German school. He wrote the operas, *Erzsike* (Budapest, Sept. 24, 1901), *Széchy Mária* (1906), and *Mila* (1913), 5 symphonies, piano concerto, violin concerto, cello concerto, 4 string quartets, piano quintet, 2 violin sonatas, and much piano music.

Majorano. See **Caffarelli.**

Makarova (măh-kăh'-rŏh-văh), **Nina Vladimirovna,** Russian composer; b. Yurin, Aug. 12, 1908. She studied with Miaskovsky at the Moscow Cons., graduating in 1935. In her early works she showed the Romantic influence of her teacher; some technical procedures bear traces of Impressionism. She has written a symphony (1938); an opera, *Courage* (1942); several song cycles, a sonatina for piano, and a series of children's songs. Makarova is married to Aram Khatchaturian.

Maklakiewicz (măh-klăh-kyeh'-vich), **Jan Adam,** Polish composer; b. Chojnaty, near Warsaw, Nov. 24, 1899; d. Warsaw, Feb. 7, 1954. He studied with Statkowski at the Warsaw Cons. and with Paul Dukas in Paris. Returning to Poland, he became instructor in harmony at the Warsaw Cons.; from 1932 he was organist at the Church of the Holy Cross; in 1934, he established the musical periodical 'Chor' and was also active as music critic. Under the influence of French modernism, Maklakiewicz wrote a number of works in an advanced style; his *4 Japanese Songs* were performed at the Oxford Festival of the International Society for Contemporary Music (July 23, 1931). Other works include a ballet, *Cagliostro in Warsaw* (Poznan, Oct. 1, 1946); a symph. poem *Grünewald* (Cracow, Sept. 1, 1945); *Uwertura praska (The Prague Overture;* Prague, May 8, 1947); cello concerto (1932); violin concerto (1933); some chamber music; many arrangements of Polish folksongs. From 1947 to his death Maklakiewicz was director of the Cons. of Cracow.

Malashkin, Leonid Dimitrievitch, Russian composer; b. 1842; d. Moscow, Feb. 11, 1902. He was an ardent song collector; his anthology *50 Ukrainian Folksongs* is valuable. His original compositions were not successful; he wrote an opera, *Ilya Murometz* (Kiev, 1879), a *Russian Symphony on Folk Themes* (Moscow, March 27, 1873), and a great deal of church music.

Malawski, Artur, Polish composer; b. Przemysl, July 4, 1904; d. Cracow, Dec. 26, 1957. He studied in Cracow and at the Warsaw Cons.; in his music he utilized Polish folksongs, but only as thematic material; the treatment is in a general modern style. His best known work is *6 Symph. Etudes,* for piano and orch. (Amsterdam Festival of the International Society for Contemporary Music, June 9, 1948). Other works include *Toccata and Fugue,* for orch. (Cracow, Sept. 4, 1945, composer conducting), 2 symphonies (1938-48; 1956); piano trio; 2 string quartets; ballet, *Wierchy* (1950); piano pieces; songs.

Malcuzynski, Witold, outstanding Polish pianist; b. Warsaw, Aug. 10, 1914. He studied with Turczynski at the Warsaw Cons.; graduated in 1936; then took lessons with Paderewski in Switzerland. After his marriage to the French pianist Colette Gaveau, he went to Paris (1939); then toured in South America (1940-42); made his American début in 1942; gave concerts in Australia in 1950. Before 1958 he made in all 14 U. S. tours, 9 South American tours, and 2 world tours (1949; 1956). He revisited Poland for the first time in 1958. He is particularly distinguished as an interpreter of Chopin. —Cf. B. Gavoty, *Witold Malcuzynski* (London, 1957).

Maldeghem, Robert Julien van, Belgian music editor; b. Denterghem, 1810; d. Brussels, Nov. 13, 1893. He studied with Fétis at the Brussels Cons., winning the Belgian Prix de Rome; obtained a post as church organist; undertook a thorough research of old Flemish music, and eventually publ. an anthology of choral works in 29 vols., *Trésor musical,* an edition of great documentary and historic importance, despite many errors of transcription; comments and rectifications were made by Charles Van den Borren, in 'Acta musicologica' (vols. 5-6) and by G. Reese, *Maldeghem and his Buried Treasure: a Bibliographical Study,* in 'Notes' (Dec., 1948).

Maldere (Malderre), Pierre van, Belgian violinist and composer; b. Brussels, Oct. 16, 1729; d. there, Nov. 3, 1768. In 1746 he became a member of the ensemble of the Royal Chapel of Brussels. From 1751 to 1753 he was in Dublin, as violinist, conductor, and composer. He then traveled to Paris (1754) and Austria (1757-58); returning to Brussels, he became conductor of the Opera, and also wrote stage works for production there. Among his operas are: *Les Amours champêtres* (1758); *Les Précautions inutiles* (1760); *La Bagarre* (1762); *Les Sœurs rivales* (1762); *Le Médecin de l'amour* (1766); *Le Soldat par amour* (1766); a number of instrumental works, of which many were published during his lifetime: 6 symphonies (Brussels, 1759), *6 sinfonie a più stromenti* (Paris, 1760), and a similar set, publ. in Paris (1768); also violin sonatas. Three of his brothers were also violinists. —Cf. S. Clercx, *Pierre van Maldere* (Brussels, 1948).

Maleingreau (măh-lin-groh'), **Paul de,** Belgian composer and organist; b. Trélon-en-Thiérache, Nov. 23, 1887. He studied with Edgar Tinel at the Brussels Cons.; in 1913, became prof. of harmony there; in 1919 appointed instructor of organ; in 1946 he was elected president of the Froissart Academy. His performances of Bach organ works were highly regarded in Belgium. Among his compositions are 2 symphonies; *Légende de St. Augustin,* for solo voices, chorus, and orch. (1934); an Easter Mass (1925); 2 Diptychs, for orch. (1947); organ works; piano pieces.

Maler, Wilhelm, German composer; b. Heidelberg, June 21, 1902. He studied with H. Grabner in Heidelberg, J. Haas in Munich, and Jarnach in Cologne. He subsequently occupied several teaching positions: at the Rheinische Musikschule in Cologne (1925-45) and at the Detmold Music Academy (since 1946); also lectured at the Univ. of Bonn. His style reflects the nationalistic movement in Germany with elements of Classical polyphony and Romantic lyricism; he made numerous arrangements of German folksongs. His original works include a concerto for harpsichord (1927); concerto grosso (1928); a violin concerto (1932); concerto for violin, cello, and orch. (1940); several string quartets; piano pieces; a number of easy ensembles for various instruments; an oratorio, *Der ewige Strom.* He publ. a manual of harmony, *Beitrag zur Harmonielehre* (1930; 3rd ed., 1951).

Malherbe (măh-lärb'), **Charles-Théodore,** French writer on music and composer; b. Paris, April 21, 1853; d. Cormeilles, Eure, Oct. 5, 1911. First he studied law, and was admitted to the bar; but then took up music under A. Danhauser, A. Wormser, and J.

Massenet. After a tour (as Danhauser's secretary) through Belgium, Holland, and Switzerland in 1880-1, to inspect the music in the public schools, he settled in Paris; in 1896, was appointed assistant archivist to the Grand Opéra, succeeding Nuitter as archivist in 1899. He edited 'Le Ménestrel,' and contributed to many leading reviews and musical journals. His collection of musical autographs, which he left to the Paris Cons., was probably one of the finest private collections in the world. —Writings: *L'Œuvre dramatique de Richard Wagner* (1886); *Précis d'histoire de l'Opéra-Comique* (1887); *Notice sur Ascanio* (1890); *Mélanges sur R. Wagner* (1891); *Histoire de la seconde Salle Favart* [Opéra-Comique] (2 vols., 1892-3, 'couronnée par l'Institut'); *Catalogue des œuvres de Donizetti* (1897); *Programmes et concerts* (1898); *Auber* (1911). Malherbe was secretary of the edition of Rameau's complete works publ. by Durand, editing the historical and biographical notices therein; also ed., with Weingartner, of the complete edition of Berlioz's works (Breitkopf & Härtel).

Malherbe (măh-lärb'), **Edmond Paul Henri,** French composer; b. Paris, Aug. 21, 1870. He studied at the Paris Cons. with Massenet and Fauré; 1898, won the Premier Second Prix de Rome, and in 1899, the Deuxième Premier Grand Prix; 3 times winner of the Prix Trémont of the Académie des Beaux-Arts (1907, 1913, 1921); in 1950 received the Grand Prix Musical of the City of Paris for the total of his works. A productive composer, he continued to write music in his 80's, but very few of his larger compositions were performed, and virtually none published. —Works: operas: *Madame Pierre* (1903; Paris, 1912); *L'Avare,* after Molière (1907); *L'Émeute* (1911; Paris, 1912); *Cléanthis* (1912); *Anna Karénine* (1914); *Le Mariage forcé,* after Molière (1924); *Néron* (1945); *L'Amour et Psyché,* lyric tragedy with ballet (1948; State Prize, 1950); *Monsieur de Pourceaugnac,* pantomime with chorus, after Molière (1930); a series of 'tableaux symphoniques' after great paintings; 3 symphonies (1948; 1956; 1957); violin concerto; nonet; sextet; many choruses, songs, piano pieces. He publ. *L'Harmonie du système musical actuel à demi-tons* (1920) and *Le Tiers-de-ton: Deux Systèmes: Tempéré et non-tempéré* (1900; 1950).

Malibran, Maria Felicità *(née* García), famous contralto; daughter of Manuel García; b. Paris, March 24, 1808; d. Manchester, Sept. 23, 1836. Taken to Naples, she played a child's part in Paër's opera *Agnese;* later she studied solfeggio with Panseron; from the age of 15, however, she was her father's pupil in singing. Her début in London (June 7, 1825), as Rosina in the *Barbiere,* procured her engagement for the season. The family then voyaged to New York, where for two years she was the popular favorite, singing in *Otello, Romeo, Don Giovanni, Tancredi, Cenerentola,* and the 2 operas which her father wrote for her, *L'Amante astuto* and *La Figlia dell'aria.* In N. Y. she married the French merchant Malibran; he soon became bankrupt, and they separated. Returning to Paris, her immense success led to an engagement at a salary of 50,000 francs; after 1829 she sang every season at London; also appeared at Rome, Naples, Bologna, and Milan. She married the violinist Bériot in 1836, only a few months before her death, which was caused by over-exertion in singing after a severe fall from her horse. As a singer and actress she exercised the fascination of a highly endowed personality over her audiences. Her voice was of extraordinary compass, but the medium register had several 'dead' tones. She was also a good pianist, and composed numerous nocturnes, romances, and chansonnettes, publ. in album form as *Dernières pensées,* etc. —Bibliography: *Cenni biografici* (Venice, 1835); G. Barbieri, *Notizie biografiche di Maria Malibran* (Milan, 1836); I. Nathan, *The Life of Mme. Maria Malibran de Bériot* (London, 1836); A. von Treskow, *Mme. Malibran* (Leipzig, 1837); Comtesse Merlin, *Loisirs d'une femme de monde* (Paris, 1838; German transl. by G. Lotz as *Maria Malibran als Weib und Künstlerin,* Leipzig, 1839; English transl., London, 1844; more romantic than trustworthy); E. Legouvé, *Maria Malibran* in *Études et souvenirs de théâtre* (Paris, 1880); E. Heron-Allen, *A Contribution Towards an Accurate Biogr. of Ch. de Bériot and Maria Malibran,* in No. 6 of 'De fidiculis opuscula' (1894); A. Pougin, *Maria Malibran: Histoire d'une cantatrice* (Paris, 1911; English transl., London, 1911); Clément Lanquine, *La Malibran* (Paris, 1911); J.-G. Prod'homme, *La Fayette and Maria Malibran,* in the 'Chesterian' (Sept., 1919); Louise Héritte-Viardot, *Une Famille de grands musiciens* (1923); Carl Engel, *Again La Fayette and Maria Malibran,* in the 'Chesterian' (Jan.-Feb., 1925); *6 Unpubl. Letters from La Fayette to Maria Malibran,* ib. (March-April, 1925); A. Flament, *Une Étoile en 1830: La Malibran* (Paris, 1928); Phyllis Crump, *Musset and*

Malibran (Cambridge, England, 1932); P. Larionoff, *Maria Malibran e i suoi tempi* (Florence, 1935); D. Bielli, *Maria Malibran* (1936); M. Lorenzi de Bradi, *La brève et merveilleuse vie de la Malibran* (Paris, 1936); G. G. Bernardi, *La Malibran a Venezia,* in 'Musica d'oggi' (Aug.-Sept., 1936); H. Malherbe, *La Passion de la Malibran* (Paris, 1937); A. Flament, *L'Enchanteresse errante, la Malibran* (Paris, 1937).

Malipiero, Francesco, Italian composer; grandfather of Gian Francesco Malipiero; b. Rovigio, Jan. 9, 1824; d. Venice, May 12, 1887. He studied with Melchiore Balbi at the Liceo Musicale in Venice. At the age of 18, he wrote an opera, *Giovanna di Napoli,* which was produced with signal success; Rossini praised it. Other operas by Malipiero were *Attila* (Venice, Nov. 15, 1845; renamed later *Ildegonda di Borgogna), Alberigo da Romano* (his best; Venice, Dec. 26, 1846), *Fernando Cortez* (Venice, Feb. 18, 1851).

Malipiero, Gian Francesco, distinguished Italian composer; b. Venice, March 18, 1882. He was raised in a musical atmosphere; his grandfather, Francesco Malipiero, wrote operas; his father, Luigi Malipiero, was also a musician. In 1898 Malipiero entered the Vienna Cons. as a student of violin, but, failing an examination, took up harmony (with Stocker). In 1899 he returned to Venice and studied there at the Liceo Musicale Benedetto Marcello with Enrico Bossi, whom he followed to Bologna in 1902; took a diploma in composition at the Liceo Musicale G. B. Martini in Bologna (1904). In 1913 he went to Paris; was greatly influenced by the ultra-modern developments in French music and adopted many advanced harmonic devices, without surrendering the basic ideas of tonality. His absorption in old Italian music determines the principal current of his own works, which are unmistakably national in essence, while cosmopolitan in technique. From 1921 to 1923 he was prof. of composition at the Univ. of Parma; then settled in Asolo (near Venice) in 1923. He was appointed director of the Liceo Musicale Benedetto Marcello, Venice, in 1939. In addition to his work as composer and educator, he established himself as a foremost editor of Italian masters. —Works: Operas: *Canossa* (Rome, Jan. 24, 1914); *Sogno d'un tramonto d'autunno* (1914); *L'Orfeide* (Düsseldorf, Nov. 5, 1925), in 3 parts *(La Morte delle maschere; Sette Canzoni; Orfeo);* the 2nd part, *Sette Canzoni* (Paris, July 10, 1920), is often performed separately; *Tre commedie goldoniane (La Bottega da caffè; Sior Todaro Brontolon; Le Baruffe chiozzotte;* 1st performance in its entirety, Darmstadt, March 24, 1926); *Filomela e l'Infatuato* (Prague, March 31, 1928); *Merlino mastro d'organi* (Rome Radio, Aug. 4, 1934); *Il mistero di Venezia,* in 3 parts *(Le Aquile di aquileia; Il finto Arlecchino; I Corvi di San Marco;* 1st performance in its entirety, Coburg, Dec. 15, 1932); *Torneo notturno* (Munich, May 15, 1931); *Il festino* (Turin Radio, Nov. 6, 1937); *La favola del figlio cambiato* (Brunswick, Jan. 13, 1934); *Giulio Cesare* (Genoa, Feb. 8, 1936); *Antonio e Cleopatra* (Florence, June 4, 1938); *Ecuba* (Rome, Jan. 11, 1941); *La vita è sogno* (Breslau, June 30, 1943); *I Capricci di Callot* (Rome, Oct. 24, 1942); *L'allegra brigata* (Milan, May 4, 1950); *Mondi celesti e infernali* (Turin Radio, Jan. 12, 1950); *Il figliuol prodigo* (Florence May Festival, May 11, 1957); *Venere prigioniera* (Florence May Festival, May 11, 1957). Ballets: *Pantea* (Venice, Sept. 6, 1932); *La mascherata delle principesse prigioniere* (Brussels, Oct. 19, 1924); *Stradivario* (in concert form, Lisbon, Feb. 28, 1951); *El mondo novo* (Rome, Dec. 16, 1951). Orchestral works: *Sinfonia degli eroi* (1905); *Sinfonia del mare* (1906); *Sinfonie del silenzio e della morte* (1908); *Impressioni dal vero* (1st part, Milan, May 15, 1913; 2nd part, Rome, March 11, 1917; 3rd part, Amsterdam, Oct. 25, 1923); *Armenia,* on Armenian folksongs (1917); *Ditirambo tragico* (London, Oct. 11, 1919); *Pause del silenzio* (1st part, his most famous orchestral work, Rome, Jan. 27, 1918; 2nd part, Philadelphia, April 1, 1927); *Per una favola cavalleresca* (Rome, Feb. 13, 1921); *Oriente immaginario,* for chamber orch. (Paris, Dec. 23, 1920); *Variazioni senza tema,* for piano and orch. (Prague, May 19, 1925); *L'Esilio dell'Eroe,* symph. suite (1930); *Concerti per orchestra* (Philadelphia, Jan. 29, 1932); *Inni* (Rome, April 6, 1933); *Sette invenzioni* (Rome, Dec. 24, 1933); *Quattro invenzioni* (Dresden, Nov. 11, 1936); *Fantasie di ogni giorni,* for orch. (Louisville, Nov. 17, 1954); symphonies: No. 1 (Florence, April 2, 1934); No. 2, *Elegiaca* (Seattle, Jan. 25, 1936); No. 3, *delle campane* (Florence, Nov. 4, 1945); No. 4, *In Memoriam* (Boston, Feb. 27, 1948); No. 5, *Concertante, in eco* (London, Nov. 3, 1947); No. 6, *Degli archi* (Basel, Feb. 11, 1949); No. 7, *Delle canzoni* (Milan, Nov. 3, 1949); No. 8, *Di un tempo* (Rome, March 21, 1951); No. 9, *Dello Zodiaco* (Lausanne, Jan. 23, 1952); violin concerto (Amsterdam, March 5, 1933); cello concerto (Belgrade, Jan. 31, 1939); 1st piano concerto (Rome, April 3, 1935); 2nd piano concerto (Duisburg, March 6, 1939); 3rd piano concerto (Louisville, March 8, 1949); 4th piano concerto (N. Y., March 29, 1951); concerto for 2 pianos and orch. (Besançon Festival, Sept. 11, 1957); *Concerto a tre,* for violin, cello, piano, and orch. (Florence, April 9, 1939). Vocal works: *San Francesco d'Assisi,* mystery for soli, chorus, and orch. (N. Y., March 29, 1922); *La Principessa Ulalia,* cantata (N. Y., Feb. 19, 1927); *La Cena,* for soli, chorus, and orch. (Rochester, N. Y., April, 1929); *La Passione,* for soli, chorus, and orch. (Rome, Dec. 15, 1935); *De Profundis,* for solo voice, viola, bass drum, and piano (1937); *Missa pro mortuis,* for baritone solo, chorus, and orch. (Rome, Dec. 18, 1938); *Quattro vecchie canzoni,* for solo voice and 7 instruments (Washington, April 12, 1941); *Santa Eufrosina* for soli, chorus, and orch. (Rome, Dec. 6, 1942); *Le sette allegrezze d'amore,* for solo voice and 14 instruments (Milan, Dec. 4, 1945); *Vergilii Aeneis,* for 11 soli, chorus, and orch. (Turin, June 21, 1946); *La Terra,* for chorus and orch. (Cambridge, Mass., May 2, 1947, with organ); *Mondi celesti,* for solo voice and 12 instruments (Capri, Feb. 3, 1949); *Le sette peccati mortali,* for chorus and orch. (Monteceneri, Nov. 20, 1949); *La festa de la Sensa,* for baritone solo, chorus, and orch. (1950); *Cinque Favole,* for solo voice and small orch. (Washington, Oct. 30, 1950); *Passer mortuus est,* for a cappella chorus (Pittsburgh, Nov. 24, 1952). Chamber music: *Ricercari,* for 11 instruments (Washington, Oct. 7, 1926); *Ritrovari,* for 11 instruments (Gardone, Italy, Oct. 26, 1929); *Rispetti e Strambotti,* 1st string quartet (1920); *Stornelli e Ballate,* 2nd string quartet (1923); *Cantari alla madrigalesca,* 3rd string quartet (1931); 4th string quartet (1934); 5th string quartet (1950); *L'arca di Noè,* 6th string quartet (1947); 7th string quartet (1950); *Epodi e giambi,* for violin, viola, oboe, and bassoon (1932); *Sonata a cinque,* for flute, violin, viola, cello, and harp (1934); *Sonata a tre,* for violin, cello, and piano (1927); cello sonatina (1942). For piano: *Six Morceaux* (1905); *Bizzarrie luminose dell' alba, del meriggio e della notte* (1908); *Poemetti lunari* (1910); *Preludi autunnali* (1914); *Poemi asolani* (1916); *Barlumi* (1917); *Risonanze* (1918); *Maschere che passano* (1918); *Tre omaggi* (1920); *Omaggio a Claude Debussy* (1920); *Cavalcate* (1921); *La siesta* (1921); *Il tarlo* (1922); *Pasqua di Risurrezione* (1924); *Preludi a una fuga* (1926); *Epitaffio* (1931); *Omaggio a Bach* (1932); *Preludi, ritmi e canti gregoriani* (1937); *Preludio e fuga* (1941); *Hortus conclusus* (1946).—Editions of works by Bassani, Cavalieri, Galuppi, Jommelli, Marcello, Tartini, Leo, Monteverdi (several individual works, and a collected edition, 16 vols., 1926-42), Vivaldi. —Publications: *L'Orchestra* (Bologna, 1920; English transl. by Eric Blom, London, 1921); *Claudio Monteverdi* (Milan, 1930); *Stravinsky* (Venice, 1945); *Antonfrancesco Doni musico, ovvero L'armonioso labirinto* (Venice, 1946); *Così va lo mondo: 1922-45* (autobiography; Milan, 1946); *La Pietra del bando* (1947); and many articles in various European and American magazines. —Bibliography: biography, Massimo Bontempelli, *Gian Francesco Malipiero* (Milan, 1942); Guido M. Gatti, ed., *L'opera di Gian Francesco Malipiero* (Bologna, 1952; a collection of articles on Malipiero, reprinted from numerous sources, and a comprehensive list of works, up to 1950, annotated by the composer, with a chronology of performances, etc.); magazine articles: H. Prunières, *G. F. Malipiero,* in the 'Mus. Quarterly' (July, 1920); G. M. Gatti, *G. F. Malipiero,* in 'Il Pianoforte' (May, 1925); G. M. Gatti, *G. F. Malipiero,* in *Musicisti moderni d'Italia e di fuori* (Bologna, 2nd ed., 1925; pp. 75-86); M. Labroca, *G. F. Malipiero,* in 'Musikblätter des Anbruch' (special Italian issue, Aug.-Sept., 1925); H. F. Redlich, *G. F. Malipiero und die neue Oper,* in 'Anbruch' (Nov.-Dec., 1929); G. Rossi-Doria, *Le Théâtre et l'oratorio de G. F. Malipiero,* in 'Musique' (Dec. 1929-Jan. 1930); S. Goddard, *Malipiero's 'L'Orfeide,'* in the 'Chesterian' (Nov., 1930); H. F. Redlich, *Francesco Malipiero, Dramaturge lyrique,* in the 'Revue Musicale' (Nov., 1931); M. Saint Cyr, *G. F. Malipiero,* in 'Rassegna dorica' (Feb., 1932); H. O. Boehm, *G. F. Malipiero,* in 'Der Aufsteig' (Sept., 1932); H. H. Stuckenschmidt, *Zu Malipieros Bühnenwerken,* in 'Melos' (Feb., 1934); special issue of the 'Rassegna musicale' for his 60th birthday (March, 1942), containing articles by Pizzetti, Casella, Labroca, and others. See also *The Sette Canzoni, An Explanation,* by Malipiero himself, in the 'Chesterian' (Dec., 1930).

Malipiero, Riccardo, Italian composer; nephew of Gian Francesco Malipiero; b. Milan, July 24, 1914. He studied at the Cons. of Milan; was active as a pianist. In 1945 he adopted the 12-tone technique, and repudiated most of his music written before then.—Works: operas, *Minnie la Candida* (Parma, Nov. 19, 1942) and *La Donna è mobile* (opera buffa, 1954); *Piccolo Concerto,* for piano and orch. (1945); a symphony (1949); violin concerto (Festival of the International Society for Contemporary Music, Haifa, June 3, 1954); *Sinfonia-Cantata* (N. Y., March 19, 1957). He publ. monographs on Debussy and Bach.—Cf. C. Sartori, *Riccardo Malipiero* (in English, Milan, 1957).

Maliszewski (mah-lў-shĕv'-skē), **Witold,** Polish composer; b. Mohylev-Podolsk, July 20, 1873; d. Warsaw, July 18, 1939. He studied piano in Warsaw and violin in Tiflis; then enrolled in the St. Petersburg Cons., in the class of Rimsky-Korsakov. He became director of the Odessa Cons. in 1908; went to Poland in 1921, and was active there mainly as a teacher; in 1932 he joined the staff of the Warsaw Cons. As a composer, he followed the Russian Romantic tradition; some of his symph. works had a modicum of success. He wrote the operas *The Mermaid* (Warsaw, 1928) and *Boruta* (1930); 4 symphonies; a piano concerto (1932); 4 string quartets; violin sonata; cello sonata; many piano pieces and songs. — Cf. E. Wrocki, *Witold Maliszewski* (Warsaw, 1932).

Malkin, Jacques, violinist; b. Slobodka, near Odessa, Russia, Dec. 16, 1876. He studied at the Odessa Music School, and later at the Paris Cons.; in 1893 was engaged as player on the viola d'amore in the Société des Instruments Anciens. In 1918 he settled in New York as a violin teacher; also was a member of the Malkin Trio with his brothers, Joseph and Manfred.

Malkin, Joseph, cellist; brother of Jacques and Manfred Malkin; b. Propoisk, near Odessa, Russia, Sept. 24, 1879. He studied at the Odessa Music School, and later in Paris, graduating in 1902 from the Paris Cons.; was first cellist of the Berlin Philharmonic (1902-08); then toured in Europe, Mexico, the U. S., and Canada as a member of the Brussels Quartet; was 1st cellist of the Boston Symph. (1914-19) and of the Chicago Symph. (1919-22); was a member of the Malkin Trio with his brothers, Jacques and Manfred. In 1933 he organized the Malkin Cons. in Boston, with a faculty of distinguished teachers; Arnold Schoenberg taught there during his first American season, 1934-35; the Malkin Cons. was closed in 1943; from 1944 until 1949, Malkin was a cellist in the N. Y. Philharmonic; then retired. He publ. a number of cello works and studies.

Malkin, Manfred, pianist; brother of Jacques and Joseph Malkin; b. Odessa, Aug. 11, 1884. He studied at the Paris Cons.; in 1905 settled in the U. S.; was member of the Malkin Trio; taught at the Institute of Musical Art (1911-14); established his own music school in N. Y. (1914-31); thereafter taught privately.

Malko, Nikolay Andreyevitch, eminent conductor; b. Brailov, Russia, May 4, 1883. He studied at the Univ. of St. Petersburg, and later at the Cons. there, with Rimsky-Korsakov, Liadov, Glazunov, and Tcherepnin; then went to Munich, where he worked for a time under Mottl. Returning to Russia, he conducted at the St. Petersburg Opera; in 1922, founded a class in conducting at the Moscow Cons.; in 1925, was appointed prof. at the Leningrad Cons.; was conductor of the Leningrad Philharmonic (1926-29); led the first performance of Shostakovitch's 1st Symph.; in 1928 he left Russia; conducted in Vienna, Buenos Aires, Prague, etc.; from 1928 to 1932 was guest conductor with the State Symph. Orch. in Copenhagen, and returned to conduct there many times in later years, being received with special enthusiasm by Danish audiences; in 1938 he visited the U. S. as lecturer; in 1940 became lecturer at De Paul Univ. School of Music, Chicago, and also appeared as guest conductor with several American orchestras; became an American citizen, May 7, 1946; established a class of conducting in Chicago; conducted a summer series of concerts in Chicago. In 1954, he became conductor of the Yorkshire Symph. Orch., England; in 1956 apponted resident conductor of the Sydney Symph. Orch., Australia. As a conductor, Malko is a convinced classicist, striving to achieve clarity and perfection of performance above all else, while bringing out colorful effects; as a teacher of conducting, in Europe and America, he influenced the young school of conductors; publ. a manual, *The Conductor and his Baton* (Copenhagen, 1950); composed various works, among them a clarinet concerto (Copenhagen, Sept. 27, 1952).

Malling, Jørgen, Danish composer; b. Copenhagen, Oct. 31, 1836; d. there, July 12, 1905. He studied with Gade; was first winner of the Ancher stipend in 1861; went to Paris and there became enthusiastic over Chevé's system of vocal notation, which he tried (unsuccessfully) to introduce in various cities in Scandinavia and Russia; was organist in Svendborg (1869-72); lived in Vienna from 1879 to 1882, and in Munich from 1882 to 1895; returned to Copenhagen in 1901; was active there as teacher and composer. He wrote the operas *Lisenka* and *Frithjof;* a cantata, *Küvala;* a string quartet; a piano trio; numerous piano pieces and songs.

Malling, Otto (Valdemar), Danish composer; b. Copenhagen, June 1, 1848; d. there, Oct. 5, 1915. He studied with Gade and J. P. E. Hartmann at the Copenhagen Cons.; conducted the Students' Choral Society (1872-84); was organist at various churches in Copenhagen (1878-1910); became conductor of the Concert Society there (1874-93); in 1885 was appointed instructor of music theory at the Copenhagen Cons.; in 1899 became its director. His published works, comprising about 100 op. numbers, include a symph.; a fantasia for violin and orch.; an *Oriental Suite, Musique de ballet;* a piano concerto; several cantatas; works for organ; numerous songs; characteristic pieces for piano; a ballet, *Askepot (Cinderella;* Copenhagen, Sept. 25, 1910); and a treatise on instrumentation.

Mallinger, Mathilde *(née* Lichtenegger), soprano; b. Agram, Croatia, Feb. 17, 1847; d. Berlin, April 19, 1920. She studied in Prague and Vienna; made her début in Munich as Norma (Oct. 4, 1866), and created the role of Eva in *Die Meistersinger* (Munich, June 21, 1868). In 1873 she appeared in the U. S.; also sang in Russia. Subsequently she was active mainly as a singing teacher, in Prague (1890-95) and, after 1895, in Berlin. She was married to Baron von Schimmelpfennig of Berlin.

Mallinson, Albert, English composer and organist; b. Leeds, Nov. 13, 1870; d. Elsinore, Denmark, April 5, 1946. He was a pupil of W. Creser; then church organist in Leeds; in 1903, married the Danish singer Anna Steinhauer, and with her made successful tours of Denmark and Germany, introducing his own songs; from 1904 until 1914 he was organist of the English Church in Dresden; at the outbreak of World War I he went to Denmark, where he remained most of his life. He wrote about 300 songs to German, English, and Danish texts.

Malotte, Albert Hay, American organist and song composer; b. Philadelphia, May 19, 1895. He was a chorister at St. James Episcopal Church; studied with W. S. Stansfield, and later in Paris with Georges Jacob; was organist in Chicago and in London; then moved to Hollywood, where he became a member of the music staff of the Walt Disney Studios; composed the scores for some of Disney's 'Silly Symphonies' and 'Ferdinand, the Bull.' He is the composer of the enormously popular setting of *The Lord's Prayer* (1935); he also set to music the 23rd Psalm and other religious texts.

Malten (real name Müller), **Therese,** German soprano; b. Insterburg, June 21, 1855; d. Neuzschieren, near Dresden, Jan. 2, 1930. She studied with Gustav Engel in Berlin; made her operatic début in Dresden in 1873, and remained for some 30 years the principal singer on the roster of the Dresden Opera; also sang in Berlin, Vienna, and London. Wagner heard her and suggested her engagement as Kundry at the première of *Parsifal* at Bayreuth in 1882. She was particularly renowned as a Wagnerian singer; in addition to being an outstanding singer, she was also a fine dramatic actress.

Mälzel. See **Maelzel.**

Mana-Zucca (mäh'-näh-zōō'-käh) (real name Augusta Zuckermann), American pianist and composer; b. New York, Dec. 25, 1890. She studied piano with Alexander Lambert in N. Y.; with Godowsky and Busoni in Berlin; composition with Hermann Spielter in London; also singing with Von zur Mühlen in London and Paris. She was exhibited in the U. S. as a piano prodigy, playing a Beethoven concerto with the N. Y. Symph. under Walter Damrosch (1899); later she played in Poland and Russia (1907), in Germany, France (1908), and England. She became a singer in light opera; made her début as soprano in the leading part of Lehár's *Count of Luxembourg* (1914); also appeared in operettas in the U. S. In 1916 she changed her name by liberally transposing its syllables and rearranging its vowels, and also dropping her first name. That was the time when she began to compose music seriously; she played her piano concerto in N. Y. on Aug. 20, 1919; wrote 2 operas, *Hypatia* and *The Queue of Ki-Lu;* a ballet, *The Wedding of the Butterflies;* several short orchestral works *(Cuban Dance, Frolic for Strings, Fugato Humoresque, Bickerings, Havana Nights,* etc.); a violin sonata, a cello sonata, a piano trio, and a number of solo violin pieces; a great amount of teaching material for piano, and a collection of 366 piano pieces under the general title *My Musical Calendar* (12 books, 1 for each month); several hundred songs, of which *I Love Life* became extremely popular; other successful songs are *There's Joy in My Heart, Big Brown Bear, Honey Lamb, Time and Time Again.* Her violin concerto, op. 224, was performed in N. Y., Dec. 9, 1955. Mana-Zucca settled in Miami, Florida, in 1940, continuing her activities as pianist and composer.

Mancinelli (mahn-chē-nĕl'-lē), **Luigi,** Italian composer and conductor; b. Orvieto, Feb. 5, 1848; d. Rome, Feb. 2, 1921. He studied piano at home and cello in Florence; was engaged for 8 years as a cello player in a theater orch., at the same time taking lessons in theory from Mabellini. In 1874 he became opera conductor in Rome; in 1881 appointed director of the Bologna Cons. He subsequently conducted in London at Drury Lane (1886-88) and during the spring seasons at Covent Garden (1888-1906); also conducted at the Royal Theater in Madrid (1888-95); from 1894 until 1902 he was conductor at the Metropolitan Opera House, N.Y.; in 1906 he inaugurated the Teatro Colón in Buenos Aires, and was there as principal conductor until 1912; then returned to Italy. He was particularly renowned as a conductor of Wagner's operas, and was called 'il Wagnerista' in Italy. He wrote several operas: *Isora di Provenza* (Bologna, Oct. 2, 1884), *Tizianello* (Rome, June 20, 1895), *Ero e Leandro* (Madrid, Nov. 30, 1897; his most famous opera, produced all over Europe, and also at the Metropolitan Opera House, N.Y.), *Paolo e Francesca* (Bologna, Nov. 11, 1907); a posthumous opera, *Sogno di una notte d'estate* (after Shakespeare's *Midsummer Night's Dream),* was not produced. He also wrote the oratorios *Isaia* (Norwich, England, Oct. 13, 1887) and *Santa Agnese* (Norwich, Oct. 27, 1905); a cinematic cantata *Giuliano l'Apostata* (Rome, 1920); and *Intermezzi sinfonici* for *Cleopatra* by Cossa, a symph. suite that became very popular. —Cf. L. Arnedo, *Luigi Mancinelli y su opera Hero y Leandro* (Madrid, 1898); G. Orefice, *Luigi Mancinelli* (Rome, 1921).

Mancini (man-chē'-nē), **Francesco,** Italian composer; b. Naples, 1679; d. there, June 11, 1739. He studied at the Cons. di San Loreto in Naples, and in 1728 became an instructor there. He wrote some 20 operas for Naples, which established him as a notable composer. His opera *Idaspe fedele* was sung in Italian at the Haymarket Theatre in London on March 23, 1710 with excellent success.

Mandić (mahn'-ditch), **Josef,** Croatian composer; b. Trieste, April 4, 1883. He studied music in Trieste, Zagreb, and Vienna; wrote mostly vocal music, in a Croatian style; his works include an opera, *Peter Svačič;* a Croatian Mass; a cantata, *Slaven i pjesma;* and numerous songs.

Mandl, Richard, Austrian composer; b. Prossnitz, May 9, 1859; d. Vienna, April 1, 1918. He studied at the Vienna Cons.; then went to Paris, where he attended the classes of Delibes at the Cons.; returned to Vienna in 1900. He wrote a one-act comic opera, *Nächtliche Werbung* (Prague, 1888); a cantata, *Griselidis;* a symph. poem, *Stimme des Orients;* a symph. rhapsody, *Algier;* a dance suite, *Viennensia;* several violin pieces; a string quintet; songs. He was married to Camilla Barda (1872-1922), who publ. a valuable pedagogical work, *Kompendium der gesamten Klaviertechnik* (3 vols.).

Mandyczewski (man-dē-chef'-skē), **Eusebius,** eminent Austrian musicologist; b. Czernowitz, Aug. 18, 1857; d. Vienna, July 13, 1929. He studied with Robert Fuchs and Nottebohm in Vienna; in 1880 he became choirmaster of the Vienna Singakademie, and archivist to the Gesellschaft der Musikfreunde; in 1896 he joined the faculty of the Vienna Cons., where he taught music history and composition. He was subsequently engaged as one of the editors of the great edition of Haydn's works, undertaken by Breitkopf & Härtel, and of the 'Volksliederbuch.' In 1897 he received the honorary degree of *Dr. phil.* from Leipzig Univ. for his work on the complete edition of Schubert. He edited Bach's arias for soprano, alto, tenor, and bass with obbligato instruments in the 'Publ. der neuen Bachgesellschaft' (vols. 10-13 and 15); collaborated in many other scholarly editions, including the complete works of Brahms, who was a personal friend of his; his correspondence with Brahms was publ. by Karl Geiringer in the 'Zeitschrift für Musikwissenschaft' (May, 1933).

Manelli, Francesco, Italian composer; b. Tivoli, 1595; d. Parma, Sept. 1667. He served as a chorister at the Cathedral of Tivoli in 1605, and continued his service there as chapel singer (1609-24); he then was maestro di cappella there (1627-28). He produced an opera, *Gelia,* in Bologna (1630); in 1636 he went to Venice, where he was chapel singer at San Marco; from 1645 to his death he was in the service of the Duke of Parma. In 1637, the Teatro San Cassiano in Venice, the first public opera house in Europe, was opened with Manelli's opera *Andromeda;* he wrote several other operas, which enjoyed considerable popularity. All the musical scores of Manelli are lost, but some librettos are preserved. His op. 4, *Musiche varie* (Venice, 1636), a collection of cantatas, arias, *canzonette* and *ciacone,* shows that he had adopted the 'parlando' recitative. —Cf. G. Radicotti, *L'Arte musicale in Tivoli nei secoli XVI, XVII e XVIII* (1907; 2nd ed., 1921).

Manén, Joan, Catalan composer; b. Barcelona, March 14, 1883. He studied both piano and violin, and was first exhibited as a piano prodigy; later appeared as a violinist; gave numerous concerts, and was particularly successful in Germany, where he spent many years (from 1908). He wrote the operas *Giovanna di Napoli* (Barcelona, 1902), *Der Fackeltanz* (Frankfurt, 1909), *Nero und Akté* (Karlsruhe, Jan. 28, 1928; a revision of an earlier opera, *Acté,* originally produced in Barcelona, 1903), and *Soledad* (Barcelona, 1952); also a 'theater symphony,' *Camino del Sol* (Brunswick, May 2, 1926); a ballet, *Triana* (1952); *Petite suite espagnole,* for violin and piano; *Nova Catalonia,* for orch.; *Fantasia-Sonata* for guitar; choral works; songs. He edited some of Paganini's compositions, and completed the sketches and orchestration of an early (1787) violin concerto of Beethoven.

Manfredini, Francesco, Italian violinist and composer; b. Pistoia, c. 1680; d. there, 1748. He was engaged as violinist in Ferrara and Bologna (1704-11); at the Munich Court in 1711; maestro di cappella at the Cathedral of Pistoia from 1734. He publ. *Concertini per camera* (1704); *12 Sinfonie da chiesa* (1709); *12 concerti grossi* (1718). His *Concerto grosso per il santissimo natale* (which includes a fine *Pastorale)* was publ. for 2 violins, string quartet, and piano (Leipzig, 1906); his 6 sonatas for 2 violins and cello appeared in London (c. 1750); Sinfonia No. 10, in Vienna (1935); Concerto grosso No. 9 was ed. for string orch. by E. Bonelli (Padua, 1948); Sinfonia No. 12, ed. by R. Nielsen (Rome, 1949).

Manfredini, Vincenzo, Italian composer; son of Francesco Manfredini; b. Pistoia, Oct. 22, 1737; d. St. Petersburg, Aug. 16, 1799. He was a pupil of his father; later studied with Perti in Bologna and with Fioroni in Milan. In 1758 he went to Russia, where he was attached to the court (until 1769); then returned to Italy; lived in Bologna and Venice; in 1798 was engaged by Paul I (who was his former pupil) to come to Russia again; he died there the following year. During his first visit to Russia he produced the following works: *Amour et Psyché,* ballet (Moscow, Oct. 20, 1762); *L'Olimpiade,* opera (Moscow, Nov. 24, 1762); *Pygmalion,* ballet (St. Petersburg, Sept. 26, 1763); *Carlo Magno,* opera (St. Petersburg, Nov. 24, 1763); wrote 6 clavecin sonatas for Catherine the Great (St. Petersburg, 1765). —Cf. *Les dernières œuvres de Vincenzo Manfredini,* in R.-Aloys Mooser, *Annales de la musique et des musiciens en Russie au XVIII*[e] *siècle* (Geneva, 1950; vol. II, pp. 28-43).

Mangold, Karl (Ludwig Amand), German composer; brother of Wilhelm Mangold; b. Darmstadt, Oct. 8, 1813; d. Oberstdorf, Aug. 5, 1889. He studied at the Paris Cons. with Berton and Bordogni; returning to Darmstadt, became a violinist in the court orch.; from 1848-69, was court music director; also conducted various choral societies there. He wrote an opera, *Tannhäuser,* which was produced in Darmstadt on May 17, 1846, only a few months after the première of Wagner's great work; in order to escape disastrous comparisons, the title was changed to *Der getreue Eckart,* and the libretto revised; the new version was produced posthumously in Darmstadt on Jan. 17, 1892. Mangold wrote two more operas, *Gudrun* and *Dornröschen;* several 'concert dramas' *(Frithjof, Hermanns Tod, Ein Morgen am Rhein, Barbarossas Erwachen);* also oratorios *(Abraham, Wittekind, Israel in der Wüste)*; chamber music; and a number of male quartets, which attained great popularity in Germany.

Mangold, (Johann) Wilhelm, German composer and violinist; brother of Karl Mangold; b. Darmstadt, Nov. 19, 1796; d. there, May 23, 1875. He studied with Rinck and Abbé Vogler; then went to Paris for lessons with Cherubini at the Paris Cons.; in 1825, became court conductor at Darmstadt; was pensioned in 1858. He wrote 3 operas, chamber music, and melodies for clarinet with piano, which were popular for a time.

Mankell, Henning, Swedish composer; b. Härnösand, June 3, 1868; d. Stockholm, May 8, 1930. He was a member of a musical family of German extraction (original ancestral name, Mangold); studied piano with Lennart Lundberg. —Works: piano concerto (1917); a piano quintet (1915); a piano trio (1915); 3 string quartets (1914-24); *Sonata pastiche* for violin and piano (1924); 3 piano sonatas; 8 ballads for piano; 24 intermezzi for piano; *Flor and Blancheflor* for baritone and orch.

Mann, Arthur Henry, English organist and editor; b. Norwich, May 16, 1850; d. Cambridge, Nov. 19, 1929. He studied at Oxford (B. Mus., 1874; D. Mus., 1882); from 1876 to his death was organist at King's College, Cambridge. He was a noted student of Handel's music; with Ebenezer Prout, he discovered at the Foundling Hospital the original wind-instrument parts of Handel's *Messiah,* and reconstructed the score in accordance with these parts; the work was performed in London in this version on June 13, 1894. Mann was co-editor (with Fuller Maitland) of the Fitzwilliam Catalogue (publ. 1893); edited Tallis' motet for 40 voices, *Spem in alium* (1888); was music editor of *The Church of England Hymnal* (1895). He composed an oratorio, *Ecce Homo* (1882), and several sacred works.

Manners, Charles (real name, Southcote Mansergh), English bass singer and impresario; b. London, Dec. 27, 1857; d. Dublin, May 3, 1935. He studied at the Dublin Royal Academy of Music; then in London and in Florence. In 1882 he made his stage début with the D'Oyly Carte company, creating the role of Private Willis in Sullivan's *Iolanthe.* In 1890 he married the soprano Fanny Moody (q.v.) and organized the Moody-Manners Opera Co. with her as a partner, for the production of grand opera in the English language; in 1902, after several successful seasons in the provincial theaters, he took his enterprise to London.

Mannes, Clara Damrosch, pianist; daughter of Leopold Damrosch; b. Breslau, Dec. 12, 1869; d. New York, March 16, 1948. At the age of 6 she began to study piano in N.Y.; then went to Dresden, where she took lessons with H. Scholtz; later also was a pupil of Busoni in Berlin (1897). On June 4, 1898, she married the violinist David Mannes, with whom she toured the U. S. and England for 20 years in joint recitals; was co-director of the Mannes School in N.Y.

Mannes, David, American violinist and conductor; b. New York, Feb. 16, 1866. He studied violin with various local teachers; spent the summer months in Europe studying with de Ahna (1891) and Halir (1892-3) in Berlin, and Ysaÿe (1903) in Brussels. He was engaged by Walter Damrosch as a violinist for the N.Y. Symph. Orch. (1891); then was concertmaster there (1898-1912); also played chamber music; in 1904, he founded the Symph. Club of N.Y. Always interested in settlement work, he took charge of the violin dept. of the Music School Settlement in N.Y. (1902) and was its director from 1910 to 1915; in 1912 he founded the Music School Settlement for Colored People; conducted a series of free symph. concerts at the Metropolitan Museum (1919-47). In 1916 he opened his own music school in N. Y., known as the David Mannes School of Music; continued to be its director until an advanced age; on his 90th birthday (1956), a special concert was organized in his honor at the Metropolitan Museum. He was co-editor (with his wife, Clara Damrosch Mannes, who was also co-director of the Mannes School) of *New Songs for New Voices.* He publ. an autobiography, *Music is My Faith* (N.Y., 1938).

Mannes, Leopold Damrosch, American pianist; son of David Mannes and Clara Damrosch Mannes; b. New York, Dec. 26, 1899; graduated from Harvard Univ. (B.A., 1920); studied at the David Mannes School and at the Institute of Musical Art, N.Y.; pupil of Elizabeth Quaile, Guy Maier, and Alfred Cortot (piano) and Schreyer, Scalero, and Goetschius (theory); won a Pulitzer Scholarship (1925) and a Guggenheim Fellowship (1926); subsequently taught composition and piano at the Institute of Musical Art and at the Mannes School; succeeded his father as its director. He temporarily abandoned music as a profession to enter the research laboratory of the Eastman Kodak Co. at Rochester; co-inventor, with Leopold Godowsky (son of the pianist), of the Kodachrome process of color photography. Among his works are a suite for 2 pianos (1924); a string quartet (1928; performed many times by Kneisel Quartet); *3 Short Pieces,* for orch. (1926); incidental music to Shakespeare's *Tempest* (1930).

Manney, Charles Fonteyn, American music editor and composer; b. Brooklyn, N.Y., Feb. 8, 1872; d. New York, Oct. 31, 1951. He was first a church singer; then studied theory with W. A. Fisher in N. Y., and with Goodrich and Goetschius in Boston. In

1898 he was engaged as music editor for the Oliver Ditson Co., and held this position until 1930; also conducted the 'Footlight Orch.' and various choral groups; after retirement, he moved to N.Y. He wrote an opera, 3 cantatas, songs, and piano pieces.

Manning, Kathleen Lockhart, composer; b. near Hollywood, Calif., Oct. 24, 1890; d. Los Angeles, March 20, 1951. She studied music with Elizabeth Eichelberger in Los Angeles, and played as a child pianist in public concerts; took lessons with Moszkowski in Paris; also appeared as an opera singer with the Hammerstein Opera Co. in London (1911-12). She wrote 2 operas (*Mr. Wu* and *For the Soul of Rafael)* and a great number of songs, some of which became popular: *Sketches of Paris* (which includes *In the Luxembourg Gardens), Sketches of London, Songs of Egypt, Sketches of New York, Autumn Leaves, Water Lily, The Lamplighter, The Street Fair,* etc.; also piano pieces *(3 Dance Impressions, In the Summer,* etc.).

Manns, Sir August (Friedrich), conductor; b. Stolzenberg, near Stettin, March 12, 1825; d. London, March 1, 1907. His talent was fostered by playing in an amateur quintet (2 violins, cello, horn, and flute) formed by his father (a poor glass-blower) his brothers, and himself; the village musician of a nearby hamlet taught him the violin, clarinet, and flute. At the age of 15 he was apprenticed to Urban, a town musician of Elbing; later he played the clarinet in a regimental band in Danzig; then was a violinist in Gungl's orch. in Berlin; subsequently conducted at Kroll's Garden (1849-51); was bandmaster of a regiment at Königsberg and Cologne (1854). In 1854 he was engaged as assistant conductor of the Crystal Palace in London; the following year he became chief conductor there. In 1856 the famous Saturday Concerts were inaugurated at the Crystal Palace, and Manns conducted them for 45 seasons until 1901; presented some 14,000 concerts in all, with an enlarged orchestra, capable of performing a regular symph. repertory. Besides these, he conducted 6 Triennial Handel Festivals (1883-1900); the Promenade Concerts at Drury Lane in 1859; and the orchestral concerts of the Glasgow Choral Union (1879-92). He was knighted in 1903. —Cf. H. S. Wyndham, *August Manns and the Saturday Concerts* (London, 1909); 'Dictionary of National Biography' (Supplement; Oxford, 1920).

Mannstädt, Franz, German conductor; b. Hagen, July 8, 1852; d. Wiesbaden, Jan. 18, 1932. He studied at the Stern Cons., in Berlin; was Hans von Bülow's assistant conductor at Meiningen, and also conducted some concerts of the Berlin Philharmonic; then was theater conductor at Wiesbaden; again conducted the Berlin Philharmonic (1893-97), and then returned to Wiesbaden as court conductor, retiring in 1924.

Manojlović (mah-noy'-loh-vitch), **Kosta,** Serbian composer; b. Krnjevo, Dec. 3, 1890; d. Belgrade, Oct. 2, 1949; studied in Munich and at Oxford Univ., receiving a bachelor's degree in 1919. He wrote a Serbian liturgy, and a cantata, *By the Waters of Babylon;* characteristic piano pieces (*Danse Fantastique,* etc.) and songs. He publ. several studies on Serbian folk music; his collection of 337 songs of East Serbia was publ. posthumously (Belgrade, 1953).

Manrique de Lara, Manuel, Spanish composer and student of folklore; b. Cartagena, Oct. 24, 1863; d. St. Blasien, Germany, Feb. 27, 1929. He entered the Spanish Army and rose to the rank of brigadier general; studied music with Chapí; became a leading authority on old Spanish ballads, including those sung by Jewish communities in the Near East. He wrote *La Orestiada,* symph. trilogy (1900); chamber music; etc.

Mansfield, Orlando Augustine, English organist and composer; b. Warminster, Nov. 28, 1863; d. Cheltenham, July 6, 1936. He studied with E. H. Turpin in London and later at Trinity Univ. in Toronto; held various positions as organist in England; from 1892 to 1912 was examiner for London College of Music. In 1912 he visited the U.S.; until 1917 was prof. of music at Wilson College, Chambersburg, Penna., and at Brenau College, Gainsville, Ga. He publ. about 600 works for piano and for organ; and some 100 arrangements of choral and other works; publ. his original compositions under the pen names of Oscar Liemann and Sofie N. Adlam. He contributed numerous articles to English and American journals; publ. *Student's Harmony* (1896), which passed through several editions.

Mansfield, Purcell James, English organist; son of Orlando Augustine Mansfield; b. Torquay, May 24, 1889. He received his entire education from his father. In 1905 he won the gold and silver medals at the Bristol Eisteddfod (Welsh Festival); then was organist at various churches in London and Glasgow; also conducted choral groups in Glasgow. He arranged 24 Scottish airs for mixed chorus; publ. 50 Miscellaneous Pieces for organ and 6 Scottish Song Books.

Manski, Dorothée, American soprano; b. New York, March 11, 1895; went to Germany as a child; appeared at Berlin in Max Reinhardt's productions; made her first American appearance with the Metropolitan Opera, N. Y., on Nov. 6, 1927, as the Witch in *Hänsel und Gretel;* remained with the Metropolitan Opera until 1941; then joined the faculty of the School of Music, Indiana Univ., as a vocal teacher.

Manskopf, (Jakob Friedrich) Nicholas, German collector of musical materials; b. Frankfurt, April 25, 1869; d. there, July 2, 1928. After extensive travels in France and England, he founded in his native city the 'Musikhistorisches Museum' containing MSS, books, documents, rare scores, theater programs, medals, caricatures, autographs, etc., of musicians from the 14th to the 20th centuries; about 30,000 items in all.

Mantovani, Tancredi, Italian writer on music; b. Ferrara, Sept. 27, 1864; d. Rome, Feb. 25, 1932. He was a pupil of A. Busi in Bologna; in 1894 he became prof. of music history and librarian at the Liceo Rossini in Pesaro; editor of the 'Cronaca musicale' (1896-1904); in 1919 appointed prof. of literature at the Academy of Santa Cecilia in Rome. —Publications: *Estetica musicale* (1892); *Orlando di Lasso* (1895); *Rossini a Lugo* (1902); *Cristoforo Gluck* (1914); *Angelo Mariani* (1921); a guide to Berlioz' *Damnation de Faust* (1923); etc.

Mantovano, Alberto. See Ripa.

Mantuani, Josef, Austrian music scholar; b. Laibach (Ljubljana), March 28, 1860; d. there, March 18, 1933. He studied composition with Bruckner and others in Vienna; musicology at the Univ. of Vienna, obtaining the degree of *Dr. phil.;* became librarian in the Vienna Library in 1893, and later chief of the music division; from 1909 taught in his native town of Laibach. He edited several volumes of the 'Denkmäler der Tonkunst in Österreich'; publ. *Tabulae codicum manuscriptorum . . . asservatorum* (2 vols., 1897 and 1899; a complete catalogue of the MSS in the Vienna Library); *Katalog der Ausstellung anlässlich der Centenarfeier D. Cimarosas* (1901); *Über den Beginn des Notendrucks* (1901); *Ein unbekanntes Druckwerk* (1902); *Geschichte der Musik in Wien. I. Teil: Von den Römerzeiten bis zum Tode des Kaisers Max I.* (1904); *Die Musikpflege Laibachs zur Zeit Schuberts,* in the 'Adler Festschrift' (1930).

Manuel, Roland. See Roland-Manuel.

Mapleson, Col. James Henry, English impresario; b. London, May 4, 1830; d. there, Nov. 14, 1901. He studied at the Royal Academy of Music in London; subsequently was engaged as a singer and a viola player; sang in Italy under the name of Enrico Mariani. In 1861 he became the manager of the Italian Opera at the Lyceum Theatre in London; then of Her Majesty's Theatre (1862-67); at Drury Lane (1868-69); in partnership with Gye at Covent Garden (1869-71); again at Drury Lane (1871-77); at the reconstructed (after the fire of 1868) Her Majesty's Theatre (from 1877). He gave several seasons of opera in the U.S. (during intervals of his London enterprises); his American ventures fluctuated between success and disaster; his last season was 1896-97 at the N.Y. Academy of Music. On March 17, 1890, he married the American singer Laura Schirmer. An exuberant personality, he dominated the operatic news both in England and America by his recurrent professional troubles and his conflicts with, and attachments to, prima donnas. He was known as 'Colonel' Mapleson by his intimates, but held no such rank. He publ. *The Mapleson Memoirs* (2 vols., London, 1888). His nephew, **Lionel S. Mapleson** (b. London, Oct. 23, 1865; d. N.Y., Dec. 21, 1937), came to the U.S. as a violinist; in 1889 joined the orchestra of the Metropolitan Opera in N.Y.; then, for half a century, was librarian there; left his own valuable library to the Metropolitan Opera including the first recordings, made by himself, ever taken of actual performances, with the voices of de Reszke, Calvé, and others.

Mara, Gertrud Elisabeth (*née* Schmeling), German soprano; b. Kassel, Feb. 23, 1749; d. Reval, Russia, Jan. 20, 1833. The daughter of a poor musician, and crippled by a fall in infancy, she played the violin by instinct; appeared in Vienna and in London as a child prodigy, arousing great admiration. In the meantime she revealed a fine singing voice; studied with Paradisi; her health also was improved; she returned to Germany and was accepted by J. A. Hiller as a student in his music school in Leipzig; soon she developed a voice with the phenomenal compass g-e^3; she sang at the Dresden

Opera between 1766-71, and then received a life appointment at the Berlin Court Opera. The caprices of a vicious husband (the cellist Mara, whom she married in 1773) and the autocratic rule of Frederick II rendered this period of her life wretched; in 1780 she was in Vienna; then, armed with letters of recommendation to Marie Antoinette, she went to Paris. From 1784 to 1802 she made her home in London, singing chiefly in concerts, and twice visited Italy; obtained a decree of separation from her husband in 1799; left London to make a long European tour, and settled in Moscow, but lost all her property in the conflagration of 1812. She then went to Reval, where she taught singing; died there at the age of 83. —Cf. G. C. Grosheim, *Das Leben der Künstlerin Mara* (Kassel, 1823); Fr. Rochlitz, *Für Freunde der Tonkunst* (Leipzig, 1824-32; in vol. I); G. Bürkli, *Gertrud Elisabeth Mara* (Zürich, 1835); *Autobiographie* (ed. by Riesemann) in the 'Allgemeine musikalische Zeitung' (Leipzig, 1875); A. Niggli, *Gertrud Elisabeth Mara,* in Waldersee's 'Sammlung musikalischer Vorträge' (Leipzig, 1881; after the autobiography); E. Wolff, *Mignon* (Munich, 1909); Rosa Kaulitz-Niedeck, *Die Mara: das Leben einer berühmten Sängerin* (Heilbronn, 1929); O. Anwand, *Die Prima Donna Friedrichs des Grossen* (Berlin, 1931).

Marais (măh-rā'), **Marin,** great French player on the viola da gamba; b. Paris, March 31, 1656; d. there, Aug. 15, 1728. He was a shoemaker's son; was apprenticed as a choirboy at the Sainte-Chapelle; studied viola da gamba with Hottemann and composition with Lully (whom he addresses as teacher in a letter published in his first book of pieces for his instrument). He then became "joueur de viole du roi" (Aug. 1, 1679). In 1686 he presented at Versailles an *Idylle dramatique;* in 1701 he was called upon to write a *Te Deum* for the convalescence of the Dauphin. Marais possessed matchless skill as a virtuoso on the viola da gamba, and set a new standard of excellence by enhancing the sonority of the instrument. He also established a new method of fingering which had a decisive influence on the technique of performance. As a composer, he followed Lully's French manner; his recitatives comport with the rhythm of French verse and the inflection of the rhyme. The purely instrumental parts in his operas were quite extensive; in *Alcione* (Paris, Feb. 18, 1706) he introduced a 'tempeste,' which is one of the earliest attempts at stage realism in operatic music. His other operas are *Alcide* (1693), *Ariane et Bacchus* (1696), and *Sémélé* (1709). He published 5 books of pieces for gamba (1686-1717); trios (or 'symphonies') for violin, flute, and viola da gamba (1692); a book of trios for violin, viola da gamba, and harpsichord under the title *La Gamme* (1723). He was married on Sept. 21, 1676 and had 19 children; in 1709 he played a concert with three of them for Louis XIV. His son Roland was also a talented gambist; he publ. 2 books of pieces for the instrument with a *basso continuo* and a *Nouvelle méthode de musique pour servir d'introduction aux acteurs modernes* (1711). —Cf. L. de La Laurencie, *L'école française de violon* (Paris, 1924); F. Lesure, *Marin Marais* and M. Barthélemy, *Les opéras de Marin Marais* (both in 'Revue Belge de Musicologie,' 1953).

Marazzoli (măh-rah-tsoh'-lē), **Marco,** Italian composer; b. Parma, c. 1600; d. Rome, Jan. 24, 1662. He was a singer in the papal chapel from about 1637; he is important in music history because he was the composer of the 1st comic opera (in collaboration with Virgilio Mazzocchi), *Chi soffre, speri,* produced in Rome on Feb. 27, 1639. He was the sole author of the serious opera *La Vita Umana* (Rome, Jan. 31, 1656), dedicated to Queen Christina of Sweden, who was then resident in Rome. For details, see A. Lowenberg, *Annals of Opera* (Cambridge, 1943).

Marbeck (Merbecke), John, English composer and theologian; b. Windsor, c. 1510; d. there, c. 1585. He was a chorister in St. George's Chapel, Windsor (1531); narrowly escaped burning as a heretic in 1544; was imprisoned, but pardoned by Henry VIII; Mus. Bac., Oxford, 1550; lay clerk, and organist of St. George's Chapel. His chief work is *The Booke of Common Praier noted* (1550), an adaptation of the plainchant of earlier rituals to the first ritual of Edward VI; reprinted in facsimile, 1939: republished in Jebb's 'Choral Responses and Litanies' (1857; vol. II). One of his hymns appears in Hawkins' *General History of the Science and Practice of Music.* Marbeck was also the compiler of a concordance of the English Bible (1550). —Cf. J. Pulver, *A Biographical Dictionary of Old English Music* (London, 1927); J. Eric Hunt, *Cranmer's First Litany, 1544, and Merbecke's Book of Common Prayer noted, 1550* (London, 1939); R. Stevenson, *John Marbeck's 'Noted Booke' of 1550,* in the 'Mus. Quarterly' (April, 1951).

Marcel, Lucille (real name Wasself), American soprano; b. New York, c. 1887; d. Vienna, June 22, 1921. She studied in N.Y.; then went to Berlin and to Paris for further study; Jean de Reszke heard her there, and recommended her for the role of Elektra for the Vienna première of Strauss' opera; accordingly she made her début in that transcendently difficult part (March 24, 1908), under Felix Weingartner; she remained at the Vienna Opera as a regular member; when Weingartner resigned the directorship in 1910, she also left, and married him the following year; was the principal soprano where Weingartner was conductor, in Hamburg (1912-14), Darmstadt (1914), and later in Vienna. She made her American début with the Boston Opera Co., as Tosca (Feb. 14, 1912); at the conclusion of her American season, returned to Vienna.

Marcelli (măhr-chĕl'-lē), **Nino,** conductor and composer; b. Santiago, Chile, Jan. 21, 1890. He studied at the National Cons. of Music there, and taught theory from 1909-13; was cellist of the Opera Orch. there (1909-10); conductor of the Santiago Symph. (1911-13); conductor of the American Headquarters Band in France (1918-19). In 1920 he was cellist of the San Francisco Symph.; director of instrumental music in the San Diego, Calif., city schools (1921); 1927 founded the San Diego Symph. Orch., of which he was conductor until 1937; in 1948 he made a tour of South America; then returned to San Diego. Among his works are a *Suite Araucana,* for orch., on old Indian themes; several orchestral marches; songs *(Solitude, Deep in the Forest, Harp of Sunset,* etc.); a light opera, *Carmelita;* teaching pieces for various instruments.

Marcello (măhr-chĕhl'-lŏh), **Alessandro,** Italian scholar and composer; brother of Benedetto Marcello; b. Venice, c. 1684; d. there, c. 1750. He publ. his works under the name of Eterico Stinfalico; extant are 6 concertos for 2 flutes or violins, 6 concertos for oboe or flute with orch., several sonatas for violin with continuo, solo cantatas, etc. Alessandro Marcello seems to have been the composer of the oboe concerto transcribed by Bach and often attributed to Benedetto Marcello. —Cf. F. C. Walker, *A Little Bach Discovery,* in 'Music & Letters' (April, 1950).

Marcello (măhr-chĕhl'-lŏh), **Benedetto,** famous composer and poet; b. Venice, July 24, 1686; d. Brescia, July 24, 1739. He received an excellent education; studied jurisprudence as well as music, was a pupil of Gasparini and Lotti; had a political career: was a member of the Council of Forty for 14 years, then 'Provveditore' at Pola for 8 years, and finally papal chamberlain at Brescia, a position he retained until his death. His masterwork is the settings of Giustiniani's paraphrases of the first 50 Psalms *(Estro poetico-armonico; Parafrasi sopra i cinquanta primi Salmi;* Venice, publ. by D. Lovisa, 1724-26, in 8 vols. folio); they are for 1, 2, 3, and 4 voices, with basso continuo for organ or clavicembalo; a few with cello obbligato, or 2 violas; they have been often republished (by Carli in Paris, etc.). He also publ. *Concerti grossi* for 5 parts (1701); *Sonate per cembalo, Sonate a cinque, e flauto solo con basso continuo* (1712), *Canzoni madrigaleschi ed Arie per camera a 2-4* (1717); a satire on operatic manners, *Il teatro alla moda, o sia Metodo sicuro e facile per ben comporre ed eseguire opere italiane in musica* (1720; 2nd ed. 1722; modern ed. by E. Fondi, Lanciano, 1913; English transl. by R. G. Pauly in the 'Mus. Quarterly,' July, 1948, and January, 1949; German transl. by A. Einstein in 'Perlen älterer romanischer Prosa,' vol. 24); the pamphlet *Lettera famigliare* (1705), a rather captious critique of Lotti, was printed incomplete, with a statement that it no longer corresponded to the views of the author. Both *Il teatro alla moda* and *Lettera famigliare* were publ. anonymously, but Marcello's authorship was never in dispute. Besides the works named above, Marcello composed several cantatas, preserved in MS in the libraries of Dresden and Vienna, and sacred works. —Bibliography: G. Sacchi, *Vita di Benedetto Marcello* (Venice, 1788; transl., with supplementary material, of F. L. Fontana's Latin biography of Marcello in vol. 9 of 'Vitae Italorum Doctrinae Excellentium,' Pisa, 1787); O. Chilesotti, *I nostri maestri del passato* (Milan, 1882; pp. 83-91); Leonida Busi, *Benedetto Marcello* (Bologna, 1884); O. Chilesotti, *Sulla Lettera Critica di Benedetto Marcello contro A. Lotti* (Bassano, 1885; contains polemics with Busi; appends a list of Marcello's publications and bibliography); E. Fondi, *La vita e l'opera letteraria del musicista Benedetto Marcello* (Rome, 1909); A. Della Corte, *La Morale d'una satira,* in 'Il Pianoforte' (1921); U. Rolandi, *I 50 salmi,* in 'Musica d'oggi' (XI, 1); A. d'Angeli, *Benedetto Marcello* (Milan, 1940); R. G. Pauly, *Benedetto Marcello's Satire on Early 18th-Century Opera,* in the 'Mus. Quarterly' (April, 1948); W. S. Newman, *The Keyboard Sonatas of Benedetto Marcello,* in 'Acta Musicologica' (Basel, 1957).

Marchand (mahr-shan'), **Louis**, French organist; b. Lyons, Feb. 2, 1669; d. Paris, Feb. 17, 1732. He was the organist of the Chapel Royal in Paris (1708-14); publ. 3 books of music for the clavecin, and one for the organ. A vol. of his organ compositions was publ. by Guilmant in 'Archives des maîtres de l'orgue.' His *Plein Jeu* (in 6 parts) appears in J. Bonnet's 'Historical Organ Recitals' (vol. 1). Marchand's name is connected with Bach's because the two organists were scheduled to meet in open competition at Dresden in 1717 and Marchand failed to appear. —Cf. A. Pirro, *Louis Marchand* in the 'Sammelbände der Internationalen Musik-Gesellschaft' (vol. 6).

Marchant, Sir **Stanley (Robert),** English organist and composer; b. London, May 15, 1883; d. there, Feb. 28, 1949. He studied organ at the Royal Academy of Music in London; occupied various posts as organist in London churches; was on the staff of the Royal Academy of Music from 1913, in executive as well as teaching capacities. He was knighted in 1943. As a composer, he confined himself to organ music, vocal works for church services, and school manuals.

Marchesi (măhr-kā'-zē), **Blanche** (Baroness André Caccamisi), famous dramatic soprano; daughter of Salvatore and Mathilde Marchesi; b. Paris, April 4, 1863; d. London, Dec. 15, 1940. She was first trained as a violinist; took lessons with Nikisch in Germany and with Colonne in Paris. In 1881 she began to study singing with her mother, and, until her marriage to Baron Caccamisi, acted as her mother's assistant. She made her début in Berlin (1895); when she sang in London (1896), the reception was so enthusiastic that she made England her home; sang the Wagner roles at Covent Garden; made tours of Russia and Central Europe; also made 2 concert tours of the U.S. (1899; 1909); gave her farewell concert in 1938. In her last years, she established herself as a highly esteemed teacher in London. She publ. her memoirs under the title *Singer's Pilgrimage* (London, 1923).

Marchesi, Luigi, celebrated male soprano, known as 'Marchesini'; b. Milan, Aug. 8, 1754; d. Inzago, Dec. 14, 1829. He was a chorister in Milan; made his début at Rome, scoring an immediate success. His fame as a sopranist grew rapidly after his visits to other Italian cities. In 1785 he was engaged as a singer at the court of Catherine the Great; on his way to St. Petersburg, he stopped over in Vienna, where he sang at the Imperial court of Joseph II. He made his Russian début in St. Petersburg, early in 1786, as Rinaldo in Sarti's opera *Armida e Rinaldo;* the Italian female soprano Luiza-Rosa Todi intrigued against him, and despite his successes, he left Russia before the expiration of his contract. On March 9, 1787, he sang in Berlin, winning great acclaim; then toured through Switzerland and Italy. He sang for the last time at the age of 66 in Naples; then returned to Milan. —Cf. R.-Aloys Mooser, *Annales de la Musique et des Musiciens en Russie au XVIIIe siècle* (Geneva, 1950; vol. II, pp. 497-98).

Marchesi de Castrone, Mathilde (*née* Graumann), famous vocal teacher; b. Frankfurt, March 24, 1821; d. London, Nov. 17, 1913. She studied singing in Vienna with Nicolai and in Paris with Manuel García (1845). In 1849 she went to London; then gave concerts in Germany, France, etc. In 1852 she married Salvatore Marchesi. Subsequently she devoted herself mainly to teaching; was on the faculty of the Vienna Cons. (1854-61 and 1869-78) and the Cologne Cons. (1865-68); also in Paris (1861-65 and from 1881). Among her famous pupils were Murska, Gerster, Melba, Eames, Calvé, Sanderson, etc. Besides a vocal method and 24 books of vocalises, she publ. *Erinnerungen aus meinem Leben* (Vienna, 1877), an autobiography, which was publ. in English, much enlarged, as *Marchesi and Music: Passages from the Life of a Famous Singing Teacher* (N.Y., 1897).

Marchesi de Castrone, Salvatore (complete name and title, Cavaliere Salvatore de Castrone, Marchese della Rajata), baritone and famous teacher; b. Palermo, Jan. 15, 1822; d. Paris, Feb. 20, 1908. Of a noble family, he was destined for a government career, and studied law in Palermo; however, he turned to music, and took lessons in singing and theory with Raimondi in Palermo, and with Lamperti in Milan. He was involved in the revolutionary events of 1848, and was compelled to leave Italy; went to New York, where he made his operatic début in Verdi's *Ernani.* He then studied with García in London; married Mathilde Graumann in 1852, and sang with her in opera on the Continent. From 1854 till 1861, they both taught at the Vienna Cons.; later at the Cologne Cons. (1865-68), and again in Vienna (1869-78); after that they resided in Paris.

Marchetti (măhr-keht'-tē), **Filippo,** Italian opera composer; b. Bolognola, near Camerino, Feb. 26, 1831; d. Rome, Jan. 18, 1902. He was a pupil of Lillo and Conti at the Royal Cons., Naples. His first opera, *Gentile da Varano* (Turin, 1856), was extremely well received, and he repeated his success with another opera, *La Demente,* for Turin (Nov. 27, 1856); however, his next opera, *Il Paria,* never reached the stage. He was not discouraged by this and wrote his *Romeo e Giulietta* (Trieste, Oct. 25, 1865), which had a pronounced success in performances at La Scala, Milan, and other Italian theaters. He achieved his greatest success with *Ruy-Blas* (La Scala, April 3, 1869), which was produced also in Germany and England; the remaining operas were *Gustavo Wasa* (La Scala, Feb. 7, 1875) and *Don Giovanni d'Austria* (Turin, March 11, 1880). In 1881 he was appointed president of the Academy of Santa Cecilia in Rome.

Marchetto da Padua, an early proponent of *Ars Nova* who flourished in the 14th century and worked in Florence; author of the important treatises *Lucidarium in arte musicae planae* (on plainsong, early 14th century) and *Pomerium artis musicae mensurabilis* (on mensural music, 1318); the latter is included (in part) in Strunk's *Source Readings in Music History* (N. Y., 1950); see also O. Strunk, *Intorno a Marchetto da Padua,* in 'Rassegna Musicale' (Oct., 1950).

Marcoux (mahr-koo'), **Vanni** (full name, Jean Émile Diogène Marcoux) dramatic baritone; b. (of French parents), Turin, June 12, 1877. He studied jurisprudence and singing; made his first appearance on the stage in Turin (1894); then went to France to continue his vocal training; his début there took place at Bayonne (Jan. 28, 1900) in Gounod's *Roméo et Juliette,* as Frère Laurent. He subsequently sang in various French theaters; also in London at Covent Garden (1905-12); obtained excellent success in his début at the Paris Opéra, when he created the role of Colonna in the première of Février's *Monna Vanna* (Jan. 13, 1909); Massenet entrusted to him the creation of the part of Don Quichotte in the première of his opera of that name (Monte Carlo, Feb. 19, 1910). He sang with the Boston Opera Co. (1912); later he became one of the prime favorites of the Chicago Opera Co., appearing there in 1913-14, in 1926-27, and for several seasons thereafter. His repertory comprised 240 roles; his portrayal of the title role in Mussorgsky's *Boris Godunov* (in French) elicited comparisons with Shaliapin. He retired from the stage about 1940; was instructor in lyric declamation and stage directing at the Paris Cons. (1938-43); stage director of the Grand Théâtre at Bordeaux (1947-51); then returned to Paris. In his professional appearances, he used the hyphenated name, Vanni-Marcoux.

Maréchal (măh-rā-shahl'), **Henri-Charles,** French composer; b. Paris, Jan. 22, 1842; d. there, May 10, 1924. He studied piano and theory at the Paris Cons.; composition with Victor Massé; won the Grand Prix de Rome (1870) with the cantata *Le Jugement de Dieu.* After his return from Rome he produced an oratorio, *La Nativité* (1875), and several operas: *Les Amoureux de Catherine* (Paris, May 8, 1876), *La Taverne des Trabans* (1881), *Calendal* (Rouen, Dec. 21, 1894), *Ping-Sin* (Paris, Jan. 25, 1918), etc.; also wrote several orchestral suites; choral works; etc. He publ. 2 vols. of reminiscences: *Rome: Souvenirs d'un musicien* (Paris, 1904; 2nd ed., 1913) and *Paris: Souvenirs . . .* (Paris, 1907); also *Monographie universelle de l'Orphéon . . .* (Paris, 1910; on singing societies); and *Lettres et Souvenirs, 1871-1874* (Paris, 1920).

Maréchal, Maurice, French cellist, b. Dijon, Oct. 3, 1892. He studied at the Dijon Cons. and then at the Paris Cons., winning first prize for cello (1911); made his début as soloist at the Lamoureux Concerts, Paris, in 1919; in London, in 1923; and in the U. S., 1926 (N. Y., Boston, Chicago, etc.); also traveled in Russia, China, and Japan. In 1942 he became prof. of cello at the Paris Cons.

Marek, Czeslaw, Polish composer and pianist; b. Przemysl, Sept. 16, 1891. He studied .at the Lwow Cons., and at the Academy of Music in Vienna with Leschetizky (piano) and with Pfitzner in Strasbourg (composition). He subsequently taught in Lwow; in 1915 went to Zürich; toured as pianist in Europe; became a Swiss citizen in 1932, and made Zürich his headquarters; taught the Leschetizky method there. — Works: *Meditations* for orch. (1911-13); a symphony (1927); *Petite Suite* for 3 wind instruments (1935); violin sonata; a number of piano pieces; *Échos de la jeunesse,* for 2 pianos (1937); several song cycles.

Marenco, Romualdo, Italian composer; b. Novi Ligure, March 1, 1841; d. Milan, Oct.

10, 1907. He played the violin, then the bassoon in the Doria Theater, Genoa, for which he wrote his first ballet, *Lo sbarco di Garibaldi a Marsala.* He studied counterpoint under Fenaroli and Mattei; traveled; and became in 1873 director of ballet at La Scala, Milan. He composed over 20 ballets (*Sieba, Excelsior, Sport,* etc.), also the operas, *Lorenzino de' Medici* (Lodi, 1874), *I Moncada* (Milan, 1880), *Le Diable au corps* (Paris, 1884), and the 'idilio giocoso' *Strategia d'amore* (Milan, 1896). A posthumous opera, *Federico Struensea,* was produced in Milan in 1908.

Marenzio, Luca, important Italian composer; b. Coccaglio, near Brescia, 1553; d. Rome, Aug. 22, 1599. He was a chorister at the Cathedral of Brescia and pupil of Giovanni Contini there. From 1572-78 he was maestro di cappella to Cardinal Madruzzo at Rome and subsequently entered the service of Cardinal Luigi d'Este, often visiting the court of the latter's brother (Alfonso d'Este) at Ferrara and other courts. He also visited Paris, and in 1588-89 was at Florence. From 1591-95 he was in the service of Cardinal Aldobrandini at Rome, and in 1596-98 at the Polish court of Sigismund III. Upon his return to Rome he was in the service of Roman noblemen. He was called 'il più dolce cigno d'Italia' and 'il divino compositore' by his contemporaries. His madrigals, which are unsurpassed, were publ. as follows: 9 books *a* 5 (1580-99); 6 books *a* 6 (1584-95); 1 book *a* 4-6 (1588); 1 book of 5-part *Madrigali spirituali* (1584); 2 books of *Mottetti a* 4 (1585, 1592); 1 book of *Mottetti* a 12 (1614); a book of *Sacri concenti a* 5-7 (1616); 5 books of *Villanelle ed Arie alla napoletana a* 3 (1584-91); 1 book of motets *a* 5-7 (1616, youthful work, ed. Giovanni Maria Piccioni); also antiphons and other church music. Some pieces in modern notation are in Proske's 'Musica divina,' Choron's 'Principes de composition,' Padre Martini's 'Counterpoint,' etc. Some of his motets have been publ. by the Universal Edition; one madrigal is to be found in A. Einstein's *The Golden Age of the Madrigal;* another in Einstein's *Beispielsammlung zur älterer Musikgeschichte,* 2 pieces in A. Schering's *Geschichte der Musik in Beispielen* (Nos. 140, 165), other selections in F. Jöde's *Alte Madrigale,* F. Blume's *Das Chorwerk* (vol. 8), and Davison and Apel, *Historical Anthology of Music* (vol. 1; Cambridge, Mass., 1947). Six books of his 5-part madrigals have been publ. in *Publikationen älterer Musik* (IV, 1, 1929; VI, 1931; ed. by Alfred Einstein). — Cf. P. Guerrini, in 'Santa Cecilia' IX and X (1908); A. Einstein, *Eine Caccia im Cinquecento,* in the 'Liliencron-Festschrift' (1910); A. Einstein, *Dante im Madrigal,* in 'Archiv für Musikwissenschaft,' III (1921); J. A. F. Orbaan, *Notizie inedite su Luca Marenzio,* in 'Bolletino bibliografico musicale,' III, 2 (1928); A. Einstein, *The Italian Madrigal* (Princeton, 1949; pp. 614-18, 628-37); H. Engel, *Luca Marenzio* (Florence, 1956; contains a bibliography and a list of works; supersedes Engel's earlier publications on Marenzio). See also G. Reese, *Music in the Renaissance* (N. Y., 1954; pp. 420-24).

Maresch (măh'-rěsh), **Johann Anton,** inventor of the Russian 'hunting-horn music,' in which each player has a horn producing a single tone; b. Chotěboř, Bohemia, 1719; d. St. Petersburg, June 10, 1794. He studied horn with Hampel in Dresden, and cello in Berlin. In 1748 he was engaged by the Russian Chancellor Bestuzhev as horn player in his private orch. in St. Petersburg, and later became chamber musician to the Russian court. In 1751 he was commissioned to organize an ensemble of hunting horns for the court; he formed a group comprising 2 complete octaves tuned chromatically, adding large drums with church bells suspended within them; also constructed wooden horns for soft accompaniment to operas. The vogue of horn orchestras in Russia continued for about 50 years after Maresch's death; the players were recruited usually from serfs. With the abolition of serfdom in 1861, the practice disappeared. —Cf. J. C. Hinrichs, *Entstehung, Fortgang und jetzige Beschaffenheit der russischen Jagdmusik* (St. Petersburg, 1796); K. Vertkov, *Russian Horn Music* (Moscow, 1948); *Les orchestres de cors russes,* in R.-Aloys Mooser, *Annales de la Musique et des Musiciens en Russie au XVIIIe siècle* (Geneva, 1951, vol. III, pp. 859-76).

Mareschall, Samuel, Flemish composer; b. Tournai, May 22, 1554; d. Basel, c. 1640. As a young man, he was organist at the Basel Cathedral; in 1576 was appointed prof. at the Univ. there. His collection of 4-part vocal settings of the Psalms (1606) became a traditional Lutheran hymn book; another book of Psalms (including hymns by Luther) appeared in 1616. He also compiled *Melodiae suaves* (1622); much earlier he publ. a disquisition, *Porta Musica, mit einem kurtzen Bericht und Anleitung zu den Violen* (Basel, 1589). —Cf. R. Kendall, *The Life and Works of Samuel Mareschall,* in the 'Mus. Quarterly' (Jan., 1944).

Marescotti, André-François, Swiss composer; b. Carouge, near Geneva, April 30, 1902. He studied at the Geneva Cons., and in Paris with Roger-Ducasse; from 1924 he was chorusmaster at the St. Joseph church in Geneva, and prof. at the Geneva Cons.—Works: *Aubade,* for orch. (Geneva, Jan. 27, 1938); *Concert Carougeois,* for orch. (1942); *Les anges du Greco,* ballet (Zürich, June 1, 1947); *Giboulées,* for bassoon and orch. (1949); *La Lampe d'argile,* dramatic legend (Strasbourg, April, 1951); numerous piano pieces. He publ. a valuable volume (in folio), *Les Instruments d'orchestre, leurs caractères, leurs possibilités et leur utilisation dans l'orchestre moderne,* with 900 musical examples (Paris, 1950).

Maretzek, Max, operatic impresario; b. Brünn, Moravia, June 28, 1821; d. Staten Island, N. Y., May 14, 1897. He studied medicine and law at the Univ. of Vienna; music with Ignaz von Seyfried (a pupil of Mozart and Haydn). He progressed rapidly, and at the age of 22 conducted his first opera, *Hamlet* (Brünn, 1843). He then traveled as theater conductor and composer of ballet music, in France and England. In 1848 he arrived in N. Y. as conductor and manager of the Italian Opera Co. He presented Adelina Patti for the first time in opera (as Lucia, 1859); in 1876 he staged his own play with music, *Baba;* conducted his pastoral opera *Sleepy Hollow; or, The Headless Horseman,* after Washington Irving (N. Y., Sept. 25, 1879). As a worldly impresario, he was extremely successful; traveled to Mexico and Cuba, but lived mostly in N. Y., and became an American citizen. He publ. a book of reminiscences, *Crotchets and Quavers, or Revelations of an Opera Manager in America* (N. Y., 1855); and a sequel, *Sharps and Flats* (N. Y., 1870).—Cf. E. Hipsher, *American Opera and Its Composers* (Philadelphia, 1934; pp. 310-12).

Margola (măhr'-gŏh-lă), **Franco,** Italian composer; b. Orzinuovi, near Brescia, Oct. 30, 1908. He studied at the Cons. of Parma and with Pizzetti, whose influence is apparent in his music; in 1945 taught composition at the Cons. of Cagliari.—Works: for orch. *Adagio e Allegro* (1928), *Il Campiello delle streghe* (1930), *Espressioni eroiche* (1933); an opera, *Il Mito di Cairo* (1940); piano concerto (Florence, Feb. 12, 1944); etc.

Maria Antonia Walpurgis, Electress of Saxony; daughter of the Elector of Bavaria (Emperor Charles VII); b. Munich, July 18, 1724; d. Dresden, April 23, 1780. She was not only a generous patroness of the fine arts, but a trained musician, pupil of Hasse and Porpora (1747-52); under the pseudonym E.T.P.A. (Ermelinda Talea Pastorella Arcada, her name as member of the Academy of Arcadians) she produced and publ. 2 Italian operas to her own librettos, *Il Trionfo della Fedeltà* (Dresden, 1754) and *Talestri* (Nymphenburg, near Munich, Feb. 6, 1760; Dresden, Aug. 24, 1763); the former was one of the earliest publications of Breitkopf & Härtel printed from their new types (1765); she also wrote texts of oratorios and cantatas for Hasse and Ristori.—Cf. K. von Weber, *Maria Antonia Walpurgis* (2 vols., Dresden, 1857); H. Drewes, *Maria Antonia Walpurgis als Komponistin* (Leipzig, 1934); A. Yorke-Long, *Music at Court: 4 Eighteenth-Century Studies* (London, 1954).

Mariani, Angelo, Italian conductor and composer; b. Ravenna, Oct. 11, 1821; d. Genoa, June 13, 1873. He studied violin and composition; had some lessons with Rossini in Bologna; made his principal career as opera conductor, first in Italy (1844-47), then in Denmark (1847-48). He took part in the Italian war of independence of 1848; then was compelled to leave Italy, and spent 4 years in Constantinople. In 1852 he returned to Italy as opera conductor; introduced Wagner's *Lohengrin* in Bologna; was also favorably known as a composer; wrote several attractive songs (*Liete e tristi rimembranze, Il Trovatore nella Liguria, Rimembranze del Bosforo,* etc.); also some orchestral music. He arranged 3 operas by Verdi (in their entirety) for string quartet: *Macbeth, I Vespri Siciliani,* and *Un Ballo in Maschera.*—Cf. T. Mantovani, *Angelo Mariani* (Rome, 1921); U. Zoppi, *Mariani, Verdi e la Stolz* (Milan, 1947).

Marie (mah-rē'), **Gabriel,** composer of light music; b. Paris, Jan. 8, 1852; d. while traveling in Spain, Aug. 29, 1928. He studied at the Paris Cons.; was chorusmaster of the Lamoureux Concerts (1881-87); conductor of the orch. concerts of the Société Nationale de Musique (1887-94); of Ste.-Cécile in Bordeaux; at Marseilles and (during the summer months) at the Casino in Vichy. He wrote a number of melodious pieces for orch., of which *La Cinquantaine* (in arrangements for violin or cello with piano) became immensely popular. He also wrote music criticism, collected in *Pour la musique* (Paris, 1930).

Marini, Biagio, Italian violinist and composer; b. Brescia, c. 1595; d. Venice, March 20, 1665. He was a pupil of Monteverdi in Mantua; then was a violinist at San Marco, Venice (1615-18); in Brescia (1620); in Parma (1622); then in the service of the courts in Neuberg and Düsseldorf (1623-45); in Milan (1649); in Ferrara (1652). He publ. some 25 op. numbers of vocal and instrumental chamber music, noteworthy for technical devices presupposing a high standard of performance. His op. 1, *Affetti musicali* (1617), contains the earliest specimen of the Italian solo violin sonata, entitled *La Gardana* (reprinted in Schering's *Geschichte der Musik in Beispielen,* No. 182); other reprints are in J. von Wasielewski, *Die Violine im 17. Jahrhundert,* L. Torchi, 'L'Arte Musicale in Italia' (vol. VIII), etc. —Cf. A. Einstein, *Italienische Musiker am Hofe der Neuberger-Wittelsbacher,* in the 'Sammelbände der Internationalen Musik-Gesellschaft' (vol. IX, 3); A. Schering, in 'Riemann-Festschrift' (1909); A. Moser, *Geschichte des Violinspiels* (p. 55 ff., 93 ff); Dora J. Iselin, *Biagio Marini, sein Leben und seine Instrumentalwerke* (dissertation; Basel, 1930).

Marinuzzi (mahr-rē-noo'-tsē), **Giuseppe (Gino),** Italian conductor and composer; b. Palermo, March 24, 1882; d. Milan, Aug. 17, 1945. He studied with Zuelli at the Palermo Cons.; began his career as conductor in Catania; conducted in Italy and Spain; went to South America on tour with the 'Teatral' Opera Co.; then was director of the Liceo Musicale in Bologna (1915-18); in 1919 conducted in Rome; in 1920 came to the U. S. as artistic director of the Chicago Opera Association; returned to Italy in 1921; was chief conductor of the Rome Opera in 1928-34, and of La Scala from 1934 to his death. He was murdered in Milan during the turbulent days after the end of World War II. He wrote 3 operas: *Barberina* (Palermo, 1903), *Jacquerie* (Buenos Aires, Aug. 11, 1918), *Palla de' Mozzi* (La Scala, Milan, April 5, 1932), and several works for orch., on Italian themes. His son, also named **Gino Marinuzzi** (b. N. Y., April 7, 1920), studied at the Milan Cons. with Renzo Bossi, graduated as pianist and composer (1941), and began his career as conductor at the Opera in Rome (1946); he also wrote numerous short works for orch. and film music.

Mario, Giovanni, celebrated tenor; b. Cagliari, Sardinia, Oct. 17, 1810; d. Rome, Dec. 11, 1883. He was of noble birth (his real name was Mario Cavaliere di Candia), and was destined for a military career; after a period of training at the Turin Military Academy, he joined the regiment of which his father was the colonel, but eloped to Paris with a ballerina in 1836; there he studied with Bordogni and Boncharde at the Cons., and made his début at the Opéra in *Robert le Diable* (Nov. 30, 1838); in 1840 he joined the roster of the Italian Opera in Paris, and won triumphs by the freshness and power of his voice and his exquisite vocal style; this was combined with a handsome figure, which made him the idol of the pleasure-loving women of Paris. In order not to embarrass his aristocratic relatives, he appeared under his Christian name, Mario, without a patronymic, achieving fame not only in opera, but also in concerts; he was as successful in London and St. Petersburg as in France. For some years, he, Tamburini, Lablache, and Giulia Grisi formed a celebrated vocal quartet; he married Grisi; retired in 1867, and lived in Paris and Rome.—Cf. L. Engel, *From Mozart to Mario* (London, 1886); Mrs. Godfrey Pearce (Cecilia Maria de Candia, Mario's daughter) and F. Hird, *The Romance of a Great Singer* (London, 1910).

Mario, Queena (real name Tillotson), American soprano; b. Akron, Ohio, Aug. 21, 1896; d. N. Y., May 28, 1951. She was a practicing journalist in N. Y. before she began to study music; took voice lessons with Oscar Saenger and Marcella Sembrich; made her début with the San Carlo Opera in N. Y. (Sept. 4, 1918); then joined the staff of the Metropolitan Opera; her first appearance there was as Micaela in *Carmen* (Nov. 30, 1922); retired from the opera stage in 1938, but continued to give concerts; taught at the Curtis Institute of Music from 1931 as successor to Marcella Sembrich. She married Wilfred Pelletier in 1925; divorced in 1936. She was the author of several mystery novels (*Murder in the Opera House,* etc.).

Mariotte (măh-rē-ŏht'), **Antoine,** French opera composer; b. Avignon, Dec. 22, 1875; d. Izieux (Loire), Nov. 30, 1944. He was trained at the Naval Academy; in 1897 he became a pupil of Vincent d'Indy at the Schola Cantorum; in 1899 was appointed conductor of the symph. concerts at St.-Etienne, Loire; from 1902 until 1919 he taught at the Cons. of Orléans; in 1920 was appointed its director; from 1936 to 1938 he was director of the Paris Opéra-Comique. —Operas: *Salomé* (Lyons, Oct. 30, 1908);

Le vieux Roi (Lyons, 1911); *Léontine Sœurs* (Paris, May 21, 1924); *Esther, Princesse d'Israël* (Paris, May 5, 1925); *Gargantua* (Paris, Feb. 13, 1935). He also wrote a symph. suite, *Impressions urbaines*, numerous teaching pieces for piano, and songs.

Mariz, Vasco, Brazilian singer and musicologist; b. Rio de Janeiro, Jan. 22, 1921. He studied with O. L. Fernandez (composition) and Vera Janacopulos (voice). He also studied law; in 1943, received the degree of Doctor of Jurisprudence at the Univ. of Rio de Janeiro. He made his operatic début as Bartolo in *Le Nozze di Figaro* (Porto Alegre, 1945). At the same time, he entered a diplomatic career; was vice-consul at Oporto, Portugal, in 1948; secretary of the Brazilian Embassy in Belgrade from 1949-51; since 1952, consul in Rosario, Argentina. He publ. the following books: *Figuras da música brasileira contemporánea* (Oporto, 1948); *Dicionário bio-bibliográfico musical* (Rio de Janeiro, 1948); *Heitor Villa-Lobos, compositor brasileiro* (Rio de Janeiro, 1949); *Vida musical (1946-1950)* (Oporto, 1950).

Markevitch (mähr-kĕh'-vich), **Igor,** brilliant composer and conductor; b. Kiev, July 27, 1912. At the age of 2 he was taken to Vevey, Switzerland, where he remained until 14; then he went to Paris to study with Nadia Boulanger; later also took lessons with Vittorio Rieti. In Paris he attracted the attention of Diaghilev, who commissioned him to write a ballet, *Rebus;* however, Diaghilev died before the ballet could be produced; Markevitch conducted a suite from it in Paris on Dec. 15, 1931. The score, modern and rhythmically fresh, was subsequently performed by major orchestras in Europe and America, and established Markevitch's reputation as one of the most talented composers of his generation; his 2nd ballet, *L'Envoi d'Icare* (Paris, June 25, 1933), was equally successful; other works are *Concerto Grosso* (Paris, Dec. 8, 1930); piano concerto (Paris, March 1, 1931); *Partita* for piano and orch. (1931); *Galop,* for piano and wind instruments (1932); *Introduction and Hymn* (N. Y., 1934); *Le nouvel âge,* for orch. (London Festival of the International Society for Contemporary Music, June 17, 1938); *Cantata,* for soprano, men's chorus and orch. (Paris, June 4, 1930); *Paradise Lost,* oratorio (London, 1932); *Psalm* (Florence Festival of the International Society for Contemporary Music, April 4, 1934); *Serenade* for violin, clarinet, and bassoon; *Lorenzo the Magnificent,* historic oratorio (Rome, April 20, 1941). During World War II he was in Italy. Although he began his career as an outstanding composer, he gradually devoted more and more time to conducting, eventually achieving the stature of a first-class interpreter, excelling particularly in modern works; he began conducting at the age of 18; studied with Scherchen; conducted in Europe; made his first appearance in the U. S. with the Boston Symph. (March 18, 1955) with exceptional success; then appeared as guest conductor with other American orchestras; also conducted in Mexico and South America. In 1957 he was appointed permanent conductor of the Lamoureux Orch. in Paris. —Cf. B. Gavoty, *Igor Markevitch* (Monaco, 1954).

Markull, Friedrich Wilhelm, German composer; b. Reichenbach, near Elbing, Prussia, Feb. 17, 1816; d. Danzig, April 30, 1887. He studied organ-playing, and in 1836 was appointed organist at a Danzig church. He also gave concerts as a pianist. His 3 operas were performed in Danzig: *Maja und Alpino* (Dec. 23, 1843), *Der König von Zion* (March 22, 1850), and *Das Walpurgisfest* (Jan. 14, 1855). He also wrote 2 oratorios, symphonies, and organ pieces.—Cf. W. Neumann, *F. W. Markull* (Kassel, 1857).

Markwort, Johann Christian, German writer; b. Reisling, near Brunswick, Dec. 13, 1778; d. Bessungen, near Darmstadt, Jan. 13, 1866. A theological student, he adopted the career of a tenor; appeared on the stage at Feldsberg, Trieste, Munich; was chorus director at Darmstadt (1810-30), then pensioned. He publ. *Umriss einer Gesammt-Tonwissenschaft überhaupt wie auch einer Sprach- und Tonsatzlehre und einer Gesang-, Ton-, und Rede-Vortraglehre* (1826); *Über Klangveredelung der Stimme* (1847); and an elementary piano method.

Marliani, Marco Aurelio, Italian composer; b. Milan, Aug., 1805; d. Bologna, May 8, 1849. He studied philosophy; took some lessons with Rossini in Paris, where he went in 1830; under Rossini's influence, he wrote several operas, which reached the stage in Paris: *Il Bravo* (Feb. 1, 1834), *Ildegonda* (March 7, 1837), *Xacarilla* (Oct. 28, 1839); a ballet, *La Gypsy* (with A. Thomas; Jan. 28, 1839). He returned to Italy in 1847; produced another opera in Bologna, *Gusmano il Buono* (Nov. 7, 1847). He was involved in the revolutionary struggle of 1848; became an important staff officer in the insurgent army; was wounded in a skirmish near Bologna, and died later as a result of his injuries.

Marmontel (mähr-mohn-těl'), **Antoine-François,** celebrated French pedagogue and pianist; b. Clermont-Ferrand, July 16, 1816; d. Paris, Jan. 17, 1898. He studied at the Paris Cons. with Zimmerman (piano), Dourlen (harmony), Halévy (fugue), and Lesueur (composition); won 1st prize for piano playing in 1832. In 1837 he became instructor in solfeggio at the Cons.; in 1848 he succeeded Zimmerman as head of a piano class, and won enduring fame as an imaginative and efficient teacher; among his pupils were Bizet, Vincent d'Indy, Th. Dubois, E. Guiraud, Paladilhe, Diémer, Planté, and Debussy. He continued to teach until 1887. He publ. numerous didactic works: *L'Art de déchiffrer* (100 easy studies); *École élémentaire de mécanisme et de style* (24 studies); *École de mécanisme;* 5 *Études de salon; L'Art de déchiffrer à 4 mains;* also sonatas, serenades, characteristic pieces, salon music, dances, etc.—His writings include *Les Pianistes célèbres* (1878); *Symphonistes et virtuoses* (1880); *Virtuoses contemporains* (1882); *Éléments d'esthétique musicale, et considérations sur le beau dans les arts* (1884); *Histoire du piano et de ses origines* (1885).

Marpurg, Friedrich, German opera composer; great-grandson of Friedrich Wilhelm Marpurg; b. Paderborn, April 4, 1825; d. Wiesbaden, Dec. 2, 1884. He played the violin and piano as a child; studied composition later with Mendelssohn and Hauptmann at Leipzig. He became conductor at the Königsberg Theater; at Sondershausen (1864); succeeded Mangold as court music director at Darmstadt (1868); at Freiburg (1873); and Laibach (1875); then went to Wiesbaden, where he became conductor of the 'Cäcilienverein.' — Operas: *Musa, der letzte Maurenkönig* (Königsberg, 1855), *Agnes von Hohenstaufen* (Freiburg, 1874), and *Die Lichtensteiner* (not performed).

Marpurg, Friedrich Wilhelm, German theorist; b. Seehausen, Brandenburg, Nov. 21, 1718; d. Berlin, May 22, 1795. While secretary to General von Rothenburg at Paris (1746-49), he became acquainted with Rameau and his theories; after a short stay in Berlin, and a prolonged sojourn in Hamburg, he was appointed director of the Prussian lottery at Berlin (1763).—Writings: *Die Kunst das Clavier zu spielen* (1750-51; 2 vols.); *Anleitung zum Clavierspielen, der schönern Ausübung der heutigen Zeit gemäss entworfen* (1755; 2nd ed., 1765; also in French and Dutch); *Abhandlung von der Fuge* (his *magnum opus;* 1753-54, in 2 parts; French ed. by Marpurg himself, 1756; revised by Sechter, Vienna, 1843, and Dehn, Leipzig, 1858); *Historisch-kritische Beyträge zur Aufnahme der Musik* (5 vols., 1754-78); *Handbuch bey dem Generalbasse und der Composition* (1755-58: 3 parts; supplement 1760; 2nd ed., 1762: French by Choron and Lafage, 1836-38); a German translation of d'Alembert's *Éléments de la musique (Systematische Einleitung in die musikalische Setzkunst* according to Rameau; 1757); *Kritische Einleitung in die Geschichte und Lehrsätze der alten und neuen Musik* (1759; only on ancient music); *Kritische Briefe über die Tonkunst* (a weekly publication appearing 1759-63); *Anleitung zur Musik überhaupt und zur Singkunst besonders* (1763); *Neue Methode, allerley Arten von Temperaturen dem Claviere aufs bequemste mitzutheilen* (1790); etc. He composed 6 keyboard sonatas, some books of piano pieces, and organ music, songs (sacred and secular), and an unfinished 4-part Mass.—Cf. H. Riemann, *Geschichte der Musiktheorie* (2nd ed., 1921, p. 496 ff.); E. Bieder, *F. W. Marpurgs System* (Berlin, 1923).

Marqués (mahr-käs') **y García, Pedro Miguel,** Spanish composer of light opera; b. Palma de Mallorca, May 20, 1843; d. there, Feb. 25, 1918. He studied in Paris with Alard and Armingaud, then at the Paris Cons. with Massart (violin) and Bazin (composition); also studied privately with Berlioz, and in 1867 at Madrid with Monasterio. From 1870-96 he was one of the most successful of 'zarzuela' composers, his most popular works being *El anillo de hierro* (1878), *El reloj de Lucerna, La monja alférez, El plato de día,* etc. He also wrote orchestral variations, and was the author of a number of books (mostly on philosophy).

Marrocco, William Thomas, American musicologist; b. West New York, New Jersey, Dec. 5, 1909; was educated in Rochester; then went to Italy, where he entered the Cons. of Naples; licentiate and master's diploma, 1930; returning to the U. S., he studied at the Eastman School of Music (B. M. in violin, 1934; M. M. in musicology, 1940); then taught at Elmira College (1936-39), the Univ. of Iowa (1945-46), the Univ. of Kansas (1946-49). In 1949, appointed associate prof. at the Univ. of California, Los Angeles; Ph. D. in musicology there,

1952. He publ. essays on old Italian music; ed. *14th-Century Italian Cacce* (Cambridge, 1942); brought out *The Music of Jacopo da Bologna* (Los Angeles, 1954; contains all extant works of Jacopo).

Marschalk, Max, German music critic; b. Berlin, April 7, 1863; d. Poberow-on-the-Ostsee, Germany, Aug. 24, 1940. He was a pupil of H. Urban; from 1894 until its dissolution in 1933, music critic of the 'Vossische Zeitung'; from 1934, music director of the publishing company 'Dreililien' in Berlin. He composed a short opera, *In Flammen* (Gotha, 1896); a 'Liederspiel,' *Aucassin und Nicolette* (Stuttgart, 1907); incidental music to Hauptmann's *Hanneles Himmelfahrt* (1894), *Die versunkene Glocke* (1898), *Und Pippa tanzt* (1906), to Maeterlinck's *Sœur Béatrice,* etc.

Marschner, Franz, pianist, pedagogue, and writer on music; b. Leitmeritz, Bohemia, March 26, 1855; d. Weisspyhra, Aug. 28, 1932. He studied with Skuherský at the Prague Cons., and with Bruckner in Vienna, where he settled as a teacher; publ. *Entwurf einer Neugestaltung der Theorie und Praxis des kunstgemässen Anschlags* (on piano touch; Vienna, 1888); *Die Grundfragen der Ästhetik im Lichte der immanenten Philosophie* (1899), etc.; wrote a violin sonata, choral works, and songs.

Marschner, Heinrich (August), German opera composer; b. Zittau, Saxony, Aug. 16, 1795; d. Hanover, Dec. 14, 1861. He entered Leipzig Univ. in 1813 as a law student; but his passion for music, and the encouragement he received from the influential music critic Rochlitz, decided his vocation. Becoming a pupil of cantor Schicht, he began composing minor pieces; in 1817 he was invited to Vienna by Count Thaddäus von Amadee, and met Beethoven. Obtaining, through the court's aid, a place as music teacher in Pressburg, he wrote his first (one-act) opera, *Der Kieffhäuserberg* (Pressburg, 1816). There followed *Saidor und Zulima* (Pressburg, Nov. 22, 1818) and *Heinrich IV. und d'Aubigné;* the latter was brought out at Dresden (July 19, 1820) by Weber, and caused him to invite Marschner there. In 1821 he went to Dresden, where, in 1823, he was made director of the German and Italian operas, jointly with Weber and Morlacchi. After Weber's death (1826), Marschner became Kapellmeister of the Leipzig theater, where he produced his operas *Der Vampyr* (March 29, 1828) and *Der Templer und die Jüdin* (Dec. 22, 1829; after Walter Scott's *Ivanhoe*), the latter carrying his fame throughout Germany. In 1831 he was appointed court Kapellmeister at Hanover, and retained this post 28 years; he retired on a pension, with the title 'General Musikdirektor,' in 1859. In 1834 the Univ. of Leipzig made him *Dr. phil.* In Hanover his greatest work, *Hans Heiling,* was written; it was first performed on May 24, 1833, at Berlin, with tumultuous applause; it is still in the repertory of most German theaters. In his operas, Marschner stands between Weber and Wagner; from Weber he retained the Romantic flavor of musical invention, and his predilection for the supernatural, and he approached Wagner in the pathos of humanized emotion and the fullness of the orchestral accompaniment. His other dramatic works are: *Der Holzdieb* (Dresden, Feb. 22, 1825); *Lucretia* (Danzig, Jan. 17, 1827); *Des Falkners Braut* (Leipzig, March 10, 1832); *Das Schloss am Ätna* (Leipzig, Jan. 29, 1836); *Der Bäbu* (Hanover, Feb. 19, 1838); *Kaiser Adolf von Nassau* (Hanover, Jan. 5, 1845); and *Austin* (Hanover, Jan. 26, 1852). A posthumous opera, *Hjarne der Sängerkönig,* was produced at Frankfurt (Sept. 13, 1863). Marschner publ. about 20 sets of songs, and 10 sets of men's choruses (*Zigeunerleben,* etc.); also piano compositions and chamber music. —Cf. M. E. Wittmann, *Heinrich Marschner* (Leipzig, 1897); G. Münzer, *Heinrich Marschner* (Berlin, 1901); G. Fischer, *Musik in Hannover* (Hanover, 1902); H. Gaartz, *Die Opern Heinrich Marschners* (Leipzig, 1912); G. Fischer, *Marschner Erinnerungen* (Hanover, 1918); A. Gnirs, *Hans Heiling* (Karlsbad, 1931); V. Köhler, *Heinrich Marschners Bühnenwerke und Verzeichnis der . . . im Druck erschienenen Werke des Komponisten* (Göttingen, 1955).

Marsh, Mrs. **Lucile.** See **Crews, Lucile.**

Marshall, John Patton, American music educator; b. Rockport, Mass., Jan. 9, 1877; d. Boston, Jan. 17, 1941. He studied music with MacDowell, Chadwick, B. J. Lang, and others; was organist at various churches; lectured on music at the Harvard Summer School. In 1903 he was appointed prof. at Boston Univ., and in 1928 became dean of the College of Music there. He publ. the teaching manuals, *Syllabus of History of Music* (1906), *Syllabus of Music Appreciation* (1911), etc.

Marsick, Armand, eminent Belgian composer; b. Liège, Sept. 20, 1877; studied with his father Louis Marsick; then with Guy

Ropartz in Nancy. In 1898 he became concertmaster at the Concerts Colonne in Paris, while continuing to study composition (with Lenepveu and Vincent d'Indy). In 1908 he obtained the position of instructor at the Cons. of Athens; he remained in Greece until 1922, when he was appointed conductor at the Music Academy of Bilbao, Spain. He returned to Belgium in 1927; became prof. at the Liège Cons.; was conductor of the Société des Concerts Symphoniques (1927-39). — Works: operas: *La Jane* (1903; Liège, March 29, 1921), *Lara* (1913), *L'Anneau nuptial* (1920); radio play, *Le Visage de la Wallonie* (1937); symph. poems, *La Source* (1908) and *Scènes de montagnes* (1910); *Tableaux grecs* for orch. (1912); *3 Morceaux Symphoniques* (1950); quartet for 4 horns (1950); several sets of songs. A catalogue of his works was publ. by the Centre Belge de Documentation Musicale (1954).

Marsick, Martin-Pierre-Joseph, distinguished violinist; b. Jupille, near Liège, Belgium, March 9, 1848; d. Paris, Oct. 21, 1924. He studied at the Liège Cons.; at the age of 12 played the organ at the cathedral; then studied violin with Léonard at the Brussels Cons. and with Massart at the Paris Cons., taking 1st prize there. In 1870 he became a pupil of Joachim in Berlin. After a brilliant début at Paris in the 'Concerts populaires' (1873), he undertook long tours in Europe; also played in the U. S. (1895-96). In 1892 he was appointed prof. of violin at the Paris Cons. Among his pupils were Karl Flesch and Jacques Thibaud. He wrote 3 violin concertos and numerous solo pieces for the violin (*Adagio scherzando; 2 Reveries; Songe; Romance; Tarentelle; Agitato; Intermezzo; Berceuse;* etc.).

Marsop, Paul, German librarian and writer on music; b. Berlin, Oct. 6, 1856; d. Florence, Italy, May 31, 1925. He studied with Hans von Bülow; from 1881 lived in Munich and (during the winter) in Italy. He founded in Munich a 'Musikalische Volksbibliothek,' which he turned over to the city in 1907; also aided in the establishment of similar libraries in other cities.— Publications: *Musikalische Essays* (1899); *Studienblätter eines Musikers* (1903); *Neue Kämpfe* (1913); *Musikalische Satiren und Grotesken* (1924); and various pamphlets dealing mostly with Wagner (*Die Aussichten der Wagnerschen Kunst in Frankreich, Der Kern der Wagnerfrage,* etc.).

Marston, George W., American organist, choral conductor, and composer; b. Sandwich, Mass., May 23, 1840; d. there, Feb. 2, 1901. He studied with local teachers; played the organ when 16. About 1859 he moved to Portland, Me., and remained there permanently as organist, choirmaster, and teacher. From 1887 he was organist at the Hale St. Congregational Church, for whose choir he wrote much excellent music.

Marteau (măhr-tŏh'), **Henri,** famous violinist; b. Reims, March 31, 1874; d. Lichtenberg, Bavaria, Oct. 3, 1934. He studied at the Paris Cons. with Léonard and Garcin; won 1st prize in 1892 for violin playing; also studied composition with Dubois. At the age of 10 he played at a concert of the Vienna Philharmonic under the direction of Hans Richter, who was also responsible for his appearance in London, at a concert in 1888. Marteau made his first American tour in 1892, scoring tremendous success; he was received with great enthusisam during his subsequent U. S. tours (1893, 1894, 1898, and 1906); also played in Scandinavia, Russia, France, Germany, and the Netherlands. In 1900 he was appointed principal prof. at the Geneva Cons. and in 1908 succeeded Joachim at the Hochschule für Musik in Berlin. In 1915 he left Berlin and went to Sweden, where he became a naturalized Swedish citizen in 1920; conducted symph. concerts in Göteborg; then taught at the German Music Academy in Prague (1921-24), at the Leipzig Cons. (1926-27); in 1928 became prof. at the Dresden Cons. Between periods of teaching he continued his concert appearances. At various times he participated in string quartets, proving himself a masterly ensemble player. Massenet, Dubois, and Reger each wrote a violin concerto for him, and his teacher Léonard left him his magnificent Maggini instrument, formerly owned by the Empress Maria Theresa. Marteau was also a composer; wrote an opera, *Meister Schwalbe* (Plauen, 1921); a symph. work, *Gloria Naturae* (Stockholm, 1918); 2 violin concertos (1912 and 1919); a cello concerto; *Sonata fantastica* for violin alone, and other violin pieces.

Martelli, Henri, French composer; b. Bastia, Corsica, Feb. 25, 1895. He took lessons with Widor and Caussade, while studying law at Paris Univ.; later was active on the Paris Radio. In his compositions he attempted to recreate the spirit of old French music in terms of modern counterpoint. He wrote an opera, *La chanson de Roland*

(1923); *Basreliefs assyriens* for orch. (1928); concerto for orch. (Boston Symph., April 22, 1932); *Ouverture pour un conte de Boccace* (1942); sinfonietta (1948); piano concerto (1948); a symphony for strings (Paris, March 13, 1955); much chamber music, including a suite for 4 clarinets (1936); wind octet (1941); 2 quintets for various instruments; 2 string quartets; violin sonata, bassoon sonata, flute sonata, and a sonatina for trumpet and piano.

Martenot, Maurice, French inventor of the electronic instrument 'Ondes musicales' (generally known as 'Ondes Martenot'); b. Paris, Oct. 14, 1898; studied composition with Gedalge at the Paris Cons.; gave the first demonstration of his 'Ondes musicales' in Paris, April 20, 1928; publ. a *Méthode d'ondes musicales.* Many French composers (Milhaud, Messiaen, Jolivet, etc.) have written special works for the instrument. His sister, **Ginette Martenot** (b. Paris, Jan. 27, 1902), became the chief exponent of the 'Ondes Martenot' and appeared as soloist with orchestras in Europe and America.

Martens, Frederick Herman, American writer on musical subjects; b. New York, July 6, 1874; d. Mountain Lakes, N.J., Dec. 18, 1932. He studied in N.Y. with local teachers; from 1907 was active mainly as a writer; publ. *Leo Ornstein: The Man, His Ideas, His Work* (1917); *Violin Mastery* (1919); *Art of the Prima Donna and Concert Singer* (1923); *String Mastery* (1923); *A Thousand and One Nights of Opera* (1926); *Book of the Opera and the Ballet* (1925); contributed articles to the 'Mus. Quarterly' and other publications.

Martienssen, Carl Adolf, German musicologist and pedagogue; b. Güstrow, Dec. 6, 1881; d. Berlin, March 1, 1955. He studied with Klindworth and Wilhelm Berger in Berlin; musicology with Kretzschmar. In 1914 he was appointed prof. of piano at the Leipzig Cons.; in 1932 became prof. at the Musical Institute for Foreigners in Berlin. He taught at Rostock from 1948 to 1950; then returned to Berlin. —Publications: *Die individuelle Klaviertechnik auf der Grundlage des schöpferischen Klangwillens* (1930); *Methodik des individuellen Klavierunterrichts* (1934); *Grundlage einer deutschen Klavierlehre* (1942); *Das Klavierkunstwerk* (1950); and shorter studies. He discovered and published, in Copenhagen, a hitherto unknown Bach cantata (1913).

Martín, Edgardo, Cuban composer; b. Cienfuegos, Oct. 6, 1915. He first studied with his maternal grandmother, the pianist Aurea Suarez; later with other teachers in Havana. In 1942 he graduated from the National Univ. of Cuba and from the Municipal Cons. of Havana. After that, he taught musical esthetics and wrote music criticism. —Works: 2 symphonies; a cantata, *Los dos abuelos* (1949); a concerto for 9 wind instruments; *La Conga de Jagua* for 2 pianos; etc.

Martin (măhr-tăn'), **Frank,** outstanding Swiss composer; b. Geneva, Sept. 15, 1890. He studied with Joseph Lauber; in 1918-20, lived in Zürich; then in Rome (1921-23). In 1923 he went to Paris, where he joined the modern movement and perfected his technique. Returning to Geneva, he taught at the Institut Jaques-Dalcroze; also was director of the 'Technicum moderne de musique' (1933-39). He went to Amsterdam in 1950; in 1952-58, taught at the Cons. of Cologne; then returned to Switzerland. His early music shows the influence of César Franck and French Impressionists; but soon he succeeded in creating a distinctive style supported by a consummate mastery of contrapuntal and harmonic writing, and a profound feeling for emotional consistency and continuity; in later works he adopted a modified 12-tone method. He has also demonstrated his ability to stylize folksong material in modern harmonies with incisive, but always authentically scanned, rhythms. —Works: opera, *The Tempest,* after Shakespeare (Vienna, June 17, 1956); incidental music to *Oedipus Rex* (1923), *Romeo and Juliet* (1927), *Athalie* (1946); oratorios, *Le vin herbé* (Zürich, March 26, 1942), *In terra pax* (Geneva, May 7, 1945), *Golgotha,* to a text by St. Augustine (Geneva, April 29, 1949); for orch.: *Symphonie pour orchestre burlesque* (1915), *Rythmes* (Geneva Festival of the International Society for Contemporary Music, April 6, 1929), piano concerto (Barcelona Festival, April 22, 1936), *Symphonie* (Geneva, March 10, 1938), *Petite Symphonie Concertante,* for harp, harpsichord, piano, and 2 string orchestras (Zürich, May 17, 1946; his best known work; numerous performances in Europe and America), concerto for 7 wind instruments, strings, and percussion (Bern, Oct. 25, 1949), violin concerto (Basel, Jan. 24, 1952), concerto for harpsichord and orch. (Paris, Nov. 6, 1955); *Ballade* for piano and orch. (1939); *Ballade* for cello and orch. (Geneva, April 4, 1951); *Etudes* for string orch. (1956); chamber music:

piano quintet (1920), piano trio, on popular Irish themes (1925), string trio (1936), string quartet (1936), 2 violin sonatas (1913 and 1931), *Ballade* for flute and piano (1939; also with orch.; Geneva, Nov. 30, 1939), *Ballade* for trombone and piano (1941; also with orch.; Geneva, Jan. 29, 1942); choral works. —Cf. R.-Aloys Mooser, *Regards sur la musique contemporaine, 1921-1946* (Lausanne, 1947); Frank Martin, *Responsabilité du compositeur,* with a list of works, in 'Polyphonie' (1948, No. 2).

Martin, Sir **George (Clement),** English organist and composer; b. Lambourne, Berks, Sept. 11, 1844; d. London, Feb. 23, 1916. He was a pupil of J. Pearson and Dr. Stainer; received the degree of Bachelor of Music at Oxford in 1868, and Mus. Doc. (Canterbury) in 1883. He was knighted in 1897. In 1888 he succeeded Stainer as organist of St. Paul's Cathedral, which post he held until his death. He publ. the primer *The Art of Training Choir Boys.*

Martin (măhr-tăn'), **Jean-Blaise,** famous French baritone; b. Paris, Feb. 24, 1768; d. Ronzières, Rhône, Oct. 28, 1837. He made his début at the Théâtre de Monsieur in 1788; sang at the Théâtre Feydeau and the Théâtre Favart until they were united as the Opéra-Comique in 1801, and there until 1823. From 1816-18 and again from 1832-37, he was a professor at the Paris Cons. His voice, while essentially a baritone in quality, had the extraordinary range of three full octaves *(C-c²).*

Martin, Riccardo (real name Hugh Whitfield Martin), American tenor; b. Hopkinsville, Ky., Nov. 18, 1874; d. New York, Aug. 11, 1952. He studied violin in Nashville and singing in N.Y.; was a pupil in composition of MacDowell at Columbia Univ.; went to Paris in 1901, where he took singing lessons with Sbriglia; made his début as Faust in Nantes (1904); American début as Canio (*Pagliacci*) with the San Carlo Opera Co. in New Orleans (1906); was a member of the Metropolitan Opera Co. from 1907 to 1913; then with the Boston Grand Opera Co. (1916-17), with the Chicago Opera Co. (1920-22); subsequently settled in N.Y. as a singing teacher.

Martín y Soler, Vicente, Spanish opera composer; b. Valencia, June 18, 1754; d. St. Petersburg, Jan. 30, 1806. He was church organist at Alicante as a youth, before going to Madrid, where he produced his first opera *I due avari* (1776). He then went to Italy, where he was known as Martini lo Spagnuolo (the Spaniard); wrote operas for Naples, Turin, and Lucca. He secured the services of Da Ponte as librettist, and produced with him the operas *Il Burbero di buon cuore (The Grumbler with a Good Heart;* Vienna, Jan. 4, 1786; much acclaimed; revived there, Nov. 9, 1789, with 2 additional airs written expressly for it by Mozart), *Una Cosa rara* (his undoubted masterpiece; Vienna, Nov. 17, 1786; numerous productions in other European capitals; Mozart borrowed a theme from this opera for his *Don Giovanni),* and *L'Arbore di Diana* (Vienna, Oct. 1, 1787). Having achieved fame in Italy, where he was favorably compared with Cimarosa and Paisiello, Martín y Soler was engaged as court composer by Catherine the Great (1788). In St. Petersburg, he produced the operas *Gorye Bogatyr Kosometovitch* (libretto by Catherine II; Feb. 9, 1789), *La Melomania* (Jan. 7, 1790), *Fedul and His Children* (Jan. 16, 1791), and *La Festa del villaggio* (Jan. 26, 1798); the ballets, *Didon abandonnée* (1792), *L'Oracle* (1793), *Amour et Psyché* (1793), and *Tancrède* (1799). In 1795 he went to London; his operas *La Scola de' maritati* (Jan. 27, 1795) and *L'Isola del piacere* (May 26, 1795), both to librettos by Da Ponte, were presented there with excellent success. In 1796 he returned to Russia, and remained there until his death. —Cf. J. R. de Lihory, *La Música en Valencia* (Valencia, 1903); R.-Aloys Mooser, *Un Musicien espagnol en Russie,* in the 'Rivista Musicale Italiana' (1936); R.-Aloys Mooser, *Annales de la musique et musiciens en Russie au XVIIIe siècle* (Geneva, 1951; vol. II, pp. 455-61).

Martinelli, Giovanni, Italian tenor; b. Montagnana, near Venice, Oct. 22, 1885. He played the clarinet in an army band; then studied singing with Mandolini. He made his concert début in Milan (Dec. 3, 1910) in Rossini's *Stabat Mater;* then sang opera in Milan, Rome, and other Italian cities; one of his signal successes was his appearance in Puccini's opera *The Girl of the Golden West,* at its European première (Rome, 1911). In 1912 he sang at Covent Garden, London; made his American début with the Metropolitan Opera Co. as Rodolfo in *La Bohème* (N.Y., Nov. 20, 1913); remained on the roster of the Metropolitan Opera until 1946; then opened an opera studio in New York.

Martinet, Jean-Louis, French composer; b. Ste.-Bazeille, Nov. 8, 1916. He studied at the Paris Cons. with Koechlin and Roger-Ducasse; received 1st prize for composition in 1943. —Works: a pantomime, *La trilogie des Promethées* (1947); *Orphée,* symph. poem (1947); *6 Chants* for chorus and orch. (1948); *Épisodes-Cantate* for chorus and orch. (1950); numerous vocal works.

Martinez (măhr-tē'-nĕts), **Marianne di,** Austrian vocalist and pianist; b. Vienna, May 4, 1744; d. there, Dec. 13, 1812. She was a pupil of Metastasio and of Haydn. She wrote oratorios, motets, psalms, symphonies, piano concertos, etc. (all MSS in possession of the Gesellschaft der Musikfreunde in Vienna).

Martini (mahr-tē'-nē), **Giambattista,** best known as Padre Martini; illustrious Italian composer and teacher; b. Bologna, April 24, 1706; d. there, Oct. 4, 1784. His musical education was conducted by his father, a violinist; he then took lessons with Padre Predieri (harpsichord and voice) and Riccieri (counterpoint). He entered the Franciscan Order at Lago, and was ordained priest in 1722; in 1725 he became maestro di cappella at the church of San Francesco in Bologna. A man of unquenchable intellectual curiosity, he studied mathematics with Zanotti, and took a course in ecclesiastical music with Giacomo Perti. He accumulated a magnificent musical library, which, after his death, went to the Liceo Musicale of Bologna and the court library in Vienna. He composed Masses and oratorios of great merit; but it was as a teacher that his name became widely known. Students of all nationalities sought his instruction (among them Gluck, Mozart, Grétry, Jommelli, Mattei), and scholars submitted complex questions regarding musical science to him for settlement. He was a member of the Accademia Filarmonica of Bologna; also of the Accademia degli Arcadi, Rome, in which his 'Arcadian' title was 'Aristosseno Anfioneo' (Aristoxenos Amphion). Of his compositions, in the style of the Roman school (of which he was a warm partisan), the following were publ.: *Litaniae atque antiphoniae finales, a 4,* with organ and instruments (1734); *12 Sonate d'intavolatura per l'organo e cembalo* (1742); *6 Sonate d'intavolatura per l'organo e cembalo* (1747); *Duetti da camera a diversi voci* (1763). In MS, 2 oratorios, Masses, a 'farsetta,' 3 'intermezzi,' etc. —His principal work is *Storia della musica* (3 vols.; Bologna, 1757, 1770, 1781), dealing only with ancient music; the *Esemplare ossia saggio fondamentale pratico di contrappunto* (2 vols.; 1774, 1775) is a collection of contrapuntal models; he also wrote *Regole per gli organisti per accompagnare il canto fermo* (1756), other learned dissertations and essays, etc. —Bibliography: G. della Valle, *Elogio del Padre Giambattista Martini* (Bologna, 1784); G. della Valle, *Memorie storiche del Padre Giambattista Martini* (Naples, 1785); F. Parisini, *Della vita e delle opere del padre Martini* (Bologna, 1887); L. Busi, *Il padre Giambattista Martini* (vol. I, Bologna, 1891); G. Gandolfi, *Elogio di Giambattista Martini* (1913); W. Reich, *Padre Martini als Theoretiker* (Vienna, 1934); A. Pauchard, *Ein italienischer Musiktheoretiker. Pater G. B. Martini* (Lugano, 1941). Martini's voluminous correspondence was publ. by F.Parisini (Bologna, 1888).

Martini (real name Schwarzendorf), **Jean Paul Égide,** German organist and composer; b. Freistadt in the Palatinate, Sept. 1, 1741; d. Paris, Feb. 10, 1816. In 1760, having studied organ, he settled in Nancy, and Italianized his name; then was attached to the retinue of King Stanislas at Lunéville (1761-66). In 1766 he went to Paris, where he won a prize for a military march for the Swiss Guard; this introduced him into army circles in France; he enlisted as an officer of a Hussar regiment, and wrote more band music; also composed an opera, *L'Amoureux de quinze ans,* which was produced with extraordinary success at the Italian Opera in Paris (April 18, 1771). Leaving the army, he became music director to the Prince of Condé, and later to the Comte d'Artois. He purchased the reversion of the office of First Intendant of the King's Music, a speculation brought to naught by the Revolution, which caused him to resign in haste his position as conductor at the Théâtre Feydeau, and flee to Lyons in 1792. He returned to Paris in 1794, and was appointed Inspector of the Paris Cons. in 1798; also taught composition there until 1802. In appreciation of his royalist record, he was given the post of Royal Intendant at the Restoration in 1814, but died 2 years later. He wrote 12 operas, a Requiem for Louis XVI, Psalms and other church music, but he is chiefly remembered as the composer of the popular air *Plaisir d'amour,* which was arranged by Berlioz for voice and orch. —Cf. A. Pougin, *J.P.E. Martini* (Paris, 1864).

Martini, Nino, tenor; b. Verona, Italy, Aug. 8, 1905; studied voice in Italy and in the U.S. with Maria Gay and Giovanni Zenatello. In 1929 he visited the U.S. as a film actor and singer; also became a popular radio performer. He made his American début as an opera singer with the Philadelphia Opera Co. (1931); appeared at the Metropolitan Opera House, N.Y., for the first time as the Duke in *Rigoletto* (Dec. 28, 1933), and remained on its roster for several seasons; also continued his career as a concert singer.

Martinon, Jean, French composer and conductor; b. Lyons, Jan. 18, 1910. He studied first at the Lyons Cons.; then at the Paris Cons., graduating as a violinist, and winning 1st prize (1928); later took lessons with Albert Roussel (composition) and Charles Munch (conducting). He was in the French army; taken prisoner in 1940, and spent 2 years in a German concentration camp; there he wrote *Stalag 9 ou Musique d'exil,* for orch., and a motet, *Absolve Domine,* in memory of French musicians killed in the war. After his release, he conducted the Concerts du Conservatoire de Paris (1944-46); in 1946 was appointed conductor of the Bordeaux Symph. Orch.; later undertook several conducting tours (England, South America); made his American début with the Boston Symph. Orch., March 29, 1957. — Works: *Symphonietta,* for strings, piano, harp, and kettledrums (1935); *Concerto giocoso,* for violin and orch. (1937-42); *Hymne à la vie* for orch. (1944); *Ode au soleil,* for narrator, chorus, and orch. (1945); *Ambohimanga,* ballet (1946); *Irish Symphony* (1948); *Concerto lyrique,* for string quartet and chamber orch. (1944); *Hécube,* opera (1954); wind quintet (1938); woodwind trio (1940); string trio (1943); piano trio (1945); string quartet (1946); also *Psalm 136* (1943; 1st prize of the City of Paris); other choral works; piano pieces. —Cf. A. Machabey, *Portraits de trente musiciens français* (Paris, 1950; pp. 121-25).

Martinu, Bohuslav, outstanding Czech composer; b. Polička, Dec. 8, 1890. He studied violin at home; in 1906 he enrolled at the Cons. of Prague, in the Organ School; in 1913 became a violinist in the Prague Philharmonic; his symph. poem *Vanishing Midnight* was performed by that orchestra in 1922. He then decided to resume his study of composition; re-entered the Prague Cons. as a pupil of J. Suk; however, he did not graduate. In 1923 he went to Paris; took a course with Albert Roussel, and began his career as a composer in full earnest. In a relatively short time his name became known through increasingly frequent performances of his chamber works, ballets, and symph. pieces in Paris, in Prague, and in America; many of his works were performed at the festivals of the International Society for Contemporary Music. He remained in Paris until June 1940, when he fled from the German invasion, and went to Portugal, and finally to America; settled in N.Y. His music is characterized by a strong feeling for Bohemian melorhythms; his stylizations of Czech dances are couched in a modern idiom without losing their simplicity. In his large works, he follows the neo-Classical trend, with some Impressionistic undertones; his mastery of modern counterpoint is extraordinary. In his stage works, his predilections are for chamber forms; his sense of operatic comedy is very strong, but he is also capable of poignant lyricism. —Works: operas: *Voják a Tenečnice (The Soldier and the Ballerina;* Brno, 1928), *Les Lames du couteau (The Knife's Edge;* Paris, 1928), *Journée de bonté* (1929), *Hry o Marii (The Miracle of the Virgin Mary;* Brno, 1934), *Hlas Lesa (The Voice of the Forest;* 1935), *Divadlo za bránou (Surburban Theater,* Brno, 1936), *Comedy on a Bridge* (1937; revised, 1950), *Juliette* (Prague, March 16, 1938), *The Marriage,* after Gogol (N.B.C. Television Opera Theater, N.Y., Feb. 7, 1953), *What Men Live By,* after Tolstoy (1953); ballets: *Istar* (Prague, 1922), *Who Is the Most Powerful in the World?* (Brno, 1924), *On tourne (They are filming;* Paris, 1925), *Revolt* (Brno, 1926), *La Revue de cuisine* (Prague, 1927), *Echec au roi (Checkmate;* 1928), *The Butterfly that Stamped,* after Kipling (1929), *Špalíček* (with voices; Prague, 1932), *The Judgment of Paris* (1935); 6 symphonies: No. 1 (Boston, Nov. 13, 1942), No. 2 (Cleveland, Oct. 28, 1943), No. 3 (Boston, Oct. 12, 1945), No. 4 (Philadelphia, Nov. 30, 1945), No. 5 (N.Y., Jan. 24, 1948), No. 6, *Fantaisies Symphoniques* (Boston, Jan. 9, 1955; his most successful symphony; numerous performances in Europe and America); other orchestral works: *Mizející pulnoc (Vanishing Midnight;* Prague, 1922), *Polička (Half-Time;* Prague Festival of the International Society for Contemporary Music, May 17, 1925), *La Bagarre* (Boston, Nov. 18, 1928), *La Rapsodie* (Boston, Dec. 14, 1928), *Jazz Suite* (1929), *Serenade* (1930), *Partita,* for strings (1931), cello concerto (Paris, 1931), concerto for string quartet and orch. (1931), *Les Rondes* (1932), *Sinfonia* for 2 orchestras (1932), piano concerto (Prague, 1935), *Tre Ricercari* (Venice, 1938), *Double Concerto,* for 2 string orchestras, piano and kettledrums (Basel, Feb. 9, 1940), *Concerto* *grosso* (Boston, Nov. 14, 1941), *Sinfonietta giocosa* (N.Y., March 16, 1942), *Memorial to Lidice* (N.Y., Oct. 28, 1943), concerto for 2 pianos and orch. (Philadelphia, Nov. 5, 1943), violin concerto (Boston, Dec. 31, 1943); *Thunderbolt P-45* (Washington, Dec. 19, 1945), *Toccata e due Canzoni* (Basel, Jan. 21, 1947), concerto for orch. (Dallas, Nov. 20, 1949), *Rhapsody-Concerto,* for viola and orch. (Cleveland, Feb. 19, 1953), *Incantation,* for piano and orch. (N.Y., Oct. 4, 1956); chamber music: 6 string quartets (1921-47), string quintet (1929), wind quintet (1930), piano trio (1930), string sextet (1931; Elizabeth Sprague Coolidge Prize), 2 violin sonatas (1931 and 1933), sonata for 2 violins and piano (1932), piano quintet (1934), string trio (1935), trio for flute, violin, and piano (1936), *Madrigals,* for oboe, clarinet, and bassoon (1937), 2 cello sonatas (1940 and 1941), piano quartet (1942), *Madrigal Sonata,* for flute, violin, and piano (1942); several piano pieces *(3 Czech Dances, Ritournelles,* etc.). —Cf. M. Šafránek, *Bohuslav Martinu,* in the 'Mus. Quarterly' (July, 1943); M. Šafránek, *Bohuslav Martinu: The Man and His Music* (N. Y., 1944); R.-Aloys Mooser, *Regards sur la musique contemporaine, 1921-1946* (Lausanne, 1947; pp. 111, 185, 321, 354, 393); Jan Löwenbach, *Martinu pozdravuje domov* (Prague, 1947); R.-Aloys Mooser, *Panorama de la musique contemporaine, 1947-1953* (Lausanne, 1954; pp. 277, 280, 358).

Martucci (mahr-tooch'-chē), **Giuseppe,** eminent Italian composer and conductor; b. Capua, Jan. 6, 1856; d. Naples, June 1, 1909. A pupil of his father (a trumpet player), he made his début as a child pianist at the age of 7; at 11 he was admitted to the Cons. di San Pietro a Maiella in Naples; there he studied piano with B. Cesi, and composition with P. Serrao, but left in 1871. Subsequently he traveled as pianist in Italy, France, Germany, and England; in 1880 he became prof. of piano at the Naples Cons.; conducted symph. concerts established by Prince d'Ardore, and was the director of the Neapolitan Società del Quartetto. From 1886 until 1902 he was director of the Bologna Cons.; in 1902 he returned to Naples, and became director of the Cons. there, a post he held until his death. His activities as a fine symph. conductor contributed much to Italian musical culture, and he was greatly esteemed by his colleagues and the public; an ardent admirer of Wagner, he conducted the Italian première of *Tristan und Isolde* (Bologna, June 2, 1888); also led performances of other operas by Wagner. In his own works, he follows the ideals of the German school; the influences of Wagner and Liszt are particularly pronounced. He wrote no operas; his works include 2 symphonies (1895 and 1904); *4 piccoli pezzi* for orch.; 2 piano concertos; piano quintet; 2 piano trios; *Momento musicale e minuetto* for string quartet; cello sonata; several sets of piano pieces; numerous songs; piano arrangements of classical works. —Cf. R. Prati, *Giuseppe Martucci* (Turin, 1914); a commemorative vol., *Capua a Giuseppe Martucci* (Capua, 1915); Perrachio, *L'opera pianistica di Martucci* in 'Il Pianoforte' (March, 1922); M. Limoncelli, *Giuseppe Martucci* (Naples, 1939); F. Fano, *Giuseppe Martucci* (Milan, 1950, contains complete chronology of life, and exact dates of first performances of works).

Martucci, Paolo, Italian pianist, son of Giuseppe Martucci; b. Naples, Oct. 8, 1883. He studied with his father; made his début at Bologna with Tchaikovsky's concerto (June 27, 1902); from 1904 to 1911 lived in England; then settled in the U.S.; was prof. at the Cincinnati Cons. (1911-13); in 1913 moved to N.Y., where he taught piano.

Marty (măhr - tē'), **Georges - Eugène,** French composer and conductor; b. Paris, May 16, 1860; d. there, Oct. 11, 1908. He attended the Paris Cons. (1872-82), winning the Grand Prix de Rome with the cantata *Edith;* in 1894 was appointed instructor at the Paris Cons.; in 1903 succeeded Taffanel as conductor of the famous 'Société des Concerts du Conservatoire.' He wrote 3 operas *(Le Duc de Ferrare, Daria,* and *La grande Mademoiselle);* a symph. poem, *Merlin enchanté;* a *Suite romantique* for orch.; choruses, songs, much piano music, etc.

Marx, Adolf Bernhard, eminent German theorist and writer; b. Halle, May 15, 1795; d. Berlin, May 17, 1866. Intended for the law, he matriculated at the Univ. of Halle, but likewise studied music with Türk, and gave up a subsequent legal appointment at Naumburg to gratify his love for art. He continued the study of composition in Berlin with Zelter; in 1824 he founded the 'Berliner Allgemeine Musikalische Zeitung' (with the publisher Schlesinger); he edited this publication with ability, and proved himself a conspicuous advocate of German music; however, the publication ceased in 1830. After taking the degree of *Dr. phil.*

at Marburg (1827), Marx lectured on music at the Berlin Univ.; was appointed prof. in 1830; became music director of the scholastic choir there in 1832. He was co-founder (with Kullak and Stern) of the Berlin Cons. (1850), retiring in 1856 to devote himself to literary and university work. He was an intimate friend of the Mendelssohn family, and advised young Mendelssohn in musical matters; their relationship became less cordial when Marx realized that Mendelssohn had little appreciation for his creative works. Indeed, these have not stood the test of time; his opera *Jery und Bätely* (after Goethe) was performed in Berlin (1825) with scant success; he also wrote several oratorios and some instrumental music. However, his writings on musical theory and esthetics are valuable; they include: *Die Lehre von der musikalischen Komposition* (4 vols., 1837-47; several times reprinted; new eds. by Hugo Riemann, 1887-90); *Allgemeine Musiklehre* (1839; 10th ed., 1884; transl. into English); *Über Malerei in der Tonkunst* (1828); *Über die Geltung Händelscher Sologesänge für unsere Zeit* (1829); *Die alte Musiklehre im Streit mit unserer Zeit* (1841); *Die Musik des 19. Jahrhunderts und ihre Pflege* (1855); *Ludwig van Beethoven, Leben und Schaffen* (1859; 6th ed., by G. Behnke, 1911); *Gluck und die Oper* (1863; 2 vols.); *Anleitung zum Vortrag Beethoven'scher Klavierwerke* (1863; new ed. by E. Schmitz, 1912; English transl., 1895); *Erinnerungen aus meinem Leben* (1865; 2 vols.); *Das Ideal und die Gegenwart* (1867). A collection of his essays was publ. by L. Hirschberg as *Über Tondichter und Tonkunst* (3 vols., 1912-22). —Cf. G. F. Selle, *Aus Adolf Bernhard Marx's litterarischem Nachlass* (Berlin, 1898); L. Hirschberg, *Der Tondichter Adolf Bernhard Marx,* in the 'Sammelbände der internationalen Musik-Gesellschaft' (1908).

Marx, (Walter) Burle, Brazilian conductor; b. São Paulo, July 23, 1902. He studied piano with his mother; played in public from the age of 11; in 1920 went to Germany, where he studied piano with Barth and Kwast; composition with F. E. Koch and Reznicek. In 1930 he returned to Brazil, where he developed an active career as conductor; also conducted elsewhere in South America; led concerts of Latin American music in Washington and N.Y.; conducted the N.Y. Philharmonic for the Brazilian government at the N.Y. World's Fair (1939); thenceforward divided his time between Brazil and the U.S.; in 1953, was engaged as instructor at the Settlement Music School in Philadelphia. He has written a number of effective orchestral pieces, including a *Fantastic Episode* (N.Y., 1939); also a symph. (1940); has contributed articles on Brazilian music to various publications.

Marx, Joseph, Austrian composer; b. Graz, May 11, 1882. He studied with Degner; musicology at the Univ. of Graz, taking the degree of *Dr. phil.* with the dissertation *Über die Funktionen von Intervallen, Harmonie und Melodie beim Erfassen von Tonkomplexen.* In 1941 he went to Vienna, where he taught at the State Academy; was its director (1922-24); then rector of the Hochschule für Musik in Vienna (1924-27); for 3 years was adviser to the Turkish government on music education, and traveled to Ankara; later resumed his teaching in Vienna; from 1947 was also prof. at the Univ. of Graz. As a composer, he styles himself a 'Romantic Realist.' —Works: *Eine Herbst-Symphonie* (1922); *Eine symphonische Nachtmusik* (1926); *Nordlandsrhapsodie* (1929); *Alt-Wiener Serenaden* (1942); *Feste im Herbst* (1946); *Castelli romani,* for piano and orch. (1931); *Verklärtes Jahr,* for voice and orch. (1932); *Quartett in Form einer Rhapsodie,* for violin, viola, cello, and piano; string quartet 'In modo antico' (1940); string quartet 'In modo classico' (1942); 2 violin sonatas; about 150 songs; etc. He publ. a book of essays, *Betrachtungen eines romantischen Realisten* (Vienna, 1947). —Cf. J. Bistron, *Joseph Marx* (Vienna, 1923); A. Liess, *Joseph Marx: Leben und Werk* (Graz, 1943).

Marx, Karl, German composer and pedagogue; b. Munich, Nov. 12, 1897; was in the German army during World War I, and was a prisoner of war in England; after the Armistice, studied with Carl Orff, Hausegger, Beer-Walbrunn, and Schwickerath. In 1924 he was appointed to the faculty of the Akademie der Tonkunst in Munich; in 1928 became the leader of the Bach Society in Munich; from 1939-46 was instructor at the Hochschule für Musikerziehung in Graz; in 1946 was appointed teacher at the Hochschule für Musik in Stuttgart. —Works: the cantatas, *Die unendliche Woge; Vom Himmel hoch, o Englein, kommt; Auf der Landstrasse;* also cantatas for special seasons; children's cantatas and the like; many pieces for amateurs; a piano concerto; a concerto for flute and strings; song cycles; many choruses. —Cf. R. von Saalfeld, *Karl Marx,* in the 'Zeitschrift für Musik' (May, 1931).

Marxsen, Eduard, German organist and teacher; b. Nienstädten, near Altona, July 23, 1806; d. Altona, Nov. 18, 1887. He was a pupil of his father, an organist; later studied with Seyfried and Bocklet in Vienna; then returned to Hamburg, where he became well known as a pedagogue. He was the first teacher of Brahms; composed about 70 works in various genres.

Maryon, Edward (full name, John Edward Maryon-d'Aulby), English composer; b. London, April 3, 1867; d. there, Jan. 31, 1954. He began to compose early in life; went to Paris, where his first opera, *L'Odalisque,* won the Gold Medal at the Exposition of 1889; however, he regarded the work as immature and destroyed the score. In 1891 he studied with Max Pauer in Dresden; later took lessons with F. Wüllner in Cologne; he then lived in France; from 1914-19 he was in Montclair, N.J., where he established a conservatory with a fund for exchange of music students between England and America; in 1933 he returned to London. Besides *L'Odalisque,* Maryon wrote the following operas: *Paolo and Francesca; La Robe de Plume; The Smelting Pot; The Prodigal Son; Werewolf; Rembrandt; Greater Love;* and *Abelard and Heloise.* His *magnum opus* was a grandiose operatic heptalogy under the title, *The Cycle of Life,* comprising seven mystical dramas: *Lucifer, Cain, Krishna, Magdalen, Sangraal, Psyche,* and *Nirvana.* He further wrote a symph. poem, *The Feather Robe,* subtitled *A Legend of Fujiyama* (1905), which he dedicated to the Emperor of Japan; and an *Armageddon Requiem* (1916), dedicated to the dead of World War I. Of his works, only the following were published: the *Beatitudes* for baritone, double chorus, and orch. (1907), *Six Melodies* for voice and piano (1907), and *The Paean of Asaph,* a festival cantata (1931). After Maryon's death, his complete manuscripts were donated by his heirs to the Boston Public Library. Maryon developed a theory of universal art, in which colors were associated with sounds; an outline of this theory was published in his pamphlet *Marcotone* (N. Y., 1919). —Cf. E. E. Hipsher, *American Opera and its Composers* (Philadelphia, 1934; pp. 313-16).

Marzo, Eduardo, Italian pianist, organist, and composer; b. Naples, Nov. 29, 1852; d. New York, June 7, 1929. As a boy of 15, he settled in N.Y., and appeared in concerts as a pianist; was accompanist to many celebrated artists, among them Carlotta Patti, Mario, and Sarasate on their American tours. From 1878 he played the organ in various New York churches. He held numerous honorary orders, conferred on him by the King of Italy; was co-founder of the American Guild of Organists. Publ. many Masses and other sacred choral works; cantatas; operettas; songs; piano pieces.

Mascagni (mas-kah'-ñē), **Pietro,** famous Italian opera composer; b. Leghorn, Dec. 7, 1863; d. Rome, Aug. 2, 1945. His father was a baker who wished Mascagni to continue in that trade, but yielded to his son's determination to study music. He took lessons with Alfredo Soffredini in his native town, until he was enabled, by the aid of an interested patron, to enter the Cons. of Milan, where he studied with Ponchielli and Saladino. However, he became impatient of the school discipline, and left the Cons. in 1884. The following year he obtained a post as conductor of the municipal band in the small town of Cerignola. He composed industriously; in 1888 he sent the manuscript of his 1-act opera *Cavalleria Rusticana* to the music publisher Sonzogno for a competition, and won first prize. The opera was performed at the Costanzi Theater in Rome on May 17, 1890, with sensational success; the dramatic story of village passion and Mascagni's emotional score, laden with luscious music, combined to produce an extraordinary appeal to opera lovers. The short opera made the tour of the world stages with amazing rapidity, productions being staged all over Europe and America with never-failing success; the opera was usually presented in 2 parts, separated by an 'intermezzo sinfonico' (which became a popular orchestral number performed separately). *Cavalleria Rusticana* marked the advent of the operatic style known as 'verismo,' in which stark realism was the chief aim, and the dramatic development condensed to enhance the impression. When, 2 years later, another 'veristic' opera, Leoncavallo's *Pagliacci,* was taken by Sonzogno, the 2 operas became twin attractions on a single bill. Ironically, Mascagni could never duplicate, or even remotely approach, the success of his first production, although he continued to compose industriously, and opera houses all over the world were only too eager to stage his successive operas. Thus, his opera *Le Maschere* was produced on Jan. 17, 1901, at six of the most important Italian opera houses simultaneously (Rome, Milan, Turin, Genoa, Venice, Verona); it was produced 2 days later in Naples. Mascagni himself conducted the première in Rome, but the opera failed to fire the imagination of the public; it was produced in a revised form in Turin 15 years later (June 7, 1916), but was not established in the repertory even in Italy. In 1902 Mascagni made a tour of the U. S., conducting his *Cavalleria Rusticana* and other operas, but owing to mismanagement, the visit proved a fiasco; a South American tour in 1911 was more successful. Mascagni also appeared frequently as conductor of symph. concerts. In 1890 he was made Knight of the Crown of Italy; in 1929 he was elected member of the Academy. At various times he also was engaged in teaching; from 1895 until 1902 he was director of the Rossini Cons. in Pesaro. His last years were darkened by the inglorious role that Mascagni assumed in his ardent support of the Fascist regime, so that he was rejected by many of his old friends, including Toscanini. He died at the age of 81. —Operas: *Pinotta* (written in 1880; score recovered after 50 years, and first produced in San Remo, March 23, 1932); *Guglielmo Ratcliff* (c. 1885; Milan, Feb. 16, 1895); *Cavalleria Rusticana* (Rome, May 17, 1890); *L'Amico Fritz* (Rome, Oct. 31, 1891; the only fairly successful opera by Mascagni after *Cavalleria Rusticana;* still performed in Italy); *I Rantzau* (Florence, Nov. 10, 1892); *Silvano* (Milan, March 25, 1895); *Zanetto* (Pesaro, March 2, 1896); *Iris* (Rome, Nov. 22, 1898); *Le Maschere* (première in 6 cities, Jan. 17, 1901); *Amica* (Monte Carlo, March 16, 1905); *Isabeau* (Buenos Aires, June 2, 1911); *Parisina* (Milan, Dec. 15, 1913); *Lodoletta* (Rome, April 30, 1917); *Scampolo* (1921); *Il piccolo Marat* (Rome, May 2, 1921); *Nerone* (Milan, Jan. 16, 1935); *I Brianchi ed i Neri* (1940). Other works include *Poema Leopardiano* (for the centenary of G. Leopardi, 1898); Hymn in honor of Admiral Dewey (July, 1899); *Rapsodia Satanica* for orch. (music for a film, Rome, July 2, 1917); *Davanti Santa Teresa* (Rome, Aug., 1923); chamber music. —Bibliography: G. Monaldi, *Pietro Mascagni: L'uomo e l'artista* (Rome, 1899); G. Marvin, *Pietro Mascagni: Biografia aneddotica* (Palermo, 1904); G. Bastianelli, *Pietro Mascagni, con nota delle opere* (Naples, 1910); E. Pompei, *Pietro Mascagni, nella vita e nell'arte* (Rome, 1912); G. Orsini, *L'arte di Pietro Mascagni* (Milan, 1912); G. Scuderi, *Iris* (1923); T. Mantovani, *Iris* (1930); A. Donno, *Modernità di Pietro Mascagni* (1931); G. Cogo, *Il nostro Mascagni* (1931); *Bibliografia delle opere di Pietro Mascagni,* in the 'Bolletino bibliografico musicale' (Milan, 1932); A. de Donno, *Mascagni nel 900 musicale* (Rome, 1935); A. Jeri, *Mascagni, 15 Opere, 1000 Episodi* (Milan, 1940); D. Cellamare, *Mascagni e la 'Cavalleria' visti da Cerignola* (Rome, 1941); *Mascagni parla* (Rome, 1945).

Maschera (măs'-kĕ-răh), **Fiorenzo,** Italian organist and composer of the late 16th century. He was a pupil of Merulo; on Aug. 1, 1557, he became organist at the Cathedral of Brescia, succeeding Merulo in this post. He publ. instrumental *Canzoni a 4 voci* (Brescia, 1584; reprinted in Venice, 1588 and 1593); in this collection are some of the earliest examples of the ensemble canzona, with sections organized in terms of repetition. One such work is included in Davison and Apel, *Historical Anthology of Music,* vol. I (Cambridge, Mass., 1947).

Mascheroni (măh-skĕ-rŏh'-nē), **Edoardo,** Italian conductor and composer; b. Milan, Sept. 4, 1852; d. Ghirla, near Varese, March 4, 1941. As a boy, he showed special interest in mathematics and literature; wrote literary essays for the journal 'La vita nuova' before he decided to study music seriously; took lessons with Boucheron in Milan, and composed various pieces. In 1883 he began a career as conductor, and it was in that capacity that he distinguished himself. He was first a theater conductor in Leghorn; then went to Rome, where he established his reputation as an opera conductor. Upon Verdi's explicit request, he was selected to conduct the première of *Falstaff* at La Scala (1893); he remained on the staff of La Scala until 1897; then conducted in Germany, Spain, and South America; also was successful as a symph. conductor. He wrote 2 operas: *Lorenza* (Rome, April 13, 1901) and *La Perugina* (Naples, April 24, 1909).

Mašek (mah'-shek), **Vincenz,** virtuoso pianist; b. Zwikovecz, Bohemia, April 5, 1755; d. Prague, Nov. 15, 1831. He was a pupil of Seegert and Dussek; became an accomplished player of the piano and harmonica; after long tours, he settled in Prague as an organist and music-dealer. —Works: Bohemian operas, Masses, symphonies, chamber music, pieces for piano and harmonica, etc. His brother **Paul Mašek** (1761-1826) was a good pianist and a teacher in Vienna.

Masetti, Enzo, Italian composer; b. Bologna, Aug. 19, 1893. He studied with Franco Alfano at the Cons. of Bologna; then went to Rome, where he devoted himself chiefly to composing for the theater and films. —Works: musical fables: *La fola delle tre ochette* (1927), *La mosca mora* (1929), etc.; for orch.: *Leggenda del padule* (1920), *Contrasti* (1921), *Ora di vespro* (1931), *Sagra* (1936), *Idillio e ditirambo* (1938), *Notturno e Vendemmiale* (1949); also *Il gioco del cucù,* for piano and orch. (1928); chamber music; piano pieces; songs. Also ed. *La musica nel film* (Rome, 1950).

Mason, Colin, English music critic; b. Northampton, Jan. 26, 1924. He studied music in London; after the war he received a Hungarian state scholarship for the purpose of writing a book on Béla Bartók, and entered as a student at the Budapest Academy of Music (1947-49). In 1950 he became music critic of the 'Manchester Guardian.' His main interests lie in modern music; he has contributed numerous articles on this subject to magazines. In 1952 he made a tour in the U. S. as lecturer.

Mason, Daniel Gregory, eminent American composer and educator; b. Brookline, Mass., Nov. 20, 1873; d. Greenwich, Conn., Dec. 4, 1953. He was a scion of a famous family of American musicians; grandson of Lowell Mason, and nephew of William Mason. His father, Henry Mason, was a co-founder of the piano manufacturing firm Mason & Hamlin. He entered Harvard Univ., where he studied with John K. Painc (B.A., 1895); after graduation he continued his studies with Arthur Whiting (piano), P. Goetschius (theory), and Chadwick (orchestration). Still feeling the necessity for improvement of his technique as composer, he went to Paris, where he took courses with Vincent d'Indy. Returning to America, he became active as teacher and composer. In 1910 he became a member of the faculty of Columbia Univ.; in 1929, appointed MacDowell Professor of Music; he was chairman of the Music Dept. until 1940, and continued to teach there until 1942, when he retired. As a teacher, he developed a high degree of technical ability in his students; as a composer, he represented a conservative trend in American music; his ideals were the German masters of the Romantic School; but there is an admixture of Impressionistic colors in his orchestration; his harmonies are full and opulent; his melodic writing expressive and songful. The lack of strong individuality, however, has resulted in the virtual disappearance of his music from the active repertory, with the exception of the overture *Chanticleer.* —Works: for orch.: Symph. No. 1, in C minor (Philadelphia, Feb. 18, 1916; revised radically, and perf. in a new version, N. Y., Dec. 1, 1922), *Chanticleer,* a festival overture (Cincinnati, Nov. 23, 1928), Symph. No. 2, in A major (Cincinnati, Nov. 7, 1930), Symph. No. 3, *Lincoln* (N. Y., Nov. 17, 1937), *Prelude and Fugue,* for piano and orch. (Chicago, March 4, 1921), *Scherzo-Caprice,* for chamber orch. (N. Y., Jan. 2, 1917), *Suite after English Folksongs* (1934), *Russians,* for baritone and orch. (1918), a choral work, *Songs of the Countryside* (1926); chamber music: quartet for piano and strings (1912), *Pastorale,* for violin, clarinet, and piano (1913), sonata for clarinet and piano (1915), string quartet on Negro themes (1919), 3 pieces for flute, harp, and string quartet (1922), Variations on a theme of John Powell, for string quartet (1926), Divertimento, for flute, oboe, clarinet, horn, and bassoon (1927), *Fanny Blair,* folksong fantasy for string quartet (1929), Serenade, for string quartet (1932), *Sentimental Sketches,* 4 short pieces for violin, cello, and piano (1935); *Variations on a Quiet Theme* (1939), etc. —Books: *From Grieg to Brahms* (1902; re-issued, 1936); *Beethoven and His Forerunners* (1904); *The Romantic Composers* (1906); *The Appreciation of Music* (1907; with T. W. Surette); *The Orchestral Instruments* (1908); *A Guide to Music* (1909); *A Neglected Sense in Piano Playing* (1912); *Great Modern Composers* (1916); *Short Studies of Great Masterpieces* (1917); *Music as a Humanity: and Other Essays* (1921); *From Song to Symphony* (1924); *Artistic Ideals* (1925); *The Dilemma of American Music* (1928); *Tune In, America!* (1931); *The Chamber Music of Brahms* (1933); *Music in My Time and Other Reminiscences* (1938); *The Quartets of Beethoven* (1927); contributed articles to the 'Mus. Quarterly'; was editor-in-chief of 'The Art of Music.' —Cf. B. C. Tuthill, *Daniel Gregory Mason,* in the 'Mus. Quarterly' (Jan., 1948); Sister Mary Justina Klein, *The Contribution of Daniel Gregory Mason to American Music* (Washington, 1957; contains a list of musical and literary works, indicating MSS and their locations).

Mason, Lowell, American composer, organist, and conductor; b. Medfield, Mass., Jan. 8, 1792; d. Orange, N. J., Aug. 11, 1872. A self-taught musician, at 16 he directed the church choir at Medfield; 1812-27, bank clerk at Savannah, Ga., also teaching and conducting; 1827, went to Boston, becoming church organist; president of the Handel and Haydn Soc. (1827-32); established classes on Pestalozzi's system, teaching it privately from 1829 and in the public schools from 1838. He founded the Boston Academy of Music in 1832, with George J. Webb; 1835, made honorary Mus. Doc. by N. Y. Univ. (one of the 1st instances of the conferring of that degree in America); studied pedagogic methods in Zürich in 1837; publ. his experiences in *Musical Letters from Abroad* (N. Y., 1853); 1851, went to N. Y.; after 1854, resided in Orange, N. J. He became wealthy through the sale of his many collections of music: 'Handel and Haydn Society's Collection of Church Music' (1822; 16 later eds.); 'Juvenile Psalmist' (1829); 'Juvenile Lyre' (1830); 'Lyra Sacra' (1832); 'Sabbath School Songs' (1836); 'Boston Academy Collection of Church Music' (1836); 'Boston Anthem Book' (1839); 'The Psaltery' (1845); 'Cantica Laudis' (1850); 'New Carmina Sacra' (1852); 'Normal Singer' (1856); 'Song Garden' (3 parts; 1864-65); etc. Many of his own hymn tunes, including *Missionary Hymn* (*From Greenland's Icy Mountains*), *Olivet, Boylston, Bethany, Hebron,* and *Olmutz,* are still found in hymnals. His valuable library, including 830 MSS and 700 vols. of hymnology, was given to Yale College after his death. —Cf. T. F. Seward, *The Educational Work of Dr. Lowell Mason* (Boston, 1885); F. J. Metcalf, *American Writers and Compilers of Sacred Music* (1925); E. B. Birge, *History of Public School Music in the U. S.* (1928); H. L. Mason, *Hymn Tunes of Lowell Mason, a Bibliography* (Cambridge, Mass., 1944); A. L. Rich, *Lowell Mason; The Father of Singing Among the Children* (Chapel Hill, N. C., 1946).

Mason, Luther Whiting, American music educator; b. Turner, Maine, April 3, 1828; d. Buckfield, Maine, July 14, 1896. He was chiefly self-taught; 1853, superintendent of music in Louisville schools, later in Cincinnati, where he invented the 'National System' of music charts and books, which had instant success, and made him famous. He settled in Boston 1865, and reformed music instruction in the primary schools; in 1879 he was invited by the Japanese government to supervise music in the schools of Japan, where he labored 3 years with notable results (school music in Japan is termed 'Mason-song'). He spent some time in Germany perfecting his principal work, *The National Music-Course.*

Mason, William, American pianist and pedagogue; b. Boston, Mass., Jan. 24, 1829; d. New York, July 14, 1908. The son of Lowell Mason, his opportunities for study were excellent; after piano lessons from Henry Schmidt in Boston, and frequent public appearances (first in Boston, March 7, 1846, at an Academy of Music concert), he studied in Leipzig (1849) under Moscheles, Hauptmann, and Richter, in Prague under Dreyschock, and under Liszt at Weimar. He played in Weimar, Prague, and Frankfurt; 1853, in London; 1854-5, in various American towns, settling 1855 in New York. With Theodore Thomas, Bergmann, Mosenthal, and Matzka, he founded the 'Mason and Thomas Soirées of Chamber Music,' a series of classic concerts continued until 1868; thereafter he won wide celebrity as a composer and teacher. In 1872 Yale College conferred on him the honorary degree of Mus. Doc.—His principal textbook for piano playing is *Touch and Technic* (op. 44); others are *A Method for the Piano,* with E. S. Hoadley (1867); *System for Beginners* (1871); and *Mason's Pianoforte-Technics* (1878). His compositions, classical in form and refined in style and treatment, include a Serenata for cello and piano; some 40 numbers for piano solo, including *Amitié pour moi, Silver Spring, Monody, Rêverie poétique,* etc.; publ. *Memories of a Musical Life* (1901).

Mason & Hamlin Co., celebrated firm of piano manufacturers. The house was founded as the M. & H. Organ Co. in Boston in 1854 by Henry Mason, a son of Dr. Lowell Mason, and Emmons Hamlin. The latter, a brilliant mechanic, turned his attention to improving the quality of the reeds and obtaining great variety of tonal color, with the result that in 1861 the firm introduced the American Cabinet Organ. The firm became internationally famous, when at the Paris Exposition of 1867 its organs were awarded the 1st prize over numerous European competitors; since then they have exhibited at every important exposition in Europe and America. In 1882 they began the construction of pianofortes, introducing a new system of stringing which found immediate favor; of several improvements patented by them the most important is the Tension-Resonator (1902; described in the 'Scientific American,' Oct. 11, 1902), a device for preserving the tension of the sounding-board. The firm subsequently became a subsidiary of the Aeolian American Corporation and eventually of the American Piano Corp. Henry Lowell Mason, son of the founder, was president of the firm until 1929. He died in Boston, Oct. 18, 1957, at the age of 93.

Massa, Juan Bautista, Argentinian composer; b. Buenos Aires, Oct. 29, 1885; d. Rosario, March 7, 1938. He studied violin and composition; became a choral conductor; moved to Rosario, where he was active as a teacher. —Works: the operas *Zoraide* (Buenos Aires, May 15, 1909), *L'Evaso* (Rosario, June 23, 1922), *La Magdalena* (Buenos Aires, Nov. 9, 1929); 3 operettas: *Esmeralda* (1903); *Triunfo del Corazón* (1910), and *La Eterna Historia* (1911); a ballet, *El Cometa* (Buenos Aires, Nov. 8, 1932); symph. poem *La Muerte del Inca* (Buenos Aires, Oct. 15, 1932); 2 Argentine Suites for orch.; other pieces on native themes. —Cf. F. C. Lange, *Juan Bautista Massa,* in 'Boletín Latino-Americano de Música' (Dec., 1938).

Massa, Nicolò, Italian composer; b. Calice Ligure, Oct. 26, 1854; d. Genoa, Jan. 24, 1894. He studied at the Milan Cons. with Bazzini; wrote the operas *Aldo e Clarenza* (Milan, April 11, 1878), *Il Conte di Chatillon* (Reggio Emilia, Feb. 11, 1882), *Salammbò* (Milan, April 15, 1886; his most successful opera), *Eros* (posthumous; Florence, May 21, 1895); also composed an *Inno al Lavoro* (1892).

Massarani, Renzo, Italian composer; b. Mantua, March 26, 1898. He was a pupil of Respighi in Rome; active as a music critic and teacher. —Works: for the stage: *Bianco e nero,* intermezzo (Rome, 1923), *Le nozze di Tachiu* (Rome, 1927), *Povero Guerino* (Darmstadt, 1928), etc.; also violin pieces. —Cf. *Renzo Massarani,* in 'Il Pianoforte' (Dec., 1924).

Massart (măhs - săhr'), **Lambert - Joseph,** eminent violinist; b. Liège, July 19, 1811; d. Paris, Feb. 13, 1892. He was a pupil of R. Kreutzer at Paris, where he was refused admission to the Cons., as a foreigner, by Cherubini, but became so celebrated as a teacher that he was appointed professor of violin there (1843-90). Wieniawski, Marsick, Sarasate, and Teresina Tua were his pupils. His wife, **Louise-Aglaë Massart** (b. Paris, June 10, 1827; d. there, July 26, 1887), was a pianist and teacher. In 1875 she succeeded Farrenc as teacher at the Paris Cons.

Massart (măhs-săhr'), **Nestor-Henri-Joseph,** Belgian tenor; b. Ciney, Oct. 20, 1849; d. Ostend, Dec. 19, 1899. He was an officer in the Belgian army when his remarkable voice attracted the attention of the royal family, through whose influence he was granted leave of absence for study. He sang with success in Brussels, Lyons, Cairo, New Orleans, San Francisco, and Mexico. His chief roles were in *La Favorita, Lohengrin, Sigurd,* etc.

Massé (măh-sā'), **Victor** (real names **Félix-Marie**), French opera composer; b. Lorient, Morbihan, March 7, 1822; d. Paris, July 5, 1884. He was a child prodigy; was accepted at the Paris Cons. at the age of 12, and studied with Zimmerman (piano) and Halévy (composition); in 1844 he won the Grand Prix de Rome with the cantata *La Renégat de Tanger.* While in Rome, he sent home an Italian opera, *La Favorita e la schiava.* After his return, his *romances* had great vogue, and his first French opera, *La Chambre gothique* (Paris, 1849), was fairly successful. In 1866 he succeeded Leborne as prof. of counterpoint at the Paris Cons.; and in 1872 he was elected member of the Institut de France, as successor to Auber. Illness forced his retirement from all activities in 1880. His most successful light opera was *Les Noces de Jeannette* (Paris, Feb. 4, 1853); the list of his other operas, performed in Paris, includes: *La Chanteuse voilée* (Nov. 26, 1850), *Galathée* (April 14, 1852), *La Reine Topaze* (Dec. 27, 1856), *La Fiancée du Diable* (June 3, 1854), *Miss Fauvette* (Feb. 13, 1855), *Les Saisons* (Dec. 22, 1855), *Fior d'Aliza* (Feb. 5, 1866), and *Le Fils du Brigadier* (Feb. 25, 1867); his last opera *Une Nuit de Cléopatre,* was performed posthumously (April 25, 1885). —Cf. L. Delibes, *Notice sur Victor Massé* (Paris, 1885); J. G. M. Ropartz, *Victor Massé* (Paris, 1887); C. Delaborde, *Notice sur la vie et les ouvrages de Victor Massé* (Paris, 1888).

Massenet (mahss-nā'), **Jules (-Émile-Frédéric),** illustrious French composer; b. Montaud, near St.-Etienne, Loire, May 12, 1842; d. Paris, Aug. 13, 1912. At the age of 9 he was admitted to the Paris Cons.; studied with Laurent (piano), Reber (harmony), Savard and Ambroise Thomas (composition); after taking 1st prizes for piano playing and fugue (1859), he carried off the Grand Prix de Rome with the cantata *David Rizzio* (1863). In 1878 he was appointed prof. of composition at the Paris Cons., and at the same time was elected member of the Académie des Beaux-Arts;

he continued to teach at the Paris Cons. until his death; among his students were Alfred Bruneau, Gabriel Pierné, and Gustave Charpentier. As a pedagogue he exercised a profound influence on French opera, and it is only with the decisive turn towards modern music that his influence began to decline. After Gounod, Massenet was the most popular French opera composer; he possessed a natural sense of graceful melody in a distinctive French style; his best operas, *Manon, Werther, Thaïs,* etc., enjoy tremendous popularity in France, and have become favorites on opera stages all over the world; the celebrated *Meditation* for violin and orch. from *Thaïs* is a regular repertory number among violinists. —Operas: *La Grand'-Tante* (Paris, April 3, 1867); *Don César de Bazan* (Paris, Nov. 30, 1872); *Le Roi de Lahore* (Paris, April 27, 1877); *Hérodiade* (Brussels, Dec. 19, 1881); *Manon* (Paris, Jan. 19, 1884); *Le Cid* (Paris, Nov. 30, 1885); *Esclarmonde* (Paris, May 14, 1889); *Le Mage* (Paris, March 16, 1891); *Werther* (Vienna, Feb. 16, 1892); *Thaïs* (Paris, March 16, 1894); *Le Portrait de Manon* (Paris, May 8, 1894); *La Navarraise* (London, June 20, 1894); *Sapho* (Paris, Nov. 27, 1897); *Cendrillon* (Paris, May 24, 1899); *Grisélidis* (Paris, Nov. 20, 1901); *Le Jongleur de Notre-Dame* (Monte Carlo, Feb. 18, 1902); *Chérubin* (Monte Carlo, Feb. 14, 1905); *Ariane* (Paris, Oct. 31, 1906); *Thérèse* (Monte Carlo, Feb. 7, 1907); *Bacchus* (Paris, May 5, 1909); *Don Quichotte* (Monte Carlo, Feb. 19, 1910); *Roma* (Monte Carlo, Feb. 17, 1912); posthumous: *Panurge* (Paris, April 25, 1913); *Cléopatre* (Monte Carlo, Feb. 23, 1914); *Amadis* (Monte Carlo, April 1, 1922). Incidental music to *Les Érynnies* (1873); *Un Drame sous Philippe II* (1875); *Nana-Sahib* (1883); *Théodora* (1884); *Le Crocodile* (1886); *Phèdre* (1900); *Le Grillon du foyer* (1904); *Le Manteau du Roi* (1907); *Perce-Neige et les sept gnomes* (1909). Ballets: *Le Carillon* (1892); *La Cigale* (1904); *Espada* (1908). Oratorios: *Marie - Magdeleine* (1873); *Ève* (1875); *La Terre Promise* (1900). Other choral works: *Narcisse; La Vierge; Biblis.* For orch.: 7 suites: No. 1 (1865); No. 2, *Scènes hongroises* (1871); No. 3, *Scènes dramatiques* (1873); No. 4, *Scènes pittoresques* (1874); No. 5, *Scènes napolitaines* (1876); No. 6, *Scènes de Féérie* (1879); No. 7, *Scènes alsaciennes* (1881); 3 overtures: *Ouverture de Concert* (1863); *Phèdre* (1873); *Brumaire* (1899); a symph. poem, *Visions* (1890); *Parade militaire* (1887); *Devant la Madone* (1897); *Marche solennelle* (1897); *Les Rosati* (1902); *Fantaisie* for cello and orch. (1897); concerto for piano and orch. (1903). About 200 songs, 12 vocal duets; piano pieces for 2 and 4 hands. Massenet completed and orchestrated Delibes' opera *Kassya* (1893). —Bibliography: E. de Solenière, *Massenet: étude critique et documentaire* (Paris, 1897); A. Bruneau, *La Musique française* (Paris, 1901); C. Fournier, *Étude sur le style de Massenet* (Amiens, 1905); L. Aubin, *Le Drame lyrique* (Tours, 1908); L. Schneider, *Massenet: l'homme et le musicien* (Paris, 1908; the most comprehensive biography; new ed., 1926); H. T. Finck, *Massenet and His Operas* (N. Y., 1910); O. Séré, *Musiciens français d'aujourd'hui* (rev. ed. Paris, 1921); A. Soubies, *Massenet historien* (Paris, 1913); A. Pougin, *Massenet* (Paris, 1914); G. Jean-Aubry, *Un mot sur Massenet,* in *La Musique française d'aujourd'hui* (Paris, 1916); René Brancour, *Massenet* (1922; 2nd ed., 1930); J. Loisel, *Manon de Massenet* (1922); C. Bouvet, *Massenet* (Paris, 1929); J. d'Udine, *L'Art du lied et les mélodies de Massenet* (1931); A. Bruneau, *Massenet* (Paris, 1935); A. Morin, *Jules Massenet et ses opéras* (Montreal, 1944). Massenet's autobiography (completed by X. Leroux) appeared shortly after his death as *Mes souvenirs* (Paris, 1912; English transl., as *My Recollections,* Boston, 1919).

Masson (mahs-sohn'), **Paul-Marie,** eminent French musicologist; b. Sète, Hérault, Sept. 19, 1882; d. Paris, Jan. 27, 1954. He received a liberal education in Montpellier and Paris; then studied music history with Romain Rolland at the Sorbonne; received his degree with the dissertation, *La Musique mesurée à l'Antique au XVIe siècle* (1907), and obtained the Thiers stipend; subsequently enrolled in the Schola Cantorum as a pupil of Vincent d'Indy; also took lessons with Koechlin. In 1910 he was appointed prof. of the history of music at the Univ. of Grenoble, and entrusted with the organization of the 'Institut français de Florence' (under the auspices of the faculty of philosophy), with the aim of publishing complete editions of works of the early Italian masters. He was in the French Army during World War I; in 1919, director of the Institut Français in Naples. In 1931 he became prof. of music history at the Sorbonne; retired in 1952. In 1937 he was elected vice-president of the Société française de musicologie, and in 1949, its president, resigning shortly before his death. He publ. valuable books:

Lullistes et Ramistes (1912), *Musique italienne et musique française* (1912), *Berlioz* (1923), *L'Opéra de Rameau* (1930); ed. *Chants de carnaval florentins . . .* (vol. I) and 5-part madrigals by Gesualdo; contributed numerous articles to European music magazines, etc. He was also a competent composer; his works include a cantata to his own words, *Chant des peuples unis;* a *Suite Pastorale,* for wind quintet; *Marche à la Justice,* for orch. (1944); several songs and piano pieces. A 2-vol. offering, *Mélanges d'histoire et d'esthétique musicale offertes à Paul-Marie Masson* (containing a brief biographical sketch and bibliography), was presented to him by his colleagues, friends, and pupils on his retirement from the Sorbonne in 1952; publ. posthumously (Paris, 1955).

Maszkowski (mahsh-kŏhv'-skē), **Raphael,** Polish conductor; b. Lemberg, July 11, 1838; d. Breslau, March 14, 1901. He studied at the Conservatories at Vienna and Leipzig; was conductor of the 'Imthurneum' at Schaffhausen (1865); music director at Koblenz (1869). In 1890 he succeeded Bruch as conductor of the Breslau Orchestral Society.

Maszynski (măh-shin'-skē), **Piotr,** Polish choral composer; b. Warsaw, July 3, 1855; d. there, Aug. 1, 1934. He studied piano and composition at the Warsaw Cons.; taught there from 1892 till his death; also conducted a choral society. He wrote several attractive choruses, two cantatas, a violin sonata, and some 100 songs; publ. textbooks for music schools; edited instructive anthologies of vocal music.

Matchavariani, Alexey Davidovitch, Georgian composer; b. Gory, Caucasus, Sept. 23, 1913. He studied at the Cons. of Tiflis, graduating in 1936; from 1940, instructor in theory there. His music is permeated with Caucasian melorhythms, particularly folk elements of his native Georgia. —Works: symph. poems, *Mumly Muhasa* (1939), *Satchidao* (1940), *On the Death of a Hero* (1948); overture, *The People's Choice* (1950); cantata, *For Peace, for Fatherland* (1951); piano concerto (1944); violin concerto (1950); patriotic opera, *Mother and Son* (Tiflis, May 1, 1945); oratorio, *The Day of My Fatherland* (1954); many songs, of which *Blue Light* (1949) achieved great popularity in Russia; *Khorumy,* a Georgian military dance, for piano (1941; very popular); *Othello,* ballet, after Shakespeare (Tiflis, 1957).

Materna, Amalie, Austrian soprano; b. St. Georgen, Styria, July 10, 1844; d. Vienna, Jan. 18, 1918. She sang at first in churches at Graz; made her début in opera in 1864. She married an actor, Karl Friedrich, and together they sang in operettas in Vienna. In 1869 she appeared as Selika in Meyerbeer's *Africaine* and won excellent success; she remained a regular member of the Vienna Opera until her retirement in 1897. Her uncommon dramatic talent, united with a voice of great power and beauty, attracted the notice of Wagner, who selected her for the role of Brünnhilde in the first Bayreuth Festival of 1876, and that of Kundry in 1882; in 1877 she was soloist at the Wagner Festival in London, under the composer's own direction; she also sang in the Wagner festivals in N. Y., Chicago, and Cincinnati. Her American operatic début took place on Jan. 5, 1885, as Elisabeth, during the first season of German opera at the Metropolitan Opera House; in 1894 she became a member of Walter Damrosch's German company. She had few equals in Wagnerian roles. In 1902 she returned to Vienna and lived there as a teacher.

Mathews, William Smythe Babcock, American organist and writer on music; b. London, N. H., May 8, 1837; d. Denver, Col., April 1, 1912. He studied music in Boston; occupied various teaching posts in Georgia, North Carolina, Alabama, Chicago, and Denver; was organist in Chicago churches; edited the 'Musical Independent' (1868-72); was music critic of the 'Chicago Tribune' (1878-86); 1891, founded and ed. the monthly magazine 'Music.' He publ. *Outlines of Musical Form* (1867); *Emerson Organ-Method,* with L. O. Emerson (1870); *Mason's Piano Techniques,* with William Mason (1876); *How to Understand Music* (2 vols., 1880 and 1888); *100 Years of Music in America* (1889); *Popular History of Music* (1889; 2nd ed., 1906); *Pronouncing and Defining Dictionary of Music* (1896); *Music, Its Ideals and Methods* (1897); *The Masters and Their Music* (1898); *The Great in Music* (3 vols., 1900-3); etc.

Mathias (măh-tyah'), **Georges (-Amédée-Saint-Clair),** French composer; b. Paris, Oct. 14, 1826; d. there, Oct. 14, 1910. He was a pupil of Savard, Bazin, Barbereau, and Halévy (composition) at the Cons., and of Kalkbrenner and Chopin (piano). From 1862-93 he was professor of piano at the Cons., then lived in retirement as a composer. —Works: symphony, op. 22; overtures to *Hamlet* and *Mazeppa;* 2 piano concertos; 6 piano trios; 5 *morceaux symphoniques* for piano and strings; piano études (*Études de style et de mécanisme,* op. 28; *Études de genre,* op. 10); *Œuvres choisis pour le piano,* a collection of excellent original pieces for 2 and 4 hands; a lyric scene, *Jeanne d'Arc;* the choral works *Prométhée enchainé* and *Olaf;* etc.

Mathieu, Émile (-Louis-Victor), composer and pedagogue; b. Lille, France (of Belgian parentage), Oct. 16, 1844; d. Ghent, Aug. 20, 1932. He studied at the Brussels Cons. with Fétis and Auguste Dupont; taught at Louvain (1867-73); then was in Paris as theater conductor; returning to Louvain, he became director of the music school there (1881-98); in 1898 was appointed director of the Ghent Cons. In 1869, and again in 1871, he won the 2nd Grand Prix de Rome in Brussels. Among his works are the cantatas, *La dernière nuit de Faust, Le Songe de Colomb, Debout, Peuple,* and *Les Bois;* the comic operas, *L'Échange* (Liège, 1863), *Georges Dandin* (Brussels, 1877), and *La Bernoise* (Brussels, 1880); grand operas, *Richilde* (Brussels, 1888) and *L'Enfance de Roland* (1895); a violin concerto, and other instrumental works; symph. poems, *Noces féodales, Le Lac,* etc.

Mátray, Gábor, Hungarian music scholar; b. Nágykáta, Nov. 23, 1797; d. Budapest, July 17, 1875. He studied law and at the same time learned to compose. In 1812, at the age of 15, he wrote the earliest Hungarian piece of stage music, *Cserni György;* also publ. a general history of music (1828-32), the first such history in the Hungarian language; wrote treatises on folk music and Gypsy music, and made arrangements of Hungarian folksongs. His own works (for piano, guitar, and chorus) are mostly salon music, but some of them are historically important because of the use of native rhythms. —Cf. P. Varnai, *Gábor Mátray* in vol. II of 'Zenetudományi Tanulmányok' (Budapest, 1954).

Matsudaira, Yoritsune, Japanese composer; b. Tokyo, May 5, 1907. He studied composition with Komatsu and A. Tcherepnin; won the Weingartner Prize in 1937. He has experimented with adapting the 12-tone technique to Japanese popular modes. —Works: *Theme and Variations* on popular Nanby District songs, for orch. (Tokyo, Dec. 17, 1939); concerto for 2 pianos (1946); *Ancient Japanese Dance,* for orch. (Berlin, Oct. 9, 1953); *Negative and Positive Figures* (Tokyo, May 28, 1954); *Metamorphosis* on an old Japanese melody, for soprano and orch. (Festival of the International Society for Contemporary Music, Haifa, June 3, 1954); piano trio (1948); 2 string quartets (1949; 1951); 2 violin sonatas (1948; 1952); suite for flute, bassoon, and piano (1950); several song cycles; piano pieces.

Mattei, Tito, Italian pianist and composer, b. Campobasso, near Naples, May 24, 1841; d. London, March 30, 1914. He studied with Parisi, Conti, and Thalberg; made rapid progress, so that at the age of 11 he obtained a nominal appointment as 'professore' of the Accademia di Santa Cecilia in Rome; received a gold medal for playing before Pope Pius XI, and was appointed pianist to the King of Italy. About 1865 he settled in London, where he was active principally as opera conductor. He himself composed several operas, *Maria di Gand* (London, 1880), *The Grand Duke* (London, 1889), *La Prima Donna* (London, 1889); a ballet, *The Spider and the Fly* (London, 1893); also songs and piano pieces.

Matteis, Nicola, Italian violinist, who settled in London in 1672, and publ. there 4 books of violin pieces (airs, preludes, fugues, allemandes, sarabands, etc.) under varying Italian and English titles; also *The False Consonances of Musick, or, Instructions for playing a true Base upon the Guitarre, with Choice Examples and clear Directions to enable any man in a short time to play all Musicall Ayres,* etc. He was likewise the author of *A Collection of New Songs* (2 vols., London, 1696). His son, also named **Nicola** (d. 1749), lived in Vienna, and in Shrewsbury, England. He was Burney's teacher.—Cf. Paul Nettl, *An English Musician at the Court of Charles VI in Vienna,* in the 'Mus. Quarterly' (April, 1942).

Matteo da Perugia, Italian church composer; b. Perugia in the 2nd half of the 14th century; date of death unknown. He was the first maestro di cappella of the Milan Cathedral; occupied this post from 1402 to 1416. He wrote 4 Glorias in 3 parts; one Gloria in 4 parts; a number of motets and other sacred works for services at the Milan Cathedral. The 1st vol. of the 'new series' of the 'Istituzioni e monumenti dell'arte musicale italiana' (1957) is devoted to music by Matteo, ed. by F. Fano; 22 pieces are transcribed in modern notation by Willi Apel in his anthology, *French Secular Music of the Late 14th Century* (Cambridge, Mass., 1950). —Cf. F. Fano in the 'Rivista Musicale Italiana' (Jan.-March, 1953); C. Sartori, *Matteo da Perugia, e Bertrand Feragut,* in 'Acta Musicologica' (1956).

Mattfeld, Julius, American organist, librarian, and musicographer; b. New York, Aug. 8, 1893. He studied at the N. Y. German Cons. In 1910 he joined the staff of the N. Y. Public Library; resigned in 1926 to become music librarian of National Broadcasting Co. (until 1929); then was librarian of the Columbia Broadcasting System; was also organist of the Fordham Lutheran Church, N. Y. (1915-32). He publ. *The Folk Music of the Western Hemisphere* (1925), *A Hundred Years of Grand Opera in N. Y.* (1927), *Variety Music Cavalcade, 1620-1950* (N. Y., 1952); composed a ballet, *Virgins of the Sun* (N. Y., 1922), etc.

Mattfeld, Victor Henry, American organist and music editor; b. Bunceton, Mo., Sept. 1, 1917. He studied at Concordia College, River Forest, Ill.; then at the Univ. of Chicago (B. A., 1942) and at the American Cons. of Music in Chicago (M. Mus., 1946); took a course in conducting with Malko; was organist and choirmaster at Zion Lutheran Church, Chicago (1938-47); instructor at the American Cons. of Music (1945-47); from 1947 till 1956 was organist and choirmaster at various churches in N. Y. and New Haven; instructor in music history at the Yale School of Music (1952-55); in 1956, succeeded Henry Clough-Leighter as Editor-in-Chief with E. C. Schirmer Music Co., Boston.

Matthay, Tobias (Augustus), eminent English pianist and pedagogue; b. London, Feb. 19, 1858; d. High Marley, near Haslemere, Surrey, Dec. 14, 1945. He began to play the piano at the age of 6; was taught by private teachers; in 1871 he entered the Royal Academy of Music as a pupil of Dorrell (piano); won the Sterndale Bennett scholarship, and continued to study piano (with Macfarren); took courses with Sterndale Bennett, and after the latter's death (1875) completed his studies with Ebenezer Prout and Arthur Sullivan; appointed sub-professor of piano at the Royal Academy of Music in 1876; sub-professor of harmony in 1878, and full professor of piano in 1880. In that year he gave his first public recital, and for the next 15 years appeared frequently on the concert platform; but his interest in teaching gradually engrossed his attention, so that in 1895 he gave up his career as concert pianist, and established his own piano school in London. The Matthay System, as his teaching method was known, became famous not only in England, but on the Continent and in America. Students flocked to him and carried his method abroad. Matthay wrote about 100 piano pieces, a *Konzertstück* for piano and orch., a piano quartet, and some other works. His didactic publications include: *The Art of Touch* (1903); *The First Principles of Pianoforte Playing* (1905); *Relaxation Studies* (1908); *Commentaries on the Teaching of Pianoforte Technique* (1911); *The Rotation Principle* (1912); *The Child's First Steps in Piano Playing* (1912); *Musical Interpretation* (1913); *Pianist's First Music Making* (3 books); *The Nine Steps towards Finger-individualization; On Memorizing;* etc. —Cf. Jessie Henderson Matthay; *The Life and Works of Tobias Matthay* (London, 1945).

Mattheson (mah'-tĕ-zon), **Johann,** famous German composer and lexicographer; b. Hamburg, Sept. 28, 1681; d. there, April 17, 1764. A student of law, and master of several languages, he studied music under Braunmüller, Praetorius, and Kellner; at the age of 9 he sang, composed, and played the organ and harpsichord; entered the chorus at the Hamburg Opera, and later sang tenor roles, also bringing out his own operas. He befriended Handel in Hamburg, and together they made a futile journey to Lübeck in 1703, to visit Buxtehude and, possibly, apply for the position as organist to succeed him. The unwritten requirement for the gaining of that position being marriage to one of Buxtehude's daughters, Mattheson declined the opportunity. In 1704 he became tutor in the English ambassador's family; 1706, secretary of legation; later ambassador *ad interim.* In 1715 he was appointed musical director and cantor at the Hamburg Cathedral; a growing deafness obliged him to resign his directorship in 1728. Of his operas, the most important is *Cleopatra,* performed at the Hamburg Opera on Oct. 20, 1704, with Mattheson acting both as singer and conductor, in alternation, Handel taking care of the direction when Mattheson was on the stage; it was during a later performance of *Cleopatra* that a quarrel arose between Mattheson and Handel when Handel refused to give up the direction even when Mattheson was back in the pit; however, they soon were reconciled and Mattheson became Handel's first German biographer. He wrote 7 other operas, which had but little success, 24 oratorios and cantatas, a Passion, a Mass, suites for harpsichord, 12 flute sonatas with violin; etc. (88 publ. works in all; some are included in Pauer's 'Old German Composers'). His importance in music history lies in the many published treatises on various musical subjects; his most significant work was the unique biographical dictionary, *Grundlage einer Ehren-Pforte, woran der tüchtigsten Capellmeister, Componisten, Musikgelehrten, Tonkünstler etc., Leben, Werke, Verdienste, etc., erscheinen sollen* (1740; new ed. by Max Schneider, with addenda, Berlin, 1910; in this work Mattheson gives himself 31 pages, as against 8 for Handel). Other publications are: *Das neu-eröffnete Orchester, oder gründliche Anleitung, wie ein 'galant homme' einen vollkommenen Begriff von der Hoheit und Würde der edlen Musik erlangen möge* (1713); *Das beschützte Orchester* (1717); *Die exemplarische Organistenprobe* (1719; 2nd ed. as *Grosse Generalbass-Schule,* 1731); *Critica musica* (2 vols.; 1722); *Der brauchbare Virtuos* (1720); *Das forschende Orchester* (1721); *De eruditione musica* (1732); *Der vollkommene Capellmeister* (1739; facsimile reprint, Kassel, 1954); *Die neueste Untersuchung der Singspiele* (1744); *Mithridat, wider den Gift einer welschen Satyre des Salvator Rosa, genannt: 'La Musica,' übersetzt und mit Anmerkungen, etc.* (1749); *Georg Friedrich Händels Lebensbeschreibung* (1761; based almost entirely on Mainwaring's English biography of Handel, publ. in London, 1760); etc. — Cf. L. Meinardus, *Mattheson und seine Verdienste um die deutsche Tonkunst,* in Waldersee's *Sammlung musikalischer Vorträge* (Leipzig, 1879); H. Schmidt, *Johann Mattheson im Lichte seiner Werke* (Erlangen, 1897); B. C. Cannon, *Johann Mattheson, Spectator in Music* (New Haven, 1947).

Matthews, (Harvey) Alexander, organist and composer; b. Cheltenham, England, March 26, 1879. He studied with his father, John A. Matthews; after serving as church organist in Cheltenham, he went to America; settled in Philadelphia; was on the faculty of the Univ. of Pennsylvania; honorary Mus. Doc. there (1925). He retired in 1954; living in Madison, Conn. He publ. *The Introits and Graduals of the Church Year* (Philadelphia, 1924) and the successful cantata, *The Story of Christmas.* His brother, **John Sebastian Matthews** (b. Cheltenham, Dec. 11, 1870; d. Pawtucket, R. I., July 23, 1934), was also an organist; settled in the U. S. early in his career; was church organist and teacher in Philadelphia and elsewhere; publ. several anthems; organ pieces; songs.

Matthias, Hermann. See **Werrekoren.**

Matthias (or **Mattheus**) **Le Maître.** See **Le Maistre.**

Matz, Rudolf, Croatian cellist and composer; b. Zagreb, Sept. 19, 1901. He studied cello and conducting; was active in Zagreb as choral conductor and teacher of cello at the Zagreb Cons. He publ. a manual for cello (Zagreb, 1951); wrote 4 string quartets, 2 cello sonatas, a cycle of 24 songs on Croatian folk poems, etc.

Matzenauer, Margarete, famous singer; b. Temesvar, Hungary, June 1, 1881. Her father was an orch. conductor, and her mother a dramatic soprano; she grew up in favorable musical surroundings, and began to study singing at an early age, first in Graz, and then in Berlin. She made her professional début in Strasbourg in 1901, and remained on the roster of the Strasbourg Opera until 1904; then sang contralto roles at the Munich Court Opera (1904-11), specializing in Wagnerian parts; also appeared in Bayreuth. She made her American début as Amneris at the Metropolitan Opera House, N. Y., on Nov. 13, 1911, and remained one of its leading members until 1930; in the interim she accepted engagements in Germany and in South America. For many years she sang both soprano and contralto parts, but from 1914 she called herself a soprano. After a farewell concert recital in Carnegie Hall, N. Y., in 1938, she retired from the stage, and lived in Santa Monica, Calif. She was married to the Italian tenor Edoardo Ferrari-Fontana (q.v.) in 1912; divorced in 1917.

Mauduit, Jacques, French composer; b. Paris, Sept. 16, 1557; d. there, Aug. 21, 1627. He served as registrar in a Paris court, and studied music by himself, progressing so well that at the age of 24 he won the 1st prize for a motet at a competition. When the poet Antoine Baïf established in Paris the Académie Française de Musique et de Poésie (1570), Mauduit became associated with him, and made several settings of Baïf's poems (Paris, 1586; reprinted by Henry Expert in 'Les Maîtres-Musiciens de la Renaissance française'). He is reputed to have saved the musical manuscripts of Le

Jeune when the latter was arrested for his Huguenot sympathies. Mauduit's 5-part Requiem, included in Mersenne's *Harmonie Universelle,* is reprinted in R. E. Chapman's English transl. of Mersenne's books on instruments (The Hague, 1957). —Cf. G. Reese, *Music in the Renaissance* (N. Y., 1954; pp. 385-86).

Mauke (mow'-kĕh), **Wilhelm,** German composer; b. Hamburg, Feb. 25, 1867; d. Wiesbaden, Aug. 24, 1930. He first studied medicine; then turned to music; was a pupil of Huber in Basel. He then established himself as a music critic in Munich; wrote the operas *Der Taugenichts* (1905), *Fanfreluche* (1912), *Die letzte Maske* (1917), *Das Fest des Lebens* (1926); other stage works; a *Romantische Sinfonie;* an oratorio, *Die Vertreibung aus dem Paradies;* a symph. poem, *Einsamkeit,* after Nietzsche; a piano concerto; 160 songs. A list of his works was publ. by F. X. Osterrieder (Munich, 1927).—Cf. W. Nagel, *Wilhelm Mauke* (1919).

Maurel (mŏh-rĕl'), **Victor,** famous French baritone; b. Marseilles, June 17, 1848; d. New York, Oct. 22, 1923. He studied with Vauthrot and Duvernoy at the Paris Cons., winning the 1st prizes (divided with Gailhard) for vocal art and opera (1867). He made his début at the Paris Opéra in 1868 as Nevers in *Les Huguenots;* then sang for several seasons in Italy, Spain, England, and Russia; also appeared in America (1874). Returning to Paris with an established international reputation, he rejoined the Opéra (1879), remaining on the roster until 1894; he sang at the Metropolitan Opera House, in N. Y., during the season of 1894-95; from 1895 until his retirement in 1904 he was a member of the Opéra-Comique. He then devoted himself to teaching; in 1909 he settled in N. Y., where he remained until his death; he also acted as stage designer, having studied painting in his youth. His voice was not exceptional, but he used it with exquisite art; his dramatic powers were so extraordinary that he won excellent success as an actor on the French stage (1901). He created the roles of Iago in Verdi's *Otello* (Milan, Feb. 5, 1887) and Falstaff (Milan, Feb. 9, 1893); he also distinguished himself in Wagnerian parts. He publ. *Le Chant renové par la science* (1892); *Un Problème d'art* (1893): *À propos de la mise-en-scène de Don Juan* (1897); *L'Art du chant* (1897); *Dix ans de carrière* (1898). — Cf. F. Rogers, *Victor Maurel: His Career and His Art,* in the 'Mus. Quarterly' (Oct., 1926).

Maurer, Ludwig (Wilhelm), German violinist and composer; b. Potsdam, Feb. 8, 1789; d. St. Petersburg, Nov. 6, 1878. A precocious child musician, he appeared in concerts at the age of 13; at 17 he went to Russia, remaining there for 10 years, giving concerts, and serving as house musician to Russian aristocrats. From 1817 until 1832 he traveled in Europe, and was successful as a violinist in Berlin and in Paris. He was in Russia again (1832-45), then lived in Dresden, eventually returning to St. Petersburg. He produced 2 operas in Hanover: *Der neue Paris* (Jan. 27, 1826) and *Aloise* (Jan. 16, 1828); also wrote many stage pieces in Russia; with Aliabiev and Verstovsky, he contributed the music to Chmelnitsky's comedy *A Novel Prank, or Theatrical Combat* (1822). Besides, he wrote a curious quadruple concerto, *Symphonie concertante,* for 4 violins with orch. (1838); 3 violin concertos; string quartets and other chamber music. His 2 sons **Vsevolod,** a violinist, and **Alexis,** a cellist, remained in Russia.

Maurice, Alphons, German composer; b. Hamburg, April 14, 1862; d. Dresden, Jan. 27, 1905. He studied with Dessoff, Krenn, and Grädener at the Vienna Cons.; wrote the operas *Josepha, Schatz,* and *Der Wundersteg; Waldestraum,* for orch.; *Spanische Serenade,* for violin and orch.; choruses; piano pieces; songs.

Maurice, Pierre, Baron de, Swiss composer; b. Geneva, Nov. 13, 1868; d. there, Dec. 25, 1936. He attended the Cons. at Geneva, then for a short time studied at Stuttgart, finishing his musical education with Lavignac and Massenet at the Paris Cons. He lived many years in Munich; composed the operas *Die weisse Flagge* (Kassel, 1903), *Misé brun* (Stuttgart, 1908), *Lanval* (Weimar, 1912), and *Kalif Storch* (not performed); a biblical drama, *La Fille de Jephthé* (Geneva, 1899); a symph. suite, *Die Islandfischer* (after Loti); *Chanson des quatre saisons,* for piano, and other piano pieces; songs.

Mauricio, José, Portuguese composer and theorist; b. Coimbra, March 19, 1752; d. Figueira, Sept. 12, 1815. He studied theology; was maestro di cappella at Santa Cruz in Coimbra; then at Santa Cecilia in Lisbon. He wrote a great deal of church music; also some instrumental works, in close imitation of Haydn. He also publ. a *Metodo de musica* (Coimbra, 1806). —Cf. J. Vasconcellos, *Os Musicos Portugueses* (Oporto, 1870; pp. 229-48).

Maurin (mŏh-ran'), **Jean-Pierre**, French violinist; b. Avignon, Feb. 14, 1822; d. Paris, March 16, 1894. He studied violin with Abillot and Habeneck at the Paris Cons., where he succeeded Alard as teacher in 1875. He was a co-founder of the 'Société des derniers quatuors de Beethoven' in Paris.

Maus (mŏhs), **Octave**, Belgian journalist and musician; b. Brussels, June 12, 1856; d. Lausanne, Nov. 26, 1919. He studied music with Louis Brassin, and as a young man became an ardent follower of Wagner's theories. He went to Bayreuth for the inauguration of the first Wagner Festival in 1876; in 1881 was a co-founder of the weekly magazine 'L'Art Moderne' (Brussels) in which he promoted progressive ideas; in 1884 became secretary of the musical society 'XX' (dissolved in 1893); in 1894 he organized in Brussels a concert group, 'Libre Esthétique,' which presented a number of chamber concerts of modern works; at the outbreak of World War I in 1914 the concerts had to be discontinued; Maus went to Switzerland, and organized an orchestra of Belgian and French musicians interned there, which he himself conducted. In the last years of his life he lived in Lausanne. He played an important role in the musical life of Belgium during the period from 1881 to 1914. His wife, Madeleine Maus, described these years in a memoir, *Trente années de lutte pour art* (Brussels, 1926). See the exhaustive monograph, *Octave Maus et la vie musicale belge,* by Albert Van Der Linden (Brussels, 1950; contains 55 letters from Vincent d'Indy to Maus).

Maxson, Frederick, American organist and composer; b. Beverly, N. J., June 13, 1862; d. Philadelphia, Jan. 21, 1934. He studied with Guilmant in Paris; for many years played organ in Philadelphia churches; was a successful teacher; publ. organ pieces, anthems, and songs.

May, Edward Collett, celebrated English organist and singing-teacher; b. Greenwich, Oct. 29, 1806; d. London, Jan. 2, 1887. He studied with C. Potter and Crivelli; was organist of Greenwich Hospital (1837-69); prof. of vocal music at Queen's College, London. A disciple of Hullah, he taught in numerous schools and private classes, doing much to popularize singing among the masses; publ. *Progressive Vocal Exercises for Daily Practice* (1853); songs.

May, Florence, English pianist and writer; daughter of Edward Collett May; b. London, Feb. 6, 1845; d. there, June 29, 1923. She studied music with her father and with an uncle, Oliver May; began a promising career as a pianist in London; in 1871 went to Germany; took lessons with Clara Schumann in Baden-Baden; there she made the acquaintance of Brahms, who gave her some lessons. She became his enthusiastic admirer; upon her return to England, she started a vigorous campaign for performances of the music of Brahms; she herself gave many first performances of his piano music in London. The important result of her dedication to Brahms was her comprehensive work, *The Life of Johannes Brahms* (2 vols., London, 1905; revised ed., publ. posthumously, 1948); she also publ. *The Girlhood of Clara Schumann* (London, 1912).

Maybrick, Michael (pseudonym, Stephen Adams), English baritone and composer; b. Liverpool, Jan. 31, 1844; d. Buxton, Aug. 25, 1913. He studied at the Leipzig Cons. with Plaidy, Moscheles, and Richter (1866-68), and was a vocal pupil of Nava at Milan. He sang at the principal concerts in London and the provinces, and toured the U. S. and Canada in 1884. Many of his songs (sung by himself) had great vogue (e.g., *Nancy Lee).* His hymn *The Holy City* is still sung in churches in England and America.

Mayer, Charles, German pianist and composer; b. Königsberg, March 21, 1799; d. Dresden, July 2, 1862. He was taken to Russia as a child; was taught by John Field, who was in Russia at the time; lived in Moscow until Napoleon's invasion in 1812; then went to St. Petersburg, and in 1814 to Paris. He returned to Russia in 1819, and formed a large class of pupils in St. Petersburg; in 1845 he made a tour of Scandinavia and Germany; in 1850 he settled in Dresden. He publ. an enormous number of piano pieces, in salon style; one of his mazurkas was once misattributed to Chopin.

Mayer, Frederick Christian, American organist; b. Columbus, Ohio, March 4, 1882. He studied at the Cincinnati Cons. of Music (graduated in 1905); then at the Stern Cons. of Berlin, and at the Cons. of Fontainebleau. Returning to America, he taught at the Cincinnati Cons. of Music and at the National Cons., N. Y. In 1911 he was appointed organist and choirmaster of Cadet Chapel, West Point Military Academy; by exception, was permitted to carry on after the retirement age of 70; resigned finally in 1954. He particularly distinguished himself as carillon architect; inspected and supervised important carillons in the U. S., Canada, and Belgium.

Mayer, Joseph Anton, German composer and pedagogue; b. Pfullendorf, Baden, Dec. 5, 1855; d. Stuttgart, Dec. 3, 1936. He studied at the Stuttgart Cons., and later in Berlin with Bargiel; then taught at the Stuttgart Cons. He wrote the operas *Der Stern von Bethlehem* and *Magdelenenbrunnen;* the choral works with orch. *Der Geiger von Gmünd, Jephtha, Würde der Frauen,* etc.; also piano pieces and songs.

Mayer, Max, pianist and pedagogue; b. Hamburg, May 31, 1859; d. Manchester, England, Oct. 26, 1931. He studied with local teachers; then with Seyfriz in Stuttgart, and finally with Liszt in Weimar. In 1883 he settled in Manchester; appeared frequently in chamber music concerts, and as accompanist in his own songs, which were first introduced by Muriel Foster. From 1908 he taught at the Royal College of Music in Manchester.

Mayer, Wilhelm (pseudonym, W. A. Rémy), pianist and pedagogue; b. Prague, June 10, 1831; d. Graz, Jan. 22, 1898. He studied with C. F. Pietsch; also took a course in law; *Dr. jur.* (1856). In 1862 he became conductor of the Graz Musical Society, resigning in 1870 to apply himself to pedagogy; he taught both piano and composition, and achieved great renown; among his pupils were Busoni, Kienzl, Reznicek, and Weingartner.

Mayer-Mahr, Moritz, pianist and teacher; b. Mannheim, Jan. 7, 1869; d. Göteborg, Sweden, July 30, 1947. After a course of study in Mannheim, he went to Berlin; in 1892, appointed prof. of piano at the Klindworth-Scharwenka Cons. In 1933 he left Germany and settled in Sweden, remaining there until his death. He publ. *Die Technik des Klavierspiels* (3 vols.) and *Der musikalische Klavier-Unterricht;* edited the studies of Czerny and Heller.

Mayer-Reinach, Albert, German musicologist; b. Mannheim, April 2, 1876. He studied in Munich and Berlin; received his *Dr. phil.* with the dissertation *K. H. Graun als Opernkomponist* (Berlin, 1899); was lecturer on music at the Univ. of Kiel (1904-30); conducted various choral societies; edited 2 vols. of works by early Königsberg composers; publ. valuable papers on German operas, etc. In 1933 he went to Sweden; in 1936 became director of a music school in Örebro.

Mayer-Serra, Otto, eminent musicologist; b. Barcelona, Spain, July 12, 1904, of German-Catalan parentage. He studied in Germany with H. Abert, Curt Sachs, J. Wolf, and E. von Hornbostel. He returned to Spain in 1933, and was music critic of the Catalan weekly, 'Mirador.' In 1936, at the outbreak of the Spanish Civil War, he was appointed head of the music division of the propaganda ministry of the Catalan Government; served in the Loyalist Army in 1938-39; after its defeat, he fled to France. In 1940 he reached Mexico, where he became active as writer, editor, lecturer, and manager. He publ. *El Romanticismo Musical* (Mexico, 1940); *Panorama de la Música Mexicana* (Mexico, 1941); *Panorama de la Música Hispano-americana* (Mexico, 1944); *Música y Músicos de Latino-América* (of fundamental importance; contains detailed biographies of Latin American musicians and descriptions of folksongs; 2 vols.; Mexico, 1947). In 1954 he founded a monthly magazine on recordings, 'Audio y Música.'

Maykapar (mī-kah-pahr'), **Samuil Moysseyevitch,** Russian pianist, composer, and teacher; b. Taganrog, Dec. 18, 1867; d. Leningrad, May 8, 1938. He studied at the St. Petersburg Cons. with B. Cesi (piano) and Soloviev (theory); then in Vienna with Leschetizky; gave concerts in Germany (1903-10). From 1910 to 1930 he was prof. at the St. Petersburg Cons. He composed almost exclusively for piano; was particularly successful in miniature forms. His piano works include: *Biriulki* (a suite of 26 pieces); 24 Miniatures; *The Marionette Theater* (an album of 7 pieces); 2 sonatinas; etc.; also piano studies and special exercises (for pedaling, for wrist actions, etc.). He publ. the books *The Musical Ear* (Moscow, 1900) and *The Years of Study and of Musical Activity* (partly autobiographical; Moscow, 1938).

Maylath (mī'-lăht), **Heinrich,** pianist and pedagogue; b. Vienna, Dec. 4, 1827; d. New York, Dec. 31, 1883. He was a pupil of his father; traveled as a concert pianist in Europe, including Russia. In 1867 he settled in America, and became a teacher in N. Y. He publ. some excellent instructive piano music, as well as concert pieces; made numerous transcriptions of various works for piano.

Maynor, Dorothy, Negro soprano; b. Norfolk, Va., Sept. 3, 1910. Her father was a Methodist minister, and she received her first musical training in the choir of his church; at 14 she entered Hampton Institute and later toured Europe with the Institute's famous Negro chorus. After graduation from Hampton she studied at Westminster Choir College, Princeton, N. J., and later privately in N. Y. In 1939 she had an audition with Koussevitzky, who was greatly impressed by her voice and engaged her to sing at the Berkshire Festival (Aug. 8, 1939). Her New York début took place at Town Hall, Nov. 19, 1939, and she later sang throughout the country.

Mayr (mīr), **Richard,** Austrian bass singer; b. Henndorf, near Salzburg, Nov. 18, 1877; d. Vienna, Dec. 1, 1935. He was a student of medicine in Vienna. At the age of 21, he enrolled in the Vienna Cons.; studied voice, and in 1902 made his operatic début at Bayreuth as Hagen. He was then engaged by Gustav Mahler at the Vienna Opera, of which he remained a member until his death. He made his American début on Nov. 2, 1927, with the Metropolitan Opera Company as Pogner. He possessed a rich and powerful voice, equally suited for tragic and comic parts; was particularly distinguished as Wotan; his performance of Baron Ochs in *Der Rosenkavalier* was also notable. —Cf. H. J. Holz, *Richard Mayr* (Vienna, 1923); Otto Kunz, *Richard Mayr* (Vienna, 1933).

Mayr (mīr), **(Johann) Simon,** outstanding composer of operas; b. Mendorf, Bavaria, June 14, 1763; d. Bergamo, Dec. 2, 1845. He was of Italian parentage; was educated at the Jesuit Seminary at Ingolstadt; went to Bergamo, where he studied with Lenzi; then to Venice, where he took lessons with Bertoni. He began his career as a composer of oratorios; several of these (*Jacob a Labano fugiens, David, Tobiae matrimonium, Sisera*) were successfully presented in Vienna. Piccinni encouraged him to write operas, and Mayr produced his 1st stage work, *Saffo, ossia I riti d'Apollo Leucadio,* in Venice with excellent success (1794). After that he wrote one opera after another for 30 years, bringing out about 60 works in all; they held the Italian stage until the success of Rossini's operatic style put Mayr's operas in the shade. Mayr possessed a fine talent for melody of the Italian type; his harmonization and orchestration followed the German model, somewhat in the tradition of Jommelli. In 1802 Mayr was appointed maestro di cappella at Santa Maria Maggiore, Bergamo, and, on the foundation of the Musical Institute there in 1805, was made its director. His most eminent pupil was Donizetti. He also founded 2 institutions for disabled musicians. After 1816 he wrote much church music; he became blind towards the end of his life.—Operas: *Lodoiska* (Venice, Jan. 26, 1796); *Che originali* (Venice, Oct. 18, 1798); *Adelaide di Guesclino* (Venice, May 1, 1799); *Il Carretto del venditore d'aceto* (Venice, June 28, 1800); *Ginevra di Scozia* (Trieste, April 21, 1801); *I Misteri eleusine* (Milan, Jan. 16, 1802); *Alonso e Cora* (Milan, Dec. 26, 1803); *Elisa* (Venice, July 5, 1804); *Adelasia e Aleramo* (Milan, Dec. 26, 1806); *La Rosa rossa e la rosa bianca* (Genoa, Feb. 21, 1813); *Medea in Corinto* (Naples, Nov. 28, 1813). He also publ. a commemorative book on Haydn, *Breve notizie istoriche della vita e delle opere di Giuseppe Haydn* (1809); compiled theoretical works, which remained in MS. His *Biografie di scrittori ed artisti musicali bergamaschi nativi ed oriundi* was ed. by A. Alessandri (Bergamo, 1875). —Cf. F. Alborghetti and M. Galli, *Gaetano Donizetti e G. Simone Mayr, notizie e documenti* (Bergamo, 1875); C. Schmidl, *Cenni biografici su G. S. Mayr* (Trieste, 1901); C. G. Scotti, *S. Mayr* (Bergamo, 1903); H. Kretzschmar, *Die musikgeschichtliche Bedeutung S. Mayrs* (Leipzig, 1904); L. Schiedermair, *Beiträge zur Geschichte der Oper um die Wende des 18. und 19. Jahrhunderts: Simon Mayr* (2 vols.; Leipzig, 1907 and 1910).

Mayseder, Joseph, Austrian violinist and composer; b. Vienna, Oct. 26, 1789; d. there, Nov. 21, 1863. He was a pupil of Suche and Wranitzky (violin); and of E. Förster (piano and composition). He joined the famous Schuppanzigh Quartet as 2nd violin; entered the court orch. in 1816; became solo violinist at the court opera in 1820, and chamber violinist to the Emperor in 1835. He never went on tours, and rarely gave concerts; yet he was a finished virtuoso, admired even by Paganini. In Vienna he was very successful as a teacher. His works include several violin concertos, 5 string quintets and 8 string quartets, trios, and solo violin pieces, all effectively written and pleasingly harmonized. About 60 of his pieces have been published.

Mayuzumi, Toshiro, Japanese composer; b. Yokohama, Feb. 20, 1929; studied at the Musical College in Tokyo.—Works: violin sonata (1946); *Divertimento* for 10 instruments (1948); *Symphonic Mood,* for orch. (1950); *Sphenogramme,* for contralto, flute, saxophone, marimba, violin, cello, and piano (Frankfurt Festival of the International Society for Contemporary Music, June 25, 1951); *Mikrokosmos,* for 7 instruments (Modern Music Festival, Karuizawa, Japan, Aug. 12, 1957).

Mazas, Jacques-Féréol, French violinist; b. Béziers, Sept. 23, 1782; d. Bordeaux, Aug. 26, 1849. He was a pupil of Baillot at the Paris Cons., winning 1st prize as violinist (1805); then played in the orch. of the Italian Opera in Paris; toured Europe (1811-29); then was a teacher in Orléans, and director of a music school in Cambrai (1837-41). He spent the last years of his life in Bordeaux. He wrote a method for violin (new ed. by J. Hřímalý) and numerous valuable studies; also a method for viola; concertos, string quartets, trios, violin duets, fantasias, variations, *romances,* etc.; also 3 operas, one of which, *Le Kiosque,* was performed at Paris in 1842. A set of 6 études was publ. in a new ed. by Hubay.

Mazzinghi (măh-tsin'-gē), **Joseph,** pianist and composer; b. London, Dec. 25, 1765; d. Downside, near Bath, Jan. 15, 1844. He was the son of Thomas Mazzinghi, of Corsican extraction, who made his home in England. Joseph Mazzinghi studied with John Christian Bach in London; he was a mere child when his father died, and he succeeded him as organist of the Portuguese Chapel. He subsequently took lessons with Anfossi and Sacchini. He wrote 2 Italian operas for the King's Theatre: *La Bella Arsena* (1795) and *Il Tesoro* (1796), and a number of light stage works to English texts: *A Day in Turkey* (1791), *The Turnpike Gate* (1799), *The Wife of Two Husbands* (1803). He also wrote a large number of arias, glees, and songs; one of them, *Tell Me Shepherds,* attained great popularity.

Mazzocchi (măh - tsŏh' - kē), **Domenico,** Italian composer; b. Veja, near Cività Castellana, Nov. 8, 1592; d. Rome, Jan. 20, 1665. A learned Roman lawyer, he studied music with Nanini; publ. a book, *Madrigali a 5 voci in partitura* (1638), in which appear, for the 1st time, the conventional symbols for crescendo < and descrescendo >, piano (*p*), *forte* (*f*), and *trillo* (*tr*), which he explains in a preface. He also composed the operas *La Catena d'Adone* (Rome, 1626) and *L'Innocenza difesa,* several oratorios, and various pieces of church music.

Mazzocchi (măh-tsŏh'-kē), **Virgilio,** Italian composer, brother of Domenico Mazzocchi; b. Veja, July 22, 1597; d. there, Oct. 3, 1646. He was chorusmaster at St. Peter's from 1629 until his death. With M. Marazzoli he composed the 1st comic opera, *Chi soffre, speri* (Rome, Feb. 27, 1639). Excerpts from this opera were publ. by H. Goldschmidt (1901); an *Argomento et allegoria* relating to it was publ. at the time of the 1st performance (a copy is in the Library of Congress, Washington). —Cf. H. Prunières, *L'Opéra italien en France avant Lulli* (Paris, 1913); A. Salza, *Mazzocchi,* in the 'Rivista Musicale Italiana' (1917); A. Cardinali, *Cenni biografici su Domenico e Virgilio Mazzocchi* (1926).

Mazzolani (măh - tsŏh - lăh'- nē), **Antonio,** Italian composer; b. Ruina, near Ferrara, Dec. 26, 1819; d. Ferrara, Jan. 25, 1900. He studied with Zagagnoni (composition) and Lodi (piano); wrote the operas *Gismonda* (Ferrara, May 17, 1854) and *Enrico Charlis* (Ferrara, Nov. 25, 1876); his choruses, with extensive soli, were very popular in Italy during his time.

Mazzoleni (măh-tsŏh-lĕh'-nē), **Ettore,** conductor and composer, of Italian and Swiss extraction; b. Brusio, Switzerland, June 18, 1905. He studied music in Oxford and London; in 1929 he was appointed teacher at Upper Canada College, Toronto; later became a member of the faculty of the Toronto Cons., and conducted concerts there; also appeared as guest conductor in other Canadian towns. He has made several transcriptions of folksongs for various instrumental and vocal groups.

Mazzucato (măh-tsoo-kăh'-toh), **Alberto,** Italian violinist, composer, and writer on music; b. Udine, July 28, 1813; d. Milan, Dec. 31, 1877. He first studied mathematics; then turned to music, his teacher being Bresciano in Padua, where his 1st opera *La Fidanzata di Lammermoor* was given (Feb. 24, 1834); he wrote 6 more operas: *Don Chisciotte* (Milan, April 26, 1836), *Esmeralda* (Mantua, Feb. 10, 1838; his most successful stage work), *I Corsari* (Milan, Feb. 15, 1840), *I Due Sergenti* (Milan, Feb. 27, 1841), *Luigi V* (Milan, Feb. 25, 1843), and *Hernani* (Genoa, Dec. 26, 1843); however, Verdi's ascendance soon put him into the shade. From 1859 till 1869 he was concertmaster in the orch. of La Scala, Milan; for several years was editor of the influential 'Gazzetta Musicale'; publ. a *Trattato d'estetica musicale.*

McArthur, Edwin, American pianist and conductor; b. Denver, Sept. 24, 1907. He studied with local teachers, and later with Rosina Lhevinne in N. Y.; became a successful accompanist, traveling with Jeritza, Pinza, Flagstad, and other celebrated singers. In 1938 he made his début as conductor with the Chicago City Opera Co.; in 1939 he conducted the San Francisco Opera; then was director of the St. Louis Municipal Opera (1945-50). In 1950 he was appointed conductor of the Harrisburg, Penna., Symphony Orchestra.

McBride, Robert Guyn, American composer; b. Tucson, Arizona, Feb. 20, 1911. He learned to play the clarinet and the saxophone, and performed in dance bands; he then entered the Univ. of Arizona (M. A., 1935). He studied composition with Otto Luening. From 1935-46 he taught at Bennington College; in 1937 he had a Guggenheim Fellowship. He toured in South and Central America in 1941 as clarinetist in a chamber music group. His compositions are mostly of a programmatic nature, often on American themes with jazz material.—Works: *Mexican Rhapsody* for orch. (1934); piano quintet (1934); *Fugato on a Well-Known Theme,* for orch. (Tucson, May 7, 1935); *Prelude to a Tragedy* (N. Y., Nov. 20, 1935); *Workout* for oboe and piano (1936); oboe quintet (1937); ballet, *Show Piece* (N. Y., Dec. 12, 1937); *Swing Stuff,* for clarinet and piano (1938); *Jam Session,* for woodwind quintet (1941); *Punch and Judy,* ballet (1941); *Stuff in G* for orch. (1942); *Side Show* for orch. (1944); *Popover* for clarinet and piano (1945; also for orch.); *Sherlock Holmes,* suite for military band (1945); violin concerto (1954). His early violin sonata (1934) is subtitled *Depression.*

McClellan, John Jasper, American organist and conductor; b. Payson, Utah, April 20, 1874; d. Salt Lake City, Aug. 2, 1925. He studied piano with A. Jonás, organ with A. A. Stanley, and composition with J. E. Schmaal. In 1900 he became organist at the Mormon Tabernacle at Salt Lake City; made a transcontinental tour with its choir. In 1905 he founded the Salt Lake City Symph. Orch., and conducted it until 1910; Bachelor of Didactics, Mormon Church; composed an *Ode to Irrigation;* organ pieces; numerous anthems.

McCorkle, Donald Macomber, American musicologist; b. Cleveland, Feb. 20, 1929. He studied clarinet, and took courses in musicology at Indiana Univ. with Willi Apel and Paul Nettl; was granted a Ph. D. degree there (1958). In 1954 he was appointed assistant prof. of musicology at Salem College, Winston-Salem, N. C.; received a special grant for study of early American music; simultaneously appointed music editor of the Moravian Church in America; since 1956, executive director of the Moravian Music Foundation. He has contributed articles to historical and musical magazines, especially on subjects dealing with early music in America and has publ. eds. of such music.

McCormack, John, famous tenor; b. Athlone, Ireland, June 14, 1884; d. near Dublin, Sept. 16, 1945. Without previous training he took part in the National Irish Festival at Dublin in 1902, and carried off the gold medal; in 1903 he became a member of the Dublin Cathedral Choir and began to study seriously with the organist and choirmaster, Vincent O'Brien; he made his début as a concert singer at a concert of the Sunday League in London (Feb. 17, 1907) and his operatic début as Turiddu in *Cavalleria Rusticana* at Covent Garden (Oct. 5, 1907), becoming instantly a prime favorite; in 1909 he sang at the San Carlo in Naples, and in the fall was engaged by Hammerstein for the Manhattan Opera House in N. Y., where he made his American début on Nov. 10, 1909, as Alfred Germont in *La Traviata;* during the 1910-11 season he was with the Boston Opera Co.; 1912-14, with Chicago Opera Co.; after that, he appeared seldom in opera, but became tremendously successful as a concert tenor. He was naturalized as an American citizen in 1919; was given the title of Count by Pope Pius XI in 1928, and named Papal Chamberlain. —Cf. L. A. G. Strong, *John McCormack* (London, 1941; reprint, 1949); Lily McCormack (his widow), *I Hear You Calling Me* (Milwaukee, 1949); L. F. X. McDermott Roe, *John McCormack, the Complete Discography* (London, 1956).

McCoy, William J., American composer; b. Crestline, Ohio, March 15, 1848; d. Oakland, Calif., Oct. 15, 1926. His family moved to California when he was a child; he began to compose at the age of 12; then was sent to N. Y. to study with William Mason; later studied at the Leipzig Cons. with Reinecke and Hauptmann. His symphony in F was conducted in Leipzig by Reinecke in 1872. He returned to California and wrote some theater music for the Bohemian Club there (*Hamadryads,*

The Cave Man, etc.); also wrote an opera, *Egypt* (2 acts presented at the Berkeley Music Festival, Sept. 17, 1921), for which he received the Bispham Medal of the American Opera Society of Chicago; *Yosemite,* overture; violin concerto; a suite from *A Masque of Apollo (Prelude, Dance,* and *The Naiad's Idyl)*; numerous songs, and a textbook, *Cumulative Harmony.* —Cf. E. E. Hipsher, *American Opera and Its Composers* (Philadelphia,1934; pp. 317-20).

McDonald, Harl, American composer; b. near Boulder, Colo., July 27, 1899; d. Princeton, N. J., March 30, 1955. He studied at the Univ. of Southern California (Mus. Bac.) and at Redlands Univ. (Mus. Doc.); also at the Leipzig Cons. He began to compose at an early age; became a professional pianist; toured in the U. S. as accompanist to various artists; appeared as soloist in his own piano concerto; taught at the Music Academy of Philadelphia and at the Univ. of Pennsylvania; was guest conductor with the Philadelphia Orch. and in Europe; was engaged in research work in the measurement of instrumental and vocal tone, recording and transmission of tone, new scale divisions, etc., under a Rockefeller grant (1930-33); publ. the results of his investigation in a book, *New Methods of Measuring Sound* (Franklin Institute, Philadelphia, 1935). In 1939 he was appointed business manager of the Philadelphia Orchestra, but continued to compose, lecture, and conduct also. Most of his works were performed for the first time by the Philadelphia Orchestra, under Stokowski and Ormandy, among them his 4 symphonies: No. 1, *The Santa Fé Trail* (Nov. 16, 1934), No. 2, *The Rhumba Symph.* (Oct. 4, 1935), No. 3, *Lamentations of Fu Hsuan,* for orch., chorus, and soprano solo (Jan. 3, 1936), No. 4, (April 8, 1938); *Festival of the Workers* (April 26, 1934); *3 Poems on Traditional Aramaic Themes* (Dec. 18, 1936); concerto for 2 pianos and orch. (April 2, 1937); violin concerto (March 16, 1945); *Saga of the Mississippi* (April 9, 1948); *From Childhood,* suite for harp and orch. (Jan. 17, 1941). Other orchestral works: 2 nocturnes for orch., *San Juan Capistrano* (Boston Symph., Oct. 30, 1939); *Arkansas Traveler,* a humoresque (Detroit, March 3, 1940); *Bataan,* a tone poem (Washington, July 3, 1942). Chamber music: 2 piano trios (1931; 1932); Fantasy for string quartet (1932); Quartet on Negro Themes (1933); many choral works. —Cf. Madeleine Goss, *Modern Music-Makers* (N. Y., 1952; pp. 303-13).

McEwen (m'c-u-en), Sir **John Blackwood,** Scottish composer and pedagogue; b. Hawick, April 13, 1868; d. London, June 14, 1948. He studied at Glasgow Univ. (M.A., 1888) and at the Royal College of Music in London, with Corder, Matthay, and Prout; taught piano in Glasgow (1895-98) and composition at the Royal College of Music in London (1898-1936); in 1924 he succeeded Alexander MacKenzie as director. He was knighted in 1931. He continued to compose until his last years; his works include several symphonies, of which one subtitled *Solway* (1911) was the best known; 4 orch. suites (1893-1941); *7 Bagatelles* for strings; a viola concerto (1901); 17 string quartets (1893-1947); 6 violin sonatas (1913-29); a viola sonata (1930); *Scottish Rhapsody* for violin and piano (1915); piano pieces; songs. He publ. *Text-Book of Harmony and Counterpoint* (1908); *The Elements of Music* (1910); *A Primer of Harmony* (1911); *The Thought in Music* (1912); *Tempo Rubato* (1928); *Introduction to the Piano Sonatas of Beethoven* (1931).—See S. Dyke's article on McEwen's string quartets in Cobbett's 'Cyclopedic Survey of Chamber Music' (London, 1930; vol. 2, pp. 105-08).

McGill, Josephine, composer and collector of American folksongs; b. Louisville, Ky., Oct. 20, 1877; d. there, Feb. 24, 1919. She studied with Alexander Lambert at the New York College of Music; collected material for and publ. *Folk Songs of the Kentucky Mountains* (1917, 1922, 1926, and 1937), and contributed the following articles to the 'Mus. Quarterly': *Music in a Mountain Land* (July, 1917), *Old Ballad Burthens* (April, 1918), *A Quaint Musical Survival: The 12 Apostles* (April, 1930); also papers on Kentucky folksongs to other magazines (several publ. posthumously).

McKay, George Frederick, American composer; b. Harrington, Wash., June 11, 1899. He studied at the Univ. of Washington, Seattle, and subsequently at the Eastman School of Music in Rochester, with Palmgren and Sinding; graduated in 1923. In 1941 he was appointed to the faculty of the Univ. of Washington. —Works: 4 sinfoniettas (1925-42); *Fantasy on a Western Folk Song* (Rochester, May 3, 1933); *Bravura Prelude,* for brass ensemble (Rochester, April 30, 1939); *To a Liberator,* symph. poem (Indianapolis, March 15, 1940); *Introspective Poem,* for strings (Philadelphia, April 3, 1941); *A Prairie Portrait* (San Francisco, Sept. 4, 1941);

Pioneer Epic (Oakland, Feb. 17, 1942); wind quintet (1930); piano trio (1931); a quintet, subtitled *American Street Scenes,* for clarinet, trumpet, saxophone, bassoon, and piano (1935); 2 organ sonatas; violin concerto (1940); cello concerto (1942); a suite on Negro folksongs for strings, entitled *Port Royal, 1861* (1939).

McKinley, Carl, American composer and organist; b. Yarmouth, Maine, Oct. 9, 1895. He studied at Knox College and Cons., and at Harvard Univ. with Hill and Nadia Boulanger; won the Boott Prize (Harvard, 1916), a Naumburg Traveling Fellowship (1917), the Flagler Prize of the N. Y. Symph. Society (1921), and 2 Guggenheim Fellowships (1927-29); 1928-29 was stage assistant at the Munich Opera; returning to the U. S. in 1929, he was appointed instructor of organ, composition, and history of music at the New England Cons., Boston. —Works: *Indian Summer Idyl,* for orch. (Boston, May 11, 1917); *The Blue Flower,* symph. poem (won the Flagler Prize; N. Y. Philharmonic, Jan. 18, 1924); *Masquerade,* an American rhapsody for orch. (his most popular work; Chicago Symph. Orch., at the Chicago North Shore Festival, May 29, 1926); *Chorale, Variations and Fugue,* for orch. (Rochester, Oct. 29, 1941); *Caribbean Holiday* (Boston, Nov. 18, 1948); *The Kid,* a cantata (Galesburg, Ill., April 24, 1955); string quartet (1941); cello sonata (1953); organ pieces; songs.

McNaught, William (Gray), English music journalist and editor; b. London, March 30, 1849; d. there, Oct. 13, 1918. He studied at the Royal Academy of Music; was active as a choral conductor; in 1892 began to edit the 'School Music Review' publ. by Novello; in 1909 became editor of the 'Mus. Times.' His son, also named **William McNaught** (b. London, Sept. 1, 1883; d. there, June 9, 1953), was assistant editor of the 'Mus. Times' when his father was editor; wrote program notes and reviews for many years; in 1944 he became editor of the 'Mus. Times,' succeeding Harvey Grace. He publ. *A Short Account of Modern Music and Musicians* (London, 1937).

McPhee, Colin, outstanding modern composer; b. Montreal, Canada, March 15, 1901. He studied composition at the Peabody Cons. with Gustav Strube, graduating in 1921; returned to Canada to study piano with Arthur Friedheim in Toronto; played his own concerto with the Toronto Symph. Orch. (1924). He then went to Paris, where he took a course in advanced composition with Paul Le Flem, and piano with Isidor Philipp. Returning to America in 1926, he joined the modern movement in N. Y.; wrote a concerto for piano and wind octet (Boston, March 11, 1929), a *Sea Shanty Suite,* for male chorus, 2 pianos, and drums; also the scores for the experimental films *H_2O* and *Mechanical Principles.* In 1934 he went to the island of Bali, where he made an extensive investigation of native music and instruments; in 1936 he was in Mexico, where he wrote his major work *Tabuh-Tabuhan,* for 2 pianos and orch., which Carlos Chávez performed with the National Orch. of Mexico City; he then returned to Bali, where he remained until 1939. He publ. a book, *A House in Bali* (N. Y., 1946), in which he gave a detailed description of his sojourn there. Other works include *Transitions,* for orch.; Symphony No. 2 (Louisville, Jan. 15, 1958; commissioned by the Louisville Orch.); *4 Iroquois Dances,* for orch.; *Invention and Kinesis* for piano; a set for 2 pianos, *Balinese Ceremonial Music* (1. *Pemoenghah.* 2. *Gambangan.* 3. *Taboeh Teloe).*

Meader, George, American tenor; b. Minneapolis, July 6, 1888. He studied law at the Univ. of Minnesota; after graduation (1908) he went to Germany, where he studied voice with Anna Schoen-René; he remained in Germany as member of the Stuttgart Opera (1911-19). Returning to America in 1919, he gave recitals before making his début with the Metropolitan Opera as Victorin in Korngold's opera *Die tote Stadt* (Nov. 19, 1921); continued his concerts in Europe; in 1931 he resigned from the Metropolitan Opera and became a successful singer in light opera; was particularly successful in Jerome Kern's *Cat and the Fiddle.*

Meck, Nadezhda Filaretovna von, friend and benefactress of Tchaikovsky; b. Znamenskoye, near Smolensk, Feb. 10, 1831; d. Wiesbaden, Jan. 13, 1894. She became interested in Tchaikovsky's music through Nicholas Rubinstein, director of the Moscow Cons., of which she was a patroness. At first offering Tchaikovsky commissions, she later granted him a yearly allowance of 6000 rubles in order that he might compose undisturbed by financial considerations. He lived for long periods in close proximity to her, at Brailov (near Kiev) and in Florence, Italy; but although they carried on an extensive and intimate correspondence (publ. in 3 vols., Moscow, 1934-

36), they never met face to face. Tchaikovsky's allowance was abruptly cut off in 1890, on the pretext of financial difficulties, leading to a complete break between him and Mme. von Meck in 1891. She also employed the youthful Debussy as pianist in her household (1880-82). —Cf. Barbara von Meck and Catherine Bowen, *Beloved Friend* (biographical romance; N. Y., 1937); Olga Bennigson, *More Tchaikovsky-von Meck Correspondence,* in the 'Mus. Quarterly' (April, 1938). See also the bibliography under Tchaikovsky.

Medinš (meh'-dinsh), **Jānis,** foremost Latvian composer; b. Riga, Oct. 9, 1890; was a pupil at the music school there; 1904-13, orch. player; 1914-16, head of the piano department of the firm of A. Diederichs in St. Petersburg; 1916-20, military bandmaster there. In 1920 he returned to Riga; conducted opera at the Latvian National Theater; also was prof. at the Riga Cons. In 1944, as the Soviet armies approached Latvia, Medinš went to Stockholm. He wrote the operas *Uguns un Nakts* (*Fire and Night;* Riga, May 26, 1921) and *Deevi un Cilveki* (Riga, May 23, 1922); symph. and chamber music; choruses.

Medtner, Nikolai Karlovitch, notable Russian composer; b. (of German parents) Moscow, Jan. 5, 1880; d. London, Nov. 13, 1951. He first studied with his uncle Theodore Goedicke; in 1892 entered Moscow Cons., where he took courses with Sapelnikov and Safonov (piano), and with Taneyev (composition); graduated in 1900, winning the gold medal; in the same year he won the Rubinstein prize in Vienna; for the next 2 years he appeared with much success as a pianist in the European capitals; returning to Russia, he taught at the Moscow Cons. for one academic year (1902-3); was again prof. there from 1918 till 1921, when he left Russia: lived in Berlin and Paris; eventually settled in London; made U. S. tours in 1924-25 and in 1929-30. In Russian music he was a solitary figure; he never followed the nationalist trend, but endeavored to create a new type of composition, rooted both in the Classical and the Romantic tradition; his sets of fairy tales in sonata form are unique examples of his favorite genre. He wrote his best compositions before he left Russia; although he continued to compose during his residence abroad, his late music lacks the verve and Romantic sincerity that distinguishes his earlier works. He wrote almost exclusively for the piano and for the voice. A revival of his music was begun in Russia after his death. —Works: 3 piano concertos (1916-18, 1927, 1943; he was soloist in the première of his 3rd concerto with the London Philharmonic, Feb. 19, 1944); string quintet (1950). For piano: *3 Mood Pictures* (1902); 3 *Improvisations* (1902); *3 Arabesques* (1905); 34 *Fairy Tales* (1905-29); *3 Dithyrambs* (1906); *Sonata-Triad* (1907); *3 Novels* (1909); 4 sonatas (1904-14); *Fairy-tale Sonata* (1912); *Sonata-Ballade* (1913); *Sonata romantica* (1930); *Sonata minacciosa* (1931); *Sonata idillica* (1935); 4 *Lyric Fragments* (1912); 3 sets of *Forgotten Melodies* (1919-20); 4 sets of *Romantic Sketches* (1933); 2 *Elegies* (1945). Vocal works: 104 songs; *Sonata-Vocalise,* for voice and piano, without words (1921); *Suite-Vocalise* (1923). Chamber music: 2 violin sonatas and various pieces for violin and piano. A collection of Medtner's literary essays was published in an English transl. by Alfred Swan, as *The Muse and the Fashion* (Haverford, Pa., 1951). —Cf. E. Newman, *N. Medtner,* in the 'Musical Times' (Jan., 1915); V. Yakovlev, *N. Medtner,* in Russian and German (Moscow, 1927); A. Swan, *Medtner and the Music of Our Time,* in 'Music & Letters' (Jan., 1927); R. Holt, *Medtner and His Music* (London, 1948); R. Holt, editor, *N. Medtner,* a symposium (London, 1956).

Meerens (mä'-rens), **Charles,** Belgian acoustician; b. Bruges, Dec. 26, 1831; d. Schaerbeek, n. Brussels, Jan. 14, 1909. He studied cello under Bessems, Dumont, and Servais; then became a tuner in his father's piano factory, and devoted himself to acoustical researches. —Writings: *Le Métromètre, ou moyen simple de connaître le degré de vitesse d'un mouvement indiqué* (1859); *Instruction élémentaire de calcul musical* (1864); *Phénomènes musico-physiologiques* (1868); *Hommage à la mémoire de M. Delezenne* (1869); *Examen analytique des expériences d'acoustique musicale de M. A. Cornu et E. Mercadier* (1869); *Le Diapason et la notation musicale simplifiées* (1873); *Mémoire sur le diapason* (1877); *Petite méthode pour apprendre la musique et le piano* (1878); *La Gamme musicale majeure et mineure* (1890); *Acoustique musicale* (1892); *L'Avenir de la science musicale* (1894); *La Science musicale à la portée de tous les artistes et amateurs* (1902).

Meerts (märts), **Lambert** (**-Joseph**), Belgian violinist and pedagogue; b. Brussels, Jan. 6, 1800; d. there, May 12, 1863. He studied with Lafont and Habeneck at Paris; from 1835, prof. at Brussels Cons. Among his important instructive works for violin are *Études pour violon avec accompagnement d'un second violon; Mécanisme du violon* (advanced studies); 12 books of studies on rhythm, on motifs by Beethoven; etc.

Mees, Arthur, American conductor; b. Columbus, Ohio, Feb. 13, 1850; d. New York, April 26, 1923. He was a pupil, at Berlin, of Kullak (piano), Weitzmann (theory), and Dorn (conducting); from 1880 to 1886, he conducted the Cincinnati May Festival Chorus; from 1888 to 1911, conductor of the Orange Mendelssohn Union; 1891-1913, conductor of the Albany Musical Association; from 1913, also conductor of the Bridgeport Oratorio Society; from 1896, assistant conductor of the Chicago Symph. Orch.; wrote analytical program notes for it, and also for the N. Y. Philharmonic Society (1887-96). He publ. *Choirs and Choral Music* (1901); also composed piano studies.

Mehrkens, Friedrich Adolf, German conductor and teacher; b. Neuenkirchen, near Ottendorf-on-Elbe, April 22, 1840; d. Hamburg, May 31, 1899. He studied at the Leipzig Cons. (1861-62), then settled in Hamburg as pianist, teacher, and conductor of singing societies. He was conductor of the Bach-Gesellschaft from 1871. He wrote a symphony, a *Te Deum,* and chamber music.

Méhul (mä-ül'), **Étienne-Nicolas,** French opera composer; b. Givet, Ardennes, June 22, 1763; d. Paris, Oct. 18, 1817. By dint of hard work, and with the friendly aid of a blind old organist, he learned to play the organ, and at the age of 10 performed the functions of organist of the Couvent des Récollets at Givet. The fame of Wilhelm Hauser, organist at Lavaldieu monastery, attracted him; the Abbot admitted him as a novice, so that he might be taught by Hauser, whose assistant he became in 1777. In 1778 he went to Edelmann in Paris for lessons in piano playing and composition. When he heard a performance of Gluck's *Iphigénie en Tauride,* he was deeply moved, and succeeded in meeting Gluck himself, by whose advice he turned towards dramatic composition. For the sake of practice he wrote 3 operas (*Psyché, Anacréon,* and *Lausus et Lydie*); a fourth early opera, *Alonzo et Cora,* though accepted by the Académie de Musique, was not performed until 1791; meanwhile *Euphrosine et Coradin, ou le Tyran corrigé,* came out at the Comédie-Italienne, on Sept. 4, 1790, and was crowned with encouraging success; good fortune likewise attended the production of *Stratonice* (May 3, 1792). There followed the operas *Le jeune sage et le vieux fou* (March 28, 1793), *Horatius Coclès* (Feb. 18, 1794), *Le Congrès des rois* (Feb. 26, 1794), *Mélidore et Phrosine* (May 6, 1794), and *Doria, ou la Tyrannie détruite* (March 12, 1795). During the turbulent years of the French Revolution, Méhul shrewdly selected subjects for his operas allegorically suitable to the times, but he also wrote in a melodious and forceful style that pleased those who sought artistic entertainment. In 1795 he was appointed one of the four inspectors of the newly established Conservatoire, and was also elected member of the Institut. For 2 years he wrote little, but he then resumed production with renewed energy, bringing out one opera after another (given mostly at the Opéra-Comique): *Le jeune Henri* (May 1, 1797); *Le Pont de Lodi* (Dec. 15, 1797); *Adrien* (June 4, 1799); *Ariodant* (Oct. 11, 1799); *Épicure* (March 14, 1800); *L'Irato, ou L'Emporté* (Feb. 18, 1801); *Une Folie* (April 5, 1802); *Le Trésor supposé* (July 29, 1802); *Joanna* (Nov. 23, 1802); *Héléna* (March 1, 1803); *Le Baiser et la quittance* (June 18, 1803); *L'Heureux malgré lui* (Dec. 28, 1803); *Les Deux Aveugles de Tolède* (Jan. 28, 1806); *Uthal* (May 17, 1806); *Gabrielle d'Estrées, ou Les Amours d'Henri IV* (June 25, 1806); *Joseph* (Feb. 17, 1807); *Le Prince troubadour* (May 24, 1813); *La Journée aux aventures* (Nov. 16, 1816); *Les Amazones* was produced at the Opéra (Dec. 17, 1811), as was *L'Oriflamme* (Jan. 31, 1814); *Valentine de Milan* was produced posthumously (Opéra-Comique, Nov. 28, 1822). Of these, the greatest was *Joseph;* after a *succès d'estime* at its initial production in Paris, performances followed in Germany, Austria, Hungary, Russia, Holland, Belgium, Switzerland, England, Italy, and America. Some of his operas were written in collaboration: *Épicure* with Cherubini; *Le Baiser et la quittance,* with Boieldieu, Kreutzer, and Isouard: *L'Oriflamme,* with Paer, Berton, and Kreutzer. The early opera *Le Congrès des rois* was the product of collaboration with 11 other composers. He wrote only a few ballets: *Le Jugement de Paris* (Opéra, March 5, 1793; music in large part from Haydn and Pleyel), *La Dansomanie* (Opéra, June 14, 1800), *Daphnis et Pandrose* (Opéra, Jan. 14, 1803), and

Persée et Andromède (Opéra, June 8, 1810). He composed also numerous pieces of incidental music, patriotic hymns, and the like, and some interesting symphonic works, rather bold in character for his time; piano sonatas; chamber music. Some of his choral works (*Chant du départ, Chant de victorie, Chant de retour,* etc.) attained a certain vogue. There is extant in MS an *Ouverture burlesque,* scored for violin, woodwind, and piano. —Cf. P. Viellard, *Méhul, sa vie et ses œuvres* (Paris, 1859); A. Pougin, *Méhul: sa vie, son génie, son caractère* (Paris, 1889); René Brancour, *Méhul* (Paris, 1912); A. L. Ringer, *A French Symphonist at the Time of Beethoven: Étienne Nicolas Méhul,* in the 'Mus. Quarterly' (Oct., 1951). See also A. Loewenberg, *Annals of Opera* (Cambridge, 1943).

Meibom (or **Meibomius, Meiboom, Meybom**), **Marcus,** erudite scholar; b. Tönning, Schleswig, c. 1620; d. Utrecht, Feb. 15, 1710. He was for some years prof. at the Univ. of Upsala; in 1674 visited England; lived thereafter principally in Utrecht, ending in such poverty that he had to sell part of his library. His chief work is *Antiquae musicae auctores septem, graece et latine, Marcus Meibomius restituit ac notis explicavit* (Amsterdam, 1652; 2 vols.); it contains treatises on music by Aristoxenos, Euclid (*Introductio harmonica*), Nicomachos, Gaudentius Philosophos, Bacchius Senior, Aristides Quintilianus, and M. Capella (Book IX of the *Satyricon*); until the publication of the new ed. of those authors by Karl Jan, Meibom's work was the only accessible source of information.

Meiland, Jakob, German composer; b. Senftenberg, Lausitz, 1542; d. Hechingen, Dec. 31, 1577; Kapellmeister in Ansbach to 1574, then in Frankfurt and Celle. Published works: *Sacrae cantiones, a* 5, 6 (1564; 3rd ed., 1573); *Newe auserlesene teutsche Liedlein, a* 4, 5 (1569); *Sacrae aliquot cantiones* (1575); *Sacrae aliquot novae cantiones* (1576; 2nd ed., 1588); *Cygneae cantiones* (1577); 3 Passions; a Mass; secular songs; etc. —Cf. R. Oppel, *Jakob Meiland* (dissertation; Munich, 1911).

Meinardus, Ludwig (Siegfried), German composer and writer; b. Hooksiel, Oldenburg, Sept. 17, 1827; d. Bielefeld, July 10, 1896. A pupil of Leipzig Cons.; also studied in Berlin, in Weimar (with Liszt), and with Marx at Berlin. 1853-65, conductor of the Singakademie at Glogau; then teacher in Dresden Cons.; from 1874 till 1887 he lived in Hamburg as a composer and critic, then going to Bielefeld. — Writings: *Kulturgeschichtliche Briefe über deutsche Tonkunst* (2d ed., 1872); *Ein Jugendleben* (1874, 2 vols.; a sort of autobiography); *Rückblick auf die Anfänge der deutschen Oper* (1878); *Mattheson und seine Verdienste um die deutsche Tonkunst* (1879); *Mozart: ein Künstlerleben* (1882); *Die deutsche Tonkunst im 18.-19. Jahrhundert* (1887); *Klassizität und Romantik in der deutschen Tonkunst* (1893); *Eigene Wege* (1895).

Meisle, Kathryn, American contralto; b. Philadelphia, Oct. 12, 1899. She studied at the Philadelphia Cons. and in N. Y. with Wm. S. Brady; 1921, concert début with the Minneapolis Symph. Orch.; 1923, opera début as Erda with the Chicago Civic Opera; 1935-38, member of the Metropolitan Opera (début as Amneris, Feb. 28, 1935).

Meitus, Yuli Sergeyevitch, Ukrainian composer; b. Elizavetgrad, Jan. 28, 1903; studied in Kharkov. In 1942-46, he worked in Turkmenia on the codification of native folksongs. —Works: operas, *Perekop* (Kiev, Jan. 20, 1939), *Gaidamaki* (Ashkhabad, Oct. 15, 1943), *The Young Guard* (Kiev, Nov. 7, 1947), *Dawn Over the Dvina* (Kiev, July 5, 1955); *Turkmenian Symphony* (1946); 5 symph. suites: *Ukrainian Suite* (1928), *Dnieprostroy* (1929), No. 3 (1939), No. 4 (1942), No. 5, on Ukrainian themes (1944); choral arrangements of Ukrainian songs.

Melani, Jacopo, Italian opera composer; b. Pistoia, July 6, 1623; d. there, 1676. He was a member of an exceptionally gifted family of Italian musicians; his 8 brothers were singers and composers. He specialized in comic operas, of which the following, performed in Florence, are the most important: *Il Podestà di Colognole* (Dec., 1656), *Ercole in Tebe* (July 8, 1661), and *Girello* (Jan. 20, 1670); regarding the last, see the discussion of its authenticity in Loewenberg's *Annals of Opera* (Cambridge, 1943; pp. 23-24). See also Hugo Goldschmidt, *Studien zur Geschichte der italienischen Oper im 17. Jahrhundert* (vol. 1, 1901).

Melartin, Erkki Gustaf, Finnish composer; b. Käkisalmi (Kexholm), Feb. 7, 1875; d. Helsinki, Feb. 14, 1937. He was a pupil of Wegelius at the Cons. in Helsinki and of Robert Fuchs in Vienna; taught theory at the Helsinki Cons. (1901-08); then conducted the symph. orch. of Viborg; 1911-22, director of the Cons. in Helsinki. —Works: The opera *Aino* (Helsinki, Dec.

10, 1909); 7 symphonies; 3 symph. poems; 3 suites for orch.; a violin concerto; 4 string quartets; a piano sonata; a violin sonata; incidental music to *Prinsessan Törnrosa* and *Hannele;* piano pieces; choruses; about 300 songs. — Cf. K. Flodin, *Finska musiker* (Stockholm, 1900); E. Marvia, *Erkki Melartin,* in *Suomen Säveltäjiä,* ed. by Sulho Ranta (Helsinki, 1945; pp. 342-59).

Melba, Nellie (stage-name of Mrs. Helen Porter Armstrong, *née* Mitchell), famous Australian coloratura soprano; b. Richmond, near Melbourne, May 19, 1861; d. Sydney, Feb. 23, 1931. Her father, who had decided objections to anything connected with the stage, was nevertheless fond of music and proud of his daughter's talent. When she was only 6 years old he allowed her to sing at a concert in the Melbourne Town-Hall, but would not consent to her having singing lessons; instead, she was taught piano, violin, and harp, and even had instruction in harmony and composition. As she grew older she frequently played the organ in a local church and was known among her friends as an excellent pianist, while all the time her chief desire was to study singing. Not until after her marriage in 1882 to Captain Charles Armstrong was she able to gratify her ambition, when she began to study with a local teacher, Cecchi; her first public appearance as a singer was in Dec., 1885, in a performance of Handel's *Messiah* in Sydney. The next year her father received a government appointment in London, and she accompanied him, determined to begin an operatic career. Her first concert in London (June 1, 1886) convinced her of the necessity of further study, and she went to Mme. Marchesi in Paris. Her début as Gilda at the Théâtre de La Monnaie in Brussels (Oct. 12, 1887) created a veritable sensation; the famous impresario Sir Augustus Harris immediately engaged her for the spring season at Covent Garden, where she appeared on May 24, 1888, as Lucia, arousing great enthusiasm; a similar success attended her appearance in Paris, where she sang Ophelia in Ambroise Thomas' *Hamlet* (May 8, 1889), St. Petersburg (1890), Milan (La Scala, 1893; immense triumph over a carefully planned opposition), Stockholm and Copenhagen (Oct., 1893), New York (Metropolitan Opera, as Lucia, Dec. 4, 1893), Melbourne (Sept. 27, 1902). From her first appearance at Covent Garden she sang there regularly with only the exception of the seasons of 1909, 1912, and 1913; besides being one of the most brilliant stars of several seasons at the Metropolitan Opera, she also sang with Walter Damrosch's Opera Co. (1897-98) and at Hammerstein's Manhattan Opera (1906-7 and 1908-9), and made several transcontinental concert-tours of the U. S. Bemberg wrote for her *Elaine* (1892) and Saint-Saëns *Hélène* (1904), in both of which she created the title roles. In 1926, she returned to Australia and retired from the stage; she then became president of the Melbourne Cons. Melba was by nature gifted with a voice of extraordinary beauty and bell-like purity; through her art she made this fine instrument perfectly even throughout its entire compass ($b\flat$-f^3) and wonderfully flexible, so that she executed the most difficult *fioriture* without the least effort. As an actress she did not rise above the conventional, and for this reason she was at her best in parts demanding brilliant coloratura (Gilda, Lucia, Violetta, Rosina, Lakmé, etc.). On a single occasion she attempted the dramatic role of Brünnhilde in *Siegfried* (Metropolitan Opera, N. Y., Dec. 30, 1896), and met with disaster. In 1918 she was created a Dame of the British Empire. She was a typical representative of the golden era of opera; a prima donna *assoluta,* she exercised her powers over the public with perfect self-assurance and a fine command of her singing voice; her popularity spread far beyond the opera stage; a brand of toast and an ice cream dessert were named after her; a motion picture, based on her life, was produced in 1953, with Patrice Munsel as Melba. She wrote an autobiography, *Melodies and Memories* (London, 1925). See also Agnes Murphy, *Melba, a Biography* (London, 1909; contains a chapter on singing written by Melba); P. Colson, *Melba; An Unconventional Biography* (London, 1931).

Mel-Bonis. Pseudonym of **Melanie Bonis.**

Melcer (mĕhl'-tsĕr), **Henryk,** Polish pianist and composer; b. Kalisch, Sept. 21, 1869; d. Warsaw, April 18, 1928. He was a pupil of Moszkowski at the Warsaw Cons. and of Leschetizky in Vienna (1891-93). After successful concert tours of Russia, Germany, and France, he taught piano for a short time at the Cons. of Helsinki; then taught in Lwow and at the Vienna Cons. (1903-06); in 1908, became conductor of the Warsaw Philharmonic Society; from 1922 to 1927 was director of the Warsaw Cons. —Works: the operas *Marja* (Warsaw, Nov. 16, 1904) and *Protasilaos and Laodamia;* a choral ballad, *Pani Twardowska;* 2 piano concertos: No. 1 in E minor (won the Rubinstein prize, 1895) and No. 2 in

C minor (won the Paderewski prize, 1898); a piano trio; a violin sonata; piano pieces; songs.

Melchers, Henrik Melcher, Swedish violinist and composer; b. Stockholm, May 30, 1882. He studied there at the Cons. and with J. Lindegren; later at the Paris Cons. He lived in Paris (1905-19), then in Brussels, and in Sondershausen. In 1925 became prof. at the Stockholm Cons.—Works: a *Swedish Rhapsody* for orch. (Stockholm, 1914), the symph. poems *Näcken* (1916), *La Kermesse* (1919), and others; a *Poem* for violin and orch. (1922); songs.

Melchior, Lauritz, celebrated tenor; b. Copenhagen, March 20, 1890. He was a boy-soprano; then studied with Paul Bang at the Royal Opera School, Copenhagen; in 1913, made his operatic début in *Pagliacci* (as a baritone) at the Royal Opera, where he was engaged from 1914-21; studied at the same time with Wilhelm Herold, and in 1918 appeared as a tenor; 1921-23, studied with Beigel in London, then with Grenzebach in Berlin and Anna Bahr-Mildenburg in Munich; made his London début at Covent Garden on May 14, 1924; studied the Bayreuth traditions under Kittel, at the invitation of Cosima and Siegfried Wagner, and made his first appearance at the Festspielhaus there on July 23, 1924, as Siegfried; sang at Bayreuth regularly till 1931, and acquired the reputation of being one of the finest Wagnerian tenors. He sang Tannhäuser at his first appearance with the Metropolitan Opera, N. Y. (Feb. 17, 1926); remained on its roster until 1950; then settled in California. He became an American citizen on June 13, 1947.

Melis (mä'-liss), **Carmen,** dramatic soprano; b. Cagliari, Sardinia, Aug. 14, 1885. She studied with Teresina Singer and Carlo Carignani in Milan, and later with Jean de Reszke in Paris; made a successful début at Naples in 1906; then sang in Rome, Milan, Venice, Cairo, Warsaw, and Odessa. She was engaged by Hammerstein for the Manhattan Opera, and made her American début there as Tosca (N. Y., Nov. 26, 1909); subsequently was a member of the Boston Opera Co. (1911-13). Later became a teacher; Renata Tebaldi studied with her for 3 years.

Melkikh, Dmitri Mikheyevitch, Russian composer; b. Moscow, Feb. 11, 1885. He studied with Yavorsky; wrote music using a Russian modal technique; was at one time influenced by French Impressionism. He wrote the symph. poems *Alladine et Palomides* (after Maeterlinck), *On the Sea,* and *Epitaph;* song cycles with orch.; etc.

Mellers, Wilfrid Howard, English musicologist and composer; b. Leamington, April 26, 1914. He pursued his musical studies privately with Egon Wellesz and Edmund Rubbra. After holding various teaching posts in England, he was appointed tutor in music at Birmingham Univ. (1948). — Works: opera, *The Tragical History of Christopher Marlowe* (1952); several cantatas (*The Song of Ruth; The White Island;* etc.); *Sinfonia ricercata* (1947); a symphony (1953); chamber music and songs. His writings include valuable articles and the following books publ. in London: *Music and Society* (1946), *Studies in Contemporary Music* (1947), *François Couperin and the French Classical Tradition* (1950), and *The Sonata Principle* and *Romanticism & the 20th Century* (1957) in the series 'Man and His Music.'

Melnikov (mĕl'-nē-kov), **Ivan Alexandrovitch,** Russian baritone; b. St. Petersburg, March 4, 1832; d. there, July 8, 1906. He was a choirboy in school; was engaged in trade, and for a time served as inspector of Volga boats; he began to study seriously late in life; took lessons with Lomakin (1862); then went to Italy, where he studied with Repetto. He made his début in Bellini's *Puritani* (St. Petersburg, Oct. 6, 1867); created the title role in Mussorgsky's *Boris Godunov* (St. Petersburg, Feb. 8, 1874).

Melton, James, American tenor; b. Moultrie, Ga., Jan. 2, 1904. He attended high school and college in Florida; later entered the Univ. of Georgia, where he played the saxophone in the college band. Subsequently, he went to Vanderbilt College, Nashville, Tenn., where he took lessons in singing with Giuseppe de Luca. He obtained several lucrative engagements on the radio; made his concert début in N. Y. on April 22, 1932; opera début with the Zoo Opera, Cincinnati, June 28, 1938. On Dec. 7, 1942 he appeared for the first time with the Metropolitan Opera, remaining on its roster until 1950; also toured the U. S. as a concert singer.

Meltzer, Charles Henry, English journalist and translator; b. London, 1852; d. New York, Jan. 14, 1936. He studied music in London and Paris; was foreign correspondent for the N. Y. 'Herald' and the Chicago

'Tribune'; settled in N. Y. in 1888; wrote drama criticism; also was assistant manager at the Metropolitan Opera (1903-7). He was an ardent proponent of opera in English, and translated the librettos of *Die Walküre* and *Das Rheingold, Les Contes d'Hoffmann,* Monteverdi's *Orfeo,* etc.

Meluzzi (mĕh-lōō'-tsē), **Salvatore,** Italian composer of church music; b. Rome, July 22, 1813; d. there, April 17, 1897. He was maestro di cappella at the basilica of St. Peter's in the Vatican, and for 45 years director of the Cappella Giulia. Thoroughly versed in the art of the old Italian masters, he emulated them in writing Masses, Requiems, antiphons, motets, hymns, psalms; among his best pieces are a fine *Stabat Mater* and a beautiful *Miserere.*

Membrée (mahn-brā'), **Edmond,** French composer; b. Valenciennes, Nov. 14, 1820; d. Château Damont, near Paris, Sept. 10, 1882. He studied at the Paris Cons. with Alkan and Zimmerman (piano) and Carafa (composition).—Works: the operas *François Villon* (Paris, April 20, 1857), *L'Esclave* (Paris, July 17, 1874), *Les Parias* (Paris, Nov. 13, 1876), and *La courte échelle* (Paris, 1879); a cantata *Fingal* (Paris, May 14, 1861); ballads, songs, etc.—Cf. L. Mention, *Un Compositeur valenciennois: Edmond Membrée* (Paris, 1908).

Menasce, Jacques de, composer and pianist; b. Bad Ischl, Austria, Aug. 19, 1905, of a French-Egyptian father and a German mother. He studied in Vienna with Sauer (piano) and with J. Marx, Paul Pisk, and Alban Berg (composition). From 1932 until 1940 he gave concerts in Europe as a pianist; in 1941 came to America, living mostly in N. Y., but continued his concert career in Europe. — Works: 2 piano concertos (1935; 1941); *5 Fingerprints,* for piano (1943); *Romantic Suite,* for piano (1950); *Divertimento,* for piano and string orch. (1940); *Le Chemin d'écume,* for soprano and orch. (Geneva, 1942); a ballet, *Status Quo* (1947); violin sonata; viola sonata (1955); songs and choruses.

Menchaca (men-chăh'-kăh), **Angel,** Paraguayan theorist; b. Asunción, March 1, 1855; d. Buenos Aires, May 8, 1924. He was trained as a jurist; was in charge of the government 'Boletín Oficial' and also taught history and literature at the National College in Buenos Aires. In 1914 he publ. a provocative book, *Sistema teórico-gráfico de la Música,* in which he proposed a new system of notation, employing a basic alphabet of 12 notes and dispensing with the established signatures, staff, etc. He toured Europe for the purpose of lecturing on this device; invented a special keyboard to facilitate its application. He was also a composer; his compositions include songs and school choruses.

Mendel, Arthur, eminent American music scholar; b. Boston, June 6, 1905. He studied at Harvard Univ. (B.A., 1925), and the École Normale de Musique in Paris; also studied privately with Nadia Boulanger. He was subsequently teacher at the Dalcroze School of Music and Diller-Quaile School, N.Y.; music critic of the 'Nation' (1930-33); literary editor of G. Schirmer, Inc. (1930-38); editor, Associated Music Publishers (1941-47). From 1937 to 1953 conducted in N.Y. the Cantata Singers, a small chorus specializing in music of the 17th and 18th centuries, performed in the style of the period. In 1952 he was appointed prof. of music and chairman of the music department at Princeton Univ. He edited (with H. David) the valuable 'documentary biography,' *The Bach Reader* (N.Y., 1945); contributed a series of articles, *Pitch in the 16th and Early 17th Centuries* to the 'Mus. Quarterly' (Jan., April, July, Oct., 1948), etc.; edited Bach's *St. John Passion* (1951), Schütz's *Christmas Story* (1949) and *Musicalische Exequien* (1957), and other works of the Baroque period.

Mendel, Hermann, German music lexicographer; b. Halle, Aug. 6, 1834; d. Berlin, Oct. 26, 1876. He was a pupil of Mendelssohn and Moscheles in Leipzig, and of Wieprecht in Berlin. In 1870 he founded and edited the 'Deutsche Musiker-Zeitung'; also edited 'Mode's Opernbibliothek' (about 90 librettos, with commentaries and biographies of composers) and a 'Volksliederbuch.' He publ. 2 small books on Meyerbeer (1868 and 1869). His great work was the 'Musikalisches Conversations-Lexikon,' which he began to publ. in 1870, but was able to continue only to the letter M; the rest was completed by August Reissmann; the entire edition was in 11 vols.; a supplementary vol. was publ. in 1883.

Mendelssohn, Arnold, German composer; son of a cousin of Felix Mendelssohn; b. Ratibor, Dec. 26, 1855; d. Darmstadt, Feb. 19, 1933. He studied law at the Univ. of Tübingen; then entered the Hochschule für Musik in Berlin, where he studied with Löschhorn (piano), Haupt (organ), Grell,

Kiel, and Taubert (composition). He was subsequently instructor in Bielefeld (1883-85); prof. at the Cologne Cons. (1885-90); then director of church music in Darmstadt. In 1912 he was appointed prof. at Hoch's Cons. in Frankfurt; among his pupils there was Hindemith. He wrote 3 operas: *Elsi, die seltsame Magd* (Cologne, 1896), *Der Bärenhäuter* (Berlin, Feb. 9, 1900), and *Die Minneburg* (Mannheim, 1909); 2 cantatas: *Aus tiefer Not* and *Auf meinen lieben Gott;* a German Mass, for 8-part chorus a cappella; 3 symphonies; a violin concerto; 2 string quartets; a cello sonata; 2 piano sonatas; several sets of songs. He edited Schütz's oratorios and some of Monteverdi's madrigals. His book on esthetics, *Gott, Welt und Kunst,* was brought out by W. Ewald (Wiesbaden, 1949). —Cf. E. O. Nodnagel, *Jenseits von Wagner und Liszt* (Königsberg, 1902); W. Nagel, *Arnold Mendelssohn* (Leipzig, 1906); H. Hering, *Arnold Mendelssohn: die Grundlagen seines Schaffens und seiner Werke* (Regensburg, 1930).

Mendelssohn, Fanny. See Hensel, Fanny Cäcilia.

Mendelssohn, Felix (full name **Jacob Ludwig Felix Mendelssohn-Bartholdy**), illustrious German composer; b. Hamburg, Feb. 3, 1809; d. Leipzig, Nov. 4, 1847. He was a grandson of the philosopher Moses Mendelssohn and son of the banker Abraham Mendelssohn, who moved to Berlin in 1812, during the French occupation of Hamburg; his mother was Lea Salomon-Bartholdy, of Berlin, and from her he received his first piano lessons, in company with his elder sister Fanny. These lessons were continued by L. Berger; Mendelssohn's other teachers were Zelter (theory) and Hennings (violin); also Mme. Bigot for a short time in 1816 at Paris, whither Mendelssohn had accompanied his father on a business trip. On April 11, 1819, he entered the Singakademie (conducted by Zelter) as an alto; on Sept. 18, 1819, a composition by Mendelssohn, the 19th Psalm, was performed by the Akademie, of which, after the change of his voice to a tenor in his 16th year, he still remained a favorite member. Mendelssohn's talent for composition was likewise fostered by the Sunday performances of a small orchestra at his father's house, his own works finding speedy production. In 1825 his father again took him to Paris, to ask Cherubini's opinion on the adoption of a musical career by Felix; this opinion was strongly affirmative, and the master even offered to undertake the boy's further training, but the elder Mendelssohn considered the home atmosphere preferable. Indeed, Mendelssohn's genius could nowhere have been more healthfully stimulated; as early as 1820 he was regularly engaged in composition. As a pianist his début was even earlier—on Oct. 24, 1818, he played at a public concert the piano part of a trio with 2 horns by Wölffl. Of the incidental music to Shakespeare's *A Midsummer Night's Dream,* the overture was written in 1826, and is a most astonishing proof of the young composer's mental maturity, showing no less mastery and finish of form than the remaining numbers composed 15 years later. On April 29, 1827, his opera, *Die Hochzeit des Camacho,* had a single performance in a small theater in Berlin, but this immature work failed to advance Mendelssohn's career as composer. But he soon proved his musicianship in an act of great cultural importance, when he brought out Bach's *St. Matthew Passion* in the Singakademie; the performance (the first anywhere since Bach's death) took place on March 11, 1829, and gave the initial impulse to the significant revival of Bach's music, in which Mendelssohn was the leading figure. He made his first journey to England in the spring of 1829; conducted his symphony in C minor seated, after the fashion of the time, at the piano; some months after this performance the London Philharmonic Society, to which he dedicated the symphony, elected him an honorary member. Later he played the *Concertstück* by Weber, and (for the first time in England) Beethoven's Emperor Concerto. Following this active concert season, a long pleasure tour through Scotland stimulated his teeming imagination and served as the inspiration of his *Fingal's Cave* (*Hebrides*) overture. In 1830-32 he traveled through Germany, Austria, Italy, and Switzerland to Paris; then made his 2nd visit to London, where he conducted the *Fingal's Cave* overture (May 14, 1832) and played his G minor concerto (May 22, 1832) and his *Capriccio brillante.* Here, too, his 1st book of 6 *Songs without Words,* finished in Venice, 1830, was published. In England, then and later, he found the musical environment more congenial than in Berlin, where, for some reason, he was not generally popular — witness his failure, in competition with Rungenhagen, to obtain the conductorship of the Singakademie on his return in 1833. And this after he had arranged a series of concerts for the benefit of the Orchestral Pension Fund, himself conducting his *Reformation* symphony, the 3 overtures, *Mid-*

summer Night's Dream, Fingal's Cave, and *Calm Sea and Prosperous Voyage,* etc. He was called to conduct the Lower-Rhine Musical Festival at Düsseldorf in May, 1833; after a short visit to London, he returned to Düsseldorf to take charge as Town Musical Director of the church music, the Municipal Opera, and 2 singing societies. He gave most of the theatrical work into the hands of Julius Rietz within 6 months; after conducting the Lower-Rhine Festival at Cologne (June 7-9, 1835), he accepted a call to the conductorship of the celebrated Gewandhaus Orchestra in Leipzig — an epoch-making event, not only in his personal career, but for the musical life of Leipzig and the world. Leipzig was not slow to respond to Mendelssohn's masterly activity as a conductor, composer, and player; the University created him, in 1836, *Dr. phil.* (*honoris causa*); he infused new life into the orchestra, and by calling the violin virtuoso Ferdinand David to his aid, gave it a concertmaster who not merely seconded his own efforts, but who, by native force of character and musicianly ability, gave a tone of precision and pliability to this body of players that became a tradition of vital force in the Gewandhaus. Mendelssohn conducted the 1st performance of his oratorio *St. Paul* at the Lower-Rhine Festival in Düsseldorf, May 22, 1836. On March 28, 1837, he married Cécile Charlotte Sophie Jeanrenaud of Frankfurt, the daughter of a French Protestant clergyman. Five children, Carl, Marie, Paul, Felix, and 'Lili' (Elisabeth), were born to them, and their union was happy. During 4 weeks of this year Mendelssohn was in England, and conducted *St. Paul* at the Birmingham Festival. In 1841 Friedrich Wilhelm IV invited Mendelssohn to Berlin to take charge of the grand orchestral and choral concerts; but Mendelssohn found the attitude of the court, musicians, and even the public, more or less openly hostile, and wished to resign in October, 1842. At the King's special request, he remained to organize the music in the cathedral; the chosen body of singers later became famous as the 'Domchor' (cathedral choir). Mendelssohn also received the title of Royal General Musical Director; residence in Berlin was not required. Late in 1842, with von Falkenstein, Keil, Kistner, Schleinitz, and Seeburg as directors, and Schumann, Hauptmann, David, Becker, and Pohlenz as teachers, Mendelssohn organized the 'Conservatorium' at Leipzig; it was officially opened on April 3, 1843. Mendelssohn himself taught when his manifold other duties permitted. The financial nucleus of the foundation was a legacy from Blümner of 20,000 Thaler, left at the disposal of the King of Saxony for the promotion of art; Mendelssohn had made a special journey to Dresden to interest the King in the Leipzig Conservatory, and the royal patronage was obtained. During his frequent absences, the Gewandhaus Concerts were conducted by Hiller (1843-44) and Gade (1844-45); in the autumn of 1845 Mendelssohn resumed the baton. During the summer of 1844 he conducted the Philharmonic Concerts in London, and took part, as a pianist, in numerous other concerts, everywhere receiving a most enthusiastic welcome. This was his 8th visit to England; his 9th was made memorable by his conducting the 1st performance of *Elijah* (at Birmingham, Aug. 26, 1846). It was in England that the Wedding March from Mendelssohn's music to *A Midsummer Night's Dream* began to be used to accompany the bridal procession; the music became particularly fashionable when it was played at the wedding of the Princess Royal in 1858. Having relinquished the direction of the Gewandhaus to Gade, and the supervision of the piano department at the Leipzig Cons. to Moscheles, he made still another visit to England, his 10th (April-May, 1847), but soon his health, always delicate, began to fail; the death of his favorite sister, Fanny (May 14, 1847), was a shock that his overwrought nervous system could not withstand; he died a few months later, at the age of 38. — The sorrow at his premature death was universal; not only in Germany and in England, where he was personally well known, but in America as well, the news of his demise was received as a great calamity to the cause of music. Numerous Mendelssohn societies were formed all over the world; in America the Mendelssohn Quintette Club was founded in 1849. A Mendelssohn Scholarship was established in England in 1856; its first recipient was Arthur Sullivan. — Mendelssohn's genius cannot be regarded as equal to that of Schubert, Schumann, or Chopin; but his influence on German, English, and American musical composition for several decades after his death was overpowering; his symphonies and his chamber music have never ceased to be part of the world repertory; it was only with the emergence of Wagnerism that Mendelssohn's star began to dim. As a dramatic composer, Mendelssohn left no mark, although he eagerly sought after a suitable libretto. Besides his early opera *Die Hochzeit des Camacho,* he left fragments of the opera *Lorelei* (an

Ave Maria, a vintage chorus, and the beautiful finale to Act I); there was also a 'Liederspiel' *Die Heimkehr aus der Fremde,* composed for the silver wedding of Mendelssohn's parents and performed at their house in Berlin (Dec. 26, 1829); it was not brought out in public until 3 years after Mendelssohn's death (Leipzig, April 10, 1851); 5 juvenile operas are extant in MS. His grandest productions are the oratorios *St. Paul* and *Elijah,* unquestionably the greatest works of their kind since the time of Handel and Haydn. Other important vocal works (with orch.) are the symphony-cantata *Lobgesang* (op. 52), also designated as symph. No. 2; the ballade, *Die erste Walpurgisnacht* (op. 60), for soli, chorus, and orch.; 2 'Festgesänge,' *An die Künstler* (for men's chorus and brass), and *Zur Säcularfeier der Buchdruckerkunst* ('Gutenberg Cantata,' for men's chorus and orch.); music to *Antigone* (op. 55), *Athalie* (op. 74), *Œdipus in Colonos* (op. 93), and *A Midsummer Night's Dream* (op. 61); Hymn for alto solo, chorus, and orch. (op. 96); *Lauda Sion,* for chorus and orch. (op. 73); *Tu es Petrus,* for chorus with orch. (op. 111); Psalms 115 (op. 31) and 95 (op. 46) for soli, chorus, and orch.; Psalms 114 (op. 51) and 98 (op. 91), for men's chorus and orch.; the prayer *Verleih' uns Frieden,* for chorus and orch.; the concert aria for soprano, *Infelice!* (op. 94). Vocal works without orch.: Psalm 42, for chorus and organ; Psalms 2, 22, and 43, *a* 8, a cappella; Funeral Song for mixed chorus (op. 116); *Kyrie eleison* for double chorus; 6 anthems ('Sprüche') for 8-part chorus (op. 79); 3 motets for soli, chorus, and organ (op. 23); 3 motets for women's chorus and organ (op. 39); 3 motets for solo and chorus a cappella (op. 69); 21 quartets for men's voices, and 28 quartets for mixed voices (among these vocal quartets are some of Mendelssohn's finest compositions); 13 vocal duets; and 83 songs for solo voice with piano (*Es ist bestimmt in Gottes Rat, Wer hat dich, du schöner Wald, O Täler weit, o Höhen,* etc.). —Orchestral works: symph. No. 1 (op. 1) in C minor (1824); symph. No. 2 (op. 52), *Lobgesang,* with voices (Birmingham, Sept. 23, 1840); symph. No. 3 (op. 56), in A minor, *Scotch* (1830-42; Leipzig, March 3, 1842); symph. No. 4 (op. 90), in A major, *Italian* (Berlin, May 13, 1833); symph. No. 5 (op. 107), in D minor, *Reformation* (1831; Berlin, Nov. 15, 1832); the concert overtures *A Midsummer Night's Dream* (op. 21), *Fingal's Cave* or *Hebrides* (op. 26), *Calm Sea and Prosperous Voyage* (*Meeresstille und glückliche Fahrt;* op. 27), *The Lovely Melusine* (*Die schöne Melusine;* op. 32), *Ruy Blas* (op. 95), and the 'Trumpet' overture (op. 101); also an overture for wind band (op. 24); *Andante, Scherzo, Capriccio and Fugue,* for string orch. (op. 81); Funeral March (op. 103) and March (op. 108); piano concerto No. 1, in G minor (op. 25), and No. 2, in D minor (op. 40); *Capriccio brillante,* for piano with orch. (op. 22); *Rondo brillante,* for piano with orch. (op. 29); *Serenade* and *Allegro giojoso,* for piano with orch. (op. 43); violin concerto in E minor (op. 64; a classic, and one of the finest for the instrument; while writing it, Mendelssohn constantly consulted and often deferred to the judgment of Ferdinand David, who performed it for the 1st time with the Gewandhaus Orch., Leipzig, on March 13, 1845); the score of a juvenile violin concerto by Mendelssohn, written at the age of 12 (1822) was rediscovered and publ. in 1952; played from MS for the 1st time by Yehudi Menuhin, N. Y., Feb. 4, 1952. —Chamber music: an octet for strings (op. 20); 2 string quintets (op. 18, 87); a piano sextet (op. 110); 7 string quartets (op. 12, 13, 44, 44a, 44b, 80, 81); 3 piano quartets (op. 1, 2, 3); 2 piano trios (op. 49, 66); 2 trios for clarinet, basset-horn, and piano (op. 113, 114); 2 sonatas for cello and piano (op. 45, 58); a sonata for violin and piano (op. 4); *Variations concertantes* (op. 17) and *Lied ohne Worte* (op. 109), for cello with piano; also an unpubl. clarinet sonata (performed in N. Y., 1939). —Piano music: 3 sonatas (op. 6, 105, 106); *Capriccio* (op. 5); *Charakterstücke* (op. 7); *Rondo capriccioso* (op. 14); Fantasia on 'The Last Rose of Summer' (op. 15); 3 Fantasias (op. 16); the original and popular *Songs without Words* (*Lieder ohne Worte*), in 8 books (op. 19b, 30, 38, 53, 62, 67, 85, 102); Fantasia in f♯ minor, or *Sonate écossaise* (op. 28); 3 Caprices (op. 33); 6 preludes and fugues (op. 35); *Variations sérieuses* (op. 54); 6 *Kinderstücke* (op. 72); Variations in E♭ (op. 82); Variations in B♭ (op. 83); 3 preludes and 3 studies (op. 104); *Albumblatt* (op. 117); *Capriccio* in E major (op. 118); *Perpetuum mobile* (op. 119); etc.; 4-hand *Allegro brillant* (op. 92); *Duo concertant* (with Moscheles) for 2 pianos on the march theme of Weber's *Preciosa;* also organ music: 3 preludes and fugues (op. 37); 6 organ sonatas (op. 65); preludes, etc. —Mendelssohn's collected works, ed. by Julius Rietz, were publ. by Breitkopf & Härtel (1874-77); the same firm publ. a *Thematisches Verzeichnis* (1846; 2nd ed., 1853;

3rd ed., 1882, with a bibliography).

BIBLIOGRAPHY. A. BIOGRAPHY (only works of documentary or interpretative value): W. A. Lampadius, *Felix Mendelssohn-Bartholdy. Ein Denkmal für seine Freunde* (Leipzig, 1848; in English, Philadelphia, 1865; 2nd greatly enlarged ed. as *Felix Mendelssohn-Bartholdy. Ein Gesammtbild seines Lebens und Wirkens,* 1886); J. Benedict, *A Sketch of the Life and Works of the late Felix Mendelssohn-Bartholdy* (London, 1850; 2nd ed., 1853); J. Schubring, *Erinnerungen an Felix Mendelssohn-Bartholdy,* in 'Daheim' (No. 26, Leipzig, 1866; English transl. in the 'Musical World,' May 12 and 19, 1866); A. Reissmann, *Felix Mendelssohn-Bartholdy. Sein Leben und seine Werke* (Berlin, 1867); S. Hensel, *Die Familie Mendelssohn* (3 vols.; Berlin, 1879; 18th ed., 1924; English transl., in 2 vols., London, 1881); W. S. Rockstro, *Mendelssohn* (London, 1884; revised ed., 1911); B. Schrader, *Mendelssohn* (Leipzig, 1898); S. Stratton, *Mendelssohn* (London, 1901; revised ed., 1934); J. C. Hadden, *Life of Mendelssohn* (London, 1904); B. Blackburn, *Mendelssohn* (London, 1904); E. Wolff, *Felix Mendelssohn-Bartholdy* (Berlin, 1906); C. Bellaigue, *Mendelssohn* (Paris, 1907); J. Hartog, *Felix Mendelssohn-Bartholdy en zijne werken* (Leyden, 1908); W. Dahms, *Mendelssohn* (Berlin, 1919); P. de Stoecklin, *Mendelssohn* (Paris, 1927); Cyril Winn, *Mendelssohn* (London, 1927); E. Vuillermoz, *Une heure avec Mendelssohn* (Paris, 1930); J. Erskine, *Song Without Words, The Story of Felix Mendelssohn* (N. Y., 1941); J. Petitpierre, *Le Mariage de Mendelssohn* (Lausanne, 1937; in English as *The Romance of the Mendelssohns;* London, 1947); B. Bartels, *Mendelssohn-Bartholdy: Mensch und Werk* (Bremen, 1947); K. H. Wörner, *Felix Mendelssohn-Bartholdy* (Wiesbaden, 1947); P. Radcliffe, *Mendelssohn* (London, 1954).

B. CRITICISM, APPRECIATION: C. Selden, *La Musique en Allemagne: Mendelssohn* (Paris, 1867); K. Mendelssohn-Bartholdy, *Goethe und Mendelssohn* (Leipzig, 1871; in English, London, 1874); E. David, *Les Mendelssohns-Bartholdy et Robert Schumann* (Paris, 1887); J. Eckardt, *Ferdinand David und die Familie Mendelssohn-Bartholdy* (Leipzig, 1888); F. G. Edwards, *The History of Mendelssohn's Oratorio Elijah* (London, 1896; 2nd ed., 1900); J. W. Hathaway, *An Analysis of Mendelssohn's Organ Works* (London, 1908); M. Clerjot and G. Marchet, *Mendelssohn et ses quatuors à cordes* (Reims, 1901); O. A. Mansfield, *Organ-parts of Mendelssohn's Oratorios, analytically considered* (London, 1907); O. A. Mansfield, *Some Characteristics and Peculiarities of Mendelssohn's Organ Sonatas,* in the 'Mus. Quarterly' (July, 1917); H. W. Waltershausen, *Mendelssohns Lieder ohne Worte* (Munich, 1920); G. Schünemann, *Die Bachpflege der Berliner Singakademie,* in the 'Bach-Jahrbuch' (1928); R. Werner, *Felix Mendelssohn-Bartholdy als Kirchenmusiker* (Frankfurt, 1930); C. Wilkinson, *How to Interpret Mendelssohn's Songs Without Words* (London, 1930); T. Armstrong, *Mendelssohn's Elijah* (London, 1931); G. Kinsky, *Was Mendelssohn Indebted to Weber?* in the 'Mus. Quarterly' (April, 1933); Schima Kaufmann, *Mendelssohn, a Second Elijah* (N. Y., 1934); H. Foss, *Felix Mendelssohn-Bartholdy* (Oxford, 1934); R. B. Gotch, *Mendelssohn and His Friends in Kensington* (including letters from F. Horley; London, 1934); J. Horton, *The Chamber Music of Mendelssohn* (Oxford, 1946); Luise and Hans Tischler, *Mendelssohn's Songs Without Words,* in the 'Mus. Quarterly' (Jan., 1948); Percy M. Young, *Introduction to the Music of Mendelssohn* (London, 1949); D. Mintz, *Melusine: A Mendelssohn Draft,* in the 'Mus. Quarterly' (Oct., 1957).

C. CORRESPONDENCE: P. Mendelssohn-Bartholdy, *Reisebriefe . . . aus den Jahren 1830-32* (Leipzig, 1861; 5th ed., 1882; English transl., by Lady Wallace, as *Letters from Italy and Switzerland*, London, 1862); P. Mendelssohn-Bartholdy, *Briefe aus den Jahren 1833-47* (Leipzig, 1863; 8th ed., 1915; English transl. by Lady Wallace, London, 1863); L. Nohl, *Musikerbriefe* (Leipzig, 1867); E. Polko, *Erinnerungen an Felix Mendelssohn-Bartholdy* (Leipzig, 1868; English transl. by Lady Wallace, London, 1869); E. Devrient, *Meine Erinnerungen an Felix Mendelssohn-Bartholdy und seine Briefe an mich* (Leipzig, 1869; English transl. by Lady Macfarren, London, 1869); *Acht Briefe und ein Faksimile* (Leipzig, 1871; English transl. in 'Macmillan's Magazine,' June, 1871); F. Hiller, *Felix Mendelssohn, Briefe und Erinnerungen* (Cologne, 1874; English transl., by M. E. von Glehn, London, 1874); F. Moscheles, *Briefe von Felix Mendelssohn an Ignaz und Charlotte Moscheles* (Leipzig, 1888; English transl. as *Letters of Felix Mendelssohn,* London, 1888); M. Friedlaender, *Briefe an Goethe,* in the 'Goethe-Jahrbuch' (1891); E. Wolff, *Felix Mendelssohn-Bartholdy. Meisterbriefe* (Berlin, 1907; 2nd augmented ed., 1909); K. Klingemann, *Felix Mendelssohn-Bartholdys Briefwechsel mit Legationsrat Karl Klinge-*

mann (Essen, 1909); G. Selden-Goth, *Mendelssohn's Letters* (selections from the letters transl. by Lady Wallace, with additional correspondence; N. Y., 1945); R. Sietz, ed., *Felix Mendelssohn-Bartholdy: sein Leben in Briefen* (Cologne, 1948). A pictorial album, *Mendelssohn im Bildnis,* was compiled by M. Fr. Schneider (Basel, 1953).

Mendelssohn, Felix Robert, German cellist; direct descendant of the famous composer; b. Berlin, Sept. 27, 1896; d. Baltimore, May 15, 1951. He studied at the Stern Cons.; later taught cello there. In 1936 he settled in the U. S.; taught in N. Y.; in 1941 joined the Baltimore Symph. Orch. He died in Cadoa Hall, Baltimore, while playing Dohnányi's *Konzertstück.*

Mengal, Jean-Baptiste, Belgian horn virtuoso and composer; b. Ghent, Feb. 21, 1792; d. Paris, Dec. 19, 1878. He learned the rudiments of music from his father, who was an experienced horn player, and from his brother Martin-Joseph Mengal, whom he succeeded as first horn player at the Ghent municipal theater. In 1812 he entered the Paris Cons., graduating with 1st prize; then played in the orchestra of the Grand Opéra. He wrote a number of works for his instrument: fantasies, duets, solos; also publ. a method of horn playing.

Mengal, Martin-Joseph, Belgian horn player and conductor; brother of Jean-Baptiste Mengal; b. Ghent, Jan. 27, 1784; d. there, July 4, 1851. He studied with his father; played in Paris orchestras; in 1825 was appointed director of the Ghent municipal theater; then was conductor at Antwerp; in 1835 became director of the Ghent Cons. He wrote a great number of sacred works; his MSS are preserved at the Ghent Cons.

Mengelberg, Karel, Dutch composer and conductor; b. Utrecht, July 18, 1902. He studied with Willem Pijper, and later took a course at the Hochschule für Musik in Berlin. He conducted theater orchestras in provincial German towns; then was active on the radio in Berlin; subsequently was conductor of the municipal band in Barcelona; then went to Kiev, Russia, where he was in charge of the music dept. in the Ukrainian film division; returned to Amsterdam in 1938; from 1945 was connected with the Amsterdam Radio. He has written the ballets *Bataille* (1922) and *Parfait Amour* (1946); a *Divertimento* for orch.; many pieces of chamber music; also songs.

Mengelberg, Kurt Rudolf, musicologist and composer, cousin of Willem Mengelberg; b. Krefeld, Feb. 1, 1892. He studied at the Leipzig Cons. with Riemann and Neitzel. In 1915 he went to Amsterdam, where he took a course of studies with Willem Mengelberg; in 1917, he was appointed editor of the programs of the Concertgebouw; wrote a biography of W. Mengelberg and one of Mahler. His works include *Missa pro Pace* (1932; often performed in Holland); *Ballade van den boer,* for narrator and orch. (1942); church music.

Mengelberg, Willem, celebrated Dutch conductor; b. Utrecht, March 28, 1871; d. Chur, Switzerland, March 21, 1951. He studied at the Cons. of Utrecht, and later at the Cologne Cons. with Seiss, Jensen, and Wüllner. He was appointed municipal music director in Lucerne in 1891, and his work there attracted so much attention that in 1895 he was placed at the head of the famous Concertgebouw Orch. in Amsterdam; during his directorship, he elevated that orchestra to a lofty position in the world of music. In addition, he became conductor of the choral society 'Toonkunst' in Amsterdam (1898); appeared frequently as guest conductor in all European countries; in England he was an annual visitor from 1913 until World War II; appeared with the N. Y. Philharmonic in 1905; came to the U. S. again in 1921, conducting the National Symph. Orch. in N. Y., which was absorbed at his suggestion by the Philharmonic Orch.; he led the Philharmonic at various intervals from 1922 till 1930; in 1928 he received the degree of Mus. Doc., Columbia Univ. (*honoris causa*); in 1933 was appointed prof. of music at Utrecht Univ. During the occupation of Holland by the Germans, Mengelberg openly expressed his sympathies with the Nazi doctrines, and lost the high respect and admiration that his compatriots had felt for him; after the liberation of Holland he was barred from professional activities there, the ban to be continued until 1951, but he died in that year in exile in Switzerland.—Mengelberg was one of the finest representatives of the Romantic tradition in symphonic conducting; his interpretations extracted the full emotional power from the music, and yet he never transgressed the limits imposed by the structural forms of classical music; his renditions of Beethoven's symphonies were inspiring. He was a great admirer of Mahler and conducted a festival of Mahler's music in Amsterdam in May, 1920; he was also a champion of works by Richard Strauss (who dedicated the score of *Ein Heldenleben* to him), Max Reger, and Debussy.—Cf. Hugo Nolthenius, *Willem Mengelberg* (Amsterdam, 1920); Rudolf Mengelberg, *Das Mahlerfest in Amsterdam* (Amsterdam, 1920); A. Van den Boer, *De Psychologische beteekenis van Willem Mengelberg als Dirigent* (Amsterdam, 1925); Edna R. Sollitt, *Mengelberg and the Symphonic Epoch* (N. Y., 1930); Edna R. Sollitt, *Mengelberg spreckt* (speeches of Mengelberg; The Hague, 1935).

Menges, Herbert, English conductor, brother of Isolde Menges; b. Hove, Aug. 27, 1902. He began to study violin as a child, and made a public appearance at the age of 4; then he turned to study of the piano; took lessons with Mathilda Verne; in composition, with Vaughan Williams at the Royal College of Music, London. He began his conducting career in Brighton; in 1931 he became music director of the Old Vic Theatre, where he wrote a number of scores for the Shakespeare plays produced there. In 1941 he became conductor at the Sadler's Wells Opera Co., returning to the Old Vic in 1944. In 1945 he was appointed conductor of the Southern Philharmonic Orch., at Southsea. In 1947 he made his first appearance in the U. S., conducting the CBS Symph. in New York.—Cf. Donald Brook, *International Gallery of Conductors* (Bristol, 1951; pp. 113-16).

Menges, Isolde, English violinist; sister of Herbert Menges; b. Hove, May 16, 1893. Her parents were violinists, and she studied at home; then for 3 years with Leopold Auer in St. Petersburg and in Dresden (1909-12); made her London début on Feb. 4, 1913; toured the U. S. in 1916-19 (début in N. Y., Oct. 21, 1916), and again in 1921. In 1931 she became prof. at the Royal College of Music; also organized the Menges Quartet; at the Brahms Centennial in 1933, the Menges Quartet presented in London a series of concerts including most of the chamber music by Brahms.

Mengewein, Karl, German composer and teacher; b. Zaunroda, Thuringia, Sept. 9, 1852; d. Berlin, April 7, 1908. From 1876 until 1886 he was a teacher at Freudenberg's Cons., Wiesbaden, and with the latter founded a Cons. at Berlin in 1886, of which he was co-director till 1896. He founded the 'Oratorienverein' (1895) and the next year the 'Madrigal' for the production of a cappella music.—Works: oratorio, *Johannes der Täufer* (1892); festival cantata, *Martin Luther;* operetta, *Schulmeisters Brautfahrt* (Wiesbaden, 1884); overture, *Dornröschen;* several 'Singspiele,' a Requiem, female choruses, etc. He also publ. *Die Ausbildung des musikalischen Gehörs* (1908).

Ménil (mā-nēl'), **Félicien de,** French musicologist; b. Boulogne-sur-Mer, July 16, 1860; d. Neuilly, near Paris, March 28, 1930. He studied with Henri Maréchal and Lenepveu at the Paris Cons.; undertook extensive travels in America, India, and Africa; returning to Paris, he was appointed prof. of history of music at the École Niedermeyer (1899). His publications include: *Monsigny* (1893); *Josquin des Près* (1897); *L'École flamande du XVe siècle* (Paris, 1895; considerably augmented and publ. as *L'École contrapuntique flamande au XVe et au XVIe siècle,* 1905); *Histoire de la danse à travers les âges* (1904). He was an ardent adherent of Esperanto, and wrote the hymn of the Esperantists (1928).

Mennicke, Karl, German writer on music; b. Reichenbach, May 12, 1880; killed during World War I in Galicia, late June, 1917. He studied music with Hugo Riemann; received his *Dr. phil.* in 1905 with the dissertation *Hasse und die Brüder Graun als Symphoniker* (with thematic catalogue); subsequently conducted choral societies in various towns; edited the Riemann 'Festschrift' (1909).

Mennin, Peter, American composer; b. Erie, Penna., May 17, 1923, of Italian parents (real name, Mennini). He studied music at the Oberlin Cons. (1940-42); then was in the Army Air Force; after demobilization he resumed his music study; received his Mus. M. at the Eastman School of Music in 1945, Ph. D. in 1947; his teachers there were Howard Hanson and Bernard Rogers; he also studied conducting with Koussevitzky at the Berkshire Music Center. He received a Guggenheim Fellowship in 1947; subsequently taught at the Juilliard School of Music, N. Y. (1947-58). In 1958 he was appointed director of the Peabody Cons. in Baltimore. —His music has a strong sense of purposeful thematic development and formal compactness; he is at best in his purely instrumental works, cast in a neo-Classical mold. — Works: 7 symphonies: No. 1 (1942), No. 2 (1944), No. 3 (N. Y., Feb. 27, 1947), No. 4, *The Cycle,* for chorus and orch. (N. Y., March 18, 1949), No. 5 (1951), No. 6 (Louisville, Nov. 18, 1953), No. 7 (1955); *Sinfonia* for chamber orch. (Rochester, May 24, 1947); *Fantasia,* for string orch. (N. Y., Jan. 11, 1948); *Folk Overture* (Washington, Dec. 19, 1945); a violin concerto (1950); piano concerto (Cleveland, Feb. 27, 1958); concertino for flute, strings, and percussion; several pieces of chamber music; a piano sonata; *The Christmas Story,* cantata for chorus, soloists, and chamber orch.; choruses for women's voices; 4 choruses based on Chinese texts for mixed voices; songs.

Mennini, Louis, American composer; brother of Peter Mennin; b. Erie, Pa., Nov. 18, 1920; studied at Oberlin Cons. 1939-42; then, after 3 years in the Army Air Force, at Eastman School of Music, Rochester, N. Y., where his teachers in composition were Bernard Rogers and Howard Hanson; 1947, B. Mus. and M. Mus.; 1948-49, assistant prof., Univ. of Texas; since 1949 teaching composition and orchestration at the Eastman School. In 1949 received a grant from the National Institute of Arts and Letters. —Works: 2 chamber operas, *The Well* (Rochester, 1951) and *The Rope,* after Eugene O'Neill (Berkshire Music Festival, Aug. 8, 1955); a ballet, *Allegro Energico* (1948); for orch.: *Andante and Allegro* (1946), *Andante and Allegro Energico* (1947), *Arioso for Strings* (1948), *Canzona for Chamber Orch.* (1949), *Cantilena* (1950), *Overtura Breve* (1952); violin sonata (1947); *Tenebrae,* for chorus a cappella (1948); sonatina for cello and piano (1952); *Proper of the Mass* (1953).

Menotti, Gian Carlo, remarkable composer; b. Cadegliano, Italy, July 7, 1911; was the sixth of 10 children. He learned the rudiments of music from his mother, and began to compose as a child, making his first attempt at an opera entitled *The Death of Pierrot,* at the age of 10. He studied for several years (1923-27) at the Milan Cons.; then came to the U. S., and entered the Curtis Institute, Philadelphia (1927-33), where he studied with Rosario Scalero; subsequently taught composition at the Curtis Institute; traveled often to Europe; made his home at Mt. Kisco, N. Y. Although Menotti has associated himself with the cause of American music, and spends most of his time in the U. S., he has retained his Italian citizenship. As a composer, he is unique on the American scene, being the first to create American opera possessing such an appeal to audiences as to become established in permanent repertory. Inheriting the natural Italian gift for operatic drama and expressive singing line, he has adapted these qualities to the peculiar requirements of the American stage and to the changing fashions of the period; his serious operas have a strong dramatic content, in the realistic style stemming from the Italian 'verismo.' He writes his own librettos, marked by an extraordinary flair for drama and for the communicative power of the English language; with this is combined a fine, though subdued, sense of musical humor. As to the musical style, Menotti makes no pretensions at extreme modernism, and does not fear to approximate the successful formulas developed by Verdi and Puccini; the influence of Mussorgsky's realistic prosody is also in evidence, particularly in recitative. When dramatic tension requires a greater impact, Menotti resorts to atonal and polytonal writing, leading to climaxes accompanied by massed dissonance. His 1st successful stage work was *Amelia Goes to the Ball,* an opera buffa in 1 act (originally to an Italian libretto by the composer, as *Amelia al Ballo),* staged at the Academy of Music, Philadelphia, on April 1, 1937. This was followed by another comic opera, *The Old Maid and the Thief,* commissioned by the National Broadcasting Co., first performed on the radio, April 22, 1939, and on the stage, by the Philadelphia Opera Co., on Feb. 11, 1941. Menotti's next operatic work was *The Island God,* produced by the Metropolitan Opera, N. Y., on Feb. 20, 1942, with indifferent success; but with the production of *The Medium* (N. Y., May 8, 1946) Menotti established himself as the foremost composer-librettist of modern opera. The imaginative libretto, dealing with a fraudulent spiritualist who falls victim to her own practices when she imagines that the ghostly voices are real, suited Menotti's musical talent to perfection; the opera had a long and successful run in N. Y., an unprecedented occurrence in the history of the American lyric theater. A short humorous opera, *The Telephone,* was first produced by the N. Y. Ballet Society, Feb. 18, 1947, on the same bill with *The Medium;* these 2 contrasting works were subsequently staged all over the U. S. and in Europe, often on the same evening. Menotti then produced *The Consul* (N. Y., March 15, 1950), his best tragic work, describing the plight of political fugitives vainly trying to escape from an unnamed country, but failing to obtain the necessary visa from the consul of an anonymous power; very ingeniously, the author does not include the title character in the cast, since the consul never appears on the stage, but remains a shadowy presence. *The Consul* exceeded

Menotti's previous operas in popular success; it had a long run in N. Y., and was produced all over the world. On Christmas Eve, 1951, the National Broadcasting Co. presented Menotti's television opera *Amahl and the Night Visitors,* a Christmas story of undeniable poetry and appeal; it became an annual television production every Christmas in subsequent years. His next opera was *The Saint of Bleecker Street,* cast in a New York locale (N. Y., Dec. 27, 1954); it won the Drama Critics Circle Award for the best musical play of 1954, and the Pulitzer Prize of 1955. A madrigal ballet, *The Unicorn, the Gorgon and the Manticore,* commissioned by the Elizabeth Sprague Coolidge Foundation, was first presented at the Library of Congress, Washington, Oct. 21, 1956. His opera *Maria Golovin,* written expressly for the International Exposition at Brussels, was staged there on Aug. 20, 1958. Menotti scored all of his operas for a small orchestra, and virtually without chorus, the ensembles of solo singers performing the function of the operatic choral groups. This modest scoring has made it possible for his operas to be performed by student groups and small operatic organizations. Among Menotti's other works are the ballets *Sebastian* (1944) and *Errand into the Maze* (N. Y., Feb. 2, 1947); piano concerto (Boston, Nov. 2, 1945); *Apocalypse,* symph. poem (Pittsburgh, Oct. 19, 1951); violin concerto (Philadelphia, Dec. 5, 1952, Zimbalist soloist); also a number of *pièces d'occasion,* such as *Trio for a House-Warming Party,* for piano, cello, and flute (1936), *Variations on a Theme of Schumann* (awarded the Lauber Composition Prize, 1931); *Pastorale* for piano and string orch.; *Poemetti per Maria Rosa* (piano pieces for children); etc. Menotti is the author of the libretto for the opera *Vanessa* by Samuel Barber, produced by the Metropolitan Opera, N. Y., on Jan. 15, 1958.

Menter, Joseph, German cellist; b. Deutenkofen, Bavaria, Jan. 19, 1808; d. Munich, April 18, 1856. He began his career as a violinist, then changed to cello as a student of P. Moralt in Munich, where he entered the orch. of the Royal Opera (1833). He made several tours in Germany, the Low Countries, and England; then returned to Munich.

Menter, Sophie, German pianist and teacher; daughter of Joseph Menter; b. Munich, July 29, 1846; d. Stockdorf, near Munich, Feb. 23, 1918. She studied in Munich with Schönchen; also with Lebert and Niest; made her professional début in 1867. After hearing her, Tausig took her as a pupil. In 1869 she met Liszt, who recognized and promoted her talent. In 1872 she married the cellist David Popper (divorced 1886). From 1883 to 1887 she was professor at the Cons. of St. Petersburg, Russia; then resided at Castle Itter, in the Tyrol. She wrote a number of attractive piano pieces, and a work for piano and orch. *Ungarische Zigeunerweisen;* Tchaikovsky orchestrated the accompaniment, and she played it under Tchaikovsky's direction in Odessa on Feb. 4, 1893 (MS of the orchestration is lost).

Menuhin, Yehudi, celebrated violinist; b. New York, April 22, 1916; taken as an infant to San Francisco, where he began the study of the violin at the age of 4 with Sigmund Anker; later became a pupil of Louis Persinger. At the age of 7 he played the Mendelssohn concerto in San Francisco at a gala concert, creating a sensation. He then went to Europe, where he studied with Adolf Busch and Enesco; played in Paris as a child of 10 with the Lamoureux orch., performing 3 violin concertos on the same program. Returning to America, he made his N. Y. début in the Beethoven concerto, with the N. Y. Symph. Society, Fritz Busch conducting (Nov. 25, 1927). The interpretative maturity and the extraordinary technique of the then 11-year-old virtuoso aroused great enthusiasm, and moved the critics to praise him without the usual reservations for child prodigies; the occasion was compared with the electrifying appearance in N. Y. of Jascha Heifetz 10 years before. During the season of 1928-29, Menuhin toured California and Europe, with increasing success. An outstanding event was his playing of concertos by Bach, Beethoven, and Brahms in one evening with the Berlin Philharmonic, under the direction of Bruno Walter. He made his London début on Nov. 4, 1929, in the Brahms concerto. He played the Mendelssohn concerto with the Gewandhaus Orch. (Nov. 14, 1931) on the occasion of the sesquicentennial of that orchestra's founding. In 1934 he completed his first world tour with concerts in 73 cities in 13 countries, including Australia. In 1936 he voluntarily withdrew from the concert stage, in order to devote himself to further study. He reappeared in 1938, and thenceforth continued his triumphant career as a full-fledged artist of the first magnitude. With his sister, **Hephzibah Menuhin** (b. San Francisco, May 20, 1920), a precocious pianist, he has given numerous sonata recitals, beginning in 1930. — Cf. B. Gavoty, *Yehudi Menuhin et Georges Enesco* in the series 'Les grands interprètes' (Geneva, 1955); Robert Magidoff, *Yehudi Menuhin; the Story of the Man and the Musician* (Garden City, 1955).

Merbecke, John. See Marbeck.

Mercadante, (Giuseppe) Saverio (Raffaele), Italian composer; b. Altamura, near Bari, Sept. (baptized Sept. 17), 1795; d. Naples, Dec. 17, 1870. He was born out of wedlock; taken to Naples at the age of 13, he enrolled at the Collegio di San Sebastiano. He studied violin; after preliminary theoretical courses with Furno and Tritto, he entered the class of Zingarelli, whose favorite pupil he became. He began to compose while still in school; wrote 2 symphonies (which were praised by Rossini), several concertos, string quartets, a Mass, etc. He began his career as a dramatic composer auspiciously with the production of his first opera, *L'Apoteosi d'Ercole* (Naples, Jan. 4, 1819). He exhibited a typical Italian dramatic flair for comedy in his next opera, *Elisa e Claudio,* produced at La Scala, Milan, on Oct. 30, 1821, and subsequently staged at all important opera houses in Europe, and, within a decade, in America. Other important operas were *Caritea, Regina di Spagna* (Venice, Feb. 21, 1826), *Gabriella di Vergy* (Lisbon, Aug. 8, 1828), *I Normanni a Parigi* (Turin, Feb. 7, 1832), *I Briganti* (Paris, March 22, 1836), *Il Giuramento* (Milan, March 10, 1837; his best work; performed many times, and in the repertory of Italian opera houses well into the 20th century), *Elena da Feltre* (Naples, Dec. 26, 1838), *Il Bravo* (Milan, March 9, 1839), *La Vestale* (Naples, March 10, 1840; successful in Italy), *Leonora* (Naples, Dec. 5, 1844), *Gli Orazi ed i Curiazi* (Naples, Nov. 10, 1846), and *Virginia* (Naples, April 7, 1866; his last opera, composed in 1851, but not staged, for political reasons; although not successful with the public, the score is regarded as of fine workmanship). Mercadante composed operas for different towns, residing, after the manner of Italian opera composers, in the city for which he was writing; thus he lived in Rome, Bologna, Madrid (1827-28), Lisbon (1828-29), and Vienna (where he produced 3 operas in 1824), as well as the cities already mentioned. In 1833 he became maestro di cappella at the Cathedral of Novara; here he lost the sight of one eye, and in 1862 total blindness ensued. In 1839 he was engaged as maestro di cappella at Lanliano; and in 1840 he succeeded Zingarelli as director of the Naples Cons. Besides his operas (about 60 in all) he wrote much chamber music; a *Messa solenne,* and some 20 other Masses; *Le 7 parole di Nostro Signore,* for 4 voices with string quartet; a *Salve Regina,* a *De profundis,* 2 *Tantum ergo,* litanies, vespers, psalms, cantatas, hymns (one to Garibaldi in 1861; to Rossini in 1866); funeral symphonies to Rossini, Donizetti, Bellini, Pacini; orchestral fantasies *(L'Aurora, La Rimembranza, Il Lamento dell'Arabo, Il Lamento del Bardo,* the last composed after he had become blind); pieces for various instruments; many songs; solfeggi for the Cons.; etc.—Cf. R. Colucci, *Biografia di Saverio Mercadante* (Venice, 1867); G. Bustico, *Saverio Mercadante a Novara,* in the 'Rivista Musicale Italiana' (1921); Guido Pannain, *Saggio su la musica a Napoli nel secolo XIX,* in the 'Rivista Musicale Italiana' (1928); G. De Napoli, *La Triade Melodrammatica Altamurana: G. Tritto, V. Lavigna, S. Mercadante* (Milan, 1931); G. Solimene, *La Patria ed i genitori di Mercadante* (Naples, 1940); B. Notarnicola, *Saverio Mercadante: biografica critica* (Rome, 1945; 3rd, much revised ed., 1951, as *Saverio Mercadante nella gloria e nella luce; Verdi non ha vinto Mercadante);* a sesquicentennial publ., *Saverio Mercadante: note e documenti* (Bari, 1945; publ. by the Committee 'Pro Mercadante'); Frank Walker, *Mercadante and Verdi,* in 'Music & Letters' (Oct., 1952; Jan., 1953).

Mercadier (mehr-kah-dyā'), **Jean Baptiste,** French music theorist; b. Belesta, Ariège, April 18, 1750; d. Foix, Jan. 14, 1815. He wrote *Nouveau système de musique théorique et pratique* (1776), a critique of Tartini's and Rameau's systems, favoring Rameau.

Mercure, Pierre, Canadian composer; b. Montreal, Feb. 21, 1927. He studied piano, bassoon, and cello at the Quebec Cons. and composition in Paris with Nadia Boulanger; played the bassoon with various orchestras in Montreal.—Works: *Kaleidoscope,* symph. fantasy (1948); *Pantomime* for 14 wind instruments and percussion (1949; New York, Oct. 16, 1953, Stokowski conducting); *Lucretia Borgia* for trumpet, harpsichord, and percussion (1949); *Emprise* for clarinet, bassoon, cello, and piano (1950).

Merian, Hans, musicologist; b. Basel, 1857; d. Leipzig, May 28, 1905. He publ. *Mozarts Meisteropern* (1900); *Geschichte der Musik im 19. Jahrhundert* (1902; 2nd ed. by A. Smolian, 1906; 3rd ed. by B. Egg as *Illustrierte Geschichte der Musik von der Renaissance bis auf die Gegenwart,* 1914); also wrote a number of guides to instrumental and operatic masterpieces.

Merian, Wilhelm, Swiss musicologist; b. Basel, Sept. 18, 1889; d. there, Nov. 15, 1952. He studied with Nef in Basel and with Rezniček in Berlin; also studied musicology at the Univ. of Berlin; *Dr. phil.,* 1915, with the dissertation, *Die Tabulatur des Organisten H. Kotter.* From 1920, music editor of the 'Basler Nachrichten'; docent (1921), then (1930) prof. of musicology, at the Univ. of Basel.—Writings: *Gedenkschrift zum 50-jährigen Bestehen der Allgemeinen Musikschule in Basel* (1917); *Basels Musikleben im 19. Jahrhundert* (1920); *Die Klaviermusik der deutschen Koloristen* (1921); *Der Tanz in den deutschen Tabulaturbüchern* (1927); *Formuntersuchung zu Mozarts Klaviersonaten,* in the 'Nef-Festschrift' (1932); *Hermann Suter: der Dirigent und der Komponist* (Basel, 1936); *Hermann Suter: ein Lebensbild als Beitrag zur schweizerischen Musikgeschichte* (Basel, 1936). He was the editor of the Basel 'Kongress-Bericht' (1924), 'Geistliche Werke des 16. Jahrhunderts,' and other publications.

Mériel (mā-r'yĕhl), **Paul,** French composer; b. Mondonbleau, Loire-et-Cher, Jan. 4, 1818; d. Toulouse, Feb. 24, 1897. As a boy, he earned his living playing the violin in theater orchestras; later studied with Napoleão in Lisbon; produced a comic opera, *Cornelius l'argentier,* in Amiens; then settled in Toulouse, where he brought out a symph. poem, *Le Tasse* (*Tasso*), a grand opera, *L'Armorique* (1854), and the comic opera *Les Précieuses ridicules* (1877).

Merikanto, Aarre, Finnish composer, son of Oskar Merikanto; b. Helsinki, July 29, 1893. He studied in Leipzig with Max Reger (1912-14) and with Vassilenko in Moscow (1916-17). In 1937 he was appointed prof. of music theory at the Cons. of Helsinki; in 1951, succeeded Palmgren as head of the dept. of composition. His works include an opera, *Juha,* a ballet on a subject from the *Kalevala,* 3 symphonies, several symph. poems, 2 piano concertos, 3 violin concertos, 2 cello concertos, and a number of smaller works. In his music he was influenced by German neo-Romanticism; superimposed are some Impressionistic colors; only a few of his works are nationalist in tendency.

Merikanto, Oskar, Finnish composer; b. Helsinki, Aug. 5, 1868; d. Hausjärvi-Oiti, Feb. 17, 1924. After preliminary study in his native city, he went to Leipzig and Berlin to continue his musical education (1887). Returning to Finland, he became organist of St. John's Church, and from 1911 till 1922 was conductor of the National Opera in Helsinki. He wrote a great number of songs, which became very popular in Finland; organ works and manuals for organ playing; various instrumental pieces; and 3 operas: *Pohjan Neiti* (*The Maid of Bothnia;* Viborg, June 18, 1908), *Elinan Surma* (*Elina's Death;* Helsinki, Nov. 17, 1910), and *Regina von Emmeritz* (Helsinki, Jan. 30, 1920). —Cf. Yrjö Suomalainen, *Oskar Merikanto* (Helsinki, 1950).

Merk (märk), **Joseph,** Austrian cellist; b. Vienna, March 18, 1795; d. Ober-Döbling, June 16, 1852. He was trained in Vienna; in 1818 became 1st cellist at the Vienna Opera; in 1823, teacher at the Cons. He wrote 2 cello concertos, fantasias, polonaises, etc.; his cello études are of value to students.

Merkel, Gustav (Adolf), German organist and composer; b. Oberoderwitz, Nov. 12, 1827; d. Dresden, Oct. 30, 1885. He studied organ with J. Schneider and theory with J. Otto; also was aided by Schumann's advice. He was organist in several churches in Dresden, and taught at the Dresden Cons. from 1861; wrote many valuable organ works: 9 sonatas (for 4 hands, with double pedal); 5 fantasias; 30 pedal studies; an organ method; also motets and songs.

Merklin, Joseph, famous organ builder; b. Oberhausen, Baden, Jan. 17, 1819; d. Nancy, France, June 10, 1905. He was trained in the workshops of his father, organ builder at Freiburg, and Walcker; established himself in Brussels, 1843; won a medal at the National Exposition of 1847; took his brother-in-law, F. Schütze, into partnership, changing the firm name to 'Merklin, Schütze & Cie.' in 1853, and to 'Merklin-Schütze' in 1858. In 1855 they bought out Ducroquet of Paris, and established a branch in that city.

Merö, Yolanda, pianist; b. Budapest, Aug. 30, 1887. She studied piano with her father, and later at the Budapest Cons.; made her 1st appearance in Dresden, playing Liszt's 1st concerto with the Dresden Philharmonic; then toured Europe; appeared in America for the 1st time with the Russian Symph. Orch., N. Y. (Nov. 3, 1909); married Herman Irion of Steinway & Sons, N. Y., and remained in the U. S.; was active in various musical societies (Musicians' Emergency Fund, Inc., etc.).

Merola, Gaetano, conductor and impresario; b. Naples, Jan. 4, 1881; d. San Francisco, Aug. 30, 1953. He studied at the Naples Cons.; came to the U. S. in 1899, and was appointed assistant conductor at the Metropolitan Opera House; also conducted with the Henry Savage English Opera, N. Y. (1903), the Manhattan Opera Co., N. Y. (1906), etc.; in 1923 became general director of the San Francisco and Los Angeles Operas. He collapsed and died while conducting a concert at Sigmund Stern Grove in San Francisco.

Merrick, Frank, English pianist and composer; b. Clifton, Bristol, April 30, 1886. He studied with his father and his mother; then was sent to Vienna to take lessons with Leschetizky. He made his London début in 1903; in 1910, won a Rubinstein award in St. Petersburg, Russia; in 1911 married the pianist, Hope Squire, with whom he appeared in duo-piano recitals. From 1911 to 1929 he taught at the Royal Manchester College of Music; in 1929 became prof. at the Royal College of Music in London; continued his career as a concert pianist; edited the Students' Edition of Chopin's works; wrote a *Celtic Suite* for small orch.; *Dream-Pageant* for string orch.; chamber music and choral works. He won a prize from the Columbia Gramophone Co. for an orchestral scherzo and finale, completing Schubert's *Unfinished Symphony* (Schubert Centennial, 1928).

Merrill, Robert, American baritone; b. Brooklyn, June 4, 1917. He studied with his mother, Lillian Miller Merrill. In 1943 he began his professional career as a popular singer at the Radio City Music Hall, N. Y.; also sang occasionally in small opera enterprises. In 1945 he won an audition with the Metropolitan Opera; made a successful début there as Germont in *La Traviata* (Dec. 15, 1945), and remained on the roster; also appeared in recitals.

Merritt, Arthur Tillman, American musicologist and pedagogue; b. Calhoun, Mo., Feb. 15, 1902. He received the A.B. degree at the Univ. of Missouri (1924) and A.M. from Harvard Univ. (1927). He then went to Europe, on the J. K. Paine traveling scholarship from Harvard, and studied in Paris with Nadia Boulanger and Paul Dukas. He taught at Trinity College, Hartford, Conn. (1930-32); in 1932 was appointed to the staff of the music dept. of Harvard; prof., 1946. He is the author of a valuable treatise, *16th Century Polyphony: a Basis for the Study of Counterpoint* (Cambridge, Mass., 1939; several subsequent reprints).

Merseburger, Carl Wilhelm, founder of the music-publishing firm in Leipzig bearing his name; b. 1816; d. 1885. In 1849 he purchased the publishing business of Carl Friedrich Meusel; specializing in school music, he brought out a great number of useful manuals and song books; also was the publisher of 'Euterpe,' a periodical on education. His successor was his brother, **Otto Merseburger** (1822-1898); the latter was succeeded by his son, **Max Merseburger** (1852-1935). The entire stock was destroyed during the air raids on Leipzig in 1945; after the end of the war, the business was resumed, with headquarters in Darmstadt, and a branch in Berlin. A centennial 'Festschrift' was publ. in Leipzig, 1949, by the grandson of the founder.

Mersenne (mär-sehn'), **Marin,** important French theorist; b. Oizé, Sept. 8, 1588; d. Paris, Sept. 1, 1648. He was a member of the Franciscan Order (from 1613); between 1640 and 1645 made 3 trips to Italy; maintained a correspondence with the leading philosophers and scientists of his time. His writings provide source material of fundamental importance for the history of 17th-century music. — Publications: *Traité de l'harmonie universelle* (1627), later expanded to *Harmonie universelle* (1636-37; 2 large folio vols. with illustrations and musical examples; includes a *Traité des instruments,* depicting and describing all instruments of the 17th century; his most important work); *Quaestiones celeberrimae in Genesim* (1623; chiefly on Hebrew music); *Questions harmoniques* (1634); *Les Préludes de l'harmonie universelle* (1634); *Harmonicorum libri XII* (1635; enlarged ed., 1648); etc. — Cf. C. Adam, *Le Père Mersenne et ses correspondants en France* (Paris, 1897); A. Pirro, *Les Correspondants du Père Mersenne,* in the 'Bulletin de la Société Internationale de Musique' (1909); P. Tannery, *Correspondance du Père Marin Mersenne* (Paris, 1933); H. Ludwig, *Marin Mersenne und seine Musiklehre* (Halle, 1934); R. Lenoble, *Mersenne ou la naissance du mécanisme* (Paris, 1943). The 7 books of the *Traité des instruments* were translated into English for the first time by Roger E. Chapman and publ. under the title, *Harmonie Universelle: The Books on Instruments* (The Hague, 1957).

Mersmann, Hans, German musicologist; b. Potsdam, Oct. 6, 1891. He studied in Munich with Sandberger and in Leipzig and Berlin with Kretzschmar; *Dr. phil.* with the dissertation *Beiträge zur Ansbacher Musikgeschichte* (1916). He subsequently occupied various teaching positions: at the Stern Cons. in Berlin, and the Technische Hochschule there, until 1933; was in charge of folksong archives of the Prussian Volksliederkommission (1917-33); also organized numerous seminars on musicology and modern music; edited the periodical 'Melos'; wrote music criticism. In 1947 he was appointed director of the Hochschule für Musik in Cologne. As a historian and analyst of modern music, Mersmann occupies an important position in contemporary research. Apart from numerous papers in German periodicals, he publ. *Angewandte Musikästhetik* (collected papers on esthetics; Berlin, 1926); *Kulturgeschichte der Musik in Einzeldarstellungen* (Berlin, 1923-25; 4 vols.: *Das deutsche Volkslied; Beethoven; Musik der Gegenwart; Mozart*); *Die moderne Musik seit der Romantik,* in Bücken's 'Handbuch der Musikwissenschaft' (1928); *Die Tonsprache der neuen Musik,* in 'Melosbücherei' (ed. by Mersmann, 1928; 2nd ed., 1930); *Das Musikseminar* (Leipzig, 1931); *Kammermusik* (*Leipzig,* 1930-34; in 4 vols.: *Die Kammermusik des 17. und 18. Jahrhunderts; Beethoven; Deutsche Romantik; Europäische Kammermusik des 19. und 20. Jahrhunderts*); *Eine deutsche Musikgeschichte* (Potsdam, 1934; enlarged to include music history of other Western nations, publ. as *Musikgeschichte in der abendländischen Kultur,* 1955); *Volkslied und Gegenwart* (Potsdam, 1936); *Musikhören* (Berlin, 1938; enlarged ed., 1952); *Neue Musik in den Strömungen unserer Zeit* (1949). — Cf. W. Wiora, ed., *Musikerkenntnis und Musikerziehung. Dankesgaben für H. Mersmann zu seinem 65. Geburtstag* (1957).

Mertens, Joseph, Belgian composer; b. Antwerp, Feb. 17, 1834; d. Brussels, June 30, 1901. He was 1st violinist at the Opéra in Brussels; violin teacher at the Cons.; conductor of the Flemish Opera there (1878-89); then inspector of the Belgian music schools, and finally director of the Royal Theater at The Hague. He composed a number of Flemish and French operettas and operas which had local success: *De zwaarte Kapitein* (The Hague, 1877); *De Vrijer in de strop* (1866); *La Méprise* (1869); *L'Egoïsa* (1873); *Thécla* (1874); *Liederik l'intendent* (1875); *Les trois étudiants; Le Vin, le jeu et le tabac; Le Capitaine Robert; Les Évincés;* etc.

Mertke, Eduard, pianist and composer; b. Riga, June 17, 1833; d. Cologne, Sept. 25, 1895. He studied with S. von Lützau (piano) and Agthe (theory); appeared in public as a child pianist; toured in Russia and Germany; in 1869, was appointed to the faculty of the Cologne Cons., where he continued to teach until his death. He wrote 3 operas: *Lisa, oder die Sprache des Herzens* (Mannheim, Feb. 24, 1872), *Resi vom Hemsensteig,* and *Kyrill von Thessalonica* (performed posthumously in Russia); 2 cantatas; many piano pieces; technical exercises and a School of Octaves for piano; he edited the works of Chopin; arranged for 2 pianos some orchestral works of Mendelssohn, Weber, and Hummel; publ. a collection, *Melodies of the Ukraine.*

Mertz (märts), **Joseph Kasper,** distinguished guitar player; b. Pressburg, Hungary, August 17, 1806; d. Vienna, Oct. 14, 1856. His parents were poor, and he was early obliged to give music lessons to support himself. In 1840 he took part in a concert at Vienna; then made a tour through Moravia, Silesia, Poland; gave concerts in 1842 at Dresden, where he met and married the pianist Josephine Plantin, with whom he played in Chemnitz, Leipzig, and Prague, before settling in Vienna.

Merula, Tarquinio, Italian composer; b. Cremona, c. 1600; date of death unknown. He was maestro di cappella at the Church of Santa Maria in Bergamo (1623); organist at the court of Sigismund III of Poland (1624); organist at Sant' Agata in Cremona and maestro di cappella of the Cathedral in Cremona (1628); again at Santa Maria in Bergamo (1639); maestro di cappella and organist of the Cathedral there (1640); then at Cremona as maestro di cappella of the Cathedral (1652). —Published works: *Canzoni a 4 per stromenti, lib. 1* (Venice, 1615); *Madrigali et altre musiche concertate a 1-5* (Venice, 1623); *Madrigaletti a 3, lib. 1,* op. 4 (Venice, 1624); *Madrigali a 4-8 voci, lib. 1,* op. 5 (Venice, 1624); *Satiro, e Corsica, dialogo* (Venice, 1626); *Concerti spirituali . . . a 2-5 voci, lib. 2* (Venice, 1628); *Canzoni, overe Sonate concertate per chiesa, lib. 2,* op. 12 (Venice, 1637); *Curtio precipitato et altri capricii*

. . ., *lib. 2,* op. 13 (Venice, 1638); *Canzoni da suonare a tre,* op. 9 (Venice, 1639); *Concerto decimo quinto . . . Messi, salmi . . . concertati, a 2-12* (Venice, 1639); *Arpa Davidica . . . Pegaso, salmi, motetti, a 2-5, lib. 3,* op. 11 (Venice, 1640); *Arpa Davidica, salmi et messa . . .,* op. 16 (Venice, 1640); *Canzoni da suonare a 2-3, lib. 4,* op. 17 (Venice, 1651); *Salmi et messa concertati a 3-4, lib. 3,* op. 18 (Venice, 1652); etc. A *Sonata cromatica* for organ was publ. by L. Torchi in 'L'Arte Musicale in Italia' (vol. 4); examples of Merula's violin music are in Riemann's *Alte Kammermusik.* —Cf. article by M. Seiffert in 'Vierteljahrsschrift für Musikwissenschaft' (VII, 410).

Merulo (real name Merlotti), **Claudio,** Italian organist and composer; called 'da Correggio'; b. Correggio, April 8, 1533; d. Parma, May 4, 1604. He was a pupil of Menon and G. Donati; organist at Brescia in 1556; on July 2, 1557, chosen 2nd organist at San Marco, Venice; in 1566, succeeded Padovano as 1st organist, and held this position until 1584, when he went to Mantua, and then to Parma, where he became court organist. He was reputed to be one of the greatest organists of his time; as composer, he was an important representative of the Venetian School; his works opened a new era of independent composition for the organ. He also produced a drama in madrigal style, *La Tragedia* (Venice, July 21, 1574); was renowned as a teacher; Conforti was one of his pupils. Most of Merulo's works were publ. posthumously; they include: *Canzoni d'intavolatura d'organo* (1592), *Toccate d'intavolatura d'organo* (1604; 2 books), and *Ricercari d'intavolatura d'organo* (1605); 4 vols. of madrigals for 3, 4, and 5 voices (1566-1604); 2 vols. of motets for 5 voices (1578), *Ricercari da cantare* for 4 voices (1607; 1608); *Canzoni alla francese* (1620). Reprints of his organ works have been publ. by C. G. Winterfeld in *Johann Gabrieli und sein Zeitalter* (1 piece), A. Catelani in *Claudio Merulo* (2 pieces), K. F. Weitzmann in *Geschichte des Klavierspiels* (1 piece), A. Reissmann in *Allgemeine Geschichte der Musik* (1 piece), A. G. Ritter in *Zur Geschichte des Orgelspiels im 14.-18. Jahrhundert* (1 piece), Torchi in 'L'Arte Musicale in Italia' IV (4 pieces), Riemann, in *Musikgeschichte in Beispielen* (1 piece), A. Einstein in the musical supplement to his *Geschichte der Musik* (1 piece), J. Wolf in *Sing- und Spielmusik aus älterer Zeit (La Leonora),* A. Schering in *Geschichte der Musik in Beispielen* (No. 149), A. T. Davison & W. Apel in *Historical Anthology of Music* (vol. 1, No. 153), etc. —Cf. A. Catelani, *Memorie della vita e delle opere di Claudio Merulo* (Milan, 1859; reprinted in the 'Bollettino bibliografico musicale,' Milan, 1930-31); Q. Bigi, *Di Claudio Merulo* (Parma, 1861); *Claudio Merulo da Correggio* (Parma, 1904; essays by 8 Italian scholars); A. Einstein, *Claudio Merulos Ausgabe der Madrigale des Verdelot,* in the 'Sammelbände der Internationalen Musik-Gesellschaft' (vol. VIII, 2; 1907); O. Kinkeldey, *Orgel und Klavier in der Musik des 16. Jahrhunderts* (1910). See also G. Reese, *Music in the Renaissance* (N. Y., 1954; pp. 540-41).

Merz (märts), **Karl,** German-American musician; b. Bensheim, near Frankfurt, Sept. 19, 1836; d. Wooster, Ohio, Jan. 30, 1890. He was a pupil of his father and F. J. Kunkel; went to the U. S. in 1854, and lived in Philadelphia as a teacher. He was a contributor to various periodicals; his collected essays, *Music and Culture,* edited by his son, Dr. Charles H. Merz, were publ. in Philadelphia (1890).

Messager (mĕhs-săh-zhā'), **André (-Charles-Prosper),** celebrated French composer and conductor; b. Montluçon, Allier, Dec. 30, 1853; d. Paris, Feb. 24, 1929. He studied at the École Niedermeyer in Paris with Gigout (composition), A. Laussel (piano), and C. Loret (organ); then took lessons with Saint-Saëns. In 1874 he became organist at St.-Sulpice; subsequently was choir director at Sainte-Marie des Batignoles (1882-84). He began his career as conductor at the Opéra-Comique (1898-1908); also directed the opera at Covent Garden, London (1901-07). From 1907 till 1915 he was the regular conductor of the Paris Opéra; was in charge of the Société des Concerts du Conservatoire from 1908 until his death; under the auspices of the French government he visited the U.S. with that orchestra, giving concerts in 50 American cities (Oct.-Dec., 1918). Returning to Paris, he again conducted at the Opéra-Comique; led a season of Diaghilev's Ballets Russes in 1924. As conductor, he played an important role in Paris concert life; he directed the première of *Pelléas et Mélisande* (1902, with 21 rehearsals), the score of which Debussy dedicated to him. His initial steps as a composer were auspicious; his symph. (1875) was awarded the gold medal of the Société des Compositeurs and performed at the Concerts Colonne (Jan. 20, 1878); his dramatic scene, *Don Juan* *et Haydée* (1876), was awarded a gold medal by the Academy of St. Quentin. He wrote several other works for orch. (*Impressions orientales, Suite funambulesque,* etc.) and some chamber music, but he was primarily a man of the theater. His style may be described as enlightened eclecticism; his music is characteristically French, and more specifically, Parisian, in its elegance and gayety. He was honored in France; in 1926 he was elected to the Académie des Beaux Arts. He was married to Hope Temple (real name, Dotie Davies, 1859-1938), who was the author of numerous songs. His operas (first performed in Paris except where otherwise indicated) include *François les-bas-bleus* (Jan. 20, 1878; score begun by F. Bernicat and completed after his death by Messager); *La Fauvette du Temple* (Nov. 17, 1885); *La Béarnaise* (Dec. 12, 1885); *Le Bourgeois de Calais* (April 6, 1887); fairy-tale, *Isoline* (Dec. 26, 1888; ballet suite from it is popular); *La Basoche* (May 30, 1890; greatly acclaimed); *Madame Chrysanthème* (after Loti; Jan. 30, 1893; to a story similar to Puccini's *Madama Butterfly* produced 11 years later; but Puccini's dramatic treatment eclipsed Messager's lyrical setting); *Le Chevalier d'Harmental* (May 5, 1896); *Véronique* (Dec. 10, 1898; successful); *Les Dragons de l'Impératrice* (Feb. 13, 1905); *Fortunio* (June 5, 1907); *Béatrice* (Monte Carlo, March 21, 1914); *Monsieur Beaucaire* (Birmingham, April 7, 1919). Among his successful operettas were *Le Mari de la Reine* (1889); *Miss Dollar* (1893); *La Fiancée en Loterie* (1896); *Les p'tites Michu* (Paris, Nov. 16, 1897; many subsequent performances); *La petite fonctionnaire,* dance-hall operetta (Paris, May 14, 1921); *Passionnément* (Paris, Jan. 15, 1926). His ballets include *Fleur d'Oranger* (1878); *Les Vins de France* (1879); *Mignons et Vilains* (1879); *Les deux Pigeons* (1886); *Scaramouche* (1891); *Amants éternels* (1893); *Le Chevalier aux Fleurs,* in collaboration with Pugno (1897); *Le Procès des Roses* (1897); *Une Aventure de la Guimard* (1900). He also wrote incidental music to Delair's *Hélène* (1891) and Moreau's and Carré's *La Montagne enchantée,* in collaboration with Leroux (1897). An autobiographical sketch and articles on Messager are found in 'Musica' (Paris, Sept., 1908); see also O. Séré, *Musiciens français d'aujourd'hui* (1911; revised ed., 1921); H. Février, *André Messager; mon maître, mon ami* (Paris, 1948); M. Augé-Laribé, *André Messager, musicien de théâtre* (Paris, 1951).

Messchaert (mehs'-hahrt), **Johannes Martinus,** Dutch baritone; b. Hoorn, Aug. 22, 1857; d. Zürich, Sept. 9, 1922. He studied violin, then changed to singing; was a pupil of Stockhausen in Frankfurt and Wüllner in Munich; began his career as choral conductor in Amsterdam; then appeared as a singer of the German repertory; lived for many years in Berlin; from 1911 to 1920 taught singing at the Hochschule für Musik; in 1920 went to teach at the Cons. of Zürich. —Cf. F. Martienssen, *Johannes Messchaert. Ein Beitrag zum Verständnis echter Gesangskunst* (Berlin, 1914; 2nd ed., 1920); id., *Johannes Messchaert, Eine Gesangsstunde;* F. Martienssen also edited 2 vols. of Schubert's songs with Messchaert's dynamic marks (Mainz, 1928).

Messiaen (mĕh-sē-yăn), **Olivier,** outstanding French composer; b. Avignon, Dec. 10, 1908. A scion of a literary family (his father was a prof. of literature; his mother a well-known poetess, Cécile Sauvage), he began to play the piano without a teacher; at the age of 11 he enrolled in the Paris Cons., where he studied with Jean and Noël Gallon, Marcel Dupré, Maurice Emmanuel, and Paul Dukas; won several prizes there for harmony, organ, improvisation, and composition; graduated in 1930. In 1931 he became organist at the Trinity Church in Paris; in 1936, jointly with Jolivet, Baudrier, and Lesur he organized the group known as 'La jeune France' with the aim of promoting modern French music; was in the French Army in World War II; was taken prisoner by the Germans, and spent 2 years (1940-41) in a prison camp at Görlitz, Silesia; repatriated in 1942, and resumed his post of organist at the Trinity Church in Paris; also appointed prof. of harmony at the Paris Cons.; from 1947 he taught esthetics and rhythm there. In 1949 he led a seminar in composition at the Berkshire Music Center in Tanglewood. —Messiaen is one of the most original modern composers and theorists; in his music he makes use of a wide range of resources, from Gregorian chants to Oriental rhythms. A mystic by nature and persuasion, he strives to find a relationship between progressions of musical sounds and religious entities; in his theory of composition, he establishes a new terminology of transposed modes, exploits asymmetrical rhythms, and applies basically triadic harmonies, often combining them in dissonant polytonal structures. Seeking new sonorities, he makes use of exotic percussion instruments and electronic wave-generators ('Ondes Martenot'). The culmination and a synthesis of the disparate elements of his musical resources is the grandiose symph. *Turangalila,* in 10 movements, the title being a Hindu word that means approximately a love-song; this work includes *Trois Talas* for piano and orch., first performed in Paris, Feb. 15, 1948. —Works: for orch.: *Le Banquet eucharistique* (1928); *Simple Chant d'une âme* (1930); *Les Offrandes oubliées* (Paris, Feb. 19, 1931); *Le Tombeau resplendissant* (Paris, Feb. 12, 1933); *Hymne au Saint Sacrement* (Paris, March 23, 1933); *L'Ascension* (1934); *Trois Petites Liturgies de la Présence Divine,* for voices and orch. (Paris, April 21, 1945); *Hymne* (N.Y., March 13, 1947); *Turangalila* (Boston Symph., Dec. 2, 1949, Leonard Bernstein conducting); *Réveil des Oiseaux,* for piano and orch. (Donaueschingen, Oct. 11, 1953); choral works: Mass for 8 sopranos and 4 violins (1933); *O sacrum convivium* (1937); *Chœurs pour une Jeanne d'Arc,* for chorus a cappella (1941); 5 *Rechants* (1949); chamber music: *Le Merle Noir,* for flute and piano; *Mort du nombre,* for soprano, tenor, violin, and piano (Paris, March 25, 1931); *Quatuor pour la fin du temps,* for violin, clarinet, cello, and piano (composed in the prison camp in Silesia and performed there, with the composer at the piano, Jan. 15, 1941); pieces for violin and piano; *La Vision de l'Amen,* for 2 pianos (1942); *20 Regards sur l'enfant Jésus,* for piano (1944); *Mode de valeurs et d'intensité,* for piano (1949); *Harawi,* 'chant d'amour et de mort' for dramatic soprano and piano; other songs; for organ: *L'Ascension* (4 meditations); *La Nativité du Seigneur* (9 meditations); *Le Banquet céleste; Les Corps glorieux* (7 visions); *Messe de la Pentecôte; Livre d'orgue* (7 pieces). —Books: *20 Leçons de solfèges modernes* (1933); *20 Leçons d'harmonie* (1939); *Technique de mon langage musical* (2 vols., 1944; English transl. under the title, *The Technique of My Musical Language,* in 2 vols.; Chicago, 1957). —Cf. B. Gavoty, *Musique et mystique: le 'cas' Messiaen* (Paris, 1945); Virginie Zinke-Bianchini, *Olivier Messiaen . . .; notice biographique; catalogue détaillé des œuvres éditées* (Paris, 1949); Claude Rostand, *Olivier Messiaen* (Paris, 1958; contains a list of works and a discography).

Messiter, Arthur Henry, organist; b. Frome, Somersetshire, England, April 12, 1834; d. New York, July 2, 1916. He was for 31 years (1866-97) organist and choirmaster at Trinity Church, N. Y.; publ. *A History of the Choir and Music of Trinity Church* (1906).

Messner, Joseph, Austrian organist and composer; b. Schwatz, Tyrol, Feb. 27, 1893. He studied in Innsbruck and Munich; 1922, became cathedral organist in Salzburg; 1926, conductor there; director of the cathedral concerts of the Salzburg Festivals (1932). —Works: 4 operas: *Hadassa* (Aachen, March 27, 1925), *Das letzte Recht* (1932), *Ines* (1933), *Agnes Bernauer* (1935); 3 symphonies; a violin concerto; a cello concerto; several works for chorus and orch.; a number of church compositions; chamber music. He edited a collection of old Salzburg masters (Bernardi, Caldara, M. Haydn, Leopold Mozart, W. A. Mozart); also Masses by Anton Bruckner.

Metallov, Vassili Mikhailovitch, Russian musicologist; b. Saratov, March 13, 1862; d. Moscow, 1927. He studied theology and Russian church music; in 1901, appointed prof. of history of Russian church singing at the Moscow Cons. His works on Russian church music possess great authority; they include *Alphabet of the Neume Songs* (Moscow, 1899); *The Synodal Singers* (1898); *Outline of the History of the Orthodox Church Song in Russia* (1893); *The Strict Style* (1897); etc. Metallov twice received awards from the Russian Academy of Science.

Metastasio, Pietro Antonio Domenico Bonaventura, famous Italian poet and opera librettist; b. Rome, Jan. 3, 1698; d. Vienna, April 12, 1782. He was the son of a papal soldier named Trapassi, but in his professional career assumed the Greek translation of the name, both Trapassi (or Trapassamento) and Metastasio meaning transition. He was a learned classicist; began to write plays as a young boy; studied music with Porpora; he achieved great fame in Italy as a playwright; in 1730 he was appointed by Emperor Charles VI court poet at Vienna. He wrote about 35 opera texts, which were set to music by Handel, Gluck, Mozart, Hasse, Porpora, Jommelli and many other celebrated composers; some of them were set to music 60 or more times. His librettos were remarkable for their melodious verse, which naturally suggested musical associations; the libretto to the opera by Niccolo Conforto, *La Nitteti* (1754; first performed in Madrid, Sept. 23, 1756), was on the same subject as *Aida,* anticipating the latter by more than a century. Metastasio's complete works were publ. in Paris (1780-82; 12 vols.), Mantua (1816-20; 20 vols.), etc. —Cf. S. Mattei, *Memorie per servire alla vita del Metastasio* (Colle, 1785); C. Burney, *Life and Letters of Metastasio* (3 vols., 1796); M. Zito, *Studio su Pietro Metastasio* (Naples, 1904); E. M. Leonardi, *Il Melodramma del Metastasio* (Naples, 1909); L. Russo, *Metastasio* (1921); A. Gustarelli, *Metastasio* (1930); M. Apollonio, *Metastasio* (1931); A. Bonaventura, *Pietro Metastasio musicista,* in 'Musica d'oggi' (1932); A. Vullo, *Confronto fra i melodrammi di Zeno e Metastasio* (Agrigento, 1935); A. Salazar, *Un Antecedente de Aida en España,* in 'Nuestra Música' (Mexico, 1950); see also A. Wotquenne, *Verzeichnis der Stücke in Versen . . . von Zeno, Metastasio und Goldoni* (Leipzig, 1905).

Metcalf, Frank J., American hymnologist; b. Ashland, Mass., April 4, 1865; d. Washington, D.C., Feb. 25, 1945. He studied at Boston Univ. (B.A., 1886); was for 42 years a clerk in the War Department. He owned a private collection of more than 2000 hymn books, including Lyon's *Urania* (1761) and other rare editions; also a MS bibliography containing about 10,000 entries. He publ. *American Psalmody* (N.Y., 1917); *American Writers and Compilers of Sacred Music* (N.Y., 1925); *Stories of Hymn Tunes* (N.Y., 1928); also numerous articles.

Methfessel (māt'-fĕs-sĕl), **Albert Gottlieb,** German composer; b. Stadtilm, Thuringia, Oct. 6, 1785; d. Heckenbeck, near Gandersheim, March 23, 1869. From 1832 until 1842 he was court composer at Brunswick, then retired on pension. —Works: the opera *Der Prinz von Basra;* oratorio, *Das befreite Jerusalem;* sonatas and sonatinas for piano; part-songs, publ. in his *Liederbuch, Liederkranz,* and other collections. —Cf. W. H. Riehl, *Musikalische Charakterköpfe* (Stuttgart, 1879; vol. 3). His brother, **Friedrich Methfessel** (b. Stadtilm, Aug. 27, 1771; d. there, May, 1807), publ. songs with guitar accompaniment.

Metner, Nikolai. See **Medtner.**

Métra, (Jules-Louis-) Olivier, French composer of light music; b. Reims, June 2, 1830; d. Paris, Oct. 22, 1889. An actor's son, he became an actor himself as a boy; was first taught music by Ed. Roche; then was a pupil at the Paris Cons. of Elwart (1849-54). He played violin, cello, and double-bass at Paris theaters; then conducted at various dance halls; the masked balls at the Opéra-Comique (1871); the orch. at the Folies-Bergère (1872-77); the balls at the Théâtre de la Monnaie, Brussels (1874-76); finally the balls at the Paris Opéra. His waltzes, mazurkas, polkas, quadrilles, etc. were extremely popular; at the Folies-Bergère he produced 19 operettas and ballet divertissements; and at the Opéra the ballet *Yedda* (1879).

Métru, Nicolas, French organist and composer; b. Bar-sur-Aube, c. 1600; d. Paris, c. 1670. He was organist at St.-Nicolas-des-Champs in Paris; was Lully's teacher. Ballard publ. his *Fantaisies* in 2 parts for string instruments (1642), 2 books of airs (1646), and an *Air sur la paix et le mariage du roy* (1662).

Mettenleiter, Dominicus, German music historian, brother of Johann Georg Mettenleiter; b. Tannenhausen, Württemberg, May 20, 1822; d. Regensburg, May 2, 1868; *Dr. theol.* and *phil.* He wrote *Musikgeschichte der Stadt Regensburg* (1866), *Musikgeschichte der Oberpfalz* (1867); and contributed to his brother's *Enchiridion.* His fine music library was united with Proske's in the Bishop's Library at Regensburg.

Mettenleiter, Johann Georg, German church composer, brother of Dominicus Mettenleiter; b. St. Ulrich, near Ulm, April 6, 1812; d. Regensburg, Oct. 6, 1858, as choirmaster and organist at the cathedral. An erudite church composer, he publ. *Manuale breve cantionum ac precum* (1852) and an *Enchiridion chorale . . .* (1855), both with added organ accompaniments; also Psalm 95, for 6 male voices (1854); other works in MS (Masses; a *Stabat Mater;* 2 *Miserere; Ave Maria* for double chorus, etc.). His brother wrote his biography, *Johann Georg Mettenleiter, ein Künstlerbild* (1866).

Metzler, Valentin, music publisher and instrument dealer in London; b. Bingen, Germany; d. London, 1833. He settled in London about 1788 and opened a shop for the sale of musical instruments; after his death, his son George Richard Metzler (1797-1867) became the owner, and the name of the firm was G. Metzler & Co. In 1816 the firm began to publish music; in 1867 G. Metzler entered into partnership with Frank Chappell; the firm continued to carry on its business in London until 1930.

Meulemans (moi'-lĕh-mans), **Arthur,** Flemish composer, b. Aarschot, May 19, 1884. He studied with Edgar Tinel; then became a teacher in provincial Belgian towns. From 1930 to 1942, he was conductor of the orch. of the Brussels Radio. In 1954 he was elected president of the Royal Flemish Academy of Sciences, Literature, and Fine Arts. An exceptionally prolific composer, he wrote 14 symphonies between 1931 and 1954; 3 operas: *Vikings* (1919), *Adriaen Brouwer* (1926), and *Egmont* (1944); 3 violin concertos; 2 cello concertos; a piano concerto; a flute concerto; an oboe concerto; a trumpet concerto; a harp concerto; 5 string quartets; quartet for saxophones; quartet for trombones; many works for various instrumental combinations; 4 piano sonatas; 2 dance suites for piano; much choral music; etc. A catalogue of his works was publ. by the Centre Belge de Documentation Musicale in 1954.

Mey (mī), **Kurt Johannes,** German musicologist; b. Dresden, June 24, 1864; d. there, Sept. 21, 1912. He studied with K. A. Fischer in Dresden and with Spitta at the Univ. of Berlin; after filling various positions as répétiteur in provincial opera houses, he returned to Dresden. He publ. *Der Meistergesang in Geschichte und Kunst* (1892; revised ed., 1901); *Die Musik als tönende Weltidee* (part I, *Die metaphysischen Urgesetze der Melodik,* 1901); etc.

Meybom, Marcus. See **Meibom.**

Meyer, Ernst Hermann, German musicologist; b. Berlin, Dec. 8, 1905. After a brief career in business, he studied musicology at the Univ. of Berlin with Johannes Wolf, Curt Sachs, Friedrich Blume, Hornbostel, and others; then at the Univ. of Heidelberg with Besseler; received his *Dr. phil.* in 1930 with a thesis on the polyphonic German sonata of the 17th century; in 1930 became a music critic; also continued his studies and took lessons in modern composition with Hanns Eisler and Hindemith. In 1931 he received a scholarship to undertake research on early instrumental music in Europe, for which he visited France and England. With the advent of the Nazi regime in 1933, he established himself in London, working in the film industry; also conducted a workers' chorus in Cambridge. In 1948 he went back to Germany, and became prof. at Humboldt Univ. in Berlin. He publ. *English Chamber Music . . . from the Middle Ages to Purcell* (London, 1946); *Musik im Zeitgeschehen* (Berlin, 1952); contributed numerous papers on musical sociology (from the Marxist standpoint) to various magazines.

Meyer, Leopold von (called **Leopold de Meyer**), celebrated piano virtuoso; b. Baden, near Vienna, Dec. 20, 1816; d. Dresden, March 5, 1883. He studied with Czerny and Fischhof; from the age of 19, embarked on a series of pianistic tours in Europe, and in America (1845-47). At his concerts, he invariably included his own compositions, written in a characteristic salon style; his agents spread sensational publicity about him in order to arouse interest. A *Biography of Leopold de Meyer* was publ. in London in 1845.

Meyer-Beer, Kathi, musicologist; b. Berlin, July 27, 1892; studied piano there with Frieda Kwast-Hodapp and G. Bertram; then musicology at the Univ. of Berlin with Kretzschmar, Riemann, and Johannes Wolf. In 1922 she became librarian of the Paul Hirsch Music Library in Frankfurt (transferred in 1936 to Cambridge, England); was music critic for the 'Frankfurter Zeitung' (1923-33). In 1936 she went to Paris; in 1939 settled in N. Y., where she was active as librarian, teacher, and writer. She publ. *Der chorische Gesang der Frauen* (Leipzig, 1917), *Das Konzert* (Stuttgart, 1925), *Bedeutung und Wesen der Musik* (Strasbourg, 1932), and a great number of valuable articles in German and American magazines; edited the catalogue of the Hirsch Library in 4 vols.; brought out new editions of Bottrigari's *Il Desiderio* (1924), etc.

Meyer-Helmund, Erik, composer; b. St. Petersburg, April 25, 1861; d. Berlin, April 4, 1932. He studied music with his father; then in Berlin with Kiel; was first a singer, and traveled extensively in Europe, introducing his own songs; from 1911 he lived in Berlin. He is best known as a song composer; more than 200 of his light vocal numbers were published; also composed 5 operas: *Margitta* (Magdeburg, 1889), *Der Liebeskampf* (Dresden, 1892), *Taglioni* (Berlin, 1912), *Traumbilder* (Berlin, 1912), and *Die schöne Frau Marlies* (Altenburg, 1916); also the operettas *Trischka* (Riga, 1894) and *Lucullus* (Riga, 1905); the ballet *Rübezahl* (Leipzig, 1893); male choruses; and piano pieces in a Romantic vein (*Wonnetraum, Sérénade rococo,* etc.); a *Fantasie* for violin and orch.; etc.

Meyer-Olbersleben, Max, German pianist and composer; b. Olbersleben, near Weimar, April 5, 1850; d. Würzburg, Dec. 31, 1927. He first studied with his father; then with Müller-Hartung and Liszt at Weimar. On Liszt's recommendation he received a liberal allowance from the Duke for further study; took lessons in Munich with Cornelius and Rheinberger. In 1876 he became teacher of piano and theory at Wüllner-Hartung's orchestra school in Weimar; in 1877, was appointed to the staff of the Würzburg Cons., of which he became director in 1907; also conducted the famous 'Liedertafel' from 1879. He was a composer of talent and ability; his chamber music is effectively and competently written; he also publ. songs and piano pieces. His 'romantic opera' *Clare Dettin* was produced in Würzburg (1896); the comic opera *Der Haubenkrieg,* in Munich (1902).

Meyerbeer, Giacomo, famous dramatic composer; b. Berlin, Sept. 5, 1791; d. Paris, May 2, 1864. Of Jewish family, his real name was Jakob Liebmann Beer; a wealthy relative made him his heir on condition that he should prefix the name 'Meyer' to his patronymic; and 'Giacomo' (Jacob Italianized) was later assumed as an artist name. He was a piano pupil of Lauska and Clementi, and played in public at 7; began the study of theory under Zelter, but soon left this strict master for Anselm Weber, and from 1810-12 lived and studied with Abbé Vogler at Darmstadt, C. M. von Weber and Gänsbacher being his fellow pupils. There he wrote an oratorio, *Gott und die Natur* (Berlin, May 8, 1811), and 2 operas, *Jephthas Gelübde* (Munich, Dec. 23, 1812), and *Wirt und Gast, oder Aus Scherz Ernst* (Stuttgart, Jan. 6, 1813); the first two were failures, but *Wirt und Gast,* later known as *Alimelek,* was accepted for Vienna, and Meyerbeer followed his opera there. Already a brilliant pianist, Hummel's suave style so impressed him that he deferred his own début at Vienna for several months, successfully working to acquire the same fluent ease and finish. His opera was rather coolly received in Vienna (and later in Prague and Dresden); still, despite pianistic triumphs, he felt dramatic composition to be his real vocation. Acting on Salieri's suggestion that Italian melody would prove a corrective for his heavy contrapuntal style, Meyerbeer went to Venice in 1815; the vogue of Rossini's operas indicated the path to popularity, and Meyerbeer entered it with a series of operas in the Italian vein—*Romilda e Costanza* (Padua, July 19, 1817), *Semiramide riconosciuta* (Turin, Jan., 1819), *Emma di Resburgo* (Venice, June 26, 1819; in Germany as *Emma von Leicester*), *Margherita d'Angiù* (Milan, Nov. 14, 1820), *L'Esule di Granata* (Milan, March 12, 1822), and *Il Crociato in Egitto* (Venice, March 7, 1824), this last with immense success. While writing it, he had visited Berlin with the vain hope of bringing out a 3-act German opera, *Das Brandenburger Thor,* and embraced the opportunity to call on his old friend Weber, in Prague, whose strong remonstrances against Meyerbeer's Italian transformation of himself seem to have borne fruit. Certain it is, that for six years Meyerbeer produced no more operas. In 1826 he went to Paris to prepare the first representation of *Il Crociato.* After this, his father's death, his own marriage, and the death of two of his children, also serve to explain his silence. But at this time he was also (according to Mendel) immersed in the study of French opera, from Lully onward; the result being Meyerbeer's third style of operatic composition, in which 'he united to the flowing melody of the Italians and the solid harmony of the Germans the pathetic declamation and the varied, piquant rhythm of the French.' Combining with these Meyerbeer's undeniable fecundity and originality of orchestral effect, and the theatrical ability and routine of his librettist, Scribe, it is no wonder that Meyerbeer's first French 'grand opera,' *Robert le Diable* (Nov. 21, 1831), fairly electrified the Parisians, and caused the Opéra to prosper financially. *Les Huguenots* followed on Feb. 29, 1836, and was recognized by cultured critics as vastly superior to *Robert;* though the general public, enjoying the flamboyant unrealities of *Robert,* was disappointed at first. Two years later Meyerbeer began the composition of *L'Africaine,* which was destined to occupy him through life; irritated by the composer's continued demand for changes, Scribe after a while testily withdrew the libretto, but was mollified by Meyerbeer's entering heart and soul into the composition of another of his texts, *Le Prophète,* finished in 1842-3. After the production of *Les Huguenots* at Berlin, 1842, Meyerbeer was called to that city by King Friedrich Wilhelm IV as General Musical Director. Here his opera, *Ein Feldlager in Schlesien* (Dec. 7, 1844), achieved only moderate success until Jenny Lind assumed the role of Vielka in 1847. He visited Vienna and London in 1847; on his return to Berlin, he brought out Wagner's *Rienzi.* In 1849, *Le Prophète* was at last produced at the Grand Opéra, Paris, on April 16; on

Feb. 16, 1854, it was followed by *L'Étoile du Nord* at the Opéra-Comique (much of the music taken from *Ein Feldlager in Schlesien*), where *Dinorah, ou le Pardon de Ploërmel* was brought out in 1859. Last in the series was *L'Africaine* (Grand Opéra, April 28, 1865), just a year after his death; he had returned to Paris to take charge of the rehearsals in the spring of 1864. Other works: incidental music to *Struensee* (tragedy by Michael Beer, his brother; Berlin, Sept. 19, 1846), one of his finest works; choruses to Aeschylus' *Eumenides;* festival play *Das Hoffest von Ferrara;* monodrama *Thevelindens Liebe,* for soprano solo, chorus, and clarinet obbligato (Munich, Nov. 9, 1817); *Gutenberg* cantata; cantata *Maria und ihr Genius,* for the silver wedding of Prince and Princess Carl of Prussia; serenade *Brautgeleite aus der Heimat,* for the wedding of Princess Luise of Prussia; cantata *Der Genius der Musik am Grabe Beethovens;* ode to Rauch (the sculptor), for soli, chorus, and orch.; 7 sacred odes by Klopstock, for 4 voice parts a cappella; *Festhymnus* for the King of Prussia's silver wedding, for 4 voices and chorus; *Freundschaft,* for 4-part men's chorus; Psalm 91, *a* 8; *Pater noster a* 4 with organ; in MS are 12 Psalms for double choir, a *Te Deum,* a *Stabat Mater,* and a *Miserere. Quarante mélodies à une et plusieurs voix* were published in Paris; other works are *Neben dir,* for tenor with cello obbligato; *Des Jägers Lied,* for bass with horns obbligato; *Des Schäfers Lied,* for tenor with clarinet obbligato; *A Venezia,* barcarolle; *Dichters Wahlspruch,* canon for 3 voices. —Instrumental: 4 *Fackeltänze* for wind band (also scored for orch.); Grand March for the Schiller Centenary (1859); overture in march form (for opening of London Exhibition, 1862); Coronation March for King Wilhelm I (1863); piano music in MS. Meyerbeer left by will 10,000 Thaler ($7,500) for the foundation of a Meyerbeer Scholarship; only Germans under 28, and pupils of the Berlin Hochschule, the Stern Cons., and the Cologne Cons., could compete.—BIBLIOGRAPHY: A. de Lasalle, *Meyerbeer, sa vie et le catalogue de ses œuvres* (Paris, 1864); A. Pougin, *Meyerbeer* (Paris, 1864); H. Blaze de Bury, *Meyerbeer, sa vie, ses œuvres et son temps* (1865); H. Mendel, *G. Meyerbeer* (Berlin, 1868); the same in epitome, *Meyerbeer, sein Leben und seine Werke* (Paris, 1869); A. Kohut, *Meyerbeer* (Leipzig, 1890); J. Weber, *Meyerbeer, Notes et souvenirs d'un de ses secrétaires* (Paris, 1898); H. de Curzon, *Meyerbeer. Biographie critique* (Paris, 1910); H. Eymieu, *L'Œuvre de Meyerbeer* (Paris, 1910); L. Dauriac, *Meyerbeer* (Paris, 1913; 2nd ed., 1930); A. Hervey, *G. Meyerbeer* (London, 1913); H. Abert, *G. Meyerbeer,* in 'Jahrbuch Peters' (1918); J. Kapp, *G. Meyerbeer* (Berlin, 1920; rev. ed., 1930); E. Istel, *Meyerbeer's Way to Mastery,* in the 'Mus. Quarterly' (Jan., 1926); J. F. Cooke, *Meyerbeer* (Philadelphia, 1929); H. Becker, *Der Fall Heine-Meyerbeer. Neue Dokumente revidieren ein Geschichtsurteil* (Kassel, 1958).

Meyerowitz, Jan, German-American composer; b. Breslau, April 23, 1913. In 1927 he went to Berlin, where he studied with Zemlinsky at the Hochschule für Musik. Compelled to leave Germany in 1933, he went to Rome, where he studied composition with Respighi, Casella, and Molinari. In 1938 he went to Belgium; then to Southern France, where he remained until 1946, emigrating to the U. S. afterwards (American citizen, 1951). He married the French singer Marguerite Fricker in 1946. In the U. S. he taught at the Berkshire Music Center in Tanglewood, and later at Brooklyn College. He held a Guggenheim Fellowship twice (in 1956 and 1958). His music is marked by a flow of expansive emotionalism, akin to that of Mahler; in his theater works, there is present a dramatic element in the tradition of 19th-century grand opera (Meyerbeer, Verdi). His technical idiom is modern insofar as it incorporates progressions of unresolved dissonances, but the tonal foundation remains firm. —Works: operas: *The Barrier* (N. Y., Jan. 18, 1950), *Eastward in Eden* (Detroit, Nov., 1951), *Simoon* (Tanglewood, 1949), *Bad Boys in School* (Tanglewood, 1953), *Esther* (Univ. of Illinois, March 17, 1957); choral works: *The Glory Around His Head* (N. Y. Philharmonic, April 14, 1955), *Missa Rachel Plorans* (N. Y., Nov. 5, 1955), *Midrash Esther* (N. Y. Philharmonic, Jan. 31, 1957), several cantatas to English words (among them *Emily Dickinson Cantata);* woodwind quintet (1954); string quartet (1955); cello sonata (1946); piano sonata; trio for flute, cello, and piano (1946); songs to German, French, and English texts.

Meyrowitz, Selmar, German conductor; b. Bartenstein, East Prussia, April 18, 1875; d. Toulouse, May, 1941. He studied at the Cons. of Leipzig, and later with Max Bruch in Berlin; in 1897, became assistant conductor at the Karlsruhe Opera under Mottl, with whom he went to America as conductor at the Metropolitan Opera House (1903); subsequently conducted in Prague

(1905-06), Berlin (1907-10), and Hamburg (1913-16), where he was also director of the Cons. In 1917 he returned to Berlin; was conductor at the State Opera (1924-27); toured with the German Grand Opera Co. in the U. S. (1929-31); after a brief sojourn in Germany, he went to France in 1933, and remained there until his death.

Mézeray (māz-rä'), **Louis-Charles-Lazare-Costard de,** conductor and composer; b. Brunswick, Nov. 25, 1810; d. Asnières, near Paris, April, 1887. As a young man he conducted theater orchestras in Strasbourg and elsewhere; at 17, obtained the post of conductor at the Liège Theater; at 20, became conductor at the Court Theater in The Hague, where he brought out his heroic opera *Guillaume de Nassau;* subsequently studied with Reicha in Paris; again traveled as theater conductor in France, and also appeared as baritone singer; finally, in 1843, he became chief conductor at the Grand Théâtre in Bordeaux, and brought the standard of performance there to a very high level, establishing a fine reputation for himself.

Miaskovsky (myăh-skŏv'-skē), **Nikolai Yakovlevitch,** eminent Russian composer; b. Novogeorgievsk, near Warsaw, April 20, 1881; d. Moscow, Aug. 9, 1950. His father was an officer of the dept. of military fortification; the family lived in Orenburg (1888) and in Kazan (1889-93). In 1893 he was sent to a military school in Nizhny-Novgorod; in 1895 he went to a military school in St. Petersburg, graduating in 1899. At that time he developed an interest in music, and tried to compose; took lessons with the composer Kazanli; his first influences were Chopin and Tchaikovsky. In 1902-03 he was in Moscow, where he studied harmony with Glière. Returning to St. Petersburg in 1903, he took lessons with Kryzhanovsky, from whom he acquired a taste for modernistic composition in the Impressionist style. In 1906, at the age of 25, he entered the St. Petersburg Cons. as a pupil of Liadov and Rimsky-Korsakov, graduating in 1911. At the outbreak of World War I in 1914, Miaskovsky was called into active service in the Russian army; in 1916 he was removed to Reval to work on military fortification; he remained in the army after the Soviet Revolution of 1917; in 1918 he became a functionary in the Maritime Headquarters in Moscow; was finally demobilized in 1921. In that year he became prof. of composition at the Moscow Cons., remaining at that post to the end of his life. A composer of extraordinary ability, a master of his craft, Miaskovsky wrote 27 symphonies, much chamber music, piano pieces, and songs; his music is marked by structural strength and emotional élan; he never embraced extreme forms of modernism, but adopted workable devices of tonal expansion short of polytonality, and freely modulating melody short of atonality. His style was cosmopolitan; only in a few works did he inject folkloric elements. —Works: symphonies (all first performed in Moscow, unless otherwise indicated); No. 1, C minor (1908; Pavlovsk, June 2, 1914); No. 2, C# minor (July 24, 1912); No. 3, A minor (Feb. 27, 1915); No. 4, E minor (Feb. 8, 1925); No. 5, D major (July 18, 1920); No. 6, E♭ minor (May 4, 1924); No. 7, B minor (Feb. 8, 1925); No. 8, A major (May 23, 1926); No. 9, E minor (April 29, 1928); No. 10, F minor (April 7, 1928); No. 11, B♭ minor (Jan. 16, 1933); No. 12, G minor (June 1, 1932); No. 13, B minor (world première, Chicago, Nov. 15, 1934); No. 14, C major (Feb. 24, 1935); No. 15, D minor (Oct. 28, 1935); No. 16, D minor (Oct. 24, 1936); No. 17, C# minor (Dec. 17, 1937); No. 18, C major (Oct. 1, 1937); No. 19, E♭ major (Feb. 15, 1939); No. 20, E major (Nov. 28, 1940); No. 21, F# minor (Nov. 16, 1940; performed by the Chicago Orch. as a commissioned work, on Dec. 26, 1940, under the title *Symphonie-Fantasie*); No. 22, subtitled *Symphonie-Ballade* (Tiflis, Jan. 12, 1942); No. 23, A minor, *Symphony-Suite* (July 20, 1942); No. 24, F minor (Dec. 8, 1943); No. 25, D♭ major (March 15, 1947); No. 26, C major (1948; on old Russian themes; regarded as unsuccessful, and not performed); No. 27, C minor (performed posthumously, Moscow, Dec. 9, 1950). Other orchestral works: *Silence,* symph. poem after Edgar Allan Poe (Moscow, June 13, 1911); *Alastor,* symph. poem after Shelley (Moscow, Nov. 18, 1914); *Serenade,* for small orch. (Moscow, Oct. 7, 1929); *Lyric Concertino,* for small orch. (Moscow, Oct. 7, 1929); *Sinfonietta,* for string orch. (Moscow, May, 1930); violin concerto (Leningrad, Nov. 14, 1938); *Salutatory Overture,* on Stalin's 60th birthday (Moscow, Dec. 20, 1939); cello concerto (Moscow, March 17, 1945). Also cantata, *Kirov is With Us* (1942); marches for military band; choruses; 13 string quartets; 2 cello sonatas; violin sonata; 9 piano sonatas; several sets of piano pieces; song cycles; etc. —Cf. Miaskovsky's *Autobiographical Notes,* in 'Sovietskaya Musica' (June, 1936); L. Sabaneyev, *Modern Russian Composers* (N. Y., 1927);

A. Ikonnikov, *Miaskovsky, His Life and Work* (Moscow, 1944; English transl., N. Y., 1946); T. Livanova, *Miaskovsky* (Moscow, 1953); V. Vinogradov, *Guide to the Symphonies of N. Miaskovsky* (Moscow, 1954).

Michael, David Moritz, German wind-instrument player, violinist, and composer; b. Kienhausen, near Erfurt, Oct. 27, 1751; d. Neuwied, on the Rhine, 1825. From 1796 till 1814 he lived in the Moravian settlements at Nazareth and Bethlehem, Pennsylvania, and was the leading spirit in the musical performances in both towns. A list of programs of the Collegium Musicum at Nazareth beginning with 1796 is preserved in the Moravian Historical Society at Nazareth. Michael's compositions are listed in 'A Catalogue of Music by American Moravians,' compiled by A. G. Rau and H. T. David (Bethlehem, Pa., 1938). They include 16 *Partien* or suites for 5, 6, and 7 wind-instruments, among them one written for a boat ride on the Lehigh. —Cf. H. T. David, *Background for Bethlehem: Moravian Music in Pennsylvania,* in 'American Magazine of Art' (April, 1939).

Michaelides, Solon, Greek musicologist and composer; b. Nicosia, Cyprus, Nov. 12, 1905. He studied in Paris with Nadia Boulanger; upon his return to Cyprus he established a cons. at Limassol and inaugurated a series of concerts there. He gave lectures on Greek music in England (1946-48) and published a paper, *The Neo-Hellenic Folk Music* (Limassol, 1948); wrote an opera to his own libretto, *Ulysses;* several orchestral suites based on Greek themes; songs.

Micheelsen, Hans Friedrich, German composer of sacred music; b. Hennstedt, Dithmarschen, June 9, 1902. He studied in Hamburg and Berlin; was active as church organist and chorusmaster in Berlin until 1938; then was in the German army; after demobilization settled in Hamburg as a teacher; 1954, prof. at the Hochschule für Musik. —Works: *Abendkantate* (1934); *Sommerkantate* (1935); *Luther Mass* (1933); oratorio *Die Weihnachtsbotschaft* (1938); a German Requiem, *Tod und Leben* (1938); many other choral works; a concerto for organ, *Es sungen drei Engel* (1943), and numerous smaller organ pieces; sonatina for flute and piano (1939); violin sonata (1940); variations and fugue for 3 violins (1945); partita for string orch. (1951); a Singspiel, *Münchhausen;* teaching pieces for piano; also some light operas and songs in the Hamburg dialect.

Michi (mē'-kē), **Orazio,** called **della Arpa** (because of his virtuosity on the harp), Italian composer; b. Alifa Caserta, c. 1595; d. Rome, Oct. 27, 1641. From 1614 till 1623 he was in the service of Cardinal Montalto in Rome; after that, with Cardinal Maurice of Savoy. Until 1914 nothing was known of his works except 5 arias publ. in Bianchi's 'Raccolta d'arie' (Rome, 1640) and a 6th one publ. by Torchi in vol. 5 of 'L'Arte Musicale in Italia.' Then, A. Cametti publ., in the 'Rivista Musicale Italiana' (April, 1914), a full description and complete thematic catalogue of 43 pieces for 1-3 voices with continuo (chiefly arias) by Michi which he had discovered in various Italian libraries, and which prove that Michi was one of the earliest and most important Roman masters of the monodic style.

Middelschulte, Wilhelm, eminent organist; b. Werne, near Dortmund, April 3, 1863; d. there, May 4, 1943. He studied at the Institut für Kirchenmusik in Berlin with Löschhorn (piano), Haupt (organ), Commer and Schröder (composition). After serving as organist at the Church of St. Luke in Berlin (1888-91), he went to America and settled in Chicago; was organist there at the Cathedral of the Holy Name (1891-95); prof. of organ at the Wisconsin Cons. of Music, Milwaukee. He was greatly distinguished as a Bach player and pedagogue; in 1935 became instructor of theory and organ at the Detroit Foundation Music School; in 1939 returned to Germany. —Cf. J. J. Becker, *Wilhelm Middelschulte,* in the 'Mus. Quarterly' (April, 1928).

Mielck, Ernst, Finnish composer; b. Viborg, Oct. 24, 1877; d. Locarno, Italy, Oct. 22, 1899 (shortly before his 22nd birthday). He studied piano in St. Petersburg, and composition with Max Bruch in Berlin. Although he did not live long enough for his talent to reach its full development, his works exhibit considerable technical skill and inventive power of a high order. He wrote a *Finnish Symphony;* a string quartet; a string quintet; several choral works. —Cf. K. Flodin, *Finska musiker* (Stockholm, 1900); W. Mauke, *Ernst Mielck. Ein kurzes Künstlerleben* (Leipzig, 1901); A. P. Virtanen, *Ernst Mielck,* in *Suomen Säveltäjiä* (Helsinki, 1945; pp. 378-83).

Mielke (mēl'-kĕ), **Antonia,** German dramatic soprano; b. Berlin, c. 1852; d. there, Nov. 15, 1907. At first she sang chiefly coloratura roles, but gradually assumed the great dramatic parts, for which she was particularly gifted. She sang the Wagner heroines at the Metropolitan Opera during the season of 1890-91 (succeeding Lilli Lehmann); also toured the U. S. in concert recitals; returning to Germany, she continued her operatic career until 1902, when she settled in Berlin as a teacher.

Miersch, Paul Friedrich Theodor, cellist and composer; b. Dresden, Jan. 18, 1868; d. New York, March 1, 1956. He studied at the Munich Academy with Werner (cello) and Rheinberger (composition); came to the U. S. in 1886, and lived in Washington; during Tchaikovsky's American tour in 1891, he played the cello part in Tchaikovsky's trio in Washington, in the composer's presence. In 1892 he moved to N. Y., was 1st cellist of the N. Y. Symph. Orch. (1893-98); then in a similar post at the Metropolitan Opera (1898-1912). After retirement from concert life, he remained in N. Y. as a teacher. He wrote a number of compositions, 46 of which have been publ. —Works: *Indian Rhapsody,* for orch. (N. Y., 1932); *Theme and Variations,* for string quartet; *Pleasant Memories,* for string orch.; pieces for cello and piano; songs.

Mies, Paul, German musicologist and pedagogue; b. Cologne, Oct. 22, 1889. He studied musicology in Bonn; *Dr. phil.* with the dissertation *Über die Tonmalerei* (1912); then returned to Cologne, where he taught mathematics (until 1939), while continuing his work in music; in 1946 he was appointed director of the dept. of school music in Cologne (retired, 1954). His writings include the books *Stilmomente und Ausdrucksstilformen im Brahms'schen Lied* (1923); *Die Bedeutung der Skizzen Beethovens zur Erkenntnis seines Stiles* (1925; in English, 1929); *Musik im Unterricht der höherer Lehranstalten* (2 vols.; 1925-26); *Skizzen aus Geschichte und Ästhetik der Musik* (1926); *Das romantische Lied und Gesänge aus Wilhelm Meister; Musik und Musiker in Poesie und Prosa* (2 vols.; 1927); *Noten und Bücher. Ein Wegweiser durch die musikalische Buch- und Notenliteratur für den Musikfreund; Schubert,* (1930); *Der Charakter der Tonarten* (1948); *Wege zur modernen Musik* (1949); *Das kölnische Volks- und Karnevalslied* (1951). He edited Nottebohm's *Zwei Skizzenbücher von Beethoven* (1924) and brought out 'Reihenfolge,' a collection for school and home orchestras (30 vols.).

Mignone, Francisco, eminent Brazilian composer; b. São Paulo, Sept. 3, 1897. He studied music with his father, and then entered the Cons. at São Paulo. In 1920 he went to Italy for further study with V. Ferroni in Milan. Returning to Brazil, he became prof. of piano and harmony at the National Cons. at Rio de Janeiro (1929). In 1942 he toured the U. S. as conductor-composer. His music shows the influence of the modern Italian technique; his piano compositions are of virtuoso character. In most of his works, the subject matter is Brazilian, and he employs with natural skill the indigenous melorhythms. —Works: operas: *O Contractador dos diamantes* (Rio de Janeiro, Sept. 20, 1924), *L'Innocente* (Rio de Janeiro, Sept. 5, 1928); ballets: *Maracatú de Chico-Rei* (Rio de Janeiro, Oct. 29, 1934), *Quadros Amazonicos* (Rio de Janeiro, July 15, 1949); for orch.: *Suite campestre* (Rio de Janeiro, Dec. 16, 1918), *Congada,* from the opera, *O Contractador dos diamantes* (São Paulo, Sept. 10, 1922; his most celebrated work), *Scenas da Roda,* symph. dance (São Paulo, Aug. 15, 1923), *Festa dionisiaca* (Rome, Oct. 24, 1923), *Intermezzo lirico* (São Paulo, May 13, 1925), *Momus,* symph. poem (Rio de Janeiro, April 24, 1933), *Suite Brasileira* (Rio de Janeiro, Dec. 9, 1933), *Sonho de um Menino Travesso* (São Paulo, Oct. 30, 1937), *4 Fantasias Brasileiras,* for piano and orch. (1931-37), *Seresta,* for cello and orch. (Rio de Janeiro, March 31, 1939), *Miudinho,* symph. dance (São Paulo, June 28, 1941), *Festa das Igrejas* (NBC Orch., April 22, 1942), *Caramurú, No Sertão, Suite asturiana,* 6 preludes; oratorio, *Alegrias de Nossa Senhora* (Rio de Janeiro, July 15, 1949); sextet for wind-instruments and piano (1934); other chamber music; numerous piano pieces; many songs. —Cf. N. Slonimsky, *Music of Latin America* (N. Y., 1945; pp. 134-36); Luiz Heitor Correa de Azevedo, *Francisco Mignone,* in 'Música Brasileña Contemporánea' (Rosario, Argentina, 1952; pp. 125-57).

Migot (mē-gōh'), **Georges,** French composer and writer on music; b. Paris, Feb. 27, 1891. He studied composition at the Paris Cons. with Widor; music history with Maurice Emmanuel; orchestration with Vincent d'Indy, and organ with Gigout and Guilmant; won various awards, including the Lili Boulanger prize (1918) and that of the Blumenthal Foundation for French Art and Thought (1921). Of versatile gifts, he also was a painter; wrote numerous literary essays and books on music. In his style, he attempts to recapture the old French spirit of polyphonic writing, emphasizing the national continuity of art. —Works: for the stage: *Hagoromo*, 'symphonie chorégraphique et lyrique' (Monte Carlo, 1922), *Le Rossignol en amour*, chamber opera (1924); for orch.: *Le Paravent de laque aux 5 images* (Paris, Jan. 21, 1923); *3 Épigrammes; 3 Guirlandes sonores*, for string orch.; *Le Livre de danceries; Prélude pour un poète; Prélude, salut et danse; Le Tombeau de Du Fault, joueur de luth; La Victoire de Rameau entendue à l'orchestre; La Jungle* for organ and orch. (Paris, Jan. 9, 1932); 5 symphonies for small instrumental ensembles; several suites for solo instruments with orch.; *7 Petits Images du Japon*, for voice and orch.; chamber music: *Concert* for flute, cello, and harp; *Le Premier Livre de divertissements français* (5 pieces for various ensembles); trio for violin, viola, and piano; trio for oboe, clarinet, and bassoon; quartet for flute, violin, clarinet, and harp; *Les Agrestides*, for 2 violins, viola, cello, and piano; *Serenade* for oboe, clarinet, horn, bassoon, and string quintet; flute sonata; horn sonata; also *Ève et le Serpent*, suite for flute solo; numerous piano pieces; songs; Psalm XIX (Paris, Dec. 11, 1936); oratorio, *Le Sermon sur la Montagne* (Paris, June 9, 1937). —Cf. Léon Vallas, *Georges Migot, musicien français* (Paris, 1917); P. B. Wolff, *La Route d'un musicien: Georges Migot* (Paris, 1933); R. Aigrain, *Georges Migot et la musique religieuse* (Paris, 1944). Migot's writings were publ. in Paris, 1932 (3 vols.).

Miguez (mē-ges'), **Leopoldo**, Brazilian composer; b. Rio de Janeiro, Sept. 9, 1850; d. there, July 6, 1902. He was a conductor, and was associated with various theatrical enterprises; began to compose marches and waltzes; won 1st prize for his *Hymn of the Republic* (1889). In 1890 he was appointed director of the Instituto Nacional de Musica in Rio de Janeiro, retaining this post until his death. In his theater works, he pursued Wagnerian ideas, but his technique was insufficient for adequate orchestration. —Operas: *Pelo Amor* (Rio de Janeiro, Aug. 24, 1897) and *Os Saldunes* (Rio de Janeiro, Sept. 20, 1901); overtures; songs; marches. —Cf. *Leopoldo Miguez e o Instituto Nacional de Musica*, in the 'Revista Brasileira de Musica' (1940).

Mihalovich, Edmund (Ödön) von, Hungarian composer; b. Fericsancze, Sept. 13, 1842; d. Budapest, April 22, 1929. He studied with Mosonyi in Budapest, and with Hauptmann in Leipzig; also took lessons with Peter Cornelius in Munich. From 1887 to 1919 he taught at the Hungarian Academy of Music in Budapest. In his music he was an ardent Wagnerite; was opposed to Hungarian musical nationalism; the melodic materials of his own works are entirely Germanic. —Works: operas: *Hagbart und Signe* (Dresden, March 12, 1882), *Eliane* (Budapest, Feb. 16, 1908), *Toldi szerelme* (*Toldi's Love;* Budapest, March 18, 1893); 4 symphonies (1879, 1892, 1900, 1902); *Hero and Leander*, symph. poem (1875); *Faust*, a fantasy for orch. (1880); violin sonata; piano pieces; songs.

Mihalovici (mē-hăh-lŏh-vē'-tzē), **Marcel**, composer; b. Bucharest, Oct. 22, 1898. He studied in Rumania, and later in Paris with Vincent d'Indy; remained in Paris. —Works: operas: *L'Intransigeant Pluton; Phèdre* (1948); radio opera, *Die Heimkehr* (Frankfurt, June 17, 1954); *Karagueuz*, marionette ballet (Paris, 1925); for orch.: *Introduction au mouvement symphonique* (Enesco Prize, 1925); *Fantaisie* (Liège Festival of the International Society for Contemporary Music, Sept. 6, 1930); *Capriccio roumain; Concerto quasi una Fantasia*, for violin and orch. (Barcelona Festival of the I. S. C. M., April 22, 1936); *Prelude and Invention* (Warsaw Festival of the I. S. C. M., April 21, 1939); *Symphonies pour le Temps présent* (1944); *Sequences*, for orch. (1949); *Sinfonia giocosa* (Basel, Dec. 14, 1951); *Sinfonia-Partita* (1952); *Étude*, for piano, wind instruments, and percussion (Donaueschingen Music Festival, Oct. 6, 1951); sonata for cello solo; 3 string quartets; songs.

Mikorey (mĭ'-kŏ-rī), **Franz**, German composer and conductor; b. Munich, June 3, 1873; d. there, May 11, 1947. He studied in Munich with Thuille and H. Levi; later in Berlin with H. von Herzogenberg; conducted in Bayreuth (1894); then in Prague, Regensburg, Elberfeld, and Vienna; in 1902 was engaged as court conductor in Dessau; appointed music director there in 1912. He conducted opera at Helsinki from 1919 to 1924; then returned to Germany. —Works: the opera *Der König von Samarkand* (Dessau, 1910); 2 symphonies (*Tragische; An der Adria*); *Sinfonia Engadiana*, for soli, chorus, and orch.; a piano concerto; a piano quintet; a piano trio; male choruses; songs; publ. *Grundlagen des Dirigierens* (1929). —Cf. E. Hamann, *Franz Mikorey* (Leipzig, 1907).

Miksch, Johann Aloys, famous baritone and singing teacher; b. Georgental, Bohemia, July 19, 1765; d. Dresden, Sept. 24, 1845. He was a chorus boy in Dresden; then singer at the Court Church (1786), baritone in the Italian Opera of Dresden (1797), chorusmaster of the German Opera (1820); pensioned in 1831. He was greatly renowned as a teacher; among his pupils was Schröder-Devrient. —Cf. A. Kohut, *J. Miksch* (Leipzig, 1890).

Mikuli, Karl, Polish pianist and composer; b. Czernowitz, Oct. 20, 1821; d. Lwow, May 21, 1897. He first studied medicine in Vienna, but his pronounced talent for music made him decide to go to Paris for serious study; there he became a pupil of Chopin (1844); also studied composition with Reicha. After the outbreak of the revolution of 1848, he left Paris and made several tours in Russia and Austria; was appointed director of the Lwow Cons. (1858); 30 years later he established a music school of his own there. His edition of Chopin's works contains numerous emendations made by Chopin himself as marginal remarks in Mikuli's student copies. He publ. a number of piano pieces of his own, greatly influenced by Chopin's style; also *43 Airs nationaux roumains* for piano.

Mila, Massimo, Italian writer on music; b. Turin, Aug. 14, 1910. He studied literature at the Univ. of Turin, and also took music lessons; for his dissertation at the Univ. of Turin he presented *Il Melodramma di Verdi* (1931; publ. 1933). He became a regular contributor to the 'Rassegna Musicale' and other magazines; publ. several books on music and esthetics: *Cent' anni di musica moderna* (1944); *W. A. Mozart* (1945); *Breve storia della musica* (1946); *L'Esperienza musicale e l' estetica* (1950).

Milán (mē-lahn'), **Luis,** Spanish musician, courtier, and poet; b. Valencia, c. 1500; d. after 1561. He was a favorite at the vice-regal court of Valencia under Germaine de Foix and her third husband, Don Fernando of Aragón. In 1535-36 he brought out his most important work, *Libro de música de vihuela de mano intitulado El Maestro,* intended as an instruction-book for learning to play the 'vihuela' (large six-stringed guitar). This was the first book of its kind to be publ. in Spain, and it is valuable for its many musical examples ('tientos,' fantasias, pavanes, and solo songs with guitar accomp.: 'villancicos,' 'romances,' and 'sonetos'), which reveal Milán's high qualities as a composer. Milán also publ. *El Cortesano* (1561), giving a description of courtly life at Valencia in his day. *El Maestro,* with the original tablature and the transcription into modern notation, was edited by Leo Schrade in the 'Publikationen älterer Musik' (Leipzig, 1927); selections are also found in Morphy's 'Les Luthistes espagnols du XVIe siècle' (Leipzig, 1902). —Cf. J. B. Trend, *L. Milán and the Vihuelistas* (London, 1925).

Milanov (*née* Kunc), **Zinka,** famous soprano; b. Zagreb, Yugoslavia, May 17, 1906. She studied with Milka Ternina in Zagreb, and made her professional début there (1927); then sang opera in Hamburg and Vienna; in 1937 was soloist in Verdi's Requiem under the direction of Toscanini. She made her American début at the Metropolitan Opera House, N. Y., on Dec. 17, 1937, in *Il Trovatore;* remained on the roster for many seasons. In 1937 she married Predrag Milanov; divorced in 1946; married Ljubomir Ilic in 1947.

Milde, Hans Feodor von, opera baritone; b. Petronek, near Vienna, April 13, 1821; d. Weimar, Dec. 10, 1899. He studied singing with Manuel García; was a life member of the Weimar Court Opera, and created the role of Telramund in *Lohengrin* (1850). His wife, **Rosa Agthé** (b. Weimar, June 25, 1827; d. there, Jan. 26, 1906), created the role of Elsa, and sang at Weimar until 1876. They were members of the Weimar circle of musicians, and were particularly friendly with Cornelius. —Cf. Natalie von Milde, *P. Cornelius. Briefe . . . an Feodor und Rosa von Milde* (Weimar, 1901).

Mildenberg, Albert, American composer; b. Brooklyn, N. Y., Jan. 13, 1878; d. there, July 3, 1918. He was a member of a musical family; studied piano with his mother; then took lessons with Rafael Joseffy (piano) and Bruno Oscar Klein (composition). In 1905 he went to Rome, where he studied with Sgambati; later in Paris with Massenet; in 1907 he made a public appearance in Paris as a conductor. Returning to America, he became dean of the dept. of music of Meredith College at Raleigh, N. C. He wrote a number of songs, many of them to his own texts; also wrote his own opera librettos. His style was in the Italian tradition; Massenet commended his gift of melody. His light opera *The Wood*

Witch was produced in N. Y. on May 25, 1903; another comic opera, *Love's Locksmith,* was given in N. Y. in 1912. —Cf. E. E. Hipsher, *American Opera and its Composers* (Philadelphia, 1934, pp. 320-22).

Mildenburg, Anna von, famous dramatic soprano; b. Vienna, Nov. 29, 1872; d. there, Jan. 27, 1947. She studied at the Vienna Cons. with Rosa Papier and Pollini; made her opera début in Hamurg, where her fine voice and acting ability attracted a great deal of attention; in 1897 she was engaged to sing in Bayreuth; in 1898 she became a member of the Vienna Opera; retired from the stage in 1917; went to Munich, where she taught singing at the State Academy; later taught in Berlin; eventually returned to Vienna. Her repertory included all the great Wagner roles. In 1909 she married the playwright Hermann Bahr, with whom she wrote *Bayreuth und das Wagner Theater* (Leipzig, 1910; English transl., London, 1912); she also publ. *Erinnerungen* (1921) and *Darstellung der Werke Richard Wagners aus dem Geiste der Dichtung und Musik* (vol. 1, *Tristan und Isolde;* Leipzig, 1936). Bahr alone wrote *Parsifalschutz ohne Ausnahmegesetz* (Berlin, 1912). —Cf. P. Stefan, *Anna Bahr-Mildenburg* (Vienna, 1922).

Milder-Hauptmann, Pauline Anna, dramatic soprano; b. Constantinople, Dec. 13, 1785; d. Berlin, May 29, 1838. She was the daughter of an Austrian diplomatic official; in Vienna she attracted the notice of Schikaneder, who recommended her to Tomaselli and Salieri, who taught her opera singing. She made her début at the Vienna Opera on April 9, 1803, and soon became so well regarded as an artist and a singer that Beethoven wrote the role of Fidelio for her. Her voice was so powerful that Haydn reportedly said to her: 'Dear child, you have a voice like a house.' In 1810 she married a Vienna merchant, Hauptmann. In 1812 she went to Berlin, where she created a sensation, particularly as Gluck's heroines (*Iphigenia, Alcestis, Armida*); in 1829 she left the Berlin Opera on account of personal difficulties with Spontini; then sang in Russia, Sweden, and Austria.

Mildner, Poldi, Austrian pianist; b. Vienna, July 27, 1915; studied with Hedwig Rosenthal; made her début in Vienna at the age of 12; then appeared in European cities; made her American début in 1931; in 1938, toured South America and Australia.

Miles, Maurice, English conductor; b. Epsom, Feb. 25, 1908. He studied piano and violin at home; then at the Royal Academy of Music, with Clifford Curzon (piano) and Sir Henry J. Wood (conducting). Later he took lessons with Clemens Krauss in Salzburg. Returning to England, he conducted the summer orch. at Buxton, and the regular season at Bath; in 1939 made a South American tour. He was in the British Army from 1940 till 1943, when he was placed in charge of overseas music broadcasts at the B.B.C. In 1947 he was appointed conductor of the newly formed Yorkshire Symph. Orch. —Cf. Donald Brook, *International Gallery of Conductors* (Bristol, 1951; pp. 117-20).

Miles, Philip Napier, English composer; b. Shirehampton, Jan. 21, 1865; d. Kingsweston, Bristol, July 19, 1935. He studied music in Dresden, and later in London with Parry and Dannreuther; founded the Bristol Madrigal Society, the Shirehampton Choral Society (on his own estate), and other groups; organized festivals elsewhere as well. His works include the operas: *Westward Ho!* (London, 1913), *Queen Rosamond, Markheim, Good Friday,* and *Demeter; Ode to Autumn* (after Keats), for baritone, oboe, clarinet, and string quartet; and many songs. —Cf. H. C. Colles, *Philip Napier Miles —Composer,* in 'Music & Letters' (1936).

Milford, Robin, English composer; b. Oxford, Jan. 22, 1903. He studied with Holst, Vaughan Williams, and R. O. Morris, at the Royal College of Music in London. Still as a student, he composed a number of works, mostly in small forms, in a clear rhythmic manner, with thematic materials suggesting English folk music. —Works: ballet *The Snow Queen,* after Hans Christian Andersen (1946); oratorio, *The Pilgrim's Progress,* after John Bunyan (1932); *The Forsaken Merman,* after Matthew Arnold, for tenor, women's chorus, strings, and piano (1938-50); *A Litany to the Holy Spirit,* after Robert Herrick (1947); suite for chamber orch. (1924); *Miniature Concerto* for strings (1933); *Ariel,* for small orch. (1940); *Miniature Concerto* for harpsichord and chamber orch. (1927); violin concerto (1937); *Elegiac Meditation,* for viola and strings (1947); *Fantasia* for string quartet (1945); trio for clarinet, cello, and piano (1948); trio for 2 violins and piano (1949); flute sonata (1944); violin sonata (1945); piano pieces; songs; other works in various forms.

Milhaud (mē-yŏh'), **Darius,** eminent French composer; b. Aix-en-Provence, Sept. 4, 1892; descendant of an old Jewish family, settled in Provence for many centuries. His father was a merchant of almonds; there was a piano in the house, and Milhaud improvised melodies as a child; then began to take violin lessons. He entered the Paris Cons. in 1909, almost at the age limit for enrollment; studied with Berthelier (violin), Lefèvre (ensemble), Leroux (harmony), Gedalge (counterpoint), Widor (fugue), Vincent d'Indy (composition), and Paul Dukas (orchestration); received 1st 'accessit' in violin and counterpoint, and 2nd in fugue; won the Prix Lepaulle for composition. Still as a student, he wrote music in a bold modernistic manner; became associated with Erik Satie, Jean Cocteau, and Paul Claudel. When Claudel was appointed French minister to Brazil, he engaged Milhaud as his secretary; they sailed for Rio de Janeiro early in 1917; returned to Paris (via the West Indies and New York) shortly after the Armistice of Nov. 1918. Milhaud's name became known to a larger public as a result of a newspaper article by Henri Collet in 'Comœdia' (Jan. 16, 1920), grouping him with 5 other French composers of modern tendencies (Auric, Durey, Honegger, Poulenc, and Germaine Tailleferre) under the sobriquet 'Les Six,' even though the association was stylistically fortuitous. In 1922 Milhaud visited the U. S.; lectured at Harvard Univ., Princeton, and Columbia; appeared as pianist and composer in his own works; in 1925, traveled in Italy, Germany, Austria, and Russia; returning to France, he devoted himself mainly to composition and teaching. At the outbreak of World War II, he was in Aix-en-Provence; in July, 1940, came to the U. S.; taught for several years at Mills College, Oakland, Calif. In 1947 he returned to France; was appointed prof. at the Paris Cons., but continued to visit the U. S. as conductor and teacher almost annually, despite his illness (arthritis), which compelled him to conduct while seated. Exceptionally prolific since his student days, he has written a great number of works in every genre; introduced a modernistic type of music drama, 'opéra à la minute,' and also the 'miniature symphony.' He has experimented with new stage techniques, incorporating cinematic interludes; has also successfully revived the Greek type of tragedy with vocal accompaniment; has composed works for electronic instruments, and has demonstrated his contrapuntal skill in such compositions as his 2 string quartets (No. 14 and No. 15) that can be played together as a string octet. He was the first to exploit polytonality in a consistent and deliberate manner; has applied the exotic rhythms of Latin America and the West Indies in many of his lighter works; of these, his *Saudades do Brasil* are particularly popular; Brazilian movements are also found in his *Scaramouche* and *Le Bœuf sur le toit;* in some of his works he has drawn upon the resources of jazz. Despite this variety of means and versatility of forms, Milhaud has succeeded in establishing a style that is distinctly and identifiably his own; his melodies are nostalgically lyrical or vivaciously rhythmical, according to mood; his instrumental writing is of great complexity and difficulty, and yet entirely within the capacities of modern virtuoso technique; he has arranged many of his works in several versions each (e. g., for orch., for piano, for 2 pianos). —Works: Operas: *La Brebis égarée,* 'roman musical' (1910-15; Paris, Dec. 10, 1923); *Agamemnon* (1913; Paris, April 16, 1927); *Le pauvre matelot,* 'complainte en trois actes' (1916; Paris, Dec. 12, 1927); *Les Choéphores* (Paris, June 15, 1919, in concert form; stage performance, Brussels, March 27, 1935); *Les Euménides* (1922; Antwerp, Nov. 27, 1927); *Les Malheurs d'Orphée* (Brussels, May 7, 1926); *Esther de Carpentras,* 'opéra-bouffe' (1925; Paris, Feb. 1, 1938); 3 'minute operas': *L'Enlèvement d'Europe* (Baden-Baden, July 17, 1927), *L'Abandon d'Ariane,* and *La Délivrance de Thésée* (Wiesbaden, April 20, 1928); *Cristophe Colomb,* grand opera in 26 scenes, to a book by Paul Claudel (Berlin, May 5, 1930); *Maxmilien* (Paris, Jan. 4, 1932); *Médée* (Antwerp, Oct. 7, 1939); *Bolivar* (1943; Paris, May 12, 1950); *Le Jeu de Robin et Marion,* mystery play after Adam de la Halle (Wiesbaden, Oct. 28, 1951); *David,* opera in 5 acts and 12 scenes (Jerusalem, June 1, 1954; for the 3,000th anniversary of Israel); 'jeux d'enfants' (short plays with music) for voice and instruments: *À propos de bottes* (1932), *Un petit peu de musique* (1933), *Un petit peu d'exercise* (1937). Ballets: *L'Homme et son désir* (Paris, June 6, 1921); *Le Bœuf sur le toit* (Paris, Feb. 21, 1920); *Les Mariés de la Tour Eiffel* (Paris, June 19, 1921; with Honegger, Auric, Poulenc, and Tailleferre); *La Création du monde* (Paris, Oct. 25, 1923); *Salade,* 'ballet chanté' (Paris, May 17, 1924); *Le Train bleu,* 'danced operetta' (Paris, June 20, 1924); *Polka* for a ballet, *L'Éventail de Jeanne,* homage to Jeanne Dubost, patroness of music (other numbers by Ravel, Ibert, Roussel, etc.; Paris, June 16, 1927); *'adame Miroir* (Paris, May 31, 1948); *Jeux de printemps* (Martha Graham, Library of Congress, Washington, Oct. 30, 1944); *The Bells,* after Poe (Chicago, April 26, 1946). For orch.: *Suite symphonique* No. 1 (Paris, May 26, 1914); *Suite symphonique* No. 2 (from incidental music to Paul Claudel's *Protée;* Paris, Oct. 24, 1920); 5 symphonies for small orch.: No. 1, *Le Printemps* (1917), No. 2, *Pastorale* (1918), No. 3, *Sérénade* (1921), No. 4, *Dixtuor à cordes* (1921), No. 5, *Dixtuor d'instruments à vent* (1922); 8 symphonies for large orch.: No. 1 (Chicago, Oct. 17, 1940; composer conducting); No. 2 (Boston, Dec. 20, 1946, composer conducting); No. 3, *Hymnus ambrosianus* with chorus (Paris, Oct. 30, 1947); No. 4 (Paris, May 20, 1948, composer conducting); No. 5 (Paris, 1955); No. 6 (Boston, Oct. 7, 1955; composer conducting); No. 7 (Chicago, March 3, 1956); No. 8, subtitled *Rhodanienne* (Univ. of California, Berkeley, Festival, April 22, 1958); *Cinéma-Fantaisie sur le Bœuf sur le toit,* for violin and orch. (Paris, Dec. 4, 1920); *Caramel mou,* a shimmy, for jazz band (1920); *Cinq études,* for piano and orch. (Paris, Jan. 20, 1921); *Saudades do Brasil,* suite of dances (also for piano; 12 numbers; 1920-21); *Ballade* for piano and orch. (1921); *3 Rag Caprices* (Paris, Nov. 23, 1923); *Le Carnaval d'Aix,* for piano and orch. (N. Y., Dec. 9, 1926, composer soloist); *Deux hymnes* (1927); violin concerto (1927); viola concerto (Amsterdam, Dec. 15, 1929); concerto for percussion and small orch. (Paris, Dec. 5, 1930); piano concerto No. 1 (Paris, Nov. 23, 1934); *Concertino de printemps,* for violin and orch. (Paris, March 21, 1935); cello concerto No. 1 (Paris, June 28, 1935); *Suite provençale* (Venice Festival, Sept. 12, 1937); *L'Oiseau* (Paris, Jan. 30, 1938); *Cortège funèbre* (N. Y., Aug. 4, 1940); piano concerto No. 2 (Chicago, Dec. 18, 1941, composer soloist); concerto for 2 pianos and orch. (Pittsburgh, Nov. 13, 1942); *Opus Americanum* (San Francisco, Dec. 6, 1943); clarinet concerto (1941; Washington, Jan. 30, 1946); *Suite française* (Goldman Band, N. Y., June 13, 1945; for orch., N. Y. Philharmonic, July 29, 1945); *Cain and Abel,* for narrator and orch. (Hollywood, Oct. 21, 1945); *Le Bal martiniquais* (N. Y., Dec. 6, 1945, composer conducting); *2 Marches* (C. B. S., N. Y., Dec. 12, 1945); *Fête de la Victoire* (1945); cello concerto No. 2 (N. Y., Nov. 28, 1946); suite for harmonica and orch. (1942; Paris, May 28, 1947, Larry Adler, soloist; also for violin and orch., Philadelphia, Nov. 16, 1945, Zino Francescatti, soloist); concerto No. 3 for piano and orch. (Prague, May 26, 1946); violin concerto No. 2 (Paris, Nov. 7, 1948); *L'Apothéose de Molière,* for harpsichord and strings (Capri, Sept. 15, 1948); *Kentuckiana* (Louisville, Jan. 4, 1949); concerto for marimba, vibraphone, and orch. (St. Louis, Feb. 12, 1949); piano concerto No. 4 (Boston, March 3, 1950); *West Point Suite,* for band (West Point, May 30, 1952); *Concertino d'hiver,* for trombone and string orch. (1953); *Ouverture méditerranéenne* (Louisville, May 22, 1954); concerto for harp and orch. (Venice Festival, Sept. 17, 1954). Chamber music: 15 string quartets (nos. 14 and 15 playable together, forming an octet; first performed in this form at Mills College, Aug. 10, 1949); 2 violin sonatas (1911; 1917); sonata for piano and 2 violins (1914); *Le Printemps,* for piano and violin (1914); sonata for piano, flute, clarinet, and oboe (1918); sonatina for flute and piano (1922); *Impromptu,* for violin and piano (1926); *3 Caprices de Paganini,* for violin and piano (1927); sonatina for clarinet and piano (1927); *Pastorale,* for oboe, clarinet, and bassoon (1935); suite for oboe, clarinet, and bassoon (1937); *La Cheminée du Roi René,* suite for flute, oboe, clarinet, horn, and bassoon (1939); sonatina for 2 violins (1940); *Sonatine à trois,* for violin, viola, and cello (1940); sonatina for violin and viola (1941); *Quatre Visages,* for viola and piano (1943); 2 viola sonatas (1944); *Élégie,* for cello and piano (1945); *Danses de Jacarémirim* for violin and piano (1945); sonata for violin and harpsichord (1945); duo for 2 violins (1945); string trio (1947). Vocal works: 3 albums of songs to words of Francis Jammes (1910-12); *7 Poèmes de la Connaissance de l'Est,* to words by Paul Claudel (1913); *3 Poèmes romantiques,* for voice and piano (1914); *Le Château,* song cycle (1914); *4 Poèmes,* for baritone, to words by Paul Claudel (1915-17); *8 Poèmes juifs* (1916); *Child poems,* to Tagore's words (1916); *Trois poèmes,* to words by Christina Rossetti (1916); *Le Retour de l'enfant prodigue,* cantata for 5 voices and orch. (1917; Paris, Nov. 23, 1922, composer conducting); *Chansons bas,* to Mallarmé's words, for voice and piano (1917); *2 Poèmes de Rimbaud* for voice and piano (1917); *Psalm 136,* for baritone, chorus, and orch. (1918); *Psalm 129,* for baritone and orch. (1919); *Les Soirées de Pétrograd,* in 2 albums: *L'ancien régime* and *La Révolution* (1919);

Machines agricoles, for voice and 7 instruments, to words from a commercial catalogue (1919); *3 Poèmes de Jean Cocteau,* for voice and piano (1920); *Catalogue de fleurs,* for voice with piano or 7 instruments (1920); *Feuilles de température,* for voice and piano (1920); *Cocktail,* for voice and 3 clarinets (1921); *Psalm 126,* for chorus a cappella (1921); *4 Poèmes de Catulle,* for voice and violin (1923); *6 Chants populaires hébraïques,* for voice and piano (1925); *Hymne de Sion,* for voice and piano (1925); *Pièce de circonstance,* to words by Jean Cocteau, for voice and piano (1926); *Cantate pour louer le Seigneur,* for soli, choruses, and orch. (1928); *Pan et Syrinx,* cantata (1934); *Les Amours de Ronsard,* for chorus and small orch. (1934); *Le Cygne,* for voice and piano, to words by Paul Claudel (1935); *La Sagesse,* for voices and small orch., to words by Paul Claudel (1935; Paris Radio, Nov. 8, 1945); *Cantate de la Paix,* to words by Paul Claudel (1937); *Cantate nuptiale,* after *Song of Songs* (Marseilles, Aug. 31, 1937); *Les deux cités,* cantata a cappella (1937); *Chanson du capitaine,* for voice and piano (1937); *Les quatre éléments,* for soprano, tenor, and orch. (1938); *Récréation,* children's songs (1938); *Trois élégies,* for soprano, tenor, and strings (1939); *Incantations,* for male chorus (1939); *Quatrains valaisans,* for chorus a cappella, to Rilke's words (1939); *Cantate de la guerre,* for chorus a cappella, to Paul Claudel's words (1940); *Le Voyage d'été,* suite for voice and piano (1940); *Quatre chansons de Ronsard,* for voice and orch. (1941); *Rêves,* song cycle (1942); *La Libération des Antilles,* for voice and piano (1944); *Kaddisch,* for voice, chorus, and organ (1945); *Sabbath Morning Service,* for baritone, chorus, and organ (1947); *Naissance de Vénus,* cantata for mixed chorus a cappella (Paris Radio, Nov. 30, 1949); *Ballade-Nocturne,* for voice and piano (1949); *Barba Garibo,* 10 French folksongs with orch. (for the celebration of wine harvest in Menton, 1953); etc. For piano: *Le Printemps,* suite (1915-19); 2 sonatas (1916 and 1949); *Saudades do Brasil,* 12 numbers in 2 books (1921); *Trois Rag Caprices* (1922; also for small orch.); *L'Automne,* suite of 3 pieces (1932); *Quatre Romances sans paroles* (1933); 2 sets of children's pieces: *Touches noires; Touches blanches* (1941); *La Muse ménagère,* suite of 15 pieces (1944; also for orch.); *Une Journée,* suite of 5 pieces (1946); *L'Enfant aimé,* suite of 5 pieces (also for orch.; 1948); *Le Candélabre à sept branches,* piano suite (Ein Gev Festival, Israel, April 10, 1952); *Scaramouche,* a version for 2 pianos (1939); *Le Bal martiniquais,* a version for 2 pianos (1944); etc. *Paris,* suite of 6 pieces for 4 pianos (1948); film music; incidental music for plays by Claudel, Romain Rolland, etc. —Bibliography: Paul Landormy, *Darius Milhaud,* in 'Le Ménestrel' (Aug. 14, 21, 28, 1925); Géa Augsbourg, *La Vie de Darius Milhaud en images* (Paris, 1935); Ernst Krenek, *Darius Milhaud,* in *The Book of Modern Composers,* ed. by David Ewen (N. Y., 1942); Marion Bauer, *Darius Milhaud,* in the 'Mus. Quarterly' (April, 1942); Paul Collaer, *Darius Milhaud* (Antwerp, 1947); Georges Beck, *Darius Milhaud: étude suivie du catalogue chronologique complet* (Paris, 1949; a detailed list of works, with dates of composition and performance; with a supplement, publ. 1957); Colin Mason, *The Chamber Music of Milhaud,* in the 'Mus. Quarterly' (July, 1957); Milhaud himself publ. a collection of essays, *Études* (Paris, 1926), and an autobiography, *Notes sans musique* (Paris, 1949; in English, as *Notes Without Music,* London, 1952; N. Y., 1953); also *Entretiens avec Claude Rostand* (Paris, 1952).

Millard, Harrison, American composer; b. Boston, Nov. 27, 1829; d. there, Sept. 10, 1895. He sang in the chorus of the Handel and Haydn Society as a child; then went to Italy to study voice; was a concert tenor for several years, and made tours in England with the Irish soprano Catherine Hayes. Returing to America in 1854, he became a vocal instructor, first in Boston, then (from 1856) in N. Y. He publ. about 350 songs; wrote also many church works, and an opera, *Deborah,* to an Italian libretto (not performed). He also set to music *Uncle Tom's Cabin* by Harriet Beecher Stowe.

Miller, Dayton Clarence, American physicist and flutist; b. Strongsville, Ohio, March 13, 1866; d. Cleveland, Feb. 22, 1941. After graduation from Baldwin Univ. and Princeton (D. Sc., 1890), he became prof. of physics at Case School of Applied Science (from 1893). An early interest in the flute led to his experimentation with various versions of the instrument (including a double-bass flute); he accumulated an extensive collection of flutes and various materials relating to the flute, which he left to the Library of Congress, Washington. A leading authority in the field of acoustics and light, he was president of the American Physical Society (1925-26), and of the Acoustical Society of America (1931-32), and vice-president of the American Musicological Society (1939). He publ. *The Science of Musical Sounds* (1916; revised 1922; reprinted, 1934); *Catalogue of Books and Literary Material relating to the Flute and Other Musical Instruments* (1935); *Anecdotal History of Sound* (1935); *Sound Waves, Their Shape and Speed* (1937); etc. He also transl. and annotated Böhm's *The Flute and Flute Playing* (Cleveland, 1908; revised ed., 1922). —Cf. H. Fletcher, *Biographical Memoir of Dayton Clarence Miller* (Washington, 1944; contains an extensive list of writings).

Miller, Mildred, American opera singer; b. Cleveland, Dec. 16, 1924. Her parents came from Germany; the original family name was Mueller. She studied at the Cleveland Institute of Music (B. M., 1946), then with Sundelius at the New England Cons. in Boston. In 1949 she went to Germany; sang with the Stuttgart Opera (1949-50) and with the Munich Opera (1950-51); her performance of Carmen was praised by the Munich critics. In Stuttgart she married the American pilot Wesley W. Posvar (May 1, 1950). Returning to the U. S., she made her début with the Metropolitan Opera Co., N. Y., as Cherubino in *Le Nozze di Figaro* (Nov. 17, 1951).

Miller, Philip Lieson, American librarian and musicologist; b. Woodland, N. Y., April 23, 1906. He studied at the Manhattan Music School and the Juilliard School of Music, N. Y.; from 1927, in the Music Division of the N. Y. Public Library; since 1946, assistant chief. Has publ. many articles and reviews, dealing especially with singers and singing, and a book, *Vocal Music,* in the series 'The Guide to Long-Playing Records' (N. Y., 1955).

Millet (mil-yeht'), **Luis,** Catalan composer and conductor; b. Masnou, near Barcelona, April 18, 1867; d. Barcelona, Dec. 7, 1941. He studied with Vidiella and Pedrell; then became a choral conductor. In 1891 he founded the famous choral society 'Orfeó Català,' which he continued to lead until the last years of his life; was also director of the municipal music school in Barcelona; composed several orchestral fantasies on Catalan folksongs and many choral works; publ. two books on folk music: *De la canción popular catalana* and *Pel nostre ideal* (1917). —Cf. Baltasar Sampler, *Luis Millet* (Barcelona, 1926).

Milligan, Harold Vincent, American organist and composer; b. Astoria, Oregon, Oct. 31, 1888; d. New York, April 12, 1951. He studied with Carl and Noble; was church organist in Portland, Ore., before coming to N. Y. in 1907; then taught organ at various schools and colleges; was church organist in Brooklyn and N. Y.; also lectured on American music. He publ. 4 collections of early American songs: *Pioneer American Composers* (2 vols.); *Washington Garland; The First American Composer; Colonial Love Lyrics;* also a biography of Stephen Foster (N. Y., 1920); *Stories of the Famous Operas* (N. Y., 1950); and with G. Souvaine, edited *The Opera Quiz Book* (N. Y., 1948).

Millöcker, Karl, Austrian operetta composer; b. Vienna, May 29, 1842; d. Baden, near Vienna, Dec. 31, 1899. His father was a jeweler, and Millöcker was destined for that trade, but showed irrepressible musical inclinations and learned music as a child; played the flute in a theater orchestra at 16; later took courses at the Cons. of the Gesellschaft der Musikfreunde in Vienna. Upon the recommendation of Franz von Suppé, he received a post as theater conductor in Graz (1864); produced his operettas *Der tote Gast* and *Die beiden Binder* there (both in 1865). In 1866 he returned to Vienna; from 1869 to 1883 was conductor of the Theater an der Wien; there he presented a number of his operettas, among them *Drei Paar Schuhe* (Jan. 5, 1871); *Wechselbrief und Briefwechsel,* or *Ein nagender Wurm* (Aug. 10, 1872); *Ein Abenteuer in Wien* (Jan. 20, 1873); *Gräfin Dubarry* (Oct. 31, 1879); *Apajune der Wassermann* (Dec. 18, 1880); *Die Jungfrau von Belleville* (Oct. 29, 1881); *Der Bettelstudent* (Dec. 6, 1882; his most successful work; popular also in England and America as *Student Beggar;* N. Y., Oct. 29, 1883); *Gasparone* (Jan. 26, 1884); *Der Vice-Admiral* (Oct. 9, 1886); *Die sieben Schwaben* (Oct. 29, 1887); *Der arme Jonathan* (Jan. 4, 1890; new version by Hentschke and Rixner, 1939; quite successful); *Das Sonntagskind* (Jan. 16, 1892); *Der Probekuss* (Dec. 22, 1894); *Das Nordlicht* (Dec. 22, 1896). Millöcker possessed a natural gift for melodious music; although his popularity was never as great as that of Johann Strauss or Lehár, his operettas captured the spirit of Viennese life.—Cf. C. Preiss, *Karl Millöcker* (Vienna, 1905).

Mills, Charles, American composer; b. Asheville, N. C., Jan. 8, 1914. He studied with Aaron Copland, Roy Harris, and Roger Sessions; has written 2 symphonies (1940 and 1942); a flute concerto (1939); a piano concerto (1948); *Theme and Variations* for orch. (N. Y., Nov. 8, 1951); 3 string quartets; a piano trio; 5 sonatas for unaccompanied flute; a sonata for flute and piano; 2 cello sonatas; a violin sonata; an oboe sonata; 2 piano sonatas; etc. He received first prize from Columbia Univ. for his *Concerto sereno* for woodwind octet (1948); holder of a Guggenheim Fellowship (1952).

Milojević (mē-loh-yā'-vich), **Miloje,** Serbian composer and writer on music; b. Belgrade, Oct. 27, 1884; d. there, June 16, 1946. He was taught piano by his mother; then entered the Serbian school at Novi Sad. Returning to Belgrade after graduation (1904), he became a student of literature at Belgrade Univ., and a pupil at the Serbian School of Music. In 1907 he married the singer Ivanka Milutinović; they settled in Munich until 1910; Milojević served at the headquarters of the Serbian Army in 1914. From 1917-19 he was in France; from 1919 again in Belgrade. He publ. a school manual, *Elements of the Art of Music* (1922). As a composer, he wrote mostly in small forms; was influenced successively by Grieg, Strauss, Debussy, and Russian modernists; his music contains an original treatment of Balkan folksongs. His piano suite, *Grimaces rythmiques* (in a modern vein), was performed at the Paris Festival on June 26, 1937. His list of works contains 89 opus numbers. —Cf. P. Konjović, *Miloje Milojević,* in Serbian, with a summary in French (Belgrade, 1954).

Milstein, Nathan, violinist; b. Odessa, Russia, Dec. 31, 1904. He studied violin at the Odessa Music School; then went to St. Petersburg, where he became a pupil of Leopold Auer at the Cons. As a very young man, he supported himself by giving concerts in Russia with Vladimir Horowitz. He left Russia in 1925 and went to Paris, where he established his reputation. He arrived in the U. S. in 1928; made his American début with the St. Louis Symph. Orch. (Nov. 29, 1929); since then has appeared with major orchestras in the U. S. and in Europe, eliciting much praise for his virtuoso technique and discriminating taste in the interpretation of classical violin concertos. — Cf. B. Gavoty, *Nathan Milstein* (Geneva, 1956).

Milton, John, father of the poet; b. Stanton St. John, near Oxford, c. 1563; d. London, March, 1647. He was a chorister at Christ Church, Oxford (1573-77); apparently remained at Oxford for several years, and in 1585 went to London, where he was admitted to the Scriveners' Company in 1600; in that year he married Sarah Jeffrey. His fine 6-part madrigal *Fayre Oriana in the Morn* was publ. in Morley's 'Triumphes of Oriana' (1601); 4 anthems were publ. in Leighton's 'Teares or Lamentacions' (1614); a motet and 5 anthems in Myriell's 'Tristitiae remedium' (1616); and 3 psalm settings in Ravenscroft's 'Whole Booke of Psalms' (1621); 3 fantasias for 5 viols, and other works, are in MS. —Cf. E. Brennecke, Jr., *John Milton the Elder and His Music* (N. Y., 1938; with bibliography and 16 musical examples).

Minoja, Ambrosio, Italian composer and singing teacher; b. Ospedaletto, near Lodi, Oct. 22, 1752; d. Milan, Aug. 3, 1825. He taught composition at the Cons. of Milan (1814-24); publ. celebrated books of solfeggi and *Lettere sopra il canto* (Milan, 1812); wrote sacred music; a symphony; an opera, *Tito nelle Gallie* (Milan, 1787).

Miolan-Carvalho. See **Carvalho-Miolan.**

Mirecki (mē-reht'-skē), **Franz,** Polish composer and singing teacher; b. Cracow, April 1, 1791; d. there, May 29, 1862. He was a pupil of Hummel in Vienna (1814) and of Cherubini in Paris (1817); lived in Milan (1822-26), in Genoa (1831-38); and after that in Cracow, where he was director of a singing school. —Works: the operas *Cyganie* (Warsaw, May 23, 1822), *Evandro in Pergamo* (Genoa, Dec. 26, 1824), *I due forzati* (Lisbon, March 7, 1826), *Cornelio Bentivoglio* (Milan, March 18, 1844), and *Nocleg w Apeninach (A Night in the Apennines;* Cracow, April 11, 1845); numerous piano pieces; also publ. (in 12 vols.) 50 psalms of Benedetto Marcello with added instrumental accompaniment.

Mirouze, Marcel, French composer and conductor; b. Toulouse, Sept. 24, 1906; d. Aude (in an automobile accident), Aug. 1, 1957. He studied with Busser at the Paris Cons.; conducted the Paris Radio Orch. (1935-40) and in Monte Carlo (1940-43). He wrote an opera, *Geneviève de Paris,* for the 2,000th anniversary of the foundation of the City of Paris; it was produced first as a radio play with music in 1952, and on the stage in Toulouse in the same year; also composed 2 ballets, *Paul et Virginie* (1942) and *Les Bains de Mer* (1946); 2 symph. tableaux, *Afrique* (1936) and *Asie* (1938); piano concerto (1948); film music; piano pieces; songs.

Miry, Karel, Belgian composer; b. Ghent, Aug. 14, 1823; d. there, Oct. 5, 1889. He studied with Gevaert in Brussels; then taught at the Ghent Cons.; in 1859 became its director. He cultivated the national Flemish style of composition; he wrote 18 operas and operettas, in French and in Flemish; his opera *Bouchard d'Avesnes* (Ghent, Feb. 5, 1864) was particularly successful. But he owes his fame to the patriotic song, *De Vlaamse Leeuw,* which he wrote at the age of 22, and which became the Flemish anthem of Belgium.

Mischakov, Mischa, violinist; b. Proskurov, Russia, April 3, 1895. He studied with Korguev and Auer at the St. Petersburg Cons. (graduated 1914); was until 1920 prof. at the Cons. of Nizhny-Novgorod; then left Russia; came to the U. S. in 1922; was concertmaster of the N. Y. Symph. Orch. (1924-27), the Philadelphia Orch. (1927-29), and the Chicago Symph. Orch. (1930-37); in 1937 he became concertmaster of the N. B. C. Symph. Orch. under Toscanini; after 1945 remained in N. Y. as teacher. In 1951 he was appointed concertmaster of the Detroit Symph. Orch.

Misón (mē-sohn'), **Luis,** Spanish musician; b. Barcelona; d. Madrid, Feb. 13, 1766. He was a flutist in the Royal Chapel and the Royal Opera, Madrid (from 1748), and composed stage music; was the first to introduce the 'tonadilla escénica,' a sort of miniature comic opera that developed from the musical interludes in early Spanish plays; also wrote 'sainetes' (dramatic dialogues) and 'zarzuelas' (operettas); his sonatas for flute and bass are in MS. —Cf. J. Subirá, *La Música en la Casa de Alba* (Madrid, 1927); J. Subirá, *Tonadillas teatrales ineditas* (Madrid, 1932; with musical examples); J. Subirá, *Los Maestros de la tonadilla escénica* (Barcelona, 1933; with musical examples).

Missa, Edmond Jean Louis, French opera composer; b. Reims, June 12, 1861; d. Paris, Jan. 29, 1910. He studied with Massenet at the Paris Cons.; received an honorable mention for the Prix de Rome in 1881; then served as organist at St. Thomas d'Aquin. —Operas: *Babette* (London, Oct. 22, 1900); *Muguette,* based on Ouida's *Two Little Wooden Shoes* (Paris, March 18, 1903; his most successful work; also performed in Germany and England); *Maguelone* (London, July 20, 1903); several other operas were produced in Paris and Reims.

Mitchell, Donald, English music critic; b. London, Feb. 6, 1925. He studied music briefly at Durham Univ.; after 1945 was a schoolmaster; at the same time made a thorough study of modern music, in which he specialized. He was editor and founder of the quarterly 'Music Survey' (1947-52). He publ. a number of articles in British magazines; with Hans Keller, edited the symposium, *Benjamin Britten: a Commentary on all his Works from a Group of Specialists* (London, 1952); and, with H. C. Robbins Landon, *The Mozart Companion* (N. Y., 1956).

Mitchell, Howard, American cellist and conductor; b. Lyons, Nebraska, March 11, 1911. His family moved to Sioux City, Iowa, when he was a child, and he studied piano, and also trumpet, before taking up the cello at Peabody Cons. in Baltimore; in 1930 he enrolled in the Curtis Institute, Philadelphia, as a cello student of Felix Salmond, graduating in 1935. Still at Curtis, he was engaged as first cellist in the National Symph. Orch. in Washington; in 1944 became assistant conductor; appointed permanent conductor in 1949. —Cf. Hope Stoddard, *Symphony Conductors of the U. S. A.* (N. Y., 1957; pp. 119-25).

Mitchell, William John, American musicologist; b. New York, Nov. 21, 1906. He studied at Columbia Univ. (M.A., 1938); on its faculty from 1932, he became associate prof. in 1947, prof. in 1952; special lecturer at the Univ. of Calif. 1950 and 1957. He publ. *Elementary Harmony* (N. Y., 1939; 2nd ed., 1948); translated K. P. E. Bach's *Versuch über die wahre Art das Clavier zu spielen* (publ. N. Y., 1949, as *Essay on the True Art of Playing Keyboard Instruments);* contributed essays to the 'Mus. Quarterly' and other periodicals.

Mitjana (mēt-yăh'-năh) **y Gordón, Rafael,** eminent Spanish music historian; b. Málaga, Dec. 6, 1869; d. Stockholm, Aug. 15, 1921. He studied music with Eduardo Ocón in Málaga, Felipe Pedrell in Madrid, and Saint-Saëns in Paris; was employed in the Spanish diplomatic service in Russia, Turkey, Morocco, and Sweden. His most important work is the extensive contribution on the history of Spanish music in Lavignac's 'Encylopédie de la Musique' (Paris, 1920; Part I, vol. IV). He also wrote numerous valuable works of a critical or historical nature, including: *L'Orientalisme musical et la musique arabe; El Cancionero de Upsala; Catalogue critique et descriptif* *des imprimés de musique des XVIe et XVIIe siècles conservés à la Bibliothèque de l'Université Royale d'Upsala* (vol. 1 only; Upsala, 1911; vols. 2 and 3 completed by A. Davidsson); *Don Fernando de Las Infantas teólogo y músico* (Madrid, 1918); *Estudios sobre algunos músicos españoles del siglo XVI* (Madrid, 1918); *Francisco Guerrero* (Madrid, 1922); *Cristóbal Morales* (Madrid, 1922); etc.

Mitropoulos, Dimitri, celebrated conductor; b. Athens, March 1, 1896. He studied with Armand Marsick, the Belgian musician who spent many years in Athens, at the Athens Cons.; wrote an opera after Maeterlinck, *Sœur Béatrice,* which was performed at the Cons. (1919); in 1920, after graduation from the Cons., he went to Brussels, where he studied with Paul Gilson, and in 1921 to Berlin, where he took piano lessons with Busoni; served as répétiteur at the Berlin Opera (1921-25); then returned to Greece, where he became conductor of the municipal orch. in Athens. In 1930 he was invited to conduct a concert of the Berlin Philharmonic; when the soloist Egon Petri became suddenly indisposed, Mitropoulos substituted for him as soloist in Prokofiev's piano concerto No. 3, conducting from the keyboard (Feb. 27, 1930). He played the same concerto in Paris in 1932, as pianist-conductor, and later in the U. S. His Paris début as conductor (1932) obtained a spontaneous success; he conducted the most difficult works from memory, which was a novelty at the time; also led rehearsals without a score. He made his American début with the Boston Symph. in 1936; in 1937 he was engaged as permanent conductor of the Minneapolis Symph. Orch.; there he frequently performed modern music, including works by Schoenberg, Alban Berg, and other representatives of the atonal school; the opposition that naturally arose was not sufficient to offset his hold on the public as a conductor of great emotional power. He resigned from the Minneapolis Symph. in 1949 to accept the post of conductor of the N. Y. Philharmonic; shared the podium with Stokowski for a few weeks, and in 1950 became musical director. In 1956 Leonard Bernstein was engaged as associate conductor with Mitropoulos, and in 1958 succeeded him as musical director. With the N. Y. Philharmonic, Mitropoulos continued his policy of bringing out important works by European and American modernists; he also introduced the innovation of programming modern operas (*Elektra, Wozzeck*) in concert form. A musician of astounding technical ability, Mitropoulos has become successful with the general public as well as with the musical vanguard whose cause he so boldly espoused. While his time was engaged mainly in the U. S., Mitropoulos continued to appear as guest conductor in Europe; also appeared on numerous occasions as conductor at the Metropolitan Opera House and at various European opera theaters. He became an American citizen in 1946. Apart from his early opera, he wrote a *Concerto Grosso* (Paris, March 12, 1933, composer conducting) and has made arrangements of Bach's organ works.

Mitsukuri, Shukichi, Japanese composer; b. Tokyo, Oct. 21, 1895. He was graduated from the Univ. of Tokyo in 1939; then went to Berlin, where he took courses in chemistry at the Kaiser-Wilhelm Institut, and studied composition with Georg Schumann. In 1954 he was appointed a prof. at the Music Academy in Tokyo. —Works: *Sinfonietta classica* (Paris, March 6, 1936); *10 Haikai de Basho* (Paris, Dec. 10, 1937); a symphony (Tokyo, Aug. 22, 1951); concertino for piano and orch. (Tokyo, Aug. 22, 1953); piano concerto (Tokyo, April 23, 1955); violin sonata (1935); piano quintet (1955); 3 albums of Japanese folksongs (1950; 1954; 1955).

Mitterer, Ignaz Martin, Austrian composer of church music; b. St. Justina, Feb. 2, 1850; d. Brixen, Aug. 2, 1924. He studied singing with his uncle, Anton Mitterer; piano and organ with B. Huber; was ordained priest in 1874; studied again (1876-77) at the Kirchenmusikschule in Regensburg with F. X. Haberl; Kapellmeister at the Cathedral there (1882-84); then at the Cathedral in Brixen. He won for himself a distinguished place among modern masters of the Palestrina style; wrote more than 200 opus numbers for the church; publ. *Praktischer Leitfaden für den römischen Choralgesang* (1896), *Die wichtigsten kirchlichen Vorschriften für Kirchenmusik* (4th ed., 1905), *Praktische Chor-Singschule* (4th ed., 1908), *Vademecum für Harmoniumspieler,* etc.

Mitterwurzer, Anton, famous Austrian baritone; b. Sterzing, April 12, 1818; d. Döbling, near Vienna, April 2, 1876. He was a nephew of Gänsbacher, and studied with him; after serving as chorister at St. Stephen's, Vienna, he sang in Austrian provincial theaters. In 1839 he was engaged by the Dresden Court Opera, and remained there for 30 years until he was pensioned in 1870. He was particularly notable in Wagnerian roles.

Mittler, Franz, Austrian composer and pianist; b. Vienna, April 14, 1893; studied there with Heuberger and Prohaska; later in Cologne with Fritz Steinbach and Carl Friedberg. From 1921 to 1938 he lived in Vienna as pianist and accompanist; in 1939 went to America, and settled in N. Y. —Works: opera, *Rafaella* (Duisburg, 1930); piano trio; a number of piano pieces. In America he wrote numerous popular songs (*In Flaming Beauty, From Dreams of Thee, Soft Through My Heart, Over the Mountains*); also light piano suites: *Manhattan Suite, Suite in 3/4 Time, Newsreel Suite, Boogie-Woogie, Waltz in Blue, One-Finger Polka.*

Mittmann, Paul, German composer of choral music; b. Habelschwerdt, June 18, 1868; d. Breslau, Jan. 11, 1920. He studied with G. Kothe at the seminary in Habelschwerdt, and later with Riemenschneider; served as church organist in Breslau; also music critic for the 'Breslauer Zeitung.' He wrote a number of fine male and mixed choruses (several in Silesian dialect), and some 150 opus numbers for the church.

Miyagi, Michio, Japanese virtuoso on the *koto* and composer; b. Kobe, April 7, 1894; d. near Tokyo (in a railroad accident), June 26, 1956. He lost his eyesight at the age of 7; instructed in *koto* playing by a blind musician named Nakajima; in 1908 went to Korea; in 1917 moved to Tokyo, where he remained most of his life. In 1918 he introduced a *koto* with 17 strings. He was named a member of the Academy of Fine Arts in Tokyo in 1948; was the Japanese delegate at the Folk Music and Dance Festival in Europe in 1953. He composed more than 1,000 works for the *koto* and for other Japanese instruments; all of these are descriptive of poetic moods, or suggest a landscape. His concerto for *koto,* flute, and orch., entitled *Haru no Umi (Sea at Springtime)* was presented by André Kostelanetz with the N. Y. Philharmonic on Dec. 31, 1955, with Shinichi Yuize, a member of the Kabuki Dance Group, as soloist on the *koto.* Other works are: *Variations on Etenkagu,* for *koto* and orch. (1925); *Ochiba no Odori (Dance of Falling Leaves)* for *koto* solo; etc. He also publ. a book, *Ame no Nembutsu (Prayers for Rain).*

Mizler (mits'-lĕr), **Lorenz Christoph,** German music scholar; b. Heidenheim, Württemberg, July 25, 1711; d. Warsaw, March, 1778. He was a pupil of J. S. Bach (clavier and composition) from 1731 to 1734; *magister* of Leipzig Univ. with his *Dissertatio, quod musica ars sit pars eruditionis philosophiae* (1734; 2nd ed., 1736); lecturer in philosophy at Leipzig Univ. from 1736; established the 'Societät der musikalischen Wissenschaften' (1738); from 1743, private tutor in Warsaw; was ennobled by the Polish Court as Mizler von Kolof. His 'Neu eröffnete musikalische Bibliothek . . .' (1736-54) was one of the earliest musical periodicals. He publ. *Die Anfangsgründe des Generalbasses, nach mathematischer Lehrart abgehandelt* (1739); a translation of Fux's *Gradus* as *Gradus ad Parnassum, oder Anführung zur regelmässigen musikalischen Composition* (1742); etc. —Cf. F. Wöhlke, *Lorenz Christoph Mizler* (Berlin, 1940).

Mlynarski, Emil, Polish conductor and composer; b. Kibarty, July 18, 1870; d. Warsaw, April 5, 1935. He studied at the St. Petersburg Cons. (1880-89) with Auer (violin), Anton Rubinstein (piano), and Liadov (composition); made his début as violinist in St. Petersburg (1899), then played concerts in Germany and England. In 1893 he was 2nd conductor at the Warsaw Opera; from 1894 to 1897 taught violin at the Odessa Music School; in 1897, appointed 1st conductor at the Warsaw Opera; conducted the Warsaw Philharmonic (1901-05); was director of the Warsaw Cons. (1904-09). After a series of appearances as conductor with various orchestras in Europe, he became permanent conductor of the Scottish Orch. (Glasgow and Edinburgh), visiting London every season. In 1915 he returned to Russia; in 1919 was again in Warsaw as opera conductor and director of the Cons. In 1922 he went abroad, conducting in England, France, and Austria. He was engaged to teach conducting at the Curtis Institute of Music in Philadelphia (1929-31); then returned to Warsaw. He wrote a symph., *Polonia;* 2 violin concertos, of which the 1st won the Paderewski prize in Leipzig (1898); effective pieces for violin and piano; also a comic opera, *Noc letnia (Summer Night;* Warsaw, March 29, 1924).

Moberg, Carl Allan, Swedish musicologist; b. Östersund, June 5, 1896. He attended the Univ. of Upsala, where he studied with Norlind (1917-24); then with Alban Berg in Vienna (1924) and Peter

Wagner in Freiburg, Switzerland (1924-27). In 1927, was appointed docent of musicology at the Univ. of Upsala; in 1946, prof. In 1943 he undertook a journey to Lapland in order to collect native songs. —Writings: *Über die schwedischen Sequenzen* (2 vols., Upsala, 1927); *Über mehrstimmige mittelalterliche Musik in Schweden während der Reformations-Zeit,* in the 'Kirchenmusikalisches Jahrbuch' (1932); *Kyrkomusikens historia* (1932); *Tonkonstens historia i Västerlandet* (2 vols.; 1935); *Från Kyrko- och Hovmusik till Offentlig Konsert* (Upsala, 1942); *Buxtehude* (1945); *Die liturgische Hymnen in Schweden* (1947); *Bachs Passioner och Höga Mässa* (1949).

Mocquereau (mŏhk-roh'), Dom **André,** distinguished French scholar; authority on Gregorian chant; b. La Tessoualle, near Cholet (Maine-et-Loire), June 6, 1849; d. Solesmes, Jan. 18, 1930. In 1875 he joined the Order of Benedictines at the Abbey of Solesmes, devoted himself to the study of Gregorian chant under the direction of Dom Pothier, and became teacher of choral singing in the Abbey. After the expulsion, in 1903, of the Order from France they found a refuge on the Isle of Wight (Quarr Abbey, Ryde), where Mocquereau then became prior; later he returned to Solesmes. Founder and editor of the great work 'Paléographie musicale,' published serially since 1889. The following volumes have appeared: I, *Le Codex 339 de la Bibliothèque de Saint-Gall (Xe siècle): Antiphonale Missarum Sancti Gregorii* (1899); II and III, *Le Répons-Graduel "Justus ut palma"* (1891-2; 1892-3); IV, *Le Codex 121 de la Bibliothèque d'Einsiedeln (X^e^-XIe siècle): Antiphonale Missarum S. Gregorii* (1893-6); V and VI, *L'Antiphonaire Ambrosien,* Codex add. 34209 of the British Museum (1896-9; 1897-1900); VII and VIII, *Le Codex H. 159 de la Bibliothèque de l'École de Médecine de Montpellier (XIe siècle): Antiphonarium Tonale Missarum* (1901-5); IX, *Le Codex 601 de la Bibliothèque capitulaire de Lucques [Lucca] (XIIe siècle): Antiphonaire monastique* (1905-09); X, *Le Codex 239 de la Bibliothèque de Laon (IXe-Xe siècle): Antiphonale Missarum S. Gregorii* (1909-12); XI, *Le Codex 47 de la Bibliothèque de Chartres (Xe siècle): Antiphonale Missarum S. Gregorii* (1912-21); XII, *Codex F. 160 de la Bibliothèque de la Cathédral de Worcester (XIIIe siècle): Antiphonaire monastique* (1922-5); XIII, *Le Codex 903 de la Bibliothèque Nationale de Paris (XIe siècle): Graduel de Saint-Yrieix* (1925-30); XIV, *Le Codex 10673 de la Bibliothèque Vaticane, Fonds Latin (XIe siècle): Graduel Bénéventain* (1931-36); XV, *Codex VI 34 de la Bibliothèque Capitulaire de Bénévent (XIe-XIIe siècle): Graduel Bénéventain avec Prosaire et Tropaire* (1937-39, 1951); XVI, *L'Antiphonaire du Mont-Renaud (Xe siècle)* (1955). Series 2, I, *No. 390-391 de la Bibliothèque de Saint-Gall (Xe siècle): L'Antiphonaire du B. Hartker* (1900-01); Series 2, II, *Le Codex 359 de la Bibliothèque de Saint-Gall (IXe siècle): Cantatorium* (1924-25). Mocquereau also edited the series 'Monographies grégoriennes.' —Other works by Mocquereau include *Le Nombre musical grégorien ou Rythmique grégorienne* (very valuable; 1908-27); *L'Art grégorien, son but, ses procédés, ses caractères; Petit traité de psalmodie; La Psalmodie romaine et l'accent tonique latin* (1895); *Notes sur l'influence de l'accent et du cursus tonique latins dans le chant ambrosien* (1897); *Méthode de chant grégorien* (1899); *De la transposition sur lignes des notations neumatique et alphabétique à propos du répons Tua sunt* (with G. Beyssac), in the 'Riemann-Festschrift' (1909). —Cf. F. Kosch, in the 'Zeitschrift für Musikwissenschaft' (vol. XII, p. 312 ff.); J. Ward, *De greg. Zangen naar Dom Mocquereau* (Doornik, 1929); J. A. de Donostia, *À propos du nombre musical grégorien de Dom Mocquereau* (Paris, 1930); Maurice Blanc, *L'Enseignement musical de Solesmes* (Paris, 1953; chapter 3); see also special issues of the 'Gregorian Review' (Toledo, Ohio, Jan.-Feb., 1955) and 'Revue grégorienne' (Jan.-April, 1955).

Moeck, Hermann, German music publisher and instrument maker; b. Lüneburg, July 9, 1896. He established his business in Lüneburg (1920), then moved it to Celle (1925). He was influential in the revival of the vertical flute (recorder); manufactured also violas da gamba, quintfidels, other old stringed instruments; publ. a number of arrangements and authentic pieces by old and modern composers for various recorder ensembles; also for the fidels. The firm possesses one of the great collections of old instruments. **Hermann Moeck,** Jr. (b. Celle, Sept. 16, 1922) joined the firm in 1947; wrote a dissertation, *Ursprung und Tradition der Kernspaltflöten der europäischen Folklore und die Herkunft urgeschichtlichen Kernspaltflötentypen* (1951; publ. Leipzig, 1956).

Moeller, Mathias, organ builder; b. Bornholm, Denmark, Sept. 29, 1855; d. Hagerstown, Md., April 13, 1937. He came to the U. S. in 1872 and established his factory in Hagerstown. It became the largest organ factory in the world and built the organs at West Point, the New York Hippodrome, etc. Moeller contributed a number of important improvements to the construction of the organ.

Moeran, Ernest John, English composer of Irish descent; b. Heston, Middlesex, Dec. 31, 1894; d. Kenmare, County Kerry, Ireland, Dec. 1, 1950. His father was a clergyman, and he learned music from hymn-books; then studied at the Royal College of Music; was an officer in the British army in World War I, and was wounded. Returning to London, he took lessons in composition with John Ireland (1920-23); also became interested in folk music; collected numerous folksongs in Norfolk, some of which were publ. by the Folksong Society (1922). Most of his music is inspired by simple folk patterns; his folksong arrangements are aptly made and are authentic in feeling. —Works: 2 Rhapsodies for orch. (1st, Manchester, 1924; 2nd, Norwich Festival, 1924); symph. in G minor (London, Jan. 13, 1938); violin concerto (London, July 8, 1942); *Rhapsody* for piano and orch. (London, Aug. 19, 1943); cello concerto (Dublin, Nov. 25, 1945; with Moeran's wife, Peers Coetmore, as soloist); *Serenade* in G major for orch. (London, Sept. 2, 1948); quartet for oboe and strings (1946); cello sonata (1947); piano and organ works; many songs.

Moeschinger, Albert, Swiss composer; b. Basel, Jan. 10, 1897. He studied in Bern, Leipzig, and Munich. In his works he shows influences of German neo-Romanticism and French Impressionism. A prolific composer, he has written some 100 opus numbers; his works include 3 symphonies; 3 piano concertos; violin concerto; 6 string quartets; 2 piano trios; quintet for clarinet and strings; 2 trios for flute, clarinet, and bassoon; 2 cello sonatas; sonata for violin and organ; many pieces for piano, organ, etc.; cantatas and other choral works.

Moffat, Alfred Edward, Scottish music editor and arranger; b. Edinburgh, Dec. 4, 1866; d. London, June 9, 1950. He studied with L. Bussler in Berlin (1882-88); then went to London, where he became active as editor of violin music by old English composers; publ. the series 'Old English Violin Music' (London) and 'Meisterschule der alten Zeit' (Berlin); numerous arrangements: 'The Minstrelsy of Scotland' (200 Scottish songs); 'The Minstrelsy of Ireland'; '40 Highland Reels and Strathspeys'; 'Songs and Dances of All Nations' (with J. D. Brown); various other editions of string and vocal music; etc.

Mohaupt (moh'-howpt), **Richard,** German composer; b. Breslau, Sept. 14, 1904; d. Reichenau, Austria, July 3, 1957. He studied with J. Prüwer and R. Bilke; began his musical career as an opera conductor; also gave concerts as pianist. After the advent of the Nazi regime in 1933, he was compelled to leave Germany because his wife was Jewish; settled in New York in 1939, and continued to compose; was also active as a teacher. In 1955 he returned to Europe. —Works: operas: *Die Wirtin von Pinsk* (Dresden, Feb. 10, 1938), *Die Bremer Stadtmusikanten* (Bremen, June 15, 1949), *Double Trouble* (Louisville, Dec. 4, 1954), *Der grüne Kakadu* (Hamburg, Jan., 1958); ballets: *Die Gaunerstreiche der Courasche* (Berlin, Aug. 5, 1936), *Lysistrata* (1946), *The Legend of the Charlatan,* pantomime (1949), *Max und Moritz,* dance-burlesque, after Wilhelm Busch (Karlsruhe, Dec. 18, 1950); a symphony (N. Y. Philharmonic, March 5, 1942), *Stadtpfeifermusik* (London Festival of the International Society for Contemporary Music, July 7, 1946), *Bucolica,* for double chorus and orch. (1948), *Trilogy* for contralto solo and orch. (1951), violin concerto (N. Y. Philharmonic, April 29, 1954); chamber music; songs; piano pieces.

Moiseiwitsch (moĭ-sā'-ĭ-vich), **Benno,** pianist; b. Odessa, Feb. 22, 1890; studied there, and won the Anton Rubinstein prize at the age of 9; went to Vienna, where he studied with Leschetizky. He made his début in Reading, England, on Oct. 1, 1908, and subsequently made London his home; also toured many times in the U. S., Australia, India, Japan, etc. He represents the traditional school of piano playing, excelling mostly in Romantic music. He revisited the U. S. in 1958 and gave recitals in N. Y.

Mojsisovics (moĭ-sē'-soh-vitch), **Roderich von,** Austrian composer; b. Graz, May 10, 1877; d. there, March 30, 1953. He studied with Degner in Graz, with Wüllner and Klauwell at the Cologne Cons., and with Thuille in Munich. He conducted a choral group in Brno (1903-7); then taught in various Austrian towns; in 1912 returned to Graz; was director of the Graz Cons. from 1920 till 1934. In his music he was a decided follower of Wagnerian precepts. He wrote 8 operas; 5 symphonies; a symph. poem, *Stella;* 2 overtures; a violin concerto; numerous chamber works; songs; publ. the biographies, *Max Reger* (1911) and *E. W. Degner* (1919); *Bachprobleme* (1930); etc. —Cf. M. Morold, *Roderich Mojsisovics* (1924); F. Stichtenoth, in the 'Zeitschrift für Musik' (1942).

Mokranjac (moh-krah'-nyats), **Stevan,** Serbian composer; b. Negotin, Jan. 9, 1856; d. Skoplje, Sept. 29, 1914. He studied in Munich with Rheinberger, and in Leipzig with Jadassohn and Reinecke; in 1887 became director of the Serbian Choral Society in Belgrade, with which he also toured. In 1899 he founded a Serbian Music School in Belgrade, and remained its director until his death. He wrote 15 choral rhapsodies on Serbian and Macedonian melodies; a Liturgy of St. John Chrysostomos (publ. in Leipzig, 1901; also with an English transl. as *Serbian Liturgy,* London, 1919); a Funeral Service ('Opelo'); compiled a large collection of church anthems according to the Serbian usage and derived from old Byzantine modes; wrote a collection of songs for mixed chorus, *Rukoveti (Bouquets).*

Mokroussov (mŏh-krŏh-ŏŏ'-sŏv), **Boris Andreyevitch,** Russian composer; b. Nizhny-Novgorod, Feb. 27, 1909. He studied at the Moscow Cons. with Miaskovsky, graduating in 1936. Still as a student, he wrote an orchestral suite, *The Pioneers* (1933); a quartet for 2 trumpets and 2 trombones (1934); and a trombone concerto (1935). His graduation piece was a politically inspired work, *Anti-Fascist Symphony,* for orch., chorus, and military band (Moscow, Aug. 1, 1937). He has also written an opera, *Tchapayev,* depicting the life of a Soviet hero.

Moldavan, Nicolas, viola player; b. Kremenetz, Russia, Jan. 23, 1891; studied at the Odessa Cons.; then at the St. Petersburg Cons., graduating in 1912. In 1918 he left Russia and went on a tour of the Far East; settled in the U. S.; was a member of the Flonzaley Quartet (1925-29); then played in the Coolidge Quartet and in the NBC orch. in N. Y.; also active as a teacher.

Moldenhauer, Hans, musicologist; b. Mainz, Germany, Dec. 13, 1906. He studied there with Hans Rosbaud; left Germany in 1933; in 1939 settled in Spokane, Washington. He was in the U. S. Army in 1943; obtained the degree of Doctor of Fine Arts at Chicago Musical College (1951). He is the author of a valuable compendium, *Duo-Pianism* (Chicago, 1950).

Molina, Antonio J., Philippine composer and conductor; b. Quiapo, Manila, Dec. 26, 1894; received his primary education at the Boys' Catholic School in his native town; then studied violin with Bibiano Morales in Manila; founded and directed a string group, 'Rondalla Ideal'; also was engaged as conductor of various theater and cinema orchestras in Manila; wrote popular waltzes; then began to compose more ambitious theater music; conducted at Manila the première of his lyric drama *Ritorna Vincitor* (March 10, 1918) and his zarzuelas, *Panibugho* (*Jealousy;* April 16, 1918) and *Ang Ilaw* (Nov. 23, 1918). He was graduated from the Cons. of Music, Univ. of the Philippines, as cellist (1923); traveled as conductor and cellist in Indochina (1924-25); in 1925 became teacher of harmony at the Univ. of the Philippines; in 1934 joined the staff of the President's Committee on Filipino Folksongs and Dances; wrote a Christmas carol for mixed chorus and orch., *The Living Word* (Manila, Dec. 18, 1936); a quintet for piano and strings, based on native folksongs (Manila, Jan. 21, 1950); also numerous piano pieces and songs.

Molinari, Bernardino, eminent Italian conductor; b. Rome, April 11, 1880; d. there, Dec. 25, 1952. He studied with Falchi and Renzi at the Liceo di Santa Cecilia in Rome; in 1912, became conductor of the Augusteo orch. in Rome; also conducted throughout Europe and South America. In 1928, made his American début with the N. Y. Philharmonic, which he conducted again during the 1931-32 season; also appeared with other American orchestras. He was a champion of the modern Italian school, and brought out many works by Respighi, Malipiero, and other outstanding Italian composers; publ. a new ed. of Monteverdi's *Sonata sopra Santa Maria* (1919) and concert transcriptions of Carissimi's oratorio *Giona,* Vivaldi's *Le quattro stagioni,* etc.; also orchestrated Debussy's *L'Isle joyeuse.* —Cf. E. Mucci, *Bernardino Molinari* (Lanciano, 1941).

Molique (mŏh-lēk), **Wilhelm Bernhard,** German violinist and composer; b. Nuremberg, Oct. 7, 1802; d. Cannstadt, near Stuttgart, May 10, 1869. He first studied with his father; King Maximilian I, hearing of his uncommon gifts, sent him to Munich (1816) to study with Rovelli, concertmaster of the Munich Court orch.; he succeeded Rovelli in that post in 1820; in 1826 he became concertmaster of the Stuttgart orch., with the title of 'Musikdirektor.' He won fame abroad with extended tours in Holland, Russia, England, and France. The political crisis of 1849 caused him to settle in London, where he remained until 1866; then returned to Germany. His works include 6 violin concertos; 8 string quartets; pieces for violin and piano, and for violin and flute; fantasias, rondos, etc., for solo violin; etc. —Cf. Fritz Schröder, *Bernhard Molique und seine Instrumentalkompositionen* (Stuttgart, 1923).

Molitor, Raphael, German musicologist; b. Sigmaringen, Feb. 2, 1873; d. Beuron, Oct. 14, 1948. He was the son of Johann Baptist Molitor, cathedral organist; studied philosophy and theology in the Benedictine Monastery of Beuron; ordained priest in 1897; lectured there on canon law (1898-1904); prior (1904); abbot (1906) of Benedictine Monastery, St. Joseph, near Coesfeld, Westphalia; in 1904, was appointed a member of the advisory board of the 'Editio Vaticana.' He was one of the foremost authorities on Gregorian Chant. —Writings: *Reformchoral* (1901), *Die nach-tridentinische Choralreform zu Rom* (2 vols., 1901; 1902), *Choralwiegendrucke, Der gregorianische Choral als Liturgie und Kunst, Josef Rheinberger,* etc.; contributed important articles to the 'Gregoriusblatt,' 'Kirchenmusikalisches Jahrbuch,' 'Sammelbände der Internationalen Musik-Gesellschaft,' etc.

Möllendorff, Willi von, German pianist and composer; b. Berlin, Feb. 28, 1872; d. Stettin, April 27, 1934. He studied with Bargiel at the Berlin Hochschule für Musik (1891-93); was subsequently active as pianist and theater conductor in Giessen, Berlin, and finally Stettin. He was known especially for his experimentation with quarter-tones, for the exposition of which he invented a bichromatic harmonium with a new keyboard. For this instrument he composed an *Adagio religioso* (with cello solo); also *5 kleine Stücke.* In addition, he wrote operas, a ballet, 2 symphonies, choral works, etc.

Mollenhauer, Eduard, German violinist; b. Erfurt, April 12, 1827; d. Owatoma, Minnesota, May 7, 1914. He was a violin pupil of Ernst (1841) and Spohr (1843); after a brief concert career in Germany, he went to London, where he joined Jullien's Orch., of which an older brother, **Friedrich Mollenhauer** (1818-85), also a violinist, was a member; after Jullien's tour with his orch. in the U. S. (1853), the brothers settled in New York as teachers; Eduard Mollenhauer also appeared as a soloist with the N. Y. Philharmonic Society. He wrote the operas *The Corsican Bride* (N. Y., 1861) and *Breakers* (N. Y., 1881); 3 symphonies; a violin concerto; solo pieces for violin (*La Sylphide,* etc.); songs.

Mollenhauer, Emil, American violinist and conductor; son of Friedrich Mollenhauer; b. Brooklyn, Aug. 4, 1855; d. Boston, Dec. 10, 1927. He studied violin with his father; as a child, appeared at the old Niblo's Garden in N. Y.; in 1872 entered Theodore Thomas' orch. as a first violin, remaining there for 8 years; then joined the Damrosch Orch.; from 1885 to 1888 was a member of the Boston Symph. Orch.; then assumed the conductorship of the Boston Festival Orch., and toured the U. S. with it, featuring many celebrated soloists (Calvé, Nordica, Melba, Campanari, Joseffy, Ysaÿe, Marteau, etc.). In 1899 he was elected conductor of the Boston Handel and Haydn Society, which he led until 1927; from 1900 was also conductor of the Apollo Club (men's chorus) in Boston, and from 1915, of the Brookline Choral Society. See the article on Mollenhauer in the 'Dictionary of American Biography' (vol. 13).

Mollenhauer, Henry, cellist; brother of Eduard Mollenhauer; b. Erfurt, Germany, Sept. 10, 1825; d. Brooklyn, N. Y., Dec. 28, 1889. In 1853 he was a member of the Royal Orch. in Stockholm; toured the U. S. from 1856-58 with Thalberg, Gottschalk, and Carlotta Patti; then settled in Brooklyn as teacher; founded the Henry Mollenhauer Cons., which later flourished under the direction of his sons Louis, Henry, and Adolph.

Mollenhauer, Louis, American violinist; son of Henry Mollenhauer; b. Brooklyn, Dec. 17, 1863; d. there, Feb. 9, 1926. He was a pupil of his uncle, Eduard Mollenhauer; was a member of the Mollenhauer Quintet Club; after his father's death, was director of his Cons. (1889-91); then founded his own Cons. in Brooklyn.

Möller, Heinrich, German musicologist; b. Breslau, June 1, 1876. He studied musicology with Riemann, Kretzschmar, and Friedlaender; lived in New York from 1914 to 1921; then returned to Germany. From 1937 till 1945 he was docent at the

Univ. of Jena; in 1953, appointed instructor at the Hochschule für Musik in Weimar. He was editor of the valuable collection, *Das Lied der Völker* (14 vols.); also translated the librettos of operas of Mussorgsky and Rimsky-Korsakov into German.

Moller (or **Möller**), **Joachim.** See **Burgk.**

Moller, John Christopher, German composer and organist; date and place of birth unknown; d. New York, Sept. 21, 1803. In 1790 he appeared in New York as a harpsichordist, but left immediately after his concerts for Philadelphia, where (in 1791-92) he took part in the City Concerts (with Reinagle, and later Henri Capron) both as manager and performer. Apparently he was also proficient as pianist, violist, and 'harmonica'-player. In 1793 he was organist at the Zion Church, Philadelphia, and at the same time joint proprietor, with Capron, of a music store, which he also used as a music school. In 1796 he succeeded Hewitt in the management of the New York City Concerts with the Van Hagens. His attempt to continue this subscription series by himself, when Van Hagen later left for Boston, was unsuccessful. His known compositions include *6 Quartettos* (publ. in London by J. Betz); *Progressive Lessons for the Harpsichord* (op. 6, London); *Compleat Book of Instruction for the Pianoforte* (op. 6, London); *6 Sonatas for the forte piano or harpsichord, with a violin or violoncello accompaniment* (London); *12 Variations pour le clavecin* (1798); and *Sinfonia, Rondo, Overture, Quartetto* for 'harmonica' (Benjamin Franklin's *armonica* or musical glasses), 2 violas, and cello, and *Duetti* for clarinet and piano in the first issue of Moller & Capron's *Monthly Numbers* (1793). —Cf. J. T. Howard, *Our American Music* (N. Y., 1939).

Molloy, James Lyman, Irish composer of light music; b. Cornalaur, King's County, Aug. 19, 1837; d. Wooleys, Bucks, Feb. 4, 1909. His operettas (*Students' Frolic, My Aunt's Secret, Very Catching*), numerous songs (*Love's Old Sweet Song, London Bridge, The Kerry-dance, The Postilion, Punchinello,* etc.), and Irish melodies with new accompaniments enjoyed great popularity. —Cf. 'Dictionary of National Biography' (Supplement; Oxford, 1920).

Molnár, Antal, Hungarian musicologist; b. Budapest, Jan. 7, 1890. He studied violin; then played the viola in the Waldbauer String Quartet and later in the Dohnányi Piano Quartet (1915-17). In 1919 he was appointed instructor of harmony at the Budapest Academy of Music, and continued to teach there for nearly 40 years. He publ. (in Hungarian) a *History of European Music before 1750* (1920); *Sociology of Music History* (1923); *The New Hungarian Music* (1926); *Jazzband* (1928); a monograph on Kodály (Budapest, 1936); *Music and Life* (1946); *The Spirit of New Music* (1948); etc. He was also a prolific composer; among his works are *Hungarian Dances* for orch. (1917); *Hungarian Comedy Overture* (1931); a cello concerto; 3 string quartets; church music.

Molnár, Géza, Hungarian musicologist; b. Budapest, 1872; d. there, 1933. He was prof. of music theory at the Budapest Academy of Music; publ. numerous treatises on Hungarian music (*Acoustics of the Hungarian Scale; Hungarian Dances of the 16th Century;* etc.).

Moltchanov (mol-chăh'-nov), **Kirill Vladimirovitch,** Russian composer; b. Moscow, Sept. 7, 1922. He studied at the Moscow Cons. with Anatoly Alexandrov. His graduation work was the opera *The Stone Flower,* based on Ural folk tales (Moscow, Dec. 10, 1950). Other works: cantata, *Song of Friendship* (Moscow, May 18, 1955); 3 piano concertos (1945, 1947, 1953); songs; film music.

Momigny (moh-mē-ñē'), **Jérôme-Joseph de,** French music theorist; b. Philippeville, Jan. 20, 1762; d. Paris, July, 1838. At 12, he was organist at St. Omer, later at Ste.-Colombe, and 1785 at Lyons; established a music business in Paris, 1800; lived later in Tours, but returned to Paris. —Writings: *Cours complet d'harmonie et de composition d'après une théorie neuve* (3 vols., 1806; bases the scales on the overtone series up to 13); and other books supporting his theories. In this work he lays the foundations of the theory of phrasing. Lussy, Westphal, and Hugo Riemann elaborated the principles laid down by Momigny. He also wrote the musical articles for vol. II (1818) of Framéry's and Ginguené's 'Encyclopédie méthodique,' presenting in condensed form the theories advanced in his *Cours complet* (under *Mesure, Motif, Période, Phrase, Ponctuation, Proportion, Rythme*); wrote chamber music and an opera.

Mompou, Federico, Spanish composer; b. Barcelona, April 16, 1893. He studied at the Barcelona Cons.; in 1911 went to Paris, where he studied with S. S. Rousseau (composition) and Isidor Philipp (piano). From 1914 to 1921 he lived in Barcelona; then in Paris, until 1941, when he returned to Barcelona. He writes almost exclusively for piano and for voice; his thematic material is derived mainly from Catalan folk melodies, but the treatment is thoroughly modern. —Works for piano: *6 Impressions intimes* (1911-14), *Scènes d'enfants* (1915), *Suburbis* (1916-17), *3 Pessebres* (1918), *Canço i dança* (1918-28), *Cants magics* (1919), *Festes Llunyanes* (1920), *6 Charmes* (1921), *3 Variations* (1921), *Dialogues* (1923), and *9 Preludes* (1928-44); for voice and piano: *L'Hora grisa, Cançoneta incerta, 4 Mélodies, Le Nuage,* and *3 Comptines* (also orchestrated). —Cf. S. Kastner, *Federico Mompou* (Madrid, 1946).

Monaco, Mario del. See **Del Monaco, Mario.**

Monasterio, Jesús, famous Spanish violinist and pedagogue; b. Potes, near Santander, March 21, 1836; d. Casar del Periedo, Sept. 28, 1903. He made his début in 1845 in Madrid, as an infant prodigy; studied at Brussels Cons. with Bériot (violin) and with Fétis (theory). In 1857 he returned to Madrid; was appointed prof. of violin at the Madrid Cons., and taught there for many years; was its director from 1894 to 1897; conducted the Sociedad de Conciertos (1869-76), and was influential in forming a taste for classical music in Spain. He publ. a number of violin pieces, some of which (e.g., *Adíos a la Alhambra*) were very popular. —Cf. J. M. Alonso, *Jesús de Monasterio* (Santander, 1954; contains a list of works).

Moncada, Eduardo Hernández. See **Hernández Moncada, Eduardo.**

Moncayo, Pablo, Mexican composer; b. Guadalajara, June 29, 1912; d. Mexico City, June 16, 1958. A pupil of Chávez; with Ayala, Contreras, and Galindo he formed the so-called Group of Four (1935) created for the purpose of furthering the cause of Mexican music. Moncayo composed an opera, *La Mulata de Córdoba* (Mexico City, Oct. 23, 1948), an effective orch. dance *Huapango* (1941), and some chamber music.

Mondonville (mŏhn-dŏhn-vēl), **Jean-Joseph Cassanea de** (de Mondonville was his wife's maiden name), French violinist and composer; b. Narbonne, Dec. (baptized Dec. 25), 1711; d. Belleville, near Paris, Oct. 8, 1772. He appeared as a violinist in the Concert Spirituel, Paris (1737); wrote numerous motets for that organization; succeeded Gervais in 1744 as intendant of the 'musique de la chapelle' at Versailles; was musical director of the Concert Spirituel from 1755 till 1762. He produced several operas and pastorales: *Isbé* (Paris, April 10, 1742), *Le Carnaval du Parnasse* (Sept. 23, 1749; included ballet scenes), *Titon et l'Aurore* (Paris, Jan. 9, 1753), *Daphnis et Alcimadure* (Fontainebleau, Oct. 29, 1754); also wrote some instrumental music: *Pièces de clavecin en sonates* (with violin; 1734), *Les Sons harmoniques,* for violin and continuo (1736), and various other works. —Cf. L. Galibert, *Jean-Joseph Cassanea de Mondonville* (Narbonne, 1856); F. Hellouin, *Feuillets d'histoire* (Paris, 1903); L. de La Laurencie, *L'École française de violon de Lulli à Viotti* (Paris, 1922-24); A. Moser, *Geschichte des Violinspiels* (1923; p. 377 ff.); A. Tessier, *Madame de Mondonville,* in the 'Revue Musicale' (July, 1926).

Monestel, Alejandro, Costa Rican composer; b. San José, April 26, 1865; d. there, Nov. 3, 1950. He studied music at the Brussels Cons.; returning to Costa Rica in 1884, he was organist at the San José Cathedral (1884-1902); then lived in New York (1902-37), where he was active as church organist and composer. He wrote 14 Masses, 4 Requiems, 5 cantatas on the life of Jesus; also *Rapsodia Costarricense* for orch. (San José, Aug. 28, 1935); and publ. arrangements of Costa Rican songs.

Moniuszko (moh-nyush'-koh), **Stanislaw,** outstanding Polish composer; b. Ubiel, province of Minsk, Russia, May 5, 1819; d. Warsaw, June 4, 1872. He studied with August Freyer in Warsaw (1827-30) and with Rungenhagen in Berlin (1837-39); served as church organist in Vilna (1840-58), where he also produced a number of his operas. In 1858 he settled in Warsaw; was prof. at the Warsaw Cons. He wrote about 20 operas and operettas; his masterpiece was *Halka,* the first genuinely national Polish opera, which attained a lasting success in Poland, Russia, and to some extent in Germany. It was first presented in 2 acts in Vilna, by an amateur group (Jan. 1, 1848); then expanded to 4 acts, and produced ten years later in Warsaw (Jan. 1, 1858). Other operas are: *Loterya* (Warsaw, Sept. 12, 1846), *Jawnuta* (Vilna, May 20, 1852), *Flis* (*The Raftsman;* Warsaw,

Sept. 24, 1858), *Hrabina* (*The Countess;* Warsaw, Feb. 7, 1860), *Verbum nobile* (Warsaw, Jan. 1, 1861), *Straszny dwór* (*The Haunted Castle;* Warsaw, Sept. 28, 1865), *Paria* (Warsaw, Dec. 11, 1869), *Beata* (Warsaw, Feb. 2, 1872); also wrote about 270 songs (some of which are very popular in Poland); choral works; a symph. poem, *Bajka* (*Fairy Tale*); etc. Several biographies of Moniuszko have been publ. in Polish: by A. Walicki (1873); J. Karlowicz (1885); B. Wilczynski (1900); A. Koehler (1919); Z. Jachimecki (1921); H. Opienski (1924); S. Niewiadomski (1928); E. Wrocki (1930); T. Joteyko (1932); W. Hulewicz (1933); K. Stromenger (1946). Witold Rudzinski publ. a comprehensive biography with a complete list of works (Warsaw, 1952) and also brought out an *Almanach moniuszkowski 1872-1952,* on the 50th anniversary of Moniuszko's death (Warsaw, 1952). Se also Z. Jachimecki, *Stanislaw Moniuszko,* in the 'Mus. Quarterly' (Jan., 1928).

Monk, Edwin George, English organist and music editor; b. Frome, Somerset, Dec. 13, 1819; d. Radley, near Oxford, Jan. 3, 1900. He studied with G. A. Macfarren; Mus. Bac., Oxford, 1848; Mus. Doc., 1856. From 1858 till 1883 he was organist of York Minster. He edited 'The Anglican Chant Book,' 'The Anglican Choral Service Book,' 'The Anglican Hymn Book' (with Singleton), 'The Psalter and Canticles pointed for chanting' (with Ouseley), and 'Anglican Psalter Chants' (with Ouseley).

Monk, William Henry, English music editor; b. London, March 16, 1823; d. there, March 1, 1889. He was a pupil of T. Adams, J. A. Hamilton, and G. A. Griesbach; served as organist in various London churches; taught music at King's College, London; at the School for the Indigent Blind, at the National Training School, etc. He edited for the Church of Scotland 'The Book of Psalms in Metre,' 'Scottish Hymnal,' 'The Psalter,' and 'Book of Anthems'; was the music editor of 'Hymns, Ancient and Modern,' and composed many popular hymn tunes (*Eventide,* etc.); edited 'The Parish Choir.' —Cf. 'Dictionary of National Biography' (vol. 13).

Monleone, Domenico, Italian opera composer; b. Genoa, Jan. 4, 1875; d. there, Jan. 15, 1942. He studied at the Cons. of Milan; from 1895 to 1901 was active as theater conductor in Amsterdam and in Vienna. He attracted attention by producing in Amsterdam (Feb. 5, 1907) an opera, *Cavalleria Rusticana,* to a libretto by his brother Giovanni, on the same subject as Mascagni's celebrated work; after its first Italian performance (Turin, July 10, 1907), Mascagni's publisher Sonzogno brought a lawsuit against Monleone for infringement of copyright; Monleone was forced to change the title; his brother rewrote the libretto, and the opera was produced as *La Giostra dei falchi* (Florence, Feb. 18, 1914). Other operas were: *Una Novella di Boccaccio* (Genoa, May 26, 1909); *Alba eroica* (Genoa, May 5, 1910); *Arabesca* (Rome, March 11, 1913; won 1st prize at the competition of the City of Rome); *Suona la ritrata* (Milan, May 23, 1916); *Il Mistero* (Venice, May 7, 1921); *Fauvette* (Genoa, March 2, 1926); *La Ronda di notte* (Genoa, March 6, 1933); also an opera in Genovese dialect, *Scheûggio Campann-a* (Genoa, March 12, 1928). For some of his works he used the pseudonym W. di Stolzing.

Monn, Georg Matthias, Austrian composer; b. Lower Austria, 1717; d. Vienna, Oct. 3, 1750. For many years he was organist of the Karlskirche there. He wrote instrumental works marking a transition from the Baroque to the new style perfected by Johann Stamitz. A selection of his extant works appears in the 'Denkmäler der Tonkunst in Österreich,' vol. XV, part 2, ed. by Horwitz and Riedel: 3 symphonies, of which one, in E♭, may possibly be by a younger relative, Johann Christoph Monn or Mann (1726-1782), and a trio sonata; in vol. XIX, part 2, ed. by W. Fischer and Arnold Schoenberg: 5 symphonies, cello concerto in G minor, and harpsichord concerto in D (together with thematic catalogue of instrumental works of Georg Matthias Monn and Johann Christoph Monn). The Quartet Fugues reprinted by Albrechtsberger are by Johann Christoph Monn. Schoenberg transcribed G. M. Monn's harpsichord concerto in D for cello and orch. (1932).

Monnikendam, Marius, Dutch composer; b. Haarlem, May 28, 1896. He studied at the Amsterdam Cons. with Sem Dresden (composition) and de Pauw (organ and piano); in 1924 went to Paris on a government scholarship, and studied with Vincent d'Indy at the Schola Cantorum. Returning to Holland, he became a teacher at the Rotterdam Cons.; also wrote music criticism. He wrote a number of church works, in which he revived the most ancient forms of plainchant, but injected asymmetric rhythms in a modern style; in his larger works, he employed the resources of advanced harmony, including polytonality. He publ. books on César Franck (Amsterdam, 1949) and Igor Stravinsky (Haarlem, 1951). —Works: *Missa nova* (1928); *Te Deum; 7 Penitent Psalms* (1934); *Missa antiphonale* (1939); oratorios: *Noah* (1937), *Samson* (1938), *Solomon* (1939); *Sinfonia Sacra,* for men's voices and orch. (1947); *Passion,* for chorus, speaker, and orch. (1948); etc. —Cf. Cor Backers, *Nederlandse Componisten van 1400 tot op Onze Tijd* (The Hague, 1949; pp. 147-52).

Monsigny (mohn-sē-ñē), **Pierre-Alexandre,** French opera composer; b. Franquembergues, near St.-Omer, Oct. 17, 1729; d. Paris, Jan. 14, 1817. He was forced at an early age, by his father's death, to support his family; abandoned his study of music, and took a position as clerk in the Bureaux des Comptes du Clergé (1749); then became 'maître d'hotel' (majordomo) to the Duke of Orléans; in 1754, a performance of Pergolesi's *Serva padrona* so fired his imagination that he decided to try his own skill at comic opera. He took a rapid course of harmony with the double-bass player Gianotti, and soon completed his first stage work, *Les Aveux indiscrets,* produced at the Théâtre de la Foire Saint-Germain (Feb. 7, 1759). In quick succession, and with increasing success, the same theater brought out 3 more of Monsigny's operas: *Le Maître en droit* (Feb. 13, 1760), *Le Cadi dupé* (Feb. 4, 1761), and *On ne s'avise jamais de tout* (Sept. 14, 1761). The members of the Comédie-Italienne, alarmed at the rising prestige of its rival enterprise, succeeded in closing it, by exercise of vested privilege. and took over its best actors. Monsigny thereafter wrote exclusively for the Comédie-Italienne; a few of his operas, however, were first presented at the private theater of the Duke of Orléans, at Bagnolet. The operas produced at the Comédie-Italienne in Paris were: *Le Roi et le fermier* (Nov. 22, 1762), *Rose et Colas* (March 8, 1764), *Aline, reine de Golconde* (April 15, 1766), *L'Ile sonnante* (Jan. 4, 1768), *Le Déserteur* (March 6, 1769), *Le Faucon* (March 19, 1772), *La belle Arsène* (Aug. 14, 1775), and *Félix, ou l'enfant trouvé* (Nov. 24, 1777). Here Monsigny stopped abruptly, perhaps (as he himself modestly explained it) for lack of ideas. After the Revolution, he lost the stewardship of the estates of the Duke of Orléans, but the Opéra-Comique allowed him a pension of 2,400 francs; in 1800 he was made Inspector of Instruction at the Cons. (resigning in 1802). In 1813 he was elected to Grétry's chair in the Institut de France. Monsigny possessed an uncommon and natural melodic invention, and sensibility in dramatic expression, but his theoretical training was deficient; still, his works attained the foremost rank among the precursors of the French comic opera. —Cf. Quatremère de Quincy, *Notice historique sur la vie et les ouvrages de Monsigny* (Paris, 1818); M. Alexandre, *Éloge historique de Pierre Alexandre Monsigny* (Arras, 1819); M. Hédouin, *Éloge de Monsigny* (Paris, 1820); F. de Ménil, *Les grand musiciens du Nord: Monsigny* (Paris, 1893); A. Pougin, *Monsigny et son temps* (Paris, 1908); P. Druilhe, *Monsigny, sa vie et son œuvre* (Paris, 1955).

Montagu-Nathan, Montagu, English writer on music; b. Banbury, Sept. 17, 1877. His real name was Montagu Nathan; he changed it legally to Montagu Montagu-Nathan on March 17, 1909. He studied in Birmingham; then took violin lessons with Ysaÿe in Brussels, with Heermann in Frankfurt, and Wilhelmj in London. He appeared as a violinist in Belfast and Leeds, but soon abandoned concerts in favor of music journalism. He learned the Russian language and wrote several books on Russian music: *A History of Russian Music* (1914), *Handbook to the Piano Works of A. Scriabin* (1916; reprinted 1922); *Contemporary Russian Composers* (1917); and monographs on Glinka, Mussorgsky, and Rimsky-Korsakov. In 1951 he became editor of the periodical 'Music.'

Montani, Nicola Aloysius, American choral conductor and composer; b. Utica, N. Y., Nov. 6, 1880; d. Philadelphia, Jan. 11, 1948. He studied with American teachers till 1900; then with Lorenzo Perosi and others in Rome; Gregorian music under Dom Mocquereau and Dom Eudine on the Isle of Wight (1905-06); was organist and choirmaster of the Church of St. John the Evangelist, Philadelphia (1906-23); choirmaster at St. Paul's Church, N. Y. (1923-24); from 1925 instructor at various music schools in N. Y. and Philadelphia. In 1914 he founded the Society of St. Gregory of America (officially recognized by Pope Benedict XV) for the restoration of Gregorian Chant and the early polyphonic style recommended in the 'Motu Proprio' of Pius X; edited the 'Catholic Choirmaster.' Montani was also, for a time, editor-in-chief of the liturgical musc department of G. Schirmer, Inc., and of the Boston Music Co. He wrote

8 Masses; a *Stabat Mater;* motets, songs, etc.; publ. *Essentials of Sight Singing* and *The Art of A Cappella Singing;* 'St. Gregory Hymnal'; 'Catholic Choir Book' (1920; also publ. in Braille type, for use by the blind). The 'Caecilia' devoted its Aug., 1935 issue to Montani, listing biographical data and a catalogue of works.

Monte, Philippe de (Filippo di Monte, or Philippe de Mons), great Belgian contrapuntist; b. Malines, 1521; d. Prague, July 4, 1603. From about 1541-54 he was in Naples as tutor in the Pinelli family, and while there struck up a friendship with Roland de Lassus. In 1554 was in Rome for a brief sojourn, but soon went to Antwerp, and then to England, as singer in the choir of Philip II, husband of Queen Mary Tudor. In Sept., 1555, he left England and went to Italy again. In 1567 he was in Rome, and in 1568 he was appointed maestro di cappella to the Emperor Maximilian II in Vienna, holding this position until his death, which occurred while the court was at Prague during the summer. In 1572 he was appointed treasurer of Cambrai Cathedral, and in 1577, canon (without being required to reside there). He publ. Masses and many books of motets and madrigals; numerous others are in MS. In his *General History,* Hawkins reprinted a madrigal for 4 voices by Monte; Dehn's 'Sammlung' and Commer's 'Collectio' each contains a motet; a Mass for 6 voices, *Benedicta es,* was reproduced by A. Smijers in the 'Publications of the Vereeniging voor Nederlandsche Muziekgeschiedenis' (vol. 38); 3 madrigals for 5-7 voices are in the 'Denkmäler der Tonkunst in Österreich' (vol. 41). Publication of a collected ed. of Monte's works, under the editorship of Charles Van den Borren and J. van Nuffel, was begun in 1927 (26 vols. appeared, the latest dated 1935). —Cf. G. van Doorslaer, *Philippe de Monte* (Malines, 1895); G. van Doorslaer, *Philippe de Monte: la vie et les œuvres* (Brussels, 1921); P. Bergmans, *Quatorze lettres inédites du compositeur Philippe de Monte* (Brussels, 1921); A. Einstein, *Philippe de Monte als Madrigalkomponist* (in the report of the Liège Congress, 1930); J. van Nuffel, *Philippe de Monte,* in the 'Proceedings' of the Music Association (vol. 57; 1931). See also G. Reese, *Music in the Renaissance* (N. Y., 1954; pp. 395-96 and 406-08).

Monte, Toti dal (real name Antonietta Meneghel), Italian coloratura soprano; b. Mogliano, Treviso, June 27, 1893. She studied with Barbara Marchisio; appeared in various Italian theaters; sang at the Metropolitan Opera, N. Y. (1924-25); also made world-wide tours.

Montéclair (mohn-tā-klär'), **Michel Pignolet de,** French composer; b. Andelot, Dec. (baptized Dec. 4), 1667; d. near St. Denis, Sept. 27, 1737. He was one of the earliest players of the modern double-bass; from 1707 to his death he played in the orch. of the Académie Royale de Musique; there he produced his ballet-opera *Les Fêtes de l'été* (June 12, 1716) and a lyric tragedy *Jephté,* in 5 acts (Feb. 28, 1732), the first stage work on a biblical subject to be presented at the Académie. He also wrote a Requiem, 6 trio sonatas, flute duets, and 'brunettes' (French love songs); publ. a *Nouvelle Méthode pour apprendre la musique* (Paris, 1700; revised eds., 1709, 1736), *a Méthode facile pour apprendre à jouer du violon* (Paris, 1712; a pioneer violin method); and *Principes de musique* (Paris, 1736). —Cf. E. Voillard, *Essai sur Montéclair* (Chaumont, 1879); J. Carlez, *Un Opéra biblique au XVIII*[e] *siècle* (on *Jephté;* Paris, 1879); A. Moser, *Geschichte des Violinspiels* (1923; p. 176 ff.); M. Pincherle, *Elementary Musical Instruction in the 18th Century: an Unknown Treatise by Montéclair,* in the 'Mus. Quarterly' (Jan., 1948).

Montella, Giovanni Domenico, Italian lutenist and composer; b. Naples, c. 1570; d. there, 1607. In 1591 he was engaged as lutenist in the Royal Chapel, Naples; was also organist and harpist. He wrote psalms and other church music; publ. 2 vols. of *villanelle,* a vol. of motets, and 10 vols. of madrigals. Some of his sacred music is included in 'Istituzioni e Monumenti dell'arte musicale italiano' (vol. V, 1934).

Montemezzi, Italo, Italian composer; b. Vigasio, near Verona, Aug. 4, 1875; d. there, May 15, 1952. He was a pupil of Saladino and Ferroni at the Milan Cons., and graduated in 1900; his graduation piece, conducted by Toscanini, was *Cantico dei Cantici,* for chorus and orch. He then devoted himself almost exclusively to opera. In 1939 he went to the U. S.; lived mostly in California; also made several appearances as conductor of his operas. In 1949 he returned to Italy. Montemezzi's chief accomplishment is the maintenance of the best traditions of Italian dramatic music, without striving for realism or overelaboraton of technical means. His masterpiece in this genre is the opera *L'Amore dei tre re* (Milan, La Scala, April 10, 1913), which has become a standard work in the repertory of opera houses all over the world. Other operas are: *Giovanni Gallurese* (Turin, Jan. 28, 1905), *Hellera* (Turin, March 17, 1909), *La Nave* (libretto by Gabriele d'Annunzio; Milan, Nov. 1, 1918), *La Notte di Zoraima* (Milan, Jan. 31, 1931), *L'Incantesimo* (radio première, NBC, Oct. 9, 1943, composer conducting); he also wrote the symph. poems *Paolo e Virginia* (Rome, 1930) and *Italia mia!* (1944), etc. —Cf. L. Tretti and L. Fiumi, eds., *Omaggio a Italo Montemezzi* (Verona, 1952).

Monteux (mohn-tö'), **Pierre**, celebrated French conductor; b. Paris, April 4, 1875. He studied at the Paris Cons. with Berthelier (violin), Lavignac (harmony), and Lenepveu (composition); received 1st prize for violin (1896); then was viola player in the Colonne Orch., and later chorusmaster there; also played viola in the orch. of the Opéra-Comique. He then organized his own series, 'Concerts Berlioz,' at the Casino de Paris. In 1911 he became conductor for Diaghilev's Ballets Russes; his performances of modern ballet scores established him as one of the finest technicians of the baton. He led the world premières of Stravinsky's *Petrouchka, Le Sacre du Printemps,* and *Le Rossignol,* Ravel's *Daphnis et Chloé,* and Debussy's *Jeux;* conducted at the Paris Opéra (1913-14); founded the Société des Concerts Populaires in Paris (1914); appeared as guest conductor in London, Berlin, Vienna, Budapest, etc. In 1916-17 he toured the U. S. with the Russian Ballet; in 1917, conducted the Civic Orch. Society, N. Y.; in 1917-18, at the Metropolitan Opera House. In 1919 he was engaged as conductor of the Boston Symph. Orch., and held this post until 1924 (succeeded by Koussevitzky); introduced many works of the modern French school there; also gave the first American performance of *Le Sacre du Printemps.* In 1925 he became guest conductor of the Concertgebouw Orch., Amsterdam; in 1929 he founded the Orchestre Symphonique de Paris, and was its principal conductor until 1938. From 1936 until 1952 he was conductor of the reorganized San Francisco Symph. Orch.; then continued to conduct in Europe and America; was a frequent guest conductor with the Boston Symph. (conducted it on his 80th birthday, April 4, 1955); also led its concerts at Tanglewood; shared the podium with Munch during the European tour of the Boston Symph. in 1956 (which included Russia). As an interpreter, Monteux strives to bring out the inherent essence of the music, without imposing his own artistic personality; unemotional and restrained in his podium manner, he nonetheless succeeds in producing brilliant performances.

Monteverdi, Claudio (Giovanni Antonio), great Italian composer; founder of modern opera; renowned madrigalist; b. Cremona (baptized May 15), 1567; d. Venice, Nov. 29, 1643. He was a chorister at the Cathedral of Cremona and studied there under the choirmaster Marc' Antonio Ingegneri, learning to play the organ and the viol. His first published work (a collection of 3-part motets) dates from 1582, when he was only 15. About 1590 he entered the service of Vincenzo Gonzaga, Duke of Mantua, as viol player and madrigal singer. With him, he traveled to Hungary (1595) and Flanders (1599). In the meantime he had publ. a collection of *canzonette a* 3 (1584) and the first three books of madrigals (1587, 1590, 1592). 1602, maestro di cappella to the Duke; the 4th and 5th books of madrigals appeared in 1603 and 1605; and on Feb. 22, 1607, his first musical drama, *Orfeo,* was performed at Mantua with instant success. Also in 1607 he publ. the *Scherzi musicali a tre voci.* In 1608 he set to music Rinuccini's tragedy, *Arianna,* for the wedding of Francesco, Prince of Mantua (May 28, 1608). The music is lost, except the *Lamento d'Arianna,* which Monteverdi publ. separately (1623) as well as in a 5-part arrangement in book 6 of his madrigals (Venice, 1614); this aria, unsurpassed in its expressive melancholy, is one of Monteverdi's finest creations. He also wrote a ballet-opera, *Il Ballo delle Ingrate* (Mantua, June 4, 1608). In 1610 he wrote a Mass and Vespers, and took them to Rome in quest of assistance from Pope Paul V; when this proved futile, he returned to Mantua; after the death of his patron Vincenzo (1612), he lost his Mantuan position, but in 1613 was elected to succeed Martinengo as maestro di cappella at San Marco, Venice, at a salary of 300 ducats (raised to 500 in 1616), and a house, besides traveling expenses. He remained in Venice until his death, composing mainly for the church, but not neglecting the stage and the secular madrigal forms. The 7th book of madrigals was publ. in 1619. In 1624 he brought out, at the palace of Senator Mocenigo, his great dramatic scene, *Il Combattimento di Tancredi e Clorinda,* in which a narrator ('testo') connects the dialogue. In 1627 he composed 5 dramatic intermezzi for the plays *Melissa e Bradamente* and *Didone e gli Argonauti,* for the court of Parma; and in 1630 the opera *Proserpina rapita,* for the wedding of Mocenigo's daughter. In 1632 he took holy orders, out of gratitude for having escaped the terrible plague of the previous year. The *Madrigali guerrieri et amorosi,* the 8th book of madrigals, was publ. in 1638. In 1637 the first opera house was opened in Venice, the Teatro di S. Cassiano (up to that time, operas were presented at the palaces of the nobility); other theaters were soon established. Monteverdi produced *Il Ritorno di Ulisse in patria* at the Teatro di S. Cassiano (1641); two operas at the Teatro SS. Giovanni e Paolo: *Le Nozze di Enea con Lavinia* (1641) and (his last) *L'Incoronazione di Poppea* (1642). The authenticity of the opera *Adone* (Venice, Dec. 21, 1639), attributed to Monteverdi, is in dispute; the music is lost, but according to the libretto, the composer is Francesco Manelli.—The role of Monteverdi in music history is of great magnitude. He established the type of modern opera, conceived as true drama; he enlarged the orchestra, selected and skillfully combined the instruments accompanying the voices; he was among the first, if not the first, to employ the tremolo for strings, and also pizzicato; his recitative assumes a new dramatic power, at times expanding to an arioso. Even his early works show a remarkably advanced style of composition; the harmonic progressions reveal a strong sense of modern tonality, and the dominant seventh and other dissonances are used without preparation. In all this, he ran counter to the established tradition, and became involved in a bitter polemical exchange with Giovanni Maria Artusi of Bologna, who published several pamphlets attacking Monteverdi as a representative of the 'musica moderna.' —*Orfeo* (first publ., 1609) was reproduced by Sandberger (1927; facsimile of the 1616 ed.); modern eds. by Eitner in 'Publikationen . . . der Gesellschaft für Musikforschung' (1881), G. Orefice (1909), Vincent d'Indy (1915), G. F. Malipiero (1923), J. A. Westrup (1925), Respighi (1935), Redlich (1936), Orff (1940, very free), and Benvenuti (1942). A facsimile of the MS of *L'Incoronazione di Poppea* has been published (1938); the score was republished by Goldschmidt in his *Studien zur Geschichte der italienischen Oper* (vol. II, 1904); by d'Indy (1908), Charles van den Borren (1914), Westrup (1927), Malipiero (1937), Krenek (1937), Benvenuti (1937), Redlich (1939), and Ghedini (1953). A reprint of *Il Ballo delle Ingrate* appears in 'L'Arte musicale in Italia' by L. Torchi (vol. 6, 1897); newly ed. by Carl Orff as *Tanz der Spröden* (1929), by A. Toni (Milan, 1932), and by E. J. Dent (London, 1945). *Il Combattimento di Tancredi e Clorinda* has been reproduced by L. Torchi in 'L'Arte musicale in Italia' (vol. 6, 1897); modern editions by A. Toni (1921), Malipiero (1931), and Redlich (1946). *Il Ritorno d'Ulisse* was publ. by R. Haas in the 'Denkmäler der Tonkust in Österreich' (vol. 57, 1922); new editions by Vincent d'Indy (1927), Charles Van den Borren (1927), J. A. Westrup (1927), and Luigi Dallapiccola (1942). A 9th book of madrigals was publ. posthumously in 1651. Numerous madrigals and sacred works have been reprinted in modern eds., e.g., a 4-part Mass by Tirabassi and Charles van den Borren (1914); Vespers (1610) by Redlich (Vienna, 1949), Ghedini (Milan, 1952), Schrade (N. Y., 1953); chamber duets by Landshoff (in *Alte Meister des Bel Canto,* 1927), etc. A Mass *a* 6, Masses *a* 4, psalms *a* 1-8, with litanies to the Virgin and *Selva morale e spirituale* (containing Masses, psalms, hymns, Magnificats, motets, *Salve,* and a *Piano della Madonna* on the *Lamento* from *Arianna*) have been preserved; the arioso *Cruda Amarilli* (from the 5th book of madrigals) is included in many anthologies. The collected ed., in 16 vols., was assembled and edited by G. F. Malipiero (1926-42). — Cf. S. Davari, *Notizie biografiche del distinto maestro di musica Claudio Monteverdi* (Mantua, 1885); E. Vogel, *Claudio Monteverdi,* in the 'Vierteljahrsschrift für Musikwissenschaft' (1887); G. Sommi Picenardi, *Claudio Monteverdi a Cremona* (Milan, 1896); A. Heuss, *Die Instrumentalstücke des 'Orfeo',* in 'Sammelbände der internationalen Musik-Gesellschaft' (1903); H. Leichtentritt, *Claudio Monteverdi als Madrigalkomponist* (ibid., 1910); A. Heuss, *Claudio Monteverdi als Charakteristiker in seinen Madrigalen,* in the 'Liliencron-Festschrift' (1910); R. Mitjana, *Claudio Monteverdi y los orígines de la ópera italiana* (Málaga, 1911); L. Schneider, *Claudio Monteverdi* (Paris, 1920); A. Tessier, *Les deux styles de Monteverdi,* in the 'Revue Musicale' (1922); H. Prunières, *La Vie et l'œuvre de Claudio Monteverdi* (Paris, 1924; English transl., 1926); Charles Van den Borren, *'Il Ritorno d'Ulisse' de Claudio Monteverdi* (Brussels, 1925); A. Striggio, *L'Orfeo di Monteverdi* (Bologna, 1928; reprint of the libretto); issue of the 'Rassegna Musicale' devoted to Monteverdi (Oct., 1929); G. F. Malipiero, *Monteverdi* (Milan, 1930); K. F. Müller, *Die Technik der Ausdrucksdarstellung in Monteverdi's monodischen*

Frühwerken (Berlin, 1931); H. Redlich, *Claudio Monteverdi: vol. I: Das Madrigalwerk* (Berlin, 1932); G. F. Malipiero, *Monteverdi,* in the 'Mus. Quarterly' (July, 1932); G. Cesari, *La Musica in Cremona,* in 'Istituzioni e Monumenti dell'arte musicale italiano' (vol. VI, 1939); J. A. Westrup, *Monteverdi's 'Lamento d'Arianna',* in 'Music Review' (April, 1940); J. A. Westrup, *Monteverdi and the Orchestra,* in 'Music & Letters' (July, 1940); D. de Paoli, *Claudio Monteverdi* (Milan, 1945); M. Bukofzer, *Music in the Baroque Era—from Monteverdi to Bach* (London, 1948); H. F. Redlich, *Claudio Monteverdi, Leben und Werk* (Olten, 1949; in English, *Monteverdi, Life and Works,* London, 1952); L. Schrade, *Monteverdi, Creator of Modern Music* (N. Y., 1950); M. Le Roux, *Claudio Monteverdi* (Paris, 1951); C. Sartori, *Monteverdiana,* in the 'Mus. Quarterly' (July, 1952); C. Sartori, *Monteverdi* (Brescia, 1953); Anna Amalie Abert, *Claudio Monteverdi und das musikalische Drama* (Lippstadt, 1954); H. F. Redlich, *Claudio Monteverdi: Some Problems of Textual Interpretation,* in the 'Mus. Quarterly' (Jan., 1955); W. Osthoff, *Monteverdi-Funde,* in 'Archiv für Musikwissenschaft' (1957).

Monteverdi, Giulio Cesare, Italian organist and composer; brother of Claudio Monteverdi; b. Cremona, Jan. 31, 1573; date of death unknown. He wrote the important 'Dichiarazione' appended to Monteverdi's *Scherzi musicali a 3 voci* (1607), in which he expounded the musical ideas of his brother, and gave a vigorous reply to the attacks on Monteverdi by Artusi. Only a few madrigals by Giulio Cesare Monteverdi are extant. See bibliography under Claudio Monteverdi.

Moodie, Alma, Australian violinist; b. Brisbane, Sept. 12, 1900; d. Frankfurt, Germany, March 7, 1943. She studied with César Thomson in Brussels (1907-10); played at a concert as a child prodigy (with Max Reger); gave concerts in Germany, where she lived most of her life; taught at the State Academy of Music at Frankfurt. Her prestige as a musician was high in Germany; she performed many new works; Pfitzner wrote his violin concerto for her.

Moody, Fanny (Manners), English dramatic soprano; b. Redruth, Cornwall, Nov. 23, 1866; d. Dundrum, County Dublin, July 21, 1945. She studied singing with Mme. Sainton-Dolby; after several appearances in the provinces, she sang Micaela at Drury Lane, London (April 30, 1887). She married Charles Manners, the singer and impresario, on July 5, 1890, and thereafter accompanied her husband on his tours. She was at her best in lyric roles; also appeared successfully in Wagnerian parts (Elsa, Elizabeth, etc.).

Moór (mohr), **Emanuel,** Hungarian pianist and inventor; b. Kecskemét, Feb. 19, 1863; d. Mont Pèlerin, near Montreux, Switzerland, Oct. 21, 1931. He studied in Budapest and Vienna; toured the U. S. from 1885 to 1887, as director of the 'Concerts artistiques,' for which he engaged Lilli Lehmann, Ovide Musin, and other celebrated artists, and also acted as their accompanist. He then lived in London, Lausanne, and Munich. He invented the Moór-Duplex piano, consisting of a double keyboard with a coupler between the two manuals (an octave apart). With the introduction of this piano a new technique was made possible, facilitating the playing of octaves, tenths, and even chromatic glissandos. Some piano manufacturers (Steinway, Bechstein, Bösendorfer) have put the Moór mechanism into their instruments. Moór's second wife, **Winifred Christie** (b. Stirling, Feb. 26, 1882), English pianist, aided him in promoting the Moór keyboard, and gave many performances on it in Europe and America. She publ. (in collaboration with her husband) a manual of technical exercises for the Moór piano. Moór was also a composer; his works include 5 operas: *La Pompadour* (Cologne, Feb. 22, 1902), *Andreas Hofer* (Cologne, Nov. 9, 1902), *Hochzeitsglocken* (Kassel, Aug. 2, 1908; in London, under the title *Wedding Bells,* Jan. 26, 1911), *Der Goldschmied von Paris,* and *Hertha;* 8 symphonies and other orchestral works; 4 piano concertos; 3 violin concertos; 2 cello concertos; a triple concerto for violin, cello, and piano; concerto for 2 cellos and orch.; 2 piano quintets; 2 string quartets; 2 piano trios; suite for 4 cellos; 12 violin sonatas; 7 cello sonatas; 3 piano sonatas; Hungarian Dances for piano; harp sonata; a sonata for 4 harps; a great number of songs. —Cf. L. Deutsch, *Die Technik der Doppelklaviatur Moór* (Leipzig, 1932); W. Reich, *Das Moórsche Doppelklavier,* in 'Die Musik' (XXIV, 4); D. Tovey, *The Pianoforte of Emanuel Moór,* in 'Music & Letters' (Jan., 1922).

Moor, Karel, Czech composer; b. Bělohrad, Dec. 26, 1873; d. Prague, March 30, 1945. He wrote the operas *Viy,* after Gogol (Prague, Dec. 26, 1903), and *Hjoerdis*

(Prague, Oct. 22, 1905); several symph. poems; chamber music.

Moore, Douglas Stuart, distinguished American composer and music educator; b. Cutchogue, N. Y., Aug. 10, 1893. He studied at Yale Univ. with D. S. Smith and Horatio Parker; wrote several university songs, among them the football song *Good Night, Harvard;* after obtaining his B. A. (1915) and Mus. Bac. (1917), he joined the Navy and served as a lieutenant; then studied in Paris, with Vincent d'Indy, at the Schola Cantorum (1919-21), and with Tournemire (organ), Nadia Boulanger, and Ernest Bloch. In 1921 he received the post of director of music and organist at the Cleveland Museum of Art. From 1923 to 1925, he served as organist at Adelbert College, Western Reserve Univ.; in 1925 received the Pulitzer Traveling Scholarship in Music, and spent a year in Europe. In 1926 he was appointed associate prof. of music at Columbia Univ.; in 1940, succeeded Daniel Gregory Mason as head of the music dept.; also conducted the univ. orch.; lectured at the Metropolitan Museum of Art, N. Y. (1927-29); was guest conductor with several American orchestras; was a recipient of the Guggenheim Fellowship (1934). In 1946 he was elected president of the National Institute of Arts and Letters. His understanding of American folklore and regional melorhythms enables him to create works of typical American flavor, such as his 'folk opera' *Ballad of Baby Doe* (1956). Operas: *The Headless Horseman* (1936); *The Devil and Daniel Webster* (N. Y., May 18, 1939); *White Wings,* chamber opera (Hartford, Feb. 2, 1949); *The Emperor's New Clothes* (N. Y., Feb. 19, 1949); *Giants in the Earth* (N. Y., March 28, 1951; awarded the Pulitzer prize); *Ballad of Baby Doe* (Central City, Col., July 7, 1956); *Gallantry,* a 'soap opera' (N. Y., March 15, 1958); for orch.: *Pageant of P. T. Barnum,* suite in 5 movements (Cleveland, April 15, 1926); *Moby Dick,* symph. poem (1928); *A Symphony of Autumn* (1930); *Overture on an American Tune* (N. Y., Dec. 11, 1932, composer conducting); *Village Music,* suite in 4 movements (N. Y., Dec. 18, 1941); *In Memoriam* (Rochester, April 27, 1944); symph. in A major (Paris, May 5, 1946; received honorable mention by the N. Y. Music Critics Circle, 1947); *Farm Journal,* for chamber orch. (N. Y., Jan. 19, 1948); violin sonata (1929); string quartet (1933); quintet for woodwinds and horn (1942); quintet for clarinet, 2 violins, viola, and cello (1946); piano trio (1953).—Books: *Listening to Music* (N. Y., 1932; revised and enlarged ed., 1937); *From Madrigal to Modern Music: A Guide to Musical Styles* (N. Y., 1942).

Moore, Earl Vincent, American organist and teacher; b. Lansing, Mich., Sept. 27, 1890; he studied at the Univ. of Michigan (B. A., 1912; M. A., 1915); then in Europe with Widor, Holst, and Heger; served as organist and teacher at the Univ. of Michigan (1913-23); from 1923, prof.; in 1940 appointed dean of the School of Music there; 1928, elected vice-president of the Music Teachers' National Association; its president (1936-37); etc. He wrote the children's cantatas *The Voyage of Arion* and *The Bird Man.*

Moore, Gerald, English pianist; b. Watford, July 30, 1899. After a brief career as a concert pianist, he devoted himself almost exclusively to the art of accompaniment, in which he attained the foremost rank; also made transcriptions for piano of many songs and other works. He publ. an entertaining book, *The Unashamed Accompanist* (London, 1943), and *Singer and Accompanist: The Performance of 50 Songs* (London, 1953).

Moore, Grace, American soprano; b. Jellico, Tenn., Dec. 5, 1901; d. Copenhagen, Jan. 26, 1947. She studied at the Wilson Greene School of Music in Washington, and with Marafioti; first appeared in musical comedy in N. Y. (1921-26); then studied in France. Upon returning to America, she made her operatic début as Mimi at the Metropolitan Opera House (Feb. 7, 1928); made successful appearances also at the Paris Opéra-Comique (1928); at Covent Garden, London (1935); and at other European centers; also sang with the Chicago City Opera (1937); appeared in several motion pictures. She was killed in an airplane accident, on a flight from Copenhagen to Stockholm. Publ. an autobiography, *You're Only Human Once* (1944).

Moore, John Weeks, pioneer American musicologist and lexicographer; b. Andover, N. H., April 11, 1807; d. Manchester, N. H., March 23, 1889. He was a newspaper publisher and editor at Bellows Falls, Vt., where he publ. the 'Bellows Falls Gazette' (1838-55); also was for a time editor of the musical journals 'World of Music' and 'Musical Library.' His *magnum opus* is the *Complete Encyclopedia of Music, Elementary, Technical, Historical, Biographical,*

Vocal, and Instrumental (Boston, 1854; 1004 pages; Appendix, 1875); also *Dictionary of Musical Information* (1876); publ. the collections *Sacred Minstrel* (1842), *American Collection of Instrumental Music* (1856), and *The Star Collection of Instrumental Music* (1858); also *Puritanism of Music in America* (18 numbers), *Musical Record* (5 vols.; 1867-70), *Song and Song Writers of America* (200 numbers; 1859-80), etc. See 'Dictionary of American Biography.'

Moore, Mary Carr, American composer; b. Memphis, Tenn., Aug. 6, 1873; d. Ingleside, California, Jan. 11, 1957. In 1885 the family moved to California, where she studied singing; then theory with her uncle, John Harraden Pratt, H. B. Pasmore, and others. She began to compose as a child; her first publ. work was a lullaby, written at 16. She sang the leading part in her operetta, *The Oracle* (San Francisco, 1894); other stage works are: *The Flaming Arrow,* 'Indian intermezzo' (San Francisco, March 27, 1922, composer conducting); *Narcissa* (1912; San Francisco, Sept. 7, 1925; the first grand opera by an American woman, performed under her own direction); *Rizzio* (Los Angeles, May 26, 1932); *Los Rubios* (Los Angeles, Sept. 10, 1931). In 1930 she received the David Bispham Memorial Medal for her *Narcissa;* publ. songs (*My Dream,* etc.) and piano pieces (*Murmur of Pines,* etc.). —Cf. E. E. Hipsher, *American Opera and Its Composers* (Philadelphia, 1934; pp. 328-36).

Moore, Thomas, famous Irish poet, ballad singer, and song composer; b. Dublin, May 28, 1779; d. there, Feb. 25, 1852. He had no regular musical training, but learned to play the piano with the aid of the organist William Warren. He was in London from 1799 to 1803; then received a position as a government functionary in Bermuda; however, he stayed there only a few months; then returned to London by way of the U. S. and Canada. In London he became extremely popular as a ballad singer in the houses of aristocracy; in 1807 he publ. a volume of poetry, *Irish Melodies,* set to music by Sir John Stevenson. In 1817 he issued his celebrated poem, *Lalla Rookh.* An ardent Irish nationalist, he played an important role in the creation and revival of Irish poetry and music. Among his own melodies are *Love thee, dearest, When midst the gay, One dear smile,* and *The Canadian Boat-Song.* He freely borrowed his musical materials from popular Irish tunes, and in some cases modified them sufficiently to produce apparently new songs. He also composed short concerted vocal pieces; the terzetto *O lady fair,* and the 3-part glee *The Watchman* won wide popularity. In 1895 Sir Charles Stanford publ. *The Irish Melodies of Thomas Moore; the Original Airs Restored.* See the article on Moore in the 'Dictionary of National Biography.'

Moos (mohs), **Paul,** German writer on esthetics; b. Buchau, March 22, 1863; d. Raeren, Belgium, Feb. 27, 1952. He studied with Thuille, Rheinberger, and others in Munich; publ. *Moderne Musikästhetik in Deutschland* (1902; 2nd ed., 1922, entitled *Die Philosophie der Musik von Kant bis Eduard von Hartmann*); *Richard Wagner als Ästhetiker* (1906); *Die psychologische Ästhetik in Deutschland* (1919); *Die deutsche Ästhetik der Gegenwart* (vol. I, 1929; vol. II, 1931); also contributed many valuable essays to German music magazines.

Mooser, Aloys, Swiss organ manufacturer; b. Niederhelfenschwyl, June 27, 1770; d. Freiburg, Dec. 19, 1839. He studied with his father, an Alsatian organist; attained fame as one of the greatest masters in organ building; the quality of the 'Vox humana' in his organs was particularly admired.

Mooser, R.-Aloys, Swiss writer on music; great-grandson of the preceding; b. Geneva, Sept. 20, 1876. He studied with his father and Otto Barblan in Geneva. In 1896 he went to St. Petersburg, where he took courses with Balakirev and Rimsky-Korsakov; wrote music criticism for the 'Journal de St. Petersbourg' and made an extensive study of Russian music in the archives: his books on the subject possess great authority. In 1909 he returned to Geneva and became active as music critic there. His reviews were collected in the volumes: *Regards sur la Musique Contemporaine: 1921-46* (Lausanne, 1946); *Panorama de la Musique Contemporaine: 1947-1953* (Geneva, 1953); *Aspects de la Musique Contemporaine: 1953-1957* (Geneva, 1957). Books on Russian music: *L'Opéra-comique français en Russie au XVIIIe siècle* (Geneva, 1932; 2nd ed., 1954); *Violonistes-compositeurs italiens en Russie au XVIIIe siècle* (Milan, 1938-50); *Opéras, intermezzos, ballets, cantates, oratorios joués en Russie durant le XVIIIe siècle* (Geneva, 1945; 2nd ed., 1955); *Annales de la musique et des musiciens en Russie au XVIIIe siècle* (of prime importance for new, detailed, and accurate documentation; 3 vols.; Geneva, 1948-51).

Morales, Cristóbal de, eminent Spanish composer; b. Seville, c. 1500; d. Málaga, 1553 (between Sept. 4 and Oct. 7). He was a pupil of Fernández de Castilleja, who was chapel master at the Seville Cathedral. From 1526 to 1530, Morales was choirmaster of the Avila Cathedral. In 1535 he entered the papal choir in Rome (until 1540); he composed much sacred music during this period. After a brief journey to Spain, he returned to Rome and increased his productivity as composer; he also traveled in the retinue of the Pope to various towns in Italy. From 1545 to 1547 he was choirmaster at the cathedral of Toledo; in 1551 he obtained a similar post at Málaga, where he remained until his death. Morales was one of the outstanding masters of the polyphonic style; he was greatly esteemed by contemporary musicians; Bermudo described him as 'the light of Spain in music.' 2 books of Masses, many motets, Magnificats, and Lamentations were publ. during his lifetime. Modern reprints are found in Eslava's 'Lira sacro-hispana'; Pedrell's 'Hispaniae Schola musica sacra'; Martini's 'Esemplare'; Rochlitz's 'Sammlung'; etc. The 1st vol. of his collected works, containing 'Missarum Liber Primus' (originally publ. in Rome, 1544), appeared in the series 'Monumentos de la Música Española,' ed. by H. Anglès (Madrid, 1951). —Cf. H. Collet, *Le Mysticisme musical espagnol au XVIe siècle* (Paris, 1913); R. Mitjana, *Cristóbal de Morales, Estudio critico-biográfico* (Madrid, 1920); F. R. Piqueras, *Música y músicos toledanos* (Toledo, 1922); J. B. Trend, *Cristóbal Morales,* in 'Music & Letters' (Jan., 1925); Elústiza and Castrillo Hernández, *Antología Musical* (Barcelona, 1933); R. Stevenson, *Cristóbal Morales, A Fourth-Centenary Biography,* in the 'Journal of the American Musicological Society' (Spring, 1953).

Morales, Melesio, Mexican composer; b. in Mexico City, Dec. 4, 1838; d. San Petro de los Pinos, May 12, 1908. He began to compose salon music for piano and soon acquired sufficient technique to write for the stage; produced two operas, *Romeo y Julieta* (Mexico City, Jan. 27, 1863) and *Ildegonda* (Mexico City, Jan. 27, 1866); then went to France and Italy for additional study. Returning to Mexico after 4 years abroad, he presented two more operas: *Gino Corsini* (Mexico City, July 14, 1877) and *Cleopatra* (Mexico City, Nov. 14, 1891). Despite his passionate advocacy of national music, he followed conventional Italian models in his own works.

Morales, Olallo Juan Magnus, writer and composer; b. (of a Spanish father and Swedish mother) Almeria, Spain, Oct. 15, 1874; d. Tällberg, May, 1957. Taken to Sweden as a child, he received his education there, first at Göteborg, then at the Stockholm Cons. with W. Stenhammar and others (1891-99), and in Berlin with H. Urban (composition) and Teresa Carreño (piano). In 1901 he returned to Sweden; wrote music criticism; was conductor of the Göteborg Symph. Orch. (1905-09). From 1909 he lived in Stockholm; was prof. at the Stockholm Cons. (1917-39); secretary of the Academy of Music (1918-40). With T. Norlind he compiled a history of the Royal Academy of Music on its sesquicentennial (1921); also publ. a handbook of conducting (Stockholm, 1946). His works include a symph.; several overtures; a violin concerto (1943); a string quartet; a piano sonata; *Balada andaluza,* for piano (1946); *Nostalgia,* and other character pieces for piano; choral works; songs.

Moralt, Joseph, the eldest brother and 1st violin in a famous Munich string quartet of brothers; b. Schwetzingen, Aug. 5, 1775; d. Munich, c. 1836. **Johann Baptist Moralt,** the 2nd violin (b. Mannheim, Jan. 10, 1777; d. Munich, Oct. 7, 1825), wrote symphonies and string quartets; **Philipp Moralt,** the cellist (b. Munich, 1780; d. there, 1847), also played in the Munich municipal band; **Georg Moralt,** the viola player (b. Munich, 1781; d. there, 1818), was a member of the quartet until his death.

Moran-Olden, Fanny, German soprano; b. Oldenburg, Sept. 28, 1855; d. Berlin, Feb. 13, 1905. She took lessons with Götze in Dresden, where she made her début as Fanny Olden (her real name was Tappenhorn) in the role of Norma (1877); she then was at the Frankfurt Opera (1878-83), at the Leipzig City Theater (1884-91), and at the Munich Opera (1892-93); sang in New York during the 1888-89 season. She was twice married: in 1879 to the tenor Karl Moran, and in 1897 to Bertram, court singer in Munich.

Morawetz, Oscar, composer; b. Svetla, Czechoslovakia, Jan. 17, 1917. He studied in Prague with Jaroslav Křička; in 1940 went to Canada; joined the faculty of the Toronto Cons. —Works: *Carnival Overture* (Toronto, July 1, 1945); a Serenade for strings (1947); *Anthem to Canada,* for chorus and orch. (1951); many piano pieces.

Moreau (mŏh-rŏh'), **Jean-Baptiste,** French composer; b. Angers, 1656; d. Paris, Aug. 24, 1733. He was a chorister at the Cathedral of Angers; then was choirmaster at the Cathedral of Langres. After a year in Dijon, he went to Paris in 1686; was introduced at the French court by the Dauphine, and was commissioned by Louis XIV to write several divertissements, among them *Les Bergers de Marly* (1687). He won great success with his musical interludes (recitatives and choruses) for Racine's *Esther* (1698) and *Athalie* (1691), performed at the royal school of St.-Cyr, where Moreau was maître de chapelle; also wrote music for Racine's *Cantiques spirituels,* for performance at St.-Cyr. His success at court was marred by his dissolute habits; however, he was greatly esteemed as a teacher of singing and composition; among his pupils were Montéclair, J. F. Dandrieu, Clérambault, and the singers Louise Couperin and his own daughter Marie-Claude Moreau. The music to *Esther* and *Athalie,* and the *Cantiques spirituels,* were publ. in the music supplement to P. Mesnard's 'Oeuvres de J. Racine' (Paris, 1873).—Cf. Th. Lavallée, *Histoire de la maison royale de St.-Cyr* (Paris, 1856); A. Taphanel, *Le Théâtre de St.-Cyr* (Paris, 1876); J. Tiersot, *Les Chœurs d'Esther et d'Athalie de Moreau,* in the 'Revue Musicale' (Jan., 1903); Kathi Meyer, *Der chorische Gesang der Frauen* (Leipzig, 1917); N. Demuth, *A Musical Backwater,* in the 'Mus. Quarterly' (Oct., 1954).

Moreau, Léon, French composer; b. Brest, July 13, 1870; d. Paris, April 11, 1946. He studied at the Paris Cons., won the Grand Prix de Rome in 1899. Among his works are the operas *Myriade* and *Pierrot décoré;* the symph. poems *Sur la mer lointaine* and *Dionysos;* a piano concerto; many songs.

Moreira, Antonio, Portuguese composer; b. Lisbon, c. 1750; d. there, Nov. 21, 1819. He studied at a seminary in Lisbon, and in 1775 became an instructor there. He wrote a number of operas in Italian, and 2 in Portuguese, for production at the Teatro San Carlos, where he was conductor until 1800. His Italian opera *Il Disertore* was given at La Scala, Milan (1800).

Morel, Auguste-François, French composer; b. Marseilles, Nov. 26, 1809; d. Paris, April 22, 1881. He lived in Paris from 1836 to 1850; then returned to Marseilles, and became director of the Cons. there; produced a grand opera *Le Jugement de Dieu* (1860); wrote a great deal of chamber music of excellent quality, for which he won the 'Prix Chartier' twice; also 2 symphonies and a number of overtures.

Morel, François d'Assise, Canadian composer; b. Montreal, March 14, 1926. He studied at the Quebec Provincial Cons. in Montreal; obtained a diploma as piano teacher.—Works: *Esquisse,* for orch. (1947); string quartet (1948); *4 Chants japonais,* for voice and piano (1949); *3 Miniatures,* for flute and piano (1950); *Antiphonie* (1951; N. Y., Oct. 16, 1953).

Morel, Jean, conductor; b. Abbeville, France, Jan. 10, 1903; studied in Paris with I. Philipp (piano), N. Gallon (theory), M. Emmanuel (history of music), R. Hahn (lyric repertory), and G. Pierné (composition). Taught at the American Conservatory in Fontainebleau (1921-36) and Brooklyn College (1940-43). From 1934 to 1939, conducted various French orchestras. Conducted opera in Rio de Janeiro, Mexico, and the New York City Center. Since 1949, teacher at the Juilliard School of Music, N. Y., and conductor of the Juilliard Orch.; also, since 1956, conductor at the Metropolitan Opera House.

Morelli, Carlo (real name Carlos Zanelli), baritone; b. Valparaiso, Chile, Dec. 25, 1897. He studied voice in Bologna with Angelo Queize, and in Florence with Leopoldo Mugnone; made his début in 1922; was then engaged for 7 seasons at La Scala, Milan; toured South America (1925-31); made his first U. S. appearance with the Chicago City Opera (1932), and remained on its roster for 4 seasons; 1935-40, with the Metropolitan Opera Co. His brother, Riccardo Zanelli, also a baritone, made his début at the Metropolitan Opera as Amonasro in 1919 and sang there for several seasons.

Morelli, Giacomo, Italian librarian and music scholar; b. Venice, April 14, 1745; d. there, May 5, 1819. He was librarian at San Marco; discovered fragments of the *Art of Rhythm* by Aristoxenos, and published them in 1785.

Morelot (mohr-loh'), **Stéphen,** French scholar; authority on sacred music; b. Dijon, Jan. 12, 1820; d. Beaumont, Oct. 7, 1899. He was dean of the faculty of jurisprudence at Dijon Univ.; was co-editor (from 1845) of the 'Revue de la musique religieuse, populaire et classique'; went to Italy in 1847 to study church music. He publ. numerous essays on the subject, among them *De la musique au XVe siècle . . .* (1856), *Éléments de l'harmonie appliqués à l'accompagnement du plain-chant, d'après les traditions des anciennes écoles* (1861). His *Manuel de Psalmodie en fauxbourdons à 4 voix . . .* (1855) is an ingenious attempt to revive the ancient style of harmonization.

Morena (real name Meyer), **Berta,** German soprano; b. Mannheim, Jan. 27, 1878; d. Rottach-Eggern, Oct. 7, 1952. Her great beauty attracted the attention of the famous painter von Lenbach; at his behest, she was engaged (after brief training under Sophie Röhr-Brajnin in Munich) to sing Agathe in *Der Freischütz* at the Munich Opera (1898), and was immediately successful. She remained at the Munich Opera for more than 20 years; made her American début with the Metropolitan Opera, N. Y., as Sieglinde (March 4, 1908), and remained a favorite for 5 consecutive seasons. Her talent as an actress greatly helped her in her career; she was regarded in Germany as one of the most intelligent and musicianly singers; excelled particularly in the Wagnerian parts (Elisabeth, Elsa, Eva, Isolde, the three Brünnhildes, etc.).—Cf. A. Vogl, *Berta Morena und ihre Kunst* (Munich, 1919).

Morera, Enrique, Spanish composer; b. Barcelona, May 22, 1865; d. there, March 11, 1942. As a child, he was taken to Argentina, and studied in Buenos Aires; then took courses at the Cons. of Brussels. Returning to Barcelona, he studied piano with Albéniz and harmony with Felipe Pedrell. In 1896 he founded a choral society, 'Catalunya Nova,' which he conducted for several years; taught at the Escuela Municipal de Música in Barcelona (1910-28). He was an ardent propagandist of Catalan music, and wrote a number of songs to Catalan words; also collected 193 melodies of popular origin. His opera *Emporium,* originally to a Catalan text, was performed first in Italian (Barcelona, Jan. 20, 1906); he wrote more than 50 other stage works (lyric comedies, zarzuelas, operettas, intermezzos, etc.); several symph. poems (*Atlántida, Traidoría,* etc.); a cello concerto; some chamber music; a set of 5 sardanas (national dances of Catalonia) for piano, etc. — Cf. I. Iglesias, *E. Morera* (Barcelona, 1921; in Catalan).

Moreschi (moh-res'-kē), **Alessandro,** the last of the artificial male sopranos; b. Rome, Nov. 11, 1858; d. there, April 21, 1922. He studied with Capocci in Rome; from 1883 to 1913 was sopranist at the Sistine Chapel in the Vatican. His voice was of such purity and beauty that he was nicknamed 'l'angelo di Roma.' — Cf. Angus Heriot, *The Castrati in Opera* (London, 1956; appendix; pp. 225-27).

Morgan, Maud, American harpist; b. New York, Nov. 22, 1860; d. there, Dec. 2, 1941. She received her musical training from her father, George Washbourne Morgan (1823-1892); then studied in London; made her public début in 1875 in a concert with Ole Bull, and appeared as a soloist in various cities of the U. S. In 1895 she became harpist at Grace Church, N. Y., continuing in that post until 1920. In 1925 she founded a harp school in Staten Island, N. Y., and made her residence there until her death.

Mori, Frank, English musician; son of Nicolas Mori; b. London, March 21, 1820; d. Chaumont, France, Aug. 2, 1873. He received his education from his father; wrote light music; his operetta *The River-Sprite* (London, Feb. 9, 1865) was fairly successful.

Mori, Nicolas, English violinist and music publisher (of Italian extraction); b. London, Jan. 24, 1796; d. there, June 14, 1839. He studied violin with Barthélemon and Viotti; gave many concerts as a soloist at an early age; also was a member of the London Philharmonic. He brought out the English editions of works by Mendelssohn, and other music. An eccentric, he wrote flamboyant advertisements about his career, and shortly before his death, announced his own memorial concert, punning on his name ('Memento Mori'). See E. W. Duffin, *Particulars of the Illness and Death of the Late Mr. Mori* (London, 1839).

Morillo, Roberto García, Argentinian composer; b. Buenos Aires, Jan. 22, 1911. He studied with Aguirre and J. J. Castro; later with Gaito and Ugarte. In 1926-30 was in Paris. Returning to Argentina, he became a teacher at the National Cons., and music critic of 'La Nación.' His music is marked by propulsive rhythm and a strong contrapuntal sense, along polytonal lines. His first important work was a symph. poem, *Bersaerks* (Buenos Aires, Dec. 29, 1932); other works: piano concerto (Buenos Aires, Nov. 7, 1940); *Las Pinturas Negras de Goya,* for 6 instruments (Montevideo, May 27, 1940); *The Fall of the House of Usher,* after Poe (Buenos Aires, May 12, 1943); piano pieces.

Morin, Gösta, Swedish musicographer; b. Stockholm, April 14, 1900. He studied with T. Norlind at Upsala Univ., and later in Germany, Austria, and Italy; in 1937 visited the U. S. He held the position of librarian at Upsala Univ.; then at the Royal Music Academy in Stockholm; editor-in-chief of the valuable new edition of *Sohlmans Musik Lexikon* (Stockholm, 1948-53; 4 vols.).

Morini, Erica (originally, Erika), violinist; b. Vienna, Jan. 5, 1904. Her father was Italian, her mother Viennese. She studied at her father's school of music in Vienna; then with Ševčik; made her professional début as a child prodigy, at the age of 12; played with the Gewandhaus Orch. in Leipzig, under the direction of Nikisch (1918). She made her U. S. début in N. Y. on Jan. 26, 1921; in subsequent years, played with virtually all major American orchestras; also toured South America, Australia, and the Orient; eventually settled in New York.

Morlacchi (mŏhr-lăhk'-kē), **Francesco,** Italian composer; b. Perugia, June 14, 1784; d. Innsbruck, Oct. 28, 1841. He was a pupil of Caruso in Perugia, and of Zingarelli at Loreto; received the diploma of 'maestro compositore' from the Liceo Filarmonico of Bologna (1805). At the time of graduation, he wrote a cantata for the coronation of Napoleon as King of Italy (1805); even earlier he wrote church music and an opera. His first stage work to be performed was an operetta *Il Poeta spiantata, o il Poeta in campagna* (Florence, 1807); he showed his contrapuntal skill in the composition of a Miserere in 16 parts; then produced a comic opera, *Il Ritratto* (Verona, 1807), and a melodrama, *Il Corradino* (Parma, 1808). His first signal success as an opera composer was the production of *Le Danaide* in Rome (Feb. 11, 1810). He was engaged as musical director of the Italian Opera in Dresden in 1811; wrote there several operas and, in 1814, a Mass in celebration of the return of the King of Saxony to Dresden; also wrote music for the Russian governor of Dresden during the occupation, and other occasional pieces. He continued to compose operas, for Naples, Milan, Venice, and Genoa, among them *Gianni di Parigi* (Milan, May 30, 1818), *Tebaldo ed Isolina* (Venice, Feb. 4, 1822; his most famous work; produced also in London, Paris, Leipzig, Prague, etc.), and *Colombo* (Genoa, June 21, 1823). When the King of Saxony died in 1827, Morlacchi wrote a Requiem, one of his finest works. He spent the last years of his life partly in Dresden and partly in Italy; he died on his way to Italy, at Innsbruck. —Cf. G. B. Rossi-Scotti, *Della vita e delle opere del cav. Francesco Morlacchi . . . memorie istoriche* (Perugia, 1860); E. Magni-Dufflocq, *Francesco Morlacchi,* in the 'Bolletino bibliografico musicale' (1934, No. 4).

Morley, Thomas, famous English composer; b. 1557; d. Oct., 1602; was a pupil of Byrd; Mus. Bac., Oxford, 1588; organist at St. Paul's Cath.; Gentleman of the Chapel Royal, 1592, also Epistler and Gospeller.—Publ. compositions: *Canzonets, or Little Short Songs to three voyces* (1593); *Madrigalls to Foure Voyces* (1594); *The First Booke of Ballets to fiue Voyces* (1595; reprinted 1842 in score by the Musical Antiquarian Society); *The First Booke of Canzonets to Two Voyces* (1595); *Canzonets, or Little Short Aires to fiue and sixe voices* (1597); *The First Booke of Aires or Little Short Songs to sing and play to the Lute with the Base-Viol* (1600; contains the song *It was a lover and his lass* from 'As you like it,' reprinted in Knight's 'Shakespeare' and Chappell's 'Popular Music of the Olden Time'; the entire book was republ. by E. H. Fellowes, London, 1932).—Morley's works are unusually melodious, and many of the madrigals and ballets are still popular; the canzonets *a* 3-4 and madrigals were publ. in modern score by Holland and Cooke; 5 sets of harpsichord lessons are in 'Queen Elizabeth's Virginal Book'; services and anthems are in Barnard's and Boyce's collections. The complete secular works were publ. by E. H. Fellowes in *The English Madrigal School* (4 vols., 1914 ff.; I. *Canzonets to 2 voices* [1595] and *Canzonets to 3 voices* [1593]; II. *Madrigals to 4 voices* [1594]; III. *Canzonets to 5 and 6 voices* [1597]; IV. *Ballets to 5 voices* [1600]). Morley edited 'Canzonets or Little Short Songs to Four Voyces. Collected out of the best and approued Italian Authors' (1598); 'Madrigals to fiue voyces [ditto]' (1598); and 'The Triumphes of Oriana, to five and six voyces composed by divers seuerall aucthors' (1601; reprinted in score by Wm. Hawes).—He wrote the first regular treatise on music publ. in England: *A Plaine and Easie Introduction to Practicall Musicke* (1597; reprinted by E. H. Fellowes, London, 1937; modernized ed., by R. Alec Harman, London, 1952); ed. the collection of instrumental music, 'The First Booke of Consort Lessons, made by divers exquisite Authors for sixe Instruments to play together, viz. the Treble Lute, the Pandora, the Citterne, the Base Violl, the Flute, and the Treble Violl' (1599; revised ed. 1611;

new ed. by Sidney Beck, N. Y., 1958). — Cf. O. Becker, *Die englischen Madrigalisten W. Bird, Th. Morley und J. Dowland* (Bonn, 1901); E. H. Fellowes, *The English Madrigal Composers* (London, 1921; 2nd ed., 1948); Margaret Glyn, *About Elizabethan Virginal Music and Its Composers* (London, 1924); E. H. Fellowes, *The English Madrigal* (London, 1925) and *The English Madrigal School, a Guide to Its Practical Use* (London, 1926). See also J. E. Uhler's *Morley's Canzonets for Two Voices* (Univ. of Louisiana, Baton Rouge, 1954) and *Morley's Canzonets for Three Voices* (Baton Rouge, 1957), with facsimile eds., transcriptions of texts, and commentaries.

Mornington, Garrett Colley Wellesley, Earl of; the father of the Duke of Wellington; b. Dangan, Ireland, July 19, 1735; d. London, May 22, 1781. He was a glee composer. In 1776 and 1777 the Catch Club awarded him prizes for catches; and in 1779 for the glee *Here in a cool grot.* Sir Henry Bishop edited a complete collection of his glees and madrigals (1846). Mornington was Mus. Doc., Dublin, and prof. at Dublin Univ. from 1764 to 1774.

Moroi, Saburo, Japanese composer; b. Tokyo, Aug. 7, 1903. He studied literature at Tokyo Univ.; later took courses at the Hochschule für Musik in Berlin. Upon his return to Japan, he became a superintendent of music schools. He has written 4 symphonies: No. 1 (Berlin, Oct. 2, 1934); No. 2 (Tokyo, Oct. 12, 1938); No. 3 (Tokyo, May 26, 1950); No. 4 (Tokyo, March 26, 1951); 2 piano concertos (1927; 1934); cello concerto (1936); violin concerto (1939); chamber music; songs. His son, **Makoto Moroi** (b. Tokyo, Dec. 17, 1930), is also a composer; has written a partita for solo flute (1952); piano sonata (1953); *Alpha and Beta,* for piano (1954); and *Développements raréfiants,* for piano (Festival of Modern Music, Karuizawa, Japan, Aug. 12, 1957).

Moross, Jerome, American composer; b. Brooklyn, Aug. 1, 1913. He studied at N. Y. Univ.; became interested in ballet music; has written several ballet scores for various dance groups in N. Y.: *Paul Bunyan* (1934), *American Pattern* (1937), *Frankie and Johnnie* (1938), *Guns and Castanets* (1939), *Robin Hood* (1946); ballet-operas: *Susanna and the Elders* (1940), *Willie the Weeper* (1945), *The Eccentricities of Davy Crockett* (1946); also a symphony (Seattle, Oct. 18, 1943); *Biguine,* for orch. (N. Y., Nov. 21, 1934); *A Tall Story,* for orch. (C.B.S. commission; broadcast, Sept. 25, 1938); choral works; piano pieces.

Morphy, Guillermo, Conde de, Spanish courtier and musician; b. Madrid, Feb. 29, 1836; d. Baden, Switzerland, Aug. 28, 1899. He was taken to Germany as a child; there he studied music; took courses with Fétis in Brussels, where he wrote an orchestral *Serenata española,* which had several performances. In 1864 he was named 'chamber gentleman' to the Prince of Asturias, the future Alfonso XII, and then became his secretary; received his nobiliary title in 1885. He spent much time in Vienna and Paris, and took up the study of Spanish tablature music of the 16th century. His transcriptions (marred by inaccuracies) were publ. posthumously, with an introduction by Gevaert, as 'Les Luthistes espagnols du XVIe siècle' (2 vols., Leipzig, 1902; German text by Riemann). In his influential position at the Spanish court, Morphy helped many talented musicians; was instrumental in procuring a stipend for Albéniz to enable him to study in Brussels.

Morris, Harold, American composer and pianist; b. San Antonio, Texas, March 17, 1890. He studied at the Univ. of Texas (B.A.) and the Cincinnati Cons.; lectured at the Rice Institute of Houston, Texas (1933), at Duke Univ. (1939-40), etc.; was on the faculty of Juilliard School of Music (1922-39); Teachers College, Columbia Univ. (1939-46); received many awards (National Federation of Music Clubs, Philadelphia Music Guild Award, etc.); was one of the principal founders of the Amer. Music Guild (N. Y., 1921). In his music, he reveals himself as a neo-Romanticist; in the main direction of his creative development, he was influenced by Scriabin. Many of his works are of programmatic content; some of them include American thematic material. — Works: for orch: *Poem,* after Tagore's *Gitanjali* (Cincinnati, Nov. 29, 1918); *Dum-A-Lum,* variations on a Negro spiritual, for chamber orch. (1925); piano concerto (Boston, Oct. 23, 1931, composer soloist; very successful); Symph. No. 1, after Browning's *Prospice* (1934); *Passacaglia and Fugue* (1939); suite, for chamber orch. (N. Y., Nov. 1, 1941); violin concerto (N. Y., May 25, 1939); *American Epic* (1942); Symph. No. 2, subtitled *Victory* (Chicago, Dec. 23, 1952); *Heroic Overture* (1943); Symph. No. 3, subtitled *Amaranth,* after Edwin A. Robinson (Houston, March 13, 1948); chamber music: 2 piano trios, 2 string quartets, 2 piano quintets, violin sonata, *Prologue and Scherzo,* for flute, violin, cello, and piano, *Rhapsody,* for flute, cello, and piano; 4 piano sonatas; other piano pieces.

Morris, Reginald Owen, English composer and eminent pedagogue; b. York, March 3, 1886; d. London, Dec. 14, 1948. He studied at the Royal College of Music, with Charles Wood; was music critic of the 'Nation'; from 1920, taught at the Royal College of Music, with the exception of 2 years (1926-28), when he taught theory at the Curtis Institute of Music in Philadelphia. His works include a symph. in D major (London, Jan. 1, 1934), a *Concerto Piccolo* for 2 violins and string orch., a set of songs, etc. It is mainly as an excellent teacher that Morris established himself; he gave considerable freedom to his students in expressing their individuality without adhering too closely to academic dogma. He publ.: *Contrapuntal Technique in the XVIth Century* (1922); *Foundations of Practical Harmony and Counterpoint* (1925); *Preparatory Exercises in Score Reading* (with H. Ferguson; 1931); *Figured Harmony at the Keyboard* (1933); *The Structure of Music* (1935); *The Oxford Harmony* (vol. 1 only; 1946). —Cf. E. Rubbra, *R. O. Morris: an Appreciation,* in 'Music & Letters' (Jan., 1949).

Morse, Charles Henry, American organist; b. Bradford, Mass., Jan. 5, 1853; d. Boston, June 4, 1927. He studied at the New England Cons. and at the Boston Univ. College of Music, with J. K. Paine; then taught at various Boston schools, at Minneapolis, and in Brooklyn, before returning to Boston. He publ. a number of anthems, Christmas carols, etc.; many arrangements for organ, and several valuable compilations ('The Contemporary Organist,' 'The Church Organist,' 'The Junior Church Organist,' etc.).

Mortari, Virgilio, Italian composer and pianist; b. Passirana di Lainate, near Milan, Dec. 6, 1902; he studied in Milan with Bossi and Pizzetti; after some years of concertizing, he became instructor at the Cons. Benedetto Marcello in Venice (1933-40); in 1940 became prof. at the Santa Cecilia in Rome.—Works: operas: *Secchi e Sberlecchi* (Udine, 1927), *La Scuola delle moglie* (1930), and *La Figlia del diavolo* (Milan, March 24, 1954); also completed Mozart's *L'Oca del Cairo* from fragments of Mozart's other works (Salzburg, Aug. 22, 1936); wrote a ballet, *L'Allegra piazzetta* (Rome, 1945); for orch.: *Fantasia,* for piano and orch. (1933), concerto for string quartet and small orch. (1937), *Notturno incantato* (1940), piano concerto (1952); vocal works: *Trittico* for soprano, mezzo soprano, and orch. (1939), *Ritorni e ritornelli,* for voice and piano (1940), *Stabat Mater,* for 2 voices and orch. (1947), *2 Funeral Psalms,* in memory of Alfredo Casella, for voice and instruments (1947), etc.; chamber music: sonatina for harp (1938), *Piccola serenata,* for cello solo (1946), *Piccola serenata,* for violin solo (1947); also arrangements of operas and oratorios by Galuppi (*Filosofo di campagna, L'Amante dell'onore*), Pergolesi (*Flaminio*), and Monteverdi; publ. *La Tecnica dell'orchestra contemporario* (in collaboration with Casella; Milan, 1950).

Mortelmans, Ivo, Belgian composer; son of Lodewijk Mortelmans; b. Antwerp, May 19, 1901. He studied at the Antwerp Cons., and later in Brussels; then became a music critic; also conducted opera in Holland, and taught theory at the Antwerp Cons. He has written several pieces of stage music; choruses for women's voices; also several Masses; arrangements of Flemish folksongs; etc.

Mortelmans, Lodewijk, Belgian composer; b. Antwerp, Feb. 5, 1868; d. there, June 24, 1952. He was a chorister in the Dominican Church; then studied with Benoit in Antwerp. In 1889 he won the 2nd Belgian Prix de Rome; gained 1st prize with his cantata *Lady Macbeth,* in 1893; then taught at the Antwerp Cons. In 1921 he made a tour in the U. S.; was director of the Antwerp Cons. from 1924 to 1933. —Works: opera, *De Kinderen der Zee* (Antwerp, 1920); symph. poems, *Helios* (1894), *Mythe du Printemps* (1895), *Avonlied* (1928), *Weemoedig Aandenken* (1942), *Eenvoud* (1950); church cantata *Jong Vlaanderen* (1907); *Symphonie homérique* (1898); 4 elegies for orch.: *In memoriam* (1917), *Elevation du Cœur* (1917), *Solitude* (1919), *Treurdicht* (1925); 3 sets of *Miniatures* for piano; *27 Old Flemish Folksongs,* for piano; a number of songs to Flemish words, which are his finest creations. Paul Gilson has called him 'Prince of the Flemish song.' The Belgian Center of Musical Documentation publ. a complete catalogue of his works, with a brief biography in Flemish, French, and English (Brussels, 1954). See also: J. L. Broeckx, *Lodewijk Mortelmans* (Antwerp, 1945).

Morton, Robert, English composer; b. c. 1440; d. 1475. He was clerk of the chapel of Philip the Good and Charles the Bold of

Burgundy; possibly identical with Robertus Anglicus (1485), a singer at St. Peter's, Rome. Some of his compositions are preserved in the 'Kopenhagener Chansonnier,' publ. by K. Jeppesen (1927); several MSS are in Belgian archives.

Mosca, Giuseppe, Italian composer of operas; b. Naples, 1772; d. Messina, Sept. 14, 1839. He studied with Fenaroli; was engaged as répétiteur at the Théâtre Italien, Paris (1803-09); then was maestro di cappella in Palermo (1817-21); director of music at the Messina Theater (after 1823). He was a prolific composer; wrote 44 operas, which were produced on leading Italian stages; also ballets and other theatrical pieces.

Mosca, Luigi, Italian composer; brother of Giuseppe Mosca; b. Naples, 1775; d. there, Nov. 30, 1824. He was a pupil of Fenaroli; served as maestro al cembalo at the San Carlo Theater in Naples; later taught singing. He produced 14 operas, of which *I Pretendenti delusi* (Milan, Sept. 7, 1811) was the most successful.

Moscheles (mŏh'-shĕ-less), **Ignaz,** eminent pianist, pedagogue, and composer; b. Prague, May 30, 1794; d. Leipzig, March 10, 1870. Of a well-to-do family (his father was a Jewish merchant), he was trained in music as soon as his ability was discovered; his 1st piano teacher was Dionys Weber at the Prague Cons.; at the age of 14, Moscheles performed publicly a concerto of his own composition. On his father's death, shortly after, he went to Vienna to study under Albrechtsberger and Salieri, at the same time earning his living as a teacher. His conspicuous talents won him access to the best circles; he prepared the piano score of Beethoven's *Fidelio* under the master's supervision, and entered into friendly rivalry with Meyerbeer, then a brilliant pianist, and Hummel. At concerts in Munich, Dresden, and Leipzig (1816), and in Paris (1820), his remarkable playing was much applauded; he was a pioneer in developing various modifications of tone by touch, afterwards exploited by Liszt. In 1821 Moscheles settled in London; made frequent trips to the Contient, and gave Mendelssohn piano lessons at Berlin in 1824. The teacher and the pupil became close friends; on July 13, 1829, they gave the first performance in London of Mendelssohn's concerto for 2 pianos and orch. After the foundation of the Leipzig Cons. in 1846, Mendelssohn invited Moscheles to join its staff. There, a host of pupils from all quarters of the globe were trained by him with sympathetic consideration, and yet with unflinching discipline in musical matters. He was noted for his energetic, brilliant, and strongly rhythmical playing; his virtuosity equalled his emotional absorption in the music; his romantic pieces for piano expressed clearly his ideas of the extent and the limitations of the instrument. He wrote 8 piano concertos, of which Nos. 3, 5, and 6 were favorites; also wrote, for piano and orch., *Marche d'Alexandre, Souvenirs d'Irlande, Souvenirs de Danemark,* etc.; a *Grand Septuor,* for piano, violin, viola, clarinet, horn, cello, and double-bass; a *Grand Sextuor,* for piano, violin, flute, 2 horns, and cello; a piano trio; piano duos with violin, with horn, and with guitar; for 2 pianos, *Hommage à Haendel;* for 2 pianos, 8 hands, *Les Contrastes;* for piano, 4 hands, *Sonate symphonique;* for piano solo, *Sonate mélancolique, Allegro di bravura, La Tenerezza, Les Charmes de Paris;* also excellent studies (*Characteristic Studies,* in 2 books; 54 *Études de concert*; the études *L'Ambition* and *L'Enjouement,* etc.). His output totals 142 opus numbers. Moscheles translated Schindler's biography of Beethoven into English (with numerous additions), publ. as *The Life of Beethoven* (2 vols., London, 1841). His wife, **Charlotte Moscheles,** *née* Embden (d. Detmold, Dec. 13, 1889), wrote *Aus Moscheles' Leben* (Leipzig, 1872; 2 vols.; English transl., London, 1873). His correspondence with Mendelssohn was publ. by his son, F. Moscheles, who also publ. his father's memoirs, as *Fragments of an Autobiography* (London, 1899). See G. Servières, *Moscheles,* in the 'Revue Pleyel' (Paris, Dec., 1926); H. Engel, *Die Entwicklung des deutschen Klavierkonzertes von Mozart bis Liszt* (1927).

Moscona, Nicola, Greek bass singer; b. Athens, Sept. 23, 1907. He studied at the Athens Cons. and sang opera in Greece and Egypt (1931-37); then went to Milan; was engaged to sing at the Metropolitan Opera, and made his American début in *Aida* (Dec. 13, 1937).

Mosel, Ignaz Franz von, Austrian composer, conductor, and writer on music; b. Vienna, April 2, 1772; d. there, April 8, 1844. He began his career as an opera conductor, and was the first in Vienna to use a baton (1812). In 1816 he conducted the first concert of the 'Gesellschaft der Musikfreunde.' In 1820 he was appointed vice-director of the court theaters in Vienna, and in 1829, custodian of the Imperial Library.

3 of his operas were produced at the Court Opera in Vienna: *Die Feuerprobe* (April 28, 1811), *Salem* (March 5, 1813), and *Cyrus und Astyages* (June 13, 1818); publ. 3 collections of songs. — Writings: *Versuch einer Ästhetik des dramatischen Tonsatzes* (1813); *Über das Leben und die Werke des Anton Salieri* (1827); *Über die Originalpartitur des Requiems von W. A. Mozart* (1839); *Geschichte der kaiserl. königl. Hofbibliothek zu Wien* (1835); and *Die Tonkunst in Wien während der letzten fünf Dezennien* (1818, in the Vienna 'Allgemeine musikalische Zeitung'; separate reprint, 1840). —Cf. R. Batka, *Moseliana*, in 'Musikbuch aus Österreich' (1911 and 1912).

Mosenthal (moh'-zĕn-tăhl), **Joseph,** violinist and composer; b. Kassel, Nov. 30, 1834; d. New York, Jan. 6, 1896. He was a pupil of his father and Spohr, and played in the court orch. of Kassel under Spohr's direction. He emigrated to America in 1853; was organist at the Calvary Church, N. Y. (1860-87); from 1867, was conductor of the N. Y. Mendelssohn Glee Club; also was a violinist in the N. Y. Philharmonic (for 40 years). He publ. several anthems, hymns, and other sacred works for the Episcopal Church, and part-songs for male chorus (*Thanatopsis, Blest pair of Sirens, Music of the Sea,* etc.); *Sunday Lyrics* (6 songs); psalm, *The Earth is the Lord's;* numerous songs.

Moser, Andreas, notable German violinist and music scholar; b. Semlin, Hungary, Nov. 29, 1859; d. Berlin, Oct. 7, 1925. He studied first in Zürich, with Hegar; also took courses in engineering and architecture in Stuttgart; in 1878 he became a violin pupil of Joachim in Berlin; in 1883 was concertmaster in Mannheim; in 1884 settled in Berlin. In 1888 he was appointed teacher at the Hochschule für Musik, a post he held until his death; made prof. in 1900. He publ. a number of valuable studies on the history of the violin. — Writings: *Joseph Joachim. Ein Lebensbild* (1899; 2nd enlarged ed., in 2 vols., 1908; 1910); *Methodik des Violinspiels* (2 parts; 1920); *Geschichte des Violinspiels* (1923; also in English); *Technik des Violinspiels* (2 vols.; 1925); collaborated with Joachim in a 3-vol. *Violinschule* (1902-5; French by Marteau; English by Moffat); ed. *Johannes Brahms im Briefwechsel mit Joseph Joachim* (1908; vols. V and VI of the Brahms correspondence) and, with Johannes Joachim, *Briefe von und an Joseph Joachim* (3 vols., 1911-13); edited (with Joachim) Beethoven's string quartets and Bach's partitas for violin; also various other violin works. —Cf. H. J. Moser, *Andreas Moser,* in Ebel's 'Berliner Musikjahrbuch' (1926, p. 106 ff.).

Moser, Hans Joachim, eminent German musicologist; son of Andreas Moser; b. Berlin, May 25, 1889. He studied violin with his father; musicology with Kretzschmar and Johannes Wolf in Berlin, with Jenner and Schiedermair in Marburg, with Riemann and Schering in Leipzig; also took courses in singing with Oskar Noë and Felix Schmidt; composition with H. van Eyken and Robert Kahn; he received his *Dr. phil.* at the Univ. of Rostock, with the dissertation *Die Musikergenossenschaften im deutschen Mittelalter* (1910). Returning to Berlin, he was active as a concert singer (bass baritone); was in the German army during World War I. In 1919, he became privatdozent of musicology at the Univ. of Halle; 1922, prof. there; 1925, prof. at the Univ. of Heidelberg; 1927, honorary prof. at the Univ. of Berlin; from 1927 to 1933, director of the State Academy for Church- and School-music in Berlin; in 1931 he received the degree of *Dr. theol.,* Königsberg. During World War II he worked in Berlin as music editor; in 1947 became prof. at Jena Univ. and the Hochschule für Musik in Weimar; in 1950, appointed director of the Berlin Cons. As a music historian and lexicographer, he is preëminent; particularly important are his writings on German church music. — Publications: *Technik der deutschen Gesangskunst* (after Oskar Noë; 1911; 3rd ed., 1955); *Geschichte der deutschen Musik* (3 vols.: I. 1920, 5th ed. 1930; II. 1922, 5th ed. 1930; III. 1924, 2nd ed. 1928); *Musikalischer Zeitenspiegel* (1922); *Musikalisches Wörterbuch* (1923); *Die evangelische Kirchenmusik in volkstümlichem Überblick* (1926); *Paul Hofhaimer* (1929); *Das Studium der Musikwissenschaft in Deutschland* (1929); *Die Epochen der Musikgeschichte* (1930; 2nd ed., 1956); *Die mehrstimmige Vertonung des Evangeliums* (2 vols.; 1931, 1934); *Corydon; das ist: Geschichte des mehrstimmigen Generalbassliedes und des Quodlibets im deutschen Barock* (2 vols., 1933); *Die Melodien der Lutherlieder* (1935); *Tönende Volksaltertümer* (1935); *J. S. Bach* (1935; 2nd ed., 1956); *Heinrich Schütz* (1936; 2nd ed., 1954); *Lehrbuch der Musikgeschichte* (1936; 12th ed., 1954); *Das deutsche Lied seit Mozart* (1937); *Kleine deutsche Musikgeschichte* (1938; 4th ed., 1955); *Kleines Heinrich-Schütz-Buch* (1940; 2nd ed., 1950); *Allgemeine Musiklehre* (1940; 2nd ed., 1954); *G. F. Händel* (1941; 2nd ed., 1952); *Chr.*

W. Gluck (1940); *C. M. von Weber* (1941; 2nd ed., 1955); *Bernhard Ziehn* (1949); *Musikgeschichte in 100 Lebensbildern* (1952); *Die evangelische Kirchenmusik in Deutschland* (1954); *Dokumente der Musikgeschichte* (1954); *Die Musikleistung der deutschen Stämme* (1955); *Die Tonsprachen des Abendlandes* (1956); *Robert Schumann* (1956); numerous articles in German music magazines, some publ. separately; pamphlets for various occasions. His major work is the *Musik Lexikon* (1931; 2nd ed., 1943, withdrawn; 3rd ed., 1951; 4th ed., in 2 vols., 1956; despite the inevitable errors, and conspicuous omissions, a very scholarly and serviceable reference work). Moser was editor (from 1926) of a projected collected ed. of Weber's works (2 vols. only appeared, 1926-28); wrote an entirely new libretto for Weber's *Euryanthe* and produced the opera under the title *Die sieben Raben* (Berlin, March 5, 1915); edited 'Alte Meister des deutschen Liedes' (1912; 2nd ed., 1931); 'Minnesang und Volkslied' (1925; 2nd enlarged ed., 1933); 'Lutherlieder' (1930); 5 works of Heinrich Schütz, discovered by Moser; facsimile editions of German music and old treatises; a collection of Alsatian songs; etc. He also wrote a number of songs and choruses; a school opera, *Der Reisekamerad,* after Andersen; fictional works (*Die verborgene Symphonie, Ersungenes Traumland, Der klingende Grundstein,* etc.). On the occasion of his 65th birthday (1954) a symposium of articles dedicated to him by his friends and students was publ. in Berlin.

Moser, Rudolf, Swiss composer; b. Niederuzwyl, St. Gall, Jan. 7, 1892. He studied theology at Basel Univ. and musicology (with Nef); then at the Leipzig Cons. (1912-14), with Max Reger, Sitt, and Klengel; further with Huber in Basel and Lauber in Geneva. He became conductor of the cathedral choir in Basel; also active as a pedagogue. —Works: *Der Rattenfänger,* dance play (1950); *Concerto grosso,* for string orch. (Basel, June 26, 1927); several suites for orch.; 3 violin concertos; organ concerto; concerto for violin, viola, and cello; piano concerto; viola concerto; 4 string quartets; piano trio; string sextet; *Das Lied von der Sonne,* for soli, chorus, orch., and organ; *Odes of Horace,* for baritone, chorus, and orch.; other vocal music; organ pieces; etc.

Mosewius, Johann Theodor, German conductor and musicologist; b. Königsberg, Sept. 25, 1788; d. Schaffhausen, Sept. 15, 1858. He began his career as an opera singer in Königsberg, and later in Breslau. In 1829, he became music director at the Univ. of Breslau; in 1831, director of the Institute for Church Music there. By establishing the Singakademie (1825), and giving competent performances of works from Bach to Beethoven, he exercised cultural influence on the musical life of Breslau. He also publ. articles on composers; of these, 2 were reprinted separately: *J. S. Bach in seinen Kirchencantaten und Choralgesängen* (1845) and *J. S. Bachs Matthäus Passion* (1852). — Cf. A. Kempe, *Erinnerungen an J. T. Mosewius* (Breslau, 1859).

Moskowa, Prince de la, **Joseph Napoléon,** eldest son of Marshal Ney; French musician; b. Paris, May 8, 1803; d. St.-Germain-en-Laye, July 25, 1857. A senator, and brigadier general under Napoleon III, he was also a talented musician. In 1843 he established the 'Société de musique vocale, religieuse et classique' (for the performance of works of the 16th-17th centuries), himself conducting the concerts in his palace; the society publ. 11 volumes of these works, as 'Recueil des morceaux de musique ancienne, etc.' which included works by Allegri, Arcadelt, Bach, Bononcini, Carissimi, the 2 Gabrielis, Gesualdo, Orlando Gibbons, Gluck, Handel, Haydn, Janequin, Josquin Des Prez, Lotti, Marcello, Orlando Lasso, Palestrina, Scarlatti, Stradella, Victoria, etc. He composed 2 comic operas, *Le Cent-Suisse* (Paris, June 7, 1840) and *Yvonne* (Paris, March 16, 1855); also a Mass with orch. in 1831.

Mosonyi, Mihály (real name Michael Brandt), Hungarian composer; b. Frauenkirchen, Sept. 4, 1814; d. Budapest, Oct. 31, 1870. He learned to play violin, double-bass, and organ as a child; then took some lessons with Karl Turányi in Pressburg; subsequently earned his living as a private tutor in aristocratic families in Hungary and Vienna; he also played double-bass in various orchestras. Although he was a product of the Classical school of composition he became enamored of Hungarian national music; began to write in the Hungarian idiom, although his harmonies remained Germanic. Liszt took great interest in his works, and proposed to bring out Mosonyi's German opera *Kaiser Max auf der Martinswand* (1857), but Mosonyi delayed the final revision of the work, and it never reached performance. His 2nd opera, *Szêp Llon* (*Pretty Helen*), was produced at Budapest on Dec. 19, 1861; another opera, *Almos,* was not staged until Dec. 6, 1934, many years after Mosonyi's death. He further wrote 5 Masses and other church music; 2 symphonies; 6 string quartets; several choruses for men's voices; songs. His *Funeral Music for Széchenyi* employs the so-called Hungarian mode, and its strong national character established Mosonyi as one of the founders of the Hungarian School. —Cf. K. Ábrányi, *Mosonyi* (Budapest, 1872); J. Káldor, *Michael Mosonyi* (Dresden, 1936); Béla Bartók, *Three Unpublished Liszt Letters to Mosonyi,* in the 'Mus. Quarterly' (Oct., 1921).

Mossolov, Alexander Vassilievitch, Russian composer; b. Kiev, Aug. 10, 1900. He studied at the Moscow Cons. with Glière and Miaskovsky. In his earliest works he experimented with modern techniques; wrote songs to texts from newspaper advertisements. His ballet entitled *Zavod* (*The Factory*) was performed in Moscow on Dec. 4, 1927; the orchestration included a metal sheet, shaken so as to imitate the sound of a factory at work; the section containing this effect was frequently performed abroad (in the U. S. usually under the title *Iron Foundry*). When modern music came under criticism in Russia, Mossolov repudiated his experimental phase, and adopted a more orthodox Russian style; also traveled in Turkestan and collected folksongs. He wrote a patriotic cantata, *Minin and Pozharsky; Kirghiz Rhapsody,* for mezzo-soprano, chorus, and orch. (1933); *Turkmenian Suite* (1933), for orch.; 4 symphonies (1928; 1934; 1937; 1941); 2 piano concertos; cello concerto; harp concerto; some chamber music and songs.

Moszkowski (mŏhsh-kŏhf'-skē), **Alexander,** music critic; brother of Moritz Moszkowski; b. Pilica, Poland, Jan. 15, 1851; d. Berlin, Sept. 26, 1934. He lived most of his life in Berlin; wrote criticism for various publications there; was also editor of 'Lustige Blätter' (a humorous magazine); publ. the entertaining booklets, *Anton Notenquetschers Neue Humoresken* (1893; 9th ed., 1904), *Anton Notenquetschers heitere Dichtungen* (1894); etc. A serious work is *Die Kunst in 1000 Jahren* (1910).

Moszkowski (mŏhsh-kŏhf'-skē), **Moritz,** famous pianist, teacher, and composer; b. Breslau, Aug. 23, 1854; d. Paris, March 4, 1925. He studied at the Dresden Cons.; later at the Stern Cons. and at the Kullak Academy in Berlin; then became a teacher at the latter institution. He gave his first public concert in Berlin in 1873; then played elsewhere in Germany, and in Paris, where he established his reputation as a pianist; in 1897, he made Paris his headquarters. As a composer, he is most widely known by his pieces in the Spanish vein, particularly the two books of *Spanish Dances,* for piano solo, or piano duo; also popular were his études, concert waltzes, gavottes, *Skizzen,* a tarantella, a *Humoresque,* etc. In larger forms he essayed an opera, *Boabdil der Maurenkönig* (Berlin, April 21, 1892), which contains a ballet number that became popular; also wrote a ballet, *Laurin* (1896); a symph. poem, *Jeanne d'Arc; Phantastischer Zug* for orch.; *Aus aller Herren Länder* for orch.; a violin concerto; a piano concerto.

Motta, José Vianna da. See **Da Motta.**

Mottl, Felix, celebrated conductor; b. Unter-St. Veit, near Vienna, Aug. 24, 1856; d. Munich, July 2, 1911. After preliminary studies at a seminary, he entered the Vienna Cons., and studied there with Door (piano), Bruckner (theory), Dessoff (composition), and Hellmesberger (conducting), graduating with high honors. In 1876 he acted as one of the assistants at the first Wagner festival at Bayreuth, and thereafter became a confirmed propagandist for Wagner, and conductor of Wagner's music dramas. Even before his journey to Bayreuth, he had conducted a Wagner society in Vienna. In 1880 he succeeded Dessoff as court conductor at Karlsruhe; in 1893 was appointed general musical director there. He conducted *Tristan und Isolde* at the Bayreuth festival in 1886; led a Wagner concert in London in 1894, and gave the entire *Ring* tetralogy at Covent Garden in 1898. In 1903 he was engaged to conduct the projected performances of *Parsifal* at the Metropolitan Opera in N. Y., but withdrew owing to the protests of the Wagner family, leaving the direction of the work to Alfred Hertz. However, he conducted some other Wagner operas at the Metropolitan Opera House during the season of 1903-1904. Mottl secured recognition for Peter Cornelius' *Der Barbier von Bagdad* by re-orchestrating the score, and producing it first at Karlsruhe, on Feb. 1, 1884; additional changes were made by him with Hermann Levi, and in this form the work finally became established in the opera repertory. In Dec., 1905, he conducted, also in Karlsruhe, the 1st complete performance of both parts of Berlioz's *Les Troyens* (in German); he orchestrated Wagner's *Fünf Gedichte,* and edited Wagner's early overtures; his complete vocal scores of Wagner's dramatic works were publ. posthumously in the 'Edition Peters' (1914). Mottl's original works show excellent craftsmanship, but they are devoid of invention; he composed 3 operas: *Agnes Bernauer* (Weimar, 1880), *Rama*, and *Fürst und Sänger;* a string quartet; numerous songs. Among his arrangements, that of Chabrier's *Bourrée fantasque* enjoys continued popularity in the concert hall.

Moulaert (moo-lart), **Raymond,** Belgian composer; b. Brussels, Feb. 4, 1875. He studied at the Brussels Cons. with Arthur de Greef (piano) and Edgar Tinel (theory); became an assistant in the harmony class, and continued to teach there for 43 years (1896-1939); from 1913-38 he was director of his own music school in St.-Gilles. —Works: *Symphonie de valses* (1936); *Symphonie de fugues* (1944); *Variations symphoniques* (1952); piano concerto (1938); *Rapsodie écossaise* for clarinet and orch. (1940); *Eroica* for horn and orch. (1946); *Légende* for flute and orch. (1951); sextet for piano, flute, oboe, clarinet, horn, and bassoon (1925); suite for 3 trombones (1939); 5 sets of *Poèmes de la vieille France* (1917-43); a Mass (1949); a song cycle *L'Eau passe* (1952); many choral works. A catalogue of his works was publ. by the Centre Belge de Documentation Musicale (Brussels, 1954).

Mount-Edgcumbe, Richard, British nobleman (second Earl of Mount-Edgcumbe) and music amateur; b. Plymouth, Sept. 13, 1764; d. Richmond, Surrey, Sept. 26, 1839. He was the author of a book, *Musical Reminiscences, containing an Account of the Italian Opera in England from 1773,* which he publ. anonymously in 1825. He also wrote an opera, *Zenobia* (in Italian), which was produced at London in 1800.

Mouquet (moo-kā'), **Jules,** French composer; b. Paris, July 10, 1867; d. there, Oct. 25, 1946. He studied at the Paris Cons. with Leroux (harmony) and Dubois (composition); won 1st Prix de Rome in 1896 with his cantata *Mélusine,* the Prix Trémont in 1905, and the Prix Chartier (for chamber music) in 1907; in 1913 became prof. of harmony at the Paris Cons. —Works: the oratorios *Le Sacrifice d'Isaac* and *Le Jugement dernier;* the symph. poems, *Diane et Endymion* and *Persée et Andromède; Danse grecque* for orch.; *Divertissement grec,* for flute and harp; sonata for flute and piano; pieces for oboe and piano, bassoon and piano, saxophone and piano, etc.; a septet for wind instruments; *Études antiques* for piano solo. He also publ. a *Cours complémentaire d'harmonie.*

Mouret, Jean Joseph, French composer; b. Avignon, April 11, 1682; d. Charenton, Dec. 20, 1738. He was attached to the court in Paris; produced an opera-ballet, *Les Festes de Thalie* (Paris, Aug. 19, 1714); an opera, *Ariane* (Paris, April 6, 1717); *Les Amours des dieux,* opera-ballet (Paris, Sept. 14, 1727). He was director of the Concert Spirituel (1728-34); wrote motets for performances there; also divertissements for the Comédie-Italienne; about 50 of his chamber pieces were publ. during his lifetime. —Cf. R. Viollier, *J. J. Mouret, le musicien des grâces* (Paris, 1950).

Moussorgsky. See **Mussorgsky.**

Mouton (moo-tohn'), **Jean,** important French composer; b. Haut-Wignes (Holluigue), near Boulogne, c. 1470; d. St.-Quentin, Oct. 30, 1522. At the age of 7 he became a 'chantre écolâtre' (chorister) in the choir of Notre Dame at Nesle, near St. Quentin; in 1500, was in charge of the choirboys at the Cathedral of Amiens; in 1501, in a similar position at the Cathedral of Grenoble. In 1513 he became a chapel singer to Louis XII, and later to Francis I; then served as canon at Thérouanne, and later at St. Quentin. He was the teacher of Willaert. He wrote almost exculsively sacred music, and was one of the greatest masters of counterpoint of the period; in his works he followed the precepts of Josquin Des Prez; excelled particularly in the art of canon. His Masses and motets were publ. between 1508 and 1540 (in collections by Petrucci, Attaignant, and others); his canons are cited by Glareanus in his *Dodecachordon* (republ. by P. Bohn, 1889); other examples of his works are found in the histories of Burney, Forkel, Hawkins, and Busby; in Commer's 'Collectio'; etc. A Mass, *Alma Redemptoris,* was republished by H. Expert in his 'Maîtres Musiciens' (vol. IX). —Cf. F. Lesure, *Un Document sur la jeunesse de Jean Mouton,* in the 'Revue belge de musicologie' (1956); see also G. Reese, *Music in the Renaissance* (N. Y., 1954, pp. 280-85).

Moyzes, Alexander, Slovak composer; son of Mikuláš Moyzes; b. Klaštor pod Znievom, Sept. 4, 1906. He studied at the Prague Cons. (1925-28); in 1929, became prof. of composition at the Cons. of Bratislava; in 1949, appointed prof. at the Academy of Music there. His music uses the melodic resources of Slovak folksongs. —Works: 6 symphonies; a concertino for piano and orch.; a string quartet; a wind quintet; 2 scenic cantatas; incidental music for 2 plays of Shakespeare; folksong arrangements.

Moyzes, Mikuláš, Slovak composer; b. Velká Slatina, Dec. 6, 1872; d. Prešov, April 2, 1944. He studied at the Budapest Academy of Music; in 1907 became director of the Municipal School of Music in Prešov, where he remained. He wrote a *Missa Solemnis;* many choruses; a wind quintet; a wind sextet; made arrangements of Slovak songs. His popular overture *Naše Slovensko* (*Our Slovakia*) was reorchestrated by his son Alexander Moyzes.

Mozart, (Maria) Anna (nickname **Nannerl**), daughter of Leopold Mozart and sister of Wolfgang Amadeus Mozart; b. Salzburg, July 30, 1751; d. there, Oct. 29, 1829. Taught by her father from her earliest childhood, she quickly developed into an excellent pianist, and appeared in public with her brother; after their trip to Vienna in 1768, she remained mostly at home, helping to support the family by teaching. In 1784 she married Baron von Berchthold zu Sonnenburg; after his death, she resumed her teaching, until her eyesight failed in 1820.

Mozart, (Johann Georg) Leopold, the father of Wolfgang Amadeus, and himself an important musician; b. Augsburg, Germany, Nov. 14, 1719; d. Salzburg, Austria, May 28, 1787. A poor bookbinder's son, he learned music as a chorister in Augsburg; went to Salzburg to study at the Univ. there; at the same time learned to play the violin; was in the service of Count Thurn and Taxis at Salzburg (1740-43); then entered the private orch. of the Archbishop of Salzburg (1743); appointed court composer (1757); then became Vice-Kapellmeister (1762). He married Anna Maria Pertl of Salzburg in 1747; of their 7 children only two, 'Nannerl' and Wolfgang, passed the age of one year. He dedicated himself to the musical education of his children wholeheartedly; his methods of presentation of their concerts at times approached frank exploitation, and his advertisements of their appearances were often in poor taste, but there is no denying that he succeeded in fostering and developing his son's genius. Leopold Mozart was a noteworthy composer in his own right; among his works are operas, pantomimes, 12 oratorios, other sacred music; many symphonies (18 publ.), serenades, divertimentos (the *Musikalische Schlittenfahrt* was publ.), concertos, chamber music (6 trio sonatas for 2 violins with basso continuo were publ.), organ music, piano music (12 pieces, *Der Morgen und der Abend,* were publ.). He was probably the author of the *Kindersonfonie* (*Toy Symphony*) usually attributed to Haydn (see E. F. Schmid, *Leopold Mozart und die Kindersonfonie,* in the 'Mozart Jahrbuch' for 1951). His most signal accomplishment, however, is the publication of a violin method, *Versuch einer gründlichen Violinschule* (Augsburg, 1756; 2nd, revised ed., 1770; transl. into several languages; English transl. by Editha Knocker, London, 1948; a facsimile ed. was publ. in Vienna, 1922; another facsimile ed., by H. J. Moser, Leipzig, 1956). A selection from his works was publ. by M. Seiffert in 'Denkmäler der Tonkunst in Bayern' (vol. IX, 2). His 'Nannerls Musikbuch' was republished in Munich, 1956, with an introduction by E. Valentin. —Cf. M. Friedlaender, *Leopold Mozarts Klaviersonaten* in 'Die Musik' (IV, 1; 1901); J. E. Engl, *Aus Leopold und des Sohns Wolfgang Mozarts irdischem Lebensgange* (Salzburg, 1902); H. Abert, *Leopold Mozarts Notenbuch von 1762,* in the 'Gluck-Jahrbuch' (1917); A. Schurig, *Leopold Mozart: Reise-Aufzeichnungen 1763 bis 1771* (1920); A. Moser, *Geschichte des Violinspiels* (1923; p. 354ff.); E. L. Theiss, *Die Instrumentalwerke Leopold Mozarts* (Giessen, 1942). His letters to his wife are publ. in Schiedermair's ed. of *Mozart's Letters;* those to his daughter, ed. by O. E. Deutsch und B. Paumgartner (Salzburg, 1936); English transl. of all them in Emily Anderson, *Letters of Mozart and His Family,* 3 vols. (London, 1938). See also the literature on Mozart, in which Leopold Mozart is constantly referred to.

Mozart (moh-tsahrt), **Wolfgang Amadeus** (baptismal names **Johannes Chrysostomus Wolfgangus Theophilus**), was born in Salzburg, Jan. 27, 1756; d. in Vienna, Dec. 5, 1791. In his fourth year he manifested such eager and intelligent interest in his sister's harpsichord lessons that his father began teaching him, as well; he also composed little pieces. His progress was so rapid that in January, 1762, the father ventured to introduce his children to the public on a concert trip to Munich, and in September to Vienna; the Emperor, Francis I, frequently invited the children to the palace, where Wolfgang was wholly at his ease amid the brilliant assemblage, caring only for the approval of connoisseurs. Some of the pieces he played were sonatas by D.

Paradies and J. C. Bach, and a concerto by Lucchesi. While in Vienna, a small violin was given him, on which he learned to play without instruction; he learned the organ in the same manner, after the use of the pedals had been explained. A longer journey, to Paris, was undertaken in 1763; the brother and sister gave private and public concerts on the way, and in Frankfurt Wolfgang played concertos both on the harpsichord and the violin, accompanied symphonies on the harpsichord, and ended with long improvisations. (The clavichord and harpsichord were his principal keyboard instruments while he was in Salzburg, where pianos were still scarce, but from 1774 on, when visiting places like Munich and Paris, where the new instruments were plentiful, and after he settled in Vienna, he played on, and wrote for, the piano.) In Paris the pair played before the royal family, and gave two brilliant public concerts. Here Wolfgang's first publ. compositions appeared, op. 1 and 2, each comprising *II Sonates pour le clavecin* (2 harpsichord sonatas) with violin *ad libitum*. The travelers' reception in England (1764) was so cordial that they remained there about 15 months; the King tried Mozart's faculty for sight-reading with works by J. C. Bach, Handel, Abel, etc., and greatly admired his playing. Here Wolfgang composed several sonatas for violin and harpsichord, and his first symphonies, which were performed repeatedly. Of his marvelous progress his father wrote home: "Our high and mighty Wolfgang knows everything in this, his eighth year, that one can require of a man of forty." On the return journey they passed through Lille, The Hague, Paris, Dijon, Bern, Zürich, Donaueschingen, Ulm, Munich, etc.; and arrived in Salzburg in November 1766, having been absent three years. After an interval of rest and serious study, during which Mozart composed his first oratorio (1767), they revisited Vienna in 1768, and Mozart wrote, at the Emperor's request, his first opera, *La finta semplice;* its production was prevented by intrigues, although Hasse and Metastasio declared that thirty operas, in no way equal to the boy's, had been given there (it was brought out at Salzburg in 1769). However, the 'Liederspiel' *Bastien und Bastienne* was privately performed; and Mozart made his first appearance at a large public concert as a conductor, directing his own Solemn Mass (Dec. 7, 1768). Returning to Salzburg, he was appointed Konzertmeister to the Archbishop. For the purpose of broadening his son's education, Leopold Mozart decided on an Italian tour, leaving home in Dec., 1769. The program of a concert at Mantua, Jan. 16, 1770, exhibits Mozart's versatility at the age of 14: 'A Symphony of his own composition; a harpsichord concerto, which will be handed to him, and which he will immediately play *prima vista;* a Sonata handed him in like manner, which he will provide with variations, and afterwards repeat in another key; an Aria, the words for which will be handed to him, and which he will immediately set to music and sing himself, accompanying himself on the harpsichord; a Sonata for harpsichord on a subject given him by the leader of the violins: a Strict Fugue on a theme to be selected, which he will improvise on the harpsichord; a Trio, in which he will execute a violin part *all'improvviso;* and finally, the latest Symphony composed by himself.' It was in Rome that Mozart, after twice hearing Allegri's famous *Miserere,* wrote out the entire score from memory, without a mistake. The journey was a veritable triumphal progress; his concerts were crowded, his genius recognized by the highest musical authorities; the Pope conferred on him the order of the Golden Spur, and he was elected a member of the Bologna Philharmonic Academy, after passing the required examinations. At Milan his 3-act opera seria *Mitridate, rè di Ponto* was enthusiastically received on Dec. 26, 1770, and had 20 consecutive performances under Mozart's own direction. He returned to Salzburg in March, 1771; but in August again visited Milan to bring out a 'theater serenade,' *Ascanio in Alba,* written for the wedding festivities of Archduke Ferdinand (Oct. 17, 1771); it quite eclipsed Hasse's festival opera *Ruggiero.* Next year his friendly protector, the Archbishop of Salzburg, died; the unmusical successor, Hieronymus, Count of Colloredo, cared little for Mozart's genius, and in the end heaped indignities upon him. It was for his installation (1772) that Mozart's 'dramatic serenade' *Il Sogno di Scipione* was penned. *Lucio Silla* (Milan, Dec. 26, 1772) and *La finta giardiniera* (Munich, Jan. 13, 1775) were the occasion of trips to those cities for their production. On April 23, 1775, *Il Rè pastore* was brought out at Salzburg during Archduke Maximilian's visit. Mozart obtained leave of absence in 1777, and, accompanied by his mother, repaired to Munich, in hopes of obtaining an appointment commensurate with his abilities; disappointed there, and also in Augsburg and Mannheim, they journeyed to Paris, where a symphony of Mozart's was performed at a Concert Spirituel. But the war between the Gluckists and Piccinnists was at its height, and little attention was paid to the young composer. He had the further misfortune to lose his mother, who died in Paris, July 3, 1778. His expectations unrealized, Mozart resumed his function of Konzertmeister at Salzburg, also succeeding Adlgasser as court organist in 1779, with a salary of 400 florins. The opera *Idomeneo* (Munich, Jan. 29, 1781) was the first dramatic work in his mature style. In the summer of that year Mozart definitively left the service of the Archbishop, whose treatment had grown unbearable, and settled in Vienna. Commissioned by the Emperor to write an opera, Mozart composed *Belmonte und Constanze, oder Die Entführung aus dem Serail,* which was most successfully produced, despite the machinations of the theatrical clique, on July 16, 1782; a month later he married Constanze Weber, the sister of his youthful flame Aloysia, whom he had met in Mannheim. A period of real poverty set in. His wife was a careless housekeeper, and he himself an improvident liver, fond of pleasant company and fine dress, of dancing, bowling, billiards, and kindred pleasures (but, despite allegations to the contrary, never dissipated or dissolute); the meager receipts for compositions and concerts were quickly spent and, though an indefatigable worker, he was never free from pecuniary anxieties. A musical comedy, *Der Schauspieldirektor,* was produced at Schönbrunn, Feb. 7, 1786; on May 1, 1786, his fine opera buffa *Le Nozze di Figaro* (*The Marriage of Figaro*) came near failing in Vienna through the intentional lapses of the jealous Italian singers (at that time the works of Paisiello, Sarti, and Cimarosa set the standard of musico-dramatic taste in Vienna). But the hearty and spontaneous welcome accorded to this masterpiece and its author in Prague partially made up for this rebuff; he was invited to lodge in the palace of Count Thun, and every attention was bestowed on him. Next year, the unexampled success of his grandest work, *Don Giovanni* (*Don Juan*), at Prague (Oct. 29, 1787), coupled with the fear that Mozart might accept favorable offers to go to England, moved the Emperor to show tardy and scanty recognition of his genius by appointing him 'chamber composer' at 800 florins annually (Gluck, just deceased, as court composer had 2,000 florins). In this year (1788) Mozart ceased giving public concerts at Vienna, appearing there but once more, in 1791. In 1789 he accompanied Prince Carl Lichnowsky to Berlin, on the way playing before the Dresden court, and in the Thomaskirche at Leipzig. According to an unverified story, King Friedrich Wilhelm II, after hearing him at Potsdam, offered him the post of 1st Royal Kapellmeister, with a salary of 3,000 Thaler a year; but Mozart with simple trust in and loyalty to the Austrian Emperor refused the benevolent offer—his last opportunity, as it proved, of ridding himself of money troubles. For the Emperor's only response to the news of the King's offer was an order for a new opera (*Così fan tutte;* Vienna, Jan. 26, 1790), which seems to have made little impression beside the fashionable Italian works. In October Mozart attended the coronation of Emperor Leopold II at Frankfurt, full of joyful anticipations which, as usual, were not realized. He came back to Vienna in time to bid farewell to his fatherly friend Haydn, then about to set out for London. For the coronation of Leopold II at Prague, as King of Bohemia, Mozart was invited to write a festival opera; and *La Clemenza di Tito* was performed on Sept. 6, 1791, the eve of the ceremony. Already suffering from illness, overwork, and the excitement and fatigue of the journey, he returned to Vienna, and still, at Schikaneder's entreaty, composed *Die Zauberflöte* (*The Magic Flute*) (Vienna, Sept. 30, 1791). The writing of his last work, the Requiem, was interrupted by fainting fits. The Requiem was uncompleted when he died (it was finished by Süssmayr). The immediate cause of his death is believed to have been malignant typhus; the funeral was in the open air, near St. Stephen's Cathedral, and the coffin was accompanied by a few friends only part way to the cemetery of St. Marx, where he was buried in the ground allotted to paupers. Thus even his last resting place is not exactly known. A monument was erected to his memory in the above cemetery in 1859; Salzburg had honored him with a grand monument in 1841.

Mozart is one of the brightest stars in the musical firmament. In his melody, German depth of emotion is expressed with Italian frankness, making his great dramatic works perennially fresh. Among his symphonies the 'Jupiter' in C, and those in G minor and E♭ (1788), are prominent. His productivity was astounding, and embraced all departments of musical composition. The first complete edition of Mozart's works (528 compositions in 24 series), prepared by Köchel, Nottebohm, Rietz, Espagne, Reinecke, Brahms, and others, was issued by Brietkopf & Härtel from 1876 to 1886; it contains (1) Church Music (Series 1-4):

15 Masses, 4 litanies, 1 *Dixit,* 1 Magnificat, 4 Kyries, a madrigal, a *Veni Sancte,* a *Miserere,* an antiphon, 3 *Regina coeli,* a *Te Deum,* 2 *Tantum ergo,* 2 German church songs, 9 offertories, a *De profundis,* an aria, a motet for soprano solo, a 4-part motet, a Gradual, 2 hymns, a Passion cantata, and the cantatas *Davidde penitente* and (Masonic) *Maurerfreude* and *Kleine Freimaurercantate.* —(2) STAGE WORKS: (Series 5): *Die Schuldigkeit des ersten Gebotes* (sacred play with music), *Apollo et Hyacinthus* (Latin comedy with music), *Bastien und Bastienne, La finta semplice, Mitridate, Ascanio in Alba, Il Sogno di Scipione, Lucio Silla, La finta giardiniera, Il Rè pastore, Zaïde* (German opera; unfinished), *Thamos, König in Ägypten* (heroic drama; choruses and entr'actes); *Idomeneo, rè di Creta, Die Entführung aus dem Serail, Der Schauspieldirektor, Le Nozze di Figaro, Don Giovanni, Così fan tutte, La Clemenza di Tito, Die Zauberflöte.* English transls. of the most important librettos have been made by E. J. Dent and others. —(3) VOCAL CONCERT MUSIC (Series 6): 27 arias, and 1 rondo, for soprano with orchestra; 1 alto aria; 8 tenor arias; 5 arias and an arietta for bass; a German war-song; a duet for 2 sopranos; a comic duet for soprano and bass; 6 terzets; 1 quartet. —(4) SONGS, ETC. (Series 7): 34 songs for solo voice with piano; a song with chorus and organ; a 3-part chorus with organ; a comic terzet with piano; 20 canons *a* 2-12. —(5) ORCHESTRAL WORKS (Series 8-11): 49 symphonies, 2 symphonic movements, 31 divertimentos, serenades, and cassations, 9 marches, 25 dances, *Masonic Funeral Music; Ein musikalischer Spass* (satirical; employs deliberate discords, consecutive fifths, etc.) for strings and 2 horns; also (for various instruments) a sonata for bassoon and cello, an Adagio for 2 basset-horns with bassoon, an Adagio for 2 clarinets and 3 basset-horns, an Adagio for harmonica, Adagio and Allegretto for harmonica, flute, oboe, viola, and cello, a fantasy and an Andante for a clockwork organ. —(6) CONCERTOS AND SOLO PIECES WITH ORCH. (Series 12 and 16): 6 violin concertos, 6 solos for violin, a *Concertone* for 2 violins, a *Concertante* for violin and viola, a bassoon concerto, a concerto for flute and harp, 2 flute concertos, an Andante for flute, 4 horn concertos, a clarinet concerto, 25 piano concertos, a Concert Rondo for piano, a double concerto for 2 pianos, a triple concerto for 3 pianos. —(7) CHAMBER MUSIC (Series 13-15, 17, 18): 7 string quintets (with 2 violas); a quintet for violin, 2 violas, horn (or cello), and cello; a quintet for clarinet and strings; 26 string quartets; *Eine kleine Nachtmusik* for strings (including double-bass); Adagio and Fugue for string quartet; a quartet for oboe with string trio; a divertimento for string trio; 2 duos for violin and viola; 1 duo for 2 violins; a quintet for piano, horn, oboe, clarinet, and bassoon; 2 piano quartets; 7 piano trios; 1 trio for piano, clarinet, and viola; 42 violin sonatas; an Allegro for piano and violin; 2 sets of variations for piano and violin. —(8) PIANO MUSIC (Series 19-22): (a) 4 hands: 5 sonatas, and an Andante with variations; (b) for 2 pianos: a Fugue, and a Sonata; (c) solo pieces: 17 sonatas; a Fantasia and fugue; 3 Fantasias; 15 sets of variations; 35 cadenzas to piano concertos; several minuets; 3 rondos, a suite, a fugue, 2 Allegros, an Allegro and Andante, Andantino, Adagio, Gigue. —(9) FOR ORGAN (Series 23): 17 sonatas, mostly with 2 violins and cello; —SUPPLEMENT (Series 24): unfinished works, doubtful works, and arrangements.

Mozart's works are designated by the numbers in the Köchel Catalogue ('K. numbers'), which have been universally accepted.

Since the publication of the B. & H. ed., Wyzewa and St.-Foix and other authorities have shown that certain works published in that ed. are not original works of Mozart but copies in his handwriting of works by other composers. These works include the Symphony No. 3 (Köchel 18), which is by K. F. Abel, and Symphony No. 37 (K. 444), by Michael Haydn (except the Introduction). Among other works listed by Köchel, the following are spurious: Symphony in B♭ (K. 17); Sonatas for piano and violin (K. 55-60); *Salve Regina* (K. 92); Symphony in F (K. 98); *Tantum ergo* (K. 142); 2 Small Fugues (K. 154a); *Tantum ergo* (K. 197); 2 canons, *O Schwestern traut dem Amor nicht* and *O wunderschön ist Gottes Erde* (K. 226-7); Kyrie (K. 340); 9 Country Dances or Quadrilles (K. 510). The following are by other composers: Minuet and Trio in C major (K. 25a), probably by Beethoven; Sonata for piano and violin (K. 61), by H. F. Raupach; *De profundis clamavi* (K. 93), by C. G. Reutter; *Offertorium sub exposito venerabili* (K. 177 and 342), by Leopold Mozart; Kyrie (K. 221), by J. E. Eberlin; Fugue in D (K. 291), by M. Haydn, finished by S. Sechter; *Justum deduxit Dominus,* hymn (K. 326), by Eberlin; *Adoramus te,* hymn (K. 327), by Q. Gasparini; *Wiegenlied, Schlafe, mein Prinzschen* (K. 350), by B. Flies; Rondo in B♭ (K. 511a), probably by Beethoven; *Momento Domine David*

(K. Anh. 22), by Reutter; *Lacrimosa* (K. Anh. 21), by Eberlin. The first four piano concertos (K. 37, 39, 40, 41) are arrangements of sonata movements, by Honauer, Raupach, Schobert, Eckard, and K. P. E. Bach; the 5th piano concerto (K. 107) consists of arrangements of 3 sonatas by Joh. Chr. Bach. —Cf. A. Einstein's latest revised ed. of the Köchel Catalogue (1947).

A new Complete Edition of Mozart's works ('Neue Mozart-Ausgabe'), under the general editorship of Ernst Fritz Schmid, began publication in 1955.

Mention should be made here of the Mozarteum at Salzburg, a celebrated municipal musical institute founded in 1842 in memory of Salzburg's greatest son; it consists of an orchestral society, pledged to perform Mozart's church music in the 14 churches of the town, and to give 12 concerts yearly; a music school, in which the musicians of the orchestra give instruction; and an interesting museum of Mozart relics, etc. From 1880 a yearly report was issued. A series of summer courses, given by outstanding teachers in all musical branches during the Salzburg Festival in July and August, was also founded by the Mozarteum. Under the collective title of 'Internationale Mozartgemeinde' branches were established in 1888 in Austria and Germany, of which those in Berlin and Dresden were especially active.

BIBLIOGRAPHY: A. BIOGRAPHY: Fr. v. Schlichtegroll, *Mozart,* in his 'Nekrolog auf das Jahr 1791' (new ed. by L. Landshoff, 1924); F. Niemtschek, *W. A. Mozarts Leben, nach Originalquellen beschrieben* (Prague, 1798; 2nd augm. ed., 1808; facsimile reprint of this ed., 1905; English transl., London, 1956); J. F. Arnold, *Mozarts Geist* (Erfurt, 1803); G. N. von Nissen, *Biographie W. A. Mozarts* (Leipzig, 1828); A. D. Oulibisheff, *Nouvelle biographie de Mozart* (Moscow, 1843; German transl., 3 vols., Stuttgart, 2nd ed. augm. by L. Gantter, 4 vols., 1859); E. Holmes, *Life and Correspondence of Mozart* (London, 1845; 2nd ed., 1878; reprint, 1912); O. Jahn, *W. A. Mozart* (4 vols., Leipzig, 1856-9; 2nd ed., 2 vols., 1867; 3rd ed., 1891-3; 4th ed., rev. and augm. by H. Deiters, 1905, 1907; Engl. transl. by P. D. Townsend, London, 1882 [3 vols.]; the most exhaustive and standard biography; entirely rewritten and revised by H. Abert in 2 vols., 1919 and 1921; this ed. further revised by A. A. Abert, 1956); L. Nohl, *Mozarts Leben* (Leipzig, 1863; 3rd ed. by P. Sakolowski, Berlin, 1906; Engl. transl. by Lady Wallace, London, 1877); L. Nohl, *Mozart nach den Schilderungen seiner Zeitgenossen* (Leipzig, 1880); V. Wilder, *Mozart, l'homme et l'artiste* (Paris, 1880; 4th ed., 1889; English transl., London, 1908, 2 vols.); L. Meinardus, *Mozart, Ein Künstlerleben* (Leipzig, 1882); F. Gehring, *Mozart* (London, 1883; new ed., 1911); L. Klasen, *W. A. Mozart. Sein Leben und seine Werke* (Vienna, 1897); O. Fleischer, *Mozart* (Berlin, 1899); E. J. Breakspeare, *Mozart* (London, 1902); E. Prout, *Mozart* (London, 1903); L. Mirow, *Mozarts letzte Lebensjahre. Eine Künstlertragödie* (Leipzig, 1904); C. Belmonte, *Die Frauen im Leben Mozarts* (Augsburg, 1905); C. Bellaigue, *Mozart* (Paris, 1906); F. Lentner, *Mozarts Leben und Schaffen* (Innsbruck, 1906); H. von der Pfordten, *Mozart* (Leipzig, 1908); K. Storck, *Mozart, Sein Leben und Schaffen* (Stuttgart, 1908); L. Schmidt, *W. A. Mozart* (Berlin, 1912); Th. de Wyzewa and G. de Saint-Foix, *W. A. Mozart. Sa vie musicale et son œuvre de l'enfance à la pleine maturité* (5 vols., Paris, 1912-1946; the most valuable work since Jahn-Abert, especially on the origin and development of Mozart's style; the last three vols. were written by St.-Foix alone); A. Schurig, *W. A. Mozart. Sein Leben und sein Werk* (2 vols., Leipzig, 1913; 2nd ed., 1923; French transl., 1925); J. Kreitmaier, *Mozart* (1919); L. Schiedermair, *Mozart* (Munich, 1922); E. K. Blümml, *Aus Mozarts Freundes und Familien Kreis* (Vienna, 1923); O. Keller, *W. A. Mozart* (Berlin, 1926); B. Paumgartner, *Mozart* (Berlin, 1927; 4th ed., 1945); D. Hussey, *Mozart* (London, 1928; 2nd ed., 1933); M. Morold, *Mozart* (1931); R. Tenschert, *Mozart* (1931); E. Buenzod, *Mozart,* in 'Maîtres de la Musique' (1931); S. Sitwell, *Mozart* (N. Y., 1932); R. Haas, *Mozart* (Potsdam, 1933; 2nd ed., 1950); Marcia Davenport, *Mozart* (N. Y., 1932; reprinted, 1956); A. il Mantovano, *Mozart fra noi* (Milan and Rome, 1933); H. Ghéon, *Promenades avec Mozart* (Paris, 1933; English transl. as *In Search of Mozart,* London, 1934); J. E. Talbot, *Mozart* (London, 1934); E. F. Schmid, *Mozart* (Lübeck, 1934); A. Boschot, *Mozart* (Paris, 1935); E. Blom, *Mozart* (London, 1935; 2nd ed., 1947); Ch. Perriolat, *Mozart, révélateur de la beauté artistique* (Paris, 1935); A. Kolb, *Mozart* (Vienna, 1937); H. de Curzon, *Mozart* (Paris, 1938); W. J. Turner, *Mozart, The Man and His Works* (N. Y., 1938); P. Nettl, *Mozart in Böhmen* (1938); I. Gyomai, *Le Cœur de Mozart* (Paris, 1939); W. Goetz, *Mozart: sein Leben in Selbstzeugnissen, Briefen und Berichten* (Berlin, 1941); E. Komorzynski,

Mozart (Berlin, 1941; Vienna, 1955); G. Schaeffner, *W. A. Mozart* (Bern, 1941); E. Valentin, *Wege zu Mozart* (Regensburg, 1942); A. Albertini, *Mozart. La vita, le opere* (Milan, 1942); *Augsburger Mozartbuch* (Augsburg, 1943); A. Einstein, *Mozart: His Character, His Work* (N. Y., 1945); L. Parrot, *Mozart* (Paris, 3rd ed., 1945); P. Espil, *Les Voyages de Chérubin, ou l'enfance de Mozart* (Bayonne, 1946); M. Mila, *W. A. Mozart* (Turin, 1946); E. Valentin, *Mozart* (Hameln, 1947); E. F. Schmid, *Ein schwäbisches Mozartbuch* (Stuttgart, 1948); R. Tenschert, *W. A. Mozart* (Salzburg, 1951; English transl., London, 1952); M. Kenyon, *Mozart in Salzburg* (London, 1952); K. Röttger, *W. A. Mozart* (Stuttgart, 1952); L. Biancolli, ed., *The Mozart Handbook* (N. Y., 1954); E. Schenk, *Mozart* (Zürich, 1955); N. Medici and R. Hughes, *A Mozart Pilgrimage* (London, 1955); J. Dalchow, *W. A. Mozarts Krankheiten, 1756-1763* (Bergisch Gladbach, 1955); M. Brion, *Mozart* (Paris, 1955); A. Ostoja, *Mozart e l'Italia* (Bologna, 1955); C. Fusero, *Mozart* (Turin, 1956); D. Kerner, *W. A. Mozarts Krankheiten und sein Tod,* in the 'Neue Zeitschrift für Musik' (Dec., 1956; see also E. Blom, *Mozart's Death,* in 'Music and Letters,' Oct., 1957).

B. Criticism, Appreciation: F. Lorenz, *W. A. Mozart als Clavier-Componist* (Breslau, 1866); K. F. Pohl, *Mozart und Haydn in London* (Vienna, 1867); W. Pole, *The Story of Mozart's Requiem* (London, 1879); E. Sauzay, *Haydn, Mozart, Beethoven, Étude sur le quatuor* (Paris, 1884); K. Prieger, *Urteile bedeutender Dichter, Philosophen und Musiker über Mozart* (Wiesbaden, 1886); A. Farinelli, *Don Giovanni: Note critiche* (Turin, 1896); A. J. Weltner, *Mozarts Werke und die Wiener Hofheater: Statistisches und Historisches* (Vienna, 1896); D. Schultz, *Mozarts Jugendsinfonien* (Leipzig, 1900); E. von Komorzynski, *Mozarts Kunst der Instrumentation* (Stuttgart, 1906); A. Cametti, *Mozart a Roma* (Rome, 1907); K. Söhle, *Mozart. Dramatisches Zeitbild* (Leipzig, 1907); G. Schünemann, *Mozart als achtjähriger Komponist. Ein Notenbuch Wolfgangs* (1908; English transl., 1909); W. Nagel, *Mozart und die Gegenwart* (Langensalza, 1912); E. J. Dent, *Mozart's Operas. A Critical Study* (London, 1913; 2nd ed., 1947); A. Leitzmann, *Mozarts Persönlichkeit* (Leipzig, 1914); H. Cohen, *Die dramatische Idee in Mozarts Operntexten* (1916); E. Lert, *Mozart auf dem Theater* (Berlin, 1918; 4th ed., 1922); R. Lach, *Mozart als Theoretiker* (1919); H. W. von Waltershausen, *Die Zauberflöte* (1921); A. Lorenz, *Das Finale in Mozarts Meisteropern,* in 'Die Musik' XIX, 9; H. Mersmann, *Mozart* (1925); F. H. Marks, *Questions on Mozart's Pianoforte-sonatas* (London, 1929); E. Schenk, ed., *Bericht über die musikwissenschaftliche Tagung der Internationalen Stiftung Mozarteum in Salzburg, 1931* (Leipzig, 1932); V. P. Heinrich, *Komik und Humor bei Mozart* (Vienna, 1931); O. Beer, *Mozart und das Wiener Singspiel* (Vienna, 1932); G. de Saint-Foix, *Les Sinfonies de Mozart* (Paris, 1932; English transl., 1947); S. Anheisser, *Die Urfassung des Figaro,* in the 'Zeitschrift für Musikwissenschaft,' XV (p. 301 ff.); N. Broder, *The Wind Instruments in Mozart's Symphonies,* in the 'Mus. Quarterly' (July, 1933); H. G. Farmer and H. Smith, *New Mozartiana* (Glasgow, 1935); C. M. Girdlestone, *Mozart's Piano Concertos* (in French, 2 vols., Paris, 1939; in English, 1 vol., London and Norman, Okla., 1948); A. Einstein, *Two Missing Sonatas of Mozart* (with music) in 'Music & Letters' (Jan., 1940); P. A. Hirsch, *Some Early Mozart Editions,* reprinted from 'Music Review' (1940); N. Broder, *Mozart and the 'Clavier,'* in the 'Mus. Quarterly' (Oct., 1941); P. J. Jouve, *Le Don Juan de Mozart* (Freiburg, 1942; 3rd ed., Paris, 1948; English transl., London, 1957); E. A. Ballin, *Die Klavierlieder Mozarts* (Bonn, 1943); L. Conrad, *Mozarts Dramaturgie der Oper* (Würzburg, 1943); H. Socnik, *Das Pedal bei Mozart* (Danzig, 1943); M. Mila, *Saggi Mozartiani* (Milan, 1945); F. C. Benn, *Mozart on the Stage* (N. Y., 1946); A. Hutchings, *A Companion to Mozart's Piano Concertos* (London, 1948); J. Chantavoine, *Mozart dans Mozart* (Paris, 1948); G. Hausswald, *Mozarts Serenaden* (Leipzig, 1951); H. Dennerlein, *Der unbekannte Mozart: Die Welt seiner Klavierwerke* (Leipzig, 1951); S. Levarie, *Mozart's Le Nozze di Figaro* (Chicago, 1952); D. Lauener, *Die Frauengestalten in Mozarts Opern* (Zürich, 1954); A. Hyatt King, *Mozart in Retrospect* (London, 1955); K. G. Fellerer, *Mozarts Kirchenmusik* (Salzburg, 1955); R. Dumesnil, *Le Don Juan de Mozart* (Paris, 1955); A. Greither, *Die sieben grossen Opern Mozarts* (Heidelberg, 1956); R. Giazotto, *Annali Mozartiani* (Milan, 1956); G. Barblan and A. Della Corte, eds., *Mozart in Italia* (Milan, 1956); H. C. Robbins Landon and D. Mitchell, eds., *The Mozart Companion* (N. Y., 1956); P. Nettl, *Mozart and Masonry* (N. Y., 1957); A. Della Corte, *Tutto il teatro di Mozart* (Turin, 1957); H. Albrecht, ed., *Die Bedeutung der Zeichen Keil, Strich, und Punkt bei Mozart* (Kassel,

1957). See also A. Einstein, *Essays on Music* (N. Y., 1956).

C. CORRESPONDENCE AND ICONOGRAPHY: L. Nohl, *Mozarts Briefe nach den Originalen herausgegeben* (Salzburg, 1865; 2nd augm. ed., Leipzig, 1877; English transl. by Lady Wallace, London, 1866); G. Nottebohm, *Mozartiana* (Leipzig, 1880); H. de Curzon, *Nouvelles lettres des dernières années de la vie de Mozart* (Paris, 1898); K. Storck, *Mozarts Briefe in Auswahl* (Stuttgart, 1906); M. Weigel, *Mozarts Briefe* (Berlin, 1910); A. Leitzmann, *Mozarts Briefe ausgewählt* (Leipzig, 1910); H. Leichtentritt, *Mozarts Briefe* (Berlin, 1912); L. Schiedermair, *Die Briefe W. A. Mozarts und seiner Familie. Erste kritische Gesamtausgabe* (5 vols., of which the last is an iconography; Munich, 1914); also correspondence ed. by H. de Curzon (in French, Paris, 1928), H. Mersmann (1928, in English and German), and H. Leichtentritt (Berlin, 1936); Emily Anderson, *The Letters of Mozart and His Family* (3 vols., London and N. Y., 1938, the most complete collection in English); R. Tenschert, *Mozarts Leben in Bildern* (Leipzig, 1935); E. H. Müller von Asow, *Briefe und Aufzeichnungen der Familie Mozart,* 5 vols. (Berlin, 1942); I. Voser-Hoesli, *W. A. Mozarts Briefe* (Zürich, 1948); R. Bory, *The Life and Works of W. A. Mozart in Pictures* (Geneva, 1948; also publ. in French and German); E. H. Mueller von Asow, *W. A. Mozart Briefwechsel und Aufzeichnungen,* 2 vols. (1769-79 only; Lindau im Bodensee, 1949).

D. CATALOGUES, YEAR-BOOKS: *W. A. Mozart, Verzeichnis alle meiner Werke,* facsimile ed. by O. E. Deutsch, (Oxford, 1938); another ed. by E. H. Müller von Asow (Vienna, 1943); see also A. André, *Thematischer Katalog wie Mozart solchen von 1784-91 eigenhändig geschrieben hat* (Offenbach, 1805; 2nd augm. ed., 1828); L. von Köchel, *Chronologisch-thematisches Verzeichniss sämmtlicher Tonwerke W. A. Mozarts* (Leipzig, 1862; supplements 1864 [by Köchel in the 'Allgemeine Musik Zeitung'] and 1889; 2nd ed., rev. and augm. by P. von Waldersee, 1905. An entirely new ed., greatly enlarged and containing the latest information on Mozart's works, was published by Alfred Einstein, 1937; this was again revised by Einstein, Ann Arbor, Mich., 1947); K. Moyses, *Systematischer Katalog der im Mozarteum . . . befindlichen Autographe Mozarts* (Salzburg, 1862); J. Horner, *Katalog des Mozarts-Museums zu Salzburg* (Salzburg, 1882; 2d ed., by J. Engl, 1898); H. de Curzon, *Revue critique des ouvrages relatifs à W. A. Mozart et ses œuvres. Essai de bibliographie mozartienne* (Paris, 1906); also works on Mozart bibliography by P. Hirsch (1905), R. Tenschert (1925), and O. Keller (1927). — 'Jahresbericht des Mozarteums' (from 1880); 'Mitteilungen für die Mozart-Gemeinde' (Berlin, from 1895); 'Bericht des Dresdener Mozart-Vereins' (from 1897); 'Mozarteums-Mitteilungen' of Salzburg (1918-21; quarterly); 'Mozart-Jahrbuch' (1st series, ed. by H. Abert, Munich, 1923, 1924, 1929; 2nd series, ed. by E. Valentin, Regensburg, 1941-43; 3rd series, Salzburg, from 1950); 'Acta Mozartiana' (from 1954; a quarterly publ. by the Deutsche Mozart-Gesellschaft).

The bicentennial celebration in 1956 produced a flood of books, articles, special editions, etc. Only the most important of the books are included in the above lists. See also the special Mozart issues of the 'Mus. Quarterly' (April, 1956), the 'Schweizerische Musikzeitung' (vol. 96, no. 2; 1956), the 'Neue Zeitschrift für Musik' (Jan., 1956), 'High Fidelity' (Jan., 1956), etc.

Mozart, Wolfgang Amadeus, son of the great composer; b. Vienna, July 26, 1791; d. Karlsbad, July 29, 1844. He studied with Hummel and Salieri in Vienna; gave a concert as pianist at the age of 13; lived many years as a private tutor in Lwow, where he founded the Cecilia Society. He wrote 2 piano concertos, a string quartet, a piano trio, a violin sonata, many pieces for piano. — Cf. J. Fischer, *W. A. Mozart* (Karlsbad, 1888); Karl Geiringer, *W. A. Mozart the Younger,* in the 'Mus. Quarterly' (Oct., 1941); W. Hummel, *W. A. Mozarts Söhne* (Kassel, 1956).

Mraczek (mrăh'-chehk), **Joseph Gustav,** Czech composer; b. Brno, March 12, 1878; d. Dresden, Dec. 24, 1944. He received his first instruction from his father, the cellist Franz Mraczek; was a chorister in various churches in Brno before going to Vienna, where he studied with Hellmesberger, Stocker, and Löwe at the Cons.; from 1897 to 1902, was concertmaster at the Stadttheater in Vienna; then taught violin in Brno (until 1918). In 1919, he went to Dresden to teach composition at the Cons. there; conducted the Dresden Philharmonic (1919-24); remained in Dresden to the end of his life. He wrote 6 operas: *The Glass Slipper* (Brno, 1902); *Der Traum* (Brno, Feb. 26, 1909), *Aebelö* (Breslau, 1915), *Ikdar* (Dresden, 1921), *Herrn Dürers Bild,* or *Madonna am Wiesenzaun* (Hanover, Jan. 29, 1927), *Der Liebesrat* (not produced); his most successful piece was a symph. burlesque,

Max und Moritz (Brno, 1911; also widely played through Germany, and in the U. S.); other works include: *Oriental Sketches* for small orch. (1918); symph. poem, *Eva* (1922); *Oriental Dance Rhapsody* (1931); a piano quintet; a string quartet; piano pieces; songs. — Cf. E. H. Müller, *J. G. Mraczek* (Dresden, 1918).

Mravinsky, Eugene Alexandrovitch, Russian conductor; b. St. Petersburg, June 4, 1903. He studied at the Cons. there; in 1938 became conductor of the Leningrad Philharmonic. He is regarded in Russia as a proponent of the modern Soviet school; has given numerous first performances of works by Shostakovitch and other Soviet composers; also distinguished himself as conductor of classical Russian operas; awarded the Stalin Prize in 1946. —Cf. V. M. Bogdanov-Berezovsky, *E. A. Mravinsky* (Leningrad, 1956).

Muck (mŏŏk), **Karl,** great German conductor; b. Darmstadt, Oct. 22, 1859; d. Stuttgart, March 3, 1940. He received his first musical instruction from his father; also studied piano with Kissner in Würzburg; later pursued academic studies (classical philology) at the Univ. of Heidelberg and at Leipzig; received his *Dr. phil.* in 1880. He also attended the Leipzig Cons., and shortly before graduation made a successful début as pianist with the Gewandhaus Orch. However, he did not choose to continue a pianistic career; obtained a position as chorusmaster at the municipal opera in Zürich; his ability soon secured him the post of conductor there; in subsequent years he was theater conductor in Salzburg, Brünn, and Graz; there Angelo Neumann, impresario of a traveling opera company, heard him, and engaged him as conductor for the Landestheater in Prague (1886), and then as Seidl's successor for his traveling Wagner Co. It was during those years that Muck developed his extraordinary qualities as a masterful disciplinarian and faithful interpreter, possessing impeccable taste. In 1889 he conducted the Wagner tetralogy in St. Petersburg, and in 1891 in Moscow. In 1892 he was engaged as first conductor at the Berlin Opera, and also frequently conducted symph. concerts of the Royal Chapel there. From 1894 to 1911 he led the Silesian Music Festivals; in 1899 he conducted the Wagner repertory at Covent Garden; from 1903 to 1906, he conducted the concerts of the Vienna Philharmonic (alternating with Mottl); besides, he appeared with outstanding success in Paris, Rome, Brussels, Madrid, Copenhagen, and other European centers. In 1901 he was selected to conduct the performances of *Parsifal* at Bayreuth. In 1906 he was engaged as conductor of the Boston Symph. Orch., and led it for 2 seasons, returning to Berlin in 1908, as general music director. He returned to America in the autumn of 1912 and assumed the post of permanent conductor of the Boston Symph. His farewell appearance at the Berlin Opera, conducting *Tristan und Isolde,* was made the occasion of a tumultuous demonstration. During the 20 years of his activity in Berlin he conducted 1,071 performances of 103 operas, of which 35 were novelties. With the entry of the U. S. into the war in the spring of 1917, Muck's position in Boston became ambiguous; he was known as a friend of Wilhelm II, and did not temper his intense German nationalism. Protests were made against the retention of Muck as conductor in Boston, and despite the defense offered by Major Higginson, the founder of the Boston Symph., Muck was arrested at his home on March 25, 1918, and interned as an enemy alien until the end of the war. In 1919 he returned to Germany; conducted the Hamburg Philharmonic from 1922 until 1933; then went to Stuttgart. —Cf. Irving Lowens, *L'Affaire Muck,* in 'Musicology' (vol. I, No. 3, 1947).

Muczynski, Robert, American composer (of Polish descent); b. Chicago, March 19, 1929. He began to study piano as a child, and received his formal training at De Paul Univ. with Alexander Tcherepnin. For his graduation, he played his own *Divertimento* for piano and orch. (1950). Other works include: piano concerto (Louisville, Jan., 1955; composer soloist); a symphony; *Music for Brass Sextet and Timpani;* suite for clarinet and piano; Fantasy for violin and piano; for piano solo: *5 Sketches* (1952); 6 Preludes (1954); sonata No. 1 (1957). His style follows the trend of French neo-Classicism, without chromatic elaboration, but containing some polytonal usages.

Mudarra, Alonso, Spanish lutenist; b. between 1506 and 1510; d. Seville, April 1, 1580. He was appointed canon of the Seville Cathedral in 1566. His important work, *Tres libros de música en cifra para vihuela* (i.e., lute music in tablature), originally publ. in Seville in 1546, was printed in modern notation by Emilio Pujol (Barcelona, 1946); this edition contains 77 works by Mudarra and his contemporaries, a biographical sketch, and commentary.

Mudge, Richard, English composer; b. Bideford, 1718; d. Great Packington, near Birmingham, April 3, 1763. He publ. 6 concertos for strings, and also an adagio for string orch. with a finale for voices singing the melody of Byrd's canon *Non Nobis Domine*. He entered Pembroke College, Oxford, in 1735 (B.A., 1738; M.A., 1741); ordained curate at Great Packington. See S. R. Flint, *Mudge Memoirs* (1883; privately printed).

Mudie, Thomas Mollison, English composer and organist; b. London, Nov. 30, 1809; d. there, July 24, 1876. He studied at the Royal Academy of Music with Crotch and Potter; then taught piano there (1832-34); was organist at Galton, Surrey (1834-44); then taught at Edinburgh (1844-63), eventually returning to London. He wrote 4 symphonies; a piano quintet; a piano trio; and some vocal works.

Mueller von Asow, Erich Hermann, German musicologist; b. Dresden, Aug. 31, 1892. He studied at the Univ. of Leipzig with Hugo Riemann (1912-15); theory with Richard Hofmann. During World War I he was engaged as army conductor; then lived in Dresden and Berlin; from 1926 to 1932, was in charge of the Pädagogium der Tonkunst in Dresden; in 1936, he went to Austria; from 1940 to 1944, in Salzburg; was briefly under arrest by the Gestapo in 1943; in 1945, returned to Germany; living mostly in Berlin. He edited the valuable 'Deutsches Musiker Lexikon' (1929) and its 2nd ed., as 'Kürschners Deutscher Musiker-Kalender' (1954). —Publications: *Die Mingottischen Opernunternehmungen 1732-1756* (dissertation; Dresden, 1915); *Angelo und Pietro Mingotti* (1917); *J. G. Mraczek* (1918); *Heinrich Schütz* (1922); *Heinrich Schütz, Gesammelte Briefe und Schriften* (1931); *An die unsterbliche Geliebte: Liebesbriefe berühmter Musiker* (1934; 2nd ed., 1942); *The Letters and Writings of G. F. Handel* (London, 1935; in German, 1949); *J. S. Bach, Gesammelte Briefe und Schriften* (1940; 2nd ed., 1950); *Egon Kornauth* 1941); the correspondence and documents of the Mozart family (complete ed., 5 vols., 1942; 1769-79 only, 2 vols., 1949); other books on Mozart; *Johannes Brahms und M. Wesendonck* (1943); *Max Reger und seine Welt* (1944); numerous articles in music magazines; facsimile eds. of works by Bach, Schütz, etc. A 'Festschrift' on the occasion of his 50th birthday was publ. in Salzburg (1942); and a compendium, *Epistolae et Musica,* on his 60th birthday (Hamburg, 1952); for a complete list of his writings, see the article in 'Kürschners Deutscher Musiker-Kalender' (1954).

Muffat, Georg, important organist and composer; b. Megève, Alsace, baptized June 1, 1653; d. Passau, Feb. 23, 1704. He was named organist at the Molsheim Cathedral on March 31, 1671; in 1674, went to Austria, 1678, entered the service of the Archbishop of Salzburg. In 1681 he was in Italy; studied with Corelli and Pasquini in Rome; also spent several years in Paris, when he made a careful study of Lully's music. In 1687 he was appointed organist to the Bishop of Passau; in 1690, became Kapellmeister there. He was a significant composer; developed the German type of concerto grosso; publ. organ works, sonatas for various instruments, orchestral suites, etc. — Publications: *Armonico tributo,* polyphonic sonatas (1682; partly reprinted in the 'Denkmäler der Tonkunst in Österreich,' XI, 2); *Florilegium,* orchestral suites in the style of Lully (2 vols., 1695-96; reprinted by Rietsch in the 'Denkmäler der Tonkunst in Österreich,' I, 2 and II, 2); *Apparatus musico-organisticus,* toccatas for organ (1690; reprinted by Lange, 1888, and by Kaller-Valentin, 1933); 12 concerti grossi, publ. under the title *Auserlesener . . . Instrumentalmusik erste Versamblung* (1701; reprinted in the 'Denkmäler der Tonkunst in Österreich,' XI, 2); a toccata is included in J. Bonnet's 'Historical Organ Recitals' (vol. 1). —Cf. L. Stollbrock, *Die Komponisten Georg und Gottlieb Muffat* (Rostock, 1888); F. Raugel, *Georg Muffat en Alsace,* in the 'Revue de Musicologie' (Dec., 1954).

Muffat, Gottlieb (Theophil), Austrian organist and composer; son of Georg Muffat; b. Passau, April (baptized April 25), 1690; d. Vienna, Dec. 10, 1770. In 1704 he went to Vienna, where he studied with J. J. Fux; from 1714, was in charge of the accompaniment of operas, church festivals, and chamber music at the Vienna court; became 2nd court organist in 1717; 1st organist, 1751; retired on a pension in 1763. — Works: *72 Versetl samt 12 Toccaten,* for organ (1726; reprinted by Guido Adler, in the 'Denkmäler der Tonkunst in Österreich,' XXIX, 2); *Componimenti musicali,* for harpsichord (ibid., vol. III, 3; includes an essay on ornaments; Handel used this material for ornamental phrases in his oratorios). — Cf. L. Stollbrock, *Die Komponisten Georg und Gottlieb Muffat* (Rostock, 1888); H. Knöll, *Die Klavier- und Orgelwerke von Theophil Muffat* (Vienna, 1916); F. Chrysander in ***Supplemente, enthaltend***

Quellen zu Händels Werken (vol. 5 of the complete ed. of Handel's works).

Mugellini (moo-jěhl-lē'-nē), **Bruno,** Italian composer; b. Potenza, Dec. 24, 1871; d. Bologna, Jan. 15, 1912. He studied with Busi and Martucci in Bologna; appeared as a concert pianist in Italy; then was appointed prof. of piano at the Liceo Musicale in Bologna (1898), and succeeded Martucci as its director in 1911. He wrote an opera, *Catullo;* a symph. poem, *Alla Fonte del Clitumno;* a piano quartet; a cello sonata; several sonatas and other pieces for piano; church music.

Mugnone (mŏŏ-ñoh'-nĕ), **Leopoldo,** Italian conductor; b. Naples, Sept. 29, 1858; d. there, Dec. 22, 1941. He studied with Cesi and Serrao at the Naples Cons.; began to compose as a young student; when he was 16, he produced a comic opera, *Don Bizarro e le sue figlie* (Naples, April 20, 1875); other operas were *Il Biricchino* (Venice, Aug. 11, 1892; fairly successful) and *Vita Bretone* (Naples, March 14, 1905). He also composed an attractive Neapolitan song, *La Rosella,* and other light music. But it was as a fine opera conductor that Mugnone achieved fame; his performances of Italian stage works possessed the highest degree of authority and an intense musicianly ardor. He also brought out Wagner's music dramas in Italy; conducted the first performance of Mascagni's *Cavalleria Rusticana* (Rome, 1890) and other premières; was guest conductor at Covent Garden, London, in 1905-6, and made some appearances elsewhere in Europe.

Mühlfeld, Richard, famous German clarinetist; b. Salzungen, Feb. 28, 1856; d. Meiningen, June 1, 1907. He first studied the violin and played in the Meiningen court orch.; then practiced on the clarinet without a teacher, and in 1876, at the age of 20, became 1st clarinetist at Meiningen. From 1884 to 1896 he was 1st clarinetist at the Bayreuth Festivals. Brahms wrote for him the trio, op. 114 (clarinet, cello, and piano), the quintet, op. 115 (clarinet, 2 violins, viola, and cello), and the 2 clarinet sonatas, op. 120.

Mühling, August, German organist and composer; b. Raguhne, Sept. 26, 1786; d. Magdeburg, Feb. 3, 1847. He was for many years organist at the Magdeburg Cathedral; wrote the oratorios *Abbadona, Bonifazius, David, Die Leidensfeier Jesu;* 2 symphonies; a concerto for bassoon and orch.; 3 string quartets; a quintet for flute, 2 violins, viola, and cello; sacred duets and songs.

Mulè (mŏŏ-lā'), **Giuseppe,** Italian composer; b. Termini, Sicily, June 28, 1885; d. Rome, Sept. 10, 1951. He studied at the Cons. of Palermo; graduated as a cellist as well as in composition. In 1922 he was engaged as director of the Cons. of Palermo (until 1925); in 1926 he succeeded Respighi as director of Santa Cecilia in Rome. He wrote mostly for the stage, and was particularly successful in providing suitable music for revivals of Greek plays. He composed numerous operas, in the tradition of the Italian 'verismo': *La Baronessa di Carini* (Palermo, April 16, 1912), *La Monacella della fontana* (Trieste, Feb. 17, 1923), *Dafni* (Rome, March 14, 1928), *Liolà* (Naples, Feb. 2, 1935); the oratorio *Il Cieco di Gerico;* the symph. poems *Sicilia canora* (1924) and *Vendemmia* (1936); also *Tre canti siciliani,* for voice and orch. (1930); a string quartet and other chamber music; songs.

Mule (mül), **Marcel,** French saxophone player; b. Aube, June 24, 1901. He studied clarinet and saxophone with his father; was a member of the Garde Républicaine (1923-36); in 1929 he formed the Quatuor de Saxophones de Paris; in 1942 was appointed instructor of the newly established saxophone class at the Paris Cons. In 1957-58 he made his first American tour, appearing as soloist with the leading American orchestras in concertos by modern French composers.

Müller, Adolf, Sr., opera composer; b. Tolna, Hungary, Oct. 7, 1801; d. Vienna, July 29, 1886. He began his career as a singer; in 1828 became conductor at the Theater an der Wien, and brought out there a number of 'Singspiele,' musical farces, etc.; also 2 operas: *Domi, der amerikanische Affe* (Jan. 28, 1831; fairly successful) and the comic opera *Das Zauberrütchen* (Dec. 2, 1831).

Müller, Adolf, Jr., Austrian composer and conductor; son of the preceding; b. Vienna, Oct. 15, 1839; d. there, Dec. 14, 1901. After completing his education in Vienna, he was engaged as theater conductor in the provinces; was conductor of the German Opera at Rotterdam (1875-83); after that at the Theater an der Wien, where his father had directed before him. He produced there a number of operas: *Der*

Pfarrer von Kirchfeld (Nov. 5, 1870), *Heinrich der Goldschmidt, Waldmeisters Brautfahrt, Van Dyke,* etc.; and the operettas *Der Hofnarr* (Nov. 20, 1886; his greatest success), *Des Teufels Weib* (Nov. 22, 1890), *Der Millionen-Onkel* (Nov. 5, 1892), *General Gogo* (Feb. 1, 1896), and *Der Blondin von Namur* (Oct. 15, 1898).

Müller, August Eberhard, German organist and composer; b. Nordheim, Hanover, Dec. 13, 1767; d. Weimar, Dec. 3, 1817. He was an organist at various churches at Magdeburg and Leipzig; in 1800 he became assistant to Johann Adam Hiller at the Thomasschule in Leipzig, and succeeded him as cantor there in 1804; also was music director of the Thomaskirche and Nikolaikirche. In 1810 he became court conductor in Weimar. He wrote 3 piano concertos, and 18 piano sonatas; 11 flute concertos; 11 church cantatas; a practical piano method (1805; really the 6th ed. of Löhlein's *Pianoforte-Schule,* revised by Müller; Kalkbrenner's method is based on it; Czerny publ. the 8th ed. in 1825); a method for the flute. He also publ. cadenzas for and a guide to the interpretation of Mozart's concertos; arranged piano scores of Mozart's operas (very popular in his time). —Cf. G. Haupt, *A. E. Müller's Leben und Klavierwerke* (Leipzig, 1926).

Müller, Erich H. See **Mueller von Asow.**

Müller, Franz (Karl Friedrich); German writer on Wagner and other subjects; b. Weimar, Nov. 30, 1806; d. there, Sept. 2, 1876. He was a government councillor in Weimar; was closely connected with the growing Wagner movement, and publ. a number of pamphlets on Wagner's operas: *Tannhäuser* (1853), *Richard Wagner und das Musikdrama* (1861), *Der Ring des Nibelungen* (1862), *Tristan und Isolde* (1865), *Lohengrin* (1867), and *Die Meistersinger von Nürnberg* (1869), the last three at the express command of King Ludwig II of Bavaria; also *Im Foyer* (1868; on theatrical affairs in Weimar).

Müller, Friedrich, German clarinetist, conductor, and composer; b. Orlamünde, Dec. 10, 1786; d. Rudolstadt, Dec. 12, 1871. In 1803 he entered the royal orch. at Rudolstadt as clarinet player; in 1831, became its conductor; pensioned in 1854. He wrote 2 symphonies; 2 clarinet concertos and other music for clarinet; also clarinet studies; a quartet for clarinet and strings; etc.

Müller, Georg Gottfried, 'Moravian' minister, violinist, and composer; b. Gross Hennersdorf, Saxony, May 22, 1762; d. Lititz, Pennsylvania, March 19, 1821. He came to America in 1784, and spent the major part of his life at Lititz, as a member of the culturally important group of 'Moravians' in America. His works are listed by A. G. Rau and H. T. David in 'A Catalogue of Music by American Moravians' (Bethlehem, 1938), and his music is represented in vol. I of the series, 'Music by the Moravians in America,' publ. by the N. Y. Public Library (1938).

Müller, Gottfried, German composer; b. Dresden, June 8, 1914. He studied with Sir Donald Tovey in Edinburgh and with Straube in Leipzig; was instructor at the Hochschule für Musik in Leipzig (1942-45), cantor in Glaubitz, near Riesa (1945-52); after 1952, organist in Berlin. He wrote a set of variations for orch. on a German folksong, which became popular; a *Deutsches Heldenrequiem* (1934); a concerto for orch. (1939); a number of works for organ; church music.

Müller, Hans, German musicologist; son of the poet Wolfgang Müller von Königswinter; b. Cologne, Sept. 18, 1854; d. Berlin, April 11, 1897. He was appointed prof. of history of music at the Hochschule für Musik, Berlin, in 1889; publ. *Hucbalds echte und unechte Schriften über Musik* (1884); *Abhandlung über Mensuralmusik in der Karlsruher Handschrift St. Peter Pergamen, 29a* (Leipzig, 1886); etc.

Müller, Heinrich Fidelis, German composer and choral leader; b. Fulda, April 23, 1827; d. there, Aug. 30, 1905. He was for many years choirmaster at the Cologne Cathedral; composed the oratorios *Weihnachtsoratorium, Die heilige Elisabeth, Die Passion unseres Herrn;* several Masses, motets, choruses, etc.

Müller, Hermann, German music editor and ecclesiastic; b. Dortmund, Oct. 1, 1868; d. Paderborn, Jan. 17, 1932. He studied theology (*Dr. theol.;* 1891, priest), later church music with Haberl and Haller in Regensburg (1894); from 1894, cathedral choirmaster in Paderborn; specialist in church music. —He publ. *Der feierliche Gottesdienst der Karwoche* (9th ed., 1928); *Gänge durchs Kirchenlied* (1926); numerous articles on church music in special publications; ed. the Masses of Lotti in the 'Denkmäler deutscher Tonkunst' (vol. 60), etc.

Müller, Iwan, clarinetist and instrument maker; b. Reval, Estonia, Dec. 14, 1786; d. Bückeburg, Feb. 4, 1854. He invented the clarinet with 13 keys, also the 'Altclarinet' (superseding the basset-horn). In 1809 he went to Paris, where he established a clarinet workshop; although he faced the opposition of conservative instrument makers, his improved clarinet eventually won general popularity. He spent the last years of his life at Bückeburg as court musician; publ. a method for his new instruments; 3 quartets for clarinet and strings; a concertante for 2 clarinets; pieces for clarinet and piano; 6 flute concertos; etc. —Cf. F. G. Rendall, *The Clarinet* (London, 1954; *passim*).

Müller, Joseph, collector of musicians' portraits; b. Frankfurt, April 23, 1877; d. Closter, N. J., May 9, 1939. He studied at the Cons. of Ostend, Belgium, graduating in 1893; settled in N. Y. in 1933, and in 1934 became curator of musical iconography at the N. Y. Public Library; publ. *The Star Spangled Banner: Words and Music issued between 1814-64,* an annotated bibliographical list of the different versions, with many facsimiles (N. Y., 1935); contributed articles on musical iconography to the 'Mus. Quarterly' and other publications.

Müller, Karl Christian, organist and teacher, b. Saxe-Meiningen, July 3, 1831; d. New York, June 4, 1914. He studied piano and organ with Heinrich Pfeiffer, composition with Andreas Zöllner. He went to New York in 1854; worked in a piano factory, then played violin in the orch. of the Barnum Museum. From 1879 to 1895 he taught harmony at the N. Y. College of Music; transl. Sechter's *Grundsätze der musikalischen Composition* (entitled *Fundamental Harmony,* N. Y., 1871; 9 subsequent eds.); also supplemented it by 4 sets of tables, on modulation, chord succession, and harmonization (1882-93). —Works: *Pleasant Recollections* and *Golden Hours* for piano; 3 organ sonatas; sonata for violin and piano; a string quartet; choruses; songs; *March of the Crusaders* and *Resignation* for organ; several large works in MS.

Müller, Maria, lyric soprano; b. Leitmeritz, Austria, Jan. 29, 1898; d. Bayreuth, March 13, 1958. Studied in Prague; later with Max Altglass, N. Y.; was a member of the Prague Opera (1921-23), Munich Opera (1923-24), and Metropolitan Opera (1924-35; début as Sieglinde, Jan. 21, 1925). In 1926 she joined the Berlin State Opera; also sang at the Wagner Festivals in Bayreuth.

Müller, Paul, Swiss conductor and composer; b. Zürich, June 19, 1898. He studied at the Zürich Cons. (1917-20); in Paris and Berlin. In 1927 he was appointed to the faculty of the Zürich Cons. His early works show Romantic influences; later he turned to a modern contrapuntal style. —Works: 2 cantatas; viola concerto (1935); violin concerto (1936); *Sinfonia* for string orch. (1945); 2 string quartets; 2 violin sonatas; works for organ, piano, etc.

Müller, Peter, German composer; b. Kesselstadt, near Hanau, June 9, 1791; d. Langen, Aug. 29, 1877. He taught music at various schools in Germany; wrote his renowned 'Jugendlieder,' male choruses, organ pieces, etc. In 1839 he became pastor at Staden. His opera (after Bulwer-Lytton), *Die letzten Tage von Pompeii,* was produced at Darmstadt, Dec. 25, 1853; he also wrote 7 string quintets and other chamber music.

Müller, Sigfrid Walther, German composer; b. Plauen, Jan. 11, 1905; d. in the autumn of 1946, in a Russian prison camp. He studied at the Leipzig Cons. with Karg-Elert and Martienssen; also church music and organ with Straube; taught at the Leipzig Cons. (1929-32) and at the Hochschule für Musik in Weimar (1940-41); then was in the German army on the eastern front. His output comprised 62 op. numbers, mostly chamber music and organ works; also an opera, *Schlaraffenhochzeit* (Leipzig, 1937); *Böhmische Musik,* for orch.; *Gohliser Schlossmusik,* for small orch.; a concerto for flute and chamber orch. (1941).

Müller, Wenzel, Austrian composer; b. Tyrnau, Moravia, Sept. 26, 1767; d. Baden, near Vienna, Aug. 3, 1835. He studied with Dittersdorf; conducted theater orchestras in provincial towns; was director of the Prague Opera from 1808 to 1813; then went to Vienna as conductor at the Leopoldstadt Theater, a post he held almost to the end of his life. He wrote an enormous amount of stage music, and his 'Singspiele' were very popular in their day; among them were the following, which he brought out at the Leopoldstadt Theater: *Das Sonnenfest der Braminen* (Sept. 9, 1790); *Kaspar der Fagottist, oder die Zauberzither* (June 8, 1791); *Das Neusonntagskind* (Oct. 10, 1793); *Die Schwestern von Prag* (March

11, 1794); *Die Teufelsmühle am Wienerberg* (an Austrian fairy-tale; Nov. 12, 1799; his most popular stage work). A full list of his operas is given in the 2nd supplement to Riemann's *Opernhandbuch* (Leipzig, 1887). —Cf. W. Krone, *Wenzel Müller* (Berlin, 1906); L. Raab, *Wenzel Müller* (Vienna, 1928); R. Haas, *Wenzel Müller,* in 'Mozart-Jahrbuch 1953' (1954).

Müller Quartets. Two famous German string quartets, the first to undertake regular concert tours, their members being:

(1) The brothers **Karl** (1797-1873); **Gustav** (1799-1855); **Theodor** (1802-1875); and **Georg** (1808-1855); they were all born in Brunswick and belonged to the orchestra there, Karl as concertmaster, Theodor as cellist, Gustav as violist, and Georg as conductor. Their artistic tours included not only all large German cities, but also Vienna and Paris (1833), Copenhagen (1838), St. Petersburg in 1845, and Holland in 1852. —Cf. L. Köhler, *Die Gebrüder Müller und das Streichquartett* (Leipzig, 1858); E. Stier, *Das Streichquartett der Gebrüder Müller,* in 'Braunschweigisches Archiv' (July, 1913).

(2) The four sons of Karl, all b. in Brunswick (this quartet was organized in 1855, after the death of two members of the first one); **Karl,** 1st violin, b. April 14, 1829; d. Stuttgart, Nov. 11, 1907; **Hugo,** 2d violin, b. Sept. 21, 1832; d. Brunswick, June 26, 1886; **Bernhard,** viola, b. Feb. 24, 1825; d. Rostock, Sept. 4, 1895; and **Wilhelm,** cello, b. June 1, 1834; d. New York, Sept., 1897. For ten years they held the position of court quartet at Meiningen; then, after extended and successful travels, they settled in Rostock as members of the orch., Karl being appointed music director. The quartet was broken up by the appointment of Wilhelm (1873) to succeed Sweerts as 1st cello in the Royal Orch. at Berlin, and prof. in the Hochschule. Karl lived from then on at Stuttgart and Hamburg; was also a noted composer.

Müller von Kulm, Walter, Swiss composer; b. Kulm, Aug. 31, 1899. He studied in Basel and Zürich; in 1947 was appointed director of the Basel Cons. He has written a number of stage works, among them an opera, *Der Erfinder* (1944); a ballet, *Die blaue Blume* (1936); an oratorio, *Vater unser* (1945); a symphony (1928); and several works of chamber music. He has also publ. a manual of harmony, *Grundriss der Harmonielehre* (Basel, 1948).

Müller-Blattau, Joseph Maria, musicologist; b. Colmar, Alsace, May 21, 1895; studied music with Friedrich Ludwig at the Univ. of Strasbourg; with Pfitzner (composition) and Ernst Münch (piano and organ) at the Strasbourg Cons.; was in the German Army during World War I; then studied with Wilibald Gurlitt at the Univ. of Freiburg-im-Breisgau (1919-20); assistant at the Musicological Institute of the Univ. of Freiburg (1920-22); lecturer at Königsberg Univ. (1922-35); professor at the Univ. of Frankfurt (1935-38); successor to Wilibald Gurlitt at the Univ. of Freiburg (1937-39); from 1939 to 1942 was in military administration; lectured at Strasbourg Univ. (1942-45); then taught at Kusel (Pfalz) and Coesfeld; in 1952 appointed director of the State Cons. at Saarbrücken. He was editor of the abortive 12th ed. of Riemann's *Musiklexikon* (as successor to Alfred Einstein; 1937-39; only a few issues appeared). —Writings: *Das Elsass, ein Grenzland deutscher Musik* (1922); *Grundzüge einer Geschichte der Fuge* (1923; 2nd and augmented ed., 1930); *Musikalische Erneuerung* (collected essays; 1928); *Grundlagen der musikalischen Gestaltung* (1928); *Geschichte der Musik in Ost- und Westpreussen* (1931); *Hamann und Herder in ihren Beziehungen zur Musik* (1931); *Einführung in die Musikgeschichte* (1932); *Das deutsche Volkslied* (1932); *Johannes Brahms* (1933); *G. Fr. Händel* (1933); *J. S. Bach* (1935; 2nd ed., 1950); *Geschichte der deutschen Musik* (1938; 2nd ed., 1953); *Hans Pfitzner* (1940); *Gestaltung-Umgestaltung: Studien zur Geschichte der musikalischen Variation* (1950); *Das Verhältnis von Wort und Ton in der Geschichte der Musik* (1952); *Musikalisches Taschenlexikon* (1952); edited Forkel's *J. S. Bach* (1924); brought out a modern ed. of Heinrich Albert's cantata *Musikalische Kürbis-Hütte* of 1645 (1932), a collection, *Musica reservata* (1952), and other works.

Müller-Hartmann, Robert, German composer; b. Hamburg, Oct. 11, 1884; d. Dorking, Surrey, Dec. 15, 1950. He studied at the Stern Cons. in Berlin; was lecturer on music at Hamburg Univ. (1923-33); in 1937 settled in England, where he worked mainly as an arranger and translator. He wrote a number of symph. works, some of which were first performed by Richard Strauss and Karl Muck (a symphony, a symph. ballad, several sets of variations, etc.); a trio for flute, violin, and viola; 2 violin sonatas; many organ works; piano pieces.

Müller-Hermann, Johanna, Austrian composer and pedagogue; b. Vienna, Jan. 15, 1878; d. there, April 19, 1941. She studied with Karl Nawratil, Josef Labor, Guido Adler, Zemlinsky, and J. B. Foerster; began to compose at an early age, in a Romantic vein, influenced chiefly by Mahler and Max Reger; was regarded as one of the foremost European women composers of orchestral and chamber music. She wrote an oratorio, *In Memoriam,* to Walt Whitman's words; a symphony for voices with orch.; a symph. fantasy on Ibsen's play *Brand;* a string quartet; a string quintet; a piano quintet; a violin sonata; a cello sonata; a piano sonata; several song cycles.

Müller-Reuter, Theodor, German conductor and composer; b. Dresden, Sept. 1, 1858; d. there, Aug. 11, 1919; studied with Alwin Wieck (piano) and Meinardus (composition) in Dresden; later with Clara Schumann in Frankfurt. He taught piano and theory at Strasbourg Cons. (1879-87); then at Dresden (1887-92) and (as conductor) in Krefeld (1893-1918), returning to Dresden, after a brief professorship at the Leipzig Cons., shortly before his death. He wrote the operas *Ondolina* (Strasbourg, 1883) and *Der tolle Graf* (Nuremberg, 1887), and many choruses; publ. a valuable *Lexikon der deutschen Konzert-Literatur* (vol. I, 1909; supplement, 1921); also *Bilder und Klänge des Friedens; musikalische Erinnerungen und Aufsätze* (1919).

Munch (münch), **Charles,** eminent conductor; b. Strasbourg, Sept. 26, 1891. The original spelling of his name was Münch; he was a son of Ernst Münch (1859-1928), choral conductor in Alsace. He studied violin at the Strasbourg Cons., in Paris with Lucien Capet, and in Berlin with Karl Flesch; conducting with Furtwängler in Leipzig. He was sergeant of artillery in the German army during World War I; was gassed at Peronne, and wounded at Verdun. In 1918, as an Alsatian, he became a French citizen; was concertmaster of the municipal orch. of Strasbourg (1919-26); also taught at the Strasbourg Cons.; then joined the Gewandhaus Orch. in Leipzig as concertmaster. He made his professional début as symph. conductor on Nov. 1, 1932, in Paris, with the Straram Orch.; subsequently was guest conductor with the Lamoureux Orch. Although he began his career as a conductor at the age of 41, he quickly rose to eminence; organized his own orch. in Paris, the Orchestre de la Société Philharmonique (1935-38), featuring modern French works. In 1938 he was engaged to conduct the Société des Concerts du Conservatoire de Paris, and led it brilliantly for 8 years, including the difficult time of the German occupation. He received the French Legion of Honor in 1945. He made his American début with the Boston Symph. Orch., on Dec. 27, 1946; conducted the N. Y. Philharmonic in several concerts during the season of 1947-48. In 1948 he also made a transcontinental tour of the U. S. with the French Radio Orch. In 1949 he was selected as permanent conductor of the Boston Symph., to succeed Koussevitzky. In 1952 he traveled with the Boston Symph. in Europe; this was its first European tour. In 1956 the Boston Symph., with Munch and Monteux as conductors, made another European tour which included Russia. As an interpreter, Munch combines a distinct individuality with a fine sense of authentic color and stirring rhythm; in classical works, he takes a broad line, with careful regard to the formal proportions of the music. In his repertory, modern French music occupies a prominent place; he has brought out a number of new works by Roussel, Milhaud, Honegger, and others. He publ. a book, *Je suis chef d'orchestre* (Paris, 1954; English transl. by L. Burkat, *I am a Conductor,* N. Y., 1955; also publ. in several other languages). —Cf. Hope Stoddard, *Symphony Conductors of the U. S. A.* (N. Y., 1957; pp. 136-46).

Münch, Hans, conductor; b. Mulhouse, Alsace, March 9, 1893. He studied with Schweitzer, and later at the Basel Cons. with Huber; from 1918-27, taught piano at the Basel Cons.; then conducted various choral societies there; chiefly distinguished as a choral conductor, but also led symph. performances. He wrote several cantatas, chamber music, and songs.

Münchinger, Karl, German conductor; b. Stuttgart, May 29, 1915; studied in Leipzig. In 1945 he founded the Stuttgart Chamber Orch.; made his U. S. début in San Francisco, Feb., 1953; toured in the U. S. with his Stuttgart orch. during 1953-54.

Münnich, Richard, German musicologist; b. Berlin, June 7, 1877. He studied with his father (piano) and with Otto Hutschenreuter (cello); then at the Univ. of Berlin with Max Friedlaender and Karl Stumpf (1897-1901); composition with Martin Grabert; later took courses at the Univ. of Leipzig with Hugo Riemann, and in Berlin with Kretzschmar. He then held various teaching posts in Berlin (1902-4) and Stettin (1904-8); in 1908, was again in Berlin as teacher and choral director; taught theory at the Klindworth-Scharwenka Cons. (1910-35); in 1925, was appointed director (with Kestenberg) of school courses of music instruction in Prussia; from 1928 was joint editor (with Jöde, Martens, and Susanne Trautwein) of 'Zeitschrift für Schulmusik'; in 1935 he became prof. at the Hochschule für Musik in Weimar; retired in 1949. —Publications: *Johann Kuhnau* (part I: *Kuhnaus Leben*), in 'Sammelbände der Internationalen Musik-Gesellschaft' (III, p. 473 ff.); *Wiederholungsbüchlein für den Musikunterricht an höheren Schulen* (4th ed., 1928); *Jale, ein Beitrag zur Tonsilbenfrage und zur Schulmusik-Propädeutik,* in which he evolved a new and ingenious solmisation system (1930); *Die Suite,* in 'Musikalische Formen in historischen Reihen' ed. by Martens. A 'Festschrift' was publ. for his 70th birthday, with articles by H. J. Moser and others (1947).

Munsel, Patrice Beverly, American soprano; b. Spokane, Wash., May 14, 1925. She studied with William Herman and Renato Bellini in N. Y.; won an audition at the Metropolitan Opera, and made a successful professional début there on Dec. 4, 1943 (the youngest singer ever accepted by the Metropolitan); subsequently sang in Scandinavia and elsewhere in Europe. On June 10, 1952, she married Robert Charles C. Schuler. Her best roles are Gilda, Lucia, Rosina, Violetta, Lakmé. She portrayed Melba in a motion picture on Melba's life (1953).

Munz, Mieczyslaw, pianist; b. Cracow, Poland, Oct. 31, 1900. He studied at the Academy of Music in Vienna; later in Berlin. In 1922 he settled in New York; in 1933 embarked on an extensive tour to Australia, the Far East, South America, and Europe, returning to the U. S. in 1938. In 1941 he was appointed prof. of piano at the Curtis Institute of Music in Philadelphia.

Münzer, Georg, German writer on music and teacher; b. Breslau, Sept. 4, 1866; d. Berlin, April 24, 1908. He studied with various teachers in Breslau; then in Berlin with Klindworth (piano) and Helmholtz (acoustics); also musicology with Bellermann and Spitta; received his *Dr. phil.* with the dissertation *Beiträge zur Konzertgeschichte Breslaus;* lived in Breslau and Berlin. —Writings: *Zur Einführung in Richard Wagners 'Ring des Nibelungen'* (1900), *Heinrich Marschner* (1901), *Die Notation der Meistersinger* (1907; in the report of the Basel Congress of the International Music Society); numerous essays in music journals; ed. *Das Singebuch des Adam Puschmann* (1907).

Muradeli, Vano Ilitch, Russian composer; b. Gori, Georgia, April 6, 1908. As a child, he improvised songs accompanying himself on the mandolin (there was no piano in his home); he did not learn to read music until he was 18, when he entered the Tiflis Cons.; after graduation (1934) he went to the Moscow Cons., where he studied first with Shekhter and then with Miaskovsky. His early compositions were influenced by his native folk music; he wrote a *Georgian Suite* for piano (1935) and incidental music to plays on Caucasian subjects. His first important work was a symphony in memory of the assassinated Soviet dignitary Kirov (Moscow, Nov. 28, 1938); his 2nd symphony (1946) received a Stalin prize. The performance of his opera *Great Friendship* (Moscow, Nov. 7, 1947) gave rise to an official condemnation of modernistic trends in Soviet music, culminating in the resolution of the Central Committee of the Communist Party of Feb. 10, 1948, which described the opera as "chaotic, inharmonious and alien to the normal human ear." Muradeli's reputation was rehabilitated by his subsequent works, *The Path of Victory* for orch., and a series of choruses (*Stalin's Will Has Led Us; Song of the Fighters for Peace; Hymn to Moscow,* which received a Stalin prize in 1951; etc.).

Muratore (mü-rah-tohr'), **Lucien,** French tenor; b. Marseilles, Aug. 29, 1876; d. Paris, July 16, 1954. He studied at the Cons. of Marseilles, graduating with honors in 1897, but began his career as an actor. Later he studied opera at the Paris Cons.; made his opera début at the Opéra-Comique, Dec. 16, 1902, in Hahn's *La Carmélite* with extraordinary success. Muratore also sang in the premières of several operas by Massenet: *Ariane* (1906), *Bacchus* (1909), and *Roma* (1912), Février's *Monna Vanna* (1909), Giordano's *Siberia* (1911), etc. In 1913 he made his American début with the Boston Opera Co.; on Dec. 15, 1913, he sang Faust with the Chicago Opera Co. In 1914 he joined the French Army; in 1917 sang at the Teatro Colón in Buenos Aires; then returned to the Chicago Opera

Co. In 1922 he went back to France; for 7 years he served as mayor of the town of Biot. In 1943, settled in Paris as voice teacher. He was married three times; his first two marriages (to Marguerite Bériza, a soprano, and to the famous prima donna Lina Cavalieri) ended in divorce; his third wife was Marie Louise Brivaud.

Muris, Johannes (Jean) de, important musical theorist, astronomer, and mathematician; b. (probably in Normandy) c. 1290; d. c. 1351. He is often confused with a certain Julianus de Muris, rector of the Sorbonne in Paris, who was appointed to that post in 1350. It was also believed that Johannes de Muris was the author of the famous treatises *Speculum musicae* and *Summa musicae,* but it has since been established that the author of the *Speculum musicae* was Jacques de Liège (q. v.); indeed the conservatism of this treatise is quite inconsistent with the progressive views held by Muris. But he did write the *Musica Speculativa,* which bears the inscription 'abbreviata Parisiis in Sorbona A.D. 1323,' and another important treatise, *Ars novae music e,* in which his forward-looking ideas are especially manifest (this treatise may be pieced together from material in Gerbert's 'Scriptores,' III). In 1344 he was canon of Mezières (near Bourges), and he was one of the astronomers who took part in the reform of the calendar under the auspices of Pope Clement VI at Avignon. He does not appear to have been active as a composer. There is extant a letter of his to Philippe de Vitry (q. v.). —Cf. Hugo Riemann, *Geschichte der Musiktheorie* (2nd ed., 1921; p. 234 ff.); J. Wolf, *Geschichte der Mensuralnotation von 1250-1460* (1905); W. Grossmann, *Die einleitenden Kapitel des Speculum musicae* (1924; erroneous in ascribing the authorship of *Speculum musicae* to Johannes de Muris); H. Besseler, *Studien zur Musik des Mittelalters,* in 'Archiv für Musikwissenschaft' (VII, p. 180 ff., and VIII, p. 207 ff.). A partial transl. into English of *Ars novae musice* is found in O. Strunk, *Source Readings in Music History* (N. Y., 1950).

Murphy, Lambert, American tenor; b. Springfield, Mass., April 15, 1885; d. Hancock, N. H., July 24, 1954. He studied at Harvard Univ. (A.B., 1908); took singing lessons with T. Cushman in Boston and Luckstone in N. Y.; was soloist in various Boston churches (until 1910); made tours with the Boston Festival Orch.; appeared at many music festivals; from 1910 to 1914, was a member of the Metropolitan Opera.

Murray, Bain, American composer and musicologist; b. Evanston, Ill., Dec. 26, 1926. He studied composition with Herbert Elwell, Randall Thompson, Walter Piston, and Nadia Boulanger; musicology with Otto Gombosi, Suzanne Clercx, Stephen Tuttle, and A. Tillman Merritt. M.A., Harvard (1952). He received a Fulbright Grant to Belgium (1953-54) and a teaching fellowship at Harvard (1954-55). Under U. S. Government auspices he has recorded, notated, and lectured on American Indian music. Since 1955, teaching theory at Oberlin Conservatory. —Works: Ballad for orch. (1950); ballet, *Peter Pan* (1952); 2 string quartets (1950; 1953); *Song Cycle,* after Sara Teasdale (1956); other songs; choruses; piano pieces. Has contributed articles to the 'Mus. Quarterly' and other periodicals.

Murrill, Herbert Henry John, English composer; b. London, May 11, 1909; d. there, July 24, 1952. He studied at the Royal Academy of Music with York Bowen, Stanley Marchant, and Alan Bush; then at Oxford Univ., with Ernest Walker and Sir Hugh Allen, taking the degrees of M.A. and Mus. Bac. He occupied various posts as organist and choral conductor; in 1933 appointed prof. of composition at the Royal Academy of Music, remaining at that post until his death. His relatively small output is in a modern vein: a 'jazz opera,' *Man in Cage* (London, 1930); incidental music to various plays; the ballet *Picnic* (1927); several choral works; *3 Hornpipes,* for orch. (1932); *Set of Country Dances,* for strings (1945); 2 cello concertos (1935 and 1950); a string quartet; a sonata for recorder and harpsichord (1950); several arrangements of folksongs for piano; some songs and piano pieces.

Murschhauser, Franz Xavier Anton, German theorist; b. Zabern, near Strasbourg, June (baptized July 1), 1663; d. Munich, Jan. 6, 1738. He studied with J. K. Kerll in Munich; from 1691 was music director of the Frauenkirche there. He wrote the theoretical treatise *Academia musico-poetica bipartita, oder Hohe Schule der musikalischen Composition,* the first part of which appeared in 1721, provocatively described as being intended 'to give a little more light to the excellent Herr Mattheson.' The latter retaliated with such devastating effect in his *Melopoetische Lichtscheere* (*Critica* *musica,* 1722; pp. 1-88) that Murschhauser refrained from publishing the second part of his work. His compositions for organ are reprinted in the 'Denkmäler deutscher Tonkunst' (2nd series, XVIII, ed. by M. Seiffert, with a biographical sketch). —Cf. M. Vogeleis, *F. X. A. Murschhauser,* in the 'Kirchenmusikalisches Jahrbuch' (1901).

Murska (mŏŏrs'-kăh), **Ilma di,** dramatic soprano; b. in Croatia, 1836; d. (suicide by poison) Munich, Jan. 14, 1889. She studied with Mathilde Marchesi in Vienna, and later in Paris; made her début in Florence (1862). After a European tour, she was engaged at the Vienna Opera. She made her London appearance for the first time as Lucia (May 11, 1865) and was favorably received there for several seasons (until 1873); toured America and Australia (1873-76); was again in London in 1879. She taught at the National Cons., N. Y., in 1880. She led a turbulent life; was married 3 times; towards the end of her career, settled in Munich.

Musard (mü-zahr'), **Philippe,** famous French dance composer; b. Tours, 1793; d. Auteuil (Paris), March 30, 1859. He studied music privately with Reicha; first came into public view at the promenade concerts in Paris, begun in Nov., 1833, in a bazaar of the Rue St. Honoré; there he introduced Dufresne, a remarkable player on the cornet, and wrote special solo pieces for him, which became a great attraction; he also conducted balls at the Paris Opéra (1835-36), at which his orch. of 70 musicians won great acclaim. His quadrilles and galops enjoyed immense popularity, and he earned the sobriquet 'le roi des quadrilles.' In London he conducted the promenade concerts at Drury Lane during the season of 1840-41, and appeared at other concerts in England. His son **Alfred Musard** (1828-81) was likewise a composer of quadrilles, and a bandleader.

Musin (mü-zăn'), **Ovide,** Belgian violinist; b. Nandrin, near Liège, Sept. 22, 1854; d. Brooklyn, N. Y., Nov. 24, 1929. He studied with Heynberg and Léonard at the Liège Cons., taking 1st violin prize at the age of 13; following Léonard to the Paris Cons., he won the gold medal at 15; toured Europe from 1874 to 1882 with remarkable success. In 1883 he went to America; between 1892 and 1897 he made two world tours. From 1897 to 1908 he taught at the Cons. of Liège; in 1908 he established himself in N. Y., and opened his own school of music. He publ. a number of brilliant violin pieces; also instructive works, *System of Daily Practice* (1899) and *The Belgian School of the Violin* (4 vols.; 1916; a combination of his own methods with those of his teacher Léonard); also a book, *My Memories* (1920). His wife, **Annie Louise Tanner-Musin** (b. Boston, Oct. 3, 1856; d. there, Feb. 28, 1921), was a well known coloratura soprano. See the article on Musin in the 'Dictionary of American Biography.'

Musiol, Robert Paul Johann, German writer on music and pedagogue; b. Breslau, Jan. 14, 1846; d. Fraustadt, Posen, Oct. 19, 1903. He attended the Seminary at Liebenthal, Silesia; in 1873 became teacher and cantor at Röhrsdorf, near Fraustadt; pensioned in 1891. —Publications: *Musikalisches Fremdwörterbuch; Katechismus der Musikgeschichte* (2nd ed., 1888); edited Tonger's *Konversations-Lexikon der Tonkunst* (1881-85) and *Musikerlexikon* (1890); contributed to music periodicals; wrote choruses, organ pieces, piano pieces, songs.

Mussolini, Cesare, Italian composer and theorist; b. Romagna, 1735; d. probably in London, where he went in 1780; publ. (in English) *A New and Complete Treatise on the Theory and Practice of Music, with Solfeggios* (London, 1795); also canzonets. He was an ancestor of Benito Mussolini.

Mussorgsky, Modest Petrovitch, great Russian composer; b. Karevo, district of Pskov, March 21, 1839; d. St. Petersburg, March 28, 1881. He received his first instruction on the piano from his mother; at the age of 10 he was taken to St. Petersburg, where he had piano lessons with Anton Herke. In 1852 he entered the cadet school of the Imperial Guard; composed a piano piece entitled *Porte enseigne Polka,* which was published (1852); after graduation, he joined the regiment of the Guard. In 1857, he met Dargomyzhsky, who introduced him to Cui and Balakirev; he also became friendly with the critic and chief champion of Russian national music, Vladimir Stasov. These associations prompted Mussorgsky's decision to become a professional composer. He played and analyzed piano arrangements of works by Beethoven and Schumann; Balakirev helped him to acquire a knowledge of form; he tried to write music in a classical style, but without success; his inner drive was directed towards 'new shores,' as Mussorgsky himself expressed it. The liquidation of the family estate made it imperative for Mussorgsky to take a paying job; he became a clerk in the Ministry of Communications (1863), resigning 4 years later. During this time, he continued to compose, but his lack of technique compelled him time and again to leave his various pieces unfinished. He eagerly sought professional advice from his friends Stasov (for general esthetics) and Rimsky-Korsakov (for problems of harmony); to the very end of his life, he regarded himself as being only half-educated in music, and constantly acknowledged his inferiority as a craftsman. But he yielded to no one in his firm faith in the future of national Russian music. When a group of composers from Bohemia visited St. Petersburg in 1867, Stasov published an article in which he for the first time referred to the 'mighty handful of Russian musicians' pursuing the ideal of national art. The expression was picked up derisively by some journalists, but it was accepted as a challenge by Mussorgsky and his comrades-in-arms, Balakirev, Borodin, Cui, and Rimsky-Korsakov, the 'mighty five' of Russian music. In 1869, Mussorgsky once more entered government service, this time in the forestry department. He became addicted to drink, and had epileptic fits; he died a week after his 42nd birthday. — The significance of Mussorgsky's genius did not become apparent until some years after his death. Most of his works were prepared for publication by Rimsky-Korsakov, who corrected some of Mussorgsky's harmonic crudities, and reorchestrated the symphonic works. Original versions of Mussorgsky's music were preserved in manuscript, and eventually published and performed. But despite the availability of the authentic scores, Mussorgsky's works continue to be performed in Rimsky-Korsakov's editions, made familiar to the whole musical world. — In his dramatic works, and in his songs, Mussorgsky draws a boldly realistic vocal line, in which inflections of speech are translated into a natural melody. His first attempt in this genre was an unfinished opera, *The Marriage,* to Gogol's comedy; here Mussorgsky also demonstrated his penetrating sense of musical humor. His ability to depict tragic moods is revealed in his cycle, *Songs and Dances of Death;* his understanding of intimate poetry is shown in the children's songs. His greatest work is the opera *Boris Godunov* (to Pushkin's tragedy), which has no equal in its stirring portrayal of personal destiny against a background of social upheaval. In it, Mussorgsky created a true national music drama, without a trace of the Italian conventions that had theretofore dominated the operatic works by Russian composers. Mussorgsky wrote no chamber music, perhaps because he lacked the requisite training in contrapuntal technique. Of his piano music, the set of pieces, *Pictures at an Exhibition* (somewhat after the manner of Schumann's *Carnaval*), is remarkable for its vivid representation of varied scenes (it was written to commemorate his friend, the painter Victor Hartmann, whose pictures were the subjects of the music); the work has been made famous by the brilliant orchestration of Ravel. — Although Mussorgsky was a Russian national composer, his music influenced profoundly many composers outside Russia (Debussy, Manuel de Falla, Italian opera composers, etc.), and he came to be regarded as the most potent talent of the 'mighty five.' — Works: operas: *The Marriage* (1864; only the first act completed; produced, Petrograd, Oct. 26, 1917; completed and orchestrated by Alexandre Tcherepnin; performed in this form for the first time, Essen, Sept. 14, 1937); *Boris Godunov* (St. Petersburg, Feb. 8, 1874; revised and reorchestrated by Rimsky-Korsakov in 1896; produced in this new form, St. Petersburg, Dec. 10, 1896, and subsequently all over the world; Mussorgsky's original score, ed. by Paul Lamm, publ. in 1928); *Khovanshtchina* (on a historical subject from the time of Peter the Great; completed and orchestrated by Rimsky-Korsakov; first performed, St. Petersburg, Feb. 21, 1886); *The Fair at Sorotchinsk* (unfinished, completed by Cui; St. Petersburg, Oct 26, 1917; also arranged and orchestrated by Nicolas Tcherepnin, and produced at Monte Carlo, March 17, 1923); choral works: *The Destruction of Sennacherib,* after Byron, for chorus and orch. (St. Petersburg, March 18, 1867) and *Joshua,* for contralto, bass, chorus, and piano (1874-77); for orch.: *Scherzo* (St. Petersburg, Jan. 23, 1860), *Intermezzo in modo classico* (1867), *A Night on the Bald Mountain* (1860-66; reorchestrated by Rimsky-Korsakov and performed posthumously, St. Petersburg, Oct. 27, 1886); for piano: *Scherzo* (1858), *Jeux d'enfants - les quatre coins* (German subtitle *Ein Kinderscherz;* 1859), *Impromptu passionné* (1859), sonata, for piano, 4 hands (1860), *Souvenirs d'enfance* (1865), *Rêverie* (1865), *La Capricieuse* (1865), *Intermezzo in modo classico* (piano version of the orch. piece; 1867), *Pictures at an Exhibition* (1874: *Promenade; Gnomus; Il vecchio castello; Tuileries; Bydlo; Ballet des poussins dans leurs coques; Deux juifs, l'un riche et l'autre pauvre; Promenade; Limoges —Le Marché; Catacombae; Cum mortuis in lingua mortua; La Cabane sur des pattes de poule; La grande porte de Kiev;* French titles by Mussorgsky), *En Crimée* (1880), *Méditation* (1880), *Une Larme* (1880), piano transcriptions of dances from the opera *The Fair at Sorotchinsk,* many incomplete fragments of youthful works, etc.; songs: *King Saul* (1863), *Cradle Song* (1865), *Darling Savishna* (1866), *The Seminarist* (1866), *Hopak* (1866), *On the Dnieper* (1879), *Hebrew Song* (1879), *The Classicist* (satirical; 1867), *The Garden by the Don* (1867), *The Nursery,* children's song cycle (1868-72), *Rayok* (*The Peep-show;* a musical lampoon at assorted contemporaries; 1870), *Sunless,* song cycle (1874), *Forgotten* (1874), *Songs and Dances of Death,* a cycle of 4 songs (1875-77), *Mephistopheles' Song of the Flea* (1879), a number of other songs. In 1931, to mark the 50th anniversary of Mussorgsky's death, the Soviet State Edition, under the direction of Paul Lamm, undertook the publication of his complete works, including variants, fragments, notations of folksongs, etc. —Bibliography: V. Stasov, *M.* (St. Petersburg, 1881); V. Baskin, *M.* (Moscow, 1887); Pierre d'Alheim, *M.* (Paris, 3rd ed., 1896); Marie Olénine-d'Alheim, *Le Legs de Mussorgski* (Paris, 1908); M.-D. Calvocoressi, *M.* (Paris, 1907; 2nd French ed., 1911; English transl., London, 1919); Rosa Newmarch, *M.'s Operas,* in the 'Mus. Times' (July, 1913); M. Montagu-Nathan, *M.* (London, 1916); Oskar von Riesemann, *M.* (Munich, 1925; in English, N. Y., 1935); Alfred Swan, *M. and Modern Music,* in the 'Mus. Quarterly' (April, 1925); Kurt von Wolfurt, *M.* (Stuttgart, 1927); R. Godet, *En marge de Boris Godunov* (Paris, 1927); Igor Glebov, *M.* (Leningrad, 1928); H. van Dalen, *M.* (The Hague, 1930); Y. Keldish, *Lyricism in M.'s Songs* (Moscow, 1933); M. D. Calvocoressi, *M.'s Musical Style,* in the 'Mus. Quarterly' (Oct., 1932); M. D. Calvocoressi, *M.'s Youth,* in the 'Mus. Quarterly' (Jan., 1934); V. Fedorov, *M.* (Paris, 1935); Maria Tibaldi Chiesa, *M.* (Milan, 1935); Gerald Abraham and M. D. Calvocoressi, *M.,* in *Masters of Russian Music* (London, 1936; pp. 178-248); C. Barzel, *M.* (Paris, 1939); G. Orlov, *Chronicle of the Life and Works of Mussorgsky* (Moscow, 1940); G. Gavazzeni, *M. e la musica russa dell' 800* (Florence, 1943); R. Garcia Morillo, *M.* (Buenos Aires, 1943); M. D. Calvocoressi, *M.* (completed by Gerald Abraham, London, 1946); R. Hofmann, *M.* (Paris, 1952); M. D. Calvocoressi, *M. M., His Life and Works* (London, 1956; ed. by Gerald Abraham; a completely different book from the earlier ones by Calvocoressi); numerous publications in Russian, pertaining to various aspects of Mussorgsky's life and works; special numbers of Russian magazines. A collection of letters and documents was publ. by A. Rimsky-Korsakov (Moscow, 1932); materials, largely taken from this volume, were transl. and ed. by J. Leyda and S. Bertensson, as *The M. Reader* (N. Y., 1947). The paintings of Victor Hartmann that inspired Mussorgsky's *Pictures at an Exhibition* were reproduced by Alfred Frankenstein in his article on the subject in the 'Mus. Quarterly' (July, 1939); Frankenstein also brought out an illustrated edition of the work (1951).

Mustel (müs-tehl'), **Victor,** celebrated French builder of harmoniums; inventor of the celesta; b. Le Havre, June 13, 1815; d. Paris, Jan. 26, 1890. He began as a carpenter; went to Paris in 1844, where he worked in several shops, becoming foreman in Alexandre's harmonium factory; established himself in 1853, the following year invented 'the double expression,' which won the first prize at the Paris Exposition of 1855; from 1866 the firm became famous as 'V. Mustel et ses Fils.' He also constructed an instrument consisting of graduated tuning forks in a resonance box, operated by a keyboard; this was patented in 1886 by his son Auguste (1842-1919) as 'Celesta.' Tchaikovsky heard the celesta in Paris, and became so enchanted with it that he used it (for the first time in any score) in his ballet *The Nutcracker.*

Müthel, Johann Gottfried, German organist and composer; b. Möllin, Jan. 17, 1718; d. Riga, Jan. 17, 1788. He studied at Lübeck and became court organist at Schwerin. In 1750 he traveled to Leipzig to see Bach, with whom he remained through several weeks before Bach's death. He then journeyed to Potsdam, where he formed a friendship with Karl Philipp Emanuel Bach. In 1753 he went to Riga as organist at the Lutheran Church there. He had the reputation of a very excellent organist; his compositions for the organ were highly praised. He publ. several piano works in Riga, including a duet, the title of which includes for the first time the word 'Fortepiano.'

Muzio (moo'-tsyŏh), **Claudia,** Italian dramatic soprano; b. Pavia, Feb. 7, 1889; d. Rome, May 24, 1936. Her baptismal name was Claudina Muzzio, but she adopted the altered form Claudia Muzio early in her career. She studied with Mme. Casaloni in Turin; made her début as Manon at Arezzo

(Feb. 7, 1912), then sang in Italy, South America, France, and England; made her first American appearance at the Metropolitan Opera as Tosca (Dec. 4, 1916); from 1922 to 1933 was a member of the Chicago Opera; after returning to the Metropolitan Opera for a season, she went back to Italy in 1934. —Cf. H. M. Barnes, *Claudia Muzio; a Biographical Sketch and Discography* (Austin, Texas, 1947).

Muzio (moo'-tsyŏh), **Emanuele,** Italian composer; b. Zibello, Aug. 25, 1825; d. Paris, Nov. 27, 1890. He studied piano with Margherita Barezzi (Verdi's first wife), and composition with Verdi himself, one of the very few pupils Verdi ever had. In 1852 he was engaged as conductor of the Italian Opera in Brussels; later traveled to England and America; settled in Paris in 1875 as a singing teacher. Carlotta Patti and Clara Louise Kellogg were his pupils. He wrote several operas: *Giovanna la pazza* (Brussels, April 8, 1851), *Claudia* (Milan, Feb. 7, 1853), *Le due Regine* (Milan, May 17, 1856), *La Sorrentina* (Bologna, Nov. 14, 1857); also many songs and piano pieces. —Cf. A. Belforti, *Emanuele Muzio, l'unico alievo di G. Verdi* (Milan, 1896); L. A. Garibaldi, ed., *Giuseppe Verdi nelle lettere di Emanuele Muzio ed Antonio Barezzi* (Milan, 1931).

Myer, Edmund J., American teacher of singing; b. York Springs, Pa., Jan. 21, 1846; d. Los Angeles, Jan. 25, 1934. He studied in Philadelphia and N. Y.; founded the National Summer School of Music at Lake Chautauqua and Round Lake, N. Y.; publ. a number of books and pamphlets on the voice: *Truths of Importance to Vocalists* (1883); *The Voice From a Practical Standpoint* (1886); *Voice Training Exercises* (1888); *Vocal Reinforcement* (1891); *Position and Action in Singing* (1897); *The Renaissance of the Vocal Art* (1902); *The Vocal Instructor* (1913); *A Revelation to the Vocal World* (1917).

Myers, Rollo, English writer on music; b. Chislehurst, Kent, Jan. 23, 1892. He studied briefly at the Royal College of Music in London; then was music correspondent for English papers in Paris (1919-34); member of the staff of the B.B.C. in London (1935-44); active as music journalist and editor; publ. the books: *Modern Music: its Aims and Tendencies* (London, 1923); *Music in the Modern World* (London, 1939); *Erik Satie* (London, 1948); *Debussy* (London, 1949); *Introduction to the Music of Stravinsky* (London, 1950); numerous articles on music.

Mysliveczek (mĭs-lĭ-vĕt'-shĕk), **Joseph,** Bohemian composer; called 'Il Boemo' or 'Venatorini' in Italy; b. Ober-Sárka, near Prague, March 9, 1737; d. Rome, Feb. 4, 1781. He studied with Habermann and Seeger in Prague; in 1763, went to Venice in order to perfect himself as a composer. After traveling through Italy, he wrote the opera *Bellerofonte* for Naples, and it was produced there with extraordinary success, on Jan. 29, 1767. This was followed by a mock-exotic opera *Montezuma* (Florence, Jan., 1771), and *Ezio* (Naples, 1775). In 1777 he went to Munich, where he wrote the oratorio *Abramo ed Isacco;* there he fell desperately ill, but survived, and went back to Italy; presented a new opera in Naples, *Olimpiade,* on Nov. 4, 1778; his last opera was *Armida* (Milan, Dec. 26, 1779); there were at least 25 operas by him in addition to the above; he also wrote a set of 6 symphonies, named after the first six months of the year; concertos, clavier sonatas, etc. Mozart had genuine admiration for him. —Cf. G. de Saint-Foix, *Un ami de Mozart,* in the 'Revue Musicale' (March, 1928); Paul Nettl, *Mozart in Böhmen* (Prague, 1938); J. Čeleda, *Josef Mysliveček* (Prague, 1946; in Czech).

Mysz-Gmeiner (müsh-gmī'-nĕr), **Lula,** noted contralto; b. Kronstadt, Transylvania, Aug. 16, 1876; d. Schwerin, Aug. 7, 1948. She studied violin in her native town, and singing in Berlin with Etelka Gerster and Lilli Lehmann; made her début there in 1900; then traveled in Europe as concert singer; was greatly praised for her interpretations of German lieder. She married an Austrian officer, Ernst Mysz (1900).

N

Nabokov (năh-bŏ'-kŏv), **Nicolas,** composer; b. near Lubcha, Novogrudok district, Minsk region, Russia, April 17, 1903. His family moved to St. Petersburg in 1911; after the Revolution, he went to Southern Russia; took lessons in composition in Yalta, with Rebikov; then went to Berlin, where he studied with Busoni; subsequently was in Paris; was introduced to Diaghilev, who commissioned him to write a cantata to words by Lomonosov, Russian 18th-century poet. In 1933 he settled in the U. S.; taught at Wells College (1936-41), and at the Peabody Cons. of Music, Baltimore (1947-52). In 1947 he was appointed chief editor of the Russian Section of the International

Broadcast Div. of the State Dept.; in 1952 he became secretary-general of the Congress for Cultural Freedom; in this capacity, he organized the Paris Festival of 20th Century Music (1952); subsequently lived mostly in Paris. —Works: opera, *The Holy Devil,* on the subject of Rasputin (Louisville, April 18, 1958); *Ode, or Meditation at Night on the Majesty of God, as revealed by the Aurora Borealis* (Ballets Russes, Monte Carlo, June 6, 1928); a symphony (Paris, Feb. 16, 1930; Boston, Oct. 31, 1930); *Union Pacific,* ballet (Philadelphia, April 6, 1934); an orch. suite, *Vie de Polichinelle* (1934); *Le Fiancé,* for orch. (1934); incidental music to Milton's *Samson Agonistes* (Wells College, May 14, 1938); *Sinfonia Biblica* (N. Y., Jan. 2, 1941); symph. suite of marches, for band (1945); *The Return of Pushkin,* an elegy for voice and orch. (Boston, Jan. 2, 1948); *Vita Nuova,* for soprano, tenor, and orch. (Boston, March 2, 1951); a cello concerto, subtitled *Les Hommages* (Philadelphia, Nov. 6, 1953); an oratorio, *Job* (1933); *Collectionneur d'échos,* for soprano, bass, and 9 percussion instruments (1933); a string quartet (1937); a sonata for bassoon and piano (1941), 2 piano sonatas (1926 and 1940); piano concerto (1932); flute concerto (1948); a group of piano pieces; songs. He publ. an entertaining volume of reminiscences and essays, *Old Friends and New Music* (Boston, 1951); contributed numerous articles to various magazines in Europe and America.

Nachbaur, Franz, German tenor; b. Giessen, near Friedrichshafen, March 25, 1830; d. Munich, March 21, 1902. He studied in Stuttgart and was a pupil of Pischek there; sang as a chorister at Basel, then in opera at Mannheim, Hanover, Prague, Vienna, and other musical centers. In 1866 he joined the roster of the Munich Opera, and remained there until his retirement in 1890. He was the first to sing the part of Walther in *Die Meistersinger* (1868); sang Lohengrin in Rome (1878); appeared in London with a German opera company (1882).

Nachez (năh'-chĕz), **Tivadar (Theodor Naschitz)**, Hungarian violinist; b. Budapest, May 1, 1859; d. Lausanne, May 29, 1930. He studied in Berlin with Joachim, and in Paris with Léonard. After a series of transcontinental tours in Europe, he settled in London in 1889; in 1916 went to live at Santa Barbara, Calif.; then returned to London, and presented his farewell concert there in 1926. He wrote a number of violin pieces derived from Hungarian folksongs; also a string quartet, and 2 concertos (publ. 1895; 1908); edited 2 violin concertos of Vivaldi (1913).

Nadel, Arno, composer and writer; b. Vilna, Oct. 3, 1878; d. in a concentration camp in Germany, c. 1945. He studied in Königsberg with Birnbaum and Schwalm; 1895-1900, at the Jewish Seminary in Berlin with Loewengard and L. Mendelssohn; music critic of 'Vossische Zeitung,' 'Freiheit,' and 'Vorwärts,' Berlin; from 1916 choral conductor of the Jewish community there; arranged Jewish folksongs and synagogue services. —He publ.: *Jontefflieder* (10 vols., 1919); *Jüdische Volkslieder,* in 2 vols.; *Der Ton* (Leipzig, 1921; new ed., 1926); and an essay on Jewish music in the vol. *Juderna* of the 'Nationernas Bibliothek' (1920). Composed chamber music, songs, etc.

Nadermann, François Joseph, French harp virtuoso and composer; b. Paris, 1773; d. there, April 2, 1835. He was a pupil of Krumpholtz; from 1816 member of the Royal Chapel; from 1825 prof. at the Cons., also joining his brother **Henri** (b. 1780) in managing the harp-making business founded by their father. —He composed 2 harp concertos and much chamber music for harp with various instruments; also sonatas and pieces for solo harp.

Nagel, Wilibald, German musicologist; b. Mülheim-on-Ruhr, Jan. 12, 1863; d. Stuttgart, Oct. 17, 1929. He was a pupil of Ehrlich, Spitta, Bellermann, etc., in Berlin. He established himself as instructor at the Univ. of Zürich; lived 1893-96 in London, studying early English music; in 1898 he settled in Darmstadt as lecturer on musical science at the Technical Academy; conducted the Academy Singing Society; 1917, prof. at the Stuttgart Musikhochschule; 1917-21, editor of the 'Neue Musikzeitung'; was also a concert pianist. —Works: *Geschichte der Musik in England* (2 vols., 1894, 1897; down to Purcell's death); *Annalen der englischen Hofmusik, 1509-1649* (1894); *Geschichte der Musik am Darmstädter Hof, 1570-1800* (1901); *Beethoven and seine Klaviersonaten* (2 vols., 1903, 1905; 2nd ed., 1923, 1924); *Studien zur Geschichte der Meistersänger* (1909); *Christoph Graupner als Sinfoniker* (1912); *Die Klaviersonaten von Brahms* (1915); *Wilhelm Mauke* (1919); *Johannes Brahms* (1924). He revised and edited the 6th ed. of Köstlin's *Geschichte der Musik im Umriss* (1910).

Nägeli, Johann (Hans) Georg, Swiss publisher, writer, and composer; b. Wetzikon, near Zürich, May 26, 1773; d. there, Dec. 26, 1836. He was a music publisher at Wetzikon (established 1792); founder and president of the Swiss Association for the Cultivation of Music; singing teacher at a primary school, applying the Pestalozzian system. As a song composer he is best known by *Freut euch des Lebens* (Life let us cherish). He wrote *Gesangsbildungslehre nach Pestalozzischen Grundsätzen* (with M. Pfeiffer; 1810; popular ed., 1811); *Christliches Gesangbuch* (1828); *Vorlesungen über Musik mit Berücksichtigung der Dilettanten* (1826); *Musikalisches Tabellwerk für Volksschulen zur Herausbildung für den Figuralgesang* (1828); a polemical pamphlet against Thibaut (q.v.); *Der Streit zwischen der alten und der neuen Musik* (1826); etc. Nägeli publ. (from 1803) a periodical, 'Répertoire des clavecinistes,' in which he brought out piano pieces by contemporary composers, including the first publication of Beethoven's sonatas, op. 31. With Beethoven he was on intimate terms despite disagreements. —Biographical sketches of Nägeli were written by Ott (1838), Bierer (1844), Keller (1848), and Schneebeli (1873). —Cf. H. Kling, *Beethoven et ses relations avec Nägeli* (1912); R. Hunziker, *H. G. Nägeli* (Zürich, 1938); A. E. Cherbuliez, *Der unbekannte Nägeli* (Chur, 1938); I. I. Hassan, *Die Welt- und Kunstanschauung Hans Georg Nägelis* (Zürich, 1947). Willi Reich ed. a collection of Nägeli's articles under the title, *Von Bach zu Beethoven* (Basel, 1945).

Naginski, Charles, composer; b. Cairo, Egypt, May 29, 1909; d. by drowning, Lenox, Mass., Aug. 4, 1940. He was brought to America at an early age; studied piano with his father and other teachers; 1928-33 held a fellowship at the Juilliard Graduate School as pupil in composition of Rubin Goldmark. Won the American Prix de Rome in 1938. — Works: for orch.: suite (1931), 2 symphs. (1935; 1937), *1936,* orchestral poem (1936), sinfonietta (1937), *3 Movements,* for chamber orch. (1937), *The Minotaur,* ballet for orch. (1938), *Nocturne and Pantomime* (1938), *5 Pieces from a Children's Suite* (Boston, 1940), *Movement,* for strings; 2 string quartets (1933); songs.

Nancarrow, Conlon, American composer; b. Texarkana, Ark., Oct. 27, 1912; studied trumpet and played in jazz orchestras; took courses at Cincinnati Cons.; then in Boston with Nicolas Slonimsky and Walter Piston. In 1937 he joined the Abraham Lincoln Brigade, during the Spanish Civil War; returned to the U. S. in 1939; in 1940 settled in Mexico City. In his music he is preoccupied mainly with problems of rhythm and sonority; in order to make possible faithful execution, he composes music by perforating player-piano rolls according to notes and rhythms; such pieces are not playable except on player-pianos. Some of his piano works are publ. by the 'New Music Quarterly.'

Nanino (Nanini), Giovanni Bernardino, Italian composer, brother and pupil of Giovanni Maria Nanino; b. Vallerano, c. 1550; d. Rome, 1623. From 1591 he was maestro di cappella at San Luigi de' Francesi; later at San Lorenzo in Damaso. Proske printed 4 Psalms *a* 4 in 'Musica divina.' —Nanino publ. 3 books of madrigals *a* 5 (1588-1612); 4 books of motets *a* 1-5, with organ (1608-18); Psalms *a* 4 and 8 (1620); and a *Venite exultemus* a 3, with organ (1620). Many other works are in manuscript.

Nanino (Nanini), Giovanni Maria, Italian composer; b. Tivoli, c. 1545; d. Rome, March 11, 1607. He was a pupil of Palestrina; after completing his studies, he officiated in Vallerano as maestro di cappella; but on Palestrina's resignation as maestro at Santa Maria Maggiore, Rome, he was called there in 1571. Resigning in 1575, he founded the first public school of music opened in Rome by an Italian, in which his brother, Giovanni Bernardino, and Palestrina were active instructors. Nanino's compositions were performed at the Sistine Chapel; in 1577 he became a member of the papal choir, and, in 1604, maestro di cappella of the Sistine Chapel. His works are among the best of the Palestrina epoch; the 6-part motet *Hodie nobis coelorum rex* is still sung annually on Christmas morning in the Sistine Chapel. Haberl publ. a sketch of Nanino in the 'Kirchenmusikalisches Jahrbuch' for 1891, with 5 hitherto unpubl. Lamentations *a* 4. Other printed works are motets *a* 3-5 in canon form with cantus firmus (1586); 4 books of madrigals *a* 5 (1578-86); canzonets *a* 3 (1587-99); psalms in Constantini's 'Psalmi a 8 voci'; other motets and madrigals in collections of the time. 3 motets *a* 3, one *a* 4, and a Miserere are in Proske's 'Musica divina'; 4 pieces in L. Torchi 'L'Arte musicale in Italia' (vol. 2); detached numbers in the collections of Rochlitz, Tucher, Lück. An admirable work in MS is the *Cento cinquanta sette contrappunti e canoni a 2-11 voci, sopra del canto fermo, intitolata la base di Costanzo Festa;* also a *Trattato di contrappunto.* —Cf. G.

Radiciotti, *Giovanni Maria Nanino, musicista tiburtino . . . Vita ed opere* (Pesaro, 1909); G. Reese, *Music in the Renaissance* (N. Y., 1954; pp. 424 f., 482 f.).

Napier, William, British music publisher; b. 1740; d. London, 1812. He was a violinist in the Chapel Royal; established a music-publishing business; Haydn arranged 2 books of Scottish songs for him, with accompaniment for piano, violin, and cello (1792). — Cf. F. Kidson, *British Music-publishers* (1900).

Napoli, Gennaro, Italian composer; b. Naples, May 19, 1881; d. there, June 26, 1943. He was a pupil of d'Arienzo and de Nardis at the Royal Cons. in Naples; 1906, won the 'Pensionato nazionale per la musica'; 1912, teacher of composition at the Liceo Musicale, Naples; 1915, at the Royal Cons.; 1926, assistant director; editor of 'L'Arte pianistica.' —Works: the opera *Jacopo Ortis;* the dramatic scene *Armida abbandonata* (1906); *In montagna,* orchestral suite (1906); symph. in D minor; *Il Sole risorto,* for soli, chorus, and orch. (1909); piano pieces, songs, etc. Author of *Bassi imitati e fugati* (1915).

Napoli, Jacopo, Italian composer; son of Gennaro Napoli; b. Naples, Aug. 26, 1911. He studied at the Cons. San Pietro a Maiella, Naples, with his father and S. Cesi; subsequently appointed to the faculty, and eventually became director. He specialized in opera, often with a Neapolitan background, which gave him the opportunity to use Neapolitan songs in his scores. The list of his operas includes: *Il Malato immaginario* (Naples, 1939); *Miseria e nobilità* (Naples, 1945); *Il Tesoro* (1948); *Un curioso accidente* (Bergamo, 1950); *Masaniello* (1951; won a prize of La Scala, Milan); *I Peccatori* (1954).

Napravnik, Eduard, celebrated Russian conductor of Czech origin; b. Býšt, near Hradec Králové, Bohemia, Aug. 24, 1839; d. St. Petersburg (Petrograd), Nov. 23, 1916. He studied music at home, and at Prague; also took lessons with J. B. Kittl. In 1861 he was engaged by the Russian nobleman Yussupov to lead his private orch. in St. Petersburg; in 1863 he became a répétiteur at the Imperial Opera; 2nd conductor in 1867, and chief conductor in 1869. He held this post for 47 years, until his death, and became greatly renowned as a thorough musician, possessing a fabulous sense of pitch and rhythm, and exceptional ability as a disciplinarian. His reputation and influence were very great in Russian operatic affairs; Dostoyevsky in one of his novels uses Napravnik's name as a synonym for a guiding spirit. Napravnik conducted the première of *Boris Godunov* and of many other Russian operas; his interpretations of the Russian repertory established a standard emulated by other Russian conductors; yet he was deficient in emotional inspiration; his performances of symphonic works were regarded as competent but not profound. He was himself a composer of several operas, in the Russian style, imitative of Tchaikovsky; one of them, *Dubrovsky* (St. Petersburg, Jan. 15, 1895), has become part of the active repertory in Russia. Other operas were: *Nizhegorotzy* (St. Petersburg, Jan. 8, 1869); *Harold* (St. Petersburg, Nov. 23, 1886); *Francesca da Rimini* (St. Petersburg, Dec. 9, 1902). He also wrote 4 symphonies, some chamber music, piano pieces, etc. — Cf. P. Weymarn, *E. Napravnik* (St. Petersburg, 1881); N. Findeisen, *E. Napravnik* (St. Petersburg, 1898).

Nardini, Pietro, Italian violinist; b. Leghorn, April 12, 1722; d. Florence, May 7, 1793. He was a pupil of Tartini at Padua; from 1753-67, solo violinist in the court orch., Stuttgart; lived with Tartini until the latter's death in 1770; then maestro of the court music at Florence. Both Leopold Mozart and Schobert praised his playing. Among his works are 6 violin concertos; 6 sonatas for violin and bass; 6 violin solos; 6 violin duets; 6 string quartets; 6 flute trios. Sonatas are in Alard's 'Les Maîtres classiques' and David's 'Hohe Schule des Violinspiels'; others in Jensen's 'Klassische Violinmusik'; also numerous new eds. —Cf. A. Moser, *Geschichte des Violinspiels* (p. 269 ff.); C. Pfäfflin, *Pietro Nardini* (Stuttgart, 1935; with a thematic catalogue of works).

Nares, James, English composer and organist; b. Stanwell, Middlesex, 1715 (baptized April 19); d. London, Feb. 10, 1783. He was a chorister in the Chapel Royal under Gates; also studied with Pepusch. Deputy organist of St. George's Chapel, Windsor; organist of York Cathedral, 1734; in 1756 he succeeded Greene as organist and composer to the Chapel Royal; Mus. Doc., Cambridge, 1757; Master of the Children at the Chapel Royal, 1757-80. He publ. a dramatic ode, *The Royal Pastoral;* a collection of catches, canons, and glees (1772); methods for harpsichord, organ, and singing; etc. Detached pieces are in Arnold's 'Cathedral Music,' Page's 'Harmonia Sacra,' and Stevens' 'Sacred Music.' —Cf. 'Dictionary of National Biography,' XL.

Narvaez (nahr-văh'-eth), **Luis de,** Spanish guitar virtuoso of the 16th century. He was a native of Granada; chamber musician to Philip II. He publ. *Los seys libros del Delphin de música de cifra para tañer vihuela* (Vallodolid, 1538; in tablature), containing the earliest examples of variation form publ. in Spain; reprinted in modern notation by E. Pujol in 'Monumentos de la Música Española' (vol. 3, Barcelona, 1945); some selections in Morphy's 'Les Luthistes espagnols du XVIe siècle' (Leipzig, 1902); one in A. T. Davison and W. Apel, 'Historical Anthology of Music' (vol. 1, Cambridge, Mass., 1946). See E. M. Torner, 'Collección de Vihuelistas españoles del siglo XVI' (Madrid, 1924) and J. B. Trend, *Luis Milán and the Vihuelistas* (1925).

Nat, Yves, French pianist; b. Béziers, Dec. 29, 1890; d. Paris, Sept. 1, 1956. He studied at the Paris Cons. with Diémer; appointed prof. of piano there in 1934. He gave numerous recitals in France, where his reputation was very high; made an American tour as accompanist in 1911 and in 1914 (with Luisa Tetrazzini); taught at Texas Women's College, Forth Worth (1914-15).

Nathan, Isaac, English composer; b. Canterbury, 1792; d. Sydney, Australia, Jan. 15, 1864. He studied under D. Corri. — Works: music to the comedy *Sweethearts and Wives* (1823, very popular); an opera, *The Alcaid* (1824); an operetta, *The Illustrious Stranger* (1827); *Hebrew Melodies* (Byron), with Braham (1822, 1861); songs; *Musurgia Vocalis, an essay on the History and Theory of Music, and on the Qualities, Capabilities, and Management of the Human Voice* (1823; 2nd ed., 1836); *Memoirs of Madame Malibran de Bériot* (1836). —Cf. 'Dictionary of National Biography,' XL.

Natorp, Bernhard Christoph Ludwig, German pedagogue; b. Werden-on-Ruhr, Nov. 12, 1774; d. Münster, Feb. 8, 1846. He studied theology and pedagogics at Halle Univ.; pastor at Essen, 1798; counsellor of the Consistory at Potsdam, 1808; general superintendent at Münster, 1819. — He publ. *Anleitung zur Unterweisung im Singen für Lehrer in Volksschulen* (2 courses, 1813, 1820; often republ.); *Lehrbüchlein der Singekunst* (2 courses, 1816, 1820); *Über den Gesang in den Kirchen der Protestanten* (1817); *Über den Zweck, die Einrichtung und den Gebrauch des Melodienbuchs für den Gemeindegesang in den evangelischen Kirchen* (1822), followed by the *Melodienbuch* (1822); *Choralbuch für evangelische Kirchen* (1829; harmonized in 4 parts with preludes and interludes by Rinck; 4th ed., 1885); and *Über Rincks Präludien* (1834). —Cf. H. Knab, *B. C. L. Natorp* (Kassel, 1933).

Nau, Maria Dolores Benedicta Josefina, operatic soprano; b. New York (of Spanish parentage), March 18, 1818; d. Levallois, near Paris, Jan., 1891. She was a pupil of Cinti-Damoreau at the Paris Cons.; from 1836-42 sang minor parts at the Paris Opéra, then appeared in Brussels and London; from 1844 she sang again at the Opéra, in leading roles; 1849-50 in London; 1850 and 1854-56 in the U. S.; she returned to Paris in 1856 and retired from the stage.

Naudin (noh-dăn'), **Emilio,** tenor, b. (of French parentage) Parma, Oct. 23, 1823; d. Boulogne-sur-Mer, May 5, 1890. He was a pupil of Panizza in Milan; début at Cremona, c. 1845; appeared in Vienna, St. Petersburg, London, Madrid, and Paris (from 1862 at the Théâtre Italien). He created the role of Vasco da Gama in *L'Africaine* (in accordance with a stipulation in Meyerbeer's will); retired in 1879.

Naujalis (now-yah'-lĭs), **Juozas,** Lithuanian composer; b. Raudondvaris, near Kaunas, 1869; d. Kaunas, Sept. 10, 1934. He studied at the Warsaw Musical Institute (graduated 1889); organist in various Lithuanian towns; 1894, studied theology at the Kirchenmusikalische Hochschule at Regensburg; thereafter cathedral organist and lecturer at the theological seminary in Kaunas, where he founded a Lithuanian chorus; 1919, director of the Music School, later of the State Musical Institute. His compositions include Masses, a Lithuanian Church Hymn; also piano and organ works; etc. He edited a collection of contemporary organ masters (6 vols.).

Naumann (now'-man), **Emil,** German composer and writer, grandson of Johann Gottlieb Naumann; b. Berlin, Sept. 8, 1827; d. Dresden, June 23, 1888. He was a pupil of Schnyder von Wartensee at Frankfurt; of Mendelssohn, 1842; studied at the Leipzig Cons., 1843-4; then attended Bonn Univ. In 1848 his oratorio *Christus der Friedensbote* was produced at Dresden; also the opera *Judith.* In 1856 his treatise on *Die Einführung des Psalmengesanges in die evangelische Kirche* procured his appointment as music director in the court church, Berlin, for which he composed motets, psalms, etc., publishing *Psalmen auf alle Sonn- und Feiertage des evangelischen Kirchenjahres* (vols. VIII-X of Commer's 'Musica sacra'). The Univ. of Berlin conferred on him the title of *Dr. phil.* for *Das Alter des Psalmengesangs;* his master work is *Die Tonkunst in ihren Beziehungen zu den Formen und Entwickelungsgesetzen alles Geisteslebens* (2 vols.; 1869, 1870). He went to Dresden in 1873, and lectured on musical history at the Cons.—Other writings: *Deutsche Tondichter, von Sebastian Bach bis auf die Gegenwart* (1871; often republ.); *Italienische Tondichter, von Palestrina bis auf die Gegenwart* (1876; 2nd ed., 1883); *Illustrierte Musikgeschichte* (2 vols., 1883-85; English transl. by F. Praeger, 1886; new German ed., brought up to date, by E. Schmitz, 1908, often republ.; 2nd revised ed. in German by A. Loeven, as *Allgemeine Musikgeschichte,* 1927); *Musikdrama oder Oper?* (1876; *contra* Wagner); *Zukunftsmusik und die Musik der Zukunft* (1877); etc.

Naumann, Johann Gottlieb, German composer, b. Blasewitz, near Dresden, April 17, 1741; d. Dresden, Oct. 23, 1801. Intended for a school teacher, he was trained in the Dresden Kreuzschule, where he learned singing. In 1757 a Swedish musician named Weeström took him to Italy. He received lessons from Tartini in Padua, and in 1761 he went to Rome and Naples with the violinist Pitscher to study dramatic composition; studied counterpoint later with Padre Martini at Bologna; brought out his first opera, *Il Tesoro insidiato,* in 1763 at the San Samuele Theater, Venice; and returned to Dresden in 1763, receiving next year the appointment of court composer of sacred music, and of 'chamber composer' in 1765. On a second Italian tour he brought out several operas; then, after refusing an offer from Frederick the Great, he was appointed Kapellmeister at Dresden (1776). In 1777 he was also invited to Stockholm to reorganize the orch., and brought out operas then and in 1780. In all he produced 24 operas; also a ballet, 11 oratorios, 21 Masses, cantatas and other sacred music (including the fine *Vater unser,* after Klopstock); an elegy, *Klopstocks Grab;* 18 symphonies; sonatas for piano, violin, and harmonica; songs (complete ed. by Breitkopf & Härtel); etc. H. F. Mannstein publ. a catalogue of Naumann's compositions. —Cf. A. G. Meissner, *Bruchstücke zur Biographie J. G. Naumanns* (2 vols.; Prague, 1803-4; 2nd ed., Vienna, 1814); *Des sächsischen Kapellmeisters Naumann's Leben* (Dresden, 1841); G. Schweizer, *Biographie von Johann Gottlieb Naumann* (3 vols.; Zürich, 1843-45); M. J. Nestler, *Der kursächsische Kapellmeister Naumann aus Blasewitz* (Dresden, 1901); R. Engländer, *Johann Gottlieb Naumann als Opernkomponist* (Leipzig, 1922); T. Norlind, in 'Svensk Tidskrift for Musikforskning' V, 1 (1923).

Naumann, Karl Ernst, German organist and music editor, grandson of Johann Gottlieb Naumann; b. Freiberg, Saxony, Aug. 15, 1832; d. Jena, Dec. 15, 1910. He studied in Leipzig (1850) under Hauptmann, Richter, Wenzel, and Langer; took the degree of *Dr. phil.* at the Univ. in 1858 for his dissertation *Über die verschiedenen Bestimmungen der Tonverhältnisse und die Bedeutung des pythagoreischen oder reinen Quinten-Systemes für unsere heutige Musik;* studied for 2 years in Dresden under Johann Schneider (organ), soon afterward being called to Jena as music director and organist; prof. in 1877; retired in 1906. Composed chiefly chamber music; publ. many valuable revisions and arrangements of classical works, especially for the Bach-Gesellschaft.

Nauwach, Johann, German composer; b. Brandenburg, about 1595; d. about 1630. He was a chamber musician at the Electoral court of Saxony in Torgau; from 1612-18 he studied in Florence and Turin; he was one of the first German followers of Caccini. He publ. *Libro primo di arie passeggiate a una voce per cantar e sonar nel chitarrone* (Dresden, 1623), and *Erster Theil teutscher Villanellen mit 1, 2, und 3 Stimmen auf der Tiorba* (Dresden, 1627). —Cf. 'Sammelbände der Internationalen Musik-Gesellschaft,' XII (article by A. Einstein); H. Kretzschmar, *Geschichte des neuen deutschen Liedes,* I (1912); also H. Volkmann, in 'Zeitschrift für Musikwissenschaft,' IV (1922; biographical).

Nava (nah'-văh), **Gaetano,** Italian singing master; b. Milan, May 16, 1802; d. there, March 31, 1875. He was taught by his father (Antonio Maria Nava, 1775-1826), and Pollini; then at Milan Cons. 1817-24 by Orlandi, Ray, Piantanida, and Frederici. From 1837 prof. of solfeggio at the Cons. and of choral singing from 1848. Wrote a great number of excellent solfeggi and vocalises; also a *Metodo pratico di vocalizzazione.*

Navarro, Juan, Spanish composer; b. Marchena, c. 1530; d. Palencia, Sept. 25, 1580. He was perhaps a pupil of Fernández de Castilleja in Seville; in 1554 applied unsuccessfully for the post of maestro de capilla at Málaga (F. Guerrero was the successful candidate); 1567-70, maestro at the Cathedral of Salamanca; 1570-78, at the Cathedral of Ciudad Rodrigo, and then at the Cathedral in Palencia. Navarro's *Psalmi, Hymni ac Magnificat totius anni . . . 4, 5 ac 6 v.* were publ. at Rome, 1591. A book, *Liber in quo 4 Passiones Christi Domini continentur . . . 8 Lamentationes: Oratioque Hieremiae Prophetae,* is by another Juan Navarro, a Franciscan monk born in Cádiz and serving in Mexico. —Extant MSS: *Antifona a San Sebastian* (in Málaga), part of a Magnificat (in Seville), 8 pieces (in Toledo), *Recuerde el alma dormida,* madrigal *a* 5 (in the Valencia 'Collección del Patriarca'); madrigals: 7 for 4 voices, 1 for 5 voices (Biblioteca Medinaceli and Biblioteca Nacional, Madrid). The madrigal *Ay de mí, sin ventura,* was printed by Pedrell in 'Cancionero Musical Popular Español' III: Eslava printed 3 Magnificats and 2 psalms; several motets are in the 'Antología Musical' ed. by Elústiza and Castrillo Hernández (Barcelona, 1933; with biography). —Cf. G. Chase, *Juan Navarro Hispalensis and Juan Navarro Gaditanus* in the 'Mus. Quarterly' (April, 1945).

Navas, Juan, important Spanish composer of the 2nd half of the 17th century; wrote numerous secular works, including some interesting *Pasacalles* with guitar accompaniment; also some sacred music. —Cf. F. Pedrell, *Teatro lírico español anterior al siglo XIX,* vols. III and IV (1897).

Navrátil, Karl, Czech composer; b. Prague, April 24, 1867; d. there, Dec. 23, 1936. He was a pupil of Ondříček (violin) and G. Adler (theory); lived in Prague. — Works: the lyric drama *Hermann;* opera, *Salammbô;* the symphonic poems *Der weisse Berg, Lipany, Jan Hus, Žižka,* and *Žalco;* a symph.; a violin concerto; 2 piano concertos; sonata for violin; sonata for viola; men's choruses; songs. — He wrote a biography of Smetana, essays on Hugo Wolf, etc.

Naylor, Edward Woodall, English organist and composer, son of John Naylor; b. Scarborough, Feb. 9, 1867; d. Cambridge, May 7, 1934. He was a pupil of his father, and from 1888-92, of the Royal College of Music; Mus. Doc., Cambridge, 1897; organist at St. Mary's, Kilburn, 1896-8; from 1908, organist at Emanuel College, Cambridge. — Works: An opera, *The Angelus* (London, Jan. 27, 1909; won the Ricordi prize); men's choruses; sacred music; overture, *Tokugawa,* for orch. (Tokyo, 1919); chamber music; etc. Author of *Shakespeare and Music* (London, 1896), *An Elizabethan Virginal Book* (London, 1905), *The Poets and Music* (London, 1928).

Naylor, John, English composer; b. Stanningley, near Leeds, June 8, 1838; d. at sea, May 14, 1897. He was a choirboy at Leeds Parish Church; Mus. Doc., Cambridge, 1872; organist of various churches in England; 1883, organist and choirmaster of York Minster, and also (1892) conductor of York Musical Society. — Works: 4 cantatas: *Jeremiah, The Brazen Serpent, Meribah,* and *Manna;* church services, anthems, hymns, part-songs, organ pieces, and a well-known book of chants.

Neal, Heinrich, composer, son of the American painter David Neal; b. Munich, Sept. 8, 1870; d. Heidelberg, June 9, 1940. He was a pupil of Rheinberger in Munich and Draeseke in Dresden. In 1894 he was co-founder of a cons. in Heidelberg, where he taught until 1920; afterwards he taught privately. — His works are mostly for piano: 24 Études in all keys as an introduction to modern music, op. 75; other études (op. 80, 81); Studies for polyphonic playing, op. 90; several German Rhapsodies; *Kinderouvertüre* for 2 pianos, 8 hands, op. 36; etc.

Neate, Charles, English musician; b. London, March 28, 1784; d. Brighton, March 30, 1877. He was a pupil of W. Sharp (cello), John Field (piano), and Wölfl (composition); appeared with great success as a pianist in 1800 at London; in 1815 he spent 8 months in Vienna, making the acquaintance of Beethoven and profiting from the master's advice; then spent 5 months in Munich, where he took a course in counterpoint with Winter. He was one of the founders of the London Philharmonic Society (1813), and frequently appeared at its concerts as performer and conductor. He publ. 2 piano sonatas (C minor and D minor); a quintet for piano, woodwind, and double-bass; 2 piano trios; a fantasia for cello and piano; also *An Essay on Fingering* (1855).

Nebra, José de, Spanish composer; b. c. 1688; d. Madrid, July 11, 1768. He was organist at the Convent of the Descalzas Reales in Madrid; was appointed 2nd organist to the Royal Chapel in 1724, and music director there in 1739. Together with Literes (q.v.) he was engaged to reconstruct and compose new music when the archives of the Royal Chapel were destroyed in the fire of 1734. He was a prolific composer; wrote about 20 operas, a great deal of sacred music. His Requiem for Queen Barbara (1758) is reproduced in Eslava's 'Lira Sacro-Hispana.' —Cf. M. Soriano-Fuertes, *Historia de la música española,* IV (Madrid, 1859); E. Cotarelo y Mori, *Historia de la Zarzuela,* chap. III (Madrid, 1934).

Necil Kazim, Akses. See **Akses.**

Nedbal, Karel, Czech conductor and composer, nephew of Oskar Nedbal; b. Dvur Králové, near Prague, Oct. 28, 1888. He studied with Novák in Prague and Foerster in Vienna; conductor at the theater of Moravska-Ostrava, then of the Vinohrady Choral Society in Prague, and in 1914 of the Vinohrady Theater (with Ostrčil); 1921-28, opera director at Olomouc; 1928-38, at Bratislava; 1938-40, at Brno; from 1940 in Prague as radio and opera conductor.

Nedbal, Oskar, Czech composer and conductor; b. Tábor, Bohemia, March 26, 1874; d. (suicide) Zagreb, Dec. 24, 1930. He was a pupil of Bennewitz (violin), Knittl and Stecker (theory), and Dvořák (composition) at the Prague Cons., where he graduated in 1892. From 1891 to 1906 he played viola in the famous Bohemian String Quartet (Karl Hoffmann, Josef Suk, Nedbal, Hans Wihan); 1896-1906 also conducted concerts of Bohemian music in Prague and Vienna; 1906-19, conductor of the 'Tonkünstler-Orch.' in Vienna; also of the 'Volksoper' there for a time; from 1919, guest conductor in Czechoslovakia, Austria, and Yugoslavia. —Works: the ballets *Der faule Hans* (1902), *Grossmütterchens Märchenschätze* (1908), *Prinzessin Hyazintha* (1911), *Des Teufels Grossmutter* (1912), *Andersen* (1914); the operettas *Die keusche Barbara* (Prague, 1910), *Polenblut* (Vienna, Oct. 25, 1913; successfully revived, Oct. 10, 1954); *Die Winzerbraut* (Vienna, Feb. 11, 1916), *Die schöne Saskia* (Vienna, Nov. 16, 1917), and *Eriwan* (Vienna, Nov. 29, 1918); an opera, *Sedlák Jakub* (*Farmer James;* Brno, Oct. 13, 1922); also instrumental works. —Cf. J. Květ, *In memoriam Oskar Nedbal* (Bratislava, 1931).

Neefe (nā'-fĕ), **Christian Gottlob,** German composer and conductor; b. Chemnitz, Feb. 5, 1748; d. Dessau, Jan. 26, 1798. While a law student in Leipzig, he had music lessons with A. Hiller; was conductor at Leipzig and Dresden, then of Seyler's traveling opera troupe, and (1779) of the Grossmann-Hellmuth company at Bonn, where he was appointed deputy organist and succeeded van den Eeden as Electoral music director in 1782, also as Beethoven's teacher. In 1796 he became conductor of the Dessau opera. —Works: 8 vaudevilles and operas for Leipzig and Bonn; Klopstock's ode *Dem Unendlichen,* for 4 voices and orch.; double concerto for violin, piano, and orch.; sonatas, variations, and fantasias for piano; songs; etc. —Cf. Irmgard Leux, *Christian Gottlob Neefe* (Leipzig, 1925); L. Schiedermair, in *Der junge Beethoven* (1925); H. Abert, in *W. A. Mozart* (vol. I, p. 925 ff.); I. Leux, in 'Zeitschrift für Musikwissenschaft,' VII. A. Einstein republ. Neefe's autobiography (originally publ. in 'Allgemeine musikalische Zeitung,' I).

Neel, Boyd, English conductor; b. Blackheath, Kent, July 19, 1905. He was educated at Cambridge Univ., studying medicine; he served as an intern at a London hospital, and did some social work, at the same time studying music. In 1933 he organized the Boyd Neel String Orch., with a contingent of music students; he made a signal success of this venture; gave a concert of English music with his group at the Salzburg Festival in 1937. His musical activity was suspended during World War II, but after 1945 he reassembled the orch. and developed an extensive schedule of concerts in England; then made a tour of Australia. He also conducted operas and ballets with the Sadler's Wells Opera; published a book, *The Story of an Orchestra* (London, 1950). Since 1953, dean of the Royal Cons. of Music in Toronto, Canada. —Cf. Donald Brook, *International Gallery of Conductors* (London, 1951; pp. 125-28).

Nef (nĕhf), **Albert,** brother of Karl Nef; Swiss conductor and composer; b. St. Gall, Oct. 30, 1882. He studied at the Leipzig Cons. and with Kretzschmar in Berlin (*Dr. phil.,* 1906); from 1907 opera conductor in Lübeck, Neustrelitz, and Rostock; since 1912 in Bern, also conductor of the Orchestral Society since 1922; from 1920 president of the Swiss Stage Artists Alliance. Author of *Das Lied in der deutschen Schweiz im letzten Drittel des 18. und am Anfang des 19. Jahrhunderts* (1909); also *50 Jahre Berner Theater* . . . (Bern, 1956; includes opera). He composed a singspiel, *Graf Strapinski* (Bern, 1928); *Appenzeller Tänze* for orch.

(1926); *Wanderschaft,* song cycle for tenor, mixed chorus, and orch. (Bern, 1924); choruses; piano pieces; songs.

Nef, Karl, Swiss musicologist; b. St. Gall, Aug. 22, 1873; d. Basel, Feb. 9, 1935. He entered the Leipzig Cons. in 1891, studying with Reckendorf (piano), Julius Klengel (cello), and Jadassohn (theory); attended the lectures on musicology by Kretzschmar at the Univ., and in 1896 became *Dr. phil.* with his dissertation *Die Collegia musica in der deutschen reformierten Schweiz* (publ. St. Gall, 1897). He settled in Basel in 1897; 1898-1909, editor of 'Schweizerische Musikzeitung'; 1900, Privatdozent for musicology at the Univ.; 1909, associate prof.; 1923, prof. — Publications: *Ferdinand Fürchtegott Huber* (1898); *Zur Geschichte der deutschen Instrumentalmusik in der zweiten Hälfte des 17. Jahrhunderts* (1902; in 'Beihefte der Internationalen Musik-Gesellschaft,' No. 5); *Die Musik im Kanton St. Gallen, 1803-1903* (1903); *Katalog der Musikinstrumente im historischen Museum zu Basel* (1906); *Schriften über Musik und Volksgesang* (1908, bibliography of books and essays by Swiss writers); *Einführung in die Musikgeschichte* (1920; 3rd ed., 1945; in French 1925, 2nd ed. 1931; in English as *Outline of the History of Music,* N. Y., 1935); *Geschichte der Sinfonie und Suite* (1921); *Geschichte unserer Musikinstrumente* (1926; new ed., 1949); *Die 9 Sinfonien Beethovens* (1928); *Aufsätze* (posthumous; Basel, 1936). Also edited J. Rosenmüller's *Kammersonaten* (vol. 18 of 'Denkmäler deutscher Tonkunst') and 'Sammlung musikwissenschaftlicher Abhandlungen' (Strasbourg). A dedicatory vol., *Karl Nef zum 60. Geburtstag,* was publ. at Basel in 1933.

Neff, Fritz, German composer, b. Durlach, Baden, Nov. 20, 1873; d. Munich, Oct. 3, 1904. He was a pupil of Thuille and Mottl in Karlsruhe; a composer of great promise unfulfilled.—Publ. choral works: *Ein schön teutsch Reiterlied, Chor der Toten, Schmied Schmerz, Die Weihe der Nacht;* songs (*Die Polenschänke,* etc.).

Neidhardt (Nithart) von Reuenthal, famous Minnesänger of the 12th-13th centuries; probably the earliest German composer whose songs are extant. These are found in MSS of the late 14th century, also in 15th-century sources (a complete list of sources is given in Hagen's *Minnesinger,* vol. 4; 1838). —Cf. Fr. M. Böhme, *Geschichte des Tanzes* (1888); Erk-Böhme, *Deutscher Liederhort* (1893-94); H. Rietsch, *Die deutsche Liedweise* (1904); H. J. Moser, *Geschichte der deutschen Musik,* I (1926); Johannes Wolf, *Musikalische Schrifttafeln* (1927; contains one song in facsimile). The following collections contain songs in modern notation: H. Riemann, *10 Mailieder und Winterklagen* (1897); M. Friedlaender, *Volksliederbuch für gemischten Chor* (1915); B. Paumgartner, *Das Taghorn* (1922); K. Ameln and W. Rössle, *Tanzlieder Neidhardts von Reuenthal* (1927). A new ed. of all the songs, with fascsimile reproductions and transcriptions in modern notation, was publ. by Wolfgang Schmieder in 'Denkmäler der Tonkunst in Österreich' XXXVII, 1 (vol. 71).

Neidlinger, William Harold, American composer, b. Brooklyn, July 20, 1863; d. East Orange, N. J., Dec. 5, 1924. He was a pupil of Dudley Buck and C. C. Müller in New York (1880-90, composition and orchestration), and of E. Dannreuther in London (1896-8). Until 1896 he was an organist in Brooklyn; conductor of the 'Amphion Male Chorus' and 'Cecilia Women's Chorus' in Brooklyn, and the 'Treble Clef Club' and 'Mannheim Glee Club' in Philadelphia; then lived in London and Paris as singing teacher until 1901; returning to the U. S., he settled in Chicago, where for several years he was one of the most prominent singing teachers. The remarkable success of *Small Songs for Small Singers* (1896), which became a standard work for kindergartens, turned his special attention to that line of composition and to the study of child psychology; the latter pursuit gradually absorbed his interest to such an extent that he practically abandoned music, and established a school for sub-normal children in East Orange, N. J. He is best known for his books of children's songs: *Earth, Sky and Air in Song* (1900; 2 books); *The Owl and the Woodchuck; The Squirrel and the Crow; Little Folks' Song Book;* and his Christmas song, *The Birthday of a King.*

Neitzel, Otto, German composer and writer; b. Falkenburg, Pomerania, July 6, 1852; d. Cologne, March 10, 1920. He was a pupil at Kullak's Academy, Berlin; studied also at the Univ. (*Dr. phil.,* 1875); then made a concert tour, as pianist, with Pauline Lucca and Sarasate; in 1878 became conductor of the 'Musikverein' at Strasbourg, where (1879-81) he likewise conducted in the City Theater. Until 1885 he taught at the Moscow Cons.; then at the Cologne Cons.; from 1887, also critic for the 'Kölnische Zeitung'; visited the U. S. in 1906-

07 as lecturer, pianist, and conductor; 1919, member of the Academy of Arts, Berlin. Among his works are the operas *Die Barbarina* (Wiesbaden, Nov. 15, 1905) and *Der Richter von Kaschau* (Darmstadt, March 31, 1916), a piano concerto (1900), etc. He wrote *Führer durch die Oper des Theaters der Gegenwart* (3 vols., 1890-93; 4th ed., 1908); *Beethovens Symfonien nach ihrem Stimmungsgehalt erläutert* (1891; 6th ed., 1924); *Saint-Saëns* (1899); *Aus meiner Musikantenmappe* (1914). —Cf. A. Dette, *Die Barbarina* (Fulda, 1913; guide to Neitzel's opera; contains biographical sketch).

Nejedlý, Vít, Czech composer; son of Zdeněk Nejedlý; b. Prague, June 22, 1912; d. Dukla, Slovakia (of typhoid fever), Dec. 30, 1944. He studied at the Univ. of Prague, obtaining his Ph.D. in 1936; was active as opera conductor in the provinces; in the summer of 1939 he went to Russia, where he continued his studies; joined the Czechoslovak contingent of the Red Army in 1943, and reached his country shortly before he died. —Works: opera, *The Weavers* (1938); 3 symphonies (1931; 1934; 1938); many songs and choruses. A memorial brochure was publ. at Prague in 1948.

Nejedlý (ně-yěhd'-lē), **Zdeněk,** Czech musicologist; b. Litomysl, Bohemia, Feb. 10, 1878. He studied music with Zdenko Fibich in Prague, and musicology at the Univ. there with O. Hostinský; *Dr. phil.*, 1900; established himself as instructor of musicology there in 1905; from 1909, associate prof.; later prof. He edited the musical journal 'Smétana' and the quarterly 'Hudební Slovník.' 1939, in Moscow; 1945-46 and again since 1948, minister of education of Czechoslovakia; later, vice president. —Writings (in Czech): *History of Bohemian Music* (1903; in the form of a catechism); *History of Music in Bohemia* (3 vols.: I. *History of pre-Hussite Hymnology,* 1904; II. *The Beginnings of Hussite Hymnology,* 1907; III. *History of Hussite Hymnology in the time of the Hussite Wars,* 1913); *Smetana's Operas* (1909); *The Modern Bohemian Opera since Smetana* (1911); *Gustav Mahler* (1912; extensive biography); *Richard Wagner* (1917); *Vitězslav Novák* (1921); biographical sketches of Hostinský, Smetana, Fibich, and J. B. Foerster; guides to Beethoven's string quartets and Strauss's *Rosenkavalier* and *Ariadne auf Naxos.* His fundamental work on Smetana (7 vols.) was brought out in a 2nd ed. in 1950-54. A collection of his writings, *Sebrané Spisi,* appeared in 27 parts after 1948.

Nelle, Wilhelm, German authority on church music; b. Schwöbler, near Hameln, May 9, 1849; d. Münster, Oct. 18, 1918. From 1861-67 he was organist at Godesberg; 1867-71 studied theology in Halle and Tübingen, where he also studied music with Robert Franz and Otto Scherzer. From 1872 he was active as a priest in various German cities (from 1886 in Hamm); in 1905 he received the degree of *Dr. theol.* from Breslau. In 1895 he founded the Evangelischer Kirchengesang - Verein für Westfalen. He was prominent in the reform and organization of Evangelical church music in Germany. Publ. *Das Evangelische Gesangbuch von 1835* (1883); *Liederbüchlein, 25 geistliche und weltliche Lieder* (1891); *Choralbuch zum Rheinisch-Westfälischen Evangelischen Gesangbuch* (with Hollenberg, 1892; 3rd ed., 1908); *Die Festmelodien des Kirchenjahres charakterisiert* (1895; 2nd ed., 1904, as *Aus dem Evangelischen Melodienschatz,* I); *Geschichte des deutschen evangelischen Kirchenliedes* (1904; 3rd ed., 1928); *Chorbuch* (with J. Plath, 1917).

Nemiroff, Isaac, American composer; b. Cincinnati, Feb. 16, 1912. He studied at the Cincinnati Cons.; later with Stefan Wolpe at the N. Y. College of Music; was instructor at the School of Music of the Brooklyn Musical Society (1946-48); Contemporary Music School in N. Y. (1948-52); in 1952 appointed to the staff of the Greenwich House Music School. —Works: incidental music for modern dance and ballet (*Calamity Jane, Scarlet Letter, Ebb Tide, Odyssey, Antigone*); *Ghost Wind,* a piece for violin and symph. band; a concerto for oboe and strings (1955); a fantasy for oboe and piano; 2 string quartets; 2 sonatas for violin and piano; chamber music; songs; piano pieces.

Nenna, Pomponio, Italian madrigalist; b. Bari, near Naples, c. 1550; d. Rome, c. 1618. Held in high regard by his contemporaries, he was created a Knight of the Golden Spur in 1603; publ. 8 books of madrigals for 5 voices from 1582 to 1618, and a book of madrigals *a* 4 (1613; 2nd ed., 1621). Several responds are printed in 'Istituzione e monumenti dell'arte musicale italiana,' vol. 5 (pp. LIII-LX); madrigals, ed. by E. Dagnino, in 'Pubblicazioni dell' Istituto italiano per la storia della musica' (Monumenti, II).

Nepomuceno, Alberto, important Brazilian composer; b. Fortaleza, July 6, 1864; d. Rio de Janeiro, Oct. 16, 1920. He studied in Rome, Berlin, and Paris, returning to Brazil in 1895. In 1902 he was appointed director of the Instituto Nacional de Musica in Rio de Janeiro, holding this post until 1916. In 1910 he conducted Brazilian music at the International Exposition in Brussels. In some of his music he introduced thematic material from Brazilian folk music. —Works: *Artemis,* lyric drama (Rio de Janeiro, June 14, 1898); *O Garatuja,* opera (Rio de Janeiro, Oct. 26, 1904); *Abul,* opera (Buenos Aires, June 30, 1913); a symphony (early work; publ. posthumously, 1937); *Suite Brasileira* for orch. (contains a popular *Batuque*); songs; piano pieces.

Neri, Saint **Filippo,** one of the greatest spiritual leaders of the Renaissance; b. Florence, July 21, 1515; d. Rome, May 25, 1595. He went to Rome as a youth and in 1551 took holy orders. He began by giving lectures on religious subjects and holding spiritual exercises in the oratory of the church of San Girolamo della Carità, and soon attracted a large following. These meetings invariably ended with the singing of hymns, or 'laudi spirituali,' for which the poet Ancina wrote many of the texts, while Giovanni Animuccia, maestro di cappella at the Vatican, and music director of the Oratory, set them to music. In 1575 the Congregation of the Oratory, as a seminary for secular priests, was officially recognized by Pope Gregory XIII, and in 1578 the Congregation transferred its headquarters to the church of Santa Maria in Vallicella. But the founder himself remained at S. Girolamo until 1583; from 1578 the great Spanish polyphonist Victoria lived with him there, as chaplain at this church. Another Spanish musician who was prominently associated with the Oratorio was Francisco Soto de Langa. S. Filippo was friendly with Palestrina, whose spiritual adviser he was, but there is no evidence that the latter succeeded Animuccia as music director of the Oratory. From the musical practice of the Oratory there eventually developed the form that we know as 'oratorio.' Contrary to general belief, this form did not make its first appearance in Cavalieri's *Rappresentazione di anima e di corpo,* performed at S. Maria in Vallicella in 1600, but in Giov. Francesco Anerio's *Teatro Armonico spirituale di madrigali a 5, 6, 7 e 8 voci,* dating from 1619 and consisting of musical settings of the Gospels and of stories from the Bible. It was not until about 1635-40 that this form actually began to receive the title of 'oratorio,' from the place where the performances were given. —Cf. P. G. Bacci, *Vita di San F. Neri* (Naples, 1855; English transl. 2 vols., St. Louis, 1903); L. Ponnelle and L. Bourdet, *St. Ph. Neri et la société romaine de son temps* (Paris, 1918; English transl., London, 1932); P. Pasquetti, *L'Oratorio musicale in Italia* (Florence, 1906), chapters 4-8; L. Pastor, *Geschichte des Päpste* (Freiburg, 1886-1930; cf. English transl., London, 1930, vol. 19, chapter 4); D. Alaleona, *Storia dell'Oratorio Musicale in Italia* (Milan, 1945; chaps. 3-9).

Nerini, Émile, French composer; b. Colombes, near Paris, Feb. 2, 1882. Son of a piano manufacturer, he studied with Decombes, Diémer, Lenepveu, and Caussade at the Paris Cons.; living in Paris as composer and teacher. —Works: the lyric dramas *Manoël* (Paris, May 11, 1905), *Le Soir de Waterloo* (Paris, April 17, 1910), *L'Épreuve dernière* (Monte Carlo, March 16. 1912), *Mazeppa* (Bordeaux, 1925); *Bacchus,* for chorus and orch.; programmatic pieces for orch. (*Parmi les roses, Solitude, Rêve oriental,* etc.); chamber music; instrumental sonatas; songs; etc.; publ. a *Traité d'Harmonie.*

Neruda, Franz Xaver, Bohemian cellist, brother of Wilma Maria Francisca Neruda; b. Brünn, Dec. 3, 1843; d. Copenhagen, March 19, 1915. At an early age he appeared in concerts with his father and sister; 1864-76, member of the Royal Orch. in Copenhagen, where in 1868 he founded the 'Society for Chamber Music'; succeeded Gade in 1892 as conductor of a similar organization in Stockholm; made 'prof.' in 1894. —Works: *Aus dem Böhmerwald* and *Slovakische Märsche* for orch.; a cello concerto; string quartets; pieces for cello, for piano, for organ; songs.

Neruda (Lady **Hallé**), **Wilma Maria Francisca,** Czech violinist; b. Brünn, March 21, 1839; d. Berlin, April 15, 1911. Her father was an organist. She studied under Jansa, and first played in public at Vienna, 1846, with her sister Amalie, a pianist; thence making a tour with her father, sister, and brother Franz (see above) through Germany. On June 11, 1849, played at a Philharmonic concert in London; after prolonged travels on the Continent, chiefly in Russia, she played at Paris in 1864, and there married Ludwig Norman (died 1885). She returned to London in 1869, and played at the Popular Concerts, the Philharmonic, the Crystal Palace, Hallé's recitals and the Manchester Concerts, etc. On July 26, 1888, she married Sir Charles Hallé, and with him made triumphal tours to Europe, Australia, and South Africa until her husband's death in 1895. When she announced her intention of retiring, a number of admirers, headed by the Prince of Wales (Edward VII), raised a subscription and presented to her a palace at Asolo, near Venice. But after the death (1898) of her only son she resumed her concert work with an American tour in 1899; after 1900 she made her headquarters in Berlin; in 1901 Queen Alexandra conferred upon her the title of 'Violinist to the Queen.' She was regarded as the rival of the greatest masters of her instrument. Her violin, a Stradivarius dated 1709, considered one of the finest in existence, was presented to her in 1876 by the Duke of Saxe-Coburg and Gotha, Earl Dudley, and Earl Hardwicke. —Cf. 'Dictionary of National Biography' (Supplement, 1901-11), II, p. 190.

Nessler, Victor E., Alsatian composer, b. Baldenheim, Jan. 28, 1841; d. Strasbourg, May 28, 1890. A student of theology and music (Th. Stern) at Strasbourg, he produced a successful opera, *Fleurette,* in 1864; then studied further in Leipzig, where he became chorusmaster at the City Theater and conductor of the 'Sängerkreis'; the same theater brought out his romantic fairy opera *Dornröschens Brautfahrt* (1867), and the operettas *Die Hochzeitsreise* (1867), *Nachtwächter und Student* (1868), and *Am Alexandertag* (1869); then followed the operas *Irmingard* (1876), *Der Rattenfänger von Hameln* (March 19, 1879), *Der wilde Jäger* (1881), *Der Trompeter von Säkkingen* (Leipzig, May 4, 1884; New York, 1888; this work and the *Rattenfänger* were the most successful), *Otto der Schütz* (1886), and *Die Rose von Strassburg* (Munich, 1890).

Nestyev, Israel, Russian musicologist; b. Kerch, Crimea, April 17, 1911. He studied at the Moscow Cons.; served as military correspondent during World War II; then was active as music commentator at the Moscow Radio. He is the author of the basic biography of Prokofiev (Moscow, 1945; N. Y., 1946; new Russian ed., Moscow, 1957), and several essays on Soviet composers.

Nettl, Bruno, American musicologist, son of Paul Nettl; b. Prague, March 14, 1930; brought to the U. S. in 1939; studied at Indiana Univ. (A.B., 1950; M.A., 1951; Ph. D., 1953); since 1953, teaching at Wayne Univ., Detroit; 1956-58, visiting lecturer, under a Fulbright grant, at the Univ. of Kiel. Publications: *North American Indian Musical Styles* (diss., Philadelphia, 1954); *Music in Primitive Culture* (Cambridge, Mass., 1956); many articles on ethnomusicological subjects.

Nettl, Paul, musicologist; b. Hohenelbe, Bohemia, Jan. 10, 1889. He studied law in Prague (LL.D., 1913), then musicology with H. Rietsch (*Dr. phil.,* 1915) and theory with Keussler; 1913-14, music editor of the paper 'Deutsche Arbeit'; from 1920, instructor at the Musicological Institute of the German Univ. in Prague; from 1937, music director of the radio broadcasting station 'Prague II'; in 1939 (Nov.) came to the U. S. and joined the faculty of the Westminster Choir School, Princeton, N. J. From 1946, teaching at the Univ. of Indiana. Editor of 'Denkmäler der Tonkunst in Österreich' vol. 56 (*Wiener Tanzmusik in der 2. Hälfte des 17. Jahrhunderts*). His writings include: *Über den Ursprung der Musik* (Prague, 1920); *Alte jüdische Spielleute und Musiker* (Prague, (1923); *Musik und Tanz bei Casanova* (Prague, 1924); *Das Wiener Lied in Zeitalter des Barock* (Vienna, 1934); *Mozart in Böhmen,* after Prochazka's *Mozart in Prag* (Prague, 1938); *The Story of Dance Music* (N. Y., 1947); *Luther and Music* (Philadelphia, 1948); *The Book of Musical Documents* (N. Y., 1948); *Casanova und seine Zeit* (Esslingen, 1949); *Forgotten Musicians* (N. Y., 1951); *Beethoven Encyclopedia* (N. Y., 1956); *Mozart and Masonry* (N. Y., 1957).

Neubaur (noi'-bowr), **Franz Christoph,** Czech violinist and composer; b. Hořin, Bohemia, 1760; d. Bückeburg, Oct. 11, 1795. A violinist, taught by the village schoolmaster, he led a wandering life; produced an operetta, *Ferdinand und Yariko,* at Munich in 1784; then went to Vienna, where he met Mozart and Haydn; in 1789, Kapellmeister to Prince Weilburg; later court composer and Johann Christoph Friedrich Bach's successor as court Kapellmeister at Bückeburg. —Publ. 12 symphonies; 10 string quartets; concertos for piano, for flute, and for cello; songs; etc. —Cf. F. von Schlichtegroll, *Musiker-Nekrologe* (ed. R. Schaal, Kassel, 1953).

Neuendorff (noi'-en-dorf), **Adolf,** conductor; b. Hamburg, June 13, 1843; d. New York, Dec. 4, 1897. He went to America in 1854; pupil of G. Matzka and J. Weinlich (violin), and Dr. Schilling (piano). Made his début as pianist in 1859; 1861, toured Brazil as violinist; 1863, music director of German theater, Milwaukee; 1864-77, conductor of German opera in New York (*Lohengrin* given for the first time in America, April 3, 1871; *Walküre* given first time, April 2, 1877); 1878, conducted New York Philharmonic; 1884-89, concert director in Boston; 1885, first conductor of the Music Hall Promenade Concerts (later Boston Pops); 1889-91, conductor of the Juch English Opera Co.; 1892, of English grand opera, New York; 1893-95, in Vienna, where his wife, Georgine von Januschowsky, was prima donna at the Imperial Opera; then returned to New York, becoming (1896) director of music in the Temple Emanu-El; 1897, conductor of the Metropolitan Permanent Orch., succeeding Seidl. —Cf. 'Dictionary of American Biography,' vol. XIII.

Neukomm (noi'-kom), **Sigismund Ritter von,** composer and conductor; b. Salzburg, July 10, 1778; d. Paris, April 3, 1858. He was a pupil of the organist Weissauer, and of Michael Haydn for composition; at 15, Univ. organist; at 18, chorusmaster at the opera. From 1798 he studied at Vienna under Joseph Haydn, who showed him fatherly care. In 1806 he passed through Stockholm, where he was elected a member of the Academy, to St. Petersburg, there becoming conductor of the German opera. 1809 found him in Paris, an intimate of Grétry and Cherubini, and pianist to Talleyrand after Dussek. For his Requiem in memory of Louis XVI (Vienna, 1814), Louis XVII ennobled him in 1815, decorating him with the cross of the Legion of Honor. In 1816 he went to Rio de Janeiro, and was appointed court music director by Emperor Dom Pedro, whom he accompanied to Lisbon on the outbreak of the revolution in 1821. He was in Talleyrand's service until 1826; then traveled for many years; and finally resided alternately in London and Paris. He was extremely popular in England before Mendelssohn's advent in 1837. Despite his almost continuous travels, he was a most industrious composer. Besides much church music, he produced 10 German operas; a symphony, 5 overtures, and 7 fantasias for orch.; chamber music; a piano concerto and many piano pieces; 57 organ pieces; about 200 French, English, Italian, and German songs; etc. —His autobiography was publ. as *Esquisses biographiques de Sigismond Neukomm* (Paris, 1859). See also Gisela Pellegrini, *Sigismund Ritter von Neukomm: ein vergessener Salzburger Musiker* (Salzburg, 1936).

Neumann (noi'-mahn), **Angelo,** tenor; b. Vienna, Aug. 18, 1838; d. Prague, Dec. 20, 1910. He began a mercantile career, but deserted it after vocal lessons from Stilke-Sessi, and after his début as a lyric tenor in 1859; sang at theaters in Cracow, Ödenburg, Pressburg, Danzig, and the Vienna court opera (1862-76); from 1876-82 he was manager of the Leipzig opera under Förster; then gathered together a traveling company for producing Wagner operas, journeying as far as Italy; from the end of 1882 to 1885 he was manager of the Bremen opera; then until his death, of the German opera in Prague (Landestheater). —Publ. *Erinnerungen an Richard Wagner* (1907; English transl. by E. Livermore, 1908).

Neumann (noi'-mahn), **Franz (Frantizek),** Czech conductor and composer; b. Přerov, Moravia, June 16, 1874; d. Brno, Feb. 24, 1929. He was a pupil at the Leipzig Cons.; repetiteur in Karlsruhe and Hamburg; Kapellmeister in Regensburg, Linz, and Reichenberg; 1904, 2nd Kapellmeister in Frankfurt; 1919, 1st conductor of the Czech National Opera, Brünn; 1925, its director. —He composed the operas *Die Brautwerbung* (Linz, 1901), *Liebelei* (Frankfurt, Sept. 18, 1910), *Herbststurm* (Berlin, April 9, 1919), *Beatrice Caracci* (Brno, April 29, 1922; in Czech), and *Leyer und Schwert* (publ. 1901; not produced); 2 ballets; men's choruses; etc.

Neumark, Georg, German hymn-writer; b. Mühlhausen, March 16, 1621; d. Weimar, July 8, 1681. He was the author of the words and music of the hymn *Wer nur den lieben Gott lässt walten,* used by Bach in several of his cantatas, and by Mendelssohn in the oratorio *St. Paul.* Neumark publ. several vols. of verse, some with his own tunes; the most important is *Poetisch-musikalisches Lustwäldchen* (Jena, 1652; enlarged ed., as *Fortgepflanztes Lustwäldchen,* 1657). —Cf. Franz Knauth, *Georg Neumark, Leben und Dichten* (Langensalza, 1881).

Neupert (noi'-pert), **Edmund,** piano pedagogue, b. Christiania, April 1, 1842; d. New York, June 22, 1888. He was (1858) a student, later a teacher, at Kullak's Academy in Berlin; afterwards he taught at the Stern Cons., and in 1868 became piano teacher at the Copenhagen Cons.; in 1881 he succeeded N. Rubinstein as principal piano teacher in the Moscow Cons.; in 1883 he settled in New York. His instructive pieces for piano are of value: *Technical Studies; Concert-Études,* op. 17; *Octave Studies,* op. 18; *Studies in Style,* op. 19 and 20; *Poetical Études,* op. 25; *Poetiske Etuder,* op. 51; *Exercises for the Various Hand Movements and Modes of Touch,* op. 77.

Nevada, Emma, stage name of **Emma Wixom,** operatic soprano; b. Alpha, near Nevada City, Calif., Feb. 7, 1859; d. Liverpool, June 20, 1940. She studied from 1877 with Marchesi in Vienna. Made her début in London, May 17, 1880, in *La Sonnambula;* sang at Trieste in the autumn; then in Florence, Leghorn, Naples, Rome, and Genoa, and at La Scala, Milan. Her first appearance in Paris was at the Opéra Comique, May 17, 1883, as Zora in F. David's *Perle du Brésil.* During the season of 1884-5 she was a member of Col. Mapleson's company at the old Academy of Music in New York, singing on alternate nights with Patti. She sang in Chicago at the Opera Festival, 1885, and again in 1889. She then sang again in Europe. Married a British physician, Dr. Raymond Palmer, in Paris on Oct. 1, 1885.

Nevada, Mignon Mathilde Marie, daughter of Emma Nevada; operatic soprano; b. Paris, Aug. 14, 1886. She made her début at the Costanzi Theater, Rome, as Rosina in *Il Barbiere di Siviglia;* then sang a season at the San Carlos in Lisbon; after a season at the Pergola Theater in Florence, she made her London début in Covent Garden as Ophelia (Oct. 3, 1910), and sang there in subsequent seasons; also appeared at La Monnaie, Brussels, and (1923) at La Scala, Milan; during World War II she engaged in war work at Liverpool, England; 1954, living in London.

Neveu, Ginette, French violinist; b. Paris, Aug. 11, 1919; d. in an airplane disaster at the Azores Islands, Oct. 28, 1949. She was of a musical family; a grandniece of Widor; studied with her mother, and later with Karl Flesch; first played in public with the Colonne Orch. in Paris at the age of 7. After graduating from the Paris Cons. with a 1st prize, she won the Wieniawski Grand Prize at the International Contest in Warsaw in 1934. Her American début took place with the Boston Symph., Oct. 24, 1947; her success was immediate and unmistakable. She was at the height of her career as the most remarkable woman violinist of modern times, and was flying to the U. S. for her third annual tour, when she perished. Numerous appreciations were publ. after her death. —Cf. M. J. Ronze-Neveu, *Ginette Neveu; la fulgurante carrière d'une grande artiste* (Paris, 1952; in English, London, 1956).

Nevin, Arthur Finley, American teacher and composer, brother of Ethelbert Nevin; b. Edgeworth, Penn., April 27, 1871; d. Sewickley, Penn., July 10, 1943. He received his first instruction in music from his father; from 1891-3 was a pupil at the New England Cons. in Boston, and from 1893-7 of K. Klindworth (piano) and O. B. Boise (composition) in Berlin; 1915-20, prof. of music at the Univ. of Kansas; 1920-22, director of the municipal music department of Memphis, Tenn.; also conductor of the Memphis Orch.; hon. Mus. Doc., Univ. of Pittsburgh, 1935; in 1938, lived for a time on the Montana reservations, engaged in research on Indian music. —Works: the opera *Poia* (Berlin, April 23, 1910; only four performances; the composer attributed the fiasco to the anti-American faction in Berlin); a one-act opera, *A Daughter of the Forest* (Chicago, Jan. 5, 1918); 2 orchestral suites, *Lorna Doone* and *Love Dreams;* 2 cantatas; a piano trio; a string quartet; choruses; songs; piano pieces; etc. —Cf. E. E. Hipsher, *American Opera and Its Composers* (Philadelphia, 1934; pp. 337-43).

Nevin, Ethelbert Woodbridge, popular American composer; b. Edgeworth, Penn., Nov. 25, 1862; d. New Haven, Conn., Feb. 17, 1901. He was a pupil of von der Heide and W. Günther (piano) at Pittsburgh; of von Boehme (voice) at Dresden (1877-8); of Pearce (New York) and Lang and Emery (Boston); and of Bülow, Klindworth, and K. Bial at Berlin (1884-6). He lived at various times in Boston, New York, Berlin, Paris, Venice, and Florence. His works consist chiefly of piano pieces and songs, which show a fine melodic talent and marked individuality. Of the former *Narcissus* (op. 13, no. 4), and of the latter *The Rosary* and *Mighty Lak' a Rose,* achieved immense popularity. A pantomime, *Lady Floriane's Dream,* was produced in New York in 1898. —Cf. V. Thompson, *The Life of Ethelbert Nevin* (Boston, 1913); F. Rogers, *Some Memories of Ethelbert Nevin,* in the 'Mus. Quarterly' (July, 1917); J. T. Howard, *Our American Music* (N. Y., 1939 and later eds.); J. T. Howard, *Ethelbert Nevin* (N. Y., 1935).

Nevin, Gordon Balch, American composer; b. Easton, Penn., May 19, 1892; d. New Wilmington, Penn., Nov. 15, 1943. He studied organ and theory in N. Y.; was organist at various churches in Pennsylvania; also in Cleveland; publ. numerous songs (*In Memoriam, Song of Sorrow, Moonlight Serenade,* etc.); contributed to music magazines.

Newcomb, Ethel, American pianist; b. Whitney Point, N. Y., Oct. 30, 1879. She went to Vienna in 1895, and studied with Leschetizky until 1903; served as his assistant from 1904 to 1908; made her début on Feb. 28, 1903, with the Vienna Philharmonic Orch.; continued to give concerts in Europe; returning to America, she appeared in recitals; then settled at her home in Whitney Point; presented private concerts there (1955).

Newlin, Dika, American writer on music and composer; b. Portland, Ore., Nov. 22, 1923; studied at the Univ. of California, Los Angeles, and at Columbia Univ.; took private lessons with Roger Sessions and with Schoenberg in California, and acquired a thorough knowledge of the 12-tone technique. She taught at Western Maryland College, Westminster, Maryland (1945-49); at Syracuse Univ. (1949-51); Fulbright research scholar in Vienna (1951-52); in 1952 established the dept. of music at Drew Univ., Madison, N. J. —Compositions: *Sinfonia* for piano (1947); piano trio (1948); chamber symph. for 12 solo instruments (1949); *Fantasia* for piano (1957); most of these in the 12-tone idiom; publ. a valuable analytical study *Bruckner-Mahler-Schoenberg* (N. Y., 1947); transl. Schoenberg's *Style and Idea* (N. Y., 1951).

Newman, Ernest, English music critic; b. Liverpool, Nov. 30, 1868. He prepared himself for the Indian Civil Service, but entered business in Liverpool, pursuing his musical studies as a favorite avocation. In 1903 he accepted an instructorship in the Midland Institute, Birmingham, and took up music as a profession; 1905, in Manchester as critic of the 'Guardian'; 1906-19, in Birmingham as critic for the 'Daily Post'; 1919-20, in London as critic for the 'Observer'; since March 1920 on the staff of the London 'Sunday Times'; from 1923, also contributor to the 'Glasgow Herald'; 1924-25, guest critic of the New York 'Evening Post.' One of the best equipped and most influential of the English music critics. He continued to write his regular column in the 'Sunday Times' in his 90th year. —Publications: *Gluck and the Opera* (1895); *A Study of Wagner* (1899); *Wagner* (1904); *Musical Studies* (1905; 3rd ed., 1914); *Elgar* (1906); *Hugo Wolf* (1907; German transl., 1910); *Richard Strauss* (1908); *Wagner as Man and Artist* (1914); *A Musical Motley* (1919); *The Piano-Player and Its Music* (1920); *A Musical Critic's Holiday* (1925); *The Unconscious Beethoven* (1927); *What to Read on the Evolution of Music* (1928); *Stories of the Great Operas* (3 vols., 1929-31); *Fact and Fiction about Wagner* (1931); *The Man Liszt* (1934); *The Life of Richard Wagner* in 4 vols. (1933; 1937; 1941; 1946); *Opera Nights* (1943; U. S. ed. as *More Stories of Famous Operas); Wagner Nights* (1949; U. S. ed. as *The Wagner Operas*); *More Opera Nights* (1955; U. S. ed. as *17 Famous Operas*); *From the World of Music: Essays from 'The Sunday Times'* (selected by F. Aprahamian, London, 1956); *More Musical Essays* (2nd selection from 'The Sunday Times,' London, 1958). Newman translated Felix Weingartner's book *Über das Dirigieren* (Leipzig, 2nd ed., 1925), Schweitzer's *J. S. Bach* (Leipzig, 1911), and Rolland's *Beethoven the Creator* (London, 1929; New York, 1937); for Breitkopf & Härtel's complete ed. of Wagner's works he wrote entirely new and remarkably fine translations. He edited *Fifty Songs of Hugo Wolf* (with critical introduction); editor of 'The New Library of Music' (historical and bibliographical monographs); editor of a new revised ed. (in English) of Berlioz's 'Memoirs' (1932); contributor to numerous English and American journals. —Cf. H. van Thal, ed., *Fanfare for Ernest Newman* (London, 1955).

Newman, William S., American pianist, musicologist, and composer; b. Cleveland, April 6, 1912; studied piano with Riemenschneider and Arthur Loesser; composition with Elwell and Shepherd; then at Western Reserve Univ. (Ph.D., 1939); musicology with Paul H. Lang at Columbia Univ. (1940); taught at a high school in Cleveland; then was in the Army Air Forces (1942-46); appeared as piano soloist with the Cleveland Orch.; in 1946 appointed assistant prof. of music history at the Univ. of North Carolina, Chapel Hill. —Publications: *The Pianist's Problems* (N.Y., 1950); *Understanding Music* (N. Y., 1953); ed. *13 Keyboard Sonatas of the 18th and 19th Centuries* (1947) and *Sons of Bach: 3 Sonatas for Keyboard* (1947). Compositions: piano sonata (1929); cello sonata (1935); operetta, *Freddy and His Fiddle* (1936); string quartet (1937); *Little Symphony* (1940); *An American Tragedy,* overture for orch. (1941); various pieces for band.

Newmarch, Rosa Harriet (*née* Jeaffreson), English writer on musical subjects; b. Leamington, Dec. 18, 1857; d. Worthing, April 9, 1940. Growing up in an artistic atmosphere, she entered the Hetherley School of Art to study painting, but after a time abandoned that career for literary pursuits; settled in London in 1880 as contributor to various journals. There she married Henry Charles Newmarch in 1883. During her first visit to Russia in 1897 her association with some of the foremost Russian musicians led her to study with Vladimir Stasov; she revisited Russia many times thereafter, and became an authority on the music of that country; 1908-20, wrote the analytical notes for the programs of the Queen's Hall Orch.; edited the series 'Living Masters of Music'; gave many lectures. —Works: *Tchaikovsky* (1900); *Henry J. Wood* (1904); *Jean Sibelius* (1906; German transl., 1906); *Songs to a Singer* (1906); *Poetry and Progress in Russia* (1907); *The Russian Opera* (1914; in French, 1922); *The Russian Arts* (1916); *A Book of Spiritual Wisdom* (1918); *The Devout Russian* (1919); *The Concert-Goer's Library* (collection of program notes; 6 vols., London, 1928-48); *The Music of Czechoslovakia* (1942). She transl. Deiters' *Brahms* (1888); Habets' *Borodin et Liszt* (1895); *The Life and Letters of Tchaikovsky* (1908; abridged from Modest Tchaikovsky's biography); Vincent d'Indy's *César Franck* (1910); and K. Hoffmeister's *Dvořák* (1928).

Ney, Elly, German pianist; b. Düsseldorf, Sept. 27, 1882. She studied with Böttcher and Seiss at the Cons. of Cologne, and with Leschetizky and Sauer in Vienna; won the Mendelssohn and Ibach prizes; made her début in Vienna in 1905; toured the U. S. and Europe, appearing in recital and with the leading orchestras; taught for a time at the Cologne Cons.; lived in Bonn, from 1932 near Munich. 1911-27, wife of Willem van Hoogstraten (q. v.); in 1928 married to P. F. Allais of Chicago. She wrote an autobiography, *Ein Leben für die Musik* (Darmstadt, 1952; 2nd ed. as *Erinnerungen und Betrachtungen; mein Leben aus der Musik,* 1957). —Cf. C. von Pidoll, *Elly Ney* (Leipzig, 1942); Zenta Maurina, *Begegnung mit Elly Ney* (Memmingen, 1956).

Ney, Joseph Napoléon. See **Moskowa,** Prince de.

Nibelle (nē-běhl'), **Adolphe - André,** French composer of operettas; b. Gien, Loiret, Oct. 9, 1825; d. Paris, March 11, 1895. He was a pupil at the Paris Cons. His numerous light operas had considerable vogue in Paris. Among the most successful were *Le Loup-Garou* (1858), *Les Filles du Lac* (1858), *L'Arche-Marion* (1868), *La Fontaine de Berny* (1869), *Le 15 Août* (1869), *Les quatre cents femmes d'Ali-Baba* (1872), *L'Alibi* (1873); also publ. *Heures musicales* (24 songs).

Niccolo. See **Isouard.**

Nicholl, Horace Wadham, organist and composer; b. Tipton, near Birmingham, England, March 17, 1848; d. New York, March 10, 1922. He was a pupil of his father and of the organist Samuel Prince. Organist at Dudley, near Birmingham, 1867-70; at Stoke-on-Trent, 1870-1; in the latter year he was induced by an American gentleman to accompany him to Pittsburgh, where he became organist at St. Paul's Cathedral (4 or 5 years), later at the Third Presbyterian Church, and also teacher at the Female College. Going to New York in 1878, he became editor of the organ department in Freund's 'Music Trades Review'; 1879-80, organist at St. Mark's. From 1888-95, prof. of harmony and ensemble playing at Miss Porter's school, Farmington, Conn. He composed a cycle of biblical oratorios; 2 symphonies; *Hamlet,* a 'psychic sketch' for orch.; piano pieces; 12 Grand Preludes and Fugues for organ; etc.

Nicholl, Joseph Weston, English composer; b. Halifax, Yorkshire, May 7, 1875; d. there, May, 1925. He studied in Berlin, Munich, and Paris; pupil of Rheinberger and Guilmant; 1906, conductor of the Yorkshire Military Band, later of the Black-Dyke Band. —Works: for orch.: Concert Overture (with organ); *Alastor,* symph. poem; *In English Seas,* tone poem; for band: *The Viking,* tone picture and Festival Overture (1913); also choral works, songs, etc.

Nicholls, Agnes, English soprano; b. Cheltenham, July 14, 1877. She studied singing with Visetti at the Royal College of Music from 1894 to 1900; then with John Acton in Manchester. She made her operatic début at the Lyceum Theater, Nov. 20, 1895, as Dido (in a revival of Purcell's opera); concert début at the Gloucester Festival, 1897. In spite of her success she continued her regular studies, postponing the real beginning of her professional career until May 14, 1901, when she sang the Dewman in *Hänsel und Gretel* at Covent Garden; from 1904-08 she sang there every season. On July 15, 1904, she married the conductor Hamilton

Harty. She was very successful in oratorio and concert. In 1904 she toured the U. S.; then settled in London.

Nicodé, Jean-Louis, pianist and composer; b. Jerczik, near Posen, Aug. 12, 1853; d. Langebrück, near Dresden, Oct. 5, 1919. He was taught by his father and the organist Hartkäs; entered Kullak's Academy in Berlin, 1869, where he studied piano with Kullak, harmony with Wüerst, and counterpoint and composition with Kiel. He lived for some years in Berlin as a teacher and pianist; made a concert tour (1878) with Mme. Artôt through Galicia and Rumania; 1878-85, piano teacher at Dresden Cons.; till 1888, conductor of the Philharmonic Concerts; established the 'Nicodé Concerts' in 1893, and, in order to enlarge their scope by the production of larger choral works (chiefly those seldom heard), formed the 'Nicodé Chorus' in 1896. In 1900 he abandoned these concerts, retired to Langebrück, and devoted himself to composition, with only occasional appearances as conductor of his own works. In 1897, temporary conductor of Leipzig 'Riedel-Verein,' succeeding Kretzschmar. —Composed works for voices and orchestra; a symph.; symphonic poems; 2 sonatas for cello and piano; many piano pieces; songs. —Cf. Th. Schäfer, *Jean-Louis Nicodé. Ein Versuch kritischer Würdigung und Erläuterung seines Schaffens* (Berlin, 1907); O. Taubmann, *Jean-Louis Nicodé,* in 'Monographien moderner Musiker' (vol. III, Leipzig, 1909).

Nicolai, Otto, German opera composer; b. Königsberg, June 9, 1810; d. Berlin, May 11, 1849. A piano pupil of his father, a singing teacher, he escaped from parental tyranny at the age of 16, and found a protector in Justizrat Adler of Stargard, who sent him to Berlin in 1827 to study under Zelter and Klein. He had developed excellent ability as a teacher, when the Prussian Ambassador at Rome, von Bunsen, appointed him (1833) organist of the embassy chapel at Rome, where he also studied the old Italian masters under Baini. Going to Vienna in 1837, he was Kapellmeister at the Kärnthnerthor Theater till Oct., 1838, when he returned to Rome and took up Italian opera composition. He had a great vogue, bringing out *Rosmonda d'Inghilterra* (Turin, 1838; at Trieste, 1839, as *Enrico II d'Inghilterra*), *Il Templario* (after *Ivanhoe;* Turin, Feb. 11, 1840; at Naples, autumn, 1843, as *Teodosia;* at Vienna as *Der Templer*), *Odoardo e Gildippe* (Turin, 1841), and *Il Proscritto* (Milan, March 13, 1841; in Vienna as *Die Heimkehr des Verbannten,* Feb. 3, 1844). Succeeding Kreutzer as court Kapellmeister at Vienna, 1841-47, he founded the Philharmonic Society in 1842. He began to compose *Die lustigen Weiber von Windsor,* the opera upon which his fame rests, in Vienna; but was called to Berlin (1847) as Kapellmeister of the Opera and of the newly established 'Domchor.' His last-mentioned opera (in English *The Merry Wives of Windsor*) came out in Berlin, March 8, 1849, only two months before his death by a stroke of apoplexy. —Nicolai's other works are a Mass (dedicated 1843 to Friedrich Wilhelm IV); a Festival Overture on *Ein' feste Burg* (1844); a piano concerto; piano pieces; 2 symphonies; a string quartet; a cello sonata; a Requiem; a *Te Deum;* songs (op. 6, 16) and part-songs. —Cf. H. Mendel, *Otto Nicolai: eine Biographie* (Berlin, 1866); G. R. Kruse, *Otto Nicolai. Ein Künstlerleben* (Berlin, 1911); B. Schroeder, *Otto Nicolai's Tagebücher, nebst biographischen Ergänzungen* (Leipzig, 1892); *Otto Nicolai's Briefe aus den Jahren 1832-48* in the 'Deutsche Rundschau' (Jan., 1897); G. R. Kruse, *Otto Nicolai als Symphoniker,* in the 'Allgemeine Musik-Zeitung' (1908); G. R. Kruse, *Otto Nicolai's italienische Opern,* in 'Sammelbände der Internationalen Musik-Gesellschaft' (XII, 2; 1911); G. R. Kruse, *Otto Nicolai's musikalische Aufsätze* (Regensburg, 1913); *Otto Nicolai: Briefe an seinen Vater,* ed. by W. Altmann (Regensburg, 1924); *Otto Nicolai's Tagebücher,* ed. by W. Altmann (Regensburg, 1937).

Nicolau, Antonio, Catalonian composer and conductor; b. Barcelona, June 8, 1858; d. there, Feb. 26, 1933. He studied in Barcelona with Balart and Pujol; also in Paris, where he lived for 8 years; then became conductor of the Sociedad de Conciertos de Barcelona, with which he gave many important 1st performances in Spain; was director of the Barcelona Municipal Music School from 1896 and teacher of many of the leading Catalan musicians, including Lamote de Grignon. —Works: the operas *El Rapto* (Madrid, 1887) and *Constanza* (Barcelona); the dramatic scene *La Tempestad* (Barcelona); the symph. poems *El Triunfo de Venus* (Paris, 1882) and *Spes;* choral works: *Captant* (1904), *La Mort del Escolà, Entre flors, La Mare de deu;* songs. —Cf. R. Mitjana, *Para música vamos!* (Valencia, 1909).

Nicolini, stage name of **Ernest Nicolas,** French dramatic tenor; b. Saint-Malo, Feb.

23, 1834; d. Pau, Jan. 19, 1898. He studied at the Paris Cons.; made his début in July, 1857, in Halévy's *Mousquetaires de la Reine,* at the Opéra-Comique, where he was engaged till 1859; then went to Italy, and sang as 'Nicolini' with moderate success. From 1862-70 he sang at the Salle Ventadour, Paris, visiting London in 1866. In 1871 he sang in opera at Drury Lane; from 1872 for several years at Covent Garden. After touring with Adelina Patti, he married her, on Aug. 10, 1886.

Nicolò. See **Isouard.**

Niecks (nēks), **Friedrich (Frederick),** pedagogue and writer on music, b. Düsseldorf, Feb. 3, 1845; d. Edinburgh, June 24, 1924. He studied the violin under Langhans, Grünewald, and Auer, and piano and composition with J. Tausch; début (as violinist) at Düsseldorf in 1857; until 1867 he was a member of the orch. there, the last years as concertmaster; in 1868, organist at Dumfries, Scotland, and viola player in a quartet with A. C. Mackenzie. After 2 terms in Leipzig Univ. (1877), and travels in Italy, he won a position in London as critic for the 'Monthly Musical Record' and 'Musical Times'; in 1891, appointed Reid Prof. of music at Edinburgh Univ. In 1901 Niecks founded the Music Education Society. He was made Mus. Doc. (*hon. c.*) by Dublin Univ. in 1898; LL.D. by Edinburgh Univ. After his retirement in 1914 he lived in Edinburgh. —Works: *A Concise Dictionary of Musical Terms* (2nd ed., 1884); *Frédéric Chopin as a Man and Musician* (1888; 3rd ed., 1902; German ed., 1890; a valuable work); a monograph on the history of accidentals, *The Flat, Sharp and Natural* (1890; in 'Proceedings' of the Musical Association); *The Two Keys to the Theory and Practice of Harmony* (1903; in 'Proceedings' of the Musical Association); *Programme Music in the Last Four Centuries* (1907); *R. Schumann* (posthumous, 1925).

Niedermeyer, Louis, composer; b. Nyon, Switzerland, April 27, 1802; d. Paris, March 14, 1861. He was a pupil in Vienna of Moscheles (piano) and Förster (composition); in 1819, of Fioravanti in Rome, and Zingarelli in Naples. He lived in Geneva as an admired song-composer, and settled in Paris in 1823; there he brought out four unsuccessful operas (*La Casa nel bosco,* May 28, 1828; *Stradella,* March 3, 1837; *Marie Stuart,* Dec. 6, 1844; *La Fronde,* May 2, 1853). He then bent his energies to sacred composition, and reorganized Choron's Institute for Church Music as the 'École Niedermeyer,' which eventually became a flourishing institution with government subvention; he also founded (with d'Ortigue) a journal for church music, 'La Maîtrise'; and publ. with him a *Méthode d'accompagnement du plain-chant* (1856; 2nd ed., 1876; English transl. by W. Goodrich, N. Y., 1905). His Masses, motets, hymns, etc. were well received; his romances (*Le Lac; Le Soir; La Mer; L'Automne;* etc.) are widely known; he also publ. organ preludes, piano pieces, etc. —Cf. A. Niedermeyer, *Louis Niedermeyer, Son œuvre et son école* (Paris, no date); Anon., *Vie d'un compositeur moderne* (by Niedermeyer's son; Fontainebleau, 1892; reprinted Paris, 1893, with preface by Saint-Saëns); M. Galerne, *L'École Niedermeyer* (Paris, 1928).

Nielsen, Alice, American soprano; b. Nashville, Tenn., June 7, 1876; d. New York, March 8, 1943. She was a pupil of Ida Valerga in San Francisco; made her début with the Burton Stanley Opera Co. as Yum-Yum (*The Mikado*) in Oakland, Calif., 1893; from 1896-8 she was the leading lady of the famous Bostonians; 1898-1901, the star of her own light opera company. While she was singing in *The Fortune Teller* in London, Henry Russell, later director of the Boston Opera Co., heard her, and upon his advice she went for further study to Rome; début as a grand opera singer at the Bellini Theater in Naples, Dec. 6, 1903, as Marguerite; sang at Covent Garden 1904-5; made her American début in grand opera in New York, Nov. 10, 1905 (Casino Theater); 1908, joined Russell's San Carlo Opera Co. in New Orleans; member of the Boston Opera Co., 1909-13, appearing also with the Metropolitan and Chicago companies; later, toured the United States and Canada with the '3 Star' Opera Co.; also made numerous concert tours; then lived in New York.

Nielsen, Carl (August), outstanding Danish composer; b. Nörre-Lyndelse, June 9, 1865; d. Copenhagen, Oct. 2, 1931. He studied at the Cons. of Copenhagen, with V. Tofte (violin) and O. Rosenhoff (composition); also had lessons with Gade. He played violin in a theater orch. (1886-90); then received the Ancker stipend and spent a year studying in Germany, France, and Italy. Returning to Copenhagen, he continued to be employed as an orchestral violinist; was in the court orch. in Copenhagen (1890-1905); then conductor at the

Copenhagen Opera (1908-14) and of the Copenhagen Musical Society (1915-27); also conducted concerts in Germany, Holland, Sweden, and Finland. While thus engaged, he composed industriously; his early style was determined by the combined influences of Gade, Grieg, and Liszt. His later works display the powerful impact of modern music; he adopted many devices of Impressionism; his harmonic procedures verged on polytonality, but his melodic lines always remained clear; chromaticism remained an integral part of Nielsen's idiom, but he reserved the simple diatonic progressions, often in folksong manner, for his major climaxes. His orchestral writing is opulent and rich in instrumental color. As a symphonist, he adopted a programmatic genre, giving subtitles, expressive of mood, to his symphonies; his stature as a major composer continued to grow after his death; festivals of his music have been presented in Denmark, but elsewhere in the world his music is little known. —Works: the operas *Saul and David* (Copenhagen, Nov. 28, 1902) and *Maskarade* (Copenhagen, Nov. 11, 1906); 6 symphonies: No. 1 (1892-94); No. 2, *The Four Temperaments* (Copenhagen, Dec. 1, 1902); No. 3, *Sinfonia Espansiva* (Copenhagen, Feb. 28, 1912); No. 4, *The Inextinguishable* (Copenhagen, Feb. 1, 1916); No. 5, his best-known work (Copenhagen, Jan. 24, 1922); No. 6, *Sinfonia Semplice* (Copenhagen, Dec. 11, 1925); *Little Suite for strings* (1888); *Helios,* overture (Copenhagen, Oct. 8, 1903); *Pan and Syrinx,* symph. poem (Copenhagen, Feb. 11, 1918); violin concerto (Copenhagen, Feb. 28, 1912); flute concerto (Paris, Oct. 21, 1926); clarinet concerto (Copenhagen, Oct. 2, 1928); vocal works: *Hymnus Amoris,* for soli, chorus, and orch. (Copenhagen, April 27, 1897), *Søvnen* (*Sleep*), for chorus and orch. (Copenhagen, March 21, 1905), 10 cantatas for various occasions; *Fynsk Foraar,* lyric humoresque, for soli, chorus, and orch. (Copenhagen, July 8, 1922); 4 string quartets; string quintet; *Serenata in vano,* for clarinet, bassoon, horn, cello, and double-bass (1914); quintet for flute, oboe, clarinet, bassoon, and horn (1922); 2 violin sonatas; for piano: 5 pieces (1890), *6 Humoresques-Bagatelles* (1897), *Theme and Variations* (1916), 3 pieces (1928); organ preludes; harmonizations of Danish folksongs; original songs to Danish words; incidental music to various plays; etc. He publ. the books *Levende Musik* (Copenhagen, 1925; publ. in English transl., as *Living Music,* London, 1953); and *Min Fynske Barndom* (reminiscences of his childhood, Copenhagen, 1927; publ. in English under the title *My Childhood,* London, 1953). —Cf. Hugo Seligmann, *Carl Nielsen* (Copenhagen, 1931); Knud Jeppesen, *Carl Nielsen: A Danish Composer,* in 'Music Review' (1946); T. Meyer and F. S. Petersen, *Carl Nielsen* (2 vols.; Copenhagen, 1947-48); L. Dolleris, *Carl Nielsen* (Odense, 1949); H. Madsen, *Carl Nielsens Fyn* (Odense, 1950); R. Simpson, *Carl Nielsen, Symphonist* (London, 1952).

Nielsen, Ludolf, Danish composer; b. Nørre-Tvede, Jan. 29, 1876; d. Copenhagen, May 11, 1939. He was a pupil at the Copenhagen Cons. of V. Tofte (violin), A. Orth (piano), Bondesen (harmony), O. Malling and F. P. E. Hartmann (composition); during the winter of 1903-4 at the Leipzig Cons.; as winner of the Ancker stipend traveled in 1907 in Germany, Austria, and Italy. From 1897-1907 solo viola and assistant conductor of the Tivoli Orch., and viola of the Björvig Quartet; then lived in Copenhagen as teacher and composer; subsequently resided in Hellerup, Denmark. —Works: the operas *Isabella* (Copenhagen, Oct. 8, 1915), *Uhret* (*The Clock*), and *Lola* (Copenhagen, 1920); the ballet *Reisekameraden;* 3 symphonies; other orchestral works; chamber music; choruses; songs; piano pieces; etc.

Nielsen, Riccardo, Italian composer; b. Bologna, March 3, 1908. He graduated from the Liceo there, then studied in Milan with Carlo Gatti. His music is neo-Classic in form. —Works: *Sinfonia concertante* for piano and orch. (1932); violin concerto (1933); *Sinfonia* in G (1934); *Divertimento* for clarinet, bassoon, trumpet, violin, viola, and cello (1934); concerto for orch. (1935); *Adagio e Allegro* for cello and 11 instruments; trio for oboe, bassoon, and piano; sonatas for piano, for violin, and for cello; etc.

Niemann, Albert, German tenor; b. Erxleben, near Magdeburg, Jan. 15, 1831; d. Berlin, Jan. 13, 1917. Endowed with a good natural voice, he appeared at Dessau (1849) in minor roles, and sang in the chorus; he was then taken in hand by F. Schneider, and the baritone Nusch; after this training he sang at Hanover, then went to study under Duprez at Paris, sang with success in Halle and other towns, and was engaged at Hanover as dramatic tenor, 1860-6; from then, until his retirement in 1889, at the court opera in Berlin. Wagner engaged him to create the roles of Tannhäuser at Paris, March 13, 1861, and Siegmund at Bayreuth, 1876. During the seasons of 1886-8 he was a member of the Metropolitan Opera Co., making his début as Siegmund (Nov. 10, 1886); there he sang at the American premières the roles of Tristan (Dec. 1, 1886) and Siegfried in *Götterdämmerung* (Jan. 25, 1888). —Cf. R. Sternfeld, *Albert Niemann* (Berlin, 1904); Niemann's correspondence with Wagner was publ. by W. Altmann (Berlin, 1924).

Niemann, Walter, German writer on music and composer; b. Hamburg, Oct. 10, 1876; d. Leipzig, June 17, 1953. He was a pupil of his father, Rudolf Niemann, and of Humperdinck (1897); 1898-1901 studied at the Leipzig Cons. with Reinecke and von Bose, and at the Univ. with Riemann and Kretzschmar (musicology); *Dr. phil.* in 1901, with the dissertation *Über die abweichende Bedeutung der Ligaturen in der Mensuraltheorie der Zeit vor Johannes de Garlandia* (publ. Leipzig, 1902); 1904-6, editor of 'Neue Zeitschrift für Musik,' in Leipzig; 1906-7, teacher at the Hamburg Cons.; 1907-17, again in Leipzig as writer and critic of the 'Neueste Nachrichten'; then gave up this position to devote himself to composition. Besides a violin sonata (op. 70) and a few works for orch. and string orch., he wrote numerous interesting piano pieces (over 150 opus nos.). —Books: *Musik und Musiker des 19. Jahrhunderts* (1905); *Die Musik Skandinaviens* (1906); *Das Klavierbuch* (1907; 5th ed., 1920); *Edvard Grieg* (1908; with G. Schjelderup); *Die musikalische Renaissance des 19. Jahrhunderts* (1911); *Taschenlexikon für Klavierspieler* (1912; 4th ed., 1918); *Die Musik seit Richard Wagner* (1913; later editions as *Die Musik der Gegenwart*); *Jean Sibelius* (1917); *Klavier-Lexikon* (1917); *Die nordische Klaviermusik* (1918); *Die Virginalmusik* (1919); *Meister des Klaviers* (1919); *Brahms* (1920; English transl. N. Y., 1929); etc. He virtually rewrote the 4th ed. of Kullak's *Ästhetik des Klavierspiels* (1905); revised the 2nd ed. of Klauwell's *Formen der Instrumentalmusik* (1918); edited Ph. E. Bach's *Versuch über die wahre Art das Klavier zu spielen* (1906; critical reprint) and early works for piano and organ.

Niemtschek (Niemetschek, Něměček), Franz Xaver, Czech writer on music; b. Sadská, near Poděbrady, July 24, 1766; d. Vienna, March 19, 1849. He was prof. of philosophy at the Univ. of Prague from 1802, and is known in musical annals for his biography of Mozart, whom he greatly admired and evidently knew personally: *Leben des k. k. Kapellmeisters Wolfgang Gottlieb Mozart* (Prague, 1798; 2nd ed., 1808; in English, London, 1956).

Niessen-Stone, Matja von, soprano; b. Moscow, Dec. 28, 1870; d. New York, June 8, 1948. At the age of 6 she was taken by her mother to Germany, where she was educated, first in Weimar, then in Dresden; studied singing with Adolf Jansen in Dresden (1886-9); then in Berlin with Lilli Lehmann, Mme. Souvestre-Paschalis, Etelka Gerster, and George Fergusson; her concert début took place in Dresden (1890); she then toured Germany, Austria, Hungary, and Russia; 1896-1901, prof. of singing in Riga. In 1905 she sang in Belgium and England; American début in recital in March, 1906. During the season of 1908-9 she sang at the Metropolitan Opera House; 1910-17, head of the vocal department at the Inst. of Musical Art, New York; 1917-22, had her own studio in New York; 1922, returned to Europe and taught in Berlin until 1938, when she re-established a vocal studio in New York.

Nietzsche, Friedrich, the philosopher; b. Röcken, near Lützen, Oct. 15, 1844; d. Weimar, Aug. 25, 1900, after 11 years of insanity. Prof. of classical philology at the Univ. of Basel 1869-79; he was at first a warm partisan of Wagner, whom he championed in *Die Geburt der Tragödie aus dem Geiste der Musik* (1872; 2nd ed., 1874) and *Richard Wagner in Bayreuth* (1876). In *Der Fall Wagner* and *Nietzsche contra Wagner* (both 1888) and *Götzendämmerung* (1889) he turned against his former idol and became a partisan of Bizet. Nietzsche was also a trained musician; he publ. 17 songs (1864) and *An das Leben* for chorus and orch. (1887); in MS are piano pieces (2 and 4 hands) and songs. A complete ed. of his compositions was undertaken by G. Göhler (vol. I, 1924). —Bibliography: E. Förster-Nietzsche, *Das Leben F. N.s* (2 vols., Leipzig, 1895-1904; English transl. [condensed], N. Y., 1912-15); J. Zeitler, *N.s Ästhetik* (Leipzig, 1900); Th. Lessing, *Schopenhauer, Wagner, N.* (Munich, 1906); H. Bélart, *F. N. und Richard Wagner* (Berlin, 1907); P. Lasserre, *Les Idées de N. sur la musique. La Période Wagnérienne (1871-6)* (Paris, 1907; new ed., 1930); E. Eckertz, *N. als Künstler* (Munich, 1910); H. Bélart, *F. N.s Freundschaftstragödie mit R. Wagner* (Dresden, 1912); E. Förster-Nietzsche, *Wagner und N.*

zur Zeit ihrer Freundschaft (Munich, 1915); *Wagner and N. The Beginning and End of Their Friendship,* in the 'Mus. Quarterly' (July, 1918; selection from E. Förster-Nietzsche's book, transl. by C. V. Kerr); W. Dahms, *Die Offenbarung der Musik. Eine Apotheose F. N.s* (1922); L. Griesser, *N. und Wagner* (1923); K. Hildebrandt, *Wagner und N., ihr Kampf gegen das 19. Jahrhundert* (Breslau, 1924); H. Baugh, *N. and His Music,* in the 'Mus. Quarterly' (April, 1926); J. M. Verweyen, *Wagner und N.* (Stuttgart, 1926); E. Gürster, *N. und die Musik* (1929); J. G. Huneker, *Essays* (N. Y., 1929); G. B. Foster, *F. N.* (N. Y., 1931); P. G. Dippel, *N. und Wagner* (1934); E. Ruprecht, *Der Mythos bei Wagner und N.* (Berlin, 1938). See also *F. N.s gesammelte Briefe* (Berlin, 1900-1908; vol. III, 2, contains letters to Bülow, H. von Senger, and M. von Meysenbug; vol. IV, letters to P. Gast) and H. Daffner's ed. of *N.s Randglossen zu Bizets 'Carmen'* (Regensburg, 1912). P. Gast's letters to N. were publ. in 1924 (vol. I).

Niewiadomski (nē-v'yah-dom'-skē), **Stanislaw,** Polish composer and music critic; b. Soposzryn, Galicia, Nov. 4, 1859; d. Lwow, Aug. 16, 1936. He studied in Lwow (with Mikuli), Vienna (F. Krenn), and Leipzig (Jadassohn); 1886-87 and 1918-19, manager of the Lwow Opera; 1885-1914, music critic there; 1887-1914, teacher at the Lwow Cons.; 1918-21, editor of 'Gazeta Muzyczna'; from 1919, music critic in Warsaw and teacher at the Cons. there; 1929, director of the Warsaw Music Institute. He composed numerous songs and piano pieces (about 500 works). Author of biographies of Chopin and Moniuszko.

Nigg, Serge, French composer; b. Paris, June 6, 1924. He studied with Olivier Messiaen at the Paris Cons., and with René Leibowitz; evolved an extremely complex musical idiom, rooted in dodecaphonic procedures. In 1948, under the influence of Russian developments in music, he denounced atonality, and adopted a simplified style of composition suitable for mass listening; also wrote workers' choruses. —Works: symph. poem, *Timour* (1944); *Variations* for piano and 10 instruments (Paris, Jan. 29, 1947); piano concerto (Paris, Jan. 10, 1955); numerous vocal pieces.

Niggli, Arnold, Swiss writer and editor; b. Aarburg, Dec. 20, 1843; d. Zürich, May 30, 1927. He studied law at Heidelberg, Zürich, and Berlin. 1875-1909, secretary to the town council at Aarau; 1890-98, editor of the 'Schweizerische Musikzeitung'; later, lived in Zürich. He publ. a valuable work, *Die Schweizerische Musikgesellschaft; eine musik- und kulturgeschichtliche Studie* (1886), a *Geschichte des Eidgenössischen Sängervereins, 1842-92,* and short studies of a number of great composers and performers (some of them in Waldersee's 'Sammlung musikalischer Vorträge').

Nikisch, Arthur, celebrated conductor; b. Szent-Miklós, Hungary, Oct. 12, 1855; d. Leipzig, Jan. 23, 1922. His father was head bookkeeper to Prince Lichtenstein. Nikisch attended the Vienna Cons., studying with Dessoff (composition) and Hellmesberger (violin), graduating in 1874. While still a student he had the honor of playing among the first violins (under Wagner's direction) at the laying of the cornerstone of the Bayreuth Theater (1872). He was at first engaged as a violinist in the court orch. (1874); then by Angelo Neumann in 1878 (début Feb. 11) as 2nd conductor in the Leipzig Theater (he began by conducting operettas in the Old Theater, without score), later being placed on an equality with Seidl and Sucher. From 1882-9 he was 1st Kapellmeister under Stägemann's management; then (1889-93) greatly distinguished himself as conductor of the Boston Symph. Orch. From 1893-95 he was director of the Royal Opera in Budapest, and conducted the Philharmonic Concerts there; from 1895, conductor of the Gewandhaus Concerts, Leipzig, succeeding Reinecke, and of the Philharmonic Concerts, Berlin. From 1897 he was in constant demand as visiting conductor, and made a number of extended tours with the Berlin Philharmonic Orch.; directed many of the concerts of the London Philharmonic Society, and works of Wagner and Richard Strauss at Covent Garden; in 1912 he made a tour of the U. S. with the entire London Symphony Orch. (85 performers). From 1902-7 he was director of studies at the Leipzig Cons.; 1905-6, general director of the Stadttheater; made 'Royal Prof.' in 1901. He was a conductor of the widest sympathies, penetrating insight, and extraordinary magnetism; he conducted the most intricate music without score. He had in MS an orchestral fantasy on themes from Nessler's *Trompeter von Säkkingen,* a symph., a string quartet, a violin sonata, and a cantata, *Christnacht.* —Cf. F. Pfohl, *Arthur Nikisch als Mensch und als Künstler* (Leipzig, 1900; new ed., 1925); I. Lipaiev, *Arthur Nikisch* (Moscow, 1904; in Russian); E. Segnitz, *Arthur Ni-*

kisch (1920); A. Dette, *Arthur Nikisch* (1922); H. Chevalley, *Arthur Nikisch, Leben und Wirken* (1922; 2nd ed., 1925). —His son **Mitja Nikisch** (b. Leipzig, May 21, 1899; d. Venice, Aug. 5, 1936) was an excellent pianist; toured South America in 1921; U. S. début in New York, Oct. 23, 1923.

Nikolaidi, Elena, contralto; b. Smyrna, Turkey, of Greek parents, June 13, 1914. She studied voice with Thanos Mellos, whom she married on April 27, 1936; made her operatic début at the Vienna State Opera, Dec. 16, 1936; later sang in Salzburg, London, Prague, and Cairo; American début (in a concert), N. Y., Jan. 20, 1949.

Nikolayev, Leonid Vladimirovitch, Russian pianist and pedagogue; b. Kiev, Aug. 13, 1878; d. Tashkent, Oct. 11, 1942. He was a pupil of Sergey Taneyev and Ippolitov-Ivanov at the Moscow Cons.; then settled in St. Petersburg, where he became prof. of piano at the Cons. in 1906, achieving a fine reputation as a teacher; among his piano pupils was Shostakovitch. Nikolayev went to Tashkent, Central Asia, after the German invasion of Russia in 1941, and died there shortly afterwards. He composed several symph. works; a *Hymn to Beauty* for soli, chorus, and orch.; a cello sonata; a violin sonata; a number of piano works (sonata, *Tarantella,* etc.); also a suite for 2 pianos; made arrangements for piano of organ works by Buxtehude and Pachelbel.

Nikolayeva, Tatiana Petrovna, Russian pianist and composer; b. Bezhitz, May 4, 1924. She studied at the Moscow Cons. with Goldenweiser (piano) and Golubev (composition). After a highly successful series of concerts in Russia, she appeared in Prague (1948); at the bicentennial Bach festival in Leipzig (1950) she won 1st prize for her playing of Bach's clavier works. In 1953 she visited Iceland as a member of the Soviet delegation; in the same year also toured Siberia. Among her works is a cantata, *Song of Happiness* (1949), a piano concerto (1951; received 1st Stalin prize); a vocal cycle, *Iceland* (1953); many piano pieces.

Niles, John Jacob, American folk singer and authority on folk music; b. Louisville, Ky., April 28, 1892. He studied at the Cincinnati Cons. and in France (Univ. and Cons. of Lyons; Schola Cantorum, Paris); pupil of A. Bimboni and Edgar Stillman Kelley. He has made a special study of American folk material and is an authority on the music of the Southern Appalachians; he also makes his own instruments (dulcimers and lutes) and arrangements of folk melodies, which to date include about 1000 songs, and has concertized extensively as a singer and player of this material throughout the U. S. and Europe. He has also composed songs and choral works in folk style. Publ. *7 Kentucky Mountain Songs* (1929); *7 Negro Exultations* (1929); *Songs of the Hill Folk* (1934); *10 Christmas Carols* (1935); *More Songs of the Hill Folk* (1936); *Ballads and Tragic Legends* (1937); *The Anglo-American Ballad Study Book* (1945); *The Anglo-American Carol Study Book* (1948); *The Shape-Note Study Book* (1950); etc. Also the song collections *Singing Soldiers* (1927) and *Songs My Mother Never Taught Me* (with Douglas Moore, 1929).

Nilsson, Kristina (Christine), Swedish soprano; b. Sjöabol, near Vexiö, Aug. 20, 1843; d. Stockholm, Nov. 22, 1921. Her teachers were Baroness Leuhausen, and F. Berwald at Stockholm; with him she continued study in Paris, and on Oct. 27, 1864, made her début, as Violetta in *La Traviata,* at the Théâtre Lyrique, where she was engaged for three years. After successful visits to London, she was engaged 1868-70 at the Paris Opéra; then made long tours with Strakosch in America (1870-2), and sang in the principal Continental cities. In 1872 she married Auguste Rouzaud (d. 1882); her second husband (married 1887) was the Spanish count Angel Vallejo y Miranda (d. 1902). She revisited America in the winters of 1873, 1874, and 1884. Her voice was not powerful, but sweet and brilliant. She excelled as Marguerite and Mignon. —Cf. B. Carlsson, *Kristina Nilsson* (Stockholm, 1922); T. Norlind, *Kristina Nilsson* (Stockholm, 1923); H. Headland, *Christine Nilsson, the Songbird of the North* (Rock Island, Ill., 1943).

Nin (y Castellanos), Joaquín, Spanish composer and pianist; b. Havana, Sept. 29, 1879; d. there, Oct. 24, 1949. He studied piano with Carlos Vidiella in Barcelona, and M. Moszkowski in Paris; composition with d'Indy at the Schola Cantorum; 1906-8, prof. there; 1908-10, in Berlin; then briefly in Havana and Brussels; lived for many years in Paris; member of the French Legion of Honor, Spanish Academy, etc. He made numerous successful pianistic tours of Europe; was especially noted as an interpreter of early piano music. —Works:

A 'mimodrama,' *L'Autre;* for piano: *Suite de valses lyriques, Danza Ibérica, Message à Claude Debussy, '1830': Variations on a Frivolous Theme,* etc.; for violin and piano: *En el jardín de Lindaraja, Suite espagnole,* etc.; *Chants d'Espagne,* for cello; etc.; publ. several essays on general problems of esthetics, among them *Pour l'art* (Paris, 1909; English transl., London, 1915, as *In the Service of Art*), *Idées et Commentaires* (1912), *Clavecin ou Piano* (1921), and *Las Tres Grandes Escuelas.* He edited 2 valuable collections of Spanish keyboard music: *16 sonates anciennes d'auteurs espagnols* (Paris, 1925) and *17 sonates et pièces anciennes d'auteurs espagnols* (Paris, 1929); also 10 violin pieces by Herrando, etc. —Cf. R. Villar, *Músicos Españoles* (vol. II); H. Collet, *L'Essor de la musique espagnole au XXe siècle* (Paris, 1929).

Nin-Culmell, Joaquín, Cuban-Spanish pianist and composer, son of Joaquín Nin; b. Berlin, Sept. 5, 1908. He was a pupil of Falla in Granada, 1930-34; then of Paul Dukas at the Paris Cons.; has concertized in Spain, France, England, Denmark, Italy, Cuba, and the U. S. (N. Y. début, 1936). 1940-49, on the music faculty of Williams College, Williamstown, Mass.; 1949 to 1954, chairman of the music department at the Univ. of California, Berkeley. Served in the Cuban army, 1943. —Works: piano concerto (Williamstown, Mass., Dec. 9, 1946, Rochester Philharmonic, composer soloist); piano quintet (International Society for Contemporary Music Festival, London, 1938); *Tres Impresiones* (1931) and a sonata (1934) for piano; *Dos Canciones* for voice and piano (or string quartet).

Nisard (nē-zahr'), **Théodore,** pen name of Abbé **Théodule-Eléazar-Xavier Normand,** French authority on Gregorian Chant; b. Quaregnon, near Mons, Jan. 27, 1812; d. Jacqueville, Seine-et-Marne, Feb. 29, 1888. He was a chorister at Cambrai, and also studied music at Douay; attended the priests' seminary at Tournai; and in 1839 was appointed director of Enghien Gymnasium, occupying his leisure with the study of church music. In 1842 he became 2nd chef de chant and organist at St. Germain des Prés, Paris; but soon devoted himself wholly to literary work; he publ. the first transcription of the Antiphonary of Montpellier (neumes and Latin letter notation from A to P), discovered by Danjou in 1847. Of his numerous books on plainchant the most important are a revised ed. of Jumilhac's *La science et la pratique du plain-chant* (1847; with Le Clercq) and *Dictionnaire liturgique, historique et pratique du plain-chant et de musique d'église au moyen âge et dans les temps modernes* (1854; with d'Ortigue). He also publ. *De la notation proportionelle au moyen âge* (1847); *Études sur les anciennes notations musicales de l'Europe* (1847); *Études sur la restauration du chant grégorien au XIXe siècle* (1856); *Du rythme dans le plain-chant* (1856); *Les vrais principes de l'accompagnement du plain-chant sur l'orgue d'après les maîtres des XVe et XVIe siècles* (1860); *Des chansons populaires chez les anciens et chez les Français* (1867); *L'archéologie musicale et le vrai chant grégorien* (1890; 2nd ed., 1897).

Nissen, Georg Nikolaus, Danish Councillor of State; b. Hadersleben, Jan. 22, 1761; d. Salzburg, March 24, 1826. He married Mozart's widow in 1809, and collected materials for a biography of Mozart publ. by his widow in 1828 as *Biographie W. A. Mozarts nach Originalbriefen.*

Nissen, Hans Hermann, German baritone; b. near Danzig, May 20, 1896. After a brief business career, he went to Berlin in 1916, where he studied voice with Raatz-Brockmann; 1920, début in recital, then active as a concert and oratorio singer; 1924, operatic début at the Berlin Volksoper; from 1924, member of the Munich Opera; guest appearances in various European opera houses; 1930-32, member of the Chicago Civic Opera; Nov. 23, 1938, début at the Metropolitan Opera House as Wotan.

Noack, Friedrich, German musicologist; b. Darmstadt, July 10, 1890; d. there, Jan. 21, 1958. He studied musicology in Berlin with Kretzschmar, Stumpf, and J. Wolf; 1916, *Dr. phil.,* Leipzig; also pupil of M. Schneider (composition); 1920, docent of musicology at the Univ. of Darmstadt; 1927, associate prof.; teacher for several years at Hoch's Cons. and prof. at the Pädagogische Akademie in Frankfurt; librarian of the court library, music critic, and choral director in Darmstadt. Edited vols. 51 and 52 of 'Denkmäler deutscher Tonkunst' (*Ausgewählte Kirchenkantaten von Chr. Graupner*); vol. 10 (overtures) of the works of Telemann (Kassel, 1955); also revised vol. 1 (on the symphony) of Kretzschmar's *Führer durch den Konzertsaal* (1932). —Publications: *Chr. Graupners Kirchenmusiken* (Leipzig, 1916); *Briegel als Liederkomponist,* in 'Zeitschrift für Musikwissenschaft' I; *Lullys Musik zu*

Molières M. de Pourceaugnac, in 'J. Wolf-Festschrift'; *Bach und Graupner,* in 'Archiv für Musikwissenschaft' II; etc. —**Elizabeth Noack,** his sister (pupil of Wolf and Kretzschmar; *Dr. phil.*), was docent at the Pädagogische Akademie in Kiel. Her writings include *G. Chr. Strattner,* in 'Archiv für Musikwissenschaft' III and *Die Bibliothek der Michaeliskirche in Erfurt,* in 'Archiv für Musikwissenschaft' VII.

Noack, Sylvain, violinist; b. Rotterdam, Aug. 21, 1881; d. Los Angeles, Oct. 26, 1953. He was a pupil (1898-1900) of Elderling at the Cons. in Amsterdam; 1903, teacher at the Cons.; 1906, concertmaster at Aix-la-Chapelle; from 1908, member of Boston Symph. Orch; then concertmaster of the St. Louis Symph. Orch., and lastly, of the Los Angeles Philharmonic.

Nobel, Felix de, Dutch composer and conductor; b. Haarlem, May 27, 1907. He studied piano and composition at the Amsterdam Cons.; has toured as accompanist with Dutch soloists. His works include *5 Irish Folksongs, 3 Old Dutch Songs* for women's chorus, and *5 Jewish Folksongs;* also melodramas for voice and piano.

Noble, Thomas Tertius, organist and composer; b. Bath, England, May 5, 1867; d. Rockport, Mass., May 4, 1953. From 1884-89, he was a pupil at the Royal College of Music of Parratt (organ), J. F. Bridge (harmony, counterpoint), and Stanford (composition). Organist at All Saints', Colchester, 1881-89; assistant organist at Trinity College, Cambridge, 1890-92; organist at Ely Cathedral, 1892-98; in 1898 he founded the York Symphony Orch., which he conducted until 1912; at York Minster, 1898-1913; then organist and choirmaster at St. Thomas' Episcopal Church, New York, until 1947. He made a recital tour of the Eastern States and Canada in 1913; gave recitals at the Panama Exposition in San Francisco, 1915; 1922-24, president of the National Association of Organists; on Feb. 26, 1947, he gave a final organ recital of his works. —Works: a comic opera, *Killibegs* (York, 1911); *Morris Dance* for orch.; *Introduction and Passacaglia* for orch. (Seattle, 1934); suite for violin and orch. (MS); *Gloria Domini,* cantata; Concerto in G minor for organ; *Toccata and Fugue* in F minor for organ; *Solemn March* in E minor for organ; Theme in D♭ with variations, for organ; etc.; anthems, services, and hymns; pieces for violin and piano; choruses; songs; piano pieces. Also publ. *The Training of the Boy Chorister* (N. Y., 1943).

Nobutoki, Kiyoshi, Japanese composer; b. Osaka, Dec. 29, 1887. He studied at the Tokyo Music Academy and in Germany; was prof. at the Academy until 1932; primarily concerned with educational activities. Among his works are a cantata, *Kaido Tosei* (Tokyo, Nov. 26, 1940), other choral works, and several songs.

Nodermann, Preben (Magnus Christian), Danish composer; b. Hjörring, Jan. 11, 1867; d. Lund, Nov. 14, 1930. He was a pupil of O. Malling in Copenhagen (1888-90); 1899-1903, organist in Malmö; then Kapellmeister at the Cathedral in Lund. —Works: the operas *King Magnus* (Hamburg, 1898), *Gunnlögs Saga* (publ. but not produced), *Rokoko* (Leipzig, 1923); an operetta, *Prinz Inkognito* (Copenhagen, 1909; publ. as *Die Jungfernstadt*); motets; sacred and secular choruses; pieces for violin and piano; organ preludes; etc. He made a new vocal score of Gluck's *Orfeo* (1906). Publ. *Tragedien om Orpheus och Eurydice af J. Celcius* (1901) and *Studier i svensk hymnologi* (1911; very valuable).

Nodnagel, (Ernst) Otto, German critic and teacher; b. Dortmund, May 16, 1870; d. Berlin, March 25, 1909. While studying jurisprudence in Heidelberg (1888-90) he also studied music with Ph. Wolfrum; 1890-2, pupil at the Hochschule in Berlin; 1899-1903, prof. of singing at the Cons., and critic of the 'Ostpreussische Zeitung' in Königsberg. He wrote *Jenseits von Wagner und Liszt* (1902), *Stimmbildung und Staat* (1903), *Aus dem Gemerke* (1904); etc.; also orchestral works and songs.

Noël, Victoire. See **Stoltz, Rosine.**

Noël-Gallon. See **Gallon, Noël.**

Noelte, A. Albert, critic and composer; b. Starnberg, Bavaria, March 10, 1885; d. Chicago, March 2, 1946. He went to the U. S. in 1901 and studied music and literature in Boston; critic of the 'Boston Advertiser'; 1908, returned to Munich, where he was critic of the 'Augsburger Abendzeitung'; frequently visited the U. S. as guest teacher, and in 1931 settled there; later, prof. of music at Northwestern Univ., Evanston, Ill.; composed *Prologue to a Romantic Drama* (Chicago, Jan. 16, 1941).

Nohl, (Karl Friedrich) Ludwig, German writer on music; b. Iserlohn, Westphalia, Dec. 5, 1831; d. Heidelberg, Dec. 16, 1885. He studied jurisprudence at Bonn (1850), Heidelberg, and Berlin; and entered the legal profession against his own desire, to please his father. In music he was instructed by Dehn, later (1857) by Kiel, in Berlin. Having embraced music as his profession, he became lecturer at Heidelberg, 1860; associate prof. at Munich, 1865-8; retired to Badenweiler till 1872, when he settled in Heidelberg as a private lecturer, becoming prof. in 1880. —Publications (most also in English): *Mozarts Briefe* (1865; 2nd ed., 1877); *Briefe Beethovens* (1865); *Musikalisches Skizzenbuch* (1866); *Musiker-Briefe* (1867); *Beethovens Leben* (3 vols., 1867-77); *Neues Skizzenbuch* (1869); *Gluck und Wagner* (1870); *Die Beethoven-Feier und die Kunst der Gegenwart* (1871); *Beethoven, Liszt, Wagner* (1874); *Beethoven nach den Schilderungen seiner Zeitgenossen* (Stuttgart, 1877; in English as *Beethoven as depicted by his Contemporaries,* London, 1880); *Mozart nach den Schilderungen seiner Zeitgenossen* (1880); *R. Wagners Bedeutung für die nationale Kunst* (1883); *Das moderne Musikdrama* (1884); *Die geschichtliche Entwickelung der Kammermusik* . . . (1885). For Reclam's 'Universal-Bibliothek' he wrote *Allgemeine Musikgeschichte* and biographies of Beethoven, Mozart, Wagner, Haydn, Weber, Spohr, and Liszt; in addition, he wrote a number of biographies of composers for other publishers.

Nono, Luigi, Italian composer; b. Venice, Jan. 29, 1924; studied with Bruno Maderna and Hermann Scherchen. He adopted the 12-tone system from his earliest works. His list of compositions includes *Variazioni canoniche,* for orch., based on the tone-row of Schoenberg's op. 41 (Darmstadt, Aug. 27, 1950); *Polifonica, Monodia, Ritmica* for flute, clarinet, bass clarinet, saxophone, horn, piano, and percussion (Darmstadt, July 10, 1951); *España en el corazón* (to words by F. G. Lorca) for voices and instruments (Darmstadt, July 21, 1952); ballet *Der rote Mantel* (Berlin, Sept. 20, 1954); *Canti* for 13 instruments (Paris, March 26, 1955); *Incontri* for 24 instruments (Darmstadt, May 30, 1955); *Varianti,* for violin solo, strings, and woodwinds (Donaueschingen, Oct. 20, 1957); *La Terra e la compagna,* for soli, chorus, and instruments (Hamburg, Jan. 13, 1958). The extremely radical idiom of Nono's works frequently caused disturbances among audiences in protest against their ultra-modern effects.

Norden, Norris Lindsay, American composer and theorist; b. Philadelphia, April 24, 1887; d. there, Nov. 3, 1956. He studied with C. Rybner at Columbia Univ. (Mus. Bac., 1910; M. A., 1911); held various positions as church organist in Philadelphia, and conducted choral societies. He wrote several large works for chorus and orch.: *Thanatopsis* (1922); *Te Deum* (1923); *Charity* (1928); overtures; symph. poems, *Silver Plume* (1924), *The White Swan* (1936), etc.; publ. about 150 choral arrangements of sacred works by Russian and Scandinavian composers; also articles on music theory.

Nordica, Lillian (stage name of Lillian Norton), distinguished American soprano; b. Farmington, Maine, May 12, 1857; d. Batavia, Java, May 10, 1914. She studied with John O'Neal at the New England Cons., Boston; made her concert début in Boston, 1876, and toured with the Handel and Haydn Society. In 1877 she made her New York début with Gilmore's Band and in 1878 traveled to Europe as soloist with this band. She then studied operatic roles with Antonio San Giovanni in Milan, who suggested the stage name Nordica, which she used for her operatic début there on March 8, 1879, as Elvira in *Don Giovanni.* In St. Petersburg, she sang for Czar Alexander II a week before he was assassinated in March, 1881; she sang again in Russia early in 1882. After making appearances in several German cities, she made her Paris début on April 22, 1882, as Marguerite, at the Opéra, and in the same year she married Frederick A. Gower. With him she returned to America and made her American début with Colonel Mapleson's company at the Academy of Music (New York) as Marguerite, Nov. 23, 1883, then sang under Mapleson's management in various cities for the next 4 years. In 1883 proceedings begun by her for a separation were suspended on account of her husband's mysterious disappearance while attempting to cross the English Channel in a balloon. She sang for the first time at Covent Garden, London, on March 27, 1887, as Violetta. She first sang at the Metropolitan Opera House, New York, on March 27, 1890, and in Dec., 1893, she became a regular member of the company, which included Melba, Calvé, Eames, the De Reszkes, Plançon. In 1894 she sang Elsa in Bayreuth, and her emphatic success in that part caused her to take up the greater Wagner roles. After careful study with J. Kniese at Bayreuth she was heard for the first time as Isolde (to De Reszke's Tristan) at the Metropolitan Opera House on Nov. 27, 1895, scoring an overwhelming success. From then on she sang chiefly Wagner roles. With short intermissions, she remained at the Metropolitan Opera House until 1908, when she began to make extended concert tours throughout the world, appearing only occasionally in opera. Her farewell appearance was in a recital at Carnegie Hall, New York, on April 24, 1913. In 1896 she married the Hungarian tenor Zoltan Doeme, from whom she was divorced in 1904; on July 30, 1909, she married the banker George W. Young in London. She died while on a trip around the world that was to be her 'farewell tour.' —Cf. O. Thompson, *The American Singer* (New York, 1937); also 'Dictionary of American Biography,' vol. XIII.

Nordoff, Paul, American composer; b. Philadelphia, June 4, 1909. He studied at the Philadelphia Cons. of Music from 1923 (piano with Ezerman and Samaroff), and at the Juilliard School from 1929 (fellowship in piano and composition); received Guggenheim Fellowships in 1933 and 1935. In 1938 he became head of the composition department at the Philadelphia Cons. of Music; resigned in 1943. Assistant prof. of music at Michigan State Coll. (1945-46), then teaching privately in New York. — Works: opera in one act, *The Masterpiece* (Philadelphia, Jan. 24, 1941); a secular Mass for mixed chorus and orch. (1934); *The Sun,* cantata with eurhythmic ballet (1945); suite for orch. (St. Louis, Dec. 6, 1940); violin concerto (1940); 2 piano concertos; various compositions for piano (*Bavarian Variations, Preludes and 3 Fugues,* etc.); 2 string quartets and other chamber music; 2 song-cycles (1943); etc.

Nordquist, Johan Conrad, Swedish conductor; b. Vänersborg, April 11, 1840; d. there, April 16, 1920. He was a pupil of the Music Academy in Stockholm (1856); joined the court orch. in 1859 as viola player; 1864, regimental bandmaster; 1876, chorus master at the Royal Opera; 1885, court conductor; 1888-92, general director. Differences with the singers led to his resignation, but popular demand brought about his reinstatement in 1897. From 1870-2, and again from 1880-1900, he was prof. of harmony at the Cons.; in 1875, organist at the Storkyrka. In 1908 he practically retired, retaining only the ensemble classes and conductorship of the pupils' orch. at the Cons. He was one of the most distinguished of Scandinavian conductors. He wrote a funeral march for the obsequies of Charles XV (1872) and a festival march for the golden wedding of Oscar II (1897), besides piano pieces and songs.

Nordraak, Rikard, the composer of the Norwegian national hymn, *Ja, vi elsker;* b. Christiania, June 12, 1842; d. Berlin, March 20, 1866. He was a pupil of Kiel and Kullak in Berlin; composer of strong Norwegian nationalist tendency; a close friend of Grieg, upon whom he exerted a considerable influence and who wrote a funeral march in his memory. His death at the age of 23 was a grievous loss to Norway's music. Besides the Norwegian national anthem, he wrote music to Björnson's *Mary Stuart in Scotland;* also songs and piano pieces. —Cf. L. Greni, *Rikard Nordraak* (Oslo, 1941); A. van E. Sein, *Rikard Nordraak* (Oslo, 1942); also articles by Ö. Anker in 'Norsk Musikkgranskning' for 1940.

Noren, Heinrich Gottlieb, Austrian composer; b. Graz, Jan. 6, 1861; d. Rottach, Bavaria, June 6, 1928. He was a violin pupil of Massart in Paris; after having filled various posts as violinist in Belgium, Spain, Russia, and Germany, he studied composition with Gernsheim in Berlin; 1896-1902, director of his own Cons. in Crefeld; 1902-7, prof. at Stern's Cons. in Berlin; 1907-11, lived in Loschwitz, near Dresden, as composer; then in Berlin; 1915, retired in Rottach. He attracted considerable attention in 1907 with his orchestral variations *Kaleidoskop,* op. 30 (on a theme from *Ein Heldenleben*). Although it was intended as an act of homage to Strauss, the latter instituted a law suit, which in the end proved to be a most valuable advertisement for Noren. He also composed an opera, *Der Schleier der Beatrice;* symph. in B minor; concerto for violin and orch.; chamber music; pieces for violin; pieces for piano; numerous men's choruses and songs.

Norena, Eide (real name Kaja Hansen Eide), Norwegian soprano; b. Horten, April 26, 1884. She studied voice in Oslo, then in Weimar, London, and Paris; pupil of Raimund von Zur Mühlen; began her career as a concert singer in Scandinavia, later joining the Oslo Opera Co.; sang at La Scala, Milan, then at Covent Garden; 1926-32, member of the Chicago Civic Opera; from 1932, of the Metropolitan Opera Company (début as Mimi, Feb. 9, 1933); from 1935, of the Paris Opéra; toured the U. S. in concert.

Norlind, (Johan Henrik) Tobias, Swedish musicologist; b. Hvellinge, May 6, 1879; d. Upsala, Aug. 13, 1947. He was a pupil of F. Rothstein (piano) and A. Berg (theory) in Lund; of von Bose (piano) and Jadassohn (composition) at the Leipzig Cons., 1897-8; of L. Thuille (composition) in Munich, 1898-9, and at the same time of A. Sandberger (musicology) at the Univ.; the following winter he continued his studies in musicology at the Univ. of Berlin with O. Fleischer and M. Friedlaender. Returning in 1900 to his native country, he attended the universities of Upsala and Lund, and from the latter obtained the degree of *Dr. phil.* in 1909 for his dissertation *Skolsäng och Soekengäng i Sverige.* From 1907-14 he was director of the high school in Tomelilla; also (from 1909) instructor in history of literature and music at Lund Univ.; 1921, appointed prof. of music history at the Royal Academy of Music, Stockholm. At various times he received stipends from the government for extended travels for research in Austria, Italy, England, and Switzerland. —Writings: *Svensk musikhistoria* (1901; German transl., abridged, 1904; 2nd ed., 1918); *Musiken vid svenska skolor under 1600 talet* (1906-07); *Beethoven* (1907; 2nd ed., 1923); *Latinska skolsånger i Sverige och Finland* (1909); *Studier i svensk folklore* (1911); *Svenska allmogens lif* (1912; 2nd ed., 1926); *Allmänt Musiklexikon* (2 vols., 1916; 2nd ed., 1927; very valuable for Scandinavian and Finnish music); *Erik Gustav Geijer som musiker* (1919); *Jenny Lind* (1919); *Allmän Musikhistoria* (1920); *Wagner* (1923); *Kristina Nilsson* (1923); *Beethoven och hans Tid* (1924; a different book from his earlier and much smaller Beethoven monograph); *Kungl. Hovkapellets historia 1526-1926* (with E. Trobäck, 1926); *Konzert- und Opernlexikon* (1928); *Die schwedische Hofkapelle in der Reformationszeit,* in 'Johannes Wolf-Festschrift' (1929); *Några livsbilder och Kulturbilder ur musikens wärld* (1929); *Svensk Folkmusik och folkdans* (1930); *Systematik der Saiteninstrumente* (2 vols., 1936, 1939); *Dansens historia* (1941); *Musikinstrumentens historia* (1941); *Bilder ur svenska musikens historia* in 4 vols.: *Från äldsta tid till medeltidens slut* (1 vol., 1947); *Från Tyska kyrkans glansdagar* (3 vols., 1944-45); numerous articles on Swedish music in various European publications. —Cf. C. A. Moberg, *Tobias Norlind och svensk musikhistorisk forskning,* in 'Svensk Tidskrift för Musikforskning' (1929, vol. II, pp. 5-30; contains a list of Norlind's publications).

Norman, (Fredrick Vilhelm) Ludvig, Swedish conductor; b. Stockholm, Aug. 28, 1831; d. there, March 28, 1885. Under the patronage of Prince (later King) Oscar, Jenny Lind, and Lindblad, he was sent to Leipzig Cons., where he studied with Moscheles, Hauptmann, and Rietz (1848-52); returning to Stockholm, he became (1859) conductor of the new Philharmonic Society, in 1861 prof. of composition in the Swedish Academy, and conductor of the Opera; also president of the Music Academy; retired in 1879. He married the violinist Wilma Neruda in 1864 (divorced 1869). Publ. *Musikaliska Uppsatser och Kritiker,* 1880-85 (Stockholm, 1888); wrote 4 symphonies; a piano concerto; a string octet; a piano sextet; other chamber music; 11 books of songs; piano pieces. —Cf. L. Lagerbielke, *Svenska tonsättare* (Stockholm, 1908).

Norris, Homer Albert, American organist; b. Wayne, Maine, Oct. 4, 1860; d. New York, Aug. 14, 1920. He was a pupil of Marston; a graduate of the New England Cons., where he received instruction from Turner, Emery, and Chadwick; studied 4 years in Paris under Guilmant, Dubois, Godard, and Gigout (chiefly composition and theory). He was organist at the Ruggles St. Baptist Church, Boston, for 12 years; 1904-14, organist and choirmaster at St. George's Church, New York. —He publ. *Practical Harmony on a French Basis* (Boston, 1896); *The Art of Counterpoint* (1899).

Norton, Eunice, American pianist; b. Minneapolis, June 30, 1908. She studied piano there, then with T. Matthay in London (1930) and A. Schnabel (1931-33); made her début in Queen's Hall, London, 1924; concertized in Germany, France, and Holland; 1932, American début in New York; appeared as soloist with leading American orchestras and in recital.

Norton, Lillian B. See **Nordica.**

Norton, William Wellington, American music educator; b. Elmira, N. Y., Feb. 16, 1881. He attended the Univ. of Nebraska, Teachers College, N. Y., Sioux Falls College and the Univ. of Minnesota; 1909, B. A.; 1910, M. A.; 1936, Mus. Doc.; head of music department at Sioux Falls College (1899-1903) and Univ. of North Dakota (1910-19); from 1921 musical and executive organizer of the Community Music Association, Flint, Mich.; also, from 1922, conductor of the Flint Symph. Orch.; president of the North-Central Music Educators Conference (1932-33), etc. He edited the *Minnesota Song Book* (1911).

Noskowski (nos-kŏhv'-skē), **Sigismund (Zygmunt von)**, Polish conductor and composer; b. Warsaw, May 2, 1846; d. Wiesbaden, July 23, 1909. He was a pupil at the Warsaw Musical Institute, 1864-7. After his invention of a music notation for the blind, the Music Society sent him (1873) to study under Kiel and Raif at Berlin. 1876, conductor of the Bodau Society, Konstanz; 1881-92, director of the Music Society at Warsaw, and (1888) prof. at the Cons. there; in 1904 appointed 2nd conductor of the Warsaw Philharmonic Society, and in 1906 2nd conductor at the opera. —Works: the operas *Livia Quintilla* (Lemberg, 1898) and *Wyrok* (Warsaw, 1907); 3 symphonies; *Z życia (From Life)*, variations on the theme of Chopin's Prelude in A; *Die Steppe*, symphonic poem; cantatas; 3 string quartets; a piano quartet; pieces for piano; songs; etc. Also publ. 2 collections of folk melodies and (with M. Zawirski) a book on harmony and counterpoint (Warsaw, 1909).

Notker (Balbulus), a monk at the Monastery of St. Gall; b. Elgg, near Zürich (or Jonschwyl, near St. Gall) c. 840; d. April 6, 912. One of the earliest and most important composers of Sequences. Several short musical treatises in Latin and German are traditionally inscribed to him; but these should be more correctly attributed to a certain **Notker Labeo**, who was also a monk at St. Gall, but who flourished about a century later than Notker 'Balbulus' (a nickname meaning 'the stammerer'). It has also been established that he was not the author of the *Media in vita in morte sumus* (cf. P. Wagner, *Das Media vita*, in 'Schweizerisches Jahrbuch für Musikwissenschaft' I). Gerbert ('Scriptores,' I) publ. 4 of the abovementioned treatises, together with a commentary on the so-called 'Romanian' letters (this is probably a forgery). Two of these treatises, also a fifth one (presumably also by N. Labeo), are included in Riemann's *Studien zur Geschichte der Notenschrift*. All 5 treatises were publ. by Piper in 2 vols. as part of the projected collected edition of Notker Labeo's works. —Cf. A. K. Henschel, *Zehn Sequenzen des Notker Balbulus, aus den ältesten Quellen übertragen und mit der Überlieferung verglichen* (dissertation, Erlangen, 1924); R. van Doren, *Étude sur l'influence musicale de l'Abbaye de St. Gall* (1925); H. Husmann, *Die St. Galler Sequenztradition bei Notker und Ekkehard*, in 'Acta Musicologica' (vol. 26; 1954).

Nottebohm, Martin Gustav, German musicologist; b. Lüdenscheid, Westphalia, Nov. 12, 1817; d. Graz, Oct. 29, 1882. He was a pupil of Berger and Dehn at Berlin, 1828-9; of Schumann and Mendelssohn at Leipzig, 1840; and 1846 of Sechter at Vienna, where he settled as a music teacher and writer (a Beethoven specialist). —Works: *Ein Skizzenbuch von Beethoven* (1865); *Thematisches Verzeichniss der im Druck erschienenen Werke von Beethoven* (2nd ed., 1868; reprint 1913); *Beethoveniana* (2 vols., 1872, 1887); *Beethovens Studien* (vol. I, 1873; Beethoven's exercises, etc., under Haydn, Albrechtsberger, and Salieri, after the original MSS); *Thematisches Verzeichniss der im Druck erschienenen Werke von Franz Schubert* (1874); *Mozartiana* (1880); *Ein Skizzenbuch von Beethoven aus dem Jahre 1803* (1880). Paul Mies republished 2 of Nottebohm's eds. of Beethoven's sketchbooks as *Zwei Skizzenbücher von Beethoven aus den Jahren 1801 bis 1803* (Leipzig, 1924).

Nouguès (noo-gäs'), **Jean**, French composer; b. Bordeaux, April 25, 1875; d. Auteuil, Aug. 28, 1932. He showed remarkable precocity as a composer, having completed an opera, *Le Roi du Papagey*, before he was 16. After regular study in Paris he produced his opera *Yannha* at Bordeaux in 1897. On reaching his majority, he came into a considerable fortune, the greater part of which he squandered in a few years, during which he did nothng with his music beyond retouching his early opera (Bordeaux, 1901). The next two operas, *Thamyris* (Bordeaux, 1904) and *La Mort de Tintagiles* (Paris, 1905), were brought out without much success; but after the production of his spectacular *Quo Vadis* (text by H. Cain after Sienkiewicz's famous novel; Nice, Feb. 9, 1909) he suddenly found himself famous. The work was given in Paris on Nov. 26, 1909, in New York on April 4, 1911; had numerous revivals in subsequent years. His later operas failed to measure up to *Quo Vadis;* they included *L'Auberge rouge* (Nice, Feb. 21, 1910), *La Vendetta* (Marseilles, 1911), *L'Aiglon* (Rouen, Feb. 2, 1912), and *Le Scarabée bleu* (1931).

Nourrit (noo-rē'), **Adolphe**, French tenor; b. Paris, March 3, 1802; d. Naples, March 8, 1839. He was trained by García, who persuaded his father to let him become a singer; his début at the Paris Opéra (Sept.

10. 1821) as Pylades in Gluck's *Iphigénie en Tauride,* was successful. In 1826 he succeeded his father (**Louis Nourrit,** 1780-1831) as leading tenor, creating important roles in operas by Rossini, Auber, Meyerbeer, etc. In 1837, discontented by the popular success of his rival Duprez, he left the Opéra and decided to study Italian methods of singing. After touring the French provinces he went to Italy and in March, 1838, began to study with Donizetti. He planned to make his Italian début in the latter's *Polyeucte,* but the censor forbade the production. He was given only mediocre roles to sing at La Scala in Milan, although he achieved a fine success at Naples. But the combination of disappointment and overwork led to a state of dejection, and he committed suicide by leaping from the roof of his dwelling. He was an exceptionally endowed singer, and an excellent teacher (in the Paris Cons. for ten years). The roles of Robert, Masaniello, Arnold, Eléazar, Raoul, and many others, were written expressly for Nourrit. —Cf. L. M. Quicherat, *Adolphe Nourrit* (3 vols., Paris, 1867); E. Boutet de Monvel, *Un artiste d'autrefois. Adolphe Nourrit* (2 vols., Paris, 1903); F. Rogers, *Adolphe Nourrit,* in the 'Mus. Quarterly' (Jan., 1939).

Nováček (nŏh'-vah-chĕhk), **Ottokar (Eugen),** violinist and composer; b. Fehértemplom (Weisskirchen), Hungary, May 13, 1866; d. New York, Feb. 3, 1900. He was a pupil of his father, Martin Joseph Nováček; then of Dont in Vienna and of Schradieck and Brodsky at the Leipzig Cons., graduating in 1885 with the Mendelssohn prize. In Leipzig he joined the Brodsky Quartet as 2nd violin (later viola). In 1891 he was engaged by Nikisch to join the Boston Symph. Orch. as a violinist; in 1892-93 he played the viola in the Damrosch Orch., N. Y. He was forced to abandon work in 1899, because of a heart disease, and died shortly afterwards at the age of 33. He is known as a composer chiefly through his *Perpetuum mobile* for violin and orch. (or with piano), which became a standard virtuoso piece in the violin repertory. His piano concerto (1896) was introduced by Busoni; he also wrote a Sinfonietta for 8 woodwind instruments; 3 string quartets; 2 Concert Caprices for piano; 8 Concert Caprices for violin and piano; *Bulgarian Dances* for violin and piano; and songs.

Novaës (no-vī'-es), **Guiomar,** Brazilian concert pianist; b. São João da Boã Vista, Feb. 28, 1895. At the age of 4 she began to play by ear; at 7 she was placed under Prof. Chiafarelli in São Paulo, under whom her progress was so rapid that in 1904 she was exhibited as a prodigy; for the next 5 years she continued her studies, but also made frequent appearances in public. In 1909 she entered the competition for a scholarship at the Paris Cons., winning the first place over 380 rivals; studied there for 2 years with I. Philipp, graduating in 1911 as winner of the 1st prize; the same year, made a highly successful début in Paris; until 1913 she toured France, Germany, England, Italy, and Switzerland; then appeared at São Paulo and Rio de Janeiro. Her début in the U. S. took place at New York, Nov. 11, 1915; she has appeared as soloist with all the major American orchestras. In 1922 she married the Brazilian composer and architect Octavio Pinto (q.v.).

Novák (nŏh'-vahk), **Vitězslav,** Czech composer; b. Kamenitz, Bohemia, Dec. 5, 1870; d. Skutec (Slovakia), July 18, 1949. He studied under Jiránek, Stecker, and Dvořák at the Prague Cons.; 1909-20, prof. of composition there; from 1920 prof. of composition at the Czech State Cons.; 1912-22, rector of that institution. Brahms was the first to discover the extraordinary talent of Novák and recommended his works to Simrock for publication. Novák's earlier compositions show the influence of German Romanticism, but later he became one of the foremost exponents of nationalism. As a teacher he had a strong influence on young Czech composers. In 1946 he received the title of national artist of the Republic of Czechoslovakia.—Works: the operas *Karlštejn* (Prague, Nov. 18, 1916), *Burgkobold* (*The Sprite of the Castle;* Prague, Oct. 10, 1915), *Lucerna* (Prague, May 13, 1923), *Jano der Geiger* (Brno, Jan. 16, 1926); the ballets *Signorina Gioventù* (Prague, March 8, 1930) and *Nikotina* (Prague, March 8, 1930); for orch.: *Maryša,* dramatic overture (1898); *In der Tatra,* symph. poem (1902); *Von ewiger Sehnsucht,* symph. poem (1904); *Toman und die Waldfee,* symph. poem (1907); op. 36, *Serenade; Lady Godiva,* overture (1907); *De Profundis,* symph. poem (Brno, Nov. 20, 1941); vocal music: *Der Sturm* for soli, chorus, and orch. (1910); *Die Totenbraut* for soli, chorus, and orch. (1913); *Dvanáct Ukolébavek* (12 Lullabies), variations on a poem for women's voices (Prague, 1938); chamber music: op. 1, piano trio in G minor; op. 7, piano quartet in C minor; op. 12, piano quintet in A minor; op. 22, string quartet in G; op. 27, *Trio quasi una ballata,* in D minor; op. 35, string quartet in D; op. 68, sonata for viola, cello, and piano; for piano: op. 2, *Ballade;* op. 9, *Serenaden;* op. 10, *Barkarolen;* op. 11, *Eklogen;* op. 15, *3 Czech Dances;* op. 24, *Sonata eroica;* op. 30, *Winternachtgesänge;* op. 32, *Slovácká suita* (also orch.); op. 43, *Pan,* tone poem (5 movements; also orch.); op. 45, *Suite exoticon* (also orch.); *Christmas Sonatina;* op. 73, *St. Wenceslas Triptych* for organ; songs; etc. —Cf. Z. Nejedlý, *Vitězslav Novák* (in Czech; 1921); H. Holländer, *Vitězslav Novák,* in the 'Schweizerische Musikzeitung' (Feb., 1931); Rosa Newmarch, in the 'Chesterian' (July, 1931); K. Hoffmeister, *Tvorba V. Nováka, z let 1941-1948* (Prague, 1949); G. Carritt, *Vitězslav Novák,* in the 'Monthly Musical Record' (July, 1950).

Novello, Clara Anastasia, daughter of Vincent Novello; English soprano; b. London, June 10, 1818; d. Rome, March 12, 1908. Having studied piano and singing in London, she entered the Paris Cons. in 1829, but returned home the following year because of the revolution. After a successful début on Oct. 22, 1832, at Windsor, she was engaged for the Philharmonic Society, the Antient Concerts, and the principal festivals. In 1837 Mendelssohn engaged her for the Gewandhaus concerts; she then sang in Berlin, Vienna, Düsseldorf, St. Petersburg, etc.; in 1839 she prepared herself for the stage under Micheroux in Milan, making her operatic début in Padua (July 6, 1841); sang with great success in the principal Italian cities, and appeared at Drury Lane in 1843. On Nov. 22, 1843, she married Count Gigliucci, withdrawing to private life for several years; reappeared in 1850, singing in concert and opera (chiefly in England and Italy). After her farewell appearance in London in 1860 (*Messiah*), while still at the height of her powers, she retired to Rome. —Cf. Valeria Gigliucci, *Clara Novello's Reminiscences, compiled by her daughter* (London, 1910; with memoir by A. D. Coleridge); Averil Mackenzie-Grieve, *Clara Novello* (London, 1955).

Novello, Joseph Alfred, English music publisher, son of Vincent Novello; b. London, Aug. 12, 1810; d. Genoa, July 17, 1896. He was also a bass singer, organist, and composer; choirmaster at Lincoln's Inn Chapel. He entered his father's business at 19. He inaugurated an important innovation, the printing of separate vocal parts for choir use; did much to popularize classical music in England by publishing cheap oratorio scores. Retired in 1856 to Nice, later to Genoa. —See **Novello & Co.**

Novello, Vincent, English music publisher; b. London, Sept. 6, 1781; d. Nice, Aug. 9, 1861. He was a chorister in the Sardinian Chapel, Duke St., under Webbe; later deputy organist to Webbe and Danby, and 1797-1822 organist at the chapel of the Portuguese Embassy. Pianist to the Italian Opera, 1812; co-founder of the Philharmonic Society, sometimes conducting its concerts; 1840-43, organist at the Roman Catholic Chapel, Moorfields. In 1811 he founded the great London music publishing firm of Novello & Co. Himself a composer of sacred music (Masses, motets, anthems, Kyries, etc.), he gathered together and published excellent collections: 'A Collection of Sacred Music' (1811; 2 vols.); 'Purcell's Sacred Music' (1829; 5 vols.); 'Croft's Anthems'; 'Greene's Anthems'; 'Boyce's Anthems'; Masses by Haydn, Mozart, Beethoven; etc. He retired to Nice in 1849. —See **Novello & Co.** —Cf. Mary Cowden-Clarke, *Life and Labours of Vincent Novello* (London, 1862); W. Barclay Squire, *Some Novello Correspondence,* in the 'Mus. Quarterly' (April, 1917); 'Dictionary of National Biography,' vol. XLI; also N. Medici and R. Hughes, *A Mozart Pilgrimage* (London, 1955; travel diaries of Vincent Novello and his wife).

Novello & Co., prominent firm of music publishers, founded in 1811 at London by Vincent Novello (q.v.). Under the management of his eldest son, Joseph Alfred (q.v.), the business increased enormously, and after the latter's retirement in 1856 **Henry Littleton** (d. London, May 11, 1888), who for some years had been a partner, assumed the general management, becoming sole proprietor in 1866. The following year he acquired the business of Ewer and Co., and in 1867 changed the name of the firm to 'Novello, Ewer & Co.' On his retirement in 1887 he was succeeded by his sons, Alfred H. and Augustus J. Littleton, and his sons-in-law, George T. S. Gill and Henry W. Brooke. In 1898 the house was formed into a limited company, under the name of 'Novello & Co., Ltd.' In 1846 they acquired 'Mainzer's Mus. Times' (established 1844), which they have publ. since then as the 'Mus. Times.' The New York branch, established in 1850, was taken over in 1906 by H. W. Gray & Co. —See J. Bennett, *A Short History of Cheap Music as Exemplified in* *the Records of the House of Novello, Ewer & Co.* (1887); *The Novello Centenary,* in the 'Musical Times' (June, 1911).

Novello-Davies, Clara, Welsh singing teacher and choral conductor; b. Cardiff, April 7, 1861; d. London, March 1, 1943. Her real surname was Davies; her father (who was also her first teacher) called her 'Clara Novello' after the celebrated singer of that name, and she adopted the combined name professionally. She sang at concerts from 1872; in 1881 she turned to choral conducting; organized a Royal Welsh Ladies' Choir, with which she traveled with fine success in Great Britain, France, America, and South Africa; at the World's Fair in Chicago (1893) and at the Paris Exposition of 1900 the chorus was awarded 1st prize. She was commended by Queen Victoria (1894) and by King George and Queen Mary (1928). She publ. a number of successful songs *(A Voice from the Spirit Land, The Vigil, Comfort,* etc.). Author of the book *You Can Sing* and an autobiography, *The Life I Have Loved* (London, 1940). — Her son, **Ivor Novello** (b. 1893; d. London, March 6, 1951), wrote (at her request) the song *Keep the Home Fires Burning,* immensely popular during the World War of 1914-18.

Noverre (nŏh-vär'), **Jean-Georges,** the introducer of dramatic action into the ballet (ballet-pantomime); b. Paris, April 29, 1727; d. St.-Germain-en-Laye, Nov. 19, 1810. He was a solo dancer at Berlin; ballet master at the Opéra-Comique, Paris, 1749; at London, 1757-75; at Lyons, Stuttgart, Vienna, Milan, and (1775-80) at the Grand Opéra, Paris. —He publ. *Lettres sur la danse, et sur les ballets* (1760, several eds.; English transl., London, 1782, 1930, 1951). —Cf. C. E. Noverre, *Life and Works of the Chevalier Noverre* (London, 1882); H. Abert, *Jean Georges Noverre und sein Einfluss auf die dramatische Ballet-Komposition,* in 'Jahrbuch Peters' (1908); H. Niedecken, *J. G. Noverre; sein Leben und seine Beziehungen zur Musik* (Halle, 1914); D. Lynham, *The Chevalier Noverre* (London, 1950).

Novotna, Jarmila, Czechoslovak soprano; b. Prague, Sept. 23, 1903. She studied with Emmy Destinn; made her début in *La Traviata* (Prague, June 27, 1926); in 1928, joined the roster of the Berlin State Opera. She made her American début at San Francisco, in *Madama Butterfly* (Oct. 18, 1939); first sang at the Metropolitan Opera, N. Y., in *La Bohème,* Jan. 5, 1940; also appeared at La Scala, Milan; Teatro Colón, Buenos Aires; and other opera houses in Europe and America.

Novotný, Václav Juda, Bohemian composer; b. Wesetz, near Počatek, Sept. 17, 1849; d. late July, 1922. He studied at the Prague Organ School with Skuherský; for many years editor of the Bohemian musical paper 'Dalibor'; composed pieces for violin and songs; made a large collection of Bohemian folksongs; transl. into Bohemian about 100 opera texts, among them all the dramatic works of Wagner.

Nowak, Leopold, Austrian musicologist; b. Vienna, Aug. 17, 1904. He studied at the Univ. there *(Dr. phil.,* 1932); docent, 1939; prof. 1946; from 1946 to 1954, director of the music division of the National Library in Vienna. From 1954, editor of the Collected Works of Bruckner. —Writings: *Grundzüge einer Geschichte des Basso ostinato in der abendländischen Musik* (Vienna, 1932); *Franz Liszt* (1936); *Te Deum laudamus* (on the music of Bruckner; Vienna, 1947); *Joseph Haydn* (Zürich, 1951). Also edited a collection of German Renaissance part-songs in the 'Denkmäler der Tonkunst in Österreich' (vol. 72).

Nowak, Lionel, American composer and pianist; b. Cleveland, Sept. 25, 1911. He studied theory and composition with Roger Sessions, Quincy Porter, and Herbert Elwell; piano with Beryl Rubinstein and Edwin Fischer; has been active as conductor, lecturer, and teacher; was on the faculty of the music dept. of Syracuse Univ. (1946-48) and from 1948 has taught at Bennington College. —Works: modern dance scores: *On My Mother's Side* (1939), *Flickers* (1941), *House Divided* (1943), *Story of Mankind* (1945); concertino for piano and small orch. (1944); sonata for unaccompanied violin (1950); *Fantasia* for 3 instruments (1951); suite for 4 wind instruments (1945); quartet for oboe and strings (1952); suite for clarinet, cello, and piano (1953); piano trio (1954); piano pieces; songs.

Nowowiejski (nŏh-vŏh-v'yĕh'y-skē), **Felix,** Polish composer; b. Wartenburg, Ermeland, Feb. 7, 1877; d. Poznan, Jan. 23, 1946. He was a pupil of Bussler at Stern's Cons. in Berlin; won a prize for composition in London (1899), and the Paderewski Prize (Bonn, 1903). He lived as teacher of composition and conductor of various choral societies in Berlin; from 1909, director of the Musical Society and conductor of the symph. concerts in Cracow; also conductor of the Warsaw Philharmonic Orch.; 1914, returned to Berlin, where he lived during the war; 1920-27, prof. of organ and church music at the State Cons. in Poznan. In 1935 he won the Polish State Music Prize. The oratorio *Quo Vadis* (after Sienkiewicz) is his best-known work. Also wrote operas, orchestral works, organ pieces, oratorios, choruses, songs, etc.

Nucius (Nucis), Johannes, German composer and theorist; b. Görlitz, c. 1556; d. Himmelwitz, March 25, 1620. In 1591 he became a Cistercian monk in the monastery of Rauden; from 1609, abbot of the monastery of Himmelwitz in Silesia. He publ. *Modulationes sacrae,* 5-6 voices (1591), and 2 books of *Sacrae cantiones* (1609); 2 of his Masses are in MS. Also publ. a theoretical work, *Musices poeticae sive De compositione cantum praeceptiones ultissimae* (1613). —Cf. B. Widmann, *Johannes Nucius, Abt von Himmelwitz* (Bregenz, 1921); E. Kirsch, *Von der Persönlichkeit und dem Stil des . . . Johannes Nucius* (1926).

Nuitter, Charles Louis Etienne, French writer on music; b. Paris, April 24, 1828; d. there, Feb. 24, 1899. He was a lawyer by profession; then became interested in the theater; was custodian of the archives of the Paris Opéra. He changed his real name, Truinet, to Nuitter by anagrammatic transposition of letters, and under that name wrote librettos for many operas and operettas, including some by Offenbach; also translated librettos of operas by Weber, Mozart, Wagner, and Verdi; wrote scenarios for Delibes (*Coppélia*) and others. He publ. *Le nouvel opéra* (1875); *Les Origines de l'opéra français* (1886; with Thoinan); many articles in music magazines.

Nunn, Edward Cuthbert, English organist, conductor, and composer; b. Bristol, Feb. 23, 1868; d. London, Nov. 26, 1914. He studied at the Royal Academy of Music; then served as organist at various churches, and conducted opera. He composed a ballet suite, *Fête Champêtre;* a cantata, *Everyman;* the children's operas: *Kamar-al-Zaman, The Fairy Slipper, The Shepherdess and the Sweep, The Garden of Paradise, The Wooden Bowl.*

Nunó, Jaime, Spanish bandmaster; composer of the Mexican national anthem; b. San Juan de las Abadesas, Sept. 8, 1824; d. Auburndale, N. Y., July 18, 1908. He studied with Mercadante in Italy; in 1851 went to Cuba, and in 1853 to Mexico, where he was appointed chief of military bands; was commissioned to write a national anthem for Mexico; it was sung for the 1st time on Sept. 15, 1854. Subsequently he was active as impresario for Italian opera companies in Cuba, Mexico, and the U. S. In 1870 he settled in Buffalo as organist and teacher; composed a number of sacred works.

Nussio, Otmar, composer; b. Grosseto, Italy, Oct. 23, 1902. He was a student of Respighi in Rome; then went to Switzerland; taught flute at the Zürich Cons.; in 1938 became music director of Radio Monte Ceneri. He has conducted a number of concerts of light music; composed numerous orchestral suites: *Suite ticinese* (his best), *Escapades musicales, Danza di Mallorca;* a flute concerto, a piano concerto, a violin concerto; also a children's opera, *Hans im Märchenland.* His suite for harpsichord, flute, violin solo, and strings, *Rubensiana,* was performed for the first time in the Rubens House in Antwerp, on May 21, 1950.

Nyiregyházi (nĭ'-rĕh-zh'hah-zē), **Erwin,** Hungarian pianist; b. Budapest, Jan. 19, 1903. He studied with Dohnányi, Thomán, and Székely; then with Lamond in Berlin. From early infancy he showed a phenomenal musical ability, so that his sense of pitch and other faculties were made the subject of study, publ. in a volume by G. Révész, *Erwin Nyiregyházi; Psychologische Analyse eines musikalisch hervorragenden Kindes* (Leipzig, 1916; in English as *The Psychology of a Musical Prodigy,* 1925). In 1930 he came to the U. S., and settled in Hollywood as a film studio pianist.

Nystedt, Knut, Norwegian composer; b. Oslo, Sept. 3, 1915. He studied organ with A. Sandvold in Oslo and with E. White in N. Y.; composition with B. Brustad in Oslo, and Aaron Copland in America. —Works: *Norge mitt land,* for chorus and orch. (1946); *Spenningens Land* (*The Land of Suspense*), symph. fantasy (Oslo, Sept. 29, 1948); string quartet (1939); violin sonata (1942); *Introduzione e Passacaglia* for organ (1944); vocal pieces.

Nystroem, Gösta, Swedish composer; b. Silvberg, Oct. 13, 1890. He studied piano with his father; composition with Lundberg in Stockholm. In 1920 he went to Paris, where he took lessons from Vincent d'Indy. He also studied painting, and had several art exhibitions in Scandinavia. In 1932 he returned to Sweden, where he continued to be active as composer, painter, and critic. His music is marked with Romantic tendencies, with some touch of Impressionism and, in some instances, neo-Classicism. —Works: ballet, *Ungersvennen och de sex Prinsessorna* (*Young Men and Six Princesses;* 1951); radio drama, *De Blinda* (*The Blind,* 1949); for orch.: symph. poem, *Babels Torn* (*The Tower of Babel,* 1928), *Regrets,* a lyric suite (1929), *Sinfonia breve* (1929-31), *Sinfonia espressiva* (1932-35), viola concerto (1941), *Sinfonia concertante,* for cello and orch. (1945), *Sinfonia del mare* (1948), symph. suite, *Palettskrap* (*Palette Jottings,* 1951); chamber music; songs.

O

Oakeley, Sir **Herbert Stanley,** English composer; b. Ealing, Middlesex, July 22, 1830; d. London, Oct. 26, 1903. He studied at Oxford; later attended the Leipzig Cons.; also took organ lessons in Dresden and Bonn. In 1865 he was appointed prof. of music at Edinburgh Univ., and held this post until 1891; was influential in the musical affairs of Scotland in general. He wrote a cantata, *Jubilee Lyric;* a *Suite in the Olden Style,* for orch.; many pieces of church music; choruses, arrangements of Scottish national melodies, etc. —Cf. E. M. Oakeley, *The Life of Sir H. S. Oakeley* (London, 1904).

Ober, Margarete, German soprano; b. Berlin, April 15, 1885. She studied with various teachers in Berlin; made her operatic début as Azucena in Frankfurt (Aug. 20, 1906); was then a member of the Berlin Opera; appeared with the Metropolitan Opera, N. Y., as Ortrud, on Nov. 21, 1913; continued to sing there until 1916; then settled in Berlin as a teacher; was still active in 1954. In 1910 she married her former teacher, Arthur Arndt.

Oberhoffer, Emil, conductor; b. near Munich, Aug. 10, 1867; d. San Diego, Calif., May 22, 1933. He received his musical training from his father, an organist; learned to play violin and organ; later studied piano in Paris with Isidor Philipp. He then came to the U. S.; in 1897 settled in St. Paul, Minnesota; became conductor of the Philharmonic Choral Society in Minneapolis (1901); succeeded in securing an endowment for the establishment of a permanent orch.; gave his first concert with the newly organized Minneapolis Symph. Orch. on Nov. 5, 1903; led it until 1923; made several appearances with other orchestras; then retired, and lived in California.

Oberthür, Karl, German harp player and composer; b. Munich, March 4, 1819; d. London, Nov. 8, 1895. He studied with Elise Brauchle and G. V. Röder in Munich; after playing at various theaters in Switzerland and Germany, he went to London in 1844; established himself as a teacher in London. He wrote 2 operas; several cantatas; a symph. legend, *Lorelei,* for harp and orch.; a nocturne for 3 harps; many elegant soli for harp (*Élégie, Pensées musicales, Réveil des elfes, Miranda, Le Sylphe,* etc.).

Obin (oh-ban'), **Louis-Henri,** French bass singer; b. Ascq, near Lille, Aug. 4, 1820; d. Paris, Nov. 11, 1895. From 1844 till 1869 he was a renowned singer at the Paris Opéra; after his retirement from the stage, he taught at the Paris Cons. (1871-91).

Oborin, Lev Nikolayevitch, Russian pianist; b. Moscow, Sept. 11, 1907. He studied at the Moscow Cons. with Igumnov, graduating with honors in 1926; in 1928, was appointed instructor in piano there; in 1935, was named prof.; received various prizes as pianist, but dedicated himself mainly to teaching.

Obouhov (oh'-bŏŏ-**hov**), **Nicolas,** Russian composer; b. Moscow, April 22, 1892; d. Paris, June 13, 1954. He studied at the St. Petersburg Cons. with Nicolas Tcherepnin and Maximilian Steinberg; after the Revolution he settled in Paris, where he took some lessons with Ravel. He devoted his entire life to his major work, of great dimensions, *Le Livre de Vie,* for solo voices, chorus, 2 pianos, and orch. The score (never published) is some 2,000 pages long, and it employs a new notation devised by Obouhov, with accidentals represented by crosses; its introductory section was performed by Koussevitzky in Paris, June 3, 1926. In 1934 he supervised the construction of an electronic instrument, 'croix sonore' (sounding cross), in the form of a cross; wrote several pieces for it, which were performed by Mme. Aussenac de Broglie. A mystic, he signed some of his works 'Nicolas l'illuminé' and used his own blood for sectional marks in his scores. He publ. *Traité d'harmonie tonale, atonale et totale* (Paris, 1946). Several French musicians adopted his new notation; Honegger publ. a piano piece in this notation. A special Prix Obouhov was established in 1957 for the best piece written in the Obouhov notation. —Cf. Boris de Schloezer, *Nicolas Obouhov,* in the 'Revue Musicale' (1921).

Oboussier, Robert, Swiss composer; b. Antwerp (of Swiss parents), July 9, 1900; d. (stabbed to death), Zürich, June 9, 1957. He studied at the Cons. of Zürich, with Volkmar Andreae and Philipp Jarnach (composition); then with Siegfried Ochs in Berlin (conducting). He then lived in Florence (1922-28); was music editor of the 'Deutsche allgemeine Zeitung' but in 1938 political conditions in Germany impelled him to leave for Switzerland; in 1942 he became director of the Central Archive of Swiss Music. Of cosmopolitan background, he combined in his music the elements of both Germanic and Latin cultures. —Works: opera, *Amphitryon* (Berlin, March 13, 1951); *Trilogia sacra,* for chorus and orch. (1929); piano concerto (1933; rev., 1944); symphony (1936); *Antigone,* cantata (1939); violin concerto (1953); *3 Psalms,* for soli, chorus, and orch. (1947); *Vie et mort,* song cycle for contralto; piano pieces. —Cf. K. H. Wörner, *Robert Oboussier,* in 'Musica' (Kassel, Oct., 1954).

Obrecht (Hobrecht, Obreht, Obertus, Hobertus), Jacob, famous Netherlands contrapuntist; b. Berg-op-Zoom, Nov. 22, 1452; d. Ferrara, 1505 (of the pestilence). The son of a city trumpeter, he received his rudimentary musical training in his native town; he entered the Univ. of Louvain on Aug. 17, 1470; then returned to Berg-op-Zoom; took holy orders, and said his first Mass as ordained priest there on April 23, 1480. He was named *maître des enfants* at Cambrai on July 28, 1484; was in Bruges from 1485 to 1487; at the request of the Duke of Ferrara, he obtained a leave of absence for 6 months to travel to Italy; arrived in Ferrara in Dec. 1487; returned to Bruges in 1488, and remained there until 1491, when he became music director at Notre-Dame in Antwerp; he visited Berg-op-Zoom in 1496-97, after which he went again to Bruges; at various times was also in Antwerp. In 1504 he once more entered the service of the ducal court at Ferrara, where he remained until his death. He was a prolific composer; his Masses, motets, hymns, etc., are found in various collections of the period, and also in MSS in the Munich Library and the Archives of the Papal Chapel. He was well known in Italy during his lifetime; Petrucci publ. a collection 'Missae Obrecht' (1503), containing the Masses *Je ne demande, Grecorum, Fortuna desperata, Malheur me bat, Salve diva parens;* the collection *Missae diversorum* (vol. I) includes Obrecht's Mass *Si dedero.* The extensive edition of Obrecht's works (30 vols.) ed. by Johannes Wolf (1908-21, Amsterdam and Leipzig), contains 24 Masses, 22 motets, chansons, and the famous 4-part Passion according to St. Matthew, the oldest known polyphonic setting of this text. Since the publication of this edition, additional works by Obrecht have been brought to light. On the other hand, some works formerly attributed to him have been proved to be spurious; thus another Passion, long thought to have been by Obrecht, was apparently by a chapel singer in the court of King Louis XII of France, named Longueval. Vol. I of *Opera omnia,* edited by A. Smijers, was publ. at Amsterdam in 1953.—Cf. P. Wagner, *Geschichte der Messe* (I, p. 114 ff.); O. J. Gombosi, *Jakob Obrecht* (Leipzig, 1925); E. H. Juten, *Obrecht,* in 'Annales' of the Académie royale d'archéologie de Belgique (Ser. 7, vol. 7, Antwerp, 1930); A. Smijers, *Vijftiende en zestiende eeuwsche Muziekhandschriften in Italië met werken van Nederlandsche Componisten* and *De Matthaeus-Passie van Jacob Obrecht,* in 'Tijdschrift der Vereeniging voor Nederlandsche Muziekgeschiedenis' (vol. 14, 3; pp. 165-184); H. Anglès, *Un manuscrit inconnu avec polyphonie du XVᵉ siècle . . . ,* in 'Acta musicologica' (1936); A. W. Ambros, *Geschichte der Musik* (vol. III, p. 182 ff.; vol. V contains 6 examples); Anny Piscaer, *Jacob Obrecht* (Berg-op-Zoom, 1938); G. Reese, *Music in the Renaissance* (N. Y., 1954; pp. 186-205); Bain Murray, *New Light on Jacob Obrecht's Development,* in the 'Mus. Quarterly' (Oct., 1957). See also the article on Obrecht in 'Dictionnaire des musiciens,' ed. by René Vannes (Brussels, 1947).

Obrist, Aloys, conductor and music editor; b. San Remo, March 30, 1867; d. (by suicide, after having killed the singer Anna Sutter out of jealousy) Stuttgart, June 29, 1910. He studied at the Univ. of Berlin; received his *Dr. phil.* (1892) with the dissertation *Melchior Franck.* He filled posts as conductor in Rostock, Augsburg, etc.; then became court conductor at Stuttgart; from 1900, was custodian of the Liszt Museum in Weimar, and chairman of the editorial board for the publication of Liszt's works. He was a connoisseur of old instruments, and owned a valuable collection, which passed to the Bach Museum in Eisenach.

Obuchov. See **Obouhov.**

O'Carolan, Turlough. See **Carolan.**

Očenáš, Andrej, Czech composer; b. Selce, near Banská Bystrica, Jan. 8, 1911. He studied first at Bratislava, and then with Novák in Prague. He taught at the Bratislava Cons. (1940-45); then was engaged as music director of the Bratislava Radio. Among his works are a musical play *Rok na dedine* (*Year in a Village*), produced in Bratislava (Dec. 11, 1948); a symph. trilogy, *Resurrection* (1945); several overtures and orchestral suites; piano pieces; harmonizations of folksongs.

Ochs, Siegfried, German choral conductor and composer; b. Frankfurt, April 19, 1858; d. Berlin, Feb. 6, 1929. He studied medicine and chemistry, and also attended the Hochschule für Musik in Berlin; took private lessons with Friedrich Kiel and Heinrich Urban; also became a protégé of Hans von Bülow. In 1882 he organized a choral union, the 'Philharmonischer Chor.' He trained it with such competence and efficiency that the chorus became one of the best in Germany; the membership grew to 400 singers; in 1920 it was merged with that of the Berlin Hochschule, and Ochs continued to conduct it. He wrote a comic opera, *Im Namen des Gesetzes* (Hamburg, 1888), 2 operettas, vocal canons, and several song cycles; publ. an autobiography, *Geschehenes, Gesehenes* (1922); a history of German choral singing, *Der deutsche Gesangverein* (4 vols., Berlin, 1923-28); and *Über die Art, Musik zu hören* (1926; 2nd ed., 1928); ed. Bach's cantatas and *St. Matthew Passion,* etc.; publ. choral arrangements of German folksongs. —Cf. M. Stappenbeck, *Chronik des Philharmonischen Chores in Berlin* (1932); K. Singer, *Siegfried Ochs, der Begründer des Philharmonischen Chors* (1933).

Ockeghem (or **Okeghem, Okenghem, Ockenheim,** etc.), **Johannes** (or **Jean de**), great Flemish contrapuntist and teacher; b. probably in the village of Ockeghem, near Dendre, Flanders, 1430; d. Tours, 1495. He was probably a pupil of Binchois; boy chorister at Antwerp Cath., 1443-44; chorister in the chapel of Duke Charles of Bourbon, 1446-48; in 1449, pupil of Dufay in Cambrai; in 1452-53, chorister in the royal chapel; from 1454, composer and first chaplain to three successive kings of France: Charles VII, Louis XI, and Charles VIII; was treasurer of the Abbey of St.-Martin at Tours; 1465, 'maître de la chapelle du roy'; in 1469 he traveled to Spain, and in 1484 to Flanders, at the King's expense. Upon Ockeghem's death, Guillaume Crétin wrote a poetic 'Déploration,' and Josquin Des Prez (his greatest pupil) and Lupi composed musical epitaphs. — Important both as teacher and composer, Ockeghem was the leader of the 2nd generation of the great Franco-Flemish school of the 15th century (which includes Busnois, Regis, Caron, Faugues, etc.; to the first belonged Dufay, Binchois, etc.). His art expresses the mysticism of the Netherlands in the late Middle Ages; his technical skill in the development of purely formal resources, while very important, is not the most prominent characteristic of his style, as most historians have asserted. At the same time, Ockeghem's achievements in the art of imitative counterpoint unquestionably make his music a milestone on the way to the a cappella style of the coming generations. — Extant works: 16 Masses and individual sections of Masses; 9 motets; a ninefold canon-motet, *Deo gratias,* in 36 parts (of doubtful authenticity); about 20 chansons, and 1 canon (*Fuga a 3 in epidiatessaron*=the chanson *Prenez sur moi*). Burney, Forkel, Kiesewetter, Schlecht, Ambros-Kade, Wooldridge, and P. Wagner have printed fragments of the Mass *Cujusvis toni* (*ad omnem tonum*); Bellermann (*Die Mensuralnoten und Taktzeichen*), a fragment of the *Missa Prolationum;* Riemann, in *Musikgeschichte in Beispielen* (1912; No. 16) and in *Handbuch der Musikgeschichte* (II, 1), fragments of the Mass *Pour quelque peine* (probably not by Ockeghem); the Masses *Caput* and *Le Serviteur* (which is probably a work of V. Faugues, according to Tinctoris [Coussemaker, 'Scriptores' IV, 146a]) are publ. in entirety in 'Denkmäler der Tonkunst in Österreich' (XIX, 1); the Mass *Mi mi* (ed. for practical use by H. Besseler), is in F. Blume's *Das Chorwerk* (1928); 2 sections of the Mass *L'Homme armé* are in A. T. Davison and W. Apel, 'Historical Anthology of Music' (Cambridge, Mass., 1947); a motet, *Alma redemptoris mater,* in *Altniederländische Motetten* (Kassel, 1929), ed. by H. Besseler; another motet, *Ut heremita solus,* in Schering's *Geschichte der Musik in Beispielen* (1931; No. 52); the 'Déploration' on the death of Binchois, *Mort tu as navré,* in J. Marix's *Les Musiciens de la cour de Bourgogne au XVe siècle* (1937; No. 54); the motet *Intemerata Dei Mater* in Smijers' *Muziekgeschiedenis in Voorbeelden,* I (1939); the canon-motet in 36 parts, in Riemann's *Handbuch der Musikgeschichte* II, 1. Regarding the chansons, there are 4 in Ambros-Kade's *Geschichte,* V; 4 in O. Gombosi's *Jacob Obrecht* (1925); 1 in J. Wolf's *Sing- und Spielmusik aus älterer Zeit* (1926); 8 in *Trois Chansonniers français du XVe siècle,* I (1927), ed. by Droz-Rokseth-Thibault; 2 in K. Jeppesen's *Der Kopenhagener Chansonnier* (1927); and 2 in Davison and Apel, 'Historical Anthology of Music' (Cambridge, Mass., 1947). A 3-part chanson, *O rosa bella,* by Hert, with a new discantus added to it by Ockeghem, is in 'Denkmäler der Tonkunst in Österreich' (VII; *Trienter Codices,* I). The *Fuga in epidiatessaron* has been discussed, reprinted, and solved with more or less success by innumerable writers; the latest reprints are to be found in Jeppesen, Droz-Rokseth-Thibault, and J. S. Levitan (see below). A complete ed. of Ockeghem's works, edited by D. Plamenac, was begun in 1927 in the 'Publikationen älterer Musik' of the Deutsche Musikgesellschaft, with a vol. containing 8 Masses; new ed. of this vol., N. Y., 1958; vol. 2, containing 8 Masses and Mass sections, N. Y., 1947.

BIBLIOGRAPHY: L. de Burbure, *J. de Ockeghem* (1853; 2nd ed. 1868); E. Thoinan, *Déploration de Guillaume Crétin sur le trépas de J. Ockeghem* (Paris, 1864); M. Brenet, *J. de Ockeghem* (Paris, 1893; 2nd ed. in 'Musique et musiciens de la vieille France,' 1911; with bibliography; important); A. Schering, *Ein Rätseltenor Ockeghem's* ('Kretzschmar-Festschrift,' 1918); D. Plamenac, *J. Ockeghem als Motetten- und Chansonkomponist* (Vienna, 1924); id., *Autour d' Ockeghem,* in 'Revue Musicale' (Feb., 1928); M. Cauchie, *Les véritables nom et prénom d'Ockeghem,* in 'Revue de Musicologie' (1926); W. Stephan, *Die burgundisch-niederländische Motette zur Zeit Ockeghems* (Heidelberg, 1937); J. S. Levitan, *Ockeghem's Clefless Compositions,* in the 'Mus. Quarterly' (Oct., 1937); Ernst Krenek, *J. Ockeghem* (N. Y., 1953). See also Ambros' *Geschichte* III, p. 170 ff.; Riemann's *Handbuch* II, 1, p. 225 ff.; H. Leichtentritt's *Geschichte der Motette* (1908; p. 31 ff.); P. Wagner's *Geschichte der Messe,* I (1913; p. 101 ff.); H. Besseler's *Die Musik des Mittelalters und der Renaissance* (1931-34; p. 230 ff.); G. Reese, *Music in the Renaissance* (N. Y., 1954; p. 118 ff.).

O'Connell, Charles, American conductor and music executive; b. Chicopee, Mass., April 22, 1900. He studied at the Catholic School and College of the Holy Cross (B. A., 1922); also organ in Paris with Widor; was guest conductor of the Philadelphia Orch. and in summer seasons of the N. Y. Philharmonic (Lewisohn Stadium) and Boston Pops. From 1930 to 1944 he was head of the artist and repertory dept. of the R.C.A.-Victor Co.; then music director of Columbia Masterworks (1944-47). He publ. *The Victor Book of the Symphony* (1934; new ed., 1948); *The Victor Book of the Opera* (1937); *The Other Side of the Record* (relating personal experiences in dealing with musical celebrities; N. Y., 1947); *The Victor Book of Overtures, Tone Poems and Other Orchestral Works* (1950).

Odak, Krsto, Croatian composer; b. Siverić, Dalmatia, March 20, 1888. He studied music in Prague with Novák. Upon his return, he was appointed prof. at the Zagreb Cons. He wrote 2 symphonies, 3 string quartets, a violin sonata, a flute sonata, several choral works, and an opera, *Dorrit Dances* (1934), based on native melodies. Odak emphasizes the polyphonic element in all of his works, while his melodic material remains tonal. He publ. a manual of instrumentation, *Poznavanje instrumenata* (Zagreb, 1956).

Odaka, Hisatada, Japanese composer; b. Tokyo, Sept. 26, 1911; d. there, Feb. 16, 1951. He received his education in Europe; was one of the most prolific Japanese composers. —Works: *Japanese Suite No. 1* (Budapest, Nov. 8, 1938); *Japanese Suite No. 2* (Vienna, Nov. 3, 1939); symph. poem, *Midare* (Berlin, Dec. 10, 1939); cello concerto (Tokyo, May 23, 1943); *Rhapsody* for piano and orch. (Tokyo, Dec. 10, 1943); *Fatherland,* for orch. (Tokyo, Oct. 22, 1945); concerto for flute and orch. (March 5, 1951).

Odington, Walter (Walter of Evesham), a Benedictine monk at the monastery of Evesham; he was at Oxford in 1316, and at Merton College there in 1330. He is one of the chief medieval writers on mensural notation; his *De speculatione musices* (MS in Corpus Christi College, Cambridge) was printed by Coussemaker in 1864 ('Scriptores' I). This work is particularly valuable for the light it throws on musical rhythm as practiced in the late 13th century; it also discusses intervals, notation, musical instruments, and musical forms ('rondellus,' 'motet,' etc.). His views on consonance and dissonance are interesting for their acceptance of thirds and sixths as legitimate consonances. He was also noted as an astronomer. —Cf. Hugo Riemann, *Geschichte der Musiktheorie* (p. 119 ff. and p. 197 ff.); J. Wolf, *Early English Musical Theorists,* in the 'Mus. Quarterly' (Oct., 1939). See also

G. Reese, *Music in the Middle Ages* (N. Y., 1940, p. 273 ff.).

Odnoposoff, Ricardo, Argentinian violinist; b. Buenos Aires, Feb. 24, 1914. He studied with Aaron Klasse in Buenos Aires (1919-26), Rudolph Deman in Berlin (1927-28), and Karl Flesch in Berlin (1928-32). He was a child prodigy; appeared at a public concert in Buenos Aires at the age of 5; played with the Berlin Philharmonic at 17; won the 1st prize at the International Contest for Violinists in Vienna (1932) and the State Prize at the Ysaÿe Competition in Brussels (1937); after 1945 made tours in Europe and America; living for the most part in New York.

Odo de Clugny (klü-ñē'), (Saint), important musical theorist of the 10th century (not to be confused with Odilo de Clugny, 994-1048); d. Clugny, Nov. 18, 942. A pupil of Remy d'Auxerre in Paris, he took holy orders at 19, and in 899 was canon and choir-singer at Tours; in 909 he entered the Benedictine monastery at Baume, near Besançon, and then was successively abbot at Aurillac, Fleuri, and (from 927) Clugny. He is reputedly the author of the *Dialogus de musica* (also known as *Enchiridion musices*), though this work may simply have been written under his supervision (it is printed in Gerbert's 'Scriptores,' I; English transl. in O. Strunk's *Source Readings in Music History,* N. Y., 1950). In the development of pitch notation through letter-names, he was the first to give a complete series (2 octaves and a fifth) of letter-names (Γ, A, B, C, D, E, F, G, etc.) corresponding to our modern series; but whereas we change from capital to lower-case letters at *c* to designate the pitches of the 2nd octave, in Odo's system the change was made at *a*. He was also the first to add the sign *gamma* (Γ, Greek 'G') to designate the note corresponding to G on the first line of our bass clef. He distinguished between b♭ and b♮ (b *rotundum* and b *quadratum*), but only at one point in the gamut, namely, the note lying one degree below middle C in our system. —Cf. Th. Nisard, *St.-Odo de Clugny* (Paris, 1866); H. Riemann, *Geschichte der Musiktheorie* (p. 55 ff.).

O'Dwyer, Robert, composer and conductor; b. Bristol, England, Jan. 27, 1862; d. Dublin, Jan. 6, 1949. He was conductor of the Carl Rosa Opera Co. in London and on tour (1891); then with the Arthur Rousbey Opera Co. in England and Ireland (1892-96); organist at various churches in Dublin; in 1899, became musical director at the Univ. of Ireland, Dublin; from 1914 to 1939, prof. of Irish music there; musical director (from 1901) of the Gaelic League choir, for which he arranged many Irish songs. He wrote one of the earliest operas with a Gaelic text, *Eithne,* produced in Dublin on May 16, 1910; also composed songs with Gaelic words; organ pieces. He left a book in MS, *Irish music and its traditions.*

Oesterlein, Nikolaus, Austrian music scholar, specialist in Wagner; b. Vienna, May 4, 1842; d. there, Oct. 8, 1898. His perusal of Wagner's *Oper und Drama* awakened such enthusiasm in him that he began collecting everything relating to the master. His collection, known as the 'Wagner Museum,' was subsequently given to the town of Eisenach; the catalogue, publ. by Breitkopf & Härtel (1882-95), fills 4 vols. Oesterlein also publ. a volume, entitled *Bayreuth,* on the inauguration of the festival plays in 1876, and *Über Schicksale des Wagner-Museums in Wien* (1892).

Oetting, William H., American organist and pedagogue; b. Pittsburgh, Oct. 14, 1875; studied in Berlin with Riemann, Egidi, Boise, and Hutcheson; while there, he taught at the Klindworth-Scharwenka Cons. In 1901 he returned to the U. S., and for half a century was organist at various churches in Pittsburgh. He publ. *Preparatory Exercises for Manuals and Pedals* (2nd ed., 1953).

Oettingen, Arthur Joachim von, German physicist and musical theorist; b. Dorpat, Russia, March 28, 1836; d. Leipzig, Sept. 6, 1920. He studied physics at the Univ. of Dorpat; then in Paris and Berlin; from 1863 to 1893, was prof. of physics at the Univ. of Dorpat; from 1894 to 1919, at the Univ. of Leipzig. He publ. *Das Harmoniesystem in dualer Entwicklung* (1866; revised ed. as *Das duale Harmoniesystem,* 1913), reconciling and developing the systems of Helmholtz and Hauptmann; *Die Grundlage der Musikwissenschaft* (Leipzig, 1916); etc. Thürlings, Hostinský, and Hugo Riemann were among his followers.

Offenbach, Jacques, the creator of French burlesque opera; b. Cologne, June 20, 1819; d. Paris, Oct. 5, 1880. He was the son of a Jewish cantor, whose original surname was Eberst; Offenbach was the town where his father lived. He went early to Paris; studied cello with Vaslin at the Cons.

(1833-34); then played the cello in the orch. of the Opéra-Comique; composed various pieces for his instrument. In 1849 he was engaged as conductor at the Théâtre Français; wrote a *Chanson de Fortunio* for the production of Alfred de Musset's *Chandelier* (1850); the song proved tremendously popular; he then undertook the composition of operettas, a genre in which he became a master. He wrote a 1-act operetta, *Pepito* (Théâtre des Variétés, Oct. 28, 1853); in 1855 he ventured to open a theater of his own, the old Théâtre Comte, in the Passage Choiseul, which under a new name, Bouffes-Parisiens, became celebrated; he carried on the enterprise until 1866, producing a number of his most popular pieces, among them *Les deux aveugles,* for the opening of the Bouffes-Parisiens (July 5, 1855), *Le Violoneux* (Aug. 31, 1855), *Madame Papillon* (Oct. 3, 1855), *Ba-ta-clan* (Dec. 29, 1855), *La Bonne d'enfants* (Oct. 14, 1856), *Les trois baisers au diable* (Jan. 15, 1857), *Le Mariage aux lanternes* (Oct. 10, 1857), *Mesdames de la Halle* (March 3, 1858), *Orphée aux enfers* (one of his most celebrated pieces; Oct. 21, 1858), *Geneviève de Brabant* (Nov. 19, 1859), *Daphnis et Chloé* (March 27, 1860), *Barkouf* (Dec. 24, 1860), *La Chanson de Fortunio* (a new operetta to Musset's *Chandelier*), *Le Pont des soupirs* (March 23, 1861), *Monsieur et Madame Denis* (Jan. 11, 1862), etc. Having abandoned the management of the Bouffes-Parisiens, he produced several operettas in Ems, Germany; and an opera-ballet *Die Rheinnixen,* in Vienna (Feb. 8, 1864); then returned to Paris, where he staged, at the Variétés, one of his most spectacular successes, *La belle Hélène* (Dec. 17, 1864), an operetta that was soon taken over by theater enterprises all over the world; another fabulously successful operetta was *La Vie parisienne* (Palais Royal, Oct. 31, 1866); subsequent productions were *La Grande Duchesse de Gérolstein* (Variétés, April 12, 1867), *La Périchole* (Variétés, Oct. 6, 1868; one of the most enduringly popular operas of Offenbach; recurring revivals in many countries), and *Les Brigands* (Variétés, Dec. 10, 1869). In 1870, the Franco-Prussian War interrupted his activities in Paris; he resumed the production of operettas with *Boule-de-neige* (Bouffes-Parisiens, Dec. 14, 1871); in 1873 he took over the management of the Théâtre de la Gaîté, and produced there a new enlarged version of *Orphée aux enfers,* as an 'opéra-féerique' (Feb. 7, 1874). In 1877 he undertook a tour in America, which was not wholly successful; he described his impressions in *Notes d'un musicien en voyage* (Paris, 1877) and in *Offenbach en Amérique* (Paris, 1877; in English, 1877, as *Offenbach in America;* republished as *Orpheus in America* by the Indiana Univ. Press, Bloomington, Indiana, 1957). His last operetta produced in his lifetime was *La Fille du tambour-major* (Paris, Folies-Dramatiques, Dec. 13, 1879). A posthumous work, *La belle Lurette,* was revised by Delibes, and staged in Paris on Oct. 30, 1880. His only grand opera, and his real masterpiece, *Les Contes d'Hoffmann,* remained unfinished at his death; recitatives were added by Ernest Guiraud. The famous barcarolle was taken from Offenbach's opera-ballet *Die Rheinnixen* (1864), where the tune was used for a ghost song. *Les Contes d'Hoffmann* was produced at the Opéra-Comique on Feb. 10, 1881 with immediate and decisive success; presented in N. Y. on Oct. 16, 1882; also all over Europe. —Offenbach's music is characterized by an abundance of flowing, rollicking melodies, seasoned with a sprightly and ironic humor, and perfectly suitable to the extravagant burlesque of the situations. His irreverent treatment of mythological characters gave Paris society a salutary shock; his art mirrored the atmosphere of gayety during the Second Empire. — Bibliography: E. de Mirecourt, *Offenbach* (Paris, 1867); A. Martinet, *Offenbach* (Paris, 1887); H. Berlioz, *Les Musiciens et la Musique* (ed. by A. Hallays, Paris, 1903); P. Bekker, *Offenbach* (Berlin, 1909); E. Rieger, *Offenbach und seine Wiener Schule* (Vienna, 1920); L. Schneider, *Offenbach* (Paris, 1923); R. Brancour, *Offenbach* (Paris, 1929); A. Henseler, *Jakob Offenbach* (Berlin, 1930); H. Kristeller, *Der Aufstieg des Kölners Jacques Offenbach* (Berlin, 1931); S. Kracauer, *Jacques Offenbach* (Paris, 1937; in English, London, as *Offenbach and the Paris of His Time;* N. Y., as *Orpheus in Paris,* 1938); S. Sitwell, *La Vie Parisienne: a Tribute to Offenbach* (London, 1937); J. Brindejont-Offenbach, *Offenbach, mon grand-père* (Paris, 1940). For details of productions see A. Loewenberg, *Annals of Opera* (Cambridge, 1943; 2nd ed., 1955).

Oginski, Prince **Michael Cleophas,** Polish composer; b. Guzow, near Warsaw, Sept. 7, 1765; d. Florence, Oct. 18, 1833. He was a Polish nobleman of a musical family; his uncle, Michael Casimir Oginski (1731-1803), was an amateur composer of some talent. He pursued the career of diplomacy; as a Polish patriot, he left Poland after its partition, and agitated in Turkey and

France for the Polish cause. In 1799 he wrote an opera, *Zelis et Valcour ou Bonaparte au Caire,* to ingratiate himself with Napoleon; it was revived in a radio performance in Cracow on June 29, 1953. Of historical interest are his polonaises, many of which were publ.; the one in A minor, known as *Death Polonaise,* became extremely popular; he also wrote mazurkas and waltzes for piano, and a patriotic Polish march (1825).

Ogiwara, Toshitsugu, Japanese composer; b. Osaka, June 6, 1911. He studied at Tokyo Univ. with Matsudaira and Tcherepnin; won the Weingartner Prize (1939). He has written several dance suites, among them *Spring* (Tokyo, Dec. 3, 1935) and *The Three Worlds* (Tokyo, Jan. 29, 1937); 3 string quartets (1940; 1949; 1953).

Ogura, Rō, Japanese composer; b. Kyushu, Jan. 19, 1916. He was a pupil of S. Fukai, M. Sugawara, and T. Ikenouchi. —Works: a piano concerto (Tokyo, March 24, 1946); Symphony in F (Tokyo, April 25, 1951); 3 string quartets (1941; 1946; 1954); a violin sonata (1950); etc.

O'Hara, Geoffrey, American composer of songs; b. Chatham, Ontario, Canada, Feb. 2, 1882. He settled in the U. S. in 1904; became an American citizen in 1922. He studied with Homer Norris and J. Vogler; played organ in the Chatham Episcopal Church at the age of 12; then acted in vaudeville, as pianist, singer, and composer; wrote the song *Your eyes have told me* for Caruso. In 1913 he was appointed instructor in American Indian music as part of the program of the Secretary of Interior; in 1917, became an army song leader; was instructor in community singing at Teachers College, Columbia Univ. (1936-37); charter member of the American Society of Composers, Authors and Publishers (1914); a director of that organization in 1942-45. He wrote several operettas, among them *Peggy and the Pirate, Riding down the Sky, The Count and the Co-ed, The Smiling Sixpence;* about 300 songs, of which the following were extremely popular: *K-K-K-Katy, I Love a Little Cottage, Wreck of the Julie Plante, Leetle Bateese, The Living God, I Walked Today Where Jesus Walked, Give a Man a Horse He Can Ride, Where Heaven Is, Tomasso Rotundo, A Little Close Harmony, The Old Songs, Sing Awhile Longer, Forward to Christ, One World,* etc.; publ. a collection of Canadian folksongs.

Oistrakh, David Feodorovitch, famous Russian violinist; b. Odessa, Sept. 30, 1908. He began to study violin as a child of 5 with Stolarsky; then entered the Odessa Music School (graduated, 1926); made a tour in the Ukraine; played Glazunov's violin concerto under the composer's direction in Kiev (1926); won first prize in the Kharkov contest (1930); in 1933 appeared for the first time in Moscow. In 1934 he was appointed instructor at the Moscow Cons.; later became prof. there. He made a tour of Poland, Turkey, and Sweden in 1935-36. His name attracted universal attention in 1937, when he won first prize at the International Competition in Brussels, among 68 violinists from 21 countries. He played in Paris and London in 1953 with extraordinary success; made his first American appearances in 1955, with orchestras and in recital, winning enthusiastic acclaim. His son and pupil, **Igor Oistrakh** (b. 1931), is also an extremely talented violinist; received first prize at the International Festival of Democratic Youth in Budapest (1949) and the Wieniawski Contest in Poznan (1952). In 1953 he played in London and was judged by some critics as equal to his father in virtuosity. A biography of David Oistrakh, by V. Bronin, was publ. at Moscow in 1954.

Okeghem. See **Ockeghem.**

Oki, Masao, Japanese composer; b. Shizuoka, Oct. 3, 1901. After studying at the Osaka Engineering College, he turned to music; won the Weingartner Prize (1939). —Works: symph. suite with chorus, *Shinano Way* (Tokyo, Nov. 24, 1933); a symphony (1950); a symph. fantasy, *Atomic Bomb* (Tokyo, Nov. 6, 1953); 6 pieces for string quartet (1936); etc.

Olczewska (ŏhl-chĕv'-skăh), **Maria** (real name Marie Berchtenbreiter), contralto; b. near Augsburg, Aug. 12, 1892. She was first an operetta singer; in 1920 made her début at the Leipzig Opera, thereafter appearing as guest at Covent Garden, London; also in other European centers and in South America; engaged at the Vienna State Opera (1920-23, and from 1925); member of the Chicago Civic Opera (1928-32) and of the Metropolitan Opera from 1932-35 (début as Brangäne, Jan. 16, 1933). From 1947 she was prof. at the Vienna Cons.

Oldberg, Arne, American composer; b. Youngstown, Ohio, July 12, 1874. He studied in Chicago with A. Hyllested (piano) and W. Middelschulte (composition); then went to Vienna, where he was a piano pupil of Leschetizky (1893-95); also took courses with Rheinberger in Munich. Returning to America in 1899, he became head of the piano dept. at Northwestern Univ., Evanston, Ill.; retired in 1941. Most of his orchestral works were performed by the Chicago Symph. Orch., among them *Paolo and Francesca* (Jan. 17, 1908), *At Night* (April 13, 1917), symph. No. 4 (Dec. 31, 1942), symph. No. 5 (Jan. 19, 1950), and *St. Francis of Assisi,* for baritone and orch. (Ravinia Festival, July 16, 1954). Other works are: *Academic Overture* (1909); *The Sea,* symph. poem (1934); 2 piano concertos, of which the second won the $1000 Hollywood Bowl prize and was performed there (Aug. 16, 1932); a violin concerto (1933; Chicago, Nov. 7, 1946); 2 rhapsodies for orch.; chamber music; piano pieces.

Oldham, Arthur, English composer; b. London, Sept. 6, 1926. He studied at the Royal College of Music with Herbert Howells, and privately with Benjamin Britten. From 1945 he was active as musical director of various London theaters. He has written the ballets *Mr. Punch* (1946), *The Sailor's Return* (1947), *Circus Canteen* (1951), and *Bonne-Bouche* (1952); a symph. poem, *The Apotheosis of Lucius* (1952); violin sonata; songs.

Oldman, Cecil Bernard, English music librarian; b. London, April 2, 1894. He studied at Exeter College, Oxford; in 1920 received an appointment in the Dept. of Printed Books in the British Museum; in 1948 became Principal Keeper. His specialty was documentation on Mozart; he publ. and annotated the letters of Constanze Mozart to J. A. André, in the 3rd vol. of Emily Anderson's *Letters of Mozart and his Family* (1938); contributed numerous valuable papers to British, German, and Dutch publications. In 1951 he became chairman of the Council of the British Union Catalogue of Music.

Oldroyd, George, English organist and composer; b. Healey, Yorkshire, Dec. 1, 1886; d. London, Feb. 26, 1951. He studied organ and music theory with Eaglefield Hull; violin with Frank Arnold. After a year in Paris as organist of the English Church there (1915), he played at various London churches; taught at the Trinity College; in 1949 succeeded Stanley Marchant as prof. at London Univ. He wrote a number of sacred works, of which a *Stabat Mater* is notable; publ. *The Technique and Spirit of Fugue: An Historical Study* (London, 1948); *Polyphonic Writing for Voices, in 6 and 8 Parts* (London, 1953); and some essays on Gregorian Chant.

Olenin, Alexander Alexeyevitch, Russian composer, brother of the singer Olénine d'Alheim; b. Istomino, district of Riazan, June 13, 1865; d. Moscow, Feb., 1944. He studied with P. Pabst and with Erdmannsdörfer; lived most of his life in Moscow. He wrote an opera in a folk style, *Kudeyar* (Moscow, Nov. 26, 1915); a symph. poem, *After the Battle; Préludes prairiales,* for 2 oboes, violin, and piano (1927); a piano sonata; a violin sonata; several song cycles (*The Street, The Peasant's Son, The Autumn, Home,* etc.), and 52 songs to texts by Heine. —Cf. V. Belaiev, *Olenin's Reminiscences of Balakirev,* in the 'Mus. Quarterly' (Jan., 1930).

Olénine d'Alheim, Marie, Russian soprano; b. Istomino, Riazan district, Oct. 2, 1869. She studied in Russia and later in Paris. Through her brother, the composer Alexander Olenin, she met Stasov, Balakirev, and Cui, and became interested in Russian vocal music. In 1893 she married the French writer Pierre d'Alheim (1862-1922), translator of the text of *Boris Godunov;* together they organized, in Moscow and in Paris, numerous concerts and lectures on Russian music, particularly on Mussorgsky; she was an outstanding interpreter of Russian songs; publ. a book, *Le Legs de Mussorgsky* (Paris, 1908). In 1935 she settled in Paris as voice teacher, and was still active in that capacity in 1954.

Olibrio, Flavio Anicio. See **J. F. Agricola.**

Oliphant, Thomas, British composer; b. Condie, Perthshire, Dec. 25, 1799; d. London, March 9, 1873. Of Scottish birth, he settled in London in 1830 and became a member of the Madrigal Society of London; publ. *A Brief Account of the Madrigal Society* (1835), *A Short Account of Madrigals* (1836), and *La Musa Madrigalesca* (1837; the words of 400 madrigals, chiefly of the Elizabethan period); also wrote English words for Italian madrigals; publ. several collections of glees, catches, and rounds. See the article on him in the 'Dictionary of National Biography.'

Olitzka, Rosa, contralto; b. Berlin, Sept. 6, 1873; d. Chicago, Sept. 29, 1949. She studied with Désirée Artôt and Julius Hey;

sang at Berlin (1891); then was engaged at the Hanover Opera (1892-93); at Covent Garden, London (1894), and in New York with the German Opera Co., conducted by Damrosch (1895-97); later also with the Metropolitan Opera. She married Boris J. Sinai of Chicago in 1908; after a season with the Chicago Opera Co. (1910-11), she left the stage and was active as vocal teacher in Chicago. In her prime, she was a distinguished Wagnerian contralto.

Olitzki, Walter, baritone; b. Hamburg, March 17, 1903; d. Los Angeles, Aug. 2, 1949. After a career in Germany, he appeared as Beckmesser at the Metropolitan Opera, N. Y. (Dec. 2, 1939); specialized in Wagnerian roles; was with the Metropolitan Opera until 1947. He was the nephew of Rosa Olitzka (q.v.).

Oliver, Henry Kemble, American composer; b. Beverly, Mass., Nov. 24, 1800; d. Salem, Aug. 12, 1885. He was a chorister at Park Street Church in Boston; graduated from Dartmouth College in 1818; played the organ in various churches in Salem and Boston; in 1826, founded and managed the Salem Mozart Association; subsequently went to Lawrence, Mass., where he was mayor in 1859; later was also mayor of Salem; from 1861-65, was treasurer of the State of Massachusetts. He was given B.A. and M.A. degrees by Harvard Univ. (1862) and was made Mus. Doc. by Dartmouth College (1883). He wrote many well-known hymn tunes (*Federal Street, Morning, Harmony Grove, Beacon Street, Hudson*), motets, chants, and a *Te Deum;* publ. *The National Lyre* (1848; with Tuckerman and Bancroft; contains many of his own compositions), *Oliver's Collection of Hymn and Psalm Tunes* (1860), and *Original Hymn Tunes* (1875). —Cf. F. J. Metcalf, *American Writers and Compilers of Sacred Music* (1925; pp. 230-33); 'Dictionary of American Biography' (vol. XIV).

d'Ollone, Max (full name, **Maximilien-Paul-Marie-Félix**), French composer and writer on music; b. Besançon, June 13, 1875. He studied with Lavignac, Massenet, and Lenepveu at the Paris Cons.; received the Grand Prix de Rome in 1897 with his cantata *Frédégonde;* prof. at the Paris Cons. for many years, retiring in 1942; was active as opera conductor in Paris and the French provinces. A prolific composer, he wrote 5 operas: *Le Retour* (Angers, Feb. 13, 1913), *Les Uns et les autres* (Paris, Nov. 6, 1922), *L'Arlequin* (Paris, Dec. 24, 1924), *George Dandin,* after Molière (Paris, March 19, 1930), and *La Samaritaine* (Paris, June 25, 1937); *Dans la cathédrale,* for orch. (1906); *Fantaisie* for piano and orch. (1899); chamber music; many songs; contributed to French magazines on musical subjects; publ. a book, *Le Théâtre lyrique et le public* (Paris, 1955).

Olmeda de San José, Federico, Spanish musicologist and composer; b. Burgo de Osma, 1865; d. Madrid, Feb. 11, 1909. He studied violin and music theory at Burgos; was appointed organist at the Cathedral of Burgos in 1888; in 1908 went to Madrid as choirmaster of the Convent of Las Descalzas Reales; founded and edited the review 'La Voz de la Música' (1907); publ. manuals of solfeggio; the essays, *Folklore de Burgos* (Burgos, 1902), *Pio X y el canto romano* (Burgos, 1904), etc. and an important study on the 12th-century Codex of Calixtus II, in *Viaje Musical a Santiago de Galicia* (1895). He wrote 4 symphonies; a symph. poem, *Paraíso perdido;* an *Oda* for string orch.; several church works: *32 Rimas* for piano (1890-91); organ pieces, etc. (altogether some 350 works). —Cf. H. Collet, *L'Essor de la musique espagnole au XXe siècle* (Paris, 1929).

Olsen, Ole, Norwegian composer; b. Hammerfest, July 4, 1850; d. Oslo, Nov. 10, 1927. He studied with J. Lindeman; was active as organist and theater conductor in Trondhjem and other provincial towns; in 1870 went to Leipzig, where he studied with Richter and Reinecke; returning to Norway in 1874, he became a piano teacher in Oslo; was conductor of the Music Society there (1878-81), instructor of music at the Military Academy (1887-1903), and inspector of military music (1899-1919). He wrote the operas *Stig Hvide* (1876), *Stallo* (1902), *Klippeøerne* (1905), which were not produced, and *Lajla* (Oslo, Oct. 8, 1908); also some incidental music; a symph. (1878); the symph. poems *Aasgaardsreien* (1878) and *Alfedans* (*Elf Dance;* 1880); concerto for horn and orch. (Oslo, April 1, 1905); numerous choruses; songs; piano music.

Olsen, Sparre, Norwegian composer; b. Stavanger, April 25, 1903. He studied composition with Fartein Valen in Oslo, with Butting in Berlin, and with Grainger in London; was violinist in the Oslo Symph. Orch. (1923-33); and in Bergen (1934-40); then was active as conductor. His music is partly in the folksong tradition. —Works:

Draumkvedet (*Dream Ballad*) for narrator, solo voices, chorus, and orch. (Bergen, April 19, 1937); *Symph. Fantasy,* in one movement (Oslo, Sept. 21, 1939); *Nidarosdomen* (*The Cathedral*), for orch. (N. Y., 1948); *Ver Sanctum,* for chorus and orch. (1949); *Pastorale and Dance* (1949); sacred choruses; chamber music; songs.

Olsson, Otto Emanuel, eminent Swedish organist and composer; b. Stockholm, Dec. 19, 1879. He studied with Lagergren and Dente at the Stockholm Cons. (1897-1901); from 1908 until 1945, taught there; also filled various posts as church organist. Among his works are a *Te Deum,* for chorus and orch. (1906); several cantatas for various occasions; 6 Latin hymns; other church music; 3 string quartets; numerous organ and piano pieces.

Ondříček (ŏhn'-drzhi-chĕhk), **Emanuel,** Czech violinist; son of Jan Ondříček and brother of Franz Ondříček; b. Pilsen, Dec. 6, 1882. He studied with his father and with Ševčik at the Prague Cons.; after a series of concerts in Europe, he settled in the U. S. in 1912; became an eminent teacher in Boston and N. Y.; publ. a manual, *Mastery of Tone Production and Expression on the Violin.*

Ondříček, Franz, Czech violinist; b. Prague, April 29, 1859; d. Milan, April 13, 1922. He studied with his father, Jan Ondříček, and later with Bennewitz at the Prague Cons., winning 1st prize (1876-79); and with Massart at the Paris Cons., where he also won 1st prize (1879-81). He undertook extensive concert tours of Europe, America, Siberia, and the Far East before settling in Vienna (1907), where he founded the celebrated Ondříček Quartet (with Silbiger, Junck, and Jelinek); was prof. of the 'Neues Wiener Kons.' (1910-19); from 1919 taught at the Prague Cons. In 1885 he married Anna Hlavaček, a singer at the National Theater of Prague. As a concert player, he impressed his audiences with his fiery temperament, but in his later years developed a grand classical style, marked by dignified repose. He publ. *Rapsodie bohème,* for violin and orch.; a cadenza to the violin concerto of Brahms; numerous pieces for violin with piano. In collaboration with S. Mittelmann, he publ. *Neue Methode zur Erlangung der Meistertechnik des Violinspiels auf anatomisch-physiologischer Grundlage* (2 parts, 1909) with 15 of his own études.

Ondříček, Jan, Czech violinist; b. Běleč, near Bratronice, May 6, 1832; d. Prague, March 13, 1900. He was the son of a village violinist, and studied with him; played in various orchestras, and also conducted; was a friend of Dvořák. He had 9 children, all of whom were musicians.

Onégin, Sigrid (*née* Hoffmann; full name, **Elizabeth Elfriede Emilie Sigrid**), contralto; b. Stockholm (of a German father and a French mother), June 1, 1889; d. Magliaso, Switzerland, June 16, 1943. She studied in Frankfurt with Resz, in Munich with E. R. Weiss, and with di Ranieri in Milan. She made her first public appearance, using the name Lilly Hoffmann, in Wiesbaden, Sept. 16, 1911, in a recital, accompanied by the Russian pianist and composer **Eugene Onégin** (b. St. Petersburg, Oct. 10, 1883; d. Stuttgart, Nov. 12, 1919; real name Lvov; he was a grandnephew of Alexis Lvov, author of the Russian Tsarist hymn), whom she married on May 25, 1913; after his death, she married a German doctor, Fritz Penzoldt (Nov. 20, 1920). She made her first appearance in opera, as Carmen, in Stuttgart, on Oct. 10, 1912; American operatic début at the Metropolitan Opera House, N. Y., as Amneris, on Nov. 22, 1922; revisited America several times, her last tour (in recitals) being in 1938. From 1931 she lived mostly in Switzerland. —Cf. Fritz Penzoldt, *Alt-Rhapsodie; Sigrid Onegin—Leben und Werk* (Neustadt, 1953; includes several chapters written by Sigrid Onégin herself, originally publ. 1939, Magdeburg).

O'Neill, Norman, English conductor and composer; b. London, March 14, 1875; d. there, March 3, 1934. He was a direct descendant of the composer John Wall Callcott; his father was a painter. He studied in London with Arthur Somervell, and later with Knorr in Frankfurt. Returning to London in 1899, he married the pianist Adine Rückert (1875-1947). He wrote incidental music for the Haymarket Theatre, of which he was musical director from 1908 to 1919; also produced the ballets *Before Dawn* (1917); *Punch and Judy* (1924), *Alice in Lumberland* (1926), etc.; overture *In Autumn* (1901); *Miniatures* for small orch. (1904); *Theme and Variations on an Irish Air* (1910); *A Scotch Rhapsody* (1911); *Two Shakespearean Sketches* (1928); some chamber music; violin pieces; a cello sonata; several sets of dances for piano; an album of Irish songs, *Echoes of Erin* (1926); numerous other songs. —Cf. D. Hudson, *Norman O'Neill: A Life of Music* (London, 1945).

Onofri, Alessandro, Italian organist and composer; b. Spoleto, May 29, 1874; d. Varese, Aug. 27, 1932. He studied in Rome with Mascagni, Rossi, and others; in 1904 settled in Boston, where he was church organist. He wrote the operas *Biancospino* (Venice, March 31, 1910) and *Assiuolo* (Rome, Sept. 25, 1912); the light operas *La Famiglia modello* (Leghorn, 1913) and *Il Bocciuolo di rosa* (Rome, 1916). During his stay in the U. S., he wrote a set of American dances for piano.

Onslow, George (full name, **André Georges Louis Onslow**), French composer; b. Clermont-Ferrand, July 27, 1784; d. there, Oct. 3, 1853. He was the grandson of the first Lord Onslow, studied in London with Hüllmandel, Dussek, and Cramer (piano) and in Paris with Reicha (composition). He wrote 3 comic operas, produced in Paris: *L'Alcalde de la Vega* (Aug. 10, 1824), *Le Colporteur* (Nov. 22, 1827), and *Le Duc de Guise* (Sept. 8, 1837); 4 symphonies, and some other orchestral music. However, these works failed to maintain interest; Onslow's real achievement was the composition of a great number of chamber works, in which he demonstrated an uncommon mastery of counterpoint; he wrote 34 string quintets; 36 string quartets; 6 piano trios; a sextet for flute, clarinet, horn, bassoon, double-bass, and piano (the double-bass part was expressly written for the famous virtuoso Dragonetti); a nonet, for violin, viola, cello, double-bass, flute, oboe, clarinet, bassoon, and horn; a septet, for flute, oboe, clarinet, horn, bassoon, double-bass, and piano; violin sonatas; cello sonatas; piano sonatas 4-hands; a number of piano pieces. As a result of a hunting accident in 1829, when a stray bullet injured him, he became deaf in one ear; his quintet No. 15, subtitled *Le Quintette de la balle* (*Quintet of the bullet*), was the musical rendering of this episode. —Cf. L. Halévy, *Notice sur George Onslow* (Paris, 1855).

Opienski (ŏh-pyĕhn'-skē), **Henryk,** eminent Polish music scholar and composer; b. Cracow, Jan. 13, 1870; d. Morges, Switzerland, Jan. 22, 1942. He studied with Zelenski in Cracow, with Vincent d'Indy in Paris, and with H. Urban in Berlin; then went to Leipzig, where he studied musicology with Riemann and conducting with Nikisch. In 1907 he was appointed instructor at the Warsaw Musical Society; from 1908 to 1912 he conducted the Warsaw Opera; in 1912, went again to Germany, where he took his degree of *Dr. phil.* (Leipzig, 1914). He spent the years of World War I at Morges, Switzerland; returning to Poland, he was director of the Cons. of Poznan (1919-26); then settled again in Morges. —Works: the operas *Maria* (1904; Poznan, April 27, 1923) and *Jakub lutnista* (*Jacob the Lutenist;* 1916-18; Poznan, Dec. 21, 1927); the oratorio *The Prodigal Son* (1930); the symph. poems *Lilla Weneda* (1908) and *Love and Destiny* (1912); *Scènes lyriques en forme de quatuor,* for string quartet; violin pieces; songs; an album of 15 Polish songs (with French words; 1928) and another album of 15 Polish songs publ. with English words (1936). He publ. several books and essays on Chopin (Lwow, 1910; 2nd ed., 1922; Warsaw, 1911; Warsaw, 1912, etc.); also the collected letters of Chopin, in Polish, German, French, and English (1931); other writings include a history of music in Polish (Warsaw, 1912; 2nd ed., 1922); *La Musique polonaise* (Paris, 1918; 2nd ed., 1929); a valuable monograph on Moniuszko (Warsaw, 1924); a monograph on Paderewski (Lwow, 1910; 2nd ed., Warsaw, 1928; in French, Lausanne, 1928; 2nd ed., 1948). —Cf. A. Fornerod, *H. Opienski* (Lausanne, 1942).

Orbón, Julián, Cuban composer; b. Aviles, Spain, Aug. 7, 1925. He studied with his father and later at the Cons. of Oviedo; settled in Havana, where he wrote music criticism and participated in concerts of modern Cuban music. He has written a symphony (1945); quintet for clarinet and strings (1944); a piano sonata, and other pieces. His *3 Symphonic Variations* received a 2nd prize of $5,000 at the Caracas Music Festival in 1956.

Orchard, William Arundel, English-Australian conductor and pianist; b. London, April 13, 1867. He studied in London and in Durham. In 1903 he emigrated to Australia, where he became conductor of the Sydney Symph. Orch. (1909) and several choral societies. He was director of the New South Wales State Cons. (1923-43); later taught at the Univ. of Tasmania. He wrote 2 books on Australian music: *The Distant View* (Sydney, 1943) and *Music in Australia* (Melbourne, 1952); composed an opera, *The Picture of Dorian Gray* (after Oscar Wilde), a violin concerto, madrigals, and songs.

Orefice (ŏh-rĕh-fē'-chĕ), **Giacomo,** Italian composer; b. Vicenza, Aug. 27, 1865; d. Milan, Dec. 22, 1922. He studied with Mancinelli and Busi in Bologna; in 1909, became prof. at the Verdi Cons. in Milan; also wrote music criticism. —Works: operas: *Mariska* (Turin, Nov. 19, 1889), *Consuelo* (Bologna, Nov. 27, 1895); *Il Gladiatore* (Madrid, March 20, 1898), *Chopin* (Milan, Nov. 25, 1901), *Cecilia* (Vicenza, Aug. 16, 1902), *Mosè* (Genoa, Feb. 18, 1905), *Il Pane d'altrui* (Venice, Jan. 19, 1907), *Radda* (Milan, Oct. 25, 1912), *Castello dei sogni* (unfinished); a ballet, *La Soubrette* (Milan, 1907); a symph.; the orchestral suites *Sinfonia del bosco* (1898), *Anacreontiche,* and *Laudi francescane* (1920); chamber music; piano pieces; etc. He arranged Monteverdi's *Orfeo* (produced, Milan, Nov. 30, 1909); publ. a monograph on his teacher Mancinelli (Rome, 1921).

Orel, Alfred, Austrian musicologist; b. Vienna, July 3, 1889. He studied law in Vienna; then musicology with Guido Adler; 1919, *Dr. phil.* (dissertation: *Die Hauptstimme in den Salve Regina der Trienter Codices*); from 1918, librarian of the music division of the municipal library, Vienna, and of the Musicological Institute of the Univ.; later (1936) also associate prof. at the Univ. —Books: *Ein Wiener Beethoven-Buch* (1921); *Unbekannte Frühwerke Anton Bruckners* (with a reprint of the G minor Overture; Vienna, 1921); *Anton Bruckner: Das Werk - Der Künstler - Die Zeit* (Vienna, 1925); *Beethoven* (Vienna, 1927); *Der junge Schubert* (Vienna, 1940); *Mozarts deutscher Weg; Eine Deutung aus Briefen* (Vienna, 1940; 2nd ed., 1943); *Grillparzer und Beethoven* (Vienna, 1941); *Mozart in Wien* (Vienna, 1944); *Hugo Wolf* (Vienna, 1947); *Johannes Brahms* (Olten, 1948); *Goethe als Operndirektor* (Bregenz, 1949); *Bruckner-Brevier: Briefe, Dokumente, Berichte* (Vienna, 1953); *Musikstadt Wien* (Vienna, 1953); *Mozart, Gloria Mundi* (Salzburg, 1956). He ed. selections from the Trent Codices, in 'Denkmäler der Tonkunst in Österreich' XXVII, 1 (with R. Ficker), and the collected works of Bruckner (with R. Haas; 1934 ff.). He also brought out pictorial biographies of Beethoven, Schubert, and Brahms.

Orel, Dobroslav, Czech ecclesiastical music scholar; b. Ronov, near Prague, Dec. 15, 1870; d. Prague, Feb. 18, 1942; studied music with Novák and Hostinský in Prague, later musicology with Guido Adler in Vienna; 1914, *Dr. phil.* there (dissertation: *Der Mensuralkodex Speciálník, ein Beitrag zur Geschichte der Mensuralmusik und der Notenschrift in Böhmen bis 1540*); ordained priest; prof. at the Prague Cons. (1907-19); 1909-18, ed. of the Prague church music periodical 'Cyrill'; 1921-38, prof. of musicology at the Komensky Univ., Bratislava; conductor of various choral societies in Bratislava. His writings, some in Czech, some in German, include: *Handbook of the Roman Plainchant* (1899); *The Franus Cantional of 1505* (1921); *Czech Hymnal* (1921); *Old Czech Rorate Songs* (1922); *J. L. Bella,* a biography (1924); *Stilarten der Mehrstimmigkeit des 15. und 16. Jahrhunderts in Böhmen,* in the 'Adler Festschrift' (1930). Edited (with M. Springer) the liturgical works: *Graduale parvum* (Regensburg, 1912) and *Proprium Provinciae Pragensis ad Grad. Rom.* (1913); and (with Hejčl) *Marian Folk-Vespers* (1912).

Orem, Preston Ware, American composer, conductor, and teacher; b. Philadelphia, 1865; d. there (while conducting a school orch.) May 26, 1938. He studied at the Univ. of Pennsylvania; taught at Combs Cons., Philadelphia (1896-1905); in 1900, became editor for the Theodore Presser Co. and conductor of the Presser Choral Society. He publ. a harmony book for beginners; composed an *American Indian Rhapsody* for piano (also for orch.); a symph. sketch, *Out of the West;* chamber music; piano pieces; songs.

Orff, Carl, outstanding German composer; b. Munich, July 10, 1895. He studied at the Academy of Music in Munich and with Heinrich Kaminski; was one of the founders of the Günter School in Munich, organized to promote rhythmical education; also conducted a Bach Society there; from 1950, prof. at the Hochschule für Musik in Munich. In connection with his new methods of music education, he publ. a set of elementary exercises, *Schulwerk* (1930-33). In his own music he sought to revive the old monodic forms, and adopt them to modern tastes by means of dissonant counterpoint, with lively rhythm in asymmetrical patterns. His most famous work is the scenic oratorio, *Carmina Burana* (Frankfurt, June 8, 1937; numerous productions in Europe and America); the words (in Latin and German) are from 13th-century student poems discovered in the monastery of Benediktbeuren in Bavaria ('Burana' is the Latin adjective of the locality). Other works: *Der Mond,* opera, after a fairy-tale by Grimm (Munich, Feb. 5, 1939; revised version, Munich, Nov. 26, 1950); *Die Kluge,* opera after a fairy-tale by Grimm (Frankfurt, Feb. 20, 1943); *Catulli Carmina,* scenic cantata after Catullus (Leipzig, Nov. 6, 1943); *Die Bernauerin,* a musical play (Stuttgart, June 15, 1947); *Antigonae,* musical play after Sophocles (Salzburg, Aug. 9, 1949); *Trionfo di Afrodite* (3rd part of a triology under the general title *Trionfi,* the 1st and 2nd parts being *Carmina Burana* and *Catulli Carmina;* Milan, Feb. 13, 1953); *Astutuli,* opera-ballet (Munich, Oct. 20, 1953); dance play, *Der Feuerfarbene* (1925); *Präludium* for orch. (1925); concertino for wind instruments and harpsichord (1927); *Entrata,* for orch., based on melodies of William Byrd (1928; revised 1940); festival music for chamber orch. (1928); *Bayerische Musik* for small ensemble (1934); *Olympischer Reigen,* for various instruments (1936); revised versions of Monteverdi's *Orfeo* (Mannheim, April 17, 1925; 2nd version, Munich, Oct. 13, 1929; 3rd version, Dresden, Oct. 4, 1940) and Monteverdi's *Ballo delle Ingrate, Lamento d'Arianna,* and *L'Incoronazione di Poppea.* —Cf. A. Liess, *Carl Orff* (Zürich, 1955); E. Helm, *Carl Orff,* in the 'Mus. Quarterly' (July, 1955).

Orgeni, Aglaja (real name Görger St. Jorgen), Hungarian coloratura soprano; b. Roma Szombat, Dec. 17, 1841; d. Vienna, March 15, 1926. She was a pupil of Mme. Viardot-Garcia at Baden-Baden; made her début on Sept. 28, 1865, as Amina, at the Berlin Opera; first appearance in London, April 7, 1866, as Violetta, at Covent Garden; she sang later in Vienna, Dresden, Berlin, Copenhagen, etc.; from 1886, taught singing at the Dresden Cons.; was made 'Royal Professor' in 1908 (the first case of the title being conferred on a woman). In 1914 she settled in Vienna. Among her distinguished pupils were Erika Wedeking and Edyth Walker. —Cf. Erna Brand, *Aglaja Orgeni* (Munich, 1931).

Orlov, Nikolay Andreyevitch, Russian pianist; b. Eletz, Feb. 26, 1892. He studied at the Moscow Cons. with Igumnov; also privately with Taneyev; in 1921, left Russia and gave concerts throughout Europe; also appeared in the U. S.; made his headquarters mainly in Paris.

Ormandy, Eugene (real name Blau); outstanding conductor; b. Budapest, Nov. 18, 1899; studied violin with his father; entered the Royal Academy of Music in Budapest at the age of 5; began studying with Hubay at 9; received an artist's diploma for violin in 1914; received a teacher's certificate at the Royal Academy in 1917; then was concertmaster of the Blüthner Orch. in Germany; also gave recitals and played with orchestras as soloist; in 1921, came to the U. S., obtained the position of concertmaster of the Capitol Theater Orch., N. Y., and remained there for 2½ years; made his début as conductor with that orch. in Sept. 1924; in 1925, became its associate music director; 1929, conducted the N. Y. Philharmonic at Lewisohn Stadium; 1930, guest conductor with the Robin Hood Dell Orch., Philadelphia; on Oct. 30, 1931, conducted the Philadelphia Orch. In 1931, he was appointed permanent conductor of the Minneapolis Symph. Orch.; in 1936, engaged as associate conductor of the Philadelphia Orch. (with Stokowski); in 1938, permanent conductor; traveled with it on transcontinental tours in 1937, 1946, and in 1948; in 1949, made an extended tour in England; in the spring of 1955, presented concerts with the Philadelphia Orch. in 10 European countries; in the summer of 1958 he led it in another European tour (including Russia). He appeared on numerous occasions as guest conductor with European orchestras; in Australia (summer of 1944); South America (summer of 1946), etc. He is an officer of the French Legion of Honor (1952); Knight of the Order of the White Rose of Finland (1955); holder of the medal of the Bruckner Society (1936); honorary Mus. Doc., Univ. of Pennsylvania; etc. In his interpretations, Ormandy reveals himself as a Romanticist; he excels in the works of Beethoven, Schumann, and Richard Strauss; his renditions of music by Debussy and of the moderns are marked by color without extravagance; he conducts all his scores from memory. —Cf. Hope Stoddard, *Symphony Conductors of the U. S. A.* (N. Y., 1957; pp. 147-59).

Ornithoparchus (Greek form of his real name, Vogelsang), **Andreas,** German music scholar; b. Meiningen, c. 1485; d. Münster, c. 1535; led a wandering life; about 1516, *magister artium* at Tübingen. He was the author of a valuable theoretical treatise, *Musice active micrologus* (1517; 6th ed., 1540; English transl. by Dowland, London, 1609). —Cf. J. W. Lyra, *Andreas Ornithoparchus und dessen Lehre von den Kirchenakzenten* (Gütersloh, 1877).

Ornstein, Leo, notable pianist and composer; b. Krementchug, Russia, Dec. 11, 1895. The son of a synagogal cantor, he studied music at home; then with Vladimir Puchalski in Kiev; at the age of 10 he was accepted as a pupil at the St. Petersburg Cons. As a consequence of anti-Semitic disturbances in Russia, the family decided to emigrate; arrived in the U. S. in 1907. He studied piano with Mrs. Bertha Feiring Tapper at the New England Cons., Boston, and with Percy Goetschius; also attended the Institute of Musical Art, N. Y. He gave his first concert in N. Y., as pianist, on March 5, 1911; then played in Philadelphia and other cities. About 1913 he began to compose; experimented with percussive sonorities, in dissonant harmonies; made a European tour in 1913; played in Norway, Denmark, and in Paris; appeared in London on March 27, 1914, in a piano recital announced as 'futuristic music' and featuring his sonata and other works. Returning to the U. S. early in 1915, he gave a series of recitals at the Bandbox Theatre, N. Y., comprising works by Debussy, Ravel, Schoenberg, Scriabin, and other modern composers; also his own music; acquired considerable notoriety, and became a self-styled 'enfant terrible' of ultramodern music, with critics of the vanguard welcoming him as a harbinger of a new art, and others declaring him to be a musical anarchist. After a few years, he ceased to attract attention; then settled in Philadelphia as a teacher. —Works: for orch.: *3 Moods*: *Anger, Peace, Joy* (1914); *The Fog*, symph. poem (1915); piano concerto (Philadelphia Orch., Feb. 13, 1925, composer soloist); *Lysistrata Suite* (1933); a symphony (1934); *Nocturne and Dance of Fates* (St. Louis, Feb. 12, 1937); *3 Russian Choruses,* a cappella (1921), a piano quintet; a string quartet; a violin sonata; a cello sonata; *Nocturne* for clarinet and piano; 4 piano sonatas; many pieces for piano: *À la chinoise, Wild Men's Dance, Poems of 1917* (10 pieces), *6 Water Colors, Suite russe;* songs (*The Corpse*, etc.). —Cf. Carl Van Vechten, *Music and Bad Manners* (N. Y., 1916; pp. 229-43); Ch. L. Buchanan, *Ornstein and Modern Music,* in the 'Mus. Quarterly' (April, 1918); F. H. Martens, *Leo Ornstein*: *The Man, His Ideas, His Work* (N. Y., 1918); Paul Rosenfeld, in *Musical Chronicle, 1917-1923* (N. Y., 1923); Paul Rosenfeld, in *An Hour with American Music* (N. Y., 1929).

Orr, Charles Wilfred, English composer; b. Cheltenham, July 31, 1893. He began his music studies relatively late in life; wrote songs in the style of German lieder; publ. several song cycles to words by English poets; his set of 7 songs to poems from Housman's *A Shropshire Lad* is particularly notable. —Cf. S. Northcote, *The Songs of C. W. Orr,* in 'Music & Letters' (1937).

Orrego Salas, Juan, Chilean composer; b. Santiago, Jan. 18, 1919. He studied architecture and received his diploma in 1943; at the same time took composition lessons with Allende and Domingo Santa Cruz; and later with Randall Thompson and Aaron Copland in the U. S.; took courses in musicology with Paul Henry Lang at Columbia Univ. In 1942 he was appointed prof. of music history at the Conservatorio Nacional in Santiago; in 1949 he became editor of the foremost Chilean music magazine, 'Revista Musical Chilena.' —Works: *Cantata de Navidad* (Christmas cantata; 1945); symph. suite, *Escenas de cortes y pastores* (1946); *Canciones castellanas* for soprano and 8 instruments (1947; 1st National Prize of Chile); *Obertura festiva* for orch. (1947; his most successful work); the ballets *Juventud* (1948) and *Umbral del sueño* (1951); symph. No. 1 (1949); symph. No. 2 (1954; Minneapolis, Feb. 17, 1956); piano concerto (1950); opera-oratorio *El Retablo del rey pobre* (1952); *Concerto da camara* for wind quartet, 2 horns, harp, and strings (1952); sextet for clarinet, piano, and string quartet (1954); string quartet (1958); violin sonata (1944); *Sonata a duo* for violin and viola (1945); *Canciones castellanas,* for soprano and instruments (1947); *Cantos de Advenimiento,* for mezzo-soprano, cello, and piano (1948); choral works; songs; piano pieces. —Cf. Vicente Salas Viu, *La Creación musical en Chile 1900-1951* (Santiago, 1952; pp. 295-337).

Orsi, Romeo, Italian clarinetist and manufacturer of wind instruments; b. Como, Oct. 18, 1843; d. Milan, June 11, 1918. He studied at the Royal Cons. of Milan (1856-64); in 1873 became prof. of clarinet there; for 40 years was 1st clarinetist of La Scala (1871-1911); gave concerts in Italy and in Paris. In 1881 he constructed a combination clarinet capable of performing both B♭ and A clarinet parts; it had a temporary acceptance among orchestral players; also manufactured a bass clarinet in A for use in Verdi's *Otello;* publ. a method for the saxophone.

Orth (ohrt), **John,** American organist and composer; b. Annweiler, Bavaria, Dec. 2, 1850; d. Boston, May 3, 1932. His parents settled in Taunton, Mass., when he was a year old; he studied organ with his father; then went to Germany, where he took courses with Kullak and Deppe (piano); also had lessons with Liszt; composition with Faiszt, Weitzmann, Kiel, and P. Scharwenka. In 1875 he settled in Boston as pianist and teacher; became a propagandist for Liszt's music in America, in lecture-recitals. In 1883, he married his pupil, Lizette E. Blood, known as **L. E. Orth** (d. Boston, Sept. 14, 1913), who was herself a composer of songs and piano pieces. Orth publ. a number of teaching pieces for piano.

Orthel, Leon, Dutch pianist and composer; b. Roosendaal, North Brabant, Oct. 4, 1905. He studied at The Hague with J. Wagenaar and in Berlin with Paul Juon. In 1941 he became a member of the faculty of the Royal Cons. in The Hague. He has written 3 symphonies (of which the third has had several performances abroad); a cello concerto; 2 violin sonatas; numerous songs and piano pieces.

d'Ortigue, Joseph-Louis, French musicologist; b. Cavaillon, Vaucluse, May 22, 1802; d. Paris, Nov. 20, 1866. He studied law in Aix-en-Provence; in 1829, settled in Paris, where he wrote articles on music for various journals. In 1857 he founded 'La Maîtrise' (with Niedermeyer) and in 1862 the 'Journal des Maîtrises' (with F. Clément), both periodicals for church music; in 1863 he became editor of 'Le Ménestrel'; succeeded Berlioz as critic for the 'Journal des Débats.' In his various positions he exercised considerable influence on musical life in Paris. —Principal writings: *Le Balcon de l'opéra* (Paris, 1833; a book of essays); *De l'École musicale italienne et de l'administration de l'Académie Royale de Musique* (1839; republ. 1840 as *Du Théâtre italien et de son influence . . .*); *Abécédaire du plain chant* (1844); *Dictionnaire liturgique,* etc. (1854); *Introduction à l'étude comparée des tonalités, et principalement du chant grégorien et de la musique moderne* (1853); *La Musique à l'église* (1861); *Traité théorique et pratique de l'accompagnement du plain-chant* (with Niedermeyer; 1856; English transl. by W. Goodrich, N. Y., 1905). —Cf. M. Barber, *Joseph-Louis d'Ortigue* (Paris, 1919).

Ortiz (ŏhr-tēth'), **Diego,** Spanish composer; b. Toledo, c. 1525; date of death unknown; in the service of the Duke of Alba at the vice-regal court in Naples from 1555 until 1570. He was one of the earliest masters of variations (divisions). His greatest work is *Tratado de glosas sobre clausulas y otros géneros de puntos en la música de violones* (Rome, 1553; modern ed. by M. Schneider, Berlin, 1913; 2nd ed., Kassel, 1936), containing early examples of instrumental variations and ornamental cadenzas (for viola da gamba alone with harpsichord). An Italian version of this work was also publ. at Rome in 1553 (*Il primo libro de Diego Ortiz Toletano, etc.*). In addition, Ortiz publ. a vol. of sacred music at Venice in 1565 (hymns, motets, psalms, etc., for 4-7 voices). Some motets by him (in lute tablature) were included in Valderrábano's *Silva de Sirenas* (1547). Modern reprints of his sacred music are in the collections of Proske, Eslava, and Pedrell. —Cf. J. Subirá, *La Música en la Casa de Alba* (Barcelona, 1927).

Ortmann, Otto Rudolph, American music pedagogue; b. Baltimore, Jan. 25, 1889; attended Peabody Cons. there (1913-17) and Johns Hopkins Univ. (1918-20); appointed to the staff of Peabody Cons. in 1913; from 1928 to 1935 was director there. He publ. *The Physical Basis of Piano Touch and Tone* (1925); *The Physiological Mechanics of Piano Technique* (1929); and articles in musical and psychological magazines; also instructive pieces for piano.

Orto, Marbriano (Marbrianus) de, Netherlands composer and singer; b. Ortho, near Laroche; d. Nivelles, Feb., 1529. As a young man he was a singer in the papal choir at Rome (1484-89); then went to Nivelles, and lived there most of his life; in 1505 he was in the service of Philip the Fair of Burgundy; went to Spain with him in 1506, and was ennobled. In 1515, he was in the chapel of Archduke Charles (later Emperor Charles V). Petrucci publ. a book of 5 Masses by him (1505), also 11 chansons for 4 voices in the *Odhecaton* (1500-1503), and a Lamentation in *Lamentationum Jeremias prophetae liber I* (1506); several MSS are in the Vienna Library and at the Univ. of Jena; Ambros reproduced an *Agnus* from the so-called 'Mi-mi' Mass (based on the theme of 2 notes, E, A) in the supplement of his *Geschichte der Musik.* —Cf. G. van Doorslaer, *La Chapelle de Philippe le Beau;* K. E. Roediger, *Die geistlichen Musikhandschriften der Universitäts-Bibliothek Jena* (2 vols.; 1935); G. Reese, *Music in the Renaissance* (N. Y., 1954; pp. 264-66).

Orvieto. See **Ugolino de Orvieto.**

Osborn-Hannah, Jane, American soprano; b. Wilmington, Ohio, July 8, 1873; d. New York, Aug. 13, 1943. She received her first singing lessons from her mother; then went to Europe where she studied with Marchesi and Sbriglia in Paris; was engaged at the Leipzig Opera (1904-7); then sang in Dresden, Berlin, and Munich; appeared in London in 1908; made her American début at the Metropolitan Opera House as Elisabeth (Jan. 5, 1910); was a member of the Chicago Opera Co. (1910-14); was particularly notable in Wagnerian roles; after 1914 lived mostly in N. Y. She was married to Frank Hannah, American consul at Magdeburg.

Osborne (real name Eisbein), **Adrienne,** American contralto; b. Buffalo, Dec. 2, 1873; d. Zell am Ziller, Austria, June 15, 1951. She studied with August Götze and Max Stägemann in Leipzig; later with Felix von Kraus (q.v.), whom she married in 1899. She sang at the Municipal Opera in Leipzig; in 1908 settled in Munich, where she received the rank of Royal Chamber Singer. After the death of her husband in 1937, she went to live in Zell am Ziller, and remained there until her death.

Osgood, George Laurie, American singer and vocal teacher; b. Chelsea, Mass., April 3, 1844; d. Godalming, England, Dec. 12, 1922. He studied at Harvard Univ.; led the Glee Club there; then went to Germany, where he studied singing and interpretation with Haupt and Robert Franz; gave concerts in Germany; in 1872 returned to the U. S., and settled in Boston as a successful vocal teacher; conducted the Boylston Club (200 voices) from 1875-1893. He subsequently lived in Switzerland and England. He publ. *Guide in the Art of Singing,* which went through 8 editions; also anthems, choruses, and some 50 songs. —Cf. 'Dictionary of American Biography' (vol. XIV).

Osgood, Henry Osborne, American music journalist; b. Peabody, Mass. March 12, 1879; d. New York, May 8, 1927. He was educated in Boston; also studied music in Germany, Italy, and France; was correspondent in Munich and Paris for the 'Musical Courier' of N. Y.; returning to the U. S. in 1914, he became associate editor of the 'Musical Courier.' He publ. *So This Is Jazz* (N. Y., 1926); composed *The Rouge Bouquet* (words by Joyce Kilmer) for men's chorus; also songs.

Osterc (ohs'-tärts), **Slavko,** Yugoslav composer; b. Verzej, June 17, 1895; d. Ljubljana, May 23, 1941. He studied at the Prague Cons. with Jirák and Novák (1925-27); took a course in the quarter-tone system with Alois Hába; returning to Yugoslavia, he became prof. at the Cons. of Ljubljana. He was associated with the modern movement in Europe; experimented with various techniques, including quarter-tone writing. —Works: ballets, *The Masque of the Red Death* (after Edgar Allan Poe; 1930), *Illegitimate Mother* (1940), *Illusions* (1941); symph. poem, *Mermaid* (1924); *Nocturne,* for strings (1940); sonata for 2 clarinets (1929); quintet for wind instruments (1932); saxophone sonata (1941); a number of piano pieces. The following works by him were performed at the festivals of the International Society for Contemporary Music: concerto for piano and wind instruments (Prague, Sept. 1, 1935), *Mouvement symphonique* (London, June 24, 1938), and *Passacaglia-Chorale* for orch. (Warsaw, April 14, 1939).

Osthoff, Helmuth, German musicologist; b. Bielefeld, Aug. 13, 1896. He studied music with Brecher, Klatte, and Kwast at the Stern Cons., Berlin; musicology with Johannes Wolf at the Univ. of Berlin (*Dr. phil.,* 1922); was subsequently coach at the Leipzig Opera (1923-26); assistant in musicology at Arnold Schering's seminar in Halle (1926-28); then in a similar post at the Univ. of Berlin (1928-32); was privat-docent there (1932-38); in 1938 appointed prof. at the Univ. of Frankfurt. —Principal writings: *Der Lautenist Santino Garsi da Parma* (1926); *Adam Krieger, neue Beiträge zur Geschichte des deutschen Liedes in 17. Jahrhundert* (1929); *Die Niederländer und das deutsche Lied* (1938); edited works by Jacob Regnart, J. S. Kusser, Frederick the Great, and others; contributed numerous articles to various musical periodicals.

Ostrčil (ohs'-trchil), **Otakar,** eminent Czech conductor and composer; b. Smichov, near Prague, Feb. 25, 1879; d. Prague, Aug. 20, 1935. He studied languages at the Univ. of Prague, and then taught at a school there (until 1920); at the same time took courses in piano with Adolf Mikeš (1893-95); and composition privately with Fibich (1895-1900). From 1909 till 1922 he conducted an amateur orch. in Prague; also conducted opera there (1914-19); in 1920 he succeeded Karel Kovařovic as principal conductor at the Prague National Theater. In his compositions, Ostrčil continues the Romantic tradition of Czech music, with some modern elaborations revealing the influence of Mahler. —Works: the operas: *Vlasty Skon* (*The Death of Vlasta;* Prague, Dec. 14, 1904); *Kunálovy oči* (*Kunala's Eyes;* Prague, Nov. 25, 1908); *Poupě* (*The Bud;* Prague, Jan. 25, 1911); *Legenda z Erinu* (*The Legend of Erin;* Brno, June 16, 1921); *Honzovo království* (*Johnny's Kingdom;* Brno, May 26, 1934); a symph. (1905); Sinfonietta (1921); *Summer,* 2 symph. movements

(1926); *Calvary,* a set of variations (1928); several cantatas; a string quartet; a trio for violin, viola, and piano; several song cycles. —Cf. J. Bartoš, *Otakar Ostrčil* (Prague, 1936).

O'Sullivan, Patrick, American pianist and pedagogue; b. Louisville, Ky., Aug. 23, 1871; d. Los Angeles, March 18, 1947. He studied piano with Harold Bauer in Paris and Ph. Scharwenka in Berlin; composition with Wilhelm Berger in Berlin; returning to America, he occupied various posts as choral conductor and teacher; was prof. at the Louisville Cons. (1915-39) and at the Cons. of Memphis, Tenn., conducted by Roman Catholic sisters. Among his works are: *Heraklius,* for orch.; *Fantaisie irlandaise,* for piano and orch.; *Epithalamium,* for chorus and string quartet; also publ. a collection of 65 Irish melodies for 2 voices.

Otaño (oh-tahn'-yoh), **(José María) Nemesio,** Spanish composer and musicologist; b. Azcoitia, Dec. 19, 1880; d. San Sebastián, April 29, 1957. He studied with V. Arregui and V. Goicoechea; became a Jesuit priest; founded the Schola Cantorum at Comillas and, in 1907, the journal 'Música Sacro-Hispana,' of which he was editor until 1922. He supported energetically the study of Spanish folk music; made a study of the Spanish 'villancico'; from 1940 till 1951 was director of the Madrid Cons. He publ. an important collection of old and new Spanish organ music, *Antología de organistas españoles;* an essay on folklore, *El Canto popular montañés;* a collection of Spanish military music of the 18th century (Burgos, 1939); also composed a number of sacred works; wrote a book, *La Música religiosa y la legislación eclesiástica* (Barcelona, 1912).

Otescu, J. Nonna, Rumanian composer; b. Bucharest, Dec. 3, 1888; d. there, March 25, 1940. He studied at the Bucharest Cons. with Kiriak and Castaldi; then with Widor at the Paris Cons. and with Vincent d'Indy at the Schola Cantorum; in 1913 he was appointed teacher of composition at the Bucharest Cons.; in 1918, its director; also conducted opera at the National Theater; from 1927, led the concerts of the Bucharest Philharmonic. —Works: the operas *L'Ilderim* (libretto by Queen Marie of Rumania; 1919) and *De la Matei cetire* (1928); the ballets *Ileana Cosinzeana* (1918) and *Le Rubin enchanté* (1920); the symph. poems *Le Temple de Gnide* (1907), *Narcisse* (1909), *Légende de la rose rouge* (1910), and *Impressions d'hiver* (1913); *Diu batrani,* orchestral piece on Rumanian themes (1912); etc.

Othegraven (ŏh'-te-grăh-ven), **August von,** German composer; b. Cologne, June 2, 1864; d. Wermelskirchen, March 11, 1946. He studied at the Cons. of Cologne; from 1889 taught there; prof., 1914. He composed chiefly for chorus; his oratorio *Marienleben* (Cologne, 1919) was fairly successful; also wrote a musical fairy tale *Die schlafende Prinzessin* (Cologne, 1907) and an operetta, *Poldis Hochzeit* (Cologne, 1912). —Cf. B. Voss, *August von Othegraven, Leben und Werk* (Cologne, 1955).

Othmayr, Kaspar, German composer; b. Amberg, March 12, 1515; d. Nuremberg, Feb. 4, 1553. He studied at the Univ. of Heidelberg; in 1536 became 'magister' and then rector of the monastery school at Heilsbronn near Ansbach; in 1548 became provost in Ansbach. He was celebrated not only for his sacred works, but also for his ingenious polyphonic settings of secular songs; of the latter, the most important are *Reutterische und jegerische Liedlein,* for 4 voices (1549). Sacred works include: *Cantilenae* (1546); *Epitaphium Lutheri* (1546); *Bicinia sacra* (1547); *Symbola Principum* (1547; new ed. by H. Albrecht, 1941); *Tricinia* (1549). —Cf. H. Albrecht, *Kaspar Othmayr, Leben und Werk* (Kassel, 1950).

Otis, Philo Adams, American writer and composer of sacred music; b. Berlin Heights, Ohio, Nov. 24, 1846; d. Chicago, Sept. 23, 1930. He studied music with Dudley Buck in N. Y., and with Clarence Eddy in Chicago. He served as chorusmaster at the First Presbyterian Church in Chicago (1905-12); publ. *The First Presbyterian Church, 1833-1913* (a history, 1913); *Impressions of Europe, 1873-1874. Music, Art and History* (1922); *The Chicago Symphony Orchestra* (a history, 2 vols., 1925); *The Hymns You Ought to Know* (1928); composed 2 sacred cantatas: *Wondrous Words of Love* and *The Risen Christ;* a *Pastorale,* for violin, cello, double-bass, harp, and organ; many hymns and anthems.

Otterloo, Willem van. See **Van Otterloo.**

Öttingen. See **Oettingen.**

Otto, (Ernst) Julius, German choral conductor and composer; b. Königstein, Sept. 1, 1804; d. Dresden, March 5, 1877. He studied with Weinlig in Dresden; then was a teacher there. In 1830 he was appointed cantor at the Kreuzkirche, and held this position for 45 years; his choir became one of the most celebrated in Germany; he also conducted several choral societies. His best works are the excellent male choruses in his collection *Ernst und Scherz,* which became extremely popular (*Burschenfahrten, Gesellenfahrten, Soldatenleben, Der Spinnabend, Der Sängersaal,* etc.); 2 grand operas and 4 comic operas for amateur performance (*Die Mordgrundbruck bei Dresden* is the best); 3 oratorios; many songs for solo voice (*In die Ferne, Des deutschen Rheines Braut,* etc.); piano sonatas, rondos, etc. —Cf. A. R. Scheumann, *Julius Otto* (Dresden, 1904).

Oudin, Eugène (Espérance), American baritone; b. New York, Feb. 24, 1858; d. London, Nov. 4, 1894. He was of French extraction; studied law at Yale Univ.; was an amateur singer, and made his début in N. Y. on Aug. 30, 1886, in an operetta. On Jan. 31, 1891 he created the role of Ivanhoe in Arthur Sullivan's opera of that name, and won immediate acclaim. He remained in England most of his life, but also made several appearances in Europe, including Russia; scored notable successes in Wagnerian roles (Wolfram, Telramund, etc.).

Oudrid (y Segura), Cristóbal, Spanish composer; b. Badajoz, Feb. 7, 1829; d. Madrid, March 15, 1877. He studied music with his father; acquired his craft by arranging works of Haydn and Mozart for wind instruments; in 1844 went to Madrid, where he took lessons with Saldoni. He showed a decided talent for writing melodious zarzuelas; produced his first theatrical work in 1847; among his successful zarzuelas were: *Buenas noches, Señor Don Simon* (Madrid, April 16, 1852), *El Postillon de la Rioja* (Madrid, June 7, 1856), *El último mono* (Madrid, May 30, 1859), and *El Molinero de Subiza* (1870). —Cf. A. Pena y Goni, *La Opera española en el siglo XIX* (Madrid, 1881).

Oulibishev, Alexander Dimitrievitch, Russian official and music amateur; b. Dresden, April 13, 1794; d. Nizhny-Novgorod, Feb. 10, 1858. He studied violin at home in Dresden, where his father was Russian ambassador; was educated in Germany. When the family returned to Russia after 1812, he was employed in the Ministry of Finance, and later in that of Foreign Affairs (1816-30). He was the editor of the French periodical, 'Journal de St. Petersbourg' (1812-30); retired to his estate in Nizhny-Novgorod in 1830. His greatest admiration was for Mozart; his magnum opus is *Nouvelle Biographie de Mozart, suivie d'un aperçu sur l'histoire générale de la musique* (3 vols., Moscow, 1843; 2nd German ed., 1859; Russian transl. by M. Tchaikovsky, Moscow, 1890). By way of praising Mozart, he inserted deprecating remarks on Beethoven's later style; when he was taken to task for this lack of appreciation (by Lenz and others), he publ. *Beethoven, ses critiques et ses glossateurs* (Leipzig and Paris, 1857), in which he emphatically reiterated his sharp criticism of Beethoven's harmonic and formal procedures.

Oury, Anna Caroline (*née* Belleville), German pianist; b. Landshut, Bavaria, June 24, 1808; d. Munich, July 22, 1880. Her father, a French nobleman named Belleville, was director of the Munich Opera. She studied with Czerny in Vienna; made her début there; then gave concerts in Munich and in Paris; settled for many years in London, where she married the violinist **Antonio James Oury** (b. London, c. 1800; d. Norwich, July 25, 1883) in 1831; toured with him in Russia, Germany, Austria, and France. She wrote a number of piano pieces in the salon style, of which nearly 200 were published.

Ouseley, Sir **Frederick Arthur Gore,** English composer and theorist; b. London, Aug. 12, 1825; d. Hereford, April 6, 1889. He was the son of Sir Gore Ouseley, ambassador to Persia; studied at Oxford Univ. (B.A. 1846; M.A. 1849). He was ordained priest in 1849; was curate of St. Paul's, Knightsbridge (1849-51). In 1855 he succeeded Sir Henry Bishop as prof. of music at Oxford Univ. He was a fine organist, and excelled in fugal improvisation. His works include 2 oratorios, *The Martyrdom of St. Polycarp* (1855) and *Hagar* (1873); 11 church services; 70 anthems; 'The Psalter, arranged for Chanting, with Appropriate English Chants,' 'Anglican Psalter Chants,' 'Cathedral Services by English Masters' (2 vols.). He also publ. *Treatise on Harmony* (1868), *Counterpoint, Canon and Fugue,* after Cherubini (1868), *Musical Form and General Composition* (1875). He left his fine music library to St. Michael's College, Tenbury. —Cf. F. T. Havergal, *Memorials of F. A. G. Ouseley, Bart.* (London, 1889); F. W. Joyce, *Life of Rev. Sir F. A. G. Ouseley, Bart,* etc. (London, 1892; revised, 1896, with an appendix by J. S. Bumpus, containing a list of all of Ouseley's extant works); M. F. Alderson and H. C. Colles, *History of*

St. Michael's College, Tenbury (London, 1943).

Ozawa, Hisato, Japanese composer, b. Kobe, Aug. 1, 1907. He studied piano in his native city; in 1930 he went to Boston, where he took courses with Converse at the New England Cons. of Music. In 1934 he went to Paris; presented a concert of his works there with the Pasdeloup Orch. (Nov. 8, 1935); in 1936 he returned to Japan. He has written 3 symphonies, 2 piano concertos, and numerous songs.

P

Paap, Wouter, Dutch composer and writer on music; b. Utrecht, May 7, 1908. He studied piano with local teachers, and then became a pedagogue and music journalist; publ. monographs (in Dutch) on Beethoven, Bruckner, Toscanini, etc. Self-taught in composition, he has written some orchestral music in Classical forms (Passacaglia, Sinfonietta, etc.), cantatas, piano pieces, and a curious work for narrator and orch., *De Drukkunst (The Art of Printing;* 1940).

Pabst, Louis, German pianist and composer; b. Königsberg, July 18, 1846; d. Moscow, after 1903. He made his first appearance as pianist in his native city in 1862; was in England from 1867 to 1869; then established a music school in Riga, Russia (1869-75); subsequently toured Australia; there he founded the Academy of Music of Melbourne (1887); revisited London in 1894; in 1897 went to Russia; became instructor at the music school of the Philharmonic Society in Moscow in 1899; 1903, court councillor of the Ministry of the Interior. He publ. a number of piano pieces.

Pabst, Paul, German pianist; brother of Louis Pabst; b. Königsberg, May 27, 1854; d. Moscow, June 9, 1897. He studied with Liszt; went to Russia, and taught at the Moscow Cons. He made a number of effective paraphrases for piano of operatic works; particularly well known is the one on *Eugene Onegin.*

Pacchiarotti (păh-k'yah-rŏh'tē) (**Pacchierotti**), **Gaspare,** famous Italian male soprano; b. Fabriano, near Ancona, 1740; d. Padua, Oct. 28, 1821. He studied under Bertoni at St. Mark's in Venice; from 1769, sang at the principal Italian theaters with brilliant success; 1778, went to London with Bertoni, returning there in 1780-84 and 1790. In 1792 he retired and settled in Padua; sang for Napoleon when the latter passed through Padua in 1796. A. Calegari publ. *Modi generali del canto* (1836), based on Pacciarotti's method.—Cf. G. C. Pacchiarotti (his adopted son), *Cenni biografici intorno a Gaspare Pacchiarotti* (Padua, 1844); R. Sassi, *Un celebre musico fabrianese Gaspare Pacchiarotti* (Fabriano, 1935); A. Heriot, *The Castrati in Opera* (London, 1956; pp. 163-71).

Pacchierotti, Ubaldo, Italian composer and conductor; b. Cervarese-Croce (Padua), Oct. 30, 1875; d. Milan, April 18, 1916. He studied at the Cons. S. Pietro a Majella in Naples; conducted in Leghorn and Buenos Aires; composed the operas *La Lampada* (Buenos Aires, 1899), *L'Albatro* (Milan, 1905), *Eidelberga mia!* (Genoa, Feb. 27, 1908; in N. Y. as *Alt Heidelberg,* 1910), *Il Santo* (Turin, 1913); and other works. —Cf. C. M. Rietmann, *Ubaldo Pacchierotti,* in 'Pensiero Mus.' (Nov.-Dec., 1926).

Pache, Joseph, conductor; b. Friedland, Silesia, June 1, 1861; d. Baltimore, Dec. 7, 1926. Pupil at the Munich Cons., 1879-83; studied with Klindworth in Berlin, 1883-85; composition with Max Bruch in Breslau, 1885-86; further study in Berlin with H. Barth (piano) and J. Hey (voice). Came to the U. S. in 1891; from 1894, conductor of the Oratorio Society in Baltimore; later he founded there the Woman's Philharmonic Chorus, and the Oratorio Society in York, Pa. He published choruses and songs.

Pachelbel (also **Perchival**), **Carl Theodorus,** son of Johann Pachelbel; b. Stuttgart, Nov. 24, 1690; d. Charleston, S. C., Sept. 14, 1750. He emigrated to Boston in the 1730's and in 1733 assisted in the erection of the organ in Trinity Church, Newport, R. I., of which he became organist for about a year. On Jan. 21, 1736 he advertised a concert in N. Y., the first there of which details have been recorded, and on March 8, a second one. He then moved to Charleston, became organist of St. Philip's Church, and on Nov. 22, 1737 gave a public concert in his home. An 8-part Magnificat, the only known composition of Pachelbel's, is in the State Library, Berlin (publ. N. Y., 1937). —Cf. O. G. Sonneck, *Early Concert-Life in America (1731-1800)* (in English, Leipzig, 1907); J. T. Howard, *Our American Music* (N. Y., 1939 and later eds.); V. L. Redway, *A New York Concert in 1736,* in the 'Mus. Quarterly' (April, 1936); V. L. Redway: *C. T. Pachelbel, Musical Emigrant,* in 'Journal of the American Musicological Society' (spring, 1952).

Pachelbel, Johann, German organist and composer; b. Nuremberg (baptized Sept. 1), 1653; d. there, March 3, 1706. He studied at Nuremberg, Altdorf, and Regensburg; organist at St. Stephen's Cathedral in Vienna, 1674; court organist at Eisenach, 1677; of the Predigerkirche at Erfurt, 1678; court organist at Stuttgart, 1690; at Gotha, 1692. Organist at St. Sebald's, Nuremberg, 1695.—Several organ pieces by Pachelbel are printed by Commer in 'Musica sacra,' vol. I; others by G. W. Körner in 'Der Orgelvirtuose'; by Winterfeld in 'Evangelischer Kirchengesang,' vol. II; by Trautwein (a chaconne with 13 variations, a fugue, and a fughetta, for clavier, Berlin, 1860); by A. Schering in *Geschichte der Musik in Beispielen* (No. 243); by A. Einstein in the vol. of examples to his *Geschichte der Musik;* by A. G. Ritter in *Geschichte des Orgelspiels im 14.-18. Jahrhundert;* J. Bonnet in 'Historical Organ Recitals' (vol. I); etc. H. Botstiber and M. Seiffert publ. 94 fugues on the Magnificat in the 'Denkmäler der Tonkunst in Österreich' (VIII, 2; with biography); M. Seiffert edited *Hexachordon Apollinis,* 4 arias with variations, *Musikalische Sterbensgedanken,* 6 chaconnes, 4 fantasies, 19 suites, and 7 fugues in 'Denkmäler der Tonkunst in Bayern' (II, 1 and IV, 1; with introduction and biography by A. Sandberger); K. Matthaei publ. a practical ed. of Pachelbel's organ works, in 4 vols. (1930-36). —Cf. G. Beckmann, *J. Pachelbel als Kammerkomponist,* in 'Archiv für Musikwissenschaft' I, 2 (1919); M. Seiffert, *Pachelbel's Sterbensgedanken,* in 'Sammelbände der Internationalen Musik-Gesellschaft' V; M. Seiffert, *Geschichte des Klavierspiels* (p. 196 ff.); Ph. Spitta, *J. S. Bach* (vol. I, p. 106 ff.); E. Born, *Die Variation als Grundlage handwerklicher Gestaltung im musikalischen Schaffen Johann Pachelbels* (Berlin, 1941); H. H. Eggebrecht, *J. Pachelbel als Vokalcomponist,* in 'Archiv für Musikwissenschaft' XI (1954).

Pachelbel, Wilhelm Hieronymus, son of preceding; b. Erfurt, 1685; d. Nuremberg, 1764. He was an organist, from 1706, at the Jakobkirche in Nuremberg; from 1725, at St. Sebald's there. Publ. *Musikalisches Vergnügen* (1725; prelude, fugue, and fantasia for organ or clavier); also a prelude and fugue in C; all reprinted by M. Seiffert in 'Denkmäler der Tonkunst in Bayern' (II, 1 and IV, 1; as supplement to his father's works). A toccata in G was publ. by Keller-Valentin in *Liber organi,* V (Mainz, 1933).

Pachler-Koschak, Marie Leopoldine, Austrian pianist; b. Graz, Oct. 2, 1792; d. there, April 10, 1855. She was an enthusiastic admirer of Beethoven, who wrote to her in 1817: 'I have found no one, not excepting the great pianists, who interprets my compositions as well as you.' In 1816 she married Dr. Karl Pachler, a lawyer in Graz. In their house Franz Schubert spent several weeks in the summer of 1827. Schubert wrote a little four-hand march for the son, Faust Pachler, who publ. *Beethoven und M. Pachler-Koschak* (Berlin, 1866), which contains valuable details concerning Beethoven's last days.

Pachmann, Vladimir de, pianist; b. Odessa, July 27, 1848; d. Rome, Jan. 6, 1933. He was a pupil of his father (prof. at Vienna Univ. and a good violinist), and from 1866 of Dachs at the Cons. Although he met with considerable success on his first concert-tour of Russia (1869), he was not satisfied, and retired for 8 years; in 1877 he played in Berlin, Leipzig, and other German cities. After another period of retirement he reappeared in Vienna and Paris in 1880; he then made phenomenally successful tours of all Europe and America (first visit 1891); his farewell American tour took place in 1924-25. In 1885, on his tour of Denmark, he was made Knight of the Order of Danebrog; in 1916 the London Philharmonic Society awarded him the much-coveted Beethoven medal. In 1884 he married his former pupil, Maggie Oakey, a fine pianist, who accompanied him on his first American tour, and who was also heard in her own recitals; about 1895 she obtained a divorce, and later married the famous French lawyer, Fernand Labori; she ed. several Chopin *Études* with Pachmann's fingering.—Pachmann was a player of a highly poetic temperament, refined sensibilities, and extraordinary personal magnetism. He was at his best in the smaller compositions of Chopin and in works demanding extreme delicacy of touch, for there he could legitimately display his marvelous velvety tone and ethereal pianissimo. From the very beginning of his career Pachmann was eccentric, indulging in undignified grimaces, gestures, and audible comments—a habit in which he became more and more confirmed with advancing years.

Pachulski (păh-hŏŏl'-skē), **Heinrich Albertovitch,** pianist; b. Lasa, Poland, Oct. 16, 1857; d. c. 1921. Pupil of Strobel, Zelenski, and Moniuszko at Warsaw; of Taneyev (composition), N. Rubinstein, and Pabst at the Moscow Cons., where he taught from 1886 to 1917.—He made fine piano arrangements of Tchaikovsky's orchestral works. His own works include a suite for orch. (publ. 1897), a *Marche solennelle* (1900), a piano sonata, and other piano pieces.

Pacini (pah-chē'-nē), **Giovanni,** Italian composer; b. Catania, Feb. 17, 1796; d. Pescia, Dec. 6, 1867. He was a pupil of Marchesi and Padre Mattei at Bologna, and of Furlanetto at Venice; his first opera was *Annetta e Lucinda* (Venice, 1813); up to 1835 he had produced over 40 operas on various Italian stages, when the failure of *Carlo di Borgogna* at Venice temporarily checked the flow of dramatic composition; he went to Viareggio, near Lucca, and established a very successful school of music there, for which he wrote several short treatises—*Corso teoretico-pratico di lezioni di armonia* (1863), *Cenni storici sulla musica e trattato di contrappunto* (1864)—and built a private theater. Later he removed the school to Lucca. In 1840 Pacini, who prided himself on rapid work, wrote his dramatic masterpiece, *Saffo,* in 28 days (Naples, Nov. 29, 1840; enthusiastically received). Forty more operas followed up to 1867; the best were *Medea* (Palermo, Nov. 28, 1843), *La Regina di Cipro* (Turin, Feb. 7, 1846), and *Niccolò de' Lapi* (Florence, Oct. 29, 1873; posthumous production). Pacini also wrote numerous oratorios, cantatas, Masses, etc.; a *Dante* symphony; an octet; 6 string quartets; other chamber music; vocal duets and arias. He was an active contributor to several musical papers; and publ. memoirs, *Le mie memorie artistiche* (Florence, 1865; enlarged by Cicconetti, 1872; rev. by F. Magnani, 1875). —Cf. Anon., *G. Pacini* (Pescia, 1896); M. Davini, *Il Maestro Pacini* (Palermo, 1927); A. Cametti, *Il Corsaro di Pacini* (1931). —His brother, **Emilio Pacini,** b. 1810; d. Neuilly, near Paris, Dec. 2, 1898, was a distinguished librettist.

Pacini, Leonardo, Italian composer; b. near Pistoia, May 26, 1885; d. Viareggio, April 13, 1937. He was a pupil of Pizzetti at Florence; in 1921, graduated from the Liceo Martini of Bologna. —His works include the operas *Alla Muda* (1924; Viareggio, 1925) and *Mirta;* the operetta *Il Pirata* (Viareggio, 1927); the oratorios *Transitus Divi Dominici* (Bologna, 1921) and *Frate Francesco* (Viareggio, 1929); the cantatas *La Sagra dei Caduti* (1922), *Portiuncola Pia,* and *Clara Discipula* (Viareggio, 1924); *Sinfonia del giglio,* for chorus and orch.; psalms, motets, and other church music; chamber music; songs; etc. He was a Franciscan friar.

Pacius (pah'-s'yŏŏs), **Fredrik (Friedrich),** composer; b. Hamburg, March 19, 1809; d. Helsinki, Jan. 9, 1891. He was a pupil of Spohr; music director at the Univ. of Helsinki from 1834. In 1835 he organized a choral society there and in 1845 established regular symphony concerts. In his own compositions he laid the foundations of the national Finnish school. On March 24, 1852 his opera *Kung Karlsjakt,* the first Finnish opera, was produced at Helsinki (in Swedish) and was received with immense enthusiasm. In recognition of his services he was made Knight of the Order of Vasa in 1856, prof. in 1860, and *Dr. phil.* (*hon. c.*) in 1877. Many of his songs (*Finland's Song, Our Land, The Soldier-boy,* etc.) became nationally famous. He also wrote a second opera, *Lorelei* (Helsinki, April 28, 1887); incidental music to Topelius' *Princess of Cypria* (1860); a fantasy for violin and orch.; a violin concerto; men's and mixed choruses. —Cf. M. Collan-Beaurain, *F. Pacius* (Helsinki, 1921); Otto E. Andersson, *Den unge Pacius* (Helsinki, 1938); I. Meyer-Lüne, *F. Pacius,* in 'Zeitschrift für Musik' (July, 1941); J. Rosas, *F. Pacius som tonsättare* (Åbo, 1949).

Paderewski (pah-dĕh-reff'skē), **Ignace Jan,** celebrated Polish pianist and composer; b. Kurylówka, Podolia (Russian Poland), Nov. 18, 1860; d. New York, June 29, 1941. His father was administrator of some large estates, and was artistically inclined; his mother died soon after his birth. From the age of 3 he began to be attracted by the piano, and about that time received his first music lessons from an itinerant violinist. His father was ruined by the revolution of 1863, and thereafter Paderewski's boyhood was spent in poverty. His second teacher was a certain Peter Sowinski, who taught him some operatic arrangements for 4 hands, which he played with his sister. He also filled a notebook with his own childish compositions. His first public appearance was in a charity concert with his sister, at the age of 12. His playing aroused the interest of wealthy patrons, who took him to Kiev, where he heard his first concerts. He was then sent to the Cons. at Warsaw;

there his first teacher discouraged him from taking up the piano; he studied various instruments and played the trombone in the Cons. orchestra. Nevertheless, he continued his piano studies under Schlozer, Strobl, and Janota. Owing to a dispute about rehearsals, he was expelled from the Cons. after a year; in 1877 he made a tour of some of the smaller Russian towns with a violinist. He was then readmitted to the Cons., studied piano, counterpoint, and composition, and after his graduation, in 1878, was engaged as instructor of piano there. In 1880 he married a young student named Antonina Korsak, who died in childbirth a year later. In 1881 he went to Berlin to study composition with Kiel; there he met Rubinstein, who encouraged his attempts at composition. In 1883 he gave up his position at Warsaw and returned to Berlin, studying orchestration with Urban. While on a vacation in the Tatra Mountains in Slovakia (which inspired his *Tatra Album* for piano), he met the famous actress Modjeska, who urged him to take up a pianistic career and provided him with funds to begin study in Vienna under Leschetizky, with whom he remained from 1884-87 (except for 1 year of teaching at the Strasbourg Cons.). His first important appearance as a pianist was at a concert with Pauline Lucca at Vienna in 1887. In March, 1888, he gave his first recital in Paris, at the Salle Érard, and was enthusiastically received. After some further study with Leschetizky he made his début as soloist in Vienna in 1889, with immense success. He was also obtaining recognition as a composer, for Mme. Essipov played his piano concerto under the baton of Hans Richter in Vienna. His English début took place in London on May 9, 1890; his American début in New York on Nov. 17, 1891, was followed by a series of 117 concerts. He had made a tour of Germany in 1890, and, in spite of critical hostility in Berlin, soon won over the public of that country also. His subsequent numerous tours of Europe, North and South America, South Africa, and Australia were an uninterrupted succession of triumphs. In 1909 he accepted the directorship of the Warsaw Cons. (succeeding Mlynarski); 1913, came to the U. S., and in 1914 bought a ranch at Paso Robles, Calif.; the entire proceeds of his concerts given from 1914-18 were used for the benefit of Polish sufferers; 1918-19, diplomatic representative in Washington for the new Polish State; 1919, first premier of the Polish Republic; 1920, retired from politics, resuming his pianistic career with tours of Europe and America in 1922-23 and 1923-24 (for the benefit of World War victims). His last tour of the U. S. was in 1939. After the invasion of Poland he joined the Polish government in exile in France and was appointed president of its parliament on Jan. 23, 1940. He returned to the U. S. Nov. 6, 1940, and immediately resumed his efforts in behalf of his native country as well as of Great Britain and Greece. At the order of President Roosevelt, he was given state interment at the Arlington National Cemetery. Paderewski received the following honorary degrees: *Dr. phil.* from the Univs. of Lwow (1912), Cracow (1919), Poznan (1924); LL.D. from Columbia (1922), Southern Calif. (1923), Glasgow (1925); Mus. Doc. from the Univs. of Yale (1917) and Cambridge (1926); D.C.L. from Oxford Univ. (1920). He held the Grand Cross of the French Legion of Honor (1922) and many other decorations. In 1936 he played in a motion picture entitled *The Moonlight Sonata*.

No other instrumentalist, not even Paganini or Liszt, earned such large sums of money. In 1898 he bought the beautiful Châlet de Riond-Bosson on Lake Geneva, near Morges, where he spent his time when not on tour, and in that year he married Helena Gorska, Baroness von Rosen. An outstanding trait of the artist was his ardent patriotism. In the year of the Chopin centenary (1910) he donated $60,000 to the Chopin Memorial Hall in Warsaw, and in the same year he unveiled a colossal statue of King Jagiello, commemorating the latter's victory over the Teuton Knights in 1410, which he had erected at a cost of $100,000.

Paderewski began to compose in his seventh year, and his earliest ambition—and one that never left him—was to win laurels as a composer. His Menuet in G (one of a set of 6 Humoresques for piano) has attained extraordinary popularity. His opera *Manru* (1897-1900), dealing with life in the Tatra Mountains, was successfully produced at Dresden on May 29, 1901 (Metropolitan Opera, N. Y., Feb. 14, 1902). His Symphony in B minor was first performed at Boston on Feb. 12, 1909 (inspired by the 40th anniversary of the revolution of 1863). Other works: For piano: op. 1, *Prelude and Capriccio, Minuetto* in G minor; op. 2, Three Pieces (*Gavotte, Mélodie, Valse mélancolique*); op. 4, *Élégie;* op. 5, 3 Polish Dances; op. 6, *Introduction and Toccata;* op. 8 *Chants du Voyageur* (5 pieces); op. 9, 6 Polish Dances; op. 10, *Album de mai* (5 pieces); op. 11, Variations and Fugue in A minor; op. 12, *Tatra Album* (also for 4 hands); op. 14, *6 Humoresques de Concert* (with the famous Menuet in G); op. 15, *Dans le désert,* toccata; op. 21, Sonata in E♭ minor; op. 23, Variations in E♭ minor; etc. For orch.: op. 17, Piano Concerto in A minor; op. 19, *Fantaisie polonaise* for piano and orch.; op. 24, Symphony in B minor; also a sonata for violin and piano (op. 13), and songs. A complete list of his compositions was publ. in the 'Bollettino bibliografico musicale' (Milan, 1932). —Paderewski ed. the complete works of Chopin for the Chopin Institute (Warsaw, 1949-58). —Cf. H. T. Finck, *Paderewski and his Art* (N. Y., 1895); E. A. Baughan, *I. J. Paderewski* (London, 1908); J. C. Hadden, *Modern Musicians* (Boston, 1913); *To I. J. Paderewski* (Kosciusko Foundation; N. Y., 1928); J. F. Cooke, *I. J. Paderewski* (Philadelphia, 1928); H. Opienski, *Paderewski* (Lausanne, 1928; new ed., 1948); A. Henderson, *Contemporary Immortals* (N. Y., 1930); C. Phillips, *Paderewski* (N. Y., 1933); R. Landau, *Paderewski* (N. Y., 1934); L. T. Wolkowicz, *Paderewski's Diamond Anniversary* (N. Y., 1936); Mary Lawton, in collaboration with Paderewski, publ. *The Paderewski Memoirs* (to 1914 only; N. Y., 1938); A. Gronowicz, *Paderewski, Pianist and Patriot* (Edinburgh, 1943); S. Giron, *Le Drame Paderewski* (Geneva, 1948); A. Baumgartner, *Le Vérité sur le prétendu drame Paderewski* (Geneva, 1948); A. Strakacz, *Paderewski as I knew him* (New Brunswick, N. J., 1949); C. Kellogg, *Paderewski* (N. Y., 1956). —In 1900, by a deed of trust, Paderewski established a fund of $10,000 (original trustees were Wm. Steinway, Major H. L. Higginson, and Dr. Wm. Mason), the interest to be devoted to triennial cash prizes 'to composers of American birth without distinction as to age or religion,' in the following forms: symph. works for orchestra; compositions for solo instruments with orchestra; chamber music.

Padilla (pah-dil'yah), **Lola Artôt de,** soprano; daughter of the Spanish baritone Mariano Padilla; b. Sèvres, near Paris, Oct. 5, 1885; d. Berlin, April 12, 1933. She was trained solely by her mother, Désirée Artôt. After singing in *salons* and concerts, she was engaged by Albert Carré for the Opéra-Comique in 1903. Later toured as concert singer through Europe; engaged at the Komische Oper, Berlin, 1905-08, as prima donna; 1909-27, member of the Royal Opera, Berlin; then retired.

Padilla y Ramos, Mariano, Spanish baritone; b. Murcia, 1842; d. Paris, Nov. 23, 1906. He studied with Mabellini in Florence; made his début in Messina; sang in opera with great success in Italy, Austria, Germany, and Russia. In 1869 he married the singer Désirée Artôt (q.v.).

Paër (păh-är), **Ferdinando,** composer; b. Parma, June 1, 1771; d. Paris, May 3, 1839. He was a pupil of Fortunati and Ghiretti. His career as an opera composer began in 1792, when he produced the operas *Circe* (Venice) and *Le Astuzie amorose* (Parma). In that year he was also appointed honorary maestro di cappella to the court of Parma. In Vienna, 1797-1802, his style, doubtless influenced by Mozart's masterpieces, underwent a change, both harmony and orchestration showing increased variety and fullness; *Camilla, ossia il sotterraneo* (Vienna, Feb. 23, 1799) is considered his best opera. Paër succeeded Naumann as court Kapellmeister at Dresden in 1802; *Leonora, ossia l'amore conjugale* (Dresden, Oct. 3, 1804) is identical in subject with Beethoven's *Fidelio.* In 1807 he went to Paris, becoming 'maître de chapelle' to Napoleon and conductor of the Opéra-Comique; later (1812) he succeeded Spontini at the Italian Opera, where he remained, through the vicissitudes of Catalani's domination and the joint conductorship of Rossini (1824-26), his successful rival on the stage, until his forced resignation in 1827 (he was held to blame for the poor financial condition of the theater). In 1828 he received the cross of the Legion of Honor; was elected to the Institut in 1831; and in 1832 was appointed conductor of the royal chamber music. Although some of his 43 operas were successful — e.g. *Sargino* (Dresden, May 26, 1803) and *Agnese* (first performed privately, near Parma, Oct., 1809)—they have all disappeared from the repertory, except for *Le Maître de chapelle* (Paris, March 29, 1821), occasionally performed in France; he also wrote 2 oratorios and a Passion, 10 cantatas, and much other vocal music; a *Symphonie bacchante* and variations on *Vive Henri IV,* for full orch.; 4 grand military marches; many piano variations; etc.—Cf. T. Massé and A. Deschamps, *Paër et Rossini* (Paris, 1820); C. de Colobrano, *Funérailles de F. Paër* (Paris, 1893); A. Della Corte, *L'Opera comica . . .* (II, p. 199; 1923); R. Engländer, in 'Neues Beethoven-Jahrbuch' IV (1929).

Paesiello. See **Paisiello.**

Paganelli, Giuseppe Antonio, Italian composer; b. Padua, March 6, 1710; d. Madrid, 1760. He was probably a pupil of Tartini;

was employed as a cembalo player in an Italian opera company; was in Venice (1732); then at Bayreuth (1737-39). In 1755 he went to Madrid. He wrote several operas; but his historical importance lies in his works for the harpsichord. His *Divertissement de le Beau Sexe* (6 sonatas) was publ. by Gino Tagliapietra (Milan, 1936). —Cf. F. Torrefranca, *Poeti minori del clavicembalo,* in the 'Rivista Musicale Italiana' (1910); E. Schenk, *G. A. Paganelli* (Salzburg, 1928).

Paganini, Niccolò, most famous of violin virtuosos; b. Genoa, Oct. 27, 1782; d. Nice, May 27, 1840. His father, a poor shopkeeper with little musical knowledge, but loving the art, taught him to play on the mandolin, and then procured abler teachers for his gifted son; under G. Servetto, and after him the maestro di cappella G. Costa, Niccolò's progress in violin playing was rapid; at 8 he composed a sonata for violin; in 1793 he appeared in public; from 1795 he studied with Ghiretti and Alessandro Rolla at Parma, and began to compose seriously. His career as an independent virtuoso dates from 1798, when he ran away from his father after a concert at Lucca, and made a tour by himself to Pisa and other places. Though only 16, he was passionately fond of gambling, and addicted to all forms of dissipation; at Leghorn he had to part with his violin to pay a gambling debt, but a French merchant named Levron lent him a fine Guarnerius violin, and was so charmed with his playing that he made him a present of it. In 1804 he went home, and spent a year in assiduous practice; set out again on his travels in 1805, arousing unbounded enthusiasm; was soon appointed court solo violinist at Lucca (where his novel performances on the G-string began), and stayed there until 1808; then up to 1827 he traveled throughout Italy, his renown spreading from year to year, and his vast technical resources maturing and augmenting so that victory over would-be rivals (Lafont at Milan, 1816, and Lipinski at Piacenza, 1817) was easy. When he left Italy for the first time in 1828, his opening concert, at Vienna, was a veritable triumph; from the municipality he received the great gold medal of St. Salvator; from the Emperor the (honorary) title of court virtuoso. He reached Berlin in March, 1829, Paris in March, 1831; and played for the first time in London on June 3, 1831. Within a year he accumulated a fortune in Britain. The winter of 1833-34 was passed in Paris; he then retired for a time to his villa at Parma, though often visiting Paris; his health had already begun to fail seriously, as a result of life-long dissipation and excitement. He spent the winter of 1838 in Paris, where his chief disorder, laryngeal phthisis, was aggravated by the climate and by chagrin at financial losses; he lived for several months at Marseilles with a friend, but finding no relief, repaired to Nice for the winter, and died there the following spring. —Paganini's stupendous technique (in double stops, left-hand pizzicato, staccato, harmonics), great power and perfect control of tone, the romantic passion and intense energy of his style, quite apart from his personal eccentricities (which were numberless) and mere tricks of virtuosity (such as tuning up the A-string by a semitone or playing the *Witches' Dance* on one string after severing the other three on the stage, in sight of the audience, with a pair of scissors), made him the marvel of his time. He never controlled his individuality so far as to become even a good quartet-player; he was an artist quite *sui generis,* whose dazzling genius held his audiences spellbound, and impressed musicians and amateurs alike. —Works: 24 *Capricci per violino solo* (op. 1; piano transcriptions by Schumann and Liszt); 6 *Sonate per violino e chitarra* (op. 2); do. (op. 3); 6 *Gran quartetti a violino, viola, chitarra e violoncello* (op. 4, 5); concerto in B minor, *La Campanella,* with rondo 'à la clochette' (op. 7); *Le Streghe,* variations on theme by Süssmayr (op. 8); Variations on *God Save the King* (op. 9); *Il Carnevale di Venezia,* 20 variations (op. 10); the concert allegro *Moto perpetuo* (op. 11); Variations on *Non più mesta* (op. 12); Variations on *Di tanti palpiti* (op. 13); *Variazioni di bravura* on airs from *Mosè;* 60 studies in 60 progressive variations on the air *Barucabà.* Of these only op. 1-5 were publ. during his life (the others posthumously). A number of works are still in MS. —BIBLIOGRAPHY: J. M. Schottky, *Paganini's Leben und Treiben als Künstler und als Mensch* (Prague and Hamburg, 1830; reprinted 1909); L. F. L'Héritier, *Notice sur le célèbre violiniste N. Paganini* (Paris, 1830; English transl., London, 1830); F. C. J. Schuetz, *Leben, Charakter und Kunst des Ritters N. Paganini* (Illmenau, 1830); K. F. Guhr, *Über Paganini's Kunst, die Violine zu spielen* (Mainz, 1831; English transl. by S. Novello, London, 1831); F. J. Fétis, *Notice biographique sur N. Paganini* (Paris, 1851; English transl., London, 1852); G. Conestabile, *Vita di N. Paganini* (Perugia, 1851; new ed., Milan, 1936); O. Bruni, *N. Paganini, Racconto storico* (Florence, 1873; new ed., 1903); A. Niggli, *N. Paganini,* in Waldersee's 'Sammlung musikalischer Vorträge' (Leipzig, 1882); S. S. Stratton, *N. Paganini; His Life and Work* (London, 1907); J.-G. Prod'homme, *Paganini* (Paris, 1907; English transl., N. Y., 1911); A. Bonaventura, *N. Paganini* (Modena, 1911); J. Kapp, *N. Paganini* (Berlin, 1913; rev. ed., 1928); E. Istel, *Paganini* (1919); J. Siber, *Paganini* (Berlin, 1920); G. Kinsky, *Paganinis musikalischer Nachlass,* in the Heyer Catalogue IV (pp. 402-47); L. Day, *Paganini* (N. Y., 1929); A. Günther, *Paganini in Lucca* (Munich, 1929); A. Montanelli, *Paganini a Forlì* (Forlì, 1930); E. Istel, *The Secret of Paganini's Technique,* in the 'Mus. Quarterly' (Jan., 1930); J. Pulver, *Paganini, the Romantic Virtuoso* (London, 1936); R. de Saussine, *Paganini le magicien* (Paris, 1938; English transl., N. Y., 1954); I. Pizzetti, *N. Paganini* (Turin, 1940); N. Podenzani, *Il Romanzo di N. Paganini* (Milan, 1944); M. Tibaldi Chiesa, *Paganini, la vita e l'opera* (3rd ed., Milan, 1944); H. Spivacke, *Paganiniana* (Washington, 1945); T. Valensi, *Paganini* (Nice, 1950); A. Mell, *Paganiniana in the Muller Collection of the New York Public Library,* in the 'Mus. Quarterly' (Jan., 1953); G. I. C. de Courcy, *Paganini: the Genoese* (Norman, Okla., 1957). A very important documentary compilation, *Paganini intimo,* was brought out by A. Codignola (Genoa, 1935).

Page, John, English tenor; b. c. 1760; d. London, Aug. 16, 1812. He was a lay clerk at St. George's, Windsor, 1790; Gentleman of Chapel Royal; Vicar-choral at St. Paul's, 1801.—Publ. 'Harmonica sacra' (1800; 3 vols.; a collection of 74 anthems in score, by eminent English composers of the 16th-18th centuries; new ed. by Rimbault); 'Festive Harmony . . .' (1804; 4 vols.; madrigals, glees, and elegies); 'Collection of Hymns . . .' (1804); 'The Burial Service, Chant, Evening Service, Dirge and Anthems App. to be Perf. at the Funeral of Lord Nelson' (1806); anthems, psalms, etc.

Page, Kate Stearns, American pedagogue; b. Brookline, Mass., Aug. 21, 1873; taught at the Denison House Settlement in Boston for 10 years and at the Parke School, Brookline, Mass., for 5 years; from 1933 piano teacher at the Diller-Quaile School of Music, N. Y. Publ. valuable pedagogical material, some of it in collaboration with Angela Diller.

Page, Nathaniel Clifford, American editor, b. San Francisco, Oct. 26, 1866; d. Philadelphia, May 12, 1956. He was a pupil of E. Stillman Kelley; 1905-09, editor for O. Ditson Co. in Boston; from 1909, for C. C. Birchard & Co., Carl Fischer, Theo. Presser, etc.; then again for O. Ditson Co.; 1921-29, conducted summer classes in orchestration at Columbia Univ. He made a special study of Oriental music.—Works: a light opera, *The First Lieutenant* (San Francisco, 1889); other stage works; many band and orchestral pieces; cantatas; songs; etc. He publ. over 400 vocal and instrumental arrangements.

Pahissa (păh-ēs'-săh), **Jaime,** Catalan composer; b. Barcelona, Oct. 7, 1880. He was a practicing architect for 4 years before turning to music as a profession; studied composition with Morera in Barcelona. He associated himself with the Catalan nationalist movement in art, obtaining his first important success with the romantic opera *La Presó de Lleida (The Prison of Lérida)* in 1906, which had 100 consecutive performances in Barcelona; it was later rewritten and produced in Barcelona on Feb. 8, 1928 under the title *La Princesa Margarita,* again obtaining a notable success. Other operas produced in Barcelona were *Gala Plácida* (Jan. 15, 1913) and *Marianella* (March 31, 1925); among his orchestral works the most remarkable is *Monodía,* written in unisons, octaves, double octaves, etc., without using any other intervals, and depending for its effect only on instrumental variety (Barcelona, Oct. 12, 1925); in a different vein is his *Suite Intertonal* (Barcelona, Oct. 24, 1926), based on his own method of free tonal and polytonal composition. In 1935 Pahissa emigrated to Argentina, settling in Buenos Aires, where he continued to compose; also established himself as a teacher and writer there. He publ. in Buenos Aires the books: *Espíritu y cuerpo de la música* (1945); *Los grandes problemas de la música* (1945; new ed., 1954); *Vida y obra de Manuel de Falla* (Buenos Aires, 1947; also in English, London, 1954); *Sendas y cumbres de la música española* (1955). A detailed account of Pahissa's career in Barcelona is found in the 'Diccionario de la Música Ilustrado' (1930).

Pahlen, Kurt, writer on music; b. Vienna, May 26, 1907. He studied at the Vienna Cons., and also at the Univ. of Vienna (with Guido Adler, Lach, and Orel), graduating in 1929. In 1939 he settled in Buenos Aires, where he became a successful teacher and writer on musical subjects; publ. a music history: *Historia gráfica uni-*

versal de la música (Buenos Aires, 1944; in English as *Music of the World,* N. Y., 1949); also a general manual of musical knowledge, *Síntesis del saber musical* (Buenos Aires, 1948); *Ins Wunderland der Musik* (Zürich, 1948); *Manuel de Falla und die Musik in Spanien* (Olten, 1953).

Paine, John Knowles, American composer and teacher; b. Portland, Me., Jan. 9, 1839; d. Cambridge, Mass., April 25, 1906. His father kept a music store in Portland, and conducted the local band. His first music teacher was H. Kotzschmar. He then went to Berlin and studied under Haupt (counterpoint), Fischer (singing), and Wieprecht (instrumentation), 1858-61. After organ concerts in Berlin and various American cities, he settled in Boston as organist of the West Church, Cambridge St. In 1862 he became teacher of music at Harvard Univ., and organist at Appleton Chapel, Cambridge, Mass.; from 1875 until his death he occupied the newly created professorship of music at Harvard, the first in any American university. In 1866-67 he toured Germany and conducted his Mass at Berlin. M. A. *(hon. c.),* Harvard, 1869; Mus. Doc. *(hon. c.),* Yale, 1890. He was one of the most notable pioneers in American musical development. Among his many pupils were J. A. Carpenter, A. Foote, E. B. Hill, F. S. Converse, H. T. Finck, D. G. Mason.—Works: *Domine salvum fac,* for men's chorus and orch., op. 8 (1863); Mass in D for soli, chorus, and orch., op. 10; oratorio, *St. Peter,* op. 20; *Centennial Hymn* in D, for chorus and orch., op. 27 (Philadelphia, 1876); music to *Œdipus tyrannus* (Sophocles), for men's voices and orch., op. 35; *The Realm of Fancy,* cantata for soprano solo, chorus and orch., op. 36; *Phœbus, arise; The Nativity,* cantata for soli, chorus, and orch., op. 38; *Song of Promise,* cantata for soprano, chorus, and orch., op. 43; incidental music to *The Birds* of Aristophanes; *Columbus March and Hymn,* for the Chicago Exposition (1893); *Hymn of the West,* for the St. Louis Exposition (1904); 2 symphonies, op. 23 in C minor and op. 34 in A (*Spring Symphony;* Cambridge, Mass., March 10, 1880); 2 symphonic poems, op. 31 in D minor, on *The Tempest,* and op. 44 in G♯ minor and A♭, *An Island Fantasy;* overture to *As You Like It; Duo concertante* for violin and cello with orch., in A, op. 33; string quartet, op. 5; piano trio, op. 22; Larghetto and Scherzo for piano, violin, and cello, op. 32; Romanza and Scherzo for piano and cello, op. 30; sonata for piano and violin, op. 24; characteristic pieces for piano; variations and fantasias for organ; motets, part-songs, and songs. An opera, *Azara* (text by himself), was publ. in 1901, and had a concert performance in Boston in 1907. Also wrote *The History of Music to the Death of Schubert* (posthumous, 1907). His *Lecture Notes* were publ. in 1885.—Cf. 'Mus. Times' (June, 1906); G. T. Edwards, *Music and Musicians of Maine* (1928); M. A. DeW. Howe, *J. K. Paine,* in the 'Mus. Quarterly' (July, 1939); see also 'Dictionary of American Biography,' vol. XIV.

Paisible, Louis Henri, French violinist and composer; b. Paris, 1745; d. St. Petersburg, March 30, 1782 (suicide). He studied with Gaviniès; played in the orch. of the Concert Spirituel in Paris; then traveled through Europe; in 1778, was engaged at the Russian court in St. Petersburg. Although well received at first, he was unable to make headway with a series of concerts for which he solicited subscriptions; deprived of resources, he shot himself. Twelve of his string quartets and 2 violin concertos have been publ. in Paris and London. —Cf. A. Mooser, *Annales de la Musique et des Musiciens en Russie au XVIIIe siècle* (Geneva, 1950; vol. II, pp. 274-78).

Paisiello, Giovanni, Italian dramatic composer; b. Taranto, May 9, 1740; d. Naples, June 5, 1816. From the age of 5 he studied at the Jesuit school in Taranto, where he was taught by a priest, Resta, and where his singing so delighted Guaducci, maestro at the Capuchin church, that he advised the boy's father to place him in the Cons. di S. Onofrio at Naples. There he studied under Durante, Cotumacci, and Abos, from 1754 to 1759, remaining 4 years longer as a teacher, and occupying himself with sacred composition (Masses, oratorios, etc.). But a comic intermezzo performed at the Cons. in 1763 disclosed such dramatic talent that he was commissioned to write an opera for the Marsigli Theater at Bologna; here his first comic opera was produced, *La Pupilla, ossia Il Mondo alla rovescia* (1764). For 12 years, during which he brought out no less than 50 operas, his successes were many, and reverses few, even in rivalry with Piccinni and Cimarosa. Important works of this period are *Le finte Contesse* (Rome, Feb., 1766), *L'Idolo cinese* (Naples, spring, 1767), and *La Frascatana* (Venice, Nov., 1774). Invited to St. Petersburg by Empress Catherine II in 1776, he lived there 8 years on a princely salary, produced several operas, including *Il Barbiere di Siviglia* (St.

Petersburg, Sept. 26, 1782), which became so popular in Italy that it still stood as a rival to Rossini's masterpiece in 1816. During the next 15 years he acted as maestro di cappella to Ferdinand IV of Naples (1784-99); *Il Re Teodoro in Venezia* (Vienna, Aug. 23, 1784; perhaps his best opera), *Le Gare generose* (Naples, spring, 1786), *L'Amor contrastato* (later called *La Molinara;* Naples, summer, 1788), *Nina, o La Pazza per amore* (Caserta, June 25, 1789; a charming 'opera semiseria,' a genre in which Paisiello excelled), and *I Zingari in fiera* (Naples, Nov. 21, 1789) are especially noteworthy. During the revolutionary period of 1799-1801 Paisiello stood well with the republican government, but lost the favor of the King, together with his place and salary. From 1802-03 he was Napoleon's maître de chapelle at Paris. From 1803 to the Bourbon restoration of 1815, he held his former position at Naples, and other posts of importance, all of which latter he lost on Ferdinand's return in 1815, being retained solely as maestro di cappella.—Paisiello was an extraordinarily productive composer, and one of the most popular of his time; yet of his 100 or more operas only a few are ever revived nowadays. His vein of melody was original, fresh, and natural; although he introduced instrumental effects that were novel in Italy, he carefully avoided the over-elaborate numbers common to the period, obtaining his effect by the grace, beauty, and dramatic truthfulness of his melody. Seven operas were published: *Il Marchese di Tulipano, La Serva padrona, Il Barbiere, Il Re Teodoro, La Molinara, Nina,* and *Proserpine.*—Church music: a Passion oratorio (Warsaw, 1784); 3 solemn Masses for double choir and 2 orchestras; *Te Deum* for the same; Requiem for 4 voices and orch. (performed at his own funeral); 30 Masses for the same; two 5-part Masses; *Dixit,* Magnificat, *Miserere,* about 40 motets with orch.; etc.—12 symphonies; funeral march for Gen. Hoche; 6 piano concertos; 12 piano quartets; 6 string quartets; sonata and concerto for harp; 2 vols. of sonatas, caprices, etc. for piano.—Bibliography: I. F. Arnold, *G. Paisiello seine kurze Biographie* (Erfurt, 1810); J. F. Lesueur, *Notice sur Paisiello* (Paris, 1816); Gagliardo, *Onori funebri . . . di Paisiello* (Naples, 1816); Quatremère de Quincy, *Notice historique de Paisiello* (Paris, 1817); F. Schizzi, *Della vita e degli studi di G. Paisiello* (Milan, 1833); C. G. Pupino, *Paisiello* (Naples, 1908); S. Panareo, *Paisiello in Russia* (Trani, 1910); H. Abert, *Paisiello's Buffokunst und ihre Beziehungen zu Mozart,* in 'Archiv für Musikwissenschaft' I, 3 (1919); A. Della Corte, *Settecento italiano: Paisiello* (Turin, 1922); F. Barberio, *I primi dieci anni di vita artistica di Paisiello,* in the 'Rivista Musicale Italiana' (1922); A. Cametti, *Paisiello e la corte di Vienna* (Rome, 1929); G. C. Speciale, *G. Paisiello* (Naples, 1931); P. Petrosellini, *Il Barbiere di Siviglia di G. Paisiello* (1932); A. Loewenberg, *Paisiello's and Rossini's 'Barbiere di Siviglia,'* in 'Music & Letters' (April, 1939); E. Faustini-Fasini, *Opere teatrali, oratori e cantate di G. Paisiello* (Bari, 1940).

Paladilhe (păh-lăh-dēl'), **Émile,** French composer; b. Montpellier, June 3, 1844; d. Paris, Jan. 7, 1926. He entered the Paris Cons. in 1853; pupil of Marmontel (piano), Benoist (organ), and Halévy (counterpoint); 1st prize for piano and organ, 1857; won the Grand Prix de Rome in 1860 with the cantata *Le Czar Ivan IV* (Opéra, 1860). He brought out the 1-act comedy-opera *Le Passant,* at the Opéra-Comique (April 24, 1872), followed by *L'Amour africain* (May 8, 1875), *Suzanne* (Dec. 30, 1878), *Diana* (Feb. 23, 1885), the 5-act opera *Patrie* (Opéra, Dec. 20, 1886); and *Les Saintes Maries de la mer,* a sacred lyric drama (Montpellier, 1892). He also produced 2 Masses, a symph. in E♭, some sacred music, and numerous songs (*Mandolinata, Premières pensées, Mélodies écossaises*). In 1892 he succeeded Guiraud as member of the Institut de France.

Palau, Manuel, Spanish composer and conductor; b. Valencia, Jan. 4, 1893. He studied first at the Cons. of Valencia; later in Paris, where he took lessons from Koechlin and Ravel. Returning to Valencia, he established himself as teacher, conductor, and composer. Most of his thematic material is inspired by Catalan folksongs; his instrumental music usually bears programmatic content; his technique of composition follows the French Impressionist procedures. —Works: 'zarzuelas': *Beniflors, Amor torna,* etc.; *Gongoriana,* orch. suite (1927); 2 symphonies; *Concierto levantino,* for guitar and orch.; *Homenaje a Debussy,* for orch.; sonata for guitar solo; numerous songs of a popular nature; piano pieces: *Valencia, Levantina, Sonatina Valenciana, Tres Impresiones fugaces, Campanas y paisaje balear, Danza hispalense, Danza iberica, Evocación de Andalucía,* etc. —Cf. A. Mingote, *Manuel Palau* (Valencia, 1946); F. J. León Tello, *La Obra pianistica de Manuel Palau* (Valencia, 1956).

Palester, Roman, Polish composer; b. Sniatyn, Dec. 28, 1907. He studied with Soltys at the Cons. of Lwow, and with Sikorski at the Warsaw Cons.; went to France in 1925; then returned to Poland for a few years; settled in Paris in 1947. In his music, Palester adopts the modernistic features of neo-Classicism, in a lucid diatonic style, enlivened by a strong sense of rhythm. Several of his works were performed at festivals of the International Society for Contemporary Music: *Symphonic Music* (London, July 27, 1931), *Danse polonaise,* for orch. (Barcelona, April 22, 1936), violin concerto (London, July 14, 1946); other works: opera, *The Living Stones* (1944); ballet, *Song of the Earth* (1937); 4 symphonies (1936, 1942, 1947, 1952); *Requiem* (1948); concerto for saxophone and string orch.; sonatina for 3 clarinets (1936); concertino for piano and orch. (1942); Serenade for 2 flutes and string orch. (Cracow, Nov. 9, 1947); 3 string quartets; a string trio; piano pieces.

Palestrina (Giovanni Pierluigi, called **da Palestrina)**, the greatest composer of the Catholic Church and of the Roman School, b. Palestrina, near Rome, c. 1525; d. Rome, Feb. 2, 1594. He was a chorister at the Cathedral of his native town c. 1532, and in 1534, when Cardinal della Valle, Bishop of Palestrina, was made Archbishop of S. Maria Maggiore in Rome, he took Palestrina with him and entered him in the choir school of that church. In 1537 we find him listed as an elder choir-boy, and in 1539, his voice having broken, he left the choir and returned home. But by 1540, or soon after, he was back in Rome, studying music; his teacher may have been Firmin Le Bel, choirmaster of S. Maria Maggiore. In 1544 he was appointed organist and choirmaster at the Cathedral of St. Agapit in Palestrina; the bishop there was Cardinal del Monte, who in 1550 became pope under the name of Julius III, and who in 1551 bestowed upon Palestrina the post of maestro of the Cappella Giulia. Meanwhile, Palestrina had married (June 12, 1547) and had become the father of two sons. In 1554 he publ. his first book of Masses, dedicated to Julius III, who rewarded him by making him a member of the Pontifical Choir (Jan., 1555); this aroused much resentment, for Palestrina was admitted without taking the entrance examination, and it is said that he had a poor voice. A few months later he was dismissed with a small pension by the new pope, Paul IV, on the ground that he was a married man. He then received the appointment of maestro at the church of St. John Lateran, for which he wrote his celebrated *Lamentations*. In 1560 he resigned this post, and in March of the following year he became maestro of S. Maria Maggiore. In 1563 his first book of motets was published. About this time the Council of Trent concerned itself with the reform of church music, decreeing the exclusion of all profane and impure elements; contrapuntal music, which lent itself to many abuses, might also have been forbidden, had it not been for the determined opposition of the Emperor Ferdinand I. Palestrina's role in influencing the decisions of the Council, especially as regards the proposed exclusion of contrapuntal music, has been grossly exaggerated and misrepresented by most historians, beginning with Baini. Palestrina's famous *Missa Papae Marcelli* is undoubtedly a model of the purest religious style; but there is no evidence that it played much part in shaping the fate of church music at that time. From 1565 to 1571 Palestrina was music director at the new Roman Seminary, where his two elder sons were students. In 1567 he resigned his post at S. Maria Maggiore and entered the service of Cardinal Ippolito d'Este (d. 1572). In 1568 the Emperor Maximilian offered him the post of maestro at the court of Vienna, but Palestrina demanded so high a salary that the matter was dropped. In 1571 he resumed his old post as maestro of the Cappella Giulia, retaining this office until his death. In 1576 Pope Gregory XIII issued a decree for the revision of the Gradual, which was to be carried out by Palestrina and Annibale Zoilo; but the revised version, known as the 'Medicean Gradual,' was not printed until 20 years after Palestrina's death (1614). In 1580, having suffered several family bereavements, including the death of his wife, Palestrina decided to enter the priesthood; but soon he changed his mind, and on March 28, 1581, he married the widow of a prosperous furrier. He then took a partner and successfully carried on the fur business. In 1583 he was invited to become maestro at the court of Mantua, but again his terms were rejected as too high. In 1584 he brought out his settings of the *Song of Solomon,* and in 1589 his harmonized version of the Latin Hymnal was published. At his death he was buried in the Cappella Nuova of old St. Peter's Church. —In his music Palestrina aimed at technical smoothness and beauty of sound rather than at forceful expression and originality. In the 'Motu Proprio' of Pope Pius X on sacred music (1903), his works are recommended as 'of excellent quality from a liturgical and musical standpoint.' A monumental edition of his complete compositions was publ. by Breitkopf & Härtel in 33 volumes (1862-94); vols. I-III edited by Theodor de Witt and J. N. Rauch; vols. IV-VIII by Franz Espagne; vol. IX by Fr. Commer; and vols. X-XXXIII by Fr. X. Haberl. The contents of these volumes is as follows: vols. I-VII, 179 motets (*a* 4-12); vols. VIII, IX, 113 hymns and offertories (*a* 4-5); vols. X-XXIV, 93 Masses (*a* 4-8); vol. XXV, 9 Lamentations (each in several settings *a* 4-8); vol. XXVI, 10 litanies, 4 psalms, 2 motets (*a* 4-12); vol. XXVII, 35 Magnificats (*a* 4-8); vol. XXVIII, 83 Italian secular madrigals (*a* 3-6); vol. XXIX, 56 Italian sacred madrigals (*a* 4-6); vols. XXX-XXXII, miscellaneous compositions (many doubtful); vol. XXXIII, index, documents, facsimiles, etc. After the completion of this great edition the same firm began the separate publication of several of the most famous works (in treble and bass clefs). Breitkopf & Härtel also publ. a special catalogue. A new collected edition, in 34 vols. (compiled on the basis of the original texts, and using modern notation), was begun in 1938 under the editorship of R. Casimiri; vols. I-XXIII were publ. to 1958 (vols. I-XVI ed. by Casimiri, vol. XVII by L. Virgili, vols. XVIII-XIX by K. Jeppesen, and vols. XX-XXIII by L. Bianchi): vols. I, IV, VI, X, XV, XVIII, XIX, XXI—Masses; vols. II, IX, XXII, XXIII—madrigals; vols. III, V, VII, VIII, XI, XII—motets; vol. XIII—Lamentations; vol. XIV—hymns; vol. XVI—Magnificats; vol. XVII—offertories; vol. XX—litanies. — BIBLIOGRAPHY: G. Baini, *Memorie storico-critiche della vita e delle opere di G. P. da Palestrina* (Rome, 1828, 2 vols.; German transl., abridged, Leipzig, 1834); K. von Winterfeld, *Joh. P. von Palestrina* (Breslau, 1832); W. Bäumker, *Palestrina* (Freiburg, 1877); P. Wagner, *Palestrina als weltlicher Komponist* (Strasbourg, 1890); F. X. Haberl, *Die Kardinals-Kommission von 1564 und Palestrina's 'Missa Papae Marcelli,'* in 'Kirchenmusikalisches Jahrbuch' (1892); Ph. Spitta, *Palestrina im 16. und 19. Jahrhundert,* in 'Deutsche Rundschau' (July, 1894); F. X. Haberl, *G. P. da Palestrina e il Graduale romanum officiale dell'editio medicaea (1614)* (Regensburg, 1894); A. Cametti, *Cenni biografici di G. P. da Palestrina* (Milan, 1895); G. Félix, *Palestrina et la musique sacrée (1594-1894)* (Lille, 1896); C. Respighi, *Nuovo studio su G. P. da Palestrina e l'emendazione del Graduale romano* (Rome, 1899); A. Cametti, *Un nuovo documento sulle origini di G. P. da Palestrina* in the 'Rivista Musicale Italiana' (1903); Michel Brenet, *Palestrina* (Paris, 1905); J. Gloger, *Die 'Missa Prima.' Eine Studie über den Palestrinastil* (Leobschütz, 1910); E. Schmitz, *G. P. Palestrina* (Leipzig, 1914); K. Weinmann, *Palestrina's Geburtsjahr* (Regensburg, 1915); R. Casimiri, *G. P. da Palestrina. Nuovi documenti biografici* (Rome, 1918); id., *Il 'Codice 59' dell' archivio musicale lateranense'* (Rome, 1919); Zoë K. Pyne, *G. P. da Palestrina, His Life and Times* (London, 1922); A. Cametti, *G. P. da Palestrina e il suo commercio di pelliccerie* (Rome, 1922); id., *G. P. da Palestrina e le sue alleanze matrimoniali,* in the 'Rivista Musicale Italiana' (1923); id., *Le Case dei Pierluigi in Palestrina* (Rome, 1925); id., *Palestrina* (Milan, 1925); id., *Bibliografia palestriniana,* in 'Bollettino bibliografico musicale' (Sept., 1926); K. Jeppesen, *The Style of Palestrina and the Dissonance* (Danish, 1923; German, 1925; English, 1927; 2nd English ed., 1946); id., in the 'P. Wagner-Festschrift' (1926), 'Adler-Festschrift' (1930), and 'Liège Kongress-Bericht' (1931); L. P. Manzetti, *Palestrina,* in the 'Mus. Quarterly' (July, 1928); K. G. Fellerer, *Palestrina* (Regensburg, 1930); F. Raugel, *Palestrina* (Paris, 1930); W. Widmann, *Die 6-stimmigen Messen Palestrina's,* in 'Kirchenmusikalisches Jahrbuch' (1930-31); O. Ursprung, *Die katholische Kirchenmusik* (1933); H. Coates, *Palestrina* (London, 1938); O. Strunk, *Guglielmo Gonzaga and Palestrina's 'Missa Dominicalis,'* in the 'Mus. Quarterly' (April, 1947); J. Samson, *Palestrina ou La poésie de l'exactitude* (Geneva, 1950); K. Jeppesen, *The Recently Discovered Mantova Masses of Palestrina,* in 'Acta Musicologica' (1950); A. I. M. Kat, *Palestrina* (Haarlem, 1951); G. Reese, *Music in the Renaissance* (N. Y., 1954). For Palestrina's correspondence with the Duke of Mantua see 'Kirchenmusikalisches Jahrbuch' (1886).

Pallantios, Menelaos, Greek composer; b. Piraeus, Feb. 11, 1914. He studied in Rome with Casella; returning to Greece, became instructor at the Athens Cons. He has written incidental music to several ancient Greek tragedies; a *Greek Overture* (1946); a symphony (1948); violin pieces and songs.

Pallavicini (or **Pallavicino**) (păl-lăh-vĭh-chē'-nē), **Carlo,** Italian composer; b. Salò, near Brescia, 1630; d. Dresden, Jan. 26, 1688. He was vice-Kapellmeister in 1667, and Kapellmeister in 1672, to the Dresden court; after a stay in Italy, he became Kapellmeister of the new Italian Opera at Dresden (1686). Composed over 20 operas for Italian theaters and Dresden. A scene from *Le Amazoni nell'isole fortunate* (Piazzola, near Padua, Nov. 11, 1679) was publ. in the 'Sammelbände der Internationalen Musik-Gesellschaft' (vol. 2), and the complete score of *La Gerusalemme liberata* (Venice, Jan. 3, 1687) was ed. by Abert in the 'Denkmäler deutscher Tonkunst' (vol. 55).

Pallavicino, Benedetto, Italian composer; b. Cremona; d. Mantua, May 6, 1601. He was a court singer in Mantua from 1582 and maestro di cappella to the Duke from 1596. Monteverdi mentions Pallavicino's death in a letter applying for his post to the Duke of Mantua in Nov., 1601. Pallavicino publ. 1 book of madrigals *a* 4 (1579), 8 books *a* 5 (1581, ?, 1585, 1588, 1593, 1600, 1604, 1612), 1 book *a* 6 (1587), and other madrigals in collections; also a book of motets *a* 8, 12, and 16 (1595). —Cf. D. de Paoli, *Monteverdi* (Milan, 1945); G. Sartori, *Monteverdiana,* in the 'Mus. Quarterly' (July, 1952).

Pallemaerts, Edmundo, composer; b. Malines, Belgium, 1867; d. Buenos Aires, April 20, 1945. He studied with De Greef and Kufferath at the Brussels Cons.; settled in Buenos Aires in 1889, and founded there the Conservatorio Argentino, of which he was the first director (1894). He wrote a *Fantasia Argentina* for orch.; many minor works for piano; also songs.

Palma, Athos, Argentine composer; b. Buenos Aires, June 7, 1891; d. Miramar, Argentina, Jan. 10, 1951. He studied with C. Troiani (piano) and other teachers in Buenos Aires; in 1904, went to Europe, returning to Buenos Aires in 1914. There he was busily engaged as a teacher. His music follows the Italian tradition, although the subject matter is derived from South American history and literature. He wrote the operas *Nazdah* (Buenos Aires, June 19, 1924) and *Los Hijos del Sol* (*The Sons of the Sun,* after an Inca legend; Buenos Aires, Nov. 10, 1928); *Cantares de mi tierra,* for strings (1914); the symph. poems *Jardines* and *Los Hijos del Sol;* a violin sonata; a cello sonata; a piano sonata; many songs; pedagogical works: *Teoría razonada de la música* and *Tratado completo de armonía.* —Cf. N. Lamuraglia, *Athos Palma: vida, arte, educación* (Buenos Aires, 1954).

Palmer, Geoffrey (Molyneux), Anglo-Irish organist and composer; b. Staines, Middlesex, Oct. 8, 1882. He studied at the Royal College of Music in London; in 1910, settled in Ireland as a church organist; wrote cantatas, songs, and an Irish opera *The Sea of Moyle,* produced in Dublin (in the Gaelic language) on July 25, 1923.

Palmer, Horatio Richmond, American pedagogue; b. Sherburne, N. Y., April 26, 1834; d. Yonkers, N. Y., Nov. 15, 1907. He was taught by his father and sister, later by various teachers in New York, Berlin, and Florence. Began composing at 18, and chorus-conducting at 20. In 1857, head of the music dept., Rushford Academy; settled in Chicago after the Civil War; from 1873 he had charge, for many years, of the New Church Choral Union, giving concerts with as many as 4,000 singers; from 1877-91 dean of the Summer School of Music at Chautauqua. Mus. Doc. (Chicago Univ. and Alfred Univ.). Of his collections, 'The Song Queen,' 'The Song King,' 'The Song Herald,' and 'Concert Choruses' had great success; also publ. *Theory of Music, Class Method* (of elementary teaching), *Manual for Teachers* (in public schools), etc. —Cf. 'Dictionary of American Biography' vol. XIV (1934).

Palmer, Robert, American composer; b. Syracuse, N. Y., June 2, 1915. He studied at the Eastman School of Music, Rochester, with Howard Hanson and Bernard Rogers; later took some lessons with Roy Harris and Aaron Copland; taught music at the Univ. of Kansas (1940-43); in 1943, appointed instructor at Cornell Univ., Ithaca. In many of his works he builds his thematic material on the scale of alternating whole tones and semitones. —Works: for orch.: *Poem* for violin and chamber orch. (1938), concerto for small orch. (1940), concerto for orch. (1943), *K 19,* symph. elegy for Thomas Wolfe (1945), Variations, Chorale and Fugue for orch. (1947-54), chamber concerto No. 1 for violin, oboe, and strings (1949), symphony (1953); chamber music: 3 string quartets (1939; 1943-47; 1954), Concerto for Five Instruments (1943), piano quartet (1947), piano quintet (1950), viola sonata (1951), quintet for winds (1951), quintet for clarinet, piano, and strings (1952); choral music: *Abraham Lincoln Walks at Midnight* (1948), *Slow, Slow, Fresh Fount* (1953), *The Trojan Women*

(1955); 2 piano sonatas (1938-46; 1942-48), sonata for piano, 4-hands (1952), sonata for 2 pianos (1944), shorter piano pieces; ballet music. —Cf. W. Austin, *The Music of Robert Palmer* in the 'Mus. Quarterly' (Jan., 1956).

Palmgren, Selim, Finnish composer; b. Björneborg, Feb. 16, 1878; d. Helsinki, Dec. 13, 1951. After completing the course at the Cons. in Helsinki (1895-99), he continued his pianistic studies in Berlin with K. Ansorge, W. Berger, and F. Busoni; from 1902 to 1904, conductor of a choral society in Helsinki; from 1909 to 1912, led the Music Society in Åbo; 1921, made a tour of the U. S., and from 1923-26 was prof. of piano and composition at the Eastman School of Music, Rochester, N. Y.; then returned to Helsinki. He made several pianistic tours of Finland and Scandinavia, appearing also as visiting conductor. In 1909 he married the Finnish soprano Maikki Pakarienen (after she had been divorced from A. Järnefelt; she died in 1929); in 1930 he married Minna Talwik. —Works: 2 operas, *Daniel Hjort* (Åbo, April 15, 1910) and *Peter Schlemihl;* 5 piano concertos; a symph. poem, *Floden; Metamorphoses* (1916); *April* (1927); for piano: 2 sonatas; op. 3, suite; op. 6, *Fantasia;* op. 17, 24 Preludes; op. 18, *Ballade* (in the form of a theme with variations); op. 22, *Finnische Lyrik* (12 pieces); op. 24, *Finnische Suite* (The Seasons); op. 36, *Maskenball,* suite; etc.; songs and men's choruses. —He publ. a book, *Minusta Tuli Muusikko* (Helsinki, 1948).

Panassié, Hugues, French music critic, expert on jazz; b. Paris, Feb. 27, 1912. He founded the 'Hot Club de France' (1932); lectured on jazz at the Sorbonne in 1937, and in America in 1938; publ. *Le Jazz Hot* (basic treatise on the subject, Paris, 1934; in English, as *Hot Jazz,* N. Y., 1936); *The Real Jazz* (N. Y., 1942; in French, *La véritable musique de Jazz,* Paris, 1946); *La Musique de jazz et le swing* (Paris, 1945); *Douze années de Jazz (1927-1938)* (Paris, 1946); *Louis Armstrong* (Paris, 1947); *Jazz panorama* (Paris, 1950); *Discographie critique* (Paris, 1951); *Dictionnaire du jazz* (with Madeleine Gautier; Paris, 1954; in English as *Dictionary of Jazz,* London, 1956; American ed., Boston, 1956, as *Guide to Jazz).*

Panizza (păh-nĭt'-săh), **Ettore,** Argentine conductor and composer of Italian extraction; b. Buenos Aires, Aug. 12, 1875. He studied at the Cons. of Milan, Italy, graduating in 1898 with prizes for piano and composition; began his career as operatic conductor in Italy in 1899, and continued successfully for more than half a century. From 1907 to 1913 he conducted Italian operas at Covent Garden, London; then at La Scala, Milan (1916-26); in 1934 joined the staff of the Metropolitan Opera, N. Y., as conductor of the Italian repertory; then conducted at the Berlin State Opera (1938); also led symph. concerts in Europe, the U. S., and South America. He publ. an autobiography, *Medio siglo de vida musical* (Buenos Aires, 1951). —Operas: *Il Fidanzato del mare* (Buenos Aires, Aug. 15, 1897); *Medio evo latino* (Genoa, Nov. 17, 1900); *Aurora* (Buenos Aires, Sept. 5, 1908); *Bisanzio* (Buenos Aires, July 25, 1939); also *Il Re della foresta,* for soli, chorus, and orch.; *Tema con Variaciones,* for orch.; violin sonata; cello sonata; string quartet; piano pieces; songs.

Pannain, Guido, distinguished Italian musicologist; b. Naples, Nov. 17, 1891. He studied composition with C. de Nardis at Naples; upon graduation, devoted himself mainly to research, into both old and new aspects of music. —Publications: *La Teoria musicale di G. Tinctoris* (1913); *Le Origini della scuola musicale napoletana* (1914); *Le Origini e lo sviluppo dell' arte pianistica in Italia dal 1500 al 1700 circa* (1917); *Lineamenti di storia della musica* (1922; 4th ed., 1936); *Musica e musicisti in Napoli nel secolo XIX* (1922); *Storia del Conservatorio di Napoli* (1942); *La Vita del linguaggio musicale* (1947); *Ottocento musicale italiano* (1952); collaborated with A. Della Corte in *Storia della musica,* in 3 vols. (1936; 3rd ed., 1952). Beginning in 1928, he was one of the chief contributors to the 'Rassegna musicale' (essays on modern composers; publ. as *Musicisti dei tempi nuovi,* Turin, 1932; English transl. by Bonavia, London, 1932, as *Modern Composers*); also composed the operas *L'Intrusa* (1926; Genoa, 1940) and *Beatrice Cenci* (Naples, 1942); several symph. poems; a violin concerto; chamber music; songs. Edited *L'Oratorio dei Filippini e la scuola musicale di Napoli* (1934; vol. 5 of 'Istituzioni e monumenti dell'arte musicale italiana').

Panofka, Heinrich, singing teacher; b. Breslau, Oct. 3, 1807; d. Florence, Nov. 18, 1887. He began as a violinist, studying with Strauch and Forster; at ten he played in a concert, and from 1824 to 1827 studied at Vienna under Mayseder and Hoffmann;

then gave concerts, went to Munich in 1829, thence to Berlin, and settled in Paris (1834), playing at the Cons. concerts, and studying the art of singing and vocal instruction under Bordogni, with whom he founded, in 1842, an 'Académie de chant,' which failed in competition with the Prince of Moskowa's 'Société de concerts.' Lived 1844-52 at London, becoming famous as a singing teacher; was also Lumley's assistant conductor at His Majesty's Theatre in 1847, during Jenny Lind's appearances; returned to Paris, 1852; settled in Florence, 1866. Published instructive vocal works, etc.

Panseron (păhns-rŏhn'), **Auguste-Mathieu,** French singing teacher; b. Paris, April 26, 1795; d. there, July 29, 1859. His father, who orchestrated many operas for Grétry, taught him until he entered the Paris Cons. in 1804; he studied under Gossec, Levasseur, and Berton, winning the Prix de Rome in 1813. After study in Bologna, Rome, Naples, Vienna (with Salieri), and Munich, he returned to Paris in 1818, taught singing, was accompanist at the Opéra-Comique, and wrote three 1-act operas; became prof. of solfeggio at the Cons. in 1826, prof. of vocalisation in 1831, and prof. of singing in 1836. From 1825-40 he brought out some 200 charming *romances;* he also composed church music, but attained real eminence as a vocal teacher and as a writer of instructive works on singing.

Panufnik, Andrzej, Polish composer; b. Warsaw, Sept. 24, 1914. His mother was an Englishwoman who studied violin in Warsaw, his father a manufacturer of string instruments. Panufnik studied at the Warsaw Cons.; graduated in 1936; then went to Vienna, where he took courses in conducting with Weingartner. In 1945 he was appointed conductor of the Cracow Philharmonic; in 1946, became conductor of the Warsaw Orch.; also conducted concerts in Western Europe. In July, 1953 he settled in England. In 1957 he was appointed conductor of the Birmingham Symph. Orch. As a composer, he belongs to the vanguard group among Polish musicians; he makes use of advanced techniques, including quarter-tones, which he employs in his instrumental *Berceuse.* Even in the matter of notation, he is an innovator; in several of his orchestral scores he leaves blank spaces instead of rests in the inactive instrumental parts. —Works: *5 Folksongs,* for children's voices (London Festival of the International Society for Contemporary Music, July 12, 1946); *Berceuse,* for 29 string instruments and percussion (Paris, April 26, 1948); *Tragic Overture,* in memory of the victims of the Warsaw uprising of 1942 (N. Y., March 24, 1949); *Sinfonia Rustica* (Warsaw, May 13, 1949); *Old Polish Suite,* for string orch. (1950); *Symphony of Peace* (1951); *Heroic Overture* (Helsinki, Olympiad, July 27, 1952, composer conducting; received the gold medal award). —Cf. Scarlett Panufnik (his wife), *Out of the City of Fear* (recounting Panufnik's flight from Poland; London, 1956).

Panum, Hortense, Danish musicologist; b. (of Danish parents) Kiel, March 14, 1856; d. Copenhagen, April 26, 1933. Her father, who had been prof. of physiology at Kiel Univ., returned to Copenhagen in 1864. There she studied composition; later she won a stipend, and studied history of music with W. Tappert in Berlin (1886-87). After her return she devoted herself to historical studies (especially concerning old instruments); 1907, prof. of history of music at the Copenhagen Cons. —Works: *Illustreret Musikhistorie* (1895-1905; Part II by W. Behrend); *Musiken og musiklivet i Danmark för anno 1800* (1904); do. *efter anno 1800* (1906); *Haydn, Mozart, og Beethoven* (1908); *Middelalderens Strengeinstrumenter og dares Forlöbere i Oldtiden* (profusely illustrated; I, 1915; II, 1928; III, 1931; English ed., in 1 vol., by J. Pulver, as *The Stringed Instruments of the Middle Ages, their Evolution,* etc., London, 1939); *Af Musikhistoriens Billedbog* (1916; 2nd ed., 1930); *Langelegen som dansk Folkeinstrument* (1918); *Illustreret Musiklexikon* (Copenhagen, 1924-26; with W. Behrend and O. M. Sandvik; new ed., 1940). Also contributed valuable papers to the 'Sammelbände der Internationalen Musik-Gesellschaft' *(Harfe und Lyra im alten Nordeuropa)*, etc.

Panzéra, Charles, French baritone; b. Hyères, Feb. 16, 1896. He studied at the Paris Cons.; made his début at the Opéra-Comique in 1919; then gave concerts in Europe and America; also taught at the Juilliard School, N. Y. In 1949 he was appointed prof. at the Paris Cons. He publ. a manual, *L'Art de chanter* (Paris, 1945).

Panzner, Karl, conductor; b. Teplitz, Bohemia, March 2, 1866; d. Düsseldorf, Dec. 17, 1923. He studied piano and composition at the Dresden Cons.; then private pupil of A. Rubinstein, who advised him to adopt the career of a concert pianist. Instead, he became a theater conductor; in 1893 he succeeded E. Paur as Kapellmeister at the Leipzig Stadttheater, where he remained 6 years. In 1899 he was called to Bremen to conduct the 'Philharmonic' and (in 1904) also the 'Lehrer Gesangverein,' with which he made several successful tours (notably to Paris in 1907); from 1907 to 1909 he filled numerous engagements as visiting conductor in Barcelona, Paris, St. Petersburg, Moscow, Rome, and New York (Philharmonic Society, 1906). From 1909 he was municipal music-director in Düsseldorf; also conductor of the Philharmonic Society concerts at Hamburg. —Cf. W. Gareiss, *K. Panzner,* in 'Monographien moderner Musiker' III (Leipzig, 1909).

Papandopulo (păh-păhn-doh'-pŏŏ-lô), **Boris,** Croatian composer; b. Honef-on-the-Rhine, Feb. 25, 1906. He studied music with Bersa in Zagreb, and later in Vienna. He then became a choral conductor; in 1949 appointed opera conductor at Sarajevo. —Works: 2 operas, *Amphytrion* (1940) and *Sunflower* (1942); a ballet, *Gold;* a cantata, *Stojanka;* 2 symphonies; a sinfonietta for strings (frequently performed in Europe); 2 piano concertos; a violin concerto; 2 string quartets; choral works; piano pieces.

Papi, Gennaro, conductor; b. Naples, Dec. 21, 1886; d. New York, Nov. 29, 1941. He studied with de Nardis at the S. Pietro a Majella Cons. in Naples (graduated, 1904); assistant conductor in Warsaw (1909-10), Turin (1911), London (Covent Garden, 1911-12), Milan, Odessa, and Buenos Aires; 1913-16, assistant to Toscanini at the Metropolitan Opera House; 1916-25, conductor of Russian and Italian opera there; 1925-32, conductor of the Chicago Civic Opera; then made appearances in Milan, Mexico City, and Buenos Aires until 1935, when he was re-engaged at the Metropolitan.

Papier, Rosa, Austrian mezzo-soprano; b. Baden, near Vienna, Sept. 15, 1858; d. Vienna, Feb. 9, 1932. She sang at the Imperial Opera, Vienna. Owing to an infection of the throat, she was obliged to retire in 1891; then prof. of singing at the Vienna Cons. Married Dr. Hans Paumgartner, a pianist and music critic (1843-96), in 1881.

Pâque (pahk), **Désiré,** a remarkable Belgian composer; b. Liège, May 21, 1867; d. Bessancourt, France, Nov. 20, 1939. He began to compose as a child; wrote a Mass at the age of 12; studied at the Liège Cons.; lived in Sofia, Athens, Lisbon, and Geneva, settling in Paris in 1914. He wrote 144 op. numbers, among them: one-act opera *Vaima* (1903); 8 symphonies (1895; 1905; 1912; 1916; 1919; 1927; 1934; 1936); 2 piano concertos (1888; 1935); cello concerto (1893); *Ouverture sur 3 thèmes bulgares* (Ostende, Aug. 17, 1895); *Ouverture libre* (1899; Munich, Dec. 29, 1911); *Requiem* (1900); 10 string quartets (1892-1939); 3 piano quintets (1896; 1924; 1938); 2 sextets (1909; 1919); 5 suites for piano, violin, and viola (1891-96); 3 piano trios (1903-30); 4 violin sonatas (1890-1934); 4 piano sonatas (1911); viola sonata (1915); 13 albums of piano pieces; choral works. His production falls into 3 periods: cosmopolitan and formal (1886-1908); freely episodic, in an 'adjonction constante' of recurrent themes (1909-18); atonal and polytonal (1919-39). His last manner is exemplified by *10 pièces atonales pour la jeunesse* for piano (1925). Only a few of his works are published; the bulk of his music remains in MS.

Parać (pah'-ratch), **Ivo,** Croatian composer; b. Split, June 24, 1890. He studied in Italy with Alaleona and Pizzetti; wrote mostly for voice, combining Croatian melodies with rich Italian harmonies. Among his larger works are an opera, *Adele's Song* (1941), and a 'symphonic song' *The Spell of the Night.*

Paradies (or **Paradisi**), **Pietro Domenico,** Italian composer and harpsichordist; b. Naples, 1707; d. Venice, Aug. 25, 1791. He was a pupil of Porpora; brought out operas in Italy, went to London in 1747, and lived there many years as a harpsichord-teacher. —Publ. 12 *Sonate di gravicembalo* (London, 1746). Some pieces are in Pauer's 'Old Italian Masters'; many in MS in the Fitzwilliam Collection; eds. of the sonatas have been brought out by G. Benvenuti and D. Cipollini (Milan, 1920); other pieces by M. Vitali, B. Cesi, etc.

Paradis, Maria Theresia von, Austrian pianist and composer; b. Vienna, May 15, 1759; d. there, Feb. 1, 1824. Blind from her fifth year, she was taught by Richter and Koželuh (piano), Salieri and Righini (singing), and Friberth and Abbé Vogler (composition), becoming an excellent pianist and organist; played in Paris in 1784, and made a tour to London, Brussels, and German capitals in 1786. By the aid of a system of notation invented by a friend, she became a skillful composer, her chief works being a melodrama, *Ariadne und Bacchus* (Vienna, 1791), an operetta, *Der Schul-*

kandidat (1792), the fairy opera *Rinaldo und Alcina* (Prague, summer, 1797), a funeral cantata on the death of Louis XVI (1794), a piano trio, sonatas and variations for piano, songs, etc. In her last years she taught singing and piano playing. —Cf. F. Niecks, in the 'Monthly Mus. Record' (Jan., 1913); H. Ullrich, *M. T. Paradis and Mozart,* in 'Music & Letters' (Oct., 1946); E. Komorzynski, *Mozart und M. T. Paradis,* in 'Mozart-Jahrbuch' (Salzburg, 1952).

Paranov, Moshe, American pianist and conductor; b. Hartford, Conn., Oct. 28, 1895. He studied piano with Julius Hartt and Harold Bauer, composition with Ernest Bloch and Rubin Goldmark. He married Julius Hartt's daughter, Pauline; was co-founder of the Julius Hartt School of Music, Hartford, in 1920; dean, 1932; in 1938, became its director; in 1957, was named president of the Julius Hartt Musical Foundation of the Univ. of Hartford. He conducted the Hartford Symph. from 1947 to 1953; in 1954 was appointed musical director of the Brockton, Mass., Orch.; conductor of the Hartt Opera Guild since its establishment in 1942; as pianist, appeared with many American orchestras; gave numerous recitals in Hartford and elsewhere.

Paray, Paul, French conductor; b. Le Tréport, May 24, 1886; received his musical education at home, from his father, an amateur musician and church organist; as a small child, played drums in a local band conducted by his father; later studied at a choir school in Rouen; at 17, became a church organist there. In 1904 he entered the Paris Cons.; studied with Leroux, Caussade, Lenepveu, and Vidal; received the 1st Grand Prix de Rome with his cantata *Yanitza* (1911). He was called into the French army at the outbreak of World War I; became a prisoner of war and was interned at Darmstadt; after the Armistice, returned to Paris, where he made his début as conductor on Feb. 29, 1920; became assistant conductor of the Concerts Lamoureux, and succeeded Chevillard as 1st conductor in 1923. After 5 seasons with the Lamoureux Orch., he was engaged as conductor of the Municipal Orch. of the Casino of Monte Carlo; also led concerts of the Colonne Orch. in Paris. After the occupation of Paris by the German army, he went to Marseilles, where he led radio concerts; in 1942 he went again to Monte Carlo. After the liberation of Paris, he returned there; resumed his conductorship of the Colonne Orch. (Oct. 22, 1944); continued as its head until 1952, when he was engaged as permanent conductor of the Detroit Symph. Orch. On Oct. 18, 1956, he inaugurated the new Ford Auditorium in Detroit, conducting his own *Mass of Joan of Arc.* Paray's compositions include a ballet, *Artémis troublée* (Paris Opéra, April 28, 1922); *Fantaisie,* for piano and orch. (Paris, March 25, 1923); 2 symphonies; chamber music; piano pieces. The world première of his *Mass of Joan of Arc* took place at Rouen in May, 1931, on the occasion of the 500th anniversary of Joan of Arc's martyrdom. —Cf. W. L. Landowski, *Paul Paray* (Lyons, 1956); Hope Stoddard, *Symphony Conductors of the U.S.A.* (N. Y., 1957; pp. 160-70).

Parelli, Attilio (real last name Paparella), Italian conductor and composer; b. Monteleone d'Orvieto, near Perugia, May 31, 1874; d. there, Dec. 26, 1944. He studied at the Santa Cecilia in Rome; graduated in 1899; held various posts as conductor in Italy and France; went to the U. S. as assistant conductor to Campanini at the Manhattan Opera, N. Y. (1906); also conducted for the Chicago Grand Opera Company. In 1925 he returned to Europe, and organized the music department of the Milan Radio. He wrote the operas *Hermes* (Genoa, Nov. 8, 1906), *I dispettosi amanti* (Philadelphia, March 6, 1912), and *Fanfulla* (Trieste, Feb. 11, 1921); a symphony; an orchestral suite, *Rapsodia umbra;* a symph. poem, *La Chimera;* songs.

Parent (pah-răhn), **Armand,** Belgian violinist; b. Liège, Feb. 5, 1863; d. Paris, Jan. 19, 1934. He was a pupil at the Liège Cons. of L. Massart (violin) and S. Dupuis (harmony). From 1883 to 1889, concertmaster with the Colonne Orch.; from 1900 prof. of violin at the Schola Cantorum. In 1892 he founded (with Loiseau, Vieux, and Fournier) the 'Quatuor Parent,' which for many years enjoyed international fame. Parent wrote 2 string quartets, a string quintet, a violin sonata, and a number of minor pieces for violin and piano; also *Gymnastique du violon, 20 Études de virtuosité, Études pour violon, Exercises pour le violon d'après les 17 quatuors de Beethoven,* and a 5-part *Méthode complète.*

Parepa-Rosa *(née* Parepa de Boyescu), **Euphrosyne,** soprano; b. Edinburgh, May 7, 1836; d. London, Jan. 21, 1874. Her father was a native of Bucharest; her mother, Elizabeth Seguin, was a well-known singer, undertaking her daughter's musical education at first. After her father's death she was trained for the stage; made her début at 16, as Amina, in Malta; then sang in Naples, Genoa, Rome, Florence, Madrid, and Lisbon, appearing in London as Elvira in *I Puritani* on May 21, 1857. She became a great favorite there, singing frequently in opera and oratorio up to her American tour in 1865 with Carl Rosa, whom she married on their second American tour in 1867, when they organized an opera company, with Parepa as leading lady, and gained great success. On her third visit to America, in 1871, Parepa sang with Santley and Wachtel in Italian opera; returned to England in 1873, intending to give *Lohengrin* in English at Drury Lane the following March, a project defeated by her fatal illness. —Cf. 'Dictionary of National Biography,' vol. XLIII.

Paribeni (pah-rĭ-bā'nē), **Giulio Cesare,** Italian teacher and critic; b. Rome, May 27, 1881; studied there at the Univ. and at the Liceo di S. Cecilia; was first a conductor, then, from 1911-15, head of the publishing firm of Sonzogno; from 1914 teacher of composition and harmony at the Royal Cons., Milan; from 1922 opera critic of 'L'Ambrosiano,' Milan. Author of *Storia e teoria della antica musica greca* (Milan, 1912) and *Muzio Clementi,* a biography (Milan, 1921). Composer of orchestral works, chamber music, and church music.

Parish-Alvars, Elias, English harpist; b. Teignmouth, Feb. 28, 1808; d. Vienna, Jan. 25, 1849. He studied harp with Bochsa; from 1831-36 gave concerts in Germany. While in Leipzig he was associated with Mendelssohn. In 1847 he settled in Vienna. His compositions for harp enjoyed a certain popularity during his lifetime.

Parker, Henry Taylor, American critic and writer on music; b. Boston, April 29, 1867; d. there, March 30, 1934. 1886-89, attended Harvard Univ.; was N. Y. correspondent of the 'Boston Transcript' for 7 years; then London correspondent of the same paper and of the 'N. Y. Globe'; 1903, drama and music critic of the 'Globe' in N. Y. for 2 years, after which he held a similar post on the staff of the 'Boston Transcript' until his death. Publ. a collection of essays on music, *Eighth Notes* (N. Y., 1922). —Cf. D. T. W. McCord, *H. T. P.; Portrait of a Critic* (N. Y., 1935).

Parker, Horatio William, eminent American composer; b. Auburndale, Mass., Sept. 15, 1863; d. Cedarhurst, L. I., Dec. 18, 1919. He was a pupil, in Boston, of Emery (theory), J. Orth (piano), and Chadwick (composition); organist at Dedham and Boston; studied in Munich (1882-85) with Rheinberger (organ and composition) and L. Abel (conducting), bringing out a cantata, *King Trojan,* in 1885. Returning to America, he became organist and prof. of music at the Cathedral School, Garden City, L. I.; 1886, organist and choirmaster at St. Andrew's, N. Y.; 1888, at the Church of the Holy Trinity, Boston. The first performance (N. Y., May 3, 1893) of his oratorio *Hora Novissima* attracted wide attention and in 1894 he was called to the chair of music at Yale Univ., where he remained until his death. There he reorganized a choral society and founded the New Haven Symph. Orch., of which he was conductor. He conducted performances of his works at English festivals in 1900 and 1902. M.A. (*hon. c.*), Yale Univ., 1894; Mus. Doc. (*hon. c.*), Cambridge Univ., 1902. In 1911 his opera *Mona* won the $10,000 prize offered by the Metropolitan Opera and was produced there on March 14, 1912; two years later his second opera, *Fairyland,* won a similar prize offered by the National Federation of Women's Clubs and was produced at Los Angeles on July 1, 1915. The books of both operas are by Brian Hooker.

WORKS: For the stage: *Mona,* opera (N. Y., March 14, 1912); *Fairyland,* opera (Los Angeles, July 1, 1915); *Cupid and Psyche,* masque for the 50th anniversary of the founding of the Yale Art School (New Haven, June 16, 1916); music for the Yale Pageant (Oct., 1916). —For orch.: op. 4, overture in E♭ (not publ.); op. 5, overture, *Regulus* (not publ.); op. 7, symph. in C minor (not publ.); op. 12, *Venetian Overture,* in B♭ (not publ.); op. 13, scherzo in G minor (not publ.); op. 46, *A Northern Ballad* (not publ.); op. 55, concerto for organ and orch. in E minor (Boston, Dec. 26, 1902); op. 56, symph. poem. —Choral music (for mixed voices unless otherwise indicated): op. 1, *Mountain Shepherd's Song,* for men's voices; op. 2, 5 choruses (not publ.); op. 3, *The Lord is My Shepherd,* for women's voices and organ; op. 6, *The Ballad of a Knight and His Daughter,* with orch.; op. 8, *King Trojan,* for soli, chorus, and orch.; op. 14, *Blow, Blow, Thou Winter Wind,* for men's voices; op. 15, *Idylle* with orch.; op. 16 (also listed as op. 69) *The Norsemen's Raid,* for men's voices and orch.; op. 18, *Morning and Evening Service in E;* op. 21, *The Kobolds,* with orch.; op. 26, *Harald*

Harfager; op. 27, 2 choruses for women's voices; op. 30, *Hora Novissima,* oratorio (N. Y., May 3, 1893); op. 31, *Dream-King and His Love,* cantata; op. 33, *6 Part-Songs,* for men's voices; op. 37, *The Holy Child,* Christmas cantata; op. 39, *4 Part-Songs,* for men's voices; op. 42, *Ode for Commencement Day at Yale Univ.,* for men's voices and piano; op. 43, *The Legend of St. Christopher,* oratorio; op. 45, *Adstant Angelorum Chori,* motet (prize of Musical Art Society, N. Y., 1899); op. 48, *3 Part-Songs,* for men's voices; op. 50, *A Wanderer's Psalm,* with orch.; op. 53, *Hymnos Andron,* ode (on Greek text) for the bicentenary celebration of the founding of Yale Univ. (1901); op. 54, *A Star Song,* for soli, chorus, and orch. (Paderewski Prize, 1901); op. 57, *The Office for the Holy Communion,* in B♭, with organ; op. 61, *Spirit of Beauty,* ode for the dedication of the Albright Art Gallery in Buffalo (1905); op. 64, *King Gorm the Grim,* ballad with orch.; op. 66, *School Songs;* op. 72, *Collegiate Overture,* for men's chorus and orch.; op. 73, *A Song of Times,* cantata; op. 74, *7 Greek Pastoral Scenes,* for soli, women's chorus, strings, harp, and oboe; op. 75, *The Leap of Roushan Beg,* ballad for tenor solo, men's chorus, and orch.; op. 79, *Morven and the Grail,* oratorio; op. 82, *The Dream of Mary,* a morality for soli, chorus, and orch. (Norfolk Festival, 1918). —Chamber music: op. 11, string quartet in F (not publ.); op. 35, suite for violin, cello, and piano; op. 38, string quartet in D minor (not publ.); op. 41, suite for violin and piano (not publ.). —Organ works: op. 17, 4 pieces; op. 20, 4 pieces; op. 28, 4 pieces; op. 32, *5 Sketches;* op. 36, *4 Compositions;* op. 65, sonata in E♭; op. 67, *4 Compositions;* op. 68, *5 Short Pieces.* — Piano works: op. 9, *5 Morceaux caractéristiques.* —For voice and piano: op. 10, *3 Love Songs;* op. 22, 3 sacred songs; op. 24, 6 songs; op. 25, 2 songs; op. 29, 6 songs; op. 34, 3 songs; op. 40, *Cáhal Mór of the Wine-Red Hand,* for baritone and orch.; op. 47, *6 Old English Songs;* op. 51, 4 songs; op. 52, 3 songs; op. 58, *3 Sacred Songs;* op. 59, 4 songs; op. 60, *Union and Liberty,* patriotic song with orch. for the inauguration of Theodore Roosevelt (1905); op. 62, *Crépuscule,* for mezzo-soprano and orch.; op. 70, 7 songs; op. 76, songs (not publ.); op. 83, *The Red Cross Spirit Speaks,* for contralto and orch. (Worcester Festival, 1917). Many compositions, some publ., are without opus numbers. — Parker also publ. *The Progressive Music Series* (8 vols.) and *Music and Public Entertainment* (1911). —Cf. W. S. Pratt's American Supplement to Grove's 'Dictionary'; G. W. Chadwick, *Horatio Parker* (N. Y., 1921); *A Brief Tribute to the Life and Work of Horatio Parker* (1925); D. S. Smith, *A Study of Horatio Parker,* in the 'Mus. Quarterly' (April, 1930); J. T. Howard, *Our American Music* (1931 and subsequent eds.); 'Dictionary of American Biography,' vol. XIV (1934); Isabel Parker Semler, *Horatio Parker, A Memoir for His Grandchildren* (N. Y., 1942; with complete list of works).

Parker, James Cutler Dunn, American organist and composer; b. Boston, June 2, 1828; d. Brookline, Mass., Nov. 27, 1916. He studied law in Boston, and music in Leipzig (1851-54) under Moscheles (piano), Hauptmann and Richter (composition); then lived in Boston; organist and choir-director of Trinity Church 1864-91, and for many years organist of the Handel and Haydn Society; was prof. at the Boston Univ. College of Music, and Examiner for the New England Cons.—His choral works include *Redemption Hymn* (1877); cantata *The Blind King* (1886); *St. John; The Life of Man* (oratorio); several church services; etc. Translated Richter's *Manual of Harmony,* publ. an original *Manual of Harmony* (1855) and *Theoretical and Practical Harmony* (1870).—Cf. 'Dictionary of American Biography,' vol. XIV (1934).

Parkhurst, Howard Elmore, American organist; b. Ashland, Mass., Sept. 13, 1848; died (accidentally drowned) Lavalette, N. J., Aug. 18, 1916. He publ. (besides books on botany and ornithology) *A Complete System of Harmony* (1908), *A Complete Method for the Modern Organ* (1911), *The Church Organist* (1913), *The Beginnings of the World's Music* (1915), *Rambles in Music-Land* (1914); also wrote an oratorio, a cantata, an orchestral overture, and church music.

Parlow, Kathleen, Canadian violinist; b. Calgary, Sept. 20, 1890. When she was 5 years old her family moved to San Francisco, where she began to study the violin with a cousin; in 1906 went to St. Petersburg, Russia, to study with Auer; gave a recital there in 1908; then toured in Scandinavia and Germany; appeared frequently in the U. S., and founded the Parlow String Quartet; later, joined the faculty of Mills College, Oakland, Calif.; 1957, living in Toronto.

Parodi, Lorenzo, Italian pedagogue and composer; b. Genoa, Aug. 10, 1856; d. there, March 28, 1926. He studied in Genoa and with Guiraud and Massenet in Paris. He taught esthetics and history of music at the Liceo Amilcare Zanella in Genoa, of which he was also director. —Works: the oratorios *Joannes Baptista* and *Calvario;* Masses and hymns; cantatas; a *Stabat Mater; Suite greca* and *Ouverture triomphale* for orch.; pieces for violin, and for piano; songs. Also publ. *Musicologia, L'Estetica del canone,* and a treatise on instrumentation.

Parratt, Sir **Walter,** English organist, b. Huddersfield, Feb. 10, 1841; d. Windsor, March 27, 1924. He was a pupil of his father; at 7 played his first church service; at 11, organist at Armitage Bridge, and passed through successive similar positions to Magdalen College, Oxford (1872) and St. George's Chapel, Windsor (1882), succeeding Elvey. Mus. Bac., Oxon., 1873; organ prof. at Royal College of Music, 1883; knighted in 1892; Master of Music in Ordinary to the Queen, 1893; do. to King Edward VII (1901) and King George V (1910); from 1908, prof. of music at Oxford (resigned on Jan. 1, 1918); from 1916 dean of music at London Univ.; Mus. Doc. (*hon. c.*), Oxford, 1894; Commander of the Victorian Order; etc. —Works: music to Aeschylus' *Agamemnon* and *Orestes; Elegy to Patroclus* (1883); anthems, songs, music for organ and piano. —Cf. 'Mus. Times' (July, 1902); 'Dictionary of National Biography' (Suppl., 1922-30; pp. 655-7); Sir Donald Tovey and G. Parratt, *Walter Parratt, Master of Music* (London, 1941).

Parrish, Carl, American musicologist and composer; b. Plymouth, Pa., Oct. 9, 1904. After receiving his Ph.D at Harvard (1939), he taught at Wells College (1929-41), Fisk Univ. (1941-45), Westminster Choir College (1945-49), Pomona College (1949-53); from 1953 prof. at Vassar College. Publ. *The Notation of Medieval Music* (N. Y., 1957). In collaboration with John F. Ohl, he publ. *Masterpieces of Music before 1750* (N. Y., 1951); has written choral settings of folksongs; a string quartet; a song cycle; piano pieces.

Parrott, Ian, British composer; b. London, March 5, 1916. He studied at Harrow and at the Royal College of Music; received his B. Mus. and Dr. Mus. degrees at Oxford; served in the Middle East and North Africa in the Royal Corps of Signals during World War II; was lecturer in music at Birmingham Univ. (1947-50); then prof. of music at Aberystwyth Univ. He has written much theater music, including the comic *The Sergeant-Major's Daughter* (1943); a ballet, *Maid in Birmingham* (1949); a symph. prelude, *El Alamein* (1944); a symph. impression, *Luxor* (1948); concerto for piano and string orch. (1948); wind quintet (1948); *Fantasy Trio* for piano, violin, and cello (1950); opera *The Black Ram* (in the Welsh language, 1951-53); piano pieces; choral works; publ. *Pathway to Modern Music* (London, 1947); *A Guide to Musical Thought* (London, 1955); *Method in Orchestration* (London, 1957). — Cf. H. F. Redlich, *A New Welsh Folk Opera,* in 'Music & Letters' (April, 1956).

Parry, Sir **Charles Hubert Hastings,** eminent English composer and pedagogue; b. Bournemouth, Feb. 27, 1848; d. Knight's Croft, Rustington, Oct. 7, 1918. While at Eaton, from 1861, he studied composition with G. Elvey; took part in the concerts of the Musical Society as a pianist, organist, vocalist, and composer. At 19, while still a student at Eton, he took the degree of Mus. Bac. at Oxford. Entered Exeter College, Oxford, in 1867; was a founder of the 'University Mus. Club,' and took the degree of M.A. in 1874. There he began to study music in earnest under Bennett and Macfarren, also taking piano lessons from Dannreuther (1872-79). His public career as a composer began with the production of an *Intermezzo religioso* for strings at the Gloucester Festival of 1868. In 1883 Perry was appointed Choragus of Oxford Univ.; in that year Cambridge conferred on him the hon. degree of Mus. Doc., followed by Oxford (1884) and Dublin (1891). In 1894 he succeeded Sir George Grove as director of the Royal College of Music, which post he held until his death; 1899-1908, prof. of music at Oxford Univ.; knighted in 1898. —Works: the opera *Guinevere* (1885-86); for orch.: 4 symphonies (1878-82; 1883; 1889; 1889), overture *Guillem de Cabestanh* (1878-79), *Overture to an Unwritten Tragedy* (1893), piano concerto in F♯ (1878-79), *Suite moderne* (1886), *Lady Radnor's Suite,* for strings (1894), *An English Suite* (publ. posthumously, 1921), symph. fantasy in B minor, *1912* (1912), symph. poem, *From Death to Life* (1914), etc.; choral works: the oratorios *Judith* (Birmingham, 1888), *Job* (Gloucester, 1892; his best work), and *King Saul* (Birmingham, 1894), *Scenes from Shelley's Prometheus Unbound* (Gloucester, 1880), choral song *Jerusalem* (publ.

1916), many anthems, hymns, motets, odes, part-songs, etc.; chamber music: 3 string quartets (1867; 1868; 1878-80), 3 piano trios (1878; 1884; 1884-90), string quintet (1884), piano quartet (1879), nonet for winds (1877), fantasy-sonata for violin and piano (1878), cello sonata (1883), etc.; songs; organ pieces; piano pieces. —His published writings include numerous excellent articles in Grove's Dictionary, *Studies of Great Composers* (1886; 8th ed., 1904), *The Art of Music* (1893; enlarged as *The Evolution of the Art of Music,* 1896; new rev. ed. by H. C. Colles, N. Y., 1930), *Summary of the History and Development of Medieval and Modern European Music* (1893), *The Music of the 17th Century* (vol. III of the 'Oxford History of Music,' 1902; 2nd ed., 1938, ed. by E. J. Dent), *J. S. Bach* (1909; rev. ed., 1934), *Style in Musical Art* (1911). His college addresses were publ. by H. C. Colles (1920). —Cf. R. O. Morris, *H. Parry* in 'Music & Letters' (April, 1920); Ch. L. Graves, *H. Parry, His Life and Works* (2 vols., London, 1926); G. M. Greene, *Two Witnesses* (N. Y., 1930); J. A. Fuller-Maitland, *The Music of Parry and Stanford* (Cambridge, 1934).

Parry, John, blind Welsh bard; b. Ruabon, N. Wales; d. as harper to Sir W. W. Wynne at Wynnstay, Oct. 7, 1782.—Publ. 'Antient British Music . . .' (tunes of the Cambro-Britons, 1742); 'Collection of Welsh, English and Scotch Airs' (1716); 'Cambrian Harmony; a Collection of Antient Welsh Airs . . .' (1781).

Parry, John (called 'Bardd Alaw,' master of song), Welsh musician; b. Denbigh, Feb. 18, 1776; d. London, April 8, 1851. He played clarinet in a band; then was bandmaster; composer to Vauxhall, 1809; conductor of 'Eisteddfodau' in Wales for years; was critic for the 'Morning Post' (1834-48), and treasurer of the Royal Society of Musicians (1831-49). —Works: 'The Welsh Harper' (1839-48; collection of Welsh music, with historical introduction); various other collections; also much original music (incidental music to several plays, harp sonatas, glees, songs, part-songs, etc.). —Cf. 'Dictionary of National Biography,' vol. XLIII (1895).

Parry, Joseph, Welsh composer; b. Merthyr Tydvil, May 21, 1841; d. Penarth, near Cardiff, Feb. 17, 1903. His parents emigrated to America, but he returned to Britain, won Eisteddfod prizes for songs, and entered the Royal Academy of Music in 1868, studying under Bennett, Garcia, and Steggall. Mus. Bac., Cambridge, 1871; then appointed prof. of music at the Univ. College, Aberystwith; Mus. Lecturer at Univ. College of S. Wales, Cardiff. Also F. R. A. M. —Works: 5 operas: *Blodwen* (Aberdare, 1878); *Virginia* (Aberdare, 1883); *Arianwen* (Cardiff, 1890); *Sylvia* (Cardiff, 1895); *King Arthur* (finished 1897); the oratorios *Emmanuel* (1880) and *Saul of Tarsus* (1892); the cantatas *The Prodigal Son, Nebuchadnezzar, Cambria,* and *The Maid of Cefu Idfa; Druids' Chorus;* an orchestral ballade, overtures, a string quartet, piano music, anthems, songs.—Cf. 'Dictionary of National Biography' (Suppl., 1901-11; vol. III, pp. 73-74).

Parsley (Parseley, Persleye, Parcele, etc.), **Osbert,** English church-music composer; b. 1511; d. 1585. Lay clerk at Norwich Cathedral for about 50 years. 'Tudor Church Music' (vol. 10) contains reprints of 5 of his works; MSS in the British Museum include several motets; *Perslis clocke,* for 5 voices; etc. —Cf. 'Dictionary of National Biography,' vol. XLIII (1895).

Parsons, Albert Ross, American piano pedagogue; b. Sandusky, O., Sept. 16, 1847; d. Mt. Kisco, N. Y., June 14, 1933. From 1863 to 1866 he studied with F. L. Ritter in New York; 1867-69 at Leipzig Cons. with Moscheles, Reinecke, Wenzel, and Papperitz (piano), and Richter and Paul (counterpoint and fugue); later with Tausig, Kullak, Weitzmann, and Wüerst at Berlin. Settled in N. Y. 1871, holding various positions as organist; prominent as a piano pedagogue. In 1889, president of the Music Teachers National Association. Publ. *Science of Pianoforte Practice* (1886); *Parsifal, or the Finding of Christ through Art* (1890); *The Virtuoso Handling of the Pianoforte* (1917); transl. Wagner's *Beethoven* and O. Lessmann's *Liszt* into English; etc. Composed vocal quartets, songs, etc. Cf. 'Dictionary of American Biography,' vol. XIV (1934).

Partos, Ödön, composer; b. Budapest, Oct. 1, 1907; studied violin with Hubay, composition with Kodály; 1928-33, in Berlin; 1933-36, in Budapest; since 1938, in Israel as violinist in the Tel Aviv Philharmonic Orch. —Works: *Yiskor (In Memoriam),* for viola solo and string orch. (1946); *Song of Praise,* for viola and orch. (Tel Aviv, Jan. 22, 1949); songs.

Pasdeloup (păh-d'loo'), **Jules-Étienne,** French conductor; b. Paris, Sept. 15, 1819; d. Fontainebleau, Aug. 13, 1887. He was a piano pupil, at the Conservatoire, of Laurent and Zimmerman; 1841, répétiteur of a solfeggio class; 1847-50, teacher of a piano class, which he gave up to organize the celebrated symphony concerts of the 'Société des jeunes élèves du Cons.' (1851), developing (1861) into the 'Concerts populaires de musique classique' at the 'Cirque d'hiver,' a pioneer series of good cheap popular concerts which were a success from the start. Not only classic music, but the best modern French and foreign composers had a hearing. Pasdeloup also taught a vocal ensemble class at the Cons., 1855-68; he unsuccessfully attempted the direction of the Théâtre-Lyrique, 1868-69, and his popular concerts gradually lost ground in competition with Colonne and Lamoureux, ceasing in 1884; he revived them just before his death, in 1886-87. A grand popular mus. festival at the Trocadéro, instituted for his benefit, netted him nearly 100,000 francs. The 'Concerts Pasdeloup' were revived by Rhené-Baton in 1920.

Pashkevitch (păsh-kyĕh'-vich), **Vassily Alexeyevitch,** Russian violinist and composer; b. c. 1740; d. 1800. In 1763 he was admitted as a violinist in the 2nd court orch. in St. Petersburg; in 1779 was engaged as a theater conductor there. His Russian opera *A Carriage Accident* was performed in St. Petersburg on Nov. 7, 1779; in 1782 he presented 2 comic operas in Russian: *The Miser* (Moscow) and *The Pasha of Tunis* (St. Petersburg). In 1783 he was transferred to the 1st court orch.; in 1786, was commissioned by Catherine the Great to write a comic Russian opera, *Fevey,* for which the Empress herself wrote the libretto. It was produced in St. Petersburg on April 19, 1786, and Pashkevitch received an award of 1,000 rubles. In 1789, he was appointed chief of ball music at the Imperial Palace, and simultaneously was elevated to the rank of concertmaster of the 1st court orch. In 1790 he collaborated with Sarti and Canobbio in another Russian opera to a text of Catherine the Great, *The Early Reign of Oleg,* which was first produced at the palace, and publicly performed in St. Petersburg on Nov. 2, 1790. In collaboration with Martín y Soler, he wrote still another comic opera to a text by the Empress, *Fedul and his Children* (performed at the palace, Jan. 27, 1791; publicly, St. Petersburg, March 2, 1791). He was given the honorary rank of colonel. A Mass according to the Russian ritual by him was publ. in Moscow in 1796. —Cf. R.-Aloys Mooser, *Annales de la Musique et des Musiciens en Russie au XVIIIe siècle* (Geneva, 1950; vol. II, pp. 55-57).

Pashtchenko, Andrey Filippovitch, Russian composer; b. Rostov, Aug. 15, 1883. He studied at the St. Petersburg Cons. with Vitols and Steinberg, graduating in 1917. He first appeared as a composer in 1915, when the St. Petersburg Philharmonic played his fantasy-scherzo, *Harlequin and Columbine;* from that time on he continued to compose symph. music, operas, and choral works. In his early compositions, he followed the traditions of the Russian National School; later, experienced the influence of Scriabin and the French Impressionists. —Works: operas: *Eagles in Revolt* (Leningrad, Nov. 7, 1925), *King Maximilian* (satirical; 1927), *The Black Cliff* (Leningrad, June 12, 1931), *The Pompadours* (comic; 1939), *Jester Balakirev* (1949), *The Capricious Bride* (1956), *Radda and Loyko,* after Maxim Gorki (1957); symphonies: No. 1 (1915), No. 2, *Komsomol* (1929), No. 3, *Pioneer* (1933), No. 4, *Youth* (1938; revised, 1955), No. 5 (1952), No. 6 (1954), No. 7 (1956), No. 8 (1957); 3 other symphonies were destroyed by the composer; symph. poem, *Giants* (1913); *Oriental Legend* for orch.; symph. poem, *Tchapayev* (1957); *Song of the Sun-Bearer,* for chorus and orch. (1928); *The Song for the Dead,* for chorus (1942; written during the siege of Leningrad); a violin concerto; 2 string quartets; about 60 songs; piano pieces; orchestral ensembles for folk instruments.

Paskhalov, Viatcheslav Viktorovitch, Russian writer on musical ethnography; b. Moscow, May 13, 1873; d. Leningrad, Dec. 26, 1951. He studied literature, philosophy, and music in Moscow; 1916, prof. at the Moscow People's Cons.; from 1919 head of the ethnographic division of the Rumianzov Museum (now the State Library). —Writings: *Survey of the Musical Structure of the Russian Songs of the Province of Voronezh* (1914); *The Musical Structure of the Songs of Crimea* (1924); *Songs of the Orient* (a theoretical analysis; 1925); he harmonized *12 Songs of the Province of Voronezh* (1912); also Polish, Oriental, and Russian songs. His compositions include an overture; a string quartet; songs.

Pasmore, Henry Bickford, American singing teacher and composer; b. Jackson, Wis.,

June 27, 1857; d. San Francisco, Feb. 23, 1944. He studied in San Francisco; then went to Leipzig and London, where he took courses in singing with various teachers. Returning to America, he taught singing at the Univ. of the Pacific, San José; at Stanford Univ., and at Mills College. He wrote an exotic opera, *Lo-ko-rah;* another opera on a libretto based on Californian history, *Amor y Oro;* an overture, *Miles Standish;* a symph. poem, *Gloria California;* a Mass; several cantatas; church music; songs.

Pasquali (**Pascale, Paschali**), **Francesco,** Italian composer, one of the earliest musicians to write instrumental pieces with figured bass; b. Cosenza, c. 1590; d. after 1633. He studied in Rome, and remained there for most of his life. Between 1615 and 1633 he brought out 3 books of madrigals for 4 and 5 voices, and several vols. of secular and sacred songs for 1, 2, 3, 4, and 5 voices.

Pasquali, Nicolò, Italian violinist and composer; place and date of birth unknown; d. Edinburgh, Oct. 13, 1757. He settled in Edinburgh in 1740; was in Dublin between 1748 and 1752; then briefly in London, before returning to Edinburgh. He publ. sonatas for violin with accompaniments, 12 overtures, and an instructive book, *Thorough-bass Made Easy* (Edinburgh, 1757).

Pasquini (pah-skwē'-nē), **Bernardo,** Italian organist and composer; b. Massa di Valdinievole, Tuscany, Dec. 7, 1637; d. Rome, Nov. 21, 1710. He was a pupil in Rome of Vittori and Cesti; was long organist of S. Maria Maggiore; chamber musician to Prince Giambattista Borghese. Durante and Gasparini were his pupils. —Works: 10 operas, 8 oratorios, etc.; harpsichord pieces were publ. in 'Toccates et suites pour le clavecin de MM. Pasquini, Poglietti et Gaspard Kerle' (Paris, 1704); a sonata is in Pauer's 'Old Italian Composers'; other clavier works have been publ. by J. S. Shedlock, L. Torchi in 'L'Arte Musicale in Italia' (vol. III), W. Danckert (Kassel, 1931), Cesi, G. Tagliapietra in 'Antologia di musica antica e moderna per pianoforte'; vocal works have been publ. by F. Boghen (1923, 1930). —Cf. J. S. Shedlock, *The Pianoforte Sonata* (London, 1895; p. 71 ff.); V. Virgili, *B. Pasquini* (Pescia, 1908); A. Bonaventura, *B. Pasquini* (Ascoli Piceno, 1923); F. Boghen, *L'Arte di B. Pasquini* (1931); G. Roncaglia, *Il Tirinto di B. Pasquini e i suoi intermezzi,* in 'Rassegna Musicale' (Nov., 1931).

Pasquini, Ercole, Italian organist and composer; b. Ferrara; d. Rome, between 1608 and 1620. He studied with Alessandro Milleville; was organist in Ferrara and later at St. Peter's in Rome, retiring in 1608. His set of *Canzone francese per cembalo* is reprinted by Torchi in 'L'Arte Musicale in Italia' (vol. III). —Cf. Fr. Superbi, *Apparato degli Huomini illustri della città di Ferrara* (1620).

Passereau, French composer of the first part of the 16th century; curate of St. Jacques de la Boucherie, Paris; 1509, chapel-singer to the Duke of Angoulême (Francis I). 23 of his chansons appear in various anthologies published between 1533 and 1547; 2 of them reprinted in F. Lesure, ed., 'Anthologie de la Chanson parisienne au XVIe siècle' (Monaco, 1953).

Passy (păh'-sü), **(Ludvig Anton) Edvard,** Swedish pianist and pedagogue; b. Stockholm, Sept. 4, 1789; d. Drottningholm, Aug. 16, 1870. He received his first music instruction from his brother; then studied with L. Piccinni (who was Kapellmeister in Stockholm from 1796-1801), with J. Field (piano) in St. Petersburg, and with Eggert in Stockholm. After several successful pianistic tours of Germany he settled in his native city as a highly esteemed teacher, and organist of the court chapel. —Works: 2 piano concertos; a fantasy for piano and orch.; 3 string quartets; 2 piano trios; organ fugues; piano pieces songs; etc.

Pasta (*née* Negri), **Giuditta,** Italian dramatic soprano; b. Saronno, near Milan, April 9, 1798; d. at her villa on Lake Como, April 1, 1865. At first a pupil of Asioli at Milan Cons., she sang without success, after her début in 1815, in Italy, London, and Paris; returned to Italy for further serious study under Scappa, and reappeared at Paris in 1822 as a vocal phenomenon; the compass of her voice was from *a* to d^3, and in power, dramatic intensity, and truth of expression she had then no rival, though her voice, even in her best days, was not perfectly equalized. By 1829 she had acquired a fortune in London and Paris, and sang but little thereafter (in London 1837 and 1850; in St. Petersburg 1840; etc.), since her singing rapidly deteriorated. For her Bellini wrote *La Sonnambula* and *Norma,* Donizetti his *Anna Bolena,* Pacini his *Niobe;* she excelled in the leading roles of the Italian operas then in vogue. —Cf. Maria Ferranti Giulini, *Giuditta Pasta e i suoi tempi* (Milan, 1935).

Pasternack, Josef Alexander, conductor; b. Czenstochowa, Poland, July 1, 1881; d. Chicago, April 29, 1940. He studied at the Warsaw Cons. with Michalowski (piano) and Noskowski (composition); came to America in 1895; played the viola in the Metropolitan Opera orch. (1900-10); was assistant conductor there during the season of 1909-10; then was conductor of various opera companies in New York and Chicago; composed popular orchestral pieces and songs; made numerous arrangements.

Pasterwitz, Georg von, German church composer; b. Bierhütten, near Passau, June 7, 1730; d. Kremsmünster, Jan. 26, 1803. He studied music with Eberlin in Salzburg; after touring Europe, entered the order of the Benedictines in 1755; was choirmaster at the monastery in Kremsmünster (1767-82); lived in Vienna (1782-95); in 1795 resumed his post in Kremsmünster. He publ. 24 organ fugues and 300 *Themata und Versetten zum Präambulieren*. In MS: about 20 Masses, numerous psalms, offertories, vespers, motets, etc.; also several operas, 'intermezzi,' and detached arias interpolated in various operas of other composers. —Cf. G. Huemer, *Die Pflege der Musik im Stifte Kremsmünster* (Wels, 1877); A. Kellner, *Musikgeschichte des Stiftes Kremsmünster* (Kassel, 1956).

Pastou (păhs-tōō'), **Étienne-Jean Baptiste,** French vocal educator; b. Vigan, Gard, May 26, 1784; d. Ternes, near Paris, Oct. 8, 1851. He founded a singing school in Paris in 1819; was made prof. at the Paris Cons. in 1836; publ. a method for ensemble singing, *École de la lyre harmonique* (Paris, 1822).

Patey, Janet Monach (*née* Whytock); English contralto; b. London, May 1, 1842; d. Sheffield, Feb. 28, 1894. She was married to the bass singer, John Patey (1835-1901). After singing at various English festivals, she made an American tour in 1871; also sang in Australia (1890). In her prime she was regarded as the foremost English contralto.

Patiño, Carlos, Spanish ecclesiastic and composer; b. Galicia, date unknown; d. Madrid, 1683. In 1632 he received a grant from King John IV of Portugal; in 1633 was appointed successor to Romero as chapelmaster at the Spanish court; was at the royal chapel until 1648; from 1660, was chapelmaster of the Royal Cloister of the Incarnation. He was one of the most important 17th-century composers of sacred music; particularly excelled in polyphonic works for 8-12 voices; also wrote some dramatic pieces; most of his music is in MS, preserved in the archives of El Escorial and in Salamanca. His *Missa in Devotione* for double chorus is found in Eslava's *Lira sacro-hispana;* Felipe Pedrell transcribed some of Patiño's *Tonos humanos* in vols. 3 and 4 of *Teatro Lírico Español anterior al siglo XIX*. See also Varela Silvari, *Galeria biográfica de músicos gallegos* (Coruna, 1874); V. Torres, *Galeria de gallegos ilustres* (Madrid, 1875; vol. 5).

Paton, Mary Ann, Scottish soprano; b. Edinburgh, Oct., 1802; d. Bulcliffe Hall, Chapelthorpe, July 21, 1864. Of a musical family, she sang in concerts as a child; made her first operatic appearance as Susanna in the *Marriage of Figaro* (London, Aug. 3, 1822); she sang the part of Rezia in the première of Weber's *Oberon* in London (April 12, 1826) and was greatly praised by Weber himself. She had a very fine voice, and could sing lyric and coloratura parts with equal brilliance. She was married to Joseph Wood, the tenor. —Cf. *Miss Paton,* in 'Quarterly Mus. Magazine and Review' (London, 1823); also *Memoir of Mr. and Mrs. Wood . . .* (Philadelphia, 1840).

Patterson, Annie Wilson, Irish collector of folksongs and writer on music; b. Lurgan, Oct. 27, 1868; d. Cork, Jan. 15, 1934. She studied organ at the Royal Irish Academy of Music with Sir R. Stewart; was organist at various churches in Dublin; in 1909, settled in Cork; was awarded the degree of Mus. Doc. by the National Univ. of Ireland. She organized the 'Feis Ceoil,' Irish Music Festival, held annually since 1897. —Publ. works: *6 Original Gaelic Songs; Rallying Song of the Gaelic League* (with orch.); *The Bells of Shandon,* for chorus; *Ivernia,* arrangement of Irish airs. In MS: 2 Irish operas, *The High-King's Daughter* and *Oisin;* cantatas; symph. poems; etc. —Writings: *The Story of Oratorio* (1902); *Schumann* (1903; in 'Master Musicians'; new rev. ed., 1934); *Chats with Music-Lovers* (1908); *How to Listen to an Orchestra* (1913; new ed., 1928); *Great Minds in Music; Beautiful Song and the Singer; The Music of Ireland; The Profession of Music* (1926); etc.

Patterson, Franklin Peale, American composer and writer; b. Philadelphia, Jan. 5, 1871. He studied at the Univ. of Pennsylvania, and later in Munich with Thuille and Rheinberger. In 1911 he went to California, where he played the viola in the Los Angeles Orch.; then lived in New York, where he was on the editorial staff of the 'Musical Courier.' His opera, *The Echo,* produced in Portland, Ore., on June 9, 1925, was awarded the David Bispham Memorial Medal and the medal award of the National Federation of Music Clubs. Other works: the short operas *Beggar's Love* (*A Little Girl at Play*), *Mountain Blood,* and *The Forest Dwellers;* and the grand operas *Through the Narrow Gate* and *Caprice.* He also publ. various instructive pamphlets: *How to Write a Good Tune* (1924), *Practical Instrumentation* (1923), *Leit-Motives of the Nibelungen Ring* (1896), *The Perfect Modernist* (1921), etc. —Cf. E. Hipsher, *American Opera and its Composers* (Philadelphia, 1934; pp. 355-58).

Patti, Adelina (Adela Juana Maria), one of the greatest coloratura singers of the 19th century, both in opera and concert; b. Madrid, Feb. 19, 1843; d. Brecknock, Wales, Sept. 27, 1919. Daughter of two Italian singers, she was taken to New York at an early age; from 1851-55 sang in many concerts there. She was taught piano by her sister Carlotta, and singing by her half-brother Ettore Barili; her formal début was made at New York on Nov. 24, 1859, as Lucia (under the stage-name of 'the little Florinda'). In London she first appeared in *La Sonnambula* on May 14, 1861, at Covent Garden, her success rivalling that of the Grisi; her Paris début was in the same role, at the Théâtre Italien, on Nov. 19, 1862. In Paris she married the Marquis de Caux in 1868, from whom she separated in 1877, and was divorced in 1885. She sang for the first time in Italy at La Scala, Milan, Nov. 3, 1877, Violetta in *La Traviata* being the role selected. She sang in all the chief cities of Europe, and was everywhere received with enthusiasm. After 1882 she never sang for less than $5,000 a performance. She retired from the stage in 1895, but continued to appear in concerts, giving an official 'farewell' concert at Albert Hall, London, on Dec. 1, 1906. Her last public appearance was at a benefit concert for the Red Cross in the same hall, on Oct. 20, 1914. Her second husband, the tenor Nicolini, whom she married in 1886, died in 1898; she married a Swedish nobleman, Baron Cederström, in 1899. Her voice was not powerful; but it had a wide range (c^1-f^3), wonderful flexibility, and perfect evenness throughout; it probably excelled that of any other singer in voluptuous sweetness and bell-like purity. Her vocalization and technical skill were above all criticism, and the ease with which she took the highest notes was astonishing. But she was a poor actress, she lacked temperament, and her musical intelligence was ordinary. Her operatic repertory included about 30 roles in the operas of Rossini, Bellini, Donizetti, Meyerbeer, Gounod, Auber, and Verdi (earlier works). —Cf. Th. de Grave, *Biographie d' A. Patti* (Paris, 1865); G. de Charnacé, *A. Patti* (Paris, 1868); G. M. Dalmazzo, *A. Patti's Life* (London, 1877); L. Lauw, *Fourteen Years with A. Patti* (London, 1884); E. Hanslick, *A. Patti,* in *Musikalische Stationen* (Berlin, 1885; English transl. in Hanslick, *Vienna's Golden Years of Music,* N. Y., 1950, pp. 187-208); A. Weissmann, *Die Primadonna* (1919); H. Klein, *The Reign of Patti* (N. Y., 1920).

Patti, Carlotta, sister of Adelina Patti; b. Florence, Oct. 30, 1835; d. Paris, June 27, 1889. Her father and mother were her first teachers in singing; she had piano lessons with Henri Herz, at Paris. Her early youth was spent in New York. Lameness prevented success on the stage, but she was more fortunate as a concert singer, making her début in New York, 1861, followed by an American tour with the impresario Ullmann. Here, and in Europe, she became a favorite on the concert stage, more especially as a coloratura vocalist of exquisite technique united with great sentiment. In 1871 she married the cellist De Munck, with whom her artistic tours were continued.

Pattison, John Nelson, American pianist and composer; b. Niagara Falls, Oct. 22, 1845; d. New York, July 27, 1905. He studied piano in Germany with celebrated teachers (Thalberg, Henselt, Hans von Bülow) and also had lessons from Liszt. He gave a series of concerts in the U. S., and toured as accompanist for Parepa-Rosa, Louise Kellogg, Albani, Pauline Lucca, and others. He wrote a symph. work, *Niagara;* marches and overtures for military band; a concerto-fantasia for piano and orch.; and some 200 pieces for piano solo. —Cf. *Memoir of J. N. Pattison* (N. Y., 1868).

Pattison, Lee, American pianist; b. Grand Rapids, Wis., July 22, 1890. He first studied at the New England Cons. of Music; later in Berlin with Schnabel. In 1917 he formed a duo piano team with Guy Maier; they gave a number of successful concerts, until

1931, when the partnership was dissolved. From 1932 till 1937 he was head of the piano dept. of Sarah Lawrence College; also taught at the Juilliard Summer School; lived mostly in N. Y. His compositions include *Florentine Sketches* for piano and a piano suite of 7 pieces, *Told in the Hills.*

Patton, Willard, American singer and composer; b. Milford, Maine, May 26, 1853; d. Minneapolis, Dec. 12, 1924. He studied with Dudley Buck and others in N. Y.; was active as a tenor in oratorios; in 1883, settled in Minneapolis as vocal teacher. He wrote an oratorio, *Isaiah* (1897); the operettas *The Gallant Garroter* (1882) and *La Fianza* (1889); a grand opera, *Pocahontas* (Minneapolis, Jan. 4, 1911); 2 'musical epics,' *The Star of Empire* (1900) and *Foot-Stones of a Nation* (1906); also a symph. fantasy, *The Spirit of 1861* (1915).

Patzak, Julius, tenor; b. Vienna, April 9, 1898; studied at the Univ. and School of Music there; pupil of Adler, Mandyczewski, and Maeschart; 1926, début at the State Opera, Reichenberg; 1927-28, member of the Brünn Opera; from 1928 of the Munich Opera; guest appearances with the Vienna and Berlin State Operas, in Barcelona (1930), at the Salzburg Festival, etc.; has also appeared in recital and as soloist with orchestras; American début, Cincinnati, 1954.

Pauer (pow'ĕr), **Ernst,** Austrian pianist; b. Vienna, Dec. 21, 1826; d. Jugenheim, near Darmstadt, May 9, 1905. Pupil of Theodor Dirzka until 1839; 1839-44, of W. A. Mozart, Jr. (piano), and Sechter (composition); 1845-47, of Fr. Lachner, Munich. 1847-51, director of the music societies at Mainz; settled in London, 1851; prof. at the Royal Academy of Music 1859-64; in 1861, began his historical performances of harpsichord and piano music in chronological order (3 series). 1867, principal prof. at the National Training School; 1883, at the Royal College of Music. In 1878, member of the Board of Mus. Studies at Cambridge Univ., and Examiner in 1879. He was appointed pianist to the Austrian court in 1866. He retired to Jugenheim in 1896. —Publ. primers on *The Art of Pianoforte-playing, Musical Forms,* and *The Elements of the Beautiful in Music; A Dictionary of Pianists and Composers for the Pianoforte;* 'Alte Klaviermusik,' 12 books, and 'Alte Meister,' 65 numbers, contain keyboard works of old English, Italian, French, and German masters; etc. —Educational: *The New Gradus ad Parnassum* (100 selected studies): *Classical Companion* (100 pieces); *Celebrated Concert-studies* (50); *Culture of the Left Hand* (4 books). He also publ. many original studies and pieces for piano; a symphony in C minor; chamber music; etc. Also excellent arrangements of Beethoven's and Schumann's symphonies, for solo piano, 4 and 8 hands; and Mendelssohn's orchestral works (4 and 8 hands).

Pauer, Max, son of the preceding; distinguished pianist and teacher; b. London, Oct. 31, 1866; d. Jugenheim, May 12, 1945. Pupil of his father till 1881; then of V. Lachner at Karlsruhe (theory) till 1885; made concert tours, settled in London, and in 1887 was called to the Cologne Cons. as piano prof. In 1893, chamber virtuoso to the Grand Duke of Hesse; in 1897, prof. at Stuttgart Cons.; from 1908, director of the Städtische Hochschule für Musik at Mannheim; retired in 1934 and returned to Stuttgart. On his first American tour, 1913-14, he met with great success. He publ. piano pieces, and arrangements of Mozart's and Haydn's symphonies for 2 and 4 hands; ed. piano works of Schumann; and brought out a new ed. of Lebert-Stark's *Klavierschule* (1904). —Cf. his *Unser seltsames Ich . . .* (Stuttgart, 1942).

Paul (powl), **Oscar,** German theorist; b. Freiwaldau, April 8, 1836; d. Leipzig, April 18, 1898. Student of theology at Leipzig Univ., 1858, but chose music for a profession, studying at the Cons., with private lessons from Plaidy (piano), and Hauptmann and Richter (theory). He took the degree of *Dr. phil.* in 1860, and in 1866 qualified as lecturer at Leipzig Univ. with the treatise *Die absolute Harmonik der Griechen* (Leipzig, 1866). Teacher in the Cons., 1869; after publishing his translation of Boetius' *De Musica,* 1872, he was appointed prof. extraordinarius at the Univ. A disciple of Hauptmann, he publ. the latter's *Lehre von der Harmonik* (1868), of which his own *Lehrbuch der Harmonik* (1880) is a practical adaptation (English transl., N. Y., 1885). He also wrote a *Geschichte des Klaviers* (Leipzig, 1868); *Handlexikon der Tonkunst* (Leipzig, 1873); *Musikalische Instrumente* (Brunswick, 1874).

Paulli (pow'lē), **Holger Simon,** Danish conductor; b. Copenhagen, Feb. 22, 1810; d. there, Dec. 23, 1891. Studied violin with Schall and Wexschall; entered the court orch. as violinist in 1828; was appointed concertmaster and assistant conductor in 1849; 1864-83, chief conductor, in which capacity he conducted the first performances in Denmark of *Lohengrin* (1870), *Meistersinger* (1872), and *Tannhäuser* (1875); he also conducted the concerts of the Music Society (1865-70) and of the Cecilia Society (1872-77). On the founding of the Copenhagen Cons. in 1866 he was appointed co-director with Gade and Hauptmann; founded the Chamber Music Society in 1868, and was its president until his death. Besides a number of successful ballets, he wrote a 'Singspiel,' *Lodsen* (*The Pilot*), staged in Copenhagen on Sept. 25, 1851; a concert overture, studies for violin, and songs. —Cf. F. Bendix, *Af en Kapelmusikers Erindringer* (Copenhagen, 1913).

Paulson, Gustaf, Swedish organist and composer; b. Hälsingborg, Jan. 22, 1898. He studied at Stockholm, Copenhagen, and Paris. Since 1929 he has been a church organist in Hälsingborg. His compositions include 5 symphonies; piano concerto (1940); cello concerto (1944); oboe concerto (1950); 5 string quartets; etc.

Paulus (pow'-loos), **Olaf,** Norwegian composer; b. Christiania, Jan. 25, 1859; d. Stavanger, June 29, 1912. Pupil of C. Cappelen and J. Svendsen, and at the Leipzig Cons.; from 1889 he was organist at the Cathedral in Stavanger; made a trip to the U. S. in 1902, directing choral concerts in Minneapolis and St. Paul. In his native country he is highly esteemed as a national composer; his men's choruses are in the repertory of all Norwegian societies; also wrote songs and piano pieces, and ed. a collection of songs, *De 1,000 hjems sange* (*Home Songs;* 1888).

Pauly (pow'-lē), **Rosa,** soprano; b. Eperjes, Hungary, March 15, 1895; studied voice in Vienna with Rosa Papier; operatic début as Aïda in Hamburg, then sang at the Cologne Opera, at the Kroll Opera in Berlin (1927-31), and at the Vienna State Opera. She made her American début as Elektra on March 18, 1937 in a concert performance with the N. Y. Philh.; her first appearance with the Metropolitan Opera (of which she became a member) on Jan. 7, 1938, and her débuts at Covent Garden and with the San Francisco Opera in the same year, were also in this rôle. She has made numerous guest appearances throughout Germany, also in Budapest, Paris, Rome, Salzburg, etc.; has toured the U. S. and Canada in concert; 1939, guest appearances at the Teatro Colón, Buenos Aires.

Paumann (pow'-man), **Conrad,** born blind at Nuremberg, c. 1410; d. Munich, Jan. 24, 1473. Famous as the greatest organist of his time; also a virtuoso on the harp, theorbolute, and flute; author of the oldest extant organ-book, *Fundamentum organisandi,* containing exercises or preludes, and other pieces (not all by Paumann); it was publ. by Arnold in Chrysander's 'Jahrbücher' (2nd year, 1867); a facsimile reprint was publ. by K. Ameln (1925). Arnold also publ. some other compositions (MSS at Wernigerode). An example, in tablature with 7 lines for the right hand and letters for the left, is found in A. Schering's *Geschichte der Musik in Beispielen* (No. 48). —Cf. H. Abele, *Erinnerungen an einen grossen Münchener Tonmeister . . .* (Munich, 1910); A. Schering, *Studien zur Musikgeschichte der Frührenaissance* (1914); O. Kade, in 'Monatshefte für Musik-Geschichte' IV; H. Schnoor, in 'Zeitschrift für Musikwissenschaft' IV; G. Reese, *Music in the Renaissance* (N. Y., 1954; pp. 658-60).

Paumgartner, Bernhard, Austrian musicologist, composer, and conductor; b. Vienna, Nov. 14, 1887. Son of Dr. **Hans Paumgartner** (b. Kirchberg, Austria, 1843; d. Vienna, May 23, 1896; chorusmaster for 20 years at the Vienna Court Opera, critic and composer), and Rosa Papier (q.v.). Pupil of Bruno Walter; teacher at the Staatsakademie für Musik and conductor of the Vienna Tonkünstler Orch.; 1917-38, director of the Mozarteum in Salzburg; and, from 1945, also conductor of the Salzburg symph. concerts; guest-conductor in Vienna and elsewhere. —Works: *Rossini in Neapel* (Zürich, March 27, 1936; very successful) and 2 other operas; incidental music for the Reinhardt production of *Faust* (Salzburg Fest.); *Ouvertüre zu einem ritterlichen Spiel,* for orch.; suite in G minor, after sketches by old French masters; divertimento on old English dances; etc. Edited Leopold Mozart's *Violinschule* (1922); (in collaboration with A. Rottauscher) *Das Taghorn* (poems and tunes of the Bavarian and Austrian Minnesingers; Vienna, 1922); etc.—Author of biographies of Mozart (1927; 4th ed., 1945), Schubert (1943; 2nd ed., 1947), and Bach (vol. 1, 1950).

Paur (powr), **Emil,** conductor; b. Czernowitz, Bukovina, Aug. 29, 1855; d. Mistek, Czechoslovakia, June 7, 1932. Taught by his father, at 8 he played the violin and piano in public; in 1866 he entered the Vienna Cons., studying under Dessoff (composition) and Hellmesberger (violin). In 1870, after graduating with first prizes, he joined the court opera orch. as first violin and assistant soloist. Became Kapellmeister at Kassel (1876), Königsberg, and Mannheim (1880); conductor of the Leipzig City Theater, 1891; from 1893-98 of the Boston Symphony Orch., succeeding Nikisch; 1898-1902, conductor of the N. Y. Philh. Society, succeeding Seidl; 1899-1900, conductor of the Wagner works at the Metropolitan Opera; 1902-04, in Europe as visiting conductor; 1904-10, conductor Pittsburgh Symph. Orch. (also appearing as pianist). In 1912 he succeeded Karl Muck as Kapellmeister at the Royal Opera in Berlin, but owing to differences with the intendancy resigned after 2 months; then in Berlin as concert conductor. From 1899-1902 he also was director of the National Cons. in N. Y. (succeeding Dvořák).—Works: a symphony, *In der Natur;* violin concerto; string quartet; violin sonata; piano pieces; songs. —In 1882 he married the pianist **Marie Bürger** (b. Gengenbach, Baden, 1862; d. New York, April 27, 1899).

Payne, Albert, German publisher; b. Leipzig, June 3, 1842; d. there, April 1, 1921. From 1858-61, pupil at the Leipzig Cons. of David (violin), Dreyshock (piano), E. Fr. Richter and Hauptmann (theory); then for a short time of Massart in Paris. In 1862 he entered the publishing firm of his father; under the title 'Payne's Kleine Kammermusik Partiturausgabe' he began in 1886 the publication of a low-priced pocket edition of the chamber music of the Classic masters, which immediately met with pronounced favor, so that he soon added the works of the Romanticists; in 1892 he sold the edition (212 numbers) to Ernst Eulenburg (q.v.), who enlarged its scope still further.

Paz, Juan Carlos, Argentine composer; b. Buenos Aires, Aug. 5, 1897. He studied composition with Constantino Gaito; in 1929, with several young composers of radical tendencies, he organized in Buenos Aires the 'Grupo Renovación,' and in 1937 began a series of concerts of new music. His early works are marked by strong polyphony, in a neo-Classical style; about 1927, he adopted atonal and polytonal procedures; in 1934 he began to compose almost exclusively in the 12-tone idiom; after 1950, he moderated his musical language, and occasionally wrote pieces in simplified harmony. —Works: for orch.: *Canto de Navidad* (1927), *Movimiento Sinfónico* (1930), suite for Ibsen's play *Julian the Emperor* (1931), *3 Piezas (Moderato; Animato; Moderadamente animato;* 1932), overture for 12 instruments, *Passacaglia,* for 12 violas, 10 cellos, and 10 double-basses (1936; Paris Festival of the International Society for Contemporary Music, June 25, 1937), *Preludio y fuga* (1940), *Rítmica constante* (1952), *Seis superposiciones* (1954); chamber music: *Tema y transformaciones,* for 11 wind instruments (1929), octet for wind instruments (1930), sonatina for clarinet and piano (1930), *Concierto No. 1,* for flute, oboe, clarinet, bassoon, trumpet, and piano (1932), sonatina for flute and clarinet (1932), *Concierto No. 2,* for oboe, trumpet, 2 French horns, bassoon, and piano (1934), *Composición dodecafónica,* for flute and piano (1935), *Composición dodecafónica,* for clarinet and piano (1937), trio, for flute, clarinet, and bassoon (1937), string quartet No. 1 (1938), trio for clarinet, trumpet, and saxophone (1938), trio for flute, oboe, and bass clarinet (1940), string quartet (1943), trio for flute, saxophone, and piano (1943), *Dédalus 1950,* for flute, clarinet, violin, cello, and piano (1951); *Continuidad,* for percussion (1954); for piano: sonata No. 1 (1923), sonata No. 2 (1925), *6 baladas* (1927-29), *Tema con transformaciones* (1928), *3 movimientos de jazz* (1932), *3 invenciones a dos voces* (1932), sonata No. 3 (1935), *10 piezas sobre una serie dodecafónica* (1936), *Canciones y baladas* (1937), *5 piezas de carácter* (1937), *Música 1946* (1946); songs. He publ. the books *La Música en los Estados Unidos* (1952), *Arnold Schoenberg o el fin de la era tonal* (1954), and *Introducción a la música de nuestro tiempo* (1955); contributed articles on modern music to numerous publications. —Cf. Hector J. Gallac, *La Obra Musical de Juan Carlos Paz,* in vol. I of the 'Boletín Latino-Americano de Música'; F. C. Lange, *Juan Carlos Paz,* in vol. IV of the same 'Boletín.'

Peace, Albert Lister, English organist and composer; b. Huddersfield, Jan. 26, 1844; d. Liverpool, March 14, 1912. He played organ in the parish church as a child; in 1865, became organist in Glasgow; then studied at Oxford Univ. (Mus. Bac., 1870; Mus. Doc., 1875). From 1879 to 1897 he was organist at Glasgow Cathedral; in 1897, became successor to W. T. Best as organist of St. George's Hall in Liverpool. He wrote a cantata, *St. John the Baptist; Psalm 138* for soli, chorus, and orch.; many organ pieces; anthems; church services.

Pearce, Stephen Austen, organist and composer; b. London, Nov. 7, 1836; d. Jersey City, N. J., April 9, 1900. He was a graduate of Oxford Univ. (Mus. Bac., 1859; Mus. Doc., 1864). In 1872 he settled in America; taught vocal music at Columbia College, N. Y.; also at the Peabody Institute, Baltimore. He wrote an opera, *La belle Américaine;* a dramatic oratorio, *Celestial Visions;* a church cantata, *The Psalm of Praise;* piano pieces; songs; compiled 'A Pocket Dictionary of Musical Terms . . .' (in 21 languages; N. Y., 1889); ed. various piano methods; wrote music criticism for the N. Y. 'Evening Post.'

Pears, Peter, English tenor; b. Farnham, June 22, 1910. He studied at the Royal College of Music in London; in 1936-37 toured the U. S. as a member of a group called the New English Singers. From 1943 to 1945 he was on the roster of the Sadler's Wells Opera. In 1946 he joined Benjamin Britten, to initiate song recitals in programs of works by Britten and other English composers, with Britten acting as his accompanist. Together, they undertook numerous tours in Europe and America. Pears sang leading tenor parts in the premières of Britten's operas: *Peter Grimes, The Rape of Lucretia, Albert Herring, Billy Budd, Gloriana,* and *The Turn of the Screw.* He was co-editor, with Britten, of some vocal works by Purcell.

Pearsall, Robert Lucas de, English composer; b. Clifton, March 14, 1795; d. Wartensee, on Lake Constance, Aug. 5, 1856. He studied law and music; as a boy of 13 wrote a cantata, *Saul and the Witch of Endor.* He lived many years in Germany, where he publ. many of his compositions; was in London on several extended visits; in 1842, purchased a castle on Lake Constance, and remained there for the rest of his life. As a composer, he was at his best in many ingenious madrigals; particularly popular were his part-songs, *Sir Patrick Spens, The Hardy Norseman,* and *O who will o'er the downs so free;* he edited old church music in Germany; publ. an *Essay on Consecutive Fifths and Octaves in Counterpoint.* —Cf. W. Barclay Squire, *Letters of R. L. Pearsall,* in the 'Mus. Quarterly' (April, 1919).

Pedrell (pĕh-drĕhl'), **Carlos,** composer; b. Minas, Uruguay, Oct. 16, 1878; d. Montrouge, near Paris, March 3, 1941. He studied in Madrid with his uncle, Felipe Pedrell; later went to Paris, where he took lessons with Vincent d'Indy and Bréville at the Schola Cantorum. Returning to South America, he was inspector of music in the Buenos Aires schools; lectured at the Univ. of Tucumán; in 1921 he went to Paris, where he remained for the rest of his life. His works are cast in a French style, but the rhythmic elements are related to Spanish and South American sources; his songs, with richly developed accompaniments, are the best among his works. He wrote the operas *Ardid de Amor* (Buenos Aires, June 7, 1917), *Cuento de Abril,* and *La Guitare* (Madrid, 1924); the ballets *La Rose et le gitan* (Antwerp, 1930) and *Alleluia* (Buenos Aires, 1936); for orch.: *Une Nuit de Schéhérazade* (1908), *Danza y canción de Aixa* (1910), *En el estrado de Beatriz* (1910), *Fantasia Argentina* (1910), *Ouverture Catalane* (1912), *Pastorales,* for voice and orch. (Paris, 1928); choruses; songs. —Cf. A. Suarès, *Carlos Pedrell,* in the 'Revue Musicale' (June, 1931).

Pedrell (pĕh-drĕhl'), **Felipe,** eminent Spanish musicologist and composer; b. Tortosa, Feb. 19, 1841; d. Barcelona, Aug. 19, 1922. A chorister in the Cathedral of Tortosa, his musical studies were guided by J. A. Nin y Serra; began to compose from the age of 15; 1873-74, 2nd conductor of an operetta company in Barcelona. His prolific literary career began in 1867, with articles in various mus. reviews; his first opera, *El último Abencerrage,* was produced at Barcelona in 1874. After a visit to Italy and a sojourn in Paris, he settled in Barcelona (1882), where he founded the 'Salterio Sacro-Hispano' for the publication of contemporary religious music, and the weekly review 'Notas Musicales y Literarias,' both of which ceased publication in 1883. In 1888 he founded the 'Ilustración Musical Hispano-Americana,' which he edited until its demise in 1896. In 1889-91 he composed his great dramatic trilogy, *Los Pirineos,* and as a sort of introduction to this work he wrote his famous pamphlet *Por nuestra música,* a plea for the creation of a national lyric drama on the basis of the national folksong. In 1891-92, critic for the 'Diario de Barcelona'; in 1894 he went to Madrid, where he was made a member of the Royal Academy of Fine Arts; also prof. at the Madrid Cons. (1895-1903) and lecturer on music history at the Madrid Ateneo. He was also invited to direct the reform of religious music in Spain; ed. the review 'Música religiosa,' 1896-99. At the end of 1904 he returned to Barcelona as artistic director for the publishing firm of Vidal y Llimona, which revived the 'Salterio Sacro-Hispano.' There he spent the rest of his life, writing, teaching, and composing. Among his pupils were Albéniz, Granados, Manuel de Falla, and Gerhard. Though highly praised by contemporary critics, his music has not obtained recognition outside of Spain; but the importance of his achievement in bringing to light the treasures of Spain's musical past is universally recognized, and he is considered the leading spirit of the modern Spanish nationalist revival in music. On his 70th birthday Pedrell was honored by the publication (under the auspices of the 'Orfeó Tortosí,' the choral society of his native city) of a 'Festschrift,' *Al Maestro Pedrell: Escritos heortásticos,* with contributions from the foremost musical scholars throughout the world. —Works: The operas *El último Abencerrage* (Barcelona, April 14, 1874); *Quasimodo* (Barcelona, April 20, 1875); *Mazeppa* and *Tasse à Ferrare* (both on 1-act French texts, Madrid, 1881); *Cléopâtre* (4-act, French text); *Los Pirineos,* his most ambitious effort, a trilogy consisting of a Prologue and the 3 dramas *El Conde de Foix, Rayo de Luna,* and *La Jornada de Panissars* (the Prologue produced separately in Venice, March 12, 1897; the entire work, Barcelona, Jan. 4, 1902); *La Celestina* (not produced); *Matinada* (really a dramatic cantata; produced scenically, Barcelona, Oct. 27, 1905). For orch.: The symph. poems *Excelsior* (after Longfellow); *El Conde Arnau* and *Glosa* (both with chorus); *Cant de la Montanya,* 'symph. scenes'; *I Trionfi,* suite after Petrarch; *Marcia a Mistral.* Vocal works: *Canço latina* for chorus and orch.; *Messa di Gloria* for soli, chorus, organ, and orch.; Requiem a cappella; *Hymne à Ste. Thérèse;* motets and antiphons; songs (from V. Hugo's *Les Orientales,* Th. Gauthier's *Consolations,* etc.). Also string quartet, etc.; 302 opus numbers in all. —He edited the collections 'Hispaniae Schola musica sacra,' works of Morales, Guerrero, Victoria, Cabezón, Ginés Pérez, Diego Ortiz (8 vols.); 'Teatro lírico español anterior al siglo XIX' (5 vols., 1897-98); 'Salterio Sacro-Hispano' (1905); 'Antología de organistas clásicos de España' (2 vols., 1905, 1908); the complete works of Victoria (8 vols., 1903-13; with biography in vol. VIII); 'Cancionero popular español' (Barcelona, 1919-20, 4 vols.; new ed., 2 vols., 1936). —Writings: *Diccionario técnico de la música* (1894); *Teatro lírico español anterior al siglo XIX . . .* (1897-98; 5 vols. in 1); *Prácticas preparatorias de instrumentación* (1902); *Emporio científico e histórico de organografía musical antigua española* (1901); *Musicalerías* (1906); *Catàlech de la Biblioteca musical de la Diputació de Barcelona* (2 vols., 1908, 1909); *Jean I. d'Aragon, compositeur de musique* (1909; in 'Riemann-Festschrift'); *Tomás Luis de Victoria* (1918; reprinted from vol. VIII of collected works); *P. Antonio Eximeno* (1921). Of a valuable *Diccionario biográfico y bibliográfico de músicos y escritores de música españoles, portugueses y hispano-americanos antiguos y modernos,* only vol. I appeared (A-G; 1894-97). He publ. a book of reminiscences, *Jornadas de Arte* (Paris, 1911). His collected essays and critical writings were publ. in Paris in 3 vols., *Orientaciones, Musiquerías, Lírica nacionalizada* (1911-13). A complete list of Pedrell's works was publ. by A. Reiff in 'Archiv für Musikwissenschaft' III, 1 (1921). —Cf. G. Tebaldini, *Felipe Pedrell ed il dramma lirico spagnuolo* (Turin, 1897); R. Mitjana, *La Música contemporanea en España y Felipe Pedrell* (Málaga, 1901); H. de Curzon, *Felipe Pedrell et 'Les Pyrénées'* (Paris, 1902); *Felipe Pedrell,* in 'La Nouvelle Revue' (Jan., 1912); A. Reiff, *Felipe Pedrell,* in 'Zeitschrift für Musikwissenschaft' (Feb., 1921); Manuel de Falla, *Felipe Pedrell,* in the 'Revue Musicale' (Feb., 1923); E. Istel, *Felipe Pedrell,* in the 'Mus. Quarterly' (April, 1925).

Pedrollo, Arrigo, Italian composer; b. Montebelli, near Vicenza, Dec. 5, 1878. He studied at the Cons. of Milan (1891-1900); at his graduation wrote a symphony, which was performed by Toscanini. In 1914 he won the Sonzogno competition with his opera *Juana.* His other operas include *Terra promessa* (Cremona, 1908); *La Veglia* (Milan, Jan. 2, 1920); *L'Uomo che ride* (Rome, March 6, 1920); *Maria di Magdala* (Milan, 1924); *Delitto e castigo,* after Dostoyevsky's *Crime and Punishment* (La Scala, Milan, Nov. 16, 1926); *L'Amante in trappola* (Verona, Sept. 22, 1936); *Il Giglio di Ali* (1948). He also wrote music for voice and orch.; chamber works; a violin sonata. He was also active as educator; taught at the Cons. of Milan (from 1930); after 1945, appointed director of the Istituto Musicale in Padua.

Pedrotti, Carlo, Italian composer and conductor; b. Verona, Nov. 12, 1817; d. there, Oct. 16, 1893 (suicide). He was a pupil of Domenico Foroni; obtained an excellent success with his first opera, *Lina* (Verona, 1840); was then engaged as conductor of the Italian Opera at Amsterdam; he wrote 2 operas there, *Mathilde* (1841) and *La Figlia del Arciere* (1844). He returned to Verona in 1845 and presented there his operas *Romea di Monfort* (1846), *Fiorina* (1851), *Il Parrucchiere della reggenza* (1852), and *Tutti in maschera* (Nov. 4, 1856; his principal work; many revivals in Italy; also performed in Paris); the following were given in Milan: *Gelmina* (1853), *Genoveffa del Brabante* (1854), *La Guerra in quattro* (1861); also *Isabella d'Arragona* (Turin, 1859), *Mazeppa* (Bologna, 1861), *Marion Delorme* (Trieste, 1865), *Il Favorito* (Turin, 1870), and *Olema la schiava* (Modena, 1872). In 1868 he settled in Turin as teacher and conductor of popular symphonic concerts.

Peellaert (pā'-lahrt), **Augustin-Philippe-Marie-Ghislain,** Baron **de,** Belgian composer; b. Bruges, March 12, 1793; d. Brussels, April 16, 1876. He studied in Paris with Momigny; entered the army in 1814, but devoted himself assiduously to musical composition; in 1832, became a member of the executive board of the Brussels Cons. He wrote Masses and other sacred works; chamber music; songs; several operas, of which the following were produced in Brussels: *L'Heure du rendez-vous* (1821), *Agnès Sorel* (Aug. 30, 1823), *Le Barmécide* (1824), *Teniers ou La Noce flamande* (Feb. 21, 1825), *L'Exilé* (1827), *Faust* (1834), *Le Coup de pistolet* (1836), *Louis de Male* (1838); publ. an autobiography, *Cinquante ans de souvenirs* (Brussels, 1867).

Peerce, Jan (real name Jacob Pincus Perelmuth), American tenor; b. New York, June 3, 1904. He played the violin in dance bands, and sang at various entertainment places in N. Y. In 1933 he was engaged as a singer at the Radio City Music Hall; made his operatic début in Philadelphia as the Duke in *Rigoletto* (May 14, 1938); gave his first recital in N. Y. on Nov. 7, 1939; as a consequence of his growing reputation, he was engaged by the Metropolitan Opera Co.; made his first appearance there as Alfredo in *La Traviata,* on Nov. 29, 1941.

Peeters, Flor, Belgian organist and composer; b. Thielen, July 4, 1903. He studied with J. Brandt and Mortelmans. In 1925 he was appointed prof. of organ at the Lemmens Institute in Malines. He became greatly renowned as an improviser, and gave innumerable concerts in Europe; made 5 tours of the U. S.; during his 5th tour in 1956, he presented special recitals in American churches and colleges. He wrote a Mass; a cantata, *William Tell;* many organ works; publ. a manual of organ playing, *Ars Organi* (3 vols., Brussels, 1953-55), with text in Flemish, French, English, and German. —Cf. Piet Visser, *Flor Peeters, Organist* (Turnhout, 1950; in Flemish).

Pelemans, Willem, Flemish composer and music critic; b. Antwerp, April 6, 1901; studied there; then joined a theater group and began to write music for its productions. An exceptionally prolific composer, Pelemans wrote 6 symphonies within 3 years (1936-39); 8 ballades for orch. (1933-35); a harpsichord concerto (1931); 2 piano concertos (1945; 1950); violin concerto (1954); 3 concertinos for small orch. (1948-50); 3 violin sonatas (all written in 1942); 2 viola sonatas (1946; 1949); 2 piano trios; string trio; 2 trios for oboe, clarinet, and bassoon; 5 string quartets (1942-44); a quintet for flute, oboe, clarinet, bassoon, and horn (1948); 16 piano sonatas (1935-48); 2 sonatas for 2 pianos (1947; 1954); an album of 98 'petites études' for piano, of which *3 Flemish Dances* (1926) are popular; numerous songs and choral works; for the theater: 2 opera-oratorios, *Le Juif errant* (1932) and *Flores et Blanchefleur* (1939), a fairy-tale opera, *Le petit soldat de plomb* (1945), 2 chamber operas, *Le Combat de la vierge et du diable* (1949) and *De Mannen van Smeerop* (1952), and a ballet, *Miles Gloriosus* (1945). Virtually all of his works are in MS. A catalogue was publ. by the Centre Belge de Documentation Musicale (Brussels, 1954). He has publ. 2 essays on esthetics (in Flemish): *Architectonische Muziek* (1927) and *Geest en Klank* (1943); many articles in various publications.

Pelissier (peh-lis-s'yā'), **Victor,** horn virtuoso and composer. His name appears first in 1792 on Philadelphia concert programs as 'first horn of the Theatre in Cape François.' In 1793 he went to New York, where he lived for many years, and became the principal horn-player, also composer and arranger, of the Old American Co.—Known works: the operas *Edwin and Angelina* or *The Banditti* (N. Y., John Street Theater, Dec. 19, 1796), *Ariadne Abandoned by Theseus in the Isle of Naxos* (N. Y., 1797), and *Sterne's Maria* or *The Vintage* (1799); incidental music to about 18 plays performed in N. Y. (mostly in 1794-96), including *Fourth of July* or *Temple of American Independence* (1799), *Castle of Otranto* (adaptation of *Sicilian Romance*), etc.; various pantomimes performed in Philadelphia; a quartet; and a few separate pieces. In 1811 he publ. the collection 'Columbian Melodies,' which contains 3 songs from *Sterne's Maria.* —Cf. O. G. Sonneck, *Early Opera in America* (N. Y., 1915); J. T. Howard, *Our American Music* (N. Y., 1939 and later eds.); 'Sammelbände der Internationalen Musik-Gesellschaft' VI, 475.

Pellegrini, Vincenzo, Italian composer and organist; b. Pesaro, late 16th century; d. Milan, 1636. He was a canon at Pesaro (1603) and maestro di cappella at the cathedral of Milan (1611-31). His extant works include *Canzoni da intavolatura d'organo fatte alla francese* (Venice, 1599); *Missarum a 4 e 5 voci* (Venice, 1603); sacred vocal pieces with organ accompaniment, published under the title *Concerti ecclesiastici da 1, 2, 3, 5 e 6 voci* (Venice, 1619); other compositions are in the collections *Parnassus musicus Ferdinandoeus* (Venice, 1615); 2 canzone (*La Serpentina* and *La Capricciosa*) in Torchi's 'L'Arte Musicale in Italia' (vol. III).

Pelletier (pĕl-lĕh-t'yā'), **Wilfred,** conductor; b. Montreal, June 20, 1896. He studied with his father; at the age of 17 became assistant conductor at the Montreal Opera; won a scholarship in 1914, and went to Paris, where he studied with Isidor Philipp and Widor. Returning to America in 1917, he became a coach at the Metropolitan Opera, N. Y.; then was assistant conductor there; in 1932 was appointed a principal conductor. From 1921 to 1931 he conducted the Ravinia Opera and the San Francisco Opera; after 1935 divided his activities between N. Y. and Montreal; was the founder of the Concerts Symphoniques in Montreal; became director of the Cons. of Montreal in 1942; also director of a music school in Quebec (since 1943). In 1951 he became conductor of the Orchestre Symphonique in Quebec; 1954-57, he also conducted children's concerts of the N. Y. Philharmonic. He married the singer Queena Mario in 1925; divorced in 1936; in 1937 married Rose Bampton, soprano.

Pelton-Jones, Frances, American harpsichord player; b. Salem, Oregon, Dec. 6, 1863; d. New York, April 24, 1946. She studied piano with Carl Faelten at the New England Cons. in Boston; organ with Dudley Buck and William C. Carl in N. Y.; after filling various posts as organist in Portland, Ore., she settled in N. Y. in 1904. Meeting Arnold Dolmetsch, she became interested in the harpsichord, and under his instruction developed into a highly proficient player on that instrument; gave numerous recitals, including a special series in N. Y., 'Salons Intimes,' begun in 1923, which she continued for some 20 years.

Pembaur, Joseph, Sr., Austrian composer and teacher; b. Innsbruck, May 23, 1848; d. there, Feb. 19, 1923. He studied at the Vienna Cons. with Bruckner and in Munich with Rheinberger and others. In 1874 he was appointed director of the Innsbruck Music School; retired in 1918. —Works: opera, *Der Bauer von Langwall* (Innsbruck, May 2, 1898); a symph. tableau, *In Tirol;* a Requiem (in memory of the Tyrolese fallen in World War I; 1916); an organ sonata; numerous male choruses a cappella; also publ. *Harmonie- und Modulationslehre* (1910) and *Über das Dirigieren* (1907).

Pembaur, Joseph, Jr., Austrian pianist; son of the preceding; b. Innsbruck, April 20, 1875; d. Munich, Oct. 12, 1950. He was a pupil of his father; then studied with Rheinberger and Thuille at the Munich Academy of Music; was prof. of piano at the Munich Musikschule (1897-1900); subsequently was on the faculty of the Leipzig Cons. (1902-21); in 1921, appointed prof. at the Munich Academy of Music. He wrote a violin sonata; a number of songs; publ. *Von der Poesie des Klavierspiels* (1910; 2nd ed., 1911; in Dutch, 1930) and *Beethovens Sonaten Op. 31, No. 2, und Op. 57* (Cologne, 1915). —Cf. C. Werner, *Joseph Pembaur d. j. zum 60. Geburtstag* (Berlin, 1935).

Pembaur, Karl Maria, Austrian organist and conductor; son of Joseph Pembaur, Sr.; b. Innsbruck, Aug. 24, 1876; d. Dresden, March 6, 1939. He studied with his father; then with Rheinberger at the Munich Academy of Music. In 1901 he went to Dresden, where he became court organist and choral conductor; also conducted at the Dresden Opera. He wrote several Masses; *Ständchen,* for men's chorus with orch.; the 'Singspiel' *Seien Sie vorsichtig; Geistliche Sonette* for 5 solo voices and piano; *Bergbilder,* for woodwind quintet and piano; marches; songs. Publ. *Drei Jahrhunderte Kirchenmusik am sächsischen Hofe* (Dresden, 1920).

Peña Costa, Joaquín, Spanish musicologist; b. Barcelona, March 1, 1873; d. there, June 25, 1944. He studied law at the Univ. of Barcelona, but devoted himself mainly to musical journalism; translated librettos of Wagner's operas into Catalan; arranged vocal scores of *Tristan und Isolde, Lohengrin, Tannhäuser,* and *Die Meistersinger;* ed. 5 vols. of songs of Beethoven, Schubert, Fauré, etc. under the title *Canconer selecte.* In 1940 he began work on a large music dictionary in Spanish; it was completed by H. Anglès, and publ. by the Labor publishing firm as *Diccionario de Música Labor* (Barcelona, 1954; 2 vols.; of limited value owing to a multitude of errors).

Peña y Goñi, Antonio, Spanish writer on music; b. San Sebastian, Nov. 2, 1846; d. Madrid, Nov. 13, 1896. He studied at the Cons. of Madrid; for 30 years was music critic of the periodical 'Imparcial,' in which he carried on earnest propaganda for Wagner, whom he knew personally. He composed a cantata, *Viva Hernani* (1875), and some minor choral and piano works; publ. the important historical book, *La Opera española y la música dramática en España en el siglo XIX* (1881); also *La Obra maestra de Verdi* (1875), *Impresiones musicales* (1878), *Charles Gounod* (1879), guides to Wagner's operas, etc.

Penfield, Smith Newell, American organist and teacher; b. Oberlin, Ohio, April 4, 1837; d. New York, Jan. 7, 1920. After preliminary study of the piano in N. Y., he went to Leipzig, where he took lessons from Moscheles, Reinecke, Plaidy, and Papperitz (piano), Richter (organ), and Hauptmann (theory). Returning to America, he conducted various choral societies; from 1882 was active in N. Y. as church organist and teacher. He wrote a piano sonata, subtitled *Poem of Life;* some sacred music; songs; piano pieces.

Penha, Michael, violoncellist; b. Amsterdam, Dec. 14, 1888. He studied at the Cons. there; then in Frankfurt with Hugo Becker, and in Paris with J. Salmon. He made successful tours of the principal cities of Europe and South America; American début in N. Y. (Oct. 13, 1916); conducted the Bach Society of Pasadena (1937-42); then settled in Los Angeles as teacher.

Penn, Arthur A., composer; b. London, England, Feb. 13, 1875; d. New London, Conn., Feb. 6, 1941. He was educated in private schools in England; came to the U. S. in 1903 and settled in New London as composer and teacher. —Works: the comic operas (of which he composed both librettos and music) *Yokohama Maid, Your Royal Highness, The Lass of Limerick Town, Captain Crossbones, Mam'zelle Taps, The China Shop;* the songs *Carissima, The Magic of Your Eyes, Smilin' Through, Sunrise and You, The Lamplit Hour, When the Sun Goes Down, Across the River,* etc.

Penna, Lorenzo, Italian composer; b. Bologna, 1613; d. Imola, Oct. 20, 1693. In 1656 he was maestro di cappella at Casale Monferrato; entered the Carmelite Order, and then was at the Carmelite Monastery in Parma; later, at Imola Cathedral. He publ. 2 books of Masses for 4 voices, with instruments *ad libitum* (1670); 2 books of Psalms for 4 voices; *Psalmi per tutto l'anno . . . ,* with a fauxbourdon Mass, antiphons, and litanies (1669); and treatises: *Li primi albori musicali per li principianti della musica figurata* (1656; 5th ed., 1696); *Albori musicali per li studiosi della musica figurata* (1678); *Direttorio del canto fermo* (1689).

Pennario, Leonard, American pianist; b. Buffalo, July 9, 1924. He was taken to California as a child; studied piano there, and appeared in public at the age of 7; was soloist with the Dallas Symph. Orch. at 12, and with the Los Angeles Philharmonic at 15. He subsequently continued his studies (with Guy Maier); served in the U. S. Army Air Corps during World War II; then resumed his career, appearing with major American orchestras, and in recital. In 1951 and afterwards he made European tours, with excellent success.

Penny, George Barlow, American organist and composer of sacred music; b. Haverstraw, N. Y., June 30, 1861; d. Rochester, N. Y., Nov. 15, 1934. He studied in N. Y. with Dudley Buck (organ) and Percy Goetschius (composition); from 1890 to 1911 filled various positions as teacher and organist in Kansas; in 1911 was appointed director of the Rochester Cons., connected with the Eastman School of Music there. He made 9 European and 2 Oriental tours as organist, lecturer, and conductor; publ. several services for the Episcopalian Church, and other sacred music.

Pente, Emilio, Italian violinist and music editor; b. Padua, Oct. 16, 1860; d. Sachsa, Germany, May 14, 1929. He studied at the Milan Cons.; made a special study of the works of Tartini, and recovered about 40 Tartini MSS, which he arranged for publication in Germany; also presented 'concerti Tartiniani' in Florence and Milan;

toured in Europe as violinist; from 1909 to 1928 taught at the Guildhall School of Music in London; then went to Germany. He edited the following works of Tartini: 6 sonatas for 2 violins and cello (arranged as piano quartets); 4 sonatas for 2 violins and cello; 5 trios for 2 violins and piano; 2 string quartets; *Allegro festoso* for violin and piano; *Preludio e Variazioni* in A minor; concerto in D minor, for violin and string orch.; concerto in G major, for violin and orch.; 6 sonatas for violin and piano (in collaboration with C. Angelelli); 11 sonatas and a *Minuetto variato* for violin and piano (with M. Zanon); edited works by Albinoni, Geminiani, Giardini, Nardini, and Vivaldi. He also wrote some original violin pieces (17 opus numbers).

Pentenrieder, Franz Xaver, German composer; b. Kaufbeuren, Bavaria, Feb. 6, 1813; d. Munich, July 17, 1867. He studied with Kalcher and Stunz; became conductor at the court opera; wrote a successful opera, *Die Nacht zu Paluzzi* (Munich, Oct. 2, 1840; performed widely in Germany), and a comic opera, *Das Haus ist zu verkaufen* (Leipzig, 1846); a number of church works; songs. As the result of an accident, he became insane, and spent the last few years of his life in an asylum.

Pepin, Clermont, Canadian composer; b. St. Georges de Beauce, May 15, 1926. He studied in Quebec and Montreal; then with Scalero at the Curtis Institute, Philadelphia; also in Paris with Honegger (1949-51). —Works: symph. No. 1 (1948); 2 piano concertos (1946; 1949); symph. poem *Guernica,* after Picasso (Quebec, May 17, 1953); 2 string quartets (1948); a piano sonata (1947); études for piano; songs.

Pepöck, August, Austrian operetta composer; b. Gmunden, May 10, 1889; studied in Vienna with Heuberger and R. Fuchs; was conductor of theater music; then began to write operettas: *Mädel ade!* (Vienna, Oct. 5, 1930), *Der Reiter der Kaiserin* (Vienna, April 30, 1941), etc.; also composed chamber music and sacred choruses.

Pepping, Ernst, German composer; b. Duisburg, Sept. 12, 1901. He studied with Gmeindl in Berlin; then taught at the Church Music School in Berlin-Spandau; was elevated to the rank of prof. in 1947; subsequently taught at the Hochschule für Musik. Through his long association with Lutheran church culture, he acquired a profound understanding of the proper style of vocal polyphonic music to German texts; wrote a *Deutsche Choralmesse* (1930); *Choralbuch* (1931); *Deutsche Messe* (1938); *Spandauer Chorbuch,* a collection of choral works for the entire church year, in 20 vols. (1934-41); Te Deum (1956); also secular works a cappella: *Sprüche und Lieder* (1930); *Das Jahr* (1942); *Der Morgen* (1942); 33 folksongs for children's voices (1947); 3 symphonies (1939; 1943; 1947); partita for orch. (1934); a suite for trumpet, saxophone, and trombone (1926); 2 string quartets; string trio; 4 piano sonatas; organ works (*Grosses Orgelbuch,* 4 vols.); songs; books: *Stilwende der Musik* (1934) and *Der polyphone Satz* (1943; 2nd ed., 1950; Part II, 1957). —Cf. Karl Laux, *Ernst Pepping,* in *Musik und Musiker der Gegenwart* (Essen, 1949; pp. 193-201).

Pepusch (pā'pŏŏsh), **John Christopher (Johann Christoph),** composer; b. Berlin, 1667; d. London, July 20, 1752. For a year he was taught by Klingenberg (theory) and Grosse (organ), but was obliged to complete his musical education by private study. He had a position at the Prussian court 1681-97; then went to Holland, and thence (1700) to London, joining the Drury Lane orch. as violinist, later as cembalist and composer; from 1707 adapting Italian airs to English operas, adding recitatives and songs. In 1710 he founded (with Needler, Gates, Galliard, and others) the 'Academy of Ancient Music,' famous for the revival of 16th-century compositions; 1712, organist and composer to the Duke of Chandos, preceding Handel; 1713, Mus. Doc., Oxford; for many years director of Lincoln's Inn Theatre, for which he wrote the masques *Venus and Adonis* (1715), *Apollo and Daphne* (1716), *The Death of Dido* (1716), *The Union of the Three Sister-Arts* (1723), and arranged music to the ballad-operas *The Beggar's Opera, Polly,* and *The Wedding.* In 1724 his scheme for founding a college in the Bermudas with Dr. Berkeley was frustrated by shipwreck. In 1730 a fortune of £10,000, brought him by marriage with the singer Marguerite de l'Épine, rendered him independent. From 1737 till death he was organist of the Charterhouse. Pepusch was a learned, though conservative, musician, and a high authority in England before Handel. He publ. a *Treatise on Harmony* (1731), the final attempt of the kind to revive solmisation; an essay on the 3 genera of the Greeks is in the 'Philosophical Transactions' of 1746. His odes and cantatas, and the concertos and sonatas for strings and wind, are of slight importance.

—Cf. 'Dictionary of National Biography' (vol. XLIV); C. W. Hughes, *J. C. Pepusch*, in the 'Mus. Quarterly' (Jan., 1945).

Perabo, (Johann) Ernst, pianist; b. Wiesbaden, Germany, Nov. 14, 1845; d. Boston, Oct. 29, 1920. The family moved to New York in 1852. He studied with his father; then at the Leipzig Cons. with Moscheles (piano), Reinecke (composition), and others. Returning to America in 1865, he established himself as a concert pianist, and a highly successful teacher in Boston; had nearly 1,000 pupils, among them well-known musicians (Mrs. H. H. A. Beach was one of his pupils). He publ. a number of piano pieces: *Moment musical; Scherzo; Prelude; Waltz; Pensées; Circumstance, or Fate of a Human Life; Prelude, Romance, and Toccatina.* See the 'Dictionary of American Biography' (vol. XIV).

Peragallo, Mario, Italian composer; b. Rome, March 25, 1910. He studied with Casella; adopted a radical, quasi-dodecaphonic style. —Works: operas: *Ginerva degli Almieri* (Rome, Feb. 13, 1937), *Lo Stendardo di S. Giorgio* (1941), *La Gita in campagna* (La Scala, Milan, March 24, 1954); scenic cantata, *La Collina* (1947); concerto for orch. (1940); piano concerto; violin concerto (Conference of 20th Century Music, Rome, April 9, 1954; received the prize of 12,000 Swiss francs); double string quartet (1948); piano music.

Pereira-Salas, Eugenio, Chilean musicologist; b. Santiago, May 19, 1904. He studied in Santiago, at the Sorbonne in Paris, and later (on a Guggenheim Fellowship) at the Univ. of California, Berkeley (1933-34). Returning to Chile, he became prof. of American history at the Univ. of Chile. He publ. the important books on Chilean music: *Los Orígenes del arte musical en Chile* (1941) and *Juegos y alegrías coloniales de Chile* (1947), and various essays in music journals.

Pérez (pĕh'-rĕhth), **David,** composer of operas; b. Naples (of Spanish parents), 1711; d. Lisbon, Oct. 30, 1778. He was a pupil of Galli (violin) and Mancini (theory) at the Cons. di Loreto in Naples; presented his first opera, *Siroe,* at the San Carlo in Naples, on Nov. 4, 1740; in 1741, went to Palermo as maestro of the court orch., remaining there until 1748. He then lived the life of a traveling composer, visiting various cities in Italy, until 1752, when he was engaged as maestro di cappella at the royal chapel in Lisbon. In 1755 he visited London. Among his best operas are *Alessandro nell' Indie* (Genoa, Dec. 26, 1745), *Demetrio* (Venice, Spring, 1751), and *Solimano* (Lisbon, 1757; his most important dramatic work). As an opera composer, he was considered a worthy rival of Jommelli. He also wrote several Masses; a Miserere for 5 voices with bassoons obbligati and organ; *Mattutino de' morti,* for chorus and orch. (London, 1774); etc. —Cf. E. Soares, *David Pérez, Subsídios para a biografía do célebre mestre* (Lisbon, 1935); H. Kretzschmar, *Geschichte der Oper* (pp. 188-89).

Pérez Casas, Bartolomeo, Spanish conductor and composer; b. Lorca, near Murcia, Jan. 24, 1873; d. Madrid, Jan. 15, 1956. He studied at the Madrid Cons.; played the clarinet in various military bands; also was a bandmaster. He then established himself in Madrid as a teacher at the Cons.; from 1915 to 1936, conducted the Orquesta Filarmónica de Madrid. He wrote a lyric drama in one act, *Lorenzo;* an orchestral suite, *A mi tierra* (an early work, which became fairly popular); a string quartet; pieces for band.

Perfall, Karl von, German composer and conductor; b. Munich, Jan. 29, 1824; d. there, Jan. 14, 1907. He was a student of law; filled minor government positions before he began to study music; took music lessons with Hauptmann in Leipzig (1848-49); became conductor of the Munich 'Liedertafel' (1850); founded the Oratorio Society (1854); in 1864, was appointed intendant of the court music, and abandoned his activities as conductor. From 1867 to 1893 he was intendant of the court theater in Munich. Of his operas (all produced in Munich), *Raimondin* (March 27, 1881) and *Junker Heinz* (April 9, 1886) were fairly successful. He publ. *25 Jahre Münchener Hoftheater-Geschichte* (1892; covering the period from 1867); *Ein Beitrag zur Geschichte des königlichen Theaters in München* (1894); *Die Entwickelung des modernen Theaters* (1899).

Pergament, Moses, composer; b. Helsinki, Finland, Sept. 21, 1893. He studied at the St. Petersburg Cons.; 1913-15, was violinist in the Helsinki Symph. Orch. In 1915 he settled in Sweden; active as music critic in Stockholm since 1923. —Works: string quartet (1918); violin sonata (1920); ballet, *Vision* (1923); *Swedish Rhapsody,* for orch. (1940); violin concerto (1950); over 100 songs. Publ. a book on Jenny Lind (Stockholm, 1945).

Perger, Richard von, Austrian composer and conductor; b. Vienna, Jan. 10, 1854; d. there, Jan. 11, 1911. He studied cello and theory; was in the Austrian army during the campaign in Bosnia (1878); then received a stipend, and took lessons with Brahms (1880-82); was director of the Cons. of Rotterdam, Holland (1890-95); returning to Vienna, conducted the 'Gesellschaftskonzerte'; from 1899 to 1907, was director of the Vienna Cons. His music bears unmistakable evidence of the profound influence of Brahms. —Perger wrote the text and music of a comic opera, *Der Richter von Granada* (Cologne, 1889); the 'Singspiel' *Die 14 Nothhelfer* (Vienna, 1891); the musical fairy tale, *Das stählerne Schloss* (Vienna, 1904); also a violin concerto; some chamber music; songs; publ. a biography of Brahms (1908; new ed. by Hernried, 1934). His *Geschichte der K. K. Gesellschaft der Musikfreunde in Wien* was publ. posthumously (1912).

Pergolesi (per-goh-la'-zē), **Giovanni Battista,** remarkable Italian composer; b. Jesi, near Ancona, Jan. 4, 1710; d. Pozzuoli, March 16, 1736. The family's original name was Draghi; the surname Pergolesi was derived from the town of Pergola, where Pergolesi's ancestors lived. He was the only surviving child of his parents, three having died in their infancy. He studied music with Francesco Santi, choir director at Jesi Cathedral; was given a stipend by the Marchese Cardolo Pianetti, which enabled him to enter the Conservatorio dei Poveri at Naples; there, he was a pupil of Domenico de Matteis (violin) and Gaetano Greco (theory); later also studied with Durante and Feo. He became proficient as a violinist, and played on various occasions during the carnivals. His first performed work was an oratorio, *La Conversione di S. Guglielmo d'Aquitania* (which included a comic section in the Neapolitan dialect), presented at the monastery of S. Agnello Maggiore in Naples in the summer of 1731; another oratorio, *La Fenice sul rogo,* was performed in the same year; this was followed by a serious opera, *Salustia,* and an opera buffa, *Lo Frate 'nnamorato* (Naples, Sept. 23, 1732). In Dec., 1732 he was commissioned by the municipal authorities of Naples to write a solemn Mass as a votive offering after a series of severe earthquakes. On Aug. 28, 1733 Pergolesi presented a serious opera, *Il Prigionier superbo;* it contained a comic intermezzo, *La Serva padrona,* which was to become his most celebrated work. After a brief sojourn in Rome (May, 1734) to conduct his Mass at the San Lorenzo Church, he returned to Naples; there his new opera *Adriano in Siria* was produced, on Oct. 25, 1734, with an intermezzo, *Livietta e Tracollo* (performed at various times under different titles, *La Contadina astuta, La finta Polacca,* etc.). During another trip to Rome he performed his serious opera *L'Olimpiade* (Jan. 8, 1735), directing from the harpsichord, but it had little success. His last opera was a comic play, *Il Flaminio* (Naples, autumn, 1735). At that time his health was undermined by consumption; early in 1736 he went to Pozzuoli, where he died at the age of 26; he was buried in the common grave. His last completed work was a masterpiece of sacred music, *Stabat Mater.* Several dramatic works ascribed to Pergolesi and published under his name, notably *Il Maestro di musica* and *Il Geloso schernito,* are spurious.—The revival of his comic intermezzo *La Serva padrona* in Paris (1752) precipitated the so-called 'querelle des bouffons' between the supporters of the Italian and the French factions. Pergolesi's instrumental music is less known, and there are grave doubts as to the authenticity of many of these works published under his name: 14 trio sonatas (of these, 3 were ed. by Riemann, Berlin, 1900); 6 concertini for strings (publ. in London as works by Carlo Ricciotti); 3 'sinfonie' (string quartets); 2 concertos for flute and strings; sonata for violin and strings; 5 harpsichord sonatas. Stravinsky used some of these instrumental works for his ballet *Pulcinella,* but most of the borrowed material is not by Pergolesi. *La Serva padrona* was publ. in new editions by Abert (1911), Karl Geiringer, and others; *Flaminio* was ed. by Mortari (1942); the spurious *Il Maestro di musica* (which is in reality a pasticcio publ. in Paris in 1753) was orchestrated and ed. by Schering (1924); the intermezzo *La finta Polacca* was issued by Radiciotti (1914); the *Stabat Mater* was publ. by Eulenburg in A. Einstein's edition. Among other extant works attributed to Pergolesi are the oratorios, *Il Pentimento, La Morte d'Abel,* and *Septem verba;* 10 chamber cantatas; at least 5 Masses; still doubtful is the authenticity of many arias, including the popular *Tre giorni son che Nina.* A complete ed. of Pergolesi's works, *Opera Omnia,* was brought out in Rome (1940-42), in 5 vols. (148 works, of which 129 publ. for the first time; many are spurious). —Bibliography: P. Boyer, *Notices sur la vie et les ouvrages de Pergolèse,* in 'Mercure de France' (July, 1772); Marchese di Villarosa, *Lettera biografica intorno alla patria ed alla vita di G. B. Pergolesi* (Naples, 1831; 2nd ed., 1843); F. Villars, *La Serva padrona, son apparition à Paris en 1752, son influence, son analyse* (Paris, 1863); A. Gianandrea, *Pergolesiana* (Jesi, 1885); E. Faustini-Fasini, *G. B. Pergolesi attraverso i suoi biografi e le sue opere* (Milan, 1900); G. Radiciotti, *G. B. Pergolesi; vita, opere ed influenza su l'arte* (Rome, 1910; 2nd ed., Milan, 1935; in German, Zürich, 1954); A. Della Corte, *G. B. Pergolesi,* in *L'Opera comica italiana nel 1700* (vol. I, pp. 49-75; Bari, 1923); G. Radiciotti, *Tre giorni,* in 'Musica d'oggi' (July, 1925); A. Della Corte, *Pergolesi* (Turin, 1936); R. Giraldi, *G. B. Pergolesi* (Rome, 1936); G. de Saint-Foix, *Le deuxième centenaire de Pergolesi,* in 'Revue de Musicologie' (1936); special issues of 'Rassegna Musicale' (1936) and 'Musica d'oggi' (1936); H. Claydon, *Three String Quartets Attributed to Pergolesi,* in 'Music & Letters' (Oct., 1938); F. Schlitzer, *G. B. Pergolesi* (Turin, 1940); S. A. Luciani, *G. B. Pergolesi: note e documenti* (Siena, 1942); E. J. Luin, *Fortuna e influenza della musica di Pergolesi in Europa* (Siena, 1943); F. Walker, *Two Centuries of Pergolesi Forgeries and Misattributions,* in 'Music & Letters' (Oct., 1949); C. L. Cudworth, *Notes on the Instrumental Works Attributed to Pergolesi,* in 'Music & Letters' (Oct., 1949); F. Walker, *Pergolesi Legends,* in 'Monthly Mus. Record' (1952); F. Walker, *'Orazio': The History of a Pasticcio,* in the 'Mus. Quarterly' (July, 1952). For a complete list of pamphlets publ. in Paris during the 'querelle des bouffons' see L. Reichenburg, *Contribution à l'histoire de la Querelle des Bouffons* (Philadelphia, 1937); for details of performances, alternative titles, etc., consult A. Loewenberg, *Annals of Opera* (Cambridge, 1943; new ed., 1955).

Peri, Jacopo, Italian composer; called 'Il Zazzerino' from his abundant hair, b. Florence, Aug. 20, 1561; d. there, Aug. 12, 1633. Of noble family, he studied at Lucca under Cristoforo Malvezzi; was maestro at the court of Ferdinando I and Cosimo II de' Medici, and from 1601 at the court of Ferrara. A participant in the Florentine circle at the houses of Counts Bardi and Corsi, where the revival of ancient Greek musical declamation was planned, Peri set to music Rinuccini's text of *Dafne* (1597). It was first performed at Corsi's palace in Florence, and played again at Pitti's palace. Peri followed it with a setting of Rinuccini's *Euridice* for the wedding of Maria de' Medici with Henry IV of France (produced Oct. 6, 1600). *Dafne* was the first 'opera,' or drama set to music in monodic style (i. e., vocal soli supported by instruments); this style was termed 'stile rappresentativo.' In 1608 Peri wrote for Mantua the recitatives of *Ariadne* (text by Rinuccini), while Monteverdi composed the arias. In the same year he submitted in Mantua an opera *Tetide* (text by Cini), which, however, was not produced. With Grazie, Signorini, and del Turco he wrote *Guerra d'amore* (Florence, 1615). No records are available showing that *Adone* (text by Cicognini), composed 1620, ever had a public performance. *La Precedenza delle dame* was produced at Florence in 1625, and Peri also collaborated with Gagliano on *La Flora* (Florence, Oct. 11, 1628). He published in 1609 *Le varie musiche . . .* in 1-3 parts, some to be sung with harpsichord or chitarrone, others to be played on the organ. Kiesewetter printed 3 madrigals *a* 4 in *Schicksale und Beschaffenheit des weltlichen Gesanges* (1841). Fragments from *Euridice* are in several histories of music; a complete ed. was publ. by Guidi in Florence, and by Torchi in vol. VI of 'L'Arte Musicale in Italia'; a facsimile reprint was publ. in Milan, 1934; A. Schering's *Geschichte der Musik in Beispielen* contains 3 excerpts (Nos. 171a-c). —Cf. G. O. Corazzini, *Commemorazione della Riforma melodrammatica,* in the annual report of the 'Reale Instituto di Musica' (Florence, 1895); A. Solerti, *Le Origini del melodramma* (3 vols., Florence, 1905); O. G. Sonneck, *Dafne, the First Opera,* in 'Sammelbände der Internationalen Musik-Gesellschaft,' vol. XV (1913); M. Mila, *J. Peri,* in 'Rassegna Musicale' IV (1933). For details of productions of Peri's operas, see A. Loewenberg, *Annals of Opera* (Cambridge, 1943).

Périer, Jean, French tenor; b. Paris, Feb. 2, 1869; d. there, Nov. 3, 1954. He studied at the Paris Cons., obtaining 1st prize for singing (1892); was engaged at the Opéra-Comique. He created the role of Pelléas at the première of Debussy's opera (1902), and sang the leading tenor parts in several other premières of French operas; a talented comedian, he also appeared in variety shows in Paris. He publ. an instructive album, *Mes Exercises, tirés des chansons populaires de France.*

Perinello, Carlo, Italian editor and composer; b. Trieste, Feb. 13, 1877; d. Rome, Jan. 6, 1942. He studied music in Trieste and Leipzig; then taught at the Trieste Cons. (1904-14) and at the Milan Cons. He served on the staff of the Istituto Editoriale Italiano, and collaborated in the preparation of its publications.

Perini, Flora, Italian mezzo-soprano; b. Rome, Nov. 20, 1887. She studied with Zaira Falchi at the Santa Cecilia in Rome, where she graduated in 1907 as winner of the gold medal; made her début at La Scala, Milan, in 1908; then sang in Venice (1909), in Madrid and Buenos Aires (1910); in Bari, Rome, Montevideo, and Rio de Janeiro (1911); in Barcelona and Palermo (1912); in Turin and St. Petersburg (1913); in Trieste and Turin (1914); American début at the Metropolitan Opera House in Puccini's *Manon Lescaut,* Nov. 27, 1915; then was a regular member of the Metropolitan Opera Co. (1915-24). In 1924 she returned to Italy.

Perkins, Charles Callahan, American musician and painter; b. Boston, March 1, 1823; d. Windsor, Vt., Aug. 25, 1886. He was educated at Harvard Univ.; also studied in Italy and in Paris. In 1850 he became the head of the Handel and Haydn Society, in which position he exercised considerable influence on musical affairs in Boston; compiled (with John S. Dwight) vol. I of *History of the Handel and Haydn Society of Boston* (Boston, 1883). See the article on him in the 'Dictionary of American Biography' (vol. XIV).

Perkins, Francis Davenport, American music critic; b. Boston, Nov. 18, 1897. He studied at the New England Cons., at Trinity College, Cambridge, England, and at Harvard Univ. (B. A. *cum laude,* 1918). In 1919 he became exchange editor of the N. Y. 'Tribune' (which in 1924 became the N. Y. 'Herald Tribune'), from 1922 assistant music critic; also contributed numerous articles to various musical publications.

Perkins, Henry Southwick, American vocal teacher; b. Stockbridge, Vt., March 20, 1833; d. Chicago, Jan. 20, 1914. He studied voice at the Boston Music School (graduated in 1861); later, in Italy. He filled various administrative and educational posts in Iowa, Kansas, and Illinois; in 1890, founded the Chicago National College of Music; was active as director of music festivals and conventions across the country, from Maine to California. He was one of the organizers of the Music Teachers National Association in 1876; edited 30 song books, hymn books, class books; etc.; composed vocal quartets and songs.

Perkins, (David) Walton, American pianist and music critic; b. Rome, N. Y., Nov. 16, 1847; d. Chicago, Feb. 6, 1929. He was a pupil of Th. Kullak and Anton Rubinstein in Berlin; upon his return to America, he settled in Chicago; with William H. Sherwood, organized the Sherwood Music School in Chicago (1897); was its director until 1901. In 1906, became president of the Chicago Cons. of Music. He wrote music criticism in various Chicago newspapers; publ. *Piano Technique;* also piano pieces and songs; edited collections of choruses, and composed choral works.

Perkins, William Oscar, American vocal teacher and composer; brother of Henry Southwick Perkins; b. Stockbridge, Vt., May 23, 1831; d. Boston, Jan. 13, 1902. He studied voice in Milan; lived in Boston as a teacher; publ. about 40 collections of songs, anthems, etc., including many of his own pieces.

Perkowski, Piotr, Polish composer; b. Oweczacz, Nov. 17, 1902. He studied in Warsaw with Statkowski and in Paris with Albert Roussel. After 1945 he taught at the Warsaw Cons. —Works: ballet *Swantewit* (Poznan, June 19, 1948); 2 symphonies (1925; 1949); a sinfonietta; a piano concerto (1925); a violin concerto (1933); numerous sets of stylized Polish dances for piano; songs. In his early years he was influenced by abstract musical ideas; his *Geometrical Suite* for orch. (1930) is typical of that trend; later he followed the folkloric style.

Perle, George, American composer; b. Bayonne, N. J., May 6, 1915; studied with La Violette at De Paul Univ.; also took private lessons with Ernst Krenek. He was lecturer in music history at City College, N. Y. (1948); in 1949, was appointed instructor in music history and composition at the Univ. of Louisville. —Works: 2 symphonies, 3 string quartets, sonata for solo viola, works for band, piano sonatas, etc. In most of his music he follows the 12-tone technique of composition. He has contributed valuable articles on old music to various publications. —Cf. G. Chase, *America's Music* (N. Y., 1955; p. 611 ff.).

Perlea, Jonel, Rumanian conductor; b. Ograda, Dec. 13, 1900, of a German mother and a Rumanian father. He studied music in Munich and Leipzig; held posts as conductor in Leipzig and Rostock; from 1934-44 was conductor at the Bucharest Opera. During the last year of World War II he was interned in a German concentration camp. After 1945, he conducted opera in Italy, including regular appearances at La Scala. He made his American début at the Metropolitan Opera House, Dec. 1, 1949, in *Tristan und Isolde;* also was guest conductor with several American and European symphony orchestras. In 1955 he was appointed conductor of the Connecticut Symph. Orch. He has written a violin concerto, several orchestral works, and chamber music.

Perne (pärn), **François Louis**, French music scholar; b. Paris, Oct. 4, 1772; d. there, May 26, 1832. He studied with Abbé d'Haudimont at the maîtrise of St.-Jacques-de-la-Boucherie; was chorus singer at the Paris Opéra in 1792; double-bass player in the orch. there, 1799. His profound skill in composition was illustrated by his writing a triple fugue, to be sung backwards on reversing the page; his knowledge of old music was extraordinary. In 1813 he became prof. of harmony at the Paris Cons., as successor to Catel; he became inspector-general of the Cons. in 1816, and librarian in 1819. In 1822 he went into retirement, at an estate near Laon; returned to Paris shortly before his death. He publ. *Exposition de la séméiographie, ou notation musicale des Grecs* (1815), *Cours d'harmonie et d'accompagnement* (1822), *Chansons du Châtelain de Coucy* (1830), and a great number of articles on Greek and medieval music publ. in vols. I-IX of the 'Revue Musicale' edited by Fétis. He also wrote several pieces of sacred music.

Perosi, Don **Lorenzo,** distinguished Italian composer of church music; b. Tortona, Dec. 20, 1872; d. Rome, Oct. 12, 1956. He studied music at the Cons. of Milan (1892-93); also took courses at Haberl's School for Church Music at Regensburg (1894); became maestro di cappella at Imola, and then at San Marco in Venice. He was ordained priest in 1896; in 1898 became musical director of the Sistine Chapel, and leader of the papal choir; he resigned this post in 1915 owing to a severe mental disturbance; spent some time in a sanitarium (1922-23). Regaining his health after treatment, he returned to active service as choral conductor and composer. Shortly after his 80th birthday, he led a performance of his oratorio *Il Natale del Redentore* at the Vatican, before Pope Pius XII (Dec. 28, 1952). He was a self-denying and scholarly worker for the cause of the cultivation of a pure church style, both in composition and in performance, and was esteemed above all others as a church musician by his colleagues and at the Vatican. His *magnum opus,* the sacred trilogy *La Passione di Cristo* (I. *La Cena del Signore;* II. *L'Orazione al monte;* III. *La Morte del Redentore*), was produced in Milan, Dec. 2, 1897, at the Italian Congress for Sacred Music, and had numerous performances elsewhere in Europe and America. Other oratorios are: *La Trasfigurazione del Nostro Signore Gesù Cristo* (Venice, March 20, 1898); *La Risurrezione di Lazaro* (Venice, July 27, 1898, in La Fenice Theater, by special permission); *La Risurrezione di Cristo* (Rome, Dec. 13, 1898); *Il Natale del Redentore* (Como, Sept. 12, 1899); *L'Entrata di Cristo in Gerusalemme* (Milan, April 25, 1900); *La Strage degli innocenti* (Milan, May 18, 1900); *Mosè* (Milan, Nov. 16, 1901); *Dies Iste* (Rome, Dec. 9, 1904); *Transitus Animae* (Rome, Dec. 18, 1907); *In Patris memoriam* (Naples, May 15, 1919); *Giorni di Tribulazione* (Milan, Oct., 1916). He wrote further some 40 Masses with organ; a Requiem with instrumental accompaniment; a *Stabat Mater* for solo voices, chorus, and orch.; *Vespertina Oratio,* for solo voices, chorus, and orch.; about 150 motets, Psalms, etc.; 2 symph. poems, *Dovrei non piangere* and *La Festa del villaggio;* a series of 8 orchestral pieces, each named after an Italian city: *Roma, Firenze, Milano, Venezia, Messina, Tortona, Genoa, Torino;* other orchestral works; a piano concerto; a violin concerto; chamber music; many organ works. —Bibliography: I. Seytre, *L'Abbé Perosi: sa biographie, son œuvre* (Nice, 1901); Romain Rolland, *Don Lorenzo Perosi,* in *Musiciens d'aujourd'hui* (Paris, 1914; in English, N. Y., 1915); A. Damerini, *Lorenzo Perosi* (Rome, 1924); E. Carabella, *L'Oratorio musicale e la 'Risurrezione di Cristi' di Lorenzo Perosi* (Milan, 1924); Z. Musmeci, *Don Lorenzo Perosi e le sue opere* (Acireale, 1932); A. Della Corte, *Lorenzo Perosi* (Turin, 1936); A. Paglialunga, *Lorenzo Perosi* (Rome, 1952); M. Glinski, *Lorenzo Perosi* (Milan, 1953).

Perotin (called **Perotinus Magnus**), celebrated composer of the 12th century; the greatest master (after Leonin) of the Notre Dame School, representing the flowering of the 'Ars antiqua.' He was maître de chapelle at 'Beatae Mariae Virginis' (before the erection of Notre-Dame), Paris. Among his extant works are 'organa' in 2, 3, and 4 parts. His melodic writing differs from the practice of Leonin in that he employs triadic progressions; there is also a suggestion of rudimentary canonic procedures. His most famous quadruple organum, *Sederunt principes,* was publ. by R. Ficker in 1930, and appears in several collections of medieval music. Other works are in Coussemaker's 'L'Art harmonique au XIIe et XIIIe siècles'; vol. I of 'Oxford History of Music'; Y. Rokseth, 'Motets du XIIIe siècle' (1936); Davison and Apel, 'Historical Anthology of Music' (vol. 1, 1946); etc. —Cf. R. Ficker, in 'Neue Musikzeitung' (1928, 2); J. Handschin, in 'Schweizerisches Jahrbuch für Musikwissenschaft' (vol. II); F. Ludwig, in the 'Riemann-Festschrift' (1909), the 'Archiv für Musikwissenschaft' (vol. III), the 'Zeitschrift für Musikwissenschaft' (vol. V), Guido Adler's 'Handbuch der Musikgeschichte' (1930), and the 'Adler-Festschrift' (Vienna, 1930). See also H. Besseler, *Die Musik des Mittelalters und der Renaissance* (Potsdam, 1931-35); G. Reese, *Music in the Middle Ages,* chap. 11 (N. Y., 1940); J. Chailley, *Histoire musicale du moyen-âge* (Paris, 1950); W. Waite, *The Rhythm of Twelfth-Century Polyphony* (New Haven, 1954).

Perrin, Harry Crane, British organist and pedagogue; b. Wellingborough, Aug. 19, 1865; d. Exeter, England, Nov. 6, 1953. Pupil in Dublin of Sir R. Stewart, Dr. C. W. Pearce, and Dr. F. Bates; Mus. Bac., Dublin, 1890; F.R.C.O., 1892; Mus. Doc., 1901; 1892-98, organist and choirmaster at St. Michael's, Coventry; 1898-1908, at Canterbury Cathedral, and conductor of the Cathedral Musical Society; 1908-30, prof. of music and director of the Cons., McGill Univ., Montreal, Canada (from 1920, dean of the faculty there); 1930, retired as dean-emeritus, and returned to England. —Works: cantatas; overture and suite for orch.; numerous church services and anthems; song cycles, part-songs, etc.

Perrin (pĕhr-ran'), **Pierre,** French poet; b. Lyons, c. 1616; d. Paris, April 25, 1675. Author of the librettos for the first French operas (so called): Cambert's *La Pastorale* (1659), *Pomone* (1671), and *Ariane* (1672). The privilege obtained from Louis XIV by Perrin and Cambert to organize an 'Académie de musique' (1668) was revoked in Lully's favor (1672). —Cf. A. Pougin, *Les vrais créateurs de l'opéra français, Perrin et Cambert* (Paris, 1881); H. Prunières, *Lully and the Académie de Musique et de Danse,* in the 'Mus. Quarterly' (Oct., 1925).

Perry, Edward Baxter, American pianist; b. Haverhill, Mass., Feb. 14, 1855; d. Camden, Maine, June 13, 1924. He early lost his sight; was taught by J. W. Hill at Boston; studied later in Germany under Kullak, Clara Schumann, Pruckner, and Liszt. Returning to America, he originated the 'lecture-recital'; visited every state of the Union, appearing in over 3,000 piano recitals, and an equal number of 'lecture-recitals'; 1881-83, prof. of music at Oberlin College; 1897-98, concertized in Europe; 1917, appointed dean of fine arts and director of music at the Woman's College, Montgomery, Alabama. —Works: a *Loreley* fantasia, *The Lost Island,* and other piano pieces; a string quartet; wrote *Descriptive Analyses of Piano Works* (1902) and *Stories of Standard Teaching Pieces* (1910). —Cf. 'Dictionary of American Biography,' vol. XIV (1934).

Perry, George, English composer; b. Norwich, 1793; d. London, March 4, 1862. He was a choir boy at the Cathedral of Norwich; moved to London in 1822, and became director of the music at the Haymarket Theatre; then organist of Quebec Chapel; 1832-47, concertmaster of the Sacred Harmonic Society orch. —Works: the oratorios *Elijah and the Priests of Baal* (1818), *The Fall of Jerusalem* (1830), *The Death of Abel* (1846), *Hezekiah* (1847); a cantata, *Belshazzar's Feast* (1836); 2 operas, *Morning, Noon and Night* (1822), *Family Quarrels* (1830); overture to *The Persian Hunters;* anthems, songs, piano pieces. —Cf. 'Dictionary of National Biography,' vol. XLV (1896).

Persiani (*née* Tacchinardi), **Fanny,** Italian coloratura soprano; b. Rome, Oct. 4, 1812; d. Paris, May 3, 1867. Her father, the tenor Nicola Tacchinardi, was her teacher. After a successful début at Leghorn in 1832, she sang in the principal cities of Italy; from 1837-47 she appeared in London and Paris with brilliant success; also visited Holland and Russia, but returned to Paris in 1858. —In 1830 she married Giuseppe Persiani (1804-69), a composer of 11 operas. —Cf. G. Tebaldini, *G. Persiani e F. Tacchinardi, memorie ed appunti,* in the 'Rivista Musicale Italiana' (vol. 12).

Persichetti, Vincent, outstanding American composer; b. Philadelphia, June 6, 1915. He studied piano with Alberto Jonás and Olga Samaroff; composition with Paul Nordoff and Roy Harris; conducting with

Fritz Reiner. In 1942 he was appointed head of the dept. of composition at the Philadelphia Cons.; in 1948, joined the staff of the Juilliard School of Music, N. Y.; wrote (with Flora Rheta Schreiber) the monograph *William Schuman* (N. Y., 1954). Persichetti's music is remarkable for its contrapuntal compactness, in a synthetic style, amalgamating the seemingly incompatible idioms of different historical epochs; the basis is tonal, but the component parts often move independently, creating polytonal combinations; the rhythmic element is always strong and emphatic; the melody is more frequently diatonic than chromatic or atonal. —Works: 4 symphonies: No. 1 (1942; Rochester, Oct. 21, 1947); No. 2 (1942); No. 3 (Philadelphia, Nov. 21, 1947); No. 4 (Philadelphia, Dec. 17, 1954); concertino for piano and orch. (Rochester, Oct. 23, 1945); *Dance Overture* (Tokyo, Feb. 7, 1948); *Fables,* for narrator and orch. (Philadelphia, April 20, 1945); *The Hollow Men,* for trumpet and string orch. (Germantown, Dec. 12, 1946); *Divertimento* for band (N. Y., June 16, 1950); *Fairy Tale,* for orch. (1950); *Pageant,* for band (Miami, March 7, 1953); *Symphony for Strings* (Louisville, Aug. 28, 1954); a series of serenades for various groups: No. 1, for 10 wind instruments (1929); No. 2, for piano (1929); No. 3, for violin, cello, and piano (1941); No. 4, for violin and piano (1945); No. 5, for orch. (Louisville, Nov. 15, 1950); No. 6, for trombone, viola, and cello (1950); No. 7, for piano (1952); No. 8, for piano, 4 hands (1954); *King Lear,* ballet music for 7 instruments (Martha Graham Co., Montclair, N. J., Jan. 31, 1949); 2 string quartets (1939; 1944); suite for violin and cello (1940); sonata for solo violin (1940); 2 piano quintets: No. 1 (1940); No. 2 (Library of Congress, Washington, Kroll String Quartet and the composer, Feb. 4, 1955; his most remarkable chamber music work); violin sonata (1941); *Pastoral* for woodwind quintet (Philadelphia, April 20, 1945); *Vocalise* for cello and piano (1945); sonata for unaccompanied cello (1952); 9 piano sonatas; 6 piano sonatinas; 3 sets of *Poems* for piano; sonata for 2 pianos (1940); concerto for piano 4 hands (1952); *The Little Piano Book* (1953); Magnificat for chorus and organ (1940); *Two Chinese Songs* (1945); *3 Canons for Voices* (1947); several choruses; harpsichord sonata (1951); a sonatina for organ (pedals alone); etc. —Cf. Robert Evett, *The Music of Vincent Persichetti,* in the 'Juilliard Review' (Spring, 1955).

Persinger, Louis, American violinist and teacher; b. Rochester, Ill., Feb. 11, 1887. He studied with Hans Becker at the Leipzig Cons., 1900-04, making his début at a Cons. concert on March 23, 1904; then went for further study to Ysaÿe in Brussels (1905-08); also coached with J. Thibaud in Paris; 1909-11, he made successful tours of Germany, Austria, and Scandinavia; 1912-13, first extended American tour; 1913-14, another tour of Germany; 1914-15, concertmaster of the Berlin Philharmonic; 1915-17, with the San Francisco Symph. Orch.; 1916-28, director and 1st violin of 'The Chamber-Music Society of San Francisco'; 1929-30, prof. of violin at the Cleveland Institute of Music; 1930, succeeded Leopold Auer at the Juilliard Graduate School, N. Y. His pupils include Yehudi Menuhin and Guila Bustabo. He has publ. transcriptions and arrangements for violin. In 1913 he married the pianist Angela Gianelli (d. 1954); remarried in 1956.

Perti, Jacopo Antonio, Italian composer; b. Crevalcore, near Bologna, June 6, 1661; d. there, April 10, 1756. A pupil of Padre Petronio Franceschini, as early as 1680 he brought out a Mass, and next year was elected a member of the Accademia Filarmonica, of which he was five times the president. After spending several years as an opera composer at Parma, he became maestro at San Pietro in Bologna (1690), and in 1696 maestro at San Petronio. He wrote 24 operas, the most successful of which was *Il Furio Camillo* (Venice, 1692), and 19 oratorios; publ. the oratorio *Abramo vincitor de' propri affetti* (1687), *Cantate morali e spirituali* (1688), and *Messe e salmi concertati* (1735). His MSS were dispersed; Abbate Santini possessed a valuable collection. Extant works include 4 Passions and 8 oratorios at Bologna, an *Adoramus Te* in the Fitzwilliam Collection, Cambridge, 2 fine choruses in Novello's 'Sacred Music,' and other compositions in various collections. —Cf. L. Mancini, *J. A. Perti* (Bologna, 1813); G. Atti, *Orazione in lode di I. A. Perti* (1844); an extended biography of Perti is found in L. Busi's *Il Padre Giamb. Martini* (Bologna, 1891; vol. I, p. 61 et seq.); F. Giegling, *G. A. Perti,* in 'Die Musikforschung' (1955, No. 4).

Pessard (pĕhs-sahr'), **Émile-Louis-Fortuné,** French composer; b. Paris, May 29, 1843; d. there, Feb. 10, 1917. Pupil in the Paris Cons. of Bazin (harmony), Laurent (piano), Benoist (organ), and Carafa (composition); won the 1st harmony-prize in 1862, and the

Grand Prix de Rome in 1866 with the cantata *Dalila* (Opéra, 1867). In 1881 he was appointed professor of harmony at the Paris Cons. —Works: *La Cruche cassée* (Opéra-Comique, 1870); *Le Char* (Opéra-Comique, 1878); *Le Capitaine Fracasse* (1878); *Tabarin* (Opéra, 1885); *Tartarin sur les Alpes* (1888); *Don Quichotte* (1889); *Les Folies amoureuses* (Opéra-Comique, April 15, 1891; his most successful comic opera); *Une Nuit de Noël* (1893); *Mlle. Carabin* (1893); *Le Muet* (1894); *La Dame de trèfles* (1898); *L'Armée des Vierges* (1902); *L'Épave* (1903); etc. Also Masses, orchestral suites, a piano trio, piano pieces, etc. He enjoyed considerable regard as a composer of fine songs. Debussy copied Pessard's song *Chanson d'un fou,* and the MS in Debussy's handwriting was publ. erroneously as Debussy's own.

Pessl, Yella (real Christian names **Gabriela Elsa**), harpsichordist, organist, and pianist; b. Vienna, Jan. 4, 1906. She studied with Alexander Wunderer; joined the Vienna Bach Society, of which Wunderer was president, and played the organ at its concerts at an early age; later was engaged as a harpsichordist at various performances in Vienna. She made her first American appearance in 1931; with the exception of a few tours of Europe, established herself in N. Y.; taught at Columbia Univ.; in 1937 founded the Bach Circle in N. Y.; one of her specialties was the integral performance of Bach's *Musical Offering.*

Pestalozzi, Heinrich, Swiss composer; b. Wädenswil, near Zürich, Aug. 26, 1878; d. Zürich, Aug. 10, 1940. He studied theology and music in Berlin; was singing teacher there (1902-12); then pastor in Arosa, Switzerland; in 1917 was appointed voice teacher at the Zürich Cons. His many songs and choral works have enjoyed great popularity in Switzerland; a full list is found in Refardt's 'Musikerlexikon der Schweiz.' Pestalozzi publ. several manuals on singing: *Individuelle Stimmbildung; Kehlkopfgymnastik; Die deutsche Bühnenaussprache im Gesang; Geheimnisse der Stimmbildung; Der Weg zu einer schönen Stimme.*

Petchnikov, Alexander, violinist; b. Elets, Russia, Feb. 20, 1873; d. Buenos Aires, Nov. 3, 1949. He was a pupil of Hřimalý at the Moscow Cons., where he won the gold medal; then toured Europe and (1906-07) America; lived several years in Berlin; 'royal prof.' in 1910; 1913-21, prof. at the Royal Academy in Munich; then returned to Berlin, where he founded a string quartet in 1924; 1927, made prof. at the Stern Cons. there. He concertized frequently with his wife, Lily, also an excellent violinist.

Peter, Johann Friedrich, organist and composer; b. Heerendijk, Holland (of German parentage), May 19, 1746; d. Bethlehem, Pa., July 13, 1813. Was educated in Holland and Germany; came to America in 1770. A 'Moravian,' he served his church in various capacities in Nazareth, Bethlehem, and Lititz, Pa., and in Salem, N. C. (1779-89), where he married. He spent the rest of his life mostly in Bethlehem as organist of the church. He was the most conspicuous figure among the Moravians in America. His collection of copies of instrumental works by Stamitz, J. C. F. Bach, and J. Ch. Bach, Abel, Boccherini, and Haydn (preserved in the Archives of the Moravian Church) proves his knowledge of contemporary music. He began to compose in 1770. While at Salem he wrote (in 1789) a set of six quintets for 2 violins, 2 violas, and cello (his only secular works), which appear to be the oldest preserved examples of chamber music composed in America; they were publ., under the editorship of H. T. David, in 1955, for the N. Y. Public Library series, 'Music of the Moravians in America.' His anthems (more than 80) for chorus and with strings and organ, or with woodwinds, strings and organ, are well written, often quite expressive, and evidently constitute the finest and most elaborate concerted church music written in America at that time. Those preserved in the Archives of the Moravian Church at Bethlehem are listed in A. G. Rau's and H. T. David's 'A Catalogue of Music by American Moravians' (Bethlehem, Pa., 1938). —Cf. A. G. Rau, *J. F. Peters,* in the 'Mus. Quarterly' (July, 1937); H. T. David, *Musical Life in the Pennsylvania Settlements of the Moravians,* in 'Proceedings' of the Moravian Historical Society (Bethlehem, 1939); H. T. David, *Background for Bethlehem: Moravian Music in Pennsylvania,* in 'Magazine of Art' (April, 1939). See also 'Dictionary of American Biography' XIV.

Peter, Simon, 'Moravian' composer; brother of Johann Friedrich Peter; b. Heerendijk, Holland (of German parentage), April 2, 1743; d. Salem, N. C., May 29, 1819. With his brother, he was educated at Moravian Brethren's schools in Holland and Germany; came to America in 1770. His ministry was spent in both the Northern and Southern Provinces of the Moravian Church.

From 1784 to 1819 he lived in North Carolina as pastor of several congregations, and was a member of the governing board of the Church. He composed only a few sacred anthems, but one of these, *O Anblick, der mirs Herze bricht,* may well be one of the most expressive of all Lenten songs written in America. —Cf. H. T. David, *Musical Life in the Pennsylvania Settlements of the Unitas Fratrum,* in 'Transactions of the Moravian Historical Society' (1942).

Peterkin, Norman, English composer; b. Liverpool, Dec. 21, 1886. He studied piano and violin; lived in China, where he participated in theatrical activities as composer and conductor. From 1925 till 1947, he was on the staff of the music department of the Oxford Univ. Press. He wrote several ballets, a piano concerto, a piano trio, and other music, some of which has been published.

Peters (pā'-tĕrs), **Carl Friedrich,** German music publisher; b. Leipzig, March 30, 1779; d. there, Nov. 20, 1827. In 1814 Peters purchased Kühnel & Hoffmeister's 'Bureau de Musique' (established in 1800; Hoffmeister left the firm in 1805; Kühnel was the sole owner from 1805 to his death in 1813). The firm was thenceforward known as 'C. F. Peters, Bureau de Musique.' Its rich catalogue contained the first edition of collected works of J. S. Bach; it also included music by Beethoven, who entrusted to the 'Bureau de Musique' the publication of his 1st symph., piano concerto, op. 19, septet, op. 20, piano sonata, op. 22, and other works. Later on C. F. Peters acquired works by Weber, Spohr, Czerny, Chopin, Schumann, Wagner, Liszt, and Brahms. In more recent times the works of Mahler, Grieg, Hugo Wolf, Max Reger, Richard Strauss (his 7 symph. poems), and others were publ. From 1868, classical works were publ. in the inexpensive and reliable 'Edition Peters.' Its large and important musical library was opened to the public in 1893 as the 'Bibliothek Peters.' Scholarly annual books ('Peters Jahrbuch') were publ. until 1941, containing articles by eminent musicologists, current bibliography, etc. Dr. Max Abraham (q.v.) was sole proprietor from 1880 to 1900. After his death in 1900, his nephew, Heinrich Hinrichsen (b. Hamburg, Feb. 5, 1868; d. Belgium, Sept., 1942), became head of the firm; from 1927 to 1932 he shared the ownership with his son, Max Hinrichsen (b. Leipzig, July 6, 1901); soon afterwards, two other sons joined the firm—in 1933 Walter Hinrichsen (b. Leipzig, Sept. 23, 1907), and in 1934 Hans Hinrichsen (b. Leipzig, Aug. 22, 1909; d. Perpignan, France, 1941). The Litolff catalogue was acquired by Peters in 1938. Heinrich Hinrichsen was still in charge in 1939, when the Nazi regime finally forced him into exile, and Johannes Petschull was appointed manager in his stead. After World War II the firm was divided into three separate but closely affiliated companies—Peters Edition, London, under the direction of Max Hinrichsen; C. F. Peters Corporation, New York, owned by Walter Hinrichsen; and the German firm, since 1950 in Frankfurt, under the management of Johannes Petschull. See **Hinrichsen, Max,** and **Hinrichsen, Walter.**

Peters, Roberta, American soprano; b. New York, May 4, 1930. She studied singing with William Pierce Herman; made her operatic début with the Metropolitan Opera, N. Y., as Zerlina in *Don Giovanni* on Nov. 17, 1950 (as a substitute on short notice) and subsequently remained on the roster, singing with excellent success such roles as Rosina in *Il Barbiere di Siviglia,* Susanna in *Le Nozze di Figaro,* and Gilda in *Rigoletto.* She was married to Robert Merrill in 1952 (divorced); married Bertram Fields in 1955.

Petersen, Wilhelm, composer; b. Athens, March 15, 1890; d. Darmstadt, Dec. 18, 1957. He studied in Germany, at the Munich Academy with Mottl, Klose, and others (1908-12); was opera coach in Lübeck for a season (1913-14); was in the German army during World War I; then music critic in Munich (1919-22); in 1922 settled in Darmstadt; was instructor in music theory at the Akademie der Tonkunst there (1927-35); in 1935 became prof. of theory at the Cons. of Mannheim; then was again in Darmstadt; from 1945, taught privately in Heidelberg. —Works: opera, *Der goldne Topf* (Darmstadt, March 29, 1941); 4 symphonies: No. 1 (Nuremberg, 1921), No. 2, *Ostersinfonie* (Kassel, 1923), No. 3 (Darmstadt, 1934), No. 4 (Ludwigshafen, 1941); sinfonietta, after the 1st string quartet (1934); *Eine Trauermusik* (1913); 3 string quartets; 2 violin sonatas; a Mass (1929); many sacred works; songs.

Petersilea, Carlyle, American pianist and teacher; b. Boston, Jan. 18, 1844; d. Tropico, near Los Angeles, June 11, 1903. He studied at the Leipzig Cons. with Moscheles, Reinecke, and others, winning a prize. After a tour in Germany, he returned to Boston; established there the 'Petersilea Academy of Music' (1871); after 15 years, he closed his own school to become a teacher at the New England Cons. (1886); in 1892, went to California. He spent the spring of 1884 with Liszt at Weimar. He publ. technical studies and various pieces for piano.

Peterson, Franklin Sivewright, Scottish music pedagogue; b. Edinburgh, Feb. 24, 1861; d. Melbourne, July, 1914. He studied in Germany; returned to Edinburgh in 1884, and taught there; in 1901 went to Australia; was prof. of music at Melbourne Univ. He publ. *Elements of Music* (1895; 9th ed., 1899); *Introduction to the Story of Music* (1897); *Pianist's Handbook* (1899); *Catechism of Music* (1900).

Peterson-Berger, (Olof) Wilhelm, Swedish composer; b. Ullånger, Feb. 27, 1867; d. Östersund, Dec. 3, 1942. He studied with J. Dente and O. Bolander at the Stockholm Cons. (1886-89); then in Dresden with H. Scholtz (piano) and E. Kretschmer (composition). After 2 years in Dresden as a music teacher, he settled in Stockholm, where he became music critic of 'Dagens Nyheter' (1896). He was stage director for the Wagner repertory at the Stockholm Opera (1908-10); translated into Swedish some of Wagner's literary works. In Sweden he enjoyed a great reputation both as composer of national music and as critic. A symposium of articles was publ. in Stockholm on the occasion of his 70th birthday (1937). —Works: *Sveagaldrar,* a festival play for the silver jubilee of the accession of Oscar II (1897); a fairy opera, *Lyckan* (*Luck;* Stockholm, 1903); the music dramas, all produced at Stockholm, *Ran* (May 20, 1903), *Arnljot* (April 13, 1910), *Domedagsprofeterna* (1919), *Adils och Elisiv* (Feb. 27, 1927); 5 symphonies with programmatic subtitles: *Baneret* (Stockholm, Feb. 23, 1904), *Sunnanfärd* (Göteborg, March 22, 1911), *Same-Ätnam* (Stockholm, Dec. 11, 1917), *Holmia* (Stockholm, April 9, 1930), *Solitudo* (Stockholm, April 11, 1934); violin concerto (Stockholm, Feb. 6, 1929); orchestral ballads; *Carnival in Stockholm,* for orch.; several cantatas; 2 violin sonatas and other chamber music; several song cycles. —Writings: *Svensk Musikkultur* (1911); *Richard Wagner som kulturföreteelse* (*Wagner as a Phenomenon of Civilization,* 1913; in German as *Richard Wagner als Kulturerscheinung,* 1917). A selection of his essays was publ. in Stockholm in 2 vols. (1923); another, in 1 vol., in Östersund (1951). His reminiscences were publ. posthumously (Upsala, 1943). —Cf. B. Carlberg, *Peterson-Berger* (Stockholm, 1950).

Petit (pŭ-tē'), **Raymond,** French music critic and composer; b. Neuilly-sur-Seine, July 6, 1893. He studied music with Tournemire in Paris; lived there most of his life; contributed numerous articles on modern music to the 'Revue Musicale' and criticism to 'Le Ménestrel' as well as to some American publications. He wrote an opera, *La Sulamithe; Suite grave* for orch. (1920); *2 Méditations* for string quartet (1921); *Dialogue* for 2 violins; *Hymnus* for voice and flute (1924); *Il Cantico del sole,* for voice and wind instruments (Frankfurt Festival of the International Society for Contemporary Music, July 3, 1927); songs.

Petrassi, Goffredo, outstanding Italian composer; b. Zagarolo, near Rome, July 16, 1904. He worked as a clerk in a music store in Rome, studying musical compositions in his leisure time; began taking lessons at 21, first with Vincenzo di Donato and then with Alessandro Bustini at the S. Cecilia Academy in Rome; in 1939 was appointed prof. there. Despite the late beginning, Petrassi has acquired a solid technique of composition; the chief influence on him was that of Casella; later he became interested in 12-tone procedures. In 1955-56 he made a tour in the U. S. —Works: operas, *Il Cordovano* (La Scala, Milan, May 12, 1949) and *La Morte dell'Aria* (Rome, Oct. 24, 1950); ballets, *Ritratto di Don Chisciotte* (1945) and *La Follia di Orlando* (La Scala, Milan, April 12, 1947); for orch.: *Overture da concerto* (1931), *Partita* (1932), piano concerto (1939), 5 concertos for orch.: No. 1 (1934), No. 2 (1951), No. 3, subtitled *Recréation Concertante* (1953), No. 4, for strings (1954), No. 5 (commissioned by the Boston Symph. Orch. for its 75th season and performed in Boston, Dec. 2, 1955), *Invenzione concertata,* for brass, strings, and percussion (1957); chamber music: *Introduzione e Allegro* for violin and piano (1933; also for violin and 11 instruments), *Preludio, Aria e Finale,* for cello and piano (1933), *Sonata da Camera* for cembalo and 10 instruments (1948), *Dialogo angelico* for 2 flutes (1948), *Musica a due* for 2 cellos (1952); vocal works: *Psalm IX* (1936), *Magnificat* (1940), *Coro di Morti,* dramatic madrigal (1941), *Quattro Inni Sacri* for voice and organ (1942; also with orch., 1950), *Noche Oscura,* cantata with Spanish and Italian words (1950), *Nonsense* (to words by Edward Lear), for chorus a cappella (1952); also songs; *Invenzioni* for piano (1944). —See John S. Weissmann, *Goffredo Petrassi* (Milan, 1957; in English).

Petrauskas, Kipras, Lithuanian tenor; b. Vilna, Nov. 23, 1885. He studied with his brother, the composer Mikas Petrauskas; appeared in his brother's opera, *Birute* (Vilna, Nov. 6, 1906); then became a singer at the Imperial Opera, St. Petersburg (1911-20); also appeared in Berlin, Paris, Milan, and made a tour of the U. S. He returned to Lithuania before World War II, and remained there; in 1950 received the Stalin Prize.

Petrauskas, Mikas, Lithuanian composer; b. Kaunas, Sept. 29, 1873; d. there, March 23, 1937. He studied organ with his father; was church organist at the age of 15; then went to St. Petersburg, where he studied with Rimsky-Korsakov at the Cons. During the abortive revolution of 1905 he became implicated in various political activities and was imprisoned; he was briefly in Vilna, where he produced his opera *Birute* (Nov. 6, 1906); in 1907 he emigrated to America; settled in Boston in 1914, and founded the Lithuanian Conservatory in South Boston; with the aid of a Lithuanian chorus there, he produced his operas *The Devil Inventor* (3 acts; South Boston, May 20, 1923) and *Egle, Queen of the Snakes* (6 acts; South Boston, May 30, 1924; Petrauskas himself sang the part of the King of the Snakes); cantatas; etc. The Lithuanian Conservatory publ. the piano scores of his operas *The King of the Forest* (1918) and *Egle;* he also publ. arrangements of Lithuanian songs in the periodical 'Kankles' (Boston, 1917-21); further publ. a brief dictionary of musical terms in Lithuanian (Boston, 1916) and an album of Lithuanian songs (Boston, 1922). In 1930 he went back to Lithuania.

Petrella, Errico, Italian opera composer; b. Palermo, Dec. 1, 1813; d. Genoa, April 7, 1877. He studied at the Naples Cons. (Collegio di S. Sebastiano) as a pupil of Costa, Bellini, Ruggi, and Zingarelli. His first theatrical attempt was the 2-act opera buffa *Il Diavolo color di rosa* (Naples, 1829). Being successful, it was followed by some 20 operas, both comic and serious; *Le Miniere di Freibergh* (Naples, 1839) was his finest buffo work; *Elnava, o l'Assedio di Leida* (Milan, March 4, 1856), the best in the serious style. *Marco Visconti* (Naples, Feb. 9, 1854) obtained immediate popularity in Italy, and *La Contessa d'Amalfi* (Turin, March 8, 1864) also had a notable success. Other operas were *Ione,* after Bulwer Lytton's novel, *The Last Days of Pompeii* (Milan, Jan. 26, 1858), *Giovanni II di Napoli* (Naples, Feb. 27, 1869), *I promessi sposi* (Lecco, Oct. 2, 1869), and *Bianca Orsini* (Naples, April 4, 1874). During a quarter of a century he vied with Verdi in Italian favor, but his lack of a true sense of dramatic development and his dependence on Bellini and Donizetti as models caused his operas to appear old-fashioned without a redeeming freshness. Despite his many productions, he died in poverty. —Cf. F. Guardione, *Di Errico Petrella e della traslazione della salma da Genova a Palermo* (Palermo, 1908); G. Siciliano, *Di Errico Petrella, musicista palermitano* (Palermo, 1913).

Petrelli, Eleanora, Swedish soprano; b. Simtuna, April 9, 1835; d. Chicago, Feb. 21, 1904. Her maiden name was Wigström; while touring Finland as a member of a small theatrical company, she married a wealthy Russian named Petrov, and Italianized her married name to Petrelli. She studied in Milan with Lamperti, and in Paris with Mme. Viardot-Garcia. After her husband died in 1869, she virtually abandoned the stage, but continued to give concerts in Russia, Germany, and Scandinavian countries. In 1886 she settled in Stockholm, but soon went to Chicago, where she established a school for vocal culture. She publ. a number of songs.

Petri, Egon, distinguished pianist; b. Hanover, March 23, 1881; he was educated in a musical family; his father was the Dutch violinist, Henri Wilhelm Petri (1856-1914). He studied violin before he began to take piano lessons with Teresa Carreño. As a boy he played 2nd violin in a string quartet organized by his father in Dresden. He then went to Berlin, where he became a pupil of Busoni, who influenced Petri's own conception of piano playing as the fullest representation, by a single instrument, of the sonorities of an orchestra; he played with Busoni in London in 1921, in a concert for 2 pianos; made an extensive tour in Russia in 1923. He established himself as an eminent pedagogue in Europe; was teacher of piano at the Hochschule für Musik in Berlin (1921-26); presented a series of concerts in the U. S. (American début, N. Y., Jan. 11, 1932); then lived in Zakopane, Poland; in 1939 he settled in the U. S.; taught at Cornell Univ. (1940-46); in 1947 became prof. of piano at Mills College, Oakland, Calif. In the autumn of 1957 he returned to Europe, to teach advanced piano classes at the Academy of Music of Basel.

Petridis, Petro, Greek composer; b. Nigdé, Asia Minor, July 23, 1892. He studied at the American College in Constantinople and at the Univ. of Paris (political science); participated in the Balkan war of 1911-12 as a member of the Greek army; then returned to Paris, where he took lessons with Albert Wolff and Albert Roussel. He first essayed composition in 1917, with his songs, *Le Rayon* and *Berceuse;* continued to live in Paris, but also visited London and other European centers. In 1939 he went back to Athens; wrote there the oratorio *Saint Paul,* to celebrate the 1900th anniversary of St. Paul's sojourn in Greece. —Works: opera, *Zemphyra* (1923-25); oratorio, *St. Paul* (Athens, June 29, 1951, composer conducting); *A Byzantine Requiem* (1952); 5 symphonies (1928, 1940, 1941, 1943, 1951); *Panighiri,* suite of Greek tableaux for orch.; *Suite grecque; Suite ionienne;* piano concerto; chamber music; a number of songs.

Petrov (pět-rŏhv'), **Ossip Afanassievitch,** Russian basso; b. Elizavetgrad, Nov. 15, 1807; d. St. Petersburg, March 14, 1878. The intendant of the Imperial Opera accidentally heard him in 1830, singing with an inferior company at a fair in Kursk, and immediately engaged him. Petrov made his début in St. Petersburg as Sarastro in *The Magic Flute.* The enormous compass of his voice, its extraordinary power and beautiful quality, combined with consummate histrionic skill, secured for him recognition as one of the greatest of Russian bassos; this place he held throughout his long career (he appeared on the stage for the last time March 10, 1878, 4 days before his death). He created the roles of Sussanin in Glinka's *Life for the Tsar* (1836), Russlan in *Russlan and Ludmilla* (1842); the Miller in Dargomyzhsky's *Russalka* (1856), and Varlaam in Mussorgsky's *Boris Godunov* (1874).—Cf. *Recollections of the 50th Anniversary of O. A. Petrov* (St. Petersburg, 1876); V. Stassov, *O. A. Petrov,* in vol. III of his collected works (St. Petersburg, 1894); A. Kompaneisky, *A Great Russian Singer,* in 'Russkaya Muzykalnaya Gazeta' (1903, No. 9); E. Lastotchkina, *Ossip Petrov* (Moscow, 1950).

Petrucci (pěh-trōōch'-chē), **Ottaviano dei,** Italian music-publisher, the first to print a complete collection of part-songs from movable type; b. Fossombrone, June 18, 1466; d. there, May 7, 1539. In 1498 he received from the Council of the Republic of Venice the privilege of printing music by this new method for 20 years, and worked there industriously 1501-11, then ceding the business to A. Scotto and N. da Rafael, and removing to Fossombrone, with a 15-year privilege for printing within the Papal States. His editions, printed with great neatness, are rare and highly prized specimens of early press-work. In Fossombrone he labored from 1513-23. His publications appeared at the most flourishing epoch of the Netherlands School, and his first work, *Odhecaton* (1501), contains 96 numbers (modern ed. by Helen Hewitt, Cambridge, Mass., 1942), *Canti B.* (1502) and *Canti C.* (1503), 49 and 137, respectively, by famous composers before 1501. Petrucci's last publications were 3 books of Masses (1520-23) printed in folio as chorus books. Books I and IV of the 9 books of *frottole* publ. in Venice from 1504-08 by Petrucci were ed. by R. Schwartz in Jg. 8 of Th. Kroyer's 'Publikationen älterer Musik' (Leipzig, 1933-35). —Cf. A. Schmid, *O. d. Petrucci . . .* (Vienna, 1845; contains full list of works known at the time; Italian by B. Revel, in 'Bollettino bibliografico musicale,' Milan, 1931-33); A. Vernarecci, *O. d. Petrucci . . .* (Bologna, 2nd ed., 1882); J. B. Weckerlin, *Petrucci Harmonice musices odhecaton* (Paris, 1885); E. Vogel, *Der erste . . . Notendruck für Figuralmusik,* in 'Jahrbuch Peters' (1895; full list of contents of *Odhecaton*); M. Cauchie, *L'Odhecaton, recueil de musique instrumentale,* in 'Revue de musicologie' (Nov., 1925) and *A propos des trois receuils instrumentaux de la série de l'Odhecaton,* ib. (May, 1928); J. Marix, *Harmonice Musices Odhecaton. A,* ib. (Nov., 1935); K. Jeppesen, *Die neuentdeckten Bücher der Lauden des O. d. Petrucci,* in the 'Zeitschrift für Musikwissenschaft' (Nov., 1929); G. Reese, *The First Printed Collection of Part-Music: The Odhecaton,* in the 'Mus. Quarterly' (Jan., 1934); A. Catelani, *Due stampe ignote di O. Petrucci* (1856; reprinted in 'Bollettino bibliografico musicale,' Milan, 1932); C. Sartori, *A Little-Known Petrucci Publication,* in the 'Mus. Quarterly' (April, 1948); C. Sartori, *Bibliografia delle opere musicali stampate da O. Petrucci* (Florence, 1948). A facsimile ed. of the *Odhecaton* was publ. by the 'Bollettino bibliografico musicale' (Milan, 1932).

Petrus Platensis. See **La Rue.**

Petrželka (pěh-trzhěhl'-kăh), **Vilém,** noted Czech composer; b. Královo Pole, near Brno, Sept. 10, 1889. He studied in Brno with Janáček and in Prague with Novák. In 1910 he became Janáček's assistant at the School for Organists in Brno; in 1919, was appointed to the faculty of the Cons. of Brno.

In his compositions Petrželka continued the national tradition of modern Moravian music; he was mainly influenced by Janáček; but he expanded his resources, and upon occasion made use of jazz rhythms, quarter-tones, and other modernistic devices. —Works: *Věčný Návrat* (*Eternal Return*), symph. poem (Brno, Feb. 10, 1924); *Námořník Mikuláš* (*Mariner Nicholas*), symph. drama for recitation, soli, chorus, organ, jazz band, and orch., employing quarter-tones (Brno, Dec. 9, 1930); *Dramatic Overture* (Brno, March 26, 1933); *Partita*, for string orch. (Brno, May 3, 1935); *Sinfonietta* (Brno, Jan. 22, 1942); violin concerto (1942); 4 string quartets; *Z intimnich chvil* (*From Intimate Moments*) for violin and piano (1918); *Modlitba k slunci* (*Hymn to the Sun*) for chorus and orch. (Brno, Feb. 13, 1922); *Cesta* (*The Way*), song cycle for tenor and small orch. (also with piano; 1924); *Štafeta* (*The Courier*), songs with string quartet (1927); an opera, *Horník Pavel* (1935-38; not performed); a number of choruses; of these, the patriotic part-song for male chorus *To Je Má Zem* (*This Is My Land*), written and performed in 1940, is well known; also arrangements of folksongs; piano pieces. —Cf. L. Firkušný, *Vilém Petrželka* (Prague, 1946).

Petschnikoff. See **Petchnikov.**

Pettis, Ashley Burnett, American pianist and music scholar; b. Sutter Creek, Calif., Nov. 13, 1892. He studied in San Francisco, New York, and Berlin; taught at the Eastman School of Music, Rochester (1925-31) and later at Sarah Lawrence College, Bronxville, N. Y. In 1935 he established in N. Y. the Composers Forum Laboratory, as part of the educational program of the Federal Music Project; as its director for 15 years, he presented periodical concerts, each dedicated to works by one or two American composers. In 1951 he entered the priesthood of the Roman Catholic Church; resided in Rome. He publ. a book, *Music: Now and Then* (N. Y., 1955); collaborated with C. V. Bos in writing *The Well-Tempered Accompanist* (Bryn Mawr, 1949).

Petyrek, Felix, composer; b. Brno, May 14, 1892; d. Vienna, Dec. 1, 1951. He studied piano with Godowsky and Sauer; composition with Schreker at the Vienna Univ. (graduated in 1919). He taught piano at the Salzburg Mozarteum (1919-21); then at the Orchestral School of the Berlin Hochschule für Musik (1921-23); lived in Italy (1923-26); taught composition at the Odeon Athenon, in Athens (1926-30); from 1930 to 1939, at the Stuttgart Akademie für Musik; then went to Leipzig (until 1944); after 1945, settled in Vienna. Among modern composers, he occupied a fairly advanced position; in his melodic writing, he adopted the scale of alternating whole tones and semitones as a compromise between tonality and atonality. —Works: *Der Garten des Paradieses*, opera after Andersen (1923-41; Leipzig, Nov. 1, 1942); *Die arme Mutter und der Tod*, fairy play after Andersen with small orch. (Winterthur, 1923); the pantomimes *Tahi* and *Komödie; Die Litanei*, for boys' chorus, 2 trumpets, 2 harps, and percussion (Zürich Festival of the International Society for Contemporary Music, June 21, 1926); *Sinfonietta; Divertimento* for 8 wind instruments; piano trio; *Tänze*, for 2 flutes; sextet for clarinet, string quartet, and piano (Donaueschingen Festival, July 30, 1922); piano trio; songs; piano pieces.

Petz (Pez), Johann Christoph, German composer; b. Munich, Sept. 9, 1664; d. Stuttgart, Sept., 1716. He was employed as a chorister in Munich while still a child (1676-86); then resided in Liège and in Bonn (until 1705); in 1706 was appointed court conductor at Stuttgart, where he remained until his death. He publ. a set of 12 sonatas (Augsburg, 1696) under the title *Duplex Genius sive Gallo-italus Instrumentorum Concentus;* also a Psalm. Two of his operas were produced in Bonn. Instrumental and vocal works were publ. by B. A. Wallner in the 'Denkmäler der Tonkunst in Bayern' (vol. 27-28; 1928).

Petzet, Walter, German pianist, composer, and music editor; b. Breslau, Oct. 10, 1866; d. Dresden, Aug. 13, 1941. He studied with Kleffel in Augsburg; later at the Munich Academy with Rheinberger and others; in 1887 went to Minneapolis, where he taught piano until 1890; from 1891 to 1896 taught piano at the Scharwenka Cons. in N. Y.; in 1896 succeeded Busoni as prof. at the Helsingfors Cons.; from 1898 to 1910, was prof. at the Cons. of Karlsruhe; subsequently taught at the Weimar Cons. (1910-13), at the Klindworth Scharwenka Cons. in Berlin (1913-16), and at the Dresden Cons. (1917-21); lived mostly in Dresden. He wrote 2 piano concertos, numerous piano pieces, etc.; wrote music criticism for the 'Signale für die musikalische Welt.'

Petzold, Rudolf, composer and teacher; b. Liverpool, England (of a German father and English mother), July 17, 1908. He studied with Jarnach in Cologne; in 1946 was appointed teacher at the Hochschule für Musik there. He has written a number of orchestral works; also church music; a string trio; 2 string quartets; song cycles; pedagogical works.

Petzoldt, Richard, German musicologist; b. Plauen, Nov. 12, 1907. He studied in Berlin with Abert, Schering, Moser, Sachs, Hornbostel, Schünemann, and Blume; received his *Dr. phil.* with the dissertation *Die Kirchenkompositionen und weltlichen Kantaten Reinhard Keisers* (Düsseldorf, 1935). In 1934 he became editor of the 'Allgemeine musikalische Zeitung'; in 1939 went to Leipzig; in 1945 joined the faculty of the Univ. there; was editor of the periodical 'Musik in der Schule' (1949-54). —Publications: *Beethoven* (1938; 4th ed., 1947); *Schubert* (1940; 2nd ed., 1947); *Schumann* (1941; 2nd ed., 1947); *Mozart* (1948); *J. S. Bach und Leipzig* (1950); *Die Oper in ihrer Zeit* (1956); compiled iconographies of Bach (1950), Schubert (1953), Beethoven (1953), Tchaikovsky (1953); Handel (1955), Glinka (1955), Schumann (1956), Mozart (1956); wrote numerous articles for German publications.

Peuerl (Peurl, Bäwerl, Bäurl, Beurlin), Paul, Austrian organist; b. c. 1570; d. c. 1624. He was organist at Horn, Lower Austria (1602) and of the Protestant church school in Steyer (1609-24). He is generally acknowledged to be the originator of the German variation-suite; following the example of the lutenists, he expanded the earlier combination of pavane and galliard into a new 4-movement form for string quartet. He edited *Newe Padouan, Intrada, Däntz und Galliarda* (1611); *Weltspiegel, das ist: Neue teutsche Gesänge* (1613); *Ettliche lustige Padovanen, Intrada, Galliard, Couranten und Däntz sampt zweyen Canzon zu 4 Stimmen* (1620); *Gantz Neue Padouanen, Auffzüg, Balletten, Couranten, Intraden und Däntz* (1625). Selections from his works, ed. by Karl Geiringer, appeared in the 'Denkmäler der Tonkunst in Österreich' (vol. 70). —Cf. E. Noack, *Ein Beitrag zur Geschichte der älteren deutschen Suite,* in the 'Archiv für Musikwissenschaft' (vol. II, 2); P. Nettl, *Zur Lebensgeschichte Paul Peuerls,* in the 'Bulletin de la Société Musicologique' (vol. V, 1); K. Geiringer, *Paul Peuerl,* in 'Studien zur Musikwissenschaft' (vol. XVI; Vienna, 1929; pp. 32-69); E. Mohr, *Die Allemande* (Zürich, 1932; p. 70 ff.); H. J. Moser, *Die Musik im frühevangelischen Österreich* (Kassel, 1953; p. 37 ff.).

Pevernage, Andries, Flemish composer; b. Courtrai, 1543; d. Antwerp, July 30, 1591. He was a boy chorister in Courtrai; then was chorusmaster at Bruges (1563); returned to Courtrai and help the post of chorusmaster at a church there from 1564 until 1585, when he went to Antwerp as master of the choristers at the Cathedral. He was greatly honored there, and was buried in the Cathedral itself. He wrote a number of vocal works, sacred and secular. Three books of his spiritual chansons were publ. in 1589, 1590, and 1591; other collections were publ. posthumously. —Cf. J. A. Stellfeld, *Andries Pevernage* (Louvain, 1943).

Peyko, Nicolay Ivanovitch, Russian composer; b. Moscow, March 25, 1916. He studied with Miaskovsky at the Moscow Cons., graduating in 1939. He then was commissioned to collect folksong materials in the remote Yakutsk district of Siberia; wrote a *Suite on Yakutsk* themes for orch. (1941); then investigated Bashkir music, and composed a Bashkir opera, *Aykhylu;* also a Tartar ballet, *Spring Winds* (1950). Other works include 3 symphonies (1944; 1946; 1950) and a *Suite on Russian Themes* for orch. (1949); *Festive Overture* on Kabardin themes (1951); a *Concert Fantasy* on Finnish themes, for violin and orch. (1953); piano concerto (1954); piano pieces; songs. His most successful work is a *Moldavian Suite,* for orch. (Moscow, Dec. 14, 1950).

Peyser, Ethel Rose, American writer on music; b. New York, March 6, 1887. She was educated at Vassar College, Barnard College, and Teachers College, N. Y.; was a member of the editorial dept. of the N. Y. 'Tribune' (1912-14), N. Y. 'Evening Mail' (1914); music critic of the 'Musical Leader' (1926-34). She wrote *How to Enjoy Music* (N. Y., 1933), *The Book of Culture* (1934), and *The House That Music Built* (on Carnegie Hall; N. Y., 1936). Together with Marion Bauer, she publ. the successful books on music history *How Music Grew* (N. Y., 1925; 2nd rev. ed., 1946) and *Music Through the Ages* (N. Y., 1932); also *How Opera Grew* (N. Y., 1956).

Peyser, Herbert Francis, American music critic, b. New York, Aug. 6, 1886; d. there, Oct. 19, 1953. He studied in Germany and

France; returning to America, he took the B. A. degree at Columbia Univ. (1909). From 1909 to 1920 he was music critic of 'Musical America'; then assistant to Henry T. Finck on the N. Y. 'Evening Post' and (from 1924 to 1940) associate music critic of the N. Y. 'World Telegram.' In 1930 he became foreign music correspondent of the N. Y. 'Times' in Berlin, Vienna, and Paris (until 1939). In 1940 he returned to N. Y. For 4 seasons (1949-53) he was program annotator for the N. Y. Philharmonic; collaborated with L. Biancolli in the book *Masters of the Orchestra* (N. Y., 1953).

Pezel (Petzold, Petzel, Pezelius, etc.), **Johann Christoph,** German musician; b. Calau, 1639; d. Bautzen, Oct. 13, 1694. He was a municipal trumpeter in Leipzig (1664-81) and Bautzen; publ. several collections of pieces for wind instruments: *Musica vespertina Lipsica* (1669); *Hora decima* (1670); *Intraden* (1676); *Deliciae musicales* (1678), etc. His most interesting work is *Fünffstimmigte blasende Musik* (Frankfurt, 1685; 3 pieces arranged for modern brass ensemble by Robert D. King, and publ. in Wakefield, Mass.). Selections from various of his works were ed. by A. Schering in 'Denkmäler deutscher Tonkunst' (vol. 63).

Pfannstiehl, Bernhard, German organist; b. Schmalkalden, Dec. 18, 1861; d. Freiberg, Oct. 21, 1940. He became blind in infancy, and was educated at the Institute for the Blind in Leipzig; studied piano at the Leipzig Cons.; was thrice winner of the Mendelssohn Prize. Following Liszt's advice, he made a specialty of the organ; was church organist in Leipzig (1896-1903), in Chemnitz (1903-11), and at the Kreuzkirche, Dresden (1912-34). He enjoyed a great reputation as an interpreter of Bach. —Cf. K. Hasse, *Bernhard Pfannstiehl,* in 'Die Orgel' (1910).

Pfatteicher, Karl Friedrich, American specialist in church music and pedagogue; b. Easton, Pa., Sept. 22, 1882; d. Philadelphia, Sept. 29, 1957. He studied theology (Th. D. from Harvard Univ.); then went to Germany (Ph. D. from the Univ. of Freiburg); taught Latin and German at Lafayette College; in 1912 became prof. of music at Phillips Academy, Andover; held this post until 1947; in 1947-48, was lecturer in music, Trinity Univ., San Antonio, Texas; 1948-49, at Franklin and Marshall College, Lancaster, Pa.; in 1949, became lecturer in musicology at the Univ. of Pennsylvania. —Publications: *John Redford* (in English; Kassel, 1934); *The Christian Church Year in Chorals* (1917); *The Christian Church Year in Part Songs* (1915); *Thesaurus musicae sacrae* (1920); *The Oxford American Hymnal* (1930); was co-editor of *The Office Hymns of the Church in their Plainsong Settings* and *The Church Organist's Golden Treasury.*

Pfeiffer, Georges-Jean, French composer; b. Versailles, Dec. 12, 1835; d. Paris, Feb. 14, 1908. He began his career as a pianist; then was active as music critic in Paris; was a member of the firm Pleyel, Wolff et Cie., piano makers at Paris. —Works: operetta, *Capitaine Roche* (1862); 1-act opera, *L'Enclume* (Paris, 1884); comic opera, *Le Légataire universel* (Paris, 1901); an oratorio, *Hagar;* a symph. poem, *Jeanne d'Arc; Légende,* symph. fantasy for piano and orch.; many pieces of chamber music; also piano pieces.

Pfeiffer, Theodor, German pianist and pedagogue; b. Heidelberg, Oct. 20, 1853; d. Baden-Baden, Nov. 9, 1929. He studied piano with Hans von Bülow at Raff's Cons. in Frankfurt. In 1889 he settled in Baden-Baden as private teacher. He publ. a number of valuable studies: *Studien nach Kreutzerschen Violin-Etüden gebildet; Tonleiterschule; Virtuosen-Studien* (in part preparatory studies for Bülow's editions); also wrote a Mass, songs, men's choruses, and piano pieces (*Albumblatt, Dryadenspiel, Mazurka-Caprice, Konzert-Etüde,* etc.). His recollections of Bülow's remarks in teaching specific works were publ. as *Studien bei Hans von Bülow* (1894; 6th ed., 1909).

Pfitzner, Hans (Erich), eminent German composer; b. Moscow (of German parents), May 5, 1869; d. Salzburg, May 22, 1949. He studied at Hoch's Cons. in Frankfurt with James Kwast (piano) and Iwan Knorr (composition); married Kwast's daughter in 1899. He taught piano and theory at the Cons. of Coblenz (1892-93); was assistant conductor of the Municipal Theater in Mainz (1894-96); teacher at Stern's Cons. in Berlin (1897-1906); conductor in the Theater des Westens (1903-06). During the 1907-08 season he led the renowned Kaim Concerts in Munich. From 1908 to 1916 he was in Strasbourg as municipal music director and director of the Cons.; from 1910 to 1916, also 1st conductor at the Strasbourg Opera; conducted some concerts of the Munich Konzertverein (1919-20); then led a master class at the Berlin Academy of Arts (1920-29); prof. of composition at the Akademie der Tonkunst in Munich (1930-33); after that he devoted himself chiefly to composition, appearing frequently as guest conductor of his own works, and accompanist in recitals of his songs. In 1944 he went to Vienna; stricken by poverty and illness, he was taken to a home for the aged in Munich, and later to Salzburg. Charged with active participation in the cultural propaganda of the Nazi regime, he appeared before the Denazification Court in Munich in 1948, but was exonerated. —Pfitzner enjoyed great esteem in Germany as a national composer; his initial successes were considerable. When he presented a concert of his works in Berlin on May 12, 1893, he was hailed by the press as a talent of the first magnitude. After the 1st performance of his opera, *Der arme Heinrich,* in Mainz on April 2, 1895, the critics (Humperdinck among them) praised the work in extravagant terms; even more successful was his opera *Palestrina* (to his own libretto), produced in Munich on June 12, 1917. A Pfitzner Society was formed in Munich as early as 1904; and a Hans Pfitzner Association, in Berlin in 1938, with Furtwängler as president. Although his music was traditional in style and conservative in harmony, he was regarded as a modernist, a comrade-in-arms of Richard Strauss; very soon, however, his fame began to dwindle; there were fewer performances of his operas, and still fewer of his instrumental works; he himself bitterly complained of this lack of appreciation. Revivals of some of his best music (*Palestrina,* songs, etc.) were not supported by public interest. Outside Germany, his compositions are virtually unknown. —Works: operas: *Der arme Heinrich* (Mainz, April 2, 1895), *Die Rose vom Liebesgarten* (Elberfeld, Nov. 9, 1901), *Das Christelflein* (Munich, Dec. 11, 1906; revised version, Dresden, Dec. 11, 1917), *Palestrina* (Munich, June 12, 1917), *Das Herz* (Munich, Nov. 12, 1931); for orch.: 3 preludes from *Palestrina* (1917), symph. no. 1, in C♯ minor (arranged from string quartet no. 2, 1933), *Kleine Sinfonie* (1939), *Elegie und Reigen* (1940), symph. no. 2, in C major (1940), *Fantasie* (1947), piano concerto (1922), violin concerto (1923), 2 cello concertos (1935; 1944); chamber music: cello sonata (1890), piano trio (1896), 3 string quartets (1903; 1925; 1942), piano quartet (1908), violin sonata (1918), sextet for clarinet, violin, viola, cello, double-bass, and piano (1945); vocal works: *Der Blumen Rache,* ballad for contralto, women's voices, and orch. (1888), *Columbus,* for chorus a cappella (1905), *Gesang der Barden,* for men's chorus with instruments (1906), *Von deutscher Seele,* cantata for soli, chorus, orch., and organ (1921), *Das dunkle Reich,* for soprano, baritone, chorus, orch., and organ (1929), *Fons salutifer* for chorus and orch. (1942), *Herr Oluf,* ballad for baritone and orch. (1891), *Die Heinzelmännchen,* for baritone and orch. (1903); *Zwei deutsche Gesänge,* for baritone, men's chorus, and orch. (1916), *Lethe,* for baritone and orch. (1926), 106 songs for voice and piano. He further publ. arrangements and new editions of musical works by E. T. A. Hoffmann, Schumann, Marschner, and Loewe; also numerous essays and pamphlets, polemical in nature, with virulent attacks against modern ideas in theory; these were publ. as *Gesammelte Schriften* (Augsburg, 1926; 2 vols.; new ed. in 3 vols., Munich, 1929); also *Eindrücke und Erinnerungen* (Hamburg, 1947); *Über musikalische Inspiration* (Berlin, 1940); *Philosophie und Dichtung in meinem Leben* (Berlin, 1944). A list of Pfitzner's works was publ. by A. Berrsche (Munich, 1919; 2nd ed., 1926). —Bibliography: P. N. Cossmann, *Hans Pfitzner* (Munich, 1904); R. Louis, *Hans Pfitzners 'Die Rose vom Liebesgarten'—Eine Streitschrift* (Munich, 1904); R. Louis, *Hans Pfitzner* (Leipzig, 1907); A. Berrsche, *Hans Pfitzners 'Der arme Heinrich'* (1910); A. Seidl, *Hans Pfitzner* (1921); C. Wandrey, *Hans Pfitzner, seine geistige Persönlichkeit und das Ende der Romantik* (1922); W. Lütge, *Hans Pfitzner* (1924); E. Kroll, *Hans Pfitzner* (1924); 'Pfitzner-Festschrift' (1930); W. Abendroth, *Hans Pfitzner* (1935; basic biography); E. Valentin, *Hans Pfitzner: Werk und Gestalt eines Deutschen* (Regensburg, 1939); J. Müller-Blattau, *Hans Pfitzner* (Potsdam, 1940); H. Lindlar *Hans Pfitzners Klavierlied* (Würzburg, 1940); W. Abendroth, *Hans Pfitzner: sein Leben in Bildern* (Leipzig, 1941); J. Bahle, *Hans Pfitzner und der geniale Mensch* (Constance, 1949); Hans Rutz, *Hans Pfitzner: Musik zwischen den Zeiten* (Vienna, 1949); a symposium of articles, *Hans Pfitzner zum 75. Geburtstag* (Cologne, 1944); *Hans Pfitzner, ein Bild in Widmung, anlässlich seines 75. Geburstages,* ed. by W. Abendroth (Leipzig, 1944); *In Memoriam Hans Pfitzner* (Vienna, 1950).

Pflughaupt, Robert, German pianist; b. Berlin, Aug. 4, 1833; d. Aix-la-Chapelle, June 12, 1871. He studied with Dehn in Berlin, Henselt in St. Petersburg, and Liszt in Weimar. He wrote a number of agreeable piano pieces (*Petite valse, Mazurka, Galop de concert, Invitation à la Polka,* etc.). His wife, **Sophie Pflughaupt** (née Shtchepin; b. Dvinsk, Russia, March 15, 1837; d. Aix-la-Chapelle, Nov. 10, 1867), was also an excellent pianist, a pupil of Henselt and Liszt.

Pfohl, Ferdinand, writer on music; b. Elbogen, Bohemia, Oct. 12, 1862; d. Hamburg, Dec. 16, 1949. He studied law in Prague; in 1885, went to Leipzig, where he took private lessons in music with Oscar Paul. In 1892 he became the music critic of the influential 'Hamburger Nachrichten,' holding this important post until his retirement in 1932; also taught (from 1908) music theory and esthetics at Vogt's Cons. in Hamburg. —Publications: *Die moderne Oper* (1894); *Die Nibelungen in Bayreuth* (1897); *Arthur Nikisch als Mensch und Künstler* (Leipzig, 1900; 2nd ed., 1925); *Karl Grammann. Ein Künstlerleben* (Berlin, 1910); *Richard Wagner. Sein Leben und Schaffen* (1911; 4th ed., 1924); *Beethoven* (1922); also descriptions of African music: *Quer durch Afrika* (1891) and *West-Östliche Fahrten* (1902); publ. guides to Wagner's operas. His original compositions include the symph. poems *Die versunkene Glocke, Pierrot lunaire,* and *Frau Holle;* a symph. fantasy, *Das Meer;* male choruses; piano pieces; songs.

Pfordten, Hermann Ludwig von der, German writer on music; b. Munich, July 5, 1857; d. there, Nov. 16, 1933. He was the son of a Bavarian minister; studied in Munich and in Leipzig; became prof. of music history at the Univ. of Munich; he specialized in writing about Wagner's music. —Publications: *Handlung und Dichtung der Bühnenwerke Richard Wagners* (1893; 8th ed., 1922); *Musikalische Essays* (2 vols.; 1897; 1899); *Deutsche Musik* (1917; 3rd ed., 1922); *Der Musikfreund,* an introductory book on music (1923; 8th ed., 1928); *Einführung in Wagners Werke und Schriften* (3rd ed., 1925); popular biographies of Beethoven (1907; 4th ed., 1922), Mozart (1908; 3rd ed., 1926), Schubert (1916; 3rd ed., 1928), Weber (1919), Schumann (1920), and Robert Franz (1923).

Pfrogner, Hermann, Austrian musicologist; b. Graz, Jan. 17, 1911; studied law at the Univ. of Vienna; held various positions in financial institutions; studied musicology with E. Schenk (1945-47); in 1948 settled in Stuttgart. He has contributed numerous articles on modern harmony to various periodicals; publ. a fundamental essay dealing with 12-tone composition, *Die Zwölfordnung der Töne* (1953); also *Musik, Geschichte ihrer Deutung* (1954).

Pfundt, Ernst Gotthold Benjamin, celebrated German timpani player; b. Dommitzsch, near Torgau, June 17, 1806; d. Leipzig, Dec. 7, 1871. He studied theology, and at the same time developed an extraordinary ability as a drummer; was called by Mendelssohn in 1835 to join the Gewandhaus Orch., and remained there as drummer until his death; achieved legendary fame for his rhythmic skill. He was the inventor of the pedal kettledrums; publ. a method for drums (1849; 3rd ed., enlarged to include the snare-drum, by H. Schmidt, 1894).

Phalèse (făh-lehz'), **Pierre (Petrus Phalesius),** Flemish music publisher; b. Louvain, c. 1510; d. there, c. 1573. He established a music publishing business in 1545; the printing was done elsewhere, and it was not until 1553 that Phalèse began to print on the premises in Louvain. From 1570 he worked in association with Jean Bellère of Antwerp. After the death of Pierre Phalèse, the business was moved to Antwerp (1581), and was managed by his sons, Pierre Jr. and Corneille; continued under the management of the heirs until about 1674. Two compositions by Pierre Phalèse, the elder, are found in A. Schering's *Geschichte der Musik in Beispielen* (No. 134). —Cf. A. Goovaerts, *Notice biographique sur Phalèse* (1869); A. Goovaerts, *Histoire et bibliographie de la typographie musicale dans le Pays-Bas* (1880).

Phelps, Ellsworth C., American organist and composer; b. Middletown, Conn., Aug. 11, 1827; d. Brooklyn, N. Y., Nov. 29, 1913. Self-taught in music, he became organist in New London at the age of 19; settled in Brooklyn in 1857; held various positions as organist and taught in the public schools. He wrote several symphonic works in a programmatic genre, usually on American subjects: *Hiawatha* (1878), *Emancipation* (1880), etc.; pieces for military band (performed by Gilmore and Sousa), etc.; more than 200 pieces in all, in every style.

Phile (Fyles, Pfeil, Phyla, etc.), **Philip,** violinist and teacher; b. Germany, c. 1734; d. Philadelphia, between Aug. 1 and Nov. 9, 1793, in a yellow-fever epidemic. He served in the Pennsylvania German Regiment during the Revolutionary War; was transferred in July 1778 to the Invalid Regiment; discharged on Jan. 4, 1783; pension granted, July 11, 1785. He was active in Philadelphia and New York; gave concerts; played in theater orchestras; conducted the orchestra of the Old American Co. of Comedians. He was probably the composer of the music of the *President's March,* to which Joseph Hopkinson (son of Francis Hopkinson) wrote the words *Hail Columbia.* He also wrote a piece entitled *Harmony Music* for the series of summer concerts at Gray's Gardens in Philadelphia. —Cf. O. G. Sonneck, *Report on the 'Star Spangled Banner,' 'Hail Columbia,' etc.* (Washington, 1909); J. T. Howard, *Our American Music* (N. Y., 1931 and later eds.).

Philidor (real name **Danican**), famous family of French musicians.—(1) **Jean Danican-Philidor,** d. Paris, Sept. 8, 1679, as 'Phiphre de Grande Écurie' (piper in the King's military band).—(2) **André Danican-Philidor** (*l'aîné*), d. Dreux, Aug. 11, 1730. As a youth, he was cromorne player in the above band, later of the King's private band (oboe, cromorne, trompette marine, and bassoon). As assistant librarian of the Royal Music Library at Versailles, he made a fine MS collection of old instrumental pieces performed at court since the time of François I. A MS copy (35 vols.) of this collection is in the Library of Congress, Washington. He composed masques and ballets for the court, and military music (marches, etc.).—Publ. works: *Mascarade des Savoyards* (1700); *Mascarade du roi de la Chine* (1700); *Suite de danses pour les violons et hautbois . . .* (1699); *Pièces à deux basses de viole, basse de violon et basson . . .* (1700); *Marches et batteries de tambour . . . avec les airs de fifres et de hautbois.* — (3) **Anne Danican-Philidor,** André's eldest son; b. Paris, April 11, 1681; d. there, Oct. 8, 1728. A flute player, he composed pastoral operas (*L'Amour vainqueur,* 1697; *Diane et Endymion,* 1698; *Danaë,* 1701), and publ. music for flutes, violins, and oboes. He founded the Concert Spirituel (1725). —(4) **Pierre Danican-Philidor,** flute player; b. Paris, Aug. 22, 1681; d. there, Sept. 1, 1731. Publ. 3 books of suites for 2 transverse flutes (1717, 1718), and flute trios. —(5) **François André Danican-Philidor,** last and greatest of the family, the youngest son of André; b. Dreux, Sept. 7, 1726; d. London, Aug. 24, 1795. Campra was his teacher in music, but chess was for a long time his master passion, and after vanquishing many celebrated Continental players, he wrote an *Analyse du jeu d'échecs,* which he publ. in London in 1749, where he commenced a series of victories at the London Chess Club, later receiving a pension from the Club. From 1756 he appeared in the unexpected role of a successful composer of comic operas. His first stage work was *Le Diable à quatre,* an opera-pot-pourri, in 3 acts, arranged from popular airs. It was produced at the Opéra-Comique on Aug. 19, 1756; there followed the opera-ballet *Le Retour du printemps;* these were succeeded by several one-act pieces (*Blaise le savetier,* 1759; *L'Huitre et les plaideurs,* 1759; *Le Quiproquo ou Le Volage fixé,* 1760; *Le Soldat magicien,* 1760; *Le Jardinier et son seigneur,* 1761); then one of his best, in 2 acts, *Le Maréchal ferrant* (1761), performed over 200 times; followed by more one-act pieces (*Sancho Pança,* 1762; *Le Bûcheron, ou Les trois souhaits,* 1763). Then came *Le Sorcier,* in 2 acts (Jan. 2, 1764) and *Tom Jones,* in 3 acts (Feb. 27, 1765); the latter had great vogue, and contained a noteworthy novelty, a quartet a cappella. In 1767 appeared his finest effort, the grand opera *Ernelinde, princesse de Norvège* (Nov. 24, 1767; revised in 1769 as *Sandomir, prince de Danemark*). *Le Jardinier de Sidon* (1768), *L'Amant déguisé* (1769), *La nouvelle école des femmes* (1770), *Le bon fils* (1773), *Zémire et Mélide* (1773), *Berthe* (Brussels, 1775, with Gossec and Botson), *Les Femmes vengées* (1775), *Le Puits d'amour* (1779), *Persée* (1780), *L'Amitié au village* (1785), *Thémistocle* (1786), *La belle esclave* (1787), and *Le Mari comme il les faudrait tous* (1788) close the long list. A posthumous opera, *Bélisaire,* finished by Berton, was produced in 1796. —Philidor surpassed his rivals Grétry and Monsigny both in skilfulness of orchestration and richness and correctness of harmony, though he was their inferior in dramatic expression and melodic charm. He was adored by the Parisians; but his love for chess caused him to forsake them at frequent intervals for the neighbors across the Channel. He also wrote church music; a set of 12 *Ariettes périodiques* (in alternation with Trial) for vocal solo with violin, bass, oboe, and horn; *L'Art de la modulation,* quartets for 2 violins, oboe, and bass; etc. —Cf. J. Lardin, *Philidor peint par lui-même* (Paris, 1847); G. Allen, *The Life of Philidor* (Philadelphia, 1858); A. Pougin, *Philidor,* in 'Chronique musicale' (1874-75); Ch. Piot, *Particularités inédites concernant les œuvres musicales de Gossec et de Philidor,* in 'Bulletins de l'Académie royale de Belgique' (Brussels, 1875); G. E. Bonnet, *L'Œuvre de Philidor,* in the 'Revue Musicale' (Oct., 1921); G. E. Bonnet, *Philidor et l'évolution de la musique française au XVIIIe siècle* (1921); also 'Dictionary of National Biography,' XLV. For details on his operas, see A. Loewenberg's *Annals of Opera*.

Philipp (fĭ-lēp'), **Isidor,** eminent French pianist; b. Budapest, Sept. 2, 1863; d. Paris, Feb. 20, 1958 (as a result of injuries received from a fall in the subway). He was brought to Paris at the age of 3; entered the Paris Cons. at 16 as a pupil of Georges Mathias; won 1st piano prize in 1883; then took lessons with Saint-Saëns, Stephen Heller, and Ritter for about 4 years. He appeared as a soloist with several French orchestras; also in London and elsewhere in Europe; established a concert trio with Loeb and Berthelier; also was an active participant in the programs of the 'Société des instruments à vent' in Paris. In 1903 he was appointed prof. of piano at the Paris Cons.; as a teacher he met with extraordinary success. After the outbreak of World War II, he went to the U. S., arriving in New York on May 20, 1941; despite his advanced age, he continued to teach privately and in various schools in N. Y. and also in Montreal (until 1955); played the piano part in the Franck violin sonata at his farewell appearance in N. Y. (March 20, 1955); afterwards divided his time between France and N. Y. He composed a *Rêverie mélancolique* and a *Sérénade humoristique* for orch. and some piano pieces. Among his technical works for piano that have won high esteem are *Exercises journaliers, École d'octaves, Problèmes techniques, Études techniques basées sur une nouvelle manière de travailler, La Gamme chromatique,* etc.; also publ. numerous arrangements for 2 pianos of works by Bach, Mendelssohn, Saint-Saëns, and others; *La Technique de Liszt* (2 vols., Paris, 1932); wrote memoirs, etc. —Cf. Henry Bellamann, *Isidor Philipp,* in the 'Mus. Quarterly' (Oct., 1943).

Philippe de Mons. See **Monte.**

Philippe de Vitry. See **Vitry.**

Philips, Peter, important English composer and organist; b. 1561; d. Brussels, 1628. He belonged to a Catholic family; was probably a chorister at St. Paul's Cathedral; was befriended by a Catholic almoner, Sebastian Westcote, and received a bequest upon the latter's death in 1582. In that year, Philips left England; on Aug. 18, 1582 he arrived at Douai, where he presented himself at the English College; then proceeded to Rome, where he entered the service of Cardinal Alessandro Farnese; also was for 3 years organist at the English College in Rome (1582-85). In the autumn of 1585 Philips joined the household of Lord Thomas Paget in Rome, and subsequently traveled with him through Spain, France, and the Netherlands. From early 1587 until June 1588, Philips was with Paget in Paris; then went to Antwerp, remaining there until early 1589; also made visits to Brussels. After Paget's death in 1590, Philips settled in Antwerp, and was active there as teacher of keyboard playing. In 1593 Philips went to Amsterdam, where he met Sweelinck. On his return trip to Antwerp, he was detained at Middelburgh, was charged with planning the assassination of Queen Elizabeth, and was alleged to have participated with Lord Paget in the act of burning the queen in effigy in Paris. He stood trial in The Hague in Sept. 1593, but was released for lack of evidence. Late in 1593 he was back in Antwerp. In 1597 he moved to Brussels, entering the service of the Archduke Albert, as organist of the Royal Chapel. After Albert's marriage to Isabella of Spain (1599) Philips was officially designated as 'Organist to their Serene Highnesses the Archduke Albert and Isabella.' On March 9, 1610 he received a canonry at Soignies, but continued to reside in Brussels. On Jan. 5, 1621 he exchanged his title at Soignies for a chaplainship at Tirlemont; in 1623 he is also described as canon of Béthune. However, he continued to be designated canon of Soignies for many years afterwards, even in posthumous editions of his works, possibly because he was best known in that nominal post. Philips was highly esteemed in his day, and his works were printed in many collections; his music shows mixed Italian and Netherlandish characteristics; he excelled in madrigals and motets; his pieces for the virginals reveal a kinship with Sweelinck. Published works include: 4 madrigals in *Melodia Olympica di diversi eccellentissimi musici* (Antwerp, 1591); 2 vols. of madrigals for 6 voices (1596; 1603); 1 vol. of madrigals for 8 voices (1598); motets for 5 voices (1612); motets for 8 voices (1613); *Gemmulae sacrae,* for 2-3 voices, with continuo (1613); *Les Rossignols spirituels,* for 2-4 voices (1616); *Deliciae sacrae,* for 2-3 voices (1622); litanies for 4-9 voices (1623); *Paradisus sacris cantionibus conditus* (1628); other works listed in the catalogue of the library of King João IV of Portugal, publ. by Vasconcellos in 1873. W. B. Squire edited the madrigals *Amor che vuoi* for 4 voices (London, 1890) and *Dispiegate guancie amate,* for 8 voices in *Ausgewählte Madrigale* (Leipzig, 1906), and the motets *Hodie Sanctus Benedictus* for 5 voices (London, 1899) and *Ego sum panis vivus* (London, 1902); Sir Richard Terry, who contributed greatly to a revival of the music by Philips, publ. 4 motets for 5 voices in the collection 'Downside Motets' (London, 1904-05). 19 keyboard pieces are included in the 'Fitzwilliam Virginal Book,' .vol. 1 (1889); other keyboard pieces are found in various anthologies. — Cf. P. Bergmans, *L'Organiste des archiducs Albert et Isabelle, Peter Philips* (Ghent, 1903); C. Hughes, *Peter Philips; an English Musician in the Netherlands,* in 'Papers of the American Musicological Society, 1940' (Oberlin, 1946).

Phillipps, Adelaide, English contralto; b. Stratford-on-Avon, Oct. 26, 1833; d. Karlsbad, Oct. 3, 1882. When she was a child, her family went to America, settling in Boston; there she appeared as a dancer at the Tremont Theater (Jan. 12, 1842). She showed an early gift as a vocalist, and was introduced to Jenny Lind during the latter's American tour (1850); Lind started a subscription to enable her to study singing. She took lessons with Manuel Garcia in London; made her professional début in Milan, Dec. 17, 1854, as Rosina. Returning to Boston in 1855, she sang in light opera in English; her first appearance on the grand opera stage in America was as Azucena in Verdi's *Il Trovatore* (Academy of Music, N.Y., March 17, 1856). In 1861 she went to Europe; appeared in Paris, Madrid, Barcelona, and in various cities in Hungary and Holland, singing the Italian repertory. In 1879 she joined the 'Boston Ideal Opera Company,' with which she appeared for the last time on Nov. 30, 1880. Her final stage appearance took place in Cincinnati in Dec., 1881. She was advised to go to Karlsbad for her health in 1882, but died shortly after her arrival there. During her European engagements she sang under the name Signorina Filippi. —Cf. A. C. L. Waterston, *Adelaide Phillipps* (Boston, 1883).

Phillips, Burrill, American composer; b. Omaha, Nov. 9, 1907. He studied music with Edwin Stringham in Denver; and with Howard Hanson and Bernard Rogers at the Eastman School of Music, Rochester, N. Y.; upon graduation, appointed to the faculty of the Eastman School. He held a Guggenheim Fellowship (1942); also received a grant for creative work from the American Academy of Arts and Letters (1944). He writes in a neo-Classical style; successfully exploits American rhythms. In 1958 he was teaching at the University of Illinois. —Works: the ballets: *Play Ball* (Rochester, April 29, 1938) and *Step Into My Parlor* (1941); for orch.: *Selections from McGuffey's Reader* (Rochester, May 3, 1934), *Sinfonia Concertante* (Rochester, April 3, 1935), *American Dance,* for bassoon and strings (Rochester, April 25, 1940), *3 Satiric Fragments* (Rochester, May 2, 1941), piano concerto (1943), *Scherzo* (1944), *Tom Paine Overture* (N. Y., May 15, 1947); chamber music: a trio for trumpets (1937), a string quartet (1939), a violin sonata (1942), a cello sonata (1946), *Partita* for violin, viola, cello, and piano (Rochester, May 7, 1948), *Four Figures in Time,* for flute and piano (1953); *Declaratives* for women's voices and small orch. (1943); for piano: *Nine by Nine,* a set of 9 variations, each one in a meter of 9 (1942), *Toccata* (1944), *3 Informalities* (1945), *3 Divertimenti* (1946), etc.

Phillips, Montague Fawcett, English composer; b. London, Nov. 13, 1885. He studied composition with F. Corder at the Royal Academy of Music; subsequently was active as a church organist; also taught harmony at the Royal Academy of Music. He wrote a light opera, *The Rebel Maid* (London, 1921), which enjoyed some success; *The Song of Rosamund,* for soprano and orch.; *The Death of Admiral Blake,* for baritone, chorus, and orch.; *Charles II,* overture; a symphony; the orchestral suites, *Surrey, The World in the Open Air, In May Time, Dance Revels,* etc.; *A Shakespearean Scherzo* for orch.; 2 piano concertos; chamber music; choruses; piano pieces. Later works included *Empire March* for orch. (1941) and an overture, *In Praise of My Country* (1944).

Piastro, Josef, Russian-American violinist; b. Kerch, Crimea, Feb. 17, 1889. He studied with Auer at the St. Petersburg Cons.; then toured in Russia; came to the U. S. in 1920; became a citizen in 1926; was concertmaster of the Los Angeles Philharmonic; conducted children's concerts in Hollywood; also successful as a teacher. In America, he assumed the pseudonym Borissoff, to avoid confusion with his brother, Michel Piastro. He composed a *Crimean Rhapsody* for violin and piano (1920; orchestrated, and performed by the San Francisco Symph. Orch. Oct. 5, 1938).

Piastro, Michel, Russian-American violinist; brother of Josef Piastro; b. Kerch, Crimea, June 19, 1891; studied with Auer at the St. Petersburg Cons.; was in the Far East from 1914-19; settled in the U. S. in

1920; was concertmaster of the San Francisco Symph. Orch. (1925-31); and of the N. Y. Philharmonic under Toscanini (1931-37). In 1941 he became conductor of the radio orch. 'Longines Symphonette.'

Piatigorsky, Gregor, famous Russian cellist; b. Ekaterinoslav, April 20, 1903. He first studied with his father, a violinist; then took cello lessons with Alfred von Glehn; played in various orchestras in Moscow. In 1921 he left Russia; remained for some time in Warsaw; then went to Berlin, where he took lessons with Julius Klengel. He entered a competition for the first cello desk of the Berlin Philharmonic, and won it; held this position from 1924 to 1928; then devoted himself entirely to the career of a virtuoso; played the solo part in *Don Quixote* by Strauss under the composer's direction; made his American début with the N. Y. Philharmonic, on Dec. 29, 1929, playing the Dvořák concerto; after that he appeared with virtually every important orchestra in the U. S., in Europe, in South America; gave world premières of several cello concertos commissioned by him (Hindemith, Dukelsky, Castelnuovo-Tedesco, and others). From 1924 he taught advanced classes at the Curtis Institute of Music in Philadelphia; in 1957, engaged to teach a master class at Boston University.

Piatti, Alfredo Carlo, Italian cellist and composer; b. Bergamo, Jan. 8, 1822; d. there, July 19, 1901. Son of the violinist Antonio Piatti; pupil at first of Zanetti, and 1832-37 of Merighi at Milan Cons. Concert début at Milan, 1834; in 1838 his concert tours began; he played (1843) with Liszt at Munich, and next year in Paris. The same year he visited London, where he created a profound impression; after playing in Italy and Russia he returned to England in 1846, and met with such enthusiasm that he became an annual visitor; from 1846-49 he was 1st cello at the Italian opera, and from 1859-98 a leading figure in the Monday and Saturday Popular Concerts of chamber music. He combined marvelous technical skill with profound musicianship, and his influence on contemporary cellists may well be compared with that of Joachim on violinists.—Works: op. 18, concertino for cello and orch.; 2 concertos for cello and orch. (op. 24, in B♭; op. 26, in D minor); 6 sonatas for cello and piano (op. 28, C; op. 29, D; op. 30, F; op. 31, G, *idillica;* 2 others in MS); smaller pieces for cello and piano. Also edited 6 string sonatas by Boccherini and Locatelli, a sonata (op. 2) by B. Marcello, etc., Kummer's method for cello. —Cf. M. Latham, *Alfredo Piatti* (London, 1901).

Piccinni (Piccini) (pē-chēn'-nē), **Niccolò,** Italian opera composer; b. Bari, Jan. 16, 1728; d. Paris, May 7, 1800. Piccinni's father was a violinist at the Basilica di San Nicola in Bari, and his maternal uncle, Gaetano Latilla (1713-83), a well-known operatic composer. The innate ability of young Piccinni attracted the attention of the Archbishop of Bari, Muzio Gaeta, who arranged for him to enroll at the Cons. di Sant' Onofrio in Naples; there, at the age of 14, he began studying under the celebrated masters Leo and Durante; continued as a student for 13 years, and then became instructor at the same Cons. His first work, *Le Donne dispettose,* an opera buffa in the style made popular in Naples by Logroscino, was produced at the Teatro dei Fiorentini in 1754. He wrote 139 operas; in 1761 alone he produced 10 operas; 7 more followed in 1762. An instinct for the theater made him select librettos rich in dramatic content. His melodic invention was fresh, and his arias were written in a pleasing style eminently suitable to the voice. He elaborated the conventional climactic scenes so that dramatic interest was sustained to the end. He varied the tempos and the harmonies in the ensembles, which further contributed to the general effect. After modest successes in Naples with *Le Gelosie* (1755) and *Il Curioso del proprio danno* (1756), he went to Rome, where he produced his opera *Alessandro nelle Indie* (Jan. 21, 1758); later wrote another setting to the same subject (Naples, Jan. 12, 1774). Piccinni's greatest success in Rome was his comic opera *La buona figliuola,* to Goldoni's libretto based on Richardson's *Pamela* (Feb. 6, 1760; also produced in Italy as *La Cecchina nubile*); Piccinni wrote a sequel to it, *La buona figliuola maritata* (Bologna, June 10, 1761). Other operas produced in Rome were: *Le Contadine bizarre* (Feb. 10, 1763); *Gli Stravaganti* (Jan. 1, 1764; also performed under the title *La Schiava riconosciuta*); *Il Barone di Torreforte* (Jan. 10, 1765); *La Pescatrice* (Jan. 9, 1766); *Antigone* (1770); and *Le finte gemelle* (Jan. 2, 1771). Piccinni's fortunes declined with the rising popularity in Rome of a powerful rival, Anfossi; not wishing to compete, Piccinni returned to Naples, where he staged his opera *I Viaggiatori* with excellent success.—Piccinni's historical role was destined to be played on the international scene in Paris, where he went with his family in

Dec. 1776. His arrival in Paris precipitated one of the most famous controversies in music history, the 'querelle célèbre,' which was in essence a continuation of the 'Guerre des Bouffons' of 1752. In the later case, the Parisian public was sharply divided into two warring factions, one supporting the Italian operatic art as practiced by Piccinni, the other championing the operatic realism of Gluck. Piccinni himself had the highest regard for Gluck, and never encouraged the frenzied outbursts of the "Piccinnists." Gluck left Paris in 1780; at his death in Vienna (1787) Piccinni made plans to organize annual concerts in Paris in Gluck's memory, but failed to find financial support for his project. Piccinni's first opera in French, *Roland* (Jan. 27, 1778), had considerable success; he continued to use French librettos, producing several operas in close succession, of which the following were fairly well received: *Le Fat méprisé* (Paris, May 16, 1779); *Atys* (Paris, Feb. 22, 1780); *Iphigénie* (Paris, Jan. 23, 1781; fairly successful, despite the fact that Gluck's masterpiece on the same subject was produced 2 years before); *Didon* (Fontainebleau, Oct. 16, 1783; his most enduring work; separate arias have been reprinted many times); *Le Dormeur éveillé* (Paris, Nov. 14, 1783); *Le faux Lord* (Paris, Dec. 6, 1783); and *Pénélope* (Fontainebleau, Nov. 2, 1785). In 1778 Piccinni became director of the Italian troupe in Paris; in 1784 he was appointed 'maître de chant' at the newly-founded 'École royale de chant et de déclamation lyrique' in Paris, but lost this position after the Revolution and returned to Naples, where he subsisted on a small pension granted him by the King of Naples; went back to Paris in 1798, where he was received with public honors, and given a purse of 5,000 francs for immediate necessities; an honorary position of a 6th inspector was granted to him by the Paris Cons. (formerly 'Ecole royale de chant et de déclamation lyrique'). But Piccinni was too ill for active life; he retired to Passy, where he spent the last months of his life. Piccinni's operas are rarely performed in their entirety: *La Cecchina* was revived in Bari on his bicentenary, Feb. 7, 1928. —Bibliography: Ph. Coquéau, *Entretiens sur l'état actuel de l'opéra de Paris* (Paris, 1779; a discussion of the relative merits of Piccinni and Gluck in dialogue form); P. L. Ginguené, *Notice sur la vie et les ouvrages de Nicolas Piccinni* (Paris, 1800); G. Desnoiresterres, *Gluck et Piccinni* (Paris, 1872); E. Thoinan, *Notes bibliographiques sur la guerre musicale des Gluckistes et Piccinnistes* (Paris, 1878); H. Curzon, *Les dernières années de Piccinni à Paris* (Paris, 1890); H. Abert, *Piccinni als Buffokomponist,* in 'Jahrbuch Peters' (1913); G. de Napoli, *Nicola Piccinni nel secondo centenario della nascita* in the 'Rivista Musicale Italiana' (1928); A. Parisi, *Intorno al soggiorno di Nicola Piccinni in Francia* (ib., 1928); A. Della Corte, *Piccinni* (Bari, 1928); P. La Rotella, *Niccolò Piccinni* (Bari, 1928); N. Pascazio, *L'Uomo Piccinni e la 'Querelle célèbre'* (Bari, 1951). A complete list of Piccinni's operas is given by A. Cametti under the title *Saggio cronologico delle opere teatrali di Niccolò Piccinni* in vol. VIII of the 'Rivista Musicale Italiana' (also separately, Turin, 1901). See also A. Loewenberg, *Annals of Opera.*

Pichl, Wenzel, Bohemian violinist and composer; b. Bechin, Aug. 25, 1741; d. Vienna, June 4, 1804. He studied violin with Pokorny and composition with Seeger in Prague. In 1775 he was appointed chamber composer to Archduke Ferdinand at Milan; went with him to Vienna in 1796; also supplied musical entertainment to Viennese noblemen; he died during a concert at the palace of Prince Lobkowitz. He wrote about 700 works, including 12 operas, some 20 Masses, 89 symphonies (of which 66 are publ.), 13 serenades (3 of which were publ.), a great number of concertos for violin and other instruments with orch., 7 octets, 7 septets, 6 sextets, 21 quintets, 172 string quartets (of which 163 were publ.), 148 works for baryton, piano pieces, etc. His 6 fugues with a fugal prelude for violin alone became fairly popular (reprint, ed. by Kocian and Gardavsky, Prague, 1951).—Cf. R. Kolisko, *Wenzel Pichls Kammermusik* (Vienna, 1918).

Pick-Mangiagalli, Riccardo, Italian composer; b. Strakonice, Bohemia, July 10, 1882; d. Milan, July 8, 1949. He was of mixed Italian and Bohemian parentage; studied at the Cons. Giuseppe Verdi in Milan with Appiani (piano) and Ferroni (composition). He began his career as a successful concert pianist, but later turned exclusively to composition. In 1936 he succeeded Pizzetti as director of the Cons. Giuseppe Verdi, and held this post until his death.—Works: operas: *Basi e Bote* (Rome, March 3, 1927), *Casanova a Venezia* (La Scala, Milan, Jan. 19, 1929; an orchestral suite from it, entitled *Scene carnevalesche,* was performed in Milan, Feb. 6, 1931), *L'Ospite inatteso* (Milan-Turin-Genoa Radio network, Oct. 25, 1931; the first opera to be given a world première by radio anywhere), *Il Notturno romantico* (Rome, April 25, 1936); for the dance: *Il Salice d'oro,* mimo-drama (Milan, Sept. 18, 1918), *Sumitra* (Frankfurt, 1922), *Mahit,* ballet-fable with singing (La Scala, Milan, March 20, 1923), *La Berceuse* (San Remo, Feb. 21, 1933), *Variazioni coreografiche* (San Remo, April 13, 1935); for orch.: *Sortilegi,* symph. poem for piano and orch. (Milan, Dec. 13, 1917), *Notturno e rondo fantastico* (Milan, May 6, 1919), *Due preludi* (Rome, March 1, 1921), *Quattro poemi* (Milan, April 24, 1925), *Piccola suite* (Milan, June 12, 1927), *Preludio e fuga* (Rome, March 11, 1928), *Preludio e scherzo sinfonico* (Milan, Oct. 22, 1938); a violin sonata; a string quartet; piano pieces; songs. —Cf. G. M. Gatti, *Musicisti moderni d'Italia e di fuori* (2nd ed., Bologna, 1925); D. de Paoli, in the 'Bollettino bibliografico musicale' (1928).

Picka, František, Czech organist, conductor, and composer; b. Strašice, near Hořovice, May 12, 1873; d. Prague, Oct. 18, 1918. Of a musical family, he received a solid education in Prague; held several posts as chorus master and opera conductor. His opera, *Malíř Reiner* (*The Painter Reiner*), was produced in Prague (April 28, 1911) without success; the bulk of his works consists of church music, including 9 Masses and many other works in a traditional but effective contrapuntal style.

Pierné (p'yar-nā'), **(Henri-Constant-) Gabriel,** French composer, conductor, and organist; b. Metz, Aug. 16, 1863; d. Ploujean, near Morlaix, July 17, 1937. He studied at the Paris Cons. (1871-82), where his teachers were Marmontel (piano), César Franck (organ), and Massenet (composition); won 1st piano prize (1879), 1st prize for counterpoint and fugue (1881), and 1st prize for organ (1882); awarded the Grand Prix de Rome (1882) with the cantata *Édith;* succeeded César Franck as organist at Ste.-Clothilde, where he remained until 1898. In 1903 he was appointed assistant conductor to Colonne, and in 1910 his successor (until 1932); elected a member of the Académie des Beaux-Arts in 1925. He was a prolific composer, but of his many works only the oratorio *La Croisade des Enfants* and the piano piece, *Marche des petits soldats de plomb,* became popular. —Works: the operas *La Coupe enchantée,* (Royan, Aug. 24, 1895; revised verision, Opéra-Comique, Paris, Dec. 26, 1905), *Vendée* (Lyons, March 11, 1897), *La Fille de Tabarin* (Opéra-Comique, Paris, Feb. 20, 1901), *On ne badine pas avec l'amour* (Opéra-Comique, Paris, May 30, 1910), *Sophie Arnould,* 1-act lyric comedy, based on episodes from the life of the famous singer (Opéra-Comique, Feb. 21, 1927); ballets and pantomimes: *Le Collier de saphirs* (1891), *Les joyeuses commères de Paris* (1892), *Bouton d'or* (1893), *Le Docteur Blanc* (1893), *Salomé* (1895), *Cydalise et le chèvre-pied* (1919; Paris Opéra, Jan. 15, 1923; as an orchestral suite, 1926), *Impressions de Music-Hall,* 'ballet à l'Américaine' (Opéra, April 6, 1927), *Giration* (1934), *Fragonard* (1934), *Images,* 'divertissement sur un thème pastoral' (Opéra, June 19, 1935); the oratorios *La Croisade des enfants,* for mixed choir of children and adults (Paris, Jan. 18, 1905), *Les Enfants à Bethléem,* for soloists, children's chorus, and orch. (Amsterdam, April 13, 1907), and *Les Fioretti de St. François d'Assise* (1912); for orch: *Suite de concert* (1883), *Première suite d'orchestre* (1883), *Ouverture symphonique* (1885), *Marche solonnelle* (1889), *Pantomime* (1889), *Ballet de cour* (1901), *Paysages franciscains* (1920), *Gulliver au pays de Lilliput* (Paris Festival of the International Society for Contemporary Music, June 23, 1937), piano concerto (1887), *Scherzo-Caprice* for piano and orch. (1890), *Poème symphonique* for piano and orch. (1901), *Konzertstück* for harp and orch. (1901), *L'An mil,* symph. poem with chorus (1897); chamber music: *Pastorale variée dans le style ancien,* for wind instruments (also for piano), *Berceuse* for violin and piano, *Caprice* for cello and piano, *Canzonetta* for clarinet and piano, *Solo de concert* for bassoon and piano, *Variations libres et Finale* for flute, violin, viola, cello, and harp; for piano: *15 Pièces* (1883); *Étude de concert; Album pour mes petits amis,* containing the famous *Marche des petits soldats de plomb; Humoresque; Rêverie; Ariette dans le style ancien; Pastorale variée; Sérénade à Colombine; Sérénade vénitienne; Barcarolle* for 2 pianos; song cycles: *Contes* (1897), *3 Adaptations musicales* (1902), and *3 Mélodies* (1904); 38 other songs; harp music, folksong arrangements, etc. He contributed the section *Histoire de l'instrumentation* to Lavignac's 'Encyclopédie de la Musique.' —Cf. W. Weber, *Gabriel Pierné;* H. Eymieu, *Gabriel Pierné,* in the 'Revue illustrée' (Paris, March 15, 1897); L. Schneider, *Gabriel Pierné* in 'Le Théâtre' (Paris, March, 1901); O. Séré, *Musiciens français d'aujourd'hui* (Paris, 1921).

Pierné, Paul, French composer, cousin of Gabriel Pierné; b. Metz, June 30, 1874; d. Paris, March 24, 1952. He studied at the Paris Cons. with Lenepveu and Caussade; wrote a number of works, which were occasionally performed in Paris: the operas *Le Diable galant* (1913), *Emilde,* and *Mademoiselle Don Quichotte;* a ballet, *Le Figurinaï;* 2 symphonies and several symph. poems of a programmatic nature (*Jeanne d'Arc, Cléopâtre, De l'ombre à la lumière, Nuit évocatrice, Rapsodie Lorraine,* etc.); choral works; organ pieces; a song cycle, *Schéhérazade;* piano pieces.

Pierre (p'-yär), **Constant,** French writer on music; b. Paris, Aug. 24, 1855; d. there, Jan., 1918. He was a pupil at the Paris Cons.; played the bassoon in various Paris orchestras; from 1881 devoted himself mainly to musical journalism; was for many years editor of 'Le Monde musical.' —Writings: essays on *Les Noëls populaires* (1866) and *La Marseillaise* (1887); *La Facture instrumentale à l'Exposition universelle de 1889* (1890); *Les Facteurs d'instruments de musique, les luthiers* (1893); *L'École de chant de l'Opéra (1672-1807)* . . . (1895); *B. Sarrette et les origines du Conservatoire national de musique et de déclamation* (1895); *Notes inédites sur la musique de la Chapelle Royale* (*1532-1790*) . . . (1899); *Le Conservatoire national de musique et de déclamation* (1900); *Le Concert Spirituel 1725-1790* (1900; very valuable); *Les Hymnes et chansons de la Révolution* (1904); compiled *Musique des fêtes et cérémonies de la Révolution française* . . . (1899; of documentary value).

Pierson, Henry Hugh, English composer; b. Oxford, April 12, 1815; d. Leipzig, Jan. 28, 1873. He was educated at Cambridge; in 1839 went to Germany, where he studied music with Tomaschek and Reissiger; entered the circle of Mendelssohn in Leipzig; after a brief term as prof. of music at the Univ. of Edinburgh (1844), he returned to Germany, where he remained for the rest of his life; married Caroline Leonhardt, who wrote the German librettos for his operas. He changed his name from the original form Pearson to Pierson in order to secure proper pronunciation by Germans; used the pen name Edgar Mansfeldt for his published music. —Works: operas: *Leila* (Hamburg, Feb. 22, 1848) and *Contrarini oder Die Verschwörung zu Padua* (Hamburg, April 16, 1872; revived in Dessau, April 24, 1883, under the title *Fenice*); oratorio *Jerusalem* (Norwich Festival, Sept. 23, 1852); incidental music to the 2nd part of Goethe's *Faust;* overtures to Shakespeare's *Macbeth, As You Like It,* and *Romeo and Juliet.* His music was totally submerged in Mendelssohn's style. —Cf. H. G. Sear, *Faust and Henry Hugo Pierson,* in the 'Music Review' (1949).

Pijper (pī'-pĕr), **Willem,** eminent Dutch composer; b. Zeist, Sept. 8, 1894; d. Leidschendam, March 19, 1947. He received rudimentary education from his father, an amateur violinist; then went to the Utrecht Music School, where he studied composition with J. Wagenaar and piano with Mme. H. J. van Lunteren-Hansen; from 1918 to 1923, was music critic of the 'Utrecht Dagblad'; also taught at various schools; from 1925 to 1928, was prof. of composition at the Amsterdam Cons.; in 1930, director of the Rotterdam Cons.; was co-editor of the monthly 'De Muziek' (1926-29); also active in the International Society for Contemporary Music; was president of its Dutch section. In his music, Pijper was influenced from the very first by the new harmonies and melodic patterns of the French Impressionists, but he was able to transmute these elements into a language of his own; adopted a scale of alternating whole tones and semitones in many of his works, and regarded it as his own, not realizing that it was used (independently) by several other modern composers (Ludomir Rogowski, Felix Petyrek, and the Dutch composer Anthon van der Horst); his chamber music is of a very high quality. —Works: the operas: *Halewijn* (Amsterdam, June 13, 1933) and *Merlijn* (unfinished; 1939-46); incidental music to Sophocles' *Antigone* (1920-22), Euripides' *Bacchantes* (1922) and *The Cyclops* (1925), Shakespeare's *The Tempest* (1930), and Vondel's *Phaëton* (1938); for orch.: symph. No. 1 (1917), symph. No. 2 (1921), symph. No. 3 (his best; Amsterdam, Oct. 28, 1926; many performances abroad), *6 Symphonic Epigrams* (1928), *6 Adagios* (1940), piano concerto (1927), cello concerto (1936), violin concerto (1938); chamber music: 2 piano trios (1914, 1921), 4 string quartets (1914, 1920, 1923, 1928), septet for flute, oboe, clarinet, bassoon, horn, double-bass, and piano (1920), sextet for wind instruments and piano (1923), trio for flute, clarinet, and bassoon (1927), quintet, for flute, oboe, clarinet, bassoon, and horn (1929), 2 violin sonatas (1919, 1922), 2 cello sonatas (1919, 1924), flute sonata (1925), sonata for violin unaccompanied (1931), sonata for 2 pianos (1935); *3 Aphorisms* for piano

(1915), 3 piano sonatinas, piano sonata (1930), 3 Old Dutch Dances, for piano (1926), etc.; 2 works for voice and orch., to words by Verlaine: *Fêtes galantes* (1916) and *Romance sans paroles* (1919); 2 choruses a cappella for 8 voices: *Heer Halewijn* (1920) and *Heer Danielken* (1925); for voice and piano: 8 Old Dutch Songs (2 sets; 1924, 1935), 8 Old Dutch Love Songs (1920), *8 Vieilles Chansons de France* (1918), *8 Noëls de France* (1919); etc. He also publ. two collections of his articles, *De Quinten-Cirkel* (Amsterdam, 1929) and *De Stemvork* (Amsterdam, 1930). —Cf. M. D. Calvocoressi, *Willem Pijper*, in the 'Monthly Mus. Record' (London, 1924); H. Antcliffe, *Two Modern Dutch 'Nationals,'* in 'Eolus' (Jan., 1929); P. F. Sanders, *Moderne Nederlandsche Componisten* (The Hague, 1931); Cor Backers, *Nederlandse Componisten van 1400 tot op onze tijd* (The Hague, 1941; new ed., 1948; pp. 123-31); A. L. Ringer, *Willem Pijper and the Netherlands School of the 20th Century*, in the 'Mus. Quarterly' (Oct., 1955).

Piket, Frederick, composer; b. Constantinople, Jan. 6, 1903; son of an Austrian physician resident in Turkey. He attended the Vienna State Cons., and later studied with Schreker in Berlin; won the Mendelssohn State prize for his *Triple Fugue* for woodwinds in 1931. In 1940 he came to America and settled in N. Y. —Works: an overture, *Curtain Raiser for an American Play* (Minneapolis, Dec. 30, 1948); piano concerto; violin concerto; saxophone concerto; concerto for string orch.; orchestral suite, *The Funnies* (after 'Superman' and 'Little Orphan Annie'); *Sea Charm* for chorus a cappella; chamber music.

Pilati, Mario, Italian composer; b. Naples, Oct. 16, 1903; d. there, Dec. 10, 1938. He studied at the Naples Cons.; was instructor there (1930-38). —Works: *Notturno* for orch. (1923); *La Sera* for women's voices and orch. (1926); flute sonata (1926); *Il Battesimo di Cristo* for soli, chorus, and orch. (1927); piano quintet (1928); violin sonata (1929); cello sonata (1929); string quartet (1930); piano pieces; also transcriptions for piano of works by Pizzetti and Casella. —Cf. G. Gavazzeni, *M. Pilati*, in his *Il Suono è stanco* (Bergamo, 1950).

Pilger, Karl. See **Spazier.**

Pilkington, Francis, English composer; b. c. 1562; d. Chester, 1638. He received a B. Mus. degree at Lincoln College in Oxford; was successively lay clerk (1602), minor canon (1612), curate (1616), and precentor of the Chester Cathedral (1623). He publ. *The First Booke of Songs or Ayres of 4 parts* (1604), reprinted by Arkwright in the 'Old English Edition' (Nos. 18-20) and by Fellowes in 'The English School of Lutenist Song Writers' (vols. 7, 15); *The First Set of Madrigals and Pastorals of 3, 4, and 5 parts* (1614) and *The Second Set of Madrigals and Pastorals of 3, 4, 5, and 6 parts* (1624), reprinted by Fellowes in 'The English Madrigal School' (vols. 25, 26). Pilkington also contributed 2 songs to Sir William Leighton's collection, 'The Teares or Lamentacions of a Sorrowful Soule' (1614). —Cf. E. H. Fellowes, *The English Madrigal Composers* (London, 1921; 2nd ed., 1948).

Pillois (pĭl-wăh'), **Jacques,** composer; b. Paris, Feb. 14, 1877; d. New York, Jan. 3, 1935. He studied with Widor and Vierne at the Paris Cons.; taught at various schools there; from 1921 to 1929 was on the faculty of the American Cons. at Fontainebleau; wrote articles on music for the 'Revue Musicale' and other journals. He taught at N. Y. Univ. (1927-30); then became acting director of the music dept. at Smith College. He wrote *L'Anémone et la rose*, lyric scene for soli, chorus, and orch. (1913); *Rosène*, symph. prelude (1923); *Croisière*, a Mediterranean rhapsody for small orch. (1927); a number of songs, some with orch. accompaniment; sacred and secular choruses; *5 Haï-kaï*, for flute, violin, viola, cello, and harp; *Bucoliques*, for flute and piano; etc. In some of his works he used the pen-name Jacques Desky.

Pilss, Karl, Austrian composer; b. Vienna, April 7, 1902. He studied at the Vienna Music Academy with Franz Schmidt (composition) and with Dirk Fock (conducting). He subsequently filled various positions as chorusmaster in Vienna; also was active as a teacher. —Works: trumpet concerto (1934); piano concerto (1940); 2 wind octets (1941, 1947); *Serenade*, for wind quintet (1942); trumpet sonata (1935); violin sonata (1945); oboe sonata (1946); sonatina for oboe and guitar (1942); piano pieces and choral works.

Pincherle (păn'-shărl'), **Marc,** noted French musicologist; b. Constantine, Algiers, June 13, 1888; studied in Paris with Pirro, Laloy, and Rolland. He served in both World Wars; a captain in the second, he was a prisoner of war in Germany from June 1940 to March 1941. Prof. of history of the violin at the École Normale, Paris; he has been president of the Société française de musicologie; artistic director of the Pleyel Piano Co.; music critic of the 'Nouvelles Littéraires.' —His writings include: *Les Violonistes compositeurs et virtuoses* (Paris, 1922); *Feuillets d'histoire du violon* (ib., 1927; 2nd ed., 1935); *Corelli* (Paris, 1933); *Les Musiciens peints par eux-mêmes* (160 letters of famous composers from his own autograph collection; Paris, 1939); *Antonio Vivaldi et la musique instrumentale* (2 vols., Paris, 1948); *Les Instruments du quatuor* (Paris, 1948); *L'Orchestre de chambre* (Paris, 1948); *Jean-Marie Leclair l'aîné* (Paris, 1952); *Petit lexique des termes musicaux d'usage courant* (Paris, 1953); *Corelli et son temps* (Paris, 1954; English transl. as *Corelli, His Life, His Work,* N. Y., 1956); *Vivaldi* (Paris, 1955; English transl., N. Y., 1957); *Albert Roussel* (Paris, 1957). Pincherle has ed. works by Leclair, Mondonville, Torelli, and others.

Pingoud, Ernest, composer; b. St. Petersburg, Russia, Oct. 14, 1888; d. Helsinki, June 1, 1942. He studied at the St. Petersburg Cons. and then in Germany at the Leipzig Cons. with Max Reger. In 1918 he settled in Finland, where he served as managing director of the Helsinki Symph. Orch. In his own music, he was influenced by the Russian modern school, particularly by Scriabin; composed 2 symphonies, several symph. poems with characteristically evocative titles (*La Flamme éternelle, Le Chant d'espace,* etc.); chamber music; piano pieces; songs. —Cf. A. Rudnev, *Ernest Pingoud,* in *Suomen Säveltäjiä* (Helsinki, 1945; pp. 487-500).

Pinkham, Daniel, American composer; b. Lynn, Mass., June 5, 1923. He studied organ and harmony with Carl F. Pfatteicher at Phillips Academy, Andover (1937-1940); then at Harvard Univ. with A. Tillman Merritt, Walter Piston, and Archibald T. Davison (A.B., 1943; M.A., 1944); also studied harpsichord with Putnam Aldrich and Wanda Landowska, and organ with E. Power Biggs; at Tanglewood he took courses with Aaron Copland, Arthur Honegger, and Nadia Boulanger. He subsequently taught music history at Simmons College and harpsichord at Boston Univ.; visiting lecturer in music at Harvard Univ. (1957-58). In 1950 he received a Fulbright Fellowship; co-founder (with Robert Brink) and conductor of the Cambridge Festival Orch. The formal design of his music is strong; contrapuntal texture and the rhythmic element, rather than considerations of harmony and color, govern his writing. —Works: piano concertino (Cambridge, Mass., May 3, 1950); Concertante No. 1 for violin and harpsichord soli, strings, and celesta (Boston, Dec. 16, 1954); concerto for celesta and harpsichord soli (N. Y., Nov. 19, 1955); violin concerto (Falmouth, Mass., Sept. 8, 1956); Concertante No. 2 for violin and strings (Boston, May 9, 1958); *Cantilena and Capriccio,* for violin and harpsichord; divertimento for oboe and strings; other chamber music; 2 cantatas: *Wedding Cantata* (Cambridge, Mass., Sept. 22, 1956) and *Christmas Cantata* (*Sinfonia Sacra;* Boston, Dec. 10, 1957); songs to words by William Blake, Ben Jonson, W. H. Auden, etc.; he arranged and supplemented Gay's *Beggar's Opera* (Cambridge Drama Festival, 1956).

Pinsuti, Ciro, celebrated Italian singing teacher; b. Sinalunga, near Florence, May 9, 1829; d. Florence, March 10, 1888. His talent developed so rapidly that at 11 he was elected an honorary member of the Accademia Filarmonica, Rome. Taken to England soon after by Henry Drummond, he studied the piano under C. Potter, and the violin under Blagrove; returned to Bologna, 1845, and studied at the Liceo, also privately with Rossini, soon becoming assistant teacher of a piano class. In 1848 he went back to England; appointed prof. of singing at the Royal Academy of Music in 1856. He divided his time between London and Italy; brought out an opera, *Il Mercante di Venezia,* at Bologna (Nov. 9, 1873), another, *Mattia Corvino,* at Milan (1877), and a third, *Margherita,* at Venice (1882). In 1871 he represented Italy at the opening of the London Exhibition, for which he composed the hymn *O people of this favoured land.* As a recipient of the order of the Italian Crown, he was styled 'Cavaliere' Pinsuti. Besides his operas, he wrote some 200 songs to English and Italian texts.

Pinto, Octavio, Brazilian composer; b. São Paulo, Nov. 3, 1890; d. there, Oct. 31, 1950. He was trained as an architect; built apartment houses in Brazil; also studied piano with Isidor Philipp. In 1922 he married the Brazilian pianist, Guiomar Novaës; Villa-Lobos wrote his suite, *Prole do Bébé,* for their children. Pinto publ. a number of effective piano miniatures, of which the *Scenas Infantis* (1932) and *Children's Festival* (1939) are best known.

Pinza, Ezio (real baptismal name **Fortunio**), celebrated bass singer; b. Rome, May 18, 1892; d. Stamford, Conn., May 9, 1957. The family moved to Ravenna when he was an infant; he studied engineering; also was active in sports. He began to study voice at the age of 18 with Ruzza and Vizzani, at the Cons. of Bologna; served in the Italian artillery during World War I; made his opera début as King Mark in *Tristan und Isolde* at the Teatro Reale in Rome (1920); then sang for 3 seasons at La Scala, Milan; was selected by Toscanini for the leading part in the world première of Boito's *Nerone* (May 1, 1924). He made his American début at the Metropolitan Opera House as Pontifex Maximus in Spontini's *La Vestale* (1926); remained with the Metropolitan until 1948; appeared also in San Francisco, Chicago, etc.; sang in Europe and in South America; his most celebrated roles were Méphistophélès in Gounod's *Faust,* Don Giovanni, and Boris Godunov. In 1949 he appeared as a musical comedy star in *South Pacific,* and immediately became successful in this new career; also appeared in films.

Pipkov, Lubomir, Bulgarian conductor and composer; b. Lovetch, Sept. 6, 1904. He studied piano in Sofia; composition with Paul Dukas in Paris (1926-32). From 1932 till 1947, he was assistant conductor at the State Opera House in Sofia; then prof. of music at the National Academy. —Works: the operas *Nine Brothers of Yanina* (Sofia, Sept. 19, 1937) and *Momtchil* (Sofia, April 24, 1948); a cantata, *Marriage* (1934); piano trio; piano quartet; 2 string quartets; choral works.

Pirani, Eugenio, Italian pianist and composer; b. Bologna, Sept. 8, 1852; d. Berlin, Jan. 12, 1939. A pupil of Colinelli at the Bologna Liceo Musicale, he graduated in 1869; then studied in Berlin with Th. Kullak (piano) and Kiel (composition); taught in Kullak's Academy 1870-80, also touring Italy (1873, 1876), England and Germany, France and Russia. He lived in Heidelberg till 1895, and then settled in Berlin. From 1905, lived in Brooklyn, N. Y., where, with the singer Alma Webster-Powell, he founded the Powell-Pirani Music Institute; returned to Berlin. He publ. concert studies and many pieces for piano solo; songs; duets; etc.; also *Die Hochschule des Klavierspiels,* op. 88 (in German and English). Author of *Secrets of the Success of Great Musicians* (Philadelphia, 1922).

Pirro, André, distinguished French musicologist; b. St.-Dizier, Haute-Marne, Feb. 12, 1869; d. Paris, Nov. 11, 1943. Pupil of his father, an organist; from 1896 prof. at the Schola Cantorum, and member of the board of directors; from 1904 also lecturer on the history of the theory of music at the École des Hautes Études Sociales; in 1912 he succeeded R. Rolland as prof. of the history of music at the Sorbonne. —Writings: *L'Orgue de J.-S. Bach* (1897; won prize of the Académie des Beaux-Arts; preface by Widor; English transl. by J. W. Goodrich, N. Y., 1902); *J. S. Bach* (1906, in 'Maîtres de musique'; 6th ed., 1924; English transl., N. Y., 1957); *Descartes et la musique* (1907); *L'Esthétique de J.-S. Bach* (1907; a most valuable work); *Dietrich Buxtehude* (1913); *Heinrich Schütz* (1913; German transl. by W. Gurlitt, 1914); *Les Clavecinistes* (1925); *L'Art des organistes* (in Lavignac's 'Encyclopédie du Conservatoire'; Part II, vol. 2); *La Musique à Paris . . . 1380-1422* (Strasbourg, 1930); *L'Exécution musicale 1380-1450* (1930, in 'Liège Kongress-Bericht'); *Musiciens allemands et auditeurs françaises 1350-1422* (1930, in 'Adler-Festschrift'); *L'Enseignement de la musique aux universités françaises* (1930, in Bulletin of the 'Union musicologique' II, 1); *Pour l'histoire de la musique* (1931, in 'Acta musicologica' III, 2); *Léon X et la musique* (Paris, 1934; in English as *Leo X and Music,* in the 'Mus. Quarterly,' Jan., 1935); *Histoire de la musique de la fin du XIV*^e^ *siècle à la fin du XVI*^e^ (Paris, 1940). For Guilmant's 'Archives des Maîtres de l'Orgue' he wrote a number of biographies of early French organists (Titelouze, Daquin, Couperin, Marchand, etc.); contributed valuable essays to various musical publications.

Pirrotta, Nino, musicologist; b. Palermo, Italy, June 13, 1908. He studied at the Florence Cons., graduating as organist in 1931; taught history of music at the Cons. of Palermo (1936-48); in 1948 was appointed librarian of Santa Cecilia, Rome; 1954-56, visiting prof. at Princeton Univ. and Columbia Univ.; 1956, appointed prof. at Harvard Univ. His principal fields of specialization are 14th-century polyphony and Baroque opera. —Publications: *Il Sacchetti e la tecnica musicale del trecento italiano* (with E. Li Gotti; Florence, 1935); *Il Codice Estense lat. 568 e la musica francese in Italia al principio dell '400* (Palermo, 1946); numerous valuable articles in the 'Mus. Quarterly,' 'Rivista Musicale Italiana,' etc.; edited 'The Music of 14th-Century Italy' (vol. 1, Amsterdam, 1954).

Pisa, Agostino, Italian music scholar; flourished in Rome c. 1600, in which year he was *Dr. jur.* there. He publ. the earliest known treatise on conducting, *Breve dichiariazione, della battuta musicale* (Rome, 1611); a 2nd augmented ed. was publ. in the same year, also in Rome, as *Battuta della musica dichiarata.* —Cf. R. Schwartz, *Zur Geschichte des Taktschlagens,* in 'Jahrbuch Peters' (1907); G. Schünemann, *Geschichte des Dirigierens* (Leipzig, 1913).

Pisador, Diego, Spanish lutenist; b. Salamanca, c. 1508; d. after 1557. In 1526 he entered the priesthood; in 1552 he publ. in Salamanca a *Libro de música de vihuela,* containing madrigals, a set of Spanish ballads, and transcriptions of secular and sacred works by Josquin Des Prez and others; the collection is reprinted by A. Morphy in 'Les Luthistes espagnols du XVIe siècle.'

Pisari (Pizari), Pasquale, Italian composer; b. Rome, 1725; d. there, March 27, 1778. He was a pupil of Giovanni Biordi; in 1752 he was taken into the papal chapel, being a fine bass singer; he wrote most of his sacred works for it, and the MSS are preserved in the archives of the papal chapel; they include several Masses, motets, 2 Te Deums for 8 voices, one Te Deum for 4 voices (his most remarkable work); also a *Dixit* in 16 parts, for 4 choirs, and a series of motets for the entire year, written for the Lisbon court. Padre Martini called Pisari the 'Palestrina of the 18th century.'

Pischna, Josef, famous Bohemian pianist and pedagogue; b. Erdischowitz, June 15, 1826; d. Prague, Oct. 19, 1896. He was a pupil at the Prague Cons.; taught for many years in Moscow; then at the Prague Cons. His pedagogical work, *60 Exercises* for piano, became a standard method in Europe and has been reprinted in many editions; enlarged ed. by W. Rehberg; simplified ed. by B. Wolff.

Pisendel (pē'-zĕn-dĕl), **Johann Georg,** German violinist and composer; b. Kadolzburg, Dec. 26, 1687; d. Dresden, Nov. 25, 1755. He studied violin with Torelli at Ansbach, and music theory with Pistocchi; later (1716) took lessons in Venice from Vivaldi, who dedicated several works to him. He held the post of violinist in the Dresden court chapel orch. (1712); traveled with the Elector of Saxony to Paris, Berlin, Italy, and Vienna (1714-18); in 1728 became concertmaster in Dresden; 1731, appointed to a similar post in the orch. of the Dresden Opera. It seems certain that Bach wrote his partitas for unaccompanied violin for Pisendel. In his own works, Pisendel combined characteristics of German, French, and Italian music; many of his MSS are extant in the Dresden archives, among them 8 violin concertos, 3 concertos for 2 oboes and string orch., 2 *concerti grossi,* a symphony, and 2 solo pieces for violin with bass; a violin concerto is reprinted in 'Denkmäler deutscher Tonkunst' (vols. 29/30). —Cf. A. Moser, *Geschichte des Violin-Spiels* (p. 316ff.); H. R. Jung, *J. G. Pisendel,* in 'Musica' (Kassel, Nov., 1955).

Pisk, Paul Amadeus, composer and teacher; b. Vienna, May 16, 1893. He studied there with J. Epstein (piano), Schreker and Schoenberg (theory), Hellmesberger (conducting), and G. Adler (musicology); 1918, *Dr. phil.,* Univ. of Vienna; wrote music criticism for the 'Wiener Arbeiterzeitung'; was co-editor (with Paul Stefan) of 'Musikblätter des Anbruch'; in 1936 emigrated to the U. S.; was prof. of music, Univ. of Redlands (1937-51) and director of the School of Music there (1948-51); in 1951, appointed prof. at the Univ. of Texas, Austin. A prolific composer, he has written about 100 opus numbers in all genres. —Works: for the stage: *Schattenseite,* monodrama (1931) and *American Suite,* ballet (Redlands, Calif., Feb. 19, 1948); *Die neue Stadt,* a 'cantata for the people' (Vienna, Nov. 1926; on the occasion of completion of a workers' settlement); *Der grosse Regenmacher,* scenic ballad for narrator and orch. (1931); *Requiem* for baritone and orch. (1942); for orch.: *Partita* (Prague Festival of the International Society for Contemporary Music, May 17, 1925), *Suite on American Folksongs* for 24 instruments (1944), *Passacaglia* (1944), *Bucolic Suite* for string orch. (Saratoga Springs, Sept. 10, 1946), *Rococo Suite,* for viola and orch. (1953), *Baroque Chamber Concerto,* for violin and orch. (1953); chamber music: 3 songs with string quartet (Salzburg, Aug. 10, 1922), string quartet (1924), 3 violin sonatas (1921, 1927, 1939), *Fantasy,* for clarinet and piano (1925), *Rondo* for violin and piano (1932), trio for violin, viola, and guitar (1933), *Moresca Figures,* for violin, clarinet, and piano (1934), *3 Sonnets* for voice and string quartet (1936), piano trio (1939), suite for 4 clarinets (1940), *Four Beasts,* after Belloc, for voice and string quartet (1942), woodwind quartet (1945), clarinet sonata (1947), suite for oboe and piano (1947), quartet for 2 trumpets, horn, and trombone (1951); organ sonata; piano pieces; etc. Pisk has contributed many musicological essays to German and American publications; ed. Masses by Jacobus Gallus for the 'Denkmäler der Tonkunst in Österreich' (vol. 78). —Cf. Boris Kremenliev, *Paul A. Pisk,* in 'Music of the West Magazine' (July, 1952).

Pišna, Johann. See **Pischna, Josef.**

Pistocchi (pĭs-tŏh'-kē), **Francesco Antonio,** founder of the famous School of Singing at Bologna; b. Palermo, 1659; d. Bologna, May 13, 1726. Taken to Bologna very young, his first work was publ. there in 1667: *Capricci puerili saviamente composti e passeggiati in 40 modi sopra un Basso da un balletto, per il clavicembalo ed altri instrumenti,* when he was but 8 years old. His teacher in theory was G. A. Perti; he studied singing under Padre Vastamigli and B. Monari. As a lad he became maestro at the church of San Giovanni in Monte; later a priest in the Oratorian order; from 1697-99 was Kapellmeister at the court of Ansbach; and returned to Bologna, *via* Vienna and Venice, about 1700. There he founded, soon after his return, the first school of music in which vocal instruction was given systematically in the several classes. In this school were trained many eminent singers (Bernacchi, Bertolino da Faenza, Minelli, Pio Fabri, etc.); similar institutions soon sprang up in other Italian cities. Pistocchi was twice elected president of the Accademia Filarmonica (1708 and 1710).

Piston, Walter, outstanding American composer; b. Rockland, Maine, Jan. 20, 1894. The family name was originally Pistone; his grandfather was Italian. He received his education in Boston; first studied painting at the Mass. Normal Art School, graduating in 1916; then took lessons in piano with Harris Shaw, and in violin with Fiumara, Theodorowicz, and Winternitz; played in restaurants and places of public entertainment as a youth; was in the Navy during World War I; after the Armistice, entered Harvard Univ., graduating in musical subjects in 1924, *summa cum laude;* also conducted concerts of the Univ. orch., the Pierian Sodality. He was awarded a John Knowles Paine Fellowship and went to Paris, where he took a course in composition with Nadia Boulanger (1924-26); upon his return to the U. S., was appointed to the faculty of Harvard Univ.; 1944, prof. of music. In 1934 he received a Guggenheim Fellowship. Both as composer and teacher, Piston occupies a high position in American music. In general, he follows a cosmopolitan course in his style, adhering to classical forms, while extending his harmonic structures towards a maximum within a firmly tonal framework; his counterpoint is masterly; although he never professed the tenets of American nationalism, he employs upon occasion syncopated rhythms of a jazz type. Many American composers have been his pupils (Leonard Bernstein, Harold Shapero, etc.). —Works: ballet *The Incredible Flutist* (Boston Pops, May 30, 1938); for orch.: symph. No. 1 (Boston, April 8, 1938, composer conducting), symph. No. 2 (Washington, March 5, 1944; received the N. Y. Music Critics Circle Award, 1945), symph. No. 3 (Boston, Jan. 9, 1948; received the Pulitzer Prize), symph. No. 4 (Minneapolis, March 30, 1951), symph. No. 5 (commissioned by the Juilliard School of Music for its 50th anniversary; N. Y., Feb. 24, 1956), symph. No. 6 (Boston, Nov. 25, 1955), *Symphonic Piece* (Boston, March 23, 1928), *Suite* (Boston, March 28, 1930, composer conducting), *Concerto for Orchestra* (Cambridge, Mass., March 6, 1934, composer conducting), *Prelude and Fugue* (Cleveland, March 12, 1936), *Concertino* for piano and chamber orch. (N. Y., June 20, 1937), violin concerto (N. Y., March 18, 1940), *Sinfonietta* (Boston, March 10, 1941), *Prelude and Allegro* for organ and strings (Boston, Oct. 29, 1943), *Fanfare for the Fighting French* (Cincinnati, Oct. 23, 1942), *Fugue on a Victory Tune* (N. Y., Oct. 21, 1944), *Symphonic Suite* (Dallas, Feb. 29, 1948), *Toccata* (Orchestre National de France, Munch conducting, Bridgeport, Conn., Oct. 14, 1948), *Fantasy* for English horn, strings, and harp (Boston, Jan. 1, 1954), *Serenata* (Louisville, Oct. 24, 1956); chamber music: quintet for flute and strings (1942), *Partita* for violin, viola, and organ (1944), sonatina for violin and harpsichord (1945), *Divertimento* for 9 instruments (N. Y., May 18, 1946), 3 string quartets, *Carnival Song,* for men's chorus and 11 brass instruments (Harvard Glee Club, Cambridge, Mass., March 7, 1940); quintet for horn and woodwinds (1956). Piston publ. valuable and practical books: *Harmony* (N. Y., 1941); *Counterpoint* (N. Y., 1947); *Orchestration* (N. Y., 1955). —Cf. N. Slonimsky, *Walter Piston* in Henry Cowell's *American Composers on American Music* (1933); Israel Citkowitz, *Walter Piston—Classicist,* in 'Modern Music' (Jan.-Feb., 1936); E. Carter, *Walter Piston,* in the 'Mus. Quarterly' (July, 1946); Madeleine Goss, *Modern Music Makers* (N. Y.,

1952); W. Austin, *Piston's Fourth Symphony,* in 'Mus. Review' (May, 1955).

Pitfield, Thomas Baron, English composer; b. Bolton, April 5, 1903. He studied at the Royal Manchester College of Music; became instructor there in 1947; also studied engineering and painting; was a book illustrator; wrote verse. In his music, he adopts a simple style, in folksong manner. His works include a cantata, *The Rhyming Shopman;* a piano concerto; various pieces of chamber music; a set of piano pieces under the general title *Ballet in Education;* also humorous pieces for piano (*Limusicks,* etc.). —Cf. A. K. Holland, *T. B. Pitfield,* in the 'Monthly Mus. Record' (May, 1939).

Pitoni, Giuseppe Ottavio, Italian composer of church music; b. Rieti, March 18, 1657; d. Rome, Feb. 1, 1743. He began music studies at 5, under Pompeo Natale in Rome; at 8 was chorister at S. Giovanni de' Fiorentini, later at the S. S. Apostoli, and studying counterpoint under Foggia. In 1673, maestro di cappella at Terra di Rotondo; in 1674, at Assisi; in 1676, at Rieti; finally, in 1677, he became maestro at the Collegio di S. Marco, Rome, retaining this post until death, though simultaneously engaged at San Apollinare (1686), San Lorenzo in Damaso (1686), San Giovanni in Laterano (1708-19), and also at St. Peter's (1719), also in some minor Roman churches. He was an excellent teacher, and taught after the same method by which he himself rose to eminence as a composer, e.g., the writing out in score of Palestrina's works to study his style. Durante, Leo, and Feo were his greatest pupils. As a composer, he cultivated a distinct feature of the Roman school, the writing in many parts; his finest works are a *Dixit a* 16 (for 4 choirs), still sung yearly at St. Peter's during Holy Week, and 3 Masses based on popular airs, *Li Pastori a Maremme, Li Pastori a Montagna,* and *Mosca.* Of Masses and psalms he composed over 40 *a* 12 (for 3 choirs) and over 20 *a* 16 (for 4 choirs), psalms and motets *a* 24 and 36; and left an unfinished Mass *a* 48. He also wrote for St. Peter's a set of Masses, vespers, etc., for the entire year, besides motets *a* 3-8, hymns, etc. Only one book of motets, *a* 2, was publ. (Rome, 1697) during his lifetime, probably because he insisted that music written for one church should not be performed in any other. Proske, in his 'Musica divina' (1855, *et seq.*), printed a Mass, a Requiem, 6 motets, a psalm, a hymn, and a *Christus factus est.* In the Vatican Library is a MS work by Pitoni, *Notizie dei maestri di cappella sì di Roma che oltramontani . . .* from 1500-1700; and a fragmentary *Guida armonica* (108 printed pages). —Cf. M. Tiberti, *G. O. Pitoni,* in 'Musica d'oggi' (1941).

Pitt, Percy, English conductor and composer; b. London, Jan. 4, 1870; d. there, Nov. 23, 1932. He went to France as a youth; studied music in Germany, at the Leipzig Cons. (with Jadassohn and Reinecke) and at the Akademie der Tonkunst in Munich (with Rheinberger). He returned to England in 1893; held various subordinate positions at London opera houses; in 1907 became conductor and musical director of the Grand Opera Syndicate, at Covent Garden (until 1915); then conductor of the Beecham Opera Co. (1915-18) and, subsequently, artistic director of the British National Opera Co. (1920-24). In 1922 he was appointed musical director of the British Broadcasting Co., and held this post until 1930. He composed a number of works, of which a *Ballade* for violin and orch. (1900) was performed by Ysaÿe; a clarinet concerto (1897); several orchestral suites; choruses; incidental music for several plays. —Cf. J. D. Chamier, *Percy Pitt of Covent Garden and the B.B.C.* (London, 1938).

Pittaluga, Gustavo, Spanish composer; b. Madrid, Feb. 8, 1906. He studied law at the Univ. of Madrid and composition with Oscar Esplá; participated in the Paris group of modern musicians, 'Triton' (1935); from 1936 to 1939 was a member of the staff of the Spanish Embassy in Washington (for the Loyalist Government); then remained in the U. S.; was in charge of the film library at the Museum of Modern Art, N. Y. (1941-43). —Works: *La Romería de los Cornudos,* ballet, after F. G. Lorca (Madrid, 1933); a zarzuela, *El Loro* (Madrid, 1933); *Concerto militaire* for violin and orch. (Barcelona, 1933); *Petite suite* for 10 instruments (Paris, 1935; also for piano as *3 Pièces pour une espagnolade*); *Capriccio alla romantica,* for piano and orch. (Paris, 1936); *6 Danses espagnoles en suite* for piano (1935); *Vocalise-étude,* for voice and piano (1932); *Berceuse* for violin and piano (1935); *Ricercare,* for violin, clarinet, bassoon, and trumpet (1934); *5 Canciones populares* for chorus and 10 instruments (1939); *Habanera* for violin and piano (1942); *Lament* for Federico Garcia Lorca, for narrator and orch. (1942).

Pittrich, George Washington, German composer; b. Dresden, Feb. 22 (Washington's birthday), 1870; d. Nuremberg, April 28, 1934. He studied at the Dresden Cons. with Draeseke and others; was active as conductor in Dresden (1890-98), Hamburg (1898), Cologne (1899-1901), Frankfurt (1901-04), Dresden (1904-12), and Berlin (from 1912). He wrote a 1-act opera, *Marga* (Dresden, Feb. 8, 1894); incidental music to Shakespeare's *As You Like It* and to several classical German plays; Christmas musical plays *Der Stern von Bethlehem, Der Zauberschleier, Mäusekönigin;* a clarinet concerto; a fantasia for piano with string orch.; many songs.

Pitzinger, Gertrude, mezzo-soprano; b. Krasna Hora, Czechoslovakia, Aug. 15, 1904. She studied general musical subjects at the Vienna Singakademie, with Joseph Marx; singing with various teachers; made a prolonged tour of Czechoslovakia in 1930; then gave recitals in Berlin; was coached for interpretation by Julia Culp; in 1938 received her first American engagement; gave a N. Y. recital on Jan. 17, 1938 with excellent success; acquired a fine reputation as a singer of German lieder. Her repertory includes about 400 songs and the leading parts of all the major oratorios.

Piutti, Karl, German composer; b. Elgersburg, April 30, 1846; d. Leipzig, June 17, 1902. He studied at the Leipzig Cons.; in 1880 became organist at the Thomaskirche. He wrote a great number of organ works, including a *Hochzeit Sonata;* about 200 organ preludes; psalms and motets a cappella; songs. He also publ. *Regeln und Erläuterungen zum Studium der Musiktheorie.*

Pixis, Johann Peter, German pianist; b. Mannheim, Feb. 10, 1788; d. Baden-Baden, Dec. 22, 1874. Of a musical family (his father and his brother were good musicians), he received his primary education at home; went to Munich in 1809, and to Paris in 1825; established himself as a teacher, and was greatly esteemed in the Paris musical world. In 1845 he settled in Baden-Baden, where he continued to teach. He wrote several operas: *Almazinde, oder Die Höhle Sesam* (Vienna, April 11, 1820), *Bibiana, oder Die Kapelle im Walde* (Aachen, Oct. 8, 1829), etc.; a piano concerto; a piano quartet; a piano quintet; a string quintet; 7 piano trios; sonatas, variations, transcriptions, etc. for piano solo; altogether about 150 opus numbers. Together with Liszt, Chopin, Thalberg, Czerny, and Herz, he wrote *Hexaméron* (a series of brilliant variations on the march from Bellini's opera, *I Puritani*). —Cf. R. Batka, *Aus J. P. Pixis's Memoiren,* in *Kranz. Gesammelte Blätter über Musik* (Leipzig, 1903).

Pizzetti, Ildebrando, prominent Italian composer; b. Parma, Sept. 20, 1880. He studied piano with his father; at the age of 15 entered the Parma Cons., where his teacher was Telesforo Righi; graduated with honors in 1901; then devoted himself to composition and teaching; was on the faculty of the Cons. of Parma (1907-09); prof. of composition at the Istituto Musicale in Florence; in 1917 became its director; in 1925, left Florence, and was appointed director of the Cons. G. Verdi in Milan; in 1936, became prof. of composition at the Santa Cecilia Academy in Rome; was its director from 1948 to 1951. In 1914 he founded (with G. Bastianelli) in Florence the magazine 'Dissonanza' as an organ for contemporary Italian music; was also critic, for several years, of the 'Secolo' (Milan) and 'Nazione' (Florence); co-ed. of the 'Raccolta nazionale delle musiche italiane.' Pizzetti made his first visit to the U. S. in 1930, when Toscanini conducted his *Rondo veneziano* with the N. Y. Philharmonic; in 1931 Pizzetti conducted his opera *Fra Gherardo* at the Teatro Colón in Buenos Aires. Pizzetti's music represents the Romantic trend in modern Italy; in his many works for the theater, he presents the modern counterpart of medieval mystery plays; the mystical element is very strong in his own texts for his operas. He employs astringent chromatic harmony, but the mainstream of his melody flows along pure diatonic lines. —Works: operas: *Fedra* (Milan, March 20, 1915), *Debora e Jaele* (1915-21; Milan, Dec. 16, 1922), *Lo Straniero* (1922-25; Rome, April 29, 1930), *Fra Gherardo* (1925-27; Milan, May 16, 1928; his most famous work; N. Y., March 21, 1929, at the Metropolitan Opera), *Orsèolo* (Florence, May 5, 1935), *L'Oro* (1938-42; Milan, Jan. 2, 1947), *Vanna Lupa* (Florence, May 4, 1949), *Ifigenia* (1950; Turin Radio, Sept. 18, 1950; 1st stage performance, Florence, May 4, 1951), *Cagliostro* (La Scala, Milan, Jan. 24, 1953), *La Figlia di Jorio* (Naples, Dec. 4, 1954); *Assassinio nella cattedrale,* after T. S. Eliot's *Murder in the Cathedral* (Milan, La Scala, March 1, 1958; highly acclaimed); incidental music: to the tragedy by Gabriele d'Annunzio *La Nave* (1905), to d'Annunzio's *La Pisanella* (Paris, June 11, 1913), *La sacra rappresentazione di Abram e d' Isaac,* mystery play (Florence, 1917; expanded and produced at Turin, March 11, 1926), to *Agamemnon,* by Aeschylus (Greek Theater at Syracuse, 1930), *The Trachiniae,* by Sophocles (Greek Theater, Syracuse, 1936), *As You Like It* by Shakespeare (Florence, May, 1938); choral works: *Requiem* (1922), *De Profundis* (1983), *Cantico di gloria,* for a treble chorus, 24 wind instruments, 2 pianos, and percussion (1948); for orch.: *Ouverture per una farsa tragica* (1911), *Concerto dell' estate* (N. Y., Toscanini conducting; Feb. 28, 1929), *Rondo veneziano* (N. Y., Feb. 27, 1930; as a ballet, La Scala, Milan, Jan. 8, 1931), cello concerto (Venice, Sept. 11, 1934), symph. in A (1940), violin concerto (Rome, Dec. 9, 1945), *Canzone di beni perduti* (Venice, Sept. 4, 1950); chamber music: 2 string quartets (1906; 1933), piano trio (1925), violin sonata (1919), cello sonata (1921); for piano: *Da un autunno già lontano* (1911; 3 pieces), *Sonata 1942;* songs: *Tre liriche* (1904), *Sera d'inverno* (1906), *I Pastori* (his most remarkable song; poem by Gabriele d'Annunzio; 1908), *La Madre al figlio lontano* (1910), *Erotica* (1911), *Due canti popolari greci* (1912), *Tre sonetti di Petrarca* (1922), *E il mio dolore io canto* (1940); transcriptions of madrigals by Gesualdo, of Veracini's sonatas for violin and continuo, etc.; books: *La Musica dei Greci* (Rome, 1914), *Musicisti contemporanei* (Milan, 1914), *Intermezzi critici* (Florence, 1921), *Paganini* (Turin, 1940), *Musica e dramma* (Rome, 1945), *La Musica italiana dell' 800* (Turin, 1946); numerous articles in Italian magazines. —Bibliography: R. Fondi, *I. Pizzetti e il dramma musicale italiano d'oggi* (Rome, 1919); G. M. Gatti, *I. Pizzetti,* in the 'Mus. Quarterly' (Jan., April, 1923); M. Pilati, *'Fra Gherardo' di Pizzetti* (Milan, 1928); M. Rinaldi, *L'Arte di Pizzetti e 'Lo Straniero'* (Rome, 1930); G. Tebaldini, *I. Pizzetti* (Parma, 1931); G. M. Gatti, *I. Pizzetti* (Turin, 1934; in English, London, 1951; a basic biography, with a list of works; new Italian ed., 1955); G. Bastianelli, *Pizzetti,* in 'Il Convegno' (March-April, 1921); M. Castelnuovo-Tedesco, *I. Pizzetti e la sua musica corale,* in 'Il Pianoforte' (Aug. 15, 1921; a Pizzetti issue); G. Gavazzeni, *Tre studi su Pizzetti* (Como, 1937); a special Pizzetti number of the 'Rassegna Musicale' (Oct. 1940); M. Castelnuovo-Tedesco, *I. Pizzetti,* in David Ewen's *The Book of Modern Composers* (N. Y., 1945); a symposium, *Firenze a I. Pizzetti* (Florence, 1947).

Pizzi (pit'-sē), **Emilio,** Italian composer; b. Verona, Feb. 1, 1861; d. Milan, Nov. 27, 1940. He studied at the Istituto Musicale of Bergamo and at the Cons. of Milan (with Ponchielli and Bazzini); received 1st prize for his 1-act opera, *Lina* (1885); in 1897, was appointed director of the Istituto Musicale at Bergamo; from 1900 lived for some time in London. —Operas: *Guglielmo Ratcliff* (Bologna, Oct. 31, 1889), *Gabriella* (world première, Boston, Nov. 25, 1893, with Adelina Patti in the title role), *La Rosalba* (Turin, May 31, 1899), *Vendettà* (in German, Cologne, Dec. 1, 1906; in Italian, as *Ivania,* Bergamo, Sept. 14, 1926); also a comic opera in English, *Bric-à-Brac Will* (London, 1895); he further wrote a *Messa solenne* for soli, chorus, and orch.; a Requiem; violin pieces; piano pieces; songs.

Pizzini, Carlo Alberto, Italian composer; b. Rome, March 22, 1905. He studied with Respighi at the Rome Cons. (graduated in 1929); remained in Rome as composer and teacher. —Works: opera *Dardanio* (Rome, 1928); for orch.: *Sinfonia in istile classico* (1930); *Il Poema delle Dolomiti* (1931); *Strapaese,* a symph. suite (1932); *Al Piemonte,* symph. triptych (1941); *Grotte di Postumia,* divertimento in variation form (1941); chamber music; piano pieces.

Plaidy (plä'-dē), **Louis,** famous German piano teacher; b. Wermsdorf, Nov. 28, 1810; d. Grimma, March 3, 1874. He began his professional career as a violinist, and performed in public in Dresden and Leipzig; at the same time he took piano lessons from Agthe, and became greatly proficient as pianist, so that Mendelssohn engaged him in 1843 as piano teacher at the Leipzig Cons. Plaidy concentrated on the technical problems of piano pedagogy; taught at the Leipzig Cons. until 1865; then continued to give private lessons. He publ. a number of instructive piano studies which are still widely used; his *Technische Studien für das Pianoforte-Spiel* is a standard manual; he also publ. a booklet, *Der Klavierlehrer* (1874; British ed. as *The Pianoforte Teacher's Guide;* American ed., transl. by J. S. Dwight, as *The Piano-Teacher*).

Plamenac (plăh'-mĕh-năts), **Dragan,** eminent musicologist; b. Zagreb, Croatia, Feb. 8, 1895. He began his studies in composition, piano, and violin in his native city; then studied law at the Univs. of Zagreb and Vienna; LL.D. (Zagreb); took composition lessons with Franz Schreker at the State Academy of Music in Vienna, and with Novák in Prague. In 1919 he went to Paris under a French Government Scholarship; studied musicology with André Pirro at the Sorbonne; then in Vienna under Guido Adler; received his Ph.D. from Vienna Univ. in 1925, with the dissertation *Joh. Ockeghem als Motetten- und Chansonkomponist.* From 1925 to 1927 he was coach and assistant conductor at the Berlin City Opera; 1928 to 1939, taught musicology at the Univ. of Zagreb; in Sept., 1939, came to the U. S. as a representative of Yugoslavia at the International Musicological Congress; remained in the U. S.; American citizen, 1946; taught at the St. Louis Institute of Music (1940-43); then was connected with the Office of War Information; was awarded a Guggenheim Fellowship in 1947; in 1955 appointed prof. of musicology at the Univ. of Illinois. He edited the collected works of Ockeghem (vol. 1, 1927, publ. by Breitkopf & Härtel; vol. 2, 1947, publ. by the American Musicological Society); and *Odabrani Moteti* (selected motets) by Ivan Lukačić (Zagreb, 1935).—Important writings: *La Chanson de l'Homme armé* . . . in 'Rapport sur le congrès archéologique et historique,' Bruges, 1925; *Autour d'Ockeghem,* in the 'Revue Musicale' (Feb., 1928); *Zur l'Homme armé-Frage,* in the 'Zeitschrift für Musikwissenschaft' (1928-29); *Tomaso Cecchini,* a bio-bibliographical study (Bulletin of the Yugoslav Academy of Sciences and Arts, 1938); *Music of the 16th and 17th centuries in Dalmatia* in 'Papers Read at the International Congress of Musicology . . . New York . . . 1939' (N. Y., 1944); *New Light on the Last Years of C.P.E. Bach,* in the 'Mus. Quarterly' (Oct., 1949); *A Reconstruction of the French Chansonnier in the Biblioteca Colombina, Seville,* in the 'Mus. Quarterly' (Oct., 1951, and Jan., 1952); *Keyboard Music of the 14th Century in Codex Faenza 117,* in the 'Journal of the American Musicological Society' (1951); *Deux pièces de la Renaissance tirées de fonds florentins,* in the 'Revue Belge de Musicologie' (1952); *An Unknown Composition by Dufay?* in the 'Mus. Quarterly' (April, 1954); numerous other articles in European and American publications. He contributed the section 'Music in the Adriatic Coastal Areas of the Southern Slavs' to G. Reese's *Music in the Renaissance.*

Planchet (plăhn - shā'), **Dominique-Charles,** French composer and pedagogue; b. Toulouse, Dec. 25, 1857; d. Versailles, July 19, 1946. He studied at the École Niedermeyer in Paris; was for many years organist at the Cathedral in Versailles; in 1898 appointed organist at the Ste.-Trinité, Paris; taught at the École Niedermeyer; was active as general secretary of the Société des Compositeurs; in 1905, won the Prix Chartier for chamber music. He wrote an opera, *Le Fils du Croisé* (privately performed in Versailles, 1885); 2 cello concertos; *Esclavage africain,* cantata for male voices; much sacred music; organ pieces; a piano trio; a violin sonata; songs; contributed the section 'L'Art du maître de chapelle' to Lavignac's 'Encyclopédie de la Musique.' On his chamber music, see the entry in 'Cobbett's Cyclopedic Survey of Chamber Music' (London, 1930).

Plançon (plăhn-sŏhn'), **Pol (-Henri),** famous French bass singer; b. Fumay, June 12, 1851; d. Paris, Aug. 12, 1914. He was destined by his parents for a commercial career in Paris, but showed a natural vocal ability, and began to study singing with Sbriglia; made his operatic début in Lyons (1877); then appeared in Paris (Feb. 11, 1880); after a season in Monte Carlo, he made a highly successful appearance at the Paris Opéra as Méphistophélès in Gounod's *Faust* (June 23, 1883); sang that role more than 100 times during his 10 seasons at the Opéra, and was regarded as unrivaled in his dramatic delivery and vocal power. On June 3, 1891, he sang Méphistophélès in London; his American début, in the same role, took place at the Metropolitan Opera House on Nov. 29, 1893. He then resigned from the Paris Opéra and remained a member of the Metropolitan Opera until his retirement in 1906. He had an imposing physique, mobile features, and an innate acting ability. His repertory consisted of about 50 roles in French, Italian, German, and English. In some operas he sang more than 1 part, as in *Roméo et Juliette* (Capulet and Friar), *Aida* (Ramfis and King), *Les Huguenots* (St.-Bris and Marcel), etc. Of Wagnerian roles, he sang the Landgrave, King Henry, and Pogner.

Planquette (plăhn-kĕhtt'), **Jean-Robert,** French composer of operettas; b. Paris, July 31, 1848; d. there, Jan. 28, 1903. He studied at the Paris Cons. with Duprato; wrote chansonnettes and 'saynètes' for the cafés-concerts in Paris; then composed a 1-act operetta, *Paille d'avoine* (1874); and others. He achieved his first great success with the production of *Les Cloches de Corneville,* a comic opera in 3 acts (Folies-Dramatiques, April 19, 1877); it was performed for the 1000th time there in 1886, and became one of the most popular works of its genre; in English, given as *The*

Chimes of Normandy (N. Y., Oct. 22, 1877; London, Feb. 23, 1878). Other operettas were *Le Chevalier Gaston* (Monte Carlo, Feb. 8, 1879), *Rip Van Winkle* (London, Oct. 14, 1882; very successful), *Nell Gwynne* (1884), *Surcouf* (1887; in English as *Paul Jones*), *La Cocarde tricolore* (1892), *Le Talisman* (1893), *Panurge* (1895), *Mam'zelle Quat'Sous* (1897). A posthumous operetta, *Le Paradis de Mahomet* (orchestrated by Louis Ganne), was produced at the Variétés in Paris in 1906.

Plantade, Charles-Henri, French composer; b. Pontoise, Oct. 14, 1764; d. Paris, Dec. 18, 1839. As a child, he studied singing and the cello in the Royal School for the 'pages de musique'; afterwards he took lessons with Honoré Langlé (theory), Hüllmandel (piano), and Petrini (harp). In 1797 he became singing teacher at the Campan Institute at St.-Denis, where Hortense de Beauharnais, the future queen of Holland, was his pupil. He subsequently was in the service of Queen Hortense as her representative in Paris; was prof. at the Paris Cons. from 1799 to 1807, and again in 1815-16 and 1818-28. From 1812 he also held the post of maître de chambre at the Paris Opéra. He received the ribbon of the Legion of Honor from Louis XVIII (1814). Losing his various positions after the revolution of 1830, he retired to Batignolles. He wrote several operas, of which *Le Mari de circonstances* (Opéra-Comique, March 18, 1813) was the most successful; 2 other operas, *Palma, ou Le Voyage en Grèce* (1798) and *Zoé, ou La Pauvre Petite* (1800), were also performed. He further composed Masses, motets, etc. for the Chapelle Royale; publ. 20 sets of *romances,* 3 books of vocal duets (nocturnes), and a harp sonata.

Planté (plăhn-tā'), **Francis,** French pianist; b. Orthez, Basses-Pyrénées, March 2, 1839; d. St. Avit, near Mont-de-Marsan, Dec. 19, 1934. From 1849 he was a pupil of Marmontel at Paris Cons.; won 1st prize after 7 months' tuition. After a course in harmony in Bazin's class (1853), he retired for private study during ten years, and then reappeared as a pianist of finished technique and style. About 1900 he suddenly vanished from concert life, vowing that he should 'never be seen again in public.' He created a sensation in 1915 when he was heard again in several concerts in Paris; but, in order to keep his strange vow, he was hidden from the view of the audience by a screen. Made excellent transcriptions of classic pieces (Gluck, Mozart), but publ. no original compositions.—Cf. O. Comettant, *Francis Planté* (Paris, 1874); A. Dandelot, *Francis Planté* (Paris, 1920; 3rd ed., 1930); A. Lenoir and Jean de Nahuque, *Francis Planté: Doyen des pianistes* (Paris, 1931).

Plass, Ludwig, German trombonist and historian of military music; b. Osterode, March 13, 1864; d. Berlin, Sept. 16, 1946. He studied trombone at the Hochschule für Musik in Berlin; in 1893 became solo trombonist of the Royal Chapel; in 1905, court bandleader; collected materials on military music in Germany; wrote 28 pieces for wind instruments; publ. interesting historical essays on the German post-horn; also *Bachs Clarintrompeter* (1927); *Was bliesen unsere Reiter?* (1934); etc.

Platania, Pietro, Italian composer; b. Catania, April 5, 1828; d. Naples, April 26, 1907. He studied with P. Raimondi at the Naples Cons.; was director of the Palermo Cons. (1863); later maestro di cappella at Milan, and director of the Royal College of Music at Naples (1888). —Operas: *Matilde Bentivoglio* (Palermo, 1852); *Piccarda Donati* (Palermo, March 3, 1857); *La Vendetta slava* (Palermo, Feb. 4, 1865); *Spartaco* (Naples, March 29, 1891). He also wrote a symphony, *L'Italia;* a festival symphony with choruses to welcome King Umberto in 1878; *Pensiero sinfonico;* a Requiem; Psalm 67 for chorus and orch.; etc.; and *Trattato d'Armonia* (1872). —Cf. F. Guardione, *Pietro Platania* (Milan, 1908).

Plato, the great Greek philosopher (427-347 B.C.); formulated in his 'Timaeus' a system of musical harmony, eruditely interpreted by Th.-Henri Martin in his *Études sur le Timée de Platon* (Paris, 1841). R. von Westphal, in his *Harmonik und Melopöie der Griechen* (Leipzig, 1865), von Jan in *Die Harmonie der Sphären* (in 'Philogus,' vol. LII), and H. Abert's *Die Lehre vom Ethos in der griechischen Musik* (Leipzig, 1899) may also be consulted. Plato's thoughts on music are collected in an essay by Deyk in Weber's 'Cäcilia' (1828). Plato likened the movements of music to those of the soul, whose development may therefore be influenced by musical art. —Cf. J. Regner, *Platos Musik-Theorie* (Halle, 1923).

Platti, Giovanni, Italian composer; b. Venice, 1690; d. Würzburg, Jan. 11, 1763. He was attached to the Würzburg court in 1724; was active there as tenor, violinist, composer, and teacher; regarded by some music historians as the first composer to employ the classical sonata form, but this contention is debatable. 12 keyboard sonatas by Platti were edited by L. Hoffmann-Erbrecht (Leipzig, 1953-54); one is included in W. S. Newman, '13 Keyboard Sonatas of the 18th and 19th Centuries' (Chapel Hill, N. C., 1947); a *Miserere* was transcribed by Molinari and performed in Rome (March 15, 1936); a flute sonata was edited by Jarnach (1936). —Cf. F. Torrefranca, *La Creazione della sonata drammatica moderna rivendicata all'Italia: Giovanni Platti, il grande,* in the 'Rivista Musicale Italiana' (XVII, 309); O. Kaul, *Geschichte der Würzburger Hofmusik im 18. Jahrhundert* (Würzburg, 1924).

Playford, John, English music publisher; b. Norfolk, 1623; d. London, Nov., 1686. He was in business for 36 years (1648-84); publ. 'The Dancing Master' (1651; 12th ed., 1703; modern ed. by M. Dean-Smith, London, 1958); Hilton's 'Catch that catch can' (1652); 'Select Musical Ayres and Dialogues' (1653); 'Musick's Recreation on the Lyra Violl' (1652; in a collection); 'Briefe Introduction to the Skill of Musick for Song and Violl' (1654; enlarged ed. 1655, with an essay on *The Art of Descant* by Dr. Thos. Campion, which was revised by Purcell in the 10th ed. of 1683; this very popular work, written by John Playford himself, ran through 19 numbered eds. up to 1730, besides 6 or more unnumbered eds.); 'Psalms and Hymns in Solemn Musick of four parts . . .' (1671); 'The Whole Book of Psalms, with the usual Spiritual Songs' *a* 3 (1673; 20th ed., 1757); 'The Musical Companion' (1673; Book I, catches and rounds *a* 3; Book II, dialogues, glees, ayres, and songs *a* 2-4); 'Choice Ayres, Songs and Dialogues to be sung to the theorbo . . .' (5 books; 1676-84); 'Musick's Delight on the Cithern' (1666); 'The Division Violin' (variations for violin over a basso ostinato; 2nd ed., 1685); etc.—His son and successor, **Henry Playford** (b. May 5, 1657; d. 1720), publ. 'The Theatre of Musick' (with R. Carr; 4 books; 1685-87; 'the newest and best songs'); 'Banquet of Music' (6 books; 1688-1692); Purcell's 'Orpheus Britannicus' (1698-1702) and 'Ten Sonatas' with Te Deum and Jubilate for St. Cecilia's Day (1697); Blow's 'Amphion Anglicus' (1700) and Ode on Purcell's death; etc. —Cf. F. Kidson, *J. Playford and 17th Century Music Publishing,* in the 'Mus. Quarterly' (Oct., 1918); J. Pulver, *J. Playford,* in the 'Mus. News and Herald' (May, 1927); C. L. Day and Eleanore Murrie, *English Song-Books, 1651-1702, and Their Publishers* (London, 1936; reprint from 'Transactions of the Bibliographical Society,' March, 1936).

Plessis, Hubert du, South African composer; b. Cape Province, June 7, 1922. He studied composition with W. H. Bell, and later at the Rhodes Univ. College in Cape Town; in 1946, was appointed instructor there; in 1951, he went to London. Many of his works are based on South African themes; he writes mostly in smaller forms; among his compositions is a serenade for strings (1952); a string quartet (1953); piano pieces; songs.

Pleyel (plā-yĕl'), **Camille,** French pianist, son of Ignaz Pleyel; b. Strasbourg, Dec. 18, 1788; d. Paris, May 4, 1855. He was a pupil of his father, had some success as a composer, but is chiefly noteworthy as a piano manufacturer, entering his father's firm in 1821. Kalkbrenner was his partner for a time; Auguste Wolff, his successor. —His wife, **Marie-Félicité-Denise** (b. Paris, Sept. 4, 1811; d. St.-Josse-ten-Noode, March 30, 1875), was a pianist; pupil of Henri Herz, Moscheles, and Kalkbrenner. In her fifteenth year, as Mlle. Moke, her virtuosity created a sensation in Belgium, Austria, Germany, and Russia. Before her marriage, Berlioz was in love with her (1830). From 1848-72 she was prof. of piano at the Brussels Cons.

Pleyel, Ignaz Joseph, pianist, composer, and piano manufacturer; b. Ruppertsthal, near Vienna, June 1, 1757; d. on his estate near Paris, Nov. 14, 1831. His piano teacher till his 15th year was Wanhal; Count Erdödy, his patron, then placed him under Haydn's care, with whom he lived 5 years. The count then appointed him his private Kapellmeister, but granted leave of absence for further study in Rome, together with means of maintenance. Pleyel remained in this congenial atmosphere until 1781, then making a brief visit to Vienna, and returning to Rome, departing for the second time, in 1783, to become 2d Kapellmeister at the Strasbourg Cathedral. He was advanced to 1st Kapellmeister in 1789; lost his position owing to the Revolution, and went to London in the winter of 1791-92 on an invitation to conduct the Professional Concerts, a rival enterprise (though Pleyel did not know it) to his old teacher Haydn's concerts under Salomon's management. These Professional Concerts were successful in themselves, but did not overwhelm the rival enterprise; after conducting them for a few years, Pleyel returned to his property near Strasbourg, but was subjected to such annoyances from the revolutionists that he sold his place in 1795 and went to Paris. There he began business as a music seller, and in 1807 founded a piano factory, the growing prosperity of which gradually absorbed his attention and caused him to give up composition. The firm, now known as 'Pleyel et Cie.,' is one of the most important in France. Pleyel was an extremely prolific instrumental composer; he publ. 29 symphonies; a quantity of chamber music (5 books of string quintets; 45 string quartets; 6 quartets for flute and strings, etc.); 2 violin concertos; 4 cello concertos; 2 piano concertos; 6 grand sonatas for piano solo; etc. His music is entirely in the style of Haydn, whose disciple and admirer he was. —Cf. L. de Fourcaud, *La Salle Pleyel* (Paris, 1893).

Plotnikov, Eugene, Russian conductor; b. Odessa, Aug. 29, 1877; d. New York, Sept. 28, 1951. He studied at the Moscow Cons.; was coach and assistant conductor at the Moscow Opera; also conducted at the Paris Opéra (1921). In 1922 he settled in the U. S.; conducted Russian operas in N. Y. and other American cities with Shaliapin; in 1934 became conductor of the N. Y. Federal Symph. Orch.

Plüddemann, Martin, German composer; b. Kolberg, Sept. 29, 1854; d. Berlin, Oct. 8, 1897. He studied at the Leipzig Cons.; later took singing lessons with Hey in Munich; in 1889 was engaged as singing teacher at the Styrian Music School in Graz. He wrote a number of popular male choruses and ballads; publ. pamphlets of Wagnerian tendency. —Cf. R. Batka, *M. Plüddemann und seine Balladen* (Prague, 1896); L. Schemann, *M. Plüddemann und die deutsche Ballade* (1930).

Plutarch, famous Greek writer; b. Chæronea, Bœotia, 50 A. D.; d. there, 120. Among his treatises ('Moralia') one, *De musica,* contains important historical data concerning music (Latin transl. by R. Volkmann; German transl., with parallel Greek text, and commentary, by R. Westphal, 1865; also by Weil and Reinach, with commentary, 1900).

Pocci (pŏhch'-chē), **Franz,** Graf von, composer; b. (of an old Italian noble family) Munich, March 7, 1807; d. there, May 7, 1876. Possessing versatile talents, he wrote plays with music for a puppet theater in Munich, for which he also designed the scenery. He was at his best in pieces for children (*Blumenlieder, Bildertöne für Klavier, Soldatenlieder, Jägerlieder, Alte und neue Kinderlieder,* etc.). His 2 piano sonatas were praised by Schumann for their poetic expression and fine romantic spirit. An opera, *Der Alchemist,* was produced in Munich (1840); his grandson F. Pocci publ. a collection: *Franz Poccis Lustiges Komödienbüchlein* (Munich, 1921). —Cf. K. Pastor, *Franz Pocci als Musiker* (Munich, 1932); L. Hirschberg, *F. Pocci, der Musiker,* in the 'Zeitschrift für Musikwissenschaft' (1918).

Pochon (poh-shohn'), **Alfred,** Swiss violinist; b. Yverdon, July 30, 1878. At the age of 11 he appeared in public concerts; at the recommendation of Joachim, he went to the Liège Cons. to study with César Thomson; in 1898 became a teacher there; also played 2nd violin in Thomson's string quartet. In 1902 he was requested by the philanthropist E. de Coppet to organize a string quartet, which became famous as the Flonzaley Quartet, so named after Coppet's summer residence near Lausanne; Pochon remained a member (as 2nd violin) throughout its existence; traveled with it all over Europe, and gave notable concert cycles in the U. S., until its disbandment in 1929; after that he became a member of the Stradivarius Quartet of N. Y. In 1938 he returned to Switzerland; in 1941 was elected director of the Cons. of Lausanne, retiring in 1957. —Publ. *A Progressive Method of String-Quartet Playing* (N. Y., 1924) and several essays on musical subjects.

Poglietti, Alessandro, Italian composer; from 1661 court organist in Vienna; killed in July 1683 at the siege of Vienna by the Turks. His compositions include 12 ricercari, suites for harpsichord (*On the Hungarian Rebellion, Nightingale Suite,* etc.), and other instrumental pieces, some of which appear in *Toccates et Suites,* publ. by Roger (Amsterdam); also church music. H. Botstiber publ. some reprints in the 'Denkmäler der Tonkunst in Österreich' (vol. 27); some dance music publ. ibid., vol. 56. —Cf. A. Koczirz, *Zur Lebensgeschichte Alexander Pogliettis,* in the 'Studien zur Musikwissenschaft' (1916; pp. 116-27).

Pohl, Karl Ferdinand, German writer on music; b. Darmstadt, Sept. 6, 1819; d. Vienna, April 28, 1887, where he had been archivist and librarian to the 'Gesellschaft der Musikfreunde' from 1866. During 3 years' residence in London (1863-66) he gathered all available facts concerning the residence there of Mozart and Haydn, embodying them in his *Mozart und Haydn in London* (1867; 2 vols.). Pohl also began an extended biography of Haydn, but publ. only one vol. (in 2 parts: 1875, 1882); the work was finished by Hugo Botstiber. Other publications: *International Exhibition of 1862. Cursory Notices on the . . . History of the Glass Harmonica* (London, 1862); an interesting historical review, *Die Gesellschaft der Musikfreunde . . . und ihr Conservatorium* (1871); *Denkschrift aus Anlass des 100 jährigen Bestehens der Tonkünstler-Sozietät in Wien* (1871); *Bibliographie der Musiksammelwerke des 16. und 17. Jahrhunderts* (with R. Eitner and A. Lagerberg; 1877).

Pohl, Richard, German writer on music; b. Leipzig, Sept. 12, 1826; d. Dec. 17, 1896, at Baden-Baden, where he had lived since 1846. Study at Göttingen and Leipzig, and a long friendship with Liszt at Weimar, showed their influence in Pohl's sturdy advocacy of neo-German tendencies, both in the 'Neue Zeitschrift für Musik,' of which he was joint editor for some years, and in his writings: *Akustische Briefe für Musiker und Musikfreunde* (1853); *Bayreuther Erinnerungen* (1877); *Autobiographisches* (1881); *Richard Wagner* (1883; in Waldersee's 'Vorträge'); *Richard Wagner, Studien und Kritiken* (1883); *Franz Liszt* (1883); *Hector Berlioz, Studien und Erinnerungen* (1884); *Die Höhenzüge der musikalischen Entwickelung* (1888). He also publ. *Gedichte* (1859; 2nd ed., 1883); a comedy, *Musikalische Leiden* (1856); a German transl. of Berlioz's Collected Writings; wrote connecting text for Schumann's *Manfred* and Liszt's *Prometheus;* and wrote the melodrama *Die Wallfahrt nach Kevelaar,* an *Abendlied* for string orch., a *Wiegenlied* for violin with piano, ballads, songs, men's choruses, etc. —From his notes and collected materials his second wife, Luise, compiled *Hector Berlioz' Leben und Werke* (1900) and a novel, *Richard Wiegand. Episoden aus dem Leben eines grossen Meisters* (1904; modeled closely after the life of Richard Wagner). —His first wife, **Johanna Pohl** (*née* Eyth; b. Karlsruhe, March 19, 1824; d. Baden-Baden, Nov. 25, 1870), was a harp virtuoso.

Pohlig, Karl, German conductor; b. Teplitz, Feb. 10, 1858; d. Brunswick, June 17, 1928. A pupil of Liszt in Weimar, Pest, and Rome, he began his career as a pianist, touring Germany, Austria, Russia, Scandinavia, and Italy; became 1st Kapellmeister at Graz, then assistant conductor to Mahler at the Vienna court opera, and conductor at Covent Garden (1897, 1898); until 1900 1st Kapellmeister at the Hoftheater in Coburg; 1900-07, at the Hoftheater in Stuttgart, and conductor of the symph. concerts; in 1907, engaged as conductor of the Philadelphia Orch.; directed it for 5 seasons, emphasizing the German repertory, and particularly Wagner, of whom he was an impassioned admirer. In 1912 he returned to Germany, and became conductor of the Brunswick Opera. He wrote a symph. poem, *Per Aspera ad Astra* (Stuttgart, 1902), several choral works, and songs.

Poirée (pwăh-rā'), **(Élie-Émile-) Gabriel,** French writer on music; b. Villeneuve-St.-Georges, near Paris, Oct. 9, 1850; d. Paris, May 25, 1925. Wrote for various papers, was librarian of the Ste. Geneviève library, and publ. *L'Évolution de la musique* (1884); an essay on *Tannhäuser* (1895; with Alfred Ernst); *Essais de technique et d'esthétique musicales* (No. 1, Wagner's *Meistersinger,* 1898; No. 2, *Étude sur le discours musical,* 1899; new ed. 1922); *Le Chant gnostico-magique des sept voyelles* (1901; with Ch.-E. Ruelle); *Une nouvelle interprétation du second hymne delphique* (1901); *Chopin* (1907); *R. Wagner* (1921); also publ. a string quartet (1908).

Poise (pwăz), **(Jean Alexandre) Ferdinand,** French composer of comic operas; b. Nîmes, June 3, 1828; d. Paris, May 13, 1892; studied at the Paris Cons. with A. Adam and Zimmerman, taking 2nd Grand Prix de Rome in 1852. He composed a number of light operas, all produced in Paris: *Bonsoir, voisin* (Sept. 18, 1853); *Le Thé de Polichinelle* (May 4, 1856); *Don Pèdre* (April 30, 1858); *Le Jardinier galant* (March 4, 1861); *Le Corricolo* (Nov. 28, 1868); *Les deux billets* (Feb. 19, 1870); *Les trois Souhaits* (Oct. 29, 1873); *La Surprise de l'amour* (Oct. 31, 1877); *L'Amour médicin* (Dec. 20, 1880); *Joli Gilles* (Oct. 10, 1884).

Poissl, Johann Nepomuk, German composer; b. Haukenzell, Bavaria, Feb. 15, 1783; d. Munich, Aug. 17, 1865. He was a pupil of Danzi in Munich; from 1825 to 1848 was in charge of the court music. He wrote about 12 operas; of these the following had a modicum of success: *Athalia* (Munich, June 3, 1814), *Der Wettkampf zu Olympia* (Munich, April 21, 1815), and *Nittetis* (Darmstadt, June 29, 1817); also several oratorios, a Mass, and other works for the church. —Cf. E. Reipschläger, *Schu-*

baur, Danzi und Poissl (Berlin, 1911); also L. Schrott in 'Die Musik' (1940; pp. 299-303).

Pokrass (pŏh-krăhs'), **Dimitri Yakovlevitch,** Russian composer of popular music; b. Kiev, Nov. 7, 1899. He studied piano at St. Petersburg Cons. (1913-17); in 1919 he joined the Soviet Cavalry during the Civil War, and wrote the song, *The Red Cavalry.* This was the first of a series of many songs that have acquired great popularity, among them *If War Comes Tomorrow* (1938), *March of the Tank Brigade, Farewell,* etc. He also wrote music for films.

Polacco, Giorgio, conductor; b. Venice, April 12, 1875. Taught at first in St. Petersburg, he continued in Venice at the Liceo B. Marcello, and graduated from the Cons. G. Verdi in Milan. After conducting in various Italian cities, he was 4 seasons at the Teatro Colón in Buenos Aires, and 7 in Rio de Janeiro; then in Italy again; in 1906 appeared for the first time in the U. S. (San Francisco). On Nov. 11, 1912, he made his début at the Metropolitan Opera House (with Puccini's *Manon Lescaut*); following Toscanini's resignation (1915), Polacco was principal conductor of the Italian, French, and Russian works until 1917; 1918-30, chief conductor of the Italian repertory of the Chicago Opera Co.; then settled in N. Y., where he was still living in 1958.

Poldini, Ede (Eduard), Hungarian composer; b. Budapest, June 13, 1869; d. Vevey, Switzerland, June 29, 1957. He studied at the Budapest Cons., and later with Mandyczewski (theory) and Julius Epstein (piano) in Vienna. In 1908 he went to live at Vevey. In 1935 he received the order of the Hungarian Cross; in 1948 was awarded the Hungarian Pro Arte Prize. He composed the comic operas *The Vagabond and the Princess* (Budapest, Oct. 17, 1903), *The Carnival Marriage* (Budapest, Feb. 16, 1924; produced in London under the title, *Love Adrift,* 1926), and *Himfy* (Budapest, 1938); wrote in all 156 opus numbers, most of them for piano; his *Poupée valsante* became an international favorite; other popular piano pieces are *Arlequinades, Morceaux pittoresques, Images, Moments musicaux, Marionnettes,* etc.

Poldowski (pen name of Irene Regine Wieniawska; by marriage, Lady Dean Paul), composer; b. Brussels, May 16, 1880; d. London, Jan. 28, 1932. She was a daughter of the Polish violinist Henryk Wieniawski; her mother was an Englishwoman. She studied at the Brussels Cons. with Gevaert, and later in London with Percy Pitt; married Sir Aubrey Dean Paul; took additional courses in composition with Gedalge and Vincent d'Indy in Paris; began writing songs to French words, in the Impressionist style; set 21 poems by Paul Verlaine, and 8 poems by others; her songs have been frequently performed at recitals; other compositions are: *Caledonian Market,* a suite of 8 pieces for piano; *Berceuse de l'enfant mourant* for violin and piano; *Tango* for violin and piano; *Suite miniature de chansons à danser* for woodwind instruments; 2 symph. sketches (*Nocturnes* and *Tenements*); and an operetta, *Laughter.*

Pole, William, English writer on music; b. Birmingham, April 22, 1814; d. London, Dec. 30, 1900. He was a prof. of civil engineering at University College, London; also a student of music (Mus. Doc., Oxon., 1864), and examiner in music for London Univ., 1876-90. Publ. *Philosophy of Music* (1879; 6th ed., 1924). Also contributor to the original ed. of Grove's 'Dictionary.'

Polignac (poh-lē-ñak'), **Armande de,** French composer; b. Paris, Jan. 8, 1876. She studied with Gabriel Fauré and Vincent d'Indy; married the Comte de Chabannes; her salon in Paris became a center of artistic and musical activities. She composed the operas *Morgane* and *L'Hypocrite sanctifié;* a dramatic scene, *Judith de Béthulie* (Paris Opéra, March 23, 1916); *La Source lointaine,* Persian ballet (Paris, 1913); *Les mille et une nuits,* Arabian ballet (Paris, 1914); *Chimères,* Greek ballet (Paris Opéra, June 10, 1923); *Urashima,* Japanese ballet; also a Chinese ballet for small orch., *La Recherche de la vérité; Petite suite pour le clavecin* (1939); etc. In 1958 she was living on her country estate at Neaufles le Vieux (Seine-et-Oise).

Polinski, Alexander, Polish music historian; b. Wlostow, June 4, 1845; d. Warsaw, Aug. 13, 1916. He was a pupil of Noskowski, Zelenski, and Minchejmer in Warsaw; 1899, music critic for the 'Warsaw Courier'; from 1904, prof. of history of music at the Warsaw Cons. Publ. (in Polish) *Concerning Church-music and Its Reform* (1890), *The Song 'Bogarodzica' from the Viewpoint of Music* (1903), *History of Polish Music* (1907).

Polívka, Vladimir, Czech pianist and composer; b. Prague, July 6, 1896; d. there, May 11, 1948. He studied at the Prague

Cons., and became a successful pianist; traveled in Europe and America with a chamber music group; from 1923 to 1930 taught piano in Chicago. Returning to Prague (1939), he was appointed prof. at the Cons. there. He wrote many picturesque piano pieces: *Days in Chicago* (1926); *Landscapes in the Years of Occupation* (1941); etc., also several collections of children's pieces; publ. a book of travels, describing his world tour (Prague, 1945).

Polko (*neé* Vogel), **Elise**, German singer and writer on music, b. Leipzig, Jan. 13, 1822; d. Munich, May 15, 1899. Gifted with a fine mezzo-soprano voice, she studied under García at Paris for the stage; but after a few appearances at Frankfurt, she married the railway engineer Eduard Polko (d. 1887), and thenceforward sang only occasionally on the concert stage. In musical circles she became widely known by the *Musikalische Märchen* (publ. in the 'Signale'; later in book-form, 3 vols., 1852; also in English); then followed *Faustina Hasse* (a novel in 2 vols., 1860; 2nd ed., 1870); *Die Bettleroper* (3 vols., 1864); *Alte Herren* (1865; Bach's 6 predecessors at the Thomaskirche, Leipzig); *Verklungene Akkorde* (1868; 3rd ed., 1873); *Erinnerungen an F. Mendelssohn-Bartholdy* (1868; in English, 1869); *Nicolo Paganini und die Geigenbauer* (1876; also Italian transl.); *Vom Gesange* (1876); *Aus der Künstlerwelt* (1878); *Die Klassiker der Musik* (1880); *Meister der Tonkunst* (1897).

Pollack, Egon, Czech conductor; b. Prague, May 3, 1879; d. (of a heart attack during a performance) there, June 14, 1933. Pupil of K. Knittl at the Cons. in Prague; began his career as chorus master at the Landestheater there; in 1905 he was called to the Bremen Opera as 1st Kapellmeister; went to Leipzig in 1910 in the same capacity; 1912-17, 1st Kapellmeister at the Frankfurt Opera; from 1915, conductor of the Wagner works with the Chicago Opera Co.; 1917-32, 1st Kapellmeister at the Hamburg Opera; 1932, conductor at Cairo, Egypt; also guest-conductor at the Vienna State Opera (1933) and in other European cities. In Germany he was regarded as one of the foremost interpreters of R. Strauss.

Pollak, Robert, violinist; b. Vienna, Jan. 18, 1880; studied there and in Leipzig; teacher of violin in Geneva and Lausanne (1905-14), Moscow (1919), Vienna (1919-24); 1926, teacher at the San Francisco Cons.; 1929, went to Japan; 1930-37, prof. at the Imperial Cons. of Tokyo; 1937, returned to California; became an American citizen in 1943. In 1941 he was appointed prof. of violin at the Los Angeles Cons.

Pollaroli, Antonio, Italian composer; son of Carlo Francesco Pollaroli; b. Venice, 1680; d. there, May 4, 1746. He studied with his father, and became his assistant at San Marco in Venice, 1702; in 1723 he was 2nd maestro di cappella there; in 1740, 1st maestro. He wrote the operas *Aristeo* (Venice, 1700) and *Leucippo e Teonoe* (1719), among others.

Pollaroli, Carlo Francesco, Italian organist and composer; b. Brescia, 1653; d. Venice, 1722. He was a pupil of Legrenzi. In 1665 he became a chorister at San Marco, Venice; in 1690, 2nd organist; in 1692, 2nd maestro di cappella. He wrote the oratorios *Jefte, La Rosinda,* and *Jesabel,* and many operas for Venice: *La Forza della virtù* (1693), *Ottone* (1694); *Gl'Inganni felici* (1695), *Faramondo* (1699), *Semiramide* (1714), and *Ariodante* (1716). His *Sonata per organo o cembalo* is reprinted in Torchi's 'L'Arte musicale in Italia' (vol. III).

Pollini, Bernhard (real name Baruch Pohl), German impresario; b. Cologne, Dec. 16, 1838; d. Hamburg, Nov. 27, 1897. A tenor singer, he made his début at Cologne, 1858, as Arturo in Bellini's *I Puritani;* later sang baritone roles in an Italian opera-troupe, of which he subsequently became manager and artistic director. He then undertook the management of the Lemberg Theater, later of the Italian opera at St. Petersburg and Moscow. His fame dates from his assumption, in 1874, of the directorship of the Hamburg City Theater; in 1876 he also became manager of the Altona Theater and in 1894 of the Thalia Theater in Hamburg.

Pollini, Cesare, Cavaliere **de',** Italian writer on music; b. Padua, June 13, 1858; d. there, Jan. 26, 1912. After legal studies at the Univ. of Padua, he took a 2-year course in music with Bazzini in Milan (1881-83); from 1883-85 director of the chief Cons. at Padua; resigned to devote himself to writing and composition. Publ. a *Terminologia musicale tedesco-italiana;* a *Teoria generale della musica; La Musica italiana nelle sue principali fasi storiche;* etc. —Cf. G. Sacerdoti, *C. Pollini* (Padua, 1912); S. Leoni, *C. Pollini nella vita e nell' arte* (Padua, 1917).

Pollini, Francesco (Giuseppe), Austrian pianist; b. Laibach (Ljubljana), of Italian parents, 1763; d. Milan, Sept. 17, 1846. He was a pupil of Mozart (who dedicated a violin rondo to him) at Vienna, later of Zingarelli at Milan, where he was appointed prof. of piano shortly after the opening of the Cons. (1809). He was the first to write piano music on 3 staves, imitated therein by Liszt, Thalberg, and others; a specimen of this style being one of his *32 Esercizi in forma di toccata* (op. 42), a central melody surrounded by passagework for both hands; publ. a method and many pieces for piano; wrote an opera buffa, *La Casetta nei boschi* (Milan, Feb. 25, 1798).

Pollitt, Arthur W., English organist; b. Liverpool, Nov. 27, 1878; d. there, Feb. 3, 1933. He studied at the Royal College of Music in Manchester, where he became assistant organist at the Cathedral; 1900-17, organist at the Liverpool Church, and at the School for the Blind; 1918, chorus director of the Liverpool Philharmonic Society. Publ. *The Necessity of Music in a School Curriculum; The Self-reliant Musician; The Enjoyment of Music;* etc.

Polovinkin, Leonid, Russian composer; b. Kurgan, Aug. 13, 1894; d. Moscow, Feb. 2, 1949. He studied at the Moscow Cons. with Glière and Vassilenko; began his career as a composer by writing theater music in Moscow after the revolution of 1917; adopted a modernistic idiom; emphasized the element of humor. Later, however, he devoted more time to instrumental music; wrote 9 symphonies, 4 string quartets, 2 piano trios, several overtures on folk themes; 5 piano sonatas; 24 postludes for piano; songs.

Ponce (pŏhn'-sĕh), **Manuel María,** distinguished Mexican composer; b. Fresnillo, Dec. 8, 1882; d. Mexico City, April 24, 1948. He studied piano with his older sister; in 1905, went to Europe, where he took lessons in composition with Enrico Bossi at Bologna and in piano with Martin Krause in Berlin. Upon his return to Mexico, he taught piano at the National Cons. He gave a concert of his compositions in Mexico on July 7, 1912, which included a piano concerto. During World War I he lived in N. Y. and in Havana; then went to Paris for additional study, and took lessons with Paul Dukas. His contact with French music wrought a radical change in his style of composition; his later works are more polyphonic in structure and more economical in form. He possessed a great gift of melody; one of his songs, *Estrellita,* became a universal favorite, often mistaken for a folksong. In 1941 he made a tour in South America, conducting his own works. He was the first Mexican composer of the 20th century to employ an identifiably modern musical language; his place in the history of Mexican music is a very important one. His works are often performed in Mexico; a concert hall was named after him in the Instituto de Bellas Artes. —Works: for orch.: *Estampas nocturnas* (1923), *Canto y danza de los antiguos Mexicanos* (1933), *Chapultepec,* symph. triptych (Mexico, Aug. 25, 1929; revised version, Mexico, Aug. 24, 1934), *Suite en estilo antiguo* (1935), *Poema elegiaco* (Mexico, June 28, 1935), *Ferial* (Mexico, Aug. 9, 1940), *Concierto del Sur,* for guitar and orch. (Montevideo, Oct. 4, 1941), violin concerto (Mexico, Aug. 20, 1943); piano trio (1911), *4 Miniaturas,* for string quartet (1929), *Pequeña suite en estilo antiguo,* for violin, viola, and cello (1933), sonata for violin and viola (1935), cello sonata (1922); numerous piano pieces, some based on Mexican rhythms; about 30 songs; 34 arrangements of Mexican folksongs. A collection of his articles was publ. posthumously in 1948. —Cf. Otto Mayer-Serra, *Música y músicos de Latino-América* (Mexico, 1947; vol. 2, pp. 782-86); D. López Alonso, *Manuel M. Ponce: ensayo biográfico* (Mexico, 1950); J. C. Romero, *Efemérides de Manuel Ponce* in 'Nuestra Música' (No. 2, 1950).

Ponchielli (pŏhn-kyĕhl'-lē), **Amilcare,** Italian composer; b. Paderno Fasolaro, Cremona, Aug. 31, 1834; d. Milan, Jan. 16, 1886. He studied at the Milan Cons. (1843-54); his first dramatic work (written with 3 other students) was the operetta *Il Sindaco Babbeo* (Milan, March 3, 1851). Leaving the Cons., he was organist at S. Ilario in Cremona; then became bandmaster. He brought out the opera *I promessi sposi* at Cremona (Aug. 30, 1856), followed by *La Savoiarda* (Cremona, Jan. 19, 1861; revised as *Lina,* Milan, Nov. 17, 1877), and *Roderico, re de' Goti* (Piacenza, Dec. 26, 1863). His first striking success was achieved with a revised version of *I promessi sposi* (Milan, Dec. 5, 1872); continuous good fortune attended the production of his operas *I Lituani* (La Scala, March 7, 1874; revised and revived in 1884 as *Aldona*), *La Gioconda* (his most famous work; Milan, April 8, 1876), *Il Figliuol prodigo* (Milan, Dec. 26, 1880), and *Marion Delorme* (Milan, March 17, 1885). An unfinished opera, *I Mori di Venezia,* in the orchestration by A.

Cadore, was produced posthumously in Monte Carlo (March 17, 1914). Ponchielli also brought out a musical farce, *Il Parlatore eterno* (Lecco, Oct. 18, 1873) and the ballets *Le due gemelle* and *Clarina* (both in 1873); a cantata in honor of Donizetti; a funeral march, *Il 29 Maggio,* for Manzoni; a fine patriotic hymn, *Inno in memoria di Giuseppe Garibaldi.* Of his operas, *La Gioconda* established itself in the repertory everywhere; the ballet number from it, *Dance of the Hours,* is extremely popular at concerts of light orchestral music. Ponchielli also wrote sacred music, for use at the Cathedral of Bergamo, where he was maestro di cappella from 1881 to 1886. —Cf. A. Mandelli, *Le Distrazioni di A. Ponchielli* (Cremona, 1897); G. Cesari, *A. Ponchielli nell' arte del suo tempo* (Cremona, 1934); G. de Napoli, *A. Ponchielli* (Cremona, 1936); A. Damerini, *A. Ponchielli* (Turin, 1940).

Pond, Sylvanus Billings, American music publisher and composer; b. Milford, Vt., April 5, 1792; d. Brooklyn, March 12, 1871. He was a prominent musician of his time; conducted the N. Y. Sacred Musical Society and the N. Y. Academy of Sacred Music; wrote songs for Sunday School; ed. and publ. *Union Melodies* (1838), *The U. S. Psalmody* (N. Y., 1841), and *The Book of Praise,* for the Reformed Dutch Church in America (N. Y., 1866); composed the hymn tunes *Armenia* (1835) and *Franklin Square* (1850). Early in life, he went to Albany; established a piano workshop; from 1820, was partner of the publishing house of Meacham and Pond there; in 1832 he joined Firth & Hall of N. Y., and the firm's name became Firth, Hall & Pond; 1848, reorganized as Firth, Pond & Co., one of the principal publishers of Stephen Foster's songs; in 1850, S. B. Pond retired, and his son, William A. Pond, became the owner; upon the withdrawal of Firth in 1863, the firm became known as William A. Pond & Co.; W. A. Pond's elder son, William A. Pond, Jr., was taken into partnership, but died in 1884; William A. Pond Sr. died the following year, and his 2 sons, Albert Edward and George Warren Pond, succeeded him. In 1934, Joseph Fletcher acquired the catalogue; in 1946, it was purchased by Carl Fischer, Inc. For the dealings of Firth, Pond & Co. with Stephen Foster, see J. T. Howard, *Stephen Foster, America's Troubadour* (N. Y., 1934); consult also H. Dichter and E. Shapiro, *Early American Sheet Music, Its Lure and Its Lore, 1768-1889* (N. Y., 1941).

Poniatowski, Josef (Michal Xawery Franciszek Jan), Prince of Monte Rotondo, Polish composer; b. Rome, Feb. 20, 1816; d. Chiselhurst, England, July 3, 1873. He was a member of the Polish nobility; his uncle was a marshal in Napoleon's army. He studied in Florence, and appeared on the stage as a tenor; then wrote operas (to Italian and French librettos); in 1848 he went to Paris and was elevated to the rank of Senator by Napoleon III; after the fall of the Second Empire, he went to England. —Operas: *Giovanni da Procida* (Florence, 1838); *Don Desiderio* (Pisa, Dec. 26, 1840); *Ruy Blas* (Lucca, 1843); *Malek-Adel* (Genoa, June 20, 1846); *Esmeralde* (Florence, June 27, 1847); *Pierre de Médicis* (Paris, March 9, 1860); *Au travers du mur* (Paris, May 9, 1861); *L'Aventurier* (Paris, Jan. 26, 1865); *La Contessina* (Paris, April 28, 1868); *Gelmina* (London, June 4, 1872). Also composed a Mass in F.

Poniridis, Georges, Greek composer and violinist; b. Constantinople, of Greek parents, Oct. 8, 1892. He studied violin at the Brussels Cons., winning 1st prize; composition with Vincent d'Indy at the Schola Cantorum in Paris. After that he lived mostly in France; returned to Greece at the outbreak of World War II, and was appointed head of the music dept. of the Ministry of Education. —Works: *Triptyque symphonique* (Athens, Nov. 22, 1937); symph. No. 2 (Athens, Feb. 1, 1948); incidental music to ancient Greek plays; arrangements of Greek folksongs.

Pons (pohns), **Charles,** French composer; b. Nice, Dec. 8, 1870; d. Paris, April, 1957. He studied organ, and earned his living as church organist in his youth; then turned to theater music, and produced a long series of operas: *L'Épreuve* (Nice, 1904), *Laura* (Paris, 1906), *Mourette* (Marseilles, 1909), *Le Voile du bonheur* (Paris, April 26, 1911), *Françoise* (Lyons, 1913), *Loin du bal* (Paris, 1913), *Les Fauves* (Paris, 1917), *Le Drapeau* (Paris, 1918), *Le Passant de Noël* (Nice, 1935), *L'Envol de la Marseillaise* (Marseilles, 1947); further wrote an overture, *Pyrrhus;* a symph. poem, *Heures vendéennes;* a *Symphonie tragique;* several orchestral suites; an oratorio, *La Samaritaine* (Nice, 1900), and other vocal works with orch.: *La Mort de Démosthène* (Paris, 1928) and *Dans la forêt normande* (1934); chamber music; songs. He wrote music criticism for 'Paris-Presse' and other publications.

Pons, Lily (baptismal names, **Alice Joséphine**), famous coloratura soprano; b. Draguignan, France, April 12, 1904. She entered the Paris Cons. at the age of 13; first studied piano; appeared at the Théâtre des Variétés in Paris as a singer at 15; made her operatic début in *Lakmé* at Mulhouse; subsequently studied in Paris with Alberto de Gorostiaga; was engaged at the Metropolitan Opera, and sang Lucia (Jan. 3, 1931) with excellent success; while in N. Y., continued her vocal studies, with Maria Gay and G. Zenatello. She became one of the most celebrated stars; her most brilliant roles were Lakmé, Lucia, Gilda, Rosina, and Marie in *La Fille du Régiment;* also appeared in motion pictures. She was married to August Mestritz, a publisher, in 1923; divorced, 1933; in 1938 she married the conductor André Kostelanetz; toured with him all over the world, making their home at Silvermine, Conn.

Ponselle (real name, Ponzillo), **Carmela**, American mezzo-soprano, sister of Rosa Ponselle; b. Schenectady, N. Y., June 7, 1892. She began to study singing rather late in life; made her professional début in 1923; first appearance at the Metropolitan Opera House as Amneris in *Aida* (Dec. 5, 1925); remained on its roster until 1928; was re-engaged for the seasons 1930-35; then devoted most of her time to teaching.

Ponselle (real name, Ponzillo), **Rosa**, American soprano; b. Meriden, Conn., Jan. 22, 1897. She sang in various entertainment places in New Haven; then appeared with her sister Carmela in vaudeville in Pittsburgh. She made her first appearance as an opera singer at the Metropolitan Opera, N. Y., in the role of Leonora in *La Forza del Destino,* opposite Caruso (Nov. 15, 1918); remained with the Metropolitan Opera until 1936; received praise for her opulent voice, with fine low tones; her interpretations of the Italian roles were particularly impressive. —Cf. O. Thompson, *The American Singer* (N. Y., 1937; pp. 335-46).

Ponte, Lorenzo da. See **Da Ponte.**

Pontécoulant (pŏhn-tā- kŏŏ-lăhn'), **Louis-Adolphe de Doulcet,** Comte de, French writer on music; b. Paris, 1794; d. Bois-Colombe, near Paris, Feb. 20, 1882. After an adventurous career, he began the study of music history and the construction of instruments; publ. the following: *Essai sur la facture musicale considérée dans ses rapports avec l'art, l'industrie, et le commerce* (1857; 2nd augmented ed., as *Organographie* in 2 parts, 1861); *Musée instrumental du Conservatoire de musique* (1864); *La Musique à l'Exposition universelle de 1867* (1868); and *Les Phénomènes de la musique* (1868).

Pontoglio (pŏhn-tŏhl'-yŏh), **Cipriano,** Italian composer; b. Grumello del Piano, Dec. 25, 1831; d. Milan, Feb. 22, 1892. He was a pupil of Ant. Cagnoni in Milan, and P. Serrao in Naples; then opened a music school in Milan. He composed 5 operas: *Lamberto Malatesta* (Pavia, 1857), *Tebaldo Brusato* (Brescia, 1865; rewritten as *L'Assedio di Brescia,* Rome, June 15, 1872), *La Schiava greca* (Bergamo, 1868), *La Notte di Natale* (Bergamo, Aug. 29, 1872), and *Edoardo Stuart* (Milan, May 21, 1887); publ. songs, piano pieces, etc.

Poole, Elizabeth, English mezzo-soprano; b. London, April 5, 1820; d. Langley, Bucks, Jan. 14, 1906. She made her début at Drury Lane in 1834; sang in Italian opera in the U. S. (appearing with Malibran). Until her retirement in 1870 she was immensely popular as a ballad singer. Balfe wrote for her *'Tis gone, the past is all a dream,* which she introduced into *The Bohemian Girl.*

Poot (pŏht), **Marcel,** Belgian composer; b. Vilvorde, near Brussels, May 7, 1901. He received his first musical training from his father; then studied at the Brussels Cons. and at the Flemish Cons. of Antwerp; later took courses with Paul Gilson; was an original member (1925) of a group of Belgian composers, the 'Synthétistes,' dedicated to propaganda of new musical ideas. In 1930 he received the Rubens prize, which enabled him to study with Paul Dukas in Paris. Returning to Belgium, he held several teaching posts; also wrote music criticism; taught at the Brussels Cons.; became its director in 1949. The most striking element of his music is its rhythmic vivacity; he generally adheres to a basic tonal design, pursuing the aim of artistic utilitarianism. —Works: opera *Moretus* (1943); ballets: *Paris et les trois divines* (1933), *Camera* (1937), *Pygmalion* (1952); 3 symphonies (1929; 1938; 1952); symph. sketches *Charlot* (inspired by Charlie Chaplin's films; 1926); *Poème de l'espace* for large orch. (glorifying the Lindbergh flight; Liège Festival of the International Society for Contemporary Music, Sept. 4, 1930); *Jazz Music* (Brussels, Feb. 21, 1932); *Ouverture* *joyeuse* (1934); *Danse laudative* for orch. (1937); *Légende épique* for piano and orch. (1938); *Sinfonietta* (Chicago, Oct. 22, 1946); *Mouvement perpétuel* for orch. (1953); oratorio *Icare* (1945); piano quartet (1932); scherzo for 4 saxophones (1941); octet for wind and string instruments (1948); string quartet (1952); also music for radio and for films. A catalogue of his works, with a biographical sketch, was publ. by the Centre Belge de Documentation Musicale in 1953.

Popov (pŏh-pohff'), **Gavriil Nikolayevitch,** Russian composer; b. Novotscherkask, Sept. 12, 1904. He studied at the St. Petersburg Cons. with Nikolayev (piano) and Vladimir Shtcherbatchev (composition). From his student days, he adopted the procedures of modern music; his septet (Moscow, Dec. 13, 1927) was written in a system of dissonant counterpoint then fashionable in Western Europe; his 1st symph. (1927-34) was in a similar vein. When modern music became the target of attack in Russia, Popov modified his style towards a more popular conception, following the tenets of 'socialist realism'; wrote several film scores, among them *Communist Youth Union, Leader of Electrification* (1932; also as a symph. suite). —Other works: symph. No. 2, subtitled *Fatherland* (Moscow, Feb. 15, 1944); symph. No. 3, for string orch., on Spanish themes (Moscow, Jan. 31, 1947); symph. No. 4, *Glory Be to the Fatherland* (1949); choral works; film music.

Popper, David, famous cellist and composer; b. Prague, June 16, 1843; d. Baden, near Vienna, Aug. 7, 1913. He was a pupil of Goltermann at the Prague Cons.; made his first appearance as soloist at the Karlsruhe Music Festival (March 29, 1865), and in subsequent years played with great success in many European music centers. From 1868 to 1873 he was 1st cellist of the Vienna Court Orch. In 1872 he married the pianist Sophie Menter (divorced, 1886). From 1896 until the year of his death he taught at the Budapest Cons. The diploma making him a 'Hofrat' of the Austro-Hungarian Empire reached him on the morning of his death. Many of his compositions for his instrument have become great favorites with cello players; while not strikingly original, they are melodious, pleasing, and eminently idiomatic. —Works: 4 cello concertos; solo cello pieces: *Sérénade orientale,* op. 18, *Gavotte* in D, op. 23, *Tarentelle,* op. 33, *Elfentanz,* op. 39, *Im Walde,* suite, op. 50, *Ungarische Rhapsodie,* op. 68; *Requiem* for 3 cellos (performed by him with Delsart and Howell, London, Nov. 25, 1891); publ. the cello methods, *Hohe Schule des Violoncellspiels* (40 studies), op. 73; *10 mittelschwere grosse Etüden* (preparatory studies to op. 73), op. 76.

Poradowski, Stefan Boleslaw, Polish composer; b. Wloclawek, Aug. 16, 1902. He studied at the Cons. of Poznan with Opienski; in 1930, appointed instructor there. He wrote 5 symphonies; an oratorio, *Odkupienie* (*Redemption*); a *Concerto antico,* for viola d'amore and strings; a double-bass concerto; a *Polish Rhapsody,* for violin and orch.; several string quartets and string trios; violin sonata; piano pieces; publ. textbooks on harmony, composition, and orchestration.

Porges, Heinrich, writer on music; b. Prague, Nov. 25, 1837; d. Munich, Nov. 17, 1900. He was a pupil of Cölestin Müller (piano) and Zwonař (theory). In 1863 he became co-editor with Brendel of the 'Neue Zeitschrift für Musik,' and was in close intercourse with Wagner and Cornelius; lived for a time in Vienna, and in 1867 was called to Munich by King Ludwig II, for whom he had written a study on *Tristan und Isolde* (publ. 1906 by Hans von Wolzogen). There he was literary editor of the 'Süddeutsche Presse'; from 1880, music critic for the 'Neueste Nachrichten.' He organized the 'Porges'scher Gesangverein' in 1886. —Writings: *Die Aufführung von Beethovens 9. Symphonie unter Richard Wagner in Bayreuth* (1872), *Die Bühnenproben zu den 1876er Festspielen* (1877), and other essays on Wagner in German periodicals.

Porpora, Nicola Antonio, Italian composer; b. Naples, Aug. 17, 1686; d. there, March 3, 1768. The son of a bookseller, he entered the Cons. dei Poveri at Naples at the age of 10 and studied with Gaetano Greco, Matteo Giordano, and Ottavio Campanile. Porpora's first opera, *Agrippina,* was presented at the Royal Palace of Naples (Nov. 4, 1708); Cardinal Grimani attended the performance and wrote a libretto on the same subject for Handel. This episode gave rise to the incorrect statement (by Fétis and others) that Handel heard Porpora's opera in Rome in 1710. Porpora produced in Naples 2 more operas: *Flavio Anicio Olibrio* (1711) and *Basilio, re d'oriente* (1713). From 1711 until 1725, he held the title of maestro di cappella to Philip, Landgrave of Hesse-Darmstadt. He gained a great reputation as a singing teacher, and numbered among his pupils the famous castrati Farinelli, Caffarelli, Antonio Uberti (who called himself 'Porporino' out of respect for his teacher), and Salimbeni. Metastasio, who wrote librettos for several of Porpora's operas, was also his pupil. Porpora's career as a singing teacher was divided between Naples and Venice. In Naples he taught at the Conservatories of Sant' Onofrio (1715-22 and 1760-61) and Santa Maria di Loreto (1739-41 and 1758-60); in Venice he gave lessons at the Ospedali degli Incurabili (1726-33 and 1737-39), the Ospedali della Pietà (1742-46), and the Ospedaletto (1746-47). In 1718 Porpora collaborated with Domenico Scarlatti in the writing of the opera *Berenice, regina d'Egitto,* produced in Rome (1718). At about this time he succeeded in obtaining support from the Austrian court. His opera *Temistocle* was produced in Vienna on the Emperor's birthday (Oct. 1, 1718); his next opera, *Faramondo,* was staged in Naples (Nov. 19, 1719). He continued to write operas for theaters in Naples and Rome: *Eumene* (Rome, 1721); *Adelaide* (Rome, 1723); *Semiramide, regina dell' Assiria* (Naples, 1724); *Didone abbandonata* (his first opera to a libretto by Metastasio; produced at Reggio, 1725). In 1725 Porpora was in Vienna; in 1726 he settled in Venice. He wrote the following operas during the next 8 years: *Meride e Selinunte* (Venice, 1726); *Siroe, re di Persia* (Rome, 1727); *Semiramide riconosciuta* (Venice, 1729); *Mitridate* (Rome, 1730); *Tamerlano* (1730); *Poro* (Turin, 1731); *Germanico in Germania* (Rome, 1732); *Issipile* (Rome, 1733). In 1733 he applied for the post of maestro di cappella at San Marco in Venice, but failed to obtain it. In the same year he was engaged by the directors of the 'Opera of the Nobility' in London (organized as a rival company to that of Handel). For this venture Porpora wrote 5 operas: *Arianna in Nasso* (Dec. 29, 1733), *Enea nel Lazio* (May 11, 1734), *Polifemo* (Feb. 1, 1735), *Ifigenia in Aulide* (May 3, 1735), and *Mitridate* (Jan. 24, 1736; a different score from the earlier opera of the same title). For a while he competed successfully with Handel, but soon the 'Opera of the Nobility' began to falter, and Porpora left London on the eve of the company's collapse. From 1747-51, he was in Dresden as singing teacher to the Electoral Princess. There he became Hasse's competitor for the position of musical director. Although Hasse himself conducted Porpora's 'pastoral drama' *Filandro* (Dresden, July 18, 1747), their relationship was made difficult by the intrigues of Hasse's wife, the singer Faustina Bordoni. In 1751 Porpora left Dresden for Vienna, where he became the teacher of Haydn, who paid for his lessons by serving Porpora as accompanist and personal helper. Porpora returned to Naples in 1758. His last stage work, *Il Trionfo di Camilla* (Naples, May 30, 1760; a revision and adaptation to a new text of an earlier opera of the same title produced in Naples on Jan. 20, 1740), was unsuccessful; nor could he regain his former teaching positions. His last years were spent in poverty. —Porpora wrote 44 operas in all, 11 oratorios, and numerous Masses and motets. His instrumental music includes 6 *sinfonie da camera* (London, 1735), 12 violin sonatas (Vienna, 1754), a cello concerto, and a cello sonata (the latter two exist in modern reprints). The fugues in Clementi's *Practical Harmony* are from Porpora's violin sonatas, some of which have been publ. by A. Schering, F. David, D. Alard, and A. Moffat. A trio sonata was publ. in Riemann's *Collegium Musicum* (no. 23). —Bibliography: Marchese di Villarosa, *Memorie dei compositori di musica del regno di Napoli* (Naples, 1840); F. Clément, *Les Musiciens célèbres depuis le XVIe siècle* (Paris, 1868); S. Fassini, *Il Melodramma italiano a Londra* (Turin, 1914); S. di Giacomo, *I quattro antiche Conservatorii di musica di Napoli* (Palermo, 1925); F. Walker, *A Chronology of the Life and Works of Nicola Porpora,* in 'Italian Studies' (vol. 6, Cambridge, 1951); U. Prota-Giurleo, *Per una esatta biografia di Nicolo Porpora,* in 'La Scala' (Jan., 1957; establishing for the first time his dates of birth and death).

Porporino. See **Uberti.**

Porrino, Ennio, Italian composer; b. Cagliari, Sardinia, Jan. 20, 1910; studied at the Santa Cecilia in Rome with Mulè, and later took an additional course with Respighi. He subsequently taught at Santa Cecilia; in 1954 became prof. of composition at the Naples Cons. —Works: 1-act opera *Gli Orazi* (Milan, 1941); the ballet *Altair* (Naples, 1942); for orch.: *Tartarin de Tarascon,* overture (Rome, 1933), *Sardegna,* symph. poem, based on Sardinian folk themes (Rome, 1933; his most popular work), *3 Canzoni italiane; Sonata drammatica* for piano and orch.; *I Canti della Sardegna* for voice and orch. (1948); songs.

Porro, Pierre-Jean, famous French guitar virtuoso; b. Béziers, 1750; d. Montmorency, 1831. Through his influence the guitar became a fashionable instrument in Paris; he had a class of pupils there; also was editor and publisher of 'Journal de Guitarre' (1787-1803). He publ. a guitar method, *Tableau Méthodique,* numerous divertissements, sonatas, canzonets, for guitar solo and with other instruments; also a 'Collection de musique sacrée' for 4 mixed voices and organ. —Cf. F. Donnadieu, *Porro, compositeur et éditeur de musique* (Béziers, 1897).

Porsile, Giuseppe, Italian composer; b. Naples, 1680; d. Vienna, May 29, 1750. He served as maestro di cappella in Naples and later in Barcelona; from 1720 to 1740, was singing master at the Vienna court, and composer to the Austrian Empress Amalia. He wrote the operas *Meride e Selinunte* (performed at Laxenburg, near Vienna, Aug. 28, 1721), *Spartaco* (Vienna, Feb. 21, 1726), and 4 others; 12 oratorios, various cantatas; instrumental pieces.

Porta, Costanzo, important Italian composer; b. Cremona, c. 1529; d. Padua, May 26, 1601. He studied with Willaert in Venice; was chorusmaster at Osimo, near Ancona, from 1552 to 1564. In 1564 he became choirmaster at the Basilica of St. Anthony in Padua; in 1567, received a similar post at the Cathedral of Ravenna; in 1575 was in Loreto, returning to Padua in 1585. He was highly esteemed as a master contrapuntist; wrote not only sacred music but also madrigals; combined great technical skill with a characteristically Italian grace of melodic line. —Works: books of motets *a* 4 (1559), *a* 5 (1555), *a* 6 (1585), *a* 4-8 (1580); 1 book of Masses for 4, 5, 6 voices (1578); 2 books of Introits for 5 voices (1566, 1588); 4 books of madrigals for 4, 5 voices (1555-85); hymns for 4 voices (posthumous, 1602); vesper psalms and canticles for 8 voices (1605); in MS are various madrigals, Lamentations, a treatise on counterpoint, etc. Reprints are in Torchi's 'L'Arte musicale in Italia' (vol. 1), Einstein's *The Golden Age of the Madrigal* (N. Y., 1942), etc. —Cf. G. Reese, *Music in the Renaissance* (N. Y., 1954; pp. 493-95); A. Garbelotto, *Il Padre Costanzo Porta da Cremona* (Rome, 1955; a documented biography).

Porter, Cole, American composer of popular music; b. Peru, Ind., June 9, 1893. He was educated at Yale Univ. (B.A. 1913); then took an academic course at the Harvard Law School, and later at the Harvard School of Music. While at Yale Univ., he wrote football songs (*Yale Bull Dog Song, Bingo Eli Yale,* etc.); also composed music for college functions. His first production in N. Y. was *See America First* (N. Y., 1916). In 1916 he joined the Foreign Legion, but later was transferred to the French Army. After the armistice he remained in Paris and studied music at the Schola Cantorum. Returning to America, he devoted himself entirely to the writing of musical comedies, of which the following are notable: *Hitchy-Koo* (1919), *50 Million Frenchmen* (1929), *Gay Divorcee* (1932), *Anything Goes* (1934), *Jubilee* (1935), *Red, Hot, and Blue* (1936), *Leave It to Me* (1938), *Dubarry was a Lady* (1939), *Panama Hattie* (1940), *Let's Face It* (1941), *Something for the Boys* (1943), *Mexican Hayride* (1944), *Kiss Me, Kate* (1948), *Out of This World* (1950), *Can-Can* (1953), and *Silk Stockings* (1955). Of his many songs, at least a dozen became great favorites: *Begin the Beguine, It's De-Lovely, Night and Day, My Heart Belongs to Daddy, Don't Fence Me In, Wunderbar,* etc.

Porter, Quincy, American composer; b. New Haven, Conn., Feb. 7, 1897. He was brought up in an intellectual atmosphere; his father and his grandfather were professors at Yale Univ. He studied with David Stanley Smith and Horatio Parker at the Yale School of Music (Mus. Bac., 1921); submitted a violin concerto for the American Prix de Rome, received an honorable mention; also won the Steinert and Osborne prizes. After graduation he went to Paris, where he took courses with Lucien Capet (violin) and Vincent d'Indy (composition). Returning to America, he earned a living as a violinist in theater orchestras in N. Y.; then took an additional course in composition with Ernest Bloch. He taught at the Cleveland Institute of Music (1922-28 and 1931-32); played the viola in the Ribaupierre String Quartet there; spent 3 years in Paris on a Guggenheim Fellowship (1928-31); was prof. at Vassar College, and conductor of the Vassar Orch. (1932-38); in 1938, succeeded Frederick Converse as dean of the New England Cons., Boston; from 1942 to 1946, was its director. In 1946 he was appointed prof. at Yale Univ. His music is built on strong contrapuntal lines, with incisive rhythms; his harmonic procedures often reach stridently polytonal sonorities; the general idiom combines the influences of both the modern German and the modern French styles. —Works: *Ukrainian Suite,* for string orch. (Rochester, N. Y., May 1, 1925); *Suite in C minor* for orch.

(1926); *Poem and Dance,* for orch. (Cleveland, June 24, 1932, composer conducting); *Dance in Three-Time,* for chamber orch. (St. Louis, July 2, 1937); symph. no. 1 (N. Y., April 2, 1938, composer conducting); *Music for Strings* (1941); *Fantasy on a Pastoral Theme,* for organ and string orch. (1942); viola concerto (Columbia Univ. Festival, N. Y., May 16, 1948); *Fantasy* for cello and small orch. (1950); *The Desolate City,* for baritone and orch. (1950); *Concerto Concertante* for 2 pianos and orch. (Louisville, March 17, 1954; awarded the Pulitzer Prize); *New England Episodes,* symph. suite (commissioned for the Inter-American Music Festival, Washington, D. C., April 18, 1958); 8 string quartets (1923, 1925, 1930, 1931, 1935, 1937, 1943, 1950); *In Monasterio,* for string quartet (1927); quintet for clarinet and strings (1929); *Quintet on a Childhood Theme,* for flute and strings (1940); string sextet on Slavic folk tunes (1947); 2 violin sonatas (1926, 1929); *Little Trio,* for flute, violin, and viola (1928); suite for viola alone (1930); sonata for French horn and piano (1946); 4 pieces for violin and piano (1947); duo for violin and viola (1954); duo for flute and harp (1957); piano sonata (1930); *Canon and Fugue* for organ (1941); *6 Miniatures* for piano (1943); *Day Dreams* for piano (1957); several songs. —Cf. H. Elwell, *Quincy Porter,* in 'Modern Music' (vol. 23, no. 1); H. Boatwright, *Quincy Porter,* in the 'Bulletin of American Composers Alliance' (No. 3, 1957).

Portnoff, Mischa, composer; b. Berlin (of Russian parents), Aug. 29, 1901. He studied with his father, Leo Portnoff; toured in Scandinavia as pianist; settled in N. Y. in 1924, and devoted himself to teaching piano and composition. He has written mainly for piano; also many works for 2 pianos. His piano concerto was performed by the N. Y. Philharmonic on Feb. 23, 1941.

Portugal (Portogallo), Marcos Antonio da Fonseca (real name, Ascenção), Portuguese composer; b. Lisbon, March 24, 1762; d. Rio de Janeiro, Feb. 7, 1830. A pupil at the ecclesiastical seminary at Lisbon, his musical education was continued under the operatic singer Borselli (singing and composition), by whose influence he was appointed cembalist at the Madrid opera in 1782. Between 1784 and 1791 he wrote for Lisbon 17 stage works, mostly ephemeral. His reputation was made in Italy, where, with the exception of a short visit to Lisbon, he lived from 1793 to 1799, bringing out 22 Italian operas. From 1799 to 1810 he acted as conductor at the San Carlos Theater, Lisbon, producing Italian and Portuguese operas. His *Il Filosofo seducente, ossia Non irritar le donne* (Venice, Dec. 27, 1798), was selected by Napoleon for opening the Théâtre Italien at Paris in 1801. In 1807 the royal family fled to Brazil before the French invasion; Portugal remained until the San Carlos Theater was closed in 1810, and then followed the court to Rio de Janeiro, where he was made general music director. The royal theater of São João, after its inauguration in 1813, produced several new operas by Portugal. In that year he became director of the new Cons. at Vera Cruz, jointly with his brother Simão; visited Italy in 1815, returned to Rio de Janeiro, and passed his last years there as an invalid. His masterpiece is generally assumed to be *Fernando nel Messico* (Venice, Jan. 16, 1798; written for the famous English singer Elizabeth Billington; produced in London, in Italian, March 31, 1803); other Italian operas that had a favorable reception were *Demofoonte* (Milan, Feb. 8, 1794); *Le Donne cambiate* (Venice, Oct. 22, 1797); of Portuguese operas, *A Castanheira* (The *Chestnut Seller*), produced in Lisbon in 1790, enjoyed considerable popular success. He further wrote about 100 sacred works. —Cf. Manoel Carvalhães, *Marcos Portugal na sua musica dramatica* (Lisbon, 1910).

Posselt, Ruth, American violinist; b. Medford, Mass., Sept. 6, 1914. She studied with Emanuel Ondricek; has given numerous recitals in America and Europe; gave the world premières of violin concertos by Walter Piston, Vladimir Dukelsky, Edward Burlingame Hill, and others. On July 3, 1940 she married Richard Burgin (q.v.).

Poston, Elizabeth, English pianist and composer; b. Highfield, Hertfordshire, Oct. 24, 1905. She studied piano with Harold Samuel; in 1940 she became director of music in the European service of the British Broadcasting Corporation; after 1945 devoted herself mainly to composition. In her music she shows a strong predilection for the Elizabethan period; her stylizations of old song patterns are made adroitly and preserve an archaic flavor.

Pothier (poh-t'yā'), Dom **Joseph,** learned authority on Gregorian chant, b. Bouzemont, near Saint-Dié, Dec. 7, 1835; d. Conques, Belgium, Dec. 8, 1923. He became a Benedictine monk in 1859 at Solesmes; 1862, sub-prior; 1866, prof. of theology at the Solesmes Monastery; 1895, prior at the Benedicine monastery of St.-Wandrille; 1898, abbot there. When the religious orders were banned from France, he moved to Belgium. In 1904 he was appointed by Pius X president of the publication committee of the 'Editio Vaticana.' —Writings: *Les Mélodies grégoriennes* (highly important source book, based on the study of original MSS; Tournai, 1880; 3rd ed., 1890; in German, 1881; in Italian, 1890); *Méthode du chant grégorien* (Paris, 1902). Was a chief editor of *Liber Gradualis* (Tournai, 1883); *Hymni de Tempore et de Sanctis* (Solesmes, 1885); *Processionale Monasticum* (Solesmes, 1888); *Liber Antiphonarius* (Solesmes, 1891); *Liber Responsorialis* (Solesmes, 1895); *Cantus Mariales* (Paris, 1902). He contributed many valuable articles to the 'Revue du Chant Grégorien.' —Cf. F. Velluz, *Étude bibliographique sur les mélodies grégoriennes de Dom Joseph Pothier* (Grenoble, 1881); N. Rousseau, *L'École grégorienne de Solesmes* (Tournai, 1911); A. Le. Guennant, *Précis de rythmique grégorienne d'après les principes de Solesmes* (Paris, 1948); M. Blanc, *L'Enseignement musical de Solesmes* (Paris, 1953; chap. 2).

Potter, Philip Cipriani Hambly, English pianist and composer; b. London, Oct. 2, 1792; d. there, Sept. 26, 1871. He studied music first with his father; then with Attwood, Callcott, and Crotch; also took piano lessons with Woelffl during the latter's sojourn in England. In 1817 he went to Vienna, where he studied composition with Aloys Förster; he met Beethoven, who gave him good advice. He traveled in Germany and Italy; returned to London in 1821; the following year he became piano teacher at the Royal Academy of Music; succeeded Crotch as principal in 1832; retired in 1859. From 1855 to 1870 he was conductor of the Madrigal Society. He frequently appeared in London as pianist; introduced 3 of Beethoven's concertos (Nos. 1, 3, 4) to England. He publ. a number of piano pieces, including a set of variations under the title *The Enigma* comprising 'variations in the style of 5 eminent artists.' This early anticipation of the famous work by Elgar was not known to Elgar himself. In MS are 9 symphonies, 4 overtures, 3 piano concertos, and other pieces. Wagner conducted one of Potter's symphonies during his engagement with the London Philharmonic Society in 1855. Potter ed. for Novello a series of Mozart's piano works. —Cf. 'Dictionary of National Biography' (vol. 46).

Poueigh (pŏŏ-ā'), **Jean** (**Marie-Octave-Géraud**), French composer and writer on music; b. Toulouse, Feb. 24, 1876. After music study in his native city, he entered the Paris Cons. as a student of Caussade, Lenepveu, and Gabriel Fauré; also received advice from Vincent d'Indy; settled in Paris. He harmonized and edited a number of folksongs of Languedoc and Gascogne in 'Les Chansons de France' (1907-8), *3 Chansons des Pays d'Oc,* and *14 Chansons anciennes;* also ed. the collection *Chansons populaires des Pyrénées françaises* (vol. 1, 1926). His original compositions include the operas *Les Lointains* (1903), *Le Meneur de louves* (1921), *Perkin,* a Basque legend (Bordeaux, Jan. 16, 1931), *Le Roi de Camargue* (Marseilles, May 12, 1948), *Bois-brûlé* (1956); ballets: *Fünn* (1906), *Frivolant* (Paris Opéra, May 1, 1922), and a Moroccan ballet, *Chergui;* a symph. tableau, *La Basilique aux vainqueurs;* piano pieces and songs. Under the pen-name of Octave Séré he publ. *Musiciens français d'aujourd'hui* (Paris, 1911; 7th ed., 1921); contributed numerous articles to various French periodicals.

Pougin (poo-zhăn'), **Arthur** (pen name of François-Auguste-Arthur Paroisse-Pougin), French writer and critic; b. Châteauroux, Indre, Aug. 6, 1834; d. Paris, Aug. 8, 1921. He was a pupil of Alard (violin) and Reber (harmony) at the Paris Cons.; 1855, conductor of the Théâtre Beaumarchais; 1856-59, assistant conductor of the Folies-Nouvelles; till 1863, violinist in the Opéra-Comique orch.; then devoted himself to letters. Active contributor to leading French musical papers; and music critic for 'Le Soir,' 'La Tribune,' 'L'Evénement,' and the 'Journal Officiel.' He started the 'Revue de la Musique' in 1876, but it appeared only 6 months. Publ. many biographical sketches and essays: *André Campra* (1861), *Gresnick* (1862), *Dezèdes* (1862), *Floquet* (1863), *Martini* (1864), *Devienne* (1864; all six are collected as *Musiciens français du XVIIIe siècle*), *Meyerbeer* (1864), *F. Halévy, écrivain* (1865), *William Vincent Wallace* (1866), *Léon Kreutzer* (1868), *Bellini* (1868), *A. Grisar* (1870), *Rossini* (1871), *Auber* (1873), *Notice sur Rode* (1874), *Boieldieu* (1875), *Rameau* (1876), *Adolphe Adam* (1876), *Verdi* (1886; in English, 1887); further, an *Almanach de la musique* (1866, 1867, 1868; the last two with necrological supplements); *De la littérature musicale en France* (1867); *De la situation des compositeurs de musique et de l'avenir de l'art musical en France*

(1867); *Figures de l'Opéra-Comique: Elleviou, Mme. Dugazon, la tribu des Gavaudan* (1875); *Les vrais créateurs de l'opéra français* (1881); *Dictionnaire historique et pittoresque du théâtre* (1885); *Viotti et l'école moderne de violon* (1888); *Méhul* (1889; 2nd ed., 1893); *L'Opéra-Comique pendant la Révolution* (1891); *Essai historique sur la musique en Russie* (1896; 2nd ed., 1904; in English, 1915); *Acteurs et actrices d'autrefois* (1897); *J.-J. Rousseau, musicien* (1901); *Pierre de Jélyotte et les chanteurs de son temps* (1905); *Hérold* (1906), *Monsigny et son temps* (1908); *Musiciens du XIXe siècle* (1911); *Marie Malibran* (in English, 1911); *Marietta Alboni* (1912); *Madame Favart* (1912); *Massenet* (1914); *Un Directeur d'opéra au XVIIIe siècle* (1914); *Giuseppina Grassini* (1920); *Le Violon, les violonistes, et la musique de violon du XVIe au XVIIIe siècle* (posthumous, 1924). Pougin wrote for Larousse's 'Grand Dictionnaire Universel' all the articles on music. He likewise edited the supplement to Fétis' 'Biographie universelle' (2 vols., 1878-80), and the new edition of the 'Dictionnaire lyrique, ou histoire des opéras' of Félix Clément and P. Larousse (Paris, 1898; with supplement up to 1904).

Poulenc (poo-lank), **Francis,** brilliant French composer; b. Paris, Jan. 7, 1899. He studied piano with Ricardo Viñes and composition with Koechlin; at the age of 18 he joined a group of progressive French musicians, which presented concerts as 'Nouveaux Jeunes,' out of which developed the 'Groupe des Six.' Poulenc was mainly influenced by Satie and Ravel; his early works pursued the aim of sophisticated entertainment; a professional pianist himself, he developed in his piano pieces a highly idiomatic style in a modern vein; like Ravel, he successfully revived the classical keyboard style in a new guise. His songs are also notable; the melodic line is always lucid, while the accompaniments, although elaborate, are never obtrusive. He frequently appeared in joint recitals with the tenor Pierre Bernac, in Europe and in America; first tour in the U. S., 1948-49. —Works: *Le Gendarme incompris,* comédie-bouffe (1920); *Les Mamelles de Tirésias,* opéra-bouffe (Opéra-Comique, June 10, 1947); *Les Dialogues des Carmélites,* religious opera (La Scala, Milan, Jan. 26, 1957); *Les Biches,* ballet (Diaghilev's Ballets Russes, Monte Carlo, Jan. 6, 1924); *Animaux modèles,* ballet (Paris Opéra, Aug. 8, 1942); *Figure humaine,* cantata (London, March 25, 1945); *Rapsodie nègre,* for small orch. (1917); *Aubade,* for piano and 18 instruments (Paris, June 19, 1929); *Deux Marches et un Intermède,* for chamber orch. (BBC, London, June 6, 1938); *Concert champêtre,* for harpsichord and small orch. (Paris, May 3, 1929); concerto for 2 pianos and orch. (1932); concerto for organ, string orch., and kettledrums (Paris, June 10, 1941); piano concerto (Boston, Jan. 6, 1950, composer soloist); chamber music: sonata for 2 clarinets (1918), *Le Bestiaire,* for voice, flute, clarinet, bassoon, and string quartet (1919); sonata for clarinet and bassoon (1922), sonata for horn, trumpet, and trombone (1922), trio for oboe, bassoon, and piano (1926), sextet for flute, oboe, clarinet, bassoon, horn, and piano (1930-32), *Le Bal masqué,* for voice with instruments (1932), string quartet (1946), violin sonata (1943); choral works: Mass (1937), 4 motets (1939), *Exultate Deo* (1941), *Salve Regina* (1941), *Un Soir de neige,* for chorus a cappella (1945), 2 books of traditional French songs, arranged for chorus a cappella (1945), *Stabat Mater,* for chorus a cappella (Strasbourg Festival, June 13, 1951); incidental music for plays; film scores; many piano pieces, of which the earliest, *Mouvements perpétuels* (1918), is the most popular; other piano pieces are *Promenades, 12 Improvisations, Suite française,* etc.; sonata for 2 pianos (1918); song cycles: *Le Bestiaire* (1919), *Cocardes* (1919), *Poèmes de Ronsard* (1925), *Chansons gaillardes* (1926), *Airs chantés* (1928), *8 Chansons polonaises* (1934), *4 Chansons pour enfants* (1935), *Tel Jour telle nuit* (1937), *Fiançailles pour rire* (1939), *Banalités* (1940), *Chansons villageoises* (1942); separate songs: *Épitaphe, Ronsard à sa guitare, Miroirs brûlants, Le Portrait, La Grenouillère, Priez pour paix, Ce donc petit visage, Bleuet, Les Chemins d'amour, Montparnasse et Hyde Park; Histoire de Babar le petit éléphant,* for narration and piano (1940); etc. —Cf. L. Durey, *Francis Poulenc,* in the 'Chesterian' (1922); A. Georges, *Francis Poulenc,* in the 'Chesterian' (1925); D. Milhaud, *Études* (Paris, 1927); H. Prunières, *Francis Poulenc,* in the 'Sackbut' (1928); J. Bruyr, *L'Écran des musiciens* (Paris, 1930); A. Schaeffner, *Francis Poulenc, musicien français,* in 'Contrepoints' (1946, No. 1); Henri Hell, *La Musique religieuse de Francis Poulenc,* in the 'Revue Musicale' (April, 1952); I. Vein, *Francis Poulenc,* in the 'Chesterian' (1954); C. Rostand, *Francis Poulenc: Entretiens avec Claude Rostand* (Paris, 1954); Henri Hell, *Poulenc, musicien français* (Paris, 1958).

Poulet (pōō-lā'), **Gaston,** French violinist and conductor; b. Paris, April 10, 1892. He studied violin at the Paris Cons., gaining 1st prize; organized a string quartet, and gave concerts in Europe; from 1927 to 1936 conducted the Concerts Poulet at the Théâtre Sarah-Bernhardt in Paris; also taught at the Paris Cons.; in 1932 became director of the Cons. of Bordeaux and conducted the Orchestre Philharmonique there; from 1940 to 1945 conducted the Concerts Colonne in Paris; guest conductor with the London Symph. (1947) and in Germany (1948); also in South America. He played the violin in the 1st performance of Debussy's violin sonata with Debussy himself at the piano.

Poulet, Gérard, French violinist, son of Gaston Poulet; b. Bayonne, Aug. 12, 1938. He entered the Paris Cons. at the age of 11 in the class of André Asselin, and won 1st prize at 12; in the same year (1950) he played 3 violin concertos with the Orchestre Colonne, under his father's direction; then appeared with other Paris orchestras; subsequently gave concerts and played with orchestras in England, Holland, Germany, Italy, Austria, and Holland. In 1956 he won 1st Grand Prix at the Paganini competition of Geneva, and was given the honor of performing on Paganini's own violin, the famous Guarneri del Jesù.

Pouplinière. See La Pouplinière.

Pourtalès, Guy de, French writer on music; b. Geneva, Aug. 4, 1881; studied in Bonn, Berlin, and Paris; was in the French army during World War I; then settled in Paris as a music critic. He publ. a number of successful biographies of composers: *La Vie de Franz Liszt* (1925); *Chopin, ou le poète* (1927; 2nd ed., 1946; in English, as *Chopin: a Man of Solitude,* London, 1930); *Wagner, histoire d'un artiste* (1932; revised and augmented ed., 1942); *Berlioz et l'Europe romantique* (1939).

Powell, John, American pianist and composer; b. Richmond, Va., Sept. 6, 1882. His father was a schoolmaster, his mother an amateur musician; he acquired elementary musical education at home, taking lessons with an elder sister; then studied piano with a Liszt pupil, F. C. Hahr; entered the Univ. of Virginia (B. A., 1901) and then went to Vienna, where he became a pupil of Leschetizky (1902-07) and studied composition with Navrátil (1904-07); made a successful début as pianist in Berlin (1908); then played in Paris and London; returning to America, he gave a piano recital in N. Y. (1912) and then toured the country. In 1917 he was commissioned by Modest Altschuler, conductor of the Russian Symph. Orch. in N. Y., to write a work for piano and orch.; this proved to be his most famous composition, *Rapsodie Nègre* (inspired by Joseph Conrad's *Heart of Darkness*); Powell played the piano part in its world première, with the Russian Symph. Orch. (N. Y., March 23, 1918), and afterwards performed it with many orchestras in the U. S.; in 1920 went with the N. Y. Symph. Orch. (under Walter Damrosch) to Europe as soloist in this piece. The titles of many of his works disclose a whimsical state of mind (*Sonate Virginianesque, Sonate psychologique, Sonata Teutonica,* etc.); folksongs, particularly from the South, underlie much of his music. He was the organizer of the Virginia State Choral Festival; also active in the annual White Top Mountain Folk Music Festival; collector of folklore materials; an amateur astronomer (discovered a comet). —Works: Symphony in A (commissioned by the National Federation of Music Clubs in 1932, but not completed until 1947; première at the Music Clubs Convention, Detroit, April 23, 1947); 2 piano concertos; violin concerto; *Rapsodie Nègre,* for piano and orch.; *In Old Virginia,* overture (1921); *Natchez on the Hill,* 3 Virginian country dances (1932); *A Set of Three,* for orch. (1935); numerous vocal and choral arrangements of folksongs; a string quartet; Variations and Double-Fugue on a Theme of F. C. Hahr, for piano; *Sonata Virginianesque,* for violin and piano (1919); another sonata for violin and piano; 3 piano sonatas: *Sonate psychologique, Sonate noble, Sonata Teutonica; In the South,* suite for piano; *At the Fair,* suite for piano (also for orch., 1925); *In the Hammock,* for 2 pianos 8 hands; *Dirge,* for 2 pianos; a number of songs; also an opera, *Judith and Holofernes.*

Powell, Laurence, composer and conductor, b. Birmingham, England, Jan. 13, 1899. He studied at Ratcliffe College, Leicester (1909-15), Ushaw College, Durham (1915-17); was in the British Army and the Royal Air Force during World War I; in 1923, came to the U. S. (citizen, 1936); studied at the Univ. of Wisconsin (M. A., 1926); held various teaching positions: at the Univ. of Wisconsin (1924-26), Univ. of Arkansas (1926-34), Little Rock Junior College (1934-39); also conducted the Little Rock Symph. Orch. (1934-39), the Grand Rapids WPA Symph. Orch. (1939-41), etc. In 1947 he became director of music at St. Joseph's

High School in Victoria, Texas. —Works: for orch.: *The Ogre of the Northern Fastness* (1921), *Keltic Legend* (Bournemouth, England, Aug. 27, 1924, composer conducting; revised version, Madison, Wis., May 20, 1931), *Charivari,* suite (1925), 2 symphonies (1929, 1943), *Deirdre of the Sorrows* (1933; Little Rock, March 18, 1937, composer conducting), *The County Fair,* suite (1936), *Suite,* for string orch. (1931; Grand Rapids, May 9, 1940, composer conducting), *Picnic,* an 'Arkansas pastoral' for string orch. (Oklahoma City, March 21, 1936), *Variations* (Rochester, N. Y., Oct. 28, 1941), *Duo Concertante* for recorders and orch. (1941), *The Santa Fe Trail,* for baritone, narrator, and orch. (Rio Grande Symph. Orch., Santa Fe, New Mexico, April 22, 1958); *Halcyone,* dramatic poem for chorus and orch. (1923), *Alleluya,* cantata for chorus and orch. (1926); *The Seasons* (after poems by Blake) for chorus a cappella (1928); 2 Masses; songs; piano quartet (1933); quartet for clarinets (1936); piano pieces; etc.

Powell, Maud, American violinist; b. Peru, Ill., Aug. 22, 1868; d. Uniontown, Pa., Jan. 8, 1920. Her father, a writer of English-Welsh stock, and her mother, an amateur musician of Hungarian parentage, settled in Aurora, Ill., in 1870. Maud Powell received her primary instruction at home; then studied with William Lewis of Chicago, with Schradieck in Leipzig, and with Charles Dancla at the Paris Cons. She then played in England and Germany. Returning to America in 1885, she toured the country for a number of seasons; when the N. Y. Arion Society went to Germany in 1892 for the quadricentennial celebration of the discovery of America, she went along as a 'representative American violinist'; also played at the Chicago World's Fair in 1893. In 1894 she organized the Maud Powell String Quartet, with which she made a transcontinental tour; from 1898, resumed her career as a concert violinist; traveled in Europe and in South Africa (1905-06); in 1910 settled definitely in the U. S. She was considered the leading woman virtuoso on the violin; introduced to American audiences the violin concertos by Dvořák and Sibelius; also was the first violinist to make recordings in America (for the Victor Talking Machine Co.).

Powell, Mel, American composer; b. New York, Feb. 12, 1923; studied piano with Nadia Reisenberg; played in dance bands and in radio orchestras; was a member of the Army Air Force Band. In 1948 he entered the Yale School of Music, and studied with Hindemith (B. M., 1952); subsequently taught at the Mannes Music School in N. Y. and at Queens College; 1958, appointed instructor at Yale. His works include music for documentary films; a string quartet; sonata for harpsichord; 2 piano sonatas; divertimento for violin and harp.

Power, Lionel (Lionel, Leonell Polbero, Powero, etc.), Engish composer; date of birth unknown; d. Winchester, June 5, 1445. He was a contemporary of Dunstable, whose style he so closely approximated that authorship of works of the two composers has often been confused (some authorities claim, without foundation, that Power and Dunstable were identical). Details of his life are unknown. He wrote a treatise 'Upon the Gamme' (c. 1450, transcribed by J. Wylde, in the British Museum; reprinted by Hawkins in 'History of the Science and Practice of Music' vol. 2; also by S. B. Meech in 'Speculum,' July, 1935; pp. 242-58; and in part by M. Bukofzer, *Geschichte des englischen Diskants und des Fauxbourdons . . .* 1936); 2 *Ave Reginas,* a *Salve Regina,* a *Mater ora filium* and 21 pieces (mostly parts of Masses) for 3-4 voices appear in the 'Denkmäler der Tonkunst in Österreich' (vol. 14-15), 'Sammelbände der Internationalen Musik-Gesellschaft' (vol. 2, p. 378), Stainer's 'Early Bodleian Music,' and 'The Old Hall Manuscript' (3 vols., ed. by A. Ramsbotham; Burnham, Bucks, 1933-38); see also A. Schering, *Geschichte der Musik in Beispielen* (no. 37) and Davison and Apel, *Historical Anthology of Music* (vol. 1, no. 63). Other pieces preserved in MS at Bologna, Modena, Oxford, Vienna, and London (British Museum), include a *Missa Rex Saeculorum* (with *Kyrie*), a 4-voiced *Ave Regina* and part of a *Kyrie.* 2 Masses attributed to Power were publ. in the 'Documenta polyphoniae liturgicae S. Ecclesiae Romanae' (ser. 1, nos. 2 and 9). —Cf. H. Riemann, *Geschichte der Musiktheorie,* p. 143; W. Korte, *Die Harmonik des 15. Jahrhunderts* (1929; p. 23).

Pownall, Mary Ann, English actress and singer, b. 1751; d. Charleston, S. C., Aug. 11, 1796. She was known first as Mrs. Wrightson (her 1st husband was a prompter in a London theater); made her début in 1770 in *The Recruiting Officer,* in London; from 1776 to 1788 was a Vauxhall favorite. In 1792 she first appeared in Boston with the Old American Co., of which she was a leading artist; later she sang in subscription concerts in N. Y., and joined John Henry's New York Co. She composed the text and music of numerous songs—including *Advice to the Ladies of Boston, Washington* (in honor of George Washington), and *Primroses*—some of which appeared in a book of songs that she compiled with J. Hewitt (publ. in N. Y.). Her 2nd husband was A. Pownall. —Cf. J. T. Howard, *Our American Music* (N. Y., 1931; and later eds.).

Pozniak, Bronislaw, pianist and pedagogue; b. Lwow, Aug. 26, 1887; d. Halle, April 20, 1953. He studied at the Cons. of Cracow; then in Berlin with Barth; established a trio, and traveled in Germany; then settled in Breslau as piano teacher; in 1946 moved to Leipzig, and eventually to Halle. He publ. *ABC des Klavierspielers* (1939; 2nd ed., 1948); *Praktische Anweisungen für das Studium der Chopinschen Werke* (Halle, 1949); was editor of a new edition of Chopin's piano works for Peters.

Praetorius, Ernst, German musicologist; b. Berlin, Sept. 20, 1880; d. Ankara, March 27, 1946. He studied violin in Breslau and Halle; history and theory in Berlin with Friedlaender, Fleischer, and Stumpf; 1905, *Dr. phil.* with his dissertation, *Die Mensuraltheorie des Franchinus Gafurius* (publ. Leipzig, 1905); in 1906, appointed director of the famous Heyer Museum in Cologne; held this post until 1909, when he joined the staff of the Cologne Opera, first as coach, then as conductor. Subsequently, he held similar positions in Bochum (1912), Leipzig (1913), Lübeck (1914), Breslau (1915), and Berlin (1922). From 1924 until 1933 he was general musical director in Weimar; in 1934, went to Turkey, where he was active in the educational field and on the radio; remained in Ankara until his death.

Praetorius (Latinized from Schulz or Schulze), **Hieronymus,** German composer, b. Hamburg, Aug. 10, 1560; d. there, Jan. 27, 1629. He studied with his father, Jacobus Schulze, organist of the Jacobikirche; then in Cologne. He became town cantor in Erfurt in 1580; assistant organist to his father in 1582, and his successor in 1586. He brought out a *Hamburger Melodeyen-Gesangbuch* (1604; with his son Jacobus, J. Decker, and D. Scheidemann). His works were publ. in 5 collections in 1622-25, under the general title, *Opus musicum novum et perfectum*: I, *Cantiones sacrae a* 5-12; II, *Magnificats a* 8-12; III, *Liber missarum,* 6 Masses *a* 5-8; IV, *Cantiones variae, a* 5-20, containing Latin and German motets; V, *Cantiones novae officiosae, a* 5-15, also containing Latin and German motets. A selection of his works (a Mass, a Magnificat, and some motets) was publ. by Hugo Leichtentritt in the 'Denkmäler deutscher Tonkunst' vol. 23). —Cf. Hugo Leichtentritt, *Geschichte der Motette* (1908; page 309 ff.); B. Friedrich, *Der Vokalstil des Hieronymus Praetorius* (Hamburg, 1932).

Praetorius, Jacobus, German composer and organist; son of Hieronymus Praetorius; b. Hamburg, Feb. 8, 1586; d. there, Oct. 22, 1651. He studied with Sweelinck in Amsterdam; in 1603 was appointed organist at the Peterskirche in Hamburg. He contributed several motets to his father's collection, *Hamburger Melodeyen-Gesangbuch.*

Praetorius, Michael, great German musician, composer, and theorist; b. Kreuzberg, Thuringia, Feb. 15, 1571; d. Wolfenbüttel, Feb. 15, 1621. His real family name was Schultheiss (German for magistrate, or praetor), which he Latinized as Praetorius. He was the son of a preacher; attended the Latin school of Torgau; studied organ in Frankfurt; then was in the service of the Duke of Brunswick (from 1604); was also prior of the Ringelheim monastery, although without actual residence there. In 1612 he succeeded Mancinus as Kapellmeister in Wolfenbüttel and remained there until his death. —Compositions: *Musae Sioniae,* a collection of 1244 vocal numbers in 9 parts, in note-against-note counterpoint (1605-10; 2nd ed. of Part IX, as *Bicinia et tricinia,* 1611); *Musarum Sioniarum motetae et psalmi 4-16 vocae* (1607); *Eulogodia Sionia* (1611); 60 motets *a* 2-8 for the 'close of the Divine Service'; *Missodia Sionia* (1611), *Hymnodia Sionia* (1611; hymns *a* 2-8); *Megalynodia* (1611; madrigals and motets *a* 5-8); *Terpsichore* (1612; dance pieces *a* 4-6, by Praetorius and some French composers); *Polyhymnia caduceatrix et panegyrica* (1619; songs of peace and rejoicing *a* 1-21); *Polyhymnia exercitatrix* (1620; *a* 2-8); *Uranodia* or *Uranochordia* (1613; 19 songs *a* 4); *Kleine und grosse Litaney* (1613); *Epithalamium* (1614); *Puericinium* (1621; 14 church songs *a* 3-12). —Writings: *Syntagma musicum . . . ,* his major work, of which 3 volumes were printed: vol. I (1615), in 2 parts, is a historical and descriptive treatise in Latin on ancient and ecclesiastical music, and ancient secular instruments; vol. II (1618), written in German, in 5 parts and an Appendix (1620), is the most important extant source of information on musical instruments of the period, describing their form, compass, tone quality, etc., the organ, in particular, being treated at great length; the Appendix contains 42 woodcuts of the principal instruments enumerated (vol. II has been reprinted as vol. XIII of the publications of the 'Gesellschaft für Musikforschung'; facsimile reprint, with introduction by W. Gurlitt, Kassel, 1929); vol. III (1619) contains a valuable and interesting account of secular composition at that time, and a treatise on solmisation, notation, etc., etc. A reprint of vol. III was publ. by E. Bernouilli (1916). Other reprints: organ works by W. Gurlitt, in the 'Archiv für Musikwissenschaft' (1921); also by K. Matthäi (Brunswick, 1930); Psalm 116, by R. Holle (Mainz, 1933); 2 pieces by A. Schering in *Geschichte der Musik in Beispielen* (Nos. 161, 162); various numbers reprinted by G. Tucher, L. Schöberlein, F. Riegel, K. Ameln, etc. A complete ed. of Praetorius' works was issued in 20 vols. under the editorship of Friedrich Blume (1927-42). —Cf. W. Gurlitt, *Michael Praetorius (Creuzburgensis), sein Leben und seine Werke* (Leipzig, 1915); F. Blume, *Michael Praetorius Creuzburgensis* (Wolfenbüttel, 1929); P. Zimmermann, *Zur Biographie des Michael Praetorius,* in 'Braunschweigischer Geschichtsverein Jahrbuch' (1930); R. Unger, *Die mehrchörige Aufführungspraxis bei Michael Praetorius und die Feiergestaltung der Gegenwart* (Wolfenbüttel, 1941); G. Ilgner, *Die lateinischen liturgischen Kompositionen von Michael Praetorius Creuzburgensis* (Kiel, 1944).

Pratella, Francesco Balilla, Italian composer and writer of radical tendencies; b. Lugo, Romagna, Feb. 1, 1880; d. Ravenna, May 18, 1955. He studied with Ricci-Signorini, then at the Liceo Rossini in Pesaro with Cicognani and Mascagni; taught in Cesana (1908-09); director of the Istituto Musicale, Lugo (from 1910), of the Liceo Musicale G. Verdi, Ravenna (1927-45); co-editor of the 'Raccolta nazionale delle musiche italiane.' — Writings: *Cronache e critiche* (1905-17); *Evoluzione della musica* (1910-18); *Saggio di gridi, canzoni, cori e danze del popolo italiano* (1919); *Il Canzioniere dei canterini romagnoli* (1923); *Scritti vari di pensiero, di arte e di storia musicale* (Bologna, 1932); *Luci ed ombre* (1933); *Il Vino e la musica* (1937); *Linee di storia della musica* (1946). He joined the Italian futurist movement in 1910 (Russolo's manifesto of 1913 was addressed to 'Balilla Pratella, grande musicista futurista'), and in 1913 wrote his first composition in this idiom, the choral *Inno alla vita.* —Works: operas: *Lilia* (won honorable mention in the Sonzogno Contest, 1903; performed in Lugo, Nov. 13, 1905), *La Sina d'Vargöun,* to his own libretto (Bologna, Dec. 4, 1909); *L'Aviatore Dro* (also to his own libretto; Lugo, Sept. 4, 1920); *La Ninna nanna della bambola,* children's opera (Milan, May 21, 1923); *Dono primaverile,* comedy with music (Bologna, Oct. 17, 1923); *Fabiano,* opera (Bologna, Dec. 9, 1939); incidental music; for orch.: *Romagna, La Guerra, 5 Poemi musicali;* chamber music; etc. —Cf. A. Toni, *La Sina d'Vargöun di Francesco Balilla Pratella,* in the 'Rivista Musicale Italiana' (1910); G. Bastianelli, *Musicisti d'oggi e di ieri* (Milan, 1914); G. M. Gatti, *Musicisti moderni d'Italia e di fuori* (Bologna, 1920); A. Ghigi, *F. B. Pratella* (Ravenna, 1929); *F. B. Pratella, Appunti biografici e bibliografici* (Ravenna, 1931).

Pratt, Silas Gamaliel, American composer, b. Addison, Vt., Aug. 4, 1846; d. Pittsburgh, Oct. 30, 1916. Both his parents were church singers. The family moved to Chicago when he was a child, and he received his primary music education there; at 22 he went to Berlin, where he studied piano with Kullak and theory with Kiel (1868-71). He then returned to Chicago, where he served as organist of the Church of the Messiah; in 1872, established the Apollo Club. In 1875 he went to Germany once more; studied orchestration with Heinrich Dorn, and also took some piano lessons with Liszt. On July 4, 1876, he conducted in Berlin his *Centennial Overture,* dedicated to General Grant; also at the Crystal Palace in London, when General Grant was visiting there; another work that he presented in London was a *Homage to Chicago March.* Returning to Chicago, he conducted his opera, *Zenobia, Queen of Palmyra* (to his own libretto) in concert form, on June 15, 1882 (stage performance, Chicago, March 26, 1883; New York, Aug. 21, 1883). The opera was received in a hostile manner by the press, partly owing to the poor quality of the music, but mainly as a reaction to Pratt's exuberant and immodest proclamations of its merit in advance of the production. Nothing daunted, Pratt unleashed a vigorous campaign for native American opera; organized the Grand Opera Festival of 1884, which had some support. The following year he visited London again, and conducted there his symph. work, *The Prodigal Son* (Oct. 5, 1885). Returning to Chicago, he revised his early lyric opera *An-*

tonio, renamed it *Lucille,* and produced it on March 14, 1887. In 1888 he moved to N. Y.; there he presented, during the quadricentennial of the discovery of America, his opera, *The Triumph of Columbus* (in concert form, Oct. 12, 1892); also produced a scenic cantata *America,* subtitled *Four Centuries of Music, Picture, and Song* (Nov. 24, 1894; with stereopticon projections). Other works were a *Lincoln Symphony;* a symph. poem, *The Tragedy of the Deep* (1912; inspired by the Titanic disaster), and a cantata, *The Last Inca;* also pub. a manual, *Pianist's Mental Velocity* (N. Y., 1903). In 1906 he settled in Pittsburgh; established there the Pratt Institute of Music and Art, and remained its director until his death. —Pratt was a colorful personality; despite continuous and severe setbacks, he was convinced of his own significance. The story of his salutation to Wagner at their meeting: 'Herr Wagner, you are the Silas G. Pratt of Germany' may be aprocryphal, but is very much in character. —Cf. E. E. Hipsher, *American Opera and Its Composers* (Philadelphia, pp. 361-63); see also 'Dictionary of American Biography' (vol. 15).

Pratt, Waldo Selden, distinguished American music historian and pedagogue; b. Philadelphia, Nov. 10, 1857; d. Hartford, Conn., July 29, 1939. Graduate of Williams College (1878); then spent 2 years in post-graduate work at Johns Hopkins, specializing the first year (1878-79) in Greek and classical archæology, the second as Fellow in esthetics and art; studied music with B. C. Blodgett in Pittsfield, Mass., but chiefly self-taught. From 1880-82 he was assistant director of the Metropolitan Museum of Art, N. Y.; from 1882 on faculty of Hartford Theological Seminary (now Hartford Seminary Foundation), Hartford, Conn.; from 1889, as prof. of music and hymnology, and from 1917, as prof. of public worship and allied subjects; 1891-1906, instructor in elocution at Trinity College, Hartford; also lecturer on music history at Smith College (1895-1908), Mt. Holyoke College (1896-99), Institute of Musical Art, N. Y. (1905-20), and Y. W. C. A. Training School (1908-12); organist and choirmaster in North Adams, Mass. (1873-76), Williams College (1876-78), and Hartford (1882-90); president of the Music Teachers National Association, 1906-08; ed. of its 'Proceedings,' 1906-15; 1882-90, conductor of the Hosmer Hall Choral Union, Hartford; made Mus. Doc. by Syracuse Univ. in 1898, L. H. D. by Williams College in 1929. —Publ. *Musical Ministries in the Church* (1901; 4th enlarged ed., 1915), *The History of Music* (1907; enlarged eds., 1927 and 1935), *Class Notes in Music-History* (1908; enlarged, 1915), *The Music of the Pilgrims* (1921; concerning Ainsworth's Psalter [1612] as brought to Plymouth in 1620, with the tunes in full), *The Importance of the Early French Psalter* in the 'Mus. Quarterly' (Jan., 1935); publ. *The Music of the French Psalter of 1562* (1939); ed. 'St. Nicholas Songs' (1885), 'Aids to Common Worship' (1887), 'Songs of Worship for the Sunday School' (1887), music section of 'Century Dictionary' (1892; also of the supplement, 1909), American supplement to Grove's 'Dictionary' (with Chas. N. Boyd, 1920; enlarged, 1928), 'New Encyclopedia of Music and Musicians' (1924; enlarged, 1929); contributor to 'Parish Problems' (1887; 5 chapters), 'International Encyclopedia' (1891; article *Music*), 'Standard Bible Dictionary' (1908; rev. 1925). —Cf. Otto Kinkeldey, *Waldo Selden Pratt,* in the 'Mus. Quarterly' (April, 1940).

Predieri, Antonio, Italian composer; b. Bologna, Sept. 13, 1688; d. there, 1767. He was maestro di cappella at San Petronio in Bologna and a member of the Accademia dei Filarmonici there; in 1739 was appointed 2nd Kapellmeister at the court chapel in Vienna; in 1746 became 1st Kapellmeister there; retired in 1751. His opera *Il Sogno di Scipione* was performed at the Emperor's palace in Laxenburg, near Vienna, on Oct. 1, 1735. He also wrote oratorios and instrumental works for festive occasions.

Preger, Leo, Corsican composer; b. Ajaccio, Jan. 27, 1907. He studied composition with Nadia Boulanger in Paris; acquired a considerable mastery of counterpoint in the old style; has devoted himself mainly to choral music on religious subjects. —Works: cantatas, *La Reine Isaure; Cantate de l'arc; Arrestation de Jésus; Cantique de St. Jean de la Croix;* psalms, etc.

Preindl, Joseph, Austrian composer; b. Marbach, Jan. 30, 1756; d. Vienna, Oct. 26, 1823. He was a pupil of Albrechtsberger; in 1809 was appointed cantor at St. Stephen's. He publ. 5 Masses and other church works; brought out a *Gesanglehre* (singing manual) and a book of melodies by old German composers; wrote pieces for organ. His method *Wiener Tonschule* was publ. after his death, ed. by Seyfried (Vienna, 1827; 2nd ed., 1832).

Preiss, Cornelius, Austrian writer on music; b. Troppau, May 20, 1884; d. Linz,

April 1, 1944. He studied in Olmütz and Graz (*Dr. phil.,* 1907); taught in Graz (1908-24) and Linz (from 1924). He publ. the valuable survey, *Zur Geschichte der Operette* (1908); the monographs, *K. Millöcker* (1905), *L. C. Seydler* (1908), *Meyerbeer-Studien* (1907-14), *J. Drechsler* (1910), *R. Volkmann* (1912), *R. Stöhr* (1914), *K. Zeller* (1928), *F. X. Süssmayr* (1933); a collection of Austrian folksongs, *Österreichischer Liederquell* (3 vols., 1930-32); and the manual, *Sing- und allgemeine Musiklehre* (1933). Preiss was also a composer; wrote mainly vocal music.

Preobrazhensky, Anton Viktorovitch, Russian musicologist; b. 1870; d. Leningrad, Feb. 17, 1929. Educated in Kazan; 1898-1902, teacher in Moscow; from 1902 librarian of the Court Chapel in St. Petersburg and prof. at the Cons. there. —Publications: *Dictionary of Russian Hymns* (Moscow, 1897); *Bibliography of Hymns* (Moscow, 1900); *The Monodic Hymn in the Russian Church of the 17th Century* (St. Petersburg, 1904); *Ecclesiastical Music* (1924), and numerous studies on Russian church music.

Presser, Theodore, American music publisher; b. Pittsburgh, Pa., July 3, 1848; d. Philadelphia, Oct. 27, 1925. He studied music at the New England Cons. in Boston with S. Emery, G. E. Whiting, J. C. D. Parker, and B. Lang; then at the Leipzig Cons. with Zwintscher and Jadassohn; in 1883 he founded in Philadelphia 'The Etude,' a well-known music monthly of which he was the editor until 1907; James F. Cooke was its editor from 1908 to 1949; it discontinued publication in 1957. Shortly after the foundation of 'The Etude' Presser established a publishing house, 'Theo. Presser Co.,' for music and books about music, which has come to be one of the important firms in the U. S. In 1906 he founded the 'Presser Home for Retired Music Teachers,' which in 1908 moved to fine new quarters in Germantown (accommodations for 65 guests). In 1916 he established the 'Presser Foundation' to administer this Home, also to provide for the relief of deserving musicians and to offer scholarships in more than 75 colleges and universities in the U. S. James Francis Cooke was president of the Foundation from 1918. —Presser wrote instructive pieces and studies for piano, and transl. several foreign textbooks on music; was a co-founder of the Music Teachers National Association (1876). —Cf. 'Dictionary of American Biography' (vol. 15).

Previtali, Fernando, Italian conductor; b. Adria, Feb. 16, 1907. He studied cello, piano, and composition at the Cons. of Turin; 1928-36, was conductor in Florence; then radio conductor in Rome; 1953, appointed artistic director of the Santa Cecilia Orch.; made annual appearances with various European orchestras; American début with the Cleveland Orch. (Dec. 15, 1955); N. Y. début with the N. Y. Philharmonic (Dec. 5, 1957). He has written a ballet, *Allucinazioni* (1945), and other music; publ. *Guida allo studio della direzione d'orchestra* (Rome, 1951).

Prévost (prā-vōh'), **Eugène-Prosper,** conductor and composer; b. Paris, April 23, 1809; d. New Orleans, Aug. 19, 1872. He studied at the Paris Cons. with Lesueur, winning the Grand Prix de Rome in 1831 with the cantata, *Bianca Cappello.* He conducted theatrical music in Le Havre (1835-38), then went to New Orleans, where he conducted until 1862; was active in Paris (1862-67) before returning to New Orleans as a singing master. He produced several operas in Paris, of which *Cosimo* (Opéra-Comique, Oct. 13, 1835) was the most successful, and one (*Blanche et René*) in New Orleans; also wrote oratorios and Masses.

Preyer, Carl Adolph, pianist, composer, and teacher; b. Pforzheim, Baden, July 28, 1863; d. Lawrence, Kansas, Nov. 16, 1947. He studied at the Stuttgart Cons.; then with Navrátil in Vienna, and with H. Urban and H. Barth in Berlin. In 1893 he settled in the U. S.; became piano teacher at the School of Fine Arts, Univ. of Kansas, and remained with that institution throughout his life. He publ. several instructive collections for piano, *20 Progressive Octave Studies, Melodious Pieces in the Form of Etudes, 12 Wrist Studies, 16 Studies for Rhythm and Expression, 12 Etudes for the Left Hand;* also some character pieces. —Cf. Howard F. Gloyne, *Carl A. Preyer; the Life of a Kansas Musician* (Lawrence, Kansas, 1949).

Preyer (prī'ehr), **Gottfried von,** Austrian organist and composer; b. Hausbrunn, March 15, 1807; d. Vienna, May 9, 1901. He studied with Sechter; in 1835 became organist of the Lutheran Church in Vienna; in 1838, prof. of music theory at the Vienna Cons., of which he was director from 1844 to 1848. In 1853 he became music director at St. Stephen's; pensioned in 1876. He wrote 3 operas; the oratorio, *Noah* (often performed in Vienna); a symph.; several Masses and other church music.

Price, Enrique (Henry), conductor and composer; b. London, May 5, 1819; d. New York, Dec. 12, 1863. He settled in Colombia, and established the Philharmonic Orch. of Bogotá (Nov. 11, 1846); was its first conductor. He wrote numerous pieces making use of native melodies.

Price, Jorge Wilson, Colombian musician, son of Enrique Price; b. Bogotá, May 20, 1853; d. there, Oct. 9, 1953 (at the age of 100). He was educated in New York; returning to Colombia, he founded the National Academy (1882) and taught violin. —Cf. J. I. Perdomo Escobar, *Historia de la Música en Colombia* (Bogotá, 1945).

Příhoda, Váša, noted Czech violinist; b. Vodnany, Aug. 24, 1900. He received his first instruction from his father, a professional violinist; made his public début at the age of 13 in Prague; made a successful Italian tour in 1920; in 1921 appeared in the U. S.; in 1927, in England; then played in recitals throughout Europe. During World War II he taught at the Mozarteum in Salzburg; after the war, resumed his career as a concert artist, giving recitals in Paris and London.

Prill, Emil, eminent German flutist; brother of Karl and Paul Prill; b. Stettin, May 10, 1867; d. Berlin, Feb. 28, 1940. He studied with his father; finished his musical education at the Hochschule für Musik in Berlin; in 1888 taught in Kharkov, Russia; then played 1st flute with the Hamburg Philharmonic; in 1892 became 1st flutist at the Berlin Opera; in 1903 was appointed instructor at the Hochschule. He publ. the methods *Schule für die Böhm-Flöte* and *Flötenschule;* also a valuable practical collection of flute passages from orchestral works, *Orchesterstudien* (7 books).

Prill, Karl, German violinist; brother of Emil and Paul Prill; b. Berlin, Oct. 22, 1864; d. Vienna, Aug. 18, 1931. He studied violin with Joachim at the Berlin Hochschule für Musik; played in various orchestras, including that of the Gewandhaus (1891-97); in 1897 became concertmaster of the court opera in Vienna; also taught violin at the Vienna Academy. He organized the Prill String Quartet, which was famous in his day.

Prill, Paul, German cellist and conductor, brother of Emil and Karl Prill; b. Berlin, Oct. 1, 1860; d. Bremen, Dec. 21, 1930. He studied with Manecke (cello) and Sturm (theory); was solo cellist in various German orchestras; conducted opera in Rotterdam (1886-89), in Hamburg (1889-92), in Nuremburg (1892-1901), and in Schwerin (1901-6); conducted the Mozart Orch. in Berlin (1906-08); then settled in Munich as conductor of the Konzertverein.

Primrose, William, eminent viola virtuoso; b. Glasgow, Aug. 23, 1903. He studied violin in Glasgow with Camillo Ritter; then at the Guildhall School of Music, London, and in Belgium with Eugène Ysaÿe (1925-27), who advised him to become a viola player; from 1930 to 1935, traveled in Europe, the U. S., and South America as violist of the London String Quartet; also appeared as soloist. In 1937 he was engaged by Toscanini as a first violist in the N.B.C. Symph. Orch., and held that post until 1942; in 1939 he established the William Primrose Quartet; also made numerous appearances as soloist with major symph. orchestras in Europe and America; was knighted by Queen Elizabeth II (Feb. 24, 1953). He commissioned a viola concerto from Béla Bartók, but the work was not completed at the time of Bartók's death. In 1956 he became violist in the Festival String Quartet (with Babin, Goldberg, and Graudan).

Pringsheim, Klaus, German conductor and composer; b. Munich, July 24, 1883. He studied in Munich with Stavenhagen and Thuille, and in Vienna with Gustav Mahler; became operatic coach in Vienna; then conducted opera in Geneva, Prague, Breslau, and Bremen (1907-17); in 1918 was appointed music director at the Grosses Schauspielhaus, Berlin, during the artistic directorship of Max Reinhardt; wrote music criticism in the Berlin 'Vorwärts' (1927-31). He left Germany in 1931 and transferred his activities to Japan; was prof. of composition and choral director at the Ueno Academy of Music in Tokyo (1931-37); musical adviser to the Royal Dept. of Fine Arts, Bangkok, Thailand (1937-38); director of the Tokyo Chamber Symph. Orch. (1941-46). In 1947-51 he was in Hollywood; also toured the U. S. as lecturer; in 1951 returned to Tokyo, and was appointed music director of the Musashino Academy of Music. As a composer, he endeavored to combine Japanese melodic material with European harmonic and contrapuntal resources; wrote a *Symphonic Concert Piece* (Tokyo, Sept. 27, 1936, composer conducting); piano concerto in C (Tokyo, Oct. 13, 1935); chamber music; contributed numerous articles on Japanese and Siamese music to publications in German and English.

Printz, Wolfgang Kaspar, German composer and writer; b. Waldthurn, Oct. 10, 1641; d. Sorau, Oct. 13, 1717. Originally a theological student, he later led a roving life, and then was cantor successively at Promnitz, Triebel, and (from 1665) Sorau. He brought out a *Historische Beschreibung der edelen Sing- und Kling-Kunst* (Dresden, 1690), a work of some importance for the history of music of the 17th century. His other theoretical writings include *Anweisung zur Singkunst* (1666; 2nd ed., 1671; 3rd ed., 1685); *Compendium ad Oden componendam* (1668); *Musica modulationis vocalis* (1678); *Exercitationes . . . de concordantiis* (1687-89); also a curious satire on music theory, *Phrynis Mytilenaeus oder Satyrischer Componist* (1676-77; 2nd ed., 1696); also wrote 3 musical stories, characterizing different types of musicians. According to his own statement, the MSS of his numerous compositions were destroyed in a fire. —Cf. E. Schmitz, *Studien über W. Printz als Musikschriftsteller,* in 'Monatshefte für Musik-Geschichte' (1904).

Proch (prŏh), **Heinrich,** Austrian conductor, composer, and singing teacher; b. Böhmisch-Leipa. July 22, 1809; d. Vienna. Dec. 18, 1878. He studied law and at the same time took violin lessons; became conductor of the Josephstadt Theater, Vienna, in 1837; from 1840 to 1870 conducted at the Vienna Opera; pensioned in 1870. Among his voice pupils were Materna, Tietjens, and Peschka-Leutner. He wrote many songs that were popular for a time; his set of variations for coloratura soprano with flute obbligato was particularly well known. Also brought out in Vienna a comic opera, *Ring und Maske* (Dec. 4, 1844), and 3 one-act operas, *Die Blutrache* (Dec. 5, 1846), *Zweiter und dritter Stock* (Oct. 5, 1847), and *Der gefährliche Sprung* (Jan. 5, 1849)

Procházka (prŏh-hăhz'-kăh), **Rudolf,** Freiherr **von,** Bohemian writer on music and composer; b. Prague, Feb. 23, 1864; d. there, March 23, 1936. While pursuing the study of jurisprudence at the Univ. of Prague, he studied violin with Wittich and composition with Grünberger and Fibich; in Prague he was music inspector, and archivist of the 'Verein zur Beförderung der Tonkunst in Böhmen' and of the Cons. In May, 1911, he arranged an important musical exposition in Prague in commemoration of the centenary of the founding of the Cons., and wrote its official catalogue, *Aus fünf Jahrhunderten.* In the same year he brought about the establishment of a commission for the examination and licensing of all music teachers in Bohemia, and was appointed its head. —Writings: *Die böhmischen Musikschulen* (1890); *Mozart in Prag* (very valuable; 1892; revised by Paul Nettl in 1938 as *Mozart in Böhmen*); *Robert Franz* (1894); *Arpeggien: Musikalisches aus alten und neuen Tagen* (1897; 2nd ed. as *Musikalische Streiflichter,* 1901); *Johann Strauss* (1900; 2nd ed., 1903); *Das romantische Musik-Prag* (1914); *Der Kammermusikverein in Prag* (1926); also ed. the 8th (1909; practically rewritten) and 11th (1920) editions of Kothe's *Musikgeschichte.* —Compositions: an allegorical opera, *Das Glück* (Prague, 1898); oratorio, *Die Palmen; Haffner-Variationen über ein Thema von Mozart,* for orch.; *Sinfonische Lieder,* for orch.; *Deutsch-böhmische Reigen,* for piano 4 hands; pieces for solo piano; many choruses and songs. —Cf. C. Hunnius, *Rudolf von Procházka, Ein deutscher Tondichter Böhmens* (Leipzig, 1902); E. Janetschek, *Rudolf von Procházka,* in the 'Neue Zeitschrift für Musik' (Dec., 1915).

Prod'homme, Jacques-Gabriel, French writer on music; b. Paris, Nov. 28, 1871; d. there, June 18, 1956. Having completed his course at the Lycée Condorcet, he studied philology and history of music at the École des Hautes Études Sociales (1890-94). In 1895 he began his career as music critic of 'L'Enclos,' and until 1912 held similar positions with 'La Revue Socialiste,' 'Droits de l'Homme,' 'Messidor,' 'Paris-Journal,' etc. From 1897 to 1900 he lived in Munich as ed. of the 'Deutsch-französische Rundschau.' From 1898 to 1916, was secretary of the French section of the International Musical Society; archivist of the Paris Opéra Museum (from 1931); librarian of the Paris Cons. (from 1934); etc. In 1917, with La Laurencie, he founded the Société Française de Musicologie. —Publications: *Le Cycle Berlioz,* in 2 vols.: *La Damnation de Faust* (1896) and *L'Enfance du Christ* (1898); *Hector Berlioz. Sa vie et ses œuvres* (1905; in German, 1906); *Les Symphonies de Beethoven* (1906; 15th ed., 1938; awarded prize by the French Academy); *Paganini* (1907; in English, 1911); *Écrits de musiciens . . .* (1912); *La Jeunesse de Beethoven* (1921); *Richard Wagner et la France* (1921); *L'Opéra, 1669-1925* (1925); *Pensées sur la musique et les musiciens* (1926); *Beethoven raconté par ceux qui l'ont vu* (1927); *Mozart raconté par ceux qui l'ont vu* (1928); *Schubert raconté par ceux qui l'ont vu* (1928); *Wagner raconté par ceux qui l'ont vu* (1929); *Les Sonates pour piano* *de Beethoven* (1937; in German, 1948); *L'Immortelle bien-aimée de Beethoven* (1946); *Gluck* (1948); *Gossec* (1949); contributed a number of articles to the 'Mus. Quarterly.' In collaboration with Ch. Bertrand, he publ. *Guide musical et étude analytique de la Götterdämmerung* (1902); with A. Dandelot, *Gounod. Sa Vie et ses œuvres d'après des documents inédits* (2 vols., 1911); with E. Crauzat, *Les Menus plaisirs du roi; l'École royale et le Conservatoire de Paris* (1929). Together with Fr. Holl, F. Caille, and L. van Vassenhove he transl. Wagner's prose works, *Œuvres en prose,* in 13 vols. (1908-25); also transl. A. Schurig's *Mozart* (1925); ed. *Souvenirs de voyage de Berlioz* (1932); transl. and ed. *Cahiers de conversation de Beethoven, 1819-1827* (1946).

Profe, Ambrosius, German organist and music editor; b. Breslau, Feb. 12, 1589; d. there, Dec. 27, 1661. He studied theology at Wittenberg; then was cantor in Silesia; from 1633, he was church organist in Breslau. He edited important collections of German sacred music: *Geistliche Concerte und Harmonien,* for 1-7 voices (1641-46), *Corollarium geistlicher Collectaneorum* (a supplement to the previous vol.; 1649); a collection of Christmas songs, *Cunis solennibus Jesuli recens-nati sacra genethliaca* (1646); also brought out Heinrich Albert's *Arien* (1657).

Prohaska, Felix, Austrian conductor, son of Karl Prohaska; b. Vienna, May 16, 1912. He studied theory with his father and Hanns and Egon Kornauth, violin with G. Feist, piano with F. Wührer and E. Steuermann, and musicology at the University of Vienna. Since 1936 he has been conductor at various opera houses, including Graz (1936-39), Duisberg (1939-41), Strasbourg (1941-43), Vienna (from 1945), and Frankfurt (since 1955).

Prohaska, Karl, Austrian composer; b. Mödling, near Vienna, April 25, 1869; d. Vienna, March 28, 1927. He was a pupil in Vienna of Anny Assmayer (piano) and Franz Krenn (composition); then in Berlin of Eugen d'Albert (piano) and H. von Herzogenberg (composition); from 1901 to 1905, was conductor of the Warsaw Philharmonic; in 1908, appointed prof. at the Akademie der Tonkunst in Vienna. — Works: opera, *Madeleine Guimard;* oratorio, *Frühlingsfeier; Passacaglia,* for orch.; chamber music; 6 songs to Giraud's *Pierrot Lunaire;* motet *Aus dem Buch Hiob;* some fine choruses.

Prokofiev (prŏh-kŏh'-fyĕf), **Sergey Sergeyevitch,** outstanding Russian composer; b. Sontzovka, near Ekaterinoslav, April 23, 1891; d. Moscow, March 5, 1953. His mother was an amateur pianist, and he received his first training from her. He improvised at the piano; in June 1900, at the age of 9, he completed the piano score of an opera, *The Giant;* then wrote an overture and 3 tableaux for an opera entitled *On Desert Islands* (1902). He was taken to Taneyev in Moscow, who referred him to Glière for serious study. Under Glière's guidance he wrote a symphony in G major, and 2 operas, *Feast During the Plague,* after Pushkin (1903), and *Ondine* (1904). At the age of 13 he entered the St. Petersburg Cons., where he studied composition with Rimsky-Korsakov, Wihtol, and Liadov; piano with Mme. Essipova, and conducting with Nicolas Tcherepnin. He graduated from the Cons. in 1914; received the Anton Rubinstein Prize (a grand piano) as a pianist, for his performance of his 1st piano concerto. Even before graduation, he appeared before various modern music societies in St. Petersburg, playing his own piano pieces, and soon earned a reputation as a youthful 'futurist.' He developed a novel piano idiom, explicitly demonstrated in his *Sarcasms* and *Visions Fugitives,* percussive and sharp, yet not without a lyric charm. Grotesquerie and irony animated Prokofiev's early works; he also felt a strong attraction towards subjects of elemental or primitive character. His first important orchestral composition, the *Scythian Suite,* or *Ala and Lolly,* draws upon the ancient Russian sun-worship. While a parallel with Stravinsky's *Le Sacre du Printemps* may exist, there is no similarity between the styles of the two works. Another score, primitivistic in its inspiration, was *Seven, They Are Seven,* an incantation from an old Sumerian ritual. During the same period, Prokofiev wrote his famous *Classical Symphony,* which he completed at the age of 26. In it he successfully recreated the formal style of the 18th century; while the structure was indeed classical, the sudden modulatory shifts and a subtle element of grotesquerie betrayed a 20th-century hand. He conducted the first performance of the *Classical Symphony* in the spring of 1918, and then left Russia, proceeding through Siberia and Japan to America; gave concerts of his music in New York, Chicago, and other cities. In 1920 he went to Paris, where he became associated with Diaghilev, who produced Prokofiev's ballets *Chout* (French transliteration of the Russian word for buffoon), *Le Pas d'acier,* and *L'Enfant prodigue.* Koussevitzky, who became Prokofiev's publisher, commissioned several works from him for his concerts in Paris, and subsequently in Boston. In 1921 Prokofiev again visited the U. S. for the production by the Chicago Opera Co. of his opera, *Love for Three Oranges.* In 1927 he played a series of concerts in Russia; then lived in Europe (mostly in Paris); late in 1933 he returned to Russia, establishing himself as a Soviet citizen; however, he continued to make occasional tours in Europe and America; he visited the U. S. for the last time in 1938. In Russia he wrote some of his most popular works: the symph. fairy-tale, *Peter and the Wolf* (for a children's theater in Moscow), the cantata *Alexander Nevsky* (originally for a film), the ballet *Romeo and Juliet,* the opera *War and Peace,* the 5th, 6th, and 7th symphonies; several piano sonatas; songs; etc. Although Prokofiev was the target of sharp criticism on the part of the Soviet press for his 'decadent' practices in adopting certain modernistic procedures, his status on the whole remained very high; virtually all of his works were published; his music became a major influence on the young generation of Soviet composers. Outside Russia, too, Prokofiev enjoyed enduring fame; his *Classical Symphony,* his 3rd piano concerto, *Peter and the Wolf,* the march from *Love for Three Oranges,* the suite from *Lieutenant Kijé,* and many of the piano works have become repertory pieces all over the world. —Prokofiev never departed from the tonal system despite occasional excursions into modernistic practices (polytonality, atonality). He had an innate sense of sharp rhythm, often in asymmetrical patterns; in his melodic writing, he was equally adept in simple lyricism, along modal lines, and in a modern manner spanning large intervals; he was a master of instrumentation, developing an individual method of treating orchestral sonorities. Above all, his music shows a professional care for the performer, never reaching beyond the practicable limits of execution. —Works: Operas: *Magdalena,* op. 13 (1913); *The Gambler,* op. 24, after Dostoyevsky (1915-16; revised 1927; première, Brussels, April 29, 1929); *Love for Three Oranges,* op. 33, after Carlo Gozzi (Chicago, Dec. 30, 1921, composer conducting); *The Flaming Angel,* op. 37 (1919; 2 fragments performed at a Koussevitzky concert, Paris, June 14, 1928; complete performance in concert form was given over the Paris Radio, Jan. 13, 1954); *Simeon Kotko,* op. 81 (1939; Moscow, June 23, 1940); *Betrothal in a Convent,* op. 86, after Sheridan's *Duenna* (1940; Leningrad, Nov. 3, 1946); *War and Peace,* op. 91, after Tolstoy (1941-52; 1st version, Leningrad, June 12, 1946; 2nd version, Leningrad, April 1, 1955); *A Tale about a Real Man,* op. 117 (1947-48; privately performed, Leningrad, Dec. 3, 1948; severely censured by Soviet critics and not produced in public). Ballets: *A Tale of a Buffoon Who Outwitted Seven Buffoons,* op. 21 (usually performed outside Russia as *Chout;* 1920; Paris, May 17, 1921); *Le Pas d'acier,* op. 41 (1924; Paris, June 7, 1927); *L'Enfant prodigue,* op. 46 (1928; Paris, May 21, 1929); *Sur le Boristhène,* op. 50 (1930; Paris, Dec. 16, 1932); *Romeo and Juliet,* op. 64 (1935-36; Leningrad, Jan. 11, 1940); *Cinderella,* op. 87 (1940-44; Moscow, Nov. 21, 1945); *A Tale of the Stone Flower,* op. 118 (1948-50; Moscow, Feb. 12, 1954). Incidental music to *Boris Godunov,* op. 70-bis (1936), *Eugene Onegin,* op. 71 (1936), *Hamlet,* op. 77 (1937-38). Music for films: *Lieutenant Kijé* (1933); *The Queen of Spades,* op. 70 (1938); *Alexander Nevsky* (1938); *Ivan the Terrible,* op. 116 (1942-45). Choral works: 2 poems for women's chorus with orch., op. 7, *The White Swan* and *The Wave* (1909); *Seven, They Are Seven,* cantata for tenor, chorus, and orch., op. 30 (1917-18; Paris, May 29, 1924); cantata for the 20th anniversary of the October Revolution, for 2 choruses, military band, accordions, percussion, to texts by Marx, Lenin, and Stalin, op. 74 (1937; not performed); *Songs of Our Days* op. 76, suite for solo voices, mixed chorus, and orch. (Moscow, Jan. 5, 1938); *Alexander Nevsky,* op. 78, cantata for mezzo-soprano, mixed chorus, and orch. (Moscow, May 17, 1939); *Salute,* op. 85, cantata for mixed chorus and symph. orch., for Stalin's 60th birthday (Moscow, Dec. 21, 1939); *Ballad of a Boy Who Remained Unknown,* op. 93, cantata for soprano, tenor, chorus, and orch. (Moscow, Feb. 21, 1944); *Hymn to the Soviet Union,* op. 98 (1943; submitted to the competition for a new Soviet anthem but failed to win; a song by Alexander Alexandrov was selected); *Flourish, Powerful Land,* op. 114, cantata for the 30th anniversary of the October Revolution (Moscow, Nov. 12, 1947); *Winter Bonfire,* op. 122, suite for narrators, boys' chorus, and symph. orch. (Moscow, Dec. 19, 1950); *On Guard for Peace,* op. 124, oratorio for mezzo-soprano narrators, mixed chorus, boys' chorus, and symph. orch. (Moscow, Dec. 19, 1950). For orch.: *Sinfonietta,* op. 5 (1914; Petrograd, Nov. 6, 1915); *Rêves,* op. 6, symph. tableau

(St. Petersburg, Dec. 5, 1910); *Autumn,* op. 8, symph. tableau (Moscow, Aug. 1, 1911); 1st piano concerto, op. 10 (Moscow, Aug. 7, 1912, composer soloist); 2nd piano concerto, op. 16 (Pavlovsk, Sept. 5, 1913, composer soloist; 2nd version, Paris, May 8, 1924, composer soloist); 1st violin concerto, op. 19 (1916-17; Paris, Oct. 18, 1923); *Scythian Suite,* op. 20 (1914; Petrograd, Jan. 29, 1916); *Chout,* op. 21-bis, symph. suite from the ballet (Brussels, Jan. 15, 1924); *Classical Symphony,* op. 25 (1916-17; Petrograd, April 21, 1918, composer conducting); 3rd piano concerto, op. 26 (1917-21; Chicago, Dec. 16, 1921, composer soloist); *Love for Three Oranges,* op. 33-bis, symph. suite from the opera (Paris, Nov. 29, 1925); symph. no. 2, op. 40 (1924; Paris, June 6, 1925; 2nd version, op. 136; not completed); *Le Pas d'acier,* op. 41-bis, symph. suite from the ballet (1926; Moscow, May 27, 1928); overture for chamber orch., op. 42 (Moscow, Feb. 7, 1927; also for large orch., 1928; Paris, Dec. 18, 1930); *Divertissement,* op. 43 (1925-29; Paris, Dec. 22, 1929); symph. no. 3, op. 44 (1928; Paris, May 17, 1929); *L'Enfant prodigue,* op. 46-bis, symph. suite from the ballet (1929; Paris, March 7, 1931); symph. no. 4, op. 47 (Boston, Nov. 14, 1930; 2nd version, op. 112, not performed); *Sinfonietta,* op. 48, a new version of op. 5 (1929; Moscow, Nov. 18, 1930); *4 Portraits,* op. 49, symph. suite from the opera, *The Gambler* (1931; Paris, March 12, 1932); *On the Dnieper,* op. 51-bis, symph. suite from the ballet (1933); 4th piano concerto, op. 53, for left hand alone (1931; Berlin, Sept. 5, 1956); 5th piano concerto, op. 55 (Berlin, Oct. 31, 1932, composer soloist); *Symphonic Song,* op. 57 (Moscow, April 14, 1934); 1st cello concerto, op. 58 (1933-38; Moscow, Nov. 26, 1938); *Lieutenant Kije,* op. 60, symph. suite from film music (1934; Paris, Feb. 20, 1937, composer conducting); *Egyptian Nights,* op. 61, symph. suite (1934; Moscow, Dec. 22, 1938); 2nd violin concerto, op. 63 (1935; Madrid, Dec. 1, 1935); *Romeo and Juliet,* op. 64-bis, 1st suite from the ballet (Moscow, Nov. 24, 1936); *Romeo and Juliet,* op. 64-ter, 2nd suite from the ballet (Leningrad, April 15, 1937); *Peter and the Wolf,* op. 67, symph. fairy-tale (Moscow, May 2, 1936); *4 Marches,* op. 69, for military band (1935-37); *Russian Overture,* op. 72 (Moscow, Oct. 29, 1936); *Hamlet,* op. 77, symph. suite from the film score (1938; Moscow, Nov. 25, 1954); *Symphonic March,* op. 88 (1941); *The Year 1941,* op. 90 (1941; Sverdlovsk, Jan. 21, 1943); *March* for military orch., op. 99 (Moscow, April 30, 1944); symph. no. 5, op. 100 (1944; Moscow, Jan. 13, 1945); *Romeo and Juliet,* op. 101, 3rd suite from the ballet (Moscow, March 8, 1946); *Ode on the End of the War,* op. 105, for 8 harps, 4 pianos, military band, percussion ensemble, and double-basses (1945; Moscow, Nov. 12, 1945); *Cinderella,* op. 107, 108, 109, 3 suites from the ballet (1946); *Waltzes,* op. 110, suite for orch. (1946; Moscow, May 13, 1947); symph. no. 6, op. 111 (1945-47; Leningrad, Oct. 11, 1947); *Festive Poem,* op. 113 (Moscow, Oct. 3, 1947); *Ivan the Terrible,* op. 116, suite for orch. (1942-45); *Pushkin Waltzes,* op. 120 (1949); *Summer Night,* op. 123, symph. suite on themes from the opera, *Betrothal in a Convent* (1950); 2nd cello concerto, op. 125 (1950-52; Moscow, Feb. 18, 1952); *Wedding Scene,* op. 126, suite from the ballet, *A Tale of the Stone Flower* (Moscow, Dec. 12, 1951); *Gypsy Fantasy,* op. 127, from the ballet, *A Tale of the Stone Flower* (Moscow, Nov. 18, 1951); *Ural Rhapsody,* op. 128, from the ballet, *A Tale of the Stone Flower* (1951); *The Mistress of the Copper Mountain,* op. 129, suite from the ballet, *A Tale of the Stone Flower* (incomplete); *The Meeting of the Volga with the Don River,* op. 130 (for the completion of the Volga-Don Canal; 1951; Moscow, Feb. 22, 1952); symph. no. 7, op. 131 (1951-52; Moscow, Oct. 11, 1952); *Concertino* for cello and orch., op. 132 (1952); concerto for 2 pianos and string orch., op. 133 (1952; incomplete). Chamber music: *Humorous Scherzo* for 4 bassoons, op. 12-bis (1912; London, Sept. 2, 1916); *Ballade* for cello and piano, op. 15 (1912); *Overture on Hebrew Themes,* op. 34, for clarinet, 2 violins, viola, cello, and piano (N. Y., Jan. 26, 1920); quintet for oboe, clarinet, violin, viola, and double-bass, op. 39 (1924; Moscow, March 6, 1927); 1st string quartet, op. 50 (Washington, April 25, 1931); sonata for 2 violins, op. 56 (Moscow, Nov. 27, 1932); 1st violin sonata, op. 80 (1938-46; Moscow, Oct. 23, 1946); 2nd string quartet, op. 92 (1941; Moscow, Sept. 5, 1942); sonata for flute and piano, op. 94 (Moscow, Dec. 7, 1943); 2nd violin sonata, op. 94-bis (transcription of the flute sonata; Moscow, June 17, 1944); sonata for violin unaccompanied, op. 115 (1947); cello sonata, op. 119 (1949; Moscow, March 1, 1950). Piano music: 10 sonatas: no. 1, op. 1 (1909); no. 2, op. 14 (1912); no. 3, op. 28 (1917); no. 4, op. 29 (1917); no. 5, op. 38 (1923); no. 6, op. 82 (1940); no. 7, op. 83 (1942); no. 8, op. 84 (1944); no. 9, op. 103 (1947); no. 10 (incomplete), op.

137 (1953); 2 sonatinas, op. 54 (1931-32); 4 études, op. 2 (1909); 4 pieces, op. 3 (1911); 4 pieces, op. 4 (1912); toccata, op. 11 (1912); 10 pieces, op. 12 (1913); *Sarcasms,* op. 17, a suite of 5 pieces (1912-14); *Visions fugitives,* op. 22, a suite of 20 pieces (1915-17); *Tales of an old Grandmother,* op. 31, 4 pieces (1918); 4 pieces, op. 32 (1918); *Schubert's Waltzes,* transcribed for 2 pianos (1911); March and Scherzo from the opera, *Love for Three Oranges,* op. 33-ter (1922); *Things in Themselves,* op. 45 (1928); 6 pieces, op. 52 (1930-31); 3 pieces, op. 59 (1934); *Pensées,* op. 62 (1933-34); *Children's Music,* op. 65, 12 easy pieces (1935); *Romeo and Juliet,* op. 75, 10 pieces from the ballet (1937); 3 pieces from the ballet *Cinderella,* op. 95 (1942); 3 pieces, op. 96 (1941-42); 10 pieces from the ballet *Cinderella,* op. 97 (1943); 6 pieces from the ballet *Cinderella,* op. 102 (1944). Songs: 2 poems, op. 9 (1911); *The Ugly Duckling,* op. 18, after Andersen (1914); 5 poems, op. 23 (1915); 5 poems, op. 27 (1916); *5 Songs Without Words,* op. 35 (1920; also for violin and piano, op. 35-bis); 5 poems, op. 36 (1921); 6 songs, op. 66 (1935); *3 Children's Songs;* op. 68 (1936); 3 poems, op. 73 (1936); 3 songs from the film *Alexander Nevsky,* op. 78 (1939); 7 songs, op. 79 (1939); 7 mass songs, op. 89 (1941-42); 6 transcriptions of folksongs, op. 104 (1944); 2 duets, op. 106 (1945); *Soldiers' March Song,* op. 121 (1950). — Bibliography: M. Montagu-Nathan, *S. Prokofiev,* in the 'Mus. Times' (Oct., 1916); M. Montagu-Nathan, *Prokofiev's First Pianoforte Concerto,* in the 'Mus. Times' (Jan., 1917); M. Montagu-Nathan, *Contemporary Russian Composers* (N. Y., 1917); L. Sabaneyev, *Modern Russian Composers* (N. Y., 1927); N. Slonimsky, *S. Prokofiev,* in the 'Quarterly on the Soviet Union' (N. Y., April, 1939); Gerald Abraham, *8 Soviet Composers* (London, 1943); S. Prokofiev, *The War Years,* in the 'Mus. Quarterly' (Oct., 1944); I. Nestyev, *S. Prokofiev* (Moscow, 1946; in English, N. Y., 1946; enlarged Russian ed., Moscow, 1957); Rena Moisenko, *Realist Music: 25 Soviet Composers* (London, 1949; pp. 173-87); N. Nabokov, *Old Friends and New Music* (Boston, 1951; pp. 141-83); S. I. Schlifstein, ed., *S. Prokofiev, Materials, Documents, Reminiscences* (Moscow, 1956; of prime documentary value; contains Prokofiev's autobiography and a complete catalogue of Prokofiev's works, with exhaustive commentaries and dates of composition and performance).

Proksch, Josef, Bohemian pianist and pedagogue; b. Reichenberg, Aug. 4, 1794; d. Prague, Dec. 20, 1864. He studied with Koželuch; in 1811, he lost his eyesight, but still learned Logier's system, and in 1830 founded a 'Musikbildungsanstalt' (school of piano playing) in Prague. He publ. a useful piano manual, *Versuch einer rationellen Lehrmethode im Pianofortespiel;* also a *Musikalisches Vademecum; Aphorismen über katholische Kirchenmusik; Allgemeine Musiklehre;* made for his pupils transcriptions, for 2, 3, 4, and even 8 pianos, of orchestral works; composed a concerto for 3 pianos, sonatas and other works; also vocal music. His son, **Theodor Proksch** (1843-1876), and a daughter, **Marie Proksch** (1836-1900), managed the school after his death; the last director of the Proksch school was **Robert Franz Proksch,** a great-grand-nephew of Josef Proksch; he died in 1933. —Cf. R. Müller, *Josef Proksch* (Prague, 1874); H. P. Kraus, *Musikbibliothek Josef Proksch* (Vienna, 1934).

Prony, Gaspard-Claire-François-Marie-Riche, Baron **de,** French harpist and music theorist; b. Chamelot, Rhône, July 12, 1755; d. Paris, July 29, 1839. As a member of the Académie, he was in charge of educational information; publ. a report on Érard's double-pedal harp, *Rapport sur la nouvelle harpe à double mouvement* (1815); other reports are: *Note sur les avantages du nouvel établissement d'un professorat d'harpe à l'école royale de musique* (1825); *Instruction élémentaire sur les moyens de calculer les intervalles musicaux* (1832; employing Euler's system of logarithms).

Proske, Karl, German authority on sacred music; b. Gröbnig, Feb. 11, 1794; d. Regensburg, Dec. 20, 1861. He was a medical student, regimental physician during the war of 1813-15; took the degree of M. D. at Halle in 1817, and practiced at Oberglogau and Oppeln. In 1823 he renounced medicine for theology, and studied at Regensburg; was ordained in 1826, became vicar-choral in 1827, and canon and Kapellmeister of the Church of Our Lady at Regensburg in 1830. After diligent research in Germany and Italy, he began his life-work, the publication of sacred classics, the first being Palestrina's *Missa Papae Marcelli* (Palestrina's original version, and arrangements by Anerio *a* 4 and Suriano *a* 8), followed by the famous collection 'Musica divina,' containing chiefly Italian masterworks of the 16th-17th centuries: vol. I, 12 Masses *a* 4 (1853); vol. II, motets for the entire church-year

(1855); vol. III, fauxbourdons, psalms, Magnificats, hymns, and antiphons (1859); vol. IV, Passions, Lamentations, responses, Te Deums, litanies (1863; edited by Wesselack); publication continued by Schrems and Haberl; also a 'Selectus novus missarum' *a* 4-8 (1855-59). His valuable library was purchased for the Episcopal Library at Regensburg; in 1909, when Dr. Karl Weinmann was appointed librarian, it was opened to musicians and music students. —Cf. Dom. Mettenleiter, *Karl Proske* (Regensburg, 1868; 2nd ed., 1895); K. Weinmann, *Karl Proske, der Restaurator der klassischen Kirchenmusik* (Regensburg, 1909); K. Weinmann, *Die Proskesche Musikbibliothek in Regensburg,* in the 'Riemann Festschrift' (Leipzig, 1909); O. Ursprung, *Restauration und Palestrina-Renaissance in der katholischen Kirchenmusik* (Augsburg, 1924; p. 32 ff.).

Prosniz, Adolf, Austrian pianist and pedagogue; b. Prague, Dec. 2, 1829; d. Vienna, Feb. 23, 1917. He was a pupil of Proksch and Tomaschek; 1869-1900, prof. of piano at the Vienna Cons.; then retired and lived in Vienna. — Publications: *Kompendium der Musikgeschichte* (vol. I, 1889; 3rd ed., 1920; vol. II, 1900; vol. III, 1915); *Handbuch der Klavierliteratur* (vol. I, 1450-1830, 1884; 2nd ed., 1908; vol. II, 1830-1904, 1907); *Elementarmusiklehre* (6 eds.); *Historische Klavierliteratur aus dem 16., 17. und 18. Jahrhundert. Ausgewählte Beispiele zu jedem Handbuch der Klavierliteratur* (9 vols.).

Prota-Giurleo, Ulisse, Italian musicologist; b. Naples, March 13, 1886; living in Ponticelli, near Naples. At first an art critic, he took up the study of musicology and devoted himself chiefly to Neapolitan music. His publications (all printed in Naples) are valuable for their new documentation; they include: *Musicisti napoletani alla corte di Portogallo* (1923); *Musicisti napoletani in Russia* (1923); *Paisiello ed i suoi primi trionfi a Napoli* (1923); *Nicola Logroscini, 'il dio dell' opera buffa'* (1927); *La grande orchestra del R. Teatro San Carlo nel settecento* (1927); *La Famiglia e la giovinezza di Salvator Rosa* (containing 52 unpublished documents; 1929); *Notizie sul musicista belga Jean Macque,* in the 'Report of the First Congress of the International Society for Musical Research' (Burnham, 1930); *Sacchini non nacque a Pozzuoli* (1952); *Nuovi contributi alla biografia di Domenico Cimarosa* and *Nuovi contributi alle biografie di Nicola Porpora e Giuseppe Porsile* (both published serially in 'La Scala' during 1955-56); numerous essays publ. in the Italian periodicals 'Samnium,' 'Vita Musicale Italiana,' 'Nostro Tempo,' etc.

Protheroe, Daniel, American conductor and composer; b. Ystradgynlais, S. Wales, Nov. 24, 1866; d. Chicago, Feb. 24, 1934. From 1884-86, conductor of the Choral Society at Ystradgynlais; choral conductor in Scranton, Pa., 1886-94; singer and teacher in Milwaukee, 1894-1909; then lived in Chicago as mus. director of the Central Church. —Publ. a symph. poem, *In the Cambrian Hills,* op. 59; a string quartet in A minor, op. 52; works for men's chorus; songs. Author of a *Course in Harmony and Choral Conducting.*

Prout, Ebenezer, eminent English theorist and teacher; b. Oundle, Northamptonshire, March 1, 1835; d. London, Dec. 5, 1909. Excepting some piano lessons as a boy, and a later course with Charles Salaman, he was wholly self-taught. His father had him trained for a school-teacher, and he took the degree of B. A. at London Univ. in 1854; but in 1859 went over definitely to music; was organist at Union Chapel, Islington, 1861-73; prof. of piano at the Crystal Palace School of Art, 1861-85; prof. of harmony and composition at the National Training School from 1876, and took Sullivan's class at the Royal Academy of Music in 1879; also conducted the Hackney Choral Association 1876-90, bringing it to a high state of efficiency; edited the 'Monthly Mus. Record' 1871-74, was critic on the 'Academy' 1874-79, and on the 'Athenæum' 1879-89. To Grove's 'Dictionary' he contributed 53 articles. In 1894 he was called to Dublin Univ. as prof. of music, succeeding Sir R. Stewart; in 1895 both Dublin and Edinburgh Universities conferred on him the degree of Mus. Doc. (*hon. c.*). His valuable theoretical works are the following: *Instrumentation* (Novello primer, 1876; German transl.; 3rd ed., 1904); *Harmony, Its Theory and Practice* (1889; 20th ed., entirely rewritten, 1903); *Counterpoint, Strict and Free* (1890); *Double Counterpoint and Canon* (1891); *Fugue* (1891); *Fugal Analysis* (1892); *Musical Form* (1893); *Applied Forms* (1895); all of which have passed through two or more editions; *The Orchestra* (2 vols., 1898-99; in German, 1905-06); and *Some Notes on Bach's Church-Cantatas* (1907). He reorchestrated Handel's *Messiah,* and this version is still in use. Besides, he wrote a number of compositions: 4 symphonies; 2 overtures; 2 organ concertos; a piano quintet; 2 string quartets; 2 piano quartets; clarinet sonata; the cantatas *Hereward, Alfred, The Red Cross Knight;* a considerable amount of church music; *Freedom,* ode for baritone solo and orch.; organ arrangements.

Provenzale, Francesco, one of the founders of the Neapolitan Opera School; b. Naples, 1627; d. there, Sept., 1704. From 1663 he was maestro at the Cons. di Santa Maria di Loreto; 1673-1701, director of the Cons. della Pietà de' Turchini; c. 1680 associate conductor of the Royal Chapel; 1686-1699, conductor at the Tesoro di San Gennaro, Naples. Romain Rolland believed him to be identical with Francesco della Torre. —Works: operas (all performed in Naples): *Ciro* (1653), *Serse* (1655), *Artemisia* (1657), *Teseo o L'Incostanza trionfante* (1658), *L'Eritrea* (1659), *Lo Schiavo di sua moglie* (1671), *La Stellidaura vendicata,* or *Diffendere l'offensore* (1678), and *Candaule re di Lidia* (1679); also oratorios; motets; a 9-voiced hymn with instrumental accompaniment, *Pange lingua;* and cantatas. —Cf. R. Rolland, *Histoire de l'opéra avant Lully et Scarlatti* (1895); H. Riemann, 'Handbuch der Musikgeschichte' II, 2, p. 385 ff.; H. Goldschmidt, *F. Provenzale als Dramatiker,* in 'Sammelbände der Internationalen Musik-Gesellschaft' VII, 4; G. Pannain, *F. Provenzale e la lirica del suo tempo,* in 'Rivista Musicale Italiana' (1925).

Prudent (prü-dăhn), **Émile,** French pianist; b. Angoulême, Feb. 3, 1817; d. Paris, May 13, 1863. Early orphaned, he was adopted by a piano-tuner; studied at the Paris Cons. with Zimmerman (piano) and Laurent (harmony), taking 1st prize in 1833. He made tours as a pianist in France, Belgium, England, and Germany; then settled in Paris, and was greatly esteemed there as a teacher. He wrote a number of piano works; contemporary critics ranked him between Thalberg and Döhler; his paraphrase of *Lucia di Lammermoor* enjoyed considerable success; he publ. *6 études de salon,* and other effective piano pieces (*L'Hirondelle, La Berceuse, Chanson sicilienne, Le Réveil des fées,* etc.).

Prüfer, Arthur, German musicologist; b. Leipzig, July 7, 1860; d. Würzburg, June 3, 1944. He was a law student; then turned to music; studied at the Leipzig Cons. (1887-88), also attending the lectures on musicology of Paul and Kretzschmar at the Univ.; studied further in Berlin (1888-89) with Spitta and Bargiel; took the degree of *Dr. phil.* (Leipzig, 1890), with the dissertation *Über den ausserkirchlichen Kunstgesang in den evangelischen Schulen des 16. Jahrhunderts;* qualified 1895 as lecturer at Leipzig Univ. with the essay *Johann Hermann Schein;* 1902 as associate prof., with the lecture *J. S. Bach und die Tonkunst des 19. Jahrhunderts.* Further publications: *Briefwechsel zwischen K. von Winterfeld und Ed. Krüger* (1898); *Die Bühnenfestspiele in Bayreuth* (1899; 2d ed., completely rewritten and greatly enlarged, as *Das Werk von Bayreuth,* 1909); *Joh. Herm. Schein und das weltliche deutsche Lied des 17. Jahrhunderts* (1908); *R. Wagner in Bayreuth* (1910); *Einführung in R. Wagners 'Feen'* (1912); *R. Wagner und Jakob Grimm* (1913); *Liszt und das Schiller-Goethe-Denkmal in Weimar* (1917); *Die Musik als tönende Faust-Idee* (1920); *Tristan und Isolde* (3rd ed., 1928); *Deutsches Leben im Volkslied und Wagners Tannhäuser* (1929); *Tannhäuser und der Sängerkrieg* (1930); many other essays on Wagner. Ed. of the first collected ed. of Schein's works, publ. 1901-23 by Breitkopf & Härtel (8 vols. appeared); publ. separately selections of 20 'weltliche Lieder' and instrumental pieces of Schein. —Cf. Paul Bülow, *A. Prüfer,* in 'Neue Zeitschrift für Musik' (1930).

Prume, F. H. See **Jehin-Prume.**

Prumier (prü-myā'), **Antoine,** French harpist; b. Paris, July 2, 1794; d. there, Jan. 20, 1868. He studied at the Paris Cons.; played the harp in the orch. of the Opéra-Comique (from 1835); succeeded Nadermann as harp prof. at the Cons. He wrote about 100 fantasies, rondos, and airs with variations, for harp. His son, **Ange-Conrad Prumier** (b. Paris, Jan. 5, 1820; d. there, April 3, 1884), succeeded him at the Opéra-Comique, and became prof. at the Cons. in 1870. He publ. études for harp; nocturnes for harp and horn; sacred songs.

Prunières (prü-ñär'), **Henry,** eminent French musicologist; b. Paris, May 24, 1886; d. Nanterre, April 11, 1942. He studied history of music with R. Rolland; *Dr. ès lettres,* 1913; 1909-14, instructor at the École des Hautes Études Sociales in Paris; 1919, founded the important journal 'La Revue Musicale,' of which he was editor-in-chief until 1939; 1921, organized the concerts at the Théâtre du Vieux Colombier; was head of the French section of the International Society for Contemporary Music. —Publications: *Lully* (1910; 2nd ed., 1927), *L'Opéra italien en France avant Lully* (1913; important), *Le Ballet de cour en France avant Benserade et Lully* (1914), *Monteverdi* (1924, enlarged 1926; 2nd ed., 1931; also in English, valuable), *La Vie illustre et libertine de J.-B. Lully* (1929), *Cavalli et l'opéra vénitien au XVII*[e] *siècle* (1931), *Nouvelle histoire de la musique* (2 vols., 1934, 1936; in English, 1 vol., 1943); and the following valuable essays: *La Musique de la Chambre et de l'Écurie sous le règne de François I,* in the 'Année musicale' (I, 1911), *Jean de Cambeford, Surintendant de la musique de la chambre du roy,* ib. (II, 1913); *Notes sur la vie de Luigi Rossi,* in 'Sammelbände der Internationalen Musik-Gesellschaft' (XII, 1), *Notes sur l'origine de l'ouverture,* ib. (XII, 4), *Les Représentations du 'Palazzo d'Atlante' de Luigi Rossi,* ib. (XIV, 2); *Lecerf de Viéville et le classicisme musical,* in 'Bulletin de la Société Internationale de Musique' (June, 1908), *La Jeunesse de Lully* (with L. de La Laurencie), ib. (March-April, 1909), *Lully fils de meunier,* ib. (June, 1912); *Recherches sur les années de jeunesse de J.-B. Lully,* in 'Rivista Musicale Italiana' (XVII, 3); *Lully and the Académie de Musique et de Danse,* in the 'Mus. Quarterly' (Oct., 1925); *Albert Roussel and the 80th Psalm,* ib. (Jan., 1930), *Opera in Venice in the 17th Century,* ib. (Jan., 1931), *Musical Symbolism,* ib. (Jan., 1933); etc. Publ. a new ed. of Stendhal's *Vie de Rossini* (1922). He was general editor of a complete ed. of Lully's works (10 vols., Paris, 1930-39). —Cf. the special issue of the 'Revue Musicale' dedicated to Prunières (1952-53).

Prüwer (prü'-věr), **Julius,** Austrian conductor; b. Vienna, Feb. 20, 1874; d. New York, July 8, 1943. He studied in Vienna with A. Friedheim and M. Rosenthal (piano), also profited greatly from his association with Brahms. He began his career as conductor at Bielitz; then was conductor at the Cologne Opera (1894-96); conductor at the Municipal Theater in Breslau (1896-1923), where he distinguished himself by producing many modern works; conductor of the Weimar Opera (1923-24); prof. at the Berlin Hochschule für Musik and conductor of the popular concerts of the Berlin Philharmonic (1924-33). In 1933 he was compelled to leave Germany; conducted opera in Russia; then was in Austria; in 1939, settled in New York. He publ. with O. Röse a guide to *Elektra* by Richard Strauss (Berlin, 1909).

Ptolemy, Claudius, the celebrated Alexandrian astronomer, geographer, and mathematician, early in the 2nd century wrote a very important treatise on music, a poor Latin version of which was made by Gogavinus (1562); Wallis publ. the original Greek text in 1682; O. Paul gives a fragment in Greek, with German transl., in his 'Boëtius.' A new ed. of this work was publ. by Ingemar Düring (Göteborg, 1930), with excellent commentary and explanation. —Cf. I. Düring, *Ptolemaios und Porphyrios über die Musik* (Göteborg, 1934); M. Shirlaw, *Claudius Ptolemy as Musical Theorist,* in the 'Music Review' (Aug., 1955).

Puccini (pŏŏch-chē'-nē), **Giacomo,** celebrated Italian composer; b. Lucca, Dec. 22, 1858; d. Brussels, Nov. 29, 1924. Beginning with his great-great-grandfather, **Giacomo** (1712-81), all his ancestors in the direct line were musicians of local prominence: **Antonio** (1747-1832), **Domenico** (1771-1815), **Michele** (1813-64). As a child Puccini showed neither inclination nor special talent for music; but his mother, determined to continue the family tradition, sent him to the Istituto Musicale of Lucca (founded by Pacini), where Carlo Angeloni, a pupil of Michele Puccini, became his teacher. After Angeloni's untiring patience had aroused interest, and then enthusiasm, in his pupil, progress was rapid, and Puccini soon was a good pianist and organist. About 1875 he became organist at the church in a near-by village, Muligliano, and soon after was also appointed organist at San Pietro in Somaldi. In 1877 he submitted a cantata, *Juno,* to a competition held at Lucca, but failed to win the prize. Nevertheless, he produced the work, which won considerable local success, so that the young composer brought out, also with success, a motet for the feast of Santa Paolina. These successes fired his ambition, and when he became acquainted about that time with *Aida* he resolved to win laurels as a dramatic composer. Assistance from a grand-uncle and a stipend granted by Queen Margherita enabled him to enter the Milan Cons., where he spent 3 years (1880-83) in serious study with Antonio Bazzini and Amilcare Ponchielli. For his graduation he wrote a *Capriccio sinfonico,* which at its performance at one of the Cons. concerts, and later by Faccio, elicited unstinted praise from the critics. In the same year Ponchielli introduced Puccini to the librettist Fontana, who furnished him the text of a 1-act opera; in a few weeks the score was finished and sent to the Sonzogno competition. It did not win the prize, but on May 31, 1884, *Le Villi* was produced at the Teatro dal Verme, in Milan, with gratifying success. Ricordi, who was present, considered the work sufficiently meritorious to commission the young composer to write a new opera for him; but 5 years elapsed before this work, *Edgar* (3 acts, text by Fontana), was produced at La Scala on April 21, 1889, scoring only a moderate success. By this time Puccini had become convinced that, in order to write a really effective opera, he needed a better libretto than Fontana had provided. Accordingly, he commissioned Domenico Oliva to write the text of *Manon Lescaut;* during the composition, however, Puccini and Ricordi practically rewrote the entire book, and in the publ. score Oliva's name is not mentioned. With *Manon Lescaut* (4 acts), first produced at the Teatro Regio in Turin on Feb. 1, 1893, Puccini won a veritable triumph, which was even surpassed by the next work, *La Bohème* (4 acts; text by Illica and Giacosa), produced at the same theater on Feb. 1, 1896. These two works not only carried their composer's name throughout the world, but also have found and maintained their place in the repertory of every opera-house. With fame came wealth, and in 1900 he built at Lago del Torre, where he had been living since 1891, a magnificent villa. The next opera, *Tosca* (3 acts; text by Illica and Giacosa), produced at the Teatro Costanzi in Rome on Jan. 14, 1900, is Puccini's most dramatic work; it has become a fixture of the standard repertory and contains some of Puccini's best-known arias. At its première at La Scala on Feb. 17, 1904, *Madama Butterfly* (2 acts; text by Illica and Giacosa) was hissed. Puccini thereupon withdrew the score and made some slight changes (division into 3 acts, and addition of the tenor aria in the last scene). This revised version was greeted with frenzied applause in Brescia on May 28 of the same year. Puccini was now the acknowledged ruler of the Italian operatic stage, his works rivaling those of Verdi in the number of performances. The first performance of *Madama Butterfly* at the Metropolitan Opera House (Feb. 11, 1907) took place in the presence of the composer, whom the management had invited specially for the occasion. It was then suggested that he write an opera on an American subject, the première to take place at the Metropolitan Opera House. He found his subject when he witnessed a performance of Belasco's *The Girl of the Golden West;* he commissioned C. Zangarini and G. Civinini to write the libretto, and in the presence of the composer the world première of *La Fanciulla del West* occurred, amid much enthusiasm, at the Metropolitan Opera House on Dec. 10, 1910. But the enthusiasm subsided quickly; the following season the work had a few more performances, and then disappeared from the repertory; it shared the same fate in Italy (1st Italian performance Teatro Costanzi, Rome, June 12, 1911) and other European countries. Puccini then brought out *La Rondine* (3 acts; Monte Carlo, March 27, 1917) and the 3 1-act operas *Il Tabarro* (after Didier Gold's *La Houppelande*), *Suor Angelica,* and *Gianni Schicchi* (all performed at the Metropolitan Opera House, Dec. 14, 1918). His last opera, *Turandot* (after Gozzi), was left unfinished; the final scene was completed by Franco Alfano and the work first performed at La Scala, Milan, on April 25, 1926; it was also given at the Metropolitan Opera House, Nov. 16, 1926.—All operas but *Edgar* have been performed in the U. S.: *Le Villi* (Metropolitan Opera House, Dec. 17, 1908); *Manon Lescaut* (Hinrichs Co., Philadelphia, July 29, 1894); *La Bohème* (Los Angeles, Oct. 18, 1897); *Tosca* (Metropolitan Opera House, Feb. 4, 1901); *Madama Butterfly* (Washington, Oct. 15, 1906). Puccini also composed the *Inno a Roma* (1919), for use in the schools of Rome.—BIBLIOGRAPHY: M. Virgilio, *Della Decadenza dell' opera in Italia* (Milan, 1900); A. Brüggemann, *Madama Butterfly e l'arte di G. Puccini* (Milan, 1904); Wakeling Dry, *G. Puccini* (London, 1906); F. Torrefranca, *G. Puccini e l'opera internazionale* (Turin, 1912); D. C. Parker, *A View of G. Puccini,* in the 'Mus. Quarterly' (Oct., 1917); A. Weissmann, *G. Puccini* (Munich, 1922); A. Cœuroy, *La Tosca* (Paris, 1924); A. Bonaventura, *G. Puccini: L'Uomo, l'artista* (Leghorn, 1924); A. Fraccaroli, *La Vita di G. Puccini* (Milan, 1925; also in German); G. Marotti and F. Pagni, *G. Puccini intimo* (Florence, 1926); A. Neisser, *Puccini* (Leipzig, 1928); F. Salerno, *Le Donne pucciniane* (Palermo, 1928); G. M. Gatti, *The Works of G. Puccini,* in the 'Mus. Quarterly' (Jan., 1928); R. C. Merlin, *Puccini* (Milan, 1930); R. Specht, *Puccini* (Berlin, 1931; in English, N. Y., 1933); W. Maisch, *Puccinis musikalische Formgebung* (Neustadt, 1934); G. Adami, *Puccini* (Milan, 1935; in German, 1943); M. Carner, *The Exotic Element in Puccini,* in the 'Mus. Quarterly' (Jan., 1936); K. G. Fellerer, *G. Puccini* (Potsdam, 1937); V. Seligman, *Puccini Among Friends* (correspondence; N. Y., 1938); G. Marotti, *Giacomo Puccini intimo* (Florence, 1942); F. Thiess, *Puccini, Versuch einer Psychologie seiner Musik* (Berlin, 1947); A. Bonaccorsi, *Giacomo Puccini e i suoi antenati musicali* (Milan, 1950);

G. Marek, *Puccini: a Biography* (N. Y., 1951); Dante del Fiorentino, *Immortal Bohemian: an Intimate Memoir of Giacomo Puccini* (N. Y., 1952); V. Terenzio, *Ritratto di Puccini* (Bergamo, 1954); A. Machard, *Une Vie d'amour: Puccini* (Paris, 1954); L. Ricci, *Puccini interprete di se stesso* (Milan, 1954). G. Adami publ. letters of Puccini (Milan, 1928; in English, London, 1931).

Puccitta, Vincenzo. See Pucitta.

Puchalsky, Vladimir Viatcheslavovitch, Russian pianist and composer; b. Minsk, April 2, 1848; d. Kiev, Feb. 23, 1933. He studied at the St. Petersburg Cons. with Leschetizky (piano) and Zaremba (theory); in 1876 appointed instructor at the Kiev Cons.; remained in Kiev until his death. He wrote an opera, *Valeria;* piano pieces and songs.

Puchat (pŏŏ'-hăht), **Max,** German composer and pianist; b. Breslau, Jan. 8, 1859; d. (killed in a fall in the Karwendel Alps) Aug. 12, 1919. He studied with Kiel in Berlin, winning the Mendelssohn prize in 1884. From 1886 to 1903 he was active as choral conductor in German provinces; then went to Milwaukee, where he conducted the local Musikverein (1903-05); returned to Germany; lived in Munich; in 1910, settled in Breslau, where established his own music school. He wrote several symph. works: *Euphorion* (1888), *Leben und Ideal* (1892), *Tragödie eines Künstlers* (1894), *Ouvertüre über ein nordisches Thema,* etc.; a piano concerto; a string quartet; songs.

Pucitta, Vincenzo, Italian composer; b. Civitavecchia, 1778; d. Milan, Dec. 20, 1861. He studied with Fenaroli in Naples; traveled through Europe, and was successful as an opera composer in Italy, Austria, France, and England; wrote about 30 operas, of which the best were *La Burla fortunata* (Venice, April 9, 1804) and *La Vestale* (London, May 3, 1810).

Puente, Giuseppe Del, baritone; b. Naples, Jan. 30, 1841; d. Philadelphia, May 25, 1900. He first studied cello at the Naples Cons. but later began to cultivate his voice, making his operatic début at Jassy; was then engaged for the Teatro San Carlo in Naples, and for appearances in France, Germany, Russia, Spain, and England (début at Covent Garden, 1873; became very popular there); first American engagement under Strakosch at the N. Y. Academy of Music in 1873-74; became a member of the first Metropolitan Opera company and sang the role of Valentin in the inaugural performance of *Faust* on Oct. 22, 1883. In 1885 he returned to the Academy of Music under Mapleson's management, taking part in the American première of *Manon* on Dec. 23 of that year; he was also a member of the opera troupes of Patti and Hinrichs; with the latter's company he sang in the American première of *Cavalleria Rusticana* (Philadelphia, Sept. 9, 1891). He married the mezzo-soprano Helen Dudley Campbell.

Puget (pü-zhā'), **Louise,** French composer of songs; b. Paris, Feb. 11, 1810; d. Pau, 1889. She was an amateur, whose songs acquired an extraordinary vogue in Paris; particularly popular were *Ave Maria, Le Soleil de ma Bretagne, Mon pays, Les Rêves d'une jeune fille;* she also wrote a 1-act opera, *Le mauvais œil* (Paris, Oct. 1, 1836), and an operetta, *La Veilleuse* (Paris, Sept. 27, 1869). She was married to the song writer Lemoine.

Puget (pü-zhā'), **Paul-Charles-Marie,** French composer; b. Nantes, June 25, 1848; d. Paris, March 14, 1917. He studied at the Paris Cons. with Marmontel (piano) and Massé (composition); won 1st Grand Prix de Rome in 1873 with the cantata *Mazeppa;* wrote much theater music; his opera *Beaucoup de bruit pour rien,* after Shakespeare (Paris, March 24, 1899), had a moderately good reception.

Pugnani (pŏŏ-ñah'-nē), **Gaetano,** celebrated Italian violinist and composer; b. Turin, Nov. 27, 1731; d. there, July 15, 1798. He studied with Somis; on April 19, 1748, was appointed violinist in the Royal Chapel of Turin; in 1749 was sent to Rome for additional study; then traveled in Europe; was in London in 1768 as concertmaster of the Italian Opera there; also played in Paris at the Concert Spirituel. In 1770 he was back in Turin, as teacher and conductor; had a school of his own; among his violin pupils were Viotti, Conforti, Bruni, and Polledro. His style approaches that of Tartini; he wrote effective music for the violin; Fritz Kreisler publ. a purported arangement for violin of a piece by Pugnani, *Preludio e Allegro e Tempo di Minuetto,* but this is actually an original work by Kreisler himself.—Pugnani composed 9 violin concertos; 12 octets (*sinfonie*) for strings, 2 oboes, and 2 horns; 6 quintets for 2 violins, 2 flutes, and cello; 6 string quartets; 3 sets of trios for 2 violins and cello;

2 sets of violin duets; 14 violin sonatas (one is reprinted in Jensen's 'Klassische Violin-Musik'). He also wrote several operas: *Nanetta e Lubino* (London, 1769), *Issea* (Turin, 1771), *Aurora* (Turin, 1775), *Adone e Venere* (Naples, 1784), *Demetrio a Rodi* (Turin, 1789); his last opera was *Werther,* after Goethe (Vienna, March 22, 1796).—Cf. F. Fayolle, *Notices sur Corelli, Tartini, Gaviniès, Pugnani et Viotti* (Paris, 1810); Dom. Carutti, *Della famiglia di Gaetano Pugnani,* in 'Miscellanea di storia italiana' (3rd series, vol. II, Turin, 1895); S. Cordero di Pamparato, *Gaetano Pugnani* (Turin, 1930); A. Della Corte, *Notizie di Gaetano Pugnani, musicista torinese* (Turin, 1931); E. M. von Zschinsky-Troxler, *Gaetano Pugnani* (Berlin, 1939; contains a thematic catalogue); A. Müry, *Die Instrumentalwerke Gaetano Pugnanis* (Basel, 1941).

Pugni (pōō'-ñe), **Cesare,** Italian composer; b. Milan, 1805; d. St. Petersburg, Jan. 26, 1870. He studied violin with Alessandro Rolla and composition with Asioli at the Cons. of Milan; began his career as composer for the stage with the ballet *Elerz e Zulmida* (Milan, May 6, 1826) and the opera *Il Disertore svizzero* (Milan, May 28, 1831), followed by several other operas: *La Vendetta* (Milan, Feb. 11, 1832), *Ricciarda di Edimburgo* (Trieste, Sept. 29, 1832), *Il Contrabbandiere* (Milan, June 13, 1833), *Un Episodio di S. Michele* (Milan, June 14, 1834), etc.; also wrote an ingenious *Sinfonia a canone* for 2 orchestras playing the same music, but with the 2nd orch. coming in one measure later than the first (this musical legerdemain enchanted Meyerbeer); he then lived in Paris, where he produced the ballets *La Fille de marble* (Oct. 20, 1847), *Le Violon du diable* (Jan. 19, 1849), etc. In 1851 he was appointed ballet composer for the Imperial Theater in St. Petersburg; wrote about 300 ballet scores; of these, *Esmeralda* (originally produced in Milan, 1845) and *Konyok-Gorbunok* (*Le Cheval enchanté,* St. Petersburg, 1864) still retain their popularity in Russia.

Pugno (pōō-ñoh), **Raoul,** celebrated French pianist; b. (of an Italian father) Montrouge, Seine, June 23, 1852; d. (while on a concert tour) Moscow, Jan. 3, 1914. From early childhood he showed unusual talent for the piano and appeared in public at an early age. Prince Poniatowski was impressed by his talent, and procured for him a scholarship at the École Niedermeyer; afterwards (1866-69) he studied at the Paris Cons. with G. Mathias (piano) and Ambroise Thomas (composition); won several prizes, but his Italian citizenship barred him from competition for the Prix de Rome. He began a career as organist at the St.-Eugène Church in 1871; maître de chapelle there in 1878; taught harmony at the Paris Cons. (1892-96) and subsequently was prof. of piano there (1896-1901). In the meantime he gave numerous recitals, and gradually rose to the rank of a great virtuoso; appeared in England in 1894; in America, in 1897-98. He was equally remarkable as an ensemble player; his sonata recitals with Ysaÿe became world-famous. He was responsible for making the name of César Franck known to a wide public. Pugno was also a composer; wrote several operas: *Ninetta* (Paris, Dec. 23, 1882), *Le Sosie* (1887), *Le Valet de cœur* (1888), *Le Retour d'Ulysse* (Paris, Feb. 1, 1889), *La Vocation de Marius* (1890), etc.; ballet, *La Danseuse de corde* (Paris, Feb. 5, 1892); piano pieces; songs. His score for *La Ville morte* (after Gabriele d'Annunzio), left incomplete at his death, was finished by Nadia Boulanger.

Pujol, Francesc, Catalan composer; b. Barcelona, May 15, 1878; d. there, Dec. 24, 1945. He studied at the Barcelona Cons., also with Millet; assistant conductor (1900-41), then musical director (1942-45) of the Orfeó Catalá, Barcelona. Composer of 40 sardanas, church music, orchestral works, etc. Publ. valuable studies on Catalan songs: On the *Chant de la Sibila; L'Œuvre du 'Chansonnier populaire de la Catalogne'* (Report of the International Musicological Congress, Vienna, 1927); *Observacions, apéndix i notes al Romancerillo catalán de Manuel Milá y Fontanals* (with Joan Punti; 1927 ff.); Catalan folksongs with piano accompaniment (Madrid, 1921).

Pujol, Juan, Catalan church musician; b. Barcelona, c. 1573; d. there, May, 1626. From 1593 to 1595 he was maestro de canto in Tarragona; 1595-1612, maestro at Nuestra Señora del Pilar in Saragossa; then at Barcelona Cathedral until his death. His Masses, motets, Passions, psalms, and 'villancicos' are preserved in MS. A collected ed. of Pujol's works was undertaken by H. Anglès, of which 2 vols. appeared: I, biography, and Office of St. George's Day (1926); II, Offices and Masses (1932). An Introit (1614) was publ. in Schering's *Geschichte der Musik in Beispielen* (No. 179).

Puliti, Leto, Italian scholar; b. Florence, June 29, 1818; d. there, Nov. 15, 1875. He publ. valuable essays in the Proceedings of the Royal Institute of Music in Florence, especially *Cenni storici della vita del serenissimo Ferdinando de' Medici* (1884; printed separately), with information concerning Cristofori, the inventor of the piano.

Pulver, Jeffrey, English violinist and musicologist; b. London, June 22, 1884; studied with Ševčik (Prague), Heermann (Frankfurt), Marteau (Geneva), and A. Moser (Berlin). He made a specialty of old English music, and played the viola d'amore, the tenor viola, and other old string instruments. —Publications: *A Dictionary of Musical Terms* (1913); *A Dictionary of Old English Music and Musical Instruments* (1923); *Johannes Brahms* (1926); *A Biographical Dictionary of Old English Music* (1927); *Paganini, the Romantic Virtuoso* (1936); etc.; articles in the 'Monthly Mus. Record,' 'Sackbut,' 'Strad,' the 'Mus. Quarterly,' etc. His lectures before the Mus. Association, London, are printed in their 'Proceedings': *The Ancient Dance Forms* (2 parts; 1912, 1914); *The Intermezzi of the Opera* (1917); *The Viols in England* (1920); *The Music of Ancient Egypt* (1921); etc.

Punto, Giovanni. See **Stich.**

Puppo, Giuseppe, Italian violinist; b. Lucca, June 12, 1749; d. Florence, April 19, 1827. He was a successful violin virtuoso at an early age; traveled in Spain; was inEngland until 1784, when he settled in Paris; was a fashionable teacher there; in 1811, abandoned his family in Paris, went to Naples, and then to Florence, dying in poverty. He publ. 3 violin concertos, 8 études for the violin, and 6 piano fantasias.

Purcell (pur'-sĕl), **Daniel,** brother of Henry Purcell; b. London, c. 1660; d. there, Dec. 12, 1717. He became organist of Magdalen College, Oxford, in 1688; took his brother's place as dramatic composer in 1695, and was organist of St. Andrew's, Holborn, from 1713.—Works: incidental music to 30 dramas; several odes (e.g., funeral ode for his brother); publ. *The Psalm Tunes set full for the Organ or Harpsichord . . .*; also songs in collections. Six anthems are in the choirbooks of Magdalen College chapel.

Purcell (pur'-sĕl), **Henry,** one of the greatest of English composers; b. London (?), c. 1659; d. Dean's Yard, Westminster, Nov. 21, 1695. Until recently it was believed that his father was Henry Purcell (d. 1664), Gentleman of the Chapel Royal and Master of the choristers at Westminster Abbey. But the latest evidence indicates that he was the son of Henry's brother, Thomas Purcell, who was also a Gentleman of the Chapel Royal and held other important posts at the court. From 1669 he was a chorister of the Chapel Royal under Cooke and Humfrey, also receiving instruction from Dr. Blow. When his voice broke in 1673, he was appointed assistant 'Keeper of the Instruments.' In 1677 he was appointed composer to the King's band, and in 1679 he succeeded Blow as organist of Westminster Abbey. In 1682 he became one of the 3 organists of the Chapel Royal as Lowe's successor; in 1683, Keeper of the King's wind-instruments. His first printed composition is a song in vol. I (1675) of Playford's 'Choice Ayres'; vol. II (1679) contains several other songs, and an elegy on the death of Matthew Locke. In 1680 Purcell wrote the first of 29 'Odes' and 'Welcome Songs.' His first publ. chamber music dates from 1683, *Sonatas of III Parts: two violins and bass: to the Organ or Harpsichord* (with engraved portrait), 12 numbers, based on Italian models, each having an Adagio, a Canzone (fugue), a slow movement, and an air. *The Yorkshire Feast Song,* called by D'Urfey, the author, 'one of the finest compositions he ever made,' was composed and produced in 1690. This is one of the 29 'Welcome Songs,' which he wrote (on an average of 2 annually) in his capacity of 'composer-in-ordinary.' Although the texts are almost invariably stupid or bombastic, Purcell wrote some of his finest music for these occasional odes. During the last five years he developed extraordinary activity in theatrical composition, to which he had given some attention since 1680, when he began to write some incidental dances and occasional airs for various dramas. In spite of this close connection with the stage, he wrote only one opera, *Dido and Aeneas,* produced in 1689. He lies in the north aisle of Westminster Abbey, and his burial-tablet well expresses contemporary estimation of his worth: 'Here lyes Henry Purcell, Esq.; who left this life, and is gone to that blessed place where only his harmony can be exceeded.' His church music shows an original melodist, and a master of form, harmony, and all contrapuntal devices; his music for the stage is equally rich in invention, dramatic instinct, and power of characterization; his chamber works surpass those of his predecessors and contemporaries. —Works: Besides the compositions mentioned there were publ. during Purcell's life a theoretical treatise, *The Art of Descant,* in the 10th ed. of Playford's 'Briefe Introduction of the Skill of Musick' (1683); Playford also publ. several airs and 'symphonies' (written for various dramas) in 'The Theatre of Musick' (1685), anthems and sacred songs in 'Harmonia Sacra' (1688), and pieces for harpsichord in 'Musick's Handmaid' (part II, 1689); of the incidental music to plays there appeared *Amphitryon* (1690; the airs in the text, the instrumental pieces in 'Ayres for the Theatre'), *Dioclesian* (1691), and 'Select ayres' from the *Fairy Queen* (1692). The stage pieces for which Purcell wrote music include the following: 1680, Lee's *Theodosius,* D'Urfey's *The Virtuous Wife* (1694?); 1681, Tate's arrangement of Shakespeare's *Richard II,* D'Urfey's *Sir Barnaby Whigg;* 1682, Beaumont and Fletcher's *The Double Marriage* (1685?); 1685, Davenant's *Circe,* Lee's *Sophonisba;* 1688, D'Urfey's *A Fool's Preferment;* 1689, Betterton's *Dioclesian,* Settle's *Distressed Innocence,* Southerne's *Sir Anthony Love,* Dryden's *Amphitryon,* Lee's *The Massacre of Paris;* 1691, Dryden's *King Arthur, The Gordian Knot Untyed* (author unknown), Dryden's *The Indian Emperor,* Southerne's *The Wives' Excuse;* 1692, Dryden's *Cleomenes, The Fairy Queen* (an arrangement of the *Midsummer Night's Dream*), D'Urfey's *The Marriage-hater Matched,* Crowne's *Regulus,* Shadwell's *The Libertine,* Bancroft's *Henry II,* Dryden's *Aureng-Zebe,* Dryden and Lee's *Oedipus;* 1693, Congreve's *The Old Bachelor,* D'Urfey's *The Richmond Heiress,* Southern's *The Maid's Last Prayer,* Wright's *The Female Virtuosos* (after Molière), Congreve's *The Double Dealer,* Shadwell's *Epsom Wells,* Fletcher's *Rule a Wife and Have a Wife;* 1694, D'Urfey's *Don Quixote* (part I), Dryden's *Love Triumphant,* Crowne's *The Married Beau,* Southerne's *The Fatal Marriage,* Ravenscroft's *The Canterbury Guests,* D'Urfey's *Don Quixote* (part II), Shadwell's arr. of *Timon of Athens,* Dryden's *The Spanish Friar,* Dryden's *Tyrannic Love;* 1695, Behn's *Andelazer,* Beaumont and Fletcher's *Bonduca,* Howard and Dryden's *Indian Queen,* Scott's *The Mock Marriage,* Norton's *Pausanias,* Gould's *The Rival Sisters,* Southerne's *Oroonoko,* Davenant and Dryden's arrangement of *The Tempest,* D'Urfey's *Don Quixote* (part III). In this list only *Dioclesian, The Fairy Queen, The Indian Queen,* and *King Arthur* are provided with sufficient music to be possibly classed as 'semi-operas'; the music for other dramas usually includes overtures, airs, and instrumental dances. Purcell's widow, who survived him till 1706, publ. *A Choice Collection of Lessons for the Harpsichord or Spinet* (1696), *Ten Sonatas in Four Parts* (1697), *Orpheus Britannicus: A Collection of the choicest Songs . . . with Symphonies for Violins or Flutes . . .* (Part I, 1698, 2nd ed., 1706; Part II, 1702; 2nd ed., 1711; both parts in 1 vol., with the addition of several new numbers, 1721). Many compositions were publ. in Playford's 'Harmonia Sacrae' (1688-93), Walsh's 'The Catch Club, or Merry Companions' (c. 1730), Boyce's 'Cathedral Music' (3 vols., 1760-73), Arnold's continuation of the same (4 vols., 1790), Page and Sexton's 'Harmonia Sacra' (3 vols., 1800). Vincent Novello collected all services, anthems, hymns, and sacred songs, and publ. them as *Purcell's Sacred Music* (4 vols., 1829-32; very inaccurate). The Musical Antiquarian Society publ. *Dido and Aeneas* (ed. G. A. Macfarren, 1840), *Bonduca* (ed. E. F. Rimbault, 1842; with historical sketch of dramatic music in England), *King Arthur* (ed. E. Taylor, 1843), *Ode for St. Cecilia's Day* (ed. E. F. Rimbault, 1847). In 1876 the Purcell Society was formed in London for the purpose of publishing the first complete ed. of Purcell's works; 26 vols. were brought out from 1878-1928; a 27th in 1957; 4 final vols. were in preparation in 1958. The Purcell Society also began to publ. a 'Popular Edition of Selected Works' (vol. 1: *15 Songs and Airs;* London, 1939). Various selections have been publ. by P. Warlock (*Fantasias* in 3, 4, and 5 parts; some publ. for the 1st time; London, 1927), G. Jensen, A. Egidi, A. Moffat and H. David (trio sonatas), W. Barclay Squire (harpsichord pieces), A. Schering in *Geschichte der Musik in Beispielen* (Nos. 246-48a), F. Blume in *Das Chorwerk* (5 sacred choruses), E. Dent (*Let the Dreadful Engines*), W. Gillies Whittaker (22 sonatas; Eds. de l'Oiseau-Lyre, Paris), etc.—The so-called *Trumpet Voluntary,* ascribed to Purcell, and made popular through an orchestral transcription by Sir Henry Wood, is not by Purcell but by Jeremiah Clarke (q.v.); for details, see C. L. Cudworth, *Some New Facts About the Trumpet Voluntary,* in the 'Mus. Times' (Sept., 1953).

Bibliography: W. H. Cummings, *Purcell* (London, 1881; 3rd ed., 1911; pop. ed., 1923); W. Barclay Squire, *Purcell's Dramatic Music,* in 'Sammelbände der Internationalen Musik-Gesellschaft' V, 4 (1904); J. F. Runciman, *Purcell* (London,

1909); G. E. Arkwright, *Purcell's Church Music,* in the 'Mus. Antiquary' (July, 1910); P. A. Scholes, *H. Purcell: Sketch of a Busy Life,* in the 'Mus. Quarterly' (July, 1916); W. Barclay Squire, *Purcell's 'Dido and Aeneas,'* in the 'Mus. Times' (June, 1918); H. Dupré, *Purcell* (Paris, 1927; in English, N. Y., 1928); D. Arundell, *H. Purcell* (London, 1927; in German, 1929); E. Dent, *Foundations of the English Opera* (1928); A. K. Holland, *H. Purcell, the English Musical Tradition* (London, 1932); F. de Quervain, *Der Chorstil H. Purcells* (Leipzig, 1935); J. A. Westrup, *Purcell* (London, 1937); S. Favre-Lingorow, *Der Instrumentalstil von Purcell* (Bern, 1950); S. Demarquez, *Purcell* (Paris, 1951); G. van Ravenzwaaÿ, *Purcell* (Haarlem, 1954); R. Sietz, *Henry Purcell: Zeit, Leben, Werk* (Leipzig, 1955).

Puschmann, Adam, German meistersinger; b. Görlitz, 1532; d. Breslau, April 4, 1600. He was a pupil of Hans Sachs; brought out *Gründlicher Bericht des deutschen Meistergesanges* (1571; new ed., Halle, 1888); his songs were publ. by Georg Münzer in 1906. His brother Zacharias Puschmann (with whom he is often confused) was a cantor in Görlitz.

Pustet, Friedrich, German publisher; b. Hals, near Passau. In 1826 he founded a publ. firm for church music in Regensburg. For 30 years he had the exclusive right of printing, with privilege of the Pope, the chant books according to the 'Editio Medicaea.' In 1921 Pustet's firm merged with the publ. house of Kösel, retaining, however, the original name. Pustet publ. Proske's *Musica divina;* Peter Wagner's *Elemente des gregorianischen Gesanges;* Johner's *Cantus ecclesiastici;* 'Kirchenmusikalisches Jahrbuch' (from its founding in 1886 through the vol. for 1935); etc.

Pyamour, John, English composer; date of birth unknown; d. 1431. He was a clerk of the Chapel Royal in 1419, and Master of Children in 1420; was commissioned to find boys with good voices for the royal service; traveled with King Henry V and the chapel on the Continent, and probably remained in Normandy for several years. His motet *Quam pulchra es* is extant in MS.—Cf. John Harvey, *Gothic England* (London, 1947).

Pycard, English singer and composer, who flourished c. 1400. The 'Old Hall Manuscript' contains 6 works by him; his contrapuntal skill was out of the ordinary, and he used complicated canonic forms in sections of the Mass. —Cf. M. Bukofzer, *Studies in Medieval and Renaissance Music* (N. Y., 1950).

Pylkkänen, Tauno Kullervo, Finnish composer; b. Helsinki, March 22, 1918. He studied at the Helsinki Cons., and for a brief time in France and Italy. Returning to Finland, he edited the periodical, 'Musiikki' (1947-50); was active on the Finnish Radio. —Works: operas: *Jaakko Ilkka* (1937), *Bathsheba Saarenmaalla* (1940), *Mare ja hänen poikansa* (1945), *Simo Hurtta* (1948), *Varjo* (1952); a symphony (1945); symph. poems, *Sommar i Lappland* (1941) and *Ultima Thule* (1949); *Marathon Overture* (1947); *Bilder fran Lappland* (1948); songs. His radio opera, *Suden Morsian* (*The Wolf Bride*), won a prize in Turin (1950). —Cf. *Suomen Säveltäjiä* (Helsinki, 1945; pp. 726-31).

Pyne, James Kendrick, English organist; b. Bath, Feb. 5, 1852; d. Ilford, Essex, Sept. 3, 1938. Pupil of his father, James K. Pyne (for 53 years organist at Bath Abbey); then of Dr. S. S. Wesley, organist at Winchester Cathedral. He held positions as church organist from the age of 11; was engaged as organist at St. Mark's, Philadelphia for a year (1875); returning to England was organist at the Manchester Cathedral (1876-98); in 1877 became organist of Town Hall Corporation, Manchester; celebrated his 50 years of tenure (1927) by giving 3 organ recitals on the jubilee day. He also lectured on church music at the Univ. of Manchester (from 1901); prof. of organ at the Royal College of Music, Manchester (from 1893). He composed organ music; also a Communion Service and other sacred works. —Cf. S. Lucas, *J. K. Pyne,* in 'Mus. Opinion' (Nov., 1927).

Pythagoras, the Greek philosopher and mathematician; b. Samos, c. 582 B. C.; d. Metapontum, c. 500 B. C. His doctrines on the musical ratios are preserved in the writings of his followers, no books by Pythagoras himself having come down to us. The Pythagoreans (Archytas, Didymos, Eratosthenes, Euclid, Ptolemy, etc.) reckoned only the fifth and octave as pure consonances (the fourth being the fifth below); their system recognized only intervals reached by successive skips of pure fifths, the major third being the 4th fifth above (ratio 64:81, instead of the modern 64:80, or 4:5), their minor third the 3rd fifth below; etc. Their thirds and sixth were, consequently, dissonant intervals.

Q

Quagliati (quăhl-yah'tē), **Paolo,** Italian composer and excellent cembalist; b. Chioggia, c. 1555; d. Rome, Nov. 16, 1628. He publ. *Carro di fedeltà d'amore,* one of the earliest mus. dramas, containing not only monodies, but ensemble numbers up to 5 voices (Rome, 1611); also motets and 'dialogues' *a* 2-8 (3 vols.; 1612, 1620, 1627); etc. Reprints are found in H. Riemann's *Musikgeschichte in Beispielen* and L. Torchi's 'L'Arte Musicale in Italia' III. —Cf. A. Cametti, *Paolo Quagliati, organista e compositore,* in the 'Rassegna dorica' (Dec. 20, 1930; pp. 28-34); 'Zeitschrift für Musikwissenschaft' (vol. 13, p. 558).

Quaile, Elizabeth, piano pedagogue; b. Omagh, Ireland, Jan. 20, 1874; d. South Kent, Conn., June 30, 1951. She came early to N. Y., where she was educated; studied with Franklin Robinson; for 5 years taught at the Music School Settlement, N. Y.; from 1916-19, was head of the piano dept. of the David Mannes School; studied with Harold Bauer in Paris, and from 1916 was his assistant for about 10 years; 1921, founded, with Angela Diller (q.v.), the Diller-Quaile School of Music, N. Y., of which she was also co-director. She publ. much valuable teaching material, some of it written by her alone, and some in collaboration with Angela Diller. In the former group are: *First Book of Technical Exercises* and *A Pre-Czerny Book* (2 vols.).

Quantz, Johann Joachim, famous German flutist and composer; b. Oberscheden, Hanover, Jan. 30, 1697; d. Potsdam, July 12, 1773. Naturally musical, at 8 he played the double-bass at village festivals. His father died when he was but 10, and Quantz was apprenticed to an uncle, then 'Stadtmusikus' at Merseburg, in 1708, learning various instruments, among them the harpsichord with Kiesewetter. His apprenticeship ended, he went to Radeburg, Pirna, and in 1716 joined the town orch. of Dresden, under Heine. In 1717, during 3 months' leave of absence, he studied counterpoint with Zelenka and Fux at Vienna; in 1718 he became oboist in the Royal Polish orch. of Warsaw and Dresden, but soon took up the flute, which he studied under Buffardin. In 1724 he was sent to Italy in the suite of the Polish ambassador; studied counterpoint under Gasparini at Rome; went to London *via* Paris in 1726; and returned to Dresden in 1727, resuming his position as orchestral flute-player in 1728. In this year he played before Frederick the Great (then Crown Prince) at Berlin, and so pleased him that he engaged Quantz to teach him the flute, and to make two long yearly visits to Berlin for that purpose. Frederick ascended the throne in 1740, and next year called Quantz to Berlin and Potsdam as chamber musician and court composer at a salary of 2,000 Thaler, besides an honorarium for each composition furnished, and 100 ducats for each flute supplied by Quantz. Here he remained until his death. He left in MS 300 concertos for one and two flutes, and some 200 other flute pieces (solos, duets, trios, and quartets). —Publ. *Sei sonate* with bass (1734); *Sei duetti* (1759); *Neue Kirchenmelodien* (1760; settings of 22 odes by Gellert as chorales); *Versuch einer Anweisung, die Flöte traversiere zu spielen* (1752; this famous flute method also contains valuable information on 18th-century performance practices; 2nd and 3rd eds., 1780, 1789; French, 1752; Dutch, 1755); and *Application pour la flûte traversière à deux clefs* (an account of his invention of a 2nd key applied to the flute for just intonation, and also of the tuning barrel for the instrument). —Cf. A. Quantz, *Leben und Werke des Flötisten J. J. Quantz* (Berlin, 1877); R. Schäfke, *Quantz als Ästhetiker. Eine Einführung in die Musikästhetik des galanten. Stils,* in 'Archiv für Musikwissenschaft' VI, 2 (1924). His autobiography is found in Marpurg's *Historisch-kritische Beyträge zur Aufnahme der Musik* (Berlin, 1755); reprinted in Willi Kahl, *Selbstbiographien deutscher Musiker des XVIII. Jahrhunderts* (Cologne, 1948).

Quarenghi, Guglielmo, Italian cellist; b. Casalmaggiore, Oct. 22, 1826; d. Milan, Feb. 4, 1882. Pupil at Milan Cons., 1839-42; from 1850, 1st cello at La Scala Theater; 1851, prof. of cello-playing at the Cons.; from 1879, maestro di cappella at Milan Cathedral. —Works: an excellent cello method, and original pieces and transcriptions for cello; church music; and an opera, *Il Dì di S. Michele* (Milan, 1863).

Quarles, James Thomas, American organist and educator; b. St. Louis, Nov. 7, 1877; d. Saugus, Calif., March 4, 1954. He studied organ with local teachers; then with Widor in Paris. He was church organist in St. Louis (1897-1913); then taught at Cornell Univ. (1913-23) and at the Univ. of Missouri (1923-43). He gave nearly 1000 organ recitals in various parts of the U. S.; composed anthems, organ pieces, and songs.

Quatremère de Quincy (kăht'r-mär' dŭ kăn-sē'), **Antoine-Chrysostome,** French writer; b. Paris, Oct. 28, 1755; d. there, Dec. 28, 1849. Secretary of the Académie des Arts. Publ. *De la nature des opéras bouffons italiens* (Paris, 1789; pamphlet) and eulogies of Catel, Boieldieu, Gossec, Méhul, Monsigny, Paisiello, and other deceased members of the Académie (in *Recueil de notices historiques* . . . 1834-37, 2 vols.; also printed separately).

Quef, Charles, French organist and composer; b. Lille, Nov. 1, 1873; d. there, July 2, 1931. He studied at the Lille Cons. and at the Paris Cons. with Guiraud, Th. Dubois, Guilmant, and Widor (1898, won 1st prize for organ and improvisation); organist in Paris at Ste. Marie, St. Laurent, and (from 1901) of La Trinité, succeeding Guilmant; concertized in France and England. Publ. sacred choruses and other works.

Querol Gavaldá, Miguel, Spanish musicologist; b. Ulldecona, Tarragona, April 22, 1912. He studied music at the Benedictine Monastery of Monserrat (1926-36) and later in Barcelona with Juan Lamote de Grignon. —Publications: *La Música en las obras de Cervantes* (Barcelona, 1948), *La Escuela estética catalana contemporánea* (doctoral dissertation; Madrid, 1953); edited the *Cancionero musical de la casa de Medinaceli* (2 vols.; Barcelona, 1949-50); also wrote some church music; chamber music; a *Sonata romántica catalana* for piano; etc.

Quilter, Roger, English composer; b. Brighton, Nov. 1, 1877; d. London, Sept. 21, 1953. He studied at Eton College, later in Frankfurt with Iwan Knorr. He is principally known for his artistic settings of Shakespearian lyrics. —Works: for orch.: *Serenade* (1907); *3 English Dances,* for small orch. (1910); *A Children's Overture* (1920); incidental music to *Where the Rainbow Ends,* fairy-play (1911) and Shakespeare's *As You Like It* (1922) (both also as orchestral suites); *The Sailor and his Lass,* for soprano, baritone, chorus, and orch. (1948); part-songs; several sets of piano pieces; numerous songs and song cycles (*To Julia, 7 Elizabethan Lyrics, Songs of Sorrow, 3 Songs of the Sea, 4 Shakespeare Songs,* etc.). He also wrote a light opera, *Julia* (London, Dec. 3, 1936). —Cf. L. Woodgate, *Roger Quilter,* in the 'Mus. Times' (Nov., 1953).

Quinault (kē-noh'), **Jean-Baptiste-Maurice,** singer and actor at the Théâtre Français, Paris, 1712-33, then retiring to Gien, where he died 1744. He set to music over 20 *intermèdes,* ballets, etc.; also a grand 4-act ballet *Les Amours des déesses* (Paris Opéra, 1729).

Quinault (kē-noh'), **Philippe,** b. Paris, June 3, 1635; d. there, Nov. 26, 1688; French dramatic poet; was Lully's librettist. —Cf. G. A. Crapelet, *Notice sur la vie et les ouvrages de Quinault* (Paris, 1824); E. Richter, *Philippe Quinault. Sein Leben, seine Tragödien, seine Bedeutung für das Theater Frankreichs und des Auslandes* (Leipzig, 1910); Etienne Gros, *Philippe Quinault, sa vie et son œuvre* (Paris, 1926); J. B. A. Buijtendorp, *Philippe Quinault, sa vie, ses tragédies et ses tragi-comédies* (Amsterdam, 1928).

Quinet (kē-nā'), **Fernand,** Belgian cellist and composer; b. Charleroi, Jan. 29, 1898; studied there with Biarent (composition), later with Dubois at the Brussels Cons. (won 2 prizes for cello playing); 1921, won the Belgian Prix de Rome with his cantata, *La Guerre;* for a time was cellist of the Pro Arte Quartet; wrote incidental music to *Le Conte d'été;* a suite for 3 clarinets; a string quartet and songs. In 1938 he was appointed director of the Liège Cons.

Quinet, Marcel, Belgian composer; b. Binche, July 6, 1915. He studied at the Cons. of Mons, and later at the Brussels Cons. (with Léon Jongen and Jean Absil). In 1943 he was appointed instructor at the Brussels Cons. —Works: cantata, *La Vague et le sillon* (1945; received the Belgian Grand Prix de Rome); *3 Esquisses concertantes,* for violin and orch. (1946); *3 Pièces pour orchestre* (Festival of the International Society for Contemporary Music, Salzburg, June 21, 1952).

Quiroga (kē-roh'-gah), **Manuel,** Spanish violinist; b. Pontevedra, April 15, 1890; studied at the Royal Cons. in Madrid and at the Paris Cons.; toured Western Europe and the U. S. with success, appearing also as soloist with leading symph. orchestras. After a street accident in N. Y. in 1937, he abandoned his career; went to a sanitarium in Madrid, where he was still living in 1958. He composed some violin pieces and a 'sainete,' *Los Amos del Barrio* (Madrid, Sept. 7, 1938).

Quittard (kē-tahr'), **Henri Charles Étienne,** French musicologist; b. Clermont-Ferrand, May 13, 1864; d. Paris, July 21,

1919. He was a pupil of César Franck, then turned to musicology and made a specialty of 16th- and 17th-century French music; wrote music criticism in 'Le Matin' and 'Le Figaro' (from 1909); from 1912 archivist at the Opéra. —Publ.: *Henry du Mont: un musicien en France au XVIIe siècle* (1906); *Les Couperins* (1913); and many studies in musical periodicals; left a work on Guillaume de Machault, incomplete. He ed. Méhul's *Uthal* and works of Carissimi, Couperin, etc. —Cf. the 'Bulletin' of the Société Française de Musicologie (vol. 3, 1919, pp. 242-45).

R

Raabe, Peter, German writer on music and conductor; b. Frankfurt-on-the-Oder, Nov. 27, 1872; d. Weimar, April 12, 1945. He studied at the Hochschule für Musik in Berlin (with Bargiel); in 1894, began a career as theater conductor, in Königsberg, Zwickau, and Elberfeld; in 1899 appointed conductor of the Netherlands Opera in Amsterdam; held this post until 1903; then conducted the Kaim Orch. in Munich (1903-06) and the newly established Kaim Orch. in Mannheim (1906-07); in 1907 became 1st Kapellmeister in Weimar; in 1910, custodian of the Liszt Museum there; from 1920 till 1934, conductor of the Municipal Orch. at Aachen; in 1935, became head of the Reichsmusikkammer and the Deutscher Tonkünstlerverein. He held these posts until his death. He received his *Dr. phil.* at the Univ. of Jena (1916) with the thesis *Entstehungsgeschichte der ersten Orchesterwerke Franz Liszts.*—Publications: *Festschrift zum Jubiläum des 50-jährigen Bestehens der Abonnementskonzerte der Grossherzoglichen Hofkapelle in Weimar* (1909); *Grossherzog Karl Alexander und Liszt* (Leipzig, 1918); *Franz Liszt: Leben und Schaffen* (Stuttgart, 1931; 2 vols.; vol. 2 contains an annotated catalogue of Liszt's works); *Die Musik im dritten Reich* (Berlin, 1935; an exposition of the musical ideology of the Third Reich); *Kulturwille im deutschen Musikleben* (Berlin, 1936); *Deutsche Meister* (Berlin, 1937); *Wege zu Weber* (Regensburg, 1942); *Wege zu Liszt* (Regensburg, 1943); *Wege zu Bruckner* (Regensburg, 1944); edited Liszt's songs and Hungarian Rhapsodies for the collected ed.; wrote some songs and piano pieces of his own. —Cf. *Festschrift zu Peter Raabes 70. Geburtstag* (Leipzig, 1942).

Raaff, Anton, German singer, a friend of Mozart; b. Gelsdorf, near Bonn, May 6, 1714; d. Munich, May 27, 1797. He studied with Ferrandini in Munich and Bernacchi in Bologna; sang in Italy; then in Bonn, Vienna, and at various German courts (1742-52); in Lisbon (1753-55), Madrid (1755-59), and Naples, returning in 1770 to Germany, where he was attached to the court of the Elector Karl Theodor at Mannheim. In 1778 he went to Paris with Mozart; in 1779 was in Munich. Mozart wrote the role of Idomeneo for him, and also the aria, *Se al labbro mio non credi,* K. 295. —Cf. H. Freiberger, *Anton Raaff: sein Leben und Wirken* (Cologne, 1929).

Raalte, Albert van, Dutch conductor; b. Amsterdam, May 21, 1890; d. there, Nov. 23, 1952. He studied at the Cologne Cons. with Bram Eldering (violin) and Waldemar von Baussnern (theory); later in Leipzig with Nikisch and Max Reger; was theater conductor in Brussels (1911) and Leipzig (1912); conducted Wagner's operas at the Municipal Opera in Leipzig (1914-15); then at the Dutch National Opera in The Hague (1915-22); then formed his own opera enterprise there. He remained in Holland during the German Occupation, conducted the radio orch. at Hilversum; was sent to a concentration camp as a person with Jewish associations; after the Liberation in 1945, he returned to his post at Hilversum, building the radio orch. to a high degree of efficiency.

Raasted, Niels Otto, Danish organist and composer; b. Copenhagen, Nov. 26, 1888. He studied at the Copenhagen Cons. (1909-12); then at the Cons. of Leipzig, with Max Reger, Karl Straube, and R. Teichmüller (1913-14); returning to Denmark, he became cathedral organist; also conducted the Bach Society (1925-46). —Works: 3 symphonies (1914, 1938, 1944); several orch. suites, among them *Pictures from Finland* (1928) and *Hans Christian Andersen Suite* (1940); *Sinfonia da chiesa* (1944); 3 string quartets (1914, 1918, 1920); 5 violin sonatas; 6 organ sonatas; an oratorio, *Saul* (1923); cantatas (all performed on the Copenhagen Radio); *Sangen om København* (June 27, 1934), *Thylands pris* (May 12, 1941); *Kong Vaar* (Oct. 20, 1947).

Rabaud (răh-bŏh'), **Henri,** French composer and conductor; b. Paris, Nov. 10, 1873; d. there, Sept. 11, 1949. The son of Hippolyte Rabaud (1839-1900), professor of cello at the Paris Cons., he was a pupil of Gedalge and Massenet; won the Premier

Grand Prix de Rome in 1894 with his cantata *Daphné;* in 1908 he became conductor at the Paris Opéra and at the Opéra-Comique; from 1914 to 1918, director of the Opéra. In 1918 he was engaged to conduct the Boston Symph. Orch., succeeding Karl Muck; conducted only one season (1918-19) and was followed by Pierre Monteux; returned to Paris and was appointed director of the Paris Cons. in 1922 (following Gabriel Fauré's resignation); he held this post until 1941. —Works: the operas *La Fille de Roland* (Opéra-Comique, March 16, 1904), *Le premier glaive* (Béziers, 1908), *Marouf, Savetier du Caire* (Opéra-Comique, May 15, 1914; his most successful opera), *Antoine et Cléopâtre,* after Shakespeare (1916-17), *L'Appel de la mer* (1 act; Opéra-Comique, April 10, 1924; in German, Leipzig, May 6, 1927), *Le Miracle des loups* (Opéra-Comique, Nov. 14, 1924), *Rolande et le mauvais garçon* (Opéra, May 28, 1934), *Le Jeu de l'Amour et du Hasard* (1948; produced posthumously at Monte Carlo, 1954); an oratorio, *Job* (1900); Psalm 4 for soli, chorus, and orch.; *Hymne à la France éternelle* (1916); *L'Été,* for 4-voice choir; also for orch.; 2 symphonies; *La Procession nocturne,* symph. poem after Lenau's *Der nächtliche Zug* (his most famous orchestral work; first performed Paris, Jan. 15, 1899); *Églogue,* 'poème virgilien'; *Divertissement sur des chansons russes; Suite anglaise,* for string quartet; *Concertino* for cello and piano; *Allegro de concert,* for cello and piano; piano pieces; songs; etc. —Cf. Max d' Ollone, *Rabaud* (Paris, 1958).

Rabich (rah'-biyh), **Ernst,** German choral conductor and composer; b. Herda, May 5, 1856; d. Gotha, Feb. 1, 1933. After study with local teachers, he became in 1880 church organist and conductor of the Liedertafel (900 singers) in Gotha; from 1897, editor of 'Blätter für Haus- und Kirchenmusik' and later of the 'Musikalisches Magazin' (a large collection of excellent monographs to which he contributed); retired in 1918. He composed several choral works with orch.: *Die Martinswand; Die Frühlingsfeier; Des Volkes Gruss; Das hohe Lied der Arbeit; Dornröschen;* etc.; brought out 'Psalter und Harfe,' a collection of motets (5 books); 'Thüringer Liederkranz.'

Rabin, Michael, American violinist; b. New York, May 2, 1936. His father was a violinist in the N. Y. Philharmonic; his mother, a pianist. He studied with Ivan Galamian; progressed rapidly; made his professional début at the age of 14; appeared with a number of American orchestras; also made several European tours and played in Australia.

Rabl, Walter, Austrian conductor and composer; b. Vienna, Nov. 30, 1873; d. Klagenfurt, July 14, 1940. He was a pupil of J. F. Hummel, the director of the Mozarteum at Salzburg, and later of Navratil in Vienna; studied musicology with Guido Adler in Prague (*Dr. phil.,* 1897). He conducted at the Düsseldorf Opera (1903-06), and at the Municipal Theaters in Essen, Dortmund, and Magdeburg (1915-24); wrote an opera, *Liane* (Strasbourg, 1903); a symphony; a quartet for clarinet, violin, cello, and piano (1st prize of the Vienna Tonkünstlerverein, 1897); a violin sonata; several song cycles. —Cf. A. Eccarius-Sieber, *Walter Rabl,* in vol. II of 'Monographien moderner Musiker' (Leipzig, 1907).

Rachmaninoff (răh-măh'-nē-nŏhf), **Sergey Vassilievitch,** famous Russian composer; b. on his father's estate at Oneg, district of Novgorod, April 1, 1873; d. Beverly Hills, Calif., March 28, 1943. He was of a musical family; his grandfather was an amateur pianist, a pupil of John Field; his father also played the piano; Rachmaninoff's *Polka* was written on a theme improvised by his father. After financial setbacks, the family estate was sold, and in 1882 Rachmaninoff was taken to St. Petersburg; became a piano pupil of Demiansky at the Cons. there (1882-85); acting on the advice of his cousin, the well-known pianist and conductor Alexander Siloti, Rachmaninoff went to Moscow and studied piano with Zverev (1885-88) at the Moscow Cons.; in 1888 he began to study piano with Siloti and composition with Taneyev and Arensky. He met Tchaikovsky, who appreciated Rachmaninoff's talent, and gave him friendly advice. At the age of 19 he wrote his Prelude in C♯ minor (op. 3, No. 2), which became one of the most celebrated piano pieces in the world. He graduated as pianist in 1891, and as composer in 1892, receiving the gold medal for his opera in one act, *Aleko,* after Pushkin (1892). His 1st symph. was given in Moscow in 1897, with little success. Discouraged, Rachmaninoff destroyed the MS; however, the orchestral parts were preserved, and after Rachmaninoff's death the score was restored and performed in Moscow (1945). He toured with the Italian violinist Teresina Tua in Russia (1895); gave his own piano recitals, and soon became known as a piano virtuoso; in 1899 he gave a concert of his orchestral works with the Philharmonic Society of London. He continued to compose for orch., for piano, and for voice; in 1901 he gave the 1st performance of his 2nd piano concerto in Moscow, at a concert conducted by Siloti; this concerto became the most celebrated work of its genre written in the 20th century, and its singular charm has never abated since; it is no exaggeration to say that it became a model for piano concertos by a majority of modern Russian composers, and also of semi-popular virtuoso pieces for piano and orch. written in America. In 1902 Rachmaninoff married his cousin Natalie Satina; they spent some months in Switzerland; then returned to Moscow. Rachmaninoff was engaged to conduct opera at the Bolshoy Theater for two seasons (1904-06), and proved himself a very efficient conductor. From 1906 to 1909 he lived mostly in Dresden; spent the summers in his Russian country home near Novgorod. In 1909 he made his 1st American tour; his initial public appearance in the U. S. took place at Smith College, Northampton, Mass., on Nov. 4, 1909. His fame was such that the Boston Symph. Orch. offered him the post of permanent conductor, but he declined; the offer was repeated in 1918, but then, too, Rachmaninoff decided against acceptance. From 1910 to 1917 he lived in Moscow; conducted the Philharmonic Society Orch. there (1911-13). After the October Revolution of 1917, he left his native country, never to return; lived on his small estate on Lake Lucerne, Switzerland; made annual tours in Europe and in the U. S.; in 1935 made N. Y. his home; later settled in Los Angeles. He became an American citizen a few weeks before his death. —Among Russian composers Rachmaninoff occupies a very important place. The sources of his inspiration lie in the Romantic tradition of 19th-century Russian music; the link with Tchaikovsky's lyrical art is very strong; melancholy moods prevail, and minor keys predominate in Rachmaninoff's compositions, as in Tchaikovsky's; but there is an unmistakable stamp of Rachmaninoff's own individuality in the broad, rhapsodic sweep of the melodic line, and particularly in the fully expanded sonorities and fine resonant harmonies of his piano writing; its technical resourcefulness is unexcelled since Liszt. Despite the fact that Rachmaninoff was an émigré, and stood in avowed opposition to the Soviet regime (until the German attack on Russia in 1941 impelled him to modify his stand), his popularity never wavered in Russia; his works were constantly performed; after his death Russian musicians paid spontaneous tribute to him. Rachmaninoff's music is much less popular in Germany, France, and Italy; on the other hand, in England and America it constitutes a potent factor on the concert stage. —Works: Operas: *Aleko*, after Pushkin's *The Gypsies* (Moscow, May 9, 1893); *The Miserly Knight* (Moscow, Jan. 24, 1906, composer conducting); *Francesca da Rimini* (Moscow, Jan. 24, 1906, composer conducting). For orch.: symph. No. 1 (St. Petersburg, March 27, 1897); symph. No. 2 (St. Petersburg, Feb. 8, 1908, composer conducting); symph. No. 3 (Philadelphia, Nov. 6, 1936); *Andante and Scherzo* for string orch. (Moscow, Feb. 24, 1891); *Prince Rostislav*, symph. poem (1891); *Intermezzo* (Moscow, Oct. 31, 1892); *The Rock*, symph. fantasy (1893; Moscow, March 20, 1896); *Caprice bohémien*, for orch. (1894); *The Isle of the Dead*, symph. poem, inspired by Böcklin's painting (Moscow, May 1, 1909, composer conducting); *Symph. Dances* (Philadelphia, Jan. 3, 1941); 4 piano concertos: No. 1, in F♯ minor (1890-91; revised, 1917); No. 2, in C minor, one of his most famous works (Moscow, Oct. 27, 1901, composer soloist); No. 3, in D minor (N. Y., Nov. 28, 1909, composer soloist); No. 4, in G minor (Philadelphia, March 18, 1927); *Rhapsody on a Theme* by Paganini, for piano and orch. (Baltimore, composer soloist with the Philadelphia Orch., Nov. 7, 1934). Chamber music: *Trio élégiaque*, in memory of Tchaikovsky (1893); *Romance* and *Danse hongroise*, for violin and piano (1893); cello sonata (1901). Choral works: *The Spring*, for baritone, chorus, and orch. (Moscow, March 24, 1902); *Liturgy of St. John Chrysostom*, for chorus a cappella (Moscow, Nov. 25, 1910); *The Bells*, after Edgar Allan Poe, for orch., chorus, and soloists (St. Petersburg, Dec. 13, 1913, composer conducting); Vesper Mass, for chorus a cappella (Moscow, March 10, 1915); *3 Russian Songs*, for chorus and orch. (Philadelphia, March 18, 1927). For piano: *5 Morceaux de fantaisie*, op. 3: *Élégie*, *Prélude* (the famous one, in C♯ minor), *Mélodie*, *Polichinelle*, *Sérénade* (1892); *7 Morceaux de salon*, op. 10 (1894); *6 Moments musicaux*, op. 16 (1896); Variations on a theme by Chopin, op. 22 (1903); 10 Preludes, op. 23 (1904); sonata No. 1, in D minor, op. 28 (1907); 13 Preludes, op. 32 (1910); *6 Études-Tableaux*, op. 33 (1911); *Polka V.R.*, on a theme by the composer's father, Vassily Rachmaninoff (1911); sonata No. 2, in B♭ minor (1913); *9 Études-Tableaux*, op. 39 (1916-17; orchestrated by Respighi,

1931); 6 Duets for piano, 4 hands, op. 11 (1894); *Fantasy* (suite No. 1) for 2 pianos, op. 5 (1893); suite No. 2, op. 17 (1901); arrangements for piano of *Prelude, Gavotte,* and *Gigue* from Bach's violin partita in E major; of Mendelssohn's *Scherzo* from *A Midsummer Night's Dream,* Mussorgsky's *Hopak,* Rimsky-Korsakov's *Flight of the Bumble-Bee,* Fritz Kreisler's *Liebesfreude* and *Liebeslied,* and of his own song, *Lilacs.* Several sets of songs (all written before 1916): 6 songs, op. 4; 6 songs, op. 8; 12 songs, op. 14, of which *Spring Waters* is well known; 12 songs, op. 21 (including *Fate,* on Beethoven's 5th symph., and *Lilacs*); 15 songs, op. 26 (including *Christ is Risen*); 14 songs, op. 34 (including *Vocalise*); 6 songs, op. 38. —Bibliography: Ivan Lipayev, *S.R.* (in Russian; Saratov, 1913); M. Montagu-Nathan, *Contemporary Russian Composers* (N. Y., 1917); V. Belaiev, *R.* (Moscow, 1924); V. Belaiev, *S.R.,* in the 'Mus. Quarterly' (July, 1927); Oskar von Riesemann, *R.'s Recollections* (N. Y., 1934); Eric Brewerton, *R.'s Songs,* in 'Music & Letters' (1934); Watson Lyle, *R.: a Biography* (London, 1939); Alfred and Katherine Swan, *R.: Personal Reminiscences,* in the 'Mus. Quarterly' (Jan. and April, 1944); A. Gronowicz, *S.R.* (N. Y., 1946); Sophie Satin, ed., *In Memory of R.* (N. Y., 1946, in Russian); Igor Boelza, ed., *R. and Russian Opera* (Moscow, 1947); J. Culshaw, *S. R.* (London, 1949); J. Andriessen, *R.* (Amsterdam, 1950); V. Seroff, *R.* (N. Y., 1950; in French, Paris, 1953); A. Alexeyev, *S. R.* (Moscow, 1954); S. Bertensson and J. Leyda, *S. R.* (N. Y., 1956); Z. Apetian, ed., *Reminiscences about R.* (Moscow, 1957). See also the Rachmaninoff issue of 'Tempo' (London, Winter, 1951-52).

Rachmilovich, Jacques, conductor; b. Odessa, Russia, Oct. 8, 1895. He studied at the St. Petersburg Cons.; came to America in 1925; settled in California. He made numerous appearances as guest conductor, specializing in modern music. In 1945 he organized the Santa Monica Symph. Orch.

Radecke, Ernst, German musicologist, son of Robert Radecke; b. Berlin, Dec. 8, 1866; d. Winterthur, Switzerland, Oct. 8, 1920. He studied with his father, with Bussler, and others; took the degree of *Dr. phil.* at the Univ. of Berlin with the dissertation, *Das deutsche weltliche Lied in der Lautenmusik des 16. Jahrhunderts* (publ. Leipzig, 1891); in 1893 settled in Winterthur, as teacher; from 1908 lectured at the Univ. of Zürich. He publ. a monograph on Robert Kahn (Leipzig, 1894); wrote an analysis of Beethoven's *Eroica* for Schlesinger's 'Musikführer,' etc.

Radecke, Robert, German conductor and composer; b. Dittmannsdorf, Oct. 31, 1830; d. Wernigerode, June 21, 1911. He studied violin, piano, and organ at the Leipzig Cons.; held various posts as player; then established himself in Berlin as choral conductor and teacher; from 1871 to 1887 was music director of the court opera; from 1892 till 1907 taught at the Institute for Church Music. On the occasion of his 75th birthday his friends and former students established the 'Robert Radecke Stiftung' (7000 marks) for scholarships. Radecke wrote a 1-act 'Liederspiel,' *Die Mönkgüter* (Berlin, May 1, 1874); a symphony; 2 overtures, *König Johann* and *Am Strande;* 2 piano trios; many excellent choruses and songs; particularly successful was his song *Aus der Jugendzeit,* op. 22, which attained such popularity in Germany that it was commonly mistaken for a folksong.

Radecke, Rudolf, German conductor, pedagogue, and composer; brother of Robert Radecke; b. Dittmannsdorf, Sept. 6, 1829; d. Berlin, April 15, 1893. He studied in Breslau; then at the Leipzig Cons.; settled in Berlin in 1859; taught at the Stern Cons. (1864-71); founded the Radecke Choral Society (1868) and a music school (1869). He wrote a number of part-songs.

Radiciotti (răh-dē-chŏht'-tē), **Giuseppe,** Italian writer on music; b. Jesi, Le Marche, Jan. 25, 1858; d. Tivoli, April 4, 1931. He was a music pupil of his uncle, G. Faini; after finishing a course of studies at the Univ. of Rome, he taught in secondary schools there; in 1895 appointed prof. at the Liceo in Tivoli. He made a specialty of the music and musicians of his native region, Le Marche. —Publications: *Teatro, musica e musicisti in Sinigaglia* (1893); *Contributi alla storia del teatro e della musica in Urbino* (1899); *Il Teatro e la musica in Roma nel secondo quarto del secolo XIX* (1904); *Teatro, musica e musicisti in Recanati* (1904); *L'Arte musicale dei Marchigiani* (1905); *L'Arte musicale in Tivoli nei secoli XVI, XVII e XVIII* (1907); *G. B. Pergolesi* (1910; in German, 1954); *Rossini* (1914); *La Cappella musicale del duomo di Pesaro* (1914); *G. Rossini: Vita documentata, opere ed influenza sul'arte* (a monumental biography in 3 vols., 1927-29); *Aneddoti rossiniani autentici* (Rome, 1929); also numerous essays in various journals. —Cf. L. Parigi, *G. Radiciotti,* in 'Critica musicale' (1918); V. Scotti, *G. Radiciotti* in the 'Bollettino bibliografico musicale' (1931).

Radnai, Miklós, Hungarian critic and composer; b. Budapest, Jan. 1, 1892; d. there, Nov. 4, 1935. He studied violin, piano, and composition at the Academy of Music; then traveled in Europe. In 1925 he was appointed director of the Budapest Opera. He wrote a ballet, *The Birthday of the Infanta,* after Oscar Wilde (Budapest, April 26, 1918); a *Symphony of the Magyars,* for chorus and orch.; a violin concerto; some chamber music; a textbook of harmony; contributed critical essays to Hungarian publications.

Radó, Aladár, Hungarian composer; b. Budapest, Dec. 26, 1882; killed in battle near Belgrade, Sept. 7, 1914. He studied in Budapest and Berlin; wrote 2 operas: *The Black Knight* (1911) and *Golem* (1912); a symphony (1909); *Hungarian Concerto* for cello and orch. (1909); 2 string quartets and a string quintet; publ. several albums of piano pieces and song cycles.

Radoux (răh-dŏŏ'), **Charles,** Belgian composer, writer on music, and pedagogue; son of Jean-Théodore Radoux; b. Liège, July 30, 1877; d. there, April 30, 1952. He studied with his father; in 1907 received the Belgian Prix de Rome with the cantata *Geneviève de Brabant;* in 1911, appointed prof. at the Liège Cons.; wrote music criticism for the 'Journal de Liège'; was active in folksong research. —Works: the operas *Les Sangliers des Ardennes* (Liège, 1905) and *Oudelette* (Brussels, April 11, 1912); choral compositions with orch.: *Adieu-Absence-Retour, Chanson d'Halewyn, Les Fées;* orch. sketches: *Danse tzigane, Burlesque, Vision, Triptique champêtre; Scène grecque* for cello and orch.; *Variations* for violin and orch; *Lamentation* (on a Bach prelude) for English horn and piano; piano pieces; folksong albums (*5 Noëls liégeois, 7 Chansons populaires de l'ancien Hainaut, Cramignons liégeois,* etc.). He used the surname Radoux-Rogier in his works.

Radoux, Jean-Théodore, Belgian composer and pedagogue; b. Liège, Nov. 9, 1835; d. there, March 21, 1911. He studied bassoon with Daussoigne-Méhul at the Cons. of Liège, where he became teacher of bassoon in 1856; won the Belgian Prix de Rome with the cantata *Le Juif errant* (1859); then went to Paris for additional study with Halévy. In 1872 he was appointed director of the Cons. of Liège. —Works: the operas *Le Béarnais* (Liège, March 14, 1866) and *La Coupe enchantée* (Brussels, 1872); oratorio, *Cain* (1877); symph. poems, *Ahasvère* and *Le Festin de Balthasar;* a patriotic overture, *Épopée nationale;* church music; publ. a monograph, *Vieuxtemps. Sa vie, ses œuvres* (1891).

Radoux-Rogier, Charles. See **Radoux, Charles.**

Radziwill, Prince **Anton Heinrich,** musical amateur and excellent singer; b. Vilna, June 13, 1775; d. Berlin, April 8, 1833. He was governor of Posen and a patron of art. —Works: incidental music to Goethe's *Faust* (publ. 1835); *Complainte de Maria Stuart,* with cello and piano; French *romances* (1802), vocal duets (1804), men's quartets (for Zelter's 'Liedertafel'), etc. To him Beethoven dedicated the *Namensfeier* overture, op. 115; he was also Chopin's patron.

Raeli, Vito, Italian writer and editor; b. Tricase, July 8, 1880; educated in Naples; studied music privately; since 1905 living in Rome; 1920, founded the 'Rivista Nazionale di Musica,' of which he is editor. Publ.: *Collezioni e archivi romani di stampe a manoscritti musicale* (Tricase, 1919); *La Collezione Corsini di antichi codici musicali,* in 'Rivista Musicale Italiana' (1918-19); *Nel secolo di P. L. Palestrina; alla cappella della Basilica Liberiana 1550-1600* (Rome, 1920); *Da V. Ugolini ad O. Benevoli, 1630-46* (1920); *Maestri Compositori pugliesi* (Tricase, 1925); etc.

Raff, Joseph Joachim, composer; b. Lachen, Lake of Zürich, May 27, 1822; d. Frankfurt, June 25, 1882. The son of an organist, he was educated at Wiesenstetten, Württemberg, and at the Jesuit Lyceum in Schwyz; being too poor to take a University course, he then became a school teacher, but continued the study of composition, and of the piano and violin by himself. In 1843 he sent some MS works to Mendelssohn; the latter recommended them to Breitkopf & Härtel, who publ. Raff's op. 2-14, all piano pieces. Thus encouraged, he gave up school teaching for the career of a composer, and worked hard, though without improving his material condition for some time. Liszt invited him to accompany him on a concert tour; Raff went as far as Cologne (1846), where he remained for a time, writing reviews for Dehn's 'Cäcilia,' and composing industriously. His hopes of remunerative employment by the Viennese publisher, Mechetti, were dashed by the latter's death; Raff returned to Wiesenstetten, but often visited Stuttgart, and there met von Bülow, who greatly aided his reputation by publicly playing his *Konzertstück;* Raff's opera, *König Alfred,* was also accepted for performance at the court theater; but the Revolution of 1848 again frustrated his hopes. In 1850 he joined Liszt at Weimar; entered heart and soul into the new German movement, which he championed in the 'Neue Zeitschrift für Musik,' and had the satisfaction of seeing his opera, *König Alfred,* brought out in revised form at Weimar (March 9, 1851) by Liszt; though it never got any further. Until his death he always remained in close contact with Liszt, and rendered very material assistance in the instrumentation of several of Liszt's symphonic poems. He published (1854) a book, *Die Wagnerfrage.* In 1856 he followed the actress, Doris Genast, to Wiesbaden, and married her in 1859. In Wiesbaden he was in great demand as a piano teacher. In 1863 his first symphony, *An das Vaterland,* won the prize of the Viennese 'Gesellschaft der Musikfreunde' over 32 competitors; on April 9, 1870 a second opera, *Dame Kobold* (comic), was produced at Weimar; and in 1877 he was appointed director of Hoch's Cons. at Frankfurt, where he remained till his death (from apoplexy). —Raff was a composer of prodigious fertility of invention, an inexhaustible vein of melody, and thorough mastery over the technical and formal requirements of composition. He wrote over 230 works of very unequal value; they include 11 symphonies, of which the 3rd (*Im Walde;* 1869; Weimar, April 17, 1870) and 5th (*Lenore;* Sondershausen, Dec. 13, 1872) are the best; 5 overtures; 2 violin concertos; a cello concerto; a piano concerto; 8 string quartets; 4 piano trios; 5 violin sonatas; many choruses, songs, and piano pieces. The finest of these won him a leading place among contemporary composers. But soon after his death his popularity began to wane rapidly; by the end of the century even the best of the orchestral works had fallen into complete oblivion. —Cf. A. Schäfer, *Chronologisch-systematisches Verzeichnis der Werke Joachim Raffs* (Wiesbaden, 1888); R. Gandolfi, *La Musica di G. Raff,* in 'Note illustrative di due accademic . . .' (Florence, 1904); Helen Raff, *Joachim Raff. Ein Lebensbild* (Regensburg, 1925).

Rahlwes, Alfred, German conductor and composer; b. Wesel, Oct. 23, 1878; d. Halle, April 20, 1946. From 1893-99 pupil of Wüllner, G. Hollaender, and W. Hess at the Cologne Cons.; was Kapellmeister in Stuttgart, Liegnitz, and Königsberg; in 1913 succeeded O. Reubke as Univ. music-director in Halle; 1917, prof. there.

Raida, Karl Alexander, composer; b. (of German parents) Paris, Oct. 4, 1852; d. Berlin, Nov. 26, 1923. He studied at the Conservatories of Stuttgart and Dresden; was Kapellmeister from 1878-92 at the Viktoria Theater in Berlin, where he founded an 'Akademie für dramatischen Gesang' (1882) and the 'Gesellschaft der Opernfreunde' (1887); 1895-97 director of the new 'Deutsches Theater' in Munich; a successful composer of light operas, operettas, ballets, farces, etc.

Raimann, Rudolf, Hungarian composer; b. Veszprem, May 7, 1861; d. Vienna, Sept. 26, 1913. He entered the service of Prince Esterházy as music director; wrote an opera, *Enoch Arden,* after Tennyson (Budapest, May 8, 1894), and about a dozen operettas, produced in Vienna: *Das Waschermädel* (April 19, 1905); *Paula macht alles* (March 27, 1909), *Die Frau Gretl* (April 7, 1911), *Unser Stammhalter* (Nov. 15, 1912), etc.

Raimondi, Ignazio, Italian composer; b. Naples, c. 1737; d. London, Jan. 14, 1813. He left Italy about 1770; conducted concerts in Amsterdam; then went to Paris, and eventually (1790) to London, where he remained until the end of his life. —Works: a symphony titled *Les Aventures de Télémaque* (Amsterdam, Jan. 15, 1777); opera, *La Muta* (Paris, Nov. 12, 1789); a symphony titled *The Battle* (1785; very popular in England); several string quartets; string trios; various other instrumental pieces.

Raimondi, Pietro, Italian composer; b. Rome, Dec. 20, 1786; d. there, Oct. 30, 1853. For six years he studied under La Barbara and Tritto at the Cons. della Pietà de' Turchini, Naples; lived for a time at Rome and Florence, and in 1807 brought out an opera buffa, *Le Bizzarie d'amore,* at Genoa, where he had established himself as a teacher and composer. It was followed by about 60 other dramatic works, which were generally successful, and 21 ballets, for whose production he went from place to place (Florence, Naples, Rome, Messina, Milan, etc.); from 1824-32 he was director of the royal theaters at Naples, also, from

1825, prof. of counterpoint at the Cons.; from 1832-52, prof. of counterpoint at Palermo Cons.; on Dec. 12, 1852, he succeeded Basili as maestro di cappella at St. Peter's, Rome. —Raimondi was a contrapuntist of remarkable originality, and of a skill in combination rivalling that of the masters of the contrapuntal epoch; he publ. 4 fugues *a* 4, which could be combined as a quadruple fugue *a* 16; 6 fugues *a* 4, to be combined as a sextuple fugue *a* 24; in the *24 Fughe a 4, 5, 6 e 8 voci* publ. by Ricordi, there is one such quadruple fugue *a* 16, and a quintuple fugue *a* 20; further, 6 fugues *a* 4, performable as a sextuple fugue *a* 24; and a fugue *a* 64, for 16 choirs *a* 4. His most astounding feat in combination, however, was the sacred trilogy *Giuseppe* (Joseph), comprising 3 oratorios, *Putifar, Giuseppe, Giacobbe,* performed at the Teatro Argentina, Rome, Aug. 7, 1852, at first separately, and then simultaneously, the ensemble of 400 musicians on the stage and in the orchestra presenting a most striking effect, and arousing great curiosity among professional musicians. —Cf. F. Cicconetti, *Memorie intorno a Pietro Raimondi* (Rome, 1867); Cecil Gray, *Pietro Raimondi,* in the 'Mus. Review' (Jan., 1940).

Rainier, Priaulx, South African composer; b. Howick, Natal, Feb. 3, 1903. She studied at the South African College of Music; in 1920, went to London, where she took courses with McEwen at the Royal Academy of Music; in 1942, was appointed prof. there. —Works: *Incantation* for clarinet and orch. (1933); *Sinfonia da camera* for strings (1947); viola sonata (1945); *Barbaric Dance Suite* for piano (1949); 3 string quartets. —Cf. John Amis, *Priaulx Rainier,* in the 'Mus. Times' (July, 1955).

Rains, Leon, American operatic bass; b. New York, Oct. 1, 1870; d. Los Angeles, June 11, 1954. He studied with Saenger in N. Y. (1891-96) and with Bouhy in Paris; made a concert tour with Melba in the U. S. (1898); then was a member of the court opera at Dresden (from 1899); made his first appearance with the Metropolitan Opera Company in 1908; then returned to Dresden, and continued to sing there for several years, eventually returning to America.

Raisa, Rosa, soprano; b. Bialystok, Poland, May 30, 1893. In order to escape the horrors of anti-Semitic persecutions she fled to Naples at the age of 14; on Lombardi's advice she entered the Cons. San Pietro a Maiella, where she studied under Barbara Marchisio; début at Parma, Sept. 6, 1913, in Verdi's *Oberto, Conte di San Bonifacio* (revived for the Verdi centenary); then sang 2 seasons at the Costanzi in Rome; 1914 at Covent Garden; 1914-15, with the Chicago Opera Co.; sang with increasing success in Rio de Janeiro, Montevideo, São Paulo, and Milan; on her reappearance with the Chicago company she scored a triumph as Aida (Nov. 13, 1916); was leading soprano of the Chicago Civic Opera Co. for many seasons.

Raison, André, French composer and organist, active in Paris c. 1687-1714. He received instruction at Nanterre; was organist of the Jacobins and at the church of Ste. Geneviève in Paris; apparently the teacher of L. N. Clérambault; publ. 2 books of organ pieces (1688, 1714), of which the first was reprinted by Guilmant ('Archives des Maîtres de l'Orgue,' vol. 2, Paris, 1899).

Raitio, Väinö, Finnish composer; b. Sortavala, April 15, 1891; d. Helsinki, Sept. 10, 1945. He studied in Helsinki with Melartin and Furuhjelm and in Moscow with Ilynsky; also in Berlin (1921) and Paris (1925-26). He wrote 5 operas to Finnish librettos: *Jephtha's Daughter* (1931), *Princess Cecilia* (1931), *Väinämöinen's Courtship* (1935), *The King of Lydia* (1938), and *Two Queens* (1944; Helsinki, 1945); symph. poems, *Fantasia estatica* and *Fantasia poetica;* a symph. tableau, *Moonlight on Jupiter;* a piano concerto; a double concerto for violin and cello with orch.; chamber music. His style of composition combines the elements of German Romanticism and French Impressionism. —Cf. Sulho Ranta, ed., *Suomen Säveltäjiä* (Helsinki, 1945; pp. 514-21).

Rajičič (rī'-ĭh-chich), **Stanojlo,** Serbian composer; b. Belgrade, Dec. 16, 1910. He studied music in Vienna, Berlin, and Prague; has appeared as a pianist but has devoted most of his time to composing and teaching. He has written 5 symphonies, 2 overtures, a piano concerto, a cello concerto, 2 string quartets, a piano trio; also ballet music, miscellaneous piano pieces, and songs. His early works are in a radical idiom of atonal music; later he adopted a more traditional style with emphasis on national folksongs.

Ralf, Torsten, Swedish tenor; b. Malmö, Jan. 2, 1901; d. Stockholm, April 27, 1954. He studied at the Stockholm Cons. and in

Berlin. Made his début as Cavaradossi in Stettin (1930); then sang in Frankfurt (1933-35), Dresden (1935-44), London (1935-39), New York (Metropolitan Opera House, 1945), and Buenos Aires (1946).

Ramann, Lina, German writer on music; b. Mainstockheim, near Kitzingen, June 24, 1833; d. Munich, March 30, 1912. She was a pupil of Franz and Frau Brendel at Leipzig; founded (1858) a music seminary for women teachers, at Glückstadt, Holstein; in 1865, with Ida Volkmann, a music school at Nuremberg, which they sold in a most flourishing condition to August Göllerich (q.v.) in 1890. from then until her death she lived in Munich, devoting herself entirely to literary work.—Publ. *Die Musik als Gegenstand der Erziehung* (1868); *Aus der Gegenwart* (1868); *Allgemeine Erzieh- und Unterrichtslehre der Jugend* (1869; 3rd ed., 1898); *Bach und Händel* (1869); *Fr. Liszts Oratorium 'Christus'; eine Studie zur zeit- und musikgeschichtlichen Stellung desselben* (1880); *Franz Liszt als Künstler und Mensch* (3 vols., 1880-94; vol. 1 in English, 1882); *Franz Liszt als Psalmensänger* (1886); she transl. and ed. Liszt's literary works, 'Gesammelte Schriften' (6 vols., 1880-83); also wrote a *Grundriss der Technik des Klavierspiels,* in 12 books. Composed 4 sonatinas (op. 9) and other piano music; ed. 'Liszt-Pädagogium' (5 vols. of Liszt's piano compositions with Liszt's own changes, additions, remarks, etc.). —Cf. M. Ille-Beeg, *Lina Ramann* (1914).

Rameau (răh-moh'), **Jean-Philippe,** the creator of the modern science of harmony, and a distinguished dramatic composer, was baptized at Dijon, Sept. 25 (probably born the same day), 1683; died Paris, Sept. 12, 1764. Of a musical family, at 7 he could play at sight, on the harpsichord, any music given him; from 10 to 14 he attended the Jesuit College at Dijon; then devoted himself to music, and in 1701 was sent to Italy; but after a brief stay at Milan he joined the orchestra of a traveling French opera-troupe as violinist. In 1702 he was assistant organist at Notre-Dame in Avignon; in June of that year he became organist at Clermont-Ferrand. In 1706 he publ. his first *Livre de pièces de clavecin* in Paris, where he probably had been living since the spring of 1705. Until 1708 he remained in Paris as church organist. In 1709 he became his father's successor at the Cathedral in Dijon; in 1714 he was organist in Lyons. Then he became organist of the Cathedral at Clermont-Ferrand, where he wrote his famous *Traité de l'Harmonie* (Paris, 1722). This epoch-making work, though little understood at the time, attracted considerable attention and roused opposition, so that when he settled definitely in Paris (1723) he was by no means unknown. The fact that he failed in 1727 in a competition for the position of organist at St.-Vincent-de-Paul did not injure his reputation, for it was generally known that Marchand (probably out of jealousy) had exerted his powerful influence in favor of Daquin, who was in every respect inferior to Rameau. He became organist at Sainte-Croix-de-la-Bretonnerie, and soon was recognized as the foremost organist in France. In 1726 appeared his *Nouveau système de musique théorique,* an introduction to the *Traité.* The leading ideas of his system of harmony are (1) chord-building by thirds; (2) the classification of a chord and all its inversions as one and the same, thus reducing the multiplicity of consonant and dissonant combinations to a fixed and limited number of root-chords; (3) his invention of a fundamental bass ('basse fondamentale'), which does not correspond to our thorough-bass, but is an imaginary series of root-tones forming the real basis of the varied chord-progressions employed in a composition. The stir that these novel theories occasioned, and his reputation as the foremost French organist, by no means satisfied Rameau's ambition; his ardent desire was to bring out a dramatic work at the Opéra. He had made a modest beginning with dramatic music in 1723, when he wrote some dances and divertissements for Alexis Piron's fairy burlesque *L'Endriague,* which was produced at the Théâtre de la Foire St.-Germain. In 1726 he brought out at the same theater two light operas by the same poet, *L'Enrôlement d' Arlequin* (Feb. 28) and *La Robe de dissension, ou le Faux Prodigue* (autumn). He then became music-master to the wife of the 'fermier-général' La Pouplinière, and the latter obtained of Voltaire a libretto on *Samson,* which Rameau set to music; but it was rejected on account of its biblical subject. A second libretto, by Abbé Pellegrin, was accepted, and *Hippolyte et Aricie* was produced at the Opéra in 1733; its reception was cool, despite undeniable superiority (over the operas of Lully and his following) in the rich and varied harmony and instrumentation, and Rameau almost renounced dramatic composition. But the persuasions of his friends, who also influenced public opinion in his favor, were effective; in 1735 he brought out the successful opera-ballet *Les Indes galantes,* and in 1737 his masterpiece, *Castor et Pollux,* a work that for years held its own beside the operas of Gluck. A career of uninterrupted prosperity commenced; he was recognized as the leading theorist of the time, and his instruction was eagerly sought; for the next 30 years his operas dominated the French stage; he was named composer of the King's chamber music, and just before his death he was granted a patent of nobility.—From the beginning of his dramatic career Rameau roused opposition, and at the same time found ardent admirers. The first war of words was waged between the 'Lullistes' and the 'Ramistes.' This had scarcely been ended by a triumphant revival of *Pygmalion* in 1751, when the production of Pergolesi's *La Serva padrona* (1752) caused a more prolonged and bitter controversy between the adherents of Rameau and the 'Encyclopédistes,' a struggle known as 'La Guerre des Bouffons,' in which Rameau participated by writing numerous essays defending his position. Practically the same charges were made against him as a century later against Wagner: unintelligible harmony, lack of melody, preponderance of discords, noisy instrumentation, etc. But when 25 years later the war between Gluckists and Piccinnists was raging, Rameau's works were praised as models of beauty and perfection. It is a matter for regret that Rameau was indifferent to the quality of his librettos; he relied so much upon his musical inspiration that he never could be brought to a realization of the importance of a good text; hence the inequality of his operas. Nevertheless, his operas mark a decided advance over Lully's in musical characterization, expressive melody, richness of harmony, variety of modulation, and individuality of instrumentation. —WRITINGS: *Traité de l'harmonie . . .* (1722); *Nouveau système de musique théorique* (1726); *Plan abrégé d'une nouvelle méthode d'accompagnement* (1730); *Les différentes méthodes d'accompagnement pour le clavecin ou pour l'orgue* (1732); *Génération harmonique* (1737); *Démonstration du principe de l'harmonie* (1750); *Nouvelles réflexions de M. Rameau sur sa démonstration . . .* (1752); *Réflexions . . . sur la manière de former la voix . . .* (1752); *Observations sur notre instinct pour la musique* (1754); *Code de musique pratique . . .* (1760); also numerous pamphlets, polemical or otherwise, and 3 works in MS.—WORKS: Theatrical entertainments to which Rameau contributed music: *L'Endriague* (Paris, Feb. 3, 1723); *L'Enrôlement d'Arlequin* (Paris, Feb., 1726); *La Robe de dissension* (1726); *Les Jardins de l'Hymen ou la Rose* (1726; Paris, March 5, 1744); *Les Courses de Tempé* (1734). Operas: *Hippolyte et Aricie* (Paris, Oct. 1, 1733); *Les Indes galantes,* 'ballet héroïque' (Paris, Aug. 23, 1735); *Castor et Pollux* (Paris, Oct. 24, 1737); *Les Fêtes d'Hébé,* ballet (Paris, May 21, 1739); *Dardanus* (Paris, Nov. 19, 1739); *La Princesse de Navarre,* ballet (Versailles, Feb. 23, 1745); *Platée* (Versailles, March 31, 1745); *Les Fêtes de Polymnie,* ballet (Paris, Oct. 12, 1745); *Le Temple de la Gloire,* ballet (Versailles, Nov. 27, 1745); *Les Fêtes de l'Hymen et de l'Amour,* 'ballet héroïque' (Versailles, March 15, 1747); *Zaïs,* 'pastorale héroïque' (Paris, Feb. 29, 1748); *Pygmalion,* ballet (Paris, Aug. 27, 1748); *Les Surprises de l'Amour,* ballet (Versailles, Nov. 27, 1748); *Naïs,* 'pastorale héroïque' (Paris, April 22, 1749); *Zoroastre* (Paris, Dec. 5, 1749); *La Guirlande,* ballet (Paris, Sept. 21, 1751); *Acante et Céphise,* 'pastorale héroïque' (Paris, Nov. 9, 1751); *Daphnis et Eglé* (Fontainebleau, Oct. 30, 1753); *Les Sybarites,* ballet (Fontainebleau, Nov. 13, 1753); *La Naissance d'Osiris,* ballet (Fontainebleau, Oct. 12, 1754); *Anacréon,* ballet (Fontainebleau, Oct. 23, 1754); *Les Paladins* (Paris, Feb. 12, 1760); *Abaris ou les Boréades* (1764). Most of the above were publ. in short score (voice, violin, and bass, with the ritornelli in full).—Other publ. music: *Premier livre de pièces de clavecin* (1706); *Pièces de clavecin avec une méthode pour la mécanique des doigts* (n. d.; with important notes); *Pièces de clavecin avec une table pour les agréments* (1731); and *Nouvelles suites de pièces pour clavecin avec des remarques sur les différents genres de musique* (n. d.; Farrenc publ. these last two in his 'Trésor des pianistes,' 1861); *Pièces de clavecin en concerts* (1741; with accomp. of violin, flute, and viola or 2nd violin); detached numbers of the above are in Pauer's 'Old French Composers' and 'Popular Pieces by Rameau'; Hugo Riemann edited a complete ed. of the clavecin compositions (publ. by Steingräber). —In 1895 Durand & Cie. began the publication of a monumental edition under the editorship of C. Saint-Saëns and Ch. Malherbe; after the latter's death (1911) his part of the work was divided between M. Emmanuel and M. Teneo. 18 vols. appeared up to 1914: I, *Pièces de clavecin;* II, *Musique instrumentale;* III, *Cantates;* IV, *Motets* (1st series); V, *Motets* (2nd series); VI, *Hippolyte et Aricie;* VII, *Les Indes galantes;* VIII, *Castor et Pollux;*

IX, *Les Fêtes d'Hébé;* X, *Dardanus;* XI, *La Princesse de Navarre, Les Fêtes de Ramire, Nélée et Myrthis, Zéphire;* XII, *Platée;* XIII, *Les Fêtes de Polymnie;* XIV, *Le Temple de la Gloire;* XV, *Les Fêtes de l'Hymen et de l'Amour;* XVI, *Zaïs;* XVII, *Pygmalion, Les Surprises de l'Amour;* XVIII, *Naïs, Anacréon, Les Sybarites.* No vols. have been added since 1914.

BIBLIOGRAPHY: A. BIOGRAPHY: Ch. Poisot, *Notice biographique sur J.-P. Rameau* (Paris, 1864); Th. Nisard, *Monographie de J.-P. Rameau* (Paris, 1867); A. Pougin, *Rameau* (Paris, 1876); R. Garraud, *Rameau* (Paris, 1876); H. Grigne, *Rameau* (Dijon, 1876); M. Brenet, *Notes et croquis sur J.-P. Rameau,* in the 'Guide Musical' (1899) and *La Jeunesse de Rameau,* in 'Rivista Musicale Italiana' (1902-03); H. Quittard, *Les Années de jeunesse de Rameau,* in 'Revue d'histoire et de critique musicale' (1902); L. de La Laurencie, *Quelques documents sur J.-P. Rameau et sa famille* (Paris, 1907) and *Rameau* (Paris, 1908); L. Laloy, *Rameau* (Paris, 1908); L. de la Laurencie, *Rameau et ses descendants,* in 'Sammelbände der Internationalen Musik-Gesellschaft' (1911); M. M. Mayer, *J.-P. Rameau; J. S. Bach* (Chambéry, 1946); Y. Tiénot, *J.-P. Rameau, esquisse biographique* (Paris, 1954); H. Charlier, *J.-P. Rameau* (Lyons, 1955); P. Berthier, *Rameau* (Paris, 1957); C. Girdlestone, *Rameau* (London, 1957). —B. CRITICISM AND HISTORY: L. Danjou, *Rameau, son influence sur l'art musical* (Paris, 1866); J. Carlez, *Grimm et la musique de son temps* (Paris, 1872); R. de Récy, *La Critique musicale au siècle dernier; Rameau et les Encyclopédistes,* in 'Revue des Deux Mondes' (July, 1886); A. Jullien, *La Musique et les philosophes au XVIIIe siècle* (Paris, 1873); E. Newman, *Gluck and the Opera* (London, 1895); H. Imbert, *L'Œuvre de J.-P. Rameau,* in the 'Guide Musical' (1896); H. Riemann, *Geschichte der Musiktheorie* (2nd ed., 1921; p. 459 et seq.); E. Dacier, *L'Opéra au XVIIIe siècle,* in the 'Revue Musicale' (1902); E. Hirschberg, *Die Encyklopädisten und die französische Oper im 18. Jahrhundert* (Leipzig, 1903); R. Rolland, *Musiciens d'autrefois* (Paris, 1908); A. Jullien, *Musiciens d'hier et d'aujourd'hui* (Paris, 1910); P.-M. Masson, *Lullistes et Ramistes,* in 'L'Année Musicale' (1911); J. Rivière, *Études* (Paris, 1911); J.-G. Prod'homme, *Écrits de musiciens, XVe au XVIIIe siècle* (Paris, 1912); L. Striffling, *Le Goût musical en France au XVIIIe siècle* (Paris, 1913); G. Cucuel, *La Pouplinière et la musique de chambre au XVIIIe siècle* (Paris, 1913); M. Shirlaw, *The Theory of Harmony* (London, 1917); J. Tiersot, *Rameau,* in the 'Mus. Quarterly' (Jan., 1928); P. Lasserre, *Philosophie de goût musical* (Paris, 1928; new ed., 1931); P. M. Masson, *L'Opéra de Rameau* (1930; 2nd ed., 1932), *Rameau et Beethoven,* in the Liège 'Kongressbericht' (1930), and *Rameau and Wagner,* in the 'Mus. Quarterly' (Oct., 1939); G. Migot, *Rameau et le génie de la musique française* (Paris, 1930); J. Gardien, *J.-P. Rameau* (Paris, 1949); P. M. Masson, *Les deux versions du 'Dardanus' de Rameau,* in 'Acta Musicologica' (Jan.-July, 1954). —A comprehensive bibliography was publ. by M. Brenet in 'Le Courrier musical' (1908).

Ramin, Günther, German conductor, organist, and composer; b. Karlsruhe, Oct. 15, 1898; d. Leipzig, Feb. 27, 1956. He studied at the Leipzig Cons. with Karl Straube (organ), Robert Teichmüller (piano), and Stephan Krehl (theory). In 1918 he was appointed organist at the Thomaskirche; conducted choral groups in Leipzig; in 1939 succeeded Straube as cantor at the Thomasschule; from 1933 to 1942 conducted the Philharmonic Chorus in Berlin; from 1945 to 1951, the Gewandhaus Chorus in Leipzig; remained in Leipzig as choral conductor, teacher, and composer. His works include an *Orgelchoral-Suite* and many other organ pieces; a violin sonata; etc. He edited several collections of organ works and publ. the manual *Gedanken zur Klärung des Orgelproblems* (1929). —Cf. L. von Koerber, *Der Thomanerchor und sein Kantor* (Hamburg, 1954).

Ramos (Ramis) de Pareja (rah'mohs dĕh pah-rĕh'hăh), **Bartolomé,** Spanish theorist; b. Baeza, c. 1440; d. after 1491. After lecturing at Salamanca, he went to Bologna (but he did not occupy a chair of music there, as is often stated), where in 1482 he publ. his Latin treatise *Musica practica* (modern ed. by Joh. Wolf, Leipzig, 1901; extract in English in O. Strunk, *Source Readings in Music History,* N. Y., 1950), one of the important landmarks in the science of harmony. In 1491 he was in Rome. He established the mathematical ratios 4:5 and 5:6 for the intervals of the major and minor third, thus completing the definition of the consonant triad and laying the basis of our harmonic system. He was also the first to set forth the theory of equal temperament, probably based on the practice of the early Spanish guitarists (vihuelistas), since the frets on the guitar were placed a semitone apart, and the scale was composed of equal semitones (cf. the treatises of Bermudo, Milán, etc.). The Bolognese theorist Giovanni Spataro was Ramos's pupil. —Cf. H. Riemann, *Handbuch der Musikgeschichte,* 2, I, p. 429.

Randegger, Alberto, conductor; b. Trieste, April 13, 1832; d. London, Dec. 18, 1911. A pupil of Lafont (piano) and Ricci (composition); after conducting in various Italian theaters, about 1854 settled in London, where he became famous as a singing teacher. In 1868 he was appointed prof. of singing at the Royal Academy of Music. From 1879-85 he conducted with the Carl Rosa Company; 1887-98 at Drury Lane and Covent Garden. He composed operas, etc.

Randegger, Alberto, Jr., nephew of the preceding; b. Trieste, Aug. 3, 1880; d. Milan, Oct. 7, 1918. In 1896 he appeared in London as a violinist at an orchestral concert conducted by his uncle; then studied at the Royal Academy of Music; 1897-1901, pupil at the Milan Cons.; lived for some years in London as a composer; then resided in Trieste, later in Milan. —His works include the 1-act opera *L'Ombra di Werther* (Trieste, 1899), a violin concerto (London, 1902), many piano pieces and songs.

Randegger, Giuseppe Aldo, pianist and pedagogue; b. Naples, Feb. 17, 1874; d. New York, Nov. 30, 1946. From 1888-93 pupil at the Cons. in Naples; 1893-97, appeared as pianist in Atlanta, Ga., and other Southern cities; after a year in England and 2 years in Italy, he returned to the U. S.; was director of music at Hamilton College, Lexington, Ky., and Belmont College, Nashville, Tenn.; then settled in New York, as pianist and teacher. Composed a 1-act opera, *The Promise of Medea,* songs, etc.

Randolph, Harold, American pianist and educator; b. Richmond, Va., Oct. 31, 1861; d. Northeast Harbor, Me., July 6, 1927. He studied at the Peabody Cons. of Music, Baltimore; début at Baltimore, 1885, with the Peabody Symph. Orch., then appeared with the principal orchestras and in numerous recitals throughout the U. S.; also gave recitals for 2 pianos with Ernest Hutcheson; in 1898 he succeeded Asger Hamerik as director of the Peabody Cons., which under his administration came to be one of the foremost music schools in the U. S. —Cf. D. Leedy, *H. Randolph, the Man and Musician,* in the 'Mus. Quarterly' (April, 1944).

Rangström, Ture, remarkable Swedish composer; b. Stockholm, Nov. 30, 1884; d. there, May 11, 1947. He studied singing in Berlin and Munich with Julius Hey (1905-7); then composition with Lindegren in Stockholm and Pfitzner in Munich. Returning to Sweden, he became music critic of the 'Stockholms Dagblad' (1910-14) and the 'Svenska Dagbladet' (1907-09, and after 1927). From 1922 to 1925 he was conductor of the Göteborg Symph. Orch.; then became stage director at the Stockholm Opera. His music is permeated with a lyrical sentiment, and his forms are rhapsodic; in his symphonies he achieves great intensity by a concentrated development of the principal melodic and rhythmic ideas; his songs are also appreciated. —Works: operas: *Kronbruden (The Crown Bride)*, after Strindberg (première, Stuttgart, in German, as *Die Kronbraut,* Oct. 21, 1919), *Middelalderlig* (Stockholm, 1921), *Gilgamesh* (left incomplete; finished and orchestrated by John Fernström; Stockholm, Nov. 20, 1952); for orch.: 4 symphonies (I, *In memoriam A. Strindberg,* 1915; II, *My Country,* 1919; III, *Song Under the Stars,* 1931; IV, *Invocatio,* 1936); the symph. poems *Dithyramb* (1909; revised in 1949 by Atterberg), *En höstsang (Ode to Autumn,* 1912), *Havet sjunger (The Sea Sings,* 1914), *Gamla Stockholm* (1939); *Festpreludium 1944,* for the 50th anniversary of the Stockholm Opera Theater (1944); *Divertimento elegiaco,* for strings (1918); *Un petit rien,* for string orch. (1937); *Ballad* for piano and orch. (1937); *Poem-Capriccio amoroso,* for violin and orch. (1944); *Ein Nachtstück in E.T.A. Hoffmanns Manier,* for string quartet (1909); other chamber music; piano pieces; about 60 fine songs, to Swedish texts. —Cf. the special issue of 'Musikrevy' (vol. 5, no. 2; Stockholm, 1950).

Ranki, György, Hungarian composer; b. Budapest, Oct. 30, 1907. He studied with Kodály at the Academy of Music in Budapest (1926-30); then worked at the Ethnographic Museum. He presented his first work, a piano quintet, in 1929, at the Budapest Academy of Music; his ballet *Snowmen* was performed at London in 1939; other works are a cantata, *On The Edge of the City* (1947); 2 piano sonatas; chamber music; many film scores. His music derives its inspiration chiefly from Hungarian folksong.

Rankl, Karl, conductor and composer; b. Gaaden, near Vienna, Oct. 1, 1898. He studied in Vienna with Schoenberg and Anton von Webern; was opera coach at the Vienna Volksoper (1921) and chorusmaster there (1922); subsequently served as conductor at the Stadtheater in Reichenberg (1924), at the East Prussian Broadcasting Co., Königsberg (1926), assistant to Klemperer at the Kroll Opera House, Berlin (1928-31), opera conductor at Graz (1932-37), and conductor at the German Theater in Prague (1937-39). In 1939 he went to England, and became successful there; was conductor at Covent Garden, London (1946-51); in 1952, appointed conductor of the Scottish Orch., Glasgow. He wrote an opera, *Deirdre of the Sorrows,* which received a prize at the Festival of Britain in 1951; 4 symphonies; many choruses. —Cf. Donald Brook, *International Gallery of Conductors* (London, 1951; pp. 140-44).

Ranta, Sulho, eminent Finnish composer and writer on music; b. Peräseinäjoki, Aug. 15, 1901. He studied at the Helsinki Cons. and later in Germany, France, and Italy. Since 1934 he has taught at the Sibelius Academy in Helsinki; is also active as a music critic. He edited a comprehensive biographical dictionary of 90 Finnish composers, *Suomen Säveltäjiä* (Helsinki, 1945), and a general biographical survey of performers, *Sävelten Taitureita* (Helsinki, 1947); also a compendium of music history in Finnish. —Works: *Sinfonia programmatica* (1931); *Sinfonia piccola* (1932); symph. poem, *Images boréales* (1933); cantata, *Kalevala* (1935); symph. poem, *En Folksaga* (1940); *Sinfonia dell'arte* (1947); chamber music; piano pieces.

Rapee (răh-pā'), **Erno,** conductor, b. Budapest, June 4, 1891; d. New York, June 26, 1945. He studied piano with Emil Sauer at the National Academy in Budapest; gave concerts as pianist; appeared as conductor with various European orchestras; in 1912 came to America as accompanist; in 1913 was engaged as musical director of the Hungarian Opera Co., N. Y.; then became conductor for S. L. Rothafel (Roxy) at his motion picture theaters in N. Y.; after several years at the Roxy Theater (1926-31) he became music director of the N.B.C.; then at the Radio City Music Hall, again under Rothafel's management. He introduced classical works into his programs, mostly in the form of potpourris, but upon occasion also in full version; ed. collections of mood music for silent motion pictures (N. Y., 1924, 1925).

Raphael, Günther, German composer; b. Berlin, April 30, 1903. He was a son of the organist and choral conductor Georg Raphael; studied in Berlin with Max Trapp (piano), Walter Fischer (organ), and Robert Kahn (composition). He was on the faculty of the Leipzig Cons. (1926-34); then lived in Meiningen (1934-44); in Laubach (1945-48); in 1949 appointed teacher of theory at the Duisburg Cons. —Works: 4 symphonies; violin concerto; cello concerto; organ concerto; a number of sacred works for chorus a cappella; clarinet quintet; piano quintet; 5 string quartets; sonata for viola unaccompanied; piano trio; 2 violin sonatas; viola sonata; cello sonata; other chamber music; several piano sonatas and other pieces for piano.

Raphling, Sam, American composer; b. Fort Worth, Texas, March 19, 1910. He studied piano in Chicago and, as an exchange fellowship student, in Germany. Returning to the U. S., he was active in Chicago as a teacher and pianist; publ. a number of compositions in various genres: *Abraham Lincoln Walks at Midnight,* for orch.; *Cowboy Rhapsody,* for violin and orch.; *American Album,* for two pianos (1946); sonatina, for 2 clarinets (1948); *Prelude and Toccata,* for trumpet and trombone (1949); *Lyric Prelude,* for trombone and piano (1950); *Dance Suite,* for 2 trumpets (1950); *Variations* for 2 flutes unaccompanied (1955; also for flute and clarinet); sonatina for 2 trombones (1955; also for 2 bassoons); *Sonata, Variations, Introduction and Workout,* for French horn unaccompanied (1955); *Nocturnal Prelude,* for piano (1955); *Duograms,* for 2 oboes (1955); trio for 3 oboes (1955); *Pastorale,* for oboe and piano (1955); etc.

Rappold, Marie (*née* Winterroth), dramatic soprano; b. London, of German parents, c. 1873; d. North Hollywood, Calif., May 12, 1957. She appeared on the London stage as a child entertainer at the age of 5; shortly afterwards the family moved to America, settling in Brooklyn. As a young girl she sang with various local groups in and around N. Y.; studied with Oscar Saenger; later was a member of the Amberg German Opera Co., N. Y. She made her opera début at the Metropolitan Opera, N. Y., on Nov. 22, 1905; remained on the roster until 1919; also appeared in Europe. She was married to Dr. Julius Rappold; when he objected to her stage career, she divorced him; married the tenor Rudolf Berger in 1913; she appeared with him at the Metropolitan Opera.

Rappoldi, Eduard, Austrian violinist and composer; b. Vienna, Feb. 21, 1831; d. Dresden, May 16, 1903. He studied at the Vienna Cons.; then played violin in opera orchestras in Vienna and Rotterdam; conducted opera in Lübeck and Prague; was 2nd violinist in the Joachim Quartet in Berlin (1871-77); concertmaster of the Court Opera in Dresden (1878-98); from 1893 till his death, prof. of violin at the Dresden Cons. He publ. 2 violin sonatas; chamber music; piano pieces; songs. His wife, **Laura Rappoldi-Kahrer** (b. Mistelbach, near Vienna, Jan. 14, 1853; d. Dresden, Aug. 17, 1925), was an excellent pianist, a pupil of Liszt; from 1890 taught piano at the Dresden Cons.

Rasbach, Oscar, American composer; b. Dayton, Ky., Aug. 2, 1888. He studied academic subjects in Los Angeles; music with Ludwig Thomas, Julius Albert Jahn, José Anderson, and A. J. Stamm. He was first engaged in business; then went to Vienna, where he took piano lessons with Leschetizky and studied theory with Hans Thornton. He returned to the U. S. in 1911 and settled in San Marino, Calif. He wrote 2 operettas, *Dawn Boy* and *Open House,* and a number of songs, of which *Trees,* to Joyce Kilmer's poem, became enormously popular.

Rascher, Sigurd M., German saxophone virtuoso; b. Elberfeld, May 15, 1907. He studied at the Stuttgart Cons.; gave concerts as saxophone soloist; taught at the Cons. of Copenhagen (1933-38); in 1939 went to the U. S.; taught at the Manhattan School, N. Y. (1940-42); was soloist with orchestras in special works written for him by Jacques Ibert, Frank Martin, and others. Publ. studies for his instrument.

Raselius (Rasel), Andreas, German composer and theorist; b. Hahnbach, near Amberg, c. 1563; d. Heidelberg, Jan. 6, 1602. Son of a Lutheran preacher; from 1581-84 studied at Leipzig Univ.; then appointed cantor at the Gymnasium in Regensburg; remained there till 1600, when he returned to Heidelberg as Hofkapellmeister to the Elector Palatine Frederick IV. In 1589 he publ. a music instruction book, *Hexachordum seu Quaestiones musicae practicae.* Other publ. works: *Teutsche Sprüche* (2 vols.: *a* 5, 1594; *a* 5-9, 1595); *Regensburgischer Kirchenkontrapunkt* (5-voiced Lutheran chorales; 1599); in MS: motets and Magnificats. A selection of his Latin and German motets was ed. by L. Roselius in the 'Denkmäler der Tonkunst in Bayern' (vol. 29-30). —Cf. J. Auer, *A. Raselius* (1892); L. Roselius, *A. Raselius als Motettenkomponist* (Berlin, 1924).

Rasse, François, Belgian composer; b. Helchin, near Ath, Jan. 27, 1873; d. Brussels, Jan. 4, 1955. He studied violin with Eugène Ysaÿe at the Brussels Cons., winning the Belgian Grand Prix de Rome in 1899; from 1925 to 1938 was director of the Liège Cons. —Works: operas, *Déidamia* (1905) and *Sœur Béatrice* (1938); ballet, *Le Maître à danser* (1908); for orch.: *Symphonie romantique* (1901), *Symphonie mélodique* (1903), *Symphonie rythmique* (1908), tone poems, *Douleur* (1911), *Joie* (1925), *Aspiration* (1946), a violin concerto (1906), *La Dryade* for clarinet and orch. (1943), *Lamento* for cello and orch. (1952); 2 string quartets (1906; 1950); a piano quartet (1941); numerous piano pieces; choral works; songs. A catalogue of his works was publ., with a biographical sketch, by the 'Centre Belge de Documentation Musicale' (1954).

Rastrelli, Joseph, German composer and conductor; b. Dresden, April 13, 1799; d. there, Nov. 15, 1842. He was a pupil of his father, the Italian musician Vincenzo Rastrelli (1760-1839); then studied with Mattei in Bologna. In 1830 he was appointed court conductor in Dresden; was Wagner's predecessor in this post. His opera, *Salvator Rosa, oder Zwey Nächte in Rom* (Dresden, July 22, 1832), was the first new German opera produced in Dresden after the disbanding of the Italian Opera Co. there.

Rasumovsky. See **Razumovsky.**

Ratez (răh-tā'), **Émile-Pierre,** French composer; b. Besançon, Nov. 5, 1851; d. Lille, May 19, 1934. He studied at the Paris Cons. with Bazin and Massenet (1872-81); played the viola in the orch. of the Opéra-Comique; in 1891 was appointed director of the Lille branch of the Paris Cons.; also conducted popular concerts there (1893-1906). He wrote the operas *Lydéric* (Lille, 1895) and *Paula* (Besançon, 1904); a ballet, *La Guivre* (Paris, 1925); a cantata, *Scènes héroïques* (1899); chamber music; publ. *Traité élémentaire de contrepoint et de fugue* and *Traité d'harmonie théorique et pratique.*

Rath (raht), **Felix vom,** German composer; b. Cologne, June 17, 1866; d. Munich, Aug. 25, 1905. He studied piano with Reinecke in Leipzig and composition with

Thuille in Munich, where he settled. A composer of more than ordinary abilities, he publ. a piano concerto, a piano quartet, a violin sonata, and a number of piano pieces.

Rathaus, Karol, composer; b. Tarnopol, Poland, Sept. 16, 1895; d. New York, Nov. 21, 1954. He studied composition with Schreker in Berlin and in Vienna; taught in Berlin; in 1932 went to Paris, and in 1934 to London. In 1938 he settled in New York; in 1940 was appointed to the faculty of Queens College, and remained in that capacity until his death. His music is distinguished by a firm sense of contrapuntal development; the harmonies are maintained within a general tonal framework; the esthetic attitude is that of late Romanticism. Several of his works were performed at festivals of the International Society for Contemporary Music.—Works: ballet, *Der letzte Pierrot* (Berlin, May 7, 1927); opera, *Fremde Erde* (Berlin, Dec. 10, 1930); 3 symphonies (1922; 1923; 1942); *Suite for Orch.* (Liège Festival, Sept. 6, 1930); piano concerto (Berkeley, Calif., Festival, Aug. 1, 1942); *Jacob's Dream* for orch. (1941); Adagio for strings (1941); *Polonaise symphonique* (N. Y., Feb. 26, 1944); *Vision dramatique,* a symph. movement (Tel Aviv, April 4, 1948); 5 string quartets; *Serenade* for clarinet, violin, viola, cello, and piano; *Eine kleine Serenade* for 4 wind instruments and piano; clarinet sonata; violin sonata; 4 piano sonatas; Psalm 23; *Diapason,* for mixed chorus, baritone solo, and orch., to texts by Dryden and Milton. In 1953 he was commissioned to revise Mussorgsky's original orchestration of *Boris Godunov* for production at the Metropolitan Opera, which took place in March, 1953. —Cf. Boris Schwarz, *Karol Rathaus,* in the 'Mus. Quarterly' (Oct., 1955).

Ratzenberger, Theodor, German pianist; b. Grossbreitenbach, April 14, 1840; d. Wiesbaden, March 8, 1879. He was a pupil of Liszt (piano) and Cornelius (composition); publ. some salon pieces for piano.

Raucheisen, Michael, German pianist; b. Rain-on-the-Lech, Bavaria, Feb. 10, 1889. He was educated in Munich; studied piano with Bussmeyer, and theory with Thuille. In 1913 he began to appear in Germany as accompanist; toured in the U. S. (1922-24); was accompanist to Fritz Kreisler. He married the American soprano Marion Talley on June 30, 1932 (marriage annulled, Jan. 28, 1933); he then married the Austrian soprano Maria Ivogün (1933).

Rauchenecker, Georg Wilhelm, German violinist and composer; b. Munich, March 8, 1844; d. Elberfeld, July 17, 1906. He studied violin with Joseph Walter; filled various posts as a theater violinist in France; then lived in Switzerland; conducted the Berlin Philharmonic for a season (1884). In 1889 he established a music school in Elberfeld, and conducted an orchestral society there until his death. He wrote the operas (all produced in Elberfeld): *Die letzten Tage von Thule* (1889), *Ingo* (1893), *Don Quixote* (1897), *Sanna* (1898), *Zlatorog* (1903), *Der Florentiner* (posthumous; Strasbourg, 1910); a symphony; *Orientalische Fantasie* for solo violin with string quintet; 6 string quartets; a string sextet; an octet for woodwind instruments.

Raudenbush, George King, American conductor; b. Jersey Shore, Pa., March 13, 1899; d. San Diego, Calif., May 26, 1956. He studied at the Detroit Cons., the New England Cons. and the American Institute of Applied Music; also in Germany; pupil of Chadwick, R. Huntington Woodman, M. Wilson, Schradieck, Volpe, Ysaÿe, and Th. Spiering; he made his début as a violinist in 1921 at Aeolian Hall, N. Y.; music director of the Theater Guild, and for Winthrop Ames and Walter Hampden; 1922-29, member of the N. Y. Symph. Orch.; 1929, founded the Harrisburg Symph. Orch. and conducted it until 1950; also founder (1939) and conductor (until 1943) of the Toledo Symph. Orch., and of the York, Pa., Symph. Orch.

Raugel (roh-zhĕhl'), **Félix,** French musicologist; b. Saint-Quentin, Nov. 27, 1881. While attending the Lycée at Lille he studied music with Ch. Queste and F. Lecocq; continued his studies in 1900 in Paris with H. Libert and at the Schola Cantorum with Vincent d'Indy. Together with E. Borrel he founded in 1908 the 'Société Haendel' for the cultivation of early music. —Writings: *Les Orgues de l'abbaye de St. Mihiel* (1919); *Recherches sur quelques maîtres de l'ancienne facture d'orgues française; Le Cantique français* (Tourcoing, 1920); *Les Organistes* (1923); *Les grandes orgues des églises de Paris et du département de la Seine* (1927); *Palestrina* (1930); *Les grandes orgues de Notre Dame* (1934); *Le Chant choral* (1948); *L'Oratorio* (1948); ed. organ works of Handel, Scarlatti, Buxtehude, etc.

Ravanello, Oreste, Italian composer; b. Venice, Aug. 25, 1871; d. Padua, July 1,

1938. Pupil of P. Agostini and A. Girardi, and later at the Liceo Benedetto Marcello; 1893, 2nd organist at San Marco; 1895, 1st organist; 1898, maestro di cappella at San Antonio, Padua; 1902, prof. of organ at the Liceo Benedetto Marcello; 1914 again in Padua as director of the Istituto musicale; was for 3 years ed. of 'Il Repertorio pratico dell' Organista liturgico.' He composed more than 30 Masses *a* 1-6 (some with orch.), numerous motets *a* 2-8; 2 cantatas; a string quartet; a piano trio; a sonata for violin and organ; many pieces for organ and for piano; also publ. *Il Ritmo del Canto Gregoriano, Cento Studi ed Esercizi per il Organo,* etc.

Ravasenga, Carlo, Italian composer; b. Turin, Dec. 17, 1891; pupil of Cravero (composition), Navone (violin), and Vogliazzo (piano); composer and teacher in Turin; ed. of 'L'Araldo mus.' (Milan).—Works: the operas *Una Tragedia fiorentina,* after O. Wilde (Turin, 1916) and *Il Giudizio di Don Giovanni* (1916); *Un Giorno di festa,* orchestral suite (1916); *Giuditta e Oloferno,* symph. suite; *Variazioni pittoresche* for string quartet; *Contrasto burlesco-sentimentale,* for piano; violin sonata; piano sonata; etc.

Ravel (răh-vĕhl'), **Maurice (Joseph),** famous French composer; b. Ciboure, Basses-Pyrénées, March 7, 1875; d. Paris, Dec. 28, 1937. His father was a Swiss engineer, and his mother of Basque origin; Ravel was able to speak the Basque language fluently. The family moved to Paris when he was an infant. He began to study piano at the age of 7 with Henri Ghis (q.v.) and harmony at 12 with Charles-René. In 1889 he entered the Paris Cons.; studied piano with Anthiome; won 1st medal in 1891, and passed to the advanced class of Charles de Bériot; studied harmony with Émile Pessard. Still as a student he wrote and publ. a *Menuet antique* for piano and *Habanera* for 2 pianos (later included in the *Rapsodie espagnole* for orch.); these pieces, written at the age of 20, already reveal great originality in the treatment of old modes and of Spanish motifs; however, he continued to study; in 1897 he entered the classes of Gabriel Fauré (composition) and Gedalge (counterpoint and fugue); his well-known *Pavane pour une Infante défunte* for piano was written during that time (1899). On May 27, 1899, he appeared in public as conductor, in a performance of his overture *Shéhérazade* with the Société Nationale in Paris. The work was never published, but some elements were incorporated in Ravel's song cycle of the same title (1903). In 1901 he won the 2nd Prix de Rome with the cantata *Myrrha;* but the ensuing attempts to win the Grand Prix de Rome were unsuccessful; at his last try (1905) he was eliminated in the preliminaries, and so was not allowed to compete; the age limit then set an end to his further effort to enter. Since 6 prizes all went to pupils of Lenepveu, suspicion was aroused of unfair discrimination; Jean Marnold publ. an article, *Le Scandale du Prix de Rome,* in the 'Mercure de France' (June, 1905) in which he brought the controversy into the open; this precipitated a crisis at the Paris Cons.; its director, Théodore Dubois, resigned, and Gabriel Fauré took his place. By that time, Ravel had written a number of his most famous compositions, and was regarded by most French critics as a talented disciple of Debussy. No doubt Ravel's method of poetic association of musical ideas paralleled that of Debussy; his employment of unresolved dissonances and the enhancement of the diatonic style into pandiatonicism were techniques common to Debussy and his followers; but there were important differences: whereas Debussy adopted the scale of whole tones as an integral part of his musical vocabulary, Ravel resorted to it only occasionally; similarly, augmented triads appear much less frequently in Ravel's music than in Debussy's; in his writing for piano Ravel actually anticipated some of Debussy's usages; in a letter addressed to Pierre Lalo and publ. in 'Le Temps' (April 9, 1907) Ravel pointed out that at the time of the publication of his piano piece *Jeux d'eau* (1902) Debussy had brought out only his suite *Pour le Piano* which had contained little that was novel. In Paris, in France, and soon in England and other European countries, Ravel's name became well known, but for many years he was still regarded as an ultra-modernist. A curious test of audience appreciation was a 'Concert des auteurs anonymes' presented by the Société Indépendante de Musique on May 9, 1911; the program included Ravel's *Valses nobles et sentimentales,* a set of piano pieces in the manner of Schubert; yet Ravel was recognized as the author. Inspired evocation of the past was but one aspect of Ravel's creative genius; in this style are written the *Pavane pour une Infante défunte, Le Tombeau de Couperin,* and *La Valse*; luxuriance of exotic colors marks his ballet *Daphnis et Chloé,* his opera *L'Heure espagnole,* the song cycles *Shéhérazade* and *Chansons madécasses* and his virtuoso pieces for piano,

Miroirs and *Gaspard de la nuit;* other works are deliberately austere, even ascetic in their pointed Classicism: the piano concertos, the piano sonatina, and some of his songs with piano accompaniment. His association with Diaghilev's Ballets Russes was most fruitful; for Diaghilev he wrote one of his masterpieces, *Daphnis et Chloé;* another ballet, *Boléro,* commissioned by Ida Rubinstein and performed at her dance recital at the Paris Opéra on Nov. 22, 1928, became Ravel's most spectacular success as an orchestral piece. —Ravel never married, and lived a life of semi-retirement, devoting most of his time to composition; he accepted virtually no pupils, although he gave friendly advice to Vaughan Williams and to others; he was never on the faculty of any school. As a performer, he was not brilliant; he appeared as pianist only in his own works, and often accompanied singers in programs of his songs; although he accepted engagements as conductor, his technique was barely sufficient to secure a perfunctory performance of his music. When the war broke out in 1914, he was rejected because of his frail physique, but he was anxious to serve; his application for air service was denied, but he was received in the ambulance corps at the front; his health gave way, and in the autumn of 1916 he was compelled to enter a hospital for recuperation. In 1922 he visited Amsterdam and Venice, conducting his music; in 1923 he appeared in London; in 1926 he went to Sweden, England, and Scotland; in 1928 he made an American tour as conductor and pianist; in the same year he received the degree of D. Mus. *honoris causa* at Oxford Univ. In 1929 he was honored at his native town of Ciboure by the inauguration of the Quai Maurice Ravel. Shortly afterwards, he began to experience difficulties in muscular coordination, and suffered from attacks of aphasia, symptoms indicative of a cerebral malady; a brain operation was performed on Dec. 19, 1937, but was not successful, and he died 9 days later. —Works: 1-act opera, *L'Heure espagnole,* text by Franc-Nohain (Paris, Opéra-Comique, May 19, 1911; Metropolitan Opera House, N. Y., Nov. 7, 1925); the 'fantaisie lyrique' *L'Enfant et les sortilèges,* libretto by Colette (Monte Carlo, March 21, 1925); the ballets *Daphnis et Chloé* (Paris, June 8, 1912), *Adélaide ou le langage des fleurs,* after the *Valses nobles et sentimentales* (Paris, April 22, 1912), *Ma Mère l'Oye,* elaborated from the piano suite (Paris Opéra, March 11, 1915), *Le Tombeau de Couperin,* choreographic poem from the orchestral suite (Ballets Suédois, Paris, Nov. 8, 1920); *La Valse* (Paris, Dec. 12, 1920), *Boléro* (Ida Rubinstein's dance recital, Paris, Nov. 22, 1928). For orch.: overture *Shéhérazade* (1898); *Pavane pour une infante défunte* (1899); *Alborada del gracioso* (*Serenade of a Clown;* 1905); *Rapsodie espagnole* (Paris, March 19, 1908); *Daphnis et Chloé,* 2 suites from the ballet (1909-11); *Ma Mère l'Oye,* after the piano duet (1912); *Le Tombeau de Couperin* (1917); *La Valse* (1920); *Tzigane,* for violin and orch. (also with piano accompaniment; 1924); *Boléro* (1928; 1st American performance, N. Y., Nov. 14, 1929); piano concerto in D for left hand alone, written for the one-armed pianist Paul Wittgenstein, who gave its first performance (Vienna, Nov. 27, 1931); piano concerto in G (Paris, Jan. 14, 1932, Ravel conducting, Marguerite Long, pianist). Chamber music: string quartet in F (1903); *Introduction et Allegro,* for harp, string quartet, flute, and clarinet (Paris, Feb. 22, 1907); piano trio (1914); sonata for violin and cello (1920-22); *Berceuse sur le nom de Fauré,* for violin and piano (1922); violin sonata (1923-27); *Tzigane,* for violin and piano (London, April 26, 1924, Jelly d'Aranyi, violinist; Ravel at the piano, in a concert of Ravel works). Vocal works: *Shéhérazade,* song cycle for solo voice and orch. (Paris, May 17, 1904); *Trois Poèmes de Mallarmé,* for voice, piano, 2 flutes, 2 clarinets, and string quartet (1913); *Trois chansons,* for mixed chorus a cappella (1916); *Chansons madécasses,* for voice, flute, cello, and piano (1926); *Don Quichotte à Dulcinée,* 3 songs with orchestral accompaniment (Paris, Dec. 1, 1934). Songs: *Ballade de la Reine morte d'aimer* (1894); *Un grand sommeil noir* (1895); *Sainte* (1896); *Deux Épigrammes de Clément Marot* (1896); *Si morne* (1899, unpublished); *Manteau de fleurs* (1903); *Le Noël des jouets,* text by Ravel (1905); *5 Mélodies populaires grecques* (1905; another Greek melody was publ. in the 'Revue Musicale,' Dec., 1938); *Les grands vents venus d'outre-mer* (1906); *Histoires naturelles* (1906); *Sur l'herbe* (1907); *Vocalise en forme d'habanera* (1907); *4 Chants populaires* (1910); *2 Mélodies hébraïques* (1914); *Ronsard à son âme* (1924); *Rêves* (1927). For piano: *Sérénade grotesque* (1894); *Menuet antique* (1895); *Pavane pour une Infante défunte* (1899); *Jeux d'eau* (1901); *Miroirs* (5 pieces): *Noctuelles, Oiseaux tristes, Une Barque sur l'océan, Alborada del Gracioso, La Vallée des cloches* (1905); *Sonatine* (1903-5); *Gaspard de la nuit: Ondine, Le Gibet, Scarbo* (1908); *Menuet sur le nom d'Haydn*

(1909); *Valses nobles et sentimentales* (1911); *Prélude* (1913); *À la manière de . . . Borodine, Chabrier* (1913); *Le Tombeau de Couperin* (1914-17); *Les Sites auriculaires,* for 2 pianos (1895-96): *Habanera* and *Entre cloches; Ma Mère l'Oye,* 5 'pièces enfantines' for piano 4 hands, written for Christina Verger, age 6, and Germaine Duramy, age 10, and performed by them (Paris, April 20, 1920). Ravel was commissioned by Koussevitzky to make an orchestration of Mussorgsky's *Pictures at an Exhibition;* it was first performed by Koussevitzky at one of his concerts (Paris, Oct. 19, 1922) and subsequently became one of the most popular orchestral suites; Ravel also orchestrated Chabrier's *Menuet pompeux,* arranged Debussy's *Prélude à l'après-midi d'un faune* for 2 pianos, etc. —Bibliography: O. Séré, *Musiciens français d'aujourd'hui* (1911); Roland-Manuel, *Maurice Ravel et son œuvre* (1914; rev. ed., 1926; in English, London, 1941); M. O. Morris, *Maurice Ravel,* in 'Music & Letters' (July, 1921); A. Cœuroy, *La Musique française moderne* (1922); E. Vuillermoz, *Musiques d'aujourd'hui* (1923); E. B. Hill, *Modern French Music* (N. Y., 1924); F. H. Shera, *Debussy and Ravel* (London, 1925); Cecil Gray, *A Survey of Contemporary Music* (London, 1925); Roland-Manuel, *Ravel et son œuvre dramatique* (1928); M. D. Calvocoressi, *Music and Ballet* (London, 1933); Roland-Manuel, *À la gloire de Ravel* (1938); V. Jankélévitch, *Maurice Ravel* (Paris, 1939); R. Wild, ed., *Ravel par quelques-uns de ses familiers* (Paris, 1939); P. Landormy, *Maurice Ravel,* in the 'Mus. Quarterly' (Oct., 1939); M. Goss, *Bolero: The Life of Maurice Ravel* (N. Y., 1940); M. D. Calvocoressi, *Ravel's Letters to Calvocoressi,* in the 'Mus. Quarterly' (Jan., 1941); K. Akeret, *Studien zum Klavierwerk von Maurice Ravel* (Zürich, 1941); H. Jourdan-Morhange, *Ravel et nous* (Geneva, 1945); A. Machabey, *Maurice Ravel* (Paris, 1947); N. Demuth, *Ravel* (London, 1947); Roland-Manuel, *Ravel* (Paris, 1948; a new work); W.-L. Landowski, *Maurice Ravel, sa vie, son œuvre* (Paris, 1950); L. La Pegna, *Ravel* (Brescia, 1950); José Bruyr, *Maurice Ravel, ou le Lyrisme et les sortilèges* (Paris, 1950); W. Tappolet, *Maurice Ravel: Leben und Werk* (Olten, 1950); V. Perlemuter, *Ravel d'après Ravel* (Lausanne, 1953); V. Seroff, *Maurice Ravel* (N. Y., 1953); Marcelle Gerrar and René Chalupt, eds., *Ravel au miroir de ses lettres* (Paris, 1956). See also the special Ravel issues of the 'Revue Musicale' (April, 1925; Dec., 1938).

Ravenscroft, John, English composer; b. London; d. there, c. 1708. In 1695 he was in Rome, where he publ. a set of 'sonate a trè' under the Italianized name Giovanni Ravenscroft. He apparently was a pupil of Corelli, whose style he imitated. His op. 2, containing 6 sonatas for 2 violins with continuo, was publ. posthumously in London. —Cf. W. S. Newman, *Ravenscroft and Corelli,* in 'Music & Letters' (Oct., 1957).

Ravenscroft, Thomas, English composer and music editor; b. c. 1590; d. c. 1633. He was a chorister at St. Paul's Cathedral under Edward Pearce; in 1607 received his Mus. B. at Cambridge; from 1618 to 1622 he was music master at Christ's Hospital, London. —Publications: *Pammelia: Musick's Miscellanie: or Mixed Varietie of Pleasant Roundelayes and Delightful Catches of 3-10 Parts in one* (1609; the first collection of rounds, catches, and canons printed in England; 2nd ed., 1618); *Deuteromelia: or the Second Part of Musick's Melodie . . .* (1609); *Melismata: Musicall Phansies, Fitting the Court, Citie, and Countrey Humours, to 3, 4 and 5 Voyces* (1611); *A Briefe Discourse of the true (but neglected) use of Charact'ring the Degrees by their Perfection, Imperfection, and Diminution in Mensurable Musicke . . .* (1614); and *The Whole Booke of Psalmes: With the Hymnes Evangelicall and Songs Spirituall Composed into 4 parts by Sundry Authors . . .* (1621; 2nd ed., newly corrected and enlarged, 1633; his best-known and most valuable work, containing numbers by 15 leading British composers, and some by Ravenscroft himself). —Cf. G. Reese, *Music in the Renaissance* (N. Y., 1954; p. 832 ff.).

Ravina, Jean-Henri, French composer; b. Bordeaux, May 20, 1818; d. Paris, Sept. 30, 1906. He studied at the Paris Cons. with Zimmerman (piano) and Laurent (theory); taught at the Cons. (1834-36); then made a concert tour as pianist in Russia (1858); later traveled in Spain; lived chiefly in Paris. He wrote elegant and attractive salon pieces for piano, which enjoyed considerable vogue, and eventually became part of the piano repertory: *Nocturne in D♭,* op. 13; *Douce pensée,* op. 41; *Jour de bonheur,* op. 55; *Petit boléro,* op. 62; *Câlinerie,* op. 86; also *Études de style et de perfectionnement,* op. 14; *Études harmonieuses,* op. 50; etc.; a piano concerto. He publ. 4-hand arrangements of all of Beethoven's symphonies.

Rawsthorne, Alan, English composer; b. Haslingden, May 2, 1905. He went to a dentistry school; did not begin to study music until he was 20, when he entered the Royal Manchester College of Music; later studied piano with Egon Petri in Berlin. Returning to England in 1932, he occupied various teaching posts; then devoted himself mainly to composition; settled in London. In 1935 he married the violinist, Jessie Hinchliffe. His music is essentially a revival of the contrapuntal style of the past, without much harmonic elaboration; but the rhythm is vigorous, and the melodic patterns are extremely fluid, often departing from the tonal center. —Works: *Symphonic Studies* (Warsaw Festival of the International Society for Contemporary Music, April 21, 1939); *Cortèges,* fantasy overture (London, July 23, 1945); concerto for strings (1949); symphony (1950); *Concertante pastorale,* for flute, horn, and strings (1951); *A Canticle of Man,* for baritone, chorus, flute, and strings (1952); clarinet concerto (1936); violin concerto (1947); oboe concerto (1947); piano concerto no. 1 (London, Dec. 7, 1946); piano concerto no. 2 (London, June 17, 1951); trio for flute, oboe, and piano (1936); *Theme and Variations* for 2 violins (1937); *Theme and Variations* for string quartet (1939); clarinet quartet (1948); viola sonata (1938); cello sonata (1949); several song cycles, to French and English words; *Practical Cats,* 'an entertainment for children,' for speaker and orch., to a text by T. S. Eliot (Edinburgh, Aug. 26, 1954); *Madame Chrysanthème,* ballet suite (London, Aug. 31, 1957); *Overture Hallé,* for the centennial of the Hallé Orch. (Manchester, Feb. 16, 1958). —Cf. K. Avery, *Alan Rawsthorne,* in the 'Monthly Mus. Record' (Feb., 1948); H. Howells, *A Note on Alan Rawsthorne,* in 'Music & Letters' (Jan., 1951); A. E. F. Dickinson, *The Progress of Alan Rawsthorne,* in the 'Music Review' (May, 1951); A. Frank, *Modern British Composers* (London, 1954; pp. 74-79).

Razumovsky, Count (from 1815, Prince) **Andrey Kyrillovitch,** Russian diplomat and music lover; b. St. Petersburg, Nov. 2, 1752; d. Vienna, Sept. 23, 1836. He was the Russian ambassador at Vienna from 1793 to 1809; from 1808 to 1816 he maintained the celebrated Razumovsky Quartet (1st violin, Schuppanzigh; 2nd violin, Razumovsky; viola, Weiss; cello, Lincke), later known as the Schuppanzigh Quartet, with Sina as 2nd violin. Razumovsky's name was immortalized through the dedication to him of Beethoven's 3 string quartets, op. 59, and (with Prince Lobkowitz) Fifth and Sixth Symphonies. He was a munificent and prodigal patron of art, but after the destruction by fire of his Vienna palace in 1815, he gave up the quartet, and disappeared from musical history.

Read, Daniel, American composer; b. Attleboro, Mass., Nov. 16, 1757; d. New Haven, Dec. 4, 1836. He worked on a farm as a youth; studied mechanics, and was employed as surveyor at 18; began to compose at 19. He served in the Continental army as a private; at 21 he settled at New Stratford, then going to New Haven. In 1782-83, he maintained a singing school on the North River. He also was a combmaker. At his death, he left a MS collection of some 400 tunes by him and other composers. —Publications: *The American Singing Book, or a New and Easy Guide to the art of Psalmody, devised for the use of Singing Schools in America* (New Haven, 1785; subsequent eds., 1786, 1792, 1793, 1795); *The American Musical Magazine* (with Amos Doolittle, New Haven, 12 numbers, May, 1786 to Sept., 1787); *Supplement to The American Singing Book* (New Haven, 1787); *The Columbian Harmonist,* in 3 books: no. 1 (New Haven, 1793), no. 2 (New Haven, 1794; 2nd ed., with numerous additions, 1798; 3rd ed., with further additions, 1801), no. 3 (New Haven, 1795); all 3 books in 1 vol. (New Haven, 1795; 2nd ed. completely revised, Dedham, 1804; 3rd ed., Boston, 1807; 4th ed., Boston, 1810). Shortly before his death he completed the compilation, *Musica Ecclesia, or Devotional Harmony,* but it remained unpublished. Many of his tunes—e.g., *Sherburne, Windham,* and *Lisbon*—achieved great popularity. —Cf. G. Hood, *Daniel Read,* in the 'Musical Herald' (N. Y., Oct., 1882); F. J. Metcalf, *American Composers and Compilers of Sacred Music* (N. Y., 1925); I. Lowens, *Daniel Read's World,* in 'Notes' (March, 1952). See also the 'Dictionary of American Biography.'

Read, Gardner, American composer; b. Evanston, Ill., Jan. 2, 1913. He studied theory at the Northwestern Univ. School of Music; conducting with Bakaleinikoff, and composition at the Eastman School of Music with Paul White, Bernard Rogers, and Howard Hanson (Mus. Bac., 1936; M.M., 1937); traveled in Europe on a Cromwell Fellowship (1938-39) for study with Pizzetti in Rome and Sibelius in Finland, the latter cut short owing to the imminence of war. Returning to the U. S.

he studied with Aaron Copland at the Berkshire Music Center; taught composition at the St. Louis Institute of Music (1941-43), at the Kansas City Cons. of Music (1943-45), and at the Cleveland Institute of Music (1945-48); appointed composer-in-residence and prof. of composition, Boston Univ. College of Music, in 1948. He was awarded a State Dept. grant in 1957 for lecturing and conducting in Mexico. A prolific composer (more than 100 op. numbers), he has written in every genre except opera. —Works: For orch.: *The Lotus-Eaters* (Interlochen, Mich., Aug. 12, 1932); *Sketches of the City,* symph. suite after Carl Sandburg (Rochester, April 18, 1934); *The Painted Desert* (Interlochen, Mich., July 28, 1935); symph. No. 1 (1936; N. Y., Nov. 4, 1937; awarded 1st prize of $1,000 in the American Composer's Contest sponsored by the N. Y. Philharmonic); *Fantasy,* for viola and orch. (Rochester, April 22, 1937); *Prelude and Toccata* (Rochester, April 29, 1937); *Suite* for string orch. (N. Y., Aug. 5, 1937); *Passacaglia and Fugue* (Chicago, June 30, 1938); *The Golden Journey to Samarkand,* for chorus, soloists, and orch. (1936-39); *Pan e Dafni* (1940); *American Circle* (Evanston, March 15, 1941); *First Overture* (Indianapolis, Nov. 6, 1943); symph. No. 2 (awarded 1st prize of $1,000, Paderewski Fund Competition, 1942; Boston, Nov. 26, 1943, composer conducting); *Night Flight,* tone-poem after Antoine de St.-Exupéry (Rochester, April 27, 1944); cello concerto (1945); *Threnody,* for flute and strings (Rochester, Oct. 21, 1946); *A Bell Overture* (Cleveland, Dec. 22, 1946); *Partita* for small orch. (Rochester, May 4, 1947); *Pennsylvaniana Suite* (Pittsburgh, Nov. 21, 1947); symph. No. 3 (1948); *Quiet Music for Strings* (Washington, May 9, 1948); *Dance of the Locomotives* (Boston, June 26, 1948); *Sound Piece,* for brass and percussion (Boston, May 11, 1949); *The Temptation of St. Anthony,* dance-symph. after Flaubert (Chicago, April 9, 1953); *Toccata Giocosa* (Louisville, March 13, 1954); *Vernal Equinox* (Brockton, Mass., April 12, 1955); symph. No. 4 (1958). Vocal works: *4 Nocturnes* for voice and orch. (Rochester, April 3, 1935); *From a Lute of Jade,* for voice and orch. (Rochester, March 15, 1937); *Songs for a Rainy Night,* for voice and orch. (Rochester, April 27, 1942); many songs and choruses. Chamber music: *Suite* for string quartet (1936); piano quintet (1945); *Sonata Brevis,* for violin and piano (1948); *Nine by Six* for wind sextet (1951); string quartet No. 1 (1957); *Sonoric Fantasia,* for celesta, harp, and harpsichord (1958). For organ: *Passacaglia and Fugue* (1937); *Suite for Organ* (co-winner, 1st prize of $1,000, Penn. College for Women, Pittsburgh, 1950); *8 Preludes on Old Southern Hymns* (1951). Piano music: *3 Satirical Sarcasms* (1941); *Driftwood Suite* (1943); *Dance of the Locomotives* (1944); *Sonata da Chiesa* (1948); *Touch Piece* (1949). He has publ. a valuable and unique reference work, *Thesaurus of Orchestral Devices* (N. Y., 1953).

Reading, John, English organist; d. Winchester, 1692. Lay-vicar of Lincoln Cathedral, 1667, and Master of the Choristers, 1670; organist of Winchester Cathedral, 1675-81; then of Winchester College, for which he composed the well-known song '*Dulce Domum*' (publ. in Hayes' 'Harmonia Wiccamica').

Reading, John, son of preceding; b. 1677; d. London, Sept. 2, 1764. Chorister of the Chapel Royal, under Blow; organist of Dulwich College, 1700-02; lay-vicar at Lincoln Cathedral 1702, and Master of the Choristers, 1703; later organist in several London churches. —Publications: *A Book of New Anthems* and *A Book of New Songs with Symphonies and a Thorough Bass fitted to the Harpsichord.*

Rebel, François, French composer; b. Paris, June 19, 1701; d. there, Nov. 7, 1775. He became an excellent violinist under the tutelage of his father, Jean-Féry Rebel. He was in charge of the '24 violins' of the King and master of the royal chamber-music. From 1757 to 1767 Rebel and his lifelong friend and collaborator, François Francœur, were directors of the Académie Royale de Musique (the Opéra). The operas composed jointly by Rebel and Francœur and produced at Paris include *Pirame et Thisbé* (Oct. 17, 1726) and *Scanderberg* (Oct. 27, 1735). —Cf. L. de La Laurencie, *Une Dynastie de musiciens aux XVII*[e] *et XVIII*[e] *siècles: Les Rebel,* in 'Sammelbände der Internationalen Musik-Gesellschaft' (vol. 7).

Rebello, João Lourenço (João Soares), Portuguese composer; b. Caminha, 1609; d. San Amaro, Nov. 16, 1661. He was maestro to King John IV of Portugal, who dedicated to Rebello his *Defensa de la música moderna* (1649). Psalms *a* 16, Magnificats, Lamentations, and Misereres by Rebello were publ. at Rome (1657).

Reber (rŭ-bär'), **Napoléon-Henri,** French composer; b. Mulhouse, Alsace, Oct. 21,

1807; d. Paris, Nov. 24, 1880. Pupil of Reicha and Le Sueur at the Paris Cons.; became prof. of harmony in 1851, succeeded Halévy as prof. of composition in 1861 (being succeeded in turn by Saint-Saëns in 1880), and was also inspector of the branch conservatories from 1871. —Works: ballet, *Le Diable amoureux* (1840); the comic operas *La Nuit de Noël* (1848), *Le Père Gaillard* (1852), *Les Papillottes de M. Benoist* (1853), and *Les Dames capitaines* (1857), all produced at the Opéra-Comique; also 4 symphonies; chamber music; piano pieces for 2 and 4 hands; 33 songs; vocalises for soprano or tenor (op. 16), etc.; and a *Traité d'harmonie* (1862, and several later eds.). —Cf. Saint-Saëns, *Notice sur H. Reber* (Paris, 1881).

Řebiček (r'zhā'-bĭ-chĕhk), **Josef,** Czech conductor and composer; b. Prague, Feb. 7, 1844; d. Berlin, March 24, 1904. He studied violin at the Prague Cons.; was violinist in the court orch. in Weimar; then played in theater orchestras in Prague and Wiesbaden; conducted opera in Warsaw, Budapest, etc.; from 1897 till 1903 was conductor of the Berlin Philharmonic, succeeding Franz Mannstädt. He wrote *Huldigungsfestklänge* (on old Dutch themes) for orch.; a symphony; a violin sonata; many pieces for violin.

Rebikov (rĕh'-bē-kŏhv), **Vladimir Ivanovitch,** Russian composer; b. Krasnoyarsk, Siberia, May 31, 1866; d. Yalta, Dec. 1, 1920. He studied at the Moscow Cons. with Klenovsky; then in Berlin and Vienna. He then went to Odessa, where his first opera, *In the Thunderstorm,* was produced in 1894. In 1898 he moved to Kishinev, Bessarabia, where he organized a branch of the Imperial Russian Musical Society. In 1901 he settled in Moscow, remaining there until 1919; he spent his last year of life in the Crimea. His early works (op. 1-9) are very much under the influence of Tchaikovsky; but beginning with op. 10 (*Esquisses* for piano) he made a decisive turn towards a modern style; he became particularly fond of the whole-tone scale and its concomitant, the augmented triad; claimed priority in this respect over Debussy and other European composers; his piano piece, *Les Démons s'amusent,* is based entirely on the whole-tone scale. He declared that music is a language of emotion, and therefore could not be confined to set forms, or to arbitrarily defined consonances. An entirely new departure is represented by his *Mélomimiques* (op. 11, 15, 17), short lyric pieces for piano, in which mimicry and suggestion are used in an Impressionistic manner. He also wrote several vocal 'melomimics' (op. 1, 16, 19, 20), 3 'rhythmo-declamations' for piano (op. 32), and 20 for voice and piano. In these compositions he abandoned cohesive form in favor of a free association of melodic and rhythmic phrases, scantily harmonized; prevalence of esthetic theories over musical substance made his experiments ephemeral. A melodious waltz from his children's opera, *The Christmas Tree,* is his most popular composition. —Works: the operas *In the Thunderstorm* (Odessa, Feb. 27, 1894) and *The Christmas Tree* (Moscow, Oct. 31, 1903); a musico-psychological pantomime, *Little Snow White* (Tiflis, 1909); a 2-act fairy opera, *Prince Charming;* scenic fables after Krylov: *The Grasshopper and the Ant, A Dinner with a Bear, The Ass and the Nightingale, The Funeral, The Liar* (Moscow, Dec. 27, 1903); several 'musico-psychological tableaux': *Slavery and Freedom, Songs of the Harp, The Nightmare,* etc.; numerous piano pieces (*Scènes bucoliques, Silhouettes, Dans la Forêt, Chansons blanches, Idylles, Les Danses, Les Démons s'amusent,* etc.); a suite for 4 hands; etc. He publ. numerous articles on musical esthetics, particularly relating to modern music; translated into Russian Gevaert's *Traité d'Instrumentation.* —Cf. M. Montagu-Nathan, *Contemporary Russian Composers* (N. Y., 1917); N. Nabokov, *Old Friends and New Music* (Boston, 1951; pp. 148-50).

Rebling, Gustav, German organist; b. Barby (Magdeburg), July 10, 1821; d. Magdeburg, Jan. 9, 1902. He was a pupil of Fr. Schneider at Dessau, 1836-39; then organist of the French church, Magdeburg, and teacher in the seminary in 1847; 1853, conductor of the cathedral choir, and singing teacher at the Gymnasium; 1856, 'Royal Music-Director'; 1858, organist of the Johanniskirche; retired in 1897. —Works: Psalms *a* 4-8; motets; pieces for organ and piano; choruses and songs; 2 cello sonatas; etc.

Rebner, Adolf, Austrian violinist; b. Vienna, Nov. 21, 1876. Pupil of Grün at the Cons. there, graduating in 1891 as winner of the 1st prize; continued his studies under Marsick in Paris. Settled in 1896 in Frankfurt, where he was for some years concertmaster at the opera, succeeded Heermann in 1904 as professor of violin at Hoch's Cons. He became especially renowned as leader of his own quartet; with it, he made successful tours of Germany, France, Spain, and England. In 1934 he left Germany and went to Vienna. —His son **Edward Wolfgang Rebner** (b. Frankfurt, Dec. 20, 1910), an excellent pianist and accompanist (toured with E. Feuermann), settled in the U. S. in 1939. He has written some chamber music and piano pieces.

Rechid, Djemal. See **Rey, Cemal Reshid.**

Redford, John, English organist, composer, and poet; d. London, 1547. He was one of the vicars-choral of St. Paul's Cathedral in London. Surviving in MS are a number of fantasias on plainsong melodies (2 of which are printed in Davison and Apel, *Historical Anthology of Music,* vol. I, Cambridge, Mass., 1946) and 3 motets. —Cf. C. F. Pfatteicher, *John Redford* (Kassel, 1934) and 'Grove's Dictionary' 5th ed.

Redhead, Richard, English composer of church music; b. Harrow, March 1, 1820; d. Hallingley, April 27, 1901. He served as organist in various churches in London; wrote much vocal music; edited the collections 'Cathedral and Church Choir Book,' 'Parochial Church Tune Book,' and 'The Universal Organist.'

Redlich, Hans Ferdinand, musicologist; b. Vienna, Feb. 11, 1903. He received his higher education at the universities of Vienna, Munich, and Frankfurt; *Dr. phil.,* Frankfurt, with the dissertation, *Das Problem des Stilwandels in Monteverdis Madrigalwerk* (publ. Leipzig, 1931); conducted opera in Charlottenburg-Berlin (1924-25) and at the Municipal Theater of Mainz (1925-29). In 1939 he went to England, settling at Letchworth (British subject, 1947). He was engaged as conductor at various provincial schools, and also in London; lectured at Cambridge Univ. (from 1942); was also active in radio work for the BBC, while continuing his main work, musicology; edited compositions by Monteverdi; composed a *Concerto grosso* (1927), *Hölderlin Trilogy* for tenor and orch. (1946), etc. In 1955 he was appointed lecturer at Edinburgh Univ. —Books: *Gustav Mahler: eine Erkenntnis* (1919); *Claudio Monteverdi, I: Das Madrigalwerk* (1932); *Claudio Monteverdi: Leben und Werk* (Olten, 1949; in English, London, 1952); *Bruckner and Mahler* (N. Y., 1955); *Alban Berg: The Man and His Music* (London, 1957).

Redman, Harry Newton, American organist and composer; b. Mount Carmel, Ill., Dec. 26, 1869. He studied organ and composition with Chadwick; from 1897 taught at the New England Cons., Boston; publ. 2 string quartets, 2 violin sonatas, an *Octave Method* and studies for piano; 2 albums of songs, etc. About 1925 he abandoned music and devoted himself chiefly to painting; exhibited in Boston as late as 1957.

Rée (rā), **Anton,** Danish pianist and pedagogue; b. Aarhus, Oct. 5, 1820; d. Copenhagen, Dec. 20, 1886. He studied with Karl Krebs in Hamburg; had a few lessons with Chopin in Paris. In 1842 he returned to Denmark and settled in Copenhagen as a teacher. He publ. *Musikhistoriske Momenter* and a book of exercises, *Bidrag til Klavierspillets Teknik; Danses caractéristiques* for piano; etc.

Rée, Louis, pianist; cousin of Anton Rée; b. Edinburgh, Oct. 15, 1861; d. Vienna, Feb. 28, 1939. He was a pupil of Leschetizky in Vienna; settled there as a teacher; gave duo-piano concerts with his wife, Susanne Pilz-Rée (1865-1937). He wrote a concerto for 2 pianos (1925); publ. transcriptions for 2 pianos and various other works.

Reed, Herbert Owen, American composer and teacher; b. Odessa, Mo., June 17, 1910. He studied at the Univ. of Missouri and Louisiana State Univ.; subsequently entered the Eastman School of Music, under Howard Hanson and Bernard Rogers (Ph. D., 1939). In 1939 he was appointed instructor at Michigan State Univ., and later became chairman of the theory dept. there. —Works: a 'folk opera,' *Michigan Dream* (1955); ballet-pantomime, *The Masque of the Red Death,* after Poe (1936); symph poem, *Evangeline* (Rochester, March 30, 1938); symph. No. 1 (Rochester, April 27, 1939); *Overture* (Rochester, Oct. 27, 1941); *Spiritual,* for band (1947); a cello concerto (1949); a string quartet (1937); *Scherzo* for clarinet and piano (1947); *La Fiesta Mexicana,* a folk-song symph. for concert band (1956); several piano pieces; songs and choruses. He publ. *A Workbook in the Fundamentals of Music* (N. Y., 1946); *Basic Music* (N. Y., 1954).

Reed, Thomas German, versatile English musician; b. Bristol, June 27, 1817; d. London, March 21, 1888. Under the guidance of his father, he appeared in Bath as a child of 10 in the various capacities of singer, pianist, and actor. After the family moved to London (1832), he was active as teacher and arranger. In 1838 he succeeded his father as conductor of the Haymarket Theatre, remaining at that post until 1851. In 1844 he married Priscilla Horton (b. Birmingham, Jan. 1, 1818; d. Bexley Heath, March 18, 1895), an actress and a singer. Together they started the celebrated series 'Mr. and Mrs. German Reed's Entertainment' (1855), which included productions of operettas by Offenbach, Balfe, Clay, Sullivan, etc. These entertainments enjoyed great success, and were continued by his son Alfred German Reed, who died in London on March 10, 1895, a few days before the death of his mother.

Reed, William Henry, English violinist and composer; b. Frome, July 29, 1876; d. Dumfries, July 2, 1942. He studied at the Royal Academy of Music in London; was a violinist in the London Symph. Orch. at its foundation in 1904; then taught violin at the Royal College of Music; was concertmaster of the London Symph. Orch. from 1912 to 1935. He was a close friend of Elgar, and publ. a book, *Elgar as I Knew Him* (1936). His works include the orchestral sketches *The Lincoln Imp* (Hereford Festival, 1921) and *Aesop's Fables* (Hereford Festival, 1924); a violin concerto; *Rhapsody* for violin and orch.; 5 string quartets; violin pieces; songs; etc.

Reed, William Leonard, English composer; b. London, Oct. 16, 1910. He studied at the Royal College of Music in London with Herbert Howells; received the degrees of M. A. and D. Mus. at Oxford. He toured in the U. S. in 1947. —Works for orch.: *Recitative and Dance* (1934); *Jig* (1935), *Pantomime* (1935), *Scherzo* (1937), *Hornpipe* (1939), *Doctor Johnson's Suite,* for strings (1944), *Suite* for clarinet and strings (1942); various pieces for piano quintet, string quartet, and other chamber groups; suites for violin and piano, and viola and piano; piano pieces; songs.

Reese, Gustave, eminent American musicologist; b. New York, Nov. 29, 1899; studied at N. Y. Univ. (LL.B. and Mus. Bac.), where he has taught, with varying titles, since 1927 (except in the season 1933-34 and from the season 1937-38 to that of 1944-45), full prof., 1955; from 1933 to 1944 associate editor, 1944-45 editor, of the 'Mus. Quarterly'; 1935, co-founder of the American Musicological Society (secretary, 1935-46; vice-president, 1946-50; president, 1950-52); 1954, was one of the organizers of the Renaissance Society of America; 1940-45, head of publication dept., G. Schirmer, Inc.; 1945-55, director of publication of Carl Fischer, Inc., with which firm he is still (1958) connected in an advisory capacity. Mus. Doc. (*hon.c.*), Chicago Musical College, 1947; guest teacher at Univ. of Southern California (1953), Univ. of Michigan (1951, 1952), Harvard Univ. (1958). Author of *Music in the Middle Ages* (N. Y., 1940); *Music in the Renaissance* (N. Y., 1954); *Fourscore Classics of Music Literature* (N. Y., 1957); publ. valuable articles in the 'Mus. Quarterly,' 'Notes,' 'Journal of the American Musicological Society,' etc.; contributor to the 4th ed. of Grove's 'Dictionary of Music and Musicians' and Thompson's 'International Cyclopedia of Music and Musicians.'

Reeve, William, English composer; b. London, 1757; d. there, June 22, 1815. Pupil of Richardson; organist at Totness, Devon, 1781-83; returned to London, and composed operettas, pantomimes, and incidental music for plays, for Astley's Circus and Covent Garden (1791); in 1792, organist of St. Martin's, Ludgate Hill; from 1802, part-proprietor of Sadler's Wells Theatre. Besides music to some 40 plays, he composed glees and songs; the song 'I am a friar in orders grey,' in the play of *Merry Sherwood,* was very popular.

Reeves, John Sims, English tenor; b. Shooter's Hill, Kent, probably Sept. 26 (baptized Oct. 25), 1818; d. Worthing, London, Oct. 25, 1900. Learned to play several instruments; had lessons with J. B. Cramer (piano) and W. H. Callcott (harmony). Début (as a baritone) at Newcastle-on-Tyne, in the role of Rodolfo (*Sonnambula*), in 1839. Studied further and sang minor tenor parts at Drury Lane, 1842-3; studied in Paris under Bordogni, and in Milan under Mazzucato, appearing at La Scala, 1846, as Edgardo (*Lucia*). He retired in 1891, but reappeared in concerts in 1893, and even made a successful tour in South Africa in 1896. Publ. *Sims Reeves; His Life and Recollections Written by Himself* (London, 1888); *My Jubilee, or Fifty Years of Artistic Life* (London, 1889); *Sims Reeves On the Art of Singing* (1900). —Cf. H. S. Edwards, *The Life and Artistic Career of Sims Reeves* (London, 1881); Ch. E. Pearce, *Sims Reeves: Fifty Years of Music in England* (1924). See also 'Modern English Biography' vol. VI.

Refardt, Edgar, eminent Swiss musicologist and bibliographer; b. Basel, Aug. 8,

1877. He studied law; obtained the degree of *Dr. jur.;* in 1915 was appointed librarian and cataloguer of the musical collection of the Municipal Library of Basel; publ. valuable bibliographical works on Swiss music; also essays on various literary and musical subjects. —Publications: *Verzeichnis der Aufsätze zur Musik in den nichtmusikalischen Zeitschriften der Universitätsbibliothek Basel . . .* (Leipzig, 1925); *Historisch-biographisches Musikerlexikon der Schweiz* (1928); *Hans Huber: Leben und Werk eines Schweizer Musikers* (1944; definitive biography of Huber; supersedes Refardt's previous writings on Huber); *Johannes Brahms, Anton Bruckner, Hugo Wolf: drei Wiener Meister des 19. Jahrhunderts* (1949); *Musik in der Schweiz* (collection of articles; 1952); *Thematischer Katalog der Instrumentalmusik des 18. Jahrhunderts in den Handschriften der Universitätsbibliothek Basel,* ed. by Hans Zehntner (Basel, 1957); etc.

Refice (rĕh-fē'-chĕh), **Licinio,** Italian composer of sacred music; b. Patrica, near Rome, Feb. 12, 1883; d. Rio de Janeiro, Sept. 11, 1954 (while conducting his mystery play, *Santa Cecilia*). He studied with Falchi and Renzi at Santa Cecilia in Rome; in 1910 became teacher of church music at the Scuola Pontifica Superiore di Musica Sacra. In 1947 he toured the U. S. as director of the Roman Singers of Sacred Music (99 concerts). His works include the operas *Cecilia* (Rome, 1934) and *Margherita da Cortona* (Milan, 1938); the cantatas *La Vedova di Naim* (1912), *Maria Magdalena* (Rome, 1917), and *Il Martirio di S. Agnese* (Rome, 1919); *Stabat Mater* (1917); *Te Deum* (1918); *Missa Jubilaei* (1925), *Missa Italica* (1944); the choral symph. poems *Dantis poetae transitus* (Ravenna, 1921) and *Il Trittico francescano* (Assisi, 1925); a Requiem; the sacred play ('azione sacra') *Santa Cecilia* (Rome, Feb. 15, 1934); the oratorios *Cananea* and *La Samaritana* (very successful); hymns; motets; etc.

Regamey, Constantin, composer; b. Kiev, Jan. 28, 1907. He studied at the Warsaw Cons. (philology), and taught Sanskrit at the Univ. of Warsaw; edited the periodical 'Muzyka polska' (1937-39); in 1944 settled in Lausanne as prof. of Slavonic languages at the Univ. As a composer, he adopted the advanced technique of atonal music. —Works: *Chansons persanes,* for baritone and orch. (1943); quintet for violin, clarinet, bassoon, cello, and piano (1944); other chamber music. —Cf. H. Jaccard, *Initiation à la musique contemporaine: trois compositeurs vaudois: Raffaele d'Alessandro, Constantin Regamey, Julien-François Zbinden* (Lausanne, 1955).

Reger (rā'-gĕr), **Max,** eminent German composer; b. Brand, Bavaria, March 19, 1873; d. Leipzig, May 11, 1916. In 1874 his father, a school teacher and good organist (d. 1905 in Munich), removed to Weiden, where Reger attended the Realschule. Although he was intended for the schoolmaster's career, he received thorough instruction on the piano and harmonium from his father, and on the organ and in theory from Lindner. At an early age he began to write piano pieces and chamber music, and after hearing *Die Meistersinger* and *Parsifal* in Bayreuth (1888) he gave expression to the emotions created in him by those masterpieces in an ambitious symphonic poem, *Héroïde funèbre* (score lost). In 1889 he passed the entrance examination for the teachers' seminary. But by that time music had taken such complete possession of him that he submitted a number of MSS to H. Riemann, who immediately recognized the young man's unusual talent. Accordingly, Reger became Riemann's pupil at the Sondershausen Cons. in April, 1890, and in 1891 followed him to the Wiesbaden Cons., where he continued his studies till 1895, and also taught piano and organ (till 1896). Having served a year in the army, he settled in Weiden as composer, writing the works up to about op. 50. However, he did not attract general attention until 1901, when he removed to Munich, whence he undertook pianistic tours through Germany, Austria, and Switzerland. During 1905-06 he was prof. of counterpoint at the Königliche Akademie der Tonkunst, and conductor of the 'Porges'scher Gesangsverein'; in 1907 he was called to Leipzig as Musikdirektor at the Univ. (also conductor of the Univ. chorus 'St. Pauli') and prof. of composition at the Cons.; the former post he resigned in 1908, but the latter he retained till his death; 1911-15, Hofkapellmeister in Meiningen; then in Jena and Leipzig. He died suddenly of paralysis of the heart. In 1908 he was made *Dr. phil.* (*hon. c.,* Univ. of Jena); in 1911 Hofrat, and in 1913 General-Musikdirector. —Reger won the greatest number of admirers through his remarkably fine works for organ. A German Max Reger Society was founded in 1920, with branches in many cities; another society was established in Austria. The Max Reger Archives (containing most of his MSS) are at Weimar. A complete ed. of Reger's works was begun in 1954 by Breitkopf & Härtel.

WORKS: For orch.: Op. 90, *Sinfonietta;* op. 95, *Serenade;* op. 100, *Variationen und Fuge über ein lustiges Thema von J. A. Hiller;* op. 108, *Symphonischer Prolog zu einer Tragödie;* op. 120, *Eine Lustspielouvertüre;* op. 123, *Konzert im alten Stil;* op. 125, *Romantische Suite;* op. 128, *Vier Tondichtungen nach Böcklin;* op. 130, *Ballet-Suite;* op. 132, *Variationen und Fuge über ein Thema von Mozart;* op. 140, *Eine vaterländische Ouvertüre;* op. 50, *Zwei Romanzen* for violin and orch.; op. 101, violin concerto in A; op. 114, piano concerto in F minor. —Vocal works with orch.: Op. 21, *Hymne an den Gesang* (men's chorus); op. 71, *Gesang der Verklärten* (mixed chorus *a* 5); op. 106, Psalm 100 (mixed chorus and organ); op. 112, *Die Nonnen* (mixed chorus and organ); op. 119, *Die Weihe der Nacht* (alto solo and mixed chorus); op. 124, *An die Hoffnung* (also solo); op. 126, *Römischer Triumphgesang* (men's chorus). —Chamber music: Op. 118, string sextet in F; op. 64, piano quintet in C minor; op. 113, piano quartet in D minor; 5 string quartets: op. 54 (G minor and A), op. 74 (D minor), op. 109 (E♭), op. 121 (F♯ minor); 2 piano trios: op. 2 (B minor, for piano, violin, and viola), op. 102 (E minor); op. 77a, *Serenade* for flute, violin, and viola; op. 77b, trio for flute, violin, and viola; op. 103a, Suite for flute and piano (A minor); 9 violin sonatas: op. 1 (D minor), op. 3 (D), op. 41 (A), op. 72 (C), op. 84 (F♯ minor), op. 103b (*Zwei kleine Sonaten,* D minor and A), op. 122 (E minor), op. 139 (C minor); op. 93, *Suite im alten Stil* for violin and piano; 4 cello sonatas: op. 5 (F minor), op. 28 (G minor), op. 78 (F), op. 116 (A minor); 3 clarinet sonatas: op. 49 (A and F minor), op. 107 (B♭); op. 42, 4 sonatas for violin solo; op. 117, *Präludien und Fugen* for violin solo; op. 131, 3 suites for cello solo.—For organ: Op. 16, Suite in E minor; op. 27, Fantasy on *Ein' feste Burg;* op. 29, *Fantasie und Fuge* in C minor; op. 30, Fantasy on *Freu dich sehr, o meine Seele;* op. 33, Sonata in F♯ minor; op. 40, 2 Fantasies on *Wie schön leucht' uns der Morgenstern* and *Straf mich nicht in deinem Zorn;* op. 46, *Fantasie und Fuge über* BACH; op. 52, 3 Fantasies on *Alle Menschen müssen sterben, Wachet auf! ruft uns die Stimme,* and *Hallelujah! Gott zu loben;* op. 57, *Symphonische Phantasie und Fuge;* op. 60, Sonata in D minor; op. 67, 52 *Vorspiele* to the chorales in general use; op. 73, *Variationen und Fuge über ein Originalthema;* op. 92, Suite in G minor; op. 127, *Introduktion, Passacaglia und Fuge* in E minor; numerous minor pieces: op. 7, 56, 59, 63, 65, 69, 79, 80, 85, 129. —For piano: 4 hands: op. 9, *Walzer-Capricen;* op. 10, *Deutsche Tänze;* op. 22, *Sechs Walzer;* op. 34, *Cinq pièces pittoresques;* op. 58, *Sechs Burlesken;* op. 94, *Sechs Stücke;* op. 96, *Introduktion, Passacaglia und Fuge;* for piano solo: op. 17, *Aus der Jugendzeit* (20 pieces); op. 18, *Improvisationen* (8 pieces); op. 20, *Fünf Humoresken;* op. 24, *Six Morceaux;* op. 25, *Aquarellen;* op. 26, *Sieben Fantasiestücke;* op. 32, *Sieben Charackterstücke;* op. 36, *Bunte Blätter* (9 pieces); op. 44, *Zehn kleine Vortragsstücke;* op. 45, *Sechs Intermezzi;* op. 53, *Silhouetten* (7 pieces); op. 81, *Variationen und Fuge über ein Thema von Bach;* op. 82, *Aus meinem Tagebuche* (22 pieces); op. 89, 2 *Sonatinen* (F, A); op. 99, *Sechs Präludien und Fugen;* op. 115, *Episoden* (2 books); op. 134, *Variationen und Fuge über ein Thema von Ph. Telemann;* for 2 pianos: op. 86, *Variatonen und Fuge über ein Thema von Beethoven.*—Mixed choruses a cappella, op. 6, 39 (*a* 6); men's choruses do., op. 38, 83; women's choruses do., op. 111b; duets, op. 14, 111a; about 300 songs, op. 3, 4, 5, 12, 15, 23, 31, 35, 37, 43, 48, 51, 55, 62, 66, 68, 70, 75, 76 (60 *Schlichte Weisen*), 88, 97, 98, 104.—Sacred music: Op. 19, *Zwei geistliche Gesänge;* op. 61, *Leicht ausführbare Kompositionen zum gottesdienstlichen Gebrauch in der katholischen Kirche* (38 motets for mixed voices); op. 105, *Zwei geistliche Lieder;* op. 110, Motets for mixed chorus a cappella (*a* 5); op. 137, *Zwölf geistliche Lieder.*—Without opus number: *Der evangelische Kirchenchor* (I. 40 mixed choruses for all festivals [4 series]; II, Cantata *O wie selig* for mixed chorus, string orch., and organ; III, Cantata, *O Haupt voll Blut und Wunden* (for alto and tenor soli, mixed chorus, violin and oboe soli, and organ). Men's and mixed choruses, and songs (sacred and secular).—For piano: 2 books of canons in all major and minor keys; 4 *Spezialstudien für die linke Hand allein;* minor pieces.—Transcriptions: For organ: *Schule des Triospiels* (with K. Straube; Bach's 2-part Inventions); 15 clavier compositions of Bach. For piano 4 hands: Bach's Prelude and Fugue (D), Toccata and Fugue (D minor); Fantasia (G), Prelude and Fugue (G), Prelude and Fugue (A minor), Fantasia and Fugue (G minor), Toccata and Fugue (E), Prelude and Fugue (E minor); Bach's orchestral Suites and Brandenburg Concertos.—For piano solo: H. Wolf's overture to *Penthesilea* and *Italienische Serenade;* d'Albert's overture to *Esther;* songs of Jensen, Brahms, H. Wolf, and R. Strauss.—Arrangements: 5 *Spezialstudien* (Chopin); 12 madrigals for men's chorus (Hassler, Lully, Donati, Morley, Praetorius, Meyland); 6 madrigals for mixed chorus (Gastoldi, Morley, Lully).—He also wrote *Beiträge zur Modulationslehre* (1903).—BIBLIOGRAPHY: R. Braungart, *Max Reger,* in vol. II of 'Monographien moderner Musiker' (Leipzig, 1907); G. Robert-Tornow, *Max Reger und Karl Straube* (Göttingen, 1907); V. Junk, *Max Reger als Orchesterkomponist* (Leipzig, 1910); W. Fischer, *Über die Wiedergabe der Orgelkompositionen Max Regers* (Cologne, 1911); M. Hehemann, *Max Reger. Eine Studie über moderne Musik* (Munich, 1911; 2nd ed., 1917); F. Rabich, *Regerlieder: Eine Studie* (Langensalza, 1914); H. Grace, *The Late Max Reger as Organ Composer,* in the 'Mus. Times' (June, 1916); H. Poppen, *Max Reger* (1917); E. Isler, *Max Reger* (Zürich, 1917); R. Würz, ed., *Max Reger: eine Sammlung von Studien* (4 vols.; Munich, 1920-23); H. Unger, *Reger* (1921 and 1924); K. Hasse, *Max Reger* (1921); E. Segnitz, *Max Reger* (1922); E. Brennecke, *The Two Reger-Legends,* in the 'Mus. Quarterly' (July, 1922); A. Lindner (his teacher), *Max Reger, Ein Bild seines Jugendlebens und künstlerischen Werdens* (Stuttgart, 1922; 3rd ed., 1938); G. Bagier, *Reger* (Stuttgart, 1923); A. Spemann, *Max Reger-Brevier* (1923); H. Unger, *Max Reger* (Bielefeld, 1924); E. Gatscher, *Die Fugentechnik Regers in ihrer Entwicklung* (Stuttgart, 1925); S. Kallenberg, *Max Reger* (1929); E. C. Ebert-Stockinger, *Max Reger* (1930); G. R. Dejmek, *Der Variationszyklus bei Max Reger* (Essen, 1930); P. Coenen, *Max Regers Variationsschaffen* (Berlin, 1935); R. Huesgen, *Der junge Max Reger und seine Orgelwerke* (Schramberg, 1935); H. E. Rahner, *Regers Choralfantasien für die Orgel* (Kassel, 1936); E. Brand, *Max Reger im Elternhaus* (Munich, 1938); F. W. Stein, *Max Reger* (Potsdam, 1939); F. W. Stein, *Max Reger, Sein Leben in Bildern* (1941); E. H. Müller von Asow, *Max Reger und seine Welt* (Berlin, 1945); K. Hasse, *Max Reger: Entwicklungsgang eines deutschen Meisters* (Leipzig, 1946); H. M. Poppen, *Max Reger* (Leipzig, 1947); R. Braungart, *Freund Reger; Erinnerungen* (Regensburg, 1949); A. Kalkoff, *Das Orgelschaffen Max Regers* (Kassel, 1950); G. Wehmeyer, *Max Reger als Liederkomponist* (Regensburg, 1955); E. Otto, *Max Reger: Sinnbild einer Epoche* (Wiesbaden, 1957). A collection of articles about Reger (*Max Reger. Festschrift*) was publ. at Leipzig in 1953; see also the special Reger issue of the 'Zeitschrift für Musik' (March, 1953). His widow, Elsa Reger, wrote *Mein Leben für und mit Max Reger* (1930). Reger's letters were publ. by Else von Hase-Koehler under the title *Briefe eines deutschen Meisters* (1928). W. Altmann publ. a complete catalogue of Reger's works in 1917 (2nd ed., 1926); Fritz Stein ed. a Thematic Catalogue (Leipzig, 1934).

Regis, Johannes, noted composer and organist; b. in Flanders; d. Soignies, May 16, 1502. He was 'magister puerorum' at the Cathedral of Antwerp (1460-64); then was clerk to Dufay at Cambrai, and finally canon at Soignies. He wrote 2 Masses on the melody of *L'Homme armé;* a 5-part motet, *O admirabile commercium,* and other choral pieces. His collected works were publ. in 2 vols. by the American Institute of Musicology in Rome (1956), under the editorship of C. W. H. Lindenburg. —Cf. C. W. H. Lindenburg, *Het Leven en de werken van Johannes Regis* (Amsterdam, 1938).

Regli (rĕh-lyē), **Francesco**, Italian lexicographer; b. Milan, 1802; d. Turin, March 10, 1866. He founded a theatrical publication, 'Il Pirata,' in 1835; publ. a *Dizionario biografico dei più celebri poeti ed artisti melodrammatici che fiorirono in Italia dal 1800 al 1860* (Turin, 1860); *Storia del violino in Piemonte* (Turin, 1863); *Elogio a G. Rossini* (Turin, 1864); *Elogio a Felice Romani* (Turin, 1865).

Régnal, Frédéric. Pen-name of **Frédéric d'Erlanger.**

Regnart (or **Regnard**) (rĕh-ñahr'), **Jacob,** one of five brothers active as musicians; b. probably in or near Douai, c. 1540; d. Prague, Oct. 16, 1599. He was trained as a chorister and alumnus at the Imperial Chapel in Vienna, and was a tenor singer there from 1564; in 1568-70 he was in Italy; from 1576 second Kapellmeister at the Imperial Court in Prague; from 1582-95 Vice Kapellmeister to the Archduke Ferdinand of Innsbruck, and then in Prague again as Vice-Kapellmeister. Publ. (1574-1611) a great number of Masses, motets, canzone, villanelle, and German songs (many books of these last went through 7 editions; in a collection of 1590 are some songs by his brothers, Franz, Karl, and Pascasius). In the 'Monatshefte für Musikgeschichte' (vol. XII, p. 97) is a full list of his works. Reprints have been publ. by L. Lechner (villanelle), R. Eitner (do., in 'Publikation älterer . . . Musikwerke,' vol. 19), H. Osthoff (5-voiced German songs), A. Schering in *Geschichte der Musik in Beispielen* (No. 139), A. Einstein (a madrigal), etc.—Cf. H. Osthoff, *Die Niederländer und das deutsche Lied* (Berlin, 1938, pp. 343-422).

Rehberg, Walter, Swiss pianist and writer; b. Geneva, May 14, 1900; d. Zürich, Oct. 22, 1957. He studied with his father, Willy Rehberg (1863-1937); then in Berlin with Ernst Toch and Eugen d'Albert; began a career as pianist; in 1934 appointed prof. at the Music Academy in Zürich. Publ. (with his wife Paula Rehberg) popular biographies of Brahms (1944), Schubert (1946), Chopin (1949), and Schumann (1954).

Reich, Willi, Austrian writer on music; b. Vienna, May 27, 1898. He studied at the Univ. of Vienna; Ph. D. (1934) with the dissertation *Padre Martini als Theoretiker und Lehrer;* also studied privately with Alban Berg; ed. a modern music magazine, '23.' In 1938 he settled in Switzerland; in 1948, became music critic of the 'Neue Zürcher Zeitung.' —Books: *Alban Berg* (Vienna, 1937; basic biography); *Bekenntnis zu Mozart* (Lucerne, 1945); *Joseph Haydn* (Lucerne, 1946); *Hugo Wolf-Rhapsodie* (Zürich, 1947); *Richard Wagner* (Olten, 1948); *Anton Bruckner: ein Bild seiner Persönlichkeit* (Basel, 1953).

Reicha, Anton, Czech composer; b. Prague, Feb. 26, 1770; d. Paris, May 28, 1836. Nephew and pupil of Joseph Reicha (*recte* Rejcha; composer and violinist, leader and later Kapellmeister, of the Electoral orch. at Bonn). From 1788, flutist in the Bonn orch., in which Beethoven was a viola-player; 1794-99, piano teacher in Hamburg, writing an opera, and going to Paris in hopes of producing it; but had to content himself with the successful performance of two symphonies. From 1801-08 he lived in Vienna, intimate with Beethoven, and associating with Haydn, Albrechtsberger, and Salieri. After the French invasion he went to Paris; brought out the moderately successful comic operas *Cagliostro* (1810), *Natalie* (1816), and *Sapho* (Dec. 16, 1822); but gained a high reputation as a theorist and teacher (some of his pupils were Liszt, Elwart, Gounod, Lefebvre, and Dancla), also as an instrumental composer. Among his best works are 4 sets of 6 woodwind quintets each (op. 8, 91, 99, 100). In 1818 he succeeded Méhul as prof. of counterpoint and fugue at the Cons.; was naturalized in 1829; and succeeded to Boieldieu's chair in the Institute in 1835.—Writings: *Études ou théories pour le pianoforte, dirigées d'une manière nouvelle* (1800); *Traité de mélodie, abstraction faite de ses rapports avec l'harmonie* (1814; 2nd ed., 1832); *Cours de composition musicale . . .* (1818); *Traité de haute composition musicale* (1824, 1826; 2 vols.; edited 1834 by Czerny together with the *Cours de composition musicale* in German as *Vollständiges Lehrbuch . . .*, 4 vols.); *Art du compositeur dramatique . . .* (1833); *Petit traité d'harmonie pratique* (n. d).—Cf. J. A. Delaire, *Notice sur Reicha* (Paris, 1837); E. Bücken, *Anton Reicha; sein Leben und Kompositionen* (Munich, 1912) and *Beethoven und A. Reicha,* in 'Die Musik' (March, 1913); A. Hnilička, *Portraite* (Prague, 1922); J. G. Prod'homme, *From the Unpublished Autobiography of A. Reicha,* in the 'Mus. Quarterly' (July, 1936); M. Emmanuel, *A. Reicha* (Paris, 1937).

Reichardt, Johann Friedrich, German composer and writer; born Königsberg, Nov. 25, 1752; d. Giebichenstein, near Halle, June 27, 1814. A pupil of C. G. Richter (piano and composition) and Veichtner (violin), he later studied philosophy at the Univs. of Königsberg and Leipzig; in 1775 obtained the post of Kapellmeister to Frederick the Great. He founded (1783) the 'Concerts spirituels' for the performance of new works, for which he wrote short analytical programs. Dismissed in 1794 because of his sympathy with the French Revolution, Reichardt lived in Altona till 1797; was then appointed inspector of the salt works at Giebichenstein. The French invasion drove him to Königsberg in 1806, and on Jerome Napoleon's threat to confiscate his property Reichardt joined him at Kassel, and became his court conductor. On account of disagreements with the authorities, Reichardt was soon granted leave of absence, which he extended by visiting Vienna to produce his operas and Singspiele; the trip was unsuccessful, and he returned to Giebichenstein, where he remained until his death.—For Berlin and Potsdam Reichardt composed numerous Italian and German operas, incidental music to plays, and German Singspiele, the latter exercising considerable influence on the development of German opera. As a song-composer (cf. Lindner, *Geschichte des deutschen Liedes*) he ranks high (he set about 60 of Goethe's lyrics to music); his instrumental music includes 7 symphonies, 14 piano concertos, 2 piano quartets, 6 string trios, a violin concerto, 11 violin sonatas, 12 piano sonatas, etc. An extremely diligent writer, he edited a number of musical periodicals; and publ.

the books *Über die deutsche komische Oper* (1774), *Über die Pflichten des Ripienviolinisten* (1776), *Briefe eines aufmerksamen Reisenden, die Musik betreffend* (2 parts; 1774, 1776), *Schreiben über die Berlinische Musik* (1775), *Vertraute Briefe aus Paris* (1804, 1805; 3 parts), *Vertraute Briefe, geschrieben auf einer Reise nach Wien* (2 vols.; 1810). Autobiography in the 'Berlinische musikalische Zeitung' (1805; Nos. 55-89).—His wife **Juliane** (*née* **Benda;** b. Berlin, 1752; d. there, May 9, 1783) was a fine pianist, who also publ. a number of songs.—Cf. H. M. Schletterer, *J. F. Reichardt, Sein Leben und seine musikalische Tätigkeit* (Augsburg, 1865; only vol. I publ.); C. Lange, *J. F. Reichardt* (Halle, 1902); W. Pauli, *J. F. Reichardt, Sein Leben und seine Stellung in der Geschichte des deutschen Liedes* (Berlin, 1902); M. Faller, *Reichardt und die Anfänge der musikalischer Journalistik* (Kassel, 1929); P. Sieber, *Reichardt als Musikästhetiker* (Strasbourg, 1930); H. Dennerlein, *Reichardt und seine Klavierwerke* (Münster, 1930); J. Müller-Blattau, *Musik zur Goethezeit,* in 'Euphorion' (1930); F. Flössner, *Beiträge zur Reichardt-Forschung* (Frankfurt, 1933); E. Neuss, *Das Giebichensteiner Dichterparadies; J. F. Reichardt und die Herberge der Romantik* (Halle, 1949).

Reichardt, Luise, daughter of the preceding; b. Berlin, April 11, 1779; d. Hamburg, Nov. 17, 1826. She composed a number of beautiful songs, of which a selection was publ. by G. Rheinhardt (Munich, 1922).—Cf. M. G. W. Brandt, *Leben der Luise Reichardt* (Karlsruhe, 1858).

Reichel, Friedrich, German composer; b. Oberoderwitz, Jan. 27, 1833; d. Dresden, Dec. 29, 1889. He studied with Wieck and Rietz in Dresden. Chief among his 32 publ. works is a *Frühlingssymphonie;* he also wrote an operetta, *Die geängsteten Diplomaten;* part-songs for men's voices; and some motets.

Reicher-Kindermann, Hedwig, German dramatic soprano; b. Munich, July 15, 1853; d. Trieste, June 2, 1883. Daughter of the baritone A. Kindermann; sang in the Court Theater, then in the Gärtnerplatz Theater at Munich; later at Hamburg; from 1880-82 at Leipzig; then in A. Neumann's Wagner troupe. She married the opera singer Reicher.—Cf. A. Neumann, *Erinnerungen an R. Wagner* (Leipzig, 1907; in English, N. Y., 1908).

Reichert, Arno Julius, German writer on music; b. Dresden, May 31, 1866; d. there, Feb. 10, 1933. After studying at the Dresden Cons. he was appointed teacher of music at the Freimaurer-Institut, Dresden; 1894-1904, at R. L. Schneider's Musikschule; from 1904 head of the music division of the Dresden Royal Library. He arranged about 450 folksongs for men's and mixed chorus; publ. *50 Jahre Sinfonie-Konzerte* (a record of the works produced in Dresden from 1858-1908) and *Die Original-Musik-Handschriften der sächsischen Landesbibliothek* (Leipzig, 1923).

Reichert, Johannes, German conductor and composer; b. Dresden, June 19, 1876; d. Teplitz, Feb. 15, 1942. Pupil of Draeseke (1893), and of Nicodé and Buchmayer (1894-98). From 1896-1900, conductor of the orch. class at the Dresden Musikschule; 1902-06, also répétiteur at the court theater; founded in 1899 the 'Volkssingakademie' (a mixed chorus recruited exclusively from the working classes); 1905-13, private teacher of the crown prince of Saxony; 1906-22, municipal Musikdirektor in Teplitz-Schönau, then living in retirement in Teplitz. —He arranged Handel's *Samson* and *Belshazzar.*

Reichmann, Theodor, German baritone; b. Rostock, March 15, 1849; d. Marbach, on Lake Constance, May 22, 1903. Pupil of Mantius and Elsler (Berlin), Ress (Prague), and Lamperti (Milan). After singing in various theaters, he was at the Court Opera, Vienna (1882-89); in 1882 he created the role of Amfortas at Bayreuth. Sang in German opera at the Metropolitan Opera House, 1889-91; made extended tours; and was re-engaged at Vienna in 1893.

Reichwein, Leopold, Austrian conductor; b. Breslau, May 16, 1878; d. (suicide) Vienna, April 8, 1945. He was theater conductor in Breslau, Mannheim, and Karlsruhe; then on the staff of the Vienna Opera (1913-21); music director of the Gesellschaft der Musikfreunde in Vienna (1921-26); music director in Bochum (1926-38); returned to Vienna in 1938; conducted at the State Opera, and taught conducting at the Vienna Academy. He committed suicide at the end of the war, when he was accused of Nazi affiliations. He was also a composer; wrote the operas *Vasantasena* (Breslau, 1903) and *Die Liebenden von Kandahar* (Breslau, 1907); incidental music to Goethe's *Faust;* songs.

Reid, General **John,** b. Straloch, Perthshire, Feb. 13, 1721; d. London, Feb. 6, 1807. A musical amateur, he left £52,000 to found a chair of music in Edinburgh Univ., also providing that an annual concert of his own compositions should be given. The 'Reid' professors since the foundation (1839) have been John Thomson; Sir Henry Bishop, 1842; Henry Hugh Pearson, 1844; John Donaldson, 1845; Sir Herbert Stanley Oakeley, 1865; Frederick Niecks, 1891; and Donald Francis Tovey, from 1914 until his death in 1940.

Reimann, Heinrich, German writer on music, son of Ignaz Reimann; b. Regersdorf, Silesia, March 14, 1850; d. Berlin, May 24, 1906. He was taught by his father; attended the Glatz Gymnasium, and studied philology at Breslau Univ. (1870-74), also conducted the academic Gesangverein 'Leopoldina.' From 1887 he lived in Berlin, where he was assistant librarian at the Royal Library, organist to the Philharmonic Society, teacher of organ and theory at the Scharwenka-Klindworth Cons.; critic for the 'Allgemeine Musikalische Zeitung'; composed organ sonatas and studies, etc. He publ. a biography of Schumann (1887); *Zur Theorie und Geschichte der byzantinischen Musik* (in 'Vierteljahrsschrift für Musikwissenschaft,' 1889); *Joh. Brahms* (1897; 3rd ed., 1903; in 'Berühmte Musiker,' of which series he was ed.); *Musikalische Rückblicke* (2 vols., 1900); *H. von Bülow* (1909, posth.); *J. S. Bach* (1912; completed by B. Schrader). He revised vol. II of Ambros' *Musikgeschichte* for a new ed. (1892); publ. a collection of old songs, arranged for concert performance, 'Das deutsche Lied' (4 vols.; originally collected for Amalie Joachim), and the collections 'Internationales Volksliederbuch' (3 vols.) and 'Das deutsche geistliche Lied' (6 vols.); also ed. Bach's St. John Passion (1903). His 'program books' for the Berlin Philharmonic concerts were models for all similar analyses.

Reimann, Ignaz, German church-composer; b. Albendorf, Silesia, Dec. 27, 1820; d. Regensdorf, June 17, 1885. Publ. 18 Masses, 4 Requiems, 3 Te Deums, 48 offertories, 40 graduals; many others, also instrumental works, in MS.

Reimers (rī'mers), **Paul,** tenor; b. Lunden, Schleswig-Holstein, March 14, 1878; d. New York, April 14, 1942. He studied with Prof. Spengel in Hamburg, Georg Henschel and Raymund von zur Mühlen in London, and Jean Criticos in Paris. Début as Max (*Freischütz*) in Hamburg, 1902; then devoted himself to oratorio and lieder-singing; after his first tour of the U. S. (1913) he was a regular visitor; then settled in New York; taught singing at the Juilliard Graduate School.

Rein (rīn), **Walter,** German composer and pedagogue; b. Stotternheim, near Erfurt, Dec. 10, 1893; d. Berlin, June 18, 1955. He studied composition with Erwin Lendvai; joined the Jöde youth movement in music, and wrote many instructive choral works; in 1935 became prof. at the Hochschule für Musik-Erziehung in Berlin (until 1945). His folksong arrangements were publ. in Jöde's *Musikant* and the *Lobeda-Chorbuch.*

Reinach, Théodore, French musicologist; b. St. Germain-en-Laye, July 3, 1860; d. Paris, Oct. 28, 1928. Was first a lawyer, then turned to musicology and specialized in old Greek music. He was a prof. at the École du Louvre, a member of the Institut, and from 1888 ed. of 'Revue des études grecques.' —Works: *Le second hymne delphique à Apollon* (with L. Boëllmann; 1897); a study of Plutarch's treatise on music (with H. Weil; Paris, 1900); on pseudo-Aristotelian musical problems, in 'Revue des études grecques' (with Eichtal; 1902); *La Musique grecque* (Paris, 1926); the article, *Musica,* in 'Dictionnaire des antiquités grecques' (Paris); etc. He also wrote the libretto for the opera-ballet, *La Naissance de la lyre* (after Sophocles; music by A. Roussel; Paris Opéra, 1925) and for the lyric tragedy *Salamine* (after Aeschylus; music by M. Emmanuel; ibid., June 19, 1929).

Reinagle, Alexander, b. Portsmouth, England (of Austrian parents), baptized April 23, 1756; d. Baltimore, Sept. 21, 1809. He studied in Edinburgh with Raynor Taylor; in London for a time; also visited Lisbon and other Continental cities. From his correspondence he appears to have been an intimate friend of K. P. E. Bach. Came to New York early in 1786, settling in the same year in Philadelphia, where he taught, managed subscription concerts (also in N. Y.), and was active as singer, pianist, conductor, and composer; 1787, introduced 4-hand piano music to America; associated, possibly as harpsichordist, with the Old American Co., and most likely took part in their 1788-89 season in N. Y.; in 1793, he was engaged as musical director of a stock company for the production of plays and comic operas, with Thomas Wignell as general director; also built the New Theatre, which opened on Feb. 2, 1793, with Reinagle acting as composer, singer, and director; later also managed a company in Baltimore. — Wrote: 'Collection of Most Favorite Scots Tunes with Variations for Harpsichord' (London; probably issued in Glasgow); *6 Sonatas . . . with Accompaniment for Violin* (London, c. 1780); *Miscellaneous Quartets* (Philadelphia, 1791); *Concerto on the Improved Pianoforte with Additional Keys* (1794); *Preludes* (1794); accompaniments and incidental music to *The Sicilian Romance* (1795), *The Witches of the Rock,* pantomime (1796), and various English plays; *Masonic Overture* (1800); sonatas (in Library of Congress, Washington; Sonata No. 2 publ. in abridged form by J. T. Howard in *A Program of Early American Piano-Music,* N. Y., 1931); also 'Collection of Favorite Songs'; and music to Milton's *Paradise Lost* (incomplete). —Cf. J. R. Parker's *Musical Reminiscences,* in 'Euterpeiad' (Jan. 19, 1822); O. G. Sonneck, *Early Concert Life in America* (Leipzig, 1907; in English); id., *Early Opera in America* (N. Y., 1915); E. C. Krohn, *A. Reinagle as Sonatist,* in the 'Mus. Quarterly' (Jan., 1932); J. T. Howard, *Our American Music* (N. Y., 1939 and later eds.); O. G. Sonneck and W. T. Upton, *Bibliography of Early Secular American Music* (Washington, 1945); 'Sammelbände der Internationalen Musik-Gesellschaft' XI; 'Dictionary of American Biography.'

Reinecke, Carl (Heinrich Carsten), German pianist and composer; b. Altona, June 23, 1824; d. Leipzig, March 10, 1910. He was a pupil of his father, a music teacher. His first concert tour was to Denmark and Sweden in 1843; he then went to Leipzig, learned much through meetings with Mendelssohn and Schumann, made a second tour through North Germany, and was from 1846-48 court pianist to Christian VIII at Copenhagen. Then, after spending some years in Paris, he became teacher at the Cologne Cons. in 1851, music director at Barmen 1854-59, at Breslau, 1859-60, and from 1860-95 conductor of the Gewandhaus Concerts at Leipzig. At the same time he was prof. of piano playing and free composition at the Leipzig Cons. An eminent pianist, he excelled as an interpreter of Mozart, made concert tours almost yearly, and was enthusiastically welcomed in England, Holland, Scandinavia, Switzerland, and throughout Germany; among his pupils were Maas, Kwast, and Joseffy. As a composer, and teacher of composition, Reinecke was the leader in Leipzig for a quarter of a century; his numerous works, classic in form and of a refined workmanship, do not entirely escape from the influence of Wagner and Brahms. In his writings he showed himself an extreme conservative. Besides the Leipzig letters for the 'Monthly Musical Record' and essays for various journals, he wrote *Was sollen wir spielen?* (1886), *Zur Wiederbelebung der Mozartschen Klavierkonzerte* (1891), *Die Beethovenschen Klaviersonaten* (1896; 9th ed., 1924; in English, 1898), *Und manche liebe Schatten steigen auf* (1900), *Meister der Tonkunst* (1903), *Aus dem Reich der Töne* (1907). He composed a great many works in every genre: the operas *König Manfred* (Wiesbaden, July 26, 1867); *Ein Abenteuer Händels* (Schwerin, 1874); *Auf hohen Befehl* (Hamburg, 1886); *Der Gouverneur von Tours* (Schwerin, 1891); several musical fairy tales, for solos, chorus, and piano: *Nussknacker und Mausekönig, Schneewittchen, Dornröschen, Aschenbrödel, Die wilden Schwäne, Glückskind und Pechvogel,* etc.; the oratorio *Belsazar;* several choral works with orch.: *Sommertagsbilder, Schlachtlied, Der deutsche Sang,* etc.; numerous choruses for mixed voices; for orch.: 3 symphonies, 9 overtures, smaller works; 4 piano concertos; a violin concerto; a cello concerto; a harp concerto; a flute concerto; chamber music: octet for wind instruments; sextet for wind instruments; 6 string quartets; piano quintet; 2 piano quartets; 6 piano trios; trio for piano, oboe, and horn; trio for piano, clarinet, and horn; violin sonata; 3 violin sonatinas; 3 cello sonatas; a sonata for flute and piano; numerous character pieces for piano; a sonata for piano, left hand; a suite, *Biblische Bilder;* 3 sonatas for 2 pianos; altogether about 300 op. numbers. He wrote cadenzas to 42 movements of piano concertos by Bach, Mozart, Beethoven, and Weber; some of these cadenzas are often used. —Cf. J. von Wasielewski, *Carl Reinecke. Ein Künstlerbild* (Leipzig, 1892); E. Segnitz, *Carl Reinecke* (Leipzig, 1900); M. Steinitzer, *Das Leipziger Gewandhaus im neuen Heim unter Carl Reinecke* (Leipzig, 1924); N. Topusov, *Carl Reinecke; Beiträge zu seinem Leben* (dissertation; Berlin, 1943).

Reiner, Fritz, eminent conductor; b. Budapest, Dec. 19, 1888; studied there with Koessler and Thomann at the Music Academy; also law at the Univ.; 1909, coach at the Comic Opera, Budapest; then operatic conductor in Laibach (1910) and at the Budapest People's Opera (1911-14); 1914-21, music director of the Dresden Opera, also appearing in guest engagements in Hamburg, Berlin, and Vienna; 1921-22, guest conductor in Rome and Barcelona; 1922-31, conductor of the Cincinnati Symph. Orch.; from 1931, he taught conducting at the Curtis Institute of Music, Philadelphia; has appeared as guest conductor of many major orchestras in the U. S. and Europe; has conducted opera at San Francisco (1935-38), Covent Garden (1936-37), and in Philadelphia; 1938-48, conductor of the Pittsburgh Symph. Orch.; from 1949 conductor at the Metropolitan Opera House; since 1953 conductor of the Chicago Symph. Orch. He is especially admired by musicians as a master of the technique of conducting.

Reiner, Karel, Czech composer; b. Žatec, June 27, 1910. He studied law; then applied himself to music, taking courses with Suk and a seminar with Alois Hába (quartertone music). During World War II he was interned at the Dachau concentration camp. After his release, he became active in the Union of Czech Composers. —Works: opera, *Tale of an Enchanted Song* (1949); piano concerto (1937); violin concerto (1947); nonet (1946); 2 piano sonatas; etc.

Reinhardt (rīn'-hart), **Heinrich,** operetta composer; b. Pressburg, April 13, 1865; d. Vienna, Jan. 31, 1922. Pupil of M. Mocker and A. Bruckner in Vienna; was music critic for several papers. —Works: the operettas *Das süsse Mädel* (Vienna, Oct. 25, 1901, his greatest success), *Der liebe Schatz* (Vienna, Oct. 30, 1902), *Der General-Konsul* (Vienna, Jan. 28, 1904), *Krieg im Frieden* (Vienna, Jan. 20, 1906), *Die süssen Grisetten* (Vienna, 1907), *Ein Märchen für alles* (Munich, 1908), *Die Sprudelfee* (Vienna, 1909), *Napoleon und die Frauen* (Vienna, April 28, 1911), *Prinzessin Gretl* (Berlin, 1914), *Des Königs Gäste* (Vienna, 1916), *Die erste Frau* (Munich, 1918); also wrote 2 operas, *Die Minnekönigin* and *Der Schuster von Delft;* author of *Die Entwicklung der Operette* and *Virtuosentum und Künstlerschaft.*

Reinhold (rīn'hŏlt), **Hugo,** Austrian composer; b. Vienna, March 3, 1854; d. there, Sept. 4, 1935. Choir-boy in the Hofkapelle; then pupil of J. Epstein (piano), O. Dessoff and A. Bruckner (composition) at the Vienna Cons., graduating in 1874 as winner of the silver medal; until 1925, prof. of piano at the Akademie der Tonkunst. A composer of pronounced melodic gift and highly poetic conception. —Works: *Präludium, Menuett und Fuge* for string orch.; Symph. in C; *Konzert-Ouvertüre*; violin sonata; piano pieces (2 and 4 hands); men's choruses and songs.

Reinken, Jan Adams, organist; b. Wilshausen, Alsace, April 27, 1623; d. Hamburg, Nov. 24, 1722. Pupil of Sweelinck in Amsterdam. In 1658 he became assistant, and in 1663 successor, to Scheidemann, organist at the Katharinenkirche, Hamburg. One of the foremost among North German organists; J. S. Bach several times walked the 30 miles from Lüneburg to Hamburg to hear him. —Works: *Hortus musicus* for 2 violins, viola, and bass (1687), and *Partite diverse* (both republ. by Riemsdijk in the 'Maatschappij tot bevordering der Toonkunst'; vols. 13 and 14). Some of his compositions have been published by R. Buchmayer, Seiffert in 'Organum,' A. Schering in *Geschichte der Musik in Beispielen* (No. 207), etc. —Cf. A. Pirro, *Notes pour servir, éventuellement, à la biographie de Reinken,* in the 'Scheuerleer-Festschrift' (1925); id., *Reinken et la musique en Alsace au XVIIe siècle,* in 'Annuaire' of the Club vosgien (Strasbourg, vol. 3, 1935).

Reinthaler (rīn'tah-ler), **Karl (Martin),** German composer; b. Erfurt, Oct. 13, 1822; d. Bremen, Feb. 13, 1896. He studied with G. A. Ritter and Marx in Berlin, and for 3 years in Rome; taught singing at the Cologne Cons. (1853); from 1857, municipal music director in Bremen. —Works: 2 operas, *Edda* (Bremen, 1875) and *Käthchen von Heilbronn* (Frankfurt, 1881); an oratorio, *Jephtha,* repeatedly performed in Germany and elsewhere; the famous *Bismarck-Hymne;* choral works; a symph.; songs; psalms.

Reisenauer (rī'-zehn-ow-ĕhr), **Alfred,** German pianist; b. Königsberg, Nov. 1, 1863; d. (on a concert tour) Liebau, Oct. 3, 1907. Pupil of L. Köhler and Liszt. Début at Cardinal Hohenlohe's palace, Rome, with Liszt (1881); after a concert tour (London, Leipzig), he studied law at Leipzig Univ. 1881-82, but in 1886 resumed his career of pianist, and visited almost every region of the globe (even Siberia and Central Asia); 1900-06 prof. at the Leipzig Cons. —He publ. a number of fine songs: 6 *Gesänge aus Wilhelm Meister,* 5 *Traurige Lieder* (Heine), *Wanderlieder* (Uhland), *Sieben Gedichte* (op. 12); 6 *Balladen und Romanzen* (op. 13); *Reisebilder* (op. 14; for piano 4 hands); 50 *Übungsstücke* for piano. —Cf. J. Schwerin, *Erinnerungen an A. Reisenauer* (Königsberg, 1909).

Reiser, Alois, composer; b. Prague, April 6, 1887. He attended the Univ. of Prague and also studied with Dvořák. He toured Europe as a cellist; then came to the U. S.; was a cellist with the Pittsburgh Symph. Orch. and the N. Y. Symph.; conducted the orch. at the Strand Theater, N. Y. (1918-29); in 1929 settled in Hollywood as studio conductor and composer for films.—Works: for orch.: *Evening of Summer,* symph. idyll (Prague, 1911); *Slavic Rhapsody* (Los Angeles, March 8, 1931, composer conducting); cello concerto (Los Angeles, March 23, 1933); *Erewhon* (Los Angeles, Jan. 24, 1936, composer conducting); chamber music: piano trio (1910); string quartet in E minor (E. S. Coolidge Prize; Pittsfield Festival, 1918); string quartet in C major (NBC Prize); piano trio; violin sonata; songs; light operas; etc.

Reiss (rīs), **Albert,** German dramatic tenor; b. Berlin, Feb. 22, 1870; d. Nice, June 19, 1940. He was an actor before making his début as a singer in Königsberg (Sept. 28, 1897); then sang in various German towns; on Dec. 23, 1901, made his American début at the Metropolitan Opera House in the minor roles of the Sailor and Shepherd in *Tristan und Isolde;* then sang more important parts in Wagner's operas. In 1919 he returned to Berlin; in 1938 retired from the stage and lived in Nice.

Reiss, Józef Wladyslaw, Polish musicologist; b. Dembica, Aug. 4, 1879. He studied musicology with Guido Adler at the Univ. of Vienna; *Dr. phil.* with a dissertation on the Polish composer Gomólka (1912); in 1922 he became prof. of musicology at Cracow Univ., remaining at that post for 30 years. —Publications: (in Polish) *The Psalm Melodies of Nicolaus Gomólka, 1580* (1912; a German version in 'Zeitschrift der Internationalen Musik-Gesellschaft,' vol. 13); *The Problem of Meaning in Music* (1915; 2nd ed., 1922); *A History of Music* (1919); *Beethoven* (1920); *Henryk Wieniawski* (1931); several school manuals; a *Formenlehre* appeared in German (Leipzig, 1917).

Reisserová, Julie, Czech composer; b. Prague, Oct. 9, 1888; d. there, Feb. 25, 1938. She studied with J. B. Foerster; also with Albert Roussel in Paris. Among her works are *Pastorale maritime* for orch. (1933); *Esquisses* for piano; several albums of songs. —Cf. J. Vacková, *Julie Reisserová* (Prague, 1948).

Reissiger, Karl Gottlieb, German composer; b. Belzig, near Wittenberg, Jan. 31, 1798; d. Dresden, Nov. 7, 1859. A pupil of Schicht at the Thomasschule, Leipzig, from 1811; went to Vienna in 1821 and thence to Munich (1822), pursuing the study of dramatic composition under Winter; taught at the Berlin Royal Institute for Church Music, and in 1826 was invited to The Hague to organize a conservatory. In the same year he succeeded Marschner as music director of the German Opera at Dresden, and soon after was appointed court Kapellmeister as Weber's successor. —Reissiger was a prolific composer (over 200 op. numbers), writing with great facility, but with little originality. —The waltz for piano, *Weber's Last Thought,* long misattributed to Weber, was proved to be a composition by Reissiger; many of his songs also became popular.—Cf. H. Pfiel, *K. G. Reissiger* (1879); K. Kreiser, *K. G. Reissiger* (Dresden, 1918).

Reissmann, August, German writer on music; b. Frankenstein, Silesia, Nov. 14, 1825; d. Berlin, July 13, 1903. Pupil there of H. Jung, and in Breslau of Mosewius and Baumgart (theory), E. L. Richter (piano and organ), Lüstner (violin), and Kahl (cello). His first compositions were well received; but two years' residence in Weimar with Liszt (1850-52) developed a strong literary vein. He lived in Halle, and from 1863-80 in Berlin, lecturing 1866-74 at the Stern Cons. on the history of music; then in Leipzig (where the Univ. conferred on him the degree of *Dr. phil.* in 1875), in Wiesbaden, and again in Berlin. —Writings: *Katechismus der Gesangskunst* (1853; after Sieber); *Von Bach bis Wagner* (1861); *Das deutsche Lied in seiner historischen Entwicklung* (1861; rev. ed., 1874, as *Geschichte des deutschen Liedes;* considered his best and most original work); *Allgemeine Geschichte der Musik* (3 vols., 1863-64); *Allgemeine Musiklehre* (1864; 2nd ed., 1864); *Robert Schumann* (1865; 3rd ed., 1879; in English, 1886); *Grundriss der Musikgeschichte* (1865); *Lehrbuch der musikalischen Komposition* (3 vols., 1866-71); *Felix Mendelssohn-Bartholdy* (1867; 2nd ed., 1871); *Schubert* (1873); *Die königliche Hochschule für Musik in Berlin* (1875); *Klavier- und Gesangschule für den ersten Unterricht* (1879); *Joseph Haydn* (1879); *Zur Ästhetik der Tonkunst* (1879); *Illustrierte Geschichte der deutschen Musik* (1881); *J. S. Bach* (1881); *Händel* (1882); *Gluck* (1882); *Die Hausmusik* (1884); *Weber* (1886); *Die Oper in ihrer kunst- und kulturhistorischen Bedeutung* (1885); edited Gathy's 'Musikalisches Conversationslexikon' (1870), and vols. VII-XI of Mendel's ditto (1876; also Supplement of 1881, and an epitome, *Handlexikon der Tonkunst,* in 1882). He wrote 3 operas, *Gudrun* (Leipzig, 1871), *Die Bürgermeisterin von Schorndorf* (Leipzig, 1880), and *Das Gralspiel* (Düsseldorf, 1895); several cantatas; a violin concerto; chamber music; and many songs. —Cf. J. Göllrich, *A. Reissmann als Schriftsteller und Komponist* (Leipzig, 1884).

Reiter (rī'-ter), **Josef,** Austrian composer; b. Braunau, Jan. 19, 1862; d. Vienna, June 2, 1939. He received his first instruction from his father, who was the schoolmaster and organist of the little town; after that entirely self-taught; from 1886-1907 he lived in Vienna as teacher in the elementary schools; 1908-11, director of the Mozarteum in Salzburg; then lived again in Vienna. In 1899 a number of admirers formed the 'J. Reiter Verein' for the propagation of his works. His reputation rests chiefly on his numerous, and mostly excellent, men's choruses. —Cf. M. Morold, *J. Reiter* (1904); L. Etzmansdorfer, *J. Reiter* (Vienna, 1924).

Reizenstein, Franz, pianist and composer; b. Nuremberg, June 7, 1911. He studied with Leonid Kreutzer (piano) and Hindemith (composition); in 1934 settled in London, where he took a course with Vaughan Williams. He has written 2 radio operas: *Men Against the Sea* (1949) and *Anna Kraus* (1952); *Jolly Overture* (1952); a cello concerto (1936); a piano concerto (1941); a violin concerto (1953); much chamber music; piano sonata; etc.

Relfe, John, English theorist and composer; b. Greenwich, 1763; d. London, c. 1837. Member of the King's Band, 1810; also an esteemed teacher of piano and harmony. —Works: airs, sonatas, lessons, divertimentos, etc., for harpsichord or piano; songs; *Guida Armonica . . .* (3 parts, 1798; 2nd ed. as *The Principles of Harmony . . .* 1817); *Remarks on the Present State of Musical Instruction* (1819); *Lucidus ordo . . .* (1821). He proposed a reformed thorough-bass figuring, marking the root-chord r., and the inversions ′ and ″.

Rellstab, Johann Karl Friedrich, German writer on music; b. Berlin, Feb. 27, 1759; d. there, Aug. 19, 1813. Pupil of Agricola and Fasch; succeeded his father as head of a printing establishment, adding a music printing and publishing department and a circulating library of music; founded short-lived amateur concerts in 1787; lost his property in the war of 1806, and gave music lessons, lectured on harmony, and wrote criticisms for the 'Vossische Zeitung.' Compositions unimportant. —Writings: *Versuch über die Vereinigung der musikalischen und oratorischen Deklamation* (Vienna, 1785); *Anleitung für Klavierspieler, den Gebrauch der Bach'schen Fingersetzung, die Manieren und den Vortrag betreffend* (1790); and a polemical pamphlet, *Über die Bemerkungen eines Reisenden* [Reichardt], *die Berlinischen Kirchenmusiken, Konzerte, Opern und die königliche Kammermusik betreffend* (1789). —Cf. O. Guttmann, *J. K. F. Rellstab* (Berlin, 1910).

Rellstab, (Heinrich Friedrich) Ludwig, the noted novelist, son of the preceding; b. Berlin, April 13, 1799; d. there, Nov. 27, 1860. Artillery officer, teacher of mathematics and history in the Brigade School, Berlin, retired from the army in 1821, and lived as a writer in Berlin from 1823. Editor and music critic of the 'Vossische Zeitung' from 1826. Publ. the satirical pamphlets *Henriette, oder die schöne Sängerin, eine Geschichte unserer Tage von Freimund Zuschauer* (1826; on Henriette Sontag's triumphs), and *Über mein Verhältniss als Critiker zu Herrn Spontini als Componisten und General-Musikdirector in Berlin, nebst einem vergnüglichen Anhang* (1827; directed against Spohr's truckling to virtuosity in *Agnes von Hohenstaufen*), for each of which he suffered a period of imprisonment, though his opinions were eventually upheld both in official circles and by the public. From 1839-41 Rellstab edited a musical periodical, 'Iris im Gebiet der Tonkunst'; he also contributed to several other papers. In his 'Gesammelte Schriften' are biographies of Liszt, Ludwig Berger, Bernhard Klein, Nanette Schechner, and others; vol. I contains criticisms, on opera and concert, which came out in the 'Vossische Zeitung' 1826-48. He wrote an autobiography, *Aus meinem Leben* (1861, 2 vols.). —Cf. L. R. Blengert, *L. Rellstab* (Leipzig, 1918).

Reményi (rĕh'-mā-ñē), **Eduard,** eminent violinist; b. Miskolcz, Hungary, July 17, 1830; d. San Francisco, May 15, 1898. Pupil of Böhm at the Vienna Cons. (1842-45). Banished from Austria for participation in the Hungarian Revolution of 1848, he began the career of a wandering violinist in America; returned to Europe in 1853, profited by Liszt's counsels, and in 1854 became solo violinist to Queen Victoria. In 1860 he was amnestied, and appointed solo violinist to the Emperor of Austria; in 1865, commenced a brilliant tour, visiting Paris, Germany, Belgium, and Holland; then proceeded to London (1877), and to America in 1878, traveling in the U. S., Canada, and Mexico; in 1886 he began a new concert tour around the world, visiting Japan, China, South Africa, etc. Some MS notes on his trip to the Far East are in the N. Y. Public Library. He died of apoplexy on his last American tour. —His technique was prodigious; in vigor, passion, and pathos he was unexcelled. He made skilful transcriptions of Field's Nocturnes, Chopin's Waltzes, Polonaises, and Mazurkas, and pieces by Bach, Schubert, etc.; these are united under the title of 'Nouvelle École du violon.' He composed a violin concerto, and some solos for violin. —Cf. G. Kelley and G. Upton, *Eduard Reményi. Musician, Littérateur, and Man* (Chicago, 1906); E. Sas, *Reményi* (Budapest, 1934).

Remoortel, Edouard van, Belgian conductor; b. Brussels, May 30, 1926; was a pupil at the Brussels Cons. (1945-49); studied conducting at the Cons. of Geneva, and privately with Josef Krips. Returning to Belgium, he started an auspicious career by conducting the Concerts Populaires in Brussels; subsequently was guest conductor in Paris, Rome, and London. In 1951 he was appointed chief conductor of the Belgian National Orch. He made a successful American début in Washington (Dec., 1956). In 1958 he was appointed permanent conductor of the St. Louis Symph. Orch. He is a nephew of the Belgian statesman, Paul-Henri Spaak.

Rémusat (rā-mü-zăh'), **Jean,** French flutist; b. Bordeaux, May 11, 1815; d. Shanghai, Sept. 1, 1880. He studied with Tulou. After successful concert giving, he became 1st flutist at the Queen's Theatre, London; from 1853 was flutist at the Théâtre-Lyrique, Paris. He publ. a flute method and solo pieces for flute.

Remy, Alfred, writer on music and editor; b. Elberfeld, March 16, 1870; d. New York, Feb. 26, 1937. Came to the U. S. in 1882; attended the College of the City of N. Y. (graduated 1890); then studied piano with Bruno Oscar Klein from 1890-96, and violin with C. Palm; 1895-97, music critic of 'Vogue' and the 'Looker-On'; lectured on history of music at N. Y. College of Music (1896-98), and on modern languages at the Brooklyn Commercial High School (1899-1911); 1905, M.A. at Columbia Univ., where he was extension lecturer on musicology from 1906-15. 1901, was staff member of the 'International Enyclopedia'; 1907, assisted in the preparation of the 'International Yearbook.' He was the editor of the 3rd ed. of Baker's Biographical Dictionary of Musicians (N. Y., 1919).

Remy, W. A. See **Mayer, Wilhelm.**

Renaud (rü-nŏh'), **Maurice,** French baritone; b. Bordeaux, July 24, 1861; d. Paris, Oct. 16, 1933. He studied in Paris and Brussels; sang at the Théâtre de la Monnaie, Brussels (1883-90); at the Opéra-Comique, Paris (1890-91); and the Paris Opéra (1891-1902). He made his American début in New Orleans, on Jan. 4, 1893. From 1906 till 1909 he sang at the Manhattan Opera House, where he became a favorite; then appeared in Chicago for a season, and at the Metropolitan Opera House (1910-12); thereafter, was active chiefly in France. He sang baritone and bass parts in some 60 operas.

Renié (rü-nyā'), **Henriette,** French harpist and composer; b. Paris, Sept. 18, 1875; d. there, March 1, 1956. She studied with Alphonse Hasselmans at the Paris Cons.; received 1st prize for harp at the age of 11; then entered the classes of Lenepveu and Dubois in harmony and composition. She performed her concerto for harp and orch. at the Concerts Lamoureux, Paris, on March 24, 1901; further wrote *Pièce symphonique,* for harp and orch.; *Légende et Danse caprice,* for harp and orch.; publ. numerous pieces for harp solo: *Promenades matinales, Feuilles d'automne, Ballade fantastique, Légende, Contemplation, Défilé lilliputien, Danse des lutins,* etc.; also works for the harp sextet she formed in Paris; a trio for harp, violin, and cello; a trio for harp, flute, and bassoon; several songs. She taught for many years at the Paris Cons.; among her students was Marcel Grandjany.

Renner, Josef, German choral conductor; b. Schmatzhausen, near Landshut, Bavaria, April 25, 1832; d. Regensburg, Aug. 11, 1895. Taught by his father; later by Mettenleiter and Proske. From 1858-92, choral conductor and teacher at the Aula Scholastica, Regensburg; founder, about 1865, and until 1882 director, of a Music Institute. To revive the German part-songs of the 16th-17th centuries, he organized the Regensburg Madrigal Quartet. Edited and publ. 'Auswahl deutscher Madrigale von Meistern des 16. Jahrhundert,' 'Neue Regensburger Sängerhalle,' 'Regensburger Oberquartette,'

'Mutter Donau,' 'Männerquartette von der Donau' (242 numbers), etc.

Rensburg, Jacques E., Dutch cellist; b. Rotterdam, May 22, 1846; d. Bonn, Dec. 1910. A pupil of J. Giese, D. de Lange, and E. Hegar, he took up music relatively late; made a successful début as soloist at the Gewandhaus in Leipzig in 1872, and then toured Germany; shortly afterwards a nervous affection compelled him to abandon his concert career; returned to Rotterdam in 1874; in 1880 he established himself in business in Bonn. —His works include several pieces for cello and orch. and some for cello and piano.

Resinarius, Balthasar (possibly identical with Balthasar Harzer or Hartzer), b. Jessen, c. 1480. Was chorister in the Emperor's Chapel and pupil of Isaac; 1543, became bishop of Leipa, Bohemia. He was one of the finest of early Protestant composers. —Publ. 118 'Responsories' (Wittenberg, 1543; 80 printed by Rhaw and reprinted by Bärenreiter and Concordia, 1957); 30 choral pieces in Rhaw's *Neue deutsche geistliche Gesenge für die gemeinen Schulen* (1544; ed. by J. Wolf in 'Denkmäler deutscher Tonkunst' vol. 39); 4 motets, in Offices collected by Rhaw; 3 bicinia, in Rotenbucher's *Diphona amoena et florida* (Nuremberg, 1549). —Cf. I. M. Schröder, *Die Responsorienvertonungen des B. Resinarius* (Kassel, 1954).

Resnik, Regina, American soprano; b. New York, Aug. 30, 1922. She studied in New York; made her concert début at the Brooklyn Academy of Music (Oct. 27, 1942); sang in opera in Mexico (1943); won an annual audition at the Metropolitan Opera in 1944, and appeared there in *Il Trovatore* (Dec. 6, 1944); sang the leading part in Beethoven's *Fidelio* (March 17, 1945). In 1953 she appeared in Bayreuth as Sieglinde. Later, she sang mezzo-soprano parts; appeared as Marina in *Boris Godunov* at the Metropolitan Opera, on Feb. 15, 1956. She married Harry W. Davis, a lawyer, in New York, on July 16, 1946.

Respighi (rĕh-spē'-gē), **Ottorino,** eminent Italian composer; b. Bologna, July 9, 1879; d. Rome, April 18, 1936. He studied violin with F. Sarti at the Liceo Musicale of Bologna; composition with L. Torchi and G. Martucci. In 1900 he went to Russia, and played 1st viola in the orch. of the Imperial Opera in St. Petersburg; there he took lessons with Rimsky-Korsakov, which proved a decisive influence in Respighi's coloristic orchestration. In 1902 he studied with Max Bruch in Berlin. From 1903 to 1908 he was active as a concert violinist; also played the viola in the Mugellini Quartet of Bologna. In 1913 he was engaged as prof. of composition at the Santa Cecilia in Rome; in 1923, appointed its director, but resigned in 1925, retaining only a class in advanced composition; subsequently devoted himself to composing and conducting. He was elected a member of the Italian Royal Academy on March 23, 1932. In 1925-26 and again in 1932 he made tours of the U. S. as pianist and conductor. —His style of composition is a highly successful blend of songful melodies with full and rich harmonies; he was one of the best masters of modern Italian music in orchestration. His power of evocation of the Italian scene and his ability to sustain interest without prolixity is incontestable. Although he wrote several operas, he achieved his greatest success with 2 symph. poems, *Le Fontane di Roma* and *I Pini di Roma,* each consisting of 4 tone paintings of the Roman landscape. —Works: Operas: *Re Enzo* (Bologna, March 12, 1905); *Semirama,* lyric tragedy in 3 acts (Bologna, Nov. 20, 1910); *La bella addormentata nel bosco,* musical fairy tale (Rome, April 13, 1922, performed by Vittorio Podrecca's marionettes, Teatro dei Piccoli, with singers off stage); *Belfagor,* lyric comedy (Milan, April 26, 1923); *La Campana sommersa,* after Hauptmann's *Die versunkene Glocke* (Hamburg, Nov. 18, 1927); *Maria Egiziaca,* mystery play in 1 act (N. Y., March 16, 1932); *La Fiamma* (Rome, Jan. 24, 1934); a free transcription of Monteverdi's *Orfeo* (Milan, March 16, 1935); *Lucrezia* (posthumous, Milan, Feb. 24, 1937). Ballets: *La Boutique Fantasque,* on themes by Rossini (London, June 5, 1919); *Scherzo veneziano* (Rome, Nov. 27, 1920); *Belkis, regina di Saba* (Milan, Jan. 23, 1932). For orch.: *Notturno* (1905); *Sinfonia drammatica* (1915); *Fontane di Roma,* symph. poem in 4 movements (Rome, March 11, 1917); *Antiche arie e danze per liuto,* 3 sets, the 3rd for string orch. (1916; 1923; 1931); *Ballata delle gnomidi* (Rome, April 11, 1920); *Pini di Roma,* symph. poem in 4 movements (Rome, Dec. 14, 1924); *Rossiniana,* suite from Rossini's piano pieces (1925); *Vetrate di chiesa,* symph. impressions in 4 movements (Boston, Feb. 25, 1927); *Impressioni brasiliane* (1927); *Trittico Botticelliano,* for chamber orch. (commissioned by E. S. Coolidge; 1927); *Gli Uccelli,* suite for small orch. on themes by Rameau, B. Pasquini, and others (1927); *Feste romane,* symph. poem in 4 movements (N. Y. Philharmonic, Toscanini conducting, Feb. 21, 1929); *Metamorphoseon modi XII,* theme and variations (commissioned by the Boston Symph.; Boston, Nov. 7, 1930); *Concerto gregoriano,* for violin and orch. (Rome, Feb. 5, 1922); *Concerto in modo misolidio,* for piano and orch. (N. Y., Dec. 31, 1925, composer soloist); *Concerto a cinque,* for violin, oboe, trumpet, double-bass, piano, and strings (1932). Choral works: *La Primavera,* cantata for soloists, chorus, and orch. (Rome, March 4, 1923) and *Lauda per la Natività del Signore,* for soloists, chorus, and orch. (1930). Chamber music; 11 pieces for violin and piano (1904-07); string quartet in D major (1907); *Quartetto dorico,* for string quartet (1924); *Il Tramonto,* after Shelley, for mezzo-soprano and string quartet (1917); violin sonata (1917). Also *Huntingtower Ballad,* for band (Sousa memorial concert, Washington, April 17, 1932); 45 songs; 3 vocalises without words; arrangements of works by Monteverdi, Vitali, Pergolesi, Cimarosa, Marcello, etc., and of several *Etudes-Tableaux* by Rachmaninoff; co-author, with S. A. Luciani, of *Orpheus*: *iniziazione musicale, storia della musica* (Florence, 1925). —His wife, **Elsa Olivieri Sangiacomo Respighi** (b. Rome, March 24, 1894), was his pupil; wrote a fairy opera, *Fior di neve,* the symph. poem *Serenata di maschere,* and numerous songs; was also a concert singer herself. She publ. Respighi's biography, *Ottorino Respighi*: *Dati biografici ordinati* (Milan, 1954.) —Cf. S. A. Luciani, in the 'Bolletino bibliografico musicale' (1926); M. Saint-Cyr, *Ottorino Respighi,* in 'Musicisti contemporanei' (1932); M. Mila, *Probleme di gusto ed arte in Ottorino Respighi,* in the 'Rassegna Musicale' (1933); R. de Rensis, *Ottorino Respighi* (Turin, 1935).

Restori, Antonio, Italian musicologist; b. Pontremoli, Massa Carrara, Dec. 10, 1859; d. Genoa, June 30, 1928. Studied philology at the Univ. of Bologna, and taught in secondary schools in various Italian cities; from 1897 prof. of Romance languages at the Univ. of Messina. He publ. *Notazione musicale dell' antichissima Alba bilingue* (1892), *Musica allegra di Francia nei secoli XII e XIII* (1893), *La Gaîté de la Tor, aubade del secolo XIII* (1904); *La Musique des chansons françaises,* in Juleville's 'Histoire de la langue et de la littérature françaises' (1895), etc.

Reszke, Édouard. See **De Reszke.**

Reszke, Jean de. See **De Reszke.**

Rethberg, Elisabeth (real name Elisabeth Sattler), soprano; b. Schwarzenberg, Saxony, Sept. 22, 1894; studied piano at the Dresden Royal Cons.; later trained her voice. 1915-22, member of the Dresden State Opera; on Nov. 22, 1922, made her début as Aida at the Metropolitan Opera House, of which she remained a leading member until 1942. She also sang, in opera and in recital, in many American and European cities; in 1936 she toured in joint recital with Ezio Pinza, appearing throughout America, Europe, and Australia; in 1938 they toured South America together. She created the title role of Strauss' *Die Aegyptische Helena* at the world première in Dresden, 1927. —Cf. Henschel and Friedrich, *E. Rethberg* (Schwarzenberg, 1928).

Réti (reh'tē), **Rudolf,** pianist and composer; b. Užice, Serbia, Nov. 27, 1885; d. Montclair, N. J., Feb. 7, 1957; studied at the Cons. in Vienna, where he lived as music critic of 'Echo' and composer; *Dr. phil.* He was one of the founders of the International Society for Contemporary Music (Salzburg, 1922); came to the U. S. in 1938; in 1943 married the Canadian pianist, Jean Sahlmark (b. Saltcoats, Saskatchewan, May 19, 1911); in 1950 settled in Montclair. Publ. *The Thematic Process in Music* (N. Y., 1951); another book, *Tonality, Atonality, Pantonality,* was publ. posthumously (N. Y., 1958). His works include the opera, *Ivan and the Drum* (after Tolstoy; not performed); ballet-opera *David and Goliath* (1935); piano concerto (Detroit, 1948; Jean Réti soloist); a string quartet; piano pieces; songs.

Rettich, Wilhelm, German composer and conductor; b. Leipzig, July 3, 1892; studied at Leipzig Cons. with Max Reger; was a prisoner of war in Siberia during World War I; then was in China. Returning to Leipzig in 1921, he became music director of the local synagogue, occuped various posts as theater conductor until 1933, when he left Germany and settled in Amsterdam. An exceptionally industrious composer; his works total some 110 opus numbers, including 3 symphonies, many choral works, chamber music, and songs.

Reubke (roib'kĕ), **Adolf,** German organ builder at Hausneindorf, near Quedlinburg; b. Halberstadt, Dec. 6, 1805; d. there, March 3, 1875. Built the organs in the cathedral (88 stops) and the Jacobikirche (53 stops) at Magdeburg. —His son **Emil** (b. Hausneindorf, March, 1836; d. there 1885) succeeded his father, and introduced various improvements (pneumatic tubes). —**Julius Reubke,** son of Adolf (b. Hausneindorf, March 23, 1834; d. Pillnitz, June 3, 1858), was a pupil of Kullak and Marx, in Berlin, and later of Liszt; a fine pianist, whose few compositions show great talent (a piano sonata, an organ sonata entitled 'The 94th Psalm,' other piano pieces, and songs).—**Otto Reubke,** the youngest son of Adolf (b. Hausneindorf, Nov. 2, 1842; d. Halle, May 18, 1913), was a pupil of von Bülow and Marx, lived in Halle as a music teacher; conductor of the Robert Franz Singakademie, 1867-1911; from 1892, musical director at the University.

Reuchsel, Amédée, French organist; b. Lyons, March 21, 1875. Pupil at the Brussels Cons. of J. Dupont (organ), A. Mailly (harmony), and E. Tinel (composition); then of G. Fauré in Paris, where he was organist at St.-Denis for a number of years; won the Prix Chartier for chamber music in 1908. Wrote *Théorie abrégée de la musique* and *L'Education musicale populaire,* and ed. the collection 'Solfège classique et moderne' for the Paris Cons. (18 books).

Reuchsel, Maurice, French violinist and composer, brother of the preceding; b. Lyons, Nov. 22, 1880. Pupil of his father and at the Paris Cons. Made successful tours of France, England, and Italy; 1903, ed. of the 'Express musical de Lyon'; 1915, won the Institute prize for chamber music. —Wrote *La Musique à Lyon* (2nd ed., 1903), *L'École classique du violon* (1905; 3rd ed., 1906), *Un Violoniste en voyage* (3rd ed., 1907), etc.

Reuling (roi'-link), **(Ludwig) Wilhelm,** German conductor and composer; b. Darmstadt, Dec. 22, 1802; d. Munich, April 19, 1879. He studied with Rinck and Seyfried; was theater conductor in Vienna (1829-54). He composed 37 operas and operettas, and 17 ballets, produced mostly in Vienna; in addition, he wrote overtures, chamber music, and songs. A complete list of his operas produced in Vienna, with dates of premières, is found in Anton Bauer, *Opern und Operetten in Wien* (Vienna, 1955).

Reusner (Reussner), Esajas, German lute player and composer; b. Löwenberg, Silesia, April 29, 1636; d. Berlin, May 1, 1679. He was a pupil of his father, a lutenist, and at the age of 15 was engaged as musician to Countess Radziwill in Breslau; at 19, lutenist at Brieg; in 1674 became lutenist at the court of the Elector of Brandenburg in Berlin. He publ. several suites for the lute: *Deliciae testudinis* (1667; new ed., 1697, as *Erfreuliche Lautenlust); Neue Lautenfrüchte* (1676); a book of 100 religious melodies arranged for the lute, and publ. in tablature (1678). Reprints of suites and chorale settings by Reusner are in the 'Reichsdenkmale,' vol. XII. —Cf. A. Sparmann, *Esaias Reusner und die Lautensuite* (dissertation, Berlin, 1926); K. Koletschka, *E. Reussner der Jüngere und seine Bedeutung für die deutsche Lautenmusik des XVII. Jahrhunderts,* in 'Studien zur Musikwissenschaft' (vol. 15; 1928).

Reuss (rois), **August,** composer; b. Liliendorf, Moravia, March 6, 1871; d. Munich, June 18, 1935. Pupil of L. Thuille in Munich; after a brief activity as Kapellmeister in Augsburg (1906) and Magdeburg (1907) he lived in Berlin; then in Munich; 1927, co-director of the Trapp Music School; 1929, prof. at the Akademie der Tonkunst. —His works include a comic opera, *Herzog Philipps Brautfahrt* (Graz, 1909); a piano concerto; a string quartet; etc.

Reuss, Eduard, pedagogue; b. New York, Sept. 16, 1851; d. Dresden, Feb. 18, 1911. From 1862-69 pupil of E. Krüger in Göttingen; then went to Liszt, and also studied with Savard (1876-77) in Paris; 1880-96, teacher in Karlsruhe; 1896-1902 in Wiesbaden, where in 1899 he was director of the Cons.; accompanied his wife, Luise Royce-Belce (q. v.), on her American tour (1902-03), and then settled in Dresden as prof. at the Cons. Publ. *Franz Liszt. Ein Lebensbild* (1898), *Liszts Lieder* (1906), and *Franz Liszt in seinen Briefen* (1911).

Reuss, Wilhelm Franz, German conductor; son of Eduard Reuss and Luise Reuss-Belce; b. Karlsruhe, March 17, 1886; d. in a Russian prison, in Königsberg, May 15, 1945. He was a pupil of Draeseke and Max von Schillings; conducted in Berlin (1923-27) and Kassel (1927-33); in 1935 went to Königsberg.

Reuss-Belce, Luise, soprano; b. Vienna, Oct. 24, 1860; d. Aibach, Germany, March 5, 1945 (was found dead in a refugee train). Pupil of J. Gänsbacher in Vienna and Fritz Planck in Karlsruhe; début as Elsa at the Hoftheater in Karlsruhe in 1881; from 1882, at Bayreuth; 1896-99, in Wiesbaden; 1900 at Covent Garden; 1902-03, in the Wagner parts at the Metropolitan Opera House; 1903-11 in Dresden. In 1885 she married Eduard Reuss (q. v.), after whose death (1911) she removed to Berlin, where she established a singing-school. In 1913 she was stage manager at the festival performances in Nuremberg (the first woman to act in that capacity on a German stage).

Reuter (roi'-ter), **Florizel von,** violinist and composer; b. Davenport, Iowa, Jan. 21, 1890; studied with M. Bendix (Chicago), Sauret (London), C. Thomson (Brussels), and Marteau (Geneva); toured successfully throughout Europe and the U. S.; 1931-33, prof. of violin at the Vienna Academy of Music; settled in Munich, 1934. Author of *Führer durch die Solo-Violinmusik* (Berlin, 1926); *Psychical Experiences of a Musician* (London, 1928). His opera *Postmaster Wynn,* after Pushkin, was produced at the Berlin Staatsoper in 1947.

Reuter, Rudolph Ernest, American pianist; b. New York, Sept. 21, 1888; studied at the Royal Academy of Music, Berlin (1908, won the Mendelssohn Prize); 1909, made his début with the Hamburg Philh. Orch.; 1910-13 prof. at the Imperial Academy of Music, Tokyo, which he reorganized on western academic lines; 1913-21, teacher at the Chicago Musical College. Toured Europe twice, also appearing throughout the U. S. in recital and as soloist with leading orchs.; 1935-37, president of the Society of American Musicians.

Reutter (roi'-tĕr), **Georg von,** Sr., Austrian organist and composer; b. Vienna, 1656; d. there, Aug. 29, 1738. He was a pupil of Johann Kaspar Kerll; in 1686, became organist at St. Stephen's Cathedral in Vienna; from 1697 to 1703, theorbo player at the Imperial Court Chapel. In 1700 he became court and chamber organist, and in 1715, 1st Kapellmeister at St. Stephen's Cathedral, a post that he held until his death. A ricercar and 6 capriccios publ. under his name in the 'Denkmäler der Tonkunst in Österreich' (vol. XIII, 2), are really by Strungk. —Cf. N. Hofer, *Die beiden Reutter als Kirchenkomponisten* (Vienna, 1915); G. Frotscher, *Geschichte des Orgelspiels* (Berlin, 1934-35; vol. I).

Reutter, Hermann, outstanding German composer; b. Stuttgart, June 17, 1900. He studied with Walter Courvoisier (composition) and Franz Dorfmüller (piano) in Munich; in 1932, appointed prof. at the Hochschule für Musik in Frankfurt; in 1945, returned to Stuttgart. In his music Reutter follows the line of neo-Classicism, and in his technical procedures comes close to Hindemith. The basic thematic material of many of his compositions is inspired by German folk music. —Works: operas: *Saul* (Baden-Baden, July 15, 1928), *Der verlorene Sohn,* after André Gide (Stuttgart, March 20, 1929), *Doktor Johannes Faust* (Frankfurt, May 26, 1936), *Odysseus* (Frankfurt, Oct. 7, 1942), *Don Juan und Faust* (Stuttgart, June 11, 1950), *Ballade der Landstrasse* (Stuttgart, July 21, 1952), *The Bridge of San Luis Rey,* after Thornton Wilder's novel (Frankfurt Radio, June 20, 1954); *Die Witwe von Ephesus* (Cologne, June 23, 1954); choral works: oratorio, *Der grosse Kalender* (1933; very successful), *Der glückliche Bauer,* cantata (1944), *Pandora* (1949), *Die Rückkehr des verlorenen Sohnes,* chamber oratorio after André Gide, a new version of the opera *Der verlorene Sohn* (Munich, Feb. 15, 1952); *Der Himmlische Vagant,* a lyrical portrait of François Villon, for 2 voices and instruments (Donaueschingen Music Festival, Oct. 6, 1951); *Prozession,* for cello and orch. (Wiesbaden, Dec. 6, 1957); 4 piano concertos; violin concerto; a string quartet; a violin sonata; a cello sonata; *Fantasia apocalyptica,* for piano; *Antagonismus,* for 2 pianos; 3 vols. of Russian songs, arranged and harmonized; other minor pieces. —Cf. Karl Laux, *Musik und Musiker der Gegenwart* (Essen, 1949; pp. 203-15).

Reutter (roi'-tĕr), **Johann Adam Karl Georg von,** Jr., Austrian composer; son of Georg von Reutter, Sr.; b. Vienna, April 6, 1708; d. there, March 11, 1772. He studied with his father, and upon the latter's death (1738) succeeded him as Kapellmeister at St. Stephen's Cathedral in Vienna. He became 2nd court Kapellmeister in 1746 (the 1st being Antonio Predieri), and acting 1st Kapellmeister in 1751 (after Predieri's retirement). In 1740 he was ennobled by Maria Theresa with the title 'Edler von Reutter.' He wrote several operas, oratorios, and much church music (a Mass, a Requiem, etc. were publ. in the 'Denkmäler der Tonkunst in Österreich,' vol. 88; 1952; a symphony, *Servizio di tabula,* in vol. 31; 1908). Reutter was the choir leader who engaged young Haydn as a chorister at St. Stephen's and who, according to some accounts, treated him harshly. —Cf. N. Hofer, *Die beiden Reutter als Kirchenkomponisten* (Vienna, 1915).

Révész, Géza, Hungarian psychologist; b. Siófek, Dec. 9, 1878; first studied law (1901, LL.D) then experimental psychology at

Göttingen (1905, *Dr. phil.*) and Budapest (1908); 1910, teacher of psychology at the Univ. of Budapest; 1921, director of the Psychological Institute of the Univ. of Amsterdam. —Books: *Zur Grundlegung der Tonpsychologie* (Leipzig, 1913); *Erwin Nyiregyházi. Psychologische Analyse eines musikalisch hervorragenden Kindes* (Leipzig, 1916; in English, as *The Psychology of a Musical Prodigy,* London, 1925); *Das frühzeitige Auftreten der Begabung und ihre Erkennung* (Leipzig, 1921); *Musikgenuss bei Gehörlosen* (with Prof. Katz; Leipzig, 1926); *Inleiding tot de musiekpsychologie* (Amsterdam, 1944; in German, Bern, 1946; in English, as *Introduction to the Psychology of Music,* N. Y., 1953); numerous articles on psychological aspects of music.

Revueltas, Silvestre, Mexican composer; b. Santiago Papasquiaro, Dec. 31, 1899; d. Mexico City, Oct. 5, 1940. He studied violin at the Mexico Cons.; with Felix Borowski in Chicago (1916) and with Ševčik in N. Y. (1922); conducted theater orchestras in Texas (1926-28); in 1929 returned to Mexico City and became assistant conductor to Carlos Chávez of the Orquesta Sinfónica de Mexico; only then did he begin to compose. In 1937 he went to Spain, where he was active in the cultural affairs of the Loyalist Government during the civil war. His health was ruined by exertions and irregular life, and he died of pneumonia. He possessed an extraordinary natural talent and intimate understanding of Mexican music, so that despite a lack of academic training in composition, he succeeded in creating works of great originality, melodic charm, and rhythmic vitality. —Works: the ballets *El Renacuajo paseador* (Mexico City, Oct. 4, 1940) and *La Coronela* (left unfinished at his death; completed by Galindo and Huízar; produced posthumously, Nov. 20, 1941); for orch.: *Esquinas* (Mexico City, Nov. 20, 1931), *Ventanas* (Nov. 4, 1932); *Cuauhnahuac* (June 2, 1933), *Janitzio* (Oct. 13, 1933), *Colorines* (N. Y., Nov. 4, 1933), *Homenaje a Federico García Lorca* (Madrid, Sept. 22, 1937, composer conducting); 7 scores of film music; of these, *Redes* (Barcelona, Oct. 7, 1937) was arranged as a symph. suite; 2 string quartets; for piano: *Canción* and *Allegro;* songs.—Cf. O. Mayer-Serra, *Silvestre Revueltas,* in the 'Mus. Quarterly' (April, 1941); N. Slonimsky, *Music of Latin America* (N. Y., 1945; pp. 247-51); G. Contreras, *S. Revueltas* (Mexico, 1954).

Revutsky (rā-vŏŏt'-skē), **Lev Nikolayevitch,** Ukrainian composer; b. near Poltava, Feb. 20, 1889. He studied in Kiev with Lisenko and Glière; then was engaged as instructor at the Musico-Dramatic Institute in Kiev (1924-41); during the occupation of Kiev by the Germans, he went to Tashkent, where he taught at the Cons.; in 1944 resumed his post in Kiev. His works include 2 symphonies (1915; 1926); 2 piano concertos (1914; 1934); a number of choral pieces to Ukrainian words; arrangements of Ukrainian folksongs.

Rey, Cemal Reshid, Turkish composer; b. Istanbul, Oct. 25, 1904. Son of a poet who was also twice Minister of the Interior, he studied in Paris with Laparra (composition) and Marguerite Long (piano); gave piano recitals in Paris, returning to Istanbul in 1923, where he taught at the Cons. He was the 1st conductor of the Istanbul Municipal Orch. in 1934; from 1938 to 1940, was musical director of Radio Ankara; in 1949, appointed musical director of Radio Istanbul. — Works: *Faire sans dire,* 1-act opera (1920); *Yann Marek,* 3-act opera (1922); *Sultan Cem,* 5-act opera (1923); *Zeybek,* 3-act opera (1926); *La Légende du Bebek,* for orch. (Paris, Dec. 15, 1929); *Karagueuz,* symph. poem (Paris, Feb. 14, 1932; composer conducting); *Scènes turques,* for orch. (Paris, March 6, 1932); *Concerto chromatique,* for piano and orch. (Paris, March 12, 1933, composer soloist); violin concerto (1939); symphony in D minor (1941; Ankara, April 2, 1948, composer conducting); *L'Appel,* symph poem (1950; Paris, April 3, 1952, composer conducting); chamber music; military marches; choruses.

Rey, Jean-Baptiste, French conductor and composer; b. Tarn-et-Garonne, Dec. 18, 1734; d. Paris, July 15, 1810. He studied at Toulouse and became a theater conductor in the provinces. In 1776 he was appointed court musician to Louis XVI, as 'surintendant de la chapelle.' He conducted the Concert Spirituel (1782-86); then was in charge of the musical performances at the Paris Opéra. In 1799 he became prof. at the Paris Cons. He taught according to the principles of Rameau and became embroiled in an academic controversy with the followers of the more modern method of Catel. He played an important role in producing operas by Gluck, Grétry, and others; wrote some stage music himself.

Rey, Louis Charles Joseph, French composer and cellist; brother of Jean-Baptiste Rey; b. Lauzerte, Oct. 26, 1738; d. Paris, May 12, 1811. He was trained as a cellist, and was in the orch. of the Paris Opéra from 1766 until 1806; composed music for cello and other instruments.

Reyer (rā-yär') (real name, Rey), **Louis-Étienne-Ernest,** French composer; b. Marseilles, Dec. 1, 1823; d. Le Lavandou, near Hyères, Jan. 15, 1909. From 6 to 16 he studied in the free municipal school of music; then took a place in the government financial bureau at Algiers, and while there composed a solemn Mass (for the arrival of the French governor in Algiers; performed 1847) and publ. several songs. He definitely embarked upon a musical career in 1848, studying at Paris with his aunt, the wife of Aristide Farrenc (q.v.). In 1866 he became librarian at the Opéra, and followed d'Ortigue as music critic of the 'Journal des Débats'; his collected essays were publ. in 1875 as *Notes de musique;* also in *Quarante ans de musique* (posthumous, 1909). He was elected to David's chair in the Institut in 1876; chevalier of the Legion of Honor, 1862; Grande-Croix, 1906. Although Reyer was an avowed admirer of Wagner, his music does not betray specific Wagnerian influences; both in form and in harmonic progressions Reyer adheres to the classical French school of composition, with a certain tendency towards exoticism in his choice of librettos. —Works: for the stage: *Le Sélam,* text by Gautier (labeled a 'symphonie orientale' but actually a 4-act opera; Paris, April 5, 1850), *Maître Wolfram,* 1-act opera (Paris, May 20, 1854), *Sacountale,* ballet pantomime (Paris, July 14, 1858), *La Statue,* opera (in 3 acts, Paris, April 11, 1861; recast in 5 acts, Feb. 27, 1903), *Erostate,* opera (Baden-Baden, Aug. 21, 1862, by the Paris Opéra troupe), *Sigurd,* opera (Brussels, Jan. 7, 1884; his most popular work; 300 performances up to 1925 in Paris and many abroad), *Salammbô,* opera (Brussels, Feb. 10, 1890); a cantata, *Victoire* (1859); a hymn, *L'Union des arts* (1862); men's choruses (*L'Hymne du Rhin, Le Chant du paysan, Chœur des buveurs, Chœur des assiégés*); a dramatic scene, *La Madeleine au désert* (1874); also some church music. —Cf. A. Jullien, *E. Reyer* (Paris, 1909); H. Roujon, *Notice sur la vie et les travaux de E. Reyer* (Paris, 1911); H. de Curzon, *E. Reyer, sa vie et ses œuvres* (Paris, 1923).

Rezniček (rĕhz'-nĭ-chĕhk), **Emil Nikolaus von,** Austrian composer; b. Vienna, May 4, 1860; d. Berlin, Aug. 2, 1945. He studied law at Graz and music with Wilhelm Mayer (W. A. Rémy); later took a brief course with Reinecke and Jadassohn at the Leipzig Cons. He was subsequently engaged as theater conductor in Graz, Zürich, Berlin, Jena, Mainz, Stettin, and Weimar; was Kapellmeister at the court theater in Mannheim (1896-99). After a short residence in Wiesbaden, he settled in Berlin, and in 1902 established there a very successful series of concerts for chamber orch., 'Orchester-Kammerkonzerte'; in 1906 he was appointed prof. at the Scharwenka Cons. in Berlin; conducted the Warsaw Opera during the 1907-08 season; then became conductor of the Komische Oper, Berlin (1909-11); from 1920 to 1926, he taught at the Hochschule für Musik; retired from teaching in 1919. —Works: operas: *Donna Diana,* to his own libretto (Prague, Dec. 16, 1894; very successful; the overture frequently performed in concerts); *Till Eulenspiegel* (Karlsruhe, Jan. 12, 1902); *Ritter Blaubart* (Darmstadt, Jan. 29, 1920); *Holofernes* (Berlin, Oct. 27, 1923); *Spiel oder Ernst* (Dresden, Nov. 11, 1930); *Der Gondoliere des Dogen* (Stuttgart, Oct. 29, 1931). He wrote 5 symphonies; 3 symph. poems; a *Symphonietta* (also known as the *Ironische Symphonie;* Berlin, March 30, 1905, composer conducting); violin concerto (Berlin, Feb. 26, 1925); *Nachtstück,* for cello, harp, 4 horns, and string quartet; piano pieces; songs.—Cf. O. Taubmann, *Emil Nikolaus von Rezniček* (Leipzig, 1907); Max Chop, *E. N. von Rezniček: sein Leben und seine Werke* (Vienna, 1920); R. Specht, *E. N. von Rezniček: eine vorläufige Studie* (Leipzig, 1923).

Rhaw (**Rhau**), **Georg,** German publisher and composer; b. Eisfeld, Franconia, 1488; d. Wittenberg, Aug. 6, 1548. Cantor of the Thomasschule, Leipzig, from 1518 to 1520, bringing out a Mass *a* 12 and a Te Deum at the disputation of Luther and Eck, then settled in Eisleben as a schoolmaster; later, went to Wittenberg, where in 1524 he established a publishing business, issuing many first eds. of Luther's writings and numerous collections of musical works, mostly Protestant, including *Sacrorum Hymnorum Liber Primus* (1542; modern ed. by R. Gerber in 'Das Erbe deutscher Musik,' vols. 21, 25); *Newe deutsche Gesenge für die gemeinen Schulen* (1544; reprinted by Joh. Wolf as vol. 34 of the 'Denkmäler deutscher Tonkunst'), *Bicinia gallica, latina et germanica* (1545, contains the earliest known version of the *Ranz des vaches;* selections were republ. in F. Jöde's 'Musikantengilde,' 1926; also ed. by K. Ameln, Kassel, 1934), etc. Wrote an *Enchiridion musices* (Part I, 1518, on

Musica choralis; Part II, 1520, on *Musica mensuralis*). —Cf. W. Wölbing, *G. Rhaw* (diss., Berlin, 1922); W. Gosslau, *Die religiöse Haltung in der Reformationsmusik . . .* (Kassel, 1933).

Rheinberger, Josef (**Gabriel**), pedagogue; b. Vaduz, Liechtenstein, March 17, 1839; d. Munich, Nov. 25, 1901. He played piano at 5, and was a good organist at 7. In 1851 he entered the Munich Cons., where until 1854 he studied piano with J. E. Leonhard, organ with J. G. Herzog, and composition with J. J. Maier. After graduating with the highest honors he studied further with Franz Lachner, earning his livelihood with private lessons and acting as accompanist of the Munich Gesangverein, of which he became conductor in 1864. From 1860-66 he was organist at St. Michael's, and from 1865-67 répétiteur at the court opera. In 1859 he succeeded his teacher Leonhard as professor of piano at the Cons.; 1860, appointed prof. of composition (later also of organ). When Bülow completely reorganized the institution (1867) as the 'Königliche Musikschule,' Rheinberger retained his professorship, and also was made inspector of the instrumental and theory classes. In 1877 he declined an invitation to become director of Hoch's newly founded Cons. in Frankfurt. For this act of loyalty he was appointed Wüllner's successor as conductor of the 'Kgl. Kapellchor,' celebrated for its performances of early music, and King Ludwig made him Knight of St. Michael; the bestowal of the 'Zivilverdienstorden' in 1894 raised him to the rank of the nobility, and the Univ. of Munich made him *Dr. phil.* (*hon. c.*) in 1899; he also was elected member of the Berlin Akademie. —As a teacher Rheinberger's reputation was second to none; pupils flocked to him from all parts of the world. As a composer, his dignity, formal finish, and consummate technical mastery compel respect and admiration. The 20 organ sonatas are undoubtedly his highest achievement, and must be ranked among the greatest works in organ literature. —Cf. Th. Kroyer's necrology in Bettelheim's 'Jahrbuch' (1901); P. Molitor, *J. Rheinberger und seine Kompositionen für die Orgel* (Leipzig, 1904); T. Kroyer, *J. Rheinberger* (Regensburg, 1916); Harvey Grace, *The Organ Works of Rheinberger* (London, 1925; 2nd ed., 1932).

Rhené-Baton (real name René Baton), French conductor; b. Courseulles-sur-Mer, Calvados, Sept. 5, 1879; d. Le Mans, Sept. 23, 1940. He attended for 2 years the advanced class for piano at the Paris Cons.; then studied composition as a private pupil with A. Bloch and A. Gedalge. He began his career as chef du chant at the Opéra-Comique (1 year), then was conductor at various concert-series in Paris and Bordeaux; 1918-32, conductor of the Pasdeloup Concerts; also of Diaghilev's Russian Ballet, etc.; many tours; also active as composer.—Cf. D. Sourdet, *Douze chefs d'orchestre* (Paris, 1924).

Riadis, Emile, Greek composer; b. Salonica, May 13, 1890; d. there, July 17, 1935. He studied in Munich with Felix Mottl; in 1910, went to Paris, where he appeared as composer under the name Riadis, formed from the ending of his mother's maiden name, Elefteriadis (his father's real name was Khu). In 1915 he became piano teacher at the Cons. of Salonica. He wrote a number of songs, distinguished by an expressive melodic line, somewhat Oriental in its intervallic pattern; his harmonizations are in the French manner. He composed a Byzantine Mass; an orch. suite; *Biblical Dances;* a symph. poem, *Sunset in Salonica;* a string quartet; a piano quartet; a cello sonata; *3 Greek Dances,* for piano; and several sets of songs: *Jasmins et minarets, Les étranges pèlerinages,* etc.

Riaño, Juan Facundo, an authority on Spanish art; b. Granada, Nov. 24, 1828; d. Madrid, Feb. 27, 1901. He was the founder and director of the 'Museo de reproducciones artísticas.' He publ. (in English) *Critical and Bibliographical Notes on Early Spanish Music* (London, 1887), a valuable work containing many reproductions of old Spanish instruments, descriptions of medieval musical MSS, etc. He developed the theory that the neumes of the Mozarabic notation were derived from the characters of the Visigothic alphabet.

Ribera (**Maneja**) (rē-beh'rah), **Antonio,** Spanish conductor; b. Barcelona, May 3, 1873; d. Madrid, March 4, 1956; studied with Riemann and Mottl in Leipzig and Munich; conducted the Wagner Society in Barcelona (1901-04); then theater conductor in Lemberg (1905-12); again in Barcelona (1912-25), and finally in Madrid (from 1925).

Ribera (**y Tarragó**) (rē-beh'-rah), **Julián,** Spanish scholar and musicologist; b. Carcagente, near Valencia, Sept. 19, 1858; d. Madrid, 1936. For many years prof. of Hispanic-Arabic literature at the Univ. of

Madrid; member of the Spanish Royal Academy and of the Academy of History. He is known chiefly for his study of the *Cantigas* of Alfonso the Wise, the famous collection of songs to the Virgin Mary dating from the 13th century. Ribera maintained that the key to the musical interpretation of the *Cantigas* was to be found in the music and the metrical forms of the Arabs. Under the auspices of the Spanish Academy he publ. *La Música de las Cantigas. Estudio sobre su origen y naturaleza* (Madrid, 1922; English version published as *Music in Ancient Arabia and Spain,* London, 1929). Another important work is *La Música andaluza medieval en las canciones de Trovadores, Troveros y Minnesinger* (3 vols., Madrid, 1923-25), containing 356 transcriptions from medieval MSS (51 harmonized). Other writings: *Historia de la Música árabe medieval y su influencia en la española* (Madrid, 1927); *La Música de la jota aragonesa* (1928), etc. —Cf. H. Spanke, *Die Theorie Riberas über Zusammenhänge zwischen frühromanischen Strophenformen und andalusisch-arabischer Lyrik des Mittelalters,* in *Volkstum und Kultur der Romanen,* III, pp. 258-78; V. Castañeda, *Don J. Ribera y Tarragó,* in 'Boletín de la Academia de la Historia' (Madrid, 1934; vol. 104, pp. 401-16).

Ricci (rĭch-chē), **Corrado,** Italian writer; b. Ravenna, April 18, 1858; d. Rome, June 5, 1934. From 1906-19, general director of the dept. of Fine Arts in the Ministry of Education at Rome; it was through his efforts that the Augusteo was transformed into a concert hall. Besides several opera librettos, he wrote *I Teatri di Bologna nei secoli XVII e XVIII* (Bologna, 1888); *Mozart a Bologna* (with unpubl. documents), in the 'Gazzetta Musicale' (Aug., 1891; reprinted, with other essays, in Ricci's *Figure e figuri del mondo teatrale,* Milan, 1920); *Arrigo Boito* (Milan, 1919); *Burney, Casanova e Farinelli in Bologna* (ib., 1890); *Claudio Monteverdi e la Corte di Mantova,* in 'Cronaca Bizantina' (June, 1886); etc.

Ricci (rĭch-chē), **Federico,** Italian composer; b. Naples, Oct. 22, 1809; d. Conegliano, Dec. 10, 1877. Pupil of Furno, Zingarelli, and Raimondi at the Royal Cons. di San Sebastiano. He produced 19 operas, at least 4 of which were written in collaboration with his elder brother Luigi; these 4 were his first, *Il Colonnello* (Naples, March 14, 1835), *Il Disertore per amore* (Naples, Feb. 16, 1836), *L'Amante di richiamo* (Turin, 1846), and *Crispino e la comare* (Venice, Feb. 28, 1850). On March 13, 1838 his *La Prigione d'Edimburgo* had great success in Trieste; *Corrado d'Altamura* was well received at La Scala, Milan (Nov. 16, 1841). He was invited to St. Petersburg in 1853 as musical director of the imperial theaters; in 1869 *Una Follia a Roma* (as *Une Folie à Rome*) had 77 consecutive representations at the Fantaisies-Parisiennes, so that Ricci went to Paris in hopes of further good fortune; but his subsequent dramatic ventures failed, and in 1876 he retired to Conegliano. 6 Masses, a cantata, and numerous smaller vocal works, were also written by him. —Cf. F. de Villars, *Notice sur Luigi et Federico Ricci . . .* (Paris, 1866); L. de Rada, *I Fratelli Ricci* (Florence, 1878).

Ricci, Luigi, Italian composer; brother of Federico Ricci; b. Naples, July 8, 1805; d. Prague, Dec. 31, 1859. Eminent dramatic composer; pupil of Furno and Zingarelli at the Cons. di S. Sebastiano, Naples, also taking private lessons with Generali. His first stage work was the opera buffa *L'Impresario in angustie* (Cons. theater, 1823); he wrote in all about 30 operas, several in collaboration with his brother. In 1836 he was appointed maestro di cappella of the cathedral at Trieste, and chorusmaster at the theater. In 1844 he married the singer Lidia Stolz, of Prague. Shortly after producing his last opera, *Il Diavolo a quattro* (Trieste, 1859), symptoms of insanity developed, and he was sent to an asylum in Prague, where he died. Among his operas may be mentioned *Il Colombo* (Parma, June 27, 1829), *L'Orfanella di Ginevra* (Rome, 1829), *Chiara di Rosemberg* (Milan, Oct. 11, 1831), *Il nuovo Figaro* (Parma, Feb. 15, 1832), *Chi dura vince* (Rome, Dec. 27, 1834), *Il Birraio di Preston* (Florence, Feb. 4, 1847), *Crispino e la comare* (with Federico; Venice, Feb. 28, 1850; Metropolitan Opera, N. Y., Jan. 18, 1919), *La Festa di Piedigrotta* (Naples, 1852), and *Il Diavolo a quattro* (Trieste, 1859). —His son (by his wife's identical twin sister Francesca Stolz), **Luigi Ricci,** Jr. (b. Trieste, Dec. 27, 1852; d. Milan, Feb. 10, 1906), was also a composer of operas.

Ricci, Ruggiero, American violinist; b. San Francisco, July 24, 1920. He studied with Louis Persinger; made his 1st public appearance in San Francisco at the age of 8, playing the Mendelssohn concerto; N. Y. début, Oct. 20, 1929; in 1932 he made a European tour, playing with excellent success in London, Berlin, and Vienna; returned to America in 1934. He successfully negotiated the transition from a child prodigy to a serious artist; became a virtuoso violinist; in 1957 made a world tour.

Riccitelli (rēch-chē-tehl'-lē), **Primo,** Italian composer; b. Campli, Aug. 9, 1875; d. Giulianova, March 27, 1941; pupil of Mascagni at the Liceo Rossini, Pesaro. He wrote the operas *Maria sul Monte* (1911; Milan, July 8, 1916), *I Compagnacci* (1-act; Rome, April 10, 1923; Metropolitan Opera, N. Y., Jan. 2, 1924), and *Madone Oretta* (Rome, Feb. 3, 1932); also songs.

Riccius (rĭ'-tsyŏŏs), **August Ferdinand,** German composer; b. Bernstadt, Feb. 26, 1819; d. Karlsbad, July 5, 1886. He was conductor of the Euterpe Concerts in Leipzig (from 1849); then at the City Theater there (1854-64); in 1864 went to Hamburg, where he conducted opera, and wrote music criticism for the 'Hamburger Nachrichten.' He composed an overture to Schiller's *Braut von Messina;* a cantata, *Die Weihe der Kraft;* piano music; choruses; songs.

Riccius, Karl August, German violinist, conductor, and composer, nephew of August Ferdinand Riccius; b. Bernstadt, July 26, 1830; d. Dresden, July 8, 1893. He studied in Dresden with Wieck, and in Leipzig with Mendelssohn, Schumann, and Ferdinand David. In 1847 he became violinist in the Dresden Court Orchestra, and later also conductor. He wrote a comic opera, *Es spukt* (Dresden, 1871); several ballets; music to various plays; publ. piano pieces and songs.

Rice, William Gorham, American writer on music; b. Albany, N. Y., Dec. 23, 1856; d. there, Sept. 10, 1945. His writings include *Carillons of Belgium and Holland; The Carillon in Literature; Tower Music of Belgium and Holland* in the 'Mus. Quarterly' (April, 1915); etc.

Richafort, Jean, Flemish composer; b. c. 1480; d. 1548. Probably a pupil of Josquin, he was chapelmaster at St. Rombaut, in Mechlin, from 1507 to 1509; in 1531, in the service of Mary of Hungary, regent of the Netherlands; 1542-47, chapelmaster at St. Gilles in Bruges. Surviving are Masses, Magnificats, motets, and chansons. —Cf. G. Van Doorslaer, *Jean Richafort,* in 'Bulletin' of the Académie royale d'archéologie de Belgique, 1929 (1930; p. 103ff.). See also G. Reese, *Music in the Renaissance* (N. Y., 1954).

Richards, (Henry) Brinley, British composer and pianist; b. Carmarthen, Wales, Nov. 13, 1817; d. London, May 1, 1885. Pupil of the Royal Academy of Music, winning the King's Scholarship in 1835 and 1837. He resided in London, highly esteemed as a concert pianist and teacher. —Wrote the popular hymn *God bless the Prince of Wales* (1862), etc.

Richards, Lewis Loomis, American pianist, harpsichordist, and music educator; b. St. Johns, Mich., April 11, 1881; d. East Lansing, Mich., Feb. 15, 1940. Studied at the Brussels Cons.; concert tours in Europe, 1908-14; returned to the U. S. in 1923, and in 1927 became head of the dept. of music, Michigan State College; was also director of Michigan State Institute of Music and Allied Arts.

Richardson, Alfred Madeley, organist; b. Southend-on-Sea, Essex, England, June 1, 1868; d. New York, July 23, 1949. He received his classical education at Keble College, Oxford (A.M., 1892), and studied at the Royal College of Music under Sir C. H. H. Parry, Sir W. Parratt, and E. Pauer; Mus. Doc., Oxon., 1897; 1897-1908, organist and choirmaster at Southwark Cathedral. From 1909 to 1910 he was organist and choirmaster at St. Paul's, Baltimore; from 1912 in New York as instructor in theory at the Institute of Musical Art. —Publ. *Choir Training Based on Voice Production* (1897); *The Psalms; Their Structure and Musical Rendering* (1903); *Church Music* (1904); *The Southwark Psalter* (1904); *Modern Organ Accompaniment* (1907); *The Choir-Trainer's Art* (1914); *The Southwark Canticles* (1918); *Extempore Playing* (1922); *Helps to Fugue Writing* (1930); *The Medieval Modes* (1933); *Fundamental Counterpoint* (1936).

Richault (rē-shoh'), **Charles-Simon,** French publisher, b. Chartres, May 10, 1780; d. Paris, Feb. 20, 1866. In 1805 he founded a well-known music-publishing house, the first issues of which were Mozart's concertos and Beethoven's symphonies in score. His sons **Guillaume-Simon** (1806-77) and **Léon** (1839-95) carried on the business, publishing works by eminent French composers, and also excellent editions of German classics. Later the stock was bought by the publisher Costallat of Paris.

Riche, Antoine le. See **Divitis.**

Richter, Alfred, German pedagogue, son of Ernst Friedrich Richter; b. Leipzig, April 1, 1846; d. Berlin, March 1, 1919. Teacher in the Leipzig Cons., 1872-83; then lived in London, but returned to Leipzig in 1897; 1898-99, conductor of the choral society 'Arion'; later went to Berlin. —Publ. an *Aufgabenbuch* (English ed. as *Additional Exercises,* N. Y., 1882) supplementary to his father's *Lehrbuch der Harmonie;* a supplement to his father's *Lehrbuch des Kontrapunkts* (English transl., N. Y.); *Die Elementarkenntnisse der Musik* (1895; 6th ed., 1920); *Die Lehre von der thematischen Arbeit* (1896); *Das Klavierspiel für Musikstudierende* (1898; 2nd ed., 1912); *Die Lehre von der Form in der Musik* (1904; 2nd ed., 1911). He also brought out numerous new editions of his father's books. Composed piano pieces, songs, and choruses.

Richter, Ernst Friedrich (Eduard), German theorist and composer; b. Gross-Schönau, Saxony, Oct. 24, 1808; d. Leipzig, April 9, 1879. Son of a schoolmaster, and educated in the Zittau Gymnasium; matriculated 1831 as student of theology at Leipzig Univ., but gave his chief attention to musical study under Weinlig, and on the foundation of the Cons. (1843) became Hauptmann's coadjutor as teacher of harmony and composition; from 1843-47, conductor of the Singakademie; 1851, organist of the Petrikirche; 1862, of the Neukirche, going in a short time to the Nikolaikirche, and in 1868 succeeding Hauptmann as music director of the Nikolai- and Thomaskirche, and cantor of the last-named. —He is best known by his eminently practical and very popular *Lehrbuch der Harmonie* (1853; 26th ed., 1910; in English, N. Y., 1867; transl. by Th. Baker from the 25th German ed., N. Y., 1912; also in Swedish, Russian, Polish, Italian, French, Spanish, Dutch); its continuations are the *Lehrbuch des einfachen und doppelten Kontrapunkts* (1872; 13th ed., 1913; in English, London, 1874 and N. Y., 1884); and *Lehrbuch der Fuge* (1859; 7th ed., 1911; in English, London, 1878). Richter was a skilful contrapuntist, and his vocal music, more especially the a cappella motets, psalms, etc., is pleasing; he also composed string quartets, organ music, violin sonatas, piano sonatas, etc.

Richter, Ferdinand Tobias, Austrian organist and composer; b. Würzburg, 1649; d. Vienna, 1711. He was court organist in Vienna from 1683, and enjoyed a great reputation as a theorist and composer. The following works are extant at Vienna in MS: 2 stage pieces: *L'Istro ossequioso* (Vienna, Jan. 6, 1694) and *Le Promesse degli dei* (Vienna, June 9, 1697); 5 *Sepulcri* (a special type of Viennese oratorio performed in semi-operatic manner during Holy Week); 4 oratorios; sonata for 7 instruments; 2 sonatas for 8 instruments; etc. Modern reprints of his suites, toccatas, and versets are found in 'Denkmäler der Tonkunst in Österreich' (vol. 27).

Richter, Francis William, American organist; nephew of Hans Richter; b. Minneapolis, Feb. 5, 1888; d. Los Angeles, Dec. 25, 1938. He became blind at the age of 3; showed musical ability, and was sent to Vienna, where he studied with the blind pianist Joseph Labor; also took lessons with Leschetizky (piano) and Karl Goldmark (theory); subsequently studied organ with Guilmant in Paris. Returning to the U. S., he was active as church organist and teacher. In 1930 he settled in Portland, Oregon; then moved to Los Angeles.

Richter, Franz Xaver, composer; b. Holleschau, Moravia, Dec. 1, 1709; d. Strasbourg, Sept. 12, 1789. In 1740 member of the chapel of the Prince-Abbot at Kempten; in 1747 he joined the electoral orch. at Mannheim; 1769 till his death Kapellmeister at Strasbourg Cathedral. A prolific composer of decided originality, one of the chief representatives of the new instrumental style of the Mannheim school. —In the library of Strasbourg Cathedral are the MSS of 28 Masses, 2 Requiems, 16 psalms, 38 motets, 2 cantatas, 2 Passions, Lamentations for Holy Week, etc. (the greater part with orch.). An oratorio, *La Deposizione della Croce,* was produced in Mannheim (1748). Publ. works: 69 symphonies (4 reprinted by Riemann in 'Denkmäler der Tonkunst in Bayern' III, 1 and VII, 2), 6 string quartets (reprinted by Riemann, ib., XV, 1); 8 trios for flute (or violin), cello, and piano (G minor reprinted by Riemann, ib., XVI, 2; A in 'Collegium musicum'); 12 trio sonatas for 2 violins with basso continuo; 6 duets for flute; 6 sonatas for flute with basso continuo; 6 piano concertos with string orch. Almost all the chamber music was originally publ. in London. A treatise, *Harmonische Belehrung oder gründliche Anweisung zur musikalischen Tonkunst* (MS in library of Brussels Cons.), was publ. in transl. by Ch. Kalkbrenner as *Traité d'harmonie et de composition* (1804). —Cf. F. X. Mathias, *Thematischer Katalog der im Strassburger Münsterachiv aufbewahrten kirchenmusikalischen Werke Fr. X. Richters,* in 'Riemann Festschrift' (Leipzig, 1909).

Richter, Hans, conductor; b. Raab, Hungary, April 4, 1843; d. Bayreuth, Dec. 5, 1916. In 1853, choirboy in the Court Chapel, Vienna; from 1860-65 he studied composition under Sechter, violin under Heissler, and the French horn under Kleinecke at the Cons. From 1862-66, horn-player in the orch. at the Kärnthnerthor-Theater; from 1866-67 in Lucerne (Triebschen) with Wagner, making for him a fair copy of the *Meistersinger* score and recommended by him for the position of chorusmaster at the Munich Opera (Dec., 1867); from Aug. 25, 1868, to Sept. 1, 1869, court conductor under Bülow. Conducted rehearsals and initial performances of *Lohengrin* at Brussels, March 22, 1870; Kapellmeister at the Pest National Th. 1871-75, then at the Imperial Opera, Vienna, becoming 1st Kapellmeister in 1893. From 1875-97 he conducted, concurrently with the opera, the concerts of the Vienna Philh. Society, and from 1880-95 he also conducted the concerts of the 'Gesellschaft der Musikfreunde,' excepting the season of 1883-84. He was chosen by Wagner to conduct the *Ring des Nibelungen* at Bayreuth in 1876, and at the close of the festival was decorated with the Maximiliansorden by the King of Bavaria and the Falkenorden by the Grand Duke of Weimar. In 1877 (May 7-19) he conducted, alternately with the master himself, the great Wagner Festival at Albert Hall, London. The success of a second festival (May 5-12, 1879), conducted by Richter alone, led to the establishment of an annual series in May, known at first as 'Orchestral Festival Concerts,' later simply as 'Richter Concerts,' which were given regularly until 1897. In that year Richter settled definitely in Manchester as conductor of the Symph. (Hallé) Orch., but did not by any means limit his activity to that city; he still gave occasional 'Richter Concerts' in London, and was regular conductor of the Birmingham Festival (1885-1911) and of the season of Wagner opera at Covent Garden (1903-10); in 1882 he conducted at Drury Lane the English premières of *Meistersinger* (May 30) and *Tristan und Isolde* (June 20). Throughout his life he remained in closest touch with Bayreuth, spending a part of every summer there as conductor-in-chief of the festivals. The last concert he conducted was his farewell concert with the Manchester Symph. Orch. on April 11, 1911, having bidden farewell to London the day before at a special concert of the London Symph. Orch.; he then directed a few performances at the Hofoper in Vienna, and after directing with all the fire of youth the superb *Meistersinger* performances at Bayreuth in the summer of 1912 he retired from all activities, spending his last years in Bayreuth. Among the world's conductors the figure of Richter is one of the most imposing. A pioneer and unsurpassed interpreter of Wagner's art, he espoused with equal devotion the cause of Brahms, the majority of whose orchestral works had their first performance in Vienna (and later also in England) under Richter's baton. A musician of universal sympathies and master of all styles, his interpretation of classic or modern works was equally convincing and authoritative. —Cf. F. Klickmann, *Dr. H. Richter* in 'Windsor Magazine' (Sept., 1896); also L. Karpath, *Wagners Briefe an Hans Richter* (Vienna, 1924); W. Kienzl, in Bettelheim's 'Nekrolog' (1930).

Richter, Sviatoslav Teofilovitch, outstanding Russian pianist; b. Zhitomir, March 20, 1914. The family moved to Odessa when he was a child; he grew up in a musical atmosphere (his father was a pianist); studied symph. literature, and developed exceptional skill in playing orchestral scores at the piano; gave his 1st concert as pianist at 20, at the Sailors' Collective Circle in Odessa. He entered the Moscow Cons. in 1937, studying piano with H. Neuhaus; graduated in 1947; but even before graduation, he won 1st prize at the national contest in 1945; was awarded the Stalin Prize in 1949; was soloist in Prokofiev's 5th piano concerto in Leningrad with the Philadelphia Orch. during its Russian tour, in the spring of 1958. His virtuoso technique and extraordinary interpretative powers, in a wide repertory, place him in the front rank among Russian pianists.

Ricordi & Co., G., famous music-publishing firm of Milan; founded by **Giovanni Ricordi**, b. Milan, 1785; d. there, March 15, 1853. As first violinist and conductor at the old Fiando theater, he also earned small sums as a music copyist, and in 1807 went to Leipzig to learn music engraving in Breitkopf & Härtel's establishment. Returning, he opened a little shop, and began publishing in 1808, the first works being engraved by himself. He was an intimate of Rossini, whose operas he published; also recognized Verdi's genius when the latter was still unknown. His son **Tito Ricordi** (b. Milan, Oct. 29, 1811; d. there, Sept. 7, 1888) succeeded to the business. In 1845 he established the 'Gazzetta Musicale,' one of the most important Italian musical papers; also introduced the 'Edizioni economiche,' and under his able administration the house became the largest music-publishing firm in Italy. With Verdi he was on terms of intimate friendship, and that composer's works (especially *Aida*) made a fortune for both publisher and author. Owing to ill health he withdrew from active management in 1887. —His successor was his son **Giulio Ricordi** (b. Milan, Dec. 19, 1840; d. there, June 6, 1912), a man of extraordinary business ability, who continued the policy of expansion. In 1888 he bought, and consolidated with his own, the important firm of Francesco Lucca. It was he who discovered Puccini. A trained musician, he publ., under the pseudonym of J. Burgmein, much elegant salon-music (160 opus numbers). Until his death (when it ceased publication) he was ed. of the 'Gazzetta Musicale.' Cf. E. di S. M. Valperga, *Ricordi* (Rome, 1943); G. Adami, *G. Ricordi, l'amico dei musicisti italiani* (Milan, 1945). —His son **Tito** (b. 1865; d. Milan, March 30, 1933), a remarkable pianist, was the subsequent head of the house. The present administrators (1958) are Eugenio Clausetti and Guido Valcarenghi. The catalogue contains over 120,000 numbers, and in the archives are the autograph scores of more than 550 operas by the most famous Italian composers. The firm has branches in New York (established 1897), several European countries, Canada, Australia, Mexico, and South America. —Cf. O. Vergani, *Piccolo viaggio in un archivio* (Milan, 1953).

Rider-Kelsey, Mme. **Corinne,** American soprano; b. on a farm near Batavia, N. Y., Feb. 24, 1877; d. Toledo, Ohio, July 10, 1947. She attended Oberlin College; then studied voice in Chicago and N. Y.; made her professional début in Handel's *Messiah* (St. Louis, Nov. 24, 1904); then appeared in the same work with the N. Y. Oratorio Society almost every season from 1905. She made her 1st operatic appearance as Micaëla in *Carmen,* at Covent Garden, London, on July 7, 1908. In 1926 she married the violinist Lynell Reed, who wrote her biography under the title *Be Not Afraid* (N. Y., 1955).

Ridout, Godfrey, Canadian composer; b. Toronto, May 6, 1918. He studied with H. Willan; in 1939 was engaged as a teacher at the Royal Cons., Toronto, and since 1948, also at the Univ. of Toronto. —Works: a dramatic symphony, *Esther,* for soli, chorus, and orch. (Toronto, April 29, 1952); *Ballade,* for viola and string orch. (Toronto, May 29, 1939); *Festal Overture* (1939); *Comedy Overture* (1941); *Folksong Fantasy* for violin, cello, and piano (1951); songs.

Riechers (rē'-hěrs), **August,** German violin-maker; b. Hanover, March 8, 1836; d. Berlin, Jan. 4, 1893. He was trained in the making and repairing of violins by Bausch of Leipzig; Joachim entrusted his violins to Riechers' hands. He publ. a valuable pamphlet, *Die Geige und ihr Bau* (1893; in English as *The Violin and the Art of its Construction; a Treatise on the Stradivarius Violin,* 1895), with 4 plates of full-size diagrams exhibiting the structure and exact dimensions of the model Stradivarius violin.

Riedel, Karl, German choral conductor; b. Kronenberg, near Elberfeld, Oct. 6, 1827; d. Leipzig, June 3, 1888. He was a silk-dyer by trade; the Revolution of 1848 upset his business and turned his thoughts to the serious study of music. He became a pupil of Carl Wilhelm at Krefeld, and entered the Leipzig Cons. in 1849. In 1854 he organized the 'Riedelverein,' a singing society which later became famous for the performance of ancient church music. The first public concert was given in 1855; in 1868, Riedel was elected president, of the 'Allgemeiner deutscher Musikverein,' and founded the Leipzig branch. A powerful advocate of the Wagner Festivals, he also became president of the 'Wagnerverein.' —Even after its founder's death the 'Riedelverein' maintained its reputation as one of the finest choral organizations in Germany; successive conductors were H. Kretzschmar (1888-97), G. Göhler (1897-1907 and 1909-13, R. Hagel (1907-09), R. Wetz (1913-15), F. Mayerhoff (1915), M. Ludwig (1919). —Publ. the collections, 'Altböhmische Hussiten- und Weihnachtslieder' and '12 altdeutsche Lieder'; a skilful reduction of Schütz's 4 Passions to one; and editions of Schütz's *Sieben Worte,* J. W. Franck's *Geistliche Melodien,* Eccard's *Preussische Festlieder,* Praetorius' *Weihnachtslieder.*—Cf. A. Göhler, *Der Riedelverein zu Leipzig* (Leipzig, 1904; includes a brief biographical sketch of Riedel).

Riedt, Friedrich Wilhelm, German flutist; b. Berlin, Jan. 24, 1712; d. there, Jan. 5, 1784. He studied with Graun; in 1741 became chamber musician to Frederick the Great; 1750, director of the 'Musikalische Gesellschaft' in Berlin. He wrote 6 trios for 2 flutes and continuo; sonatas for 2 flutes; a sonata for flute and cello; publ. a *Versuch über die musikalischen Intervalle* (1753); contributed various articles (critical and polemical) to Marpurg's 'Historisch-kritische Beyträge zur Aufnahme der Musik.'

Riegel (rē'gĕl), **Heinrich (Henri) Joseph,** composer; b. Wertheim, Franconia, Feb. 9, 1741; d. Paris, May, 1799. Pupil of F. X. Richter in Mannheim and Jommelli in Stuttgart; settled in Paris in 1768; from 1782-86 conductor of the Concert Spirituel. On the title page of several works publ. in Paris his name appears as Rigel (which form his son [q.v.] adopted). He is one of the earliest composers who wrote ensemble music with piano (e.g., piano quartets; and 'symphonies' for 2 violins, cello, 2 horns, and piano); also composed the operas (all produced in Paris) *Le Savetier et le financier* (1778), *L'Automat* (1779), *Rosanie* (1780), *Blanche et Vermeille* (1781), *Lucas* (1785), *Les Amours du Gros-Caillou* (1786), *Alix de Beaucaire* (1791). A 'symphony' in D was republ. by R. Sondheimer in 1923. —Cf. G. de Saint-Foix, *Rigel,* in the 'Revue Musicale' (June, 1924); R. Sondheimer, *H. J. Rigel,* in the 'Music Review' (Aug., 1956).

Riegger, Wallingford, outstanding American composer; b. Albany, Georgia, April 29, 1885. He received his primary education at home; his mother was a pianist; his father a violinist. The family moved to New York in 1900, and Riegger began serious study with Percy Goetschius (theory) and Alwin Schroeder (cello) at the Institute of Musical Art; after graduation (1907), he went to Berlin, where he took courses at the Hochschule für Musik; conducted opera in Würzburg and Königsberg (1915-16); also led the Bluethner Orch. in Berlin (1916-17). He returned to America in 1917 and became teacher of theory and cello at Drake Univ., Des Moines (1918-22); in 1922 received the Paderewski Prize for his piano trio; in 1924 he was awarded the E. S. Coolidge Prize for his setting of Keats' *La Belle Dame sans Merci;* in 1925 he was given the honorary degree of Dr. of Music by the Cincinnati Cons. He taught at the Institute of Musical Art, N. Y. (1924-25) and at the Ithaca Cons. (1926-28); then settled in N. Y., where he became active as composer and participant in various modern music societies; took part in the development of electronic instruments (in association with Theremin), and learned to play an electronic cello. His music is of a highly advanced nature; a master craftsman, he wrote in disparate styles with an equal degree of proficiency; used numerous pseudonyms for certain works (William Richards, Walter Scotson, Gerald Wilfring Gore, John H. McCurdy, George Northrup, Robert Sedgwick, Leonard Gregg, Edwin Farell, Edgar Long, etc.). After a long period of non-acceptance on the part of the public and the critics, he began to receive recognition; his 3rd symph. was the choice of the N. Y. Music Critics Circle (1948); member of The National Institute of Arts and Letters (1953). —Works: for orch.: *American Polonaise* (1923), *Rhapsody* (N. Y., Oct. 29, 1931), *Fantasy and Fugue* for organ and orch. (1931), *Passacaglia and Fugue* (Washington, March 19, 1944), Symph. No. 1 (1935), Symph. No. 2 (1946), Symph. No. 3 (N. Y., May 16, 1948), Symph. No. 4 (Univ. of Illinois, April 12, 1957), *Scherzo* (N. Y., Jan. 30, 1933), *Dichotomy* (Berlin, March 10, 1932), concerto for piano and woodwinds (Washington, Feb. 19, 1954), *Dance Rhythms* (Atlanta, March 4, 1955), *Music for Orchestra* (Cleveland, March 22, 1956), *Overture* (1956), *Preamble and Fugue* (1956), *La Belle Dame sans Merci,* for 4 solo voices and chamber orch. (Pittsfield, Mass., Sept. 19, 1924); *Study in Sonority,* for 10 violins or multiples of 10 (1927); suite for solo flute (1929); 3 canons for flute, oboe, clarinet, and bassoon (1930); *Divertissement* for flute, harp, and cello (N. Y., Dec. 11, 1933); *Music for Brass Choir;* duos for 3 woodwind instruments; 2 string quartets; *Whimsy,* for cello and piano; sonatina for violin and piano; piano quintet (1950); nonet for brass (1951); *New and Old,* 12 pieces for piano in various styles; several stage works for dance, scored for various instrumental ensembles (*Theater Piece, Chronicle, Case History, Trojan Incident,* etc.); a 'Suite for Younger Orchestras'; *The Dying of the Light,* song to words by Dylan Thomas (1956); etc. —Cf. H. Cowell, ed., *American Composers on American Music* (1933); R. F. Goldman, *The Music of Wallingford Riegger,* in the 'Mus. Quarterly' (Jan., 1950; with a list of works).

Riehl, Wilhelm Heinrich von, German writer on music; b. Biebrich-on-Rhine, May 6, 1823; d. Munich, Nov. 16, 1897. He studied at the Univ. of Munich, where he became (1854) prof. of political economy; also lectured on music history. He publ. the valuable compendium, *Musikalische Charakterköpfe* (3 vols., 1853-61; 6th ed., 1879; 3rd vol. contains the essays *Die Kriegsgeschichte der deutschen Oper* and *Die beiden Beethoven*), and 2 vols. of original songs, *Hausmusik* (1856; 1877). Posthumous publications: *Zur Geschichte der romantischen Oper* (Berlin, 1928); *Musik im Leben des Volkes,* a collection of Riehl's articles, compiled and ed. by J. Müller-Blattau (Kassel, 1936).—Cf. H. Simonsfeld, *Heinrich Riehl als Kulturhistoriker* (Munich, 1899).

Riem (rēm), **Friedrich Wilhelm,** German organist and composer; b. Kölleda, Thuringia, Feb. 17, 1779; d. Bremen, April 20, 1857. He was a pupil of J. A. Hiller in Leipzig; organist at the Thomaskirche (1807-14), then in Bremen. He wrote an oratorio, *Der Erlöser;* a string quintet, a piano quartet, 3 string quartets, 4 violin sonatas, 6 piano sonatas; also publ. a collection of organ pieces for concert and church.

Riemann, (Karl Wilhelm Julius) Hugo, distinguished German musicologist; b. Grossmehlra, near Sondershausen, July 18, 1849; d. Leipzig, July 10, 1919. He was trained in theory by Frankenberger at Sondershausen, studying the piano with Barthel and Ratzenberger; took the gymnasial course in the Rossleben 'Klosterschule,' 1865-68, and studied at first law, then philosophy and history, at Berlin and Tübingen; and, after passing through the campaign of 1870-71, entered the Leipzig Cons. In 1873 he took the degree of *Dr. phil.* at Göttingen with the dissertation *Musikalische Logik* (publ.); was active as a conductor and teacher at Bielefeld until 1878, when he qualified as University lecturer on music at Leipzig; taught music at Bromberg 1880-81, then at the Hamburg Cons. till 1890, at the Sondershausen Cons. for a short time, and at the Wiesbaden Cons. until 1895, when he resumed his lectures at Leipzig. In 1905 he was made prof.; in 1908 director of the newly established 'Collegium Musicum,' and in 1914 also director of the newly established 'Forschungsinstitut für Musikwissenschaft.' He was made Mus. Doc. (*hon. c.*) by the Univ. of Edinburgh (1899). On his 60th birthday he was honored by the publication of a 'Festschrift' (ed. by Karl Mennicke) containing contributions from the world's foremost scholars, many of whom were Riemann's pupils. The second Riemann 'Festschrift' was publ., after his death, in 1919. —The mere bulk of Riemann's writings, covering every branch of musical science, constitutes a monument of indefatigable industry, and is proof of enormous concentration and capacity for work. When one takes into consideration that much of this work is the result of painstaking research and of original, often revolutionary, thinking, one must share the great respect and admiration in which Riemann was held by his contemporaries. Although many of his ideas are now seen in a different light, his works treating of harmony were considered to constitute the foundation of modern musical theory. His researches in the field of music history have solved a number of vexed problems, and thrown light on others. And, finally, in formulating the new science of musicology, the labors of Riemann have been a most important factor.—WORKS (a partial list): Theory: *Musikalische Syntaxis* (1877); *Skizze einer neuen Methode der Harmonielehre* (1880); rewritten as *Handbuch der Harmonielehre* (1887; 8th ed., 1920); *Elementarmusiklehre* (1882); *Neue Schule der Melodik* (1883); *Vergleichende Klavierschule* (1883); *Musikalische Dynamik und Agogik* (1884); *Praktische Anleitung zum Phrasieren* (1886; rewritten as *Vademecum der Phrasierung,* 1900); *Systematische Modulationslehre* (1887); *Lehrbuch des einfachen, doppelten und imitierenden Kontrapunkts* (1888; 6th ed., 1921; in English, 1904); *Die Elemente der musikalischen Ästhetik* (1900); *Grosse Kompositionslehre* (vol. I, *Der homophone Satz,* 1902; vol. II, *Der polyphone Satz,* 1903; vol. III, *Der Orchestersatz und der dramatische Vokalstil,* 1913); *System der musikalischen Rhythmik und Metrik* (1903); *Grundriss der Musikwissenschaft* (1908; 4th ed. edited by J. Wolf, 1928); *Analyse von Beethovens Klaviersonaten* (3 vols., 1915-19). —History: *Studien zur Geschichte der Notenschrift* (1878); *Die Entwickelung unserer Notenschrift* (1881); *Die 'Martyriai' der byzantinischen liturgischen Notation* (1882); *Notenschrift und Notendruck* (1896); *Geschichte der Musiktheorie im 9-19. Jahrhundert* (1898); *Epochen und Heroen der Musikgeschichte* (1900); *Geschichte der Musik seit Beethoven* (1901); *Handbuch der Musikgeschichte* (5 vols., 1904-13); as supplement to this, a *Musikgeschichte in Beispielen* (1912; a collection of 150 compositions, 13th-18th century; 4th ed., with introduction by A. Schering, 1929); *Die byzantinische Notenschrift im 10.-15. Jahrhundert* (vol. I, 1909; vol. II, 1915); *Kompendium der Notenschriftkunde* (1910); *Folkloristische Tonalitätsstudien* (1916). —Lexicography: *Musiklexikon* (1882; revised and largely rewritten periodically, it has long been recognized as one of the world's standard reference-works on music; 9th to 11th eds. by A. Einstein, 1919-29; in English, 1893-96 [4th ed., 1908]; also in Danish [1888-92; abridged], French [1896 ff.], Russian [1902 ff.]); *Opernhandbuch* (1884; with 2 supplements, 1887, 1893). —To Schlesinger's 'Meisterführer' he contributed analyses of Beethoven's string quartets (vol. XII, 1910), and some of the orchestral works of Brahms (vol. III, 1908), Schumann (vol. XIII, 1911), and Tchaikovsky (vol. XIV, 1911); revised Marx's *Lehre* *von der musikalischen Komposition* (4 vols.; 1887-90); ed. vols. IV (1907) and V (1908) of Deiters' transl. of Thayer's *Beethoven,* and revised vols. II and III (1910, 1911). He publ. in various journals innumerable (many very important) articles and essays; of these some were collected and publ. as *Präludien und Studien* (3 vols., 1895, 1900, 1901). —He ed. numerous works of early composers in the 'Denkmäler der Tonkunst in Bayern' and in the 'Denkmäler deutscher Tonkunst'; also the collections 'Alte Kammermusik' (4 vols.); 'Collegium musicum' (50 books), 'Hausmusik aus alter Zeit' (96 madrigals, canzone, etc., of the 14th and 15th centuries), etc. —He composed many instructive piano pieces; also chamber music, choruses, and songs. —Cf. the biographical sketch by K. Mennicke in 'Riemann-Festschrift' (Leipzig, 1909); R. Heuler, *Dr. H. Riemann als Volksschulgesangpädagog,* in 'Sonde' (Würzburg, 1910); Riemann issue of the 'Zeitschrift für Musikwissenschaft' (July, 1919); H. Grabner, *Die Funktionstheorie Riemanns* (Munich, 1923); H. L. Denecke, *Die Kompositionslehre Hugo Riemanns* (Kiel, 1937); W. Gurlitt, *H. Riemann* (Wiesbaden, 1951). A new revised ed. of the *Musiklexikon,* prepared under the editorship of W. Gurlitt, was publ. in 3 vols. in 1958-59.

Riemann, Ludwig, German writer on music; b. Lüneburg, March 25, 1863; d. Essen, Jan. 25, 1927. Pupil of his father; also of O. von Königslöw and H. Schröder (violin), H. Grüters and A. Löschhorn (piano), J. Alsleben, A. Haupt, and W. Bargiel (composition) at the Königliche Institut für Kirchenmusik in Berlin; from 1889, teacher of singing at the Gymnasium in Essen; 1918, prof. Publ. *Populäre Darstellung der Akustik in Beziehung zur Musik* (1896), *Über eigentümliche, bei Natur- und orientalischen Kulturvölkern vorkommende, Tonreihen und ihre Beziehungen zu den Gesetzen der Harmonie* (1899), *Das Wesen des Klavierklanges und seine Beziehungen zum Anschlag* (1911; valuable), *Das Erkennen der Ton- und Akkordzusammenhänge in Tonstücken klassischer und moderner Literatur* (1925), *Kurzgefasste praktische Modulationsübungen* (2nd ed., 1924), etc.

Riemenschneider, Albert, American organist; b. Berea, O., Aug. 31, 1878; d. Akron, O., July 20, 1950; studied at Baldwin Wallace College (B.A., 1899), in Cleveland with Ch. Clemens and J. H. Rogers, in Vienna with R. Fuchs and H. Reinhold, and in Paris with Widor and Guilmant; 1905-17, conductor of the chorus and orch. of Baldwin Wallace Cons.; 1933, president of the Music Teachers National Association; director of the Baldwin-Wallace Cons.; 1949, acting pres. of the College. He was a Bach specialist.—Publ. the following eds. of Bach: *Liturgical Year* (the *Orgelbüchlein;* 1933); *Chorales* (120 chorales in original clefs and with the original orchestral parts; 2 vols., 1939; with Ch. N. Boyd); *371 Harmonized Chorales and 69 Chorale Melodies with Figured Bass* (1941); *'Schübler' Chorales* (1942).

Riepel, Joseph, Austrian composer and theorist, b. Hörschlag, Jan., 1709 (baptized Jan. 23); d. Regensburg, Oct. 23, 1782. Principal work: *De rhythmopoeia* (1752). —Cf. W. Twittenhoff, *Die musiktheoretischen Schriften J. Riepels* (Halle, 1935); E. Schwarzmaier, *Die Takt- und Tonordnung J. Riepels* (Wolfenbüttel, 1936); J. Merkl, *J. Riepel als Komponist* (Kallmünz, 1937).

Ries (rēs), **Ferdinand** (eldest son of Franz 'der alte Ries' [1775-1846], concertmaster and music director to the Elector Max Franz at Bonn), b. Bonn, Nov. 29, 1784; d. Frankfurt, Jan. 13, 1838. Piano pupil of Beethoven, his father's friend at Bonn, from 1801-05 at Vienna; studied theory with Albrechtsberger. He lived 2 years in Paris, made pianistic tours in North Germany, Scandinavia, and Russia, and resided in London 1813-24, prominent as a player, teacher, and composer. He then retired to an estate at Godesburg, near Bonn; and from 1830 resided in Frankfurt, though he was town music director at Aix, 1834-36. He is best known by his *Biographische Notizen über L. van Beethoven* (1838; reprinted by A. Kalischer, 1906), which his intimacy with the great man renders extremely valuable. He was an excellent pianist, and a prolific composer; among his works are 52 well-written piano sonatas (in which the method, but not the spirit, of Beethoven is apparent). —Cf. L. Überfeldt, *F. Ries' Jugendentwicklung* (Bonn, 1915).

Ries, Franz, German publisher; son of Hubert Ries; b. Berlin, April 7, 1846; d. Naumburg, June 20, 1932. Violin-pupil of his father, and of Massart at the Paris Cons. (1866-68); excellent concert violinist, but gave up playing in 1875 on account of nervousness, and entered the music-publishing business; co-founder and director, from 1882-1924, of the firm of Ries & Erler, Berlin. In 1924 his son, Robert, became the proprietor. —As a composer (pupil of Kiel), he wrote fine orchestral and chamber music.

Ries, Hubert, German violinist; brother of Ferdinand Ries; b. Bonn, April 1, 1802; d. Berlin, Sept. 14, 1886. Studied at Kassel under Spohr (violin) and Hauptmann (composition); in 1836, concertmaster of the royal orch., Berlin; in 1851 teacher at the Royal 'Theaterinstrumentalschule'; pensioned 1872. Publ. excellent instructive works for violin: *Violinschule* (also in English); *Erzählungen aus alter Zeit* (30 instructive duets); *15 Violinstudien von mässiger Schwierigkeit,* op. 26; *30 Violinstudien für den ersten Unterricht,* op. 28; *50 Intonationsübungen, 12 Violinstudien in Form von Konzertstücken,* op. 9; duets, exercises, etc.; also 2 violin concertos (op. 13 and 16).

Riesemann, (Bernhard) Oskar von, musicologist; b. Reval, Feb. 29, 1880; d. St. Niklausen, near Lucerne, Sept. 28, 1934. Studied music and musicology in Munich (Lipps, Riehl, Sandberger, Thuille), Moscow (1899-1900), Berlin (Fleischer, Friedlaender), and Leipzig (Riemann); 1907, *Dr. phil.,* Leipzig; 1912-13, traveled in South America, then lived, until 1915, in Moscow as music critic and conductor (Koussevitzky concerts, 1913-14); fled during the Revolution to Munich, where he lived for a time.—Publ. *Die Notation des alt-russischen Kirchengesanges* (1908); *Monographien zur russischen Musik* (I, 1923; II, 1928, *Mussorgsky* [in English, N. Y., 1929]); *Rachmaninoff's Recollections . . .* (N. Y., 1934); translated into German Scriabin's *Prometheische Phantasien* (1924), Sabaneiev's *Geschichte der russischen Musik* (1926), Rimsky-Korsakov's *Chronik meines musikalischen Lebens* (1928), etc.

Rieter-Biedermann, J. Melchior, Swiss publisher; b. Winterthur, May 14, 1811; d. there, Jan. 25, 1876. He founded a successful music-publishing house in 1849 in Winterthur, with a branch at Leipzig in 1862, which gradually became more important than the original house, so that the latter was dissolved in 1884. After the death of the last proprietor, Robert Astor (d. Leipzig, April 14, 1917), the firm was bought by C. F. Peters. Brahms was the most famous composer in their catalog (see Brahms' *Briefwechsel,* vol. 14).

Rieti (rē-yĕh'-tē), **Vittorio,** composer; b. Alexandria, Egypt (of Italian parents), Jan. 28, 1898. He studied with Frugatta in Milan and Respighi in Rome. After 1925 he lived mostly in France; in 1939 came to the U. S.; became an American citizen (June 1, 1944); was instructor at the Peabody Cons. in Baltimore (1948-49); then at Roosevelt College, Chicago (1950); in 1958 at Queens College, N. Y.; also made prolonged sojourns in Europe. His style of composition represents an effective synthesis of cosmopolitan modern ideas; he is particularly successful in his ballet music. —Works: *Orfeo,* a lyric tragedy (1928); *Teresa nel bosco,* chamber opera (Venice Festival, Sept. 15, 1934); *Don Perlimplin,* opera in 1 act (1949; première, Univ. of Illinois, March 30, 1952); *The Pet Shop,* opera in 1 act (N. Y., April 14, 1958); ballets: *L'Arca di Noè* (1922), *Barabau,* with chorus (Ballets Russes, London, Dec. 11, 1925), *Le Bal* (Monte Carlo, 1929); *David triomphant* (Paris, 1937), *Waltz Academy* (Boston, 1944), *The Mute Wife,* on themes by Paganini (N. Y., 1944), *Trionfo di Bacco e Arianna* (N. Y., 1948), *Unicorn* (1950); oratorio, *Viaggio d'Europa* (Rome, 1954); 5 symphonies; of these No. 4 is subtitled *Sinfonia Tripartita* (St. Louis, Dec. 16, 1944); *Concerto du Loup* (named after the Loup River in Southern France) for chamber orch. (Los Angeles, Aug. 8, 1942); concerto for 5 wind instruments and orch. (Prague Festival, May 31, 1924); 2 piano concertos (1926; 1937); violin concerto (1928); harpsichord concerto (1930); cello concerto (1935); concerto for 2 pianos and orch. (Cincinnati, 1952); quintet for woodwinds (N. Y., 1958); sonata for flute, oboe, bassoon, and piano (1924); 3 string quartets (1926; 1942; 1953); *Madrigal* for 12 instruments; songs; piano pieces. —Cf. G. Rossi Doria, in 'Il Pianoforte' (1924).

Rietsch (rēch), **Heinrich,** musicologist and composer, b. Falkenau-on-Eger, Sept. 22, 1860; d. Prague, Dec. 12, 1927. Studied in Vienna under F. Krenn, E. Mandyczewski, R. Fuchs (composition) and E. Hanslick, G. Adler (musicology). 1895, Privatdozent for musicology at Vienna Univ.; 1900, succeeded G. Adler at the German Univ. in Prague; 1909, full prof. and director of the Institute for Musicology. In the 'Denkmäler der Tonkunst in Österreich' he ed. G. Muffat's *Florilegium* (I, 2 and II, 2), songs of Frauenlob, Reinmar von Zweter, and Alexander (XX, 2), and J. J. Fux's *Concentus musico-instrumentalis* (XXIII, 2). Author of *Die Mondsee-Wiener Liederhandschrift und der Mönch von Salzburg* (1886; with F. A. Mayer), *Die Tonkunst in der 2. Hälfte des 19. Jahrhunderts* (1900; 2nd ed., 1906), *Die deutsche Liedweise* (1904), *Die Grundlagen der Tonkunst* (1907; 2nd ed., 1918), etc.

—Cf. autobiographical sketch in 'Neue Musikzeitung' (1915); P. Nettl, *Verzeichnis der wissenschaftlichen und künstlerischen Arbeiten von Rietsch bis 1920,* in 'Zeitschrift für Musikwissenschaft' II (p. 736); see also ib. X (p. 193; valuable).

Rietschel (rēt'shĕl), **Georg Christian,** German theologist; b. Dresden, May 10, 1842; d. Leipzig, June 13, 1914. Studied theology and after filling several pastorates in various cities became prof. of theology at Leipzig Univ. in 1899. Wrote *Die Aufgabe der Orgel im Gottesdienste bis in das 18. Jahrhundert* (1892; valuable), and *Lehrbuch der Liturgik* (2 vols., 1900, 1909).

Rietz, Julius, German conductor and editor; b. Berlin, Dec. 28, 1812; d. Dresden, Sept. 12, 1877. His father was the royal chamber-musician Johann Friedrich Rietz (d. 1828); his brother Eduard (1802-32) was Mendelssohn's intimate friend, a talented violinist, and the founder of the Berlin Philharmonic Society. —Julius was a cello pupil of Schmidt, B. Romberg, and M. Ganz; in 1828 he joined the orch. of the Königstädt'sches Theater in Berlin. In 1834 he became 2nd conductor at the Düsseldorf opera under Mendelssohn, whom he succeeded as 1st in 1835, next year becoming town music director. In 1847 he was called to Leipzig as theater-Kapellmeister (resigned 1854) and conductor of the Singakademie; in 1848 also conductor of the Gewandhaus Concerts, and prof. of composition at the Cons. He became court Kapellmeister at Dresden in 1860; later he was made artistic director of the Cons., and received the title of 'General-Musikdirektor' in 1874. A conductor of great ability, and a scholarly musician, Rietz's editorial work was of high value; his last work was the complete edition of Mendelssohn for Breitkopf & Härtel (1874-77); he also edited the St. Matthew Passion and the B minor Mass in the complete ed. of Bach, Mozart's operas and symphonies, Beethoven's symphonies and overtures, etc. As a composer he belonged to the Mendelssohn school. —Cf. *Pauline Viardot-Garcia to J. Rietz, Letters of Friendship,* in the 'Mus. Quarterly' (July, 1915, to Jan., 1916); P. A. Merbach, *Briefwechsel zwischen Eduard Devrient und J. Rietz,* in 'Archiv für Musikwissenschaft' III (1921).

Riezler (rēts'-lĕr), **Walter,** German musicologist; b. Munich, Oct. 2, 1878; studied music with Max Reger and Felix Mottl (1904-06). He was at first interested principally in art; he was director of the Stettin Museum of Fine Arts (1910-33); in 1934 he returned to Munich; since 1946, prof. of music history at the Univ. of Munich. He publ. an excellent monograph on Beethoven (1936) which went through 7 German editions up to 1951 and was also translated into English (N. Y., 1938).

Rigel (rē-zhĕl'), **Henri-Jean,** French composer; son and pupil of Heinrich Joseph Riegel (q.v.); b. Paris, May 11, 1772; d. Abbeville, Dec. 16, 1852. From 1798-1800, chef d'orchestre of the French Opera in Cairo; 1808, chamber pianist to Napoleon. Composed operas, oratorios, chamber music, etc.

Righini, Vincenzo, Italian composer; b. Bologna, Jan. 22, 1756; d. there, Aug. 19, 1812. Pupil of Bernacchi (singing) and Padre Martini (counterpoint). Stage-début as a tenor singer at Parma, 1775; went to Prague in 1776, where he also began composing; in 1780 he became singing-master to the Archduchess Elizabeth at Vienna, and conductor at the Opera Buffa; from 1788-92, Electoral Kapellmeister at Mainz; and in 1793, after the successful production of his opera *Enea nel Lazio* at Berlin, he was appointed Kapellmeister at the Court Opera. —Works: some 20 operas, including *Il Convitato di pietra* (Vienna, Aug. 21, 1777; one of the early settings of the Don Giovanni story) and *Gerusalemme liberata* and *La Selva incantata* (a single work consisting of 2 2-act operas; Berlin, Jan. 17, 1803); a series of very fine vocal exercises (1806).

Rignold, Hugo, English conductor; b. Kingston-on-Thames, May 15, 1905. His father was a theatrical conductor; his mother an opera singer. He was taken to Canada as a child, and studied violin in Winnipeg; in 1920 he returned to England on a scholarship to the Royal Academy of Music. During World War II he was stationed in Cairo, where he trained a radio orch. in performances of symph. music. Returning to England, he was a ballet conductor at Covent Garden (1947); from 1948 to 1950 was conductor of the Liverpool Philharmonic. —Cf. Donald Brook, *International Gallery of Conductors* (Bristol, 1951; pp. 151-54).

Riisager, Knudage, Danish composer; b. Port Kunda, Estonia, March 6, 1897. He studied economics at the Univ. of Copenhagen; then music with Peder Gram and Otto Malling; subsequently took lessons with Albert Roussel and Paul Le Flem in Paris. In 1937 he was elected president of the Danish Composers' Union. —Works: opera buffa, *Susanne* (Copenhagen, Jan. 7, 1950); ballets: *Benzin* (Copenhagen, Dec. 26, 1930), *Qarrtsiluni,* on Eskimo themes (Copenhagen, Feb. 21, 1942), *Phoenix* (Copenhagen, May 12, 1946), *Etude,* based on Czerny's studies (Copenhagen, Jan. 15, 1948); incidental music to 2 plays by Munk: *Niels Ebbesen* (Copenhagen, Sept. 1, 1945) and *Pilatus* (Copenhagen, Feb. 20, 1947); *Danish Psalm,* for chorus and orch. (Copenhagen, Sept. 18, 1945); 4 symphonies (1925, 1927, 1935, 1940); orchestral suite *Tivoli-Tivoli* (Copenhagen, Aug. 15, 1943); concerto for trumpet and strings (London Festival of the International Society for Contemporary Music, June 20, 1938); concertino for saxophone and orch. (1939); several overtures; *Sinfonia serena,* for strings and percussion (1950); *Suite dionysiaque,* for chamber orch. (1924); wind quintet (1921); *Divertimento,* for 5 wind instruments and string quartet (1925); 6 string quartets (1918, 1920, 1922, 1926, 1932, 1943); concertino for oboe, clarinet, and bassoon (1932); *Serenade,* for flute, violin, and cello (1936); 2 violin sonatas (1917, 1923); piano sonata (1931); *Quatre épigrammes,* for piano (1921); and other pieces. He publ. a collection of essays, *Det usynlige Mønster* (Copenhagen, 1957).—Cf. S. Berg, *Knudåge Riisager* (Copenhagen, 1950; contains a list of works).

Rimbault, Edward Francis, English writer and editor; b. London, June 13, 1816; d. there, Sept. 26, 1876. Son of Stephen Francis Rimbault, organist and composer (1773-1837); pupil of his father, of Samuel Wesley and Dr. Crotch; organist of the Swiss Church, Soho, in 1832. He began giving lectures on English musical history in 1838; in 1840 he founded, with E. Taylor and W. Chappell, the Musical Antiquarian Society; received the degree of *Dr. phil.* from Göttingen. He composed various songs, of which *Happy Land* became a popular favorite. —His writings include: *Bibliotheca Madrigaliana* (1847; English poetry and compositions publ. during the reigns of Elizabeth and James I); *The Organ, Its History and Construction* (1855 and other eds.; it is the first part of the Appendix to Hopkins' *The Organ: its History*); *The Pianoforte; Its Origin, Progress and Construction* (1860); *The Early English Organ-builders and Their Works* (1864); *J. S. Bach* (after Hilgenfeldt and Forkel; 1869); a *Singing Tutor* (after Lablache), etc. He edited many collections of sacred and secular music, especially by English composers of the 16th-18th centuries.

Rimsky-Korsakov, Andrey Nikolayevitch, son of the composer; b. St. Petersburg, Oct. 17, 1878; d. there (Leningrad), May 23, 1940. He studied philology at the Univ. of St. Petersburg, and later in Strasbourg and Heidelberg (*Dr. phil.,* 1903); returning to Russia, he undertook his important investigations of Russian music history and biography. In 1915 he began the publication of the illustrated magazine, 'Musikalny Sovremennik' ('The Musical Contemporary'); it was suspended in 1917. He was subsequently active in various bibliographical and lexicographical pursuits. He was married to the composer Julia Weissberg. —Publications: *N. A. Rimsky-Korsakov; Life and Works,* in 5 issues (Moscow, 1933, 1935, 1936, 1937; vol. 5, 1946, ed. by Vladimir Rimsky-Korsakov); *Maximilian Steinberg* (Moscow, 1928); edited *M. P. Mussorgsky, Letters and Documents* (1932; extremely valuable); edited and annotated his father's *Chronicle* (Moscow, 1935); compiled *Musical Treasures of the Manuscript Dept. of the Leningrad Public Library* (1938); contributed numerous articles to Russian and foreign journals.

Rimsky-Korsakov, Georgy Mikhailovitch, grandson of the composer and nephew of Andrey Rimsky-Korsakov; b. St. Petersburg, Dec. 26, 1901. He studied at the St. Petersburg Cons.; in 1923, founded a society for the cultivation of quarter-tone music; composed some works in that system; publ. the articles *Foundations of the Quarter-Tone System* (Leningrad, 1925) and *The Deciphering of the 'Luce' Part in Scriabin's Prometheus,* in the Russian magazine 'De musica' (1927); then became active in work on electronic musical instruments; was co-inventor of the 'Emeriton' (1930), capable of producing a complete series of tones at any pitch and of any chosen or synthetic tone color; wrote solo pieces for it; also an octet for 2 emeritons, 2 clarinets, bassoon, violin, viola, and cello (1932). In 1953 he was appointed prof. of orchestration at the Leningrad Conservatory.

Rimsky-Korsakov, Nikolay Andreyevitch, celebrated Russian composer; b. Tikhvin, near Novgorod, March 18, 1844; d. Liubensk, near St. Petersburg, June 21, 1908. He remained in the country until he was 12 years old; in 1856 he entered the Naval School in St. Petersburg, graduating in

1862. As a child he took piano lessons with provincial teachers, and later with a professional musician, Théodore Canillé, who introduced him to Balakirev; he also met Cui and Borodin. In 1862 he was sent on the clipper Almaz on a voyage that lasted 2½ years; returning to Russia in the summer of 1865, he settled in St. Petersburg, where he remained most of his life. During his travels he maintained contact with Balakirev, and continued to report to him the progress of his musical composition. He completed his 1st symphony (which was also the earliest work in this form by a Russian composer), and it was performed in St. Petersburg under Balakirev's direction on Dec. 31, 1865, at a concert of the Free Music School in St. Petersburg. In 1871 Rimsky-Korsakov was engaged as prof. of composition and orchestration at the St. Petersburg Cons., even though he was aware of the inadequacy of his own technique. He remained on the faculty until his death, with the exception of a few months in 1905, when he was relieved of his duties as prof. for his public support of the rebellious students during the revolution of that year; the roster of his pupils testifies to his importance as a teacher: Glazunov, Liadov, Arensky, Ippolitov-Ivanov, Gretchaninov, N. Tcherepnin, Steinberg, Stravinsky, etc. In 1873 he abandoned his naval career, but was appointed to the post of inspector of military orchestras of the Russian Navy, until it was abolished in 1884. From 1883 to 1894 he was also assistant director of the Court Chapel, and led the chorus and the orchestra there. Although he was not a gifted conductor, he gave many performances of his own orchestral works; made his début at a charity concert for the victims of the Volga famine, in St. Petersburg, March 2, 1874; the program included the 1st performance of his 3rd symph. From 1886 until 1900 he conducted the annual Russian Symphony concerts organized by the publisher Belaiev; in June 1889 he conducted 2 concerts of Russian music at the World Exposition in Paris; in 1890 he conducted a concert of Russian music in Brussels; led a similar concert there in 1900. His last appearance abroad was in the spring of 1907, when he conducted in Paris 2 Russian historic concerts arranged by Diaghilev; in the same year he was elected corresponding member of the French Academy to succeed Grieg. These activities, however, did not distract him from his central purpose as a national Russian composer. His name was grouped with those of Cui, Borodin, Balakirev, and Mussorgsky as the 'Mighty Five' and he maintained an intimate friendship with most of them; at Mussorgsky's death he collected his manuscripts and prepared them for publication; he also revised Mussorgsky's opera *Boris Godunov;* it was in Rimsky-Korsakov's version that the opera became famous. In the 20th century, strong criticism was voiced against Rimsky-Korsakov's reduction of Mussorgsky's original harmonies and melodic lines to an academically acceptable standard. He had decided influence in the affairs of the Belaiev publ. firm, and was a permanent member of the Belaiev Prize Jury. He thus helped publish a great number of works by Russian composers of the St. Petersburg group; only a small part of these sumptuously printed scores represents the best in Russian music, but culturally Rimsky-Korsakov's solicitude was of great importance. Although he was far from being a revolutionary, he freely expressed his disgust at the bungling administration in Czarist Russia; he was particularly indignant about the attempts of the authorities to alter Pushkin's lines in his own last opera, *Le Coq d'or,* and refused to compromise; he died, of angina pectoris, with the situation still unresolved; the opera was produced posthumously, with the censor's changes; the complete text was not restored until the revolution of 1917. —Rimsky-Korsakov was one of the greatest masters of Russian music. His source of inspiration was Glinka's operatic style; he made use of both the purely Russian idiom and coloristic Oriental melodic patterns; such works as his symph. suite *Scheherazade* and *Le Coq d'or* represent Russian Orientalism at its best; in the purely Russian style the opera *Snow Maiden* and the *Russian Easter Overture* are outstanding examples. The influence of Wagner and Liszt in his music was small; only in his opera, *The Legend of the Invisible City of Kitezh* are there perceptible echoes from *Parsifal.* In the art of orchestration Rimsky-Korsakov had few equals; his treatment of instruments, in solo passages and in ensemble, was invariably idiomatic. In his treatise on orchestration he selected only passages from his own works to demonstrate the principles of practical and effective application of registers and tone colors. Although Rimsky-Korsakov was an academician in his general esthetics, he experimented boldly with melodic progressions and ingenious harmonies that pointed towards modern usages. He specifically favored the major scale with the lowered submediant; in *Mlada* he had a part for an ocarina tuned in a scale of alternating semitones and whole tones; in *Le Coq d'or* and *Kashchey the*

Immortal he applied dissonant harmonies in unusual superpositions; but he set for himself a definite limit in innovation, and severely criticized Richard Strauss, Debussy, and Vincent d'Indy for their practices. — Works: Operas: *Pskovityanka (The Maid of Pskov;* 1868-72; revised, 1891; St. Petersburg, Jan. 13, 1873; last version, St. Petersburg, April 18, 1895); *Maiskaya Notch (May Night;* St. Petersburg, Jan. 21, 1880); *Sniegurotchka (Snow Maiden;* St. Petersburg, Feb. 10, 1882); *Mlada* (St. Petersburg, Nov. 1, 1892); *Notch pered Rozhdestvom (Night Before Christmas;* St. Petersburg, Dec. 10, 1895); *Sadko* (Moscow, Jan. 7, 1898; Metropolitan Opera, N. Y., Jan. 29, 1929); *Mozart i Salieri,* on Pushkin's play dealing with Salieri's supposed poisoning of Mozart (Moscow, Dec. 7, 1898); *Boyarynia Vera Sheloga* (Moscow, Dec. 27, 1898; originally written as a prologue to *Pskovityanka;* N. Y., May 9, 1922); *Tsarskaya Neviesta (The Tsar's Bride;* Moscow, Nov. 3, 1899); *Tsar Saltan* (Moscow, Nov. 3, 1900); *Servilia* (St. Petersburg, Oct. 14, 1902); *Kaschey Bezsmertny (Kashchey the Immortal;* Moscow, Dec. 25, 1902); *Pan Voyevoda (The Commander;* St. Petersburg, Oct. 16, 1904); *Skazanie o nevidimom gradie Kitezhie (The Legend of the Invisible City of Kitezh;* St. Petersburg, Feb. 20, 1907); *Zolotoy Pietushok (The Golden Cockerel;* usually performed under the French title, *Le Coq d'or;* posthumous; Moscow, Oct. 7, 1909; the only opera of Rimsky-Korsakov often produced abroad). For orch.: op. 1, symph. no. 1 in E minor (originally in E♭ minor; later rewritten and transposed); op. 5, *Sadko,* symph. poem (1867; revised 1869 and 1891); op. 6, *Fantasy on Serbian themes* (1867; revised 1888); op. 9, symph. no. 2, *Antar* (1868; revised 1876 and 1897; also as a symph. suite); op. 28, *Overture on Russian Themes* (1866; revised 1880); op. 29, *Conte féerique* (1880); op. 30, piano concerto in C♯ minor (1882-83); op. 31, *Symphoniette* in A minor (on Russian themes; 1879); op. 32, symph. no. 3 in C major (1873-74; revised 1885-86); op. 33, *Fantaisie de concert sur des thèmes russes* for violin and orch. (1886); op. 34, *Capriccio espagnol* (1887); op. 35, *Scheherazade,* symph. suite (St. Petersburg, Nov. 3, 1888); op. 36, *Grande pâque russe (Russian Easter Overture;* 1888); suite from the opera, *Tsar Saltan* (1903; includes the famous musical tableau, *The Flight of the Bumblebee*); op. 59, *Pan Voyevoda,* suite from the opera (1903); op. 61, *Nad mogiloï (At the Grave;* in memory of Belaiev; 1904); op. 62, *Chanson russe (Dubinushka,* 1905, with chorus *ad lib.*); without op. numbers: *Night on Mount Triglav,* from the opera, *Mlada* (1907); suite from the opera, *Le Coq d'or* (1907). Chamber music: op. 12, string quartet in F (1875); op. 37, *Serenade* for cello and piano (1903); without op. numbers: string sextet in A (1876); quintet in B♭ for flute, clarinet, horn, bassoon, and piano (1876); first movement of a string quartet on B-la-f (Belaiev; other movements by Liadov, Borodin, and Glazunov; 1886); string quartet in G (1897); trio in C minor, for violin, cello, and piano (1897). Vocal works with orch.: op. 20, *Stikh ob Alexeye (Poem about Alexis),* folksong for mixed chorus (1877); op. 21, *Slava (Glory),* for mixed chorus (1876-80); op. 44, *Svitezyanka,* cantata for soprano and tenor solo and mixed chorus (1897); op. 53, *Strekozy (Dragonflies)* for women's voices (1897); op. 58, *Piesnia o veshchem Olegye (Poem of Oleg the Wise),* for men's chorus; op. 60, *From Homer,* for women's voices (1899); op. 49, 2 ariosos for bass, *Antchar (The Upas Tree)* and *Prorok (The Prophet)* (1897); choruses a cappella, op. 13, 14, 16, 18, 19, 23; 77 songs; 5 vocal duets; a vocal trio. Piano pieces: op. 10, 6 variations on BACH; op. 11, 4 pieces; op. 15, 3 pieces; op. 17, 6 fugues. He edited a collection of 100 Russian folksongs, op. 24 (1876); harmonized 40 folksongs. After Dargomyzhsky's death, he orchestrated his posthumous opera, *Kamennyi Gost (The Stone Guest)*; also orchestrated Borodin's *Prince Igor;* his greatest task of musical reorganization was the preparation for publication and performance of Mussorgsky's works; he reharmonized the cycle, *Songs and Dances of Death,* the symph. picture, *Night on the Bald Mountain;* orchestrated the opera, *Khovanshchina;* revised *Boris Godunov* (in melody and harmony, as well as in orchestration). Among his pedagogical works, the book on harmony (St. Petersburg, 1884; numerous subsequent eds. in Russian; in English, N. Y., 1930) is widely used in Russian music schools; publ. *Foundations of Orchestration* (2 vols., St. Petersburg, 1913; ed. by Maximilian Steinberg; also available in French and in English); collected articles were publ. in 1911, ed. by M. Gnessin. His autobiographical book, *The Chronicle of My Musical Life* (posthumous, 1909; 5th ed. by his son Andrey, supplemented and annotated, 1935) is a valuable document of the most important period of Russian music; it is publ. also in English (N. Y., 1924; new ed., 1942), in French (Paris, 1938), etc. The centennial of his birth (1944) was marked by the inauguration of a complete edition of his works (about 50 vols. planned). —Bibliography: V. Yastrebtzev, *R.-K.* (1900; 2nd ed. with a complete list of works, 1908); N. Findeisen, *R.-K.* (1908); I. Lapshin, *Philosophical Motives in the Works of R.-K.* (1911); N. van Gilse van der Pals, *R.-K.* (Leipzig, 1914); M. Montagu-Nathan, *History of Russian Music* (London, 1915; pp. 179-236); Rosa Newmarch, *The Russian Opera* (London, 1915; pp. 281-333); M. Montagu-Nathan, *R.-K.* (London, 1916); Igor Glebov, *R.-K.* (1922); E. Istel, *R.-K., the Oriental Wizard,* in the 'Mus. Quarterly' (July, 1929); N. van Gilse van der Pals, *R.-K.'s Opernschaffen* (Leipzig, 1929); A. Rimsky-Korsakov, *R.-K., Life and Works* (fundamental biography; 5 fascicles; Moscow, 1933, 1935, 1936, 1937, 1946; last vol. ed. by Vladimir Rimsky-Korsakov); Igor Markevitch, *R.-K.* (Paris, 1935); G. Abraham and M. D. Calvocoressi, *Masters of Russian Music* (London, 1936); G. Abraham, *R.-K.; a Short Biography* (London, 1949); D. Brook, *6 Great Russian Composers* (London, 1946); M. O. Yankovsky, *R.-K. and the Revolution of* 1905 (Moscow, 1950); A. Solovtzov, *Symphonic Works of R.-K.* (Moscow, 1953); D. Kabalevsky, ed., *R.-K., Materials and Letters* (Moscow, 2 vols., 1953 and 1954); M. F. Gnessin, *Reflections and Reminiscences about N.A. R.-K.* (Moscow, 1956); A. Gozenpud, *N.A. R.-K., Sources and Ideas of his Operas* (Moscow, 1957); numerous brochures and papers dealing with individual compositions by Rimsky-Korsakov. Correspondence is found in V. A. Kiselev, *R.-K.* (Moscow, 1951).

Rinaldo di Capua, Italian opera composer; b. Capua, c. 1710; d. Rome, after 1770. He came from the vicinity of Naples and seems to have been active chiefly in Rome, where Burney knew him in 1770, and where most of his operas were given (others were produced in Florence, Venice, London, and Paris). His career as a dramatic composer probably began in 1737. Thereafter he produced about 30 theatrical works with varying success, among them, *Ciro riconosciuto* (Rome, 1737), *Vologeso re de' Parti* (Rome, 1739), and *La Zingara* (Paris, June 19, 1753; his best work). He also composed a *Cantata per la Natività della Beata Vergine* (1747). —Cf. Charles Burney, *Present State of Music in France and Italy* (1771); Ph. Spitta's study of Rinaldo di Capua in 'Vierteljahrsschrift für Musikwissenschaft' (vol. III, 1887); G. Radiciotti, in 'Musica d'oggi' (July, 1925). See also A. Loewenberg, *Annals of Opera* (Cambridge, 1943; p. 113).

Rinck, Johann Christian Heinrich, famous German organist; b. Elgersburg, Feb. 18, 1770; d. Darmstadt, Aug. 7, 1846. He studied under Bach's pupil Kittel in Erfurt (1786-89); was town organist at Giessen (1790), and at Darmstadt (1805); became court organist there in 1813, and chamber musician in 1817. One of the foremost players of the time, he made frequent concert tours. He wrote many organ works. —Cf. his *Selbstbiographie* (Breslau, 1833); M. J. Fölsing, *Züge aus dem Leben und Wirken des Dr. C. H. Rinck* (Erfurt, 1848); F. Clément, *Musiciens célèbres* (Paris, 1868; 4th ed., 1887); F. W. Donat, *C. H. Rinck und die Orgelmusik seiner Zeit* (1933).

Ringwall, Rudolph, American violinist and conductor; b. Bangor, Maine, March 19, 1891; studied at the New England Cons.; graduated in 1913; later studied in Vienna. From 1913 to 1915 and from 1917 to 1920 he was a violinist in the Boston Symph. Orch.; taught at the New England Cons. (1916-20). In 1926 he was appointed assistant conductor, in 1934 associate conductor of the Cleveland Orch.; resigned in 1956.

Rinuccini (rē-nōōch-chē'-nē), **Ottavio,** great Italian poet and librettist; b. Florence, Jan. 20, 1562; d. there, March 28, 1621. He wrote several librettos for the Florentine creators of opera: the text of the intermezzo *Apollo e il pitone,* set to music by Marenzio in 1589, and subsequently the famous *Dafne,* set to music by Peri, Caccini, and Corsi in 1594; the latter is considered the first 'opera.' Rinuccini's *Euridice,* with music by Peri, was performed in 1600; another setting, by Caccini, in 1602. He also wrote the libretto of Monteverdi's *Arianna* (1608). These texts were republished by A. Solerti in vol. II of *Gli Albori del melodramma* (Milan, 1905). —Cf. F. Meda, *Ottavio Rinuccini* (Milan, 1894); A. Civita, *Ottavio Rinuccini ed il sorgere del melodramma in Italia* (Mantua, 1900); F. Raccamadoro-Ramelli, *Ottavio Rinuccini, studio biografico e critico* (1900); A. Solerti, *Le Origini del melodramma* (Turin, 1903); A. Solerti, *Musica, ballo e drammatica alla corte medicea dal 1600 al 1637* (Florence, 1905); O. G. Sonneck, *Dafne, the First Opera,* in 'Sammelbände der internationalen Musik-Gesellschaft' (1913); A. Della Corte, *Ottavio Rinuccini librettista* (Turin, 1925); U. Rolandi, *Didascalie sceniche in un raro libretto dell' Euridice del Rinuccini,* in the 'Rivista Musicale Italiana' (1926); M. Schild, *Die Musikdramen O. Rinuccinis* (Würzburg, 1933).

Riotte, Philipp Jakob, German conductor and composer; b. St. Mendel, Trier, Aug. 16, 1776; d. Vienna, Aug. 20, 1856. He studied with André in Offenbach; in 1808 settled in Vienna, where he conducted at the Theater an der Wien; produced there 48 works of his own, including operas, ballets, and minor pieces; also wrote a symphony, 9 piano sonatas, 6 violin sonatas, etc. He was the author of the 'tone picture,' *Die Schlacht bei Leipzig (The Battle of Leipzig)* for piano, which achieved extraordinary popularity in Germany.

Ripa, Alberto da (called Alberto Mantovano), Italian lutenist; b. Mantua; d. there, 1551. Little is known about his life; from 1529 he was in the service of Francis I of France. —Works: *Tablature de Luth* in 6 books publ. by his pupil Guillaume Morlaye (1553-58); pieces in Phalèse's publications of 1546 and 1574; also in Francesco da Forli's 'Intavolatura di liuto' (1536). —Cf. M. Brenet, in 'L'Année musicale' (1911); J. G. Prod'homme, *Guillaume Morlaye, éditeur d'Albert de Ripe,* in 'Revue de musicologie' (1925).

Rischbieter, Wilhelm Albert, German music theorist and pedagogue; b. Brunswick, July 20, 1834; d. Dresden, Feb. 11, 1910. He studied with Hauptmann; was violinist in Leipzig, Bremen, Nuremberg, and Liegnitz. In 1862 he was appointed teacher of harmony and comp. at the Dresden Cons. and held this position for nearly 40 years, until 1900. He publ. *Über Modulation, Quartsextakkord und Orgelpunkt* (1879); *Erläuterungen und Aufgaben zum Studium des Kontrapunkts* (1885); and *Die Gesetzmässigkeit der Harmonik* (1888).

Riseley, George, English organist and conductor; b. Bristol, Aug. 28, 1845; d. there, April 12, 1932. He was a chorister at the Bristol Cathedral from the age of 7, and studied with the cathedral organist, John Davis Corfe; in 1876 succeeded him at that post; in 1877 he organized a series of orchestral concerts in Bristol which contributed greatly to Bristol's musical life; also conducted the Bristol festival (1896-1911). In 1898 he was appointed conductor of the Queen's Hall Choral Society in London. He wrote a Jubilee Ode (Bristol, 1887), part-songs, and pieces for organ. For an account of his career see the 'Mus. Times' (Feb., 1899).

Risler (rēs-lär'), **Édouard,** pianist; b. Baden-Baden (of a German mother and Alsatian father), Feb. 23, 1873; d. Paris, July 21, 1929. He studied at the Paris Cons. with Diémer (piano) and Dubois (theory). After graduation, he continued his piano studies with Klindworth, Stavenhagen, and Eugène d'Albert. In 1906 he was appointed member of the 'Conseil supérieur' of the Paris Cons. He continued to make tours in Europe, where he acquired a very high reputation as a fine musician as well as virtuoso pianist; he made a specialty of cycles of one composer's works (Beethoven's 32 sonatas, both books of Bach's *Well-Tempered Clavier,* Chopin's complete works, etc.). He was also greatly esteemed as teacher.

Rist, Johann, German poet and composer; b. Ottensen, near Hamburg, March 8, 1607; d. Wedel-on-Elbe, Aug. 31, 1667. He studied theology at the universities of Hamburg and Bremen; later became a pastor in Mecklenburg and Wedel. In 1644 he was made poet-laureate by the Emperor, and in 1653 elevated to the rank of nobleman. He organized in Hamburg a 'Liederschule,' for which he secured the cooperation of many important composers of the day, among them Schiedemann and Thomas Selle. He has been described as the 'organizer of the German Parnassus' and indeed his role in the development of a purely national type of secular song, of German folk inspiration, was historically significant. He also wrote a number of sacred songs: *O Ewigkeit, du Donnerwort; O Traurigkeit; O Herzeleid; Werde munter, mein Gemüte;* etc., which are still sung in Lutheran churches in Germany. He compiled valuable collections of German sacred songs. —Cf. Th. Hansen, *Johann Rist und seine Zeit* (Halle, 1872); W. Krabbe, *Johann Rist und das deutsche Lied* (Bonn, 1910); O. Kern, *Johann Rist als weltlicher Lyriker* (Marburg, 1919); O. Heins, *Johann Rist und das niederdeutsche Drama des 17. Jahrhunderts* (1930).

Ristori, Giovanni Alberto, Italian composer; b. Bologna, 1692; d. Dresden, Feb. 7, 1753. He received his education from his father, a violinist in an Italian opera company; with him he went to Dresden (1715) and obtained the post of director of the Polish chapel there; then was appointed chamber organist to the court of Saxony (1733), church composer (1746), and assistant conductor (1750). He wrote a number of operas for the Italian Opera in Dresden. His *Calandro,* staged at Pillnitz, near Dresden, on Sept. 2, 1726, was one of the earliest Italian comic operas produced in

Germany, and so possesses historical significance beyond its intrinsic worth; other operas produced in Dresden and in court theaters near Dresden were *Don Chisciotte* (Feb. 2, 1727), *Cleonice* (Aug. 15, 1718), *Le Fate* (Aug. 10, 1736), *Arianna* (Aug. 7, 1736), etc. He also wrote 3 oratorios, 16 cantatas, 11 Masses; some instrumental music; many of his MSS were destroyed during the siege of Dresden (1760). —Cf. C. R. Mengelberg, *G. A. Ristori* (Leipzig, 1916).

Ritter, Alexander, German composer and poet, b. Narva, Estonia (of German parents), June 27, 1833; d. Munich, April 12, 1896. He was taken to Dresden in 1841; there he studied violin with Franz Schubert (namesake of the great composer), who was concertmaster of the Dresden opera; then studied at the Leipzig Cons. (1849-51) with Ferdinand David (violin) and E. F. Richter (theory). In 1854 he married Wagner's niece, Franziska Wagner, and settled in Weimar, where he entered into a close association with Liszt, von Bülow, Cornelius, Raff, and others. He was conductor at the opera in Stettin (1856-58), where his wife was engaged as soprano; he then lived in Dresden (1858-60), Schwerin (1860-62), and Würzburg (1863-82). When Bülow became conductor at the Hofkapelle in Meiningen (1882) Ritter settled there and played the violin in the orch.; after Bülow's departure from Meiningen in 1886, Ritter moved to Munich. He wrote 2 operas, *Der faule Hans* (Munich, Oct. 15, 1885) and *Wem die Krone?* (Weimar, June 8, 1890), to his own librettos, and several symph. poems in an intensely Romantic manner (*Seraphische Phantasie, Erotische Legende, Karfreitag und Frohnleichnam,* and *Kaiser Rudolfs Ritt zum Grabe*); a string quartet; about 60 songs; piano pieces. Ritter's significance derives, however, not from these well-made but ephemeral compositions, but from his profound influence on young Richard Strauss; it was Ritter who encouraged Strauss in the creation of a new type of philosophical tone-poem along the lines of 'Musik als Ausdruck' (music as expression), a modern development of the art of Liszt, Wagner, and Berlioz. Ritter wrote the poem printed in the score of *Tod und Verklärung.* —Cf. S. von Hausegger, *Alexander Ritter. Ein Bild seines Charakters und Schaffens* (Berlin, 1907).

Ritter, August Gottfried, German organist; b. Erfurt, Aug. 25, 1811; d. Magdeburg, Aug. 26, 1885. He was a pupil of Fischer at Erfurt, Hummel at Weimar, and Rungenhagen at Berlin; filled various posts as organist at Erfurt, Merseburg, and Magdeburg; edited the 'Urania' (1844-48); co-editor of the 'Orgelfreund' and 'Orgelarchiv'; publ. a valuable book, *Zur Geschichte des Orgelspiels . . . im 14. bis zum Anfange des 18. Jahrhunderts* (1884; new ed. by Frotscher, 1933ff.), and *Die Kunst des Orgelspiels,* (2 vols.; 9 eds.; in English, N. Y., 1874); also organ pieces; 4 books of chorales; a piano concerto, a piano quartet, 2 symphonies, 3 overtures, etc.

Ritter, Frédéric Louis, music historian and choral conductor; b. Strasbourg, June 22, 1834; d. Antwerp, July 4, 1891. He was of Spanish extraction, his original family name being Caballero, which was translated into German as Ritter (knight). He studied in Strasbourg with Schletterer and in Paris with J. G. Kastner. In 1856 he went to Cincinnati, where he organized the Philharmonic Orch., but left for New York in 1861; was active mainly as a choral conductor; in 1867 became prof. of music at Vassar College. He publ. several manuals and music histories; *History of Music* (2 vols.; Boston, 1870, 1874; 2nd ed., 1880); *Music in England* (N. Y., 1883); *Music in America* (N. Y., 1883; 3rd ed., 1893); *Music in Its Relation to Intellectual Life* (N. Y., 1891); etc. His wife, **Fanny Raymond Ritter** (b. Philadelphia, 1840; d. Poughkeepsie, N. Y., Oct. 26, 1890), was the author of *Woman as a Musician, an Art-Historical Study* (1876), *Some Famous Songs* (1878), etc.; transl. into English Schumann's *Music and Musicians.*

Ritter, Hermann, the inventor of the viola alta; b. Wismar, Sept. 16, 1849; d. Würzburg, Jan. 25, 1926. He studied at the Hochschule für Musik in Berlin; attended courses at the Univ. of Heidelberg; turning his attention to musical instruments, he began a series of experiments for the purpose of improving the muffled tone of the ordinary viola; profiting by some practical hints in A. Bagatella's book, *Regole per la Costruzione di Violini* (Padua, 1786), he constructed a slightly larger model possessed of better resonance and a more brilliant tone. Exhibiting this new 'viola alta' in 1876, he attracted the attention of Wagner, who invited his cooperation for the Bayreuth festival; after that engagement he made successful tours of all Europe as viola virtuoso; from 1879, prof. of viola and history of music at the Musikschule in Würzburg; in 1905 he founded the 'Ritterquartett' (violin, W. Schulze-Prisca; viola alta, Ritter; viola tenore, E. Cahnbley; viola bassa, H. Knöchel).—Publications: *Die Viola Alto: ihre Geschichte, ihre Bedeutung und die Principien ihres Baues* (1876; 3rd ed., 1885); *Repetitorium der Musikgeschichte* (1880); *Aus der Harmonielehre meines Lebens* (1883); *Elementartheorie der Musik* (1885); *Ästhetik der Tonkunst* (1886); *Studien und Skizzen aus Musik- und Kulturgeschichte, sowie Musikästhetik* (Dresden, 1892); *Katechismus der Musikästhetik* (2nd ed., 1894); *Katechismus der Musikinstrumente* (1894); *Volksgesang in alter und neuer Zeit* (1896); *Schubert* (1896); *Haydn, Mozart, Beethoven* (1897); *Die fünfsaitige Geige und die Weiterentwicklung der Streichinstrumente* (1898); *Allgemeine illustrierte Encyklopädie der Musikgeschichte* (6 vols., 1901-02). Also publ. numerous original compositions and transcriptions for viola and piano, and *Elementartechnik der Viola alta.* —Cf. G. Adema, *Hermann Ritter und seine Viola alta* (Würzburg, 1881; 2nd ed., 1894).

Ritter, Peter, German composer; b. Mannheim, July 2, 1763; d. there, Aug. 1, 1846. He studied violin and cello with his father; completed his theoretical studies under Abbé Vogler. He entered the Mannheim court orch. as a cellist, but later became its concertmaster, and, in 1803, conductor. He brought out in Mannheim his first opera, *Der Eremit auf Formentera* (Dec. 14, 1788; text by the celebrated poet A. von Kotzebue), which attained considerable vogue in Germany; some 20 more operas and Singspiele followed, but were not successful. In 1787 he married the famous actress Katharina Baumann (to whom Schiller had proposed); in 1790 both were employed at the Hoftheater; his wife retired on a pension in 1819, and Ritter himself in 1823. Besides his operas, he wrote a fine chorale, *Grosser Gott dich loben wir* (1792); an oratorio, *Das verlorene Paradies;* and much chamber music (selections publ. by Riemann in vol. XVI, 2, of the 'Denkmäler der Tonkunst in Bayern'). 24 autograph scores, including 2 symphonies, several concertos, etc., are in the Library of Congress in Washington.—Cf. W. Schulze, *Peter Ritter* (Berlin, 1895).

Ritter (real name Bennet), **Théodore,** French pianist and composer; b. near Paris, April 5, 1841; d. Paris, April 6, 1886. He was a pupil of Liszt; made successful European tours; publ. numerous solo pieces for piano, of which *Les Courriers* was a favorite; his operas, *Marianne* (Paris, 1861) and *La Dea risorta* (Florence, 1865), were unsuccessful.

Rivé-King, Julie, American pianist; b. Cincinnati, Oct. 31, 1857; d. Indianapolis, July 24, 1937. She received her primary instruction from her mother; then studied in New York with William Mason and in Leipzig with Reinecke; also was for a time a pupil of Liszt. She played Liszt's piano concerto No. 1 at her American début, with the N. Y. Philharmonic (April 24, 1875); this was the beginning of an active career; she gave about 4,000 concerts in the U. S., retiring only a year before her death. In 1876 she married Frank King of Milwaukee. From 1905 till 1936 she was piano instructor at the Bush Cons. in Chicago. She wrote some attractive piano pieces *(Impromptu, Polonaise héroïque, Bubbling Spring,* etc.).

Rivier (rē-viā'), **Jean,** French composer; b. Villemonble, July 21, 1896. He was in the French army in World War I, and did not begin his musical studies until 1918, when he entered the Paris Cons. and studied with Caussade; participated in various modern music societies in Paris; formed a style of composition that combined the elements of French Classicism and Impressionism. His music, always logical and attractive in its fluid development, has had numerous performances in France. —Works: opera, *Vénitienne* (Paris, July 8, 1937); for orch.: 5 symphonies: No. 1 (Paris, Jan. 29, 1933); No. 2, for strings (1937); No. 3 (1937; Paris, Nov. 25, 1940); No. 4 (Paris, 1947); No. 5 (Strasbourg, June 24, 1951); piano concerto (1941); violin concerto (1942); *3 Pastorales* (Paris, Feb. 7, 1929); *Adagio,* for string orch. (Paris, March 1, 1931); *Ouverture pour une opérette imaginaire* (Paris, Dec. 13, 1931); *Concertino* for alto and orch. (Paris, Feb. 15, 1936); *Jeanne d'Arc à Domrémy,* symph. tableau (Paris, Jan. 31, 1937); *Ballade des amants désespérés,* for orch. (1945); *Rapsodie provençale* (Aix-en-Provence, July 22, 1949); 2 string quartets; *Petite Suite,* for oboe, clarinet, and bassoon; violin pieces; piano pieces; several song cycles.

Roberton, Sir Hugh S., Scottish composer and choral conductor; b. Glasgow, Feb. 23, 1874; d. there, Oct. 7, 1952. In 1906 he founded the Glasgow Orpheus Choir, which contributed to a large extent to the cultivation of choral music in Scotland. He disbanded it in 1951. He publ. about 300 vocal pieces, including *The Faux Bourdon Series of Psalm Tunes; Songs of the Isles,* and a *Concert Edition of Scottish Songs;* also a pamphlet, *Prelude to the Orpheus* (London, 1947).

Robertson, Leroy, American composer; b. Fountain Green, Utah, Dec. 21, 1896. He studied in Provo; then in Boston with Chadwick and Converse at the New England Cons.; subsequently went to Europe, where he took courses with Ernest Bloch in Switzerland and with Hugo Leichtentritt in Berlin. Returning to America, he became instructor of music at Brigham Young Univ. at Provo; in 1948, was appointed head of the music dept., Univ. of Utah. In 1947 his symph. work *Trilogy* received the 1st prize of $25,000 in a contest sponsored by Henry H. Reichhold of Detroit; it was performed by the Detroit Symph. Orch. on Dec. 11, 1947, but despite the attendant publicity, the work was not successful, and there were few subsequent performances. Other works: *The Book of Mormon,* oratorio (Salt Lake City, Feb. 18, 1953); *Prelude, Scherzo, Ricercare,* for orch. (1940); *Rhapsody,* for piano and orch. (1944); *Punch and Judy Overture* (1945); violin concerto (1948); piano quintet (1933); string quartet (1940; N. Y. Music Critics Circle Award, 1944); *American Serenade,* for string quartet (1944); other chamber music; piano pieces; songs.

Robertson, Rae, pianist; b. Ardersier, Scotland, Nov. 29, 1893; d. Los Angeles, Nov. 4, 1956. He studied with F. Niecks at Edinburgh Univ.; then at the Royal Academy of Music, London, with Matthay and F. Corder; married Ethel Bartlett, pianist, with whom he gave numerous concerts in Europe and America as duo-pianists. With her he edited an Oxford Univ. Press series of works for 2 pianos.

Robeson, Lila, American contralto; b. Cleveland, April 4, 1880. She studied singing with Isidor Luckstone and Oscar Saenger in N. Y.; made her operatic début as Ortrud with the Aborn Opera Co. (Boston, April 4, 1911); from 1912 till 1920 she was a member of the Metropolitan Opera Co.; then devoted herself mainly to teaching; in 1953 taught voice at Western Reserve Univ., Cleveland.

Robeson, Paul, Negro bass singer; b. Princeton, N. J., April 9, 1898. He first studied law (1919, B.A., Rutgers Univ.; 1923, LL.B, Columbia Univ.); when his talent for singing and acting was discovered, he appeared in plays in the U. S. and England; acted the part of Emperor Jones in Eugene O'Neill's play and of Porgy in the Negro folk play by Du Bose and Dorothy Heyward. In 1925 he gave his first Negro spiritual recital in N. Y.; then toured in Europe. In 1930, he appeared in the title role of Shakespeare's *Othello* in London. Returning to the U. S., he continued to give recitals, but his radical political beliefs interfered with the success of his career. In 1952 he was awarded the International Stalin Peace Prize ($25,000). During the summer of 1958 he made an extensive European tour.—Cf. E. G. Robeson, *Paul Robeson, Negro* (N. Y., 1930); S. Graham, *Paul Robeson* (N. Y., 1946); Marie Seton, *Paul Robeson* (London, 1958); autobiography, *Here I Stand* (London, 1958.)

Robinson, Earl, American composer; b. Seattle, Wash., July 2, 1910; studied at the Univ. of Washington (B.M., 1933); then took lessons with Aaron Copland. In 1934 he joined the Federal Theater, for which he wrote incidental music for several plays; his *Ballad for Americans* from the revue *Sing for Your Supper* became nationally famous (1939). He received a Guggenheim Fellowship in 1940; in 1943 went to Hollywood to compose film music.

Robinson, Franklin Whitman, American organist and teacher; b. New York, June 27, 1875; d. Northeast Harbor, Maine, Sept. 16, 1946. He studied with MacDowell and Rybner at Columbia Univ. (M.A., 1907); in 1908 became instructor at the Institute of Musical Art, N. Y.; publ. *Anthems and Chant Forms* (1908-14) and *Aural Harmony* (N. Y., 1914; revised ed., 1936).

Robinson, Stanford, English conductor; b. Leeds, July 5, 1904. He played piano in hotel orchestras in London before entering the Royal College of Music; there he studied conducting under Sir Adrian Boult; at the age of 20 he became an assistant conductor with the B.B.C. (1924); organized the London Wireless Chorus, and conducted its programs for many years. In 1936 he became a director of the opera dept. of the B.B.C.; was conductor of the B.B.C. Theatre Orch. until 1946; in 1949 he was put in charge of the BBC Opera Orch. for broadcasting symph. music. —Cf. Donald Brook, *International Gallery of Conductors* (Bristol, 1951; pp. 155-58).

Robles (rŏh'-blĕs), **Daniel Alomias,** Peruvian composer and folksong collector; b. Huánuco, Jan. 3, 1871; d. Chosica, near Lima, July 17, 1942. He was of Indian blood; traveled through Indian villages of Peru, Bolivia, and Ecuador and collected many hundreds of melodies, of which the

Himno al Sol was notated by him as sung by a 117-year-old Indian. From 1919 to 1934 he lived mostly in the U. S.; then returned to Lima. He had no formal education and little musical technique; his melodic and rhythmic material was arranged by various composers for performances. In this manner he brought out an operetta, *El Condor Pasa;* several orchestral suites (*El Resurgimiento de los Andes, El Indio, Danza Huanca,* etc.). 5 melodies collected by Robles are reproduced in *La Musique des Incas et ses survivances* by Raoul and Marguerite d'Harcourt (Paris, 1925). —Cf. N. Slonimsky, *Music of Latin America* (N. Y., 1945; p. 275).

Robyn, Alfred George, American pianist, organist, and composer; b. St. Louis, April 29, 1860; d. New York, Oct. 18, 1935. He studied with his father, an organist; traveled with Emma Abbott at the age of 16, as pianist and accompanist; filled numerous posts as church organist in N. Y. He wrote the light operas, *The Yankee Consul* (1903), *The Gypsy Girl* (1905), *The Yankee Tourist* (1907), *Fortune Land* (1907), *All for the Ladies* (1912), etc.; the oratorios *The Ascension, Love Unending, Praise and Thanksgiving;* a symph. poem, *Pompeii;* a piano concerto; a piano quintet; 4 string quartets; numerous piano pieces; songs. Some of his songs and piano pieces sold extremely well.

Rocca, Lodovico, Italian composer; b. Turin, Nov. 29, 1895. He studied with Orefice at the Cons. of Milan; also attended the Univ. of Turin; then taught at Verona. In 1940 he was appointed director of the Cons. of Turin. —Works: operas: *In Terra di leggenda* (Milan, Sept. 28, 1933), *Il Dibuc* (Milan, March 24, 1934), *La Morte di Frine* (Milan, April 24, 1937), *Monte Ivnor* (Rome, Dec. 23, 1939), *L'Uragano* (Milan, Feb. 8, 1952); for orch.: *Contrasti* (1919), *Aurora di morte* (1920), *La Foresta delle samodive* (1921), *L'Alba del malato* (1922), *Le Luci* (1923), *Chiaroscuri* (1924), *La Cella azzurra* (1925); *Biribù, occhi di rana,* for voice and string quartet (1937); *Schizzi francescani,* for tenor and 8 instruments (1942); other songs with piano accompaniment. —Cf. G. Bas, in 'Musica d'oggi' (1925 and 1927); M. Castelnuovo-Tedesco in 'Il Pianoforte' (1925); A. Damerini, in 'Il Pianoforte' (1927).

Rochberg, George, American composer; b. Paterson, N. J., July 5, 1918. He studied piano with George Szell and Leopold Mannes (1939-41) in N. Y.; then at the Curtis Institute, Philadelphia, with Scalero and Menotti (1945). He received a Fulbright Fellowship (1950-51) and spent a year at the American Academy in Rome; also a Guggenheim Fellowship (1956). His symph. poem *Night Music* won the George Gershwin Memorial Award in 1953, and was performed by Mitropoulos and the N. Y. Philharmonic in the same year. From 1948 to 1954, he taught at the Curtis Institute; in 1955, appointed editor for the Theodore Presser Company. He has elaborated a system of composition with 12 tones that differs considerably from orthodox dodecaphony. —Works: *Capriccio* for 2 pianos (1949); symph. No. 1 (1949-55; Philadelphia, March 28, 1958); *Cantio Sacra,* for chamber orch. (1953); *Fantasia* for violin and piano (1955); *Sinfonia Fantasia* (1956); *Waltz Serenade* for orch. (Cincinnati, Feb. 14, 1958); string quartet; clarinet sonata (1958); 2 piano sonatas; a number of small piano pieces; songs. He publ. *The Hexachord and Its Relation to the 12-Tone Row* (1955).

Rochlitz, Johann Friedrich, German writer on music; b. Leipzig, Feb. 12, 1769; d. there, Dec. 16, 1842. A pupil of Doles in the Thomasschule, he entered the Univ. of Leipzig as a theological student; publ. some novels and sketches; his 2 pamphlets, *Blicke in das Gebiet der Kunst . . .* and *Einige Ideen über Anwendung des guten Geschmacks* (both 1796), treat in part of music. In 1798 he founded the 'Allgemeine musikalische Zeitung,' which he edited till 1818, and contributed to until 1835. From 1805 he was a director of the Gewandhaus Concerts. His best-known work is *Für Freunde der Tonkunst* (4 vols., 1824-32; 3rd ed., 1868), which contains biographies, essays, analyses of compositions, etc.; vol. IV has an outline *Geschichte der Gesangmusik,* which Rochlitz supplemented by a 'Sammlung vorzüglicher Gesangstücke' in 3 vols., from Dufay to Vallotti. Müller-Blattau compiled Rochlitz's essays on Bach under the title *Wege zu Bach* (1926). Rochlitz composed songs for men's chorus; also a setting of the 23rd Psalm; wrote texts for operas, oratorios, cantatas, etc. —Cf. Ernst Rychnovsky, *L. Spohr und F. Rochlitz* (Prague, 1904); J. Gensel, *Aus Rochlitzs Briefen an Henriette Voigt* (Leipzig, 1906); H. Ehinger, *J. F. Rochlitz als Musikschriftsteller* (Leipzig, 1929).

Röckel, August, Austrian writer on music; b. Graz, Dec. 1, 1814; d. Budapest, June

18, 1876. He was a pupil of his father, the impresario Joseph August Röckel, and of J. N. Hummel (his uncle); was for some years Kapellmeister in Weimar and Bamberg; then music director in Dresden (1843-48). There his opera *Farinelli* was to have been produced, but his admiration for Wagner's music, and the realization of his own inferiority, caused him to withdraw the score and abandon composition forever. Condemned to death for participation in the revolution of 1848, his sentence was commuted, and he spent 13 years in the prison in Walkheim; after his release he lived in Frankfurt, Munich, and Vienna, engaged in literary activity. —Cf. La Mara, *Richard Wagners Briefe an August Röckel* (Leipzig, 1894; 2nd ed., 1912; in English, Bristol, 1897).

Rockstro (real name Rackstraw), **William Smyth,** English music scholar; b. North Cheam, Surrey, Jan. 5, 1823; d. London, July 2, 1895. He studied at the Leipzig Cons. under Mendelssohn, Plaidy, and Hauptmann. Returning to London, he taught piano and singing; wrote a popular ballad, *Queen and Huntress;* publ. piano arrangements of numerous operas; devoted himself to a close study of ecclesiastical music, and became an acknowledged authority on plainchant; became a Roman Catholic in 1876. —Publications: *History of Music for Young Students* (1879); *Practical Harmony* (1881); *Rules of Counterpoint* (1882); *Life of G. F. Handel* (1883); *Mendelssohn* (1884); *General History of Music* (1886; 3rd ed., 1897); *Jenny Lind, the Artist* (1891; with Canon Scott Holland); *Jenny Lind, her Vocal Art and Culture* (1894; with Otto Goldschmidt); also publ. 'Festival Psalter, Adapted to the Gregorian Tones'; 'Accompanying Harmonies to the Ferial Psalter'; and 'Harmonies for Additional Chants and the Ambrosial Te Deum.'

Roda y López, Cecilio de, Spanish writer on music; b. Albuñol, near Granada, Oct. 24, 1865; d. Madrid, Nov. 27, 1912. From 1904 he was president of the music division of the Ateneo in Madrid; elected member of the Academy in 1906. He was the author of *Los Instrumentos, las Danzas y las Canciones en el Quijote* (1905), *La Evolución de la Música* (1906), *Un Quaderno di autografi di Beethoven del 1825* (Turin, 1907), etc.

Rode (rŏhd), **(Jacques-) Pierre (-Joseph),** French violinist; b. Bordeaux, Feb. 26, 1774; d. Château-Bourbon, near Damazan, Nov. 25, 1830. He was a pupil of Fauvel; from 1787, of Viotti at Paris; made his début in 1790 in a concerto by Viotti, at the Théâtre Feydeau; after tours in Holland and Germany and a short visit to London he was appointed prof. of violin at the newly opened Paris Cons. During a visit to Spain in 1799 he met Boccherini, who wrote concertos for him. In 1800 he was solo violinist to Napoleon; from 1803 to 1808 was in Russia with Boieldieu; became 1st violinist to the court of Alexander I; then spent 3 years in Paris, after which he toured Germany and Austria (at Vienna Beethoven wrote for him the *Romance,* op. 50); lived for a time in Berlin, where he married in 1814; then retired and lived in Bordeaux. His final appearance in Paris (1828) was a disheartening failure.—Works: 13 violin concertos; the famous *24 Caprices en forme d'études, dans les 24 tons de la gamme;* 12 études; 3 books of violin duos; etc.; and a *Méthode du violon* (with Baillot and Kreutzer). —Cf. A Pougin, *Notice sur Rode* (Paris, 1874); H. Ahlgrimm, *Pierre Rode* (Vienna, 1929).

Röder, Carl Gottlieb, German printer of music; b. Stötteritz, near Leipzig, June 22, 1812; d. Gohlis, Oct. 29, 1883. He founded the great Leipzig establishment for engraving and printing music, starting in 1846 with one engraver's apprentice; the business became one of the largest in the world. A book printing department was added later. In 1872 Röder's sons-in-law C. L. H. Wolff and C. E. M. Rentsch became partners in the firm; Röder himself retired in 1876. After Rentsch's death (Feb. 19, 1889) his heirs withdrew from the firm, but a son-in-law of Wolff, Karl Johannes Reichel (b. Aug. 15, 1853; d. Leipzig, Sept. 9, 1927), became a partner, and after Wolff's death (1915), head of the firm. On the 50th anniversary of its foundation the firm issued a 'Festschrift,' to which Hugo Riemann contributed a valuable essay, *Notenschrift und Notendruck;* a second 'Festschrift' (on the 75th anniversary), took the form of a study by W. von zur Westen entitled *Musiktitel aus 4 Jahrhunderten* (1921).

Röder, Martin, composer and singing teacher; b. Berlin, April 7, 1851; d. Boston, June 7, 1895. After studying music in Berlin, he went to Milan, where he organized the 'Società del Quartetto Corale' (1875), giving performances of vocal quartets; then occupied various posts as singing teacher in Berlin (1881-87), Dublin (1887-92), and finally at the New England Cons. in Boston (1892). He wrote 3 operas, of which only one, *Vera,* was performed (Hamburg, 1881); 2 symph. poems, *Azorenfahrt* and *Leonore;* the overture *Attila;* chamber music; publ. *Studî, critici, raccolti* (Milan, 1881) and *Dal Taccuino di un direttore di orchestra* (1881; in German as *Aus dem Tagebuche eines wandernden Kapellmeisters,* 1884).

Rodgers, Richard, American composer of popular music; b. New York, June 28, 1902; studied at Columbia Univ. (1919-21) and at the Institute of Musical Art, N. Y. (1921-23). He collaborated for 18 years with the lyricist Lorenz Hart in highly successful musical comedies: *The Girl Friend* (1926), *A Connecticut Yankee* (1927), *On Your Toes* (1936), *Babes in Arms* (1937), *I Married an Angel* (1938), *The Boys From Syracuse* (1938), *Pal Joey* (1940), and *By Jupiter* (1942). *The Rodgers and Hart Song Book* (N. Y., 1951) contains their most famous tunes. After Hart's death in 1943, Rodgers was associated with Oscar Hammerstein II (q.v). Together they wrote the greatly celebrated musical play *Oklahoma!* (1943; Pulitzer Prize, 1944; 2,248 performances); this was followed by many productions, scarcely less successful: *Carousel* (1945), *Allegro* (1947), *South Pacific* (1948; enormously popular; Pulitzer Prize, 1950), *The King and I* (1951), *Me and Juliet* (1953), *Pipe Dream* (1955); and *The Flower Drum Song* (1958). In 1952 Rodgers wrote the musical score for the documentary film, *Victory at Sea* (arranged as a symph. suite by Robert Russell Bennett), for which he was awarded the Distinguished Public Service Award by the U. S. Navy in 1953. —Cf. Deems Taylor, *Some Enchanted Evenings: The Story of Rodgers and Hammerstein* (N. Y., 1953); David Ewen, *Richard Rodgers* (N. Y., 1957; contains a full list of productions and a bibliography of magazine articles).

Rodio, Rocco, contrapuntist of the early Neapolitan school; b. Calabria, c. 1530; date of death unknown. He publ. *Regole per far contrapunto solo e accompagnato nel canto fermo* (1st ed., 1600; 3rd ed., 1626); also a collection (Naples, 1580) of 9 Masses; the last, *Missa de Beata Virgine* (*a* 5) is remarkable, because it can be sung by 4 or 3 voices by omitting the *quintus* or that voice and the *superius* (soprano), and also by the 3 highest voices if *quintus* and *bassus* are omitted.

Rodolphe, Jean Joseph, French composer; b. Strasbourg, Oct. 14, 1730; d. Paris, Aug. 18, 1812. He studied the French horn with his father; then the violin with Leclair in Paris; composition with Traetta in Parma, and with Jommelli in Stuttgart; wrote ballet music for Jommelli's productions there. In 1764 he was in Paris once more; brought out his 1st opera, *Le Mariage par capitulation* (Comédie-Italienne, Dec. 3, 1764); another opera, *L'Aveugle de Palmyre* (Comédie-Italienne, March 5, 1767), obtained considerable success. The famous balletmaster Noverre produced several of Rodolphe's ballets at the Paris Opéra. Mozart met Rodolphe in Paris in 1778, and spoke of him highly. 3 of Rodolphe's ballets are printed in the 'Denkmäler deutscher Tonkunst' (vol. 43/44). From 1784 to 1802 Rodolphe taught composition and solfège at the Paris Cons.; publ. the manuals, *Solfèges* and *Théorie d'accompagnement.*

Rodrigo, Joaquín, Spanish composer; b. Sagunto, Nov. 22, 1902. He studied in Valencia, and in Paris with Dukas; in 1939 settled in Madrid. —Works: for orch.: *Juglares* (1923); *5 Piezas infantiles* (1924); *Preludio para un poema a la Alhambra* (1926); *2 Miniaturas andaluses* (1939); *Concierto de Aranjuez,* for guitar (Barcelona, Nov. 9, 1940); *Concierto heroico,* for piano and orch. (Lisbon, April 5, 1943); *Concierto de estio,* for violin and orch. (Lisbon, April 11, 1944); *Concierto in modo galante,* for cello and orch. (Madrid, Nov. 4, 1949); concerto for harp and orch. (1954); *Fantasía para un gentilhombre* for guitar and orch. (1955). —Cf. F. Sopeña, *Joaquín Rodrigo* (Madrid, 1946).

Rodrigo de Ledesma, Mariano, Spanish composer; b. Zaragoza, Dec. 14, 1779; d. Madrid, March 28, 1848. He served as a chorister at the Cathedral of Zaragoza; was organist and chorusmaster at Vinaroz (1799-1802); then tenor singer in Madrid; in 1807 he was appointed conductor of the Madrid opera theater, but the French invasion forced him to flee, and he took refuge in Seville. In 1812 he was in Cádiz; there he composed an anti-Bonaparte hymn, *En tan infausto día,* while Joseph Bonaparte was king of Spain; fled to England, where he established himself as a singing teacher in London. With the restoration of legitimate monarchy in Spain, he returned there, and received a court appointment; publ. *40 Ejercicios de vocalización* (Madrid, 1820; Paris, 1827; also in English). He was again in England from 1823 to 1831; heard

Weber conduct his operas in London, and was profoundly impressed; thenceforth he tried to emulate Weber, writing music in a Romantic manner. Back in Spain once more, he became maestro to Queen María Cristina. He wrote chiefly church music: 3 solemn Masses, 9 Lamentations, a Stabat Mater; also some secular songs and instrumental pieces. Eslava reprinted 5 motets for 4 voices and orch. by Rodrigo in the 'Lira sacro-hispana.' —Cf. R. Mitjana, *El Maestro Rodrigo de Ledesma y sus Lamentaciones de Semana Santa* (Málaga, 1909).

Rodriguez, Augusto, Puerto Rican composer; b. San Juan, Feb. 9, 1904. He studied literature at the Univ. of Puerto Rico; music at Harvard with E. B. Hill and Walter Piston; since 1934, professor at the Univ. of Puerto Rico; organized a chorus, which achieved a high degree of excellence; gave a concert with it in New York in 1949. He published several songs, and dance suites.

Rodriguez, Felipe, Catalan composer; b. 1759; d. 1814. He was a member of the Monserrat School; ordained priest, 1778; served as organist in Madrid. He wrote organ pieces, some of which are printed in *Música instrumental,* ed. by D. Pujol (vol. 2, Montserrat, 1946), and church music; his *Rondo* for piano is printed by J. Nín in the collection *17 Sonates et pièces anciennes d'auteurs espagnols* (Paris, 1929).

Rodriguez, Vicente, Spanish organist and composer; b. Valencia, about 1685; d. there, 1761. He was a cleric, served as organist of the Valencia Cathedral from 1716 to his death; wrote several Masses; also keyboard music; his *Sonata in F* (1744), printed by Joaquín Nín in his collection, *17 Sonates et pièces anciennes* (Paris, 1929), is in the style of Domenico Scarlatti.

Rodríguez de Hita (rŏh-drē'-geth deh ē'tăh), **Antonio,** Spanish composer; date of birth unknown; d. Madrid, Feb. 21, 1787. In 1757 he was chorusmaster at the Cathedral of Palencia, where he publ. a book of advice to his pupils, *Consejos que a sus discípulos da don Antonio Rodríguez de Hita.* Then he became music director at the Convent of the Incarnation in Madrid. From 1768 he collaborated with the dramatist Ramón de la Cruz in a series of notable stage works impregnated with Spanish atmosphere; the best are the comic operas (zarzuelas) *Las Segadoras de Vallecas* (Madrid, Sept. 3, 1768) and *Las Labradoras de Murcia* (Madrid, Sept. 16, 1769). He also composed the Spanish opera *Briseida* (Madrid, July 11, 1768), various hymns for 4 and 8 voices; etc. —Cf. E. Cotarelo y Mori, *Don Ramón de la Cruz* (with music examples); E. Cotarelo y Mori, *Historia de la Zarzuela* (Madrid, 1934).

Rodzinski (roh-dzhin'-skē), **Artur,** eminent conductor; b. Spalato, Dalmatia, Jan. 2, 1894; studied law at the Univ. of Vienna (LL.D.); later at the Vienna Academy of Music. During World War I he served in the Austrian army; was wounded in action in 1917. He made his conducting début in Lwow in 1921; was for 5 seasons conductor of Polish operas in Warsaw; also conducted concerts of the Warsaw Philharmonic. In 1926 he was engaged as assistant conductor to Leopold Stokowski with the Philadelphia Orch.; also became head of the opera and orch. departments of the Curtis Institute. In 1929 he was appointed permanent conductor of the Los Angeles Philharmonic; after 4 seasons there he became conductor of the Cleveland Orch. (1933); introduced the novel custom of staging operas in concert form (*Parsifal, Elektra,* etc.); gave the American première of Shostakovitch's opera, *Lady Macbeth of Mtzensk* (Cleveland, Jan. 31, 1935). In 1936 he conducted at the Salzburg Festival; in the spring of 1937, was guest conductor of the N. Y. Philharmonic for 8 weeks; in the same year he organized and trained the N.B.C. Symph. Orch. for Toscanini; also conducted a number of its concerts. In 1943 he was engaged as permanent conductor of the N. Y. Philharmonic, obtaining excellent success; but after a series of conflicts with the management on account of Rodzinski's independent artistic policy, he was forced to resign in the middle of his 4th season (Feb. 3, 1947). A few days later he was engaged as conductor of the Chicago Symph. Orch.; but there too a conflict rapidly developed between him and the management, and he was dismissed during his first season (Jan. 13, 1948). Rodzinski subsequently conducted mostly in Europe and South America; was particularly successful in Italy; settled in Rome. He was engaged to conduct 2 productions for the Lyric Opera in Chicago in the autumn of 1958, his first American appearance after 10 years of absence. —Cf. Donald Brook, *International Gallery of Conductors* (Bristol, 1951; pp. 159-64).

Roeckel. See **Röckel.**

Roentgen. See **Röntgen.**

Roesgen-Champion, Marguerite, Swiss harpsichordist and composer; b. Geneva, Jan. 25, 1894. She studied at the Cons. of Geneva with Ernest Bloch and Jaques-Dalcroze, graduating in 1913. She settled in Paris; appeared as a pianist; then made a specialty of the harpsichord; gave numerous recitals on that instrument in France and elsewhere; also wrote harpsichord pieces. —Works: *Nymphes chasseresses,* for chorus and orch. (Geneva, 1926); *Faunesques,* 3 symph. poems (Paris, 1929); *Concerto moderne* for harpsichord and orch. (Paris, Nov. 15, 1931, composer soloist); symph. suite *Aquarelles* (Paris, Nov. 26, 1933); harp concerto (1944; Paris, March 28, 1954).

Rogatis, Pascual de, Italian-Argentine composer; b. Teora, May 17, 1881. He was taken to Buenos Aires as an infant; studied piano and composition with Alberto Williams at the Cons. there; violin with Pietro Melani and Rafael Albertini; taught violin at the Cons. —Works: operas (all first performed in Buenos Aires): *Anfion y Zeto,* Greek tragedy (Aug. 18, 1915), *Huémac,* to a story of ancient Mexico (July 22, 1916), *La Novia del hereje* (*The Heretic's Bride;* June 13, 1935); symph. poem, *Atipac* (Buenos Aires, April 7, 1928); *Canciones Argentinas,* a cycle of 5 songs in the native vein; piano pieces.

Rogel (rŏh-hĕl'), **José,** Spanish composer of light opera; b. Orihuela, Alicante, Dec. 24, 1829; d. Cartagena, Feb. 25, 1901. At a very early age he was taught music by the organist J. Cascales, and at 10 composed a Mass, which he conducted himself. After he finished his law studies in Valencia, he studied counterpoint with Pascual Pérez; subsequently conducted at various theaters in Madrid, and in 1854 began his unusually successful career as composer of zarzuelas, of which he wrote about 75 (some in collaboration). Among his best works are *El Joven Telémaco, Las Amazones del Tormes, El Rey Midas, Los Infiernos de Madrid, Genoveva de Brabante, Pablo y Virginia.*

Roger (rŏh-zhä'), **Gustave-Hippolyte,** famous French tenor; b. La Chapelle St.-Denis, near Paris, Dec. 17, 1815; d. Paris, Sept. 12, 1879. He was a pupil of Morin at the Paris Cons.; made his début at the Opéra-Comique in 1838; then at the Paris Opéra, where he created the role of the Prophète in Meyerbeer's opera (1848); later toured in Germany. While hunting in the fall of 1859 the accidental discharge of his gun injured his right arm so severely that it had to be amputated. An artificial arm proved unsuccessful, and he was obliged to retire from the stage in 1861, when he settled in Paris as a singing teacher. From 1868 until his death he was prof. of singing at the Cons. —Cf. his memoirs, publ. as *Le Carnet d'un Ténor* (Paris, 1880); also A. Laget, *G.-H. Roger* (Paris, 1865).

Roger (roh-zhä'), **Victor,** French composer of operettas; b. Montpellier, July 21, 1854; d. Paris, Dec. 2, 1903. He studied at the École Niedermeyer; wrote light music; composed some 30 operettas, of which the following were fairly successful: *Sa Majesté l'Amour* (1896), *l'Auberge du Tohu-Bohu* (1897), *Les Fêtards* (1897), *L'Agence Crook & Co.* (1898), *La petite Tâche* (1898), and *Poule blanche* (1899). After his death 3 completely finished scores were found: *La Fille de Fra Diavolo, La Princesse de Babylone,* and *Adélaïde.*

Roger-Ducasse (rŏh-zhā'-dü-kähs'), **Jean-Jules Aimable,** French composer; b. Bordeaux, April 18, 1873; d. Le-Taillan-Médoc, near Bordeaux, July 20, 1954. He studied at the Paris Cons. with Fauré (composition), Pessard (harmony), Gedalge (counterpoint) and with de Bériot. In 1902 he won the 2nd Prix de Rome for the cantata *Alcyone;* in 1909, appointed inspector of singing in the Paris schools; subsequently prof. of ensemble at the Paris Cons.; from 1935 to 1940 taught composition there; then retired to Bordeaux. His 1st work to be played in public was a *Petite Suite* for orch. (Paris, March 5, 1898). He adopted a pleasing style of Impressionism; his symph. pieces enjoyed considerable success, without setting a mark for originality. —Works: comic opera, *Cantegril* (Opéra-Comique, Feb. 9, 1931); a mimodrama, *Orphée* (St. Petersburg, Jan. 31, 1914); for orch.: *Variations plaisantes sur un thème grave* (Paris, Jan. 24, 1909), *Suite française* (1909), *Prélude d'un ballet* (1910), *Le joli jeu de furet,* orchestral scherzo (1911), *Nocturne de printemps* (Paris, Feb. 14, 1920), *Symphonie sur la Cathédrale de Reims, Le petit faune* (Bordeaux, May 22, 1954), etc.; *Sarabande,* symph. poem with voices (1911); *Au Jardin de Marguerite,* for soloists, chorus, and orch. (1901-05); *Sur quelques vers de Virgile,* for chorus and orch.; piano quartet (1899-1912); string quartet (1900-09); piano pieces (*Le Cœur de l'eau, Noëls des roses, 7 Préludes,* études, arabesques, etc.); pedagogic works (*Solfèges,* 3 vols.; *Dictée musicale,* 4 vols.; *Exercises de piano,* 3 vols.; etc.). His autobiography was publ. in

L'Écran des musiciens (1930). —Cf. L. Ceillier, *Roger-Ducasse* (Paris, 1920); A. Cœuroy, *La Musique française moderne* (Paris, 1922).

Rogers, Bernard, American composer; b. New York, Feb. 4, 1893. He studied architecture before devoting himself to music. His first teacher was Arthur Farwell; he subsequently studied with Ernest Bloch in Cleveland. His symph. composition, *To the Fallen,* was performed by the N. Y. Philharmonic on Nov. 13, 1919; on the strength of it, he won a Pulitzer Traveling Scholarship and went to Europe for further study; in 1927 he received a Guggenheim Fellowship; took courses with Nadia Boulanger in Paris and Frank Bridge in London. When he returned from Europe in 1929 he was engaged as instructor at the Eastman School of Music, Rochester; he has remained there, teaching orchestration and composition. His lyric drama, *The Marriage of Aude,* was brought out in a festival of American music at the Eastman School, on May 22, 1931. The Metropolitan Opera Co. produced his 1-act opera, *The Warrior* (to the story of Samson and Delilah), on Jan. 11, 1947, but it was not successful; another opera, *The Veil,* was produced at the Univ. of Indiana on May 18, 1950. Other works: for orch.: *The Faithful* (1918), *Adonais* (Rochester, April 29, 1927), *Prelude to Hamlet* (1928), symph. No. 2 (Rochester, Oct. 24, 1930), *3 Japanese Dances* (Rochester, May 3, 1934), *Once Upon a Time,* 5 fairy tales for small orch. (Rochester, April 4, 1935), *The Supper at Emmäus* (Rochester, April 29, 1937), symph. No. 3 (Rochester, Oct. 27, 1937), *The Colors of War* (Rochester, Oct. 25, 1939), *The Song of the Nightingale* (Cincinnati, March 21, 1940), *The Dance of Salome* (Rochester, April 25, 1940), *The Plains,* 'landscapes for orch.' (N. Y., May 3, 1941), *Invasion* (N. Y., Oct. 17, 1943); *Characters from Hans Christian Andersen* (Rochester, April 28, 1945), *In Memory of Franklin Delano Roosevelt* (N. Y., April 11, 1946), *Amphitryon,* symph. overture (N. Y., March 10, 1947), symph. No. 4 (Rochester, May 4, 1948), *Dance Scenes* (Louisville, Oct. 28, 1953), *Fantasy,* for flute, viola, and orch. (Rochester, April 25, 1938), *Soliloquy,* for flute and strings (1922), *Soliloquy,* for bassoon and string orch. (Rochester, Oct. 18, 1938), *The Silver World,* for flute, oboe, and strings (1950), *Leaves from the Tale of Pinocchio,* suite for narrator and small orch. (1950); vocal works: *The Passion,* oratorio in 6 scenes, for soloists, mixed chorus, and orch. (Cincinnati, May 12, 1944; his most significant work), *The Raising of Lazarus,* for soloists, chorus, and orch. (1928), *The Exodus,* sacred poem, for soloists, chorus, and orch. (1932); a string quartet and other chamber music. He publ. a valuable manual, *The Art of Orchestration* (N. Y., 1951). —Cf. E. E. Hipsher, *American Opera and Its Composers* (Philadelphia, 1934; pp. 369-70); David Diamond, *Bernard Rogers,* in the 'Mus. Quarterly' (April, 1947).

Rogers, Clara Kathleen (née Barnett); English soprano; b. Cheltenham, Jan. 14, 1844; d. Boston, March 8, 1931. She was the daughter of the composer John Barnett; studied at the Leipzig Cons. with Moscheles and Plaidy (piano), Papperitz and Richter (theory), David and Rietz (ensemble playing); singing with Goetz in Berlin and with Sangiovanni in Milan. She made her début in Turin (1863) as Isabella in *Robert le Diable* (stage name 'Clara Doria'); came to America in 1871 with the Parepa-Rosa Co.; début, N. Y., in *Bohemian Girl* (Oct. 4, 1871); later settled in Boston as a teacher; from 1902 was prof. of singing at the New England Cons.; married a Boston lawyer, Henry M. Rogers, in 1878. She publ. *The Philosophy of Singing* (1893); *Dreaming True* (1899); *My Voice and I* (1910); *English Diction in Song and Speech* (1912); *The Voice in Speech* (1915); *Memories of a Musical Career* (Boston, 1919) and its sequel, *The Story of Two Lives* (Norwood, Mass., (1932); also a number of songs and violin pieces.

Rogers, Francis, American baritone; b. Roxbury, Mass., April 14, 1870; d. New York, May 15, 1951. He studied singing with W. L. Whitney in Boston, Vannuccini in Florence, Bouhy in Paris, and Luckstone in N. Y.; appeared in concert and oratorio throughout the U. S.; from 1924 member of the faculty of the Juilliard Graduate School, N. Y. He publ. *Some Famous Singers of the 19th Century* (N. Y., 1914).

Rogers, James Henderson, American organist and song composer; b. Newark, N. Y., 1852; d. St. Petersburg, Fla., May 30, 1933. He studied music in N. Y.; was a church organist; composed a quantity of anthems and other church pieces, later collected in a book under the title, 'The Church Chorus Series.'

Rogers, James Hotchkiss, American organist and composer; b. Fair Haven, Conn., Feb. 7, 1857; d. Pasadena, Calif., Nov. 28, 1940. He studied with Clarence

Eddy in Chicago; in Berlin under Loeschhorn and Ehrlich (piano), Rohde (theory), and Haupt (organ); in Paris under Fissot (piano), Guilmant (organ), and Widor (theory). Returning to the U. S., he settled in Cleveland (1883) as organist; eventually retired to California. He publ. about 150 works: a Lenten cantata, *The Man of Nazareth;* an Easter cantata, *The New Life*; anthems, secular part-songs, songs, piano pieces, studies for piano and organ. Among his most popular songs are *The Star* and *At Parting.*

Roget (rŏh-zhā'), **Henriette,** French composer and organist; b. Bastia, Corsica, Jan. 9, 1910; studied at the Paris Cons.; received the Premier Second Prix de Rome in 1933.—Works: *Montanyas del Rosello,* for organ and orch. (Paris, April 6, 1933, composer soloist); *Cathérinettes,* ballet (1937); *Hymne à l'aviation* (1937; awarded a prize at the Paris Exhibition); *3 Ballades françaises* (Paris, Jan. 11, 1936); *Rythmes* for orch. (Paris, Jan. 23, 1937); *Sinfonia andorrana* (1939); *Symphonie pour rire* (1947); *Concerto classique* for cello and orch. (1944); *Concerto sicilien* for piano and orch. (1945); chamber music; organ pieces; choral works; songs. —Cf. A. Machabey, *Portraits de trente musiciens français* (Paris, 1949).

Rogowski (rŏh-gŏv'-skē), **Ludomir,** Polish composer; b. Lublin, Oct. 3, 1881; d. Dubrovnik, Yugoslavia, March 14, 1954. Of a musical family, he received his early training at home; in 1906 went to Leipzig and took a course with Hugo Riemann. Returning to Poland, he conducted the Vilna Symph. Orch., which he founded (1910); in 1911 was in Paris; from 1912 to 1914, was a theater conductor in Warsaw. He was again in France (1917-19); in Poland (1919-26), finally settling in Dubrovnik, Yugoslavia (1927), where he remained for the rest of his life, with only occasional engagements as conductor in Warsaw (1935 and 1938). —Works: operas: *Tamara* (1918), *Un grand chagrin de la petite Ondine* (1919), *La Sérénade inutile* (1921), *Królewicz Marko* (1930); the ballets *Bajka* (1922) and *Kupala* (1925); 6 symphonies: no. 1, *Offering* (1921), no. 2, *Rejoicing* (1936), no. 3 (1940), no. 4 (1943), no. 5 (1947), no. 6 (1949); other symphonic works: *Images ensoleillées* (1918), *Villafranca* (1919), *Les Saisons* (1933), *Les Sourires* (1933), *Poème du travail* (1936), *Fantômes* (1937), 4 rhapsodies on Slavonic themes (1945), *Dubrovnik Impressions* (1950); 6 works for violin and orch.; 2 string quartets; short pieces for various instruments; numerous arrangements of Slavonic songs for chorus. In some of his works he made use of the so-called Slavonic scale (Lydian mode with the lowered 7th) and the scale of alternating whole tones and semitones.

Roguski, Gustav, Polish composer and pedagogue; b. Warsaw, May 12, 1839; d. there, April 5, 1921. He studied in Germany with Kiel; then went to Paris, where he became a pupil of Berlioz. Returning to Warsaw in 1873, he was appointed prof. at the Cons. He wrote a symphony, 2 string quartets, a quintet for wind instruments and piano, many piano pieces, choruses, and songs; publ. a manual of harmony in Polish (with L. Zelenski). He was greatly esteemed as a teacher of composition; Paderewski was his pupil.

Rohde, (Friedrich) Wilhelm, Danish violinist and composer; b. Altona, Dec. 11, 1856; d. Gentofte, near Copenhagen, April 6, 1928; pupil at the Leipzig Cons. of H. Schradieck and F. David (violin), J. Röntgen (piano), E. F. Richter (composition), and H. Kretzschmar. He lived in Chicago (1878-85) as teacher; after one season as violist in the Boston Symph. Orch. and prof. at the New England Cons., he returned to Germany; lived in Schwerin; from 1914, in Copenhagen. He composed several symph. poems; a serenade for strings; *Höller-Galopp* for violin, cello, flute, horn, and piano; a number of male choruses; piano pieces.

Rohloff, Ernst, German music historian; b. Graudenz, April 17, 1899. He studied in Leipzig with Straube (organ), Schering and Abert (musicology); received his *Dr. phil.* for the dissertation *Studien zum Musiktraktat des Johannes de Grocheo* (publ. Leipzig, 1925); settled in Weissenfels as teacher and organist. Publ. several papers on medieval music.

Röhr, Hugo, German conductor and composer; b. Dresden, Feb. 13, 1866; d. Munich, June 7, 1937. He was a pupil at the Dresden Cons. of A. Blassmann (piano) and F. Wüllner (composition); began his career as Kapellmeister in Augsburg; after filling similar positions in Prague and Breslau he was called in 1892 as Hofkapellmeister to Mannheim; appointed Hofkapellmeister at the court opera in Munich (1896), and (from 1912) also conductor of the Lehrergesangverein; 1924-34, teacher of conducting at the Munich Academy of Music; then retired. He wrote several 1-act operas: *Das*

Vaterunser (Munich, 1904), *Frauenlist* (Leipzig, 1917), *Cœur-Dame* (1927); a dramatic poem *Ekkehard,* for soli, chorus, and orch.; chamber music; songs.

Röhrig, Emil, German composer; b. Rettert, Oct. 31, 1882; d. Aachen, July 22, 1954. After studying violin in Chemnitz, he became engaged as violinist and conductor in Krefeld and Aachen. He wrote much music for brass; also concertos for double-bass, viola, trumpet, etc.; cantatas and other choral works.

Rojo (rŏh'-hŏh), **Casiano,** Spanish authority on Gregorian Chant; b. Acinas, near Burgos, Aug. 5, 1877; d. at the monastery of Santo Domingo de Silos, Burgos, Dec. 4, 1931. He entered the monastery school at Silos in 1890; ordained priest in 1901; taught organ until 1913; was chorus leader until 1922. He studied music with Dom Pothier; devoted himself to the study of Gregorian Chant. He publ.: *Le Chant grégorien en Espagne,* in the Strasbourg 'Kongressbericht' (1905); *Método de canto gregoriano* (Valladolid, 1906); *Antiphonarium Mozarabicum de la Catedral de León* (with G. Prado; León, 1928); *El Canto mozárabe. Estudio histórico-critico de su antigüedad y estado actual* (with G. Prado; Barcelona, 1929); articles in 'Revue du chant grégorien,' etc.

Rokseth, Yvonne (*née* Rihouët), French musicologist and organist; b. Maisons-Laffitte, near Paris, July 17, 1890; d. Paris, Aug. 23, 1948. She studied at the Paris Cons.; with d'Indy and Roussel at the Schola Cantorum; and with Pirro at the Sorbonne; *Dr. ès lettres* (dissertation: *La Musique d'orgue au XVe siècle et au début du XVIe*; Paris, 1930); held various positions as organist in Paris (1920-25); was later librarian at the Paris Cons. and in the music division of the Bibliothèque Nationale; prof. of musicology at the Univ. of Strasbourg (from 1937); publ. a biography of Grieg (Paris, 1933); edited *Deux livres d' orgue parus chez P. Attaingnant en 1531,* in the 'Publications de la Société française de musicologie' (1925); *Treize motets et un prélude pour orgue,* ib. (1930); *Polyphonies du XIIIe siècle: Le Manuscrit Montpellier H 196* (facsimile, transcription, and commentary, 4 vols., 1935-39); also organ works of Marc Antonio da Bologna of 1523; etc.; co-editor of *Trois Chansonniers français du XVe siècle* (Paris, 1927). —Cf. G. Thibault, *Yvonne Rokseth,* in 'Revue de Musicologie' (1948).

Roland-Manuel, Alexis (real name Roland Alexis Manuel Lévy), French composer and writer; b. Paris, March 22, 1891. He was a pupil of Albert Roussel and Vincent d'Indy; also studied privately with Ravel; was engaged as music critic of the 'Eclair.' In 1947 he became prof. at the Paris Cons. In his compositions he adopted the French neo-Classical style, close to Roussel's manner; however, it is not as a composer but as a perspicacious critic that he is chiefly known. He publ. 3 books on Ravel: *Maurice Ravel et son œuvre* (1914), *Maurice Ravel et son œuvre dramatique* (1928), *Maurice Ravel* (1938; in English, London, 1947); also monographs on Honegger (1925) and Manuel de Falla (1930). —Works: *Isabelle et Pantalon,* opéra-bouffe (Paris, Dec. 11, 1922); *Le Diable amoureux,* light opera (1929); *L'Écran des jeunes filles,* ballet (Paris Opéra, May 16, 1929); *Elvire,* ballet on themes of Scarlatti (Paris Opéra, Feb. 8, 1937); piano concerto (1938); *Cantique de la sagesse,* for chorus and orch. (1951); chamber music; songs.

Roldán, Amadeo, Cuban violinist and composer; b. Paris (of Cuban parents), July 12, 1900; d. Havana, March 2, 1939. He studied violin at the Madrid Cons. with Fernández Bordas, graduating in 1916; won the Sarasate violin prize; subsequently studied composition with Conrado del Campo in Madrid and with Pedro Sanjuán. In 1921 he settled in Havana; in 1924, became concertmaster of the Orquesta Filarmónica there; 1925, assistant conductor; from 1932, conductor. In his works he employed with signal success the melorhythms of Afro-Cuban popular music; as a mulatto, he had an innate understanding of these elements. Of his works, the most powerful is the ballet, *La Rebambaramba,* employing a number of Cuban percussion instruments in the score; a suite from this ballet was performed in Havana on Aug. 12, 1928. Other works: *Obertura sobre témas cubanos* (Havana, Nov. 29, 1925); *El Milagro de Anaquillé* (Havana, Sept. 22, 1929); *Danza Negra,* for voice and 7 instruments (1929); *Motivos de Son,* for voice and 9 instruments (1930); 3 *Toques* for chamber orch. (1931); and 6 *Rítmicas* for a percussion ensemble.

Rolla, Alessandro, Italian violinist, Paganini's teacher; b. Pavia, April 6, 1757; d. Milan, Sept. 15, 1841. He was a pupil of Renzi and Conti; from 1782 till 1802 he was concertmaster of the ducal orch. in Parma; Paganini studied with him there. In

1805 he was appointed violinist to the French Viceroy Eugène Beauharnais, in Milan; prof. at the Cons. of Milan from its foundation in 1807. He wrote several ballets: *Adelasia* (Milan, 1779), *Iserbeck* (Padua, 1802), *Eloisa e Roberto* or *Il Conte d'Essex* (Rome, 1805), *Pizzarro* (Milan, 1807), *Abdul* (Vienna, 1808), *Achilles auf Skyros* (Vienna, 1808); symphonies; 3 violin concertos; 4 viola concertos; 6 string quartets; trios for violin, viola, and cello, also for 2 violins and cello; duos for violin, also for violin and viola, etc.

Rolla, Antonio, Italian violinist; son of Alessandro Rolla; b. Parma, April 18, 1798; d. Dresden, May 19, 1837. He studied with his father; was concertmaster of the orch. of the Italian Opera Co. in Dresden (1823-35); composed a number of violin pieces.

Rolland (rŏh-lahn'), **Romain,** famous French author and musicologist; b. Clamecy, Nièvre, Jan. 29, 1866; d. Vézelay, Yonne, Dec. 30, 1944. He was educated at the École de Rome; *Dr. ès lettres* (1895) with two theses, *Cur ars picturae apud Italos XVI saeculi deciderit* and the very valuable *Les Origines du théâtre lyrique moderne (Histoire de l'opéra en Europe avant Lully et Scarlatti;* 3rd ed., 1931); the latter was awarded the Prix Kastner-Bourgault by the Academy in 1896, and at the same time won him the professorship in the history of music at the École Normale. In 1900 he organized the 1st international congress for the history of music in Paris, and read a paper on *Les Musiciens italiens en France sous Mazarin et 'l'Orfeo' de Luigi Rossi* (publ. 1901); with J. Combarieu he ed. the transactions and the papers read as *Documents, mémoires et vœux* (1901). In Oct., 1901, he founded, with J. Combarieu (editor), P. Aubry, M. Emmanuel, L. Laloy, and himself as principal contributors, the fortnightly 'Revue d'Histoire et Critique musicales.' In 1903 the Univ. of Paris commissioned him to organize the music section of the newly founded École des Hautes Études Sociales, of which he was the 1st president, and where he lectured on the history of music; resigned in 1909, devoting his entire time to literary work. From 1913 he resided in Switzerland, but in 1938 returned to France and took up his residence at Vézelay. —Rolland's writings exhibit sound scholarship, broad sympathy, keen analytical power, well-balanced judgment, and intimate acquaintance with the works of the composers. The book by which he is most widely known is *Jean-Christophe,* a musical novel remarkable for its blending of historical accuracy, psychological and esthetic speculation, subtle psychological analysis, and romantic interest; for it he received the Nobel prize (1915). The 1st volume was publ. in 1905, the last (10th) in 1912; English transl. by G. Cannan, N. Y., 1910-13; German transl. by E. Grautoff, Frankfurt, 1913-15 (new ed., 1931). Rolland's other works include *Paris als Musikstadt* (1904; in Strauss' series 'Die Musik'; rewritten and publ. in French as *Le Renouveau* in *Musiciens d'aujourd'hui); Beethoven* (1903; English transl. by B. Constance Hull, with brief analyses of the symphs., quartets, and sonatas by A. E. Hull, 6th ed., 1927; in German, Zürich, 1918); *Haendel* (1910; English transl. by A. E. Hull, 1916); *Voyage musical au pays du passé* (1920; in English, 1922); *Beethoven: Les grandes époques créatrices* (1928; English transl. by Ernest Newman entitled *Beethoven the Creator,* 1929; in German, 1930); *Goethe et Beethoven* (1930; in English, 1931); *Beethoven: Le Chant de la Résurrection* (1937; on the *Missa solemnis* and the last sonatas); essays in various journals he collected and publ. in 2 vols. as *Musiciens d'autrefois* (1908; 6th ed., 1919; in English, 1915) and *Musiciens d'aujourd'hui* (1908; 8th ed., 1947; in English, 1914); *Essays on Music* (a selection from some of the above books; N. Y., 1948); contributed the chapters on Italian, French, English, and German opera in the 17th century to Lavignac's 'Encyclopédie de la Musique' (1913). —Cf. P. Seippel, *Romain Rolland: l'Homme et l'œuvre* (Paris, 1913); Stefan Zweig, *Romain Rolland: der Mann und das Werk* (Frankfurt, 1921; in English, N. Y., 1921); J. Bonnerot, *Romain Rolland, sa vie, son œuvre* (Paris, 1921); E. Lerch, *Romain Rolland und die Erneuerung der Gesinnung* (Munich, 1926); M. Lob, *Un grand Bourguignon, Romain Rolland* (Auxerre, 1927); Chr. Sénéchal, *Romain Rolland* (Paris, 1933); M. Doisy, *Romain Rolland* (Brussels, 1945); R. Argos, *Romain Rolland* (Paris, 1950); W. T. Starr, *A Critical Bibliography of the Published Writings of Romain Rolland* (Evanston, Ill., 1950).

Rolle, Johann Heinrich, German composer; b. Quedlinburg, Dec. 23, 1716; d. Magdeburg, Dec. 29, 1785. He played the viola and the organ in the Berlin court orch. (1741); went to Magdeburg in 1746 as church organist; in 1752 became his father's successor as town music director there. He wrote 4 Passions, 20 oratorios, several church services for the entire year; *Odes of Anacreon* for voice and harpsichord; other secular pieces. —Cf. W. Kawerau, *J. H. Rolle. Ein musikalisches Characterbild* (Magdeburg, 1885); H. von Hase, *J. H. Rolle, in* 'Zeitschrift für Musikwissenschaft' (vol. 2); R. Kaestner, *J. H. Rolle* (Kassel, 1932).

Röllig, Karl Leopold, Austrian composer and inventor; b. Vienna, c. 1735; d. there, March 4, 1804. He was a harmonica player; invented the 'Orphika' and 'Xänorphika' (pianos with bows instead of hammers), and made many tours, in an attempt to popularize them. In 1797 he settled in Vienna. He wrote a comic opera, *Clarisse* (Hamburg, Oct. 10, 1771); publ. the pamphlets *Über die Harmonika* (1787) and *Über die Orphika* (1795).

Rolón, José, Mexican composer; b. Ciudad Gusmán, Jalisco, June 22, 1883; d. Mexico City, Feb. 3, 1945. He studied in Paris with Moszkowski, and later with Nadia Boulanger and Dukas. In Mexico he was active as a teacher. —Works: symph. poem *Cuauhtémoc* (Mexico City, Jan. 10, 1930); symph. suite *Zapotlán* (Mexico City, Nov. 4, 1932); piano concerto (Mexico City, Sept. 4, 1942); many effective piano pieces.

Roman, Johan Helmich, important Swedish composer; b. Stockholm, Oct. 26, 1694; d. Haraldsmala, near Kalmar, Oct. 19, 1758. At 16, violinist in the court orch. in which his father was concertmaster; studied composition with Ariosti and Pepusch in London (1714) and entered the service of the Duke of Newcastle (1717), winning a high reputation; returned to Stockholm in 1720; became court conductor in 1729; lived in Italy, France, and England (1735-37); elected member of the Swedish Academy in 1740; retired in 1745. Of his numerous compositions, only 2 sets were published during his life, *12 Sonate a flauto traverso, violone e cembalo* (1727) and *Assaggio a violino solo* (1740). In MS in various libraries are preserved a Swedish Mass, motets, hymns, and about 80 psalms; 21 *sinfonie,* 2 *sinfonie da chiesa,* 6 overtures, 5 suites, 2 concerti grossi, 5 violin concertos, about 20 violin sonatas, 17 trio sonatas, etc. Modern editions of Roman's instrumental works were brought out by P. Vretblad, H. Rosenberg, and V. Söderholm. Roman is called 'the father of Swedish music,' for he was the first in Sweden to write choral and instrumental music that could compare favorably with German and Italian products. His style shows the influence of Handel, whom he knew personally in England. —Cf. P. Vretblad, *J. H. Roman Svenska musikens fader* (2 vols., Stockholm, 1914; vol. II contains complete thematic catalogue); C. A. Moberg, *J. H. Roman* (Stockholm, 1944); I. Bengtsson, *J. H. Roman och hans Instrumentalmusik . . .* (Upsala, 1955).

Romani, Carlo, Italian composer; b. Avellino, May 24, 1824; d. Florence, March 4, 1875. He studied with Palafuti (piano) and Picchianti (composition); completed his studies under his uncle, Pietro Romani; set to music the recitatives of *Der Freischütz* for its first Italian performance (Florence, Feb. 3, 1843); wrote the operas (all produced at Florence): *Tutti amanti* (1847), *Il Mantello* (1852; successful), *I Baccanali di Roma* (1854), *Ermellina ossia Le Gemme della corona* (1865); an oratorio, *San Sebastiano* (1864); various patriotic songs.

Romani, Felice, Italian librettist; b. Genoa, Jan. 31, 1788; d. Moneglia, Jan. 28, 1865. Abandoning the legal profession, he turned to literature, becoming the foremost librettist of his time. He wrote about 100 librettos for Mayr, Winter, Vaccai, Rossini, Bellini, Donizetti, Pacini, Ricci, etc. —Cf. F. Regli, *Elogio a Felice Romani* (Turin, 1865); L. Lianovosani, *Saggio bibliografico relativo ai melodrammi di Felice Romani* (Milan, 1878); E. Branca (Romani's wife), *Felice Romani ed i più riputati maestri di musica del suo tempo* (Turin, 1882); C. Paschetto, *Felice Romani monografia* (Turin, 1907).

Romani, Pietro, Italian composer; b. Rome, May 29, 1791; d. Florence, Jan. 6, 1877. He studied with Fenaroli; became conductor at the Teatro della Pergola in Florence; taught singing at the Istituto Musicale there. He wrote 2 operas, *Il Qui pro quo* (Rome, 1817) and *Carlo Magno* (Florence, 1823); also ballet music; but he is remembered chiefly for his aria *Manca un foglio* for Bartolo in *Il Barbiere di Siviglia* which he wrote for the production of the opera in Florence in 1816, as a substitute for Rossini's original aria *A un dottor della mia sorte,* which presented some vocal difficulties. Romani's aria was long retained in many productions of the opera.

Romano, Giulio. See **Caccini.**

Romberg, Andreas (Jacob), German violinist and composer; b. Vechta, near Münster, April 27, 1767; d. Gotha, Nov. 10, 1821. He was the son of the clarinetist and music director Gerhard Heinrich Romberg (1745-

1819); played in public at 7; in 1784 made a concert tour with his cousin Bernhard Romberg through Holland and France, remaining in Paris as soloist for the Concert Spirituel during that season. From 1790 to 1793 he played in the Electoral orch. at Bonn with Bernhard; toured in Italy with him; lived many years in Hamburg (1801-15), and then succeeded Spohr as court Kapellmeister at Gotha. His numerous compositions include the operas: *Der Rabe* (Hamburg, April 7, 1794), *Die Ruinen zu Paluzzi* (Hamburg, Dec. 27, 1811), *Die Grossmut des Scipio* (Berlin, March 4, 1818); Singspiele; choral works with orch.; church music; 10 symphonies (4 published); 23 violin concertos (4 published); 33 string quartets (25 published), 8 flute quintets with strings, 1 clarinet quintet, 2 string quintets, 1 piano quartet, 3 violin sonatas, 11 rondos and caprices for violin, a concertante for violin and cello with orch., etc. His *Toy Symphony* was popular for a time, as was his setting of Schiller's *Lied von der Glocke*. —Cf. Rochlitz's *Für Freunde der Tonkunst* (vol. 1, Leipzig, 1824); K. Stephenson, *Andreas Romberg* (Hamburg, 1938).

Romberg, Bernhard, German cellist and composer; b. Dinklage, Nov. 11, 1767; d. Hamburg, Aug. 13, 1841. He was the son of Anton Romberg, famous bassoonist (1742-1814), who took him to Paris in 1781; he remained there for 2 years; played in the court orch. at Bonn (1790-93); then traveled in Spain; was the constant companion of his cousin Andreas Romberg; in 1796 they played at a concert with Beethoven in Vienna. Romberg was appointed prof. of cello playing at the Paris Cons. in 1801, but resigned in 1803. He was then in Hamburg and Berlin; in 1807 toured in Russia; paid a visit to England (1814); then was court Kapellmeister in Berlin (1815-19); was subsequently in Vienna (1822-25) and again in Russia (1825); lived in Paris (1839-40) before retiring to Hamburg. For the cello he wrote 9 concertos, 3 concertinos, and a fantasia with orch., 4 sets of Russian airs with orch., caprices and fantasias on Swedish, Spanish, and Rumanian airs, and polonaises. In Paris he publ. a cello method (1840); also brought out several operas: *Ulysses und Circe* (Berlin, July 27, 1807), *Rittertreue* (Berlin, Jan. 31, 1817), *Alma* (Copenhagen, May 15, 1824), etc.; 11 string quartets; other chamber music. —Cf. H. Schäfer, *Bernhard Romberg* (Münster, 1931).

Romberg, Sigmund, famous operetta composer; b. Szeged, Hungary, July 29, 1887; d. New York, Nov. 9, 1951. He studied at the Univ. of Bucharest and in Vienna (with Heuberger); in 1909 came to the U. S. as an engineer, later turning to composition; settled in N. Y. in 1913. He composed over 70 operettas, including *The Midnight Girl* (Feb. 23, 1914; his first success); *The Blue Paradise* (with E. Eysler; N. Y., Aug. 5, 1915); *Maytime* (N. Y., Aug. 16, 1917); *Blossom Time* (on Schubert's melodies; N. Y., Sept. 29, 1921); *The Rose of Stamboul* (March 7, 1922); *The Student Prince* (N. Y., Dec. 2, 1924); *The Desert Song* (N. Y., Nov. 30, 1926); *My Maryland* (N. Y., Sept. 12, 1927); *The New Moon* (Sept. 19, 1928); *Up in Central Park* (N. Y., Jan. 27, 1945). —Cf. E. Arnold, *Deep in My Heart* (a biography in the form of a novel, but containing a list of shows and songs; N. Y., 1949).

Romero, Mateo, Spanish composer; date and place of birth unknown; d. Madrid, May 10, 1647. He was a soldier (called 'El Maestro Capitán'). After serving with the army in Flanders, he became a cantor in the Chapel Royal, Madrid (1594), and was maestro from 1598 till his retirement in 1633 (succeeded by Patiño). He was ordained in 1609; in 1638 he went to Portugal as emissary to the Duke of Braganza (the future João IV). He was esteemed highly as a composer of both sacred and secular music. 22 works by Romero for 3 and 4 voices are included in the 'Cancionero de Sablonara' (modern ed. by J. Arcoa, Madrid, 1918); other compositions in Diego Pizarro's collection, *Libro de tonos humanos* (MS in the Madrid Library), and in Pedrell's 'Teatro lírico español' III (La Coruña, 1896-98); a motet, *Libera me*, was included by Eslava in his collection 'Lira sacro-hispana.'

Romeu, Luis, Spanish composer; b. Vich, near Barcelona, June 21, 1874; d. there, Sept. 23, 1937. A priest, he was first choirmaster, then organist, at the cathedral in Vich. His works, which show the influence of Catalan folksong, include a Mass for the *Mare de Deu de Nuria* and *Cants catequistics et Marianes* (3 collections). He publ. a book on Catalan church music, *La Versio auténtica dels Goigs del Roser de tot l'any* (vol. I of *Obra del Cançoner popular de Catalunya;* Barcelona, 1928). The total number of his works, secular and sacred, is 331.

Römhildt, Johann Theodor, German organist and composer; b. Salzungen, Sept.

23, 1684; d. Merseburg, Oct. 26, 1757. He studied with Schelle and Kuhnau at the Thomasschule in Leipzig; was cantor at Spremberg, Freystadt, and Merseburg; in 1735, was appointed cathedral organist at Merseburg. He wrote about 250 church cantatas, numerous works for chorus and for organ; also a *St. Matthew Passion,* which was publ. by Paulke in 1922. —Cf. Karl Paulke, *J. Th. Römhildt,* in the 'Archiv für Musikwissenschaft' (vol. 1, 1919).

Ronald, Sir **Landon** (real name L. R. Russell; son of the composer, Henry Russell, Sr.; brother of the impresario Henry Russell, Jr.), English conductor; b. London, June 7, 1873; d. there, Aug. 14, 1938. He was a pupil at the Royal College of Music of Franklin Taylor (piano), Henry Holmes (violin), and Sir Charles Parry (composition); also attended for a time the classes of Sir Charles Stanford and Sir Walter Parratt. He made a successful début as pianist in London in 1890, but soon abandoned that career to conduct comic operas in the provinces; toured the U. S. in 1894 with Mme. Melba as her accompanist. From 1898 to 1902 he was conductor at the Lyric Theatre in London, and during that time began his series of summer symphony concerts at Blackpool; also conducted in Germany, Austria, and Holland. In 1908 he was appointed permanent conductor of the New Symph. Orch. (later the Royal Albert Hall Orch.) in London; instituted a series of Promenade Concerts in Birmingham; in 1910 was appointed principal of the Guildhall School of Music and held that position almost until his death. He was knighted in 1922. At various times he acted as music critic for 'The Artist,' 'The Onlooker,' 'The Tatler,' 'Musical News,' 'The News Chronicle.' —Works: an operetta, *A Capital Joke;* 2 dramatic scenes, *Adonais* and *The Lament of Shah Jehan;* 2 ballets, *Britannia's Realm* (1902; for the coronation of Edward VII) and *Entente cordiale* (1904); symph. poem, *A Winter's Night;* about 300 songs; was the editor of 'Who's Who in Music' (London, 1937); publ. 2 autobiographical books, *Variations on a Personal Theme* (London, 1922) and *Myself and Others* (London, 1931).

Roncaglia (rohn-cal'-yah), **Gino,** Italian musicologist; b. Modena, May 7, 1883. He studied with Sinigaglia; devoted himself to music history and biography.—Publications: *Giuseppe Verdi* (Naples, 1914); *La Rivoluzione musicale italiana* (Milan, 1928); *Rossini l'Olimpico* (Milan, 1946); *Invito alla musica* (Milan, 1947; 4th ed., 1958); *Invito all' opera* (Milan, 1949; 2nd ed., 1954); *L'Ascensione creatrice di Giuseppe Verdi* (Florence, 3rd ed., 1951); *La Cappella musicale del Duomo di Modena* (Florence, 1957).

Ronconi, Domenico, famous Italian tenor and singing teacher; b. Lendinara, July 11, 1772; d. Milan, April 13, 1839. He was a successful opera tenor; sang in Italy, France, Germany, and Russia. In 1829 he opened a singing school in Milan; publ. vocal exercises that were widely used. His son, **Giorgio Ronconi** (b. Milan, Aug. 6, 1810; d. Madrid, Jan. 8, 1890), was a well-known baritone; spent some years in New York (from 1867).

Ronga, Luigi, eminent musicologist; b. Turin, June 19, 1901. He studied at the Univ. of Turin and in Dresden; in 1926 became prof. at the Cons. of Palermo; later joined the faculty of Santa Cecilia, Rome. He publ. an excellent monograph on Frescobaldi (Turin, 1930); also one on Rossini (Florence, 1939) and essays on other Italian composers; *Bach, Mozart, Beethoven; tre problemi critici* (Venice, 1956); *Arte e gusto nella musica, dell' ars nova a Debussy* (Milan, 1956); *The Meeting of Poetry and Music* (N. Y., 1956).

Rongé (rohn-zhā'), **Jean-Baptiste,** Belgian composer and translator; b. Liège, April 1, 1825; d. there, Oct. 28, 1882. He was a pupil at the Liège Cons.; won the 2nd Belgian Prix de Rome (1851); wrote occasional cantatas and other pieces; a meeting with the poet André van Hasselt directed his interests towards literary work; in collaboration they translated into French the librettos of *Don Giovanni, Zauberflöte, Freischütz, Barbiere di Siviglia,* and other famous operas. After van Hasselt's death (1874), Rongé returned to composing, producing a comic opera, *La Comtesse d'Albany* (Liège, 1877); also wrote some choruses and songs, and *24 Études rythmiques* (for voice).

Ronger, Florimond. **See Hervé.**

Röntgen, Julius, pianist and composer; b. Leipzig, May 9, 1855; d. Utrecht, Sept. 13, 1932. He studied music with his father, Engelbert Röntgen (1829-97); later with Plaidy and Reinecke in Leipzig and Fr. Lachner in Munich. In 1878 he settled in Amsterdam as teacher; was conductor of the Society for the Promotion of Music (1886-98); was a co-founder (1885) of the Amsterdam Cons., and its director from 1914 to 1924. He was a friend of Brahms and Grieg; edited the letters of Brahms to Th. Engelmann (1918); publ. a biography of Grieg (1930). An astonishingly industrious composer, he wrote an enormous amount of music in every genre, cast in an expansive Romantic style: 12 symphonies; 3 piano concertos; 3 operas *(Agnete, Samum,* and *Der lachende Kavalier);* much chamber music; etc.; edited old Dutch keyboard compositions (vol. 37 of the publs. of the Vereeniging voor Nederlandsche Muziekgeschiedenis) and 14 songs by Adrianus Valerius. His correspondence was publ. by his widow (1934).

Roos, Robert de, Dutch composer; b. The Hague, March 10, 1907. He studied with Johan Wagenaar; then in Paris with Milhaud, Monteux, and Koechlin; later worked with Sem Dresden in Holland. In 1948 he was named attaché at the Netherlands Embassy in Paris. His works include the ballet *Kaartspel (Card Game;* 1934); *Cinq Études* for piano and small orch. (1929); *Mouvement symphonique* (1930); *Chant funèbre* (1931); a chamber oratorio after Omar Khayyám (1928); violin concerto (1939); viola concerto (1941); *Sinfonia romantica* (1943); piano concerto (1944); 4 string quartets.

Root, Frederick Woodman, American organist and writer on music, son of George Frederick Root; b. Boston, June 13, 1846; d. Chicago, Nov. 8, 1916. He was taught by his father, then by Dr. B. C. Blodgett and William Mason in New York. In 1863 became organist of the Third Presbyterian Church, Chicago; in 1865, of the Swedenborgian Church. In 1869-70, traveled and studied in Europe, studying singing with Vannuccini in Florence. Returning, he wrote for 'The Song Messenger,' which he edited for some years; publ. *The Technic and Art of Singing, Methodical Sight-Singing, Introductory Lessons in Voice Culture, The Polychrome Lessons in Voice Culture, Resources of Musical Expression, A Study of Musical Taste, The Real American Music;* composed anthems, cantatas, songs.

Root, George Frederick, American composer and publisher; b. Sheffield, Mass., Aug. 30, 1820; d. Bailey's Island, Maine, Aug. 6, 1895. He was a pupil of George J. Webb in Boston; then lived in New York; was organist of the 'Church of the Strangers.' He went to Paris for a year's study in 1850. Going to Chicago in 1859, he joined the music publishing firm of Root and Cady established in 1858 by his elder brother, E. T. Root, and C. M. Cady; it was dissolved in 1871. He wrote many popular songs *(Battlecry of Freedom, Tramp, tramp, tramp, Just before the battle, Mother);* publ. numerous collections of church music and school songs. For some of his earlier compositions he used the German transl. of his name, 'Friedrich Wurzel,' as a pseudonym. —Cf. his autobiography, *The Story of a Musical Life* (Cincinnati, 1891); D. J. Epstein, *Music Publishing in Chicago before 1871: The Firm of Root and Cady, 1858-1871,* in 'Notes' (June, 1944 through June, 1946).

Rootham, Cyril Bradley, English organist and composer; b. Bristol, Oct. 5, 1875; d. Cambridge, March 18, 1938. He studied music with his father, Daniel Rootham (1837-1922); won classical and musical scholarships at St. John's College (Mus. Bac., 1900; A. M., 1901; Mus. Doc., 1910); finished at the Royal College of Music under Sir Charles Stanford and Sir Walter Parratt. From 1901 till his death he was organist at St. John's College, Cambridge; also conductor of the Univ. Musical Society there (1912-36); lectured at the Univ. from 1913. His career as composer was also bound with the musical life in Cambridge; he brought out there his opera *The Two Sisters,* on Feb. 14, 1922; *For the Fallen* for chorus and orch. (1919); *Brown Earth* (performed by the musical societies of Oxford and Cambridge Universities, Albert Hall, London, March 14, 1923); *Ode on the Morning of Christ's Nativity* (Milton), for soli, chorus, and orch. (1930); etc. A 2nd symph. (with a choral ending) was performed posthumously by the B. B. C., March 17, 1939. Other works include *Pan,* rhapsody for orch. (1912); a string quintet (1909); a string quartet (1914); a septet for viola, flute, oboe, clarinet, bassoon, horn, and harp (1930); piano trio (1931).

Ropartz (rŏh-pǎhrts'), **(Joseph) Guy (Marie),** French composer; b. Guingamp, Côtes du Nord, June 15, 1864; d. Lanloup, Nov. 22, 1955. He studied law at Rennes and was admitted to the bar, but decided against a legal career; entered the Paris Cons. as pupil of Dubois and Massenet; then took lessons in organ and composition from César Franck, who remained his chief influence in composition; from 1894 until 1919, director of the Cons. and conductor of the symph. concerts at Nancy; from 1919 to 1929 conducted the Municipal Orch. in Strasbourg; after that lived in retirement in

Paris. He received the Prix Cressent (for opera) in 1906, and the Prix Chartier (for chamber music) in 1919. His most important stage work is the 3-act opera *Le Pays* (Nancy, Feb. 1, 1912; Paris Opéra, April 14, 1913); other stage works: incidental music for Pierre Loti's *Pêcheur d'Islande* (1889-91) and *Le Miracle de St.-Nicolas,* legend in 13 scenes (1905); for orch.: 5 symphonies: No. 1 (1895), No. 2 (1900), No. 3, with chorus (1906), No. 4 (1910), No. 5 (1945), *La Cloche des morts* (1887), *Les Landes* (1888), *Marche de Fête* (1888), *5 Pièces brèves* (1889), *Carnaval* (1889), *Sérénade* (1892), *Dimanche breton* (1893), *À Marie endormie* (1912), *La Chasse du prince Arthur* (1912), *Soir sur les Chaumes* (1913), *Divertissement* (1915), *Sérénade champêtre* (Paris, Feb. 24, 1934), *Pastorale et danse,* for oboe and orch. (1907), *Romanza e scherzino,* for violin and orch. (1926), *Rapsodie* for cello and orch. (Paris, Nov. 3, 1928); sacred music for chorus: 5 motets a cappella (1900), 3 Masses, Requiem for soloists, chorus, and orch. (Paris, April 7, 1939), *De Profundis* for solo voice, chorus, and orch. (1942), etc.; chamber music: 5 string quartets (1893, 1912, 1925, 1934, 1940), piano trio (1918), string trio (1935), 3 violin sonatas, 2 cello sonatas; for piano: *Dans l'ombre de la montagne* (1913), *Musiques au jardin* (1917), *Croquis d'été* (1918), *Croquis d'automne* (1929), *Jeunes filles* (1929); *3 Nocturnes,* etc.; many organ pieces; songs *(Chrysanthèmes, La Mer, Paysage, Tes yeux, De tous les temps, Poème d'adieu, En mai, Chanson de bord, Il pleut, Au Bord d'un ruisseau, Douloureux mensonge, La vieille maison,* etc.); pedagogic works: *Enseignement du Solfège, Leçons d'harmonie,* etc.; *Notations artistiques* (essays; Paris, 1891); also 3 vols. of poems and a play, *La Batte.* —Cf. A. Cœuroy, *La Musique française moderne* (1922); M. Boucher, *Guy Ropartz,* in the 'Revue Musicale' (1924); F. Lamy, *J. G. Ropartz, l'homme et l'œuvre* (Paris, 1948); L. Kornprobst, *J. G. Ropartz* (Strasbourg, 1949).

Roquet (roh-kā'). See **Thoinan.**

Rore, Cipriano de, celebrated composer; b. Mechlin or Antwerp, 1516; d. Parma, 1565. He was a pupil of Willaert, maestro at San Marco, Venice; and in 1542 publ. his 1st book of madrigals *a* 5. From about 1547 to 1558 he was in the service of the Duke of Ferrara, Ercole II; visited Antwerp in 1558, and in 1561 was appointed maestro di cappella to Duke Ottavio Farnese at Parma. Upon Willaert's death in 1562, Rore was appointed his successor, but soon resigned and returned to the court of Parma (July, 1564). —Publications: 8 books of madrigals, 3 of motets, a Passion according to St. John, 'Fantasie e ricercari.' Motets and madrigals are in collections by Susato, Phalèse, and others. —In MS (Munich Library) are 3 Masses: *Vivat Felix Hercules a* 5, *Praeter rerum seriem a* 7, and a *Missa a note nere a* 5; also motets and madrigals. Reprints in A. Einstein's *The Italian Madrigal* (5 madrigals in vol. 3); A. Schering's *Vier Meister-Madrigale aus dem 16. Jahrhundert* (Leipzig, 1916); Davison's and Apel's *Historical Anthology of Music* (vol. 1, no. 131); F. Blume's *Das Chorwerk* (madrigals ed. by W. Wiora in vol. 5; 1930); Madrigals *a* 3 and *a* 4, ed. by Gertrude P. Smith (Northampton, Mass., 1943); G. Tagliapietra's *Antologia di musica antica e moderna per pianoforte* (Milan, 1931); Ph. de Monte's complete works: vols. 4 (1928), 8 (1929), 23 (1933); A. Schering's *Geschichte der Musik in Beispielen* (no. 106); A. Einstein's *The Golden Age of the Madrigal* (1942); reprints of motets by Commer, Burney, Hawkins, Kiesewetter, Dehn, etc. —Cf. R. van Aerde, *Notice sur la vie et les œuvres de Cipriano de Rore* (Mechlin, 1909); J. Musiol, *Cipriano de Rore, ein Meister der venezianischen Schule* (Breslau, 1932); A. Einstein, *The Italian Madrigal* (Princeton, 1949; vol. 1, p. 384 ff.); A. Johnson, *The Masses of Cipriano de Rore,* in 'Journal of the American Musicological Society' (Fall, 1953).

Rorem, Ned, American composer; b. Richmond, Ind., Oct. 23, 1923. He received his musical training in Chicago; won a scholarship at the Curtis Institute, Philadelphia, in 1942; studied there and later at the Berkshire Music Center, Tanglewood; also at the Juilliard School of Music, N. Y., with Wagenaar, obtaining his M. M. degree in 1948; studied privately with Aaron Copland and Virgil Thomson. In 1948 he received the Gershwin Memorial Award; in 1950, the Lili Boulanger Award; in 1951, a Fulbright Fellowship; from 1951 to 1955 lived in Europe; in 1955, returned to the U. S.; living mostly in N. Y. —Works: opera, *A Childhood Miracle,* for 6 voices and 13 instruments (N. Y., Punch Opera Co., May 10, 1952); opera, *The Robbers* (N. Y., April 14, 1958); symph. No. 1 (Vienna, 1951); symph. No. 2 (La Jolla, Calif., Aug. 5, 1956); *Design,* for orch. (Louisville, May 28, 1955); 2 piano concertos (1950; 1951); *Sinfonia* for woodwinds and percussion (Pittsburgh, July 14, 1957); *The Poets' Requiem,* for chorus, soprano solo, and orch., on 8 contemporary poems (1954-55; N. Y., Feb. 15, 1957); 2 string quartets; 2 piano sonatas; *A Quiet Afternoon,* a set of 9 piano pieces; *Sicilienne,* for 2 pianos; *From an Unknown Past,* a cycle of 7 choruses; *5 Prayers for the Young,* for chorus; many songs.

Rosa, Carl (real name Karl Rose), famous opera impresario; b. Hamburg, March 21, 1842; d. Paris, April 30, 1889. At 12 he made tours as violinist in England, Denmark, and Germany; studied further in the Conservatories of Leipzig (1859) and Paris; was concertmaster at Hamburg (1863-65); gave a concert at the Crystal Palace, London (March 10, 1866), and toured in the U. S. with Mr. Bateman, meeting the singer Euphrosyne Parepa (see **Parepa-Rosa**) and marrying her at New York in 1867. They organized an English opera company, and toured America until 1871, then returned to London. After his wife's death in 1874, he produced opera in English in various London theaters, forming the Carl Rosa Opera Co., which under various managements continued to be an important factor in English musical life for many years.

Rosa, Salvatore, Italian painter, poet, and musician; b. Arenella, near Naples, June 21, 1615; d. Rome, March 15, 1673. He studied music and became an expert lute player; from 1635 to 1640 he divided his time between Rome and Naples, and from 1640 to 1649 was court painter to the Medici at Florence; then lived in Rome. The pieces credited to Rosa by Burney and others have been proved to be spurious; it is doubtful whether Rosa ever composed music. His *Satire,* written about 1640 and containing sharp criticism of Italian church music of his day, was publ. posthumously in 1695, and was reprinted several times; Matheson attacked Rosa's views in his *Mithridat, wider den Gift einer welschen Satyre des Salvator Rosa. . .* (1749). —Cf. N. d'Arienzo, *S. Rosa musicista,* in the 'Rivista Musicale Italiana' (1894); D. Battesti, *Saggio sulla vita e le satire di Salvatore Rosa* (Bourges, 1913); F. Gerra, *Salvatore Rosa e la sua vita romana dal 1650 al 1672. . .* (a summary of 200 letters written by Rosa; Rome, 1937); Frank Walker, *Salvatore Rosa and Music,* in the 'Monthly Mus. Record' (Oct., 1949 and Jan.-Feb., 1950).

Rosbaud, Hans, eminent Austrian conductor; b. Graz, July 22, 1895. He studied at the Hoch Cons. in Frankfurt; was director of the municipal music school in Mainz (1923-30); then radio conductor in Frankfurt and Münster; was active in Strasbourg during World War II; in 1945 was appointed director of the Munich Konzertverein; in 1948 he became music director of Baden-Baden; also conducted concerts in Switzerland and elsewhere in Europe; he particularly distinguished himself as a conductor of modern works.

Rösch, Friedrich, German composer; b. Memmingen, Dec. 12, 1862; d. Berlin, Oct. 29, 1925. He was a law student at Munich; studied music with Rheinberger; lived in Berlin, St. Petersburg, and Munich. In 1898 he, with Hans Sommer and Richard Strauss, organized the 'Genossenschaft deutscher Tonsetzer' (dissolved in 1937). —Works: *Antonius,* a burlesque oratorio; numerous choral pieces in a humorous vein; 4-part madrigals for men's chorus; songs; a book, *Musikästhetische Streitfragen* (Leipzig, 1897).

Rosé (roh-zā'), **Arnold (Josef),** distinguished violinist; b. Jassy, Rumania, Oct. 24, 1863; d. London, Aug. 25, 1946. He studied under Karl Heissler at the Vienna Cons.; made his professional début at the Gewandhaus, Leipzig, Oct. 30, 1879; in 1881 was appointed concertmaster of the Vienna Philh. and Opera orch.; held this post for 57 years, until 1938, when he was forced to leave Vienna; spent his last years in London. In 1882 he founded the Rosé Quartet (Rosé, P. Fischer, A. Ruzitska—later, Morawetz—and F. Buxbaum, who was succeeded by J. Walther in 1921), which won a high reputation throughout Europe; the Quartet made its American début at the Library of Congress, Washington, on April 28, 1928. In 1902 Rosé married Justine Mahler, a sister of Gustav Mahler.

Rose, John, British composer; b. London (of Dutch parents), Sept. 23, 1928. His family moved to South Africa in 1940, and he studied in Cape Town. In 1946 he went back to England for a course at the Royal Academy of Music in London; later studied with Rubbra and Wellesz. —Works: *Slow Music* for strings and harp (1951); a choral symph. (1952).

Rose, Leonard, American cellist; b. Washington, D. C., July 27, 1918. He studied at the Curtis Institute of Music with Felix Salmond; was subsequently a member of the N. B. C. Orch. under Toscanini, in the Cleveland Orch., and then 1st cellist of the N. Y. Philharmonic. Since 1951 he has devoted himself to solo performances. He is also a member of the faculty of the Juilliard School and head of the cello department at the Curtis Institute.

Roseingrave, Thomas, English organist and composer; b. Winchester, 1690; d. Dunleary, June 23, 1766. He was the son and pupil of the organist Daniel Roseingrave (1650-1727); went to Italy in 1710 on a stipend from the Chapter of St. Patrick's Cathedral in Dublin and at Venice met Alessandro and Domenico Scarlatti; traveled with the latter to Rome and Naples. In 1720 he was at London, where he produced Domenico Scarlatti's opera *Narciso;* from 1725 to 1737 he was organist of St. George's, Hanover Square; then lived at Hampstead, and about 1749 returned to Dublin. —Publ. works: *15 Voluntarys and Fugues, made on Purpose for the Organ or Harpsichord* (1730); *12 Solos for the German Flute, with a Thorough Bass for the Harpsichord; 8 Suites of Lessons for Harpsichord; 6 Double Fugues* for organ or harpsichord (1750); etc. —Cf. V. Butcher, *Thomas Roseingrave,* in 'Music & Letters' (July, 1938).

Rösel, Artur, German violinist and composer; b. Münchenbernsdorf, Aug. 23, 1859; d. Weimar, April 3, 1934. He studied violin and composition in Weimar; was violinist in various theater orchestras in Hamburg, Lugano, and Rotterdam. In 1888 he became concertmaster of the Weimar court orch. — Works: 'lyric stage play' *Halimah* (Weimar, 1895); symph. poem, *Frühlingsstürme;* 2 violin concertos; viola concerto; 2 string quartets; violin pieces.

Roselius, Ludwig, German composer; b. Kassel, Aug. 2, 1902; studied in Berlin with Abert and Wolf (musicology) and with Georg Schumann (composition); then settled in Bremen as music critic and teacher. —Works: the operas *Doge und Dogaressa* (Dortmund, Nov. 14, 1928), *Godiva* (Nuremberg, Aug. 17, 1933), *Gudrun* (Graz, April 29, 1939); choruses; piano pieces; songs. Edited motets by Andreas Raselius in the 'Denkmäler der Tonkunst in Bayern' (vol. 29/30).

Rosellen, Henri, French pianist and composer; b. Paris, Oct. 13, 1811; d. there, March 18, 1876. He studied at the Paris Cons. with Zimmerman (piano) and Halévy (composition); later became a pupil of Henri Herz, under whose influence he began to compose salon music for piano. His *Rêverie* was fantastically popular for many years; he further composed *Nocturne et Tarentelle; 12 Études brillantes;* 76 fantasias on operatic airs; variations for piano; chamber music. He was a highly successful teacher in Paris, and publ. a *Manuel des pianistes.*

Rosen, Jerome, American composer; b. Boston, July 23, 1921; studied with Roger Sessions and William Denny at the Univ. of California, Berkeley; took courses with Darius Milhaud in Paris (1949-51). Upon his return to the U. S., he became instructor at the Univ. of California. He has written mostly chamber music (sonata for clarinet and cello; string quartet, etc.).

Rosen, Max, American violinist; b. Dorohoi, Rumania, April 11, 1900; d. New York, Dec. 17, 1956. Before he was a year old, his parents settled in New York. His father, an amateur violinist of some ability, was his 1st teacher; he then studied with David Mannes at the Music School Settlement, N. Y. In 1912 he began taking lessons with Leopold Auer in Germany; made his début in Dresden, Nov. 16, 1915; this was followed by a successful tour of Scandinavia (1916-17); his American début was with the N. Y. Philharmonic (Jan. 12, 1918); he subsequently toured the U. S. (until 1921); 1921-25, in Europe; 1926, returned to the U. S.

Rosenberg, Hilding (Constantin), eminent Swedish composer; b. Bosjökloster, June 21, 1892. He studied at the Royal Academy of Music in Stockholm; then in Dresden with Buchmayer and K. Striegler. Returning to Sweden, he assumed the post of assistant conductor at the Stockholm Opera. In 1948 he visited the U. S. to conduct the American première of his 4th symphony, *The Revelation of St. John.* He employs the neo-Classical idiom in an individual manner, occasionally introducing elements of melodic atonality. —Works: operas: *Resan till America (Journey to America;* Stockholm, Nov. 24, 1932), *Marionettes* (1933; Stockholm, Feb. 14, 1939), *De tva Kungadöttrarna (The Two Princesses;* Stockholm Radio, Sept. 19, 1940), *Lycksalighetens (Isle of Felicity,* Stockholm, Feb. 1, 1945); 5 symphonies: No. 1 (1919), No. 2, *Sinfonia grave* (1928-35), No. 3, *De fyra tidsaldrarna (The Four Ages of Man,* 1939), No. 4, *Johannes Uppenbarelse (The Revelation of St. John),* with chorus (1940), No. 5, *Örtagardsmästaren (The Keeper of the Garden;* 1944); *Sinfonia da chiesa* No. 1 (1923); *Sinfonia da chiesa* No. 2 (1924); *Sinfonia concertante* (Paris Festival of the International Society for Contemporary Music, June 22, 1937); *Overtura piccola* (1942); *Overtura bianca-nera,* for strings (1948); *The Louisville Concerto* (Louisville, March 12, 1955); violin concerto (1924); trumpet concerto (1928); cello concerto (1939); viola concerto (1942); 5 string quartets; sonata for unaccompanied violin; songs and minor pieces. —Cf. M. Pergament, *Hilding Rosenberg: a Journey in Modern Swedish Music,* in 'Music & Letters' (July, 1947).

Rosenbloom, Sydney, British pianist and composer; b. Edinburgh, June 25, 1889; studied at the Royal Academy of Music in London; after teaching in the English provinces, he went to South Africa (1920); in 1921 was appointed prof. at the Harrison Cons. in Johannesburg. In 1930 he visited the U. S., and gave piano recitals in California. Upon returning to South Africa, he settled in East London. His works are mostly for piano, written in an ingratiating and highly pianistic manner, along Romantic lines: *Caprice Impromptu, Valse-Etude, 3 Concert Studies, 6 Preludes, 2 Scherzos, Romance Triste, Etchings, From My Sketch Book, Falling Snow,* etc.; 2 violin sonatas; *Variations and Fugue* for 2 pianos; songs.

Rosenfeld, Leopold, Danish composer and writer on music; b. Copenhagen, July 21, 1850; d. there, July 19, 1909. He studied at the Copenhagen Cons. and was for some years music critic of 'Musikbladet'; wrote several choral works with orch., of which *Henrik og Else* (Copenhagen, Feb. 7, 1885) had considerable success; he also publ. a number of piano pieces and about 200 songs to German and Danish texts.

Rosenfeld, Paul, American author and music critic; b. New York, May 4, 1890; d. there, July 21, 1946. He studied at Yale Univ. (B. A., 1912) and at Columbia Univ. School of Journalism (Litt. B., 1913). He then associated himself with progressive circles in literature and music; wrote music criticisms for 'The Dial' (1920-27); contributed also to other literary and music magazines. Although not a musician by training, Rosenfeld possessed a penetrating insight into musical values; he particularly championed the cause of modern American music; his incisive literary style enhanced the influence of his articles; he collected the most significant of them in his books: *Musical Portraits* (on 20 modern composers; 1920); *Musical Chronicle,* covering the New York seasons 1917-23 (1923); *An Hour with American Music* (1929); *Discoveries of a Music Critic* (1936). —Cf. J. Mellquist and L. Wiese, ed., *Paul Rosenfeld, Voyager in the Arts* (N. Y., 1948).

Rosenhain, Jacob (Jacques), German pianist and composer; b. Mannheim, Dec. 2, 1813; d. Baden-Baden, March 21, 1894. He was a child prodigy; made his 1st public appearance at the age of 11 in Mannheim; studied there with Schmitt, and in Frankfurt with Schnyder von Wartensee. In 1837 he went to Paris and London; continued to travel until 1870, when he settled as a teacher in Baden-Baden. —Works: the operas *Der Besuch im Irrenhause* (Frankfurt, Dec. 29, 1834), *Le Démon de la nuit* (Paris, March 17, 1851), *Le Volage et Jaloux* (Baden-Baden, Aug. 3, 1863); 3 symphonies; 3 string quartets; 4 piano trios; many piano pieces; *12 Études caractéristiques* for piano; etc. He publ. *Erinnerungen an Paganini* (1893). —Cf. E. Kratt-Harveng, *Jacques Rosenhain* (Baden-Baden, 1891). —His brother **Eduard Rosenhain** (b. Mannheim, Nov. 16, 1818; d. Frankfurt, Sept. 6, 1861) was also a noteworthy pianist and teacher; publ. a serenade for cello and piano, and piano pieces.

Rosenmüller, Johann, German composer; b. Ölsnitz, c. 1620; d. Wolfenbüttel, Sept. 10, 1684. He graduated from the Univ. of Leipzig in 1640; from 1642 was master at the Thomasschule; later deputy cantor for Tobias Michael; in 1651 he was appointed organist of the Nicolai-Kirche. Imprisoned for a moral offense in 1655, he escaped and fled to Hamburg, thence to Venice; but in 1674 he was appointed ducal Kapellmeister at Wolfenbüttel. —Publ. *Kernsprüche mehrenteils aus Heiliger Schrift,* for 3 to 7 parts with continuo (2 vols., 1648, 1652); *Studentenmusik mit 3 und 5 Violen* (dance music; 1654); *12 Sonate da camera a 5 stromenti* (Venice, 1670; reprinted by Karl Nef in the 'Denkmäler deutscher Tonkunst;' vol. 18); *Sonate a 2-5 stromenti d'arco* (Nuremberg, 1682); 6 Mass-sections; 2 Magnificats; many sacred choruses. Rosenmüller's setting of *Welt ade* was used by Bach in his church cantata No. 27, *Wer weiss wie nahe mir mein Ende.* —Cf. A. Horneffer, *Johann Rosenmüller* (Berlin, 1898); F. Hamel, *Die Psalmkompositionen Johann Rosenmüllers* (Strasbourg, 1933).

Rosenstock, Joseph, conductor; b. Cracow, Jan. 27, 1895. He studied at the Cracow Cons.; then with Schreker in Vienna; graduated from the Vienna Academy of Music in 1920; conducted opera in Darmstadt

(1922-25), Wiesbaden (1925-27), and Mannheim (1930-33); in 1933 he was disqualified in Germany as a Jew; conducted operatic performances of the Jewish Kulturbund in Berlin until 1936, when he was appointed conductor of the Nippon Philharmonic Orch. in Tokyo; was successful there until 1941; then went to the U. S.; conducted in Tokyo again in 1945-46; in 1948 was engaged as conductor and music director of the N. Y. City Opera (till 1955); 1958, appointed music director of the Cologne Opera.

Rosenthal, Manuel, French composer and conductor; b. Paris, June 18, 1904, of a Russian mother and French father. He studied violin and composition at the Paris Cons., graduating in 1924; also took some lessons with Ravel. He was mobilized in 1939, and taken prisoner of war; remained in Germany for a year, returning to France in March, 1941. After conducting various orchestras in Europe, he made a tour of the U. S. in the autumn of 1946; in 1948, appointed instructor in composition at the College of Puget Sound, Tacoma, Wash. In 1949, he was engaged as conductor of the Seattle Symph. Orch,; was dismissed summarily for moral turpitude in Oct., 1951 (the soprano who appeared as soloist with the Seattle Symph. Orch. under the name of Mme. Rosenthal was not his legal wife). He has written a number of works in an entertaining manner, expertly orchestrated: *Bootleggers,* a satirical operetta (Paris, May 2, 1933); *La Poule noire,* 1-act operetta (Paris, 1937); *Les petits métiers,* for orch. (St. Louis, March 3, 1936); *La Fête du vin,* choreographic poem (1937; N. Y., Dec. 5, 1946, composer conducting); *St. Francis of Assisi,* for chorus, orch., and vibraphone (Paris, Nov. 1, 1944, composer conducting); *Musique de table,* symph. suite (N. Y., Oct. 10, 1946). He arranged for L. Massine, choreographer, a ballet, *Gaîté Parisienne* (from Offenbach; Monte Carlo, April 5, 1938; highly successful).

Rosenthal, Moriz, famous pianist; b. Lwow, Dec. 19, 1862; d. New York, Sept. 3, 1946. He received his 1st instruction on the piano from a local teacher, Galath; Karl Mikuli, Chopin's pupil and director of the Lwow Cons., undertook his further musical education; in 1872 the two played in public Chopin's Rondo in C for 2 pianos. In 1875, after his parents moved to Vienna, Rosenthal became a pupil of R. Joseffy, who taught him according to Tausig's method. His début at Vienna in 1876 was eminently successful, and he was accepted by Liszt as a pupil, studying with him in Weimar and Rome (1876-78). He then withdrew from the concert stage and studied philosophy and esthetics at the Univ. of Vienna; reappeared as pianist in 1884 and thereafter toured regularly, establishing a reputation as one of the world's greatest virtuosos; nicknamed (because of his small stature and great power) 'little giant of the piano.' Beginning in 1887 he made 12 tours of the U. S.; in 1938 he took up permanent residence in the U. S. He publ. (with L. Schytte) a *Schule des höheren Klavierspiels.* —His wife, Hedwig Kanner-Rosenthal (q.v.), is a distinguished piano teacher.

Rosenwald, Hans, musicologist, b. Bünde, Germany, Jan. 14, 1907. He studied in Berlin with Arnold Schering and Johannes Wolf, and at the Univ. of Heidelberg with H. J. Moser and Besseler, receiving his Ph.D. in 1929 with the dissertation *Geschichte des deutschen Liedes zwischen Schubert und Schumann* (Berlin, 1930). In 1936 he emigrated to the U. S.; was appointed instructor of music history at the Chicago Musical College; in 1943 became dean; in 1953, moved to New York. —Publications: *Handbook of Music History* (Chicago, 1940; 5 subsequent eds.); ed. *Who Is Who In Music* (Chicago, 1940); from 1944 to 1953, publ. the periodical 'Music News.'

Rosetti, Francesco Antonio (real name Franz Anton Rössler), composer; b. Niemes, Bohemia, Oct. 26, 1746; d. Ludwigslust, Germany, June 30, 1792. He was a theological student; in 1773, became a string player in the orch. of Prince Öttingen-Wallenstein; in 1785, Kapellmeister; from 1789, court Kapellmeister in Ludwigslust. Rosetti, who has been described as 'a German Boccherini,' was a prolific composer; wrote some fine chamber music. —Works: a Requiem (1776); 2 oratorios, *Der sterbende Jesus* (publ.) and *Jesus in Gethsemane;* several operas, including *Das Winterfest der Hirten* (1789); more than 30 symphonies and other orchestral works; 9 string quartets; 4 flute concertos; 5 oboe concertos; 3 clarinet concertos; 4 bassoon concertos; 5 horn concertos; 5 concertos for 2 horns; etc. Oskar Kaul publ. 5 symphonies in vol. 12, and chamber music in vol. 25, of the 'Denkmäler der Tonkunst in Bayern.' —Cf. W. Riehl, in 'Musikalische Charakterköpfe' (vol. 1, 1853, p. 191 ff.); Oskar Kaul, *Die Vokalwerke Anton Rosettis* (Cologne, 1911); L. Schiedermair, in the 'Sammelbände der internationalen Musik-Gesellschaft' (IX; p. 92 ff.).

Rösler, Johann Josef, Hungarian composer; b. Schemnitz, Aug. 22, 1771; d. Prague, Jan. 25, 1813. He served as Kapellmeister for Prince Lobkowitz in Prague; brought out an opera, *Elisene, Prinzessin von Bulgarien* (Prague, Oct. 18, 1807), which was the 1st original stage work to be produced at the German opera theater in Prague; wrote a great amount of instrumental music. A movement from one of his piano concertos was erroneously attributed to Beethoven. —Cf. H. Engel, *Der angeblich Beethovensche Klavierkonzertsatz,* in 'Neues Beethovenjahrbuch' (1925).

Ross, Hugh, choral conductor and organist; b. Langport, England, Aug. 21, 1898. He studied at the Royal College of Music, where he won 1st prize in organ and was made a Fellow in 1915; went to Canada; became conductor of the Winnipeg Male Voice Choir (1921); organized and conducted the Winnipeg Symph. Orch. (1923-27); in 1927, appointed conductor of the Schola Cantorum, N. Y.; choral director at the Berkshire Music Center, Tanglewood (since 1941); gave performances of many choral works. In 1958 he was appointed musical director of the National Chorus of America.

Rossellini, Renzo, Italian composer; b. Rome, Feb. 2, 1908. He studied composition with Sallustio and Setaccioli; taught at the Liceo Musicale in Pesaro (1940-42); in 1942 appointed prof. at the Cons. in Rome. — Works: *Alcassino e Nicoletta,* a 4-act opera (1928-30); *La Danza di Dâssine,* ballet (San Remo, Feb. 24, 1935); *Suite in tre tempi,* for orch. (1931); *Roma cristiana,* cantata (1940); *Stornelli della Roma bassa,* for orch. (1946); wrote film music.

Rossi, Abbate **Francesco,** Italian composer; b. Bari, about 1645; canon there, 1680. — Works: the operas *Bianca di Castiglia* (Milan, 1674), *Il Sejano moderno della Tracia* (Venice, 1680), *La Pena degli occhi* and *La Clorilda* (both in Venice, 1688), *Mitrane* (Venice, 1689); oratorio *La Caduta degli angeli;* Requiem; psalms; etc.

Rossi, Giovanni Gaetano, Italian composer; b. Borgo S. Donnino, Parma, Aug. 5, 1828; d. Genoa, March 30, 1886. He studied at the Milan Cons.; from 1851 was concertmaster at the Teatro Regio, Parma; also court organist and (1864-73) director of the Istituto Musicale. From 1873 to 1879 he conducted at the Teatro Carlo Felice in Genoa; then was director of the Liceo Musicale. — Works: 4 operas; an oratorio, *Le sette parole;* overture, *Saulo;* a Requiem, 3 Masses, etc.

Rossi, Giulio, Italian bass singer; b. Rome, Oct. 27, 1865; d. Milan, Oct. 9, 1931. He had a tenor voice until he was 19, when an unintentional plunge into the Tiber in December induced an illness, after which his voice lowered to the range of *basso profondo.* He then began vocal study under Oreste Tomassoni; made his début at Parma, Oct. 20, 1887. In 1889 he toured South America with Adelina Patti, and also appeared in London; sang 3 seasons at La Scala, Milan; 3 seasons at Madrid, 2 at Barcelona, and 4 at St. Petersburg; 6 in South America; 3 in Mexico; made a tour of the U. S. and 2 tours of Mexico and California with Luisa Tetrazzini; from 1908 till 1913 sang at the Metropolitan Opera. His repertory included about 80 Italian operas.

Rossi, Lauro, Italian dramatic composer; b. Macerata, Feb. 19, 1810; d. Cremona, May 5, 1885. He was a pupil of Furno, Zingarelli, and Crescentini at Naples, bringing out a comic opera, *Le Contesse villane* there (1829) with fair success. He became maestro at the Teatro Valle, Rome, in 1832; with his tenth opera, *La Casa disabitata o I falsi monetari,* produced at La Scala, Milan, Aug. 16, 1834, he won a veritable triumph; it made the rounds of Italy, and was given in Paris. In 1835 he went to Mexico as conductor and composer to an Italian opera troupe, becoming its director in 1837, and going to Havana (1839) and New Orleans (1842), returning to Italy in 1844. He brought out a new opera, *Il Borgomastro di Schiedam* (Milan, June 1, 1844), with indifferent success; his opera *Il Domino nero* (Milan, Sept. 1, 1849) fared a little better. His most successful opera was *La Contessa di Mons* (Turin, Jan. 31, 1874). He wrote 29 operas in all. In 1850 he was given the post of director of the Milan Cons.; in 1870 he succeeded Mercadante as director of the Naples Cons.; resigned in 1878, and retired to Cremona in 1882. —Cf. F. Florimo, *La Scuola musicale di Napoli* (1882).

Rossi, Luigi (Latinized as **Aloysius Rubeus**), Italian composer and singer; b. Torremaggiore, Foggia, 1597; d. Rome, Feb. 19, 1653. He studied in Naples with J. de Macque; then went to Rome, where his opera *Il Palazzo d'Atlante incantato* was produced (Feb. 22, 1642). In 1646 he was called by Mazarin to Paris with 20 other singers, and there staged his most important work, *Orfeo* (March 2, 1647), the 1st Italian opera expressly written for a Paris production. He wrote besides the oratorio *Giuseppe* and some 100 cantatas; reprints of some of these appear in Gevaert's *Les Gloires de l'Italie,* Riemann's *Kantatenfrühling* and Landshoff's *Alte Meister des Bel Canto.* Riemann also publ. several da capo arias by Rossi in the 'Handbuch der Musik-Geschichte' (Vol. II, 2). —Cf. A. Wotquenne, *Étude bibliographique sur Luigi Rossi* (Brussels, 1909); Henry Prunières, *Notes sur la vie de Luigi Rossi,* in 'Sammelbände der internationalen Musik-Gesellschaft' (vol. XII); Henry Prunières, *Les Réprésentations du Palazzo d'Atlante,* ibid. (vol. XIV); Henry Prunières, *Notes bibliographiques sur les cantates de Luigi Rossi au Conservatoire de Naples,* in the 'Zeitschrift der internationalen Musik-Gesellschaft' (vol. XIV); Henry Prunières, *L'Opéra italien en France avant Lulli* (Paris, 1913; pp. 86-150); Romain Rolland, *Le premier opéra joué à Paris: l'Orféo de Luigi Rossi,* in *Musiciens d'autrefois* (1912); A. Cametti, *Alcuni documenti inediti su la vita di Luigi Rossi,* in 'Sammelbände der internationalen Musik-Gesellschaft' (vol. XIV); A. Cametti, *Luigi Rossi: Organista a S. Luigi dei Francesi,* in 'La Critica Musicale' (1919); A. Ghislanzoni, *Luigi Rossi* (Rome, 1954).

Rossi, Michel Angelo, Italian composer; b. Rome, c. 1600. He was a pupil of Frescobaldi; among his compositions are an opera, *Erminia sul Giordano* (Rome, 1635), and a set of *Toccate e Correnti per organo o cembalo* (2nd ed., Rome, 1657). The complete keyboard works of Rossi were publ. by A. Toni (Milan, 1920); the 1657 ed. of *Toccate* etc. by L. Torchi, in 'L'Arte Musicale in Italia' (vol. 3; faulty); 10 *correnti* by F. Boghen (Milan, 1923); 2 toccatas and 3 *correnti* by Béla Bartók (N. Y., 1930); etc. —Cf. Alceo Toni, *M. A. R.,* in 'Bollettino Bibliografico Musicale' (June, 1927).

Rossi, Salomone (Salamone), Italian composer of Jewish origin (called himself **Ebreo**); b. Mantua, 1587; d. there, c. 1630. Nothing is known of the circumstances of his life, except that he was in the service of the court of Mantua, and publ. 13 books of madrigals and instrumental works. He also wrote some synagogue music. As composer of instrumental works, he demonstrated technical procedures in advance of his time; particularly notable are his variations on popular Italian melodies. —Works: canzonettas for 3 voices (1589); madrigals (5 books; 1600, 1602, 1603, 1610, 1622); sonatas (4 books: I, II, *Sinfonie e gagliarde a* 3-5, 1607, 1608; III, IV, *Varie sonate, sinfonie,* etc. 2nd ed., 1623; 1622, 2nd ed., 1636); madrigals for 4-5 voices (1614); *cantici,* psalms, hymns, and *laudi* for 3-8 voices (1620); *madrigaletti* for 2-3 voices, with basso continuo (1628). He also wrote an intermezzo to the drama *L'Idropica* (1608) and music to a sacred play, *Maddalena.* Naumbourg and Vincent d'Indy prepared a new ed. of selected sacred and secular works by Rossi (2 vols.; Paris, 1877); examples of Rossi's instrumental music appear in Riemann's *Alte Kammermusik, Musikgeschichte in Beispielen* (no. 81), and 'Handbuch der Musikgeschichte' (II, 2). Six duets are reprinted in Landshoff's *Alte Meister des Bel Canto.* Lazare Saminsky remodelled Rossi's *Adon Olam* in conformity with modern choral sonorities, retaining his harmonic texture, as part of his *Sabbath Evening Service* (N. Y., 1930). —Cf. D. Maggid, *Die Dreihundertjahrfeier des Salomon de Rossi* (1887); E. Birnbaum, *Jüdische Musiker am Hofe zu Mantua von 1542-1628* (1893); Paul Nettl, *Alte jüdische Spielleute und Musiker* (Prague, 1923); B. Selwyn, *The Gonzaga Lords of Mantua* (London, 1927); A. Einstein, *S. Rossi as Composer of Madrigals,* in 'Hebrew Union College Annual' (vol. 23; Cincinnati, 1950/51).

Rossi-Lemeni, Nicola, Italian bass singer; b. Constantinople, Nov. 11, 1922, of an Italian father and a Russian mother. He was educated in Italy; studied law and planned a diplomatic career. In 1943 he decided to become a professional singer, but the war interfered with his plans, and his début did not take place until 1946. He first appeared in America as Boris Godunov, with the San Francisco Opera (Oct. 2, 1951); also sang Mefistofele (Boito), William Tell, etc.; in 1955, he was engaged at La Scala, Milan.

Rossini, Gioacchino (Antonio), great Italian composer; b. Pesaro, Feb. 29, 1792; d. Paris, Nov. 13, 1868. His father was a town trumpeter at Pesaro, and also played the horn and trumpet in provincial theaters, his mother singing opera as *seconda donna.* For a time Rossini was left in a home in Bologna while his parents performed in various theaters in Italian cities; there he acquired some knowledge of music, and learned to play the harpsichord and to sing; he studied with Angelo Tesei; at the age of 15 he entered the Liceo Comunale of Bologna, where he took courses with Padre Mattei (theory) and Cavedagni (cello); at that time he had already written a number of pieces of chamber music, and on Aug. 8, 1808, his cantata *Il Pianto d'armonia per la* *morte d'Orfeo* was performed at the Liceo, and also won a prize. He abandoned his study of counterpoint with Mattei when an opportunity presented itself for the composition of an opera commissioned by the San Moisè theater in Venice, for which he wrote his first opera buffa, *La Cambiale di matrimonio;* after its production in Venice (Nov. 3, 1810) he returned to Bologna, and brought out there a 2-act opera buffa, *L'Equivoco stravagante.* Two more comic operas were ordered by the San Moisè theater in Venice, and produced there in 1812, and there were further commissions from other theaters. In 1813 he obtained his first grand success, with the opera *Tancredi* at the Fenice Theater in Venice, followed by *L'Italiana in Algeri,* another opera buffa, produced at the San Benedetto Theater in Venice. Encouraged by a steady demand, Rossini ventured to set to music an Italian version of the famous play of Beaumarchais, *Le Barbier de Séville,* despite the fact that an opera on the same subject by Paisiello, *Il Barbiere di Siviglia,* produced as early as 1782, was still enjoying great success. Rossini's opera was brought out at the Argentina Theater in Rome on Feb. 20, 1816, under the title *Almaviva ossia l'inutile precauzione;* he himself stated that he wrote the score in 13 days, using the overture from his earlier opera, *Elisabetta, regina d'Inghilterra.* Rossini himself conducted; the opera was hissed on the first night, but the second performance was very favorably received, and the opera became Rossini's greatest triumph. From 1815 to 1823 he was under contract to write 2 operas annually for the famous impresario Barbaja, who managed the theaters of Naples, La Scala of Milan, and the Italian opera in Vienna. During these 8 years he composed no fewer than 20 operas, beginning with *Elisabetta, regina d'Inghilterra;* in that opera he replaced the traditional *recitativo secco* (that is, recitative accompanied by the cembalo) by *recitativo stromentato* (accompanied by strings). On March 16, 1822, he married Barbaja's mistress, the Spanish soprano Isabella Colbran. He spent the next season in Vienna; then returned with his wife to Bologna. In 1823, disappointed at the cool reception in Venice of his opera *Semiramide,* in which his wife sang, he accepted a favorable offer from Benelli, the manager of the King's Theatre in London. After a brief stay in Paris, Rossini arrived in London, and was received by the king. Although the manager Benelli failed to keep the terms of his contract, Rossini earned during 5 months in London the sum of about £7,000, from concerts given for the nobility at generous fees. He then agreed to undertake the management of the Théâtre-Italien in Paris, and produced several operas of his own as well as one by Meyerbeer. After the expiration of his contract he was given a more or less nominal post as 'premier compositeur du roi,' and another of 'inspecteur-général du chant en France' at the combined salary of 20,000 francs. He produced at the Paris Opéra several French versions of his earlier Italian pieces; the glorious culmination of his Paris seasons was the production of his great dramatic work *Guillaume Tell,* presented at the Opéra on Aug. 3, 1829, with a magnificent cast, winning immense applause. With this grand work, Rossini abruptly closed his career as a composer of operas, at the age of 37. The reasons for this decision were never made clear by Rossini, who was otherwise outspoken and articulate in supplying information about his work and even about his personal habits. The revolution of 1830 invalidated the agreement made with Rossini by the court of Charles X, which guaranteed 15,000 francs for each opera, biennially, to be written exclusively for the French stage; he had to appeal to the courts to secure a pension of 6,000 francs, which was finally granted him in 1835. With the exception of a brief visit to his father in Bologna (1830) and a trip to Madrid (1831) he stayed in Paris until 1836. In 1837 he separated from his wife, and after her death in 1845, married Olympie Desguilliers (Aug. 21, 1846). He lived in Bologna from 1836 till 1848, and accepted the honorary presidency of the Liceo Musicale, where he also taught singing to some exceptionally talented pupils; was briefly in Paris in 1843 for a gallstone operation; in 1848 he settled in Florence, and in 1855, decided to return to Paris, where he remained for the rest of his life. His villa in Passy became the magnet of the artistic world in Paris; Rossini and his wife entertained gladly and lavishly. He was a great gourmet, and invented recipes for Italian food that were enthusiastically adopted by French chefs. His wit was fabulous, and his sayings were eagerly collected and reported. He did not abandon composition entirely during his last years of life; in 1864 he wrote a *Petite Messe Solennelle;* as a token of gratitude to the government of the Second Empire, he composed a *Hymne à Napoléon III;* of greater interest are the numerous piano pieces, songs, and instrumental works which Rossini called *Péchés de vieillesse (Sins of Old Age).* The Rossini Foundation in Pesaro brought out in 1954-56 a series of 'Quaderni Rossiniani' (6 vols.) comprising the following theretofore unpublished compositions: vol. 1: 6 sonatas for 2 violins, cello, and double-bass (juvenilia); vol. 2: piano pieces; vol. 3: Prelude, Theme and Variations for horn and piano; vol. 4: *Melodie italiane* for voice and piano; vol. 5: *Melodie francesi* for voice and piano; vol. 6: chamber music. Operas: *Demetrio e Polibio* (Rome, May 18, 1812); *La Cambiale di matrimonio* (Venice, Nov. 3, 1810); *L'Equivoco stravagante* (Bologna, Oct. 29, 1811); *L'Inganno felice* (Venice, Jan. 8, 1812); *La Scala di seta* (Venice, May 9, 1812); *La Pietra del paragone* (Milan, Sept. 26, 1812); *L'Occasione fa il ladro, ossia Il Cambio della valigia* (Venice, Nov. 24, 1812); *Il Signor Bruschino, ossia Il Figlio per azzardo* (Venice, Jan., 1813); *Tancredi* (Venice, Feb. 6, 1813); *L'Italiana in Algeri* (Venice, May 22, 1813); *Aureliano in Palmira* (Milan, Dec. 26, 1813); *Il Turco in Italia* (Milan, Aug. 14, 1814); *Sigismondo* (Venice, Dec. 26, 1814); *Elisabetta, regina d'Inghilterra* (Naples, Oct. 4, 1815); *Torvaldo e Dorliska* (Rome, Dec. 26, 1815); *Il Barbiere di Siviglia* (1st performed in Rome, Feb. 20, 1816, as *Almaviva o sia l'inutile precauzione;* 1st performed under the title *Il Barbiere di Siviglia* at Bologna, Aug. 10, 1816); *La Gazzetta* (Naples, Sept. 26, 1816); *Otello, ossia il Moro di Venezia* (Naples, Dec. 4, 1816); *Cenerentola, ossia La Bontà in trionfo* (Rome, Jan. 25, 1817); *La Gazza ladra* (Milan, May 31, 1817); *Armida* (Naples, Nov. 11, 1817); *Adelaida di Borgogna* (Rome, Dec. 27, 1817); *Mosè in Egitto* (Naples, March 5, 1818); *Adina, o Il Califfo di Bagdad* (Lisbon, June 22, 1826); *Ricciardo e Zoraide* (Naples, Dec. 3, 1818); *Ermione* (Naples, March 27, 1819); *Edoardo e Cristina* (Venice, April 24, 1819); *La Donna del lago* (Naples, Sept. 24, 1819); *Bianca e Faliero, ovvero Il Consiglio dei tre* (Milan, Dec. 26, 1819); *Maometto II* (Naples, Dec. 3, 1820); *Matilde di Shabran, ossia Bellezza e cuor di ferro* (Rome, Feb. 24, 1821); *Zelmira* (Naples, Feb. 16, 1822); *Semiramide* (Venice, Feb. 3, 1823); *Il Viaggio a Reims* (Paris, June 19, 1825); *Le Siège de Corinthe* (new version of *Maometto II;* Paris, Oct. 9, 1826); *Moïse* (new version of *Mosè in Egitto;* Paris, March 26, 1827); *Le Comte Ory* (Paris, Aug. 20, 1828); *Guillaume Tell* (Paris, Aug. 3, 1829). Cantatas: *Il Pianto d'armonia sulla morte d'Orfeo* (1808); *La Morte di Didone* (1811); *Egle ed Irene* (1814); *Inno agli Italiani* (1815); *Le Nozze di Teti e Peleo* (1816); *Igea* (1819); *Partenope* (1819); *Voto filiale* (1820); *La Riconoscenza* (1821); *La santa alleanza* (1822); *Il vero omaggio* (1822); *L'Augurio felice* (1822); *Il Bardo* (1822); *Omaggio pastorale* (1823); *Il Pianto delle muse in morte di Lord Byron* (1824); *I Pastori* (1825); *Il Serto votivo* (1829); *Giovanna d'Arco* (1832); *Inno popolare* (1846); *Inno nazionale* (1848); *Inno alla pace* (1848); *Il Fanciullo smarrito* (1861); *Coro di cacciatori* (1861). For orch.: an early overture (1808); variations for clarinet and orch. (1809); marches; fanfares. Chamber music: 5 string quartets (1808); *Tema con variazioni,* for flute, clarinet, bassoon, and horn (1812); *Rondeau fantastique,* for horn and piano (1856). Rossini's melodies have been used by many composers as themes for various works: Respighi utilized Rossini's *Quelques Riens* in his ballet *La Boutique fantasque,* and other themes in his orchestral suite *Rossiniana.* An opera entitled *Rossini in Neapel* was written by Bernhard Paumgartner (1936). Benjamin Britten made use of Rossini's music in his orch. suites, *Soirées musicales* and *Matinées musicales.* The most famous arrangement of Rossini's music is the Prayer from *Mosè* transcribed for violin by Paganini. —Bibliography: Stendhal, *Vie de Rossini* (Paris, 1824; often republished; German ed. with corrections and additions, Leipzig, 1824; 3rd ed., 1929; in English, London, 1824, 1956); G. Carpani, *Le Rossiniane* (Padua, 1824); J. d'Ortigue, *De la guerre des dilettanti ou de la révolution opéree par Rossini dans l'opera français* (Paris, 1829); H. Blaze de Bury, *Vie de Rossini* (Paris, 1854); M. and L. Escudier, *Rossini* (Paris, 1854); E. de Mirecourt, *Rossini* (Paris, 1855); A. J. Azevedo, *G. Rossini* (Paris, 1864); F. Hiller, *Plaudereien mit Rossini,* in *Aus dem Tonleben unserer Zeit* (Leipzig, 1868); H. S. Edwards, *Life of Rossini* (London, 1869; condensed in 'Great Musicians,' 1881); A. Pougin, *Rossini: Notes, impressions, souvenirs, commentaires* (Paris, 1870); O. Moutoz, *Rossini et son Guillaume Tell* (Bourg, 1872); S. Silvestri, *Della vita e delle opere di G. Rossini* (Milan, 1874); A. Zanolini, *Biografia di G. Rossini* (Bologna, 1875); J. Sittard, *G. A. Rossini* (Leipzig, 1882); C. Thrane, *Rossini og operaen* (Copenhagen, 1885); A. Kohut, *Rossini* (Leipzig, 1892); G. Mazzatinti, *Lettere inedite e rare di Rossini* (Pesaro, 1892); E. Checchi, *Rossini* (Florence, 1898); G. Tebaldini, *Da Rossini a Verdi* (Naples, 1901); G. Mazzatinti and G. Manis, *Lettere di G. Rossini* (Florence, 1902); L. Dauriac, *Rossini* (Paris, 1906); E. Michotte, *Souvenirs personnels* (Paris,

1906); E. Corradi, *G. Rossini* (Rome, 1909); A. Testoni, *G. Rossini: Quattro episodi della sua vita* (Bologna, 1909); F. Cowen, *Rossini* (N. Y., 1912); H. de Curzon, *Rossini* (Paris, 1920; 2nd ed., 1930); R. Fauchois, *Rossini* (Lyons, 1922); G. M. Gatti, *Le 'Barbier de Séville' de Rossini* (Paris, 1926); G. Radiciotti, *G. Rossini: vita documentata, opere ed influenza su l'arte* (3 vols.; Tivoli, 1927-29; basic biography); G. Radiciotti, *Aneddoti Rossiniani autentici* (Rome, 1929); H. de Curzon, *Une heure avec Rossini* (Paris, 1930); Lord Derwent, *Rossini and Some Forgotten Nightingales* (London, 1934); F. Toye, *Rossini: A Study in Tragi-Comedy* (London, 1934); H. Gerigk, *Rossini* (Potsdam, 1934); A. Bonaventura, *Rossini* (Florence, 1934); G. Monaldi, *Rossini nell' arte, nella vita, negli aneddoti* (Milan, 1936); L. d'Amico, *Rossini* (Turin, 1938); A. Fraccaroli, *Rossini* (Milan, 1941; 4th ed., 1944); R. Bacchelli, *G. Rossini* (Turin, 1941; 2nd ed., 1945); F. Bonavia, *Rossini* (London, 1941); G. Roncaglia, *Rossini, l'olimpico* (Milan, 1946); K. Pfister, *Das Leben Rossinis: Gesetz und Triumph* (Vienna, 1948); C. van Berkel, *Rossini* (Haarlem, 1950); E. J. Dent, *Rossini* in *The Heritage of Music,* Vol. III (London, 1951); special issue of the 'Rassegna Musicale' (Sept., 1954) devoted to the collection of 1100 pages of Rossini's manuscript works in the Pesaro archives; F. Schlitzer, *Rossiniana: contributo all'epistolario di G. Rossini* (Siena, 1956); Luigi Rognoni, *Rossini* (Modena, 1956).

Rosslavetz, Nikolay Andreyevitch, Russian composer; b. Suray, near Tchernigov, Jan 5, 1881. He studied violin with Jan Hřímalý, and composition with Ilyinsky and Vassilenko, at the Moscow Cons.; won the silver medal for his cantata *Heaven and Earth* (after Byron). A composer of advanced tendencies, he publ. a remarkable violin sonata in 1913, which stands as the first atonal work by a Russian composer. He continued to develop his style along ultramodern lines until 1925; but at that time the trend in Soviet Russia, political and artistic, changed towards traditionalism, and Rosslavetz was severely criticized in the press for persevering in his modernism. About 1930 he attempted to write light theater music, but without success; soon he disappeared from the musical scene. Besides the early violin sonata, he wrote the symph. poems *Man and the Sea,* after Baudelaire (1921), and *End of the World,* after Paul Lafargue (1922); also a violin concerto (1925).

Rössler, F. A. See **Rosetti, F. A.**

Rostropovitch (rŏs-trŏh-pŏh'-vich), **Mstislav Leopoldovitch,** remarkable Russian cellist; b. Baku, March 27, 1927. His father was prof. of cello at the Cons. of Baku; his mother, a pianist. After preliminary study at home, he entered the Moscow Cons. in 1937; his studies were interrupted by the war in 1941, but in 1943 he resumed his work, studying cello with Kozolupov and composition with Shebalin; in 1948 he graduated, and became instructor at the Moscow Cons., and in 1957, professor. He won 1st prize at the international festival in Prague (1950); subsequently gave concerts in Europe and America with outstanding success.

Roswaenge, Helge, Danish tenor; b. Copenhagen (of German parents), Aug. 29, 1897; studied engineering and voice; then sang in Germany, Austria, and Scandinavia, attaining great renown in opera and concert. Since 1949, mostly at the Berlin State Opera. In his prime his lyric and dramatic qualities were often compared with Caruso's. He publ. an autobiography, *Skratta Pajazzo* (1945).

Rota, Nino, Italian composer; b. Milan, Dec. 3, 1911. At the age of 11 he composed an oratorio which had a public performance, and at 14 a lyric comedy in 3 acts, *Il Principe porcaro,* after Andersen (1926); later studied with Casella and Pizzetti at Santa Cecilia, Rome, graduating in 1930; then went to the U. S. to enter the Curtis Institute of Music, Philadelphia, where he studied composition with Rosario Scalero and conducting with Fritz Reiner. Returning to Italy, he taught at the Liceo Musicale in Taranto (1937-38); from 1939 was instructor at the Liceo Musicale in Bari; in 1950 appointed its director. —Works: viola sonata (1934-35); *Canzona* for 11 instruments (1935); quintet for flute, oboe, viola, cello, and harp (1935); symph. No. 1 (1936-39); violin sonata (1937); sonata for flute and harp (1938-39); symph. No. 2 (1938-43); the opera *Ariodante* (Parma, 1942); harp concerto (1948); radio opera, *I due timidi* (1950); songs; etc. He has also written a number of film scores.

Roters, Ernst, German composer; b. Oldenburg, July 6, 1892. He studied at the Klindworth-Scharwenka Cons., in Berlin, with Moritz Mayer-Mahr (piano), Hugo Leichtentritt (theory), and Georg Schumann (composition); from 1914 to 1916, taught piano at the Cons. of Danzig; was in the

German army during World War I; in 1920 settled in Hamburg, where he was active as lecturer and music critic; in 1930 went to Berlin as radio conductor; then worked in the films; was again in the German army during the last year of World War II (1944-45); after the cessation of hostilities, he returned to Berlin, where he conducted the Deutsches Theater (1945-47). A highly prolific composer (150 op. numbers before 1955), he wrote an opera, *Die schwarze Kammer* (Darmstadt, 1928); incidental music for 15 plays; about 50 radio works; 3 piano concertos; numerous pieces of chamber music and songs (some with orch.).

Roth (roht), **Bertrand,** Swiss pianist; b. Degersheim, Feb. 12, 1855; d. Bern, Jan. 25, 1938. He studied at the Leipzig Cons. and later in Weimar with Liszt; then lived in Frankfurt, where he founded (with Schwarz and Fleisch) the Raff Cons. (1882); from 1885 to 1890, taught at the Cons. of Dresden; in 1901, he established there the 'Musiksalon Bertrand Roth,' Sunday matinées at which were performed works by contemporary composers. He publ. songs and piano pieces.

Roth, Feri, eminent violinist; b. Zvolen, Czechoslovakia, July 18, 1899; studied at the State Academy, Budapest; organized the Budapest String Quartet in 1923 (Roth, Schiff, Spitz, Franke), with which he toured Europe and Africa (1925) and which established itself as one of the finest quartets in the world. Left the Budapest in 1926 and organized the Roth Quartet (Roth, Jenö Antal, Ferenc Molnar, Janos Scholz). Their American début took place at the Pittsfield Music Festival on Sept. 21, 1928.

Roth, Herman, German musicologist; b. Hornberg, Baden, Feb. 15, 1882; d. Berlin, Feb. 1, 1938. He studied philology and philosophy; then took courses in music with Philipp Wolfrum in Heidelberg (1902) and Hugo Riemann in Leipzig (1905). He was music critic in Leipzig (1907-10) and Munich (1910-21); taught at the Cons. of Baden (1921-24) and at the Hochschule für Musik at Stuttgart (1925-32); after 3 years of musical journalism in Hamburg (1932-35) he settled in Berlin. His German translations of the Italian librettos of operas of Handel, Mozart, and Rossini are used in many German opera houses. He publ. the books *Heinrich Kaspar Schmid* (Munich, 1921) and *Elemente der Stimmführung* (Stuttgart, 1926); edited works by Bach, Handel, etc.

Rothier (roh-tyä'), **Léon,** French bass singer; b. Reims, Dec. 26, 1874; d. New York, Dec. 6, 1951. He studied at the Paris Cons. with Crosti (singing), Lhérie (opéra-comique), and Melchissedec (opera), winning 1st prizes in all 3 classes upon graduation. He made his operatic début as Jupiter in Gounod's *Philémon et Baucis* at the Opéra-Comique, where he remained until 1903; then was active at Marseilles (1903-07), Nice (1907-09), and Lyons (1909-10). On Dec. 10, 1910, he made his American début at the Metropolitan Opera, N. Y. as Méphistophélès; after retirement (1939), he remained in N. Y. as a teacher.

Rothmüller, Marko, Yugoslav baritone; b. Trnjani, Dec. 31, 1908. He studied at the Music Academy in Zagreb; then took courses at the Vienna Cons., and had lessons in composition from Alban Berg. He made his operatic début in Hamburg (1932); then sang in Zagreb (1932-34) and Zürich (1935-47). His first signal success came with his appearances in England with the New London Opera Co., which he joined in 1947; he also sang at the Vienna State Opera.

Rothwell, Walter Henry, conductor; b. London, Sept. 22, 1872; d. Santa Monica, Calif., March 12, 1927. He studied at the Vienna Cons. (1881-88) with J. Epstein (piano), R. Fuchs (theory), and Bruckner (composition); took further courses in Munich with Thuille and Schillings. In 1895 he became assistant conductor to Mahler at the Hamburg Opera; then conducted the German opera in Amsterdam (1903-04) and (1904-08) the Savage Opera Co. in the U. S., with which he gave performances of *Parsifal* in English. He then was conductor of the St. Paul Symph. Orch. (1908-14); after several years in N. Y. as teacher, he was engaged by W. A. Clark (1919) to organize and conduct the Los Angeles Philh. Orch., which he led until his death. He was married (Sept. 10, 1908) to the soprano Elisabeth Wolff.

Rottenberg, Ludwig, conductor and composer; b. Czernowitz, Bukovina, Oct. 11, 1864; d. Frankfurt, May 6, 1932. He studied music with A. Hřímalý, R. Fuchs, and E. Mandyczewski in Vienna; was Kapellmeister at the Stadttheater in Brünn (1891-92) and at the Frankfurt opera (1893-1926); retired in 1927. In 1912 and 1913 he conducted the Wagner performances at Covent Garden, London. He publ. a collection of 30 songs, a violin sonata, and piano variations; his opera, *Die Geschwister,* was produced in

Frankfurt on Nov. 30, 1915. —Rottenberg was the father-in-law of Paul Hindemith.

Rouart-Lerolle & Cie., French publishing house, founded in 1905 at Paris by Alexander Rouart (1869-1921), through the purchase of the firms of Meuriot and Baudoux. When, in 1908, Jacques Lerolle (b. 1880), son of the famous painter, became his associate, the firm acquired the catalogue of the publ. house of Gregh (founded in 1840). After the death of Rouart in 1921, Lerolle became director, Mme. Rouart, the founder's widow, a partner, and François Hepp (b. 1887), son-in-law of Rouart, co-director. In 1942, the entire stock of Rouart-Lerolle & Cie. was sold to Salabert (q. v.).

Rouget de l'Isle (roo-zhā' dŭ lēl'), **Claude-Joseph,** composer of the *Marseillaise;* b. Lons-le-Saulnier, Jura, May 10, 1760; d. Choisy-le-Roy, June 27, 1836. He composed the famous national hymn in 1792, while stationed in Strasbourg as a military engineer. The original title of the *Marseillaise* was *Le Chant de guerre de l'armée du Rhin,* and it was designed to be a patriotic song at the time of the war with Austria; it was taken up by the Marseilles soldiers marching towards Paris, and so assumed its universally known title. Rouget de l'Isle was himself not a revolutionary; he was in fact imprisoned for refusing to take the oath against the crown. He went to Paris after Robespierre's downfall, and composed a *Hymne dithyrambique sur la conjuration de Robespierre* (1794), *Chant des vengeances* (1798), and a *Chant du combat* for the army in Egypt (1800). He publ. 50 *Chants français* in 1825; wrote several opera librettos. Maurice de La Fuye and Émile Guéret, in their book *Rouget de l'Isle, inconnu* (Paris, 1943), argued that he wrote only the words and not the music of the *Marseillaise,* and suggested that the composer was Ignace Pleyel. A. Loth, in his pamphlet *Le Chant de la Marseillaise* (Paris, 1886), claimed that the composer was one Grisons. See also J. Tiersot, *Rouget de l'Isle: son œuvre, sa vie* (Paris, 1892); A. Köckert, *Rouget de l'Isle* (Leipzig, 1898); A. Lanier, *Rouget de l'Isle* (Besançon, 1907); J. Tiersot, *Histoire de la Marseillaise* (Paris, 1915); R. Brancour, *La Marseillaise et le Chant du départ* (1916); E. Istel, *Is the Marseillaise a German Composition?,* in the 'Mus. Quarterly' (April, 1922); V. Helfert, *La Marseillaise,* in the 'Rivista Musicale Italiana' (1922); A. Becker, *La Marseillaise* (Brunswick, 1930); G. de Froidcourt, *Grétry, Rouget de Lisle et la Marseillaise* (Liège, 1945).

Rousseau (rŏŏs-sŏh'), **Jean-Jacques,** great philosopher and author; b. Geneva, June 28, 1712; d. Ermenonville, near Paris, July 2, 1778. Without other musical training than desultory self-instruction, Rousseau made his début as a music scholar at the age of 29, reading a paper before the Académie in Paris (1742), which was revised and publ. as a *Dissertation sur la musique moderne* (1743). His opera, *Les Muses galantes,* had only one private representation, at the house of La Pouplinière in 1745; his revision of the intermezzo *La Reine de Navarre* (by Voltaire and Rameau) was a failure in Paris; but his opera *Le Devin du village* (Fontainebleau, Oct. 18, 1752; Paris Opéra, March 1, 1753) was very successful, and remained in the repertory for 75 years. In the meantime his musical articles for the 'Encyclopédie' had evoked scathing criticism from Rameau and others; improved by revision and augmentation, they were republished as his *Dictionnaire de musique* (Geneva, 1767). In 1752 commenced the dispute, known as the 'guerre des bouffons,' between the partisans of French and Italian opera; Rousseau sided with the latter, publishing a *Lettre à M. Grimm au sujet des remarques ajoutées à sa lettre sur Omphale* (1752), followed by the caustic *Lettre sur la musique française* (1753, to which the members of the Opéra responded by burning him in effigy and excluding him from the theater), and *Lettre d'un symphoniste de l'Académie royale de musique à ses camarades* (1753). He wrote 2 numbers for the melodrama, *Pygmalion* (1770; Paris, Oct. 30, 1775). Publ. posthumously were six new arias for *Le Devin du village,* and a collection of about 100 *romances* and duets, *Les Consolations des misères de ma vie* (1781), and fragments of an opera, *Daphnis et Chloé* (1780). All his writings on music have been often republished in eds. of his 'Collected Works' (1782; many eds. since). —Bibliography: A. Jensen, *J.-J. R. Fragments inédits, recherches biographiques* (Paris, 1882); A. Jansen, *J.-J. R. als Musiker* (Berlin, 1884); A. Pougin, *J.-J. R., musicien* (Paris, 1901); E. Istel, *J.-J. R. als Komponist seiner lyrischen Szene 'Pygmalion'* (Leipzig, 1901); F. Hellouin, *J.-J. R. et la psychologie de l'orchestre,* in *Feuillets d'histoire musicale française* (Paris, 1903); E. Schütte, *J.-J. R. Seine Persönlichkeit und sein Stil* (Leipzig, 1910); J. Tiersot, *J.-J. R.* (Paris, 1912); E. Faguet, *Rousseau artiste* (Paris, 1913); A. L. Sells, *The Early Life of Rousseau: 1712-40* (London, 1929); R. Gérin, *J.-J. R.* (Paris, 1930); M. Moffat, *Rousseau et le théâtre* (Paris,

1930); J. Tiersot, *Concerning J.-J. R., the Musician,* in the 'Mus. Quarterly (July, 1931); *Correspondance générale de J.-J. R.,* ed. by Dufour and Plan, in 20 vols. (Paris, 1924-34); H. V. Somerset, *J.-J. R. as a Musician,* in 'Music & Letters' (1936); L. Richebourg, *Contributions à l'histoire de la 'querelle des bouffons'* (Paris, 1937); A. Pochon, *J.-J. R., musicien, et la critique* (Montreux, 1940); E. Kisch, *Rameau and Rousseau,* in 'Music & Letters' (1941); A. R. Oliver, *The Encyclopaedists as Critics of Music* (N. Y., 1947); Jean Senelier, *Bibliographie générale des œuvres de J.-J. R.* (Paris, 1949). For details of productions, see A. Lowenberg, *Annals of Opera* (Cambridge, 1943; 2nd ed., 1955).

Rousseau, Marcel (-Auguste-Louis), French composer; b. Paris, Aug. 18, 1882; d. there, June 11, 1955. He studied with his father, Samuel Rousseau; then entered the Paris Cons. as a student of Lenepveu; won the Deuxième Premier Grand Prix de Rome with the cantata *Maia* (1905). Later in his professional career he added his father's first name to his own, and produced his works as Samuel-Rousseau. —Works: the operas (all produced in Paris) *Tarass Boulba,* after Gogol (Nov. 22, 1919), *Le Hulla* (March 9, 1923), *Le bon roi Dagobert* (Dec. 5, 1927; his most successful work), *Kerkeb* (April 6, 1951); the ballets *Promenade dans Rome* (Paris, Dec. 7, 1936) and *Entre deux rondes* (Paris, April 27, 1940); orchestral tableaux, *Solitude triste* and *Impression dolente;* etc. In 1947 he was elected to the Académie des Beaux-Arts.

Rousseau, Samuel-Alexandre, French composer; father of Marcel Samuel-Rousseau; b. Neuve-Maison, Aisne, June 11, 1853; d. Paris, Oct. 1, 1904. He studied at the Paris Cons. with César Franck (organ) and Bazin (composition); won the Grand Prix de Rome with the cantata *La Fille de Jephté* (1878); also the Prix Cressent with the 1-act comic opera *Dianora* (Opéra-Comique, Dec. 22, 1879). His opera *Mérowig* was awarded the Prize of the City of Paris, and was performed in concert form at the Grand Théâtre there on Dec. 12, 1892. In 1892 he was appointed conductor at the Théâtre-Lyrique; was for 10 years chorusmaster at the Société des Concerts du Conservatoire; also taught harmony at the Paris Cons. On June 8, 1898, his lyric drama *La Cloche du Rhin* was staged at the Paris Opéra with considerable success, but had only 9 performances in all; this was followed by the music dramas *Milia* (Opéra-Comique, 1904) and *Léone* (Opéra-Comique, March 7, 1910).

Roussel (roos-sehl'), **Albert (Charles Paul),** outstanding French composer; b. Tourcoing, Département du Nord, April 5, 1869; d. Royan, Aug. 23, 1937. Orphaned as a child, he was educated by his grandfather, mayor of his native town, and after the grandfather's death, by his aunt. He studied academic subjects at the Collège Stanislas in Paris; music with the organist Stoltz; then studied mathematics in preparation for entering the Naval Academy; at the age of 18 he began his training in the navy; from 1889 to Aug., 1890 he was a member of the crew of the frigate Iphigénie, sailing to Indo-China. This voyage was of great importance to Roussel, since it opened for him a world of Oriental culture and art, which became one of the chief sources of his musical inspiration. He later sailed on the cruiser Dévastation; received a leave of absence for reasons of health, and spent some time in Tunis; was then stationed in Cherbourg, and began to compose there. In 1893 he was sent once more to Indo-China. He resigned from the navy in 1894 and went to Paris, where he began to study music seriously with Eugène Gigout. In 1898 he entered the Schola Cantorum in Paris as a pupil of Vincent d'Indy; continued this study until 1907, when he was already 38 years old, but at the same time he was entrusted with a class in counterpoint, which he conducted at the Schola Cantorum from 1902 to 1914; among his students were Paul Le Flem, Erik Satie, Stan Golestan, Roland-Manuel, Guy de Lioncourt, and Edgard Varèse. In 1909 Roussel and his wife Blanche Preisach-Roussel undertook a voyage to India, where he became acquainted with the legend of the queen Pâdmâvatî, which he selected as a subject for his famous opera-ballet. His choral symph. *Les Évocations* was also inspired by this tour. At the outbreak of war in 1914, Roussel applied for active service in the navy but was rejected and volunteered as an ambulance driver. After the Armistice of 1918, he settled in Normandy and devoted himself to composition. In the autumn of 1930 he visited the U. S. —Roussel began his work under the influence of French Impressionism, with its dependence on exotic moods and poetic association. However, the sense of formal design asserted itself in his symphonic works; his *Suite en fa* (1927) signalizes a transition towards neo-Classicism; the thematic development is vigorous, and the rhythms are clearly delineated, despite some asymmetrical progressions; the orchestration, too, is in the Classical tradition. Roussel possessed a keen sense of the theater; he was capable of fine characterization of exotic or mythological subjects, but also knew how to depict humorous situations in lighter works. An experiment in a frankly modernistic manner is exemplified by his *Jazz dans la nuit* for voice and piano. —Works: For the stage: *Le Marchand de sable qui passe,* incidental music (Le Havre, Dec. 16, 1908); *Le Festin de l'araignée,* ballet-pantomime in 1 act (Paris, April 3, 1913); *Pâdmâvatî,* opera-ballet in 2 acts (1914-18; Paris, June 1, 1923); *La Naissance de la lyre,* lyric opera in 1 act (Paris, July 1, 1925); *Bacchus et Ariane,* ballet in 2 acts (Paris, May 22, 1931); *Le Testament de la tante Caroline,* opéra-bouffe (1932-33; Olomouc, Czechoslovakia, Nov. 14, 1936; Paris, March 11, 1937); *Aeneas,* ballet with chorus, in 1 act (Brussels, July 31, 1935). For orch.: 4 symphonies: No. I, *Le Poème de la forêt* (1904-06; Brussels, March 22, 1908), No. II, *Symphonie en si bémol* (1919-21; Paris, March 4, 1922), No. III, *Symphonie en sol mineur* (commissioned by the Boston Symph. Orch.; performed there by Koussevitzky, Oct. 24, 1930), No. IV, *Symphonie en la majeur* (1934; Paris, Oct. 19, 1935); *Suite en fa* (Boston, Jan. 21, 1927); *Sinfonietta* for strings (Paris, Nov. 19, 1934); *Résurrection,* symph. poem (Paris, May 17, 1904); *Évocations,* suite in 3 movements (Paris, May 18, 1912); *Pour une fête de printemps* (Paris, Oct. 29, 1921); *Rapsodie flamande* (Brussels, Dec. 12, 1936); *Concert pour petit orchestre* (Paris, May 5, 1927); *Petite suite pour orchestre* (Paris, Feb. 6, 1930); piano concerto (Paris, June 7, 1928); *Concertino* for cello and orch. (Paris, Feb. 6, 1937); *Le Bardit des Francs,* for male chorus, brass, and percussion (Strasbourg, April 21, 1928); *Psaume LXXX,* for tenor, chorus, and orch. (Paris, April 25, 1929); symph. suites from theater works: *Le Festin de l'araignée* (1912), *Pâdmâvatî* (1914-18), *La Naissance de la lyre* (1922-24), *Bacchus et Ariane* (1930). Chamber music: a piano trio (1902); *Divertissement* for flute, oboe, clarinet, bassoon, horn, and piano (1906); *Sérénade,* for flute, violin, viola, cello, and harp (1925); trio for flute, viola, and cello (1929); string quartet (1932); trio for violin, viola, and cello (1937); 2 violin sonatas (1908; 1924); *Joueurs de flûte,* suite for flute and piano (1924); *Andante et Scherzo,* for flute and piano (1934). For piano: *Des Heures passent,* a cycle of 4 pieces (1898); *Rustiques,* a cycle of 3 pieces (1904-06); suite of 3 pieces (1910); sonatina (1912); *Petit canon perpétuel* (1913); *Prélude et fugue (Hommage à Bach);* etc. Songs: *Adieux* (1907); *Jazz dans la nuit* (1928); *Deux idylles* (1931); 3 sets of *Poèmes chinois* (1908; 1927; 1932); etc. — A complete catalogue of works, with a biographical notice and annotations, was publ. in Paris, 1947, and constitutes a primary source of information. —Bibliography: Roland-Manuel, *A. R.,* in the 'Revue Musicale' (Nov., 1922); L. Vuillemin, *A. R. et son œuvre* (Paris, 1924); Roussel issue of the 'Revue Musicale' (May-June, 1929); H. Prunières, *A. R. and the 80th Psalm,* in the 'Mus. Quarterly' (Jan., 1930); R. Dumesnil, *L'Œuvre symphonique de A. R.,* in 'Musique Française' (Feb., 1933); R. Petit, *A. R.,* in 'Modern Music' (Nov.-Dec., 1937); A. Hoérée, *A. R.* (Paris, 1938); P. Landormy, *A. R.,* in the 'Mus. Quarterly' (Oct., 1938); N. Demuth, *A. R.: a Study* (London, 1947); R. Bernard, *A. R.: sa vie, son œuvre* (Paris, 1948); Marc Pincherle, *A. R.* (Paris, 1957).

Roussier, Abbé **Pierre-Joseph,** French writer on music; b. Marseilles, 1716; d. as canon at Ecouis, Normandy, c. 1790. —Publ. *Observations sur différents points d'harmonie* (1755); *Sentiment d'un harmoniphile sur différents ouvrages de musique* (1756); *Traité des accords, et de leur succession* (1764; supplemented by *L'harmonie pratique . . . .,* 1775); *Mémoire sur la musique des anciens* (1770); *Notes et observations sur le mémoire du P. Amiot concernant la musique des chinois* (1779); *Mémoire sur la nouvelle harpe de M. Cousineau* (1782); *Mémoire sur le clavecin chromatique* (1782); *Lettre sur l'acceptation des mots 'basse fondamentale'* . . . (1783; 'Journal encyclopédique,' vol. I); etc.

Rovelli, Pietro, Italian violinist; b. Bergamo, Feb. 6, 1793; d. there, Sept. 8, 1838. He studied with R. Kreutzer; then played in various orchestras in Italy; was concertmaster of the court orch. in Munich (1817-19). He publ. excellent études and caprices for violin; also *Variazioni* for violin and orch.

Rovsing Olsen, Paul, Danish composer and pianist; b. Copenhagen, Nov. 4, 1922. He studied with Jeppesen at the Cons. of Copenhagen, and later with Nadia Boulanger in Paris; from 1949 was music critic in Copenhagen. Among his works are an orchestral suite, *Miniatures* (1949), a *Serenade,* for violin and piano (1950), and a number of piano pieces and songs.

Rowbotham, Rev. **John Frederick,** British music historian; b. Edinburgh, April 18, 1854; d. Sutton-Cheney, Oct. 20, 1925. He took the Balliol Scholarship, Oxford, at 18; studied music there, and at the Stern Cons. (Berlin), Dresden, Paris, and Vienna; ordained in 1891, he held various appointments as vicar and rector until 1910, when he founded 'The Bard,' of which he was editor. He traveled on the Continent to collect materials for his *History of Music,* publ. in 3 vols. (London, 1885-87); also publ. *How to Write Music Correctly* (1889); *A Short History of Music* (1891); *Private Life of the Great Composers* (1892); *The Troubadours, and the Courts of Love* (1895); *A History of Music to the Time of the Troubadours* (1899); *Story Lives of Great Musicians* (1908); etc.

Rowley, Alec, English composer; b. London, March 13, 1892; d. there, Jan. 10, 1958. He studied at the Royal Academy of Music; upon graduation, became a teacher and examiner. Among his works are a pantomime, *The Princess Who Lost a Tune;* 2 piano concertos; a rhapsody for viola and orch.; a concerto for oboe and orch.; *Phyllis and Corydon,* for string quartet; *From Faerie,* for string quartet; *Little Jesus,* for voice, piano, and string quartet; *Watercolours,* for piano, violin, viola, and cello; *Pastel Portraits,* for piano, violin, and cello; 3 little trios for piano, violin, and cello: *The Puppet Show, 4 Contrasts, A Short Suite;* also piano pieces for children.

Roy, Klaus George, composer, critic, and musicologist; b. Vienna, Jan. 24, 1924. He studied piano and composition with F. C. Schreiber; in 1939 went to England; then settled in the U. S. (naturalized in 1944); took courses with Karl Geiringer (musicology) at Boston Univ. (Mus. B., 1947); then with Walter Piston (composition), A. T. Davison and A. T. Merritt (music history) at Harvard Univ. (M. A., 1949). He was librarian at the Boston Univ. College of Music (1948-57); also a contributing music critic for the 'Christian Science Monitor,' Boston (1950-57); also wrote for other publications; 1958, appointed ed. of the program book and assistant manager of the Cleveland Orch. —Works: 2 chamber operas: *Sterlingman* (Boston Univ., April 18, 1957) and *The Easter Guest* (1956); cantata, *St. Francis's Canticle of the Sun* (Boston, Nov. 5, 1951); *Tripartita,* for brass ensemble (1949); sonata for trombone and piano (1951); *3 Songs of Praise* (1952); *Trialogue and Choreia,* for violin and harpsichord (1952); *3 Folksong Settings* (Dutch, Greek, Slovakian), for mixed chorus a cappella (1955); string trio (1956); *2 Rhapsodic Pieces,* for viola and piano (1957); *Serenade* for solo violin (1957); several choruses; songs; piano pieces.

Royce, Edward, American composer and teacher; b. Cambridge, Mass., Dec. 25, 1886. He studied at Harvard Univ. (B. A., 1907), later at the Stern Cons. in Berlin; 1913, founded the music dept. at Middlebury College, Vermont; then head of the theory dept. at the Ithaca Cons. (1916-21); from 1923 till 1947 prof. of theory at the Eastman School of Music, Rochester, N. Y. —Works: 2 tone poems, *The Fire Bringers* (Rochester, April 23, 1926) and *Far Ocean* (Rochester, June 3, 1929, composer conducting); piano pieces, songs.

Royer (rwăh-yā'), **Étienne,** French composer; b. Grenoble, April 12, 1882; d. Paris, March 2, 1928. He studied with Vincent d'Indy and Sérieyx at the Schola Cantorum in Paris; was a cello pupil of L. Revel; wrote music criticism and publ. pedagogical works. He composed a *Danse mystique* for orch.; *Cantus memorialis,* for violin and orch.; *Pour le temps de la moisson* and *Pour les fêtes de mai,* for string quartet (based on French folk tunes); songs; piano pieces, etc.

Royer (rwăh-yā'), **Joseph-Nicolas-Pancrace,** French composer; b. 1700; d. Paris, Jan. 11, 1755. He was a native of Burgundy, and settled in Paris in 1725. In 1739 he became a member of the court orch.; 1748, lessee and director of the Concert Spirituel; 1753, inspector of the Paris Opéra and 'maître de musique de la chambre du roy.' —Works: the operas *Pyrrhus* (Paris, 1730), *Zaïde* (1739), *Le Pouvoir de l'amour* (1743), *Almasis* (1747), *Myrtil* (1750); also *Pandore,* after Voltaire, which was not produced. He publ. sonatas and a book of pieces for the clavecin. —Cf. M. Brenet, *Les Concerts en France sous l'ancien régime* (Paris, 1900).

Rôze (rohz), **Marie-Hippolyte** (*née* Roze-Ponsin), famous French soprano; b. Paris, March 2, 1846; d. there, June 21, 1926. She studied at the Paris Cons. with Mocker and later with Auber, winning 2 prizes in 1865; made her début at the Opéra-Comique in the title role of Hérold's *Marie* (Aug. 16, 1865); sang there for 3 seasons; then appeared at the Paris Opéra as Marguerite in Gounod's *Faust* (Jan. 2, 1879); after several engagements in Belgium and Holland, she made her London début at Drury Lane as Marguerite (1872), achieving extraordinary success; continued to sing in England for many years. She visited America twice, in 1877-78 and 1880-81. In 1874 she married an American bass singer, Julius E. Perkins, who died the following year; later she married the impresario, Col. J. H. Mapleson, but the marriage ended in divorce. In 1890 she settled in Paris as a teacher; appeared occasionally in England, the last time in 1903.

Rôze, Raymond (J. H. Raymond Rôze-Perkins), English composer; son of Maria Rôze; b. London, 1875; d. there, March 31, 1920. He studied at the Brussels Cons., where he won 1st prize; was musical director to Sir Henry Irving at the Lyceum Theatre, and later at His Majesty's Theatre. He wrote overtures and incidental music to many plays, including several of Shakespeare's and *Trilby*. In the fall of 1913 he conducted at Covent Garden a season of opera in English, during which he brought out his own opera *Joan of Arc* (Oct. 31, 1913); another opera by him, *Arabesque,* was produced at the Coliseum, London, in 1916.

Rozkošný (rŏz-kŏsh'-nē), **Josef Richard,** Czech composer; b. Prague, Sept. 21, 1833; d. there, June 3, 1913. He studied painting and music in Prague; his teachers were Tomaschek (piano) and Kittl (composition). His songs and choruses became popular, and he successfully attempted the composition of operas to Czech librettos; 8 operas were produced in Prague, among them: *Svatojanské proudy (The Rapids of St. John;* Oct. 3, 1871), *Popelka (Cinderella;* May 31, 1885), *Černé jezero (The Black Lake;* Jan. 6, 1906). He also publ. a number of piano pieces.

Rózsa (roh'-zhah), **Miklós,** composer; b. Budapest, April 18, 1907. He studied piano and composition in Leipzig, with Hermann Grabner; musicology with Theodor Kroyer. In 1932 he settled in Paris, where he became successful as a composer; his works were often performed in European music centers. In 1935 he went to London as a writer for the films; in 1939 emigrated to the U. S., and settled in Hollywood. His orchestral and chamber music is cast in the advanced modern idiom in vogue in Europe between the two wars; neo-Classical in general content, it is strong in polyphony and incisive rhythm; for his film music, he employs a more Romantic and diffuse style, relying on a Wagnerian type of grandiloquence. —Works: for orch.: *Nordungarische Bauernlieder und Tänze* (1929); symphony (1930); *Serenade* for small orch. (1932); *Scherzo* (1933); *Thema, Variationen und Finale* (1933); *Capriccio, pastorale e danza* (1938); *Variations on a Hungarian Peasant Song* (N. Y., Nov. 14, 1943); *Concerto,* for string orch. (Los Angeles, Dec. 28, 1944); violin concerto (Dallas, Jan. 5, 1956, Heifetz soloist); sonata for 2 violins; etc.

Rózycki (rŏh-zhit'-skē), **Ludomir,** Polish composer; b. Warsaw, Nov. 6, 1883; d. Katowice, Jan. 1, 1953. He studied piano with his father, a teacher at the Warsaw Cons.; theory with Noskowski at the Cons., graduating with honors in 1903. He then went to Berlin, where he took lessons with Humperdinck. In 1908 he was appointed conductor of the opera theater in Lwow and instructor at the Lwow Cons.; in 1912, he went to Warsaw to supervise the production of his opera *Meduza;* then undertook a European tour; settled in Berlin, where he remained through the years of World War I, continuing to compose. In 1920 he returned to Warsaw; after 1945, lived mostly in Katowice. He was highly regarded in Poland as a national composer of stature; his style of composition was a successful blend of German, Russian, and Italian ingredients, yet the Polish characteristics were not obscured by the cosmopolitan harmonic and orchestral dress. —Works: the operas *Boleslaw smialy (Boleslaw the Bold;* Lwow, Feb. 11, 1909), *Meduza* (Warsaw, Oct. 22, 1912), *Eros und Psyche* (Breslau, March 10, 1917; in German), *Casanova* (Warsaw, June 8, 1923), *Beatrice Cenci* (Warsaw, Jan. 30, 1927), *Mlyn diabelski (The Devilish Mill,* Poznan, Feb. 21, 1931), *Lili chce spiewac,* comic opera (Poznan, March 7, 1933); the ballets: *Pan Twardowski* (Warsaw, May 9, 1921; his most successful work; more than 800 performances in Warsaw) and *Apollon et la belle* (1937); for orch.: the symph. poems *Stanczyk* (1903), *Anhelli* (1909), *Warszawianka* (1910), *Mona Lisa Gioconda* (1910), *Pietà* (1942), *Warszawa wyzwolona (Warsaw Liberated;* 1950); 2 piano concertos (1918; 1942); violin concerto (1944); piano quintet (1913); string quartet (1916); violin sonata (1903); cello sonata (1906); a number of piano pieces; several song cycles. —Cf. A. Wieniawski, *Ludomir Rózycki* (Warsaw, 1928); M. Kaminski, *Ludomir Rózycki* (Katowice, 1951).

Rubbra, Edmund, English composer; b. Northampton, May 23, 1901. His parents were musical, and he was taught to play the piano by his mother. He left school as a young boy and was employed in various factories; at the same time he continued to study music by himself, and attempted some composition; organized a concert devoted to the works of his favorite composer, Cyril Scott (Northampton, 1918); subsequently took lessons from him in London; in 1919 he studied with Holst; also took courses at the Royal College of Music with R. O. Morris; his other teachers in composition were John Ireland, Eugene Goossens, and Vaughan Williams. He compensated for a late beginning in composition by an extremely energetic application to steady improvement of his technique; finally elaborated a style of his own, marked by sustained lyricism and dynamic Romanticism; his harmonic language often verges on polytonality. —Works: 1-act opera, *Bee-Bee-Bei* (1933); ballet, *Prism* (1938); for orch.: *Double Fugue* (1924), *Triple Fugue* (1929), symph. No. 1 (London, April 30, 1937), symph. No. 2 (London, Dec. 16, 1938), symph. No. 3 (Manchester, Dec. 15, 1940), symph. No. 4 (London, Aug. 14, 1942), symph. No. 5 (London, Jan. 26, 1949), symph. No. 6 (London, Nov. 17, 1954), symph. No. 7 (Birmingham, Oct. 1, 1957), *Sinfonia Concertante,* for piano and orch. (London, Aug. 10, 1943), *Soliloquy,* for cello and orch. (London, Jan. 1, 1945), viola concerto (London, April 15, 1953); chamber music: *Fantasy* for 2 violins and piano (1925), *Lyric Movement,* for piano quintet (1929), 2 string quartets (1933; 1952), piano trio (1950), 2 violin sonatas (1925; 1931), cello sonata (1946); choral works: *The Sacred Hymnody* (1921), *La Belle Dame sans merci* (1925), *The Morning Watch* (1941), *Te Deum* (1951); a number of madrigals and motets for unaccompanied chorus; songs with orch. *(Ballad of Tristram, 4 Medieval Latin Lyrics, 5 Sonnets,* etc.); songs with piano; miscellaneous pieces for various instruments. —Cf. Edwin Evans, *Edmund Rubbra,* in the 'Mus. Times' (Feb.-March, 1945; with a list of works); Colin Mason, *Rubbra's 4 Symphonies,* in 'Music Review' (Jan., 1941); Alan Frank, *Modern British Composers* (London, 1953; pp. 53-57).

Rubens, Paul Alfred, English composer of light music; b. London, April 29, 1875; d. Falmouth, Feb. 5, 1917. He was educated at Oxford; studied law; in 1899 he contributed some numbers to the famous musical revue *Floradora,* and this success induced him to abandon the law and devote himself to the composition of light operas. The following stage works by him were produced: *Lady Madcap* (1904), *Miss Hook of Holland* (1907), *My Mimosa Maid* (1908), *Dear Little Denmark* (1909), *The Balkan Princess* (1910), *The Sunshine Girl* (1912); he also wrote numerous songs and ballads.

Rubenson, Albert, Swedish composer; b. Stockholm, Dec. 20, 1826; d. there, March 2, 1901. He studied at the Leipzig Cons. (1844-48) with Ferdinand David (violin), Hauptmann (counterpoint), and Gade (composition). Returning to Stockholm, he wrote music criticism; in 1872 became inspector at the Stockholm Cons., and from 1888 till his death was its director. He wrote an overture, *Julius Cæsar;* a symph.; several orchestral suites; a string quartet; many songs. His style was derived from Mendelssohn and Schumann, but he attempted to inject some elements of Swedish folksong into his music, and in doing so contributed to the rise of musical nationalism in Sweden.

Rubini, Giovanni Battista, celebrated Italian tenor; b. Romano, near Bergamo, April 7, 1794; d. there, March 2, 1854. His teacher was Rosio of Bergamo; after an auspicious début in Pavia (1814), he sang for a time in Naples; there he married (1819) a singer, Mlle. Chomel, known under the professional name of La Comelli. On Oct. 6, 1825 he sang in Paris, where he scored his first triumphs in Rossini's operas at the Théâtre-Italien; his performances of the leading parts in the operas of Bellini and Donizetti were also very successful, and there is reason to believe that Rubini's interpretations greatly contributed to the rising fame of both of those composers. Between 1831 and 1834 he sang in Paris and London; in 1843 he undertook a tour with Liszt, traveling with him in Holland and Germany; in the same year he sang in Russia with tremendous acclaim; visited Russia again in 1844; then returned to Italy, bought an estate near his native town, and remained there until his death; for some years he gave singing lessons. He publ. *12 Lezioni di canto moderno per tenore o soprano* and an album of 6 songs, *L'Addio.* —Cf. C. Traini, *G. B. Rubini* (Romano, 1954).

Rubinstein, Anton Grigorievitch, celebrated Russian composer and pianist; brother of Nicholas Rubinstein; b. Vykhvatinetz,

Podolia, Nov. 28, 1829; d. Peterhof, near St. Petersburg, Nov. 20, 1894. He was of a family of Jewish merchants who became baptized in Berdichev in July, 1831. His mother gave him his first lessons in piano; the family moved to Moscow, where his father opened a small pencil factory. A well-known Moscow piano teacher, Alexandre Villoing, was entrusted with Rubinstein's musical education, and was in fact his only piano teacher. In 1839 Villoing took him to Paris, where Rubinstein played before Chopin and Liszt; remained in Paris until 1841; then made a concert tour in Holland, Germany, Austria, England, Norway, and Sweden, returning to Russia in 1843. Since Anton's brother, Nicholas, evinced a talent for composition, the brothers were taken to Berlin in 1844, where, on Meyerbeer's recommendation, Anton too studied composition, with Dehn; subsequently he made a tour through Hungary with the flutist Heindl. He returned to Russia in 1848 and settled in St. Petersburg. There he enjoyed the enlightened patronage of the Grand Duchess Helen, and wrote 3 Russian operas, *Dmitri Donoskoy* (1852), *Sibirskie Okhotniki (The Siberian Hunters;* 1853), and *Fomka Duratchok (Thomas the Fool;* 1853). In 1854, with the assistance of the Grand Duchess, Rubinstein undertook another tour in Western Europe. He found publishers in Berlin, and gave concerts of his own works in London and Paris, exciting admiration as both composer and pianist; on his return in 1858, he was appointed court pianist and conductor of the court concerts. He assumed the direction of the Russian Musical Society in 1859; in 1862 he founded the Imperial Cons. in St. Petersburg, remaining its director until 1867. For 20 years thereafter he held no official position; from 1867 until 1870 he gave concerts in Europe, winning fame as a pianist second only to Liszt. During the season of 1872-73, he made a triumphant American tour, playing in 215 concerts, for which he was paid about $40,000; appeared as soloist and jointly with the violinist Wieniawski. He produced a sensation by playing from memory, which was a novel procedure at the time. Returning to Europe, he elaborated a cycle of historical concerts, in programs ranging from Bach to Chopin; the last concert of a cycle he usually devoted to Russian composers (Glinka, Rimsky-Korsakov, Tchaikovsky, etc.). In 1887 he resumed the directorship of the St. Petersburg Cons., resigning again in 1891, when he went to Dresden (until 1894). He returned to Russia shortly before his death. —In 1890 Rubinstein established the Rubinstein Prize, an international competition open to young men between 20 and 26 years of age. Two prizes of 5,000 francs each were offered, one for composition, the other for piano playing. Quinquennial competitions were held in St. Petersburg, Berlin, Vienna, and Paris. —Rubinstein's role in Russian musical culture is of the greatest importance. He introduced European methods into education, and established high standards of artistic performance. He was the first Russian musician who was equally prominent as composer and interpreter. According to contemporary reports, his playing possessed extraordinary power (his octave passages were famous) and insight, revealed particularly in his performance of Beethoven's sonatas. His renown as a composer was scarcely less. His *Ocean Symphony* was one of the most frequently performed orchestral works in Europe and in America; his piano concertos were part of the standard repertory; his pieces for piano solo—the *Melody in F, Romance, Kamennoi Ostrow,* etc.—became perennial favorites. Rubinstein's style of composition was unabashedly Romantic; he was cosmopolitan as well as conservative; his reputed remark: "For the Christians I am a Jew; for the Jews, a Christian; for the Russians, a German; for the Germans, a Russian" sums up fairly well his position in the musical world. After his death, his orchestral works all but vanished from concert programs, as did his operas (with the exception of *The Demon,* which is still performed in Russia); his piano concerto no. 4, in D minor, is occasionally heard. —Works: operas: *Dmitri Donskoy* (St. Petersburg, April 30, 1852), *Sibirskie Okhotniki (The Siberian Hunters;* 1853), *Fomka Duratchok (Thomas the Fool;* St. Petersburg, May 23, 1853), *Die Kinder der Heide,* 5-act German opera (Vienna, Feb. 23, 1861), *Feramors,* after the poem *Lalla Rookh* of Th. Moore (Dresden, Feb. 24, 1863), *The Demon,* after Lermontov (St. Petersburg, Jan. 25, 1875), *Die Makkabäer* (Berlin, April 17, 1875), *Nero* (Hamburg, Nov. 1, 1879), *Kupets Kalashnikov (The Merchant Kalashnikov;* St. Petersburg, March 5, 1880), *Sulamith* and *Unter Räubern* (both performed Hamburg, Nov. 8, 1883), *Der Papagei (The Parrot;* Hamburg, 1884), *Goriusha* (St. Petersburg, Dec. 3, 1889); oratorios: *Paradise Lost* (Weimar, 1858; revised and arranged as a sacred opera, Düsseldorf, 1875), *The Tower of Babel* (Königsberg, 1870), *Moses* (1892), *Christus* (1893); ballet, *Die Rebe (The Vine;* 1885); 2 cantatas, *Die Nixe,* for alto solo and famale chorus, and *Der Morgen,* for male chorus; scene and aria for soprano, *E dunque ver?;* 2 scenes for alto and orch., *Hecuba* and *Hagar in der Wüste;* 6 symphonies (No. 2, *Ocean;* No. 4, *Dramatic;* No. 5, *Russian); Ouverture triomphale; Ouverture de concert;* 3 'character pictures': *Faust, Ivan the Terrible, Don Quixote;* a 'morceau symphonique' *La Russie;* 5 piano concertos; *Fantaisie* for piano and orch.; *Konzertstück,* for piano and orch.; violin concerto; 2 cello concertos; octet for piano, strings, and winds; sextet for strings; quintet for piano, flute, clarinet, horn, and bassoon; string quintet; piano quintet; 10 string quartets; piano quartet; 5 piano trios; 2 violin sonatas; 2 cello sonatas; piano works: 4 sonatas; *Kamennoi Ostrow; Soirées à St. Petersburg; Album de Péterhof; Soirées musicales;* 6 *Barcarolles; Sérénade russe;* polkas, mazurkas, etc.; about 100 songs (of these, *Asra* is popular). —Writings: *Memoirs* (St. Petersburg, 1889; in English, as *Autobiography of Anton Rubinstein,* Boston, 1890); *Music and its Representatives* (Moscow, 1891; in English as *Music and its Masters;* N. Y., 1892; also publ. as *A Conversation on Music); Leitfaden zum richtigen Gebrauch des Pianoforte-Pedals* (posthumous; Leipzig, 1896; in French, Brussels, 1899); *Gedankenkorb, Litterarischer Nachlass* (posthumous; Stuttgart, 1896); *Die Meister des Klaviers* (posthumous; Berlin, 1899). —Bibliography: A. McArthur, *Anton Rubinstein* (London, 1889); E. Zabel, *Anton Rubinstein* (Leipzig, 1892); A. Soubies, *Anton Rubinstein* (Paris, 1895); I. Martinov, *Épisodes de la vie de Rubinstein* (Brussels, 1895); J. Rodenberg, *Meine persönlichen Erinnerungen an Anton Rubinstein, nebst Briefen,* in 'Deutsche Rundschau' (vol. 21; Berlin, 1895; in English in 'Music' vol. 8, Chicago, 1905); E. Wessel, *Some Explanations, Hints and Remarks of Anton Rubinstein from His Lessons in the St. Petersburg Cons.* (St. Petersburg, 1901; in German, Leipzig, 1904); N. Findeisen, *Anton Rubinstein* (Moscow, 1907); La Mara, *Anton Rubinstein,* in *Musikalische Studienköpfe* (vol. 3, 7th ed., Leipzig, 1909; separately, Leipzig, 1911); N. Bernstein, *Anton Rubinstein* (Leipzig, 1911); A. Hervey, *Anton Rubinstein* (London, 1913); K. Preiss, *Anton Rubinsteins pianistische Bedeutung* (Leipzig, 1914); Igor Glebov, *Anton Rubinstein in his Musical Activities and Opinions of his Contemporaries* (Moscow, 1929); C. D. Bowen, *'Free Artist': the Story of Anton and Nicholas Rubinstein* (N. Y., 1939; fictionalized account, but accurate as to actual events; with a complete list of works and a detailed bibliography, compiled by Otto E. Albrecht); O. Bennigsen, *The Brothers Rubinstein and Their Circle,* in the 'Mus. Quarterly' (Oct., 1939); L. Barenboym, *A. G. Rubinstein,* vol. I (Moscow, 1957).

Rubinstein, Artur, celebrated pianist; b. Lódz, Poland, Jan. 28, 1886. He performed in public at a very early age; after taking lessons with A. Rózycki in Warsaw, he was sent to Berlin, where he studied with Heinrich Barth (piano) and with Robert Kahn and Max Bruch (theory). He made his European début playing a Mozart concerto in Berlin, with Joachim as conductor; then toured in Russia with Koussevitzky's orch. In 1906 he made his American début with the Philadelphia Orch. During World War I he played recitals in England with Eugène Ysaÿe; in 1916 toured Spain, and later gave concerts in South America. In 1932 he married a daughter of Emil Mlynarski. Rubinstein is one of the finest interpreters of Chopin's music, for which his fiery temperament and poetic lyricism are particularly suitable. After his concerts in Spain and South America, he became one of the most ardent exponents of Spanish music. His popularity with audiences continued through the decades of his active career; he was equally successful in France, Spain, the U. S., and South America, appearing in recitals and with major symph. orchestras. His style of playing tends towards bravura in Classical compositions, but he rarely indulges in mannerisms. He appeared in several films made in Hollywood, as pianist, representing himself. In 1946 he became an American citizen. In 1958 he revisited Poland after 20 years, obtaining immense success. —Cf. B. Gavoty, *A. Rubinstein* (Geneva, 1955; in English, 1956).

Rubinstein, Beryl, American pianist and composer; b. Athens, Ga., Oct. 26, 1898; d. Cleveland, Dec. 29, 1952. He studied piano with his father and Alexander Lambert; toured the U. S. as a child (1905-11); then went to Berlin to study with Busoni and Vianna da Motta. He was appointed to the faculty of the Cleveland Institute of Music in 1921; became its director in 1932. He wrote an opera, *The Sleeping Beauty,* to a libretto by John Erskine (Juilliard School of Music, N. Y., Jan. 19, 1938); 32 piano studies; 3 dances for piano; transcriptions from Gershwin's *Porgy and Bess.* He conducted his orchestral *Scherzo* with the Cleveland Orch. on March 17, 1927; performed his piano concerto in C with the same orch. on Nov. 12, 1936.

Rubinstein, Joseph, Russian pianist; b. Starokonstantinov, Feb. 8, 1847; d. (committed suicide) Lucerne, Sept. 15, 1884; studied in Vienna with Hellmesberger, Dachs, and Liszt. He was an ardent partisan of Wagner, whom he knew personally; in 1874 he was the pianist at the preliminary rehearsals of *The Ring des Nibelungen* at Bayreuth; made piano transcriptions of it and also of *Parsifal.*

Rubinstein, Nicholas (Nicolay Grigorievitch), Russian pianist and pedagogue; brother of Anton Rubinstein; b. Moscow, June 14, 1835; d. March 23, 1881. He began to study piano with his mother at the age of 4, when his brother, 6 years older than he, was already on the road to fame as a child prodigy; was taken to Berlin with his brother, and there studied with Kullak (piano) and Dehn (composition). The brothers met Mendelssohn and Meyerbeer; returning to Moscow in 1846, he began to take lessons with Alexandre Villoing. He also studied law, and received a degree from the Univ. of Moscow (1855); subsequently was a minor functionary in the government; earned his living by giving private lessons. In 1858 he began his concert career; appeared in Russia, and also in London. In 1859, when he was only 24 years old, he became head of the Moscow branch of the Russian Music Society; in 1866 this Society opened the Moscow Cons., of which Nicholas Rubinstein was director until his death. From 1860 he was the regular conductor of the Moscow concerts of the Imperial Russian Musical Society. In 1878 he conducted 4 Russian concerts at the Paris Exposition; at the first and the fourth of the series he performed Tchaikovsky's piano concerto No. 1 (which he had criticized so sharply when Tchaikovsky first submitted it to him in 1874). Anton Rubinstein declared that Nicholas was a better pianist than himself; however, this generous appreciation was not accepted by the public. As an educator, however, Nicholas Rubinstein played perhaps a greater role than his famous brother. Among his pupils were Taneyev, Siloti, and Emil Sauer. —Cf. N. Findeisen, *Nicholas Rubinstein,* in 'Russkaya Muzÿkalnaya Gazeta' (1901, No. 10); C. D. Bowen, *'Free Artist': the Story of Anton and Nicholas Rubinstein* (N. Y., 1939); Olga Bennigsen, *The Brothers Rubinstein and Their Circle,* in the 'Mus. Quarterly' (Oct., 1939).

Rubio Piqueras (roo'-bē-oh pē-keh'-rahs), **Felipe,** Spanish musicologist; b. Valera de Arriba, Sept. 13, 1881; d. Toledo, 1936. He was ordained priest in 1904, and served as organist at the Cathedral of Badajoz until 1917; then went to Toledo as church organist. He publ. valuable works on music in Toledo: *Códices polifónicos toledanos* and *Música y Músicos toledanos* (1923); wrote some church music.

Rubner. See **Rybner.**

Rubsamen, Walter (Howard), American musicologist; b. New York, July 21, 1911. He studied the flute with Georges Barrère; musicology at Columbia Univ. under Paul H. Lang (B. A., 1933); then went to Germany (on a Clarence Barker Music Scholarship); studied at the Univ. of Munich with R. von Ficker and Otto Ursprung; received his Ph. D. there with the dissertation *Pierre de la Rue als Messenkomponist* (1937). From 1938 to 1942, instructor in music at the Univ. of California, Los Angeles; 1942-48, assistant prof.; 1948-55, associate prof.; 1955, prof. —Publications: *Literary Sources of Secular Music in Italy c. 1500* (1943); articles in the 'Mus. Quarterly,' 'Notes,' the 'Rivista Musicale Italiana,' etc.

Rückauf, Anton, an outstanding composer of German songs; b. Prague, March 13, 1855; d. Schloss Alt-Erla, Austria, Sept. 19, 1903. A pupil of Proksch, he became a teacher at the Proksch Institute in Prague; subsequently studied composition in Vienna (under Nottebohm and Nawrátil), where he settled permanently. He owed much to the artistic cooperation of the noted singer Gustav Walter, who constantly performed his songs, and whom Rückauf himself accompanied at the piano. He publ. about 80 songs; of these the following were particularly well liked: *Ballade* (to Uhland's poem), *Hafis,* 5 *Minnelieder, Zigeunerlieder, Flammen und Asche, Lenz und Liebe, Lieder der Liebe in Völkerstimmen, Aus der Wanderzeit, Grüsse;* also wrote chamber music; an opera, *Die Rosenthalerin* (Dresden, 1897); set 5 Russian folk poems for mixed chorus with 4-hand piano accompaniment.

Ruckers, celebrated family of harpsichord makers at Antwerp. **Hans** the elder (b. Mechlin, c. 1550; d. Antwerp, c. 1625), was the first to make instruments. He was admitted to the Guild of Saint Luke in 1579, and his 1st known instrument is a harpsichord dated 1581; his last, 1620. **Hans** the younger, also known as **Jean** (baptized Antwerp, Jan. 15, 1578; d. there, April 24, 1643), was the second son of the founder.

He was greatly esteemed by his contemporaries, and was exempted from Civic Guard duties in appreciation of his artistry. **Andreas** the elder (baptized Antwerp, Aug. 20, 1579; d. after 1651), manufactured harpsichords in 1601-44. **Andreas** the younger, son of the elder Andreas (baptized Antwerp, March 31, 1607; d. after 1667), made instruments between 1637 and 1667. Another member of the same family was **Christopher Ruckers**, who flourished about 1600. For a list of surviving instruments and other particulars, see Donald H. Boalch, *Makers of the Harpsichord and Clavichord, 1440 to 1840* (N. Y., 1956). See also Georg Kinsky, *Die Familie Ruckers,* in the 'Zeitschrift für Musikwissenschaft' (vol. IV); André M. Pols, *De Ruckers en de klavierbouw in Vlaanderen* (Antwerp, 1942).

Rüdel, Hugo, German horn player and choral conductor; b. Havelberg, Feb. 7, 1868; d. Berlin, Nov. 27, 1934. He studied at the Berlin Hochschule für Musik; was horn player at the Royal Opera; director of the Berlin opera chorus (1901); choral conductor at the Bayreuth Festivals (1906); in 1909 succeeded Prüfer as conductor of the famous Berlin 'Domchor,' with which he toured extensively; also conductor of the Berlin 'Lehrergesangsverein' (1916).

Rudersdorff, Hermine, dramatic soprano; b. Ivanovsky, Ukraine, Dec. 12, 1822; d. Boston, Feb. 26, 1882. A pupil of Bordogni at Paris and of de Micherout at Milan; she sang at first in Germany (1840-54); then in London (1854-65). Engaged at the Boston Jubilee of 1869, she settled in Boston, becoming renowned as a teacher (Emma Thursby was her pupil). In 1844 she married Dr. Küchenmeister, from whom she was divorced, then married in 1850 an English merchant, Maurice Mansfield. Their son was the famous actor, Richard Mansfield (1857-1907).

Rudhyar, Dane (real name Daniel Chennevière), composer and writer; b. Paris, March 23, 1895. He studied at the Sorbonne, and, for a short time, at the Paris Cons.; very early began to be interested in modern music, philosophy, and literature; publ. a book on Debussy at the age of 18 (Paris, 1913). In 1916 he came to the U. S. for a performance of his dance poems for orch., *Poèmes ironiques* and *Vision végétale,* at the Metropolitan Opera House, N. Y., on April 4, 1917; remained in the U. S. and became an American citizen; lived in California, New Mexico, and N. Y. In 1922 his tone poem *Soul Fire* won the $1000 prize of the Los Angeles Philharmonic. He became deeply interested in theosophy, and adopted the Hindu pseudonym Rudhyar; has publ. several books on mystical philosophy, contributed to astrological journals; also exhibited his paintings. His music derives from Scriabin, with whose cosmic philosophy Rudhyar finds himself in sympathy. —Works: *Ouranos,* a 'syntony' in 3 movements scored for orch. and 3 pianos (1919-26); *The Surge of Fire,* symph. trilogy (Los Angeles, Oct. 22, 1925); *Sinfonietta* (1927); *To the Real,* symph. triptych (Paris, Feb. 21, 1932); several sets of piano pieces: *3 Pæans, Tetragrams, Chants of Formation,* etc. —Cf. Paul Rosenfeld, *An Hour with American Music* (N. Y., 1929; pp. 71-78); A. Morang, *Dane Rudhyar, Pioneer in Creative Synthesis* (N. Y., 1939).

Rüdinger, Gottfried, German composer; b. Lindau, Aug. 23, 1886; d. Gauting, near Munich, Jan. 17, 1946. He studied in a local school, of which his father was director; in 1907 went to Eichstätt, where he studied philosophy and theology; at the same time took courses with Max Reger at the Leipzig Cons. (1907-09); in 1910 he settled in Munich, where he became instructor in theory at the Academy. He composed prolifically; brought out a 'peasant play-opera,' *Tegernseer im Himmel,* op. 100; the children's operas *Benchtesgadener Sagenspiel, Musikantenkomödie, König Folkwart,* etc.; several string quartets; 2 piano trios; a trio for viola, saxophone, and piano; pieces for small brass ensembles, in the style of old townpiper music; a *Nordisches Fest* for 3 zithers; many choruses; a *Muttergottes-Messe,* op. 143; also many instructive piano pieces.

Rudnick, Wilhelm, German composer; b. Damerkow, Dec. 30, 1850; d. there, Aug. 7, 1927. He studied at Kullak's Akademie der Tonkunst in Berlin; subsequently occupied various posts as church organist in Landsberg and Liegnitz; was also active as choral conductor. He wrote numerous organ works of excellent quality; a fantasy on *Ein' feste Burg, Trinitatis-Sonate, Pfingsten-Sonate, Konzert-Phantasie, Choralvorspiele;* etc. Also vocal works (sacred and secular).

Rudnicki (rood-nits'-skē), **Marian Teofil,** Polish composer; b. Cracow, March 7, 1888; d. there, Dec. 31, 1944. He was conductor at the Cracow Operetta Theater (1916-19) and at the Warsaw Municipal Opera (1919);

wrote incidental music to *Antony and Cleopatra, The Return of Ulysses, Caligula,* etc.; choral works; piano pieces; songs.

Rudnitsky, Antin, pianist, conductor, and composer; b. Luka, Galicia, Feb. 7, 1902. He studied in Berlin with Schnabel and Petri (piano), Schreker (composition), Abert and Curt Sachs (musicology); Ph. D. at the Univ. of Berlin, 1926. In 1927 he went to Russia, where he conducted the State Opera of Kharkov (1927-30) and the State Opera of Kiev (1930-32); from 1932 to 1937, was conductor at the Municipal Opera and prof. at the Academy of Music in Lwow and Warsaw. In 1937 he settled in the U. S.; toured as accompanist for his wife, Maris Sokil, soprano; in 1939 made his permanent home in N. Y. His works include an opera, *Dovbush* (1937); a ballet, *Storm over the West* (1932); 3 symphonies (1936; 1941; 1942); a cello concerto (1942); chamber music.

Rudolf, Max, eminent conductor; b. Frankfurt, June 15, 1902. He studied cello with Maurits Frank, piano with Eduard Jung, and composition with Bernhard Sekles at the Hoch Cons. in Frankfurt; then was coach at the Municipal Opera in Freiburg (1922-23) and Darmstadt (1923-25); traveled in Italy (1926-27); 1st conductor at the Darmstadt Opera (1927-29); later conducted in Prague (1929-35). From 1935 until 1940 he was conductor of the Göteborg, Sweden, Symph. Orch. and of the Swedish Broadcasting Co. In 1940 he came to the U. S. (American citizen, 1946); in 1945, joined the managerial staff at the Metropolitan Opera House, N. Y.; 1950, became its artistic administrator; also gave many distinguished performances of standard operas. In 1958 he was appointed permanent conductor of the Cincinnati Symph. Orch. He is the author of *The Grammar of Conducting* (N. Y., 1949).

Rudorff, Ernst Friedrich Karl, German pianist; b. Berlin, Jan. 18, 1840; d. there, Dec. 31, 1916. He studied with Bargiel in Berlin and with Moscheles, Plaidy, and Reinecke in Leipzig. After a few years of teaching in Cologne (1865-68), he was appointed head of the piano dept. at the Hochschule für Musik in Berlin, and held this post for 41 years (1869-1910); also conducted the Stern Gesangverein (1880-90). He edited the piano concertos and piano sonatas of Mozart; brought out the full score of Weber's *Euryanthe;* etc. He was a friend of Brahms, whose letters to him were publ. in vol. III of the Brahms correspondence (Berlin, 1907); Rudorff's correspondence with Joachim was publ. in vol. III of *Briefe von und an Joseph Joachim* (1913). He composed 3 symphonies; piano pieces. —Cf. Elisabeth Rudorff, ed., *Aus den Tagen der Romantik, Bildnis einer deutschen Familie* (Leipzig, 1938).

Rudzinski, Witold, Polish composer; b. Sebesh, Russia, March 14, 1913. He studied with T. Szeligowski at the Cons. of Vilna; in 1938 he went to Paris, where he studied with Nadia Boulanger. Returning to Poland, he taught at the Vilna Cons. (1941) and the Lodz Cons. (1946); then settled in Warsaw. Among his works are 2 symphonies, 2 piano concertos, 2 string quartets; piano music; songs. He also publ. some books on music appreciation, and a biography of Moniuszko (Cracow, 1955; 2nd ed., 1957).

Rue, Pierre de la. See La Rue.

Ruelle, Charles Émile, French musicologist, authority on Greek music; b. Paris, Oct. 24, 1833; d. there, Oct., 1912. He was chief librarian of the Bibliothèque de Ste. Geneviève, Paris, from 1898 to 1905; translated into French the treatises of Aristoxenus (1871), Nicomachus (1881), etc.; publ. the valuable treatises *Études sur l'ancienne musique grecque* (1875 and 1900); *Le Monocorde* (1891); *Sextus Empiricus* (1899); *De la musique des Grecs modernes et en particulier de leur musique ecclésiastique* (1876); contributed to the 'Dictionnaire des antiquités grecques.'

Rufer, Josef, Austrian music scholar; b. Vienna, 1893; studied with Schoenberg; was his assistant at the Akademie der Künste in Berlin (1925-33); with Stuckenschmidt, ed. the monthly magazine 'Stimmen' in Berlin (1947-49). Publ. a valuable treatise, *Die Komposition mit zwölf Tönen* (Berlin, 1952; English transl. by Humphrey Searle as *Composition with 12 Notes related only to one another,* London, 1954).

Rüfer, Philippe (-Barthélemy), pianist and composer; b. Liège, June 7, 1844 (of German parents); d. Berlin, Sept. 15, 1919. He studied at the Cons. of Liège; in 1871, settled in Berlin, where he taught piano at Stern's Cons., Kullak's Akademie der Tonkunst, and (from 1881) at Scharwenka's. He wrote the operas *Merlin* (Berlin, Feb. 28, 1887) and *Ingo* (Berlin, 1896); a symphony; 3 overtures; piano music; songs. —Cf. P. Magnette, *Philippe Rüfer. Étude biographique et critique* (Liège, 1910).

Ruffo, Titta, famous Italian baritone; b. Pisa, June 9, 1877; d. Florence, July 6, 1953. His real name was Ruffo Cafiero Titta, but he found it convenient to transpose his first and last names for professional purposes. He studied with Persichini at the Santa Cecilia in Rome, then with Cassini in Milan. He made his operatic début in Rome as the Herald in *Lohengrin* (1898); then sang in Rio de Janeiro; returning to Italy, he appeared in all the principal theaters; also sang in Vienna, Paris, and London. He made his American début in Philadelphia as Rigoletto (Nov. 4, 1912) with the combined Philadelphia-Chicago Opera Co.; 1st appearance with the Metropolitan Opera, as Figaro in *Il Barbiere di Siviglia* (N. Y., Jan. 19, 1922). He left the Metropolitan in 1929 and returned to Rome. In Oct., 1937, he was briefly under arrest for opposing the Mussolini regime; then went to Florence, where he remained until his death. He publ. a book of memoirs, *La mia parabola* (Milan, 1937); a sequel to it remains in manuscript. —Cf. M. A. Barrenechea, *Titta Ruffo; notas de psicologia artistica* (Buenos Aires, 1911).

Ruger, Morris Hutchins, American composer; b. Superior, Wis., Dec. 2, 1902. He studied at Columbia Univ. (A. B., 1924), Fontainebleau, France (1925-26), Northwestern Univ. (1930), the Juilliard School of Music (1934); piano with Isidor Philipp in Paris (1926); composition with Seth Bingham in N. Y. and André Bloch in Paris. In 1945, appointed assistant director of the Los Angeles Cons. He publ. a number of choral works; a textbook, *Harmony, a Creative Approach to Four-Part Writing* (1947); composed a string quartet, a piano quintet, a violin concerto. His opera, *Gettysburg,* was produced at the Hollywood Bowl in 1938.

Ruggi (roo'-jē), **Francesco,** Italian composer, b. Naples, Oct. 21, 1767; d. there, Jan. 23, 1845. He studied at the Cons. di S. Loreto in Naples under Fenaroli; became prof. of composition at the Cons. di San Pietro a Maiella; Bellini and Carafa were his pupils there. He wrote the operas *L'Ombra di Nino* (Naples, 1795), *La Guerra aperta* (Naples, 1796), and *Sofì tripponi* (Milan, 1804); much sacred music.

Ruggles, Carl, American composer; b. Marion, Mass., March 11, 1876. He studied with Christian Timner and Joseph Claus; then with Walter Spalding and J. K. Paine at Harvard Univ. In 1912 he organized the Winona Symph. Orch. in Minneapolis, which he conducted for some years; then lived in Arlington, Vt.; in 1937 was appointed to the faculty of the Univ. of Miami, Florida, as instructor in modern composition. In 1954 he was elected to the National Institute of Arts and Letters. In his music he adopted a radical idiom, powerfully dissonant, and atonal in its melodic patterns. He wrote only a few works, rarely performed; nonetheless, he appears a strong figure on the American musical scene. In the last decades of his active life, he devoted himself mainly to painting, and exhibited his pictures in New York and elsewhere. —Works: *Men and Angels,* symph. suite, for 5 trumpets and 1 bass trumpet (N. Y., Dec. 17, 1922; revised for brass or strings, and renamed *Angels;* Miami, April 24, 1939, composer conducting); *Men and Mountains,* symph. suite in 3 movements: *Men, Lilacs, Marching Mountains* (N. Y., Dec. 7, 1924; revised for larger orch.; N. Y., March 19, 1936); *Portals,* for string orch. (N. Y., Jan. 24, 1926); *Sun-Treader,* after Browning, for large orch. (Paris, Feb. 25, 1932); *Polyphonic Composition* for 3 pianos (1940); *Evocations,* 4 chants for piano (1945); *Organum,* for large orch. (N. Y., Nov. 24, 1949). —Cf. Paul Rosenfeld, *An Hour with American Music* (N. Y., 1929; pp. 101-06); C. Seeger, *Carl Ruggles,* in the 'Mus. Quarterly' (Oct., 1932); Lou Harrison, *About Carl Ruggles* (Yonkers, N. Y., 1946).

Rühlmann, Frans, Belgian conductor; b. Brussels, Jan. 11, 1868; d. Paris, June 8, 1948. He studied at the Cons. of Brussels; filled engagements as conductor at the Théâtre de la Monnaie in Brussels, and also in Liège, Antwerp, etc. In 1905 he appeared at the Opéra-Comique in Paris; in 1914 became conductor of the Paris Opéra; also led a series of popular concerts in Antwerp.

Rühlmann, Franz, German musicologist; b. Chemnitz, Dec. 7, 1896; d. in a camp for prisoners of war, Landsberg, June 15, 1945. He was in the German army in both wars; studied in Leipzig and Kiel; *Dr. phil.,* 1924, with the dissertation, *Richard Wagner und die deutsche Opernbühne;* was instructor of theater music at the Hochschule für Musik in Berlin (from 1933). He publ. various essays on Wagner's operas, and on German oratorios; brought out vocal scores of *Der Freischütz,* Mozart's *Requiem,* Gluck's operas, etc.

Rühlmann, (Adolf) Julius, German writer on music; b. Dresden, Feb. 28, 1816; d.

there, Oct. 27, 1877. He played the trombone in the court orch. of Dresden, where he founded the Dresden 'Tonkünstlerverein' (1855); taught piano and music history at the Dresden Cons. He prepared a valuable *Geschichte der Bogeninstrumente,* which was publ. posthumously by his son, Dr. Richard Rühlmann (1882); he also wrote *Die Urform der Bogeninstrumente* (1874).

Rumford, Robert Henry Kennerley, English baritone; b. London, Sept. 2, 1870; d. North Stoke, Oxford, March 9, 1957. He studied voice with George Henschel in London and with Sbriglia in Paris; in 1900, married the celebrated contralto Clara Butt, with whom he toured the world in 1913-14. He lived most of his life in England.

Rummel, Christian, German composer and conductor; b. Brichsenstadt, Nov. 27, 1787; d. Wiesbaden, Feb. 13, 1849. He was an able performer on the piano, violin, and clarinet; served as municipal conductor in Wiesbaden from 1815 until 1841; publ. a clarinet concerto, 2 quintets, etc. His son, **Joseph Rummel** (b. Wiesbaden, Oct. 6, 1818; d. London, March 25, 1880), was court pianist to the Duke of Nassau, and publ. piano music; another son, **August Rummel** (b. Wiesbaden, Jan. 14, 1824; d. London, Dec. 14, 1886), also was a good pianist.

Rummel, Franz, pianist, son of Joseph Rummel, grandson of Christian Rummel; b. London, Jan. 11, 1853; d. Berlin, May 2, 1901. He studied with Louis Brassin at the Brussels Cons., winning the 1st prize in 1872; toured in America 3 times (1878, 1886, 1898). He married a daughter of S. F. B. Morse, inventor of the telegraph.

Rummel, Walter Morse, distinguished pianist, son of Franz Rummel, and grandson of S. F. B. Morse, inventor of the telegraph; b. Berlin, July 19, 1887; d. Bordeaux, May 2, 1953. He studied with Leopold Godowsky (piano) and Hugo Kaun (composition). In 1908 he went to Paris, where he became acquainted with Debussy, and devoted himself to propagandizing Debussy's piano works, of which he was a foremost interpreter. He was also a composer; publ. transcriptions of Bach's organ works for piano. He was married twice, to the pianist Thérèse Chaigneau, with whom he appeared in 2-piano recitals (later divorced), and to Sarah Harrington (also divorced).

Runciman, John F., English music critic; b. 1866; d. London, April 7, 1916. He was a church organist before he joined the staff of the 'Saturday Review' in London, 1894, as music critic; held this position till his death; also was editor of 'The Chord' (quarterly) and the 'Musician's Library.' His criticisms were remarkable for their unabashed violence in denouncing composers and performers whom he did not like; on some occasions he became involved in libel suits. He publ. selected essays in 1899 under the title of *Old Scores and New Readings,* a biographical study of Haydn (1908), one of Purcell (1909), and *Richard Wagner, Composer of Operas* (1913).

Rung, Frederik, Danish composer, son of Henrik Rung; b. Copenhagen, June 14, 1854; d. there, Jan. 22, 1914. He studied with his father; became conductor at the Copenhagen Opera (1884); also led the 'Cecilia Society' (founded by his father); taught at the Copenhagen Cons. from 1881 till 1893. —Works: the operas: *Det hemmelige Selskab (The Secret Party;* Copenhagen, Feb. 9, 1888) and *Den trekantede Hat (The Three-cornered Hat;* Copenhagen, Nov. 7, 1894); symph.; a rhapsody for orch.; *Danse des papillons* for orch.; a serenade for 9 instruments; a piano quintet; 2 string quartets; a violin sonata; piano pieces; songs.

Rung, Henrik, Danish conductor and composer; father of Frederik Rung; b. Copenhagen, March 3, 1807; d. there, Dec. 13, 1871. He founded the 'Cecilia Society' in 1891; wrote a number of choral works and popular songs. —Cf. C. Thrane, *Caeciliaföreningen og dens Stifter* (Copenhagen, 1901).

Runge, Paul, German musicologist; b. Heinrichsfeld, Posen, Jan. 2, 1848; d. Colmar, Alsace, July 4, 1911. Studied with J. Schneider and at the Royal Institute for Church Music in Berlin; lived from 1873 as organist and teacher in Colmar. His writings, which are of importance especially in connection with the music of the Minnesingers and Mastersingers, are *Die Sangesweisen der Colmarer Handschrift und die Liederhandschrift Donaueschingen* (1896), *Die Lieder und Melodien der Geissler des Jahres 1349* (1900), *Die Lieder des Hugo von Montfort mit den Melodien des Burk Mangolt* (1906), *Die Notation des Meistergesanges* (1907; in the report of the Basel Congress of the Internationale Musik-Gesellschaft); with R. Batka he publ. *Die Lieder Mülichs von Prag* (1905), etc.

Rungenhagen, Karl Friedrich, German composer; b. Berlin, Sept. 27, 1778; d. there, Dec. 21, 1851. Pupil of Benda; in 1815 vice-conductor of the Singakademie, succeeding Zelter in 1833 as first conductor; member of the Berlin Academy, and teacher in the School of Composition. —Works: 4 operas, 3 oratorios, a *Te Deum,* 30 motets, 30 4-part songs, over 100 sacred and 1,000 secular songs; also symphonies, quartets, etc.

Runolfsson, Karl Otto, Icelandic composer; b. Reykjavik, Oct. 24, 1900. He studied trumpet and composition in Copenhagen; then played the trumpet in the radio orchestra in Reykjavik; in 1939, appointed teacher at the Cons. there. He wrote a set of Icelandic songs for voice and orch. (1938); many choruses on Icelandic themes; a violin sonata; songs.

Runze (roohn'tseh), **Maximilian,** German writer and editor; b. Woltersdorf, Pomerania, Aug. 8, 1849; d. Berlin, May 9, 1931. Studied philosophy and theology at the Univs. of Greifswald and Berlin; from 1882, rector of St. Johannis-Moabit, Berlin, and lecturer at the Humboldt-Akademie. His writings on the life and works of Karl Loewe are valuable: *Karl Loewe, eine ästhetische Beurteilung* (1884), *Loewe redivivus* (1888), *Ludwig Giesebrecht und Karl Loewe* (1894), *Goethe und Loewe* (1901), *Karl Loewe* (1905; a biography); also *Die musikalische Legende* (1902), *Volkslied und Ballade* (1907). Edited *Arien aus ungedruckten Opern und Oratorien Loewes* (1892; 3 vols.), *Loewe-Hohenzollern Album* (1898; 2 vols.), *Gesamtausgabe der Balladen, Legenden und Gesänge Loewes* (1899-1903; 17 vols.).

Ruolz-Montchal (rü-öhls' möhn-shahl'), **Henri (-Catherine-Camille),** comte **de,** French composer; b. Paris, March 5, 1808; d. there, Sept. 30, 1887. He was a pupil of Berton, Lesueur, Paër, and Rossini; had won some success as a composer when the loss of his fortune (1840) induced him to abandon music and devote himself to the study of chemistry. —Works: the operas *Attendre et courir* (with F. Halévy; Opéra-Comique, 1830), *Lara* (Naples, Nov. 22, 1835; was highly praised by Alexandre Dumas in the 'Gazette Musicale de Paris'), *La Vendetta* (Opéra, 1839), *La jolie fille de Perth,* and *Manfred;* a Requiem; *Cantate en honneur de Jeanne d'Arc;* a string quartet; 2 piano trios; motets; songs.

Russell, George Alexander, American organist and song composer; b. Franklin, Tenn., Oct. 2, 1880; d. Dewitt, N. Y., Nov. 24, 1953.. The son of a Presbyterian minister, he studied at home; his mother, Felicia Putnam Russell (a direct descendant of General Israel Putnam of Revolution fame), taught him piano; the family moved to Texas, where he studied academic subjects; entered the College of Fine Arts, Syracuse Univ., studying organ with George A. Parker and composition with William Berwald; subsequently studied in Europe with Leopold Godowsky and Harold Bauer (piano), and with Widor (organ). Returning to America in 1908, he toured as accompanist to various artists; in 1910 he became director of the Auditorium concerts at Wanamaker's in N. Y.; in 1917 was appointed prof. in the newly-founded chair of music at Princeton Univ.; assembled the famous Rodman Wanamaker Collection of old Italian string instruments. He wrote the songs *Sunset, The Sacred Fire, In Fountain Court, Lyric from Tagore, Expectation, Puer Redemptor,* etc.; the piano pieces *Theme and Variations, Contrapuntal Waltz,* etc. —Cf. J. T. Howard, *Alexander Russell* (N. Y., 1925).

Russell, Henry, English singer and composer; b. Sheerness, Dec. 24, 1812; d. London, Dec. 8, 1900. He studied in Italy as a young boy; took a few lessons from Rossini in Naples; sang in London in 1828; then was in Canada (1833); served as organist of the First Presbyterian Church of Rochester, N. Y. (1833-41). He returned to England in 1841, and became extremely popular there as a composer and singer of dramatic and topical songs, of which *Woodman, Spare that Tree* attained immense popularity; other songs were *Old Arm Chair, Oh, Weep Not!, A Life on the Ocean Wave* (official march of the Royal Marines), *Cheer, Boys, Cheer, Ivy Green, The Gambler's Wife, Old Bell, The Maniac,* etc. He publ. a book of reminiscences, *Cheer, Boys, Cheer* (London, 1895) and *L'Amico dei cantanti,* a treatise on singing. He was the father of Henry Russell, the impresario, and of Sir Landon Ronald (q. v.), the composer and conductor, whose real name was L. R. Russell.

Russell, Henry, English impresario; son of the preceding; b. London, Nov. 14, 1871; d. there, Oct. 11, 1937. He studied singing at the Royal College of Music, and devised an original method of vocal instruction, which attracted the attention of Mme. Melba, who sent him a number of her good pupils. Owing to his wide acquaintance with singers, he was invited in 1903 to manage a season of opera at Covent Garden; in 1905 he brought his company to the U. S., where Boston was the principal field of his operations; his success there resulted, in 1909, in the formation of the Boston Opera Co., of which he was general manager until its dissolution in 1914. Just before the outbreak of World War I, he had taken the entire Boston troupe to Paris, where he gave a successful spring season at the Théâtre des Champs-Élysées. He then lived mostly in London. He publ. a book of memoirs, *The Passing Show* (London, 1926).

Russell, Louis Arthur, American organist and pianist; b. Newark, N. J., Feb. 24, 1854; d. there, Sept. 5, 1925. He studied music in N. Y.; then singing with William Shakespeare and George Henschel in London. Returning to America in 1878, he was active as church organist in Newark; founded the College of Music there (1885) and organized the Newark Symph. Orch. (1893). He publ. several instructive books: *The Embellishments of Music; How to Read Modern Music; Problems of Time and Tune; Development of Artistic Pianoforte Touch;* etc.

Russolo, Luigi, Italian futurist composer; b. Portogruaro, May 1, 1885; d. Cerro, Feb. 6, 1947. In 1909 he joined the futurist movement of Marinetti; formulated the principles of the 'Art of Noises,' on which subject he publ. a book, *L'Arte dei rumori* (Milan, 1916); constructed a number of noise-making instruments ('intonarumore'), with which he gave concerts in Milan (April 21, 1914), Paris (June 18, 1921), etc. In his futurist manifesto, issued at Milan on March 11, 1913, he classified the futurist orch. into 6 groups of noises, ranging from explosions and clashes to shrieks and groans; this manifesto is reproduced in English transl. in N. Slonimsky's book, *Music Since 1900* (3rd ed., pp. 642-48).

Rust (rōōst), **Friedrich Wilhelm,** German violinist and composer; b. Wörlitz, near Dessau, July 6, 1739; d. Dessau, March 28, 1796. Student of law at Leipzig until 1762; then a pupil of the violinist Höckh at Zerbst and (1763) of Franz Benda at Berlin, under the patronage of Prince Leopold III of Anhalt-Dessau, whom he accompanied to Italy (1765-66), and who appointed him court music director in 1775. He brought out several stage pieces, wrote incidental music to plays and considerable instrumental music. David Singer and Wilhelm Rust publ. several of his violin pieces. —Cf. W. Hosäus, *F. W. Rust und das Dessauer Musikleben* (Dessau, 1882); E. Prieger, *F. W. Rust* (Cologne, 1894; with list of works); R. Czach, *F. W. Rust* (Essen, 1927). His son, **Wilhelm Karl Rust** (b. Dessau, April 29, 1787; d. there, April 18, 1855), was organist at Vienna (1819-27); then teacher in Dessau. Publ. pieces for piano and organ.

Rust, Wilhelm, German organist and editor; b. Dessau, Aug. 15, 1822; d. Leipzig, May 2, 1892. Pupil of his uncle, W. K. Rust (piano and organ); later of Fr. Schneider (1843-46). He went to Berlin in 1849, taught there, and entered the Singakademie; joined the Leipzig Bach-Verein in 1850, played in numerous concerts, became organist of St. Luke's in 1861, conductor of the Berlin Bach-Verein from 1862-74, 'Royal Music Director' in 1864, and received the title of *Dr. phil. (hon. c.)* from Marburg Univ. in 1868; in 1870, teacher of theory and composition at the Stern Cons.; in 1878, organist of the Thomaskirche at Leipzig, and teacher in the Cons. there; in 1880 he succeeded Richter as cantor of the Thomasschule. —As ed. of several vols. of the Bach edition prepared by the Bach-Gesellschaft, he displayed great erudition.

Ruthardt (roo'tahrt), **Adolf,** German editor and composer; b. Stuttgart, Feb. 9, 1849; d. Leipzig, Sept. 12, 1934. Pupil of the Stuttgart Cons.; music-teacher in Geneva 1868-85; from 1886-1914, prof. of piano at the Leipzig Cons.; retired in 1914. —Works: piano pieces and valuable studies (op. 40, *Trillerstudien;* op. 41, *Oktavenstudien;* op. 53, *Terzen-Etüden;* op. 54, *Sexten-Etüden;* etc.); and an *Elementar-Klavierschule* (op. 44); edited a selection of Cramer's Studies (1909), a collection of Old Dances (2 vols., 1913), and a 'Klavierbuch nordischer Komponisten' (2 vols., 1913); wrote *Das Klavier: ein geschichtlicher Abriss;* a *Chormeisterbüchlein* of short biographies; and prepared the 3rd-10th eds. (1925) of Eschmann's *Wegweiser durch die Klavier-Literatur;* also a *Wegweiser durch die Literatur des Männergesanges* (1892).

Ruthström, (Bror Olaf) Julius, Swedish violinist; b. Sundsvall, Dec. 30, 1877; d. Stockholm, April 2, 1944. He studied at the Stockholm Cons. (1894-99) and the Berlin Hochschule für Musik (1901-03); pupil of A. Moser, J. Joachim, and W. Burmester; toured Scandinavia and Central Europe; publ. valuable pedagogic works for the violin: *Mechanics of Passage-Playing* (1914); *The Art of Bowing* (1921); *Double-Note Studies* (1924); *Violin School* (1928).

Rutz, Ottmar, German writer on voice; b. Fürth, July 15, 1881; d. Garmisch, Sept. 8, 1952. He was the son of Josef Rutz and Klara Rutz, vocal teachers in Munich, whose ideas on various physiological aspects of singing (especially as regards the position of trunk muscles in singing different types of songs) he expounded in several important books: *Neue Entdeckungen von der menschlichen Stimme* (Munich, 1908); *Musik, Wort und Körper als Gemütsausdruck* (Leipzig, 1911); *Typenstimmbildung, zugleich die neue Ausdruckskunst für Bühne und Konzert* (with Klara Rutz; 1920); *Menschheitstypen und Kunst* (1921); *Vom Ausdruck des Menschen* (1926). —Cf. 'Zeitschrift der Internationalen Musik-Gesellschaft' XI, p. 180 ff. and p. 311 ff.

Ruygrok, Leo (Leonard Petrus), Dutch cellist, conductor, and composer; b. Utrecht, May 8, 1889; d. Hilversum, Jan. 3, 1944. He studied composition with Johan Wagenaar and cello with Ed. Ferrée; was active as cellist; then conductor at Arnhem (1915-19) and in The Hague (1919-40). He wrote 2 symphonies, 4 overtures, works for voice, etc.

Ruyneman, Daniel, Dutch composer; b. Amsterdam, Aug. 8, 1886. He studied at the Amsterdam Cons.; in 1918 was co-founder of the Society for Modern Dutch Composers. He made a special study of Javanese instruments, and introduced them in some of his works; also used for the first time a 2-octave set of cup bells (cast by J. Taylor & Co., England) in his work *Hieroglyphs,* for 3 flutes, harp, celesta, piano, 2 mandolins, 2 guitars, and percussion; other works include *Sonata in F,* for chorus a cappella without words; *3 Parthematologies,* for piano; 9 piano sonatas; numerous songs on Dutch and Chinese texts; also stage works. —Cf. A. Petronio, *Daniel Ruyneman et son œuvre* (Liège, 1922); C. Bérard, *Daniel Ruyneman,* in the 'Chesterian' (London, 1928); A. Hoérée, *Daniel Ruyneman,* in the 'Revue Musicale' (March, 1949).

Ryan, Thomas, American musician and composer; b. Ireland, 1827; d. New Bedford, Mass., March 5, 1903. He settled in the U. S. in 1844, and in 1849 was a co-founder of the 'Mendelssohn Quintette Club,' playing the viola (and upon occasion, the clarinet), with August Fries (1st violin), Francis Riha (2nd violin), Eduard Lehmann (viola and flute), and Wulf Fries (cello). With this club he traveled all over the U. S., doing missionary work in bringing good music to remote communities; he also acted as its manager; arranged classical sonatas and other works for it; after half a century, Ryan was the sole remaining original member of the organization; publ. a book of memoirs, *Recollections of an Old Musician* (N. Y., 1899).

Ryba, Jan Jakub, Czech composer; b. Přeštice, Oct. 26, 1765; d. Rožmitál, April 8, 1815. He studied academic subjects in Prague; in 1788 was appointed rector at a school in Rožmitál; remained there until his death (suicide). A very prolific composer, he left about 120 Masses, 100 motets, 30 pastorals (Christmas cantatas to Latin and Czech words); also many songs to Czech words; of these latter, 2 albums were publ. during his lifetime; other works were a symphony, several string quartets, sonatas. There is a growing realization in Czechoslovakia of Ryba's importance as an early representative of the national art song. —Cf. J. Němeček, *Jan Jakub Ryba* (Prague, 1947).

Rybner, (Peter Martin) Cornelius, pianist, conductor, and composer; b. Copenhagen, Oct. 26, 1855; d. New York, Jan. 21, 1929. His original name was Rubner, but he changed it to Rybner about 1920. He studied at the Copenhagen Cons. with Gade and J. P. Hartmann; then at the Leipzig Cons. with Ferdinand David (violin) and Reinecke (piano); finished his pianistic studies under Hans von Bülow and Anton Rubinstein. After a series of concerts in Europe as pianist, he settled in Karlsruhe; succeeded Mottl in 1892 as conductor of the Philharmonic Society there, and held this position until 1904, when he emigrated to the U. S., succeeding MacDowell as head of the music dept. at Columbia Univ. (1904-19). His works include a ballet, *Prinz Ador* (Munich, 1902); a symph. poem, *Friede, Kampf und Sieg;* a violin concerto; numerous choruses; piano pieces; songs; also some chamber music.

Rychnovsky (rih-nōhv'-skē), **Ernst,** Czech music critic; b. Janovice, June 25, 1879; d. Prague, April 25, 1934. He studied law in Prague; then music with Rietsch; became music critic of the 'Prager Tageblatt.' He publ. monographs on Spohr and Rochlitz (1904), Kittl (2 vols.; 1904, 1905), Blech (1905), Haydn (1909), Schumann (1910), Liszt (1911), Smetana (1924), etc.; compiled a bibliography on German intellectual life in Bohemia (1906-09).

Ryder, Arthur Hilton, American organist and composer; b. Plymouth, Mass., April 30, 1875; d. Newton, Mass., July 18, 1944. He studied at Harvard Univ. with Walter Spalding (theory) and J. K. Paine (composition); subsequently was church organist and choir director in Boston and neighboring towns. In 1935 he developed a system of 'Radical Harmony' which he taught at Univ. Extension Courses in Boston; also publ. songs.

Ryder, Thomas Philander, American organist and composer; b. Cohasset, Mass., June 29, 1836; d. Somerville, Mass., Dec. 2, 1887. He was for many years organist at Tremont Temple in Boston; publ. a number of piano pieces in a light vein.

Ryelandt (rī'-lahnt), **Joseph,** Belgian composer; b. Bruges, April 7, 1870. He studied composition with Tinel in Brussels; in 1924 was appointed director of the Bruges Cons.; was still living there in 1955. He wrote several oratorios: *The Coming of the Lord* (Rotterdam, 1909), *Maria* (Ghent, 1919), *Agnus Dei* (Brussels, 1921), and *Christus Rex* (Brussels, 1925); etc.; 5 symphonies; 3 string quartets; 7 violin sonatas; 11 piano sonatas; numerous organ pieces and songs.

Rytel, Piotr, Polish composer; b. Vilna, May 16, 1884; studied with Michalowski and Noskowski at the Warsaw Cons.; in 1918 appointed prof. of harmony there. In 1948 he conducted at the Warsaw Opera House. Among his major works are the operas: *Andrzej z Chelmna* (1942-43); *Ijola* (Warsaw, Dec. 14, 1929); *Koniec Mesjasza* (1935-36); *Krzyzowcy* (1940-41); the symph. poems *Grazyna, The Corsair* (after Byron), *The Legend of St. George, The Dream of Dante,* etc.

S

Saar, Louis Victor (Franz), composer and teacher; b. Rotterdam, Dec. 10, 1868; d. St. Louis, Nov. 23, 1937. He studied with Rheinberger in Munich (1886-89); spent one winter with Brahms in Vienna; lived in Leipzig and Berlin; in 1894 he settled in America; was accompanist for the Metropolitan Opera (1894-96); taught theory at the National Cons., N. Y. (1896-98); then at the N. Y. College of Music (1898-1906). From 1906 till 1917, he was head of the theory dept. at the Cincinnati College of Music; from 1917 to 1933, at the Chicago Musical College; from 1934 until his death, at the St. Louis Institute of Music. As a composer, he won the Mendelssohn Prize (Berlin, 1891), the Tonkünstlerpreis (Vienna, 1892), etc. He was a prolific composer; wrote about 150 op. numbers; for orch.: *Rococo Suite; From the Mountain Kingdom of the Great North West* (1922); *Along the Columbia River* (1924); *Old German Masters,* suite for string orch. (1930); *Gondoliera,* for violin and string orch.; etc.; choral works: *Hallowe'en Night, A Song of Consolation, Ave Maria,* etc.; a cycle, *Persian Love-Songs;* violin pieces; arrangements for men's chorus of 'Swedish Folk-Songs,' 'Cycle of Somerset Folk-Songs,' 'Old English Songs,' and an 'Album of Church Classics.'

Sabaneyev (sah-bah-nyĕh'-yehv), **Leonid Leonidovitch,** Russian writer on music; b. Moscow, Nov. 19, 1881. He studied at the Moscow Cons. with Taneyev; also took a course in mathematics at the Univ. of Moscow. In 1920 he joined the board of the newly-organized Moscow Institute of Musical Science; left Russia in 1926, and lived in Paris; eventually settled in Nice. —Publications (in Russian): *Richard Wagner and the Synthesis of Arts* (1913); *The Development of the Harmonic Idea* (1913); *Medtner* (1913); *The Relationship of Color and Sound* (1914); *Scriabin* (1916; 2nd rev. ed., 1923); *Rhythm, an Esthetic Inquiry* (1917); *The 53-Degree Gamut and the Prospects of Musical Composition* (1921); *Music of Speech* (1922); *The Hebrew National School of Music* (1924); *History of Russian Music* (1924; German ed., 1926); *General History of Music* (1924); *Modern Russian Composers* (in English; N. Y., 1927); *What is Music* (1928); *Taneyev* (Paris, 1930; in Russian); *Music for the Films* (in English; London, July, 1935); also *The Jewish National School in Music,* in the 'Mus. Quarterly' (July, 1929); *Musical Tendencies in Contemporary Russia,* in the 'Mus. Quarterly' (Oct., 1930); etc. He wrote 2 piano trios (1907; 1923), a violin sonata, and some other works.

Sabata, Victor de, outstanding Italian conductor and composer; b. Trieste, April 10, 1892. He studied with Saladino and Orefice at the Cons. of Milan (1901-11), winning the gold medal for his graduation; then became conductor of the Monte Carlo Opera; also conducted symph. concerts at La Scala, Milan, and at the Augusteo, Rome. In 1927 he made his American début as guest conductor of the Cincinnati Symph. Orch., and afterwards visited the U. S. frequently as guest conductor; also conducted opera and symph. orchs. in England. As conductor of

Verdi's operas he had few equals after Toscanini; he also excels in interpretations of Beethoven's symphonies. —Works: the opera, *Il Macigno* (La Scala, Milan, March 31, 1917; renamed *Driada* for its radio performance, 1935); the symph. poems *Juventus* (1919), *La Notte di Platon* (1924), and *Gethsemani* (1925; N. Y., Jan. 21, 1926); other works for orch.; chamber music. —Cf. R. Mucci, *Victor de Sabata* (Lanciano, 1937).

Sabatier. See **Unger, Karoline.**

Sabbatini, Galeazzo, Italian composer and theorist; b. Pesaro; d. there, 1662; was maestro di cappella in Pesaro 1626; from 1630-36 maestro to the Duke of Mirandola. His last publ. work appeared in 1639 (Venice). Author of a treatise on thorough-bass, *Regola facile e breve per sonare sopra il basso continuo* (Venice, 1628; 3rd ed., Rome, 1669). —Publ. 2 books of madrigals *a* 2-4 (1625, 1626; other eds.); 2 books of *Sacrae laudes a* 2-5 (1637, 1641); 1 with organ (1642); 3 books of *Madrigali concertati a* 2-5 (with instruments; 1627, 1630, 1636); Hymns to the Virgin Mary *a* 3-6 (1638); *Sacri laudi e motetti a voce sola* (1639).

Sabbatini, Luigi Antonio, Italian theorist; b. Albano Liziale, near Rome, 1739; d. Padua, Jan. 29, 1809. Pupil of Padre Martini at Bologna, and Vallotti at Padua, succeeding the latter as maestro at the Antonius Basilica in 1780. —Publ. *Elementi teorici della musica colla pratica de' medesimi in duetti, e terzetti a canone* (1789; part transl. into French by Choron); *La vera idea delle musicali numeriche segnature* (1799; gives an epitome of Vallotti's system); *Trattato sopra le fughe musicali* (1802; with fine examples by Vallotti); and *Notizie sopra la vita e le opere del R. P. Fr. A. Vallotti* (1780).

Sabin, Wallace Arthur, English organist; b. Culworth, Dec. 15, 1860; d. Berkeley, Calif., Dec. 8, 1937. Pupil of M. J. Monk at Banbury and T. W. Dodds at Oxford; F. R. C. O., 1890. Coming to the U. S., he settled in San Francisco, where he was organist at St. Luke's (1894-1906), at Temple Emanu-El (from 1895), and at the First Church, Scientist (from 1906). His settings of the Hebrew liturgy were publ. in Stark's 'Service Book.' He composed many partsongs for men's voices. —Cf. R. R. Rinder, *Tribute to W. A. Sabin* (San Francisco, 1938).

Sacchetti, Liberius Antonovitch, Russian writer on music and pedagogue; b. Kenzar, near Tambov, Aug. 30, 1852; d. St. Petersburg, March 11, 1916. He studied with Rimsky-Korsakov and others at the St. Petersburg Cons.; in 1878 was appointed to its faculty, as lecturer on musical esthetics; in 1895 became assistant librarian at the Imperial Public Library in St. Petersburg. He publ. an *Outline of General Music History* (St. Petersburg, 1882); *A Brief Anthology of Musical History* (St. Petersburg, 1896); manuals on esthetics for use at the St. Petersburg Cons., etc. He was highly regarded as a scholar and teacher in Russia.

Sacchi (sahk'-kē), **Don Giovenale,** Italian scholar; b. Barfio, Como, Nov. 22, 1726; d. Milan, Sept. 27, 1789. He was a member of the Barnabite monastic order, and an assiduous student of ancient music; also was distinguished as a biographer. —Publications: *Del numero e delle misure delle corde musiche e loro corrispondenze* (1761); *Della divisione del tempo nella musica, nel ballo e nella poesia* (1770); *Della natura e perfezione dell' antica musica de' Greci* (1778); *Delle quinte successive nel contrappunto e delle regole degli accompagnamenti* (1780); *Vita del Cav. Don Carlo Broschi, detto Farinelli* (1784); *Don Placido, dialogo dove cercasi se lo studio della musica al religioso convenga o disconvenga* (1786); etc.; translated Cardinal Fontana's *Vita di Benedetto Marcello* (1788).

Sacchini (săhk-kē'-nē), **Antonio (Maria Gasparo Gioacchino),** Italian opera composer; b. Florence, June 14, 1730; d. Paris, Oct. 6, 1786. He entered the Cons. of Santa Maria di Loreto at Naples as a pupil of Francesco Durante (composition), Nicola Fiorenza (violin), and Gennaro Manna (singing). His intermezzo *Fra Donato* was performed at the Cons. in 1756; he subsequently wrote music for various stage productions in Naples; then proceeded to Rome, where his opera *Semiramide* was successfully produced in 1762. This success marked the beginning of his career as an operatic composer; thereafter he produced operas every year: *Alessandro nell' Indie* (Venice, 1763), *Lucio Vero* (Naples, Nov. 4, 1764), *La Contadina in corte* (Rome, 1765), and *L'Isola d'amore* (Rome, 1766). In 1768 he succeeded Traetta as director of the Cons. dell'Ospedaletto in Venice; his oratorio *Caritas omnia vincit* was brought out there on April 16, 1769. He then went to Munich and produced there his operas *L'Eroe cinese*

(1769) and *Scipione in Cartagena* (1770). In 1772 he traveled to London with Venanzio Rauzzini, and while there presented the following operas: *Tamerlano* (1773), *Montezuma* (1775), *Erifile* (1776), *L'Amore soldato* (May 5, 1778), *Il Calandrino e l'avaro deluso* (1778), and *Enea e Lavinia* (1779). In 1781 he received an invitation from Marie Antoinette, through the 'intendant des menus-plaisirs,' to come to Paris. His name was already known in France, since his opera *Isola d'amore*, arranged as *La Colonie* ('comic opera imitated from the Italian'), had been produced in Paris on Aug. 16, 1775. He arrived in Paris in August, 1781, and was forthwith commissioned to write 3 works at a fee of 10,000 francs each. For this purpose he adapted his Italian opera *Armida e Rinaldo* (Milan, 1772) to a French text as *Renaud*, 'tragédie lyrique' in 3 acts (produced at the Académie Royale de Musique, Feb. 25, 1783) and his opera *Il Gran Cid* (Rome, 1769) as *Chimène* (Fontainebleau, Nov. 18, 1783); the 3rd opera, *Dardanus*, was a new work; it was staged at the Trianon, Versailles, Sept. 18, 1784, in the presence of Louis XVI and Marie Antoinette. In Paris Sacchini found himself in unintended rivalry with Piccinni as a representative of Italian music in the famous artistic war against the proponents of the French operas of Gluck; Sacchini's most successful opera, however, was to the French text, *Oedipe à Colonne*, first presented at Versailles (Jan. 4, 1786) and produced at the Paris Opéra (Feb. 1, 1787) after Sacchini's death. It held the stage for half a century, and there were sporadic revivals later on. His last opera, also to a French libretto, *Arvire et Evelina*, was left unfinished, and was produced posthumously (Paris Opéra, April 29, 1788; 3rd act added by J. B. Rey). Sacchini's music was a typical product of the Italian operatic art of his time. It possessed melodious grace, but was lacking in dramatic development. The undistinguished style of Sacchini's productions was probably the reason for the disappearance of his operas from the active repertory; Piccinni fared much better in comparison. —Cf. A. Jullien, *La Cour et l'opéra sous Louis XVI: Marie Antoinette et Sacchini* (Paris, 1878); J.-G. Prod'homme, *Écrits de musiciens des XVe-XVIIIe siècles* (Paris, 1912); J.-G. Prod'homme, *Un Musicien napolitain à la cour de Louis XVI*, in 'Le Ménestrel' (Dec. 11 and Dec. 18, 1925); V. Morelli, *Antonio Sacchini*, in 'Vita musicale italiana' (1926, Nos. 7-8); U. Prota-Giurleo, *Sacchini non nacque a Pozzuoli* (Naples, 1952, proving that Sacchini was born in Florence and not in the vicinity of Naples); F. Schlitzer, *Antonio Sacchini: schede e appunti per una sua storia teatrale* (Siena, 1955). See also A. Loewenberg, *Annals of Opera* (Cambridge, 1943; 2nd ed., Geneva, 1955).

Sacher, Paul, Swiss conductor; b. Basel, April 28, 1906. He studied with Karl Nef (music theory) and Weingartner (conducting). In 1926 he founded the Kammer Orchester in Basel; commissioned special works from a number of celebrated contemporary composers (among them Richard Strauss, Hindemith, Honegger, etc.) and presented them for the first time with his ensemble; in 1933, founded the Schola Cantorum Basiliensis; from 1941, was leader of the Collegium Musicum in Zürich; publ. *Alte und Neue Musik* (Zürich, 1951), annotated catalogue of the 25 years of the Basel Kammer Orchester. Sacher made his American début in N. Y. on April 3, 1955, conducting a concert of the Collegiate Chorale at Carnegie Hall.

Sachs, Curt, eminent musicologist and authority on musical instruments; b. Berlin, June 29, 1881. While attending the Gymnasium there, he studied piano and composition with L. Schrattenholz and clarinet with Rausch; entered Berlin Univ.; studied history of music with Oskar Fleischer, and also history of art; *Dr. phil.*, 1904; after some years as art critic, he turned to musicology, and studied with Kretzschmar and Joh. Wolf; specialized in the history of musical instruments; in 1919 appointed curator of the Museum of Musical Instruments in Berlin, and in 1920, prof. of the National Academy of Music there; also prof. at the Univ. of Berlin. In 1933 he was compelled to leave Germany; went to Paris as Chargé de Mission at the Musée de l'Homme; was visiting prof. at the Sorbonne. In 1937 he settled in the U. S.; was lecturer at the Graduate School of Liberal Arts of N. Y. Univ. (1937-38); consultant to the N. Y. Public Library (1937-52); adjunct prof., Columbia Univ. (from 1953); president of the American Musicological Society (1948-50). In 1956, he was made *Dr. phil.* (*honoris causa*) of West Berlin Univ.—Publications: *Musikgeschichte der Stadt Berlin bis zum Jahre 1800* (1908); *Musik und Oper am kurbrandenburgischen Hof* (1910); *Reallexikon der Musikinstrumente* (1913; very valuable); *Systematik der Musikinstrumente* (with E. von Hornbostel, in the 'Zeitschrift für Ethnologie,' 1914); *Die Musikinstrumente Indiens und Indonesiens*

(1915); *Die litauischen Musikinstrumente* ('Internationales Archiv für Ethnographie,' 1915); *Handbuch der Musikinstrumentenkunde* (1920; 2nd ed., 1930; very valuable); *Die Musikinstrumente des alten Ägyptens* (1921); *Katalog der Staatlichen Instrumentensammlung* (1922); *Das Klavier* (1923); *Die Musikinstrumente* ('Jedermanns Bücherei,' 1923); *Die modernen Musikinstrumente* (1923); *Musik des Altertums* ('Jedermanns Bücherei'; 1924); *Die Musik der Antike* (in Bücken's 'Handbuch der Musikwissenschaft'; 1928); *Geist und Werden der Musikinstrumente* (1929); *Vergleichende Musikwissenschaft in ihren Grundzügen* (1930); *Eine Weltgeschichte des Tanzes* (1933; in English as *World History of the Dance*, N. Y., 1937); *Les Instruments de musique de Madagascar* (Paris, 1938); *The History of Musical Instruments* (N. Y., 1940); *The Rise of Music in the Ancient World* (N. Y., 1943); *The Commonwealth of Art* (N. Y., 1946); *Our Musical Heritage* (N. Y., 1948; 2nd ed., 1955); *Rhythm and Tempo, a Study in Music History* (N. Y., 1953); valuable essays in various European and American periodicals; compiled and edited *The Evolution of Piano Music* (N. Y., 1944).—Cf. E. Hertzmann, *Alfred Einstein and Curt Sachs*, in the 'Mus. Quarterly' (April, 1941); K. Hahn, *Verzeichnis der wissenschaftlichen Arbeiten von Curt Sachs*, in 'Acta Musicologica' (vol. XXIX, pp. 94-106).

Sachs (zăhks), **Hans**, foremost poet of the Meistersinger; b. Nuremberg, Nov. 5, 1494; d. there, Jan. 19, 1576. He wrote over 4,000 poems ('Meisterschulgedichte'), 1,700 tales, etc., and 208 dramatic poems; also invented numerous 'Weisen' (melodies). He is the central figure in Wagner's opera, *Die Meistersinger von Nürnberg*. The original melodies of a large number of the poems are preserved in *Das Singebuch des Adam Puschmann* (ed. by G. Münzer, 1907).—Cf. Ch. Schweitzer, *Un Poète allemand au XVI*e *siècle: Étude sur la vie et les œuvres de H. Sachs* (Nancy, 1889); K. Drescher, *Studien zu H. Sachs* (Marburg, 1891); R. Genée, *H. Sachs und seine Zeit* (Leipzig, 1894; 2nd ed., 1901); B. Suphan, *H. Sachs: Humanitätszeit und Gegenwart* (Weimar, 1895); K. Drescher, *Nürnberger Meistersinger-protokolle von 1575-1689* (2 vols.; Tübingen, 1898); K. Mey, *Der Meistergesang* (1901); H. Holzschuher, *H. Sachs in seiner Bedeutung für unsere Zeit* (Berlin, 1906); E. Mummenhoff, *Musikpflege und Musikaufführungen im alten Nürnberg* (Leipzig, 1908); H. Nutzhorn, *Mestersangeren H. Sachs* (Copenhagen, 1911); F. H. Ellis, *H. Sachs Studies* (Bloomington, Ind., 1941).

Sachs, Léo, composer; b. Frankfurt, Germany, April 3, 1856; d. Paris, Nov. 13, 1930. He was active in the field of modern music in Paris; composed several symph. poems (*Retour des cloches; Sur l'eau; Lamento*); a piano quintet; 2 string quartets; a piano trio; 3 violin sonatas; a viola sonata; a cello sonata; a *Petite suite* for string quartet; 24 preludes for piano. His total output amounts to nearly 200 op. numbers. His style of composition was mildly modernistic.

Sachse, Leopold, opera stage director; b. Berlin, Jan. 5, 1880; studied at the Cons. of Cologne; then in Vienna; in 1902 joined the Strasbourg Opera as baritone; in 1907, general manager of the Stadttheater in Münster; in 1913 organized the Sachse Opera in Berlin; from 1922 to 1933 was with the Hamburg Staatsoper. In 1935 he was engaged as stage director of Wagner's operas at the Metropolitan Opera House, N. Y., retiring in 1943; in 1945, became stage director of the N. Y. City Opera; in 1951, organized the 'Opera in English' Co. at Cooper Union, N. Y. From 1936 to 1943 he taught stage technique at the Juilliard Graduate School, N. Y.

Sack, Erna, German coloratura contralto; b. Spandau-Berlin, Feb. 6, 1906. She studied in Prague and in Berlin; made her 1st operatic appearance at the Municipal Theater in Bielefeld; then with the Breslau and Dresden Operas; also at the Charlottenburg-Berlin Opera; sang at the Salzburg festivals, in Italy, and in England; made her first American appearance as concert singer in 1937-38, and revisited the U. S. in 1954. In 1953 she gave a series of concerts in Australia.

Sacrati, Francesco (Paolo), Italian composer; b. Parma, c. 1600; d. Modena, May 20, 1650. He was one of the earliest composers for the opera theaters that began to be opened in Venice after 1637; was also a pioneer of 'opera buffa' before the rise of the Neapolitan school. He wrote an opera, *La Delia*, for the opening of the Teatro Grimani dei Santi Giovanni e Paolo in Venice (Jan. 20, 1639); there followed *La finta pazza* (Teatro Novissimo, Venice; Jan. 14, 1641); this was also one of the earliest Italian operas performed in Paris (Salle du Petit Bourbon, Dec. 14, 1645); other operas by Sacrati were: *Bellerofonte* (1642), *Ve-*

nere gelosa (Padua, 1643), *Ulisse errante* (1644), *Proserpina rapita* (1644), *La Semiramide in India* (1648), *L'Isola d'Alcina* (Bologna, 1648). In 1649 he was appointed maestro di cappella at the court of Modena, but died a few months after the appointment. —Cf. Henry Prunières, *L'Opéra italien en France avant Lully* (Paris, 1913). See also A. Loewenberg, *Annals of Opera* (Cambridge, 1943; pp. 10-11).

Sadero, Geni, Italian singer; b. Trieste, May 12, 1886. She specialized in collecting and singing regional folksongs of Italy; made a début in opera at Milan (1914), but did not pursue a dramatic career. In 1919 she went to Paris, where she gave lecture-recitals on Italian popular music; in 1936, returned to Italy and devoted herself to teaching; joined the staff of the Academy of Santa Cecilia in Rome. She publ. 2 collections of Italian songs (in Milan and N. Y.); also original songs with piano accompaniment. —Cf. I. Schwerké, *Kings Jazz and David* (Paris, 1927).

Saenger, Gustav, American music editor and arranger; b. New York, May 31, 1865; d. there, Dec. 10, 1935. He studied violin with Leopold Damrosch and others; was an orchestral violinist; then conducted theater orchestras in N. Y.; in 1897 was engaged as arranger for Carl Fischer, Inc., and in 1909 became editor-in-chief of Fischer's publications; also edited the Fischer periodicals, the 'Metronome' (from 1900) and the 'Mus. Observer' (1904-29). Besides a vast number of arrangements, he publ. pieces for violin and piano *(5 Silhouettes; 3 Concert Miniatures;* etc.); also a *New School of Melody.*

Saenger, Oscar, American singing teacher; b. Brooklyn, Jan. 5, 1868; d. Washington, April 20, 1929. He sang in church as a boy; studied voice with J. Bouhy at the National Cons. in N. Y., and taught there from 1889 to 1897; made his début with the Hinrichs Grand Opera Co. in 1891; after a brief tour in Germany and Austria, returned to America, and devoted himself entirely to teaching. Among his students were many well-known singers (Marie Rappold, Paul Althouse, Mabel Garrison, etc.).

Saerchinger, César, editor and writer; b. Aachen, Germany, Oct. 23, 1884. He studied singing with his mother (a pupil of G. B. Lamperti); settled in America in 1902, and continued his musical education in N. Y. Still as a young man, he began writing biographical articles for various American encyclopedias; was managing editor and contributor to 'The Art of Music' (14 vols., 1915-17); from 1919 to 1930 was foreign correspondent of the 'N. Y. Evening Post' and the 'Musical Courier'; lived in Berlin (1920-25) and London (1925-37); then returned to N. Y. He edited 'International Who's Who in Music and Musical Gazetteer' (N. Y., 1918); publ. *Voice of Europe* (N. Y., 1937); *Artur Schnabel* (London, 1957).

Saeverud, Harald, prominent Norwegian composer; b. Bergen, April 17, 1897. He studied at the Bergen Music Academy with B. Holmsen and at the Hochschule für Musik in Berlin with F. E. Koch; conducting with Clemens Krauss. He began to compose very early, and at the age of 15 conducted in Bergen a program of his symph. pieces (Dec. 12, 1912). —Works: 7 symphonies (1919, 1923, 1926, 1937, 1941, 1943, 1944), of which the 6th, *Sinfonia Dolorosa* (Bergen, May 27, 1943), is the best known; the 7th *Psalm Symph.,* is with chorus; cello concerto (1930); oboe concerto (1938); divertimento for flute and strings (1939); numerous *Slåtter* (dances in the Norwegian folk manner) for piano (also for orch.); new music for Ibsen's *Peer Gynt* (Oslo, March 2, 1948). —Cf. S. Lind, *Harald Saeverud,* in 'Nordisk Musikkultur' (Oslo, 1952, no. 4; with a list of works).

Safonov (sah-foh'-nov), **Vassily Ilyitch,** eminent Russian pianist, conductor, and pedagogue; b. Ishtcherskaya, Caucasus, Feb. 6, 1852; d. Kislovodsk, March 13, 1918. He studied at the Cons. of St. Petersburg with Leschetizky and Brassin (piano) and Zaremba (theory); made his début as pianist with the Imperial Russian Music Society in St. Petersburg, on Nov. 22, 1880; then taught piano at the St. Petersburg Cons. (1881-85); in 1885 was appointed to the faculty of the Moscow Cons., and in 1889 became its director, resigning in 1905; also conducted the symph. concerts of the Imperial Russian Music Society in Moscow; was the first modern conductor to dispense with the baton; achieved international fame as a forceful and impassioned interpreter of Russian music; conducted in almost all the capitals of Europe; on March 5, 1904, was engaged as guest conductor of the N. Y. Philharmonic, obtaining sensational success; as a consequence, was appointed regular conductor for 3 seasons (1906-09; was succeeded by Gustav Mahler); at the same time he was also director of the National Cons. in N. Y. After his return to Russia, he was appointed permanent conductor of the Imperial Russian Music Society in St. Petersburg. He publ. *A New Formula for the Piano Teacher and Piano Student* (Boston, 1916).

Safranek-Kavić (shaf-rah'-nek-kah'-vitch), **Lujo,** Croatian composer; b. Zagreb, Oct. 12, 1882; d. there, July 18, 1940. He wrote a symph. suite for violin and orch., *Guslar* (inspired by the playing of the gusla, the Slovakian national instrument), 2 operas (*Hasanaginica* and *The Queen of Medvedgrad*), chamber music, and songs.

Sagittarius. See **Schütz.**

Saint-Foix (săn-fwăh'), **Georges (du Parc Poullain,** comte) **de,** eminent French musicologist; b. Paris, March 2, 1874; d. Aix-en-Provence, May 26, 1954. He was a pupil of d'Indy at the Schola Cantorum. His researches in the music of the 18th century brought to light some very important facts. He publ. *Un Maître inconnu de Mozart* (with T. de Wyzewa), in 'Zeitschrift der Internationalen Musik-Gesellschaft' (Nov., 1908); *Contribution à l'histoire de la symphonie française vers 1750* (with L. de La Laurencie), in 'L'Année musicale' (1911); *Chronologie de l'œuvre instrumentale de J. B. Sammartini,* in 'Sammelbände der Internationalen Musik-Gesellschaft' XV (1914); *M. Clementi; Un Quatuor d'airs dialogués de Mozart; Mozart, disciple de Bach et Haendel* (all in 'Bulletin de la Société Union Musicologique,' 1918-21); *Les Débuts de Gluck à Milan; Le dernier concèrto pour violon de Mozart* (ib. II, 1 [1922]); *Quatre quatuors inconnus de Mozart* (ib. III, 2 [1923]); *Clementi, Forerunner of Beethoven,* in the 'Mus. Quarterly' (Jan., 1931); the section *Sonate et symphonie* in Lavignac's 'Encyclopédie' (Part II, vol. 5; 1930); other articles in various journals. His most valuable book, and one of the most important on Mozart since Jahn, is *W. A. Mozart, Sa vie musicale et son œuvre de l'enfance à la pleine maturité* (1756-77) (2 vols., 1912; with T. de Wyzewa; 3rd vol. [1777-84] by Saint-Foix alone, publ. 1937; 4th vol. [1784-88], publ. 1940; 5th vol. [1788-91], publ. 1946); also publ. *Les Symphonies de Mozart* (Paris, 1932; in English, London, 1947).

Saint-George, George, notable player on the viola d'amore; b. (of English parents) Leipzig, Nov. 6, 1841; d. London, Jan. 5, 1924. He studied piano, violin, and theory in Dresden and Prague; his violin teacher, Moritz Mildner of Prague, had a fine viola d'amore, which he lent to Saint-George for practicing; he made such progress on this little-used instrument that he decided to adopt it as a specialty. About 1862 he settled in London and became a manufacturer of string instruments; gave performances on the Welsh crwth for the 'Hon. Soc. Cymmrodorion'; also played the viola d'amore in duos with his son, Henry Saint-George, who assisted him on the viola da gamba.

Saint-George, Henry, son of the preceding; b. London, Sept. 26, 1866; d. there, Jan. 30, 1917. He studied the violin with his father, with whom he subsequently gave concerts, playing works for old instruments; was editor of 'The Strad' for 4 years; publ. *The Bow: Its History, Manufacture and Use* (1895; 3rd ed., 1922); *The Place of Science in Music* (1905); *Fiddles: Their Selection, Preservation and Betterment* (1910).

Saint-Georges (san-zhohrzh'), **Joseph Boulogne** Chevalier **de,** violinist; b. Guadeloupe, Dec. 25, 1745; d. Paris, June 12, 1799. He studied with Leclair in Paris; acquired notoriety by eccentric behavior at concerts; wrote an opera, *L'Amant anonyme* (1780), 5 violin concertos, and several violin sonatas with bass.—Cf. L. de La Laurencie, *L'École française de violon,* vol. 2.

Saint-Luban (săn-lü-băn'), **Léon de,** violinist and composer; b. Turin, July 5, 1805; d. Berlin, Feb. 13, 1850. After filling various positions as a theater violinist, he pursued further studies with Spohr; was concertmaster at the Josephstadt Theater in Vienna (1827-30); then held a similar position at the Königstadt Theater in Berlin (1830-47). He composed 2 operas, *König Branors Schwert* and *Der Vetter des Doctor Faust;* 5 violin concertos; 2 string quintets, 2 piano trios, a violin sonata, and 19 string quartets. He lacked originality, but possessed a solid craft of composition.

Saint-Requier (reh-k'yā'), **Léon,** French composer, conductor, and music editor; b. Rouen, Aug. 8, 1872; studied with Vincent d'Indy, Guilmant, and Charles Bordes; taught harmony at the Schola Cantorum (1900-34) and at the École César Franck (1934-44); was active as choral conductor at various Paris churches; edited the collection 'Palestrina' (sacred songs of the 16th, 17th, and 18th centuries). He composed a Christmas motet *Il est né le divin enfant* (using some folk melodies; 1924); the oratorio, *La Mort du doux Jésus* (1932); *Messe* *de grande louange* (1946); *Le Sermon sur la montagne* (1949); *Messe de St. Jean Apôtre* (1957); other religious works.

Saint-Saëns (sän-sahns'), **(Charles-) Camille,** celebrated French composer; b. Paris, Oct. 9, 1835; d. Algiers, Dec. 16, 1921. His widowed mother sent him to his great-aunt, Charlotte Masson, who taught him to play piano. He proved exceptionally gifted, and gave a performance in a Paris salon before he was 5; at 6 he began to compose; at 7 he became a private pupil of Stamaty; so rapid was his progress that he made his pianistic début at the Salle Pleyel on May 6, 1846, playing a Mozart concerto and a movement from Beethoven's C minor concerto, with orch. After studying harmony with Pierre Maleden, he entered the Paris Cons., where his teachers were Benoist (organ) and Halévy (composition). He won the 2nd prize for organ in 1849, and the 1st prize in 1851. In 1852 he competed unsuccessfully for the Grand Prix de Rome, and failed again in a second attempt in 1864, when he was already a composer of some stature. His *Ode à Sainte Cécile* for voice and orch. was awarded the 1st prize of the Société Sainte-Cécile (1852). On Dec. 11, 1853, his 1st symph. was performed; Gounod wrote him a letter of praise, containing a prophetic phrase regarding the 'obligation de devenir un grand maître.' From 1853 to the end of 1857 Saint-Saëns was organist at the church of Saint-Merry in Paris; in 1858 he succeeded Lefébure-Wély as organist at the Madeleine. This important position he filled with distinction, and soon acquired a great reputation as virtuoso on the organ and a master of improvisation. He resigned in 1877, and devoted himself entirely to composition and conducting; also continued to appear as pianist and organist. From 1861 to 1865 he taught piano at the École Niedermeyer; among his pupils were André Messager and Gabriel Fauré. Saint-Saëns was one of the founders of the Société Nationale de Musique (1871), established for the encouragement of French composers, but withdrew in 1886 when Vincent d'Indy proposed to include works by foreign composers in its program. In 1875 he married Marie Truffot; their 2 sons died in infancy; they separated in 1881, but were never legally divorced; Madame Saint-Saëns died in Bordeaux on Jan. 30, 1950, at the age of 95. In 1891 Saint-Saëns established a museum in Dieppe (his father's birthplace), to which he gave his manuscripts and his collection of paintings and other art objects. On Oct. 27, 1907, he witnessed the unveiling of his own statue (by Marqueste) in the court foyer of the opera house in Dieppe. He received many honors: in 1868 he was made Chevalier of the Legion of Honor; in 1884, Officer; in 1900, Grand-Officer; and in 1913, 'Grand-Croix' (the highest rank); in 1881 he was elected to the Institut de France; was also a member of many foreign organizations; received an honorary Mus. D. degree at Cambridge Univ. He visited the U. S. for the 1st time in 1906; was a representative of the French government at the Panama Exposition in 1915, and conducted his choral work with orch., *Hail California* (San Francisco, June 19, 1915), written for the occasion. In 1916, at the age of 81, he made his 1st tour of South America; continued to appear in public as conductor of his own works almost to the time of his death. He took part as conductor and pianist in a festival of his works in Athens, Greece, in May, 1920. He played a program of his piano pieces at the Saint-Saëns museum in Dieppe on Aug. 6, 1921. For the winter he went to Algiers, where he died. —The position of Saint-Saëns in French music was very important. His abilities as a performer were extraordinary; he aroused the admiration of Wagner during the latter's stay in Paris (1860-61) by playing at sight the entire scores of Wagner's operas; curiously, Saint-Saëns achieved greater recognition in Germany than in France during the initial stages of his career. His most famous opera, *Samson et Dalila,* was produced in Weimar (in 1877), under the direction of Edouard Lassen, to whom the work was suggested by Liszt; it was not performed in France until nearly 13 years later, in Rouen. He played his 1st and 3rd piano concertos for the first time at the Gewandhaus in Leipzig. Solidity of contrapuntal fabric, instrumental elaboration, fullness of sonority in orchestration, and a certain harmonic saturation were the chief characteristics of his music, qualities as yet not fully exploited by French composers at the time, and the French public preferred the lighter type of music. However, Saint-Saëns overcame this initial opposition, and towards the end of his life was regarded as an embodiment of French traditionalism. The shock of the German invasion of France in World War I made him abandon his former predilection for German music, and he wrote virulent articles against German art. He was unalterably opposed to modern music, and looked askance at Debussy; he regarded later manifestations of musical modernism as outrages, and was outspoken in his opinions. That Saint-Saëns possessed a fine sense of musical characterization, and true Gallic wit, is demonstrated by his instrumental suite, *Carnival of the Animals,* which he wrote in 1886 but did not allow to be published during his lifetime. He also possessed a considerable literary talent; publ. 2 books of poetry. — Works: Operas: *La Princesse jaune* (Paris, June 12, 1872), *Le Timbre d'argent* (Paris, Feb. 23, 1877), *Samson et Dalila* (Weimar, Dec. 2, 1877; Rouen, March 3, 1890; Paris Opéra, Nov. 23, 1892; New Orleans, Jan. 4, 1893; Metropolitan Opera, N. Y., Feb. 8, 1895), *Étienne Marcel* (Lyons, Feb. 8, 1879), *Henry VIII* (Paris, March 5, 1883), *Prosperpine* (Paris, March 16, 1887), *Ascanio* (Paris, March 21, 1890), *Phryné* (Paris, May 24, 1893), *Les Barbares* (Paris, Oct. 23, 1901), *Hélène* (Monte Carlo, Feb. 18, 1904), *L'Ancêtre* (Monte Carlo, Feb. 24, 1906), *Déjanire* (Monte Carlo, March 14, 1911). Incidental music: *Antigone* (Paris, Nov. 21, 1893), *Andromaque,* by Racine (Paris, Feb. 7, 1903), *On ne badine pas avec l'amour,* by Alfred de Musset (Paris, Feb. 8, 1917); a ballet, *Javotte* (Lyons, Dec. 3, 1896). For orch.: symph. No. 1 (Paris, Dcc. 18, 1853); symph. No. 2 (Leipzig, Feb. 20, 1859); symph. No. 3 (with organ, London, May 19, 1886); *Le Rouet d'Omphale,* symph. poem (1869; Paris, Jan. 9, 1872); *Marche héroïque* (Paris, Dec. 10, 1871); *Phaéton,* symph. poem (Paris, Dec. 7, 1873); *Danse macabre,* symph. poem (one of his most successful works; Paris, Jan. 24, 1875); *La Jeunesse d'Hercule,* symph. poem (Paris, Jan. 28, 1877); *Suite algérienne* (Paris, Dec. 19, 1880); *Une Nuit à Lisbonne* (Paris, Jan. 23, 1881); *Le Carnaval des Animaux* (contains, as its 13th section, the popular *Swan;* Paris, Feb. 26, 1922); 5 piano concertos (all 1st performed by Saint-Saëns): No. 1, D major (Leipzig, Oct. 26, 1865), No. 2, G minor (Paris, May 6, 1868), No. 3, E♭ major (Leipzig, Nov. 25, 1869), No. 4, C minor (Paris, Oct. 31, 1875), No. 5, F major (Paris, June 3, 1896); 3 violin concertos: No. 1 *(Concertstück),* A major (Paris, April 4, 1867); No. 2, C major (1877); No. 3, B minor (Paris, Jan. 2, 1881); *Introduction et Rondo Capriccioso,* for violin and orch. (1863; 1st performance 50 years later, Paris, Nov. 6, 1913); 2 cello concertos: No. 1, A minor (Paris, Jan. 19, 1873; still extremely popular; No. 2, D minor (1902); *Africa,* fantasy for piano and orch. (Paris, Oct. 25, 1891). Chamber music: piano quintet (1858), 2 piano trios (1869; 1892), piano quartet (1875), septet for trumpet, strings, and piano (1881), 2 string quartets (1899; 1919), 2 violin sonatas (1885; 1896), 2 cello sonatas (1873; 1905), oboe sonata (1921), clarinet sonata (1921), bassoon sonata (1921). Choral works: *Oratorio de Noël* (1863), *Le Déluge,* oratorio (Paris, March 5, 1876), *Hail California,* for chorus and orch. (1915), *Hymne à la Paix,* for chorus and orch. (1919); numerous choruses a cappella; song cycles: *Mélodies persanes* (1870) and *La Cendre rouge* (1915); about 100 other songs; *La Fiancée du timbalier,* for voice and orch. (Paris, Feb. 19, 1888); études and various other pieces for piano; also pieces for piano, 4-hands and 2 pianos; 169 op. numbers in all. Saint-Saëns completed Guiraud's opera *Frédégonde* (Paris Opéra, Dec. 18, 1895); publ. numerous arrangements of works by Classical and Romantic composers; edited Gluck's *Armide, Orphée,* and *Écho et Narcisse* in the Pelletan edition (1875-1902), the Durand ed. of Rameau's works (from 1895), and Mozart's piano sonatas (1915). —Writings: *Notice sur H. Reber* (1881); *Matérialisme et musique* (1882); *Harmonie et mélodie* (1885; a collection of essays, chiefly on Wagner); *Notes sur les décors de théâtre dans l'antiquité romaine* (1886); *Ch. Gounod et le Don Juan de Mozart* (1894); *Problèmes et mystères* (1894); *Portraits et souvenirs* (1899); *Essai sur les Lyres et Cithares antiques* (1902); *École buissonnière* (1913); *Au Courant de la vie* (1914); *Germanophilie* (1916); *Les Idées de M. Vincent d'Indy* (1919); *Outspoken Essays on Music* (London and N. Y., 1922; transl. of several of preceding).—BIBLIOGRAPHY: C. Kit and P. Loanda, *Musique savante. Sur la musique de M. S.-S.* (Lille, 1889); Blondel, *C. S.-S. et son cinquantenaire artistique* (Paris, 1896); C. Bellaigue, *C. S.-S.* (Paris, 1899); E. Solenière, *C. S.-S.* (Paris, 1899); O. Neitzel, *C. S.-S.* (Berlin, 1899); P. Locard, *Les Maîtres contemporains de l'Orgue* (Paris, 1900); A. Hervey, *French Music in the 19th Century* (London, 1903); E. Baumann, *Les grandes formes de la musique: L'Œuvre de S.-S.* (Paris, 1905; new ed., 1923); L. Aubin, *Le Drame lyrique* (Tours, 1908); R. Rolland, *Musiciens d'aujourd'hui* (Paris, 1908; English transl., 1914); A. Jullien, *Musiciens d'hier et d'aujourd'hui* (Paris, 1910); O. Séré, *Musiciens français d'aujourd'hui* (rev. ed., 1921); J. Bonnerot, *C. S.-S.* (Paris, 1914; 2nd ed., 1922); L. Augé de Lassus, *S.-S.* (Paris, 1914); J. Montargis, *C. S.-S.* (Paris, 1919); *Funerailles de S.-S.* (collection of speeches, Paris, 1921); J. Chantavoine, *L'Œuvre dramatique de C. S.-S.* (Paris, 1921); A. Hervey, *S.-S.* (London, 1921); W. Lyle, *C. S.-S., His Life and Art* (London, 1923); G. Servières, *S.-S.* (Paris, 1923; 2nd ed., 1930); L. Laloy,

Cinquante ans de musique français, 1874-1923 (1924); A. Dandelot, *S.-S.* (Paris, 1930); J. Handschin, *C. S.-S.* (Zürich, 1930); J. Normand, *S.-S.* (1930); L. Schneider, *Une Heure avec S.-S.* (1930); J. Langlois, *C. S.-S.* (Moulins, 1934); R. Dumaine, *Les Origines normandes de C. S.-S.* (Rouen, 1937); René Fauchois, *La Vie et l'œuvre prodigieuse de C. S.-S.* (Paris, 1938); D. Brook, *Five Great French Composers* (London, 1946); J. Chantavoine, *C. S.-S.* (Paris, 1947). See also 'Le Monde musical' (Oct. 31, 1901) and 'Musica' (June, 1907), special numbers devoted entirely to S.-S., containing numerous portraits and essays by eminent writers. —Durand publ. *Catalogue général et thématique des œuvres de C. S.-S.* (1897; revised ed., 1907).

Sainton (sän-tohn'), **Prosper**, violinist; b. Toulouse, June 5, 1813; d. London, Oct. 17, 1890. He was a pupil of Habeneck at the Paris Cons., winning 1st prize for violin playing in 1834; was prof. at the Cons. of Toulouse (1840-44); went to England in 1844; appointed prof. at the Royal Academy of Music in 1845; became concertmaster of the London Philharmonic (1846-54), at Covent Garden (1847-71), and at Her Majesty's Theatre (1871-80). He married (1860) **Charlotte Helen Dolby**, a contralto (b. London, May 17, 1821; d. there, Feb. 18, 1885). Sainton wrote 2 violin concertos and several violin solos; his wife composed some songs and choruses.

Sala, Nicola, Italian composer and theorist; b. Tocco-Gaudio, near Benevento, April 7, 1713; d. Naples, Aug. 31, 1801. He was a pupil of Fago, Abos, and Leo at the Cons. della Pietà de' Turchini, Naples; apparently was not engaged as a teacher there until his old age; was appointed 2nd maestro when he was 74, in 1787, and 1st maestro 6 years later; continued to teach until 1799. It was during his tenure at the Cons. that he publ. his most celebrated theoretical work, *Regole del contrappunto prattico* (3 vols., 1794; reprinted by Choron in Paris, 1808, as *Principii di composizione delle scuole d'Italia)*. He brought out several operas: *Vologeso* (Rome, 1737), *Zenobia* (Naples, Jan. 12, 1761), *Demetrio* (Naples, Dec. 12, 1762), and *Merope* (Naples, Aug. 13, 1769); also an oratorio, *Giuditta* (1780), Masses, litanies, and other religious works.

Salabert, Francis, French music publisher; b. Paris, July 27, 1884; d. in an airplane crash at Shannon, Ireland, Dec. 28, 1946. The Editions Salabert was founded by his father, Édouard Salabert, in 1896; at the latter's death in 1903, Francis Salabert took over the management. A professional musician and composer in his own right, he made a series of practical arrangements for small orch. of numerous classical and modern works, which were widely used. Editions Salabert expanded greatly through the purchase of the stock of orchestral and other music of the firms Gaudet (1927), Mathot (1930), Senart (1941), Rouart-Lerolle (1942), and Deiss (1946). On the death of Francis Salabert, his widow assumed the directorship.

Salaman, Charles Kensington, English pianist; b. London, March 3, 1814; d. there, June 23, 1901. He studied with Charles Neate in London and with Henri Herz in Paris. Returning to London, he took active part in musical affairs; in 1853 he founded, with Lucas Blagrove and others, the 'Concerti da camera'; from 1837 to 1855 was an associate of the Philharmonic Society; in 1849 he was a founder of an amateur choral society in London; co-founder, in 1858, of the Musical Society of London; was one of the founders of the Musical Association in 1874. He wrote a comic opera, *Pickwick* (London, 1889); about 100 choral works for the synagogue; many anthems, part-songs, piano pieces; also many songs to English, Latin, Grek, and Hebrew texts.

Salas Viú, Vicente, Spanish-Chilean musicologist; b. Madrid, Jan. 29, 1911. He studied academic subjects at the Univ. of Madrid; music with Rodolfo Halffter; wrote for various literary and musical publications until 1939, when he emigrated to Chile; settled in Santiago. He published a very valuable book, *La Creación musical en Chile 1900-1951* (Santiago, 1952), in 2 sections, embracing a general account of musical activities in Chile and detailed biographies of 40 Chilean composers; also *La última luz de Mozart* (Santiago, 1949); *Momentos decisivos en la música* (Buenos Aires, 1957).

Salazar, Adolfo, eminent Spanish musicologist; b. Madrid, March 6, 1890; studied with Manuel de Falla and Pérez Casas. In 1914 he became editor-in-chief of the 'Revista Musical Hispano-Americana' (until 1918); from 1918 to 1936 was music critic of the influential Madrid daily 'El Sol'; was founder and later secretary of the Sociedad Nacional de Música (1915-22). During the final period of the Spanish Civil War he was cultural attaché at the Spanish embassy in Washington (1938-39); then settled in

Mexico City as writer and teacher. —Publications: *Música y músicos de hoy* (Madrid, 1928), *Sinfonía y ballet* (Madrid, 1929); *La Música contemporánea en España* (Madrid, 1930), *La Música actual en Europa y sus problemas* (Madrid, 1935), *El Siglo romántico* (Madrid, 1935; new ed. as *Los grandes compositores de la época romántica,* 1955); *La Música en el siglo XX* (Madrid, 1936); *Música y sociedad en el siglo XX* (Mexico, 1939), *Las grandes estructuras de la música* (Mexico, 1940), *La Rosa de los vientos en la música europea . . .* (Mexico, 1940; reissued in 1954 as *Conceptos fondamentales en la historia de la música*); *Forma y expresión en la música; ensayo sobre la formación de los géneros en la música instrumental* (Mexico, 1941), *Introducción en la música actual* (Mexico, 1941), *Los grandes periodos en la historia de la música* (Mexico, 1941), *Poesía y música en lengua vulgar y sus antecedientes en la edad media* (Mexico, 1943), *La Música en la sociedad europea* (Mexico, 1942-46; a monumental work; 4 vols.; covers the entire period of music history until modern times), *La Música moderna* (Buenos Aires, 1944; in English as *Music in Our Time,* N. Y., 1946), *Música, instrumentos y danzas en las obras de Cervantes* (Mexico, 1948), *La Danza y el ballet* (Mexico, 1949), *La Música, como proceso histórico de su invención* (Mexico, 1950), *J. S. Bach* (Mexico, 1951), *La Música de España* (Buenos Aires, 1953); several other smaller works, brochures and pamphlets on a variety of subjects. Salazar is also a composer; wrote 3 symphonic works: *Paisajes, Estampas,* and *Don Juan de los Infernos;* songs to words by Verlaine; piano pieces.

Saldoni, Baltasar, Spanish composer and lexicographer; b. Barcelona, Jan. 4, 1807; d. Madrid, Dec. 3, 1889. He was a pupil of Mateo Ferrer at Montserrat and of Carnicer in Madrid. In 1826 he produced in Madrid his light opera, *El Triunfo del amor,* and a series of Italian operas: *Saladino e Clotilde* (1833), *Ipermestra* (1838), and *Cleonice regina di Siria* (1840); also 2 Spanish operas, *Boabdil* (1845) and *Guzmán el Bueno* (1855). He achieved his best successes with the zarzuelas *El Rey y la costurera* (1853), *La Corte de Mónaco* (1857), and *Los Maridos en las máscaras* (1864). In 1840 he was appointed prof. of singing at the Madrid Cons. His *magnum opus* as a scholar was the *Diccionario biográfico-bibliográfico de efemérides de músicos españoles,* in 4 vols. (Madrid, 1868-81), to which a supplementary volume was added, in the form of a chronology of births and deaths of Spanish musicians, day by day, year by year, with exhaustive biographical notes. This monumental compilation, upon which Saldoni worked nearly 40 years, contains (inevitably) a number of errors, but in the absence of other musicographical works on Spanish musicians, it still retains considerable documentary value.

Sales, Pietro Pompeo, Italian composer; b. Brescia, 1719; d. Hanau, Germany, 1797. Little is known about his early life; when a devastating earthquake destroyed his home in Italy, he went to Germany; in 1763 was in the service of the Prince-Bishop of Augsburg as Kapellmeister; from 1768 occupied a similar position with the Elector at Coblenz, where Burney met him in 1772. After the French invasion of 1797 he fled to Hanau, where he died shortly afterwards. He also visited London. His operas had performances in Germany and Italy, as well as in London; he also composed oratorios, church music, instrumental works; a piano sonata is reprinted in Haffner's 'Raccolta musicale.' —Cf. F. Collignon, *Pietro Pompeo Sales* (Bonn, 1923).

Saleski (zah-lĕs'-kē), **Gdal,** cellist; b. Kiev, Feb. 11, 1888; sang in a synagogue choir there; then went to Leipzig, where he studied cello with Julius Klengel, graduating in 1911; while a student, he played in the cello section of the Gewandhaus orch. under Nikisch. He was in Scandinavia from 1915 till 1921; then settled in the U. S.; was a member of the NBC orch. under Toscanini (1937-48). He publ. a biographical compilation, *Famous Musicians of a Wandering Race* (N. Y., 1927; revised ed. under the title *Famous Musicians of Jewish Origin,* N. Y., 1949); both editions include Bizet, Ravel, Saint-Saëns, and others in the mistaken belief that they were Jews; there are many other factual errors, but the material on performers is serviceable; also publ. some pieces for cello.

Saléza, Albert, French tenor; b. Bruges, near Bayonne, Oct. 18, 1867; d. Paris, Nov. 26, 1916. He studied at the Paris Cons., taking the 1st prize in singing, 2nd in opera; made his début at the Opéra-Comique on Sept. 19, 1888, as Mylio in *Le Roi d'Ys* by Lalo; then sang at Nice (1892-94), at the Paris Opéra (1892-94), at Monte Carlo (1895-97), returning to the Paris Opéra in 1897; sang at the Théâtre de la Monnaie, Brussels (1898-99); also appeared at Covent

Garden, London; was engaged at the Metropolitan House, N. Y., from 1899 to 1901; returned to sing in Paris in 1901. In 1911 he became prof. of singing at the Paris Cons. —Cf. H. de Curzon, *Croquis d'artistes* (Paris, 1898).

Salieri, Antonio, Italian composer; b. Legnago, near Verona, Aug. 18, 1750; d. Vienna, May 7, 1825. He studied music with his brother, Francesco, who was a violinist, and also took lessons from the organist Simoni. His father died in 1765, and Salieri was taken to Venice by a wealthy patron; there he studied harmony with Pescetti and singing with Pacini. Gassmann, the Viennese composer, who was in Venice at the time, took Salieri to Vienna in 1766, and provided there for his education. While Gassmann was in Rome (1770), Salieri took his place as conductor at the Burg Theater in Vienna, and brought out there his 1st opera, *Le Donne letterate,* with marked success. From that time until 1774 he produced 9 more operas of his own, all in the Italian style, the last being *La Calamità dei cuori.* When Gassmann died in 1774, Salieri became his successor as court composer. He began a serious study of Gluck's style under the master's own direction; Gluck recommended Salieri to the administration of the Académie de Musique in Paris for the composition of a French opera; this was produced in Paris as *Les Danaïdes,* based on an Italian libretto, *Ipermestra,* by Calzabigi; the opera was advertised as composed by Gluck in collaboration with Salieri, but after the 12th performance Gluck declared that the work was entirely by Salieri; it remained in the repertory of the Paris Opéra for many years. Salieri then returned to Vienna, where he produced a comic opera, *La Grotta di Trofonio* (Oct. 12, 1785), with much success. His French opera, *Les Horaces,* was produced in Paris on Dec. 7, 1786, and proved a failure, but his next French opera, *Tarare* (Paris Opéra, June 8, 1787), made a sensation, and was performed on all the principal stages in Europe; Lorenzo Da Ponte made a revised Italian version of it as *Axur, Re d'Ormus,* which was produced in Vienna on Jan. 8, 1788, with enormous acclaim. In 1788 Salieri succeeded Bonno as court Kapellmeister at Vienna, retaining this post until 1824, but he did not conduct operatic performances after 1790, confining himself to the concerts of the 'Hofsängerkapelle'; was also conductor of the 'Tonkünstler-Sozietät' (founded in 1771 by Gassmann) until 1818. In Vienna he enjoyed great renown as a teacher; Beethoven studied with him, and acknowledged himself willingly as Salieri's pupil; Schubert and Liszt were also his pupils. Salieri was undoubtedly a master of the Italian method of composition, and his technique in harmony and counterpoint was of the highest. He had a reputation for selfishness and unscrupulousness; it seems certain that he intrigued against Mozart at the Vienna court, and this gave rise to the fantastic story of his poisoning of Mozart (Pushkin publ. a drama, *Mozart and Salieri,* based on this story, and Rimsky-Korsakov set it to music). In all, Salieri wrote 39 operas, of which 6 remained unproduced; 11 cantatas, 6 Masses, 4 Te Deums, a Requiem, many other pieces of church music; 2 symphonies; 2 piano concertos; various other instrumental works. —Cf. I. von Mosel, *Über das Leben und die Werke des Anton Salieri* (Vienna, 1827); A. von Hermann, *Antonio Salieri* (Vienna, 1897); H. de Curzon, *Salieri,* in 'Le Ménestrel' (1925); C. Serini, *Antonio Salieri,* in the 'Rivista Musicale Italiana' (1926); R. Nützlader, *Salieri als Kirchenmusiker,* in 'Studien zur Musikwissenschaft' (vol. 14, Vienna, 1927); G. Magnani, *Antonio Salieri* (Legnago, 1934); A. Della Corte, *Un Italiano all' estero, Antonio Salieri* (Turin, 1936); E. J. Juin, *Documenti inediti sul Salieri come maestro di F. Liszt e di altri,* in the 'Rivista Musicale Italiana' (1936); W. Bollert, *Aufsätze zur Musikgeschichte* (Bottrop, 1938, pp. 43-93); G. Barblan, *Il primo operista della Scala,* in 'La Scala: Rivista dell' Opera' (May, 1950).

Salinas, Francisco de, Spanish organist and theorist; b. Burgos, March 1, 1513; d. Salamanca, Jan. 13, 1590. He became blind at the age of 10; was taught organ playing, and studied languages at the Univ. of Salamanca. In 1538 he was taken to Italy by Cardinal Sarmiento; from 1553-58, was organist to the Duke of Alba at the vice-regal court of Naples, where Diego Ortiz (q.v.) was maestro. In 1561 Salinas returned to Spain, and from 1567 until his retirement in 1587 was prof. of music at the Univ. of Salamanca. He wrote the theoretical treatise *De musica libri septem . . .* (Salamanca, 1577), chiefly valuable for the examples of Spanish folk music it contains. It was to Salinas that Luis de León dedicated his famous 'Ode to Music.' —Cf. Otto Kinkeldey, *Orgel und Klavier in der Musik des 16. Jahrhunderts* (Leipzig, 1910); F. Pedrell, *Lírica nacionalizada* (Paris, 1913; pp. 211-63; contains musical examples); J. B. Trend, *Francisco de Salinas,* in 'Music & Letters' (Jan., 1927).

Salmhofer, Franz, Austrian composer; b. Vienna, Jan. 22, 1900. He was a chorister at the Admont Monastery in Styria until 1914; then studied composition with Schreker at the Vienna Academy, and musicology with Guido Adler at the Vienna Univ. In 1923 he married the pianist Margit Gál. In 1929 he became conductor at the Hofburg Theater, for which he composed incidental music, ballets, and operas; he resigned in 1939. In 1945, he became conductor at the Vienna State Opera. —Works: operas: *Dame in Traum* (Vienna, Dec. 26, 1935), *Iwan Sergejewitsch Tarassenko* (Vienna, March 9, 1938), *Das Werbekleid* (Vienna, June 25, 1946); ballets: *Das lockende Phantom, Der Taugenichts in Wien, Weihnachtsmärchen, Österreichische Bauernhochzeit;* 2 symphonies (1947; 1955); the overtures *Der Ackermann und der Tod* and *Heroische Ouvertüre;* trumpet concerto; cello concerto; *Der geheimnisvolle Trompeter,* symph. poem for narrator and orch., after Walt Whitman's *The Mystic Trumpeter* (1924); *Kammersuite,* for 16 instruments (Vienna, May 10, 1923); string quartet; piano quartet; viola sonata; cello sonata; songs; piano pieces.

Salmon, Alvah Glover, American composer and pianist; b. Southold, N. Y., Sept. 23, 1868; d. Boston, Sept. 17, 1917. He studied at the New England Cons. in Boston, graduating in 1888; then with Goetschius and MacDowell in N. Y.; went to Russia, where he took lessons from Glazunov and became deeply interested in Russian music; collected a valuable library of works by Russian composers (about 3000 vols.) and an extensive collection of autographs; publ. numerous essays. His compositions are chiefly for piano *(Valse arabesque, Scherzo, Novelette, Fileuse, Impromptu, Tarentelle fantastique),* etc.

Salmond, Felix, distinguished cellist; b. London, Nov. 19, 1888; d. New York, Feb. 19, 1952. He studied at the Royal College of Music with W. E. Whitehouse, and in Brussels with Édouard Jacobs; made his début in London (1909), accompanied at the piano by his mother, Mrs. Norman Salmond. He gave the world première of Elgar's cello concerto under Elgar's direction, on Oct. 27, 1919; after a European tour, he settled in America (début, N. Y., March 29, 1922); was head of the cello dept. at the Curtis Institute of Music in Philadelphia (1925-42) and taught cello at the Juilliard Graduate School of Music in N. Y. from its opening in 1924. He enjoyed the reputation of a fine chamber-music player and an excellent teacher.

Salò, Gasparo da. See **Gasparo.**

Saloman, Siegfried, composer; b. Tondern, Schleswig, Oct. 2, 1816; d. Stockholm, July 22, 1899. He studied composition with J. P. Hartmann in Copenhagen, and violin with Lipinski in Dresden. He lived in Copenhagen for many years and produced 2 operas there, *Tordenskjold I Dynekilen* (May 23, 1844) and *Diamantkorset (The Diamond Cross;* March 20, 1847); toured Russia and Holland (1847-50); married the singer Henriette Nissen, and traveled with her; in 1859, settled in Russia; one of his operas, to a German libretto, was produced in Russian as *Karpatskaya Roza* in Moscow, Jan. 7, 1868; several other operas were produced in Stockholm, where he went in 1879 after the death of his wife. Some of his violin pieces and songs have been published.

Salomon (Salomonis). See **Elias Salomon.**

Salomon, Johann Peter, German violinist, composer, and impresario; b. Bonn (baptized Feb. 2), 1745; d. London, Nov. 28, 1815. He was a member of the Electoral orch. at Bonn (1758-65); after a successful concert tour he was engaged as concertmaster and composer to Prince Henry of Prussia at Rheinsberg. When the orch. was disbanded Salomon went to Paris and then to London, where he settled in 1781; made himself known as a violinist and conductor; introduced symphonies by Haydn and Mozart in a series of concerts he gave in 1786. In 1790 he went to Italy to engage singers for the Italian Opera in London, and from there went to Vienna, where he saw Haydn and persuaded him to accept an engagement in London. At Salomon's behest Haydn wrote the works familiarly known as his 'Salomon Symphonies'; it is through his association with Haydn's 2 visits to London, in 1791 and 1794, that Salomon's name remains in the annals of music. He was a founder of the Philharmonic Society in London (1813). His own works are of merely antiquarian interest; they include the operas *Les Recruteurs* (Rheinsberg, 1771), *Le Séjour du bonheur* (Rheinsberg, 1773), *Titus* (Rheinsberg, 1774), *La Reine de Golconde* (Rheinsberg, 1776), *Windsor Castle,* or *The Fair Maid of Kent* (London, 1795); also violin sonatas. —Cf. *Memoir of Johann Peter Salomon,* in the 'Harmonicon' (London, Feb., 1830).

Salter, Mary Elizabeth Turner (Mrs. Sumner Salter), American soprano; b. Peoria, Ill., March 15, 1856; d. Orangeburg, N. Y., Sept. 12, 1938. She studied in Burlington, Iowa, and Boston; from 1874 to 1893, sang in churches in Boston and N. Y.; she married Sumner Salter in 1881, and settled with him in Williamstown, Mass. She publ. a number of song cycles, and was still composing at the age of 80 *(Christmas Song,* 1936). —Song cycles: *Love's Epitome, A Night in Naishapur, Lyrics from Sappho, From Old Japan;* about 80 songs publ. separately *(The Cry of Rachel, The Pine Tree, Für Musik, Die stille Wasserrose,* etc.); duets, some part-songs, and church music.

Salter, Sumner, American organist and arranger; b. Burlington, Iowa, June 24, 1856; d. New York, March 5, 1944. After graduating from Amherst College he studied at the New England Cons.; then taught at various schools in Boston and elsewhere; from 1905 to 1923, was director of music at Williams College; then retired. He edited 'The Pianist and Organist' (official organ of the American Guild of Organists) from 1895 to 1898; publ. church music and numerous organ arrangements of various works. In 1881 he married Mary E. Turner, the singer and composer.

Salvayre (sahl-vär'), **(Gervais-Bernard-) Gaston,** French composer; b. Toulouse, June 24, 1847; d. St. Ague, near Toulouse, May 16, 1916. He was a pupil at the Cons. of Toulouse; then entered the Paris Cons., studying organ with Benoist and composition with Ambroise Thomas. After failing to win the Prix de Rome for 5 consecutive years, he finally obtained it in 1872 with the cantata *Calypso.* He was subsequently chorusmaster at the Opéra-Populaire in 1877. —Works: operas: *Le Bravo* (Paris, April 18, 1877), *Richard III* (St. Petersburg, Dec. 21, 1883), *Egmont* (Paris, Dec. 6, 1886), *La Dame de Monsoreau* (Paris, Jan. 30, 1888), *Solange* (Paris, March 10, 1909); ballets: *Le Fandango* (Paris, Nov. 26, 1877), *La Fontaine des fées* (Paris, 1899), *L'Odalisque* (Paris, 1905); for orch.: *Le Jugement dernier* (Paris, Dec. 3, 1876, under the title *La Résurrection), Ouverture symphonique* (Paris, March 22, 1874), *Air et Variations* for string orch. (1877).

Salviucci, Giovanni, Italian composer; b. Rome, Oct. 26, 1907; d. there, Sept. 5, 1937. He studied with Respighi and Casella; developed a fine style of instrumental writing; his works were performed by Italian orchestras with increasing frequency, but his early death cut short his promising career. His overture in C♯ (1932) received a national prize. —Works: the symph. poem *La Tentazione e la preghiera* (1931); *Sinfonia italiana* (1932; Rome, Feb. 25, 1934); *Introduzione, Passacaglia e Finale* (1934); *Serenata* for 9 instruments (1937); also *Psalm of David,* for soprano and chamber orch. (Rome, 1935); *Alcesti,* after Euripides, for chorus and orch. (1937). —Cf. F. Ballo, *Giovanni Salviucci,* in 'Rassegna Musicale' (Jan., 1937).

Salzedo (originally Salzédo) (sahl-zā'-doh), **Carlos,** eminent harpist and composer; b. Arcachon, France, April 6, 1885. He studied at the Cons. of Bordeaux (1891-94), winning 1st prize in piano; then entered the Paris Cons., where his father, Gaston Salzédo, was prof. of singing; studied with Charles de Bériot (piano), gaining 1st prize in 1901, and with Hasselmans (harp), also receiving 1st prize. He began his career as a concert harpist upon graduation; traveled all over Europe (1901-05); was solo harpist of the 'Association des Premiers Prix de Paris' in Monte Carlo (1905-09); in 1909 settled in N. Y.; was 1st harpist in the orch. of the Metropolitan Opera Co. (1909-13). In 1913 he formed the 'Trio de Lutèce' (from Lutetia, ancient name for Paris), with Georges Barrère (flute) and Paul Kéfer (cello). In 1921 he was co-founder with Edgard Varèse of the International Composers' Guild in N. Y., with the aim of promoting modern music; this organization presented many important contemporary works; in the same year he founded a modern music magazine, 'Eolian Review,' later renamed 'Eolus' (discontinued in 1933). He became an American citizen in 1923; was elected president of the National Association of Harpists; held teaching positions at the Institute of Musical Art, N. Y., and the Juilliard Graduate School of Music; organized and headed the harp dept. at the Curtis Institute of Music in Philadelphia. In 1931 he established the Salzedo Harp Colony at Camden, Maine, for teaching and performing during the summer months. Salzedo introduced a number of special effects, and publ. special studies for his new techniques; designed a 'Salzedo Model' harp, capable of rendering novel sonorities (Eolian Flux, Eolian chords, gushing chords, percussion, etc.). His own compositions are rhythmically intricate and contrapuntally elaborate, and require a virtuoso technique. —Works: *Terres enchan-*

tées, for orch. with harp solo (performed under the title *The Enchanted Isle* by Salzedo with the Chicago Symph. Orch., Nov. 28, 1919); *5 Poetical Studies* for harp solo (1918); *3 Poems* for soprano, 6 harps, and 3 wind instruments (1919); *Bolmimerie* for 7 harps (1919); *4 Preludes to the Afternoon of a Telephone,* for 2 harps (1921); *Sonata* for harp and piano (1922); *3 Poems by Mallarmé,* for soprano, harp, and piano (1924); concerto for harp and 7 wind instruments (N. Y., April 17, 1927; composer soloist); *Pentacle,* 5 pieces for 2 harps (1928); *Préambule et Jeux,* for harp, 4 wind instruments, and 5 string instruments (Paris, 1929); *Scintillation* for harp solo (1936); *Panorama,* suite for harp solo (1937); *10 Wedding Presents,* for harp solo (1946-52); etc.; many transcriptions for harp of various works by Bach, Corelli, Rameau, Haydn, Brahms, etc. He publ. *Modern Study of the Harp* (N. Y., 1921), *Method for the Harp* (N. Y., 1929); *The Art of Modulating* (in collaboration with Lucile Lawrence; N. Y., 1950).

Salzer, Felix, theorist and musicologist; b. Vienna, June 13, 1904; studied there with Schenker and Weisse (theory and composition), Malvine Bree (piano), and Guido Adler (musicology); Ph. D., Univ. of Vienna; taught at the Vienna Cons. (1935-38); then came to America and (1940-56) was on the faculty of the Mannes College of Music in New York (from 1948, director); 1956-58, at Queens College there. —Publ. *Sinn und Wesen der abendländischen Mehrstimmigkeit* (Vienna, 1935); *Structural Hearing* (2 vols.; N. Y., 1952; in German, 1958); contributed various articles to the musical press; was co-editor of the monthly 'Der Dreiklang' (Vienna, 1937).

Samara, Spiro, Greek composer; b. Corfu, Nov. 29, 1861; d. Athens, March 25, 1917. He was a pupil of Enrico Stancampiano in Athens; later of Léo Delibes at the Paris Cons. He won considerable success with his 1st opera, *Flora Mirabilis* (Milan, May 16, 1886), and devoted himself almost exclusively to dramatic composition. Other operas were *Medgè* (Rome, 1888), *Lionella* (Milan, 1891), *La Martire* (Naples, May 23, 1894), *La Furia domata* (Milan, 1895); *Storia d'amore* (Milan, 1903; in Gotha, 1906, as *La Biondinetta), Mademoiselle de Belle-Isle* (Genoa, Nov. 9, 1905), *Rhea* (Florence, April 11, 1908), *La Guerra in tempo di guerra* (Athens, 1914). He publ. *Scènes orientales,* suite for piano (4 hands); many pieces for piano solo; songs.

Samaroff, Olga (*née* Hickenlooper), American pianist and educator; b. San Antonio, Texas, Aug. 8, 1882; d. New York, May 17, 1948. She studied as a child with her mother and grandmother (Mrs. L. Grünewald, a former concert pianist); subsequently studied in Paris (with Delaborde), Baltimore (with Ernest Hutcheson), and Berlin (with Ernst Jedliczka). She made her concert début in N. Y. (Jan. 18, 1905) with the N. Y. Symph. Society; appeared with other orchestras in the U. S. and Europe; gave joint recitals with Fritz Kreisler, Zimbalist, and other violinists. In 1911 she married Leopold Stokowski; divorced in 1923; for 2 seasons was music critic for the 'N. Y. Evening Post' (1927-29); taught at the Juilliard Graduate School and at the Philadelphia Cons. of Music; from 1930, gave master courses in N. Y.; lectured extensively on music appreciation; publ. *The Layman's Music Book* (N. Y., 1935); *The Magic World of Music* (N. Y., 1936); *A Music Manual* (N. Y., 1937); *An American Musician's Story* (autobiography; N. Y., 1939); *The Listener's Music Book* (N. Y., 1947; enlarged and revised ed. of *The Layman's Music Book;* 12 printings).

Samazeuilh (sah-mah-zö'y), **Gustave,** French composer; b. Bordeaux, June 2, 1877. He studied music with Chausson and at the Schola Cantorum with Vincent d'Indy; also took some lessons from Paul Dukas. In his music he absorbed the distinct style of French Impressionism, but despite its fine craftsmanship, performances were few and far between. He is much better known as a writer on musical subjects; publ. *Un Musicien français: Paul Dukas* (Paris, 1913; augmented ed., 1936); *Musiciens de mon temps: chroniques et souvenirs* (Paris, 1947). —Works: for orch.: *Étude symphonique* (1907), *Nuit* (Paris, March 15, 1925), *Naïades au soir* (Paris, Oct. 18, 1925); *L'Appel de la danse* (1946); for orch. with chorus: *Le Sommeil de Canope* (1908), *Chant d'Espagne* (Paris, Jan. 10, 1926), *Le Cercle des heures* (Paris, Feb. 17, 1934); string quartet (1911); *Suite en trio,* for strings (1938); etc.; many transcriptions for piano of orchestral works by d'Indy, Debussy, Franck, Dukas, Fauré, etc.

Saminsky, Lazare, composer, conductor, and writer on music; b. Odessa, Nov. 8, 1882. He studied mathematics and philosophy at the Univ. of St. Petersburg; composition with Rimsky-Korsakov and Liadov, conducting with Nicolas Tcherepnin at the St. Petersburg Cons. (graduated, 1910). He was in the military service at Tiflis in 1911; conducted the symph. concerts there (1915-18); taught at the People's Cons. in Tiflis (1917-18); left Russia in 1919; traveled in Palestine; then was in Paris and London; emigrated to the U. S. in 1920, settling in N. Y.; in 1923 was a co-founder of the League of Composers; in 1924 appointed music director of Temple Emanu-El, N. Y.; established annual Three-Choir Festival there in 1936, presenting old and new music; conducted many American works; also was guest conductor with major European orchestras; lectured and conducted in the U. S., Canada, South America, and Europe. A versatile scholar and musician, he wrote essays on mathematics and philosophy, as well as on music. In his compositions he follows the Romantic tradition; Hebrew subjects and styles play an important part in some of his music. He was married to an American writer, Lillian Morgan Buck, who died in 1945. On Feb. 15, 1948, he married the American pianist Jennifer Gandar. —Works: operas: *The Vision of Ariel* (1916), *Gagliarda of a Merry Plague,* chamber opera (N. Y., Feb. 22, 1925), *The Daughter of Jephta* (1929), *Julian, the Apostate Caesar* (1933-38); 5 symphonies: No. 1, *Of the Great Rivers,* in 'E-Frimoll' (free minor mode; Petrograd, Feb. 25, 1917, composer conducting), No. 2, *Symphonie des Sommets* (1918; Amsterdam, Nov. 16, 1922), No. 3, *Symphony of the Seas* (Paris, June, 1925, composer conducting), No. 4 (Berlin, April 19, 1929, composer conducting), No. 5, *Jerusalem, City of Solomon and Christ,* with chorus (1929-30; performed many years later, N. Y., April 29, 1958); *Vigiliae,* a symph. triptych (Moscow, Feb. 20, 1913, composer conducting); *Lament of Rachel,* suite from a ballet (Boston, March 3, 1922); *Litanies of Women,* for voice and chamber orch. (Paris, May 21, 1926); *Venice,* a 'poem-serenade' for chamber orch. (Berlin, May 9, 1928); *Ausonia,* orch. suite (1930; Florence, Feb. 24, 1935); *Three Shadows,* poems for orch. (N. Y., Feb. 6, 1936); *Pueblo, a Moon Epic* (Washington, Feb. 17, 1937); *Stilled Pageant,* for orch. (Zürich, Aug., 1938); *Eon Hours,* suite of 4 rondos for 4 voices and 4 instruments (N. Y., Nov. 28, 1939); *Requiem,* in memory of Lillian M. Saminsky (N. Y., May 20, 1946); *A Sonnet of Petrarch,* for 3 voices and 3 instruments (1947); *To a New World,* for orch. (1932; N. Y., April 16, 1951); *East and West,* suite for violin and orch. (1943); *To Zion,* a choral fanfare (1948); *4 Sacred Choruses* (1913); *10 Hebrew Folksongs and Folk Dances; 3 Hebrew Song Cycles; 6 Songs of the Russian Orient; Sabbath Morning Service; Holiday Service; By the Rivers of Babylon,* for chorus; a group of piano pieces; etc. —Books: *Music of Our Day* (N. Y., 1932); *Music of the Ghetto and the Bible* (N. Y., 1934); *Living Music of the Americas* (N. Y., 1949); *Essentials of Conducting* (N. Y., 1958); *Physics and Metaphysics of Music and Essays on the Philosophy of Mathematics* (The Hague, 1957). —Cf. *Lazare Saminsky, Composer and Civic Worker,* a collection of essays by Domenico de Paoli, Leigh Henry, L. Sabaneyev, Joseph Yasser, and Léon Vallas (N. Y., 1930).

Sammarco, (Giuseppe) Mario, Italian baritone; b. Palermo, Dec. 13, 1873; d. Milan, Jan. 24, 1930. He studied singing with Antonio Cantelli, making a successful début at Milan (1894); then sang in Brescia, Madrid, Lisbon, Brussels, Moscow, Warsaw, Berlin, and Vienna. After his triumphant début as Scarpia in *Tosca* at Covent Garden, London (Oct. 19, 1905) he sang there every season until the outbreak of World War I. He made his American début as Tonio (Feb. 1, 1908) at the Manhattan Opera House, N. Y.; in 1910 joined the Chicago Opera Co.; also sang several seasons at the Teatro Colón in Buenos Aires (from 1897). He sang in Russian, Spanish, Italian, French, and English.

Sammartini (or **San Martini**), **Giovanni Battista,** significant Italian composer; b. Milan, 1701; d. there, Jan. 15, 1775. Younger brother of Giuseppe (see below). He was organist of several churches in Milan, and from 1730-70 maestro di cappella at the convent of Santa Maria Maddalena. Gluck was his pupil from 1737-41. An extremely prolific composer (said to have written over 2,000 works), and a precursor of Haydn in the development of the symph. style; produced his first symph. in 1734. He was also a pioneer in the cultivation of chamber music. His publ. instrumental works include 24 symphonies; 6 trio sonatas for 2 violins with bass (London, 1744); Nocturnes for the same (op. 7); sonatas for flute, 2 violins, and bass (op. 9); *concerti grossi;* flute duets; sonatas for cembalo, etc. Also composed 2 operas, an oratorio, and church music. Modern eds. of various works have been publ. by Prunières (concerto), G. Salomon (2 trio sonatas), Riemann (Trio in E♭), A. Moffat (2 sonatas for violin and piano), etc. —Cf. F. Torrefranca, in 'Rivista Musicale Italiana' (1913, 1915); G. de Saint-Foix, in 'Sammelbände der Internationalen Musik-Gesellschaft' XV (1914); R. Sondheimer, *G. B. Sammartini,* in 'Zeitschrift für Musikwissenschaft' III (1920); H. G. Mishkin, *Five Autograph String Quartets by G. B. Sammartini,* in 'Journal of the American Musicological Society' (Summer, 1953).

Sammartini (San Martini), **Giuseppe,** called 'il Londinese' to distinguish him from his brother, 'il Milanese'; b. Milan, c. 1693; d. London, c. 1770. In 1727 he went to London, where he became oboist at the Opera; later director of the chamber concerts in the household of the Prince of Wales. He gave concerts with Arrigoni at Hickford's Rooms in 1732; was an oboe virtuoso. Burney heard him play in 1744, and according to Hawkins he was still living in 1770. —He publ. sonatas for 2 flutes (1738), 12 *concerti grossi,* 12 violin sonatas, 8 overtures, harpsichord concertos, solos for flute, etc. A sonata *a* 3 was ed. by Riemann in his 'Collegium musicum.'

Sammons, Albert Edward, English violinist and composer; b. London, Feb. 23, 1886; d. there, Aug. 24, 1957. He studied with his father and other teachers in London; was 1st violinist of the London String Quartet (1907-16); also concertmaster of the London Philharmonic; edited the violin concerto by Delius; composed a *Phantasy Quartet* for strings and other works; taught violin at the Royal College of Music.

Sampson, George, English organist and conductor; b. Clifton, July 24, 1861; d. Brisbane, Australia, Dec. 23, 1949. He studied with George Riseley and Harford Lloyd; was organist at various churches in Bristol; in 1898, went to Australia, where he was organist at St. John's Cathedral in Brisbane; in 1907 he organized and conducted the Sampson Orch. there, which later became the Queensland State and Municipal Orch. His works include a *Berceuse* for organ and strings, church music, and a *Romance* for violin and piano. Author of *The Pianoforte; Rhythm; Elements of Music; Queensland Manual of Music; A Day with Felix Mendelssohn* (1910); *Seven Essays* (Cambridge, 1947).

Samuel (sah-mü-ehl'), **Adolphe,** Belgian composer; b. Liège, July 11, 1824; d. Ghent, Sept. 11, 1898. He was educated at the Cons. of Liège and that of Brussels, winning the Belgian Grand Prix de Rome (1845); taught harmony at the Brussels Cons. (1860-70); in 1871 was appointed director of the Ghent Cons. He founded the Brussels Popular Concerts in 1865; in 1869 organized the 1st annual musical festivals, with an orch. of 450 and a chorus of 1200. —Works: 5 operas: *Il a rêvé* (1845), *Giovanni da Procida* (1848), *Madeleine* (1849), *Les deux prétendants* (1851), *L'Heure de la retraite* (1852); 7 symphonies; overtures; string quartets; piano pieces; publ. *Cours d'harmonie pratique et de basse chiffrée; Livre de lecture musicale* (400 national airs). —Cf. E. L. V. Mathieu, *Notice sur Adolphe Samuel* (1922).

Samuel, Harold, famous English pianist; b. London, May 23, 1879; d. there, Jan. 15, 1937. He studied at the Royal College of Music with Dannreuther (piano) and Stanford (composition); later was on its faculty. He was particularly distinguished as an interpreter of Bach; in 1921 gave 6 successive Bach recitals in London and a similar cycle in New York; toured the U. S. regularly from 1924. He wrote a musical comedy, *Hon'ble Phil,* and some piano pieces.

Samuel-Rousseau, Marcel. See **Rousseau, Marcel Samuel.**

Sanborn, (John) Pitts, American music critic; b. Port Huron, Mich., Oct. 19, 1879; d. New York, March 7, 1941. He studied at Harvard Univ. (B. A., 1900; M. A., 1902); was music editor of the 'N. Y. Globe' (1905-23), 'N. Y. Evening Mail' (1924-31), and 'N. Y. World Telegram' (from 1931). He publ. *Prima Donna—A Novel of the Opera* (London, 1929); *The Metropolitan Book of the Opera* (with Emil Hilb; N. Y., 1937); a pamphlet, *Beethoven and His Nine Symphonies* (1939); etc.

Sanchez de Fuentes, Eduardo, important Cuban composer and educator; b. Havana, April 3, 1874; d. there, Sept. 7, 1944. He studied music with Ignacio Cervantes and Carlos Anckermann. He occupied an influential position in the artistic affairs of Cuba; wrote 6 operas and many other works, but is known outside Cuba chiefly by his popular song, *Tú,* which he publ. at the age of 18. —Operas (all produced in Havana): *El Náufrago,* after Tennyson's *Enoch Arden* (Jan. 31, 1901), *Dolorosa* (April 23, 1910), *Doreya* (Feb. 7, 1918), *Kabelia,* to his own libretto after a Hindu legend (June 22, 1942); *Bocetos cubanos,* for orch., women's chorus, and soprano solo (Barcelona, 1922); *Temas del patio,* symph. prelude; songs (*Mírame así,* etc.); piano pieces; publ. *El Folk-lore en la música* *cubana* (1923), *Folklorismo* (1928), *Viejos ritmos cubanos* (1937), etc. —Cf. O. Martínez, *Eduardo Sánchez du Fuentes: in Memoriam* (Havana, 1944); M. Guiral, *Un grand musicógrafo y compositor cubano: Eduardo Sánchez de Fuentes* (Havana, 1944); A. Carpentier, *La Música en Cuba* (Mexico, 1946; pp. 213-17).

Sancta Maria. See **Santa María, Tomás de.**

Sandberg, Mordecai, composer; b. Rumania, March, 1897. He studied in Vienna; went to Jerusalem in 1922, remaining there until 1938; in 1939, he was in London; in 1940, settled in New York. A musician of extraordinary ambition, he set to music the complete Book of Psalms, as part of a grandiose project of writing a musical score for the entire Bible. In several of his works he employs fractional tones in order to secure greater expressiveness; apart from 2 symphonies, chamber music, piano pieces, etc., he wrote 2 oratorios, *Ruth* (N. Y., May 22, 1949) and *Ezkerah (I Remember;* N. Y., April 22, 1952).

Sandberger, Adolf, eminent German musicologist; b. Würzburg, Dec. 19, 1864; d. Munich, Jan. 14, 1943. He studied composition at the Royal School of Music there, and at Munich; also musicology at the Universities of Würzburg and Berlin (under Spitta); *Dr. phil.,* 1887; spent the next 2 years in further study in Austria, Italy, France, England, and Russia. In 1889 provisional, 1892 regular, custodian of the music department of the Munich Library, also lecturer at the Univ. from 1894; made associate prof. in 1900, and regular prof. in 1909; prof. emeritus in 1930. Editor of 'Denkmäler der Tonkunst in Bayern' and of Breitkopf & Härtel's monumental edition of the complete works of Roland de Lassus; from 1924 ed. of the 'Neues Beethoven-Jahrbuch'; 1927, brought out a facsimile ed. of Monteverdi's *Orfeo.* Sandberger was a specialist in Haydn; discovered in the Esterházy archives some theretofore unknown works by Haydn (string trios, etc.); brought out a new edition of the 1828 Haydn biography by Fröhlich (1926). —Writings: *Leben und Werke des Dichtermusikers Peter Cornelius* (1887; dissertation); *Beiträge zur Geschichte der bayerischen Hofkapelle unter Orlando di Lasso* (planned in 3 vols.: I. Life, 1894; III, Documents, 1895; II, not publ.); *Zur Geschichte des Haydnschen Streichquartetts* (1899); *Über zwei ehedem Mozart zugeschriebene Messen* (1907); *Lasso und die geistigen Strömungen seiner Zeit* (Munich Akademie der Wissenschaft, 1924-26); *Neue Haydniana,* in 'Jahrbuch Peters' (1933); other valuable essays. His collected essays were publ. in 3 vols.: I, Biography of Lassus, On old Italian keyboard music, etc. (1921); II, On Beethoven (1924); III, On the history of opera (1934). —In 1918 a 'Sandberger Festschrift' appeared, contributed to by his pupils, and ed. by Th. Kroyer; in 1929 a second Festschrift was publ., containing many valuable articles. —Cf. L. Schiedermair, *A. S.,* in 'Zeitschrift für Musikwissenschaft' (Jan., 1935); E. I. Luin, *In memoria di A. S.,* in 'Rivista Musicale Italiana' (1943, pp. 418-23).

Sandby, Herman, Danish cellist and composer; b. Sandby, near Holbaek, March 21, 1881. He studied cello with Hugo Becker and composition with Iwan Knorr in Frankfurt (1895-1900); gave concerts in Scandinavia, England, and Germany; in 1912 settled in America as 1st cellist of the Philadelphia Orch.; moved to N. Y. in 1916; returned to Denmark in 1930. —Works: cello concerto (Philadelphia, Feb. 5, 1916); *The Woman and the Fiddler,* symph. suite; 3 symphonies (1930, 1938, 1942); *Serenade,* for strings (1940); 3 string quartets; string sextet; string quintet; piano quintet; piano trio; etc.

Sander, Constantin. See **Leuckart.**

Sanders, Paul F., Dutch composer; b. Amsterdam, Dec. 21, 1891. He studied with Sem Dresden and Willem Pijper; contributed to various Dutch publications; was co-founder (with Pijper) of the magazine 'De Muziek'; in 1947 was N. Y. correspondent of Dutch newspapers. —Works: *Pierrot aan de lantaarn,* ballet for recitation and chamber orch. (1923); *Rataplan,* ballet for chamber orch. (1925); *Mara,* for chorus and orch.; string quartet; sonata for solo violin (1933); *Little Suite,* for piano 4 hands; songs; etc. He publ. *De Piano* (Amsterdam, 1926); *Moderne Nederlandsche Componisten* (The Hague, 1933).

Sanders, Robert L., American composer; b. Chicago, July 2, 1906; attended the Bush Cons. there (Mus. B., 1924; Mus. M., 1925); in 1925 received a fellowship of the American Academy in Rome; there he studied with Respighi; also in Paris with Guy de Lioncourt. Returning to America in 1929, he taught at the Chicago Cons. and conducted its orch.; also taught at Univ. of Chicago and Meadville Theological School; was for many years organist-director, First

Unitarian Church; in 1938, became dean of the School of Music at Indiana Univ.; in 1947, appointed prof. at Brooklyn College; held a Guggenheim Fellowship in 1954-55. —Works: *L'Ag'ya,* choreographic drama (Hollywood Bowl, summer 1944; danced by Katherine Dunham); *Scenes of Poverty and Toil,* a choreographic suite for orch. (1934-35; first performed under the title *The Tragic Muse,* Chicago, Jan. 30, 1936, composer conducting); *Suite* for orch. (Rome, May 31, 1929, composer conducting); *Little Symphony* No. 1 (N. Y., Feb. 26, 1939); *Little Symphony* No. 2 (Louisville, 1954); Symphony in A (1954-55); violin concerto (1936; Rochester, N. Y., April 28, 1945); a symph. for band (1943); *An American Psalm,* for women's voices and organ (1945); *The Mystic Trumpeter* for baritone solo, chorus, and orch. (1947); *A Celebration of Life,* cantata for soprano solo, chorus, and chamber orch. (1956); 23rd Psalm, for soprano and organ; *Recessional* for mixed voices and organ; numerous other choral works; chamber music: piano trio (1925), violin sonata (1927-28), string quartet (1929); cello sonata (1931), *The Imp* for clarinet quartet (or for clarinet and piano; 1941), quintet for brass instruments (1942), Rhapsody for woodwind quartet (1943), sonata for trombone and piano (1945), suite for brass quartet (1949), Scherzo and Dirge for 4 trombones (1949), *Fugue on a Noël* for woodwind quartet (1949); Variations on an Original Theme, for pipe organ pedals only (1956); etc.

Sanderson, Sibyl, American soprano; b. Sacramento, Calif., Dec. 7, 1865; d. Paris, May 15, 1903. She was educated in San Francisco, where her musical talent attracted attention; taken to Paris by her mother at the age of 19, she studied at the Cons. with Massenet; also with Sbriglia and Mathilde Marchesi. Massenet was charmed with her voice, and wrote the leading part in *Esclarmonde* for her; she created it at the Opéra-Comique, on May 14, 1889; the role of Thaïs (Paris Opéra, March 16, 1894) was also written by Massenet for her. Other French composers were equally enchanted with her voice, her appearance, and her passionate lyricism; Saint-Saëns wrote *Phryné* for her (1893). She made her American début at the Metropolitan Opera, N. Y., as Manon (Jan. 16, 1895); sang there again in 1901, but had little success with the American public. In 1897 she married a wealthy Cuban, Antonio Terry, who died in 1900. —Cf. J. Massenet, *Mes Souvenirs* (Paris, 1912).

Sandi, Luis, Mexican composer; b. Mexico City, Feb. 22, 1905. He studied violin; later specialized in choral music; was active in the administration of musical affairs; in 1938 founded the Coro de Madrigalistas; compiled collections of choral pieces for schools. —Works: symph. suite *Norte* (Mexico City, Aug. 15, 1941); 1-act opera *Carlota* (Mexico City, Oct. 23, 1948); ballet *Bonampak* (Mexico City, Nov. 2, 1951); film music. —Cf. C. Chávez, *Luis Sandi,* in 'Nuestra Música' (July, 1949).

Sándor, Arpád, pianist; b. Budapest, June 5, 1896; studied there with Bartók and Kodály at the Royal Academy, graduating in 1914; after several years in Berlin, he toured the U. S. as accompanist in 1922; then returned to Germany, and wrote art criticism in the 'Berliner Tageblatt.' In 1933 he settled permanently in the U. S.; was accompanist to Jascha Heifetz, Lily Pons, and other celebrated artists. He became an American citizen in 1943.

Sándor, György, pianist; b. Budapest, Sept. 21, 1912. He studied at the Royal Academy of Music there, with Bartók (piano) and Kodály (composition). After a series of concerts in Europe (1930-38), he settled in the U. S. in 1939; was soloist in the première of Bartók's posthumous piano concerto No. 3, with the Philadelphia Orch. (Feb. 8, 1946); traveled in Australia in 1951. He made brilliant transcriptions of several modern orchestral works, including *L'Apprenti sorcier* by Paul Dukas.

Sandoval, Miguel, pianist, conductor, and composer; b. Guatemala City, Nov. 22, 1903; d. New York, Aug. 24, 1953. He settled in the U. S. in 1919, and became an American citizen in 1925; was active as conductor and pianist; wrote a symph. poem, *Recuerdos en un paseo,* and publ. numerous piano works and songs in the Latin American vein.

Sandt, Maximilian van de, Dutch pianist and composer; b. Rotterdam, Oct. 18, 1863; d. Cologne, July 14, 1934. He was a pupil of Liszt in the last years of the master's life; toured in Europe with conspicuous success; taught at the Stern Cons. in Berlin (1889-94) and at the Cons. of Cologne (1896-1906); from 1910 taught at Bonn. He composed many brilliant piano pieces (*Concert-étude, 4 kleine Tonbilder, Auf dem See,* etc.); also wrote cadenzas to Beethoven's piano concertos.

Sandvik, Ole Mörk, Norwegian musicologist; b. Hedemarken, May 9, 1875. He studied theology, and in 1916 was appointed teacher of liturgy and church music at the Theological Seminary of the Univ. of Oslo, retiring in 1945. —Writings: *Norsk Kirkemusik* (1918), *Folkemusikk i Gudbrandsdalen* (1919; 2nd ed., 1948), *Norsk Folkemusikk* (1921), *Norges Musikkhistorie* (1921, with G. Schjelderup); *Norsk Koralhistorie* (1930); *Østerdalsmusikken* (1943); *Gregoriansk sang . . .* (1945); a centennial biography of Agathe Backer-Gröndahl (1948); a monograph on L. M. Lindeman (1950); compiled the Gradual for the Norwegian Church; publ. albums of regional folksongs, etc. A symposium of articles in his honor was publ. on the occasion of his 70th birthday (Oslo, 1945).

Sanford, Harold Bryant, American conductor and arranger; b. Florence, Mass., Sept. 5, 1879; d. Springfield, Mass., Jan. 19, 1945. He studied violin with Emil Mollenhauer in Boston, and theory with Goetschius; was employed as a violinist, conductor, and arranger by Victor Herbert in N. Y. City (1906-24); conducted recordings for various phonograph companies; also on the radio.

Sanford, Samuel Simons, American pianist; b. Bridgeport, Conn., 1849; d. New York, June 6, 1910. He studied with William Mason; went to Europe in 1868, where he took lessons with Anton Rubinstein, who had a high opinion of Sanford's abilities. However, Sanford did not undertake a pianistic career; in 1894 he became prof. of applied music at Yale Univ., developing the music dept. in collaboration with Horatio Parker.

Sangiovanni (sahn-joh-vahn'-nē), **Antonio,** celebrated Italian singing teacher; b. Bergamo, Sept. 14, 1831; d. Milan, Jan. 6, 1892. He studied at the Cons. of Milan; in 1854, was appointed prof. of singing there, and acquired considerable fame as a builder of voices. Two generations of Italian and foreign singers were his pupils.

Sanjuán (sahn-hwahn'), **Pedro,** Spanish composer and conductor; b. San Sebastian, Nov. 15, 1886. He studied composition with Turina; after conducting in Europe, he went to Havana, where he organized the Havana Philharmonic (1926); was also teacher of composition there; Roldán, Caturla, and other Cuban composers were his pupils; in 1932 he went back to Spain; was in Madrid (1932-36); from 1939 until 1942, he was again conductor of the Havana Philharmonic; in 1942 was appointed prof. of composition at Converse College, Spartanburg, S. C.; American citizen, 1947. —Works: *Rondo fantástico* (Havana, Nov. 29, 1926); *Castilla,* suite for orch. (Havana, June 12, 1927); *Sones de Castilla,* for small orch.; *La Macumba,* a 'ritual symphony' (St. Louis, Dec. 14, 1951, composer conducting); *Antillean Poem* for band (N. Y., Aug. 11, 1958, composer conducting); choral works; piano pieces.

San Martini. See **Sammartini.**

Sanromá, Jesús María, brilliant pianist; b. Carolina, Puerto Rico (of Catalonian parents), Nov. 7, 1903. At the age of 14 he was sent to the U. S. by the governor of Puerto Rico; studied piano with Antoinette Szumowska at the New England Cons.; 1920, won the Mason & Hamlin piano prize; then went to Europe, where he studied with Alfred Cortot (in Paris) and Artur Schnabel (in Berlin); from 1926 till 1944 he was pianist of the Boston Symph. Orch.; taught at the New England Cons.; gave annual concerts in the U. S., Canada, and South America; also played in Europe. In 1951 he was appointed chairman of the music dept. at the Univ. of Puerto Rico. He excels particularly in the works of modern composers, and has given several world premières of contemporary concertos (by Hindemith, etc.). —Cf. E. S. Belaval, *El Niño Sanromá* (San Juan, Puerto Rico, 1952).

San Sebastián, Padre **José Antonio de.** See **Donostia.**

Santa Cruz Wilson, Domingo, foremost Chilean composer; b. La Cruz, near Quillota, July 5, 1899. He studied law at the Univ. of Chile; served as 2nd secretary of the Chilean Legation in Spain (1921-24); in music, received his training with Enrique Soro in Santiago and with Conrado del Campo in Madrid. Returning to Chile, he became prof. at the National Cons. in Santiago (1928); dean of the faculty of fine arts of the Univ. of Chile (1933); president of the Instituto de Extensión Musical (1940). His role in the promotion of musical culture in Chile, in the publishing of music by Chilean composers, and in the organization of educational activities is very important; he traveled in Europe and in South America; visited the U. S. several times as lecturer. In his works he accepts the international tradition of neo-Classical music; only in a few instances does he employ identifiable Chilean melodies. —Works (all first performed in Santiago): *Cantata de los ríos de Chile,* for chorus and orch. (Nov. 27, 1942); *5 Piezas breves,* for string orch. (May 31, 1937); *Variaciones,* for piano and orch. (June 25, 1943); *Sinfonía concertante,* for flute, piano, and string orch. (Nov. 29, 1945); symph. no. 1, for strings, celesta, and percussion (May 28, 1948); symph. no. 2, for strings (Nov. 26, 1948); *Egloga,* for soprano, chorus, and orch. (Nov. 24, 1950); *Cantares de la Pascua,* for chorus a cappella (Dec. 7, 1950); 2 string quartets; many songs; piano pieces. —Cf. N. Slonimsky, *Music of Latin America* (N. Y., 1945, pp. 162-64); Otto Mayer-Serra, *Música y Músicos de Latinoamérica* (Mexico City, 1947; vol. 2, pp. 892-99); special issue of the 'Revista Musical Chilena' (Dec., 1951); Vicente Salas Viu, *La Creación musical en Chile 1900-1951* (Santiago, 1952; pp. 367-422).

Santa María, Fray **Tomás de,** important Spanish organist and composer; b. Madrid, c. 1510; d. Valladolid, 1570. A Dominican monk, and a pupil of Antonio de Cabezón; publ. *Libro llamado Arte de tañer fantasía* (Valladolid, 1565), a treatise on playing fantasias on keyboard instruments and on the guitar or lute (German transl., with critical and biographical introduction, by E. Harich-Schneider and R. Boadella, Leipzig, 1937). —Cf. Pedrell, *Hispaniae schola musica sacra* (vol. 6); Villalba, *Antología de organistas clásicos españoles,* I; O. Kinkeldey, *Orgel und Klavier in der Musik des 16. Jahrhunderts* (Leipzig, 1910; with mus. examples); H. Collet, *Le Mysticisme musical espagnol au XVIe siècle* (Paris, 1913); J. Bonnet, 'Historical Organ Recitals' VI (1940); G. Reese, *Music in the Renaissance* (N. Y., 1954; pp. 629-30).

Santelmann, William Henry, violinist and band conductor; b. Offensen, Hanover, Sept. 24, 1863; d. Washington, D.C., Dec. 17, 1932. He studied at the Leipzig Cons.; in 1887 settled in America; played the baritone in the U. S. Marine Band in Washington (1887-95); was its conductor from 1898 until 1927, when he retired. He wrote the suite *Pocahontas,* for band; marches and dances; made numerous transcriptions. His son, **William F. H. Santelmann** (b. 1902), studied the violin, joined the U. S. Marine Band in 1923, became its assistant conductor in 1935, and conductor in 1940; president of the American Bandmasters Association, 1953-54; retired in 1955.

Santi, Padre **Angelo de,** Italian Jesuit priest and music scholar; b. Trieste, July 12, 1847; d. Rome, Jan. 28, 1922. He took a leading part in the reform of Catholic church music, his views being embodied in the *Motu proprio* of Pius X on sacred music (1903). He founded the Schola Cantorum of the Vatican Seminary. —Publications: *Il Maestro Filippo Capocci e le sue composizioni per organo* (1888); *L'Origine delle feste natalizie* (1907); also articles in 'Rassegna Gregoriana,' etc.

Santini, Abbate **Fortunato,** Italian music scholar and composer; b. Rome, Jan. 5, 1778; d. there, 1862. He was noted as the collector of one of the finest music libraries ever formed; ordained priest in 1801; as early as 1820 he publ. a catalogue of the MSS then in his possession, *Catalogo della musica antica, sacra e madrigalesca . . .,* listing 1,000 titles by more than 700 composers. The valuable collection is now in the library of the Univ. of Münster, Westphalia. His original compositions (all MS) include a Requiem, a *Stabat Mater,* many motets. —Cf. V. Stassov, *L'Abbé Santini et sa collection musicale à Rome* (Florence, 1854; biography and summary of Santini's own catalogue); Mendelssohn's *Reisebriefe* (Leipzig, 1861; 5th ed., 1882; English transl. by Lady Wallace as *Letters from Italy and Switzerland,* London, 1862); J. Killing, *Kirchenmusikalische Schätze der Bibliothek des Abbate F. Santini* (Düsseldorf, 1910); K. Fellerer, *Verzeichnis der kirchenmusikalischen Werke der santinischen Sammlungen,* in the 'Kirchenmusikalisches Jahrbuch' (Regensburg, 1931 ff.).

Santley, Sir **Charles,** English baritone; b. Liverpool, Feb. 28, 1834; d. Hove, near London, Sept. 22, 1922. He studied with Nava in Milan; then with Garcia in London; made his professional début as Adam in Haydn's *Creation,* on Nov. 16, 1857. His stage début was at Covent Garden, Oct. 1, 1859; he joined the Carl Rosa Company in 1875, and toured with it for several years; visited America in 1871 and 1891; Australia in 1889-90. In 1887 he was made Commander of the Order of St. Gregory by Pope Leo XIII; in 1907, was knighted. His songs were publ. under the pseudonym 'Ralph Betterton'; he also publ. *Student and Singer* (London, 1892; a vol. of reminiscences); *The Singing Master* (2 parts; London, 1900); *The Art of Singing and Vocal Declamation* (London, 1908); *Reminiscences of My Life* (London, 1909). —Cf. J. J. M. Levien, *Sir Charles Santley* (London, 1930).

Santoliquido, Francesco, Italian composer; b. San Giorgio a Cremano, Naples, Aug. 6, 1883. He studied at the Santa Cecilia in Rome; graduated in 1909; in 1912 he went to live in Hammamet, a village in Tunisia, spending part of each year in Rome; about 1950 made his home in Anacapri. Many of his compositions contain melodic inflections of Arabian popular music. —Works: the operas *La Favola di Helga* (Milan, Nov. 23, 1910), *Ferhuda* (Tunis, Jan. 30, 1919), *La Bajadera dalla maschera gialla* (Rome, 1923), *La Porte verde,* musical tragedy in 4 acts (Bergamo, Oct. 15, 1953); for orch.: *Crepuscolo sul mare* (Nuremberg, Jan. 19, 1909; composer conducting), *Il Profumo delle oasi sahariane* (Tunis, April 17, 1918; also in Rome, March 5, 1922), *Acquarelli* (Rome, April 11, 1923), symph. in F (1924), *La Sagra dei morti,* heroic elegy for the victims of World War I (Rome, 1929), *Tre miniature per i piccoli* (1933), *Preludio e Burlesca,* for string orch. (Rome, 1938), *Alba di gloria,* symph. prelude (Rome, Nov. 13, 1940), *Grotte di Capri,* 5 pieces for orch. (1943), *Santuari asiatici,* symph. sketches (Naples, 1952); a string quartet; a violin sonata; *Aria antica,* for cello and piano; *Chiarità lunare,* for violin and piano; *2 Pezzi* for 5 wind instruments; *Piccola ballata* for piano; 2 *Acqueforti tunisine* for piano; a cycle of songs to words by Pierre Louys; *Messa facile* for chorus; publ. *Il Dopo-Wagner; Claudio Debussy e Richard Strauss* (Rome, 1909); also books of verse; wrote short stories in English.

Santoro, Claudio, Brazilian composer; b. Manaos, Nov. 23, 1919. He studied at the Cons. of Rio de Janeiro; also took lessons with Koellreutter, who gave him instruction in modern techniques, particularly the 12-tone method; held a Guggenheim Fellowship in 1946. Under the influence of Soviet ideas about realistic music, Santoro abandoned atonal music and adopted the diatonic style; this orientation is expressed in his work *Symphony of Peace,* which he conducted by special invitation in Moscow (March 21, 1955). Among his works written in an atonal idiom are a wind quintet (1942), 3 string quartets, 3 violin sonatas, 2 cello sonatas, and his 1st and 2nd symphonies (1940; 1945); his 3rd symphony (1948), *Ode to Stalingrad* (1947), ballet *The Factory* (1949), and a marionette opera, *Zée Brasil,* are in the diatonic style.

Santucci (san-tooch'-chē), **Marco,** Italian composer; b. Camajore, Tuscany, July 4, 1762; d. Lucca, Nov. 29, 1843. He was Anfossi's successor (1797-1808) as maestro at S. Giovanni in Laterano, Rome; in 1808 was appointed canon at the Cathedral of Lucca. A motet *a* 16, for 4 choirs, received a prize from the Accademia Napoleone in 1806 because of the 'entirely new and original' combination of voices. Baini publ. an energetic protest against this award, pointing out that such polyphonic writing was common in works by Italian composers of the 16th and 17th centuries. Santucci also wrote Masses, motets, psalms, canons in up to 7 parts, symphonies, organ sonatas, etc.; publ. a treatise *Sulla melodia, sull'armonia e sul metro* (1828). —Cf. G. Rinuccini, *Biografia di Marco Santucci* (Milan, 1851).

Sanz, Gaspar, Spanish 17-century guitarist; b. Calanda (Aragón); studied at Salamanca Univ., taking degrees in theology and philosophy; became maestro to the Spanish Viceroy at Naples. He was guitar teacher to Don Juan of Austria, for whom he wrote an *Instrucción de música sobre la guitarra española* (Zaragoza, 1674; 2nd ed., 1697), containing examples of contemporary Spanish dance music and folksong.

Sanzogno, Nino, outstanding Italian conductor and composer; b. Venice, April 13, 1911. He studied composition with Malipiero; conducting with Scherchen; appeared as opera conductor at the Teatro La Fenice in Venice and La Scala in Milan; also in South America. Among his compositions are the symph. poems *I quattro cavaliere dell'-Apocalisse* (1930) and *Vanitas* (1931); a viola concerto (1935); cello concerto (1937); songs.

Sapelnikov, Vassily, Russian pianist; b. Odessa, Nov. 2, 1868; d. San Remo, March 17, 1941. He was a pupil of L. Brassin and Sophie Menter at the St. Petersburg Cons.; in 1888, made his début at Hamburg with the Tchaikovsky concerto in B♭ minor, under the composer's direction; then made tours throughout Europe; 1897-99, prof. at the Moscow Cons.; then resigned to continue his concert tours. Later, he lived chiefly in Germany, also for a time in Florence; 1916, returned to Russia, remaining there until 1922; from 1923, again in Germany and Italy. He wrote an opera, *Der Khan und sein Sohn,* and pieces for piano (*Petite Mazourka, Danse des elfes, Valse-Caprice, Impromptu, Solitude*).

Saperton, David, American pianist; b. Pittsburgh, Oct. 29, 1889. He received his first instruction on the piano from his grandfather, a former tenor at the Brünn Opera, while his father, a physician and former concert bass, superintended his theoretical studies. At the age of 10 he made his first public appearance with orch. in Pittsburgh; in 1905 he gave a recital in New York; in 1910-12, toured Germany, Austria, Hungary, Italy, Russia, and Scandinavia; then returned to the U. S. In 1921, he married Vanita Godowsky (daughter of Leopold Godowsky); 1924, joined the piano faculty of the Curtis Institute, Philadelphia.

Sapio, Romualdo, singing teacher; b. Palermo, Sept. 8, 1858; d. New York, Sept. 22, 1943; studied at the Palermo Cons.; made his début as conductor in Milan (1883); conducted Patti's tours of North and South America; also operatic and concert tours of Albani and Nordica; in 1892, settled in New York as teacher of singing and head of the vocal dept. at the National Cons.; the same year he married the concert singer Clementine de Vere (q.v.).

Sapp, Allen Dwight, American composer; b. Philadelphia, Dec. 10, 1922. He studied piano with Robert Elmore and theory with William Hoppich, in Philadelphia (1935-39); subsequently at Harvard Univ., with Walter Piston (composition) and E. B. Hill (orchestration); A.B., 1942; A.M., 1949; graduate studies there with A. T. Davison, A. T. Merritt, Irving Fine, and Randall Thompson; also took courses with Aaron Copland and Nadia Boulanger. He was chief cryptanalyst in the Civil Censorship Division of the U.S. Army, and chief of Code Research (1943-48). In 1949, appointed to the faculty of Harvard Univ. His music is cast in a Classical framework, with contrapuntal and harmonic elements treated as of equal importance; the main influences are Stravinsky, Piston, and Copland; in some works, he applies, freely, methods of serial thematic composition derived from Schoenberg's theories.—Works: for orch.: *Andante* (1941), 2 suites (1949; 1957), *The Double Image* (1957), *The Septagon* (1957); chamber music: 2 violin sonatas (1942; 1948), viola sonata (1949), piano trio (1949), string quartet (1951), string trio (1956), *Ricercare for Viols* (1956); for piano: 4 sonatas, 2 sonatinas, *Dialogues* for 2 pianos (1952); 5 *Landscapes* for chorus (1950); *The Marriage Song,* after Donne, for chorus and orch. (1951); 4 motets for chorus (1953); *The Little Boy Lost,* after William Blake, for chorus and orch. (1954); songs (*The Lady and the Lute, 7 Epigrams* for bass, etc.).

Saran, Franz Ludwig, German writer on music; b. Altranstädt, near Lützen, Oct. 27, 1866; d. Erlangen, April 24, 1931. He studied languages in Halle, Leipzig, and Freiburg; 1896, instructor in German language and literature at the Halle Univ.; 1905, prof.; from 1913, prof. at the Univ. of Erlangen. His works having to do with music include the revision and editing of R. Westphal's *Aristoxenos' von Tarent Melodik und Rhythmik* (2 vols., 1893) and the editing and transcription of the famous Jena MS of *Minnelieder* (2 vols.; with G. Holz and E. Bernouilli, 1901; vol. 2 includes a systematic treatise on the rhythm of medieval songs). Also publ. *Der Rhythmus des französischen Verses* (1904).

Sarasate, Pablo de (Pablo Martín Melitón Sarasate y Navascuez), celebrated Spanish violin virtuoso; b. Pamplona, March 10, 1844; d. Biarritz, Sept. 20, 1908. At the age of 10 he played before Queen Isabella, who presented him with a fine Stradivarius. After successful concerts in Spain he studied at the Paris Cons. under Alard, taking 1st prize in the violin class in 1857, and a 'premier accessit' in 1859. His playing was noted for its extraordinary beauty of tone, impeccable purity of intonation, perfection of technique, and grace of manner; but his repertory consisted almost exclusively of fantasies on operatic airs (mostly arranged by himself). Later his taste changed, and he turned to the masterpieces of violin literature. His tours, extending through all Europe, North and South America, South Africa, and the Orient, were an uninterrupted succession of triumphs. He bequeathed to his native city the gifts that had been showered upon him by admirers throughout the world; the collection was placed in a special museum. For him Lalo wrote his *Symphonie espagnole*; Bruch, the *Schottische Fantasie;* Mackenzie, the *Pibroch* suite. Sarasate's compositions, exclusively for violin, are pleasing and effective. —Works: for violin and orch.: *Zigeunerweisen* (his best and most popular work), *Navarra,* for 2 violins, *Peteneras,* caprice, *Jota de San Fermín,* Spanish dances; also Spanish dances for violin and piano, etc. —Cf. M. L. van Vorst, *Sarasate* in 'Scribner's Magazine' (March, 1896); Julio Altadill, *Memorias de Sarasate* (Pamplona, 1909); A. Hartmann, *The Perfect Virtuoso,* in 'Musical America' (March 25, 1940); León Zárate, *Sarasate* (Barcelona, 1945); G. Woolley, *Pablo Sarasate: His Historical Significance* in 'Music & Letters' (July, 1955); Angel Sagardia, *Pablo Sarasate* (Palencia, 1956).

Sargeant, Winthrop, American music critic; b. San Francisco, Dec. 10, 1903; studied violin with Elkus in San Francisco, Prohaska in Vienna, and Capet in Paris; was violinist of the San Francisco Symph. (1922-24), the N. Y. Symph. (1926-28), and the N. Y. Philh. (1928-30); 1931-34, on the editorial staff of 'Musical America'; 1934-36, music critic of the 'Brooklyn Daily Eagle'; 1936-37, chief music critic of the 'N. Y. American'; 1937-53, music editor of 'Time' magazine; since 1954, of the 'New Yorker'; author of *Jazz, Hot and Hybrid* (N. Y., 1938; new ed., 1946); *Geniuses, Goddesses, and People* (N. Y., 1949); *Listening to Music* (N. Y., 1958).

Sargent, Sir (Harold) Malcolm (Watts), eminent English conductor; b. London, April 29, 1895. He studied organ at the Royal College of Organists, London, winning the Sawyer Prize in 1910; then was articled to Dr. Keeton, organist of the Peterborough Cathedral (1911-14); served in the infantry during World War I; after the Armistice, studied piano with Moiseiwitsch. He made his début as conductor in 1921, at the Promenade Concerts in London, in a performance of his own piece, *Impression on a Windy Day;* organized the Leicester Symph. (1922); conducted 2 seasons with the D'Oyly Carte Opera Co.; conducted the Llandudno Orch. (1926-28); filled engagements with Diaghilev's Ballets Russes (1927-30); was conductor of the Royal Choral Society, London (from 1928), the Courtauld-Sargent Concerts (from 1929); led various choruses in England, and won great distinction as choral conductor. In 1945, made his American début in a series of concerts with the NBC Symph.; toured Australia for the Australian Broadcasting Commission (1945-46). He was knighted in 1947. In 1950 he was appointed conductor of the B.B.C. Symph. Orch.; resigned in 1957. —Cf. Donald Brook, *International Gallery of Conductors* (Bristol, 1951; pp. 159-64).

Sarly, Henry, Belgian composer; b. Tirlemont, Dec. 28, 1884; studied there with his father, then at Louvain, and with Huberti, Tinel, Gilson, and Du Bois at the Brussels Cons.; in 1921 was appointed inspector of music education in the Belgian schools. —Works: *Scènes brabançonnes,* for orch.; *La Chanson d'Hallewijn,* for soli, chorus, and orch.; *Le Cœur d'Hjalmar,* for voice and orch.; piano quintet; *Poème,* for piano trio; violin sonata; *2 Danses antiques,* for piano; songs. Author of *Cours théorique et pratique d'harmonie.*

Sarnette, Eric Antoine Joseph André, French inventor of musical instruments; b. Tarbes, Hautes-Pyrénées, Nov. 28, 1898. He studied at Marseilles, and later at the Paris Cons.; also took lessons with Adolphe Sax, the son of the inventor of the saxophone. He became interested in acoustical problems; was active on the staff of the French Radio; manufactured new musical instruments (the sax trumpet, alto clarinet, etc.); publ. *La Musique et le micro* (Paris, 1934) and *L'Orchestre moderne à la Radio* (Paris, 1940).

Saro (zah'-ro), **J. Heinrich,** German bandmaster and composer; b. Jessen, Jan. 4, 1827; d. Berlin, Nov. 27, 1891. In 1859 he became bandmaster in Berlin; in 1867 his band won the international competition at the Paris Exposition; in 1872 he was awarded a gold medal for his performance at the Boston Jubilee. He wrote a number of brilliant pieces of military music, and also some symph. works; publ. *Lehre vom musikalischen Wohlklang und Tonsatz,* and *Instrumentationslehre für Militärmusik.*

Sarrette (săhr-rĕht'), **Bernard,** founder of the Paris Conservatoire; b. Bordeaux, Nov. 27, 1765; d. Paris, April 13, 1858. A captain in the national guard at Paris, he brought together, after the 14th of July, 1789, 45 musicians to form the nucleus of the Parisian band of the national guard. In 1790 the City of Paris assumed the expenses of this band, which was increased to 70 members, among them artists of distinction. In 1792 the financial embarrassments of the Commune led to the suspension of payment; but Sarrette held the band together, and, with the aid of the municipality, established a free school of music employing all the members as teachers. From this school came the musicians employed in the fourteen armies of the Republic. Its energetic principal soon had it converted into a national Institute of Music; and in Sept., 1795, it was definitely organized as a Conservatory. Sarrette, having gained his end, assumed the captaincy of the 103rd Regiment; but the board of directors (5 inspectors and 4 professors) proved so incompetent that he was recalled to the directorship of the Conservatoire in 1796. By introducing advanced methods of instruction, establishing the school of declamation, the concert hall, the grand library, etc., he raised the Cons. to an institution of the first rank. At the Restoration in 1814 he was deprived of his position; nor would he accept it after the revolution of 1830, not wishing to oust his friend

Cherubini. —Cf. Pierre Constant, *B. Sarrette et les origines du Conservatoire national de musique et de déclamation* (Paris, 1895).

Sarti, Giuseppe, Italian composer (nicknamed 'Il Domenichino'); b. Faenza (baptized Dec. 1), 1729; d. Berlin, July 28, 1802. He was a pupil of Padre Martini at Bologna. As a young man he was organist in the Cathedral of his native town (1748-50); appointed director of a theater there in 1752; produced there his earliest opera, *Pompeo in Armenia* (1752); in the following year he brought out a new opera, *Il Rè pastore,* in Venice, with excellent success. In 1755 he was engaged as conductor of an Italian opera company in Denmark. The opera performances were terminated after 2 seasons, but Sarti received the appointment of court conductor, and remained in Copenhagen. In 1765 he was sent by the Danish government to Italy in order to engage singers for a new opera season in Copenhagen, but the project was put off; Sarti remained in Italy until 1768; returned to Copenhagen, and conducted at the Danish court theater (1770-75). As a result of political intrigue in the palace, Sarti was dismissed. He returned to Italy with his wife, the singer Camilla Pasi, whom he had married in Copenhagen. He was director of the Cons. dell' Ospedaletto at Venice (1775-79); then entered the competition for the post of maestro di cappella at the Cathedral of Milan, and won it, defeating a number of competitors including Paisiello. He assumed his position at the Milan Cathedral in 1778; his prestige as a scholar and composer was very high; he was also renowned as a teacher; Cherubini was one of his students; his operas were produced in rapid succession in Copenhagen, Venice, Rome, Florence, and Vienna. In 1784 he was engaged by Catherine the Great as court musician. On the way to Russia he passed through Vienna, where he was received with honors by the Emperor Joseph II; he also met Mozart, who quoted a melody from Sarti's opera *Fra i due litiganti il terzo gode* in *Don Giovanni.* His greatest success in St. Petersburg was *Armida e Rinaldo* (1786; remodelled from an earlier opera, *Armida,* originally produced in Copenhagen, 1759); the leading part was sung by the celebrated Portuguese mezzo-soprano, Luiza Todi; but she developed a dislike of Sarti, and used her powerful influence with Catherine the Great to prevent Sarti's re-engagement. However, he was immediately engaged by Prince Potemkin, and followed him to southern Russia and Moldavia during the military campaign against Turkey; on the taking of Otchakov, Sarti wrote an ode to the Russian liturgical text of thanksgiving, and it was performed in January 1789 at Jassy, Bessarabia, with the accompaniment of cannon shots and church bells. Potemkin gave him a sinecure as head of a musical academy in Ekaterinoslav, but the academy was never established in fact. After Potemkin's death in 1791, his arrangements with Sarti were honored by the court of St. Petersburg; in 1793 Sarti was finally reinstated as court composer. He retained his position during the reign of the Emperor Paul, and only after the latter's death decided to leave Russia. He died on his way to Italy, in Berlin. Although Sarti enjoyed a great reputation during his lifetime, and wrote music comparing favorably with that by other Italian composers, his productions sank into oblivion almost immediately after his death; only his sacred works continued to be heard in Italy; he also wrote some instrumental music. —Operas: *Pompeo in Armenia* (Faenza, 1752); *Il Rè pastore* (Venice, 1753); *Vologeso* (Copenhagen, 1754); *Gram og Signe* (Copenhagen, Feb. 21, 1757); *Ipermestra* (Rome, 1766); *La Contadina fedele* (Vienna, 1771); *La Successione in Sidone* (Copenhagen, April 4, 1771); *Deucalio e Pyrrha* (Copenhagen, March 19, 1772); *Le Gelosie villane* (Venice, Nov., 1776); *Medonte, Rè di Epiro* (Florence, Sept. 8, 1777); *I Contrattempi* (Venice, Nov., 1778); *Giulio Sabino* (Venice, Jan., 1781); *Fra due litiganti il terzo gode* (Milan, Sept. 14, 1782); *I finti eredi* (St. Petersburg, Oct. 19, 1785); *Armida e Rinaldo* (St. Petersburg, 1786); *Ena nel Lazio* (Gatchina, near St. Petersburg, Oct. 15, 1799); contributed some numbers to the Russian opera *The Early Reign of Oleg* (St. Petersburg, Oct. 22, 1790). —Cf. G. Pasolini-Zanelli, *Giuseppe Sarti* (Faenza, 1883); A. Untersteiner, *Giuseppe Sarti,* in the 'Gazzetta Musicale di Milano' (July 24, 1902); C. Rivalta, *Giuseppe Sarti, musicista faentino del secolo XVIII* (Faenza, 1928); G. Fesetchko, *Giuseppe Sarti,* in 'Sovietskaya Musica' (Dec., 1950); R.-Aloys Mooser, *Annales de la Musique et des Musiciens en Russie au XVIIIe siècle* (vol. II; Geneva, 1951; pp. 415-50, 463-79).

Sartori, Claudio, Italian musicologist; b. Brescia, April 1, 1913. He studied in Pavia and Strasbourg; in 1942 was appointed chief librarian of the Cons. of Milan; publ. important bibliographical works, among them *Bibliografia delle opere musicali stampate da Ottaviano Petrucci* (1948) and *Bibliografia* *della musica strumentale stampata in Italia fino al 1700* (1952); also *La Notazione italiana del trecento* (1938), *Il Regio Conservatorio di musica 'G. B. Martini' di Bologna* (1942), a monograph on Monteverdi (1950), etc.

Sartorio, Antonio, Italian composer; b. Venice, c. 1620; d. there, after 1685. From 1666 to 1675 he was court Kapellmeister at Hanover; in 1676 appointed maestro di cappella at San Marco in Venice, holding that post until 1685. He was a leading representative of the Venetian school; produced 14 operas, of which the best were *Seleuco* (Venice, Jan. 16, 1666), *L'Adelaide* (Venice, Feb. 19, 1672), and *Orfeo* (Venice, Dec. 14, 1672); publ. a Psalm for 8 voices (1780), cantatas, and motets.

Sartorius, Paul, German organist and composer who flourished at the turn of the 17th century. He publ. a book of madrigals in 1600 and a collection of German songs, *Neue teutsche Liedlein* (1601); also wrote motets.

Sás, Andrés, composer; b. Paris, April 6, 1900, of French-Belgian parents. He studied at the Brussels Cons. with Marchot (violin), Ernest Closson (music history), and Maurice Imbert (counterpoint). In 1924 he was engaged by the Peruvian government to teach violin at the National Academy of Music in Lima; in 1928 he returned temporarily to Belgium; the following year, settled in Lima permanently; married the Peruvian pianist Lily Rosay, and with her established the Sás-Rosay Academy of Music. He became profundly interested in Peruvian folk music, and collected folk melodies; made use of many of them in his own compositions. —Works: incidental music to Molière's *Le Malade imaginaire* (1943); the ballets, *La Señora del pueblo* (Viña del Mar, Chile, Jan. 20, 1946), *El Hijo prodigo* (1948); for orch.: *Canción India* (1927), *Tres Estampas del Perú* (1936); *Poema Indio* (1941), *Sueño de Zamba* (1943), *Danza Gitana* (1944), *La Patrona del pueblo* (1945), *La Parihuana* (1946), *Las Seis Edades de la Tía Conchita* (1947), *La Leyenda de la Isla de San Lorenzo* (1949); *Recuerdos,* for violin and piano (also for orch.; 1927); *Rapsodia Peruana,* for violin and piano (also for orch.; 1928); *Sonata-Fantasía,* for flute and piano (1934); string quartet (1938); *Cantos del Perú,* for violin and piano (1941); for piano: *Aires y Danzas del Perú* (2 albums; 1930 and 1945), *Suite Peruana* (1931), *Himno y Danza* (1935), *Sonatina Peruana* (1946); numerous choruses and songs. —Cf. N. Slonimsky, *Music of Latin America* (N. Y., 1945; pp. 275-76).

Saslavsky, Alexander, violinist; b. Kharkov, Russia, Feb. 8, 1876; d. San Francisco, Aug. 2, 1924. He studied in his native town with local violin teachers; then with Jakob Grün in Vienna; after a Canadian tour in 1893 he joined the N. Y. Symph. Orch.; in 1903 became its concertmaster; was also concertmaster of the Russian Symph. Orch. in N. Y.; in 1919, became concertmaster of the newly organized Los Angeles Philharmonic. See 'Dictionary of American Biography.'

Sassòli, Ada, Italian harpist; b. Bologna, Sept. 25, 1886; d. Rome, Dec. 3, 1946. She studied at the Cons. of Bologna; then entered the class of A. Hasselmans at the Paris Cons., winning 1st prize for harp playing in 1902. She toured with Mme. Melba in England and Australia (1904-05); made several tours of the U. S.; appeared as soloist with the Boston Symph. and other American orchestras; returned to Europe in 1916; was appointed prof. of harp at the Santa Cecilia in Rome, and lived there until her death.

Satie (sah-tē'), **Erik (-Alfred-Leslie),** French composer; b. Honfleur, May 17, 1866; d. Paris, July 1, 1925. At the age of 8 he received his first musical instruction from a local organist, Vinot (pupil of Niedermeyer); at 13 he settled in Paris, where his father was a music publisher; attended the Paris Cons. for an academic year (1883-84), took some lessons with Guilmant, but then abandoned systematic study; played in various cabarets in Montmartre; publ. some piano pieces in 1887 (which he, to mislead, marked op. 62). A meeting with Josephin Péladan, a writer and mystic, led him to join a Rosicrucian Society in Paris (1892); he also composed music to Péladan's plays. He was nearly 40 years old when he decided to resume serious study of composition, and entered the Schola Cantorum, in the classes of Vincent d'Indy and Albert Roussel. In 1898 he moved to Arcueil, near Paris; became friendly with many leaders of the modern movement in literature, opera, dance, and music. He had devoted admirers among musicians; Milhaud, Sauguet, and the conductor Desormière organized (without facetious intent) the 'École d' Arcueil' to honor Satie as master and leader. Satie's eccentricity was not merely a pose, but an esthetic creed which he proclaimed in the face of ridicule and public contempt. His influence on French composers of the first quarter of the 20th century was profound, and had lasting consequences even after a change of style made his once-daring ideas obsolete. Hence, the flow of books and articles on Satie, and repeated attestations by French musicians to his erratic genius. — Works: the 'symph. drama' *Socrate,* after Plato, for 4 sopranos and small orch. (Paris, Société Nationale de Musique, Feb. 14, 1920); a lyric comedy, *Le Piège de Méduse* (1913); the ballets: *Parade* (Paris, May 18, 1917), *Mercure* (Paris, June 15, 1924), *Relâche* (Paris, Nov. 29, 1924); incidental music to Péladan's *Le Fils des Étoiles* (1891; prelude orchestrated by Ravel) and *Le Prince de Byzance* (1891), to H. Mazel's *Le Nazaréen* (1892), to J. Bois' *La Porte heroïque au ciel* (1893), to M. de Féraudy's *Pousse l'Amour* (1905); numerous piano pieces, notable chiefly for their extravagant titles: *Pièces froides, Prélude en tapisserie, Trois Préludes flasques, Descriptions automatiques, Embryons desséchés, Heures séculaires et instantanées, Crépuscule matinal, Obstacles vénimeux, Trois Morceaux en forme de poire,* etc. His early piano suite, *Gymnopédies* (1888), was orchestrated by Debussy; his posthumous pieces, *Jack in the Box* (title in English) and *Cinq Grimaces pour le 'Songe d'une nuit d'été,'* were orchestrated by Milhaud. —Cf. Erik Satie, *Mémoirs d'un amnésique* (facetious autobiographical notice, in the bulletin of the Société Internationale de Musique, Paris, 1912); G. Jean-Aubry, *La Musique française d'aujourd'hui* (Paris, 1916); Carl van Vechten, *Erik Satie,* in *Interpreters and Interpretations* (N. Y., 1917); R. D. Chennevière, *Erik Satie and the Music of Irony,* in the 'Mus. Quarterly' (Oct., 1919); A. Cœuroy, *La Musique française moderne* (Paris, 1922); W. W. Roberts, *The Problem of Satie,* in 'Music & Letters' (Oct., 1923); 2 special issues of the 'Revue Musicale' (March, 1924; June, 1952); G. M. Gatti, *Musicisti moderni d'Italia e di fuori* (Bologna, 1925); W. Dankert, *Der Klassizismus Erik Saties und seine geistesgeschichtliche Stellung,* in 'Zeitschrift für Musikwissenschaft' (Nov., 1929); P.-D. Tamplier, *Erik Satie* (Paris, 1932); D. Milhaud, *Notes sur Erik Satie, in* 'Les Œuvres Nouvelles' (vol. 6, N. Y., 1946); W. H. Mellers, *Studies in Contemporary Music* (London, 1947); Rollo H. Myers, *Erik Satie* (London, 1948).

Satter, Gustav, pianist and composer; b. Vienna, Feb. 12, 1832; d. Savannah, Ga., 1879. He studied in Vienna and Paris; undertook a pianistic tour in the U. S. and Brazil (1854-60) with surprising success; went back to Paris, where Berlioz warmly praised his music; then lived in Vienna, Dresden, Hanover, and Stockholm. He wrote an opera, *Olanthe;* the overtures *Lorelei, Julius Cæsar, An die Freude;* 2 symphonies; a symph. poem, *George Washington;* much chamber music; 3 sonatas, studies, waltzes, etc., for piano; about 160 opus numbers in all. —Cf. *The Life and Works of Gustav Satter* (Macon, Georgia, 1879).

Sattler (zat'-lär), **Heinrich,** German organist and teacher; b. Quedlinburg, April 3, 1811; d. Brunswick, Oct. 17, 1891. He devoted himself mainly to teaching; from 1861, was on the staff of the Oldenburg Seminary. He publ. a treatise, *Die Orgel* (5 eds.); a book, *Erinnerung an Mozart's Leben und Werke* (1856); composed an oratorio, *Die Sachsentaufe;* and 2 cantatas, *Triumph des Glaubens and Pfingstkantate;* sacred works; chamber music; many organ pieces.

Satz (sahts), **Ilya,** Russian composer; b. Tchernobyl, Kiev district, April 30, 1875; d. St. Petersburg, Dec. 12, 1912. He studied cello in Kiev; then took lessons in composition with Taneyev in Moscow; his general education was desultory. He traveled in Europe in 1900; then made a tour as a cellist through Siberia. He returned to Moscow in 1903; in 1905 became music director of the Studio of the Moscow Art Theater, and wrote incidental music for new plays, including Maeterlinck's *Blue Bird* and Andreyev's *A Man's Life;* also composed ballet music for Salome's dance; the ballet *The Goat-Footed* (a *Dance of the Satyrs* was reorchestrated and prepared for performance by Glière). Satz had a talent for the grotesque; a lack of technique prevented his development into a major composer. A memorial volume, *Ilya Satz,* with articles by Glière and several members of the Moscow Art Theater, was publ. at Moscow in 1923.

Sauer (zow'-ër), **Emil von,** eminent pianist; b. Hamburg, Oct. 8, 1862; d. Vienna, April 28, 1942. He studied with Nicholas Rubinstein in Moscow (1879-81), and Liszt in Weimar (1884-85); made numerous European tours; played in the U. S. in 1898-99 and 1908. From 1901 till 1907, and again from 1915, was prof. at the 'Meisterschule für Klavierspiel' in Vienna; from 1908 till 1915 he lived in Dresden; appeared in concerts until 1936, and then retired to Vienna. He wrote 2 piano concertos,

2 piano sonatas, many studies for piano; edited the complete works of Brahms and pedagogical works of Pischna, Plaidy, Kullak, etc. He publ. an autobiography, *Meine Welt* (1901).

Sauguet, Henri, French composer; b. Bordeaux, May 18, 1901. He was a pupil of Joseph Canteloube; in 1922 he went to Paris, where he studied with Koechlin; became associated with Erik Satie, and formed a group designated as the École d'Arcueil (from the locality where Satie lived near Paris). In conformity with the principles of utilitarian music, he wrote sophisticated works in an outwardly simple manner; his first conspicuous success was the production of his ballet, *La Chatte,* by Diaghilev in 1927. —Works: operas: *Le Plumet du colonel* (Paris, April 24, 1924), *La Contrebasse,* after Tchekhov (Paris, 1932); *La Chartreuse de Parme* (Paris, March 16, 1939), *La Gageuse imprévue* (Paris, July 4, 1944), *Les Caprices de Marianne* (Aix-en-Provence, July 20, 1954); ballets: *La Chatte* (Monte Carlo, April 30, 1927), *Paul et Virginie* (Paris, April 15, 1943), *Les Mirages* (Paris, Dec. 15, 1947), *Cordelia* (Paris, May 7, 1952); *Les Saisons et les jours,* 'allegoric symph.' (Paris, Dec. 15, 1946); *Symphonie expiatoire,* in memory of innocent war victims (Paris, Feb. 8, 1948); *Orphée,* for violin and orch. (Aix-en-Provence, July 26, 1953); much incidental music; film music; chamber music; piano pieces; songs.

Sauret (soh-rā'), **Émile,** French violinist; b. Dun-le-Roi (Cher), May 22, 1852; d. London, Feb. 12, 1920. He studied with Vieuxtemps at the Paris Cons. and with Bériot in Brussels; was a child prodigy, and made his London début at the age of 14. He was 20 when he was engaged for an American tour (1872); gave concerts in America again in 1874, 1876, 1877, and 1895. From 1903 till 1906 he taught at the Chicago Musical College; returning to Europe, he lived in Geneva and Berlin; was at various times prof. of violin in London and Berlin. In 1872 he married the pianist Teresa Carreño (divorced in 1877). He was a typical representative of the French school of violin playing, distinguished by grace, elegance, and excellent taste. He composed for violin and orch. *Souvenir de Moscou, Rapsodie russe, Rapsodie suédoise, Farfalla,* and *Élégie et rondo;* for violin and piano, *Feuilles d'album, Pensées fugitives, Scènes champêtres, 20 grandes études, 12 Études artistiques, 24 Études-caprices;* publ. a method, *Gradus ad Parnassum du violoniste* (in 4 parts, with annotations in French and German); also made about 25 transcriptions.

Sauveur (soh-vör'), **Joseph,** French acoustician; b. La Flèche, March 24, 1653; d. Paris, July 9, 1716. A deaf-mute, learning to speak in his 7th year, he became a remarkable investigator in the realm of acoustics; in 1696, member of the Académie. — Works (all publ. in the *Mémoires* of the Académie): *Principes d'acoustique et de musique* (1700-01); *Application des sons harmoniques à la composition des jeux d'orgue* (1702); *Méthode générale pour former des systèmes tempérés . . .* (1707); *Table générale des systèmes tempérés* (1711); *Rapports des sons des cordes d'instruments de musique aux flèches des cordes* (1713). He was the first to calculate absolute vibration numbers, and to explain scientifically the phenomenon of overtones.—Cf. H. Scherchen, *Vom Wesen der Musik,* chap. I (Zürich, 1946; in English as *The Nature of Music,* Chicago, 1950).

Sauzay (soh-zā'), **(Charles-) Eugène,** French violinist and composer; b. Paris, July 14, 1809; d. there, Jan. 24, 1901. He studied with Baillot at the Paris Cons., and was a member of Baillot's string quartet; taught violin at the Paris Cons. from 1860 to 1892. He publ. a *Symphonie rustique; Études harmoniques,* for violin; numerous transcriptions; also *Haydn, Mozart, Beethoven, étude sur le quatuor* (Paris, 1861; 2nd ed., 1884); and *L'École de l'accompagnement* (Paris, 1869).

Savage, Henry Wilson, American impresario; b. New Durham, N. H., March 21, 1859; d. Boston, Nov. 29, 1927. He started in business as a real estate operator in Boston, where he built the Castle Square Theater; later went into theatrical enterprise himself and in 1897 opened a season of opera in English. His 'Castle Square Opera Co.' flourished, and he undertook tours of other cities. In 1900 he formed the 'English Grand Opera Co.' and engaged several artists from the Carl Rosa Co. of London. In 1904-05 he organized a special troupe, producing *Parsifal* in English in the principal cities of the East and Middle West; in 1906-07 the same company made a tour with Puccini's *Madama Butterfly;* he also produced light opera with another company, which, among other operettas, introduced Lehár's *The Merry Widow* to the U. S. (1906). Cf. 'Dictionary of American Biography.'

Savard (sah-vahr'), **(Marie-Gabriel-) Augustin,** French music educator; b. Paris, Aug. 21, 1814; d. there, June, 1881. He studied with Leborne and Bazin; in 1843 became prof. of solfège, later of harmony and thorough-bass, at the Paris Cons. —Publications: *Cours complet d'harmonie* (1853); *Principes de la musique* (1861; 14th ed., 1913) and its abridge version, *Premières notions de musique* (1866; 25th ed., 1897); *Études d'harmonie pratique;* etc.

Savard, (Marie-Emmanuel-) Augustin, French composer and pedagogue; son of the preceding; b. Paris, May 15, 1861; d. Lyons, Dec. 6, 1942. He studied at the Paris Cons. with Durand, Taudou, and Massenet; won the Prix de Rome in 1886 with the cantata *La Vision de Saul;* 1892-93 was chorusmaster at the Opéra; director of the Cons. in Lyons from 1902 until 1921, when he retired. —Works: a lyric drama, *La Forêt* (Paris Opéra, 1910); 2 symphonies; an overture, *Roi Lear; Poème* for voice and orch.; a string quartet; a violin sonata; etc.

Savart (sah-vahr'), **Félix,** French acoustician; b. Mézières, June 30, 1791; d. Paris, March 17, 1841. He was prof. of acoustics at the Collège de France; in 1827, was elected member of the Académie. — Writings (publ. in the 'Annales de physique et de chimie'): *Mémoire sur la construction des instruments à cordes et à archet* (1819, separate reprint; in German, 1844); *Sur la communication des mouvements vibratoires entre les corps solides* (1820); *Sur les vibrations de l'air* (1823); *Sur la voix humaine* (1825); *Sur la communication des mouvements vibratoires par les liquides* (1826); *Sur la voix des oiseaux* (1826); etc.

Saville, Frances, American soprano; b. San Francisco, Jan. 6, 1862; d. Burlingame, Calif., Nov. 8, 1935. She went early to Australia, where she made her début in oratorio; continued her studies in Paris with Marchesi; in 1892 made her operatic début in Brussels; also appeared with the Carl Rosa Co. in England, at the Paris Opéra-Comique, in Vienna, Berlin, St. Petersburg, Warsaw, etc.; on Nov. 18, 1895, she made her début as Juliette (with Jean de Reszke) at the Metropolitan Opera House, on whose roster she remained through the season 1899-1900 later she reappeared at the Vienna Opera; then lived in retirement in California.

Savine, Alexander, conductor, composer, and singing teacher; b. Belgrade, April 26, 1881; d. Chicago, Jan. 19, 1949. He studied in Belgrade with S. Mokranjac, and later at the Vienna Cons. (singing with Pauline Lucca). He then was engaged as opera conductor in Berlin (1905-07); taught singing at the Musical Academy in Winnepeg, Canada (1908-12); later settled in the U. S.; was director of the opera dept. at the Institute of Musical Art, N. Y. (1922-24); in 1929 moved to Chicago. He was married (1914) to the soprano Lillian Blauvelt. — Works: the opera *Xenia* (Zürich, May 29, 1919); 4 symph. poems; choruses; songs.

Sax, (Antoine-Joseph-) Adolphe, inventor of the saxophone; b. Dinant, Belgium, Nov. 6, 1814; d. Paris, Feb. 7, 1894. He was the son of Charles-Joseph Sax, the instrument maker, and acquired great skill in manipulating musical instruments from his early youth; his practical and imaginative ideas led him to undertake improvements of the clarinet and other wind instruments. He studied the flute and clarinet at the Brussels Cons.; in 1842 he went to Paris with a wind instrument of his invention, which he called Saxophone, made of metal, with a single-reed mouthpiece and conical bore. He exhibited brass and woodwind instruments at the Paris Exposition of 1844, winning a silver medal; his father joined him in Paris, and together they continued the manufacture of new instruments; evolved the saxhorns (improved over the bugle-horn and ophicleide by replacing the keys by a valve mechanism), and the saxotromba, a hybrid instrument producing a tone midway between the bugle and the trumpet. Conservative critics and rival instrument makers ridiculed Sax's innovations, but Berlioz and others warmly supported him; he also won praise from Rossini. His instruments were gradually adopted by French military bands. Sax won a gold medal at the Paris Industrial Exposition of 1849. Financially, however, he was unsuccessful, and was compelled to go into bankruptcy in 1852. He exhibited his instruments in London (1862) and received the Grand Prix in Paris (1867) for his improved instruments. In 1857 the Paris Cons. engaged him as instructor of the saxophone; with some interruptions, saxophone instruction was continued at the Paris Cons. for a whole century. He publ. a method for his instrument. Although Wieprecht, Červený, and others disputed the originality and priority of his inventions, legal decisions gave the rights to Sax; the saxophone became a standard instrument; many serious composers made use of it in their scores (Bizet's

L'Arlésienne, etc.). The instrument fell into desuetude after Sax's death; but about 1918 a spectacular revival of the saxophone took place, when it was adopted in jazz bands; its popularity became world-wide; numerous methods were publ. and special schools established; and there appeared saxophone virtuosos for whom many composers wrote concertos. —Cf. O. Comettant, *Histoire d'un inventeur au XIX*e *siècle* (Paris, 1860); Th. Lajarte, *Instruments Sax et fanfares civiles* (Paris, 1876); Albert Remy, *La Vie tourmentée d'Adolphe Sax* (Brussels, 1939); L. Kochnitzky, *Adolphe Sax and His Saxophone* (N. Y., 1949).

Sax, Charles-Joseph, Belgian instrument maker; b. Dinant-sur-Meuse, Feb. 1, 1791; d. Paris, April 26, 1865. He established an instrument factory at Brussels in 1815, manufacturing not only wind instruments, but also pianos, harps, and guitars; his specialty, however, was brass instruments. He joined his son Adolphe Sax in Paris, and helped him to launch his revolutionary inventions.

Sayão (sah-yahn'-oh), **Bidú,** Brazilian soprano; b. Rio de Janeiro, May 11, 1902. She studied with Jean de Reszke in Nice (1923-25); sang at the Opéra-Comique in Paris, at the Royal Opera in Rome, and at La Scala, Milan. In 1935 she made her American dèbut in a recital in N. Y.; opera début with the Metropolitan Opera Co. on Feb. 14, 1937, as Manon; also made several South American tours.

Saygun, Ahmed Adnan, Turkish composer; b. Izmir, Sept. 7, 1907; studied in Paris with Le Flem and Vincent d'Indy at the Schola Cantorum. Returning to Turkey in 1931, he was active as teacher and conductor in Istanbul; in 1946 appointed prof. at the Cons. of Ankara. He visited the U.S. in 1950 and again in 1958. —Works: 1-act opera, *Tas Bebek* (Ankara, Dec. 27, 1934); 3-act opera, *Kerem* (Ankara, March 1, 1953); *Yunus Emre,* oratorio (Ankara, May 25, 1946); piano concerto (1952); quartet for clarinet, saxophone, percussion, and piano (1933); 2 string quartets (1947 and 1958); symphony (1953); an orchestral suite of national dances, *Zeybek, Interlude and Horon* (Ankara, April 14, 1951); cello sonata (1935); violin sonata (1942).

Sayn-Wittgenstein-Berleburg, Count **Friedrich Ernst,** German composer; b. Castle Sannerz, Fulda, June 5, 1837; d. Meran, April 16, 1915. He pursued a military career; also studied music with Julius Rietz in Leipzig; publ. *Szenen aus der Frithjofsage* for voice and orch., and songs; wrote 2 operas, *Die Wolfenbraut* (Graz, 1879) and *Antonius und Kleopatra* (Graz, 1883).

Sayve, Lambert de, Flemish composer; b. Sayve, near Liège, 1549; d. Prague, Feb. 1614. As a youth he went to Vienna, where he became a singer in the Imperial chapel; in 1569 he was choirmaster at the monastery of Melk, near Linz, a post he retained until 1577 (made a trip to Spain in 1570). In 1582 he entered the service of the Archduke Charles in Graz; in 1583 he joined the retinue of Archduke Matthias, King of Bohemia, and lived in Prague. He publ. during his lifetime *Il primo libro delle canzoni a la Napolitana a 5 voci* (Vienna, 1582); *Teutsche Liedlein mit 4 Stimmen* (Vienna, 1602); and (his most important works) a collection *Sacræ Symphoniæ* (1612), containing 141 pieces *a* 4 to 16 in 12 books. Modern reprints by F. Blume in 'Das Chorwerk' (vol. 51) and by A. Einstein in 'Denkmäler der Tonkunst in Österreich' (vol. 77). 6 Masses by Sayve (*a* 5 to 16) are in Austrian libraries. —Cf. R. Bragard, *Lambert de Sayve* (Liège, 1934); H. Osthoff, *Die Niederländer und das deutsche Lied* (Berlin, 1938); H. Federhofer, *L. de Sayve an der Grazer Hofkapelle,* in 'Revue Belge de Musicologie' (vol. 3; 1949).

Sbriglia (sbrēl'-yăh), **Giovanni,** celebrated singing teacher; b. Naples, June 23, 1832; d. Paris, Feb. 20, 1916. He sang as a tenor at the San Carlo Theater in Naples; was heard in Italy by Maretzek, the impresario, who engaged him for a season at the Academy of Music, N. Y., where Sbriglia appeared with Adelina Patti (1860); he then made a grand tour of the U. S. with Parodi and Adelaide Phillipps; also sang in Mexico and Havana. He returned to Europe in 1875 and settled in Paris, where he became a highly successful vocal teacher. Jean, Joséphine, and Édouard de Reszke studied with him when they were already professional artists; Sbriglia trained the baritone voice of Jean de Reszke, enabling him to sing tenor roles. Pol Plançon, Nordica, and Sibyl Sanderson were also his pupils.

Scalchi (skahl'-kē), **Sofia,** celebrated Italian mezzo-soprano; b. Turin, Nov. 29, 1850; d. Rome, Aug. 22, 1922. She made her début at Mantua in 1866 as Ulrica in Verdi's *Ballo in Maschera;* then sang throughout Italy; appeared in concert in London (Sept. 16, 1868) and at Covent Garden (Nov. 5,

1868) as Azucena, obtaining enormous success. She visited the U. S. for the first time in 1882 with Mapleson's opera company; sang in the opening season of the Metropolitan Opera (1883-84) and again in 1891-96. She then toured with unfailing success in Russia, Austria, Spain, and South America. She married Count Luigi Lolli in 1875; in 1896 she retired to her estate in Turin; in 1921 went to Rome, where she remained until her death. Her voice had a range of 2½ octaves; it was essentially a contralto voice, but with so powerful a high register that she successfully performed soprano parts.

Scalero, Rosario, eminent Italian pedagogue and composer; b. Moncalieri, near Turin, Dec. 24, 1870; d. Settimo Vittone, near Turin, Dec. 25, 1954. He studied violin with Sivori in Genoa, and in London with Wilhelmj; general subjects with Mandyczewski in Vienna. In 1896 he was engaged as violin teacher in Lyons, France; then was instructor at Santa Cecilia, Rome, and examiner at the Naples Cons., and later at the Cons. of Parma. In 1919 he came to the U. S., and was head of the composition classes at the David Mannes School, N. Y.; in 1928 joined the faculty of the Curtis Institute of Music, Philadelphia; among his students there were Samuel Barber, Gian Carlo Menotti, and Lukas Foss. He wrote a violin concerto; *Neapolitan Dances,* for violin and piano; chamber music; sacred songs; etc.

Scaria, Emil, Austrian bass singer; b. Graz, Sept. 18, 1838; d. Blasewitz, near Dresden, July 22, 1886. He studied with Netzer at Graz, with Lewy at Vienna, and with Garcia in London. After singing in opera in Dessau (1862), Leipzig (1863), and Dresden (1864), he acquired a fine reputation; in 1872 he was engaged as a member of the Court Opera of Vienna. He excelled in Wagner's operas; created the role of Gurnemanz in *Parsifal.* —Cf. A. Neumann, *Erinnerungen an Richard Wagner* (Leipzig, 1907; English transl., N. Y., 1908).

Scarlatti, Alessandro, founder of the 'Neapolitan School' of music; b. Palermo, May 2, 1660; d. Naples, Oct. 24, 1725. He was brought to Rome in 1672, and was a pupil there of Carissimi; in 1679 he conducted his first known opera, *L'Errore innocente,* at Rome; then followed a performance there of *L'Onestà negli amori* at the palace of Queen Christina of Sweden (Feb. 6, 1680); on the score of another opera, *Il Pompeo* (Rome, Jan. 25, 1683), he is styled maestro di cappella to the Queen. In 1694 he was maestro to the Viceroy at Naples. In 1703 he became assistant maestro to Foggia at S. Maria Maggiore, Rome, and succeeded him as 1st maestro in 1707, resigning in 1709 and returning to Naples, where he subsequently became maestro of the royal chapel. He also taught music; was briefly engaged at the Cons. di Santa Maria di Loreto, Naples (1689), but never had prolonged tenure; among his private pupils was Hasse, who studied with him in 1724. Scarlatti wrote approximately 115 operas (about 50 are still extant); *La Rosaura* (Rome, 1690), ed. by Eitner, was printed by the 'Gesellschaft für Musikforschung,' vol. XIV; in *Teodora Augusta* (Rome, Jan. 3, 1693) he uses an incipient *recitativo obbligato* accompanied by the entire orchestra; also several arias with the first part sung *da capo,* a style that was later generally adopted by opera composers. —An aria and a duet from *Laodicea e Bernice* (Naples, 1701) have been publ. by J. J. C. Maier, also a terzet and quartet from *La Griselda* (Rome, 1721), with German transl. by Wolzogen; in *Il Tigrane,* his most celebrated opera, marked in the libretto as his 106th work for the stage (Naples, Feb. 16, 1715), the orch. comprises violins, violas, cellos, double-basses, 2 flutes, 2 oboes, 2 bassoons, and 2 horns; *Il Trionfo dell'onore,* his only comic opera (Naples, Nov. 26, 1718), was transl. into English by Geoffrey Dunn (London, July 23, 1937). Other important operas are: *Olimpia vendicata* (Naples, Dec. 23, 1685); *La Statira* (Rome, Jan. 5, 1690); *Pirro e Demetrio* (Naples, Jan. 28, 1694); *Il Prigioniero fortunato* (Naples, Dec. 14, 1698). 14 oratorios are also known; he is said to have written over 200 Masses (up to ten parts), besides much other sacred music (*Concerti sacri,* motets *a* 1-4, with 2 violins, viola, and organ, were publ. at Amsterdam as op. 1 and 2; a few separate numbers are in the collections of Choron, the Prince of Moskowa, Commer [a *Tu es Petrus*], Dehn, Proske, and Rochlitz; Choron also publ. a Requiem, and Proske a Mass); his secular vocal music includes madrigals (one *a* 4, is in Padre Martini's 'Esempli di contrappunto fugato'), serenatas, duets, and a vast number of cantatas (Dent gives a list of 600 with basso continuo and 61 with instruments). The Cons. Library at Paris has 8 vols. of these in MS. He also composed 12 symphonies (concertos) for small orch., a string quartet, a sonata for 3 flutes and one for 2 flutes, 2 violins, and continuo, one for flute, 2 violins, and continuo, 2 suites for flute and harpsichord, variations on Corelli's *La Follia,* toccatas for harpsichord, etc. Some of his works have been publ. by G. Bas and F. Nekes (a 4-voiced *Missa ad voces æquales),* Lenzewski (concertos for strings and continuo), Tebaldini (sonata for flute and strings), J. S. Shedlock (toccatas for harpsichord; 9 vols.), Tagliapietra, Longo (keyboard compositions), etc. —Cf. E. J. Dent, *The Operas of A. S.,* in 'Sammelbände der Internationalen Musik-Gesellschaft' (IV, 1); id., *A. S. His Life and Works* (London, 1905); Ch. Van den Borren, *A. S. et l'esthétique de l'opéra napolitain* (1922); A. Lorenz, *A. S.s Opern in Wien,* in 'Zeitschrift für Musikwissenschaft' IX, 2 (1926); id., *A. S.s Jugendopern* (2 vols., Augsburg, 1927); E. Jaloux, *Sur un air de S.* (Maastricht, 1928); A. Cametti, in 'Musica d'oggi' (Feb., 1931); P. Fienga, *La véritable patrie et la famille d'Alessandro Scarlatti,* in the 'Revue Musicale' (Jan., 1929); *Gli Scarlatti* (Siena, 1940); O. Tiby, *La Famiglia Scarlatti: nuove ricerche e documenti* (Rome, 1947).

Scarlatti, (Giuseppe) Domenico, famous Italian composer and harpsichordist; son of Alessandro Scarlatti; b. Naples, Oct. 26, 1685; d. Madrid, July 23, 1757. A pupil of his father, he was named organist and composer at the royal chapel in Naples when he was 16; two years later his first operas, *Ottavia restituita al trono* and *Il Giustino,* were produced in Naples (Dec. 19, 1703). In 1705 he was sent by his father to Venice, where he studied with Gasparini. In 1709 he was back in Rome, where he engaged in a friendly contest with Handel, who was adjudged his superior on the organ, while Scarlatti held his own on the harpsichord. From 1709-14 he was maestro di cappella to Queen Maria Casimira of Poland, for whose private theater (in her palace at Rome) he composed 7 operas and an oratorio. He had been appointed in 1713 assistant to Bai, the maestro di cappella at the Vatican, and upon the latter's death in 1714 succeeded him as maestro; resigned in 1719. During this time was also maestro to the Portuguese Ambassador to the Holy See. There is no evidence that Scarlatti went to London in 1720, as is usually stated. But in that year his opera *Amor d'un ombra e gelosia d'un'aura* (rewritten as *Narciso)* was produced there at the Haymarket Theatre under Roseingrave's direction (May 30), and his brother Francesco gave a concert there in September. Scarlatti went to Lisbon in 1719 or 1720, where he was engaged as maestro of the royal chapel and music-teacher to the Princess Maria Barbara, for whom he composed his famous *Esercizi per gravicembalo,* of which the first were publ. in 1738. In 1729 the princess married the heir to the Spanish throne, and Scarlatti accompanied her to Madrid, where he spent the rest of his life. When Maria Barbara became queen in 1746, he was appointed her 'maestro de cámara.' After leaving Italy he returned only twice, once for a brief visit to his father at Naples in 1724, and the other time to marry Maria Catalina Gentili on May 15, 1728, in Rome. In Madrid, Scarlatti does not appear to have composed operas; but he founded an instrumental school in Spain, the chief representative being P. Antonio Soler (q.v.), his pupil. He composed over 600 sonatas and pieces for harpsichord, besides operas, cantatas, and sacred music (2 Misereres *a* 4; a Stabat Mater; a Salve Regina for soprano and strings [1756], his last work); a *Fuga estemporanea per orchestra* (MS) in the library of the Univ. of Münster. The principal MS source for the harpsichord works of Scarlatti is the collection of the Biblioteca Marciana at Venice, which belonged originally to the Queen of Spain and at her death was brought to Italy by Farinelli. —Domenico Scarlatti's special claim to renown rests upon his harpsichord music; he studied the peculiarities of the instrument, and adapted his compositions to them, being one of the finest writers in the 'free style' (the homophonic 'song form' with graceful ornamentation, in contrast to the former—contrapuntal—vocal or organ style). He also obtained effects by the frequent crossing of the hands; runs in thirds and sixths; leaps wider than an octave; broken chords in contrary motion; tones repeated by rapidly changing fingers; etc. He has been called the founder of modern piano technique. —During Scarlatti's lifetime some of his keyboard pieces were printed in various eds. at London and Paris. Later editions include a collection by Czerny, of 200 pieces; Breitkopf, 60; Pauer, 50; Köhler, 12 sonatas and fugues; Tausig, 3 sonatas; Bülow, 18 pieces in suite-form; Schletterer, 18; André, 28; Banck, 30; Farrenc, 100 (in 'Trésor des pianistes'); Sauer, 25; Barth, 70; Gerstenberg, 5 sonatas (not included in the Longo ed.); Buonamici, 22 (in Schirmer's Library, vol. 73). Ricordi publ. Scarlatti's 'complete' harpsichord works, ed. by A. Longo, in 11 vols. (1 vol. as supplement; 1906 ff.), also a Thematic Index (Milan, 1937). 60 sonatas ed. by Ralph Kirkpatrick were publ. by G. Schirmer. —The most important publication dealing with the life and works of Domenico Scarlatti is Ralph Kirkpatrick's book, publ. in Princeton and London in 1953. Apart from clearing up biographical data, Kirkpatrick gives a new chronological numbering of works, which has been widely accepted and promises to supersede Longo's catalogue. Cf. also E. J. Dent, in the 'Monthly Mus. Record' (1906); id., in 'Auftakt' (1922); A. Longo, *D. Scarlatti e la sua figura nella storia della musica* (Naples, 1913); G. F. Malipiero, *D. Scarlatti,* in the 'Mus. Quarterly' (July, 1927); F. Torrefranca, *Le Origini italiane del romanticismo musicale* (Turin, 1930); W. Gerstenberg, *Die Klavierkompositionen D. Scarlattis* (1933); S. Sitwell, *A Background for D. Scarlatti* (London, 1935); U. Rolandi, *Per una bio-bibliografia di Scarlatti,* in 'Bolletino dei Musicisti' (Nov., 1935); C. Valabrega, *D. Scarlatti, il suo secolo, la sua opera* (with 233 musical examples; Modena, 1937); S. A. Luciani, *D. Scarlatti* (biographical and bibliographical notes; valuable), in the 'Rassegna Musicale' (Dec., 1938; Jan. and Feb., 1939; also reprinted separately); *Gli Scarlatti* (Siena, 1940); A. Solar Quintes, *Documentos sobre la familia de Domenico Scarlatti,* in the 'Anuario Musical' (Barcelona, 1949).

Scarlatti, Giuseppe, Italian composer, grandson of Alessandro Scarlatti; b. Naples, 1718; d. Vienna, Aug. 17, 1777. He was in Rome in 1739, and later in Lucca, where he married Barbara Stabili, a singer (1747). He went to Vienna in 1757, and remained there for 20 years until his death. He wrote 31 operas, produced in Rome, Florence, Lucca, Turin, Venice, Naples, Milan, and Vienna; of these the most successful was *L'Isola disabitata* (Venice, Nov. 20, 1757). Another Giuseppe Scarlatti (a nephew of Alessandro Scarlatti), whose name appears in some reference works, was not a musician. —Cf. H. Springer, *Das Partitur-Autograph von Giuseppe Scarlatti's bisher verschollener Clemenza di Tito,* in 'Beiträge zum Bibliotheks- und Buchwesen' (1913); *Gli Scarlatti* (Siena, 1940); O. Tiby, *La Famiglia Scarlatti: nuove ricerche e documenti* (Rome, 1947); Frank Walker, *Some Notes on the Scarlattis,* in 'Music Review' (Aug., 1951).

Scarmolin, (Anthony) Louis, composer and conductor; b. Schio, Italy, July 30, 1890; came to the U. S. as a boy; graduated from the N. Y. College of Music in 1907; served in the U. S. Army during World War I; returning to America, he settled in Philadelphia; then resided in Union City, N. J. He wrote 6 operas; numerous symph. poems, including *Night* (1937); *Overture on a Street Vendor's Ditty* (1938); *Dramatic Overture* (1938); *The Ambassador Overture* (1938); *Mercury Overture* (1939); *Visions,* a symph. impression (1939); *Dramatic Tone Poem* (Chicago, June 2, 1939); *Miniature Symphony* (Cleveland, Feb. 7, 1940); *The Clockmaker* for small orch. (N. Y., March 25, 1933). His works aggregate about 200 op. numbers.

Scarpini, Pietro, Italian pianist; b. Rome, April 6, 1911. After study in Rome, he made several tours in Europe; in 1940 was appointed teacher at the Florence Cons. He made his U. S. début with the N. Y. Philharmonic on Nov. 4, 1954. He specializes in modern works, but is also successful in the standard repertory.

Scelsi, Giacinto, Italian composer; b. La Spezia, Jan. 8, 1905. He studied in Rome and in France. Influenced by Schoenberg, he adopted the 12-tone method after 1930. — Works: for orch.: *Rotatives* (1930), *Rapsodie* (1931), concertino for piano and orch. (1934), *Ballade,* for cello and orch. (1945), *La Naissance du verbe,* cantata for chorus and orch. (Brussels, International Festival for Contemporary Music, June 28, 1950); string quartet; piano trio; piano sonata; songs.

Schaab, Robert, German organist and composer; b. Rötha, near Leipzig, Feb. 28, 1817; d. Leipzig, March 18, 1887. He studied with C. F. Becker and Mendelssohn; became organist of the Johanniskirche in Leipzig; publ. a great number of works for organ; his 60 *Choralvorspiele* (op. 118, 119, 121) are of value.

Schaaf, Edward Oswald, American composer; b. Brooklyn, Aug. 7, 1869; d. Newark, N. J., June 25, 1939. He was a physician; M. D., Bellevue Hospital Medical College, N. Y., 1894; studied at the Univ. of Vienna (1894-96); musically an autodidact, through intensive study of classical masterworks. He wrote a grand opera, 8 smaller operas, 2 symphonies, 4 string quartets, 2 Masses, 70 songs, 20 military band pieces, and 90 works for the player-piano. He publ. *A Study of Modern Operatic Art; The Art of Playing Piano Transcription;* etc.; lived most of his life in Newark.

Schachner, Rudolf Joseph, German pianist and composer; b. Munich, Dec. 31, 1821; d. Reichenhall, Aug. 15, 1896. He was a pupil of J. B. Cramer; appeared in concert in Vienna, Paris, Leipzig, etc.; in 1853, settled in London as a teacher; later went to Vienna. He composed 2 piano concertos and a number of pieces for piano solo: *Poésies musicales, Romance variée, Ombres et rayons, La Chasse,* etc.

Schacht, Matthias Henriksen, music lexicographer; b. Viborg, Jütland, April 29, 1660; d. Kierteminde, Aug. 8, 1700. He was a pedagogue; served as rector; left in MS a music dictionary, *Bibliotheca musica* (publ. by G. Skjerne as *Musicus danicus,* Copenhagen, 1928), which Gerber utilized for his lexicon.

Schacht, Theodor von, German composer; b. Strasbourg, 1748; d. Regensburg, June 20, 1823. He studied in Stuttgart with Jommelli; then went to Regensburg (1773), where he became music director of the town theater; wrote numerous operas in German and Italian; also symphonies, concertos, and chamber music. He was a minor master of the contrapuntal art; wrote an amusing series of 84 canons, under the title *Divertimento del bel sesso nel soggiorno di Baden* (1811). —Cf. S. Färber, *Das Regensburger fürstlich Thurn und Taxissche Hoftheater und seine Oper* (Regensburg, 1936).

Schack (Žak), Benedikt, tenor and composer; b. Mirowitz, Bohemia, 1758; d. Munich, Dec. 11, 1826. He studied in Prague and Vienna; made his operatic début in Salzburg (1786); became acquainted with Mozart's librettist Schikaneder, and through him met Mozart in Vienna (1789) and became friendly with him; he was the singer (if contemporary reports are to be trusted) who sang passages from the Requiem for the dying composer. Mozart wrote piano variations (K. 613) on an aria from Schack's opera *Die verdeckten Sachen.* Among Schack's theatrical pieces the following were performed in Vienna: *Der dumme Gärtner aus dem Gebirge* (July 12, 1789), *Die wiener Zeitung* (Jan. 12, 1791), *Die Antwort auf die Frage* (Dec. 16, 1792), *Die beiden Nannerin* (July 26, 1794).

Schad, Joseph, pianist and composer; b. Steinach, Germany, March 6, 1812; d. Bordeaux, July 4, 1879. He studied at the Würzburg Cons. and later with Aloys Schmitt at Frankfurt. In 1834 he became organist at Morges, Switzerland; in 1847, settled in Bordeaux, where he gained high repute as a piano teacher. He publ. a great number of melodious piano pieces which enjoyed some success during his lifetime: *Le Soupir, La Gracieuse, La Rose des Alpes, Fleur des Alpes, Tarentelle,* etc.; fantasias, transcriptions.

Schadewitz, Carl, German composer; b. St. Ingbert, Jan. 23, 1887; d. Reppendorf, near Kitzingen, March 27, 1945. Studied in Würzburg, and lived there most of his life as choral conductor and teacher. He was a prolific composer; his works include a musical fairy tale, *Johannisnacht;* a 'Romantic' oratorio,' *Kreislers Heimkehr;* an opera, *Laurenca;* a tone poem, *Heldengedenken* (1943); a number of songs, of which the cycle *Die Heimat* (1934) is outstanding; much chamber music; choruses. —Cf. A. Maxsein, *Carl Schadewitz* (Würzburg, 1954).

Schaefer, Karl Ludolf, German physiologist, physicist, and acoustician; b. Rostock, July 2, 1866; d. Berlin, Feb. 12, 1931. He obtained his M. D. diploma in 1889; then studied with Carl Stumpf; taught vocal physiology at the Berlin Hochschule. He publ. *Musikalische Akustik* (1902; 2nd ed., 1912), *Einführung in die Musikwissenschaft auf physikalischer, physiologischer und psychologischer Grundlage* (Leipzig, 1915); and numerous other studies on acoustics and tone psychology.

Schaeffner, André, French musicologist; b. Paris, Feb. 7, 1895. He studied at the Schola Cantorum with Vincent d'Indy; at the same time pursued research in ethnology; contributed numerous articles on folk music and on modern composers to French magazines; publ. an important monograph on Stravinsky (1931); *Origine des instruments de musique* (1936); *Les Instruments de musique en pays Kissi* (1949); etc.

Schäfer, Dirk, eminent Dutch composer, pianist, and pedagogue; b. Rotterdam, Nov. 23, 1873; d. Amsterdam, Feb. 16, 1931. He studied in Rotterdam and at the Cons. of Cologne; after a European tour as a pianist, he settled at The Hague (1895-1904); from 1904, mostly in Amsterdam, where he was active as pianist and teacher. —Works: *Rapsodie javanaise,* for orch. (1904); *Suite pastorale,* for orch. (1906); 2 violin sonatas; piano quintet; cello sonata; *Sonate inaugurale,* for piano; other piano works; songs. —Cf. *Herinnering aan Dirk Schäfer* (Amsterdam, 1932); Cor Backers, *Nederlandse Componisten van 1400 tot op onze tijd* (Amsterdam, 1942; pp. 110-12).

Schäffer, August, German composer; b. Rheinsberg, Aug. 25, 1814; d. Baden-Baden, Aug. 7, 1879. Pupil, from 1833, of Mendelssohn at Berlin, where he spent most of his life. His humorous duets and quartets won great popularity; he also composed symphonies, string quartets, piano pieces, etc., and produced a few operas: *Emma von Falkenstein* (Berlin, 1839), *José Riccardo* (Hanover, 1857), *Junker Habakuk* (Hanover, 1861).

Schäffer, Julius, German choral conductor and writer; b. Krevese, near Osterburg, Sept. 28, 1823; d. Breslau, Feb. 10, 1902. He studied theology at Halle, where friendship with Franz, and musicians in the nearby city of Leipzig, won him over to music. In 1850 he went to Berlin to study under Dehn; 1855, to Schwerin, where he founded and conducted the 'Schlosskirchenchor,' modelled after the Berlin cathedral choir. In 1860 he became conductor of the 'Singakademie,' Breslau. —Works: chorale-books (1866; 1880); songs and part-songs; in defence of Franz's 'additional accompaniments' to scores by Bach and Handel, Schäffer wrote, *versus* Chrysander, *Zwei Beurteiler Robert Franz's* (1863), *Fr. Chrysander in seinen Klavierauszugen zur deutschen Händel-Ausgabe* (1876), and *R. Franz in seinen Bearbeitungen älterer Vokalwerke* (1877); also *Die Breslauer Singakademie* (1875). —Cf. E. Bonn, *J. Schäffer* (Breslau, 1903).

Schaffrath, Christoph, German composer; b. Hohenstein-on-Elbe, 1709; d. Berlin, Feb. 17, 1763. As harpsichordist he entered the service of Frederick the Great in 1735 (while the latter was still Crown Prince) at Rheinsberg, and in 1740 followed that monarch to Berlin. He wrote concertos and sonatas for harpsichord, chamber music, etc.

Schafhäutl, Karl Franz Emil von, German acoustician; b. Ingolstadt, Feb. 16, 1803; d. Munich, Feb. 25, 1890, as prof. of mining, etc., custodian of the State geological collections, etc. He was also a student of acoustics, and intimate with Theobald Böhm (q.v.), whom he advised and aided in the construction of his instruments. —Publ. *Theorie gedackter, zylindrischer und konischer Pfeifen und der Querflöten* (1833, in the 'Neue Annalen der Chemie'); *Über Schall, Ton, Knall und einige andere Gegenstände der Akustik* (1834, in the same; both separately printed); *Über Phonometrie* (1854); *Abt Georg Jos. Vogler; Sein Leben, Charakter und musikalisches System* (1888); also, in the 'Allgemeine musikalische Zeitung,' 1879, investigations into the phenomena of 'Klangfarbe' (tone color), with results at variance with Helmholtz's theory. —Cf. *Erinnerungen an K. Ett und K. von Schafhäutl,* in 'Kirchenmusikalisches Jahrbuch' (1891).

Schalk, Franz, Austrian conductor; b. Vienna, May 27, 1863; d. Edlach, Sept. 2, 1931. Pupil and friend of Anton Bruckner; 1888, Kapellmeister in Reichenbach; 1889-95, in Graz; 1895-98, in Prague; guest conductor at Covent Garden in 1898, 1907, and 1911; 1898-99, succeeded A. Seidl at the Metropolitan Opera House; 1899, conductor of the Berlin Royal Opera; from 1900 at the Vienna Hofoper; 1904-21, also conductor of the Vienna Gesellschaft der Musikfreunde and prof. of the classes in conducting at the Royal Academy of Music; from 1918 director of the Vienna State Opera (succeeded Gregor; 1919-24, co-director with R. Strauss; thereafter sole director). A tireless worker, he contributed much to the high artistic standards of the Vienna Opera. His book, *Briefe und Betrachtungen,* was brought out posthumously (Vienna, 1935).

Schalk, Josef, Austrian pianist and writer on music; brother of Franz Schalk; b. Vienna, March 24, 1857; d. there, Nov. 7, 1911. Studied with Bruckner and Epstein; piano teacher at the Vienna Cons. His arrangements of the Bruckner symphonies for piano 4 hands did much to make these works known, and his book, *Anton Bruckner und die moderne Musikwelt* (1885), effectively upheld Bruckner's music. He was also a friend of Hugo Wolf, whom he championed in an article in 1890.

Schall, Klaus, Danish composer; b. Copenhagen, April 28, 1757; d. near Copenhagen, Aug. 10, 1835. He was a violinist and theater conductor; wrote many instrumental pieces and 7 operas to Danish librettos, of which the following (all produced in Copenhagen) were the most successful: *Claudine af Villa Bella* (Jan. 29, 1787), *Kinafarerne* (March 2, 1792), *Domherren i Milano* (March 16, 1802), and *De tre Galninger* (March 19, 1816).

Scharfe, Gustav, German singing teacher; b. Grimma, Saxony, Sept. 11, 1835; d. Dresden, June 25, 1892. He was a baritone at the Dresden Court Opera for 11 years; teacher of singing at the Cons. (1874); professor (1880). —Publications: *Die methodische Entwickelung der Stimme,* a standard work; also choruses and songs.

Scharfenberg, William, editor; b. Kassel, Germany, Feb. 22, 1819; d. Quogue, Long Island, N. Y., Aug. 8, 1895. A pupil of Hummel at Weimar till 1837; returned to Kassel, playing 2nd violin in Spohr's quartet; went to New York in 1838, making his début as a pianist in Hummel's septet, and at once took a leading position in the city as a teacher and concert player. He was successively secretary, vice-president, treasurer, and (1863) president of the Philharmonic Society. For many years he was music editor and adviser to the firm of G. Schirmer, and did excellent editorial work.

Scharrer, August, composer and conductor; b. Strasbourg, Oct. 18, 1866; d. Fürth, Oct. 24, 1936. As a young man he was sent on a business trip to the U. S.; in Salt Lake City he visited the Mormon Tabernacle, and was granted permission to play on the magnificent organ; after improvising for hours he resolved to devote himself entirely to music. He studied in Strasbourg, and Berlin (composition with H. Hofmann and Ph. Rüfer, musicology with Spitta and Bellermann). In 1897-98 he was Mottl's assistant in Karlsruhe; 1898-1900, Kapellmeister at the Stadtheater in Regensburg; 1900-04, 2nd conductor of the Kaim Orch. in Munich; 1904-07, conductor of the Philharmonic Orch. in Berlin; 1907-14, director of the Strasbourg Cons.; 1914-25, conductor of the 'Lehrer-Gesangverein' in Nuremberg. He wrote an opera, *Die Erlösung* (Strasbourg, Nov. 21, 1895); a symph. poem, *Per Aspera ad Astra;* overtures; songs with orch. accompaniment.

Scharrer, Irene, English pianist; b. London, Feb. 2, 1888. She studied at the Royal Academy of Music under Tobias Matthay; début in 1901; then appeared in numerous recitals and with all the great English orchestras; successful tours in Europe and the U. S.; then taught at the Matthay School in London.

Scharwenka, (Ludwig) Philipp, composer and pedagogue; b. Samter, Posen, Feb. 16, 1847; d. Bad Nauheim, July 16, 1917. After a gymnasial course at Posen, he entered Kullak's Academy at Berlin in 1865, studying chiefly under Wüerst and H. Dorn; in 1870, teacher of theory and composition at the Academy. In 1881 he founded, with his brother, Xaver, the 'Scharwenka Cons.'; also accompanied his brother to New York in 1891, but returned in 1892, joining Goldschmidt in the direction of the Cons., which was amalgamated with the Klindworth Cons. in 1893. In 1880 he married the violinist Marianne Stresow (1865-1918), who then taught in his Cons. —Works: For orch.: op. 19, *Serenade;* op. 20, *Zwei polnische Volkstänze;* op. 37, *Wald und Berggeister,* intermezzo; op. 38, *Polnische Tanzweisen;* op. 40, *Liebesnacht,* 'Fantasiestück'; op. 43, *Festouvertüre;* op. 76, *Arkadische Suite;* op. 87, *Frühlingswogen,* symph. poem; op. 92, *Traum und Wirklichkeit,* do.; op. 95, violin concerto in G; op. 96, symphony in D minor; op. 108, *Dramatische Fantasie;* op. 115, *Symphonia brevis* in E♭. Chamber music: piano quintet; 2 string quartets; 3 piano trios; trio for violin, viola, and piano; 2 violin sonatas; viola sonata in G minor; cello sonata. Minor pieces for violin and piano, and for cello and piano; numerous piano pieces (op. 61, 3 sonatas; op. 85, *Zwei Rhapsodien;* etc.); choruses; cantatas; songs.

Scharwenka, (Franz) Xaver, brother of the preceding; b. Samter, Jan. 6, 1850; d. Berlin, Dec. 8, 1924. Pianist and composer; pupil of Kullak and Wüerst at Kullak's Academy, graduating in 1868, when he was appointed teacher there. First public concert at the Singakademie, 1869, very successful; for about 10 years he gave an annual series of 3 chamber concerts there (with Sauret and H. Grünfeld); also arranged and conducted orchestral subscription concerts. In 1874 he gave up his position as teacher, and made pianistic tours through Europe and America. In 1881 he founded the Berlin 'Scharwenka Cons.,' of which he was director till 1891, then establishing his Cons. in New York; made his American début as pianist playing his own concerto, N. Y., Jan. 24, 1891. In 1898 he returned to Berlin, as co-director of the Klindworth-Scharwenka Cons., and head of the piano classes; resigned in 1914, and established his own 'Meisterschule' for piano in Berlin. He revisited the U. S. in 1913-14. Scharwenka was court pianist to the Emperor of Austria. —Works: opera *Mataswintha* (Weimar, Oct. 4, 1896; Metropolitan Opera, N. Y., April 1, 1907); 4 piano concertos; many effective piano pieces (Polish Dances, etc.); numerous songs; church music; technical works, *Beiträge zur Fingerbildung* (op. 77), *Studien im Oktavenspiel* (op. 78), *Meisterschule des Klavierspiels* (a collection of famous études progressively arranged). Also many arrangements; and a critical edition of Schumann's piano works.—Author of *Methodik des Klavierspiels* (1907; with A. Spanuth) and *Klänge aus meinem Leben: Erinnerungen eines Musikers* (Leipzig, 1922).

Schatz, Albert, b. Rostock, Germany, May 19, 1839; d. there, Oct. 18, 1910. From earliest youth he was especially interested in opera and its history; although a merchant, he spent much time collecting materials for a history of the opera. After living for 7 years in San Francisco he returned in 1873 to his native city, where he took over the music business of Ludwig Trutschel. In 1867 he formed the plan of writing the history of opera from original sources, and began to collect the original librettos of the first performances; after almost half a century he had in his possession about 12,000; the statistical material he had entered on about 80,000 cards, each containing the title of an opera, name of composer and librettist, city, theater, and date, not only of first performance (world première), but also of first performances in other cities. In 1908 he sold his valuable collection of librettos, one of the largest in the world, to the Library of Congress in Washington, where it is kept intact as a separate unit. —Cf. O. G. Sonneck's preface to *Catalogue of Opera Librettos printed before 1800* (2 vols.; Washington, 1914).

Schaub (schowp), **Hans Ferdinand,** German composer, conductor, and teacher; b. Frankfurt, Sept. 22, 1880. He studied at the Hoch Cons. there with Iwan Knorr (theory) and Carl Friedberg (piano); with Arnold Mendelssohn in Darmstadt, and with Humperdinck in Berlin; also took lessons with Richard Strauss. He then became instructor at the Cons. of Breslau (1903-06); in 1906, settled in Berlin as teacher at Benda's Cons. and editor of the 'Deutsche Musikerzeitung.' In 1916 he moved to Hamburg as music critic and pedagogue. After 1951 he lived in Hanstedt. —Works: *Passacaglia,* for orch. (1928); *3 Intermezzi,* for small orch.; *Capriccio,* for violin and piano; the cantata *Den Gefallenen* (1940); oratorio, *Deutsches Te Deum* (1942).

Schauffler, Robert Haven, American writer on music; b. Brünn, Moravia (of American parents), April 8, 1879. He was educated at Princeton Univ., and also took courses at the Univ. of Berlin; studied cello with B. Steindel, A. Schroeder, and A. Hekking. —Books: *The Musical Amateur* (Boston, 1911); *Fiddler's Luck, the Gay Adventures of a Musical Amateur* (Boston, 1920); *Beethoven: The Man who Freed Music* (N. Y., 1929; abridged ed. 1932 as *The Mad Musician;* new ed., 1937); *The Unknown Brahms* (N. Y., 1933); *The Magic of Music; an Anthology . . .* (N. Y., 1935); *Florestan: the Life and Work of Robert Schumann* (N. Y., 1945); *Franz Schubert: The Ariel of Music* (N. Y., 1949); also *Fiddler's Folly and Encores* (N. Y., 1942); various smaller publications.

Schaum, John W., American piano pedagogue; b. Milwaukee, Jan. 27, 1905; studied at Milwaukee State Teachers College, at Marquette Univ. (B.M., 1931), and Northwestern Univ. (M.M., 1934). He established a successful piano teaching class in Milwaukee and publ. several piano methods and many collections of piano pieces that sold an enormous number of copies: *The Schaum Piano Course* (9 vols.); *The Schaum Adult Piano Course* (3 vols.); *The Schaum Duet Albums* (2 vols.); also theory books, *The Schaum Theory Lessons* (2 vols.) and *The Schaum Note Spellers* (2 vols.)

Schebek (shā'-bek), **Edmund,** writer on music; b. Petersdorf, Moravia, Oct. 22, 1819; d. Prague, Feb. 11, 1895, as Imperial councillor and secretary of the Chamber of Commerce. He wrote the official (Austrian) report on the musical instruments at the Paris Exposition of 1855 (separate reprint 1858); *Der Geigenbau in Italien und sein deutscher Ursprung* (1875; in English, London, 1877); and *Zwei Briefe über J. J. Froberger* (1874).

Schebest (shā'-best), **Agnese,** noted mezzo-soprano; b. Vienna, Feb. 10, 1813; d. Stuttgart, Dec. 22, 1869. She studied at Dresden, and sang in the opera there; publ. an autobiography, *Aus dem Leben einer Künstlerin* (1857).

Schechter, Boris. See **Shekhter, Boris.**

Scheel (shāl), **Fritz,** conductor; b. Lübeck, Germany, Nov. 7, 1852; d. Philadelphia, March 13, 1907. His grandfather and father were orchestral conductors, and at 10 the boy played the violin in his father's orch.; 1864-69, pupil of F. David in Leipzig. At 17 he began his career as concertmaster and conductor at Bremerhaven; in 1873, solo violin and conductor of the summer concerts in Schwerin; succeeded Hans Sitt in 1884 as conductor of the Chemnitz municipal orch.; 1890-3, conductor of orchestral concerts in Hamburg. Came to America in 1893, and after conducting some orchestral concerts in New York went to Chicago in 1894 as conductor of the Trocadero concerts at the Columbian Exposition; in 1895 he established the San Francisco Symph. Orch., which he conducted for 4 seasons; then accepted an engagement to conduct a series of summer concerts at Woodside Park, Philadelphia. His playing of Beethoven's symphonies induced influential music-lovers to organize the 'Philadelphia Orchestral Association,' which established in the fall of 1900 the

Philadelphia Orchestra, of which Scheel was conductor until his death. —Cf. Frances A. Wister, *25 Years of the Philadelphia Orchestra 1900-1925* (Philadelphia, 1925); John H. Mueller, *The American Symphony Orchestra* (Bloomington, Ind., 1951, pp. 125-27); also 'Dictionary of American Biography' XVI.

Scheff, Fritzi, celebrated soprano; b. Vienna, Aug. 30, 1879; d. New York, April 8, 1954. She studied singing with her mother, Hortense Scheff, of the Vienna Opera, and adopted her last name, having previously appeared under her father's name, Yager. She made her operatic début in Frankfurt (1899); appeared at the Metropolitan Opera, N. Y., as Marzelline in *Fidelio* (Dec. 28, 1900), and continued for 3 seasons as a member of the company. Later she shifted to light opera, and it was in this field that she became famous. She created the role of Fifi in Victor Herbert's operetta *Mlle Modiste* (Trenton, N. J., Oct. 7, 1905); her singing of Fifi's waltz song 'Kiss Me Again' became a hallmark of her career. Her 3 marriages (to Baron Fritz von Bardeleben, the American writer John Fox Jr., and the singer George Anderson) ended in divorce.

Scheffler, Siegfried, German composer; b. Ilmenau, May 15, 1892. He studied at the Leipzig Cons. with Max Reger, Stephan Krehl, Hans Sitt, and others; at the Univ. of Leipzig with Hugo Riemann and Arnold Schering; then in Berlin with Humpderdinck and Kretzschmar. From 1919 till 1924 he filled various positions as theater conductor; in 1924 settled in Hamburg, where he became the music critic of the 'Hamburger Nachrichten.' —Works: *Wunderhorn Lieder* (1914); *Rokoko-Novelle,* for orch. (1923); *Morgen im Walde,* for male chorus a cappella (1953); incidental music to various plays; etc. He publ. *Richard Wagner* (2 vols.; Hamburg, 1928) and *Melodie der Welle* (Berlin, 1933).

Scheibe, Johann Adolf, German theorist and composer; b. Leipzig, May 3, 1708; d. Copenhagen, April 22, 1776. Law-student at Leipzig, but on his father's death had recourse to his musical training to support himself; failing to obtain the post of organist at the Thomaskirche in the competition (adjudicated by Bach, among others) with Görner, he traveled for a time, and settled in Hamburg, publishing a paper, 'Der critischer Musicus,' from 1737-40 (in No. 6 is a sharp attack on Bach). In 1740 he became Kapellmeister to the Margrave of Brandenburg-Culmbach; in 1744, court conductor at Copenhagen, where he was pensioned in 1758. He had continued the publication of 'Der critischer Musicus,' issuing an enlarged edition in 1745, containing discussions of topics broached in that paper. —Publ. *Abhandlung vom Ursprung und Alter der Musik, insonderheit der Vocalmusik* (1754; maintains that part-songs originated with Northern peoples); an *Abhandlung über das Recitativ* (1764-65); *Über die musikalische Composition* (only vol. 1, of the 4 projected, was publ. in 1773); etc. —His publ. compositions include a Danish opera, *Thusnelda* (Copenhagen, 1749); tragic cantatas *a* 2, with clavier; songs; *Musikalische Erquickungstunden* (6 sonatas for flute with continuo); 3 sonatas for flute with harpsichord. In MS he left 2 oratorios, about 200 church works, 150 flute concertos, 30 violin concertos, etc. —Cf. E. Reichel, *Gottsched und J. A. Scheibe,* in 'Sammelbände der Internationalen Musik-Gesellschaft' (II, 1901); E. Rosenkaimer, *J. A. Scheibe als Verfasser seines 'Critischen Musicus'* (dissertation, Bonn, 1923); K. A. Storch, *J. A. Scheibes Anschauungen von d. musikalischen Historie, Wissenschaft und Kunst* (diss., Leipzig, 1923).

Scheibler (shī'-bler), **Johann Heinrich,** inventor and writer on music; b. Montjoie, near Aix-la-Chapelle, Nov. 11, 1777; d. Krefeld, Nov. 20, 1837. A silk manufacturer at Krefeld, he became interested in acoustic phenomena, and invented an apparatus consisting of 56 tuning forks, for tuning fixed-tone instruments acording to the equally tempered scale. He publ. several pamphlets to explain his invention: *Der physikalische und musikalische Tonmesser* (1834); *Anleitung, die Orgel vermittelst der Stösse (vulgo Schwebungen) und des Metronoms correct gleichschwebend zu stimmen* (1834); etc., all united as *Schriften über physikalische und musikalische Tonmessung . . .* (1838). His system is more clearly explained by Töpfer (1842), Vincent (1849), and Lecomte (1856). At the Stuttgart Congress of physicists in 1834, Scheibler proposed the pitch of $a^1 = 440$ (vibrations) at 69 degrees Fahrenheit, which was adopted (hence called the 'Stuttgart pitch'). —Cf. J. J. Löhr, *Über die Scheibler'sche Erfindung überhaupt und dessen Pianoforte- und Orgel-Stimmung insbesondere* (Krefeld, 1836).

Scheidemann (shī'-dŭh-man), **Heinrich,** German composer; b. Hamburg, c. 1596; d. there, 1663. Important organist; pupil and successor of his father, Hans Scheidemann, organist of the Katherinenkirche; also studied under Sweelinck at Amsterdam. His successor was Reinken. Of his works very little was publ., but many works for organ and harpsichord were preserved in MS. Modern eds. by M. Seiffert in his 'Organum' (15 preludes and fugues for organ), K. Straube and F. Dietrich (other organ works), R. Buchmayer, and G. Tagliapietra. —Cf. M. Seiffert's essay in 'Vierteljahrsschrift für Musikwissenschaft' (1891); R. Buchmayer, *Musikgeschichtliche Ergebnisse einer Reise nach Lüneburg,* in 'Dresdener Anzeiger' (July 5-26, 1903).

Scheidemantel (shī'-dŭh-man-tel), **Karl,** German baritone; b. Weimar, Jan. 21, 1859; d. there, June 26, 1923. He was a pupil of Bodo Borchers, and sang at the court theater in Weimar, 1878-86, also studied with Stockhausen in the summers of 1881-83. Member of the Dresden court opera from 1896-1911; 1911-20, prof. at the 'Grossherzogliche Musikschule' in Weimar; 1920-22, director of the Landesoper in Dresden. In 1909 the Dresden Opera brought out Mozart's *Così fan tutte* with an entirely new text by Scheidemantel (as *Dame Kobold).* His new transl. of *Don Giovanni* won the prize of the 'Deutscher Bühnenverein' (1914). He publ. *Stimmbildung* (1907; 4th ed. as *Gesangsbildung,* 1913; in English, 1910); also ed. a collection of songs, 'Meisterweisen' (1914; 6 parts). —Cf. P. Trede, *K. Scheidemantel* (Dresden, 1911).

Scheidt (shīt), **Samuel,** famous German organist and composer; b. Halle-on-Saale (baptized Nov. 4), 1587; d. there, March 24, 1654; pupil of Sweelinck in Amsterdam; organist of the Moritzkirche, and Kapellmeister to Margrave Christian Wilhelm of Brandenburg, at Halle. He was among the first to treat the working-out of the chorale artistically, and in true organ style. Principal work, *Tabulatura nova* (1624, 3 vols.; republ., 1892, as vol. I of 'Denkmäler deutscher Tonkunst'; contains figured chorales, toccatas, fantasias, passamezzi, a Mass, Magnificats, psalms, hymns); further a *Tabulaturbuch* (1650); 100 psalms *a* 4; *Cantiones sacrae a 8* (1620); *Concerti sacri 2-12 voc., adjectis symphoniis et choris instrumentalibus* (1621; 1622); *Ludi musici* (2 parts, 1621, 1622; Paduane, Gagliarde, etc.); *Liebliche Kraft-Blümlein* (1635); *Newe geistliche Conzerten a* 2-3 with figured bass (1631); the same, Part II (1634); Part III (1635); Part IV (1640); *70 Symphonien auf Conzerten-Manier a* 3 with figured bass (1644). The collected ed. of Scheidt's works begun by G. Harms and continued by C. Mahrenholz embraces 5 vols. (1923-37). —Cf. M. Seiffert in 'Vierteljahrsschrift für Musikwissenschaft' (vol. 7, 1891); A. Werner, *Samuel und Gottfried Scheidt,* in 'Sammelbände der Internationalen Musik-Gesellschaft' (1900); C. Mahrenholz, *S. Scheidt* (1924); R. Hünicken, *S. Scheidt* (Halle, 1934); W. Serauky, *S. Scheidt in seinen Briefen* (ib., 1937); C. Mahrenholz, *Aufgabe und Bedeutung der 'Tabulatura nova,'* in 'Musica' (March, 1954). See also the 'Festschrift' in honor of his 350th birthday (Wolfenbüttel, 1937).

Schein (shīn), **Johann Hermann,** important German composer; born Grünhain, Saxony, Jan. 20, 1586; d. Leipzig, Nov. 19, 1630. On the death of his father, the pastor at Meissen, in 1599, he entered the Electoral Chapel at Dresden as a soprano; studied at Schulpforta from 1603-07, then at Leipzig Univ. (jurisprudence); became 'Praeceptor' and 'Hausmusikmeister' to Captain von Wölffersdorf at Weissenfels; court Kapellmeister at Weimar in 1615; and succeeded Calvisius as cantor of the Thomasschule at Leipzig in 1616. He was among the first to make artistic adaptations of chorales for the organ; together with Praetorius and Schütz he shares the distinction of being among the pioneers to introduce into German music the newly developed monodic and instrumental style of the Italians. His most important work is *Cantional oder Gesangbuch Augspurgischer Confession . . . a* 4-6 (1627; 2nd ed., 1645; 312 German and Latin sacred songs and psalms). He also wrote other church music, sacred and secular madrigals, and 20 suites for strings (*Banchetto musicale,* 1617; among the earliest instrumental ensemble works in Germany). The complete edition of his works in 7 vols., ed. by Arthur Prüfer, and publ. by Breitkopf & Härtel (1901-23), is as follows: I, *Venus Kräntzlein* (1609) and *Banchetto musicale* (1617); II, *Musica Boscareccia* (1621, 1626, 1628); III, *Diletti Pastorali* (1624); and *Studenten-Schmauss* (1626, 1634); IV, *Cymbalum Sionium* (1615); V-VII, *Opella nova; geistliche Konzerte* (1618-26). —Cf. A. Prüfer, *J. H. Schein* (Leipzig, 1895); A. Prüfer, *J. H. Schein und das weltliche deutsche Lied des 17. Jahrhunderts,* in 'Beihefte der Internationalen Musik-Gesellschaft' (1908).

Scheinpflug, Paul, German violinist and composer; b. Loschwitz, near Dresden, Sept. 10, 1875; d. Memel, March 11, 1937. He studied violin with Rappoldi and composition with Draeseke at the Dresden Cons.; in 1898 went to Bremen as concertmaster of the 'Philharmonie' and conductor of the 'Liederkranz'; then was conductor of the Musikverein in Königsberg (1909-14); conducted the Blüthner Orch. in Berlin (1914-19); was music director in Duisburg (1920-28); in 1930 settled in Berlin, but continued to fill engagements as guest conductor. He wrote a symph. poem, *Frühling;* an *Ouvertüre zu einem Lustspiel;* piano quartet; string quartet; violin sonatas; many male choruses; *Worpswede,* song cycle for voice, piano, violin, and English horn; many song albums. —Cf. F. Dubitzky, *Paul Scheinpflug* (Leipzig, 1907).

Schelble, Johann Nepomuk, German singer and pedagogue; b. Hüfingen, Black Forest, May 16, 1789; d. Frankfurt, Aug. 7, 1837. He studied with Weisse in Donaueschingen, with Vogler in Darmstadt, and with Krebs in Stuttgart. From 1813 to 1816 he was in Vienna and became an intimate friend of Beethoven; then settled in Frankfurt, where he founded the famous Cäcilien-Verein (1818). His methods for teaching the musical rudiments and training the sense of absolute pitch were much admired; he enjoyed the esteem of many musicians of his time; Mendelssohn paid tribute to him in his correspondence. —Cf. K. Lanz, *Die Gehörsentwicklungs-Methode von Schelble* (Brunswick, 1873); O. Bormann, *J. N. Schelble* (dissertation; Frankfurt, 1926).

Schelle, Karl Eduard, German music critic; b. Biesenthal, near Berlin, May 31, 1816; d. Vienna, Nov. 16, 1882. In 1864 he succeeded Hanslick as music critic for the Vienna 'Presse'; also lectured on music history at the Vienna Cons. He publ. *Der Tannhäuser in Paris* (1861) and a valuable monograph, *Die päpstliche Sängerschule in Rom, genannt die Sixtinische Kapelle* (1872).

Schelling, Ernest (Henry), American conductor, composer, and pianist; b. Belvidere, N. J., July 26, 1876; d. New York, Dec. 8, 1939. He first appeared in public as a child prodigy playing the piano at the age of 4½ at the Academy of Music in Philadelphia. He was then sent to Paris, where he studied, still as a small child, with Mathias (a pupil of Chopin) in Paris, and also with Moszkowski; his other teachers were Leschetizky, Hans Huber, Barth, and finally Paderewski at Morges, Switzerland (1898-1902). Extended tours in Europe (from Russia to Spain) followed; he also toured in South America; settled permanently in the U. S. in 1905, and devoted most of his energies to conducting and composing. He conducted the young people's symph. concerts in N. Y. (from 1924), in Philadelphia, Boston, Cincinnati, Los Angeles, San Francisco, etc.; for 2 seasons (1936-38) he was regular conductor of the Baltimore Symph. Orch.; also made frequent appearances as conductor in Europe. Among his works the most successful was *A Victory Ball,* orchestral fantasy after the poem by Alfred Noyes, first performed by Stokowski with the Philadelphia Orch., on Feb. 23, 1923; other works are *Légende Symphonique* (Philadelphia, Oct. 31, 1913); *Suite Fantastique,* for orch. (Amsterdam, Oct. 10, 1907); *Impressions from an Artist's Life,* symph. variations for piano and orch. (Boston, Dec. 31, 1915, composer soloist); violin concerto (Boston Symph., Providence, R. I., Oct. 17, 1916, Fritz Kreisler soloist); *Morocco,* symph. tableau (N. Y., Dec. 19, 1927, composer conducting); symph. in C-sharp minor; Divertimento, for piano and string quartet; *Tarantella,* for string quartet; piano pieces; songs.

Schenck, Jean (Johann), German gamba virtuoso; b. Elberfeld (baptized Feb. 20), 1656; became chamber musician to the Elector-Palatine at Düsseldorf; later at Amsterdam, where he publ. toward the end of the 17th century, *Kunst-Oeffeningen . . .,* 15 sonatas for gamba with continuo (1688); *Il Giardino armonico,* sonatas for 2 violins, gamba, and continuo (1692); *Scherzi musicali* for gamba; 18 sonatas for violin with continuo (1693); etc.; also *Sang-Arien van d'opera Ceres en Bacchus.* —Cf. A. Einstein, *Zur deutschen Literatur für Viola da Gamba im 16. und 17. Jahrhundert* (Leipzig, 1905, pp. 32-35); H. Bol, *'Le Nymphe di Rheno' van Johann Schenck,* in 'Mens en Melodie' (Dec., 1954).

Schenck, Pyotr Petrovitch, Russian composer; b. St. Petersburg, Feb. 23, 1870; d. Perkiarvy, Finland, July 5, 1915. He studied piano at the Cons. of St. Petersburg; composition with Solovyev. He gave some concerts as pianist; then devoted himself to conducting; appeared in several European countries. His works are entirely under the influence of Tchaikovsky. He wrote 2 operas: *Acteya,* from Etruscan life, which had a concert performance, conducted by the composer, in St. Petersburg (Dec. 3, 1899) and *The Miracle of Roses* (St. Petersburg, Oct. 7, 1913); also ballet music; 3 symphonies; an orchestral fantasy, *Dukhy (Ghosts)*; a symph. poem, *Hero and Leander;* instrumental pieces; choruses; songs.

Schenk, Erich, Austrian musicologist; b. Salzburg, May 5, 1902. He took courses with Sandberger in Munich, at the Akademie der Tonkunst and at the Univ.; *Dr. phil.,* 1925; in 1929 became lecturer at the Univ. of Rostock; in 1940, prof. of musicology at the Univ. of Vienna; settled there as music editor and pedagogue. He publ. the following books: *G. A. Paganelli* (diss., Salzburg, 1928); *Johann Strauss* (Potsdam, 1940); *Musik in Kärnten* (Vienna, 1941); *Beethoven zwischen den Zeiten* (Bonn, 1944); *950 Jahre österreichische Musik* (Vienna, 1946); *Kleine wiener Musikgeschichte* (Vienna, 1946); *W. A. Mozart* (Zürich, 1955); edited works by Friderici, Keiser, Vivaldi, Fux, Gabrieli, Vitali, Porpora, etc.

Schenk, Johann, Austrian composer; b. Wiener-Neustadt, Nov. 30, 1753; d. Vienna, Dec. 29, 1836. He studied with Wagenseil in Vienna. In 1778 he had a Mass performed, which made his reputation; it was followed by other pieces of sacred music; then he began composing light operas, some of which enjoyed great popularity. It was from Schenk that Beethoven took surreptitious lessons while studying with Haydn. Operettas (all produced in Vienna): *Die Weinlese* (Oct. 12, 1785); *Die Weihnacht auf dem Lande* (Dec. 14, 1786); *Im Finstern ist nicht gut tappen* (Oct. 12, 1787); *Das unvermutete Seefest* (Dec. 9, 1789); *Das Singspiel ohne Titel* (Nov. 4, 1790); *Der Erntekranz* (July 9, 1791); *Achmet und Almanzine* (July 17, 1795); *Der Dorfbarbier* (Vienna, Oct. 30, 1796; his most popular work; originally staged as a comedy, June 18, 1785); *Die Jagd* (May 7, 1799); *Der Fassbinder* (Dec. 17, 1802). In 1819 he wrote his last works, the cantatas *Die Huldigung* and *Der Mai.* He also wrote 6 symphonies, string quartets, string trios, and songs. The score of *Der Dorfbarbier* was publ. by R. Haas in the 'Denkmäler der Tonkunst in Österreich' (vol. 66). —Cf. F. Staub, *Johann Schenk. Eine Skizze seines Lebens* (Vienna, 1901). A short biographical sketch was publ. in 'Studien zur Musikwissenschaft' (1924).

Schenker, Heinrich, outstanding Austrian theorist; b. Wisniowczyki, Galicia, June 19, 1868; d. Vienna, Jan. 14, 1935. He studied with Anton Bruckner at the Vienna Cons.; composed songs and piano pieces; Brahms liked them sufficiently to recommend Schenker to the publisher Simrock; for a while Schenker toured as accompanist of Messchaert, the baritone; then returned to Vienna and devoted himself entirely to the development of his theoretical research; gathered around him a group of enthusiastic disciples (Otto Vrieslander, Hermann Roth, Hans Weisse, Anthony van Hoboken, Oswald Jonas, Felix Salzer, John Petrie Dunn, and others). He endeavored to derive the basic laws of musical composition from a penetrating analysis of the standard masterworks. The result, in his middle and later writings, is the theory that each composition by a master is a horizontalization, through various stages, of a single triad. Schenker brought out editions for piano of works by Bach and Handel and the complete piano sonatas of Beethoven (also, separately, special analytical editions of the last five sonatas); supervised the publication of a facsimile of the original MS of Beethoven's Piano Sonata, op. 27, no. 2; etc. —Publications: *Neue musikalische Theorien und Fantasien:* I. *Harmonielehre* (1906; in English, ed. by O. Jonas, Chicago, 1954); II. *Kontrapunkt,* in 2 vols.: *Cantus Firmus und zweistimmiger Satz* (1910); *Drei- und mehrstimmiger Satz, Ubergänge zum freien Satz* (1920); III, *Der freie Satz* (1935; new ed. by O. Jonas, 1956); *Ein Beitrag zur Ornamentik* (based on K. P. E. Bach; 1908; new ed., 1954); a monograph on Beethoven's Ninth Symphony (1912) and one on his Fifth Symphony (1925); *Der Tonwille* (a periodical containing articles and analyses by Schenker and appearing at irregular intervals from 1921 to 1924); *Das Meisterwerk in der Musik* (a continuation of *Der Tonwille* in the form of an annual; 3 vols., 1925, 1926, 1930); *5 Urlinie-Tafeln* (N. Y., 1932); *Johannes Brahms: Oktaven und Quinten* (Vienna, 1933). —Cf. W. Riezler, *Die Urlinie,* in 'Die Musik' (April, 1930); I. Citkowitz, *The Role of H. Schenker,* in 'Modern Music' (vol. 11, 1933); O Jonas, *Das Wesen des musikalischen Kunstwerkes; eine Einführung in die Lehre H. Schenkers* (Vienna, 1934); R. Sessions, *H. Schenker's Contribution,* in 'Modern Music' (vol. 12, 1935); A. T. Katz, *H. Schenker's Method of Analysis,* in the 'Mus. Quarterly' (July, 1935); A. Waldeck and N. Broder, *Musical Synthesis as Expounded by H. Schenker,* in the 'Mus. Mercury' (Dec., 1935); A. T. Katz, *Challenge to Musical Tradition* (N. Y., 1945); F. Salzer, *Structural Hearing* (N. Y., 1952; a development of the Schenker theories).

Schenkman, Edgar, American conductor; b. New Market, N. J., May 9, 1908. He was a pupil at the Juilliard School of Music; conducted the Juilliard Orch.; then was conductor of the Toledo Friends of Music Orch. (1943-46); in 1948, appointed conductor of the Norfolk, Va., Orch.; in 1950, became director of the Virginia Music Festivals; in 1957, engaged as conductor of the Richmond, Va., Orch., while retaining his post at Norfolk.

Scherchen, Hermann, eminent German conductor; b. Berlin, June 21, 1891. He was self-taught in music; played the viola in the Berlin Philharmonic (1907-10); in 1911-12, toured with Arnold Schoenberg. In 1914 he obtained an engagement as symph. conductor in Riga; at the outbreak of World War I, he was interned in Russia; after the Armistice he returned to Berlin; founded and directed the 'Neue Musikgesellschaft' there (1918); edited the music periodical 'Melos' (1920-21); conducted numerous concerts at modern music festivals, in Donaueschingen, Frankfurt, etc.; conducted symph. concerts of the Collegium Musicum in Winterthur, Switzerland (1932-38); from 1928 till 1933, was in charge of the music of the Königsberg Radio. In 1933 he left Germany; edited the periodical 'Musica Viva' in Brussels (1933-36); conducted at music festivals in Barcelona (1936), Paris (1937), etc.; from 1936 also conducted in Winterthur. He distinguished himself as a scholarly exponent of modern music; conducted many world premières of ultra-modern works; publ. the valuable manual on conducting, *Lehrbuch des Dirigierens* (Leipzig, 1929; in English as *Handbook of Conducting,* London, 1933; 6th ed., 1949); *Vom Wesen der Musik* (Zürich, 1946; in English as *The Nature of Music,* London, 1947; Chicago, 1950); *Musik für Jedermann* (Winterthur, 1950).

Scheremetiev. See **Sheremetiev.**

Schering (shā'-ring), **Arnold,** eminent German musicologist; b. Breslau. April 2, 1877; d. Berlin, March 7, 1941. Having completed the course at the Gymnasium in Dresden, he matriculated at Berlin Univ., continuing his musical studies there with Joachim (violin) and Succo (composition); then took courses at the Univs. of Munich and Leipzig; *Dr. phil.* (Leipzig, 1902) with the dissertation *Geschichte des Instrumentalkonzerts* (as far as Vivaldi; continuation, 1905; 2nd ed., 1927); instructor for esthetics and history of music at Leipzig Univ. in 1907; associate prof., 1915; from 1903-06 ed. of 'Neue Zeitschrift für Musik.' From 1909-23 prof. of music at the Leipzig Cons.; 1920, prof. at the Univ. of Halle; 1928, prof. at the Univ. of Berlin, and head of the Board of the German 'Denkmäler'; 1933, president of the German Musicological Society. A noted Bach scholar, he edited the 'Bach-Jahrbuch' from its inception in 1904 through 1939. In 1908 he discovered in Upsala Schütz's long-lost work, *Weihnachtsoratorium* (publ. as supplement to Spitta's complete ed., 1909). He was the first to develop the theory that in early *a cappella* music the 'tenor' was performed by the organ. In his history of the oratorio he emphasized the importance of the *lauda* as one of the sources. —Works: *Bach's Textbehandlung* (1900); *Geschichte des Instrumentalkonzerts bis auf die Gegenwart* (1905; 2nd ed., 1927); *Die Anfänge des Oratoriums* (1907); *Geschichte des Oratoriums* (1911); *Musikalische Bildung und Erziehung zum musikalischen Hören* (1911; 4th ed., 1924); *Die niederländische Orgelmesse im Zeitalter des Josquin* (1912); *Studien zur Musikgeschichte der Frührenaissance* (1914); *Tabellen zur Musikgeschichte* (1914; 4th ed., 1934); *Deutsche Musikgeschichte im Umriss* (1917); *Die metrisch-rhythmische Grundgestalt unserer Choralmelodien* (1924); 2 additional vols. to R. Wustmann's *Musikgeschichte Leipzigs* (1927, 1941); *Geschichte der Musik in Beispielen* (1931); *Aufführungspraxis alter Musik* (1931); *Beethoven in neuer Deutung* (1934; aroused a considerable controversy because of its attempt to explain some of Beethoven's compositions as related to modern political trends); *Beethoven und die Dichtung* (1936); *J. S. Bachs Leipziger Kirchenmusik* (1936); *Von grossen Meistern der Musik* (1940); *Das Symbol in der Musik* (1941); *Über Kantaten J. S. Bachs* (posthumous, 1942); *Vom musikalischen Kunstwerk* (posthumous, 1949); also prepared a new ed. of von Dommer's *Handbuch der Musikgeschichte* (1914). He ed. about 12 vols. of works of early composers (Hasse, Quantz, Schütz, etc.); also composed music to Goethe's *Faust* and a violin sonata. —Cf. 'Festschrift Arnold Schering zum 60. Geburtstag' (Berlin, 1937).

Scherman, Thomas, American conductor; b. New York, Feb. 12, 1917; son of Harry Scherman, founder and president of the Book-of-the-Month Club. He attended Columbia Univ. (B. A., 1937); then studied piano with Isabelle Vengerova, theory with Hans Weisse, and conducting with Carl Bamberger and Max Rudolf. He served in the Army (1941-45), entering as a private and reaching the rank of captain in the Signal Corps. In the summer of 1947 he was assistant conductor at the National Opera in Mexico City. In 1947 he organized in New

York the Little Orchestra Society for the purpose of presenting new works and reviving forgotten music of the past; inaugurated his 1st season of 8 concerts in Town Hall, Oct. 20, 1947; the new venture became extremely successful, and concerts outside N. Y. City were added to the schedule, as well as special performances of small operas and oratorios. In 1948 Scherman started a series of children's concerts at Hunter College Assembly Hall.

Scherzer (shehr'-tser), **Otto,** German violinist and composer; b. Ansbach, March 24, 1821; d. Stuttgart, Feb. 23, 1886. After studying with Molique, he became violinist in the Stuttgart court orch. (1838-54); was music director at Tübingen Univ. (1860-77); publ. a number of songs and piano pieces. —Cf. Anon., *Otto Scherzer. Ein Künstlerleben* (Stuttgart, 1897).

Schetky, Johann Georg Christoff, German cellist and composer; b. Darmstadt, 1740; d. Edinburgh, Nov. 29, 1824. The original family name was Von Teschky; Schetky's ancestors were from Transylvania. He traveled in Germany; in 1768 was in Hamburg; in 1772, settled in Edinburgh, where he was 1st cellist of the concerts in St. Cecilia's Hall. He married Maria Anna Teresa Reinagle, sister of Alexander Reinagle (q.v.). He publ. 6 string quartets; 6 string trios; 6 duos for violin and cello; 6 cello sonatas with bass; 6 flute duos; 6 cello duos; 6 sonatas for violin and cello; harpsichord sonatas; songs. In MS he left 3 symphonies, 4 cello concertos, and an oratorio. —His son, **J. George Schetky** (b. Edinburgh, June 1, 1776; d. Philadelphia, Dec. 11, 1831), was the 2nd of 11 children; emigrated to America in 1792; naturalized in Philadelphia on Nov. 19, 1806. He appeared as a cellist in Philadelphia; about 1800, entered into partnership with Benjamin Carr in the music publ. business; was a co-founder of the Musical Fund Society in Philadelphia. His arrangement for military band of Kotzwara's *Battle of Prague* was much played. —Cf. Madeira, *Music in Philadelphia* (Philadelphia, 1896); O. G. Sonneck, *Bibliography of Early American Secular Music* (Washington, 1905); O. G. Sonneck, *Early Concert Life in America* (Leipzig, 1907; in English); Laurance Oliphant Schetky, *The Schetky Family; A Compilation of Letters, Memoirs and Historical Data* (privately publ., Portland, Ore., 1942; of great documentary value, establishing correct factual data from family archives; the author was a grandson of J. George Schetky).

Scheurleer (shör-lär), **Daniel François,** Dutch musicologist; b. The Hague, Nov. 13, 1855; d. there, Feb. 6, 1927. Although a banker, he took an active part in musical affairs; was president, for many years, of the 'Vereeniging voor Nederlandsche Muziekgeschiedenis'; made *Dr. phil.* (*hon. c.*) by the Univ. of Leyden in 1910; he was the owner of a valuable musical library (catalogue publ. in 1885; 2 supplements, 1903 and 1910) and collection of instruments (catalogue publ. 1885 and 1887; now in the Museum of The Hague); 1921, founded the 'Union musicologique.' He publ. *Het Muziekleven in Nederland in de tweede helft der 18ᵉ eeuw . . .* (The Hague, 1909) and other studies; ed. Fruytier's *Ecclesiasticus* (1563), etc. —Cf. *Gedenkboek aangeboden an Dr. D. F. Scheurleer op zijn 70sten Verjaardag* (1925; contains a complete bibliography of his works).

Schibler, Armin, Swiss composer; b. Kreuzlingen, Nov. 20, 1920. He studied with Willy Burkhard in Zürich; since 1944, music director at the Kanton Gymnasium there. Much of his music is cast in neo-Classical forms; some works employ a modified form of the 12-tone technique. —Works: Operas: *Der spanische Rosenstock* (Bern, April 9, 1950); *Der Teufel im Winterpalais* (1950-53); *Das Bergwerk von Falun* (1953); *Die Füsse im Feuer* (Zürich, April 25, 1955; aroused considerable interest). For orch.: concertino for piano and chamber orch. (1943); *Fantasy* for viola and small orch. (1945); *Fantasy* for oboe, harp, and small orch. (1946); symph. No. 1 (1946); *Passacaglia* (1949); Symph. Variations (1950); *Concertante Fantasie* for cello and orch. (1951); symph. No. 2 (1953; *Concerto for Amateur Orchestra* (1953); symph. No. 3 (Winterthur, Nov. 13, 1957). Cantatas: *Die Hochzeit* (1946); *Gefährten* (1946); *Weil Alles erneut sich begibt* (1949); *Mondlicht* (1950). Chamber music: solo sonata for flute (1944); suite for cello alone (1945); *Little Concerto* for viola alone (1947); 2 string quartets (1945; 1951); *Trio Concertante* for trumpet, violin, and piano (1948); *Duo Concertante* for violin and piano (1950); *Dodecaphonic Studies* for piano. —Cf. K. H. Wörner, *Armin Schibler; Werk und Persönlichkeit* (Amriswil, 1953).

Schicht, Johann Gottfried, German composer; b. Reichenau, Saxony, Sept. 29, 1753; d. Leipzig, Feb. 16, 1823. In 1776, already well trained as an organist and pianist, he matriculated at Leipzig as a law student, but became pianist at Joh. Adam Hiller's 'Liebhaber-Konzerte,' and at the 'Gewandhaus Concerts' evolved from them in 1781, succeeding Hiller as conductor in 1785. In 1810 he became cantor at the Thomasschule. His works comprise the oratorios *Die Feier der Christen auf Golgatha, Moses auf Sinai,* and *Das Ende des Gerechten;* Masses, motets, Te Deums, the 100th Psalm; several chorale-motets (*Nach einer Prüfung kurzer Tage, Jesus meine Zuversicht, Herzlich lieb hab' ich dich, o Herr,* etc.); 9 settings of Leo's Miserere *a* 4-8; an excellent book of chorales (1819; of 1,285 melodies, 306 are original); a concerto, sonatas, caprices, etc., for piano; and *Grundregeln der Harmonie* (Leipzig, 1812). —Cf. P. Langer, *Chronik der Leipziger Singakademie* (Leipzig, 1902).

Schick, George, conductor; b. Prague, April 5, 1908. He studied at the Prague Cons.; was assistant conductor at the Prague Opera from 1927 until 1938. He settled in the U. S. in 1939; was conductor of the San Carlo Opera (1943); then conducted in Chicago; from 1948 to 1950 was conductor of the Little Symph. of Montreal; from 1950 to 1956, associate conductor of the Chicago Symph. Orch.

Schick (*née* Hamel), **Margarete Luise,** noted German soprano; b. Mainz, April 26, 1773; d. Berlin, April 29, 1809. She studied with Steffani at Würzburg, later with Righini at Mainz, where her stage début took place in 1791. Her favorite roles were Susanna (*Figaro*) and Zerlina (*Don Giovanni*). From 1794 she sang at the Royal Opera, Berlin, having great success in operas by Gluck. Her contemporaries regarded her as the equal of the famous Mara. In 1791 she married the violinist Ernst Schick. —Cf. K. Levezow, *Leben und Kunst der Frau Margarete Luise Schick* (Berlin, 1809).

Schiedermair (shē'-der-mīr), **Ludwig,** eminent German musicologist; b. Regensburg, Dec. 7, 1876; d. Bensberg, near Cologne, April 30, 1957. He studied in Munich with Sandberger and Beer-Walbrunn; 1901, *Dr. phil.,* for the dissertation *Künstlerische Bestrebungen am Hofe des Kurfürsten Ferdinand Maria von Bayern;* studied further with Riemann in Leipzig and with Kretzschmar in Berlin. In 1906 he became instructor of musicology at the Univ. of Marburg; in 1912, lecturer at the Univ. of Bonn (1920, prof.). In 1927, on the occasion of the Beethoven centennial, he was appointed director of the Beethoven-Haus Research Institute in Bonn. —Writings: *Gustav Mahler* (Leipzig, 1901); *Beiträge zur Geschichte der Oper um die Wende des 18. und 19. Jahrhunderts* (2 vols., Leipzig, 1907, 1910); *Bayreuther Festspiele im Zeitalter des Absolutismus* (Leipzig, 1908); *Die Briefe Mozarts und seiner Familie* (5 vols.; Munich, 1914; vol. 5 is an iconography); *W. A. Mozarts Handschrift* (facsimiles, Bückeburg, 1919); *Einführung in das Studium der Musikgeschichte* (Munich, 1918; new ed., Bonn, 1947); *Mozart* (Munich, 1922; 2nd ed., Bonn, 1948); *Der junge Beethoven* (Leipzig, 1925; 3rd ed., Bonn, 1951); *Beethoven: Beiträge zum Leben und Schaffen* (Leipzig, 1930); *Die deutsche Oper* (Leipzig, 1930); *Die Gestaltung weltanschaulicher Ideen in der Vokalmusik Beethovens* (Leipzig, 1934); *Musik am Rheinstrom* (Cologne, 1947); *Musikalische Begegnungen; Erlebnis und Erinnerung* (Cologne, 1948); *Deutsche Musik im Europäischen Raum* (Münster, 1954). A 'Festschrift,' *Beethoven und die Gegenwart,* was publ. in honor of Scheidermair's 60th birthday (Berlin, 1937). —Cf. J. Schmidt-Görg, *Ludwig Schiedermair,* in 'Die Musikforschung' (No. 2, 1957).

Schiedermayer (shē'dĕr-mī-ĕr), **Johann Baptist,** German composer; b. Pfaffenmünster, Bavaria, June 23, 1779; d. Linz, Austria, Jan. 6, 1840, as cathedral organist.—Works: the 'Singspiele' *Wellmanns Eichenstämme* (Linz, 1815), *Das Glück ist kugelrund* (Linz, 1816); *Die Rückkehr ins Vaterhaus* (Linz, 1816); 16 Masses and much other sacred music; also symphonies, string trios, organ pieces, etc.; a *Theoretisch-praktische Chorallehre zum Gebrauch beim katholischen Kirchenritus* (1828); and an abridged ed. of Leopold Mozart's violin method.

Schiedmayer. The name of 2 well-known firms of piano makers in Stuttgart, i.e., 'Schiedmayer & Söhne' and 'Schiedmayer Pianofortefabrik.' —**Balthasar Schiedmayer** (1711-81) began manufacturing musical instruments in Erlangen about 1740; at his death in 1781, his son **Johann David Schiedmayer** (1753-1805) assumed the management; he was succeeded by his 19-year-old son **Johann Lorenz Schiedmayer** (1786-1860), with whom he had moved about 1800 from Erlangen to Nuremberg. Johann Lorenz ended the business at Nuremberg after 2 years, and went to Vienna for a brief time; in 1809 he was in Stuttgart, where he set up business in partnership with a young piano maker, Karl Dieudonné (d. 1825); from 1825, he carried on the business alone, until 1845, when his eldest sons, **Adolf Schiedmayer** (1819-90) and **Hermann**

Schiedmayer (1820-91), entered the firm, which was then called 'J. L. Schiedmayer & Söhne.' In 1853 Johann Lorenz Schiedmayer provided his two younger sons, **Julius** (1822-78) and **Paul** (1829-90), with their own separate factory, producing harmoniums. After their father's death, they turned to piano making, and their business became known as 'Schiedmayer Pianofortefabrik.' Upon Paul Schiedmayer's death in 1890, his son, Max Julius, became head of the firm.—Cf. A. Eisenmann, *Schiedmayer und Söhne* (1909).

Schikaneder, Emanuel (Johann), Mozart's librettist; b. Straubing, Sept. 1, 1751; d. Vienna, Sept. 21, 1812. His baptismal names were Johannes Joseph; he assumed the name Emanuel later in life. He was a member of a troupe of itinerant players when he met Mozart at Salzburg. In 1784 he reached Vienna, where he was an actor and an impresario. He was not successful until he persuaded Mozart to set to music his play *Die Zauberflöte,* which recouped his fortunes; it was produced on Sept. 30, 1791, shortly before Mozart's death; Schikaneder himself took the part of Papageno. He wrote librettos for 58 'Singspiele'; with Zitterbarth he was the manager of the Theater an der Wien, which he directed from its foundation (1801) until 1806. He died insane after a series of financial setbacks. —Cf. O. E. Deutsch, *Das Freihaustheater auf der Wieden, 1787-1801* (Vienna, 1937); Egon von Komorzynski, *Der Vater der Zauberflote: Emanuel Schikaneders Leben* (Vienna, 1948); Egon von Komorzynski, *Emanuel Schikaneder: ein Beitrag zur Geschichte des deutschen Theaters* (Vienna, 1951). For a complete list of his librettos see Anton Bauer, *Opern und Operetten in Wien* (Vienna, 1955).

Schiller, Friedrich von, great German poet; b. Marbach, Nov. 10, 1759; d. Weimar, May 9, 1805. Many musicians have turned to his works for inspiration. —Cf. M. Berendt, *Schiller bis Wagner* (Berlin, 1901); J. Baltz, *Beethoven und Schiller* (Arnsberg, 1905); A. Kohut, *F. Schiller in seinen Beziehungen zur Musik* (Stuttgart, 1905); H. Knudsen, *Schiller und die Musik* (Greifswald, 1908); G. Adler, *Schiller und Schubert* (Vienna, 1910). The Schiller number of 'Die Musik' (May, 1905) contains essays by W. Golther *(Schiller und Wagner),* M. Runze *(Schiller und die Balladenmusik),* R. Hohenemser (*Schiller als Musikästhetiker*).

Schilling, Gustav, German musical lexicographer; b. Schwiegershausen, near Hanover, Nov. 3, 1803; d. Nebraska, March, 1881. He studied theology at Göttingen and Halle; headed a music school in Stuttgart, and published a number of works dealing with various aspects of music. In 1857 he emigrated to America; lived in N. Y., later was in Montreal; finally settled in Nebraska. His most important work was the *Enzyklopädie der gesammten musikalischen Wissenschaften oder Universal-Lexikon der Tonkunst* (6 vols.; 1835-38; 2nd ed., 7 vols., 1840-42). Other publications are *Versuch einer Philosophie des Schönen in der Musik* (1838); *Lehrbuch der allgemeinen Musikwissenschaft* (1840); *Geschichte der heutigen oder modernen Musik* (1841); *Die musikalische Europa . . .* (1842); *Musikalische Dynamik; oder, Die Lehre vom Vortrage in der Musik* (1843); *Der Pianist* (1843); *Franz Liszt* (1844); *Sicher Schlüssel zur Klaviervirtuosität* (1844); *Die schöne Kunst der Töne* (1847); *Musikalische Didaktik* (1851); *Allgemeine Volksmusiklehre* (1852); *Akustik oder die Lehre vom Klange* (2nd ed., 1856); also a revised ed. of K. P. E. Bach's *Versuch über die wahre Art, das Klavier zu spielen* (1857); etc.

Schillinger, Joseph, composer and theorist; b. Kharkov, Aug. 31, 1895; d. New York, March 23, 1943. He studied at the St. Petersburg Cons. with Tcherepnin, Wihtol, and others; from 1918 to 1922, taught at the State Academy of Music in Kharkov; also conducted an orch. there; from 1926 to 1928 was active in Leningrad as teacher and composer. In 1929 he came to America, settling in N. Y.; taught at the New School for Social Research; then established private classes, teaching his own system of composition, based on rigid mathematical principles; also taught by correspondence. He became highly successful as instructor; George Gershwin took lessons from him for a considerable time; many other established composers, and particularly composers of popular music, became his students. After Schillinger's death, his correspondence lessons were organized by Lyle Dowling and Arnold Shaw and publ. in 2 vols. by Carl Fischer, Inc. under the title, *The Schillinger System of Musical Composition* (N. Y., 1946); this was followed by *The Mathematical Basis of the Arts* (N. Y., 1947); a short volume of musical patterns, *Kaleidophone,* was publ. previously (N. Y., 1940). Schillinger was also a composer in his own right; his works include a *March of the Orient,* for orch. (Leningrad, May 12, 1926); *First Airphonic Suite,* for the theremin with orch. (Cleveland, Nov. 28, 1929; Leo Theremin, the inventor, as soloist); piano pieces; etc. See Frances Schillinger, *Joseph Schillinger: a Memoir by his Wife* (N. Y., 1949); Vernon Duke, *Gershwin, Schillinger, and Dukelsky,* in the 'Mus. Quarterly' (Jan., 1947).

Schillings, Max von, German composer and conductor; b. Düren, April 19, 1868; d. Berlin, July 23, 1933. While attending the Gymnasium at Bonn he studied violin with O. von Königslöw, and piano and composition with K. J. Brambach. He then entered the Univ. of Munich, where he studied law, philosophy, literature, and art. He became associated with Richard Strauss, and under his influence decided to devote himself entirely to music. In 1892 he was engaged as assistant stage director at the Festival Theater in Bayreuth; in 1902 became chorusmaster; in 1908 he moved to Stuttgart as general music director; on the occasion of the inauguration of the new opera theater there, he was given the rank of nobility, and added the nobiliary particle 'von' to his name; he remained in Stuttgart until 1918; was intendant of the Berlin State Opera (1919-25). He made several visits as conductor to the U. S. In 1923 he married the soprano Barbara Kemp. As a composer, he trailed in the path of Wagner, barely avoiding direct imitation. One of his operas, *Mona Lisa* (Stuttgart, Sept. 26, 1915), enjoyed considerable success; it was produced by the Metropolitan Opera, N. Y. on March 1, 1923. Other works include the operas *Ingwelde* (Karlsruhe, Nov. 13, 1894), *Der Pfeifertag* (Schwerin, Nov. 26, 1899), and *Moloch* (Dresden, Dec. 8, 1906); incidental music to *Orestie* of Aeschylus (1900) and to Part 1 of Goethe's *Faust;* a symph. prologue to *Oedipus Rex* of Sophocles; also several melodramas with orch.: *Kassandra, Das eleusische Fest, Das Hexenlied,* and *Jung Olaf; Dem Verklärten,* for baritone solo, chorus, and orch.; *Glockenlieder,* for solo voice and orch.; *Hochzeitsglocken,* for baritone, chorus, and orch.; *Die Perle,* after Goethe, for soprano, tenor, and orch.; 4 duets from Goethe's *Westöstlicher Divan,* for soprano, tenor, and orch.; 2 symph. fantasies, *Meergruss* and *Seemorgen;* a violin concerto; a string quartet; a string quintet; pieces for violin and piano; men's choruses a cappella; songs; piano pieces. A complete catalogue of his works, compiled by J. Beck, was publ. at Berlin in 1934. —Cf. R. Louis, *Max Schillings* (Leipzig, 1909); A. Richard, *Max Schillings* (Munich, 1922); W. Raupp, *Max von Schillings* (Hamburg, 1935).

Schimon (shē'-mon), **Adolf,** noted singing teacher and composer; b. Vienna, Feb. 29, 1820; d. Leipzig, June 21, 1887. He studied with Berton, Halévy, and others at the Paris Cons.; studied the Italian method in Florence, bringing out his opera, *Stradella,* there in 1846; was 'maestro al cembalo' at Her Majesty's Theatre, London (1850-52), then at the Italian Opera in Paris. In 1858 Flotow brought out Schimon's 1-act comic opera *List um List* at Schwerin. His works further include Italian and French songs; German lieder; 2 string quartets; a piano trio; a violin sonata; piano music; etc. He was married to the soprano Anna Regan.

Schimon-Regan, Anna, distinguished German soprano; b. Aich, near Karlsbad, Sept. 18, 1841; d. Munich, April 18, 1902. In 1859 she had her first singing lessons from Mme. Schubert in Karlsbad; the next year her aunt, the famous Caroline Unger, took her to Florence and taught her till 1864; she was then engaged at the court opera in Hanover (1864-67); during the winter of 1867-68 she sang in Berlioz's concerts in St. Petersburg. She made her first visit to England in 1869, appearing in concerts with Caroline Unger; gave song recitals there every winter till 1875. In 1872 she married Adolf Schimon (q.v.) and settled in Munich.

Schindelmeisser, Ludwig, German composer; b. Königsberg, Dec. 8, 1811; d. Darmstadt, March 30, 1864. He was an opera conductor at Salzburg, Innsbruck, Graz, Berlin, Budapest, and Darmstadt; wrote 7 operas, including *Melusine* (Darmstadt, 1861); overture to *Uriel Acosta;* oratorios on *Schleswig-Holstein, meerumschlungen* and *Rule Britannia; Concertante* in E-flat for 4 clarinets and orch.; concertino for clarinet and orch.; 2 piano sonatas; minor piano pieces and songs.

Schindler, Anton Felix, Beethoven's faithful friend and biographer; b. Meedl, Moravia, June 13, 1795; d. Bockenheim, near Frankfurt, Jan. 16, 1864. He was the son of a schoolteacher; studied law at the Univ. of Vienna, and at the same time learned to play the violin. He was a violinist and conductor at the Josephstadt Theater and at the Kärtnertor Theater in Vienna (1825); conducted performances of several of Beethoven's symphonies. He met Beethoven in 1814; in 1819 became Beethoven's secretary and helper, and lived in the same house with him until their break in 1824, when Beethoven unjustly accused him of disloyalty. A few months before Beethoven's death, Schindler was called back and never left him again. From 1831 till 1835 Schindler was Kapellmeister at the Cathedral of Münster; from 1835 to 1837 at Aachen; later moved to Bockenheim, remaining there until his death. His intimacy with Beethoven lends peculiar value to his *Biographie Ludwig van Beethovens* (Münster, 1840; 2nd, enlarged ed., 1845; 3rd ed., 1860). The biography was publ. in English, transl. by Moscheles (London, 1841); modern German eds. were brought out by Kalischer (1909) and Fritz Volbach (1927). His diaries of his sojourns in Paris and Berlin (1841-43) were edited by Marta Becker (Frankfurt, 1939). His pamphlet, *Beethoven in Paris* (1842), is an account of the production of Beethoven's works at the Concert Spirituel; it formed an appendix to the 2nd ed. of his biography. After Schindler's death, his papers, comprising the invaluable conversation books and sketch books of Beethoven, as well as a vast amount of personal notes of all kinds, passed to the Royal Library of Berlin. —Cf. E. Hüffer, *A. F. Schindler, der Biograph Beethovens* (diss., Münster, 1909); R. Zimmermann, in 'Allgemeine Musikzeitung,' Nos. 38-39 (1925).

Schindler, Kurt, choral conductor and music editor; b. Berlin, Feb. 17, 1882; d. New York, Nov. 16, 1935. He studied piano with Ansorge and composition with Bussler, Gernsheim, and L. C. Wolf, in Berlin; then in Munich with Thuille; was at various times assistant conductor to Richard Strauss in Berlin and to Mottl in Munich; after a season as theater conductor in Stuttgart (1902-03) and another season in Würzburg (1903-04), he emigrated to America; was assistant conductor at the Metropolitan Opera House (1905-07); in 1907 became reader for G. Schirmer, Inc. In 1909 he founded in N. Y. the MacDowell Chorus, whose name was changed in 1910, with the enlargement of the scope of its work, to Schola Cantorum, Schindler remaining as conductor until 1927; with this group Schindler introduced many new works, and also produced arrangements of the folk music of various nations; was particularly interested in Spanish and Russian music. He also taught at various schools; publ. about 80 songs. —Editions: '6 Old French Christmas Carols' (1908), 'Century of Russian Song from Glinka to Rachmaninov' (50 songs, with English transl.; 1911), 'The Development of Opera' (examples of various periods; 1912), 'Songs of the Russian People' (1915), '10 Student Songs of Finland' (1915), 'A Cappella Choruses from the Russian Liturgy' (1913-17), 'Masters of Russian Song' (2 vols., 1917), 'Old Spanish Sacred Motets' (1918), 'Modern Spanish Choral Works' (1918), '60 Russian Folk-Songs' (3 vols., 1918-19); 'Folk Music and Poetry of Spain and Portugal' (N. Y., 1941; posthumous; about 1,000 musical examples; text in English and Spanish).

Schiøler (shö-lěhr), **Victor,** prominent Danish pianist; b. Copenhagen, April 7, 1899. He studied with his mother, Augusta Schiöler (1868-1946); then with Ignaz Friedman and Artur Schnabel; made his piano début in 1914; from 1919 toured in Europe; first American tour, 1948-49. He also was active as conductor in Denmark.

Schiøtz, Aksel, Danish tenor; b. Roskilde, Sept. 1, 1906. He studied languages at the Univ. of Copenhagen; then was a school teacher. It was not until 1939 that he made his début as an opera singer; in 1942 he began to give concerts and became known in Denmark as a singer of lieder. In 1946 he made appearances in England, and in 1948 was in the U. S. In 1958 was appointed to the faculty of the Royal Cons. of Music in the Univ. of Toronto. —Cf. G. Schiøtz, *Kunst og Kamp: Gerd og Aksel Schiøtz* (Copenhagen, 1951).

Schipa (skē'-pah), **Tito** (real baptismal names, **Raffaele Attilio Amedeo**), famous Italian tenor; b. Lecce, Jan. 2, 1889; studied composition with A. Gerunda, and began his career as a composer of piano pieces and songs; then turned to singing, and in 1911 made his début at Vercelli. After numerous appearances in Europe, he was engaged by the Chicago Civic Opera (1920-32); made his 1st appearance with the Metropolitan Opera on Nov. 23, 1932 as Nemorino in *L'Elisir d'amore;* made extensive tours of Europe and South America, as well as in the U. S.; lived in California until 1941, when he went back to Italy. On Sept. 28, 1946, he married Teresa Borgna of São Paulo, Brazil. He toured the U. S. again in 1947. He publ. an operetta, *La Principessa Liana* (1935; performed in Rome), *Hosanna,* a Mass (1929), and several songs.

Schippers, Thomas, American conductor; b. Kalamazoo, Mich., March 9, 1930. He gave a public concert as a pianist at the age of 6; was church organist at 14. He studied at the Curtis Institute, Philadelphia (1944-45) and privately with Olga Samaroff (1946-47). In 1948 he won 2nd prize in the young conductors' contest of the Philadelphia

Orch. His début as conductor was with the Lemonade Opera Co., N. Y., in 1948; he directed the première of Menotti's opera *The Consul* (N. Y., 1950) and the television première of *Amahl and the Night Visitors* (Dec. 25, 1951). He became a staff member of the New York City Opera Co. in 1951. On March 26, 1955, he led the N. Y. Philharmonic as guest conductor, the youngest to conduct this organization. In the fall of 1955 he made his début at the Metropolitan Opera, also the youngest musician to conduct there; was guest conductor at La Scala, Milan, in 1955.

Schirmer, the family of music publishers. The first of the family to be connected with music was Johann Georg Schirmer, who settled in Sondershausen and was married there on July 18, 1781. He was a cabinetmaker, a native of Gäuroden, and made musical instruments. His son, Ernst Ludwig Rudolf Schirmer (b. Sondershausen, May 8, 1784), emigrated to New York with his wife and children in 1840. There his son **(Friedrich) Gustav (Emil) Schirmer** (b. Königsee, Thuringia, Sept. 19, 1829; d. Eisenach, Aug. 5, 1893) found employment in the music store of Scharfenberg & Luis, and after several years entered the employ of Kerksieg & Breusing, music dealers, becoming manager in 1854. In 1861 he took over the business with a partner, and acquired sole control in 1866, establishing the house of G. Schirmer (q.v.). Schirmer was an enlightened and progressive publisher; he entered into personal relations with noted European composers, especially those of the Weimar circle, and was among the original patrons of the Bayreuth project. He was an amateur pianist and had a real love for music. The diary of Tchaikovsky's visit to N. Y. in 1891 makes repeated mention of Schirmer and his family. Schirmer married an American, Mary Fairchild, by whom he had 5 daughters and 2 sons.

The younger of these sons, **Gustave Schirmer** (b. New York, Feb. 18, 1864; d. Boston, July 15, 1907), organized in 1885 the Boston Music Company, which gained prominence especially through the publication of Ethelbert Nevin's music. Shortly afterwards, with his brother, he became a partner in the firm founded by his father in N. Y., and after the latter's death in 1893 he managed the business jointly with his brother, retaining independent control of the Boston Music Co. His brother, **Rudolph Edward Schirmer** (b. New York, July 22, 1859; d. Santa Barbara, Calif., Aug. 19, 1919), was educated in N. Y. public schools and from 1873-75 lived at Weimar with his mother, brother, and 4 sisters; studied violin and piano there with Helene Stahl and came in contact with the Liszt circle. In 1876 entered College of New Jersey (later Princeton Univ.), and after graduation in 1880 studied law for 4 years at Columbia College, being admitted to the bar in 1884. In 1885 he took the place of his brother Gustave in his father's music-publishing business (see **G. Schirmer, Inc.**). Later he was rejoined by Gustave, and upon their father's death in 1893, he became president of the firm, assuming sole control from 1907. In 1915 he founded the 'Mus. Quarterly.' He was a director of the N. Y. Oratorio Society and the N. Y. Symph. Society, and a trustee of the Institute of Mus. Art, N. Y. His second wife was the singer Ann Swinburne (married 1916), by whom he had one son. **Gustave Schirmer,** 3rd (b. Boston, Dec. 29, 1890), son of Gustave Schirmer and grandson of the founder of G. Schirmer, Inc., inherited the Boston Music Co. from his father and acquired the Willis Music Co. of Cincinnati. He was president of G. Schirmer, Inc. 1919-21 and 1944-57. Rudolph E. Schirmer's son, also named **Rudolph Edward Schirmer** (b. Santa Barbara, Calif., June 8, 1919), in 1949 became vice-president of G. Schirmer, Inc.

Schirmer, Ernest Charles, American music publisher; b. Mt. Vernon, N. Y., March 15, 1865; d. Waban, Massachusetts, Feb. 15, 1958. His father, Edward Schirmer (1831-85), a native of Thuringia, Saxony, was a brother of the famous music publisher, Gustav Schirmer of New York, the brothers emigrating to the U.S. in 1840. Ernest Schirmer entered apprenticeship in the music store of Gustav Schirmer, N. Y., in 1878. In Oct., 1891, he became business manager of the Boston Music Co.; admitted to partnership in Jan., 1902. In 1917 he withdrew from the Boston Music Co., and in 1921 founded the E. C. Schirmer Music Co., with the stated purpose of promoting good music. In 1956 he was still active in the affairs of the E. C. Schirmer Co. The publications of the firm include the Concord Series, the Choral Repertory of the Harvard Univ. Glee Club, Radcliffe, Vassar, and Wellesley College Choral Music, the Polyphonic and 'A Cappella' Libraries, the St. Dunstan Edition of Sacred Music, and treatises on harmonic analysis, musical theory, and music appreciation. The firm enjoys a world market for its publications with agencies at London and Berlin. The catalogue includes several important works by American composers (Randall Thompson, Walter Piston, Douglas Moore, Aaron Copland, etc.).

Schirmer, G., Inc., music-publishing house at New York. It is an outgrowth of the business founded in 1848 by Kerksieg & Breusing, of which Gustav Schirmer became manager in 1854. With a fellow-employee, Bernard Beer, Schirmer took over the business in 1861, the firm becoming known as 'Beer & Schirmer.' In 1866 Schirmer acquired complete control, establishing the house of 'G. Schirmer, music publishers, importers and dealers.' Until 1880 the business was located at 701 Broadway, then it was moved to 35 Union Square, and in 1910 it was transferred to a 7-story building at 3 East 43rd St., which it occupies at present. In 1891 Schirmer founded his own engraving and printing plant in East 16th St., which in 1916 developed into a large factory located at Woodside, L. I. After the death of Gustav Schirmer in 1893, the business was incorporated under the management of his sons, Rudolph Edward (president) and Gustave (secretary). Upon the death of Rudolph in 1919, he was succeeded by his nephew, Gustave Schirmer, 3rd (resigned in 1921). Then W. Rodman Fay became president, with O. G. Sonneck (q.v.) as vice-president. On May 7, 1929, Carl Engel (q.v.) was made president and continued in that office—except for one year (1933), when his place was taken by Hermann Irion —up to his death in 1944, when Gustave Schirmer, 3rd, became president again, retiring in 1957. He was succeeded by Rudolph Tauhert. The firm has branches in Cleveland and Los Angeles. The catalogue comprises about 40,000 titles. In 1892 the firm began publication of the 'Library of Musical Classics,' notable for careful editing and general typographical excellence; and the same year it launched the 'Collection of Operas' (vocal scores with original text and English transl., also historical and critical introductions). A large number of Masses, oratorios, and cantatas are included in the catalogue. The 'American Folk-Song Series' offers authentic folk material. The firm has publ. compositions by Charles T. Griffes, Victor Herbert, Loeffler, Granados, Ernest Bloch, Percy Grainger, Arnold Schoenberg, etc.; also by many of the younger and most prominent American composers (Roy Harris, Samuel Barber, William Schuman, Gian Carlo Menotti, Paul Creston, Leonard Bernstein, etc.). Other publications are 'Baker's Biographical Dictionary of Musicians,' first issued in 1900, and Pratt's 'History of Music' (revised ed., 1935), both recognized as standard works in their respective fields. In 1915 'The Musical Quarterly' was founded under the editorship of O. G. Sonneck. Its subsequent editors have been Carl Engel (1929-44), Gustave Reese (1944-45), and Paul Henry Lang (since 1945). This periodical, containing contributions by the foremost scholars of Europe and America, occupies a preëminent place among musical journals in the English language.

Schiske, Karl, composer; b. Györ (Raab), Hungary, Feb. 12, 1916. He studied at Vienna Univ. (Ph. D., 1942); in 1952 appointed prof. at the Vienna Academy of Music. —Works: 3 symphonies (1942; 1948; 1951); an oratorio, *Vom Tode* (1946); piano concerto; 2 string quartets; quintet for wind instruments; numerous piano works and songs.

Schiuma, Alfredo, Argentine composer; b. Buenos Aires, June 25, 1885. He studied with Romaniello in Buenos Aires; later founded his own music school there; wrote in various musical genres. —Operas (all performed in Buenos Aires): *Amy Robsart*, based on Walter Scott's novel *Kenilworth* (April 24, 1920); *La Sirocchia* (April 23, 1922); *Tabaré* (Aug. 6, 1925); *Las Virgenes del Sol* (June 20, 1939); *La Infanta* (Aug. 12, 1941). Orchestral works: symph. in F (Buenos Aires, June 15, 1928); *Pitunga*, symph. tableau (Buenos Aires, March 31, 1929); *Los Incas* (Buenos Aires, April 26, 1931); choral works, chamber music, and songs.

Schjelderup (shehl'-de-roop), **Gerhard**, Norwegian composer and writer; b. Christiansand, Nov. 17, 1859; d. Benediktbeuren, Bavaria, July 29, 1933. He went to Paris in 1878, and studied with Franchomme (cello) and Massenet (composition); in 1888 settled in Germany; lived in Dresden (from 1896); then moved to Benediktbeuren, where he remained till his death. He wrote music influenced partly by Wagner, partly by Grieg; publ. a biography of Grieg (in Norwegian, 1903; German ed., with Walter Niemann, 1908) and a monograph on Wagner (in Norwegian, 1908; in German, 1913). —Works: operas: *Sonntagmorgen* (Munich, May 9, 1893), *Norwegische Hochzeit* (Prague, March 17, 1900), *Frühlingsnacht* (Dresden, May 1, 1908; in Norwegian, as *Vaarnat*, Oslo, Aug. 31, 1915), *Sturmvögel* (Schwerin, Sept. 19, 1926); mus. fairy-tale, *Sampo*; *Weihnacht-Suite*, for orch.; 2 symph. poems, *Eine Sommernacht auf dem Fjord* and *Brand* (after Ibsen); *In Baldurs Hain* for violin and piano; *Fantasiestück* for cello and piano; songs. —Cf. O. M. Sandvik, *G. Schjelderup,* in 'Schweizerische Musikzeitung' (Oct., 1948).

Schladebach, Julius, German physiologist and musician; b. Dresden, 1810; d. Kiel, Sept. 21, 1872. He publ. vol. 1 of a *Neues Universal-Lexikon der Tonkunst* (1854), completed by Bernsdorf; also *Die Bildung der menschlichen Stimme zum Gesang* (1860).

Schläger, Hans, Austrian composer; b. Filskirchen, Dec. 5, 1820; d. Salzburg, May 17, 1885. He was a pupil of Preyer at Vienna; chorusmaster of the Männergesangverein (1844-61); then Kapellmeister of Salzburg Cathedral, and director of the Mozarteum, resigning on his marriage with Countess Zichy in 1867. He wrote the operas *Heinrich und Ilse* (Salzburg, 1869) and *Hans Haidekukuk* (Salzburg, 1873); the symph. tone-picture *Waldmeisters Brautfahrt;* symphonies; string quartets; etc.

Schlegel (shlā'-gel), **Leander,** Dutch composer; b. Overveen, near Haarlem, Feb. 2, 1844; d. there, Oct. 20, 1913. He was a pupil at the Cons. in The Hague and of Reinecke at the Leipzig Cons. After making several tours (as pianist) with Wilhelmj, he settled in Haarlem as director of a music school (1871-98); in 1898 he moved to Overveen, where until his death he was director of his own Cons. A composer of solid attainments and serious tendencies, he followed in the footsteps of Brahms. He publ. a piano quartet, a string quartet, and a number of piano pieces: 2 *Ballades, Rhein und Loreley, Der arme Peter, Zwei fantastische Studien, Sechs Fantasien;* songs: *An die Nacht, Deutsche Liebeslieder,* etc.; in MS are a piano concerto, *Rhapsodie* for piano; *Aus Toggenburgs Sage,* symph. poem; a symphony; violin concerto; etc.

Schleinitz (shlī'-nitz), **Heinrich Conrad,** German lawyer and musician; b. Zschaitz, near Döbeln, Oct. 1, 1802; d. Leipzig, May 13, 1881. As a pupil of the Thomasschule he had an excellent musical education; was a member of the Gewandhaus Board of Managers when they called Mendelssohn to Leipzig, and became a fast friend of the latter, giving up his legal practice on Mendelssohn's death to undertake the direction of the Conservatorium, an office he filled with conservative zeal until his death.

Schlesinger, Adolf Martin, German music publisher. In 1810 he founded the 'Schlesinger'sche Buch- und Musikalienhandlung' at Berlin; was one of Beethoven's German publishers. The firm was carried on after his death by his son Heinrich Schlesinger, who began publishing (1851) the influential music periodical 'Echo'; the business was sold in 1864 to R. Lienau (1838-1920), whose sons took it over at his death. The firm was further enlarged by the acquisition of several other catalogues, such as those of Haslinger of Vienna (1875), Krentzlin of Berlin (1919), Vernthal of Berlin (1925), and Köster of Berlin (1928). —Cf. Max Unger, *Ludwig van Beethoven und seine Verleger S. A. Steiner und T. Haslinger in Wien, A. M. Schlesinger in Berlin* (Berlin, 1921).

Schlesinger, Kathleen, musicologist; b. Hollywood, near Belfast, Ireland, June 27, 1862; d. London, April 16, 1953. She was educated in Switzerland; then settled in England; became interested in musical instruments; publ. *The Instruments of the Modern Orchestra* (2 vols., London, 1910). Her chief work is *The Greek Aulos* (London, 1939), containing not only a description of ancient Greek instruments, but also propounding an original theory of the formation of Greek modes, which aroused much controversy; the weight of learned opinion inclined against her hypotheses.

Schlesinger, Maurice Adolf, music publisher; son of Adolf Martin Schlesinger; b. Berlin, c. 1800; d. Baden-Baden, Feb., 1871. He moved to Paris in 1819, and was at first engaged in book selling. In 1834 he established a music publishing business, and launched the publication of the 'Gazette musicale,' soon united with the 'Revue musicale' (continued publication until 1880). He became one of the most important Paris publishers; publ. full scores of operas by Meyerbeer, Donizetti, and others; also Berlioz's *Symphonie fantastique* and much of Chopin's music. In 1846 he sold the catalogue to Brandus and Dufour; later it was acquired by Joubert.

Schlesinger, Sebastian Benson, German composer; b. Hamburg, Sept. 24, 1837; d. Nice, Jan. 8, 1917. He went to the U. S. at the age of 13; studied music at Boston, chiefly under Otto Dresel; was for 17 years German Consul at Boston; then lived for a time in London, and during his last years in Paris. He was a gifted composer; publ.

about 120 songs which received praise from Max Bruch and Robert Franz; wrote several piano pieces in a Romantic vein *(Novelette, Albumblatt, Impromptu-Caprice,* etc.).

Schletterer, Hans Michel, German conductor and writer on music; b. Ansbach, May 29, 1824; d. Augsburg, June 4, 1893. He studied with local teachers; then became a pupil of Spohr at Kassel and Ferdinand David in Leipzig. After filling a number of teaching posts in provincial towns, he taught at the Univ. of Heidelberg (1854-58); then was choral conductor and singing teacher in Augsburg, where he founded an oratorio society and a music school. He publ. 17 books of choral music a cappella; a selection of Lutheran church music, *Musica sacra* (2 vols., 1887; 3rd ed., 1927); *Das deutsche Singspiel* (1863); *J. Fr. Reichardt* (1865); *Geschichte der geistlichen Dichtung und kirchlichen Tonkunst* (1869); *Studien zur Geschichte der französischen Musik* (3 vols.; 1884-85; mostly borrowed from Castil-Blaze); etc.

Schlick, Arnolt, the elder, blind organist and lutenist; b. in Bohemia, c. 1460; d. after 1517. He was organist to the Count Palatine at Heidelberg (possibly from 1496 or even earlier), and since he bore the title of Imperial organist, he may have also served at one time at the court of Friedrich III. He toured Germany and Holland as organist, appearing in Worms (1495), Torgau, Hagenau, etc. —Works: *Spiegel der Orgelmacher und Organisten* (1511; reprinted by R. Eitner as a supplement to 'Monatshefte für Musik-Geschichte,' 1869; by E. Flade, 1932; by P. Smets, 1937, and Flade again, 1951); *Tablaturen etlicher Lobgesang und Lidlein uff die Orgeln und Lauten* (1512; new ed. by G. Harms, 1924; reprints by R. Eitner in 'Monatshefte für Musik-Geschichte,' 1869; A. G. Ritter, *Zur Geschichte des Orgelspiels,* II, 96, 1884; and Wm. Tappert, *Sang und Klang aus alter Zeit, Berlin,* 1906). —Cf. R. Eitner in 'Monatshefte für Musik-Geschichte,' XXI, 192; F. Stein, *Zur Geschichte der Musik in Heidelberg* (containing index of *Spiegel der Orgelmacher;* 1912; 2nd ed., 1921); A. Pirro, *Orgues et organistes de Haguenau,* in 'Revue de musicologie' (1926); R. Kendall, *Notes on A. Schlick,* in 'Acta Musicologica' (1939); H. H. Lenneberg, *The Critic Criticized: Sebastian Virdung and his Controversy with A. Schlick,* in the 'Journal of the American Musicological Society' (Spring, 1957). See also A. Mendel, *Pitch in the 16th and Early 17th Centuries,* in the 'Mus. Quarterly' (Jan., 1948).

Schlieder, Frederick William, American organist and composer; b. Foreston, Ill., Jan. 22, 1873; d. New York, Jan. 13, 1953. He studied at Syracuse Univ. (M. M., 1915); later took organ lessons in Paris with Guilmant; returning to America in 1905, he was active as concert organist; from 1910 till 1923, was organist at the Collegiate Church of St. Nicholas, N. Y.; also taught harmony at the Philadelphia Cons. He publ. *Lyric Composition through Improvisation: First Year's Training in Formal Self-expression* (Boston, 1927); a sequel was publ. by the Schlieder Book Foundation, Decatur, Ill. (1946); he further publ. *Beyond the Tonal Horizon of Music,* a collection of aphorisms (Decatur, Ill., 1948).

Schloezer, Boris de, writer on music; b. Vitebsk, Russia, Dec. 8, 1884; studied at the Brussels Cons. and in Paris; his sister, Tatiana Schloezer, was Scriabin's second wife; he was associated with Scriabin for many years beginning in 1905; lived in Moscow as music critic and lecturer; went to Kiev in 1918; in 1920, left Russia and settled in Paris; contributed to literary and musical magazines; lectured in France and Switzerland. —Books: *Scriabin* (vol. 1; Berlin, 1923; in Russian; vol. 2 was planned but not publ.); *Igor Stravinsky* (Paris, 1929; in French); *Introduction à J. S. Bach* (Paris, 1947).

Schlögel, Xavier, Belgian composer; b. Brillonville, Famène, July 14, 1854; d. Ciney, near Namur, March 23, 1889. He studied with Ledent at the Liège Cons. —Works: *Scènes champêtres* for orch.; *Ballade des épées* for voice and orch.; *Messe solennelle* for male chorus, organ, and orch.; string quartets and piano trios.

Schlösser, (Karl Wilhelm) Adolf, pianist, son and pupil of Louis Schlösser; b. Darmstadt, Feb. 1, 1830; d. Great Bookham, England, Nov. 10, 1913. He made his début at Frankfurt in 1847; after concert tours in Germany, France, and England, he settled in London (1854); taught (until 1903) at the Royal Academy of Music. —Works: piano quartet; piano trio; 24 studies and many other pieces for piano.

Schlösser, Louis, German composer; b. Darmstadt, Nov. 17, 1800; d. there, Nov. 17, 1886. He was a pupil of Rinck at Darmstadt; Seyfried, Mayseder, and Salieri at Vienna, and Le Sueur and Kreutzer at the Paris Cons.; was court conductor in Darmstadt. —Works (about 70 opus numbers publ.): the operas *Granada* (Vienna, 1826), *Das Leben ein Traum* (1839), *Die Jugend Karls II. von Spanien* (1847), *Die Braut des Herzogs* (1847), and *Benvenuto Cellini;* an operetta, *Kapitän Hector;* the melodrama *Die Jahreszeiten;* music to *Faust;* ballets, entr'actes, symphonies, overtures, string quartets, concertino for horn with orch., piano pieces, songs, etc.

Schlottmann, Louis, German pianist and composer; b. Berlin, Nov. 12, 1826; d. there, June 13, 1905. He studied with Taubert and Dehn; gave successful concerts in London and elsewhere, and settled in Berlin as a teacher. —Works: overtures to *Romeo and Juliet* and *Wallenstein's Lager; Trauermarsch, Rezitativ und Finale,* symph. scene for orch.; *Concertstück* for piano; chamber music; piano pieces *(3 Capricettes; Polonaise de concert; Andantino; Jugendspiegel);* choruses and songs.

Schlusnus, Heinrich, German baritone; b. Braubach, Aug. 6, 1888; d. Frankfurt, June 19, 1952. He studied with Louis Bachner in Berlin; was a member of the Nuremberg Opera (1915-17); on the roster of the Berlin State Opera (from 1917); made appearances with the leading opera companies of Europe; also with the Chicago Opera Co.; toured the U. S. as concert singer.

Schmedes (shmā-des), **Erik,** Danish tenor; b. Gjentofte, near Copenhagen, Aug. 27, 1868; d. Vienna, March 23, 1931. He studied piano, then turned to singing; studied with Mme. Artôt in Paris; made his operatic début as baritone in Wiesbaden (Jan. 11, 1891), as the Herald in *Lohengrin;* then sang baritone roles in Nuremberg and Dresden (1894-97). After a course of study with A. Iffert in Dresden, he developed a definite tenor voice, and appeared as Siegfried at the Vienna Opera (Feb. 11, 1898); remained as a tenor with the Vienna Opera until 1924. He was a member of the Metropolitan Opera Co. during the season of 1908-09; made his début as Siegmund (Nov. 18, 1908).

Schmeling, Gertrud. See **Mara.**

Schmelzer, Johann Heinrich, Austrian composer; b. Vienna, c. 1623; d. there, June 30, 1680. In 1649-70, violinist at the Vienna court chapel; 1671, assistant conductor; 1679, first conductor. He may have been the teacher of the famous violinist, Heinrich Biber. Composed valuable chamber music, including *Duodena selectarum sonatarum* (12 trio sonatas, 1659); *Sacro-profanus concentus musicus* (sonatas, for 2-8 instruments, 1662); *Sonate unarum fidium* (6 solo violin sonatas, 1664; one reprinted in the supplement to G. Beckermann's *Das Violinspiel in Deutschland vor 1700);* also the trumpet fanfares to Bertali's Festspiel, *La Contesa dell' aria* (1667), publ. as *Arie per il balletto a cavallo* (ed. by P. Nettl in 'Denkmäler der Tonkunst in Österreich,' vol. 56) and a *Missa nuptialis* (ed. by G. Adler in 'Denkmäler der Tonkunst in Österreich,' vol. 49). Other MSS of vocal and instrumental works by Schmelzer are in Vienna, Kromeriz, Paris, and Upsala. —Cf. E. Wellesz, *Die Ballett-Suiten von J. H. und A. A. Schmelzer* (Vienna, 1914); A. Moser, *Geschichte des Violinspiels* (p. 126 ff.); P. Nettl in 'Studien zur Musikwissenschaft' VIII.

Schmelzl (Schmeltzl, Schmaelzl), Wolfgang, b. Kemnat, Upper Palatinate, c. 1500; was at first a Protestant cantor at Amberg, where he married; then, c. 1540, a teacher in Vienna and singer at the S. Salvator Chapel, and finally a Catholic priest at St. Lorenz at Steinfeld, near Vienna, where he died c. 1561. He is known for a collection of 4-5 voiced quodlibets and folksongs of the period, published in 1544. Reprint by Schering in *Geschichte der Musik in Beispielen* (No. 111). —Cf. Elsa Bienenfeld, *W. S., sein Liederbuch (1544) und das Quodlibet des XVI. Jahrhunderts,* in 'Sammelbände der Internationalen Musik-Gesellschaft' VI, 1 (1904); R. Eitner, in 'Monatshefte für Musik-Geschichte' III, 201.

Schmid, Adolf, conductor and arranger; b. Hannsdorf, Austria, Nov. 18, 1868; d. Engelwood, N. J., Feb. 12, 1958. He studied at the Vienna Cons. (graduated, 1897); from 1901 to 1915 was music director of His Majesty's Theatre, London; in 1915 settled in the U. S.; conducted a season of the Boston Grand Opera Co. (1915-16) and the Pavlova Ballet Russe (1916-18); from 1930 to 1945, was chief arranger for the National Broadcasting Co.; made innumerable orchestral arrangements of various works, especially for schools; also wrote some incidental music for the theater; a *Caravan Dance;* a *Bacchanal Dance;* etc. He taught at the Juilliard School of Music, N. Y.; retired in 1953, and lived in Leonia, N. J. He publ. *The Language of the Baton* (N. Y., 1937).

Schmid, Anton, b. Pihl, near Leipa, Bohemia, Jan. 30, 1787; d. Baden, near Vienna, July 3, 1857. Was custodian of the music section in the Vienna Library. Publ. the monographs *Ottaviano dei Petrucci da Fossombrone, der erste Erfinder des Musiknotendruckes mit beweglichen Metalltypen, und seine Nachfolger im 16. Jahrhundert* (1845); *J. Haydn und N. Zingarelli* (1847; to prove that Haydn composed *Gott erhalte Franz den Kaiser); Christoph Willibald, Ritter von Gluck* (1854); and *Beiträge zur Literatur und Geschichte der Tonkunst* (in Dehn's 'Cäcilia,' 1842-46).

Schmid, Ernst Friedrich (Fritz), eminent German musicologist; b. Tübingen, March 7, 1904; studied natural science there and in Göttingen; music at the Munich Academy with Courvoisier (composition) and Sandberger (musicology); then at the Univ. of Freiburg-im-Breisgau; and in Vienna (under Lach and Robert Haas); *Dr. phil.* (Tübingen, 1929). In 1934 he went to Graz, where he organized a seminar in musicology; then was prof. at the Univ. of Tübingen (1935-37); was in the German army (1940-45). In 1948 he settled in Augsburg, where he developed numerous activities, as music critic, president of the Mozart Gesellschaft, general ed. of the 'Neue Mozart Ausgabe,' etc. His research in the field of Baroque music and in establishing the authenticity or the spuriousness of works of Haydn and Mozart is of the highest caliber. —Books: *C.Ph.E. Bach und seine Kammermusik* (Kassel, 1931); *Joseph Haydn: ein Buch von Heimat und Vorfahren* (Kassel, 1934); *W. A. Mozart* (Lübeck, 1935); ed. of *Ein schwäbisches Mozartbuch* (Stuttgart, 1947); edited numerous works by German and Austrian 18th-century composers; contributed valuable articles to musical periodicals, to 'Die Musik in Geschichte und Gegenwart,' etc.

Schmid, Heinrich Kaspar, German composer; b. Landau, Sept. 11, 1874; d. Odlung, near Munich, Jan. 8, 1953. He was a chorister at Regensburg, and studied there with J. Mitterer; in 1899 he entered the Munich Academy, where he was a pupil of Thuille and Bussmeyer. In 1903 he went to Athens, where he taught at the Odeon; in 1905 returned to Munich, taught at the Munich Academy (until 1921); then was director of the Karlsruhe Cons. (1921-24), director of the Augsburg Cons. (1924-32); from 1933 he occupied various positions in the Dept. of Education. His eyesight failed him, and he was totally blind during the last years of his life. As a composer, he continued the Romantic tradition of the Bavarian School; was at his best in lieder, of which he wrote a great number; also composed folk-like singspiele *(Finden und Meiden, Vilsbiburger Liebfrauenspiel,* etc.); *Tanzbilder aus unserer Zeit,* for men's voices and a dance ensemble; chamber music. —Cf. H. Roth, *H. K. Schmid* (Munich, 1921); W. Zentner, *H. K. Schmid,* in 'Neue Musikzeitschrift' (Aug.-Sept., 1949).

Schmid, Otto, German writer on music and editor; b. Dresden, May 6, 1858; d. there, Sept. 12, 1931. He abandoned the study of jurisprudence in Leipzig, and became a private pupil of Ed. Kretschmer in Dresden; 1912-24, prof. of history of music at the Cons. there; was also critic for the 'Dresdener Journal' and 'Sächsische Staatszeitung.' Publ. biographies of Koschat (1887) and Kretschmer (1890); also *Merkblätter zur Musikgeschichte* (1912); *Die Heimstätten der Sächsischen Landestheater* (1919); *R. Wagners Opern und Musikdramen in Dresden* (1919); *Der Mozart-Verein zu Dresden* (1921); *Geschichte der Staatsoper in Dresden* (2 vols., 1926-27). He ed. the important collection 'Musik am sächsischen Hofe' (10 vols.; compositions by Hasse, J. C. Schmidt, J. A. and C. S. Binder, Naumann, Petzold, etc., and members of the royal house); also 'Orgelwerke altböhmischer Meister' (2 vols.).

Schmidl, Carlo, Italian music publisher and lexicographer; b. Trieste, Oct. 7, 1859; d. there, Oct. 7, 1943. He was the son and pupil of the Hungarian composer Antonio Schmidl (1814-80). In 1872 he entered the employ of the music publisher Vicentini, and in 1889 he established his own business at Trieste; also directed the Leipzig branch of the Ricordi Co. (1901-06). He compiled and publ. an important biographical music dictionary, 'Dizionario universale dei musicisti' (Milan, 1887-89; 2nd ed., 1926-29; supplement 1938), containing scrupulously accurate data on Italian musicians, exact dates of performance of major works, and other information testifying to independent research. Schmidl also wrote biographies of Schumann (1890) and G. S. Mayr (1901).

Schmidt, Arthur Paul, music publisher; b. Altona, Germany, April 1, 1846; d. Boston, May 5, 1921. He settled in Boston in 1866, and entered the music firm of George D. Russell & Co. In 1876 he established a business of his own; for some years maintained branches in New York and Leipzig. Henry R. Austin became president of the firm in 1949. The A. P. Schmidt Co. won prominence by publication of the works of

MacDowell; brought out virtually the complete output of Arthur Foote (more than 150 items); also works by Chadwick, Hadley, Paine, and Mrs. Beach.

Schmidt, Franz, important Austrian composer; b. Pressburg, Dec. 22, 1874; d. Perchtoldsdorf, near Vienna, Feb. 11, 1939. He studied organ, piano, and cello at the Vienna Cons.; a pupil of Anton Bruckner (composition) and Robert Fuchs (theory); also took piano lessons with Leschetizky. From 1896 to 1911 he played cello in the Vienna Philharmonic Orch.; also taught at the Cons. (both cello and piano). From 1925 till 1927 he was director of the Vienna Academy of Music, and from 1927 to 1931, rector of the Hochschule für Musik; retired in 1937. While engaged in pedagogical activities, he continued to compose; his music is steeped in Viennese Romanticism, and the influence of Bruckner is particularly pronounced. Although he is regarded in Austria as a very important symphonic composer, his music is almost totally unknown elsewhere. —Works: operas, *Notre Dame* (Vienna, April 1, 1914; an orchestral suite from it entitled *Zwischenspiel aus einer unvollständigen romantischen Oper* was performed by the Vienna Philharmonic, Dec. 6, 1903); *Fredigundis* (Berlin, Dec. 19, 1922); oratorio, *Das Buch mit sieben Siegeln* (Vienna, June 15, 1938); 4 symphonies: No. 1 (Vienna, Jan. 25, 1902); No. 2 (Vienna, Dec. 3, 1913); No. 3 (Vienna, Dec. 2, 1928); No. 4 (Vienna, Jan. 10, 1934); *Konzertante Variationen über ein Thema von Beethoven* (piano concerto No. 1), for piano, left hand alone, and orch. (Vienna, Feb. 2, 1924, Paul Wittgenstein soloist); piano concerto No. 2, left hand alone (Vienna, Feb. 10, 1935, Wittgenstein soloist); *Chaconne,* for orch. (Vienna, Jan. 29, 1933); 2 string quartets; piano quintet; 2 clarinet quintets; several works for organ. —Cf. Andreas Liess, *Franz Schmidt. Leben und Schaffen* (Graz, 1951); Carl Nemeth, *Franz Schmidt. Ein Meister nach Brahms und Bruckner* (Vienna, 1957).

Schmidt, Gustav, German conductor and composer; b. Weimar, Sept. 1, 1816; d. Darmstadt, Feb. 11, 1882. While theater conductor at Frankfurt, he produced his operas *Prinz Eugen* (1845) and *Die Weiber von Weinsberg* (1858); other operas were *La Réole* (Breslau, 1863) and *Alibi.* He also wrote songs, ballads, and popular male choruses.

Schmidt, Heinrich, German editor; b. Kirchenlamitz, near Bayreuth, April 30, 1861; d. Bayreuth, May 23, 1923. Pupil of Rheinberger, Kellermann, and Riehl at the Königliche Akademie der Tonkunst in Munich; *Dr. phil.* (Univ. of Munich, 1897) with the dissertation *Joh. Mattheson, ein Förderer der deutschen Tonkunst, im Lichte seiner Werke* (Leipzig, 1897); from 1898 teacher at the seminary in Bayreuth. —He ed. 'Streichorchester für Mittelschulen' (8 vols.; selections of classical pieces), 'Der Männerchor auf natürlicher Grundlage' (1913), 'Der Chorgesang für Mittelschulen' (1918), and a new ed. of Hohmann's *Violinschule.* Publ. *Die Orgel unserer Zeit in Wort und Bild* (1904; 2nd ed., 1922) and *Richard Wagner in Bayreuth* (1909; with U. Hartmann).

Schmidt, Johann Philipp Samuel, German composer; b. Königsberg, Sept. 8, 1779; d. Berlin, May 9, 1853. He wrote operas for Königsberg and Berlin; many cantatas; 9 oratorios and Masses; symphonies; quintets and quartets for strings, etc.; also contributed to musical periodicals of Berlin and Leipzig.

Schmidt, John Henry, organist, composer, and singing teacher; b. in Germany; lived in Radevormwald, near Düsseldorf until Dec., 1783, when he arrived in Gouda, Holland; was appointed organist of the Cathedral of St. John at Schiedam on Oct. 23, 1785; held this office until 1790, when he sailed for Rio de Berbice, British Guiana. In 1793 he arrived in New York; in June, 1796 he appeared in Charleston and advertised as a singing teacher and piano manufacturer; towards the end of 1796 he settled in Philadelphia, where he became organist of St. Peter's Church (1797); also announced concerts in Baltimore (1796) and Albany (1797). He composed a *Sonata for Beginners.* —Cf. O. G. Sonneck, *Bibliography of Early Secular American Music* (Washington, 1905); O. G. Sonneck, *Early Concert Life in America* (Leipzig, 1907; in English); J. T. Howard, *Our American Music* (N. Y., 1939, and subsequent eds.).

Schmidt, Joseph, Rumanian tenor; b. Bavideni, Bukovina, March 4, 1904; d. Zürich, Nov. 16, 1942. He studied at the Berlin Cons.; in 1928 began his career as a radio singer, and won great popularity in Germany. In 1933 he went to Belgium; in 1938 was briefly in America; then settled in Switzerland. His voice was regarded as of great lyric expressiveness; but being almost a dwarf (he stood only 4 feet 10 inches in height), he was unable to appear in opera.

Schmidt, Karl, German music scholar; b. Friedberg (Hesse), July 10, 1869; d. there, Feb. 28, 1948. He studied in Leipzig; was active in school music in Laubach and Friedberg; publ. the valuable paper, *Quaestiones de musicis scriptoribus romanis imprimis Cassiodoro et Isidoro* (Leipzig, 1898).

Schmidt, Leopold, German writer on music; b. Berlin, Aug. 2, 1860; d. there, April 30, 1927. In 1880 he entered the Königliche Hochschule in Berlin, at the same time matriculating as a student of philosophy at the Univ. Was Kapellmeister in Heidelberg (1887), at the Friedrich Wilhelmstädtisches Theater in Berlin (1888), in Zürich (1891) and Halle (1895); *Dr. phil.,* Rostock (1895); from 1897 critic for the 'Berliner Tageblatt'; 1900-12, prof. of history of music at Stern's Cons.; from 1912, at the Klindworth-Scharwenka Cons. — Writings: *Zur Geschichte der Märchenoper* (dissertation, 1895); *G. Meyerbeer* (1898); *Haydn* (1898; 3rd ed., 1914; in Reimann's 'Berühmte Musiker'); *Geschichte der Musik im 19. Jahrhundert* (1901); *Moderne Musik* (being vol. III of *Die neue Kunst,* 1905); *Meister der Tonkunst im 19. Jahrhundert* (1908; 3rd ed., 1921); *Mozart* (1909; 2nd ed., 1913; in Reimann's 'Berühmte Musiker'); *Beethoven* (1914); collected criticisms publ. in 3 vols. (1909, 1913, 1922); ed. *Beethovenbriefe* (1909, 1922) and *Brahms Briefwechsel* (vol. 7, 1910); he also wrote several guides (Strauss' *Salome* and *Ariadne auf Naxos,* Gluck's *Orfeo,* etc.).

Schmidt-Görg, Joseph, German musicologist; b. Rüdinghausen, near Dortmund, March 13, 1897. He studied musicology with Schiedermair in Bonn; *Dr phil.,* 1926; became Schiedermair's assistant in the Beethoven Archives at Bonn on Beethoven's centennial in 1927; in 1945 was appointed director; also taught musicology at the Univ. of Bonn (from 1930). —Books: *Unbekannte Manuskripte zu Beethovens weltlicher und geistlicher Gesangsmusik* (Bonn, 1928); *Das rheinische Volkslied* (Düsseldorf, 1934); *Katalog der Handschriften des Beethoven-Hauses und Beethoven-Archivs* (Bonn, 1935); *Nicolas Gombert* (Bonn, 1938),

Schmieder, Wolfgang, German musicologist; b. Bromberg, May 29, 1901; studied with Kroyer and Moser; was keeper of the archives for Breitkopf & Härtel in Leipzig; 1942, appointed chief of the Music Division of the State Library in Frankfurt. He compiled the valuable *Thematisch-systematisches Verzeichnis der musikalischen Werke von J. S. Bach* (Leipzig, 1950), also ed. the songs of Neidhart von Reuental, in 'Denkmäler der Tonkunst in Österreich' (vol. 71).

Schminke, Oscar Eberhard, American organist and composer; b. New York, Dec. 12, 1881. He suffered from partial deafness since his childhood, and after taking piano lessons, decided to change to another profession; entered the N. Y. College of Dentistry, graduating in 1903; however, he continued to study music after 1909; took organ lessons with Gaston Déthier in N. Y. He publ. several works for organ *(Marche russe, Poème exotique,* etc.); piano pieces *(Chameleon, Moods,* etc.); about a dozen songs. After a long period of inactivity, he returned to music in 1948, using an electronic hearing aid; wrote a piano quintet; a flute quintet; a *Concertante,* for flute, clarinet, and piano; a piano trio; lived at Kenoza Lake, N. Y.

Schmit, Camille, Belgian composer; b. Aubange, March 30, 1908. He studied at the Brussels Cons.; later became instructor of harmony at the Cons. of Liège. He wrote for orch. a *Triptyque* and *Préludes joyeux* (Festival of the International Society for Contemporary Music, Copenhagen, June 2, 1947); also a wind quintet; piano pieces; songs.

Schmitt, Aloys, German pianist and eminent teacher; b. Erlenbach, Aug. 26, 1788; d. Frankfurt, July 25, 1866. He was the son and pupil of a cantor; studied composition with André at Offenbach; settled in Frankfurt in 1816, remaining there except for a few years in Berlin and Hanover. He wrote 4 operas, *Der Doppelgänger* (Hanover, 1827), *Valeria* (Mannheim, 1832), *Das Osterfest zu Paderborn* (Frankfurt, 1843), and *Die Tochter der Wüste* (Frankfurt, 1845); 2 oratorios *(Moses* and *Ruth);* church music; etc.; but he is known as a composer only through his valuable works for piano: a method; studies; rhapsodies; rondos; sonatinas; etc.; he also wrote 4 piano concertos, several piano quartets, and piano trios. —Cf. H. Henkel, *Leben und Wirken von Dr. Aloys Schmitt* (Frankfurt, 1873).

Schmitt, Florent, outstanding French composer; b. Blâmont, Sept. 28, 1870; d. Neuilly, near Paris, Aug. 17, 1958. He had his first music lessons from H. Hess (piano) and G. Sandré (harmony) in Nancy. In 1889 he went to Paris, where he studied with Dubois and Lavignac (harmony), Massenet and Fauré (composition). He won the 2nd Prix de Rome in 1897 with the cantata *Frédégonde* and the 1st prize in 1900 with the cantata *Sémiramis,* which was performed at a Colonne concert on Dec. 11, 1900. He spent the years 1901-04 in the Villa Medicis in Rome, sending to the Académie several important instrumental and choral works (1st movement of a piano quintet, *Le Palais hanté* [symph. sketch after Edgar Allen Poe], and Psalm XLVII), as 'envois de Rome'; then spent 2 years traveling in Germany, Austria, Hungary, and Turkey. In 1906 he settled permanently in Paris, devoting himself entirely to composition. He served as a member of the executive committee of the 'Société Musicale Indépendante' since its foundation in 1909; was also a member of the 'Société Nationale de Musique.' His formative years were spent in the ambient of French symbolism in poetry and Impressionism in music, and he followed these directions in his programmatically conceived orchestral music; but he developed a strong, distinctive style of his own, mainly by elaborating the contrapuntal fabric of his works and extending the rhythmic design to unprecedented asymmetrical combinations; he also exploited effects of primitivistic percussion, in many respects anticipating the developments of modern Russian music. He was not averse to humor; several of his works have topical allusions. The catalogue of his works is very long, and he continued to compose until his death at the age of 87; attended the première of his symphony, given at the Strasbourg Festival of the International Society for Contemporary Music, June 15, 1958. He visited the U. S. in 1932 as soloist in his *Symphonie concertante* with the Boston Symph. He was an influential music critic, writing regularly for 'Le Temps' (1919-39). —Works: Ballets: *La Tragédie de Salomé* (Paris, Nov. 9, 1907); *Le Petit Elfe Ferme-l'œil,* after Hans Christian Andersen (Opéra-Comique, Feb. 29, 1924); *Oriane la sans-égale* (Paris Opéra, Jan. 7, 1938); incidental music to *Antoine et Cléopâtre,* after Shakespeare (Paris Opéra, June 14, 1920); *Reflets* (Opéra-Comique, May 20, 1932). Vocal music with orch.: *Musique sur l'eau* (1898); *Psaume XLVII,* for soprano, chorus, orch., and organ (1904; Paris, Dec. 27, 1906); *Danse des Devadasis,* for solo voice, chorus, and orch. (1900-08); *Tristesse au Jardin* (1897-1908); *Chant de Guerre,* for tenor, male chorus, and orch. (1914); *Kerob-Shal,* for tenor and orch. (1920-24); *Fête de la lumière,* for soprano, chorus, and orch. (1937); *L'Arbre entre tous,* for chorus and orch. (1939); *À contre-voix,* for mixed chorus (1943); motets and choruses a cappella. For orch.: *En été* (1894); *Feuillets de voyage* (1903-13); *Reflets de l'Allemagne,* suite of waltzes (1905); *Puppazzi,* suite in 8 movements (1907); *Musiques de plein-air* (1897-99); *Sélamlik,* symph. poem for military band (1906); *Le Palais hanté,* symph. study after Poe (1900-04); *Trois Rapsodies* (1903-04); *Scherzo vif,* for violin and orch. (1903-10); *La Tragédie de Salomé,* from the ballet of the same title (Paris, Jan. 8, 1911); *Légende,* for viola (or saxophone) and orch. (1918); *Mirages: Tristesse de Pan, La tragique Chevauchée* (1921); *Fonctionnaire MCMXII: Inaction en Musique* (1924; Paris, Jan. 16, 1927); *Danse d'Abisag* (1925); *Salammbô,* 6 symph. episodes after Flaubert, from film music (1925); *Ronde burlesque* (1927; Paris, Jan. 12, 1930); *Çançunik* (humorous phonetic spelling of *Sens unique,* i.e., one-way street; Paris, Feb. 15, 1930); *Symphonie Concertante,* for piano and orch. (Boston, Schmitt soloist, Nov. 25, 1932); *Suite sans esprit de suite* (Paris, Jan. 29, 1938); *Branle de sortie* (Paris, Jan. 21, 1939); *Janiana,* for strings (1941); *Habeyssée,* for violin and orch. (phonetic representation of ABC, as pronounced in French; Paris, March 14, 1947); symphony (1957; Strasbourg, June 15, 1958). Chamber music: *Scherzo-pastorale,* for flute and piano (1889); *Quatre pièces,* for violin and piano (1901); *Andante et Scherzo,* for harp and string quartet (1906); piano quintet (1901-08); *Lied et Scherzo,* for double wind quintet (1910); *Sonate libre en deux parties enchainées,* for violin and piano (1919); *Suite en rocaille,* for flute, violin, viola, cello, and harp (1934); *Sonatine en trio,* for flute, clarinet, and harpsichord (1935); *Minorités,* for flute, violin, and piano (1938); *Hasards,* for violin, viola, cello, and piano (1939); *À tours d'anches,* for flute, clarinet, bassoon, and piano (1939); quartet for saxophones (1941); string trio (1944); quartet for flutes (1944); string quartet (1945-48). For piano: *Soirs* (10 preludes); *Ballade de la neige* (1896); *Musiques intimes* (2 sets; 1890-1900 and 1898-1904); *Nuits romaines* (1901); *Puppazzi,* 8 pieces (1907; also for orch.); *Pièces romantiques* (6 pieces; 1900-08); *Trois Danses* (1935; also for orch.); *Feuillets de voyage* (1903; also for orch.); *Suite sans esprit de suite* (1938; also for orch.); *Clavecin obtempérant,* suite (1945); etc. *Reflets de l'Allemagne,* 8 waltzes for piano, 4 hands (1905; also for orch.). Songs: *Soir sur le lac* (1898); *Quatre lieds,* to words by Richepin, Maeterlinck, etc.; *Kerob-Shal,* 3 songs (also for voice and orch.). —Cf.

M. D. Calvocoressi, *Œuvres de Florent Schmitt,* in 'L'Art Moderne' (Jan. 6, 1907); O. Séré, *Musiciens français d'aujourd'hui* (rev. ed., Paris, 1921); G. Jean-Aubry, *La Musique française d'aujourd'hui* (Paris, 1916); A. Cœuroy, *La Musique française moderne* (Paris, 1922); P. O. Ferroud, *Autour de Florent Schmitt* (Paris, 1927); Eric Blom, *Florent Schmitt,* in the 'Chesterian' (March, 1932); Yves Hucher, *Florent Schmitt, l'homme et l'artiste* (Paris, 1953).

Schmitt, Georg Aloys, son and pupil of Aloys Schmitt; b. Hanover, Feb. 2, 1827; d. (suddenly, during a rehearsal) Dresden, Oct. 15, 1902. He studied theory with Vollweiler at Heidelberg. After pianistic tours in Germany, France, Belgium, and Algiers, he visited London, became theater conductor at Aix-la-Chapelle, Würzburg, etc., and 1857-92 court conductor at Schwerin; from 1893, director of the 'Mozartverein,' Dresden, which flourished under his sway (chorus of 1,400 and its own orch.). He wrote 3 operas; also incidental music to plays; overtures and other orch. works; string quartets; piano trios; piano pieces; songs. He revised and completed Mozart's Mass in C minor (1901), and orchestrated compositions by Handel and Mozart. —He was married to the singer **Cornelia Czanyi** (b. Debreczin, Dec. 6, 1851; d. Wismar, Oct. 11, 1906).

Schmitt, Hans, piano teacher; b. Koben, Bohemia, Jan. 14, 1835; d. Vienna, Jan. 14, 1907. At first an oboist at Bucharest and Vienna, throat-trouble compelled him to give up that instrument, and he studied the piano under Dachs at the Vienna Cons., 1860-62, taking the silver medal, and being appointed teacher at the Cons. —His instructive works for piano include *300 Studies without Octave-stretches; Vademecum; Fundament der Klaviertechnik; Zirkelübungen in Skalen und Akkorden; 120 kleine Vortragsstücke; Repertoirestudien; Das Pedal des Klaviers* (1875, after Louis Köhler; in English, 1893).

Schmitt, Jacob (Jacques), brother and pupil of Aloys Schmitt; b. Obernburg, Bavaria, Nov. 2, 1803; d. Hamburg, June, 1853. Piano teacher; of some 370 works, his sonatinas for piano (2 and 4 hands) are especially useful; also the *Musikalisches Schatzkästlein,* a collection of 133 short pieces; his method, op. 301, and studies, rondos, and nocturnes were also popular.

Schmitz, Arnold, German musicologist; b. Sablon, near Metz, July 11, 1893; studied in Bonn (with Schiedermair), in Munich and Berlin (with Kaun and Beer-Walbrunn); 1921-28, on the faculty of the Univ. of Bonn; 1929-39, in Breslau; 1939-45 in the military service; in 1947, appointed prof. at the Univ. of Mainz. —Writings: *Beethovens 'zwei Prinzipe'* (1923); *Das romantische Beethovenbild* (1927); *Die Bildlichkeit der wortgebundenen Musik J. S. Bachs* (1950).

Schmitz, Elie Robert, eminent pianist; b. Paris, Feb. 8, 1889; d. San Francisco, Sept. 5, 1949. He studied at the Paris Cons. with Diémer, winning 1st prize in piano; in 1908 toured as accompanist of Slezak, Emma Eames, and other celebrated singers; in 1912, organized the Association des Concerts Schmitz in Paris, which he led until 1914; in 1919, toured the U. S. as pianist; in 1920 founded the Franco-American Music Society in N. Y. (incorporated in 1923 as Pro Musica), of which he was president from its inception; toured again in the U. S. and Europe (1921-29), and the Orient (1929-30 and 1932-33); eventually settled in San Francisco as a teacher. He publ. a book on his system of piano study, *The Capture of Inspiration* (N. Y., 1935; 2nd ed., 1944) and a valuable technical analysis with commentary, *The Piano Works of Claude Debussy* (N. Y., 1950).

Schmitz, Eugen, German musicologist; b. Neuberg, Bavaria, July 12, 1882. He entered the Univ. of Munich to study law, but soon went over to musicology under A. Sandberger and Th. Kroyer at the Univ. and theory under A. Beer-Walbrunn; *Dr. phil.* in 1905 with the dissertation *Leben und Wirken des Nürnberger Komponisten Johann Staden* (publ. 1906). 1908, critic for the 'Münchener Zeitung' and ed. of 'Neue musikalische Rundschau'; 1910, instructor for musicology at the Univ. In 1914-15 he was director of the Mozarteum in Salzburg; then settled in Dresden as music ed. of 'Dresdener Nachrichten'; 1916, instructor at the Dresden Technische Hochschule; 1918, prof. From 1939 to 1953 he was director of the Musikbibliothek Peters in Leipzig. —Writings: *Hugo Wolf* (Leipzig, 1906); *Richard Strauss als Musikdramatiker* (Munich, 1907); *Richard Wagner* (1909; 2nd ed., 1918); *Harmonielehre als Theorie* (1911); *Palestrina* (1914; 2nd ed., 1954); *Geschichte der Kantate und des geistlichen Konzerts* (1914); *Musikästhetik* (1915); *O. di Lasso* (1915); *Das Madonnen-Ideal in der Tonkunst* (1919); *Klavier, Klaviermusik und Klavierspiel* (1919); *Richard*

Wagner; wie wir ihn heute sehen (1937); *Schuberts Auswirkung auf die deutsche Musik*... (1954); *Geschichte der weltlichen Solokantate* (2nd ed., 1955); etc. Edited works of Johann Staden (vols. VII, 1 and VIII, 1 of 'Denkmäler der Tonkunst in Bayern'). Also publ. original choruses and songs.

Schmuller, Alexander, violinist; b. Mozyr, Russia, Dec. 5, 1880; d. Amsterdam, March 29, 1933. Pupil of Ševčik, Hřimaly, and Auer; from 1908 he taught at the Stern Cons. in Berlin, and from 1914 at the Amsterdam Cons. For several years he gave concerts with Max Reger, whose music he was one of the first to champion; made many concert tours in Europe and the U. S.

Schnabel (shnah'-bel), **Artur,** celebrated pianist and pedagogue; b. Lipnik, Austria, April 17, 1882; d. Axenstein, Switzerland, Aug. 15, 1951. After taking lessons for two years from Hans Schmitt, he studied in Vienna with Leschetizky (1891-97); appeared in public as a child prodigy; lived many years in Berlin, where he gave joint recitals with the violinist Karl Flesch; formed (1912) a trio with A. Wittenberg (violin) and A. Hekking (cello); from 1925 until 1933 he taught at the Hochschule für Musik in Berlin; after the advent of the Nazi regime he went to Switzerland, where he organized his famous master classes during summer seasons. He made his American début in 1921, and revisited the U. S. several times; lived in N. Y. after 1939, but eventually returned to Europe. It was as an interpreter of Beethoven that he reached his greatest heights; he was distinguished also in his performances of the piano music of Brahms. His pedagogical method was strict in the observance of every detail of the music, but at the same time he inspired his pupils by encouraging an individual treatment in the matter of dynamics and formal concept. Schnabel was also a composer; in his works he pursued an uncompromisingly modernistic idiom, thriving on dissonance, and tracing melodic patterns along atonal lines. —Works: symph. No. 1 (1938-40; Minneapolis, Dec. 13, 1946); Rhapsody for orch. (Cleveland, April 15, 1948); a piano concerto; chamber music. He publ. *Reflections on Music* (Manchester, 1933; N. Y., 1934) and *Music and the Line of Most Resistance* (Princeton, 1942); edited the piano sonatas of Beethoven. —Cf. César Saerchinger, *Artur Schnabel* (London, 1957).

Schnabel, Joseph Ignaz, German composer of sacred music; b. Naumburg-on-Queiss, Silesia, May 24, 1767; d. Breslau, June 16, 1831. He was appointed Kapellmeister at the Cathedral of Breslau (1804) and remained in Breslau for the rest of his life; from 1812 taught at the Roman Catholic Seminary and was director of the Royal Institute for Church Music. He wrote many sacred works; publ. 5 Masses, 4 Graduals, 2 offertories, hymns, etc., also wrote marches for military band; a quintet for guitar and strings; and a clarinet concerto. His brother, **Michael Schnabel** (b. Naumburg, Sept. 23, 1775; d. Breslau, Nov. 6, 1842), founded a piano factory in Breslau (1814); his son, **Carl Schnabel** (1809-1881), who was an excellent pianist and composer of operas and piano music, carried on the business after Michael Schnabel's death. —Cf. H.E. Guckel, *Joseph Ignaz Schnabel,* part 2 of *Katholische Kirchenmusik in Schlesien* (Leipzig, 1912).

Schnabel, Karl Ulrich, pianist and composer; son of Artur Schnabel; b. Berlin, Aug. 6, 1909. He studied piano with Leonid Kreutzer and composition with Paul Juon in Berlin; after a series of appearances as soloist in Europe, including Russia, he made an American tour (début, N. Y., Feb. 23, 1937); played 2-piano recitals with his father; also gave duo-piano concerts (4 hands at 1 piano) with his wife, Helen Fogel. He has written piano pieces and chamber music.

Schnéevoigt (shnā'-voiht), **Georg Lennart,** conductor; b. Viborg, Finland, Nov. 8, 1872; d. Malmö, Nov. 28, 1947. He studied cello with Karl Schröder in Sondershausen and Julius Klengel in Leipzig; appeared as cellist; in 1900 began his career as conductor; from 1904 to 1908 conducted the Kaim Orch. in Munich; from 1909 to 1920, the Riga Symph.; in 1912, founded a symph. orch. in Helsinki, which became known as the Municipal Orch. in 1914; from 1915 to 1924 he led the 'Konsertförening' in Stockholm; in 1919 founded the Oslo Symph. Orch.; also conducted in Germany; conducted the Los Angeles Philharmonic (1927-29); was general director of the National Opera in Riga (1929-32); then went to Malmö, Sweden. In 1907 he married the pianist, Sigrid Sundgren (q.v.).

Schneider, Alexander, violinist; b. Vilna, Dec. 21, 1908. He studied at the Frankfurt Cons.; was concertmaster of the Frankfurt Symph. Orch. (1925-33); 2nd violin of the Budapest Quartet (1933-44 and since 1957); after 1933 lived mostly in the U. S.

In 1950 he established, with Casals, annual summer festivals at Prades, France; and from 1957, collaborated with Casals in the spring festivals in Puerto Rico. He has done much teaching, and has organized, and at times conducted, special concerts.

Schneider, Edward Faber, American pianist, composer, and pedagogue; b. Omaha, Oct. 3, 1872; d. Santa Clara, Calif., July 1, 1950. He studied with local teachers in California; with X. Scharwenka in N. Y., and with H. Barth in Berlin; then settled in San Francisco as piano teacher; subsequently taught at Mills College for 25 years. Several of his orchestral works were performed in San Francisco: *In Autumn Time* (1913), *Sargasso Sea* (1922), and *Thus Spake the Deepest Stone* (1938); he further wrote many piano pieces and songs.

Schneider, Friedrich, German organist and composer; b. Alt-Waltersdorf, Saxony, Jan. 3, 1786; d. Dessau, Nov. 23, 1853. Son and pupil of Johann Gottlob Schneider (b. 1753; d. as organist at Gersdorf, May 3, 1840); attended the Zittau Gymnasium and (1805) Leipzig Univ. As the pupil of Unger at Zittau, he early began composing, and publ. 3 piano sonatas in 1803; was appointed organist of the Thomaskirche at Leipzig in 1812, and in 1817 music director of the City Theater. In 1820 his oratorio, *Das Weltgericht,* made him famous, and he was called to Dessau in 1821 as court Kapellmeister. Here he founded a celebrated school of music in 1829, which was not closed until 1854; among his pupils were R. Franz, F. Spindler, and Karl Anschütz. He also conducted many music festivals. In 1830 the degree of *Dr. phil.* was conferred on him by Halle Univ. —His oratorios were often performed. Other works: 14 Masses; 13 motets and psalms; 25 cantatas; 5 hymns; 7 operas; 23 symphonies; many overtures; 7 concertos with orch.; piano quartets; trios; sonatas for violin (or flute); 400 men's choruses; 200 songs; piano sonatas for 2 and 4 hands, etc. (complete ed. of his piano works publ. at Halberstadt). Also publ. *Elementarbuch der Harmonie und Tonsetzkunst* (1820; etc.; in English, 1828); *Vorschule der Musik* (1827); *Handbuch des Organisten* (1829-30; in 4 parts). — Cf. F. Kempe, *F. Schneider als Mensch und Künstler* (Dessau, 1859; 2nd ed., Berlin, 1864); K. Hoede, *F. Schneider und die Zerbster Liedertafel zur Hundertjahrfeier 1927* (Zerbst, 1927); A. Schering, in *Geschichte des Oratoriums* (p. 347 ff.).

Schneider, Georg Abraham, German horn virtuoso and composer; b. Darmstadt, April 19, 1770; d. Berlin, Jan. 19, 1839. He was a member of the royal orch. at Berlin; from 1820 was Kapellmeister of the Court Opera and 'Musikmeister' of all regiments of the Guards. —Works: the operettas *Der Orakelspruch, Aucassin und Nicolette, Die Verschworenen, Der Traum, Der Währwolf;* 13 ballets; music to numerous plays, melodramas, etc.; 2 oratorios; cantatas, orchestral Masses; 54 entr'actes for orch.; symphonies and overtures; concertos for horn, flute, oboe, English horn, bassoon, etc.; quintets, quartets, and other chamber music for wind instruments (over 100 works were publ.).

Schneider, Johann, outstanding German organist; brother of Friedrich Schneider; b. Alt-Gersdorf, near Zittau, Oct. 28, 1789; d. Dresden, April 13, 1864. He was a pupil at the Zittau Gymnasium, and later 'regens chori' there; matriculated in 1810 at Leipzig as a law student, but next year succeeded his brother as Univ. organist (at the Paulinerkirche), and in 1812 became organist of the Church of Saints Peter and Paul at Görlitz, also founding a singing society there, and giving organ concerts at Dresden, Leipzig, Liegnitz, etc. In 1825 he was appointed court organist at Dresden. He was praised by Mendelssohn as one of the finest German organ virtuosos of the period; was famous as a teacher; among his pupils were Berthold (his successor as court organist), G. Merkel, F. G. Jansen, K. E. Naumann, Willem Nicolai, and Van Eycken. —Works: fugues, fantasias, and preludes, for organ; songs with organ obbligato.

Schneider, (Johann) Julius, German organist, choral conductor, and composer; b. Berlin, July 6, 1805; d. there, April 3, 1885. He was a pupil of A. W. Bach, Türrschmidt, and L. Berger (piano), Hausmann (organ), and B. Klein (composition). In 1829, organist and cantor of the Friedrichwerder Church (where he organized a liturgical choir in 1852); 1835-58, singing teacher at the Municipal Industrial School; 1854, teacher of organ, singing, and composition at the Royal Institute for Church Music. — Works (few publ.): church music; 200 men's choruses; organ pieces; a piano concerto and piano sonatas; chamber music; etc.

Schneider, Karl Ernst, German writer on music; b. Aschersleben, Dec. 29, 1819; d. Dresden, Oct. 25, 1893. He was a teacher at a music school at the time of his death.

—Publications: *Das musikalische Lied in geschichtlicher Entwickelung* (1863-65; 3 vols.); *Zur Periodisierung der Musikgeschichte* (1863); and *Musik, Klavier und Klavierspiel* (1872).

Schneider, Louis, French writer on music; b. Lyons, June 23, 1861; d. Grenoble, Aug. 21, 1934. He lived in Paris as music and drama critic of 'La Paix,' 'Gaulois,' 'New York Herald,' 'Revue de France,' etc. Author of *Schumann, sa vie et ses œuvres* (1905; in collaboration with Mareschal); *Massenet* (1908; 2nd ed., 1926); *Monteverdi* (1921); *Offenbach, Hervé, Charles Lecocq, maîtres de l'opérette française* (2 vols., 1924); also of a vol. of humorous musical chronicles under the pen-name 'Le Pompier de service.'

Schneider, Marius, Alsatian musicologist; b. Hageneau, July 1, 1903. He studied in Strasbourg, Paris, and Berlin; from 1931 till 1939 was in charge of the recording section at the Ethnological Museum in Berlin; from 1944 to 1951, lived in Barcelona; in 1951, appointed prof. at the Univ. of Cologne. —Publications: *Die Ars nova des 14. Jahrhunderts in Frankreich und Italien* (diss., Wolfenbüttel, 1931); *Geschichte der Mehrstimmigkeit* (2 vols., 1934, 1935); *El Origen musical de los animales-simbolos in la mitología y la escultura antiguas* (Barcelona, 1946); *La Danza de espadas y la tarantela* (Barcelona, 1948); *Singende Steine* (1955); contributed numerous articles to musical and ethnological publications.

Schneider, Max, eminent German musicologist; b. Eisleben, July 20, 1875. While a student at the Gymnasium in Weimar he devoted much time to music; studied musicology at Leipzig Univ. under Paul, Riemann, and Kretzschmar, and composition under Jadassohn (1895-97); 1897-1901, Kapellmeister at the Stadttheater in Halle. Owing to an injury to his foot he declined an appointment as chorusmaster at the Hofoper, Munich (1901), and returned to his studies in musicology under Kretzschmar; when the latter became prof. at the Berlin Univ. in 1904, he followed him and was appointed librarian of the musical seminary at the Univ.; 1907-14 he was also Kopfermann's assistant in the music division of the Royal Library; 1909-15, teacher of orchestration and score-reading at the 'Royal Academic Institute for Church Music'; 1915, associate prof. at the Univ. in Breslau; 1920, prof.; 1928, succeeded Schering as prof. at the Univ. of Halle. From 1912-14 he was ed., with H. Springer and W. Wolffheim, of 'Miscellanea musicae bio-bibliographica,' supplement to Eitner's 'Quellenlexikon'; from 1933 ed. of the 'Zeitschrift für Musikwissenschaft'; 1936 through 1938 ed., with R. Steglich, H. Besseler, and G. Schünemann, of the 'Archiv für Musikforschung' (continuation of the 'Zeitschrift'). —Writings: *Die Anfänge des Basso continuo* (1918); *Der deutsche Kantor* (1920); *Seltene Musikinstrumente* (in 'Schlesien's Vorzeit,' Breslau, 1928); *Beiträge zu einer Anleitung Clavichord und Cembalo zu spielen* (Strasbourg, 1934); *Beiträge zur Musikforschung* (vol. I, Halle, 1935); numerous smaller essays in various journals; publ. reprints of Mattheson's *Ehrenpforte* (1910; with bibliographical additions) and Diego Ortiz's *Tratado de glosas sobre cláusulas* (1913, with transl.; 2nd ed., Kassel, 1936). In the 'Denkmäler deutscher Tonkunst' he ed. works by Telemann (vol. 28; with biography) and Keiser (vols. 37 and 38); revised Bach's *St. Matthew Passion* (Leipzig, 1936); co-ed. of the Neue Bachgesellschaft editions; ed. of 'Altbachisches Archiv' (vol. I: motets and choral songs; vol. II: cantatas; Leipzig, 1935); ed., with Th. Siebs, of 'Schlesische Volkslieder mit Bildern und Weisen' (Breslau, 1924); also ed. the works of H. Schütz, etc. —Cf. 'Festschrift Max Schneider zum 60. Geburtstag' (Halle, 1935); 'Festschrift Max Schneider zum 80. Geburtstag' (Leipzig, 1955).

Schneider, Theodor, cellist and conductor; son of Friedrich Schneider; b. Dessau, May 14, 1827; d. Zittau, June 15, 1909. He studied with his father, and with Drechsler (cello); in 1845 was cellist in the Dessau court orch.; in 1854, cantor and choir director of the court and city churches; from 1860-96 served as cantor and music director at the Jakobikirche in Chemnitz; also conductor of the 'Singakademie' and of a 'Männergesangverein' which he founded in 1870. He retired in 1898.

Schneider-Trnavský, Mikuláš, Slovak composer; b. Trnava, May 24, 1881; d. Bratislava, May 28, 1958. He studied in Budapest, Vienna, and Prague; was chorusmaster at the Cathedral of Trnava; in 1918 appointed school inspector of music in Slovakia. He brought out (in 1904) excellent arrangements of Slovak songs for voice and piano (revised in 1922 and 1935-40); also wrote a *Slovak Sonata* for piano; some symph. works; church music, including several Masses (*Missa 'Stella Matutina,' Missa facilis, Missa pastoralis,* etc.).

Schnerich (shnā'-riyh), **Alfred,** Austrian musicologist; b. Tarvis, Carinthia, Oct. 22, 1859; d. Vienna, April 29, 1944. He studied history of art at the Institut für österreichisches Geschichtsforschung in Vienna; *Dr. phil.* in 1888; from 1889, librarian at Vienna Univ.; 1921, Hofrat; retired in 1923. Was a member of the editorial commission of the 'Denkmäler der Tonkunst in Österreich.' —Works: *Der Messentypus von Haydn bis Schubert* (1892); *Die Frage der Reform der katholischen Kirchenmusik* (1902; a reply to the attacks of the 'Cäcilienverein'); *Messe und Requiem seit Haydn und Mozart* (1909); *Unsere Kirchenmusik und P. M. Horn. Eine Abwehr* (1911); *Jos. Haydn und seine Sendung* (1922; 2nd ed., 1926); *Die kirchliche Tonkunst* (1927); articles. Publ. in facsimile the autograph score of Mozart's Requiem (1913; with explanatory notes).

Schnitger (Schnitker), Arp, German organ builder; b. Golzwarden, Oldenburg, July 2, 1648; d. Neuenfelde, July 24, 1719. His organs are in the Nikolai- and Jakobikirche, Hamburg; the Cathedral and Stephanskirche at Bremen; the Johanniskirche at Magdeburg; the Nikolaikirche at Berlin; etc. —His son **Franz Kaspar** (d. 1729) worked with an elder brother at Zwolle, Holland, building the organ at Zwolle (63 stops), and that at Alkmar (56 stops). —Cf. P. Rubardt, *Arp Schnitger* (Freiberg, 1928); G. Fock, *Schnitger und seine Schule* (Kiel, 1931).

Schnoor, Hans, German writer on music; b. Neumünster, Oct. 4, 1893. He studied with H. Riemann and A. Schering at the Univ. of Leipzig; became a music critic in Dresden (1926-45); in 1949 settled in Bielefeld. —Publications: *Die Musik der germanischen Völker im XIX. und XX. Jahrhundert* (Dresden, 1926); *Weber auf dem Welttheater* (Dresden, 1942); *Weber: ein Lebensbild aus Dresdner Sicht* (Dresden, 1947); *400 Jahre deutscher Musikkultur; zum Jubiläum der Staatskapelle und zur Geschichte der Dresdner Oper* (Dresden, 1948;) *Geschichte der Musik* (1953); *Weber; Gestalt und Schöpfung* (1953); *Oper, Operette, Konzert; ein praktisches Nachschlagsbuch* (1955).

Schnorr von Carolsfeld, Ludwig, German tenor; b. Munich, July 2, 1836; d. Dresden, July 21, 1865. Son of the noted painter; pupil of J. Otto at Dresden, and of the Leipzig Cons.; then of Ed. Devrient at Karlsruhe, making his début there, followed by engagement in 1858. From 1860, leading tenor at Dresden. He created the role of Tristan in Wagner's *Tristan und Isolde* at Munich, June 10, 1865, his wife singing Isolde. He died shortly afterwards, of heart failure, at the age of 29. —Cf. R. Wagner, *Meine Erinnerungen an Ludwig Schnorr von Carolsfeld,* in vol. VIII of 'Gesammelte Schriften und Dichtungen'; C. H. N. Garrigues, *Ein ideales Sängerpaar, Ludwig Schnorr von Carolsfeld und Malwine Schnorr von Carolsfeld* (Copenhagen, 1937).

Schnorr von Carolsfeld *(née* Garrigues), **Malwine,** soprano; wife of the preceding; b. Copenhagen, Dec. 7, 1832; d. Karlsruhe, Feb. 8, 1904. She created Isolde on June 10, 1865, in Munich, her husband singing Tristan; after his death she sang in Hamburg, and later in Karlsruhe; after her retirement from the stage she taught. In 1867 she publ. a volume of poems by her husband and herself. —Cf. C. H. N. Garrigues, *op. cit.* (above).

Schnyder von Wartensee, Xaver, composer; b. Lucerne, April 16, 1786; d. Frankfurt, Aug. 27, 1868. A pupil at Vienna of J. C. Kienlen; joined the campaign against the French in 1815; taught at the Pestalozzian Institute, Yverdun; and in 1817 settled in Frankfurt. —His works include cantatas; sacred and secular songs; Swiss songs for men's chorus; etc.; *System der Rhythmik* (posthumous publ. by B. Widmann). —Cf. *Lebenserinnerungen von X. Schnyder von Wartensee* (Zürich, 1887; contains an autobiography and a complete list of works; new ed. by Willi Schuh, Berlin, 1940).

Schoberlechner, Franz, pianist and composer; b. Vienna, July 21, 1797; d. Berlin, Jan. 7, 1843. He studied with Hummel and E. A. Förster at Vienna, and at 10 played in public Hummel's 2nd Concerto, written for him. On a pianistic tour to Italy he produced his opera *I Virtuosi teatrali* at Florence (1814), and the next year became maestro di cappella to the Duchess of Lucca, producing there a second opera, *Gli Arabi nelle Gallie* (1816); returned to Vienna in 1820, where he brought out an opera in German, *Der junge Onkel* (Jan. 14, 1823); made a trip to Russia in 1823, and there married the singer Sophie dall' Occa (1807-63), with whom he made further tours to Italy and Vienna. He purchased a villa in Florence in 1831, and retired to it some years later. Besides his operas, he composed overtures, string quartets, a piano trio, and many piano pieces (sonatas, variations, fantasias, etc.).

Schobert, Johann, composer; b. Silesia, c. 1720; d. Paris, Aug. 28, 1767 (with his entire family, except one child, from eating poisonous mushrooms). From 1760, he was chamber musician to the Prince de Conti in Paris. His works show the general characteristics of the Mannheim school, although it cannot be proved that he ever was in that city. The slow movement of Mozart's Clavier Concerto in B♭, K. 39, is based on music by Schobert. A selection of Schobert's works (with thematic catalogue) was publ. by H. Riemann in vol. 39 of 'Denkmäler deutscher Tonkunst' (1909). —Publ. works: op. 1, 2, 3, sonatas for clavecin and violin; op. 4, 5, 16, 17, sonatas for clavecin solo; op. 6, 8, clavecin trios; op. 9, 10, 11, 12, 18, clavecin concertos; op. 13, *Concerto pastoral* for clavecin; op. 14, 15, 6 symphonies for clavecin, violin, and 2 horns. (The same works reprinted by Hummel in Amsterdam with different op. numbers.) A 'Singspiel,' *Le Garde-chasse et le braconnier,* was produced in Paris (1765) with little success. —Cf. G. de Saint-Foix, *J. Schobert,* in the 'Revue Musicale' III, 10 (1922); K. Schalscha, *Zur Würdigung Schoberts* (1923); H. T. David, *J. Schobert als Sonatenkomponist* (1928).

Schoeck, Othmar, eminent Swiss composer and conductor; b. Brunnen, Sept. 1, 1886; d. Zürich, March 8, 1957. He was the son of a painter; studied at the Zürich Cons. with Nägeli and Freund; later, with Reger in Leipzig; 1907-15, conductor of the men's chorus 'Aussersihl' in Zürich; 1911-17, of the Lehrergesangverein; from 1917, of the symph. concerts at St. Gall; made hon. *Dr. phil.* by Zürich Univ. in 1928. A Schoeck Festival was held at Bern in April, 1934. Schoeck is acknowledged as a foremost song composer of Switzerland. —Works: the operas *Don Ranudo de Colibrados* (Zürich, April 16, 1919), *Das Wandbild* (libretto by Busoni; Halle, Jan. 2, 1921); *Venus* (Zürich, May 10, 1922); *Penthesilea* (Dresden, Jan. 8, 1927); *Massimilla Doni* (Dresden, March 2, 1937); *Das Schloss Dürande* (Berlin, April 1, 1943). Also choral and orch. works: violin concerto (1911-12), cello concerto (1947), horn concerto (1951), *Festlicher Hymnus* for orch. (1950), etc.; chamber music (2 string quartets, 2 violin sonatas, etc.). Song-cycles: op. 36, *Elégie* (voice and chamber orch.; 1924); op. 38, *Gaselen* (voice and chamber orch.); op. 40, *Lebendig vegraben* (bass and large orch.; 1927); op. 45, *Wanderung im Gebirge* (voice and piano; 1930); op. 47, *Notturno* (bass and string quartet); over 120 songs. A thematic index of his works was publ. by W. Vogel (Zürich, 1956). —Cf. W. Schuh, *Der harmonische Stil O. Schoecks,* in 'Neue Musikzeitung,' Jg. 49 (1928); E. Isler, *Führer durch 'Penthesilea'* (1928); H. Corrodi, *O. Schoeck* (Frauenfeld, 1931; new ed., much enlarged and revised, 1936); W. Schuh, *O. Schoeck* (Zürich, 1934); also articles in the 'Schweizerische Musikzeitung' (special Schoeck issue, March, 1943), 'Festgabe der Freunde zum 50. Geburtstag,' ed. by W. Schuh (Erlenbach-Zürich, 1936); W. Vogel, *Wesenszüge von Othmar Schoecks Liedkunst* (Zürich, 1950).

Schœlcher, Victor, French statesman and music amateur; b. Paris, July 21, 1804; d. Houilles, Dec. 24, 1893. During the Second Empire he lived in England because of his radical politics, and became an enthusiastic admirer of Handel's music; publ. *The Life of Handel* (1857) in an inadequate English translation from the original French MS (the first 4 chapters in the original French were publ. in 'La France musicale,' 1860-62; the entire MS was bought for the library of the Paris Cons. in 1881). Schœlcher accumulated a fine collection of Handel materials, which he donated to the Paris Conservatory.

Schoemaker, Maurice, Belgian composer; b. Anderlecht, near Brussels, Dec. 27, 1890. He studied theory with Théo. Ysaÿe, Martin Lunssens, and Paul Gilson. He was one of the founders of the group of modern Belgian composers known as 'Synthétistes,' whose aim was to promote modern music. While assimilating the general European tendencies, Schoemaker drew for his thematic material on native folk music. —Works: the opera *Swane* (1933); 2 comic operas, *Arc-en-ciel* (1937) and *De Toverviool* (1954); the ballets: *Breughel-Suite* (1928) and *Pan* (1937); symph. poems: *Feu d'artifice* (1924) and *Médée la magicienne* (1936); concerto for trombone and orch. (1939); *2 Danses flamandes* for orch. (1944); concerto for bassoon and orch. (1947); piano trio (1934); *Suite champêtre* for oboe, clarinet, and bassoon (1940); string quartet (1945); numerous piano pieces; also music for radio.

Schoenberg, Arnold, renowned composer; b. Vienna, Sept. 13, 1874; d. Los Angeles, July 13, 1951. As a pupil of the Realschule, in Vienna, he learned to play the violin and also the cello. His father's death left him in needy circumstances at the age of 16; he eked out his existence as a bank clerk, but continued to study music. When he was 20 he began taking lessons in counterpoint with Alexander von Zemlinsky, whose sister he married in 1901; played the cello in Zemlinsky's orchestral group 'Polyhymnia.' He also accepted various jobs of arranging operettas and popular songs. His first original work to obtain public performance was a string quartet in D major (1897), which was favorably received in Vienna; but when his early songs, cast in a more individual style, were presented in public (1898) there were outbursts of protest in the hall, premonitory of the opposition that increased in vehemence throughout his career as a composer. In 1899 he wrote his string sextet *Verklärte Nacht,* a fine work, deeply imbued with the spirit of Romantic poetry, and in its harmonic idiom stemming from Wagner; it remains Schoenberg's most frequently performed composition. About 1900 Schoenberg was engaged as conductor of several amateur choral groups in Vienna suburbs; this increased his interest in vocal music. He then began work on a choral composition, *Gurre-Lieder,* after the poem of the Danish writer Jens Peter Jacobsen. For sheer dimensions, it surpassed the most formidable orchestral edifices of Mahler and Strauss; it calls for 5 solo voices, a speaker, 3 male choruses, an 8-part mixed chorus, and a very large orchestra. To write out the score, he had to order special music paper of 48 staves. He completed the first 2 parts of *Gurre-Lieder* in the spring of 1901; only the concluding chorus remained unfinished; this was delayed by 10 years; since the prospect of a performance was remote, there was no compelling reason to have the work ready. In 1901 Schoenberg moved to Berlin; joined E. von Wolzogen, F. Wedekind, and O. Bierbaum, who launched an 'Überbrettl' (a sort of artistic cabaret), which created a brief sensation; Schoenberg conducted light music there, and himself composed a cabaret song with trumpet obbligato; later he met Richard Strauss, through whom he obtained the Liszt stipendium (1902) and a position as teacher at the Stern Cons. In the summer of 1903 he returned to Vienna, where he found the support of Mahler, who became a sincere advocate of Schoenberg's music; Mahler's influence was then at its zenith, and performers were aroused sufficiently to give Schoenberg a hearing. In March, 1904, Schoenberg organized the 'Vereinigung schaffender Tonkünstler' with Alexander Zemlinsky and others, for the purpose of promoting modern music; under the auspices of this society Schoenberg conducted the 1st performance of his symph. poem *Pelleas und Melisande* (Jan. 26, 1905); in this work is found the first example of a trombone glissando. His *Kammersymphonie* was performed in Vienna on Feb. 8, 1907, producing much consternation, because of the decided departure from traditional tonal harmony, the use of chords built on fourths, and the cultivation of dissonances without immediate resolution. In the same year Schoenberg also turned to painting; in his art, as in his music, he adopted the tenets of Expressionism. His fame as a leading modernist attracted progressively minded students, among them Alban Berg, Anton von Webern, and Egon Wellesz, whose own music developed according to Schoenberg's precepts. Schoenberg's string quartet no. 2 (with soprano solo), finished in 1908, was his last work with a designated key signature (F♯ minor), except for the *Suite* for strings, in G major, written for school use in 1934. In 1910 Schoenberg was appointed teacher of composition at the Vienna Academy; in 1911 he completed his important book, *Harmonielehre,* dedicated to the memory of Mahler; this manual presents a traditional exposition of chords and progressions, but also offers illuminating ideas regarding new musical developments. In 1911 he was again in Berlin, where he lectured at the Stern Cons. and taught privately; a small but enthusiastic group of admirers and disciples followed him there. In 1912 he brought out two works that aroused much controversy: *5 Orchester-Stücke,* first performed by Sir Henry Wood in London, and a cycle of 21 songs with instrumental accompaniment, *Pierrot Lunaire,* in which Schoenberg used the 'Sprechstimme,' substituting a gliding speech-song for precise pitches; the work was given, after some 40 rehearsals, in Berlin, on Oct. 16, 1912, and the reaction was startling, the critics drawing upon the strongest invective in their vocabulary. On Feb. 23, 1913, the *Gurre-Lieder* was finally performed in Vienna under the direction of Franz Schreker. Meanwhile, Schoenberg was appearing as conductor of his own works in various European cities (Amsterdam, 1911; St. Petersburg, 1912; London, 1914). During World War I he was engaged in periods of military service; in 1918 he settled in Mödling, near Vienna, holding a composition seminar, which attracted many new pupils. In Nov., 1918, Schoenberg organized in Vienna a 'Verein für musikalische Privataufführungen' (Society for Private Musical Performances), from which newspaper critics were excluded and which forbade applause (the English translation of a statement of aims is found in N. Slonimsky, *Music Since 1900,* N. Y., 1949, pp. 649-54). In 1925 Schoenberg was appointed prof. of a master class at the Prussian Academy of Arts in Berlin, but was dismissed from that post in May, 1933, by order of the German Ministry of Education under the Nazi regime; he then went to Paris, where, in a symbolic gesture, he reassumed his original Jewish faith, which he had abandoned in 1921. On Oct. 31, 1933, he arrived in the U. S. at the invitation of Joseph Malkin, to direct a master class at the Malkin Cons. in Boston. After teaching in Boston for a season, he settled in Hollywood; in 1935 he became prof. of music at the Univ. of Southern California, and in 1936 accepted a similar position at the Univ. of California in Los Angeles. He became an American citizen on April 11, 1941; in 1947 he received the Award of Merit for Distinguished Achievement from the National Institute of Arts and Letters. In the U. S. he changed the original spelling of his name, Schönberg, to Schoenberg. —In 1924 Schoenberg's creative evolution reached the all-important point where he found it necessary to establish a new governing principle of tonal relationship; a 'method of composing with 12 tones,' adumbrated in Schoenberg's music as early as 1914 and used partly in *5 Klavierstücke,* op. 23, and *Serenade,* op. 24, was employed for the first time throughout a work in the Suite for Piano, op. 25 (1924), in which the thematic material is based on a group of 12 different notes stated in a certain order; such a 'tone row' was henceforth Schoenberg's mainspring of thematic invention; development was provided by presenting the basic series in inversion, retrograde, and retrograde inversion; allowing for transposition, 48 forms were obtainable in all, with counterpoint and harmony, as well as melody, derived from the basic tone row; the realm of rhythm remaining free, and immediate repetition of single notes freely admitted. As with many revolutionary innovations, the 12-tone technique was not the creation of Schoenberg alone, but rather a result of many currents of musical thought. Josef Matthias Hauer specifically claimed priority in laying the foundations of the 12-tone method; among others who had essayed similar ideas simultaneously with Schoenberg was Jef Golyscheff in his '12 Tondauer-Musik.' Instances of themes composed of 12 different notes are found in Liszt (in the *Faust Symphony)* and Strauss *(Also sprach Zarathustra,* in the section *On Science).* Schoenberg's great accomplishment was to establish the 12-tone row and its changing forms as fundamentals of a new musical language, and to write music of great expressiveness and power, which, in spite of the difficulties of performance and slowness of public comprehension, has become one of the strongest influences in the art. In Europe the 12-tone method is often termed 'dodecaphony.' The most explicit works of Schoenberg couched in the 12-tone idiom are *Begleitungsmusik zu einer Lichtspielscene* (1930), the violin concerto (1936), piano concerto (1942), and *Klavierstück,* op. 33a (1929). Among adherents to Schoenberg's method are Alban Berg, Anton von Webern, Egon Wellesz, Krenek, Leibowitz, Roberto Gerhard, Humphrey Searle, and Luigi Dallapiccola. These men and many other composers all over the world—even in the Orient—have adapted the 12-tone technique to their own creative purposes; the sole exception among the nations is Russia, where Schoenberg's theories are unacceptable on ideological grounds. Stravinsky, too, when he was about 70, began to use a serial method, in a manner close to that of Anton von Webern, in his works. —Works: For the stage: *Erwartung,* monodrama, op. 17 (1909; Prague, June 6, 1924); *Die glückliche Hand,* drama with music, to Schoenberg's own libretto, op. 18 (1910-13; Vienna, Oct. 14, 1924); *Von Heute auf Morgen,* opera in 1 act, op. 32 (1928; Frankfurt, Feb. 1, 1930); *Moses und Aron,* biblical drama to the composer's libretto (2 acts completed, 1932; resumed 1951, but not finished; radio performance of 2 acts, Hamburg, March 12, 1954; stage performance, Zürich Festival of the International Society for Contemporary Music, June 6, 1957). For orch.: *Pelleas und Melisande,* symph. poem after Maeterlinck, op. 5 (1902; Vienna, Jan. 26, 1905); *Kammersymphonie,* for 15 instruments, op. 9 (1906; Vienna, Feb. 8, 1907; 2nd version for large orch., 1935); *5 Orchester-Stücke,* op. 16 (1909; London, Sept. 3, 1912; revised, 1949); Variations, op. 31 (Berlin, Dec. 2, 1928); *Begleitungsmusik zu einer Lichtspielscene (Accompaniment to a Cinema Scene),* op. 34 (1930); Suite in G for strings (1934; Los Angeles, May 18, 1935); violin concerto, op. 36 (1936; Philadelphia, Dec. 6, 1940); Second Chamber Symph., op. 38 (N. Y., Dec. 15, 1940); piano concerto, op. 42 (1942; N. Y., Feb. 6, 1944); *Theme and Variations,* op. 43 (1943; Boston, Oct. 20, 1944; also and originally for band). For chorus: *Gurre-Lieder,* for soli, mixed chorus, and orch. (1901; Vienna, Feb. 23, 1913); *Friede auf Erden,* op. 13 (1907); 4 pieces for mixed chorus, op. 27 (1925); *3 Satires,* op. 28 (1925); 6 pieces for men's chorus, op. 35 (1930); *Kol Nidre,* for speaker, chorus, and orch., op. 39 (1938); *A Survivor from Warsaw,* cantata for narrator, chorus, and orch., op. 46 (1947; Albuquerque, Nov. 4, 1948); *3 German Folksongs,* for chorus a cappella, op. 49 (1948); *Dreimal Tausend Jahre,* for chorus a cappella, op. 50a (1949); *De Profundis,* for chorus a cappella, to Hebrew text, op. 50b (1951). The oratorio *Die Jacobsleiter,* begun in 1913, remained unfinished. Chamber music: string quartet in D major (1897; not numbered; presumed lost, but brought to the U. S. by Schoenberg; revived at the Library of Congress, Washington, Feb. 8, 1952); *Verklärte Nacht (Transfigured Night),* sextet for strings, op. 4 (1899; arranged for string orch., 1917; revised, 1943); string quartet No. 1, in D minor, op. 7 (1904; Vienna, Feb. 15, 1907); string quartet No. 2, in F♯ minor, op. 10, with voice (1907); *Serenade* for clarinet, bass clarinet, mandolin, guitar, violin, viola, and cello, op. 24 (4th movement with a sonnet by Petrarch for baritone; 1923; Vienna, July 20, 1924); quintet for flute, oboe, clarinet, horn, and bassoon, op. 26 (1924); suite for 2 clarinets, bass clarinet, violin, viola, cello, and piano, op. 29 (1927); string quartet No. 3, op. 30 (Vienna, Sept. 19, 1927); string quartet No. 4, op. 37 (1936); *Ode to Napoleon,* after Byron, for speaker, strings, and piano. op. 41 (1942; N. Y., Nov. 23, 1944); string trio, op. 45 (1946); *Fantasia,* for violin and piano (1949). Songs: op. 1, 2 songs; op. 2, 4 songs; op. 3, 6 songs; op. 6, 8 songs (1905); op. 8, 6 songs (with orch.; 1904); op. 12, 2 ballads (1907); op. 14, 2 songs; op. 15, cycle of 15 poems from Stefan George's *Das Buch der hängenden Gärten* (1908); op. 20, *Herzgewächse,* after Maeterlinck, for soprano with celesta, harmonium, and harp (1915); op. 21, *Pierrot lunaire,* 21 poems by Albert Giraud, for 'Sprechstimme' with piano, flute (interchangeable with piccolo), clarinet (interchangeable with bass clarinet), violin (interchangeable with viola), and cello (Berlin, Oct. 16, 1912); op. 22, 4 songs (with orch., 1914-15); op. 48, 3 songs. For piano; op. 11, *3 Klavierstücke* (1909; No. 2 arranged for concert performance by Busoni); op. 19, *6 kleine Klavierstücke* (1911); op. 23, *5 Klavierstücke* (1923); op. 25, *Suite* (1924); op. 33a, *Klavierstück* (1929); op. 33b, *Klavierstück* (1932). For organ: op. 40, *Variations on a Recitative* (1940). Arrangements and transcriptions: 2 chorale preludes, by Bach, for large orch.; organ prelude and fugue in E♭ major, by Bach, for orch.; piano quartet in G minor by Brahms, for orch.; cello concerto, transcribed from a harpsichord concerto by G. M. Monn; concerto for string quartet and orch. after Handel's Concerto grosso, op. 6, no. 7. —Books: *Harmonielehre* (Vienna, 1911; abridged English transl., N. Y., under the title *Theory of Harmony,* 1947); *Models for Beginners in Composition* (N. Y., 1942); *Style and Idea* (N. Y., 1950); numerous essays in German and American publications. —Bibliography: *A. S.,* a collection of essays by 11 admirers (Munich, 1912); E. Steinhard, *Die Kunst A. S.s,* in 'Neue Musikzeitung' (1912, No. 18); J. G. Huneker, *S.,* in *Ivory Apes and Peacocks* (N. Y., 1915); Egon Wellesz, *S. and Beyond,* in the 'Mus. Quarterly' (Jan., 1916); Egon Wellesz, *A. S.* (Leipzig, 1921; English transl. London, 1925); C. Gray, *A. S., a Critical Study,* in 'Music & Letters' (Jan., 1922); E. Stein, *Praktischer Leitfaden zu S.s Harmonielehre* (Vienna, 1923); S. issue of 'Anbruch' (Vienna, 1924); Paul Stefan, *A. S.* (Vienna, 1924); K. Westphal, *A. S.s Weg zur Zwölftöne-Musik,* in 'Die Musik' (July, 1929); Carl Engel, *Discords Mingled* (pp. 84-97, *S.'s Pierrot Lunaire;* N. Y., 1931); *A. S. zum 60. Geburtstag,* a collection of articles by friends and pupils (Vienna, 1934); H. E. Wind, *Die Endkrise der bürgerlichen Musik und die Rolle A. S. s* (Vienna, 1935); R. S. Hill, *S.'s Tone-Rows and the Tonal System of the Future,* in the 'Mus. Quarterly' (Jan., 1936); D. J. Bach, *A Note on A. S.,* in the 'Mus. Quarterly' (Jan., 1936); M. Armitage (ed.), *A. S.* (N. Y., 1937; contains essays by Sessions, Krenek, E. Stein, Carl Engel, Otto Klemperer, Paul Pisk, Paul Stefan, etc., also 2 by Schoenberg himself: *Tonality and Form* and *Problems of Harmony);* Darius Milhaud, *To A. S. on his 70th Birthday,* in the 'Mus. Quarterly' (Oct., 1944); H. Jalowetz, *On the Spontaneity of S.'s Music,* in the 'Mus. Quarterly' (Oct., 1944); R. Leibowitz, *S. et son école* (Paris, 1947; English transl., N. Y., 1949); Dika Newlin, *Bruckner, Mahler, S.* (N. Y., 1947); R. Leibowitz, *Introduction à la musique de douze sons; les Variations pour orchestre, op. 31, d'A. S.* (Paris, 1949); W. H. Rubsamen, *S. in America,* in the 'Mus. Quarterly' (Oct., 1951); H. H. Stuckenschmidt, *A. S.* (Zürich, 1951); J. Rufer, *Die Komposition mit zwölf Tönen* (Berlin, 1952; English transl., by Humphrey Searle, as *Composition with 12 Notes Related to One Another,* London, 1954); Roman Vlad, *Storia della dodecafonia* (Milan, 1958); Egon Wellesz, *The Origin of S.'s 12-Tone System* (Washington, 1958).

Schoenefeld, George, American harpsichordist and teacher; son of Henry Schoenefeld; b. Chicago, June 24, 1887. He studied piano and harmony with his father; then in Berlin with Martin Krause and in Paris with Harold Bauer. He became interested in old keyboard instruments; made his début in Los Angeles on June 13, 1913 as a harpsichord player; later specialized exclusively in old music. He was also a noted teacher in Los Angeles; after 1953, lived in Sunland, Calif.

Schoenefeld, Henry, American pianist and composer; b. Milwaukee, Oct. 4, 1857; d. Los Angeles, Aug. 4, 1936. He studied at the Leipzig Cons. with Papperitz (piano), Richter (theory), Reinecke (composition), and Schradieck (conducting); took an additional course in composition with Lassen in Weimar. On his return to America, he settled in Chicago; conducted a German male chorus there (1891-1902). In 1904 he moved to Los Angeles, where he conducted various German choral societies and also the Women's Symph. Orch. He was one of the earliest American composers who recognized the artistic possibilities of the employment of Indian musical resources. He wrote a grand opera *Atala,* or *The Love of Two Savages* (not produced); *Suite caractéristique,* for string orch. (on Indian themes); *Wachicanta,* an Indian pantomime; *2 Indian Legends,* for orch.; *Rural Symphony* (won $500 prize offered by the National Cons. of N. Y., 1892); *Danse américaine,* for piano, and many other piano pieces *(Little Soldiers' March, Valse élégante, Mystics of the Woods, Valse noble, etc.).* —Cf. Rupert Hughes, *Contemporary American Composers* (Boston, 1900; pp. 128-35).

Schoen-René, Anna E., noted singer and teacher; b. Coblenz, Germany, Jan. 12, 1864; d. New York, Nov. 13, 1942. She studied singing with Pauline Viardot-Garcia, and sang in opera before coming to America in 1895; she devoted herself to teaching in the U. S., first in Minneapolis and then in N. Y., where she joined the faculty of the Juilliard School of Music. She publ. a book of memoirs, *America's Musical Heritage* (N. Y., 1941).

Schöffler, Paul, German baritone; b. Dresden, Sept. 15, 1897. He studied at the Dresden Cons. and in Milan; was on the roster of the Dresden Opera from 1925 to 1937; then joined the Vienna Opera; also appeared at Covent Garden, London (1930-38); made his American début at the Metropolitan Opera House in *Salome* (Jan. 26, 1949).

Scholes (skohls), **Percy Alfred,** eminent English writer on music; b. Leeds, July 24, 1877; d. Vevey, Switzerland, July 31, 1958. He took his B.Mus. at Oxford in 1908 and later the M.A., D.Litt., and Hon.D. Mus., as also the Hon.Litt.D., Leeds. *Dr. ès lettres,* Univ. of Lausanne (1934); was organist at various churches until 1905; extension lecturer at the Univs. of Oxford, Cambridge, London, and Manchester; in 1908, founded the Home Music Study Union, and until 1921 edited its organ, the 'Music Student' and 'Music and Youth'; toured the U. S. as lecturer in 1915 and on 4 later occasions; critic of the 'London Evening Standard' and the 'Observer' (1920-27), and for the BBC (1923-29); 1925-30, edited the Audiographic Series of Pianola and Duo Art Rolls; 1928, organized the Anglo-American Music Education Conferences (Lausanne, 1931, 1933); music editor of 'Radio Times' (1932-36); lived in Oxford, and for periods in Switzerland, where he later settled permanently. A writer of great literary attainments and stylistic grace, he succeeded in presenting music 'appreciation' in a manner informative and stimulating to the layman and professional alike. His *Oxford Companion to Music* is unique in the lexicographical field in its vividness of presentation and its comprehensiveness. His scholarly biographies of Burney and Hawkins are among the finest of the genre. —Books: *Everyman and His Music* (1917); *An Introduction to British Music* (1918); *The Listener's Guide to Music* (1919; 10th ed., 1942); *Music Appreciation, Why and How?* (1920; 4th ed., 1925); *The Book of the Great Musicians* (3 vols., 1920; many eds.); *New Works by Modern British Composers* (2 series; 1921, 1924); *The Beginner's Guide to Harmony* (1922; several further eds.); *The Listener's History of Music* (3 vols.; 1923-28; 4th ed., 1933); *Crotchets* (1924); *Learning to Listen by Means of the Gramophone* (1925); *Everybody's Guide to Broadcast Music* (1925); *The Appreciation of Music by Means of the Pianola and Duo Art* (1925); *A Miniature History of Music* (1928); *The Columbia History of Music Through Eye and Ear* (5 albums of records with accompanying booklets; 1930-39; eds. in Japanese and Braille); *Music and Puritanism* (Vevey, 1934); *The Puritans and Music in England and New England* (London, 1934); *Music: The Child and the Masterpiece* (1935; American ed.: *Music Appreciation, Its History and Technics); Radio*

Times Music Handbook (1935; 3rd ed., 1936; American ed. as *The Scholes Music Handbook,* 1935); *The Oxford Companion to Music* (encyclopedia; London and N. Y., 1938; 9th completely revised ed., 1955; contains a pronouncing glossary and over 1,100 portraits and pictures); *God Save the King; Its History and Romance* (London, 1942; new ed. as *God Save the Queen! The History and Romance of the World's First National Anthem,* London, 1954); *The Mirror of Music, 1844-1944, A Century of Musical Life in Britain as Reflected in the Pages of the 'Musical Times'* (London, 1947); *The Great Dr. Burney* (2 vols.; London, 1948); *Sir John Hawkins: Musician, Magistrate, and Friend of Johnson* (London, 1952); *The Concise Oxford Dictionary of Music* (London, 1952); *The Oxford Junior Companion to Music* (London, 1954); various pamphlets, e.g., *Song of Supper,* publ. by the London Vegetarian Society (1948); innumerable articles in the musical press; contributions to encyclopedias and dictionaries, etc.

Scholtz, Herrmann, German pianist and composer; b. Breslau, June 9, 1845; d. Dresden, July 13, 1918. He studied in Breslau; then with Plaidy in Leipzig, with Hans von Bülow and Rheinberger in Munich; taught at the Munich Hochschule für Musik (1870-75); then went to Dresden. He was an accomplished pianist; excelled especially in Chopin's works; had a reputation as a fine teacher; also wrote a number of piano pieces in a fashionable style: *Albumblätter, Mädchenlieder, Lyrische Blätter, Stimmungsbilder, Ballade,* etc. He edited Chopin's works for Peters; also edited the piano concerto, op. 15, of Brahms.

Scholz, Bernard E., German conductor and composer; b. Mainz, March 30, 1835; d. Munich, Dec. 26, 1916. He studied with Ernst Pauer in Mainz and with Dehn in Berlin; after teaching in Munich, he was engaged as court Kapellmeister in Hanover (1859-65); then conducted the Cherubini Society in Florence (1865-66); led the concerts of the Breslau Orch. Society (1871-82), and in the spring of 1883, succeeded Raff as director of the Hoch Cons. in Frankfurt; retired in 1908. He wrote the operas *Carlo Rosa* (Munich, 1858), *Ziethen'sche Husaren* (Breslau, 1869), *Morgiane* (Munich, 1870), *Golo* (Nuremberg, 1875), *Der Trompeter von Säkkingen* (Wiesbaden, 1877), *Die vornehmen Wirte* (Leipzig, 1883), *Ingo* (Frankfurt, 1898), *Anno 1757* (Berlin, 1903), and *Mirandolina* (Darmstadt, 1907); a great many choral works with orch.; 2 symphonies; a piano concerto; 2 string quartets; string quintet; piano quartet; 2 piano trios; 3 violin sonatas; 5 cello sonatas; numerous piano pieces and songs. — Writings: *Lehre vom Kontrapunkt und der Nachahmung* (1897); *Wohin treiben wir?* (1897; collection of essays); *Musikalisches und Persönliches* (1899); *Verklungene Weisen* (1911); edited Dehn's *Lehre vom Kontrapunkt, dem Kanon und der Fuge* (1859; 2nd ed., 1883).

Schönberg, Arnold. See **Schoenberg.**

Schonberg, Harold C., American music critic; b. New York, Nov. 29, 1915. He studied at Brooklyn College (A. B., 1937) and N. Y. Univ. (A. M., 1938). From 1942 to 1946 he was in the army; then was on the staff of the N. Y. 'Sun' (1946-50); in 1950 appointed to the music staff of the N. Y. 'Times'; also has contributed to various musical magazines. He publ. *Chamber and Solo Instrument Music,* in the series 'The Guide to Long-Playing Records' (N. Y., 1955).

Schönberger, Benno, pianist and composer; b. Vienna, Sept. 12, 1863; d. Wisborough Green, Sussex, March 9, 1930. He studied with Anton Door (piano), Bruckner and Volkmann (composition) at the Vienna Cons.; then took lessons with Liszt. After a European concert tour, he went to London, where he taught at the Royal Academy of Music and appeared in chamber music concerts. He wrote 3 sonatas, 3 rhapsodies, a bolero, and a polonaise, for piano, and about 40 songs.

Schondorf, Johannes, German choral conductor and composer; b. Röbel, July 1, 1833, d. Güstrow, Oct. 4, 1912. He studied at the Stern Cons. in Berlin; then was a singing teacher at the Cathedral School in Güstrow; also conducted a choral society there. He publ. *Vaterländische Gesänge,* for mixed voices; many school songs; also piano pieces.

Schönstein, Karl, Austrian singer and government official; b. Ofen, June 26, 1797; d. Vienna, July 16, 1876. Before he assumed office, he had a career as a concert singer; was one of the earliest interpreters of Schubert's songs; Schubert's song cycle, *Die schöne Müllerin,* is dedicated to him.

Schopenhauer, Arthur, the great German philosopher; b. Danzig, Feb. 22, 1788; d. Frankfurt, Sept. 21, 1860. Although his excursions into the realm of music are neither remarkable nor very valuable, they are stimulating, and have inspired a number of valuable contributions by modern investigators, especially in the field of musical esthetics. Wagner was influenced to a considerable extent by Schopenhauer's philosophical system. —Cf. K. Fuchs, *Präliminarien zu einer Kritik der Tonkunst* (Greifswald, 1870); F. von Hausegger, *Richard Wagner und Arthur Schopenhauer* (Leipzig, 1878; 2nd ed., 1892); H. Dinger, *Die Weltanschauung Wagners in den Grundgedanken ihrer Entwickelung* (Leipzig, 1893; traces especially the influence of Hegel and Schopenhauer); M. Seydel, *Arthur Schopenhauers Metaphysik der Musik* (Leipzig, 1895); E. Zoccoli, *L'Estetica di Schopenhauer* (Milan, 1901); G. Melli, *La Filosofia di Schopenhauer* (Florence, 1905; treats the relations between Schopenhauer and Wagner); Th. Lessing, *Schopenhauer, Wagner, Nietzsche* (Munich, 1906); A. Mäcklenburg, *Schopenhauer und seine Stellung zur Musik,* in 'Die Musik' (Dec., 1908); F. J. Wagner, *Beiträge zur Würdigung der Musiktheorie Schopenhauers* (dissertation, Bonn, 1910); A. von Gottschalk, *Beethoven und Schopenhauer* (Blanckenburg, 1912); L. Dunton Green, *Schopenhauer and Music,* in the 'Mus. Quarterly' (April, 1930); V. Bennett, *Referring to Schopenhauer,* in 'Mus. Review' (Aug., 1950).

Schorr, Friedrich, baritone; b. Nagyvarád, Hungary, Sept. 2, 1888; d. Farmington, Conn., Aug. 14, 1953. He studied law at the Univ. of Vienna, and also took private lessons in singing; appeared with the Chicago Opera Co. (1911-12); then was a member of the opera companies in Graz (1914-16), Prague (1916-18), Cologne (1918-23), and of the Berlin State Opera (1923-31). He sang Wolfram at the Metropolitan Opera on Feb. 14, 1924, and continued as a member till the season 1942-43; sang Wotan at the Bayreuth Festivals in 1925, 1927, 1928, and 1930; specialized in Wagnerian opera. He sang the leading roles of the American premières at the Metropolitan Opera of Krenek's *Jonny Spielt Auf* (1929) and Weinberger's *Schwanda* (1931).

Schott, Anton, German tenor; b. Castle Staufeneck, June 24, 1846; d. Stuttgart, Jan. 6, 1913. He was in the Prussian army; after the Franco-Prussian War, he sang at the Munich Opera (1871) and the Berlin Opera (1872-75); then in London and in Italy; made his American début at the Metropolitan Opera, N. Y., as Tannhäuser (Nov. 17, 1884). He excelled as an interpreter of Wagnerian roles. He publ. a polemical brochure, *Hie Welf, hie Waibling* (1904).

Schott, Bernhard, the founder of the German music publishing firm, **B. Schott's Söhne;** b. 1748; d. Mainz, 1817. He founded the firm in 1773; after his death the business was carried on by his sons **Andreas Schott** (1781-1840) and **Johann Joseph Schott** (1782-1855) under the firm name of B. Schott's Söhne. The 2 sons of Andreas Schott, **Franz Philip Schott** (1811-74) and **Peter Schott** (d. Paris, Sept. 20, 1894), succeeded to the business; Peter Schott was manager of the Paris and Brussels branches; subsequently Peter Schott, Jr., took over the directorship, together with Ludwig Strecker and Franz von Landwehr. B. Schott's Söhne published the journals 'Cäcilia' (1824-48), 'Süddeutsche Musikzeitung' (1852-69), and 'Melos' (1920-34 and from 1946). Dr. Ludwig Strecker, son of the director of the same name, and Heinz Schneider Schott, Dr. Strecker's son-in-law, are the present directors (1958); the main office is at Mainz, and a principal branch is at London. (Schott Frères at Brussels is now an entirely different firm.) The catalogue of Schott is one of the richest in the world; it includes works by Beethoven, (last quartets, 9th symph.), operas by Donizetti, Rossini, etc.; Wagner's *Meistersinger, Ring des Nibelungen,* and *Parsifal;* virtually all works by Hindemith and a great number of other contemporary works. Schott is the publisher of the Riemann Musik-Lexikon. —Cf. W. Altmann, *Richard Wagners Briefwechsel mit seinen Verlegern* (Leipzig, 1911; vol. II contains correspondence with Schott); L. Strecker, *Richard Wagner als Verlagsgefährte* (Mainz, 1951); *Der Musikverlag B. Schott* (Mainz, 1954).

Schouwman, Hans, Dutch pianist and composer; b. Gorinchem, Aug. 8, 1902. He began his career as an accompanist; then developed a singing voice, and gave recitals accompanying himself on the piano. —Works: a trio for clarinet, bassoon, and piano; 2 series of old Dutch songs with string accompaniment; arrangements of folksongs for various instruments; teaching pieces for piano; vocal duets; solo songs.

Schrade, Leo, eminent musicologist; b. Allenstein, Germany, Dec. 13, 1903. He studied with Hermann Halbig at the Univ. of Heidelberg (1923-27), with Adolf Sandberger at the Univ. of Munich, and with Theodor Kroyer at the Univ. of Leipzig; *Dr. phil.,* 1927; was appointed instructor at the Univ.

of Königsberg in 1929; in Bonn, 1932; in 1937 he settled in America; joined the faculty of Yale Univ. in 1938; prof., 1948; in 1958, prof. at the Univ. of Basel. —Writings: *Die ältesten Denkmäler der Orgelmusik als Beitrag zu einer Geschichte der Toccata* (dissertation, Leipzig, 1926; publ. 1928); *Die handschriftliche Überlieferung der ältesten Instrumentalmusik* (1931); *Mozart und die Romantiker* (1931); *Das Haydn-Bild in den ältesten Biographien* (1932); *Beethoven in France* (New Haven, 1942); *Monteverdi: Creator of Modern Music* (N. Y., 1950); *Bach; the Conflict between the Sacred and the Secular* (N. Y., 1955); many valuable articles. Edited Luis Milán's *Libro de musica de vihuela* (Leipzig, 1927); Virdung's *Musica getutscht* (Kassel, 1931); etc. His ed. of the complete *Polyphonic Music of the 14th Century* began to appear in 1956.

Schradieck, Henry, noted violinist; b. Hamburg, April 29, 1846; d. Brooklyn, March 25, 1918. He studied at the Brussels Cons. with Léonard (1854-58) and with Ferdinand David in Leipzig (1859-61). He was concertmaster of the Philharmonic Concerts at Hamburg (1868-74), and of the Gewandhaus Orch. in Leipzig (1874-83). In 1883 he came to America; taught violin at the Cincinnati College of Music, and conducted symph. concerts there; after a visit to Germany, he returned to the U. S.; was active as violinist and teacher in N. Y. He publ. valuable technical studies for the violin: *25 grosse Studien für Geige allein; Scale-studies; Technical Studies; Guide to the Study of Chords; Finger Exercises; Schule der Violintechnik* (3 parts; also adapted for viola).

Schreck, Gustav, German composer and teacher; b. Zeulenroda, Sept. 8, 1849; d. Leipzig, Jan. 22, 1918. He studied at the Leipzig Cons. with Plaidy, Papperitz, and Jadassohn; after a few years of teaching in Finland, he returned to Leipzig, and joined the faculty of the Cons. there in 1887. His works are mostly vocal; he wrote an oratorio, *Christus der Auferstandene,* and other sacred works; also a sonata for bassoon and piano; a sonata for oboe and piano; *Divertimento,* for 9 woodwinds; piano pieces; songs.

Schreiber (shrī'-ber), **Frederick C.,** composer; b. Vienna, Jan. 13, 1895; studied piano, cello, and composition at the Vienna Academy of Music, and also at the Vienna Univ.; was on the faculty of the Vienna Cons. of Music (1927-38), teaching music theory; also was active as opera conductor. In 1939 he emigrated to the U. S.; became an American citizen in 1945; settled in N. Y., as organist and choir director at a Reformed Protestant Church. He has written about 125 works, among them 7 symphonies (1927; 1933; 1936; 1951; 1952; 1956; 1957); the 2nd symph. was performed at the Vienna Radio Music Festival, on Sept. 25, 1934; the 4th symph., at Raleigh, N. C., April 26, 1956. Other works are: *The Beatitudes,* a symph. trilogy for orch. and mixed chorus (1950); 2 violin concertos; a cello concerto; *Concerto Grosso* (1936; Chicago, March 3, 1955); *Sinfonietta in G* (Philadelphia, Nov. 18, 1949); numerous choral compositions; chamber music; organ pieces; piano pieces.

Schreiber (shrī'-ber), **Friedrich Gustav,** German organ teacher and composer; b. Bienstedt, Gotha, Aug. 5, 1817; d. Mühlhausen, Thuringia, July 14, 1889. He studied with E. Kast and L. Gebhardt in Erfurt; taught organ in Prague (1840-47); settled at Erfurt in 1851 as municipal music director and cantor at St. Blasius's; founded and conducted a choral society with which he produced oratorios. —Works: *Borussia,* for male chorus and orch.; *Pestalozzi-Kantate* and *Der deutsche Geist* for soli, male chorus, and orch.; songs.

Schreker, Franz, eminent composer and teacher; b. Monaco, March 23, 1878; d. Berlin, March 21, 1934. He spent his early childhood in Monaco, where his father, a native of Austria, was court photographer. He was 10 when his father died, and the family moved to Vienna; there he studied violin with Rosé and theory with Robert Fuchs. In 1908 he organized the Vienna Philharmonic Chorus, and conducted many new works with it. In 1912 he was appointed prof. of composition at the Akademie der Tonkunst. In 1920 he went to Berlin, where he was director of the Hochschule für Musik (until 1932); there he had many talented pupils who later became well-known composers (Krenek, Rathaus, Alois Hába, and others). In 1932 became prof. of a class for advanced students at the Prussian Academy of Arts, but lost this post with the advent of the Nazi regime (1933), when he was forced to resign; he died a year later. As a composer, he led the neo-Romantic movement in the direction of Expressionism, emphasizing psychological conflicts in his operas; in his harmonies he expanded the basically Wagnerian sonorities to include many devices associated with

Impressionism. He exercised considerable influence on the German and Viennese schools of his time, but with the change of direction in modern music towards economy of means and away from mystical and psychological trends, Schreker's music suffered an irreversible decline. —Works: operas: (all to his own librettos): *Der ferne Klang* (Frankfurt, Aug. 18, 1912), *Das Spielwerk und die Prinzessin* (Vienna, March 15, 1913; revised and produced as a mystery play, *Das Spielwerk*, Munich, Oct. 30, 1920), *Die Gezeichneten* (Frankfurt, April 25, 1918), *Der Schatzgräber* (Frankfurt, Jan. 21, 1920; very successful), *Irrelohe* (Cologne, March 27, 1924), *Der singende Teufel* (Berlin, Dec. 10, 1928), *Der Schmied von Gent* (Berlin, Oct. 29, 1932), *Christophorus* (Freiburg, 1932); ballet, *Der Geburtstag der Infantin*, after Oscar Wilde (Vienna, 1908); *Rokoko*, dance suite (1908); *Der Wind*, pantomime (1908); *Ekkehard*, overture for orch. and organ (1903); *Romantische Suite* for orch. (1903); *Phantastische Ouvertüre* (1903); *Vorspiel zu einem Drama* (1913; used as a prelude to his opera *Die Gezeichneten)*; *Kammersymphonie* (Vienna, March 12, 1917); *Kleine Suite* for small orch. (Breslau, Jan. 17, 1929); *Vom ewigen Leben*, for soprano and orch., after Walt Whitman (1929); 23 songs. —Cf. Paul Bekker, *Franz Schreker* (Berlin, 1919); R. S. Hoffmann, *Franz Schreker* (Leipzig, 1921); J. Kapp, *Franz Schreker* (Munich, 1921); F. X. Bayerl, *Franz Schrekers Opernwerk* (Erlangen, 1928); special issues of 'Musikblätter des Anbruch' (1920; 1928, in honor of Schreker's 50th birthday).

Schrems, Joseph, German music scholar and choral leader; b. Warmensteinach, Oct. 5, 1815; d. Regensburg, Oct. 25, 1872. He was appointed Kapellmeister of the Cathedral at Regensburg in 1839, and held this position almost until his death; revived much early church music in performance; succeeded Proske as editor of 'Musica divina.' Through his efforts the library of the Regensburg Cathedral became one of the largest collections of early church music in existence.

Schröder, Alwin, cellist; brother of Karl Schröder; b. Neuhaldensleben, June 15, 1855; d. Boston, Oct. 17, 1928. He studied piano with his father, and violin with De Ahna; then devoted himself to the cello; became successor of his brother as 1st cellist in the Gewandhaus orch. in Leipzig. In 1891 he went to America; joined the Boston Symph. Orch. (until 1925). He was also for a time the cellist in the Kneisel Quartet. His publications include *Violoncello Studies, Technical Studies, New Studies in Scale-playing*, as well as collections of classical pieces adapted for cello.

Schröder, Hermann, German violinist and composer; brother of Alwin Schröder; b. Quedlinburg, July 28, 1843; d. Berlin, Jan. 31, 1909. He studied with A. Ritter at Magdeburg; from 1885 was teacher at the Royal Institute for Church Music in Berlin; also had a music school of his own. He publ. *Untersuchung über die sympathischen Klänge der Geigeninstrumente* (1891); *Die symmetrische Umkehrung in der Musik* (1902); *Ton und Farbe* (1906); chamber music for instructive purposes: *6 instruktive Quartette, 3 kleine Trios*, etc.; a violin method, *Die Kunst des Violinspiels* (1887); etc.

Schröder, Karl, German cellist and composer; brother of Alwin Schröder; b. Quedlinburg, Dec. 18, 1848; d. Bremen, Sept. 22, 1935. He studied with Drechsler and Kiel; in 1871 he formed a string quartet with his brothers Hermann, Franz, and Alwin. He was solo cellist in the Gewandhaus orch. in Leipzig (1874-81); afterwards held 8 successive posts as conductor in Germany and Holland, finally settling in Berlin as cello teacher at Stern's Cons. (1911-24). He then retired and lived in Bremen. Among his works are 2 operas, *Aspasia* (1892) and *Asket* (1893), 2 string quartets, and other chamber music. He compiled 3 pedagogical manuals, *Katechismus des Dirigierens und Taktierens* (1889), *Katechismus des Violinspiels* (1889), and *Katechismus des Violoncellspiels* (1890), which were also publ. in English (1893, 1895, 1896). His collections of classical works for the cello, especially *Vortragsstudien* (60 pieces), are of value.

Schröder-Devrient (-dŭ-vryahn'), **Wilhelmine**, celebrated German soprano; b. Hamburg, Dec. 6, 1804; d. Coburg, Jan. 26, 1860. She received an early training for the stage from her father, a baritone, and from her mother, Antoinette Sophie Bürger, a well-known actress; she herself played children's parts and was an actress until her 17th year. After the death of her father in 1818, she followed her mother to Vienna, where she studied with Mazatti; made her début as Pamina in Mozart's *Zauberflöte;* then sang Agathe in *Der Freischütz* under the direction of Weber himself (Vienna, March 7, 1822). She sang Leonore when *Fidelio* was revived in Vienna (1822) in the presence of Beethoven. In 1823 she was engaged at the Court Opera in Dresden; there she married the actor Karl Devrient (divorced 1828). She sang in Paris in 1831 and 1832 with spectacular success; in the summer of 1832 she appeared in London. She returned to Germany in 1837; continued to sing in Dresden until 1847; also appeared as a concert singer, evoking praise from critics and musicians alike; Wagner expressed his admiration for her; she created the roles of Adriano Colonna in *Rienzi* (Oct. 20, 1842), Senta in *Der fliegende Holländer* (Dresden, Jan. 2, 1843), and Venus in *Tannhäuser* (Dresden, Oct. 19, 1845). She contracted 2 more marriages: to Döring (divorced) and von Bock (1850). —Cf. C. von Glümer, *Erinnerungen an Wilhelmine Schröder-Devrient* (Leipzig, 1862; reprinted in Reclam's ed., 1905); A. von Wolzogen, *Wilhelmine Schröder-Devrient* (Leipzig, 1863); G. Bonacci, *G. Schröder-Devrient e Gasparo Spontini,* in 'Nuova Antologia' (Rome, 1903); C. Hagemann, *Wilhelmine Schröder-Devrient* (Berlin, 1904); E. Schuré, *Précurseurs et revoltés* (Paris, 1904). A purported autobiography, publ. anonymously in many editions since about 1870, as *Aus den Memoiren einer Sängerin* or *Memoires d'une chanteuse allemande,* is in fact a pornographic fantasy whose real author is unknown. A novel based on her life, by Eva von Baudissin, *Wilhelmine Schröder-Devrient*: *Der Schicksalsweg einer grossen Künstlerin,* was publ. in Berlin, 1937. See also Richard Wagner's *Über Schauspieler und Sänger* (dedicated to her memory), in vol. IX of his 'Gesammelte Schriften und Dichtungen,' and his numerous references to her in *Mein Leben.*

Schröter, Christoph Gottlieb, German organist and theorist; b. Hohenstein, Saxony, Aug. 10, 1699; d. Nordhausen, Nov. 2, 1782. Chorister under Schmidt, and pupil of the Kreuzschule, Dresden. In 1717 he began the study of theology in Leipzig, but in the same year became Lotti's music copyist at Dresden; traveled (1720-24) in Germany, Holland, and England with a German baron; lectured on music at Jena Univ., became organist at Minden in 1726, and at Nordhausen in 1732. —Works: 7 sets of church cantatas for the entire church year; a Passion, *Die sieben Worte Jesu,* for which he wrote the poem; 4 other Passions; secular serenades and cantatas; symphonies, overtures, concertos, sonatas; fugues and preludes for organ; etc. —Writings: *Umständliche Beschreibung eines neuerfundenen Clavierinstruments, auf welchem man in unterschiedenen Graden stark und schwach spielen kann* (1763, in Marpurg's 'Kritische Briefe,' vol. II), in which he claims the invention, in 1717, of a hammer action for keyed stringed instruments, a model of which (so he says) he laid before the Saxon court in 1721; his claim of priority in the invention of the pianoforte action rests, however, on this bare assertion, and it is not sufficiently weighty to disturb the priority of Cristofori (q.v.); *Deutliche Anweisung zum Generalbass . . .* (1772; the first book to represent the major and minor triads as the sole fundamental chords); *Letzte Beschäftigung mit musikalischen Dingen; nebst sechs Temperatur-Planen und einer Notentafel* (1782); critical and polemical letters in Mizler's 'Bibliothek' and Marpurg's 'Kritische Briefe.'

Schröter, Corona (Elisabeth Wilhelmine), celebrated German soprano; b. Guben, Jan. 14, 1751; d. Ilmenau, Aug. 23, 1802. She was trained in music by her father, Johann Friedrich Schröter, who was an oboe player. About 1764 she appeared in a 'grand concert' in Leipzig and was engaged there till 1771. On Nov. 23, 1776 she sang at the court of Weimar, and was appointed Kammersängerin to the Dowager Duchess of Weimar. She was also active on the dramatic stage; Goethe esteemed her highly as an actress. She composed some songs, publ. in 2 vols. (1786 and 1794); among them, the first setting of Goethe's *Erlkönig.* —Cf. R. Keil, *Corona Schröter. Eine Lebensskizze* (Leipzig, 1875); H. Düntzer, *Charlotte von Stein und Corona Schröter* (Ilmenau, 1902); H. Stümcke, *Corona Schröter* (Bielefeld, 1904).

Schröter, Johann Samuel, pianist and composer; brother of Corona Schröter; b. Warsaw, between 1750 and 1753; d. London, Nov. 1, 1788. He traveled with his father and sister to London, where they gave concerts together. He remained in London, and in 1782 was appointed successor of John Christian Bach as music master to the Queen. 12 piano concertos and 7 trios were publ. in London, also in Paris. His widow became attached to Haydn during the latter's stay in London (1790-91) and sent him many impassioned letters, of which copies made by Haydn are extant. —Cf. Konrad Wolff, *Johann Samuel Schroeter,* in the 'Mus. Quarterly' (July, 1958).

Schröter, Leonhart, German contrapuntist; b. Torgau, c. 1532; d. Magdeburg, c. 1601. From 1561 to 1576 he was cantor at

Saalfeld; then librarian at Wolfenbüttel (1572-73); cantor of the Old Latin School in Magdeburg (1576-95). He was an important composer of Lutheran church music; publ. *55 geistliche Lieder* (1562), a German Te Deum for 8 voices (1571; publ. 1576; reprinted by Kade in vol. V of Ambros' *Geschichte der Musik); also* a Latin Te Deum (1584); 16 *Weihnachtsliedlein* for 4-8 voices (1587; reprinted by Engelke in 1914 for Peters); 28 *Hymni sacri* (1587). 4 *Weihnachtsliedlein* are found in Schlesinger's 'Musica sacra' (No. 11), other pieces in Jöde's 'Das Chorbuch' I and IV; further reprints by W. Ehmann (Göttingen, 1932), G. Hormann (1933), and E. Lendvai (1934). —Cf. G. Hofmann, *Leonhart Schröter, ein lutherischer Kantor zu Magdeburg* (dissertation; Altdorf, 1934).

Schryock, Buren, American composer and conductor; b. Sheldon, Iowa, Dec. 13, 1881; at the age of 7, moved to West Salem, Oregon, where he studied music, and played organ in a church; occupied various teaching posts in Michigan, Texas, Nebraska, and California; was conductor of the San Diego Symph. Orch. (1913-20) and of the San Diego Opera Co. (1920-36); then settled in National City, near San Diego. —Works: 5 operas to his own librettos: *Flavia* (1930-46), *Mary and John* (1948), *Nancy and Arthur* (1951), *Malena and Nordico* (1954), *Tanshu and Sanchi* (1955); a symphony; chamber music; piano pieces.

Schubart, (Christian Friedrich) Daniel, German poet and musician; b. Sontheim, April 13, 1739; d. Stuttgart, Oct. 10, 1791. Organist at Ludwigsburg in 1768; founded a paper, the 'Deutsche Chronik,' in 1774; from 1777-87 imprisoned at Hohenasperg for political reasons. After his release, he was made music director of the Stuttgart theater and court poet. He was the author of the words of Schubert's famous song *Die Forelle.* His own compositions are unassuming, but he was historically important in contributing to the creation of the German lied of the folk-like type; his song, *Schaf wohl, du Himmelsknabe du,* rivalled real folksongs in popularity. He also wrote piano pieces. His son, Ludwig Schubart, edited his philosophical disquisition, *Ideen zu einer Aesthetik der Tonkunst* (1806; new ed., 1924), written in the extravagant vein characteristic of his whole life. —Cf. *Schubarts Leben und Gesinnungen von ihm selbst, im Kerker, aufgesetzt* (2 vols.; Stuttgart, 1791-93); F. D. Strauss, *Schubarts Leben in seinen Briefen* (2 vols.; Berlin, 1849); G. Hauff, *Schubart in seinen Leben und seinen Werken* (Stuttgart, 1885); H. Solcher, *Schubart der Gefangene auf dem Hohenasperg* (Bamberg, 1895); E. Holzer, *Schubart als Musiker* (Stuttgart, 1905); H. Hesse and K. Isenberg, *Schubart: Dokumente seines Lebens* (Berlin, 1927); R. Hammerstein, *Schubart, ein Dichter-Musiker der Goethe-Zeit* (Freiburg-im-Breisgau, 1943); E. Thorn, *Genius in Fesseln: Schubarts Leben* (2nd ed., Geislingen, 1956).

Schubaur (shoo'bour), **Johann Lukas,** German composer; b. Lechfeld, Dec. (baptized 23), 1749; d. Munich, Nov. 15, 1815. While studying medicine in Vienna he earned his livelihood by giving music lessons; began to practice in 1775 in Neuburg but soon moved to Munich, where he became physician to the court and president of the medical commission. He was one of the earliest and most successful composers of German 'Singspiele.' The following were produced in Munich: *Melida* (1781; lost), *Die Dorfdeputierten* (1783), *Das Lustlager* (1784; lost), *Die treuen Köhler* (1786); also composed Psalm 107, and a cantata, *Il Sacrifizio.* —Cf. E. Reipschläger, *Schubaur, Danzi und Poissl als Opernkomponisten* (Berlin, 1911).

Schubert, Ferdinand, brother of the great composer; b. Lichtenthal, near Vienna, Oct. 18, 1794; d. Vienna, Feb. 26, 1859, as director of the Normal School of St. Anna. He was devoted to his gifted brother, and inherited the latter's literary remains. — Publ. a Tantum ergo, a Regina coeli, a German Requiem *a* 4 with organ, part-songs, etc.; wrote much other church music, a Requiem for Franz, 2 children's operas, etc. (most in MS).

Schubert, Franz, violinist, son and pupil of the Konzertmeister **Franz Anton Schubert** (1768-1824); b. Dresden, July 22, 1808; d. there, April 12, 1878. Also taught by Rottmeier and L. Haase; then, with a stipend from the King, by Lafont at Paris. Entered the royal orch. at Dresden in 1823; succeeded Lipinski as 1st Konzertmeister in 1861. —Publ. études for violin, op. 3; duo for piano and violin, op. 8; a fantasia for violin with orch.; 2 concertanti for violin and cello (with Kummer); numerous other violin pieces, including the popular *L'Abeille (The Bee).*

Schubert, Franz (Peter), great Viennese composer; b. Lichtenthal (then a suburb of Vienna; now a part of that city), Jan. 31, 1797; d. Vienna, Nov. 19, 1828. He came of Moravian and Silesian peasant stock. By his father, the schoolmaster at Lichtenthal and an amateur cellist, the gifted boy was taught violin playing at the age of 8; and by choirmaster Holzer, in addition, the piano, organ, singing, and thorough-bass, becoming first soprano in the church choir in his tenth year. In 1808 he was admitted into the Vienna court choir as a singer, and also entered the 'Konvict,' the training school for the court singers. His teachers in theory were Ruzicka and Salieri (the latter from 1812 until at least 1816). He also played in the school orchestra, finally as 1st violin. His earliest extant song, *Hagars Klage* (dated March 30, 1811), and several others of the period, show that Zumsteeg was his model at this time; he also cultivated instrumental composition, especially chamber music; his first symphony was written in 1813. In this year, his voice having broken, he left the 'Konvict.' His first Mass was completed in 1814 and successfully performed. Meantime he fitted himself for the post of elementary teacher in his father's school, and taught there until 1816. During these three years, the future supreme exponent of the German lied devoted his leisure to obtaining a thorough mastery of vocal expression. His usual method of composition was to jot down the melody with a sketch of the harmony, and then to write out the piece in full, following this first version by a second for the elimination of faults; when the second failed to satisfy him, the song was subjected to a third, or even a fourth, revision (e.g., *Erlkönig* and *Die Forelle)*. Such masterworks as *Gretchen am Spinnrade* (Oct. 19, 1814) and *Erlkönig* (1815) mark the swift and unique development of his genius. In the year 1815 he composed as many as 144 songs; in one day (Oct. 15) he wrote eight. From 1814-16 he also composed 2 operettas, 3 Singspiele, and 3 other (fragmentary) stage pieces, none of which were then performed; 4 Masses, other church music, etc. In 1816 his application for the musical directorship of the new State Normal School at Laibach was rejected. The following year he left his place in the Lichtenthal school, and from 1818 made Vienna his home, with the exception of two summers (1818 and 1824) spent at Zelész, Hungary, as music teacher in Count Esterházy's family. From 1817 his friend Franz von Schober (1796-1882) generously aided him; often sharing lodgings and purse with the struggling artist. Through him, Schubert became acquainted with the famous baritone Michael Vogl, one of the first and greatest interpreters of his songs; through his influence Schubert's musical farce, *Die Zwillingsbrüder,* was brought out at the Kärnthnerthor Theater (June 14, 1820), but made little impression. In 1821, however, when he had already written over 600 compositions, his *Erlkönig* was sung at a public concert of the 'Musikverein' with great applause, and others followed at other concerts; so that Cappi & Diabelli were induced to publish on commission 20 songs *(Erlkönig* was the first), which were so successful that Diabelli assumed the risk of further publications; from 1826 his songs and piano music had good sales. Efforts to obtain a salaried post were unsuccessful; that of vice-Kapellmeister to the court, for which he applied in 1826, was given to Weigl; his friends failed to obtain a similar position for him in Hamburg; and the conductorship of the Kärnthnerthor Theater was also refused him in 1827. Not until March 26, 1828, did he give a public concert of his own works (the E♭ trio, a movement from the D minor quartet, songs, etc.), which was an artistic and pecuniary success. Excepting such occasional and momentary good fortune, his life was a continual battle for the daily means of subsistence; although his genius was fully recognized by musicians like Salieri, Weigl, and the singer Vogl, and his songs were highly praised by Beethoven, he was wretchedly underpaid by his publishers, and his greatest works were almost totally neglected. His wonderful gifts, and genial and buoyant disposition, won many friends; chief among them the poet Mayrhofer, the family von Sonnleithner (at whose house Schubert's compositions were often performed long before their introduction to the public), Baron von Schönstein (whose singing aided in bringing Schubert's lyrical songs into vogue), Moritz Schwind, and Anselm Hüttenbrenner. Two visits which Schubert paid to Beethoven are recorded; but they were never intimate. For months previous to his death, Schubert had been failing; his final illness was brought to a fatal termination by an attack of typhus. He was buried, at his own desire, in the 'Ostfriedhof' at Währing, his grave being the third from Beethoven's. When, in 1888, the remains of both masters were transferred to the 'Zentralfriedhof' the new graves also were only a few feet apart. In 1897 Brahms was buried close by.

Schubert was the least 'schooled' of all great German musicians. For this lack of training, his keen musical intuition and inexhaustible resources of melody amply compensated. The spontaneity and fecundity of his song-compositions are not more astounding than the perfection with which the music—melody and accompaniment—fits the poem. He is regarded as the creator of the modern German lied. His known songs for solo voice with piano accompaniment number 634. As to his alleged carelessness in choice of subjects for musical setting, the fact is that he took 72 poems by Goethe, 46 by Schiller, 44 by Wilhelm Müller, 28 by Matthison, 23 by Hölty, 22 by Kosegarten, 13 by Körner, etc.—that is, the best at his command. He also set 47 poems by Mayrhofer and 12 by Schober, both his warm personal friends. Of Heine (then a newcomer) he composed only 6 numbers (in the 'Schwanengesang'). Equally inspired is his transference of the 'Liedform' to the piano in the 'Moments musicaux' and Impromptus—a miniature form of piano composition extensively copied. In larger forms, his symphony in C (1828) and the unfinished symphony in B minor are equal to the best after Beethoven—and Schubert was but 31 when he died. Only his operas have had no success.

A complete critical edition of Schubert's works in 40 vols. (21 series), edited by E. Mandyczewski (assisted by Brahms, Brüll, Hellmesberger, J. N. Fuchs, etc.), was publ. from 1888-97 by Breitkopf & Härtel. Since the publication of the monumental edition Max Friedlaender discovered the MSS of about 100 lost songs, which were first publ. in Peters' complete ed. of the songs (7 vols.). A thematic index of all of Schubert's works, listed in chronological order, was publ. by O. E. Deutsch (N. Y., 1951). There are numerous editions of Schubert's favorite songs with English translations.

WORKS

Operas and Other Stage Music: *Die Zauberharfe,* 3-act melodrama (Vienna, Aug. 19, 1820); *Alfonso und Estrella,* 3-act opera (1821-22; first produced Weimar, June 24, 1854, by Liszt); *Die Verschworenen,* later called *Der häusliche Krieg,* 1-act operetta (1823; Frankfurt, Aug. 29, 1861); *Fierabras,* 3-act opera (1823; Karlsruhe, Feb. 9, 1897); incidental music to the drama *Rosamunde von Cypern* (overture from *Die Zauberharfe*) (Vienna, Dec. 20, 1823); *Die Bürgschaft* (1816); etc.—Choral Works: 6 Latin Masses; *Deutsche Messe* (for 4-part mixed chorus with organ); oratorio *Lazarus* (fragment); Psalm 92 (for baritone solo and mixed chorus); 2 Tantum ergo (for 4-part mixed chorus with orch.); 2 Stabat Mater (4 voices with orch.); several Salve regina; *Miriams Siegesgesang* (for soprano solo, chorus, and orch.); prayer *Vor der Schlacht* (for soli, mixed chorus, and piano); hymn *Herr unser Gott* (for 8-part men's chorus with wind instruments); *Hymne an den Heiligen Geist* (for 8-part men's chorus with orch.); *Morgengesang im Walde* (for 4-part men's chorus with orch.); *Nachtgesang im Walde* and *Nachthelle* (for 4-part men's chorus and horns); *Schlachtlied* (8-part men's chorus with piano); *Glaube, Hoffnung und Liebe* (for mixed chorus and wind); numerous part-songs. —For Orch.: 8 symphonies (No. 8 is the 'unfinished'); Schubert is supposed to have written another symphony, the 'Gastein,' in 1825, but no trace of it has been found; 7 overtures (2 in 'the Italian style'); *Concertstück* for violin with orch.; etc.—Chamber Music: Octet for strings, horn, bassoon, and clarinet, op. 166; piano quintet in A, op. 144 (the 'Forellenquintet,' with double-bass); string quintet in C, op. 163 (with 2 cellos); 15 string quartets; 2 piano trios; string trio in B♭; for piano and violin: a *Rondo brillant* in B minor, op. 70, a *Phantasie* in C, op. 159, a sonata in A, op. 162, 3 sonatinas, op. 137; Introduction and Variations for flute and piano, op. 160; etc.—For Piano (2 hands): 22 sonatas (including op. 42, in A minor; op. 53, D; op. 78 (fantasia), G; op. 120, A; op. 122, E♭; op. 143, A minor; op. 147, B; op. 164, A minor; and 3 grand posthumous sonatas in C minor, A, and B♭); 8 *Impromptus,* op. 90, 142; 6 *Moments musicaux,* op. 94; Adagio and Rondo, op. 145; Fantasia, op. 15, in C; sets of variations (op. 10, E minor, on a French air; op. 35, in A♭; on a Diabelli waltz, in C minor; op. 82, in C, on Hérold's *Marie;* etc.); many waltzes (op. 9, 18, 33, 50 [34 *Valses sentimentales*], 67 [*Hommage aux belles Viennoises*], 77 [10 *Valses nobles*], 91 [12 *Grätzer Walzer*], etc.); *Wanderer-Fantasie* in C, op. 15 (arr. for piano and orch. by Liszt); 2 Scherzos; 5 *Klavierstücke;* etc. —For piano 4 hands; 2 sonatas (op. 30, B♭; op. 140, C); *Divertissement à l'hongroise,* op. 54; *Divertissement* in E minor, op. 63; Fantasia in F minor, op. 103; Grand rondo in A, op. 107; *Notre amitié,* rondo in D, op. 138; Andantino and rondo, op. 84; *Lebensstürme, allegro caractéristique,* op. 144; Fugue in E minor, op. 52; Polonaises, op. 61, 75; Variations, op. 10, 35, 82; 3 Waltzes, op. 33; 4 Ländler; Marches (op. 27, 40, 51, 55 [*Trauermarsch*], 66 [*héroïque*], 121.—Songs: *Erlkönig,* op. 1; *Gretchen am Spinnrade,* op. 2; *Heidenröslein,* op. 3; *Der Wanderer* and *Der du von dem Himmel bist,* in op. 4; 3 *Gesänge des Harfners,* op. 12; *Erster Verlust, Der Fischer,* and *Es war ein König in Thule,* in op. 5; the Suleika songs, op. 14, 31; *An Schwager Kronos,* in op. 19; Mignon's songs, op. 62; *Über allen Gipfeln ist Ruh'*, in op. 96 (all the above by Goethe); further, the grand song-cycles by Wilhelm Müller, *Die schöne Müllerin*, op. 25, and *Die Winterreise*, op. 89, containing 20 and 24 numbers respectively; 7 songs from Scott's *Lady of the Lake (Fräulein vom See)*, op. 52, and 9 songs from Ossian; *Der Tod und das Mädchen; Nähe des Geliebten; Des Mädchens Klage; Gruppe aus dem Tartarus; Nur wer die Sehnsucht kennt; Frühlingsglaube; Die Forelle; Du bist die Ruh'*; the Barcarolle *Auf dem Wasser zu singen*; 6 songs by Heine, in the *Schwanengesang*; and many more of surpassing beauty.

BIBLIOGRAPHY. (Note: Many of the books listed here under 'Biography' also deal with the works.) A. BIOGRAPHY: H. Kreissle von Hellborn, *F. S., eine biographische Skizze* (Vienna, 1861; 2nd, greatly enlarged, ed. as *F. S.*, 1865; in English, London, 1866); H. Barbedette, *F. S. Sa vie, ses œuvres, son temps* (Paris, 1865); La Mara, *F. S.*, in vol. I of *Musikalische Studienköpfe* (Leipzig, 1868; 9th ed., 1894; reprinted separately, 1912); A. Audley, *F. S., sa vie et ses œuvres* (Paris, 1871); A. Reissmann, *F. S. Sein Leben und seine Werke* (Berlin, 1873); G. L. Austin, *The Life of F. S.* (Boston, 1873); H. F. Frost, *S.* (N. Y., 1881); M. Friedlaender, *Beiträge zu einer Biographie F. S.s* (Rostock, 1887); A. Niggli, *S.* (Leipzig, 1890); H. Ritter, *F. S.* (Bamberg, 1896); F. Skalla, *F. S.* (Prague, 1897); H. Frost, *S.* (London, 1899); M. Zenger, *F. S.s Wirken und Erdenwallen* (Langensalza, 1902); R. Heuberger, *S.* (Berlin, 1902; 2nd ed., 1908); E. Duncan, *S.* (London, 1905); W. Klatte, *S.* (Berlin, 1907); L.-A. Bourgault-Ducoudray, *S.* (Paris, 1908; new ed., 1926); H. Antcliffe, *S.* (London, 1910); W. Dahms, *S.* (Berlin, 1912); O. E. Deutsch, *F. S. Die Dokumente seines Lebens und Schaffens* (3 vols. planned; only 2 publ.; Munich, 1913-14); R. Heuberger, *F. S.* (vol. 14 of Riemann's 'Berühmte Musiker'; 1921); K. Kobald, *S. und Schwind* (Zürich, 1921); Th. Gerold, *S.* (Paris, 1923); O. Bie, *F. S.* (Berlin, 1925; in English, N. Y., 1929); M. Friedlaender, *S.; Skizze seines Lebens und Wirkens* (Leipzig, 1928); A. Weiss, *F. S.* (Vienna, 1928); P. Stefan, *F. S.* (Berlin, 1928; new ed., Vienna, 1947); P. Landormy, *La Vie de S.* (Paris, 1928); J.-G. Prod'homme, *S.* (Paris, 1928); J.-G. Prod'homme, *S. raconté par ceux qui l'ont vu* (Paris, 1928); C. Whitaker-Wilson, *F. S.* (London, 1928); E. Roggeri, *S.* (Turin, 1928); E. H. Bethge, *F. S.* (Leipzig, 1928); H. Eulenberg, *S. und die Frauen* (Hellerau, 1928); N. Flower, *F. S.* (London and N. Y., 1928; new ed., 1949); K. Kobald, *F. S. und seine Zeit* (Zürich, 1928; new ed., 1948; in English, N. Y., 1928); G. R. Kruse, *F. S.* (Bielefeld, 1928); R. Pitrou, *F. S.* (Paris, 1928); A. K. Glazunov, *S.* (Leningrad, 1928); R. Pecio Agüero, *S.* (in Spanish; Paris, 1929); M. Tibaldi Chiesa, *S.* (Milan, 1932; 2nd ed., 1936); R. Bates, *F. S.* (London, 1934); W. Vetter, *F. S.* (Potsdam, 1934); E. Duncan, *S.* (revised ed. N. Y., 1934); G. Schünemann, *Erinnerungen an S.* (Berlin, 1936); E. Buenzod, *F. S.* (4th ed., Paris, 1937); J. Bruyr, *F. S.* (Brussels, 1938); A. Silvestrelli, *F. S.* (Salzburg, 1939); A. Orel, *Der junge S.* (Vienna, 1940); A. Kolb, *F. S., sein Leben* (Stockholm, 1941); K. Höcker, *Wege zu S.* (Regensburg, 1942); R. Tenschert, *Du holde Kunst: Ein kleiner S.-Spiegel* (Vienna, 1943); B. Paumgartner, *F. S.* (Zürich, 1943; 2nd ed., 1947); W. & P. Rehberg, *F. S.* (Zürich, 1946); O. E. Deutsch, *S.; A Documentary Biography* (London, 1946; a transl. and revision of *F. S. Die Dokumente seines Lebens*; a work of fundamental importance; American ed. as *The S. Reader*, N. Y., 1947); A. Hutchings, *S.* (London, 1947; 3rd ed., 1956); C. Weingartner, *F. S.* (Alten, 1947); R. H. Schauffler, *F. S.: the Ariel of Music* (N. Y., 1949); H. Malherbe, *F. S., son amour, ses amitiés* (Paris, 1949); A. Einstein, *S.: A Musical Portrait* (N. Y., 1951); H. Rutz, *S., Dokumente seines Lebens und Schaffens* (Munich, 1952); H. Goldschmidt, *F. S.* (Berlin, 1954); P. Mies, *F. S.* (Leipzig, 1954); O. E. Deutsch, ed., *S.: Die Erinnerungen seiner Freunde* (Leipzig, 1957; in English, as *S.: Memoirs by His Friends*, N. Y., 1958); M. J. E. Brown, *S.: A Critical Biography* (London, 1958). —B. CRITICISM, APPRECIATION: J. Rissé, *F. S. in seinen Liedern* (2 vols.; Hanover, 1872); E. Mandyczewski, *F. S.s Werke*, in series XX of B. & H.'s complete ed. (Leipzig, 1895); M. Friedlaender, *F. S. zu seinen 100. Geburtstage* (Berlin, 1897); H. de Curzon, *Les Lieder de F. S.* (Brussels, 1899); O. E. Deutsch, *S.-Brevier* (Berlin, 1905); M. Vancsa, *S. und seine Verleger* (Vienna, 1905); L. Scheibler, *S.s einstimmige Lieder mit Texten von Schiller*, in 'Die Rheinlande' (1905); A. Nathansky, *Bauernfeld und S.* (Trieste, 1906); D. G. Mason, *The Romantic Composers* (N. Y., 1906); M. Gallet, *S. et le Lied* (Paris, 1907); A. Schnerich, *Messe und Requiem seit Haydn und Mozart* (Vienna, 1909); O. Wissig, *F. S.s Messen* (Leipzig, 1909); G. H. Clutsam, *S.* (N. Y., 1912); M. Bauer, *Die Lieder F. S.s* (Leipzig, 1915); H. von der Pfordten, *S. und das deutsche Lied* (1916; 2nd ed., Leipzig,

1920); W. Kahl, *Das lyrische Klavierstück S.s,* in 'Archiv für Musikwissenschaft' III (1921); O. E. Deutsch, *Die Originalausgaben von S.s Goethe-Lieder* (Vienna, 1926); H. Költzsch, *F. S. in seinen Klaviersonaten* (Leipzig, 1927); Felicitas von Kraus, *Beiträge zur Erforschung des malenden und poetisierenden Wesens in der Begleitung von F. S.s Liedern* (Mainz, 1927); P. Mies, *S., der Meister des Liedes* (Berlin, 1928); F. Günther, *S.s Lied* (Stuttgart, 1928); F. V. Damian, *F. S.s Liederkreis, Die schöne Müllerin* (Leipzig, 1928); K. Kobald, *Der Meister des deutschen Liedes, F. S.* (Vienna and Leipzig, 1928); F. Weingartner, *S. und sein Kreis* (Zürich, 1928); C. Lafite, *Das Schubertlied und seine Sänger* (Vienna, 1928); R. Capell, *S.'s Songs* (London, 1928); K. Huschke, *Das 7 Gestirn der grossen S.'schen Kammermusikwerke* (Pritzwalk, 1928); H. Biehle, *S.s Lieder als Gesangsproblem* (Langensalza, 1929); A. Farinelli, *Beethoven e S.* (Turin, 1929); Th. Werner, *S.s Tod,* in 'Joh. Wolf-Festschrift' (1929); *Bericht über den Internationalen Kongress für Schubertforschung* (Augsburg, 1929); H. Bosch, *Die Entwicklung des Romantischen in S.s Liedern* (Leipzig, 1930); H. J. Therstappen, *Die Entwicklung der Form bei S.* (Leipzig, 1931); E. Laaff, *F. S.s Sinfonien* (Wiesbaden; Part I, 1933); T. Archer, *The Formal Construction of 'Die schöne Müllerin,'* in the 'Mus. Quarterly' (Oct., 1934); H. Eschmann, *S.-Beethoven* (Cologne, 1934); P. Egert, *Die Klaviersonate im Zeitalter der Romantik* (Berlin, 1934); E. G. Porter, *The Songs of S.* (London, 1937); E. Schaeffer, *S.'s 'Winterreise,'* in the 'Mus. Quarterly' (Jan., 1938); G. Abraham, ed., *The Music of S.* (N. Y., 1947); O. E. Deutsch, *The Discovery of S.'s Great C Major Symphony: a Story in 15 Letters,* in the 'Mus. Quarterly' (Oct., 1952); W. Vetter, *Der Klassiker S.* (2 vols., Leipzig, 1953); M. J. E. Brown, *S.'s 'Winterreise,' Part I,* in the 'Mus. Quarterly' (April, 1953); E. Schmitz, *S.s Auswirkung auf die deutsche Musik bis zu Hugo Wolf und Bruckner* (Leipzig, 1954). —C. CORRESPONDENCE, ETC.: O. E. Deutsch, *F. S.s Briefe und Schriften* (Munich, 1922; 4th ed., Vienna, 1954; English transl. with foreword by E. Newman, London, 1928); O. E. Deutsch, *S.s Tagebuch* (1928). —D. CATALOGUES, ICONOGRAPHY, ETC.: G. Nottebohm, *Thematisches Verzeichniss der im Druck erschienenen Werke von F. S.* (Vienna, 1874); A. Trost, *F. S.-Bildnisse* (Vienna, 1893); H. de Curzon, *Bibliographie critique de F. S.* (Brussels, 1900); W. Kahl, *Verzeichnis des Schrifttums über F. S., 1828-1928* (Regensburg, 1938); A. Orel, *F. S. Sein Leben in Bildern* (Leipzig, 1939); O. E. Deutsch, in collaboration with Donald R. Wakeling, *S.: Thematic Catalogue of all his Works in Chronological Order* (London, 1951).

The centenary of Schubert's death in 1928 gave rise to a flood of articles in the musical press. See especially the Schubert numbers in that year of the 'Mus. Quarterly' (Oct.), 'Zeitschrift für Musikwissenschaft,' 'Music & Letters,' 'Die Musik,' the 'Chesterian,' etc. E. Decsey dramatized Schubert's life in a play entitled *Der unsterbliche Franz* (music by J. Bittner; Vienna, 1930). The musical score of the popular operetta *Blossom Time* (Romberg) is based on melodies by Schubert.

Schubert, Louis, German violinist; b. Dessau, Jan. 27, 1828; d. Dresden, Sept. 17, 1884. He went to St. Petersburg at the age of 17; then was concertmaster of the City Theater in Königsberg for 6 years; eventually settled in Dresden and became a singing teacher. He produced the operettas *Aus Sibirien* (Königsberg, 1865), *Die Rosenmädchen* (Königsberg, 1860), *Die Wahrsagerin* (Dresden, 1864), *Die beiden Geizigen* (Altenburg, 1879), and *Faustina Hasse* (Altenburg, 1879); publ. a method for violin and a *Gesangschule in Liedern.*

Schuberth, Julius (Ferdinand Georg), founder of the firm of 'J. Schuberth & Co.' of Leipzig and New York; b. Magdeburg, July 14, 1804; d. Leipzig, June 9, 1875. Established the Hamburg business in 1826; opened a branch at Leipzig, 1832, and at New York, 1850. His brother, **Friedrich Wilhelm** (b. 1817) took over the Hamburg house in 1853 (firm-name 'Fritz Schuberth'). Schuberth publ. the 'Kleine Hamburger Musikzeitung' (1840-50), the 'New Yorker Musikzeitung' (from 1867), and 'Schuberth's kleine Musikzeitung' (1871-72). In 1872 he founded the music library at Weimar known as the 'Liszt-Schuberth-Stiftung.'—In 1891 the business was purchased by Felix Siegel (d. Leipzig, July 4, 1920), the originator of the 'Musikalische Universalbibliothek.'

Schuberth, Karl, German cellist; b. Magdeburg, Feb. 25, 1811; d. Zürich, July 22, 1863. He studied in Magdeburg and Dessau; after a European tour, which included Russia (1835), was engaged as court musician in St. Petersburg, and remained there for 20 years. He then went to Switzerland for his health, and died there. He publ. 2 cello concertos, variations for cello with orch.; a string octet; 2 string quintets; 4 string quartets; and a cello sonata.

Schubiger, Anselm (baptismal names, **Josef Allis**), learned Swiss writer on music; b. Uznach, March 5, 1815; d. at the Monastery of Einsiedeln, March 14, 1888. He took holy orders in 1835, and assumed the clerical name Anselm. —Publications: *Die Sängerschule St. Gallens* (Einsiedeln, 1858); *Die Pflege des Kirchengesanges und der Kirchenmusik in der deutschen katholischen Schweiz* (Einsiedeln, 1873); *Musikalische Spicilegien . . .* (Berlin, 1876; a collection of miscellaneous essays on medieval music); also various papers publ. in special magazines.

Schuch (shooh), **Ernst von,** eminent Austrian conductor; b. Graz, Nov. 23, 1846; d. Dresden, May 10, 1914. After studying violin in Graz and Vienna, he became theater conductor in Breslau (1867); then conducted in Würzburg, Graz, and Basel; his first important engagement was with the Dresden Opera in 1872; he became court conductor there in 1873, and remained at that post without interruption for over 40 years, until his death. In 1897 he was given the rank of hereditary nobility, entitling him to add the nobiliary particle 'von' to his name. In Dresden he was a worthy continuator of the traditions established by Weber and Wagner, and earned a reputation as one of the finest opera conductors. He was moreover a man of great general culture and of progressive ideas. He brought out the operas *Feuersnot, Salome, Elektra,* and *Rosenkavalier* by Strauss, which had their world premières at the Dresden Opera; also included in his repertory operas by Puccini, then new to Germany. He seldom left Dresden, and his most extensive journey was undertaken for a brief appearance in New York in the spring of 1900 to direct 3 orchestral concerts. In 1875 he married **Clementine Proska** (real name, Procházka; b. Ödenburg, Feb. 12, 1850; d. Kötzschenbroda, June 8, 1932), who was the principal coloratura soprano under Schuch's direction from 1873 till her retirement in 1904. Their daughter **Liesel von Schuch** (b. Dresden, Dec. 12, 1891) was coloratura soprano at the Dresden Opera from 1914, and was in 1935 appointed Kammersängerin. —Cf. L. Hartmann, *Ernst Schuch und das moderne Kapellmeistertum* in 'Nord und Süd' (May, 1896; Breslau); P. Sakolowski, *Ernst von Schuch* (Leipzig, 1901); F. von Schuch, *Richard Strauss, Ernst von Schuch und Dresdens Oper* (2nd ed., Leipzig, 1953).

Schucht, Jean F., German writer on music; b. Holzthalleben, Thuringia, Nov. 17, 1822; d. Leipzig, March 30, 1894. He studied with Hauptmann and Spohr at Kassel, and with Schnyder von Wartensee at Frankfurt; from 1868 was in Leipzig as critic for the 'Neue Zeitschrift für Musik.' He publ. a *Wegweiser in der Tonkunst* (1859); *Kleines Lexikon der Tonkunst; Partiturenkenntniss; Meyerbeers Leben und Bildungsgang* (1869); *Grundriss einer praktischen Harmonielehre* (1876); a biography of Chopin (1880); wrote piano pieces and songs.

Schuecker, Edmund, Austrian harpist; b. Vienna, Nov. 16, 1860; d. Bad Kreuznach, Nov. 9, 1911. After studying with Zamara at the Vienna Cons., he played the harp in various orchestras; taught at the Leipzig Cons. (1884). In 1891 he went to America as harpist of the newly organized Chicago Symph.; was a member of the Pittsburgh Symph. (1903-04) and of the Philadelphia Orch. (1904-09). He wrote pieces for harp, of which a *Mazurka* became popular; also published the harp manuals *Etüden- und Melodien-Album* (4 books), *Etüdenschule* (3 books), *6 Virtuosenetüden, Orchestra-Studies* (5 books), *The Most Important Parts from Wagner's Operas* (2 books).

Schuecker, Heinrich, Austrian-American harpist, brother of Edmund Schuecker; b. Vienna, Nov. 25, 1867; d. Boston, April 17, 1913. He studied at the Vienna Cons. (1878-84) with Zamara. In 1885 he was engaged as 1st harpist of the Boston Symph. Orch., and held this position until his death. He also taught harp at the New England Cons., Boston.

Schuecker, Joseph E., harpist, son of Edmund Schuecker; b. Leipzig, May 19, 1886; d. Los Angeles, Dec. 9, 1938. He studied with his father, and later at the Vienna Cons. with Zamara. From 1904 to 1909 he was 1st harpist of the Pittsburgh Symph. Orch.; in 1909 succeeded his father as harpist in the Philadelphia Orch.; from 1915 till 1920 taught at the Carnegie Institute at Pittsburgh; from 1926 till 1930, again played in the Pittsburgh Symph.; then lived in California. He was the author of a *History of the Harp.*

Schueller, Rudolf, conductor; b. Böhmisch-Leipz, Czechoslovakia, July 31, 1884; d. Cleveland, Aug. 1, 1949. He studied at the Univ. of Prague; conducted opera in Berlin (1909-14); after World War I was engaged at the Rumanian Opera at Cluj (1920-24); in 1925 he settled in America; was head of the Opera School of the Cleveland Institute of Music; wrote operas and orchestral works.

Schuh, Willi, Swiss musicologist; b. Basel, Nov. 12 1900. He studied in Munich with Courvoisier, Sandberger, and Beer-Walbrunn, and in Bern with Ernst Kurth; *Dr. phil.,* 1927; settled in Zürich as music critic for the 'Neue Züricher Zeitung'; joined the faculty of the Zürich Cons. —Books: *Das Volkslied in der Schweiz* (1932); *Othmar Schoeck* (1934); *Ludwig Senfl* (1938); *Über Opern von Richard Strauss* (1947); *Zeitgenossische Musik* (1947); *Schweizer Musik der Gegenwart* (1948); *Von neuer Musik* (a collection of reviews, etc.; 1955); brought out (with Refardt) the *Schweizer Musikbuch* (2 vols., 1939); edited music by Swiss composers; contributed numerous articles to various musical periodicals.

Schulhoff, Erwin, composer and pianist; great-grandnephew of Julius Schulhoff; b. Prague, June 8, 1894; d. in a concentration camp, Wülzburg, Germany, Aug. 18, 1942. He studied in Prague and in Vienna (1902-08); then in Leipzig with Max Reger and others (1908-10) and in Cologne (1910-14). Settling in Prague, he became a piano teacher; at the same time was active in modern-music circles; together with Alois Hába, he worked on the problems of quarter-tone music; traveled through France, England, and Russia as pianist. In his music (mostly for piano) he followed the modernistic ideas of the period between the two wars, emphasizing the grotesque and making use of atonal and polytonal devices. Several of his pieces were performed at the festivals of the International Society for Contemporary Music: string quartet (Venice, Sept. 3, 1925); violin sonata (Geneva, April 7, 1929); *La Somnambule,* a ballet (Oxford, July 24, 1931). His opera *Plameny (Flames)* was performed in Brno on Jan. 27, 1932.

Schulhoff, Julius, noted pianist and composer; b. Prague, Aug. 2, 1825; d. Berlin, March 13, 1898. He studied in Prague; proceeded to Paris, where he gave concerts under the patronage of Chopin, to whom he dedicated his first composition, an *Allegro brillant.* He made a long tour through Austria, England, Spain, and Southern Russia; returning to Paris, he was a successful teacher; after the outbreak of the Franco-Prussian War (1870) he settled in Dresden; moved to Berlin shortly before his death. He publ. excellent salon music for piano; his *Galop di bravura* and *Impromptu Polka* were great favorites.

Schuller, Gunther, American horn player and composer; b. New York, Nov. 22, 1925. He played the French horn in the Cincinnati Symph. Orch.; was soloist in his horn concerto there (1944); later moved to New York and was engaged as 1st horn of the Metropolitan Opera Orch. —Works: cello concerto (1945); suite for woodwind quintet (1945); *Vertiges d'Héros* for orch. (1945); cello sonata (1946); *Fantasia Concertante,* for 3 oboes and piano (1947); *Fantasia Concertante* for 3 trombones and piano (1947); quartet for 4 double-basses (1947); trio for oboe, horn, and viola (1948); quintet for 4 horns and bassoon (1949); symph. for brass and percussion (1950); *Dramatic Overture* (1951); 5 pieces for 5 horns (1952); *Recitative and Rondo* for violin and piano (1953); quartet for flute and strings (1953); *12 by 11* for chamber orch. and jazz improvisation (1955); *Contours* for chamber orch. (1956).

Schulthess, Walter, Swiss conductor and composer; b. Zürich, July 24, 1894. He studied with Andreae in Zürich, with Courvoisier in Munich, and with Ansorge in Berlin; in 1918 settled in Zürich. As a composer, he excelled in lyric songs, in a style resembling Othmar Schoeck's. He also wrote 2 violin sonatas; *Variationen* for cello and orch.; concertino for piano and orch.; piano pieces. He was married to the pianist Stefi Geyer (1888-1956).

Schultz, Edwin, German baritone; b. Danzig, April 30, 1827; d. Tempelhof, near Berlin, May 20, 1907. He studied singing with Brandstätter in Berlin; conducted choral societies and concerts. In 1880 the Prussian Ministry of War commissioned him to compile a book of soldiers' songs. He publ. many male choruses, songs, duets, and the collection *Meisterstücke für Pianoforte.*

Schultz, Helmut, German musicologist; b. Frankfurt, Nov. 2, 1904; killed in battle, Waldburg, April 19, 1945. He studied musicology with Kroyer in Leipzig; in 1933 was appointed to the faculty of the Univ. of Leipzig. He publ. several books: *Johann Vesque von Püttlingen* (Regensburg, 1930); *Instrumentenkunde* (Leipzig, 1931), *Das Madrigal als Formideal* (1939); edited (with Robert Haas) the works of Hugo Wolf; also was editor of works by Haydn, Rosetti, etc.

Schultz, Svend, Danish composer; b. Nykobing, Dec. 30, 1913; he studied at the Royal Cons. in Copenhagen (1933-38); became active as choral conductor; was music critic of *Politiken* (1942-49). In his music, he developed a neo-Classical style characterized by simplicity of form and a cumulative rhythmic drive. —Works: 3 operas, *Bag Kulisserne* (Copenhagen, May 26, 1949), *Solbadet* (Aarhus, Nov. 26, 1949), and *Host* (1950); a *Sinfonia piccola* (1941); an oratorio, *Job* (1945); woodwind quintet; 3 violin sonatas; piano pieces.

Schultze, Norbert, German composer of popular music; b. Brunswick, Jan. 26, 1911. He studied in Cologne and Munich; was theater conductor and composer of theatrical pieces; wrote the operettas *Schwarzer Peter* (Hamburg, Dec. 6, 1936; highly successful); the ballets: *Der Struwwelpeter* (1937), *Max und Moritz* (1938), etc., also film music. He is the composer of the celebrated song *Lili Marlene,* which was tremendously popular during World War II on both sides.

Schulz, August, German violinist, conductor, and composer; b. Lehre, near Brunswick, June 15, 1837; d. Brunswick, Feb. 12, 1909. He studied violin with Joachim; was violinist in the court orch. at Brunswick; then concertmaster at Detmold; returned to Brunswick as conductor of symphony concerts and choral societies. —Works: an opera, *Der wilde Jäger* (Brunswick, 1887); for chorus and orch.: *Eine Sommernacht, Prinzessin Ilse,* etc.; many male choruses; altogether nearly 200 opus numbers.

Schulz, Bartholomäus, Hieronymus, Jacob, and **Michael.** See **Praetorius.**

Schulz, Ferdinand, German choral conductor and composer; b. Kossar, near Krossen, Oct. 21, 1821; d. Berlin, May 27, 1897. He was a pupil of A. W. Bach and Dehn in Berlin; after serving as chorister, he became conductor of the Cäcilien-Verein in 1856. He wrote motets and other church music; publ. male choruses, songs, and piano pieces.

Schulz, Johann Abraham Peter, German composer; b. Lüneburg, March 31, 1747; d. Schwedt, June 10, 1800. He studied with Kirnberger in Berlin; from 1768 to 1773 was music master to a Polish princess; from 1776 to 1778, was music director of the French theater in Berlin; then was Kapellmeister to Prince Heinrich at Rheinsberg (1780-87); from 1787 to 1795 he was court conductor at Copenhagen; finally returned to Germany, where he was director of an opera troupe. A song composer of marked ability, he publ. in 1779 *Gesänge am Clavier,* in 1782 *Lieder im Volkston,* both printed together, with augmentations, as *Lieder im Volkston* in 1785; a 3rd book was publ. in 1790. His sacred songs are *Uzens lyrische Gedichte* (1784) and *Religiöse Oden und Lieder* (1786). *Chansons italiennes* (1782), *4 Lieder* with piano, and a *Rundgesang* (round) for mixed voices, were also published. Among his stage works are: *Das Opfer der Nymphen* (Berlin, 1774); operetta, *La Fée Urgèle* (1782; in German as *Was den Damen gefällt);* operetta, *Clarisse, oder das unbekannte Dienstmädchen* (1783); tragic melodrama, *Minona* (1786; publ.); *Le Barbier de Séville* (Rheinsberg, 1786); the opera, *Aline, reine de Golconde* (Rheinsberg, 1787); the following were produced in Copenhagen: *Høstgildet (The Harvest Home,* Sept. 16, 1790); *Indtoget (Entry;* Feb. 26, 1793); *Peters Bryllup (Peter's Wedding;* Dec. 12, 1793). He further wrote church music, small instrumental works, a piano sonata, and various other pieces for piano *(Musikalische Belustigung, Musikalische Badinage, Musikalischer Luftball,* etc.); publ. *Entwurf einer neuen und leichtverständlichen Musiktablatur . . .* (1786; merely the old organ tablature); *Gedanken über den Einfluss der Musik auf die Bildung eines Volks* (1790); and claimed authorship of *Wahre Grundsätze zum Gebrauch der Harmonie* (1773; publ. as Kirnberger's). —Cf. K. Klunger, *J. A. P. Schulz in seinen volkstümlichen Liedern* (Leipzig, 1909); O. K. Riess, *J. A. P. Schulz' Leben* (dissertation, Leipzig, 1913); J. F. Reichardt, *J. A. P. Schulz* (new ed., Kassel, 1948).

Schulz, Johann Philipp Christian, German conductor and composer; b. Langensalza, Feb. 1, 1773; d. Leipzig, Jan. 30, 1827. He studied with Schicht at Leipzig; from 1810 was conductor of the Gewandhaus concerts. He published overtures to *Faust* and *Die Jungfrau von Orleans;* dances interpolated into *Faust* (arranged for piano); a *Salvum fac regem* for 4 voices with brass; marches, etc.; songs with piano.

Schulz, Leo, cellist; b. Posen, March 28, 1865; d. La Crescenta, Calif., Aug. 12, 1944. He was a child prodigy, and appeared in public at the age of 5; then studied at the Hochschule für Musik in Berlin; was 1st cellist with the Berlin Philharmonic (1885) and the Gewandhaus Orch. in Leipzig (1886-89); then settled in America; was 1st cellist of the Boston Symph. (1889-98), of the N. Y. Philharmonic (1899-1906); taught in various schools; wrote overtures, string quartets, and some cello music; edited *Cello Classics* (2 vols.), *Cello Album* (2 books), and *Cello Composers* (2 vols.).

Schulz-Beuthen (-boi'ten), **Heinrich,** German composer; b. Beuthen, June 19, 1838; d. Dresden, March 12, 1915. He was destined for the career of civil engineer; while a student at the Univ. of Breslau, he learned to play the piano and attempted composition; produced a 'Singspiel,' *Fridolin* (Breslau, 1862), then went to study at the Leipzig Cons., with Moscheles (piano) and Hauptmann (composition). In 1866 he went to Zürich, where he remained until 1880; then lived in Dresden (1880-93) and Vienna 1893-95); finally settled in Dresden, where he became prof. at the Cons. He was an ardent disciple of Liszt and Wagner; during his lifetime he was regarded as a significant composer. —Works: 8 symphonies: No. 1, *Dem Andenken Haydns;* No. 2, *Frühlingsfeier;* No. 3, *Sinfonia maestosa;* No. 4, *Schön Elsbeth;* No. 5, *Reformationssymphonie* (with organ); No. 6, *König Lear* (with male chorus); No. 7 (expanded from a string quartet); No. 8, *Siegessymphonie;* the symph. poems *Mittelalterliche Volksszene, Des Meeres und der Liebe Wellen, Beethoven-Hymnus, Ein Pharaonenbegräbnis, Wilhelm Tell, Sturmesmythe;* overtures; orch. suites; *Symphonisches Konzert* for piano and orch.; a string quintet; a wind octet; a string trio; etc.; a number of piano works *(Heroische Sonata, Erinnerung an die Jugendzeit, Präludium und Fuge);* several sacred choral works; the opera *Aschenbrödel* (Zürich, 1879; text by Mathilde Wesendonk) and 4 other operas. —Cf. K. Mey, *H. Schulz-Beuthen* (Leipzig, 1909); A. Zosel, *H. Schulz-Beuthen* (Würzburg, 1931).

Schulz-Dornburg, Rudolf, German conductor; b. Würzburg, March 31, 1891; d. Gmund-am-Tegernsee, Aug. 16, 1949. He studied in Cologne, where he became a choral director; then conducted opera in Mannheim, Münster, and Essen; in 1934 settled in Berlin as radio conductor; from 1945 till 1948 was general music director in Lübeck. He arranged for performance the opera *Seelewig* by S.T. Staden (q.v.).

Schulz-Evler, Andrey, Polish pianist; b. Radom, Dec. 12, 1852; d. Warsaw, May 15, 1905. He studied at the Warsaw Cons., and later with Tausig in Berlin; was prof. of piano at the Kharkov Music School (1888-1904); publ. 52 piano pieces and songs; his transcription of the *Blue Danube Waltz* was very popular with pianists for a time.

Schulz-Schwerin, Karl, German pianist; b. Schwerin, Jan. 3, 1845; d. Mannheim, May 24, 1913. He studied at the Stern Cons. in Berlin (1862-65) with Hans von Bülow, Stern, and Weitzmann. He was court pianist to the Grand Duke of Mecklenburg; then taught at Stern's Cons. in Berlin (1885-1901); from 1901 lived in Mannheim. —Works: a symphony, overtures to *Torquato Tasso* and *Die Braut von Messina; Serenata giocosa, In Memoriam,* and *Jubiläums-Festmarsch* for orch.; *Sanctus, Osanna, Benedictus, Ave Maria,* etc., for soli, chorus, and orch.; piano pieces.

Schuman, William Howard, eminent American composer; b. New York, Aug. 4, 1910. He studied at the Malkin Cons. in N. Y., with Max Persin (harmony); then took lessons in counterpoint with Charles Haubiel; in 1933 he entered Teachers College, Columbia Univ. (B. S. 1935; M. A. 1937); attended the Mozarteum Academy in Salzburg during the summer of 1935; returning to N. Y., he became instructor at Sarah Lawrence College; on March 27, 1936, married Frances Prince. In 1936 he also began taking courses with Roy Harris at a summer session of the Juilliard School of Music. He began to spring into national prominence when his *American Festival Overture* was given by Koussevitzky and the Boston Symph. (1939), and his 3rd string quartet by the Coolidge String Quartet (1940); in 1941 Koussevitzky performed his 3rd symphony, and in 1942 Rodzinski his 4th at Cleveland; in a brief interval Schuman became one of the leading American composers; held 2 Guggenheim Fellowships, in 1939 and in 1940. He continued to teach at Sarah Lawrence College until 1945, when he became director of publication for G. Schirmer, Inc. (resigned in 1952); in 1945, too, he was appointed president of the Juilliard School of Music. He has won many awards: the Koussevitzky Music Foundation Award, the first Pulitzer Prize in music, Music Critics Circle of N. Y. Award, the Composition Award of the American Academy of Arts and Letters, etc. His music is characterized by great emotional tension, and rhythmic vivacity; the contrapuntal structures reach great complexity. In several of his works he employs explicit American melorhythms, but his general style is cosmopolitan in its thematic content and treatment. —Works: a 'baseball opera' *The Mighty Casey* (Hartford, Conn., May 4, 1953); ballets: *Undertow* (choreographer: Antony Tudor; N. Y., April 10, 1945), *Night Journey* (Martha Graham, Cambridge, Mass., Feb. 17, 1948),

Judith, choreographic poem for orch. (Martha Graham, Louisville, Ky., Jan. 4, 1950); for orch.: symph. no. 1 (N. Y., Oct. 21, 1936), symph. no. 2 (N. Y., May 25, 1938), symph. no. 3 (Boston, Oct. 17, 1941), symph. no. 4 (Cleveland, Jan. 22, 1942), *Symphony for Strings* (his 5th symph.; Boston, Nov. 12, 1943), symph. no. 6 (Dallas, Feb. 27, 1949), *American Festival Overture* (Boston, Oct. 6, 1939), concerto for piano and small orch. (N. Y., Jan. 13, 1943), *Prayer in Time of War* (Pittsburgh, Feb. 13, 1943), *William Billings Overture* (N. Y., Feb. 17, 1944), *Circus Overture* (Philadelphia, July 20, 1944), violin concerto (1947; Boston, Feb. 10, 1950, Isaac Stern soloist; revised 1954 and 1958), *Credendum* (Cincinnati, Nov. 4, 1955), *New England Triptych* (Miami, Oct. 28, 1956); for band: *Newsreel* (also orch.; 1941), *George Washington Bridge* (1950), *Chester,* overture (1956); choral works: *4 Canonic Choruses* (original title, *Chorale Canons*) for mixed voices (1932-33), *Pioneers!* for 8-part mixed chorus, after Walt Whitman (1937), *Choral Etude,* for mixed chorus (1937), *Prologue,* for mixed chorus and orch. (1939), *Prelude* for women's voices (1939), *This is Our Time,* secular cantata for mixed chorus and orch. (1940), *Requiescat,* for women's chorus (1942), *Holiday Song,* for mixed chorus (1942), *A Free Song,* secular cantata for mixed chorus and orch., after Walt Whitman (Boston, March 26, 1943), *Te Deum,* for mixed chorus (1944), *Truth Shall Deliver,* for men's voices (1946), *4 Rounds on Famous Words* (1957), *The Lord Has a Child,* hymn (1957); *The Earth is Born,* music for a film (1957); 4 string quartets (1936, 1937, 1939, 1950); *Quartettino* for 4 bassoons (1939); *3-Score Set* for piano (1943); *Voyage,* a cycle of 5 pieces for piano (1953); songs. —Cf. N. Broder, *The Music of William Schuman,* in the 'Mus. Quarterly' (Jan., 1945); F. R. Schreiber and V. Persichetti, *William Schuman* (N. Y., 1954).

Schumann, Camillo, German organist and composer, brother of Georg Schumann; b. Königstein, March 10, 1872; d. Gottleuba, Dec. 29, 1946. He learned the rudiments of music from his father, then studied with Jadassohn and Reinecke at the Leipzig Cons. After further study with Adolf Bargiel in Berlin (1894-96) he became organist at the church in Eisenach. For some years before his death he lived in retirement at Gottleuba. He was a prolific composer, especially noted for his organ works (5 sonatas and numerous smaller pieces); also wrote 6 cantatas, 3 piano trios, 5 cello sonatas, 2 clarinet sonatas, 2 violin sonatas, and 30 albums of piano pieces. About 60 of his compositions have been published.

Schumann, Clara (*née* Wieck), famous pianist, wife of Robert Schumann; b. Leipzig, Sept. 13, 1819; d. Frankfurt, May 20, 1896. She was the daughter of Friedrich Wieck; trained by her father from her fifth year; played in public for the 1st time on Oct. 20, 1828; made tours from 1832, and during a sojourn in Vienna (1836) received the title of Imperial Chamber Virtuoso. At Paris she had great success in 1839. On Sept. 12, 1840, she was married to Schumann, despite the stubborn opposition of her father to this union. With Schumann she made a tour of Russia as a pianist (1844); appeared with Jenny Lind in Vienna (1846). After Schumann's death (1856) she went with her children to Berlin, living for some years with her mother, who had been divorced from Wieck and had married the music teacher Adolf Bargiel (d. Feb. 4, 1841). From 1856 till 1888 she played regularly in England. In 1863 she moved to Lichtenthaler, near Baden-Baden. In 1878-79 she taught piano in Hoch's Cons. at Frankfurt. She was a masterly and authoritative interpreter of her husband's compositions; later she became an equally admirable interpreter of Brahms, her lifelong friend. She was completely free of all mannerisms, and impressed her audiences chiefly by the earnestness of her regard for the music she played. She was a composer in her own right; wrote a piano concerto and numerous character pieces for piano; also some songs; Schumann made use of her melodies in several of his works. She wrote cadenzas to Beethoven's concertos in C minor and G major; edited the Breitkopf & Hartel ed. of Schumann's works, and some of his early correspondence; also edited finger exercises from Czerny's piano method. —Cf. A. von Meichsner, *Friedrich Wieck und seine Töchter Clara und Marie* (Leipzig, 1875); La Mara, *Clara Schumann,* in vol. V of *Musikalische Studienköpfe* (Leipzig, 1882; 3rd ed., 1902); B. Litzmann, *Clara Schumann, Ein Künstlerleben nach Tagebüchern und Briefen* (3 vols., Leipzig, 1902-08; English transl. in 2 vols., abridged, London, 1913); W. Kleefeld, *Clara Schumann* (Bielefeld, 1910); Florence May, *The Girlhood of Clara Schumann* (London, 1912); F. Schumann, *Brahms and Clara Schumann,* in the 'Mus. Quarterly' (Oct., 1916); Eugenie Schumann, *Erinnerungen* (1925; English transl., 1927); B. Litzmann,

Letters of Clara Schumann and Johannes Brahms (2 vols.; Leipzig, 1927; English transl., N. Y., 1927); K. Höcker, *Clara Schumann* (1938); J. N. Burk, *Clara Schumann* (N. Y., 1940); A. De Lara, *Clara Schumann's Teaching,* in 'Music & Letters' (Jan., 1945); L. Henning, *Die Freundschaft Clara Schumanns mit Johannes Brahms* (Zürich, 1952); W. Quednau, *Clara Schumann* (Berlin, 1955); Margaret and Jean Alley, *A Passionate Friendship; Clara Schumann and Brahms* (London, 1956; contains a selection of letters). See also the bibliography under Robert Schumann.

Schumann, Elisabeth, noted soprano; b. Merseburg, June 13, 1885; d. New York, April 23, 1952. She studied in Berlin and Hamburg; made her début at the Hamburg Opera in 1910; on Nov. 20, 1914 she made her American début as Sophie in *Der Rosenkavalier* at the Metropolitan Opera, N. Y.; then returned to Germany; sang in Munich in 1919; in 1921 she toured with Richard Strauss in the U. S.; subsequently was engaged at the Vienna Opera. In 1938 she settled in the U. S.; taught at the Curtis Institute of Music, Philadelphia; became an American citizen in 1944. —Publ. *German Song* (London, 1948).

Schumann, Georg (Alfred), German composer and choral conductor; b. Königstein, Oct. 25, 1866; d. Berlin, May 23, 1952. He studied with his father, the town music director, and with his grandfather, a cantor; then took courses in Dresden and at the Leipzig Cons. with Reinecke and Jadassohn; received the Beethoven Prize in 1887. He conducted a choral society in Danzig (1890-96) and the Bremen Philharmonic Orch. (1896-99). In 1900 he became conductor of the Singakademie, Berlin; in 1934 he was elected president of the Berlin Akademie der Künste. —Works: for orch.: *Zur Karnevalszeit* suite; *Liebesfrühling,* overture; *Lebensfreude,* overture; 2 symphonies; chamber music: 2 violin sonatas, 2 piano quintets, cello sonata, piano trio, piano quartet; choral works with orch.: the oratorio *Ruth* (1909), *Amor und Psyche, Totenklage, Sehnsucht, Das Tränenkrüglein;* numerous songs; for piano: *Stimmungsbilder, Traumbilder, Fantasie-Etüden, Harzbilder.* —Cf. P. Hielscher, *Georg Schumann,* in vol. 1 of 'Monographien moderner Musiker' (Leipzig, 1906); H. Biehle, *Georg Schumann* (Münster, 1925).

Schumann, Robert (Alexander), great German composer; b. Zwickau, Saxony, June 8, 1810; d. Endenich, near Bonn, July 29, 1856. He was the youngest son of a bookseller, and his first music lessons (about 1818) were on the piano from the organist of the Zwickau Marienkirche. His attempts at composition date from his seventh year; in his eleventh, without instruction, he wrote choral and orchestral works. He attended the Zwickau Gymnasium from 1820-28, toward the end of his term developing a marked predilection for the romantic works of Byron and Jean Paul Richter. In 1826 his father wished him to study under Carl M. von Weber, but Weber died, as did Schumann's father shortly thereafter. In 1828 Schumann matriculated at Leipzig Univ. as *studiosus juris,* though he gave more attention to the philosophical lectures. In 1829 he went to Heidelberg, drawn thither chiefly by the fame of Thibaut (prof. of law, but a profound student of music), and began to apply himself seriously to musical study, aided by his dexterity as a pianist. In the autumn of 1830 he obtained his mother's permission to return to Leipzig in order to devote himself to music. He lived with Friedrich Wieck, under whom he studied the piano; and also took a course in composition under H. Dorn, though his industry was principally concentrated on piano practice. An unfortunate experiment (the endeavor to obtain independence of the fingers by suspending the fourth finger of the right hand in a sling while practicing with the others) ended in 1832 his bright prospects as a piano virtuoso. Thenceforward he gave himself up to composition and literary work. As a composer, his published works (op. 1-23) up to the beginning of 1840 (an important date) are exclusively for the piano; Liszt, Henselt, and Clara Wieck (the daughter of his instructor and host) played them in public. In 1834 Schumann founded, with J. Knorr, L. Schunke, and Wieck, the 'Neue Zeitschrift für Musik,' which Schumann edited alone from 1835-44. It entered the field as an exponent of liberal and progressive musical art, in opposition to the vapid productions of the Italian stage, to the then fashionable pianists, and to all shallow or retrograde tendencies. Schumann's numerous essays and criticisms (signed Florestan, Eusebius, Meister Raro, or with the numerals '2' and '12') show what musical journalism can be when actuated by the loftiest motives, and based on real and intimate knowledge of the subjects treated. During the succeeding decades it exercised a potent influence for good; Schumann was among the first to herald Chopin's genius (1834); and one of his last papers was the famous 'Neue Bahnen' (1853) on Brahms.

In the meantime he had fallen in love with Clara Wieck; owing to her father's determined opposition their marriage did not take place until 1840, the year in which the degree of *Dr. phil.* was conferred upon Schumann by the University of Jena. He had spent one year, 1838-39, in Vienna, hoping to better his fortunes by establishing himself and his paper in that city, an attempt which failed. From his marriage year, too, dates the beginning of his career as a song composer, and some of his finest lyrical gems were then produced, including the song-cycles to poems by Heine (op. 24) and Eichendorff (op. 39), the *Frauenliebe und Leben* (op. 42), and the *Dichterliebe* to Heine's words (op. 48). In 1841 he wrote his first symphony, speedily followed by three string quartets, op. 41, the piano quintet, op. 44, and the piano quartet, op. 47, also his most beautiful choral work, *Das Paradies und die Peri* (1843). In 1843 he was invited by Mendelssohn to assume the position of teacher (piano, composition, and playing from score) at the newly founded Conservatorium in Leipzig; Schumann introduced the pedal-piano, for preparatory organ practice, into the Cons., which possessed no organ for ten years. In January, 1844, he undertook a concert tour to Russia with his wife; in the autumn of the same year he moved to Dresden; his duties in the Leipzig Cons. were uncongenial, and it is probable that Mendelssohn, whom Schumann greatly admired, did not fully appreciate the latter's genius. Schumann likewise retired from the editorship of the 'Neue Zeitschrift,' being succeeded in 1845 by K. F. Brendel. In Dresden he lived until 1850, giving private lessons and composing industriously; to this period belong the great C major symphony op. 61 (1846), the opera *Genoveva* (1848), and the piano trio op. 80 (1847; one of the finest of its class). In 1847 he became the conductor of the 'Liedertafel,' and in 1848 organized the 'Chorgesang-Verein.' He was called to Düsseldorf in 1850 to succeed Ferdinand Hiller as town musical director (conductor of the Subscription Concerts and the Musical Society). He held this position until the autumn of 1853, when signs of insanity, which had appeared as far back as 1833, and still more alarmingly in 1845, compelled him to resign; for some time his assistant (and successor) Tausch had relieved him of much of the work. On Feb. 6, 1854, the disorder reached a climax; he abruptly left the room in which some friends were assembled, and threw himself into the Rhine; rescued from drowning, he had to be conveyed to an asylum at Endenich, near Bonn, remaining here, with but few lucid intervals, until the end. In 1880 a monument was erected on his grave in the churchyard at Bonn, opposite the Sternentor. Schumann was a leader of the German Romantic school, and perhaps its most powerful promoter as both a composer and a writer. At the very outset, his individuality found full expression. His mastery of detail, his concentrated passion and profound emotion, are displayed to best advantage in the smaller forms, the piano pieces and songs—the most suitable mediums for presenting the subtle shadings and artistic refinements characteristic of his lyrical genius. Yet—to name but a few—the first two symphonies and the piano concerto are unsurpassed in the post-Beethoven epoch; the piano quintet, the *Études symphoniques,* the C major Fantasie, the F♯ minor and the G minor piano sonatas, rank with the grandest works of their kind. Together with Chopin and Liszt he must be regarded as the founder of the modern piano technique, exploiting the utmost possibilities of the instrument.—A complete edition of his compositions, in 34 vols., edited by Clara Schumann, was publ. by Breitkopf & Härtel (1886-93); in 1893 Brahms edited a supplementary volume.

WORKS

FOR THE STAGE: opera, *Genoveva,* op. 81 (Leipzig, June 25, 1850); music to Byron's *Manfred,* op. 115; scenes from Goethe's *Faust.* — VOCAL WITH ORCH.: cantata *Das Paradies und die Peri,* op. 50, for solo, chorus, and orch. (after T. Moore's *Lalla Rookh*); *Adventlied,* op. 71, for soprano, chorus, and orch.; *Beim Abschied zu singen,* op. 84, for chorus with woodwind or piano; *Requiem für Mignon,* op. 98b; *Nachtlied,* op. 108, for chorus and orch.; for soli, chorus, and orch.: cantata *Der Rose Pilgerfahrt,* op. 112; ballade *Der Königssohn,* op. 116; ballade *Des Sängers Fluch,* op. 139; four ballades *Vom Pagen und der Königstochter,* op. 140; ballade *Das Glück von Edenhall,* op. 143, for men's chorus and orch.; *Neujahrslied,* op. 144, for chorus and orch.; *Missa sacra,* op. 147, with orch.; Requiem Mass, op. 148, with orch. —CHORUSES A CAPPELLA: 6 4-part songs for men's voices, op. 33; 5 songs (Burns) for mixed chorus, op. 55; 4 songs for mixed chorus, op. 59; 3 songs for men's chorus, op. 62; 7 *Ritornelle* in canon form, for men's voices, op. 65; 5 Romances and Ballades for chorus (2 sets), op. 67 and 75; 6 Romances for women's voices, with piano *ad lib.* (2 sets), op. 69 and 91; motet (Rückert) *Verzweifle nicht im Schmerzenstal,* for double men's chorus, organ *ad lib.,* op. 93 (revised with orch., 1852); 5 *Jagd-*

lieder (Laube) for men's chorus, 4 horns *ad lib.*, op. 137; 4 songs for double chorus, op. 141.—VOCAL WITH PIANO: 3 poems by Geibel, op. 29 (No. 1, for 2 sopranos; No. 2, for 3 sopranos; No. 3, for small chorus); 4 duets for soprano and tenor, op. 34, and 4 duets, op. 78; 3 2-part songs, op. 43; *Spanisches Liederspiel* for one voice or S.A.T.B., op. 74; *Minnespiel* from Rückert's 'Liebesfrühling,' for one or several voices, op. 101; *Mädchenlieder,* for 2 sopranos, op. 103; 3 songs for 3 women's voices, op. 114; ten *Spanische Liebeslieder* for one or several voices, with 4-hand accompaniment, op. 138; the ballads *Belsazar* (op. 51), *Der Handschuh* (op. 87), *Schön Hedwig* (op. 106; for declamation with piano), and *Zwei Balladen,* op. 122 (No. 1, *Ballade vom Haideknaben;* No. 2, *Die Flüchtlinge;* both for declamation with piano); *Liederkreis* (Heine), song-cycle, op. 24, and *Liederkreis,* 12 poems by Eichendorff, op. 39; *Myrthen,* op. 25; *Lieder und Gesänge,* 5 sets (op. 27, 51, 77, 96, 127); 3 poems by Geibel, op. 30; 3 songs, op. 31; 12 poems (Kerner), op. 35; 6 poems (Rückert), op. 36; 12 poems (Rückert), composed with Clara Schumann, op. 37; 5 songs for low voice, op. 40; *Frauenliebe und -Leben,* op. 42; *Dichterliebe,* op. 48; *Romanzen und Balladen,* 4 sets (op. 45, 49, 53, 64); *Liederalbum für die Jugend,* op. 79; 6 songs, op. 89; 6 poems by Lenau, and *Requiem,* op. 90; 6 songs from Byron's 'Hebrew Melodies,' op. 95 (with piano or harp); nine *Lieder und Gesänge* from Goethe's *Wilhelm Meister,* op. 98a; 7 songs, op. 104; 6 songs, op. 107; 4 *Husarenlieder* for baritone, op. 117; 3 *Waldlieder,* op. 119; *5 heitere Gesänge,* op. 125; *Gedichte der Königin Maria Stuart,* op. 135; 4 songs, op. 142; *Der deutsche Rhein* (no opus number).—FOR ORCH.: 4 symphonies: No. 1, op. 38, in B♭; No. 2, op. 61, in C; No. 3, op. 97, in E♭ ('Rhenish' symphony); No. 4, op. 120, in D minor; *Ouvertüre, Scherzo und Finale,* op. 52; 4 concert overtures (*Die Braut von Messina,* op. 100; *Festouvertüre,* op. 123; *Julius Caesar,* op. 128; *Hermann und Dorothea,* op. 136); piano concerto in A minor, op. 54; *Konzertstück* (Introduction and Allegro appassionato) in G, for piano and orch., op. 92; *Konzert-Allegro* for piano and orch., in D minor, op. 134; *Konzertstück* for 4 horns, op. 86; cello concerto, op. 129; *Fantasia* for violin with orch., op. 131; violin concerto (1853; publ. 1937).—CHAMBER MUSIC: piano quintet in E♭, op. 44; 3 string quartets, in A minor, F, and A, op. 41; piano quartet in E♭, op. 47; 3 piano trios (No. 1, in D minor, op. 63; No. 2, in F, op. 80; No. 3, in G minor, op. 110); 4 *Fantasiestücke* for piano, violin, and cello, op. 88; Adagio and Allegro for piano and horn, op. 70; 3 *Fantasiestücke* for piano and clarinet, op. 73; 3 *Romanzen* for piano and oboe, op. 94; *5 Stücke im Volkston* for piano and cello, op. 102; 2 sonatas for piano and violin (No. 1, in A minor, op. 105; No. 2, in D minor, op. 121); 4 *Märchenbilder* for piano and viola, op. 113; 4 *Märchenerzählungen* for piano and clarinet, op. 132.—For organ (or pedal-piano): 6 studies in canon-form, op. 56; *Skizzen für den Pedalflügel,* op. 58; six fugues on B-A-C-H, op. 60.—FOR PIANO: op. 1, Variations on A-B-E-G-G; op. 2, *Papillons;* op. 3, Studies after Paganini's Caprices; op. 4, *Intermezzi;* op. 5, Impromptus on theme by Clara Wieck; op. 6, *Davidsbündlertänze;* op. 7, *Toccata;* op. 8, *Allegro;* op. 9, *Carnaval;* op. 10, six Studies on Paganini's Caprices; op. 11, Sonata No. 1, in F♯ minor; op. 12, *Fantasiestücke* (2 books); op. 13, *Études symphoniques;* op. 14, Sonata No. 2, in F minor; op. 15, thirteen *Kinderscenen;* op. 16, *Kreisleriana;* op. 17, *Fantasie* in C; op. 18, *Arabeske;* op. 19, *Blumenstück;* op. 20, *Humoreske;* op. 21, *Novelletten* (4 books); op. 22, Sonata No. 3, in G minor ('Concert sans orchestre'); op. 23, *Nachtstücke;* op. 26, *Faschingsschwank aus Wien*; op. 28, three *Romanzen;* op. 32, *Scherzo, Gigue, Romanze und Fughette;* op. 68, *Album für die Jugend;* op. 72, four Fugues; op. 76, four Marches; op. 82, *Waldscenen;* op. 99, *Bunte Blätter;* op. 111, three *Fantasiestücke;* op. 118, three Sonatas for the Young; op. 124, *Albumblätter;* op. 126, seven pieces in fughetta-form; op. 133, *Gesänge der Frühe;* also a *Scherzo* (original in Sonata op. 14), a *Presto passionato* (original finale of Sonata op. 22); and a canon on *An Alexis.*—PIANO 4 HANDS: op. 66, *Bilder aus dem Osten;* op. 85, *12 vierhändige Klavierstücke für kleine und grosse Kinder;* op. 109, *Ballszenen;* op. 130, *Kinderball;* op. 46, Andante and Variations in B♭ (for 2 pianos, 4 hands). —WRITINGS: 'Gesammelte Schriften über Musik und Musiker,' a collection of his articles in the 'Neue Zeitschrift' (1854; 4 vols.; 5th ed. revised by M. Kreisig, 1914; English transl., London, 1877). A judicious selection from the complete writings, edited by H. Simon, was publ. under the same title as the original ed. (3 vols.; Leipzig, 1888-89); a selection of Schumann's critical reviews, transl. into English by P. Rosenfeld, was publ. in N. Y., 1946.

BIBLIOGRAPHY.—A. BIOGRAPHY: J. W. von Wasielewski, *R. S.* (Dresden, 1858; 4th ed., 1906; English transl., Boston, 1871); A.

Reissmann, *R. S. Sein Leben und seine Werke* (Berlin, 1865; 3rd ed., 1879; English transl., London, 1886); La Mara, *S.*, in vol. I of *Musikalische Studienköpfe* (Leipzig, 1868; 10th ed., reprinted separately, 1911); A. Niggli, *R. S.* (Basel, 1879); P. Spitta, *Ein Lebensbild R. S.'s* (Leipzig, 1882); J. A. Fuller-Maitland, *S.* (London, 1884; new ed., 1913); H. Erler, *R. S.'s Leben aus seinen Briefen,* 2 vols. (Berlin, 1887; 2nd ed., 1912); H. Reimann, *R. S.* (Leipzig, 1887); R. Batka, *S.* (Leipzig, 1893); H. Abert, *R. S.* (Berlin, 1903; 3rd ed., 1918); A. W. Paterson, *S.* (London, 1903; revised ed., 1934); L. Schneider and M. Mareschal, *S. Sa vie et ses œuvres* (Paris, 1905); E. J. Oldmeadow, *S.* (London, 1905); C. Mauclair, *S.* (Paris, 1906); E. Wolff, *R. S.* (Berlin, 1906); J. Hartog, *R. A. S. en sijne werken* (Haarlem, 1910); A. Steiner, *S.* (Zürich, 1911); M. D. Calvocoressi, *S.* (Paris, 1912); W. Dahms, *S.* (Berlin, 1916); *H. v. d. Pfordten, R. S.* (1920); F. Niecks, *R. S.* (London, 1925; valuable); H. Bedford, *R. S.* (N. Y., 1925); R. Pitrou, *La Vie intérieure de R. S.* (Paris, 1925); V. Basch, *S.* (Paris, 1926); V. Basch, *La Vie douloureuse de S.* (Paris, 1928; in English, N. Y., 1931); H. Tessmer, *R. S.* (Stuttgart, 1930); Eugenie Schumann, *R. S. ein Lebensbild meines Vaters* (Leipzig, 1931); A. Colling, *La Vie de R. S.* (Paris, 1931); M. Beaufils, *S.* (Paris, 1932); C. Valabrega, *S.* (Modena, 1934); W. Gertler, *R. S. sein Leben in Bildern* (Leipzig, 1936); W. Korte, *R. S.* (Potsdam, 1937); E. Bücken, *R. S.* (Cologne, 1940); W. Boetticher, *R. S., Einführung in Persönlichkeit und Werk* (Berlin, 1941); W. Boetticher, *R. S. in seinen Schriften und Briefen* (Berlin, 1942); R. H. Schauffler, *Florestan: The Life and Works of R. S.* (N. Y., 1945); R. Petzoldt, *R. S.* (Leipzig, 1947); J. Chissell, *S.* (London, 1948); P. Sutermeister, *R. S., sein Leben nach Briefen* (Zürich, 1949); K. H. Wörner, *R. S.* (Zürich, 1949); A. Cœuroy, *R. S.* (Paris, 1950); E. Müller, *R. S.* (Olten, 1950); P. & W. Rehberg, *R. S.* (Zürich, 1954); M. Brion, *S. et l'âme romantique* (Paris, 1954; in English as *S. and the Romantic Age,* London, 1956); G. Eismann, *R. S. ein Quellenwerk über sein Leben und Schaffen* (2 vols., Leipzig, 1956); R. Münnich, *Aus R. S.s Briefen und Schriften* (Weimar, 1956); Percy M. Young, *Tragic Muse: The Life and Works of R. S.* (London, 1957); also P. J. A. Möbius, *Über R. S.s Krankheit* (Halle, 1906).— B. Criticism, Appreciation: A. W. Ambros, *R. S.s Tage und Werke,* in *Kultur-historische Bilder aus dem Musikleben der Gegenwart* (Leipzig, 1860); H. Deiters, *S. als Schriftsteller,* in 'Allgemeine musikalische Zeitung' (Nos. 47-49; 1865); L. Mesnard, *Un Successeur de Beethoven; Étude sur R. S.* (Paris, 1876); S. Bagge, *R. S. und seine Faustszenen,* in Waldersee's 'Sammlung' (Leipzig 1879); P. Graf von Waldersee, *Über S.s Manfred,* in Waldersee's 'Sammlung' (Leipzig, 1880); F. G. Jansen, *Die Davidsbündler. Aus R. S.s Sturm- und Drangperiode* (Leipzig, 1883); J. W. von Wasielewski, *Schumanniana* (Bonn, 1883); B. Vogel, *R. S.s Klaviertonpoesie* (Leipzig, 1886); E. David, *Les Mendelssohn-Bartholdy et R. S.* (Paris, 1887); V. Joss, *Fr. Wieck und sein Verhältniss zu R. S.* (Dresden, 1900); M. d'Albert, *R. S. son œuvre pour piano* (Paris, 1904); F. Kerst, *S.-Brevier* (Berlin, 1905); H. Kretzschmar, *R. S. als Ästhetiker,* in 'Jahrbuch Peters' (1906); D. G. Mason, *The Romantic Composers* (New York, 1906); M. Katz, *Die Schilderung des musikalischen Eindrucks bei S.* (Giessen, 1910); Marie Wieck, *Aus dem Kreise Wieck-S.* (Dresden, 1912; 2nd ed., 1914); L. Hirschberg, *R. S.s Tondichtungen balladischen Charakters* (Langensalza, 1913); E. V. Wolff, *R. S.s Lieder in ersten und späteren Fassungen* (Leipzig, 1914); R. Pugno, *Leçons écrites sur S.* (Paris, 1914); R. Hohenemser, *Formale Eigentümlichkeiten in R. S.s Klaviermusik,* in 'Sandberger-Festschrift' (1919); W. H. Hadow, *Studies in Modern Music,* 1st series (London, 1892; 11th ed., 1926); P. Frenzel, *R. S. und Goethe* (Leipzig, 1926); G. Minotti, *Die Enträtselung des Sch.schen Sphinx-Geheimnisses* (Leipzig, 1926); G. Minotti, *Die Enträtselung des Sch.schen Abegg-Geheimniss,* in 'Zeitschrift für Musik' (July-Aug., 1927); O. Bie, *Das deutsche Lied* (Berlin, 1926; pp. 75-131); J. A. Fuller-Maitland, *S.'s Piano Works* (London, 1927); J. A. Fuller-Maitland, *S.'s Concerted Chamber Music* (London, 1929); M. Ninck, *S. und die Romantik in der Musik* (Heidelberg, 1929); H. H. Rosenwald, *Geschichte des deutschen Liedes zwischen Schubert und S.* (Berlin, 1930); W. Schwarz, *R. S. und die Variation* (Kassel, 1932); H. Kötz, *Der Einfluss Jean Pauls auf R. S.* (Weimar, 1933); G. Wilcke, *Tonalität und Modulation im Streichquartett Mendelssohns und S.s* (Leipzig, 1933); G. Minotti, *Die Geheimdokumente der Davidsbündler* (Leipzig, 1934); R. Hernried, *Four Unpublished Compositions by R. S.,* in the 'Mus. Quarterly' (Jan., 1942); G. Abraham, ed., *S.* (N. Y., 1951); G. Abraham, *Schumann's Jugendsinfonie in G minor* in the 'Mus. Quarterly' (Jan., 1951); M. Beaufils, *La Musique de piano de S.* (Paris,

1951); also Eugenie Schumann, *Erinnerungen* (1925; in English, London, 1927).—C. CORRESPONDENCE: Clara Schumann, *S.s Jugendbriefe. Nach den Originalen mitgeteilt* (Leipzig, 1885; 4th ed., 1912; in English, London, 1888); F. G. Jansen, *R. S.s Briefe* (Leipzig, 1886; augmented ed., 1904; in English, London, 1890); J. Gensel, *S.s Briefwechsel mit Henriette Voigt* (Leipzig, 1892); K. Storck, *S.s Briefe in Auswahl* (Stuttgart, 1906; in English, London, 1907); M. Crémieux, *Lettres choisies de R. S.* (Paris, 1909); A. Schumann, *Der junge S., Dichtungen und Briefe* (Leipzig, 1910); *Aus S.s Kreisen* (unpubl. letters from and to S.) in 'Die Musik' (No. 14; 1914).—D. CATALOGUE, ETC.: A. Dörffel, *Thematischer Katalog der Werke R. S.s* (Leipzig, 1870); M. Kreisig, *Stammbaum der Familie Sch.* (genealogy; 1931); R. Petzoldt, *R. S., sein Leben in Bildern* (Leipzig, 1956). See also H. S. Drinker, *Texts of the Vocal Works of R. S. in English Translation* (N. Y., 1947).

Schumann-Heink *(née* Rössler), **Ernestine,** famous contralto; b. Lieben, near Prague, June 15, 1861; d. Hollywood, Calif., Nov. 17, 1936. Her father was an officer in the Austrian army; her mother an Italian amateur singer. In 1872 she was sent to the Ursuline Convent in Prague, where she sang in the church choir; after lessons from Marietta von Leclair in Graz, she made her first public appearance, singing the contralto solo in Beethoven's 9th symphony (1876); made her opera début at the Dresden Court Opera (Oct. 13, 1878) as Azucena; continued her studies with Karl Krebs and Franz Wüllner. In 1883 she was engaged to sing at the Hamburg City Opera; when the company was taken to Covent Garden, London, in 1892, she sang Erda; subsequently specialized in the Wagnerian roles; took part in the Bayreuth Festivals from 1896 until 1903, in 1905 and 1906; also sang with the Berlin Opera. She made her American début as Ortrud on Nov. 7, 1898 in Chicago; appeared in the same role with the Metropolitan Opera, N. Y., on Jan. 9, 1899; cancelled her contract with the Berlin Opera in order to remain a member of the Metropolitan Opera Co. (until 1904); created the role of Klytemnestra in *Elektra* (Dresden, Jan. 25, 1909); made her last operatic appearance as Erda at the Metropolitan Opera on March 11, 1932. She became an American citizen in 1908. During the last years of her life she was active mainly as a teacher. Her operatic repertory included about 150 parts; her voice, of an even quality in all registers, possessed great power, making it peculiarly suitable to Wagnerian roles. She was married in 1882 to Ernst Heink of Dresden, from whom she was later divorced; in 1893 she married the actor Paul Schumann in Hamburg; he died in 1904; she assumed the names of both Schumann and Heink. Her 3rd husband was a Chicago lawyer, William Rapp, Jr., whom she married in 1905 (divorced 1914). —Cf. M. Lawton, *Schumann-Heink, the Last of the Titans* (N. Y., 1928).

Schünemann, Georg, German musicologist; b. Berlin, March 13, 1884; d. there, Jan. 2, 1945. He studied flute at Stern's Cons. in Berlin, and played in various orchestras; then took courses in musicology at the Univ. of Berlin with Kretzschmar; *Dr. phil.,* 1907, with the dissertation *Zur Frage des Taktschlagens in der Mensuralmusik.* In 1919 he joined the faculty of the Univ. of Berlin; from 1920 to 1928 was also prof. at the Hochschule für Musik in Berlin and later, director. In 1933 he was appointed curator of the State Collection of Instruments, and in 1935 was made chief of the music division of the Prussian State Library; was active in many correlated fields of musical research. —Publications: *Geschichte des Dirigierens* (1913; a standard work); *Das Lied der deutschen Kolonisten in Russland* (1923); *Geschichte der deutschen Schulmusik* (1928); *Carl Friedrich Zelter* (1932); *Führer durch die deutsche Chorliteratur* (2 vols., 1935-36); *Geschichte der Klaviermusik* (1940; 2nd ed. by H. Gerigk, 1953); *Die Violine* (1940); *Die Singakademie zu Berlin* (1941). He edited Mozart's sketchbook of 1764 (1908); publ. for the first time Robert Schumann's Concerto for violin and orch. in D minor (1937); brought out *Musiker-Handschriften von Bach bis Schumann* (1936), Beethoven's conversation-books (3 vols., 1941-43), a facsimile edition of *Der Freischütz* (1942), and of Beethoven's 5th symphony; contributed numerous essays to German music magazines.

Schunke, Karl, German pianist; b. Magdeburg, 1801; d. Paris (suicide), Dec. 16, 1839. He studied music with his father, the horn player Michael Schunke (1780-1821); then took lessons with Ferdinand Ries, whom he accompanied to London. In 1828 he settled in Paris, where he became a fashionable teacher. He publ. a number of brilliant transcriptions for piano of operatic airs.

Schunke, Ludwig, German pianist; b. Kassel, Dec. 21, 1810; d. Leipzig, Dec. 7, 1834. He studied with his father, the horn player Gottfried Schunke (1777-1840); then went to Paris, where he was a pupil of Kalkbrenner and Reicha; gave concerts there, and also in Vienna, Prague, etc. He settled in Leipzig in 1833, and became the intimate friend of Schumann; was associated with him in founding the 'Neue Zeitschrift für Musik.' His early death was greatly mourned; his few works (for piano) were full of promise: op. 3, sonata in G minor; op. 9, *Caprice;* op. 10, 2nd *Caprice;* op. 13, *Charakterstücke;* op. 14, *Variationen.* See Schumann's *Gesammelte Schriften* for several passages of appreciative comment.

Schuppanzigh, Ignaz, Austrian violinist, friend of Beethoven; b. Vienna, Nov. 20, 1776; d. there, March 2, 1830. He learned to play the violin and the viola; in 1798 became conductor of the Augarten concerts; Beethoven played several times at these concerts. In 1794-95 he was 1st violin in the quartet that played regularly for Prince Lichnowsky. In 1808 he founded the private quartet of Prince Razumovsky (with Mayseder, Linke, and Weiss), interpreting the Beethoven quartets under the master's eye, and also playing quartets of Haydn and Mozart. After a fire in Razumovsky's palace (1815), the Schuppanzigh quartet went on a tour in Germany, Poland, and Russia, returning to Vienna in 1824. Schuppanzigh then became a member of the court orch.; also was director of the German Opera in 1928. He publ. a *Solo brillant* for violin with string quartet; solo variations on a Russian theme; 9 variations for 2 violins. —Cf. G. Kinsky, *Beethoven und das Schuppanzigh-Quartette,* in the 'Rheinische Musik- und Theater-Zeitung' (XXI, p. 235 ff.). See also the literature on Beethoven.

Schuré (shü-rā'), **Edouard,** Alsatian writer on music; b. Strasbourg, Jan. 21, 1841; d. Paris, April 7, 1929. He studied law and philology in Strasbourg; lived in Bonn, Berlin, and Munich; in 1867, settled in Paris. In his writings (in French) he was an avowed propagandist of German music, and particularly Wagner. —Publications: *Histoire du Lied; ou, La Chanson populaire en Allemagne* (Paris, 1868; new ed. with a study *Le Réveil de la poésie populaire en France,* 1903); *Le Drame musical* (Paris, 1875; 12th ed., 1914; German transl. by Hans von Wolzogen as *Das musikalische Drama;* 3rd ed., 1888; part II is devoted to an appreciation of Wagner); *Souvenirs sur Richard Wagner* (Paris, 1900); *Précurseurs et révoltés* (Paris, 1904); *The Musical Idea in Wagner* (English transl. from French, Hampstead, 1910). —Cf. J. Mainor, *Édouard Schuré* (Angers, 1905); A. Roux and R. Veyssié, *Édouard Schuré, son œuvre et sa pensée* (Paris, 1913); R. A. Schuler, *Édouard Schuré à travers son écriture* (Paris, 1928); A. Roux, *In memoriam Schuré* (Paris, 1931).

Schuricht, Carl, German conductor; b. Danzig, July 3, 1880. He studied at home, his father being an organ manufacturer and his mother a pianist. He then took lessons with Humperdinck at the Hochschule für Musik in Berlin, and later in Leipzig with Max Reger. He subsequently conducted theater orchestras in Germany; in 1912 he became municipal music director in Wiesbaden, and held this post until 1944, when he moved to Frankfurt as choral conductor. In 1953 he conducted in France and Switzerland. He composed some piano music and an orchestral suite, *Drei Herbststücke.* —Cf. B. Gavoty, *Carl Schuricht* (Geneva, 1955).

Schurig, Arthur, German writer on music; b. Dresden, April 24, 1870; d. there, Feb. 15, 1929. He studied in Dresden, Berlin, and Leipzig; followed a military career; upon retirement, devoted much of his leisure to writing on music; publ. an excellent biography of Mozart: *W. A. Mozart; sein Leben und sein Werk* (2 vols.; 1913; 2nd ed., 1923); edited Leopold Mozart's *Reise-Aufzeichnungen* (1920) and Constanze Mozart's *Briefe, Aufzeichnungen, Dokumente* (1922).

Schurig, Volkmar (Julius Wilhelm), German organist and composer; b. Aue-on-the-Mulde, March 24, 1822; d. Dresden, Jan. 31, 1899. He studied in Dresden, where he played organ in the English Church (1844-56); subsequently filled various other posts as organist, singing teacher, and cantor. He publ. organ fantasias, organ preludes, sacred choruses to English texts; children's songs; brought out a useful collection, 'Liederperlen deutscher Tonkunst.'

Schürmann, Georg Kaspar, German composer; b. Hanover, c. 1672; d. Wolfenbüttel, Feb. 25, 1751. He was a singer (alto-falsetto) at the Hamburg Opera (1693-97); was then engaged as court Kapellmeister to the Duke of Brunswick in Wolfenbüttel; traveled in Italy for further study; from 1703 to 1706, was court Kapellmeister in Meiningen; returned to Wolfenbüttel in 1707 and remained there most of his life. He wrote about 20 operas for the Duke of Brunswick; they were produced in Wolfenbüttel and Hamburg; only a few fragments are extant; his church music is also lost. The following were produced in Brunswick: *Heinrich der Vogler* (Part I, Aug. 1, 1718; Part II, Jan. 11, 1721); *Die getreue Alceste* (1719); *Ludovicus Pius* (1726); this last opera, under the German title, *Ludwig der Fromme,* is partly reproduced in Eitner's 'Publikationen älterer Musikwerke'; a suite from *Alceste* and 3 books of arias publ. by G. F. Schmidt (Wolfenbüttel, 1934). —Cf. G. F. Schmidt, *Die frühdeutsche Oper und die musikdramatische Kunst G. C. Schürmanns* (2 vols., Regensburg, 1933-34; expanded from dissertation, Munich, 1913).

Schuster, Bernhard, German publisher and composer; b. Berlin, March 26, 1870; d. there, Jan. 13, 1934. He studied piano, organ, and violin; was active for a time as a theater conductor. In 1901 he founded the fortnightly review, 'Die Musik,' which from its inception ranked with the foremost musical journals of Germany; was its editor-in-chief until 1933. In 1905 he founded the publ. house 'Schuster und Loeffler' (Berlin and Leipzig), which brought out a number of important works on music (the business was acquired by the Stuttgart Deutsche Verlags-Anstalt in 1922). Schuster publ. 2 books of songs; also composed the operas *Der Jungbrunnen* (Karlsruhe, 1920) and *Der Dieb des Glücks* (Wiesbaden, March 10, 1923); a symphony; a string quartet; sacred choruses.

Schuster, Josef, German composer; b. Dresden, Aug. 11, 1748; d. there, July 24, 1812. He spent 4 years in Italy (1765-69) for study, and after 5 years in Dresden, went to Italy again; took lessons with Padre Martini at Bologna; wrote Italian operas, and was made honorary maestro to the King of Naples; after another 2 years in Dresden, he made a third visit to Italy (1778-81), finally establishing himself in Dresden as theatrical conductor; from 1787, he was associated with Seydelmann as court Kapellmeister. He composed a number of operas, mostly to Italian texts; also cantatas, oratorios, symphonies, etc.; publ. piano pieces for 2 and 4 hands, divertissements for piano and violin, etc. —Cf. R. Engländer, *Die Opern Josef Schusters,* in the 'Zeitschrift für Musikwissenschaft' (1928); R. Engländer, *Les Sonates de violon de Mozart et les 'Duetti' de J. Schuster,* in 'Revue de Musicologie' (1939).

Schuster, Joseph, cellist; b. Constantinople, May 23, 1903. He studied at the St. Petersburg Cons. and later at the Hochschule für Musik in Berlin; was 1st cellist in the Berlin Philharmonic (1926-31); emigrated to America in 1934; played in a string quartet, made his concert début in N. Y. on March 15, 1935; from 1936 to 1944 was 1st cellist of the N. Y. Philharmonic; also appeared as soloist with it; taught at various schools.

Schütt, Eduard, pianist and composer; b. St. Petersburg, Oct. 22, 1856; d. Obermias, near Merano, Italy, July 26, 1933. He studied at the St. Petersburg Cons. with Petersen and Stein; at the Leipzig Cons. with Richter, Jadassohn, and Reinecke (1876-78). He then went to Vienna, where he was a private pupil of Leschetizky (piano); in 1880, made a concert tour of Austria with Mme. Norman-Neruda; in 1881, a tour of Hungary with Leopold Auer. Returning to St. Petersburg, he played his 1st piano concerto in G minor, at the concert of the Russian Musical Society (Jan., 1882); then settled definitely in Vienna and became an Austrian subject. His piano pieces retained their popularity for a long time. —Works: comic opera, *Signor Formica* (Vienna, Nov. 19, 1892); Serenade in D for string orch.; 2 piano concertos; piano quartet; violin sonata; 2 piano trios; *Walzermärchen* for violin, cello, and piano; *Andante Cantabile und Scherzino* for 2 pianos; numerous piano pieces (*Scènes de bal, Thème varié et Fugato, Silhouetten-Portraits, Poésies d'Automne, Carnaval mignon,* etc.).

Schütz (Sagittarius), Heinrich, great German composer; b. Köstritz, Oct. 8, 1585; d. Dresden, Nov. 6, 1672. In 1599 he became a choir boy in the court chapel at Kassel, also studying at the Collegium Mauricianum there, and entering Marburg Univ. in 1609, at his parents' desire, to study law; but was sent to Venice in the same year, by Landgrave Moritz of Hesse-Kassel, to study under Giovanni Gabrieli, remaining there till after the latter's death in 1612. Returning to Kassel, he became court organist; in 1617 he was appointed Kapellmeister to the Elector of Saxony at Dresden, after having acted in that capacity since 1615. He repeatedly revisited Italy; from 1631, amid the distractions of the 30 Years' War, he made protracted visits to Copenhagen (in 1633-35, 1637-38, and 1642-45), where he officiated as court conductor, the Dresden court orch. having been wholly dissolved during 6 years (1633-39), and then reorganized with only ten instrumentalists and singers; after 1645 it attained the former standard of efficiency. —Standing at the parting of the ways between Palestrina and Bach, Schütz was of peculiar importance in German art through having applied the grand Italian choral style, and the new dramatico-monodic style (of Monteverdi and his predecessors), to the development of a semi-dramatic church music which is not merely of historical interest as preparing the mightier Bach epoch, but of pleasing and powerful effect at the present day. Schütz was also the composer of the first German opera, *Dafne,* set to Opitz's translation of Rinuccini's libretto (produced at Hartenfels Castle in Torgau, April 23, 1627, at the wedding of Princess Sophie of Saxony), and of a ballet, *Orpheus und Eurydice* (1638, on the wedding of Johann Georg II, of Saxony); the music of both is lost. Karl Riedel did much to awaken appreciation of Schütz's merits by publishing and producing *Die 7 Worte Christi am Kreuz,* and by bringing out other of his works, notably a Passion consisting of selections from Schütz's *Historia des Leidens . . . Jesu Christi.* From 1885-94 Breitkopf & Härtel publ. a complete edition of Schütz's works in 16 vols., ed. by Philipp Spitta: Vol. I, *Die evangelischen Historien und die Sieben Worte Jesu Christi;* the *Historien* being (1) *Die Historia des Leidens und Sterbens unsers Heylandes Jesu Christi* (4 Passions after the Evangelists; MS in the Dresden Library) and (2) *Historia der fröhlichen und siegreichen Auferstehung unsers einigen Erlösers und Seligmachers Jesu Christi* (first publ. 1623; similar to the Passions); vols. II-III, *Mehrchörige Psalmen mit Instrumenten,* with continuo (first publ. 1619); vol. IV, *Cantiones sacrae a 4* with continuo; vol. V, *Symphoniae sacrae,* Part I; vol. VI, *Kleine geistliche Konzerte a 1-5;* vol. VII, *Symphoniae sacrae,* Part II; vol. VIII, sacred choral music, containing *Musicalia ad chorum sacrum,* with continuo (1648); vol. IX, *Italienische Madrigale,* containing his first publ. work, sent home from Italy, and dedicated to the Landgrave, *Il primo libro dei Madrigali* (1611; 18 madrigals *a* 5 and a Dialog *a* 8); vol. X-XI, *Symphoniae sacrae,* Part III; vol. XII-XV, *Gesammelte Motetten, Konzerte, Madrigale und Arien;* vol. XVI, *Psalmen Davids deutsch durch Cornelium Beckern in 4 Stimmen gestellt;* index, etc. A supplementary vol. was publ. in 1909, containing the long-lost Christmas Oratorio *(Historia von der Geburt Jesu Christi),* discovered in 1908 by Schering in the Univ. of Upsala (new ed. by A. Mendel, N. Y., 1950); a 2nd supplementary vol. (1927), containing motets, madrigals, and arias, was ed. by Heinrich Spitta. A new ed. of Schütz's complete works began to appear in 1955 (Bärenreiter, Kassel). —BIBLIOGRAPHY: W. Schäfer, *H. S.* (1854); F. Chrysander, *Geschichte der Braunschweig-Wolffenbüttelschen Kapelle und Oper,* in 'Jahrbuch für musikalische Wissenschaft' I, p. 159 ff. (1863); Fr. Spitta, *Gedächtnisrede auf S.* (1886); Fr. Spitta, *Die Passionen nach den 4 Evangelien von H. S.* (1886); Ph. Spitta, *S.,* in 'Allgemeine deutsche Biographie' and 'Musikgeschichtliche Aufsätze' (1894); M. Seiffert, *Anecdota Schütziana,* in 'Sammelbände der Internationalen Musik-Gesellschaft' I, p. 213 ff.; A. Werner, *Städt. und fürstliche Musikpflege in Weissenfels* (1911); A. Pirro, *S.* (Paris, 1913; 2nd ed., 1924; German transl. by W. Gurlitt, 1914); A. Schering, *Zur Metrik der Psalmen von S.,* in 'Kretzschmar-Festschrift' (1918); E. H. Müller, *H. S. Leben und Werke* (tabulated; Dresden, 1922); E. H. Müller, *H. S.* (Leipzig, 1925); Fr. Spitta, *H. S., ein Meister der Musica sacra* (1925); J. Müller-Blattau, *Die Kompositionslehre H. Schützens in der Fassung seines Schülers Christoph Bernhard* (1926); F. Blume, *Das monodische Prinzip in der protestantischen Kirchenmusik* (1925); W. Schuh, *Formprobleme bei H. S.* (Leipzig, 1928); A. Einstein, *H. S.* (Kassel, 1928); R. Gerber, *Das Passionsrezitativ bei S.* (Gütersloh, 1929); H. Birtner, *Zur S.-Bewegung,* in 'Musik und Kirche' (1932); W. Dilthey, *H. S.* (1932); H. Hoffmann, *H. S. in unserer Zeit* (Leipzig, 1933); W. Kreidler, *H. S. und der stile concitato von Claudio Monteverdi* (Stuttgart, 1934); A. A. Abert, *Die stilistischen Grundlagen der 'Cantiones sacrae' von H. S.* (Berlin, 1935); H. J. Moser, *H. S.* (Kassel 1936; 2nd ed., 1954); K. Gudewill, *Das sprachliche Urbild bei S.* (Kassel, 1936); L. Reitter, *Doppelchortechnik bei H. S.* (Derendingen, 1937); J. Piersig, *Das Weltbild des H. S.* (Kassel, 1949); A. Adrio, *Bekenntnis zu H. S.* (a collection of articles; Kassel, 1954); *Festschrift zur Ehrung von H. S.* (Weimar, 1954). Schütz's writings and correspondence were edited by E. H. Müller (Regensburg, 1931).

Schützendorf, four brothers, all baritones: **Gustav** (b. Cologne, 1883; d. Berlin, April 27, 1937), the best known, studied singing in Milan; sang at the Munich Opera, in Berlin, and in Leipzig; made his American début as Faninal in *Der Rosenkavalier* at the Metropolitan Opera, N. Y., Nov. 17, 1922, and remained on its roster until 1935; then returned to Germany. In 1929 he married the soprano Grete Stückgold. —**Alfons** (b. Vught, Holland, May 25, 1882; d. Weimar, Aug., 1946) was distinguished as a Wagnerian singer, and took part in the

Bayreuth Festivals; in 1932 settled in Berlin as a singing teacher. —**Guido** (b. Herzogenbusch, April 22, 1880) sang with the German Opera Co. on its tour in the U. S. in 1929-30. —**Leo** (b. Cologne, May 7, 1886; d. Berlin, Dec. 18, 1931) was a member of the Berlin State Opera from 1920 to 1929, and made numerous appearances abroad.

Schuyt (Schuijt), Cornelis, Netherlands composer; b. Leyden, 1557; d. there (buried June 12), 1616; studied at first with his father, an organist, and then in Italy. In 1593 was appointed organist in his native city. Publ. madrigals *a* 5 (1600) and *a* 6 (1611); 12 pavans and galliards in the 12 modes and 2 *canzone alla francese* (1611). The 5-part madrigals were reprinted by A. Smijers (2 vols., 1937-38). —Cf. M. Seiffert, *Cornelis Schuijt,* in 'Tijdschrift der Vereeniging voor Noord-Nederlands Musiekgeschiedenis' (vol. 5; 1897).

Schuyten (shoi'-ten), **Ernest Eugene,** composer and teacher; b. Antwerp, Nov. 7, 1881. He studied composition with Flor Alpaerts at the Brussels Cons. (graduated 1900). In 1915 he emigrated to America, settling in New Orleans; in 1919 he founded the New Orleans Cons. of Music; from 1932 to 1952 he was dean of the College of Music of Loyola Univ. (affiliated with the New Orleans Cons.); in 1952 dean emeritus, but continued as president and director of the New Orleans Cons. Among his works are a piano concerto, a violin concerto, a *Solemn Mass to St. George* (1935); symph in F♯ minor (New Orleans, Jan. 2, 1951, composer conducting); chamber music; vocal works.

Schwalb, Miklós, Hungarian-American pianist; b. Budapest, Feb. 20, 1909. He studied with Dohnányi; appeared with the Budapest Philharmonic at the age of 14; then toured in Europe. He made his American début in 1942; in 1946 he joined the faculty of the New England Cons., Boston.

Schwalm, Oskar, German music critic and composer; b. Erfurt, Sept. 11, 1856; d. Berlin, Feb. 11, 1936. He studied at the Leipzig Cons. with Reinecke, Jadassohn, and others; was engaged in music publishing; wrote an overture, *König Drosselbart;* piano pieces; etc.; publ. collections of school songs.

Schwalm, Robert, German composer; brother of Oskar Schwalm; b. Erfurt, Dec. 6, 1845; d. Königsberg, March 6, 1912. He studied at the Leipzig Cons.; in 1875 settled in Königsberg, where he conducted several choral societies. —Works: opera *Frauenlob* (Leipzig, 1885); male choruses with orch.: *Morgengrauen, Bismarck-Hymne, An Deutschland, Mila, Wikingerfahrt, Gotenzug, Festgesang, Der Goten Todesgesang, Abendstille am Meer, Thermopylae,* etc.; several biblical cantatas; piano pieces; songs.

Schwanenberg, Johann Gottfried, German composer; b. Wolfenbüttel, Dec. 28, 1740; d. Brunswick, April 5, 1804. He studied with Latilla and Saratelli at Venice; was aided by Hasse. —Works: 12 Italian operas in imitation of Hasse's style; cantatas; piano concertos; violin concertos; 3 sonatas for piano.

Schwartz, Rudolf, eminent German musicologist; b. Berlin, Jan. 20, 1859; d. Halle, April 20, 1935. He studied philosophy at the Univ. of Berlin and musicology with Ph. Spitta; *Dr. phil.,* Leipzig Univ. (1892) with the dissertation *H. L. Hassler unter dem Einfluss der italienischen Madrigalisten* (publ. in the 'Vierteljahrsschrift für Musikwissenschaft,' 1893). In 1901 he became librarian of the 'Musikbibliothek Peters' and editor of the Peters 'Jahrbuch,' to which he contributed many valuable essays. A memorial issue of the 'Jahrbuch' (1936) contains a complete list of his writings. He compiled a new ed. of the catalogue of the 'Musikbibliothek Peters' (vol. I, 1910; very valuable); ed. a selection of secular works of H. L. Hassler, for the 'Denkmäler der Tonkunst in Bayern' (vols. IV, 2, and XI, 1); motets by Dulichius, for the 'Denkmäler deutscher Tonkunst' (vols. 31, 41); and Petrucci's 1st and 4th books of *frottole,* for the 'Publikationen älterer Musik' (vol. 8).

Schwarz, Bianca. See **Bianchi.**

Schwarz, Boris, violinist, teacher, and musicologist; b. St. Petersburg, March 13, 1906. He studied with Flesch in Berlin and with Thibaud in Paris; musicology with Schering, Sachs and J. Wolf in Berlin (1930-36); came to the U. S. in 1936; was concertmaster of the Indianapolis Symph. Orch. (1937-38); then a member of the NBC Symph. (1938-39). In 1941 he was appointed to the faculty of Queens College; chairman of its music department 1949-52, 1953-56; associate prof.; received a Ph. D. degree from Columbia Univ. 1950.

Schwarz, Rudolf, Austrian conductor; b. Vienna, April 29, 1905; studied piano and violin; played viola in the Vienna Philharmonic. In 1923, became assistant conductor at the Düsseldorf Opera, and later was conductor at the Karlsruhe Opera. Deprived of this post in 1933, he became music director of the Jüdischer Kulturbund in Berlin. He was arrested by the Nazi authorities in 1939, but released in 1940; then rearrested and sent to the Belsen concentration camp. He survived, and went to Sweden in 1945; then settled in England, where he pursued a successful career; was conductor of the Bournemouth Municipal Orch. (1947-50) and of the Birmingham Orch. (1950-57). In 1957 he received the important post of conductor of the BBC Symph. Orch. —Cf. Donald Brook, *International Gallery of Conductors* (Bristol, 1951; pp. 179-87).

Schwarz, Wilhelm, German singing teacher; b. Stuttgart, May 11, 1825; d. Berlin, Jan. 4, 1878. He was a theologian and teacher; became a singer and teacher of singing in Hanover and Berlin; publ. *System der Gesangkunst nach physiologischen Gesetzen* (1857) and *Die Musik als Gefühlssprache im Verhältniss zur Stimm- und Gesangbildung* (1860).

Schwarzkopf, Elisabeth, German soprano; b. Jarotschin, near Poznan, Dec. 9, 1915; studied in Berlin with Maria Ivogün; made her début in a minor part in *Parsifal* at the Berlin Opera in 1938; then joined the roster of the Vienna Opera; appeared also at Covent Garden, London, and La Scala, Milan. She sang the part of Anna Trulove in the world première of Stravinsky's opera *The Rake's Progress* (Venice, Sept. 11, 1951); gave a number of recitals in the U. S.; also appeared as soloist with major American orchestras.

Schwedler, (Otto) Maximilian, German flutist; b. Hirschberg, March 31, 1853; d. Leipzig, Jan. 16, 1940. He studied in Dresden; played flute in various German orchestras; in 1881, joined the Gewandhaus Orch. in Leipzig; also taught at the Leipzig Cons. He was the inventor of the 'Schwedler flute' (1885), fully described in his *Katechismus der Flöte und des Flötenspiels* (Leipzig, 1897); made numerous transcriptions for flute, and publ. a flute method.

Schweitzer (shvī'-tser), **Albert,** great humanitarian, physician, and organist, and an authority on Bach; b. Kaysersberg, Alsace, Jan. 14, 1875. He was the son of a Günsbach vicar; studied organ with Eugen Münch at Mulhouse, with Ernst Münch at Strasbourg, and with Widor in Paris (from 1893); was organist of the Bach Concerts in Strasbourg from 1896; studied theology and philosophy at the Universities of Strasbourg, Paris, and Berlin; in 1902 joined the faculty of the Univ. of Strasbourg; while teaching there, he completed the full medical course (M.D., 1912), with the intention of becoming a medical missionary in Africa, to which task he subsequently devoted most of his time and energy, making occasional concert tours as organist in Europe to raise funds for his hospital work among the African natives. In 1952 he was awarded the Nobel Peace Prize. His philosophical and theological writings had established his reputation as one of the foremost thinkers of our time. In the field of music, he distinguished himself as the author of one of the most important books on Bach, greatly influencing the interpretation of Bach's music, and contributing to the full understanding of Bach's symbolic treatment of various musical devices. In 1906 he became organist of the 'Société J. S. Bach' in Paris; in 1909 he presided over the conferences on organ building at the Congress of the International Music Society in Vienna, which led to the adoption of international regulations, and read a paper, *Die Reform unseres Orgelbaues,* urging the simplification of the modern organ to correct faulty tone quality caused by extreme wind pressure (full report in the 'Wiener Kongressbericht der Internationalen Musik-Gesellschaft,' 1909, pp. 581-679). With Widor, he edited the first 5 vols. of the Schirmer critico-practical edition of Bach's organ works (editions in English, French, and German) and with Edouard Nies-Berger, the remaining 3 vols. He holds the degrees of *Dr. theol.* and *Dr. phil.;* also the honorary degrees of D.D. (Oxon.) and Litt. D. (St. Andrews). —Books on music: *Deutsche und französische Orgelbaukunst und Orgelkunst* (Leipzig, 1906; 2nd ed., 1927) and *Jean Sébastian Bach, le musicien-poète* (Paris, 1905; German enlarged ed., 1908; English transl. by Ernest Newman, Leipzig, 1911; re-issued, 1923); publ. an autobiography, *Aus meinem Leben und Denken* (Leipzig, 1931; English transl. as *My Life and Thought,* London, 1933; revised ed., as *Out of My Life and Thought,* N. Y., 1949; selections in German publ. as a school textbook, with an introduction in English, N. Y., 1949); also *African Notebook* (N. Y., 1939); *On the Edge of the Primeval Forest* (combined ed. of various previous vols. in German and English; N. Y., 1948). See also C. R. Joy, ed., *Music in the Life of A. S.* (selections from his writings; N. Y., 1951). —Bibliography: C. T. Campion,

A. S.: Philosopher, Theologian, Musician, Doctor (N. Y., 1928); Jan Eigenhuis, *A. S.* (Haarlem, 1929); H. Christaller, *A. S.* (1931); John D. Regester, *A. S.: The Man and His Work* (N. Y., 1931); Magnus C. Ratter, *A. S.* (London, 1935; revised ed., 1950); A. A. Roback, ed., *The A. S. Jubilee Book* (Cambridge, Mass., 1946; a collection of essays); G. Seaver, *A. S.: the Man and his Mind* (London, 1947); O. Kraus, *A. S.: his Work and his Philosophy* (N. Y., 1947); H. Hagedorn, *Prophet in the Wilderness: the Story of A. S.* (N. Y., 1947); R. Grabs, *A. S.: Weg und Werk eines Menschenfreundes* (Berlin, 1953); R. Sonner, *S. und die Orgelbewegung* (Colmar, 1955); numerous articles in the musical and general press.

Schweitzer, Anton, German composer; b. Coburg (baptized June 6), 1735; d. Gotha, Nov. 23, 1787. He was a chorister and later viola player in Hildburghausen; in 1764 went to Italy for serious study; returning to Germany, he was appointed (in 1766) music director of the ducal theater in Weimar; in 1769 became conductor of Seyler's operatic troupe, which was engaged by the Duke of Weimar in 1772. After the destruction by fire of the Weimar Theater in 1774, Schweitzer went to Gotha; there he was appointed court conductor in 1778. Schweitzer was one of the earliest composers to write serious operas to German texts. He produced in Weimar his operas *Die Dorfgala* (June 30, 1772) and *Alceste* (May 28, 1773; libretto by Wieland); there followed another opera, *Rosamunde* (Mannheim, Jan. 20, 1780); Mozart expressed appreciation of Schweitzer's operas. But it was as a composer of 'Singspiele' that Schweitzer achieved popularity in his day; he was also important historically as the first composer of a melodrama in German, after Rousseau's *Pygmalion* (Weimar, 1772). —Cf. J. Maurer, *Anton Schweitzer als dramatischer Komponist* (Leipzig, 1912). See also A. Loewenberg, *Annals of Opera* (1943; 2nd ed., 1955).

Schwencke, Christian Friedrich Gottlieb, German composer; son of the bassoonist Johann Gottlieb Schwencke (1744-1823); b. Wachenhausen, Harz, Aug. 30, 1767; d. Hamburg, Oct. 27, 1822. He studied with Marpurg and Kirnberger; succeeded K. P. E. Bach as town cantor and music director at the Katharinenkirche, Hamburg. Wrote cantatas, sacred and secular; 2 oratorios; church music; 6 organ fugues; 3 violin sonatas; piano sonatas. He rescored Handel's *Messiah* and Bach's Mass in B minor; wrote much for the Leipzig 'Allgemeine Zeitung.'

Schwencke, Friedrich Gottlieb, pianist and organist; son and pupil of Johann Friedrich Schwencke; b. Hamburg, Dec. 15, 1823; d. there, June 11, 1896. He gave organ concerts in Paris (1855); succeeded his father in 1852 as organist of the Nikolaikirche in Hamburg. —Works: 3 fantasias for organ, trumpet, trombone, and kettledrums; sacred songs for female chorus with organ; in 1886 he publ. a new and unabridged ed. of his father's chorale preludes.

Schwencke, Johann Friedrich, German organist and composer; son and pupil of Christian Friedrich Gottlieb Schwencke; b. Hamburg, April 30, 1792; d. there, Sept. 28, 1852. He was organist at the Nikolaikirche in Hamburg; composed numerous cantatas; over 500 preludes and postludes for organ; a septet for 5 cellos, double-bass, and kettledrums; harmonized about 1,000 chorales and 73 Russian folksongs; publ. the popular *Hamburgisches Choralbuch;* made many transcriptions; orchestrated Beethoven's *Adelaide,* and various works by other composers.

Schwerké, Irving, American writer on music; b. Appleton, Wis., July 21, 1893. He was educated at the Univ. of Wisconsin and at Charleston College, S. C.; studied music privately in Europe; from 1921 to 1934, was music critic for the Paris ed. of the Chicago 'Daily Tribune'; from 1932 to 1940 was the European representative for the N. Y. 'Musical Courier.' After the outbreak of World War II he lived in Switzerland; then returned to the U. S. and settled in his home town, Appleton. —Books: *Kings Jazz and David* (Paris, 1927); *Alexandre Tansman, compositeur polonais* (Paris, 1931; in French); *Views and Interviews* (Paris, 3rd ed., 1936); contributed several articles on French composers to the 'Mus. Quarterly.'

Schwieger, Hans, conductor; b. Cologne, June 15, 1906. He studied at the Cologne Hochschule für Musik; was assistant conductor at the Berlin State Opera (1927-30); at the Kassel Opera (1930-31); in Mainz (1932-34) and in Danzig (1936-37). In 1937 he went to Japan, where he conducted the Tokyo Symph. Orch. In March, 1938 he arrived in the U. S.; organized and conducted the Southern Symph. Orch. at Columbus (1938-41); then was conductor of the Fort Wayne Symph. (1944-48). In 1948 he was appointed conductor of the Kansas City Philharmonic. —Cf. Hope Stoddard, *Symphony Conductors of the U. S. A.* (N. Y., 1957; pp. 182-89).

Schytte (shüt'-te), **Ludvig (Theodor),** Danish composer; b. Aarhus, April 28, 1848; d. Berlin, Nov. 10, 1909. He was a pharmacist as a young man; then began to study piano with Anton Rée and composition with Gade, finishing under Taubert in Berlin and Liszt in Weimar. He settled in Vienna in 1887 as a teacher; moved to Berlin in 1907; taught there at Stern's Cons. A master of the miniature forms, he wrote a number of attractive piano pieces, some of which became extremely popular; about 200 were publ., among them *Promenades musicales, Rapsodie norwégienne, Aus froher Kinderzeit, Spanische Nächte, Valse piquante, Waldbilder, Aus der Heimat und Fremde;* numerous piano studies *(6 brillante Vortragsetüden, Melodische Spezialetüden, Studien in Ornamentik und Dynamik);* for piano 4 hands: *Bajaderntänze, Kindersymphonie, Musikalische Wandelbilder, Reiseblätter, Kindersuite,* etc.; also a 1-act opera, *Hero* (Copenhagen, Sept. 25, 1898); the operetta *Der Mameluk* (Vienna, Dec. 22, 1903); a piano concerto; chamber music; a song cycle, *Die Verlassene.*

Scontrino, Antonio, Italian composer and teacher; b. Trapani, May 17, 1850; d. Florence, Jan. 7, 1922. He studied at the Palermo Cons.; was a virtuoso on the double-bass, and gave concerts; went to Munich for a special study of German music at the Musikschule (1872-74); after various engagements as an orch. player and teacher, he settled in Florence in 1892, and taught composition at the Istituto Musicale there. He wrote 5 operas: *Matelda* (Milan, June 19, 1879), *Il Progettista* (Rome, Feb. 8, 1882); *Il Sortilegio* (Turin, June 21, 1882), *Gringoire* (Milan, May 24, 1890), and *La Cortigiana* (Milan, Jan. 30, 1896); incidental music to Gabriele d'Annunzio's *Francesca da Rimini;* a *Sinfonia marinaresca;* a *Sinfonia romantica;* a concerto for double-bass and orch.; 3 string quartets; church music; songs. A biographical brochure, *Antonio Scontrino nella vita e nell' arte,* was publ. in his native town of Trapani in 1935. A detailed analysis of his instrumental works is found in Cobbett's 'Cyclopedic Survey of Chamber Music' (vol. II, pp. 395-408).

Scott, Charles Kennedy, English choral conductor and composer; b. Romsey, Nov. 16, 1876. He studied organ at the Brussels Cons., taking 1st prize (1897). In 1898, he settled in London; in 1904 he established the Oriana Madrigal Society there, in 1919 the Philharmonic Choir. and in 1922 the Euterpe String Players. He publ. *Madrigal Singing* (London, 1907; new enlarged ed., 1931); a vocal method, *Word and Tone* (London, 1933; 2 vols.); *The Fundamentals of Singing* (N. Y., 1954); edited old carols and choral music of the 16th century. —Cf. S. de B. Taylor, *C. K. Scott,* in the 'Mus. Times' (Nov., 1951).

Scott, Cyril Meir, noted English composer; b. Oxton, Cheshire, Sept. 27, 1879. He was a scion of a cultured family, his father being a classical scholar, his mother a musician. At the age of 12 he was placed at Hoch's Cons. in Frankfurt; studied piano there; then traveled back to England and continued his study in Liverpool; in 1895 he went to Frankfurt again and studied composition with Iwan Knorr. In 1898 he settled in Liverpool as a piano teacher, and also began to compose music and to write poetry. He was attracted to descriptive music and poetic legends; his first important orchestral work, *Heroic Suite,* was conducted by Hans Richter at Liverpool in 1900, and in the same year his 1st Symph. was given at Darmstadt. His 2nd Symph. was performed at a Promenade Concert in London on Aug. 25, 1903. In 1913 his overture to Maeterlinck's play *Princess Maleine* was given in Vienna. He was the soloist in his piano concerto at the festival of British music given in London by Beecham in 1915. His settings of Keats' *La Belle Dame Sans Merci* for chorus and orch. (1915-16) was revived at the Leeds Festival of 1934. His opera *The Alchemist,* to his own libretto, was produced in Essen on May 28, 1925. Among the works of his later years is the *Ode to Great Men* for speaker, women's chorus, and orch. (Norwich Festival, 1936). In 1921 Scott traveled in the U. S. as pianist and lecturer. Also in 1921 he married the novelist Rose Laure. He became widely known as a composer of evocative piano pieces, often under exotic titles, and employing modern technical devices; he experimented successfully with progressions of unresolved dissonant chords; made frequent use of the whole-tone scale; his harmonic apparatus is impressionistic; there is an aura of vague poetic inspiration in his melodies; the mood created by his music is communicative; besides, the pianistic idiom is expert, and the success of his pieces early in the century is understandable. From his youth he was a student of occult philosophy; wrote also on the relationship between music and colors; in his writings he opposed modern music beyond Impressionism, and inveighed violently against jazz. —Works: Chamber music: piano quartet (1903); piano trio (1922); 3 string quartets; 2 string trios;

concerto for oboe and strings (London, Sept. 13, 1948); cello sonata (1949); clarinet quintet (1951); *Sonata melodica,* for violin and piano (1951). Piano pieces: *Chinese Serenade, Lotus Land* (1905; very popular; arranged for violin and piano by Fritz Kreisler); *Russian Dance; Sphinx; Danse nègre* (one of his most popular pieces); *Berceuse; Autumn Idyll; Impressions of the Jungle Book,* after Kipling (highly successful); *Little Russian Suite; Indian Suite; Spanish Dance; Badinage;* etc.; over a hundred songs. —Books: *My Years of Indiscretion* (1924); *The Philosophy of Modernism in its Connection with Music* (1917); *The Influence of Music on History and Morals, a Vindication of Plato* (1928); *Music, its Secret Influence Throughout the Ages* (1933; new and extended ed., 1950). —Cf. A. Eaglefield Hull, *Cyril Scott: Composer, Poet, and Philosopher* (London, 1918).

Scott, Marion Margaret, English writer on music; b. London, July 16, 1877; d. there, Dec. 24, 1953. She studied at the Royal College of Music in London (1896-1904). With Gertrude Eaton she organized in 1911 the Society of Women Musicians; contributed to the 'Mus. Times,' 'Mus. Quarterly,' and other musical journals. She specialized in Haydn research and publ. a number of articles on Haydn; compiled a complete catalogue of Haydn's quartets, publ. in 'Music & Letters' (July, 1930); participated in the revision of the Haydn article for the 5th ed. of Grove's Dictionary. — Books: *Beethoven,* in the 'Master Musicians' series (London, 1934; revised ed., 1951) and *Mendelssohn* (London, 1938).

Scott, Tom, American folk singer and composer; b. Campbellsburg, Ky., May 28, 1912. His full name was Thomas Jefferson Scott; he studied violin with an uncle; played in dance bands; wrote songs; then went to Hollywood, where he took theory lessons with George Antheil; subsequently studied with Harrison Kerr and Wallingford Riegger. —Works: opera, *The Fisherman* (1956); for orch.: *Song with Dance* (1932); *Plymouth Rock* (1938); *Hornpipe and Chantey* (1944); symph. No. 1 (Rochester, N. Y., Oct. 22, 1946); *From the Sacred Harp* (1946); *Ballad of the Harp Weaver,* for narrator, harp, chorus, and string quartet (N. Y., Feb. 22, 1947); *Johnny Appleseed* (N. Y., March 1, 1948); *Lento* for saxophone and strings (1953); chamber music: 2 string quartets (1944; 1956); *Emily Dickinson Suite,* for violin and harp (1955); chanteys for chorus; a number of solo songs; arrangements of folksongs; etc. —Cf. J. Ringo, *Some Notes on Tom Scott's Music,* in the 'Bulletin of the American Composers Alliance' (Winter, 1957; with a list of works).

Scotti, Antonio, celebrated Italian baritone; b. Naples, Jan. 25, 1866; d. there, Feb. 26, 1936. He studied with Francesco Lamperti; made his début as Amonasro in Malta (Nov. 1, 1889); then sang in Italy, Russia, Spain, and South America; made his London début at Covent Garden on June 8, 1899, as Don Giovanni, and appeared in the same role with the Metropolitan Opera, N. Y. (Dec. 27, 1899). He remained with the Metropolitan Opera for 33 years; made his farewell appearance on Jan. 20, 1933. He also toured in America with his own company. He possessed great histrionic ability, and was especially noted for his dramatic roles (Scarpia, Rigoletto, Falstaff, Don Giovanni).

Scotus (Scot), Joannes (called **Erigena**), noted philosopher; b. c. 815; d. c. 877. His work, *De divisione naturae,* contains a definition of music, with a description of musical practice in his day. —Cf. J. Handschin, *Die Musikanschauung des Johannes Scotus (Erigena),* in 'Deutsche Vierteljahrsschrift für Literaturwissenschaft und Geistesgeschichte' (vol. V, 2).

Scriabin (skryah'-bin), **Alexander Nikolayevitch,** remarkable Russian composer; b. Moscow, Jan. 6, 1872; d. there, April 27, 1915. His mother died when he was a child; his father remarried. Scriabin received his education mainly from his aunt, who was a musician; she taught him the rudiments of music until he was 12, when he began to take regular piano lessons with George Conus, and later with Zverev. In 1885 he took private lessons in composition with Taneyev. He entered the Moscow Cons. in 1888, enrolling in the piano class of Safonov. Although he practiced assiduously, he never became a virtuoso; at his piano recitals he played mostly his own works. Graduating with a gold medal from Safonov's class, Scriabin remained at the Cons. to study fugue with Arensky, but failed to pass the required examination and left the Moscow Cons. without a diploma for composition. By that time he had written several piano pieces in Chopin's manner. The publisher Belaiev heard him play some of them and offered him a contract. Belaiev also financed Scriabin's European tour in 1895-96; on Jan. 15, 1896 Scriabin gave in Paris a concert of his own music. Returning to Russia, he completed his first major work, a piano concerto; on Oct. 23, 1897 he gave its first performance with the Odessa Philharmonic Orch., conducted by Safonov. In the same year he married the pianist Vera Isakovitch. They spent some time abroad; on Jan. 31, 1898 they gave a joint recital in Paris in a program of Scriabin's works. From 1898 until 1903 Scriabin taught piano at the Moscow Cons. His first orchestral work, *Rêverie,* was performed in Moscow by Safonov (March 24, 1899), who also conducted the première of Scriabin's 1st symph. (March 29, 1901). The 2nd symph. was brought out by Liadov in St. Petersburg (Jan. 25, 1902). After the death of Belaiev in 1904, Scriabin received an annual grant of 2,400 rubles from the wealthy Moscow merchant Morozov, and settled in Switzerland, where he began work on his 3rd symph., *The Divine Poem.* A special concert was arranged in Paris for its première on May 29, 1905, Arthur Nikisch conducting. At that time Scriabin separated from Vera Isakovitch and established a household with Tatiana Schloezer (sister of the music critic Boris Schloezer). In Dec., 1906, Scriabin went to America at the invitation of Modest Altschuler, conductor of the Russian Symphony Society in N. Y.; appeared as soloist at Altschuler's concerts and gave piano recitals of his works in New York, Chicago, Detroit, and other cities. Tatiana Schloezer joined him in N. Y. in Jan., 1907, but they were warned that charges of moral turpitude might be brought against them. To forestall this eventuality, they left America in March, 1907, for Paris. On Dec. 10, 1908 Altschuler gave in N. Y. the world première of Scriabin's new symph. work, *The Poem of Ecstasy;* the Russian première came later in St. Petersburg (Feb. 1, 1909). In the spring of 1908 Scriabin met Serge Koussevitzky, who became one of the most ardent supporters of his music. He gave Scriabin a 5-year contract with his newly established publishing house 'Éditions Russes' at a guarantee of 5,000 rubles a year; in the summer of 1910 he engaged Scriabin as soloist for a tour in a chartered steamer down the Volga River. Scriabin wrote for Koussevitzky his most ambitious symph. work, *Prometheus* or *The Poem of Fire,* with an important piano part. The score included a special color keyboard *(clavier à lumières)* intended to project changing colors according to the scale of the spectrum. The construction of such an instrument however, presented insurmountable difficulties, and when Koussevitzky gave the world première of *Prometheus* (Moscow, March 15, 1911) with Scriabin at the piano, it was without the color organ. A performance with colored lights thrown on a screen was given at Carnegie Hall, N. Y., on March 20, 1915, by Altschuler, but the effect was disappointing. Meanwhile, the intimate association between Scriabin and Koussevitzky came to a sudden end owing to financial and personal disagreement. In 1912 Scriabin signed a contract with the Moscow publisher Jurgenson, who guaranteed him 6,000 rubles annually. In 1914 Scriabin visited London and was soloist in his piano concerto and in *Prometheus* at a concert led by Sir Henry Wood (March 14, 1914); he also gave a recital of his own works there (March 20, 1914). His last public appearance was in a recital in Petrograd on April 15, 1915; upon his return to Moscow, an abscess developed on his lip, leading to blood poisoning; he died after a few days' illness. His 3 children (of the union with Tatiana Schloezer) were legitimized at his death. His son Julian, an exceptionally gifted boy, was accidentally drowned at the age of 11 in the Dnieper River at Kiev (June 22, 1919); Julian's 2 piano preludes, written in the style of the last works of his father, were publ. in a Scriabin memorial volume (Moscow, 1940). —Scriabin was a genuine innovator in harmony. After an early period of strongly felt influences (Chopin, Liszt, and Wagner), he gradually evolved his own melodic and harmonic style, marked by extreme chromaticism; in his piano piece *Désir,* op. 57 (1908) the threshold of polytonality and atonality is reached; the key signature is dispensed with in his subsequent works; chromatic alterations and compound appoggiaturas create a harmonic web of such complexity that all distinction between consonance and dissonance vanishes. Building chords by fourths rather than by thirds, Scriabin constructed his 'mystic chord' of 6 notes (C, F♯, B♭, E, A, and D), which is the harmonic foundation of *Prometheus.* In his 7th piano sonata (1913) appears a chordal structure of 25 notes (D♭, F♭, G, A, and C, repeated in 5 octaves) which was dubbed 'a 5-story chord.' These harmonic extensions were associated in Scriabin's mind with theosophic doctrines; he aspired to a universal art in which the impressions of the senses were to unite with religious experience. He made plans for the writing of a 'mystery play' designed to accomplish such a synthesis, but only the text of a preliminary poem *(L'Acte préalable)* was completed at his death. —Scriabin never wrote chamber music, songs, or choral works. His catalogue includes the following: For orch.:

concerto for piano and orch., op. 20 (1897); *Rêverie,* op. 24 (1899); symph. No. 1, op. 26 (1900); symph. No. 2, op. 29 (1901); symph. No. 3 *(The Divine Poem),* op. 43 (1905); *The Poem of Ecstasy,* op. 54 (1908); *Prometheus (The Poem of Fire),* op. 60 (1911). For piano: 10 sonatas (op. 6, 19, 23, 30, 53, 62, 64, 66, 68, 70); 79 preludes in 15 sets (op. 11, 13, 15, 16, 17, 22, 27, 31, 33, 35, 37, 39, 48, 67, 74); 24 etudes in 4 sets (op. 2, 8, 42, 65); 6 impromptus (op. 10, 12, 14); 21 mazurkas (op. 3, 25, 40); 2 nocturnes (op. 5); *Prelude and Nocturne* for the left hand alone (op. 9); *Polonaise* (op. 21); *Fantaisie* (op. 28); *Poème tragique* (op. 34); *Poème satanique* (op. 36); *3 Morceaux* (op. 49); *4 Morceaux* (op. 51); *3 Morceaux* (op. 52); *4 Morceaux* (op. 56); *2 Morceaux* (op. 57); *Feuillet d'album* (op. 58); *2 Morceaux* (op. 59); *Poème-Nocturne* (op. 61); *2 Poèmes* (op. 63); *Vers la flamme* (op. 72); *2 Danses* (op. 73). —Bibliography: 'Musikalnyi Sovremennik,' special Scriabin number (Petrograd, 1915); L. Sabaneyev, *S.* (Moscow, 1916; 2nd ed., 1923); A. E. Hull, *S.* (London, 1916); A. E. Hull, *A Survey of the Pianoforte Works of S.,* in the 'Mus. Quarterly' (Oct., 1916); A. E. Hull, *The Pianoforte Sonatas of S.,* in the 'Mus. Times' (Nov.-Dec., 1916); M. Montagu-Nathan, *A Handbook of the Pianoforte Works of S.* (Boston, 1916); M. Montagu-Nathan, *Contemporary Russian Composers* (London, 1917); A. E. Hull, *S.'s Scientific Derivation of Harmony Versus Empirical Methods,* in 'Proceedings of the Musical Association' (London, 1917); Paul Rosenfeld, *Musical Portraits* (N. Y., 1920); Igor Glebov, *S.* (Petrograd, 1921); Boris de Schloezer, *A. S.,* in the 'Revue Musicale' (1921); O. von Riesemann, *A. S. im Lichte eigener Jugendbriefe,* in 'Die Musik' (1923); Boris de Schloezer, *S.,* (Berlin, 1923; in Russian; vol. 1 only); A. J. Swan, *S.* (London, 1923); C. Gray, *A Survey of Contemporary Music* (London, 1924); V. Yakovlev, *S.* (Moscow, 1925); Georg Rimsky-Korsakov, *The Deciphering of the 'Lumière' Part in Scriabin's 'Prometheus'* in 'De Musica' (Leningrad, 1927; in Russian); R. H. Hill, *A. S.,* in 'Fortnightly Review' (N. Y., 1928); A. J. Swan, *Music 1900-1930* (N. Y., 1929); L. Sabaneyev, *S. and the Idea of Religious Art,* in the 'Mus. Times' (1931); P. Dickenmann, *Die Entwicklung der Harmonik bei A. S.* (Leipzig, 1935); M. D. Calvocoressi and G. Abraham, *Masters of Russian Music* (N. Y., 1936); *S., Symposium on the 25th Anniversary of his Death* (Moscow, 1940); N. Slonimsky, *A. S.,* in *Great Modern Composers,* ed. by O. Thompson (N. Y., 1941); D. Brook, *Six Great Russian Composers* (London, 1946); L. Danilevitch, *S.* (Moscow, 1953). Scriabin's correspondence, ed. by L. Sabaneyev, was publ. in Moscow, 1923. For an exposition of Scriabin's principles see chapter IV in A. E. Hull's *Modern Harmony* (London, 1914) and Part I of J. L. Dunk's *Hyperacoustics* (London, 1916).

Scribe, Eugène, famous French dramatist and author of many opera librettos; b. Paris, Dec. 25, 1791; d. there, Feb. 21, 1861. He was the writer of the finest librettos set to music by Auber (*La Muette de Portici, Fra Diavolo, Le Domino noir,* etc.) and Meyerbeer (*Robert le Diable, Les Huguenots, Le Prophète, L'Africaine*). For Boieldieu he wrote *La Dame blanche;* for Halévy, *Manon Lescaut* and *La Juive;* he also wrote for less celebrated composers. In the complete edition of his *Œuvres dramatiques* (Paris, 1874-85; 76 vols.), 26 vols. are filled by his opera librettos. —Cf. J. G. Prod'homme, *Wagner, Berlioz and Monsieur Scribe,* in the 'Mus. Quarterly' (July, 1926).

Scudo, Pierre, music critic; b. Venice, June 8, 1806; d. Blois, Oct. 14, 1864. He was brought up in France; studied at Choron's school in Paris; was for a time an opera singer; played clarinet in military bands; then turned to journalism; publ. several political pamphlets; became music critic of the influential 'Revue des Deux Mondes.' A writer of considerable talent, he held reactionary views; violently attacked Berlioz, Liszt, and Wagner. He became deranged and died in an insane asylum. His articles were publ. in book form: *Critique et littérature musicale* (2 series; 1850; 1859); *L'Art ancienne et l'art moderne* (1854); *L'Année musicale, ou Revue annuelle des théâtres lyriques et des concerts* (3 vols., 1860-62); etc. He also wrote a musical novel, *Le Chevalier Sarti* (1857; not connected with the composer Giuseppe Sarti); its sequel *Frédérique* was publ. in the 'Revue des Deux Mondes.' He publ. some songs (*Le Fil de la Vierge, La Baigneuse,* etc.).

Seagle, Oscar, American baritone; b. Chattanooga, Tenn., Oct. 31, 1877; d. Dallas, Dec. 19, 1945. He sang in concerts in the U. S. from 1896 until 1905; then went to Paris for further study, with Jean de Reszke; made his Paris début in 1907, and also sang in England; returned to America at the outbreak of World War I in 1914, and settled in N. Y. as a singing teacher.

Searle, Humphrey, English composer; b. Oxford, Aug. 26, 1915. He studied classical literature at Oxford Univ. and music at the Royal College of Music in London, with John Ireland and R. O. Morris. In 1937 he went to Vienna, where he took private lessons with Anton von Webern; this study was a decisive influence in Searle's future work. He served in the British Army during World War II, and was stationed in Germany in 1946. Returning to London, he was on the music staff of the BBC (1946-48); became active in various modern-music organizations. His music reflects the trends of Expressionism, and the idiom is a modification of the 12-tone method; but he also applies purely national English melodic patterns in some of his compositions. He publ. 2 books, *The Music of Liszt* and *Twentieth Century Counterpoint* (both London, 1954), and contributed articles on musical subjects to magazines. —Works: 2 suites for strings (1942, 1944); 2 piano concertos (1944; 1955); quintet for bassoon and strings (1945); *Intermezzo* for 11 instruments (1946); *Put Away the Flutes,* for tenor and 6 instruments (1947; in memory of Anton von Webern); *Fuga Giocosa,* for orch. (1948); quartet for violin, viola, clarinet, and bassoon (1948); *Gold Coast Customs,* to Edith Sitwell's poem, for speakers, men's chorus, and orch. (1948); *The Shadow of Cain,* to Edith Sitwell's poem, for speakers, men's chorus, and orch. (1952); a symphony (1953); *Concertante,* for piano, strings, and percussion (1954); *Aubade,* for horn and strings (1955); piano pieces; songs.—Cf. E. Lockspeiser, *Humphrey Searle,* in the 'Mus. Times' (Sept., 1955).

Seashore, Carl Emil, American psychologist and musician; b. Mörlunda, Sweden, Jan. 28, 1866; d. Lewiston, Idaho, Oct. 16, 1949. He was brought to the U. S. as a child; studied at Yale Univ. (Ph. D., 1895); taught psychology at Yale (until 1902), then at Iowa State Univ.; dean of the Graduate College there in 1908; dean emeritus, 1938. He devised a widely used method for measuring musical talent ('Seashore Test') through special instruments of his own invention (audiometer, tonoscope, chronograph, etc.). —Books: *The Voice Tonoscope* (1903); *Localisation of Sound* (1903); *A Sound Perimeter* (1903); *The Tonoscope and its Use in the Training of the Voice* (1906); *The Measure of a Singer* (1912); *Seeing Yourself Sing* (1916); *Vocational Guidance in Music* (1916); *The Measurement of Musical Memory* (1917); *The Psychology of Musical Talent* (1919); *Psychology of the Vibrato* (1936); *Psychology of Music* (1938); *Pioneering in Psychology* (1942); *In Search of Beauty in Music* (N. Y., 1947) etc.; contributed articles to the 'Mus. Quarterly': *The Measurement of Musical Talent* (Jan., 1915), *Psychology in Music* (April, 1930), etc. —Cf. the special Seashore issue of the Univ. of Iowa Studies in Psychology (No. 21; Princeton, N. J., 1928).

Sebastian, George, conductor; b. Budapest, Aug. 17, 1903. He studied composition with Leo Weiner and Kodály at the State Academy of Music, graduating in 1921; then took private lessons in conducting with Bruno Walter in Munich (1922-23); was opera coach at the Munich State Opera; in 1923-24 was assistant conductor with the Metropolitan Opera, N. Y.; then conductor at the Hamburg Municipal Opera (1924-25), at the Neues Theater, Leipzig (1925-27); at the Berlin Opera (1927-31). In 1931 he went to Russia, where he was conductor of the Moscow Radio Orch. (until 1937). In 1938 he came to the U. S.; conducted the Scranton, Penn., Philharmonic Orch. (1940-45); in 1946 he went back to Europe; settled in Paris; conducted at the Opéra-Comique, and also symph. concerts.

Sebastiani, Johann, German composer; b. Weimar, Sept. 30, 1622; d. Königsberg, 1683. He was in the service of the Elector of Brandenburg at Königsberg; appointed Kapellmeister to the palace church in 1663; pensioned in 1679. He wrote a Passion, *Das Leiden und Sterben . . . Jesu Christi* (1672), employing a 5-part chorus with 6 instruments. It is noteworthy for the devotional chorales therein introduced, as in Bach's Passions. It was reprinted by Zelle in vol. 17 of the 'Denkmäler deutscher Tonkunst.' Sebastiani's *Parnass-Blumen, Geistliche und weltliche Lieder* were publ. in Hamburg in 2 vols. (1672, 1675); 13 Funeral Songs for several voices were issued separately at Königsberg between 1664 and 1680.

Šebor (shā'-bohr), **Karl,** Bohemian conductor and composer; b. Brandeis, Aug. 13, 1843; d. Prague, May 17, 1903. He was a pupil of Kittl; was conductor of the National Opera (1864-67), and military bandmaster in Vienna (from 1871). He wrote the Czech operas (all produced in Prague): *The Templars in Moravia* (Oct. 19, 1864), *Drahomira* (1867), *The Hussite's Bride* (Sept. 28, 1868), *Blanka* (1870), *The Frustrated Wedding* (Oct. 25, 1879); cantatas; overtures; songs.

Sechter (zeh'-ter), **Simon,** composer and teacher; b. Friedberg, Bohemia, Oct. 11, 1788; d. Vienna, Sept. 10, 1867. He studied with Koželuh and Hartmann in Vienna; in 1810 he obtained the position of organ instructor at the Vienna Institute for the Blind; was also active as court organist; in 1851 he became prof. of harmony and composition at the Vienna Cons. The excellence of his teaching attracted to him a number of students from all over Europe, among them Henselt, Bruckner, Nottebohm, Vieuxtemps, Thalberg, and Pauer. So great was his renown even before he held an official teaching position, that Schubert, some weeks before his death (1828), expressed a desire to study with him. He was a master contrapuntist, and wrote a vast amount of church music; publ. many fugues and preludes for organ; several intricate piano pieces (Dances in Counterpoint; 12 Contrapuntal Pieces; 4 books of amusing fugues for 4 hands on national and operatic airs; etc.); string quartets; songs. He also wrote an opera, *Ali Hitsch-Hatsch,* which was produced in Vienna on Nov. 12, 1844. His most important pedagogical work is the treatise *Die Grundsätze der musikalischen Komposition* (3 vols.; Vienna, 1853-54), on the lines of Rameau's 'basse fondamentale'; the 1st vol. was publ. in English transl. (N. Y., 1871; 12th ed., 1912). He also publ. a *Generalbass-Schule,* and a new ed. of Marpurg's *Abhandlung von der Fuge.* —Cf. K. F. Pohl, *Simon Sechter* (Vienna, 1868); G. Capellen, *Ist das System S. Sechters ein geeigneter Ausgangspunkt für die theoretische Wagnerforschung?* (Leipzig, 1902).

Seckendorff (zehk'-en-dorf), **Karl Siegmund von,** German composer; b. Erlangen, Nov. 26, 1744; d. Ansbach, April 26, 1785. He was an officer in the Austrian and Sardinian armies (1761-74); then in the diplomatic service in Weimar (1776-84); shortly before his death he was appointed Prussian ambassador in Ansbach (1784). At Weimar he was on intimate terms with Goethe, who allowed him to write music for a number of his poems before their publication (*Der Fischer, Der König in Thule,* etc.); in these songs Seckendorff caught the characteristic inflections of folk melodies. He publ. 3 collections of *Volks- und andere Lieder* (1779-82); wrote 12 string quartets, 8 divertimentos for violin and piano, 3 piano trios, and 2 piano sonatas for 3 hands (probably the earliest example of such compositions); 3 Singspiele: *Lila* (1776), *Proserpine* (1778), and *Jery und Bätely* (1780). —Cf. V. Knab, *K. S. von Seckendorff* (Ansbach, 1914); Max Friedlaender, *Gedichte von Goethe in Kompositionen seiner Zeitgenossen* (1896 and 1916); E. Herrmann, *Das Weimarer Lied in der 2. Hälfte des 18. Jahrhunderts* (dissertation, Leipzig, 1925).

Seefried, Irmgard, German soprano; b. Köngetried, Bavaria, Oct. 9, 1919. She studied voice at the Augsburg Cons.; was opera singer in Aachen (1939-43); on May 2, 1943, made her first appearance with the Vienna Opera as Eva in *Die Meistersinger;* subsequently sang in Paris, London, Zürich, and Stockholm; American début at the Metropolitan Opera House, N. Y., as Susanna in *The Marriage of Figaro* (Nov. 20, 1953).

Seeger, Charles Louis, Jr., American musicologist; b. (of American parents), Mexico City, Dec. 14, 1886. He studied at Harvard Univ., graduating in 1908; taught music at the Univ. of California (1912-19) and at the Institute of Musical Art, N. Y. (1922-33); also lectured at the New School for Social Research; in 1935, he went to Washington, D. C.; from 1941 till 1953 was Chief of the Division of Music and Visual Arts at the Pan American Union. He was one of the founders of the American Musicological Society (1934); also of the American Library of Musicology (1931). In 1931 he married the composer Ruth Crawford (q.v.). His compositions include the overture *Shadowy Waters* (after Yeats) for orch.; music for the pageants *Derdra* (1914) and *The Queen's Masque* (1915); a violin sonata; songs. In collaboration with E. G. Stricklen he publ. *An Outline of a Course in Harmonic Structure and Musical Invention* (1913) and *Harmonic Structure and Elementary Composition* (1916). Author of many articles in the 'Mus. Quarterly' and elsewhere. —Cf. Henry Cowell, ed., *American Composers on American Music* (Stanford Univ., 1933, p. 119 ff.).

Seeger (zā'-ger), **Joseph** (also known as Seegr, Segert, Zeckert, etc.), Bohemian organist; b. Repin, March 21, 1716; d. Prague, April 22, 1782. He was a pupil of Czernohorsky and Franz Benda in Prague; played the violin in a Prague church, before being appointed organist at the Kreuzherrenkirche (1745); retained this position until his death. He was greatly esteemed as a teacher; among his pupils were J. A. Koželuh, Kuchar, Mašek, Mysliveček, etc. His most celebrated organ works, *8 Toccatas and Fugues,* were publ. posthumously (1793); his organ preludes were included in Guilmant's collection *École classique de l'orgue.*

Seeling (zā'-link), **Hans,** pianist; b. Prague, 1828; d. there, May 26, 1862. He went to Italy in 1852; then traveled in the East, returning to Europe in 1857; was in Paris in 1859; then in Germany; finally went back to Prague. He publ. many salon pieces, which were successful (*Barcarolle, Lorelei,* etc.).

Seghers (sŭ-găr'), **François-Jean-Baptiste,** Belgian violinist; b. Brussels, Jan. 17, 1801; d. Margency, near Paris, Feb. 2, 1881. He studied in Brussels with Gensse, and at the Paris Cons. with Baillot; founded in Brussels the Société Ste.-Cécile in 1848, and conducted it until 1854. Its concerts of orchestral and choral works were famous; after the founder's death it rapidly declined and soon was dissolved.

Segnitz (zehg'-nitz), **Eugen,** German musicologist; b. Leipzig, March 5, 1862; d. Berlin, Sept. 25, 1927. He studied privately with Papperitz; wrote music criticism; publ. valuable biographical studies: *Carl Reinecke* (1900), *Wagner und Leipzig* (1901), *Liszt und Rom* (1901), *Goethe und die Oper in Weimar* (1908), *Franz Liszts Kirchenmusik* (1911), *Arthur Nikisch* (1920), *Max Reger* (1922).

Segovia, Andrés, famous Spanish guitar virtuoso; b. Linares, near Jaen, Feb. 17, 1893. He improvised on the guitar as a child; went to Granada, and gave his first concert there at the age of 14; then presented a series of concerts in Barcelona (1916) and Madrid; subsequently undertook a grand tour in South America. On April 7, 1924 he gave his first concert in Paris; this was the beginning of his international fame; for 35 years he traveled all over the world, arousing admiration for his artistry wherever he went. He did much to reinstate the guitar as a concert instrument capable of a variety of expression; several modern composers wrote works especially for him (Castelnuovo-Tedesco, Manuel M. Ponce, Turina, and others); Albert Roussel wrote a solo piece for guitar entitled simply *Segovia,* which Segovia played in Madrid on April 25, 1925. —Cf. R. Gelatt, *Music Makers* (N. Y., 1953).

Seiber, Mátyás, composer; b. Budapest, May 4, 1905. Of a musical family, he learned to play the cello at home; later entered the Budapest Academy of Music, where he studied with Kodály (1919-24). During the following years he traveled as a member of a ship's orch. on a transatlantic line; visited Russia as a musical correspondent. He taught at Hoch's Cons. at Frankfurt (1926-33); then was again in Budapest. In 1935 he settled in London; in 1942, was appointed to the faculty of Morley College; also gave lectures on the BBC. A prolific composer, Seiber has written works of every type: an opera, *Eva spielt mit Puppen* (1934); 2 operettas; incidental music for several plays; 2 suites for string orch.; *Transylvanian Rhapsody* for orch. (1941); *Pastorale and Burlesque* for flute and strings (1942); *Fantasia Concertante* for violin and strings (1943); *Notturno* for horn and strings (1944); 3 string quartets; short works for cello; piano pieces; arrangements of folksongs; and a handbook on jazz percussion playing, *Schule für Jazz-Schlagzeug* (1929). Seiber's early works are permeated with Hungarian idioms; later he expanded his melodic resources to include oriental modes, and also jazz, treated as folk music; eventually adopted the 12-tone method, with individual extensions; applied this method in his cantata *Ulysses,* after James Joyce (London, May 27, 1949). —Cf. H. Keller, *Mátyás Seiber,* in the 'Mus. Times' (Nov., 1955).

Seidel (zī'-del), **Friedrich Ludwig,** German organist and composer; b. Treuenbrietzen, July 14, 1765; d. Charlottenburg, May 8, 1831. He studied with Benda in Berlin; served as organist of the Marienkirche; was music director of the royal orch. (1808) and court Kapellmeister (1822). —Works: the operas *Der Dorfbarbier* (1817) and *Lila* (1818); incidental music to dramas; an oratorio, *Die Unsterblichkeit* (1797); Masses, motets, songs, piano music.

Seidel, Johann Julius, German organist; b. Breslau, July 14, 1810; d. there, Feb. 13, 1856. He was organist at St. Christopher's Church; published *Die Orgel und ihr Bau* (Breslau, 1843; 4th ed. by B. Kothe, 1885; reprinted with an appendix by H. Schmidt, 1907; in English, London, 1852).

Seidel, Toscha, violinist; b. Odessa, Nov. 4, 1899. He began to play the violin as a small child; took lessons from Max Fiedelmann in Odessa; subsequently became a pupil of Leopold Auer at the Cons. of St. Petersburg (graduated in 1912). He gave a concert in Oslo, Norway, Sept. 1, 1915; then went to America; début in N. Y. (April 14, 1918); since then he has made many tours in Europe and the U. S.; also played in Australia. He became an American citizen and made his home in Los Angeles.

Seidl (zīdl), **Anton,** noted conductor; b. Budapest, May 7, 1850; d. New York, March 28, 1898. He studied at the Leipzig Cons. (1870-72); then was engaged by Hans Richter as chorusmaster at the Vienna Opera. Richter recommended him to Wagner to assist in preparing the score and parts of the *Ring* trilogy for the Bayreuth Festival; Seidl worked in Bayreuth until 1879, when he was engaged by the impresario Angelo Neumann for a great tour of Wagner operas, continuing until 1883, the year of Wagner's death. From 1883 to 1885 Seidl conducted the Bremen Opera; in Bremen he met and married the soprano Auguste Krauss. In 1885 he was engaged by Walter Damrosch to conduct the German operas at the Metropolitan Opera House. Seidl made his American début with *Lohengrin* (Nov. 23, 1885), and he conducted the American premières of *Die Meistersinger* (Jan. 4, 1886), *Tristan und Isolde* (Dec. 1, 1886), *Siegfried* (Nov. 9, 1887), *Die Götterdämmerung* (Jan. 25, 1888), and *Das Rheingold* (Jan. 4, 1889). During the week of March 4-11, 1889, he conducted the entire *Ring des Nibelungen.* In 1891 he was engaged as permanent conductor of the N. Y. Philharmonic Society, and led it until his sudden death (of ptomaine poisoning). Seidl's seasons with the N. Y. Philharmonic were the most brilliant before the advent of Mahler. He was an excellent technician of the baton, and established a standard of perfection rare in American orchestras of that time; he introduced many new works by German composers; presented the world première of Dvořák's symphony *From the New World* (1893), conducting from manuscript in the presence of the composer. —Cf. H. E. Krehbiel, *Anton Seidl* (N. Y., 1898); H. T. Finck, ed., *Anton Seidl. A Memorial by His Friends* (N. Y., 1899).

Seidl, Arthur, German writer on music; b. Munich, June 8, 1863; d. Dessau, April 11, 1928. He studied with Spitta and Bellermann; *Dr. phil.,* Leipzig, 1887 (dissertation, *Vom Musikalisch-Erhabenen. Prolegomena zur Ästhetik der Tonkunst;* 1887; 2nd ed., 1907). From 1890 to 1893 he was in Weimar; from 1893 to 1897, in Dresden. In 1899 he went to Munich as critic for the 'Neueste Nachrichten.' From 1903 to his death, was active mostly at Dessau. —Writings: *Zur Geschichte des Erhabenheitsbegriffs seit Kant* (1889); *Hat Richard Wagner eine Schule hinterlassen?* (1892); *Richard Strauss. Eine Charakterstudie* (with W. Klatte; 1896); *Moderner Geist in der deutschen Tonkunst* (1901; 2nd ed., 1913); *Wagneriana* (3 vols., 1901-02); *Moderne Dirigenten* (1902); *Kunst und Kultur* (1902); *Die Hellerauer Schulfeste und die 'Bildungsanstalt Jaques-Dalcroze'* (1912); *Straussiana* (1913); *Ascania. Zehn Jahre in Anhalt* (1913); *Richard Wagners 'Parsifal'* (1914); *Neue Wagneriana* (3 vols., 1914); *Hans Pfitzner* (1921); *Neuzeitliche Tondichter und zeitgenössische Tonkünstler* (2 vols.; Regensburg, 1926). —Cf. L. Frankenstein, *Arthur Seidl* (Regensburg, 1913); B. Schuhmann, ed., *Musik und Kultur. Festschrift zum 50. Geburtstag Arthur Seidls* (1913).

Seifert (zī'-fert), **Uso,** German organist and composer; b. Römhild, Feb. 9, 1852; d. Dresden, June 4, 1912. He studied with Wüllner and Nicodé at the Dresden Cons.; taught there for 25 years, and was later organist of the Reformed Church. He publ. a piano method; numerous piano pieces (*Capriccietto, Valse-Impromptu, Polacca graziosa, Polonaise,* etc.); choruses; organ works (*Präludium und Doppelfuge, Einleitung und Doppelfuge, Zwanzig Orgelvorspiele,* etc.); edited classic instructive works.

Seiffert (zī'-fert), **Max,** eminent German musicologist; b. Beeskow-on-Spree, Feb. 9, 1868; d. Schleswig, April 13, 1948. He entered the Univ. of Berlin in 1886, studying musicology under Ph. Spitta; took the degree of *Dr. phil.* with the dissertation *J. P. Sweelinck und seine direkten deutschen Schüler* (publ. in 'Vierteljahrsschrift für Musikwissenschaft,' 1891). In 1914 he was elected a member of the Berlin Akademie; was editor of 'Sammelbände der Internationalen Musik-Gesellschaft' (1904-14) and of 'Archiv für Musikwissenschaft' (from 1918); publ. *Geschichte der Klaviermusik* (Berlin, 1899-1901; nominally the 3rd ed. of Weitzmann's history, but actually a new and valuable book); *Die Musik Hamburgs im Zeitalter Bachs* (1920); etc. For 'Denkmäler deutscher Tonkunst' he edited Scheidt's *Tablatura nova* (vol. I), selected works of Fr. Tunder (vol. III), selected works of M. Weckmann and Ch. Bernhardt (vol. VI), cantatas etc. by Buxtehude (vol. XIV), the collected works of F. W. Zachow (vols. XXI and XXII); J. G. Walther's organ works (vols. XXVI and XXVII), etc.; for 'Denkmäler der Tonkunst in Bayern,' selected clavier works of Joh. and W. H. Pachelbel (vol. II, 1), organ works of Joh. and W. H. Pachelbel (vol. IV, 1), *Nürnberger Meister* (vol. VI, 1), selected works of Leopold Mozart (vol. IX, 2), etc.; for 'Denkmäler der Tonkunst in Österreich,' Joh. Pachelbel's

94 fugues (for organ) on the Magnificat (vol. 17; with H. Botstiber); for the publications of the 'Vereeniging voor Nederlandsche Muziekgeschiedenis,' Sweelinck's complete works (12 vols.), A. van Noordt's *Tabulatuurboek* (vol. XIX), C. Boskoop's *Psalmen Davids* (vol. XXII), etc.; and a collection of old music under the title *Organum* (from 1924). He also edited many works by Bach and Handel for modern performance. —A 'Festschrift' for him was publ. for his 70th birthday (1938), and another for his 80th birthday (1948).

Seifriz (zī'-frits), **Max,** German violinist and composer; b. Rottweil, Württemberg, Oct. 9, 1827; d. Stuttgart, Dec. 20, 1885. He was court Kapellmeister to Prince Hohenzollern at Löwenberg (1854-69); from 1871, music director at Stuttgart. —Works: incidental music to *Die Jungfrau von Orleans;* cantata, *Ariadne auf Naxos;* a symphony; a concert overture; choruses for male and mixed voices; wrote, with E. Singer, a *Grosse theoretisch-praktische Violinschule* (2 vols., 1884-97).

Seiss (zīss), **Isidor (Wilhelm),** German composer and teacher; b. Dresden, Dec. 23, 1840; d. Cologne, Sept. 25, 1905. He was a pupil of Fr. Wieck and J. Otto; from 1870, piano teacher at Cologne Cons.; conducted the concerts of the 'Musikalische Gesellschaft' there (until 1900). He composed studies in bravura for piano and other pieces; edited classical works (Beethoven, Weber); made transcriptions.

Seitz (zīts), **Robert,** German music publisher and piano manufacturer; b. Leipzig, April 8, 1837; d. there, Sept. 26, 1889. He was a music publisher from 1866 till 1878; then, selling out, he established a piano factory, which failed in 1884, when his interesting paper, 'Das musikalische Centralblatt,' ceased to appear.

Seixas (say'-shas), **(José Antonio) Carlos de,** Portuguese musician; b. Coimbra, June 11, 1704; d. Lisbon, Aug. 25, 1742. He studied with his father, a church organist, and from the age of 16, filled positions as organist in Lisbon. He also gave harpsichord lessons there; wrote a number of sonatas, fugues, and dances for the harpsichord, as well as overtures and choral works. He knew Domenico Scarlatti personally, but was not overly influenced by the Italian manner of keyboard composition. —Cf. S. Kastner, *Carlos de Seixas* (Coimbra, 1947).

Séjan (sā-zhahn), **Nicolas,** French composer and organist; b. Paris, March 19, 1745; d. there, March 16, 1819. He was a pupil of Forqueray; organist of St.-André-des-Arts in 1760, of Notre Dame in 1772, of St.-Sulpice in 1783; in 1789, of the royal chapel, and teacher at the 'École royale de chant.' He lost his posts in the Revolution, but in 1807 became organist at the Invalides, and in 1814 (after the restoration of the monarchy) of the royal chapel. He publ. 6 violin sonatas, piano sonatas, 3 piano trios, and music for piano and for organ. —Cf. C. Bouvet, *Nicolas Séjan et G.-F. Couperin, organistes de l'Opéra,* in 'Musique et Théâtre' (1926).

Sekles (zeh'-kles), **Bernhard,** German conductor, composer, and teacher; b. Frankfurt, June 20, 1872; d. there, Dec. 15, 1934. He studied with Iwan Knorr and others at the Hoch Cons., where he became prof. of theory in 1896; from 1924 till 1933 he was director of the Cons. He wrote 2 operas, *Scheherazade* (Mannheim, Nov. 2, 1917) and *Die zehn Küsse* (Frankfurt, 1926); the ballets *Der Zwerg und die Infantin,* after Oscar Wilde (Frankfurt, 1913) and *Die Hochzeit des Faun* (Wiesbaden, 1921); a symph. poem, *Aus den Gärten der Semiramis; Serenade* for 11 solo instruments; *Kleine Suite* for orch.; *Passacaglia und Fuge* for string quartet; trio for clarinet, cello, and piano; a violin sonata; several albums of piano music.

Selby, Bertram Luard, English organist, composer, and teacher; b. Ightham, Kent, Feb. 12, 1853; d. Winterton, Dec. 26, 1918. He studied with Reinecke and Jadassohn at the Leipzig Cons.; filled various organ positions in London (until 1900); was organist at the Rochester Cathedral. —Works: 2 operas: *The Ring* (1886) and *Adela* (1888); an operetta ('duologue') *Weather or no* (London, Aug. 10, 1896; very successful; also produced in Germany as *Das Wetterhäuschen);* 2 piano quintets; a violin sonata; piano pieces; organ works.

Selby, William, organist and composer; b. England, 1738; d. Boston, Dec., 1798. He settled in the U. S. about 1771, and in 1774 was organist at Trinity Church in Newport, R. I.; from 1777, organist at King's Chapel, Boston. He kept a grocery store and was also active as teacher and concert manager. He composed songs, anthems, and some instrumental pieces. —Cf. O. G. Sonneck, *Bibliography of Early Secular American Music* (1905; 2nd ed., revised by W. T. Upton, 1945).

Seligmann, Hippolyte-Prosper, French cellist; b. Paris, July 28, 1817; d. Monte Carlo, Feb. 5, 1882. He studied at the Paris Cons., taking 1st prize in 1836; made extensive tours. He publ. *6 Études caractéristiques,* fantaisies, caprices, etc., for cello with piano; and 2 albums of songs.

Selle (zel'-leh), **Thomas,** German composer; b. Zörbig, March 23, 1599; d. Hamburg, July 2, 1663. He was rector in Wesselburen (1625); cantor in Itzehoe (1634); cantor at the Johanneum and music director of the 5 principal churches in Hamburg (from 1641). He publ. sacred and secular songs (including settings of poems by Rist), and left in MS numerous madrigals, motets, and Passions. He was an early member of the Hamburg school of German song writing. His collections include: *Concertatio Castalidum* (1624); *Deliciae pastorum Arcadiae* (1624); *Hagiodecamelhydrion* (1627-31); *Deliciorum juvenilium decas* (1634); *Monophonetica* (1636). His *Johannes-Passion* of 1642 was brought out in a modern ed. by R. Gerber (1934); reprints of separate songs publ. by H. J. Moser. —Cf. A. Arnheim, *Thomas Selle als Schulkantor in Itzehoe und Hamburg,* in the 'Liliencron—Festschrift' (1910); H. J. Moser, *Aus der Frühgeschichte der deutschen Generalbasspassion,* in the 'Jahrbuch Peters' (1920); L. Krüger, *Die Hamburgische Musikorganisation im 17. Jahrhundert* (1933; p. 64 ff.); S. Günther, *Die geistliche Konzertmusik von Thomas Selle nebst einer Biographie* (Giessen, 1935).

Sellner (zehl'-ner), **Joseph,** oboe player and teacher; b. Landau, Bavaria, March 13, 1787; d. Vienna, May 17, 1843. He played the oboe in an Austrian army regiment; then at Prague in Weber's orch. (from 1811); from 1817 at the Court Opera in Vienna. He taught at the Vienna Cons. from 1821, and conducted the student concerts there until 1838. His *Theoretisch-praktische Oboen-Schule* is a fine method for oboe; he also publ. a concerto and 3 concertinos for oboe with orch.; a concerto for 2 oboes; etc.

Selmer, Johan Peter, Norwegian composer; b. Oslo, Jan. 20, 1844; d. Venice, July 22, 1910. After studying law in Norway he went to Paris, where he took a course under Ambroise Thomas at the Paris Cons. (1868-70) and later at the Leipzig Cons. with Richter (1871-74). From 1883 till 1886 he conducted the Oslo Philharmonic. He was greatly influenced by Berlioz and Wagner; his symph. pieces bear the imprint of late Romanticism; like Grieg, he made use of Norwegian folk material. —Works: for orch. (all performed in Oslo): *Scène funèbre* (Sept. 30, 1871), *Alastor,* after Shelley (Oct. 24, 1874), *Karneval in Flandern* (Nov. 8, 1890), *In den Bergen,* suite (1892), *Prometheus,* symph. poem (his most important work; Oct. 29, 1898); choral works with orch.: *Nordens Aand (The Spirit of the North); Hilsen til Nidaros,* cantata; *Nogle politiske Sange og andre Viser (Some Political Songs and Other Airs)* for chorus in unison, and orch.; numerous male choruses a cappella; arrangements of folk melodies; songs for solo voice with piano. —Cf. P. Merkel, *Der norwegische Komponist Johan Selmer. Ein Lebensbild* (Leipzig, 1904).

Selva, Blanche, French pianist and teacher; b. Brive, Jan. 29, 1884; d. St. Amand, Tallende, Puy-de-Dome, Dec. 3, 1942. She studied piano at the Paris Cons. and composition with Vincent d'Indy at the Schola Cantorum; taught piano there from 1901 till 1922; then was on the faculty of the conservatories of Strasbourg, Prague, and Barcelona. She was one of the strongest propagandists of modern music in Paris early in the century, and her concerts attracted the musical élite of Paris; she also excelled in playing Bach. As a writer and teacher, she likewise showed a fine understanding of the problems involved. —Books: *La Sonate* (Paris, 1913); *Quelques mots sur la sonate* (Paris, 1914); *L'Enseignement musical de la technique du piano* (3 vols.; Paris, 1922); *Les Sonates de Beethoven* (Barcelona, 1927); a monograph on Déodat de Séverac (Paris, 1930); etc.

Selvaggi, Rito, Italian composer; b. Noicattaro di Bari, May 22, 1898. He studied at the Liceo Musicale in Pesaro and later with Busoni; taught at the Cons. of Parma (1934-38); then became director of the Palermo Cons. (1938-43). Among his works are the operas *Maggiolata veneziana* (Naples, 1929) and *Santa Caterina da Siena* (1947); the oratorio *Estasi francescana* (1926); *Stabat Mater* (1941); several suites in the old Italian style for orchestra.

Sembrich (zĕhm'-brih), **Marcella** (real name Praxede Marcelline Kochanska; Sembrich was her mother's maiden-name), famous coloratura soprano; b. Wisniewczyk, Galicia, Feb. 15, 1858; d. New York, Jan. 11, 1935. From the age of 4 her father, Kasimir Kochanski, gave her piano lessons; violin lessons were soon added. At 10 she appeared in public as a performer on both instruments. In 1869 her father sent her to the Lwow Cons., where she studied piano with Wilhelm Stengel. In 1874 she played and sang for Liszt, who urged her to train her voice. She then studied singing with Viktor Rokitansky in Vienna, and with G. B. Lamperti, Jr., in Milan. On May 5, 1877, she married her former teacher, Stengel (b. Lemberg, Aug. 7, 1846; d. New York, May 15, 1917), and with him went to Athens, where she made her operatic début on June 3, 1877, as Elvira in Bellini's *Puritani;* returning to Vienna, she studied the German repertory with Richard Lewy. From 1878 to 1880 she sang at Dresden. On June 12, 1880, she made her London début as Lucia; American début, at the Metropolitan Opera House, on Oct. 24, 1883. Thereafter she sang at the principal opera houses of Germany, Austria, France, Spain, Scandinavia, and Russia until 1898, then becoming a regular member of the Metropolitan Opera Company. Her farewell appearance in opera was at the Metropolitan, Feb. 6, 1909. Her repertory included 40 operatic parts, of which Violetta was the favorite. Of Wagnerian roles, she sang only Eva in *Die Meistersinger.* In 1924 she joined the faculty of the newly-founded Curtis Institute, Philadelphia; also taught at the Juilliard School, N. Y. —Cf. G. Armin, *Marcella Sembrich und Herr Prof. Julius Hey* (Leipzig, 1898); H. G. Owen, *A Recollection of Marcella Sembrich* (N. Y., 1950).

Semet (sŭ-mā'), **Théophile (-Aimé-Émile),** French composer; b. Lille, Sept. 6, 1824; d. Corbeil, near Paris, April 15, 1888. He studied with Halévy; was a drummer at the Opéra; wrote popular songs before attempting operatic composition. The following operas by Semet were produced in Paris: *Nuits d'Espagne* (Dec. 30, 1857); *Gil Blas* (March 23, 1860); *Ondine* (Jan. 7, 1863); and *La petite Fadette* (Sept. 11, 1869).

Senaillé (seh-nah-yā'), **Jean Baptiste,** French violinist and composer; b. Paris, Nov. 23, 1687; d. there, Oct. 8, 1730. He studied first with his father, a member of the '24 violons du roi'; later was a pupil of Jean Baptiste Anet; then went to Italy, where he studied with Vitali. He returned to Paris in 1720; gave many performances at the Concert Spirituel. His playing was in the Italian tradition; in his music, he was also influenced by the Italan school of Corelli and Vitali. He publ. 50 violin sonatas (with continuo) in 5 books (1710-27); modern reprints by Moffat, Jensen, Alard, etc. —Cf. L. de la Laurencie, *L'École française de violon* (Paris, 1922; vol. 1, pp. 165-79); A. Moser, *Geschichte des Violinspiels* (1923; p. 179).

Senart (seh-nahr'), **Maurice,** French music publisher; b. Paris, Jan. 29, 1878. In 1908 he founded a music publishing enterprise in partnership with Roudanez; in 1912, became sole head of the firm, which bears his name. Among his early publications was the important collection edited by Henry Expert, 'Maîtres musiciens de la Renaissance française'; there followed several other collections; many editions of classical music; collected works of Chopin, edited by Alfred Cortot. Senart was also a decided supporter of modern French music; publ. many works by Honegger and Milhaud, and works by composers of other nationalities resident in Paris (Tansman, Harsanyi, etc.). His publishing firm was acquired by Salabert in 1941.

Sendrey, Albert Richard, composer, son of Aladár Szendrei; b. Chicago, Dec. 26, 1911; studied in Leipzig, Paris, and London; was arranger for film companies in Paris (1935-37) and London (1937-44) before settling in Hollywood in 1944. Among his original works are: *Oriental Suite* for orch. (1935); 3 symphonies; piano pieces; cello pieces.

Sendrey, Alfred. See **Szendrei, Aladár.**

Senesino, Francesco (real name Bernardi; called Senesino after his birthplace), Italian male soprano; b. Siena, c. 1680; d. c. 1750. He studied in Bologna with Bernacchi; in 1719 was engaged to sing at the court theater in Dresden; Handel heard him there, and engaged him for his Italian opera company in London. He began his London appearances in Bononcini's opera *Astarto* (Nov. 30, 1720), and his success was enormous from the start. For 15 consecutive seasons he enjoyed the favor of the London public; was associated with Handel's company until 1733, when a rival organization, the 'Opera of the Nobility,' engaged him and several other celebrated Italian singers, to sing under the direction of Porpora. In 1735 he returned to Siena; in 1739, he was in Florence. It is not known where and exactly when he died. —Cf. F. Haböck, *Die Kastraten und ihre Gesangskunst* (Stuttgart, 1927); A. Heriot, *The Castrati in Opera* (London, 1956, p. 91 ff.).

Senff, Bartholf (Wilhelm), German music publisher and editor; b. Friedrichshall, near Coburg, Sept. 2, 1815; d. Badenweiler, June

25, 1900. As a young man he entered Kistner's music publishing house in Leipzig, advancing to the position of managing clerk; here he already began publishing the 'Signale für die musikalische Welt,' a trial number appearing in Dec., 1842; 1st regular number was issued on Jan. 1, 1843. This was one of the most important German music periodicals of the 19th century; it included reports of musical events, special articles, and correspondence from the music centers of the world; many celebrated musicians contributed to it, among them Hans von Bülow. Senff remained editor of the 'Signale' until his death, and publication continued (with a brief interruption in 1917-18) until 1941 (after 1907 by Simrock). Senff founded his own publishing business in 1847; his catalogue included original publications of works by Schumann, Liszt, Anton Rubinstein, Raff, Franz, etc. His niece, Marie Senff, managed the firm until 1907, when she sold it and the 'Signale' to Simrock of Berlin.

Senfl (zehn-fl), **Ludwig,** important church composer of the Renaissance; b. Zürich, c. 1490; d. Munich, early in 1543. His father was a singer from Freiburg-im-Breisgau; the family name may have been Senffl, Sänftli, Sänfly, Senfel, etc., and the ultimate origin undoubtedly German, although Ludwig Senfl was known under the appellation Schweizer (the Swiss). As a small child, from 1495, he sang in the imperial court chapel; from 1504 he was in Zürich, and shortly afterwards went to Constance, where he was a pupil of Isaac; he was Isaac's assistant at St. Ann's Church, Augsburg, and also sang in the court chapel of Maximilian I; after Isaac's death (1517), Senfl completed his teacher's *Choralis Constantinus* and became his successor as chamber composer; remained in Augsburg for some time after Maximilian's death (1519), and received a stipend from Charles V; edited the historically important *Liber selectarum cantionum* (1520), which was one of the earliest books with musical notation publ. in Germany. In 1523 he settled in Munich as 'intonator' at the Bavarian court chapel; his fame grew; he was referred to by an early contemporary as 'prince of all German music.' There is extant a letter written to Senfl by Martin Luther, dated Oct. 4, 1530, containing high praise of the composer (reprinted in F. A. Beck's *Dr. M. Luthers Gedanken über die Musik,* Berlin, 1828). —Publ. works: *5 Salutationes Domini nostri Hiesu Christi* (motets in 4 voices, Nuremberg, 1526); *Varia carminum genera, quibus tum Horatius tum alii egregii poetae . . . harmoniis composita,* for 4 voices (Nuremberg, 1534; 9 Odes are in P. Hofhaimer's *Harmonie poeticae,* 1539); *Magnificat octo tonorum,* for 4-5 voices (Nuremberg, 1537); 81 numbers by Senfl are in the collection *121 newe Lieder* (Nuremberg, 1534), and 64 numbers in *115 guter newer Liedlein* (Nuremberg, 1544); single compositions in various collections of the period (for a list, see Eitner's *Bibliographie,* Berlin, 1877, and vol. IV of the 'Publikationen älterer . . . Musikwerke'). Magnificats and a selection of 12 motets were publ. by Th. Kroyer in vol. III, 2 of 'Denkmäler der Tonkunst in Bayern.' Many MSS (sacred and secular vocal works) are in the Munich Library. Some songs have been publ. in Jöde's *Chorbuch,* and in 'Denkmäler deutscher Tonkunst' (vol. 34, ed. by J. Wolf); *Weltliche Lieder* for 4-part mixed chorus were publ. by Willi Schuh (Zürich, 1929); motets are in Schering's *Geschichte der Musik in Beispielen* (Nos. 74, 84-86); etc. 7 Masses were edited by E. Löhrer and O. Ursprung for the 'Reichsdenkmale deutscher Musik' (Leipzig, 1936), and this was taken over the following year by the 'Schweizerische Musikforschende Gesellschaft' as vol. I of the collected works of Senfl (Basel, 1937-40; vol. II, *Deutsche Lieder a* 4-6; vol. III, motets; vol. IV, *Deutsche Lieder a* 4-7; vol. V, *Deutsche Lieder a* 4-6, publ. in 1949).—Cf. Th. Kroyer, *Ludwig Senfl und sein Motettenstil* (Munich, 1902); H. J. Moser, *Instrumentalismen bei Ludwig Senfl, in* 'J. Wolf-Festschrift' (1929); H. J. Moser, *Der Altmünchner Tonmeister Ludwig Senfl,* in 'Süddeutsche Monatshefte' (1930; p. 531); E. Löhrer, *Die Messen von Ludwig Senfl* (Lichtensteig, 1938); H. Birtner, *Sieben Messen von Ludwig Senfl,* in 'Archiv für Musikforschung' (1942); see also G. Reese, *Music in the Renaissance* (N .Y., 1954; pp. 689-90).

Senilov (seh-nē'-lov), **Vladimir Alexeyevitch,** Russian composer; b. Viatka, Aug. 8, 1875; d. Petrograd, Sept. 18, 1918. He was a student of jurisprudence at the Univ. of St. Petersburg; was encouraged by Rimsky-Korsakov to cultivate his natural talent for musical composition, and went to Leipzig, where he studied with Hugo Riemann (1895-1901); continued his studies with Rimsky-Korsakov and Glazunov at the St. Petersburg Cons., graduating in 1906. His works include a lyric drama, *Vassily Buslayev;* 1-act opera *Hippolytus,* after Euripides; *In Autumn,* symph. poem; *Mtziri,* symph. poem after Lermontov; *Pan,* symph. poem; *The Scythians,* symph. poem; 3 string quartets; choral pieces; songs. His MSS are preserved in the Leningrad Public Library.

Serafin, Tullio, Italian conductor; b. Rottanova di Cavarzere, Venice, Dec. 8, 1878. He studied at the Milan Cons.; made his début as conductor in Ferrara (1900); then conducted in the major cities of Italy and in Buenos Aires. In 1924 he became one of the chief conductors at the Metropolitan Opera House; in 1935 returned to Italy, conducting principally in Rome and Milan (La Scala); also conducted opera in London and Paris; in 1952 was a guest conductor for the New York City Opera Company.

Serafino, Santo, celebrated Italian violin maker; b. Udine, c. 1650; d. Venice, c. 1740. He was a pupil of Nicolo Amati, and probably worked in Cremona; signed his name on the labels as 'Sanctus Seraphinus Nicolai Amati Cremonensis Alumnus.' His instruments contained elements characteristic of Stainer and of Nicolo Amati. His nephew Giorgio Serafino worked in Venice in the 1st half of the 18th century.

Serassi, Giuseppe ('il vecchio'), the founder of a celebrated house of Italian organ builders; b. Gordano, 1694; d. Crema, 1760. His son **Andrea Luigi** (1725-1799) carried on the business; built the cathedral organs of Crema, Parma, and Fossano. A younger member of the family, **Giuseppe** ('il giovane'; b. Bergamo, Nov. 16, 1750; d. there, May 13, 1817) upheld the reputation of the firm, and built many organs in Lombardy. His catalogue of 1815 lists 345 instruments. He publ. a description of the new organ at Como (1808), with a short history of the organ, and good rules for registration; also brought out a pamphlet, *Sugli organi* (1816). The catalogue publ. in 1852 by his sons, Carlo and Giuseppe Serassi, shows a total of 654 organs constructed.

Serato, Arrigo, Italian violinist; b. Bologna, Feb. 7, 1877; d. Rome, Dec. 27, 1948. He received his musical training from his father, a cellist; studied at the Bologna Cons. and with Joachim in Germany; from 1914 till 1921 taught at the Santa Cecilia Academy in Rome. He had a very high reputation in Italy as a teacher. —Cf. A. Della Corte, *Arrigo Serato violinista* (Siena, 1950).

Serauky, Walter, eminent German musicologist; b. Halle, April 20, 1903. He studied at Leipzig Univ. with Schering, H. J. Moser, and Prüfer; *Dr. phil.* at the Univ. of Halle, 1928, with the dissertation *Die musikalische Nachahmungsästhetik im Zeitraum von 1700 bis 1850* (publ. Münster, 1929); joined the faculty of the Univ. of Halle; 1940, prof. there; in 1949, appointed prof. at the Leipzig Univ. He contributed valuable essays to various German publications; brought out a music history of the city of Halle (5 vols.; 1935-43). In 1956, he began publication of an extensive study of Handel, *G. F. Händel; sein Leben, sein Werk;* also edited works by Handel, Türk, and Reichardt.

Séré, Octave. See **Poueigh.**

Sérieyx (sā-rē-ěks'), **Auguste,** French composer and writer on music; b. Amiens, June 14, 1865; d. Montreux, Switzerland, Feb. 19, 1949. He studied at the Schola Cantorum with Gedalge and Vincent d'Indy; taught composition there (1900-14), and collaborated with Vincent d'Indy in his monumental *Cours de Composition* (3 vols., Paris, 1897-1933); publ. a biography of d'Indy (Paris, 1913) and a short treatise, *Les trois états de la tonalité* (Paris, 1910). His compositions include *La Voie lactée,* for solo voice and orch.; the cantata *Salvete cedri libani;* violin sonata; piano pieces; songs.

Sering (zä'-ring), **Friedrich Wilhelm,** German teacher and composer; b. Fürstenwalde, near Frankfurt-on-the-Oder, Nov. 26, 1822; d. Hanover, Nov. 5, 1901. From 1871 he was head teacher in the Seminary at Strasbourg, where he organized a 'Gesangverein.' —Works: oratorio, *Christi Einzug in Jerusalem;* Psalm 72, for mixed chorus with piano; the manuals, *Gesanglehre für Volksschulen* and *Die Choralfiguration, theoretisch-praktisch;* and an elementary violin method.

Serkin, Rudolf, eminent pianist; b. Eger, Bohemia, March 28, 1903 (of Russian parentage). He studied in Vienna with Richard Robert (piano), Joseph Marx and Arnold Schoenberg (composition). After an early début at the age of 12, he began his serious concert career in 1920; appeared frequently in joint recitals with the violinist Adolf Busch (whose daughter he married); made his American début with Busch at a Coolidge Festival concert in Washington (1933); in 1939 he was appointed to the faculty of the Curtis Institute, Philadelphia. He has appeared with virtually all major orchestras in the U. S. and Europe; has given numerous recitals; taught master classes. His performances of the Viennese classics are unexcelled in authority, faithfulness of treatment, and technical virtuosity.

Serly (shăr'-lē), **Tibor,** composer and conductor; b. Losonc, Hungary, Nov. 25, 1900; taken to America as a child. He studied with his father (a theater conductor in Budapest); from 1922, with Kodály and Bartók (composition) at the Royal Academy of Music, Budapest; violin with Hubay. After graduating, he returned to the U. S.; played viola in the Cincinnati Symph. Orch., the Philadelphia Orch., and the N. B. C. Symph. Orch. In 1937 he settled in N. Y. as a teacher. —Works: viola concerto (1929); symph. no. 1 (Budapest, May 13, 1935, composer conducting); *6 Dance Designs* (Budapest, May 13, 1935); *Colonial Pageant,* symph. suite (1937); *Elegy,* for orch. (1945); *Rhapsody,* for viola and orch. (N. Y., Feb. 27, 1948); trombone concerto (Chautauqua, Aug. 17, 1952); songs; etc. Serly completed and orchestrated Bartók's unfinished viola concerto (1945).

Sermisy (sehr-mē-sē'), **Claude (Claudin) de,** French composer; b. c. 1490; d. Paris, 1562. In 1508 he was appointed 'clerc musicien' of the Sainte-Chapelle at Paris; accompanied Francis I to Italy in 1515; was present at the meeting between Francis and Henry VIII at the Field of the Cloth of Gold (1520). Sermisy composed chansons, motets, and Masses, which were printed in collections of the time and frequently republished after his death, indicating a wide popularity. Attaingnant's '31 chansons' (1529) contains 11 songs by Sermisy, which are reprinted in Expert's 'Les Maîtres musiciens'; other modern reprints include 3 chansons in Eitner's 'Publikationen älterer . . . Musikwerke' (vol. 23; Leipzig, 1899); 3 chansons in Commer's 'Collectio operum musicorum' (vol. 12); 2 chansons in Bordes, 'Chansonnier du XIVe siècle'; 4 chansons in Expert's 'Extraits des maîtres musiciens de la Renaissance.' —Cf. O. Kade, *Die ältere Passionskomposition* (Gütersloh, 1893; deals fully with Sermisy's Passion music); M. Brenet, *Les Musiciens de la Sainte-Chapelle du Palais* (Paris, 1910); G. Reese, *Music in the Renaissance* (N. Y., 1954; pp. 291-95).

Serocki (sĕh-rŏts'-kē), **Kazimierz,** Polish composer and pianist; b. Torun, March 3, 1922. He studied music in Lodz; in 1947 went to Paris, where he took a course in composition with Nadia Boulanger. Among his works are several cantatas, a piano concerto, and a *Symphony of Songs* (Warsaw, June 11, 1954).

Seroff, Victor, writer on music; b. Batum, Caucasus, Oct. 14, 1902; studied law at the Univ. of Tiflis; then piano with Moriz Rosenthal in Vienna and Theodore Szanto in Paris; eventually settled in New York and became an American citizen. —Books: *Dmitri Shostakovitch: The Life and Background of a Soviet Composer* (N. Y., 1943); *The Mighty Five; the Cradle of Russian National Music* (N. Y., 1948); *Rachmaninoff* (N. Y., 1950; French transl., Paris, 1953); *Maurice Ravel* (N. Y., 1953); *Debussy, Musician of France* (N. Y., 1956). —Cf. M. R. Werner, *To Whom It May Concern: The Story of V. I. Seroff* (N. Y., 1931).

Serov (syeh-rŏv'), **Alexander Nikolayevitch,** Russian composer; b. St. Petersburg, Jan. 23, 1820; d. there, Feb. 1, 1871. He was trained in a law school; also took cello lessons with Karl Schuberth; became a functionary in the Ministry of Justice; served in St. Petersburg (1840-45); then in Simferopol, Crimea (1845-48); in 1849 turned definitely to music, and abandoned government employ. He never took lessons in composition, except a correspondence course in counterpoint, but achieved a certain mastery in harmony and orchestration by studying the classics. In 1851 he began writing critical articles on music and soon became an important figure in Russian journalism; in 1856 he became editor of the 'Musical and Theatrical Monitor.' In 1858 he made his first trip abroad, visiting Germany and Bohemia; the following year made another German visit, and also traveled in Austria and Switzerland; during this journey he met Wagner, whose ardent admirer he became and remained to the end of his career; expounded Wagner's ideas in Russian publications and engaged in bitter polemics with those who did not subscribe to his views, including his old frend and schoolmate Vladimir Stasov. He started very late in the field of composition; inspired by the performance of a biblical play, *Judith,* by an Italian troupe at St. Petersburg in 1861, he resolved to write an opera on this subject, essaying an Italian libretto, but later deciding on a Russian text. *Judith* was produced in St. Petersburg on May 28, 1863 with excellent success; but although Serov intended to emulate Wagner in the music, the style of *Judith* was closer to Meyerbeer. Quite different was Serov's 2nd opera, *Rogneda,* written on a Russian subject, in a distinctly national idiom, with plentiful use of Russian folksongs. *Rogneda* was staged in St. Petersburg on Nov. 8, 1865, and won a spectacular success; the Tsar Alexander II attended a subsequent performance and granted Serov an annual stipend of 1000 rubles for it. He then began the composition of another Russian opera, *Vrazhya Sila (Malevolent Power),* but death (of a sudden heart failure) overtook him when the 5th act was still incomplete; the opera was finished by N. T. Solovyev, and produced posthumously in St. Petersburg on May 1, 1871. All 3 operas of Serov retain their popularity in Russia, but are unknown elsewhere. Serov wrote further an Ave Maria for Adelina Patti (1868); a Stabat Mater; incidental music to *Nero; Plyaska Zaporozhtsev (Dance of the Zaporozh Cossacks)* for orch. (1867); an *Ouverture d'une comédie* for piano 4 hands, and a few other small pieces. A selection from his writings was publ. in 4 vols. (St. Petersburg, 1892-95). —In 1863 Serov married a young Conservatory pupil, **Valentina Bergmann** (1846-1927), who was the first Russian woman to compose operas: *Uriel Acosta* (Moscow, 1885) and *Ilya Murometz* (Moscow, March 6, 1899; with Shaliapin in the title role). She helped to edit and publish Serov's posthumous works; wrote essays; published a number of piano pieces and a book of memoirs (St. Petersburg, 1914) under the name Valentina Serova. —Cf. N. Findeisen, *A. N. Serov. His Life and Work* (St. Petersburg, 1900; 2nd ed., 1904); Valentina Serova, *A. N. Serov* (St. Petersburg, 1914); G. Abraham and M. D. Calvocoressi, *Masters of Russian Music* (N. Y., 1936); G. Khubov, *The Life of A. N. Serov* (Moscow, 1950).

Serpette (sehr-peht'), **Gaston,** French composer; b. Nantes, Nov. 4, 1846; d. Paris, Nov. 3, 1904. He studied with Ambroise Thomas at the Paris Cons., taking the 1st Grand Prix de Rome in 1871 with the cantata *Jeanne d'Arc.* From 1874 he produced in Paris a steady progression of light operas of which the following enjoyed a modicum of success: *La Branche cassée* (Jan. 23, 1874); *Le Manoir du pic tordu* (May 28, 1875); *Le Moulin du vert galant* (April 12, 1876); *La petite muette* (Oct. 3, 1877); *Le petit chaperon rouge* (Oct. 10, 1885); *Adam et Eve* (Oct. 6, 1886); *Mademoiselle du téléphone* (May 2, 1891); *Shakespeare* (Nov. 23, 1899).

Serrano, Emilio, Spanish composer of light operas; b. Vitoria, March 13, 1850; d. Madrid, April 9, 1939. He studied at the Madrid Cons., and taught piano and composition there for half a century (1870-1920); also conducted symph. concerts in Madrid. He wrote 5 operas: *Mitridates* (Madrid, 1882), *Doña Juana la Loca* (Madrid, 1890), *Irene de Otranto* (Madrid, Feb. 17, 1891), *Gonzalo de Córdoba* (Madrid, Dec. 6, 1898), and *La Maja de Rumbo* (Buenos Aires, Sept. 24, 1910).

Serrao, Paolo, Italian composer; b. Filadelfia, Catanzaro, 1830; d. Naples, March 17, 1907. He studied with Mercadante at the Cons. of Naples, and taught there from 1863. He brought out his first opera, *Pergolesi,* in 1857, followed by *La Duchessa di Guisa* (1865) and *Il Figliuol prodigo* (1868); also composed an oratorio, *Gli Ortonesi in Scio;* a funeral symph. for Mercadante, *Omaggio a Mercadante;* a cantata with orch. *Le tre ore d'agonia,* and much church music.

Serres (serr), **Louis (Arnal) de,** French composer and teacher; b. Lyons, Nov. 8, 1864; d. Néronde (Loire), Dec. 25, 1942. He studied at the Paris Cons. with Taudou (harmony) and César Franck (organ); joined the faculty of the Schola Cantorum; taught there from 1900; when the institution was reorganized in 1935 as the École César Franck, he became its director. His compositions include *Les Heures claires* for voice and orch.; *Les Caresses* for orch.; choruses, motets, and songs.

Servais (sehr-vā'), **(Adrien-) François,** famous Belgian cellist; b. Hal, near Brussels, June 6, 1807; d. there, Nov. 26, 1866. He studied at the Brussels Cons.; played in a theater orch. there; then went to Paris, where he gave a concert in 1834, with brilliant success; on May 25, 1835, he played his own cello concerto with the London Philharmonic; subsequently made a grand tour of Europe; spent several years in Russia as a concert player, even reaching Siberia. He was appointed prof. at the Brussels Cons. in 1848, and taught many pupils who became distinguished artists. He wrote 3 concertos and 16 fantasias for cello with orch.; 6 études and 14 duos for cello with piano (with Gregoir); 3 duos for violin and cello (with Léonard).

Servais, François (Franz), composer and conductor; b. St. Petersburg, 1846; d. Asnières, near Paris, Jan. 14, 1901. He was an illegitimate son of Liszt and Princess Carolyne Sayn-Wittgenstein, and was adopted by Adrien-François Servais, assuming his name. He studied at the Brussels Cons. with Kufferath; won the Belgian Prix de Rome in 1873 with the cantata *Le Tasse.* As a conductor he vigorously promoted the cause of Wagner's music, and performed several of Wagner's operas in Brussels for the first time. His own opera *Iôn* (originally *L'Apollonide)* was produced at Karlsruhe in 1899. —Cf. E. Michotte, *Au souvenir de François Servais* (Paris, 1907).

Servais, Joseph, Belgian cellist; son of Adrien-François Servais; b. Hal, near Brussels, Nov. 23, 1850; d. there, Aug. 29, 1885. He was a pupil of his father; made his début in a joint recital with him in Warsaw (1867); then went to Weimar, where he played in the orch. (1868-70); in 1872, returned to Belgium, where he was prof. at the Brussels Cons. until his early death.

Servières (sehr-vyär'), **Georges,** French writer on music; b. Fréjus, Oct. 13, 1858; d. Paris, July 25, 1937. He publ. a number of informative books: *Richard Wagner jugé en France* (1887); *Le 'Tannhäuser' à l'Opéra 1861* (1895); *La Musique française moderne* (1897); *Weber* (1906); *Emmanuel Chabrier* (1912); *Épisodes d'histoire musicale* (1914); *Saint-Saëns* (1923); *Documents inédits sur les organistes français des XVII*[e] *et XVIII*[e] *siècles* (1923); *Édouard Lalo* (1925); *La Décoration artistique des buffets d'orgues* (1928); *Gabriel Fauré* (1930).

Sessions, Roger, eminent American composer; b. Brooklyn, Dec. 28, 1896. He studied music at Harvard Univ. (B. A., 1915), and at the Yale School of Music with Horatio Parker (B. M., 1917); then with Ernest Bloch in Cleveland and N. Y.; this association was a decisive one for Sessions; his early works were strongly influenced by Bloch's rhapsodic style and intense harmonic idiom. From 1917 to 1921 Sessions taught music theory at Smith College; in 1921 was appointed teacher of theory at the Cleveland Institute of Music, first as assistant to Ernest Bloch, then as its head. He held two Guggenheim Fellowships (1926, 1927), a Fellowship of the American Academy in Rome (1928-31), and the Carnegie Fellowship (1931-32). He lived mostly in Europe from 1926 to 1933 (Florence, Rome, Berlin); between 1928 and 1931 presented in N. Y. a series of concerts of modern music, in association with Aaron Copland, (Copland-Sessions Concerts), which attracted considerable attention; was also active in various international music organizations. After returning to the U. S., he taught in N. Y. and at Princeton Univ.; from 1944 till 1952 was prof. of music at the Univ. of California, Berkeley; 1952, appointed prof. at Princeton Univ.; also lectured widely in the U. S. and in Europe. While his early works reflect Romantic ideas, he soon adopted an austere style of composition, akin to that of Stravinsky's later works; developed a remarkably complex and yet compact contrapuntal idiom, presenting considerable difficulties to performers, and not easily assimilated by the public; however, with the general advance of modern music, his highly individual works commanded great respect; his name soon became known as that of a major American composer, despite the scarcity of performances. —Works: for the stage: *The Black Maskers,* incidental music to Leonid Andreyev's play (Smith College, Northampton, June, 1923); *The Trial of Lucullus,* 1-act opera (Berkeley, Calif., April 18, 1947); *Montezuma,* 4-act opera (1947); for orch.: symph. No. 1 (Boston, April 22, 1927); symph. No. 2 (San Francisco, Jan. 9, 1947); symph. No. 3 (Boston, Dec. 6, 1957); symph. No. 4 (1958); suite from *The Black Maskers* (Cincinnati, Dec. 5, 1930); violin concerto (1935; Chicago, Jan. 8, 1940); *Idyll of Theocritus* (Louisville, Jan. 14, 1956); piano concerto (N. Y., Feb. 10, 1956); string quintet (1957); 2 string quartets (1936; 1950); duo for violin and piano (1942); sonata for violin solo (1953); 2 piano sonatas (1930; 1946); *From My Diary,* a suite of 4 pieces for piano; 3 Chorale Preludes for organ (1925); *Turn O Libertad,* for chorus and piano 4-hands, after Walt Whitman (1943); Mass for unison chorus and organ (1956). He publ. the books, *The Musical Experience of Composer, Performer, Listener* (Princeton, 1950), *Harmonic Practice* (N. Y., 1951), *Reflections on the Music Life in the United States* (N. Y., 1956). —Cf. M. Brunswick, *Roger Sessions,* in 'Modern Music' (vol. 10, 1933); A. Copland, *Our New Music* (N. Y., 1941, p. 176 ff.); M. A. Schubart, *Roger Sessions,* in the 'Mus. Quarterly' (April, 1946).

Setaccioli (seh-tah-choh'-le), **Giacomo,** Italian composer and teacher; b. Corneto Tarquinia, Dec. 8, 1868; d. Siena, Dec. 5, 1925. He studied at the Liceo Santa Cecilia, Rome, and was prof. there (1922-25); in 1925 appointed director of the Cons. Cherubini in Florence. He wrote 2 operas, *La Sorella di Mark* (Rome, May 7, 1896) and *Adrienne Lecouvreur* (1907); a symphony; 2 symph. poems; *Cantica* for soli, chorus, and orch.; a Requiem; chamber music; songs; piano pieces, etc.; publ. *Debussy è un innovatore?* (1910); *Note ed appunti al Trattato d'armonia di C. de Sanctis* (1923); *Studi e conferenze di critica musicale* (1923).

Ševčik (shĕf'-chik), **Otakar,** noted Czech violinist and pedagogue; b. Horaždowitz, March 22, 1852; d. Pisek, Jan. 18, 1934. He studied violin with his father; then at the Prague Cons. with Anton Bennewitz. From 1870 to 1873 he was concertmaster of the Mozarteum in Salzburg; then held a similar post in the Theater an der Wien, Vienna. He then went to Russia, where he became prof. at the Cons. of Kiev (1875); also gave concerts in Russia, achieving great success there. In 1892 he returned to Prague; became head of the violin dept. at the Prague Cons. in 1901; continued to teach until 1906; ill health compelled him to interrupt all activities for 3 years; in 1909 he became head of the master school for violin at the Vienna Academy of Music; from 1919 to 1924 he taught again in Prague; also visited abroad as a teacher in the U. S. (1920; 1924; 1931), London (1932), etc. His method, in contradistinction to the usual diatonic system, is founded on chromatic progressions, especially valuable in securing both accuracy and facility. In various parts of the world he had thousands of pupils, among them Jan Kubelík, Kocian, Marie Hall, Baloković, Erica Morini, and Efrem Zimbalist. He publ. the following pedagogical works (in German, Bohemian, French, and Russian; most of them also printed in English): op. 1, *Schule der Violintechnik* (4 parts); op. 2, *Schule der Bogentechnik* (6 parts); op. 6, *Violinschule für Anfänger* (7 parts); op. 7, *Triller-Vorstudien und Ausbildung des Fingeranschlags* (2 parts); op. 8, *Lagenwechsel-Übungen;* op. 9, *Doppelgriff-Vorstudien;* also *Böhmische Tänze und Weisen,* for violin and piano. —Cf. V. Nopp, *Otakar Ševčik* (Prague, 1948); J. Dostál, ed., *Otakar Ševčik* (collection of essays on him; Prague, 1953). See also Paul Stoeving, *A Key to Ševčik's Works* (London, 1914).

Séverac (sā-vŭ-rahk'), **Déodat de,** French composer; b. Saint-Félix-de-Caraman, Lauraguais, July 20, 1873; d. Céret, March 24, 1921. He received his first lessons on the piano from his father, a painter and ardent lover of music. He studied music at the Cons. of Toulouse; in 1890 entered the Schola Cantorum in Paris, where he remained till 1907, studying with Magnard and Vincent d'Indy. He resided alternately in Paris and his native town. —Works: the operas *Le Cœur du moulin* (Paris, Dec. 8, 1909) and *Les Princesses d'Hokifari* (not produced); incidental music to L. Damard's *Le Mirage* (1905), E. Sicard's *Héliogabale* (1910), M. Navarre's *Muguetto* (1911), E. Verhaeren's *Hélène de Sparte* (Paris, May 5, 1912); the symph. poems *Nymphes au Crépuscule, Tryptique, Les Grenouilles qui demandent un Roi, Nausikaa; Les Muses sylvestres,* suite for double string quintet and piano; *Le Parc aux cerfs,* suite for oboe, string quintet, and piano; *Suite* in E for organ; for piano; *Petite Suite; En Languedoc,* suite; *La Nymphe émue ou le Faune indiscret; En Vacances,* album of little pieces; sonata; several collections of folksongs; solo songs. —Cf. O. Séré, *Musiciens français d'aujourd'hui* (Paris, 1921); L. Moulin, *Déodat de Séverac* (1922); B. Selva, *Déodat de Séverac* (Paris, 1930); A. Cortot, *La Musique française de piano* (vol. 2, Paris, 1932); P. Landormy, *Déodat de Séverac,* in the 'Mus. Quarterly' (April, 1934); G.Soula and I. Girard, *Hommage à Déodat de Séverac* (Toulouse, 1952).

Severn, Edmund, composer and teacher; b. Nottingham, England, Dec. 10, 1862; d. Melrose, Mass., May 14, 1942. In 1866 his father, a violinist, settled in Hartford, Conn.; Severn studied violin with him and with Bernhard Listemann in Boston; composition with Chadwick in Boston and with Ph. Scharwenka in Berlin. He lived in Springfield, Mass., in N. Y., and in Melrose, Mass. His works include 2 symph. poems, *Lancelot and Elaine* (1898) and *Eloise and Abelard* (1915); a suite, *From Old New England* (originally for violin and piano, 1912; orchestrated and conducted by the composer at the Springfield, Mass., Music Festival, May 17, 1919); *Song Celestial,* for orch. (1912); violin concerto (N. Y. Philharmonic, Jan. 7, 1916); choral works; songs.

Sevitzky, Fabien, conductor; b. Vishny Volotchok, Russia, Sept. 29, 1893; nephew of Serge Koussevitzky. He entered the St. Petersburg Cons. on a scholarship as a double-bass student, graduating in 1911 with a gold medal; joined the orch. of the Bolshoy Theater in Moscow, and began a career as concert player on the double-bass, under his original name Koussevitzky; his uncle, who was already a celebrated double-bass player himself, suggested that he adopt a truncated form of the family name, and Sevitzky complied to avoid confusion. He made his appearances as conductor in Russia under the name Sevitzky; lived in Moscow until 1922; spent a year in Poland as double-bass player in the Warsaw Philharmonic; with his wife, a Russian singer, Maria Koussevitzky (who retained her legal name), he went to Mexico in 1923; then joined the Philadelphia Orch., and in 1925 organized the Philadelphia Chamber String Sinfonietta, which he conducted until 1937. From 1934 to 1936 he conducted the People's Symph. in Boston. From 1937 to 1955 he was permanent conductor of the Indianapolis Symph. Orch.; also made guest appearances in Europe and South America. In 1956-57 he conducted in Europe.

Seybold (zī-bohlt), **Artur,** German composer; b. Hamburg, Jan. 6, 1868; d. Weissenfels, near Leipzig, Dec. 15, 1948. He studied at the Hamburg Cons.; traveled as violinist with Laube's orch. in Russia (1888); lived in Hamburg as teacher and conductor of choral societies (from 1890). His numerous compositions for violin and piano and his male choruses won considerable popularity; he also publ. a violin method, *Das neue System,* and instructive pieces.

Seydelmann (zī'-del-man), **Franz,** German composer; b. Dresden, Oct. 8, 1748; d. there, Oct. 23, 1806. He was the son of a player in the court orch., which he joined as a youth; studied in Italy with Josef Schuster (1765-69). In 1772 both he and Schuster were appointed composers of church music to the Elector in Dresden; later both became conductors at the court church, cembalists at the Italian Opera in Dresden, and in 1787, conductors there. Seydelmann wrote 7 Italian operas, and a German opera, *Arsene* (Dresden, March 3, 1779); the piano score of *Arsene* is publ.; also publ. are several numbers from his operas *Il Capriccio corretto* and *La Villanella di Misnia;* 6 piano sonatas for 4 hands; 3 sonatas for piano solo; 3 flute sonatas; 3 violin sonatas. In MS are the other Italian operas, 36 Masses, 40 psalms, 37 offertories, a Requiem, numerous other vocal works, both sacred and secular. —Cf. R. Cahn-Speyer, *Franz Seydelmann als dramatischer Komponist* (Leipzig, 1909).

Seyffardt (zī'-fahrt), **Ernst Hermann,** German choral conductor and composer; b. Krefeld, May 6, 1859; d. Partenkirchen, Dec., 1942. He studied at the Cologne Cons. with F. Hiller and G. Jensen, and at the Berlin Hochschule für Musik with Kiel; conducted the 'Liedertafel' in Freiburg (1887-92); in 1892 was appointed conductor of the 'Neuer Singverein' in Stuttgart; also taught at the Stuttgart Cons.; retired in 1929. —Works: dramatic scene *Thusnelda;* a symphony; a violin sonata; a piano quartet; a string quartet; *Schicksalsgesang* for alto solo, chorus, and orch.; *Zum Gedächtniss,* for baritone solo, male chorus, and orch.; a patriotic cantata, *Aus Deutschlands grosser Zeit;* a song cycle, *Vom Schwarzwald bis zum Rhein;* other vocal works. His operas, *Die Glocken von Plurs,* was produced at Krefeld in 1912.

Seyfried (zī'-frēd), **Ignaz Xaver,** Ritter **von,** Austrian composer; b. Vienna, Aug. 15, 1776; d. there, Aug. 27, 1841. He was a close friend of Mozart, and had some piano lessons from him; studied also with Koželuh and Haydn; afterwards with Albrechtsberger. In 1797 he became conductor at Schikaneder's theater in Vienna; then at the new Theater an der Wien when it opened in 1801, retaining this post until 1827. He was an extremely prolific composer, and some of his 'Singspiele' were very successful; one of them, *Die Ochsenmenuette,* based on Haydn's music (Vienna, Dec. 31, 1823), gave rise to the well-known anecdote about Haydn's composing an *Ox Minuet* for a butcher and receiving an ox as a gift. Seyfried also wrote an opera, *Der Wundermann am Rheinfall* (Vienna, Oct. 26, 1799), which elicited praise from Haydn. He further wrote numerous melodramas, ballets, oratorios, motets, symphonies, quartets, etc. He publ. Beethoven's exercises in thorough-bass, counterpoint, and composition (1832), with some unwarranted additions (see Thayer's *Beethoven,* III, 80); edited a complete ed. of Albrechtsberger's theoretical works; also edited Preindl's *Wiener Tonschule* (1827; 2nd ed., 1832). For a complete list of Seyfried's theatrical works and dates of performances see Anton Bauer, *Opern und Operetten in Wien* (Graz, 1955).

Seymour, John Laurence, American composer; b. Los Angeles, Jan. 18, 1893. He studied with Fannie Charles Dillon; went to Europe in 1927; took lessons with Pizzetti in Italy and with Vincent d'Indy in Paris. Returning to America, he became head of the drama dept. of Sacramento, Cal., Junior College (1926-50); wrote plays. His opera, *In the Pasha's Garden,* was produced at the Metropolitan Opera House, on Jan. 24, 1935. Other operas include *The Devil and Tom Walker* (1926); *The Snake Woman; The Protégé of the Mistress; The Affected Maids* (after Molière's *Les Précieuses ridicules); Ramona;* he also wrote several operettas *(The Bachelor Belles, Hollywood Madness,* etc.); ballets; a piano concerto; sonatas for various instruments with piano.

Sgambati, Giovanni, Italian pianist and composer; b. Rome, May 28, 1841; d. there, Dec. 14, 1914. He studied piano with

Amerigo Barbieri, and appeared in public at the age of 6; sang in church, and conducted instrumental groups. He then became a pupil of Liszt in Rome; subsequently gave orch. concerts, playing German masterpieces; performed Beethoven's *Eroica* in 1866 for the 1st time in Rome. Historically, Sgambati's concerts were important as the 1st systematic attempt to introduce to the Italian public a varied fare of symph. music. Sgambati appeared also as pianist; after a concert tour in Italy and Germany, he established in 1868 a free piano class annexed to the Accademia di Santa Cecilia in Rome, which in 1877 was formally recognized by the government as the 'Liceo Musicale'; it became the foremost music school in Italy; Sgambati taught piano there until his death. He was an ardent admirer of Wagner, whom he met in 1876; Wagner recommended Sgambati to his own publishers, Schott of Mainz, who subsequently brought out many of Sgambati's works. As pianist and teacher, Sgambati enjoyed a very high reputation in Germany and Italy; his own music betrays strong Germanic influence; unlike most Italian composers of his time, he devoted his energies exclusively to instrumental music, avoiding all service to the theater. —Works: symph. in D (Rome, March 28, 1881); symph. No. 2; *Epitalamio sinfonico* (1887); overtures; piano concerto; *Te Deum* for orch.; *Messa da Requiem;* 2 piano quintets (1876; 1877; his most enduring works); a string quartet (1884); numerous piano pieces: *Fogli volanti, Pièces lyriques, Mélodies poétiques,* 6 Nocturnes, etc.; also *Formulario del pianista* (technical exercises); songs. —Cf. Bettina Walker, *My Musical Experiences* (1892; pp. 44-84); R. A. Streatfeild, in *Masters of Italian Music* (1895; pp. 246-56); E. Segnitz, *Sgambatis Klaviermusik,* in 'Musikpädagogische Blätter' (1911, Nos. 11, 12); A. de Angelis, *G. Sgambati,* in the 'Rivista Musicale Italiana' (Jan., 1912); A. Bonaventura, *G. Sgambati,* in 'La Nuova Musica' (1914); A. Casella, *G. Sgambati,* in 'Music & Letters' (Oct., 1925); A. Casella in Cobbett's 'Cyclopedic Survey of Chamber Music' (1929; vol. 2, pp. 413-14); A. Bonaventura, *G. Sgambati,* in 'Musica d'Oggi' (1941).

Shakespeare, William, English tenor and singing teacher; b. Croydon, June 16, 1849; d. London, Nov. 1, 1931. He was a chorister and played organ in a church at 13; studied at the Royal Academy of Music with Sterndale Bennett; received a Mendelssohn Scholarship in 1871 for piano playing and composition; went to Leipzig for study with Reinecke, but soon left for Milan to cultivate his voice; studied with Lamperti there. From 1875, he appeared in England as a tenor; in 1878 appointed prof. of singing at the Royal Academy of Music in London; won a high reputation as vocal teacher. His compositions are entirely in the vein of German Romanticism, his model being Mendelssohn. He publ. *The Art of Singing* (3 parts; 1898-99; several times republ.); *Singing for Schools and Colleges* (1907); *Plain Words on Singing* (1924); and *The Speaker's Art* (1931).

Shaliapin (shah-lyah'-pēn), **Feodor Ivanovitch,** celebrated Russian bass singer; b. Kazan, Feb. 13, 1873; d. Paris, April 12, 1938. He was of humble origin; at the age of 10 was apprenticed to a shoemaker; at 14, secured chorister's work in a traveling opera company; his companion was the writer Maxim Gorky, who also sang in a chorus; this provided him with a bare existence, and he was often forced to walk the railroad tracks when he could not afford the fare. His wanderings brought him to the Caucasus, and there he was introduced to the singer Usatov (1892), who immediately recognized Shaliapin's extraordinary gifts and taught him without a fee, helping him besides with board and lodgings. Shaliapin's fortunes took a turn for the better when he became a member of a summer opera company in St. Petersburg in 1894; subsequently he sang at the Imperial Opera during the regular season. In 1896 he was engaged at Mamontov's Private Opera in Moscow, where he produced a great impression by his dramatic interpretations of the bass roles in the national Russian operas, and he soon became a prime favorite in Russia. His first foreign engagement was at La Scala, Milan, in 1901; there he made his greatest success as Mefistofele in Boito's opera; he returned to La Scala in 1904 and 1908. Following a season of Russian opera in Paris in the spring of 1906, he was engaged to sing at the Metropolitan Opera House, N. Y.; made his American début there as Mefistofele on Nov. 20, 1907, but was received with only moderate favor. In London his success was immediate, after he sang in Beecham's seasons of Russian opera at Covent Garden, beginning in the spring of 1913; he returned to Russia after the outbreak of World War I, and remained there until 1920; was given the rank of 'People's Artist' by the Soviet government; this title was withdrawn by the Soviet authorities in 1927, after Shaliapin emigrated to Paris, which he made his home until his death. He appeared at the Metropolitan Opera once more in 1921 and sang there for 8 seasons, winning wide acclaim; also sang with the Chicago Opera Co.; toured the U. S. with his own opera troupe, and gave numerous concerts. His last American recital took place in N. Y. on March 3, 1935. Shaliapin was one of the greatest singing actors of all time; he dominated every scene in which he appeared, and to the last he never failed in his ability to move audiences, even though his vocal powers declined markedly. He was especially famed for his interpretation of the role of Boris Godunov in Mussorgsky's opera; both dramatically and vocally, he created an imperishable image. He was equally great as Méphistophélès (*Faust*) and in the buffo roles of Don Basilio and Leporello. He also played the title role in a film version of *Don Quixote.* He publ. his reminiscences: *Pages from My Life* (N. Y., 1926) and *Man and Mask* (N. Y., 1932). Vol. I of a monumental ed., *F. I. Shaliapin, Literary Heritage,* with a chapter of reminiscences by his daughter, was brought out in Moscow, 1957.

Shanet, Howard, American conductor; b. Brooklyn, Nov. 9, 1918. He studied cello; took courses at Columbia Univ.; studied conducting with Koussevitzky at the Berkshire Music Center in Tanglewood; became a member of its staff in 1949; conducted the Huntington, W. V., Symph. Orch. (1951-53); in 1953 was appointed to the music faculty of Columbia Univ.; also conductor of the Columbia Univ. Orch. Publ. a guide for adult beginners, *Learn to Read Music* (N. Y., 1956).

Shapero, Harold, American composer; b. Lynn, Mass., April 29, 1920. He learned to play piano as a youth; was for several years a pianist in dance orchestras; began serious study in 1936 at the Malkin Cons. in Boston, with Nicolas Slonimsky; then studied with Krenek, with Walter Piston at Harvard Univ., with Paul Hindemith at the Berkshire Music Center, Tanglewood, and with Nadia Boulanger in Cambridge, Mass. He graduated from Harvard Univ. in 1941; received the American Prix de Rome for his *Nine-Minute Overture* (N. Y., June 8, 1941); held a Guggenheim Fellowship in 1946 and 1947; won the Gershwin Prize (1946), etc.; 1949-50, was in Rome; 1952, was appointed prof. at Brandeis Univ., Waltham, Mass. He married the painter Esther Geller in 1945. In his music he adheres to an austere Classical pattern, without excluding a highly emotional melodic line; his exceptional mastery of contrapuntal technique secures clarity of intermingled sonorities in his chamber music. In some of his early compositions he applied the dodecaphonic method. —Works: *Serenade in D* for string orch. (1945); *Symphony for Classical Orchestra* (Boston, Jan. 30, 1948); *The Travelers,* overture (1948); *Credo* for orch. (Louisville, Oct. 19, 1955); concerto for orch. (1951-58); *3 Pieces for 3 Pieces,* for flute, clarinet, and bassoon (1938); trumpet sonata (1939); string quartet (1940); *4-Hand Piano Sonata* (1941); violin sonata (1942); *3 Amateur Sonatas* for piano. —Cf. Madeleine Goss, *Modern Music Makers* (N. Y., 1952; pp. 474-78).

Shapey, Ralph, American composer; b. Philadelphia, March 12, 1921; studied with Stefan Wolpe; active as violinist and conductor. —Works: symph. no. 1 (1952); *Challenge: The Family of Man,* symph. poem (1955); concerto for clarinet and small ensemble (Strasbourg Festival, June 9, 1958); piano quintet; 5 string quartets; oboe sonata; piano pieces; songs.

Shapleigh (shap'-lē), **Bertram,** American composer; b. Boston, Jan. 15, 1871; d. Washington, D. C., July 2, 1940. He studied at the New England Cons.; went to London in 1899, and remained there until 1916; then lived in New York and Washington. He made a specialty of oriental music, and gave numerous lectures on the subject. A Bertram Shapleigh Foundation was established in Washington after his death, and his unpublished MSS were deposited there.

Shaporin (shah-poh'-rēn), **Yuri Alexandrovitch,** Russian composer; b. Glukhov, Ukraine, Nov. 8, 1889. He studied law, and graduated from the Univ. of St. Petersburg in 1913; also studied at the St. Petersburg Cons. with Sokolov (composition), graduating in 1918. He wrote theatrical music in Leningrad; moved to Moscow in 1936. He is at his best in descriptive music. —Works: opera *The Decembrists* (1930-50; Moscow, June 23, 1953); cantata *A Tale of the Battle for the Russian Land* (Moscow, April 18, 1944); incidental music to *King Lear, Tartuffe, Boris Godunov,* and to Leskov's *The Flea* (also as an orchestral suite); symphony (Moscow, May 11, 1933); symphony-cantata, *On the Field of Kulikov* (Moscow, Nov. 18, 1939); 2 piano sonatas; several song cycles. —Cf. Gerald Abraham, *Eight Soviet Composers* (London, 1942; pp. 89-98); E. A. Grosheva, *Y. A. Shaporin* (Moscow, 1957).

Sharp, Cecil James, English editor and collector of folksongs; b. London, Nov. 22, 1859; d. there, June 23, 1924. He studied music privately while attending Cambridge Univ.; in 1882 he went to Australia, settling in Adelaide, where he worked in a bank, and practiced law, becoming associate to the Chief Justice of Southern Australia; in 1889 he resigned from the legal profession and took up a musical career; was assistant organist of the Adelaide Cathedral, and co-director of the Adelaide College of Music. In 1892 he returned to England; was made music instructor of Ludgrove School (1893-1910) and also principal of the Hampstead Cons. (1896-1905). At the same time he became deeply interested in English folksongs; publ. a *Book of British Songs for Home and School* (1902); then proceeded to make a systematic survey of English villages with the aim of collecting authentic specimens of English songs; this was the beginning of a movement that was of great consequence to English music. In 1911 he established the English Folk Dance Society; also was director of the School of Folk Song and Dance at Stratford-on-Avon. During World War I he was in the U. S., collecting folk music in the Appalachian Mountains, with a view of establishing their English origin. In 1923 he received the degree of M.M. *(hon. causa)* from Cambridge Univ. In 1930 the 'Cecil Sharp House' was opened in London as headquarters of the English Folk Dance Society (amalgamated with the Folk Song Society in 1932). —Sharp publ. many collections of folksongs and dances: *English Folk Carols* (1911); *Folk-Songs from Various Counties* (1912); *English Folk-Chanteys* (1914); *One Hundred English Folk-Songs* (1916); *Folk-Songs of English Origin* (2 vols.; 1921-23); *English Folk-Songs from the Southern Appalachians* (1917; new enlarged ed., 2 vols., ed. by Maud Karpeles, posthumous, Oxford, 1932; republ. 1952); *American-English Folk-Songs* (1918-21); *The Morris Book,* in 5 parts (1907-13); *Morris Dance Tunes,* in 10 parts (1907-13); *The Country Dance Book,* in 6 parts (1909-22); *Country Dance Tunes,* in 11 parts (1909-22); *The Sword Dances of Northern England,* in 5 parts (1911-13);—Books: *English Folk Song* (London, 1907; 3rd ed., revised by Maud Karpeles, London, 1954); *The Dance: An Historical Survey of Dancing in Europe,* with A. P. Oppé (London, 1924). —Cf. A. H. Fox Strangways and M. Karpeles, *Cecil Sharp* (London, 1933; 2nd ed., London, 1955). See also W. S. Shaw, *Cecil Sharp and Folk Dancing,* in 'Music & Letters' (Jan., 1921).

Sharp, Geoffrey (Newton), English music critic; b. Leeds, June 14, 1914. He studied at Trinity College, Cambridge, and also at the Royal College of Music in London. In 1940 he began publication of the quarterly 'Music Review' in Cambridge; has also written articles on music for various journals.

Sharpe, Herbert Francis, English pianist and composer; b. Halifax, Yorkshire, March 1, 1861; d. London, Oct. 14, 1925. He studied piano at the National Training School in London; joined the faculty of the Royal College of Music in 1884; gave numerous concerts in London and elsewhere; composed many piano pieces and publ. a *Pianoforte School* (with Stanley Lucas).

Shattuck, Arthur, American pianist; b. Neenah, Wis., April 19, 1881; d. New York, Oct. 16, 1951. He studied piano with Leschetizky in Vienna (1895-1902); made his home in Paris, touring extensively in many countries including Iceland and Egypt. Returning to America, he appeared as soloist with many orchestras.

Shaverzashvili, Alexander Vasilievitch, Soviet composer; b. Tiflis, Caucasus, July 8, 1919. He studied at the Tiflis Cons. with A. Balantchivadze; from 1955, prof. at the Tiflis Cons. —Works: comic opera, *Grasshopper* (Tiflis, March 18, 1955); a symph. (1945); 2 piano concertos (1946; 1949); piano quintet (1955); string quartet; piano trio; a violin sonata; songs.

Shavitch, Vladimir, conductor; b. Russia, July 20, 1888; d. Palm Beach, Fla., Dec. 26, 1947. He studied piano with Godowsky and Busoni in Berlin, and composition with Hugo Kaun and Paul Juon (1902-12). Coming to America in 1914, he became conductor of the Syracuse, N. Y., Symph. Orch.; also conducted in Rochester, N. Y. (1923-27); appeared as guest conductor in all European capitals, and in Russia. He was married to the pianist Tina Lerner.

Shaw, Frank Holcomb, American organist and teacher; b. Paxton, Ill., May 8, 1884. He studied at Oberlin Cons. and with Widor in Paris; filled various teaching posts; in 1924, appointed director of the Oberlin Cons., retiring in 1949.

Shaw, George Bernard, famous dramatist; b. Dublin, July 26, 1856; d. Ayot St. Lawrence, England, Nov. 2, 1950. Before winning fame as a playwright, he was active as a music critic in London, writing for 'The

Star' (under the name of 'Corno di Bassetto') during the season of 1888-89 and for 'The World' from 1890 to 1894. In 1899 he publ. *The Perfect Wagnerite,* a highly individual socialistic interpretation of the *Ring of the Nibelungs.* His criticisms from 'The World' were reprinted as *Music in London* in 3 vols. (1932; new ed., 1950); those from 'The Star' as *London Music in 1888-89* (London and N. Y., 1937); selected criticisms were publ., ed. by Eric Bentley, in N. Y., 1954. Shaw's play *Arms and the Man* was made into an operetta, *The Chocolate Soldier,* by Oskar Straus (1908); his *Pygmalion* was converted into a highly successful musical comedy (1956) under the title *My Fair Lady,* with a musical score by Frederick Loewe. —Cf. W. Irvine, *G. B. Shaw's Musical Criticism,* in the 'Mus. Quarterly' (July, 1946).

Shaw, Martin, English organist and composer; b. London, March 9, 1875. He was a pupil at the Royal College of Music in London; played organ in various churches in London. In 1900 he founded the Purcell Society in London; wrote an opera, *Mr. Pepys* (London, Feb. 11, 1926); several masques and ballads; the oratorios *Easter, The Rock* (after T. S. Eliot), *The Redeemer;* sacred choruses, etc. He publ. *The Principles of English Church Music Composition* (1921); edited *The English Carol Book, Songs of Britain, The Motherland Song Book,* and (with his brother, Geoffrey Shaw) *The League of Nations Song Book.* He publ. his autobiography, *Up to Now,* in 1929. —His brother **Geoffrey Shaw** (b. London, Nov. 14, 1879; d. there, April 14, 1943) was an organist and composer; also was active in musical education.

Shaw, Mary (*née* Postans), English contralto; b. London, 1814; d. Hadleigh Hall, Suffolk, Sept. 9, 1876. She studied with Sir George Smart; made her début at London in 1834 with marked success; in 1838 sang in the Gewandhaus, Leipzig, under Mendelssohn's direction, and in other German cities. She made her operatic début at La Scala, Milan, on Nov. 17, 1839; in 1842 she sang in Covent Garden and the principal festivals in England. In 1844, at the height of her success, her career was suddenly ended when her husband (the painter Alfred Shaw, whom she had married in 1835) became insane and died; the shock affected her vocal cords, so that she was unable to sing. Some time later she remarried and went to live in the country.

Shaw, Oliver, a blind American singer; b. Middleboro, Mass., March 13, 1779; d. Providence, Dec. 31, 1848. He was a singing teacher and church organist in Providence from 1807; composer of popular psalm tunes and ballads, which he sang in public; some favorites were *Mary's Tears, The Inspiration, Sweet Little Ann,* and *The Death of Perry.* He publ. the collection 'The Social Sacred Melodist' (1835). —Cf. *Memorial of Oliver Shaw* (Providence, 1884); W. Thomas, *A Discourse of the Life and Death of Oliver Shaw* (Boston, 1851).

Shaw, Robert, American conductor; b. Red Bluff, Calif., April 30, 1916. He studied at Pomona College, graduating in 1938. In 1941 he founded the Collegiate Chorale in N. Y., giving numerous and highly praised performances of choral works of various periods (until 1954); received a Guggenheim Fellowship in 1944; was choral director at the Berkshire Music Center, Tanglewood (1942-45); on the faculty of the Juilliard School of Music, N. Y. (1946-50); in 1948 founded the Robert Shaw Chorale and toured with it in the U. S.; conductor of the San Diego, Calif., Symph. (summer seasons) from 1953; in 1956, appointed associate conductor of the Cleveland Orch.; also made guest appearances with major American orchestras.

Shebalin (sheh-bah-lēn'), **Vissarion Yakovlevitch,** Russian composer; b. Omsk, June 11, 1902. He studied at the Moscow Cons. with Miaskovsky, graduating in 1928; in 1935, appointed prof. of composition there; from 1942 till 1948 was its director. —Works: a musical comedy, *Bridegroom from the Embassy* (Sverdlovsk, Aug. 1, 1942); opera, *The Taming of the Shrew,* after Shakespeare (Moscow, Oct. 1 1955); 4 symphonies (1925, 1929, 1934, 1935); symph. poem *Lenin,* with chorus and soloists (Moscow, Jan. 21, 1933); *Russian Overture* (1941); violin concerto (1940); cantata, *Moscow* (Moscow, Dec. 14, 1946); 7 string quartets (1923, 1934, 1939, 1940, 1942, 1943, 1947); a piano trio; a viola sonata; several piano sonatas; songs. Cf. Gerald Abraham, *Eight Soviet Composers* (London, 1943; pp. 61-69); Igor Boelza, *V. Y. Shebalin* (Moscow, 1945).

Shedlock, John South, English writer on music; b. Reading, Sept. 29, 1843; d. London, Jan. 9, 1919. After graduating from London Univ. (1864) he studied composition with Lalo in Paris; upon his return to London, he devoted himself to writing; was music critic of 'The Academy' (1879-1901) and of 'The Athenæum' (from 1901). He publ. a detailed description of Beethoven's sketch book purchased by the British Museum ('Mus. Times,' June, 1892-Jan., 1893); this led him to further investigations of Beethoven memorabilia, and in 1893 he discovered in Berlin a copy of Cramer's studies with notations by Beethoven; publ. his findings as *The Beethoven-Cramer Studies* (1893); also publ. 2 vols. of Beethoven's letters in English translation, a short biography of Beethoven in Bell's 'Miniature Series' (1905), and a valuable book, *The Pianoforte Sonata, Its Origin and Development* (London, 1895); edited Kuhnau's *Biblical Sonatas* (1895) and harpsichord pieces by Frescobaldi and Froberger.

Shekhter, Boris Semionovitch, Russian composer; b. Odessa, Jan. 20, 1900. He was graduated from the Odessa Cons. in 1922; then entered the Moscow Cons., studying composition with Vassilenko and Miaskovsky; graduated in 1929. In 1940 he went to Turkestan, and became prof. of the Cons. of Ashkhabad. —Works: the operas *The Year 1905* (with A. Davidenko, 1935) and *Yusup and Akhmed* (Ashkhabad, June 12, 1942); cantatas, *Volga-Don* (1952) and *A House in Shushenskoye* (1955); 5 symphonies (1929, 1943, 1945, 1947, 1951); an orch. suite, *Turkmenia,* based on Central Asian themes (1932; his best work; given at the Florence Festival of the International Society for Contemporary Music, April 4, 1934); *Rhapsody,* for orch. (1935); piano pieces; songs.

Shelley, Harry Rowe, American organist and composer; b. New Haven, Conn., June 8, 1858; d. Short Beach, Conn., Sept. 12, 1947. He was a pupil of Dudley Buck and Dvořák in New York; from 1899 was active as church organist and teacher. His compositions include 3 operas: *Leila, Romeo and Juliet,* and *Lotus San;* the symph. poem *The Crusaders;* orch. suite *Souvenir de Baden-Baden;* the cantatas *Vexilla Regis* (N. Y., 1894), *Lochinvar's Ride* (N. Y., 1915), *Death and Life,* and *The Inheritance Divine;* much choral music and some effective piano pieces. His ballads *Minstrel Boy* and *Love's Sorrow* attained considerable success. He also edited the popular collections 'Gems for the Organ,' 'The Modern Organist,' and '101 Interludes for Organ.'

Shenshin, Alexander Alexeyevitch, Russian composer; b. Moscow, Nov. 18, 1890. He studied philology at the Moscow Univ.; then became schoolmaster; also took music lessons with Gretchaninov and Glière. His compositions, in a style reminiscent of Liadov, include an opera, *O T'ao* (1925), and a number of other stage works; also the song cycle *From Japanese Anthologies.* He was inactive after 1940. —Cf. V. Belaiev, *A. A. Shenshin* (Moscow, 1929, in Russian and German).

Shepard, Frank Hartson, American pianist and pedagogue; b. Bethel, Conn., Sept. 20, 1863; d. Orange, N. J., Feb. 15, 1913. He studied music in Boston; then took courses at the Leipzig Cons. (1886-90) with Jadassohn, Reinecke, and others. Returning to America in 1891, he established the Shepard School of Music at Orange, N. J., of which he was director until his death; also was organist at Grace Church there. He publ. *Piano Touch and Scales; Church Music and Choir Training; How to Modulate; Harmony Simplified; Children's Harmony;* etc.

Shepherd, Arthur, American composer; b. Paris, Idaho, Feb. 19, 1880; d. Cleveland, Jan. 12, 1958. He studied with G. Haessel; in 1892, entered the New England Cons., where he studied piano with Dennée and Carl Faelten, and composition with Goetschius and Chadwick. In 1897 he went to Salt Lake City, where he settled as teacher and conductor of the Salt Lake Symph. Orch.; returned to Boston in 1908, and became prof. of harmony and counterpoint at the New England Cons. (until 1917). In 1917 he joined the U. S. Army, and was bandmaster of the U. S. Field Artillery in France. From 1920 to 1926 he was assistant conductor of the Cleveland Orch., and also conducted children's concerts there; was music critic of the Cleveland 'Press' (1929-32). In 1927 he became prof. of music at Western Reserve Univ., retiring in 1950; then lived in Boston and Cleveland. A composer of national tendencies, he wrote in a grand Romantic manner, derived from an intense feeling for American melos. —Works: for orch.: the overtures *The Nuptials of Attila, Ouverture joyeuse* (Paderewski Prize, 1902), *The Festival of Youth* (1915), and *Overture to a Drama* (1919; Cleveland, March 27, 1924); *Fantaisie Humoresque,* for piano and orch. (Boston, Feb. 8, 1918); *Horizons,* 1st symph. (Cleveland, Dec. 15, 1927); *Choreographic Suite* (Cleveland, Oct. 22, 1931); 2nd symph. (Cleveland, March 7, 1940); *Fantasy on Down East Spirituals* (Indianapolis, Nov. 2, 1946); violin concerto (1946-47); *Theme and Variations* (Cleveland, April 9, 1953); *Hilaritas,* overture for concert band (1942); for chorus: *Song of the Sea Wind,* for women's voices and piano (1915); *He Came All So Still,* for women's voices a cappella (1915); *Deck Thyself My Soul,* for mixed chorus and organ (1918); *Ballad of Trees and the Master,* for mixed chorus a cappella (1935); *Song of the Pilgrims,* cantata for tenor solo, mixed chorus, and orch. (1937); *Invitation to the Dance,* for mixed chorus and piano (1937); *Grace for Gardens,* for mixed chorus a cappella (1938); *Build Thee More Stately Mansions,* for women's voices (1938); *Psalm XLII,* for chorus and orch. (1944); *Drive On,* for baritone solo and mixed chorus (1946); chamber music: 2 violin sonatas (1914, 1927); *Triptych,* for voice and string quartet (1926); 3 string quartets (1927, 1935, 1936); piano quintet (1940); *Praeludium Salutatorium,* for flute, oboe, horn, bassoon, violin, viola, and cello (1942); *Divertissement,* for flute, oboe, clarinet, bassoon, and horn (1943); for piano: 2 sonatas (1907, 1929, both in F minor); songs. He publ. a valuable handbook, *The String Quartets of Beethoven* (Cleveland, 1937). —Cf. D. Leedy, *Arthur Shepherd,* in 'Modern Music' (1939); W. S. Newman, *Arthur Shepherd,* in the 'Mus. Quarterly' (April, 1950).

Shera, Frank Henry, English writer on music; b. Sheffield, May 4, 1882; d. there, Feb. 21, 1956. He studied at the Royal College of Music in London, where his teachers were Stanford, Parratt, and Walford Davies. He was music director at Malvern College from 1916 to 1926; in 1928 he was appointed prof. of music at Sheffield Univ., retiring in 1950. He publ. *Musical Groundwork* (1922); *Debussy and Ravel* (1925) and *Elgar's Instrumental Works* (1931) in the 'Musical Pilgrim' series.

Sheremetiev (sheh-reh-meht'-yehf), **Alexander Dmitrievitch,** Count, Russian nobleman and amateur musician; b. St. Petersburg, March 12, 1859; d. Ste-Geneviève-des-Bois, near Paris, May 18, 1931. The private choir maintained by his father, Dmitri, attained wide celebrity in St. Petersburg. In 1882 Count Alexander founded a symph. orch. in his own name, and in 1884 a church choir under the direction of Archangelsky. In 1898 he instituted in St. Petersburg a series of symph. concerts at popular prices, conducted by himself and others. Thanks to his inherited wealth, he was able to engage excellent musicians; presented programs of Russian composers, thus contributing to the cause of national music. He also wrote some pieces himself (*Pathetische Fantasie,* for orch.; chamber music; etc.). After the revolution of 1917 he went to Paris, and died in poverty, in a Russian charity institution near Paris.

Sheridan, Frank, American pianist; b. New York, May 1, 1898. He studied piano with Harold Bauer; made his début with the N. Y. Philharmonic at the Lewisohn Stadium in 1924; toured in Europe in 1929-30; joined the faculty of the Mannes Music School, N. Y.; also taught at Columbia Univ.

Sherwood, William Hall, American pianist and pedagogue; b. Lyons, N. Y., Jan. 31, 1854; d. Chicago, Jan. 7, 1911. He was the son of Rev. L. H. Sherwood, the founder of Lyons Music Academy, from whom he received his primary education; spent 5 years in Germany studying with Kullak in Berlin; also took lessons with Liszt in Weimar. He returned to the U. S. in 1876; taught at the New England Cons., and later at the Chicago Cons.; in 1897 established his Sherwood Piano School in Chicago. Among his publ. compositions for piano are 2 suites and 2 sets of *Gypsy Dances.*

Shield, William, English violinist and composer; b. Whickham, Durham, March 5, 1748; d. Brightling, Sussex, Jan. 25, 1829. He was taught by his father, a singing master, on whose death he was apprenticed to a ship builder; at the same time he took lessons in music with Charles Avison, at Newcastle-on-Tyne; played violin in various small theaters in the neighborhood; in 1772 he settled in London, as violinist at the Opera; from 1773 to 1791 he played the viola there. He produced his first comic opera, *A Flitch of Bacon,* at the Haymarket Theatre in 1778; it was followed by a great number of theatrical pieces; he held the post of composer to Covent Garden Theatre from 1778 till 1791; then traveled in France and Italy, returning to Covent Garden in 1792, retaining his position until 1797. He was appointed Master of the King's Music in 1817. He wrote about 40 light operas, pantomimes, musical farces, ballad operas, etc., of which only separate numbers were ever published; he also wrote 6 string quartets; 6 string trios; 6 duets for 2 violins; other instrumental pieces; publ. *An Introduction to Harmony* (1800) and *Rudiments of Thorough-bass* (c. 1815). He had some original ideas, and was not averse to experimentation; e.g., he wrote movements in 5/4 time. —Cf. G. Hauger, *William Shield,* in 'Music & Letters' (Oct., 1950).

Shilkret, Nathaniel, American composer and conductor; b. New York, Jan. 1, 1895. He studied with Pietro Floridia; until the age of 20, he played the clarinet in various orchestras in N. Y.; in 1916 became music director of the Victor Talking Machine Co., creating the Victor Salon Orch.; held executive posts with Victor until 1935; then went to Hollywood as arranger, but continued to spend part of the season in N. Y.; led thousands of radio broadcasts. He wrote a symph. poem, *Skyward* (1928); a trombone concerto (1942); numerous descriptive pieces for orch.; commissioned Schoenberg, Stravinsky, Toch, Milhaud, Castelnuovo-Tedesco, and Tansman to write a movement each for a biblical cantata *Genesis,* to which he also contributed (1947).

Shimizu, Osamu, Japanese composer; b. Osaka, Nov. 4, 1911. He studied composition at the Tokyo Music Academy; was active in the music dept. of the Tokyo Radio Station; won Odaka Prize (1953). Among his works are symph. No. 1 (Tokyo, Dec. 8, 1951); the cantatas *Ren-nyo* (Tokyo, April 8, 1948) and *Peace* (Tokyo, April 22, 1949); an opera, *Tales of Shuzeni* (Tokyo, Nov. 4, 1954); *Ballade* for violin and piano (1941); numerous songs.

Shira (shē'-rah), **Francesco,** Italian composer and conductor; b. Malta, Aug. 21, 1808; d. London, Oct. 15, 1883. He studied at the Milan Cons. with Basili; brought out his first opera, *Elena e Malvina,* at La Scala, Milan (Nov. 17, 1832); on the strength of his success he was engaged as conductor of the Santo Carlos Theater in Lisbon (1833-42); also taught at the Lisbon Cons. In 1842, after a brief sojourn in Paris, he became conductor for the English Opera at the Princess's Theatre; then conducted at Drury Lane (1844-47); in 1848 he went over to Covent Garden but after a brief season there he returned to Drury Lane in 1852; in later years made a high reputation as a singing teacher, without abandoning composition; wrote the operas *Niccolò de' Lapi* (London, 1863), *Selvaggia* (Venice, Feb. 20, 1875), and *Lia* (Venice, 1876).

Shirinsky (shē-rēn'-skē), **Vassily Petrovitch,** Russian composer; b. Ekaterinodar, Jan. 17, 1901. He studied violin with Conus and composition with Catoire and Miaskovsky at the Moscow Cons. As violin soloist, he contributed much to early propaganda for modern Russian music, playing the 1st concerto of Prokofiev and other new works. His own music is characterized by considerable rhythmic complexity, but remains within the confines of traditional harmony. He wrote an opera, *Ivan the Terrible* (1951-54); 2 symphonies; several overtures; a piano quintet; 4 string quartets; a piano trio; a violin sonata ; a viola sonata; a cello sonata; film music; songs.

Shishakov (shē-shah-kof'), **Youri Nikolayevitch,** Russian composer; b. Moscow, Jan. 18, 1925. He studied with Zhiganov in Kazan; with Gnessin in Moscow; then became teacher of composition at the Gnessin Music School. —Works: 2 symphonies (1947; 1950); overture for folk instruments (1952); concerto for balalaika and orch. (Moscow, 1954); numerous pieces for the accordion.

Shishov, Ivan Petrovitch, Russian composer; b. Novocherkask, Oct. 8, 1888; d. Moscow, Feb. 6, 1947. He studied with Kastalsky and G. Conus; conducted choral groups; taught at the Moscow Cons. (1925-31). —Works: opera, *Painter Serf* (Moscow, March 24, 1929); 2 symphonies (1925; 1933); several song cycles; arrangements of folksongs.

Shore, John, famous English trumpeter; b. London, 1662; d. there, Nov. 20, 1752. In 1707 he succeeded his uncle William Shore as Sergeant Trumpeter to the English Court; in 1711 he was one of the 24 musicians to Queen Anne, and also a lutenist of the Chapel Royal. He is the reputed inventor of the tuning-fork. Purcell wrote for Shore trumpet obbligatos to many of his songs.

Shore, Samuel Royle, English music scholar, editor, and composer; b. Birmingham, April 12, 1856; d. Hindhead, Surrey, Feb. 19, 1946. He studied organ with A. R. Gaul, but was mostly self-educated in composition and music history. He became an authority on church music; edited 'The Cathedral Series' of music of the 16th-17th centuries; wrote numerous ecclesiastical works, among them a Te Deum, 4 Communion Services, a Requiem, anthems, etc.

Shortall, Harrington, American composer; b. Chicago, 1895. After attending Harvard Univ. and serving in World War I, he studied in Paris with Nadia Boulanger; returning to America, he became a teacher; was on the faculty of Rosary College (1940-46). In 1946 he was appointed prof. at the Chicago Theological Seminary. In 1936 his *Choral Memorial* obtained the Westminster Choir School Award. Other works include: *Wealth* *of Variations for Thomas Jefferson's Proposed Orchestra of Artisans,* for chamber orch. (1942); *Hymn for Uncle Sam's Nephews and Nieces,* for chorus and small orch. (1943); *Six Pieces in One,* for orch. (1944); *One Song from Three Poets,* for voice and string quartet (1944).

Shostakovitch (shoh - stah - koh' - vitch), **Dmitri Dmitrievitch,** celebrated Russian composer; b. St. Petersburg, Sept. 25, 1906. He studied at the St. Petersburg Cons. with Nikolayev (piano), Sokolov (harmony and counterpoint), and Maximilian Steinberg (composition), graduating as pianist in 1923, as composer in 1925. As a graduation piece, he wrote his 1st symph. at the age of 18; it was first performed by the Leningrad Philharmonic on May 12, 1926, and subsequently became his most frequently performed work all over the world. His 2nd symph., written for the 10th anniversary of the Soviet Republic and with a choral ending to a text about Lenin, was less successful, despite its political program. He then wrote a satirical opera, *The Nose* (after Gogol's whimsical story of the sudden disappearance of a government functionary's nose from his face); in this opera Shostakovitch was plainly influenced by the modernistic grotesque of new German music; there are imitative noises and highly discordant combinations in the score. *The Nose* was produced in Leningrad on Jan. 12, 1930, but was violently attacked in the Soviet press as a product of 'bourgeois decadence' and was soon withdrawn from the repertory. Somewhat in the same style was his ballet *The Golden Age* (1930), which included a celebrated *Polka,* satirizing the Geneva disarmament conference. There followed his 3rd symph., *May First,* with a choral ending dedicated to the international workers' day. Shostakovitch's declared intention was to pay homage to revolution as a creative force; despite these proclamations, the 3rd symphony, like the 2nd, failed to arouse attention. Shostakovitch then wrote a work that was to precipitate a crisis in his own career, as well as in Soviet music in general, an opera to a subject by the 19th-century Russian writer Leskov, *Lady Macbeth of the District of Mtzensk* (Leningrad, Jan. 22, 1934); the sordid story of adultery, murder, and suicide was presented by the producers as a sociological tableau in condemnation of old Russia, but it ran counter to the growing puritanism of official Soviet ideology. On the occasion of its production in Moscow, the Communist organ 'Pravda' published an editorial inveighing against Shostakovitch as a disciple of foreign modernists and a propagandist of morbid naturalism (Jan. 28, 1936). Shostakovitch immediately admitted his 'faulty' concepts, and asserted his resolve to write music in keeping with the officially accepted formula of 'socialist realism.' Another article in 'Pravda' assailed Shostakovitch for the incorrect depiction of Soviet farm life in his ballet *The Limpid Brook.* Abandoning the stage for the time, Shostakovitch turned to instrumental composition, and wrote his 4th symph., which was placed in rehearsal with the Leningrad Philharmonic, but withdrawn before the performance when it was found that the music contained numerous modernistic passages. Shostakovitch's rehabilitation came with the performance of his 5th symph. (1937), which was hailed by the critics and important officials as an example of true Soviet art, classical in formal design, lucid in its melodic and harmonic procedures, and optimistic in its philosophical connotations. Of his subsequent symphonies, the 7th was the most dramatically conceived. He began its composition during the siege of Leningrad, in the autumn of 1941; he flew from Leningrad to Moscow and later to the temporary capital on the Volga, Kuibishev, where the work was completed and performed on March 1, 1942. Its symphonic development is explicitly realistic, with the theme of the Nazi military machine in mechanical march-time, rising to monstrous proportions, but eventually overwhelmed by a victorious Russian melody. It was subsequently performed by virtually every orchestra in the Allied countries, often under the title 'Leningrad Symph.' although no such designation appears in the score. During World War II Shostakovitch was one of the most popular modern composers throughout the world. Conductors and orchestras vied with each other for the right of 1st performance of his symphonies; however, his popularity outside Russia began to wane; after the sensational success of his 'Leningrad Symph.' there were no revivals; his 8th, 9th, 10th, and 11th symphonies had only sporadic hearings; the 5th symphony retained its place in the repertory; but it was his youthful 1st symph. that enjoyed repeated performances in the U. S., in England, and on the continent of Europe, without losing its original appeal. His chamber music, his piano pieces, and his few songs have never reached a high level of popularity. In 1949 he visited the U. S. as a delegate to the World Peace Conference in N. Y. He received several Stalin prizes for his works, and on the occasion of his 50th birthday was awarded the Order of Lenin (1956). —Works: operas: *The Nose* (Leningrad, Jan. 12, 1930) and *Lady Macbeth of the District of Mtzensk* (Leningrad, Jan. 22, 1934; Metropolitan Opera, N. Y., Feb. 5, 1935); ballets: *The Golden Age* (Leningrad, Oct. 27, 1930; contains the celebrated dance number *Polka*); *Bolt* (Leningrad, April 8, 1931) and *The Limpid Brook* (Leningrad, June 4, 1935); incidental music to Mayakovsky's comedy, *The Bedbug* (1929), to *Hamlet* (1932), *The Human Comedy,* after Balzac (1934). Symphonies: No. 1 (Leningrad, May 12, 1926); No. 2, with a choral ending, dedicated to the October Revolution (Leningrad, Nov. 6, 1927); No. 3, subtitled *May First* (Leningrad, Nov. 6, 1931); No. 4 (1936; not performed); No. 5 (Leningrad, Nov. 21, 1937); No. 6 (Leningrad, Nov. 5, 1939); No. 7, 'Leningrad Symph.' (Kuibishev, March 5, 1942; 1st American performance, NBC Symph., Toscanini conducting, July 19, 1942); No. 8 (Moscow, Nov. 4, 1943); No. 9 (Leningrad, Nov. 3, 1945); No. 10 (Leningrad, Dec. 17, 1953); No. 11 (Moscow, Oct. 30, 1957). Other orchestral works: *Suite for Jazz Orch.* (Leningrad, Nov. 28, 1938); 1st piano concerto, for piano, trumpet, and strings (Leningrad, Oct. 15, 1933); 2nd piano concerto (Moscow, May 10, 1957, Maxim Shostakovitch, son of the composer, soloist); violin concerto (Leningrad, Oct. 29, 1955). Vocal works: *Leningrad,* suite for chorus and orch. (Moscow, Oct. 15, 1942); *Song of the Forests,* cantata (Moscow, Nov. 26, 1949); *Democratic Vistas,* a cycle of 10 poems by Walt Whitman, for chorus and orch. (Moscow, Oct. 10, 1951); 4 songs to texts by Pushkin (1936); 6 songs to words by Burns, Shakespeare, and Walter Raleigh (1942); cycle, *From Jewish Folk Poetry* (1948). Chamber music: 2 pieces for string octet (1925); cello sonata (1934); 6 string quartets (1938, 1944, 1946, 1949, 1952, 1956); piano quintet (1940); 3 pieces for unaccompanied violin (1940); 2 piano trios (1923; 1944). For piano: *3 Fantastic Dances* (1922); 2 sonatas (1926; 1943); *Aphorisms,* suite of 10 pieces (1927); 24 Preludes (1933); 24 Preludes and Fugues (1951). He re-orchestrated Mussorgsky's opera *Boris Godunov* (1939-40); wrote music to numerous films: *Alone* (1930); *Golden Mountains* (1931); *Passerby* (1932); *Maxim's Return* (1937); *The Days of Volotchayev* (1937); *Friends* (1938); *The Man With a Gun* (1938); *A Great Citizen* (1939); *The Great River* (1943); *The Young Guard* (1947); *Ivan Mitchurin* (1948); *Fall of Berlin* (1949); etc. —Bibliography: N. Slonimsky, *Dmitri Shostakovitch,* in the 'Mus. Quarterly' (Oct., 1942); Victor Seroff, *Dmitri Shostakovitch: The Life and Background of a Soviet Composer* (N. Y., 1943); M. Sahlberg-Vatchadze, *Chostakovitch* (Paris, 1945); Ivan Martinov, *Shostakovitch* (Moscow, 1946; in English, N. Y., 1947); L. Danilevitch, *Dmitri Shostakovitch* (Moscow, 1958).

Shudi. See **Broadwood.**

Shulman, Alan, American composer; b. Baltimore, June 14, 1915. He studied cello at the Peabody Cons. of Music in Baltimore; moved to N. Y. in 1928, and studied cello with Felix Salmond and composition with Bernard Wagenaar at the Juilliard School of Music, graduating in 1937. In 1938 he became the cellist of the newly-founded Stuyvesant String Quartet; also played the cello in the NBC Symph. (1937-54), except for the years he spent in the U. S. Maritime Service (1942-45). —Works: for orch.: *A Laurentian Overture* (N. Y., Jan. 7, 1952); *Waltzes* (1949); *Popocatepetl,* symph. picture (1952); *Theme and Variations,* for viola and orch. (N. Y., Feb. 17, 1941); *Pastorale and Dance,* for violin and orch. (N. Y., July 15, 1944); cello concerto (1948; N. Y., April 13, 1950); 2nd symph. (Great Neck, L. I., May 25, 1958); chamber music: *Rendezvous,* for clarinet and strings (1946); *Threnody,* for string quartet (1950); *Suite Miniature,* for octet of cellos (1956); suite for solo cello (1956); *Top Brass,* for 12 brass instruments (Portland, Oregon, April 25, 1958); numerous short works for violin, for cello, for piano, etc.

Sibelius (sĭ-bā'-lyoos), **Jean (Johan Julius Christian),** great Finnish composer; b. Tavastehus, Dec. 8, 1865; d. Järvenpää, Sept. 20, 1957. The son of an army surgeon, he received an excellent classical education; from childhood, showed a deep absorption in music, and began to compose without a tutor. He had piano lessons from the age of 9, and at 14 began to study the violin with Gustaf Levander, the bandmaster in his native town; soon he took part in amateur performances of chamber music. He was sent to the Univ. of Helsinki in 1885 to study law, but abandoned it before the end of his 1st semester, and entered the Cons., where he studied violin with Vasiliev and Csillag, and composition with Wegelius (1886-89). He had a suite for strings and a string quartet publicly performed in 1889, producing an excellent impression; he was then granted a government stipend for further study in Berlin. He studied with Albert Becker (counterpoint and fugue); after returning to Finland for a short stay, he went to Vienna to complete his musical training; there he was a student of Robert Fuchs and Karl Goldmark (1890-91). In 1892 he married Aino Järnefelt. At that time his path as a national Finnish composer became determined; the music he wrote was inspired by native legends, with the epic *Kalevala* as a prime source of inspiration. A symph. poem, *Kullervo,* with soloists and chorus, written by Sibelius upon his return to Finland, was performed in Helsinki on April 28, 1892. A little later he completed one of his most famous scores, the symph. poem *En Saga* (revised in 1901). In 1893 he was appointed instructor in theory at the Helsinki Cons. In 1897 the Finnish senate granted him an annual stipend of 2,000 marks for 10 years. On July 2, 1900, the Helsinki Philharmonic gave the première of the most celebrated and the most patriotic symph. work by Sibelius, *Finlandia.* So profoundly moving was the music to Finnish audiences that the Czarist government forbade its performances during times of political unrest. In 1901 Sibelius conducted his own works at the annual festival of the 'Allgemeiner deutscher Tonkünstlerverein' at Heidelberg. In 1904 he moved to a country home at Järvenpää, near Helsinki, where he remained until his death, with only occasional absences. In 1913 Sibelius accepted a commission for a new orchestral work from an American patron of music, Carl Stoeckel, to be performed at the 28th annual Norfolk, Conn., Festival; the completed work was the symph. poem *Aallottaret (The Oceanides),* and Sibelius came to the U. S. to conduct its première on June 4, 1914. The program also included several of his other works. Yale Univ. conferred on him the degree of Mus. Doc. *(hon. causa).* Returning to Finland just before the outbreak of World War I, Sibelius withdrew into seclusion, but continued to work. He made his last public appearance abroad in Stockholm, when he conducted his 7th symphony on March 24, 1924. He wrote 2 more works after that, a score for Shakespeare's *The Tempest,* and *Tapiola,* a symph. poem. After 1929 he ceased to compose; rumors of his completion of another symphony proved unfounded. Although he was cordial in receiving friends and admirers from abroad, he avoided discussion of his own musical plans. Honors were showered on him; festivals of his music were for years popular events in Helsinki; a postage stamp bearing his likeness was issued by the Finnish government on his 80th birthday; special publications, biographical, bibliographical, and photographic, were issued in Finland. Artistically, too, Sibelius attained the status of a classical composer still in his lifetime; several important contemporary composers paid him homage by acknowledging their debt of inspiration to him (Vaughan Williams, for instance). He was the last representative of 19th-century nationalistic Romanticism. He stayed aloof from modern developments, but he was not uninterested in reading scores and listening to performances on the radio of works of such men as Schoenberg, Prokofiev, and Shostakovitch. —The music of Sibelius marked the culmination of the growth of national Finnish art, in which Pacius was the protagonist, and Wegelius, the teacher of Sibelius, a worthy cultivator. Like his predecessors, Sibelius was schooled in Germanic tradition, and his early works reflect German lyricism and German dramatic thought. He opened a new era in Finnish music when he abandoned formal conventions and began to write music that seemed inchoate and diffuse, but followed a powerful line of development by variation and repetition; a parallel with Beethoven's late works has frequently been drawn. The thematic material employed by Sibelius is not modelled directly on known Finnish songs; rather he recreated the characteristic melodic patterns of folk music. The prevailing mood is somber, even tragic, with a certain elemental sweep and grandeur. His instrumentation is highly individual, with long songful solo passages, and with protracted transitions that are treated as integral parts of the music. His genius found its most eloquent expression in his symphonies and symph. poems; he wrote relatively little chamber music, and only in his earlier years. His only opera, *The Maid in the Tower* (1896), to a text in Swedish, was never published. He wrote some incidental music for the stage; the celebrated *Valse Triste* was written for Järnefelt's play *Kuolema* (1903). —WORKS: the opera *Jungfruburen (The Maid in the Tower;* Helsinki, Nov. 7, 1896); *Scaramouche,* a 'tragic pantomime' (1913; Copenhagen, May 12, 1922); incidental music to *King Christian II* (1898), *Kuolema* (1903), *Pelléas et Mélisande* (1905), *Belshazzar's Feast* (1906), *Svanevhit* (1908), *Odlan* (1909), *The Language of the Birds* (1911), *Jedermann* (1916), *The Tempest* (1926); 7 symphonies: No. 1, in E minor, op. 39 (Helsinki, April 26, 1899), No. 2, in D major, op. 43 (Helsinki, March 8, 1902, composer conducting), No. 3, in C major, op. 52 (1904-07; Helsinki, Sept. 25, 1907, composer conducting), No. 4, in A minor, op. 63 (Helsinki, April 3, 1911, composer conducting), No. 5, in E♭ major, op. 82 (Helsinki, Dec. 8, 1915, composer conducting), No. 6, in D minor, op. 104 (Helsinki, Feb. 19, 1923, composer conducting), No. 7, in C major, op. 105 (Stockholm, March 24, 1924, composer conducting); symph. poems: *Kullervo,* op. 7 (Helsinki, April 28, 1892), *En Saga,* op. 9 (Helsinki, Feb. 16, 1893); *Spring Song,* op. 16 (1894), *4 Legends from the Kalevala,* op. 22: *Lemminkaïnen and the Maidens* (1895), *Lemminkaïnen in Tuonela* (1895), *The Swan of Tuonela* (1893), *The Return of Lemminkaïnen* (1895), *Finlandia,* op. 26 (Helsinki, July 2, 1900), *Pohjola's Daughter,* op. 49 (1906), *Night Ride and Sunrise,* op. 55 (1909), *The Bard,* op. 64 (1913), *Luonnotar,* op. 70 (1913), *Aallottaret (The Oceanides),* op. 73 (Norfolk, Conn. Festival, June 4, 1914, composer conducting), *Tapiola,* op. 112 (commissioned by Walter Damrosch, and 1st performed by him, N. Y., Dec. 26, 1926); symph. suites: *Karelia,* op. 11 (1893), *Rakastava,* for strings and percussion, op. 14 (1911), *Scènes historiques,* op. 25, 1st suite (1899), *Scènes historiques,* op. 66, 2nd suite (1912), *Suite mignonne,* for 2 flutes and strings, op. 98a (1921), *Suite champêtre,* for strings, op. 98b (1921), *Suite caractéristique* for small orch., op. 100 (1923); violin concerto in D minor, op. 47 (1st version, Helsinki, Feb. 8, 1904; 2nd version, Berlin, Oct. 19, 1905); *6 Humoresques* for violin and orch., op. 87b and 89 (1917); chamber music; string quartet in B♭ major, op. 4 (1882), *Voces intimae,* op. 56, for string quartet (1909), *Malinconia,* for cello and piano, op. 20 (1901), 4 pieces for violin or cello, op. 78 (1915), 6 pieces for violin and piano, op. 79 (1915), *Sonatina* for violin and piano, op. 80 (1915), 5 pieces for violin and piano, op. 81 (1915), *Novellette,* for violin and piano, op. 102 (1923), *5 Danses champêtres,* for violin and piano, op. 106 (1925), 4 compositions for violin and piano, op. 115 (1929), 3 compositions for violin and piano, op. 116 (1929); piano sonata, op. 12 (1893); 111 piano pieces, grouped in cycles, and composed between 1894 and 1929. Choral works: *The Origin of Fire,* op. 32, for baritone, male chorus, and orch. (1902), *Oma maa,* cantata for chorus and orch., op. 92 (1918), *Maan virsi,* cantata for chorus and orch., op. 95 (1920), *The Song of Väinö,* for chorus and orch., op. 110 (1926); 85 songs; various early works, without opus numbers.—BIBLIOGRAPHY: K. Flodin, *Finska Musiker* (Helsinki, 1900); Rosa Newmarch, *Jean Sibelius, a Finnish Composer* (Leipzig, 1906); E. G. Furuhjelm, *Jean Sibelius* (Borgä, 1916); W. Niemann, *Jean Sibelius* (Leipzig, 1917); Cecil Gray, *Sibelius* (London, 1931, 2nd ed., 1938); Cecil Gray, *Sibelius: The Symphonies* (London, 1935; 5th printing, 1947); Karl Ekman, *Jean Sibelius: His Life and Personality* (in English; Helsinki, 1935; 4th Swedish ed., 1956); Bengt de Törne, *Sibelius: a Close-Up* (London, 1937); Rosa Newmarch, *Jean Sibelius* (Boston, 1939); Eino Roiha, *Die Symphonien von Jean Sibelius* (Jyväskylä, 1941); E. Arnold, *Finlandia, the Story of Sibelius* (N. Y., 1941); I. Krohn, *Der Formenbau in den Symphonien von Jean Sibelius* (Helsinki, 1942); E. Tanzberger, *Die symphonischen Dichtungen von Jean Sibelius* (Würzburg, 1943); S. Levas, *Jean Sibelius* (in Finnish; Helsinki, 1945); Bengt de Törne, *Sibelius* (in Finnish; Helsinki, 1945); *The Music of Sibelius,* ed. by G. Abraham (N. Y., 1947); I. Hannikainen, *Sibelius and the Development of Finnish Music* (London, 1948); Nils-Eric Ringbom, *Sibelius* (in Swedish; Stockholm, 1948; in English, Norman, Okla., 1954); Veikko Helasvuo, *Sibelius and the Music of Finland* (Helsinki, 1952; in English); O. Andersson, *Jean Sibelius i Amerika* (Åbo, 1955, in Swedish); S. Parmet, *Sibelius symfonier* (Helsinki, 1955). See also the following articles in the 'Mus. Quarterly': A. H. Meyer, *Sibelius: Symphonist* (Jan., 1936) and H. Askeli, *A Sketch of Sibelius the Man* (Jan., 1940).

Siboni, Erik (Anton Waldemar), Danish pianist and composer; b. Copenhagen, Aug. 26, 1828; d. there, Feb. 22, 1892. He was the son of the tenor Giuseppe Siboni (b. Forli, Jan. 27, 1780; d. Copenhagen, March 29, 1839, as director of the opera and Cons.); studied with J. P. E. Hartmann; then with Moscheles and Hauptmann at Leipzig and with Sechter at Vienna; returned to Copenhagen, and in 1864 became organist and piano professor at the Royal Academy of Music at Sorö; retired in 1883. —Works: operas, *Loreley* (Copenhagen, 1859) and *Carl II's flugt (Flight of Charles II;* Copenhagen, 1862); 2 symphonies; a piano quartet; other chamber music; the choral works *Slaget ved Murten (Battle of Murten), Stormen paa København (Storming of Copenhagen),* etc.

Sieber (zē'-ber), **Ferdinand,** famous singing teacher; b. Vienna, Dec. 5, 1822; d. Berlin, Feb. 19, 1895. He studied with Ronconi; after a brief period of singing in opera, he became a singing teacher in Dresden (1848-54), later settling in Berlin, where he had numerous pupils. He taught in the tradition of the old Italian method. He publ. valuable instructive works; *Die Kunst des Gesangs*, in 2 parts (theoretical and practical studies), with a supplement, *60 Vocalisen und Solfeggien; Vollständiges Lehrbuch der Gesangskunst für Lehrer und Schüler* (1858; 3rd ed., 1878); *Katechismus der Gesangskunst* (1862 and many subsequent eds.); *Die Aussprache des Italienischen im Gesang* (1860; 2nd ed., 1880); and a *Handbuch des deutschen Liederschatzes* (1875), containing a catalogue of 10,000 songs arranged according to vocal range; he also wrote many songs.

Siegel, C. F. W., German music publisher; d. Leipzig, March 29, 1869. He founded his company in 1846, making a specialty of choral music. His successor was Richard Linnemann (b. April 14, 1845; d. Dec. 1, 1909), a pupil of the Leipzig Cons., who in 1871 acquired control of 'Die Sängerhalle' (organ of the German singing societies), which he publ. until 1916. His sons, Carl Linnemann (b. Sept. 25, 1872) and Richard Linnemann, Jr. (b. Nov. 5, 1874; d. April 5, 1932), entered the business in 1901. The stock of E. W. Fritzsch was bought in 1901, and that of K. F. Kistner (q.v.) in 1919. From 1919 to 1927 the firm publ. the 'Archiv für Musikwissenschaft.'

Siegel, Felix. See **Schuberth, Julius.**

Siegel, Rudolf, German conductor and composer; b. Berlin, April 12, 1878; d. Munich, Dec. 4, 1948. He studied with Humperdinck in Berlin and with Thuille in Munich; in 1910 became conductor of a choral society in Munich; then was in Berlin (1912-14) and Königsberg (1914-17). From 1919 until 1930 he was music director at Krefeld; then moved to Berlin; in 1945 went to Ebing near Bamberg; eventually moved to Munich. He wrote an opera, *Herr Dandolo* (Essen, 1914); *Apostatenmarsch*, for male chorus and orch.; *Heroische Tondichtung*, for orch.; *Dem Vaterlande*, for men's chorus and orch.; made arrangements of German folksongs.

Siegl, Otto, Austrian violinist, conductor, and composer; b. Graz, Oct. 6, 1896. He studied in Vienna; was active as conductor. From 1933 till 1948 he taught in Cologne; returning to Vienna in 1948, he was appointed prof. at the Academy of Music. He wrote a piano concerto, 3 cello sonatas, a violin sonata, a viola sonata, etc., a total of more than 100 works.

Siegmeister, Elie, American composer; b. New York, Jan. 15, 1909. He studied academic subjects at Columbia Univ.; composition with Seth Bingham; in 1926 he took lessons from Wallingford Riegger; then went to Paris, where he studied with Nadia Boulanger (1927-31). Returning to N. Y., he taught at various schools. In 1940 he organized the American Ballad Singers and toured with them for 5 years. Since 1949, teaching at Hofstra College. —Works: *Doodle Dandy of the USA*, play with music (1942); *Sing Out, Sweet Land*, musical show (N. Y., 1944); *Darling Corie*, 1-act opera (Hofstra College, 1952); *Miranda and the Dark Young Man*, 1-act opera (Hartford, Conn., 1955); for orch.: *A Walt Whitman Overture* (N. Y., March 31, 1940); *Ozark Set* (Minneapolis, Nov. 7, 1944); *Western Suite* (NBC Symph., Nov. 24, 1945), *Wilderness Road* (Minneapolis, Nov. 9, 1945), *Sunday in Brooklyn* (NBC Symph., July 21, 1946), *Lonesome Hollow* (1946; Columbus, O., 1948), *Prairie Legend* (N. Y., Jan. 18, 1947), 3 symphonies (No. 1, N. Y., Oct. 30, 1947; No. 2, N. Y., Feb. 25, 1952; No. 3, 1957), *From My Window* (Erie, Pa., 1949), *Summer Night* (N. Y., Sept. 27, 1952), *Divertimento* (1953), clarinet concerto (Oklahoma City, 1956), woodwind quintet (1932); string quartet (1936); *American Sonata*, for piano (1944); 2 violin sonatas; choral works: *Abraham Lincoln Walks at Midnight* (1937), 8 American Folksongs (1940), *Freedom Train*, for men's voices with piano (1943), etc.; songs; piano pieces. He ed. *The Music Lover's Handbook* (N. Y., 1943); *A Treasury of American Song* (with Olin Downes, N. Y., 1940; revised and enlarged ed., 1943); etc.

Siepi, Cesare, Italian bass singer; b. Milan, Feb. 10, 1923; made his début in Venice, 1941, as Rigoletto; from 1946, engaged at La Scala, Milan; American début, Metropolitan Opera, N.Y., Jan. 27, 1951; also sang in Scandinavia, Spain, Switzerland, and England.

Sieveking (sē'-vĕ-king), **Martinus,** pianist; b. Amsterdam, March 24, 1867; d. Pasadena, Calif., Nov. 26, 1950. He studied piano with his father and with Julius Röntgen. He began his career as accompanist in Paris; traveled with Adelina Patti on her tour of England (1891-92); then settled in the U.S.; spent a number of years experimenting with a new method which he announced as guaranteed to achieve virtuosity in 2 years. In 1915 he established in N. Y. a school to teach his virtuoso technique. He became celebrated as a teacher, while continuing to give concerts in Europe and America; then went to California, and lived in Pasadena. He publ. a number of brilliant piano studies and salon pieces.

Siface (sē-fah'-che), **Giovanni Francesco,** famous Italian male soprano; b. Pescia, Feb. 12, 1653; d. Ferrara, May 29, 1697 (murdered by hired assassins). He was a member of the Papal Chapel from 1675-77; in Modena from 1679 till 1687; later sang at Venice and London.

Sigismondi (sē-jis-mohn'-dē), **Giuseppe;** Italian singing teacher and composer; b. Naples, Nov. 13, 1739; d. there, May 10, 1826. He was librarian at the Cons. in Naples (from 1808); wrote an opera, 4 oratorios, vocal music, and pieces for piano and organ; only a few of his works were published.

Sigtenhorst-Meyer, Bernhard van den, Dutch composer; b. Amsterdam, June 17, 1888; d. The Hague, July 17, 1953. He studied at the Amsterdam Cons.; later in Vienna and Paris; settled in The Hague as composer and writer. —Works: 2 string quartets (1919, 1944); sonata for cello solo (1926); 2 violin sonatas (1926, 1938); *6 Miniatures,* for oboe and piano (1926-46); 2 piano sonatas (1922, 1925); 3 piano sonatinas (1928, 1930, 1948); other piano pieces: *La vieille Chine* (1916), *Les Oiseaux* (1917); 2 albums, *Le Monde de contes-bleus* (1926-28); edited works by Sweelinck; publ. the valuable treatises, *Jan P. Sweelinck en zijn instrumentale Muziek* (The Hague, 1934; 2nd ed., 1946) and *De vocale Muziek van Jan P. Sweelinck* (1948). —Cf. C. Backers, *Nederlandsche Componisten* (The Hague, 2nd ed., 1948, pp. 131-37); H. Antcliffe, *Sigtenhorst Meyer: A Personal Impression,* in 'Monthly Musical Record' (Dec., 1953).

Sigwart, Botho (real name Sigwart Botho, Count of Eulenburg), German pianist and composer; son of the German diplomat and poet Count Phillip of Eulenburg; b. Berlin, Jan. 10, 1884; d. in Galicia, June 2, 1915 (from wounds received in battle). He studied piano in Vienna and musicology at the Univ. of Munich *(Dr. phil.* 1907, with the dissertation, *Erasmus Widmann);* completed his studies with Max Reger at Leipzig (1908-09). In 1909 he married the concert singer Helene Staegemann. He wrote a number of piano pieces, a string quartet, and several melodramas.

Siklós (shik'-losh), **Albert,** Hungarian composer; b. Budapest, June 26, 1878; d. there, April 2, 1942. His real name was Schönwald, but he changed it to Siklós in 1910. He studied law, and later took courses with Koessler at the Budapest Academy of Music, graduating in 1901; he taught at the Academy from 1910, and gradually became one of its most respected teachers. He was a prolific composer, but few of his works were published, and there were virtually no performances outside Hungary. He wrote the opera *The House of the Months* (Budapest, Dec. 21, 1927); a ballet, *The Mirror* (Budapest, March 28, 1923), and other stage works; 2 symphonies and an interesting *Symphonie aethérique* for 12 double-basses (1899); a cello concerto; a violin concerto; much chamber music; piano pieces. He publ. a number of instructive books, and also a music dictionary in Hungarian.

Sikorski (sē-kor'-skē), **Kazimierz,** composer; b. Zürich, June 28, 1895 (of Polish parents). He studied music in Warsaw and later in Paris; became prof. at the Warsaw Cons. in 1927. He was appointed director of the State Cons. in Lodz in 1948. His concerto, chamber music, and several choral pieces.

Silas (sē'-lahs), **Eduard,** pianist and composer; b. Amsterdam, Aug. 22, 1827; d. London, Feb. 8, 1909. He studied piano in Frankfurt and in Paris; took courses at the Paris Cons. with Halévy; won 1st prize for organ playing in competition with Saint-Saëns. In 1850 he settled in England as organist; also taught harmony at the Guildhall School in London. Among his works are 3 symphonies, 3 piano concertos, 2 string quintets, 2 piano trios, numerous piano pieces; also an oratorio, *Joash* (Norwich Festival, 1863), and a Mass.

Silbermann (zil'-bär-man), German family of organ and piano makers. (1) **Andreas Silbermann,** b. Klein-Bobritzsch, Saxony, May 16, 1678; d. Strasbourg, March 16, 1734. He settled in Strasbourg in 1703; was the builder of the organ of the Strasbourg Cathedral (1714-16) and of 29 others. (2) **Gottfried Silbermann,** brother of Andreas, b. Klein-Bobritzsch, Jan. 14, 1683; d. Dresden, Aug. 4, 1753. Apprenticed to a bookbinder, he ran away and joined his brother in Strasbourg, working as his helper. He then lived in Freiberg; built 47 organs, the finest of which is that in the Freiberg Cathedral (1714), having 3 manuals and 45 stops. He owed his fame, however, mainly to the manufacture of pianos in Germany, in which field he was a pioneer; the hammer action in his instruments was practically identical with that of Cristofori, the piano inventor. Silbermann also invented the 'cembal d'amour,' a clavichord with strings of double length, struck in the middle by the tangents, thus yielding the duplicated octave of the tone of the entire string. He supplied 3 pianos to Frederick the Great for Potsdam, and Bach played on them during his visit there in 1747. (3) **Johann Andreas Silbermann,** eldest son of Andreas; b. Strasbourg, June 26, 1712; d. there, Feb. 11, 1783. He built 54 organs; publ. a *Geschichte der Stadt Strassburg* (1775). (4) **Johann Daniel Silbermann,** brother of Johann Andreas; b. Strasbourg, March 31, 1717; d. Leipzig, May 9, 1766. He worked with his uncle Gottfried at Freiberg, and continued the manufacture of pianos after the latter's death. (5) **Johann Heinrich Silbermann,** brother of Johann Andreas and Johann Daniel; b. Strasbourg, Sept. 24, 1727; d. there, Jan. 15, 1799; made pianos at Strasbourg, similar to those of his uncle Gottfried, and introduced them into France. (6) **Johann Friedrich Silbermann,** son of Johann Heinrich; b. Strasbourg, June 21, 1762; d. there, March 8, 1817. He was an organist in Strasbourg; during the Revolution wrote a *Hymne à la Paix;* also composed some German songs. —Bibliography: L. Mooser, *Gottfried Silbermann* (Langensalza, 1857); G. Zschaler, *Gottfried Silbermann* (1898); E. Flade, *Der Orgelbauer Gottfried Silbermann* (Leipzig, 1926); H. Hullemann, *Die Tätigkeit des Orgelbauers Gottfried Silbermann im Reussenland* (Leipzig, 1937); R. Gärtner, *Gottfried Silbermann der Orgelbauer* (Dresden, 1938); J. Wörsching, *Die Orgelbauer Familie Silbermann in Strassburg* (Mainz, 1941); E. Flade, *Gottfried Silbermann. Ein Beitrag zur Geschichte des deutschen Orgel- und Klavierbau im Zeitalter Bachs* (Leipzig, 1953); Donald Boalch, *Makers of the Harpsichord and Clavichord 1440-1840* (London, 1956, pp. 112-14; contains genealogy and list of extant instruments made by members of the family).

Silcher (zil'-her), **Friedrich,** German composer; b. Schnaith, Württemberg, June 27, 1789; d. Tübingen, Aug. 26, 1860. He studied with his father and with Auberlen, an organist at Fellbach; lived for some years in Stuttgart; in 1817 was appointed music director at the Univ. of Tübingen, receiving the honorary degree of *Dr. phil.* in 1852. He was an influential promoter of German popular singing; publ. several collections of German folksongs, in which he included his own compositions; of the latter, *Lorelei (Ich weiss nicht, was soll es bedeuten,* to words by Heinrich Heine) became so popular that it was often mistaken for a folksong; his other well-known songs are *Ännchen von Tharau, Morgen muss ich fort von hier, Zu Strassburg auf der Schanz,* etc. He also publ. a *Choralbuch* for 3 voices, 3 books of hymns for 4 voices; 'Tübinger Liedertafel' (male choruses); *Geschichte des evangelischen Kirchengesanges* (1844); *Harmonie- und Kompositionslehre* (1851; 2nd ed., 1859). —Cf. A. Köstlin, *F. Silcher und Weber* (Stuttgart, 1877); A. Prümers, *F. Silcher: der Meister des deutschen Volkslieds* (Stuttgart, 1910); G. Brügel, *Kritische Mitteilungen zu Silchers Volksliedern,* in the 'Sammelbände der Internationalen Musik-Gesellschaft' (1914); A. Bopp, *F. Silcher* (Stuttgart, 1916); A. Bopp, *Liederbuch aus Schwaben* (1918); H. Kleinert and H. Rauschnabel, eds., *F. Silcher* (Stuttgart, 1935); A. Lämmle, *F. Silcher* (Mühlacker, 1956).

Siloti (zē-loh'-tē), **Alexander Ilyitch,** Russian pianist and conductor; b. Kharkov, Oct. 9, 1863; d. New York, Dec. 8, 1945. He studied piano with Zverev in Moscow, and later with Nicholas Rubinstein and Tchaikovsky at the Moscow Cons. (1876-81), winning the gold medal. He made his début as pianist in Moscow (1880); appeared with great success in Leipzig in 1883; then studied for 3 years with Liszt at Weimar. From 1887 to 1890 he was prof. at the Moscow Cons.; among his students was Rachmaninoff (his first cousin). Between 1890 and 1900 he made numerous concert tours, settling for short periods in Paris, Frankfurt, Antwerp, Leipzig, and Berlin; returned to Russia in 1901; conducted the concerts of the Moscow Philharmonic Society for the season of 1901-02. In 1903 he organized his own orch. in St. Petersburg, with which he gave an annual series of symph. concerts, playing many new works by Russian composers. His piano tours in Europe and America (from 1898) established his reputation as one of Liszt's most talented pupils. He left Russia in 1918; was in England in 1919; settled in New York in 1922; in 1925 joined the faculty of the Juilliard School of Music, N. Y., retiring in 1942. He publ. a collection of piano pieces from his concert programs (with fingering and indications for pedalling); edited concertos by Bach and Vivaldi, etc.; publ. *My Memories of Liszt* (in English; Edinburgh, 1913).

Silva, Luigi, cellist; b. Milan, Nov. 13, 1903, of a musical family; his father was a vocal teacher; his mother a Viennese singer. He studied piano with his father and composition with Respighi in Rome; cello with Arturo Bonucci in Bologna at the Liceo Musicale; graduated in 1923; was cellist in the Rome Opera orch.; received the Boccherini Prize at the First National Contest for young concert artists in Rome; was a member of the Quartetto di Roma; then taught at the Cherubini Cons. in Florence. He came to the U. S. in 1939; was head of the cello and chamber music dept. at the Eastman School of Music, Rochester (1941-49); from 1949, member of the faculty of the Juilliard School of Music, N. Y., the Mannes College of Music, and the School of Music at Yale Univ. He made transcriptions for cello of works by Boccherini, Della Ciaia, Piatti, Paganini, etc.; edited Bach's unaccompanied compositions include 3 symphonies, a clarinet cello suites.

Silva, Oscar da, Portuguese pianist and composer; b. Paranhos, near Oporto, April 21, 1870. He studied at the Lisbon Cons.; in 1892 took lessons at the Leipzig Cons. with Reinecke and Jadassohn; also for a brief time studied with Clara Schumann. Returning to Portugal, he settled in Leça da Palmeira in 1910; taught piano in Oporto; then gave concerts in America, Brazil, South Africa, and Egypt. In 1932 he went to Rio de Janeiro, remaining there until 1952, when he returned to Portugal, living in retirement at Lisbon. He wrote an opera, *Dona Mecia* (Lisbon, July 4, 1901); a symph. poem, *Alma crucificada;* a number of piano pieces: *Rapsodia portuguesa, Estudos indefinidos, Papillon dans le jardin, Paginas portuguesas* (14 numbers); songs (to French words); 2 string quartets; a piano quartet; etc. —Cf. A. Pinto, *Musica moderna portuguesa e os seus representantes* (Lisbon, 1930, pp. 114-29).

Silva, (David) Poll da, French composer; b. St.-Esprit, near Bayonne, March 28, 1834; d. Clermont, Oise, May 9, 1875. He went to Paris in 1854, and Halévy advised him to enter the Cons., but he was prevented by failure of his eyesight; when he became quite blind, his mother wrote out his compositions from dictation. Thus handicapped, he succeeded nonetheless in composing 3 operas; a ballet; 2 oratorios; cantatas and other choral works; 2 symphonies; chamber music; songs; piano pieces.

Silva Leite, Antonio da, see **Leite, Antonio da Silva.**

Silver (sil-vär'), **Charles,** French composer; b. Paris, April 16, 1868; d. there, Oct. 10, 1949. He studied with Dubois and Massenet at the Paris Cons., winning the Grand Prix de Rome in 1891 with the cantata *L'Interdit.* He wrote the operas *La Belle au bois dormant* (Marseilles, 1902); *Le Clos* (Paris, 1906); *Myriane* (Nice, 1913); *La Mégère apprivoisée* (Paris, Jan. 30, 1922); *La Grand'-mère* (Oct. 7, 1930); *Quatre-vingt-treize* (Paris, Jan. 24, 1936); also orchestral works, songs, etc.

Simandl (zē'-mahndl), **Franz,** double-bass player and composer; b. Blatna, Bohemia, Aug. 1, 1840; d. Vienna, Dec. 13, 1912. He was 1st double-bass player in the Vienna court orch.; from 1869, taught at the Vienna Cons.; publ. *Neueste Methode des Kontrabass-Spiels* (in 3 parts) and *30 Etüden für Kontrabass; Die hohe Schule des Kontrabass-Spiels,* a collection of concertos, studies, solo pieces, etc. His original compositions include a *Konzertstück, Konzert-Étude,* a concerto, fantasias, and minor pieces for his instrument.

Simila, Martti, Finnish conductor; b. Uleaborg, April 9, 1898; d. Lahti, Jan. 8, 1958. He studied in Finland; then in Paris and London; conducted the Helsinski Opera (1927-44) and the Helsinki Municipal Orch. (1945-50); became conductor of the Municipal Orch. of Lahti in 1951. He made 2 tours in the U. S. as pianist, in 1923 and 1926; was again in the U. S. in 1957, and conducted a memorial concert of the music of Sibelius with the N. Y. Philharmonic, Dec. 8, 1957.

Simmons, Homer, American pianist and composer; b. Evansville, Ind., Aug. 6, 1900. He studied piano with Homer Grunn in Los Angeles; went to Rome in 1931, where he took courses in orchestration with Respighi, and then spent some time in Switzerland, taking lessons from Paderewski at Morges; also studied counterpoint with Nadia Boulanger in Paris. His works include *Phantasmania* for piano and orch. (Hollywood Bowl, 1929, composer soloist); *California Nights,* for piano and orch.; *Impressions Basques,* for orch.; *Lyra Davidica* for 2 pianos and string quartet; *Panels from a Lacquered*

Screen for voice and string quartet; *Evenings in Old Vienna,* for 2 pianos and string quartet; numerous piano pieces and songs. He settled in Sunland, California.

Simon, Alicia, Polish musicologist; b. Lodz, Nov. 13, 1879. She studied in Warsaw and Wiesbaden; attended classes of Kretzschmar and Johannes Wolf at the Univ. of Berlin; *Dr. phil.* at Zürich (1914); in 1918 she came to the U. S.; from 1924 to 1928 was on the staff of the Library of Congress, Washington; later returned to Poland. She publ. *Polnische Elemente in der deutschen Musik bis zur Zeit der Wiener Klassiker* (Zürich, 1916); *The Polish Songwriters* (in English; Warsaw, 1936; 2nd ed., 1939); edited sonatas by Telemann.

Simon, Anton, French composer; b. 1851; d. in Russia, c. 1918. He studied at the Paris Cons. with Marmontel (piano); settled in Moscow in 1871, and taught at the Philharmonic Institute until 1891. He wrote the operas *Rolla* (Moscow, April 29, 1892), *The Song of Triumphant Love* (Moscow, Dec. 14, 1897), and *The Fishermen* (Moscow, March 7, 1899); a mimodrama, *Esmeralda* (1902); 2 ballets, *The Stars* (1898) and *Living Flowers* (1900); a piano concerto; a clarinet concerto; a symph. poem, *La Pécheresse;* chamber music, including 22 pieces for brass instruments; numerous piano pieces; about 100 songs.

Simon, James, German musicologist; b. Berlin, Sept. 29, 1880; d. in the Oswiecim concentration camp, c. 1941. He studied piano with Ansorge and composition with Max Bruch; musicology in Munich; *Dr. phil.,* 1904, with a dissertation on Vogler. He taught at the Klindworth-Scharwenka Cons. in Berlin (1907-19); in 1934 he left Germany and lived in Zürich, and later in Amsterdam, where he was arrested in 1941. He wrote an opera, *Frau im Stein* (Stuttgart, 1925); a cantata after Goethe, *Urworte;* symph. works; chamber music; songs.

Simon, Robert A., American music journalist; b. New York, Feb. 18, 1897. He graduated from the School of Journalism of Columbia Univ. in 1920; in 1925 began to contribute music criticism to the 'New Yorker' magazine (until 1945); also was active as writer of lyrics for musical comedies; author of the libretto of *Garrick,* opera with music by Albert Stoessel (N. Y., 1937). He publ. a book of comic songs, *Bronx Ballads,* for which he wrote both text and music (1927).

Simonds (sī'-mündz), **Bruce,** American pianist and pedagogue; b. Bridgeport, Conn., July 5, 1895. After studying at Yale Univ. (A.B. 1917; Mus.B., 1918; A.M., 1938), he attended the Schola Cantorum in Paris (1919-21) and the Matthay School in London (1920-21). Made his début as a pianist in Europe in 1921; in the same year returned to the U.S. and embarked on a successful career as concert pianist; also in 1921 joined the teaching staff at Yale; prof. since 1938; dean of the Yale School of Music, 1941-54. Publ. 2 organ pieces and one for violin.

Simonetti, Achille, Italian-British violinist; b. Turin, June 12, 1857; d. London, Nov. 19, 1928. He studied violin with Gamba at the Milan Cons. and with Dancla at the Paris Cons.; toured in England with the singer Marie Rôze and the double-bass virtuoso Bottesini; settled in London in 1891, but made frequent tours on the Continent. He wrote a cadenza for Brahms' violin concerto, which he played for the first time in Dresden (Dec. 11, 1896); composed numerous solo pieces for the violin.

Simpson (or **Sympson**), **Christopher,** English player of the viola da gamba and composer; b. Yorkshire, c. 1610; d. Scampton, Lincolnshire, 1669. He fought on the Royalist side in the English civil war (1643) and later entered the service of Sir Robert Bolles as music tutor to the latter's son. Simpson was famous as a composer. —Published works: *The Division Violist or an Introduction to the Playing Upon a Ground: Divided into 2 Parts* (London, 1659; 2nd ed. with title and text in Latin and English, in 3 parts, London, 1665; 3rd ed., 1712, with 2 sonatas for viola da gamba; modern ed. by Nathalie Dolmetsch, London, 1958); *The Principles of Practicle Musick . . . either in Singing or Playing upon an Instrument* (London, 1665; enlarged ed., as *Practicall Musick in 5 Parts teaching by a new and easie Method,* London, 1667); also compiled annotations to Campion's *Art of Discant* (1655). In MS: *Months and Seasons:* Fancies, Airs, Galliards, for 2 basses and a treble; Fancies for viola da gamba; etc.

Simpson, George Elliott, American music educator and composer; b. Orange, N. J., Nov. 1, 1876. He studied with Emil Mollenhauer (violin) in N. Y. (1886-90); then took composition lessons with Carl Busch in Kansas City (1894-1900); subsequently studied at the Leipzig Cons. with Jadassohn and Reinecke (1900-03). He taught in Kansas City (1903-07); then occupied various teaching and executive positions in Texas, returning to Kansas City in 1918; in 1954 was living there as counselor with a public relations firm. He wrote 12 tone-poems; 4 overtures; publ. about 50 piano pieces and 80 songs. His *American Symphony* was performed for the first time in Kansas City, on March 26, 1925.

Simpson, Robert, English writer on music and composer; b. Leamington, March 2, 1921. He studied at Durham Univ.; Mus. D., 1952; joined the staff of the B.B.C. He publ. a valuable monograph, *Carl Nielsen, Symphonist* (London, 1952), and contributed articles to various music magazines. Among his compositions are a symphony (1951), 3 string quartets (1951-54), and piano pieces.

Simpson (or **Sympson**), **Thomas,** English composer; from about 1610 he was musician to the Prince of Holstein-Schaumburg, and from 1618 in the royal chapel at Copenhagen. An outstanding instrumental composer, he publ. *Opusculum newer Pavanen* (Frankfurt, 1610); *Pavanen, Galliarden, Courtanten und Volten* (Frankfurt, 1611; reprinted in 1617 under the title *Opus newer Paduanen, Galliarden, Intraden, Canzonen,* etc.); and *Tafel-Consort, allerhand lustige Lieder von 4 Instrumenten und Generalbass* (Hamburg, 1621). —Cf. G. Oberst, *Englische Orchestersuiten um 1600* (Wolfenbüttel, 1929); E. Mohr, *Die Allemande* (Zürich, 1932).

Simrock, Nikolaus, founder of the famous publishing house in Berlin; b. Mainz, 1752; d. Bonn, 1833. He played the horn in the electoral orch. in Bonn (1774-90); then abandoned playing to establish a music business; he publ. a number of Beethoven's works. His son, **Peter Joseph Simrock** (b. Bonn, Aug. 13, 1792; d. there, Dec. 13, 1868), succeeded him, and greatly increased the prestige of the house by acquiring the early works of Brahms. He was succeeded by his son, **Fritz August Simrock** (b. Bonn, Jan. 2, 1838; d. Lausanne, Aug. 20, 1901), who moved to Berlin in 1870, and added the works of Dvořák to the catalogue. His nephew **Hans Simrock** (d. Berlin, June 26, 1910), reorganized the firm in 1902 as a stock company, and established branches in London and Paris. Fritz Auckenthaler (grandson of Fritz Simrock) was head of the firm from 1920 to 1930; in 1930 he sold the business to A. Benjamin. —Cf. W. Ottendorf-Simrock, *Das Haus Simrock* (Ratingen, 1954). See also the correspondence between Simrock and Brahms (vols. IX-XII of the Brahms correspondence).

Šín (shin), **Otakar,** eminent Czech teacher and composer; b. Rokytno, Moravia, April 23, 1881; d. Prague, Jan. 21, 1943. He studied organ at the Prague Cons., where he was appointed prof. of theory in 1919; publ. a textbook of harmony (Prague, 1922; 6th ed., 1949); also a manual on counterpoint and fugue (1936); wrote several symph. poems and overtures based on Czech national themes.

Sinclair, George Robertson, English organist; b. Croydon, Oct. 28, 1863; d. Birmingham, Feb. 7, 1917. He received his musical education in Dublin; became assistant to the organist of the Gloucester Cathedral, C. H. Lloyd (1879). In 1889 he was appointed organist of Hereford Cathedral, and also conducted the Three Choirs Festivals (1891-1912). He acquired a reputation as a master organist; the 11th variation of Elgar's *Enigma* is inscribed to Sinclair ('G. R. S.'), and portrays vividly Sinclair's virtuosity in the use of the organ pedals. — Cf. 'Mus. Times' (Oct., 1900; March, 1906; March, 1917).

Sinding, Christian, Norwegian composer; b. Kongsberg, Jan. 11, 1856; d. Oslo, Dec. 3, 1941. He studied first with L. Lindeman in Norway; then at the Leipzig Cons. with Schradieck (violin), Jadassohn (theory), and Reinecke (orchestration); after 4 years (1877-81) he returned to Norway, and had his piano quartet and a symphony performed in Oslo; a government stipend enabled him to continue his studies in Germany, and he spent 2 years (1882-84) in Munich, Berlin, and Dresden; there he wrote his 1st opera, *Titandros,* much influenced by Wagner. On Dec. 19, 1885, he gave a concert of his works in Oslo; during another stay in Germany, his piano quintet was played in Leipzig with Brodsky and Busoni among the performers (Jan. 19, 1889); Erika Lie-Nissen played his piano concerto in Berlin (Feb. 23, 1889). He publ. a number of piano pieces in Germany; of these *Frühlingsrauschen* became an international favorite. His opera to a German text, *Der heilige Berg* (1914), was not successful. In 1915 he received a pension for life of 4,000 crowns 'for distinguished service'; on his 60th birthday (1916) the Norwegian government presented him with a purse of 30,000 crowns, as a mark of appreciation for 'the greatest national composer since Grieg.' He was invited by George Eastman to teach at the Eastman School of

Music in Rochester, N. Y., during the academic season 1921-22; after this journey, he lived mostly in Oslo. He continued to compose, and toward the end of his life wrote in larger forms; his 3rd symph. was conducted by Nikisch with the Berlin Philharmonic in 1921; and his 4th symph. was performed on his 80th birthday in Oslo (1936). His works aggregate to 132 opus numbers. Most of his music is of a descriptive nature; his lyric pieces for piano and his songs are fine examples of Scandinavian Romanticism, but the German inspiration of his formative years is much in evidence; he was chiefly influenced by Schumann and Liszt. —Works: Operas *Titandros* (1884; not produced); *Der heilige Berg* (Dessau, April 19, 1914). For orch.: symph. No. 1 (Oslo, March 25, 1882); symph. No. 2 (Berlin, March 22, 1907); symph. No. 3 (Berlin, Jan. 10, 1921); symph. No. 4, subtitled *Vinter og Vaar* (Oslo, Jan. 11, 1936); *Épisodes chevaleresques,* op. 35 (1888); *Rondo infinito,* op. 42 (1889; revised, 1897); piano concerto in D-flat (Berlin, Feb. 23, 1889); 3 violin concertos (1898, 1901, 1917); *Legende* for violin and orch., op. 46 (1900); *Romanze* for violin and orch., op. 100 (1910); *Abendstimmung,* for violin and orch., op. 120 (1915); several cantatas and other choral works. Chamber music: string quartet, op. 70 (1904); piano quintet, op. 5 (1884); 3 piano trios: op. 23 (1893), op. 64 (1902), op. 87 (1908); 4 violin sonatas: op. 12 (1894), op. 27 (1895), op. 73 (1905), op. 99, subtitled *Sonate im alten Stil* (1909); 4 violin suites: op. 10 (1889), op. 14 (1891), op. 96 (1909), op. 123 (1919); *Scènes de la vie* for violin and piano, op. 51 (1900); *Cantus doloris,* variations for violin and piano, op. 78 (1906); 3 capricci for violin and piano, op. 114 (1913); etc.; *Nordische Ballade,* for cello and piano, op. 105 (1911); etc. For piano: sonata, op. 91 (1909); *Fatum,* variations, op. 94 (1909); *5 Stücke,* op. 24 (1894), *7 Stücke,* op. 25 (1895), *6 Stücke,* op. 31 (1896), *6 Stücke,* op. 32 (1896; No. 3 is the celebrated *Frühlingsrauschen), 6 Charakterstücke,* op. 33 (1896; contains *A la Menuetto* and *Ständchen), 6 Charakterstücke,* op. 34 (1896; contains *Chanson), 6 Klavierstücke,* op. 49 (1899; contains *Humoresque), Mélodies mignonnes,* op. 52 (1900), *4 Morceaux de salon,* op. 54 (1900; contains *Sérénade);* etc. Songs: *Alte Weisen,* op. 1 (1886), *Lieder und Gesänge,* op. 11 (1888; contains *Viel Träume* and *Ein Weib), Galmandssange,* op. 22 (1893; contains *Mainat), Nyinger,* op. 90 (1908), etc.; about 250 publ. songs in all. A complete list of Sinding's works was publ. by Ö. Gaukstad, in the 'Norsk Musikkgranskning' (1938).

Singelée (san-zhü-lā'), **Jean-Baptiste,** Belgian violinist and composer; b. Brussels, Sept. 25, 1812; d. Ostend, Sept. 29, 1875. He publ. 144 works (2 concertos, many solos for violin, fantasias on operatic airs, etc.).

Singer, Edmund, violinist; b. Totis, Hungary, Oct. 14, 1830; d. Stuttgart, Jan. 23, 1912. He studied in Budapest, and later at the Paris Cons.; was concertmaster in Weimar (1853-61); later, prof. at the Stuttgart Cons. He publ. a number of attractive violin pieces: *Tarantella, Rapsodie hongroise, Airs variés, etc.;* wrote cadenzas for the violin concertos of Beethoven and Brahms; edited the études of Rode, Kreutzer, Fiorillo, Rovelli, and Gaviniés; with M. Seifriz, compiled the *Grosse theoretisch-praktische Violinschule* (2 vols., 1884).

Singer, Kurt, German musicologist; b. Berent, Oct. 11, 1885; d. in the Terezin concentration camp, Jan., 1944. He studied musicology with Friedlaender in Berlin; also became a doctor of medicine; wrote criticisms for the socialist newspaper 'Vorwärts.' In 1935, deprived of his posts in German organizations, he became music director of the 'Reichsverband jüdischer Kulturbünde.' He went to Holland in 1939, but was arrested there by the invading Germans, and eventually perished. —Writings: *Richard Wagner* (1913); *Bruckners Chormusik* (1924); *Berufskrankheiten der Musiker* (1927; in English as *Diseases of the Musical Profession,* N. Y., 1932); *Heilwirkung der Musik* (1927); etc.

Singer, Otto, pianist and composer; b. Sorą, Germany, July 26, 1833; d. New York, Jan. 3, 1894. He studied piano with Moscheles in Leipzig and with Liszt in Weimar; in 1867 he emigrated to America; after a few years in N. Y., he became instructor at the Cincinnati College of Music, returning to N. Y. shortly before his death. He wrote 2 cantatas, *The Landing of the Pilgrim Fathers* (1876) and *Festival Ode* (1878); 2 piano concertos; a piano sonata and other piano music. —His son, **Otto Singer, Jr.** (b. Dresden, Sept. 14, 1863; d. Leipzig, Jan. 8, 1931), was a student of Rheinberger in Munich; was active as choral conductor in Leipzig (1892-1900 and from 1922) and Berlin (1900-19); publ. a *Konzertstück* for violin and orch.; a piano quintet; male choruses; made vocal scores of operas by Wagner and Richard Strauss.

Singer, Peter, Austrian composer and music theorist; b. Häselgehr (Lechthal), July 18, 1810; d. Salzburg, Jan. 26, 1882. He was a Franciscan monk; composed 101 Masses, about 600 offertories, etc.; publ. 'Cantus choralis in provincia Tirolensi consuetus' (1862). In 1839 he invented the 'Pansymphonikon,' a kind of orchestrion with reeds; publ. *Metaphysische Blicke in die Tonwelt, nebst einem . . . neuen System der Tonwissenschaft* (1847). —Cf. Pater Hartmann, *Peter Singer* (Innsbruck, 1910).

Singher, Martial, French baritone; b. Oloron-Sainte-Marie, Aug. 14, 1904. He sang in a boys' choir in Biarritz and later studied singing at the Paris Cons. (Premier Prix, 1929). In 1930-41, sang at the Paris Opéra; also appeared in opera houses in Sweden, Denmark, Switzerland, Belgium, and Holland; married Margareta Busch (daughter of Fritz Busch) on Jan. 10, 1940. He made his American début at the Metropolitan Opera, Dec. 10, 1943; then appeared in the U. S. and Canada in recitals and with orchestras as well as in operatic roles.

Singleton, Esther, American writer on music; b. Baltimore, Nov. 4, 1865; d. Stonington, Conn., July 2, 1930. She lived most of her life in N. Y.; publ. *A Guide to the Operas* (1899); *A Guide to Modern Opera* (1909); *The Orchestra and Its Instruments* (1917); contributed the chapter on American music to Lavignac's 'Encyclopédie de la Musique' (1915).

Sinico (sē'-nē-koh), **Francesco,** Italian choral conductor and composer; b. Trieste, Dec. 12, 1810; d. there, Aug. 18, 1865. He studied with G. Farinelli; was organist and conductor in various churches; in 1843 established his own singing school in Trieste, providing excellent training for choral singing. He produced his opera *I Virtuosi di Barcellona* in 1841. —His son, **Giuseppe Sinico** (b. Trieste, Feb. 10, 1836; d. there, Dec. 31, 1907), continued the popular singing classes at the Sinico School in Trieste; wrote several operas, which he produced there: *Marinella* (Aug. 26, 1854), *I Moschettieri* (March 26, 1859), *Aurora di Nevers* (March 12, 1861), *Alessandro Stradella* (Lugo, Sept. 19, 1863), and *Spartaco* (Nov. 20, 1886). He publ. a *Breve metodo teorico-pratico di canto elementare.* —Cf. *Una Famiglia triestina di musicisti 'I Sinico'* (Trieste, 1932).

Sinigaglia (sē-nē-gah'-lyah), **Leone,** Italian composer; b. Turin, Aug. 14, 1868; d. there, May 16, 1944. He was a pupil at the Turin Cons., studying with Giovanni Bolzoni; later in Vienna (1895-1900) with Mandyczewski, and in Prague with Dvořák. His first successful work was a violin concerto dedicated to Arrigo Serato (1900), who played it with considerable success in the principal cities of Germany. His early works were much influenced by Brahms and Dvořák; then he turned for inspiration to the music of his native Piedmont, and in this field achieved a lasting reputation. Toscanini conducted in Turin the première of Sinigaglia's suite *Danze Piemontesi* on popular themes (May 14, 1905); later he publ. a collection of songs (6 albums), *Vecchie canzoni populari del Piemonte;* another work in the folksong manner is the symph. suite *Piemonte* (1909; Utrecht, Feb. 16, 1910); he further wrote *Le Baruffe Chiozzotte,* an overture to Goldoni's comedy (Utrecht, Dec. 21, 1907); *Rapsodia piemontese,* for violin and orch.; *Romanze,* for violin and orch.; *Variations on a Theme of Brahms,* for string quartet (1901); *Serenade* for string trio (1906); cello sonata (1923). Like Sgambati, Sinigaglia did not write any music for the theater. —Cf. E. Desderi, *L. Sinigaglia,* in the 'Rivista Musicale Italiana' (1946).

Siohan, Robert, French composer and conductor; b. Paris, Feb. 27, 1894. He studied at the Paris Cons. In 1929 he founded the Concerts Siohan (suspended in 1936); conducted at the Paris Opéra (1932-47); taught at the Paris Cons. —Works: the cantatas *Cantique au frère soleil* (1928) and *Hypérion* (1945); a violin concerto; a cello concerto; piano concerto; string quartet; choral pieces. Also publ. *Horizons sonores; évolution actuelle de l'art musical* (Paris, 1956).

Siqueira, José, Brazilian composer and conductor; b. Conceição, June 24, 1907. He studied composition with Francisco Braga, and conducting with Burle Marx. His works include 2 overtures, 3 symph. poems, a symphony, 5 pieces for string orch., chamber music, piano pieces, and songs, most of them based on Brazilian folk melodies. He visited the U. S. in 1944; conducted in Russia in 1955. Publ. a *Curso de instrumentação* (Rio de Janeiro, 1945).

Širola (shē'-roh-lah), **Božidar,** Croatian musicologist and composer; b. Žakanj, Dec. 20, 1889; d. Zagreb, April 10, 1956. He studied at the Univ. of Vienna; *Dr. phil.,* 1921. He was on the faculty of the Zagreb Cons. (1935-41); in 1945, became director of the Zagreb Ethnographic Museum. —

Works: the operas: *Comedy in Stanac* (1916), *Cittern and Drum* (1930), *The Village Chaplain* (1940); 8 oratorios; 4 Masses; a symph.; 9 string quartets; 3 piano trios; *24 Inventions* for piano solo; 8 piano sonatas; several song cycles; publ. (in German) several papers on Croatian music; also arrangements of folksongs.

Sistermans, Anton, Dutch bass singer; b. Hertogenbosch, Aug. 5, 1865; d. The Hague, March 18, 1926. He studied with Stockhausen in Frankfurt; from 1895 gave concerts in Europe; his only appearance in opera was as Pogner (Bayreuth, 1899). From 1904 to 1915 he taught singing at the Klindworth-Scharwenka Cons., Berlin; then lived in The Hague.

Sitt, Hans, violinist and composer; b. Prague, Sept. 21, 1850; d. Leipzig, March 10, 1922. He studied at the Prague Cons.; held various positions as violinist and conductor of theater orchestras in Breslau, Prague, and Chemnitz. In 1881 he settled in Leipzig; organized a series of popular concerts there; was viola player in the Brodsky Quartet; conducted the 'Bachverein' (1885-1903) and other musical societies there. He wrote 3 violin concertos, a viola concerto, 2 cello concertos; publ. valuable studies for the violin; also *Praktische Violaschule; Schulausgabe neuerer Violinlitteratur* (5 books); and (with Reinecke) *Lyrica,* a collection of 30 classic and romantic pieces for violin and piano.

Sittard (zit'-tahrt), **Alfred,** German organist; son of Josef Sittard; b. Stuttgart, Nov. 4, 1878; d. Berlin, March 31, 1942. He studied with his father, and later with Wüllner at the Cologne Cons.; was organist at the Kreuzkirche in Dresden (1903-12), and then at St. Michael's in Hamburg (1912-25). In 1925 he was appointed prof. of organ at the Berlin Akademie für Kirchen- und Schulmusik, and in 1933 became Kapellmeister of the Berlin Cathedral chorus. He publ. *3 Choralstudien* for organ; also wrote *Das Hauptorgelwerk und die Hilfsorgel der Michaeliskirche in Hamburg* (1912).

Sittard, Josef, German music historian; b. Aix-la-Chapelle, June 4, 1846; d. Hamburg, Nov. 24, 1903. He studied at the Stuttgart Cons., and later joined its faculty as instructor in singing and piano; from 1885 was music critic for the Hamburg 'Correspondent.' He publ. several valuable papers dealing with German city music; *Studien und Charakteristiken* (1889, collected essays); *Geschichte des Musik- und Concertwesens in Hamburg* (1890); *Zur Geschichte der Musik und des Theaters am Württembergischen Hofe* (2 vols., 1890, 1891); etc.; also composed some choral works and songs.

Sivori, Camillo, Italian violinist; b. Genoa, Oct. 25, 1815; d. there, Feb. 19, 1894. His first teacher was Restano; he played in public at the age of 6; was presented to Paganini, who was greatly impressed and agreed to take Sivori as a pupil. Still as a child, Sivori produced a sensation at his appearances in Paris and London (1827); after a period of further study with Giacomo Costa (Paganini's teacher), Sivori resumed his concerts; at the age of 16, he undertook a grand journey through Austria, Germany, and Russia. From 1846 to 1850 he made an extensive tour through North and South America. His style of playing was modeled after Paganini's, and his virtuosity amazed musicians and audiences wherever he went. He composed 2 violin concertos; fantasies on airs from various operas for the violin; and numerous characteristic pieces: *Tarentelle napolitaine, Carnaval de Chili, Carnaval de Cuba, Carnaval américain, Folies espagnoles,* etc. —Cf. E. James, *Camillo Sivori* (London, 1845); L. Escudier, *Mes Souvenirs* (Paris, 1863); A. Pierrottet, *Camillo Sivori* (Milan, 1896).

Sixt, Johann Abraham, German organist and composer; b. Gräfenhausen, Württemberg, Jan. 3, 1757; d. Donaueschingen, Jan. 30, 1797. He was the son of a schoolmaster and organist; received his musical training at home; traveled in Germany; was in Vienna in 1784, and received a recommendation from Mozart. He then settled in Donaueschingen, and remained there for 13 years as piano teacher and chamber musician to the court, until his death. He wrote piano trios, sonatas, and other instrumental works; of particular interest are his lieder, with long introductions in the accompaniment, setting the mood of the text; some of these have been brought out in a modern ed. by Erich Fischer.

Sjöberg (shö'-behrg), **Svante Leonard,** Swedish organist, conductor, and composer; b. Karlskrona, Aug. 28, 1873; d. there, Jan. 18, 1935. He studied at the Stockholm Cons. with Nordquist and Dente; in Berlin with Max Bruch (composition). Returning to Sweden in 1901, he was organist at the Stadskyrka in Karlskrona, and conductor of the Musikförening there (1901-34). He wrote an overture to *Gustaf Vasa* (1901);

a violin sonata and other chamber music; also songs.

Sjögren (shö'-gren), **Emil,** Swedish composer; b. Stockholm, June 16, 1853; d. there, March 1, 1918. He studied composition at the Stockholm Cons. with H. Berens, in Berlin with Kiel, and in Vienna with Grädener. In 1891 he was appointed organist at St. John's Church in Stockholm. His importance as composer rests chiefly on his songs, of which he wrote about 200, to texts in Swedish, French, and German; he also wrote a festival overture; several choruses; 5 violin sonatas; a cello sonata; 2 piano sonatas; several groups of lyric pieces for piano. Nils Brodén compiled an index of all of Sjögren's publ. compositions (Stockholm, 1918). A complete ed. of his songs was undertaken by the Swedish Academy in 1950-51. —Cf. S. E. Svensson, *Emil Sjögrens vokala lyrik,* in 'Svensk Tidskrift för Musikforskning' (1935).

Skalkottas, Nikos, talented Greek composer; b. Chalcis, March 8, 1904; d. Athens, Sept. 19, 1949. He studied with his father and his uncle; then at the Odeon in Athens, graduating as a violinist in 1920. In 1921 he went to Berlin, where he studied violin with Willy Hess and composition with Kurt Weill and Jarnach. From 1927 to 1933 he studied with Schoenberg, whose instruction determined his style (dodecaphonic, but with an original approach; in his book *Style and Idea* Schoenberg mentions Skalkottas as one of his most gifted disciples). Returning to Athens in 1933, Skalkottas continued to compose despite difficult material circumstances and lack of recognition. His music attracted serious attention only after his death, and a committee was formed in Athens to promote performance and publication of his works. His orchestral suite from the folk tale *Im Maienzauber* was performed posthumously in Vienna (March 18, 1951); his *Petite Suite* for orch. at the Venice Festival (1953). He wrote further an overture, *The Return of Odysseus* (1945); symphony for wind instruments (1947); *Sinfonietta* (1948); ballet suite *La Mer grecque* (1948); 36 Greek dances for orch. (4 of these dances were publ. in full score in Athens, and have had frequent performances in Europe and America); 2 piano concertos (1933; 1938); cello concerto (1937); violin concerto (1938) and a concerto for 2 violins; 4 violin sonatinas (1930); 4 string quartets (1930-40); piano trio (1936); string trio (1938); duo for violin and viola (1940); duo for violin and cello (1947); piano pieces; songs.

Škerjanc (shkār-yants), **Lucijan Maria,** composer; b. Graz, Dec. 17, 1900; studied in Vienna, Basel, and Paris; then was prof. of composition at the Academy of Music in Ljubljana. His music reflects neo-Romantic ideas, with superimposed Impressionist effects. Between 1933 and 1945 he wrote 5 symphonies, 2 violin concertos (1940, 1943), and a *Fantasia* for piano and orch. (1944); he also composed 5 string quartets (1917-45) and several cantatas; publ. a manual on counterpoint (1951).

Skilton, Charles Sanford, American composer; b. Northampton, Mass., Aug. 16, 1868; d. Lawrence, Kansas, March 12, 1941. After graduating from Yale Univ. (B.A., 1889) he studied in New York with Harry Rowe Shelley (organ) and Dudley Buck (composition); then went to Germany, where he studied with Bargiel at the Hochschule für Musik in Berlin (1891-93). From 1893 to 1896 he was director of music at the Salem Academy and College, N. C., and conducted the local orchestra there; then filled a similar post at the State Normal School, Trenton, N. J. (1898-1903); in 1903 he was engaged as prof. of organ and theory at the Univ. of Kansas, Lawrence, where he remained most of his life. He made a detailed study of Indian music, and introduced Indian motifs into the traditional forms of a suite or a fantasy. —Works: the operas *The Sun Bride* (radio performance, April 17, 1930), *Kalopin* (not produced; received the David Bispham Memorial Medal of the American Opera Society of Chicago, 1930), *The Day of Gayomair* (1936; not produced); for orch.: *Suite Primeval,* on Indian melodies, in 2 parts: *2 Indian Dances* (originally for string quartet, 1915; Minneapolis, Oct. 29, 1916); part II (Minneapolis, Nov. 13, 1921); *Autumn Night* (Detroit, Dec. 11, 1930); *Shawnee Indian Hunting Dance* (Detroit, Dec. 11, 1930); *A Carolina Legend,* symph. poem; *Mt. Oread,* overture; *Sioux Flute Serenade,* for small orch. (1920); cantata *The Witch's Daughter* (1918); *The Guardian Angel,* oratorio (1925); *From Forest and Stream* (1930); *Midnight,* for women's voices; *The Fountain,* for women's voices; a string quartet; a sonatina for violin and piano; a *Sarabande* for wind instruments. Also publ. *Modern Symphonic Forms* (N. Y., 1927). —Cf. J. T. Howard, *Charles Sanford Skilton* (N. Y., 1929).

Skinner, Ernest M., American organ builder; b. Clarion, Pa., Jan. 15, 1866. He was the founder of the Ernest M. Skinner

Co., organ builders, originally of Dorchester, later of Methuen, Mass. Until 1905 the business was carried on by Skinner himself; it was then incorporated, with Skinner as president. From 1917 to 1932 he was technical director of the Skinner Organ Co., which in 1932 was merged with the Aeolian Co. of Garwood, N. J., and became the Aeolian-Skinner Organ Co. Skinner was especially successful in the construction of organ pipes reproducing the exact tone color of the various woodwind instruments and the French horn; among several important inventions is the 'duplex windchest,' by means of which the stops of 2 manuals are made interchangeable, and the arrangement of placing the stops on swinging sides. The Skinner Co. built the organ in the National Cathedral at Washington, D.C. Skinner publ. a valuable book, *The Modern Organ* (1915; 6th ed., 1945), and *The Composition of the Organ* (1947). He celebrated his 90th birthday on Jan. 15, 1956.

Skriabin. See **Scriabin.**

Škroup (or **Skraup**) (shkrŏh'-ŏŏp), **Franz (František)**, Czech composer and conductor; b. Osice, near Pardubice, June 3, 1801; d. Rotterdam, Feb. 7, 1862. He studied law in Prague, where he also sang in a chorus. In 1827 he became 2nd conductor at the subsidized Bohemian Theater, Prague, and 1st conductor in 1837; remained at that post until 1857, and put into performance several Wagner operas for the 1st time in Prague; also was an outstanding member of the national movement, and wrote several operas to Czech librettos, which he conducted at the Bohemian Theater: *Drátenik* (Feb. 2, 1826); *Oldřich a Božena* (Dec. 14, 1828); *Libušin snatek* (Nov. 6, 1835); also the German operas *Drahomira* (Nov. 20, 1848) and *Der Meergeuse* (Nov. 29, 1891). In 1860 Škroup took a position offered to him with a German opera troupe in Rotterdam, and died there after 2 seasons. Besides his operas, he wrote some chamber music and many popular Bohemian songs, of which *Kde domov muj* became so famous as to be mistaken for a folksong and was made into the Czech national anthem. —Cf. J. Plavec, *František Škroup* (Prague, 1946).

Škroup, Jan Nepomuk, Czech composer, brother of František Škroup; b. Osice, near Pardubice, Nov. 15, 1811; d. Prague, May 5, 1892. He was a chorusmaster at the Prague Opera; then devoted himself to church music; served as music director at various churches in Prague and finally at the Cathedral; in 1846, he was appointed teacher of singing at the Theological Seminary. He wrote manuals for church services: *Manuale pro sacris functionibus* and *Musica sacra pro populo;* also a vocal method.

Skrowaczewski (skrŏh-văh-chĕv'-skē), **Stanislaw,** Polish composer; b. Lwow, Oct. 3, 1923. He studied piano in Cracow; took composition lessons with Nadia Boulanger in Paris. Returning to Poland, he was appointed conductor of the State Philharmonic in Katowice (1948). —Works: 2 symphonies; 4 string quartets; piano sonata; violin sonata; etc.

Skuherský (skoo-hehr'-skē), **Franz (František) Zdeněk,** Czech composer, pianist, and pedagogue; b. Opočno, July 31, 1830; d. České Budějovice, Aug. 19, 1892. A student of medicine, he also had lessons in music with Kittl; from 1854 to 1866 he conducted the 'Musikverein' in Innsbruck; then returned to Prague, where he lectured at the Czech Univ., conducted the court orch., and taught at the Organ School. He also took great interest in the problem of church music in Bohemia, and participated in the movement for its reform. He publ. textbooks in Czech on musical form (1879), composition (1880-84), harmony (1882), organ (1883), etc.; some of them were translated into German. He wrote the operas *Vladimír, Bohuv Zvolenec* (Prague, Sept. 27, 1863) and *Rektor a General* (Prague, March 28, 1873), and a German opera *Der Liebesring* (Innsbruck, 1861); a symph. poem *May;* 4 Masses; *30 Orgelvorspiele in den Kirchentonarten* (without accidentals) and a similar set of organ pieces with accidentals; also many organ studies, piano pieces, and songs.

Slaughter, A. Walter, English composer; b. London, Feb., 1860; d. there, April 2, 1908. He was a chorister at St. Andrews, Wells St.; studied with A. Cellier and Jacobi. He was a conductor, successively, of the Royal Theatre, the Olympic, Drury Lane, and St. James's Theatre; wrote a number of musical stage works, among them the 3-act comic opera *Marjorie* (1889), *The Rose and the Ring* (after Thackeray; 1890), and a musical comedy, *The French Maid* (1897).

Slavenski (slah-ven'-skē), **Josip,** outstanding Yugoslav composer; b. Cakovec, May 11, 1896; d. Belgrade, Nov. 30, 1955. He went to Budapest and studied with Kodály and Herzfeld; his education was interrupted by World War I; he resumed his studies with Novák in Prague (1921-23); in 1924 he was appointed prof. at the Music Academy in Zagreb, later became prof. of theory at the Belgrade Cons. A musician of advanced ideas, he experimented with various musical systems, and devised a 'natural' scale of 53 tones to the octave. —Works: *Ursinfonie,* for orch., organ, and piano (1919-28); *Balkanophonia,* suite for orch. (Berlin, Jan. 25, 1929); a cantata, *Religionophonia;* chamber music; several albums of piano pieces on Balkan themes.

Slavík, Joseph, violinist; b. Jince, Bohemia, March 26, 1806; d. Budapest, May 30, 1833. He studied with Pixis at the Prague Cons.; from 1829 was a member of the Vienna Court orch. He wrote 2 violin concertos; double concerto for 2 violins; a string quartet; etc.

Sleeper, Henry Dike, American organist and music educator; b. Patten, Maine, Oct. 9, 1865; d. Winter Park, Fla., Jan. 28, 1948. He studied with J. K. Paine in Boston, and later in London. After teaching at various colleges, he joined the faculty of Smith College in 1898, and was head of the music dept. there from 1904 to 1924. He wrote a number of organ pieces and songs; was coeditor of *The Common Order Choir Book* (1903) and *Hymns of Worship and Service* (college edition).

Slenczynska (slen-chin'-skăh), **Ruth,** American pianist; b. Sacramento, Calif., Jan. 15, 1925. Her father, a violinist, taught her music, and she appeared in public as an infant; made her début in Berlin when she was 6, and played in Paris at the age of 7; also studied composition with Dandelot there. She aroused tremendous enthusiasm by her seemingly accomplished performances of difficult works at such an early age, and was able to give complete recitals of Classical and Romantic works without signs of fatigue; also was soloist with many orchestras. However, when she reappeared after a few years of further study, the critics found her playing mechanical and devoid of mature understanding. She thereupon abandoned her career altogether, married (later divorced), and took a job as a librarian in California. Her vindication as an artist came in 1954 when she resumed her interrupted career with excellent success. She publ. a candid book of memoirs (with Louis Biancolli), *Forbidden Childhood* (N. Y., 1957), in which she described the difficulties of a child prodigy's life.

Slezak (sleh'-zahk), **Leo,** famous tenor; b. Mährisch-Schönberg, Moravia, Aug. 18, 1873; d. Egern-on-the-Tegernsee, Bavaria, June 1, 1946. As a youth, he sang in the chorus of the Brünn Opera; made his début as Lohengrin there (March 17, 1896); the role became one of his outstanding successes. He was with the Berlin Opera for a season (1898-99); in 1901 became a member of the Vienna Opera, where he was active until 1926; also performed frequently in Prague, Milan, and Munich. Not satisfied with his vocal training, he went to Paris, where he studied with Jean de Reszke. He made his London début with marked acclaim as Otello (June 2, 1909); appeared in America for the first time also as Otello, with the Metropolitan Opera Co., N. Y. (Nov. 18, 1909); sang with the Metropolitan during its spring tour of 1910 and its summer season in Paris; subsequently sang also in Russia; gave recitals presenting distinguished programs, performed with impeccable taste. He also acted in motion pictures. He was a man of great general culture, and possessed exceptionally sharp literary wit, which he displayed in his reminiscences *Meine sämtlichen Werke* (1922) and *Der Wortbruch* (1927); both were later combined in a single volume (1935); English transl. as *Songs of Motley: Being the Reminiscences of a Hungry Tenor* (London, 1938); also publ. *Rückfall* (1930). A final book of memoirs, *Mein Lebensmärchen,* was publ. posthumously (1948).

Slonimsky, Nicolas, musicologist; b. St. Petersburg, April 27, 1894. He studied at the St. Petersburg Cons. with his aunt, Isabelle Vengerova (piano), Kalafati (harmony), and Maximilian Steinberg (orchestration). He came to the U. S. in 1923 (naturalized 1931) as opera coach at the Eastman School of Music, Rochester, N. Y.; moved to Boston in 1925, as secretary to Serge Koussevitzky (until 1927); from 1928 to 1930, conducted the Pierian Sodality, Harvard; organized the Chamber Orch. of Boston (1927-34); conducted modern American music in Paris, Berlin, Budapest, Havana, etc. (1931-33); toured South and Central America (1941-42); taught at various music schools and colleges; composed (mostly in small forms). —Books: *Music Since 1900* (N. Y., 1937; 3rd enlarged ed., 1949); *Music of Latin America* (N. Y., 1945; in Spanish, Buenos Aires, 1947); *The Road to Music* (N. Y., 1947); *Thesaurus of Scales and Melodic Patterns* (N. Y., 1947); *A Thing or Two About Music* (N. Y., 1948); *Lexicon of Musical*

Invective (N. Y., 1953); edited the 4th, 5th, 6th, and 7th eds. of Oscar Thompson's 'International Cyclopedia of Music and Musicians' (1946, 1949, 1952, 1956); edited and translated '50 Russian Art Songs, from Glinka to Shostakovitch' (N. Y., 1951); 1958, appointed to the editorial advisory board of the 'Encyclopædia Britannica' (in the field of American music). He is editor of the 5th edition (1958) of BAKER'S BIOGRAPHICAL DICTIONARY OF MUSICIANS.

Sloper, (Edward Hugh) Lindsay, English pianist and teacher; b. London, June 14, 1826; d. there, July 3, 1887. He studied with Moscheles at London, A. Schmitt at Frankfurt, and Rousselot at Paris; made his début in London (1846); became a very popular concert pianist and teacher there; also gave lectures. In 1880 was made prof. of piano playing at the Guildhall School of Music. He wrote many piano pieces; studies and textbooks for piano; songs; etc.

Smallens, Alexander, conductor; b. St. Petersburg, Jan. 1, 1889. He was brought to the U. S. as a child; graduated from the College of N. Y. (B. A., 1909); studied at the Institute of Musical Art (N. Y.) and at the Paris Cons. (1911). He was then engaged as assistant conductor of the Boston Opera (1911-14); conductor for the Anna Pavlova Ballet Co. on a tour of South America (1915-18); at the Chicago Opera Co. (1919-22); was music director of the Philadelphia Civic Opera (1924-31); assistant conductor of the Philadelphia Orch. (1927-34); conductor at the Robin Hood Dell summer concerts and at the Lewisohn Stadium concerts, N. Y., for several seasons; also with the Ballet Theater, N. Y.; from 1947 to 1950 he was musical director at the Radio City Music Hall. He was the original conductor of Gershwin's opera *Porgy and Bess,* and conducted this opera during its European tour in 1956.

Smallwood, Williams, English organist; b. Kendal, Dec. 31, 1831; d. there, Aug. 6, 1897. He studied with Dr. Camidge and H. Phillips; was organist of the Kendal Parish Church from 1847 till his death. He composed didactic piano pieces and salon music; also anthems, hymns, songs, etc. His *Pianoforte Tutor* had an immense sale.

Smareglia (smah-rehl'-yah), **Antonio,** Italian composer; b. Pola, Istria, May 5, 1854; d. Grado, near Trieste, April 15, 1929. He was trained in engineering before turning to music; studied composition with Franco Faccio at the Cons. of Milan. He became totally blind about 1905, but continued to compose by improvising on the piano with a musical amanuensis; lived in Milan until 1921, when he was appointed prof. of composition at the Tartini Cons., Trieste. —Operas: *Preziosa* (Milan, Nov. 19, 1879); *Bianca da Cervia* (Milan, Feb. 7, 1882); *Re Nala* (Venice, Feb. 9, 1887); *Il Vassallo di Szigeth* (Vienna, Oct. 4, 1889); *Cornelio Schutt* (Prague, May 20, 1893); *Nozze istriane* (Trieste, March 28, 1895; very successful); *La Falena* (Venice, Sept. 4, 1897); *Oceana* (Milan, Jan. 22, 1903); *L'Abisso* (Milan, Feb. 9, 1914). —Cf. G. Zuccoli, *A. Smareglia* (Trieste, 1923); G. D. Nacamuli, *A. Smareglia* (Trieste, 1930); A. Smareglia, *Vita ed arte di Antonio Smareglia* (Lugano, 1932); Mario Smareglia, *A. Smareglia* (Pola, 1934).

Smart, Sir George (Thomas), English organist and conductor; b. London, May 10, 1776; d. there, Feb. 23, 1867. Chorister in the Chapel Royal under Ayrton; pupil of Dupuis (organ) and Arnold (composition). Knighted 1811 at Dublin by the Lord Lieutenant, after conducting a series of concerts. Original member of the Philharmonic Society and conductor of its concerts 1813-44, introducing the works of Beethoven and Schumann. Also conducted the Lenten oratorios (1813-25). Publ. a collection of glees and canons (1863), 2 vols. of sacred music, 2 piano sonatinas, etc.; edited Orlando Gibbons' madrigals and Handel's Dettingen Te Deum. —Cf. H. B. and C. L. Cox, *Leaves from the Journals of Sir George Smart* (London, 1907); C. Maclean, *Sir George Smart, Musician-Diarist,* in 'Sammelbände der Internationalen Musik-Gesellschaft' (vol. X, 1909); A. Hyatt King, *The Importance of Sir George Smart,* in the 'Mus. Times' (Dec., 1950).

Smart, Henry, English organist; son of Sir George's brother Henry (1778-1823); b. London, Oct. 26, 1813; d. there, July 6, 1879. He was a pupil of his father and W. H. Kearns; served as organist at several London churches, finally at St. Pancras, Euston Road, in 1864, his sight failing in that year; he received a government pension in 1879. His opera, *Bertha, or the Gnome of the Hartzberg,* was produced at the Haymarket Theatre, May 26, 1855; the cantatas *The Bride of Dunkerron* (1864), *King René's Daughter* (1871), *The Fishermaidens* (1871), and *Jacob* (1873) appeared after he was blind. He wrote many songs, part-songs, and anthems; a full Morning and

Evening Service; organ music; etc. —Cf. Wm. Spark, *Henry Smart, His Life and Works* (London, 1881); W. D. Seymour, *Henry Smart* (London, 1881).

Smetana (směh'-tah-nah), **Bedřich (Friedrich)**, great Bohemian composer; b. Leitomischl, March 2, 1824; d. insane at Prague, May 12, 1884. His talent manifested itself very early, but his father's prejudice against music as a profession precluded systematic instruction. However, a friend of his schooldays, Katharina Kolař, who was studying the piano with Proksch in Prague, introduced Smetana to her master, who accepted him as a pupil (piano and theory). Kittl, the director of the Cons., procured him a position as music teacher in the family of Count Thun. After four years of earnest work Smetana gave up his position, and undertook his first concert tour, which resulted in a disastrous financial failure. In despair, he turned to Liszt, who helped him to open a piano school of his own. This flourished, and a year later (1849) he married Katharina Kolař, who had also become a fine pianist. His reputation as a performer, especially as an interpreter of Chopin, grew rapidly, but his first compositions were received coldly. When, therefore, the Philharmonic Society of Göteborg offered him the conductorship in 1856, he immediately accepted. In his first year there he wrote his first three symphonic poems, *Richard III, Wallensteins Lager,* and *Hakon Jarl* (after Öhlenschläger). As conductor and pianist he was highly appreciated. But the cold climate undermined his wife's health. For her sake he spent his vacations regularly in Prague; on the trip there in 1859, she died in Dresden. Meantime, important events were preparing at home. Škroup had made a beginning with national opera, whose chief national element was Bohemian texts, the music being practically devoid of national characteristics. The younger musicians and poets sought the establishment of a national art. After Austria had granted political autonomy to Bohemia in 1860, an agitation was begun for the erection of a national opera-house in Prague. Smetana resigned his post in Göteborg, and returned to Prague in May, 1861, assuming a leading role in the new movement. On Nov. 18, 1862, the new opera-house was opened; but the dozen Bohemian operas by Škroup, Shuherský, and Šebor could not furnish an important or varied repertory; consequently, Meyerbeer and the Italians were sung in Bohemian. Smetana therefore turned to opera, and finished his first dramatic work, *Braniboři v Čechách (The Brandenburgers in Bohemia),* in 1863. It was not produced till Jan. 5, 1866; its success, while not overwhelming, was decided. On May 30, 1866, his second opera, *Prodaná nevěsta (The Bartered Bride),* was received with immense enthusiasm. Smetana was appointed 1st conductor (replacing the Meyerbeer fanatic, Mayer), and acclaimed as Bohemia's greatest composer. This opera has also found success abroad (Austria and Germany, 1892; Scandinavia, 1894; England, 1895; Italy, 1905; Belgium, 1907; U. S., Feb. 19, 1909, at the Metropolitan Opera House). The next opera, *Dalibor* (May 16, 1868), on account of Smetana's employment of leading motifs and more elaborate treatment of the orchestra, caused several critics to charge the composer with attempting to Wagnerize the national opera. A war of words, lasting ten years, resulted. In 1871, when there was talk of crowning Emperor Francis Josef as King of Bohemia, Smetana wrote *Libussa* for the coronation festivities. But no coronation took place, and Smetana's enemies found means of preventing a production at the National Opera. Hoping to duplicate the success of his second work, he selected a comedy, *Dvě vdovy (The Two Widows),* produced on March 27, 1874, with only moderate success. Continued opposition preyed upon his mind, producing a serious nervous disorder affecting his hearing. In the spring of 1874 he had to resign his conductorship; in October he was totally deaf. Mayer, his predecessor, succeeded him at the opera, and Smetana sought forgetfulness in work. He returned to the symphonic poem, but now found inspiration in national subjects. Thus originated those six masterpieces bearing the collective title *Má Vlast (My Country): Vyšehrad* (the ancient castle of the Bohemian kings) and *Vltava (The Moldau)* in 1874; *Šárka* (a valley north of Prague, named after a mythological character) and *Z českých luhüv a hayüv* (*From Bohemia's Meadows and Groves)* in 1875; *Tábor (The Camp;* introducing the Hussite war-song) in 1878; and *Blanik* (the Bohemian 'Kyffhäuser') in 1879. To this period also belongs the famous E minor string quartet *Z mého Života (Aus meinem Leben;* 1876). But Smetana's labors on behalf of national art had already borne fruit; a reaction soon set in, and by the end of 1875 his friends again controlled the opera. Early in 1876 the master began a new opera, *Hubička (The Kiss),* produced with gratifying success on Nov. 7, 1876. *Tajemství (The Secret),* staged in Prague on Sept. 18, 1878, was hailed as a second *Bartered Bride,* and won even the opposition party. For the opening (June 11, 1881) of the new National Opera *Libussa* was unanimously chosen, and created a profound impression. His last opera, *Čertova stěna (The Devil's Wall)*, presented on Oct. 29, 1882, was a comparative failure. His health had not improved; nevertheless, he continued to create new works including an opera, *Viola*, which was never completed; early in 1884 he had to be transferred to the insane asylum. Smetana's other works are: *Richard III*, symph. poem (Prague, Jan. 5, 1862, composer conducting); *Hakon Jarl*, symph. poem (Prague, Feb. 24, 1864, composer conducting); *Písen Česká (Bohemian Song)*, for vocal quartet and orch. (1868; Prague, March 29, 1875); *Prazský Karneval (The Carnival of Prague)*, symph. poem (Prague, March 2, 1884); *Rybář (The Fisher)*, music to a tableau after Goethe, for harmonium, harp, and string quintet (Žofin, April 12, 1869); a *Festmarsch* for the Shakespeare tercentenary (1864); string quartet in D minor; piano trio; 2 pieces for violin and piano; choruses and songs; piano music (a set of Bohemian dances, 3 sets of polkas, the popular concert étude *Am Seegestade*, etc.). —Bibliography: B. Wellek, *F. Smetana. Mit einem Anhang von Korrespondenzen Smetanas an Liszt* (Prague, 1895; 2nd ed. as *F. Smetanas Leben und Wirken*, 1899); O. Hostinský, *B. Smetana* (Prague, 1901); R. Batka, *Die Musik in Böhmen* (Berlin, 1906); W. Ritter, *F. Smetana* (Paris, 1907); K. Hoffmeister, *B. Smetana* (Prague, 1914); V. Helfert, *B. Smetana* (Brno, 1924); V. Balthasar, *B. Smetana* (Prague, 1924); E. Rychnovsky, *Smetana* (Stuttgart, 1924); Z. Nejedlý, *B. Smetana*, a monumental biography in 4 vols. (Prague, 1924-33; 2nd ed. in 7 vols., 1950-54); J. Bistron, *F. Smetana* (Vienna, 1924); J. Tiersot, *Smetana* (Paris, 1926); J. Teichmann, *B. Smetana* (Prague, 1944); P. Pražák, *Smetanovy zpěvohry* (on Smetana's operas; 4 vols.; Prague, 1948); H. Boese, *Zwei Urmusikanten: Smetana, Dvořák* (Zürich, 1955). Documentary vols. containing various materials on Smetana were publ. in Prague by Mirko Očadlik (1950) and F. Bartoš (9th ed., 1954; in English as *Letters and Reminiscences*, Prague, 1955); numerous monographs on Smetana's individual works have also been publ. in Prague.

Smijers (smī'-ĕhrs), **Albert Anton,** eminent Dutch musicologist; b. Raamsdonksveer, July 19, 1888; d. Huis ter Heide, near Utrecht, May 15, 1957. He studied music with Averkamp at the Cons. of Amsterdam; was trained for the priesthood; ordained in 1912; then entered the school for church music at Klosterneuburg; took a course in musicology with Guido Adler at the Univ. of Vienna (1914-19); *Dr. phil.* with the dissertation *Karl Luython als Motettenkomponist* (1917; publ. Amsterdam, 1923). Returning to Holland, he became head of the division for church music at the Catholic seminary in Tilburg; in 1930 was appointed prof. of musicology at the Univ. of Utrecht; formed the Institute of Musicology there, which gave great impetus to musicological research in Holland. He was president of the International Musicological Society from 1952 till his death. In 1921 he undertook the preparation of a critical ed. of the complete works of Josquin Des Prez; at the time of his death, 5 volumes still remained unpublished; brought out 7 volumes of the anthology *Van Ockeghem tot Sweelinck* (Amsterdam, 1939-56); in collaboration with Charles Van den Borren and others he publ. *Algemeene Muziekgeschiedenis* (Utrecht, 1938); began an edition of the collected works of Obrecht (vol. I, Amsterdam, 1953-54). Other editions are *Missa ad modulum Benedicta es*, by Philippe de Monte (1920), Attaingnant's *13 Livres de motets* (3 vols.); etc. His writings include *Die Kaiserliche Hofmusik-Kapelle von 1543-1619*, in Adler's 'Studien zur Musikwissenschaft' (VI ff.).

Smit, Leo, American pianist and composer; b. Philadelphia, Jan. 12, 1921. He received a scholarship to the Curtis Institute of Music, Philadelphia, at the age of 9; studied piano with Isabelle Vengerova; composition with Nicolas Nabokov. In 1950 he won a Guggenheim Fellowship and a Fulbright Scholarship, and spent several years in Rome; gave piano recitals, specializing in modern music. His own style is neo-Classical; the contrapuntal fabric is particularly strong. —Works: ballet, *Virginia Sampler* (N. Y., March 4, 1947); for orch.: *Joan of Arc* (1942), *Hymn and Toccata-Breakdown* (1945), *The Parcae*, overture (1951; Boston, Oct. 16, 1953), symph. No. 1 (Boston, Feb. 1, 1957); *Capriccio*, for string orch. (Ojai, Calif., May 23, 1958); chamber music: sextet for clarinet, bassoon, and strings (1940), *Rural Elegy and Rondo*, for violin and piano (1945); *V-Shum-Roo*, for chorus and organ (1946); *5 Pieces for Young People*, for piano (1947); other piano pieces; songs.

Smith, Alice Mary (Mrs. **Meadows** White), English composer; b. London, May 19, 1839; d. there, Dec. 4, 1884. She was a pupil of Sterndale Bennett and G. A. Macfarren; married M. White in 1867. —Works: the cantatas *Rüdesheim* (1865), *Ode to the Northeast Wind* (1878), *Ode to the Passions* (1882), *Song of the Little Baltung* (1883), and *The Red King* (1884); also a symphony in C minor; 4 overtures: *Endymion, Lalla Rookh, Masque of Pandora,* and *Jason;* 2 piano quartets; 2 string quartets; a piano trio; a clarinet concerto; *Introduction and Allegro* for piano and orch.; part-songs; etc.

Smith, Bernard (Bernhard Schmidt), called 'Father Smith,' organ builder; b. in Germany c. 1630; d. London, Feb. 20, 1708. He settled in London in 1660 with 2 nephews; became organ builder in ordinary to the King and court organ builder to Queen Anne. He built organs for St. Margaret's, Westminster (1675), Durham Cathedral (1683), the Temple (1684), St. Paul's Cathedral (1697), and the Banqueting Hall, Whitehall (1699). —Cf. A. Freeman, *Father Smith* (London, 1926).

Smith, Carleton Sprague, American musicologist; b. New York, Aug. 8, 1905. He was educated at Harvard Univ. (M.A., 1928) and the Univ. of Vienna (Ph.D., 1930); was a John Harvard Fellow in 1928; from 1931-34, instructor in history at Columbia Univ.; since 1931 chief of the Music Division, N.Y. Public Library. U.S. delegate to the International Congress of Music Education at Prague, 1936. President of the American Musicological Society, 1938-40. 1940, lectured in South America under the auspices of the American Council of Learned Societies; 1943-46, in Brazil as lecturer on social history of the U.S. and cultural relations officer, Dept. of State. In July, 1946, returned to his post as chief of the Music Division, N.Y. Public Library. 1948, lectured on Latin-American civilizations at N.Y. University; since 1948, lecturer there on American music. A skillful flutist, he has frequently played in public; edited Prokofiev's flute sonata, op. 94; also edited (with Leroy Robertson) a series of records, 'Music in America.'

Smith, Cecil, American music critic; b. Chicago, July 12, 1906; d. London, May 28, 1956. He studied with H. Levy (piano) and Sowerby (composition) in Chicago; later at Harvard Univ. with Piston. He taught at the Univ. of Chicago (1929-46); was music critic of the 'Chicago Tribune' (1936-42) and editor of 'Musical America' (1948-51). He went to England in 1951 and wrote for the London 'Daily Express'; remained in London until his death. —Books: *Musical Comedy in America* (N. Y., 1950); *Worlds of Music* (Philadelphia, 1952).

Smith, David Stanley, American composer and music educator; b. Toledo, Ohio, July 6, 1877; d. New Haven, Conn., Dec. 17, 1949. He studied with Horatio Parker at Yale Univ., graduating in 1900. He then went to Europe, where he took courses in composition with Thuille in Munich and Widor in Paris. Upon his return to the U. S. he obtained the Mus. Bac. degree at Yale (1903) and was appointed instructor at the Yale School of Music; in 1916 became prof. there; in 1920, was appointed dean of the School of Music, retiring in 1946. He was conductor of the New Haven Symph. Orch. from 1920 to 1946. —Works: symph. No. 1 (1905); symph. No. 2 (1917); symph. No. 3 (Cleveland, Jan. 8, 1931, composer conducting); symph. No. 4 (Boston, April 14, 1939, composer conducting); *Prince Hal,* overture (New Haven, Dec., 1912); *Impressions,* suite for orch. (1916); *Fête Galante,* fantasy for flute and orch. (N. Y., Dec. 11, 1921); *A Satire,* orch. sketch (N. Y., Nov. 15, 1933); *Epic Poem,* for orch. (Boston, April 12, 1935, composer conducting); *Requiem,* for violin and orch. (1939); *Credo,* symph. poem (1941); 4 Pieces for string orch. (1943); *The Apostle,* symph. poem (1944); *Flowers,* suite of 4 pieces for 10 instruments (1924); *Sinfonietta,* for string orch. (1931); choral works: *Rhapsody of St. Bernard,* for mixed chorus and orch. (1915), *Visions of Isaiah,* for soprano, tenor, chorus, and orch. (1927), *The Ocean,* for bass solo, mixed chorus, and orch. (1945); chamber music: 10 string quartets, *Sonata Pastorale,* for oboe and piano, 2 violin sonatas, piano quintet, cello sonata; piano works; songs (cycle, *Songs of Three Ages,* etc.). —Cf. B. C. Tuthill, *David Stanley Smith,* in the 'Mus. Quarterly' (Jan., 1942).

Smith, Gerrit, American organist and composer; b. Hagerstown, Md., Dec. 11, 1859; d. Darien, Conn., July 21, 1912. He studied music at the Stuttgart Cons.; began his professional career as organist in Buffalo; settled in N. Y. in 1885 as church organist. He was one of the founders of the Manuscript Society, N. Y.; wrote a cantata, *King David;* many songs of a lyric inspiration; *25 Song-Vignettes* (for children), and an interesting suite, *Aquarelles,* including 8 songs and 8 piano pieces. —Cf. Rupert Hughes, *Contemporary American Composers* (Boston, 1900; pp. 309-17).

Smith, John Christopher (Johann Christoph Schmidt), organist and composer; b. Ansbach, Germany, 1712; d. Bath, England, Oct. 3, 1795. His father went to England with Handel in 1720 as his agent, and the son became Handel's pupil. When Handel's eyesight began to deteriorate, Smith helped him in playing the organ and harpsichord at performances of Handel's oratorios, and continued to supervise performances of Handel's music after Handel's death; Smith presented the MS scores of Handel, and other objects left to him by Handel, to George III in appreciation for a royal pension. He retired about 1770, and settled in Bath. He wrote several English operas, of which 2 Shakespearian pieces, *The Fairies* (1754) and *The Tempest* (1756) were publ.; also wrote the oratorios *Paradise Lost* (1760), *Judith, Redemption,* etc. —Cf. W. Coxe, *Anecdotes of G. F. Handel and J. C. Smith* (London, 1799).

Smith, John Stafford, English organist and composer; b. Gloucester, c. 1750; d. London, Sept. 21, 1836. He was a pupil of his father Martin Smith, organist of Gloucester Cathedral, and of Boyce. In 1784 he was made a Gentleman of the Chapel Royal; succeeded Arnold as organist there in 1802; from 1805 to 1817, master of the boy choristers there; also was (from 1785) lay-vicar at Westminster Abbey; he won several prizes given by the Catch Club of London. The fact that in his 5th collection of glees (1799) he publ. an arrangement of *To Anacreon in Heaven,* the tune to which Francis Scott Key later wrote *The Star-Spangled Banner,* has led to his being mistakenly regarded as the composer of the tune, whose actual origin is unknown. Smith was an excellent music scholar; he transcribed into modern notation many old MSS for Sir John Hawkins' *History of Music;* publ. *A Collection of Songs of Various Kinds for Different Voices* (1785); edited 'Musica antiqua,' containing compositions 'from the commencement of the 12th to the 18th century' (2 vols., 1812). —Cf. O. G. Sonneck, *Report on the Star-Spangled Banner* (1914).

Smith, Reed, American educator and writer on folklore; b. Washington, N. C., Jan. 16, 1881; d. Pawley's Island, S. C., July 24, 1943. He was educated at the Univ. of South Carolina and at Harvard Univ. (Ph. D., 1909); in 1910 appointed prof. of English literature at the Univ. of South Carolina; he publ. *South Carolina Ballads* (1928); also various essays on songs of the South.

Smith, Sydney, English pianist and composer; b. Dorchester, July 14, 1839; d. London, March 3, 1889. He studied piano at the Leipzig Cons. with Moscheles and Plaidy; settled in London in 1859 as a teacher; publ. many salon pieces for piano (*La Harpe éolienne, Le Jet d'eau, The Spinning-wheel,* etc.); also arrangements from operas.

Smith, Warren Storey, American music critic; b. Brookline, Mass., July 14, 1885. He studied at the Faelten Pianoforte School, Boston, where he taught from 1908 to 1919; in 1922 appointed prof. of theory and music history at the New England Cons., still retaining this post in 1958; assistant music critic of the Boston 'Evening Transcript' (1919-24); music editor of the Boston 'Post' (1924-53). He wrote for orch. a *Romance* (Boston Pops, 1916) and an *Andante Cantabile* (1920); songs: *To Helen* (1914), *The Gift of Pan, Faith, I Know a Trail* (all 1915); *A Caravan From China Comes* (1916; also with orch.); numerous instructive piano pieces; brought out a *Syllabus of the Lectures in Musical History,* for use at the New England Conservatory.

Smith, Wilson George, American pianist and composer; b. Elyria, Ohio, Aug. 19, 1855; d. Cleveland, Feb. 26, 1929. He studied in Germany with Kiel, the Scharwenka brothers, Kullak, and Moszkowski. In 1882 he settled in Cleveland as piano teacher; from 1902 was critic of the Cleveland 'Press.' He publ. a number of salon pieces for piano, *Poème d'amour, Humoresque, Schumannesque, Babbling Brook, Menuet moderne, Romanza appassionata;* several books of piano studies; about 40 songs; arrangements, transcriptions, etc. His album of 5 piano pieces, *Hommage à Edvard Grieg,* was commended for its spirit by Grieg himself. —Cf. Rupert Hughes, *Contemporary American Composers* (Boston, 1900; pp. 394-406).

Smits van Waesberghe, J. See **Waesberghe.**

Smolensky, Stepan Vassilievitch, Russian authority on church music; b. Kazan, Oct. 20, 1848; d. there, Aug. 2, 1909. While teaching at the Clerical Seminary at Kazan, he had unusual opportunities for studying the old MSS preserved in the Solovetsky Library there; in 1889, appointed director of the Synodal School and Choir in Moscow; gathered a valuable collection of MSS of Russian church music from the 15th-19th centuries, illustrating the various systems of notation. Besides numerous essays in the

'Russkaya Muzykalnaya Gazeta' he publ. *A Course of Church Chant Singing* (Moscow, 1900); *The Collection of MSS of Old Ecclesiastical Music in the Synodal School at Moscow* (1899); *The Old Russian Notations* (1901). —Cf. O. Riesemann, *Die Notationen des altrussischen Kirchengesanges* (Moscow, 1908); N. Findeisen, *To the Memory of S. Smolensky* (St. Petersburg, 1910; with a list of Smolensky's writings).

Smolian, Arthur, conductor and writer; b. Riga, Dec. 3, 1856; d. Leipzig, Nov. 5, 1911. He was a pupil of Rheinberger and Wüllner at the Munich Cons.; conducted choruses in Leipzig (from 1884); taught at the Karlsruhe Cons. (1890-1901); in 1901 settled again in Leipzig as music critic and editor; edited the works of Berlioz for Eulenburg's 'Kleine Partitur-Ausgabe.' In his writings he was an ardent proponent of Wagner's ideas. He publ. *Vom Schwinden der Gesangskunst* (1903) and *Stella del Monte* (1903; a free narrative of Berlioz's last years, i.e., the period after he completed the 'Mémoires').

Smulders (smülders), **Charles,** Belgian composer; b. Maestricht, May 8, 1863; d. Liège, April 21, 1934. He studied at the Liège Cons.; won the Belgian Prix de Rome in 1889; taught at the Liège Cons. He wrote the symph. poems *Adieu-Absence-Retour; Chant d'Amour; Le Jour; Le Crépuscule;* 2 piano concertos; Hebrew Melodies for cello and orch.; a violin sonata; a piano sonata; choruses; songs. —Cf. W. Paap, *C. Smulders en A. Diepenbrock,* in 'Mens en Melodie' (vol. 1, 1946, p. 141).

Smyth, Dame **Ethel (Mary),** foremost English woman composer; b. Foots Gray, Kent, April 23, 1858; d. Woking, Surrey, May 8, 1944. She studied at the Leipzig Cons.; then with Heinrich von Herzogenberg, following him to Berlin; her string quintet was performed in Leipzig in 1884. She returned to London in 1888; presented her orchestral *Serenade* (April 26, 1890) and an overture *Antony and Cleopatra* (Oct. 18, 1890). Her prestige as a serious woman composer rose considerably with the presentation of her Mass, for solo voices, chorus, and orch., at Albert Hall (Jan. 18, 1893). After that she devoted her energies to the theater. Her first opera, *Fantasio,* to her own libretto in German, after Alfred de Musset's play, was produced in Weimar on May 24, 1898; this was followed by *Der Wald* (Berlin, April 9, 1902), also to her own German libretto; it was produced in London in the same year, and in N. Y. by the Metropolitan Opera, on March 11, 1903. Her next opera, *The Wreckers,* was her most successful work; written originally to a French libretto, *Les Naufrageurs,* it was first produced in a German version as *Strandrecht* (Leipzig, Nov. 11, 1906); the composer herself translated it into English, and it was staged in London on June 22, 1909; the score was revised some years later, and produced at Sadler's Wells, London, on April 19, 1939. She further wrote a comic opera, in English, *The Boatswain's Mate* (London, Jan. 28, 1916), a one-act opera, described as 'a dance-dream,' *Fête Galante* (Birmingham, June 4, 1923), and *Entente Cordiale* (Bristol, Oct. 20, 1926). Other works are a concerto for violin, horn, and orch. (London, March 5, 1927); *The Prison,* for soprano and bass solo, chorus, and orch. (London, Feb. 24, 1931); choral pieces *(Hey Nonny No, Sleepless Dreams,* etc.); a group of songs; etc. Her formative years were spent in Germany, and her music never overcame the strong German characteristics, in the general idiom as well as in the treatment of dramatic situations on the stage. At the same time, she was a believer in English national music and its potentialities. She was a militant leader for woman suffrage in England, for which cause she wrote *The March of the Women,* the battle song of the W. S. P. U. After the suffrage was granted, her role in the movement was officially acknowledged; in 1922 she was made a Dame of the British Empire. She publ. a number of books, mostly autobiographical in nature: *Impressions that Remained* (2 vols., 1919; new ed., 1945); *Streaks of Life* (1921); *As Time Went On* (1936); *What Happened Next* (1940); also some humorous essays and reminiscences, *A Three-legged Tour in Greece* (1927); *A Final Burning of Boats* (1928); *Female Pipings in Eden* (1934); *Beecham and Pharaoh* (1935). —Cf. the articles by R. Boughton, in the 'Music Bulletin' (Feb., 1923) and R. Capell, in the 'Monthly Mus. Record' (July, 1923); R. A. Streatfeild, *Musiciens anglais contemporains* (Paris, 1913); Kathleen Dale, *Dame Ethel Smyth,* in 'Music & Letters' (July, 1944).

Snel, Joseph-François, Belgian violinist and composer; b. Brussels, July 30, 1793; d. Koekelberg, near Brussels, March 10, 1861. He studied violin with Baillot at the Paris Cons. In 1818 he founded in Brussels the 'Académie de musique et de chant' (with Mees); popularized in Belgium the singing-teaching methods of Galin and Wilhem;

held various positions as inspector of schools. His ballets *Frisac et le page inconstant, L'Enchantement de Polichinelle,* etc., were produced at the Brussels Opera; in 1830, durthe Belgian Revolution, he wrote the ballet *Barricades.*

Snetzler (**Schnetzler**), **Johann,** Swiss organ builder; b. Schaffhausen, April 6, 1710; d. there, Sept. 28, 1785. He went to London in 1746 and established an organ workshop there; built organs for the Moravian Churches in London and in Leeds, for Chesterfield Church, and (on the recommendation of Burney) for the Church of King's Lynn. He returned to Switzerland shortly before his death. His London factory was purchased by Ohrmann, Nutt, and Eliot. A list of his organs exported to the U.S. is found in W. L. Sumner's *The Organ* (London, 1952).

Snoer (snoor), **Johannes,** Dutch harpist; b. Amsterdam, June 28, 1868; d. Vienna, March 1, 1936; he studied with Edmund Schuecker when the latter was in Amsterdam; from 1894 to 1910, was first harpist of the Gewandhaus Orch. in Leipzig; traveled as soloist in Europe and America in 1905-06. He publ. several practical pieces for the harp and didactic works: *Praktische Harfenschule, Tägliche Übungen, Studien in Konzertform, Orchesterstudien,* etc.; also *Die Harfe als Orchesterinstrument* (Leipzig, 1898).

Sobolewski, Eduard de, German-American composer; b. Königsberg, Oct. 1, 1808, of Polish parents; d. St. Louis, May 18, 1872. He was a pupil of Weber in Dresden; became an opera conductor in Königsberg and Bremen; produced there his operas *Imogen* (1833), *Velleda* (1836), and *Salvator Rosa* (1848); his opera *Komala* was produced by Liszt in Weimar on Oct. 30, 1858. In 1859 he emigrated to the U. S., settling in Milwaukee, then a center of German musical immigrants. There he staged his opera, *Mohega,* on Oct. 11, 1859, to his own libretto in German; he selected an American subject dealing with an Indian girl saved by Pulaski from death. Sobolewski subsequently moved to St. Louis; organized a symphony orch. there, which he led until his death. He further wrote the oratorios *Johannes der Täufer, Der Erlöser,* and *Himmel und Erde;* 2 symphonies; the symph. poems *Vineta* and *Meeresphantasie;* several male choruses; publ. the pamphlets, *Reaktionäre Briefe* (1854), *Oper nicht Drama* (1858), and *Das Geheimnis der neuesten Schule der Musik* (1859). —Cf. E. E. Hipsher, *American Opera and its Composers* (Philadelphia, 1927; 2nd ed., 1934; pp. 382-85).

Soderino, Agostino, Italian organist and composer; flourished in the early 17th century. He was church organist in Milan, where he publ. his *Canzoni a 4 & 8 voci . . . Libri I, Op. 2* (1608); 2 keyboard canzonas from this publication (*La Scaramuccia* and *La Ducalina*) are reprinted in L. Torchi, *L'Arte Musicale in Italia* (vol. III).

Soderlund, Gustave Frederic, pedagogue; b. Göteborg, Sweden, Jan. 25, 1881. He studied piano in Sweden; in 1908 went to South America, and taught at the Cons. of Valparaíso, Chile (until 1913); in 1916 he settled in the U. S., where he continued to study piano (with Lhévinne) and theory (with C. S. Skilton). He taught at the Univ. of Kansas (1919-27) and then at the Eastman School of Music in Rochester (1928-52). He wrote a symph. poem, *Svithiod* (1928); chamber music; piano pieces; publ. 2 collections in the Eastman School of Music Series: *Examples Illustrating the Development of Melodic Line and Contrapuntal Style, from Greek Melody to Mozart* (1932; 3rd printing, 1945) and *Examples of Gregorian Chant and Works by Orlandus Lassus . . . for Use in Classes of Counterpoint* (1937; 3rd ed., 1946); also *Direct Approach to Counterpoint in 16th-century Style* (1947).

Söderman, (**Johan**) **August,** Swedish composer; b. Stockholm, July 17, 1832; d. there, Feb. 10, 1876. He studied piano and composition at the Stockholm Academy of Music (1847-50); then joined a theatrical company on a Scandinavian tour, as composer of operettas. In 1856 he went to Leipzig, where he studied privately with Richter, and acquired an appreciation of German vocal music; he was particularly influenced by the lyric works of Schumann, Wagner, and Liszt, an influence that is combined with Swedish national elements in his theater music. —Works: the operettas *Urdur* (1852) and *Hin Ondes första lärospan (The Devil's First Lesson;* Stockholm, Sept. 14, 1856); incidental music to about 80 plays by Shakespeare, Schiller, and Swedish writers; *Digte og Sange,* part-songs to words by Bjørnson; several songs to Swedish words; a ballad for solo voice, chorus, and orch., *Die Wallfahrt nach Kevlaar,* after Heine (1859-66); also a *Missa solemnis* (1875). —Cf. G. Jeanson, *A. Söderman: en svensk tondiktares liv och verk*

(Stockholm, 1926; includes a complete list of works).

Sodero, Cesare, conductor; b. Naples, Aug. 2, 1886; d. New York, Dec. 16, 1947. He studied with Alessandro Longo (piano) and Martucci (composition) at the Naples Cons.; in 1907 emigrated to the U. S. and settled in N. Y.; was music director of the Edison Phonograph Co., of the National Broadcasting Co., and of the Mutual Broadcasting Co.; conducted the San Carlo Grand Opera Co. and the Philadelphia Grand Opera. He wrote an opera, *Ombre russe* (Venice, June 19, 1930); ballets; chamber music; etc.

Soffredini, Alfredo, Italian composer; b. Leghorn, Sept. 17, 1854; d. Milan, March 12, 1923. He studied with Mazzucato and Sangalli at the Milan Cons.; was editor of the influential 'Gazzetta Musicale' (Milan) from 1896 to 1912; also taught composition; among his students was Mascagni. He wrote 8 operas to his own librettos: *Il Saggio* (Leghorn, Feb. 3, 1883), the 2-act children's opera *Il piccolo Haydn* (Faenza, Nov. 24, 1889; Vienna, 1897; also productions in Russia and elsewhere), *Salvatorello* (Pavia, March 25, 1894), *Tarcisio* (Milan, Nov. 23, 1895), *Aurora* (Pavia, April 21, 1897), *La Coppa d'oro* (Milan, Jan. 27, 1900), *Graziella* (Pavia, Nov. 15, 1902), *Il Leone* (Cesena, 1914). He publ. *Le Opere di Verdi* (Milan, 1901) and contributed essays on Italian music to various publications, as well as to the 'Gazzetta Musicale.'

Sofronitzky, Vladimir Vladimirovitch, Russian pianist; b. Leningrad, May 8, 1902. He studied at the Leningrad Cons. with Nikolayev, graduating in 1921. In 1928 he gave concerts in France; from 1936 to 1942 was professor at the Leningrad Cons.; since 1942 at the Moscow Cons. In 1943 he received the Stalin Prize.

Sohn, Joseph, American music critic and writer; b. New York, March 22, 1876; d. there, March 15, 1935. After graduation from the College of the City of N. Y., he went to Berlin for further musical studies; upon his return to N. Y., he became music critic of the N. Y. 'American' and 'The Forum.' He publ. *Robert Schumann, a Lyrical Poet* (1896), *Lessons of the Opera* (1903), *Music in America and Abroad* (1904), *Joseph Joachim* (1904), *Opera in New York* (1907), *The Mission of Richard Wagner* (1910).

Sokalsky, Pyotr Petrovitch, Russian writer on music; b. Kharkov, Sept. 26, 1832; d. Odessa, April 11, 1887. Having studied natural sciences at the Univ. of Kharkov, he became a teacher in the secondary schools; was secretary of the Russian Consulate in New York (1857-60); founded the Philharmonic Society in Odessa in 1864. Throughout his life he collected Russian folksongs, of which he made a profound study; his chief work, *The Russian Folk-Song in Greater and Little Russia; Its Melodic Structure and Harmonic Peculiarity,* was publ. in 1888 by his brother Ivan. He wrote some piano music and 3 operas, *Osada Dubno* (*The Siege of Dubno*), *Mazeppa,* and *Maiskaya notch* (*A Night in May*).

Sokoloff, Nicolai, conductor; b. near Kiev, Russia, May 28, 1886. He was brought to America as a young boy; studied violin with Loeffler; won a scholarship at the Yale Univ. School of Music at the age of 13; joined the Boston Symph. Orch. at 17, as violinist. He acquired his first practical experience in conducting with a theatrical company in Manchester, England; in 1916 he conducted an orchestral group in San Francisco. In 1918 he became permanent conductor of the newly organized Cleveland Orch:; the 1st concert took place under Sokoloff's direction on Dec. 11, 1918, with an orchestra of 57 men; the orchestra grew to national significance with its expanded program; modern works and music by American composers were performed. Sokoloff resigned in 1933; was then the first head of the Federal Music Project under the Works Progress Administration (1935-38); was for 2 seasons conductor of the Seattle Symph. Orch. (1938-40); then settled in La Jolla, Calif., as conductor and director of the Musical Arts Society.

Sokolov (sŏh-kŏh-lŏv'), **Nikolai Alexandrovitch,** Russian composer and pedagogue; b. St. Petersburg, March 26, 1859; d. there, March 27, 1922. He studied with Johansen and Rimsky-Korsakov at the St. Petersburg Cons., graduating in 1884; later taught harmony and counterpoint there for many years, remaining on the faculty until his death; among his pupils was Shostakovitch. He was a prolific composer; a great many of his works were publ. by Belaiev: *Elégie,* for orch.; *Divertissement,* for orch.; music for Shakespeare's *The Winter's Tale;* 3 string quartets; choruses; pieces for violin with piano; cello with piano; etc.; a number of songs.

Solano, Francisco Ignacio, Portuguese musical theorist; b. Coimbra, c. 1720; d. Lisbon, Sept. 18, 1800. He publ. *Nova* *instrucçao musical* (1764), *Nova arte e breve compendio de musica* . . . (1768; 2nd ed., 1794), *Novo tratado de musica* . . . (1779), *Dissertação sobre o caracter . . . da musica* (1780), etc.

Soldat, Marie, Austrian violinist; b. Graz, March 25, 1863; d. there, Sept. 30, 1955. She first studied in Graz, and from 1879 to 1882 with Joachim at the Hochschule für Musik in Berlin, graduating as winner of the Mendelssohn Prize; made a specialty of the Brahms violin concerto, which she performed with great authority. In 1887 she formed in Berlin her own string quartet (all women); in 1889 she married the lawyer Röger, and settled in Vienna, continuing her concert career; there she formed a new string quartet (with Elsa von Plank, Natalie Bauer-Lechner, and Leontine Gärtner); eventually retired in Graz, remaining there until her death at the age of 92.

Solenière (sohl-ñär'), **Eugène de,** French writer on music; b. Paris, Dec. 25, 1872; d. there, Dec. 4, 1904. After studying music in Germany, he settled in Paris as a writer and lecturer on musical esthetics. —Publications: *La Femme compositeur* (1895); *Rose Caron* (1896); *Notes musicales* (1896); *Massenet; Étude critique et documentaire* (1897); *Musique et religion* (1897); *Camille Saint-Saëns* (1899); *Cent années de musique française, 1800-1900* (1901); *Notules et impressions musicales* (1902).

Soler, Padre **Antonio,** Spanish composer and organist; b. Olot, near Gerona, Dec. 3, 1729; d. at the Escorial, Dec. 20, 1783. At the age of 6 he entered the school of the monastery of Montserrat, near Barcelona, where he studied the organ and harmony. In 1752 he took holy orders at the monastery of the Escorial, where he spent the rest of his life (organist and choirmaster from 1753). He was a pupil in Madrid of Domenico Scarlatti, whose influence is apparent in his harpsichord sonatas (about 75 of these are extant). Soler was a prolific composer in many forms, both sacred and secular; the catalogue of his MSS at the Escorial lists 428 numbers. Besides much church music, he wrote music for many dramatic works performed by the monks of the Escorial; also 6 concertos for 2 organs; 6 quintets for strings and organ or clavier obbligato (ed. by R. Gerhard for the 'Institut d'Estudis Catalans,' Barcelona, 1933, with an introductory essay by H. Anglès); etc. A collection of 27 'Sonatas para Clave' was printed in London by T. Birchall. Portions of a Requiem for 8 voices are in Eslava's 'Lira Sacro-Hispana' (vol. V); organ works in Pedrell's 'Antología de organístas clásicos españoles' (Madrid, 1908); 14 harpsichord sonatas were publ. by J. Nin in 'Classiques espagnoles du piano' (12 in vol. I, 1925; 2 in vol. II, 1928); 100 piano sonatas and a *Fandango,* ed. by F. Marvin, were publ. in N.Y., 1958-59; a theoretical work: *Llave de la modulación y antigüedades de la música* (Madrid, 1762). —Cf. F. Pedrell, *Music vells de la terra,* in 'Revista Musicale Catalana,' Nos. 58-61 (1908-09); J. Nin, *The Bicentenary of Antonio Soler,* in the 'Chesterian' (1930).

Solerti (soh-lehr'tē), **Angelo,** Italian historiographer; b. Savona, Sept. 20, 1865; d. Massa Carrara, Jan. 10, 1907. His contributions to the early history of opera are valuable: *Le Origini del melodramma* (a collection of contemporary documents and prefaces to the earliest operas; Turin, 1903); *Gli Albori del melodramma,* 3 vols. (Milan, 1904-05); *Musica, ballo e drammatica alla corte medicea dal 1600 al 1637* (Florence, 1905); *Ferrara e la Corte Estense nella seconda metà del secolo XVI* (contains a chapter on *Musica e canto;* Città di Castello, 1891).

Sollertinsky, Ivan Ivanovitch, Russian music critic; b. Vitebsk, Dec. 3, 1902; d. Novosibirsk, Feb. 11, 1944. He studied philology at the Univ. of Petrograd (1919-24); then taught at various schools; became interested in the theater; as music and drama critic, he showed esthetic understanding of modern music, and was the earliest supporter of Shostakovitch; publ. numerous articles on works of Soviet composers. At the outbreak of World War II he joined the staff of the Leningrad Philharmonic, which was evacuated to Novosibirsk, and presented regular lectures at symphony concerts there. His selected articles were publ. in Leningrad in 1946, with a biographical sketch and bibliography compiled by M. Druskin. Another collection of his essays was edited by Shostakovitch (Leningrad, 1956).

Solomon (real name Solomon Cutner), English pianist; b. London, Aug. 9, 1902. He made a sensational début as a child prodigy at the age of 8, playing Tchaikovsky's Concerto No. 1 in London (June 30, 1911). Later he was sent to Paris for further study, resuming his career as an adult performer in 1923. He appeared under the single name Solomon, without a patronymic; toured all over the world as a concert pianist; also played with orchestras. His interpretation of the classics is particularly fine in that he adheres strictly to the spirit of the music, without superimposing any mannerisms of his own.

Solomon, Izler, American conductor; b. St. Paul, Minn., Jan. 11, 1910. He studied violin in St. Paul and Kansas City; at the age of 14, was granted a fellowship of the Kansas City Educational Art Society; studied in Philadelphia with Myron Poliakin, and in N. Y. with Michael Press; became the latter's assistant in the music dept. of Michigan Agricultural College at Lansing; there he made his début as conductor (March 17, 1932), leading the Lansing Civic Orch.; after 4 seasons, he moved to Chicago as conductor of the American Concert Orch. there; also was conductor of the Illinois Symph. (1936-42) and the Woman's Symph. of Chicago (1939-42); guest conductor of various other orchs. During his last season in Chicago, he assumed the conductorship of the newly founded Columbus, Ohio, Philharmonic; from 1943 till 1947 he conducted the New Orleans Summer Symph.; in 1946 conducted at the Hollywood Bowl; in 1948 was engaged as guest conductor of the Israel Philharmonic; led several concerts during its American tour (1951); was resident conductor of the Buffalo Philharmonic (1952-53); guest conductor with the Indianapolis Symph. during the 1955-56 season; was chosen its permanent conductor in 1956. —Cf. Hope Stoddard, *Symphony Conductors of the U. S. A.* (N. Y., 1957; pp. 190-99).

Soloviev (sŏh-lŏh-vyŏhf'), **Nikolai Feopemptovitch,** Russian composer; b. Petrozavodsk, May 9, 1846; d. St. Petersburg, Dec. 27, 1916. He studied at the St. Petersburg Cons. with Zaremba; in 1874 was appointed prof. of harmony and music history there. His opera *Cordelia* was produced in St. Petersburg on Nov. 24, 1885, and then was staged in other Russian cities; also had a performance in Prague; another opera, *Vakula, the Smith,* had a concert performance in 1880, and later was produced by a private opera company in St. Petersburg (1899). He completed the composition of Serov's opera *The Evil Power* (with Serov's wife); wrote a cantata, *The Death of Samson* (1870); a symph. picture, *Russia and the Mongols* (1882); a choral *Prayer for Russia* (1876); a number of songs and piano pieces. He was an influential critic in St. Petersburg.

Solovyev-Sedoy, Vassily Pavlovitch, Russian composer; b. St. Petersburg, April 25, 1907; studied at the Cons. there, graduating in 1936. —Works: ballet, *Taras Bulba,* after Gogol (Leningrad, Dec. 12, 1940); musical comedies, *A Faithful Friend* (Kuibyshev, Oct. 6, 1945) and *The Dearest Thing* (Moscow, Oct. 2, 1952); a great number of popular songs on patriotic subjects; film music.

Solti, Georg, Hungarian conductor; b. Budapest, Oct. 21, 1912. He studied at the Budapest Cons. with Dohnányi (piano) and Kodály (composition); conducted at the Budapest Opera (1933-39); went to Switzerland in 1939 and was active as pianist and conductor in Zürich (1939-45); in 1947 was appointed conductor of the Munich State Opera; in 1951 became conductor at the Frankfurt Opera and of the Museum Concerts there. He made his American début with the San Francisco Opera (Sept. 13, 1953); also conducted the Opera Theater Association, Chicago (1956-57).

Soltys, Adam, Polish composer; son of Miecyslaw Soltys; b. Lwow, July 4, 1890. He studied with his father, and later with Georg Schumann in Berlin; also studied musicology at the Univ. of Berlin with Kretzschmar and Johannes Wolf (*Dr. phil.,* 1921). He wrote 2 symphonies; several overtures; ballads in the national Polish style; some chamber music; choruses.

Soltys, Miecyslaw, Polish composer; b. Lwow, Feb. 7, 1863; d. there, Nov. 12, 1929. He studied music with Krenn in Vienna and with Gigout in Paris. He became director of the Lwow Cons. in 1899, retaining this post for 30 years until his death. He wrote the operas *Rzeczpospolita Babinska* (Lwow, April 27, 1905), *Opowiesc ukrainska* (Lwow, March 8, 1910), *Panie Kochanku* (Lwow, May 3, 1924), and *Nieboska komedia* (1925); a symph. poem *The Fugitive;* a piano concerto; choruses; piano pieces; songs.

Somers, Harry Stewart, Canadian pianist and composer; b. Toronto, Sept. 11, 1925. He studied at the Royal Cons. at Toronto, and with Milhaud in Paris (1949-50). —Works: piano concerto (1947); symph. (Toronto, April 27, 1953); wind quintet; 2 string quartets; 4 piano sonatas; songs.

Somervell, Sir Arthur, English composer; b. Windermere, June 5, 1863; d. London, May 2, 1937. Entered King's College, Cambridge, in 1880, taking the classical course (B.A., 1883), and music with Sir C. V.

Stanford; studied further with Kiel and Bargiel at the Hochschule in Berlin, and with Sir H. Parry at the Royal College of Music; prof. of harmony and counterpoint at the Royal College of Music, 1893-1901; then inspector of music to the Board of Education and the Scottish Education Dept.; visited Australia and Tasmania (1900) and South Africa (1905); Mus. Doc., Cambridge, 1903. He was knighted in 1929. His works include a symph. and 2 suites for orch.; *Normandy* (symph. variations) and *Highland Concerto* for piano and orch.; *Konzertstück* for violin and orch.; an oratorio, *The Passion of Christ;* 4 children's operettas; many choral works and part-songs; song cycles (*Maud, The Shropshire Lad,* etc.) and about 40 separate songs; piano pieces; etc. He ed. 'Songs of the Four Nations' (50 folksongs of England, Scotland, Ireland, and Wales).

Somis, Giovanni Battista, Italian violinist and composer; b. Turin, Dec. 25, 1686; d. there, Aug. 14, 1763, as maestro at the court. Son and pupil of the court violinist Francesco Lorenzo Somis (called 'Ardy' or 'Ardito'; 1663-1736). In 1696 entered the orch. of the ducal chapel at Turin, and from 1703-06 was a pupil of Corelli in Rome. He then returned to Turin; in 1733 appeared as soloist at the Concert Spirituel in Paris with great success. He was the teacher of Giardini, Guignon, Pugnani, Chabran, and Leclair. He publ. 2 vols. of *Sonate a violino e violoncello o cembalo* (op. 1, Rome, 1722; op. 2, Turin, 1723), and *Trattenimenti per camera,* op. 5 (trio sonatas for 2 violins and basso continuo; Paris, 1733). Sonatas for violin solo and other works are in MS. —Cf. G. Fino, *Un grande violinista torinense ed una famiglia di violinisti, G. B. Somis,* in 'Il Momento' (Turin, Oct. 25-26, 1927).

Somis, Lorenzo Giovanni, Italian violinist; brother of the preceding; b. Turin, Nov. 11, 1688; d. there, Nov. 29, 1775. He studied in Bologna; from 1724-70 he was 2nd violin in the ducal chapel at Turin. Publ. *8 Sonate da camera a violino solo e violoncello o cimbalo,* op. 2 (publ. in Paris), and *6 Sonate a tre,* op. 3 (1725). In MS (Dresden) are a concerto for violin solo and a concerto *a* 4.

Sommer, Hans (real name Zincke), German composer and writer on music; b. Brunswick, July 20, 1837; d. there, April 28, 1922. He studied mathematics at the Univ. of Göttingen (*Dr. phil.,* 1858); later taught mathematics in Brunswick, while taking active part in musical affairs there. In 1885 he married and settled in Berlin; from 1888 till 1898 he lived in Weimar; then again in Brunswick. He was one of the original founders of the 'Genossenschaft deutscher Tonsetzer' (performing rights society) with Richard Strauss, Max Schillings, and F. Rösch. He wrote the operas *Der Nachtwächter* (Brunswick, Nov. 22, 1865); *Loreley* (Brunswick, April 11, 1891); *Saint Foix* (Munich, Oct. 31, 1894); *Der Meermann* (Weimar, April 19, 1896); *Rübezahl* (Brunswick, May 15, 1904; his strongest opera); *Riquet mit dem Schopf* (Brunswick, April 14, 1907); *Der Waldschratt* (Brunswick, March 31, 1912). His operas *Augustin, Münchhausen,* and *Das Schloss der Herzen* were not performed. His lyric songs were greatly appreciated in Germany, and often performed in England; among the best are the cycles *Der Rattenfänger von Hamelin, Der wilde Jäger, Hunold Singuf, Tannhäuser, Sapphos Gesänge, Aus dem Süden, Eliland*; also *Balladen und Romanzen,* etc. —Cf. E. Stier, *Hans Sommer,* in vol. 1 of 'Monographien moderner Musiker' (Leipzig, 1906); Erich Valentin, *Hans Sommer* (Brunswick, 1939).

Sondheimer (zohnd'-hī-mer), **Robert,** musicologist; b. Mainz, Germany, Feb. 6, 1881. He studied at the Cologne Cons., and with Humperdinck in Berlin. From 1922 to 1933 he was head of the Edition Bernoulli, music publishers. In 1933 he settled in London. He publ. *Die Theorie der Sinfonie und die Beurteilung einzelner Sinfoniekomponisten bei den Musikschriftstellern des 18. Jahrhunderts* (Leipzig, 1925) and *Haydn, A Historical and Psychological Study Based on His Quartets* (London, 1951). In London he established the Sondheimer Edition (incorporating the bulk of the Edition Bernoulli); edited works by Boccherini, Haydn, Vivaldi, John Christian Bach, and the composers of the Mannheim School (Stamitz, Richter, Beck, Cannabich, Rigel, etc.), etc.

Sonneck, Oscar George Theodore, eminent American musicologist; b. Jersey City, N. J., Oct. 6, 1873; d. New York, Oct. 30, 1928. Attended the Gelehrtenschule in Kiel (1883-89) and the Kaiser Friedrich Gymnasium in Frankfurt (1889-93), where he also took piano lessons with James Kwast; from 1893-97 he studied at Munich Univ., musicology with Sandberger and philosophy with Riehl and Lipps; private pupil in composition of M. E. Sachs; 1897-98, pupil of K. Schröder (conducting) at the Sondershausen

Cons. and Iwan Knorr (instrumentation) in Frankfurt; spent the greater part of 1899 in research work in Italy; then returned to the U. S., continuing his researches in the principal libraries. On Aug. 1, 1902, he was appointed the first Chief of the Music Division of the Library of Congress in Washington, which post he resigned on Sept. 5, 1917, to accept a position with the publishing house of G. Schirmer in New York as director of the Publication Department, managing editor of 'The Musical Quarterly' (of which he had been editor since its foundation in 1915), and personal representative of the president, Rudolph E. Schirmer; in 1921 he became vice-president. He represented the U. S. Government at the International Congresses of Music held in London and Rome in 1911. He took a leading part in the formation of the Society for the Publication of American Music, and of the Beethoven Association in N. Y. —Under Sonneck's administration the Music Division of the Library of Congress became one of the largest and most important music collections in the world. His writings, exhibiting profound and accurate scholarship and embodying the results of original research, laid the real foundation for the scientific study of music in the U. S.; his elaborate catalogues, issued by the Library of Congress, are among the most valuable contributions to musical bibliography. —Works: *Protest gegen den Symbolismus in der Musik* (1897); *Francis Hopkins and James Lyon, Two Studies in Early American Music* (1905); *Early Concert Life in America (1731-1800)* (1907); *Report on 'The Star-Spangled Banner,' 'Hail Columbia,' 'America,' 'Yankee Doodle'* (1909); *A Survey of Music in America* (1913); *The Star-Spangled Banner* (1914); *Early Opera in America* (1915); *Suum Cuique* (1916; collection of essays); *Miscellaneous Studies in the History of Music* (1921); *Beethoven, Impressions of Contemporaries* (1926); *Beethoven Letters in America* (1927); *The Riddle of the Immortal Beloved* (1927); smaller essays: *Die drei Fassungen des Hasse'schen Artaserse, 1730, 1740, 1760* ('Sammelbände der Internationalen Musik-Gesellschaft,' XIV, 2), *Psiche ed Amore, 1565* (by A. Striggio and F. Corteccia) ('Mus. Antiquary,' Oct., 1911), *Dafne the First Opera* ('Sammelbände der Internationalen Musik-Gesellschaft,' XV, 1), *The Future of Musicology in America* ('Mus. Quarterly,' July, 1929), etc. —Catalogues: *Classification of Music and Literature of Music* (1904; 2nd ed., revised and augmented, 1917); *Bibliography of Early Secular American Music* (1905; 2nd ed., revised and enlarged by W. T. Upton, 1945); *Dramatic Music* (1908); *Orchestral Music* (1912); *Opera Librettos printed before 1800* (2 vols., 1914); *First Editions of Stephen C. Foster* (1915; with W. R. Whittlesey); *First Editions of Edward MacDowell* (1917); *Dramatic Music* (2 vols., 1917; entirely new, superseding the catalogue of 1908). He also publ. 2 vols. of lyric poems, *Seufzer* (1895) and *Eine Totenmesse* (1898). Among his compositions are *Symphonischer Satz* for small orch.; a string quartet (op. 4); *Romanze* and *Rhapsodie* for violin and piano (op. 8); piano pieces; songs. —Cf. H. Putnam and R. Goldmark, *Remarks at the Funeral Services for O. G. Sonneck* in the 'Mus. Quarterly' (Jan., 1929); C. Engel, *O. G. Sonneck,* in 'Adler-Festschrift' (1930); see also the 'Mus. Quarterly' for Oct., 1933.

Sonnleithner (zŏhn'līt-nĕr), **Joseph von,** son of the amateur composer **Christoph von Sonnleithner** (1734-1786); b. Vienna, 1765; d. there, Dec. 25, 1835. A government councillor, and a founder of the 'Gesellschaft der Musikfreunde,' to which he bequeathed his books and musical instruments. Publ. an interesting 'Wiener Theateralmanach' (1794, 1795, 1796). He wrote some librettos and adapted others, including *Fidelio* for Beethoven and *Faniska* by Cherubini. In 1827 he discovered the famous Antiphonary of St. Gall of the 9th century, in neume-notation; probably a copy of the one sent thither by Charlemagne in 790. —His nephew, **Leopold von Sonnleithner,** b. Vienna, Nov. 15, 1797; d. there, March 4, 1873. The staunch friend of Schubert, he procured the publication of the *Erlkönig* (the first publ. work of Schubert's); at his father's house the *Prometheus,* the *Gesang der Geister über den Wassern,* the 23rd Psalm, and other important works by Schubert were performed from the MS. —Cf. A. Fareanu, *Leopold von Sonnleithners Erinnerungen an Franz Schubert,* in the 'Zeitschrift für Musikwissenschaft' (1919).

Sontag (zohn'-tahg), **Henriette** (real name Gertrud Walburga Sonntag), celebrated German soprano; b. Coblenz, Jan. 3, 1806; d. Mexico City (on a tour), June 17, 1854. She played children's parts on the stage; then studied at the Prague Cons. with Triebensee, Pixis, Bayer, and Frau Czegka; in 1820 she sang in Italian and German opera at Vienna, and in 1823 created the title role in Weber's *Euryanthe;* on May 7, 1824, she sang in Vienna the soprano solos in Beethoven's *Missa solemnis* and 9th Symph.;

made her first Berlin appearance on Aug. 3, 1825 in the part of Isabella in Rossini's *Italiana in Algeri;* her Paris début as Rosina in *Il Barbiere di Siviglia* (June 15, 1826) was an unqualified success and she was adjudged by many as superior to Catalani; she broke her Berlin contract in order to sing at the Italian Opera in Paris (1827); went to London in 1828, and secretly married the Sardinian ambassador to the Dutch court, Count Rossi; was ennobled by the King of Prussia (as 'Fräulein Henriette von Lauenstein'). She then interrupted her career on the stage, and settled with her husband at The Hague; also traveled with him on his diplomatic missions to Germany and Russia. She continued to give concerts as a solo singer, arousing enthusiasm wherever she went. In 1848 she resumed her operatic career; made several tours in England; in the autumn of 1852 she embarked for the U. S., and gave a number of concerts; then went to Mexico (1854), where she sang opera. She died of cholera during an epidemic there. —Cf. Théophile Gautier, *L'-Ambassadrice, Biograhpie de la comtesse Rossi* (Paris, 1850); J. Gundling, *Henriette Sontag* (2 vols.; Leipzig, 1861); W. Berger, *Berühmte Frauen* (Berlin, 1904); H. Stumcke, *Henriette Sontag* (Berlin, 1913); F. Rogers, *Henriette Sontag in New York,* in the 'Mus. Quarterly' (Jan. 1942); E. Pirchan, *Henriette Sontag* (Vienna, 1946).

Sonzogno (son-tsoh'-nyoh), **Edoardo,** Italian music publisher; b. Milan, April 21, 1836; d. there, March 14, 1920. He inherited a printing plant and bookstore founded by his father, and in 1874 began to publish popular editions of French and Italian music with marked success. In 1883 he inaugurated a series of contests for new operas; the 2nd contest, in 1888, was won by Mascagni (then unknown) with *Cavalleria rusticana.* Sonzogno established his own theater (the 'Lirico Internazionale') at Milan in 1894. From 1861 until his retirement in 1909 he was sole proprietor of the newspaper 'Il Secolo.' He was succeeded by his nephew **Riccardo Sonzogno** (d. July 8, 1915); upon the latter's death, the business was taken over by another nephew, **Renzo Sonzogno,** who had previously headed a firm of his own. He died in 1920, and in 1923 control was acquired by a group of Italian industrialists.

Sonzogno (son-tsoh'-nyoh), **Giulio Cesare,** Italian composer; b. Milan, Dec. 24, 1906. He studied with Pick-Mangiagalli and F. Vittadini. —Works: *Lago di Braies,* for orch. (1929); *La Luna e l'usignolo,* for voice and orch. (1930); *Dai Nevai dell'Ortler,* symph. poem (1931); *Quadri rustici* for small orch. (1932); *Il Negro* for cello and orch. (1933); ballet *L'Amore delle tre melarancie (Love for Three Oranges),* after Carlo Gozzi (La Scala, Milan, Feb. 1, 1936); *Regina Uliva,* legend in 3 acts (La Scala, Milan, March 17, 1949).

Sopeña, Federico, Spanish writer on music; b. Valladolid, Jan. 25, 1917. He studied music and theology at Madrid and Salamanca; in 1949 became vice-rector of the Spanish Church in Rome; in 1951 was appointed supervisor of Spanish conservatories. As a music critic, he has championed the Spanish school of modern composers; publ. monographs on Turina (1943), Joaquín Rodrigo (1946), and Stravinsky (1956); also *Historia de la música en cuadros esquemáticos* (1947), *La Música europea contemporánea* (1953).

Sopkin, Henry, American conductor; b. Brooklyn, Oct. 20, 1903. His family moved to Chicago when he was a child; there he studied violin; in 1917 he entered the American Cons., Chicago, graduating in 1924; then was appointed to its faculty; taught music in Chicago high schools (1931-37), conducted concerts with college orchestras; in 1944 was engaged as conductor of the Atlanta Youth Symph.; in 1945 this became the nucleus of a professional orch. in Atlanta, increasing the number of its concerts to 50 a season in 1955, with Sopkin as permanent conductor. —Cf. Hope Stoddard, *Symphony Conductors of the U. S. A.* (N. Y., 1957; pp. 200-06).

Sor (real name Sors), **Fernando,** celebrated Spanish guitar virtuoso; b. Barcelona, Feb. 13, 1778; d. Paris, July 8, 1839. At the age of 11 he entered the school of the monastery of Montserrat, where he studied music under the direction of Anselmo Viola; wrote a Mass; then left the monastery and returned to Barcelona, where he presented his only opera, *Telemaco nella isola di Calipso,* on Aug. 25, 1797. A few years later he went to Madrid; there he joined the French army, earning the rank of captain. When Bonapartist rule was defeated in Spain in 1813, he fled to Paris. There he met Cherubini, Méhul, and other important composers, who urged him to give concerts as a guitarist, and he soon acquired fame. In Paris he produced 2 ballets, *Cendrillon* (1823) and *Le Sicilien, ou L'Amour peintre* (1827). He was then summoned to London by the Duke of Sussex; subsequently traveled in Russia; wrote funeral music for the obsequies of Alexander I of Russia (1825). After another stay in London, he returned to Paris, settling there definitely in 1828. He wrote for the guitar a number of fantasies, minuets, and studies, as well as a method; all these works are modeled after the Classical forms, rather than on popular motifs. Selected works by Sor have been edited by G. Meier.

Sorabji, Kaikhosru (real Christian names Leon Dudley), English composer; b. Chingford, Aug. 14, 1892. His father was a Parsi, his mother of Spanish-Sicilian extraction. He was self-taught in music, but despite this seeming handicap, he developed a most complex style of music in free asymmetrical rhythms, containing elements of Oriental melody structure cast in the polyphonic forms of Western music; the resulting contrapuntal idiom is akin to that of Busoni, but enormously more intricate. Virtually the only performances of his works were by himself as a pianist. He wrote 3 symphonies, 5 piano concertos, 2 organ symphonies, 2 piano quintets, 4 piano sonatas. His most remarkable work is *Opus Clavicembalisticum* for piano solo, completed in 1930, and comprising 3 parts with 12 subdivisions, including a theme with 44 variations, and a passacaglia with 81 variations. The work, which is published, is characteristically dedicated to 'the everlasting glory of those few men blessed and sanctified in the curses and execrations of those many whose praise is eternal damnation.' Sorabji played it in Glasgow under the auspices of the Active Society for the Propagation of Contemporary Music, on Dec. 1, 1930. He is also a brilliant writer, of a somewhat polemical bent; he publ. *Around Music* (1932); *Mi contra Fa: The Immoralisings of a Machiavellian Musician* (London, 1947). —Cf. A. G. Browne, *The Music of Kaikhosru Sorabji,* in 'Music & Letters' (Jan., 1930); E. Rubbra, *Sorabji's Enigma,* in the 'Monthly Mus. Record' (Sept., 1932).

Soresina, Alberto, Italian composer; b. Milan, May 10, 1911. He studied with Paribeni and Bossi at the Milan Cons. —Works: *La Fanciulla mutata in rio,* for soprano and orch. (1939); *Il Santo,* symph. poem (1940); *Lanterna rossa,* lyric drama (Siena, 1942); *L'Amuleto,* opera in one act (Bergamo, Oct. 26, 1954).

Sorge (zŏhr'gĕ), **Georg Andreas,** German composer and theorist; b. Mellenbach, Schwarzburg, March 21, 1703; d. Lobenstein,. April 4, 1778. From his 19th year, court organist at Lobenstein for life. He publ. piano and organ works of merit; a large number of cantatas and motets are in MS. He is more important as a theorist, being one of the discoverers of the 'combinational' tones. He publ. these discoveries (before Tartini) in his most important work, *Vorgemach der musicalischen Composition* (3 vols.; 1745-47). His many other treatises are of less value.

Soriano, Francesco. See **Suriano.**

Soriano Fuertes, Mariano, Spanish music historian; b. Murcia, March 28, 1817; d. Madrid, March 26, 1880. Pupil of his father (director of the royal chamber music); 1843, prof. at Madrid Cons.; from 1844 director, successively, of music schools at Córdoba, Seville, and Cádiz; conducted opera at Barcelona, where he founded the 'Gaceta musical.' He composed some zarzuelas. Author of *Música árabe-española* (1853); *Historia de la música española desde la venida de los fenicios hasta el año de 1850* (4 vols.; 1855-59; a pioneer work, but quite unscientific and unreliable); *Memoria sobre las sociedades corales en España* (1865); *Calendario histórico musical . . .* (1872).

Sormann (zohr'-man), **Alfred (Richard Gotthilf),** German pianist and composer; b. Danzig, May 16, 1861; d. Berlin, Sept. 17, 1913. He studied at the Hochschule für Musik in Berlin with Barth, Spitta, and Bargiel; in 1885, studied with Liszt. He made his début in 1886, giving successful concerts in the chief German towns; in 1889 was court pianist to the Grand Duke of Mecklenburg-Strelitz. —Works: the operas *Die Sibylle von Tivoli* (Berlin, 1902) and *König Harald* (Stettin, 1909); a piano concerto; 2 string quartets; a piano trio; concert études and other piano pieces; songs.

Soro, Enrique, Chilean composer; b. Concepción, July 15, 1884; d. Santiago, Dec. 2, 1954. He was a son of the Italian composer, José Soro, and was educated by him; played in public as a small child. He was granted a stipend by the government of Chile for study in Italy; entered the Cons. of Milan at 14; graduated in 1904, with a grand prize in composition. Returning to Chile in 1905, he was appointed inspector of musical education in primary schools; in 1907 joined the faculty of the Cons. of Santiago; from 1919 to 1928 he was its director. He traveled as a pianist; gave concerts in Europe and

South America; also publ. a number of works. In 1948 he was awarded the Premio Nacional de Arte. —Works: For orch.: *Sinfonía romántica* (1920); piano concerto (1919); *Suite sinfónica,* no. 1, subtitled *Pensamientos intimos* (1918); *Suite sinfónica,* no. 2 (Santiago, May 9, 1919, composer conducting); *Tres preludios sinfónicos* (Santiago, July 18, 1936); *Aires chilenos,* for orch. (Santiago, 1942); *Suite en estilo antiguo* (Santiago, May 28, 1943). Chamber music: piano quintet (1919), *Impresiones líricas,* for piano and strings (1918), string quartet (1904), piano trio (1926), violin sonata, cello sonata; 3 piano sonatas (1920, 1923, 1942); a number of piano pieces in a salon genre, some of them based on Chilean melorhythms. —Cf. L. G. Giarda, *Analytische Studie über Soros 2. Sonate für Violine und Klavier A moll, das Quartett A dur und das Klavierquintett* (Santiago, 1919); Vicente Salas Viú, *La Creación musical en Chile 1900-1951* (Santiago, 1953; pp. 427-52).

Sors. See **Sor.**

Soto de Langa, Francisco, Spanish composer; b. Langa, 1539; d. Rome, Sept. 25, 1619. He spent most of his life in Rome, where he was one of the disciples of St. Philip Neri; for Neri's Congregation of the Oratorio he wrote 5 books of 'laudi spirituali' (publ. between 1583 and 1598); some specimens are reproduced in Alaleona's *Studi su la storia dell' oratorio musicale in Italia* (Turin, 1908).

Soubies (sŏŏ-bēs'), **Albert,** French writer on music; b. Paris, May 10, 1846; d. there, March 19, 1918. He studied law and was admitted to the bar; about the same time he became a pupil of Savard, Bazin, and Guilmant at the Paris Cons. In 1876 he became music critic for 'Le Soir' and in 1885 began to write for the 'Revue de l'art dramatique.' In 1874 he revived the famous old 'Almanach Duchesne' (publ. between 1752 and 1815), reissuing it as 'Almanach des spectacles' (43 vols. publ. up to 1914); for this the Académie awarded him the Prix Voirac in 1893. —Writings: *Histoire de la musique* (his principal work; issued in separate sections dealing with music in individual European nations; publ. 1896-1906); *Les grands théâtres parisiens,* in 2 parts: *67 ans à l'Opéra: 1826-1893* (1893) and *69 ans à l'Opéra-Comique: 1825-1894* (1894); *Histoire de l'Opéra-Comique* (2 vols.; 1892-93; with Charles Malherbe); *Histoire du Théâtre-lyrique 1851-1870* (1899); *L'Œuvre dramatique de Richard Wagner* (1886); *Mélanges sur Richard Wagner* (1892; with Charles Malherbe); other booklets dealing with the musical theater in Paris; monographs on French composers; etc.

Soubre (soobr), **Étienne-Joseph,** Belgian composer; b. Liège, Dec. 30, 1813; d. there, Sept. 8, 1871. He studied at the Liège Cons., and became its director (1862). —Works: opera *Isoline* (Brussels, 1855); *Symphonie triomphale* (1845); 2 cantatas; a Requiem with orch.; *Stabat Mater* and *Ave Verum,* with orch.; *Hymne à Godefroid de Bouillon,* for male chorus and orch.; church music, choruses, overtures, symphonies, etc.

Souhaitty (swä-tē'), **Jean-Jacques,** Franciscan monk and music theorist; flourished in the middle of the 17th century; lived in Paris. He was the first to employ number notation, indicating by numerals 1 to 7 the degrees of the scale, and used this system for popular vocal teaching. He publ. *Nouvelle méthode pour apprendre le plain-chant et la musique* (Paris, 1665; 2nd ed. as *Nouveaux éléments de chant . . .,* 1667) and an *Essai du chant de l'église par la nouvelle méthode des chiffres* (Paris, 1679).

Šourek (shoh'-ŏŏ-rek), **Otakar,** Czech writer on music; b. Prague, Oct. 10, 1883; d. there, Feb. 15, 1956. He was trained as an engineer, and studied music as an avocation; contributed to the leading newspapers and magazines in Prague, and then embarked on his main work, a monumental biography of Dvořák, which was issued under the title *Život a dílo Antonína Dvořáka* (vol. 1, 1916, 2nd ed., 1922; vol. 2, 1917, 2nd ed., 1928; vol. 3, 1930; vol. 4, 1933); in addition he publ. a thematic catalogue of Dvořák's works, in German and Czech (Berlin, 1917); separate publications, dealing with Dvořák's symphonies (Prague, 1922; 3rd ed., 1948), orchestral music (2 vols.; Prague, 1944, 1946), chamber music (Prague, 1943; 2nd ed., 1949); the last two works together in German (2 vols., Prague, 1954); a Dvořák reader (Prague, 1929; 3rd ed., 1946; in English, Prague, 1954); also a monograph on Rudolf Karel (Prague, 1947). An abridged German version by Paul Stefan, in 1 vol., of Šourek's biography of Dvořák was publ. as *Dvořák, Leben und Werk* (Vienna, 1935; in English as *The Life and Work of Dvořák,* N. Y., 1941). —Cf. F. Oeser, *Otakar Šourek,* in 'Musica' (April, 1956).

Souris (sŏŏ-rē'), **André,** Belgian composer; b. Marchienne-au-Pont, July 10, 1899.

He studied at the Cons. of Brussels with M. Lunssens (harmony), Closson (music history), and privately with Gilson (composition). In 1927 he won the Prix Rubens, and traveled in Italy and France. He conducted the radio orch. in Brussels from 1937 to 1946; also taught at the Cons. of Charleroi. In 1925 he joined the surrealist movement in Belgium, and wrote numerous articles on the subject; was the first to apply its esthetic principles to music composition. He was the founder of the quarterly music review, 'Polyphonie' (1947-1954). —Works: *Collage,* for orch. (1928); *Quelques airs de Clarisse Juranville,* for soprano, string quartet, and piano (Barcelona Festival of the International Society for Contemporary Music, April 21, 1936); *Hommage à Babeuf* (Paris Festival of the I. S. C. M., June 22, 1937); *Rengaines,* for wind quintet (Warsaw Festival of the I. S. C. M., April 15, 1939); *Comptines pour enfants sinistres,* for voice and instruments (1942); *Le Marchand d'images,* Walloon songs for solo voices, chorus, and orch. (1944). He collaborated with René Vannes on the *Dictionnaire des musiciens* (Brussels, 1946). —Cf. Paul Nougé, *André Souris* (1928).

Sousa (sŏŏ'ză), **John Philip,** famous American bandmaster and popular composer; b. Washington, D. C., Nov. 6, 1854; d. Reading, Pa., March 6, 1932. He was the son of a Portuguese father and a Bavarian mother. He studied violin with John Esputa and harmony with G. F. Benkert in Washington (1864-67); also acquired considerable proficiency on wind instruments; played in the Marine Band at the age of 13; led an orch. in a vaudeville theater in Washington before he was 18; in 1877 was engaged as violinist in the special orchestra in Philadelphia that was conducted by Offenbach during his American tour. In 1880 Sousa was appointed leader of the Marine Band; he resigned on Aug. 1, 1892, and organized a band of his own, with which he gave successful concerts throughout the U. S. and Canada; played at the Chicago World's Fair in 1893 and at the Paris Exposition in 1900; made 4 European tours (1900, 1901, 1903, and 1905) with increasing acclaim, and finally a tour around the world in 1910-11. His flair for writing band music was extraordinary; the infectious rhythms of his military marches and the brilliance of his band arrangements earned him the sobriquet of 'The March King'; particularly celebrated is his march, *The Stars and Stripes Forever,* which became famous all over the world. During World War I Sousa served as a lieutenant in the Naval Reserve. He continued his annual tours almost to the time of his death. He compiled for the Naval Dept. the 'National, Patriotic and Typical Airs of All Lands' (1890); publ. an autobiography, *Marching Along* (Boston, 1928), and wrote 5 novels. His publ. compositions aggregate to several hundred, including the comic operas, *The Smugglers* (1879), *Désirée* (1884), *The Queen of Hearts* (1886), *El Capitan* (Boston, April 13, 1896; his most brilliant operetta), *The Charlatan* (1897), *The Bride Elect* (1898), *Chris and the Wonderful Lamp* (1900), *The Free Lance* (1906), *The Glass-Blowers* (1911), *The American Maid* (1913), and *Victory* (1915); suites for orch. and band: *Last Days of Pompeii, Three Quotations, Sheridan's Ride, At the King's Court, Looking Upward, Impressions at the Movies,* etc.; a symph. poem, *The Chariot Race* (from *Ben Hur);* many waltzes, songs, etc.; and numerous popular military marches: *The Stars and Stripes Forever, El Capitan, The Washington Post, The High School Cadets, Thunderer, Semper Fidelis, Liberty Hall, Manhattan Beach, King Cotton, Hands Across the Sea;* publ. an instruction book for trumpet and drum, and one for violin. —Cf. *Through the Years with Sousa . . .* (excerpts from his writings; N. Y., 1910); Ann M. Lingg, *J. P. Sousa* (N. Y., 1954).

Southard, Lucien H., American composer; b. Sharon, Vt., Feb. 4, 1827; d. Augusta, Ga., Jan. 10, 1881. He studied music in Boston; from 1851 to 1858 was supervisor of public schools there. After serving in the Union Army during the Civil War, he conducted the orch. of the Peabody Cons. in Baltimore (1868-71); then lived in Boston (1871-75) and Augusta. He composed an opera, *Omano,* from Indian life, to an Italian libretto (concert performance in Boston, 1858; MS score in the Boston Public Library); church music, glees, and organ pieces; publ. a harmony manual (1855); edited collections of sacred music. —Cf. F. J. Metcalf, *American Composers and Compilers of Sacred Music* (1925).

Sowerby, Leo, prominent American composer; b. Grand Rapids, Mich., May 1, 1895. He studied in Chicago with Calvin Lampert (piano) and Arthur Olaf Andersen (theory); served in the U. S. Army during World War I. In 1921 he received the American Prix de Rome, the first such prize to be awarded for composition; stayed at the American Academy in Rome for 3 years (1921-24); in 1925 was appointed teacher of composition at the American Cons., Chicago; also was organist at St. James' Episcopal Church there (from 1927). In his music, he observes a strict formal design; his harmonic style is modern, while remaining within the bounds of traditional tonality. —Works: *Comes Autumn Time,* an overture (1916); *Irish Washerwoman,* for orch. (1916); *A Set of Four,* 'Suite of Ironics' (Chicago, Feb. 15, 1918); *King Estmere,* ballad for 2 pianos and orch. (Rome, April 8, 1923); *Money Musk,* for orch. (1924); *Vision of Sir Launfal,* for soli and mixed chorus (1926); suite, *From the Northland,* for orch. (1927); symph. No. 2 (Chicago, March 29, 1929); *Prairie,* a symph. poem (Interlochen, Mich., Aug. 11, 1929); piano concerto (Chicago, March 5, 1920, composer soloist); cello concerto (1933); concerto for organ and orch. (Boston, April 22, 1938); *Concert Overture* (1941); symph. No. 3 (commissioned by the Chicago Symph. Orch.; Chicago, March 6, 1941); *Song for America,* for chorus (1942); *The Canticle of the Sun,* after St. Francis, for chorus and orch. (N. Y., April 16, 1945; won the Pulitzer Prize); symph. No. 4 (Boston, Jan. 7, 1949); *Christ Reborn,* oratorio (Philadelphia, Nov. 1, 1953); *Fantasy-Portrait,* for orch. (Indianapolis, Nov. 21, 1953); *The Throne of God,* poem for mixed voices and orch. (Washington, Nov. 18, 1957). Chamber music: 2 string quartets (1923, 1935); 2 violin sonatas (1922, 1944); quintet for flute, oboe, clarinet, bassoon, and horn (1916); cello sonata (1921); *Pop Goes the Weasel,* for flute, oboe, clarinet, bassoon, and horn (1927); clarinet sonata (1938); *Poem* for viola and organ (1942); sonata for trumpet and piano (1945); suite for organ, brass, and kettledrums (1953); symph. for organ solo (1930). Cantatas, anthems, organ pieces, etc. —Cf. B. C. Tuthill, *Leo Sowerby,* in the 'Mus. Quarterly' (April, 1938).

Sowinski, Wojciech (Albert), Polish pianist; b. Lukaszówka, Podolia, 1803; d. Paris, March 5, 1880. He was a pupil of Czerny and Seyfried in Vienna; toured in Italy as pianist; in 1830 settled in Paris, and was a successful piano teacher there. He publ. the first dictionary of Polish musicians in a western language, *Les Musiciens polonais et slaves, anciens et modernes. Dictionnaire biographique des compositeurs, chanteurs, instrumentistes, luthiers . . .* (Paris, 1857; in Polish, Paris, 1874), and it is through this publication that his name is remembered. He also wrote 3 operas, *Lenore, Le Modèle,* and *Une Scène sous la ligne;* an oratorio, *Saint Adalbert;* several motets; a symphony; overtures on Polish subjects; a piano concerto; a piano quartet; a piano trio; numerous piano pieces in the salon genre.

Spadavecchia, Antonio, Russian composer of Italian descent; b. Odessa, June 3, 1907. He studied with Shebalin at the Moscow Cons., and also took lessons from Prokofiev. —Works: operas, *Ak-Buzat (The Magic Steed;* Ufa, Nov. 7, 1942; in collaboration with Zaimov), *The Inn Hostess,* after Goldoni (Moscow, April 24, 1949), *Pilgrimage of Sorrows,* after Alexey Tolstoy (Perm, Dec. 29, 1953); ballets, *Enemies* (Moscow, May 20, 1938); *The Shore of Happiness* (Moscow, Nov. 6, 1948); a symph. suite, *Dzangar* (1940); *Heroic Overture on Bashkir Songs* (Ufa, Nov. 6, 1942); a piano concerto (1944); *Romantic Trio* for violin, cello, and piano (1937).

Spaeth, Sigmund, American writer on music; b. Philadelphia, April 10, 1885. He studied piano and violin with A. Bachmann; then attended Haverford College (M. A., 1906); Ph. D., Princeton Univ., 1910, with the dissertation, *Milton's Knowledge of Music* (publ. 1913). He was music editor of the N. Y. 'Evening Mail' (1914-18); education director of the American Piano Co. (1920-27); president of the National Association of American Composers and Conductors (1934-37); lectured widely on music; gave popular talks on the radio; was active in musical journalism; held various posts in educational organizations. —Books (a selective list): *The Common Sense of Music* (1924); *The Art of Enjoying Music* (1933); *Music for Everybody* (1934); *Great Symphonies* (1936); *Stories Behind the World's Great Music* (1937); *Music for Fun* (1939); *Great Program Music* (1940); *At Home with Music* (1945); *A History of Popular Music in America* (N. Y., 1948); *Opportunities in Music* (N. Y., 1950); *Dedication; The Love Story of Clara and Robert Schumann* (N. Y., 1950); edited several songbooks: *Barber Shop Ballads* (1925; reprinted 1940), *Read 'em and Weep* (1926; revised 1945).

Spalding, Albert, American violinist; b. Chicago, Aug. 15, 1888; d. New York, May 26, 1953. At 7, pupil of Chiti in Florence; then of Lefort in Paris and Buitrago in N. Y. Début in Paris, June 6, 1905; American début with the N. Y. Symph. Orch. on Nov. 8, 1908, followed by tour of the U. S.; visited Scandinavia, Russia, the Netherlands, Italy, and Egypt, returning for a second

American tour in 1912; won fresh laurels in European capitals from 1912-14; from 1919 he made annual tours of the U. S., also appearing frequently in Europe; was soloist with the N. Y. Symph. Orch. on its first European tour (1920). He composed violin concertos and other works for violin and orch.; a string quartet; violin sonata; suite for violin and piano; piano pieces, songs, etc.; publ. his autobiography, *Rise to Follow* (N. Y., 1943), and a fictionalized biography of Tartini, *A Fiddle, A Sword and a Lady* (N. Y., 1953).

Spalding, Walter Raymond, American pedagogue; b. Northampton, Mass., May 22, 1865. Graduate of Harvard Univ. (B. A., 1887; M. A., 1888, with honors in music); taught classics at St. Mark's School, Southborough, Mass., 1889-92; from 1892-95 studied music in Paris (with Guilmant and Widor) and Munich (with Rheinberger); appointed instructor of music at Harvard in 1895, assistant prof. in 1903, and prof. in 1912; also prof. at Radcliffe College. In 1920-21 he lectured at 8 French universities. Publ. *Tonal Counterpoint* (1940); *Modern Harmony in Its Theory and Practice* (1905; with Arthur Foote); *Music; an Art and a Language* (1920); *Music at Harvard* (1935).

Spangenberg, Heinrich, German composer; b. Darmstadt, May 24, 1861; d. there, Sept. 27, 1925. He studied at Hoch's Cons. in Frankfurt; in 1881 for a short time pupil of N. Rubinstein (piano) in Moscow; then studied with Leschetizky (piano) and Grädener (composition) in Vienna. In 1884, Kapellmeister at the opera and instructor at the Cons. in Mainz; 1886, at Fredenberg's Cons. in Wiesbaden, and in 1888 conductor of the 'Lehrerverein'; about 1890 he founded his own Cons. there, of which he was director until 1914. He composed 3 operas; orchestral works (MS); piano pieces; songs and numerous choruses for men's voices.

Spanuth (shpah'-noot), **August,** German pianist and editor; b. Brinkum, near Hanover, March 15, 1857; d. Berlin, Jan. 9, 1920. Pupil of Heymann (piano) and Raff (composition) at Hoch's Cons. in Frankfurt; début as pianist in 1874; then lived as concert pianist and teacher in Koblenz and Bremen; toured the U. S. as pianist in 1886; taught at the Chicago Musical College, 1887-93; from 1893-1906 in N. Y. as teacher and music critic of the 'Staatszeitung'; settled in Berlin in 1906 as teacher at Stern's Cons. and (from 1907) ed. of 'Signale für die musikalische Welt.' He publ. *Preparatory Piano Exercises* and *Essential Piano Technics;* songs and piano pieces; with X. Scharwenka he wrote *Methodik des Klavierspiels* (1907); ed. 3 vols. of Liszt's piano compositions (Ditson's 'Musician's Library').

Spark, Dr. William, English organist and composer; b. Exeter, Oct. 28, 1823; d. Leeds, June 16, 1897. Chorister in Exeter Cathedral; pupil of S. S. Wesley; from 1850-80, organist at St. George's, Leeds; founder, 1851, of the Leeds Madrigal and Motet Society; borough organist of Leeds, 1860; Mus. Doc., Dublin, 1861; editor of 'The Organist's Quarterly Journal.' —Writings: *Memoir of Dr. S. S. Wesley; Henry Smart, His Life and Works* (London, 1881); *Musical Memories* (1888); and *Musical Reminiscences* (1892).

Spazier (shpăh-tsēr'), **Johann Gottlieb Karl,** German song composer; b. Berlin, April 20, 1761; d. Leipzig, Jan. 19, 1805. Student of philosophy at Halle and Göttingen; prof. at Giessen; settled in Leipzig, 1800. He wrote many songs, some of which became great favorites. Publ. the autobiographical *Karl Pilgers. Roman seines Lebens* (3 vols., 1792-96); *Freie Gedanken über die Gottesverehrung der Protestanten* (1788); *Etwas über Gluckische Musik und die Oper 'Iphigenia in Tauris'* (1795); *Rechtfertigung Marpurgs . . .* (1800, in the 'Allgemeine musikalische Zeitung'); *Über den Volksgesang* (ibid.); ed. Dittersdorf's autobiography. —Cf. M. Friedlaender, *Das deutsche Lied im 18. Jahrhundert* (1902).

Speaight, Joseph, English pianist and pedagogue; b. London, Oct. 24, 1868; d. there, Nov. 20, 1947. He studied piano with Ernst Pauer and composition with R. O. Morgan at the Guildhall School of Music; taught there from 1894 to 1919; then on the faculty of Trinity College (1919-39). He wrote 3 symphonies, a piano concerto, piano pieces, and songs.

Speaks, Oley, American baritone and song composer; b. Canal Winchester, Ohio, June 28, 1874; d. New York, Aug. 27, 1948. He studied singing with Emma Thursby and composition with Max Spicker and W. Macfarlane; sang at various churches in N. Y. (1898-1906); then devoted himself entirely to concert singing and composition. He wrote some of the most popular songs in the American repertory: *On the Road to Mandalay, Sylvia, The Prayer Perfect, Morning,*

Life's Twilight, My Homeland, The Lord is My Light, To You, etc.

Specht, Richard, Austrian writer on music; b. Vienna, Dec. 7, 1870; d. there, March 18, 1932. Trained as an architect, he turned to musical criticism at the suggestion of Brahms and Goldmark, writing at first for 'Die Zeit' (Vienna daily), and from 1908-15 for 'Die Musik.' In 1909 he founded 'Der Merker,' which he ed. until 1919 (at first with R. Batka, later with J. Bittner). 1914, Officier de l'Académie (France); 1926, professor. —Principal writings: *Kritisches Skizzenbuch* (1900); *Gustav Mahler* (1906; enlarged, 1913); *Joh. Strauss* (1909); *Das Wiener Operntheater von Dingelstedt bis Schalk und Strauss* (1919); *Richard Strauss und sein Werk,* in 2 vols. (1921); *Julius Bittner* (1921); *Wilhelm Furtwängler* (1922); *E. N. von Rezniček* (1923); *Brahms* (1928; in English, 1930); *Bildnis Beethovens* (1930, in English as *Beethoven as He Lived,* 1933); *Giacomo Puccini* (1931; in English, 1933); etc.

Speer, Daniel, German composer; b. Breslau, July 2, 1636; d. Göppingen, Oct. 5, 1707. He taught music in Stuttgart (1665-67); in 1675 he settled in Göppingen, where he was employed as town piper; he was dismissed for publishing a pamphlet mocking the authorities, and spent a year and a half in prison; was sent away to Waiblingen in 1690, but was reinstated in 1693 and recalled to Göppingen. He publ. (under assumed names and anagrams) several collections of whimsical songs; also several pieces of chamber music. —Cf. H. J. Moser, *Daniel Speer,* in 'Acta Musicologica' (vol. 9, 1937).

Speidel (spī'-dĕl), **Wilhelm,** German pianist and composer; b. Ulm, Sept. 3, 1826; d. Stuttgart, Oct. 13, 1899. Pupil at Munich of Wänner and W. Kuhe, and of Ignaz Lachner (composition); 1846-48, teacher at Thann, Alsatia; 1848-54, at Munich; 1854, music director at Ulm; 1857, conductor of the 'Liederkranz' at Stuttgart; co-founder of the Cons., and teacher of piano there until he founded his 'Künstler- und Dilettantenschule für Klavier' in 1874. On Lebert's death (1884) Speidel rejoined the Cons., uniting with it his own school.

Speier, Wilhelm. See **Speyer.**

Spelman, Timothy Mather, American composer; b. Brooklyn, Jan. 21, 1891. He studied with H. R. Shelley in N. Y. (1908), with W. R. Spalding and E. B. Hill at Harvard Univ. (1909-13), and with Walter Courvoisier at the Munich Cons. (1913-15). He returned to the U. S. in 1915, and was assistant director of band musicians' training in the War Dept. After 1918 he went back to Europe with his wife, the poetess Leolyn Everett, and settled in Florence, until 1935; then again in N. Y., until 1947, when he once more went to Florence. His works are more often performed in Europe than in America; his style of composition reflects the influences of Italian Romanticism and French Impressionism; most of his music is of a programmatic nature. —Works: *Snowdrop,* a pantomime in 4 acts (Brooklyn, 1911); *The Romance of the Rose,* a 'wordless fantasy' (Boston, 1913; revised version, St. Paul, Minn., Dec. 4, 1915); *La Magnifica,* 1-act music drama to a libretto by Mrs. Everett-Spelman (1920); *The Sunken City,* opera (1930); *The Courtship of Miles Standish,* opera after Longfellow (1943). For orch.: *Barbaresques,* suite (1922); *Saints' Days,* suite in 4 movements (1925; one movement, *Assisi, the Great Pardon of St. Francis,* was performed in Boston, March 26, 1926); *The Outcasts of Poker Flat,* symph. poem after Bret Harte (1928); Symphony in G minor (Rochester, Oct. 29, 1936); *Homesick Yankee in North Africa,* a rhapsody (1944); *Jamboree,* a 'pocket ballet' (1945); *Sunday Paper,* suite (1946); oboe concerto (1954). Chamber music: *Five Whimsical Serenades,* for string quartet (1924); *Le Pavillon sur l'eau,* for flute, harp, and strings (1925); string quartet (1953). Vocal works: *Litany of the Middle Ages,* for soprano, women's chorus, and orch. (1928); *Pervigilium Veneris,* for soprano, baritone, chorus, and orch. (Paris, April 30, 1931); *I Love the Jocund Dance,* for women's chorus and piano (1938); songs.

Spencer, Allen, American pianist and pedagogue; b. Fair Haven, Vt., Oct. 30, 1870; d. Chicago, Aug. 25, 1950. He studied piano in Rochester and Chicago; in 1892 was appointed teacher at the American Cons. in Chicago; then became its dean (1928-48). He publ. *Foundations of Piano Technique,* and 5 Concert Etudes for piano.

Spencer, S. Reid, American pianist and teacher; b. Baltimore, July 30, 1872; d. Brooklyn, July 28, 1945. He studied with P. C. Lutkin at the Northwestern Univ. School of Music, and taught there from 1895 to 1900. After teaching in various conservatories, he established his own music school in Brooklyn (1927). He publ. a textbook on harmony (1915), wrote pieces for organ and a *Sonate romantique* for piano; also church music.

Spencer, Vernon, pianist and composer; b. Belmont, Durham, England, Oct. 10, 1875; d. Los Angeles, Jan. 9, 1949. He studied at the Leipzig Cons., graduating in 1897; in 1903 he settled in the U. S.; was director of the Wesleyan Univ. Cons. of Music at Lincoln, Nebraska; from 1911 taught in Los Angeles. He publ. some songs and character pieces for piano.

Spendiarov, Alexander Afanasievitch, Russian composer; b. Kakhovka, Crimea, Nov. 1, 1871; d. Erivan, May 7, 1928. He received his early education at Simferopol, Crimea, cultivating chiefly the art of painting, but also studying violin; subsequently went to Moscow, where he took academic courses at the Univ.; in 1896 he became a private pupil of Rimsky-Korsakov in St. Petersburg. In his music he adopted the style of Russian Orientalism, making use of Armenian melodic and rhythmic elements. —Works for orch.: *Minuet* (1895); *Berceuse* (1897); *Ouverture de concert* (1900); *Les trois palmiers,* a symph. picture after a poem by Lermontov (1905); *Valse de concert* (1907); *Prélude funèbre* (1908); *Crimean Sketches,* 2 sets (1903; 1912); *2 Songs of the Crimean Tartars* (1915; Moscow, Dec. 25, 1927); *Études d'Eriwan,* on Armenian melodies (1925). Shortly before his death he undertook the composition of his only opera, *Almast,* after an Armenian legend; it was completed and revised by Maximilian Steinberg, and was performed posthumously in Moscow on June 23, 1930; revived at the Festival of Armenian music in Moscow in 1939.

Spengel, Julius Heinrich, German composer; b. Hamburg, June 12, 1853; d. there, April 17, 1936. He studied at the Cologne Cons.; later at the Berlin Hochschule für Musik with Rudorff, Joachim, Kiel, and A. Schulze; settled as a teacher in Hamburg. In 1878 he was conductor of the 'Cäcilienverein' there; organist of the Gertrudenkirche (1886); made Royal Prof. in 1906. —Works: piano quintet; Psalm 39 for 6-part chorus and wind instruments; *Zwiegesang in der Sommernacht,* for chorus and orch.; *König Alfreds Gesang,* for baritone and orch.; male and female choruses; songs.

Sperontes (real name, Johann Sigismund Scholze), German composer; b. Lobendau, Silesia, March 20, 1705; d. Leipzig, Sept. 27, 1750. Between 1736 and 1745 he brought out a collection of poems and melodies to words by Johann Christian Günther, *Singende Muse an der Pleisse in zweimal 50 Oden;* this became famous, and its success generated many imitations, by composers in Leipzig, Hamburg, and Vienna. Reprint (ed. by E. Buhle) in the 'Denkmäler deutscher Tonkunst' (vols. 35, 36). —Cf. articles by Spitta in the 'Vierteljahrsschrift für Musikwissenschaft' (vol. 1, 1885) and H. von Hase in the 'Zeitschrift der Internationalen Musik-Gesellschaft' (vol. XIV, 4); also A. Schering, *Zwei Singspiele des Sperontes,* in the 'Zeitschrift für Musikwissenschaft' (vol. VII, 4).

Speyer (shpī'-er), **Wilhelm,** German violinist and composer; b. Frankfurt, June 21, 1790; d. there, April 5, 1878. He studied in Offenbach with F. Fränzl (violin) and A. André (composition); later in Paris with Baillot (violin). After extensive travels as a concert violinist, he returned to Frankfurt, and embraced a mercantile career, but continued his associations with eminent musicians (Spohr, Mendelssohn, etc.) and began to compose. He gave the first impulse to the great festival held in Frankfurt in 1838, from the profits of which was established the Mozart Scholarship. He wrote a great deal of chamber music; his violin pieces were often played, but he achieved lasting popularity with his ballads written in a characteristically Romantic style; of these *Der Trompeter* and *Die drei Liebchen* were particularly famous. —His son, **Edward Speyer** (b. Frankfurt, May 14, 1839; d. Shenley, Hertfordshire, Jan. 8, 1934), lived most of his life in London, where he organized the Classical Concerts Society; he publ. a monograph on his father, *Wilhelm Speyer, der Liederkomponist* (Munich, 1925), and a book of reminiscences, *My Life and Friends* (posthumous, London, 1937).

Spialek, Hans, composer and arranger; b. Vienna, April 17, 1894. He studied at the Cons. of Vienna; settled in the U. S. in 1924, and became an orchestrator of musical comedies in N. Y. He wrote a number of descriptive pieces for salon orch. and for various ensembles (*Cloister Meditations, Vision, The Tall City, Manhattan Watercolors, The Danube,* etc.); also a *Sinfonietta* (N. Y., Nov. 15, 1936).

Spicker, Max, conductor, composer, and music editor; b. Königsberg, Aug. 16, 1858; d. New York, Oct. 15, 1912. He studied with Louis Köhler (piano); then at the Leipzig Cons. with Reinecke and Richter.

In 1882 he settled in N. Y., where he conducted German choral societies and taught harmony at the National Cons.; was also reader for G. Schirmer, Inc. He wrote incidental music to Schiller's *Demetrius;* a cantata, *Der Pilot;* many songs; edited 'Aus aller Herren Länder' (a collection of folksongs arranged for male chorus), 'Anthology of Sacred Song' (4 vols.), 'Operatic Anthology' (5 vols.), 'The Synagogical Service' (2 vols.; with W. Sparger); etc.

Spielter (spēl'-ter), **Hermann,** composer; b. Bremen, April 26, 1860; d. New York, Nov. 10, 1925. He studied with Reinecke and Jadassohn at the Leipzig Cons.; won the Mendelssohn Prize in 1886 with a piano trio, a violin sonata, and a cello sonata. He settled in N. Y. in 1894; from 1897 to 1911 taught theory at the N. Y. College of Music. His works include an operetta, *Die Rajahsbraut* (N. Y., 1910); *Vineta,* for baritone, male chorus, and orch.; other choral pieces; a piano sonata; a cello sonata; *Serenade* for flute and piano; many piano pieces.

Spiering (spē'-ring), **Theodore,** American violinist and conductor; b. St. Louis, Sept. 5, 1871; d. Munich, Aug. 11, 1925. He studied with Schradieck at the Cincinnati College of Music and with Joachim at the Hochschule für Musik in Berlin. Returning to America, he played the violin in the Theodore Thomas Orch. in Chicago; also organized his own quartet, with which he toured the U. S. and Canada (1893-1905); then traveled in Germany as soloist (1906-09). In 1909 he was appointed concertmaster of the N. Y. Philharmonic Orch. (under Mahler); during Mahler's last illness, he was called upon to conduct 17 concerts of the N. Y. Philharmonic in the spring of 1911. He publ. *Sechs Künstler-Etüden,* for violin; with Rudolf Ganz he edited a number of classical and modern violin pieces (Bach, Mozart, Grieg, Tchaikovsky, etc.).

Spies (shpēs), **Hermine,** eminent German contralto, b. Löhneberger Hütte, near Weilburg, Feb. 25, 1857; d. Wiesbaden, Feb. 26, 1893. She was a pupil of Stockhausen in Frankfurt; in 1883 began to give song recitals in Germany; in 1889 made an appearance in England with excellent success; also sang in Austria, Denmark, and Russia. She excelled as an interpreter of songs by Brahms, who had a high regard for her. Shortly before her death she married Dr. W. A. F. Hardtmuth of Wiesbaden. —Cf. Marie Spies, *Hermine Spies. Ein Gedenkbuch für ihre Freunde* (Stuttgart, 1894; 3rd augmented ed., 1905).

Spiess (shpēss), **Meinrad,** German composer; b. Honsolgen, Aug. 24, 1683; d. Yrsee, July 12, 1761. He was a pupil of Giuseppe Antonio Bernabei in Munich; music director at the monastery of Yrsee from 1712 to 1749; wrote several Masses and other church music; also 12 trio sonatas for violin, cello, and organ, and other instrumental works.

Spilka, František, Czech composer; b. Štěken, Nov. 13, 1887. He studied at the Prague Cons., and became conductor of the Czech Philharmonic; in 1918 was appointed administrative director of the Prague Cons. He established the 'Teachers' Choral Society' in 1908, and gave concerts with it in France and England. He wrote many choral works; an opera, *Stará práva (Ancient Rights;* Prague, May 10, 1907); a Sonata-Rhapsody, for cello and piano (1945); etc.

Spindler (shpind'-ler), **Fritz,** German pianist and composer; b. Wurzbach, Nov. 24, 1817; d. Lössnitz, near Dresden, Dec. 26, 1905. He studied with Fr. Schneider at Dessau; settled in 1841 at Dresden, where he had great success as a teacher. Most of his works (over 400 op. numbers) are salon pieces and characteristic pieces for piano; also publ. the instructive sonatinas op. 157, 290, 294, and the 4-hand sonatina op. 136.

Spinelli, Nicola, Italian composer; b. Turin, July 29, 1865; d. Rome, Oct. 17, 1909. He studied at the Naples Cons., under Serrao. In 1889 his 1-act opera *Labilia* took the 2nd prize in the famous competition instituted by the publisher Sonzogno, when Mascagni won the 1st prize with *Cavalleria rusticana;* Spinelli's opera was produced in Rome on May 7, 1890, with indifferent success. His next opera, *A basso porto,* was more fortunate; after its initial production in Cologne on April 18, 1894 (in a German version), it was staged in Rome, in Italian (March 11, 1895), and then in Budapest, St. Petersburg, etc.; it was also produced in the U. S. (St. Louis, Jan. 8, 1900; N. Y., Jan. 22, 1900). Spinelli's career was cut short by a mental illness.

Spisak, Michal, Polish composer; b. Dabrowa Górnicza, Sept. 14, 1914. He studied violin in Warsaw; in 1937, went to Paris, to study with Nadia Boulanger, and remained there. —Works: *Symphonie Concertante;* bassoon concerto (Copenhagen,

Festival of the International Society for Contemporary Music, June 2, 1947); *Toccata,* for orch.; suite for string orch.; *Divertimento,* for 2 pianos and orch.; concertino for strings; quintet for wind instruments; woodwind quartet; sonatina for oboe, clarinet, and bassoon; violin sonata; piano music.

Spitta, Friedrich, German theologian and writer on music, brother of Philipp Spitta; b. Wittingen, Jan. 10, 1852; d. Göttingen, June 8, 1924. From 1887-1918 prof. of theology at Strasbourg Univ. and from 1919 at Göttingen; from 1896 also editor (with J. Smend) of 'Monatschrift für Gottesdienst und kirchliche Kunst,' in which (Jan.-March, 1913) he publ. important facts concerning Benedictus Ducis. He publ. *Liturgische Andacht zum Luther-Jubiläum* (1883); *H. Schütz,* festival oration (1886); *Die Passionen nach den vier Evangelisten von H. Schütz* (1886); *Über Chorgesang im evangelischen Gottesdienste* (1889); *'Ein' feste Burg ist unser Gott.' Die Lieder Luthers . . .* (1905); *Studien zu Luthers Liedern* (1907); *Das deutsche Kirchenlied in seinen charakteristischen Erscheinungen* (vol. I: *Mittelalter und Reformationszeit,* 1912); *H. Schütz* (1925); also a new ed. of Mergner's *Paul Gerhardt Lieder* (1918); etc.

Spitta, (Johann August) Philipp, German musicologist; b. Wechold, Hanover, Dec. 27, 1841; d. Berlin, April 13, 1894. Student of philology at Göttingen; teacher at the 'Ritter und Domschule,' Reval, 1864-66; at Sondershausen Gymnasium till 1874; and one year at the Nikolai-Gymnasium, Leipzig, where he was a co-founder of the 'Bach-Verein' (1874); in 1875, prof. of music history at Berlin Univ., life-secretary to the Royal Academy of Arts, and teacher at, and vice-director of, the 'Hochschule für Musik.' As a teacher he had extraordinary success; among his pupils were O. Fleischer, A. Sandberger, M. Friedlaender, R. Schwartz, M. Seiffert, E. Vogel, K. Krebs, and J. Combarieu. He was one of the leading spirits in organizing the publication of the 'Denkmäler deutscher Tonkunst.' —Writings: A comprehensive life of *J. S. Bach* (2 vols., 1873, 1880), carefully and learnedly written, with valuable discussions of principal works (in English, London, 1884-85; condensed ed., Leipzig, 1935); also a short sketch of Bach in Waldersee's 'Vorträge' (1880); a short biography of Schumann for Grove's Dictionary, afterwards published separately in German ('Vorträge,' 1882); *Händel und Bach,* 2 festival orations (1885); *Zur Ausgabe der Kompositionen Friedrichs des Grossen* (1890); 2 collections of articles, *Zur Musik* (1892; 16 essays), and *Musikgeschichtliche Aufsätze* (Berlin, 1894); an essay, *Die Passionsmusiken von Sebastian Bach und Heinrich Schütz* (Hamburg, 1893); many papers in the 'Allgemeine musikalische Zeitung,' the 'Monatshefte für Musikgeschichte,' and more particularly in his own periodical, the 'Vierteljahrsschrift für Musikwissenschaft,' founded in 1884 with Chrysander and G. Adler. —Spitta also edited a critical ed. of Buxtehude's organ works (2 volumes, 1875, 1876), with valuable historical notes; the complete ed. of Schütz's works (16 vols.); and Vol. I of the 'Denkmäler deutscher Tonkunst' (1892; contains Scheidt's *Tabulatura nova* of 1624). He left in MS an almost completed *Geschichte der romantischen Oper in Deutschland.* Spitta's correspondence with Brahms was publ. by the German 'Brahmsgesellschaft' (Vol. 15).

Spitzmueller, Alexander, composer; b. Vienna, Feb. 22, 1894. He studied with Alban Berg; in 1928, settled in Paris, where he conducted radio concerts. —Works: *Sinfonietta ritmica; 40th May,* satirical suite for orch. (Amsterdam, Festival of the International Society for Contemporary Music, June 12, 1948); piano concerto No. 1 (1950); piano concerto No. 2 (Geneva, Oct. 13, 1954); violin sonata; cello sonata; variations for viola and guitar; string quartet; saxophone quartet; *Te Deum,* for chorus, organ, and orch.; *Salve Regina,* for voices and small orch.

Spivacke, Harold, American musicologist; b. New York, July 18, 1904. He studied at New York Univ. (M. A., 1925); at the Univ. of Berlin (Ph. D., *magna cum laude,* 1933); privately in Berlin with Eugen d'Albert and Hugo Leichtentritt as American-German Students Exchange Fellow (1930), and as 'Alexander von Humboldt Stiftung' Fellow (1931). Returning to the U. S., he became assistant chief of the Music Division, Library of Congress, Washington (1934-37); from 1937, chief of the Music Division. Other positions held by Spivacke include: member of the Advisory Committee on Music to the Dept. of State (1939-46); member, U. S. National Commission for Unesco from 1950; member, and from 1952, chairman of the Fulbright Advisory Selection Committee on Music; president of the Music Library Association (1951-53); member of Executive Board of the American Musicological Society, etc. As chief of the Music Division of the Library of Congress, he has been responsible for the acquisition of important materials (including a sizable collection of Schoenberg's MSS). Spivacke married the violinist Carolyn Le Fevre in 1927; divorced in 1953; married Rose Marie Grentzer in 1955. He is the author of *Paganiniana* (Washington, 1945) and numerous articles.

Spivakovsky, Tossy, outstanding violinist; b. Odessa, Feb. 4, 1907. He studied with Willy Hess in Berlin; made his concert début there at the age of 10; toured Europe (1920-33) and Australia (1933-41); then came to the U. S.; appeared with major American orchestras.

Spohr (shpor), **Ludwig (Louis),** celebrated German violinist, composer, and conductor; b. Brunswick, April 5, 1784; d. Kassel, Oct. 22, 1859. The family moved to Seesen in 1786. His father, a physician, was an amateur flute player, and his mother a singer and pianist. In this musical atmosphere Spohr's talent developed very early; at the age of 5 he began taking lessons on the violin with Rector Riemenschneider and Dufour, a French *émigré*. Spohr was then sent back to Brunswick, where he was taught by the organist Hartung and the violinist Maucourt. He had already composed various violin pieces; the duke himself became interested in Spohr, admitted him to the orch., and arranged for his further study with the violinist Franz Eck. In 1802 Eck took Spohr with him on a tour to Russia, where he made the acquaintance of Clementi and John Field; he returned to Brunswick in 1803 and resumed his post in the ducal orch. In 1804 he made his 1st tour as a violinist, giving concerts in Berlin, Leipzig, and Dresden; in 1805 he became concertmaster in the ducal orch. at Gotha; married the harp player Dorette Scheidler, and toured with her in Germany in 1807. His reputation as a violin virtuoso was established, and he began to give more attention to composition. He wrote oratorios, operas, violin concertos, symphonies, and chamber music, which obtained excellent success in Germany. In 1812 he gave a series of concerts in Vienna, and was acclaimed both as composer and violinist; accepted the position of concertmaster in the orch. of the Theater an der Wien, which he held until 1815. He then made a grand tour of Germany and Italy; played a *concertante* of his own with Paganini in Rome. In 1816 Spohr's opera *Faust* was performed by Weber in Prague. After a visit to Holland in 1817, he received the post of opera conductor in Frankfurt, where he produced one of his most popular operas, *Zemire und Azor* (1819). In 1820 he visited England; appeared with his wife at several concerts of the London Philharmonic Society; this was the 1st of his 6 tours of England, where he acquired a lasting reputation as violinist, conductor, and composer; his works continued to be performed in England for many decades after his death. On his way back to Germany, he presented several concerts in Paris in 1820, but his reception there failed to match his London successes. He then proceeded to Dresden, and was recommended by Weber for the post of court Kapellmeister in Kassel, originally offered to Weber. Spohr accepted it, and settled there in 1822. It was in Kassel that he produced his masterpiece, the opera *Jessonda* (1823), which held the stage in Europe throughout the 19th century. He conducted its performances in Leipzig and Berlin; also appeared as conductor and composer at various musical festivals (Düsseldorf, 1826; Nordhausen, 1829; Norwich, 1839; Bonn, 1845; etc.). The success of *Jessonda* was followed by the production in Kassel of his oratorio *Die letzten Dinge* (1826) and his symphony *Die Weihe der Töne* (1832), both of which elicited great praise. His wife died in 1834; he married the pianist Marianne Pfeiffer in 1836. Spohr made another journey to England in 1847; visited Frankfurt in in 1848. Returning to Kassel, he found himself in an increasingly difficult position because of his outspoken radicalism; the Elector of Hesse refused to grant him further leaves of absence, and Spohr decided to ignore the ban, which resulted in litigation with the Kassel Court. In 1853 he made his last tour of England, appearing at the New Philharmonic Concerts in London. He was retired from Kassel in 1857 on a pension; a few months later he broke his left arm, but despite this accident, at an advanced age, he made another appearance (his last) conducting *Jessonda* in Prague (1858). —Spohr's style was characteristic of the transition period between Classicism and Romanticism. He was a master of technical resources; some of his works demonstrate a spirit of bold experimentation (the *Historical Symph.;* symph. for 2 orchestras; quartet concerto; nonet, etc.); yet in his esthetics he was an intransigent conservative. He admired Beethoven's early works but confessed his total inability to understand Beethoven's last period; he also failed to appreciate Weber. It is remarkable, therefore, that he was an early champion of Wagner; in Kassel he brought out *Der fliegende Holländer* (1843) and *Tannhäuser* (1853), despite strenuous opposition of the court. He was a highly esteemed teacher; among his pupils were Ferdinand David and Moritz Hauptmann. His autobiography was publ. posthumously as *Louis Spohr's Selbstbiographie* (2 vols.; Kassel, 1860-61; in English, London, 1865 and 1878). A new ed. of his selected works, under the editorship of F. O. Leinert, began publication after World War II (Kassel, Bärenreiter-Verlag). —Works: Operas: *Die Prüfung* (Gotha, 1806); *Alruna, die Eulen-Königin* (1808); *Der Zweikampf mit der Geliebten* (Hamburg, Nov. 15, 1811); *Faust* (Prague, Sept. 1, 1816); *Zemire und Azor* (Frankfurt, April 4, 1819); *Jessonda* (Kassel, July 28, 1823); *Der Berggeist* (Kassel, March 24, 1825); *Pietro von Albano* (Kassel, Oct. 13, 1827); *Der Alchymist* (Kassel, July 28, 1830); *Die Kreuzfahrer* (Kassel, Jan. 1, 1845). Oratorios: *Das Jüngste Gericht* (Erfurt, Aug. 15, 1812); *Die letzten Dinge* (Kassel, March 25, 1826; in English, as *The Last Judgment); Des Heilands letze Stunden* (Kassel, 1835; in English as *Calvary* at the Norwich Festival, 1839); and *Der Fall Babylons* (Norwich Festival, 1842). Other vocal works: *Das befreite Deutschland,* dramatic cantata; a Mass for 5 voices and double chorus; 6 psalms; hymns, part-songs, etc.; duets; 10 books of German songs; a sonatina for voice and piano, *An sie am Klavier.* Symphonies: No. 1, in E♭ major; No. 2, in D minor; No. 3, in C minor; No. 4, *Die Weihe der Töne (Consecration of Sound),* in F major; No. 5, in C minor; No. 6, *Historical* (dedicated to the London Philharmonic Society), in G minor; No. 7, *Irdisches und Göttliches im Menschenleben,* for 2 orchestras, in C major; No. 8, in G minor; No. 9, *Die Jahreszeiten (The Seasons),* in B minor. Overtures: *Macbeth; Im ernsten Styl;* etc. 15 violin concertos (among the finest being No. 8, 'in modo d'una scena cantante,' and No. 9), all edited by Ferdinand David; a 'quartet concerto' for 2 violins, viola, and cello with orch.; 2 clarinet concertos. Chamber music: nonet for violin, viola, cello, double-bass, woodwinds, and horn; octet for violin, 2 violas, cello, double-bass, clarinet, and 2 horns; 4 double quartets for strings; septet for piano, flute, clarinet, horn, bassoon, violin, and cello; string sextet; 7 string quintets; quintet for piano, flute, clarinet, horn, and bassoon; piano quintet; 34 string quartets; 5 piano trios; 14 *duos concertants* for 2 violins; 3 *duos concertants* for piano and violin; 3 *sonates concertantes* for harp and violin; piano sonata in A♭; Rondoletto for piano; etc. —BIBLIOGRAPHY: W. Neumann, *L. Spohr. Eine Biographie* (Kassel, 1854); A. Malibran, *L. Spohr. Sein Leben und Wirken* (Frankfurt, 1860); L. Stierlin, *L. Spohr* (Zürich, 1862-63; 2 vols.); H. M. Schletterer, *L. Spohr* (Leipzig, 1881); L. Nohl, *Spohr* (Leipzig, 1882); C. Robert, *L. Spohr* (Berlin, 1883); La Mara, *Aus Spohrs Leben,* in *Klassisches und Romantisches aus der Tonwelt* (Leipzig, 1892); R. Wassermann, *L. Spohr als Opernkomponist* (Rostock, 1910); E. Istel, *5 Briefe Spohrs an Marschner,* in 'Liliencron-Festschrift' (Leipzig, 1910); F. Göthel, *Das Violinspiel L. Spohrs* (dissertation; Berlin, 1934); Edith von Salburg, *L. Spohr* (Leipzig, 1936); P. Heidelbach, *Ludwig Spohrs Prozess gegen den Kurfürst von Hessen* (in the 'Allgemeine Musikalische Zeitung,' 1936). See also F. Hiller, *M. Hauptmanns Briefe an L. Spohr und andere* (Leipzig, 1876; in English, London, 1892). For details of performances of Spohr's operas see A. Loewenberg, *Annals of Opera* (Cambridge, 1943; new ed., Geneva, 1955).

Spontini, Gasparo (Luigi Pacifico), Italian composer; b. Majolati, Ancona, Nov. 14, 1774; d. there, Jan. 24, 1851. His father, a modest farmer, intended him for the church, and gave him in charge of an uncle, a priest at Jesi, who attempted to stifle his musical aspirations. Spontini sought refuge at Monte San Vito, with another relative, who not only found a competent music teacher for him, but effected a reconciliation, so that after a year he was able to return to Jesi. In 1793 he entered the Cons. della Pietà de' Turchini in Naples, where his teachers were Tritto (singing) and Sala (composition). He rapidly mastered the conventional Italian style of his time; some of his church music performed in Naples came to the attention of a director of the Teatro della Pallacorda in Rome, who commissioned him to write an opera. This was *I Puntigli delle donne,* produced with notable success during Carnival, 1796. In his subsequent opera, *L'Eroismo ridicolo* (Naples, 1798), he was helped by Piccinni's practical advice. When the Neapolitan court fled to Palermo before the French invasion, Spontini was engaged as maestro di cappella, and wrote 4 operas in quick succession, which were produced at the Palermo court theater in 1800. He left Palermo soon afterwards, and proceeded to Rome (1801), Venice (1802), Naples and Paris (1803). In Paris he brought out 2 French operas at the Théâtre-Italien: *La petite maison* (May 12, 1804) and *Julie, ou le pot de fleurs* (March 12, 1805), in sedulous imitation of the Parisian light opera, but the attempt failed completely. Fortunately for Spontini, he met the poet Etienne de Jouy, a writer of superior accomplishments, who influenced him to change his style. The result was a one-act opera *Milton,* produced at the Théâtre Feydeau on Nov. 27, 1840. Its music showed greater expressiveness and a finer taste than Spontini's preceding works. The next libretto offered by Etienne de Jouy to Spontini (after it was rejected by Boieldieu and Méhul) was *La Vestale.* Spontini worked on the score for 3 years, repeatedly revising and rewriting in his desire to attain his best, and the final product became Spontini's masterpiece. In the meantime, the Empress Josephine had appointed him her 'compositeur particulier' and her appreciation of Spontini increased after the production of his patriotic cantata, *L'Eccelsa gara,* celebrating the victory of Austerlitz. Her powerful patronage secured a hearing for *La Vestale,* which was brought out at the Académie Impériale (Grand Opéra), despite virulent open and secret opposition on the part of influential musicians, on Dec. 16, 1807, and won triumphant success. Not only did the public receive it with acclamation; by a unanimous verdict of the judges, Méhul, Gossec, and Grétry, the prize offered by Napoleon for the best dramatic work was awarded to Spontini. Shortly after the equal success of his grand opera *Fernand Cortez* (Nov. 28, 1809), Spontini married the daughter of Jean-Baptiste Érard, and in 1810 became director of the Italian Opera, in which capacity he staged Mozart's *Don Giovanni* in its original form for the first time in Paris. He was dismissed in 1812, on charges of financial irregularity; but in 1814 Louis XVIII appointed him court composer, Spontini having refused reinstatement as operatic director in favor of Catalani. He now wrote stage pieces in glorification of the Restoration: *Pélage, ou le roi et la paix* (Aug. 23, 1814); *Les Dieux rivaux* (June 21, 1816); this was followed by *Olympie* (Paris Opéra, Dec. 22, 1819). He then accepted the appointment, by King Friedrich Wilhelm III, of court composer and general musical director at Berlin; made his début there, in the spring of 1820, with his opera *Fernand Cortez,* fairly electrifying his audiences, although, like *Julie, Milton,* and *La Vestale,* it had been heard before in Berlin. Here Spontini's remarkable ability as a conductor had freest scope; besides repeating his earlier works, he wrote for Berlin the festival play *Lalla Rookh* (1821), remodeled as the opera *Nurmahal, oder das Rosenfest von Kaschmir* (Berlin, May 27, 1822); *Alcidor* (Berlin, May 23, 1825); and *Agnes von Hohenstaufen* (Berlin, June 12, 1829); none of these, however, found favor in other German cities. In spite of his success, and the King's continued favor, Spontini's position in Berlin gradually grew untenable; he had been placed on an equality with the intendant of the Royal Theater, and there were frequent misunderstandings and sharp clashes of authority, not mitigated by Spontini's jealousies and dislikes, his overweening self-conceit and despotic temper. Partly through intrigue, partly by reason of his own lack of self-control, he narrowly escaped imprisonment for *lèse-majesté;* and was finally driven out of the theater by the hostile demonstrations of the audience. He retired in 1841, retaining his titles and full pay, but with his prestige and popularity greatly impaired. Thereafter he was inactive as a composer. He returned to Paris, but met with hostility from the director of the Opéra there. In 1844 he conducted a performance (prepared by Wagner) of *La Vestale* at Dresden. Finally, shattered in health, he retired to his native place and devoted his time to public charities. In 1844 the Pope had given him the rank and title of 'Conte de Sant' Andrea'; he was a knight of the Prussian 'Ordre pour le mérite,' member of the Berlin Akademie (1833), and the French Institute (1839), and had received from the Halle Univ. the degree of *Dr. phil.* —

Bibliography: L. de Loménie, *M. Spontini, par un homme de rien* (Paris, 1841); E. M. Oettinger, *Spontini* (Leipzig, 1843); I. Montanari, *Elogio . . .* (Ancona, 1851); Raoul-Rochette, *Notice historique sur la vie et les ouvrages de M. Spontini* (Paris 1852); C. Robert, *G. L. P. Spontini* (Berlin, 1883); Ph. Spitta, *Spontini in Berlin,* in *Zur Musik* (1892); W. Altmann, *Spontini an der Berliner Oper,* in 'Sammelbände der Internationalen Musik-Gesellschaft' (1903); E. Prout, *Spontini's La Vestale* in 'Monthly Mus. Record' (vol. 35; 1905); R. Wagner, *Erinnerungen an Spontini* (in his 'Gesammelte Schriften,' vol. V); A. Pougin, *Les dernières années de Spontini* in 'Rivista Musicale Italiana' XXIX (1922); C. Radicotti, *Spontini a Berlino* (Ancona, 1925); C. Bouvet, *Spontini* (Paris, 1930); K. Schubert, *Spontinis italienische Schule* (Strasbourg, 1932); A. Ghislanzoni, *G. Spontini* (Rome, 1951); P. Fragapane, *G. Spontini* (Bologna, 1954); 'Atti del primo congresso internazionale di studi Spontiniani . . . 1951' (Fabriano, 1954); F. Schlitzer, *Frammenti biografici di G. Spontini* (Siena, 1955); A. Belardinelli, ed., *Documenti spontiniani inediti* (Florence, 1955; 2 vols.); also letters of Spontini publ. by Radiciotti and Pfeiffer in 'Note d'archivio' (1932).

Sporck, Georges, French composer; b. Paris, April 9, 1870; d. there, Jan. 17, 1943. He studied with Guiraud and Dubois at the Paris Cons., and later with Vincent d'Indy; was officer of Public Instruction; wrote a number of symph. works of a programmatic nature, often with regional color: *Symphonie vivaraise; Islande; Boabdil; Kermesse; Paysages normandes; Esquisses symphoniques; Prélude symphonique; Méditation; Orientale;* etc.; a violin sonata; piano pieces *(Études symphoniques,* sonatina, etc.); 2 books of songs. He also publ. instructive editions of classical works (Bach, Mozart, Beethoven, Mendelssohn, Schumann, etc.).

Springer, Hermann, German musicologist; b. Döbeln, May 9, 1872; d. Feb., 1945 (killed during the fighting in eastern Germany). He studied philology and music history in Leipzig, Berlin, and Paris; *Dr. phil.,* 1894, with the dissertation *Das altprovenzalische Klagelied* (1895). He entered the Prussian Library Service in 1899, continuing in this position for nearly 40 years; was a member of various learned societies. He publ. *Beethoven und die Musikkritik* (Vienna, 1927); contributed musicographical papers to German and Austrian publications.

Springer, Max, writer on music; b. Schwendi, Württemberg, Dec. 19, 1877; d. Vienna, Jan. 20, 1954. He attended the Univ. in Prague, and studied music with Klička. In 1910 he was appointed prof. of Gregorian choral singing and organist in the section for church music of the State Academy, Klosterneuburg, near Vienna, and held this post until his retirement shortly before his death. He publ. *Die Kunst der Choralbegleitung* (1907; English transl., 1908) and manuals on liturgical choral singing; *Graduale Romanum* in modern notation (1930); *Kontrapunkt* (Vienna, 1936); composed church music.

Spross, Charles Gilbert, American organist and composer; b. Poughkeepsie, N. Y., Jan. 6, 1874. He studied piano with X. Scharwenka while the latter was in N. Y.; organ with various teachers; for nearly 40 years was organist at various churches in Poughkeepsie, Paterson, N. J., New York, etc.; was accompanist to celebrated singers (Fremstad, Schumann-Heink, Nordica, Emma Eames, etc.). He publ. about 250 songs; 5 sacred cantatas; a violin sonata and other chamber music. After his retirement about 1952, he lived in Poughkeepsie.

Spry, Walter, American pianist, pedagogue, and composer; b. Chicago, Feb. 27, 1868; d. Spartanburg, S. C., Sept. 25, 1953. He studied with Leschetizky in Vienna (1889-90), and at the Hochschule für Musik in Berlin (1890-93). In 1905 he established his own music school in Chicago; from 1917 to 1933 taught at the Columbia School of Music there, and from 1933 to his death, at the Converse College School of Music (Spartanburg, S. C.). He wrote mostly for piano; also composed songs.

Squarcialupi (skwăhr-tchă-lōō'-pē), **Antonio,** renowned Italian organist (called 'Antonio degli Organi'); b. Florence, March 27, 1416; d. there, July 6, 1480. He lived in Siena before 1450; a few years later returned to Florence, where he became organist at the church of Santa Maria del Fiore and enjoyed the protection of Lorenzo the Magnificent. He was highly esteemed by Dufay (cf. F. X. Haberl, *Dufay,* in the 'Vierteljahrsschrift für Musikwissenschaft,' 1885, p. 436). Since none of his works has survived, only oblique reports on their excellence can be adduced, but his name was immortalized by the famous 'Squarcialupi Codex,' a collection of Florentine polyphonic music of the 14th century, preserved in the Biblioteca Medicea-Laurenziana in Florence (Cod. Pal. 87). The collection was edited by Johannes Wolf and publ. in 1955. —Cf. Bianca Becherini, *Un Canta in panca fiorentino; Antonio di Guido,* in the 'Rivista Musicale Italiana' (July-Dec., 1948).

Squire, William Barclay, English musicologist; b. London, Oct. 16, 1855; d. there, Jan. 13, 1927. He received his education in Frankfurt, Germany, and at Pembroke College, Cambridge (B. A., 1879; M. A., 1902). He practiced law; in 1885 he was placed in charge of the printed music in the British Museum, retiring as Assistant Keeper in 1920; compiled catalogues of music for the British Museum (publ. in 1899 and 1912); also the catalogue of the King's Music Library (3 vols., 1927-29). He wrote music criticism in the 'Saturday Review' (1890-94); contributed biographical articles to the 'Dictionary of National Biography' and to various archeological and antiquarian periodicals; edited (with J. A. Fuller Maitland) *The Fitzwilliam Virginal Book* (2 vols., London, 1899); edited Byrd's Masses, Purcell's music for harpsichord, Elizabethan madrigals, etc.

Squire, William Henry, English cellist and composer; b. Ross, Herefordshire, Aug.

8, 1871. His father was an amateur violinist, and he received his primary music education at home; then studied with Hubert Parry at the Royal College of Music; made his début as a cellist in London on Feb. 12, 1891, and became a popular recitalist in England; wrote a cello concerto and many other cello pieces. He retired in 1941, and lived in London.

Stäblein, Bruno, German musicologist; b. Munich, May 5, 1895. He studied at the Munich Academy of Music with Beer-Walbrunn (composition) and at the Univ. of Munich with Adolf Sandberger and Theodor Kroyer (musicology). He was theater conductor in Coburg (1920-26), music teacher at Regensburg (1931-45); in 1946 appointed privatdozent at the Univ. of Erlangen. —Publications: *Hymnenstudien* (Erlangen, 1946); edited reprints of important source materials pertaining to medieval music ('Monumenta Monodica Medii Aevi,' 'Musica Divina,' etc.); contributed a number of articles to 'Die Musik in Geschichte und Gegenwart' and to musical journals.

Stade (shtah'-deh), **Friedrich,** German organist and writer on music; b. Arnstadt, Jan. 8, 1844; d. Leipzig, June 12, 1928. He studied in Leipzig with Riedel and Richter; served as church organist (1885-95); edited works by Bach; publ. *Vom Musikalisch-Schönen* (1870; 2nd ed., 1904), using the title of the celebrated treatise by Hanslick, but directed against Hanslick's ideas.

Stade, Heinrich Bernhard, German organist and composer; b. Ettischleben, near Arnstadt, May 2, 1816; d. Arnstadt, May 29, 1882. He was organist and town cantor at Arnstadt; restored the organ of St. Bonifaziuskirche, on which Bach had played (1703-07). He publ. *Der wohlvorbereitete Organist, ein Präludien-, Choral- und Postludienbuch* in 2 parts; and other organ music.

Stade, Wilhelm, German organist and composer; b. Halle, Aug. 25, 1817; d. Altenburg, March 24, 1902. He studied with Fr. Schneider in Dessau; was court organist and conductor at Altenburg (1860-91). With Liliencron he ed. 'Die Lieder und Sprüche aus der letzten Zeit des Minnesangs' (1854). He composed the celebrated *Vor Jena,* which became a favorite student song; also wrote 2 symphonies, a violin sonata, 7 books of organ pieces, an attractive and unique *Kindersonate* for piano, 4 hands; many sacred and secular choral works.

Staden, Johann, German organist and composer; b. Nuremberg, 1581; d. there (of the plague), Nov. (buried Nov. 15), 1634. He was court organist to the Margrave of Brandenburg from 1604 to 1616, at Kulmbach and Bayreuth; then returned to Nuremberg, where he was church organist until his death. He publ. 4 vols. of *Harmoniae sacrae* (1616, 1621, 1628, 1632); 2 vols. of church music (1625-26; 2nd vol. contains a brief treatise on thorough bass); 4 vols. of *Haus-Musik* (1623-28; posthumous collected ed. 1648, containing sacred songs with instrumental accompaniment); *Musicalischer Freuden- und Andachtswecker* (1630); *Hertzentrost-Musica* (1630); *Geistlicher Musik-Klang* (1633); *Davids Harfe* (1643); *Neue deutsche Lieder nach Art der Villanellen* (1616, 1609; includes some dances); 3 books of dance pieces (1618, 1625, and a posthumous ed., 1643); etc. Selected works by Staden were edited by E. Schmitz for the 'Denkmäler der Tonkunst in Bayern' (VII, 1; VIII, 1) and by K. Sannwald for Nagel's 'Musik-Archiv' (1936). —Cf. 'Monatshefte für Musikgeschichte,' XV, 104 ff.

Staden, Sigmund Theophilus, German organist and composer; son of Johann Staden; b. Nuremberg, 1607; d. there, July 30, 1655. As a youth, he studied in Augsburg with the organist Jacob Baumann, and later in Berlin with the resident English player on the viola da gamba, Walter Rowe. Returning to Nuremberg in 1627, he held the position of town piper; in 1634 succeeded his father as organist at the St. Lorenz Church. Staden wrote the earliest extant German opera, *Seelewig,* in an Italian manner; it was produced in Nuremberg in 1644. The text, and separately the music, for voices and thorough bass, were publ. in Harsdörffer's *Frauenzimmer Gesprächspiele* (vol. IV, 1644); reprinted by Eitner in vol. XIII of 'Monatshefte für Musik-Geschichte.' R. Schulz-Dornburg arranged the score for a production at Cologne in 1912. Staden edited Hans Leo Hassler's *Kirchengesänge* (1637), adding 11 songs by his father and 5 songs of his own. —Cf. E. Schmitz, *Zur Bedeutung der Harsdörfferschen 'Frauenzimmer-Gesprächspiele'* in the 'Liliencron-Festschrift' (Leipzig, 1910).

Stadler, Anton, famous Austrian clarinet player; b. 1753; d. Vienna, June 15, 1812. His name is chiefly important in connection with his friendship with Mozart, and his influence on Mozart's works: trio (K. 498), the so-called Stadler Quintet (K. 581), clarinet concerto (K. 622). Stadler was a member of the court orch. in Vienna from 1787 till 1799. —Cf. M. K. Ward, *Mozart's Clarinettist,* in 'Monthly Mus. Record' (Jan., 1955).

Stadler, Maximilian, Austrian organist and composer; b. Melk, Aug. 4, 1748; d. Vienna, Nov. 8, 1833. He was ordained priest in the Benedictine Order; was abbot at Lilienfeld (1786-96); held other church positions; settled in Vienna in 1796. He was a friend of Mozart, and took care of Mozart's MS of the Requiem, which he copied at Mozart's death. When the authenticity of the work was called into question by Gottfried Weber and others, Stadler publ. a pamphlet in its defense, *Verteidigung der Echtheit des Mozartschen Requiems* (Vienna, 1825; supplement, 1826). He was also a composer; publ. a cantata, *Die Frühlingsfeier;* much church music; sonatas for organ; songs. His oratorio, *Die Befreiung von Jerusalem* (Vienna, 1811), enjoyed considerable success. —Cf. H. Sabel, *Maximilian Stadlers weltliche Werke* (Cologne, 1940); H. Sabel, *Maximilian Stadler und W. A. Mozart,* in 'Neues Mozart-Jahrbuch' (vol. 3; 1943).

Stadtfeldt, Alexander, composer; b. Wiesbaden, April 27, 1826; d. Brussels, Nov. 4, 1853. He studied with Fétis at the Brussels Cons., winning the Belgian Prix de Rome in 1849. —Works: operas: *Hamlet* (Darmstadt, 1857), *Abu Hassan, L'Illusion,* and *La Pedrina;* 4 symphonies; overtures; 2 concertinos for piano and orch.; string quartet; piano trio; a Mass; a Te Deum; etc.

Staempfli, Edward, Swiss composer; b. Bern, Feb. 1, 1908. He studied composition with Jarnach in Cologne and Paul Dukas in Paris; returned to Switzerland in 1939; settled in Lugano. His early works are in an Impressionist style; later he adopted a modified system of 12-tone writing. —Works: the opera *Ein Traumspiel;* 3 symphonies; 3 piano concertos; 2 violin concertos; *Variations* for wind instruments (Salzburg Festival of the International Society for Contemporary Music, June 23, 1952); other chamber music; songs.

Stagno (stah'-ñoh), **Roberto,** Italian tenor; b. Palermo, 1836; d. Genoa, April 26, 1897. He studied with Giuseppe Lamperti; sang with great applause in Italy, London, Russia, Spain, etc.; appeared in the 1st season of the Metropolitan Opera Company, N. Y. (1883-84). He married his pupil, Gemma Bellincioni (q.v.), in 1881.

Stahl (shtahl), **Wilhelm,** German organist and writer on music; b. Gross Schenkenberg (Lauenburg), April 10, 1872; d. Lübeck, July 5, 1954. He studied with Stiehl in Lübeck; was organist there at St. Matthew's Church (1896-1922) and at the Lübeck Cathedral (1922-39); publ. *Die Lübecker Abendmusiken* (Lübeck, 1937); *Franz Tunder und Dietrich Buxtehude* (Leipzig, 1926); *Dietrich Buxtehude* (Kassel, 1937); *Musikgeschichte Lübecks* (with J. Hennings, Kassel, 1951-52); etc.; edited several vols. of popular dances of Northern Germany.

Stahlberg, Fritz, violinist and composer; b. Ketzin, Germany, June 7, 1877; d. Los Angeles, July 23, 1937. He studied in Stuttgart; emigrated to America in 1899, joining the Pittsburgh Symph. Orch. as a violinist; from 1908 was a member of the N. Y. Philharmonic, and in 1912 was also assistant conductor. He went to Hollywood in 1929, and was in charge of the music dept. for Metro-Goldwyn-Mayer Pictures. He wrote 2 symphonies; a symph suite, *Im Hochland;* violin pieces; songs.

Stählin, Jakob von, German music historian; b. Memmingen, 1710; d. St. Petersburg, July 17, 1785. He went to Russia in 1735 and remained there until his death. He publ. an important account, *Nachrichten von der Musik in Russland* (Leipzig, 1769-70), which is the prime source of information on Russian music of the 18th century.

Stahuljak (stăh-hōō-lyăk'), **Mladen,** Croatian composer and organist; b. Zadar, March 15, 1914. He studied in Zagreb with Odak (theory) and Dugan (organ); then became a teacher at the Cons. of Zagreb. He has written music mostly for practical use in schools, for chorus, organ, and small ensembles; also made arrangements of folksongs.

Stainer (shtī'-ner), **Jakob,** Austrian manufacturer of violins; b. Absam, July 14, 1621; d. there, 1683. The son of poor peasants, he was a shepherd-boy; as a youth he began making 'Schwegelpfeifen' and other woodwind instruments; then was apprenticed to a lute maker in Innsbruck. He sold his instruments in his native Tyrol, but soon attracted the attention of the Vienna court, and from 1648 was in the service of Archduke Ferdinand Karl. In 1658 he was given the title of violin maker to the court. His fortunes suffered an adverse turn when he was accused of Lutheran leanings, and he spent several months in prison; his mind became unbalanced and he died insane. His brother, **Markus Stainer,** made excellent violins and violas. The Stainer violins are highly prized, and differed greatly from Italian models (the oft-repeated assertions that Jakob Stainer worked in Italian shops are not substantiated), and their shape created flute-like tones of great subtlety. —Cf. S. Ruf, *Der Geigenmacher Jacobus Stainer von Absam im Tirol* (Innsbruck, 1872; 2nd ed., 1892); F. Lentner, *Jacob Stainers Lebenslauf im Lichte archivarischer Forschung* (Leipzig, 1893); E. Heron-Allen, *A Pilgrimage to the House of Jacob Stainer,* in the 'Mus. Times' (Aug., 1900); Princesse A. de la Tour et Taxis, *Le Violon de Jakob Stainer* (Paris, 1910); W. Senn, *Jakob Stainer, der Geigenmacher zu Absam* (Innsbruck, 1951).

Stainer, Sir **John,** English organist and composer; b. London, June 6, 1840; d. Verona, March 31, 1901. He was a chorister at St. Paul's Cathedral in London (1847-56); played organ there and in other churches as a youth; studied theory with Charles Steggall; filled various positions as church organist and teacher, and in 1872 was appointed organist of St. Paul's; failing eyesight compelled him to resign in 1888, in which year he was knighted. In 1889 he became prof. at the Univ. of Oxford, retaining this position until his death. —Works: the oratorio *Gideon;* the cantatas *The Daughter of Jairus* (Worcester, 1878), *St. Mary Magdalene* (Gloucester, 1882), and *The Crucifixion* (London, 1887); 4 church services; canticles, anthems, songs; publ. a treatise on harmony, another on the organ, *Dictionary of Musical Terms* (with W. A. Barrett; 1876; 4th ed., 1898), etc.; edited (with his daughter, Cecie Stainer) *Dufay and His Contemporaries* (1898; 50 selected compositions) and *Early Bodleian Music . . . from about A. D. 1185 to about A. D. 1505* (3 vols.; 1901). —Cf. F. G. Edwards, *John Stainer,* in 'Mus. Times' (1901; pp. 293-309).

Stainlein (stīn'-līn), Comte **Louis Charles Georges Corneille de,** cellist and composer; b. Hungary, July 3, 1819; d. Angleur-lez-Liège, Belgium, Nov. 22, 1867. A talented cellist, he appeared with success in Germany and France; with Sivori, Ney, and others he gave concerts of chamber music in Paris. —Works: violin sonata; piano trio; 2 string quartets; string quintet; string sextet; pieces for cello and piano, male choruses; songs.

Stainov, Petko, Bulgarian composer; b. Kazanlyk, Dec. 1, 1896. Despite an almost complete loss of sight in his infancy, he studied piano and composition by ear; went to Germany in 1920; graduated from the Dresden Cons. in 1924. In 1926, he became piano teacher at the State Institute for the Blind in Sofia. He wrote 2 symphonies and numerous choral works.

Stair, Patty, American organist and composer; b. Cleveland, Nov. 12, 1869; d. there, April 26, 1926. She studied at the Cleveland Cons. (1882-93); filled several positions as organist in Cleveland; from 1902 taught at the Cleveland Cons. She wrote 2 light operas, *The Fair Brigade* and *Sweet Simplicity;* a *Berceuse* for violin and piano; songs.

Stamaty (stah-mah'-tē), **Camille-Marie,** pianist; b. Rome, March 23, 1811; d. Paris, April 19, 1870. He was of Greek-French origin; his mother, a Frenchwoman, educated him after the death of his father in 1818, and took him to Paris, where he became a pupil of Kalkbrenner; in 1836 he went to Leipzig, where he studied with Mendelssohn. He returned to Paris the next year, and remained there, enjoying fame as a teacher; among his students were Saint-Saëns and Gottschalk. He publ. a number of didactic works: *Le Rhythme des doigts, Études progressives; Études concertantes; Esquisse; Études pittoresques; 6 Études caractéristiques sur Obéron,* and 12 transcriptions entitled *Souvenir du Conservatoire;* also publ. 3 piano sonatas, a piano trio, a piano concerto, etc.

Stamitz, (Johann) Anton, composer; son of Johann Wenzel Anton Stamitz; b. Mannheim, Nov. 24, 1754; d. Paris, before June, 1809. He studied violin and composition with his father. In 1770 he went to Strasbourg, and then to Paris, accompanied by his brother Karl, with whom he made his début at the Concert Spirituel on March 25, 1772; from 1782 he was a member of the royal orch. R. Kreutzer was his pupil. He wrote 13 symphonies; 54 quartets, trios, and duets for strings (2 quartets in 'Denkmäler der Tonkunst in Bayern' XV; a trio in vol. XVI); a violin concerto; 6 sonatas for violin, flute, and bass; concertos for piano, for cello, for bassoon, etc. —Cf. M. Pincherle, *Feuillets d'histoire du violon* (Paris, 1927; pp. 110-17).

Stamitz, Johann Wenzel Anton, violinist and one of the creators of the modern style of instrumental music; b. Deutsch-Brod, Bohemia, June 19, 1717; d. Mannheim, March 27, 1757. He received his musical education from his father, a cantor. His playing at the coronation of Emperor Charles VII at Frankfurt (1742) created a sensation, and Prince Karl Theodor, who in 1743 became Elector Palatine, engaged him as chamber musician. In 1745 he became Konzertmeister of the electoral orch. in Mannheim and 'Kammermusikdirektor.' His fame became widespread; Baron Grimm publ. in Paris a pamphlet, *Le petit prophète de Boehmisch-Broda,* satirizing Stamitz's innovations. In the winter of 1754-55 Stamitz was in Paris, where, at the Concert Spirituel, he produced a symphony in which he used clarinets. As a virtuoso and teacher he was one of the most famous of his time; among his pupils were his own sons Karl and Anton, C. Cannabich, W. Cramer, I. Fränzl, etc.; as a conductor he made the Mannheim orch. the finest in Europe, unrivalled for its perfection of dynamic shading. But these achievements were overshadowed by the importance of his new methods as a composer; he virtually established the classical sonata form through introducing the element of contrast into a single movement (primary and secondary subject), replacing the stereotyped basso continuo by skillful and effective leading of the basses and making variety and ingenuity the chief factors in the thematic development. Among the composers who adopted Stamitz's new style were his pupils, C. Cannabich, C. Toeschi, F. Beck, A. Filtz, as well as F. X. Richter, F. Schobert, Johann Christian Bach, Boccherini, Dittersdorf, Eichner, Gossec, etc. During his lifetime his music was printed in Paris, London, and Amsterdam. —His works include 74 symphonies; 10 trios for orch.; about 12 violin concertos; sonatas for violin solo, and others for violin with basso continuo; a Mass in D major; etc. A selection from his symphonies was publ. by Hugo Riemann in the 'Denkmäler der Tonkunst in Bayern' (III, 1; VII, 2; with an important introduction); chamber music in the same series (XV and XVI), and 9 orchestral trios in 'Collegium Musicum.' Two symphonies (in A major and D major) were edited by R. Sondheimer (Berlin, 1933); a symph. edited by H. T. David was publ. by the N. Y. Public Library (1937); chamber music was edited by W. Altmann (6 duos for violin and cello), Moffat, Sondheimer, etc. —Cf. the studies by P. Gradenwitz: *Johann Stamitz:das Leben* (Brno, 1936), *The Symphonies of Johann Stamitz,* in 'Mus. Review' (1940), *The Stamitz Family: some Errors, Omissions and Falsifications Corrected, in* 'Notes' (Washington, Dec., 1949); also Paul Nettl, *Der kleine 'Prophète von Böhmisch-Broda'* (Esslingen, 1953).

Stamitz, Karl (Philipp), violinist and composer; son and pupil of Johann Stamitz; b. Mannheim, May 7, 1745; d. Jena, Nov. 9, 1801. He was noted as a virtuoso on the viola and viola d'amore. In 1762 he was engaged as violinist in the Electoral orch. at Mannheim; in 1770, was at Strasbourg, and then toured widely, visiting Paris, London, and St. Petersburg; in 1785, became concertmaster to the Duc de Noailles at Paris; then traveled in Germany and Austria; lived in Nuremberg and Kassel; toured Russia again in 1790, and from 1794 was conductor in Jena. —Works: 70 symphonies, including 26 'symphonies concertantes'; a symphony for 2 orchestras; 7 violin concertos; several string quartets; 6 trios for 2 violins with bass; duos for 2 violins, for violin and cello, and viola and cello; a viola concerto; a piano concerto; etc. H. Riemann edited 2 symphonies in the 'Denkmäler der Tonkunst in Bayern' (VIII, 2) and chamber music in vols. XV and XVI of the same series; chamber music was edited by Altmann, C. Meyer, Klengel; a 'symphonie concertante' by K. Geiringer (Vienna, 1935); the viola concerto was edited by S. Beck (N. Y. Public Library, 1937). —5 letters from K. Stamitz were publ. by A. Schering in *Festschrift Fritz Stein zum 60. Geburtstag* (Brunswick, 1939).

Stanford, Sir **Charles Villiers**, eminent composer and pedagogue; b. Dublin, Sept. 30, 1852; d. London. March 29, 1924. Brought up in an intellectual atmosphere, he was a diligent student in his early youth; took organ lessons in Dublin with Robert Stewart; in 1862 was sent to London, where he studied piano with Ernst Pauer. In 1870 he entered Queen's College, Cambridge, as an organ student; in 1873 became organist at Trinity College there (resigned 1892). For two years (1875-76) he studied composition with Reinecke in Leipzig, and in 1877 with Kiel in Berlin. He received his M.A. degree in Cambridge in 1877; honorary degrees of Mus. Doc. at Oxford (1883) and at Cambridge (1888). In 1883 he was appointed prof. of composition at the Royal College of Music and conductor of the orch. there; in 1887 he also became prof. of music at Cambridge, holding both positions until his death; he was conductor of the Leeds Festivals from 1901 to 1910, and appeared as guest conductor of his own works in Paris, Berlin, Amsterdam, Brussels, etc.; was knighted in 1902. He was an extremely able and industrious composer in a distinctly Romantic style, yet unmistakably national in musical materials, both Irish and English. His music, however, remains virtually unknown outside Great Britain. —Works: Operas: *The Veiled Prophet of Khorassan* (London, Feb. 6, 1881); *Savonarola* (Hamburg, April 18, 1884); *The Canterbury Pilgrims* (London, April 23, 1884); *Much Ado About Nothing* (London, May 30, 1901); *The Critic,* or *An Opera Rehearsed* (London, Jan. 14, 1916); *The Traveling Companion* (posthumous; première, Liverpool, April 30, 1925, by an amateur group; 1st professional performance, Bristol, Oct. 25, 1926). For orch.: 7 symphonies: No. 1 (1876), No. 2, *Elegiac* (1882), No. 3, *Irish* (London, May 17, 1887), No. 4 (Berlin, Jan. 14, 1889), No. 5, inspired by *L'Allegro ed il Pensieroso* of Milton (1894), No. 6 (1905), No. 7 (1911); *5 Irish Rhapsodies* (1901-14); 2 sets of Irish Dances; *Overture in the Style of a Tragedy*; suite for violin and orch. (Berlin, Jan. 14, 1889, Joachim soloist); 2 violin concertos; 3 piano concertos; *Irish Concertino* for violin, cello, and orch. Chamber and piano music: 8 string quartets; piano quintet; 2 string quintets; 3 piano trios; 2 violin sonatas; 2 cello sonatas; piano sonata; 10 Dances for piano; 24 Preludes for piano; *Ballade,* for piano. Choral works: *Eden,* oratorio (1891); Mass (1892); 3 sets of Elizabethan pastorals; *6 Irish Folksongs; Songs of the Sea; Songs of the Fleet* (1910); a number of part-songs; also an *Ode to Discord,* musical caricature of modern composers (London, June 9, 1909); about 200 songs to English words, and 12 songs to texts by Heine, in German. He edited and arranged Moore's 'Irish Melodies'; 'Songs of Erin' (3 vols.; 130 folksongs); 'Songs of Old Ireland'; 'Irish Songs and Ballads'; for the Irish Literary Society he ed. 'The Complete Petrie Collection' (3 vols., 1902-05; 1,582 Irish airs). —Books: *Studies and Memories* (1908); *Musical Composition* (1911); *Pages from an Unwritten Diary* (1914); *A History of Music* (with Cecil Forsyth; 1916); *Interludes: Records and Reflections* (1922).—Cf. the 'Mus. Times' (Dec., 1898); R. A. Streatfeild, *Musiciens anglais contemporains* (Paris, 1913); J. F. Porte, *Sir Charles V. Stanford* (London, 1921); J. A. Fuller Maitland, *The Music of Parry and Stanford* (Cambridge, 1934); H. P. Greene, *Charles Villiers Stanford* (London, 1935).

Stange, Hermann, German organist; b. Kiel, Dec. 19, 1835; d. there, June 22, 1914. He studied at the Leipzig Cons.; subsequently served as organist at Rossal College, in England (1860-64); from 1878 was music director and from 1887 prof., at Kiel Univ. until his retirement in 1911.

Stange, Max, German singing teacher and composer; nephew of the preceding; b. Ottensen, May 10, 1856; d. Berlin, Jan. 25, 1932. He was prof. of singing at the Hochschule für Musik, Berlin. —Works: *Jauchzet dem Herrn, alle Welt* for baritone solo, chorus, and orch.; *Nachtstück,* for orch.; *An die Heimat,* overture; *Adagio* for cello and orch.; *Serenade* and *Nachtgebet* for string orch.; *Zwei Romanzen,* for string orch.; many male choruses and songs.

Stanley, Albert Augustus, American organist and composer; b. Manville, R. I., May 25, 1851; d. Ann Arbor, Mich., May 19, 1932. He studied at the Leipzig Cons. with Reinecke, Richter, and others; returning to America in 1876, he served as church organist in Providence; in 1888 appointed prof. of music at the Univ. of Michigan. He classified the valuable collection of musical instruments given to the Univ. by F. Stearns in 1898, and compiled an extensive catalogue of it (publ. 1918 and 1921). The Univ. made him Mus. Doc. in 1930. He wrote a cantata, *The City of Freedom* (Boston, 1883); a *Psalm of Victory,* for solo voices, chorus, and orch. (1906); the symph. poems *The Awakening of the Soul* (1896) and *Altis* (1898); anthems; part-songs; etc.

Stanley, John, English organist and composer; b. London, Jan. 17, 1713; d. there, May 19, 1786. Blind from early childhood, he studied organ with Maurice Greene, and soon was able to fill church positions; composed theater music, and publ. a number of instrumental works. In 1779 he succeeded Boyce as Master of the King's Band of Music. He enjoyed the friendship and esteem of Handel, after whose death he conducted the oratorio performances with J. C. Smith. —Works: oratorios: *Jephtha* (1757), *Zimri* (Covent Garden, March 12, 1760), *The Fall of Egypt* (Drury Lane, March 23, 1774); dramatic pastoral *Arcadia* (for George III's wedding; 1761); an opera, *Teraminta;* incidental music; songs; etc.; also 8 solos for flute, violin, or harpsichord; 6 concertos for strings; 10 voluntaries for organ; etc. —Cf. G. Finzi, *John Stanley,* in 'Tempo' (Spring, 1953); Mollie Sands, *The Problem of 'Teraminta'* in 'Music & Letters' (1952).

Starck, Ingeborg. See **Bronsart.**

Starczewski (star-chev'-skē), **Felix,** Polish composer; b. Warsaw, May 27, 1868; d. there, Jan. 21, 1946. He studied in Berlin and Paris; returning to Poland, he was engaged in various activities as teacher, composer, and music critic. He wrote an opera in 1 act, *Taniec kwatów* (Warsaw, April 28, 1918); a violin sonata; songs.

Starer, Robert, composer; b. Vienna, Jan. 8, 1924. He went to Jerusalem in 1938 and studied at the Cons. there; joined the British Royal Air Force during World War II. In 1947 he came to New York on a scholarship to the Juilliard School of Music; then taught there. —Works: *The Intruder,* 1-act opera (N. Y., Dec. 4, 1956); symph. No. 1 (1948); *Prelude and Dance* for orch. (1949); piano concerto (N. Y., Feb. 21, 1949, composer soloist); symph. No. 2 (1951; Tel Aviv, April 27, 1953); a concertino for two voices or instruments (1948); a string quartet; songs; piano music.

Stark (shtark), **Ludwig,** German pianist; b. Munich, June 19, 1831; d. Stuttgart, March 22, 1884. He studied with Ignaz and Franz Lachner in Munich; in 1857 was co-founder of the Stuttgart Cons., where he taught singing and theory; with Lebert he edited the *Grosse Klavierschule* (revised by M. Pauer, 1904); brought out a singing method, *Deutsche Liederschule* (1861); also publ. the *Klassischer Hausschatz* (24 transcriptions for piano of movements of classical chamber music works). He wrote a number of sacred and secular choral pieces, piano music, songs, etc.; publ. *Kunst und Welt* (1884).

Stark (shtark), **Robert,** famous German clarinetist; b. Klingenthal, Sept. 19, 1847; d. Würzburg, Oct. 29, 1922. He studied at the Dresden Cons.; began his career as an orchestral player at Chemnitz; from 1873 to 1881 played the clarinet in Wiesbaden; then was prof. at the Musikschule in Würzburg. He publ. valuable and practical pieces for his instrument: 3 concertos, *Romanze* for clarinet and orch.; also a *Ballade* for trombone and orch.; *Quintett concertante,* for flute, oboe, clarinet, horn, and bassoon; *Serenade,* for oboe and piano; instructive works: *Die Kunst der Transposition auf der Klarinette, Grosse theoretisch-praktische Klarinett-Schule,* in 2 parts, followed by Part III, *Die hohe Schule des Klarinett-Spieles* (24 virtuoso studies).

Starmer, William Wooding, English organist and expert on bells; b. Wellingborough, Nov. 4, 1866; d. Birmingham, Oct. 27, 1927. He studied at the Royal Academy of Music; in 1924 was appointed lecturer on campanology at Birmingham Univ. He publ. several informative papers on the subject of bells in the 'Proceedings of the Musical Association'; also wrote some church music and organ works.

Starokadomsky (stah-roh-kah-dom'-skē), **Mikhail Leonidovitch,** Russian composer; b. Brest-Litovsk, June 13, 1901; d. Moscow, April 24, 1954. He studied composition with Miaskovsky at the Moscow Cons., graduating in 1928. He remained in Moscow, where he became prof. of orchestration. His works follow the traditional line of Russian nationalism, but several of his early orchestral scores are purely neo-Classical, and in this respect parallel the European developments. —Works: opera, *Sot* (1933); operettas, *Three Encounters* (1942), *The Gay Rooster* (1944), and *The Sun Flower* (1947); a concerto for orch. (Paris Festival of the International Society for Contemporary Music, June 22, 1937); violin concerto (Moscow, March 20, 1939); some chamber music; and numerous songs for children, by which he is best known in Russia.

Starzer, Josef, Austrian composer; b. Vienna, 1726; d. there, April 22, 1787. He was a violinist in the court chapel at Vienna; from 1760 to 1770 he was court composer in St. Petersburg, where he produced 2 ballets: *Floras Sieg* and *L'Amore medico.* After his return to Vienna, he became very popular as a composer of ballets, of which he produced about 20; also wrote instrumental music. 2 divertimentos by Starzer are reprinted in the 'Denkmäler der Tonkunst in Österreich' (vol. 31). —Cf. L. Braun, *Die Balletkomposition von J. Starzer,* in 'Studien zur Musikwissenschaft' (vol. 13).

Stasny, Carl Richard, German pianist; b. Mainz, March 16, 1855; d. Boston, April 22, 1920. He studied with Brüll in Vienna, and later was a pupil of Liszt in Weimar (1879-81); while working as piano teacher at Hoch's Cons. in Frankfurt, he made a special study of Schumann's works with Clara Schumann. In 1891 he settled in Boston, where he taught at the New England Cons. He publ. *Finger Training, Scales, Chords and Arpeggios.*

Stasny, Ludwig, popular bandmaster; b. Prague, Feb. 26, 1823; d. Frankfurt, Oct. 30, 1883. He studied at the Prague Cons.; was bandmaster in the Austrian Army, and settled in Frankfurt in 1871. He produced 2 operas in Mainz: *Liane* (1851) and *Die beiden Grenadiere* (1879). He was noted for his popular dances (211 opus numbers) and for his potpourris from Wagner's music dramas.

Stasov, Vladimir Vassilievitch, famous Russian writer on music; b. St. Petersburg, Jan. 14, 1824; d. there, Oct. 23, 1906. He attended a law school until 1843; in 1845 he became connected with the St. Petersburg Public Library; then traveled in Italy as private secretary to Count Demidov; while in Rome, he made copies of rare works in the library of Abbate Santini (q.v.), which he later presented to the Public Library in St. Petersburg; he became assistant to the librarian there in 1854, and in 1872 was appointed director of the Dept. of Fine Arts, which post he held till his death. He played a very important role in the emergence of the Russian National School, and was to the end of his days an ardent promoter of Russian music. It was Stasov who first launched the expression 'The Mighty Company' (in an article publ. on May 24, 1867, in a St. Petersburg newspaper); although in that article he did not specifically name the so-called 'Five' (Balakirev, Borodin, Cui, Mussorgsky, Rimsky-Korsakov), these composers became identified with the cause championed by Stasov. When young Glazunov appeared on the scene, Stasov declared him a natural heir to the Five. His numerous writings, including biographies of Glinka, Mussorgsky, and others, have the value of authenticity. Those publ. between 1847 and 1886 were issued in book-form in honor of his 70th birthday (St. Petersburg, 1894) in 3 vols.; a 4th vol., containing essays written between 1886 and 1904, was brought out in 1905; among them, *Russian Music during the last 25 years,* and *Art in the 19th Century* are particularly important. His collected works, including articles on art and other subjects, were publ. in Moscow in 1952. —Cf. *To the Memory of Vladimir Stasov* (St. Petersburg, 1910); V. D. Komarova (his niece), *V. V. Stasov* (St. Petersburg, 1927; 2 vols.); T. Livanova, *Stasov and the Russian Classical Opera* (Moscow, 1957).

Stassevitch (stah-seh'-vitch), **Paul,** violinist and conductor; b. Simferopol, Crimea, May 5, 1894. He studied both violin and piano; was a pupil of Auer (violin) and Nikolayev (piano) at the St. Petersburg Cons. As a violinist, he toured in Scandinavia (1914-19); settled in the U. S. in 1919, and produced a considerable sensation at his début as violinist and pianist with the N. Y. State Symph. Orch., Dec. 16, 1924, playing Tchaikovsky's 1st piano concerto and the violin concerto of Brahms; on Jan. 31, 1930, he made his 1st appearance as conductor, at an extra concert of the N. Y. Philharmonic; also was concertmaster of the Conductorless Orch., N. Y., in 1929. However, he did not pursue his career as a virtuoso or conductor, devoting himself mainly to teaching.

Statkowski (stat-kov'-skē), **Roman,** Polish composer; b. Szczypiorna, Jan. 5, 1860; d. Warsaw, Nov. 12, 1925. He studied law at the Univ. of Warsaw, graduating in 1886. At the same time he took lessons in composition with Zelenski. In 1886 he entered the St. Petersburg Cons. as a student of Soloviev (composition) and Rimsky-Korsakov (orchestration). In 1904 he returned to Warsaw, where he became prof. of music history and later of composition, retaining these positions until his death. He wrote mainly for piano and for violin; successfully stylized Polish dances; his violin pieces retain their popularity in Poland. He further wrote the operas, *Filenis* (Warsaw, Sept. 14, 1904; won 1st prize at the International Opera Contest in London) and *Maria* (Warsaw, March 1, 1906); a *Polonaise* for orch.; a *Fantasy* for orch.; 6 string quartets. His style represents a blend of German and Russian influences.

Staudigl (shtou'-dēgl), **Josef,** Sr., famous Austrian bass singer; b. Wöllersdorf, April 14, 1807; d. insane at Michaelbeuerngrund, near Vienna, March 18, 1861. He gave up the study of medicine to join the chorus at the Vienna court opera, later becoming leading bass; then was at the Theater an der Wien (1845-48); from 1848 till 1854 was again at the court opera. He also appeared as concert singer.

Staudigl, Josef, Jr., baritone, son of the preceding; b. Vienna, March 18, 1850; d. Karlsruhe, April, 1916. He studied with Rokitansky at the Vienna Cons.; in 1884-86 was principal baritone at the Metropolitan Opera House, where he created the role of Pogner in the American première of *Die Meistersinger* (Jan. 4, 1886); then sang until his retirement in 1905 at various German theaters (Berlin, Hamburg, Bayreuth, etc.), often together with his wife, the contralto Gisela Koppmayer, whom he married in 1885. In the spring of 1898 they sang with the Damrosch-Ellis Opera Co. on an American tour.

Stavenhagen, Bernhard, German pianist; b. Greiz, Reuss, Nov. 24, 1862; d. Geneva,

Dec. 26, 1914. He studied in Berlin with Kiel; was one of the last pupils of Liszt, with whom he studied in 1885-86. After a tour as pianist in Europe and the U. S., he became court conductor at Weimar in 1895; in 1898 he obtained a similar position in Munich, where he was also for a few years director of the 'Akademie der Tonkunst' (1901-04); in 1907 he went to Geneva, where he conducted the municipal orch. He wrote 2 piano concertos and other piano works; publ. cadenzas to Beethoven's 2nd and 3rd piano concertos.

Stcherbatchev (shcher-bah-chŏv'), **Vladimir Vladimirovitch,** Russian composer; b. Warsaw, Jan. 24, 1889; d. Leningrad, March 5, 1952. He studied at the St. Petersburg Cons. with Maximilian Steinberg and Liadov, graduating in 1914. From 1924 to 1931 he was prof. at the Leningrad Cons.; among his students were Popov, Zhelobinsky, and other well-known composers. He wrote an opera, *Anna Kolosova* (1939); 5 symphonies (1914, 1926, 1932, 1935, 1948); music for films; an orchestral suite from one of them, *The Thunderstorm,* was popular at concerts in Russia; other works include a *Fairy-Tale,* for orch. (St. Petersburg, Dec. 20, 1915); a nonet (1917); several piano sonatas and other piano works.

Stearns, Theodore, American composer; b. Berea, Ohio, June 10, 1880; d. Los Angeles, Nov. 1, 1935. He studied at Oberlin Cons. and at the Cons. of Würzburg; returning to America, he conducted operetta; wrote music criticism in N. Y. (1922-26); went to Germany on a Guggenheim Fellowship (1927-28); in 1932 joined the faculty of the Univ. of California, Los Angeles. He wrote an opera-ballet in 1 act, *Snowbird,* to his own libretto, which was produced by the Chicago Civic Opera Co. on Jan. 13, 1923, and gained the Bispham Memorial Medal (1925); a lyric drama, *Atlantis* (1926); a symph. poem, *Tiberio,* and an orch. suite, *Caprese.* His orch. suite *Before the Door of the Wigwam,* from *Hiawatha,* was performed in Würzburg (April 29, 1897). He publ. *The Story of Music* (1931). —Cf. E. E. Hipsher, *American Opera and its Composers* (Philadelphia, 1934, pp. 387-91).

Stebbins, George Waring, American organist and composer; b. Albion, N. Y., June 16, 1869; d. New York, Feb. 21, 1930. He received his early education from his father, the well-known evangelist George C. Stebbins (1846-1945); then studied in N. Y. with H. R. Shelley, and in Paris with Guilmant. He filled various positions as church organist in Brooklyn and N. Y. (from 1893); publ. a number of works for organ (*Wedding Song, A Song of Joy, Scherzando,* etc.), anthems, choruses, songs.

Steber, Eleanor, American soprano; b. Wheeling, W. Va., July 17, 1916. She studied at the New England Cons., Boston, and with Paul Althouse in N. Y. In 1940 she won the Metropolitan Opera radio audition and made a brilliant début in *Der Rosenkavalier* in the same year. She created the title role in Samuel Barber's opera *Vanessa* (N. Y., Metropolitan Opera, Jan. 15, 1958).

Stecker, Karel, Czech organist and writer on music; b. Kosmanos, Jan. 22, 1861; d. Prague, March 13, 1918. He was a pupil of the Organ School in Prague; taught organ there (1885-89); became prof. of theory and organ at the Prague Cons. in 1889. He publ. a history of music (in Czech, 2 vols.; 1892, 1903); a treatise on musical form (Prague, 1905), and a volume on non-thematic improvisation (1903); composed a *Missa solemnis* and other church music; some instrumental works. —Cf. C. Sychra, *Karel Stecker* (Prague, 1948).

Štědroň, Bohumír, Czech musicologist; b. Vyškov, Dec. 30, 1905. He studied history and musicology at Brno; in 1930 became a school teacher for general subjects; also gave courses in music history at the Brno Cons.; from 1946 to 1951 he was in charge of Music Education Dept. at Brno Univ. He publ. monographs on Czech composers, and contributed to various periodicals. Edited *Leoš Janáček; Letters and Reminiscences* (in Czech, 1946; in English, 1955).

Štědroň, Vladimír, Czech composer, brother of Bohumír Štědroň; b. Vyškov, March 30, 1900. He studied law in Prague and became a judge; simultaneously he took music courses with J. B. Foerster and Suk. He has composed several symphonic works in an unassuming style inspired by native folksongs; also some chamber music.

Steele, Porter, American composer; b. Natchez, Miss., Dec. 12, 1880. He studied with Horatio Parker at Yale Univ. Having completed his law studies at Columbia Univ., he was admitted to the bar in 1905, and was a practicing lawyer in N. Y. until 1934, while devoting his spare time to composition. He made his home in Plainfield, N. J. He wrote mostly in small forms; publ.

piano pieces (*At Longwood, Poème Lyrique, At Sunset,* etc.); songs (*The Seagull,* etc.).

Stefan, Paul, writer on music; b. Brno, Nov. 25, 1879; d. New York, Nov. 12, 1943. He was educated at the Univ. of Vienna; studied music theory with Hermann Grädener. He became associated with the avant-garde in Vienna, and was appointed editor of the progressive musical periodical, 'Musikblätter des Anbruch'; was a co-founder of the International Society for Contemporary Music in 1922. In 1938 he went to Switzerland; then was in Lisbon (1939-41); arrived in the U. S. in 1941. His books on music include *Gustav Mahler* (1910; 7th ed., 1921; also in English, N. Y., 1913); *Oskar Fried* (1911); *Die Feindschaft gegen Wagner* (1919); *Das neue Haus,* a history of the Vienna Opera (1919); *Neue Musik und Wien* (1921; also in English); *Der Musiker Hoffmann* (1922); *Arnold Schönberg* (1924); *Franz Schubert* (1928); *Geschichte der Wiener Oper* (1932); *Arturo Toscanini* (1935; 3rd ed., 1937; English transl., N. Y., 1936); *Bruno Walter* (1936); brought out an abridged German transl. of Šourek's biography of Dvořák (Vienna, 1935; in English, N. Y., 1941); *Georges Bizet* (Zürich, 1952); publ. essays on *Don Giovanni* (1938) and *Die Zauberflöte* (1937) and various studies in European and American journals.

Stefani, Jan, composer and conductor; b. Prague, 1746; d. Warsaw, Feb. 24, 1829. He was Kapellmeister to Count Kinsky and violinist in the orch. of the Vienna Opera. In 1771 he entered the service of Stanislaus Poniatowski in Warsaw, and became conductor of the Warsaw Opera. He wrote several Polish operas, of which *Krakowiacy i Górale* (*The Cracovites and the Mountaineers*), produced in Warsaw on March 1, 1794, was very successful, and remained in the repertory for 65 years. Other operas (all produced in Warsaw) were: *Król w kraju rozkoszy* (Feb. 3, 1787); *Wdzieczni poddani panu* (July 24, 1796); *Frozyna* (Feb. 21, 1806); *Rotmistrz Gorecki* (April 3, 1807). He also wrote a great number of polonaises.

Stefani, Józef, Polish composer and conductor, son of Jan Stefani; b. Warsaw, April 16, 1800; d. there, 1864. He was a pupil of his father and of Chopin's teacher, Elsner; conducted ballet at the Warsaw Opera, and wrote a number of light operas, which enjoyed a modicum of success during his lifetime: *Dawne czasy* (April 26, 1826); *Lekcja botaniki* (March 15, 1829); *Figle panien* (Aug. 6, 1832); *Talizman* (Dec. 7, 1849); *Zyd wieczny tulacz* (Jan. 1, 1850); *Piorun* (May 21, 1856); *Trwoga wieczorna* (posthumous, July 25, 1872). He also wrote church music, which was often performed in religious services in Poland.

Steffan, Joseph Anton, composer; b. Kopidlno, Bohemia, March 14, 1726; d. Vienna, April 12, 1797. A pupil of Wagenseil, he settled in Vienna, where he was a renowned teacher; among his pupils were the princesses Marie Antoinette (later Queen of France) and Caroline (later Queen of Naples). He wrote some church music and numerous works for piano (divertimentos, concertos, and sonatas); he is historically important for his songs, *Sammlung deutscher Lieder* (4 books), which are among the best of that time. Specimens were publ. by M. Friedlaender in *Das deutsche Lied im 18. Jahrhundert* (1902); see also 'Denkmäler der Tonkunst in Österreich' (vol. 79).

Steffani, Abbate **Agostino,** Italian composer; b. Castelfranco Veneto, July 25, 1654; d. Frankfurt, Feb. 12, 1728. He began his musical career as a choirboy at Padua, where his beautiful soprano voice so charmed Count Tattenbach that the latter obtained permission to take him to the Electoral court at Munich, where he was trained by Kerll from 1668-71; from 1672-74 he studied at Rome with E. Bernabei at the Elector's expense, and in 1675 was appointed court organist at Munich. In 1678-79 he visited Paris, where he made an advantageous study of Lully's music. He took holy orders in 1680 and was made titular Abbot of Lepsing in 1682. In 1681 he became director of the Elector's chamber music (together with G. A. Bernabei, his former teacher's son). He composed his first opera, *Marco Aurelio,* in 1680, for Munich; other operas: *Solone* (1685), *Audacia e rispetto* (1685), *Servio Tullio* (1686), *Alarico* (1687), and *Niobe* (1688), followed; in 1688 he went to Hanover as court Kapellmeister. There he brought out the opera *Enrico detto il Leone* (Jan. 30, 1689), the orchestration of which is noteworthy (besides the string quartet, there are flutes, oboes, bassoons, 3 trumpets, and drums; all the wind instruments have obbligato passages); further, *La Lotta d'Ercole con Acheloo* (1689); *La Superbia d'Alessandro* (1690; revised in 1691 as *Il Zelo di Leonato*); *Orlando generoso* (1691); *Le Rivali concordi,* or *Atlanta* (1693); *La Libertà contenta* (1693); *I Baccanali* (1695); *Il Trionfo del fato,* or *Le Glorie d'Enea* (1695; given at Brunswick in 1716 as *Enea in Italia,* or *Didone*); *Briseide* (1696); and for Düsseldorf: *Arminio* (1707); *Tassilone* (1709); and *Amor vien dal destino ossia Il Turno Aricino* (1709). Long before this, however, his services had been more in demand as a diplomatist than as a musician; in 1696 he had brought to a triumphant conclusion the delicate negotiations for the creation of a ninth Elector of Brunswick, being rewarded by the appointment of Bishop of Spiga ('in partibus'); from 1698 he was privy councillor and papal protonotary at Düsseldorf, though still holding his position as Kapellmeister at Hanover till 1711, when he joyfully relinquished it to Handel. Some works of the later epoch were produced under the name of his copyist, Gregorio Piva. —Publ. works: *Psalmodia vespertina a* 8 (1674); *Sacer Janus Quadrifrons* (1685; motets *a* 3, with continuo; any voice may be omitted at pleasure); *Sonate da camera a 2 violini, alto e continuo* (1679); *Duetti da camera a soprano e contralto con il basso continuo* (1683; historically important and intrinsically valuable); and the pamphlet *Quanta certezza habbia da' suoi principii la musica* (Amsterdam, 1695; German by Werckmeister, 1699, and Albrecht, 1760). In MS he left 85 chamber duets with continuo (16 of these, with 2 scherzi for 1 voice with instruments and 2 church cantatas, were publ. by A. Einstein and A. Sandberger in 'Denkmäler der Tonkunst in Bayern' VI, 2); a chamber cantata for soprano and continuo (publ. by T. W. Werner in 'Zeitschrift für Musikwissenschaft' I, 8); a famous Stabat Mater for 6 voices and 2 violins, 3 violas, cello, and continuo (organ); also 4 vols. of short cantatas and arias. H. Riemann publ. *Alarico* (complete score; also full bibliography of all Steffani's operas) in 'Denkmäler der Tonkunst in Bayern' XI, 2, also selections from other operas in vol. XII, 2. —Bibliography: F. M. Rudhart, *Geschichte der Oper am Hofe zu München* (Freising, 1865); G. Fischer, *Musik in Hannover* (2nd ed., Hanover, 1902); A. Neisser, *Servio Tullio . . . von A. S.* (dissertation, Leipzig, 1902); A. Untersteiner, *A. S.*, in 'Rivista Musicale Italiana' (vol. XIV; 1907); P. Hiltebrandt, *Preussen und die römische Kurie* (Berlin, 1910; vol. I contains material concerning S.); H. Riemann, *A. S. als Opernkomponist,* in 'Denkmäler der Tonkunst in Bayern' (XII, 2; 1912); R. de Rensis, *A. S.*, in 'Musica d'oggi' (1921); T. W. Werner, *A. S.s Operntheater in Hannover,* in 'Archiv für Musikforschung' (1938); also articles on Steffani by A. Einstein in 'Kirchenmusikalisches Jahrbuch' (vol. XXIII, 1910), in 'Neue Musik-Zeitung' (1928), and in 'Zeitschrift der Internationalen Musik-Gesellschaft' X, 6; J. Loschelder, *Aus Düsseldorfs italienischer Zeit* in K. G. Fellerer, ed., *Beiträge zur Musikgeschichte der Stadt Düsseldorf* (Cologne, 1952). The authorship of *Memoirs of the Life of A. S.*, publ. in London in the 18th century, is attributed to Sir John Hawkins.

Steggall, Charles, English organist and composer; b. London, June 3, 1826; d. there, June 7, 1905. He was a pupil of Sterndale Bennett at the Royal Academy of Music; became prof. there in 1851. After 52 years of continued service, he resigned his professorship in 1903. He wrote anthems and other religious music; edited 'Church Psalmody' (1848), 'Hymns Ancient and Modern' (1889), etc. —His son, **Reginald Steggall** (b. London, April 17, 1867; d. there, Nov. 16, 1938), was also a pupil at the Royal Academy of Music, where he taught organ playing from 1895. He wrote a number of organ pieces; a Mass; a symphony; orchestral variations and overtures.

Steglich, Rudolf, German musicologist; b. Rats-Damnitz, Feb. 18, 1886; studied musicology with Hugo Riemann in Leipzig (*Dr. phil.*, 1911). He was in the German army during World War I; then was active as music critic of the Hanover 'Anzeiger' (1919-29); in 1929, appointed to the faculty of the Univ. of Erlangen. He was editor of the 'Händel-Jahrbuch' (1928-33) and of the 'Archiv für Musikforschung' (1936-40); edited works by Bach's sons, old German song collections, etc. —Publications: *Die 'Quaestiones in musica': ein Choraltraktat des zentralen Mittelalters* (Leipzig, 1911); *Die elementare Dynamik des musikalischen Rhythmus* (Leipzig, 1930); *J. S. Bach* (Potsdam, 1935); *G. F. Händel: Leben und Werk* (Leipzig, 1939); *Wege zu Bach* (Regensburg, 1949); numerous essays.

Stegmayer, Ferdinand, Austrian conductor and composer; b. Vienna, Aug. 25, 1803; d. there, May 6, 1863. He was the son of Matthaeus Stegmayer (q.v.); studied music with Seyfried; was chorusmaster at Linz and Vienna; then conductor of a German opera troupe in Paris (1829-30). After filling various engagements as theater conductor in Leipzig, Bremen, and Prague, he settled in Vienna in 1848; was teacher of singing at the Vienna Cons.; co-founder, with August Schmidt, of the Vienna 'Singakademie' (1858). He publ. some church music; piano pieces; songs.

Stegmayer, Matthaeus, Austrian actor-poet and composer; b. Vienna, April 29, 1771; d. there, May 10, 1820. He was a chorister in the Dominican church, Vienna; then after singing in small provincial theatrical companies, he returned in 1793 to Vienna, where he sang at the Josephstadt theater; made his début as a singer at Schikaneder's theater Auf der Wieden in 1796; then was briefly at the court opera; in 1804 became chorusmaster at the new Theater an der Wien. He was the first to use the term 'quodlibet' for theatrical light pieces; arranged Mozart's *Schauspieldirektor* (1814); composed an operetta, *Der Salzburger Hans und sein Sohn, der Hansl* (Vienna, Nov. 14, 1800), and contributed separate numbers to many others (mainly with Ignaz von Seyfried). He wrote the text for the quodlibet *Rochus Pumpernickel,* produced at the Theater an der Wien on Jan. 28, 1809, with music assembled by Seyfried from various works, including pieces by Haydn and Mozart. It was so successful that he followed it with a sequel, *Die Familie Pumpernickel* (Feb. 13, 1810). A complete list of his works as composer, joint composer, and librettist is found in Anton Bauer, *Opern und Operetten in Wien* (Vienna, 1955).

Stehle, J. Gustav Eduard, organist and composer; b. Steinhausen, Germany, Feb. 17, 1839; d. St. Gall, Switzerland, June 21, 1915. He was organist in Rorschach (1869-74); in 1874 he settled in Switzerland as music director at the St. Gall Cathedral. His cathedral choir of 140 voices was famous as one of the finest in Europe. For 25 years he also was editor of the 'Chorwächter.' He wrote a great deal of religious music: an oratorio, *Legende von der heiligen Cäcilia;* a cantata, *Lumen de Coelo* (to words by Pope Leo XIII); *Die Nonnen von Compiègne,* for double chorus; *Frithjofs Heimkehr,* for solo, male quartet, and mixed chorus; *Die Heinzelmännchen,* humorous choral ballad for double chorus a cappella; a symph. poem for organ, *Saul;* 438 preludes in the church modes, etc. —Cf. A. Locher, *J.-G.-E. Stehlé* (Strasbourg, 1928).

Stehle, Sophie, German soprano; b. Hohenzollern-Sigmaringen, May 15, 1838; d. Schloss Harterode, near Hanover, Oct. 4, 1921. She was a prominent member of the Munich Opera, where she created the roles of Fricka in *Das Rheingold* (Sept. 22, 1869) and Brünnhilde in *Die Walküre* (June 26, 1870). She also distinguished herself in other Wagnerian parts (Elisabeth, Elsa, Eva).

Steibelt (shtī'-belt), **Daniel,** popular pianist and composer; b. Berlin, Oct. 22, 1765; d. St. Petersburg, Oct. 2, 1823. He studied with Kirnberger (piano and theory); published sonatas for piano and violin, as op. 1 and 2, at Munich, in 1788; then gave concerts in Germany, proceeding to Paris in 1790. There he found himself in strong competition with Ignaz Pleyel, but won out, and became a favorite piano teacher in Paris. His opera *Roméo et Juliette* was produced at the Théâtre Feydeau on Sept. 10, 1793, and despite the revolutionary turmoil of the time, achieved an excellent success. He left Paris in 1796, going to Holland, and then to London; became a soloist at Salomon's Concerts; played the solo part of his 3rd piano concerto (March 19, 1798), with its famous finale *L'Orage, précédé d'un rondeau pastoral,* which as a piano solo became as popular as Koczwara's *Battle of Prague.* In London he produced an opera, *Albert and Adelaide* (Covent Garden, Dec. 11, 1798); returned to Germany in 1799; then proceeded to Vienna, where he challenged Beethoven to a contest of skill, but was easily bested. His next destination was Paris, where he produced Haydn's *Creation* (Dec. 24, 1800), with an orchestra of 156 players, in an arrangement by Steibelt himself. Napoleon was present at that performance. A ballet by Steibelt, *Le Retour de Zéphire,* was produced at the Paris Opéra on March 3, 1802; he then went to London, where he staged 2 ballets, *Le Jugement du berger Paris* (May 24, 1804) and *La belle Laitière* (Jan. 26, 1805). Returning once more to Paris, he wrote a festive intermezzo, *La Fête de Mars,* to celebrate Napoleon's victory at Austerlitz; it was produced at the Opéra on March 4, 1806. In the autumn of 1808 he gave concerts in Frankfurt and Dresden; in the spring of 1809 he went to Russia by way of Warsaw, Vilna, and Riga. In St. Petersburg he produced a new opera, *Cendrillon,* to a French libretto (Oct. 26, 1810), and 2 ballets. Although he held the position of chapelmaster at the court of Czar Alexander I, he did not prosper, and at his death a public subscription was undertaken to help his family. He publ. 5 piano concertos, 37 sonatas with violin, 29 sonatas and sonatinas for piano solo, 15 rondos, 18 fantasias, etc. His *Méthode de Piano* had considerable vogue. —Cf. G. Müller, *Daniel Steibelt, sein Leben und seine Klavierwerke* (Strasbourg, 1933).

Steigleder (shteyg'-lĕ-der), **Johann Ulrich,** German organist and composer; b. Schwäbisch-Hall, March 21, 1593; d. Stuttgart, Oct.

10, 1635. He was organist at Lindau and then at Stuttgart (1617), serving also as musician to the court of Württemberg. Two of his publications survive: *Ricercar Tabulatura, organis et organoedis . . .* (1624) and *Tabulatur-Buch,* containing 40 variations for organ and other instruments, upon the Lord's Prayer (Strasbourg, 1627). Two variations are to be found in Ritter's *Geschichte des Orgelspiels im 14.-18. Jahrhundert* (1884; new ed. by Frotscher, 1933). —Cf. E. Emsheimer, *J. U. Steigleder* (dissertation, Kassel, 1928).

Stein, Erwin, Austrian conductor and editor; b. Vienna, Nov. 7, 1885; d. London, July 17, 1958. He studied with Schoenberg; was engaged as opera conductor in Germany; from 1924 till 1938 was an editor for the Universal Edition, Vienna. He settled in London in 1938 and joined the firm of Boosey & Hawkes; wrote for music magazines; publ. a collection of essays, *Orpheus in New Guises* (London, 1953).

Stein, Fritz, eminent German musicologist; b. Gerlachsheim, Baden, Dec. 17, 1879. He studied theology in Karlsruhe, then took courses in musicology with Ph. Wolfrum in Heidelberg; subsequently went to Leipzig, where he studied conducting with Arthur Nikisch and organ with Straube; also attended Riemann's lectures at the Univ. of Leipzig; *Dr. phil.* (Heidelberg, 1910) with the dissertation *Zur Geschichte der Musik in Heidelberg* (publ. 1912; new ed. 1921, as *Geschichte des Musikwesens in Heidelberg bis zum Ende des 18. Jahrhunderts).* In 1913 he was appointed prof. of musicology at the Univ. of Jena; was in the German army during World War I, and directed a male chorus for the troops at the front. He was prof. at the Kiel Univ. from 1918 to 1925; in 1933 he became director of the Hochschule für Musik in Berlin, holding this position to the end of the war and the collapse of the Nazi regime in 1945; conducted a few concerts in Berlin-Charlottenburg in 1950. He achieved great notoriety when he discovered in the library of the Univ. of Jena the parts of a symphony, marked by an unknown copyist as a work by Beethoven. The symphony became famous as the 'Jena Symphony' and was hailed by many as a genuine discovery; the score was publ. by Breitkopf & Härtel in 1911, and performances followed all over the world; Stein publ. his own exegesis of it as *Eine unbekannte Jugendsymphonie Beethovens?,* in the 'Sammelbände der Internationalen Musik-Gesellschaft' (1912, 1). Doubts of its authenticity were often expressed, but it was not until 1957 that the American musicologist H. C. Robbins Landon finally succeeded in proving that the 'Jena Symphony' was in reality the work of Friedrich Witt (1770-1837). Stein publ. a monograph on Max Reger (Potsdam, 1939) and *Max Reger: sein Leben in Bildern* (a pictorial biography; Leipzig, 1941; 2nd ed., 1956); brought out a thematic catalogue of Reger's works (Leipzig, 1934; definitive ed., 1953); edited works by Johann Christian Bach, Telemann, Handel, Beethoven, etc.; contributed essays to numerous learned publications. A 'Festschrift' was publ. for him on his 60th birthday (1939).

Stein, Johann Andreas, inventor of the 'German' (Viennese) piano action; b. Heidelsheim, Palatinate, May 6, 1728; d. Augsburg, Feb. 29, 1792. He was trained in the Strasbourg workshop of J. A. Silbermann (1748-49). In 1751 he settled in Augsburg, where he built the organ of the Barfüsserkirche; was appointed organist there in 1757. He spent a few months in Paris in 1758 before returning to Augsburg. He experimented with various types of keyboard instruments; invented a 'polytoni-clavichordium' (1769), a 'melodika' (1772), a 'vis-à-vis,' and a 'Saitenharmonika' (1789). The business was carried on by his son, Andreas Stein, and his daughter, Nanette Stein-Streicher (wife of the Austrian piano maker, J. B. Streicher, q.v.), who moved it to Vienna in 1802. —Cf. F. Luib, *Biographische Skizze des J. A. Stein* (1886); T. Bolte, *Die Musikerfamilien Stein und Streicher* (Vienna, 1917); K. A. Fischer, *J. A. Stein* (Augsburg, 1932); Eva Hertz, *J. A. Stein: ein Beitrag zur Geschichte des Klavierbaues* (Würzburg, 1937); Donald Boalch, *Makers of the Harpsichord and Clavichord, 1440 to 1840* (London, 1956; pp. 117-18).

Stein, Richard Heinrich, German writer on music and composer; b. Halle, Feb. 28, 1882; d. Santa Brigida, Canary Islands, Aug. 11, 1942. He studied law and music; *Dr. phil.* (Erlangen, 1911) with the thesis, *Die psychologischen Grundlagen der Ethik.* From 1914 to 1919 he lived in Spain; from 1920 to 1932 taught musical subjects in Berlin. In 1933 he left Germany and went to the Canary Islands, where he remained until his death. He was a composer of experimental tendencies; his *Zwei Konzertstücke* for cello and piano, op. 26 (1906), was the first composition containing quarter-tones to be published. In 1909 he wrote a brochure giving a detailed exposition of his quarter-tone system, and in 1914 he built a quarter-tone clarinet. He composed about 100 piano pieces and about 50 songs; a *Scherzo fantastico* for orch.; publ. the books *La Música moderna* (Barcelona, 1918; in Spanish and German), *Grieg* (1921), *Tschaikowsky* (1927).

Steinbach, Fritz, German conductor; b. Grünsfeld, June 17, 1855; d. Munich, Aug. 13, 1916. He studied in Leipzig, Vienna, and Karlsruhe. In 1880 he was appointed 2nd Kapellmeister in Mainz, where his interpretations of Beethoven and Brahms won praise; Brahms recommended him as successor to Hans von Bülow at Meiningen (1886); in 1902 he went to Cologne as director of the cons. there; resigned in 1914 and settled in Munich. He made frequent appearances in London as conductor, and in the spring of 1906 was engaged by the N. Y. Philharmonic to conduct a pair of concerts.

Steinberg, Maximilian, Russian composer and pedagogue; b. Vilna, July 4, 1883; d. Leningrad, Dec. 6, 1946. He studied at the St. Petersburg Cons. with Glazunov and Rimsky-Korsakov (whose daughter he married on June 17, 1908). In 1908 he was appointed teacher of theory and composition there. His early compositions reflected the influence of his teachers, but gradually he evolved a more personal style distinguished by rhapsodic eloquence, and somewhat touched with procedures of French Impressionism. In 1934 he was appointed director of the Leningrad Cons., and maintained the high standards established before him by Rimsky-Korsakov and Glazunov. Among his pupils were Shostakovitch, Shaporin, and other prominent composers of the Soviet period. —Works: symph. no. 1 (1907); symph. no. 2 (St. Petersburg, Nov. 27, 1909); *Metamorphoses,* ballet (2nd part performed by Diaghilev, Paris, June 2, 1914); *La Princesse Maleine,* after Maeterlinck, for orch. and women's chorus (1916); *Heaven and Earth,* dramatic poem for 6 soloists and orch. (1918); symph. no. 3 (Leningrad, March 3, 1929, composer conducting); symph. no. 4 subtitled *Turksib,* to celebrate the opening of the Turkestan-Siberian railroad (Leningrad, Dec. 2, 1933); *In Armenia,* symph. picture (Leningrad, Dec. 24, 1940); a violin concerto (1946); 2 string quartets, etc. He also wrote a number of lyric songs and piano pieces. He made several arrangements of Turkmenian songs for voice and orch.; also arranged for orch. a concerto in D by K. P. E. Bach (1911) and a cello sonata by Gaillard (1924); edited Rimsky-Korsakov's *Foundations of Orchestration* (St. Petersburg, 1913; 2 vols.). —Cf. A. N. Rimsky-Korsakov, *Maximilian Steinberg* (Moscow, 1928; in Russian and German).

Steinberg, William, eminent conductor; b. Cologne, Aug. 1, 1899. He received his early instruction from his mother; studied piano and violin; began to compose as a youth; conducted his own setting for chorus and orch. of a poem from Ovid's *Metamorphoses* in school at the age of 13; then took courses with Franz Bölsche (counterpoint), Lazzaro Uzielli (piano), and Hermann Abendroth (conducting). He graduated from the Cologne Cons. in 1920, obtaining the Wüllner Prize for conducting; then became assistant to Otto Klemperer at the Cologne Opera; in 1924, became 1st conductor. In 1925, he was engaged as conductor of the German Theater in Prague; in 1929, appointed general music director of the Frankfurt Opera. At Frankfurt he brought out several modern operas, including Berg's *Wozzeck.* In 1933 he was removed from his position by the Nazi authorities, and became associated with the Jewish Culture League, conducting orchestras for Jewish audiences. In 1936 he left Germany and became one of the conductors of the Palestine Orch.; prepared the orchestra for Toscanini, who subsequently engaged him as assistant conductor of the NBC Symph., N. Y. in 1937; he was also guest conductor with major American orchestras. In 1945 he was appointed conductor of the Buffalo Philharmonic Orch.; in 1952 became conductor of the Pittsburgh Symph., and established himself as one of the leading conductors in the U. S.; in 1958 he accepted an additional position as conductor of the London Philharmonic (4 weeks in midwinter, and 4 weeks in the spring). —Cf. Hope Stoddard, *Symphony Conductors of the U. S. A.* (N. Y., 1957; pp. 207-14).

Steiner, Jakob. See **Stainer.**

Steiner, Max (Maximilian Raoul), composer and arranger; b. Vienna, May 10, 1888. He studied at the Vienna Cons. with R. Fuchs, H. Grädener, and also had lessons with Mahler. He wrote an operetta at the age of 14. He went to England in 1904 and to Paris in 1911; settled in America in 1914; conducted musical comedies in N. Y.; in 1929, moved to Hollywood as film composer and conductor. He wrote the music for the motion pictures *The Informer, Life With Father, Gone With the Wind,* etc.

Steinert, Alexander Lang, American composer, conductor, and arranger; b. Boston, Sept. 21, 1900. He graduated from Harvard Univ. (1922); studied composition with Loeffler in Boston; also with Koechlin and Vincent d'Indy in Paris; took courses in counterpoint with Gedalge at the Paris Cons. In 1927 he received the American Prix de Rome, and spent the next 3 years at the American Academy in Rome. He conducted opera in N. Y. and Los Angeles; became associated with motion picture work as conductor and arranger in Hollywood. He was in charge of music in the First Motion Picture Unit with the U. S. Army at Culver City, Cal. (1942-45); after 1945, lived mostly in California, spending some months of the year in N. Y. His music bears the imprint of French Impressionism. —Works: for orch.: *Nuit méridionale* (Boston, Oct. 15, 1926); *Leggenda sinfonica* (Rome, 1930; Boston, March 13, 1931); *Concerto sinfonico,* for piano and orch. (Boston, Feb. 8, 1935, composer soloist); *Air Corps Suite* (1942); *Flight Cycle* (1944); *Rhapsody* for clarinet and orch. (1945); *The Nightingale and the Rose,* after Oscar Wilde, for speaker and orch. (Philadelphia, March 31, 1950); choral works; chamber music (violin sonata, piano trio); piano sonata, etc.

Steingräber, Theodor, German music publisher; b. Neustadt-on-the-Orla, Jan. 25, 1830; d. Leipzig, April 5, 1904. The son of a piano maker, he founded a music publishing firm, bearing his own name, in Leipzig in 1878; later the business was located in Hanover for a short time, and in 1890 it was established in Leipzig again. Under the pseudonym Gustav Damm, Steingräber publ. a piano method (1868). From 1903 to 1916 the business was managed by Steingräber's son-in-law, Walter Friedel; from 1918-26 the latter's son-in-law, G. Heinrich, was head of the firm; in 1920 he bought the 'Neue Zeitschrift für Musik,' which he publ. thenceforth as 'Zeitschrift für Musik.' In 1926 control of the business passed to Steingräber's daughters, Clara and Mathilde. — Steingräber's son, **Johann George** (b. Berlin, Jan. 1, 1858; d. there, March 16, 1932), was a piano maker; he came to the U. S. and worked for Steinway & Sons in N. Y.; from 1907 he lived in Berlin; made excellent harpsichords.

Steingruber, Ilona, Austrian soprano; b. Vienna, Feb. 8, 1912. She studied piano and voice; was on the staff of the Vienna Opera from 1948 to 1951. In 1946 she married the composer Friedrich Wildgans (q.v.).

Steinhard, Erich, Czech musicologist; b. Prague, May 26, 1886; d. in a concentration camp in Czechoslovakia, c. 1944. He was a pupil of K. Knittl and V. Novák (theory); studied musicology with J. Wolf, H. Kretzschmar, and M. Friedlaender in Berlin; *Dr. phil.* Prague, 1911 (with a thesis on organum). He became librarian of the Univ. of Prague; from 1921, ed. of 'Der Auftakt' and from 1929 music critic for the 'Prager Tageblatt.' —Writings: *Andreas Hammerschmidt* (Prague, 1914); *Gliederung neuerer deutscher Tonkunst in der Tschechoslowakei* ('Almanach,' Prague, 1922); *Junge Musik der Tschechoslowakei* ('Die Musik,' 1925); *Zur deutschen Musik in der Tschechoslowakischen Republik* (2nd part of V. Helfert's *Geschichte der Musik in der Tschechoslowakischen Republik;* Prague, 1936); *Musikgeschichte von der Urzeit zur Gegenwart* (with G. Černušák; 1936).

Steinhardt, Milton, American musicologist; b. Miami, Okla. Nov. 13, 1909. He studied at the Univ. of Kansas; in 1929 went to Europe, where he studied at the Munich Akademie der Tonkunst and in Paris with Maurice Hewitt (violin); returning to the U. S., he enrolled in the Eastman School of Music; B.M., 1936; M.M., 1937; then studied with Otto Kinkeldey at Cornell Univ., and at N. Y. Univ. with Curt Sachs and Gustave Reese; Ph.D., 1950. Was instructor at Michigan State Univ., 1948-50; associate prof., Ohio Univ., 1950-51; from 1951, associate prof. at the Univ. of Kansas. In 1958 he received a Guggenheim Fellowship. He publ. *Jacobus Vaet and His Motets* (East Lansing, Mich., 1951); edited *Jacobus Vaet, Zwei Hymnen,* in vol. 8 of the series 'Musik alter Meister' (1958); contributed articles on various musical subjects to American and European publications.

Steinitzer, Max, writer on music; b. Innsbruck, Jan. 20, 1864; d. Leipzig, June 21, 1936. Pupil of A. Kirchner (piano) and J. Hüttner (theory) in Munich; *Dr. phil.* (Munich, 1885) with the dissertation *Über die psychologischen Wirkungen der musikalischen Formen.* He subsequently conducted theater orchestras in Germany; 1903-11, prof. at the Cons. in Freiburg, Breisgau; 1911-30, music critic of the 'Leipziger Neueste Nachrichten.' An intimate friend of Richard Strauss from boyhood, he wrote a comprehensive and authoritative biography of him. —Publications: *Die menschlichen und tierischen Gemütsbewegungen* (1889); *Musikalische Strafpredigten* (1901; 12th ed., 1926); *Musikgeschichtlicher Atlas. Eine Beispielsammlung zu* *jeder Musikgeschichte* (1908); *Merkbüchlein für Mitglieder von Männerchoren* (1908); *Richard Strauss* (1911; 2nd ed., entirely rewritten, 1914; 3rd revised ed., 1927); *Richard Strauss in seiner Zeit* (1914; 2nd ed., 1922); *Zur Entwicklungsgeschichte des Melodrams und Mimodrams* (1919); *Meister des Gesanges* (1920); *Auf Flügeln des Gesanges* (1920); *Das Leipziger Gewandhaus im neuen Heim unter Carl Reinecke* (1924); *Tschaikowsky* (1925); *Beethoven* (1927); *Pädagogik der Musik* (1929); etc.

Steinway & Sons, piano manufacturers of New York and Hamburg. The founder of the firm was **Heinrich** (or **Henry**) **Engelhard Steinweg** (b. Wolfshagen, Germany, Feb. 15, 1797; d. New York, Feb. 7, 1871). He learned cabinet making and organ building at Goslar, and in 1818 entered the shop of an organ maker in Seesen, also becoming church-organist there. From about 1820 he became interested in piano making and worked hard to establish a business of his own. He married in 1825 and his first piano was probably finished at that time. In 1839 he exhibited 1 grand and 2 square pianos at the Brunswick State Fair, winning the gold medal. The Revolution of 1848 caused him to emigrate to America with his wife, 2 daughters, and 4 of his 5 sons: **Charles** (**Christian Karl Gottlieb;** b. Seesen, Jan. 4, 1829; d. there, March 31, 1865); **Henry** (**Johann Heinrich Engelhard;** b. Seesen, Oct. 29, 1830; d. N. Y., March 11, 1865); **William** (**Johann Heinrich Wilhelm;** b. Seesen, March 5, 1835; d. N. Y., Nov. 30, 1896), and (**Georg August**) **Albert** (b. Seesen, June 10, 1840; d. N. Y., May 14, 1877), leaving the management of the German business at Seesen in charge of the eldest son, (**Christian Friedrich**) **Theodor** (b. Seesen, Nov. 6, 1825; d. Brunswick, March 26, 1889). The family arrived in N. Y. on June 29, 1850, and for about 2 years father and sons worked in various piano factories there. On March 5, 1853, they established a factory of their own under the above firm-name, with premises in Varick St. In 1854 they won a gold medal for a square piano at the Metropolitan Fair in Washington, D. C. Their remarkable prosperity dates from 1855, when they took 1st prize for a square over-strung piano with cast-iron frame (an innovation then) at the N. Y. Industrial Exhibition. In 1856 they made their first grand, and in 1862 their first upright. Among the numerous honors subsequently received may be mentioned 1st prize medal at London, 1862; 1st grand gold medal of honor for all styles at Paris, 1867 (by unanimous verdict); and diplomas for 'highest degree of excellence in all styles' at Philadelphia, 1876. In 1864 the family name (Steinweg) was legally changed to Steinway. —In 1865, upon the death of his brothers Charles and Henry, Theodore S. gave up the Brunswick business (see **Steinweg**) and became a full partner in the N. Y. firm; he built Steinway Hall on 14th St., which, in addition to the offices and retail warerooms, housed a concert hall that became a leading center of N. Y. musical life. In 1925 headquarters were established in the Steinway Building on 57th St. Theodore S. was especially interested in the scientific aspects of piano construction and made a study of the acoustical theories of Helmholtz and Tyndall, which enabled him to introduce important improvements. He returned to Germany in 1870. —On May 17, 1876, the firm was incorporated and William S. was elected president; he opened a London branch in 1875, and established a European factory at Hamburg in 1880. In the latter year he also bought 400 acres of land on Long Island Sound and established there the village of Steinway (now part of L. I. City), where since 1910 the entire manufacturing plant has been located. William S. was for 14 years president of the N. Y. 'Deutsche Liedertafel.' —Control and active management of the business, now the largest of its kind in the world, has remained in the hands of the founder's descendants. **Theodore E. Steinway** (d. N. Y., April 8, 1957), grandson of Henry E. Steinway, was president from 1927; in 1955 he was succeeded by his son, Henry Steinway. —Cf. O. Floersheim, *W. S.* (Breslau, 1894); E. Hubbard, *The Story of the Steinways* (East Aurora, N. Y., 1911); A. Dolge, *Pianos and Their Makers,* vol. I (1911); Theodore E. Steinway, *People and Pianos* (N. Y., 1953).

Steinweg. Original name of the Steinway family. Christian Friedrich Theodore Steinway continued the piano-making business established by his father (see **Steinway & Sons**) at Seesen until 1852, when he transferred it to Wolfenbüttel; in 1859 he moved it to Brunswick, carrying it on there until 1865, when he left for America. The business was then taken over by his partners, Grotrian, Helfferich, and Schulz ('Theodor Steinweg Nachfolger'). In 1886 Grotrian became sole owner, and the business was carried on by his sons Willi and Kurt, the firm-name being 'Grotrian-Steinweg.'

Stellfeld, Jean-Auguste, Belgian musicologist; b. Antwerp, Feb. 17, 1881; d. there, Sept. 16, 1952. He was a practicing lawyer, and a judge; at the same time he became associated with various musical organizations in Belgium; accumulated an enormously rich library of music, published and in MS, from the 16th, 17th, and 18th centuries. After his death, the library was purchased by the Univ. of Michigan, Ann Arbor (cf. the article by L. E. Cuyler, G. A. Sutherland, and H. T. David in 'Notes,' Dec., 1954). He publ. *Bronnen tot de geschiedenis der antwerpsche clavecimbel- en orgelbouwers in de XVIe en XVIIe eeuwen* (Antwerp, 1942); *Andries Pevernage* (Louvain, 1943); *Bibliographie des éditions musicales plantiniennes* (Brussels, 1949).

Stenborg, Carl, Swedish composer; b. Stockholm, Sept. 25, 1752; d. Djurgarden, Aug. 1, 1813. He studied at the Univ. of Upsala; from 1773 to 1806 was a singer at the Swedish Opera in Stockholm. His opera, *Konung Gustaf Adolphs Jagt* (Stockholm, June 25, 1777), is of significance as the first opera based on a Swedish historical subject.

Stendhal, famous French writer (real name, Marie-Henri Beyle); b. Grenoble, Jan. 23, 1783; d. Paris, March 23, 1842. He was a military official under Napoleon, taking part in the German and Russian campaigns; from 1815 he lived in Milan, Paris, and Rome; in 1830 became French consul at Trieste, and from 1831 in Civitavecchia. He is best known as a novelist *(Le Rouge et le noir, La Chartreuse de Parme,* etc.), but also wrote on music; under the pseudonym of 'Louis Alexandre Bombet' he publ. *Lettres écrites de Vienne, en Autriche, sur le célèbre compositeur Joseph Haydn, suivies d'une vie de Mozart, et de considérations sur Métastase et l'état présent de la musique en France et en Italie* (Paris, 1814; English transl., London, 1817; new ed. in 1817 as *Vies de Haydn, Mozart et Métastase,* by 'Stendhal'; republ. in 1914 with introduction by R. Rolland: *Stendhal et la musique;* German transl., Vienna, 1921). The life of Haydn is in part translated from Carpani's *Le Haydine;* the first 4 chapters of the life of Mozart are taken from Schlichtegroll's Necrology (1791), the last 3 from Cramer's *Anecdotes sur Mozart.* In Jan., 1824, Stendhal's life of Rossini was publ. in London as *Memoirs of Rossini,* in a transl. made from the original MS. The French version, considerably expanded, was publ. in Paris later the same year (2 vols.; German transl., Leipzig, 1824; republ. in complete ed. of Stendhal's works, Paris, 1922, with introduction by Henry Prunières: *Stendhal et Rossini,* which was also publ. in the 'Mus. Quarterly,' Jan., 1921). The oft-repeated assertion that this work was plagiarized from Carpani's *Le Rossiniane* is without foundation. *The Life of Rossini* was republ. in English, London, 1956. —Cf. A. Paupe, *Histoire des oeuvres de Stendhal* (Paris, 1903); H. Prunières, *Stendhal et la musique,* in 'Revue hebdomadaire' (1921); A. E. A. Beau, *Das Verhältnis Stendhals zur Musik* (dissertation, Hamburg, 1930); D. Maurice, *Stendhal* (Paris, 1931); P. Jourda, *Stendhal, l'homme et l'œuvre* (Paris, 1934); F. C. Green, *Stendhal* (Cambridge, England, 1939); H. Imbert, *Stendhal critique musical,* in *Symphonie,* pp. 87-124 (Paris, 1891); J. W. Klein, *Stendhal as a Music Critic,* in the 'Mus. Quarterly' (Jan., 1943).

Stenhammar, Per Ulrik, Swedish composer; b. Törnvalla, Feb. 20, 1829; d. Stockholm, Feb. 8, 1875. He received his primary musical education from A. F. Lindblad; became interested in sacred music, and wrote choral works in Mendelssohn's style; many solo songs. His oratorio, *Saul och David* (1869), was orchestrated by his son, Wilhelm Stenhammar.

Stenhammar, Wilhelm, Swedish composer, son of Per Ulrik Stenhammar; b. Stockholm, Feb. 7, 1871; d. there, Nov. 20, 1927. He studied piano, organ, and theory at the Stockholm Cons., graduating in 1890; then went to Berlin for further piano study with Karl Heinrich Barth. His first large work for solo voices, chorus, and orch., *I Rosengarden* (after K. A. Melin's collection of fairy tales, *Prinsessan och svennen),* was performed in Stockholm in 1892, attracting considerable attention; on Dec. 9, 1898, he brought out his music drama, *Tirfing,* at the Stockholm Opera; this was followed by a German opera, *Das Fest auf Solhaug* (after Ibsen), which was first heard at Stuttgart (April 12, 1899), and 3 years later in Swedish, at Stockholm (Oct. 31, 1902). Both works are music dramas of a Wagnerian type, but employing many Swedish folk tunes. From 1897 to 1900 he was conductor of the Philharmonic Society in Stockholm; later also led orchestral and choral groups in Göteborg (1917-23), where he contributed much to local musical life. The Univ. of Göteborg made him Mus. Doc. in 1916. Besides his operas, he wrote 2 symphonies, 2 piano concertos, 6 string quartets, a piano quartet, a violin sonata, 4 piano sonatas, etc.

Štěpán, Václav, Czech pianist and writer on music; b. Pečky, near Kolín, Dec. 12, 1889; d. Prague, Nov. 24, 1944. He studied musicology at the Univ. of Prague *(Dr. phil.,* 1913); was also a private pupil of Novák in composition (1905-09); from 1919 he was prof. of esthetics at the Prague Cons.; appeared as pianist in Czechoslovakia and in France; contributed valuable articles on Czech musicians to foreign encyclopedias and music dictionaries; publ. 2 vols. of Bohemian folksongs (1917) and 2 vols. of Slovak folksongs (1925); also *Das Symbol in der Programm-Musik* (1914). He wrote some chamber music and other works, but did not pursue a composer's career.

Stepanian, Aro Leonovitch, Armenian composer; b. Elisabethopol, April 24, 1897. He entered the Moscow Musical Technicum in 1923 and studied composition with Gnessin; in 1926 he went to Leningrad, where he studied with Vladimir Shtcherbatchev. He graduated in 1930, and moved to Erevan, capital of Soviet Armenia. Among his works are 5 operas on Armenian subjects, *Kadz Nazar (Brave Nazar;* Erevan, Nov. 29, 1935), *David of Sasun* (1937), *Lusabatsin (At the Dawn,* 1938), *Nune* (1947), and *Heroine* (1950). He also composed 3 symphonies (1943, 1945, 1953); 2 string quartets; 2 violin sonatas; cello sonata; about 200 songs.

Stepanov (steh-pah'-nov), **Lev Borissovitch,** Russian composer; b. Tomsk, Siberia, Dec. 26, 1908. He studied at the Moscow Cons. with Miaskovsky, graduating in 1938. He devoted himself mainly to theater works; wrote the operas *Dunia's Happiness* (1937), *Darvas Pass* (1938), *The Guards* (Tashkent, Nov. 8, 1947), *Ivan Bolotnikov* (Perm, Dec. 17, 1950); the ballet, *The Native Shore* (1941); 2 piano concertos (1947; 1955); viola concerto (1955); cello sonata (1935); viola sonata (1936); choral works; film music.

Stephan, Rudi, German composer; b. Worms, July 29, 1887; d. near Tarnopol, Galicia, Sept. 29, 1915. He studied with Sekles in Frankfurt and with R. Louis in Munich; developed a fine talent for lyric songs, combining German Romantic traits with Impressionism in instrumental coloring. —Works: *Musik für 7 Saiteninstrumente,* for string quintet, piano, and harp (1912); *Musik für Orchester* (1913); *Musik für Violine und Orchester* (1914); a ballad, *Liebeszauber,* for baritone and orch.; piano pieces. His opera, *Die ersten Menschen,* was produced posthumously in Frankfurt on July 1, 1920. —Cf. K. Holl, *Rudi Stephan* (1920); A. Machner, *Rudi Stephans Werk* (dissertation, Breslau, 1942).

Stephani, Hermann, German musicologist and composer; b. Grimma, June 23, 1877. He studied at the Leipzig Cons. with Jadassohn and Reinecke, and at the Univ. of Munich with Lipps and Sandberger; *Dr. phil.,* 1902, with the dissertation, *Das Erhabene, insonderheit in der Tonkunst, und das Problem der Form* (Leipzig, 1903; 2nd ed., 1907). He became a choral conductor; in 1921 was appointed to the faculty of the Univ. of Marburg; taught musicology there until 1946, when he retired. His scholarly publications include: *Der Charakter der Tonarten* (Regensburg, 1923); *Grundfragen des Musikhörens* (Leipzig, 1925); *Das Vierteltonproblem* (Leipzig, 1925); *Polare Harmonik bei Beethoven* (Leipzig, 1927); *Das Problem des Orgelstils* (Essen, 1942). He advocated a reform in score notation through the exclusive use of the G clef with octave indications ('Einheitspartitur') and edited Schumann's *Manfred* Overture using this system (1905). He was a prolific composer; wrote about 100 opus numbers, mostly vocal works; also contrapuntal pieces for various combinations of instruments; edited works by Handel, Weber, etc. A 'Festschrift' was presented to him on his 70th birthday (Regensburg, 1947).

Stephens, Charles Edward, English organist and teacher; b. London, March 18, 1821; d. there, July 13, 1892. He studied piano with Cipriani Potter; in 1843 he was appointed to his first church position as organist, and was active in that capacity in various churches in London until 1875. From 1850 he was associated with the Philharmonic Society, as treasurer and director. He composed a piano trio, several orchestral overtures, a string quartet, and a symphony; all these works were performed in London.

Sterkel (shtehr'kel), Abbé **Johann Franz Xaver,** German ecclesiastic and composer; b. Würzburg, Dec. 3, 1750; d. there, Oct. 12, 1817. He studied theology and became a priest; was self-taught in music, but acquired sufficient proficiency as organist to occupy various positions as music director. In 1778 he became chaplain and organist in the Elector's court at Mainz; in 1782 he was in Italy, where he produced his opera, *Farnace* (Naples, Jan. 12, 1782). Beethoven heard Sterkel play in 1791, in Aschaffenburg, and was greatly impressed by his style as both composer and pianist. When the French expelled the Elector in 1794, Sterkel left

Mainz and returned to his native city. From 1805 he was again court musician to the Elector of Mainz, until 1814, when the military campaign forced him to go back to Würzburg once more. He was a prolific composer; publ. 10 symphonies, 2 overtures, a piano quartet, a string quintet, 6 string trios, 6 piano concertos, a considerable amount of piano music. His *Rondo comique* for piano was very popular. —Cf. A. Scharnagl, *J. F. X. Sterkel: ein Beitrag zur Musikgeschichte Mainfrankens* (Würzburg, 1943).

Sterling, Antoinette, American contralto; b. Sterlingville, N. Y., Jan. 23, 1850; d. London, Jan. 9, 1904. She studied with Abella in N. Y., Mathilde Marchesi in Cologne, and with Pauline Viardot-Garcia in Baden; also took lessons with Manuel Garcia in London. Returning to America, she sang in Henry Ward Beecher's church in Brooklyn; then went to London, where she made her début at a Covent Garden Promenade Concert (Nov. 5, 1873). She introduced many favorite songs (most of which were especially composed for her), such as Arthur Sullivan's *Lost Chord* (Jan. 31, 1877), Barnby's *When the Tide Comes In,* etc. In 1875 she toured the U. S.; her permanent home was in London. —Cf. Malcolm S. MacKinlay (her son), *Antoinette Sterling and other Celebrities* (London, 1906).

Sterling, Winthrop Smith, American organist and teacher; b. Cincinnati, Nov. 28, 1859; d. there, Nov. 16, 1943. He studied in Leipzig, and later in London, where he remained for several years as organist. From 1887 to 1903 he was head of the organ dept. and teacher of singing at the Cincinnati College of Music; later taught the organ at the Univ. of Miami, Florida, for 8 years. He composed a number of organ pieces and songs.

Stern (shtern), **Adolf,** German writer; b. Leipzig, June 14, 1835; d. Dresden, April 15, 1907. He publ. several books dealing with music: *Wanderbuch* (1877; about the Bayreuth Festivals); *Die Musik in der deutschen Dichtung* (1888); *Gluck in Versailles* (1904); edited the poems of Peter Cornelius (1890) and *Liszts Briefe an K. Gille* (1903). He married (1881) the pianist Margarete Herr (b. Dresden, Nov. 25, 1857; d. there, Oct. 4, 1899), who was a pupil of Liszt, and after her death he publ. her biography (Leipzig, 1901).

Stern, Isaac, outstanding violinist; b. Kremenetz, Russia, July 21, 1920. He was brought to San Francisco as an infant. His mother was a professional singer, and he received his primary musical education at home. He studied violin with Naoum Blinder and Louis Persinger; made his professional début with the San Francisco Symph. at 11; N. Y. début, Oct. 11, 1937, producing an excellent impression; made an extensive tour in Australia in 1947; subsequently appeared regularly with American and European orchestras, and gradually advanced to the foremost ranks of contemporary virtuosos. In May, 1956, he made a spectacularly successful tour of Russia.

Stern (shtern), **Julius,** eminent German music pedagogue; b. Breslau, Aug. 8, 1820; d. Berlin, Feb. 27, 1883. He studied violin with Lüstner, and later took courses with Rungenhagen in Berlin. He was in Dresden and in Paris between 1843 and 1846; in 1847 he founded the famous 'Sternscher Gesangverein' in Berlin, conducting it until 1874. In 1850 he founded the Stern Cons. in Berlin (with Kullak and Marx); Kullak withdrew in 1855, and Marx in 1857; thenceforth Stern became the sole head of the institution; it prospered and acquired the reputation of one of the greatest music schools in Europe. Stern conducted the Berlin Sinfonie-Kapelle from 1869 to 1871, and later led the 'Reichshalle' concerts (1873-75). He was also a composer, and received commendation from Mendelssohn for his songs; publ. *Barcarolle* for voice, cello, and piano; *Les Adieux,* for violin and piano; male choruses; songs. His opera, *Ismene,* was not produced. —Cf. Richard Stern, *Erinnerungsblätter an Julius Stern* (Berlin, 1886).

Stern, Leo, English cellist; b. Brighton, April 5, 1862; d. London, Sept. 10, 1904. He studied cello at the Royal Academy of Music in London with Piatti, and later with Julius Klengel in Leipzig. He was an assistant artist in Adelina Patti's concert tour in 1888; made a tour in America in 1897-98. He publ. solo pieces for cello and songs. His second wife was Suzanne Adams, the opera singer.

Sternberg, Constantin, pianist and composer; b. St. Petersburg, July 9, 1852; d. Philadelphia, March 31, 1924. He studied at the Leipzig Cons. with Moscheles and others, and later in Berlin with Th. Kullak, visiting Liszt in the summer months. He conducted various choral societies in Germany; toured as concert pianist in Russia (1879-80), including central Asia. In 1880 he made his 1st tour in the U. S., where he eventually settled; was director of the College of Music at Atlanta (1885-89); in 1890 established the Sternberg School of Music in Philadelphia, and was its director until his death. He publ. *Danses Cosaques* for violin; *Fantasia*, for cello; more than 200 salon pieces for piano, and instructive studies. He was the author of *Ethics and Esthetics of Piano-Playing* (N. Y., 1917); *Tempo Rubato and Other Essays* (N. Y., 1920).

Sternberg, Erich Walter, Israeli composer; b. Berlin, May 31, 1898. He studied with Hugo Leichtentritt; in 1932, went to Palestine. His works are mostly inspired by Hebrew subjects; among them is the orch. set of variations, *Twelve Tribes of Israel* (Tel Aviv, May 3, 1942). He further wrote 2 string quartets; piano pieces; songs.

Sternefeld, Daniel, Belgian composer; b. Antwerp, Nov. 27, 1905. He studied flute, conducting, and composition at the Antwerp Cons.; then took courses in conducting with Clemens Krauss and Karajan in Salzburg. Returning to Antwerp, he became conductor of the local orch.; in 1944 appointed 1st conductor at the Flemish Opera there. His works include an opera, *Mater Dolorosa* (Antwerp, 1935); a symphony (1943); chamber music.

Sternfeld, Frederick William, musicologist; b. Vienna, Sept. 25, 1914. He studied at the Univ. of Vienna (1933-37); then went to the U. S., and enrolled at Yale Univ. (1940-43), obtaining his Ph. D. there. He taught at Wesleyan Univ., Conn. (1940-46); at Dartmouth College (1946-56; prof. in 1955); in 1955, at the Institute for Advanced Studies, Princeton; since 1956, lecturer at Oxford Univ. He was editor of 'Renaissance News' (1946-54); in 1954 received a Guggenheim Fellowship. He publ. a number of informative studies in the 'Mus. Quarterly' and other American and British publications; also a bibliography, *Goethe and Music* (N. Y., 1954).

Sternfeld, Richard, German writer on music; b. Königsberg, Oct. 15, 1858; d. Berlin, June 21, 1926. A thoroughly trained musician, he publ. piano pieces and songs, and valuable books concerning music: *Beethoven und Wagner* (1885); *Hans von Bülow* (1898); *Beethoven's Missa Solemnis* (1900); *Albert Niemann* (1904); *Schiller und Wagner* (1905); *Richard Wagner und die Bayreuther Bühnenfestspiele* (2 vols., 1906); *Aus Richard Wagners Pariser Zeit* (1906); *Musikalische Skizzen und Humoresken* (1919); *Berühmte Musiker und ihre Werke* (1922).

Steuerlein, Johann, German composer; b. Schmalkalden, July 5, 1546; d. Meiningen, May 5, 1613. He studied in Magdeburg; occupied various positions as a clerk; became a notary public in Meiningen in 1589; in 1604 was given the rank of poet laureate by the Emperor. At the same time he was active as a song composer, and brought out *21 Geistliche Lieder* for 4 voices (1575), *24 Weltliche Gesänge* (1575); *23 Geistliche Gesänge,* for 4-6 voices (1576), *27 Geistliche Gesänge,* for 4 voices (1588), *8 Geistliche Gesänge,* for 5 voices (1589). He was the composer of the celebrated New Year song, *Das alte Jahr vergangen ist.* —Cf. G. Kraft, *Johann Steuerlein,* in 'Zeitschrift für Musikwissenschaft' (May, 1931).

Steuermann, Eduard, pianist; b. Sambor, near Lwow, June 18, 1892. He studied with Busoni (piano) and Schoenberg (theory) in Berlin (1911-14). He was instructor at the Paderewski School in Lwow, and later at the Jewish Cons. of Cracow (1932-36). In 1937 he went to the U. S.; settled in N. Y. as teacher and pianist. He dedicated himself to the cause of modern music, and particularly to that of Schoenberg; gave several performances with leading American orchestras of Schoenberg's piano concerto; also brought out piano scores of Schoenberg's orchestral compositions; edited piano music by Brahms.

Stevens, Bernard, English composer; b. London, March 2, 1916. He studied at Cambridge Univ. and the Royal College of Music in London; later taught in the latter school. He has written a *Symphony of Liberation* (1946); *Fugal Overture* (1948); a violin concerto (1943); a piano trio (1943); songs. His music adheres to traditional concepts in harmony, while the programmatic content is often political.

Stevens, Denis (William), English musicologist, violinist, and conductor; b. High Wycombe, Buckinghamshire, March 2, 1922. He studied music at Oxford Univ. with R. O. Morris and Egon Wellesz (M. A., 1947); spent a year in Calcutta, India, as a journalist (1946); then was again in Oxford, before settling in London, 1949, when he joined the BBC. He has lectured in various American universities. He edited the *Mulliner Book* (vol. 1 of 'Musica Britannica') and publ. a commentary on that collection of keyboard works (London, 1952); also publ.

Tudor Church Music (N. Y., 1955) and a monograph on Thomas Tomkins (London, 1957). Edited compositions by Boyce, Tomkins, etc. He has contributed articles on English music to various periodicals in England and America.

Stevens, Halsey, American composer and writer on music; b. Scott, N. Y., Dec. 3, 1908; studied music with William Berwald at Syracuse Univ. and with Ernest Bloch in California. He held teaching positions at Syracuse Univ. (1935-36); Dakota Wesleyan Univ. (1937-41); Bradley Univ. (1941-46); Univ. of Redlands (1946); in 1946, appointed chairman, dept. of composition, Univ. of Southern California School of Music. He was program annotator for the Los Angeles Philharmonic (1946-51); lectured widely in the U. S.; publ. *The Life and Music of Béla Bartók* (N. Y., 1953). — Works: symph. No. 1 (San Francisco, March 7, 1946, composer conducting; revised version, Los Angeles, March 3, 1950); symph. No. 2 (1945; NBC, May 17, 1947; subsequently withdrawn by the composer); *A Green Mountain Overture* (Burlington, Aug. 7, 1948; revised version, Tallahassee, Fla., March 20, 1954); *Triskelion* for orch. (Louisville, Feb. 27, 1954); *Sinfonia Breve* (Louisville, Nov. 20, 1957); 3 string quartets; quintet for flute, piano, and strings; 3 piano trios; violin sonata (1947); viola sonata (1950); bassoon sonata (1949); horn sonata (1953); 3 piano sonatas; choral works; songs. —Cf. P. A. Pisk, *Halsey Stevens,* in 'Bulletin of the American Composers Alliance' (vol. 4, no. 2; 1954).

Stevens, Richard John Samuel, English composer of glees; b. London, March 27, 1757; d. there, Sept. 23, 1837. He was a chorister at St. Paul's Cathedral in London, and served as organist of the Temple Church (from 1786); from 1801 was prof. of music at Gresham College. He received numerous prizes for his glees, of which the most famous were *Sigh no more, Ladies; Ye spotted snakes; The cloud-capt towers; Crabbed Age and Youth,* and *From Oberon in Airy Land;* 3 sets were publ.; he also brought out 3 sonatas for harpsichord, and edited a 3-vol. collection of sacred vocal music by Italian and English composers. —Cf. J. B. Trend, *R. J. S. Stevens,* in 'Music & Letters' (vol. 14).

Stevens, Risë, American mezzo-soprano; b. New York, June 11, 1913. She studied voice with Anna Schoen-René at the Juilliard School of Music, N. Y.; later took a course with George Schick in Prague. She made her début as Mignon in Prague (1938); appeared in the same role at the Metropolitan Opera, in Philadelphia, on Nov. 22, 1938; subsequently sang on the radio, and also in motion pictures and on television. In 1939 she married the Czech actor Walter Surovy; they settled in New York.

Stevenson, Robert, American musicologist; b. Melrose, N. M., July 3, 1916; studied at Harvard and Yale Univs.; later at Rochester Univ., where he received his Ph. D. He was instructor at Westminster Choir College in Princeton (1946-49); in 1950 appointed assistant prof. of music at the Univ. of California, Los Angeles; publ. a valuable book, *Music in Mexico* (N. Y., 1952); also *Patterns of Protestant Church Music* (Durham, N. C., 1953); *Music Before the Classic Era* (London, 1955).

Stewart, Humphrey John, organist and composer; b. London, May 22, 1856; d. San Diego, Calif., Dec. 28, 1932. He studied privately in England; in 1886 emigrated to the U. S., and settled in San Francisco as church organist; he was one of the founders of the American Guild of Organists. His 3 operas were produced in San Francisco: *His Majesty* (1890), *The Conspirators* (1900), and *King Hal* (1911); the MSS of the first two were lost in the San Francisco earthquake and fire of 1906. His most successful work was the sacred music drama *The Hound of Heaven* (San Francisco, April 24, 1924); he further wrote the orchestral suites *Montezuma* and *Scenes in California;* a Mass; organ pieces; songs. —Cf. E. E. Hipsher, *American Opera and its Composers* (Philadelphia, 1934, pp. 391-94).

Stewart, Reginald, conductor and pianist; b. Edinburgh, April 20, 1900. He studied piano with Mark Hambourg and Isidor Philipp; composition with Nadia Boulanger. He appeared as piano soloist with the London Symph.; taught at the Canadian Academy of Music in 1920; was pianist in the Hambourg Trio in 1921; in 1933 he went to Canada, where he organized the Bach Society of Toronto (1933-41); inaugurated Promenade symph. concerts there, and formed the Toronto Philharmonic Orch. in 1934. In 1942 he was engaged as conductor of the Baltimore Symph. (until 1952); in 1941 he was appointed director of the Peabody Cons. of Music, resigning in the spring of 1958.

Stewart, Sir Robert Prescott, Irish organist and composer; b. Dublin, Dec. 16, 1825;

d. there, March 24, 1894. He was a chorister of Christ Church Cathedral, Dublin, and at the age of 18 was appointed organist there. In 1852 he became vicar-choral at St. Patrick's Cathedral, Dublin; in 1861 was appointed to the faculty of Dublin Univ., as teacher of harmony. He was engaged as conductor of the Dublin Philharmonic in 1873. He gave concerts as organist in England; wrote several cantatas and odes for various occasions; also anthems, glees, and miscellaneous songs. —Cf. O. Vignoles, *Memoir of Sir Robert P. Stewart* (London, 1899); J. C. Culwick, *The Works of Sir Robert Stewart* (Dublin, 1902).

Stich (stiyh), **Jan Václav** (Johann Wenzel; he Italianized his German name, Johann Stich, as 'Giovanni Punto'), famous Czech horn player; b. Žehušice, near Čáslav, 1746; d. Prague, Feb. 16, 1803. He studied in Prague, Munich, and Dresden; traveled in Germany and Hungary; visited England; then entered the service of the Elector at Mainz (1769-74); subsequently served at the court of the Prince-Bishop of Würzburg, and in 1782 became chamber musician to the Comte d'Artois (later Charles X) at Paris; in Paris he met Mozart, who wrote for him, the flutist Wendling, the oboist Ramm, and the bassoonist Ritter the *Symphonie concertante* (K. Anhang 9). During the French revolution (1789-99) Stich was in charge of the music at the Théâtre des Variétés Amusantes; returned to Germany in 1799; proceeded to Vienna in 1800; made the acquaintance of Beethoven, who was enchanted by his playing, wrote for him a sonata for horn and piano (op. 17), and played it with him at a concert on April 18, 1800. He went to Prague in 1801. His works comprise 14 horn concertos, much chamber music with horn, a method for horn (1798; a revision of one by his Dresden teacher Hampel); publ. a book of exercises for the horn (Paris, 1795).

Stiedry (stē'-drē), **Fritz,** conductor; b. Vienna, Oct. 11, 1883. He studied law at the Univ. of Vienna, and music theory at the Vienna Cons.; for 2 years he was assistant conductor to Ernst von Schuch in Dresden (1907-08); subsequently conducted operas in Germany. In 1914 he was appointed conductor of the Berlin Opera (until 1923); then led the Vienna Volksoper for 2 seasons (1923-25); after traveling as guest conductor in Italy, Spain, and Scandinavia (1925-28), he returned to Berlin as music director of the Berlin Municipal Opera (1929-33). With the advent of the Nazi regime in 1933, he left Germany, and conducted the Leningrad Philharmonic for 4 seasons (1933-37). In 1938 he settled in the U. S., as conductor of the New Friends of Music Orchestra, in N. Y. In 1946 he was engaged as conductor of the Metropolitan Opera. He is particularly distinguished as a Wagnerian conductor; but he has also presented excellent performances of the operas of Verdi; at his symph. concerts he often brought out important compositions of the modern school.

Stiehl (shtēl), **Carl Johann Christian,** German organist and music historian; b. Lübeck, July 12, 1826; d. there, Dec. 2, 1911. He was a pupil of his father, Johann Dietrich Stiehl; served as church organist in Jever (1848-58) and at Eutin (1858-77); in 1878 returned to Lübeck, where he conducted the 'Musikverein' and 'Singakademie' (until 1897); also wrote music criticism, and was in charge of the music section in the Lübeck Library. —Publications: *Zur Geschichte der Instrumentalmusik in Lübeck* (1885); *Lübeckisches Tonkünstler-Lexikon* (1887); *Musikgeschichte der Stadt Lübeck* (1891); *Geschichte des Theaters in Lübeck* (1902); ed. Buxtehude's sonatas *a* 3 and 4 (vol. 11 of the 'Denkmäler deutscher Tonkunst').

Stiehl (shtēl), **Heinrich (Franz Daniel),** German organist, choral conductor, and composer; son of Johann Dietrich Stiehl; b. Lübeck, Aug. 5, 1829; d. Reval, May 1, 1886. He studied with Moscheles, Gade, and Hauptmann at the Leipzig Cons.; in 1853 he went to St. Petersburg, where he remained for 13 years as organist at the Lutheran Church and conductor of a German choral society. He was subsequently active in Vienna (1867-69), in Italy (1869-72), London (1872-73), and Belfast (1874-77). In 1880 he was engaged as organist and conductor in Reval, Estonia, where he remained to the end of his life, with occasional appearances in St. Petersburg. He wrote in all 172 op. numbers, including 2 light operas, *Der Schatzgräber* and *Jery und Bätely; Die Vision* for orch.; 2 piano quartets; 3 piano trios; a violin sonata; a cello sonata; numerous piano pieces of programmatic content, such as *Spaziergänge im Schwarzwald, Italienische Reisebilder, Hexentanz, Musikalische Portraits,* etc.

Stiehl, Johann Dietrich, German organist; b. Lübeck, July 9, 1800; d. there, June 27, 1873. He lived virtually all his life in Lübeck, where he was organist at St. Jacobi; his sons, Heinrich and Carl Johann Christian, were also excellent organists.

Stierlin (shtēr'-lēn), **Adolf,** German composer, singer, and pedagogue; b. Adenau, Oct. 14, 1859; d. Münster, April 26, 1930. He studied singing and was engaged as bass at various theaters in Germany; in 1897 he opened his own music school in Münster. He wrote the operas *Scapina* (Münster, 1887) and *Zamora* (Halle, 1893), a ballet, *Die sieben Todsünden;* choruses.

Stigelli, Giorgio (real name Georg Stiegele), celebrated German tenor; b. 1815; d. in his villa Boschetti, near Monza, Italy, July 3, 1868. He made extensive concert tours in Europe, and appeared in America in 1864-65. He was the composer of many songs, among them the popular *Die schönsten Augen.*

Still, Wiliam Grant, American Negro composer; b. Woodville, Miss., May 11, 1895. He studied at Oberlin Cons., and later with Chadwick in Boston and Varèse in N. Y.; received a Guggenheim Fellowship (1934-35). He began his career as a practicing musician by arranging music for W. C. Handy, Paul Whiteman, and other conductors in the popular field. Determined to develop a symphonic type of Negro music, he wrote an *Afro-American Symphony* (1931), which was the first work of its kind by a Negro composer. In his music he occasionally makes use of actual Negro folksongs, but mostly he invents such themes by recreating the melo-rhythmic elements of Negro spirituals. He was the first Negro to conduct a major American orch. (Hollywood Bowl, 1936). —Works: for orch.: *From the Black Belt* (1926); *Darker America* (Rochester, Nov. 21, 1927); *From the Journal of a Wanderer* (Rochester, May 8, 1929); *Africa,* symph. poem (1930); *Afro-American Symphony* (Rochester, Oct. 29, 1931); *Three Dances,* from the ballet *La Guiablesse* (Rochester, May 5, 1933); *Kaintuck (Kentucky),* for piano and orch. (Rochester, Jan. 16, 1936); *Dismal Swamp* (Rochester, Oct. 30, 1936); *Ebon Chronicle* (Fort Worth, Nov. 3, 1936); symph. in G minor (1937); *And They Lynched Him on a Tree,* for narrator, contralto, chorus, and orch. (N. Y., June 25, 1940); *Plain Chant for Americans* for baritone and orch. (N. Y., Oct. 23, 1941); *Old California* (1941); *Pages from Negro History* (1943); *In Memoriam: The Colored Soldiers Who Died for Democracy* (N. Y., Jan. 5, 1944); *Poem* (Cleveland, Dec. 7, 1944); *Festive Overture* (Cincinnati, Jan. 19, 1945); 3rd symphony (1945); *Archaic Ritual* (1946); *Wood Notes* (Chicago, April 22, 1948); 4th symphony (1949); numerous pieces for symph. band: *From the Delta* (1945), *To You, America* (1952), etc.; vocal works: *Caribbean Melodies,* for chorus, piano, and percussion (1941), *Wailing Woman,* for soprano and chorus (1946), etc.; *Pastorela* for violin and piano (1946). In addition, he wrote several stage works: *La Guiablesse,* ballet (1927); *Sahdji,* ballet (1930); *Blue Steel,* opera in 3 acts (1935); *Lenox Avenue,* ballet (1937); *Troubled Island,* opera in 4 acts (1938); *A Bayou Legend,* opera in 3 acts (1940); *Miss Sally's Party* (1940); *A Southern Interlude,* opera in 2 acts (1942); *Costaso,* opera in 3 acts (1949). He married the writer Verna Arvey, who has collaborated with her husband in stage works. —Cf. M. Cuney Hare, *Negro Musicians and Their Music* (Washington, D. C., 1936); A. Locke, *The Negro and His Music* (Washington, D. C., 1936); Verna Arvey, *William Grant Still* (N. Y., 1939).

Stillman, Mitya, Russian-American viola player and composer; b. Ilyintza, near Kiev, Jan. 27, 1892; d. New York, April 12, 1936. He studied violin at the Kiev Cons.; theory with Glière. After the Revolution he came to the U. S. In 1921 he joined the Detroit Symph. Orch. as viola player; then was a member of the Hartmann String Quartet; from 1928 he was the first viola player of the CBS orch. As composer, Stillman adopted a strong contrapuntal idiom; his 4 songs for mezzo soprano, flute, harp, and string quartet won first prize in Detroit; he wrote 8 string quartets; No. 7 received a posthumous first prize award from the NBC Guild as the best chamber music work for 1936 (publ.). Other works are *Dnieprostroy,* a symph. poem (1933); *Cyprus* for strings, woodwinds, and percussion; string trio, *Yalta Suite;* orchestral transcriptions.

Stillman-Kelley. See **Kelley.**

Stirling, Elizabeth, English organist and composer; b. Greenwich, Feb. 26, 1819; d. London, March 25, 1895. She studied organ and piano with Edward Holmes, and harmony with J. A. Hamilton and G. A. Macfarren. She was appointed organist of All Saints', Poplar, at the age of 20, and retained this position for nearly 20 years, when she competed for one at St. Andrew's, Undershaft. She won the contest, and was organist there until 1880. In 1856 she passed the examination for the degree of Mus. Bac. at Oxford (her work was Psalm 130 for 5 voices with orch.), but the degree could not be granted to a woman; her moral victory upon acceptance of the work by Oxford Univ. as satisfactory was all the greater. In 1863 she married F. A. Bridge. She made many organ transcriptions from classical works; publ. *6 Pedal-Fugues* and other organ pieces; also part-songs, of which *All Among the Barley* won great popularity.

Stobaeus, Johann, German composer; b. Graudenz, July 6, 1580; d. Königsberg, Sept. 11, 1646. In 1595 he went to Königsberg, where from 1599-1608 he was a pupil of J. Eccard; in 1601 he entered the Electoral chapel as bass singer, and in 1602 was cantor at the Cathedral. He succeeded Krocker as Kapellmeister to the Elector of Brandenburg in 1626. He publ. *Cantiones sacrae 5-6, 7, 8 et 10 vocibus item aliquot Magnificat 5 et 6 vocibus adornatae* (Frankfurt, 1624); a new ed. of *Geistliche Lieder auf . . . Kirchen-Melodeyen* for 5 voices with some additional songs of his own (1634); and an edition of Eccard's *Preussiche Festlieder* (2 vols.; 1642, 1644; modern edition by Teschner, 1858). —Cf. R. Eitner in 'Monatshefte für Musikgeschichte' (1883); A. Mayer-Reinach, *Zur Geschichte der Königsberger Hofkapelle,* in 'Sammelbände der Internationalen Musik-Gesellschaft' VI, 1 (1904); L. Kamieński, *Johann Stobaeus z Grudziadz* (Posen, 1928).

Stock (stŏhk), **Frederick A.,** conductor; b. Jülich, Germany, Nov. 11, 1872; d. Chicago, Oct. 20, 1942. Taught by his father, a bandmaster; from 1886-91 he attended the Cologne Cons., studying violin with G. Japha and composition with Wüllner, Zöllner, and Humperdinck; 1891-95, violinist in the Cologne municipal orch.; in 1895, first viola in the Chicago Symph. Orch. (Th. Thomas); appointed assistant conductor in 1901, conducting all concerts outside of Chicago (1903-05), and elected conductor after Thomas' death in 1905. He was also conductor of the Musical Art Club (1907-09) and of the Civic Music Student Orch. (from 1920). Music director of the Century of Progress Fair, Chicago, 1933. In 1910 he was elected a member of the American Institute of Arts and Letters. He received the degree of Mus. Doc. *(hon. c.)* from Northwestern Univ. (1915), from the Univ. of Michigan (1924), from Chicago Univ. (1925), etc. In 1939 he received the medal of the Bruckner Society of America; Chevalier of the Légion d'Honneur, 1925. He became a naturalized U. S. citizen in 1919. He was also a composer; wrote a symph., overtures, string quartet, etc. His violin concerto was performed by Efrem Zimbalist at the Norfolk Festival, June 3, 1915, under Stock's direction. —Cf. P. A. Otis, *The Chicago Symphony Orchestra . . .* (Chicago, 1925).

Stockhausen, Franz, conductor and educator, brother of Julius Stockhausen; b. Gebweiler, Alsace, Jan. 30, 1839; d. Strasbourg, Jan. 4, 1926. Pupil of Alkan in Paris, and of Moscheles, Richter, and Hauptmann at the Leipzig Cons., 1860-62. From 1868, conductor of the 'Société de chant sacré' in Strasbourg (resigned 1879), and music director of the Cathedral; from 1871 until his retirement in 1907 he was director of the Strasbourg Cons.

Stockhausen, Julius, son of the harpist and composer Franz Stockhausen (1792-1868); baritone and teacher; b. Paris, July 22, 1826; d. Frankfurt, Sept. 22, 1906. Pupil of Paris Cons., and of Manuel García in London, soon winning renown as a concert singer. From 1862-67, conductor of the Philharmonic Concerts and the 'Singakademie' at Stuttgart; 1874-78, conductor of the 'Sternscher Gesangverein' at Berlin; 1878-79, teacher of singing at Hoch's Cons., Frankfurt; after Raff's death in 1882 he resumed the professorship at the Cons., retiring in 1898; after that time he gave private lessons only. As an oratorio and lieder singer he was unsurpassed; a close personal friend of Brahms, he was among the first and greatest interpreters of that master. He also was an excellent conductor. His *Gesangsmethode* (2 vols., 1886, 1887; also in English) is a standard work. Also publ. *Gesangstechnik und Stimmbildung* and several songs. —Cf. Julia Wirth-Stockhausen, *J. S. der Sänger des deutschen Liedes* (Frankfurt, 1927) and *Unverlierbare Kindheit* (Stuttgart, 1949); A. H. Fox Strangways, *J. S.,* in 'Monthly Mus. Record' (March-April, 1949).

Stockhausen, Karl Heinz (or **Karlheinz**), German composer of the advanced modernist school; b. Mödrath, near Cologne, Aug. 22, 1928. He studied piano at the Musikhochschule in Cologne (1947-50) and composition with Frank Martin during the latter's residence there (1950-51); then with Olivier Messiaen and Darius Milhaud in Paris (1951-53); also made a study of 'musique concrète' and adopted an empiric method of composition which included highly complex contrapuntal formulas and uninhibited application of dissonance as well as the simplest procedures of tonal reiteration; all this in the freest of rhythms and a great variety of instrumental color, with emphasis on percussive effects. He has also perfected a system of constructivist composition in which the subjective choice of the performer determines the succession of given thematic ingredients and their polyphonic simultaneities. Among his works are *Kreuzspiel* for orch. (1952); *Kontra-Punkte* (Cologne, May 26, 1953); *Klavierstück XI* (one of a series of constructivist pieces); *Zeitmasse,* for oboe, flute, English horn, clarinet, and bassoon (1956). Co-ed. (with H. Eimert) of 'Die Reihe,' a periodical devoted to developments in contemporary music (from 1955).

Stoeckel, Carl, son of Gustave Jakob Stoeckel; b. New Haven, Conn., Dec. 7, 1858; d. Norfolk, Conn., Nov. 1, 1925. Through his personal devotion and generous financial support he raised the annual festival of the 'Litchfield County Union,' established by Robbins Battell (b. Norfolk, Conn., April 9, 1819; d. there, Jan. 26, 1895), from an event of merely local to one of national importance. In 1899 the 'Norfolk Glee Club' and 'Winchester Choral Union' joined forces, to which later were added those of other choral groups, resulting in an aggregation of almost 700 trained voices. From 1902 the festivals were held in the 'Music Shed' (capacity 2,000 seats) on Stoeckel's estate. The festival itself came to be known as 'The Norfolk Festival.' Every year in June, 3 or 4 concerts were given, under eminent conductors with the assistance of famous soloists and an orchestra selected from the best players of Boston and New York, all expenses being met by Stoeckel. What contributed especially to the fame of these festivals was the production, annually, of 2 important new works (choral or orchestral), generally by American composers, for which Stoeckel established substantial cash prizes. Sibelius composed his tone-poem *Aallottaret* especially for the Norfolk Festival and conducted its 1st performance there in 1914. Among other composers represented were J. A. Carpenter, G. W. Chadwick, S. Coleridge-Taylor, H. F. Gilbert, P. Grainger, H. K. Hadley, E. S. Kelley, C. M. Loeffler, H. Parker, D. S. Smith, C. V. Stanford, and Deems Taylor.

Stoeckel, Gustave Jakob, pedagogue; b. Maikammer, Bavarian Palatinate, 1819; d. Norfolk, Conn., May 14, 1907. He came to America in 1847, and in 1849 became instructor of music and chapel organist at Yale Univ.; appointed Battell Prof. of Music in the newly established department of music at Yale; retired in 1896 with the title of prof. emeritus. He composed some vocal and instrumental pieces, arranged college songs, and assisted in editing the 'College Hymn-Book' for men's voices. —Cf. D. S. Smith, *G. J. Stoeckel, Yale Pioneer in Music* (New Haven, 1939).

Stoessel, Albert (Frederic), American conductor and composer; b. St. Louis, Oct. 11, 1894; d. N. Y., May 12, 1943. After preliminary study in his native city, he went to Berlin, where he studied violin with Willy Hess and theory with Kretzschmar; appeared as violin soloist with the Blüthner Orch. in Berlin on Nov. 14, 1914; made his American début with the St. Louis orch., Nov. 19, 1915. In 1921 he was appointed successor to his father-in-law, Walter Damrosch, as conductor of the N. Y. Oratorio Society; from 1923 till 1930, he was head of the music dept. of N. Y. Univ.; from 1930, director of the opera dept. of the Juilliard Graduate School, N. Y.; from 1925 he conducted music festivals in Worcester, Mass. He was stricken fatally at the annual ceremonial of the American Academy of Arts and Letters, while leading the première of the symph. sketch *Dunkirk* by Walter Damrosch. Stoessel's works include *Hispania Suite* for orch. (1921; originally for piano); *Cyrano de Bergerac,* a symph. poem (1922); *Concerto Grosso* for strings and piano (1935); *Suite Antique,* for two violins and piano (his most successful work; 1922); a violin sonata and violin pieces; many choruses; piano pieces; songs. His opera *Garrick* was produced under his direction at the Juilliard School of Music, N. Y., on Feb. 24, 1937. Publ. *The Technic of the Baton* (N. Y,. 1920; new ed., 1928).

Stoeving, (Carl Heinrich) Paul, violinist and composer; b. Leipzig, May 7, 1861; d. New York, Dec. 24, 1948. He studied violin at the Leipzig Cons. and with Léonard in Paris; gave concerts in Germany, Russia, and Scandinavia, and in 1887 visited the U. S. In 1896 he went to London, where he was prof. at the Guildhall School of Music (until 1914). At the outbreak of World War I he emigrated to the U. S., and served as teacher in various music schools in New Haven and N. Y. He wrote a violin concerto, chamber music, songs, and a 'song-play' *Gaston and Jolivette;* publ. *The Art of Violin Bowing* (London, 1902); *The Story of the Violin* (London, 1904); *Elements of Violin Playing* and *A Key to Ševčík's Works* (London, 1914); *The Mastery of the Bow and Bowing Subtleties* (N. Y., 1920); *The Violin, Cello and String Quartet* (N. Y., 1927); *The Violin: Its Famous Makers and Players* (Boston, 1928).

Stöhr, Richard, Austrian music theorist and composer; b. Vienna, June 11, 1874. He studied medicine (M. D., 1898), but then turned to music and studied with Robert Fuchs and others at the Vienna Cons. In 1904 he was appointed instructor in theory there, and during his long tenure he had many pupils who later became celebrated (Artur Rodzinski, Erich Leinsdorf, etc.). In 1938 he was compelled to leave Vienna; settled in the U. S., where he taught at the Curtis Institute of Music, Philadelphia (1939-41); then taught music and German at St. Michael's College, Winooski, Vt., retiring in 1950. He was living in Vermont in 1958. A concert of his works was given by the Vermont State Symph. Orch. on Oct. 31, 1954, including the world première of his *Vermont Suite,* an early symphony, and songs accompanied by the composer. His list of works includes 4 symphonies in all; much chamber music; piano pieces. He publ. a popular manual *Praktischer Leitfaden der Harmonielehre* (Vienna, 1909; 14th ed., 1928); also *Praktischer Leitfaden des Kontrapunkts* (Hamburg, 1911); *Modulationslehre* (1932). —Cf. R. Felber, *Richard Stöhr,* in 'Cobbett's Cyclopedic Survey of Chamber Music' (London, 1930; vol. 2, p. 458).

Stojanovits, Peter Lazar, violinist and composer; b. Budapest, Sept. 6, 1877; d. Belgrade, Sept. 12, 1957. He studied violin with Hubay at the Budapest Cons. and with J. Grün at the Vienna Cons.; in 1913 established his own school for advanced violin playing in Vienna. In 1925 he settled in Belgrade, and became director of the Belgrade Cons. His works include the operas *A Tigris (The Tiger;* Budapest, Nov. 14, 1905), *Das Liebchen am Dache* (Vienna, May 19, 1917), *Der Herzog von Reichsstadt* (Vienna, Feb. 11, 1921); an operetta, *Orlić;* 2 ballets; a symph. poem, *Heldentod;* 7 violin concertos, 2 viola concertos, a flute concerto, a horn concerto; several pieces of chamber music, including a piano trio, a piano quartet, and a piano quintet. He publ. a *Schule der Skalentechnik* for violin.

Stojowski (stoh-yohf'-skē), **Sigismund,** Polish pianist; b. Strzelce, April 8, 1869; d. New York, Nov. 5, 1946. He was a pupil of Zelenski at Cracow and of Diémer (piano) and Delibes (composition) at the Paris Cons. (1887-89), winning 1st prize for piano playing and composition; later he took a course with Paderewski. At an orchestral concert of his own works, given in Paris in 1891, he played his piano concerto; he remained in Paris until 1906, when he came to the U. S. as head of the piano dept. at the Institute of Musical Art in N. Y.; later held a similar position at the Von Ende School of Music, N. Y.; taught at the Juilliard Summer School for several years. He became a naturalized American citizen in 1938. In his prime he was extremely successful as concert pianist; and in his later years was greatly esteemed as a pedagogue. His works include, besides his piano concerto, *Prologue, Scherzo and Variations,* for piano and orch., performed by him (as piano concerto No. 2) in London, June 23, 1913, under the direction of Nikisch; many solo piano pieces; *Prayer for Poland,* for chorus and orch. (1915); 2 violin sonatas; a cello sonata.

Stokowski (stoh-kohf'-skē), **Leopold,** celebrated conductor; b. (of a Polish father and Irish mother) London, April 18, 1882. He attended Queen's College, Oxford, and also studied at the Royal College of Music, London, with Stevenson Hoyte (organ), Walford Davies (counterpoint), and Sir Charles Stanford (composition); obtained the position of organist at St. James, Piccadilly in 1900; traveled to Paris and Munich for additional studies. In 1905 he went to America; was organist and choirmaster at St. Bartholomew's, N. Y. (1905-08); his organ playing there attracted attention; during the summer of 1908 he conducted some concerts in London. In 1909 he was engaged as conductor of the Cincinnati Symph. Orch., resigning in 1912 to accept the conductorship of the Philadelphia Orch., which he brought to a brilliant standard of execution; the number of players was increased to 104, and Stokowski established a vigorous system of training with emphasis on color and dynamics. He introduced numerous modern scores new to Philadelphia audiences, including works by Schoenberg and Varèse, the performances of which aroused loud protests from the audience and an animated discussion in the press; Stokowski also resorted to lecturing the audiences as to the proper attitude towards modern music. His treatment of classical compositions was often unorthodox; in order to obtain greater sonority and novel effects, he upon occasion changed the orchestration, doubling the number of brass instruments, adding percussion sounds, etc. Always eager to promote innovations, he was the first conductor in America to introduce the Theremin; made numerous radio broadcasts applying special techniques. His orchestral transcriptions of works by Bach exhibit characteristics of musical grandiosity, but there is no denying their sonorous impact. He acted in the motion pictures *The Big Broadcast of 1937* and *One Hundred Men and a Girl,* and in 1940 supervised the music and acted in the Walt Disney film *Fantasia.* He was given the Bok Award of $10,000 as 'the person who has done the most for Philadelphia'; received several honorary degrees of Dr. of Music. In 1936 he took the Philadelphia Orchestra on a transcontinental tour; in 1938 he resigned as musical director of the Philadelphia Orchestra; however, he continued to conduct several concerts a season, until 1941, when he undertook concerts with specially assembled groups; in 1940-42 he conducted in the U. S. and in South America the All-American Youth Orchestra; during the season of 1942-43, he was associate conductor with Toscanini of the NBC Symph.; in 1945 he became musical director of the Hollywood Bowl; held a similar post in 1949-50 with the N. Y. Philharmonic, sharing the season with Mitropoulos; subsequently conducted concerts with various orchestras in Europe and America. In 1955 he was engaged as permanent conductor of the Houston Symph. He was married to Olga Samaroff (q.v.) in 1911 (divorced in 1923); to Mrs. Evangeline Brewster Johnson in 1926 (divorced in 1937); and to Gloria Vanderbilt on April 21, 1945 (divorced in 1955). He publ. *Music for All of Us* (N. Y., 1943). —Cf. Hope Stoddard, *Symphony Conductors of the U. S. A.* (N. Y., 1957; pp. 215-27).

Stoltz, Rosine (real name Victoire Noël), French mezzo-soprano; b. Paris, Feb. 13, 1815; d. there, July 28, 1903. She was the daughter of a janitor; was sent by Duchess de Berri to a convent, and in 1826 to the Choron School, which she entered under the name of Rosa Niva. She first appeared in public under the assumed name of Mlle. Ternaux; later as Mlle. Héloise Stoltz (the latter being derived from her mother's maiden name Stoll). Her first important engagement was in Brussels on June 3, 1836, when she sang Rachel in Halévy's *La Juive,* with Adolphe Nourrit, who recommended her to the administration of the Paris Opéra; made her début there as Rachel on Aug. 25, 1837. She became intimate with Leon Pillet, manager of the Opéra from 1844, and through him wielded considerable influence on appointments of new singers; after a series of attacks in the press, accusing her of unworthy intrigues, she resigned in March, 1847; fought for vindication through 3 obviously inspired pamphlets (C. Cantinjou, *Les Adieux de Madame Stoltz;* E. Pérignon, *Rosine Stoltz,* and J. Lemer, *Madame Rosine Stoltz),* all published in 1847. At the invitation of the Brazilian Emperor Don Pedro (who was romantically attached to her) she made 4 tours of Brazil between 1850 and 1859, at a salary of 400,000 francs a season. She was married to A. Lescuyer (March 2, 1837; legitimizing a son born Sept. 21, 1836); was subsequently married to the Duke Carlo Lesignano (May 18, 1872); assumed the title of Baroness von Ketschendorf, from the castle given her by Ernest Ketschendorf, Duke of Saxe-Coburg-Gotha. She publ. 6 songs (not composed by her in all probability), and her name (as Princesse de Lesignano) was used as author of a learned volume, *Les Constitutions de tous les pays civilisés* (1880), which was written in her behalf. The mystifying aspects of her private life and public career are recounted by G. Bord in *Rosine Stoltz* (Paris, 1909) and by A. Pougin in *La Verité sur Madame Stoltz,* in 'Le Ménestrel' (Aug. 28, 1909 *et seq.*).

Stoltzer, Thomas, German composer of sacred music; b. Schweidnitz, Silesia, c. 1475; d. as chaplain of the Hungarian King Louis in the battle of Mohács, Aug. 29, 1526. He entered the service of Hungary in 1522. His Latin psalms were publ. in 1538, 1545, and 1569; German songs were included in collections of 1536, 1539, and 1544. His *Octo tonorum melodiae* containing instrumental fantasies for 5 voices is a collection of instrumental pieces in all 8 church modes. Modern reprints are in the 'Denkmäler deutscher Tonkunst' (vols. 34 and 65), 'Das Chorwerk' (vol. 6), and 'Das Erbe deutscher Musik' (Series 1, vol. 22, 1942). —Cf. K. L. Hampe, *Die deutschen Psalmen des Thomas Stoltzer* (Halle, 1943); G. Reese, *Music in the Renaissance* (N. Y., 1954; pp. 723-25).

Stolz, Robert, Austrian operetta composer; b. Graz, Aug. 25, 1882. He was the pupil of his father, of Robert Fuchs in Vienna, and of Humperdinck in Berlin. He conducted at the Theater an der Wien for 12 years; also appeared with many European orchestras. In 1938 he came to the U. S., and lived in N. Y. and in Hollywood; about 1950 returned to Vienna. He wrote many operettas in a characteristic Viennese style, of which the most successful was *Zwei Herzen im ¾ Takt* (Zürich, Sept. 30, 1933). Other operettas are: *Die lustigen Weiber von Wien* (Munich, 1909), *Das Glücksmädel* (1910); *Das Lumperl* (Graz, 1915); *Lang, lang, ist's her* (Vienna, March 28, 1917); *Der Tanz ins Glück* (Vienna, Oct. 18, 1921); *Die*

Tanzgräfin (Vienna, May 13, 1921); *Mädi* (Vienna, Oct. 5, 1923); *Ein Ballroman oder der Kavalier von zehn bis vier* (Vienna, Feb. 29, 1924); *Eine einzige Nacht* (Vienna, Dec. 23, 1927); *Peppina* (1931); *Wild Violets* (1932); *Venus in Seide* (1932); *Frühling im Prater* (Vienna, Dec. 22, 1949); *Karneval in Wien* (1950); wrote music for about 100 films in Germany and the U. S.; about 1500 songs. —Cf. the biography by G. Holm, *Im ¾ Takt durch die Welt* (Linz, 1948).

Stolz, Teresa (Teresina), soprano; b. Kosteletz, Bohemia, June 2, 1834; d. Milan, Aug. 23, 1902. She studied at the Cons. of Prague, and later with Luigi Ricci in Trieste; began her operatic career in Russia; from 1865 until 1879 she appeared with brilliant success at the principal Italian opera houses. She was greatly admired by Verdi, and was famous in the role of Aida and of Leonora in *La Forza del destino.* Her farewell appearance was in Verdi's Requiem at La Scala, Milan, on June 30, 1879. —Cf. U. Zoppi, *Mariani, Verdi e Stolz* (Milan, 1947).

Stölzel (Stölz), Gottfried Heinrich, German composer; b. Grünstädtl, Jan. 13, 1690; d. Gotha, Nov. 27, 1749. He studied with the cantor Umlauf at Schneeberg, and with Melchior Hofmann at Leipzig; became a music teacher in Breslau (1710-12), where his opera *Narcissus* was performed in 1711; this was followed by productions of his operas *Valeria, Artemisia,* and *Orion* (all in 1712). After a journey to Italy, he was in Prague, where he brought out the operas *Venus und Adonis* (1714), *Acis und Galathea* (1715), and *Das durch die Liebe besiegte Glück* (1716). He subsequently went to Bayreuth, where he produced the opera *Diomedes* (1717), to Gera, and to Gotha, where he produced *Der Musenberg* (1723). Altogether he wrote 22 operas, the pastoral *Rosen und Dornen,* 14 oratorios, 8 double sets of cantatas and motets for the church year, other religious works, symphonies, serenades, concertos, etc.; a concerto grosso ed. by Schering is found in the 'Denkmäler deutscher Tonkunst' (vols. 29-30); a solo cantata for contralto was ed. by J. Bachmair (1926). His autobiography was reprinted in 'Selbstbiographien deutscher Musiker,' ed. by Willi Kahl (Cologne, 1948). —Cf. W. Schmidt-Weiss, *G. H. Stölzel als Instrumentalkomponist* (dissertation, Würzburg, 1939).

Stöpel, Franz (David Christoph), German writer on music; b. Oberheldrungen, Nov. 14, 1794; d. Paris, Dec. 19, 1836. He introduced Logier's method of piano teaching in Berlin in 1822; later taught it in other cities, finally in Paris; nowhere with striking success. —Writings: *Grundzüge der Geschichte der modernen Musik* (1821); *Beiträge zur Würdigung der neuen Methode des gleichzeitigen Unterrichts einer Mehrzahl Schüler im Pianofortespiel und der Theorie der Harmonie* (1823); *System der Harmonielehre* (after Logier; 1825); *Über J. B. Logiers System der Musikwissenschaft* (1827); etc.

Stör, Karl, German violinist and composer; b. Stolberg, June 29, 1814; d. Weimar, Jan. 17, 1889. He was a pupil of Götze and Lobe at Weimar; appointed court conductor in 1857, but in a few years failing eyesight compelled his resignation. —Works: opera *Die Flucht* (Weimar, 1843); *Tonbilder zu Schillers 'Lied von der Glocke'* for orch.; a violin concerto; several ballets; a *Ständchen* for cello with orch.; male choruses; songs.

Storace, Anna Selina (Nancy), celebrated soprano; b. London, 1766; d. there, Aug. 24, 1817. She was of Italian origin; her father Stefano Storace was a player on the double-bass; her brother Stephen Storace (q.v.) was a composer. She was a pupil of Rauzzini and of Sacchini in Venice; sang in Florence, Milan, and Parma; then went to Vienna in 1784, where she was engaged at the court opera. She created the role of Susanna in Mozart's *Nozze di Figaro* (May 1, 1786). Returning to England in 1787, she became popular as a singer in comic operas. —Cf. M. K. Ward, *Nancy Storace,* in the 'Mus. Times' (Nov., 1949).

Storace, Stephen, composer; brother of Anna Selina Storace; b. London, Jan. 4, 1763; d. there, March 19, 1796. He was a pupil of his father Stefano Storace, an excellent double-bass player of Italian descent, whose original name was Sorace. He studied violin at the Cons. di S. Onofrio in Naples. When his sister went to Vienna from Italy, he followed her; there he became acquainted with Mozart. In Vienna he brought out 2 of his operas to Italian texts: *Gli Sposi malcontenti* (June 1, 1785) and *Gli Equivoci* (Dec. 27, 1786). Back in London, he produced an Italian opera, *La Cameriera astuta* (March 4, 1788), and a number of English operas: *The Haunted Tower* (Nov. 24, 1789; his greatest success; performed many times in London and revived as late as 1922), *No Song No Supper* (April 16, 1790), *The Siege of Belgrade* (Jan. 1, 1791), *The Pi-*

rates (Nov. 21, 1792), *The Prize* (March 11, 1793), *My Grandmother* (Dec. 16, 1793), *The Cherokee* (Dec. 20, 1794), *The Three and the Deuce* (Sept. 2, 1795). An opera, *Mahmoud, or The Prince of Persia,* was not finished at his death, but was arranged by Michael Kelly, and performed posthumously on April 30, 1796. Storace wrote several other pieces of theatrical music, some of them adaptations, admitted or concealed, of works by other composers, such as Dittersdorf's *Doctor und Apotheker* and Salieri's *Grotta di Trofonio.*—Cf. R. Graves, *The Comic Operas of Stephen Storace,* in the 'Mus. Times' (Oct., 1954).

Storch (shtohrh), **M. Anton,** Austrian conductor and composer; b. Vienna, Dec. 22, 1813; d. there, Dec. 31, 1888. He was conductor at the Carl and Josephstadt Theaters in Vienna, and produced several of his operettas and opera-burlesques there: *Romeo und Julie* (Oct. 31, 1863); *Das Festkleid* (April 1, 1865), *Löwen im Dorfe* (Sept. 27, 1866), *Wiener Zugstücke* (April 26, 1868), *Prinz Taugenichts* (March 8, 1870; successful); wrote many favorite male quartets *(Letzte Treue, Grün,* etc.).

Storck, Karl, Alsatian writer on music; b. Dürmenach, April 23, 1873; d. Olsberg, May 9, 1920. He studied at the Universities of Strasbourg and Berlin *(Dr. phil.,* 1897); wrote music criticism for the 'Deutsche Zeitung' (Berlin). He publ. a unique edition, *Musik und Musiker in Karikatur und Satire* (Oldenburg, 1911), richly illustrated by numerous reproductions of caricatures on musical subjects; other publications include: *Der Tanz* (1903); *Geschichte der Musik* (1904); *Das Opernbuch* (1905; 44th printing, 1946); *Die Kulturelle Bedeutung der Musik* (1907); *Mozart* (1908; 2nd ed., 1923); *Musik-Politik* (1911); *Emil Jaques-Dalcroze* (1912). He edited selections from the letters of Beethoven (1905; 3rd ed., 1922), Mozart (1906), and Schumann (1906).

Storer, John, English organist and composer; b. Hulland, near Derby, May 18, 1858; d. Berwick-on-Tweed, May 1, 1930. He was a chorister at various churches before entering Oxford Univ. (Mus. Bac., 1878). In 1891 he became music director of the old Globe Theatre in London, and later filled similar positions in London; settled in Waterford, Ireland, as organist of the Roman Catholic Cathedral, and prof. of plainchant at St. John's Ecclesiastical College; left Waterford in 1916, and lived in Sheffield and Reading, England. He composed the operas *The Punchbowl* (London, 1887) and *Gretna Green* (London, 1889); an oratorio, *Deborah and Barak* (1881); 2 symphonies: *The Holiday* (1909) and *Vita* (1914); several Masses; church services; songs; organ pieces.

Stöwe (shtö'-veh), **Gustav,** German pianist and pedagogue; b. Potsdam, July 4, 1835; d. there, April 13, 1891. He studied at the Stern Cons. in Berlin; in 1875 founded the Potsdam Musikschule, and was its director until he died. He publ. *Die Klaviertechnik, dargestellt als musikalisch-physiologische Bewegungslehre* (1886; thorough analysis of the elements of piano touch); wrote piano pieces.

Stradal (shtrah'-dahl), **August,** pianist; b. Teplitz, Bohemia, May 17, 1860; d. Schönlinde, Germany, March 13, 1930. He studied composition with Bruckner at the Vienna Cons. and piano with Door; was a pupil of Liszt in 1884 and became an ardent propagandist for Liszt's piano music; gave concerts in Germany, Austria, France, and England; made arrangements of Liszt's orchestral works; also of Bach, Frescobaldi, etc. His original compositions consist of piano pieces *(Ungarische Rhapsodie,* etc.) and songs. He wrote *Erinnerungen an Franz Liszt* (Bern, 1929). —Cf. Hildegard Stradal, *August Stradals Lebensbild* (Bern, 1934).

Stradella, Alessandro, Italian composer; b. Montefestino, 1642; murdered in Genoa, Feb. 25, 1682. According to a story narrated in Bonnet-Bourdelot's *Histoire de la musique et de ses effets* (Paris, 1715), Stradella was engaged to compose an opera for Venice, but there met the mistress of a Venetian nobleman and ran off with her before his work was produced; the enraged nobleman thereupon engineered an attempt upon Stradella's life at Turin in 1677. Though he was one of the most famous composers of his time, details of his biography are lacking, and he has been made the subject of many legends. He is the hero of Flotow's opera *Alessandro Stradella* (Hamburg, 1844), and operas by Niedermeyer (Paris, 1837), Sinico (Lugo, 1863), etc. His murder is attributed to the jealousy of an actress. Another attempt on his life was also made in Rome. —As a composer Stradella developed the structural form and expressive power of the aria, and was one of the first to make use of the instrumental crescendo. —Works: 148 MSS in the Modena Library, including 8 oratorios and 11 dramas; cantatas in the Naples Cons. Library; 21 cantatas in the library of San Marco, Venice (10 publ. by L. Escudier, with piano accompaniment by Halévy); others in the Paris National Library, and at the Cons.; 1 motet and 8 cantatas at Christchurch Library, Oxford; a number of cantatas, madrigals, arias, duets, etc., in the British Museum; etc. Among his extant works are the oratorios *S. Giovanni Battista, Esther, S. Pelagia, S. Giovanni Crisostomo, Susanna,* and *S. Edita vergine;* the operas *Il Corispeo, Orazio Cocle sul ponte, Trespolo tutore, La Forza del amore paterno* (1678; new ed. by A. Gentili, Rome, 1931); the cantata *Il Barcheggio* (dated June 16, 1681). —The church aria *Pietà, Signore* and the arias *O del mio dolce ardor* and *Se i miei sospiri* have been wrongly attributed to Stradella. —Cf. A. Catelani, *Delle Opere di A. S. esistenti nell' archivio musicale della R. Biblioteca Palatina di Modena* (Modena, 1866); P. Richard, *A. S.* (Paris, 1866); H. Hess, *Die Opern A. S.s,* in 'Beiheft' II, 3 of 'Publikationen der Internationalen Musik-Gesellschaft' (1906); F. M. Crawford, *S.* (London, 1911); A. Einstein, *Ein Bericht über den Turiner Mordanfall auf A. S.,* in 'Sandberger-Festschrift' (1918); E. M. Dufflocq, *A. S.,* in 'Bollettino Bibliografico Musicale' (1929); A. Della Corte, in 'Musica d'oggi' (1931); A. Gentili, *A. S.* (Turin, 1936); G. Roncaglia, *Le Composizioni strumentali di A. S.,* in 'Rivista Musicale Italiana' (1940-42; also separately, 1942).

Stradivari (Stradivarius), Antonio, the most celebrated of all violin makers; b. Cremona, 1644 (according to Bacchetta, end of 1648 or beginning of 1649); d. there, Dec. 18, 1737. He was a pupil of Niccolò Amati and worked for him from about 1667-79. He purchased the house in which, for half a century, his workshop was situated, in 1680. His finest instruments were made in the period from 1700 to 1725; but he still worked up to the year of his death; his last instrument was made by him at the age of 92. His label reads: 'Antonius Stradivarius Cremonensis. Fecit Anno . . . (A ✠ S).' His cellos command even higher prices than the violins, and violas the highest of all, for he made very few of them. Stradivari had 11 children; of them **Francesco** (b. Feb. 1, 1671; d. May 11, 1743) and **Omobono** (b. Nov. 14, 1679; d. July 8, 1742), were his co-workers. Stradivari also made viols of early types, guitars, lutes, mandolins, etc. —Cf. F. J. Fétis, *A. S., luthier célèbre* (Paris, 1856; English transl., London, 1864); P. Lombardini, *Cenni sulla celebre scuola Cremonense degli stromenti ad arco . . . e sulla famiglia del sommo Antonio Stradivari* (Cremona, 1872; with genealogical table from the 13th century to date of publication); A. Reichers, *The Violin and the Art of its Construction; A Treatise on S.* (1895); H. Petherick, *A. S.* (London, 1900); W. H., A. F., and A. E. Hill, *A. S. His Life and Work* (London, 1902; the standard work); A. Mandelli, *Nuove indagini su A. S.* (Milan, 1903); H. Herrmann, *Geschichte und Beschreibung von zwei Meisterwerken des A. S.* (N. Y., 1929); R. Bacchetta, *S.* (1937); G. Hoffmann, *S. l'enchanteur* (Paris, 1938); W. D. Orcutt, *The S. Memorial at Washington . . .* (Washington, 1938); M. Boger, *Das Geheimnis des Stradivari* (Berlin, 1944); D. J. Balfoort, *A. S.* (Amsterdam, 1945; also in English); E. N. Doring, *How Many Strads? . . . a tabulation of works believed to survive, produced in Cremona by A. S. between 1666 and 1737 . . .* (Chicago, 1945); G. Ottani, S. (Milan, 1945).

Straesser, Ewald, German composer; b. Burscheid, June 27, 1867; d. Stuttgart, April 4, 1933. He studied with Wüllner at the Cologne Cons.; taught theory there until 1921; from 1922 to his death was prof. at the Stuttgart Musikhochschule. He wrote 6 symphonies, 5 string quartets, piano pieces, and songs.

Straeten. See **Van der Straeten.**

Strakosch, Maurice, pianist and impresario; b. Gross-Seelowitz, Moravia, 1825; d. Paris, Oct. 9, 1887. He studied with Sechter at the Vienna Cons.; traveled as a pianist in Europe; came to America in 1848, settling in N. Y. as a teacher; from 1856 he was active mainly as an impresario. He was the brother-in-law of Adelina Patti, and managed her concerts. He gave his first season of Italian opera in N. Y. in 1857, and in 1859 took his company to Chicago; then went to Europe. His opera *Giovanna di Napoli* was brought out in N. Y.; he also wrote salon pieces for piano; publ. *Ten Commandments of Music for the Perfection of the Voice* (posthumous; 1896) and *Souvenirs d'un Impresario* (Paris, 2nd ed., 1887). After his departure from America, his brother, Max Strakosch (1834-92), carried on the management of his enterprises.

Strang, Gerald, American composer; b. Claresholm, Canada, Feb. 13, 1908. He studied at Stanford Univ., and later at the Universities of California and Southern California; during World War II he worked as an engineer at the Douglas Aircraft Co. He joined the ranks of advanced modernists; was for a time managing editor of the 'New Music Quarterly Edition' (1935-40); was assistant to Schoenberg at the Univ. of California, Los Angeles (1936-38). His music is strongly formalistic, with a technical idea determining the content. —Works: *Intermezzo* for orch. (2nd movement of a symph.; Los Angeles, April 14, 1937, composer conducting); *Canzonet,* for strings (1942); sonatina for clarinet alone (1932); clarinet quintet (1933); *Three Pieces* for flute and piano (1933); *Percussion Music* for 3 players (1935); *Mirrorrorrim* ('mirror' in mirror spelling), for piano; etc.

Strannolyubsky, Boris Mikhailovitch, Russian composer; b. St. Petersburg, Aug. 8, 1903; studied with Gnessin and Glière in Moscow; devoted himself mainly to the study of folk music; edited the series 'Songs of the Peoples of the Soviet Union' (1949-54). —Works: 2 symphonies: I (1944); II, *The Kremlin Chimes* (1947); 2 symph. suites: *Three Elements* (1941) and *Fatherland* (1951); a cello sonata; 2 piano trios; 2 piano sonatas; *Fairy Tale* for 2 harps (1954); pieces for the mandolin, for guitar, for accordion, and other popular instruments; choruses; songs.

Stransky, Josef, orchestral conductor; b. Humpoletz, near Deutschbrod, Bohemia, Sept. 9, 1872; d. New York, March 6, 1936. While studying medicine (M. D., Prague, 1896), he also studied music, at Leipzig with Jadassohn and in Vienna with R. Fuchs, Bruckner, and Dvořák. In 1898 he was engaged by A. Neumann as 1st Kapellmeister at the Landestheater in Prague; in 1903 he went in a similar capacity to the Stadttheater in Hamburg; in 1910 he resigned from the Hamburg opera to devote himself to concert work; in the autumn of 1911 became Mahler's successor as conductor of the N. Y. Philharmonic Society, a position he held until 1923. A bequest of one million dollars to the society (by Joseph Pulitzer, 1912) enabled Stransky to carry out successfully the sweeping reforms instituted by his illustrious predecessor (chief of which was a system of daily rehearsals during the season of 23 weeks). For 2 seasons (1923-25) he was conductor of the N. Y. State Symph. Orch. Having formed a valuable picture collection of his own, he abandoned all of his musical activities, and entered the business of a prominent New York and Paris firm of dealers in oil paintings. He publ. *Symphonische Lieder;* an operetta, *Der General,* was produced in Hamburg. He also wrote some instrumental music, and publ. a new ed. of Berlioz's *Beatrice und Benedikt.*

Straram, Walther, French conductor; b. London (of French parents), July 9, 1876; d. Paris, Nov. 24, 1933. He was educated in Paris, where he studied violin; in 1892 joined the Lamoureux Orch.; in 1896 was opera coach in Lyons; in 1906 became chorusmaster at the Opéra-Comique in Paris; from 1909 to 1913, assistant of André Caplet at the Boston Opera Co. In 1926 he established the Concerts Straram in Paris, and gave several concerts every season until his death. He conducted the 1st performance of Ravel's *Boléro* for Ida Rubinstein (1928).

Strategier, Herman, Dutch composer; b. Arnhem, Aug. 10, 1912. He studied music with his father, a church organist, whom he succeeded at St. Walburgis Church at Arnhem, in 1935; the church was destroyed in war action in 1944, and he went to Haarlem, and later to Utrecht. He has written much church music; a flute concerto; a symphony; a string quartet; many solo songs; publ. a collection of folksongs.

Stratton, George (Robert), English violinist and pedagogue; b. London, July 18, 1897; d. there, Sept. 4, 1954. He studied in London; was concertmaster of the London Symph. Orch. (1933-52); also organized the Stratton String Quartet (1925-42). He publ. (in collaboration with Alan Frank) a practical book, *The Playing of Chamber Music* (London, 1935; reprinted, 1951).

Stratton, Stephen Samuel, English organist; b. London, Dec. 19, 1840; d. Birmingham, June 25, 1906. Pupil of C. Gardner (organ) and C. Lucas (composition); settled in 1866 in Birmingham, where he held various posts as organist, the last being at the Church of the Saviour (1878-82); for several years music critic of the Birmingham 'Daily Post' and contributed to the London 'Monthly Mus. Record' and 'Mus. Times.' He was the author (with J. D. Brown) of a valuable work, *British Musical Biography* (1897); also publ. *Mendelssohn* (1901; revised ed., 1934) and *Nicolo Paganini: His Life and Work* (1907). His compositions include chamber music, piano pieces, partsongs and songs.

Straube (shtrou'-beh), **Karl,** prominent German organist; b. Berlin, Jan. 6, 1873; d. Leipzig, April 27, 1950. Pupil of H. Reimann (organ) and Ph. Rüfer (composition) in

Berlin. 1897-1902, organist at the Cathedral in Wesel; from 1902 at St. Thomas' in Leipzig, having also been appointed conductor of the 'Bachverein' (1903), prof. at the Cons. (1907), and official organist at the Gewandhaus (1908). In 1918 he succeeded G. Schreck as cantor of St. Thomas'. At his suggestion the Gewandhaus chorus and the Bachverein were united in 1919, and he conducted the combined choirs until 1922. He founded the 'Kirchenmusikalisches Institut der Landeskirche Sachsens' and became its director. He conducted the Handel Festival in 1925, leading to the formation of the Handel Society. *Dr. phil.* (*hon. c.*) from Leipzig Univ., 1918. His first recital in 1894 attracted unusual attention; thereafter, until 1918, he was heard in the principal cities of Germany. He was the first to introduce the organ works of Reger, with whom he was on terms of intimate friendship. He publ. 'Alte Orgelmeister' (1904); '45 Choralvorspiele alter Meister' (1907); 'Alte Meister des Orgelspiels' (2 vols.; 1929); 'Ausgewählte Gesänge des Thomanerchors' (1930); also editions of Bach's *Magnificat* (1909), Handel's 'Dettingen' *Te Deum* (1913) and *Salomon* (1926), organ works of Liszt, etc. His *Briefe eines Thomaskantors* were publ. posthumously (Stuttgart, 1952). —Cf. G. Robert-Tornow, *Max Reger und Karl Straube* (Göttingen, 1907; new ed., Leipzig, 1929); J. Wolgast, *Karl Straube* (Leipzig, 1928). A 'Festschrift' was publ. for him on his 70th birthday (Leipzig, 1943).

Straus, Oscar, Austrian operetta composer; b. Vienna, March 6, 1870; d. Ischl, Jan. 11, 1954. He studied privately in Vienna with A. Prosnitz and H. Grädener, and with Max Bruch in Berlin. From 1895 to 1900 he conducted at various theaters in Austria and Germany; in 1901 he became conductor of the artistic cabaret 'Überbrettl' managed by Ernst von Wolzogen in Berlin, and wrote a number of musical farces for it. He remained in Berlin until 1927; then lived in Vienna and Paris; on Sept. 3, 1939, he became a French citizen. In 1940 he came to America; lived in New York and Hollywood until 1948, when he returned to Europe. He was one of the most successful composers of Viennese operettas; his most celebrated production was *Der tapfere Soldat,* based on G. B. Shaw's play, *Arms and the Man* (Vienna, Nov. 14, 1908; in N. Y. as *The Chocolate Soldier,* Nov. 13, 1909; London, Sept. 10, 1910; innumerable performances all over the world). Other operettas are: *Die lustigen Nibelungen* (Vienna, Nov. 12, 1904); *Hugdietrichs Brautfahrt* (Vienna, March 10, 1906); *Ein Walzertraum* (Vienna, March 2, 1907; revised 1951); *Didi* (Vienna, Oct. 23, 1909); *Das Tal der Liebe* (Berlin and Vienna, simultaneously, Dec. 23, 1909); *Mein junger Herr* (Vienna, Dec. 23, 1910); *Die kleine Freundin* (Vienna, Oct. 20, 1911); *Love and Laughter* (London, 1913); *Rund um die Liebe* (Vienna, Nov. 9, 1914; in N. Y. as *All Around Love,* 1917); *Die himmelblaue Zeit* (Vienna, Feb. 21, 1914); *Die schöne Unbekannte* (Vienna, Jan. 15, 1915; in N. Y. as *My Lady's Glove,* 1917); *Drei Walzer* (Zürich, Oct. 5, 1935); *Ihr erster Walzer* (Munich, March 31, 1950); *Bozena* (Munich, May 16, 1952). He further wrote a *Serenade* for string orch.; *Alt-Wiener Reigen, for* string orch.; *Suite in Tanzform* for violin, cello, and piano; *Der Traum ein Leben,* overture; many piano pieces; an album, *Bilderbuch ohne Bilder* for 4 hands. —Cf. B. Grun, *Prince of Vienna: the Life, the Times, and the Melodies of Oscar Straus* (London, 1955; N. Y., 1957).

Strauss, Eduard, brother of Johann Strauss, Jr.; b. Vienna, March 15, 1835; d. there, Dec. 28, 1916. A pupil of G. Preyer in composition, he made a successful début with his own orch. at the 'Dianasaal' in 1862; acted as Johann's substitute during the latter's tour of Russia (1865); succeeded him in 1870 as conductor of the court balls. For many years he gave concerts in the 'Volksgarten' (summer) and in the hall of the 'Musikverein' (winter); also made extended tours, visiting the U. S. in 1892 and 1901-02. He then dissolved his orch. (founded by his father in 1826), which after three-quarters of a century of uninterrupted success, had become almost a historical institution. His publ. dances comprise 318 opus numbers, but could not rival his brother's in popularity. In 1906 he published *Erinnerungen.*

Strauss, Franz, German horn virtuoso, father of Richard Strauss; b. Parkstein, Feb. 26, 1822; d. Munich, June 2, 1905. Until his retirement in 1889 he was solo hornist at the Hofoper in Munich; although a violent opponent of Wagner, the master valued him highly, and entrusted to him at the premières of *Tristan, Meistersinger,* and *Parsifal* the important solo passages; until 1896 he was prof. of his instrument at the Akademie der Tonkunst, and from 1875-96 conducted an excellent amateur orch., the 'Wilde Gungl,' in Munich. He wrote a horn concerto in C minor (op. 8); *Nocturne* (op. 7) and *Empfindungen am Meere* (op. 12) for horn and piano; 17 *Konzertetüden* and *Übungen für Naturhorn* (2 books). —Cf. F. Trenner, *Der Vater: Franz Strauss,* in 'Zeitschrift für Musik' (June, 1955).

Strauss, Johann (Sr.), 'The Father of the Waltz'; b. Vienna, March 14, 1804; d. there, Sept. 25, 1849. His father, who kept a beer-house and dance-hall, apprenticed him to a bookbinder; after Strauss had run away, his parents consented to his becoming a musician. He studied the violin under Polyschansky, and harmony under Seyfried; at 15 joined Pamer's orch. in the 'Sperl' dance-hall, and the Lanner Quartet in 1823, later acting as deputy conductor of Lanner's orch.; organized an independent orch. of 14 in 1826, playing at various resorts, and producing his first waltzes (op. 1 is the *Täuberl-Walzer,* for the garden concerts at the 'Zwei Tauben'). His renown spread, and his orch. increased rapidly in size and efficiency; from 1833 he undertook concert tours in Austria, and in 1834 was appointed bandmaster of the 1st Vienna militia regiment. His tours extended to Berlin in 1834, and to Holland and Belgium in 1836; in 1837-38 he invaded Paris with a picked corps of 28, and had immense success both there and in London. In 1845 he was made conductor of the court balls at Vienna. Among 152 published waltzes, the *Lorelei-, Gabrielen-, Taglioni-, Cäcilien-, Victoria-, Kettenbrücken-,* and *Bajaderen-Walzer,* the *Elektrische Funken, Mephistos Höllenrufe,* and the *Donau-Lieder* are prime favorites; he also wrote 24 galops, 13 polkas, 32 quadrilles, 6 cotillons and contredances, 18 marches, and 6 potpourris. Both as composer and conductor he distinctly raised the level of dance music. His complete works (251 op. numbers), edited by his son Johann, were publ. by Breitkopf & Härtel in 1889: Vols. I-V, Waltzes; vol. VI, Polkas, Galops, Marches; vol. VII, Quadrilles (piano scores only; full scores in 'Denkmäler der Tonkunst in Österreich' vols. 63, 68, and 74). —Cf. L. Scheyrer, *J.S.s musikalische Wanderung durch das Leben* (Vienna, 1851); R. Kleinecke, *J. S.* (Leipzig, 1894); F. Lange, *Josef Lanner und J. S.* (Vienna, 1904; 2nd ed., 1919); F. Farga, *Lanner und S.* (Vienna 1948); M. Schönherr and K. Reinöhl, *J. S. Vater* (Vienna, 1953).

Strauss, Johann (Jr.), greatly celebrated Austrian composer of light music, 'The Waltz-King'; b. Vienna, Oct. 25, 1825; d. there, June 3, 1899. His father intended all three of his sons for business; but the mother privately procured instruction on the violin (from Kohlmann) and in composition (Hofmann and Drexler) for Johann, who threw off paternal control, tender though it was, and appeared as conductor of his own ensemble of 15 players at Dommayer's restaurant at Heitzing (Oct. 15, 1844). His success was instantaneous, and his new waltzes won wide popularity. Despite his father's objections to this rivalry in the family, Johann Strauss continued his concerts with increasing success; after his father's death in 1849 he united his father's band with his own; made a tour through Austria, Germany, Poland, and Russia. From 1863 to 1870 he was conductor of the court balls in Vienna, resigning in favor of his brother Eduard to obtain more leisure for composition, turning from dance music, in which he had won supreme artistic and popular success, to operetta. In 1872 he accepted an invitation to visit the U. S., and directed 14 monster-concerts in Boston and 4 in N. Y. He contracted 3 marriages: to the singer Henriette Treffz, the actress Angelica Dietrich, and Adele Deutsch. He wrote almost 500 pieces of dance music (498 op. numbers); of his waltzes the greatest popularity was achieved by *An der schönen blauen Donau* (op. 314, 1867), the *Blue Danube Waltz,* whose main tune became one of the best-known in all music. Brahms wrote on a lady's fan the opening measures of it, and underneath: 'Leider nicht von Brahms' (Alas, not by Brahms); Wagner, too, voiced his appreciation of the music of Strauss. Other well-known waltzes are *Geschichten aus dem Wiener Wald* (1868), *Wein, Weib, Gesang* (1869), *Wiener Blut* (1870), *Rosen aus dem Süden* (1878); *Frühlingsstimmen* (1881), *Tausend und eine Nacht, Künstlerleben,* etc.; also numerous quadrilles, polkas, polka-mazurkas, marches, galops, etc. His finest operetta is *Die Fledermaus,* an epitome of the Viennese spirit that continues to hold the stage as one of the masterpieces of its genre. It was first staged at the Theater an der Wien on April 5, 1874, and was given within a few months in N. Y. (Dec. 29, 1874); productions followed all over the world. It was performed in Paris with a new libretto as *La Tzigane* (Oct. 30, 1877); the original version was presented there as *La Chauve-souris* on April 22, 1904. Also very successful was the operetta *Der Zigeunerbaron* (Vienna, Oct. 24, 1885). All his operettas were first produced in Vienna, with the exception of *Eine Nacht in Venedig* (Berlin, Oct. 3, 1883). A complete list of Vienna productions includes: *Indigo und die vierzig Räuber* (Feb. 10, 1871); *Der Karneval in*

Rom (March 1, 1873); *Cagliostro in Wien* (Feb. 27, 1875); *Prinz Methusalem* (Jan. 3, 1877); *Blindekuh* (Dec. 18, 1878); *Das Spitzentuch der Königin* (Oct. 1, 1880); *Der lustige Krieg* (Nov. 25, 1881); *Simplizius* (Dec. 17, 1887); *Ritter Pázmán* (Jan. 1, 1892); *Fürstin Ninetta* (Jan. 10, 1893); *Jabuka, oder Das Apfelfest* (Oct. 12, 1894); *Waldmeister* (Dec. 4, 1895); *Die Göttin der Vernunft* (March 13, 1897).—Bibliography: L. Eisenberg, *J. S.* (Leipzig, 1894); R. von Procházka, *J. S.* (Berlin, 1900); R. Specht, *J. S.* (Berlin, 1909); F. Lange, *J. S.* (Leipzig, 1912); J. Schnitzer, *Meister Johann* (2 vols.; Vienna, 1920); E. Decsey, *J. S.* (Berlin, 1922; reprinted Vienna, 1948); K. Kobald, *J. S.* (Vienna, 1925); S. Loewy, *Rund um J. S.* (Vienna, 1925); H. Sündermann, *J. S., ein Vollender* (Brixlegg, 1937); Ada B. Teetgen, *The Waltz Kings of Old Vienna* (London, 1939); A. Witeschnik, *Die Dynastie Strauss* (Vienna, 1939); H. E. Jacob, *J. S. und das 19. Jahrhundert . . .* (Amsterdam, 1937; English transl. as *J. S., Father and Son, A Century of Light Music* (N. Y., 1940); W. Jaspert, *J. S.* (Berlin, 1939); Erich Schenk, *J. S.* (Potsdam, 1940); David Ewen, *Tales from the Vienna Woods; the Story of J. S.* (N. Y., 1944); J. Andriessen, *J. S., de koning van de wals* (Amsterdam, 1950); J. Pastene, *Three-Quarter Time; the Life and Music of the Strauss Family* (N. Y., 1951); P. Kuringer, *J. S.* (Haarlem, 1952). See also *J. S. schreibt Briefe,* ed. by his third wife, Adele Strauss (Vienna, 1926). A complete catalogue of works is found in C. Flamme, ed., *Verzeichnis der sämtlichen im Drucke erschienenen Kompositionen von Johann Strauss (Vater), Johann Strauss (Sohn), Josef Strauss, und Eduard Strauss* (Leipzig, 1898) and in A. Weinmann, *Verzeichnis sämtlicher Werke von Johann Strauss, Vater und Sohn* (Vienna, 1956).

Strauss, Josef, Austrian composer of waltzes; brother of Johann Strauss, Jr., b. Vienna, Aug. 22, 1827; d. there, July 21, 1870. He was versatile and gifted, and at various times wrote poetry, painted, and patented inventions. He first appeared in public conducting in Vienna a set of his waltzes (July 23, 1853); was often asked by his celebrated brother to replace him as conductor, and accompanied him on tours to Germany, Russia, etc. He wrote 283 op. numbers, of which some are well worthy of his family's renown. His op. 173, *Dynamiden,* was used by Richard Strauss for a theme in *Der Rosenkavalier.* —Cf. A. Witeschnik, *Die Dynastie Strauss* (Vienna, 1939).

Strauss, Richard, great German composer; b. Munich, June 11, 1864; d. Garmisch-Partenkirchen, Sept. 8, 1949. His father, the well-known horn player Franz Strauss, supervised his son's education. At the age of 4, he received regular instruction from A. Tombo, the harpist of the court orch.; in his 8th year he began to study the violin with Benno Walter, the concertmaster of the court orch.; from 1875 to 1880 he studied composition with the court conductor, F. W. Meyer. His first attempt at writing music (a Polka in C) dates from the year 1870, when he was 6, and he wrote piano pieces, songs, and even orchestral overtures as a child; his op. 1, a *Festmarsch* for orch., written at the age of 12, was publ. in 1880. In the meantime he had completed an academic course of study at the Gymnasium, graduating in 1882; then attended lectures on philosophy at the Munich Univ. (1882-83). On March 30, 1881, the first major work of Richard Strauss, the Symphony in D minor, was performed in Munich by Hermann Levi; Benno Walter, Strauss's teacher, played his violin concerto (Munich, Feb. 8, 1883). These works, written in the forms of the classic masters, revealed an astonishing degree of technical mastery, and won for Strauss immediate recognition; he was only 20 when he could boast the distinction of an American première, for on Dec. 13, 1884, Theodore Thomas, then conductor of the N. Y. Philharmonic, gave the first U. S. performance of the Symphony in F minor. Strauss spent the winter of 1883-84 in Berlin, where Hans von Bülow became interested in him and engaged him as assistant conductor with Bülow's orchestra in Meiningen. When Bülow left Meiningen in 1885, Strauss became his successor. Although he remained in Meiningen for only one season (1885-86), this sojourn proved to be a turning point in his career, for in that short time he became intimately associated with the poet and musician Alexander Ritter (q.v.), who revealed to Strauss the meaning of the revolution in esthetics produced by Wagner and Liszt. Ritter urged on Strauss the concept of 'music as expression' and thenceforward Strauss became convinced of the artistic importance of music with a literary or philosophical outline. After a journey to Italy in the spring of 1886, he became one of the conductors of the Court Opera in Munich (1886-89); his duties were not onerous, and he had ample time for composition; in Munich he wrote the symph. fantasy *Aus Italien,* and his first significant works in the new style, the symph. poems *Don Juan* and *Tod und Verklärung.* In the autumn of 1889 he was appointed 1st conductor of the Weimar court orch.; there he remained until spring, 1894. In Weimar he brought out *Don Juan* on Nov. 11, 1889 and another tone-poem, *Macbeth,* on Oct. 13, 1890; on June 21, 1890, he conducted the 1st performance of *Tod und Verklärung* at the meeting of the Allgemeiner Deutscher Musik-Verein in Eisenach. These works were revelations of a talent of striking originality and boldness, and made Strauss one of the greatest figures of the nascent era of musical modernism; he was praised extravagantly by admirers, and damned violently by traditionalists. Hans von Bülow called him 'Richard the Second' as a legitimate heir to Wagner's mantle. Indeed, Strauss extended Wagner's system of leading motifs to the domain of symphonic music; his tone-poems are interwoven with motifs, each representing some relevant programmatic element. Analytical brochures, compiled especially by German commentators, illustrate the complex involvements of thematic allusions in these works. —Strauss spent the winter of 1892 in Greece, Egypt, and Sicily, writing the text and music of his first stage work, the opera *Guntram,* which he conducted in Weimar on May 12, 1894. Pauline de Ahna sang the leading part; she married Strauss on Sept. 10, 1894, and remained with him throughout his life, dying a few months after he did. Strauss was appointed successor to Bülow as conductor of the Berlin Philharmonic in the autumn of 1894, and led it during the season of 1894-95. In 1896 he conducted his own works in Brussels, Liège, and Moscow, and also in many German cities; in 1897 he visited Amsterdam, Paris, London, and Barcelona. In the meantime, he continued unremittingly to write music; in quick succession, he brought out his masterpieces of musical characterization, *Till Eulenspiegels lustige Streiche* (Cologne, Nov. 5, 1895, Wüllner conducting), the philosophical poem after Nietzsche, *Also sprach Zarathustra* (Frankfurt, Nov. 27, 1896, composer conducting), and *Don Quixote,* variations with a cello solo, after Cervantes (Cologne, March 8, 1898, Wüllner conducting). The series of his great tone poems was concluded with the autobiographical work, *Ein Heldenleben* (Frankfurt, March 3, 1899, composer conducting). For his first visit to America in the early months of 1904, Strauss wrote a new work of considerable dimensions, a *Symphonia domestica,* which he conducted at Carnegie Hall, N. Y., on March 31, 1904. The score was so naturalistic, and so frankly autobiographical, that it amused and shocked the public, but the music itself fell distinctly below the poetically charged inspiration of the preceding tone-poems. Even more literal was his last symphonic work, *Eine Alpensinfonie,* which calls for a wind machine and a thunder machine to portray a storm in the Alps; it was first performed by the composer himself in Berlin, on Oct. 28, 1915. But while his symphonic production lagged, he turned vigorously to the field of the opera, producing works of exceptional merit. After *Guntram,* he wrote *Feuersnot* (Dresden, Nov. 21, 1901), which attracted little attention. Then on Dec. 9, 1905, the Dresden Opera staged the opera *Salome,* after Oscar Wilde's French play, translated into German. In this score he went far beyond the limits of Wagnerian music drama, and created a psychological tragedy of shattering impact; the erotic subject was illustrated by sensuous music. The opera made the rounds of European theaters in quick succession, but when the Metropolitan Opera Co. produced *Salome* in N. Y. (Jan. 22, 1907), there were violent protests, and it was taken out of the repertory, not to be revived until many years later. Scarcely less forceful was the impression produced by the next opera, *Elektra* (Dresden, Jan. 25, 1909), in which the horrors of matricide were pictured with extraordinary strength. Then, as if to make a graceful concession to public taste, Strauss produced *Der Rosenkavalier* (Dresden, Jan. 26, 1911), a charming comedy, which quickly became famous. With *Elektra* and *Der Rosenkavalier,* Strauss established his fruitful collaboration with the poet Hugo von Hofmannsthal, who wrote the librettos for these works, and also for the subsequent operas *Ariadne auf Naxos* (Stuttgart, Oct. 25, 1912), *Die Frau ohne Schatten* (Vienna, Oct. 10, 1919), *Die ägyptische Helena* (Dresden, June 6, 1928), and *Arabella* (Dresden, July 1, 1933). After Hofmannsthal's death in 1929, Strauss turned to Stefan Zweig for the libretto of *Die schweigsame Frau* (Dresden, June 24, 1935), and to Josef Gregor for *Friedenstag* (Munich, July 24, 1938), *Daphne* (Dresden, Oct. 15, 1938), and *Die Liebe der Danae* (written in 1938-40; produced posthumously, Salzburg, Aug. 14, 1952). The last opera by Strauss was *Capriccio,* to a libretto by the conductor Clemens Krauss (Munich, Oct. 28, 1942). The operas after *Der Rosenkavalier* were received with deference and interest, but were not retained in the permanent repertory. It may be said, therefore, that the true creative period of Strauss ended for his stage works in 1911, with *Der Rosenkavalier;* and for his symphonic compositions in 1899 with *Ein Heldenleben.* From 1898 to 1918 Strauss was on the staff of the Berlin Opera; in 1919, he became co-director (with Franz Schalk) of the Vienna State Opera, holding this position until 1924, not on a permanent basis, however, so that he had time for extended tours, one of which took him again to America in 1922. He also spent much time at his villa in Garmisch, Bavaria. On Nov. 15, 1933, Strauss was appointed president of the Reichsmusikkammer under the Nazi regime, but resigned in June, 1935. He visited London as conductor of his own works in 1937, and received there the gold medal of the Philharmonic Society. He was the recipient of numerous other honors and decorations. In 1902 the Univ. of Heidelberg made him *Dr. phil., honoris causa.* He remained in his home at Garmisch during World War II, and wrote the mournful *Metamorphosen* (with a symbolic quotation from Beethoven's funeral march from the *Eroica*) in the last months of the war; then lived for some time in Switzerland. He was strong enough to travel to England for a series of concerts in 1947; returning to Germany, he had to face the special court at Munich, investigating collaborators with the Nazis, but was officially exonerated (June 8, 1948). —Works: Operas: *Guntram* (Weimar, May 10, 1894; new version, Weimar, Oct. 22, 1940); *Feuersnot* (Dresden, Nov. 21, 1901); *Salome* (Dresden, Dec. 9, 1905); *Elektra* (Dresden, Jan. 25, 1909); *Der Rosenkavalier* (Dresden, Jan. 26, 1911); *Ariadne auf Naxos* (Stuttgart, Oct. 25, 1912); *Die Frau ohne Schatten* (Vienna, Oct. 10, 1919); *Intermezzo* (Dresden, Nov. 4, 1924); *Die ägyptische Helena* (Dresden, June 6, 1928); *Arabella* (Dresden, July 1, 1933); *Die schweigsame Frau* (Dresden, June 24, 1935); *Friedenstag* (Munich, July 24, 1938); *Daphne* (Dresden, Oct. 15, 1938); *Die Liebe der Danae* (1938-40; Salzburg, Aug. 14, 1952); *Capriccio* (Munich, Oct. 28, 1942). Ballets: *Josephslegende* (Paris, May 14, 1914); *Schlagobers* (Vienna, May 9, 1924). For orch.: *Festmarsch* (1876); symphony in D minor (Munich, March 30, 1881); violin concerto (Munich, Feb. 8, 1883); symph. in F minor (N. Y., Dec. 13, 1884); horn concerto No. 1 (Meiningen, March 4, 1885); *Burleske,* for piano and orch. (1885); *Aus Italien,* symph. fantasy (Munich, March 2, 1887); *Don Juan,* symph. poem, after Lenau (Weimar, Nov. 11, 1889); *Tod und Verklärung,* symph. poem (Eisenach, June 21, 1890); *Macbeth,* after Shakespeare (Weimar, Oct. 13, 1890); *Till Eulenspiegels lustige Streiche,* symph. poem (Cologne, Nov. 5, 1895); *Also sprach Zarathustra,* symph. poem, after Nietzsche (Frankfurt, Nov. 27, 1896); *Don Quixote,* variations based on Cervantes (Cologne, March 8, 1898); *Ein Heldenleben,* symph. poem (Frankfurt, March 3, 1899); *Symphonia domestica* (N. Y., March 31, 1904); *Festliches Praeludium* (Vienna, Oct. 19, 1913); *Eine Alpensinfonie* (Berlin, Oct. 28, 1915); *Parergon zur Symphonia domestica,* for piano (left hand) and orch. (Leipzig, Oct. 29, 1925, Paul Wittgenstein, soloist); *München Walzer* (originally written for film, 1939; new version, 1945; performed posthumously, Vienna, March 31, 1951), *Festmusik* on the 2600th anniversary of the Japanese Empire (Tokyo, Oct. 27, 1940); *Divertimento* on pieces by Couperin (Vienna, Jan. 31, 1943); horn concerto No. 2 (Salzburg, Aug. 11, 1943); *Metamorphosen,* for 23 string instruments (Zürich, Jan. 25, 1946); oboe concerto (Zürich, Feb. 26, 1946); duet concertino, for clarinet, bassoon, strings, and harp (Radio Svizzera Italiana, April 5, 1948). Chamber music: string quartet (1879-80); cello sonata (1882-83); Serenade, for 13 wind instruments (1881); piano quartet (1884); violin sonata (1887); sonatina No. 1, for 16 wind instruments (1943); sonatina No. 2, for 16 wind instruments (1944-45). Choral works: chorus for *Electra* of Sophocles (1880); *Wanderers Sturmlied,* for chorus and orch. (1884); *Eine deutsche Motette,* for solo voices and 16-part chorus (1923); *Die Tageszeiten,* cycle for men's chorus and orch. (1928); many unpubl. choral pieces. For voice and orch.: 4 songs (1896-97); 4 Hymns for soprano (1921); *Drei Gesänge,* for high voice (1948); *Im Abendrot,* for high voice (1948). For voice and piano: 26 albums to words in German; of these songs the earliest are the most famous: *Zueignung* (1882); *Die Nacht* (1882); *Allerseelen* (1883); *Ständchen* (1885); *Barcarole* (1886); *Breit über mein Haupt* (1886); *Cäcilie, Heimliche Aufforderung,* and *Morgen* (1893-94); *Traum durch die Dämmerung* (1894); *Ich trage meine Minne* (1896). For recitation and piano: *Enoch Arden,* after Tennyson (1890) and *Das Schloss am Meer,* after Uhland (1899). For piano: 5 pieces (1881); sonata (1881); *4 Stimmungsbilder* (1883). Strauss arranged Gluck's *Iphigénie en Tauride* for production at Weimar; his version was used for the American première at the Metropolitan Opera House, N. Y., Nov. 25, 1916; translated, revised, and enlarged the *Traité d'Instrumentation* of Berlioz (1905); made a new arrangement of Beethoven's *The Ruins of Athens* (Vienna, 1927); edited

Mozart's *Idomeneo* (1930); harmonized a number of folksongs for Peters' 'Volksliederbuch für Männerchor'; edited and published his father's posthumous works for horn. He publ. his souvenirs, *Betrachtungen und Erinnerungen* (Zürich, 1949; edited by W. Schuh; in English, N. Y., 1953).

BIBLIOGRAPHY: A. BIOGRAPHY: A. Seidl and W. Klatte, *R. S. Eine Charakterskizze* (Prague, 1896); G. Brecher, *R. S. Eine monographische Skizze* (Leipzig, 1900); E. Urban, *R. S.* (Berlin, 1901); Ernest Newman, *R. S.* (London, 1908); M. Steinitzer, *R. S.* (Berlin, 1911; 17th ed., 1928); H. T. Finck, *R. S. The Man and His Works* (Boston, 1917); R. Specht, *R. S. und sein Werk* (2 vols.; Leipzig, 1921); H. W. von Waltershausen, *R. S.* (Munich, 1921); R. C. Muschler, *R. S.* (Hildesheim, 1924); W. Hutschenruyter, *R. S.* (in Dutch; The Hague, 1929); E. Gehring, ed., *R. S. und seine Vaterstadt* (Munich, 1934); F. Gysi, *R. S.* (Potsdam, 1934); R. Tenschert, *Anekdoten um R. S.* (Vienna, 1945); R. Tenschert, *R. S. und Wien* (Vienna, 1949); W. Brandl, *R. S., Leben und Werk* (Wiesbaden, 1949); K. Pfister, *R. S., Weg, Gestalt, Denkmal* (Vienna, 1949); C. Rostand, *R. S.* (Paris, 1949); O. Erhardt, *R. S. Leben, Wirken, Schaffen* (Olten, 1953); F. Trenner, *R. S. Dokumente seines Lebens und Schaffens* (Munich, 1954); E. Krause, *R. S., Gestalt und Werk* (Leipzig, 1955).—B. CRITICISM, APPRECIATION: G. Jorisienne, *R. S. Essai critique et biologique* (Brussels, 1898); E. Urban, *S. contra Wagner* (Berlin, 1902); E. Newman, *R. S. and the Music of the Future,* in *Musical Studies* (London, 1905); O. Bie, *Die moderne Musik und R. S.* (Berlin, 1906); E. Schmitz, *R. S. als Musikdramatiker* (Munich, 1907); E. Zeigler, *R. S. in seinen dramatischen Dichtungen* (Munich, 1907); J. C. Manifarges, *R. S. als Dirigent* (Amsterdam, 1907); F. Santoliquido, *Il Dopo-Wagner: C. Debussy e R. S.* (Rome, 1909); G. Tebaldini, *Telepatia musicale e proposito dell' Elektra di R. S.* (Turin, 1909); M. Steinitzer, *Straussiana und Anderes* (Stuttgart, 1910); O. Hübner, *R. S. und das Musikdrama* (Leipzig, 1910); H. Rutters, *R. S. en de S.-feesten* (Amsterdam, 1911); H. Daffner, *Salome: Ihre Gestalt in Geschichte und Kunst* (Munich, 1912); A. Seidl, *Straussiana* (Regensburg, 1913); M. Steinitzer, *R. S. in seiner Zeit* (Leipzig, 1914; 2nd ed., 1922); W. Schrenk, *R. S. und die neue Musik* (Berlin, 1924); J. Subirá, *R. S., su hispanismo* (in Spanish; 1925); K. J. Krüger, *Hugo von Hofmannsthal und R. S.* (Berlin, 1935); H. Röttger, *Das Formproblem bei R. S.* (Berlin, 1937); J. Gregor, *R. S. Der Meister der Oper* (Munich, 1939); R. Tenschert, *3 x 7 Variationen über das Thema R. S.* (Vienna, 1944); W. Schuh, *Über Opern von R. S.* (Zürich, 1947); F. von Schuch, *R. S., Ernst von Schuch und Dresdens Oper* (2nd ed., Leipzig, 1953); G. Hausswald, *R. S., ein Beitrag zur Dresdner Operngeschichte seit 1945* (Dresden, 1953); Strauss numbers of the 'Allgemeine Musikzeitung' (1939) and 'Die Musik' (vol. 4, no. 8; vol. 13, no. 17). The following books contains important chapters on various phases of Strauss' art: J. Huneker, *Mezzotints in Modern Music* (N. Y., 1899); J. Huneker, *Overtones* (N. Y., 1904); L. Gilman, *Phases of Modern Music* (N. Y., 1904); F. Draeseke, *Die Konfusion in der Musik* (Stuttgart, 1906); F. Niecks, *Program Music in the Last Four Centuries* (London, 1907); L. Gilman, *Aspects of Modern Opera* (N. Y., 1908); L. A. Coerne, *The Evolution of Modern Orchestration* (N. Y., 1908); P. Bekker, *Das Musikdrama der Gegenwart* (Stuttgart, 1909); R. Louis, *Die deutsche Musik der Gegenwart* (Munich, 1909); L. Schmidt, *Aus dem Musikleben der Gegenwart* (Berlin, 1909; with preface by Strauss); R. Mayrhofer, *Zur Theorie des Schönen* (Leipzig, 1911); R. Rolland, *Musiciens d'aujourd'hui* (Paris, 1908; in English, 1914); P. Rosenfeld, *Musical Portraits* (N. Y., 1920); C. Gray, *Survey of Contemporary Music* (London, 1927). See also vols. VI and VII of H. v. Bülow's *Briefe und Schriften* (Leipzig, 1907).—C. CATALOGUES, GUIDES: R. Specht, *Vollständiges Verzeichnis der im Druck erschienen Werke von R. S.* (Vienna, 1910; also contains valuable biographical data); E. H. Müller von Asow, *R. S. Thematisches Verzeichnis* (began publ. in 1955; a complete thematic catalogue); *Modern Music and Drama* (2 vols.; Boston, 1911, 1915; gives list of several hundred titles of articles publ. about Strauss in English and American journals); *Festschrift der R. S. Woche München* (1930); E. Blom, *The Rose Cavalier* (London, 1930); T. Armstrong, *S.'s Tonepooms* (London, 1931). Analyses of the instrumental works are found in H. Kretzschmar's *Führer durch den Konzertsaal* (Leipzig, 1887; 4th ed., 1913) and in Schlesinger's 'Musikführer' and 'Meisterführer' (Berlin); guides to the dramatic works in Schlesinger's 'Opernführer' (Berlin), Wossidlo's 'Opernbibliothek' (Leipzig), and the numerous handbooks of Kufferath, Taubmann, Chop, Roese, Gilman, Schanzer, etc. —D. CORRESPONDENCE: *R. S. Briefwechsel mit Hugo von Hofmannsthal,* ed. by Franz Strauss (S.'s son; Vienna, 1926; in

English, N. Y., 1927); *R. S. und Hugo von Hofmannsthal: Briefwechsel* (complete ed., by Franz and Alice Strauss; Zürich, 1952); *R. S. et Romain Rolland; correspondance* (Paris, 1951); *Briefe an die Eltern: 1882-1906* (Zürich, 1954); *Correspondence: Hans von Bülow and R. S.* (London, 1955); *R. S. und Josef Gregor Briefwechsel, 1934-1949* (Salzburg, 1955); *Briefwechsel zwischen R. S. und Stefan Zweig* (Frankfurt, 1957).

Stravinsky, Feodor Ignatievitch, Russian bass singer; father of Igor Stravinsky; b. in the Tchernigov district, June 15, 1843; d. Wildungen, Germany, Dec. 3, 1902. He became a member of the Imperial Opera at St. Petersburg in 1876; his interpretations of heroic and comical types in Russian operas evoked sincere praise from critics and professional musicians alike. He was famous as Méphistophélès in Gounod's *Faust;* was distinguished not only for the power of his voice, but also for his acting talent; Shaliapin emulated him in this respect. Altogether, he made 1,235 appearances in 64 operatic roles.

Stravinsky, Igor (Feodorovitch), one of the greatest masters of modern music; b. Oranienbaum, near St. Petersburg, June 17, 1882. He was the son of a famous bass singer at the Imperial Opera, Feodor Stravinsky (q.v.) and was brought up in an artistic atmosphere. He studied law, and it was not until he reached the age of 19 that a meeting with Rimsky-Korsakov in Heidelberg encouraged him to undertake a serious study of composition. Upon Rimsky-Korsakov's advice, he studied theory with Kalafati. In 1907 Stravinsky began to take regular private lessons with Rimsky-Korsakov himself in St. Petersburg. On Jan. 22, 1908, his 1st symph., already showing a mastery of technique, was performed in St. Petersburg; and on Feb. 29, 1908, his set of songs, *Le Faune et la bergère,* for mezzo-soprano and orch., was brought out in St. Petersburg with considerable success. For Maximilian Steinberg's marriage to Rimsky-Korsakov's daughter (June 17, 1908), Stravinsky wrote an orchestral fantasy *Feu d'artifice.* Rimsky-Korsakov died a few days later, and Stravinsky wrote a threnody to pay tribute to his master. On Feb. 6, 1909, Stravinsky's next orchestral work, *Scherzo fantastique,* was performed in St. Petersburg. The famous impresario, Diaghilev, heard it and became interested in the new talent. Diaghilev had just asked Liadov for a ballet to be presented at the Paris season of the Ballets Russes, but Liadov declined; Diaghilev then commissioned Stravinsky to write a suitable work on a Russian subject. The result was the production of the first of Stravinsky's ballet masterpieces, *Zhar-Ptitsa,* performed under the French title, *L'Oiseau de feu* (Paris, June 25, 1910). Here Stravinsky wrote a score of coruscating brilliance, steeped in Russian folklore, and marking a natural continuation of Rimsky-Korsakov's series of musical fairy-tales. There are numerous striking effects in orchestral treatment, such as a glissando of harmonics in the string instruments, and the rhythmic elements are exhilarating; 2 orchestral suites were extracted from the work, the more famous of which was reorchestrated by Stravinsky in 1919, to conform to his new ideas of musical economy, with a general reduction of the orchestral apparatus; but the original scoring remained a favorite with conductors and orchestras. Stravinsky's association wth Diaghilev shifted his activities to Paris, where he made his home from 1911, with sojourns in Switzerland. His 2nd ballet for Diaghilev, *Petrouchka* (Paris, June 13, 1911), was highly successful; not only was it remarkably effective on the stage, but the music, arranged in 2 orchestral suites, was so new and original that it marked a turning point in 20th-century modernism; the spasmodically explosive rhythms, the novel instrumental sonorities, with the use of the piano as an integral part of the orchestra, and the bold innovation in employing 2 different keys sounded simultaneously (C major and F♯ major — the "Petrouchka Chord") exercised a highly potent influence upon contemporary composers. Two years later Stravinsky brought out a work of even greater revolutionary import, the ballet, *Le Sacre du printemps* (*Rite of Spring;* Russian title, *Vesna Sviashchennaya,* literally *Spring the Sacred*), produced by Diaghilev and his Ballets Russes in Paris on May 29, 1913. In this score, Stravinsky severed all ties with traditional harmony, and made use of dissonant combinations without precedent in modern music; the score still stands out as one of the most daring creations of the musical mind. Its impact was tremendous; there were demonstrations at the première on the part of some of the audience who believed that a trick was being played on them; but progressive musicians accepted the work as the beginning of a new era in composition. Shortly before the outbreak of World War I, Diaghilev produced Stravinsky's lyric fairy-tale, *Le Rossignol,* after Hans Christian Andersen (Paris, May 26, 1914). The war disrupted musical activities in Europe; Stravinsky spent the years 1914-18 mostly in Switzerland, where he continued to compose; Russian subjects still dominated his creative imagination. He worked on his ballet, *Les Noces* (Russian title, *Svadebka,* literally, *Little Wedding*), scored for an unusual ensemble of chorus, soloists, 4 pianos, and 17 percussion instruments. During the last months of the war Stravinsky formulated his idea that economy in musical settings became imperative in the impoverished world. To indicate the way, he wrote a stage play, *Histoire du Soldat,* scored for only 7 players; the work includes several stylized modern dances. At the same time he wrote a work for 11 instruments entitled *Ragtime,* rhythmically derived from early American jazz music. He resumed his association with Diaghilev and wrote for him a ballet, *Pulcinella* (on themes attributed to Pergolesi, although recent investigation has shown that some of them are not by him). He also wrote for Diaghilev two 1-act operas, *Mavra,* after Pushkin, and *Renard,* to stories from Russian folk literature (both produced by Diaghilev, Paris, June 3, 1922). These two works were the last in which Stravinsky used Russian subjects. In his next significant composition, the piano concerto, commissioned by Koussevitzky, Stravinsky inaugurated the much-discussed neo-Classical trend, abandoning his erstwhile luxuriance of instrumental color and affective dissonance; but his reversion to old forms was not an act of ascetic renunciation, but rather a grand experiment in reviving Baroque practices which had fallen into desuetude. He performed it with the Boston Symph. Orch. under Koussevitzky on Jan. 23, 1925, on the occasion of his 1st American tour. The Elizabeth Sprague Coolidge Foundation commissioned him to write a pantomime for string orch.; the result was *Apollon Musagète,* given at the Library of Congress in Washington, on April 27, 1928. This score, serene and emotionally restrained, evokes the court ballets of Lully in its spirit. He continued to explore the possibilities of neo-Classical writing in the *Capriccio* for piano and orch. (Paris, Dec. 6, 1929), but in this score he produced a work of hedonistic entertainment quite modern in its impact, the rhythmic element being exploited to the utmost. A desire for tragic expression became manifest in his opera-oratorio, *Oedipus Rex,* to a Latin text (Paris, May 30, 1927). A religious feeling found utterance in the *Symphony of Psalms,* written for the 50th anniversary of the Boston Symph. and dedicated 'to the glory of God.' It is scored for chorus and orch., omitting the violins and violas, thus emphasizing the lower registers and creating an austere sonority suitable to the solemn subject. Owing to a delay of the Boston performance, the world première of the *Symphony of Psalms* took place in Brussels (Dec. 13, 1930). In 1931 Stravinsky composed a concerto for violin and orch., commissioned by the violinist Samuel Dushkin, and performed by him in Berlin on Oct. 23. On a commission from Ida Rubinstein Stravinsky wrote a ballet to a text by André Gide entitled *Perséphone,* which he conducted at the Paris Opéra on April 30, 1934. For his American tour in 1937, he wrote a 'ballet in three deals,' *Jeux de Cartes,* to his own scenario derived from an imaginary poker game, and conducted it at the Metropolitan Opera House, N. Y., on April 27, 1937. His concerto for 16 instruments, entitled *Dumbarton Oaks* (after the Washington estate of Mr. and Mrs. Robert Woods Bliss) and performed in Washington, D.C., on May 8, 1938, continued the deliberate practice of neo-Baroque composition (in Paris the work was played under the simple title *Concerto,* without the reference to Dumbarton Oaks). Stravinsky was named Charles Eliot Norton lecturer at Harvard Univ. for 1939-40. He became a French citizen on June 10, 1934, but in 1939 he left France and settled in the U. S., making his home in Hollywood; he became an American citizen on Dec. 28, 1945. He continued to conduct his works in America and in Europe; his creative energy did not abate with the advancing years. He wrote music in variegated styles and for widely different purposes: a *Circus Polka* 'composed for a young elephant' commissioned by the Ringling Bros. Circus (1942); *Ebony Concerto,* for clarinet and swing band, performed by Woody Herman in Carnegie Hall, N. Y. (March 25, 1946); a Mass for men's and boys' voices and 10 instruments (Milan, Oct. 27, 1948); as a temporary return to his Russian antecedents, he wrote an orchestral *Scherzo à la russe* (1944). At the time of his application for American citizenship, he publ. an arrangement of the *Star-Spangled Banner* and conducted it with the Boston Symph. (Jan. 14, 1944), but because of complaints on the part of some of the audience against the unorthodox harmonization, and on account of legal injunctions existing in the state of Massachusetts against intentional mutilation of the national anthem, Stravinsky reverted to the standard version. In 1951 he completed his opera *The Rake's Progress,* after Hogarth's famous series of engravings, to a libretto by W. H. Auden and C. Kallman, and conducted its world première in Venice on Sept. 11, as part of the International Festival of Contemporary Music there. The opera had tremendous repercussions in the musical world, as still another illustration of Stravinsky's capacity of changing his course towards unexpected destinations; here, the style was a conglomeration of elements of 19th-century Italian opera, early English stage plays, and French opéra comique. In his latest works he applied a method of serial composition, modelled after the creations of Anton von Webern, rather than those of Schoenberg; in this manner he wrote his *Canticum sacrum ad honorem Sancti Marci nominis,* for tenor, baritone, chorus, and orch., which he conducted at St. Mark's Cathedral in Venice on Sept. 11, 1956. In 1957 he wrote a ballet for 12 dancers, *Agon,* also based on the serial technique; it was presented in Los Angeles on the occasion of his 75th birthday, June 17, 1957. —Igor Stravinsky's influence on contemporary music has been profound. Inasmuch as his early masterpieces were produced in Paris, the impact was strongest upon French composers of the generation that grew up in the 1st quarter of the 20th century. Several American composers who studied in France experienced Stravinsky's influence to a considerable degree, as did many from Spain and South America. In England, his influence was relatively weaker, and it was not strong in Germany or Italy. Owing to Soviet opposition to modern music, Stravinsky's works were virtually banned in Russia after the Revolution; he himself was proclaimed an obscurantist and a reactionary, and evoked wrathful comment in the Soviet press. A certain relaxation of restrictions against performances of Stravinky's music came after Stalin's death (1953); the Russian pianist Gilels put Stravinsky's arrangement of *Petrouchka* on the programs of his recitals in Russia and the U. S.; Shostakovitch publicly declared the work to be a masterpiece.

WORKS: FOR THE STAGE: *Rossignol,* 'lyric tale' in 3 acts, after Andersen (Paris, May 26, 1914; also performed as a ballet, Paris, Feb. 2, 1920); *The Firebird,* ballet (Paris, June 25, 1910); *Petrouchka,* ballet (Paris, June 13, 1911); *Le Sacre du printemps,* ballet, 'scenes of pagan Russia' (Paris, May 29, 1913); *Renard,* burlesque chamber opera (Paris, June 3, 1922); *Mavra,* comic opera, after Pushkin (Paris, June 3, 1922); *Les Noces,* 'choreographic Russian scenes' (Paris, June 13, 1923); *Histoire du soldat,* for narrator and 7 instruments (Lausanne, Sept. 28, 1918); *Pulcinella,* ballet 'after Pergolesi' (Paris, May 15, 1920); *Oedipus Rex,* opera-oratorio, after Sophocles (concert performance, Paris, May 30, 1927; stage performance, Berlin, Feb. 25, 1928); *Apollon Musagète,* classic ballet (Washington, D. C., April 27, 1928); *Le Baiser de la fée,* ballet on themes by Tchaikovsky (Paris, Nov. 27, 1928); *Perséphone,* ballet with recitation and chorus, to text by André Gide (Paris, April 30, 1934); *Jeux de cartes (Card Party),* 'ballet in 3 deals' (N. Y., April 27, 1937); *Orpheus,* ballet (N. Y., April 28, 1948); *The Rake's Progress,* opera after Hogarth's engravings; libretto by W. H. Auden and C. Kallman (Venice, Sept. 11, 1951, Stravinsky conducting); *Agon,* ballet for 12 dancers (Los Angeles, June 17, 1957). FOR ORCH.: symph. in E♭ major, op. 1 (1905-07; St. Petersburg, Jan. 22, 1908); *Le Faune et la bergère,* for mezzo-soprano and orch., op. 2 (St. Petersburg, Feb. 29, 1908); *Scherzo fantastique,* op. 3 (St. Petersburg, Feb. 6, 1909); *Fireworks,* op. 4 (St. Petersburg, June 17, 1908); *Funeral Chant on the Death of Rimsky-Korsakov,* for chorus and orch. (1908); *The Firebird,* 2 orchestral suites from the ballet (1910; the 2nd reorchestrated in 1919); *Petrouchka,* orchestral suite from the ballet (1910-11); *Le Roi des étoiles,* cantata for voice and orch. (1911); *Le Sacre du printemps,* orchestral suite from the ballet (Paris, April 5, 1914); *Chant du rossignol,* suite in 3 parts from the opera (Geneva, Dec. 6, 1919; 1st performance as a ballet, Paris, Feb. 2, 1920); *Ragtime,* for 11 instruments (composed Nov. 11, 1918); *Pulcinella,* suite from the ballet (1920); *Symphonies of Wind Instruments,* in memory of Debussy (1920; London, June 10, 1921); suite no. 1 for small orch. (1917-25; orchestral arrangement of four of the *5 Pièces faciles* for piano, 4 hands: *Andante, Napolitana, Española, Balalaïka);* suite no. 2 for small orch. (1921; *March, Waltz, Polka, Galop);* concerto for piano and wind instruments (Paris, May 22, 1924); *Capriccio* for piano and orch. (Paris, Dec. 6, 1929); 4 Études for orch.: *Danse, Excentrique, Cantique, Madrid* (Berlin, Nov. 7, 1930); *Symphony of Psalms,* for chorus and orch. (Brussels, Dec. 13, 1930; Boston, Dec. 19, 1930); violin concerto (Berlin, Oct. 23, 1931); concerto for 2 pianos (Paris, Nov. 21, 1935); concerto in E♭ major, *Dumbarton Oaks,* for 16 instruments (Washington, D. C., May 8, 1938); symphony in C (Chicago, Nov. 7, 1940); *Tango,* arrangement of the violin piece (Philadelphia, July 10, 1941); *Danses concertantes* (Los Angeles, Feb. 8, 1942); *Circus Polka* (1942; Boston, Jan. 14, 1944); *Ode,* in 3 parts (Boston, Oct. 8, 1943); *Norwegian Moods,* 4 episodes (Boston, Jan. 14,

1944); *Scènes de ballet* (N. Y., Feb. 3, 1945); *Scherzo à la russe* (1944; San Francisco, March 22, 1946, composer conducting); symphony in 3 movements (N. Y., Jan. 24, 1946); *Ebony Concerto,* for clarinet and swing band (N. Y., March 25, 1946); concerto in D for string orch. (Basel, Jan. 21, 1947). CHAMBER MUSIC: *3 Poems from the Japanese,* for soprano, 2 flutes, 2 clarinets, piano, and string quartet (1912-13); 3 Pieces for string quartet (1914); *Pribautki,* songs for voice with 8 instruments (1914); *Berceuses du chat,* suite of 4 songs for female voice and 3 clarinets (1915-16); 3 Pieces for clarinet solo (1919); concertino for string quartet (1920); octet for wind instruments (Paris, Oct. 18, 1923); *Duo concertant,* for violin and piano (Berlin, Oct. 28, 1932); *Suite italienne,* for cello and piano, from *Pulcinella* (1934); *Tango,* for violin and piano (1941); *Élégie,* for unaccompanied violin or viola (1944); septet for piano and string and wind instruments (1952; Washington, D. C., Jan. 24, 1954); *3 Songs from William Shakespeare,* for mezzo-soprano, flute, clarinet, and viola (Los Angeles, March 8, 1954); *In Memoriam Dylan Thomas,* for tenor, string quartet, and 4 trombones (Hollywood, Sept. 20, 1954); 4 Russian songs for soprano, flute, guitar, and harp (1954). CHORAL WORKS: *The Saucer,* 4 Russian songs for women's voices (1914-17); *Paternoster,* for mixed chorus, a cappella (1926); *Credo* for mixed chorus, a cappella (1932); *Ave Maria,* for mixed chorus, a cappella (1934); Mass for men's and boys' voices and 10 instruments (Milan, Oct. 27, 1948); Cantata on 4 poems by anonymous English poets of the 15th and 16th centuries (Los Angeles, Nov. 11, 1952); *Canticum sacrum ad honorem Sancti Marci nominis,* for tenor, baritone, chorus, and orch. (Venice, Sept. 11, 1956, composer conducting); arrangement for chorus and orch. of J. S. Bach's *Choral-Variationen über das Weihnachtslied 'Vom Himmel hoch da komm' ich her'* (1956); *Threni,* on Lamentations of Jeremiah from the Vulgate, for solo voices, chorus, and orch. (International Festival of Contemporary Music, Venice, Sept. 23, 1958). PIANO MUSIC: 2 sonatas (1904; 1922); 4 Études (1908); *3 Pièces faciles,* for piano 4 hands (1915); *5 Pièces faciles,* for piano 4 hands (1917); Étude for pianola (1917); *Piano Rag-Music* (1920); *Les cinq doigts,* 8 melodies on 5 notes (1921); Serenade in A (1925); sonata for 2 pianos (1944). —BOOKS: *Chroniques de ma vie,* autobiography (Paris, 1935; 2 vols.; in English as *Chronicles of My Life,* London, 1936); *Poétique musicale,* the Charles Eliot Norton Lectures at Harvard Univ. (Paris, 1946; in English as *Poetics of Music,* Cambridge, Mass., 1948). —BIBLIOGRAPHY: C. Van Vechten, in *Music After the Great War* (N. Y., 1915); C. S. Wise, *Impressions of I. S.,* in the 'Mus. Quarterly' (April, 1916); M. Montagu-Nathan, *Contemporary Russian Composers* (N. Y., 1917); R. D. Chennevière, *The Two Trends of Modern Music in S.'s Works,* in the 'Mus. Quarterly' (April, 1919); B. de Schloezer, *I. S.* (Paris, 1926); A. Casella, *S.* (Rome, 1926); J. Waynkop, *I. S.* (in Russian; Leningrad, 1927); V. Belaiev, *I. S.'s Les Noces, an outline* (London, 1928; also in Russian); Igor Glebov, *S.* (Leningrad, 1929); C. F. Ramuz, *Souvenirs sur I. S.* (Paris, 1929; new ed., Lausanne, 1946); P. Collaer, *S.* (Brussels, 1930); E. W. White, *S.'s Sacrifice to Apollo* (London, 1930); H. Fleischer, *S.* (Berlin, 1931); A. Schaeffner, *I. S.* (Paris, 1931); J. Handschin, *I. S.* (Zürich, 1933); E. Evans, *The Firebird and Petrouchka* (London, 1933); D. de Paoli, *I. S.* (Turin, 1934); M. Blitzstein, *The Phenomenon of S.,* in the 'Mus. Quarterly' (July, 1935); M. Armitage (ed.), *S.,* a compendium of articles (N. Y., 1936); special S. issue of the 'Revue Musicale' (May-June, 1939); A. Kall, *S. in the Chair of Poetry,* in the 'Mus. Quarterly' (July, 1940); S. Babitz, *S.'s Symphony in C,* in the 'Mus. Quarterly' (Jan., 1941); M. D. Fardel, *S. et les ballets russes* (Nice, 1941); G. F. Malipiero, *S.* (Venice, 1945); A. Casella, *S.* (Brescia, 1947; a different work from his book publ. in 1926); E. W. White, *S., a Critical Survey* (London, 1947; N. Y., 1948); A. Tansman, *I. S.* (Paris, 1948; in English, N. Y., 1949); Theodore Stravinsky, *Le Message d'I. S.* (Lausanne, 1948; in English as *The Message of I. S.,* London, 1953); M. Lederman, ed., *S. in the Theatre* (N. Y., 1949); E. Corle, ed., *I. S.* (N. Y., 1949; a compendium of articles, including some reprinted from M. Armitage's collection of 1936); F. Onnen, *S.* (Stockholm, 1949; in English); J. E. Cirlot, *I. S.* (Barcelona, 1949); R. H. Myers, *Introduction to the Music of S.* (London, 1950); W. H. Auden *et al., I. S.* (Bonn, 1952); L. Oleggini, *Connaissance de S.* (Lausanne, 1952); H. Strobel, *I. S.* (Zürich, 1956; English version as *S.: Classic Humanist,* N. Y., 1955); 'The Score,' special number for Stravinsky's 75th birthday, 1957, with articles by Sessions, H. Keller, etc.; *I. S.: a Complete Catalogue of his Publ. Works* (London, 1957); 'Musik der Zeit' (Bonn; 1st Series, vols. 1, 12; New Series, vol. 1); H. Kirchmeyer, *I. S. Zeitgeschichte im Persönlichkeitsbild* (Regensburg, 1958).

Stravinsky, Soulima, pianist, son of Igor Stravinsky; b. Lausanne, Sept. 23, 1910. He studied in Paris with Isidor Philipp and Nadia Boulanger; then gave piano recitals in Europe and America; has appeared frequently with his father, playing his works for 2 pianos.

Streatfeild, Richard Alexander, English writer on music; b. Edenbridge, June 22, 1866; d. London, Feb. 6, 1919. He studied at Pembroke College, Cambridge; in 1889 he became assistant in the Dept. of Printed Books in the British Museum; was music critic of the 'Daily Graphic' (1898-1912). He publ. the following books: *Masters of Italian Music* (1895); *The Opera* (1897; 5th ed., enlarged, 1925); *Modern Music and Musicians* (1906); *Handel* (1909); *Life Stories of Great Composers* (Philadelphia, 1910); *Musiciens anglais contemporains* (French transl., 1913; English original not published); *Handel, Canons and the Duke of Chandos* (London, 1916); contributed many articles to English publications.

Streicher (shtrī'-her), **Johann Andreas,** piano maker; b. Stuttgart, Dec. 13, 1761; d. Vienna, May 25, 1833. During a stay at Augsburg in 1793 he married Nanette Stein (b. Augsburg, Jan. 2, 1769; d. Vienna, Jan. 16, 1835), daughter of the piano manufacturer Johann Andreas Stein; in 1802 succeeded Stein in the business and moved it to Vienna. He invented the piano action in which the hammer strikes from above. He was on friendly terms with Beethoven. —Cf. T. Bolte, *Die Musiker-Familien Stein und Streicher* (Vienna, 1917); T. von Frimmel, *Beethoven und das Ehepaar Streicher,* in 'Alt-Wiener Kalender' (1925); W. Lütge, *Andreas und Annette Streicher,* in 'Der Bär' (1927).

Streicher, Theodor, Austrian song composer, great-grandson of Johann Andreas Streicher; b. Vienna, June 7, 1874; d. Wetzelsdorf, near Graz, May 28, 1940. He studied singing with F. Jäger in Vienna and J. Kniese in Bayreuth; piano with F. Löwe in Vienna; composition with H. Schulz-Beuthen in Dresden. He lived most of his life in Vienna; wrote numerous songs in a Romantic manner, reminiscent of Hugo Wolf. He set to music 36 poems from *Des Knaben Wunderhorn;* wrote *Wanderers Nachtlied,* after Goethe, for chorus a cappella; a sextet for strings; etc. He also orchestrated the accompaniments of Karl Loewe's ballades. In 1934 a 'Theodor Streicher Gemeinde' was founded in Vienna to propagate his music.

Strelezki, Anton, pianist and composer; b. Croydon, England, Dec. 5, 1859; d. 1907. According to some sources, his real name was Burnand. He studied with Clara Schumann; settled in London, where he was very popular; place and exact date of his death are unknown. He publ. a great deal of piano music (more than 225 op. numbers), some of which was widely used: *Valse-Souvenir; Jagdstück; Valsette; Sérénade espagnole; Menuet à l'antique; Barcarolle;* also songs; publ. *Personal Recollections of Chats with Liszt* (1895).

Strelnikov, Nicolay Mikhailovitch, Russian composer; b. Plotsk, May 14, 1888; d. Leningrad, April 12, 1939. He studied music with Liadov in St. Petersburg; wrote 2 operas, *A Fugitive* (Leningrad, May 26, 1933) and *Count Nulin* (1935; after Pushkin). Other works include a piano concerto, choruses, chamber music. He publ. monographs on Glinka, Rachmaninoff, and other Russian composers.

Strens, Jules, Belgian composer; b. Ixelles, Dec. 5, 1892. He studied with Paul Gilson; was one of the founders of a group called 'Synthétistes,' endeavoring to establish a modern style of composition within the formal categories of old music. In 1931 he was appointed conductor of the Association Symphonique in Brussels. —Works: opera, *Le Chanteur de Naples* (1922); *Les Elfes,* symph. poem (1927); *Danse funambulesque,* for orch. (1930); 4 string quartets, string sextet, wind quintet, piano trio; songs.

Strepponi (strep-pŏh'-nē), **Giuseppina,** Italian soprano; b. Lodi, Sept. 18, 1815; d. Busseto, Nov. 14, 1897. She was the daughter of the opera conductor in Trieste, Felice Strepponi; having completed her studies at the Milan Cons. (1830-35), she made a successful début in Trieste, and was engaged at the Italian Opera in Vienna. Her appearances in Rome. Florence, Venice, and other Italian cities established her reputation as a foremost interpreter of dramatic roles. She created a sensation by her performance of Abigaile in Verdi's *Nabucco* (Milan, March 9, 1842). Verdi admired her greatly; after many years of intimacy they were married (1859).

Strickland, Lily Teresa, American composer; b. Anderson, S. C., Jan. 28, 1887; d. Hendersonville, N. C., June 6, 1958. She studied at Converse College, Spartanburg, S. C., later in N. Y. with A. J. Goodrich and W. H. Humiston. She married J. Courtney Anderson of N. Y. in 1912. She traveled in the Orient between 1920 and 1930, and spent several years in India; then returned to the U. S. She publ. a number of successful songs, such as *Mah Lindy Lou, Dreamin' Time, Songs of India, Song From High Hills;* piano suites *(Moroccan Mosaics, Egyptian Scenes, Himalayan Idylls,* etc.); also wrote stage works; cantatas; *Oasis* for orch. (1942); etc. Co-author (with Helen Frost) of *Oriental and Character Dances* (N. Y., 1930).

Strickland, William, American conductor; b. Defiance, Ohio, Jan. 25, 1914. He studied organ and singing; was music master at St. George's School, Newport, R. I. (1934-36). In 1946 he organized the Nashville, Tenn., Symph., of which he became permanent conductor; in 1955 appointed musical director of the N. Y. Oratorio Society

Striegler, Kurt, German composer and conductor; b. Dresden, Jan. 7, 1886; d. Wildthurn, near Landau, Aug. 4, 1958. He studied with Draeseke at the Dresden Cons. From 1912 to 1945 he was conductor at the Dresden Opera, and for 40 years (1905-45) he taught at the Musik Hochschule there. In 1945 he became director of the Cons. of Coburg. He wrote 4 symphonies; a violin concerto; a cello concerto; much chamber music; a scherzo for 7 kettledrums with orch.; numerous choruses; songs and piano pieces; also the operas *Der Thomaskantor* and *Hand und Herz* (Dresden, 1924).

Striggio (strēd'jōh), **Alessandro,** Italian lutenist, organist, and composer; b. Mantua, c. 1535; d. there, c. 1595. He lived at the court of Cosimo de' Medici in Florence, and later in Mantua as court conductor. In 1567 he was in Paris and London, and in 1574 at the court of the Emperor Maximilian. He composed 3 musical intermezzi for *Psiche ed Amore* (intermezzo for the comedy *La Cofanaria;* Florence, 1565, for the wedding of Francesco de' Medici and Princess Johanna of Austria) and also 3 intermezzi for the comedy *L'Amico fido* (not extant); also other festival music (particularly, with Merulo, Caccini, and Strozzi, a festival play for the wedding of Francesco de' Medici with Bianca Capello in 1579). Publ. several books of madrigals and *Il Cicalamento delle donne . . .* (1567; descriptive songs in the manner of Janequin; new ed. by Solerti and Alaleona in 'Rivista Musicale Italiana' XII and XIII; new ed. by B. Somma, Rome, 1947); many compositions by Striggio are found in collections of the period (1559-1634); 5 madrigals were reprinted by Torchi in 'L'Arte Musicale in Italia' (vol. I). —Letters of Striggio were publ. by Gandolfi in 'Rivista Musicale Italiana' XX, p. 527 ff.; see also A. Solerti, *Gli Albori del melodramma* (Milan, 1904); O. G. Sonneck, *A Description of A. S. and F. Corteccia's Intermedi 'Psyche and Amor,' 1565,* in *Miscellaneous Studies in the History of Music* (N. Y., 1921). —His son, **Alessandro** (called Alessandrino), was a poet, and a notable player of the violin and lyra. He was active at the court of Mantua (still there in 1628) and in 1607 wrote the libretto of Monteverdi's *La Favola d'Orfeo.* In 1596-97 he publ. 3 books of his father's madrigals for 5 voices.

Strimer, Joseph, Russian-American pianist and composer; b. Rostov-on-the-Don, Oct. 21, 1881. He studied with Rimsky-Korsakov, Liadov, Steinberg, Tcherepnin, and Glazunov at the St. Petersburg Cons.; after graduation, went to Germany, where he studied conducting with Arthur Nikisch. He lived mostly in Paris after 1920; came to N. Y. in 1941, and established himself as a teacher of piano and composition. He publ. a number of piano pieces; paraphrases of works by Rimsky-Korsakov, Borodin, Liadov, etc.; arrangements of folksongs.

Stringfield, Lamar, American composer and conductor; b. Raleigh, N. C., Oct. 10, 1897. He served in the U. S. Army during World War I; then studied with Goetschius (theory) and Georges Barrère (flute) at the Institute of Musical Art, N. Y. (1920-24); conducting with Chalmers Clifton. In 1930 he organized the Institute of Folk Music at the Univ. of North Carolina; was conductor of the North Carolina Symph. Orch. (1932-35), of the Knoxville Symph. Orch. (1946-47), and of the Charlotte Symph. Orch. (1948-49); remained in Charlotte as composer and arranger. The source material of his music is largely derived from Southern folklore; as a self-taught printer and engraver, he is able to publish his own works. He wrote a musical folk-drama, *Carolina Charcoal* (1952); for orch.: *Indian Legend* (1923), suite *From the Southern Mountains* (Pulitzer Prize, 1928; contains his best-known piece, *Cripple Creek*), *A Negro Parade* (1931), *Moods of a Moonshiner* (1934), *Mountain Dawn* (1945), *About Dixie* (1950); chamber music: *Chipmunks* for flute, clarinet, and bassoon, *From a Negro Melody,* for 12 instruments, *Indian Sketches* for flute and string quartet, *Virginia Dare Dance* for wind quintet; sacred cantata, *Peace,* for chorus a cappella; etc. He publ.

America and Her Music (Univ. of North Carolina Press, 1931).

Stringham, Edwin John, American music educator and composer; b. Kenosha, Wis., July 11, 1890. He studied at Northwestern Univ. and at Cincinnati Cons.; in 1929 went to Italy, where he took courses with Respighi. He taught at the Denver College of Music (1920-29), Teachers College of Columbia Univ. (1930-38), the Juilliard School of Music, N. Y. (1930-45), and at Queens College of the City of N. Y. (1938-46). In 1948 he settled at Chapel Hill, N. C. — Works: for orch.: *The Phantom,* symph. poem (1916); *Visions,* symph. poem (1924); *The Ancient Mariner,* after Coleridge (Denver, March 16, 1928); *Three Pastels* (Rochester, May 17, 1928); symph. No. 1 (Minneapolis, Nov. 15, 1929); 2 Nocturnes (1931; 1938); *Fantasy on American Folk Tunes,* for violin and orch. (1942). Vocal works: *The Pilgrim Fathers,* for mixed chorus a cappella (1931); *Dream Song,* for soprano, 2 contraltos, and piano (1933); also chamber music and songs. He publ. a book on music appreciation, *Listening to Music Creatively* (N. Y., 1943; revised ed., 1959); in collaboration with H. A. Murphy, *Creative Harmony and Musicianship* (N. Y., 1951).

Strobel, Heinrich, German musicologist; b. Regensburg, May 31, 1898. He studied in Munich with Sandberger and Kroyer; *Dr. phil.,* 1922, with a dissertation on Hässler. From 1927 to 1933 he was music critic of the 'Börsenkurier' in Berlin; in 1939 he went to Paris; in 1945 became music director of the radio station at Baden-Baden; also editor of the monthly magazine 'Melos.' He wrote the librettos for Rolf Liebermann's *Leonore 40/45* and *Penelope.* —Publications: *Paul Hindemith* (Mainz, 1928; revised ed., 1931; new enlarged ed., 1948; basic biography); *Claude Debussy* (Zürich, 1940; new ed., Paris, 1952); *Stravinsky: Classic Humanist* (publ. in English, N. Y., 1955).

Strobel, Otto, German musicologist; b. Munich, Aug. 20, 1895; d. Bayreuth, Feb. 23, 1953. He studied at the Univ. of Munich *(Dr. phil.,* 1924). After working as an archivist at Bayreuth, he was appointed in 1938 director of the newly created Richard Wagner Institute there. He publ. *Genie am Werk: Richard Wagners Schaffen und Wirken im Spiegel eigenhandschriftlicher Urkunden* (Bayreuth, 1934); *Richard Wagner, . . . ein Zeittafel* (Bayreuth, 1952); ed. *König Ludwig II. und Richard Wagner: Briefwechsel,* 4 vols. (Karlsruhe, 1936-37), and a supplement to this, *Neue Urkunden zur Lebensgeschichte Richard Wagners* (Karlsruhe, 1939); *Neue Wagner-Forschungen,* vol. 1 (Karlsruhe, 1943).

Strong, George Templeton, American composer; b. New York, May 26, 1856; d. Geneva, Switzerland, June 27, 1948. He was the son of the New York lawyer, G. T. Strong, who was also a music lover, and whose diary, expressing his dislike of Liszt and Wagner, was publ. in 1952. From him, and from his mother, who was an amateur pianist, Strong received his first training. In 1879 he went to Leipzig, where he studied with Jadassohn. He entered the Liszt circle at Weimar, and became an adherent of program music; from 1886 to 1889 he lived in Wiesbaden, where he became friendly with MacDowell; he returned briefly to America, and taught theory at the New England Cons., Boston (1891-92); then went back to Europe and settled in Switzerland. He expressed his indignation at the lack of recognition of American composers in their own country; most performances of his works took place in Switzerland. In 1930 he donated many of his original MSS to the Library of Congress in Washington. Toscanini performed his orch. suite *Die Nacht* with the NBC Symph. Orch., N. Y., on Oct. 21, 1939; his symph. poem, *Une Vie d'artiste* for violin and orch., was presented at the 20th festival of the Association des Musiciens Suisses at Zürich in June, 1920; he also wrote 3 symphonies; the symph. poem *Undine* and *Le Roi Arthur;* etc.

Strozzi (stroh'-tsē), **Pietro,** Florentine composer; flourished in the last quarter of the 16th century; was a member of the Bardi circle in Florence, and one of the creators of the 'stile rappresentativo,' leading to the development of opera. With Caccini, Merulo, and Striggio he wrote the festival music for the wedding of Francesco de' Medici in 1579; in 1595 he set to music Rinuccini's libretto *La Mascherata degli accecati;* 2 madrigals by Strozzi are in Luca Bati's *Secondo Libro di Madrigali* (Venice, 1598).

Strube, Gustav, composer and music educator; b. Ballenstedt, Germany, March 3, 1867; d. Baltmore, Feb. 2, 1953. He was taught the violin by his father and later by Brodsky at the Leipzig Cons.; was a member of the Gewandhaus Orch. there until 1891, when he emigrated to America; was a violinist in the Boston Symph. from 1891 to 1913; then he became head of the theory department in the Peabody Cons. at Baltimore. In 1916 he was appointed conductor of the newly organized Baltimore Symph. Orch., which he led until 1930; director of the Peabody Cons. (1916-46). He publ. a useful manual, *The Theory and Use of Chords: a Textbook of Harmony* (Boston, 1928). His works written in America include a symphony subtitled 'Lanier' (after Sidney Lanier, poet and musician; Washington, D.C., March 17, 1925, composer conducting); *Sinfonietta* (1922); *Symphonic Prologue* (Baltimore, April 24, 1927, composer conducting); 2 violin concertos (1924; 1930); *Americana,* for orch. (1930); *Harz Mountains,* symph. poem (1940); *Peace Overture* (1945); 2 string quartets (1923; 1936); 2 violin sonatas (1923); viola sonata (1924); cello sonata (1925); piano trio (1925); quintet for wind instruments (1930); also an opera, *Ramona* (1916). —Cf. G. Klemm, *Gustav Strube: The Man and the Musician,* in the 'Mus. Quarterly' (July, 1942).

Strungk (shtrŏŏnk), **Nicolaus Adam,** German violinist, organist, and composer; b. Brunswick (baptized Nov. 15), 1640; d. Dresden, Sept. 23, 1700. He studied with his father, Delphin Strungk (1601-94), whose assistant he became at the age of 12; was then organist at the Church of St. Magnus at Brunswick; studied violin at Lübeck under Schnittelbach while attending Helmstadt Univ. At 20, he became 1st violinist in the Brunswick orch., later holding similar positions at Celle and Hanover. In 1678 Strungk became music director at Hamburg; wrote and produced operas in German (in keeping with the nationalist trend of the time), among them *Der glückselig-steigende Sejanus* and its sequel *Der unglücklich-fallende Sejanus* (1678) with German librettos by Christoph Richter adapted from the Italian; *Die Liebreiche, durch Tugend und Schönheit erhöhete Esther;* and *Doris* (all in 1680); *Theseus; Semiramis;* and *Floretto* (all in 1683), etc. (The opera *Die drey Töchter Cecrops',* formerly attributed to Strungk, was written by Johann Wolfgang Franck.) Strungk was subsequently chamber organist to the Elector Ernst August of Hanover, where he won the admiration of Corelli. On Jan. 26, 1688, Strungk was appointed vice Kapellmeister in Dresden, succeeding Carlo Pallavicino, whose unfinished opera *Antiope* Strungk completed. In this post he was beset with difficulties arising from friction with Italan musicans, and only managed to maintain his authority through the intervention of his patron the Elector Johann Georg III; when Bernhard, Kapellmeister in Dresden, died in 1692, Strungk was appointed to succeed him. In 1693, he organized an opera company in Leipzig; between 1693 and 1700 he wrote 16 operas for it, among them *Alceste* (performed at the inauguration of the Leipzig opera house, May 18, 1693), *Agrippina* (1699), etc. Financially, the enterprise was a failure, but Strungk continued to receive his salary from Dresden until his retirement on a pension in 1697. He publ. the important manual *Musicalische Übung auf der Violine oder Viola da Gamba in etlichen Sonaten über die Festgesänge, ingleichen etlichen Ciaconen mit 2 Violinen bestehend* (1691). A selection of airs from his operas was publ. in Hamburg under the title *Ein hundert auserlesenen Arien zweyer Hamburgischen Operen, Semiramis und Esther. Mit beigefügten Ritornellen* (1684). Among his instrumental works, a sonata for 2 violins and viola da gamba, and several other sonatas are extant; MS No. 5056 of the Yale Univ. Music Library (Lowell Mason Collection) contains capriccios and ricercars by Strungk, among them the *Ricercar sopra la Morte della mia carissima Madre Catherina Maria Stubenrauen . . .* (Venice, 1685). Six capriccios and a ricercar by Strungk, included in the 'Denkmäler der Tonkunst in Österreich' (XIII, 2), are wrongly ascribed to Georg Reutter (Senior). —Cf. F. Zelle, *J. Theile und N. A. Strungk* (Berlin, 1891); F. Berend, *Nicolaus Adam Strungk: sein Leben und seine Werke* (dissertation; Hanover, 1915); see also G. Frotscher, *Geschichte des Orgelspiels* (Berlin, 1934-35, vol. I).

Strunk, (William) Oliver, American musicologist; b. Ithaca, N. Y., March 22, 1901. He was educated at Cornell Univ. (1917-19; also 1927, musicology with Otto Kinkeldey) and at the Univ. of Berlin (1927-28; musicology with J. Wolf); also studied privately with Sinding and Royce at the Eastman School of Music, Rochester, N. Y. From 1928 to 1932 he was on the staff of the Music Division of the Library of Congress; then was assistant chief (1932-34), and chief (1934-37); also taught at the Catholic Univ. in Washington, D. C. In 1937 he was appointed to the faculty of Princeton Univ.; prof. there since 1950; lectured at various universities in America and Europe; held a Guggenheim Fellowship in 1951. He publ. *State and Resources of Musicology in the U. S.* (Washington, 1932) and the extremely valuable compilation *Source Readings in*

Music History (N. Y., 1950), containing English translations of treatises and documents on music from the earliest times to the 19th century. He has also publ. important articles, especially in the fields of Renaissance, 18th-century, and Byzantine music.

Stuart, Leslie (real name Thomas A. Barrett), English operetta composer; b. Southport, March 15, 1866; d. Richmond, Surrey, March 26, 1928. He was church organist in various provincial towns in England; settled in London in 1895, where he soon became known as a composer of popular songs. He achieved enormous success with his operetta, *Floradora,* produced in London on Nov. 11, 1899, and subsequently performed in England and America for many seasons, but failed to duplicate this success in any of his later works, which included *The Silver Slipper* (1901), *The School Girl* (1903), *The Belle of Mayfair* (1906), *Havana* (1908), *Captain Kidd* and *The Slim Princess* (1910), and *Peggy* (1911).

Stuck, Jean Baptiste, cellist and composer of operas; b. Florence, c. 1680; d. Paris, Dec. 9, 1755. He played the cello in theater orchestras in Italy and in Paris, and also wrote incidental music for various plays; lived most of his life in Paris, except for a brief sojourn in Bavaria (1714). He wrote 3 operas to French texts: *Méléagre* (1709), *Manto la fée* (1711), *Polidore* (Feb. 15, 1720), and ballets for the Versailles Court. He publ. 4 books of cantatas (1706, 1708, 1711, 1714); a collection of airs (1709).

Stucken, Van Der. See **Van Der Stucken.**

Stuckenschmidt, Hans Heinz, eminent German music critic and writer; b. Strasbourg, Nov. 1, 1901. He studied piano and composition; from 1929 till 1933 he was music critic of the Berlin daily 'B. Z. am Mittag,' and was active as a lecturer and writer on modern music. In 1934 he was forbidden to continue journalism in Germany, and went to Prague, where he wrote music criticism until 1941, when his activities were stopped once more by the occupation authorities; was drafted into the Germany army; after the war became director of the department for new music of the radio station RIAS in Berlin; also was lecturer at the Technical Univ. there (1948). He publ. *Arnold Schönberg* (Zürich, 1951) and *Neue Musik* (as vol. 2 of the series 'Zwischen den beiden Kriegen,' Berlin, 1951; in French, Paris, 1956). With Josef Rufer, founded and edited the monthly musical magazine 'Stimmen' (Berlin, 1947-49).

Stückgold, Grete *(née* Schneidt), soprano; b. London, June 6, 1895. Her mother was English, her father German. She studied voice with Jacques Stückgold, whom she married (divorced in 1928). She was a member of the Berlin State Opera before coming to America in 1927. On Nov. 2, 1927 she made her début at the Metropolitan Opera as Eva in *Die Meistersinger,* and remained on its roster until 1939. In 1953 she opened an opera school in N. Y. Her second husband was Gustav Schützendorf (q.v.).

Stückgold, Jacques, singing teacher and writer; b. Warsaw, Jan. 29, 1877; d. New York, May 4, 1953. He studied in Venice; in 1899 settled in Germany as singing teacher; in 1933 came to the U. S., and lived in N. Y. He publ. *Der Bankrott der deutschen Gesangskunst* and *Über Stimmbildungskunst.*

Stumpf, Carl, German musicologist; b. Wiesentheid, Lower Franconia, April 21, 1848; d. Berlin, Dec. 29, 1936. He studied philosophy, theology, and the natural sciences at Würzburg and Göttingen (*Dr. phil.,* 1870), and in 1873 became full prof. at Würzburg; from 1879 at Prague, from 1884 at Halle, from 1889 at Munich, and from 1893 at Berlin; retired in 1928. A profound student of music, he wrote valuable works dealing with the physiological and psychological aspects of that subject. Ed. 'Beiträge zur Akustik und Musikwissenschaft' (1898-1924) and, with Hornbostel, the 'Sammelbände für vergleichende Musikwissenschaft' (from 1922). —Publ. *Tonpsychologie* (2 vols., 1883, 1890), extending the researches of Helmholtz; *Die pseudo-aristotelischen Probleme über Musik* (1897); *Geschichte des Konsonanzbegriffs* (1897); *Die Anfänge der Musik* (1911); *Die Sprachlaute. Experimentellphonetische Untersuchungen nebst einem Anhang über Instrumentalklänge* (1926); *Lieder der Bellakula-Indianer,* in 'Vierteljahrsschrift für Musikwissenschaft' II (1886); etc. —Cf. E. Schumann, *Die Förderung der Musikwissenschaft durch die akustischpsychologische Forschung C. Stumpfs,* in 'Archiv für Musikwissenschaft' (1923); C. Sachs, *Zu Carl Stumpfs achtzigstem Geburtstag,* in 'Zeitschrift für Musikwissenschaft' (vol. 10).

Stuntz, Joseph Hartmann, German conductor and composer; b. Arlesheim, near Basel, July 25, 1793; d. Munich, June 18,

1859. He studied in Munich with Peter Winter; succeeded him as conductor in 1826; wrote several operas produced at Munich; publ. 2 overtures; a string quartet; men's choruses.

Sturgeon, Nicholas, English divine and composer; date and place of birth unknown; d. London, May 31, 1454. In 1442 he became precentor of St. Paul's Cathedral, London. He was the owner, and possibly the scribe, of the MSS found in Old Hall, near Ware; 7 works by Sturgeon (2 not complete) are part of the Old Hall MS collection, including a curious isorhythmic motet, *Salve mater Domini,* for 3 voices, which was probably written for the journey of Henry V to France (1416), on which Sturgeon accompanied him.

Stürmer, Bruno, German composer; b. Freiburg-im-Breisgau, Sept. 9, 1892; d. Bad Homburg, May 19, 1958; studied piano at the Cons. of Karlsruhe; then organ and composition with Philipp Wolfrum at the Univ. of Heidelberg; musicology with Sandberger and Kroyer at the Univ. of Munich. After service in the German Army during World War I, he taught piano in Karlsruhe (1917-22); was theater conductor in Remscheid, Essen, and Duisburg (1922-27); in 1927 founded a music school in Homberg; then was conductor of choral societies in Kassel and elsewhere (until 1945); after 1945, lived in Darmstadt and Frankfurt. He was a prolific composer (about 150 op. numbers); wrote in a distinctively modern manner, leaning towards neo-Classicism; was particularly adept in choral writing; his most notable work was *Die Messe des Maschinenmenschen,* for baritone, male chorus, and orch. (1932). Other works: dance drama, *Die Maske der Katze;* cantatas with orch.: *Von der Vergänglichkeit, Vom Tod zum Leben, Aus Liebe, Gott in der Natur;* for voice with chamber groups: *Erlösungen, Marienlieder, Lieder der Geischa, Lieder aus den Lüften, Musikantenleben, Das Lied vom Kinde,* etc.; *Der Zug des Todes,* for 8-part chorus and percussion; *Der Rattenfänger von Hamelin,* for baritone, children's chorus, and chamber orch.; a Requiem; many choruses a cappella; for orch.: *Heitere Sinfonie, Burleske Musik, Feierliche Musik* for 2 string orchestras, *Tanzsuite* for chamber orch., suite for amateur orch., piano concerto, violin concerto, cello concerto; chamber music: quintet for wind instruments, divertimento for clarinet and string quartet, 2 string quartets, 5 piano trios, clarinet trio, violin sonata, viola sonata, cello sonata, flute sonata, oboe sonata; piano pieces.

Stutchevsky, Joachim, cellist and composer, b. Romny, Ukraine, Feb. 7, 1891. He studied cello with Julius Klengel in Leipzig (1909-12); lived in Zürich (1912-24) and Vienna (1924-38). In 1938 he settled in Palestine; visited N. Y. in 1948. He publ. *Das Violoncellspiel* (Vienna, 1932; 4 vols.) and other technical studies for his instrument; composed a *Chassidic Suite* for cello and piano (1946); several other pieces for cello; *Twilight,* duet for 2 recorders (1951); piano pieces on Jewish themes; made numerous arrangements for cello of works by Mozart, Tartini, Boccherini, etc.

Subirá (Puig), José, eminent Spanish musicologist; b. Barcelona, Aug. 20, 1882. He studied at the Madrid Cons., winning 1st prizes for piano (1900) and composition (1904). He also qualified for the practice of law in 1904 (*Dr. jur.,* 1923). From 1908-10 he studied music history and esthetics at Antwerp. In 1928 he was made Officier de la Légion d'Honneur. He specialized in the study of old Spanish theater-music, and his work in this field is extremely valuable: *La Tonadilla escénica,* 3 vols. (Madrid, 1928-30); *La Participación musical en el antiguo teatro español* (Barcelona, 1930); *Tonadillas teatrales inéditas* (Madrid, 1932); *Celos aun del aire matan, Opera del siglo XVII* (cf. **Hidalgo**; Barcelona, 1933); *La Opera en los teatros de Barcelona* (2 vols.; Barcelona, 1946); *Historia de la música teatral en España* (Barcelona, 1945); *Historia y anecdotario del Teatro Real* (Madrid, 1949); *El Compositor Iriarte . . . y el cultivo español del melólogo* (2 vols.; Barcelona, 1949-50); *El Teatro del Real Palacio* (Madrid, 1950). Other publications: *Enrique Granados* (Madrid, 1926); *La Música en la Casa de Alba* (Madrid, 1927); *Manuscritos de Barbieri existentes en la Biblioteca Nacional* (Madrid, 1936); *Historia de la música* (2 vols.; Madrid, 1947; revised ed., 1951); *La Música, etapas y aspectos . . .* (Barcelona, 1949); *Historia de la música española y hispano-americana* (Barcelona, 1953); *Sinfonismos madrileños del siglo XIX* (Madrid, 1954); *Temario de critica musical* (Madrid, 1955). With H. Anglés he publ. a *Catálogo musical de la Biblioteca nacional de Madrid* (vol. 1, Barcelona, 1946). In 1953 he was elected member of the Royal Academy of Fine Arts in Madrid. Apart from his musicological works, he publ. a novel, *Su virginal pureza* (1916) and a historic account, *Los Españoles en la guerra de 1914-1918* (4 vols.).

Such, Percy Frederick, cellist and music editor; b. London, June 27, 1878. He studied cello in Germany (1892-98); appeared frequently with the Joachim Quartet; settled in the U. S.; in 1928 became prof. of cello at Rutgers Univ., and subsequently was on the faculty of the N. Y. College of Music (1938-49). With Sir Donald Tovey he edited the cello sonatas of Beethoven; publ. about 50 cello arrangements of Classical works, and editions of old cello music.

Sucher (zōō'-her), **Joseph,** conductor; b. Döbör, Hungary, Nov. 23, 1843; d. Berlin, April 4, 1908. He studied in Vienna with Sechter; in 1876 was conductor of the Leipzig City Theater; 1877, married the soprano Rosa Hasselbeck; they were at the Hamburg Stadttheater from 1878 to 1888; Sucher then became conductor of the Berlin Opera, his wife being engaged there as prima donna. He was especially distinguished as an interpreter of the Wagner repertory. He composed several vocal works: *Aus alten Märchen,* for women's voices with orch.; *Waldfräulein,* for soprano solo, mixed chorus, and orch.; *Seeschlacht bei Lepanto* for male chorus and orch.; songs (*Ruheort,* etc.).

Sucher, Rosa *(née* Hasselbeck), operatic soprano; wife of Joseph Sucher; b. Velburg, Germany, Feb. 23, 1849; d. Eschweiler, April 16, 1927. She received her first instruction from her father, a chorusmaster; sang in Berlin and Danzig; then in Leipzig, where she married the conductor Joseph Sucher (1877); both were engaged for Hamburg (1878-88) and then at the Berlin Opera. From 1886 to 1899 she sang at every Wagner Festival in Bayreuth, and in 1895 she appeared in the great Wagner roles in Damrosch's season at the Metropolitan Opera, making her American début as Isolde (Feb. 25, 1895). Her repertory included every soprano part from Senta to Kundry in Wagner's music dramas; her interpretation of Beethoven's Fidelio was regarded as equal to that of Katharina Klafsky and Lilli Lehmann in excellence. She publ. the memoirs *Aus meinem Leben* (Leipzig, 1914).

Suchon, Eugen, Slovak composer; b. Pezinok, Sept. 25, 1908. He studied at the Bratislava Cons. (1927-31) and at the Prague Master School with Novák (1931-33). In 1933 he joined the faculty of the Bratislava Univ. He continued to compose, striving to achieve a distinct Slovak style in his music. His most important work is the opera *Krútnava* (*The Whirlpool*), produced in Bratislava on Dec. 10, 1949. He further wrote a serenade for strings, a piano quartet, a serenade for wind quintet, many choruses, piano pieces. —Cf. John Clapham, *The Whirlpool, a Slovak Opera,* in the 'Music Review' (Feb., 1958).

Suckling, Norman, English composer and writer on music; b. London, Oct. 24, 1904. He received his academic education at Queen's College, Oxford; was assistant master at Liverpool Collegiate School (1925-43); then lectured on French literature at King's College in Newcastle-on-Tyne. While thus occupied, he developed sufficient mastery of the piano to give concerts, specializing in modern French music. He publ. a biography of Gabriel Fauré in the 'Master Musicians Series' (London, 1946) and books dealing with French literature. His compositions are mostly in smaller forms (chamber music; vocal pieces).

Suda, Stanislav, blind Czech flutist and composer; b. Starý Plzenec, April 30, 1865; d. Plzen, Aug. 28, 1931. He was brought up at the Prague Institute for the Blind, and developed his innate musical abilities to the point where he could give concerts and compose operas, 3 of which were produced at Plzen: *U Božich Muk* (March 22, 1897); *Lešetínský Kovář* (April 4, 1903); and *Il divino Boemo* (Dec. 30, 1927). He also wrote an autobiographical symph. poem, *Život ve tmách (The Life in Darkness).*

Sudds, William, English composer; b. London, March 5, 1843; d. Gouverneur, New York, Sept. 25, 1920. He was taken to America as a child; was a bandmaster during the Civil War; studied violin with Eichberg in Boston; wrote over 100 piano pieces and about 75 peces of church music; many songs, etc. He publ. 2 albums of organ music, *Organ Gems* and *50 Organ Voluntaries;* also guides to violin playing, a piano method, etc.

Suggia, Guilhermina, Portuguese cellist; b. Oporto, June 27, 1888; d. there, July 31, 1950. She was a child prodigy, and played 1st cello in the Oporto Orch. at the age of 12. Under the patronage of the Queen of Portugal she was sent to Leipzig in 1904 to study with Julius Klengel; made her début with the Gewandhaus Orch. under Nikisch at the age of 17. In 1906 she married Pablo Casals (divorced 1912). Shortly afterwards she settled in London, where she continued to appear in concerts until 1949, when she went back to Portugal. She was greatly appreciated for her fine musicianship as well as virtuosity. In 1923 Augustus John painted her portrait, which became celebrated.

Suk, Josef, Czech violinist and composer; b. Křečovice, Jan. 4, 1874; d. Benešov, near Prague, May 29, 1935. He studied with his father, a chorusmaster, and at the Prague Cons.; after graduation he took a course in composition with Dvořák, whose daughter Otilie he married in 1898. In 1892 he became a 2nd violinist in the celebrated Bohemian String Quartet, continuing until 1922, when he became a prof. at the Prague Cons. He was a devoted follower of Dvořák in his style of composition; his works are cast in a characteristically Romantic vein, with the rhythmic elements drawn from Bohemian folk music. When his wife died in 1905, he was disconsolate; he expressed his sorrow in his 2nd symph., *Asrael,* dedicated to her memory and to the memory of Dvořák. He continued to compose, developing an individual manner marked by deep expressiveness and religious feeling.—Works: operatic fairy-tale, *Radúz and Mahulena* (Prague, April 6, 1898); dramatic legend, *Pod jabloní (Under the Apple Trees;* 1902; Prague, Jan. 31,.1934); for orch.: *Dramatic Overture* (Prague, July 9, 1892); symphony in E major (Prague, Nov. 25, 1899); *Prague,* symph. poem (1904); *Scherzo fantastique* (Prague, April 18, 1905); *Asrael,* 2nd symph. (Prague, Feb. 3, 1907); *Pohádka léta (A Summer Fairy-Tale;* Prague, Jan. 26, 1909); *Zrání,* symph. poem (Prague, Oct. 30, 1918); *Meditation on the Chorale 'St. Venceslas'* (1914); *Epilogue,* for solo voices, chorus, and orch. (1920-32); *Fantasy,* for violin and orch. (Prague, Jan. 9, 1904); 2 string quartets; piano quartet; piano trio; piano quintet; *Allegro giocoso,* for string quartet; other chamber music; several sets of choruses; a number of piano pieces. —Cf. *Josef Suk,* a collection of articles, ed. by J. M. Květ (Prague, 1935); V. Štěpan, *Novák a Suk* (Prague, 1945); J. Berkovec, *Josef Suk* (Prague, 1956).

Suk, Váša, Czech conductor and composer; b. Kladno, Nov. 16, 1861; d. Moscow, Jan. 12, 1933. He studied with Fibich at the Prague Cons.; then played the violin in the Warsaw Symph. (1879-81); conducted opera in Kiev and Moscow (1881-84); in 1906 joined the staff of the Moscow Opera. He was appreciated in Russia for his thoroughness in drilling the singers and the orch.; achieved a fine reputation as an operatic conductor. He wrote an opera, *The Forest King,* which he conducted at Kharkov on Feb. 16, 1900; a symph. poem, *Jan Huss;* a serenade for string orch.; a number of piano pieces and songs. —Cf. I. Remezov, *V. Suk* (Moscow, 1933).

Sulek (shoo'-lek), **Stjepan,** Croatian violinist and composer; b. Zagreb, Aug. 5, 1914. He studied violin with V. Huml; in composition mainly self-taught; yet he succeeded in becoming a composer of considerable merit. Among his works are 4 symphonies (of which the 2nd, *Eroica,* received a State Prize), a violin concerto, a cello concerto, 2 piano concertos, etc.

Sullivan, Sir **Arthur Seymour,** famous English composer; b. London, May 13, 1842; d. there, Nov. 22, 1900. In 1854 he entered the Chapel Royal as a chorister, under Helmore; publ. an anthem in 1855; was elected (the first) Mendelssohn Scholar in 1856, studying at the Royal Academy of Music from 1857 under Bennett, Goss, and O'Leary, and at the Leipzig Cons. 1858-61 under Moscheles, Hauptmann, Richter, Plaidy, etc., conducting a performance of his overture to *Lalla Rookh* in 1860, and writing string quartets and music to *The Tempest* (Crystal Palace, April 5, 1862). His cantata *Kenilworth* (Birmingham Festival, Sept. 8, 1864) stamped him as a composer of high rank. In 1864 he visited Ireland and there composed his 'Irish Symphony.' In 1866 he was appointed prof. of composition at the Royal Academy of Music. About this time he formed a life-long friendship with Sir George Grove, whom he accompanied in 1867 on a memorable journey to Vienna in search of Schubert MSS, leading to the discovery of the score of *Rosamunde.* The year 1867 was also notable for the production of the first of those comic operas upon which Sullivan's fame chiefly rests. This was *Cox and Box* (libretto by F. C. Burnand), composed in 2 weeks and performed on April 27 at the home of Arthur Lewis; later it had a long public run. Less successful were *The Contrabandista* (London, Dec. 18, 1867) and *Thespis* (London, Dec. 23, 1871); but the latter is significant as inaugurating Sullivan's collaboration with Sir W. S. Gilbert, the celebrated humorist, who became the librettist of all his most successful comic operas, beginning with *Trial by Jury* (March 25, 1875). This was produced by Richard D'Oyly Carte, who in 1876 formed a company expressly for the production of the 'Gilbert and Sullivan' operas. The first big success obtained by the famous team was with *H.M.S. Pinafore* (May 25, 1878), which had 700 consecutive performances in London, and enjoyed an enormous vogue in 'pirated' productions throughout the U. S. In an endeavor to protect their interests, Gilbert and Sullivan went to N. Y. in 1879 to give an authorized performance of *Pina-*

fore, and while there they also produced *The Pirates of Penzance* (Dec. 31, 1879). On April 25, 1881, came *Patience,* a satire on exaggerated esthetic poses as exemplified by Oscar Wilde, whose American lecture-tour was conceived as a 'publicity stunt' for this work. On Nov. 25, 1882, *Iolanthe, or The Peer and the Peri,* began a run that lasted more than a year. This was followed by the comparatively unsuccessful *Princess Ida* (Jan. 5, 1884), but then came the universal favorite of all the Gilbert and Sullivan operas, *The Mikado* (March 14, 1885). The list of these popular works is completed by *Ruddigore* (Jan. 22, 1887), *The Yeomen of the Guard* (Oct. 3, 1888); and *The Gondoliers* (Dec. 7, 1889). After a quarrel and a reconciliation, the two collaborated in 2 further works, of less popularity, *Utopia Limited* (Oct. 7, 1893) and *The Grand Duke* (March 7, 1896). Sullivan's melodic inspiration and technical resourcefulness, united to the delicious humor of Gilbert's verses, raised the light opera to a new height of artistic achievement and his works in this field continue to delight countless hearers. —Sullivan was also active in other branches of musical life. He conducted numerous series of concerts, more especially those of the London Philh. Society (1885-87) and the Leeds Festivals (1880-98). He was principal of, and prof. of composition at, the National Training School for Music from 1876 to his resignation in 1881. Received the degree of Mus. Doc. *hon. causa* from Cambridge (1876) and Oxford (1879); Chevalier of the Legion of Honor, 1878; grand organist to the Freemasons, 1887; etc. He was knighted by Queen Victoria in 1883. Parallel with his comic creations, he composed many 'serious' works, including the grand opera *Ivanhoe* (Jan. 31, 1891), which enjoyed a momentary vogue. Among his cantatas the most successful was *The Golden Legend,* after Longfellow (Leeds Festival, Oct. 16, 1886). His songs were highly popular in their day and *The Lost Chord* is still a favorite. Among his oratorios, *The Light of the World* (1873) may be mentioned. —Other stage works: *The Zoo* (1875); *The Sorcerer* (1877); *Haddon Hall* (1892); *The Chieftain* (revision of *The Contrabandista;* 1894); *The Martyr of Antioch* (Edinburgh, 1898; a stage arrangement of the cantata); *The Beauty-Stone* (with Pinero; May 28, 1898); the romantic opera *The Rose of Persia* (1900); *The Emerald Isle* (completed by E. German, 1901); 2 ballets, *L'Ile enchanté* (1864) and *Victoria and Merrie England* (1897). —BIBLIOGRAPHY: A. Lawrence, *Sir A. S. Life-Story, Letters and Reminiscences* (with complete list of works; Chicago, 1900); W. J. Wells, *Souvenir of Sir A. S.* (London, 1901); B. W. Findon, *Sir A. S. His Life and Music* (London, 1904); B. W. Findon, *Sir A. S. and His Operas* (London, 1908); F. Cellier and C. Bridgeman, *Gilbert, S., and D'Oyly Carte* (London, 1914); H. M. Walbrook, *Gilbert and S.: a History and a Comment* (1922); S. J. A. Fitz-Gerald, *The Story of the Savoy Opera* (London, 1924); A. H. Godwin, *Gilbert and S.* (1926); H. Saxe Wyndham, *A. S. S.* (1926); N. Flower and H. Sullivan, *A. S.* (1927); T. F. Dunhill, *S.'s Comic Operas* (1928); L. Bradstock, *S.* (1928); I. Goldberg, *The Story of Gilbert and S.* (1928); F. J. Halton, *The Gilbert and S. Operas; a Concordance* (N. Y., 1935); H. Pearson, *Gilbert and S.* (N. Y., 1935); G. E. Dunn, *A Gilbert and S. Dictionary* (N. Y., 1936); C. L. Purdy, *Gilbert and S.: Masters of Mirth and Melody* (N. Y., 1947); W. A. Darlington, *The World of Gilbert and S.* (N. Y., 1950); A. Jacobs, *Gilbert and S.* (London, 1951); L. Bailey, *The Gilbert and S. Book* (N. Y., 1952; new ed., 1957); A. Williamson, *Gilbert and S. Opera: a New Assessment* (N. Y., 1953).

Sulzer, Salomon, Austrian music scholar; b. Hohenems, Vorarlberg, March 30, 1804; d. Vienna, Jan. 17, 1890. He studied with Seyfried at Vienna, where he was cantor of the chief synagogue from 1825. He was prof. of singing at the Cons. 1844-47; received the gold medal for science and art; also in 1868 the Order of Franz Joseph. —Works: 'Schir Zion' (Hebrew hymns); 'Dudaim' (songs for school and home); Psalms; etc. —His son **Julius Salomon** (b. Vienna, 1834; d. there, Feb. 13, 1891) was a violinist; after long travels in the East, he became conductor at the Hofburgtheater at Vienna in 1875. He wrote several operas, a *Symphonisches Tongemälde,* piano music, songs.

Sumac, Yma (real name Emperatriz Chavarri), Peruvian soprano; b. Ichocan, Sept. 10, 1927, of Indian-Spanish ancestry. She spent her childhood in the highlands (altitude 12,000 feet), and instinctively acquired an enormously powerful voice, ranging from the low baritone to high soprano; this phenomenal compass created a sensation when she first appeared in the U. S.; she gave recitals, and sang on the radio; also took part in motion pictures. She was married to the Peruvian composer Moises Vivanco (divorced); became a U. S. citizen in 1955.

Sundelius, Marie, eminent singer and vocal teacher; b. Karlsbad, Sweden, Feb. 4, 1884; d. Boston, June 26, 1958. She was taken to America at the age of 8, and studied singing in Boston; made her début as an opera singer with the Metropolitan Opera, N. Y., on Nov. 25, 1916; made a tour of Sweden in 1924; then returned to Boston.

Sundgrén-Schnéevoigt, Sigrid Ingeborg, pianist; b. Helsingfors, June 17, 1878; d. Stockholm, Sept. 14, 1953. She studied at the Cons. of Helsingfors, and then with Busoni in Berlin (1894-97). In 1907 she married the conductor Georg Schnéevoigt (q.v.), with whom she made several tours of Scandinavia and Germany; from 1910 was for many years piano teacher at the Helsingfors Cons.; later lived in Paris; toured the U. S.

Suñol y Baulenas, Dom **Gregorio María,** learned Spanish ecclesiastic; authority on Gregorian chant; b. Barcelona, Sept. 7, 1879; d. Rome, Oct. 26, 1946. He studied at Montserrat and at the Abbey of Solesmes; became prior of the Monastery of Montserrat and president of the Asociación Gregoriana of Barcelona. During his last years he was president of the Pontificio Istituto di Musica Sacra in Rome. He publ. the valuable editions *Método completo de Canto gregoriano* (6 Spanish eds.; also in English, French, and German); *Introducció a la paleografia musical gregoriana* (Montserrat, 1925; also in French, 1935); *Els Cants dels Romeus,* in 'Analecta Montserratensia' (with examples of folk music from the 14th century); brought out *Antiphonale missarum juxta ritum sanctae ecclesiae mediolanensis* (1935).

Supervia, Conchita, Spanish mezzo-soprano; b. Barcelona, Dec. 8, 1899; d. London, March 30, 1936. She sang at La Scala, Milan, at the Paris Opéra, and at the Opéra-Comique; toured in the U. S.; in 1931 she settled in London, and appeared several times at Covent Garden.

Suppé (sŏŏp'-pā), **Franz von,** famous operetta composer; b. Spalato, Dalmatia, April 18, 1819; d. Vienna, May 21, 1895. He was of Belgian descent, and his real name was Francesco Ezechiele Ermenegildo Cavaliere Suppe-Demelli. At the age of 11 he played the flute, and at 15 wrote a Mass. He was then sent by his father to study philosophy at Padua, where he also took music courses with Cigala and Ferrari; on his father's death he went with his mother to Vienna, where he continued serious study at the Vienna Cons. with Sechter and Seyfried. He became a conductor in the theaters of Pressburg and Baden, and then was on the staff at the Theater an der Wien (until 1862), at the Carl Theater (until 1865), and subsequently at the Leopoldstadt Theater. All the while, he wrote light operas and other theater music of all degrees of levity, obtaining increasing success rivaling that of Offenbach. His music possesses the charm and gayety of the Viennese genre, but there is also an element of more vigorous and at times more vulgar popular rhythms. His most celebrated single work is the overture to *Dichter und Bauer* (*Poet and Peasant*), which still retains a firm place in the light repertory. His total output comprises about 30 comic operas and operettas and 180 other stage pieces, most of which were brought out in Vienna; of these the following obtained considerable success: *Dichter und Bauer* (Aug. 24, 1846); *Das Mädchen vom Lande* (Aug. 7, 1847); *Der Bandit* (1848; in Italy as *Cartouche*); *Paragraph 3* (Jan. 8, 1858); *Das Pensionat* (Nov. 24, 1860); *Die Kartenaufschlägerin* (April 26, 1862); *Zehn Mädchen und kein Mann* (Oct. 25, 1862); *Flotte Bursche* (April 18, 1863); *Franz Schubert* (Sept. 10, 1864); *Die schöne Galatea* (Sept. 9, 1865); *Leichte Cavallerie* (March 24, 1866; enormously popular); *Freigeister* (Oct. 23, 1866); *Banditenstreiche* (April 27, 1867); *Die Frau Meisterin* (Jan. 20, 1868); *Tantalusqualen* (Oct. 3, 1868); *Isabella* (Nov. 5, 1869); *Cannebas* (Nov. 2, 1872); *Fatinitza* (Jan. 5, 1876; extremely popular); *Der Teufel auf Erden* (Jan. 5, 1878); *Boccaccio* (Feb. 1, 1879; very popular); *Donna Juanita* (Feb. 21, 1880); *Der Gascogner* (March 22, 1881); *Herzblättchen* (Feb. 4, 1882); *Die Afrikareise* (March 17, 1883); *Bellmann* (Feb. 26, 1887); *Die Jagd nach dem Glücke* (Oct. 27, 1888); *Das Modell* (posthumous; Oct. 4, 1895); *Die Pariserin* (posthumous; Jan. 26, 1898); several other operettas were produced in Prague, Berlin, and Hamburg. In addition to his theater works, he wrote a symphony; several string quartets; songs; also a *Missa dalmatica* (1867). —Cf. G. Sabalich, *F. Suppé e l'operetta* (Zara, 1888); O. Keller, *Franz von Suppé, der Schöpfer der deutschen Operette* (Leipzig, 1905); E. Rieger, *Offenbach und seine Wiener Schule* (Vienna, 1920).

Surette, Thomas Whitney, eminent American music educator; b. Concord, Mass., Sept. 7, 1861; d. there, May 19, 1941. He studied with Arthur Foote (piano) and J. K.

Paine (theory) at Harvard Univ. (graduated 1891); was church organist at Concord (1883-93); then teacher at Pottstown, Pa., and organist at Baltimore. In 1909 he was appointed staff lecturer in the extension department of Oxford Univ.; later, a member of the advisory board of music for the Boston Public Schools. He was extremely influential in shaping the musical curriculum in New England; in 1914 he founded the Concord Summer School of Music, which attracted students from all parts of the country. With A. T. Davison he edited 'The Concord Series' of educational music, which was adopted in many schools throughout the U. S. In 1921 he became head of the music department at Bryn Mawr College; from 1937 to 1939, he taught at Black Mountain College, N. C.; then retired. His publications include *The Appreciation of Music* (with D. G. Mason; 5 vols., of which vols. 2 and 5 are by Mason alone; N. Y., 1907; 16 printings before 1950); *Course of Study on the Development of Symphonic Music* (Chicago, 1915); *Music and Life* (Boston, 1917); various other publications on music history and music appreciation. He was also a composer; his light opera *Priscilla, or The Pilgrim's Proxy,* after Longfellow, first produced at Concord, on March 6, 1889, had more than 1,000 performances in the U. S.; he also wrote an opera, *Cascabel or The Broken Tryst* (Pittsburgh, May 15, 1899).

Suriano (or **Soriano**), **Francesco,** a composer of the Roman school; b. Soriano, 1549; d. there, after 1621. Was a chorister at St. John Lateran; later a pupil of Nanino and Palestrina. In 1580, choirmaster at S. Ludovico de' Francesi; from 1581-86, in Mantua; in 1587 at S. Maria Maggiore; 1588 again at S. Ludovico, returning to S. Maria Maggiore in 1595; in 1599 at St. John Lateran, and from 1600 once more at S. Maria Maggiore (pensioned June 23, 1620). He collaborated with F. Anerio in the revision of the 'Editio Medicaea' of the Gradual (cf. Palestrina). Publ. 2 books of madrigals *a* 5 (1581, 1592); 1 book of madrigals *a* 4 (1601); motets *a* 8 (1597); Masses *a* 4-8 (1609; includes an arrangement of Palestrina's *Missa Papae Marcelli* for 8 voices); *Canoni . . . sopra l'Ave Maris Stella a 3-8 voci* (1610); 2 books of psalms and motets (1614, 1616); *Villanelle a 3* (1617); a Passion and several Magnificats (1619). —Cf. F. X. Haberl, in 'Kirchenmusikalisches Jahrbuch' (1895); R. Molitor, *Die nachtridentinische Choralreform* (1901-02).

Surinach, Carlos, Spanish composer and conductor; b. Barcelona, March 4, 1915. He studied in Barcelona with Morera (1936-39) and with Max Trapp in Berlin (1939-43). Returning to Spain in 1943, he was engaged as conductor of the Gran Teatro del Liceo in Barcelona; acted as guest conductor in Lisbon and in Paris, where he lived from 1947 to 1950; then settled in New York. — Works: *El Mozo que casó con mujer brava,* 1-act opera (Barcelona, Jan. 10, 1948); ballet, *Monte Carlo* (Barcelona, May 2, 1945); *Passacaglia Symphony* (Barcelona, April 8, 1945, composer conducting); 2nd symph. (Paris Radio, Jan. 26, 1950, composer conducting); *Sinfonietta flamenca* (Louisville, Jan. 9, 1954); *Feria magica,* overture (Louisville, March 14, 1956); also *Tres Cantos Berberes,* for flute, oboe, clarinet, viola, cello, and harp (1952); *Flamenquerías* for 2 pianos (1952); *Rítmo Jondo,* for clarinet, trumpet, xylophone, and percussion (N. Y., May 5, 1952; extended version, in ballet form, *Deep Rhythm,* was performed N. Y., April 15, 1953); *Tientos,* for English horn, harpsichord, and timpani (1953); a string quartet; songs; piano pieces.

Surzynski, Józef, Polish music scholar; b. Szrem, near Poznan, March 15, 1851; d. Koscian, March 5, 1919. He studied at Regensburg and Leipzig, then theology in Rome. In 1882 he returned to Poznan, dedicating himself to the codification of Polish sacred music; also was conductor of the cathedral chorus there. Beginning in 1885, he brought out the valuable series 'Monumenta Musices Sacrae in Polonia,' containing works by Polish composers of the 16th and 17th centuries; also publ. several manuals for use in Polish churches; wrote many choral compositions, using Gregorian modes. His two brothers, Stefan and Mieczyslaw, were also musicians.

Susato, Johannes (real name Johannes Steinwert von Soest), German composer and singing master; b. Unna, 1448; d. Frankfurt, May 2, 1506. He was a chorister at Soest, then was in Cleve and Bruges, where he studied with English musicians; was subsequently active as singing master in Cologne, Kassel, and, from 1472, Heidelberg; Virdung was one of his pupils there. He was also a physician, and about 1500 went to Frankfurt as a municipal doctor.

Susato, Tielman, German publisher and composer; probably son of Johannes Susato; b. Cologne; d. Antwerp, c. 1561. In 1529 he moved from Cologne to Antwerp, where he was a town trumpeter; then established a music printing shop (1543) and issued 13 books of chansons, 4 vols. of Masses, 4 vols. of motets, 4 books of various songs, etc.; several of these miscellaneous works were of his own composition. —Cf. P. Bergmans, *Un Imprimeur musicien: Tilman Susato,* in the 'Bulletin de la Société Bibliophile Anversoise' (Antwerp, 1923). See also A. Goovaerts, *Histoire et bibliographie de la typographie musicale dans les Pays-Bas* (Antwerp, 1880).

Susskind, Walter, conductor; b. Prague, May 1, 1913. He studied composition with Josef Suk and Alois Hába, and conducting with Szell; in 1932 made his début as conductor at the German Opera House in Prague. In 1939 he went to Holland as pianist; then to England, where he conducted the Carl Rosa Opera Co. (1942-45). After the end of the war he conducted the Sadler's Wells Opera Co. in Germany; in 1946 he was appointed conductor of the Scottish Orch. in Glasgow; held this position until 1954, when he became conductor of the Victoria Symph. Orch. in Melbourne. —Cf. Donald Brook, *International Gallery of Conductors* (Bristol, 1951; pp. 200-06).

Süssmayr, Franz Xaver, Austrian composer; b. Schwanenstadt, 1766; d. Vienna, Sept. 17, 1803. He was a pupil of Salieri, and also of Mozart, of whom he became an intimate friend; after Mozart's death his widow entrusted the completion of his Requiem to Süssmayr; he was clever in emulating Mozart's style of composition, and his handwriting was so much like Mozart's that it is difficult to distinguish between them. He was conductor at the National Theater in Vienna from 1792, and 2nd conductor at the Court Opera from 1794; wrote a number of operas and operettas, which he produced in Vienna, among them: *Moses* (May 4, 1792); *L'Incanto superato* (July 8, 1793); *Der Spiegel von Arkadien* (Nov. 14, 1794); *Idris und Zenide* (May 9, 1795); *Die edle Rache* (Aug. 27, 1795); *Die Freiwilligen* (Sept. 27, 1796); *Der Wildfang* (Oct. 4, 1797); *Der Marktschreier* (July 6, 1799); *Soliman der Zweite, oder Die drei Sultaninnen* (Oct. 1, 1799); *Gülnare (Gonora;* July 5, 1800); *Phasma* (July 25, 1801). He wrote *secco* recitatives for Mozart's opera *La Clemenza di Tito* (Prague, Sept. 6, 1791); composed several numbers for the Vienna production of Grétry's *La double épreuve,* given there under the title *Die doppelte Erkenntlichkeit* (Feb. 28, 1796). Other works include a clarinet concerto and pieces for the English horn, for guitar, and other instruments. Most of his works are in MS. —Cf. G. L. P. Sievers, *Mozart und Süssmayr* (1829); W. Pole, *Mozart's Requiem* (1879); W. Lehner, *F. X. Süssmayr als Opernkomponist,* in 'Studien zur Musikwissenschaft' (vol. 18; 1931).

Suter (zōō'-tĕr), **Hermann,** Swiss composer and conductor; b. Kaiserstuhl, April 28, 1870; d. Basel, June 22, 1926. He was a pupil of his father, an organist and cantor; then studied with Hans Huber in Basel; also took courses in Stuttgart with Faisst and in Leipzig with Reinecke (1888-91). From 1892 to 1902 he conducted choral societies in various Swiss communities; in 1896 was appointed to the faculty of the Zürich Cons.; in 1902, settled in Basel, where he was active as conductor and teacher; was director of the Basel Cons. from 1918 to 1921. His best-known work is the oratorio *Le Laudi di S. Francesco d'Assisi* (1924); he also wrote a number of other vocal works, a symph., a violin concerto, 3 string quartets, a string sextet, and 3 song cycles. —Cf. W. Merian, *Hermann Suter* (Basel, 1936).

Sutermeister, Heinrich, Swiss composer; b. Feuerthalen, Aug. 12, 1910. He studied literature in Basel and Paris, then entered the Munich Academy of Music, where he was a pupil of Courvoisier and Orff; his main endeavor was to create a type of modern opera that would be dramatically effective and melodically pleasing; in this he has largely succeeded. He wrote his own librettos. His first, and greatest, success was the Shakespearean opera *Romeo und Julia* (Dresden, April 13, 1940); there followed *Die Zauberinsel,* after Shakespeare's *The Tempest* (Dresden, Oct. 30, 1942); *Niobe* (Zürich, June 22, 1946); *Raskolnikoff,* after Dostoyevsky's *Crime and Punishment* (Stockholm, Oct. 14, 1948); and *Die Rote Stiefel* (Stockholm, Nov. 22, 1951). Especially for the radio he wrote an opera in 1 act, *Die schwarze Spinne* (1936; revised for the stage, and produced at St. Gall, on March 2, 1949); his radio ballad *Füsse im Feuer,* was also arranged for an operatic production, and staged at the Berlin City Opera (Feb. 12, 1950); a radio melodrama, *Fingerhütchen,* was produced in operatic form at St. Gall on April 26, 1950. Other works include the ballet *Das Dorf unter dem Gletscher* (1937); *Jorinde und Joringel* (1936) and *Andreas Gryphius* (1936) for chorus; a piano concerto (1944); *Orazione per orchestra,* for piano and orch. (1951); *Max und Moritz,* for vocal quartet and piano duet (1951); music for Büchner's *Wozzeck* for vocal quartet (1953); *Missa da Requiem* (Basel, June 11, 1954); a burlesque opera, *Titus Feuerfuchs* (Basel, April 14, 1958); choral pieces, songs, piano pieces.

Sutro, Florence Edith *(née* Clinton), American music educator; b. May 1, 1865; d. New York, April 29, 1906. A graduate of the N. Y. Cons. of Music, she was the first woman in the U. S. to receive the degree of Mus. Doc. In 1898 she organized the National Federation of Musical Clubs, and was its first president; for her efforts in behalf of women composers and executants she was awarded a gold medal at the Atlanta Exposition in 1895. On Oct. 1, 1884, she married Theodore Sutro, a prominent lawyer of New York. She wrote *Women in Music and Law* (N. Y., 1895).

Sutro, Rose Laura (b. Baltimore, Sept. 15, 1870; d. there, Jan. 11, 1957) and **Ottilie** (b. Baltimore, Jan. 4, 1872), American duo-pianists; daughters of Otto Sutro, a patron of art and founder of the Baltimore Oratorio Society. Both began piano lessons with their mother, and in 1889 were sent to Berlin, where they continued their studies. They made a spectacular début in London on July 13, 1894; first American appearance, Brooklyn, Nov. 13, 1894, followed by a tour of the U. S. Returning to Europe, they won fresh laurels, and were invited to play before Queen Victoria. Max Bruch wrote his concerto for 2 pianos and orch. expressly for them, and they gave its première with the Philadelphia Orch. on Dec. 29, 1916. In 1953 the sisters established a Sutro Club Room at the Maryland Historical Society in memory of their father.

Svanholm, Set, Swedish tenor; b. Västeras, Sept. 2, 1904. He studied at the Stockholm Cons.; was active at first as church organist in the provinces; in 1929 was appointed singing teacher at the Stockholm Cons. In 1930 he began to study voice with John Forsell; made his début in 1930 as a baritone in the part of Silvio in *I Pagliacci;* also sang Figaro in *The Barber of Seville;* then developed a higher range, and from 1936 on sang tenor parts exclusively; was equally successful in Wagner roles and the Italian repertory; sang in Vienna, Munich, and at La Scala in Milan. In 1946 he appeared as Tristan in Rio de Janeiro; in 1946 sang in San Francisco and at the Metropolitan Opera, N. Y. Since 1957, general music-director of the Stockholm Opera.

Svečenski (svĕh-chĕhn'-skē), **Louis,** violinist; b. Osijek, Croatia, Nov. 6, 1862; d. New York, June 18, 1926. He studied violin with J. Grün and J. Hellmesberger at the Vienna Cons.; emigrated to America in 1885 and became a member of the Boston Symph. Orchestra (1885-1903); he was also the violist throughout the entire career of the Kneisel Quartet (1885-1917); in 1917 went to live in N. Y. He publ. *25 Technical Exercises for Viola.*

Svendsen, Johan (**Severin**), Norwegian violinist and composer; b. Christiania, Sept. 30, 1840; d. Copenhagen, June 14, 1911. He acquired practical experience in music from his father, a bandmaster, and played several instruments; then conducted a band himself; also began to compose violin music without formal education. It was not before he was 23 that he began serious study at the Leipzig Cons. (with F. David, Reinecke, and others); then toured Denmark, Scotland, Iceland, Norway, and France; played in theater orchestras in Paris; wrote incidental music for Coppée's play *Le Passant* (Paris, Jan. 14, 1869), a violin concerto, and other violin works. In 1870 he went back to Leipzig; then traveled to America, and married an American lady, Sarah Levett. Returning to Norway, he became conductor of the Christiania Musical Association (1872-77 and again in 1880-83). In 1883 was appointed court conductor in Copenhagen; from 1896 also conducted at the Royal Theater there. His most popular works are the *4 Norwegian Rhapsodies* for orch. and the *Carnaval des artistes norvégiens* (also for orch.), based on genuine folk melodies; he further wrote 2 symphonies; a string quartet; a string quintet; a string octet; a cello concerto; 2 albums of songs to German, French, and Norwegian words; a *Romance* for violin and orch. (very popular); arrangements of Scandinavian melodies for string quartet; etc. —Cf. A Grönwold, *Norske musikere* (1883); G. Schjelderup, in *Norges Musikhistorie.* Letters of Svendsen were publ. by G. Hauch in 'Tilskueren' (Copenhagen, 1913).

Svetlanov (svyĕt-lah'-nof), **Evgeny Fedorovitch,** Russian conductor and composer; b. Moscow, Sept. 6, 1928. He studied composition with Gnessin and Shaporin, and conducting with Gauck; graduated from the Moscow Cons. in 1955. He was appointed conductor of the Moscow Radio in 1953, and joined the staff of the Bolshoy Theater in Moscow in 1955. —Works: cantata, *The Native Fields* (Moscow, 1949); a symph.; *Siberian Fantasy* for orch. (1953); a piano concerto (1951); a suite for string orch; a string quartet; a violin sonata; 4 piano sonatas; 5 piano sonatinas; 24 preludes for piano; several song cycles to words of Pushkin and of Soviet poets.

Sviridov (svē'-rē-dof), **Georgy Vassilievitch,** Russian composer; b. Fatezh, near Kursk, Dec. 16, 1915. He studied in Kursk; then was a pupil at the Leningrad Cons. of Youdin and Shostakovitch; in 1941-44 was in Novosibirsk, with a group of Leningrad composers and musicians evacuated there during the siege of Leningrad. In 1944, returned to Leningrad. —Works: musical comedies, *The Real Bridegroom* (1939) and *Little Flames* (Kiev, 1952); a symph. for string orch.; 2 piano concertos (1936, 1942); piano quintet (1945); 2 string quartets; a piano trio; many piano pieces and songs.

Swain, Freda, English pianist and composer; b. Portsmouth, Oct. 13, 1902. She studied at the Royal College of Music in London with the pianist Arthur Alexander, whom she married in 1921; gave duo-piano concerts in South Africa and Australia in 1940-43. —Works: piano concerto (1939); concertino for clarinet, strings, and horn (1948); 2 string quartets (1924; 1949); numerous piano pieces; transcriptions for 2 pianos of works by Bach and Chopin; songs.

Swalin, Benjamin, American violinist and conductor: b. Minneapolis, March 30, 1901. He studied violin with Franz Kneisel in N. Y., while supporting himself by playing in theater orchestras there. He subsequently took music courses at the Univ. of Vienna (1930-33); upon his return to the U. S., taught at the Univ. of North Carolina; organized the North Carolina Symph. in 1943, and became its regular conductor. He publ. a book, *The Violin Concerto: A Study in German Romanticism* (Univ. of North Carolina Press, Chapel Hill, 1941). —Cf. Hope Stoddard, *Symphony Conductors of the U. S. A.* (N. Y., 1957; pp. 228-35).

Swan, Alfred (Julius), musicologist and educator; b. St. Petersburg, Russia (of English parents), Oct. 9, 1890. After attending the German Katharinenschule (high school) in St. Petersburg, he went to Oxford in 1908 and studied at the Univ. (B. A. and M. A.); returned to Russia in 1911, and studied music at the St. Petersburg Cons. (1911-13). After service with the American Red Cross in Siberia during the civil war (1918-19), he went to the U. S.; taught at the Univ. of Virginia (1921-23); in 1926 became head of the music dept. at Swarthmore College and Haverford College, Pennsylvania, retiring from these posts in 1958. His specialty is Russian music. —Publications: *Scriabin* (London, 1923); *Music 1900-1930* (N. Y., 1930); *Znamenny Chant of the Russian Church,* in the 'Mus. Quarterly' (April, July, Oct., 1940); many other articles on Russian music and Russian composers in various magazines. He also publ. a useful brochure *The Music Director's Guide to Musical Literature* (N. Y., 1941). His compositions include a trio for flute, clarinet, and piano (1932); 2 violin sonatas (1913; 1948); 4 piano sonatas (1932-46); several albums of songs. He edited *Songs from Many Lands* (1923), *Recueil de chansons russes* (1936), etc.

Swan, Timothy, b. Worcester, Mass., July 23, 1758; d. Northfield, July 23, 1842. His only musical training consisted of 3 weeks at a singing school, and while serving in the Continental army he also learned to play the flute. From 1783 he lived in Suffield, Conn., and in 1807 moved to Northfield, Mass. Composed the hymn tunes *Poland, China, Ocean,* and *Pownal.* Publ. *The Songster's Assistant* (c. 1800); *New England Harmony* (1801); and also probably was the author of *The Songsters' Museum* (1803). —Cf. F. J. Metcalf, *American Writers and Compilers of Sacred Music* (N. Y., 1925, p. 103 ff.).

Swanson, Howard, American Negro composer; b. Atlanta, Aug. 18, 1909. He was taken to Cleveland as a child, and had to earn a living by manual labor on the railroad; served also as a postal clerk. He then entered the Cleveland Institute of Music, won a Rosenwald Fellowship for study in Europe, and went to Paris, where he took composition lessons with Nadia Boulanger. He remained in Paris until 1940; then returned to N. Y., where he obtained a job with the Internal Revenue Dept. (until 1945). He continued to compose, however, and his songs attracted attention when Marian Anderson performed them in N. Y. His first signal success came with a *Short Symphony* (1948), a work of simple melodic inspiration, which was highly praised at its première (N. Y. Philharmonic, conducted by Mitropoulos, Nov. 23, 1950); Mitropoulos performed it also at the Edinburgh Festival, on Aug. 31, 1951, and the piece was taken up by many other conductors. In 1952 it was selected as the best work of the season by the N. Y. Music Critics Circle. His other works include symph. No. 1 (1945); *Night Music* for small orch. (1950); a suite for cello and piano (1949); a number of songs; piano pieces.

Swarowsky, Hans, conductor; b. Budapest, Sept. 16, 1899. He studied in Vienna; was a pupil of Schoenberg; then devoted himself mainly to conducting; was opera conductor in Stuttgart, Hamburg, Berlin, and Zürich; led the Polish Philharmonic in Cracow (1944-46); from 1947 to 1949 he was in charge of the Graz Opera; then again in Vienna as conductor and teacher. He edited the French versions of Gluck's *Orfeo* and *Alceste;* translated into German several Italian librettos.

Swarthout, Gladys, American contralto; b. Deepwater, Mo., Dec. 25, 1904. She studied at the Bush Cons. in Chicago, also opera with L. Mugnone; made her début in a minor part with the Chicago Civic Opera in 1924, and then made regular appearances with the Ravinia Opera Co. in Chicago. On Nov. 15, 1929, she sang the part of La Cieca in *La Gioconda* at the Metropolitan Opera; she remained on its roster until 1945. She married the singer Frank Chapman in 1932. Publ. an autobiography, *Come Soon, Tomorrow* (N. Y., 1945).

Sweelinck (svā'-link), **Jan Pieterszoon,** great Dutch organist and composer; b. Deventer (or Amsterdam), 1562; d. Amsterdam, Oct. 16, 1621. Contrary to repeated assertions that Sweelinck was a pupil of Zarlino in Venice, documentary evidence proves that he remained in Amsterdam virtually all his life; this also refutes the theory that Sweelinck was the carrier of Venetian ideas and techniques in Northern Europe. About 1580 he became organist of the Old Church in Amsterdam, a position previously held by his father, Pieter Sweelinck (d. 1573). As a player and teacher he was celebrated far and wide; most of the leading organists in Northern Germany, of the next generation, were his pupils. During his lifetime only some of his vocal music was publ.; but his organ music is more remarkable and important: Sweelinck was the first to employ the pedal in a real fugal part, and originated the organ fugue built up on one theme with the gradual addition of counterthemes leading up to a highly involved and ingenious finale—a form perfected by Bach. In rhythmic and melodic freedom, his vocal compositions show an advance over the earlier polyphonic style, though replete with intricate contrapuntal devices. A complete ed. of Sweelinck's works, in 12 vols., edited by Max Seiffert for the 'Vereeniging voor Nederlandsche Muziekgeschiedenis,' was publ. by Breitkopf & Härtel (1895-1903): vol. I, works for organ and clavier; vol. II, 1st half of the First Book of Psalms (1604); vol. III, 2nd half of the same; vol. IV, 1st half of the Second Book of Psalms (1613); vol. V, 2nd half of the same; vol. VI, Third Book of Psalms (1614); vol. VII, Fourth Book of Psalms (1621); vol. VIII, *Cantiones sacrae a* 5; vol. IX, *Chansons a* 5; vol. X, *Rimes françoises et italiennes a* 2-4; vol. XI, processional compositions; vol. XII, Rules for composition, ed. by H. Gehrmann. Vols. II-VII comprise the 150 Psalms of David in the rhymed French version by Marot and Beza. —Cf. F. H. J. Tiedeman: *J. P. S., een bio-bibliografische Schets* (Amsterdam, 1876; 2nd ed., 1892); M. Seiffert, *J. P. S. und seine direkten deutschen Schüler,* in 'Vierteljahrsschrift für Musikwissenschaft' (1891); M. Seiffert, *J. P. S.,* in 'Tijdschrift' of the 'Vereeniging voor Nederlandsche Muziekgeschiedenis' (1900); D. F. Scheurleer, *Sweelinckiana,* in the same (1914); C. Van den Borren, *Les Origines de la musique de clavier dans les Pays-Bas jusque vers 1630* (Brussels, 1914); O. Gombosi, *S.,* in 'Tijdschrift' (as above) (1932); E. R. Sollitt, *From Dufay to S.* (N. Y., 1933); B. van den Sigtenhorst Meyer, *J. P. S. en zijn instrumentale muziek* (The Hague, 1934; 2nd ed., 1946); B. van den Sigtenhorst Meyer, *De vocale Muziek van J. P. S.* (The Hague, 1948); R. L. Tusler, *The Organ Music of J. P. S.* (2 vols.; Bilthoven, 1958; in English).

Swert, Jules de. See **Deswert.**

Swoboda, Adalbert (Viktor), writer on music; b. Prague, Jan. 26, 1828; d. Munich, May 19, 1902. He founded (1880) and edited till his death the 'Neue Musikzeitung' in Stuttgart; author of *Illustrierte Musikgeschichte* (2 vols., 1893).

Sygiètynski (sĭg-yĕh-tĭn'-skē), **Tadeusz,** Polish conductor and arranger; b. Warsaw, Sept. 24, 1896; d. there, May 19, 1955. He studied music in Lwow with Roman Statkowski and Henryk Melcer; later took courses with Max Reger in Leipzig and with Schoenberg in Vienna. In 1949 he organized in Poland the Mazowsze State Song and Dance Ensemble for the purpose of popularizing Polish folk music; toured with it in the Far East and in Western Europe with considerable acclaim. He made numerous arrangements of Polish folksongs for this group; in 1951 he received a State prize, and later was awarded the Banner of Labor by the State Council of Poland.

Sykora, Bogumil, cellist; b. Glinsk, Russia, Jan. 15, 1890; d. New York, Jan. 19, 1953.

He studied with Julius Klengel at the Leipzig Cons. (1909) and made his professional début there on Jan. 20, 1911; toured Russia (1913-15); then came to America; gave his 1st recital in N. Y. on Dec. 12, 1916. He toured in the Far East (1917-21), in the U. S. and Canada (1921-25), in South America (1925-33), in Spain (1934-35), etc. In 1938 he returned to N. Y. and settled there as a teacher. He composed a concerto and a number of pieces for cello.

Szabados (sah'-bah-dosh), **Béla Antal,** Hungarian composer; b. Budapest, June 3, 1867; d. there, Sept. 15, 1936. He studied with Erkel and Volkmann at the Budapest Academy of Music; later joined its staff as piano teacher and vocal coach. He wrote 2 serious operas, *Maria* (Budapest, Feb. 28, 1905; in collaboration with Arpád Szendy); and *Fanny* (Budapest, Feb. 16, 1927); 11 comic operas; 4 string quartets; a psalm and several song cycles; also publ. several vocal manuals.

Szabó (săh'-bŏh), **Ferenc,** Hungarian composer; b. Budapest, Dec. 27, 1902. He studied with Kodály; in 1932 went to Russia, and became closely associated with the ideological work of the Union of Soviet Composers in Moscow. In 1946 he returned to Hungary and was appointed prof. at the Budapest Academy of Music. In conformity with his political beliefs, Szabó emphasizes in his music folk elements and realistic subject matter. —Works: symph. poem, *Class Struggle* (Moscow, April 27, 1933); *Sinfonietta* for an ensemble of Russian national instruments (1935); *Moldavian Rhapsody* for orch. (1941); 2 string quartets, a piano trio, a string trio, 2 piano sonatas, etc.

Szabolcsi (sah'-bohl-chē), **Bence,** Hungarian musicologist; b. Budapest, Aug. 2, 1899. He studied jurisprudence at the Univ. of Budapest, music with Kodály at the Budapest Academy and with Abert at the Univ. of Leipzig; *Dr. phil.*, 1923, with the dissertation *Benedetti und Saracini. Beiträge zur Geschichte der Monodie.* In 1926 he became a member of the staff of the musical periodical 'Zenei Szemle'; its publication was suspended during World War II, but resumed in 1947; Szabolcsi became an editor again in 1950. With Aladár Tóth he brought out a music dictionary in Hungarian (1930-31); publ. a history of music (Budapest, 1940), a monograph on Beethoven (Budapest, 1948), and a number of valuable papers in Hungarian, German, Italian, and English music publications; was a member of the editorial board of 'Zenetudományi Tanulmányok' ('Studies in Musical Science'); ed. *Bartók, sa vie et son œuvre* (Budapest, 1956).

Szalkiewicz (shahl-kyā'-vich), **Cyril,** Finnish pianist; b. Helsinki, Dec. 21, 1914 (of Polish parents). He studied with Lazare Lévy and Cortot in Paris; gave concerts in France and Belgium (1931); then returned to Finland, where he is regarded as one of the country's foremost pianists.

Szalowski (shah-lov'-skē), **Antoni,** Polish composer; b. Warsaw, April 21, 1907. He studied violin with his father; in 1931 went to Paris; studied there with Nadia Boulanger; his works reflect the combined influences of Impressionism and neo-Classicism. His Overture (Warsaw Festival of the International Society for Contemporary Music, April 21, 1939) is his most successful composition; other works are: a symphony (1939); *Concertino* for strings (1942); piano concerto (1930); violin concerto (1949); flute concerto (1951); 3 string quartets; clarinet sonata; oboe sonatina (Amsterdam Festival, June 8, 1948); piano pieces; songs.

Szántó (săhn'-tŏh), **Theodor,** Hungarian pianist and composer; b. Vienna, June 3, 1877; d. Budapest, Jan. 7, 1934. He studied with Dachs (piano) and Fuchs (composition) at the Vienna Cons., and later with Busoni in Berlin (1898-1901). In 1905 he settled in Paris; from 1914 to 1921 lived in Switzerland; then divided his time between Paris and Budapest, giving frequent recitals; also played at other musical centers in Europe. His opera on a Japanese story, *Typhoon,* was produced in Mannheim, on Nov. 29, 1924, and there were a few subsequent performances in other cities. He also wrote a *Japanese Suite* for orch. (1926); several symph. works based on Hungarian folksongs; chamber music; many piano pieces (of which *Variations on a Hungarian Folksong* became fairly well known).

Szeligowski (shĕh-lē-gov'-skē), **Tadeusz,** Polish composer; b. Lwow, Sept. 13, 1896. He studied with Jachimecki in Cracow (1919-22) and with Nadia Boulanger in Paris (1929-31); then was prof. at the Vilna Cons. (1938-39). After the end of the war he became director of the State Opera School in Poznan. —Works: opera *Bunt Zakow (Rebellion of Clerks;* Wroclaw [Breslau], July 14, 1951); ballet *Paw i dziewczyna (The Peacock and the Maiden;* Wroclaw, Aug. 2, 1949); 2 violin concertos; clarinet concerto; piano concerto (Cracow, May 17,

1946); sacred choral works; symph. suites on Polish themes; several string quartets and other chamber music; piano pieces.

Szell (sehl), **George,** eminent pianist and conductor; b. Budapest, June 7, 1897. He began his career as a pianist and composer of extraordinary precocity. From his earliest childhood he studied piano with Richard Robert in Vienna, where his family had moved, and he was only 11 when he performed his Rondo for piano and orch. with the Vienna Symph. Orch.; his teacher in composition was J. B. Foerster; he also studied with Mandyczewski and Max Reger. He conducted his own symphony and played Beethoven's 'Emperor Concerto' with the Berlin Philharmonic at 17; Richard Strauss became interested in him, and recommended him for the post of conductor at the Municipal Theater in Strasbourg, where Szell remained for a season (1917-18); he subsequently was engaged as conductor of the German Opera in Prague (1919-21), at Darmstadt (1921-22), and at Düsseldorf (1922-24). In 1924 he was appointed 1st conductor at the Berlin State Opera, holding this post until 1930; also taught at the Hochschule für Musik in Berlin (1927-30); from 1930 to 1936 conducted once more at the German Opera in Prague; appeared as guest conductor in Russia and England; in 1930 he conducted for the first time in America, with the St. Louis Symph. He then became conductor of the Scottish Orchestra in Glasgow (1937-39); the outbreak of World War II caused its suspension, and Szell accepted a position as teacher at the opera workshop of the New School for Social Research in N. Y.; also taught theory at the Mannes School of Music. At the invitation of Toscanini he appeared as guest conductor of the NBC Symph.; from 1942 to 1945 he conducted at the Metropolitan Opera House; in 1946 he was engaged as permanent conductor of the Cleveland Orch.; in 1957 he took the orch. on an extended tour of European cities, with tremendous acclaim. He also filled guest engagements as symphony and opera conductor with various organizations; was on the staff of the Metropolitan Opera for occasional appearances until 1954. Szell's distinguishing characteristics as conductor are clarity of line and controlled security of emotional projection, so that the pure substance of the music is expressively brought out, and the instrumental balance, or, in opera, the vocal predominance is always preserved. He excels particularly in interpretations of the Viennese classics. —He publ. a *Lyric Overture* (1922) and Theme and Variations for orch. (1916) among other works. —Cf. Hope Stoddard, *Symphony Conductors of the U. S. A.* (N. Y., 1957; pp. 236-43).

Szendrei (sehn'-drey), **Aladár** (in the U. S. changed his name to Alfred Sendrey), conductor and composer; b. Budapest, Feb. 29, 1884. He studied with Hans Koessler at the Budapest Academy of Music (1901-05); then was active as theater conductor in Germany; conducted opera in Chicago (1911-12) and New York (1913-14); returned to Europe in 1914; was conductor at the Berlin Opera (1914-15) and at the Volksoper in Vienna (1915-16). After service in the Austrian army, he became conductor of opera in Leipzig (1918-24); then led symph. concerts there (1924-32). In 1933 he left Germany and went to Paris, where he conducted at the Radiodiffusion Française; in 1940, came to the U. S. and settled in Los Angeles as music teacher. He wrote a 1-act opera, *Das türkisenblaue Garten* (Leipzig, 1920); ballet, *Danse d'odalisque;* several orch. works, including a *Hungarian Overture;* choral music; miscellaneous pieces for various instruments; publ. *Rundfunk und Musikpflege* (Leipzig, 1931); *Dirigierkunde* (Leipzig, 1932; 2nd ed., 1952); *Bibliography of Jewish Music* (N. Y., 1951).

Szendy (sehn'-di), **Arpád,** Hungarian pianist and composer; b. Szarvas, Aug. 11, 1863; d. Budapest, Sept. 10, 1922. He studied at the Budapest Cons. and at the Academy of Music there; then became a student of Liszt (1881). In 1890 he was appointed to the faculty of the Academy of Music; enjoyed great esteem in Hungary as a piano teacher. He publ. numerous editions of piano classics; wrote an opera, *Mária* (with Béla Szabados; Budapest, Feb. 28, 1905); a string quartet; much piano music; songs.

Szenkar (sehn'-kahr), **Eugen,** Hungarian conductor; b. Budapest, April 9, 1891. He studied with his father, Ferdinand Szenkar, a prominent organist, and later at the Academy of Music in Budapest. He was successively conductor of the German Opera in Prague (1911-13); the Popular Opera in Budapest (1913-15); the Mozarteum at Salzburg (1915-16); at Altenburg (1916-20); at the Frankfurt Opera (1920-23); at the Volksoper in Berlin (1923-24); and at the Cologne Opera (1924-33). With the advent of the Nazi regime he was compelled to leave Germany, and conducted several years in Moscow. In 1939 he was engaged as permanent conductor of the Brazilian Symph. Orch. in Rio de Janeiro; in 1947, was guest conductor of the NBC Symph. Orch., N. Y.; returned to Germany in 1950, and in 1952 was appointed music director of the Düsseldorf Opera and conductor of the Düsseldorf Symphony.

Szervánsky (ser'-vahn-skē), **Endre,** Hungarian composer; b. Kistétény, Jan. 1, 1912. Of a musical family, he learned to play the clarinet as a child; studied composition with Albert Siklós at the Budapest Academy of Music, graduating in 1936; in 1948, appointed teacher there. His style is influenced mainly by Bartók; the rhythmic element is very strong; the melodic material is modeled after Hungarian folksong.— Works: string quartet (1938); 3 Divertimentos for string orch. (1939-43); violin sonata (1945); *Serenade* for strings (1947); symphony (1948); *Oriental Tale,* ballet suite (1949); *Home Guard Cantata* (1949); *Rhapsody* for orch. (1950); trio for oboe, clarinet, and bassoon (1950); trio for flute, violin, and viola (1950); sonatina for flute and piano (1952); quintet for wind instruments (1953); *Serenade* for clarinet and orch. (1954); 20 pieces for 2 violins; etc.

Szigeti (si'-geh-ti), **Joseph,** famous violinist; b. Budapest, Sept. 5, 1892. He studied in Budapest with Hubay; made his professional début in 1905; from 1906 to 1913 he lived in England; in 1917 he was appointed prof. of violin at the Geneva Cons.; subsequently devoted his time mainly to concert activities; in 1926 made his home in the U. S. (in New York and later in California). His tours covered every part of the world; he was particularly interested in promoting new music; gave the world première of Ernest Bloch's violin concerto (Cleveland, Dec. 15, 1938); played Prokofiev's violin concertos on numerous occasions; participated in many festivals of modern music; toured South America in 1954. He became an American citizen in 1951. —Publ. *With Strings Attached,* an autobiography (N. Y., 1947). —Cf. R. Gelatt, *Music Makers* (N. Y., 1953; pp. 135-48).

Szostakowicz. See **Shostakovitch.**

Szulc (shoolts), **Jósef Zygmunt,** operetta composer; b. Warsaw, April 4, 1875; d. Paris, April 10, 1956; studied at the Warsaw Cons. with Noskowski, and in Paris with Moszkowski (piano). He remained in Paris as a piano teacher; then turned to composition of light operas. His first work in this genre, *Flup* (Brussels, Dec. 19, 1913), was very successful and had thousands of performances in France and other European countries. Except for disruptions of musical life during the two wars, he continued to produce operettas at regular intervals; the last one was *Pantoufle* (Paris, Feb. 24, 1945). He also wrote a ballet, *Une Nuit d'Ispahan* (Brussels, Nov. 19, 1909).

Szumowska (shoo-mohf'-skah), **Antoinette,** Polish pianist and teacher; b. Lublin, Feb. 22, 1868; d. Rumson, N. J., Aug. 18, 1938. She studied at the Warsaw Cons. with Michalowski, and later took lessons with Paderewski in Paris (1890-95). In 1895 she came to the U. S., settling in Boston, where she taught at the New England Cons. for many years. In 1896 she married the cellist Josef Adamowski, and with him and his brother Timothée, violinist, formed the 'Adamowski Trio,' which presented numerous concerts in New England.

Szymanowska (shĭh - mah - nohf' - skah), **Maria** *(née* Wolowska), Polish pianist and composer; b. Warsaw, Dec. 14, 1789; d. St. Petersburg, July 24, 1831. She studied piano with local teachers in Warsaw, and began to play in public as a child. In 1810 she married a Polish landowner, Theophilus Joseph Szymanowski (divorced in 1820). In 1822 she toured in Russia, and was appointed court pianist; in 1823, played in Germany; in 1824, in France; then in England, Holland, and Italy (1824-25), returning to Warsaw in 1826. In 1828 she settled in St. Petersburg as pianist and teacher, and remained there until her death (of cholera). She was admired by Goethe, whom she met in Germany; his poem *Aussöhnung (Trilogie der Leidenschaft)* alludes to her (cf. Goethe's correspondence with Zelter). She publ. 24 mazurkas and several character pieces for piano, of which *Le Murmure* became popular. Her piano studies were commended by Schumann. —Cf. I. Boelza, *Maria Szymanowska* (Moscow, 1956).

Szymanowski (shi-măh-nŏhf'-skē), **Karol,** eminent Polish composer; b. Timoshovka, Ukraine, Oct. 6, 1882; d. Lausanne, March 28, 1937. The son of a cultured landowner, he grew up in a musical environment. He began to play the piano and compose very early in life. His first teacher was Gustav Neuhaus in Elisavetgrad; in 1901 he went to Warsaw, where he studied with Noskowski. His first work, 9 Preludes for piano, op. 1, was publ. in 1906 in Berlin by the Association of Young Polish Composers (later known as 'Young Poland in Music'). Szymanowski lived in Berlin from 1906 to 1908, writing symphonic and other music, much influenced by Richard Strauss. He returned to Warsaw in 1909, and his 1st symph. was performed there on March 26, 1909; however, he was dissatisfied with the score, and withdrew it from further performance. In 1911 he completed his 2nd symph., which demonstrated a stylistic change from German dominance to Russian influences, paralleling the harmonic evolution of Scriabin; it was played for the first time in Warsaw, on April 7, 1911. The pianist Artur Rubinstein was one of the earliest champions of Szymanowski's piano music and performed his 2nd piano sonata in Germany and in Vienna. From 1912 to 1914 Szymanowski lived in Vienna, where he wrote his 1-act opera, *Hagith;* the years of World War I (1914-18) he spent in Timoshovka, where he wrote his 3rd symph.; appeared in concert with the violinist Paul Kochanski in Moscow and St. Petersburg, giving 1st performances of his violin works; it was for Kochanski that he composed his violin triptych, *Mythes (La Fontaine d'Aréthuse* from this cycle is one of his best-known compositions). About this time, his music underwent a new change in style, veering towards French Impressionism. During the Russian Revolution of 1917 the family estate at Timoshovka was ruined, and Szymanowski lost most of his possessions. He lived in Elisavetgrad from 1917 to 1919, where he continued to compose industriously, despite the turmoil of the civil war. Early in 1920 he settled in Warsaw; traveled to other Polish cities, and soon established his reputation as the most important modern composer of Poland. His international renown also was considerable; his works were often performed in Europe, and figured at festivals of the International Society for Contemporary Music. He visited Paris, London, and New York (1921). In 1926 he was appointed director of the Warsaw Cons. and reorganized the system of teaching along more liberal lines. His *Stabat Mater* produced a profound impression (1928), and his ballet *Harnasie,* composed in 1926, and based on the life and music of the Tatra mountain dwellers, demonstrated his ability to treat national subjects in an original and highly effective manner. In 1933 he appeared as soloist in the first performance of his *Symphonie Concertante* for piano and orch. at Warsaw, and repeated his performances in Paris, London, and Brussels. In April, 1936, greatly weakened in health by chronic tuberculosis, he attended the première of his ballet *Harnasie* at the Paris Opéra. —Through successive influences, Szymanowski developed into a national composer whose music has universal significance also. Of particular interest is his treatment of the mazurka; though he was a lifelong admirer of Chopin, he found a way to treat this dance form in a new and personal manner. —Works: *Hagith,* opera (Warsaw, May, 1922); *Król Roger,* opera in 3 acts (1920-24; Warsaw, June 19, 1926); ballet, *Harnasie* (1926; Prague, May 11, 1935); *Concert Overture* (Warsaw, Feb. 6, 1906); 3 symphonies: No. 1 (Warsaw, March 26, 1909), No. 2 (Warsaw, April 7, 1911), No. 3, for tenor, mixed chorus, and orch. (1916); 1st violin concerto (Warsaw, 1922); 2nd violin concerto (Warsaw, Oct. 6, 1933); *Symphonie Concertante* for piano and orch. (Paris, Feb. 25, 1934, composer soloist). Vocal works with orch.: *Stabat Mater* (1929); *Veni Creator* (1929); *Litania* (1933). Chamber music: 2 string quartets (1917; 1927); violin sonata (1904); *Notturno e tarantella,* for violin and piano (1914); *Mythes,* 3 poems for violin and piano: *La Fontaine d'Aréthuse, Narcisse, Dryades et Pan* (1915). For piano: 3 piano sonatas; *Fantasy* (1905); *Métopes,* 3 poems: *L'Ile des sirènes, Calypso, Nausicaa* (1915); 12 études (1917); *Masques,* 3 poems: *Shéhérazade, Tantris le bouffon, Sérénade de Don Juan* (1917); 4 Polish dances (1926); 20 mazurkas (1924-26); etc. About 100 songs, including a set of 5 to words by James Joyce (1926), 8 Love Songs of Hafiz (also with orch.), 12 Kuprian Songs (1932). —Bibliography: Z. Jachimecki, *Karol Szymanowski,* in the 'Mus. Quarterly' (Jan., 1922); A. Tansman, *Karol Szymanowski,* in the 'Revue Musicale' (May, 1922); G. Pannain in *Modern Composers* (transl. from the Italian, N. Y., 1932); Z. Jachimecki, *Karol Szymanowski,* in the 'Slavonic and East European Review' (July, 1938); also the Szymanowski issue of 'Muzyka Polska' (Warsaw, 1937); S. Lobaczewska, *Karol Szymanowski* (Cracow, 1950; exhaustive biography and musical analysis); S. Golachowski, *Karol Szymanowski* (Cracow, 1956).

T

Tabourot, Jean. See **Arbeau.**

Tacchinardi (tăhk-kē-nahr'dē), **Nicola,** Italian tenor; b. Leghorn, Sept. 3, 1772; d. Florence, March 14, 1859. After singing on Italian stages (La Scala, Milan, 1805), he was engaged at the Théâtre Italien, Paris, 1811-14, with Crivelli; from 1822-31, 'primo cantante' in the Grand Ducal chapel at Florence, also appearing repeatedly on the stage; then lived in Florence as a teacher, one of his pupils being his daughter, Fanny Tacchinardi-Persiani (see **Persiani**). He publ. vocalises and exercises; also *Dell' Opera in Musica sul teatro italiano e de' suoi difetti.* —His son, **Guido Tacchinardi** (b. Florence, March 10, 1840; d. there, Dec. 6, 1917), was a composer and theorist; from 1891 director of the Istituto Musicale at Florence.

Tadolini, Giovanni, Italian composer; b. Bologna, 1785; d. there, Nov. 29, 1872. He studied composition with Mattei and singing with Babini; from 1811 to 1814 he was on the staff of the Théâtre des Italiens in Paris; then went to Italy, where he produced a succession of operas: *Le Bestie in uomini* (Venice, 1815); *La Principessa di Navarra* (Bologna, 1816); *Il Credulo deluso* (Rome, 1817); *Tamerlano* (Bologna, 1818); *Moctar* (Milan, 1824); *Mitridate* (Venice, 1826); *Almansor* (Trieste, 1827); from 1830 to 1839 he was again at his post at the Théâtre des Italiens. He also wrote many canzonets and romances; one of them, *Eco di Scozia,* was popular in his time.

Taffanel, (Claude-) Paul, French flutist and conductor; b. Bordeaux, Sept. 16, 1844; d. Paris, Nov. 22, 1908. He was a pupil of Dorus (flute) and Reber (composition). From 1864-90, flutist in the Paris Opéra orch.; 1867-90, flutist of the Cons. concerts, which he conducted 1890-1903; from 1892 till his death he was one of the 'chefs d'orchestre' at the Opéra; in 1893 succeeded Altès as prof. of flute-playing at the Cons. In 1879 he founded the 'Société des quintettes pour instruments à vent.' With Gaubert he wrote a *Méthode complète de flûte.*

Tag, Christian Gotthilf, German composer; b. Bayerfeld, Saxony, April 2, 1735; d. Niederzwonitz, near Zwickau, June 19, 1811. From 1749-55 he studied at the Kreuzschule in Dresden (pupil of Homilius), and from 1755-1808 was cantor at Hohenstein. —Publ. 6 Chorale-preludes with Trio and Allabreve (1783); 12 Preludes and a Symphony for organ (1795); songs (1783, 1785, 1793, 1798); 70 variations for piano on an Andantino (1785); *Der Glaube,* melody with organ (1793); *Urians Reise um die Welt* and *Urians Nachricht von der Aufklärung* (1797); *Naumann, ein Todtenopfer* (1803; voice with piano); *Melodie zum Vaterunser und den Einsetzungsworten* (1803; with organ); *Wörlitz,* an ode (1803; voice with piano); many sacred and instrumental works are in MS. —Cf. J. F. Rochlitz, *Für Freunde der Tonkunst,* vol. III (1830); H. J. Vieweg, *C. G. T.* (Leipzig, 1933).

Tagliapietra (tăhl-yăh-pi-ĕt'-răh), **Gino,** Italian pianist and composer; b. (of Italian parentage) Ljubljana, May 30, 1887; d. Venice, Aug. 8, 1954. He studied piano with Julius Epstein in Vienna and with Busoni in Berlin; in 1906 was appointed to the faculty of the Liceo Benedetto Marcello in Venice. His compositions include a ballet, *La Bella dormente nel bosco* (Venice, March 11, 1926); a piano concerto; numerous studies for piano. He edited for Ricordi an important anthology of keyboard music from Willaert to modern times, 'Antologia di musica antica e moderna' (1931-32; 18 vols., containing 519 works by 157 composers).

Tagliapietra (tăhl-yăh-pi-ĕt'-răh), **Giovanni,** Italian baritone; b. Venice, Dec. 24, 1846; d. New York, April 11, 1921. He studied naval architecture, and was a graduate from the Univ. of Padua. After a study of singing with Giovanni Corsi, he appeared in various Italian opera houses; made a tour of South America; in 1874 was engaged as member of Max Strakosch's company and sang in the U. S. In 1876 he married the famous pianist Teresa Carreño, but was divorced; his brother Arturo was married to her in 1902.

Tagliavini (tăhl'-yăh-vē'-nē), **Ferruccio,** prominent Italian tenor; b. Reggio, Aug. 14, 1913. After studying at the Cons. of Parma, he won 1st prize for singing at the May Festival in Florence (1938); made his opera début there as Rodolfo in *La Bohème* (1939); later sang at La Scala, Milan, and other opera houses in Italy; in 1946, toured South America; on Jan. 10, 1947, made a very successful 1st appearance, as Rodolfo, at the Metropolitan Opera, N. Y.; has also given recitals in the major American cities; subsequently traveled widely in both hemispheres. In 1941 he married the soprano Pia Tassinari. —Cf. C. Tedeschi, *Ferruccio Tagliavini* (Rome, 1942).

Tagore, Sir **Surindro Mohun** (Rajah **Saurindramohana Thakura**), Hindu musicologist; b. Calcutta, 1840; d. there, June 28, 1914. At the age of 17 he began to study Hindu music under Luchmi Prasad and Kshetra Mohun Gosvami, and European music under a German teacher in Calcutta; founded and endowed from his personal fortune the 'Bengal Music Soc.' (1871) and the 'Bengal Academy of Music' (1881), continuing to preside over both until his death. He perfected a new and simpler system of musical notation, which gradually replaced the older system throughout India. A connoisseur of instruments, he was at various times commissioned by the principal museums of Europe to procure for them instruments of Asiatic nations; perhaps the finest collection is that in the Metropolitan Museum of Art in N. Y. He wrote nearly 60 books on an amazing variety of subjects; those concerning music (publ. in Calcutta, in the Bengali language, and some in English) include the following: *Yantra Kosha, or A Treasury of the Musical Instruments of Ancient and Modern India* (1875); *Hindu Music, from Various Authors* (1875; 2nd ed., in 2 vols., 1882); *Short Notices of Hindu Musical Instruments* (1877); *6 Principal Ragas* (1877); *The 8 Principal Ragas of the Hindus* (1880); *The Five Principal Musicians of the Hindus, or A Brief Exposition of the Essential Elements of Hindu Music* (1881); *The Musical Scales of the Hindus with Remarks on the Applicability of Harmony to Hindu Music* (1884); *The 22 Musical Srutis of the Hindus* (1886); *Universal History of Music . . .* (1896). —Cf. F. Chrysander, *Über Tagore's 'Hindu Music'* in 'Allgemeine Musikalische Zeitung' (1879; p. 540 ff.); F. Chrysander, *Über altindische Opfermusik,* in 'Vierteljahrsschrift für Musikwissenschaft' (1885; p. 21 ff.).

Tailleferre (tī-yë-fehr'), **Germaine,** French composer; b. Pau-St.-Maur, near Paris, April 19, 1892. She studied at the Paris Cons., and later took lessons with Ravel; associated herself with the vanguard of modern musicians. She obtained wide recognition as the only feminine member of the group known as 'Les Six' (Honegger, Milhaud, Poulenc, Auric, and Durey being the other members). However she wrote comparatively little music, and performances of it were infrequent. Her style of composition is simple and unaffected; some of her songs and piano pieces possess a certain poetic charm. —Works: *Image,* for piano, flute, clarinet, string quartet, and celesta (1918); string quartet (1919); 2 violin sonatas (1921; 1951); *Jeux de plein air,* for 2 pianos (1922; also for orch.); piano concerto (1924); concertino for harp and orch. (Boston Symph. Orch., Cambridge, Mass., March 3, 1927); ballet, *Le Marchand d'oiseaux* (Paris, May 25, 1923); *Chansons françaises,* for voice and instruments (Liège Festival of the International Society for Contemporary Music, Sept. 2, 1930); *Ouverture,* for orch. (Paris, Dec. 25, 1932); concerto for 2 pianos, voice, and orch. (Paris, May 3, 1934); Pastorale, for flute and piano (1942); ballet, *Paris-Magie* (Paris, June 3, 1949); opera, *Il était un petit navire* (Paris, March 9, 1951); songs; piano pieces.

Takács (tăh'-kăch), **Jenõ,** Hungarian pianist and composer; b. Siegendorf, Austria, Sept. 25, 1902. He studied composition with Joseph Marx and Hans Gál at the Vienna Cons. In 1927 he accepted an invitation to become a teacher at the Cairo Cons. in Egypt; in 1932 went to Manilla, Philippine Islands, returning to Cairo in 1935. During his travels, he collected much material on Oriental music; his research in this field is also reflected in his own works. In 1938-39 he toured the U. S.; in 1939-42, was prof. at the Sopron (Ödenburg) Cons.; 1942-48, director of the Cons. of Pécs, Hungary; 1949-51, visiting prof. at the Cons. of Lausanne and Geneva; 1952, came to the U. S. as prof. of piano at the Cincinnati Cons.; since 1955, also visiting prof. at the Cons. of Geneva (summer sessions). —Works: ballets, *The Nile Legend* (Budapest, May 8, 1940) and *Napolitana* (1940); *Philippine Suite,* for orch. (1934); *Antiqua Hungarica,* for orch. (1941); *Folk Dances of Burgenland,* for orch. (1953); 2 piano concertos (1932; 1947); *Partita* for guitar and orch. (1950); *Gumbry,* Oriental Rhapsody for violin and piano (1930); *Sonata concertante* for violin and piano (1956); sonata for trombone and piano (1956); *Sonata Missoulana* for oboe and piano (1957); *Sonata breve* for trumpet and piano (1958); a number of piano pieces, based on Hungarian and Oriental themes; publ. the treatises *Music of the Philippines* (Manila, 1933), *Tune and Chant in Egypt* (Johannesburg, 1935), etc.

Takagi, Toroku, Japanese composer and pianist; b. Okayama, July 7, 1904. He graduated from Tokyo Academy of Music in 1928; later studied in Paris. His opera *Shunko-Den* was produced in Tokyo, Nov. 20, 1948.

Takata, Saburo, Japanese composer; b. Nagoya, Dec. 4, 1913. He studied at the Tokyo Music Academy. Among his works are *Ballade* for violin and orch. (Tokyo, Jan. 13, 1945); octet for clarinet, bassoon, trumpet, horn, and string quartet (1939); 2 piano sonatas (1935; 1941); a violin sonata (1949); a sonatina for cello and piano (1950); suite for 5 wind instruments (1952); 2 piano sonatas; other piano pieces; songs.

Takata, Shin-ichi, Japanese composer; b. Tokyo, Jan. 24, 1920. He studied at the Tokyo Academy of Music; has written a symph. poem, *In Praise of Peace* (Tokyo, Nov. 25, 1948), of which a full score has been published. The style of this work reveals the influence of Richard Strauss.

Taktakishvili, Otar, Soviet Georgian composer; b. Tiflis, July 27, 1924. He studied at the Tiflis Cons., graduating in 1947; in 1949, became prof. there. —Works: 2 symphonies (1949; 1953); 3 overtures; a piano concerto (Tiflis, Nov. 15, 1951); cello concerto (1947); many choral works; film music.

Taktakishvili, Shalva, Soviet Georgian composer; b. Kvemo-Khviti, Aug. 27, 1900. He studied violin at the Tiflis Cons.; from 1928 to 1937 taught in Batum; from 1937, prof. at the Tiflis Cons. —Works: operas *The Deputy* (1939) and *Otar's Widow* (1942); several children's operas; ballet *Maltakva* (1937); *Festive Overture* (1944); cello concerto (1932); 2 string quartets; 2 piano trios; choruses; songs.

Taku, Koji, Japanese composer; b. Sakai-City (Osaka), March 10, 1904. He studied at the École normale de musique in Paris with Nadia Boulanger, then later with Yamada in Tokyo. Among his works are the ballet, *White Flower* (1942); a string quartet; several albums of piano pieces for children.

Tal (real name, Gruenthal), **Joseph,** Israeli composer; b. Posen, German Poland, Sept. 18, 1910. He studied in Berlin with Tiessen and Trapp; settled in Palestine in 1934; in 1937 became prof. of piano and composition at the Cons. of Jerusalem. —Works: *Exodus,* choreographic poem for orch. (Tel Aviv, Dec. 14, 1947); *A Mother Rejoices,* symph. cantata (1949); *Visions,* for string orch. (1950); symphony (1952); piano concerto (1953); viola concerto (Mount Carmel Festival of the International Society for Contemporary Music, June 3, 1954); a violin sonata; an oboe sonata; piano pieces; songs.

Talbot, Howard (real name Munkittrick), operetta composer; b. Yonkers, N. Y., March 9, 1865; d. London, Sept. 12, 1928. He was taken to England at the age of 4, and studied music at the Royal College of Music under Parry, Bridge, and Gladstone; from 1900, was active as conductor in various London theaters. He was a prolific composer of light operas, all produced in London; his greatest success was *A Chinese Honeymoon* (1899); his last work was *The Daughter of the Gods* (posthumous, 1929). Other operettas: *Monte Carlo* (1896); *Three Little Maids* (1902); *The Blue Moon* (1905); *The White Chrysanthemum* (1905); *The Girl Behind the Counter* (1906); *The Three Kisses* (1907); *The Belle of Brittany* (1908); *The Arcadians* (1909); *The Pearl Girl* (1913); *A Narrow Squeak* (1913); *A Mixed Grill* (1914); *A Lucky Miss* (1914); *The Light Blues* (1915); etc.

Talich, Václav, Czech conductor; b. Kroměříž, May 28, 1883. He studied music with his father, Jan Talich (1851-1915), and then entered the Prague Cons. as a pupil of Ševčik (1897-1903); in 1904 he became concertmaster of the Odessa Orch.; made his début as conductor with that orch.; in 1905-07 he taught violin at Tiflis, Caucasus. He returned to Prague in 1907, and in 1908 became conductor of the Philharmonic Orch. at Ljubljana; in 1910 he took a course of studies with Max Reger and Hans Sitt at the Leipzig Cons., and also with Arthur Nikisch in conducting. From 1912 to 1915 he was opera conductor at Pilsen; from 1919 to 1935 he was chief conductor of the Prague Philharmonic Orch., which he brought to a high degree of excellence; toured with it in Italy and Germany, and also performed with it in Vienna, Paris, and London. In 1935 he was appointed conductor of the National Opera in Prague; he lost this position in 1945, owing to political and personal dissension; in 1949 he went to Bratislava, where he formed a Slovak Philharmonic Orch. A symposium of articles was publ. on the occasion of his 60th birthday, under the editorship of Otakar Šourek (Prague, 1943).

Talley, Marion, American soprano; b. Nevada, Mo., Dec. 20, 1907. She was educated in Kansas City, where her family moved when she was a small child; sang in church there, and attracted attention by her unusually lovely voice; appeared in a local performance of *Mignon* at the age of 15, after which funds were raised to send her to N. Y., and later to Italy, for study. At 18, she made her début at the Metropolitan Opera (Feb. 17, 1926) as Gilda in *Rigoletto,* and the occasion was exploited for sensational publicity by her fellow townsmen; she remained a member of the Metropolitan Opera for the next 3 seasons, singing coloratura roles, and also gave many recitals throughout the U. S. and Canada. However, the extravagant hopes held for her as a native talent were not fulfilled, and she failed to continue her career as an opera singer; after appearances on the radio and in several motion picture films, she settled in Beverly Hills, Calif. She married Michael Raucheisen (q.v.), June 30, 1932; marriage annulled, Jan. 28, 1933.

Tallis (or **Tallys, Talys**), **Thomas,** English organist and composer; b. c. 1505; d. Greenwich, Nov. 23, 1585. Organist or master of the choristers of Waltham Abbey until 1540; Gentleman of the Chapel Royal during the reigns of Henry VIII, Edward VI, Mary, and Elizabeth, and joint-organist with Byrd. With the latter he obtained in 1575 letters patent for the exclusive privilege of printing music and ruled music paper, the first work issued by them being 34 *Cantiones quae ab argumento sacrae vocantur, 5 et 6 partium,* in 1575 (16 motets by Tallis and 18 by Byrd). Tallis' most famous work is a 'song of 40 parts' for eight 5-part choirs: *Spem in alium non habui* (specimen page in first ed. of Grove, Vol. III, p. 274). A composer of great contrapuntal skill, he was among the first to set English words to music for the rites of the Church of England. Surviving are 2 Masses, 2 Magnificats, 2 Lamentations, 52 motets and other pieces with Latin text, 18 English anthems, 3 sets of Psalms, etc., as well as some keyboard music. —In Barnard's 'First Book of Selected Church Music' (1641) is a First Service, or Short Service (*a* 4), Preces, Responses, etc., often republished (by Rimbault, Novello, Jebb, Davison & Apel, etc.); J. Day's 'Morning and Evening Prayer' (1560), Boyce's 'Cathedral Music,' and the histories by Hawkins and Burney contain specimens of his music. Rimbault republ. the *Order of Daily Service, with the Musical Notation.* R. Terry ed. a Mass *a* 4 in 1908 (Breitkopf & Härtel), and most of Tallis' church music is in vol. VI of 'Tudor Church Music' (1928). There are many works in MS at Oxford, Cambridge, and in the British Museum. —Cf. H. B. Collins, *T. T.*, in 'Music & Letters' (1929); B. Schofield, *The Manuscripts of T.'s Forty-Part Motet,* in the 'Mus. Quarterly' (April, 1951); D. Stevens, *The Keyboard Music of T. T.,* in the 'Mus. Times' (July, 1952).

Talma, Louise, American composer; b. New York, Oct. 31, 1906. She studied at N. Y. Univ. (B. M.) and at Columbia Univ. (M. A.); studied piano with Isidor Philipp and composition with Nadia Boulanger at the Fontainebleau School of Music, France. In 1946 she received a Guggenheim Fellowship; joined the faculty at Hunter College, N. Y. In her music she adopts a strongly contrapuntal neo-Baroque style. — Works: *Toccata,* for orch. (1944); *Introduction and Rondo Giocoso* (1946); *Three Madrigals* for women's voices and string quartet (1929); *La Belle Dame Sans Merci,* for baritone solo (1929); *Terre de France,* a song cycle (1925); *Five Sonnets from the Portuguese,* song cycle (1934); piano sonata (1943); *The Divine Flame,* oratorio (1948); *Let's Touch the Sky,* cycle of poems, after e. e. cummings, for chorus and woodwind instruments (1952); piano pieces. —Cf. Madeleine Goss, *Modern Music-Makers* (N. Y., 1952).

Tamagno (tăh-măh'-ñoh), **Francesco,** famous Italian tenor; b. Turin, Dec. 28, 1850; d. Varese, near Turin, Aug. 31, 1905. He was at first apprenticed to a baker, and later to a locksmith; entered the Turin Cons. as a pupil of Pedrotti, and in 1873 made his début as 2nd tenor at the Teatro Regio there, his powerful voice immediately attracting attention. Following his appearance in *Un Ballo in maschera* at Palermo on Jan. 17, 1874, his success was rapid. In 1876-77, he sang at the Liceo of Barcelona, and from 1877 at La Scala, Milan, where in 1887 he created the role of Otello in Verdi's opera. He sang at the Metropolitan Opera House, N. Y., during the season 1894-95 (début, Nov. 21, 1894, as Arnold in Rossini's *Guillaume Tell*). Other engagements included South America, Lisbon, Madrid, Paris, and London. In 1902, having made a fortune, he retired from the stage. —Cf. E. de Amicis, *Francesco Tamagno* (Palermo, 1902); M. Corsi, *Tamagno* (Milan, 1937); E. Gara, *Francesco Tamagno,* in 'La Scala' (Jan., 1954).

Tamberlik, Enrico, famous Italian tenor; b. Rome, March 16, 1820; d. Paris, March 13, 1889. He studied singing with Zirilli in Rome and with Guglielmi in Naples, where he made his stage début in 1840. On April 4, 1850, he made his 1st London appearance, as Masaniello in Auber's *La Muette de Portici,* at the Royal Italian Opera, Covent Garden, and sang annually in London until 1864, with the exception of 1857, when he undertook an extensive European tour, including Spain and Russia. In 1860 he settled in Paris, and lived there most of his life. Verdi admired him, and wrote the part of Don Alvaro in *La Forza del destino* for him; Tamberlik sang in its world première at St. Petersburg, Russia, on Oct. 30, 1862, and this role became one of his most famous interpretations. He appeared at the

Academy of Music, N. Y., on Sept. 18, 1873, but his American season was a brief one. He was famous for his rich high notes, and his ability to sustain the high C was legendary. —Cf. H. Brody, *La Carrière d'un ténor italien* in the 'Revue Musicale' (April 15, 1904, *et seq.*).

Tamburini, Antonio, Italian baritone; b. Faenza, March 28, 1800; d. Nice, Nov. 9, 1876. First learned to play the horn as a pupil of his father; then studied singing with A. Rossi and B. Asioli; début at Cento in 1818; thereafter sang on the chief stages of Italy, being engaged by Barbaja from 1824-32. During 1832-41 he sang at the Théâtre Italien, Paris, as part of a brilliant company that included Grisi, Persiani, Viardot, Rubini, and Lablache, appearing in London in the alternate seasons; after a short stay in Italy, he remained for ten years in Russia. In 1855 he retired to his estate at Sèvres, near Paris. His greatest triumph was in Bellini's *La Straniera,* in which he created a frenzy of enthusiasm by his singing of the aria *Meco tu vieni, o misera.* In 1822 he married the singer Marietta Goja. —Cf. J. de Biez, *T. et la musique italienne* (1877).

Tamura, Hirosada, Japanese musicologist; b. Tokyo, Sept. 6, 1883. From 1904 to 1907 he studied at the Imperial Univ. of Tokyo, qualifying as tutor there in 1909 (from 1916, prof.); from 1924 also lecturer on esthetics at the Women's Univ. in Tokyo. —Writings (in Japanese): *Richard Wagner* (1916) and *Beethoven's 9th Symphony* (1924); also transl. Hanslick's *Vom Musikalisch-Schönen* into Japanese, with a commentary.

Taneyev (tah-nyĕh'-ehf), **Alexander Sergeyevitch,** Russian composer, uncle of Sergey Taneyev; b. St. Petersburg, Jan. 17, 1850; d. there, Feb. 7, 1918. He studied composition with F. Reichel in Dresden; upon his return to St. Petersburg, he took lessons with Rimsky-Korsakov. Music was his avocation; he followed a government career, advancing to the post of head of the Imperial Chancellery. The style of his music is Romantic, lapsing into sentimentalism; the main influence is that of Tchaikovsky. —Works: operas, *Cupid's Revenge* (concert performance, St. Petersburg, May 19, 1899) and *Buran* (*The Snow Storm*); a *Festival March* for orch.; 3 symphonies (1890; 1903; 1908); 2 orchestral mazurkas; *Hamlet Overture*; 2 suites for orch.; *Ballade* after a poem (*Alyosha Popovitch*) by Alexey Tolstoy, for orch.; 3 string quartets; *Arabesque* for clarinet and piano; piano pieces; songs.

Taneyev (tah-nyĕh'-ehf), **Sergey Ivanovitch,** Russian composer and pedagogue; nephew of Alexander Taneyev; b. district of Vladimir, Nov. 25, 1856; d. Moscow, June 19, 1915. He began taking piano lessons at the age of 10 at the Moscow Cons.; after attending academic school for a year, he re-entered the Cons. and studied piano with Nicholas Rubinstein and composition with Tchaikovsky, forming a lifelong friendship with the latter. He made a very successful début in Moscow as a pianist, playing the D minor concerto of Brahms (Jan. 31, 1875); after a tour of Russia with Leopold Auer, he visited Turkey, Greece, and Italy; spent the winter of 1877-78 in Paris; in the autumn of 1878 he succeeded Tchaikovsky as prof. of harmony and orchestration at the Moscow Cons.; after the death of Nicholas Rubinstein in 1881, he took over the latter's piano classes there; from 1885 to 1889 he was director; from 1889 to 1906 he taught composition. Taneyev was a first-class pianist; Tchaikovsky regarded him as one of the finest interpreters of his music; but Taneyev was not interested in a virtuoso career, and gradually confined himself to composition and pedagogy. His position as a composer is anomalous: he is one of the most respectable figures of Russian music history, and there is a growing literature about him; his correspondence and all documents, however trivial, concerning his life, are treasured as part of the Russian cultural heritage; yet outside Russia his works are rarely heard; his great treatise on counterpoint, *Podvizhnoy kontrapunkt strogavo pisma* (Florid Counterpoint in Strict Style), publ. in 1909, remains untranslated into any Western language, and therefore inaccessible to musicians outside Russia. The style of his compositions presents a compromise between Russian melos and Germanic contrapuntal writing; the mastery revealed in his symphonies and quartets is unquestionable. His most ambitious work was the trilogy *Oresteia* after Aeschylus, in 3 divisions, *Agamemnon, Choëphorai,* and *Eumenides,* first performed in St. Petersburg on Oct. 29, 1895. Other works are *John of Damascus,* cantata, after Alexey Tolstoy (1884); *At the Reading of the Psalm,* cantata (1914); symph. in C minor (1902; 2 earlier symphonies are in MS); 2 string quintets; 6 string quartets; 1 piano quartet; 2 string trios; 1 piano trio; about 50 songs, most of them of a very high quality. After his death an almost completed *Treatise on Canon and Fugue* was found among his papers and published (1929). —Cf. M. Montagu-Nathan, *Contemporary Russian*

Composers (N. Y., 1917) K. A. Kuznetzov, ed., *Memorial and Bibliography of S. I. Taneyev* (Moscow, 1925); V. Yakovlev, *S. I. Taneyev: His Musical Life* (Moscow, 1927); V. Karatygin, *To the Memory of S. I. Taneyev* in the 'Mus. Quarterly' (Oct., 1927); M. D. Calvocoressi and G. Abraham, *Masters of Russian Music* (London, 1936; pp. 439-49); V. Protopopov, ed., *Memorial of S. I. Taneyev* (Moscow, 1947); G. Bernandt, *S. I. Taneyev* (Moscow, 1950); a symposium, *S. I. Taneyev; Materials and Documents* (vol. I, 1952); Jacob Weinberg, *S. I. Taneyev,* in the 'Mus. Quarterly' (Jan., 1958).

Tango, Egisto, Italian conductor; b. Rome, Nov. 13, 1873; d. Copenhagen, Oct. 5, 1951. He first studied engineering; then entered the Naples Cons.; made his début as opera conductor in Venice (1893); conducted at La Scala, Milan (1895); then at Berlin (1903-08). He conducted at the Metropolitan Opera, N. Y., in 1909-10; in Italy (1911-12); and in Budapest (1913-19), where he gave the earliest performances of stage works by Béla Bartók. From 1920 to 1926 he was active in Germany and Austria. In 1927 he settled in Copenhagen. He was distinguished for the technical precision and interpretative clarity of his performances.

Tannenberg, David, German-American organ builder; b. Berthelsdorf, Upper Lusatia, March 21, 1728; d. York, Pa., May 19, 1804. Tannenberg came to America in 1749 and became a member of the Moravian Church settlement at Bethlehem, Pa. Following the death of his teacher and colleague, Johann Gottlob Clemm (q.v.), he established himself in Lititz, Pa.; made 32 organs for churches in Pennsylvania, New York, Maryland, Virginia, and North Carolina; he also made a few pianos. —Cf. P. E. Beck, *David Tannenberger, Organ Builder,* in 'Papers Read Before the Lancaster, Pa. Historical Society' (Jan., 1926); D. M. McCorkle, *The Moravian Contribution to American Music,* in 'Music Library Association Notes' (Dec., 1956); D. M. McCorkle, *Musical Instruments of the Moravians of North Carolina,* in the 'American German Review' (Feb.-March, 1955).

Tannhäuser, famous lyric poet and Minnesinger; flourished in the 13th century; led a wandering life typical of his calling; for a time was at the court of Friedrich II, Duke of Austria; then with Otto II of Bavaria. His name became legendary through the tale of the Venusberg, pagan intimacy with Venus, penitence, pilgrimage to Rome, and the miracle of the flowering of his pilgrim's staff. Wagner's *Tannhäuser* is based on this legend, unconnected with the actual life of the real Tannhäuser. —Cf. F. Zander, *Die Tannhäusersage und der Minnesinger Tannhäuser* (1858); J. Siebert, *Tannhäuser* (1894).

Tansman, Alexander, Polish composer; b. Lodz, June 12, 1897. He studied with Piotr Rytel in Warsaw, and piano with Lütschg; his *Sérénade symphonique* was performed by the Lodz Orch. in 1917; after a brief service in the Polish army, he resumed his studies; submitted 2 works for the National Prize, and received both 1st and 2nd prize. In 1919 he went to Paris, which became his permanent home. He first appeared in public, playing his piano works, in Paris on Feb. 17, 1920; performances of his symph. and chamber music followed in rapid succession; his *Danse de la sorcière* for chamber orch. was presented at the Zürich Festival of the International Society for Contemporary Music (June 22, 1926). He made an extensive tour of the U. S. in 1927-28 as pianist in his own works. In 1933 he toured the Far East. After the occupation of Paris by the Germans in 1940, he made his way to the U. S.; settled in Hollywood, where he wrote music for films; returned to Paris in 1946. His music is distinguished by a considerable melodic gift, fine craftsmanship, and a vivacious rhythm; his harmony is often bitonal; there are some Impressionistic traits that point to his Parisian tastes. —Works: operas: *La Nuit kurde* (1925-27; not produced) and *Le Serment* (Brussels, March 11, 1955); ballets: *Sextuor* (Paris, May 17, 1924; also in Chicago, as *The Tragedy of the Cello,* Dec. 26, 1926), *La Grande Ville* (1932), *Bric-à-Brac* (1937); for orch.: 7 symphonies: No. 1 (1925; Boston, March 18, 1927), No. 2 (1926), No. 3, *Symphonie concertante* (1931), No. 4 (1939), No. 5 (1942; Washington, Feb. 2, 1943), No. 6, *In Memoriam* (1943), No. 7 (1944; St. Louis, Oct. 24, 1947); *Danse de la sorcière* (Brussels, May 5, 1924; numerous subsequent performances); *Sinfonietta* (Paris, March 23, 1925); *Ouverture symphonique* (Paris, Feb. 3, 1927); piano concerto No. 1 (Paris, May 27, 1926, Tansman soloist); piano concerto No. 2 (Boston, Dec. 28, 1927, Tansman soloist); suite for 2 pianos and orch. (Paris, Nov. 16, 1930); viola concerto (1936); *Fantaisie* for violin and orch. (1937); *Fantaisie* for cello and orch. (1937); *Rapsodie polonaise* (St. Louis, Nov. 14, 1941); *Études symphoniques* (1943); *Concertino* for guitar and orch.

(1945); *Ricercari* (St. Louis, Dec. 22, 1949); *Capriccio* (Louisville, March 6, 1955); chamber music: 8 string quartets (No. 1, 1917; No. 8, 1956); *Danse de la sorcière*, for woodwind quintet and piano (a version of the ballet; 1925); a string sextet (1940); *Divertimento*, for oboe, clarinet, trumpet, cello, and piano (1944); violin sonata (1919); flute sonata (1925); cello sonata (1930); etc.; for piano: *20 pièces faciles polonaises* (1924); *Sonata rustica* (1925); mazurkas, and other Polish dances; *Sonatine transatlantique* (1930; very popular; contains imitations of jazz; also for orch., Paris, Feb. 28, 1931; used by Kurt Jooss for his ballet *Impressions of a Big City*, Cologne, Nov. 21, 1932); *Pour les enfants*, 4 albums for piano. He publ. a monograph on Stravinsky (Paris, 1948; in English, *Igor Stravinsky: The Man and His Music*, N. Y., 1949); contributed numerous articles on Polish music to the 'Revue Musicale' and other publications. —Cf. Irving Schwerké, *Alexandre Tansman, Compositeur polonais* (Paris, 1931); R. Petit, *Alexandre Tansman*, in the 'Revue Musicale' (Feb., 1929).

Tans'ur, William, English organist, composer, and lexicographer; b. Dunchurch (baptized, Nov. 6), 1706; d. St. Neots, Oct. 7, 1783. His real name was Tanzer, and he was the son of Edward Tanzer; he changed his name to Tans'ur (using the apostrophe). He was a church organist and taught music in various provincial towns in England. His publications include: *The Royal Melody Compleat, or the New Harmony of Sion* (2nd ed.,1760; 3rd ed., in 3 parts, 1764, 1765, 1766; at least 11 American eds. are known, publ. as *The American Harmony, or Royal Melody Complete*, or under similar, slightly varying titles); *Heaven on Earth, or the Beauty of Holiness* (1738); *Sacred Mirth, or the Pious Soul's Daily Delight* (1739); *The Universal Harmony* (1743, etc.); *The Psalm-Singer's Jewel* (1760, etc.); *Melodia sacra* (1771, 1772); *New Musical Grammar* (1746; 7th ed., 1829); an epitome of this last, *The Elements of Musick Displayed* (1772). —For details on various eds. see I. Lowens and Allen P. Britton, in 'Papers of the Bibliographical Society of America' (1955, No. 4; pp. 340-54).

Tapper, Bertha (*née* Feiring), wife of Thomas Tapper (q.v.).

Tapper, Thomas, American music educator; b. Canton, Mass., Jan. 28, 1864; d. White Plains, N. Y., Feb. 24, 1958. He studied music in Europe; from 1897 to 1905 was editor of the 'Musician'; then taught at N. Y. Univ. (1908-12); was lecturer at the Institute of Musical Art (1905-24); also filled other editorial and educational positions. His publications include *The Music Life* (1891); *The Education of the Music Teacher* (1914); *Essentials in Music History* (1914; with Percy Goetschius); *The Melodic Music Course*, 28 vols. (with F. H. Ripley); *Harmonic Music Course*, 7 vols.; *The Modern Graded Piano Course*, 19 vols.; *Music Theory and Composition*, 6 vols.; *From Palestrina to Grieg* (Boston, 1929; 2nd ed., 1946). —His wife, **Bertha Feiring Tapper** (b. Christiania, Norway, Jan. 25, 1859; d. New York, Sept. 2, 1915), was a good pianist; studied with Agathe Backer-Gröndahl in Norway and with Leschetizky in Vienna; came to America in 1881; taught piano at the New England Cons., Boston (1889-97) and at the Institute of Musical Art, N. Y. (1905-10); edited 2 vols. of Grieg's piano works; publ. piano pieces and songs. She married Thomas Tapper on Sept. 22, 1895.

Tappert, Wilhelm, German music scholar and writer; b. Ober-Thomaswaldau, Silesia, Feb. 19, 1830; d. Berlin, Oct. 27, 1907. He was trained as a schoolmaster till 1856, when he entered Kullak's Academy of Music in Berlin; studied theory privately with Dehn; settled in Berlin. He was editor of the 'Allgemeine deutsche Musikzeitung' (1876-80); collected a large assemblage of old tablatures, including unique specimens; after his death this collection and his entire valuable library was acquired by the Royal Library of Berlin. An ardent admirer of Wagner, he publ. a curious volume, *Ein Wagner-Lexikon: Wörterbuch der Unhöflichkeit, enthaltend grobe, höhnede, gehässige und verläumderische Ausdrücke welche gegen den Meister Richard Wagner, seine Werke und seine Anhänger von den Feinden und Spöttern gebraucht worden sind. Zur Gemütsergötzung in müssigen Stunden gesammelt*, a collection of anti-Wagner reviews (Leipzig, 1877); a 2nd, enlarged ed. was publ. under the title *Richard Wagner im Spiegel der Kritik* (Leipzig, 1903). Other publications: *Musik und musikalische Erziehung* (1867); *Musikalische Studien* (1868); *Das Verbot der Quintenparallelen* (1869); *Wandernde Melodien* (2nd ed., 1889); *54 Erlkönig-Kompositionen* (1898; 2nd ed., 1906); *Sang und Klang aus alter Zeit* (1906); also publ. arrangements of old German songs; 50 left-hand studies for piano; other piano pieces.

Tappolet, Willy, Swiss writer on music; b. Lindau, near Zürich, Aug. 6, 1890. He studied philology and music in Berlin, Zürich, and Geneva; in 1950, appointed to the faculty of Geneva Univ. He is the author of monographs on Honegger (Zürich, 1933; in French, Neuchâtel, 1939; enlarged German ed., Zürich, 1954); and Ravel (Olten, 1950); also wrote *La Notation musicale et son influence sur la pratique de la musique du moyen-âge à nos jours* (Neuchâtel, 1947), and articles for various publications.

Tarchi (tahr'-kē), **Angelo,** Italian composer; b. Naples, about 1755; d. Paris, Aug. 19, 1814. He studied at the Cons. dei Turchini in Naples with Fago and Sala; in 1786, was in London; in 1797 settled in Paris. He wrote about 45 operas in Italian, and 6 in French; of these the following were produced at La Scala in Milan: *Ademira* (Dec. 27, 1783); *Ariarte* (Jan., 1786); *Il Conte di Saldagna* (June 10, 1787); *Adrasto* (Feb. 8, 1792); *Le Danaidi* (Dec. 26, 1794); and *L'Impostura poco dura* (Oct. 10, 1795). In Paris he produced the French version of *Il Conte di Saldagna* as *Bouffons de la foire St. Germain* (1790), *D'Auberge en auberge* (Opéra-Comique, April 26, 1800), etc. He acquired a certain notoriety by his attempt to rewrite the 3rd and 4th acts of Mozart's *Le Nozze di Figaro* (1787); regarding this episode, see A. Einstein, *Mozart e Tarchi,* in the 'Rassegna Musicale' (July, 1935); see also C. Sartori, *Lo 'Zeffiretto' di Angelo Tarchi,* in the 'Rivista Musicale Italiana' (July, 1954).

Tarditi, Giovanni, Italian bandleader and composer; b. Acqui, March 10, 1857; d. Rome, Sept. 19, 1935. He traveled as bandleader in Europe and America; publ. manuals for band playing, such as *Segnalofono* for trumpet calls; wrote the operettas *Monte Carlo* (Genoa, March 1, 1897) and *L'Isola degli antropofagi* (Rome, June 1, 1925), military marches, etc.

Tarisio, Luigi, Italian violin-maker; b. Fontanetto, near Milan, c. 1795; d. Milan, Oct., 1854. He began life as a carpenter, and in his spare hours acquired sufficient skill on the violin to play dance music at country fairs, etc. His trade brought him into many humble homes, where he found old violins, the value of which was not suspected by their owners. Gifted with extraordinary powers of observation, he soon recognized the value of those neglected instruments, and, whenever possible, acquired them. After some time he began to imitate the models thus collected; then in the capacity of repairer, he obtained access to Italian chapels and monasteries, where he discovered many valuable instruments. In 1827 he paid his first visit to Paris, disposing of a number of Italian violins to celebrated dealers. Soon he was acknowledged as the foremost connoisseur, so that his regular visits to Paris were eagerly looked for. In 1851 he made his first trip to London. Tarisio was the first to recognize the value of the now famous Italian violins; it was he who created a market for them. He left a collection of over 200 violins, which was acquired by Vuillaume of Paris.—Cf. G. Hart, *The Violin: Famous Makers and Their Imitators* (London, 1875; 4th ed., 1887); H. R. Haweis, *Old Violins* (London, 1898); Hill, A. E. et al., *Antonio Stradivari* (London, 1909); W. A. Silverman, *The Violin Hunter* (N. Y., 1957; mostly anecdotal).

Tarp, Svend Erik, Danish composer; b. Thisted, Jutland, Aug. 6, 1908. He studied at the Conservatory of Copenhagen, in Munich, and in Innsbruck; returning to Denmark, he became editor of the 'Dania Edition' (1941). —Works: the ballets *Skyggen (The Shadow,* after Andersen, 1941-44) and *Den detroniserede Dyretæmmer (The Dethroned Tamer;* Copenhagen, Feb. 5, 1944); *Sinfonia divertente* (1945); *Pro Defunctis,* for orch. (1946); symph. in E♭ major (1949); *Mosaic,* miniature suite for orch. (1940); *The Battle of Jericho,* symph. picture (1949); much chamber music; piano pieces. His opera *Prinsessen i det Fjerne,* based on Hermann Sudermann's story, was produced in Copenhagen on May 18, 1953.

Tárrega, Francisco, Spanish guitar virtuoso; b. Villarreal, Castellón, Nov. 21, 1852; d. Barcelona, Dec. 15, 1909. The outstanding representative of the modern Spanish guitar-school; studied at the Madrid Cons. He composed many pieces for his instrument, also made many transcriptions of classical and modern works. —Cf. 'La Guitarra,' No. 1 (Buenos Aires, 1923).

Tartini, Giuseppe, Italian violinist, composer, and theorist; b. Pirano, Istria, April 8, 1692; d. Padua, Feb. 26, 1770. While studying, at his parents' desire, for the priesthood, he took violin lessons that strengthened his ardent longings for a secular career; his father finally allowed him to study law at Padua (1710), but music, especially the violin, and fencing were his passion. A charge of abduction, following on his secret marriage to a protegée of Cardinal Cornaro's, obliged him to take refuge in the Franciscan monastery at Assisi; for two years he studied the violin, also composition (under the organist Czernohorsky, called 'il Padre Boemo') and then returned to Padua, a reconciliation having been effected with the Cardinal. Shortly afterward he heard the violinist Veracini at Venice, and was stimulated to more arduous endeavor; he retired to Ancona for further study of the violin. About this time (1714) he discovered the combination-tones, and utilized them in perfecting purity of intonation. His fame then increasing, in 1721 he was appointed solo violinist and conductor of the orch. at St. Antonio in Padua. He spent the years 1723-25 as chamber musician to Count Kinsky in Prague, having been invited there to perform at the coronation of Karl VI; he then resumed his duties at Padua, and in 1728 founded a violin school there, in which were trained many distinguished violinists (Nardini, Pasqualino, Lahoussaye, etc.). Although repeatedly invited to visit Paris and London, he refused to leave Italy after his return to Padua; in 1740 he visited Rome, and on his way home made a triumphal tour of the principal Italian cities.—Tartini was one of the great masters of the violin; his style of bowing still serves as a model, and his compositions are regarded as classics. He composed about 150 concertos and 100 violin sonatas as well as some choral pieces, of which a *Salve Regina* was his last composition. Publ. works: op. 1, 6 concertos (1734; 3 republ. in Paris; 3 others republ. there with 2 viola parts added by Blainville, as *Concerti grossi*); also as op. 1, 12 violin sonatas with cello and cembalo; op. 2, 6 sonatas for the same; op. 3, 12 sonatas (incl. op. 2) for violin and bass; op. 4, *Sei concerti a violino solo, 2 violini, viola e violoncello o cembalo di concerto;* also as op. 4, 6 sonatas for violin with continuo; op. 5, 6, and 7 each comprise 6 sonatas for violin and continuo; op. 8, *Sei sonate a 3, due violini col basso;* op. 9, 6 sonatas *a* 3; and *L'Arte dell' arco* (reprinted in French by Choron in *Principes de composition,* and separately by André); the famous and oft-republished *Trillo del diavolo* was a posthumous work (it was discovered by Baillot and first publ. in Cartier's *L'Art du violon*); the concertos have been republ. in various editions and in varying combinations; sonatas have been republ. by Alard, Léonard, David, Jensen, Wasielewski, etc. —Theoretical works: *Trattato di musica secondo la vera scienza dell'armonia* (1754); *Risposta alla critica del di lui Trattato di musica di Msgr. Le Serre di Ginevra* (1767); *De' principj dell' armonia musicale contenuta nel diatonico genere* (1767); *Lettera alla signora Maddalena Lombardini inserviente ad una importante lezione per i suonatori di violino* (1770; English transl. by Burney, London, 1771; German transl., 1786); and another treatise, only in a French transl. by P. Denis, *Traité des agréments de la musique* (1782). As a theorist he follows Rameau, and derives the minor chord from an undertone series opposed to the overtone series; like Zarlino, he regards the minor chord as the opposite of the major.—BIBLIOGRAPHY: Fanzago, *Orazione . . . delle lodi di G. T.* (Padua, 1770); J. A. Hiller, *Lebensbeschreibungen berühmter Musikgelehrten und Tonkünstler* (Leipzig, 1784); F. Fanzago, *Elogi* (Padua, 1792); C. Ugoni (1802; in *Della letteratura italiana . . .*, vol. I, pp. 1-28); F. Fayolle, *Notices sur Corelli, Tartini, etc.* (Paris, 1810); G. Benedetti, *Brevi cenni su G. T.* (Trieste, 1897); M. Tamaro, *G. T.* (Parenzo, 1897; in 'Atti e memorie della Società istriana . . .' vol. XII); A. Bachmann, *Les grands violinistes du passé* (Paris, 1913); C. Bouvet, *Une Leçon de T. . . .* (Paris, 1918); M. Dounias, *Die Violinkonzerte G. T.s* (Munich, 1935); H. P. Schökel, *G. T.* (Berlin, 1936); A. Capri, *G. T.* (Milan, 1945; includes a thematic index of the Tartini MSS at Padua); A. Spalding, *A Fiddle, a Sword, and a Lady* (N. Y., 1953; a fictionalized account of Tartini's life). A thematic index of Tartini's concertos was publ. by G. Tebaldini, in 'L'Archivio mus.' (Padua, 1895).

Taskin (tăhs-kăn'), **(Émile-) Alexandre,** French baritone, grandson of Henri Joseph Taskin; b. Paris, March 8, 1853; d. there, Oct. 5, 1897. He was a pupil of Ponchard and Bussine at the Paris Cons. Début at Amiens, 1875. Sang in Lille and Geneva; returned to Paris in 1878; engaged at the Opéra-Comique in 1879, and created important parts in many new operas. He retired in 1894, and from then until his death he was prof. of lyrical declamation at the Cons. On the night of the terrible catastrophe of the burning of the Opéra-Comique (May 25, 1887) he was singing in *Mignon;* through his calmness and bravery many lives were saved, and the government decorated him with a medal.

Taskin, Pascal, manufacturer of keyboard instruments; b. Theux, near Liège, 1723; d. Paris, Feb. 1793. Went to Paris at an early age and entered Blanchet's atelier, later succeeding to the business and becoming highly celebrated as an instrument maker.

He invented the leather plectra for the harpsichord (1768), replacing the crow quills previously in use. He built his first piano in 1776. —Cf. E. Closson, *P. T.,* in 'Sammelbände der Internationalen Musik-Gesellschaft' XII, pp. 234-67. —His nephew, **Joseph Pascal Taskin** (1750-1829), was Keeper of the King's Instruments from 1772 to the Revolution. His 2nd son, **Henri Joseph** (1779-1852), was an organist and composer.

Tate, Phyllis (Margaret Duncan), English composer; b. Gerrards Cross, Bucks, April 6, 1911. She studied composition with Harry Farjeon at the Royal Academy of Music; composed a symph., a cello concerto, and several other large works, but withdrew them as immature. She adopted a neo-Classical style enlivened by modernistic dissonance and syncopated rhythms. Among her works are *Valse lointaine,* for small orch. (1941); *Prelude, Interlude and Postlude,* for chamber orch. (1942); cello concerto (1933); saxophone concerto (1944); sonata for clarinet and cello (1947; performed at the Salzburg Festival of the International Society for Contemporary Music, June 23, 1952); string quartet (1952); *Occasional Overture,* for orch. (1955). In 1935 she married Alan Frank (q.v.). —Cf. H. Searle, *Phyllis Tate,* in the 'Mus. Times' (May, 1955); M. Carner, *The Music of Phyllis Tate,* in 'Music & Letters' (April, 1954).

Tauber, Richard (real name Ernst Seiffert), eminent tenor; b. Linz, Austria, May 16, 1892; d. London, Jan. 8, 1948. He studied music at Hoch's Cons. in Frankfurt; made his début at Chemnitz as Tamino in *Die Zauberflöte* (March 2, 1913), with such success that he was engaged in the same year at the Dresden Opera; in 1915 he appeared with the Berlin State Opera at Salzburg. Later he abandoned serious opera and sang mostly in light opera; was particularly successful in the leading parts of Lehár's operettas. He made his American début on Oct. 28, 1931, in a N. Y. recital. In 1938 he went to England; became a British subject in 1940. In London he wrote an operetta, *Old Chelsea,* and took the leading role in it at its production there (Feb. 17, 1943). He made his last American appearance at Carnegie Hall, N. Y., on March 30, 1947. —Cf. H. Ludwigg, ed., *Richard Tauber* (Berlin, 1928); Diana Napier Tauber (his second wife), *Richard Tauber* (Glasgow, 1949).

Taubert (tow'-behrt), **Ernst Eduard,** German composer and music critic; b. Regenwalde, Sept. 25, 1838; d. Berlin, July 14, 1934. He studied theology in Bonn, and music there with Albert Dietrich; later with Friedrich Kiel in Berlin, where he became teacher at the Stern Cons. and music critic for the 'Berliner Post'; also contributed to various German music magazines. His works include a piano quintet; a wind quintet; a piano quartet; 5 string quartets; a piano trio; a *Ballade* for orch.; piano pieces for 2 and 4 hands; songs.

Taubert, (Karl Gottfried) Wilhelm, German composer; b. Berlin, March 23, 1811; d. there, Jan. 7, 1891. Piano pupil of Neithardt, later of L. Berger, and for composition of Bernhard Klein. Appeared early as a concert player; taught music in Berlin, became assistant conductor of the court orch. in 1831; court Kapellmeister from 1845 to 1870. He conducted his 1st symph. in Berlin at the age of 19 (March 31, 1831). His operas (all produced in Berlin) include: *Die Kirmes* (Jan. 23, 1832); *Marquis und Dieb* (Feb. 1, 1842); *Der Zigeuner* (Sept. 19, 1834); *Joggeli* (Oct. 9, 1853); *Macbeth* (Nov. 16, 1857); *Cesario,* after Shakespeare's *Twelfth Night* (Nov. 13, 1874). He composed much instrumental music but is best remembered for his *Kinderlieder* (op. 145, 160), the favorites among his 300 songs. —Cf. W. Neumann, *Wilhelm Taubert und Ferdinand Hiller* (Kassel, 1857).

Taubman, Howard, American music critic; b. New York, July 4, 1907. He studied at Cornell Univ.; joined the staff of the 'N. Y. Times' in 1930; in 1955, succeeded Olin Downes as chief music critic there. —Books: *Opera—Front and Back* (N. Y., 1938); *Music as a Profession* (N. Y., 1939); *Music on My Beat* (N. Y., 1943); *The Maestro; the Life of Arturo Toscanini* (N. Y., 1951); *How to Build a Record Library* (N. Y., 1953; new ed., 1955); *How to Bring Up Your Child to Enjoy Music* (Garden City, N. Y., 1958).

Taubmann (towb'-mahn), **Otto,** German conductor and composer; b. Hamburg, March 8, 1859; d. Berlin, July 5, 1929. After graduation from school he followed a commercial career for 3 years; then studied music under Wüllner, Rischbieter, Nicodé, and Blassmann at the Dresden Cons.; traveled a year for further study, and began his career as theater conductor; 1886-89, director of the Wiesbaden Cons.; 1891-92, theater conductor in St. Petersburg; 1892-95, conductor of the Cäcilienverein in Ludwigshafen; then settled in Berlin, where from 1898 he was music critic of the 'Börsen-Courier.' —He composed chiefly choral works, of which the most successful was

Eine Deutsche Messe for soli, double chorus, organ, and orch. (1896).

Taudou (toh-doo'), **Antoine (-Antonin-Barthélemy)**, French violinist and composer; b. Perpignan, Aug. 24, 1846; d. St.-Germain-en-Laye, July 6, 1925. He studied at the Paris Cons., winning the Grand Prix de Rome in 1869 with the cantata *Francesca da Rimini;* 1883, prof. of harmony at the Cons. —Publ. a *Marche-Ballet,* a *Chant d'automne,* and a *Marche nocturne,* for orch.; a violin concerto; a string quartet; a piano trio; a trio for flute, viola, and cello; etc.

Tausch (towsh), **Franz**, celebrated German clarinetist; b. Heidelberg, Dec. 26, 1762; d. Berlin, Feb. 9, 1817. At the age of 8 he played in the Electoral orch. at Mannheim; was engaged at Munich (1777-89), and then in the court orch. at Berlin, where he founded a school for wind instruments in 1805. Heinrich Bärmann was his pupil. He published 2 clarinet concertos, 3 concertantes for 2 clarinets, Andante and Polonaise for clarinet, clarinet duos, trios for 2 clarinets with bassoon, 6 quartets for 2 basset-horns and 2 bassoons (with 2 horns *ad. lib.),* 6 military marches, *a* 10, etc.

Tausch, Julius, German pianist; b. Dessau, April 15, 1827; d. Bonn, Nov. 11, 1895. He studied with Fr. Schneider, and at the Leipzig Cons. (1844-46), then settled in Düsseldorf; there he became conductor of the 'Künstlerliedertafel'; was Schumann's deputy from 1853, and in 1855 his successor as conductor of the Music Society and Subscription Concerts in Düsseldorf, retiring in 1890. He wrote the following cantatas: *Der Blumen Klage auf den Tod des Sängers; Dein Leben schied, dein Ruhm begann; Germanenzug; Rheinfahrt;* also *Festouvertüre* for orch., duo for piano and violin, piano pieces, male choruses, etc.

Tausig (tow'zih), **Carl**, celebrated piano virtuoso; b. Warsaw, Nov. 4, 1841; d. Leipzig, July 17, 1871. He was trained by his father, **Aloys Tausig** (1820-85), who was a pupil of Thalberg and wrote brilliant piano music; from the age of 14 he studied with Liszt, almost equalling him in grandeur of interpretation, and in technique—the latter due, in great part, to his systematic and zealous practice of his original transposing finger-exercises. His public début was made in 1858, at an orchestral concert conducted by von Bülow at Berlin. During the next two years he gave concerts in German cities, making Dresden his headquarters; then went to Vienna in 1862, giving orch. concerts with 'advanced' programs similar to Bülow's at Berlin. He settled in Berlin in 1865, and opened a 'Schule des höheren Klavierspiels.' He gave concerts in the principal towns of Germany, and at St. Petersburg and other Russian centers. He died of typhoid fever. —Works (for piano): 2 études de concert, op. 1; *Ungarische Zigeunerweisen; Nouvelles soirées de Vienne; Valses-Caprices* on themes from Strauss; *Tägliche Studien* (transposing chromatic exercises of high value; ed. by Ehrlich); also transcriptions and arrangements. —Cf. K. F. Weitzmann, *Der Letzte der Virtuosen* (Leipzig, 1868); W. von Lenz, *Die grossen Pianoforte-Virtuosen unserer Zeit* (Berlin, 1872; in English, N. Y., 1899).

Tauwitz (tow'vits), **Eduard**, German conductor and composer; b. Glatz, Silesia, Jan. 21, 1812; d. Prague, July 25, 1894. He was Kapellmeister at theaters in Vilna (1837), Riga (1840), Breslau (1843), and Prague (1846; pensioned 1863). He wrote more than 1,000 compositions, including 3 operas: *Trilby* (Vilna, 1836), *Bradamante* (Riga, 1844), and *Schmolke und Bakel* (Breslau, 1846), church music, songs, and part-songs.

Taverner, John, English composer; b. c. 1495; d. Boston, Lincolnshire, Oct. 25, 1545. He was probably a native of Tattershall, where he was a lay clerk until his appointment as master of the choristers and organist at Cardinals' College, Oxford, in 1526. In 1528 he was imprisoned for heresy, but soon released; he left Oxford in 1530, and also gave up music, spending the rest of his life in promoting religious persecution as a paid agent of Thomas Cromwell. In 1537 he was elected a member of the Guild of Corpus Christi in Boston, becoming a steward in 1543. He was one of the greatest of the early English church composers. —His church music, printed in vols. I and III of 'Tudor Church Music' (1923-24), includes 8 Masses, several sections of Masses, 3 Magnificats, a Te Deum, and 28 motets. Besides his church music, he wrote 3 secular vocal compositions for W. de Worde's 'Song-book' (1530). —Cf. H. B. Collins, *John Taverner's Masses,* in 'Music & Letters' (1924).

Taylor, David Clark, American singing teacher; b. New York, Nov. 11, 1871; d. there, Dec. 6, 1918. A graduate of the College of the City of N. Y. (B. A., 1890), he studied piano with O. W. Wilkinson (1888-94), theory with A. Remy (1893-97), and singing (1890-96) with several masters in N. Y. He was long connected with the Macmillan Co. —Publ. *The Psychology of Singing* (N. Y., 1908); *Self Help for Singers* (N. Y., 1914); *New Light on the Old Italian Method* (N. Y., 1916); *The Melodic Method in School Music* (N. Y., 1918); contributed the chapters on Voice Culture to 'The Art of Music' (14 vols.; N. Y., 1917).

Taylor, (Joseph) Deems, American composer and writer; b. New York, Dec. 22, 1885. He graduated from N. Y. Univ. (B. A., 1906); studied theory with O. Coon (1912-13). After doing editorial work for various publications and serving as war correspondent for the N. Y. 'Tribune' in France (1916-17), he became music critic for the N. Y. 'World' (1921-25), editor of 'Mus. America' (1927-29), and critic for the N. Y. 'American' (1931-32). Member of the National Institute of Arts and Letters; Mus. Doc. *(hon. c.),* N. Y. Univ., 1927; Litt. D., Juniata College, 1931. Following the success of his orchestral suite *Through the Looking Glass* (1923), he was commissioned by Walter Damrosch to compose a symph. poem, *Jurgen* (1925). Meanwhile, 2 widely performed cantatas, *The Chambered Nautilus* and *The Highwayman,* had added to his growing reputation, which received a strong impetus when his opera *The King's Henchman* (libretto by Edna St. Vincent Millay), commissioned by the Metropolitan Opera, was produced in that house on Feb. 17, 1926. Receiving 14 performances in 3 seasons, it established a record for American opera at the Metropolitan Opera House, which, however, was surpassed by Taylor's next opera, *Peter Ibbetson* (Feb. 7, 1931); this attained 16 performances in 4 seasons. From 1942 to 1948 he was president of the American Society for Composers, Authors and Publishers. —Works: *The Echo,* mus. comedy (N. Y., 1909); *The King's Henchman,* opera (N. Y., Feb. 17, 1926); *Peter Ibbetson,* opera (N. Y., Feb. 7, 1931); *Ramuntcho,* opera (Philadelphia, Feb. 10, 1942); *The Dragoon,* 1-act opera (N. Y. Univ., Feb. 6, 1958); *The Siren Song,* symph. poem (1912; N. Y., July 18, 1922); *Through the Looking-Glass,* suite for chamber orch. (1917-19; N. Y., Feb. 18, 1919; rescored for full orch., 1921-22; N. Y., March 10, 1923); *The Portrait of a Lady,* for 11 instruments (1918); *Jurgen,* symph. poem (N. Y., Nov. 19, 1925); *Circus Day,* suite (for jazz orch., 1925; for symph. orch., 1933); Ballet Music from *Casanova* for orch. (N. Y., April 18, 1937); *Marco Takes a Walk,* variations for orch. (N. Y., Nov. 14, 1942); *A Christmas Overture* (N. Y., Dec. 23, 1943, composer conducting); *Élégie,* for orch. (Los Angeles, Jan. 4, 1945); *Restoration Suite,* for orch. (Indianapolis, Nov. 18, 1950); *The Chambered Nautilus,* cantata for mixed voices and orch. (1914); *The Highwayman,* cantata for baritone, women's voices, and orch. (1914); *Lucrece,* suite for string quartet; *A Kiss in Xanadu,* pantomime for piano or 2 pianos; part-songs; songs; piano pieces; many arrangements. — Books: *Of Men and Music* (N. Y., 1937); *The Well Tempered Listener* (N. Y., 1940); *Music to My Ears* (N. Y., 1949); *Some Enchanted Evenings; the Story of Rodgers and Hammerstein* (N. Y., 1953). Also wrote numerous magazine articles. —Cf. J. T. Howard, *Deems Taylor* (N. Y., 1927).

Taylor, Franklin, English pianist and teacher; b. Birmingham, Feb. 5, 1843; d. London, March 19, 1919. Pupil of C. Flavell (piano) and T. Bedsmore (organ); also studied 1859-61 at Leipzig Cons. Returning to London, he settled there as a highly successful concert pianist and teacher; 1876-82, prof. at the National Training School, and from 1883 at the Royal College of Music.—He publ. *Primer of Pianoforte Playing* (1877); *Pianoforte Tutor; Technique and Expression in Pianoforte Playing* (1897).

Taylor, Raynor, composer; b. in England, c. 1747; d. Philadelphia, Aug. 17, 1825. He received his early training as a chorister in the Chapel Royal, and in 1765 became organist of a church in Chelmsford; that same year he was also appointed music director at Sadler's Wells Theatre, London. In 1792 he came to the U. S., going first to Baltimore and then to Annapolis, where he was organist of St. Anne's Church. Moving to Philadelphia in 1793, he became organist of St. Peter's there, and in 1820 was one of the founders of the Musical Fund Society. A gifted singer, he gave humorous musical entertainments which he called 'olios,' and in 1796 conducted an orchestral concert that included several of his own compositions. In collaboration with A. Reinagle (q.v.), who had been his pupil in London, he composed a 'Monody' on the death of Washington (1799), and a ballad opera, *Pizarro, or the Spaniards in Peru* (1800); some of his songs are in the N. Y. Public Library. —Cf. L. C. Madeira, *Annals of Music in Philadelphia* (1896); O. G. Sonneck, *Bibliography of Early American Secular Music* (1905; new ed., 1945); O. G. Sonneck, *Early Concert-Life in America* (1905); J. T. Howard, *A Program of Early American Piano Music* (1931).

Tchaikovsky, Boris Alexandrovitch, Russian composer; b. Moscow, Sept. 10, 1925. He studied at the Moscow Cons. with Shostakovitch, Shebalin, and Miaskovsky. He publ. his earliest piano works at the age of 13; wrote an opera, *The Star* (1949); a symph. (1947); a *Fantasy on Russian Themes* for orch. (1950); *Slavic Rhapsody* for orch. (1951); *Symphonietta* (1953); a string quartet; a piano trio; a violin sonata; piano pieces.

Tchaikovsky, Modest, Russian playwright and librettist; brother of the composer; b. St. Petersburg, 1850; d. Moscow, Jan. 15, 1916. He was the closest intimate of Tchaikovsky, and the author of the basic biography. His plays had only a passing success, but he was an excellent librettist; he wrote the librettos of Tchaikovsky's last 2 operas, *The Queen of Spades* and *Iolanthe.*

Tchaikovsky, Piotr Ilyitch, famous Russian composer; b. Votkinsk, district of Viatka, May 7, 1840; d. St. Petersburg, Nov. 6, 1893. The son of a mining inspector at a plant in the Urals, he was given a good education; had a French governess and a music teacher. When he was 10, the family moved to St. Petersburg, and he was sent to a school of jurisprudence, from which he graduated at 19 and became a government clerk; while at school he studied music with Lomakin (q.v.), but did not display conspicuous talent as either pianist or composer. At the age of 21 he was accepted in a musical institution, newly established by Anton Rubinstein, which was to become the St. Petersburg Conservatory. He studied with Zaremba (harmony and counterpoint) and Rubinstein (composition); graduated in 1865, winning a silver medal for his cantata to Schiller's *Hymn To Joy.* In 1866 he became prof. of harmony at the Moscow Cons. under the directorship of Nicholas Rubinstein. As if to compensate for a late beginning in his profession, he began to compose with great application. His early works —a programmatic symphony, subtitled *Winter Dreams,* some overtures and small pieces for string quartet—reveal little individuality. With his symph. poem *Fatum* (1869) came the first formulation of his style, highly subjective, preferring minor modes, permeated with nostalgic longing and alive with keen rhythms. In 1869 he undertook the composition of his overture-fantasy *Romeo and Juliet;* not content with what he had written, he profited by the advice of Balakirev, whom he met in St. Petersburg, and revised the work in 1870; but this version proved equally unsatisfactory; Tchaikovsky laid the composition aside, and did not complete it until 1879; in its final form it became one of his most successful works. A Belgian soprano, Désirée Artôt, a member of an opera troupe visiting St. Petersburg in 1868, took great interest in Tchaikovsky, and he was moved by her attentions; for a few months he seriously contemplated marriage, and so notified his father (his mother had died of cholera when he was 14 years old). But this proved to be a passing infatuation on her part, for soon she married the Spanish singer Padilla; Tchaikovsky reacted to this event with a casual philosophical remark about the inconstancy of human attachments. It is interesting to note that throughout his creative career Tchaikovsky never allowed his psychological turmoil to interfere with his work: the list of his compositions shows almost no gap in the continuous flow of music from his pen. Besides teaching and composing, he contributed music criticism to Moscow newspapers for several years (1868-74), traveled often abroad, and visited the first Bayreuth Festival in 1876, reporting his impressions for the Moscow daily 'Russkyie Vedomosti.' His closest friends were members of his own family, his brothers (particularly Modest, his future biographer) and his married sister Alexandra Davidov, at whose estate, Kamenka, he spent most of his summers. The correspondence with them, all of which was preserved and eventually published, throws a true light on Tchaikovsky's character and his life. Tchaikovsky had other intimate friends—his publisher Jurgenson, Nicholas Rubinstein, and several other musicians. The most extraordinary of his friendships was the epistolary intimacy with Nadezhda von Meck, a wealthy widow, whom he never met (except for some fleeting, accidental encounters in public places) but who was to play an extremely important role in his life. Through the violinist Kotek (q.v.) she learned about Tchaikovsky's financial difficulties, and commissioned him to write some compositions, at large fees; then arranged to pay him an annuity of 6,000 rubles. For more than 13 years they corresponded voluminously, even when they lived in the same city (Moscow, Florence); on several occasions Madame von Meck hinted that she would not be averse to a personal meeting, but Tchaikovsky invariably declined such a suggestion, under the pretext that one should not see one's guardian angel in the flesh. On Tchaikovsky's part, this correspondence had to remain within the circumscribed domain of art, personal philosophy, and reporting of daily events, without touching on the basic problem of his existence. On July 18, 1877, Tchaikovsky contracted marriage with a conservatory student named Antonina Milyukova, who had declared her love for him. This was an act of defiance of his own nature; Tchaikovsky was a deviate, and made no secret of it in the correspondence with his brother Modest (who was also abnormal in this respect). He thought that by flaunting a wife he could prevent the already rife rumors about his abnormality from spreading any further. The result was disastrous, and Tchaikovsky fled from his wife in horror. He attempted suicide by walking into the Moskva River in order to catch pneumonia, but suffered nothing more severe than simple discomfort. He then went to St. Petersburg to seek the advice of his brother Anatol, a lawyer, who made suitable arrangements with Tchaikovsky's wife for a separation. (They were never divorced; she died in an insane asylum in 1917.) Madame von Meck, to whom Tchaikovsky wrote candidly of the hopeless failure of his marriage (without revealing the true cause of that failure), made at once an offer of further financial assistance, which Tchaikovsky gratefully accepted. He spent several months during 1877-78 in Italy, in Switzerland, in Paris, and in Vienna. During these months he completed one of his greatest works, the 4th Symphony, dedicated to Mme. von Meck. It was performed for the 1st time in Moscow on March 4, 1878, but Tchaikovsky did not cut short his sojourn abroad to attend the performance. He resigned from the Moscow Cons. in the autumn of 1878, and from that time dedicated himself entirely to composition. The continued subsidy from Mme. von Meck allowed him to forget money matters. Early in 1879 he completed his most successful opera, *Eugene Onegin* ('lyric scenes,' after Pushkin); it was first produced in Moscow by a conservatory ensemble, on March 29, 1879, and gained success only gradually; the 1st performance at the Imperial Opera in St. Petersburg did not take place until 5 years later (Oct. 31, 1884). A morbid depression was still Tchaikovsky's natural state of mind, but every new work sustained his faith in his destiny as a composer, despite many disheartening reversals. His piano concerto No. 1, rejected by Nicholas Rubinstein as unplayable, was given its world première (somewhat incongruously) in Boston, on Oct. 25, 1875, played by Hans von Bülow, and afterwards was performed all over the world by famous pianists, including Nicholas Rubinstein himself. His violin concerto, criticized by Leopold Auer (to whom the score was originally dedicated) and attacked by Hanslick with sarcasm and virulence at its world première by Brodsky in Vienna (1881), survived all its detractors, to become one of the most celebrated pieces in the violin repertory. The 5th Symphony (1888) was successful from the very first. Early in 1890 Tchaikovsky wrote his 2nd important opera, *The Queen of Spades,* which was produced at the Imperial Opera in St. Petersburg in that year. His ballets *Swan Lake* (1876) and *The Sleeping Beauty* (1889) became famous on Russian stages. But at the peak of his career, Tchaikovsky suffered a severe psychological blow; Mme. von Meck notified him of the discontinuance of her subsidy, and with this anouncement she abruptly terminated their correspondence. Tchaikovsky could now well afford the loss of the money, but his pride was deeply hurt by the manner in which Mme. von Meck had acted. It is indicative of Tchaikovsky's inner strength that even this desertion of one whom he regarded as his staunchest friend did not affect his ability to work. In 1891 he undertook his first and only voyage to America. He was received with honors as a celebrated composer; he led 4 concerts of his works in N. Y. and one each in Baltimore and Philadelphia. He did not linger in the U. S., however, and returned to St. Petersburg in a few weeks. Early in 1892 he made a concert tour as conductor in Russia, and then proceeded to Warsaw and Germany. In the meantime he had purchased a house in the town of Klin, not far from Moscow, where he wrote his last symphony, the *Pathétique.* Despite the perfection of his technique, he did not arrive at the desired form and substance of this work at once, and discarded his original sketch. The title *Pathétique* was suggested to him by his brother Modest; the score was dedicated to his nephew, Vladimir Davidov. Its music is the final testament of Tchaikovsky's life, and an epitome of his philosophy of fatalism. In the 1st movement, the trombones are given the theme of the Russian service for the dead. Remarkably, the score of one of his gayest works, the ballet *The Nutcracker,* was composed simultaneously with the early sketches for the *Pathétique.* Tchaikovsky was in good spirits when he went to St. Petersburg to conduct the première of the *Pathétique,* on Oct. 28, 1893 (which was but moderately successful). A cholera epidemic was then raging in St. Petersburg, and the population was specifically warned against drinking unboiled water. Nonetheless, Tchaikovsky did exactly that, no doubt from carelessness. He showed the symptoms of cholera soon afterwards, and nothing could be done to save him. The melodramatic hypothesis that the fatal drink of water was a defiance of death, in perfect knowledge of the danger, since he must have remembered his mother's death of the same dread infection, is untenable in the light of published private letters between the attendant physician and Modest Tchaikovsky at the time. Tchaikovsky's fatalism alone would amply account for his lack of precaution. —As a composer, Tchaikovsky stands apart from the militant national movement of the 'Mighty Five.' The Russian element is, of course, very strong in Tchaikovsky's music, and upon occasion he made use of Russian folksongs in his works, but this national spirit is instinctive rather than consciously cultivated. His personal relationship with the St. Petersburg group of nationalists was friendly without being intimate; his correspondence with Rimsky-Korsakov, Balakirev, and others was mostly concerned with professional matters. Tchaikovsky's music was frankly sentimental; his supreme gift of melody, which none of his Russian contemporaries could match, secured for him a lasting popularity among performers and audiences. His influence was profound on the Moscow group of musicians, of whom Arensky and Rachmaninoff were the most talented. He wrote in every genre, and was successful in each; besides his stage works, symphonies, chamber music, and piano compositions, he composed a great number of lyric songs that are the most poignant creations of his genius. By a historical paradox, Tchaikovsky became the most popular Russian composer under the Soviet regime. His subjectivism, his fatalism, his emphasis on melancholy moods, even his reactionary political views (which included a brand of amateurish anti-Semitism), failed to detract from his stature in the new society. In fact, official spokesmen of Soviet Russia repeatedly urged Soviet composers to follow in the path of Tchaikovsky's esthetics. Tchaikovsky's popularity is also very strong in Anglo-Saxon countries, particularly in America; much less so in France and Italy; in Germany his influence is insignificant. —Works: Operas: *The Voyevode* (1867-68; Moscow, Feb. 11, 1869); *Undine* (1869); *The Opritchnik* (1870-72; St. Petersburg, April 24, 1874); *Vakula the Smith* (1874; St. Petersburg, Dec. 6, 1876); *Eugene Onegin* (1877-78; Moscow, March 29, 1879); *The Maid of Orleans* (1878-79; St. Petersburg, Feb. 25, 1881); *Mazeppa* (1881-83; Moscow, Feb. 15, 1884); *Tcherevitchky (The Little Shoes;* revised version of *Vakula the Smith;* 1885; Moscow, Jan. 31, 1887); *The Sorceress* (1885-87; St. Petersburg, Nov. 1, 1887); *The Queen of Spades* (1890; St. Petersburg, Dec. 19, 1890); *Iolanthe* (1891; St. Petersburg, Dec. 18, 1892). Ballets: *Swan Lake* (1875-76; Moscow, March 4, 1877); *The Sleeping Beauty* (1888-89; St. Petersburg, Jan. 15, 1890), *The Nutcracker* (1891-92; St. Petersburg, Dec. 18, 1892). For orch.: 6 symphonies: No. 1 *(Winter Dreams;* 1868; revised 1874; Moscow, Feb. 15, 1868); No. 2, the *Little Russian* or Ukrainian symph. (Moscow, Feb. 7, 1873); No. 3 (1875; Moscow, Nov. 19, 1875); No. 4 (1877; Moscow, March 4, 1878); No. 5 (1888; St. Petersburg, Nov. 17, 1888); No. 6 *(Pathétique;* 1893; St. Petersburg, Oct. 28, 1893); overture to Ostrovsky's play *The Storm* (1864); symph. poem *Fatum* (1868; Moscow, Feb. 27, 1869); overture *Romeo and Juliet* (1869; Moscow, March 16, 1870; final version 1880); symph. fantasy *The Tempest,* after Shakespeare (1873; Moscow, Dec. 19, 1873); 1st piano concerto (1874-75; Boston, Oct. 25, 1875); *Sérénade mélancolique,* for violin with orch. (1875; Moscow, Jan. 28, 1876); *Slavonic March* (1876; Moscow, Nov. 17, 1876); symph. fantasy *Francesca da Rimini,* after Dante (1876; Moscow, March 9, 1877); suite from the ballet *Swan Lake* (1876); *Variations on a Rococo Theme,* for cello and orch. (1876; Moscow, Nov. 30, 1877); *Valse-Scherzo,* for violin and orch. (1877; Paris, Oct. 21, 1878); suite No. 1 (1878-79; Moscow, Nov. 23, 1879); violin concerto (1878; Vienna, Dec. 4, 1881); piano concerto No. 2 (1879-80; Moscow, May 30, 1882); *Italian Capriccio* (1880; Moscow, Dec. 18, 1880); *1812 Overture* (1880; Moscow, Aug. 20, 1882); *Serenade* for string orch. (1880; Moscow, Jan. 28, 1882); suite No. 2 (1883; Moscow, Feb. 16, 1884); suite No. 3 (1884; St. Petersburg, Jan. 28, 1885); *Concert Fantasy* for piano with orch. (1884; Moscow, March 6, 1885); symphony *Manfred,* after Byron (1885; Moscow, March 23, 1886); suite No. 4, *Mozartiana* (1887; Moscow, Nov. 26, 1887); overture-fantasy, *Hamlet* (1888; St. Petersburg, Nov. 24, 1888); *Pezzo capriccioso,* for cello with orch. (1887; Moscow, Dec. 7, 1889); suite from the ballet *The Sleeping Beauty* (1889); symph. ballad, *The Voyevode,* after Pushkin's translation of Mickiewicz's ballad (1890-91; Moscow, Nov. 18, 1891); suite from the ballet *Nutcracker* (1892; St. Petersburg, March 19, 1892); 3rd piano concerto (one movement only; posthumous; St. Petersburg, Jan. 19, 1895); *Andante and Finale* for piano with orch. (1893; actually 2nd and 3rd movements of the 3rd piano concerto; posthumous; St. Petersburg, Feb.

20, 1896). Chamber music: 3 string quartets (1871; 1874; 1876); piano trio, in memory of Nicholas Rubinstein (Moscow, Oct. 30, 1882); *Souvenir de Florence,* for string sextet (1887; St. Petersburg, Dec. 7, 1892); also *Souvenir d'un lieu cher,* for violin and piano (1878); several fragments of early works. For piano: *Scherzo à la russe* (1867); *Souvenir de Hapsal,* 3 pieces (No. 3 is the famous *Chant sans paroles;* 1867); *Valse-Caprice* (1868); *Romance* in F minor (1868); *Valse-Scherzo* (1870); *Capriccio* (1870); *3 morceaux: Rêverie, Polka de Salon, Mazurka de Salon* (1870); *2 morceaux: Nocturne* and *Humoresque* (1871); 6 *morceaux: Rêverie du Soir, Scherzo humoristique, Feuillet d'album, Nocturne, Capriccioso, Thème original et variations* (1872); *6 morceaux sur un seul thème: Prelude, Fugue, Impromptu, Marche funèbre, Mazurka, Scherzo* (1873); *Grande sonate,* in G major (1879); *Les quatre saisons,* 12 characteristic pieces for each month of the year (1875-76; of these the most famous are No. 6, *Barcarole;* No. 10, *Chant d'automne;* No. 11, *En Traineau;* No. 12, *Noël); 12 morceaux* (1876-78; among them *Chanson triste* and *Danse russe*); *Album pour enfants,* 24 pieces (1878); *6 pièces* (1882); *Dumka* (1886); *18 morceaux* (1893); sonata in C♯ minor (1865; posthumous). Vocal works: cantata, *An die Freude* (Schiller), for chorus and orch. (1865); *Liturgy of St. John Chrysostom,* for mixed chorus in 4 parts (1878); Vesper Service, for mixed chorus (1882); *Moskva,* coronation cantata for solo voices, chorus, and orch. (1883); 3 Cherubic Hymns, for mixed chorus (1884); 6 Church Songs (1885); other sacred and secular vocal pieces; about 100 songs, among them such favorites as *Nur wer die Sehnsucht kennt* (after Goethe), *Berceuse,* etc.; 6 duets. He publ. a *Manual of Harmony* (Moscow, 1870; many eds. English transl. as *Guide to the Practical Study of Harmony,* 1900). The collected criticisms and reminiscences were publ. in 1898; new ed., revised and enlarged, Moscow, 1953; diaries, comprising 11 separate fragments, covering the years between 1873 and 1891, were publ. in Moscow in 1923 (English transl., N. Y., 1945). A centennial edition of the complete works, in about 70 vols., was begun in 1940, interrupted during the war years, and resumed in 1946. Most of the manuscripts, correspondence, etc. are preserved in Tchaikovsky's house in Klin (now the Tchaikovsky Museum). A complete thematic catalogue was issued by B. Jurgenson (Moscow, 1897; reprinted N. Y., 1941).

BIBLIOGRAPHY: The basic source is the 3-vol. biography by Modest Tchaikovsky, *The Life of P. I. T.* (Moscow, 1900-02), but in it the author was compelled to withhold essential facts of Tchaikovsky's life; translations were made, into German by Paul Juon (2 vols.; Leipzig, 1900, 1902) and into English by Rosa Newmarch (abridged) as *The Life and Letters of P. I. T.* (London, 1906). Chapters on Tchaikovsky are included in all music histories and books dealing specifically with Russian music. Books and articles in various languages that should be noted include: V. Tcheshikhin, *P. T. Attempt at a Characterization* (Riga, 1893); H. Laroche and N. Kashkin, *In Memory of T.* (Moscow, 1894); N. Kashkin, *Reminiscences of T.* (Moscow, 1897); E. Markham Lee, *T.,* in the 'Music of the Masters' series (N. Y., 1904); Edwin Evans, Sr., *T.* (London, 1906; revised ed., 1935); *P. I. T.,* a symposium, in the series 'The Past of Russian Music' (Petrograd, 1920), containing documents relating mainly to the Tchaikovsky Museum in Klin; Igor Glebov, *T.: an Essay of Characterization* (Petrograd, 1922); Igor Glebov, *P. I. T.: His Life and Works* (Petrograd, 1922; a different book from the preceding); H. Laroche, *Collected Musico-Critical Articles,* vol. 2 (Moscow, 1922); M. Steinitzer, *T.* (Leipzig, 1925); R. H. Stein, *T.* (Stuttgart, 1927); Eric Blom, *T.: Orchestral Works,* in the 'Musical Pilgrim' series (London, 1927); M. D. Calvocoressi and Gerald Abraham, *Masters of Russian Music* (London, 1936; pp. 249-334; this essay publ. separately, 1949); Nikolai von Pals, *P. T.* (Potsdam, 1939); H. Weinstock, *T.* (N. Y., 1943); Gerald Abraham, *T.: A Short Biography* (London, 1944); H. Célis and W.-P. Right, *T.* (Brussels, 1945); Gerald Abraham, *T.: A Symposium* (London, 1945; in the U. S. as *The Music of T.,* N. Y., 1946); D. Brook, *6 Great Russian Composers* (London, 1946); D. Shostakovitch and others, *Russian Symphony; Thoughts About T.* (N. Y., 1947); R. Hofmann, *T.* (Paris, 1947); A. Alshvang, *Analytic Essay on T.'s Creative Work* (Moscow, 1951); G. Dombayev, *Creative Work of T.* (Moscow, 1958). Numerous pamphlets dealing with Tchaikovsky's operas, ballets, orchestral works, etc. have been issued in Russia; of these, the most valuable are: N. Findeisen, *T.'s Chamber Music* (Moscow, 1930), A. Budiakovsky, *P. I. T., Symphonic Music* (Leningrad, 1935), V. Bogdanov-Berezovsky, *Operatic and Choreographic Works of T.* (Moscow, 1940), B. M. Yarustovsky, *Operatic Dramaturgy of T.* (Moscow, 1947), and N. Nikolayeva, *Sym-*

phonies of T. (Moscow, 1958). V. Yakovlev compiled a most detailed chronology (often day by day) of Tchaikovsky's life, *Days and Years of T.* (Moscow, 1940). Of the greatest importance is the publication of the complete extant correspondence between Tchaikovsky and Mme. von Meck, in 3 vols. (Moscow, 1933; 1934; 1936). Other correspondence includes *Letters to Relatives* (vol. 1, Moscow, 1940); *Correspondence with P. I. Jurgenson* (2 vols., Moscow, 1939, 1952); letters to and from S. Taneyev (Moscow, 1951); selected letters to intimates (Moscow, 1955). Magazine articles on Tchaikovsky include the following, publ. in the 'Mus. Quarterly': Olga Bennigsen, *A Bizarre Friendship: T. and Mme. von Meck* (Oct., 1936); N. Slonimsky, *Further Light on T.* (April, 1938); Olga Bennigsen, *More T.-von Meck Correspondence* (April, 1938); S. Bertensson, *The T. Museum at Klin* (July, 1944). There are several fictional biographies of Tchaikovsky; among them one written by Catherine D. Bowen and Barbara von Meck, *Beloved Friend* (N. Y., 1937); Klaus Mann, *Symphonie pathétique* (Amsterdam, 1938; in German; in English, N. Y., 1948); J. Mühlberger, *Im Schatten des Schicksals* (Esslingen, 1950).

Tcherepnin (cheh-rep-nēn'), **Alexander Nikolayevitch,** composer and pianist; son of Nicolas Tcherepnin; b. St. Petersburg, Jan. 20, 1899. He studied piano as a child with his mother (*née* Benois, a sister of the stage designer, Alexander Benois). He profited much from his father's advice, but did not take formal lessons with him; began to compose early in life; wrote a comic opera at 12, a ballet at 13, and 14 piano sonatas before he was 19 (sonata No. 13 was publ. under the title *Sonatine romantique*). In 1917 he entered the Petrograd Cons. and studied with Sokolov, but remained there only a few months; then accompanied his father to Tiflis, where the latter was appointed director of the local conservatory; gave piano recitals all over the Caucasus; in 1921 went to Paris; there he studied piano with Isidor Philipp and counterpoint with Paul Vidal; in 1922 he appeared in London as pianist and composer; subsequently gave concerts in Germany, Austria, and the U. S.; between 1934 and 1937 he made 2 visits to the Far East; played in the principal cities of China and Japan; had many pupils there; established in Tokyo a firm for the publication of serious works by Japanese composers, including a number of his own students; brought out more than 50 Japanese and Chinese compositions. He married a Chinese pianist, Lee Hsien-Ming (q.v.). In 1938 he made his home in Paris, remaining there throughout the war; resumed his international career in 1947; gave concerts in Scandinavia and elsewhere in Europe. In 1949 he and his wife joined the faculty of De Paul Univ. in Chicago. —In his music Tcherepnin follows a neo-Romantic trend, using original means of expression within the framework of traditional forms. He adopted a 9-tone scale (formed by the insertion of passing tones in an augmented triad) and applied it integrally in several of his instrumental works; at the same time he explored the latent resources of folk music; adjusted Oriental scales so as to utilize them in modern forms. He also elaborated a method of rhythmic polyphony, introducing thematic rhythmic units, and termed it 'interpunctus.' —Works: Operas: *Ol-Ol,* after Leonid Andreyev (Weimar, Jan. 31, 1928); *Die Hochzeit der Sobeide,* after Hugo von Hofmannsthal (Vienna, March 17, 1933); *The Farmer and the Fairy* (Aspen Festival, Colorado, Aug. 13, 1952); completed Mussorgsky's opera *The Marriage* (Essen, Sept. 14, 1937). Ballets: *Ajanta Frescos* (London, Sept. 10, 1923); *Training* (Vienna, June 19, 1935); *Der fahrend Schüler mit dem Teufelsbannen* (1938); *Trepak* (Mordkin Russian Ballet, Richmond, Va., Oct. 10, 1938); *La Légende de Rasin* (1941); *Déjeuner sur l'herbe* (Paris, Oct. 14, 1945); *Chota Roustaveli* (Monte Carlo, May 5, 1946); *La Colline des fantômes* (1946); *Jardin persan* (1946); *Nuit kurde* (Paris, 1946); *La Femme et son ombre,* after Paul Claudel (Paris, June 14, 1948); *Aux temps des tartares* (Buenos Aires, 1949). Cantatas: *Vivre d'amour* (1942); *Pan Kéou* (Paris, Oct. 9, 1945); *Le Jeu de la Nativité* (Paris, Dec. 30, 1945); *Les Douze,* poem by Alexander Block for narrator, strings, harp, piano, and percussion (Paris, Nov. 9, 1947). For orch.: symph. no. 1 (Paris, Oct. 29, 1927); symph. no. 2 (1945-51; Chicago, March 20, 1952); symph. no. 3 (Indianapolis, Jan. 15, 1955); *Magna Mater* (1927; Munich, Oct. 30, 1930); *Russian Dances* (Omaha, Feb. 15, 1934); 3 Pieces for Chamber Orch.: *Ouverture* (1921), *Mystère,* for cello and chamber orch. (Monte Carlo, Dec. 8, 1926), *Pour un entrainement de boxe* (1922; originally a ballet sketch); *Concerto da camera,* for flute, violin, and chamber orch. (1924); *Concertino* for violin, cello, piano, and strings (1931); *Rhapsodie georgienne* for cello and orch. (Bordeaux, 1924); 3 piano concertos (composer soloist at all performances): No. 1 (1919; Monte Carlo, 1923); No. 2 (Paris, Jan. 26, 1924); No. 3 (Paris,

Feb. 5, 1933); *Suite georgienne* for orch. (Paris, April 17, 1940); *Fantaisie* for piano and orch. (1946-49); *Evocation* (1948); *Suite* for orch. (Louisville, May 1, 1954); concerto for harmonica and orch. (Venice, Sept. 11, 1956); *Capriccio* for orch. (Chicago, Nov. 14, 1957). Chamber music: piano trio (1925); 2 string quartets (1925; 1926); piano quintet (1927); *Ode* for cello and piano (1919); 3 cello sonatas; violin sonata; *Elegy* for violin and piano; *Le Violoncelle bien temperé,* 12 preludes for cello with piano, 2 of them with drum added (Berlin, March 23, 1927); suite for cello solo (1946); *Mouvement perpétuel,* for violin and piano (1945); sonatina for kettledrums and piano (1939); *Sonatine sportive,* for bassoon and piano (1939); *Andante,* for tuba and piano (1939); trio for flutes (1939); quartet for flutes (1939); *Marche,* for 3 trumpets (1939); etc. For piano: *Scherzo* (1917); *10 Bagatelles* (1913-18); *Sonatine romantique* (1918); *Toccata* (1921); *Feuilles libres* (1920-24); *5 Arabesques* (1921); *9 Inventions* (1921); *2 Novelettes* (1922); *6 Études de travail* (1923); *4 Préludes nostalgiques* (1922); *Entretiens* (1930); *Études de piano sur la gamme pentatonique* (1935); *Autour des montagnes russes* (1937); *Badinage* (1942); *Le Monde en Vitrine* (1946); 7 songs on poems translated from the Chinese, for narrator and piano (also with orch.); several albums of songs to poems in Russian, French, and Chinese; he edited Russian songs; publ. articles on Oriental music, including *Music in Modern China,* in the 'Mus. Quarterly' (Oct., 1935).

Tcherepnin (cheh-rep-nēn'), **Nicolas (Nikolay Nikolayevitch)**, Russian composer and conductor; b. St. Petersburg, May 14, 1873; d. Issy-les-Moulineaux, near Paris, June 26, 1945. He was a pupil of Rimsky-Korsakov at the St. Petersburg Cons. (1895-98); in 1905, became prof. of the orch. class and conducting there; also conducted at the Imperial Opera. He conducted Russian operas in Paris in 1908, and until 1914 toured with the Diaghilev Ballets Russes. He then returned to Russia; after the Revolution went to Tiflis, in the Caucasus, where he remained from 1918 until 1921, as director of the Tiflis Cons.; with the occupation of the Caucasus by the Red army, he, accompanied by his son Alexander (q.v.), proceeded to Paris, where he settled permanently; also conducted in London, Madrid, etc. His music embodies the principal elements of the Russian national school; he wrote successful ballets; a number of songs, some of which are favorites in the Russian repertory. He completed Mussorgsky's unfinished opera, *The Fair at Sorochintzy* (Monte Carlo, March 17, 1923; Metropolitan Opera, N. Y., Nov. 29, 1930). His own works include the operas *The Marriage Broker, Poverty is Not a Crime,* and *Ivan the Chancellor;* the ballets *Le Pavillon d'Armide* (1903), *Narcissus and Echo* (Monte Carlo, April 26, 1911; produced by Diaghilev), *The Masque of the Red Death,* after Poe (St. Petersburg, Jan. 29, 1916); Prelude to Rostand's *La Princesse lointaine,* for orch. (1897); *Fantaisie dramatique,* for orch. (1903); *Le Royaume enchanté,* symph. tableau (1904); piano concerto (1907); chamber music: *14 Esquisses sur les images d'un alphabet russe* for piano (an orchestral version of 8 of them was performed by the Boston Symph. Orch., Nov. 27, 1931). The 1st part of his sacred work *Pilgrimage and Passions of Virgin Mary* was given in Paris (Feb. 12, 1938). — Cf. M. Montagu-Nathan, *Contemporary Russian Composers* (London, 1917).

Tcheshikhin, Vsevolod Evgrafovitch, Russian writer on music; b. Riga, Feb. 18, 1865; d. Leningrad, 1934. After completing his law studies, he became a justice of the peace; was also active as music critic, and in 1898 established the Riga branch of the Imperial Russian Music Society; later went to St. Petersburg. He publ. a very valuable *History of Russian Opera* (St. Petersburg, 1902; 2nd enlarged ed., 1905); this was to be the 1st vol. of a history of Russian music in all its branches, but the project did not advance beyond this work; his other publications were: *P. Tchaikovsky: Attempt at a Characterization* (1893); *Short Librettos* (1894); *Echoes from the Opera and Concert Hall* (1896); etc.

Tebaldi, Renata, Italian soprano; b. Langhirano, Parma, Feb. 1, 1922. She received her elementary musical education at home from her father (a cellist) and her mother (a singer). She studied with Passani in Parma; then took a thorough course in vocal training with Carmen Melis (1939-42). She made her operatic début as Desdemona in Trieste (1946); sang the same role at Covent Garden, London (1950), and at the Metropolitan Opera, N. Y. (Jan. 31, 1955); also appeared in South America (1952). Her repertory includes Aida, Madama Butterfly, Tosca, Marguerite, Violetta, etc.

Tebaldini, Giovanni, Italian music scholar; b. Brescia, Sept. 7, 1864; d. San Benedetto del Tronto, May 11, 1952. He studied with

Ponchielli and Amelli at the Milan Cons., and at the School for Church Music in Regensburg; from 1889 to 1894 he was 2nd maestro di cappella at San Marco, Venice; then at the Padua Cathedral (1894-97); from 1897 to 1902, was director of the Cons. of Parma; from 1902 to 1924, at the Cathedral of Loreto; then appointed prof. at the Cons. di S. Pietro in Naples. In 1930 he went to Genoa, as director of the Ateneo Musicale there. He publ. in modern notation the scores of Peri's *Euridice,* Cavalieri's *Rappresentazione di anima e di corpo,* and Monteverdi's *Poppea.* He wrote a number of church compositions; with Enrico Bossi, publ. an important organ method (Milan, 1894). His own writings include *La Musica sacra in Italia* (Milan, 1894); *L'Archivio musicale della Cappella Antoniana in Padova* (Padua, 1895); *L'Archivio musicale della Cappella Lauretana* (Loreto, 1921); *Ildebrando Pizzetti* (Parma, 1931); contributed numerous articles on Gregorian Chant, Palestrina, etc. to various publications. He created an uproar in musical circles with his article, *Telepatia musicale,* publ. in the 'Rivista Musicale Italiana' (March, 1909), in which he cited thematic similarities between the opera *Cassandra* by Vittorio Gnecchi (produced in 1905), and *Elektra* by Richard Strauss, written much later; he failed to prove, however, that Strauss actually plagiarized Gnecchi. —Cf. M. Pilati, in the 'Bollettino bibliografico musicale' (Milan, 1929).

Tedesco, Ignaz (Amadeus), pianist, called the 'Hannibal of octaves'; b. Prague, 1817; d. Odessa, Nov. 13, 1882. He studied with Triebensee and Tomaschek; made successful concert tours, especially in Southern Russia; settled in Odessa. He composed for piano in a salon style—mazurkas, waltzes, rhapsodies, nocturnes; made transcriptions.

Teichmüller, Robert, German pianist and teacher; b. Brunswick, May 4, 1863; d. Leipzig, May 6, 1939. He studied piano with his father and with Reinecke at the Leipzig Cons., where from 1897 until his death he taught piano; made prof. in 1908. With K. Hermann he publ. a valuable guide, *Internationale moderne Klaviermusik* (Leipzig, 1927). —Cf. A. Baresel, *R. T. als Mensch und Künstler* (Leipzig, 1922); A. Baresel, *R. T. und die Leipziger Klaviertradition* (Leipzig, 1934).

Telemann, Georg Michael, German theorist and composer; grandson of Georg Philipp Telemann; b. Plön, Holstein, April 20, 1748; d. Riga, March 4, 1831. In 1773 he went to Riga and became cantor there (pensioned in 1828). He publ. *Unterricht im Generalbass-Spielen, auf der Orgel oder sonst einem Clavier-Instrumente* (1773); *Beytrag zur Kirchenmusik* (1785; organ pieces); *Sammlung alter und neuer Kirchenmelodien* (1812); and *Über die Wahl der Melodie eines Kirchenliedes* (1821); composed a book of trio sonatas, 6 violin sonatas, organ works.

Telemann, Georg Philipp, noted German composer; b. Magdeburg, March 14, 1681; d. Hamburg, June 25, 1767. He had only an ordinary school training in the musical rudiments, and owed his later eminence to self-instruction. At 12 he wrote an opera *à la* Lully; at 14 he conducted the music for a church at Hildesheim; in 1701 he entered Leipzig Univ. as a student of law and modern languages, and in 1704 became organist at the Neukirche, enlarging his choir by a students' singing society ('Collegium musicum') organized by himself. From 1704 to 1708 he was Kapellmeister to Count Promnitz at Sorau; then Konzertmeister at the court of Eisenach, where he succeeded Hebenstreit in 1709 as court conductor, retaining title and emoluments when called to Frankfurt in 1712 as Kapellmeister at the churches of the 'Barefooted Friars' and St. Catherine. From 1721 till his death he was town musical director at Hamburg, declining, on Kuhnau's death in 1722, the proffered position of cantor of the Thomasschule at Leipzig. An astonishingly productive composer, he wrote with ease and fluency in any desired style; he was far better known in his time than Bach, though subsequently his fame suffered an eclipse. After Handel and Keiser he was the most notable of the early German dramatic composers. He wrote about 40 operas; of these the following were produced in Hamburg: *Der gedultige Socrates* (Jan. 28, 1721); *Der neu-modische Liebhaber Damon* (June, 1724); *Die ungleiche Heirat* (Sept. 27, 1725); *Miriways* (May 26, 1728); *Flavius Bertaridus König der Longobarden* (Nov. 23, 1729); 21 operas were written for Leipzig, and 4 for Weissenfels. —Other works: 12 series of cantatas and motets for the church year (about 3,000 numbers with orch. or organ); 44 Passions; 32 installation numbers for preachers; 33 *Hamburger Capitänsmusiken* (each being a cantata with instrumental introduction); 20 pieces for jubilees, consecrations, or coronations; 12 funeral services; 14 numbers of wedding music; over 600 overtures; many serenades and marches; trio sonatas and other chamber music; also cantatas, odes, and oratorios. Most of his publ. works were engraved by Telemann himself. The following are among those that have been reprinted: the opera *Pimpinone,* in the 'Erbe deutscher Musik' vol. 6 (1936); oratorio *Der Tag des Gerichts* and the 'monodrama' *Ino* (solo cantata for soprano with orch.), in the 'Denkmäler deutscher Tonkunst' (vol. 28); a violin concerto (vol. 29); trio sonata in E♭, in Riemann's 'Collegium Musicum'; a 'symphony' in Schering's 'Perlen alter Kammermusik'; a concerto for 4 violins ed. by H. von Dameck; concerto ed. by H. Engel; an oboe concerto ed. by F. Stein; a flute quartet ed. by Ermeler; *Sing-, Spiel- und Generalbassübungen,* ed. by M. Seiffert (1914); clavier fantasias ed. by Seiffert (Frankfurt, 1923); *Musique de Table* (instrumental suites), ed. by Seiffert, in the 'Denkmäler deutscher Tonkunst' (vol. 61-62); 24 Odes (vol. 57); also several cantatas, etc. A collected ed. of his works was begun in 1950 by Bärenreiter in Kassel. — Cf. Telemann's autobiography in J. Mattheson's *Grundlage einer Ehrenpforte* . . . (Hamburg, 1740; reprinted by M. Schneider, Berlin, 1910); a brief *curriculum vitae* and a letter in J. Mattheson, *Grosse General-Bass-Schule, oder der exemplarischen Organisten Probe* (2nd ed., Hamburg, 1731), reproduced in Willi Kahl, *Selbstbiographien deutscher Musiker* (Cologne, 1948); K. Ottzenn, *Telemann als Opernkomponist* (Berlin, 1902); R. Rolland, *Voyage musical au pays du passé* (1919; English transl., 1922); M. Seiffert, *Telemanns 'Musique de Table' als Quelle für Händel,* in the 'Bulletin de la Société Union Musicologique' (1924); H. Gräser, *Telemanns Instrumental-Kammermusik* (Frankfurt, 1925); R. Meissner, *G. P. Telemanns Frankfurter Kirchen-Kantaten* (Frankfurt, 1924); E. Valentin, *G. P. Telemann* (Burg, 1931; revised ed., 1952); H. Büttner, *Das Konzert in den Orch.-Suiten Telemanns* (Leipzig, 1931); L. de La Laurencie, *Telemann à Paris,* in the 'Revue Musicale' (1932); H. Hörner, *Telemanns Passionsmusiken* (Leipzig, 1933); K. Schäfer-Schmuck, *Telemann als Klavierkomponist* (Leipzig, 1934); W. Menke, *Das Vokalwerk G. P. Telemanns* (Kassel, 1942).

Tellefsen, Thomas Dyke, Norwegian pianist and composer; b. Trondheim, Nov. 26, 1823; d. Paris, Oct. 6, 1874. In 1842 he went to Paris, where he studied with Kalkbrenner; in 1844 he became a pupil of Chopin, and accompanied him to England and Scotland in 1848. He publ. an edition of Chopin's works, and played Chopin's music at recitals in Paris and in Scandinavia. His own compositions were imitative of Chopin; he wrote nocturnes, waltzes, and mazurkas, but he also made use of Norwegian folksongs in many of his works, and thus became an early proponent of national music in Norway.

Telmányi, Emil, Hungarian violinist; b. Arad, June 22, 1892. He studied with Hubay at the Academy of Music in Budapest. In 1911 he began an active career as concert player; in 1918, married a daughter of Carl Nielsen (q.v.); his 2nd wife, whom he married in 1936, is the pianist Annette Schiöler. In 1940 he settled in Aarhus, Denmark, as a teacher; he toured the U. S. in 1950. He made a number of arrangements for violin of works by Chopin, Schumann, Brahms, and others; supervised the devising of a curved bow for the playing of Bach's unaccompanied sonatas and partitas.

Temianka, Henri, violinist; b. Greenock, Scotland, Nov. 19, 1906. He studied as a child with Carel Blitz in Rotterdam; then with Willy Hess in Berlin and with Jules Boucherit in Paris. In 1926 he came to America as a student of the Curtis Institute of Music, Philadelphia, in the class of Karl Flesch. He became 1st violinist in the Paganini Quartet; toured widely in Europe and America.

Templeton, Alec, blind pianist and composer; b. Cardiff, Wales, July 4, 1909. He studied at the Royal College of Music in London until 1923 and at the Royal Academy of Music until 1931. He settled in the U. S. in 1935, becoming a citizen in 1941; was extremely successful as a radio pianist, especially with his humorous musical sketches, parodies, etc., such as *Bach Goes to Town, Mozart Matriculates,* etc. He also wrote some more ambitious works, including *Concertino lirico* (1942) and *Gothic Concerto* (N. Y., Dec. 19, 1954, composer soloist), for piano and orch. In 1950 he established in N. Y. his own music publishing firm.

Templeton, John, Scottish tenor; b. Riccarton, near Kilmarnock, July 30, 1802; d. New Hampton, July 2, 1886. He sang in various churches in Edinburgh; then went to London, where he took lessons in singing with Tom Cooke; also studied theory with Blewitt. He began to appear in theaters around London, and on Oct. 13, 1831 he made his début in a London theater; subsequently became a regular member of Drury Lane. Maria Malibran selected him as tenor for her operatic appearances in London (1833-35). In 1842 he was in Paris; during the season of 1845-46 he made an American tour announced as 'Templeton Entertainment,' singing folksongs of Great Britain; his commentaries and reminiscences were publ. as *A Musical Entertainment* (Boston, 1845). He retired in 1852. —Cf. W. H. Husk, ed., *Templeton and Malibran. Reminiscences* (London, 1880).

Tenducci (tĕn-dŏŏ'-chē), **Giusto Ferdinando,** celebrated male soprano; b. Siena, c. 1736; d. in Italy after 1800. He went to England in 1758 and was received with such enthusiasm that, with the exception of very short periods, he sang throughout the British Isles until 1791, being applauded even after his voice was almost completely gone. He scandalized and amazed the public when he married in 1767 one of his pupils, Dorothy Maunsell, but the marriage was annulled in 1775. She publ. an account of the affair under the title *A True and Genuine Narrative of Mr. and Mrs. Tenducci* (1768). He wrote a treatise on singing, *Instruction of Mr. Tenducci to his Scholars* (London, 1785); also composed music for a comic opera *The Campaign,* produced in London in 1784, and a group of *Ranelagh Songs.* —Cf. A. Heriot, *The Castrati in Opera* (London, 1956; pp. 185-89; provides an explanation of Tenducci's extraordinary marriage).

Tenschert, Roland, musicologist; b. Podersam, Bohemia, April 5, 1894. He studied at the Leipzig Cons. and in Vienna *(Dr. phil.,* 1921); from 1926 to 1931 he was librarian and teacher at the Mozarteum in Salzburg; in 1945, became prof. of music history at the Vienna Academy of Music. —Publications: *Mozart: ein Künstlerleben in Bildern und Dokumenten* (Leipzig, 1931); *Mozart* (Leipzig, 1931); *J. Haydn* (Berlin, 1932); *Vater Hellmesberger: ein Kapitel Wiener Musikerhumor* (Vienna, 1947); *Musikerbrevier* (Vienna, 1940); *Mozart: ein Leben für die Oper* (Vienna, 1941); *Dreimal sieben Variationen über das Thema Richard Strauss* (Vienna, 2nd ed., 1945); *Frauen um Haydn* (Vienna, 1946); *Salzburg und seine Festspiele* (Vienna, 1947); *Richard Strauss und Wien, eine Wahlverwandtschaft* (Vienna, 1949); *C. W. Gluck* (Olten, 1951); *W. A. Mozart* (Salzburg, 1951; in English, 1952); edited the letters of R. Strauss and Joseph Gregor (Salzburg, 1955).

Terhune, Anice (*née* Potter), American pianist and composer; b. Hampden, Mass., Oct. 27, 1873. She studied in Cleveland, in Rotterdam (with Louis Coenen), and in N. Y. (with E. M. Bowman). In 1901 she married Albert Payson Terhune, the author; in 1952, was living at Pompton Lakes, N. J. She publ. several books of songs for children *(Dutch Ditties, Chinese Child's Day, Colonial Carols, Our Very Own Book,* etc.) and a number of separate songs; also many piano pieces for children; the operas *Hero Nero* (1904) and *The Woodland Princess* (1911); a book, *Music-Study for Children* (1922), and an autobiography, *Across the Line* (N. Y., 1945).

Ternina, Milka, Croatian soprano; b. Vezisče, near Zagreb, Dec. 19, 1863; d. Zagreb, May 18, 1941. She studied voice at the Vienna Cons. with Gänsbacher; made her operatic début in Zagreb (1882); then sang in Leipzig (1883-84) and Graz (1884-86). She subsequently was a member of the Bremen Opera (1886-89), and of the Munich Opera (1890-99), where she distinguished herself as a Wagnerian singer. She was engaged by Walter Damrosch for his German Opera Co. in N. Y., and made her American début as Elsa on March 4, 1896; also appeared at Covent Garden, London, as Isolde (June 3, 1898); after a series of successes at the Bayreuth Festivals, she was engaged by the Metropolitan Opera Co., singing there every season from 1899 until 1904; sang Tosca at the American première (Feb. 4, 1901) and Kundry in *Parsifal* (Dec. 24, 1903). She retired from the stage in 1906 and settled in Zagreb, where she remained until her death.

Terrabugio (ter-rah-boo'-joh), **Giuseppe,** Italian composer; b. Fiera di Primiero, May 13, 1842; d. there, Jan. 8, 1933. He studied in Padua, and then in Munich under Rheinberger. In 1883 he settled in Milan, where, as editor of 'Musica Sacra,' he exerted a strong influence in reforming Italian church music. His publ. works (about 100 opus numbers) are almost exclusively for the church (12 Masses, a Requiem, litanies, motets, etc.); he also publ. *L'Organista pratico* (3 vols.).

Terradellas (tĕr-răh-dĕhl'-yăhs), **Domingo** (Italianized as Domenico Terradeglias), Spanish composer; b. Barcelona, 1713 (baptized Feb. 13); d. Rome, May 20, 1751. He studied with Durante at the Cons. dei Poveri di Gesù Cristo in Naples (1732-36); began his career as dramatic composer with the opera *Astarto* (Rome, Jan. 3, 1739); from 1743 to 1745, he was at S. Giacomo degli

Spagnuoli, Rome; in 1746, went to London, where he produced his operas *Mitridate* (Dec. 2, 1746) and *Bellerofonte* (April 4, 1747); returned to Italy in 1750, after traveling through Belgium and France (1748-49). There is no foundation for the story that he drowned himself in the Tiber owing to the failure of his opera *Sesostri* (Rome, 1751). 12 arias and 2 duets were publ. in 1747 by J. Walsh of London, who also publ. 'the favourite songs' from the operas *Mitridate* and *Bellerofonte*. —Cf. J. R. Carreras y Bulbena, *Domingo Terradellas* (Barcelona, 1908); H. Volkmann, *Domingo Terradellas*, in the 'Zeitschrift der Internationalen Musik-Gesellschaft' (vol. XIII, p. 306).

Terrasse (tehr-rahss'), **Claude**, French composer; b. Grand-Lemps, near Grenoble, Jan. 27, 1867; d. Paris, June 30, 1923. He studied at the Lyons Cons. and at the École Niedermeyer in Paris; from 1888 to 1895, church organist in Arcachon, then in Paris until 1899, when he began to write for the stage, producing a series of successful operettas; the best-known are *Les Travaux d'Hercule* (March 7, 1901); *Le Sire de Vergy* (April 16, 1903); *Monsieur de la Palisse* (Nov. 2, 1904); *La Marquise et le marmiton* (Dec. 11, 1907); *Le Coq d'Inde* (April 6, 1909); *Le Mariage de Télémaque* (May 4, 1910); *Les Transatlantiques* (May 20, 1911); *Cartouche* (March 9, 1912).

Terry, Charles Sanford, eminent English scholar; b. Newport Pagnell, Buckinghamshire, Oct. 24, 1864; d. Westerton of Pitfodels, near Aberdeen, Nov. 5, 1936. He became prof. of history at the Univ. of Aberdeen in 1903, and occupied himself with historical research; at the same time he devoted much of his energy to the study of Bach and his period. His biography of Bach (1928; revised ed., 1933; German transl., Leipzig, 1934) is unique in that it places Bach's life within the historical perspective of his time; the documentation is exceedingly fine, and the few errors are slight. Other books and editions dealing with Bach include: *Bach's Chorals* (3 vols., 1915-21); *J. S. Bach's Original Hymn-Tunes for Congregational Use* (1922); *J. S. Bach, Cantata Texts, Sacred and Secular* (1926); *The Four-Part Chorals of J. S. Bach* (5 vols., 1929); *The Origin of the Family of Bach Musicians* (1929); *Bach: the Historical Approach* (1930); *Bach's Orchestra* (1932); *The Music of Bach: an Introduction* (1933). To the 'Musical Pilgrim' series he contributed analyses of the B minor Mass (1924), the cantatas and oratorios (1925), the Passions (1926), and the Magnificat, Lutheran Masses, and motets (1929). He arranged and publ. a stage version of the 'Coffee Cantata' as *Coffee and Cupid* (1924); also translated into English Forkel's life of J. S. Bach (1920), and wrote a biography of Johann Christian Bach (1929).

Terry, Sir **Richard Runciman,** English music editor; b. Ellington, Northumberland, Jan. 3, 1865; d. London, April 18, 1938. In 1890 appointed organist and music master at Elstow School; 1892-96, organist and choirmaster at St. John's Cathedral, Antigua, West Indies; 1896-1901, at Downside Abbey. There he attracted attention by the revival of the Catholic church music of early English masters (Byrd, Tallis, Tye, Morley, Mundy, White, Fayrfax, etc.); 1901-24 was organist and director of music at Westminster Cathedral, continuing his labors in behalf of early English music; 1915-16, examiner for National Univ. of Ireland and Birmingham Univ. He was chairman of the committee appointed to prepare the English supplement of the Vatican Antiphonary, and mus. ed. of the 'Westminster Hymnal,' the official Roman Catholic hymnal for England. He was knighted in 1922. —Besides Masses, motets, and other church music, he composed 48 *Old Rhymes with New Tunes* (1934). Edited *The Shanty Book* (2 vols.; 1921; 1926); *Old Christmas Carols* (1923); *Hymns of Western Europe* (with Davies and Hadow; 1927); *Salt Sea Ballads* (1931); *A Medieval Carol Book* (1932); *200 Folk Carols* (1933); *Calvin's First Psalter*, 1539, harmonized (1932); also the collections of 16th-century music 'Downside Masses' and 'Downside Motets,' 'Motets Ancient and Modern,' and many separate works by the early English composers mentioned above. —Books: *Catholic Church Music* (1907); *On Music's Borders* (1927); *A Forgotten Psalter and other essays* (1929); *The Music of the Roman Rite* (1931); *Voodooism in Music and other essays* (1934). —Cf. S. Grew, *Favourite Musical Performers* (Edinburgh, 1923); H. Andrews, *Westminster Retrospect: a Memoir of Sir Richard Terry* (London, 1948).

Terschak (tehr'-shak), **Adolf,** celebrated flutist; b. Hermannstadt, Transylvania, April 6, 1832; d. Breslau, Oct. 3, 1901. He studied with Zierer at the Vienna Cons. (1850-52); made long tours, as far west as London, and east to Siberia. —Works: for flute and orch.: *Salut à la Hongrie; Konzert-Fantasie; Columbus*, an American rhapsody; *Carnaval suisse; Murillo, Allegro de concert; Le Papil-*

lon en voyage, étude-caprice; 2 suites for flute and piano, *Deutsche Soldatenbilder* and *Nordlandsbilder;* 2 sonatas; a melodrama, *Die Mutter;* numerous minor pieces for flute and piano; *École de mécanisme* and technical studies; piano pieces; songs and choruses.

Tertis, Lionel, English viola player; b. West Hartlepool, Dec. 29, 1876. He studied violin at the Leipzig Cons. and at the Royal Academy of Music in London; played the viola in various quartets, and decided to make it his chief instrument. He eventually became one of the most renowned viola players in Europe; traveled also in America. Several English composers wrote viola concertos for him. He retired in 1936. He arranged for viola Mozart's clarinet concerto, Elgar's cello concerto, and other works; publ. *Beauty of Tone in String Playing* (London, 1938) and an autobiography, *Cinderella No More* (London, 1953). In 1956 he designed a 'Tertis model' viola.

Terziani (tehr-tsyah'-nē), **Eugenio,** Italian composer; b. Rome, July 29, 1824; d. there, June 30, 1889. He studied with Mercadante at the Naples Cons.; at the age of 19, produced an oratorio, *La Caduta di Gerico* (Rome, March 31, 1844), followed by the operas *Giovanna regina di Napoli* (Rome, June 1, 1845) and *Alfredo* (Rome, Feb. 21, 1852); was conductor in Rome at the Teatro Apollo from 1850; then at La Scala, Milan (1867-71), and finally (from 1877) prof. of composition at the Accademia di Santa Cecilia in Rome. His last opera, *L'Assedio di Firenze,* was produced in Rome, Feb. 24, 1883. He was also the composer of a ballet, *Una Silfide a Pechino* (Rome, Dec. 26, 1859), and of much sacred music.

Teschner, Gustav Wilhelm, German music editor and teacher of singing; b. Magdeburg, Dec. 26, 1800; d. Dresden, May 7, 1883. He was a pupil of Zelter in Berlin and of Crescentini in Italy; mastered Italian teaching methods thoroughly and settled in Berlin as a vocal instructor, specializing in the Italian repertory. He publ. elementary vocal exercises of his own, and edited many works by Italian masters (Clari, 8 books; Crescentini, 5 books; Zingarelli, 10 books; etc.); also brought out early choral church music.

Tesi, Vittoria, famous Italian contralto; b. Florence, Feb. 13, 1700; d. Vienna, May 9, 1775. She received her instruction in Florence and Bologna; appeared on the stage at the age of 16 in Parma; then was engaged in Venice (1718) and Dresden (1719). She sang in Italy every year, and also appeared in Madrid (1739) and Vienna (1747-48). She was married to one Tramontini, a barber by trade, and adopted the professional name Tesi-Tramontini. She was remarkably free in her morals, and many stories, in which it is impossible to separate truth from invention, were circulated about her life. Her letters to a priest were publ. by Benedetto Croce in his book *Un Prelato e una cantante del secolo XVIII* (Bari, 1946).

Tessarini, Carlo, Italian violinist and composer; b. Rimini, 1690; d. c. 1765. He was a follower, if not actually a pupil, of Corelli; in 1729 he was violinist at San Marco in Venice and later served at the Cathedral of Urbino; he then went to Rome and to Fano (1742), and finally entered the service of Cardinal Hannibal in Brünn, Moravia. In 1762, already an old man, he gave concerts in Amsterdam. His violin sonatas, generally in 3 movements, contributed to the establishment of a 3-movement sonata as a norm. He publ. several trio-sonatas, duets, concertinos, concerti grossi, and a violin method, *Grammatica di musica* (Rome, 1741; also in French and English transl.). —Cf. A. Schering, *Geschichte des Instrumentalkonzerts* (Leipzig, 1905; p. 107 ff.).

Tessier (teh-syā'), **André,** French musicologist; b. Paris, March 8, 1886; d. there, July 2, 1931. He studied law, history of art, and other subjects; after attending the lectures of Romain Rolland and André Pirro at the Sorbonne, he devoted himself to musical research; was archivist in the dept. of Fine Arts, and in 1926 was elected secretary to the Société Française de Musicologie; also editor of the 'Revue de Musicologie,' in which his catalogue of the Versailles Library was publ. (Nos. 38-39). He edited the complete works of Chambonnières (with P. Brunold; 1925), and Denis Gaultier's *Rhétorique des Dieux* (facsimile, 1932; transcription, 1933). He was the author of a book on Couperin (Paris, 1926); prepared materials for the complete edition of Couperin's works, but died before his work was finished. A complete list of his writings was publ. by A. Schaeffner in the 'Revue de Musicologie' (Dec., 1953). See also P. Brunold, *Quelques souvenirs sur André Tessier,* in the 'Revue de Musicologie' (Aug., 1931).

Tessier, Charles, French lutenist and composer; b. Pézenas (Hérault), c. 1550; date and place of death unknown. He was chamber musician to Henri IV; traveled in England; his book, *Chansons et airs de cour* for 4 and 5 voices, was publ. in London (1597), dedicated to Lady Penelope Riche (Sir Philip Sidney's 'Stella'); his *Airs et villanelles,* for 3, 4, and 5 voices, were publ. in Paris (1604). —Cf. the 'Musical Antiquary' (vol. 1, p. 53; 1909).

Tessmer, Hans, German writer on music; b. Berlin, Jan. 19, 1895; d. there (killed in an air raid), March 1, 1943. He studied music in Berlin, becoming music critic of the 'Tägliche Rundschau' in 1921; also was engaged as stage director at the opera houses in Dresden (1923-27), Berlin (1928-30), Stuttgart (1934-35), and Görlitz (from 1935). —Books: *Profile und Fantasien* (1921); *Anton Bruckner* (1922); *Richard Wagner* (1930); *Robert Schumann* (1930); also a fictionalized story of Schumann, *Der klingende Weg* (1923). He revised Cherubini's opera, *Lo Sposo di tre, marito di nessuna,* and produced it under the title *Don Pistacchio, der dreifach Verlobte* (Dresden, Nov. 27, 1926).

Testore, Carlo Giuseppe, Italian instrument-maker; b. Novara, c. 1660; d. c. 1720. He was a pupil of Grancino and worked in Milan (1690-1715); made mostly cellos and double-basses, and only a few violins. His son, **Paolo Antonio** (1690-1760), made violins on the model of Guarneri. —Cf. O. A. Mansfield, *Carlo Giuseppe Testore,* in the 'British Musician' (1927; p. 38).

Testori, Carlo Giovanni, Italian theorist; b. Vercelli, March 24, 1714; d. there, May 20, 1782. He publ. *La Musica raggionata* (Vercelli, 1767), a theoretical treatise based on the system of Rameau; it was followed by 3 supplements (1771, 1773, 1782). —Cf. C. Negri, *Brevi considerazioni sull'evoluzione storica ed estetica della musica: Biografie di musicisti vercellesi* (Vercelli, 1909); R. Allorto, *La 'Musica raggionata' di Carlo Giovanni Testori,* in the 'Rivista Musicale Italiana' (July-Sept., 1951).

Tetrazzini (teh-trăh-tsē'-nē), **Eva,** Italian soprano; sister of Luisa Tetrazzini; b. Milan, March, 1862; d. Salsomaggiore, Oct. 27, 1938. After studying with Ceccherini in Florence, she made her début there in 1882, as Marguérite in *Faust.* She sang Desdemona in Verdi's *Otello* at its first American production (N. Y., April 16, 1888). On May 15, 1887 she married the conductor Cleofonte Campanini. She sang with the Manhattan Opera, N. Y., in 1908; after appearances in various European countries, she returned to Italy.

Tetrazzini (teh-trăh-tsē'-nē), **Luisa,** famous Italian coloratura soprano; b. Florence, June 28, 1871; d. Milan, April 28, 1940. At the age of 12 she had learned the words and music of several operas by listening to her elder sister, Eva (Mme. Cleofonte Campanini); she then studied at the Liceo Musicale in Florence with Ceccherini. After her début as Inez in *L'Africaine* in Florence (1895) she sang in Rome and other Italian cities; then traveled with various companies in South America and Mexico, and in 1904 created a local sensation at the Tivoli Opera House in San Francisco. On Nov. 2, 1907, she made her first London appearance (as Violetta) and was so successful during that season that Hammerstein engaged her for his Manhattan Opera House in N. Y., where she was first heard in the same role on Jan. 15, 1908; she remained with Hammerstein's company until its closing in 1910, appeared for one season (1911-12) at the Metropolitan Opera House, and then sang in concert tours and in opera in the U. S. She was one of the greatest opera stars before World War I; continued her career as a concert singer; her last American appearance was in N. Y., 1931. She wrote *My Life of Song* (London, 1921) and *How to Sing* (N. Y., 1923).

Teyber (tī'-ber), **Anton,** Austrian composer; b. Vienna, Sept. 8, 1754; d. there, Nov. 18, 1822. He studied with Padre Martini at Bologna; from 1792 was cembalist at the Imperial Opera in Vienna, and assistant of Salieri; from 1793, court composer and music master to the Imperial children. He wrote an opera, 2 oratorios, a Passion, a melodrama, many Masses, symphonies, string quartets, minuets, etc. Some of his songs are printed in 'Denkmäler der Tonkunst in Österreich' vol. 79.

Teyber (tī'-ber), **Franz,** Austrian composer; brother of Anton Teyber; b. Vienna, Nov. 15, 1756; d. there, Oct. 22, 1810. He studied with Wagenseil; after a concert tour in Southern Germany and Switzerland, he conducted Schikaneder's itinerant opera troupe; was then Konzertmeister at Karlsruhe and Bern, and from 1799 to 1810 composer to Schikaneder's Theater an der Wien. He produced a number of operas and Singspiele there and in other theaters in Vienna: *Die Dorfdeputierten* (Dec. 18, 1785); *Fer-*

nando und Jariko, or *Die Indianer* (Sept. 5, 1789); *Alexander* (June 13, 1801); *Der Schlaftrunk* (Nov. 12, 1801); *Die Neuigkeitskrämer* (May 12, 1802); *Pfändung und Personalarrest* (Dec. 7, 1803); *Scheredin und Almanzor* (Aug. 9, 1804); *Der Zerstreute* (Jan. 29, 1805); *Ruthards Abentheuer* (July 26, 1808); *Pumphia und Kulikan* (Oct. 8, 1808); *Das Spinner-Kreutz am Wienerberge* (posthumous; Aug. 24, 1811).

Teyte, Maggie (real name Tate), English soprano; b. Wolverhampton, April 17, 1888. She studied in London; then was a pupil of Jean de Reszke in Paris (1903-07). In order to insure correct pronunciation of her name in France, she changed the original spelling Tate to Teyte. She made her operatic début as Zerlina at Monte Carlo (1907); was very successful as a concert singer in Paris, and appeared with Debussy at the piano; Debussy also selected her as successor to Mary Garden in the role of Mélisande (1908). She sang at the Opéra-Comique (1908-10), with Beecham's Opera Co. in London (1910-11), with the Chicago Opera Co. (1911-14), and the Boston Grand Opera Co. (1915-17). She continued her recitals of French music in London during World War II. She publ. a book of memoirs, *Star on the Door* (London, 1958). —Cf. C. Wallis, *Maggie Teyte,* in 'Opera' (London, April, 1952).

Thadewaldt (tăh'-dĕ-văhlt), **Hermann,** German conductor and composer; b. Bodenhagen, April 8, 1827; d. Berlin, Feb. 11, 1909. He was bandmaster at Düsseldorf (1850-51) and Dieppe (1853-55); from 1857 to 1869, conductor of his own orch. in Berlin, and in 1871 of the concerts at the Zoölogical Gardens there. In 1872 he founded the 'Allgemeiner Deutscher Musikerverband,' of which he was the first president, and to whose interests he devoted his entire time until his death. He published a symph. poem, *Das Rätsel der Sphinx; Im Walde* for orch.; *Meermusik* for string orch.; *Herbstlied* for string quintet; etc.

Thalberg, Sigismond, piano virtuoso and composer; b. Geneva, Jan. 8, 1812; d. Posilipo, near Naples, April 27, 1871. His parents were Joseph Thalberg of Frankfurt and Fortunée Stein, also of Frankfurt, but resident in Geneva. Thalberg, however, pretended to be the natural son of Prince Moritz Dietrichstein, who took charge of his education. His first instructor was Mittag, the bassoonist of the Vienna Court Opera; he subsequently studied piano with Hummel and composition with Sechter. He played as a precocious pianist in the aristocratic salons of Vienna, and began to compose piano music. In 1830 he made a successful concert tour through Germany; in 1834 he was appointed court pianist in Vienna; in 1835 he went to Paris, where he perfected his playing under Kalkbrenner; from that time he became one of the most admired piano virtuosos of Paris, and soon extended his triumphs through most of Europe, including Russia. In 1843 he married the widow of the painter Boucher. In 1855 he set out on a concert tour through Brazil and the U. S. (1856); made a 2nd Brazilian tour in 1863, and in 1864 retired to Naples. —Thalberg was unexcelled as a performer of fashionable salon music and virtuoso studies. He possessed a wonderful legato, eliciting from Liszt the remark, 'Thalberg is the only artist who can play the violin on the keyboard.' His technical specialty was to play a central melody with the thumb of either hand, surrounding it with brilliant arpeggios and arabesques. To present this technique graphically in notation, he made use of the method initiated by Francesco Pollini (q.v.) of writing piano music on 3 staves. He wrote 2 operas, *Florinda* (London, July 3, 1851) and *Cristina di Suezia* (Vienna, June 3, 1855), which were not successful; but his brilliant piano pieces were the rage of his day, easily eclipsing, in popular favor, those of Chopin, his close contemporary. Among them are a group of nocturnes, several *Caprices,* 2 *Romances sans paroles; Grandes valses brillantes; Le Départ, varié en forme d'étude; Marche funèbre variée; Barcarole; Valse mélodique; Les Capricieuses; Tarentelle; Souvenir de Pest; La Cadence* (very popular); *Les Soirées de Pausilippe* (6 albums); *Célèbre Ballade; La Napolitaine;* several sonatas, many pianistic studies; fantasies on operas by Rossini, Bellini, Meyerbeer, Weber, Verdi, etc.

Thallon, Robert, organist and composer; b. Liverpool, March 18, 1852; d. Brooklyn, March 13, 1910. He was taken to N. Y. as a small child; studied in Germany, in Paris and Florence (1864-76); upon his return to the U. S., he settled in Brooklyn as organist and music teacher; publ. a number of songs and piano pieces, and some orchestral arrangements.

Thayer, Alexander Wheelock, authority on Beethoven; b. South Natick, Mass., Oct. 22, 1817; d. Trieste, July 15, 1897. After graduation at Harvard Univ. in 1843, he became assistant librarian there; during 6 years' work in the library, he matured a plan for writing a detailed and trustworthy biography of Beethoven. For preliminary study, and to collect material, he first spent 2 years (1849-51) in Germany, also writing letters for newspapers; in 1852 he joined the staff of the New York 'Tribune,' and returned to Europe in 1854, where, excepting 2 years (1856-58) spent in Boston, he remained. Dr. Lowell Mason and Mrs. Mehetable Adams (of Cambridge, Mass.) gave generous and disinterested aid at this juncture. In 1862 Thayer was attached to the American embassy at Vienna; in 1865, Abraham Lincoln appointed him consul at Trieste, a post held during life. He then publ. a *Chronologisches Verzeichniss der Werke Ludwig van Beethovens* (Berlin, 1865); in 1866 vol. I of his life-work, *Ludwig van Beethoven's Leben,* appeared in German, translated from the English MS by Deiters; vol. II was publ. in 1872; vol. III, in 1879. In 1877 he publ. *Ein kritischer Beitrag zur Beethoven-Litteratur.* Unhappily, his wonderful capacity for work was overtaxed, and vol. IV of his nobly conceived work, executed with a painstaking thoroughness and scrupulous fidelity beyond praise, was left unfinished. Though he lived for years in straitened circumstances, he resolutely refused offers from firms like Novello & Co. and G. Schirmer, hoping to recast entirely the English version of his *Beethoven,* which was publ. in 3 vols. by Krehbiel in 1921. —Cf. H. E. Krehbiel, *A. W. Thayer and His 'Life of Beethoven,'* in the 'Mus. Quarterly' (Oct., 1917); Christopher Hatch, *The Education of A. W. Thayer,* in the 'Mus. Quarterly' (July, 1956).

Thayer, Arthur Wilder, American composer and conductor; b. Dedham, Mass., Aug. 26, 1857; d. there, Nov. 17, 1934. Pupil of C. A. Guilmette and C. R. Adams (singing), Chadwick (theory and instrumentation), and Zerrahn (conducting). Conducted choral societies in Lowell, Salem, Worcester, Providence, etc.; 1882-85, superintendent of music in schools at Dedham; 1885-88 at Milton; then music director at Eliot Church, Newton. He publ. numerous songs; also church music and piano pieces.

Thayer, (Whitney) Eugene, American organist; b. Mendon, Mass., Dec. 11, 1838; d. Burlington, Vt., June 27, 1889. He began to study the organ at 14; in 1862 assisted at the opening of the great organ in the Music Hall, Boston, where he became regular organist after study (1865-66) under Haupt, Wieprecht, etc., in Germany; also conductor of the Boston Choral Union, etc. For a Festival Cantata he received the degree of Mus. Doc. from Oxford Univ. He publ. a Mass; 4 organ sonatas; part-songs; also *The Art of Organ Playing* (5 parts).

Thayer, William Armour, American organist and song composer; b. Brooklyn, N. Y., Oct. 5, 1874; d. there, Dec. 9, 1933. Pupil of J. H. Brewer (organ), D. Buck (theory), and J. D. Mehan (voice); 1893-1914, organist of St. James' Protestant Episcopal Church, Brooklyn; from 1914 of St. Mark's Methodist Episcopal Church; from 1907 also prof. of music at Adelphi College, Brooklyn. He publ. many songs, of which the best known is *My Laddie.*

Thebom, Blanche, American mezzo-soprano; b. Monessen, Pa., Sept. 19, 1918, of Swedish parents. She studied singing with Margaret Matzenauer and Edyth Walker; made her concert début in N. Y. on Jan. 12, 1944, and her operatic début at the Metropolitan Opera, N. Y., as Fricka, Dec. 14, 1944. She then sang in various opera houses, in America and Europe, with increasing success. In 1958 she appeared as a guest artist in Russia. Among her best roles are Ortrud in *Lohengrin,* Azucena in *Il Trovatore,* Amneris in *Aida,* Laura in *La Gioconda,* and Carmen.

Theile (tī'lĕ), **Johann,** German composer; b. Naumburg, July 29, 1646; d. there (buried June 24), 1724. Pupil of H. Schütz at Weissenfels; in 1673, Kapellmeister to the Duke of Holstein at Gottorp; went to Hamburg and wrote (for the opening of the Opera there in 1678) the Singspiele *Adam und Eva* (Jan. 12, 1678) and *Orontos;* he also produced a Christmas Oratorio in 1681. In 1685, Kapellmeister to the Brunswick court at Wolfenbüttel; then Kapellmeister at Merseburg. He was called by contemporaries 'the father of counterpoint.' Among his numerous pupils were Buxtehude and Zachau. —Works: a German Passion (publ. Lübeck, 1675, reprinted by Zelle in 'Denkmäler deutscher Tonkunst' vol. 17); *Noviter inventum opus musicalis compositionis 4 et 5 vocum, pro pleno choro* (20 Masses), and *Opus secundum, novae sonatae rarissimae artis et suavitatis musicae* (a collection of instrumental sonatas, preludes, courantes, airs, and sarabands *a* 2-5, in single, double, triple, and quadruple counterpoint). —Cf. F. Zelle, *Johann Theile und N. A. Strungk* (Berlin, 1891); W. Maxton, *Johann Theile* (dissertation, Tübingen, 1926).

Theodorini, Helena, Rumanian soprano; b. Craiova, March 25, 1862; d. Bucharest, March, 1926. Pupil of D. Fumagalli (piano) and A. Sangiovanni (singing) at the Cons. Verdi in Milan; début (as contralto) at Teatro Municipale in Cuneo (1879); gradually her voice changed to a mezzo-soprano of wide range; after appearing in Warsaw (1881), at La Scala, Milan (1883), and in Madrid (1884-86), she sang in the chief opera houses of Europe and South America until 1902. In 1905 she established herself as a vocal teacher in Paris; lived several years in Buenos Aires, and in 1916 settled in N. Y.; later she returned to Rumania.

Theremin, Leon (real name Termen; Gallicized as Theremin, and pronounced tair-mĕn), Russian inventor of the space-controlled electronic instrument that bears his name; b. St. Petersburg, Aug. 15, 1896. He studied physics and astronomy at the Univ. there; also cello and theory. He continued his studies in physics at the Leningrad Physico-Technical Institute, where in 1919 he became director of the Laboratory of Electrical Oscillators. In 1920 he constructed the first electronic musical instrument, giving many demonstrations during the next 4 years in Russia. In 1927 he demonstrated his new instruments in Germany, France, and the U. S., where on Feb. 28, 1928, he obtained a patent for the 'Thereminovox.' On April 29, 1930, at Carnegie Hall, he presented a concert with an ensemble of 10 of his instruments, also introducing a space-controlled synthesis of color and music. On April 1, 1932, in the same hall, he introduced the first electrical symph. orch., conducted by A. Stoessel, including Theremin fingerboard and keyboard instruments. He also invented the Rhythmicon, for playing different rhythms simultaneously or separately (introduced by Henry Cowell); and an automatic musical instrument for playing directly from specially written musical scores (constructed for Percy Grainger). Until 1938 Theremin was director of his own research laboratory in N. Y.; then returned to Russia.

Thibaud, Jacques, celebrated French violinist; b. Bordeaux, Sept. 27, 1880; d. in an airplane crash near Mt. Cemet in the French Alps, Sept. 1, 1953, en route to French Indo-China. He was taught by his father, and then entered the class of Martin Marsick at the Paris Cons., winning 1st prize in 1896. Obliged to earn his living, he played the violin at the Café Rouge, where he was heard by the conductor Colonne, who offered him a position in his orch.; in 1898 he made his début as soloist (with Colonne), with such success that he was engaged for 54 concerts in Paris in the same season. Subsequently he appeared in all the musical centers of Europe, and from 1903 visited America numerous times. With his 2 brothers, a pianist and a cellist, he formed a trio, which had some success; but this was discontinued when he joined Alfred Cortot and Pablo Casals in a famous trio. His playing was notable for its warmth of expressive tone and fine dynamics; his interpretations of Beethoven ranked very high, but he was particularly authoritative in French music. — Cf. J.-P. Dorian, ed., *Un Violon parle; souvenirs de Jacques Thibaud* (Paris, 1947).

Thibault, Geneviève (Comtesse de Chambure), French musicologist; b. Neuilly-sur-Seine, May 20, 1902. She studied at the Sorbonne, Paris, under André Pirro; then became engaged in business, but continued her great interest in musical research; assembled a fine private library, containing rare editions and MSS of the Renaissance, which she opened to research scholars; also made a collection of old instruments; initiated the Société de Musique d'Autrefois, for the purpose of presenting concerts of old music performed on old instruments; also sponsored publication of old music; from 1955, lecturer at the Sorbonne. Her own contributions to musicology (usually in collaboration with other scholars) include: *Poètes et musiciens du XVe siecle* (Paris, 1924; with E. Droz); *Trois chansonniers français du XVe siècle* (Paris, 1927; with A. Pirro, E. Droz, and Y. Rokseth); *Bibliographie des poésies de P. de Ronsard mises en musique au XVIe siècle* (Paris, 1941; with L. Perceau); *Bibliographie des éditions d'Adrien Le Roy et Robert Ballard* (Paris, 1955; with F. Lesure); also wrote articles for European and American musical periodicals.

Thibaut IV, King of Navarre and Count of Champagne, one of the most notable of the trouvères; b. Troyes, 1201; d. Pamplona, July 8, 1253. 63 of his songs were publ. by Bishop La Ravallière in 1742 as *Poésies du Roi de Navarre;* the transcription of the melodies is very faulty. In Pierre Aubry's ed. of the *Chansonnier de l'Arsenal* (Paris, 1909) there are 59 melodies by Thibaut transcribed in modern notation; see also the examples in J. Beck's transcription of the *Chansonnier Cangé* ('Les Chansonniers des Troubadours et des Trouvères'), 4 vols. (Philadelphia, 1927-38), and

A. Schering, *Geschichte der Musik in Beispielen* (1931), p. 7. —Cf. P. Aubry, *Trouvères and Troubadours* (English transl., N. Y., 1914, p. 122).

Thibaut (tē-boh'), **Anton Friedrich Justus,** b. Hameln, Jan. 4, 1774; d. Heidelberg, March 28, 1840. He studied law, and from 1806 was prof. of jurisprudence in Heidelberg, also director of a singing club there; wrote *Über Reinheit der Tonkunst* (1825; often republ.; new ed., with biography of Thibaut by R. Heuler, 1907; in English as *On Purity in Musical Art,* 1877). His valuable music library (catalogue publ. in 1842) was acquired by the Hofbibliothek in Munich. —Cf. E. Baumstark, *A. F. J. Thibaut* (Leipzig, 1841).

Thiel, Carl, German editor and pedagogue; b. Klein-Öls, Silesia, July 9, 1862; d. Bad Wildungen, July 23, 1939. Pupil of the Königliche Institut für Kirchenmusik and of Bargiel's master class at the Akademie der Künste. On a government stipend he traveled in Italy; won the Mendelssohn prize in 1894, and became organist at the Sebastiankirche in Berlin; later teacher at the Institut für Kirchenmusik, of which he was director from 1922-27 (in 1924 it became the Akademie für Kirchen- und Schulmusik). In 1930 he became director of the Kirchenmusikschule in Regensburg. He ed. old a cappella music; composed Masses, motets, cantatas. —Cf. C. A. Preising, *Carl Thiel* (Regensburg, 1951).

Thiele (tē'-le), **(Johann Friedrich) Louis,** German organist; b. Quedlinburg, Nov. 18, 1816; d. Berlin, Sept. 17, 1848. He studied with A. W. Bach at the Royal Institute for Church Music at Berlin; from 1839 was organist of the Parochialkirche. He published concert pieces, variations, preludes, etc., for organ.

Thieme (tē'-me), or **Thiémé, Friedrich,** German music pedagogue; date of birth not known; d. Bonn, June, 1802. He taught at Paris (1780-92); then at Bonn. He publ. *Éléments de musique pratique* (2nd ed., Paris, 1783); a method, *Principes abrégés de musique* for beginners on the violin; also for piano; *Nouvelle théorie sur les différents mouvements des airs . . . avec le projet d'un nouveau chronomètre* (1801); and several books of violin duos.

Thienen, Marcel van, French composer; b. Paris, Oct. 3, 1922. He studied at the Paris Cons., graduating as a violinist in 1941. In his compositions, he is influenced by Erik Satie. Among his works are an opera-farce, *Le Ferroviaire* (1951); *Brasserie* for orch. (1947); *Petite Suite digestive* for orch. (1951); piano pieces; songs.

Thierfelder (tēr'-fěl-der), **Albert (Wilhelm),** German composer and writer on music; b. Mülhausen, Thuringia, April 30, 1846; d. Rostock, Jan. 6, 1924. He studied at Leipzig Univ. 1865-69, and at the same time with Hauptmann, Richter, and Paul. 1870-87, singing teacher and cantor at Brandenburg; from 1887, music director and prof. at Rostock Univ., succeeding Kretzschmar; received title of 'Professor' in 1898.—He publ. 'Altgriechische Musik: Sammlung von Gesängen aus dem klassischen Alterthume vom 5. bis 1. Jahrhundert vor Christus nach den überlieferten Melodien mit griechischem und deutschem Texte nebst einleitenden Vorbemerkungen herausgegeben und für den Konzertvortrag eingerichtet' (3 vols.; Leipzig, 1899, 1900, 1919), being a collection of the remains of ancient Greek musik; also *System der altgriechischen Instrumentalnotenschrift* (1897).

Thiman, Eric Harding, English music educator, organist, and composer; b. Ashford, Kent, Sept. 12, 1900. He studied at the Royal Academy of Music; was prof. there from 1930 (having obtained the degree of Doctor of Music in 1927). —Publications: *A Guide to Elementary Harmony* (London, 1941); *Practical Free Counterpoint* (London, 1947); *Musical Form for Examination Students* (1951); wrote a number of organ and choral works and some light orch. music (*Dance for a Children's Party; Stirling Castle March,* etc.).

Thimus (tē'-mus), **Albert,** Freiherr **von,** German writer on music; b. Aachen, May 21, 1806; d. Cologne, Nov. 6, 1878. He publ. *Die harmonikale Symbolik des Altertums* (2 vols., 1868-76). As an introduction to this work, R. Hasenclever wrote *Die Grundzüge der esoterischen Harmonik des Altertums* (1870). —Cf. R. Haase, *Der Aachener Albert von Thimus,* in C. M. Brand, ed., *Beiträge zur Musikgeschichte der Stadt Aachen* (Cologne, 1954).

Thiriet (tē-ryā'), **Maurice,** French composer; b. Meulan, May 2, 1906. He studied with Charles Koechlin and Roland-Manuel; was engaged in radio work in Paris; also worked in the music division of a cinema company. —Works: *Le Bourgeois de Falaise,* opéra-bouffe (Paris, June 21, 1937); *La* *véridique histoire du docteur,* opéra-bouffe (1937); *La Nuit vénitienne,* ballet (Paris Opéra, March 17, 1939); *Œdipe-Roi,* incidental music to Jean Cocteau's drama (1942); *La Précaution inutile,* ballet on themes by Rossini (1946); *L'Œuf à la coque,* ballet (1949); *Le Livre pour Jean,* symph. suite (Paris, Dec. 20, 1931); *Rapsodie sur des thèmes incas,* for orch. (Lyons, Jan. 20, 1936); *Afriques,* for orch. (1949); *Le Serment de l'athlète,* for chorus and orch. (1948); *Saint-Pierre et le jongleur,* for chorus and orch. (1950); *Blues de l'horloge,* for violin and piano; songs; piano pieces. —Cf. Jean Solar, *Maurice Thiriet* (Paris, 1958).

Thoinan (twăh-năhn'), **Ernest,** French writer on music (pen-name of Antoine-Ernest Roquet); b. Nantes, Jan. 23, 1827; d. Paris, May 26, 1894. A businessman in Paris, and a thoughtful student of music. He collected a fine music library. —Publ. *La Musique à Paris en 1862* (1863); *L'Opéra Les Troyens au Père Lachaise* (1863; a satire); *Les Origines de la chapelle-musique des souverains de France* (1864); *Les Origines de l'opéra français* (1886; with Ch. Nuitter); *Déploration de Guillaume Crétin sur le trépas de Jean Ockeghem* (1864); *Maugars, célèbre joueur de viole* (1865); *Antoine de Cousu et les singulières destinées de son livre rarissime 'La Musique universelle'* (1866); *Curiosités musicales et autres trouvées dans les œuvres de Michel Coyssard* (1866); *Un Bisaïeul de Molière; recherches sur les Mazuel, musiciens des XVIe et XVIIe siècles* (1878); *Louis Constantin, roi des violons* (1878); *Notes bibliographiques sur la guerre musicale des Gluckistes et Piccinistes* (1878); *Les Hotteterre et les Chédeville* (1894); also an annotated ed. of the *Entretien des Musiciens* [1643] by Annibal Gantez (1878).

Thomas (toh-măh'), **Ambroise,** French composer; b. Metz, Aug. 5, 1811; d. Paris, Feb. 12, 1896. He entered the Paris Cons. in 1828; his teachers there were Zimmerman and Kalkbrenner (piano) and Lesueur (composition); in 1829 he won the 1st prize for piano playing, in 1830 for harmony, and in 1832 the Grand Prix de Rome with the dramatic cantata *Hermann et Ketty.* After 3 years in Italy, and a visit to Vienna in 1836, he returned to Paris, and applied himself with great energy to the composition of operas. In 1851 he was elected to the Académie. In 1871, he became director of the Paris Cons., as successor to Auber (disregarding the brief incumbency of Salvador Daniel, adherent of the Paris Commune, who was killed in battle on May 23, 1871). As composer of melodious operas in the French style, he was second only to Gounod; his masterpiece was *Mignon,* based on Goethe's *Wilhelm Meister* (Opéra-Comique, Nov. 17, 1866); this opera became a mainstay of the repertory all over the world; it had nearly 2,000 performances in less than 100 years at the Opéra-Comique alone. Scarcely less successful was his Shakespearean opera *Hamlet,* produced shortly after *Mignon* (Paris Opéra, March 9, 1868). The complete list of his operas (all produced in Paris) includes: *La double Échelle* (Aug. 23, 1837); *Le Perruquier de la régence* (March 30, 1838); *Le Panier fleuri* (May 6, 1839); *Carline* (Feb. 24, 1840); *Le Comte de Carmagnola* (April 19, 1841); *Le Guerillero* (June 22, 1842); *Angélique et Médor* (May 10, 1843); *Mina, ou le Ménage à trois* (Oct. 10, 1843); *Le Caïd* (Jan. 3, 1849); *Le Songe d'une nuit d'été* (April 20, 1850); *Raymond, ou Le Secret de la reine* (June 5, 1851); *La Tonelli* (March 30, 1853); *La Cour de Célimène* (April 11, 1855); *Psyché* (Jan. 26, 1857); *Le Carnaval de Venise* (Dec. 9, 1857); *Le Roman d'Elvire* (Feb. 4, 1860); *Mignon* (Nov. 17, 1866); *Hamlet* (March 9, 1868); *Gille et Gillotin* (April 22, 1874); *Françoise de Rimini* (April 14, 1882). He contributed an act to a ballet, *La Gipsy* (Opéra, Jan. 28, 1839), and wrote the ballets *Betty* (Opéra, July 10, 1846) and *La Tempête* (Opéra, June 26, 1889); a *Messe solennelle* (1857) and other sacred works; some chamber music; songs. —Cf. A. Hervey, *Masters of French Music* (London, 1894); J. Simon, *Ambroise Thomas,* in the 'Revue de Paris' (March-April, 1896); H. Delaborde, *Notice sur la vie et les œuvres d'Ambroise Thomas* (Paris, 1896); C. Bellaigue, *Études musicales et nouvelles silhouettes des musiciens* (Paris, 1898; in English, 1899); E. Destranges, *Ambroise Thomas,* in the 'Revue Musicale de Lyon' (1911, p. 97); H. de Curzon, *Ambroise Thomas* (Paris, 1921).

Thomas Aquinas (Saint), b. Roccasecca, near Aquino, Italy, 1227; d. Fossa Nuova, near Terracina, March 7, 1274. This famed theologian and scholastic philosopher entered the Dominican order in 1245. In 1263 Pope Urban IV commissioned him to compose a communion service, which contains the memorable numbers *Lauda Sion* (Corpus Christi sequence) and *Pange lingua, Sacra solemnis, Verbum supernum,* and *Adoro te* (hymns). An extended chapter on music is contained in his *Summa Theologica* (II, *quaestio XLI, art.* 2). See *D. Thomas Aqui-*

natis de arte musica nunc primum ex codice bibl. univ. Ticinensis ed. illustr. Sac. Guarinus Amelli (1880). —Cf. G. Amelli, *S. Tommaso e la musica* (1876); C. F. Bellet, *St. Th. d' Aquin* (Paris, 1902); J. L. Callahan, *A Theory of Esthetics According to the Principles of St. Th. Aquinas* (dissertation, Catholic Univ., Washington, D. C., 1927).

Thomas, Arthur Goring, English composer; b. Ratton Park, Sussex, Nov. 20, 1850; d. London, March 20, 1892. He was a pupil of Émile Durand in Paris (1874-77), and of Arthur Sullivan and Ebenezer Prout at the Royal Academy of Music in London; later studied orchestration in Berlin with Max Bruch. He was mainly interested in creating English operas in the best German tradition; his operas were performed in England and Germany, and he had many important supporters for his art in England, but his music totally lacked vitality, and became of only antiquarian interest after his death. In the last year of his life he suffered from a mental illness. —Operas: *The Light of the Harem* (partial performance, London, Nov. 7, 1879); *Esmeralda* (London, March 26, 1883; also in German, produced in Berlin, Hamburg, and Cologne); *Nadeshda* (London, April 16, 1885); *The Golden Web* (posthumous; Liverpool, Feb. 15, 1893); he further wrote a choral ode, *The Sun Worshippers* (Norwich Festival, 1881); the cantata *The Swan and the Skylark* (posthumous; Birmingham Festival, 1894; orchestrated by C. V. Stanford); a vocal scene, *Hero and Leander* (1880); *Out of the Deep,* anthem for soprano solo, chorus, and orch. (1878); some chamber music; songs.

Thomas (toh'-mahs), **Christian Gottfried,** German composer and writer on music; b. Wehrsdorf, near Bautzen, Feb. 2, 1748; d. Leipzig, Sept. 12, 1806. He published *Praktische Beiträge zur Geschichte der Musik . . .* (1778; chiefly for the music trade); *Unparteiische Kritik der vorzüglichsten seit 3 Jahren in Leipzig aufgeführten . . . Kirchenmusiken, Concerte und Opern* (1798, 1799); and 'Musikalische kritische Zeitschrift' (1805; 2 vols.). His compositions include a Gloria for 3 choirs, with instruments; a cantata; quartets.

Thomas (toh'-măhs), **Eugen,** conductor; b. Surabaya, Java, Jan. 30, 1863; d. Schloss Orth, near Gmunden, Aug., 1922. In 1878 he went to Delft, Holland, where he studied engineering, and at the same time music; 1882-84, conductor of the orchestral society 'Euterpe'; 1884-85, conductor of 'St. Cäcilie' (choral and orchestral society) in Semarang, Java; from 1885-87 he completed his music studies at the Vienna Cons.; 1887, theater-conductor in Pilsen; 1888, Kapellmeister of the German opera, Groningen; settled in Vienna in 1889 as pianist and composer; from 1905 director of the choral classes at the Cons.; founder (1902) and conductor of the 'Wiener a cappella Chor.' —Wrote *Die Instrumentation der 'Meistersinger' von R. Wagner* (2 vols., 1899; 2nd ed., 1907); and the *Wiener Chorschule* (1907).

Thomas (toh'-mahs), **Gustav Adolf,** German organist and composer; b. Reichenau, near Zittau, Oct. 13, 1842; d. St. Petersburg, May 27, 1870. He studied at the Leipzig Cons.; was organist at the Reformed Church in Leipzig; then succeeded H. Stiehl as organist at St. Peter's in St. Petersburg. He wrote excellent works for organ: *Konzert-Fantasie; Sechs Trios über bekannte Choralmelodien; Fuga eroica;* études; piano pieces; ed. Bach's *Kunst der Fuge* and Handel's organ concertos.

Thomas, John, celebrated Welsh harpist; b. Bridgend, Glamorganshire, March 1, 1826; d. London, March 19, 1913. He also used the name Aptommas (or Apthomas; i.e. son of Thomas) and Pencerdd Gwalia (Chief of Minstrels, bardic name bestowed on him at the Aberdare Eisteddfod in 1861). He entered the Royal Academy at 14; studied harp with Chatterton, and upon the latter's death in 1872, succeeded him as Harpist to the Queen. He gave in London a series of annual concerts of Welsh music; the first took place at St. James's Hall, July 4, 1862, with a chorus of 400, and 20 harps. He was also a leader of the Eisteddfod festivals. He wrote 2 harp concertos; the dramatic cantata *Llewelyn* (1863) and *The Bride of Neath Valley,* a Welsh scene (1866); publ. a collection of Welsh melodies (1862) and a *History of the Harp* (London, 1859); made transcriptions for harp of many classical pieces. His brother, **Thomas Thomas** (1829-1913), also a harpist, went to America in 1895, eventually settling in Ottawa.

Thomas, John Charles, American baritone; b. Meyersdale, Pa., Sept. 6, 1891. He studied at the Peabody Cons. in Baltimore; from 1913 sang in musical comedy in N. Y.; then entered the concert field, in which he achieved outstanding success. He also sang in opera; was a member of the Théâtre de La Monnaie in Brussels (1925-28); later at Covent Garden, London (début as Valentin in *Faust*). In 1930 he appeared with the Chicago Opera Co.; on Feb. 2, 1934, he sang the role of the elder Germont in *La Traviata*, at his first appearance with the Metropolitan Opera; he continued to be on its roster until 1943; then settled in California.

Thomas, John Rogers, baritone and composer of songs; b. Newport, Wales, March 26, 1829; d. New York, April 5, 1896. He was a lawyer's clerk in London; came to America in 1849, and acquired considerable success as an oratorio singer. A number of his songs enjoyed tremendous popularity in their day (*The Mother's Prayer, The Cottage by the Sea, Beautiful Isle of the Sea, Must we then meet as strangers,* etc.). He publ. an operetta, *Diamond Cut Diamond;* a children's cantata, *The Picnic;* and much sacred music.

Thomas, Kurt, German composer and organist; b. Tönning, Schleswig-Holstein, May 25, 1904. He studied at the Leipzig Cons. with R. Teichmüller (piano), M. Ludwig (theory), H. Grabner (composition), and Karl Straube (organ). From 1925 to 1934 he taught theory at the Leipzig Cons.; from 1934 to 1939 was prof. at the Berlin Hochschule für Musik; from 1939 to 1945 was at Frankfurt; in 1947 was appointed prof. at the music academy in Detmold, where he remained until 1955. In 1956 he became cantor of the Thomaskirche in Leipzig. Among his works are a Mass (1924); Psalm 137 (1925); *Goethe Cantata* (1928); cantata *Jerusalem, du hochgebaute Stadt* (1929); *Christmas Oratorio* (1931); *Resurrection Oratorio* (1934); numerous choruses a cappella (sacred and secular); piano concerto (1937); 2 violin sonatas (1925, 1933); cello sonata (1927); 3 suites for school orch. Publ. *Lehrbuch der Chorleitung* (5th ed., Leipzig, 1948).

Thomas, Theodore, renowned conductor; b. Esens, East Friesland, Germany, Oct. 11, 1835; d. Chicago, Jan. 4, 1905. Taught by his father, a violinist, he played in public at 6. In 1845 the family went to New York, where Thomas soon began to play for dances, weddings, and in theaters, helping to support the family; in 1851 he made a concert tour as soloist, and in 1853 he joined Jullien's orch. on the latter's visit to N. Y., later touring the country with **Jenny Lind,** Grisi, Sontag, Mario, etc. He became a member of the N. Y. Philh. Society in 1854. In 1855 began the Mason and Thomas chamber-music soirées (cf. **William Mason**). Up to 1861 he played in various opera-orchestras, sometimes conducting. In 1862 he organized an orch. for 'Symphony Soirées' at Irving Hall, New York, which were continued until 1878 (after 1872 in Steinway Hall); in 1866 he started summer concerts in Terrace Garden, removing in 1868 to Central Park Garden. The influence of these enterprises on musical culture in New York was enormous; Thomas' programs attained European celebrity. The first concert tour with the orch. was made in 1869, with 54 players, and for nine consecutive years he made annual tours of the East and Middle West. In 1873 he established the famous Cincinnati Biennial Festival, which he conducted till his death. He also founded the Cincinnati College of Music, of which he was president and director from 1878-80, having given up his own orch. in New York and the conductorship of the N. Y. Philh. Society (1877-78) to accept this post. After his resignation he returned to New York, where he immediately reorganized his own orch. and was re-elected conductor of the Philh. Society and the Brooklyn Philh. Orch. (having been conductor of the latter in 1862-63, 1866-68, and 1873-78). Besides conducting these orchestral bodies, he was at different times director of several choruses; from 1885-87 he was conductor and artistic director of the American Opera Co. In 1891 he settled permanently in Chicago as conductor of the Chicago Symph. Orch. In recognition of Thomas' distinguished services a permanent home, Orchestra Hall, was built by popular subscription, and formally opened in Dec., 1904, with a series of festival concerts, which were the last directed by him; a cold contracted during a rehearsal developed into pneumonia, which after a few days resulted fatally. After his death the name of the orch. was changed to 'Theodore Thomas Orch.'; in 1913 the original title was officially resumed. —The influence of Thomas upon the musical development of the U. S. has been strong and lasting. A severe, almost autocratic drillmaster, his splendid musicianship and lofty idealism invariably commanded the respect and good will of those under his direction. As an arranger of homogeneous, artistic programs he has never been excelled. The list of novelties produced by him is enormous; an indefatigable apostle of Wagner, Liszt, and Brahms, he also played for the first time in America many of the larger works of Tchaikovsky, Dvořák, Rubinstein, Bruckner, Goldmark, Saint-Saëns, Cowen, Stanford, Raff, etc.; he introduced Richard Strauss to America (Symph. in F minor, Dec. 13, 1884) before that composer had become known even in his own country. —Cf. *T. T. A Musical Autobiography,* ed. by G. P. Upton (2 vols.; Chicago, 1905); R. F. Thomas (his wife), *Memoirs of T. T.* (N. Y., 1911); C. E. Russell, *The American Orchestra and T. T.* (N. Y., 1927); *Talks About Beethoven's Symphonies,* by T. T. and F. A. Stock (N. Y., 1930); E. T. Rice, *T. and Central Park Garden,* in the 'Mus. Quarterly' (April, 1940); A. Loft, *Richard Wagner, T. T., and the American Centennial,* in the 'Mus. Quarterly' (April, 1951). See also P. A. Otis, *The Chicago Symphony Orchestra* (Chicago, 1925).

Thomas (Thomas-San Galli), Wolfgang Alexander, German writer on music; b. Badenweiler, Sept. 18, 1874; d. Baden-Baden, June 14, 1918. Studied philosophy, history, and law in Freiburg, Bonn, Munich, and Marburg (*Dr. jur.,* 1898); 1899-1908, viola player of the 'Süddeutsches Streich-Quartett' in Freiburg; 1908-11, ed. of the 'Rheinische Musik- und Theaterzeitung' in Cologne; then in Berlin as writer. In 1898 he married the pianist Helene San Galli. — Works: *Sein oder Nichtsein? Aphorismen über Ethisches und Ästhetisches* (1905); *Joh. Brahms. Eine musikpsychologische Studie* (1905); *Musik und Kultur* (1908); *Musikalische Essays* (1908); *Die 'unsterbliche Geliebte' Beethovens, Amalie Sebald* (1909; attempt to prove that the famous letter was addressed to Amalie Sebald); *Beethoven und die unsterbliche Geliebte. Amalie Sebald, Goethe, Therese Brunswick, und Anderes* (1910); *Mozart-Schatzkästlein* (1911); *Joh. Brahms* (1912; biography); *L. van Beethoven* (1913; biography). Edited *Beethovens Briefe* (1910; selection with commentary) and *Beethovens Briefe an geliebte Frauen* (1913).

Thomé (toh-mā'), **Francis** (baptismal names **Joseph-François-Luc**), French composer; b. Port Louis, Island of Mauritius, Oct. 18, 1850; d. Paris, Nov. 16, 1909. He went to Paris as a youth, and studied at the Cons. with Marmontel (piano) and Duprato (theory). He became a successful teacher; wrote the operas, *Le Caprice de la Reine* (Cannes, 1892) and *Le Château de Königsberg* (Paris, 1896); the ballets, *Djemmah* (1886), *La Folie parisienne* (1900), etc.; the religious mystery play *L'Enfant Jésus* (1891); 2 symphonic odes, *Hymne à la nuit* and *Vénus et Adonis;* etc. But he is remembered chiefly for his piano pieces, of which *Simple aveu* and *Les Lutins* became very popular.

Thompson, John Sylvanus, American pianist and teacher; b. Williamstown, Pa., March 8, 1889. He was educated at the Leefson-Hille Cons., Philadelphia, and the Univ. of Pennsylvania. He traveled through the U. S. as a concert pianist; also appeared in London and Berlin. In 1917 he settled in Kansas City. He publ. much teaching material, including the very successful *Modern Course for Piano* (*Something New Every Lesson*) (Cincinnati, 1936; 6 vols.); *The Adult Preparatory Piano Book* (Cincinnati, 1943); *Melody All the Way* (Cincinnati, 1949-51; 7 vols.; last 2 vols. are subtitled *Supplementary Piano Course).*

Thompson, John Winter, American organist and composer; b. Leland, Mich., Dec. 21, 1867; d. St. Charles, Ill., March 8, 1951. After graduating from Oberlin Cons. (1890) he went to Germany, where he studied at the Leipzig Cons. with Schreck. Returning to the U. S., he became teacher of organ at Knox College, Galesburg, Ill. He publ. organ works, motets, and anthems; also *A Course in Harmony* (Boston, 1923).

Thompson, Oscar, American music critic and editor; b. Crawfordsville, Ind., Oct. 10, 1887; d. New York, July 3, 1945. He was educated at the Univ. of Washington, Seattle; studied music with G. Campanari and others; took up journalism and in 1919 joined the staff of 'Musical America,' later becoming associate ed., and finally editor (1936-43). He was music critic for the N. Y. 'Evening Post' (1928-34); from 1937 to his death was music critic for the N. Y. 'Sun' (succeeding W. J. Henderson). In 1928 he established the first class in music criticism in the U. S., at the Curtis Institute, Philadelphia; also gave courses at the N. Y. College of Music. In 1939 he brought out 'The International Cyclopedia of Music and Musicians' in one vol. of more than 2,000 pages, with feature articles by eminent authorities. After Thompson's death, N. Slonimsky took charge of the 'Cyclopedia' as editor (from 4th ed., 1946, on). Thompson publ. the following books: *Practical Musical Criticism* (1934); *How to Understand Music* (1935); *Tabulated Biographical History of Music* (1936); *The American Singer* (1937); *Debussy, Man and Artist* (1937); ed. *Plots of the Operas* (1940) and *Great Modern Composers* (1941), both vols. being extracts from the 'Cyclopedia.'

Thompson, Randall, eminent American composer; b. New York, April 21, 1899. He was educated at Harvard Univ. (B. A.,

1920; M. A., 1922); his teachers there were Walter Spalding, E. B. Hill, and A. T. Davison; he also studied with Ernest Bloch. From 1922 to 1925 he held a fellowship at the American Academy in Rome; won a Guggenheim Fellowship twice (1929, 1930). From 1927 to 1929, and again in 1936-37, he was assistant prof. of music at Wellesley College; from 1937 to 1939, prof. of music at the Univ. of California, Berkeley; from 1939 to 1941, he was director of the Curtis Institute of Music, Philadelphia; then was head of the music division of the School of Fine Arts of the Univ. of Virginia (1941-46); and prof. of music at Princeton Univ. (1946-48). In 1948 he was appointed to the faculty of Harvard Univ. He excels in vocal composition; his *Alleluia* for chorus a cappella and *The Testament of Freedom,* to words by Thomas Jefferson, scored for men's voices with piano or orch., have attained exceptional success; of his works for orch., the most popular is the 2nd symph. In another genre are the humorous choral pieces *Americana,* to texts culled from the American press, and originally publ. in the 'American Mercury.'—Compositions: opera *Solomon and Balkis* (radio performance, N. Y., March 29, 1942; 1st stage production, Cambridge, Mass., April 14, 1942); incidental music to *The Grand Street Follies* (N. Y., June 25, 1926); incidental music to *The Straw Hat* (N. Y., Oct. 14, 1926); for orch.: *Pierrot and Cothurnus* (Rome, May 17, 1923, composer conducting), *The Piper at the Gates of Dawn,* symph. prelude (Rome, May 27, 1924, composer conducting), symph. No. 1 (Rochester, N. Y., Feb. 20, 1930), symph. No. 2 (Rochester, March 24, 1932), symph. No. 3 (N. Y., May 15, 1949), *A Trip to Nahant,* fantasy for orch. (Philadelphia, March 18, 1955), *Jazz Poem,* for piano and orch. (Rochester, Nov. 27, 1928, composer at the piano); for chorus: *5 Odes of Horace* (1924), *Pueri Hebraeorum,* for women's voices a cappella (1928), *Rosemary,* for women's voices a cappella (1929), *Americana,* for chorus and piano or orch. (1932), *The Peaceable Kingdom,* for chorus a cappella (1936), *Tarantella,* for men's voices and piano (1937), *The Lark in the Morn,* for chorus a cappella (1938), *Alleluia,* for chorus a cappella (1940), *The Testament of Freedom,* for men's voices and piano or orch. (Univ. of Virginia, April 13, 1943; numerous subsequent performances by major choral organizations and orchestras); *The Wind in the Willows,* for string quartet (1924); suite for oboe, clarinet, and viola (1940); string quartet (1941); piano pieces; several song cycles. Publ. the book, *College Music* (N. Y., 1935). —Cf. Quincy Porter, *Randall Thompson,* in 'Modern Music' (vol. 19; 1942); Elliot Forbes, *The Music of Randall Thompson,* in the 'Mus. Quarterly' (Jan., 1949).

Thomson (tŏhn-sŏhn'), **César,** eminent Belgian violinist; b. Liège, March 17, 1857; d. Lugano, Aug. 21, 1931. He entered the Liège Cons. at the age of 7, winning the Gold Medal at 11; he subsequently studied with Vieuxtemps, Léonard, Wieniawski, and Massart. For several years he was household musician to a wealthy Russian patron of arts, Baron Paul von Derwies, at Lugano; in 1879 he became concertmaster of Bilse's orch. in Berlin; in 1882 he became prof. of violin at the Liège Cons.; he left Liège for Brussels in 1898, when he succeeded Ysaÿe as prof. of violin at the Brussels Cons.; there he founded a celebrated string quartet (with Lamoureux, Vanhout, and Jacobs). In 1914 he settled in Paris as prof. at the Cons. In 1924 he visited America; taught at the Cons. of Ithaca, N. Y., and at the Juilliard School of Music, N. Y., returning to Europe in 1927. He was a famous violin teacher, emphasizing the perfection of technical and expressive performance, rather than bravura. He made arrangements for the violin of various works by early Italian composers.

Thomson, George, Scottish collector of folksongs; b. Limekilns, Dunfermline, March 4, 1757; d. Leith, Feb. 18, 1851. For 50 years (1780-1830) he was secretary to the Board of Trustees for the Encouragement of Arts and Manufactures in Scotland. An ardent collector of Scotch, Welsh, and Irish melodies, he issued a series of vols. containing authentic melodies, with piano accompaniments and instrumental arrangements by the most celebrated musicians of his time, including Beethoven, Haydn, Pleyel, and Koželuh. Each song had, in accordance with his plan, a prelude, coda, and *ad libitum* parts throughout (for violin, or flute, or cello). The collections are: *A Select Collection of Original Scottish Airs . . .* (London, 6 vols.; vol. I, 1793; vol. II, 1798; vol. III, 1799; vol. IV, 1802; vol. V, 1818-26; vol. VI, 1841); *Collection of the Songs of R. Burns, Sir W. Scott, etc.* (London, 1822; 6 vols.); *Select Collection of Original Welsh Airs . . .* (London, 1809; 3 vols.); *Select Collection of Original Irish Airs* (London, 1814-16; 2 vols.); *20 Scottish Melodies* (Edinburgh, 1839). —Cf. J. C. Hadden, *George Thomson, the Friend of Burns. His Life and Correspondence* (London, 1898;

contains full and interesting details, notably Beethoven's letters); R. Aldrich, *Beethoven and George Thomson,* in 'Music & Letters' (April, 1927); Karl Geiringer, *Haydn and the Folksong of the British Isles,* in the 'Mus. Quarterly' (April, 1949); C. B. Oldman, *Beethoven's Variations on National Themes,* in 'Music Review' (Feb., 1951).

Thomson, John, Scotch composer and writer on music; b. Sprouston, Roxburgh, Oct. 28, 1805; d. Edinburgh, May 6, 1841. He studied in Leipzig with Schnyder von Wartensee, and became an intimate of Mendelssohn, Schumann, and Moscheles. In 1839 he was appointed the first Reid prof. of music at Edinburgh Univ. At the 3rd concert given by the 'Edinburgh Professional Society' (Feb., 1837), an analytical program was issued by Thomson, then conductor; this is the first recorded instance of the use of such programs. He composed 2 operas, *Hermann, or The Broken Spear* (London, Oct. 27, 1834) and *The Shadow on the Wall* (London, April 20, 1835); also wrote incidental music to Walter Scott's *The House of Aspen* (Edinburgh, Dec. 19, 1829).

Thomson, Virgil, American composer and writer on music; b. Kansas City, Mo., Nov. 25, 1896. He graduated from Harvard Univ. in 1922; studied piano with H. Gebhard and organ with W. Goodrich in Boston; composition with Rosario Scalero in N. Y. and with Nadia Boulanger in Paris. He was organist at King's Chapel in Boston (1922-1923); in 1925 he went to Paris for a prolonged stay; there he established friendly contacts with composers of the avant-garde, as well as with modern painters and writers; his association with Gertrude Stein was particularly significant in the development of his esthetics. In the formulation of his musical ideas, he was much influenced by the example of Erik Satie, adopting an eclectic style, which he brought to a fine point; under the characteristic Parisian persiflage, there is a serious intent and considerable achievement. His most famous work is the opera *Four Saints in Three Acts,* to a text by Gertrude Stein, in which the deliberate confusion wrought by the author of the play (there are actually 4 acts and more than a dozen saints, some of them in duplicate) and the composer's almost solemn, hymn-like treatment, create a hilarious modern opera-buffa. It was first produced at Hartford, Conn., on Feb. 8, 1934, under the auspices of the 'Society of Friends and Enemies of Modern Music' of which Thomson was director (1934-37); many performances followed in the U. S., and also in Europe. Another curiosity among his compositions is a series of musical portraits, scored for various instrumental ensembles, purporting to paint in tones actual people, famous and obscure. In 1940 Thomson was appointed music critic of the N. Y. 'Herald Tribune'; resigned in 1954 to devote himself to composition and conducting. Besides *Four Saints in Three Acts,* he wrote another opera, to words by Gertrude Stein, *The Mother of Us All,* on the life of the American suffragist Susan B. Anthony (N. Y., May 7, 1947); a ballet, *Filling Station* (Hartford, Conn., Jan. 6, 1938); for orch.: *Symph. on a Hymn Tune* (1928; N. Y., Feb. 22, 1945, composer conducting); symph. No. 2 (Seattle, Nov. 17, 1941); *The Seine at Night* (Kansas City, Feb. 24, 1948); *Wheatfield at Noon* (Louisville, Dec. 7, 1948); cello concerto (Philadelphia, March 24, 1950); *5 Songs* for voice and orch., after William Blake (Louisville, Feb. 6, 1952); *Sea Piece with Birds* (Dallas, Dec. 10, 1952; also grouped with *The Seine at Night* and *Wheatfield at Noon* as *Three Pictures for Orchestra*); concerto for flute, strings, and percussion (Venice, Sept. 18, 1954); *A Solemn Music,* for band (1949); chamber music: *Sonata da chiesa* for 5 instruments (1926); *5 Portraits,* for 4 clarinets (1929); violin sonata (1930); *4 Portraits,* for violin and piano (1931; also for orch.); string quartet No. 1 (1931); string quartet No. 2 (1932); also 4 piano sonatas; 2 sets of études for piano; organ pieces; sacred choral works; *Hymns from the Old South,* for mixed chorus a cappella; songs to French and English texts. Film music: *The Plough that Broke the Plains* (1936; also an orch. suite from it); *Louisiana Story* (1948; 2 orch. suites, including *Acadian Songs and Dances).* He publ. several collections of articles: *The State of Music* (1939); *The Musical Scene* (1945); *The Art of Judging Music* (1948); *Music, Right and Left* (1951). —Cf. S. L. M. Barlow, *Virgil Thomson,* in 'Modern Music' (vol. 18; 1941); Aaron Copland; *Our New Music* (N. Y., 1941; pp. 187-201); Peggy Glanville-Hicks, *Virgil Thomson,* in the 'Mus. Quarterly' (April, 1949).

Thooft (tŏhft), **Willem Frans,** Dutch composer; b. Amsterdam, July 10, 1829; d. Rotterdam, Aug. 27, 1900. He studied with A. Dupont in Brussels and with Hauptmann at the Leipzig Cons.; then went to Rotterdam, where he organized the German Opera. —Works: an opera, *Aleida von*

Holland (Rotterdam, 1866); *Gevonden,* for baritone solo, male chorus, and orch.; 3 symphonies (including one with chorus, surnamed *Kaiser Karl V*); *In Leid und Freud,* fantasy for orch.; *Die Jungfrau von Orleans,* overture; psalms; piano pieces; songs.

Thorborg, Kerstin, Swedish contralto; b. Venjan, May 19, 1896. She studied at the Stockholm Opera School; was engaged as a regular member of the Stockholm Opera (1925-30); then sang in Berlin and Vienna. On Dec. 21, 1936, she made her American début as Fricka at the Metropolitan Opera House, N. Y.; Klytemnestra in *Elektra* was especially admired; remained with the Metropolitan Opera until 1950; gave concerts throughout the U. S. and Canada; then returned to Sweden and became a voice teacher in Stockholm.

Thorn, Edgar. Pseudonym (in early works) of **Edward MacDowell.**

Thorne, Edward Henry, English organist and composer; b. Cranbourne, Dorset, May 9, 1834; d. London, Dec. 26, 1916. He was a chorister at St. George's Chapel; served as church organist in London and vicinity from 1853 on; gave organ and piano recitals in London and elsewhere; was especially noted for his Bach programs. He was made Mus. Doc. by the Archbishop of Canterbury in 1913. He wrote a number of sacred choral works; an overture, *Peveril of the Peak* (after Walter Scott); 2 piano trios; violin sonatas; cello sonatas; publ. 7 books of organ pieces.

Thouret (too-rā'), **Georg,** German writer on music; b. Berlin, Aug. 25, 1855; d. there, Jan. 17, 1924. He studied philology and history in Tübingen, Berlin, and Leipzig. The discovery of forgotten military music in the castles of Berlin, Charlottenburg, and Potsdam led him to make a special study of the subject; for the Vienna Exposition (1892) he arranged an exhibition of German military music; publ. the collections 'Altpreussische Militärmärsche' and 'Musik am preussischen Hofe.' —Writings: *Führer durch die Fachausstellung der deutschen Militärmusik* (1892; official catalogue of the Vienna Exposition); *Katalog der Musiksammlung auf der königlichen Hausbibliothek im Schlosse zu Berlin* (1895); *Friedrich der Grosse als Musikfreund und Musiker* (1898).

Thrane (trăh'-nĕ), **Waldemar,** Norwegian composer; b. Christiania, Oct. 8, 1790; d. there, Dec. 30, 1828. He studied violin with K. Schall in Copenhagen; then went to Paris, where he was a pupil of Baillot (violin), Reicha and Habeneck (composition). Returning to Christiania, he conducted theater music; and also directed a music school. He is historically important as the composer of the 1st Norwegian opera, *Fjeldeventyret (A Mountain Adventure);* the score was publ. in 1824; the first concert performance took place in Christiania in 1827; the first stage production was given posthumously (Christiania, April 9, 1850). —Cf. J. G. Conradi, *Musikkens Udvikling i Norge* (Christiania, 1878).

Thuille (tüĕl), **Ludwig (Wilhelm Andreas Maria),** composer and pedagogue; b. Bozen, Tyrol, Nov. 30, 1861; d. Munich, Feb. 5, 1907. He studied with J. Pembaur at Innsbruck (piano and theory); then went to Munich, where he was a pupil of Karl Bärmann (piano) and Rheinberger (composition) at the Music School there; in 1883 he became prof. there. Encouraged by Alexander Ritter (q.v.), he began to compose music in the grand Wagnerian manner; wrote 3 operas, chamber music, song cycles, and choral works. But he made his mark chiefly as a fine pedagogue; with Rudolf Louis he publ. the well-known manual, *Harmonielehre* (1907; abridged ed. as *Grundriss der Harmonielehre,* 1908; new revised ed., by Courvoisier and others, 1933). —Works: operas: *Theuerdank* (Munich, March 12, 1897), *Lobetanz* (Karlsruhe, Feb. 6, 1898), *Gugeline* (Bremen, March 4, 1901); *Romantische Ouvertüre* (introduction to the opera *Theuerdank);* a symph. (1886); sextet for piano and wind instruments; piano quintet; cello sonata. —Cf. F. Munter, *Ludwig Thuille* (Munich, 1923); E. Istel, *Ludwig Thuille,* in the 'Mus. Quarterly' (July, 1932).

Thuren, Hjalmar Lauritz, Danish musical folklorist; b. Copenhagen, Sept. 10, 1873; d. there, Jan. 13, 1912. From 1899 to 1907 he taught at the Fredericksberg Folk-School and was secretary of the Danish Folklore Society. He made valuable studies of folk music in Denmark, in the Faroe Islands, and among the Eskimos. —Writings: *Dans og Kvaddigtning paa Färöerne* (1901), *Folkesangen paa Färöerne* (1908); *Tanz und Tanzgesang im nordischen Mittelalter* ('Zeitschrift der Internationalen Musik-Gesellschaft,' 1908); *The Eskimo Music* (with W. Thalbitzer; Copenhagen, 1911; in French as *La Musique chez les Eskimos,* 'Publications de la revue S. I. M.,' 1912); *Melodies From East Greenland* (1914); etc.

Thürlings (tür'-lings), **Adolf,** German writer on music; b. Kaldenkirchen, July 1, 1844; d. Bern, Feb. 15, 1915. He took the *Dr. phil.* degree in Munich with the dissertation *Die beiden Tongeschlechter und die neuere musikalische Theorie* (Berlin, 1877); publ. *Die schweizerischen Tonmeister im Zeitalter der Reformation* (1903); valuable essays in various journals; also ed. works by Senfl in 'Denkmäler der Tonkunst in Bayern' III, 2, and a selection of 5-part motets by Palestrina.

Thurner (toor'-ner), **Friedrich Eugen,** oboe virtuoso; b. Montbéliard, France, Dec. 9, 1785; d. Amsterdam, March 21, 1827. He publ. 3 symphonies, an overture, 4 oboe concertos, 4 quartets for oboe and strings, rondos and divertissements for oboe with string quartet, trio for oboe with 2 horns, duos for oboe and piano, piano music, etc.

Thursby, Emma, American soprano; b. Brooklyn, Feb. 21, 1845; d. New York, July 4, 1931. She studied with Achille Errani in N. Y.; in 1873 went to Italy, where she studied with Lamperti and San Giovanni in Milan. Upon her return to America in 1875, she was engaged by the bandleader Gilmore for his summer concerts, and toured the country with him; subsequently appeared in the European music centers; in 1903 she sang in China and Japan; then returned to the U. S., living in retirement in N. Y. —Cf. R. McC. Gipson, *The Life of Emma Thursby, 1845-1931* (N. Y., 1940).

Tibaldi Chiesa, Maria, Italian writer on music; b. Milan, April 28, 1896. She studied at the Univ. of Rome; wrote opera librettos, and publ. books of verse. Her musical publications include: *Schubert* (1932; 2nd ed., 1936); *Ernest Bloch* (1933); *Mussorgsky* (1935); *Vita romantica di Liszt* (1937); *Cimarosa e il suo tempo* (1939); *Paganini* (3rd ed., 1944); *Ciaikovsky* (1943).

Tibbett, Lawrence, American baritone; b. Bakersfield, Calif., Nov. 16, 1896. His real name was Tibbet, but it was accidentally misspelled when he appeared in opera, and the final extra letter was retained. His early ambition was to be an actor, and he made a few appearances in various plays in Los Angeles as a young man. He took vocal lessons with Basil Ruysdael in Los Angeles, sang in light operas; then went to N. Y., where his teacher was Frank La Forge. He made his operatic début in N. Y. with the Metropolitan Opera on Nov. 24, 1923, in a minor role; then sang Valentin in *Faust* (Nov. 30, 1923); achieved a striking success as Ford in the revival of Verdi's *Falstaff* (Jan. 2, 1925); from then on he became one of the most successful singers at the Metropolitan Opera, where he remained until 1950; also won wide popularity in recitals and on the radio; appeared in films.

Tiby, Ottavio, Italian musicologist; b. Palermo, May 19, 1891. He studied at the Cons. of Palermo, graduating in composition in 1921; later studied in Rome. Returning to Palermo, he held a government position; devoted himself to collecting Sicilian songs; is also an authority on Byzantine music. —Publications: *Acustica musicale e organologia degli strumenti musicali* (Palermo, 1933); *La Musica bizantina: teoria e storia* (Florence, 1938); *La Musica in Grecia e a Roma* (Florence, 1942); *La Famiglia Scarlatti,* in the 'Journal of Renaissance and Baroque Music' (1947); *The Polyphonic School in Sicily of the 16th-17th Century,* in 'Musica Disciplina' (1951); edited *Antichi musicisti italiani* (1934).

Tichatschek (ti'-hăh-chĕhk), **Joseph Aloys,** Bohemian tenor; b. Ober-Weckelsdorf, July 11, 1807; d. Dresden, Jan. 18, 1886. He was the son of a poor weaver; in 1827 went to Vienna as a medical student, but then joined the chorus at the Kärnthnerthor Theater, and had vocal instruction from Ciccimara; was soon engaged at Graz for 2 years; then sang in Vienna. His career received a new impetus after his highly successful appearance at the Dresden Opera (Aug. 11, 1837); he remained there for 33 years, retiring in 1870. He created the roles of Rienzi (Oct. 20, 1842) and Tannhäuser (Oct. 19, 1845) in Wagner's operas. Wagner mentions him often and with great praise in his autobiography.

Tieffenbrucker. See **Duiffopruggar.**

Tiehsen (tē'-zen), **Otto,** German composer; b. Danzig, Oct. 13, 1817; d. Berlin, May 15, 1849. He studied at the Royal Academy in Berlin, where he settled as a teacher. —Works: the comic opera *Annette* (Berlin, 1847); *Christmas Cantata; Kyrie* and *Gloria a* 6; songs of high merit.

Tiersch, Otto, German music theorist; b. Kalbsrieth, Sept. 1, 1838; d. Berlin, Nov. 1, 1892. He studied with J. G. Töpfer at

Weimar and with Bellermann at Berlin; taught singing at the Stern Cons. in Berlin. As a theorist he was a disciple of Hauptmann. —Publications: *System und Methode der Harmonielehre* (1868); *Elementarbuch der musikalischen Harmonie- und Modulationslehre* (1874); *Kurze praktische Generalbass-, Harmonie- und Modulationslehre* (1876); *Kurzes praktisches Lehrbuch für Contrapunkt und Nachahmung* (1879); *Kurzes praktisches Lehrbuch für Klaviersatz und Accompagnement* (1881); *Notenfibel* (1882); *Die Unzulänglichkeit des heutigen Musikstudiums an Conservatorien,* etc. (1883); *Allgemeine Musiklehre* (1885; with Erk); *Rhythmik, Dynamik und Phrasierungslehre der homophonischen Musik* (1886); articles on harmony, etc., in Mendel's 'Konversationslexikon.'

Tiersot (tyär-soh'), **(Jean-Baptiste-Élisée-) Julien,** French musicologist; b. Bourg-en-Bresse, July 5, 1857; d. Paris, Aug. 10, 1936. He was a pupil of Savard, Massenet, and César Franck at the Paris Cons.; in 1883 was appointed assistant librarian at the Cons., and in 1910, chief librarian, retiring in 1920. He dedicated himself to musical ethnography, and contributed greatly to the documentation on French folk music. He was prof. at the École des Hautes Études Sociales and president of the Société Française de Musicologie. His compositions include a Mass on the tercentenary of the death of Roland de Lassus (1894); *Danses populaires françaises* for orch. (1900); *Hellas* (after Shelley) for chorus and orch.; etc. —Writings: *Histoire de la chanson populaire en France* (1889); *Musiques pittoresques* (1889); *Rouget de Lisle, son œuvre, sa vie* (1892); *Les Types mélodiques dans la chanson populaire française* (1894); *Étude sur les Maîtres-Chanteurs . . . de Richard Wagner* (1899); *Ronsard et la musique de son temps* (1903); *Index musical pour le Romancero populaire de la France par G. Doncieux* (1904); *Hector Berlioz et la société de son temps* (1904); *Notes d'ethnographie musicale* (Part I, 1905; Part II is *La Musique chez les peuples indigènes de l'Amérique du Nord,* 1910); *Les Fêtes et les chants de la Révolution française* (1908); *Gluck* (1910); *Beethoven, musicien de la Révolution* (1910); *J.-J. Rousseau* (1912); *Histoire de la Marseillaise* (1915); *Un Demi-siècle de musique française . . . 1870-1917* (1918; 2nd ed., 1924); *La Musique dans la comédie de Molière* (1921); *La Damnation de Faust de Berlioz* (1924); *Lettres de musiciens écrites en français du XVe au XXe siècle* (2 vols.; 1924, 1936); *Smetana* (1926); *Les Couperin* (1926); *La Musique aux temps romantiques* (1930); *La Chanson populaire et les écrivains romantiques* (1931); *Don Juan de Mozart* (1933); *Lettres françaises de Richard Wagner* (1933); *J.-S. Bach* (1934); also the correspondence of Berlioz, in 3 vols.: I, *Les Années romantiques* (1904); II, *Le Musicien errant* (1919); III, *Au milieu du chemin* (1930). —Collections of music; *Chansons populaires recueillies dans les Alpes françaises* (1903); *Noëls français* (1901); *Chants populaires, pour les écoles* (3 vols., 1907-29); *44 French Folk-songs and Variants from Canada, Normandy, and Brittany* (N. Y., 1910); *60 Folksongs of France* (Boston, 1915); *Chansons de Ronsard* (1924); *Chansons populaires françaises* (1921); *Mélodies populaires des provinces de France* (1928); *Chansons nègres* (1933).—Cf. D. C. Parker, *The Work of J. Tiersot,* in the 'Mus. Standard' (1920); L. de La Laurencie, *Un Musicien bressan: J. Tiersot* (Bourg, 1932).

Tiessen (tēs'-sehn), **Heinz,** German composer and conductor; b. Königsberg, April 10, 1887. He studied music with Rüfer and Klatte in Berlin; was music critic of the 'Allgemeine Musikzeitung' (1912-17); then conducted at various Berlin theaters; led 'Der junge Chor' for children of workers (1924-32). In 1925 he was appointed to the faculty of the Hochschule für Musik in Berlin; from 1946 to 1949 was director of the Municipal Cons. of Berlin, returning in 1949 to the Hochschule. His style of composition is influenced by Richard Strauss, with whom he was friendly; he publ. a guide to Strauss' *Josephslegende* (1914); *Zur Geschichte der jüngsten Musik, 1913-28* (Mainz, 1928); and *Musik der Natur,* a study of bird songs (1953). His compositions include 2 symphonies; a piano concerto; a *Naturtrilogie* for piano solo; a septet for flute, clarinet, horn, and string quartet; a string quintet; about 60 songs; incidental music to plays. —Cf. his autobiography, *Selbstzeugnis des Künstlers,* in 'Musica' (Kassel, April, 1948).

Tietjens (tēt'-yĕns), **Therese Johanne Alexandra,** famous soprano; b. Hamburg, July 17, 1831; d. London, Oct. 3, 1877. She was trained in Hamburg and made a successful début there in 1849; sang at Frankfurt, and was engaged for the Vienna Court Opera in 1856; but went to London in 1858, and remained there until her death, for long years the reigning favorite, singing at Her Majesty's Theatre, Drury Lane, Covent Garden, and the Haymarket. She visited Paris in 1863, and America in 1874 and 1876, appearing at the Academy of Music in N. Y. under Strakosch's management.

Tigranian, Armen, Armenian composer; b. Alexandropol, Dec. 26, 1879; d. Tiflis, Feb. 10, 1950. He studied flute and theory in Tiflis; returned to Alexandropol in 1902 and organized a choral society, specializing in Armenian music; arranged Armenian folk-songs; in 1913 settled in Tiflis, where he became an esteemed music pedagogue; received the order of Lenin in 1939. —Works: the operas *Anush* (1908-12; Alexandropol, Aug. 17, 1912) and *David-bek* (Erivan, Dec. 3, 1950); *Dance Suite* for orch. (1946); cantata, *The Bloody Night* (1936); *Suite of Armenian Dances* for piano; numerous other piano pieces; songs; theater music.

Tigranian, Vartan, Armenian composer; son of Armen Tigranian; b. Alexandropol, Dec. 20, 1906. He studied at the Leningrad Cons. with Shostakovitch and others, graduating in 1941. His works include an operetta, *The Big Wedding* (1945); a cantata, *October* (1945); choruses and solo songs; preludes and other pieces for piano.

Tijardović (tē-yahr'-dŏh-vich), **Ivo,** Croatian composer; b. Split, Sept. 18, 1895. He studied in Zagreb; began his professional career by conducting theater orchestras; wrote operettas of the Viennese type; of these, *Little Floramy* (1924) became successful in Yugoslavia. His opera *Dimnjiaci Uz Jadran (The Chimneys of the Adriatic Coast)*, produced in Zagreb on Jan. 20, 1951, depicts the patriotic uprising of Yugoslav partisans during World War II. —Cf. I. B. Plamenac, *Ivo Tijardović* (Split, 1954).

Tikotsky, Evgeny Karlovitch, Russian composer; b. St. Petersburg, Dec. 25, 1893; studied composition with Deshevov; began to compose in 1924; in 1944 became musical director of the Philharmonic Concerts in Minsk. —Works: the operas *Mihas Podhorny* (Minsk, March 10, 1939) and *Alesya* (Minsk, Dec. 24, 1944); 4 symphonies (1927, 1940, 1949, 1955); *Stormy Petrel,* after Maxim Gorky, for bass, chorus, and orch. (1944); trombone concerto (1944); theater music.

Till, Johann Christian, 'Moravian' teacher, organist, and composer; b. Gnadenthal, near Nazareth, Pa., May 18, 1762; d. Bethlehem, Pa., Nov. 19, 1844. From 1793 till 1808 he was teacher and organist at Hope, N. J.; from 1813 to 1844 was organist of the Bethlehem congregation. In his later years he also made pianos. His compositions are listed in A. G. Rau and H. T. David, *A Catalogue of Music by American Moravians* (Bethlehem, 1938).

Tillyard, Henry Julius Wetenhall, English musicologist; b. Cambridge, Nov. 18, 1881. He studied at the Univ. there (1900-04) and at the English schools in Rome and Athens (1904-07), specializing in ancient and medieval music; studied Greek church music with J. T. Sakellarides in Athens. Until 1918 he was lecturer at the Univ. of Edinburgh; in 1919 he became prof. at the Univ. of Johannesburg (South Africa); in 1922 at Birmingham Univ.; and in 1926 at the Univ. of Cardiff. He publ. *Byzantine Music and Hymnology* (London, 1923); *Handbook of the Middle Byzantine Musical Notation* (Copenhagen, 1935; vol. 1 of 'Monumenta musicae byzantinae. Subsidia'); ed. the following vols. in the 'Transcripta' of the 'Monumenta musicae byzantinae': vol. 1, *Sticherarium* (with Höeg and Wellesz; Copenhagen, 1935); vol. 2, *The Hymns of the Sticherarium for November* (Copenhagen, 1938); vols. 3 and 5, *The Hymns of the Octoechus* (Copenhagen, 1940; 1949); vol. 4, *Twenty Canons from the Trinity Hirmologium* (Boston, 1952).

Tilman (til-mahn'), **Alfred,** Belgian composer; b. Brussels, Feb. 3, 1848; d. Schaerbeck, near Brussels, Feb. 20, 1895. He studied at the Brussels Cons. (1866-71); wrote the cantata *La Sirène;* 24 vocal fugues for 2 and 3 voices.

Tilmant (til-mahn'), **Théophile,** French conductor; b. Valenciennes, July 8, 1799; d. Asnières, May 7, 1878. From 1838 to 1849 he served as 2nd maître de chapelle at the Théâtre Italien; then 1st maître de chapelle at the Opéra-Comique until his retirement in 1868; was also conductor of the Cons. Concerts from 1860 to 1863.

Timanova, Vera Victorovna, Russian pianist; b. Ufa, Feb. 18, 1855; d. Leningrad, 1942. She was a pupil of Anton Rubinstein, Tausig, and Liszt; appeared as a child prodigy in Russia and Germany from the age of 9; became a prominent teacher in Leningrad, remaining there until her death.

Timm, Henry Christian, pianist, organist, and composer; b. Hamburg, July 11, 1811; d. New York, Sept. 4, 1892. After study in Germany, he settled in the U. S. in 1835; was employed as church organist in N. Y.,

Boston, etc. He was president of the N. Y. Philharmonic from 1847 to 1863. He wrote choral works, organ pieces, and some piano music; made numerous transcriptions for 2 pianos of various classical works.

Timmermans, Ferdinand, Dutch organist and carillonneur; b. Rotterdam, Sept. 7, 1891. He studied organ with J. H. Besselaar and H. de Vries. In 1924 he became the municipal carillonneur at Rotterdam and in 1926 at Schiedam. He subsequently gave exhibitions in Belgium, France, and England; soon he won the reputation of being one of the world's greatest carillonneurs. On May 5, 1954 he gave a concert in Washington playing on the 50-bell carillon presented to the U. S. by the people of Holland. He publ. *Luidklokken en beiaarden in Nederland* (Amsterdam, 1944).

Tinayre, Yves (Jean), French singer and music scholar; b. Paris, April 25, 1891. He studied voice in London and Milan; gave recitals in France, England, Austria, etc., specializing in old songs, which he edited for this purpose; also revived some medieval French, German, and Italian sacred songs. He is president of the society Les Musiciens de la Vieille France.

Tinctoris, Johannes (called **John Tinctor**), Belgian writer and composer; b. probably Nivelles, 1436; d. there, before Oct. 12, 1511. About 1475, maestro to Ferdinand of Aragon at Naples, who dispatched him in quest of singers for his chapel to France, etc., in 1487; but Tinctoris never went back, and became a canon at Nivelles. He was one of the most eminent theorists of his time, and the author of the earliest dictionary of musical terms, *Terminorum musicae diffinitorium* (Naples, 1473; reprint in Coussemaker's 'Scriptores,' IV, and, with a German transl. by H. Bellermann, in Chrysander's 'Jahrbuch,' 1863; in English, London, 1849; with a French transl., Paris, 1951). The only other work known to have been printed during his life is *De inventione et usu musicae* (after 1487); a number of treatises preserved in MS were publ. for the first time in Coussemaker's ed. of the complete works of Tinctoris (1875) and reprinted in vol. IV of the 'Scriptores.' Extant compositions are a *Missa l'homme armé* (ed. by L. Feininger in 'Monumenta polyphoniae liturgicae Sanctae Ecclesiae romanae' Series I, I-9) and some chansons in MS; other chansons and a Lamentation in Petrucci's 'Odhecaton' and collection of 1506. —Cf. G. Pannain, *La Teoria musicale di G. Tinctoris* (Naples, 1913); K. Weinmann, *Johannes Tinctoris und sein unbekannter Traktat 'De inventione et usu musicae'* (Regensburg, 1917); Ch. Van den Borren, *J. Tinctoris* (Brussels, 1931); Lucie Balmer, *Tonsystem und Kirchentöne bei J. Tinctoris* (dissertation, Bern, 1935); G. Reese, *Music in the Renaissance* (N. Y., 1954; pp. 137-50). See also René Vannes, ed., *Dictionnaire des Musiciens* (Brussels, 1947; pp. 390-92).

Tinel (tē-nehl'), **Edgar,** Belgian composer; b. Sinay, March 27, 1854; d. Brussels, Oct. 28, 1912. He was taught at first by his father, a schoolmaster and organist; entered the Brussels Cons. in 1863 as a pupil of Brassin, Dupont, Gevaert, Kufferath, and Mailly; in 1873 took 1st prize for piano playing; won the Belgian Prix de Rome in 1877 with the cantata *De Klokke Roeland.* In 1882 he became director of the Institute for Sacred Music at Mechlin; was appointed to the staff of the Brussels Cons. in 1896, and in 1909 (after Gevaert's death) became the director. —Works: *Franciscus,* oratorio (Mechlin, 1888; N. Y., 1893); *Godoleva,* music drama (Brussels, July 22, 1897); *Katharina,* sacred opera (Brussels, Feb. 27, 1909); many German and Flemish songs; *Te Deum* for mixed chorus and organ; *Missa in honorem beatae Mariae Virginis de Lourdes* for 5-part chorus a cappella; psalms; motets; sacred songs. He publ. *Le Chant grégorien, théorie sommaire de son exécution* (1890). —Cf. A. van der Elst, *Edgar Tinel* (Ghent, 1901); Paul Tinel (his son), *Edgar Tinel: le récit de sa vie et l'exégèse de son œuvre de 1854 à 1886* (Brussels, 1922); Paul Tinel, *Edgar Tinel* (Brussels, 1946).

Tippett, Michael, English composer; b. London, Jan. 2, 1905. He studied composition at the Royal College of Music with R. O. Morris, conducting with Sir Adrian Boult and Sir Malcolm Sargent. His early works were imitative of Sibelius, but he rapidly developed an individual style, essentially Romantic, but with a solid background of polyphony in an emphatically Classical manner; he often employs dance forms in his instrumental music. —Works: opera, *The Midsummer Marriage* (libretto by the composer; 1952; London, Jan. 27, 1955); oratorio, *A Child of Our Time* (London, March 19, 1944); concerto for double string orch. (1939); *Fantasia,* for piano and orch., on a theme by Handel (London, March 7, 1942); symph. No. 1 (1945); symph. No. 2 (London, Feb. 5, 1958); suite in D for orch. (1948); *Little Music,* for string orch. (1952); *Variations on a Theme by Corelli,* for string orch. (1953); piano concerto (1955); 3 string quartets (1935; 1942; 1946); sonata for 4 horns (1955); *Fantasy Sonata* for piano (1938); piano sonata (1942); several choral works; organ pieces; songs. —Cf. C. Mason, *Michael Tippett,* in the 'Mus. Times' (May, 1946).

Tirabassi, Antonio, musicologist; b. Amalfi, Italy, July 10, 1882; d. Brussels, Feb. 5, 1947. He began his career as a church organist; in 1910 went to Belgium, where he founded the Institut Belge de Musicologie (1920); brought out editions of works by Monteverdi, Corelli, and other composers. —Publ. *École flamande (1450 à 1600). La mesure dans la notation proportionelle et sa transcription moderne* (Brussels, 1927); *Grammaire de la notation proportionnelle et sa transcription moderne* (Brussels, 1930).

Tirindelli, Pier Adolfo, Italian violinist and composer; b. Conegliano, May 5, 1858; d. Rome, Feb. 6, 1937. He was a pupil at the Milan Cons. (1870-76); conducted the band at Gorizia for 3 years, then studied in Vienna under Grün, and under Massart at Paris; from 1885, prof. of violin at the Liceo Benedetto Marcello, Venice, of which he was appointed director in 1892. He made his American début with the Boston Symph. Orch. (Dec. 16, 1895); from 1896 to 1920 he taught at the Cincinnati Cons. He wrote an Italian opera, *Atenaide* (Venice, Nov. 19, 1892); and a French opera, *Blanc et noir,* which was produced in Cincinnati (Dec. 15, 1897). Some of his songs (in Italian and French) became very popular (*Mistica, Vaticinio, Je ne t'aime plus, Une Existence,* etc.). —Cf. E. Montanaro, *P. A. Tirindelli e la sua musica* (Rome, 1933).

Tischer, Gerhard, German music publisher; b. Lübnitz, Nov. 10, 1877. He studied musicology in Berlin (1899-1902); *Dr. phil.* with the dissertation *Die aristotelischen Musikprobleme* (1903); from 1904 to 1919, lectured on music history at the Handelhochschule in Cologne, and from 1919 to 1921, at the Univ. there. From 1906 he edited the 'Rheinische Musik- und Theater-Zeitung' (after 1933 known as the 'Deutsche Musik-Zeitung'). In 1910 he founded in Cologne the music-publishing firm of 'Tischer & Jagenberg,' and in 1923 bought the 'Wunderhorn Verlag' of Munich. In 1943 the firm moved to Starnberg.

Tischhauser, Franz, Swiss composer; b. Bern, March 28, 1921. He studied at the Zürich Cons.; in 1951 joined the staff of the Zürich Radio. Among his works are the ballet *Birthday of the Infanta* (1941); concertino for piano and small orch. (1945); *Divertimento* for 2 horns and string orch. (1948); choral pieces; songs.

Tita Ruffo. See **Ruffo, Tita.**

Titelouze (tēt-looz'), **Jean,** the founder of the French school of organ playing; b. St.-Omer, 1563; d. Rouen, Oct. 25, 1633. Appointed organist in 1585 at St.-Jean in Rouen; from 1588 till his death organist at the Cathedral there. His complete organ works are publ. in Guilmant's 'Archives des Maîtres de l'orgue.' —Cf. A. G. Ritter, *Zur Geschichte des Orgelspiels im 14.-18. Jahrhundert* (Leipzig, 1884); A. Pirro, *J. Titelouze* (Paris, 1898); E. von Werra, *J. Titelouze,* in 'Kirchenmusikalisches Jahrbuch' (1910).

Titl, Anton Emil, conductor and composer; b. Pernstein, Moravia, Oct. 2, 1809; d. Vienna, Jan. 21, 1882. In 1850 he became conductor at the Burgtheater in Vienna; wrote two operas: *Die Burgfrau* (Brünn, 1832) and *Das Wolkenkind* (Vienna, March 14, 1845); a Mass for 8 voices; overtures; violin pieces. His *Serenade* for violin was very popular in numerous arrangements.

Titov (tē'-tŏhv), **Alexey Nikolayevitch,** Russian composer; b. St. Petersburg, June 24, 1769; d. there, Nov. 20, 1827. He served in the cavalry, reaching the rank of major general at his retirement; was an amateur violinist, and wrote operas in the traditional Italian style; of these, the following were produced in St. Petersburg: *Andromeda and Perseus* (1802); *The Judgment of Solomon* (1803); *Nurzadakh* (June 7, 1807); *The Wedding of Filatka* (April 25, 1808); *Errant Moment* (July 10, 1812); *Emmerich Tekkely* (Dec. 13, 1812); *Intrigue in the Basket* (May 12, 1817); *Valor of the People of Kiev,* or *These are the Russians* (May 12, 1817); *The Feast of the Mogul* (Sept. 15, 1823); an opera, *The Brewer, or The Hidden Ghost of Evil,* was produced at Moscow in 1788; a ballet-pantomime, *Le nouveau Werther,* was first given in St. Petersburg, on Jan. 30, 1799. His brother **Sergey Titov** (b. 1770; date of death unknown) was a cellist who wrote the operas, all produced in St. Petersburg, *The Forced Wedding* (Sept. 4, 1789), *Credulous*

Folk (July 10, 1812), and *Old-fashioned Christmas* (Jan. 25, 1813).

Titov, Nikolay Alexeyevitch, the 'Grandfather of Russian Song,' son and pupil of Alexey Titov; b. St. Petersburg, May 10, 1800; d. there, Dec. 22, 1875. He received a military upbringing; like his father, he reached the rank of major general. He had no formal musical education; took some singing lessons, and studied a manual of thorough-bass; he was a typical dilettante, but possessed a gift of melodic invention; he knew Glinka and Dargomyzhsky, who helped him to develop his ability. He wrote about 60 songs, which were extremely popular in his time; his early song, *The Pine Tree,* publ. in 1820, is erroneously believed to be the first Russian art song, but as a matter of historical fact, it had precursors; other of his songs that were popular include *Perfidious Friend, The Blue Scarf,* and *A Tree Branch.* He wrote a curious *Quadrille* for piano 3 hands, the treble part to be played by a beginner; another interesting project was a 'musical romance in 12 waltzes' (under the general title *When I Was Young*), which remained incomplete. A waltz, entitled *Past Happiness,* the *Quadrille,* and 4 songs are reproduced in *History of Russian Music in Examples,* ed by S. Ginsburg (Moscow, 1942; vol. 2, pp. 381-93).

Tocchi, Gianluca, Italian composer; b. Perugia, Jan. 10, 1901. He studied in Rome with Respighi; his early works were written in a Romantic and Impressionist manner: a symph. poem *Il Destino,* after Maeterlinck; a *Rapsodia romantica* (1929), *Tre canzoni alla maniera popolare italiana* (1931); he then changed to contemporary subjects, exemplified by such works as *Record* (1933), *Film* (1936), and a concerto for jazz band.

Toch (tohh), **Ernst,** eminent composer; b. Vienna, Dec. 7, 1887. He was a student of medicine and philosophy, and taught himself music by studying great masterpieces; won the Mozart stipend in 1909 and the Mendelssohn stipend in 1910; also won 4 times in succession the Austrian State Prize for composition. In 1909 he went to Frankfurt, where he took piano lessons with Willy Rehberg, and in 1913 became teacher of piano in Zuschneid's Hochschule für Musik in Mannheim; *Dr. phil.,* 1921, with the thesis *Beiträge zur Stilkunde der Melodie* (publ. in Berlin as *Melodielehre,* 1923). From 1929 to 1933 he lived in Berlin, and taught piano and composition. On the advent of the Nazi regime, he left Germany and went to Paris; in 1935 settled in the U. S.; became an American citizen, July 26, 1940. He lectured at the New School for Social Research in N. Y.; in 1937 moved to Hollywood; wrote music for the films; in 1940-41, taught composition at the Univ. of Southern California, Los Angeles. His music is Romantic in inspiration; it is profoundly emotional, and yet the stylistic cohesion and formal design are always strong; the idiom is basically tonal but there is considerable freedom in the melodic flow; the rhythmic element is particularly ingenious; the orchestration is masterly. His piano works, some of transcendent difficulty, are extremely original in facture. Toch is not averse to experimentation; his suite *Gesprochene Musik* for spoken voices (1930) relies exclusively on rhythmic variety and dynamic contrasts. His string quartet, op. 74 (1957), is written in 'a free 12-tone style' of composition. —Works: for the stage: *Wegwende* (1925), *Die Prinzessin auf der Erbse* (Baden-Baden, July 17, 1927), *Egon und Emilie* (Mannheim, 1928), *Der Fächer* (Königsberg, June 8, 1930); oratorio *Das Wasser* (Berlin, June 18, 1930). For orch.: *An mein Vaterland,* with soli, chorus, and organ (1915); *Fantastische Nachtmusik* (Mannheim, March 22, 1921); *Die chinesische Flöte,* for soprano and chamber orch. (Frankfurt, June 24, 1923); *Tanz-Suite,* for small orch. (Mannheim, Nov. 19, 1923); cello concerto (Kiel, June 17, 1925); piano concerto (Düsseldorf, Oct. 8, 1926; Gieseking soloist); *Spiel,* for band (Donaueschingen, July 24, 1926); *Komödie für Orchester* (Berlin, Nov. 13, 1927); *Bunte Suite* (Frankfurt, Feb. 22, 1929); *Kleine Theater-Suite* (Berlin, Feb. 9, 1931); symph. for piano and orch. (1932; London, Aug. 20, 1934); *Big Ben,* variations on the Westminster chimes (Boston Symph., Cambridge, Mass., Dec. 20, 1934); *Pinocchio,* 'a merry overture' (Los Angeles, Dec. 10, 1936; very successful); *Hyperion,* dramatic prelude after Keats (Cleveland, Jan. 8, 1948); 4 symphonies: No. 1 (Vienna, Dec. 20, 1950); No. 2, dedicated to Albert Schweitzer (Vienna, Jan. 11, 1952); No. 3 (Pittsburgh, Dec. 2, 1955; won the Pulitzer Prize); No. 4 (Minneapolis, Nov. 22, 1957); *Notturno* (Louisville, Jan. 2, 1954); *Poems to Martha,* for voice and strings (1946); *Cantata of the Bitter Herbs,* for soli, narrator, mixed chorus, and orch. (1941); also 9 string quartets; *Serenade,* for 3 violins; *2 Divertimenti* (for violin and cello and for violin and viola); string trio; piano quintet; many piano works, among them 3 sonatas, *Burlesken, Klein-*

stadtbilder; 20 concert études for beginners; incidental music for various plays; film music (1934-37); several song cycles. He publ. a theory book, *The Shaping Forces in Music* (N. Y., 1948). —Cf. E. Beninger, *Pianistische Probleme, im Anschluss an die Klavierwerke von Ernst Toch,* in 'Melos' (1928); Paul Pisk, *Ernst Toch,* in the 'Mus. Quarterly' (Oct., 1938); H. Rutz, *Ernst Toch,* in 'Melos' (May, 1952).

Toda, Kunio, Japanese composer; b. Tokyo, Aug. 11, 1914. He studied law at Tokyo Univ. and music in Germany and in Japan with Moroi; appointed cultural attaché in the Ministry of Foreign Affairs and served in Germany and Russia. Among his works are a violin concerto (1949); 3 ballets: *Salome in Studio* (Tokyo, Nov. 23, 1951), *Cirque Rouge* (Tokyo, Nov. 4, 1953), and *Cave* (Tokyo, Nov. 7, 1954); piano trio (1947), piano concerto (1944); also a choral work, *Dona Nobis Pacem* (Tokyo, May 31, 1950).

Todi, Luiza Rosa de Aguilar, Portuguese mezzo-soprano; b. Setubal, Jan. 9, 1753; d. Lisbon, Oct. 1, 1833. She appeared on the stage at 15; married the violinist Francisco Todi at 16; studied singing with David Perez. After appearances in London (1772 and 1777) she sang in Madrid (1777), Paris (1778-79 and 1781-82), and Berlin (1782). In 1783 her rivalry with Elisabeth Mara became a sensation in musical Paris, two hostile factions being formed, the Todistes and Maratistes. In 1784 she went to Russia, where she obtained considerable success at the court of Catherine the Great; in 1787 Friedrich Wilhelm II engaged her at a high salary in Berlin; in 1789 she sang again in Paris; in 1793 she returned to Portugal; during the last years of her life she was completely blind. —Cf. J. Vasconcellos, *Luiza Todi* (Oporto, 1873); R.-Aloys Mooser, *Annales de la Musique et des Musiciens en Russie au XVIIIme siècle* (Geneva, 1948-51; vol. 2, pp. 509-13).

Toepfer, Johann Gottlob. See **Töpfer.**

Toëschi (tŏh-ĕhs'-kē), **Carlo Giuseppe (Toësca della Castella-Monte),** Italian violinist and composer; b. Padua, c. 1722; d. Munich, April 12, 1788. He was the son of Alessandro Toëschi, a member of the Mannheim Orch.; studied with Johann Stamitz; entered the Mannheim Orch. in 1752 as violinist; in 1759 became concertmaster. He followed the court to Munich in 1778, and was appointed music director in 1780. A productive composer, he wrote at least 63 symphonies; also about 60 pieces of chamber music, including quartets, quintets, sextets, trio sonatas, violin sonatas, etc. Riemann publ. his symph. *a* 8 in the 'Denkmäler der Tonkunst in Bayern' (vol. VII, 2); in the same series are reprinted a flute quartet and a flute quintet (vol. XV) and a trio (vol. XVI, which also contains a thematic catalogue, listing 60 chamber works). A symph. in D was arranged by A. Carse, and publ. in London (1936). —Cf. R. Münster, *Die Sinfonien Toeschis* (dissertation; Munich, 1956).

Toëschi, Johann Baptist (Giovanni Battista), violinist and composer; brother of Carlo Giuseppe Toëschi; b. Stuttgart, c. 1727; d. Munich, May 1, 1800. Like his brother, he was a violinist in the Mannheim Orch. (from 1755); followed the court to Munich in 1778, becoming music director after his brother's death (1788). He produced a ballet, *Arlechin, Kaiser in China,* in Mannheim (April 26, 1778) and composed 6 trio sonatas. A thematic catalogue of his works appears in the 'Denkmäler der Tonkunst in Bayern' (vol. XVI).

Tofft, Alfred, Danish composer; b. Copenhagen, Jan. 2, 1865; d. there, Jan. 30, 1931. Abandoning a commercial career, he studied music with J. Nebelong (organ) and G. Bohlmann (theory); was music critic for 'Berlingske Tidende' in Copenhagen, and president of the Danish Composers Society. He was a fine organist and a talented composer of songs (op. 2, *Heine-Album;* op. 4, *Jacobsen-Album;* etc.). Two operas were produced in Copenhagen: *Vifandaka* (Jan. 1, 1898) and *Anathema* (May 10, 1928).

Togni (toh'-ñē), **Camillo,** Italian composer; b. Gussago, Oct. 18, 1922. He studied with Casella in Rome (1939-43); then in Parma; after graduation in philosophy from the Univ. of Pavia in 1948, he devoted himself entirely to music; adopted the 12-tone method of composition. His *Variations* for piano and orch. were given at the Venice Festival in 1946; his *Psalmus CXXVII* for soli, violin, viola, and cello was presented at the Brussels Festival of the International Society for Contemporary Music on June 24, 1950; his *Fantasia Concertante,* for flute and string orch. at the Cologne Festival of 'Musik der Zeit,' March 25, 1958.

Tokatyan, Armand, operatic tenor; b. Plovdiv, Bulgaria, Feb. 12, 1899. He was educated in Alexandria, Egypt, and studied voice with N. Cairone in Milan and A. Wolf in Vienna. Operatic début at the Teatro dal Verme, Milan, in 1921; then came to the U. S. and toured with the Scotti Opera Co. He made his début at the Metropolitan Opera House on Feb. 14, 1923, as Lucio in Vittadini's *Anima Allegra,* and with the exception of a few seasons spent abroad, remained a valued member of the company up to 1946. Also sang at Covent Garden, London; at the state operas of Berlin, Vienna, etc.

Tolbecque (tŏhl-băk'), **Auguste,** French cellist; b. Paris, March 30, 1830; d. Niort, March 8, 1919. He won 1st prize for cello at the Paris Cons. in 1849; taught at the Marseilles Cons. (1865-71); later was cellist at the Paris Cons. concerts. He publ. *La Gymnastique du violoncelle* (op. 14; excellent exercises and mechanical studies), a *Konzertstück* for cello and orch., and pieces for cello and piano; produced a 1-act comic opera, *Après la valse* (Niort, 1894). Also wrote *Souvenirs d'un musicien en province* (1896), *Notice historique sur les instruments à cordes et à archet* (1898), and *L'Art du luthier* (1903).

Tolbecque, Jean-Baptiste-Joseph, Belgian violinist; b. Hanzinne, April 17, 1797; d. Paris, Oct. 23, 1869. He was a pupil of Kreutzer and Reicha at the Paris Cons.; played violin at the Théâtre Italien and then became a successful conductor at court balls, for which he wrote waltzes, galops, quadrilles, and other fashionable dances which enjoyed tremendous success. In 1851 he staged his ballet, *Vert-Vert* (in collaboration with Deldevez), at the Paris Opéra. His 3 brothers, Isidore-Joseph (1794-1871), Auguste-Joseph (1801-69), and Charles-Joseph (1806-35), were professional violinists and theater conductors.

Toldrá, Eduardo, Spanish conductor; b. Villanueva y Geltrú, Catalonia, April 7, 1895. He studied the violin, and was a member of a string quartet, with which he toured in Europe. In 1921 he became prof. of violin at the Barcelona Municipal School of Music; in 1943, was appointed conductor of the Municipal Orch. He publ. an album of pieces in the form of Catalan folk dances.

Tollefsen, Carl H., violinist; b. Hull, England, Aug. 15, 1882. He emigrated to America as a youth, and studied at the National Cons., N. Y. (1898-1902) and later at the Institute of Musical Art (1906-08), where his teachers were Franz Kneisel (violin), Goetschius and Rubin Goldmark (composition); was a violinist in various orchestras in N. Y. On Aug. 7, 1907 he married the pianist **Augusta Schnabel** (b. Boise, Idaho, Jan. 5, 1885; d. Brooklyn, April 9, 1955), and formed the Tollefsen Trio with her and with Paul Kéfer (q.v.); this trio toured the U. S. for more than 30 years (succeeding cellists were M. Penha, P. Gruppe, R. Thrane, and W. Durieux). In 1939 he founded the Brooklyn Chamber Music Society. He formed a large collection of autographs of famous musicians and MS biographies (including the biographical archives gathered by Alfred Remy, editor of the 3rd ed. of Baker's Biographical Dictionary of Musicians). In 1947 the cellist Youry Bilstin bequeathed to him a collection of old instruments.

Tomaschek (tŏh'-măh-shĕk), **Johann Wenzel** (Bohemian spelling, **Jan Václav Tomášek**), composer and teacher; born Skutsch, Bohemia, April 17, 1774; d. Prague, April 3, 1850. He learned the rudiments of singing and violin playing from Wolf, *regens chori* at Chrudim; studied as a chorister at the Minorite monastery, Iglau; took the law course at Prague Univ., 1790-93, supporting himself by giving lessons, and also studying the chief German theoretical works. Finally he applied himself wholly to music; found a patron in Count Bucquoy de Longeval; and became the most noted teacher in Prague (Dreyschock, Schulhoff, v. Bocklet, Kittl, Kuhe, Dessauer, Tedesco, Sig. Goldschmidt, Hanslick, etc., were his pupils). He was an admirable pianist and organist, and a composer of high merit, though unfortunate in being Beethoven's contemporary. Among 110 works with opus numbers are a Requiem in C minor (op. 70), a *Krönungsmesse* in E♭ (op. 81), cantatas, hymns, Bohemian and German songs, a symphony in E♭ (op. 19), a piano concerto (op. 18), a piano quartet in E♭ (op. 22), a piano trio (op. 7), and several piano compositions (sonatas, op. 14, 15, 21, 48, and a fifth in B; 6 sets of Eclogues, each having 6 numbers, op. 35, 47, 51, 63, 66, 83; 2 sets of 6 Rhapsodies, op. 40, 41; 3 *Ditirambi*, op. 65; 6 *Allegri capricciosi di bravura,* op. 52 and op. 84). His opera *Seraphine, oder Grossmut und Liebe* (Prague, Dec. 15, 1811) was well received. —Cf. his autobiography in vol. IV of 'Libussa' (Prague, 1845); E. Hanslick, *Aus meinem Leben* (Berlin, 1894; vol. I, p. 25 ff.); R. v. Procházka, *Arpeggien* (Dresden, 1897; p. 44 ff.); W. Kahl, *Aus der Frühzeit des lyrischen Klavierstücks,* in 'Zeitschrift für Musik,' 89, No. 8 (1922); K. Emingerova, *T.,* in 'Národní Kultura'

(1924); M. Tarantova, *V. J. T.* (Prague, 1946); P. Nettl, *Forgotten Musicians* (N. Y., 1951, pp. 91-109); excerpts from his memoirs were publ. in the 'Mus. Quarterly' (April, 1946).

Tomášek (toh'-mah-shěk), **Jaroslav**, Czech composer; b. Koryčany, Moravia, April 10, 1896. Pupil of V. Novák; also studied musicology at the Univ. of Prague. —Works: *A Tale of Christmas Eve,* for voice and orch.; Dances for orch.; a string quartet; sonata for flute and piano; 2 piano sonatas; song-cycles. His wife, **Jaromira Tomášková-Nováková** (b. Jaroměř, May 23, 1892), is a concert soprano, from 1920 teacher of singing at the Prague Cons.

Tomasi, Henri, French composer; b. Marseilles, Aug. 17, 1901. He studied with Paul Vidal at the Paris Cons.; won the 2nd Grand Prix de Rome for his cantata *Coriolan* (1927); was music director on the Paris Radio and in French Indo-China (1930-35); served in the French Army (1939-40); conducted the Opera in Monte Carlo (1946-50). In 1952 he was awarded the Grand Prix de Musique Française. —Works: Operas: *Don Juan de Mañara* (Munich, March 29, 1956); *Atlantide* (Mulhouse, Feb. 26, 1954); *Sampiero Corso* (Bordeaux, May, 1956). Ballets: *La Grisi* (Paris, Oct. 7, 1935); *La Rosière du village* (Paris, May 26, 1936); *Les Santons* (Paris, Nov. 18, 1938); *La Féerie cambodgienne* (Marseilles, Jan. 31, 1952); *Les Folies mazarguaises* (Marseilles, Oct. 5, 1953); *Noces de cendre* (Strasbourg, Jan. 19, 1954). For orch.: *Chants de Cyrnos,* symph. poem (Paris, Nov. 30, 1929); *Mélodies corses* (1931); *Vocero,* symph. poem (1933); *Scènes municipales* (1933); *Tam-Tam,* symph. poem (1933); *Chants laotiens* (1934); *Deux danses cambodgiennes* (1934); *Chants des geishas* (1936); *Don Juan de Mañara,* suite (Paris, March 20, 1937); *Caravanes,* or *Impressions sahariennes* (1938); *Petite suite médiévale* (1938); a symph. (Paris, May 4, 1943); *Concert asiatique,* for percussion (1939); flute concerto (1947); trumpet concerto (1949); viola concerto (1951); saxophone concerto (1951); horn concerto (1955). Chamber music: *Concert champêtre,* for oboe, clarinet, and bassoon (1939); string trio (1943); *Divertimento Corsica,* for woodwind trio (1952); wind quintet (1952); piano pieces; songs.

Tomasini, Luigi (Aloysius), Italian violinist and composer; b. Pesaro, June 22, 1741; d. Esterház, April 25, 1808. From 1756 he was a violinist at Prince Paul Anton Esterházy's residence in Eisenstadt, and was a friend of Haydn there; in 1761 became concertmaster in Haydn's orch.; remained in the household of Prince Nicholas, successor to Paul Anton Esterházy, and was pensioned in 1790. Several of Haydn's concertos were dedicated to Tomasini, who was a composer of considerable merit himself; wrote 24 divertimentos for barytone, violin, and cello, string quartets, etc. His son, **Anton Tomasini** (b. Eisenstadt, 1775; d. there, June 12, 1824), was a viola player; another son, **Luigi Tomasini,** was an excellent violinist in Haydn's orchestra, highly commended by Haydn; he went to Vienna in 1796 and to Berlin in 1808.

Tombelle, Fernand de la. See **La Tombelle.**

Tomilin, Victor Konstantinovitch, Russian composer; b. Berdichev, May 15, 1908; killed in combat near Leningrad, Dec. 9, 1941. He was a pupil of Vladimir Stcherbatchev at the St. Petersburg Cons., graduating in 1932. He wrote 2 symph. suites, *Episodes of Civil War* (1936) and *Crimean Suite* (1939); a number of songs and piano pieces.

Tomkins, Thomas, English organist and composer; b. St. David's, 1572; d. Martin Hussingtree, near Worcester, June (buried June 9), 1656. He came from a family of musicians, of whom many members flourished in the 16th and 17th centuries. He was a pupil of William Byrd; was appointed organist of the Worcester Cathedral about 1596, holding this position for half a century, until 1646. In 1607 he received the degree of Mus. B. at Oxford, and in 1621 was appointed one of the organists of the Chapel Royal. He was one of the most inspired of the English madrigalists; his ballets, his keyboard pieces, and his sacred works are also of a high quality. His publ. works include *Songs of 3, 4, 5 and 6 parts* (reprinted in the 'English Madrigal School' vol. XVIII); and *Musica Deo Sacra* (posthumous, 1668), containing 5 services and 95 anthems (services reprinted in 'Tudor Church Music' vol. VII). Other church music is in MS. His keyboard music was publ. by Stephen D. Tuttle in 'Musica Britannica' (vol. 5); 2 pieces are in Davison and Apel, 'Historical Anthology of Music' vol. 1 (Cambridge, Mass., 1946). —Cf. S. de B. Taylor, *Thomas Tomkins* (London, 1933); Denis Stevens, *Thomas Tomkins* (London, 1957). See also G. Reese, *Music in the Renaissance* (N. Y., 1954; pp. 811-13).

Tomlins, William Lawrence, music educator and choral leader; b. London, Feb. 4, 1844; d. Delafield, Wis., Sept. 26, 1930. Pupil of G. A. Macfarren and E. Silas. Settled in America, 1869; from 1875-98 conductor of the Apollo Glee Club, Chicago; having made a specialty of training children's choruses and teachers, he established in 1903 the 'National Training School for Music Teachers' in Chicago; engaged by Chicago Board of Education in 1904 to train the teachers in the public schools; went to London in 1910, but later returned to the U. S. He publ. *Children's Songs, and How to Sing Them* (1885).

Tommasini, Vincenzo, Italian composer; b. Rome, Sept. 17, 1878; d. there, Dec. 23, 1950. He studied violin with Pinelli; theory with Falchi at Santa Cecilia in Rome; then went to Berlin, where he took lessons with Max Bruch; after sojourns in Paris, London, and N. Y. he returned to Rome. He wrote music in the poetic tradition of Italian Romanticism; his operas, symph. works, and chamber music obtained immediate performances and favorable reception; however, his most successful piece, *Le Donne di buon umore (The Good-humored Ladies),* was not an original work, but a comedy-ballet written on music from sonatas by Domenico Scarlatti, arranged in a series of tableaux and brilliantly orchestrated; this was a commission for the Ballets Russes of Diaghilev, who staged it at Rome in April, 1917, and kept it in the repertory during his tours all over the world. Other works by Tommasini include the operas *Medea,* to the composer's own libretto (Trieste, April 8, 1906) and *Uguale fortuna* (Rome, 1913); for orch.: *La Vita è un sogno* (1901); *Poema erotico* (1909); *Inno alla beltà* (1911); *Chiari di luna* (Rome, 1916); *Il beato regno* (Rome, 1922); *Paesaggi toscani* (Rome, 1923); *Il Carnevale di Venezia* (N. Y., Oct. 10, 1929, Toscanini conducting); *Nápule (Naples),* a fantasy (Freiburg, Dec. 7, 1931); violin concerto (1932); *Quattro pezzi* (1934); *Le Diable s'amuse,* ballet suite on themes by Paganini (1936); concerto for string quartet and orch. (1939); *La Tempesta* (1941); *Tiepolesco,* ballet suite (1945); *Duo concertante,* for piano and orch. (1948); 3 string quartets; violin sonata; harp sonata; *Due Macchiette* for cello and piano (1940); piano pieces; publ. *La Luce invisible* (1929) and *Saggio di estetica sperimentale* (1942). —Cf. G. Gatti, *Some Italian Composers of Today: Tommasini* in the 'Mus. Times' (Nov., 1921); M. Zanotti-Bianco, *Vincenzo Tommasini,* in the 'Chesterian' (Feb., 1923); A. Casella, *Vincenzo Tommasini,* in the 'Revue Musicale' (1927); M. Rinaldi, *Vincenzo Tommasini* in the 'Rivista Musicale Italiana' (Oct.-Dec., 1951).

Toni, Alceo, Italian musicologist and composer; b. Lugo, May 22, 1884. He was a pupil of L. Torchi and E. Bossi in Bologna; then lived in Milan as critic (of the 'Popolo d'Italia'), conductor, and composer. Guest-conductor in Rome, Budapest, Lisbon, Buenos Aires, etc. He ed. numerous works by Corelli, Locatelli, Torelli, Monteverdi, Carissimi, and other old Italian composers. His compositions include a Requiem Mass, chamber music, and songs. Some of his many articles were collected in a book, *Studi critici di interpretazione* (Milan, 1923; new ed., 1955).

Tonning, Gerard, choral conductor and composer; b. Stavanger, Norway, May 25, 1860; d. New York, June 10, 1940. He studied in Munich with Rheinberger and others; in 1887 he emigrated to America, settling in Duluth, Minn., where he organized several choral societies; in 1905 he moved to Seattle, where he remained until 1917; then went to New York. —Works: a historical opera, to a Norwegian libretto, *Leif Erikson* (Seattle, Dec. 10, 1910; Brooklyn Academy of Music, Oct. 4, 1924; both performances in the Norwegian language); a 1-act romantic opera, *All in a Garden Fair* (Seattle, Nov. 1, 1913); a pantomime, *Woman's Wiles, or Love Triumphant;* a piano trio; *Suite moderne* for violin and piano; *Rapsodie norvégienne* for violin and piano; piano pieces (*Norwegian Dances,* 3 nocturnes, etc.); songs (*Arabian Love Songs* for 4 solo voices); etc. —Cf. E. E. Hipsher, *American Opera and its Composers* (Philadelphia, 1934, pp. 404-07).

Töpfer, Johann Gottlob, famous German organist and writer on organ building; b. Niederrossla, Dec. 4, 1791; d. Weimar, June 8, 1870. He studied with the cantor Schlömilch; then at Weimar with Destouches and A. E. Müller; also attended the Weimar Seminary, where he became teacher of music in 1817; from 1830 was town organist of Weimar. An expert on organ construction, he wrote *Die Orgelbaukunst* (1833); *Die Scheibler'sche Stimm-Methode* (1842); *Die Orgel; Zweck und Beschaffenheit ihrer Theile* (1843); *Lehrbuch der Orgelbaukunst* (a fundamental work, 1855; 4 vols.; 2nd ed. by M. Allihn, 1888; 3rd ed. by P. Smets, 1934-39); also a *Theoretisch-praktische Organistenschule* (1845); *Allgemeines und voll-*

ständiges Choralbuch (*a* 4, with organ interludes); a cantata, *Die Orgelweihe; Konzertstück* for organ; sonatas, fantasias, preludes, fugues, etc., for organ; piano pieces. —Cf. A. W. Gottschalg, *Johann Gottlob Töpfer* (Berlin, 1870).

Toradze, David, Soviet Georgian composer; b. Tiflis, April 14, 1922; studied at the Tiflis Cons.; then at the Moscow Cons. with Glière; in 1954, became prof. at the Tiflis Cons. —Works: opera, *The Call of the Mountains* (Tiflis, Nov. 20, 1947); ballet, *For Peace* (Tiflis, June 17, 1953); a symph. (1946); chamber music; choruses; songs.

Torchi (tŏhr'kē), **Luigi,** eminent Italian musicologist; b. Mondano, near Bologna, Nov. 7, 1858; d. Bologna, Sept. 18, 1920. He studied at the Liceo Musicale of Bologna, the Naples Cons. (composition with Serrao), and the Leipzig Cons. (Jadassohn and Reinecke); from 1885-91, prof. of music history and esthetics, also librarian, at the Liceo Musicale Rossini in Pesaro; from 1895-1916, held a similar position at Bologna Cons., also teaching composition there. He was twice elected president of the Accademia Filarmonica of Bologna. From its foundation (1894) until 1904 he was ed. of the 'Rivista Musicale Italiana,' for which he wrote many valuable essays. In 1890 he publ. *R. Wagner: Studio critico* (1890; 2nd ed., 1913). Besides a collection of 'Eleganti canzoni ed arie italiane' of the 17th century (Milan, 1894) and 'A Collection of Pieces for the Violin Composed by Italian Masters of the 17th and 18th Centuries' (London; both with piano accompaniment by Torchi), in 1897 he began publishing an important anthology, 'L'Arte Musicale in Italia,' which reached 7 vols. as follows: vol. I, sacred and secular polyphonic compositions of the 14th, 15th, and 16th centuries; vol. II, polyphonic compositions of the 16th century; vol. III, compositions for organ and cembalo of the 16th, 17th, and 18th centuries; vol. IV, madrigals, stage works, etc. of the 17th century; vol. V, compositions for 1 or more voices of the 17th century; vol. VI, Peri's *Euridice* and Monteverdi's *Combattimento di Tancredi e Clorinda* and *Ballo delle Ingrate;* vol. VII, instrumental music of the 17th century. He also compiled vols. II and III of the catalogue of the library of the Liceo Musicale of Bologna (1890-95). —Cf. F. Vatielli, *Necrologia di Luigi Torchi,* in 'Rivista Musicale Italiana' (1920).

Torelli (Torrelli), Gasparo, Italian composer; b. Borgo San Sepolcro, near Lucca, where he lived as music teacher. Publ. *Brevi concetti d'amore* (madrigals *a* 5; 1598); 4 books of *Canzonette a 3* (1593-1608); and *I fidi amanti,* 'favola pastorale' (in madrigal style, 4 voices; 1600; reprinted in Torchi's 'L'Arte Musicale in Italia' vol. 4).

Torelli, Giuseppe, Italian violinist and composer, probable originator of the solo concerto for violin; b. Verona, April 22, 1658; d. Bologna, Feb. 8, 1709. He studied in Bologna, where he was a member of the Accademia Filarmonica and viola player at the church of S. Petronio (1686-95). Made a concert tour in Germany in 1695, and became Kapellmeister to the Margrave of Brandenburg at Ansbach (1697-99). From 1699 he was in Vienna, where he produced an oratorio; returned to Bologna in 1701. He had generally been regarded as the originator of the 'concerto grosso' until Arnold Schering, in 1903, showed that Stradella, who died in 1682, had written such works. But Torelli's *Concerti grossi,* op. 8 (1709), were the first to be publ. (Corelli's op. 6 was not publ. until 1712, though composed earlier). —Publ. works: op. 1, *Balletti da camera a 3 violini e basso continuo;* op. 2, *Concerto da camera a 2 violini e basso* (1686); op. 3, *Sinfonie a 2-4 stromenti* (1687); op. 4, *Concertino per camera a violino e violoncello;* op. 5, *6 sinfonie a 3, e 6 concerti a 4* (1692); op. 6, *Concerti musicali a 4* (with organ); op. 7, *Capricci musicali per camera a violino e viola ovvero arciliuto;* op. 8, *Concerti grossi con una pastorale per il Santissimo Natale* (1709), written for 2 violini concertanti, 2 violini di ripieno, viola, and continuo. The so-called 'Christmas Eve Concerto' (op. 8, No. 6) and other works from op. 8 and op. 6 have been reprinted in modern eds. —Cf. A. Schering, *Geschichte des Instrumentalkonzerts* (1903); F. Vatielli, *Arte e vita musicale a Bologna* (Bologna, 1927); R. Brenzoni, *Giuseppe Torelli, musicista veronese,* in 'Note d'Archivio per la storia musicale' (1936); F. Giegling, *Giuseppe Torelli, Ein Beitrag zur Entwicklungsgeschichte des italienischen Konzerts* (Kassel, 1949).

Torner, Eduardo Martínez, Spanish folklore specialist; b. Oviedo, April 8, 1888; d. London, Feb. 17, 1955. He was a pupil of Vincent d'Indy at the Schola Cantorum in Paris; returned to Spain in 1914 and settled in Madrid. Publ. the folksong collections *Cancionero musical de la lírica popular asturiana* (Madrid, 1920); *40 Canciones españolas* (1924), and *Cancionero musical* (1928); also the essay, *Temas folklóricos;*

música y poesía (1935); edited and arranged for piano selected pieces from tablature books of the 16th century, and publ. them under the title *Colección de vihuelistas españoles del siglo XVI* (Madrid, 1923).

Torrance, Rev. **George William,** Irish clergyman and composer; b. Rathmines, near Dublin, 1835; d. Kilkenny, Aug. 20, 1907. Chorister at Christ Church Cathedral, Dublin; organist at St. Andrew's and St. Anne's; studied music at Leipzig, 1856; ordained as a priest, 1866; in 1869 emigrated to Melbourne, Australia, where he remained till 1897; appointed chaplain to the bishop of Ossory in 1897; in 1900 made Prebendary of Killamery, canon of St. Canice's Cathedral and librarian of St. Canice's Library, Kilkenny. Torrance's madrigal *Dry be that tear* won the Molyneux Prize and the medal of the Madrigal Society in 1903.

Torrefranca, Fausto, eminent Italian musicologist; b. Monteleone Calabro, Feb. 1, 1883; d. Rome, Nov. 26, 1955. Trained as an engineer, he took up music under E. Lena in Turin (harmony and counterpoint) and also studied by himself. It was through his initiative that the first chair of musicology was established in Italy; in 1913, lecturer at the Univ. of Rome; from 1914-24, prof. of music history at the Cons. di S. Pietro in Naples, and from 1915 also librarian there; from 1924 librarian of the Milan Cons. From 1907 he was ed. for several years of the 'Rivista Musicale Italiana.' In 1941 he was appointed prof. of music history at the Univ. of Florence. —Books: *La Vita musicale dello spirito* (Turin, 1910); *L'Intuizione musicale quale sintesi a priori estetica* (1911); *Giacomo Puccini e l'opera internazionale* (1912); *Le Sinfonie dell'Imbrattacarte, G. B. Sanmartini* (1915); *Le Origine italiane del romanticismo musicale* (1930); *Il Segreto del quattrocento* (1939).

Torri, Pietro, Italian composer; b. Peschiera, c. 1665; d. Munich, July 6, 1737. In 1689 he became organist at Munich; in 1696 he was conductor for the carnival season at Hanover; in 1703 he was appointed chamber music director at Munich, following the Elector to Brussels upon the latter's exile. In Brussels he produced the oratorio *Les Vanités du monde* (1706); from 1715 again in Munich, where he was named Kapellmeister in 1732. He was strongly influenced by A. Steffani (q.v.). He composed 26 operas, of which the following were produced by him at the Munich Court Opera: *La Merope, Lucio Vero* (Oct. 12, 1720), and *Griselda* (Oct. 12, 1723); also some chamber duets. Selections from the operas were publ. by H. Junker in 'Denkmäler der Tonkunst in Bayern' (vols. 19 and 20). —Cf. H. Junker, *Zwei 'Griselda' -Opern,* in the 'Sandberger-Festschrift' (1918); K. Kremer, *Pietro Torri und seine Kammermusikwerke* (dissertation; Munich, 1956).

Torrington, Frederick Herbert, organist and conductor; b. Dudley, Worcestershire, England, Oct. 20, 1837; d. Toronto, Canada, Nov. 19, 1917. After studying with James Fitzgerald, he became in 1853 organist and choirmaster at St. Anne's, Bewdley; from 1856-68, organist of Great St. James' Church, Montreal, Canada, giving organ recitals, also acting as solo violinist, conductor, and bandmaster; was appointed organist and music director at King's Chapel, Boston, and held the position until 1873, teaching at the New England Cons. From 1873, organist and choirmaster at the Metropolitan Church, Toronto, and conductor of the Toronto Philharmonic Society; founded the Toronto College of Music (1888). —Works: services, hymn tunes, choruses, songs, organ music, etc.

Tortelier, Paul, French cellist; b. Paris, March 21, 1914. He entered the Paris Cons., and won 1st prize for cello at the age of 16; was engaged as 1st cellist by the Boston Symph. Orch. in 1935, but went back to France in 1939; in 1955 he settled in Israel; continued to give concerts in Europe. Among his works are a cello concerto and other pieces for his instrument.

Tosar, Hector, Uruguayan composer; b. Montevideo, July 18, 1923. He studied piano and composition in his native city; traveled to Brazil in 1943 as pianist and composer. He adopted a neo-Classical idiom in his works, not neglecting the local melo-rhythms in thematic material. His works include 2 symphonies (2nd for string orch.), a concertino for piano and orch.; *Danza criolla* for orch.; Nocturne and Scherzo for violin, clarinet, and piano; piano pieces; songs.

Tosatti, Vieri, Italian composer; b. Rome, Nov. 2, 1920. He studied piano and composition with Pizzetti in Rome. In his compositions he exploits sensational or morbid subjects, setting them to pungent music, with a liberal application of special effects. —Works: *Il Concerto della demenza,* for narrator, 2 pianos, and chamber orch. (1946); music drama *Dionisio* (1947); 'paradoxical drama' *Il Sistema della dolcezza* (1949);

'boxing opera' *La Partita a pugni (Fist Fight;* Venice Festival of Contemporary Music, Sept. 8, 1953); also a piano concerto (1945), a quintet for clarinet, bassoon, violin, viola, and cello (1948), piano pieces, etc.

Toscanini, Arturo, one of the greatest conductors of modern times; b. Parma, Italy, March 25, 1867; d. New York, Jan. 16, 1957. He entered the Parma Cons. at the age of 9, studying the cello with Carini and composition with Dacci; graduated in 1885 as winner of the 1st prize for cello. In 1886 he was engaged as cellist for the Italian opera in Rio de Janeiro; on the 2nd night of the spring season (June 25, 1886) he was unexpectedly called upon to substitute for the regular conductor, when the latter left the podium at the end of the introduction after the public hissed him; the opera was *Aida,* and Toscanini led it without difficulty; he was rewarded by an ovation and was engaged to lead the rest of the season. Returning to Italy, he was engaged to conduct the opera at the Teatro Cavignano in Turin, and later conducted the Municipal Orch. there. Although still very young, he quickly established a fine reputation. For 10 seasons, between 1887 and 1898, he conducted opera and symph. orchestras in major Italian cities. On May 21, 1892 he led the world première of *Pagliacci* in Milan, and on Feb. 1, 1896, the première of Puccini's *La Bohème* in Turin. He also conducted the Italian premières of *Götterdämmerung* (Turin, 1895) and *Siegfried* (Milan, 1899). In 1898, the impresario Gatti-Casazza engaged him as chief conductor for La Scala, Milan, where he remained until 1903, and again from 1906 to 1908. In the interim, he conducted opera in Buenos Aires (1903-04 and 1906). When Gatti-Casazza became general manager of the Metropolitan Opera Company (1908), he invited Toscanini as principal conductor; Toscanini's début in N. Y. was in *Aida* (Nov. 16, 1908). While at the Metropolitan Opera, Toscanini conducted 2 world premières, Puccini's *The Girl of the Golden West* (Dec. 10, 1910) and Giordano's *Madame Sans-Gêne* (Jan. 25, 1915); he also brought out for the first time in America Gluck's *Armide* (Nov. 14, 1910), Wolf-Ferrari's *Le Donne curiose* (Jan. 13, 1912); and Mussorgsky's *Boris Godunov* (March 19, 1913). On April 13, 1913 he gave his first concert in N. Y. as a symph. conductor, leading Beethoven's 9th symph. In 1915 he returned to Italy; during the season of 1920-21 he brought the Scala Orch. on a tour of the U. S. and Canada. From 1921 to 1929 he was artistic director of La Scala; there, he conducted the posthumous première of Boito's opera *Nerone,* which he himself completed for performance (May 1, 1924). In 1926-27 he was guest conductor of the N. Y. Philharmonic Orch., returning in the following season as associate conductor with Mengelberg. After the fusion of the N. Y. Philharmonic and the N. Y. Symph. in 1928, Toscanini was engaged as permanent conductor of the newly organized ensemble; in the spring of 1930 he took the orchestra on a tour of Europe; he resigned this position in 1936. Deeply touched by the plight of the Jews in Germany, he acceded to the request of the violinist Hubermann, founder of the Palestine Symph. Orch., to conduct the inaugural concert of that orch. at Tel Aviv (Dec. 26, 1936). In the meantime he had filled summer engagements at the Salzburg Festivals (1933, 1935, 1936, 1937). Returning to the U. S., he became musical director of the NBC Symph. Orch., a radio orch. that had been organized especially for him, giving his opening concert on Dec. 25, 1937; in 1940 he took it on a tour of South America. He continued to lead the NBC Symphony until the end of his active career; he conducted his last concert from Carnegie Hall, N. Y., on April 4, 1954 (10 days after his 87th birthday), and then sent a doleful letter of resignation to the NBC, explaining the impossibility of further appearances. He died in his sleep, a few weeks before his 90th birthday. —Toscanini was a unique figure among conductors; undemonstrative in his handling of the orchestra, he possessed an amazing energy and power of command. He demanded absolute perfection, and he erupted in violence when he could not obtain from the orchestra what he wanted (a lawsuit was brought against him in Milan, when he accidentally injured the concertmaster with a broken violin bow). Despite the vituperation he at times poured on his musicians, he was affectionately known to them as 'The Maestro,' who could do no wrong. His ability to communicate his desires to singers and players was extraordinary, and even the most celebrated opera stars or instrumental soloists never dared to question his authority. Owing to extreme nearsightedness, Toscanini committed all scores to memory; his repertory embraced virtually the entire field of Classical and Romantic music; his performances of Italian operas, of Wagner's music dramas, of Beethoven's symphonies, and of modern Italian works were especially inspiring. Among the moderns, he conducted works by Richard

Strauss, Debussy, Ravel, Prokofiev, Stravinsky, Samuel Barber, Roy Harris, Howard Hanson, etc. In his social philosophy, he was intransigently democratic; he refused to conduct in Germany under the Nazi regime. He militantly opposed Fascism in Italy, but he never abandoned his Italian citizenship, despite his long years of residence in America. —Bibliography: G. M. Ciampelli, *Arturo Toscanini* (Milan, 1923); E. Cozzani, *Arturo Toscanini* (Milan, 1927); T. Nicotra, *Arturo Toscanini* (transl. from the Italian, N. Y., 1929); D. Bonardi, *Toscanini* (Milan, 1929); Paul Stefan, *Arturo Toscanini* (Vienna, 1936; in English, N. Y., 1936); L. Gilman, *Toscanini and Great Music* (N. Y., 1938); S. W. Hoeller, *Arturo Toscanini* (pictorial biography; N. Y., 1943); A. Della Corte, *Toscanini* (Vicenza, 1946); G. M. Ciampelli, *Toscanini* (Milan, 1946); D. Nives, *Arturo Toscanini* (Milan, 1946); A. Segre, *Toscanini: the First Forty Years*, and H. Taubman, *Toscanini in America*, in the 'Mus. Quarterly' (April, 1947); F. Sacchi, *Toscanini* (Milan, 1951; publ. in English under the title *The Magic Baton: Toscanini's Life for Music*, N. Y., 1957, with supplementary data); David Ewen, *The Story of Arturo Toscanini* (N. Y., 1951); H. Taubman, *The Maestro: the Life of Arturo Toscanini* (N. Y., 1951); S. Chotzinoff, *Toscanini: An Intimate Portrait* (N. Y., 1956); R. C. Marsh, *Toscanini and the Art of Orchestral Performance* (Philadelphia, 1956); also articles in every book on conductors publ. in the 20th century.

Toselli, Enrico, Italian pianist and composer; b. Florence, March 13, 1883; d. there, Jan. 15, 1926. He studied with Sgambati and Martucci; gave concerts in Italy as pianist, and composed a number of songs; of these, *Serenata* became enormously popular; also wrote the symph. poem *Fuoco* (after d'Annunzio) and an opera, *La Principessa bizzarra* (Milan, 1913). In 1907 he married the former Crown Princess Luise of Saxony, creating an international furor; wrote an account of this affair, *Il mio matrimonio con Luisa di Sassonia* (Milan, 1918).

Tosi, Pier Francesco, Italian contralto *(castrato)* and singing teacher; b. Bologna, 1647; d. Faenza, April, 1732. He studied with his father, Giuseppe Felice Tosi; sang successfully in Italy, Dresden, etc., and in 1692 settled in London, where he gave regular concerts, and was highly esteemed as a vocal teacher. He owes his fame chiefly to the work *Opinioni de' cantori antichi e moderni o sieno osservazioni sopra il canto figurato* (Bologna, 1723; in English [Galliard], 1742, as *Observations on the Florid Song*, etc.; in German [Agricola] as *Anleitung zur Singkunst*, 1757; in French [Lemaire] as *L'Art du Chant, Opinions . . .*, 1774. The Italian ed. was reprinted in 1904; the English, 1906).

Tosti, Sir Francesco Paolo, Italian singing master and vocal composer; b. Ortona, Abruzzi, April 9, 1846; d. Rome, Dec. 2, 1916. He was a pupil, from 1858, of the Collegio di S. Pietro a Majella, Naples, and was appointed sub-teacher (maestrino) by Mercadante. He visited London in 1875, had great success in concerts, and settled there as a teacher, becoming singing master to the Royal Family in 1880, and prof. of singing at the Royal Academy of Music in 1894; was knighted in 1908. In 1913 he returned to Italy, taking up his residence in Rome. Besides many original songs, both English and Italian, he published a collection of 'Canti popolari abruzzesi.' His songs were highly popular; some of the best-known are *Forever, Goodbye, Mattinata,* and *Vorrei morire.* —Cf. E. A. Mario, *Francesco Paolo Tosti* (Siena, 1947).

Totenberg, Roman, violinist; b. Lodz, Poland, Jan. 1, 1913. Pupil of Michalowicz at the Chopin Music School in Warsaw, of Flesch at the Hochschule für Musik in Berlin, and of Enesco in Paris; début with the Warsaw Philharmonic in 1925; won the Mendelssohn Prize in 1932. Made his American début at N. Y. in 1935; 1935-36, toured with K. Szymanowski (q.v.); 1937-38, toured the U. S. and South America. In 1947 he became head of the violin dept. of the Santa Barbara, Cal., Music Academy, but continued his career as concert violinist.

Tottmann, Albert (Karl), German violinist and writer on music; b. Zittau, July 31, 1837; d. Leipzig, Feb. 26, 1917. He studied in Dresden, and at the Leipzig Cons. (with Hauptmann); was a violinist in the Gewandhaus Orch. —Publications: *Kritisches Repertorium der gesammten Violin- und Bratschen-Litteratur* (1873; 3rd ed., 1900, as *Führer durch die Violin-Literatur;* a compendious and valuable work); *Abriss der Musikgeschichte* (1883); *Der Schulgesang und seine Bedeutung für die Verstandes und Herzensbildung der Jugend* (1887; 2nd ed., 1904); *Das Büchlein von der Geige* (1890; 2nd, augmented ed., 1904); *Mozart's Zauberflöte* (1908); many essays in journals, etc.; composed a melodrama, *Dornröschen,* for soli, chorus, and orch.; sacred and secular choruses; songs.

Toulmouche (tool-moosh'), **Frédéric (Michel)**, French composer; b. Nantes, Aug. 3, 1850; d. Paris, Feb. 20, 1909. He studied with Victor Massé in Paris; in 1894 became director of the theater 'Menus-Plaisirs.' He composed several opéras-comiques: *Le Moûtier de St.-Guignolet* (Brussels, 1885), *La Veillée des noces* (Paris, 1888; in London, 1892, as *The Wedding Eve*), *L'Âme de la patrie* (St. Brieuc, 1892), *La Perle du Cantal* (Paris, 1895), *La St.-Valentin* (Paris, 1895); about a dozen operettas and some ballets.

Tourel, Jennie, mezzo-soprano; b. Montreal, Canada, June 22, 1910, of Russian-French parentage. She was taken to Paris as a child, and studied voice there with Anna El-Tour (q.v.); her professional *nom de scène,* Tourel, is an anagram of her teacher's name. She made her operatic début as Carmen at the Paris Opéra-Comique in 1933; left France in June, 1940, shortly before the German occupation, and after a brief stay in Lisbon, came to the U. S.; became an American citizen in 1946; made numerous tours in the U. S. in recitals and as soloist with orchestras.

Tourjée (toor-zha'), **Eben,** American music educator; b. Warwick, R. I., June 1, 1834; d. Boston, April 12, 1891. While working in a cotton factory in Harrisville, R. I., he sang and played the organ in church; then studied music in Providence, becoming clerk in a music store there; then moved to Newport, R. I., as organist and teacher; in 1861, appointed music director of the East Greenwich Seminary; then visited Europe and had lessons from A. Haupt in Berlin; in 1864, established the Music Institute of Providence (developed from the music department of the E. Greenwich Seminary), which later became the Providence Cons. of Music; 1867, settled in Boston and founded there (with R. Goldbeck) the New England Cons. of Music, which he directed till his death. He assisted Patrick S. Gilmore (q.v.) in organizing the 2 great peace jubilees in Boston (1869, 1872). He was the first president of the Music Teachers National Association (1876), and dean of the College of Music of Boston Univ. He was made Mus. Doc. by Wesleyan Univ. —Cf. 'Dictionary of American Biography' (vol. XVIII).

Tournemire (toorn-mēr'), **Charles,** French organist and composer; b. Bordeaux, Jan. 22, 1870; d. Arcachon, Nov. 3, 1939. He was a pupil of César Franck at the Paris Cons., winning the 1st prize for organ in 1891; also studied composition with d'Indy at the Schola Cantorum. In 1898 he succeeded Pierné as organist at Ste. Clotilde. His dramatic cantata, *Le Sang de la sirène,* won the Prize of the City of Paris (performed Nov. 17, 1904). As an organ virtuoso he toured throughout Europe. He was prof. of ensemble playing at the Paris Cons. —Other works: opera, *Les Dieux sont morts* (Paris Opéra, March 19, 1924); 8 symphonies (no. 5 is the 'Mountain Symph.'); Psalm 57 for mixed chorus a cappella; sextet for piano and winds; piano quartet; for organ: 51 *Offices de l'année liturgique (L'Orgue mystique); 4 Pièces symphoniques;* etc. Also a book, *César Franck* (Paris, 1931). —Cf. F. Peeters, *L'Œuvre d'orgue de Charles Tournemire,* in 'Musica Sacra' (Bruges, 1940).

Tours (toor), **Berthold,** violinist, composer, and musical editor; b. Rotterdam, Dec. 17, 1838; d. London, March 11, 1897. Pupil of his father, Barthélemy Tours (1797-1864), Verhulst, and of the Conservatories at Brussels and Leipzig; went to London in 1861 as an orch. player; in 1878 became musical adviser to Novello & Co., and editor of their publications. —Works: services, anthems, hymn tunes; piano pieces; primers on the violin and the viola.

Tours, Frank E., son of the preceding; b. London, Sept. 1, 1877. Pupil of Stanford, Parratt, and Bridge at the Royal College of Music; from 1897-1904, conductor of various light opera companies in London, then came to N. Y. as music director of Broadway productions. Later he entered the motion-picture field and was with Paramount for 6 years (3 years in London) as composer and music director. Besides several musical plays, he wrote successful songs *(Mother o' Mine, Beyond the Sunset, Red Rose, In Flanders Fields,* etc.).

Tourte (tŏŏrt), **François,** b. Paris, 1747; d. there, April, 1835. This famous maker of violin bows was the creator of the modern bow, the model for all succeeding bow-makers. The shape and inward curve of the stick, the selection and preparation of the wood (Pernambuco), the length of the bow and all its modern fittings, are the product of his constructive genius.

Tovey, Sir Donald Francis, eminent English musical scholar; b. Eton, July 17, 1875; d. Edinburgh, July 10, 1940. He studied privately with Sophie Weisse (piano), Sir W. Parratt (counterpoint), James Higgs (composition) until 1894, when he won the

Nettleship scholarship at Balliol College, Oxford; graduated with Classical Honors (B. A., 1898). In 1900-01 he gave a series of chamber music concerts in London, at which he performed several of his own works; in 1901-02 he gave similar concerts in Berlin and Vienna; played his piano concerto in 1903 under Henry Wood and in 1906 under Hans Richter; from 1906 to 1912 he gave in London regular series of chamber music concerts, known as 'The Chelsea Concerts.' In 1914 he succeeded Niecks (q.v.) as Reid Prof. of music at Edinburgh Univ. (see **Reid, John**); there he established the 'Reid Symph. Concerts,' for which he organized in 1917 the 'Reid Symph. Orch.' of 50 musicians. He made his American début as pianist in 1925, and in 1927-28 made a tour of the U. S. He was knighted in 1935. Though highly esteemed as a composer, he was most widely known as a writer and lecturer on music, his analytical essays being models of their kind. Besides much chamber music and several piano pieces (a sonata, *Balliol Dances* for 4 hands, etc.), he composed an opera, *The Bride of Dionysus* (Edinburgh, April 25, 1932); a symph. (1913); a cello concerto (première by Pablo Casals, Tovey conducting, Edinburgh, Nov. 22, 1934); etc. He publ. a collection of 16th-century church music, *Laudate Pueri* (Part I of 'Northlands Singing Book'), and ed. Bach's *Kunst der Fuge.* He wrote most of the music articles for the 'Encyclopaedia Britannica' (from the 11th ed.). Contributed essays on Schubert (1927) and Gluck (1934) to Foss' *Heritage of Music.* —Books: *A Companion to Bach's Art of Fugue* (1931); *A Companion to Beethoven's Pianoforte Sonatas* (1931); *Musical Form and Matter* (1934); *Normality and Freedom in Music* (1936); *Essays in Musical Analysis,* 6 vols. (1935-39): I and II, orchestral works; III, concertos; IV, polyphony and illustrative music; V, vocal music; VI, supplement, index, and glossary. Posthumous publications: *Walter Parratt: Master of Music* (with G. Parratt; London, 1941); *A Musician Talks* (London, 1941); *Musical Articles from the Encyclopaedia Britannica* (London, 1944); *Beethoven* (London, 1945); *Essays in Musical Analysis: Chamber Music* (London, 1944); *Essays and Lectures on Music* (London, 1949; U. S. ed. as *The Main Stream of Music).* —Cf. M. Grierson, *Donald Francis Tovey* (London, 1952).

Townsend, Douglas, American composer and musicologist; b. New York, Nov. 8, 1921; studied at the High School of Music and Art, N. Y., graduating in 1941; then took lessons in composition with Tibor Serly, Stefan Wolpe, Felix Greissle, and Otto Luening; also with Aaron Copland in Tanglewood (1946) and with Louis Gruenberg in California (1948); became active in N. Y. as theater conductor, arranger, composer, and music editor; arranged for performance and publication works by Pergolesi, Süssmayr, Danzi, Tommaso Giordani, A. Scarlatti, Rosetti, etc. —Compositions: piano sonatina (1945); septet for brass (1947); *Sinfonietta* (1949); divertimento for string and wind instruments (1950); *Fantasy* for chamber orch. (1951); *The Infinite,* ballet (N. Y., Feb. 13, 1952); *Canzona* for flute, viola, and bassoon (1954); *Music for Recitation,* to words by Walt Whitman (1955); *Lima Beans,* chamber opera (N. Y., Jan. 7, 1956); *Ballet Suite* for 3 clarinets (1956); *Adagio for Strings* (1956); duo for violas (1957); chamber concerto No. 1, for violin and string quartet (1957); *Tower Music* for brass quintet (1957); 4 fantasies on American songs, for piano 4 hands (1957); symph. for string orch. (N. Y., Nov. 29, 1958); film music.

Toye, (John) Francis, English music critic; b. Winchester, Jan. 27, 1883. He was a pupil of S. P. Waddington and E. J. Dent; became a critic for various papers in London (from 1925 for the 'Morning Post,' and 1937-39 for the 'Daily Telegraph'); in 1923, lectured on modern music in the U. S.; 1939-46 lived in Rio de Janeiro; from 1946, in Florence. —Books: *The Well-Tempered Musician* (1925); *Giuseppe Verdi, His Life and Works* (1931); *Rossini, a Study in Tragi-comedy* (1934); *For What We Have Received* (autobiography; N. Y., 1948); *Italian Opera* (London, 1952); *Truly Thankful?* (autobiographical; London, 1957).

Toye, Geoffrey, English conductor and composer; brother of Francis Toye; b. Winchester, Feb. 17, 1889; d. London, June 11, 1942. He studied at the Royal College of Music in London; became a conductor at various theaters there; was manager of opera productions at Sadler's Wells. He wrote an opera, *The Red Pen* (broadcast from London, Feb. 7, 1927); a ballet; and some other works.

Trabaci (Trabacci), Giovanni Maria, Italian composer; b. Montepeloso, c. 1580; d. Naples, Dec. 31, 1647. He studied with Giovanni Macque; became organist at the Viceregal Chapel in Naples in 1601; after Macque's death (1614) he succeeded him as choir director there. During the rebellion of the Neapolitan populace against the fruit tax of 1647, Trabaci fled to the monastery of the Trinità degli Spagnuoli, where he died. The bulk of his music consists of psalms, Masses, motets, and madrigals. Two keyboard publications are extant: *Ricercate, canzone francese, capricci, canti fermi, gagliarde, partite diverse, etc., Libro primo* (Naples, 1603) and *Il secondo libro di ricercate ed altri varii capricci* (Naples, 1615). Some of his vocal works were publ. by Pannain in 'Istituzioni e monumenti dell'arte musicale italiana' (vol. 5); these include 12 motets *a* 5, 4 *a* 6, and 4 *a* 8; also two Masses for double chorus. Keyboard works are reprinted in L. Torchi, 'L'Arte Musicale in Italia' (vol. 3), in Tagliapietra, 'Antologia di musica antica e moderna' (vol. 5), and in Davison and Apel, 'Historical Anthology of Music.' Trabaci's canzonas include examples of rhythmic variants of a single theme ('variation canzonas'), anticipating Frescobaldi in this respect. —Cf. W. Apel, *Neapolitan Links between Cabezón and Frescobaldi,* in the 'Mus. Quarterly' (Oct., 1938).

Traetta (Trajetta), Filippo (Philip), Italian musician; son of Tommaso Traetta; b. Venice Jan. 8, 1777; d. Philadelphia, Jan. 9, 1854. Pupil of Fenaroli and Perillo at Venice, later of Piccinni at Naples. Becoming a soldier in the patriot ranks, he was captured and cast into prison; escaped 6 months afterward, and sailed to Boston, settling there in 1799. There he wrote his *Vocal Exercises,* and *Washington's Dead March.* Proceeding to New York, he wrote the cantatas *The Christian's Joy and Prophecy;* also an opera, *The Venetian Maskers.* Was manager of a traveling theatrical troupe, lived in Virginia for some years, and settled in Philadelphia c. 1828, founding the 'American Conservatorio' with his pupil, U. K. Hill. He produced 2 oratorios, *Jerusalem in Affliction* (1828) and *Daughter of Zion* (1829); later 2 cantatas, *The Nativity* and *The Day of Rest;* also instrumental and vocal quartets, trios, and duets; songs; etc.; and publ. *Rudiments of the Art of Singing* (2 vols.; 1841-43) and *An Introduction to the Art and Science of Music* (1829) for his Cons. (he was active as a singing-teacher until his death). —Cf. F. L. Ritter, *Music in America* (1883); also 'Dictionary of American Biography' XVIII (1936).

Traetta, Tommaso (Michele Francesco Saverio), Italian composer; b. Bitonto, Naples, March 30, 1727; d. Venice, April 6, 1779. He entered the Cons. di Loreto in Naples at the age of 11, and was there a pupil of Durante. His first opera, *Il Farnace,* was produced at the Teatro San Carlo with fine success, on Nov. 4, 1751; there followed several more operas in Naples, and later in other Italian cities: *Buovo d'Antona* (Venice, Dec. 27, 1758), *Ippolito ed Aricia* (Parma, May 9, 1759), etc. In 1758 he was appointed maestro to the Duke of Parma, and singing master to the princesses; his *Armida* was staged in Vienna (Jan. 3, 1761) with excellent success, and he was commissioned to write another opera for Vienna, *Ifigenia in Tauride,* which was produced there on Oct. 4, 1763. He settled in Venice in 1765, and was director of the Cons. dell' Ospedaletto there for 3 years. In 1768 he was engaged for the court of Catherine the Great as successor to Galuppi, and arrived in St. Petersburg in the autumn of that year. He staged several of his operas there (mostly versions of works previously performed in Italy); he also arranged music for various occasions (anniversary of the coronation of Catherine the Great, celebration of a victory over the Turkish fleet, etc.). He left Russia in 1775, and went to London, where he produced the operas *Germondo, Telemacco,* and *I Capricci del Sesso* (all in 1777) without much success; returned to Italy, and produced 3 more operas in Venice; he wrote 48 operas in all. In many respects, he was an admirable composer, possessing a sense of drama and a fine melodic gift. In musical realism, he adopted certain procedures that Gluck was to employ successfully later on; he was highly regarded by his contemporaries. Besides operas, he wrote an oratorio, *Salomone* (1768), a Stabat Mater, and other church music. A selection of excerpts from Traetta's operas was edited by H. Goldschmidt in the 'Denkmäler der Tonkunst in Bayern' (XIV, 1 and XVII). —Cf. V. Capruzzi, *Traetta e la musica* (Naples, 1878); C. H. Bitter, *Die Reform der Oper durch Gluck und Wagner* (Brunswick, 1884); H. Kretzschmar, *Geschichte der Oper* (1919); A. Nuovo, *Tommaso Traetta* (Rome, 1922); A. Damerini, *Un Precursore italiano di Gluck: Tommaso Traetta,* in 'Il Pianoforte' (July, 1927) and *Tommaso Traetta,* in the 'Bollettino bibliografico musicale' (July, 1927); V. Raeli, *Tommaso Traetta,* in the 'Rivista nazionale di musica' (March, 1927); A. Bonaventura, *Tommaso Traetta,* in 'Pensiero musicale' (April-May, 1927); V. Raeli, *The Bicentenary of Tommaso Traetta,* in the 'Chesterian' (1927); A. Mooser, *Annales de la musique et des musiciens en Russie au XVIIIe siècle* (Geneva, 1949-51; vol. II, pp. 87-132); F. Schlitzer, ed., *Tommaso Traetta, Leonardo Leo, Vin-*

cenzo Bellini: Notizie e documenti (Siena, 1952); E. Saracino, *Tommaso Traetta* (Bitonto, 1954).

Tragó (trah-gŏh'), **José,** Spanish pianist and pedagogue; b. Madrid, Sept. 25, 1856; d. there, Jan. 3, 1934. He studied at the Conservatories of Madrid and Paris, winning 1st prizes for piano playing at both; début in Paris, 1880; noted as a pedagogue; was prof. at the Madrid Cons. Among his pupils were Manuel de Falla and Joaquín Turina.

Trambitsky, Victor Nikolayevitch, Russian composer; b. Brest-Litovsk, Feb. 12, 1895. He studied with Kalafati at the St. Petersburg Cons. In 1925 he moved to Sverdlovsk, as prof. at the Cons. there. —Works: operas: *Gadfly* (Sverdlovsk, 1929), *Orlena* (Sverdlovsk, 1935), *Storm* (Sverdlovsk, 1942); a symph. (1945); *Symphonic Pictures* (1955); a violin concerto (1921); arrangements of Russian folksongs.

Tranchell, Peter (**Andrew**), composer; b. Cuddalore, British India, July 14, 1922. He studied at Kings College, Cambridge; Mus. Bac. (1949). Most of his works are evocative of old English balladry; yet he has also experimented with modern techniques, as in his 6 piano pieces entitled *Dodecafonia.* His opera *The Mayor of Casterbridge* was produced in Cambridge, July 30, 1951. Other works include ballets; a trio for violin, horn, and piano; a triolet for flute, clarinet, and piano; songs from Chinese poets with instrumental accompaniment; etc.

Trapp, Max, German composer; b. Berlin, Nov. 1, 1887. He studied piano with Ernst von Dohnányi and composition with Paul Juon; then taught at the Berlin Hochschule für Musik and also at the Cons. of Dortmund; in 1929, became a member of the Berlin Academy of Arts, where he taught a master class in composition (1934-45); from 1951 to 1953 he was on the staff of the Municipal Cons. in Berlin; also was active as a landscape painter. His style is neo-Classical, with a strong polyphonic texture, in the tradition of Max Reger. He wrote 6 symphonies: No. 1, *Sinfonia giocosa* (1915), No. 2 (1918), No. 3 (1924), No. 4 (1931), No. 5 (1936), No. 6 (1946); 3 concertos for orch. (1934; 1940; 1946); violin concerto (1922); piano concerto (1930); cello concerto (1935); piano quintet (1910); 3 piano quartets; 2 string quartets; piano pieces; songs; a cantata, *Vom ewigen Licht* (1942). —Cf. W. Matthes, *Max Trapp,* in 'Zeitschrift für Musik' (Oct., 1937).

Traubel, Helen, American soprano; b. St. Louis, June 20, 1899. She made her concert début at St. Louis in 1925, and appeared for the first time during the regular Metropolitan Opera season, in N. Y., as Sieglinde on Dec. 28, 1939. She made several transcontinental tours; sang in Buenos Aires in 1943; also gave numerous concerts in Europe. She was married to Louis Carpenter in 1922; they were divorced the same year, and in 1938 she married William L. Bass. In 1953 she made appearances in N. Y. night clubs; this prompted objections of the Metropolitan Opera management, and as a result she resigned from the Metropolitan. She publ. the mystery novels *The Ptomaine Canary* and *The Metropolitan Opera Murders.*

Trautwein, Traugott, founder (1820) of the music publishing business ('Trautwein'sche Buch- und Musikalien-Handlung') at Berlin, transferred in 1840 to J. Guttentag, and by him in 1858 to Martin Bahn, under whose management it became famous for new editions of early music. After Bahn's death (May 21, 1902) the firm was consolidated with A. Heinrichshofen of Magdeburg.

Travers, John, English organist and composer; b. c. 1703; d. June, 1758. Chorister of St. George's Chapel, Windsor; pupil of M. Greene and Dr. Pepusch; from 1737 organist of the Chapel Royal. Publ. *The Whole Book of Psalms for 1, 2, 3, 4 and 5 voices, with a thorough bass for the harpsichord* (2 vols., 1750) and *18 Canzonets for 2 and 3 voices, the words chiefly by Matthew Prior* (1745); 12 voluntaries for organ or harpsichord were publ. posthumously.

Travers, Patricia, American violinist; b. Clifton, N. J., Dec. 5, 1927. She studied with Jacques Gordon, and made her first public appearance with the Detroit Symph. Orch. at the age of 9; gradually developed into a mature artist, and played with numerous orchestras in the U. S. and in Europe; also in recitals.

Trebelli, Zelia (real name, Zelia Gilbert), French mezzo-soprano; b. Paris, 1838; d. Étretat, Aug. 18, 1892. Studied 5 years with Wartel; début Madrid, 1859, as Rosina in *Il Barbiere,* followed by triumphs in Germany and London (1862). She was long a favorite in London; also toured the United States (1878 and 1884); her last appearance was at Mapleson's benefit concert in London (June, 1889). —Cf. M. de Mensiaux, *Trebelli, a biographical sketch* (London, 1890).

Treharne, Bryceson, music editor and composer; b. Merthyr Tydfil, Wales, May 30, 1879; d. New York, Feb. 4, 1948. He studied at the Royal College of Music in London, under Parry, Stanford, and Davies. In 1901 he went to Australia, and was for 10 years prof. at the Univ. of Adelaide; returning to Europe in 1911, he lived in Paris, Milan, Vienna, and Munich; at the outbreak of World War I, he was interned in Germany, at Ruhleben. There he wrote nearly 200 songs and other works; an exchange of prisoners of war enabled him to return to England; in 1917 he settled in America; was music editor for the Boston Music Co. and Willis Music Co. (1928-47). Among his songs are *Ozymandias, The Fair Circassian, A Lover's Prayer, The Night, Dreams, Love's Tribute,* and *Renunciation.*

Tremblay, George, Canadian-American composer; b. Ottawa, Jan. 14, 1911; studied with his father, a church organist; in 1919 moved to the U. S., eventually settling in Los Angeles. He studied with Schoenberg; wrote his first major work, a string quartet, in the strict 12-tone system (1936). —Other works: 2 symphonies (1940; 1946), 2 wind quintets (1940), 2 piano sonatas (1938), etc.

Trend, John Brande, English hispanist; b. Southampton, Dec. 17, 1887; d. Cambridge, April 20, 1958. He received his education at Cambridge Univ.; spent several years in Spain; in 1933 was appointed prof. of Spanish at Cambridge Univ. —Books: *A Picture of Modern Spain: Men and Music* (London, 1921); *Luis Milan and the Vihuelistas* (London, 1925); *The Music of Spanish History to 1600* (London, 1926); *Manuel de Falla and Spanish Music* (N. Y., 1929).

Trento, Vittorio, Italian composer; b. Venice, 1761; d. there, 1833. Pupil of Bertoni; produced several ballets at Venice, followed by a number of cantatas, farces, and comic operas. He was cembalist at the Teatro S. Samuele, Venice, and then at La Fenice; music director of the Italian opera at Amsterdam (1806), and some years later at Lisbon. His most popular stage work was the opera buffa *Quanti casi in un sol giorno, ossia Gli assassini* (Venice, Dec., 1801), which was also given in London, as *Roberto l'Assassino* (Feb. 3, 1807). Other operas are: *Teresa vedova* (Venice, Jan. 13, 1802), *Ines de Castro* (Leghorn, Nov. 9, 1803), *Ifigenia in Aulide* (Naples, Nov. 4, 1804), *Andromeda* (Naples, May 30, 1805), and *Le Gelosie villane* (Florence, Nov. 2, 1825).

Treu (troy) (Italianized as Fedele), **Daniel Gottlieb,** German composer; b. Stuttgart, 1695; d. Breslau, Aug. 7, 1749. He studied violin with Kusser, and with Vivaldi at Venice. After bringing out 12 operas at Venice, he took an Italian opera troupe to Breslau, where from 1725-27 he produced his operas *Astarte, Coriolano, Ulisse e Telemacco,* and *Don Chisciotte* with much success. In 1727 he became Kapellmeister at Prague; then in Breslau.

Tréville, Yvonne de (real name, Edyth La Gierse), American coloratura soprano; b. (of French father and American mother) Galveston, Texas, Aug. 25, 1881; d. New York, Jan. 25, 1954. She made her début in N. Y. as Marguérite (1898); then went to Paris, where she studied with Madame Marchesi; appeared at the Opéra-Comique as Lakmé (June 20, 1902); sang in Madrid, Brussels, Vienna, Budapest, Cairo, and in Russia; from 1913, gave concert tours in the U. S. and sang in light operas. Her voice had a compass of 3 full octaves, reaching the high G.

Trial (trē-ahl'), **Jean-Claude,** French composer; b. Avignon, Dec. 13, 1732; d. Paris, June 23, 1771. He studied violin in his native city, then went to Paris, where he became associated with Rameau; was conductor at the Paris Opéra. He wrote several operas: *Silvie* (Fontainebleau, Oct. 17, 1765), *Théonis ou Le Toucher* (Paris, Oct. 11, 1767), *La Fête de Flore* (Paris, June 18, 1770); also instrumental pieces.

Triggs, Harold, American pianist and composer; b. Denver, Col., Dec. 25, 1900. He studied at the Univ. of Chicago and later at the Juilliard Graduate School, N. Y., with Joseph and Rosina Lhévinne, Rubin Goldmark, and others. In 1932 he formed a piano duo with Vera Brodsky (q.v.); settled in N. Y.; taught at Columbia Univ. His compositions include the symph. poem for string orch. *The Bright Land* (N. Y., March 29, 1942), 2 piano sonatas (1951, 1953), and 18 preludes for piano (1945).

Tritto, Giacomo, Italian composer; b. Altamura, April 2, 1733; d. Naples, Sept. 16, 1824. He studied with Cafaro at the Cons. della Pietà de' Turchini; became subteacher (primo maestrino) and Cafaro's assistant in teaching harmony, also succeeded him as concertmaster at the Teatro San Carlo. From 1799 to 1807 he was principal teacher (primo maestro) at the Cons.; followed Paisiello in 1816 as maestro of the Royal Chapel. Bellini, Spontini, Mercadante, Meyerbeer, and Conti were his pupils. His first opera, *La Fedeltà in amore,* was performed at Naples in 1764; some 50 others were produced subsequently in Naples, Rome, Venice, Milan, etc.; of these *Le Vicende amorose* (Rome, 1788) and *Gli Americani* (Naples, Nov. 4, 1802) were fairly successful. Other works included 3 cantatas, a Mass for double chorus with 2 orchestras, 7 other Masses (3 of them with orch.); 2 Passions with orch., a Te Deum, motets, etc. (none printed). He publ. *Partimenti e regole generali per conoscere qual numerica dar si deve ai vari movimenti del basso* (1821), and *Scuola di contrappunto, ossia Teoria musicale* (1823). —Cf. F. Florimo, *La Scuola musicale di Napoli,* vol. III (Naples, 1880); J. A. de la Fage, in *Miscellanées musicales* (Paris, 1844); G. de Napoli, *Giacomo Tritto,* in 'La Lettura' (Oct., 1924) and *La Triade melodrammatica altamurana* [*G. Tritto, V. Lavigna, S. Mercadante*] (Milan, 1931).

Trneček (trnĕh'-chĕhk), **Hanuš,** Czech harpist and composer; b. Prague, May 16, 1858; d. there, March 28, 1914. He studied at the Prague Cons.; was harpist at the Hoftheater in Schwerin (1882-88); from 1888 prof. of harp and piano at the Prague Cons. —Works: the operas *Der Geiger von Cremona* (Schwerin, 1886), *Amaranta* (Prague, Nov. 16, 1890; in Czech), *Andrea Crini* (Prague, Feb. 2, 1900), *Die gesühnte Schuld* (posthumous; not produced); a symphony; a piano concerto; a violin concerto; an orchestral suite; piano pieces; edited Beethoven's piano sonatas for the Prague Cons. series.

Tromlitz, Johann Georg, German flutist and flute maker; b. Gera, Feb. 9, 1726; d. Leipzig, Feb. 4, 1805. He publ. *Kurze Abhandlung vom Flötenspielen* (1786); *Ausführlicher und gründlicher Unterricht die Flöte zu spielen* (1791); *Über die Flöte mit mehreren Klappen* (1800); and articles in the 'Allgemeine Musik-Zeitung' (1799); also 3 concertos for flute and strings; 2 books of sonatas for piano and flute; 6 *Partien* for flute; songs.

Trotère, Henry (real name, Trotter), English song composer; b. London, Dec. 14, 1855; d. there, April 10, 1912. Some of his songs that enjoyed success were *Once for All, Léonore, Ever dear, Asthore, The Deathless Army, Love can wait.*

Trotter, Thomas Henry Yorke, English musical educator; b. London, Nov. 6, 1854; d. there, March 11, 1934. Educated at New College, Oxford (M. A., 1887; Mus. Doc., 1892); studied music with F. E. Gladstone and F. Bridge; principal of the London Academy of Music from 1915, developing there a new system for teaching music, based on ear-training and cultivation of the rhythmic sense; he came to the U. S. and introduced his system at the Eastman School of Music in Rochester, N. Y. —Books: *Constructive Harmony* (1911); *Rhythmic Gradus; Ear-training and Sight-reading Gradus; The Making of Musicians* (1914); *Music and Mind* (1924).

Troutbeck, Rev. John, English compiler of hymns; b. Blencowe, Cumberland, Nov. 12, 1832; d. London, Oct. 11, 1899. Graduate of Oxford (B. A., 1856; M. A., 1858); from 1865-69, precentor of Manchester Cathedral; in 1869, canon of Westminster. —Publ. 'The Manchester Psalter' (1868); 'Manchester Chant Book' (1871); 'Cathedral Paragraph Psalter'; 'Hymn Book for Use in Westminster Abbey'; *Music Primer for Schools,* with R. F. Dale (1873; often republ.); *Church Choir Training* (1879). He made translations of German, French, and Italian opera librettos publ. by Novello. —Cf. the 'Mus. Times' (May and Nov., 1899).

Truhn, Friedrich Hieronymus, German composer and writer on music; b. Elbing, Nov. 14, 1811; d. Berlin, April 30, 1886. He studied with Dehn, Klein, and Mendelssohn; wrote for the Leipzig 'Neue Zeitschrift für Musik' during Schumann's editorship; lived chiefly at Berlin, where he founded and conducted the 'Neue Liedertafel'; made a concert tour with Hans von Bülow in 1854. —Works: marionette opera, *Der baierische Hiesel* (Berlin, 1832); operetta, *Der vierjährige Posten* (1833); comic opera, *Trilby* (Berlin, May 22, 1835); melodrama, *Kleopatra* (Berlin, 1853); also wrote *Über Gesangskunst* (1885).

Truinet. See **Nuitter.**

Trunk (trŏŏnk), **Richard,** German critic and conductor; b. Tauberbischofsheim, Baden, Feb. 10, 1879. Pupil of I. Knorr at Hoch's Cons. in Frankfurt (1894-95); 1896-99, at the Royal Academy in Munich. In 1906 appointed teacher of singing at the Theresien-Gymnasium; 1907-12, music critic of the 'Münchner Post'; 1912-14, conductor of the 'Arion' in New York and of the 'Arion' in Newark. He then returned to Munich; from 1916-22, critic of the Bayreuth

'Staatszeitung'; from 1925-34, co-director of the Rheinische Musikschule in Cologne, head of the choral class at the Hochschule, and conductor of the Cologne 'Männerchorverein'; in 1934 succeeded Hausegger as director of the Akademie der Tonkunst in Munich. After 1945 he went to live in Riederau-am-Ammersee. Composed over 100 songs; also choruses, chamber music, etc.

Trutovsky, Vasily Fedorovitch, Russian composer and collector of folksongs; b. Belgorod, 1740; d. St. Petersburg, 1810. He was the son of an orthodox priest; was a court singer and player on the gusli during the reigns of Empress Elizabeth, Peter III, and Catherine II. His historic achievement was the compilation of the first comprehensive collection of Russian folksongs, in 4 issues (1776, 1778, 1779, 1795). He also was the first in Russia to publish piano pieces; the earlier publications of Russian piano music were anonymous. His *Chanson russe variée* for harpsichord or piano (St. Petersburg, 1780) was republ. in 'Old Russian Piano Music,' ed. by A. Drozdov and T. Trofimov (Moscow, 1946).

Tschaikowsky. See **Tchaikovsky.**

Tschirch, (Friedrich) Wilhelm, German choral conductor and composer; b. Lichtenau, June 8, 1818; d. Gera, Jan. 6, 1892; pupil of the Royal Institute for Church-Music, Berlin; music director at Liegnitz 1843-52; then court conductor at Gera. By invitation of the German-American choral societies, he visited the U. S. in 1869, and produced many of his celebrated men's choruses at N. Y., Philadelphia, Baltimore, Washington, Chicago, etc. He publ. salon pieces for piano under the pseudonym 'Alexander Czersky.'

Tschudi. See **Broadwood.**

Tsfasman, Alexander Naumovitch, foremost Russian conductor of jazz music; b. Alexandrovsk, Ukraine, Dec. 14, 1906. He studied piano with Felix Blumenfeld at the Moscow Cons. In 1926 he organized a jazz band in Moscow, and from 1939 to 1946 was music director of the All-Union Radio Jazzband; toured with it all over Russia. He also composed a concerto for piano and jazz band, and numerous popular songs.

Tsintsadze, Sulkhan, Soviet Georgian cellist and composer; b. Gori, Aug. 23, 1925. He studied cello in Tiflis, and later at the Moscow Cons., graduating in 1950; also studied composition there. —Works: opera, *The Golden Fleece* (1953); a symph. (1954); piano concerto on native Georgian themes (1954); violin concerto (1947); cello concerto (1947); 4 string quartets; 3 suites for string quartet, on songs of the nations of the Soviet Union; pieces for cello and piano; film music.

Tua (too'-ah), **Teresina** (real name Maria Felicità), Italian violinist; b. Turin, May 22, 1867. She studied with Massart at the Paris Cons., where she took the 1st prize in 1880; toured the Continent with brilliant success; made her English début at the Crystal Palace, London, May 5, 1883; also appeared in America (1887). In 1889 she married Count Franchi-Verney della Valetta (q.v.), and withdrew from the concert stage till the autumn of 1895, when she set out on a successful European tour, including Russia, where her accompanist and joint artist was Rachmaninoff. Franchi died in 1911; in 1913 she married Emilio Quadrio. She taught at the Milan Cons. from 1915 to 1924, and then at the Santa Cecilia in Rome; subsequently abandoned her career, and entered the convent dell'Adorazione in Rome as Sister Maria di Gesù.

Tubin, Eduard, Swedish composer; b. Tartu (of Estonian parents), June 18, 1905. He studied music with A. Kapp in Estonia and with Kodály in Budapest. In 1944 he returned to Sweden. He wrote 5 symphonies, 2 violin concertos and a double-bass concerto, 2 violin sonatas, saxophone sonatas, ballads and other works for piano, choral pieces and songs.

Tucher (too'-her), **Gottlieb,** Freiherr **von,** German writer on music; b. Nuremberg, May 14, 1798; d. Munich, Feb. 17, 1877. He was in the judicial service in Bavaria; from 1856 to 1868 was judge of the Supreme Court of Munich. His musical publications include 'Kirchengesänge der berühmtesten älteren italienischen Meister . . .' (1827; dedicated to Beethoven), and 'Schatz des evangelischen Kirchengesangs' (1848; 2 vols.); he also wrote *Über den Gemeindegesang der evangelischen Kirche* (1867).

Tucker, Richard, American tenor; b. New York, Aug. 28, 1914. He studied with Paul Althouse. On Jan. 25, 1945 he made his début at the Metropolitan Opera House in *La Gioconda;* later sang leading parts as a lyric tenor.

Tuckerman, Samuel Parkman, American organist and composer; b. Boston, Feb. 11,

1819; d. Newport, R. I., June 30, 1890. Pupil of Carl Zeuner in Boston; organist and choirmaster of St. Paul's Church, 1840; studied the organ in various English cathedral towns from 1849, received the degree of Mus. Doc., Lambeth, in 1853; returned to his Boston position, and gave lectures on early cathedral music and church music; resided in England 1856-64, and for many years in Switzerland. Wrote much church music and edited 'The Episcopal Harp' (Boston, 1844); 'The National Lyre' (Boston, 1848); 'Cathedral Chants' (1858); 'Trinity Collection of Church Music' (Boston, 1864).

Tuckey, William, English singing master; b. Somersetshire, 1708; d. Philadelphia, Sept. 14, 1781. He claimed to have been a vicar-choral at Bristol Cathedral before going to America, where he was active from 1754; in March of that year he established himself as a singing teacher in New York; he taught the charity pupils at Trinity Church there, also giving performances of church music with orch. On Jan. 16, 1770, he conducted what was probably the 1st performance in America of Handel's *Messiah* (overture and 16 numbers). He composed a 'Thanksgiving Anthem' (1760), a setting of the 97th Psalm, etc. —Cf. O. G. Sonneck, *Early Concert-Life in America* (1907).

Tudway, Thomas, English composer; b. 1650; d. Cambridge, Nov. 23, 1726. From 1660 chorister in the Chapel Royal, under Dr. Blow; lay-vicar at St. George's Chapel, Windsor, 1664; organist of King's College, Cambridge, 1670; teacher of choristers there, 1679; prof. of music, Cambridge Univ., 1704; suspended 1706-07, retired 1726. Mus. Bac., Cantab., 1681; Mus. Doc., 1705. He composed services, motets, and anthems; his 'Collection of . . . Services and Anthems used in the Church of England from the Reformation to the Restoration of King Charles II . . .,' in 6 MS vols., is in the British Museum.

Tufts, John, American minister and pioneer compiler of church music; b. Medford, Mass., Feb. 26, 1689; d. Amesbury, Mass., Aug. 17, 1750. He graduated from Harvard Univ. in 1708; was ordained minister at Newbury, Mass., in 1714; upon retirement in 1738, he moved to Amesbury, Mass., where he settled as a shopkeeper. About 1721 he publ. *A Very Plain and Easy Introduction to the Art of Singing Psalm Tunes* (no copy previous to the 1721 ed. is known to exist); in this book, letters instead of notes were used on the staff; it was very popular (at least 11 eds. publ. up to 1774; reprint, Philadelphia, 1954). —Cf. N. D. Gould, *Church Music in America* (1853); F. J. Metcalf, *American Writers and Compilers of Sacred Music* (1925); E. H. Pierce, *The Rise and Fall of the 'Fugue-Tune' in America,* in the 'Mus. Quarterly' (April, 1930); C. K. Shipton, *Sibley's Harvard Graduates* (Boston, 1937; pp. 457-61); I. Lowens, *John Tufts' Introduction to the Singing of Psalm-Tunes (1721-1744): The First American Music Textbook,* in the 'Journal of Research in Music Education' (vol. II, 1954). See also 'Dictionary of American Biography' (vol. XIX, 1936).

Tufts, John Wheeler, American organist and teacher; b. Dover, N. H., May 12, 1825; d. Camden, Maine, March 18, 1908. He went to Germany in 1846, studying in Frankfurt, and in Leipzig under Moscheles (piano) and Hauptmann (theory); returned to Bangor, Maine, in 1848; organist at the Unitarian Church and conductor of the 'Bangor Choral Society'; lived later in Portland as organist of the Union Church and conductor of the 'Haydn Association.' Settled in Boston as teacher and organist (at King's Chapel 15 years), also conductor of the 'Chelsea Choral Society.' He wrote many songs and hymn tunes, church services, piano pieces, and a book on piano technique. Author of a series of school-music works, notably the *Normal Music Course* and the *Cecilian Series of Study and Song.*

Tulou (tü-loo'), **Jean-Louis,** French flutist; b. Paris, Sept. 12, 1786; d. Nantes, July 23, 1865. He was a pupil of Wunderlich at the Paris Cons.; in 1804, 1st flute at the Italian opera; in 1813 he succeeded Wunderlich at the Opéra, resigning in 1822, but resuming the position in 1826 (with the title of 'première flûte solo'); in 1829 he was appointed flute prof. at the Cons.; retired from both positions in 1856. He won his brilliant triumphs with the old-fashioned flute, and until his retirement obstinately opposed the introduction of Böhm's improved instrument into the Paris Conservatoire. He wrote 5 flute concertos; *airs variés* for flute with orch.; a trio for 3 flutes; flute duos; many solo pieces for flute.

Tuma, Franz, Bohemian virtuoso on the viola da gamba and composer; b. Kostelecz, Oct. 2, 1704; d. Vienna, Feb. 4, 1774. He was a pupil of Czernohorsky at Prague and Fux at Vienna; from 1741, chamber composer to the dowager Empress Elisabeth. —Works: 30 Masses, a Miserere, responses, etc.; also instrumental pieces. A selection of Tuma's works was publ. by O. Schmid (choruses, Passion music, piano pieces); a symphony was ed. by P. A. Pisk. —Cf. O. Schmid, in 'Sammelbände der Internationalen Musik-Gesellschaft' II.

Tunder, Franz, celebrated German organist and composer; b. Burg auf Fehmarn, 1614; d. Lübeck, Nov. 5, 1667. From 1632-41, court organist at Gottorp, where he studied with J. Heckslauer, a pupil of Frescobaldi; 1641, organist of the Marienkirche in Lübeck, being succeeded at his death by his son-in-law, Dietrich Buxtehude (q.v.). —7 chorale fantasias for organ by Tunder were discovered in 1903 in the Lüneburg tablature-books (1 publ. by Straube, in 'Alte Meister des Orgelspiels,' new series); solo and choral cantatas ed. by M. Seiffert in 'Denkmäler deutscher Tonkunst' (vol. 3); 2 preludes and fugues for organ ed. by R. Buchmayer (1927); 4 organ preludes etc. in 'Organum.'—Cf. W. Stahl, *F. T. und D. Buxtehude* (Leipzig, 1926) and *F. T.*, in 'Archiv für Musikwissenschaft' VIII; J. Hennings, *Tunderiana,* in 'Lübeckische Blätter,' Jahrg. 75, Nr. 53 (1934). A complete ed. of Tunder's organ chorale arrangements was begun in 1958, edited by Rudolf Walter.

Turchi (toor'-kē), **Guido,** Italian composer; b. Rome, Nov. 10, 1916. He studied with Pizzetti, and his early works show a Romantic quality characteristic of his teacher; however, the chief impact on his music was made by a study of Bartók's works; his concerto for string orch. (Venice, Sept. 8, 1948) is dedicated to Bartók's memory. Among his other compositions are a trio for flute, clarinet, and viola (1945); incidental music to the *Bacchae* of Euripides (1953); *Invettiva* for small chorus and 2 pianos (1946); *2 Notturni sacri* for men's chorus and orch. (1944). —Cf. F. d'Amico, *Guido Turchi,* in 'Tempo' (Autumn, 1951).

Tureck, Rosalyn, American pianist; b. Chicago, Dec. 14, 1914. In 1928 she won first prize at a children's piano tournament in Chicago; made her début at the age of 11, playing with the Chicago Symph. Orch.; then studied with Olga Samaroff at the Juilliard School of Music, graduating in 1936; in 1943 became instructor there. In 1947 she made her first European tour, appearing in London and Scandinavia; later toured England, Scotland, and Ireland (1953-55), and in 1955-56, France, Germany, Italy, etc. She specializes in Bach; her interpretation of the *Goldberg Variations* is particularly notable.

Turina, Joaquín, prominent Spanish composer; b. Seville, Dec. 9, 1882; d. Madrid, Jan. 14, 1949. He studied with local teachers; then entered the Madrid Cons. as a pupil of Tragó (piano). In 1905 he went to Paris, where he studied composition with Vincent d'Indy at the Schola Cantorum, and piano with Moszkowski. In Paris a meeting with Albéniz and Manuel de Falla proved a turning point in his career; he determined to write national Spanish music; returning to Madrid in 1913, he produced 2 symph. works in a characteristic Spanish style: *La Procesión del rocío* and *Sinfonía sevillana,* combining Romantic and Impressionist elements in an individual manner; the same effective combination is found in his chamber music of Spanish inspiration (*Escena andaluza, La Oración del torero,* etc.) and his piano music (*Sonata romántica, Mujeres españolas,* etc.); he also wrote operas and incidental music for the theater. —Works: operas: *Margot* (Madrid, Oct. 10, 1914) and *Jardín de oriente* (Madrid, March 6, 1923); incidental music: *Navidad* (Madrid, 1916), *La Adúltera penitente* (Barcelona, 1917), *La Anunciación* (Madrid, 1924); for orch.: *La Procesión del rocío,* symph. poem (Madrid, March 30, 1913), *Evangelio,* symph. poem (Madrid, April 8, 1915), 3 *Danzas fantásticas* (1920), *Sinfonía sevillana* (San Sebastian, Sept. 11, 1920), *Rítmos,* choreographic fantasy (Barcelona, Oct. 25, 1928), *Rapsodia sinfónica,* for piano and string orch. (Madrid, March 11, 1933); chamber music: piano quintet (1907), string quartet (1911), *Escena andaluza,* for viola, string quartet, and piano (1912), *La Oración del torero,* for string quartet (1925), 2 piano trios (1926; 1933), 2 violin sonatas (1929; 1934), piano quartet (1931), *Serenata* for string quartet (1935), *Círculo,* for violin, cello, and piano (1936), *Las nueve musas* (9 pieces for various instruments; 1945); for piano: *Sevilla, suite pintoresca* (1909), *Sonata romántica* (1909), *Coins de Séville,* suite (1911), *Tres danzas andaluzas* (1912), *Album de viaje* (1916), *Mujeres españolas* (2 sets, 1917, 1932), *Cuentos de España,* 2 sets of 7 pieces each (1918; 1928), *Niñerias,* 2 sets of children's pieces (1919; 1931), *Sanlúcar de Barrameda* (1922), *El Cristo de la Calavera* (1924), *Jardines de Andalucía,* suite (1924), *La Venta de los gatos* (1925), *El Barrio de Santa Cruz* (1925); *La Leyenda de la Giralda,* suite (1927), *Dos danzas sobre temas populares españoles* (1927), *Verbena madrileña,* 5 pieces (1927), *Mallorca,* suite (1928), *Evocaciones,* 3 pieces (1929), *Recuerdos de la antigua*

España, 4 pieces (1929), *Viaje marítimo*, suite (1930), *Ciclo pianístico: Tocata y fuga, Partita, Pieza romántica, El Castillo de Almodóvar* (1930-31), *Miniaturas*, 8 pieces (1930), *Danzas gitanas*, 2 sets of 5 pieces each (1930; 1934), *Tarjetas postales* (1931), *Sonata fantasía* (1930), *Radio Madrid*, suite (1931); *Jardín de niños*, 8 pieces (1931); *El Circo*, 6 pieces (1932), *Silhuetas*, 5 pieces (1932), *En la zapatería*, 7 pieces (1933), *Fantasía italiana* (1933), *Trilogia: El poema infinito* (1933), *Ofrenda* (1934), *Hipócrates* (1934), *Rincones de Sanlúcar* (1933), *Bailete, suite de danzas del siglo XIX* (1933), *Preludios* (1933), *Fantasía sobre cinco notas* (1934), *Concierto sin orquesta* (1935), *En el cortijo*, 4 pieces (1936-40); *Prelude*, for organ (1914); *Musette*, for organ (1915); for guitar: *Sevillana* (1923), *Fandanguillo* (1926), *Ráfaga* (1930), *Sonata* (1932), *Homenaje a Tárrega*, 2 pieces (1935); songs: *Rima* (1911), *Poema en forma de canciones* (1918), 3 arias (1923), *Canto a Sevilla*, cycle (1927), *2 Canciones* (1927), *Corazón de mujer* (1927), *Tríptico* (1929), *3 Sonetos* (1930), *3 Poemas* (1933), *Homenaje a Lope de Vega* (1935); publ. an *Enciclopedia abreviada de la música* (Madrid, 1917).—Cf. C. Bosch, *Impresiones estéticas* (Madrid, 1918); H. Collet, *L'Essor de la musique espagnole au XXe siècle* (Paris, 1929); A. Salazar, *La Música contemporánea en España* (Madrid, 1930); F. Sopeña, *Joaquín Turina* (Madrid, 1943); W. Dean, *Joaquín Turina*, in the 'Chesterian' (April, 1949).

Türk, Daniel Gottlob, German organist and teacher; b. Clausnitz, Saxony, Aug. 10, 1756; d. Halle, Aug. 26, 1813. He was a pupil in harmony and counterpoint of Homilius while studying at the Kreuzschule, Dresden; he had learned to play the violin at home and after he entered Leipzig Univ. J. A. Hiller continued his instruction, and engaged him as violinist at the theater and the 'Grosses Concert.' In 1776, cantor of the Ulrichskirche, Halle, and music teacher at the Gymnasium; 1779, music director of the Univ.; on becoming organist at the Liebfrauenkirche in 1787, he resigned his positions as cantor and teacher. He publ. an important clavier method (1789; 2nd ed., 1802) and instructive pieces for piano; 18 sonatas and sonatinas for piano; songs; and theoretical works. An opera, church music, symphonies, organ pieces, are in MS. Some piano pieces for 4 hands were ed. by Doflein (1933). —Cf. H. Glenewinkel, *D. G. T.* (dissertation, Halle, 1909); G. E. Hedler, *D. G. T.* (dissertation, Leipzig, 1936); also the 'Festschrift' publ. on the 125th anniversary of his death, *Daniel Gottlob Türk* (Halle, 1938).

Turle, James, English organist and composer; b. Somerton, Somerset, March 5, 1802; d. London, June 28, 1882. He was assistant organist to Greatorex at Westminster Abbey till 1831, then succeeded him as organist and master of the choristers, resigning in 1875. He conducted the 'Antient Concerts' 1840-43; was music master at the School for the Indigent Blind 1829-56. He was a noted teacher. He composed services, anthems, chants, and hymn tunes; ed. several collections of church music (e.g., 'The Westminster Abbey Chant Book,' with Dr. Bridge).

Turner, Alfred Dudley, American pianist and teacher; b. St. Albans, Maine, Aug. 24, 1854; d. there, May 7, 1888. He studied at the New England Cons. of Music and the Boston College of Music, and later taught at these schools. —Works: 3 morceaux, for piano and cello; suite for piano and cello; *Sonate dramatique* for piano; 2 sonatas for piano and violin; sonata for piano and cello; piano pieces.

Turner, Charles, American composer; b. Baltimore, Nov. 25, 1921. He studied violin at the Curtis Institute, Philadelphia, and composition with Samuel Barber; later took courses with Nadia Boulanger. He served as a naval officer during World War II; played concerts in Europe; in 1954 received a fellowship awarded by the Italian government, and took up residence in Rome. His violin concerto was performed at the Detroit Institute of Arts in 1940; his symph. sketch *Encounter* was performed for the first time by the Cleveland Orch., Dec. 29, 1955; a ballet, *Pastorale*, was given its première in New York Jan. 14, 1957.

Turner, Godfrey, English composer; b. Manchester, March 27, 1913; d. (suicide) N. Y., Dec. 7, 1948. He studied with E. J. Dent at Cambridge Univ. (musicology) and with Nadia Boulanger in Paris. He came to the U. S. in 1936; taught at the San Francisco Cons. (1938-43); was music editor for Boosey & Hawkes, N. Y. (1944-46); then secretary of the American Music Center, N. Y. (1946-48). —Works: *Trinity Concerto*, for chamber orch.; viola concerto; *Sonata concertante*, for piano and string orch.; *Fanfare, Chorale and Finale* for brass; *Saraband and Tango; Gregorian Overture* (Columbus, Ohio, Dec. 2, 1947; winner of the Broadcast Music, Inc., Contest).

Turner, Robert Comrie, Canadian composer; b. Montreal, June 6, 1920. He studied at the Royal College of Music, London, with Herbert Howells and Gordon Jacob (1947-48), with Roy Harris at Colorado College (1947) and in Nashville (1949-50); received his Mus. Doc. degree from McGill Univ. in 1953. In 1952 he was appointed music producer for the Canadian Broadcasting Corporation in Vancouver; taught composition at the Univ. of British Columbia (1955-57). His works include: *Sinfonia* for small orch. (1953); *Opening Night,* overture (1955); *Lyric Interlude* for orch. (1956); 2 string quartets (1949; 1954); quintet for piano and woodwinds (1951); violin sonata (1956); *2 Choral Pieces* (1952); *The Seasons,* a song cycle (1954); a piano sonata (1955); a *Nocturne* for piano (1946); *4 Little Pieces* for harp (1957); *Canon, Fugue, and Chorale* for organ (1957).

Turner, Walter James, English poet and writer on music; b. Shanghai, China, Oct. 13, 1889; d. London, Nov. 18, 1946. He studied with his father (organist of St. Paul's Cathedral, Melbourne, Australia), also privately in Dresden, Munich, and Vienna. He settled in London, where he became music critic for 'The New Statesman.' Among his books on music the most valuable is *Mozart: the Man and his Work* (1938). Others are *Music and Life* (1922); *Variations on the Theme of Music* (1924); *Orpheus, or the Music of the Future* (1926); *Beethoven, the Search for Reality* (1927; new ed., 1933); *Musical Meanderings* (1928); *Music, a Short History* (1932; 2nd ed., 1949); *Facing the Music* (1933); *Wagner* (1933); *Berlioz: the Man and his Work* (1934); *Music: An Introduction to its Nature and Appreciation* (1936); *English Music* (1941); *English Ballet* (1944).

Turner, William, English composer; b. Oxford, 1651; d. London, Jan. 13, 1740. Was at first a chorister at Christ Church, Oxford, under E. Lowe, and later at the Chapel Royal under H. Cooke. He was a choir-singer at Lincoln Cathedral, a vicar choral of St. Paul's, and a lay vicar of Westminster Abbey; in 1669 he was made a Gentleman of the Chapel Royal; received the degree of Mus. Doc. from Cambridge Univ. in 1696. Composed church music, anthems, songs, catches.

Turnhout, Gérard de (real name **Gheert Jacques**), Netherlands composer; b. Turnhout, c. 1520; d. Madrid, Sept. 15, 1580. In 1545, choir-singer at Antwerp Cathedral, of which he was appointed Kapellmeister in 1563; in 1572, Philip II of Spain called him to Madrid as maestro of the Royal Chapel there. Publ. 1 book of motets *a* 4-5 (1568), 1 book of motets and chansons *a* 4-6 (1569), and 1 Mass in *Praestantissimorum divinae musices auctorum Missae X* (1570). —His son, **Jean de Turnhout,** was Kapellmeister to the Archduke Alexander Farnese, governor of the Netherlands, at Brussels from 1586; from 1611 2nd Kapellmeister, and from 1618, first, of the Royal Chapel there. He publ. 2 books of madrigals and one of motets.

Turpin, Edmund Hart, English organist and composer; b. Nottingham, May 4, 1835; d. London, Oct. 25, 1907. He was a pupil of Hullah and Pauer in London, where he settled in 1857; served as organist of various churches; publ. a collection for organ, 'Student's Edition of Classical Authors'; wrote the oratorios *St. John the Baptist* and *Hezekiah;* hymn tunes; many works for organ. He was editor of 'The Musical Standard' (from 1880) and for a time also of 'The Musical World.' —Cf. C. W. Pearce, *A Biographical Sketch of E. H. Turpin* (London, 1911).

Turski, Zbigniew, Polish composer; b. Konstantin, near Warsaw, July 28, 1908. He studied composition with P. Rytel at the State Cons. in Warsaw; was music director of the Polish Radio (1936-39); after the war, he conducted orchestras in the provinces. In 1948 his 2nd symph., *The Olympiad,* was awarded a prize by the Association of Polish Composers and the Music Jury of the 14th Olympiad in London. He writes in an advanced harmonic idiom, influenced by French modernism. His music written before 1945 was lost during the war; later works include, besides *The Olympiad* (1948), symph. No. 3 (1953); violin concerto (1951); a string quartet (1951); cantatas, *Ziemia* (1952) and *Vistula River* (1953); miscellaneous compositions for piano; songs; music for the theater, films, and radio.

Turtchaninov (tŏŏr-chăh-nē'-nŏhf), **Piotr Ivanovitch,** Russian composer of sacred music; b. Kiev, Nov. 20, 1779; d. St. Petersburg, March 16, 1856. He studied music with Sarti when the latter was at the St. Petersburg court; ordained priest in 1803; taught singing at the imperial court chapel; from 1831 to 1841 was high priest at various churches. His masterly arrangements and harmonizations of old liturgical melodies of the Russian church were publ. posthumously in 4 vols. His autobiography was publ. in St.

Petersburg in 1863. —Cf. A. Preobrazhensky, *The High Priest P. I. Turtchaninov* (St. Petersburg, 1910); V. Lebedev, *P. I. Turtchaninov* (Tambov, 1910).

Tuthill, Burnet Corwin, American composer; b. New York, Nov. 16, 1888. He was educated at Columbia Univ. (M. A., 1910); took up a business career; was general manager of the Cincinnati Cons. (1922-30); then returned to music; entered the Cincinnati College of Music, receiving the degree of Mus. M. in 1935; became prof. at Southwestern College, Memphis, and in 1937 became director of the Memphis College of Music. He began to compose very late in life, but compensated for it by increased productivity. —Works: *Bethlehem,* pastorale for orch. (Interlochen, Mich., July 22, 1934, composer conducting); *Laurentia,* symph. poem (Rochester, Oct. 30, 1936); *Come Seven,* rhapsody for orch. (1935; St. Louis, Feb. 19, 1944); *Symph. in C* (1940); clarinet concerto (1948); *Nocturne* for solo flute and strings (1933); *Intrada* for chamber orch. (1935); *Intermezzo* for 2 clarinets and basset-horn (1927); *Fantasy Sonata,* for clarinet and piano (1932); *Sonatine* for flute and clarinet (1933); piano trio (1933); Variations on *When Johnny Comes Marching Home,* for piano and woodwind quintet (1934); *Sailors' Hornpipe,* for wind quintet (1935); *Divertimento,* for wind quartet (1936); clarinet quintet (1936); violin sonata (1937); saxophone sonata (1941).

Tuukkanen, Kalervo, Finnish conductor and composer; b. Mikkeli, Oct. 14, 1909; studied with Madetoja and Krohn. He has written 3 symphonies, several suites for orch., concertos, and choral works. He is the author of a monograph on his teacher, Madetoja (Helsinki, 1947).

Tuxen, Erik, German-Danish conductor; b. Mannheim (of Danish parents) July 4, 1902; d. Copenhagen, Aug. 28, 1957. In 1916 he moved to Denmark; studied architecture and music in Copenhagen; then in Paris, Vienna, and Berlin. He conducted the Danish State Radio Orch. (1936-41); made guest appearances in the U. S. (1950-51), presenting a concert of Scandinavian music at Carnegie Hall (April 2, 1951); in the summer of 1954 he conducted in South America.

Tveitt, Geirr, Norwegian composer and pianist; b. Hardanger, Oct. 19, 1908. He studied piano in Vienna and Paris; then toured in Europe. An exceptionally prolific composer, he has written 29 piano sonatas, 5 piano concertos, a violin concerto, 3 symphonies, 3 string sextets, 2 string quartets, 4 operas, 2 ballets, and over 100 songs. — Publ. *Tonalitätstheorie des parallelen Leittonsystems* (Oslo, 1937).

Tweedy, Donald, American composer; b. Danbury, Conn., April 23, 1890; d. there, July 21, 1948. He was educated at Harvard Univ. (B. A., 1912; M. A., 1917), where his teachers were Walter Spalding and E. B. Hill; later studied composition with Goetschius at the Institute of Musical Art, N. Y. He taught at Vassar College (1914-16), the Eastman School of Music (1923-27), Hamilton College (1937-38), and Texas Christian Univ. (1945-46). He publ. a *Manual of Harmonic Technic Based on the Practice of J. S. Bach* (1928). —Works: ballet, *Alice in Wonderland* (1935); *L'Allegro,* symph. study (Rochester, May 1, 1925); *3 Dances* for orch. (1925); *Williamsburg,* suite for orch. (1941); *Anthem for Lent: Out of the Depths,* for soli with organ (1942); viola sonata (1916); violin sonata (1920); cello sonata (1930); piano pieces.

Tye, Christopher, English organist and composer; b. c. 1500; d. c. 1572. He may have been a chorister at King's College, Cambridge, in 1511 (identification uncertain, since no first name is given for a choirboy named Tye appearing on an extant list of choristers). In 1537 he received his Mus. B. from Cambridge; on Sept. 10, 1541, he was appointed organist of Ely Cathedral (resigned in 1561); Mus. Doc. at Cambridge in 1545; was ordained a priest in 1560 at Doddington. He describes himself as a gentleman of the King's Chapel in the title-page of his only publ. work, *The Actes of the Apostles, translated into Englyshe metre . . . to synge and also to play upon the Lute* (London, 1553; it includes the first 14 chapters of Acts). The hymn tunes 'Windsor or Eton' and 'Winchester Old' are adapted from tunes in this collection. Tye was an important composer of English church music; in MS he left Masses, services, motets, and anthems. The 'Euge Bone' Mass was ed. by Arkwright in 'The Old English Edition' (No. 10); other examples in 'The Oxford History of Music' (vol. II) and in Walker's 'History of Music in England.' —Cf. G. Reese, *Music in the Renaissance* (N. Y., 1954; pp. 782-83).

Tyes, John, English organist and composer who flourished early in the 15th century. A Gloria for 2 voices and one instrument and a Sanctus for 4 voices are among the works included in the 'Old Hall MSS.'

Tyndall, John, eminent physicist and acoustician; b. Leighlin Bridge, Ireland, Aug. 2, 1820; d. Hindhead, Surrey, England, Dec. 4, 1893. His 2 works in the domain of acoustics are *Sound* (1867 and many subsequent eds.), a lucid and scholarly explanation of acoustical phenomena, and *On the Transmission of Sound by the Atmosphere* (1874). He was prof. of natural philosophy at the Royal Institute from 1853. —Cf. 'Dictionary of National Biography' (vol. XIX, pp. 1358-63).

Typp, W., English singer and composer who was active in the early decades of the 15th century. An Agnus Dei, 2 Credos, and 4 Sanctus settings by him are found among the 'Old Hall MSS.'

Tyrwhitt, Gerald. See **Berners, Lord.**

Tzarth (Czarth, Zarth), Georg, Bohemian violinist; b. Hochtann, April 8, 1708; d. Mannheim, Germany, 1778. He was a friend of Franz Benda (q.v.), whom he accompanied to Warsaw; in 1734 he entered the chapel of Crown Prince Frederick at Rheinsberg; in 1758 joined the court orch. at Mannheim. He wrote symphonies, concertos, string trios, violin sonatas, etc. in the 'Mannheim School' style; examples of his works are found in the 'Denkmäler der Tonkunst in Bayern' (vols. XV-XVI, edited by Riemann).

U

Ubaldus (or **Ugbaldus, Uchubaldus**). See **Hucbald.**

Uber, Christian Friedrich Hermann, German composer; b. Breslau, April 22, 1781; d. Dresden, March 2, 1822. He was a law student at Halle, but also studied music under Türk, and became chamber musician to Prince Louis Ferdinand of Prussia. After holding various positions as violinist and conductor, he settled in Dresden. He wrote the operas *Der falsche Werber* (Kassel, 1808) and *Der frohe Tag* (Mainz, 1815); incidental music to various plays; some violin works; songs to texts in German and French.

Uberti (Hubert), Antonio, male soprano; b. (of German parents) Verona, 1697; d. Berlin, Jan. 20, 1783. He was one of the most brilliant pupils of Porpora, and was known as 'il Porporino' (little Porpora). In 1741 he entered the service of Frederick the Great in Berlin. He was greatly renowned in Germany for his singing of Italian operas.

Uccellini (ŏŏ-tcheh-lē'-nē), **Marco,** Italian composer; b. Modena, c. 1610; date and place of death unknown. He was maestro di cappella at the ducal court of Modena from 1645, and at the Modena Cathedral from 1654. From 1639 to 1667 he publ. a variety of chamber music (sonatas, arias, canzonas, etc.); his advanced violin technique calls for use of the 6th position. He also wrote an opera, *Li Eventi di Filandro ed Edessa,* which was presented in Parma in 1675 (the music is not extant); 2 ballet pieces: *Le Navi d'Enea* (1673) and *Il Giove d'Elide fulminato* (1677). Riemann publ. a sonata by Uccellini in 'Alte Kammermusik'; some pieces were publ. by Wasielewski; others by Torchi in 'L'Arte Musicale in Italia' (vol. VII).

Udbye, Martin Andreas, Norwegian composer; b. Trondheim, June 18, 1820; d. there, Jan. 10, 1889. He studied in Leipzig with Hauptmann; returning to Trondheim, he was organist at various churches. He wrote 2 operettas, *Hjemvé* (Oslo, April 8, 1864) and *Junkeren og Flubergrosen* (Oslo, Jan. 7, 1870); several cantatas; 3 string quartets; military marches; organ pieces; piano works; songs.

d'Udine, Jean (real name Albert Cozanet), French writer on music; b. Landivisiau, Finistère, July 1, 1870; d. Paris, April, 1938. He was a practicing lawyer, but also wrote music criticism. In 1909 he founded in Paris the 'École Française de Gymnastique Rythmique' for teaching the methods of Jaques-Dalcroze. —Books: *La Corrélation des sons et des couleurs en art* (1897); *Lettres paradoxales sur la musique* (Paris, 1900); *L'Orchestration des couleurs* (1903); *Paraphrases musicales* (Paris, 1904); *Gluck* (1906); *L'Art et le geste* (1912); *Les Transmutations rythmiques* (1921); *Qu'est-ce que la musique?* (1925); *Traité de géométrie rythmique* (1926). Also wrote songs: *Les Chants de la jungle* (1905), *Rondels pour après* (1924), etc.

Ugalde (ü-gahld'), **Delphine** (*née* Beaucé), French soprano; b. Paris, Dec. 3, 1829; d. there, July 19, 1910. She received her first instruction in singing from her mother, an actress; subsequently studied with Moreau-Sainti; made her début in Paris in 1848 as

Angèle in Auber's *Domino noir;* in 1866 assumed the management of the Bouffes-Parisiens, taking leading roles in Offenbach's operettas; in 1867 she appeared in her own operetta, *La Halte au moulin.* She retired in 1871, and settled down as a successful vocal teacher. She was married twice, to a Spanish musician, Ugalde, who died in 1858, and to an impresario, Valcollier.

Ugarte (ŏŏ-gahr'-tĕ), **Floro M.,** Argentine composer; b. Buenos Aires, Sept. 15, 1884. He studied in Buenos Aires, and at the Paris Cons. under Fourdrain, with whom he collaborated in writing the ballet *Sigolene.* He returned to Argentina in 1913; in 1924, became prof. of the National Cons. there; was also for several years musical director of the Teatro Colón; in that capacity he visited N. Y. in 1940, to engage singers. —Works: operatic fairy tale, *Saika* (Buenos Aires, July 21, 1920); *Entre las montañas,* symph. suite (conducted in Buenos Aires by Richard Strauss in 1923 during his guest appearances there); *La Rebelión del agua,* symph. poem (Buenos Aires, Oct. 16, 1935); *De mi tierra,* symph. suite (1927); *Piri,* choreographic poem (1944); symph. in A (1946; Buenos Aires, May 13, 1952); *Tango,* for orch. (Buenos Aires, Sept. 5, 1951); chamber music; songs; piano pieces.

Ugolini (ŏŏ-gŏh-lē'-nē), **Vincenzo,** Italian composer; b. Perugia, c. 1570; d. Rome, May 6, 1638. Pupil of B. Nanini in Rome, where from 1592 to 1603 he was choirmaster at the Church of S. Maria Maggiore; from 1609 to 1615, at the Cathedral of Benevento; then returned to Rome, and in 1616 became choirmaster of S. Luigi dei Francesi; in 1620 he succeeded Suriano as maestro of the Cappella Giulia of St. Peter's (until 1626); in 1631, he resumed his former post at S. Luigi dei Francesi, retaining it till death. He was the teacher of Benevoli. A notable representative of Palestrina's school, he publ. 4 books of motets for 1, 2, 3, and 4 voices with continuo (1616-19); 2 books of Psalms for 8 voices (1620); 2 books of Masses and motets for 8 and 12 voices (1623); 1 book of songs and motets *a* 12 (1624); 2 books of madrigals *a* 5 (1615).

Ugolino de Orvieto, Italian musical theorist; d. c. 1449. He was archpriest at the Cathedral of Ferrara from about 1440; his treatise, *De musica mensurata* (MS), is in the Biblioteca Casanatense in Rome. —Cf. U. Kornmüller, *Die Musiklehre des Ugolino de Orvieto,* in the 'Kirchenmusikalisches Jahrbuch' (1895).

Uhl, Alfred, Austrian composer; b. Vienna, June 5, 1909. He was a pupil of Franz Schmidt; was in the Austrian army (1940-43), and was severely wounded. In 1945 he was appointed teacher of composition at the Vienna Academy of Music. His music is patterned after Classical forms, with particular emphasis on contrapuntal clarity. His works include a divertimento for 4 clarinets; *Eine vergnügliche Musik,* for 8 wind instruments (1943); *Konzertante Sinfonie,* for clarinet and orch. (1944); *Sonata graziosa* for orch. (1947).

Uhlig (ŏŏ'-lih), **Theodor,** German violinist and writer on music; b. Wurzen, near Leipzig, Feb. 15, 1822; d. Dresden, Jan. 3, 1853. He studied violin with Schneider in Dessau, and in 1841 became a violinist in the Dresden Orch. He was one of the most devoted friends and admirers of Wagner; made the vocal score of *Lohengrin;* Wagner's letters to him were publ. in 1888 (English transl., 1890). Of his 84 works (symphonies, chamber music, theater pieces, etc.) only a violin concerto and some piano pieces and songs were publ. His articles are of some importance; they were publ. as *Musikalische Schriften* by L. Frankenstein (Regensburg, 1913). —Cf. M. Ahrend, *Theodor Uhlig, der früh verstorbene Wagnerianer* (Bayreuth, 1904).

Ujj (ŏŏ'-ē), **Béla,** Hungarian composer of operettas; b. Vienna, July 2, 1873; d. there, Feb. 1, 1942. He lost his sight in childhood, but studied music and composed a number of successful operettas which were produced in Vienna. They include the following: *Der Herr Professor* (Dec. 4, 1903); *Kaisermanöver* (March 4, 1905); *Die kleine Prinzessin* (May 5, 1907); *Drei Stunden Leben* (Nov. 1, 1909); *Chantecler* (Oct. 25, 1910); *Der Türmer von St. Stephan* (Sept. 13, 1912); *Teresita* (June 27, 1914); *Der Müller und sein Kind* (Oct. 30, 1917).

Ulbrich, Maximilian, Austrian composer; b. Vienna, c. 1752; d. there, Sept. 14, 1814. He studied with Wagenseil; was a government clerk and pursued music as an avocation. His Singspiel *Der blaue Schmetterling* was produced in Vienna on April 2, 1782; he also wrote an oratorio; several symphonies; church music.

Ulfrstad, Marius Moaritz, Norwegian composer; b. Borgund, Sept. 11, 1890. He studied at the Cons. of Oslo; then in Berlin (with Humperdinck), in Florence (with Pizzetti), and in Paris (with Ravel). Returning to Oslo, he founded his own music school there (1921); was music critic of the 'Morgenposten' (1922-40) and the 'Aftenposten' (1945-47). His works include 5 symphonies; several suites for orch. (*Norwegia, Islandia, Grönlandia, Svalbardia,* etc.); *Arctic Suite* for piano and orch.; 2 violin concertos (1923; 1935); much chamber music; about 250 choral pieces; nearly 1,000 songs, including arrangements of folksongs.

Ullmann, Viktor, Austrian conductor and composer; b. Teschen, Jan. 1, 1898. He studied with Schoenberg in Vienna; then lived in Prague, where he conducted theater music. He wrote 2 operas, *Peer Gynt* (after Ibsen) and *Der Sturz des Antichrist.* His 5 variations and double fugue were performed at the Festival of the International Society for Contemporary Music in Geneva (April 7, 1929); his string quartet was given at the London Festival (June 18, 1938); other chamber works were heard at concerts of modern music in Europe and America. His style is atonal, but he adheres to the Classical pattern in formal design.

Ulrich, Homer, American musicologist; b. Chicago, March 27, 1906. He studied bassoon and cello at the Chicago Musical College, and played these instruments in various orchestras; was bassoonist with the Chicago Symph. Orch. (1929-35); received his M.A. at the Univ. of Chicago with the thesis *The Penitential Psalms of Lasso* (1939). He was head of the music dept. of Monticello College (1935-38); then taught at the Univ. of Texas (associate prof., 1939; prof., 1951); also played bassoon with the San Antonio Symph. In 1953 he was appointed head of the reorganized music dept. of the Univ. of Maryland. —Books: *Chamber Music* (a valuable survey; N. Y., 1948); *Education of a Concert-Goer* (N. Y., 1949); *Symphonic Music* (N. Y., 1952); *Famous Women Singers* (N. Y., 1953); *Music; a Design for Listening* (N. Y., 1957).

Ulrich (ŏŏl'-rih), **Hugo,** German composer; b. Oppeln, Silesia, Nov. 26, 1827; d. Berlin, May 23, 1872. After studying in Breslau, he went to Berlin in 1846 and took lessons from Dehn. For a few years he taught at the Stern Cons. (1859-63); otherwise earned his living by working for publishers. He wrote 3 symphonies, of which the 2nd, entitled *Symphonie triomphale,* won a prize of 1500 francs offered by the Brussels Academy in 1853. Other works include a piano trio, a cello sonata, a string quartet, piano pieces, and songs. He made excellent arrangements of Beethoven's symphonies for piano, 4 hands.

Ulybyshev. See **Oulibichev.**

Umlauf, Ignaz, Austrian composer; b. Vienna, 1746; d. Mödling, near Vienna, June 8, 1796. In 1772 he became violinist in the court theater, and in 1778, conductor of the German Opera in Vienna; in 1789 was appointed sub-conductor (under Salieri) of the Imperial Chapel in Vienna. He was a highly popular composer of Singspiele; inaugurated the season of the German Singspiele at the Burg Theater (Feb. 17, 1778) with his piece *Bergknappen;* there followed a number of others: *Die Apotheke* (June 20, 1778); *Die pucefarbenen Schuhe, oder Die schöne Schusterin* (June 22, 1779); *Das Irrlicht, oder Endlich fand er sie* (Jan. 17, 1782); *Der Oberamtmann und die Soldaten* (1782); *Der Ring der Liebe* (Dec. 3, 1786). *Zu Steffan sprach im Traume,* an aria from *Das Irrlicht,* enjoyed great popularity; Eberl wrote a set of variations on it, which was misattributed to Mozart. The score of Umlauf's 1st Singspiel, *Die Bergknappen,* was edited by R. Haas in the 'Denkmäler der Tonkunst in Österreich' (vol. 36).

Umlauf, Michael, Austrian violinist and composer, son of Ignaz Umlauf; b. Vienna, Aug. 9, 1781; d. Baden, near Vienna, June 20, 1842. He played the violin at the Vienna Opera; conducted at court theaters; wrote piano music; brought out a Singspiel, *Der Grenadier* (Vienna, July 8, 1812). He assisted Beethoven in conducting the 9th Symphony and other works (actually led the performances, with Beethoven indicating the initial tempos).

Unger, Caroline, Hungarian contralto; b. Stuhlweissenburg, Oct. 28, 1803; d. at her villa near Florence, March 23, 1877. She studied voice in Milan with D. Ronconi, and in Vienna with Aloysia Lange (Mozart's sister-in-law) and with Johann Michael Vogl. Beethoven chose her to sing the contralto parts in the first performances of his *Missa Solemnis* and 9th Symph. (May 7, 1824); long afterwards she recounted that she turned Beethoven's head around that he might see the applause, which he could no longer hear. She went to Italy, where she changed the spelling of her name to Ungher, to secure correct pronunciation in Italian. Several Italian composers(Donizetti, Bellini, Mercadante, etc.) wrote operas especially for her. In 1833 she appeared in Paris. In 1839 she was engaged to be married to the poet Lenau, but the engagement soon was broken; in 1841 she married the French writer François Sabatier (1818-91) and retired from the stage. She publ. an album of 46 songs, under the title *Lieder, Mélodies et Stornelli.* —Cf. O. Hartwig, *Fr. Sabatier und Karoline Sabatier-Unger,* in 'Deutsche Rundschau' (May, 1897); F. Margit Polgár, *Unger-Sabatier* (Budapest, 1941).

Unger, Georg, German tenor; b. Leipzig, March 6, 1837; d. there, Feb. 2, 1887. He was originally a student of theology; made his operatic début in Leipzig at the age of 30. Hans Richter heard him in Mannheim and recommended him to Wagner for the role of Siegfried. He studied the part with Hey, and his interpretation of it made him famous.

Unger, Hermann, German composer and writer on music; b. Kamenz, Oct. 26, 1886. He studied philology in Leipzig and Munich, and received his *Dr. phil.* (1910) with a dissertation on Greek poetry; in Munich he also studied music with Edgar Istel and Joseph Haas; then went to Meiningen, where he took lessons with Max Reger (1911-13). He served in the German army in World War I; in 1919 became teacher at the Cons. of Cologne; in 1925 was appointed lecturer at the Cologne Hochschule für Musik; retired in 1945. His musical compositions include the operas *Der Zauberhandschuh* (1927) and *Richmodis von Aducht* (1928); a Christmas fairy tale, *Die Geschichten vom Weihnachtsbaum* (1943); 2 symphonies; *Japanisches Liederspiel* for mixed chorus and orch.; *Der Gott und die Bajadere* for declamation, chorus, and orch.; several symph. poems; much chamber music; choral works; song cycles; piano suites. —Books: *Musikalisches Laienbrevier* (Munich, 1921); *Max Reger* (Munich, 1921); *Musiktheoretische Laienfibel* (1922); *Musikgeschichte in Selbstzeugnissen* (Munich, 1928); *Beethovens Vermächtnis* (1929); *Musikanten gestern und heute* (Siegen, 1935); *Anton Bruckner und seine 7. Sinfonie* (Bonn, 1944).

Unger, Max, German musicologist and conductor; b. Taura, May 28, 1883. He studied at the Leipzig Cons. and attended Riemann's lectures at the Univ. (1904-06); *Dr. phil.* (1911) with the dissertation *Muzio Clementis Leben* (publ. Langensalza, 1914); wrote music criticism in the 'Neue Zeitschrift für Musik.' In 1933 he was compelled to leave Germany and settled in Zürich; then went to Volterra, Italy. He devoted his efforts mainly to Beethoven research; publ. about 150 papers on various aspects of Beethoven's life and works; of these the most important are *Auf Spuren von Beethovens unsterblicher Geliebten* (Langensalza, 1911), *Ludwig van Beethoven und seine Verleger S. A. Steiner und Tobias Haslinger in Wien, A. M. Schlesinger in Berlin* (Berlin, 1921), *Beethovens Handschrift* (Bonn, 1926), *Ein Faustopernplan Beethovens und Goethes* (Regensburg, 1952); edited the catalogue of the Bodmer Beethoven collection in Zürich, under the title *Eine Schweizer Beethovensammlung: Katalog* (Zürich, 1939).

Ungher-Sabatier. See **Unger, Caroline.**

Uninsky, Alexander, Russian pianist; b. Kiev, Feb. 2, 1910. He studied at the Kiev Cons.; then in Paris; toured in Europe until 1939; went to South America in 1940, and gave successful recitals there; then came to the U. S., where he continued his concert career. In 1955 he was appointed prof. at the Cons. of Toronto, Canada.

Untersteiner, Alfredo, Italian musicologist; b. Rovereto, April 28, 1859; d. Merano, Jan., 1918. He studied with Pembaur in Innsbruck; lived in Merano; was interned there as an enemy alien by the Austrians during World War I, and died in a concentration camp. He publ. *Storia della musica* (2 vols.; 1900; many reprints; in English as *A Short History of Music* (N. Y., 1902) and *Storia del violino, dei violinisti e della musica per violino* (1904).

Upton, George Putnam, American writer on music; b. Boston, Oct. 25, 1834; d. Chicago, May 19, 1919. He was graduated from Brown Univ. (1854); in 1855 went to Chicago, where in 1861 he joined the editorial staff of the 'Tribune,' acting also as music critic (until 1885); his were the first music reviews to appear in any Chicago newspaper. In 1872 he founded the Apollo Club there. —Books: *Letters of Peregrine Pickle* (1870); *Woman in Music* (1880); *The Standard Operas* (1886; new ed., 1928); *The Standard Oratorios* (1887; 12th ed., 1909); *The Standard Cantatas* (1888; 7th ed., 1899); *The Standard Symphonies* (1889); *Musical Pastels* (1902); *The Standard Light Operas* (1902); *E. Reményi, Musician, Littérateur and Man* (with G. D. Kelley; 1906); *The Standard Concert Guide* (1908; new eds., 1930, 1947); *Standard Concert Repertory* (1909); *Standard Musical Biographies* (1910); *The Song* (1915);

In Music's Land (1920). *The Standard Operas* was reissued in an enlarged form, ed. by Felix Borowski (1936; reprint, 1947). Upton ed. the autobiography of Theodore Thomas (1905). His own autobiography, *Musical Memories,* was publ. in 1908.

Upton, William Treat, American musicologist; b. Tallmadge, Ohio, Dec. 17, 1870. He was educated at Oberlin College and Cons. of Music; later studied piano with Leschetizky in Vienna (1896-98) and Joseph Lhévinne in Berlin (1913-14). From 1898 he taught piano at Oberlin Cons.; also was church organist in Cleveland (until 1918). —Books: *Art-Song in America* (Boston, 1930; supplement, 1938); *Anthony Philip Heinrich: A 19th-Century Composer in America* (N. Y., 1939); *William Henry Fry, American Journalist and Composer-Critic* (N. Y., 1954). He brought out a new ed. of O. G. Sonneck's *Bibliography of Early Secular American Music* (Washington, 1945).

Urbach (oor'-bah), **Otto,** German pianist and composer; b. Eisenach, Feb. 6, 1871; d. Dresden, Dec. 14, 1927. He studied with Iwan Knorr and Humperdinck in Frankfurt, with Draeseke in Dresden, and with Klindworth in Berlin. In 1898 he was appointed prof. of piano at the Dresden Cons. He wrote an opera, *Der Müller von Sans-Souci* (Frankfurt, 1896); an overture, *Bergfahrt;* a string quartet; a septet for wind instruments; piano pieces; many songs.

Urban (ŏŏr'-bahn), **Friedrich Julius,** German singing teacher and composer; brother of Heinrich Urban; b. Berlin, Dec. 23, 1838; d. there, July 17, 1918. He studied with Ries (violin) and Elsler (singing); was a successful singing teacher in Berlin; publ. a manual, *Die Kunst des Gesangs,* and some songs and choruses.

Urban (ŏŏr'-bahn), **Heinrich,** noted German pedagogue; brother of Friedrich Julius Urban; b. Berlin, Aug. 27, 1837; d. there, Nov. 24, 1901. He studied with Ries (violin) Laub, and others in Berlin; was a professional violinist; wrote much symphonic and chamber music; in 1881 he became prof. at Kullak's Academy in Berlin; acquired fame as a theory teacher; among his pupils was Paderewski. His works include a concert overture, *Scheherazade;* a symph., *Frühling;* a violin concerto; many violin pieces; songs.

Urbánek, Mojmir, Czech music publisher; b. Prague, May 6, 1873; d. there, Sept. 29, 1919. Son of the music publisher **Franz Urbánek** (1842-1919); left his father's firm and founded his own business in 1901, developing it into the largest of its kind in Czechoslovakia; included a music shop, printing plant, concert agency, and concert hall ('Mozarteum'); publ. works by Suk, Novák, Foerster, and other Czechoslovak composers, and the musical monthly 'Dalibor.'

Urfey, Thomas d' (known as Tom Durfey), English playwright and poet; b. Exeter, 1653; d. London, Feb. 26, 1723. He produced about 30 plays, the songs in some of which were set to music by Purcell (e.g., *The Comical History of Don Quixote,* in 3 parts, 1694-96). He ingratiated himself into the intimate circle of Charles II by his talent for singing his poems, adapted to popular airs of his time. Between 1683 and 1710 he publ. several collections of airs with music, and in 1719 he ed. *Songs Compleat, Pleasant and Divertive* (5 vols., his own songs assembled in vols. 1 and 2); this was reissued the same year under the better-known title, *Wit and Mirth: or Pills to Purge Melancholy* (a 6th vol. was added in 1720). —Cf. C. L. Day, *The Songs of Thomas D'Urfey* (Cambridge, Mass., 1933).

Urhan (ü-răhn'), **Chrétien,** French violinist, b. Montjoie, near Aix-la-Chapelle, Feb. 16, 1790; d. Paris, Nov. 2, 1845. He was a pupil of Le Sueur in composition; revived the viole d'amour, playing in Baillot's Quartet; from 1816 he was violinist (later soloist) in the Opéra orch. In the Cons. Concerts he employed a 5-stringed violin (*violon-alto,* with the tuning $c\text{-}g\text{-}d^1\text{-}a^1\text{-}e^2$), producing charming effects. He composed some chamber music. —Cf. P. D. Förster, *Chrétien Urhan* (Raigern, 1907); P. Garnault, *Chrétien Urhan,* in 'Revue de Musicologie' (1930).

Uriarte (oo-rē-ahr'tĕh), Father **Eustaquio de,** Spanish musicologist; b. Durango (province of Vizcaya), Nov. 2, 1863; d. Motrico, Sept. 17, 1900. In 1878 he entered the Augustinian Order at Valladolid and in 1888 went to the monastery of Silos, near Burgos, devoting himself to the study and restoration of Gregorian chant; was a promoter of the 'Asociación Isidoriana' for the reform of religious music in Spain. His fundamental work was the *Tratado teórico-práctico de canto gregoriano, según la verdadera tradición* (Madrid, 1891). His shorter studies were publ., with a biographical sketch, by L. Villalba: *Estética y crítica musical del padre Uriarte* (Barcelona, 1904).

Uribe-Holguín (ŏŏ-rē'-beh-ŏhl-gēn'), **Guillermo,** foremost composer of Colombia; b. Bogotá, March 17, 1880. He studied violin with Narciso Garay; in 1907 he went to Paris, where he studied with Vincent d'Indy at the Schola Cantorum; then took further violin lessons with César Thomson and Émile Chaumont in Brussels. He returned to Colombia in 1910 and became director of the newly reorganized National Cons. in Bogotá; there he conducted the student orch. He resigned in 1935 and devoted his time to his coffee plantation; however, he continued to compose and conduct. In 1910 he married the pianist Lucía Gutiérrez. His music bears the imprint of the modern French style, but his thematic material is often related to native musical resources; particularly remarkable are his *Trozos en el sentimiento popular* for piano, of which he wrote about 350; they are stylizations of Colombian melorhythms in a brilliant pianistic setting. He publ. an autobiography, *Vida de un músico colombiano* (Bogotá, 1941). —Works: for orch. (all performed by the composer in Bogotá): *Sinfonia del terruño* (Oct. 20, 1924); *Tres danzas* (May 27, 1927); *Marcha festiva* (Aug. 20, 1928); *Serenata* (Oct. 29, 1928); *Carnavalesca* (July 8, 1929); *Cantares* (Sept. 2, 1929); *Villanesca* (Sept. 1, 1930); *Bajo su ventana* (Oct. 20, 1930); *Suite típica* (Nov. 21, 1932); *Concierto a la manera antigua,* for piano and orch. (Oct. 15, 1939); *Bochica* (April 12, 1940); 2 violin concertos; *Furatena,* a lyric tragedy in 3 acts; *Te Deum,* for soli, chorus, and orch. (1920); *Requiem* (1926); other sacred works; a suite for guitar; 5 violin sonatas; 2 cello sonatas; 3 string quartets; a piano quartet; 2 piano quintets; piano pieces; songs. —Cf. F. C. Lange, *Guillermo Uribe-Holguín,* in the 'Boletín Latino-Americano de Música' (Bogotá, 1938).

Urich, Jean, composer and publisher; b. on island of Trinidad, Sept. 9, 1849; d. London, Dec. 14, 1939. He studied in Paris with Lenepveu (1868), and in London with Gounod during the latter's sojourn there (1871-74). In 1890 he founded the 'Édition Paul Dupont' in Paris, and edited 'Le Figaro musical.' —He composed the operas *L'Orage* (Brussels, 1879); *Flora Macdonald* (Bologna, 1885); *Le Pilote* (Monte Carlo, 1890); *Le Carillon* (Aix-les-Bains, 1895); *Hermann und Dorothea* (Berlin, 1899); *La Cigale et la fourmi* (as *The Cicada,* London, 1912); and *Tsing-Tau* (London, 1914).

Urio, Francesco Antonio, Italian church composer; b. Milan, c. 1660; date and place of death unknown. He became a Franciscan monk, and in 1690 was maestro at the Church of the 12 Apostles in Rome. Publ. *Motetti di concerto a 2, 3, e 4 voci con violini e senza,* op. 1 (Rome, 1690); *Salmi concertati a 3 voci con violini,* op. 2 (Bologna, 1697); also composed a Te Deum, from which Handel 'borrowed' numerous themes, chiefly for his 'Dettingen Te Deum,' and also for his *Saul* and *Israel in Egypt.* Urio's Te Deum was publ. by Chrysander in vol. 5 of his collection, 'Denkmäler der Tonkunst' (later publ. as Supplement 2 of Handel's complete works). —Cf. E. Prout, *Urio's 'Te Deum' and Handel's Use Thereof,* in the 'Monthly Mus. Record' (Nov., 1871); S. Taylor, *The Indebtedness of Handel to Works by Other Composers* (Cambridge, 1906); P. Robinson, *Handel and his Orbit* (London, 1908).

Urlus (ür'-lüs), **Jacques,** noted tenor; b. Hergenrath, near Aachen, Jan. 9, 1867; d. Noordwijk, June 6, 1935. When he was 10, his parents moved to Tilburg, Holland, and there he received his first instruction from an uncle, who was a choral conductor; then he studied engineering in Utrecht; subsequently studied singing with Cornelia van Zanten. He made his operatic début as Beppo in *Pagliacci* at Amsterdam (Sept. 20, 1894); sang there until 1900; then was engaged at the Stadtheater in Leipzig (1900-15). In 1911 he sang Siegmund in Bayreuth. He made his American début in Boston as Tristan (Feb. 12, 1912); sang this role at his first appearance with the Metropolitan Opera (Feb. 8, 1913); was Wagnerian tenor there until 1917. —Cf. O. Spengler, *Jacques Urlus* (N. Y., 1917; in German and English).

Urrutia Blondel, Jorge, Chilean composer; b. La Serena, Sept. 7, 1905. He studied at the Univ. of Chile; also with H. Allende and Domingo Santa Cruz. In 1928 he received a stipend from the Chilean government to study in Europe; spent 3 years in France and Germany; took lessons with Charles Koechlin, Paul Dukas, and Nadia Boulanger in Paris; and with Hindemith and Hans Mersmann at the Hochschule für Musik in Berlin. Returning to Chile he was appointed prof. of harmony at the Cons. in Santiago. His major work is the ballet *La Guitarra del diablo,* based on

Chilean folklore, and including stylized treatment of native dance tunes; it was performed in Santiago on Nov. 27, 1942; other works include 3 orchestral suites; *Danzas Agrestes,* for orch.; *Estampas de Chile,* for strings, harp, and celesta; piano trio; string quartet; *Pastoral de Alhué,* for flute, clarinet, celesta, harp, and strings; *Canciones campesinas,* for voice and strings; *Sugerencias de Chile,* for violin and piano; various piano pieces; simple choral works for children. —Cf. Vicente Salas Viú, *La Creación musical en Chile 1900-1951* (Santiago, 1952; pp. 459-67).

Urso (ŏŏr'-sŏh), **Camilla,** noted violinist; b. Nantes, France, June 13, 1842; d. New York, Jan. 20, 1902. Her father was an Italian musician from Palermo, and her mother a singer, a native of Lisbon. She began to study violin at home as a small child; was admitted to the Paris Cons. at the age of 9 as an exception, and studied there with Lambert Massart, but soon was taken by her father on a tour in the U. S., arriving in N. Y. in Sept. 1852, with Oscar Comettant as her accompanist. Her impresario went into bankruptcy, but she was engaged by Marietta Alboni as a joint artist for a few concerts. In 1853 she traveled with the Germania Society as far west as St. Louis; then gave concerts with Henrietta Sontag, playing in New Orleans, etc. In 1855, when she was 13, she withdrew from public appearances; lived mostly in Nashville. She resumed her career in 1862 (after her marriage to Frédéric Luères of Paris), dividing her time between Europe and America; appeared with P. S. Gilmore's band in New England; in 1879 and 1894 she visited Australia; in 1895, made a tour of South Africa; then settled in N. Y.; taught at the National Cons. of Music (1891-92); continued to appear in concerts at infrequent intervals. —Cf. C. Barnard, *Camilla: A Tale of a Violin, Being the Artist Life of Camilla Urso* (Boston, 1874).

Urspruch (ŏŏr'-shprŏŏh), **Anton,** German pianist and composer; b. Frankfurt, Feb. 17, 1850; d. there, Jan. 11, 1907. He was a pupil of Ignaz Lachner, and later of Raff and Liszt; was engaged as piano teacher at the Raff Cons. in Frankfurt (1887). He wrote an opera, *Der Sturm,* after Shakespeare's *Tempest* (Frankfurt, 1888), and a comic opera, *Das Unmöglichste von Allem,* after Lope de Vega's comedy *El major imposible* (Karlsruhe, Nov. 5, 1897). Other works include a symph., a piano concerto, a piano quintet, a piano trio, a violin sonata, a cello sonata; many piano pieces; a *Sonata quasi fantasia* for piano 4 hands; songs; also publ. a book, *Der gregorianische Choral* (1901).

Ursprung (ŏŏr'-shprŏŏng), **Otto,** German musicologist; b. Günzlhofen, Jan. 16, 1879. He studied philosophy and theology at the Univ. of Munich (1899-1904), and became a Catholic priest; studied musicology with Sandberger and Kroyer; *Dr. phil.* (Munich, 1911); his doctoral thesis was on Jacobus de Kerle, whose selected works he edited for the 'Denkmäler der Tonkunst in Bayern' (vol. 26). In 1932 he was appointed honorary prof. of the Univ. of Munich. —Books: *Restauration und Palestrina-Renaissance in der katholischen Kirchenmusik* (Augsburg, 1924); *Münchens Musikalische Vergangenheit* (Munich, 1927); *Die katholische Kirchenmusik* (Potsdam, 1931). He publ. articles on a variety of subjects, ranging from Catholic church music to Oriental music; brought out a posthumous ed. of Kurt Huber's lectures, under the title *Musikästhetik* (1954).

Ursuleac, Viorica, soprano, b. Cernauti, Rumania, March 26, 1899. She studied at the State Academy in Vienna; joined the Berlin Opera in 1933; was also connected with the Vienna Opera from 1934; created the role of Maria in Richard Strauss's opera *Der Friedenstag* (1938). She was the wife of the conductor Clemens Krauss (q.v.).

Usandizaga (oo-sahn-dē-thăh'-găh), **José María,** Spanish (Basque) composer; b. San Sebastián, March 31, 1887; d. Yanti, Oct. 5, 1915. He studied piano with Planté, and composition with Vincent d'Indy at the Schola Cantorum in Paris; upon his return to Spain he associated himself with the Basque musical movement, to which he gave a great impetus with his opera *Mendy-Mendiyan,* produced at Bilbao in 1910. In his next stage work, however, he abandoned the local terrain and chose a subject of universal appeal, the story of Pierrot, as embodied in a libretto by the noted playwright Martínez Sierra; this opera, entitled *Las Golondrinas* (*The Swallows*), was produced with tremendous success at the Teatro Price in Madrid on Feb. 5, 1914, being acclaimed as a milestone in the creation of a national Spanish opera. With his gift of melody and his keen sense of the theater, Usandizaga might have carried the Spanish lyric drama to great heights; but he died of tuberculosis at the untimely age of 28. His last opera was *La Llama* (*The Flame*), produced in Madrid in 1915. He also wrote several symph. pieces: *En la mar, Obertura sinfónica, Irurak-Bat, Hassan y Melihah,* etc.; *Ume Zuríza* (*The Orphan*) for soli with orch.; 2 string quartets; many piano pieces on Basque themes (*Los Reyes Magos, Rapsodia Vascongada,* etc.). —Cf. L. Villalba, *J. M. Usandizaga* (1918).

Usiglio, Emilio, Italian conductor and composer; b. Parma, Jan. 8, 1841; d. Milan, July 7, 1910. He studied with Mabellini; was a successful opera conductor; gave the first Italian performance of *Carmen.* He was married to the singer Clementina Brusa. —Works: operas: *La Locandiera* (Turin, Sept. 5, 1861); *L'Eredità in Corsica* (Milan, June 17, 1864); *Le Educande di Sorrento* (Florence, May 1, 1868); *La Scommessa* (Florence, July 6, 1870); *Le Donne curiose* (Madrid, Feb. 11, 1879); *Le Nozze in prigione* (Milan, March 23, 1881); several ballets. Also publ. some humorous verse.

Usmanbas, Ilkan, Turkish composer; b. Constantinople, Sept. 28, 1921. He studied at the Ankara Cons. with Saygun; in 1948, appointed teacher there. In 1952 he made a tour of the U. S. —Works: violin concerto (1946); symph. (Ankara, April 20, 1950); *Music* for string orch., percussion, piano, and narrator (1950); *Mortuary,* for narrator, chorus, and orch. (1952-53); clarinet quintet (1949); oboe sonata (1949); trumpet sonata (1949); piano music; choruses.

Uspensky, Victor Alexandrovitch, Russian composer; b. Kaluga, Aug. 31, 1879; d. Tashkent, Oct. 9, 1949. He was brought up in Central Asia, where his father held a government post; then served in the Russian army; learned to play the violin; entered the St. Petersburg Cons. at the age of 29, and studied composition with Liadov, graduating in 1913. In 1918 he went to Tashkent, where he organized a music school, and taught theoretical subjects. From 1932 to 1948 he was in charge of the Musical Folklore Division of Uzbekistan; worked towards the restoration of native musical instruments. In 1925-28 he took part in an ethnographical expedition in Turkmenia, collecting a number of songs. Out of this authentic material he fashioned an Uzbek opera, *Farhad and Shirin,* produced in Tashkent on Feb. 26, 1936 (new version, Moscow, Uzbek Festival, May, 1937). Other works include an orch. suite on Uzbek themes, *Mukanna* (1944); *Turkmenian Capriccio* for orch. (1945); *Uzbek Rhapsody* for orch. (1946); choral works; piano pieces; songs. He collaborated with Victor Belaiev in a scholarly treatise, *Turkmenian Music* (Moscow, 1928); publ. numerous arrangements of Uzbek songs. —Cf. Yan Pekker, *V. A. Uspensky* (Moscow, 1953).

Ussachevsky (ŏŏ-săh-chĕf'-skē), **Vladimir,** Russian-American composer; b. Hailar, Manchuria (of Russian parents), Nov. 3, 1911. He came to America in 1930; studied at Pomona, Calif., graduating from Pomona College in 1935; then at the Eastman School of Music, Rochester, with Howard Hanson and Bernard Rogers; received his Ph. D. there in 1939. He was in the American army during World War II; in 1947, was appointed to the faculty of Columbia Univ. His works include *Jubilee Cantata,* for chorus and orch. (1938); *Theme and Variations,* for orch. (1935); *Miniatures for a Curious Child,* for orch. (1950); piano concerto (1951); piano sonata (1952); songs and choruses. He became interested in electronic music; perfected an instrument capable of transforming recorded music in various ways, producing automatically repeated notes and divers dynamic effects; composed and arranged a piece called *Sonic Contours,* for tape recorder with instruments (Museum of Modern Art, N. Y., Oct. 28, 1952); with Otto Luening he composed a *Poem of Cycles and Bels,* for tape recorder and orch. (Los Angeles, Nov. 18, 1954) and other works of a similar nature.

Utendal, Alexander, Dutch composer; b. Netherlands, c. 1530; d. Innsbruck, May 8, 1581. He was court musician to the Archduke Ferdinand of Austria at Innsbruck. Publ. 7 Penitential Psalms (1570); 3 books of motets (1570-77); Masses and Magnificats (1573); and *Fröliche neue teutsche und französische Lieder* for 4-8 voices (1574 and other eds.). Reprints in Proske, 'Musica Divina' (vol. IV), and W.. Barclay Squire, 'Ausgewählte Madrigale,' etc. —Cf. H. Osthoff, *Die Niederländer und das deutsche Lied* (1938; p. 333 ff.).

Uttini, Francesco Antonio Baltassare, Italian composer; b. Bologna, 1723; d. Stockholm, Oct. 25, 1795. He studied with Perti; in 1743 he became a member of the Accademia dei Filarmonici in Bologna. He first appeared as a singer; in 1755 he went to Stockholm as conductor of an Italian opera company, and remained there until his death, except for a visit to London in 1768. He was court conductor at the Stockholm Opera from 1767 to 1787, and wrote

7 Italian and 5 French operas. Historically he is important as the composer of the earliest operas on Swedish texts; the first, *Thetis och Pelée,* was written for the inauguration of the new opera house (Jan. 18, 1773); another opera to a Swedish libretto, translated from the French, was *Aline Drotning uti Golconda* (*Aline Queen of Golconda*) produced at the Stockholm Opera on Jan. 11, 1776. Of Uttini's Italian operas the best is *Il Re pastore* (Stockholm, July 24, 1755). A great admirer of Gluck, he brought out many of that composer's works in Stockholm. He also wrote 2 oratorios, 3 symphonies (for 4, 6, and 8 instruments), 12 sonatas, 9 trios for 2 violins with continuo. 6 of his sonatas were publ. at London in 1768. —Cf. E. Sundström, *F. A. Uttini och Adolf Fredriks italienska operatrupp,* in 'Svensk Tidskrift för Musikforskning' (vol. 13; 1931).

V

Vaccai, Niccolò, Italian composer and singing teacher; b. Tolentino, March 15, 1790; d. Pesaro, Aug. 5, 1848. He went to Rome as a youth and took lessons in counterpoint with Jannaconi; then studied with Paisiello in Naples (from 1812). He became a singing teacher in Venice (1818-21), Trieste (1821-23), Vienna (1823), Paris (1829-31), and London (1832), with an ever-growing reputation; was prof. of composition at the Milan Cons. (1838-44); in 1844 he retired to Pesaro, where he remained until his death. —Operas: *Pietro il Grande* (Parma, Jan. 17, 1824); *La Pastorella feudataria* (Turin, Sept. 18, 1824); *Giulietta e Romeo,* after Shakespeare (Milan, Oct. 31, 1825; the last scene was often used in performances of Bellini's *I Capuleti e i Montecchi*); his subsequent 9 operas were failures. He publ. *Metodo pratico di canto italiano per camera;* and *12 ariette per camera, per l'insegnamento del belcanto italiano.* —Cf. G. Vaccai, *Vita di N. Vaccai* (Bologna, 1882).

Vach, Ferdinand, Moravian choral leader; b. Jažlovice, Feb. 25, 1860; d. Brno, Feb. 16, 1939. He studied at the Organ School in Prague; 1886, appointed conductor of the 'Moravian' choir at Kroměříž; also taught singing at the Pedagogium there, and from among his pupils formed the Moravian Teachers' Choir in 1903, with which he toured in Germany, Russia, and England (1919). In 1905 he became prof. at the Teachers' School in Brno; composed choruses and cantatas; church music.

Vachon (văhsh-ŏhn'), **Pierre,** violinist and composer; b. Arles, 1731; d. Berlin, 1802. Pupil of Chabran in Paris from 1751; played at the Concert Spirituel in 1758; from 1761, solo violinist to the Prince de Conti; from 1784, at the Royal Chapel in Berlin; pensioned in 1798. Besides stage works, he composed violin concertos, string quartets, trios, sonatas, etc. (publ. in Paris, London, and Berlin). —A quartet for strings and continuo (op. 5, no. 3) was ed. by Sidney Beck for the N. Y. Public Library (1937).

Vačkář, Dalibor, composer; b. Korčula, Yugoslavia, Sept. 19, 1905. He studied at the Prague Cons.; played violin on the Prague Radio; then devoted himself to composition for the films. Under the name Dalibor Faltis he published poetry and drama. Among his musical works are 4 symphonies; the 3rd bears the curious title (in English), *Smoking Symphony* (1948); he also wrote a *Smoking Sonata* (1936); a violin concerto; and a quartet for oboe, clarinet, bassoon, and piano.

Vaet (vaht), **Jacobus,** Flemish composer; b. Courtrai, 1529; d. Vienna, Jan. 8, 1567. He was a choirboy in the Church of Notre Dame at Courtrai (1543-46); after his voice changed, he received a subsidy for 2 years of further study; on Jan. 1, 1554, he was listed as Kapellmeister of the chapel of Maximilian, then the nominal King of Bohemia. His position was enhanced when his patron became Emperor Maximilian II. Vaet's music exhibits a great variety of techniques, ranging in style from those of Josquin des Prez to those of Lassus. The formative influence, however, is mainly that of Nicolas Gombert, with a characteristic florid imitation in contrapuntal parts. The extant works of Vaet comprise 82 motets and hymns, 10 Masses, 8 Magnificats, and 3 chansons; a relatively large number of his motets (at least 11) are ceremonial, written to celebrate state or court occasions. 2 vols. of his motets, *Modulationes 5 vocum* and *Modulationes 5 et 6 vocum,* were publ. in 1562 by Gardano in Venice; a 6-voice motet, *Qui operatus est Petro,* was printed in luxurious format on a large single parchment sheet by Hofhalter of Vienna in 1560 (facsimile in Haas, *Aufführungspraxis der Musik,* Potsdam, 1931, p. 129). Zacconi printed a hymn in his *Prattica di musica,* Libro I, folio 50. Vaet is represented also in the publications of Berg and Neuber (30 motets), Giovanelli (24 motets), Susato (7 motets), Gerlach (3 motets), Phalèse (3 motets, 2 chansons), Stephani (2 motets, 1 chanson), Waelrant and Laet (1 chanson), Nicolas du Chemin (1 chanson), and Rühling (1 motet in organ tablature). Reprints appear in Commer's *Collectio operum musicorum Batavorum* (20 motets) and his *Musica sacra* (1 Mass), and in Maldeghem, *Trésor musical* (1 motet). E. H. Meyer edited *Jacobus Vaet, Sechs Motetten* as vol. 2 of 'Das Chorwerk,' 1929, and Milton Steinhardt edited *Jacobus Vaet, Zwei Hymnen* as vol. 8 of 'Musik alter Meister' (1958). —Cf. Milton Steinhardt, *Jacobus Vaet and His Motets* (Michigan State College Press, 1951; thematic index and 3 complete works included); Milton Steinhardt, *The Hymns of Jacobus Vaet,* in the 'Journal of the American Musicological Society' (Fall, 1956); G. Reese, *Music in the Renaissance* (N. Y., 1954; pp. 700-01).

Vainberg, Moysey Samuilovitch, Russian composer; b. Warsaw, Dec. 8, 1919. He studied piano with Turczynski at the Warsaw Cons. and composition with Zolotarev in Minsk; he was in Tashkent in 1941-43; in 1943 settled in Moscow. —Works: opera, *The Sword of Uzbekistan* (Tashkent, 1941); ballet, *For the Fatherland* (Tashkent, 1941); cantata, *In the Native Land* (Moscow, Feb. 1, 1953); 3 symphonies (1942, 1946, 1949); *Symphonietta* (Kiev, Nov. 13, 1948); *Rhapsody on Moldavian Themes* (Moscow, Nov. 30, 1949); *Serenade* for orch. (Moscow, Nov. 7, 1954); cello concerto (1943); *Moldavian Rhapsody* for violin and orch. (Moscow, Oct. 21, 1951); piano quintet (1944); 6 string quartets; piano trio; string trio; 4 piano sonatas; 5 violin sonatas; cello sonata; clarinet sonata; flute sonata; many songs; music for films.

Valabrega, Cesare, Italian pianist and writer on music; b. Novara, Dec. 27, 1898. He studied piano at the Cons. of Pesaro and literature at the Univ. of Bologna; taught music history in Naples and Perugia; then settled in Rome as lecturer and critic. —Books: *Schumann: arte e natura; arte e vita; arte e fede* (1934; 3rd ed., 1956); *Domenico Scarlatti: il suo secolo, la sua opera* (1937; 2nd ed., 1955); *Il piccolo dizionario musicale per tutti* (1929; 2nd ed., 1952); *Johann Sebastian Bach* (1950); *La Lirica di camera di Vincenzo Davico* (1953).

Valcárcel (vahl-kahr'-sĕhl), **Teodoro,** Peruvian composer; b. Puno, Oct. 18, 1900; d. Lima, March 20, 1942. He studied at the Cons. of Milan and with Felipe Pedrell in Barcelona. Returning to Peru in 1920, he settled in Lima; in 1928 he won the National Prize for Peruvian composers, and was awarded a gold medal from the municipality of Lima for his studies in Peruvian folk music. In 1929 he went to Europe once more; presented a concert of his works in Paris (April 12, 1930). He was of pure Indian origin; as a native of the highlands, he was able to collect Indian songs unpolluted by urban influences. He publ. *30 Cantos de alma vernacular; 4 Canciones incaicas; 25 Romances de costa y sierra peruana; 180 Melodías del folklore.* Among his original works are the ballets (with singing) *Suray-Surita* and *Ckori Kancha;* a symph. poem, *En las ruinas del Templo del Sol* (1940); a violin concerto, entitled *Concierto indio* (1939); *3 Ensayos* for an ensemble of native instruments; *Fiestas andinas* for piano; *Suite autóctona* for violin and piano; songs. —A catalogue of his works was publ. by R. Holzmann in 'Boletín Bibliográfico' (Lima, Dec., 1942).

Valderrábano. See **Enriquez de Valderrábano.**

Valderrama, Carlos, Peruvian composer; b. Trujillo, Sept. 4, 1887; d. Lima, Aug. 1, 1950. He studied engineering at Cornell Univ., then decided to devote himself to music; made his début as a pianist at Carnegie Hall, N. Y. (Feb. 22, 1920). He wrote many piano pieces on old Inca themes, in a salon style (several of them published), and some ballet music.

Valdrighi (văhl-drē'gē), **Luigi Francesco,** Italian music scholar; b. Modena, July 30, 1827; d. there, April 20, 1899. For his valuable researches regarding music and musicians in Modena he was made honorary member of the Academy of Arts and Sciences there, and of the Accademia Santa Cecilia in Rome. His collection of early musical instruments, exhibited in Bologna (1899), he bequeathed to the Museum of his native city. Under the collective title 'Musurgiana' he publ. a number of monographs on the music and musicians of Modena (1879-93); in the 'Memorie della Accademia modenese' he publ. *I Bononcini di Modena* (1882), *Cappelle, concerti e musiche di casa d'Este* (1884), and *Il Phagotus d'Afranio* (1895); also publ. *Ricerche sulla liuteria e violineria modenese antica e moderna* (1878) and *Nomocheliurgografia antica e moderna* (1884; with 2 supplements, 1888 and 1894). Together with G. Ferrari-Moreni he completed A. Gandini's *Cronistoria dei teatri di Modena* (1873). —Cf. E. Zoccoli, *Il Conte L. F. V.* (Modena, 1899).

Valen, Fartein, noted Norwegian composer; b. Stavanger, Aug. 25, 1887; d. Haugesund, Dec. 14, 1952. His father was a missionary in Madagascar, and Valen spent his early youth there. Upon returning to Norway he studied with Elling in Oslo and later with Max Bruch in Berlin. His early music shows the influence of Brahms and Reger. About 1924, he developed a system of 'atonal polyphony,' completely free from traditional tonal relationships, but strongly cohesive in contrapuntal fabric and greatly varied in rhythm. He never adopted the 12-tone method of composition, but a parallelism with Schoenberg's music is observable. Valen stood apart from all nationalist developments in Norway, and was a solitary figure in this respect; however he was appreciated, and in 1935 received a state pension. A Valen Society was organized during his last year of life. His works include 5 symphonies; *Sonetto di Michelangelo* (1932; Copenhagen Festival of the International Society for Contemporary Music, June 2, 1947); *Epithalamion* (1933); *Le Cimetière marin,* symph. poem (1934); *La Isla de las calmas* (1934); *Ode to Solitude* (1939); violin concerto (1940; Amsterdam Festival of the International Society for Contemporary Music, June 12, 1948); *Mignon,* 2 songs to Goethe's words for soprano and orch. (1927); *Darest thou now, O soul* (Walt Whitman), for soprano and orch. (1928); piano trio (1924); 2 string quartets (1929; 1931); serenade for 5 wind instruments (1947); violin sonata (1916); several piano pieces, including a sonata, surnamed *The Hound of Heaven,* after Francis Thompson (1941); choral works a cappella; songs. —Cf. K. Lange, *Fartein Valen,* in 'Nordisk Musikkultur' (Feb., 1953).

Valencia, Antonio María, Colombian pianist and composer; b. Cali, Nov. 10, 1902; d. there, July 22, 1952. He studied at the Schola Cantorum in Paris (from 1923) with Vincent d'Indy and Paul Le Flem; returning to Colombia in 1930, he founded the Cali Cons., and was its director until his death, with the exception of a brief period of directorship of the Bogotá Cons. (1937-38). He gave piano recitals in Europe and America. —Works: *Chirimía y bambuco sotareño* for orch. (1942); *Egloga incaica* for flute, oboe, clarinet, and bassoon (1935); *Emociones caucanas,* for piano, violin, and cello (1938); numerous pieces for piano solo, inspired by native melorhythms *(8 Ritmos y cantos suramericanos, Sonatina boyacense,* etc.); a Requiem (1943) and other church music; choruses and songs.

Valente, Antonio (known as 'il Cieco,' i.e. the blind man), Italian organist and composer; b. Naples, about 1520. Blind from infancy, he played the organ; was organist at Sant'Angelo a Nido in Naples. His first publication, *Intavolatura de cimbalo: Recercate, fantasie et canzoni francese desminuite con alcuni tenori balli et varie sorti de contraponti . . .* (Naples, 1575), is in Spanish keyboard tablature and contains early keyboard fantasias, written out in detail; his 2nd book, *Versi spirituali sopra tutte le note, con diversi canoni spartiti per suonar negli organi, messe, vespere et altri offici divini* (Naples, 1580), represents an early type of keyboard partitura; 3 numbers were reprinted by L. Torchi in 'L'Arte Musicale in Italia' (vol. 3): —Cf. N. Caravaglios, *Una nuova 'Intavolatura de Cimbalo' di Antonio Valente Cieco,* in the 'Rivista Musicale Italiana' (vol. XXIII, p. 491); Willi Apel, *Neapolitan Links between Cabezón and Frescobaldi,* in the 'Mus. Quarterly' (Oct., 1938).

Valente, Giorgio. See **Vitalis, George.**

Valente, Vincenzo, Italian operetta composer; b. Corigliano Calabro, Feb. 21, 1855; d. Naples, Sept. 6, 1921. At the age of 15 he wrote a song, *Ntuniella,* which became popular; continued writing Neapolitan songs of great appeal *(Basta ca po', Comme te voglio amà!, Canzone Cafona, Mugliera comme fa, Ninuccia, Tiempe felice, L'Acqua,* etc.), about 400 songs in all. He also brought out numerous operettas: *I Granatieri* (Turin, Oct. 26, 1889), *La Sposa di Charolles* (Rome, March 3, 1894), *Rolandino* (Turin, Oct. 15, 1897), *L'Usignuolo* (Naples, May 10, 1899), *Lena* (Foggia, Jan. 1, 1918), *L'Avvocato Trafichetti* (Naples, May 24, 1919), *Nèmesi* (posthumous, Naples, July 23, 1923). His son, **Nicola Valente** (b. Naples, Aug. 28, 1881), was also a composer of Neapolitan songs and light operas.

Valentin, Erich, German musicologist; b. Strasbourg, Nov. 27, 1906. He studied with Otto Volkmann in Magdeburg, and with Sandberger in Munich (Ph. D., 1928); held several posts as lecturer on music and librarian. From 1957, co-editor of 'Neue Zeitschrift für Musik.' —Books: *Die Entwicklung der Tokkata im 17. und 18. Jahrhundert* (Munich dissertation; Münster, 1930); *Georg Philipp Telemann: eine Biographie* (Burg, 1931; 2nd ed., Hamelin, 1947); *Richard Wagner* (Regensburg, 1937); *Dichtung und Oper: eine Unterswchung zum*

Stilproblem der Oper (Leipzig, 1938); *Hans Pfitzner* (Regensburg, 1939); *Wege zu Mozart* (Regensburg, 1941; 4th ed., 1950); *Beethoven* (Salzburg, 1942; English transl., N. Y., 1958); *W. A. Mozart: Wesen und Wandlung* (Hamelin, 1948); *Handbuch der Chormusik* (Regensburg, 1953); *Handbuch der Instrumentenkunde* (Regensburg, 1954); contributed articles to various musical magazines; brought out editions of works by Mozart, Telemann, etc.

Valentini, Giovanni, Italian composer; b. Venice; d. Vienna, April, 1649. He was a pupil of Giovanni Gabrieli; from 1614, organist to the Archduke Ferdinand at Graz, becoming court organist at Vienna when Ferdinand ascended the throne in 1619; in 1629 succeeded Prioli as Imperial Kapellmeister. He was a renowned teacher of organ. Publ. *Motetti a 6 voci* (1611); 5 books of madrigals for 3 to 11 voices with instruments; *Musiche a 2 voci* with bass for organ (1622); *Canzoni per sonar,* 4-8 voices; in MS, Masses, Magnificats, a Stabat Mater, and sonatas. Riemann published an 'Enharmonische Sonate' in 'Alte Kammermusik' but its authenticity is disputed.

Valentini, Giuseppe, Italian violinist and composer; b. c. 1681; d. c. 1740. He was at Rome in 1700; from 1710 at Bologna in the service of the Prince di Caserta, and from 1735 at the grand-ducal court of Florence. His violin technique was highly developed (some compositions call for the 6th position). Publ. 12 *Sinfonie* for 2 violins and continuo (organ); 7 *Bizarrerie* for 2 violins and cello; 12 *Fantasie* for 2 violins and continuo; 12 *Suonate* for the same; *Idee per camera* for violin solo and cello (or cembalo); 12 *Concerti grossi* for strings and continuo; 12 *Sonate o Alletamenti* for violin and continuo. —Modern reprints ed. by O. Respighi, G. Salmon, A. Moffat, etc.

Valentini, Pier Francesco, Italian theorist and composer of the Roman School; b. Rome, c. 1570; d. there, 1654. He was a pupil of G. M. Nanini. Publ. *Canone . . . sopra le parole del Salve Regina, 'Illos tuos misericordes oculos ad nos converte,' con le resolutioni a 2, 3, 4 e 5 voci* (1629; a canon with over 2000 possible resolutions; the theme is in Kircher's *Musurgia,* I, p. 402); *Canone nel nodo di Salomone a 96 voci* (1631; also in *Musurgia,* I, p. 104); *Canone a 6, 10, 20 voci* (1645); 2 books of madrigals *a 5* with continuo ad lib. and 2 books of motets with instruments (1654); 6 books of *Canzonetti spirituali* for 1 to 4 voices (1655-56); 2 books of *Musiche spirituali* for 1 and 2 voices, *Canzoni, sonetti ed arie a voce sola,* 4 books of *Conzonette ed arie a 1, 2 voci* (all 1657); 2 books of litanies and motets for 2 to 4 voices. Also 2 stage works *(favole), La Mitra* and *La Trasformazione di Dafne* (both 1654), and several theoretical works (in MS). —Cf. L. Kurz, *Die Tonartenlehre des römischen Theoretikers und Komponisten P. F. Valentini* (dissertation; Kassel, 1937).

Valentino, Henri-Justin-Armand-Joseph, French conductor; b. Lille, Oct. 14, 1785; d. Versailles, Jan. 20, 1865. In 1820 he was 2nd conductor, and in 1824 became 1st conductor, at the Opéra in Paris; from 1831 to 1837 was conductor at the Opéra-Comique; then founded a society of popular concerts of classical music, as a rival enterprise to the Conservatory Concerts, at the Salle St.-Honoré (since called the 'Salle Valentino'), but discontinued them in 1841.

Valerius, Adrianus (Adriaan), Dutch musician; b. Middelburg, 1575; d. Veer, Jan. 27, 1625. From 1606 lived in Veer as a notary; publ. an important lute-tablature book, *Nederlandtsche Gedenckclanck* (Haarlem, 1626; reprinted in part in the publ. of the 'Vereeniging voor Nederlandsche Muziekgeschiedenis denis' II [1871]; 2nd ed., The Hague, 1893; 3rd ed., Utrecht, 1931; new ed., Amsterdam, 1942). —Cf. J. W. Enschedé, *De Wilhelmus-melodie in de Gedenckclanck van Valerius,* in the 'Tijdschrift' of the Vereeniging voor Nederlandsche Muziekgeschiedenis (vol. 5; 1897); see also 'Six Ancient Songs of the Netherlands, from A. V.' (ed. by E. Kremser; English text by Th. Baker; N. Y., 1894).

Vallas, Léon, French writer on music; b. Roanne (Loire), May 17, 1879; d. Lyons, May 9, 1956. After studying medicine in Lyons, he took up music; in 1903 founded the 'Revue Musicale de Lyon' (from 1912 to 1914 this was known as the 'Revue de Musique Française,' and from 1920 to 1929, as 'Nouvelle Revue Musicale'); in 1908 he was engaged as lecturer on music history at the Univ. of Lyons. —Books: *La Musique à l'Académie de Lyon au XVIIIe siècle* (part of his doctoral thesis, Lyons, 1908; the complete work was publ. as *Un Siècle de musique et de théâtre à Lyon, 1688-1789,* Lyons, 1932); *Le Théâtre et la ville, 1694-1712* (1919); *Les Idées de Claude Debussy, musicien français* (Paris, 1927; English transl. as *The Theories of Claude Debussy,* London, 1929); *Georges Migot* (Paris, n.d.); *Claude Debussy et son temps* (Paris, 1932; English transl. as *Claude Debussy, His Life and Works,* London, 1933); *Achille-Claude Debussy,* a brief biography (Paris, 1944); a 2-vol. biography of Vincent d'Indy: vol. 1, *La Jeunesse (1851-1886);* vol. 2, *La Maturité, la vieillesse (1886-1931),* publ. in Paris (1946; 1950); *La véritable histoire de César Franck* (Paris, 1950; in English as *César Franck,* London, 1951).

Valle de Paz. See **Del Valle de Paz.**

Valle-Riestra (vahl'-yeh-rē-ehs'-trăh), **José María,** Peruvian composer; b. Lima, Nov. 9, 1859; d. there, Jan. 25, 1925. He studied as a child in London; after his return to Lima, he continued his musical education without a teacher; as a mature musician, he went to Paris for further studies, with André Gedalge (1895-97). When the Academia Nacional de Música was organized in Lima, he was appointed prof. there. In his compositions, it was his aim to contribute towards the establishment of a national school by the employment of old Inca melodies. His opera *Ollanta* (Lima, Dec. 26, 1900) was a successful dramatization of an Inca subject. His other two operas on Inca themes were *Las Rosas de Jamaica* (1 act), and *Atahualpa* (3 acts). He also wrote *Misa de Requiem* for chorus and orch.; *En Oriente* for orch.; *Elegía* for string orch.; choruses a cappella; songs.

Valleria (real name Schoening), **Alwina,** American soprano; b. Baltimore, Oct. 12, 1848; d. Nice, Feb. 17, 1925. She studied singing in London with Luigi Arditi; made her first appearance in London (June 2, 1871); was engaged to sing Italian opera at St. Petersburg; returning to England, she became very successful in opera, including the Wagnerian repertory. She made her American début as Marguérite (N. Y., Oct. 22, 1879); sang Leonora at the Metropolitan Opera House (Oct. 26, 1883); but then retired from the stage.

Vallet (văh-lā'), **Nicolas,** French lutenist; b. Cocheni, 1583; d. Amsterdam, c. 1626. In 1615 he publ. at Amsterdam a book of French, German, and English songs, also preludes, fantasias, etc., in lute tablature: *Secretum Musarum* (2nd ed., 1618, with the title *Paradisus musicus testudinis*); also publ. *Le second livre de tabulature de luth* (1618), and *21 Psaumes de David* (in lute tablature; 1619).

Vallotti, Francesco Antonio, Italian theorist and composer; b. Vercelli, June 11, 1697; d. Padua, Jan. 10, 1780. A Franciscan monk, he was a pupil of Calegari at Padua; from 1728, maestro at the church of S. Antonio. He was one of the foremost organists of his time. —Publ. works: *Responsoria in parasceve, Resp. in Sabbato Sancto,* and *Resp. in Coena Domini,* all *a* 4 (Masses, motets, etc., in MS at Padua); and *Della scienza teorica e pratica della moderna musica,* Book 1 (Padua, 1779; republ. by Bernandino Rizzi, Padua, 1950; other 3 books unpubl.), a learned work agreeing in the main principles with Rameau and Tartini, and correcting some of their errors; Vallotti's system is explained in *La vera idea delle musicali numeriche signature,* by L. A. Sabbatini, who, like Abbé Vogler, was Vallotti's pupil. —Cf. L. A. Sabbatini, *Notizie sopra la vita e le opere di F. A. Vallotti* (Padua, 1780).

Valvasensi, Lazaro, Italian organist and composer; b. Valvasone (Udine), c. 1600; date of death unknown. In 1622, he was organist at Murano (Venice); in 1626, choirmaster at Tolmezzo (Udine); from 1634-40, organist at Valvasone. Publ. *Letanie della B. V. a 5 voci, con un Mottetto nell' ultimo concertato per sonar nell'Organo* (Venice, 1622); *Compieta concertata a 4 voci* with continuo (Venice, 1626); *Secondo giardino d'amorosi fiori* (23 solo airs and 1 duet, with instrumental accompaniment; Venice, 1634; unique copy at Christ Church, Oxford).

Valverde (văhl-věhr'-děh), **Joaquín,** Spanish composer of light opera; b. Badajoz, Feb. 27, 1846; d. Madrid, March 17, 1910. He played the flute in bands from the age of 13; then studied at the Cons. of Madrid; received a prize for his orchestral work, *Batylo* (1871). From 1871 to 1889 he conducted theater orchestras in Madrid; taught flute at the Madrid Cons., and wrote melodic studies for his instrument. In collaboration with Chueca (q.v.), he wrote a number of zarzuelas, of which the most celebrated was *La gran vía* (Madrid, July 2, 1886; produced in London on April 18, 1906 as *Castles in Spain*); it contains the march *Cádiz,* which became immensely popular. — His son, **Joaquín Valverde y San Juan,** known under his diminutive given name **Quinito** (b. Madrid, Jan. 2, 1875; d. Mexico City, Nov. 4, 1918), was also a composer; wrote some 250 light pieces for the theater; his zarzuela *El gran capitán* was especially successful. He died during an American tour which he undertook as conductor of a light opera company.

Van Aerde, Raymond (Joseph Justin), Belgian musicologist; b. Mechlin, June 4, 1876; d. there, March, 1944. He was librarian and lecturer on music history at the Cons. of Mechlin. His writings include a life of Cipriano de Rore (Mechlin, 1909); *Les Tuerlinckx, luthiers à Malines* (Mechlin, 1914); *Ménestrels communaux et instrumentistes . . . à Malines de 1311 à 1790* (Mechlin, 1911); *Musicalia; documents pour servir à l'histoire de la musique . . . à Malines* (2 vols.; Mechlin, 1925-30); *Les Ancêtres flamands de Beethoven* (Mechlin, 1928).

Van Beinum, Eduard. See **Beinum.**

Van Bree, Joannes. See **Bree.**

Van Cleve, John Smith, American pianist and composer; b. Maysville, Ky., Oct. 30, 1851; d. New York, Dec. 28, 1917. He became totally blind at the age of 9; studied with Apthorp in Boston; was active in Cincinnati as a piano teacher and music critic (1879-97); then lived in Chicago; in 1913 moved to N. Y. He publ. a *Gavotte humoresque* for piano, and some other pieces. —Cf. L. C. Elson, *The History of American Music* (N. Y., 1904; p. 331).

Van den Boorn-Coclet (koh-klā'), **Henriette,** Belgian composer; b. Liège, Jan. 15, 1866; d. there, March 6, 1945. She studied with Radoux and Dupuis at the Liège Cons., and subsequently taught harmony there. Her compositions attracted considerable attention. She wrote a symph.; a symph. poem, *Le Renouveau;* a *Sérénade,* for cello and piano; various piano pieces (*Mazurka, Caprice,* etc.); songs.

Van den Borren, Charles (-Jean-Eugène), eminent Belgian musicologist; b. Ixelles, near Brussels, Nov. 17, 1874. He studied theory with E. Closson; after receiving the degree of *Dr. juris,* he practiced law until 1905; then devoted himself to historical research in music; became one of the greatest authorities on the music of the Renaissance; was lecturer at the Univ. of Liège (1927-44); from 1926, prof. of music history at the Université Libre of Brussels; held many positions in learned societies. —Writings: *L'Œuvre dramatique de César Franck* (1907); *Les Origines de la musique de clavecin en Angleterre* (1912; English transl. as *The Sources of Keyboard Music in England,* 1914); *Les Musiciens belges en Angleterre à l'époque de la Renaissance* (1913); *Les Origines de la musique de clavecin dans les Pays-Bas (Nord et Sud) jusque vers 1630* (1914); *Les Débuts de la musique à Venise* (1914); *Orlande de Lassus* (1920); *Le Manuscrit musical M.222 C.22 de la Bibliothèque de Strasbourg* (Antwerp, 1924); *Guillaume Dufay* (1926); *Études sur le quinzième siècle musical* (Antwerp, 1941); *Peter Benoît* (Brussels, 1942); *Roland de Lassus* (Brussels, 1944); *Geschiedenis van de muziek in de Nederlanden* (2 vols.; Antwerp, 1948-51); etc. He edited 'Polyphonia sacra' (15th-century pieces; publ. London, 1932); 'Pièces polyphoniques profanes de provenance liégeoise (XVe siècle)' (Brussels, 1950); co-editor of the collected works of Philippe de Monte (1927 ff.). —A compendium, *Hommage à Charles Van den Borren* (Antwerp, 1945), contains a list of his works; cf. also A. Van der Linden, *Les septante-cinq ans de Charles Van den Borren,* in 'Revue Belge de Musicologie' (vol. 3; 1949).

Van den Eeden. See **Eeden.**

Van der Horst, Anton. See **Horst.**

Van der Linden, Cornelis, Dutch conductor and composer; b. Dordrecht, Aug. 24, 1839; d. there, May 28, 1918. He studied with Kwast (piano) and F. Böhme (theory); after sojourns in Belgium, Paris, and Germany, he conducted various choral organizations; from 1875, also led symphony concerts; he was conductor of the newly established Neederlandsche Oper in Amsterdam (1888-94); produced 2 of his own operas there: *Catharina en Lambert* (Nov. 24, 1888) and *Leiden Ontzet* (*The Relief of Leiden;* April 1, 1893); he also wrote 7 overtures, cantatas, piano sonatas, and many choral works and songs.

Van der Straeten (strāh'-ten), **Edmond,** Belgian music historian; b. Audenarde, Dec. 3, 1826; d. there, Nov. 26, 1895. He studied philosophy in Ghent; went to Brussels in 1857 as secretary to Fétis, with whom he studied counterpoint. He held a lifelong position at the Royal Library, and rarely left Belgium; was active as music critic (1859-72); wrote an opera, *Le Proscrit.* His reputation rests upon his scholarly publications, dealing with music in the Low Countries. He publ. a monumental work of reference, *La Musique au Pays-Bas avant le XIXe siècle* (1867-88; 8 vols.); other writings are: *Coup d'œil sur la musique actuelle à Audenarde* (1851); *Notice sur Charles-Félix de Hollande* (1854); *Notice sur les carillons d'Audenarde* (1855); *Recherches sur la musique à Audenarde avant le XIXe siècle* (1856); *Examen des chants populaires des*

Flamands de France, publiés par E. de Coussemaker (1858); *Jacques de Goüy, chanoine d'Embrun* (1863); *J.-F.-J. Janssens* (1866); *Wagner; Verslag aan den heer minister van binnenlandsche Zaaken* (1871); *Le Théâtre villageois en Flandre* (2 vols.; 1874, 1880); *Les Musiciens belges en Italie* (1875); *Voltaire musicien* (1878); *La Mélodie populaire dans l'opéra 'Guillaume Tell' de Rossini* (1879); *Lohengrin: instrumentation et philosophie* (1879); *Turin musical* (1880); *Jacques de Saint-Luc* (1887); *La Musique congratulatoire en 1454, etc.* (1888); *Cinque lettres intimes de Roland de Lassus* (1891); *Notes sur quelques instruments de musique* (1891); *Les Ballets des rois en Flandre; xylographie, musique, coutumes, etc.* (1892); *Nos périodiques musicaux* (1893); *Charles V musicien* (1894); *Les Willems, luthiers gantois du XVII*[e] *siècle* (1896; with C. Snoeck).

Van der Straeten, Edmund Sebastian Joseph, German cellist; b. Düsseldorf, April 29, 1855; d. London, Sept. 17, 1934. He studied cello in Cologne; in 1881 went to London, where he entered the Guildhall School of Music; in 1889 he began to study the viola da gamba, and later formed a trio with his son Ludwig and N. Greiffenhagen for the performance of music for viols by English, French, and German composers of the Baroque. —Author of *The Technics of Violoncello Playing* (1898; 2nd ed., 1905); *The Romance of the Fiddle* (1911); *History of the Violoncello, the Viol da Gamba, their Precursors and Collateral Instruments* (1915); *The History of the Violin* (2 vols.; 1933).

Van der Stucken, Frank (Valentin), American conductor; b. Fredericksburg, Texas, Oct. 15, 1858; d. Hamburg, Aug. 16, 1929. Taken by his parents to Antwerp in 1866, he studied with Peter Benoît; then spent 2 years (1876-78) in Leipzig, where he was aided in his study of composition by Reinecke, and met Grieg; was in Weimar with Liszt (1883); then returned to the U. S.; became conductor of the N. Y. Arion Society (1884-95), and took it on a tour in Germany in 1892. He was the first to conduct a concert of symph. works by American composers abroad, when at the Paris Exposition (July 12, 1889) he gave 1st European performances of works by MacDowell, Foote, Chadwick, Huss, and others; also conducted a series of concerts (including American compositions) in Germany. From 1895 to 1903 he was director of the Cincinnati College of Music; from 1895 to 1907, conductor of the Cincinnati Symph. Orch. On the sudden death of Anton Seidl (1898), he was called upon to conduct the remaining concerts of the season of the N. Y. Philharmonic. From 1907 he lived chiefly in Germany. He wrote an opera, *Vlasda* (not produced); *Pagina d'Amore,* for orch. and a number of light pieces for strings; also choruses. —Cf. 'Publications of the American Academy of Arts and Letters' No. 77 (N. Y., 1932).

Van Dieren, Bernard. See **Dieren.**

Van Doorslaer, Georges, Belgian musicologist; b. Mechlin, Sept. 27, 1864; d. there, Jan. 16, 1940. He was a physician by profession, but studied music as an avocation; wrote several valuable treatises dealing with Belgian musicians: *Herry Bredemers, 1472-1522* (Antwerp, 1915); *De Toonkunstenaars der familie Vredeman* (Antwerp, 1920); *La Vie et les œuvres de Philippe de Monte* (Brussels, 1921); and *Rinaldo del Mel* (Antwerp, 1922). Also edited 8 vols. in the collected ed. of works by Philippe de Monte.

Van Dresser, Marcia, American soprano; b. Memphis, Tenn., Dec. 4, 1877; d. London, July 11, 1937. She studied in Chicago and N. Y.; sang minor parts at the Metropolitan Opera (1903-04); then after further study in Germany, she made her European début in Dresden (1907); was a member of the Dessau Opera (1908-10) and of the Frankfurt Opera (1911-14). Returning to the U. S. in 1915, she gave a recital in N. Y. (March 22, 1915), and joined the Chicago Opera (1915-17).

Van Duyze (fan doiz), **Florimond,** Belgian music scholar and composer; b. Ghent, Aug. 4, 1843; d. there, May 18, 1910. He studied at the Ghent Cons., winning the Belgian Grand Prix de Rome in 1873 with the cantata, *Torquato Tasso's dood.* He wrote 11 operas, which he produced in Ghent and Antwerp. He made valuable studies of old Netherland vocal music and publ. the important collection 'Het oude nederlandsche Lied' (4 vols.; 1903-08), also a new ed. of Phalèse's *Duytsch musijck boeck* (1572; Leipzig, 1903). Wrote *Oude nederlandsche Liedern* (1889); *Het eenstimmig fransch en nederlandsch wereldijk Lied in de belgische gewesten, van de XI*[e] *eeuw tot heden* (1902). —Cf. P. Bergmans, *Florimond van Duyze,* in the 'Annuaire' of the Académie royale des sciences . . . (Brussels, 1919).

Van Dyck, Ernest (Marie Hubert), Belgian tenor; b. Antwerp, April 2, 1861; d.

Berlaer-lez-Lierre, Aug. 31, 1923. He studied law; was a journalist in Paris; sang in the Ninth Symph. of Beethoven at a Lamoureux concert (Dec. 2, 1883); made his operatic début as Lohengrin in the memorable French première on May 3, 1887; his performance of Parsifal in Bayreuth (1888) was highly praised; from 1888 to 1898 he was a member of the Vienna Opera; from 1898 to 1902, he sang Wagnerian roles at the Metropolitan Opera (début as Tannhäuser, Nov. 29, 1898). After his return to Europe he continued to appear as a Wagnerian tenor until 1906, when he settled down as a singing teacher in Brussels and Antwerp. In 1886 he married Augusta Servais, a sister of the famous cellist.

Van Gilse, Jan. See **Gilse.**

Van Hagen, Peter Albrecht, Dutch musician active in America; b. Holland, 1750; d. Boston, 1803. After his arrival in America from Holland in 1774, he settled in Charleston, S. C., as a music teacher; from 1789 to 1796, was in N. Y., giving concerts with his wife and son; in 1796 the family moved to Boston. He composed a *Federal Overture* (1797; not to be confused with *The Federal Overture* by B. Carr, q.v.); a *Funeral Dirge for George Washington* (1800); much theater music. His son, **Peter Albrecht, Jr.** (1781-1837), born in Charleston, was also a musician; he wrote songs and composed an overture. —Cf. O. G. Sonneck, *Early Concert-Life in America* (1907).

Van Hal. See **Wanhal.**

Van Hoogstraten, Willem. See **Hoogstraten.**

Van Hoose, Ellison, American tenor; b. Murfreesboro, Tenn., Aug. 18, 1868; d. Houston, Texas, March 24, 1936. He studied with Luckstone in N. Y., Jean de Reszke in Paris, and also in Rome and London. He made his operatic début with the Damrosch Opera Co. in Philadelphia as Tannhäuser (Dec. 11, 1897); toured with Mme. Melba in the U. S. (1903-05) and Mme. Sembrich (1906-07); toured in Europe (1908-10); was a member of the Chicago Opera Co. (1911-12); then devoted himself mainly to oratorio singing.

Van Katwijk, Paul. See **Katwijk.**

Van Lier, Bertus, Dutch composer; b. Utrecht, Sept. 10, 1906. He studied composition with Willem Pijper in Amsterdam, and conducting with Scherchen in Strasbourg; settled in Utrecht as conductor, composer, and music critic. In 1945 he became an instructor at the Rotterdam Cons. Among his works are several symphonies; *De Dijk,* for narrator and chamber orch.; chamber music; choruses; piano music. He also wrote a ballet, *Catharsis* (Utrecht, Nov. 29, 1950).

Van Lier, Jacques, Dutch cellist; b. The Hague, April 24, 1875; d. Worthing, England, Feb. 25, 1951. He studied cello with Hartog at The Hague and with Eberle in Rotterdam; joined the Berlin Philharmonic in 1897; from 1899 to 1915 was instructor of cello at the Klindworth-Scharwenka Cons. in Berlin. He was cellist in the 'Holländisches Trio,' with J. van Veen (violin) and Coenraad Bos (piano), which enjoyed a European reputation (1900-07); in 1915 settled in The Hague; after 1939 went to England. He publ. *Violoncellbogentechnik* and *Moderne Violoncelltechnik der linken und der rechten Hand;* also edited about 400 classical pieces for cello. —Cf. 'Musical Opinion' (Oct., 1931).

Van Maldeghem. See **Maldeghem.**

Van Maldere, Pierre. See **Maldere.**

Vannuccini (văhn-nŏŏch-chē'-nē), **Luigi,** noted Italian singing master; b. Fojano, Dec. 4, 1828; d. Montecatini, Aug. 14, 1911. He studied at the Cons. in Florence, where he became an opera conductor (1848); then turned to the study of the piano, and appeared as a concert pianist with excellent success; finally settled in Florence, devoted himself exclusively to vocal training, and acquired fame as a singing master. He publ. some songs and piano pieces. —Cf. L. Neretti, *Luigi Vannuccini,* in 'Musica d'Oggi' (1931).

Van Otterloo, Willem, Dutch conductor; b. Winterswijk, Dec. 27, 1907. He studied cello with Orobio de Castro and composition with Sem Dresden at the Amsterdam Cons.; played the cello in the Utrecht Orch.; 1933, assistant conductor there; 1937, associate conductor. In 1949 he became conductor of the Residentie Orch. at The Hague. His compositions include an Introduction and Allegro for orch.; a suite for string orch.; a sinfonietta for winds; *Divertimento* for brass, celesta, piano, and percussion (Holland Festival, The Hague, June 5, 1952, composer conducting); choral works; piano pieces; songs. —Cf. W. Paap, *Willem van Otterloo,* in 'Mens en Melodie' (April, 1949).

Van Raalte, Albert. See **Raalte, Albert van.**

Van Rooy (fan roh'-ē), **Anton (Antonius Maria Josephus)**, Dutch baritone; b. Rotterdam, Jan. 1, 1870; d. Munich, Nov. 28, 1932. He was a chorister in a church; studied voice with Stockhausen at Frankfurt. In 1897 he was engaged to sing at Bayreuth, and performed there the 3 Wotans with excellent success. On Dec. 14, 1898 he made his American début as Wotan in *Die Walküre* at the Metropolitan Opera, where he appeared each season until 1908, singing in the summers at Covent Garden, London, and Bayreuth. In 1908 he was engaged as a regular member of the Frankfurt Opera. He was particularly distinguished in Wagnerian roles, but also was noted for his interpretations of Escamillo in *Carmen* and Valentin in *Faust.*

Van Vactor, David, American composer and conductor; b. Plymouth, Ind., May 8, 1906. He studied at Northwestern Univ. with Arthur Kitti (flute) and Arne Oldberg, Felix Borowski and Albert Noelte (composition). After a year in Vienna (1928) he returned to Chicago, where he became a flutist in the Chicago Symph. Orch. (1931-43). He organized a woodwind quintet, and toured Latin America; went to South America as conductor in 1946. From 1943 to 1945, he was flutist and assistant conductor of the Kansas City Philharmonic; in 1947 he was appointed conductor of the Knoxville Symph. Orch. — Works: *Chaconne* for string orch. (Rochester, May 17, 1928); *5 Little Pieces for Big Orchestra* (Ravinia Park, Ill., July 5, 1931); *The Masque of the Red Death,* after Poe (1932); flute concerto (Chicago, Feb. 26, 1933); *Passacaglia and Fugue* (Chicago, Jan. 28, 1934); *Concerto grosso* for 3 flutes, harp, and orch. (Chicago, April 4, 1935); *Overture to a Comedy,* No. 1 (Chicago, June 20, 1937); *Symphonic Suite* (Ravinia Park, Ill., July 21, 1938); Symphony in D (1936-37; N. Y., Jan. 19, 1939, composer conducting; awarded prize of $1,000 in the American Composers Contest sponsored by the N. Y. Philharmonic); *Divertimento,* for small orch. (Ravinia Park, Ill., July 8, 1939); *Overture to a Comedy,* No. 2 (Indianapolis, March 14, 1941); *Variazioni Solenne* (performed under the title *Gothic Impressions* by the Chicago Symph. Orch., Feb. 26, 1942); *Music for the Marines* (Indianapolis, March 27, 1943); *5 Bagatelles,* for strings (Chicago, Feb. 7, 1938); viola concerto (Ravinia Park, Ill., July 13, 1940); chamber music: flute quintet (1932); suite for 2 flutes (1933); string quartet (1940); string trio (1942); flute sonata (1945); *Pastorale and Dance* for flute and strings (1947); choral pieces.

Van Vechten, Carl, American novelist and writer on music; b. Cedar Rapids, Iowa, June 17, 1880. He graduated from the Univ. of Chicago (1903); assistant music critic of the N. Y. Times (1906-07 and 1910-13); was its Paris correspondent in 1908-09; wrote the program notes for the N. Y. Symph. Society in 1910-11. In 1931 he occupied himself much with photography, and took a great number of pictures of musicians; his collection of photographs is at Fiske Univ. in Nashville. He publ. *5 Old English Ditties* (1904). Books wholly or largely on music: *Music After the Great War* (1915); *Music and Bad Manners* (1916); *Interpreters and Interpretations* (1917; partly republ. as *Interpreters,* 1920); *The Merry-Go-Round* (1918); *The Music of Spain* (1918); *In the Garret* (1920); *Red* (1925); *Excavations* (1926). —Cf. E. G. Lueders, *Carl Van Vechten and the Twenties* (Albuquerque, 1955).

Van Vleck, Jacob, a 'Moravian' minister; b. New York, 1751; d. Bethlehem, Pa., July 3, 1831. He was director of the Young Ladies' Seminary at Bethlehem from 1790-1800; consecrated a bishop in 1815. Among the 'Moravians' who were active as composers, he was the first American-born. —Cf. A. G. Rau and H. T. David, *A Catalogue of Music by American Moravians* (Bethlehem, 1938); H. T. David, *Background for Bethlehem: Moravian Music in Pennsylvania,* in 'Magazine of Art' (April, 1939).

Van Vliet, Cornelius, cellist; b. Rotterdam, Sept. 1, 1886. He began to study cello at 9; in 1903 went to Leipzig, where he appeared as soloist; then joined the Prague Philharmonic as 1st cellist, and traveled with it in Poland and Russia; in 1908 was engaged by Mahler as 1st cellist with the Vienna Philharmonic; in 1911 settled in the U. S. He was 1st cellist of the Minneapolis Symph. Orch. (1912-19); 1st cellist of the N. Y. Philharmonic (1919-29); 1st cellist of the Pittsburgh Symph. Orch. (1938-41); prof. of cello at the Univ. of Colorado (1948-53); in 1954 he went to Mexico.

Van Westerhout, Niccolò, Italian composer; b. (of Dutch parentage) Mola di Bari, Dec. 17, 1857; d. Naples, Aug. 21, 1898. He was a pupil of Nicola d'Arienzo at the Naples Cons.; then became a prof. of harmony there. He wrote 3 operas: *Cimbe-*

lino (Rome, April 7, 1892), *Fortunio* (Milan, May 16, 1895), and *Dona Flor* (Mola di Bari, April 18, 1896, on the opening of the Teatro Van Westerhout, named after him); another opera, *Colomba,* was produced posthumously (Naples, March 27, 1923). In addition he wrote 2 symphonies, a violin concerto; publ. many piano pieces of considerable merit, and songs.

Van Wyk, Arnold. See Wyk, Arnold van.

Van Zandt, Marie, American coloratura soprano; b. N. Y., Oct. 8, 1861; d. Cannes, Dec. 31, 1919. She studied with her mother, the well-known American soprano, Jennie van Zandt; made her début in Turin (1879); was engaged at the Opéra-Comique, Paris (1880-85); sang at the Metropolitan Opera, N. Y. during the season of 1891-92; in 1896 she rejoined the Opéra-Comique. Delibes wrote the role of Lakmé for her, and she created it at the Opéra-Comique on April 14, 1883.

Van Zanten, Cornelia, famous Dutch soprano and pedagogue; b. Dordrecht, Aug. 2, 1855; d. The Hague, Jan. 10, 1946. She studied with K. Schneider at the Cologne Cons., and in Milan with Lamperti, who developed her original contralto into a coloratura soprano voice. She made her début in Turin; then sang in Germany; toured in America in 1886-87 as a member of the National Opera Co. under the directorship of Theodore Thomas; then returned to Europe; appeared in special performances of *Der Ring des Nibelungen* in Russia; finally became a member of the Nederlandsche Oper in Amsterdam; also taught at the Amsterdam Cons. (1895-1903); subsequently lived in Berlin, highly esteemed as a singing teacher; eventually settled in The Hague. She publ. songs to German and Dutch texts; with C. E. Poser, brought out *Leitfaden zum Kunstgesang* (Berlin, 1903). —Cf. J. W. Hofstra, *C. van Zanten,* in 'Mensch en Melodie' (vol. 1; 1946).

Varèse, Edgar, remarkable composer; b. (of French and Italian parentage) Paris, Dec. 22, 1885. At the age of 12, he wrote an opera, *Martin Paz,* after Jules Verne; against his father's wishes, he gave up preparing for the École Polytechnique, and left home in 1904 in order to devote himself to music. He entered the Schola Cantorum in Paris, and studied there with Vincent d'Indy and Albert Roussel; also with Widor at the Paris Cons.; won the 'bourse artistique' (a stipend) offered by the city of Paris; founded and conducted the chorus of the Université Populaire and organized the concerts of the Château du Peuple. Going to Berlin, he organized and conducted there the 'Symphonischer Chor'; came to the U. S. in Dec. 1915 and founded in N. Y. the New Symph. Orch. for performances of modern music (1st concert, April 11, 1919); in 1921, founded (with Carlos Salzedo) the International Composers' Guild (1st concert, Dec. 17, 1922); in 1926, organized the Pan American Society for promoting music of the Americas; later conducted a choral group in N. Y.; lived in N. Y. and Paris; worked on problems of electronic music with René Bertrand, inventor of the Dynophone. —Varèse is one of the boldest innovators in 20th-century music. His early works (most of which are lost or destroyed) were of a Romantic and Impressionistic nature; these include *3 Pièces d'orchestre* (1904); *Rapsodie romaine* for orch. (1905); the symph. poems *Bourgogne* (1910), *Gargantua* (1912), *Mehr Licht* (1912), *Les Cycles du Nord* (1914); and an opera in German, to a libretto of Hugo von Hofmannsthal, *Oedipus und die Sphinx* (1910-14). After this period, he proceeded to work out an entirely new concept of musical composition, governed by considerations of functional efficiency and power of aural impact; he dispensed with thematic development, and ruled out consonant harmony; in the scores of *Amériques* and *Arcana* he employs a very large orchestra, with dynamic effects of extraordinary subtlety and rhythm of great intricacy. In *Ionisation,* for percussion instruments and 2 sirens, he uses sounds without definite pitch. In other works he sets himself a task of obtaining optimal effect with given sonorities, in keeping with his conception of music as 'organized sound.' Performances of his works in Europe and America often evoked protests and sometimes resulted in riotous demonstrations. —Works: *Offrandes,* for voice and small orch. (1922); *Hyperprism,* for wind instruments and percussion (N. Y., March 4, 1923); *Octandre* for flute, oboe, clarinet, bassoon, horn, trumpet, trombone, and double-bass (1924); *Intégrales,* for small orch. and percussion (N. Y., March 1, 1925); *Amériques* for large orch. (Philadelphia, April 9, 1926, Stokowski conducting); *Ionisation,* for 41 percussion instruments and 2 sirens (1931; N. Y., March 6, 1933, N. Slonimsky conducting); *Equatorial,* for bass voice, trumpets, trombones, organ, percussion, and thereminovox (N. Y., April 15, 1934); *Density 21.5,* for flute unaccompanied

(1935); *Deserts,* for wind instruments, percussion, and 3 interpolations of 'organized sound' electronically treated (Paris, Dec. 2, 1954); *Poème Électronique,* composed for the Philips Pavilion at the Brussels Exposition, and spatially distributed over 400 loudspeakers (1958). —Cf. H. Cowell, *The Music of Edgar Varèse,* in 'Modern Music' (Jan.-Feb., 1928); J. H. Klarén, *Edgar Varèse* (Boston, 1928); P. Rosenfeld, *An Hour With American Music* (Philadelphia, 1929; pp. 160-79); F. Waldman, *Edgar Varèse,* in the 'Juilliard Review' (Fall, 1954); O. Vivier, *Innovations instrumentales d'Edgar Varèse,* in the 'Revue Musicale' (Jan., 1956); M. Wilkinson, *An Introduction to the Music of Edgar Varèse,* in 'The Score' (March, 1957).

Varga, Tibor, violinist; b. Györ, Hungary, July 4, 1921. He studied at the Music Academy, Budapest, with Hubay, and later with Karl Flesch; gave concerts from the age of 10; lived in London and taught there at the Royal Academy of Music; in 1949 appointed prof. at the Music Academy in Detmold. He specializes in modern music.

Varlamov (vahr-lah'-mŏf), **Alexander Egorovitch,** Russian composer of songs; b. Moscow, Nov. 27, 1801; d. St. Petersburg, Oct. 27, 1848. At the age of 10 he entered the Imperial Chapel at St. Petersburg, where his fine voice attracted the attention of Bortniansky, the director, who then became his teacher. As a young man he was attached to the Russian Embassy at The Hague as leader of the Russian church choir there (1819-23); then returned to Moscow, where he taught singing and violin (1823-29); later went to St. Petersburg as a singing teacher. He wrote 223 songs (publ. in 12 vols. by Stellovsky) in the Russian folk style; one of them, *Krasny Sarafan (The Red Dress),* achieved tremendous popularity; Wieniawski made use of it in his violin piece, *Souvenir de Moscou.* He was the author of the first Russian singing method, *Shkola Penya* (Moscow, 1840).

Varnay, Astrid, soprano; b. Stockholm, April 25, 1918, of Hungarian parents, both professional singers. She was taken to America as a child, and studied first with her mother, then with Hermann Weigert (1890-1955), whom she married in 1944. She made her début as Sieglinde at the Metropolitan Opera (Dec. 6, 1941), substituting for Lotte Lehmann without rehearsal; then toured in the U. S., England, Argentina, and Mexico.

Varney, Louis, French composer; b. New Orleans, La., May 30, 1844; d. Cauterets, France, Aug. 20, 1908. His father, Pierre Joseph Alphonse Varney (q.v.), was director of a French opera company in New Orleans (1840-50). Louis Varney was taken to Paris at the age of 7 and remained there for the rest of his life. From 1876 he produced about 40 light theater works, including the comic opera *Les Mousquetaires au couvent* (Paris, March 16, 1880), which remained a standard item in the French light opera repertory.

Varney, Pierre Joseph Alphonse, French composer; b. Paris, Dec. 1, 1811; d. there, Feb. 7, 1879. He studied with Reicha at the Paris Cons.; was active as theater conductor in Belgium, Holland, and France. From 1840 to 1850 he was director of the French Opera Company in New Orleans, where he married Jeanne Aimée Andry; their son Louis Varney was born there. The family returned to Paris in 1851. Varney set to music a poem by Rouget de Lisle, *Mourir pour la patrie,* which became popular during the Paris revolution of 1848.

Varvoglis, Mario, Greek composer; b. Athens, Dec. 22, 1885. He studied at the Paris Cons. with Leroux, and later at the Schola Cantorum with Vincent d'Indy. Returning to Greece in 1922, he was appointed prof. of music history at the Athens Cons. His early music was influenced by Massenet; later he evolved a more independent style, using some Greek melodic patterns. His symph. prelude *Sainte-Barbara* (1912) was publ. by the French Institute of Athens in 1948. —Other works: incidental music to the classical Greek tragedies *Agamemnon* (1932) and *Medea* (1942); *Suite pastorale* for strings (1910); *Caprice grec* for cello solo and orch. (1914); symph. poem *Behind the Wire Fence* (1945); and a 'study in symph. contrasts' *Lauriers et cyprès* (1950). In 1937 he received the Grand Prize for Music of the Athens Academy of Arts.

Vasconcellos (văhs-kong-sĕhl'-ŏŏsh), **Joaquim de,** Portuguese lexicographer; b. Oporto, Feb. 10, 1849; d. there, March 1, 1936. From 1865 to 1869 he studied at the Univ. of Coïmbra; 1871-75, traveled in Germany, France, England, and Spain; from 1883 prof. of German at the Lyceum of Oporto, and from 1884 also director of the Museum for Industries and Commerce. He publ. the biographical dictionary *Os Musicos portuguezes . . .* (1870), containing much new matter, and many emendations of old; a monograph on *Luiza Todi* (1873; 2nd ed., 1929); *Ensajo critico sobre o catalogo del rey Don João IV* (1873); publ. a facsimile ed. of the catalogue of the Royal Library of Lisbon [destroyed by the earthquake of 1755] (1874-76; with index and commentary, 1905); also contributed to Pougin's supplement to Fétis' 'Biographie universelle.'

Vasiliev-Buglay, Dmitri Stepanovitch, Russian composer; b. Moscow, Aug. 9, 1888; d. there, Oct. 15, 1956. He studied in Moscow with Kastalsky and others at the Synod School; then was active as a choral conductor. After the revolution he became a member of the Association of Proletarian Musicians, preaching the extreme simplification of music for the masses. He wrote mostly vocal music; his choruses enjoyed some popularity. He also wrote an opera designed for performance by members of collective farms, *Fatherland Calls.*

Vásquez, Juan, Spanish composer; b. Badajoz, in the first quarter of the 16th century; place and date of death unknown. He composed many excellent 'villancicos,' for 3, 4, and 5 voices, often using folksongs for the chief melodic part. Many of these are found in Spanish tablature books of the period (e.g., those of Milán, Fuenllana, Enriquez de Valderrábano, Pisador, and Daza, from 1535 to 1576), arranged as solo songs with instrumental accompaniment. He publ. *Villancicos y canciones a 3 y a 4* (Osuna, 1551); *Recopilación de sonetos y villancicos a 4 y a 5* (Seville, 1560; modern ed. by H. Anglès in 'Monumentos de la Música Española,' Barcelona, 1946).

Vasseur (văh-sör'), **Léon (-Félix-Augustin-Joseph),** French composer; b. Bapaume, Pas-de-Calais, May 28, 1844; d. Paris, July 25, 1917. He studied at the École Niedermeyer in Paris; in 1870 became organist of the Versailles Cathedral; after a few years he turned to composing light music; also conducted theater orchestras. He wrote about 30 operettas, but his most successful one was his first production, *La Timbale d'argent* (Paris, April 9, 1872). He also publ. sacred music: 'L'Office divin' (a collection of Masses, offertories, antiphons, etc.); '20 motets des grands maîtres'; a method for organ or harmonium; transcriptions for harmonium and piano.

Vassilenko (vah-si-lĕhn'-koh), **Sergey Nikiforovitch,** Russian composer; b. Moscow, March 30, 1872; d. there, March 11, 1956. He studied law at the Univ. of Moscow, graduating in 1896; took private music lessons with Gretchaninov and G. Conus; entered the Moscow Cons. in 1895 as a student of Taneyev and Ippolitov-Ivanov, winning the gold medal upon graduation (1901) with a dramatic cantata, *Legend of the Great City of Kitezh* (Moscow, March 1, 1902; later adapted as an opera, and produced in Moscow, March 3, 1903). In 1906 he was appointed prof. of composition at the Moscow Cons.; held this position until 1950. He also organized and conducted popular symph. concerts in Moscow (1907-17); conducted concerts in Berlin (1909 and 1912) and in many Russian centers. In 1953 he received the Order of Lenin. His music reveals his profound interest in Russian and Asian folklore; there is also a considerable influence of French Impressionism, both in the selection of exotic subjects and in the idiomatic use of characteristic harmonic progressions; however, his basic style remained essentially within the 19th-century tradition. —Works: Operas: *Son of the Sun* (Moscow, May 23, 1929; deals with the Boxer Rebellion in China); *Christopher Columbus* (1933); *The Blizzard* (Tashkent, June 12, 1939); *The Grand Canal* (Tashkent, Jan. 12, 1941); *Suvorov* (Moscow, Feb. 23, 1942). Ballets, etc.: *Noya* (1923); *Joseph the Handsome* (Moscow, March 3, 1925); *Lola* (1926; revised, and produced Moscow, June 25, 1943); *The Gypsies,* after Pushkin (Leningrad, Nov. 18, 1937); *Akbilyak* (Tashkent, Nov. 7, 1943); *Mirandolina* (Moscow, Jan. 16, 1949). For orch.: 5 symphonies: No. 1 (Moscow, Feb. 17, 1907), No. 2 (Moscow, Jan. 7, 1913), No. 3, *Italian,* for wind instruments and Russian folk instruments (1925), No. 4, *Arctic* (Moscow, April 5, 1933), No. 5 (1938); *Vir,* for bass and orch. (Kislovodsk, July 6, 1896); *Three Combats,* symph. poem (1900); *Poème épique,* symph. poem (Moscow, March 14, 1903); *The Garden of Death,* symph. poem after Oscar Wilde (Moscow, May 4, 1908); *Hircus Nocturnus* (Moscow, Feb. 3, 1909; his most popular work; frequently performed abroad; N. Y., Nov. 20, 1918, by the Russian Symph. Orch.); *Incantation* for voice and orch. (1910); violin concerto (1910-13); *Au Soleil,* suite for orch. (Moscow, 1911); *Valse Fantastique* (Moscow, Jan. 16, 1915); *Zodiac,* suite on old French melodies (1914); *Exotic Suite* for tenor and 12 instruments (1916); *Chinese Suite* (Leningrad, Oct. 30, 1927); *Hindu Suite* (Moscow, 1927); *Turkmenian Suite* (Moscow, 1931); *Soviet East* (1932); *Uzbek Suite* (1942); cello concerto (1944); *Ukraine* (1945); trumpet concerto

(1945); several works for folk instruments: *10 Russian Folksongs,* for voice, oboe, balalaika, accordion, and piano (1929); concerto for balalaika and orch. (1931); a suite for balalaika and accordion (1945). Chamber music: 3 string quartets; piano trio; viola sonata; Serenade for cello and piano; *Oriental Dance,* for clarinet and piano (1923); *Japanese Suite,* for wind instruments, xylophone, and piano (1938); *Chinese Sketches,* for woodwind instruments (1938); woodwind quartet on American themes (1938); a number of songs, of which *A Maiden Sang in a Church Choir* (1908) is the best. Vassilenko publ. a book of memoirs, *Pages of Reminiscences* (Moscow, 1948) and vol. I of a manual of orchestration (1952). —Cf. Victor Belaiev, *S. N. Vassilenko* (Moscow, 1927; in Russian and German).

Vatielli, Francesco, Italian musicologist; b. Pesaro, Dec. 31, 1876; d. Portogruaro, Dec. 12, 1946. He studied philology in Bologna and Florence; music at the Liceo Musicale Rossini in Pesaro; in 1905 he was appointed instructor of music history at the Liceo Musicale in Bologna; also lectured on musicology at the Univ. there. He was cofounder of the Associazione dei Musicologisti Italiani; also edited various music journals. He wrote incidental music for several plays, piano pieces, and songs; publ. a number of important papers dealing mainly with music in Bologna: *Vita ed arte musicale a Bologna* (1922; reprinted in 1927 as *Arte e vita musicale a Bologna;* 2 vols.); also books on other subjects: *La 'Lyra Barberina' di G. B. Doni* (1908); *Primordi dell'arte del violoncello* (1918); *Materia e forme della musica* (1922; 2nd ed., 1928); *Il Principe di Venosa e Leonore d'Este* (on Gesualdo; Milan, 1941); edited a collection of 17th-century airs, 'Antiche cantate d'amore' (3 vols.; 1916-20); also 'Antiche cantate spirituali,' 'Antichi maestri bolognesi,' etc. —Cf. A. Della Corte, *Francesco Vatielli,* in 'Rivista Musicale Italiana' (April-Sept., 1947).

Vaucorbeil (voh-kohr-bāy'), **Auguste-Emmanuel,** French composer; b. Rouen, Dec. 15, 1821; d. Paris, Nov. 2, 1884. He studied with Marmontel, Dourlen, and Cherubini at the Paris Cons.; made himself known by songs and 2 string quartets; produced a comic opera, *La Bataille d'amour* (Paris, April 13, 1863); another opera, *Mahomet,* remained unperformed. His lyric scene, *La Mort de Diane,* for solo, chorus, and orch., had some success. In 1872 he became government commissioner for the Paris theaters; from 1879, director of the Opéra.

Vaughan Williams, Ralph (real last name Williams), foremost English composer; b. Down Ampney, Gloucestershire, Oct. 12, 1872; d. London, Aug. 26, 1958. He was the son of a clergyman, and received his education at Charterhouse School, London (1887-90) and at Trinity College, Cambridge (1892-95); obtained his B.Mus. in 1894, and B.A. in 1895; took the degree of Mus. Doc. at Cambridge in 1901. In 1890-92 and again in 1895-96 he studied at the Royal College of Music, London, where his teachers were Parratt (organ), Parry and Stanford (composition); in 1897-98 he studied with Max Bruch in Berlin. In 1909, when he was already a mature composer, he went to Paris to seek advice from Ravel, and had several sessions with him to advance his technique of composition still further. In 1904 he joined the English Folk Song Society, and became profoundly interested in the native materials of English music. His *3 Norfolk Rhapsodies* for orch. (he discarded Nos. 2 and 3), written in 1906, demonstrate this national trend in his work: the opera *Hugh the Drover* (1911-14) is strongly impregnated with English folk music. His *Fantasia on a Theme by Tallis* for strings (1910) indicates a widening of his concept of the English idiom by embracing music of the Tudor period, both sacred and secular; modal counterpoint in particular claimed his attention. Outstanding among his works is the *London Symphony* (1914; revised 1920), revealing the esthetic attitude of the modern period but rooted in the Elizabethan tradition. In his later works, Vaughan Williams adopted an advanced technique of harmonic writing, with massive agglomerations of chordal sonorities; parallel progressions of triads are especially favored, but there is no intention of adhering to any uniform method of composition; rather, there is a great variety of procedures integrated into a distinctively personal and thoroughly English style. A parallel with Sibelius (for whom Vaughan Williams always professed admiration and to whom he dedicated his 5th symphony) may plausibly be drawn; both are proponents of nationalism without isolationalism, and stylistic freedom without eclecticism. — During World War I Vaughan Williams served with the British Army in Macedonia and France, becoming an officer in the artillery; after the Armistice he became prof. of composition at the Royal College of Music, London; also conducted the London Bach Choir (1920-28). In 1922 he visited the U. S. to conduct his *Pastoral Symphony* at the Norfolk, Conn., Festival (June 7); in

1932, made another U. S. visit, as a lecturer at Bryn Mawr College. In 1935 he received the Order of Merit from King George V. After the death of his first wife in 1951, he married his secretary, Mrs. Ursula Wood (Feb. 7, 1953). In 1954 he made his third tour in the U. S.; lectured at Cornell and Yale. He continued to compose vigorously; completed his 9th symphony at the age of 85. —WORKS: Operas: *The Shepherds of the Delectable Mountains,* a 'pastoral episode' after Bunyan's *The Pilgrim's Progress* (London, July 11, 1922); *Hugh the Drover,* a ballad opera (1911-14; London, July 14, 1924); *Sir John in Love,* after Shakespeare's *Merry Wives of Windsor* (London, March 21, 1929); *The Poisoned Kiss,* a 'romantic extravaganza' (Cambridge, May 12, 1936); *Riders to the Sea* (London, Nov. 30, 1937); *The Pilgrim's Progress,* a 'morality' (1949; Covent Garden, London, April 26, 1951; includes material from the earlier opera *The Shepherds of the Delectable Mountains).* Ballets: *Old King Cole* (Cambridge, 1923); *On Christmas Night* (Chicago, 1926); *Job,* a masque for dancing (London, July 5, 1931). Incidental music: to Ben Jonson's *Pan's Anniversary* (1905); *The Wasps* by Aristophanes (1909); *The Mayor of Casterbridge,* by Thomas Hardy (1953). Vocal works: *Willow Wood,* for baritone, women's chorus, and orch., after Dante Gabriel Rossetti (1903; Liverpool Festival, 1909); *Towards the Unknown Region,* for chorus and orch., after Walt Whitman (1905; revised 1918); *A Sea Symphony* (symph. No. 1), for soprano, baritone, chorus, and orch., after Walt Whitman (Leeds Festival, 1910); 5 *Mystical Songs,* for baritone, chorus, and orch. (Worcester Festival, 1911); *Fantasia on Christmas Carols* (Hereford Festival, 1912); 2 motets for double chorus (1913); Mass in G minor (1923); *Sancta Civitas,* oratorio (Oxford, May 7, 1926); Te Deum, for mixed chorus and organ (1928); *Benedicite,* for soprano, chorus, and orch. (1929); *Magnificat,* for contralto, women's chorus, and orch. (1932); *Dona nobis pacem,* for soprano, baritone, chorus, and orch. (Huddersfield, Oct. 2, 1936); *5 Tudor Portraits,* for contralto, baritone, chorus, and orch. (Norwich Festival, 1936); *Flourish for a Coronation* (London, 1937); *Thanksgiving for Victory,* for soprano solo, speaker, chorus, and orch. (London, May 8, 1945); *The Sons of Light* (London Philharmonic with a chorus of 1,000 school children; May 6, 1951); *Epithalamion,* cantata (1953); *This Day,* cantata (Worcester Festival, Sept. 8, 1954); *A Vision of Aeroplanes,* motet for chorus and organ (St. Michael's, Cornhill, June 4, 1956). For orch.: *Serenade* for small orch. (1901); *Bucolic Suite* (1902); 2 Impressions: *Harnham Down* and *Boldrewood* (1902); *3 Norfolk Rhapsodies:* No. 1, in E minor (London, Aug. 23, 1906); Nos. 2 and 3 (Cardiff Festival, Sept. 27, 1907; withdrawn by the composer); *Fantasia on a Theme by Tallis,* for strings (Gloucester Festival, Sept. 6, 1910, composer conducting); symph. No. 2, *A London Symphony* (1914; revised version, London, May 4, 1920); *The Lark Ascending,* romance for violin and orch. (1914; London, June 14, 1921); symph. No. 3, *Pastoral Symphony* (London, Jan. 26, 1922); *Flos Campi,* suite for viola, small chorus, and small orch. (London, Oct. 19, 1925); *Concerto accademico,* for violin and orch. (London, Nov. 6, 1925); *Fantasy on Sussex Folk-Tunes,* for cello and orch. (1930); piano concerto (London, Feb. 1, 1933; also arranged for 2 pianos with orch.); suite for viola and orch. (London, Nov. 12, 1934); symph. No. 4, in F minor (London, April 10, 1935); *5 Variants of 'Dives and Lazarus,'* for string orch. and harp, commissioned by the British Council for the N. Y. World's Fair (N. Y. Philharmonic, June 10, 1939); symph. No. 5, in D major (London, June 25, 1943); concerto for oboe and strings (Liverpool, Sept. 30, 1944); symph. No. 6, in E minor (London, April 21, 1948); *Romance,* for harmonica and orch. (N. Y., May 3, 1952); symph. No. 7, *Sinfonia antartica* (1951-52; Manchester, Jan. 14, 1953); concerto for bass tuba and orch. (London, June 13, 1954); symph. No. 8 (Manchester, May 2, 1956); symph. No. 9 (London, April 2, 1958). Chamber music: string quartet No. 1 (1908; revised 1921); *Fantasy Quintet,* for 2 violins, 2 violas, and cello (1910); *On Wenleck Edge,* for tenor, string quartet, and piano (1909); *6 Studies in English Folksong,* for cello and piano (1927); string quartet No. 2 (1945). Also numerous songs to words by English poets; arrangements of English folksongs; some short piano pieces; Introduction and Fugue, for 2 pianos (1946); organ pieces; hymn tunes; carols. Film music: *Coastal Command* (1942); *The People's Land* (1943); *The Story of a Flemish Farm* (1943; suite for orch. from it, London, July 31, 1945); *Stricken Peninsula* (1945); *The Loves of Joanna Godden* (1947); *Scott of the Antarctic* (1949; material taken from it incorporated in *Sinfonia antartica).* —Literary works: *English Folksongs* (a lecture presented at the English Folk Dance and Song Society, London, 1912); *National Music*

(London, 1934; embodies lectures at Bryn Mawr College); *Some Thoughts on Beethoven's Choral Symphony, with Writings on Other Musical Subjects* (London, 1953; contains reprints of several of his earlier articles); *The Making of Music* (Ithaca, N. Y., 1955; lectures delivered at Cornell Univ. and Yale Univ. in 1954). Editions: '15 Folk-Songs from the Eastern Counties' for voice and piano, in the 'Journal of the Folk-Song Society' (vol. I, No. 8); Purcell's 'Welcome Odes' (vols. XV and XVIII of the Purcell Society ed.); 'The English Hymnal' (1906); 'The Oxford Carol Book' (with Percy Dearmer and Martin Shaw; 1928).—Bibliography: Monographs in the 'Musical Pilgrim' series (London): A. E. F. Dickinson, *An Introduction to the Music of R. V. W.* (1928), Frank Howes, *The Dramatic Works of R. V. W.* (1937), Frank Howes, *The Later Works of R. V. W.* (1937). Other books: Hubert Foss, *R. V. W.: a Study* (London, 1950); Percy M. Young, *V. W.*, in 'Contemporary Composers' series (London, 1953); Frank Howes, *The Music of R. V. W.* (London, 1954); S. Pakenham, *R. V. W.; A Discovery of His Music* (London, 1957). Magazine articles: in 'Music & Letters': A. H. Fox Strangways, *R. V. W.* (1920), H. Howells, *V. W.'s 'Pastoral' Symphony* (1922), E. Rubbra, *The Later V. W.* (Jan., 1937), W. Kimmel, *V. W.'s Choice of Words* (1938), H. Murrill, *V. W.'s Pilgrim* (1951); in the 'Music Review': *V. W.'s Fifth Symph.* (Jan., 1945), R. Hawthorne, *A Note on the Music of V. W.* (1948), A.E.F. Dickinson, *Toward the Unknown Region* (1948), Elsie Payne, *V. W. and Folksong* (1954); in the 'Mus. Quarterly': W. Kimmel, *V. W.'s Melodic Style* (Oct., 1941). Other magazine articles: H.C. Colles, *The Music of V. W.*, in the 'Chesterian' (1922); A.E.F. Dickinson, *A Bibliography of Works by R. V. W.*, in 'Gamut' (July, 1928); H. Howells, *V. W.* in 'The Score' (Dec., 1952); chapters in books: G. Pannain, *R. V. W.*, in *Modern Composers* (English transl. from Italian, London, 1932), D. F. Tovey, *Essays in Musical Analysis,* vols. II and IV (London, 1935-39), E. Blom, *R. V. W.*, in *The Book of Modern Composers,* ed. by David Ewen (N. Y., 1942).

Vaurabourg-Honegger, Andrée. See **Honegger, Arthur.**

Vautor, Thomas, English composer; b. c. 1590; date and place of death unknown. In 1616 he received the degree of B.Mus. at Lincoln College, and in 1619 publ. a collection of madrigals, *The First Set: Beeing Songs of divers Ayres and Natures, of 5 and 6 parts* (reprinted by Fellowes in 'The English Madrigal School' vol. XXXIV). Another work by Vautor is *An Elegie on the Death of his right worshipful Master, Sir Thomas Beaumont* (1614). —Cf. E. H. Fellowes, *The English Madrigal Composers* (1921).

Veazie, George Augustus, American music educator; b. Boston, Dec. 18, 1835; d. Chelsea, Mass., Nov. 20, 1915. From 1869 to 1903 he was supervisor of music in the public schools of Chelsea; during many years of cooperation with Luther W. Mason (q.v.) he brought about important reforms and improvements in the system of primary instruction; from 1888 till 1902 he also was a member of the faculty of the New England Cons. He composed several light operas and numerous part-songs, and edited collections of school songs.

Vecchi (vĕh-kē), **Orazio (Horatio),** Italian composer; b. Modena, 1550 (baptized Dec. 6); d. there, Feb. 19, 1605. He was a pupil of Salvatore Essenga in Modena; in 1586, having taken holy orders, he went to Reggio as choirmaster, but before the end of the year he moved on to Correggio, where he obtained a canonry. In 1596 he returned to Modena and was appointed maestro at the Cathedral (Oct. 26); 2 years later he was also maestro at the ducal court there, and music master to the young princes. On Oct. 7, 1604, he was deprived of his post as choirmaster at the Cathedral, probably through the intrigues of a former pupil, Geminiano Capilupi; this circumstance is believed to have hastened his death. Vecchi was highly regarded as a composer in his day; his works—Masses, motets, madrigals, canzonette, etc.—were chiefly printed in Venice, but editions also appeared in Germany and elsewhere. He was invited to the court of the Emperor Rudolf II at Vienna, and in 1600 went to Rome in the suite of Cardinal Alessandro d'Este. His lasting fame is due above all to his 'commedia harmonica' *L'Amfiparnasso,* performed at Modena in 1594 and printed at Venice in 1597; this is a kind of musical farce written not in the monodic style of Peri's *Dafne,* but in madrigal style, with all the text sung by several voices (i.e., a chorus *a* 4-5); it has been called a 'madrigal opera,' but it was not intended for the theater and it stood entirely apart from the path that opera was to take. *L'Amfiparnasso,* newly arranged by F. Liuzzi, was performed at the Florence Festival in 1938; modern eds. have been publ. by Eitner (vol. 26 of the 'Publikationen der Gesellschaft der Musikforschung') and Torchi ('L'Arte Musicale in Italia' vol. IV). Of special interest among Vecchi's other compositions is the *Veglie di Siena ovvero i varii humori della musica moderna a 3-6 voci* (1604; also Nuremberg, 1605, as *Noctes ludicrae;* modern ed. by B. Somma), which uses colorful devices to express a wide variety of moods and feelings. Examples of Vecchi's music are in Schering's 'Beispielen' (No. 164); Chilesotti's 'Biblioteca di rarità musicali' vol. V, Torchi's 'L'Arte Musicale in Italia' vol. II, Einstein's 'Golden Age of the Madrigal,' etc. —Bibliography: A. Catellani, *Della vita e delle opere di O. V.* (Milan, 1858); E. J. Dent, *The 'Amfiparnasso' of O. V.,* in 'Monthly Mus. Record' (1906; Nos 423-24); E. J. Dent, *Notes on the 'Amfiparnasso' of O. V.,* in 'Sammelbände der Internationalen Musik-Gesellschaft' (1910-11); L. Frati, *Un Capitolo autobiografico di O. V.,* in 'Rivista Musicale Italiana' (1915); J. C. Hol, *H. V. als weltlicher Komponist* (diss., Basel, 1917), *H. V. et l'évolution créatrice,* in 'Scheurleer-Festschrift' (1925), *H. V.,* in 'Rivista Musicale Italiana' (1930), and *H. V.s weltliche Werke* (Strasbourg, 1934); G. Roncaglia, *Il Luogo e la data di nascità di O. V.,* in the 'Rassegna Musicale' (April, 1929); C. Perinello, *L'Amfiparnasso, commedia harmonica d' H. V.,* in 'Rivista Musicale Italiana' (1937); G. Roncaglia, *O. V.,* in 'Rivista Musicale Italiana' (1949); *O. V., Precursore del melodramma,* a symposium on the 400th anniversary of Vecchi's birth (Modena, 1950); A. Lualdi, *O. V.,* in 'Rivista Musicale Italiana' (1950); G. Camillucci, *L'Amfiparnasso, commedia harmonica,* in 'Rivista Musicale Italiana' (1951); G. Roncaglia, *Gli Elementi precursori del melodramma nell' opera di O. V.,* in 'Rivista Musicale Italiana' (1953); L. Ronga, *Lettura storica dell' 'Amfiparnasso' di O. V.,* in 'Rassegna Musicale' (1953).

Vecchi, Orfeo, Italian composer of sacred music; b. Milan, 1540; d. there, c. 1603. He was maestro di cappella at Santa Maria della Scala in Milan; most of his MSS are preserved there. His extant published works include 3 collections of Masses for 5 voices (1588; 1598; 1602); 2 Magnificats; 7 Penitential Psalms for 6 voices (1601); *Cantiones sacrae,* for 6 voices (1603) and for 5 (1608), etc. —Cf. F. X. Haberl, *Orfeo Vecchi,* in the 'Kirchenmusikalisches Jahrbuch' (1907); A. Einstein, *Un Libro di canzoni spirituali di Orfeo Vecchi,* in 'Bibliofilia' (Florence, 1938).

Vecsei (veh'-chā), **Desider Josef,** Hungarian pianist; b. Budapest, Sept. 25, 1882. He studied in Budapest, and then with Emil Sauer at the Vienna Cons. He made concert appearances as a child; toured in Europe until 1915; then went to the U. S., and settled in Hollywood as a piano teacher. He wrote songs and piano pieces.

Vecsey (veh'-chā), **Franz von,** Hungarian violinist; b. Budapest, March 23, 1893; d. Rome, April 6, 1935. He received his first instruction from his father, Ludwig Vecsey, a good violinist; at the age of 8 he became a pupil of Hubay, and made such rapid progress that his parents decided to send him on a European tour as a child prodigy; he appeared in Berlin (Oct. 17, 1903), London (May 2, 1904), and N. Y. (Jan. 10, 1905); toured Italy, Scandinavia, and Russia; then lived in Germany and Italy. He composed some violin pieces.

Vega, Carlos, Argentine writer on music; b. Canuelas, near Buenos Aires, April 14, 1898. He studied at the Univ. of Buenos Aires (philosophy and literature); subsequently devoted himself mainly to folklore research in music. In 1926 he was appointed chief of the music section of the Argentine Museum of Natural Sciences; in 1933, was placed in charge of the folklore division of the literature faculty at the Univ. of Buenos Aires. He traveled throughout the rural regions of Argentina and other South American countries to collect materials on folksongs and folk dances, using the phonograph for recording them; devised a special choreographic notation. His many books are basic sources for the study of Argentine folk music. —Publications: *Danzas y canciones argentinas* (Buenos Aires, 1936); *La Música popular argentina: Canciones y danzas criollas* (1941); *Panorama de la música popular argentina* (Buenos Aires, 1944); a series of monographs on Argentinian dances (with choreographic ideograms): *La Chacarera, El Cuando, El Gato, El Triunfo, El Carnavalito, La Condición* (Buenos Aires, 1944-45); *Los Instrumentos musicales . . . de la Argentina* (Buenos Aires, 1946).

Veinus, Abraham, American musicologist; b. New York, Feb. 12, 1916. He studied at the City College of N. Y., Cornell Univ. (M.A., 1937), and Columbia Univ. (1946-48). In 1948 he joined the faculty of the Dept. of Fine Arts at Syracuse Univ. He publ. *The Concerto* (1944), *Victor Book of Concertos* (1948), and *Pocket Book of Great Operas* (with Henry Simon, 1949).

Veit (vīt), **Wenzel Heinrich,** Bohemian composer; b. Leitmeritz, Jan. 19, 1806; d. there, Feb. 16, 1864. He was a member of the judiciary, but applied himself earnestly to the study of music; was music director at Aachen. He wrote a number of works in various genres; he is remembered chiefly for his effective choruses and solo songs. —Works: *Festmesse* in D, for soli, chorus, and orch.; overtures; a symph.; 5 string quintets; 4 string quartets; a piano trio; male choruses in Czech and German; songs. —Cf. A. John, *W. H. Veit. Lebensbild eines deutschen Tondichters* (Eger, 1903); H. Ankert, *W. H. Veit als Musikdirektor in Aachen* (Leitmeritz, 1906).

Velasco Maidana, José María, Bolivian composer and conductor; b. Sucre, July 4, 1899. He studied violin in Buenos Aires; subsequently taught music history at the National Cons. of La Paz. In 1937 he conducted some of his works in Buenos Aires, and in 1938 in Berlin; in 1943, toured in South America and Mexico. His ballet *Amerindia,* on a subject from pre-Columbian history, was produced in Berlin (Dec. 6, 1938), and later in La Paz (May 27, 1940). He conducted the 1st performances of his symph. works with the La Paz Symph. Orch., of which he was regular conductor: *Cory Wara* (Oct. 6, 1941); *Los Hijos del Sol* (Feb. 6, 1942); *Vida de Cóndores* (March 14, 1942); *Los Huacos* (April 22, 1942); *Los Khusillos* and *Cuento Brujo* (April 11, 1943).

Velden, Renier van der, Belgian conductor and composer; b. Antwerp, Jan. 14, 1910. He studied with Joseph Jongen in Brussels; then was engaged as radio conductor in Antwerp. —Works: *Divertimento* for string orch. (1939); *Sinfonietta* for strings (1942); oboe concerto (1941); trio for oboe, clarinet, and bassoon (1943); sextet for wind instruments and piano (1948).

Venatorini. See **Mysliveczek.**

Venegas de Henestrosa, Luis, Spanish organist and composer of the 16th century; was in the service of Cardinal Juan Tavera in Toledo; publ. the oldest known Spanish book of organ music, *Libro de cifra nueva para tecla, harpa y vihuela* (Alcalà de Henares, 1557; modern ed. by H. Anglès, Barcelona, 1944); this contains organ pieces by Palero, P. Vila, Soto, Venegas himself, etc.; also pieces for vihuela (old Spanish guitar), transcriptions of sacred works by Morales, Josquin, Soto, etc., and solo songs with instrumental accompaniment. The book is written in Spanish organ tablature. —Cf. G. Morphy, *Les Luthistes espagnols du XVIe siècle* (Leipzig, 1902); J. B. Trend, *Luis Milan and the Vihuelistas* (London, 1925); H. Anglès, *Orgelmusik der Schola Hispanica vom XV.-XVII. Jahrhundert,* in 'Peter Wagner-Festschrift' (Leipzig, 1926); J. Ward, *The Editorial Methods of Venegas de Henestrosa,* in 'Musica Disciplina' (1952).

Vengerova (vĕhn-gĕh'-rŏh-văh), **Isabelle,** distinguished piano pedagogue; b. Minsk, Russia, March 1, 1877; d. New York, Feb. 7, 1956. She studied at the Vienna Cons. with Joseph Dachs, and privately with Leschetizky; then with Anna Essipoff in St. Petersburg. In 1906 she was appointed instructor at the St. Petersburg Cons.; in 1910, prof. there. She toured in Russia as pianist; in 1923, came to the U. S.; American début with the Detroit Symph. Orch. (Feb. 8, 1925) in Schumann's piano concerto. She became prof. at the Curtis Institute of Music in Philadelphia when it was founded in 1924; in 1950, received an honorary doctor's degree there. Among her piano pupils at the Curtis Institute were Leonard Bernstein, Samuel Barber, and Lukas Foss. She also taught privately in New York.

Venosa, Prince of. See **Gesualdo.**

Venth (vehnt), **Karl,** violinist, conductor, and composer; b. Cologne, Feb. 16, 1860; d. San Antonio, Texas, Jan. 29, 1938. His father was a German, his mother Croatian. He studied violin with his father, and later at the Cologne Cons., where he was also a pupil of Ferdinand Hiller; continued his violin studies for a year in Brussels with Wieniawski. In 1880 he emigrated to the U. S.; was concertmaster of the Metropolitan Opera orch. (1884-88); conductor of the Brooklyn Symph. Orch. (1889-1902); concertmaster of the St. Paul Symph. Orch. (1907-12); conductor of the Dallas Symph. Orch. (1911-13). In 1913 he was appointed dean of the School of Fine Arts of Texas Woman's College, Fort Worth; in 1913 organized the Fort Worth Symph. Orch., which he conducted for several years. In 1932 he joined the faculty of San Antonio Univ., remaining there until his death. —Works: for the stage: *Pan in America,* a 'lyric dance drama' (won the prize of the National Federation of Music Clubs; produced at its Biennial Convention, Asheville, N. C., June 13, 1923); *The Rebel,* a fairy opera with dance (Fort Worth, May 29,

1926); *Lima Beans,* short opera: *Alexander's Horse,* a musical play; *The Juggler,* for voices and instruments; *Dolls,* a 'musical extravaganza'; *The Sun God,* an Oriental opera; *Cathal,* short music drama; *Jack,* music drama; etc.; several symph. works *(Forest Scenes, Norse Dance, Indian Prologue,* etc.); a Mass in D; 2 string quartets; a piano trio; numerous piano compositions *(Sonata appassionata,* 2 rhapsodies, etc.); songs. His autobiography, *My Memories,* was publ. posthumously (1939). —Cf. E. E. Hipsher, *American Opera and Its Composers* (Philadelphia, 1934; pp. 416-18).

Venzano (vĕn-tsăh'-nŏh), **Luigi,** Italian composer; b. Genoa, 1814; d. there, Jan. 26, 1878. He played the cello at the Carlo Felice Theater in Genoa, and taught at the Cons. there; publ. many songs, including *Valzer cantabile,* which is often sung in the lesson-scene of *The Barber of Seville;* also composed an operetta, *La Notte dei schiaffi* (Genoa, April 25, 1873) and a ballet, *Benvenuto Cellini* (Milan, Aug. 24, 1861); publ. piano pieces and singing exercises.

Veprik, Alexander Moiseyevitch, Russian composer; b. Balta, near Odessa, June 23, 1899. While still a boy he went to Leipzig, where he studied piano with Karl Wendling, graduating in 1914. He then returned to Russia; entered the Moscow Cons. in 1923 as a pupil of Miaskovsky. From 1930 to 1942 he taught orchestration there. He was associated with the Jewish cultural movement in Russia, and wrote several works in the traditional Jewish manner: *Dances and Songs of the Ghetto,* for orch. (1927); *Kaddish,* for voice with instruments (1925); a *Jewish Communist Youth Song* (1926); later wrote music based on Ukrainian folksongs. Other works: 2 symphonies (1931, 1938); *The Song of Jubilation,* for orch. (Moscow, March 17, 1937); rhapsody for viola and piano (1929); a number of piano pieces; songs. He publ. an instructive manual, *The Treatment of Orchestral Instruments* (Moscow, 1947); *Principles of Bach's Orchestration* (Moscow, 1955).

Veracini (vĕh-răh-chē'nē), **Francesco Maria,** Italian violinist and composer; b. Florence, Feb. 1, 1690; d. near Pisa, c. 1750. Pupil of his uncle, Antonio Veracini, of Casini, and of Gasparini; an eminent virtuoso, he toured widely, and in 1714 was heard in Venice by Tartini, greatly influencing the latter's style; 1715-17, soloist at the Italian Opera in London; 1717-22, chamber virtuoso at the court of Dresden; 1735-45, in London again, producing several operas there; being eclipsed by Geminiani, he retired to Pisa about 1746, dying in extreme poverty. Publ. 24 violin sonatas with continuo (1721, 1744); in MS: concertos for violin and symphonies for strings and harpsichord, also a theoretical treatise (in the library of the Cons. Cherubini at Florence). Modern reprints by G. Jensen, L. Torchi, E. Pente, etc. —Cf. L. Torchi, in 'Revista Musicale Italiana' (1889; p. 69); M. Pincherle, *Les Violinistes* (Paris, 1924); A. Damerini, *Elogio dell' asino e monte di Stradella in un trattato di F. M. Veracini,* in 'La Scala' (March, 1956).

Verbrugghen (fehr-brüg'-gen), **Henri,** violinist and conductor; b. Brussels, Aug. 1, 1873; d. Northfield, Minn., Nov. 12, 1934. He studied with Hubay and Ysaÿe at the Brussels Cons.; in 1893 was engaged as violinist in the Scottish Orch. in Glasgow; then was concertmaster in various orchestras in Wales; also conducted summer concerts there, while retaining his position in Glasgow. In 1903 he founded the Verbrugghen String Quartet, which won a good reputation. In 1915 he went to Australia, and established the National Cons. in Sydney. In 1922-23 he was guest conductor of the Minneapolis Symph. Orch.; then became its regular conductor (until 1932).

Verdelot (vĕhr-dĕh-lŏh'), **Philippe,** noted Flemish composer; date of birth unknown; d. c. 1550. He settled in Italy while young and became a singer at San Marco in Venice about 1525; from about 1530 he was choirmaster at San Giovanni in Florence. His works were widely printed, both in Italy and France; he was one of the earliest composers of madrigals; most of his approximately 100 works of that type appeared in collections along with those by other composers. Willaert (q.v.) arranged 22 of Verdelot's madrigals as solo songs with lute accompaniment, in tablature: *Intavolatura degli Madrigali di Verdelotto de cantare e sonare nel lauto . . .* (Venice, 1536). Verdelot's last publication was a book of motets, *Electiones diversorum Motetorum distinctae* (1549). Only a single Mass by him is known, entitled *Philomena,* included in Scotto's *Liber V missarum* (1544). Verdelot added a 5th part to Janequin's *Bataille,* first publ. in Susato's 10th book of *Chansons* (Antwerp, 1545; modern reprint by Commer). Reprints of madrigals by Verdelot are in Maldeghem's 'Trésor musical'; P. Wagner's *Das Madrigal und Palestrina;* Riemann's *Handbuch der Musikgeschichte,* II,

1; Schering's 'Beispielen' (Nos. 98/98); Einstein's *The Italian Madrigal* (vol. 3); etc. See A. Einstein, *Claudio Merulo's Ausgabe der Madrigale des Verdelot,* in the 'Sammelbände der Internationalen Musik-Gesellschaft' (vol. VIII) and *The Italian Madrigal,* vol. 1 (Princeton, 1949); also G. Reese, *Music in the Renaissance* (N. Y., 1954, pp. 316-19).

Verdi, (Fortunino) Giuseppe (Francesco), illustrious Italian composer of operas; b. Le Roncole, near Busseto, Duchy of Parma, Oct. 10, 1813; d. Milan, Jan. 27, 1901. His father was an innkeeper; the son's precocious talent was trained by the village organist, Baistrocchi; his progress was so extraordinary that he often substituted for his teacher at the church organ, and as a mere boy, succeeded him at the post, receiving a regular, though modest, payment for his services. He studied with Ferdinando Provesi at Busseto for 4 years, until the age of 16, and began to compose music, which he played at a local church; an overture by him was performed at the municipal theater in 1828. A Busseto merchant named Antonio Barezzi enabled Verdi to continue his musical education in Milan. Verdi applied for admission to the Milan Cons.; being older than the average age for entrance, he had to take a special examination, which, however, he failed to pass; the registrar, Francesco Basili, reported that his piano playing was inadequate, and his hand position wrong; as to Verdi's ability in composition, the report found the presence of talent, but insufficient technical knowledge. In all probability, this judgment reflected the actual state of Verdi's musical education at that time, but the examiners showed a lack of imagination in not waiving the rigid rules in an exceptional case. Verdi then turned to private instruction with Vincenzo Lavigna, the maestro al cembalo at La Scala. Verdi labored industriously over counterpoint, canon, and fugue, and assiduously frequented the opera, absorbing the art of dramatic composition. In the summer of 1834 he was engaged as municipal maestro at Busseto, but held this post only for 6 months, going to Milan for another period of study with Lavigna. From July 1835 to Sept. 1838 he was again in Busseto, holding the posts of director of the local music school and of the Philharmonic Society, returning to Milan in 1838. On May 4, 1836, he married Barezzi's daughter, Margherita; they had 2 children who died in infancy; Margherita herself died in Milan on June 18, 1840. In Busseto Verdi wrote his 1st opera, *Oberto, conte di San Bonifacio,* which was accepted by La Scala, Milan, and performed there with success on Nov. 17, 1839. His next opera, *Un Giorno di regno* (1840), was a failure. He then set to work on a new opera, *Nabucco,* which was given at La Scala (1842) with tremendous success, Signorina Giuseppina Strepponi (q.v.) taking the leading feminine role of Abigaile; this was followed by another successful opera, *I Lombardi alla prima Crociata* (La Scala, 1843); the subject, derived from events in the First Crusade, appealed to the Milan public, arousing their national aspirations for freedom. From that time, Verdi's standing with the management of La Scala was assured, and other opera houses in Italy were open to his productions. After his domestic tragedy, he was greatly consoled by the friendship and constant companionship of Giuseppina Strepponi, whom he eventually married on Aug. 29, 1859. His opera *Ernani* (1844), after Victor Hugo's romantic play, *Hernani,* written for the Teatro La Fenice in Venice, was acclaimed and produced on 15 different stages within a year. Then followed a series of works that added little to Verdi's fame: *I due Foscari* (1844); *Giovanna d'Arco* (1845); *Alzira* (1845); *Attila* (1846); *Macbeth* (1847); *I Masnadieri* (1847); *Il Corsaro* (1848); and *La Battaglia di Legnano* (1849). *Luisa Miller* obtained some success in Naples (1849); but *Stiffelio,* produced at Trieste in 1850, was a complete failure. Despite his changing fortunes, Verdi's financial prosperity grew, and he showed considerable business acumen in dealing with publishers and impresarios. He traveled to London in 1847; spent some time in Paris in 1848; then returned to Italy. Early in 1851 he completed his first real masterpiece, *Rigoletto,* which was brought out at La Fenice in Venice; it was followed by *Il Trovatore,* produced in Rome (1853) and *La Traviata,* staged at La Fenice (1853). These 3 operas firmly established Verdi's reputation. His 1st French opera, *Les Vêpres siciliennes,* was produced at the Paris Opéra (1855) with moderate success; there followed *Simone Boccanegra,* written for Venice (1857), *Un Ballo in maschera* (Rome, 1859), *La Forza del destino,* brought out in St. Petersburg (1862), and Verdi's 2nd and last French opera, *Don Carlos* (Paris Opéra, 1867). In the meantime, Verdi became involved in the Italian struggle for independence. He was not a politician, and never participated in revolutionary agitation, beyond expressing his patriotic views. But his choice of subject for his grand opera, *Un Ballo in maschera* (originally entitled *La Vendetta in Domino),* based on a play by Scribe and describing the assassination of the Swedish king Gustav III in 1792, was ill-timed because of the recent attempted assassination of Napoleon III. Verdi was compelled to transfer the scene of action in his opera from Sweden to Massachusetts, with Gustav III becoming Governor Riccardo of Boston; this episode stirred Verdi's admirers, who linked his name with that of Victor Emmanuel, the future King of Italy. The cry 'Viva Verdi' became, by using the 5 letters of his name as initials, a political slogan: 'Viva Vittorio Emmanuele Re D' Italia.' In 1869 Verdi received an offer to write an opera on an Egyptian subject for the new theater in Cairo to celebrate the opening of the Suez Canal. The financial terms were extremely advantageous; the scenario was in French; Antonio Ghislanzoni wrote the Italian libretto, entitled *Aida*. The opera was produced in Cairo on Christmas Eve in 1871, attended by a multitude of notables and newspaper correspondents; characteristically, Verdi refused to make the journey to Cairo and hear the première, explaining that it was his art and not he personally that was important. The style of *Aida* showed a remarkable advance from his earlier masterpieces. Verdi injected here a new element of tone painting; the orchestra ceased to be a mere accompaniment and became a vital element in the drama. *Aida's* popular success fully justified the praise bestowed upon it; productions followed in Italy, all over Europe, and in America. Verdi's next work was not an opera, but the *Messa da Requiem,* written in memory of Alessandro Manzoni, and performed for the 1st time at the Milan Cathedral, on the 1st anniversary of Manzoni's death (1874). After Rossini's death (1868), Verdi conceived the idea of honoring his memory by a requiem to which 13 Italian composers were to contribute one number each, Verdi reserving for himself the last, the *Libera me*. The plan did not succeed, and Verdi incorporated his number in the 'Manzoni Requiem.' 15 years elapsed after *Aida* until the production of a new Verdi opera, *Otello* (La Scala, 1887); the libretto, after Shakespeare, was by Arrigo Boito, and it possessed a poetic value of its own; Verdi, at the age of 73, succeeded in creating for it a score of great dramatic intensity and lyric beauty. Yet he never departed from the basic Italian operatic style, which he cultivated all his life; no concession was made to the growing fashion of music drama, in the Wagner manner; clear separation of aria, recitative, and chorus were still the rule. *Otello* surprised the musical world by its power in the delineation of character. Still greater was the astonishment generated by the appearance of Verdi's last opera, *Falstaff,* also to a libretto by Boito, after Shakespeare's *The Merry Wives of Windsor,* which Verdi completed in his 80th year. The score reveals a genius for subtle comedy; in this work of Verdi's old age, he, for the first time, applied a highly developed art of counterpoint; the orchestra here has more of a symphonic character than in any of Verdi's preceding operas. Verdi's last work was a group of sacred choruses, *4 Pezzi sacri;* in one of them Verdi made use of the so-called 'scala enigmatica' (c, d♭, e, f♯, g♯, a♯, b, c). —Innumerable honors were showered upon Verdi by royalty and society. In 1860 he was elected to the 1st National Parliament of Italy (resigned in 1865); in 1875 he was nominated a Senator. After the première of *Falstaff,* the King of Italy wished to create him 'Marchese di Busseto,' but Verdi declined the honor. In 1899 he founded in Milan the 'Casa di Riposo per Musicisti' in memory of his second wife (d. 1897); for its maintenance he set aside 2,500,000 lire, and after his death the income from his works, payable for 30 years. The full extent of the provision may be estimated from the fact that during his life Verdi received in royalties from *Aida* alone the sum of 4,000,000 lire. —Verdi was unquestionably the greatest figure in Italian opera. He instinctively understood the purpose and function of music in the theater, and developed a superb craft of dramatic and lyric writing. His melodic gift was of the greatest inventiveness; in his best operas he created arias and ensembles of extraordinary affective appeal. As musical tastes changed under the impact of Wagner, Liszt, and their followers, Verdi's music lost stature; in the view of some critics, it was lowered to the level of 'barrel-organ' repertory. A movement 'back to Verdi' developed in the 2nd quarter of the 20th century, as Wagnerianism began to recede. The frequency of performances of Verdi's operas rose sharply, not only in Italy, but also in Germany and Austria, France and England, and in America, and modern composers became interested in Verdi's music as a product of pure art, unobscured by artifice. The 50th anniversary of Verdi's death was widely observed in 1951; special performances and festivals were given; Toscanini conducted a concert of Verdi's works, including the 'Manzoni Requiem,' in Carnegie Hall, N. Y., on Jan. 27, 1951. Excerpts from Verdi's operas were presented in the Roman Colosseum on Oct. 7, 1951.

WORKS

OPERAS: *Oberto, Conte di San Bonifacio* (Milan, Nov. 17, 1839); *Un Giorno di regno* (also as *Il finto Stanislao;* Milan, Sept. 5, 1840); *Nabucco* (Milan, March 9, 1842; N. Y., April 4, 1848); *I Lombardi alla prima Crociata* (Milan, Feb. 11, 1843; N. Y., March 3, 1847; Paris, Nov. 26, 1847, as *Jérusalem,* with a new libretto and a ballet); *Ernani* (after Victor Hugo's *Hernani;* Venice, March 9, 1844; London, March 8, 1845; N. Y., Park Theater, April 15, 1847; Metropolitan Opera, Jan. 28, 1902); *I due Foscari* (Rome, Nov. 3, 1844; N. Y., June 6, 1847); *Giovanna d'Arco* (Milan, Feb. 15, 1845); *Alzira* (Naples, Aug. 12, 1845); *Attila* (Venice, March 17, 1846; N. Y., March 15, 1850); *Macbeth* (Florence, March 14, 1847; N. Y., Niblo's Garden, April 24, 1850; St. Petersburg, 1854, as *Sivardo, il Sassone;* revised version, Paris, April 21, 1865); *I Masnadieri* (after Schiller's *Die Räuber;* London, July 22, 1847; Milan, Sept. 20, 1853; N. Y., June 2, 1860); *Il Corsaro* (Trieste, Oct. 25, 1848); *La Battaglia di Legnano* (Rome, Jan. 27, 1849; later as *L'Assedio d'Arlem); Luisa Miller* (Naples, Dec. 8, 1849; N. Y., Castle Garden, July 20, 1854; London, June 3, 1858; Metropolitan Opera, Dec. 21, 1929); *Stiffelio* (Trieste, Nov. 16, 1850); *Rigoletto* (after Hugo's *Le Roi s'amuse;* Venice, March 11, 1851; London, May 14, 1853; N. Y., Academy of Music, Feb. 19, 1855; Metropolitan Opera, Nov. 16, 1883); *Il Trovatore* (Rome, Jan. 19, 1853; N. Y. Academy of Music, May 2, 1855; Metropolitan Opera, Oct. 26, 1883); *La Traviata* (also given as *Violetta;* Venice, March 6, 1853; N. Y., Academy of Music, Dec. 3, 1856; Metropolitan Opera, Nov. 6, 1883); *Les Vêpres siciliennes* (libretto by Scribe; Paris, June 13, 1855; N. Y., Academy of Music, Nov. 7, 1859; Milan, Feb. 4, 1856, as *Giovanna di Guzman); Simone Boccanegra* (Venice, March 12, 1857; revised, Milan, March 24, 1881; Metropolitan Opera, Jan. 28, 1932); *Aroldo* (a revision of *Stiffelio;* Rimini, Aug. 16, 1857); *Un Ballo in maschera* (Rome, Feb. 17, 1859; N. Y., Academy of Music, Feb. 11, 1861; Metropolitan Opera, Dec. 11, 1889); *La Forza del destino* (St. Petersburg, Nov. 10, 1862; N. Y., Academy of Music, Feb. 24, 1865; Metropolitan Opera, Nov. 15, 1918); *Don Carlos* (Paris, March 11, 1867; N. Y., Academy of Music, April 12, 1877; Metropolitan Opera, Dec. 23, 1920); *Aida* (Cairo, Dec. 24, 1871; Milan, Feb. 8, 1872; N. Y., Academy of Music, Nov. 25, 1873; Metropolitan Opera, in German, Nov. 12, 1886); *Otello* (Milan, Feb. 5, 1887; N. Y., Academy of Music, April 16, 1888; Metropolitan Opera, March 24, 1891); *Falstaff* (Milan, Feb. 9, 1893; Metropolitan Opera, Feb. 4, 1895). OTHER WORKS: Requiem Mass ('Manzoni Requiem'; 1874); *4 Pezzi sacri* (1898; *Ave Maria* and *Stabat Mater* for mixed chorus a cappella; *Laudi alla Vergine Maria* for female chorus a cappella; *Te Deum* for double chorus with orch.); *Inno delle Nazioni* (for the London Exhibition of 1862); a string quartet in E minor (1873); *Ave Maria* for soprano and strings (1880); *Pater noster* for 5-part chorus a cappella (1880); *6 Romanze (Non t'accostare all' urna; More, Elisa; In solitaria stanza; Nell'orror di notte oscura; Perduta ho la pace; Deh pietosa);* 2 songs for bass, *L'Esule* and *La Seduzione; Guarda che bianca luna,* nocturne for soprano, tenor, and bass with flute obbligato; *Album di sei romanze (Il Tramonto; La Zingara; Ad una stella; Lo Spazzacamino; Il Mistero; Brindisi); Il Poveretto,* romanza; *Tu dici che non m'ami,* stornello.

BIBLIOGRAPHY. — A. BIOGRAPHY: A. Pougin, *V.: Histoire anecdotique de sa vie et de ses œuvres* (Paris, 1886; in English, N. Y., 1887); E. Hanslick, *G. V. Zur Geschichte seines Lebens, insbesondere seiner Jugendzeit,* in *Suite* (Vienna, 1885); Prince de Valori, *V. et son œuvre* (Paris, 1895); L. Parodi, *G. V.* (Genoa, 1895); F. Crowest, *V.: Man and Musician* (London, 1897); G. Monaldi, *V.* (Turin, 1899; 3rd ed., Milan, 1943; German transl. as *G. V. und seine Werke,* Stuttgart, 1898, publ. before the Italian original); G. Cavarretta, *V.: Il Genio, la vita, le opere* (Palermo, 1899); C. Perinello, *G. V.* (Berlin, 1900); M. Basso, *G. V.: La sua vita, le sue opere, la sua morte* (Milan, 1901); N. Marini, *G. V.* (Rome, 1901); E. Checchi, *G. V.* (Florence, 1901); O. Boni, *V.: L'Uomo, le opere, l'artista* (Parma, 1901; 2nd ed., 1913); E. Colonna, *G. V. nella vita e nelle opere* (Palermo, 1902); L. Sorge, *G. V.: Uomo, artista, patriota* (Lanciano, 1904); P. Voss, *G. V. Ein Lebensbild* (Diessen, 1904); F. Garibaldi, *G. V. nella vita e nell'arte* (Florence, 1904); A. Visetti, *V.* (London, 1905); G. Bragagnolo and E. Bettazzi, *La Vita di G. V. narrata al popolo* (Milan, 1905); A. d'Angeli, *G. V.* (Bologna, 1910; 2nd ed., 1912); C. Bellaigue, *V. Biographie critique* (Paris, 1912; Italian transl., Milan, 1913); G. Monaldi, *Il Maestro della rivoluzione italiana* (Milan, 1913); M. Lottici, *Bio-bibliografia di G. V.* (Parma, 1913); A. Righetti, *G. V.: Vita aneddotica* (Rome, 1913); Sir A. Mackenzie, *V.* (N. Y., 1913); M. Chop, *V.* (Leipzig, 1913); G. Roncaglia, *G. V.* (Naples, 1914); A. Neisser, *G. V.* (Leipzig, 1914); A. Weissmann, *V.* (Berlin, 1922); A. Bonaventura, *G. V.* (Paris, 1923); G. Monaldi, *V. anedottico* (Turin, 1926); F. Ridella, *V.* (Genoa, 1928); E. Gascó Contell, *V., su vida y sus obras* (Paris, 1927); F. Bonavia, *V.* (London, 1930; 2nd ed., 1947); L. A. Garibaldi, ed., *G. V. nelle lettere di E. Muzio ad A. Barezzi* (Milan, 1931); C. Gatti, *V.* (Milan, 1931; 2nd ed., 1951; English transl., N. Y., 1955); F. Toye, *G. V.* (London, 1931); A. Baresel, *Was weisst du von V.* (1931); H. Gerigk, *G. V.* (Potsdam, 1932); R. de Rensis, *Franco Faccio e V.* (Milan, 1934); R. Manganella, *V.* (Milan, 1936); L. d'Ambra, *G. V.* (Milan, 1937); D. Hussey, *V.* (London, 1940); *Verdi, studi e memorie,* ed. by G. Mulè and G. Nataletti (Rome, 1941; contains precise documentation of ascertainable facts of Verdi's life; very valuable); G. Roncaglia, *G. V.* (Florence, 1941); F. Botti, *G. V.* (Rome, 1941); K. Holl, *V.* (Vienna, 1942); U. Zoppi, *Angelo Mariani, G. V. e Teresa Stolz* (Milan, 1947); F. H. Törnblom, *V.* (Stockholm, 1948); D. Humphreys, *V., Force of Destiny* (N. Y., 1948); A Oberdorfer, *G. V.* (Verona, 1949); A. E. A. Cherbuliez, *G. V.* (Zürich, 1949); G. Cenzato, *Itinerari verdiani* (Parma, 1949; 2nd ed., Milan, 1955); L. Orsini, *G. V.* (Turin, 1949); L. Gianoli, *V.* (Brescia, 1951); F. Abbiati, ed., *G. V.* (Milan, 1951); *G. V.* (collection of articles; Siena, 1951); G. Monaldi, *V., la vita, le opere* (Milan, 1951); E. Radius, *V. vivo* (Milan, 1951); G. Stefani, *V. e Trieste* (Trieste, 1951); G. Mondini, *Nel cinquantennio della morte di G. V.* (Cremona, 1952); F. Botti, *V. e l'ospedale di Villanova d'Arda* (Parma, 1952); T. R. Ybarra, *V., Miracle Man of Opera* (N. Y., 1955); V. Sheean, *Orpheus at Eighty* (N. Y., 1958); also a biographical novel by F. Werfel, *V.* (Berlin, 1924; English transl., N. Y., 1925). —B. Criticism, Appreciation: A. Basevi, *Studio sulle opere di G. V.* (Florence, 1859); G. Bertrand, *Les Nationalités musicales étudiées dans le drame lyrique. Verdisme et Wagnérisme* (Paris, 1872); E. Hanslick, *V.,* in *Die moderne Oper* (Berlin, 1875; 8th ed., 1885); B. Roosevelt, *V., Milan and Otello* (Milan, 1887); V. Maurel, *À propos de la mise-en-scène du drame lyrique 'Otello'* (Rome, 1888); E. Destranges, *L'Évolution musicale chez V.: Aïda, Otello, Falstaff* (Paris, 1895); C. Abate, *Wagner e V. Studio critico-musicale* (Mistretta, 1896); I. Pizzi, *Ricordi verdiani inediti* (Turin, 1901; contains 11 letters); A. Soffredini, *Le Opere di G. V.: Studio critico-analitico* (Milan, 1901); G. Tebaldini, *Da Rossini a V.* (Naples, 1901); P. Bellezza, *Manzoni e V., i due grandi* (Rome, 1901); J. G. Huneker, *Overtones* (N. Y., 1904); F. Flamini, *Pagine di critica e d'arte* (Leghorn, 1905; contains a study on the operas of Verdi); J. C. Hadden, *The Operas of V.* (London, 1910); K. Regensburger, *Über den 'Trovador' des García Gutiérrez, die Quelle von Verdis 'Il Trovatore'* (Berlin, 1911); C. Vanbianchi, *Saggio di bibliografia verdiana* (Milan, 1913); A. St. John-Brenon, *G. V.,* in the 'Mus. Quarterly' (Jan., 1916); E. Istel, *The 'Othello' of V. and Shakespeare* (ib., July, 1916) and *A Genetic Study of the Aïda Libretto* (ib., Jan., 1917); L. Unterholzner, *G. V.'s Operntypus* (Hanover, 1933); P. Berl, *Die Opern V.s in ihrer Instrumentation* (diss., Vienna, 1931); A. Maecklenburg, *V. and Manzoni,* in the 'Mus. Quarterly' (April, 1931); G. Menghini, *G. V. e il melodramma italiano* (Rimini, 1931); M. Mila, *Il Melodramma di V.* (Bari, 1933); A. Parente, *Il Problema della critica verdiana* (Turin, 1933); R. Gallusser, *V.s Frauengestalten* (diss., Zürich, 1936); J. Loschelder, *Das Todesproblem in V.s Opernschaffen* (Cologne, 1938); G. Engler, *V.s Anschauung vom Wesen der Oper* (diss.; Breslau, 1938); G. Roncaglia, *L'Ascensione creatrice di G. V.* (Florence, 1940); M. Rinaldi, *V. critico* (Rome, 1951); C. Gatti, *Revisioni e rivalutazioni verdiane* (Turin, 1952); also the special V. issue of the 'Rivista Musicale Italiana' (1901).—C. Correspondence, Iconography: G. Cesari and A. Luzio, *G. V. I copialettere pubblicati e illustrati* (Leipzig, 1913); G. Monaldi, *Saggio di iconografia verdiana* (Bergamo, 1913); T. Costantini, *Sei lettere inedite* (relating to the production of *Aida* in Cairo; Trieste, 1908); J. G. Prod'homme, *Unpublished Letters from V. to Camille Du Locle (1866-76),* in the 'Mus. Quarterly' (Jan., 1921); A. Martinelli, *G. V. Raggi e Penombre. Le ultime lettere* (Trieste, 1926); *Briefe* (transl. into German by P. Stefan, Vienna, 1926); G. Morazzoni, *Lettere inedite di G. V.* (Milan, 1929); A. Alberti, *V. intimo: carteggio di G. V. con il conte O. Arrivabene* (Verona, 1931); *Sei lettere inedite a G. Bottesini* (Trieste, 1934); A. Luzio, *Il Pensiero artistico e politico di G. V. nelle sue lettere inedite al conte O. Arrivabene* (Milan); C. Gatti, *V. nelle immagini* (Milan, 1941); C. Graziani, *G. V.: Autobiografia dalle lettere* (Milan, 1941; new ed., 1951, under Graziani's real name, Aldo Oberdorfer); F. Werfel and P. Stefan, eds., *V., The Man in His Letters* (N. Y., 1942).

Vere, Clémentine Duchene de (real name Wood de Vere), noted soprano; b. Paris, Dec. 12, 1864; d. Mount Vernon, N. Y., Jan. 19, 1954. Her father was a Belgian nobleman; her mother, an English lady. Her musical education was completed under the instruction of Mme. Albertini-Baucardé in Florence, where she made her début at the age of 16 as Marguerite de Valois in *Les Huguenots;* after appearances in Europe, she was engaged as Marguerite in a concert performance of Berlioz's *Damnation of Faust* at the Metropolitan Opera House, N. Y. (Feb. 2, 1896). Her operatic roles at the Metropolitan Opera were Violetta, Gilda, Marguerite in Gounod's *Faust,* and Lucia. In 1892 she married the conductor Romualdo Sapio (q. v.); after 1914 she lived mostly in N. Y., as a private teacher. Her voice was a brilliant high soprano; she excelled in coloratura.

Veremans, Renaat, Belgian composer; b. Lierre, March 2, 1894. He studied at the Antwerp Cons.; from 1921 to 1944, was director of the Flemish Opera there. He wrote the Flemish operas *Beatrice* (1930) and *Anna-Marie* (Antwerp, Feb. 22, 1938); symph. works; chamber music; choruses; many songs.

Veress, Sándor, Hungarian composer; b. Kolozsvár, Feb. 1, 1907. He studied piano with his mother and composition with Bartók and Kodály. In 1947 he left Hungary and went to Rome; later settled in Switzerland, and was appointed prof. of composition at Bern Univ. —Works: ballet, *Terszili Katica* (1943; Stockholm, Feb. 16, 1949); violin concerto (1939; Zurich, Jan. 9, 1951); *4 Transylvanian Dances* for string orch. (1944); *Threnos* in memory of Béla Bartók (1945); concerto for piano, strings, and percussion (Baden Baden, Jan. 19, 1954, composer soloist); *Sinfonia Minneapolitana* (Minneapolis, March 12, 1954); 2 string quartets; trio for oboe, clarinet, and bassoon; sonata for violin and piano; songs. —Cf. C. Mason, *Sándor Veress,* in the 'Chesterian' (Oct., 1951); E. Doflein, *Sándor Veress,* in 'Melos' (March, 1954).

Veretti, Antonio, Italian composer; b. Verona, Feb. 20, 1900. He studied composition with Alfano at the Liceo Musicale of Bologna, graduating in 1921. He taught at the Cons. of Rome (until 1943); was director of the Conservatorio G. Rossini in Pesaro (1950-52); director of the Cons. of Cagliari (1953-55). —Works: operas: *Il Medico volante* (1928; won a prize of the newspaper 'Il Secolo,' but was never performed) and *Il Favorito del re* (La Scala, Milan, March 17, 1932); ballets: *Il galante tiratore* (San Remo, Feb. 11, 1933) and *Una Favola di Andersen* (Venice, Sept. 15, 1934); oratorios: *Il Cantico dei Cantici* (Bologna, 1922) and *Il Figliuol prodigo* (1943); *Sinfonia italiana* (Liège Festival of the International Society for Contemporary Music, Sept. 4, 1930); *Morte e deificazione di Dafni,* for voice and 11 instruments (Venice Festival, Sept. 8, 1937); *Sinfonia epica* (1939); *Divertimento,* for harpsichord and 6 instruments (1939); *Sinfonia sacra,* for male voices and orch. (1946); piano concerto (Venice International Festival, Sept. 9, 1950); *Duo strumentale,* for violin and piano (1925); cello sonata (1926); piano trio (1927); music for films. —Cf. N. Costarelli, *Antonio Veretti,* in the 'Rassegna Musicale' (Jan.-March, 1955).

Verhulst (fär-hülst'), **Johannes (Josephus Herman),** Dutch conductor and composer; b. The Hague, March 19, 1816; d. there, Jan. 17, 1891. He studied violin at The Hague and Cologne; in 1838 went to Leipzig, where he became friendly with Mendelssohn; was engaged as conductor of the 'Euterpe' concerts (until 1842); then returned to The Hague, where he became royal music director; organized music festivals in Holland between 1850 and 1883, and wrote cantatas for them. He was conductor of the renowned 'Diligentia' concerts at The Hague from 1860 until 1886; also conducted in Amsterdam and Rotterdam. He wrote a number of symph. works; chamber music, sacred songs, choruses to Dutch words.

Vermeulen, Matthijs, Dutch composer and music critic; b. Helmond, Feb. 8, 1888. He studied with Diepenbrock; then wrote music criticism in Amsterdam (1908-21); in 1921 settled in Paris, where he remained until 1946; returned to Amsterdam and became music editor of 'De Groene Amsterdammer.' He wrote 5 symphonies (1914, 1919, 1922, 1941, 1945); chamber music; songs. Publ. a collection of essays, *De twee muzieken* (2 vols., Leyden, 1918), and *Principepen der Europese muziek* (Amsterdam, 1949). —Cf. W. Paap, *De Componist Matthijs Vermeulen,* in 'Mens en Melodie' (Nov., 1949).

Verne, Mathilde, Alice, and **Adela,** English pianists, sisters of Marie Wurm (q. v.). Their real name was Wurm, but they adopted the name Verne in 1893. **Mathilde**

Verne (b. Southampton, May 25, 1865; d. London, June 4, 1936) studied with her parents, and then became a pupil of Clara Schumann in Frankfurt; was very successful in England; from 1907 to 1936 gave concerts of chamber music in London; was a renowned teacher. **Alice Verne Bredt** (b. Southampton, Aug. 9, 1868; d. London, April 12, 1958) was best known as a piano teacher; also composed pedagogical works. **Adela Verne** (b. Southampton, Feb. 27, 1877; d. London, Feb. 5, 1952) studied with her sisters, and later took lessons from Paderewski in Switzerland; returning to London, she developed a successful career, and became extremely popular as a concert player in England; also made tours in the U. S. —Cf. Mathilde Verne, *Chords of Remembrance* (London, 1936).

Verneuil, Raoul de, Peruvian composer; b. Lima, April 9, 1899. He studied in Paris with André Bloch, and lived there for many years; returned to Lima in 1940, after a brief sojourn in N. Y. On Nov. 21, 1940, he gave a concert of his chamber music in Lima. He has written a *Danza Peruana* for orch.; an *Inca Legend* for voice and 8 instruments; *Rítmos del Sol* for 12-part chorus; piano pieces.

Verrall, John, American composer; b. Britt, Iowa, June 17, 1908. He studied composition and piano with Donald Ferguson, and cello with Engelbert Roentgen; attended the Royal College of Music in London (1929-30) and the Liszt Cons. in Budapest, studying with Kodály. Returning to the U. S. in 1932, he entered the Univ. of Minnesota (B. A., 1934); later took courses with Aaron Copland at Tanglewood, Roy Harris at Colorado College, and Frederick Jacobi at the Juilliard School of Music. He received a Guggenheim Fellowship in 1946. He taught at Hamline Univ. (1934-42) and at Mount Holyoke College (1942-46); served as editor for G. Schirmer, Inc. (1947-48). In 1948 he was appointed instructor at the Univ. of Washington. —Works: operas: *The Cowherd and the Sky Maiden,* after a Chinese legend (Seattle, Jan. 17, 1952), *The Wedding Knell,* after Hawthorne (Seattle, Dec. 5, 1952), *Three Blind Mice* (Seattle, May 22, 1955); for orch.: Symph. No. 1 (Minneapolis, Jan. 16, 1940), *Portrait of Man,* symph. suite (1940), Symph. No. 2 (1943), violin concerto (1946), *Symph. for Young Orchestras* (1948), *Dark Night of Saint John* (1949), *Variations on an Ancient Tune* (1955), *Portrait of Saint Christopher,* symph. poem (1956); for band: *A Northern Overture* for band (1946), *Sinfonia Festiva* for band (1954); chamber music: cello sonata (1932), Divertimento for clarinet, horn, and bassoon (1939), trio for 2 violins and viola (1940), 6 string quartets (1940, 1943, 1948, 1949, 1952, 1956), *Concert Piece* for strings and horn (1940), sonata for horn and piano (1942), sonata for viola and piano (1942), Serenade No. 1 for wind quintet (1944), a violin sonata (1949), *Appalachian Folk Song,* for cello and piano (1953), piano quintet (1953), Serenade No. 2 for wind quintet (1954), sonata for oboe and piano (1956), Serenade and Pastorale for flute and organ (1956), Suite for brass sextet (1956), Suite for 3 clarinets (1957), Sonatina for cello and piano (1957), Nocturne for bass clarinet and piano (1958); a piano sonata (1951) and *Sketches and Miniatures* for piano (1954); several choruses; publ. *Elements of Harmony* (1937) and *Form and Meaning in the Arts* (1958). —Cf. James Beale, *The Music of John Verrall,* in the 'Bulletin of American Composers Alliance' (1958, vol. 7; also contains a full list of works).

Verstovsky, Alexey Nikolayevitch, Russian composer; b. on the family estate in the district of Tambov, March 1, 1799; d. Moscow, Nov. 17, 1862. He was sent to St. Petersburg at the age of 10; there he studied with the resident German teacher, Johann Heinrich Miller, and with John Field (piano); his other teachers were Maurer (violin), Steibelt (piano), and Tarquini (voice). His first theatrical piece was an intermezzo, *Sentimental Landlord in a Village* (1818); he then produced a number of light operas in St. Petersburg: *Grandmother's Parrot* (Aug. 10, 1819); *Quarantine* (Aug. 7, 1820); *New Mischief* (Feb. 24, 1822); *The Madhouse* (Oct. 28, 1822); and *A Charade in Action* (Jan. 15, 1823; with Maurer). In 1823 he moved to Moscow, where he was engaged as inspector of the imperial theaters. There he produced a long series of vaudevilles: *Who is Brother, Who is Sister?* (Feb. 5, 1824); *Teacher and Pupil* (May 6, 1824); *The Petitioner* (June 10, 1824); *30,000 Men* (Feb. 10, 1825); *The Caliph's Amusements* (April 21, 1825); *The Miraculous Nose* (Oct. 20, 1825); *Itinerant Doctors* (Feb. 16, 1827); *5 Years in 2 Hours* (Feb. 1, 1828); *15 Years in Paris* (Feb. 8, 1828); *Man and Wife* (June 4, 1830); *The Old Hussar* (June 17, 1831); wrote couplets and songs for various plays (mostly translations from the French) produced in Moscow. He turned to the composition of serious operatic works in 1828; wrote the following operas, all produced in Moscow: *Pan Tvardovsky* (June 5, 1828); *Vadim,* or *12 Sleeping Maidens* (Dec. 7, 1832); *Askold's Grave* (Sept. 27, 1835; his most important work; still in the repertory of Russian opera houses); *Homesickness* (Sept. 2, 1839); *Gromoboy* (Feb. 5, 1858). A contemporary of Glinka, he contributed much to the progress of operatic art in Russia; he possessed a gift of facile invention, even though he lacked originality. —Cf. V. Tcheshikhin, *History of Russian Opera* (St. Petersburg, 1905, pp. 98-108); see also the biographical sketch on Verstovsky in the modern edition of his opera-vaudeville, *Who is Brother, Who is Sister?* (Moscow, 1949).

Vesque von Püttlingen, Johann, Austrian composer; b. Opole, Poland, July 23, 1803; d. Vienna, Oct. 30, 1883. He studied law in Vienna and became a councillor of state; at the same time he studied music with Moscheles (piano) and Sechter (theory), and made his mark as a composer of operas, under the pseudonym J. Hoven. The following operas by him were produced in Vienna: *Turandot* (Oct. 3, 1838), *Johanna d'Arc* (Dec. 30, 1840), and *Abenteuer Carls des Zweiten* (Jan. 12, 1850). His opera *Der lustige Rat* was produced in Weimar on April 12, 1852. He publ. a useful book, *Das musikalische Autorrecht* (1865). —Cf. E. Hanslick, *Vesque von Püttlingen,* in 'Musikalisches Skizzenbuch' (Berlin, 1888); H. Schultz, *Johann Vesque von Püttlingen* (Regensburg, 1930).

Vetter (fĕt'-tĕr), **Walther,** German musicologist; b. Berlin, May 10, 1891. He studied with Hermann Abert in Halle and Leipzig; then wrote music criticism in Halle; taught at Danzig (1921-27), Breslau (1927), Halle (1928), at the Univ. of Hamburg (1929-34), Univ. of Breslau (1934-36), Univ. of Greifswald (1936-41), Univ. of Poznan during German occupation (1941-43); in 1946 appointed prof. of musicology at Humboldt Univ., Berlin, as successor to Arnold Schering; from 1957 ed. of 'Deutsches Jahrbuch der Musikwissenschaft.' —Books: *Das frühdeutsche Lied* (2 vols., Münster, 1928); *Franz Schubert* (Potsdam, 1934); *Antike Musik* (Munich, 1935); *J. S. Bach* (Leipzig, 1938); *Beethoven und die militärisch-politischen Ereignisse seiner Zeit* (Poznan, 1943); *Der Kapellmeister Bach* (Potsdam, 1950); *Der Klassiker Schubert* (2 vols., Leipzig, 1953); *Mythos-Melos-Musica* (Leipzig, 1957).

Viadana, Lodovico (da), Italian composer; b. Viadana, near Mantua, 1564; d. Gualtieri, May 2, 1645. His family was Grossi, but he is generally known by the name of his birthplace; pupil of Ercole Porta; became a Franciscan monk in 1596; from 1594 till 1609, was maestro di cappella at the Mantua Cathedral; from 1610 to 1612, chorusmaster at Fano (Papal States), then in Venice, and finally in Mantua again. He was formerly accredited with the invention of the basso continuo (thorough-bass); but Peri's *Euridice* (publ. 1600) has a figured bass in certain numbers, as does Banchieri's *Concerti ecclesiastici* (publ. 1595); whereas Viadana's *Cento concerti . . . con il basso continuo* did not appear till 1602 (Venice). However, he was the first to write church concertos with so few parts that the organ continuo was employed as a necessary harmonic support. A very prolific composer, he publ. numerous Masses, psalms, Magnificats, Lamentations, motets, etc. —Cf. A. Parazzi, *Della Vita e delle opere musicali di L. Grossi-Viadana* (Milan, 1876); F. X. Haberl, in 'Kirchenmusikalisches Jahrbuch' (1881) and 'Musica Sacra' (1897); M. Schneider, *Die Anfänge des Basso Continuo* (with 11 numbers from the *Cento concerti* of 1602; 1918); F. T. Arnold, *The Art of Accompaniment from a Thorough Bass* (London, 1931); F. B. Pratella, *Viadana e la sinfonia,* in 'Il Pensiero Musicale' (Sept.-Nov., 1922). See also G. Reese, *Music in the Renaissance* (N. Y., 1954; pp. 488-89).

Vianesi, Auguste-Charles-Léonard-François, conductor; b. Leghorn, Nov. 2, 1837; d. New York, Nov. 4, 1908. After studying in Italy, he went to Paris in 1857; in 1859 became conductor at Drury Lane, London; later conducted Italian Opera at Covent Garden; in 1887 became principal conductor at the Grand Opéra, Paris. He conducted the performance of *Faust* at the opening night of the Metropolitan Opera House (N. Y., Oct. 22, 1883), and was on its staff throughout its first season; also conducted during the season of 1891-92; then remained in N. Y. as a vocal teacher.

Vianna, Fructuoso, Brazilian composer; b. Itajubá, Oct. 6, 1896. He studied in Rio de Janeiro with Henrique Oswald, and later in Paris (1923). Upon his return to Brazil, he was appointed to the faculty of the Cons. of S. Paulo. He wrote a number of piano pieces based on Brazilian melodic and rhythmic modes: *Dança de Negros, Tamborzinho, Tanguinho, Corta-Jaca, 7 Minia-*

turas sobre temas brasileiros, Seresta, 5 'valsas,' 6 'toadas,' etc.; several choral works and songs; a few violin pieces.

Vianna da Motta, José. See **Da Motta.**

Viardot-García (v'yăhr-doh'-găhr-thē'ah), **Pauline,** celebrated singer; daughter of Manuel del Popolo García; b. Paris, July 18, 1821; d. there, May 18, 1910. She was taken by her parents to England and America; had piano lessons from Vega, organist at Mexico Cathedral; also (on returning to Paris in 1828) from Meysenberg and Liszt. Her father and mother both gave her vocal instruction; Reicha was her teacher in harmony. Her concert début was at Brussels in 1837; after singing in Germany and Paris, she came out in opera at London, 1839, as Desdemona in Rossini's *Otello,* and was engaged by Viardot, the director of the Théâtre Italien, Paris. She sang there until her marriage to Viardot in 1841; he then accompanied her on long tours throughout Europe. She created the role of Fides in Meyerbeer's *Le Prophète* at the Paris Opéra in 1849, and that of Sapho in Gounod's opera, 1851; after another succession of tours, she took the role of Orphée in Berlioz's revival of Gluck's opera at the Théâtre Lyrique (1859), singing the part 150 nights to crowded houses. She retired to Baden-Baden in 1863; from 1871 she lived in Paris and Bougival. Her voice was a mezzo-soprano of extraordinary compass (from *c* to *f*³). For some years she taught at the Paris Cons.; among her pupils were Désirée Artôt and Antoinette Sterling. A thoroughly trained musician, she also composed operas, one of which, *Le dernier sorcier,* was performed (in a German version) at Weimar (1869), Karlsruhe, and Riga. About 60 vocal melodies were published, and won wide popularity; also 6 pieces for piano and violin and an *École classique de chant.* She owned the holograph of Mozart's *Don Giovanni,* which she left to the Library of the Cons. in Paris. She was for many years a companion of the Russian novelist Turgenev, in Paris. —Cf. La Mara, *P. Viardot-Garcia* (Leipzig, 1882); L. H. Torrigi, *P. Viardot-Garcia. Sa biographie, ses compositions, son enseignement* (Geneva, 1901); C. H. Kaminski, *Lettres à Mlle. Viardot d'Ivan Tourgéneff* (Paris, 1907); *P. Viardot-Garcia to J. Rietz. Letters of Friendship,* in the 'Mus. Quarterly' (July, 1915-Jan., 1916); T. Marix-Spire, *Gounod and His Interpreter, Pauline Viardot,* in the 'Mus. Quarterly' (April, July, 1945); A. Rachmanowa (pseud.), *Die Liebe eines Lebens: Iwan Turgenjew und Pauline Viardot* (Frauenfeld, 1952); also the memoirs of her daughter, Louise Héritte-Viardot, *Memories and Adventures* (London, 1913; transl. from original German MS; also in French, Paris, 1923).

Vicentino (vē-chĕhn-tē'-noh), **Nicola,** Italian music theorist; b. Vicenza, 1511; d. Rome, 1572. Pupil of Willaert at Venice; then became maestro and music master to Cardinal Ippolito d'Este in Ferrara and in Rome. There his book of madrigals for 5 voices, an attempt to revive the chromatic and enharmonic genera of the Greeks, led to an academic controversy with the learned Portuguese musician Lusitano; defeated, Vicentino publ. a theoretical treatise, *L'antica musica ridotta alla moderna prattica* (1555), which contains a description of his invention, an instrument called the archicembalo (having 6 keyboards, with separate strings and keys for distinguishing the ancient genera—diatonic, chromatic, and enharmonic). He also invented and described (1561) an 'archiorgano.' In chromatic composition he was followed by Cipriano de Rore and Gesualdo. His work paved the way for the monodic style, and the eventual disuse of the church modes. —Cf. H. Riemann, *Geschichte der Musiktheorie* (Leipzig, 1898); Th. Kroyer, *Die Anfänge der Chromatik im italienischen Madrigal des XVI. Jahrhunderts* ('Beihefte der Internationalen Musik-Gesellschaft,' IV). See also G. Reese, *Music in the Renaissance* (N. Y., 1954; pp. 328-29).

Victoria, Tomás Luis de (Italianized form, Tommaso Luigi da Vittoria), the greatest of Spanish composers; b. Avila, c. 1549; d. Madrid, Aug. 27, 1611. There is no record of Victoria's early years in Avila, but in all probability he received his first musical training as a choir-boy at the Cathedral there. In 1565 he went to Rome, and to prepare himself for the priesthood entered the Collegium Germanicum, a seminary founded by St. Ignatius Loyola in 1552. In Rome his teacher may have been Palestrina, who from 1566 to 1571 was music master at the Roman Seminary, at this time amalgamated with the Collegium Germanicum. Victoria was about the same age as Palestrina's two sons, Rodolfo and Angelo, who were students at the Roman Seminary; the Italian master is known to have befriended his young Spanish colleague, and when Palestrina left the Roman Seminary in 1571, it was Victoria who succeeded him as maestro there. In 1569, Victoria had left the Collegium Germanicum to become choirmaster and organist in the Church of Sta. Maria di Montserrato; from this time on he also officiated frequently at musical ceremonies in the Church of S. Giaccomo degli Spagnuoli. In June, 1573, he returned to the Collegium Germanicum as maestro di cappella; 2 years later the Collegium moved to new quarters in the Palazzo S. Apollinare, and Victoria thereby became choirmaster of the adjoining Church of S. Apollinare. In Aug., 1575, he was ordained a priest; in Jan. of that year he had received a benefice at León from the Pope, and in 1579 he was granted another benefice at Zamora, neither requiring residence. In 1587 he resigned his post at the Collegium Germanicum and was admitted as a priest to the Church of S. Girolamo della Carità, where he lived until 1585; this was the church where St. Philip Neri held his famous religious meetings, which led to the founding of the Congregation of the Oratory in 1575. Though Victoria was not a member of the Oratory, he must have taken some part in its important musical activities, living as he did for 5 years under the same roof with its founder (St. Philip left S. Girolamo in 1583); he is known to have been on terms of the closest friendship with Juvenal Ancina, a priest of the Oratory who wrote texts for many of the 'Laudi spirituali' sung at the meetings of the Congregation. In 1583, dedicating a volume of Masses to Philip II, Victoria expressed a desire to return to his native land; but this wish does not appear to have been fulfilled until some 12 years later. He probably returned to Spain in 1594; in the dedication of his 2nd book of Masses (1592) he mentions for the first time his appointment as chaplain to the widowed Empress-Mother Maria, sister of Philip II, who in 1582 had taken up her residence in the Convent of the Descalzas Reales in Madrid. After his return to Spain, Victoria became organist and choirmaster at this convent, and when the Empress Maria died in 1603, he continued to act as chaplain to her daughter, the Princess Margaret, who was a nun in the Descalzas Reales. His last work, a Requiem Mass for the Empress Maria, regarded as his masterpiece, was publ. in 1605. — Beginning with a vol. of motets in 1572, dedicated to his chief patron, Cardinal Otto Truchsess, Bishop of Augsburg, most of Victoria's works were printed in Italy, in sumptuous editions, showing that he had the backing of wealthy patrons. A vol. of Masses, Magnificats, motets, and other church music publ. at Madrid in 1600 is of special interest because it makes provision for an organ accompaniment.—A man of deep religious sentiment, Victoria expresses in his music all the ardor and exaltation of Spanish mysticism. He is generally regarded as a leading representative of the Roman School, but it should be remembered that, before the appearance of Palestrina, this school was already profoundly marked by Hispanic influences through the work of Morales, Guerrero, Escobedo, and other Spanish composers resident in Rome. Thus Victoria inherited at least as much from his own countrymen as from Palestrina, and in its dramatic intensity, its rhythmic variety, its tragic grandeur and spiritual fervor, his music is thoroughly personal and thoroughly Spanish. —Works publ. in Victoria's lifetime: motets for 4, 5, 6, and 8 voices (Venice, 1572; contains the well-known motets *O quam gloriosum* and *O vos omnes); Liber primus qui Missas, Psalmos, Magnificat, ad Virginem Dei Matrem Salutationes, aliaque complectitur* (Venice, 1576); *Cantica B. Virginis per annum* (Rome, 1581); *Hymni totius anni* (Rome, 1581; new ed., Venice, 1600); motets for 4, 5, 6, 8, and 12 voices (Rome, 1583); *Missarum libri duo,* 4-6 voices (Rome' 1583); *Officium Hebdomadae Sanctae* (Rome, 1585); *Motecta Festorum totius anni,* 4, 5, 6, and 8 voices (Rome, 1585; new eds. printed at Milan and Dillingen in 1589); *Missae Liber secundus,* 4-8 voices (Rome, 1592); *Missae, Magnificat, Motecta, Psalmi* . . . for 8, 9, and 12 voices (Madrid, 1600; contains both old and new works); *Officium Defunctorum,* 6 voices (Madrid, 1605).—Pedrell brought out a complete modern ed. of Victoria's works in 8 vols. (Breitkopf & Härtel, 1902-13). Many selections are in Proske's 'Musica divina'; Eslava's 'Lira Sacro-Hispana' contains the Requiem and other works; the *Officium Hebdomadae Sanctae* is in Pustet's 'Repertorium musicae sacrae' vol. 2 (Regensburg, 1898); other reprints in Casimiri's 'Societas polyphonica Romana' (Rome, 1925-34), Wüllner's 'Chorübungen' (new ed. by E. Schwickerath; Munich, 1931), Schering's 'Beispielen' (No. 128), H. Bäuerle's 'Hymnen und Motetten alter Meister' (Augsburg, 1936), Davison and Apel's 'Historical Anthology of Music' (vol. 1, No. 149), etc. —BIBLIOGRAPHY: L. Celler, *La Semaine Sainte au Vatican* (Paris, 1867); H. Collet, *Le Mysticisme musical espagnol au XVIe siècle* (Paris, 1913) and *T. L. de Victoria* (Paris, 1914); G. Radiciotti, *Due musicisti spagnuoli,* in 'Sammelbände der Internationalen Musik-Gesellschaft' XIV; F. Pedrell, *T. L. de Victoria* (Valencia, 1918); R. Mitjana, *Estudi-*

os sobre algunos músicos españoles del siglo XVI (Madrid, 1918) and *La Musique en Espagne,* in 'Encyclopédie du Conservatoire,' part I, vol. IV (Paris, 1920); J. B. Trend, *T. L. de Victoria,* in the 'Mus. Times' (April, 1925); R. Casimiri, *'Il Vittoria'* (Rome, 1934); Hans von May, *Die Kompositionstechnik T. L. de Victorias* (Bern, 1943); also P. Wagner, *Geschichte der Messe* I, p. 421 ff., Hugo Leichtentritt, *Geschichte der Motette,* p. 373 ff., and G. Reese, *Music in the Renaissance,* p. 599 ff.

Victory, Gerard, Irish composer; b. Dublin, Dec. 24, 1921. He studied at the National Univ. of Ireland; became active as conductor of operettas and musical comedies and musical director at the Abbey Theatre in Dublin. —Works: 2 operettas, *Nita* (1944) and *Once Upon a Moon* (1949); ballet *The Enchanted Garden* (1950); *Marche Pittoresque* for orch. (1951); a piano concerto and numerous choral and instrumental pieces for the Dublin Radio. His opera in Gaelic, *An Fear a Phós Balbhín (The Silent Wife),* was produced with considerable success at the Abbey Theatre in Dublin, on April 6, 1953, under the composer's direction.

Vidal, Louis-Antoine, French writer on music; b. Rouen, July 10, 1820; d. Paris, Jan. 7, 1891. He studied cello with Franchomme; made a specialty of string-instrument research; publ. a valuable survey, *Les Instruments à archet, les faiseurs, les joueurs d'instruments, leur histoire sur le continent européen, suivie d'un catalogue général de la musique de chambre* (3 vols.; Paris, 1876-78; with 120 illustrative plates); sections of this work were publ. separately as *Les vieilles corporations de Paris* (1878) and *La Lutherie et les luthiers* (1889).

Vidal (vē-dahl'), **Paul,** noted French composer and pedagogue; b. Toulouse, June 16, 1863; d. Paris, April 9, 1931. He studied at the Paris Cons. and in 1883 won the Prix de Rome with his cantata *Le Gladiateur;* in 1889 he joined the staff of the Paris Opéra, as choral director; later became conductor there (until 1906). He taught elementary courses at the Paris Cons. from 1894 until 1910, when he was appointed prof. of composition; his class was one of the most important there. —Stage works: ballet, *La Maladetta* (Paris Opéra, Feb. 24, 1893); opera, *Guernica* (Opéra-Comique, June 7, 1895); a mystery play, *Noël, ou Le Mystère de la Nativité* (Galerie Vivienne, Paris, Nov. 25, 1890); operetta, *Éros* (Bouffes-Parisiens, April 22, 1892); in collaboration with André Messager, he orchestrated a dance suite from music by Chopin (1913); also arranged an orchestral suite from his mystery play *Les Mystères d'Eleusis;* composed piano pieces and songs. He publ. several instructive manuals, much used in France: *Manuel pratique d'harmonie; Notes et observations sur la composition et exécution;* compiled *52 Leçons d'harmonie de Luigi Cherubini* (3 vols.); *Solfège* (2 vols., Paris, 1922).

Vieira, Ernesto, Portuguese music historian; b. Lisbon, May 24, 1848; d. there, April 26, 1915. His main achievement was the publication of the *Diccionario biografico de musicos portuguezes* (Lisbon, 1900), which supplemented the earlier dictionary by Vasconcellos (1870).

Vierdanck (fēr'-dank), **Johann,** German organist and composer; b. c. 1610; date of death unknown. He was a chorister in Dresden, where he was a pupil of Schütz; was sent to Vienna in 1628 for further study; was church organist at the Marienkirche, Stralsund (1641-56). He publ. *Ballette und Corrente* for violin with continuo (1637; 1641); spiritual 'concertos' for 2-9 voices; of these, several were brought out in modern eds. by Hans Engel (Kassel, 1932 and 1934) and Hans Erdmann (Kassel, 1950).

Vierling (fēr'-ling), **Georg,** German organist and composer; b. Frankenthal, Bavaria, Sept. 5, 1820; d. Wiesbaden, May 1, 1901. He was a pupil of his father, the organist Jacob Vierling (1796-1867); then studied organ with Rinck in Darmstadt and composition with A. B. Marx in Berlin. He occupied various posts as organist and choral conductor in the German provinces; then settled in Berlin, where he founded and conducted the 'Bach-Verein'; became a member of the Berlin Academy in 1882. A catalogue of his works was issued in 1897; they include the secular cantatas *Der Raub der Sabinerinnen, Alarichs Tod,* and *Constantin;* the choral works (with orch.) *Hero und Leander* and *Zur Weinlese;* a symph.; several overtures *(Maria Stuart, Die Hexe, Im Frühling,* etc.); *Capriccio* for piano and orch.; *Phantasiestück* for cello and piano; 2 string quartets; a piano trio; a number of piano pieces *(Valse-Caprice,* 2 Impromptus, etc.); songs.

Vierling (fēr'-ling), **Johann Gottfried,** German organist and composer; b. Metzels, near Meiningen, Jan. 25, 1750; d. Schmalkalden, Nov. 22, 1813. His teachers were K. P. E. Bach in Hamburg and Kirnberger in Berlin, from whom he acquired contrapuntal skill in composition in the Bach style. He publ. several collections of organ pieces; a piano quartet; 2 piano trios; 8 piano sonatas; in MS there are 2 sets of church cantatas for the entire year. His theoretical manuals, *Versuch einer Anleitung zum Präludieren* (1794) and *Allgemein fasslicher Unterricht im Generalbass* (1805), are of value. —Cf. K. Paulke, *J. G. Vierling*, in 'Archiv für Musikwissenschaft' (1922).

Vierne (vyärn'), **Louis,** blind French organist and composer; b. Poitiers, Oct. 8, 1870; d. Paris, June 2, 1937. He was a pupil of César Franck and Widor at the Paris Cons., winning 1st prize for organ playing; in 1892 he became Widor's assistant at St. Sulpice, and in 1900 was appointed organist at Notre Dame, holding this position until his death (he died suddenly while playing the organ at a service there). From 1912 he taught organ at the Schola Cantorum; gave many concerts in Europe; in 1927 played in the U. S. His organ works include 5 'symphonies' and many smaller pieces. Among his pupils were Nadia Boulanger, Marcel Dupré, and Joseph Bonnet. —Cf. *In Memoriam Louis Vierne* (Paris, 1939); B. Gavoty, *Louis Vierne, la vie et l'œuvre* (Paris, 1943).

Vietinghoff-Scheel (fē'-tēn-gof shāl), **Boris Alexandrovitch,** Baron, Russian composer; b. in Latvia, 1829; d. St. Petersburg, Sept. 25, 1901. He was a student of Henselt and Dargomyzhsky in St. Petersburg. Three of his operas were produced in St. Petersburg: *Mazeppa* (May 17, 1859), *Tamara* (May 2 1886), and *Don Juan de Tenorio* (Nov. 2, 1888); 2 other operas, *Mary Stuart* and *Heliodora,* were not produced. He also wrote a *Fantastic Overture* (1859; Liszt commented with interest on the use of the whole-tone scale in the finale; see *Letters of Franz Liszt,* London, 1894; vol. 1). Vietinghoff published a bok of memoirs, *World Celebrities* (St. Petersburg, 1899).

Vieuille, Felix, French bass singer; b. Saugeon, Oct. 15, 1872; d. there, Feb. 28, 1953. He was a member of the Opéra-Comique from 1898; created the role of Arkel at the première of Debussy's *Pelléas et Mélisande* (1902).

Vieuxtemps (vyö-tahn'), **Henri,** celebrated Belgian violinist and composer; b. Verviers, Feb. 17, 1820; d. Mustapha, Algiers, June 6, 1881. His first teacher was his father, a piano tuner, who soon turned him over to Lecloux, with whom he made a concert tour at the age of 8. He then continued his studies with Bériot in Brussels (1829-30); took harmony lessons from Sechter in Vienna (1833) and Reicha in Paris (1835). In 1834 he visited London, where he appeared with the Philharmonic (June 2, 1834). In 1837 he revisited Vienna; in 1838-39 gave concerts in Russia. During his constant travels, he composed violin concertos and other violin works which became part of the standard repertory, and which he performed in Europe to the greatest acclaim. He made his first American tour in 1844-45. In 1846 he was engaged as prof. at the St. Petersburg Cons., and remained in Russia for 5 seasons; his influence on Russian concert life and violin composition was considerable. In 1853 he recommenced his concert tours in Europe; paid 2 more visits to America, in 1857 (with Thalberg) and in 1870 (with Christine Nilsson). He was prof. of violin playing at the Brussels Cons. (1871-73); a stroke of paralysis, affecting his left side, forced him to end all concert activities, but he continued to teach privately. He went to Algiers for rest, and died there; one of his most prominent pupils, Jenö Hubay, was with him at his death. In 1844, Vieuxtemps married the pianist Josephine Eder (b. Vienna, Dec. 15, 1815; d. Celle-St. Cloud, June 29, 1868).—With Bériot, Vieuxtemps stood at the head of the modern French school of violin playing; contemporary accounts speak of the extraordinary precision of his technique and of his perfect ability to sustain a flowing melody; the expression 'le roi de violon' was often applied to him in the press. Besides his 7 violin concertos (the last one being posthumous), he wrote for violin and orch.: *Fantaisie-Caprice, Souvenirs de Russie, Fantasia appassionata, Ballade et polonaise,* and *Old England,* a caprice on English airs of the 16th and 17th centuries. For violin and piano he composed *Hommage à Paganini; Grosse Fantasie über slavische Volksmelodien; Andante und Rondo;* Suite in B minor; *Marche funèbre;* etc.; numerous brilliant transcriptions of operatic airs. Also wrote 3 cadenzas to Beethoven's violin concerto; a sonata for viola (or cello) and piano. —Cf. L. Escudier, *Mes Souvenirs: Les Virtuoses* (Paris, 1868); M. Kufferath, *Henri Vieuxtemps* (Brussels, 1882); J. T. Radoux, *Vieuxtemps, sa vie, ses œuvres* (Liège, 1891); P. Bergmans, *Henri Vieuxtemps* (Turnhout, 1920).

Viganò, Salvatore, Italian composer and choreographer; b. Naples, March 25, 1769; d. Milan, Aug. 10, 1821. He was the son and pupil of a dancer; studied music with Luigi Boccherini, who was his uncle; began his career as dancer at Rome in 1786 and also produced there an opera buffa, *La Vedova scoperta;* then went to Madrid, where he married the celebrated ballerina María Medina; in 1790 returned to Italy; in 1793 was at Vienna; then made a tour of the principal European cities. He is remembered chiefly because Beethoven wrote the music for Viganò's 'heroic ballet' *Die Geschöpfe des Prometheus* (Vienna, March 28, 1801), in which Viganò danced the leading male role. —Cf. C. Ritorni, *Commentarii della vita e delle opere coreodrammatiche di Salvatore Viganò* (Milan, 1838); H. Prunières, *Salvatore Viganò,* in 'Revue Musicale' (1921); also Thayer's *Life of Beethoven.*

Vila, Pedro Alberto, Spanish composer; b. 1517; d. Barcelona, Nov. 16, 1582. He was organist and canon of the Cathedral at Barcelona; was one of the few Spanish composers who cultivated the madrigal; publ. *Odarum quas vulgo Madrigales appellamus* . . . (Barcelona, 1561) with texts in Spanish, Catalan, Italian, and French; some of his organ works are found in the tablature book of Venegas de Henestrosa (q. v.). His nephew, **Luis Ferrán Vila,** succeeded him as organist at the Barcelona Cathedral. —Cf. F. Pedrell, *Catàlech de la Biblioteca Musical de la Diputació de Barcelona* (1908-09); H. Anglès, *Orgelmusik der Schola Hispanica vom XV.-XVII. Jahrhundert,* in the 'Peter Wagner-Festschrift' (Leipzig, 1926; pp. 11-26); S. Kastner, *Contribución al estudio de la música española y portuguesa* (Lisbon, 1941).

Vilback, Renaud de, French organist and composer; b. Montpellier, June 3, 1829; d. Paris, March 19, 1884. He studied piano, organ, and composition at the Paris Cons. under Lemoine and Halévy, winning the Grand Prix de Rome at the age of 15. In 1856, became organist at St.-Eugène, Paris. He wrote 2 operas, *Au clair de lune* (1857) and *Almanzor* (1858); publ. a method for piano, and numerous well-written piano pieces (3 *Morceaux de salon, Les Amazones,* etc.) besides transcriptions from operas.

Vilboa (Villebois), Konstantin Petrovitch, Russian composer; b. St. Petersburg, May 29, 1817; d. Warsaw, July 12, 1882. He studied in a military school, and was sent by the government to collect folksongs in the country; also directed various choirs in military establishments. In 1876 he went to Warsaw as a functionary in the ministry of war, and remained there until his death. His opera *Natasha, or the Volga Brigands* was produced in Moscow on Nov. 12, 1861, and in St. Petersburg in 1863, but was not retained in the repertory, although some of its choruses were sung separately by various choral societies in Russia. Two other operas, *Taras Bulba* (after Gogol) and *Tziganka (The Gypsy),* remained unperformed. Vilboa made piano arrangements of Glinka's operas.

Vilhar (vēl'-hahr), **Franz,** Croatian composer; b. Senožeče, Jan. 5, 1852; d. Zagreb, March 4, 1928. He studied music with Skuherský in Prague; after serving as organist in various churches, he settled in Zagreb in 1891, as choirmaster at St. Mark's. He composed a Croatian opera, *Smiljana* (Zagreb, Jan. 31, 1897), *Croatian Dances,* for orch., and a number of choruses that were popular for a time.

Villa (vēya), **Ricardo,** Spanish composer and conductor; b. Madrid, Oct. 23, 1873; d. there, April 10, 1935. He studied at the Cons. of Madrid, and conducted the municipal band there, which he organized in 1909; wrote the operas *El Cristo de la Vega* and *Raimundo Lulio;* and a number of pieces for band in the Spanish vein: *La Visión de Fray Martín, Impresiones sinfónicas, Cantos regionales asturianos; Rapsodía asturiana,* for violin and orch. (played by Sarasate); *Fantasía española* for piano and orch.; also light music. —Cf. M. F. Fernández Núñez, *La Vida de los músicos españoles* (Madrid, 1925).

Villalba Muñoz, Alberto, Spanish composer; b. Valladolid, Nov. 10, 1879. At the age of 15 he entered the Augustinian Order; went to Lima, Peru, in 1906, and became interested in the study of Inca music; after a few years he left the Order and married his piano pupil Rosa Munar; subsequently went to Argentina, where he established with his wife the Cons. Clementi in Jujuy. His symph. poem *Los Andes* (1921-23) is based on Inca themes; he also wrote several other works derived from Inca sources; composed a piano sonata subtitled *Libertas,* and a number of other piano pieces. His brothers, **Enrique** (b. Valladolid, Feb. 10, 1878), **Marcelino** (1890-1925), and Padre **Luis Villalba Muñoz** (q.v.), were also musicians.

Villalba Muñoz, Padre **Luis,** Spanish musicologist and composer; b. Valladolid, Sept. 22, 1873; d. Madrid, Jan. 9, 1921. He entered the Augustinian Order at the age of 14; was chorusmaster at the monastery of the Escorial (1898-1917); also taught history and other subjects; later lived in Madrid; edited the review 'La Ciudad de Dios,' to which he contributed valuable essays on Spanish music; also edited the 'Biblioteca Sacro-Musical.' He publ. a valuable 'Antología de organistas clásicos españoles,' 10 'Canciones españolas de los siglos XV y XVI'; wrote monographs on Pedrell, Granados, and Usandizaga, and *Ultimos músicos españoles del siglo XIX* (Madrid, 1914); composed organ works; sacred choruses; chamber music.

Villa-Lobos, Heitor, foremost Brazilian composer; b. Rio de Janeiro, March 5, 1887. He studied music with his father, a writer and amateur cello player; after his father's death in 1899, he earned a living by playing the cello in cafés and restaurants. In 1905 he traveled in the northern states of Brazil, collecting popular songs; in 1907 he entered the National Institute of Music, and took lessons with Frederico Nascimento, Agnelo França, and Francisco Braga. In 1912 he undertook his fourth and longest expedition into the interior of Brazil, in the company of a musician named Donizetti; gathered a rich collection of Brazilian songs. Returning to Rio de Janeiro after 3 years of travel, he presented a concert of music there, on Nov. 13, 1915, creating a sensation by the exuberance of his melodies and rhythms and the radical character of his idiom. He met the pianist Artur Rubinstein, who became his ardent admirer, and subsequently performed his music at concerts in Europe and America, including the transcendentally difficult *Rudepoema* (dedicated to Rubinstein). In 1923 Villa-Lobos sailed for France on a stipend given by the Brazilian government; made short visits to London, Vienna, Berlin, Lisbon, but resided mainly in Paris. In 1930 he was engaged as director of musical education in S. Paulo, Brazil, and in 1932 assumed the important post of superintendent of musical and artistic education in Rio de Janeiro. He introduced bold innovations into the program of musical education, putting the main emphasis on the cultivation of Brazilian songs and dances in public schools; compiled a *Guia pratico* containing choral arrangements of Brazilian folksongs; organized 'orpheonic concentrations'—huge choruses of school children, which he conducted; in 1942 established the National Cons. of Orpheonic Song; devised a chironomic method of solfeggio. In 1944 he made his 1st tour of the U. S., conducting his works in Los Angeles, Boston, and New York. In 1945 he established in Rio de Janeiro a Brazilian Academy of Music; in 1947 he made his 2nd visit to the U. S.; in 1949 he was in Europe; subsequently continued to travel widely, while retaining Rio de Janeiro as his permanent home.—Villa-Lobos is one of the most original composers of the 20th century. His lack of formal academic training, far from hampering his development, compelled him to create a technique all his own, curiously eclectic, and yet admirably suited to his musical ideas. An ardent patriot, he resolved from his earliest steps in composition to use Brazilian song materials as the exclusive source of thematic inspiration. Occasionally he uses actual quotations from folksongs; much more often he writes melodies in an authentic Brazilian style, but of his own invention. In his desire to relate Brazilian folk resources to universal values, he has written a series of unique works, *Bachianas Brasileiras,* in which Brazilian melorhythms are treated with Bachian counterpoint. A purely Brazilian form, which Villa-Lobos has successfully cultivated, is the *chôros,* a popular dance marked by incisive rhythm and songful ballad-like melody. Villa-Lobos expanded the *chôros* to embrace a wide variety of forms, from an instrumental solo to a large orchestral work with chorus. An experimenter by nature, Villa-Lobos has devised a graphic method of composition, using as material geometrical contours of drawings and photographs; composed *The New York Skyline* for the N. Y. World's Fair from a photograph (1940). An exceptionally prolific composer, he has written operas, ballets, symphonies, chamber music, choruses, piano pieces, songs; the total number of his individual compositions exceeds 2,000. —Works: Operas: *Izaht* (1914: revised, 1932; 1st performance, in concert form, Rio de Janeiro, April 6, 1940), *Zoé* (1919), *Malazarte* (1921), *Magdalena,* light opera (Los Angeles, July 26, 1948); ballets: *Uirapurú* (Buenos Aires, May 25, 1935) and *Dança da terra* (Rio de Janeiro, Sept. 7, 1943); oratorio, *Vidapura* (Rio de Janeiro, Nov. 28, 1934). For orch.: 12 symphonies: No. 1, *Imprevisto* (Rio de Janeiro, Aug. 30, 1920), No. 2, *Ascenção* (1917), No. 3, *Guerra* (Rio de Janeiro, July 30, 1919), No. 4, *Vitória* (1920), No. 5, *Paz* (1921); No. 6, *Montanhas do Brasil* (1944), No. 7, *America* (1945), No. 8 (1950; Philadelphia, Jan.

14, 1955), No. 9 (1952), No. 10, with chorus (1954), No. 11 (Boston, March 2, 1956, composer conducting), No. 12 (Inter-American Music Festival, Washington, D. C., April 20, 1958). *Chôros:* No. 1, for guitar (1920), No. 2, for flute and clarinet (1921), No. 3, for male chorus and 7 wind instruments (1925), No. 4, for 3 horns and trombone (1926), No. 5, *Alma Brasileira,* for piano solo (1926), No. 6, for orch. (1926; Rio de Janeiro, July 15, 1942), No. 7, for flute, oboe, clarinet, saxophone, bassoon, violin, and cello (1924), No. 8, for large orch. and 2 pianos (Paris, Oct. 24, 1927), No. 9, for orch. (1929; Rio de Janeiro, July 15, 1942, composer conducting), No. 10, *Rasga o Coração,* for chorus and orch. (Rio de Janeiro, Dec. 15, 1926; also performed in Paris as a ballet, under the title *Jurupary);* No. 11, for piano and orch. (Rio de Janeiro, July 15, 1942), No. 12 for orch. (Boston, Feb. 23, 1945, composer conducting), No. 13, for 2 orchestras and band (1929), No. 14, for orch., band, and chorus (1928); also a supernumerary *Chôros bis* for violin and cello (1928). *Bachianas Brasileiras:* No. 1, for 8 cellos (Rio de Janeiro, Sept. 22, 1932, composer conducting), No. 2, for 8 cellos and soprano (1933), No. 3, for piano and orch. (1934), No. 4, for orch. (N. Y., June 6, 1942), No. 5, for voice and 8 cellos (Rio de Janeiro, March 25, 1939), No. 6, for flute and bassoon (1938), No. 7, for orch. (Rio de Janeiro, March 13, 1944), No. 8, for orch. (Rome, Aug. 6, 1947). Other orchestral works: *Dansas Africanas* (1914; Paris, April 5, 1928), *Amazonas* (1917; Paris, May 30, 1929), *Fantasy of Mixed Movements,* for violin and orch. (Rio de Janeiro, Dec. 15, 1922), *Suite Suggestiva* for orch. and voice (1929), *Momo Precoce* (Paris, Feb. 23, 1930), *Caixinha de Boãs Festas* (Rio de Janeiro, Dec. 8, 1932), *Descobrimento do Brasil* (4 suites; 1937), *The New York Skyline* (1940), *Rudepoema* (orchestral version of the piano work of that name; Rio de Janeiro, July 15, 1942, composer conducting), *Madonna,* tone poem (Rio de Janeiro, Oct. 8, 1946, composer conducting), piano concerto (Rio de Janeiro, Oct. 11, 1946), *Mandú-Carará,* symph. poem with chorus (N. Y., Jan. 23, 1948), guitar concerto (1952), *Odyssey of a Race,* symph. poem written for Israel (Mount Carmel Festival of the International Society for Contemporary Music, Haifa, May 30, 1954), 2 works commissioned by the Louisville Orch.: *Erosion,* or *The Origin of the Amazon River* (Louisville, Nov. 7, 1951) and *Dawn in a Tropical Forest* (Louisville, Jan. 23, 1954), harp concerto (Philadelphia, Jan. 14, 1955), *Grand Concerto,* for cello and orch. (1915), cello concerto No. 2 (N. Y., Feb. 5, 1955). Chamber music: 15 string quartets (1915, 1915, 1916, 1917, 1931, 1938, 1942, 1944, 1945, 1946, 1948, 1950, 1952, 1955, 1958), quartet for harp, celesta, flute, and saxophone, with female voices (1921), piano quartet (1912), piano quintet (1916), woodwind quintet (1928), *Mystic Sextet,* for flute, clarinet, saxophone, celesta, harp, and guitar (1917), nonet (1923), 3 piano trios (1911, 1916, 1918), trio for oboe, clarinet, and bassoon (1921), trio for violin, viola, and cello (1945), 4 Sonatas-Fantasias for violin and piano (1912, 1914, 1915, 1918), 2 cello sonatas (1915, 1916). For chorus: *Crianças* (1908), *Na Bahia tem* (1925), *Canção da Terra* (1925), *As Costureiras* (1932), etc. Songs: *Confidencia* (1908), *Noite de Luar* (1912), *Mal Secreto* (1913), *Fleur fanée* (1913), *Il Nome di Maria* (1915), *Sertão no Estio* (1919), *Canções tipicas brasileiras* (10 numbers; 1919), *Historiettes* (6 numbers; 1920), *Epigrammes ironiques et sentimentales* (8 numbers; 1921), *Suite* for voice and violin (1923), *Poème de l'Enfant et de sa Mère,* for voice, flute, clarinet, and cello (1923), *Serestas* (suite of 14 numbers; one of his best song cycles; 1925), *3 Poemas indigenas* (1926), *Modinhas e Canções* (2 albums, 1933, 1943). For piano: *Valsa Romantica* (1908), *Brinquedo de Roda* (6 pieces; 1912), *Primeira Suite Infantil* (1912), *Segunda Suite Infantil* (1913), *Danças Africanas* (1915), *Prole do Bebé,* suite No. 1 (8 pieces, including the popular *Polichinello;* 1918), *Fábulas Características* (3 pieces; 1914-18), *Historia da Carochinha* (4 pieces; 1919), *Carnaval das Crianças Brasileiras* (8 pieces; 1919), *Lenda do Caboclo* (1920), *Dança Infernal* (1920), *Prole do Bebé,* suite No. 2 (9 pieces; 1921), *Sul América* (1925), *Cirandinhas* (12 pieces; 1925), *Rudepoema* (1921-26), *Cirandas* (16 pieces; 1926), *Alma Brasileira* (chôros No. 5; 1926), *Prole do Bebé,* suite No. 3 (9 pieces; 1926), *Saudades das Selvas Brasileiras* (1927), *Francette et Pià* (9 pieces; 1929), *Lembrança do Sertão* (1930), *Caixinha de Música Quebrada* (1931), *Ciclo Brasileiro* (4 pieces; 1936), *As Três Marias* (1939; very popular), *Poema Singelo* (1942).—Publ. *Guia pratico,* containing arrangements of European works and Brazilian folksongs; also various instructive pamphlets.—Cf. F. C. Lange, *Villa-Lobos, Pedagogo Criador,* in the 'Boletín Latino-Americano de Música' (Montevideo, 1935; p. 189 ff.); Burle Marx, *Brazilian Portrait,* in

'Modern Music' (Oct.-Nov., 1939); special issue of 'Musica Viva' (Rio de Janeiro, 1941); N. Slonimsky, *Music of Latin America* (N. Y., 1945; pp. 142-50); O. L. Fernandez, *A Contribuição Harmonica de Villa-Lobos para a Música Brasileira,* in the 'Boletín Latino-Americano de Música' (Rio de Janeiro, 1946, pp. 183-300); O. Meyer-Serra, *Música y Músicos de Latino-América* (Mexico, 1947; vol. 2, pp. 1059-85); L. M. Peppercorn, *The History of Villa-Lobos' Birth-Date,* in the 'Monthly Mus. Record' (July-Aug., 1948); Vasco Mariz, *Heitor Villa-Lobos* (full-fledged biography; contains a detailed list of works; Rio de Janeiro, 1948); C. M. de Paula Barros, *O Romance de Villa-Lobos* (Rio de Janeiro, 1951).

Villanis, Luigi Alberto, Italian writer on music; b. San Mauro, near Turin, June 20, 1863; d. Pesaro, Sept. 27, 1906. After taking the degree of LL.D. at Turin Univ. (1887), he gave up law for music; was appointed prof. of music history at Turin Univ. (1890); in 1905 received a similar post at the Liceo Musicale Rossini in Pesaro; contributed articles to various journals, notably to the 'Gazzetta Musicale' of Milan. —Publ. *Il Contenuto nella musica* (1891); *Il Leitmotiv nella musica moderna* (1891); *Estetica del libretto nella musica* (1892); *L' Estetica e la psiche moderna nella musica contemporanea* (1895); *Come si sente e come si dovrebbe sentire la musica* (1896); *L'Arte del clavicembalo* (1901); *Lo Spirito moderno nella musica* (1902); *Un Compositore ignoto alla corte dei duchi di Savoia* (1903); *Saggio di psicologia musicale* (1904); *La Psicologia della campagna* (1905); *Piccola guida alla bibliografia musicale* (1906); *L'Arte del pianoforte in Italia (da Clementi a Sgambati)* (1907).

Villar (vē-yahr'), **Rogelio,** Spanish composer and music critic; b. León, Nov. 13, 1875; d. Madrid, Nov. 4, 1937. He studied at the Madrid Cons., and later taught ensemble there; was editor of the 'Revista Musical Hispano-Americana' (ceased publ. in 1917). He composed some symph. pieces, 2 string quartets, violin sonatas, piano sonatas, other piano works. Author of *Músicos españoles,* 2 series (biographical sketches of contemporary Spanish musicians); *La Armonía en la música contemporánea* (Madrid, 1927); *Soliloquios de un músico español* (Madrid, 1928), etc.

Villoing (vēl-wăn'), **Alexander Ivanovitch,** notable Russian pianist; b. Moscow, March 12, 1804; d. there, Sept. 2, 1878. His name is known to posterity mainly because he was the piano teacher of Anton and Nicholas Rubinstein. He traveled with them in Europe, when they gave concerts as child prodigies. His *École pratique du piano* embodies his system of instruction. He composed a piano concerto and various salon pieces.

Villoteau (vē-loh-toh'), **Guillaume-André,** French music scholar; b. Bellême, Orne, Sept. 6, 1759; d. Tours, April 23, 1839. He was a chorister at the Cathedral of Le Mans, and later at Notre-Dame in Paris. Having studied philosophy at the Sorbonne, he was qualified for election as a member of the scientific commission that accompanied Napoleon to Egypt, and made a special study of Oriental music. He contributed 4 essays to the 20-vol. edition, 'La Description de l'Égypte' (Paris, 1809-26), entitled *Mémoire sur la musique de l'antique Égypte; Dissertation sur les diverses espèces d'instruments de musique que l'on remarque parmi les sculptures qui décorent les antiques monuments de l'Égypte; De l'état actuel de l'art musical en Égypte;* and *Description historique, technique et littéraire des instruments de musique des Orientaux;* also publ. *Mémoire sur la possibilité et l'utilité d'une théorie exacte des principes naturels de la musique* (1807), being an introduction to his *Recherches sur l'analogie de la musique avec les arts qui ont pour objet l'imitation du langage* (1807; 2 vols.).

Viña (Manteola), Facundo de la, Spanish composer; b. Gijon, Feb. 22, 1876; d. Madrid, Nov. 19, 1952. He studied at the Madrid Cons. and later in Paris; his music reflects the character of Asturian regional folklore. —Works: operas: *Almas muertas, La Princesa flor de roble, La Espigadora* (Barcelona, 1927); symph. poems: *Canto de trilla, Sierra de Gredos, Covadonga, Por tierras de Castilla.* —Cf. H. Collet, *L'Essor de la musique espagnole au XXe siècle* (Paris, 1929).

Vincent (văn-săhn'), **Alexandre-Joseph-Hydulphe,** French music theorist; b. Hesdin, Pas-de-Calais, Nov. 20, 1797; d. Paris, Nov. 26, 1868. Prof. of mathematics at the Collège St.-Louis, Paris; member of the Académie; custodian of the library of learned societies at the Ministry of Public Instruction. An investigator of ancient Greek and Latin music, he advanced the idea that the Greeks used chords (harmony); he likewise sought to revive the employment of the intervals smaller than a half tone that were described in Greek theory. On these subjects he publ. a great number of essays, some of which were reprinted in pamphlet form. Especially important is his *Notice sur divers manuscrits grecs relatifs à la musique* (1847).

Vincent, Charles John, English organist; b. Houghton-le-Spring, Durham, Sept. 19, 1852; d. Monte Carlo, Feb. 28, 1934. He was a chorister at the Cathedral of Durham; studied at the Leipzig Cons. (1876-78); then was church organist in England; Mus. Bac., Oxford, 1878; Mus. Doc., 1885. He was co-editor of the 'Organist and Choirmaster.' He publ. a number of widely used textbooks: *A Year's Study at the Piano, First Principles of Music, Choral Instructor for Treble Voices,* etc.; composed an oratorio, *Ruth;* several church cantatas; a choral fugue in 8 parts, *Honour and Praise to Music;* operettas; vocal duets; more than 100 songs; chamber music; organ pieces.

Vincent, Heinrich Joseph (real name, Winzenhörlein), German singer, composer, and theorist; b. Teilheim, near Würzburg, Feb. 23, 1819; d. Vienna, May 19, 1901. He studied law, and also sang tenor parts in theaters in Vienna (1847), Halle, and Würzburg; eventually settled in Vienna as a singing teacher. He composed 2 operas, *Die Bettlerin* (Halle, 1864) and *König Murat* (Würzburg, 1870); also operettas and popular songs. As a writer, he followed the tenets of the 'Chroma' Society in championing the harmonic system based on the functional equality of the 12 notes of the chromatic scale; publ. the studies *Kein Generalbass mehr* (1860), *Die Einheit in der Tonwelt* (1862), *Die Neuklaviatur* (1874), *Die Zwölfzahl in der Tonwelt* (1885), *Ist unsere Harmonielehre wirklich eine Theorie?* (1894), *Eine neue Tonschrift* (1900), and articles on the chromatic keyboard and notation.

Vincent, Henry Bethuel, American organist and composer; b. Denver, Dec. 28, 1872; d. Erie, Pa., Jan. 7, 1941. He studied organ with W. H. Sherwood in Oberlin and Widor in Paris; settled in Erie as organist and choirmaster. He wrote an oratorio, *The Prodigal Son* (Erie, 1901), an opera, *Esperanza* (Washington, 1906), an operetta, *Indian Days;* anthems; organ pieces; songs including a cycle, *The Garden of Kama.*

Vincent, John, American composer and teacher; b. Birmingham, Ala., May 17, 1902. He studied at the New England Cons. (1922-27); at the George Peabody College in Nashville, Tenn. (B.A. and M.A., 1933); Harvard Univ., with Piston (1933-35); École Normale de Musique, Paris (1935-37); also privately with Nadia Boulanger; Ph.D. at Cornell Univ. (1942). He taught in El Paso, Texas, public schools (1927-30); George Peabody College (1930-33); Western Kentucky Teachers College (1937-46). In 1946 he was appointed to the faculty of the music dept. at the Univ. of California, Los Angeles. —Works: Symph. in D (Louisville, Feb. 5, 1955); ballet, *Three Jacks; Songs of the Chattahoochie,* symph. poem; *Miracle of the Cherry Tree,* for voice and orch.; *I Wonder as I Wander,* for baritone, chorus, and orch.; 2 string quartets; *Prelude, Canon* and *Fugue,* for flute, oboe, and bassoon; choruses; songs. He is the author of the valuable book, *The Diatonic Modes in Modern Music* (Los Angeles, 1951).

Vinci (vĭn'-chē), **Leonardo,** Italian composer; b. Strongoli, 1690; d. Naples, May 27, 1730. He studied at the Cons. dei Poveri di Gesù Cristo in Naples, where he was a pupil of Gaetano Greco. In 1725 he received the post of vice-maestro at the Royal Chapel in Naples, and remained there until his death 5 years later. He produced about 40 operas for various Italian cities (25 for Naples, 11 for Rome), of which the most important are: *Silla Dittatore* (Naples, Oct. 1, 1723); *Astianatte* (Naples, Dec. 2, 1725); *La Caduta dei Decemviri* (Naples, Oct. 1, 1727); *Artaserse* (libretto by Metastasio; Rome, Feb. 4, 1730). —Cf. E. J. Dent, *Notes on Leonardo Vinci* in the 'Mus. Antiquary' (July, 1913); A. Della Corte, *L'Opera comica italiana nel 1700,* vol. I (Bari, 1923); A. Cametti, *Leonardo Vinci e i suoi drammi in musica al Teatro delle Dame,* in 'Musica d'oggi' (Oct., 1924); U. Prota-Giurleo, *Nicola Logroscino* (Naples, 1927; appendix, *La Morte di Vinci,* pp. 61-63); K. Geiringer, *Ein Geburtstagkantate von P. Metastasio und L. Vinci,* in 'Archiv für Musikwissenschaft' (vol. 9, 1926); G. Silvestri Silva, *Illustri musici calabresi: Leonardo Vinci* (Genoa, 1935).

Vinci, Pietro, Italian composer; b. Nicosia, Sicily, 1535; d. there, 1584. He was maestro di cappella at Santa Maria Maggiore, Bergamo (1568-80); returned to Nicosia in 1580. He publ. 10 books of madrigals, motets, *Sonetti spirituali,* etc. —Cf. F. Mompellio, *Pietro Vinci, madrigalista siciliano* (Milan, 1937).

Viñes (vē-ñěs'), **Ricardo,** Spanish pianist; b. Lérida, Feb. 5, 1875; d. Barcelona, April 29, 1943. He studied in Barcelona with Juan Pujol, and with Godard at the Paris Cons., winning the 1st prize for piano in 1894. In 1895 he gave his first concert in Paris, and established himself in later years as an ardent propagandist of new French and Spanish music; he possessed particular affinity with the Impressionists, and performed their works in a colorful and imaginative manner. He gave concerts in London, Berlin, and other musical centers, but lived most of his life in Paris; contributed articles on Spanish music to publications in France and Spain.

Vinogradsky, Alexander Nikolayevitch, Russian conductor; b. Kiev, Aug. 3, 1854; d. there, Oct. 17, 1912. He studied at the St. Petersburg Cons.; in 1888 became conductor of the symph. concerts of the Imperial Russian Music Society in Kiev; also conducted in Paris, Vienna, and Berlin. He wrote 2 symphonies; a symph. fantasy, *En Bourgogne;* a symph. poem, *La Nonne;* a number of minor pieces.

Viola, Alfonso della, Italian composer; b. Ferrara, 1508; d. there, 1570; was maestro di cappella to Duke Ercole II d'Este at Ferrara. He is noteworthy as an early composer of pastorals and incidental music for the court of Ferrara: *L'Orbecche* (1541), *Il Sacrifizio* (1554), *Lo Sfortunato* (1557), and *Aretusa* (1563), all in madrigal style, the dialogue sung by a chorus. Publ. 2 books of madrigals *a* 4 (1539, 1540). He died after 1567.

Viola, Francesco, Italian 16th-century madrigalist, pupil of Adrian Willaert; was for some time in the service of Alfonso d'Este, Duke of Ferrara, whom he accompanied to Venice in 1562; publ. a book of madrigals *a* 4 at Venice in 1550; other madrigals in various collections; also edited the collection 'Musica nova,' containing motets and madrigals by Willaert.

Viole, Rudolf, German pianist and composer; b. Schochwitz, Mansfeld, May 10, 1825; d. Berlin, Dec. 7, 1867. He was a pupil of Liszt, who recommended his compositions and edited his 100 études; Viole wrote mostly for piano, including 11 sonatas, a *Caprice heroïque,* a ballade, a polonaise, etc.

Viotta, Henri (Henricus Anastasius), Dutch conductor and music scholar; son of Johannes Josephus Viotta; b. Amsterdam, July 16, 1848; d. Montreux, Feb. 17, 1933. He studied with his father and with R. Hol in Amsterdam; was a student of jurisprudence at the Univ. of Leyden; *Dr. juris* (1877) with the dissertation *Het Auteursrecht van den Componist,* but gave up legal practice; became conductor of various musical groups in Amsterdam, including the Wagner Society; edited the musical periodical 'Maandblad voor Muziek' (1888-94). In 1896 he was appointed director of the Cons. at The Hague, retaining this position until 1917; founded the Residentie Orch. there (1903); and conducted it for a number of seasons, retiring in 1917. He publ. a valuable *Lexicon der Toonkunst* (3 vols., 1881-85); *Richard Wagner* (1883); *Onze hedendaagsche Toonkunstenaars* (1893-96); and *Handboek der Muziekgeschiedenis* (1916). In 1920 he went to live in Switzerland.

Viotta, Johannes Josephus, Dutch composer; b. Amsterdam, Jan. 14, 1814; d. there, Feb. 6, 1859. He was of Italian descent; studied medicine; music was his avocation. He wrote mainly for the voice, and some of his songs in the popular vein *(De zilveren vloot, Een scheepje in de haven lag,* etc.) became exceedingly well known. In Holland he played a very important role, especially in spreading the cult of Mendelssohn and other German composers.

Viotti, Giovanni Battista, famous Italian violinist and composer; b. Fontanetto da Po, May 12, 1755; d. London, March 3, 1824. His father, a blacksmith, was an amateur musician; taught him music, and bought a small violin for him to practice on. At the age of 13 he was sent to Turin, where he gained the favor of Alfonso del Pozzo, Prince della Cisterna, who paid for his lessons with Pugnani. Viotti soon acquired a virtuoso technique, and also began to compose violin music. In 1780 he made a grand tour of Germany, Poland, and Russia with Pugnani, and was welcomed at the court of Catherine the Great. On March 15, 1782, he made his first appearance in Paris at the Concert Spirituel. He became a court musician to Marie Antoinette, and in 1788 was appointed manager of the Théâtre de Monsieur, jointly with the Queen's hairdresser Léonard; he reorganized the enterprise, and invited famous singers to participate in operatic productions. He was also successful as a teacher; among his pupils were Baillot and Rode. He was intimate with Cherubini, and lodged with him in 1785; often played in private, but shunned public appearances, being satisfied with the generous emolument from the court. He remained in Paris for 3 years after the revolution, but in 1792, when the situation became extremely dangerous for friends of the Queen, he went to London, where he was employed as conductor of Italian operas; also was soloist in his own concertos at the celebrated Salomon concerts (1794-95). In 1798 he was obliged to leave England on suspicion of political intrigue; lived for some years at Schönfeld, near Hamburg, devoting himself to composition. In 1801 he returned to London and engaged in a wine business, but sustained financial losses. After the restoration of the French monarchy, he returned to Paris; was appointed director of the Italian Opera (1819-22), but suffered repeated reverses, and in 1822 returned to London, broken in spirit and health, and heavily in debt. He died 2 years later. —Viotti's role in the history of instrumental music, both in performance and composition, was very important. He elevated performing standards from mere entertainment to artistic presentation, and may be regarded as one of the chief creators of modern violin playing. He was the first to write violin concertos in a consciously formulated sonata form, with the solo part and the orchestral accompaniment utilizing the full resources of instrumental sonority more abundantly than ever before in violin concertos. He publ. 29 violin concertos (of which No. 22, in A minor, is a great favorite); 10 piano concertos (some of which are transcriptions of violin concertos); 2 *Symphonies concertantes,* for 2 violins, strings, oboes, and horns; 21 string quartets; 36 string trios; 54 duets for 2 violins; 6 serenades for 2 violins; several duos for 2 cellos; 3 Divertissements for violin unaccompanied; 12 sonatas for violin and piano; 9 piano sonatas. His song known as 'La Polacca de Viotti' (used in Paisiello's *La Serva padrona,* 1794) acquired great popularity. —Bibliography: A. M. d'Eymar, *Anecdotes sur Viotti, précédées de quelques réflexions sur l'expression en musique* (Paris, 1792); F. Fayolle, *Notices sur Corelli . . . et Viotti* (Paris, 1810); P. M. Baillot, *Notice sur J. B. Viotti* (Paris, 1825); E. F. Miel, *Notice historique sur J. B. Viotti* (Paris, 1827); A. Pougin, *Viotti et l'école moderne de violon* (Paris, 1888); H. de Curzon, *Quelques souvenirs de Viotti,* in the 'Ménestrel' (April, 1924); L. de La Laurencie, *Les Débuts de Viotti comme directeur de l'Opéra en 1819,* in 'Revue de musicologie' (Aug., 1924); L. de La Laurencie, *L'École française de violon de Lully à Viotti* (Paris, 1922-25); M. Pincherle, *Les Violonistes compositeurs et virtuoses* (Paris, 1922); W. H. Riehl, *Viotti und das Geigenduett,* in *Musikalische Charakterköpfe* (vol. II); A. Moser, *Geschichte des Violinspiels,* p. 387 ff. (Berlin, 1923); A. Della Corte, *L'Interpretazione musicale e gli interpreti* (Turin, 1951); R. Giazotto, *G. B. Viotti* (Milan, 1956). For the rectification of Viotti's birth date (heretofore given as May 23, 1753), see 'Stampa di Torino' of Sept. 29, 1935, which publ. for the first time the text of his birth certificate; an infant brother of Viotti was born in 1753; their Christian names were identical, which led to confusion; the bicentennial of Viotti was widely celebrated in the wrong year (1953).

Virdung (fēr'dŏŏng), **Sebastian,** noted German theorist, a native of Amberg (Oberpfalz); was at first a priest in Eichstätt, and from 1500 a member of the court chapel in Heidelberg; wrote a work of importance for the history of musical instruments: *Musica getutscht und auszgezogen durch Sebastianum Virdung, Priesters von Amberg, und alles Gesang ausz den Noten in die Tabulaturen diser benannten dryer Instrumenten, der Orgeln, der Lauten und der Flöten transferieren zu lernen kurtzlich gemacht* (Basel, 1511; facsimile reprint in Eitner's 'Publikationen älterer praktischer und theoretischer Musikwerke,' vol. 11, 1882; also by L. Schrade, Kassel, 1931). Virdung's method was violently attacked by Arnolt Schlick in his *Tabulatur etlicher Lobgesänge* (1512). Four of Virdung's songs are in Schöffer's 'Teutsche Lieder mit 4 Stimmen' (1513).—Cf. B. A. Wallner, *Sebastian Virdung von Amberg,* in the 'Kirchenmusikalisches Jahrbuch' (1911); H. H. Lenneberg, *The Critic Criticized: Sebastian Virdung and his Controversy with Arnold Schlick,* in the 'Journal of the American Musicological Society' (Spring, 1957). See also G. Reese, *Music in the Renaissance* (N. Y., 1954, pp. 656-57).

Virovai, Robert, violinist; b. Daruvar, Yugoslavia, March 10, 1921. He studied with Peter Stojanovits at the Belgrade Cons.; then continued his studies with Hubay at the Budapest Cons.; in 1937 he won the international violin contest in Vienna, and was launched on an auspicious career; made his American début on Nov. 3, 1938, as soloist with the N. Y. Philharmonic; thereafter toured the U. S. and Europe.

Viscarra Monje, Humberto, Bolivian composer; b. Sorata, March 30, 1898. He studied at the National Cons., La Paz, and in Italy and France (1927-29); then taught at the Cons. of La Paz. In 1940 he was appointed director of the Academia de Bellas Artes in Cochabamba. He publ. piano pieces and songs on native Bolivian themes.

Visée, Robert de, French guitar player, lutenist, and composer; b. c. 1650; d. c. 1725. He was court musician from about 1686 to 1721; publ. 2 books of guitar pieces (1682; 1686) and *Pièces de théorbe et de luth, mises en partition* (1716).

Visetti, Alberto Antonio, Italian singing teacher; b. Salona, May 13, 1846; d. London, July 10, 1928. He studied at the Milan Cons.; first appeared as pianist; went to Paris, where he was appointed chamber musician to Empress Eugénie. After the fall of the empire in France, he settled in London, where he taught singing; also conducted the Bath Philharmonic Society (1878-90). He publ. a *History of the Art of Singing* and *Verdi* (1905); the score of his opera *Les trois mousquetaires* was lost during the siege of Paris (1871). He also wrote a cantata, *The Desert and the Praise of Song;* and a waltz-song for Adelina Patti, *La Diva.*

Vitali, Filippo, Italian composer; b. Florence, c. 1600; d. 1653. In 1631 he became a singer in the Pontifical Choir in Rome; also chamber virtuoso to Cardinal Barberini; in 1642 returned to Florence and succeeded Gagliano as maestro of the ducal chapel and of the Cathedral of S. Lorenzo; in 1648-49, maestro at Sta. Maria Maggiore in Bergamo. His 'favola in musica' *L'Aretusa,* performed on Feb. 8, 1620, at the home of Monsignor Corsini, is regarded as the first attempt at opera in Rome (publ. there in 1620). In 1622 he composed 6 intermedi for the comedy *La Finta Mora* by J. Cicognini, performed at the palace of Cardinal de' Medici in Florence (publ. there, 1623). Also publ. several books of madrigals, arias with instrumental accompaniment, psalms, motets, and hymns. Vitali was outstanding among early composers in the monodic style.

Vitali, Giovanni Battista, Italian composer; b. Cremona, c. 1644; d. Modena, Oct. 12, 1692. Pupil of M. Cazzati in Bologna; from about 1667 he played the 'viola da braccio' in the Church of S. Petronio there; from 1674 he was 2nd, and from 1684 1st, maestro di cappella at the ducal court of Modena. He was an important composer of instrumental music. Publ. *Correnti e Balletti da camera* for 2 violins and continuo (1666 and other eds.); *Sonate a 2 violini col basso cont. per l'organo* (1667, etc.); *Balletti, Correnti e Sinfonie da camera a 4 stromenti* (1667, etc.); *Balletti, Correnti, etc., a violino e violone o spinetta, con il secondo violino a beneplacito* (1668, etc.); *Sonate da chiesa a 2, 3, 4 e 5 stromenti* (1669); *Salmi concertati da 2 a 5 voci con stromenti* (1677); *Sonate a 2 violini e basso cont.; Varie sonate alla francese ed all'italiana a 6 stromenti* (1684); *Balli in stile francese a 5 stromenti* (1690); *Sonate da camera a 3 stromenti* (1692); etc.—18 pieces are in Torchi's 'L'Arte Musicale in Italia' (vol. 7).

Vitalis, George, Greek composer and conductor; b. Athens, Jan. 9, 1895. He studied with Armani in Milan; conducted light opera in Athens (1923-36) and subsequently was conductor of the Athens Radio Orch. He came to the U. S. in 1945; was guest conductor of several American orchestras; settled in N. Y. —Works: the operas *Perseus and Andromeda, The Return of the Gods,* and *Golfo* (N. Y., Jan. 1, 1949, in concert form, composer conducting); *Greek Fantasy,* for orch. (Athens, Nov. 11, 1945; his best-known work; several performances in the U. S.). He also wrote many light orchestra pieces under the pseudonym Giorgio Valente.

Vitry (vē-trē'), **Philippe de (Philippus de Vitriaco),** churchman and musician; b. Vitry, Champagne, Oct. 31, 1291; d. Meaux, June 9, 1361. There are 6 towns in Champagne named Vitry, and it is not known in which of these Vitry was born; he was ordained a deacon early in life and from 1323 held several benefices; he was canon of Soissons and archbishop of Brie. He became a clerk of the royal household in Paris, and about 1346 was made counselor of the court of requests ('maître des requêtes'); from 1346-50 he was also in the service of Duke Jean of Normandy (heir to the throne), with whom he took part in the siege of Aiguillon (1346); when Duke Jean became king in 1350, he sent Vitry to Avignon on a mission to Pope Clement VI, who on Jan. 3, 1351 appointed him bishop of Meaux.—Vitry was known as a poet and a composer, but his enduring fame rests on his *Ars Nova,* a treatise expounding a new theory of mensural notation, particularly important for its development of the principle of binary rhythm; it also gives the most complete account of the various uses to which colored notes were put. Of the 4 treatises attributed to Vitry in Coussemaker's 'Scriptores' III, only the *Ars Nova* (also publ., with corrections, in 'Musica Disciplina,' 1956) is now considered authentic. Most of Vitry's works are lost; the extant pieces were publ. by L. Schrade in vol. I of his 'Polyphonic Music of the 14th Century' (Monaco, 1956). Separate pieces were brought out in 'Denkmäler der Tonkunst in Österreich' vol. 40, by H. Besseler in his *Studien zur Musik des Mittelalters* in the 'Archiv für Musikwissenschaft' (1925), etc. —Bibliography: Hugo Riemann, *Geschichte der Musiktheorie im 9.-19. Jahrhundert* (1898); Joh. Wolf, *Geschichte der Mensuralnotation* (1904); J. Combarieu, *Histoire de la musique,* vol. I (1913); A. Coville, *Philippe de Vitry, Notes biographiques,* in 'Romania' (Oct., 1933); G. Reese, *Music in the Middle Ages* (N. Y., 1940; p. 336 ff.) L. Schrade, *Philippe de Vitry: Some New Discoveries,* in the 'Mus. Quarterly' (July, 1956); see also H. Besseler's article on 'Ars Nova' in vol. I of 'Die Musik in Geschichte und Gegenwart.'

Vittadini, Franco, Italian composer; b. Pavia, April 9, 1884; d. there, Nov. 30, 1948. He studied at the Milan Cons.; settled in Pavia, where he headed a music school. He wrote the operas *Anima allegra* (Rome, April 15, 1921; Metropolitan Opera, N. Y., Feb. 14, 1923), *Nazareth* (Pavia, May 28, 1925), *La Sagredo* (Milan, La Scala, April 26, 1930), *Caracciolo* (Rome, Feb. 7, 1938); a 'pastoral triptych' *Il Natale di Gesù* (Bari, Dec. 20, 1933); *Fiordisole,* ballet (Milan, Feb. 14, 1935); *Le sette parole di Cristo,* oratorio; 10 Masses; symph. poem, *Armonie della notte* (1925); organ pieces. —Cf. A. Baratti, *Vita del musicista F. Vittadini* (Milan, 1955).

Vittoria. See **Victoria.**

Vivaldi, Antonio, celebrated Italian violinist and composer; b. Venice, possibly on June 11, 1669 (but an uncertain date between 1675 and 1678 is usually given); d. Vienna, July (buried July 28), 1741. He was the son and pupil of Giovanni Battista Vivaldi, a violinist at San Marco in Venice; also studied with Giovanni Legrenzi. He entered the priesthood, taking the tonsure in 1693, and holy orders before 1703; because of his red hair he was called 'il prete rosso' (the Red Priest). In 1703 he was engaged as teacher at the Seminario musicale dell' Ospitale della Pietà, in Venice; from 1709 was made 'maestro de' concerti' there; held this position nominally until 1740, but traveled much in the interim; was for four years (perhaps from 1718 to 1722) maestro di cappella to Prince Philip, Landgrave of Hesse-Darmstadt, in Mantua (where the Prince was governor); in later years visited Germany and possibly France; in 1735, he resumed his position at the Pietà in Venice. Although he was a priest, he did not say Mass after the first year of service, owing to an asthmatic condition. In 1740 he went to Vienna, attracted by the opportunities presented to performers and composers at the court of Charles VI; however, he failed to prosper there, and died destitute. —Vivaldi composed about 40 operas (including pasticcios and pieces written in collaboration with others); the following were produced in Venice: *Orlando finto pazzo* (1714), *Nerone fatto Cesare* (1715), *L'Incoronazione di Dario* (1716), *L'Inganno trionfante in amore* (1725), *Farnace* (1726), *Cunegonda* (1726), *Rosilena ed Oronta* (Jan. 17, 1728), *L'Olimpiade* (1734), *Griselda* (1735), *L'Oracolo in Messenia* (1738), *Feraspe* (1739); operas produced in Florence: *Scanderbeg* (June 22, 1718), *Ipermestra* (1727), *L'Atenaide* (Dec. 29, 1728), *Ginevra principessa di Scozia* (1736); other operas were produced in Rome, Verona, Milan, etc. He also wrote 2 oratorios, *Moyses Deus Pharaonis* (Venice, 1714) and *Juditha triumphans devicta Holofernis barbarie* (Venice, 1716), 24 secular cantatas, serenades, miscellaneous arias, 14 Vespers, a Kyrie for 8 voices, and other church music. However, Vivaldi's greatness lies not in his theater or church music, but in his superb instrumental works, particularly the concerti grossi and the solo concertos. Vivaldi's concertos served J. S. Bach as a model for his concertos for clavier and orch. (but of the 16 'Concertos after Vivaldi' for clavier publ. in vol. 42 of the 'Bach Gesellschaft' ed., only 6 are transcriptions of Vivaldi).—Publ. works: *12 Sonate da camera* for 2 violins and bass or harpsichord, op. 1; 18 violin sonatas with continuo, op. 2 and 5; *L'Estro armonico,* 12 concertos for 1, 2, or 4 solo violins, solo cello, strings, and continuo, op. 3; *La Stravaganza,* 12 concertos for solo violin, strings, and continuo, op. 4; 18 concertos for 3 violins, viola, and continuo, op. 6 and 7; *Il Cimento dell'Armonia e dell' Invenzione,* including *Le quattro stagione (The Four Seasons),* 12 concertos for solo violin, strings, and continuo, op. 8; *La Cetra,* 12 concertos for solo violin, strings, and continuo, op. 9; 6 concertos for flute, strings, and organ, op. 10; 12

concertos for solo violin, strings, and organ, op. 11 and 12. Many other works remain in MS. According to Pincherle, there are all together 454 concertos, 23 *sinfonie,* 75 sonatas or trios, and 2 organ pieces. Modern reprints and arrangements of Vivaldi's works are very numerous; several concertos were edited by A. Einstein (1927-28). A complete edition of Vivaldi's works, under the general editorship of G. F. Malipiero, was begun in 1947; by 1958, 275 of the promised 550 works had appeared. —Cf. A. Schering, *Geschichte des Instrumental-Konzerts* (Leipzig, 1905); A. Gentili, *Vivaldi,* in the 'Rivista Musicale Italiana' (1917); W. Altmann, *Thematischer Katalog der gedruckten Werke Antonio Vivaldis,* in the 'Archiv für Musikwissenschaft' (1922); S. A. Luciani, *Antonio Vivaldi,* in the 'Bollettino Bibliografico Musicale' (Jan., 1928); A. Salvatori, *Antonio Vivaldi,* in the 'Rivista Mensile della Città di Venezia' (Aug., 1928); M. Pincherle, *Vivaldi and the Ospitali of Venice,* in the 'Mus. Quarterly' (July, 1938); R. Gallo, *Antonio Vivaldi,* in 'Ateneo Veneto' (Dec., 1938); A. Casella, V. Mortari, S. A. Luciani, etc., *Antonio Vivaldi: note e documenti* (Siena, 1939); M. Rinaldi, *Antonio Vivaldi* (Milan, 1943); Olga Rudge, *Lettere e dediche di Antonio Vivaldi* (Milan, 1943); M. Rinaldi, *Catalogo numerico tematico delle composizioni di Antonio Vivaldi* (Rome, 1945); S. A. Luciani, *Vivaldi, Concerti e Sonate* (Milan, 1946); M. Pincherle, *Antonio Vivaldi et la musique instrumentale* (2 vols., Paris, 1948); G. Guerrini, *Antonio Vivaldi, la vita e l'opera* (Florence, 1951); M. Rinaldi, *La Data di nascità di Antonio Vivaldi* (Siena, 1953); M. Pincherle, *Vivaldi* (Paris, 1955; English transl., N. Y., 1957); W. Kolneder, *Aufführungspraxis bei Vivaldi* (Leipzig, 1955). See also L. S. Salter, *An Index to Ricordi's Edition of Vivaldi,* in 'Notes' (June, 1954; pp. 366-74). See also F. Torrefranca, *Modernità di Antonio Vivaldi,* in 'Nueva Antologia' (Aug. 1, 1942), suggesting that Vivaldi was born June 11, 1669.

Vivell, Cölestin, German ecclesiastic; writer on Gregorian Chant; b. Wolfach, Oct. 21, 1846; d. Seckau, March 10, 1923. Having completed his university studies, he joined the order of Benedictines at Beuron; from 1883 lived in the monastery at Seckau, Styria. Author of *Der gregorianische Gesang. Eine Studie über die Echtheit seiner Tradition* (1904); *Die liturgisch gesangliche Reform Gregors des Grossen* (1904); *Erklärung der vatikanischen Choralschrift* (1906); *Vom Musiktraktate Gregors des Grossen* (1911); *Initia Tractatuum musices ex codicibus . . . .* (1912; alphabetical list of beginnings of treatises in Gerbert's and Coussemaker's *Scriptores*); *Index rerum et verborum tractatuum de musica editorum* (1915); *Fritolfi Breviarum de musica* (1919).

Vives (vē'-vĕs), **Amadeo,** Spanish composer; b. Collbató, near Barcelona, Nov. 18, 1871; d. Madrid, Dec. 1, 1932. He was a pupil of Felipe Pedrell in Barcelona; with L. Millet, founded the famous choral society 'Orfeó Català' (1891). In his first opera, *Artus* (Barcelona, 1895), he made use of Catalonian folksongs. Subsequently he moved to Madrid, where he produced his comic opera *Don Lucas del Cigarral* (Feb. 18, 1899); his opera *Euda d'Uriach,* originally to a Catalan libretto, was brought out in Italian at Barcelona (Oct. 24, 1900). Then followed his most popular opera, *Maruxa* (Madrid, May 28, 1914); other operas were *Balada de Carnaval* (Madrid, July 5, 1919) and *Doña Francisquita* (Madrid, Oct. 17, 1923). The style of his stage productions shared qualities of the French light opera and the Spanish 'zarzuela'; he wrote nearly 100 of these; also composed songs and piano pieces; publ. a book of essays, *Sofia* (Madrid, 1923).

Vivier (vē-vyā'), **Albert-Joseph,** Belgian music theorist; b. Huy, Dec. 15, 1816; d. Brussels, Jan. 3, 1903. He studied with Fétis at the Brussels Cons.; wrote an interesting *Traité complet d'harmonie* (1862, and many later eds.) in which he explained secondary chords as accidental formations through incorporation of auxiliary notes; also wrote essays on acoustics (*Des vrais rapports des sons musicaux, Éléments d'acoustique musicale,* etc.). His opera *Spadillo le tavernier* was produced in Brussels on May 22, 1857.

Vivier, Eugène-Léon, French horn virtuoso; b. Brioude, Haute-Loire, Dec. 4, 1817; d. Nice, Feb. 24, 1900. He learned to play violin, then took up the French horn. He moved to Paris, where he became successful through his connections at the French court. An eccentric, he prided himself on his ability to play 2 notes simultaneously on his instrument, through clever overblowing. He publ. a number of pamphlets on music and the theater, and also an autobiography (largely fictitious), *La Vie et les aventures d'un corniste* (Paris, 1900).

Vix, Geneviève, French soprano; b. Nantes, Dec. 31, 1879; d. Paris, Aug. 25, 1939. She studied at the Paris Cons.; won 1st prize for opera (1908); sang at the Paris Opéra, in Madrid, and in Buenos Aires; made her American début with the Chicago Opera Co. as Manon in Massenet's opera (Dec. 1, 1917); married Prince Cyril Naryshkin in N. Y. (Feb. 9, 1918). She possessed a fine lyric voice and was also adept as an actress.

Vlad, Roman, composer; b. Cernauti, Rumania, Dec. 29, 1919. He was a pupil of the Cernauti Cons.; in 1938, went to Rome, where he studied piano and composition with Casella; active in modern music groups; in 1943 he adopted the 12-tone method of composition.—Works: *La Strada sul caffé* ballet (Rome, June 9, 1945); *La Dama delle camelie,* ballet in form of 5 waltzes (Rome, Nov. 20, 1945); *Sinfonia* (Venice Festival, Sept. 8, 1948); *Divertimento* for 11 instruments (Capri, Sept. 15, 1948); *De Profundis,* for soprano, mixed chorus, and orch. (Paris, June 2, 1949); *Storia d'una mamma,* musical fable (Venice Festival, Oct. 5, 1951); 5 Elegies for voice and string orch. (1952); *Le Ciel est vide,* for chorus and orch. (Turin, Oct. 29, 1954); *Variazioni concertanti* for piano and orch. based on a series of 12 notes in Mozart's *Don Giovanni* (Venice Festival, Sept. 18, 1955); *Studi dodecafonici* for piano (1943-57); *Colinde transilvane* for chorus (1957); *Musica concertata* for harp and orch. (Turin, April 24, 1958); *Tre Invocazioni* for voice and orch. (Rome, June 6, 1958); incidental music to Shakespeare's *Macbeth,* T. S. Eliot's *Murder in the Cathedral,* Pirandello's *Favola del figlio cambiato,* etc.; film music; publ. the books *Modernità e tradizione nella musica contemporanea* (Turin, 1955), *Storia della dodecafonia* (Milan, 1958), and a monograph on Stravinsky (Turin, 1958). In 1957 he became music editor of the 'Enciclopedia dello Spettacolo.' —Cf. G. Graziosi, *Roman Vlad,* in 'Rassegna Musicale' (Jan., 1953).

Vladigerov, Pantcho, foremost Bulgarian composer; b. Shumen, March 18, 1899. He studied with Paul Juon and Georg Schumann in Berlin; conducted theater orchestras there; returned to Bulgaria in 1920, and was appointed teacher of theory at the Cons. in Sofia. After 1945 he spent several years in Russia; appeared as pianist and composer. His music is rooted in Bulgarian folksong; he artfully combines the peculiar melodic and rhythmic patterns of native material with stark modern harmonies; the method is similar to that of Béla Bartók. His works include an opera on a historic Bulgarian subject, *Tsar Kaloyan* (Sofia, April 20, 1936), a Bulgarian rhapsody for orch., *Vardar* (1934); a piano concerto; a violin concerto; a number of chamber music pieces; a series of effective suites for piano, of which *Shumen* (named after his place of birth) is the most attractive.

Vockerodt, Gottfried, German writer; b. Mühlhausen, Thuringia, Sept. 24, 1665; d. Gotha, Oct. 10, 1727, as rector of the Gymnasium. It was his opinion that excessive enjoyment of music injures the intellect, and that Nero and Caligula became totally depraved through their passion for music. He advocated these ideas in *Consultatio . . . de cavenda falsa mentium intemperatarum medicina* (1696); *Missbrauch der freien Künste, insonderheit der Musik* (1697); and *Wiederholtes Zeugnis der Wahrheit gegen die verderbte Musik und Schauspiele, Opern, etc.* (1698).

Vockner, Josef, Austrian organist, composer, and teacher; b. Ebensee, March 18, 1842; d. Vienna, Sept. 11, 1906. He was a pupil of Bruckner; became prof. of organ at the Vienna Cons. Composed an oratorio, *Das jüngste Gericht;* a cello sonata; a piano quartet; fugues and other pieces for organ; songs.

Vogel, Adolf, German bass-baritone; b. Munich, Aug. 18, 1895. He studied voice with Anna Bahr-Mildenburg and J. Kiechle; was a member of the Munich Opera from 1933 to 1937; made his American début at the Metropolitan Opera as Alberich (Dec. 3, 1937); remained on its roster for 2 seasons.

Vogel, Charles Louis Adolphe, French violinist and composer; b. Lille, May 17, 1808; d. Paris, Sept. 11, 1892. He was a grandson of Johann Christoph Vogel (q. v.); studied at the Paris Cons. with A. Kreutzer (violin) and Reicha (theory). After winning popularity with his song *Les trois couleurs* during the July Revolution (1830), he brought out a series of successful operas: *Le Podestat* (Paris, 1831), *Le Siège de Leyde* (The Hague, March 4, 1847), *La Moissonneuse* (Paris, 1853), *Rompons* (Paris, 1857), *Le Nid de Cigognes* (Baden-Baden, 1858), *Gredin de Pigoche* (Paris, 1866), and *La Filleule du roi* (Brussels, 1875). He also wrote symphonies, chamber music, sacred works; songs; piano pieces.

Vogel (fŏh'-gĕhl), **Emil,** German musicologist; b. Wriezen-on-Oder, Jan. 21, 1859; d. Nikolassee, near Berlin, June 18, 1908. He studied at Greifswald and Berlin, taking the degree of *Dr. phil.* in 1887. In 1893 he organized the Peters Music Library in Leipzig and was librarian till 1901; at the same time he also ed. the 'Peters Jahrbuch.' He publ. a monograph on Monteverdi (1887), and on Marco da Gagliano and music in Florence from 1570 to 1650 (1889), both in the 'Vierteljahrsschrift für Musikwissenschaft'; also a catalogue of *Die Handschriften nebst den älteren Druckwerken der Musikabteilung der herzoglichen Bibliothek zu Wolfenbüttel* (1890), and *Bibliothek der gedruckten weltlichen Vokalmusik Italiens aus den Jahren 1500-1700* (1892; new ed., completely revised by Alfred Einstein, publ. in 'Notes' (June, 1945-Sept., 1948).

Vogel, Friedrich Wilhelm Ferdinand, German organist and composer; b. Havelberg, Prussia, Sept. 9, 1807; d. Bergen, Norway, July 20, 1892. He studied with Birnbach in Berlin; made tours as organ virtuoso; taught at Hamburg (1838-41) and Copenhagen (1845-52); then settled in Bergen, where he founded an organ school. He publ. a number of works for organ, including 60 chorale-preludes, 10 postludes, and 2 preludes and fugues; also chamber music; overtures; choruses.

Vogel, Johann Christoph, German composer; b. Nuremberg, 1756; d. Paris, June 26, 1788. He was a pupil of Riepel at Regensburg; went to Paris in 1776, and wrote 2 operas in Gluck's style: *La Toison d'or* (Paris, Sept. 5, 1786) and *Démophon,* which he completed shortly before his untimely death at the age of 32, and which was produced posthumously (Paris, Sept. 22, 1789). He also composed a great deal of instrumental music: 3 symphonies; a bassoon concerto; 3 clarinet concertos; 6 string quartets; 6 quartets for horn and strings; 3 quartets for bassoon and strings; 6 trios for 2 violins and bass; 6 duos for 2 clarinets; 6 duos for 2 bassoons; etc.

Vogel, Wilhelm Moritz, German pianist and composer; b. Sorgau, Silesia, July 9, 1846; d. Leipzig, Oct. 30, 1922. He studied in Leipzig, and settled there as a teacher; also conducted choral societies and wrote music criticism. He publ. a series of instructive piano pieces, and a method (in 12 parts); also songs and organ works; edited 'Deutsches Schulliederbuch' (a collection of 200 part-songs); brought out a *Geschichte der Musik* (1900) and several didactic books.

Vogel (fŏh'-gĕhl), **Wladimir,** composer; b. Moscow, Feb. 29, 1896, of a German father and Russian mother. As a youth he studied music privately; was interned in Russia during World War I as a German citizen; in 1918 he went to Berlin, where he studied with Tiessen and Busoni (1920-24); left Berlin in 1933, and after a brief stay in France, settled in Ascona, Switzerland. His music reveals influences of Scriabin and Schoenberg; in some of his works he applied the 12-tone method of composition; he is very much preoccupied with philosophical expression in music. His most significant composition is the oratorio *Thyl Claes (Till Eulenspiegel)* in 2 parts: *Oppression* (Geneva, 1943) and *Liberation* (Geneva, 1947); an orchestral suite from it was given at the Palermo Festival of the International Society for Contemporary Music (April 26, 1949); other works include a cantata, *Wagadu,* for 3 solo voices, chorus, and 5 saxophones (Munich, May 19, 1931); *Deux études d'orchestre* (London Festival of the International Society for Contemporary Music, July 28, 1931); *Tripartita,* for orch. (Geneva, Nov. 21, 1935); violin concerto (1937); *Sept aspects d'une série dodécaphonique* for orch. (Venice International Festival, Sept., 1950); *Spielungen,* for orch. (Frankfurt, June 26, 1953); *Overture* (Rome, April 7, 1954; received a prize of the International Congress of Contemporary Music, Rome); *Goethe-Aphorismen,* for soprano and string orch. (Venice International Festival, Sept., 1955); *12 variétudes* for violin, flute, clarinet, cello (1940); wind quintet (1941); quintet for clarinet, piano, and strings (1948); other chamber music; many piano pieces and songs.

Vogeleis (fŏh'-gĕl-īz), **Martin,** Alsatian music scholar; b. Erstein, June 5, 1861; d. Sélestat, Aug. 11, 1930. He studied for the priesthood, and was ordained in 1885; taught music at the Episcopalian Seminary in Zillesheim (1886-91); then was chaplain and choirmaster in Grafenstaden (1891-96); pastor in Behlenheim (1896-1906); from 1908 was pastor in Schlettstadt (Sélestat). He made a special study of music in Alsace; publ. *Quellen und Bausteine zu einer Geschichte der Musik und des Theaters im Elsass 500-1800* (1911). He discovered the MS of Königshofen's *Tonarius,* which he publ. in facsimile in connection with F. X. Mathias' *Der Strassburger Chronist Königshofen als Choralist* (1903).

Vogelweide (foh'-gĕl-wī-dĕh), **Walther von der**, famous German Minnesinger and lyric poet; b. probably in Tyrol, c. 1170; d. Würzburg, c. 1230. In Wagner's *Tannhäuser* he appears as one of the rival singers at the Wartburg. He led a wandering life; was in Worms in 1198; in Frankfurt in 1212; then in Würzburg. Very few of his melodies are extant; 3 of these were found in the Münster 'Bruchstücke' (MS collection of musical fragments from the Middle Ages), including the so-called 'Palestine Song' (1228); 5 others are contained in the Colmar Codex and in the 'Singebuch' of Adam Puschmann. —Cf. R. Kralik, in the supplement to Mantuani's *Geschichte der Musik in Wien,* vol. 1 (1904); R. Wustmann, *Die Hofweise Walthers von der Vogelweide,* in the 'Liliencron-Festschrift' (1910); R. Wustmann, *Walther von der Vogelweide* (1912); R. Wustmann, *Walthers Palästinalied,* in the 'Sammelbände der Internationalen Musik-Gesellschaft' (vol. 13); R. Molitor, *Die Lieder des Münsterischen Fragmentes,* in the 'Sammelbände der Internationalen Musik-Gesellschaft' (vol. 12; with facsimiles); F. Ludwig, in Adler's *Handbuch der Musikgeschichte* (Frankfurt, 1924); F. Gennrich, *7 Melodien zu mittelhochdeutschen Minneliedern,* in the 'Zeitschrift für Musikwissenschaft' (1924-25); H. J. Moser, *Geschichte der deutschen Musik,* vol. 1 (5th ed., 1928); H. J. Moser, *Gedenkblatt auf Walther von der Vogelweide* (1929); H. Rietsch, in the 'Denkmäler der Tonkunst in Österreich' (vol. 41); C. Bützler, *Untersuchungen zu den Melodien Walthers von der Vogelweide* (Jena, 1940); H. Böhm, *Walther von der Vogelweide* (Stuttgart, 1949); J. A. Huisman, *Neue Wege zur dichterischen und musikalischen Technik Walthers von der Vogelweide* (dissertation; Utrecht, 1950); K. K. Klein, *Zur Spruchdichtung und Heimatfrage Walthers von der Vogelweide* (Innsbruck, 1952); D. Kralik, *Die Elegie Walthers von der Vogelweide* (Vienna, 1952); F. Maurer, ed., *Die Lieder Walthers von der Vogelweide unter Beifügung erhaltener und erschlossener Melodien,* vol. 1 (Tübingen, 1955).

Vogl (fogl), **Heinrich,** famous German tenor; b. Au, suburb of Munich, Jan. 15, 1845; d. Munich, April 21, 1900. He studied music with Fr. Lachner; made a successful début as Max in *Der Freischütz* at the Munich Court Opera (Nov. 5, 1865) and remained on its roster until his death. He succeeded Schnorr von Carolsfeld (q.v.) as the model Tristan in Wagner's opera and was for years considered the greatest interpreter of that role. He frequently sang at Bayreuth; created the role of Loge in *Das Rheingold* (1869) and of Siegmund in *Die Walküre* (1870). He was also a composer; wrote an opera, *Der Fremdling,* in which he sang the leading role (Munich, May 7, 1899). In 1868 he married the German soprano Therese Thoma (b. Tutzing, Nov. 12, 1845; d. Munich, Sept. 29, 1921), who sang the part of Isolde with him. —Cf. H. von der Pfordten, *Heinrich Vogl. Zur Erinnerung und zum Vermächtnis* (Munich, 1900); K. Pottgiesser, *Heinrich Vogl,* in the 'Allgemeine Musikzeitung' (May 4, 1900).

Vogl (fogl), **Johann Michael**, Austrian baritone; b. Steyr, Aug. 10, 1768; d. Vienna, Nov. 19, 1840. He studied law in Vienna; Süssmayr, then conductor of the Vienna Court Theater, discovered his voice, and persuaded him to join his opera company; Vogl remained on its roster from 1794 until 1822. He was the first professional singer to perform Schubert's songs at concerts. —Cf. A. Liess, *J. M. Vogl, Hofoperist und Schubertsänger* (Graz, 1954).

Vogler (fōg'-lĕhr), **Georg Joseph,** Abbé or Abt, noted German composer and theorist; b. Würzburg, June 15, 1749; d. Darmstadt, May 6, 1814. The son of a violin maker, he mastered the organ at an early age; studied theology and law at Würzburg and Bamberg. In 1771 he went to Mannheim; there he wrote music for a ballet and gained the favor of the Elector, who provided him with funds for study in Italy. After a brief course in Bologna with Padre Martini, he proceeded to Padua, where he studied composition with Vallotti; but soon left for Rome, and took holy orders in 1773; was made Apostolic Protonotary, Chamberlain to the Pope, Knight of the Golden Spur; also joined the Academy of the Arcadians. In 1775 he returned to Mannheim as court chaplain and 2nd Kapellmeister, and founded there the 'Mannheimer Tonschule' for teaching his own method of composition. In 1780 he followed the Electoral Court to Munich. In 1781 he was in Paris, where he submitted a paper to the Académie Royale des Sciences, *Essai de diriger le goût des amateurs de musique,* an explanation of his system of teaching (publ. Paris, 1782); in Paris he also produced his opera, *La Kermesse* (1783), which was a fiasco. From France he traveled to Spain, Portugal, England, and Denmark. In 1786 he was engaged as court conductor in Stockholm, where he founded a music school; in 1788 he spent some time in St. Petersburg; in 1790 he was in London as organist; after traveling in Poland and Germany, he returned to Stockholm in 1791. In 1794 he went to Paris, and subsequently traveled to Greece and the Near East. From 1796 to 1799 he was again in Sweden, and afterwards visited Copenhagen. In 1800 he went to Berlin; was then in Vienna and Prague. Wherever he went, he solicited interest for his system of organ construction, and exhibited a portable organ called 'orchestrion,' but was unsuccessful. After spending 2 years in Vienna, where he produced his opera *Samori* (1804), and brief sojourns in various German towns, he finally settled in Darmstadt; established a 'Tonschule'; Carl Maria von Weber and Meyerbeer became his pupils there. In teaching, Vogler found his most congenial work; his pedagogical and acoustic writings were also of importance. —Works: Operas: *Der Kaufmann von Smyrna* (Mannheim, 1771); *Albert III von Bayern* (Munich, 1781), *Erwin und Elmire,* after Goethe (Darmstadt, 1781), *La Kermesse* (Paris, Nov. 15, 1783), *Castore e Polluce* (Munich, Jan. 12, 1787), *Gustav Adolph och Ebba Brahe* (Stockholm, Jan. 24, 1788), *Samori* (Vienna, May 17, 1804); ballets, *Rendez-vous de chasse* (Darmstadt, 1772) and *Le Forgeron villageois;* other stage music. Many sacred works, including Masses and a Requiem (his masterpiece); 3 Misereres, motets, Te Deum, Stabat Mater (with orch.), about 50 hymns. Instrumental music: 6 trios for piano, violin, and bass, op. 1; 6 easy sonatas for piano, op. 2; 6 easy sonatas for violin and piano, op. 3; 6 sonatas for 2, 3, and 4 instruments, op. 4; 6 concertos for piano, op. 5; 6 piano trios, op. 6; 6 piano trios, op. 7; 12 Divertissements for piano, op. 8; a piano concerto; Nocturne for piano and strings; *Quatuor concertante* for piano, violin, viola, and bass; 6 sonatas for 2 pianos; sonata for piano 4 hands; sonata for piano and strings, called *Der eheliche Zwist; Polymelos, ou caractères de musique des différentes nations,* for piano and strings; other variations on national airs; a set of variations on *Ah que dirai-je Maman* for piano with orch.; several symphonies and overtures; 32 preludes for organ in every key (a didactic work); etc.—Also publ. *Tonwissenschaft und Tonsetzkunst* (Mannheim, 1776); *Stimmbildungskunst* (Mannheim, 1776); *Churpfälzische Tonschule* (Mannheim, 1778), all 3 republished together as *Mannheimer Tonschule;* a monthly paper 'Betrachtungen der Mannheimer Tonschule' (1778-81); *Inledning til harmoniens könnedom* (*Introduction to the Theory of Harmony;* Stockholm, 1795); Swedish methods for piano, organ, and thorough-bass (Stockholm, 1797); *Choralsystem* (Copenhagen, 1800); *Data zur Akustik* (Offenbach, 1801); *Gründliche Anleitung zum Clavierstimmen* (Stuttgart, 1807); *System für den Fugenbau* (Offenbach, 1811); *Über Choral und Kirchengesänge* (Munich, 1814). —Bibliography: J. Fröhlich, *Biographie des grossen Tonkünstlers Abt Vogler* (Würzburg, 1845); H. Künzel, *Abt Vogler* (Darmstadt, 1867); E. Pasqué, *Abt Vogler als Tonkünstler, Lehrer und Priester* (Darmstadt, 1884); K. E. von Schafhäutl, *Abt G. J. Vogler, Sein Leben, sein Charakter und musikalisches System* (Augsburg, 1888; with a list of works); M. Brenet, *L'Abbé Vogler à Paris,* in 'Archives historiques, artistiques et littéraires' (Feb., 1891); J. Simon, *Abt Voglers kompositorisches Wirken* (Berlin, 1904); E. Rupp, *Abbé Vogler als Mensch, Musiker, und Orgelbautheoretiker* (Ludwigsburg, 1922); P. Vretblad, *Abbé Vogler in Stockholm* (Würzburg, 1924); P. Vretblad, *Abbé Vogler* (1933); H. Kelletat, *Zur Geschichte der deutschen Orgelmusik in der Frühklassik* (Kassel, 1933); H. Schweiger, *Abbé G. J. Vogler's Orgellehre* (dissertation; Vienna, 1938); H. Schweiger, *Abt Vogler,* in the 'Mus. Quarterly' (April, 1939).

Vogrich, Max (Wilhelm Karl), pianist and composer; b. Szeben (Hermannstadt), Transylvania, Jan. 24, 1852; d. New York, June 10, 1916. He gave a piano concert at the age of 7; then studied at the Leipzig Cons. with Reinecke and Moscheles; traveled as pianist in Europe, South America, and the U. S.; also toured Australia. In 1886 he settled in N. Y.; then lived in Weimar (1902-08), and in London until 1914, returning to N. Y. at the outbreak of World War I. He wrote several operas to his own librettos: *Vanda* (Florence, 1875), *King Arthur* (Leipzig, Nov. 26, 1893), *Der Buddha* (Weimar, 1904), etc.; an oratorio, *The Captivity* (1884); 2 symphonies; a piano concerto; several pieces for violin, including a violin concerto subtitled *E pur si muove* (1913); 12 concert studies for piano; an *Album of Ancient and Modern Dances* for piano (20 dances, 2 books); anthems; songs. He edited the complete piano works of Schumann, Clementi's *Gradus ad Parnassum* (in progressive order), 'Modern Russian Composers,' and other collections.

Vogt, Augustus Stephen, Canadian choral conductor; b. Elmira, Ontario, Aug. 14, 1861; d. Toronto, Sept. 17, 1926. He studied at the New England Cons., and then at the Leipzig Cons. In 1888 settled in Toronto; founded and conducted the Mendelssohn Choir there (1894-97 and 1900-17); toured with it in the U. S.; principal of the Toronto Cons. (1913-26); dean, faculty of music, Univ. of Toronto (1916-26). He was an important figure in music education in Canada. Publ. several choral works: *The Sea, Crossing the Bar, An Indian Lullaby, The Lord's Prayer,* etc.; *Standard Anthem Book* (1894) and *Modern Pianoforte Technique* (1900). —Cf. A. Bridle, *Vogt, a Great Chorus Master,* in the 'Year Book of Canadian Art' (1913).

Vogt, Gustav, French oboe player and composer; b. Strasbourg, March 18, 1781; d. Paris, May 30, 1870. He studied at the Paris Cons.; was 1st oboist at the Opéra-Comique, and then at the Opéra (1814-34). He taught at the Paris Cons.; wrote 4 oboe concertos; duos for 2 oboes; potpourris and marches for military band.

Vogt, Johann (Jean), German pianist and composer; b. Gross-Tinz, near Liegnitz, Jan. 17, 1823; d. Eberswalde, July 31, 1888. He studied in Berlin and Breslau; taught piano playing in St. Petersburg (1850-55); subsequently lived in Dresden and in Berlin; visited N. Y. (1871-73). He wrote a piano trio, a string quintet, many salon pieces for piano (in all, over 150 opus numbers).

Voigt, Henriette (*née* Kunze), German pianist; b. Leipzig, Nov. 24, 1808; d. there, Oct. 15, 1839. She was a talented amateur; studied with Ludwig Berger. She married the merchant Karl Voigt, whose house was the rendezvous of the most eminent musicians of the time. Schumann dedicated to her the piano sonata in G minor (op. 22). —Cf. *Acht Briefe und ein Faksimile von F. Mendelssohn-Bartholdy* (Leipzig, 1871, English transl. in 'Macmillan's Magazine' for June, 1871); J. Gensel, *Schumanns Briefwechsel mit Henriette Voigt* (Leipzig, 1892); J. Gensel, *Aus Rochlitzens Briefen an Henriette Voigt* (Leipzig, 1906).

Voigt, Johann Georg Hermann, German organist and composer; b. Osterwieck, May 14, 1769; d. Leipzig, Feb. 24, 1811. He served for many years as organist at the Thomaskirche, Leipzig; publ. chamber music and piano pieces.

Volbach (fŏhl'-bähh), **Fritz,** German choral conductor and composer; b. Wipperfürth, near Cologne, Dec. 17, 1861; d. Wiesbaden, Nov. 30, 1940. He studied at the Cologne Cons., with Hiller, Jensen, and Seiss, and in Berlin with Taubert and Löschhorn. In 1891 he was appointed conductor of the 'Liedertafel' and the 'Damengesangverein' in Mainz; brought out many choral works by modern German composers; *Dr. phil.,* Bonn Univ., for the dissertation *Die Praxis der Händel-Aufführung* (publ. 1900). A versatile musician, he had command of almost every orchestral instrument. His musical works include the symph. poems, *Ostern* and *Es waren zwei Königskinder;* a symphony; a piano quintet; numerous choral works, among them a *Festkantate* for the 5th centenary of the birth of Gutenberg (1900); publ. valuable books: *Lehrbuch der Begleitung des gregorianischen Gesangs* (1888); *Händel* (1898; in Reimann's 'Berühmte Musiker'); *Die Zeit des Klassizismus: Beethoven* (1905: 2nd ed., 1929); *Die deutsche Musik im 19. Jahrhundert* (1909); *Das moderne Orchester in seiner Entwickelung* (1910; 2nd ed., 1919); *Die Instrumente des Orchesters* (1913; 2nd ed., 1921); *Handbuch der Musikwissenschaften,* 2 vols. (1926, 1930); *Die Kunst der Sprache* (1929); *Der Chormeister* (1931). A volume of memoirs, *Erlebtes und Erstrebtes,* was publ. posthumously (Mainz, 1956). —Cf. J. Hagemann, *Fritz Volbach,* in 'Monographien moderner Musiker' (Leipzig, 1909); G. Schwake, *Fritz Volbachs Werke* (Münster, 1921).

Volckmar (fŏlk'-mähr), **Wilhelm Valentin,** German organist and composer; b. Hersfeld, Dec. 26, 1812; d. Homberg, near Kassel, Aug. 27, 1887. In 1835 he settled at Homberg, where he taught music and played organ. He wrote several organ concertos, 20 organ sonatas, an organ symphony; publ. an *Orgelschule,* a *Schule der Geläufigkeit* for organ, pieces for piano and for violin, hymns, songs.

Volkert (fŏl'-kehrt), **Franz,** organist and composer, b. Heimersdorf, Bohemia, Feb. 2, 1767; d. Vienna, March 22, 1845. He was active as organist; was (from 1821) conductor at the Leopoldstadt Theater (Vienna); produced over 100 comic operas, Singspiele, melodramas, farces, etc., many of which were popular; also church music, chamber music, and organ pieces.

Volkmann (fohlk'-măn), **Hans,** German musicologist; grand-nephew of Robert Volkmann; b. Bischofswerda, April 29, 1875. He studied German philology and music in Munich and Berlin; undertook research in Italy and France; in 1921 settled in Dresden, where he taught music history; in 1946 became prof. at the Dresden Cons. —Writings: *Neues über Beethoven* (1904); *Emanuel d'Astorga* (2 vols.; 1911; 1919; fundamental and important biography; establishes the verifiable facts of d'Astorga's life); *Beethoven in seinen Beziehungen zu Dresden* (Dresden, 1942). He publ. the standard biography of Robert Volkmann (Leipzig, 1903; abridged ed., 1915); ed. *Briefe von Robert Volkmann* (1917), and compiled a *Thematisches Verzeichnis der Werke von Robert Volkmann* (Dresden, 1937).

Volkmann (fŏhlk'-măn), **Robert,** German composer; b. Lommatzsch, April 6, 1815; d. Budapest, Oct. 29, 1883. He studied with his father, a cantor (organ and piano); with Friebel (violin and cello) and Anacker (composition); then in Leipzig with K. F. Becker; was greatly encouraged by Schumann. After teaching music in Prague (1839-42), he settled in Budapest, where he spent the rest of his life, except 4 years (1854-58) in Vienna. In 1875 he was appointed prof. at the National Academy of Music in Budapest. His music was regarded very highly in his lifetime, but after his death it faded into oblivion; however, several publications dealing with his works, including a thematic index, were brought out by his grand-nephew, Hans Volkmann. —Works: 2 symphonies; 3 serenades for strings; 2 overtures; a cello concerto; 6 string quartets; 2 piano trios; *Konzertstück* for piano and orch.; *Chant du Troubadour* for violin and piano; *Allegretto capriccioso* for violin and piano; 2 violin sonatinas; *Konzertstück* for piano and orch.; *Romanze* for cello and piano; *Capriccio* for cello and piano; *Schlummerlied* for harp, clarinet, and horn (also arranged for piano, viola and cello; his last completed work). For piano solo: *Phantasiebilder, Dithyrambe und Toccate, Souvenir de Maróth, Nocturne,* sonata in C minor, *Buch der Lieder, Deutsche Tanzweisen, Cavatine und Barcarole, Visegrád,* 4 marches, *Wanderskizzen, Fantasie, Intermezzo,* variations on a theme of Handel, *Lieder der Grossmutter, 3 Improvisations, Am Grab des Grafen Széchenyi, Ballade und Scherzetto,* transcriptions of songs by Mozart and Schubert, etc. For piano 4 hands: *Musikalisches Bilderbuch, Ungarische Skizzen, Die Tageszeiten,* 3 marches, *Rondino und Marsch-Caprice;* transcriptions of his other works. Vocal works: 2 Masses for male chorus, 5 sacred songs for mixed chorus; offertories; Christmas carol of the 12th century; old German hymn for double male chorus; 6 duets on old German poems; alto solo with orch., *An die Nacht;* dramatic scene for soprano and orch., *Sappho; Kirchenarie,* for bass, flute, and strings; *Weihnacht,* for female chorus; *Im Wiesengrün,* for mixed chorus; etc. —Cf. B. Vogel, *Robert Volkmann* (Leipzig, 1875); H. Volkmann, *Robert Volkmann. Sein Leben und seine Werke* (Leipzig, 1903; standard biography; abridged ed., 1915); C. Preiss, *Robert Volkmann. Kritische Beiträge zu seinem Schaffen* (Graz, 1912); V. von Herzfeld, *Robert Volkmann,* in the 'Mus. Quarterly' (July, 1915).

Volkov, Feodor Grigorievitch, Russian amateur musician; b. Kostroma, Feb. 19, 1729; d. St. Petersburg, April 14, 1763. He was educated in Yaroslavl, where he organized a theatrical group, which presented performances of plays with music. In 1754 he entered a military school in St. Petersburg; in 1759 he was sent to Moscow, where he was in charge of the spectacles accompanying the coronation of Catherine II (1763). Volkov was an able practical musician, even though he totally lacked professional training. His supposed authorship of the comic opera, *Taniusha, or A Happy Encounter* (1756), is extremely doubtful; in fact, the existence of such an opera has never been proved. Volkov's role in the early history of the Russian musical stage is confined to his activities as an organizer. —Cf. V. Tcheshikhin, *History of Russian Opera from 1674 to 1903* (St. Petersburg, 1905; pp. 57-60).

Vollerthun (fohl'-ler-toon), **Georg,** German composer and conductor; b. Fürstenau, Sept. 29, 1876; d. Strausberg, Sept. 15, 1945. He studied with Tappert, Radecke, and Gernsheim; was theater conductor in Prague, Berlin, Barmen, and Mainz (1899-1905); spent 3 years in Paris (1908-10); then settled in Berlin as music critic and teacher; from 1922 lived mostly in Strausberg. He wrote the operas *Veeda* (Kassel, 1916), *Island-Saga* (Munich, Jan. 17, 1925), *Der Freikorporal* (Hanover, Nov. 10, 1931; his most successful opera; also given in Berlin, June 10, 1933), and *Das königliche Opfer* (Hanover, 1942); *Alt-Danzig Suite* for orch. (1938); cantatas and other vocal works; many German songs. —Cf. E. Krieger, *Georg Vollerthun* (Berlin, 1942).

Volpe, Arnold, conductor; b. Kovno, Lithuania, July 9, 1869; d. Miami, Fla., Feb. 2, 1940. He studied violin with Leopold Auer at the St. Petersburg Cons. (1887-91); also composition, with Soloviev (1893-97).

In 1898 he emigrated to America, settling in N. Y.; was conductor-founder of the Young Men's Symph. Orch. of N. Y. (1902-19) and of the Volpe Symph. Orch. (1904-14); director of the orch. school of the Brooklyn Institute of Arts and Sciences (1910-19). In 1918 he founded the summer concerts at the Lewisohn Stadium in N. Y., and conducted the first two seasons there, reappearing in later years as guest conductor; was subsequently conductor of the Washington, D. C., Opera Co. (1919-22); musical director of the Kansas City Cons. (1922-25); from 1926, was conductor of the Univ. of Miami Symph. Orch., which he founded. He publ. a string quartet; pieces for violin and piano; many songs *(Parting, The Brook, A Dream, Shadows,* etc.). —Cf. Marie Volpe (his widow), *Arnold Volpe, Bridge Between Two Musical Worlds* (Coral Gables, Fla., 1950).

Vomáčka (vŏh' - măch - kăh), **Boleslav,** Czech composer; b. Mladá Boleslav, June 28, 1887. He studied law in Prague; took music lessons from Novák; from 1919 to 1950 he was in the service of the Labor Ministry in Prague; wrote music criticism in several newspapers there; was editor of 'Listy Hudební Matice' (1922-35). He began to compose early in life; developed a strong national style of writing; his songs and piano pieces are well known in Czechoslovakia. —Works: operas *Vodník (Water Spirit;* Prague, Dec. 17, 1937) and *Boleslav I* (Prague, March 8, 1957); oratorio, *Živi Mrtvým (The Living to the Dead;* Prague, Feb. 24, 1929); cantata, *Strážce majáku (The Watchman of the Lighthouse;* 1931-33); *S. O. S.,* for male chorus (1927); *Czech Eroica,* a symphony (1945); violin sonata; 2 piano sonatas; many part-songs. —Cf. H. Doležil, *Boleslav Vomáčka* (Prague, 1941).

Von Blon, Franz, German composer and conductor; b. Berlin, July 16, 1861; d. there, Oct. 21, 1945. He studied in Berlin at the Stern Cons.; was active as conductor in Warsaw and Berlin; wrote several operettas *(Sub rosa, Die Amazone, Die tolle Prinzess,* etc.) and much light music for piano; also a number of military marches, of which one, *Unter dem Siegesbanner,* became extremely popular.

Von der Hoya, Amadeo, violinist; b. New York, March 13, 1874; d. Linz, Austria, April 4, 1922. He studied violin in Berlin; concertmaster of the Vienna Opera (1894-96); in 1901 appointed concertmaster of the Musikverein in Linz. He publ. *Grundlagen der Violintechnik,* a valuable method; also *Moderne Lagenstudien für Violine* and *Studienbrevier.*

Voormolen, Alexander Nicolas, Dutch composer; b. Rotterdam, March 3, 1895. He studied with Johan Wagenaar in Utrecht; became deeply interested in French music and went to Paris, where he took lessons with Ravel and Roussel; returned to Holland and was active as music critic, living in The Hague. —Works: the ballets *Le Roi Grenouille* (1918), *Baron Hop* (1926), *Diana* (1935); the melodrama *Beatrijs;* symph. poems: *Droomhuis* (1923), *Zomerlied* (1926), *De drie Ruytertjes* (variations on an old Dutch song; 1927); concerto for 2 oboes and orch. (1934); cello concerto (1941); *Arethusa,* 'symph. myth' (1947); string quartet; 3 violin sonatas; several piano albums: *Le Souper clandestin, Tableaux des Pays-Bas, Le Livre des enfants, Suite de clavecin;* songs to Dutch, German, and French texts. —Cf. Cor Backers, *Nederlandse Componisten van 1400 tot op onze Tijd* (The Hague, 1949; pp. 141-47).

Vopelius, Gottfried, German composer; b. Herwigsdorf, near Zittau, Jan. 28, 1635; d. Leipzig, Feb. 3, 1715. He was cantor of St. Nicholas at Leipzig from 1675; harmonized old German hymns and publ. a *Neu Leipziger Gesangbuch* (1682), containing 100 hymns originally brought out in Schein's *Cantional oder Gesangbuch* (1627).

Voříšek, Jan Hugo. See **Worzischek.**

Voss, Charles, German pianist; b. Schmarsow, Sept. 20, 1815; d. Verona, Aug. 29, 1882. He studied in Berlin, but made his career in Paris, where he went in 1846; enjoyed great success in Paris society as pianist and composer; publ. a great number of salon pieces, transcriptions, paraphrases, etc.; also wrote piano concertos and études. His first piano concerto, in F minor, was praised by Mendelssohn.

Voss (Vossius), Isaac, music theorist; b. Leyden, Holland, 1618; d. Windsor, England, Feb. 21, 1689. He was the son of the German scholar Gerhard Johann Voss (1577-1649), who lived in Holland. After his father's death, he went to Stockholm, where he was at the court of Queen Christina (1649-52); subsequently went to England, where he remained till his death. He publ. an important treatise in Latin, *De poematum cantu et viribus rythmi* (1673).

Vranken, Jaap, Dutch organist and composer; b. Utrecht, April 16, 1897; d. The Hague, April 20, 1956. He was the son of the organist Joseph Vranken (1870-1948), with whom he studied organ and theory. In 1916-18, he was in the U. S., studying with Percy Goetschius. He returned to Holland in 1920, and was appointed organist at the church of St. Anthonius in The Hague; acquired a fine reputation as a teacher. He composed mostly sacred music; also instrumental music in classical style; publ. a manual on counterpoint (1948). His last work was a *Missa Polyphonica* (1953).

Vredenburg, Max, composer; b. Brussels, Jan. 16, 1904, of Dutch parents; was taken to Holland as a child and received elementary education there; then went to Paris, where he became a pupil of Paul Dukas at the École Normale; upon his return to Holland he settled in The Hague as a teacher; from 1936 to 1940 was again in Paris; then was sent by the Dutch government to Java; was interned by the Japanese (1942-45) but was allowed to give concerts in Indonesia with the violinist Szymon Goldberg, who was also interned there; returned to Holland after the end of the war, and continued his activities as pianist and composer; publ. a book, *Langs de vijf Lijnen* (1947). —Works: *Suite sportive,* for violin and piano; oboe sonatina; many teaching pieces for piano; also song cycles.

Vretblad, Viktor Patrik, Swedish organist and musicologist; b. Svartnäs, April 5, 1876; d. Stockholm, Jan. 15, 1953. He studied at the Stockholm Cons. (1895-1900) and later in Berlin; wrote music criticism; acted as church organist; was an official of the Ministry of the Postal Services for 40 years (1900-40). He devoted his research mainly to early Swedish music; publ. basic biographies of J. H. Roman (Stockholm, 1914 and 1945); *Konsertlivet i Stockholm under 1700-talet* (1918); *A. Hallén* (1918); *Abbé Vogler* (1933).

Vreuls (vröls), **Victor,** Belgian composer; b. Verviers, Feb. 4, 1876; d. Brussels, July 26, 1944. He was a pupil of the Cons. of Verviers, and later studied with Sylvain Dupuis and J. T. Radoux in Liège. He then went to Paris, where he took a course with Vincent d'Indy at the Schola Cantorum; taught viola playing and elementary theory there (1901-06); subsequently was for 20 years (1906-26) director of the Luxembourg Cons. —Works: operas: *Olivier le simple* (Brussels, March 9, 1922) and *Un Songe d'une nuit d'été,* after Shakespeare (Brussels, Dec. 17, 1925); a ballet, *Le Loup-garou* (Ghent, 1937); the symph. poems *Werther, Jour de Fête, Cortège héroïque;* a symph. with violin solo (Ysaÿe Prize, 1904); *Poème* for cello and orch.; *Élégie* for flute and orch.; a string quartet; a piano quartet; 2 violin sonatas; a cello sonata; piano pieces; songs.

Vrieslander (frēs'-lahn-dehr), **Otto,** German composer and writer on music; b. Münster, July 18, 1880; d. Tegna, Switzerland, Dec. 16, 1950. After attending the Cologne Cons. he went to Munich in 1904; in 1911-12, he was in Vienna, where he studied with Heinrich Schenker, becoming one of his disciples. From 1912 he lived in Ebertsberg, near Munich; in 1929 settled in Switzerland. He wrote some highly expressive song cycles *(Lieder aus des Knaben Wunderhorn, Pierrot lunaire,* etc.); edited works by Ph. E. Bach, six of whose symphonies he arranged for piano 4 hands; publ. various studies on him: *Ph. E. Bachs Klavierstücke für Anfänger mit kompositionstechnischer Analyse* (1914); *Lieder und Gesänge von Ph. E. Bach nebst Einleitung* (1922); *Ph. E. Bach als Klavierkomponist,* in 'Ganymed' (Dresden, 1922); *Ph. E. Bach* (1923); *Ph. E. Bach als Theoretiker,* in *Von neuer Musik* (1925).

Vrionides, Christos, conductor; b. Khania, Crete, Jan. 12, 1894; studied in Athens at the Odeon, and taught theory and double-bass there (1920-22), then came to the U. S.; studied at the Institute of Musical Art, N. Y. (graduated 1929); conducted the Vrionides Sinfonietta in N. Y. (1929-35); also led the Byzantine Vocal Ensemble (1924-38); conducted the Nassau-Suffolk Federal Orch. (1935-41); in 1946 became conductor of the Babylon, N. Y., Symph. Orch.; taught Greek liturgy in N. Y. and Boston; his musical settings of the liturgy of the Greek Orthodox Church have been accepted in Greek churches in the U. S. and South America.

Vronsky, Vitya (real name Victoria Vronsky), pianist; b. Evpatoria, Crimea, Aug. 22, 1909; studied at the Kiev Cons.; then with Petri and Schnabel in Berlin, and with Cortot in Paris. Married the pianist Victor Babin (q.v.) on Aug. 31, 1933. She came to America in 1937; toured widely with Babin in 2-piano recitals.

Vroye (vrwah'), **Théodore-Joseph de,** Belgian music scholar; b. Villers-la-Ville, Aug. 19, 1804; d. Liège, July 19, 1873. He entered the priesthood in 1828, and in 1835 became canon of the Liège Cathedral. He made a profound study of Gregorian Chant; publ. *Vesperal* (1829); *Graduel* (1831); *Traité du plain-chant à l'usage des séminaires* (1839); *Manuale cantorum* (1849); *Processionale* (1849); *Rituale Romanum* (1862); *De la musique religieuse* (1866; with Elewyck).

Vuataz, Roger, Swiss composer; b. Geneva, Jan. 4, 1898. He studied with Otto Barblan and Jaques-Dalcroze at the Geneva Cons.; was active as church organist and music critic; then devoted himself to conducting and composing. —Works: oratorio, *Abraham; La Flûte de roseau* for chorus; *Le Rhône* for tenor, chorus, and orch.; *Petit concert* for orch.; *Dagmayanti,* symph. poem; *La Vie et les métiers au Péloponnèse,* for orch.; *Géqmetries* for 5 instruments; piano and organ pieces.

Vuillaume (vüē-yohm'), **Jean-Baptiste,** celebrated French violin maker; b. Mirecourt, Oct. 7, 1798; d. Paris, Feb. 19, 1875. He came of a family of violin makers, and learned the trade from his father, Claude Vuillaume (1772-1834). At 19 he went to Paris, and worked with Chanot till 1821 and from 1821-25 for Lété, with whom he then entered into partnership. After Lété's retirement in 1828, Vuillaume worked alone, and put his own name on several instruments which he had constructed with the greatest care and fine craftsmanship; but he was unable to overcome the general distrust of the native product, and began manufacturing imitations of Italian instruments. After long and patient labor he placed a 'Stradivarius' violin on the market for 300 francs, bearing the master's label, and possessing a full, sonorous tone; also built cellos priced at 500 francs. The sight of a Duiffoprugcar viola da gamba inspired him with the idea of further imitations; hence the hundreds of 'Duiffoprugcar' violins and cellos with their quaint shape, carved scrolls, inlays, and the motto 'viva fui in sylvis, etc.' By dint of indefatigable researches and experiments, Vuillaume carried the construction of these various instruments to the highest perfection. His own inventions were numerous: in 1849 the huge 'Octobasse,' a double-bass 4 meters in length, 3-stringed (CC-GG-C), with a special lever-mechanism to aid the left hand (an 'octobasse' is in the Museum of the Paris Cons.); in 1855 a viola of broader and higher model, the 'contre-alto,' with double strength of tone, but clumsy to play; in 1867 a kind of mute, the 'pédale sourdine'; also a machine for manufacturing gut strings of perfectly equal thickness. He likewise formulated the laws governing the tapering of the stick of the Tourte bow.

Vuillermoz (vüē-yehr-mohz'), **Émile,** French music critic; b. Lyons, May 23, 1878. He studied organ and piano in Lyons, and composition at the Paris Cons. with Fauré. He was one of the organizers of the Société Musicale Indépendante (1911) and edited the 'Revue Musicale S. I. M.'; eventually became music critic of the daily 'L'Excelsior' and also contributed articles to 'Le Temps.' He publ. *Musiques d'aujourd'hui* (1923), *La Vie amoureuse de Chopin* (1927), and *Histoire de la musique* (26th printing, 1949).

Vuillermoz, Jean, French composer, b. Monte Carlo, Dec. 29, 1906; d. Lobsonn, Alsace, June 21, 1940 (killed while on patrol duty in the last hours before Franco-German armistice). He studied with Busser and Rabaud at the Paris Cons.; received 2nd Prix de Rome for his cantata *Le Pardon* (1932).—Works: *Triptique* for orch. (Paris, May 31, 1932); concerto for French horn and orch. (Paris, March 11, 1934); a ballet, *Veglione* (1937); cello concerto; *Promenade zoologique* for chamber orch.; piano trio; string trio.

Vulpius (Latinized form of real name, Fuchs), **Melchior,** German composer; b. Wasungen, c. 1560; d. Weimar, 1615 (buried Aug. 7). From 1596 to his death, he was cantor in Weimar. Publ. 2 books of *Cantiones sacrae* (1602, 2nd ed., 1603; and 1604, 2nd ed., 1611); *Kirchengesänge und geistliche Lieder . . .* for 4 and 5 voices (1604); *Canticum beatissimae Virginis Mariae,* for 4-8 voices (1605); *Lateinische Hochzeitstücke* (1608); *Opusculum . . . cantionum sacrarum,* for 4-6 voices (1610); *Das Leiden und Sterben unseres Herrn . . .* (Passion after Matthew; 1613); 3 books of *Sonntägliche Evangelische Sprüche* for 4 voices (1619, 1620, 1621); also a new ed. of Heinrich Faber's *Compendiolum musicae* (1610) with a German transl. and a supplementary chapter. Modern editions are: the Matthew-Passion by Ziebler (1934); hymns by Heyden (1932); Christmas choruses by Twittenhoff and Heyden (1932); other pieces by Schöberlein, etc.—Cf. C. von Winterfeld, *Zur Geschichte heiliger Tonkunst,* I (1850); H. H. Eggebrecht, *Melchior*

Vulpius, dissertation, in 'Max Schneider Festschrift' (1955).

Vycpálek, Ladislav, Czech composer; b. Prague, Feb. 23, 1882. He studied philology at the Charles Univ., Prague; *Dr. phil.,* 1906; then studied composition with Novák (1908-12). From 1922 till 1942 he was in charge of the Mus. Department at the National Library in Prague. He wrote 2 cantatas to biblical texts, and one to Moravian folk tales; many choruses; some chamber music; songs to Czech words; made numerous arrangements of Moravian folksongs.

Vyshnegradsky, Ivan, Russian composer; b. St. Petersburg, May 5, 1893; studied at the Cons. there; in 1922 settled in Paris. He devoted his entire life to the cause of quarter-tone music; built a quarter-tone piano with 2 keyboards and publ. a textbook on quarter-tone harmony (Paris, 1933). His works for quarter-tone ensembles include *First Symphonic Fragment,* arranged for 4 pianos (2 tuned a quarter-tone higher than the others); *Ainsi parlait Zarathoustra* (1928-30), similarly arranged for 4 pianos; *Étude en forme de scherzo* (1931) for 2 pianos tuned a quarter-tone apart; a cycle, *24 Preludes in the 13-tone quasi-diatonic quarter-tone scale* for 2 pianos. On Nov. 10, 1945, he conducted in Paris the première of a 4-piano arrangement of his symph. poem *Cosmos.*

W

Waack (văahk), **Karl,** German conductor; b. Lübeck, March 6, 1861; d. Neumünster, March 7, 1922. He was a pupil of the grand-ducal Musikschule in Weimar; 1882, conductor in Åbo, Finland; settled in Riga as teacher and conductor of the 'Wagnerverein.' After the outbreak of the war in 1914, he fled to Lübeck, where he conducted the 'Verein der Musikfreunde.' He edited *Tristan und Isolde* (1904) and *Lohengrin* (1907) for Breitkopf & Härtel's 'Textbibliothek' (with leading motifs in notation, and references to the full and piano scores); also wrote historical introductions and prepared tables of motifs for all the Wagner operas in the new editions brought out by Breitkopf & Härtel (1913). He publ. *Richard Wagner, ein Erfüller und Vollender deutscher Kunst* (1918).

Waart, Hendrikus Aloysius Petrus de, Dutch composer and organist; b. Amsterdam, June 28, 1863; d. Voorburg, near The Hague, April 2, 1931. He studied in The Hague; then taught piano and organ at the Cons. there; wrote 3 symphonies, numerous choral works, a string trio, piano works, songs.

Wachs, Paul Étienne Victor, French pianist and composer; b. Paris, Sept. 19, 1851; d. St. Mandé, July 6, 1915. He studied with César Franck and Victor Massé at the Paris Cons., and won 1st prize for organ playing; subsequently was engaged as church organist in Paris. He wrote works for organ, chamber music, etc., but achieved his most signal success as composer of attractive salon pieces for piano (*Pluie d'étoiles, Le Collier de perles, Les Doigts,* etc.); also well known are his *Pastorale* and *Hosanna* for organ.

Wachtel, Theodor, German tenor; b. Hamburg, March 10, 1823; d. Frankfurt, Nov. 14, 1893. The son of a livery-stable keeper, he carried on the business from the age of 17, after his father's death. When his voice was discovered, he was sent to Hamburg for study, and soon appeared in opera. After further study in Vienna, he sang at the Berlin Opera (1865-68); in 1869 he appeared in Paris; made 2 American tours (1871 and 1875); accumulated a considerable fortune. His voice was a powerful and brilliant lyric tenor; the role in which he made himself famous was that of the postillion in Adam's *Postillon de Longjumeau,* which he sang more than 1,000 times; also was successful as Raoul in *Les Huguenots.* His sole attempt as a Wagner singer, in *Lohengrin* (Leipzig, 1876), was a dismal failure.

Wachtmeister (vaht'-mī-ster), **Axel Raoul,** Count, composer; b. London (son of the Swedish ambassador there), April 2, 1865; d. Paris, Dec. 12, 1947. He studied music with Gedalge and Vincent d'Indy. He lived mostly in Paris, going to Sweden in the summers; also spent some time in the U. S.; his cantata *Sappho* was performed in N. Y. in 1917. He also wrote 2 symphonies; a symph. poem, *Le Récit de l'horloge; Hymne à la lune,* for baritone, chorus, and orch. (Cincinnati, 1933); *Suite romantique* for piano; songs.

Wackernagel, Philipp, German historian; b. Berlin, June 28, 1800; d. Dresden, June 20, 1877. He publ. several books dealing with music: *Das deutsche Kirchenlied, von Luther bis auf N. Hermann* (1841; 2 vols.); *Bibliographie zur Geschichte des deutschen Kirchenliedes im 16. Jahrhundert* (1855);

and *Das deutsche Kirchenlied von der ältesten Zeit bis zum Anfang des 17. Jahrhunderts* (5 vols., 1864-77).

Waddington, Sidney Peine, English composer and pedagogue; b. Lincoln, July 23, 1869; d. Uplyme, Devon, June 2, 1953. He studied in London, Frankfurt, and Vienna; returning to England, he was engaged as chorusmaster at St. Mary of the Angels, Bayswater, London (1894-1905); in 1905 joined the staff of the Royal College of Music as harmony teacher. He wrote an operetta for children, *Whimland; Ode to Music* for soli, chorus, and orch.; a piano concerto; a piano quintet; a string quartet; a string trio; *Suite de Pièces* for piano 4 hands; a violin sonata; a cello sonata; etc.

Wade, Joseph Augustine, Irish composer; b. Dublin, 1796; d. London, July 15, 1845. He went to London in 1821, and established himself as a highly successful composer of popular ballads; his song *Meet me by moonlight alone* (1826) enjoyed great vogue, as did his vocal duet *I've wandered in dreams.* He also wrote an opera, *The Two Houses of Granada* (London, Oct. 31, 1826), and an operetta, *The Pupil of Da Vinci* (London, Nov. 30, 1839).

Waefelghem, Louis van, Belgian violinist and composer; b. Bruges, Jan. 13, 1840; d. Paris, June 19, 1908. He studied violin at the Brussels Cons. with Meerts; went to Germany in 1860; played violin in the orch. of the Budapest Opera; settled in Paris in 1863; often visited London as chamber music player. With Grillet, Diémer, and Delsart he founded the Société des Instruments Anciens in Paris (1895), where he played the viola d'amore; composed and arranged a number of pieces for that instrument.

Waelput (văhl'-pŏŏt), **Hendrik,** Flemish composer; b. Ghent, Oct. 26, 1845; d. there, July 8, 1885. He studied at the Brussels Cons.; won the Prix de Rome for his cantata *Het Woud (The Forest).* He was director of the Bruges Cons. (1869-71); conducted theater orchestras at The Hague, Dijon, Douai, Fécamp, and Lille (1872-76). From 1876 to 1879 he was active in Ghent; in 1879 appointed prof. of harmony at Antwerp Cons.; returned to Ghent in 1884. He wrote two operas: *La Ferme du diable* (Ghent, 1865) and *Stella* (in Flemish; Brussels, March 14, 1881); 5 symphonies, cantatas, and other works.—Cf. E. Callaert, *Levensschets van Hendrik Waelput* (1886); P. Bergmans, *Notice biographique sur Henry Waelput* (1886); E. de Vynck, *Henry Waelput* (Brussels, 1935).

Waelrant (văhl'-răhnt), **Hubert,** Flemish composer and theorist; b. Tongerloo, Brabant, c. 1517; d. Antwerp, Nov. 19, 1595. He matriculated at the Univ. of Louvain in 1534; in 1544 became a tenor singer at Notre Dame in Antwerp, where he founded a music school in 1547. In 1554 he established a music publishing business in partnership with Jean Laet, retiring in 1558. As a teacher, he abandoned the old system of solmization by hexachords and introduced a new system of the 7 tone-names, *bo ce di ga lo ma ni* (hence called 'Bocedization'; also 'Voces belgicae'). His compositions include a book of chansons, publ. by Phalèse in Louvain (1553-54), and a book of madrigals for 5 voices (Antwerp, 1558); as a publisher he brought out several sacred works by various composers; edited a collection, *Symphonia angelica . . .* containing madrigals of his own (1585).—Cf. G. Becker, *Hubert Waelrant et ses psaumes. Notice biographique et bibliographique* (Paris, 1881). See also G. Reese, *Music in the Renaissance* (N. Y., 1954, pp. 396 and 505).

Waesberghe, Joseph Smits van, Dutch musicologist; b. Breda, April 18, 1901. He studied philosophy; joined the Jesuit Order; then took courses in music with C. Huygens (church music) and Marius Monnikendam (theory); taught at the Cons. of Rotterdam (1928-43) and in 1943 was appointed to the staff of the Amsterdam Cons. —Publications: *Muziekgeschiedenis der Middeleeuwen,* a voluminous survey of medieval music history in 2 parts (Tilburg, 1935-39 and 1939-47); *Klokken en Klokkegieten in de Middeleeuwen* (1937); *Muziek en Drama in de Middeleeuwen* (Amsterdam, 1942; in English, as *Music and Drama in the Middle Ages,* Stockholm, 1947); *De Gregoriaansche Zang* (Amsterdam, 1943; in English, as *Gregorian Chant and its Place in the Catholic Liturgy,* Stockholm, 1947); *School en Muziek in de Middeleeuwen* (Amsterdam, 1949).

Wagenaar (văh'-gĕh-năhr), **Bernard,** composer and teacher; son of Johan Wagenaar; b. Arnhem, Holland, July 18, 1894. He studied music with his father; violin with Gerard Veerman in Utrecht. In 1920 he came to the U. S.; was a violinist in the N. Y. Philharmonic (1921-23). In 1927 he became instructor of composition and orchestration at the Juilliard Graduate School of Music, N. Y.—Works: *Pieces of Eight,* operatic comedy (1943; N. Y., 1944); symph. No. 1 (N. Y., Oct. 7, 1928); *Divertimento* (Detroit, Nov. 28, 1929); *Sinfonietta* (N. Y., Jan. 16, 1930); symph. No. 2 (N. Y., Nov. 10, 1932, Toscanini conducting); symph. No. 3 (N. Y., Jan. 23, 1937, composer conducting); violin concerto (1940); Triple Concerto for flute, harp, cello, and orch. (N. Y., May 20, 1941, composer conducting); symph. No. 4 (Boston, Dec. 16, 1949); *5 Tableaux* for cello and orch. (Amsterdam, Jan. 9, 1955); *3 Songs from the Chinese* (1921); violin sonata (1925); 3 string quartets; piano sonata; sonatina for cello and piano; concertino for 8 instruments.—Cf. D. Fuller, *Bernard Wagenaar,* in 'Modern Music' (May, 1944).

Wagenaar (văh'-gĕh-nāhr), **Johan,** Dutch organist and composer; b. Utrecht, Nov. 1, 1862; d. The Hague, June 17, 1941. He studied with Richard Hol in Utrecht (1875-85) and with H. von Herzogenberg in Berlin (1889); established himself as an organist at the Utrecht Cathedral; also became known as an eminent Bach player; in 1904 became director of the Utrecht Music School; from 1908 also music director at Arnhem, and from 1910 at Leyden. From 1919 to 1937 he was director of the Royal Cons. at The Hague.—Works: the operas *De Doge van Venetie* (Utrecht, 1904) and *De Cid* (Utrecht, 1916); also the burlesque opera *Jupiter Amans* (Scheveningen, 1925); humorous cantata *De Schipbreuk* (1889); the symph. poems *Levenszomer* (1901); *Saul and David* (1906), and *Elverhöt* (1940); the overtures *Koning Jan* (1889), *Cyrano de Bergerac* (1905), *De getemde feeks* (1906), *Driekoningenavond* (1927), and *De philosofische prinses* (1931); numerous choral works; songs; organ pieces. —Cf. C. Backers, *Nederlandse Componisten van 1400 tot op onze Tijd* (The Hague, 1941; pp. 96-99).

Wagenmann (vah'-gen-mann), **Josef Hermann,** German singing teacher and writer; b. Engingen, May 11, 1876; d. Berlin, July 30, 1940. He studied jurisprudence in Heidelberg and Leipzig; then studied singing with various teachers in Italy; became a renowned singing teacher in Berlin; in 1934 was appointed prof. at the Academy for Church- and School-Music there. He publ. *Neue Ära der Stimmbildung für Singen und Sprechen* (1903); *Umsturz in der Stimmbildung* (1904; 2nd ed., 1922); *Lilli Lehmanns Geheimnis der Stimmbänder* (1905; 2nd ed., 1926); *Ein automatischer Stimmbildner* (1906); *Enrico Caruso und das Problem der Stimmbildung* (1911; 3rd ed., 1924); *Heinrich Knote* (1931).

Wagenseil (văh'-gĕn-zīl), **Georg Christoph,** Austrian composer and theorist; b. Vienna, Jan. 15, 1715; d. there, March 1, 1777. He studied with J. J. Fux; was music teacher of the Empress Maria Theresa and her children; in 1739 was appointed court composer, besides holding other court positions and sinecures; remained in the Imperial services until his death. He wrote many operas in Italian; the following were produced in Vienna: *La Generosità trionfante* (1745); *Ariodante* (May 14, 1746); *La Clemenza di Tito* (1746); *Alexander der Grosse in Indien* (July 7, 1748); *Il Siroe* (1748); *L'Olimpiade* (May 13, 1749); *Andromeda* (1749); *Antigone* (May 13, 1750); *Armida placata* (1750); *Euridice* (1750); *Le Cacciatrici amanti* (1755); *Demetrio* (1760); 3 oratorios; 30 symphonies; 27 harpsichord concertos; organ works. Two symphonies and a trio-sonata are in the 'Denkmäler der Tonkunst in Österreich' (XV, 2); a divertimento was ed. by Blume. Wagenseil publ. the following: *Suavis, artificiose elaboratus concentus musicus, continens: 6 selectas parthias ad clavicembalum compositas* (1740); *18 Divertimenti di cembalo,* op. 1-3; a divertimento for 2 harpsichords; 2 divertimentos for harpsichord, 2 violins, and cello, op. 5; 10 symphonies for harpsichord, 2 violins, and cello, op. 4, 7, 8; 6 violin sonatas with harpsichord, op. 6. —Cf. K. Horwitz, *Wagenseil als Symphoniker* (dissertation, Vienna, 1906); W. Vetter, *G. C. Wagenseil, ein Vorläufer Glucks,* in the 'Zeitschrift für Musikwissenschaft' (vol. 8; 1926); W. Vetter, *Der Opernkomponist G. C. Wagenseil und sein Verhältnis zu Mozart und Gluck,* in the 'Hermann Abert-Gedenkschrift' (Halle, 1928); J. Pelikant, *Die Klavier-Werke Wagenseils* (Vienna, 1926); G. Hausswald, *Der Divertimento-Begriff bei G. C. Wagenseil,* in the 'Archiv für Musikwissenschaft' (1952).

Wagenseil (văh'-gĕn-zīl), **Johann Christoph,** German historian and librarian; b. Nuremberg, Nov. 26, 1633; d. Altdorf, Oct. 9, 1708. He publ. an important book, *De Sacri Rom. Imperii Libera Civitate Noribergensi Commentatio* (Altdorf, 1697), with a 140-page supplement (in German), *Buch von der Meister-Singer holdseligen Kunst: Anfang, Fortübung, Nutzbarkeiten und Lehr-Sätze,* containing poems and melodies by

Frauenlob, Mügling, Marner, and Regenbogen; this section was the main literary source that Wagner used in *Die Meistersinger von Nürnberg.* —Cf. K. Mey, *Der Meistergesang in Geschichte und Kunst* (2nd ed., 1901); H. Thompson, *Wagner & Wagenseil. A Source of Wagner's Opera 'Die Meistersinger'* (London, 1927).

Waghalter, Ignatz, conductor and composer, b. Warsaw, March 15, 1882; d. New York, April 7, 1949. He studied in Berlin, where he became conductor of the 'Komische Oper' (1907-11); then conducted in Essen (1911-12), and at the 'Deutsches Opernhaus' in Berlin-Charlottenburg. In 1925 he succeeded Stransky as conductor of the State Symph. Orch in N. Y. (for one season only); then returned to Berlin; in 1933 he went to Prague, and in 1934 to Vienna. He then went to America, settling in N. Y. in 1938. He was also a composer; wrote the operas *Der Teufelsweg* (Berlin, 1911), *Mandragola* (Berlin, Jan. 23, 1914; N. Y., March 4, 1925), *Jugend* (Berlin, 1917), *Der späte Gast* (Berlin, 1922), and *Sataniel* (Berlin, 1923); also operettas (*Der Weiberkrieg* and *Wem gehört Helena?); a* violin concerto; a violin sonata; a string quartet; piano pieces.—Cf. H. Leichtentritt, *Ignatz Waghalter* (N. Y., 1924).

Wagner, Cosima, wife of Richard Wagner, daughter of Franz Liszt and the Countess Marie d'Agoult; b. Bellaggio, on Lake Como, Dec. 25, 1837; d. Bayreuth, April 1, 1930. She received an excellent education in Paris; married Hans von Bülow on Aug. 18, 1857; there were two daughters of this marriage, Blandine and Daniela; the third daughter, Isolde, was Wagner's child, as was the fourth, Eva, and the son, Siegfried. A divorce followed on July 18, 1870; the marriage to Wagner took place in a few weeks, on Aug. 25, 1870. A woman of high intelligence, practical sense, and imperious character, Cosima Wagner emerged after Wagner's death as a powerful personage in all affairs regarding the continuance of the Bayreuth Festivals as well as the complex matters pertaining to the rights of performance of Wagner's works all over the world. She publ. her reminiscences of Liszt: *Franz Liszt. Ein Gedenkblatt von seiner Tochter* (Munich, 2nd ed., 1911).—Cf. M. Strauss, *Wie ich Frau Cosima Wagner sehe* (Magdeburg, 1912); E. Schuré, *Femmes inspiratrices* (Paris, 1930); W. Siegfried, *Frau Cosima Wagner* (Stuttgart, 1930); F. Blei, *Gefährtinnen* (Berlin, 1931); R. Du Moulin-Eckart, *Cosima Wagner* (Munich, 1929; English translation, in 2 vols., N. Y., 1930); M. von Waldberg, *Cosima Wagners Briefe an ihre Tochter Daniela von Bülow, 1866-85* (Stuttgart, 1933); L. Scalero, *Cosima Wagner* (Zürich, 1934); P. Pretzsch, *Cosima Wagner und H. S. Chamberlain im Briefwechsel, 1888-1908* (Leipzig, 1934); *Briefwechsel zwischen Cosima Wagner und Fürst Ernst zu Hohenlohe-Langenburg* (Stuttgart, 1937); M. von Millenkovich (M. Morold), *Cosima Wagner, ein Lebensbild* (Leipzig, 1937); E. Thierbach, ed., *Die Briefe Cosima Wagners an Friedrich Nietzsche* (Weimar, 1938-40). See also Wagner's autobiography, *Mein Leben,* and bibliography under Wagner.

Wagner, Georg Gottfried, German violinist; b. Mühlberg, Saxony, April 5, 1698; d. Plauen, March 23, 1756. He studied with Kuhnau at the Thomasschule, Leipzig (1712-19); was a violinist in Bach's orch., and was recommended by Bach for the post of cantor at Plauen, which he held from 1726 to his death. He also wrote numerous sacred works and instrumental compositions; his motet *Lob und Ehre* was misattributed to Bach by Breitkopf & Härtel (publ. 1819). —Cf. B. Hammerschmidt, *G. G. Wagner* (Chemnitz, 1912).

Wagner, Gerrit Anthonie Alexander, Dutch conductor and composer; b. Amsterdam, March 8, 1862; d. Antwerp, Nov. 24, 1892. He studied with Brandts-Buys in Amsterdam and with Benoit and Blockx in Antwerp; became a choral conductor there. He wrote an oratorio, *Babylonische Gevangenschap;* a symph. poem, *Zusterengelen;* much choral music; his promising career was terminated by an early death.

Wagner, Johanna, German soprano; b. Seelze, near Hanover, Oct. 13, 1826; d. Würzburg, Oct. 16, 1894. She was a natural daughter of Lieutenant Bock von Wülfingen of Hanover, and was adopted by Richard Wagner's brother, Albert; was thus regarded as Wagner's niece. Of a precocious talent, she acted on the stage as a small child; through Wagner she obtained a position at the Dresden Opera when she was 17; produced an excellent impression as Agathe in *Der Freischütz,* and was engaged as a regular member. She studied the part of Elisabeth in *Tannhäuser* with Wagner, and sang it in the première of the opera on Oct. 19, 1845, when she was barely 19 years old. In 1846 she went to Paris for further study, with Mme. Viardot-Garcia (1846-48); then was engaged at the Hamburg Opera (1849) and finally at the Court Opera in Berlin

(1850-61). In 1859 she married the district judge Jachmann. After 1862 she acted mainly on the dramatic stage, reappearing in opera at the Bayreuth Festival in 1876 in the parts of Schwertleite and the First Norn. In 1882 she settled in Munich as a singing teacher. —Cf. J. Kapp and H. Jachmann, *Richard Wagner und seine erste 'Elisabeth,' Johanna Jachmann-Wagner* (Berlin, 1927; in English as *Wagner and His First Elisabeth,* London, 1944).

Wagner, Josef Franz, Austrian composer of light music; b. Vienna, March 20, 1856; d. there, June, 1908. He was a popular leader of military bands in Vienna; produced the operettas *Der Herzbub* (Vienna, Feb. 7, 1895) and *Der Cognac-König* (Vienna, Feb. 20, 1897), which had little success, but achieved fame as the composer of the Austrian march *Under the Double Eagle,* which became a semi-official march of the Austro-Hungarian Empire.

Wagner, Joseph Frederick, American composer and conductor; b. Springfield, Mass., Jan. 9, 1900. He studied at the New England Cons. with Converse (until 1923); then at the College of Music of Boston Univ. (graduated 1932); also private pupil in advanced composition with Alfredo Casella in Boston (1927) and Nadia Boulanger in Paris (1934-35); conducting with Pierre Monteux in Paris and Felix Weingartner in Basel (1935). He was assistant director of music and supervisor of instrumental music in the Boston public schools from 1923 till 1944; member of the faculty of Boston Univ. College of Music (1929-40), Hunter College, N. Y. (1945-46), Brooklyn College (1945-47). In 1925 he founded the Boston Civic Symph. Orch., which he conducted until 1944, presenting many new American works; was conductor of the Duluth Symph. Orch. (1947-50) and of the Orquesta Sinfónica Nacional de Costa Rica in San José (1950-54); guest conductor in Havana, Helsinki, Stockholm, Washington, Buffalo, etc. From 1955 living mostly in N. Y. —Works: Ballets: *The Birthday of the Infanta,* after Oscar Wilde (1935), *Dance Divertissement* (1937), and *Hudson River Legend* (1941; Boston, March 1, 1944). For orch.: *Miniature Concerto* for piano and orch. (1919; Providence, June 11, 1920; revised as Concerto in G minor; New Brunswick, N. J., Aug. 3, 1930); symph. No. 1 (1943; Rochester, Oct. 19, 1944); *Variations on an Old Form* (Washington, 1941); *Four Miniatures* (N. Y., May 15, 1941); *A Fugal Triptych* for piano, percussion, and strings (Boston, May 25, 1941); symph. No. 2 (1943); *Festival Processions* (Columbus, Ohio, Dec. 16, 1946); *American Jubilee,* overture (1946); concertino for harp and orch. (1947); *Radio City Snapshots* (St. Paul, Minn., Aug. 6, 1947); *Fantasy in Technicolor* for piano and orch. (1948); *Northern Saga,* a 'landscape' for orch. (1949); concerto grosso (1949); symph. No. 3 (1951); violin concerto (1955); rhapsody for clarinet, piano, and strings (Boston, May 7, 1926); sinfonietta No. 1 (1931); sinfonietta No. 2 (Boston, Feb. 22, 1942); *From the North Shore,* '2 sea pieces' for string orch. (Boston, March 10, 1942); *Introduction and Scherzo* for bassoon and strings (1951); pieces for band. Chamber music: 3 Pastorals for oboe and piano (1941); violin sonata (1941); *Concert Piece* for clarinet and piano (1942); 2 *Silhouettes* for violin and piano (1944); Theme and Variations for flute, clarinet, violin, and cello (1950); Introduction and Scherzo for bassoon and piano (1951). For piano: sonatina (1934), *4 Landscapes* (1936); *From the Monadnock Region,* suite of 5 pieces (1942); *Radio City Snapshots* (1945; also for orch.); sonata in B minor (1946); *Pastoral and Toccata* (1948); *After-Dinner Sonata* for 2 pianos (1949); *Classical Variations* for organ. Choral Works: *Gloria in Excelsis,* a Christmas cantata (1925); *David Jazz,* for baritone, men's chorus, and small orch. (1934); Psalm XXIX, for men's chorus with orch. (1934); *The Pledge of Allegiance* (1940); *Song of All Seas, All Ships* (1946); *Ballad of Brotherhood* (1947); *Missa Brevis* (1949); various pieces for women's chorus, children's chorus, etc.; songs. Published *Orchestration: A Practical Handbook* (N. Y., 1958).

Wagner, Karl Jakob, German composer, b. Darmstadt, Feb. 22, 1772; d. there, Nov. 25, 1822. He was a French horn player and conductor in the Darmstadt Orch.; studied theory with Abbé Vogler. He wrote 4 operas, all produced in Darmstadt: *Pygmalion* (1809), *Der Zahnarzt* (1810), *Siaph und Nitetis* (1811), and *Chimene* (1821); 2 symphonies; 4 overtures; trios for violin, flute, and cello; duos for flute and violin; 40 horn duos; 3 violin sonatas; variations for piano, etc. Many of his works have been published.

Wagner, Peter (Joseph), eminent musicologist; b. Kürenz, near Trèves, Aug. 19, 1865; d. Freiburg, Switzerland, Oct. 17, 1931. From 1876-86 he was a pupil at the Catholic Music School in Trèves and chorister at the Cathedral; studied musicology at the Univ. of Strasbourg from 1886, becoming *Dr. phil.* with the dissertation *Palestrina als weltlicher Komponist* (1890); studied further in Berlin under Bellermann and Spitta; 1893, instructor of church music at the Univ. of Freiburg (Switzerland); made full prof. in 1902. In 1901 he established at the Univ. the 'Gregorianische Akademie' for theoretical and practical study of plainsong, in which field he was an eminent authority. He was a member of the Papal Commission for the 'Editio Vaticana' of the Roman Gradual, and was made a Papal Chamberlain. In the course of numerous visits to Spain he did valuable research on the Mozarabic liturgical chant (cf. *Spanische Forschungen der Görresgesellschaft,* I and II; Report of the International Musicological Congress at Vienna, 1927; 'Musica Sacra,' 1927). —Writings: *Das Madrigal und Palestrina,* in 'Vierteljahrsschrift für Musikwissenschaft' (1892); *Francesco Petrarcas 'Vergini' in der Komposition des Cipriano de Rore* (1893); *Einführung in die gregorianischen Melodien* (1895; 2nd ed. in 3 parts, I. *Ursprung und Entwicklung der liturgischen Gesangsformen bis zum Ausgang des Mittelalters* [1901; 3rd ed. 1911; Engl. transl. 1907], II, *Neumenkunde* [1905; reprint, 1912], III, *Gregorianische Formenlehre; eine choralische Stilkunde* [1921]); *Das Freiburger Dreikönigspiel* (1903); *Über traditionellen Choral und traditionellen Choralvortrag* (1905); *Der Kampf gegen die 'Editio Vaticana'* (1907); *Elemente des gregorianischen Gesanges* (1909; 2nd ed., 1916); *Geschichte der Messe* (vol. I, 1913 [to 1600]); *Einführung in die katholische Kirchenmusik* (1919); also many valuable studies (in 'Adler-Festschrift,' 'J. Wolf-Festschrift,' etc.). A 'Festschrift' for him, ed. by K. Weinmann, was publ. in 1926. He wrote organ accompaniments for the Vatican Graduale and Vesperale.

Wagner (vahg'-ner), **(Wilhelm) Richard,** illustrious German composer; creator of the music drama; b. Leipzig, May 22, 1813; d. Venice, Feb. 13, 1883 His father, clerk in the city police court, died when Wagner was but six months old; his mother, Johanna Rosina, *née* Paetz (or Beetz), was ostensibly the daughter of a baker, though it is possible she was the natural daughter of Prince Friedrich Ferdinand Constantin of Weimar; about nine months after her husband's death, Johanna married the actor and playwright Ludwig Geyer, who had been an intimate member of the family circle for some time (the possibility that Geyer was Wagner's real father cannot be excluded; Wagner himself harbored such a suspicion). The family then moved to Dresden, where Wagner entered the Kreuzschule at the age of nine, remaining there until 1827 (his stepfather Geyer died in 1821). He was interested in the study of Greek, and showed strong literary inclinations, writing a grand tragedy, *Leubald und Adelaïde,* in Shakespearian style, at the age of 14. In 1825 he began to take piano lessons from a certain Humann, and with characteristic impatience tried to play the *Freischütz* overture as soon as he had learned some 5-finger exercises; actually he made little progress on the piano; nor did he do better with the violin, which he took up with Robert Sipp. He was already beginning to be fascinated by opera, and with the idea of trying to write music for his 'tragedy' he began studying Logier's *System der Musikwissenschaft und der praktischen Komposition.* In 1827 the family settled in Leipzig, and in 1828 Wagner was sent to the Nikolaischule there (from 1830 he also attended the Thomasschule for a short time). About this time he had some lessons in theory from the organist C. G. Müller, and soon began to compose, writing a string quartet, a piano sonata, and an overture in B♭, which the conductor H. Dorn performed on Christmas Eve, 1830 (the work was received with ridicule). In 1831, after a brief plunge into the wild student life at Leipzig Univ., he received his first serious training in composition from Theodor Weinlig, cantor of the Thomasschule. The following year his op. 1 (a piano sonata) and op. 2 (4-hand *Polonaise)* were publ. by Breitkopf & Härtel; to this year (1832) also belong the Concert Overture in C (performed in Leipzig, April 30, 1832) and Symphony in C, first performed in the summer in Prague (whither Wagner had gone on a visit) and later in Leipzig (Jan. 10, 1833); these works were the result of Wagner's enthusiastic study of Beethoven's symphonies. It was likewise in 1832 that Wagner wrote his first opera libretto, *Die Hochzeit,* for which he composed an introduction, a septet, and a chorus, afterwards abandoning the work on account of objections raised by his sister Rosalie (she found the plot too 'gory'). In 1833 he began his career as a professional musician, being invited by his brother Albert, stage manager and singer at the Würzburg Theater, to take the position of chorusmaster there. He found leisure to compose a romantic opera in 3 acts, *Die Feen,* to a libretto of his own after *La Donna serpente* by Carlo Gozzi. In 1834 he was made conductor of the Magdeburg Theater; he brought out two overtures, to *Die Feen* and *Columbus,* songs to the farce, *Der Berggeist,* etc.; and finished book and score of a 2-act opera, *Das Liebesverbot* (after Shakespeare's *Measure for Measure),* the performance of which, on March 29, 1836, after hurried rehearsals, ended in chaos. He then went to Königsberg, became conductor of the theater, and married (Nov. 24, 1836) the actress Minna Planer. His sole new work here was the overture *Rule Britannia.* Next year he was appointed conductor of the Riga opera; he also conducted orchestral concerts, and completed the libretto of *Rienzi, der Letzte der Tribunen,* a tragic opera in 5 acts, of which he composed the first 2 in Riga. Inspired by the hope of equalling Meyerbeer's triumphs on the stage of the Grand Opéra at Paris, Wagner set out for that city in July, 1839, his contract at Riga having expired; the events of the stormy voyage, heightened by his previous perusal of the legend of the Flying Dutchman, made an indelible impression on his mind. During a stay in Boulogne, he met Meyerbeer, who gave him letters to musicians and publishers in Paris; he arrived there with his wife in September, and remained there until 1842. Unsuccessful in his attempts to get a hearing for *Rienzi,* he found himself in dire straits, and supported himself by hack-work, writing articles for musical papers, etc. His financial situation became desperate; on Oct. 28, 1840 he was put in the debtors' prison, and was not released until Nov. 17 of that year. In the midst of his troubles, he completed the grand *Faust-Ouvertüre,* intended for the first movement of a 'Faust Symphony'; the score of the opera *Rienzi* was finished, and sent to the Intendant of the Dresden Court Theater. Sketches for *Der fliegende Holländer* had also been submitted to the Director of the Opéra, who viewed them with approval, but the upshot was that Wagner was obliged to sell his libretto for 500 francs; it was then put into French verse by Foucher and set to music by Dietsch (produced at the Paris Opéra, Nov. 9, 1842). Meanwhile, Wagner went rapidly ahead with the composition of his own version, completing the score in 7 weeks (the overture was written later). A welcome stroke of good fortune—the acceptance of *Rienzi* at Dresden—enabled Wagner to return to Germany; in April, 1842, he was in Dresden to superintend the rehearsals, and *Rienzi* was produced there on Oct. 20, 1842, with great success. Another success—the première of *Der fliegende Holländer* at Dresden on Jan. 2, 1843—led to his appointment as music director of the Saxon Court. In this position he developed great activity for the next 6 years, bringing out the best operas *(Iphigenie in Aulis, Der Freischütz, Euryanthe, Don Giovanni, Die Zauberflöte, Fidelio,* etc.) in masterly fashion at the Dresden Court Theater; he also conducted the Dresden Liedertafel, for which he composed a 'biblical scene,' *Das Liebesmahl der Apostel,* for 3 choirs of men's voices, singing at first a cappella, finally with full orch. The 3-act opera *Tannhäuser und der Sängerkrieg auf Wartburg* (originally sketched in 1842 as *Der Venusberg)* was finished in April, 1844, and produced at Dresden on Oct. 19, 1845. Wagner then began work on the 3-act romantic opera *Lohengrin,* which was finished on April 28, 1848; but he was not able to secure its production in Dresden (only the finale to Act I was performed at the 300th anniversary of the court orch. on Sept. 22, 1848); the opera was finally produced by Liszt at Weimar in 1850 (Wagner himself did not hear the work unil 1861). In 1848 he wrote the poem of *Siegfried's Death* (3-act drama with prologue). By this time Wagner, chafing under the restrictions of bourgeois conservatism, had joined a radical political organization, the 'Vaterlandsverein,' and soon allowed himself to be drawn into active participation in the revolutionary movement that came to a head with the May uprising of 1849. He was obliged to flee in order to escape arrest, going first to Weimar, where he was given a most friendly reception by Liszt (the two had met in Paris in 1840; Liszt remained a staunch champion of Wagner's music), then to Jena, and finally to Zürich. After a brief visit to Paris, he returned to Zürich, where he was joined by his wife, Minna. He now embarked upon a period of intense literary activity, writing, among other important essays explaining his philosophy of art: *Die Kunst und die Revolution* (1849), *Das Kunstwerk der Zukunft* (1850), *Kunst und Klima* (1850), and *Oper und Drama* (1851). The ideas advanced in *Das Kunstwerk der Zukunft (Art-Work of the Future)* gave rise to the description of Wagner's music as 'Zukunftsmusik' and himself (and Liszt) as 'Zukunftsmusiker'—in derision by opponents, but accepted by Wagner, Liszt, and their disciples as honorable. In 1852 Wagner completed the poems of the Nibelung trilogy (privately printed 1853). In Jan., 1850, he made another trip to Paris with the vain hope of having an opera produced there; becoming involved in a love affair with a married woman named Jennie Laussot, he followed her to Bordeaux and planned an elopement; but the affair came to nothing and Wagner returned to Minna in Zürich; but here he met a wealthy merchant, Otto

Wesendonk, with whose wife, Mathilde, he fell deeply in love. In 1857 Wagner and Minna took up their abode in a house called the 'Asyl,' on the Wesendonks' estate. Meanwhile Wagner had completed the full score of *Das Rheingold* (1854) and that of *Die Walküre* (1856), and in 1854, while under the influence of Schopenhauer's philosophy, he had conceived the idea of *Tristan und Isolde;* in 1856-57 he was at work both on *Tristan* and on *Siegfried,* always under the spell of his love for Mathilde Wesendonk, five of whose poems he set to music about this time. This situation led to a domestic crisis; Minna left Wagner and returned to Germany, while Wagner went to Venice, where he completed the 2nd act of *Tristan* in March, 1859 (the 3rd act was finished at Lucerne in Aug. of that year). Meanwhile, in the spring of 1855, Wagner had added to his reputation as a conductor by leading 8 concerts of the London Philharmonic Society. In Paris, whither he had gone in Sept., 1859, he conducted concerts of his own music, making many enthusiastic friends, but also stirring up active opposition, and incurring heavy debts. However, powerful interests in Paris were enlisted in his favor; the Emperor Napoleon III ordered that *Tannhäuser* (with the Venusberg scene revised) should be put in rehearsal at the Opéra, and it was given on March 13, 1861, though in the face of such tumultuous opposition by a hostile clique that it was withdrawn after the 3rd performance. But Wagner's general prospects were now improved owing to the fact that he had received an amnesty in the summer of 1860, allowing him to return to Germany (except Saxony, to which the amnesty was not extended until March, 1862). In 1859 Minna had rejoined him in Paris; but in the summer of 1861 she separated from him definitely (she died at Dresden in 1866). In 1861 he went to Vienna in the hopes of having *Tristan* produced and while there heard *Lohengrin* for the first time (May 31, 1861). Back in Paris he worked on the libretto of his comic opera *Die Meistersinger von Nürnberg* (finished Jan., 1862), which he had sketched as far back as 1845. After completing the text he went to Biebrich-on-Rhine and began to compose the music, though the score was not finished until 1867. He made another visit to Vienna, where *Tristan* was finally accepted for production at the Court Opera; but after 77 rehearsals it was given up as 'impracticable.' In 1863 he gave some successful concerts in Moscow and St. Petersburg. But his financial situation had become desperate; for many years he had been harassed by debts, due largely to his extravagance, aggravated by his unstable position; an annuity received from Julie Ritter in 1851, and help from various other friends, provided only temporary relief; in March, 1864, he was forced to flee from his creditors, going to Stuttgart by way of Mariafeld. At this crisis King Ludwig II of Bavaria, who had just ascended the throne, invited Wagner to Munich with the promise of the amplest aid in carrying out his projects.

It was at this time that Wagner also reached a crisis in his emotional life. He had fallen in love with Liszt's daughter, Cosima, who was married to the conductor Hans von Bülow; the passion was reciprocated and received a further impetus after the arrival in Munich of Cosima and her husband, the latter chosen to conduct Wagner's works there (he gave the 1st performance of *Tristan* on June 10, 1865). On April 10, 1865, Isolde, the daughter of Cosima and Wagner, was born. During the summer of 1865, Wagner worked on a sketch of *Parsifal* (the idea was first conceived in 1845) and began to dictate his autobiography, *Mein Leben,* to Cosima. But court cabals, and the persistent opposition of his numerous enemies, united to the circumstances of his private life, rendered Wagner's position in Munich untenable, and in Dec., 1865, he left the city at King Ludwig's request, going to Switzerland. The following April he settled in the village of Triebschen, on Lake Lucerne, where he was soon joined by Cosima (their son Siegfried was born there on June 6, 1869). In 1867 he finished *Die Meistersinger,* which was produced in Munich on June 21, 1868; this was followed by the première of *Das Rheingold,* also in Munich, on Sept. 22, 1869; in the latter year Wagner completed the score of *Siegfried* and began *Götterdämmerung* (finished in 1874). In July, 1870, Cosima was divorced by Bülow, and on Aug. 25, 1870 she and Wagner were married. A significant episode of this period was the meeting with Nietzsche (1868), a frequent visitor at Triebschen, who was at first an ardent admirer of Wagner but later became a bitter opponent. In 1871 Wagner began the publication of his collected writings, and in that year the first 'Wagner Society' was founded at Mannheim by Emil Heckel. For many years Wagner had cherished the ambition of building his own theater for the production of his operas in a way that would meet his exacting artistic ideals. Had things gone better in Munich, he might have seen his scheme realized there; as it was, he received the offer of a site for his theater from the city of Bayreuth in

1872, and at once seized the opportunity. In April, 1872 he moved to Bayreuth; on May 22 the cornerstone of the 'Festspielhaus' was laid, the ceremony commemorated by a performance of Beethoven's 9th Symphony (this was Wagner's 59th birthday). On his 60th birthday (May 22, 1873), Wagner began to build his own home in Bayreuth, 'Wahnfried,' which was ready for occupancy in the spring of 1874. The fund required for erecting the new theater, which was built according to Wagner's original plans, was raised by private subscription, by the contributions of 'Wagner Societies' formed all over the world, and by a series of concerts arranged by Wagner in various German cities. At length, in August, 1876, the dream of his life was realized; three complete performances of *Der Ring des Nibelungen* were presented at the Bayreuth theater, attended by musical notables from the four quarters of the globe, and honored by the presence of Emperor William I and King Ludwig. Hans Richter conducted the orchestra, in which Wilhelmj led the violins. Musically a grand success, the undertaking left Wagner again heavily involved in debt; concerts given at the Albert Hall, London, in 1877, gave meager pecuniary returns; but he was finally relieved by the setting aside of the royalties derived from performances of the *Ring* at Munich. The next few years were occupied with literary work, and with the completion of his last dramatic composition, the 'Bühnenweihfestspiel' *Parsifal,* finished in 1882, and produced for the first time in Munich on July 26 of that year, other performances following through July and August, all under Wagner's personal supervision. He also made arrangements for the performances of 1883; in the autumn of 1882 ill health compelled him to seek relief in Venice, where he spent the winter; death (from an attack of angina pectoris) overtook him suddenly on Feb. 13, 1883. His remains were interred in the garden of his villa 'Wahnfried' at Bayreuth.

In comprehensiveness and grandeur of conception, originality and boldness of execution, vividness of characterization, intensity of expression and sustained power Wagner towers like a colossus above all other opera composers. From the outset he wrote his own librettos, based on his own poems. His early operas, *Die Feen, Das Liebesverbot,* and *Rienzi,* represent a formative period. With *Der fliegende Holländer* the individual Wagner, the genius, is unveiled, almost abruptly. The plain, straightforward mythical tale, a conflict of stormy emotions and the apotheosis of love and self-sacrifice, appealed directly to the heart; the music is as wildly romantic, as tenderly pathetic, and as sternly tragic, as the successive situations—and, above all, a music not written to exhibit the beauty and agility of the singers' voices but to follow the drama into its least details without the customary breaks made by set numbers (arias, duets, ensembles). The dramatic and musical unity is secured by the ingenious, and yet logical use of *Leitmotive* —leading motifs that allude to characters, objects, or abstract concepts in the music dramas (the term was popularized by Hans von Wolzogen; Wagner never used it himself). With *Tannhäuser* and *Lohengrin* (1848) Wagner's second period, the romantic, closes. In these two operas he employs substantially the same manner, though with growing variety and refinement. The third period opens six years later, with *Das Rheingold* (1854). With this work Wagner's ideas are carried out to their logical conclusion. He assumes the role of a reformer of the musico-dramatic stage; unsparingly criticizes and condemns the faulty and illogical plan of the Italian 'opera' and the French 'grand opera,' and naturally discards these titles, calling his own subsequent works 'music dramas.' To quote his own words, "the mistake in the art-form of the opera consists in this, that a means of expression (music) was made the end, and the end to be expressed (the drama) was made a means." The choice of subject is of the utmost importance, for not all subjects lend themselves to musical characterization. He formulated this conviction as follows: "The subject to be treated by the word-tone poet [Worttondichter] is the purely human, freed from all convention and from everything historically formal." The new art-work procreated its own artistic form: continuous thematic development of leading-motifs. Wagner's orchestra became an exponent of the dramatic action; the highly individualized and pregnant leading-motifs, now singly, in bold relief, now subtly intertwined and varied, plastically present the ever-changing soul-states of the characters of the drama and form the connecting links for the dramatic situations; the singing of the actors is resolved into a musical declamation, which Wagner himself described as 'Sprechsingen.'

Wagner's reform was incomparably more far-reaching in aim, import, and effect than Gluck's, whose main purpose was to counteract the arbitrary predominance of the singers; this Wagner tried to accomplish through insistence upon the drama and dramatic truth. When he rejected traditional opera, he did so with the conviction that this artificial form could never serve as a basis for true dramatic expression. In its place he gave the world a new form, the music drama. So revolutionary, so novel was Wagner's art, that he was obliged to train singers and conductors in the new style of interpretation demanded by his works. Thus he became the founder of interpretative conducting and of a new school of dramatic singing.

WORKS

Writings—Wagner spent a large amount of his enormous productive activity in writing. Besides the dramatic works he set to music, he wrote the texts of a 2-act comic opera, *Männerlist grösser als Frauenlist, oder Die glückliche Bärenfamilie* (1837), a 4-act tragic opera, *Die hohe Braut, oder Bianca und Giuseppe* (first sketch, 1836; completed 1842; composed by J. F. Kittl, and produced in Prague, 1848), and a 3-act 'grosse Heldenoper' *Siegfrieds Tod* (1848; later expanded into *Götterdämmerung*); a 2-act comedy in ancient style, *Eine Kapitulation* (1871); dramatic sketches, *Die Bergwerke zu Falun* (1841), *Die Sarazenin* (1841), *Friedrich der Rothbart* (1846; enlarged 1848), *Jesus von Nazareth* (1848), *Wieland der Schmied* (1856), *Die Sieger* (1856). He expounded his theories on music and the music drama in several works, the more important of which are *Die Kunst und die Revolution* (1849), *Das Kunstwerk der Zukunft* (1850), *Kunst und Klima* (1850), *Oper und Drama* (1851), *Eine Mittheilung an meine Freunde* (1851), *Über das Dirigieren* (1869), *Beethoven* (1870). In his later years he also touched upon a large number of religious, social, and economic subjects. The first edition of Wagner's collected writings, edited by himself, was publ. at Leipzig in 9 vols. (1871-73) as *Gesammelte Schriften und Dichtungen;* it contains the dramatic works from *Rienzi* to *Der Ring des Nibelungen,* the social and esthetic essays, besides numerous others written between 1840 and 1871. The 2nd ed. (1883), with an additional vol. (*Parsifal* and essays), was also prepared by Wagner personally; the 3rd (1887) and 4th (1897) editions are only reprints. Not contained in these editions, and publ. separately, are: *Entwürfe, Gedanken, Fragmente* (ed. by H. von Wolzogen; Leipzig, 1885); *Jesus von Nazareth* (Leipzig, 1887); *Nachgelassene Schriften und Dichtungen* (Leipzig, 1895; 2nd ed., 1902); *Gedichte* (ed. by K. F. Glasenapp; Berlin, 1905); *Entwürfe zu 'Die Meistersinger,' 'Tristan und Isolde' und 'Parsifal'* (ed. by H. von Wolzogen; Leipzig, 1907); essays and criticisms of the first Paris period ed. by R. Sternfeld as *Aus R. W.s Pariser Zeit* (Berlin, 1907); the texts of *Die Feen, Die hohe Braut, Das Liebesmahl der Apostel,* a fragment of *Die Hochzeit,* the sketch to *Die Bergwerke zu Falun,* and early essays ed. by J. Kapp as *Der junge W.* (Berlin, 1910). All these works were included in the 5th edition, ed. by H. von Wolzogen and R. Sternfeld (12 vols.; Leipzig, 1911; English transl. by W. A. Ellis, *The Prose Works of R. W.,* 8 vols.; London, 1892-1900). A popular edition of Wagner's writings (10 vols.) was publ. by Kistner and Siegel, in 1930 (2 supplementary vols. ed. by R. Sternfeld, 2 by W. Altmann, 1933).—A detailed autobiography, *Mein Leben* (only up to May, 1864) was privately printed (15 copies, 1870) for distribution among intimate friends; publ. in 2 vols. at Munich, 1911 (simultaneously in English, French, and Russian; new critical ed. by W. Altmann, Leipzig, 1933).—Very valuable and important is Wagner's voluminous published correspondence (see Bibliography, section B).—Cf. also K. F. Glasenapp and H. von Stein, *W.-Lexikon. Hauptbegriffe der Kunst- und Weltanschauung W.s in wörtlichen Ausführungen aus seinen Schriften zusammengestellt* (Stuttgart, 1883) and K. F. Glasenapp, *W.-Enzyklopädie. Haupterscheinungen der Kunst- und Kulturgeschichte im Lichte der Anschauung W.s in wörtlichen Ausführungen aus seinen Schriften dargestellt* (2 vols.; Leipzig, 1891).

Operas and Music Dramas: *Die Hochzeit* (fragment; composed 1832); *Die Feen* (composed 1833, produced Munich, June 29, 1888); *Das Liebesverbot* (Magdeburg, March 29, 1836, as *Die Novize von Palermo;* revived Munich, March 24, 1923; Berlin, Jan. 20, 1932); *Rienzi, der letzte der Tribunen* (Dresden, Oct. 20, 1842; Paris Théâtre Lyrique, April 6, 1869; N. Y., March 4, 1878; London, Jan. 27, 1879); *Der fliegende Holländer* (Dresden, Jan. 2, 1843; London, July 23, 1870; Philadelphia, Nov. 8, 1876; N. Y., Jan. 26, 1877); *Tannhäuser* (Dresden, Oct. 19, 1845; N. Y., April 4, 1859; London, May 6, 1876; 'Paris version' given at the Opéra, March 13, 1861); *Lohengrin* (Weimar, Aug. 28, 1850; N. Y., April 3, 1871; London, May 8, 1875; Paris, May 3, 1887); *Tristan und Isolde* (Munich, June 10, 1865; London, June 20, 1882; N. Y., Dec. 1, 1886); *Die Meistersinger von Nürnberg* (Munich, June 21, 1868; London, May 30, 1882; N. Y., Jan. 4, 1886).—*Der Ring des Nibelungen,* 'dramatic trilogy' in 3 parts and an introduction, the latter consisting of *Das Rheingold* (Munich, Sept. 22, 1869; London, May 6, 1882; N. Y., Jan. 4, 1889); Part I, *Die Walküre* (Munich, June 26, 1870; N. Y., April 2, 1877; London, May

6, 1882); Part II, *Siegfried* (Bayreuth, Aug. 16, 1876; London, May 8, 1882; N. Y., Nov. 9, 1887); Part III, *Götterdämmerung* (Bayreuth, Aug. 17, 1876; London, May 9, 1882; N. Y., Jan. 25, 1888; first complete performance of entire *Ring* cycle, Bayreuth, Aug. 13, 14, 16, 17, 1876; N. Y., Metropolitan Opera House, March 4, 5, 8, and 11, 1889; without cuts, Feb. 20, 22, 27, and March 1, 1900). —*Parsifal* (Bayreuth, July 26, 1882; N. Y., Dec. 24, 1903; Paris, Jan. 2, 1914; London, Feb. 2, 1914).

Orchestral Works: Overture in B♭ (composed 1830; score lost); Overture in D minor (1831; Leipzig, Feb. 23, 1832; unpubl.); Overture in C (1831); Overture to Raupach's *König Enzio* (1832; publ. 1908); Symphony in C (1832; publ. 1911); Symphony in E (1834; fragment; unpubl.); Overture to Apel's *Columbus* (1835; publ. 1904); Overture *Rule Britannia* (1836; publ. 1904); Overture *Polonia* (begun 1832, finished 1836; publ. 1904); *Eine Faustouvertüre* (1839-40; Dresden, July 22, 1844; rewritten and publ. 1855); *Trauermusik* for wind instruments, after motifs from *Euryanthe* (1844; Dresden, Dec. 14, 1844, on the arrival of Weber's remains from London; publ. 1906); *Huldigungsmarsch,* dedicated to King Ludwig II (1864; originally for military band; orchestral score begun by Wagner, finished by Raff; publ. 1869); *Siegfried-Idyll* (1870; Triebschen, Dec. 25, 1870; publ. 1877); *Kaisermarsch* (1871; Berlin, May 5, 1871; publ. 1871); *Grosser Festmarsch,* for the Philadelphia Centennial Exposition (1876; Philadelphia, May 10, 1876; publ. 1876).

Choral Works: *Neujahrskantate* for mixed chorus and orch. (1834; Magdeburg, Dec. 31, 1834; publ. 1914, arranged with a new text by Peter Cornelius as *Künstlerweihe,* and produced at Bayreuth on Wagner's 60th birthday); *Volkshymne* for mixed chorus and orch. (1837; Riga, Nov. 21, 1837; publ. 1914); *La Descente de la Courtille* for mixed chorus and orch. (1840; publ. 1914); *Weihegruss* for men's chorus and orch., for the unveiling of the statue of King Friedrich August of Saxony (1843; Dresden, June 7, 1843; vocal parts publ. 1906, full score 1914); *Das Liebesmahl der Apostel,* biblical scene for men's chorus and orch. (1843; Dresden, July 6, 1843; publ. 1844); *Gruss seiner Treuen an Friedrich August den Geliebten* for men's chorus a cappella, on the return from England of King Friedrich August of Saxony (1843; Dresden, Aug. 12, 1843; publ. 1914); *An Webers Grabe* for men's chorus a cappella, for the interment of Weber's remains (1844; Dresden, Dec. 15, 1844; publ. 1871).

Piano Works: Sonata in D minor (1829; lost); *Doppelfuge* (composed probably in 1831; 103 bars, with corrections in Weinlig's hand; publ. 1912, in 'Die Musik'); sonata in B♭ (1831; publ. 1832); *Polonaise* in D major, 4 hands (1831; publ. 1832); *Fantasie* in F♯ minor (1831; publ. 1905); sonata in A major (1831; unpubl.); *Albumsonata* in E♭ (for Mathilde Wesendonck; 1853; publ. 1877); *Züricher Vielliebchen,* waltz in E (1853; publ. 1896, in 'Musikalische Rundschau'); *Albumblatt* in C (for Countess Metternich; 1861; publ. 1871); *Ankunft bei den schwarzen Schwänen (Albumblatt* for Countess Pourtalès; 1861; publ. 1897); *Albumblatt* in E♭ (for Frau Betty Schott; 1875; publ. 1876).

Songs: *Glockentöne* (1832; unpubl.); *Sieben Kompositionen zu Goethes Faust:* 1, *Lied der Soldaten.* 2, *Bauern unter der Linde.* 3, *Branders Lied.* 4, *Lied des Mephistopheles (Es war einmal ein König).* 5, *Lied des Mephistopheles (Was machst du mir).* 6, *Gesang Gretchens (Meine Ruh ist hin).* 7, *Melodram Gretchens (Ach neige, du Schmerzensreiche)* (1832; publ. 1914); *Carnevalslied* from *Das Liebesverbot* (1835; publ. 1885); *Der Tannenbaum* (1838; publ. 1871); *Les deux grenadiers* (Heine's poem; French transl. by Heine himself; composed and publ. 1839); *Trois Romances:* 1, *Dors, mon enfant.* 2, *Attente.* 3, *Mignonne* (1839-40; publ. as supplement to Lewald's *Europa,* 1841-42); *Les Adieux de Marie Stuart* (1840; publ. 1913); *Tout n'est qu'images fugitives* (1840; publ. 1914); *Fünf Gedichte:* 1, *Der Engel.* 2, *Schmerzen.* 3, *Träume.* 4, *Stehe still.* 5, *Im Treibhaus* (Nos. 1-3 composed Dec., 1857; No. 4, Feb., 1858; No. 5, June, 1858; all publ. 1862); *Kraftliedchen* (1871; publ. in 'Wiener Illustrierte Zeitung,' Oct. 14, 1877).

Arrangements: Piano score of Beethoven's Ninth Symphony (1830; unpubl.), of Donizetti's *La Favorita* and *Elisir d'Amore* (both publ. 1840) and of Halévy's *La Reine de Chypre* and *Le Guitarrero* (both publ. 1841); Gluck's *Iphigénie en Aulide,* new translation and new close to overture (1846; Dresden, Feb. 22, 1847; full score of new close, and complete piano score [by von Bülow] publ. 1859); Palestrina's *Stabat Mater,* with indications for performance (1848; Dresden, March 8, 1848; publ. 1877); Mozart's *Don Giovanni,* version of dialogues and recitatives and, in parts, new translation (1850; not produced; unpubl.).

The first complete edition of Wagner's works was publ. by Breitkopf & Härtel (1912-22).

BIBLIOGRAPHY

(The literature on Wagner is virtually inexhaustible; the following is a selective list, divided into 15 categories: A, biographical; B, correspondence; C, personal reminiscences; D, relations with contemporaries; E, criticism, appreciation; F, Wagner's art in relation to esthetics, philosophy, and religion; G, Wagner's art in relation to theory and technique; H, Wagner and Bayreuth; I, Wagner's literary sources; J, analyses, guides, stories of the operas; K, characters; L, Wagner as writer; M, catalogues, year-books, etc.; N, iconography; O, miscellaneous.)

A—BIOGRAPHICAL: R. Wagner, *Mein Leben* (see above, WRITINGS); C. Cabrol, *R. W.* (Paris, 1861); A. de Gasperini, *La nouvelle Allemagne musicale: R. W.* (Paris, 1866); F. Filippi, *R. W.* (Leipzig, 1876); P. Lindau, *R. W.* (Paris, 1885); K. F. Glasenapp, *R. W.'s Leben und Wirken* (2 vols.; Leipzig, 1876-77; 2nd ed., 1882; 3rd ed., in 6 vols., as *Das Leben R. W.'s*, Leipzig, 1894-1911); F. Hueffer, *R. W.* (London, 1883; new ed., 1912); A. Jullien, *R. W. Sa vie et ses œuvres* (Paris, 1886; English transl., Boston, 1892, reprinted Philadelphia, 1910); G. Kobbé, *W.'s Life and Works* (2 vols., N. Y., 1890); H. T. Finck, *W. and His Works* (2 vols.; N. Y., 1893; 5th ed., 1898); H. S. Chamberlain, *R. W.* (Munich, 1896; 4th ed., 2 vols., 1912; English transl., London, 1897); W. A. Ellis, *Life of R. W.* (6 vols.; London, 1900-08; vols. I-III based on Glasenapp); W. J. Henderson, *R. W., His Life and His Dramas* (N. Y., 1901; revised, 1923); Mrs. M. Burrell, *R. W. His Life and Works from 1813 to 1834* (London, 1898; a sumptuous folio richly illustrated; with many facsimiles of original documents, etc.); R. Bürkner, *R. W. Sein Leben und seine Werke* (Jena, 1906; 6th ed., 1911); M. Koch, *R. W.* (3 vols.; Berlin, 1906, 1912, 1914; with detailed bibliography); J. Kapp, *R. W.* (Berlin, 1910; 32nd printing, 1929); F. Pfohl, *R. W. Sein Leben und Schaffen* (Berlin, 1911; 4th ed., Bielefeld, 1924); E. Newman, *W. as Man and Artist* (London, 1914; 2nd American ed., N. Y., 1924); H. Lichtenberger, *W.* (Paris, 1925); W. Wallace, *W. as He Lived* (London, 1925; new ed., 1933); L. Barthou, *La Vie amoureuse de R. W.* (Paris, 1925; in English as *The Prodigious Lover*, N. Y., 1927); V. d'Indy, *R. W. et son influence sur l'art musical français* (Paris, 1930); H. Reisiger, *Unruhiges Gestirn; die Jugend R. W.s* (Leipzig, 1930; in English as *Restless Star*, N. Y., 1932); Max Morold (pen-name of Max v. Millenkovitch), *W.s Kampf und Sieg* (Zürich, 1930); G. de Pourtalès, *R. W.* (Paris, 1932; English transl., N. Y., 1932); A. Spring, *R.W.s Weg und Wirken* (Stuttgart, 1933); P. Lalo, *R. W.* (Paris, 1933); W. J. Turner, *W.* (London, 1933); Sir W. H. Hadow, *W.* (London, 1934); M. Fehr, *R. W.s Schweizer Zeit* (2 vols., Aarau, 1934-53); R. L. Jacobs, *W.* (London, 1935); Ernest Newman, *The Life of R. W.* (4 vols.; N. Y., vol. I [1813-48], 1933; vol. II [1848-59], 1937; vol. III [1859-66], 1941; vol. IV [1866-83], 1946; the most thorough and authoritative biography); H. Malherbe, *R. W. Révolutionnaire* (Paris, 1938); E. Kretzschmar, *R. W. Sein Leben in Selbstzeugnissen, Briefen und Berichten* (Berlin, 1939); O. Strobel, *Neue Urkunden zur Lebensgeschichte R. W.s 1864-1882* (Karlsruhe, 1939; a supplement to the 4 vols. of correspondence between W. and Ludwig II; see CORRESPONDENCE); M. von Millenkovitch, *Dreigestirn: W., Liszt, Bülow* (Leipzig, 1941); W. Reich, *R. W., Leben, Fühlen, Schaffen* (Olten, 1948); K. Ipser, *R. W. in Italien* (Salzburg, 1951); T. W. Adorno, *Versuch über Wagner* (Berlin, 1952); P. A. Loos, *R. W., Vollendung und Tragik der deutschen Romantik* (Munich, 1952); O. Strobel, *R. W. Leben und Schaffen* (Bayreuth, 1952); Z. von Kraft, *R. W.: ein dramatisches Leben* (Munich, 1953); R. Dumesnil, *R. W.* (Paris, 1954); C. von Westernhagen, *R. W.: sein Werk, sein Wesen, seine Welt* (Zürich, 1956).

B—CORRESPONDENCE: *Briefwechsel zwischen W. und Liszt* (2 vols., Leipzig, 1887; 2nd ed., 1900; English transl., London, 1888; 2nd ed., 1897, with index by W. A. Ellis). These two editions contain only the letters from 1841-61, and many passages referring to persons still living at the time of publication were omitted; in the 3rd ed., prepared by E. Kloss (1 vol., 1910), all letters up to Wagner's death are included, and the omitted portions restored.—Eliza Wille, *Fünfzehn Briefe des Meisters* [to her], *nebst Erinnerungen und Erläuterungen* (Leipzig, 1887); *W.s Briefe an Dresdener Freunde* (Uhlig, Fischer, Heine; Leipzig, 1888; English transl., London, 1890); La Mara, *R. W.s Briefe an Aug. Röckel* (Leipzig, 1894; 2nd ed., 1903; English transl., London, 1897); H. S. Chamberlain, *R. W.s echte Briefe an Ferd. Praeger* (Bayreuth, 1894; 2nd ed., Berlin, 1908); E. Kastner, *Briefe von R. W. an seine Zeitgenossen* (1830-83) (Berlin, 1897; very incomplete); K. Heckel, *Briefe an Emil Heckel* (Berlin, 1898; 3rd ed., 1911; English transl., London, 1899); W. Golther, *R. W. an Mathilde Wesendonck, Tagebuchblätter und Briefe*

(Berlin, 1904; 84th printing, 1922; English transl., London, 1905); W. Altmann, *R. W.s Briefe nach Zeitfolge und Inhalt* (Leipzig, synopses of 3143 letters; new ed., 2 vols., 1933; English transl., London, 1927); W. Golther, *Briefe R. W.s an Otto Wesendonck* [1852-70] (Berlin, 1905; English transl., London, 1911); D. Spitzer, *R. W.s Briefe an eine Putzmacherin* (Vienna, 1906; in English as *R. W. and the Seamstress,* N. Y., 1941); W. Golther, *Familienbriefe von R. W.* [1832-74] (Berlin, 1906; English transl., London, 1911); K. F. Glasenapp, *Bayreuther Briefe von R. W.* [1871-83] (Berlin, 1907); E. Kloss, *R. W. an seine Künstler* (Berlin, 1908); H. von Wolzogen, *R. W. an Minna Wagner* (2 vols., Berlin, 1908; English transl., London, 1909); E. Kloss, *R. W. an Freunde und Zeitgenossen* (Berlin, 1909); T. Apel, Jr., *R. W. an Theodor Apel* (Leipzig, 1910); W. Altmann, *R. W.s Briefwechsel mit seinen Verlegern* (3 vols.; Leipzig, 1911); J.-G. Prod'homme, *W. and the Paris Opéra* (unpubl. letters from Feb. and March 1861), in the 'Mus. Quarterly' (April, 1915); E. Kloss, *Briefe an Hans von Bülow* (Jena, 1916).—Almost all the above collections were republ. in 1912 by Breitkopf & Härtel as *R. W.s Briefe* (17 vols.); a number of the letters appear in mutilated form (portions expressing political and religious views being suppressed). An unmutilated edition was begun by J. Kapp and E. Kastner, *R. W.s gesammelte Briefe* [1830-50] (2 vols.; Leipzig, 1914).—S. von Hausegger, *R. W.s Briefe an Frau Julie Ritter* (Munich, 1920); E. Förster-Nietzsche, *The Nietzsche-W. Correspondence* (N. Y., 1921); L. Karpath, *Briefe an Hans Richter* (Berlin, 1924); R. Sternfeld, *R. W. Aufsätze und Briefe des Meisters aus Paris* (Grossenwörden, 1927); W. Lippert, *R. W.s Verbannung und Rückkehr, 1849-62* (Dresden, 1927; English transl. as *W. in Exile,* London, 1930); H. Scholz, *R. W. an Mathilde Maier* (Leipzig 1930); E. Lenrow, *The Letters of R. W. to A. Pusinelli* (N. Y., 1932); J. Tiersot, *Lettres françaises de R. W.* (Paris, 1935); W. Schuh, *Die Briefe R. W.s an Judith Gautier* (Zürich, 1936); K. Geiringer, *W. and Brahms* (with unpubl. letters), in the 'Mus. Quarterly' (April, 1936); O. Strobel, *König Ludwig II und R. W.; Briefwechsel* (5 vols.; Karlsruhe, 1936-39); A. Holde, *Four Unknown Letters of R. W.,* in the 'Mus. Quarterly' (April, 1941); J. N. Burk, ed., *Letters of R. W. The Burrell Collection* (N. Y., 1950; in German, Frankfurt, 1953).

C—PERSONAL REMINISCENCES: H. von Wolzogen, *Erinnerungen an R. W.* (Leipzig, 1883; English transl., Bayreuth, 1894); A. Schilling, *Aus R. W.s Jugendzeit* (Berlin, 1898; reminiscences of Wagner's step-sister Cäcilie Avenarius); E. Schuré, *Souvenirs sur R. W.* (Paris, 1900; German transl., Leipzig, 1900); E. von Possart, *Die Separat-Vorstellungen vor König Ludwig II. Erinnerungen* (Munich, 1901); L. Schemann, *Meine Erinnerungen an R. W.* (Stuttgart, 1902); G. A. Kietz, *R. W. in den Jahren 1842-49 und 1873-75* (Dresden, 1905); A. Kohut, *Der Meister von Bayreuth* (Berlin, 1905); E. Michotte, *Souvenirs personnels* (Paris, 1906); A. Gobineau, *Ein Erinnerungsbild aus Wahnfried* (Stuttgart, 1907); A. Neumann, *Erinnerungen an R. W.* (Leipzig, 1907; English transl., N. Y., 1908); H. Schmidt and U. Hartmann, *R. W. in Bayreuth. Erinnerungen* (Leipzig, 1910); Siegfried Wagner, *Erinnerungen* (Stuttgart, 1923; extended ed., privately printed, 1935); Judith Gautier, *Auprès de R. W.; Souvenirs (1861-1883)* (Paris, 1943).

D—RELATIONS WITH CONTEMPORARIES: J. L. Craemer, *König Ludwig II. und R. W.* (Munich, 1901); F. Gerard, *Romance of King Ludwig II of Bavaria. His Relation with R. W.* (London, 1901); S. Röckel, *Ludwig II. und R. W. in den Jahren 1864-65* (Munich, 1903; 2nd ed., 1913); J. Kapp, *R. W. und Franz Liszt. Eine Freundschaft* (Berlin, 1908); H. Bélart, *Friedr. Nietzsches Freundschaftstragödie mit R. W.* (Dresden, 1912) and *R. W.'s Liebestragödie mit Mathilde Wesendonck* (Dresden, 1912); J. Kapp, *R. W. und die Frauen* (Berlin, 1912; new revised ed., 1951; in English as *The Women in W.'s Life,* N. Y., 1931); E. Förster-Nietzsche, *W. und Nietzsche zur Zeit ihrer Freundschaft* (Munich, 1915); C. Sarti, *W. and Nietzsche* (N. Y., 1915); E. Schuré, *Femmes inspiratrices* (Paris, 1930); M. Herwegh, *Au banquet des dieux: F. Liszt, R. W. et ses amis* (Paris, 1931); L. Barthou, *R. W. et Judith Gautier,* in 'Revue de Paris' (1932); P. G. Dippel, *Nietzsche und W.* (Berne, 1934).

E—CRITICISM, APPRECIATION: F. Hinrichs, *R. W. und die neuere Musik: eine kritische Skizze* (Halle, 1854); F. K. F. Müller, *R. W. und das Musik-Drama* (Leipzig, 1861); L. Nohl, *Gluck und W. Über die Entwickelung des Musikdramas* (Munich, 1870); F. Nietzsche, *Die Geburt der Tragödie aus dem Geiste der Musik* (Leipzig, 1872; in vol. I of *Nietzsches Werke,* 1895; English transl. in O. Levy's ed. of complete works, Edinburgh, 1910-14); E. Dannreuther, *R. W. His Tendencies and Theories* (London, 1873); F. Hueffer, *R. W. and the Music of the Future* (London, 1874); E. Schuré, *Le Drame musical: I.*

La Musique et la Poésie dans leur dévelopment historique. II. Wagner. Son Œuvre et son idée (Paris, 1875; 3rd ed., augmented, 1894); L. Nohl, *Das moderne Musikdrama* (Vienna, 1884); F. Nietzsche, *Der Fall W.* and *N. contra W.* (both Leipzig, 1888; in vol. VIII of *Nietzsches Werke,* 1895; English transl. in vol. XI of complete works; bitter invective in place of former admiration); H. E. Krehbiel, *Studies in the Wagnerian Drama* (N. Y., 1891); M. Kufferath, *Le Théâtre de W. de Tannhäuser à Parsifal. Essais de critique littéraire, esthétique et musicale* (6 vols.; Paris, 1891-98); H. S. Chamberlain, *Das Drama R. W.s. Eine Anregung* (Leipzig, 1892; 5th ed., 1913; English transl., London, 1915); G. Servières, *R. W. jugé en France* (Paris, 1897); G. B. Shaw, *The Perfect Wagnerite* (London 1898; also in vol. 17 of complete works, 1932); Arthur Seidl, *Wagneriana* (3 vols.; Berlin, 1901-02; continuation as *Neue Wagneriana,* Bonn, 1914); E. Istel, *Das Kunstwerk R. W.s* (Leipzig, 1910; 2nd ed., 1919); G. Adler, *R. W.* (lectures; Vienna, 1904; 2nd ed., 1922); P. Bekker, *R. W. Das Leben im Werke* (Stuttgart, 1924; English transl., London, 1931); J. Kapp, *W. und die Berliner Oper* (Berlin, 1933); J. Kapp, *Das Liebersverbot, Entstehung und Schicksale des Werkes von R. W.* (Berlin, 1933); A. Bahr-Mildenburg, *Tristan und Isolde* (Leipzig, 1936; vol. I of *Darstellung der Werke R. W.s aus dem Geiste der Dichtung und Musik);* R. C. Schuster, *R. W. und die Welt der Oper* (Munich, 1937); L. Gilman, *W.'s Operas* (N. Y., 1937); T. Mann, *Freud, Goethe, W.* (N. Y., 1937); E. Borrelli, *Estetica wagneriana* (Florence, 1940); J. Barzun, *Darwin, Marx, Wagner* (Boston, 1941); M. Doisy, *L'Œuvre de R. W. du Vaisseau fantôme à Parsifal* (Brussels, 1945); M. Beaufils, *W. et le wagnérisme* (Paris, 1947); P. W. Jacob, *Taten der Musik; R. W. und sein Werk* (Regensburg, 1952). Liszt's fine essays on *Tannhäuser* (1849), *Lohengrin* (1850), *Der fliegende Holländer* (1854), and *Das Rheingold* (1855) are in vol. III, 2, of his *Gesammelte Schriften* (Leipzig, 1899).

F—Wagner's Art in Relation to Esthetics, Philosophy, and Religion: F. von Hausegger, *R. W. und Schopenhauer* (Leipzig, 1878; 2nd ed., 1897); J. Freson, *Essais de Philosophie et de l'Art: l'esthétique de R. W.* (2 vols.; Paris, 1893); M. Hébert, *Le Sentiment religieux dans l'œuvre de R. W.* (Paris, 1894); R. Louis, *Die Weltanschauung R. W.s* (Leipzig, 1898); D. Irvine, *Parsifal and W.s Christianity* (London, 1899); M. Kufferath, *Musiciens et Philosophes: Tolstoy, Schopenhauer, Nietzsche, W.* (Paris, 1899); P. Moos, *R. W. als Ästhetiker* (Berlin, 1906); R. Richter, *Kunst und Philosophie bei R. W.* (Leipzig, 1906); H. Bélart, *F. Nietzsche und R. W.: Ihre persönlichen Beziehungen, Kunst- und Weltanschauungen* (Berlin, 1907); G. Robert, *Philosophie et drame. Essai d'une explication des drames wagnériens* (Paris, 1907); O. Schmiedel, *R. W.s religiöse Weltanschauung* (Tübingen, 1907); W. Vollert, *R. W.s Stellung zur christlichen Religion* (Wismar, 1907); L. Dauriac, *Le Musicien-poète R. W. Étude de psychologie musicale* (Paris, 1908); G. Braschowanoff, *Von Olympia nach Bayreuth* (2 vols.; Leipzig, 1911-12); F. Gross, *Die Wiedergeburt des Sehers* (Zürich, 1927); A. Drews, *Ideengehalt von W.s dramatischen Dichtungen* (Leipzig, 1931); G. Wooley, *R. W. et le symbolisme français* (Paris, 1931); F. Gross, *Der Mythos W.s* (Vienna, 1932); G. Frommel, *Der Geist des Antike bei R. W.* (Berlin, 1933); I. Wyzewska, *La Revue wagnérienne; essai sur l'interprétation esthétique de W. en France* (Paris, 1934); K. R. Karzer, *R. W. der Revolutionär gegen das 19. Jahrhundert* (1934); W. Engelsmann, *Erlösung dem Erlöser: R. W.s religiöse Weltgestalt* (Leipzig, 1936); M. Boucher, *Les Idées politiques de R. W.* (Paris, 1948; in English, N. Y., 1950); K. Overhoff, *R. W.s germanisch-christlicher Mythos . . .* (Dinkelsbühl, 1955).

G—Wagner's Art in Relation to Theory and Technique: C. Kistler, *Harmonielehre . . .* (Heilbronn, 1879; 2nd ed., greatly augmented, 1903; based on Wagner's harmonic innovations); K. Mayrberger, *Die Harmonik R. W.s* (Chemnitz, 1883); S. Jadassohn, *Melodik und Harmonik bei R. W.* (Berlin, 1899); E. Thomas, *Die Instrumentation der 'Meistersinger' von R. W.* (2 vols.; Mannheim, 1899; 2nd ed., Leipzig, 1907); G. Capellen, *Ist das System Simon Sechters ein geeigneter Ausgangspunkt für die theoretische Wagnerforschung?* (Leipzig, 1902); É. Poirée, *Le Discours musical, son principe, ses formes expressives, spécialement d'après la partition des 'Maîtres-Chanteurs' de R. W.* (Paris, 1902); E. Ergo, *Über R. W.s Harmonik und Melodik* (Leipzig, 1914); E. Kurth, *Romantische Harmonik und ihre Krise in W.s 'Tristan'* (Bern and Leipzig, 1920; 2nd ed., Berlin, 1923; valuable); A. Lorenz, *Das Geheimnis der Form bei R. W.* (4 vols.; Berlin: I, *Der Ring,* 1924; II, *Tristan,* 1926; III, *Meistersinger,* 1930; IV, *Parsifal,* 1933; valuable).

H—Wagner and Bayreuth: F. Nietzsche, *W. in Bayreuth* (Chemnitz, 1876; in vol. I of *Nietzsches Werke,* Leipzig, 1895; new ed., 1931; English transl. in complete works, Edinburgh, 1910-14); H. von Wolzogen, *Grundlage und Aufgabe des Allgem. Patronalvereins zur Pflege und Erhaltung der Bühnenfestspiele in B.* (Chemnitz, 1877); K. Heckel, *Die Bühnenfestspiele in B.* (Leipzig, 1891); H. Porges, *Die Bühnenproben zu den Festspielen des Jahren 1876* (Leipzig, 1896); F. Weingartner, *B., 1876-96* (Berlin, 1896; 2nd ed., 1904); H. S. Chamberlain, *Die ersten 20 Jahre der B. Bühnenfestspiele* (Bayreuth, 1896); E. Kloss, *Zwanzig Jahre B.* (Berlin, 1896; English transl., London, 1896); F. Hofmann, *B. und seine Kunstdenkmale* (Munich, 1902); W. Golther, *B.* (Berlin, 1904); R. Sternfeld, *R. W. und die B. Bühnenfestspiele* (2 vols.; Berlin, 1906; new ed., 1927); M. G. Conrad, *W.'s Geist und Kunst in B.* (Munich, 1906); A. Prüfer, *Das Werk von B.* (Leipzig, 1909); A. Prüfer, *R. W. in B.* (Leipzig, 1910); H. von Wolzogen, *Heinrich von Steins Briefwechsel mit H. von Wolzogen. Ein Beitrag zur Geschichte des Bayreuther Gedankens* (Leipzig, 1910); H. Bahr and A. Bahr-Mildenburg, *Bayreuth und das W.-Theater* (Leipzig, 1910; 2nd ed., 1912; English transl., London, 1921); C. V. Kerr, *The Story of Bayreuth as Told in the Bayreuth Letters of R. W.* (Boston, 1912); R. Du Moulin-Eckart, *Wahnfried* (Leipzig, 1925); P. Bülow, *R. W. und sein Werk von Bayreuth* (Frankfurt, 1927); F. Klose, *Bayreuth. Eindrücke und Erlebnisse* (Regensburg, 1929); O. Bie, *R. W. und Bayreuth* (Leipzig, 1931); J. Kneise, *Der Kampf zweier Welten um das Bayreuther Erbe* (Kassel, 1931); L. Reichwein, *Bayreuth* (Bielefeld and Leipzig, 1934); H. B. Brand, *Aus R. W.s Leben in Bayreuth* (Munich, 1935); S. Rützow, *R. W. und Bayreuth* (Munich, 1943; 2nd ed., 1953); J. Bertram, *Der Seher von Bayreuth* (Berlin, 1943); E. Ebermayer, *Magisches Bayreuth, Legende und Wirklichkeit* (Stuttgart, 1951).

I—Wagner's Literary Sources: F. Schultz, *Das neue Deutschland. Seine alten Heldensagen und R. W.* (Leipzig, 1888); E. Meinck, *Die sagenwissenschaftlichen Grundlagen der Nibelungendichtung W.'s* (Berlin, 1892); J. L. Weston, *The Legends of the Wagnerian Drama* (London, 1896; new ed., 1903); A. M. Bowen, *The Sources and Text of W.'s 'Die Meistersinger von Nürnberg'* (Munich, 1897); J. Nover, *Die Tannhäusersage und ihre poetische Gestaltung* (Hamburg, 1897); E. Wechsler, *Die Sage vom hl. Gral in ihrer Entwickelung bis auf R. W.s 'Parsifal'* (Halle, 1898); J. Nover, *Die Lohengrinsage und ihre poetische Gestaltung* (Hamburg, 1899); Hermann von der Pfordten, *Handlung und Dichtung der Bühnenwerke R. W.s nach ihren Grundlagen in Sage und Geschichte* (Berlin, 1900; 4th ed., 1908); W Golther, *Die sagengeschichtlichen Grundlagen der Ringdichtung R. W.s* (Berlin, 1902); S. Valot, *Les Héros de R. W. Études sur les origines indoeuropéennes des légendes wagnériennes* (Paris, 1903); W. C. Sawyer, *Teutonic Legends in the Nibelungenlied and the Nibelungen Ring* (Philadelphia, 1904); W. Golther, *Tristan und Isolde in den Dichtungen des Mittelalters und der neuen Zeit* (Leipzig, 1907); R. von Kralik, *Die Gralssage* (Ravensburg, 1907); E. Elster, *Tannhäuser in Geschichte, Sage und Dichtung* (Bromberg, 1908); L. von Schroeder, *Die Wurzeln der Sage vom hl. Gral* (Vienna, 1910); F. Strich, *Die Mythologie in der deutschen Litteratur von Klopstock bis W.* (2 vols.; Halle, 1910): W. Golther, *Zur deutschen Sage und Dichtung* (Leipzig, 1911); O. Rank, *Die Lohengrinsage* (Vienna, 1911); W. Golther, *Parsifal und der Gral in deutscher Sage des Mittelalters und der Neuzeit* (Leipzig, 1913); A. Bonilla y San Martín, *Las Leyendas de W. en la literatura española* (Madrid, 1913); G. Brownell, *The Wagnerian Romances* (N. Y., 1925); H. Thompson, *W. and Wagenseil: A Source of W.s Opera 'Die Meistersinger'* (London, 1927); M. Unger, *The Cradle of the Parsifal Legend,* in the 'Mus. Quarterly' (July, 1932); A. Salazar, *Parsifal in Romanic Lands,* in the 'Mus. Quarterly' (Jan., 1939); R. M. Rayner, *Wagner and 'Die Meistersinger'* (Oxford, 1940); H. Hirsch, *R. W. und das deutsche Mittelalter* (Vienna, 1944).

J—Analyses, Guides, Stories of the Operas: G. Kobbé, *R. W.s 'Tristan und Isolde'* (N. Y., 1886); A. Smolian, *The Themes of 'Tannhäuser'* (London, 1891); A. Lavignac, *Le Voyage artistique à Bayreuth* (Paris, 1897; 14th printing, 1925; English transl. as *The Music-Dramas of R. W.,* N. Y., 1898; new ed., 1932); J. Tiersot, *Études sur les Maîtres-Chanteurs de Nuremberg, de R. W.* (Paris, 1899); G. Kobbé, *W.s Music Dramas Analyzed* (N. Y., 1904); G. Kobbé, *How to Understand W.s Ring* (7th ed., N. Y., 1916); W. Dry, *Erläuterungen zur R. W.s Tondramen* (2 vols., Leipzig, 1906-07); S. H. Hamer, *The Story of 'The Ring'* (N. Y., 1907); M. Burckhardt, *Führer durch R. W.s Musikdramen* (Berlin, 1909); L. Windsperger, *Das Buch der Motive und Themen aus sämtlichen Opern und Musikdramen R. W.s* (for piano, with explanatory text; Mainz, 1921); W. Wilmshurst, *Parsifal* (London, 1922; 'Mus. Pilgrim' series); A. Cœuroy, *La Walkyrie de R. W.* (Paris, 1924); C. Winn, *The Mastersingers of W.* (London, 1925; 'Mus. Pilgrim' series); A. Himonet, *Lohengrin de R. W.* (Paris, 1925); A. E. F. Dickinson, *The Musical Design of 'The Ring'* (London, 1926; 'Mus. Pilgrim' series); E. Newman, *Stories of the Great Operas* (vol. I, *R. W.*; N. Y., 1928); A. Buesst, *R. W., The Nibelung's Ring* (London, 1932; 2nd ed., 1952); R. Grisson, *Beiträge zur Auslegung von R. W.s 'Ring des Nibelungen'* (Leipzig, 1934); V. d'Indy, *Introduction à l'étude de Parsifal de W.* (Paris, 1937); E. Hutcheson, *A Musical Guide to R. W.'s Ring of the Nibelung* (N. Y., 1940); S. A. Luciani, *Il Tristano e Isolda di R. W.* (Florence, 1942); G. Gavazzeni, *Il Siegfried di R. W.* (Florence, 1944); K. Overhoff, *R. W.s Tristan Partitur; eine musikalisch-philosophische Deutung* (Bayreuth, 1948); E. Newman, *The Wagner Operas* (N. Y., 1949); K. Overhoff, *R. W.s Parsifal* (Lindau im Bodensee, 1951).

K—Characters: C. Maude, *W.'s Heroes* (London, 1896) and W.'s *Heroines* (London, 1896); H. von Wolzogen, *R. W.s Heldengestalten erläutert* (Hanover, 1896); A. Höfler, *Wotan. Eine Studie zum 'Ring des Nibelungen'* (Vienna, 1897); H. Bélart, *Taschenbuch der Wagnerkünstlerin. W.s Frauengestalten in gesangdramatischer Beziehung* (Leipzig, 1898); E. Destranges, *Les Femmes dans l'œuvre de R. W.* (Paris, 1899); F. Schwabe, *Die Frauengestalten W.s als Typen des 'Ewig-weiblichen'* (Munich, 1902); H. Materna, *R. W.s Frauengestalten* (Leipzig, 1904); W. Broesel, *Evchen Pogner* (Berlin, 1906); H. Güntert, *Kundry* (Heidelberg, 1928).

L—Wagner as Writer: H. von Wolzogen, *Die Sprache in R. W.s Dichtungen* (Leipzig, 1878); J. Gautier, *R. W. et son œuvre poétique* (Paris, 1882); B. Vogel, *W. als Dichter. Ein Überblick seines poetischen Schaffens* (Leipzig, 1889); A. Ernst, *L'Art de W.: l'œuvre poétique* (Paris, 1893); H. Lichtenberger, *R. W., poète et penseur* (Paris, 1898; new ed., 1931; German transl., Dresden, 1899 [augmented ed. 1913]); O. Lüning, *R. W. als Dichter und Denker* (Zürich, 1900); W. Golther, *R. W. als Dichter* (Berlin, 1904; English transl., London, 1905); R. Weltrich, *R. W.s 'Tristan und Isolde' als Dichtung. Nebst einigen allgemeinen Bemerkungen über W.s Kunst* (Berlin, 1904); E. Meinck, *Fr. Hebbels und R. W.s Nibelungen-Trilogien* (Leipzig, 1905); J. Schuler, *The Language of R. W.'s 'Ring des Nibelungen'* (Lancaster, Pa., 1910); K. Reichelt, *R. W. und die englische Literatur* (Leipzig, 1912); E. von Schrenck, *R. W. als Dichter* (Munich, 1913); P. Bülow, *Die Jugendschriften R. W.s* (Leipzig, 1917); W. Ramann, *Der dichterische Stil R. W.s* (Leipzig, 1929); O. Strobel, *Skizzen und Entwürfe zur Ring-Dichtung* (Munich, 1930); H. Galli, *W. und die deutsche Klassik* (Berne, 1936).

M—Catalogues, Year-Books, etc.: E. Kastner, *Chronologisch-systematischer W.-Katalog* (Offenbach, 1878); N. Oesterlein, *Katalog einer W.-Bibliothek* (4 vols.; Leipzig, 1882, 1886, 1891, 1895; describes the treasures of the W.-Museum and contains full bibliography of books and articles publ. about Wagner during his life [10, 181 titles]); E. Kastner, *Verzeichnis der ersten Aufführungen von R. W.s dramatischen Werken* (Vienna, 1896; 2nd ed., Leipzig, 1899); H. Silège, *Bibliographie wagnérienne française [1851-1902]* (Paris, 1902); P. Pabst, *Verzeichnis von R. W.s Werken, Schriften und Dichtungen, deren hauptsächlichsten Bearbeitungen, sowie von besonders interessanter Litteratur, Abbildungen, Büsten und Kunstblättern, den Meister und seine Schöpfungen betreffend* (Leipzig, 1905); L. Frankenstein, *Bibliographie der auf R. W. bezüglichen . . . Literatur für die Jahre 1907-11* (Berlin, 1912); J. Kürschner, *R. W.-Jahrbuch* (Stuttgart, 1886; only 1 vol. publ.); L. Frankenstein, *R. W.-Jahrbuch* (Berlin, 1906, 1907, 1908, 1912, 1913); M. Burrell, *Catalogue of the Burrell Collection of W. Documents, Letters and Other Biogr. Material* (London, 1929); O. Strobel, *Führer durch die wiederholte Ausstellung einer umfassenden Auswahl von Schätzen aus dem Archiv des Hauses Wahnfried: Genie am Werk, R. W.s Schaffen und Wirken im Spiegel eigenhandschriftlicher Urkunden* (Bayreuth, 1934). The volumes of 'Bayreuther Blätter' (founded by Wagner in 1878) are of value.

N—Iconography: J. Grand-Carteret, *R. W. en caricatures* (Paris, 1892); E. Fuchs and E. Kreowski, *R. W. in der Karikatur* (Berlin, 1907; 6th ed., 1913); A. Vanselow, *R. W.s photographische Bildnisse* (Munich, 1908); E. Engel, *R. W.s Leben und Werke im Bilde* (2 vols.; Vienna, 1913; new ed., Leipzig, 1922); J. Kapp, *R. W. sein Leben, sein Werk, seine Welt in 260 Bildern* (Berlin, 1933); P. Bülow, *R. W. sein Leben in Bildern* (Leipzig, 1936); R. Bory, *R. W. sein Leben und sein Werk in Bildern* (Leipzig, 1938).

O—Miscellaneous: C. Baudelaire, *R. W. et Tannhäuser à Paris* (Paris, 1861); W. Tappert, *Wagner-Lexikon. Wörterbuch der Unhöflichkeit . . . .* (Leipzig, 1877; new augmented ed. as *R. W. im Spiegel der Kritik,* 1903; an interesting collection of adverse and abusive comments); *Über Schicksale und Bestimmung des W.-Museums* (Leipzig, 1892); E. Kloss, *Das W.-Museum in Eisenach,* in *Ein W.-Lesebuch* (Leipzig, 1904); K. Grunsky, *R. W. und die Juden* (Munich, 1921); W. Lange, *R. W. und seine Vaterstadt, Leipzig* (Leipzig, 1921); J. Marnold, *Le Cas W.: la musique pendant la guerre* (Paris, 1920); *W. et la France,* special issue of the 'Revue Musicale' (Oct., 1923); P. Stefan, *Die Feindschaft gegen W.* (Regensburg, 1918); E. Newman, *Fact and Fiction About W.* (N. Y., 1931); E. Stemplinger, *W. in Munich* (Munich, 1933); W. Golther, *R. W. Leben und Werke in urkundlichen Zeugnissen, Briefen, Schriften, Berichten* (Ebenhausen, near Munich, 1936); W. Lange, *R. W.s Sippe,* with genealogical table (Leipzig, 1938); L. Weinhold, *Handschriften von R. W. in Leipzig* (Leipzig, 1938); O. Daube, *Humor bei R. W.* (Gütersloh, 1944); L. Stein, *The Racial Thinking of R. W.* (N. Y., 1950); L. Strecker, *R. W. als Verlagsgefährte* (Mainz, 1951).

Wagner, Siegfried, son of Richard and Cosima Wagner; b. Triebschen, June 6, 1869; d. Bayreuth, Aug. 4, 1930. His parents were married on Aug. 25, 1870, and Siegfried was thus legitimatized. Wagner wrote *Siegfried Idyll* for him, and it was performed in Wagner's house in Triebschen on Christmas Day, 1870 (Cosima Wagner's birthday). He attended a polytechnic school, but the lure of music proved overwhelming, and he took up studies under Julius Kniese and Humperdinck; began to compose; also embarked on a conductorial career; appeared as a symph. conductor in Germany, Austria, Italy, and England. In 1894 he was appointed assistant conductor in Bayreuth, and in 1896 became one of the regular conductors. He conducted from memory, and left-handed. In 1909 he succeeded his mother as general supervisor of the Bayreuth Festivals. On Sept. 21, 1915, he married Winifred Williams, an adopted daughter of Karl Klindworth. In 1923-24 he visited the U. S. in order to raise funds for the reopening of the Bayreuth Festspielhaus, which had been closed in the course of World War I. In his career as composer, he was greatly handicapped by the inevitable comparisons with his father. He wrote a symph. poem *Sehnsucht,* after Schiller (1895); *Fahnenschwur* for men's chorus and orch. (1914); a violin concerto (1915); chamber music and vocal works. But his main interest was in music drama; like his father, he wrote his own librettos. —Operas: *Der Bärenhäuter* (Munich, Jan. 22, 1899); *Herzog Wildfang* (Munich, March 14, 1901); *Der Kobold* (Hamburg, Jan. 29, 1904); *Bruder Lustig* (Hamburg, Oct. 13, 1905); *Sternengebot* (Hamburg, Jan. 21, 1908); *Banadietrich* (Karlsruhe, Jan. 15, 1910); *An Allem ist Hütchen Schuld* (Stuttgart, Dec. 6, 1917); *Schwarzschwanenreich* (Karlsruhe, Nov. 5, 1918); *Sonnenflammen* (Karlsruhe, 1926); *Der Heidenkönig* (Cologne, Dec. 16, 1933); *Der Schmied von Marienburg* (Rostock, 1923). His reminiscences, *Erinnerungen,* were publ. at Stuttgart in 1923.—Cf. L. Karpath, *Siegfried Wagner als Mensch und Künstler* (Leipzig, 1902); K. F. Glasenapp, *Siegfried Wagner und seine Kunst* (Leipzig, 1911; 3rd ed., 1919); P. Pretzsch, *Die Kunst Siegfried Wagners* (1919); O. Daube, *Siegfried Wagner und sein Werk* (Bayreuth, 1925); R. Du Moulin-Eckart, *Wahnfried* (Leipzig, 1925); H. Rebois, *Lettres de Siegfried Wagner* (Paris, 1933); O. Daube, *Siegfried Wagner und die Märchenoper* (Leipzig, 1936).

Wagner-Régeny, Rudolf, composer, b. Régen, Transylvania, Aug. 28, 1903. He studied piano with Robert Teichmüller at the Leipzig Cons., conducting and theory at the Musikhochschule in Berlin. He occupied various posts as theater and cinema conductor; was in the German army during World War II; director of the Musikhochschule in Rostock (1947-50); in 1950 appointed director of the State Cons. in East Berlin. In 1934 he was commissioned (together with J. Weismann) by the Ministry of Culture to write new musical settings for *A Midsummer Night's Dream,* to replace Mendelssohn's score; his music was produced at Düsseldorf, on June 6, 1934. Other works: the operas *Moschopulus* (Gera, 1928), *Der nackte König* (Gera, 1928), *Sganarelle* (Essen, 1929), *Die heilige Courtisane* (1932), *Der Günstling* (Dresden, Feb. 20, 1935), *Die Bürger von Calais* (Berlin, Jan. 28, 1939), *Johanna Balk* (Vienna, April 4, 1941), *Das Opfer* (1942), *Der Darmenwäscher* (1950); several ballets, among them *Der zerbrochene Krug* (1937); *Mythologische Figurinen* for orch. (Salzburg Festival of the International Society for Contemporary Music, June 21, 1952); various minor pieces.—Cf. A. Burgartz, *Rudolf Wagner-Régeny* (Berlin, 1935).

Wailly, (Louis Auguste) Paul (Warnier) de, French composer; b. Amiens, May 16, 1854; d. Paris, June 18, 1933. He was a pupil of César Franck, and in his works showed himself a follower of Franck's precepts. He wrote 3 symphonies; a dramatic oratorio, *L'Apôtre* (1924); *26 Pièces* for harmonium; publ. *La Vie et l'âme de César Franck* (Paris, 1922).—Cf. A. Laurent, *Paul de Wailly: l'artiste, l'œuvre* (Paris, 1933); A. Laurent, *Paul de Wailly: le compositeur, l'artiste* (Eu, 1940).

Waisselius, Matthäus, German composer and lute player; flourished in the 2nd half of the 16th century. He was a schoolmaster in the vicinity of Königsberg; publ. several books, in tablature notation, of music for the lute, among them *Cantiones 4, 5, et 6 vocum . . .* (Frankfurt, 1573) and *Lautenbuch,* comprising instruction for the lute and a selection of dance tunes (1592).

Walcker (vahl'-kehr), **Eberhard Friedrich,** German organ-builder; b. Cannstadt, near Stuttgart, July 3, 1794; d. Ludwigsburg, Oct. 2, 1872. Trained in the workshops of his father, a skilled organ-builder, he set up for himself in Ludwigsburg in 1820, and won great renown by his excellent work and numerous inventions. After his death the business passed to his five sons, **Heinrich** (b. Oct. 10, 1828; d. Kirchheim, Nov. 24, 1903), **Friedrich** (b. Sept. 17, 1829; d. Dec. 6, 1895), **Karl** (b. March 6, 1845; d. Stuttgart, May 19, 1908), **Paul** (b. May 31, 1846; d. 1928), and **Eberhard** (b. April 8, 1850; d. 1927). In 1916 **Oscar Walcker** (son of Friedrich; b. Jan. 1, 1869; d. Nov. 4, 1948) became head of the firm; in 1932 he effected a merger with the firm Ziegler of Steinsfurt (in 1910 a merger with the firm of W. Sauer of Frankfurt had taken place). His reminiscences, *Erinnerungen eines Orgelbauers,* were publ. in Kassel, 1948. The firm has built more than 2,500 organs; some of the largest are those in Ulm Cathedral (1856; 95 speaking stops; rebuilt and enlarged in 1914 to 171), Music Hall, Boston (now removed; 1863; 86 stops); Paulskirche, Frankfurt (1833; 74 stops); St. Peter's, St. Petersburg (1840; 65 stops); Reval Cathedral (1842; 65 stops); Votivkirche, Vienna (1878; 61 stops); Riga Cathedral (1885; 124 stops); St. Stephen's Cathedral, Vienna (1886; 90 stops); St. Michael's, Hamburg (1912; 154 stops, 5 manuals and pedal).—Cf. J. Fischer, *Das Orgelbauergeschlecht Walcker* (Kassel, 1949).

Wald, Max, American composer and teacher; b. Litchfield, Ill., July 14, 1889; d. Dowagiac, Mich., Aug. 14, 1954. After studying in Chicago, he was active as theater conductor; went to Paris in 1922 to study with Vincent d'Indy, and remained in Europe until 1936; then returned to Chicago and became chairman of the theory department of the Chicago Musical College. His symph. poem *The Dancer Dead* won 2nd prize in the National Broadcasting Co. competition in 1932, and was broadcast from N. Y. on May 1, 1932. His other works include *Retrospectives* for orch. (Chicago, Jan. 15, 1926), *Comedy Overture* (1937); *In Praise of Pageantry,* for orch. (Chicago, Oct. 31, 1946); *October Moonlight,* a song cycle for soprano, string quartet, flute, clarinet, and piano (1937); 2 piano sonatas; other piano music; also an opera, *Mirandolina* (1936), and a light opera, *Gay Little World* (1942).

Waldersee (văhl'-dĕr-zā), **Paul,** Graf **von,** German music editor; b. Potsdam, Sept. 3, 1831; d. Königsberg, June 14, 1906. He was a Prussian officer (1848-71), but became absorbed in musical studies; was co-editor of Breitkopf & Härtel's collected editions of Mozart and Beethoven; edited a valuable 'Sammlung musikalischer Vorträge' (1879-84), to which he contributed *Die Gesammtausgabe der Werke Mozarts* (No. 7; 1879), *Robert Schumanns Manfred* (No. 13; 1880), *Giov. Pierluigi da Palestrina und die Gesammtausgabe seiner Werke* (No. 52; 1884). He edited the 2nd edition of Köchel's catalogue of Mozart's works.

Waldstein (văhlt'-shtīn), **Ferdinand Ernst Gabriel,** Graf **von,** amateur musician; friend of Beethoven; b. Dux, Bohemia, March 24, 1762; d. Vienna, Aug. 29, 1823. While serving his novitiate in the 'Deutscher Orden' at Bonn (1787-88), he became acquainted with Beethoven, and on several occasions aided him materially, pretending that the sums were extra allowances from the Elector; after Beethoven's departure for Vienna, Waldstein introduced him in the circles of the aristocracy there; in later life their friendship seems to have cooled. Beethoven wrote a set of variations in C for piano 4 hands on a theme of Waldstein's (publ. 1794), and later (1805) dedicated to him the great sonata in C, op. 53. Waldstein also planned the *Ritter-Ballet* (1791), to which Beethoven wrote the music (score published 1872). —Cf. J. Heer, *Der Graf von Waldstein und sein Verhältnis zu Beethoven* (Bonn, 1933).

Waldteufel (văhlt'-toi-fĕl), **Emil,** celebrated waltz composer; b. Strasbourg, Dec. 9, 1837; d. Paris, Feb. 16, 1915. He received his first instruction from his father, professor at the Strasbourg Cons.; then went to the Paris Cons., where he studied with Marmontel, leaving before completing his studies to accept a position with the piano manufacturer Scholtus. The success of his first waltzes, *Joies et Peines* and *Manola* (publ. at his own expense), determined him to devote himself entirely to writing dance music; he lived all his life in Paris, making several very successful concert tours to London, Berlin, Vienna, etc., conducting his own music. In 1865 he was appointed chamber musician to the Empress Eugénie and director of the court balls. He publ. 268 dances, mostly for orch.; a selection of the most popular ones appeared in 5 vols.; several waltzes (*Die Schlittschuhläufer* [also known as *The Skaters* and *Les Patineurs*], *Les Sirènes, Mon Rêve, Les Violettes, Estudiantina, Dolores, Toujours ou Jamais*, etc.) for a time almost rivalled in popularity those of Johann Strauss.

Waley, Simon, English pianist and composer; b. London, Aug. 23, 1827; d. there, Dec. 30, 1875. He studied in London with Moscheles and Bennett (piano); later with Molique (theory); began to compose as a child, and developed rapidly; wrote a piano concerto; 2 piano trios; and many solo pieces; 2 psalms for the synagogue service, which were publ. in vol. 1 of 'Musical Services of the West London Synagogue.' Eventually he abandoned composition, and turned to a mercantile career; became a member of the London Stock Exchange.

Walker, Edyth, American mezzo-soprano, b. Hopewell, N. Y., March 27, 1867; d. New York, Feb. 19, 1950. She studied singing with Aglaja Orgeni at the Dresden Cons.; made her début as Fides in *Le Prophète* at the Berlin Opera on Nov. 11, 1894. She then became a member of the Vienna Court Opera, where she was engaged until 1903. She made her American operatic début with the Metropolitan Opera, as Amneris (N. Y., Nov. 30, 1903); remained with the company until 1906; then sang in Germany, particularly excelling in Wagnerian roles. She sang Elektra in the London première of Strauss's opera (Feb. 19, 1910). After a period of travels in Europe, she taught at the American Cons. in Fontainebleau (1933-36). In 1936 she returned to N. Y., settling there as a singing teacher.

Walker, Ernest, English writer on music; b. Bombay, India, July 15, 1870; d. Oxford, Feb. 21, 1949. He was educated at Balliol College, Oxford; D. Mus., 1898; became director of music there (1901-25); also examiner and member of the Board of Studies for music at Oxford Univ. He publ. the valuable compendium, *A History of Music in England* (Oxford, 1907; 2nd ed., 1924; 3rd ed., revised by J. A. Westrup, 1952); a monograph on Beethoven in the 'Music of the Masters' series (1905); contributed to Grove's Dictionary of Music and Musicians and to many musical periodicals. His collection of essays, *Free Thought and the Musician,* was publ. in 1946. He was also a composer; wrote a number of choral works; 2 piano quartets; a piano quintet; a horn quintet; a cello sonata; piano pieces; songs to German and English words. —Cf. M. Deneke, *Ernest Walker* (London, 1951).

Walker, Frank, English musicologist; b. Gosport, Hampshire, June 10, 1907. He studied at Portsmouth; having attained remarkable knowledge of history, literature, and music, he addressed himself to problems of musical biography; examined primary sources, and established factual data regarding particularly the composers of the Neapolitan School; contributed valuable studies on Pergolesi; publ. an excellent biography, *Hugo Wolf* (London, 1951); wrote a number of biographical articles for the 5th ed. of Grove's Dictionary (1954).

Walker, John, English lexicographer; b. Colney Hatch, Middlesex, March 18, 1732; d. London, Aug. 1, 1807. He wrote *The Melody of Speaking Delineated* (1787; often republished) with an original notation for representing the musical inflections of the speaking voice.

Walker, Joseph Cooper, Irish writer; b. Dublin, Nov., 1760; d. St.-Valéry, France, April 12, 1810. He publ. the valuable books *Historical Memoirs on the Irish Bards,* with notès on Irish music (London, 1786), and *An Historical Account and Critical Essay on the Opera . . .* (1805).

Wallace, William, Scotch composer and music educator; b. Greenock, July 3, 1860; d. Malmesbury, Wiltshire, Dec. 16, 1940. The son of a surgeon, he studied medicine at Glasgow Univ. (M.D., 1888); specialized in ophthalmology in Vienna, and was employed in the Royal Army Medical Corps during World War I. He was self-taught in music; devoted much of his energy to the protection of the rights of British composers; served on the Composers' Copyright Committee of the Society of British Authors; also taught at the Royal Academy of Music.

His works include the symph. poems *The Passing of Beatrice* (1892), *Amboss oder Hammer,* after Goethe (1896), *Sister Helen* (1899), *To the New Century* (1901), *William Wallace* (for the 6th centenary of the death of the national hero of Scotland, and namesake of the composer; 1905), *François Villon* (1909); a symph., *The Creation* 1899); the suites for orch.: *The Lady from the Sea,* after Ibsen (1892) and *Pelléas and Mélisande,* after Maeterlinck (1900); overture, *In Praise of Scottish Poesie* (1894); *The Massacre of the Macpherson,* burlesque cantata; *The Outlaw,* scena for baritone and orch.; the *Rhapsody of Mary Magdalene,* vocal scene; *My Soul is an Enchanted Boat,* trio for voice, violin, and piano; *Spanish Songs,* vocal quartet; song cycles, *Freebooter Songs* (with orch.; his most famous work), *Lords of the Sea,* and *Jacobite Songs.* He publ. *The Threshold of Music: An Inquiry into the Development of the Musical Sense* (1908); *The Musical Faculty: Its Origins and Processes* (1914); *Richard Wagner as He Lived* (1925); *Liszt, Wagner and the Princess* (1927).

Wallace, William Vincent, Irish composer; b. Waterford, March 11, 1812; d. Château de Bagen (Haute-Garonne), France, Oct. 12, 1865. The son of a bandmaster, Wallace was brought up in a musical atmosphere. He was 15 when the family moved to Dublin, and soon entered a professional career, playing violin in theater orchestras and organ in churches. One of his earliest compositions was *The Harp in the Air,* which later became famous when he incorporated it into his opera *Maritana.* In 1831 he married Isabella Kelly. He applied himself to the study of violin, and subsequently was able to give successful concerts. With his wife he traveled in Australia, South America, Mexico, and the U. S. Returning to Europe in 1844, he toured Germany; in 1845 he was in London, where he produced his opera *Maritana* (Drury Lane, Nov. 15, 1845), which obtained excellent success; it was followed by another opera, *Matilda of Hungary* (Drury Lane, Feb. 2, 1847), which was a failure. In 1850 he resumed his wanderings and revisited the U. S.; he declared his first marriage invalid, and married an American pianist, Helen Stoepel. Back in England, he produced several operas, of which *Lurline* (Covent Garden, Feb. 23, 1860) had tremendous acclaim; his other operas were *The Amber Witch* (Haymarket, Feb. 28, 1861), *Love's Triumph* (Covent Garden, Nov. 3, 1862), and *The Desert Flower* (Covent Garden, Oct. 12, 1863); several operas remained unfinished at his death. His piano music enjoyed great vogue during his lifetime; some noted numbers are *La Gondola;* 2 Nocturnes; *Chant d'amour; Nocturne mélodique; Mélodie irlandaise; Music Murmuring in the Trees; Valse brillante de salon; Tarentelle,* etc. —Cf. A. Pougin, *W. V. Wallace, étude biographique et critique* (Paris, 1866); W. H. G. Flood, *W. V. Wallace, a Memoir* (Waterford, 1912).

Wallaschek, Richard, Austrian theorist; b. Brünn, Nov. 16, 1860; d. Vienna, April 24, 1917. He studied law and philosophy in Vienna, Heidelberg, and Tübingen; from 1890 to 1895 was in London, engaged in research work; in 1896 joined the faculty of the Univ. of Vienna; wrote music criticism. He wrote a number of essays on esthetics, primitive music, and psychology of musical perception. His publications include *Ästhetik der Tonkunst* (1886) and several books publ. in London, in English: *On the Origin of Music* (1891), *Natural Selection and Music* (1892), *On the Difference of Time and Rhythm in Music* (1893), *Primitive Music: An Inquiry into the Origin and Development of Music, Songs, Instruments, Dances and Pantomimes of Savage Races* (1893; German ed., enlarged, as *Anfänge der Tonkunst,* 1903). He also publ. *Das k. k. Hofoperntheater* (Vienna, 1909). —Cf. R. Lach, *Zur Erinnerung an Richard Wallaschek* (Vienna, 1917).

Wallenstein, Alfred, American cellist and conductor; b. Chicago, Oct. 7, 1898 (of German parents). The family moved to Los Angeles when he was a child; he studied cello; was employed in theater orchestras; then became a cellist in the San Francisco Symph.; in 1917 joined the traveling troupe of the Pavlova Ballet, with whom he toured in South America; in 1919 played in the Los Angeles Philharmonic. In 1920 he went to Europe, studied medicine at the Univ. of Leipzig, and took cello lessons with Julius Klengel; returned to the U. S., and was engaged as 1st cellist with the Chicago Symph. Orch. (1922-29); from 1929 to 1936 was 1st cellist of the N. Y. Philharmonic under Toscanini. He made his début as conductor on the radio in 1931; in 1933 he established the Wallenstein Sinfonietta; presented many radio programs of serious music, including weekly performances of Bach's cantatas, a complete series of Mozart's piano concertos, and also works by modern composers. From 1943 to 1956 he was conductor of the Los Angeles Philharmonic; from 1952 also music director of the Hollywood Bowl. In the spring of 1956, Wallenstein traveled to Japan and other countries in the Far East with the Los Angeles Philharmonic, under the auspices of the American National Theater and Academy and of the State Department. —Cf. Hope Stoddard, *Symphony Conductors of the U. S. A.* (N. Y., 1957; pp. 274-79).

Wallenstein, Martin, German pianist and composer; b. Frankfurt, July 22, 1843; d. there, Nov. 29, 1896. He studied with Dreyschock in Prague, and with Hauptmann and Rietz in Leipzig; made many successful tours as a pianist. His opera, *Das Testament,* was produced at Frankfurt in 1870; he also wrote a piano concerto; many piano studies and characteristic pieces.

Wallerstein, Anton, German violinist and composer; b. Dresden, Sept. 28, 1813; d. Geneva, March 26, 1892. He played in public as a child; joined the Dresden court orch. (1829-32) and later was a member of the Hanover orch. (1832-41). He wrote a number of popular dance compositions, of which about 300 were publ.; also violin pieces and songs.

Wallerstein, Lothar, pianist and conductor; b. Prague, Nov. 6, 1882; d. New Orleans, Nov. 13, 1949. He studied art and music in Prague and Munich; also attended the Geneva Cons., where he later taught piano; after a brief engagement as accompanist at the Dresden Opera (1909), he held the posts of conductor and stage director in Poznan (1910-14), in Breslau (1918-22), in Frankfurt (1924-26), at the Vienna State Opera (1927-29), and at La Scala of Milan (1929). He came to the U. S. in 1941, and lived in New Orleans. He brought out eds. of Mozart's *Idomeneo,* Verdi's *Don Carlos,* and other operas. —Cf. A. Berger, *Über die Spielleitung der Oper. Betrachtungen zur musikalischen Dramaturgie Dr. Lothar Wallensteins* (Graz, 1928).

Wallnöfer (văhl-nö-fĕhr), **Adolf,** Austrian tenor and composer; b. Vienna, April 26, 1854; d. Munich, June 9, 1946. He studied singing with Rokitansky; composition with Krenn and Dessoff. He began his career as a baritone, but developed his voice into a tenor in 1880; joined Neumann's Wagner troupe in 1881; then sang at Bremen and at the German Opera in Prague (1885-95); in 1896-98, appeared in the U. S.; then toured in Russia (1899); in 1906 he was engaged at the Vienna Opera; in 1908 he went to Munich, where he remained until his death. He composed an opera, *Eddystone* (Prague, 1889); several works for solo voice, chorus, and orch. *(Die Grenzen der Menschheit, Gersprenz, Hymne an die Erde,* etc.); many unaccompanied choruses; piano pieces; numerous songs and ballads, a selection of which was publ. in 5 vols. His unpubl. MSS are in the Municipal Music Library in Munich. Author of *Resonanztonlehre* (1911).

Walmisley, Thomas (Attwood), English organist and composer; son of Thomas Forbes Walmisley; b. London, Jan. 21, 1814; d. Hastings, Jan. 17, 1856. His father placed him under the guidance of Thomas Attwood, his own teacher. He showed remarkable progress, and became organist at Trinity and St. John's Colleges at Cambridge, at the age of 19. In 1836 he became a prof. of music; continued to study nonetheless; received his B.A. degree in 1838 and M.A. in 1841. He wrote several odes and anthems for Trinity College. He enjoyed the reputation of being one of the best organists in England of his day. His anthems and church services were brought out by his father, who survived him by 10 years; they were included in the vol. *Cathedral Music* (1857).

Walmisley, Thomas Forbes, English organist and composer; b. London, May 22, 1783; d. there, July 23, 1866. He was a chorister at Westminster Abbey; studied organ with Thomas Attwood; then was organist at the Female Orphan Asylum (1810-14) and at St. Martin-in-the-Fields (1814-54). He was a popular composer of glees; publ. 3 sets containing 6 glees each; also 'A Collection of Glees, Trios, Rounds and Canons' (1826); several single glees and songs.

Walsh, John, English music publisher; place and date of birth unknown; d. London, March 13, 1736. From about 1690 he had his business at the sign of the 'Golden Harp and Hoboy' in the Strand, London; in 1692 he was appointed 'musical instrument maker in ordinary to His Majesty.' He developed a flourishing trade, and achieved great renown; in England he was unquestionably the foremost publisher of music in his time. In 1711 he publ. Handel's *Rinaldo,* and remained Handel's principal publisher. He was succeeded by his son, also named **John Walsh** (d. London, Jan. 15, 1766), who maintained the firm's high standards. —Cf. F. Kidson, *Handel's Publisher, John Walsh, his Successors and Contemporaries,* in the 'Mus. Quarterly' (July, 1920); Wm. C.

Smith, *Handel's 'Rinaldo': An Outline of the Early Editions,* in the 'Mus. Times' (Aug., 1935); W. C. Smith, *A Bibliography of the Musical Works Published by J. Walsh during the Years 1695-1720* (London, 1948).

Walter, Arnold, composer; b. Hannsdorf, Austria, Aug. 30, 1902; studied at the Univ. of Prague and Berlin Univ. (with H. Abert, Joh. Wolf, and Curt Sachs). He taught at Brno (1928-30); then was music critic of the daily newspaper 'Vorwärts' in Berlin (1930-33); in 1933 went to Barcelona; in 1937 settled in Canada as teacher and opera conductor at the Royal Cons., Toronto. His works include a symph. in G minor (Toronto, Feb. 1, 1944); *For the Fallen,* cantata (1949); chamber music.

Walter, Bruno (real name B. W. Schlesinger), eminent German conductor; b. Berlin, Sept. 15, 1876. He studied at Stern's Cons., Berlin with H. Ehrlich, L. Bussler, and R. Radecke. At the age of 17 he became opera coach at the Municipal Opera of Cologne; also did occasional conducting there; in the following year he was engaged as assistant conductor at the Hamburg Stadttheater, under Gustav Mahler; this contact was decisive in his career, and he became in subsequent years an ardent champion of Mahler's music; conducted the premières of the posthumous symph. No. 9 and *Das Lied von der Erde.* During the season 1896-97 Walter was engaged as 2nd conductor at the Stadttheater in Breslau; then became principal conductor in Pressburg, and in 1898 at Riga, where he conducted for two seasons. In 1900 he received the important engagement of conductor at the Berlin Opera under a 5-year contract; however he left this post in 1901 when he received an offer from Mahler to become his assistant at the Vienna Opera. He established himself as an efficient opera conductor; also conducted in England (first appearance, March 3, 1909, with the Royal Philharmonic Society, London). He remained at the Vienna Opera after the death of Mahler; on Jan. 1, 1914, he became court conductor and music director in Munich; under his guidance, the Munich Opera enjoyed brilliant performances, particularly of Mozart's works. Seeking greater freedom for his artistic activities, he left Munich in 1922, and gave numerous performances as guest conductor with European orchestras; from 1922 he also conducted summer concerts of the Salzburg festival; his performances of Mozart's music there set a standard. He also appeared as pianist in Mozart's chamber works. On Feb. 15, 1923, he made his American début with the N. Y. Symph. Society, and appeared with it again in 1924 and 1925. From 1925 till 1929 he was conductor of the Städtische Oper in Berlin-Charlottenburg; in 1929 he succeeded Furtwängler as conductor of the Leipzig Gewandhaus Orch., but continued to give special concerts in Berlin. On Feb. 25, 1932, he was guest conductor of the N. Y. Philharmonic, acting also as soloist in a Mozart piano concerto; was reengaged during the next 3 seasons as associate conductor with Toscanini. He was also guest conductor in Philadelphia, Washington, and Baltimore. With the advent of the Nazi regime in Germany his engagement with the Gewandhaus Orch. was cancelled, and he was also prevented from continuing his orchestral concerts in Berlin. He filled several engagements with the Concertgebouw in Amsterdam, and also conducted in Salzburg. In 1936 he was engaged as music director of the Vienna Opera; this was terminated with the annexation of Austria in 1938. Walter with his family then went to France, where he was granted French citizenship. After the outbreak of World War II he sailed for America, establishing his residence in California, and eventually becoming an American citizen. He was guest conductor with the NBC Symph. Orch. (1940); also conducted many performances of the Metropolitan Opera, N. Y. (début in *Fidelio* on Feb. 14, 1941). From Feb. 1947 to 1949 he was conductor and musical adviser of the N. Y. Philharmonic. —Walter achieved the reputation of a perfect Classicist among contemporary conductors; his interpretations of the masterpieces of the Vienna School are particularly notable. He is acknowledged as a foremost conductor of Mahler's symphonies. His own compositions include 2 symphonies; *Siegesfahrt* for solo voices, chorus, and orch.; a string quartet; a piano quintet; a piano trio; several albums of songs. He publ. the books *Von den moralischen Kräften der Musik* (Vienna, 1935), *Gustav Mahler* (Vienna, 1936; English transl., London, 1937; new transl. with additions, N. Y., 1958), and *Theme and Variations,* an autobiography (N. Y., 1946). —Cf. M. Komorn-Rebhan, *Was wir von Bruno Walter lernten* (Vienna, 1913); Paul Stefan, *Bruno Walter* (Vienna, 1936); Thomas Mann, *To Bruno Walter on his 70th Birthday,* in the 'Mus. Quarterly' (Oct., 1946); Donald Brook, *International Gallery of Conductors* (Bristol, 1951; pp. 207-20); B. Gavoty, *Bruno Walter* (Geneva, 1956).

Walter, Fried, German composer; b. Ottendorf-Okrilla, near Dresden, Dec. 19, 1907; studied in Dresden; filled various posts as opera coach and conductor in Germany; in 1949 became a chief of the light music dept. at the Berlin Radio. —Works: operas, *Königin Elizabeth* (Stockholm, Nov. 24, 1939), *Andreas Wolfius* (Berlin, Dec. 19, 1940), and *Dorfmusik* (Wiesbaden, Nov. 1, 1943); a dance drama, *Kleopatra* (Prague, 1943); a dance fairy tale, *Der Pfeil* (Berlin, Dec. 22, 1946); a *Kleine Sinfonie* (1942); numerous dramatic ballads; chamber music; songs.

Walter, Friedrich Wilhelm, German writer on music; b. Mannheim, Sept. 3, 1870. He studied in Heidelberg; *Dr. phil.*, 1892; lived most of his life in Mannheim, and publ. a number of valuable monographs dealing with musical life there: *Die Entwickelung des Mannheimer Musik- und Theaterlebens* (1897), *Geschichte des Theaters und der Musik am kurpfälzischen Hofe* (1898), and *Archiv und Bibliothek des Grossherzoglichen Hof- und National-Theaters in Mannheim* (2 vols.; 1899).

Walter, Georg A., composer and teacher; b. Hoboken, N. J., Nov. 13, 1875 (of German parents); d. Berlin, Sept. 13, 1952. He studied singing in Berlin, Milan, and London; composition with Wilhelm Berger in Berlin; made a career as a singer, particularly distinguishing himself in the works of Bach and Handel. He was prof. at the Stuttgart Hochschule (1925-34); then taught in Berlin until 1945. He wrote a number of songs; brought out new editions of works by the sons of Bach, Schütz, etc.

Walter, George William, American organist; b. New York, Dec. 16, 1851; d. Washington, March 11, 1911. At the age of 5 he played the organ at Trinity Chapel; studied with J. K. Paine in Boston and with S. P. Warren in N. Y.; settled in Washington in 1869. He enjoyed a high reputation as an improviser; accumulated a musical library which was one of the finest in America.

Walter (Walther) (real name Blanckenmüller), **Johann (Johannes),** one of the earliest composers for the Lutheran church; b. Kahler, Thuringia, 1496; d. Torgau, March 25, 1570. In 1517 he entered the chapel of the Elector Friedrich the Wise of Saxony as a bass singer (the Elector divided his residence betwen Altenburg and Torgau). In 1524, at Wittenberg, he publ. the *Geystlich Gesangk-Buchleyn* for 3-5 voices, the first Protestant singing-book. In 1525 he was summoned to Wittenberg by Luther to assist in the composition and regulation of the German Mass. Shortly after the death of the Elector Friedrich (1525) his chapel was disbanded, and Walter became cantor of the Municipal Latin-School in Torgau and director of the 'Stadtkantorei' (community choir) there (1526-48). In 1548 he was called upon by the new Elector, Moritz, of Saxony, to organize the court chapel in Dresden, and remained there as Kapellmeister until 1554, when he retired to Torgau on a pension. He publ. *Cantio septem vocum in laudem Dei omnipotentis et Evangelii ejus* (1544); *Magnificat 8 tonorum* (1557); *Ein newes christliches Lied* (1561); *Ein gar schöner geistlicher und christlicher Bergkreyen* (1561); *Lob und Preis der himmlischen Kunst Musica* (1564); *Das christlich Kinderlied Dr. Martin Luthers, 'Erhalt uns Herr bei deinem Wort'* (1566), etc. The *Geystlich Gesangk-Buchleyn* was reprinted in vol. VII of the 'Publikationen der Gesellschaft für Musikforschung' (1878); a list of other reprints is found in W. Ehmann's article *Johann Walter, der erste Kantor der protestantischen Kirche,* in 'Musik und Kirche' (vol. VI, 1934). Instrumental works by Walter were discovered in the library of the Thomasschule in Leipzig by B. Engelke in 1912 (examples in A. Schering's 'Geschichte der Musik in Beispielen,' Nos. 80 and 81). A complete ed. of Walter's works was begun by Otto Schröder and Max Schneider with the publ. of the *Geystlich Gesangk-Buchleyn* in 3 vols. (Kassel, 1953-55). —Cf. O. Kade, *Johann Walthers Wittenbergisch geistlig Gesangbuch von 1524* (1878); H. Holstein, *Der Lieder- und Tondichter Johann Walther,* in 'Archiv für Literaturgeschichte' (1884); A. Aber, *Die Pflege der Musik unter den Wettinern . . .* (1921); R. Haas, *Zu Walthers Choralpassion nach Matthäus,* in 'Archiv für Musikwissenschaft' IV (1922); A. Schmitz, in 'Siebs-Festschrift' (1933); W. Gurlitt, *Johannes Walter und die Musik der Reformationszeit,* in 'Luther-Jahrbuch' (1933); O. Michaelis, *Johann Walther, der Musiker-Dichter in Luther's Gefolgschaft* (Leipzig, 1939); C. Gerhardt, *Die Torgauer Walter-Handschriften; eine Studie zur Quellenkunde der Musikgeschichte der deutschen Reformationszeit* (Kassel, 1949). See also G. Reese, *Music in the Renaissance* (N. Y., 1954; pp. 677-78).

Walter, Karl, German organist and campanologist; b. Cransberg, Oct. 27, 1862; d.

Montabaur, Dec. 4, 1929. He studied at the Seminary in Montabaur, where he became instructor in 1893; in 1899, appointed diocesan inspector for the building of organs and bells. In 1903, became instructor of church music at Limburg Seminary. He wrote organ music and sacred works; publ. several manuals on organ building, and on the construction of bells, a field in which he was an authority. —Publications: *Kleine Orgelbaulehre* (1904); *Orgelbegleitung zu den Melodien des Gesangbuchs für das Bistum Limburg* (1907; 2nd ed., 1911); *Glockenkunde* (1913); *Kleine Glockenkunde* (1916).

Walter, Thomas, American clergyman and author of singing books; b. Roxbury, Mass., Dec. 13, 1696; d. there, Jan. 10, 1725. He was the son of a clergyman and a nephew of Cotton Mather; educated at Harvard College (M.A., 1713); on Oct. 29, 1718, he was ordained; was assistant pastor to his father at Roxbury. With the aim of correcting what he described as 'an horrid medley of confused and disorderly sounds' prevailing in the singing in New England churches, he publ. *The Grounds and Rules of Musick Explained; or, an Introduction to the Art of Singing by Note; Fitted to the meanest capacities* (Boston, 1721; several other eds. up to 1764). It was the 2nd singing-book to be publ. in America, following that of John Tufts (q.v.). He also publ. *The Sweet Psalmist of Israel* (1722). —Cf. F. J. Metcalf, *American Writers and Compilers of Sacred Music* (1925); E. H. Pierce, *The Rise and Fall of the 'Fugue-Tune' in America,* in the 'Mus. Quarterly' (April, 1930); M. B. Jones, *Bibliographical Notes on Thomas Walter's 'Grounds and Rules . . .'* in 'Proceedings of the American Antiquarian Society' (Oct., 1932; also reprinted separately, Worcester, Mass., 1933).

Waltershausen (vähl'-tërs-how-zen), **(Hermann) Wolfgang von,** German composer and writer on music; b. Göttingen, Oct. 12, 1882; d. Munich, Aug. 13, 1954. He was a pupil of M. J. Erb in Strasbourg and of Ludwig Thuille in Munich, where he settled. In 1917 he established there a seminar for operatic dramaturgy; prof. and assistant director at the Akademie der Tonkunst (1920-23); then director (1923-33). After 1933 he remained in Munich as private teacher; in 1948 established a seminar for all musical subjects in Munich. In his own music he adopted a neo-Romantic style, rather advanced in harmonic treatment. His most successful work was the opera *Oberst Chabert,* to his own libretto after Balzac (Frankfurt, Jan. 18, 1912; also several productions in other German cities). Other operas are *Else Klapperzehen* (Dresden, May 15, 1909), *Richardis,* a dramatic mystery (Karlsruhe, Nov.14, 1915), *Die Rauensteiner Hochzeit* (Karlsruhe, 1919), *Die Gräfin von Tolosa* (1934). He further wrote an *Apokalyptische Symphonie* (1924), the symph. poem, *Hero und Leander* (1925), *Krippenmusik* for chamber orch. with harpsichord (1926), an orchestral partita (1928), piano pieces, and songs. Having lost his right arm in a childhood accident, he developed a piano technique for the left hand alone, and publ. studies and transcriptions for left hand which he performed in public. He also publ. a number of valuable writings on music: *Musikalische Stillehre in Einzeldarstellungen* (1920-23); *R. Strauss* (1921); *Musik, Dramaturgie, Erziehung* (1926); *Dirigenten-Erziehung* (1929); *Der stilistische Dualismus in der Musik des 19. Jahrhunderts,* in the 'Adler-Festschrift' (Vienna, 1930); *Die Kunst des Dirigierens* (1943; 2nd ed., 1954); also publ. a book of poetry (1952).

Walther, Johann Gottfried, noted German composer and musicographer; b. Erfurt, Sept. 18, 1684; d. Weimar, March 23, 1748. He was a pupil of J. Bernhard Bach at Erfurt, where he was appointed organist of the Thomaskirche in 1702; in 1707, town organist at Weimar, and music master to the children of the ducal family; from 1720, court musician. He stands next to Bach as a master of chorale-variations for organ. His greatest work is the *Musikalisches Lexikon oder Musikalische Bibliothek,* the first music encyclopedia of biography, bibliography, and terms (Leipzig, 1732; facsimile ed., Kassel, 1953, by R. Schaal, with bibliographical notes); he had previously publ. the 64-page *Alte und neue musikalische Bibliothek, oder Musikalisches Lexikon* (1728; only entries under letter A printed, as a preliminary to the main work). His published musical compositions include: *Clavierconcert* (unaccompanied; 1741); Prelude and Fugue (1741); 4 chorale-variations *(Jesu meine Freude, Meinen Jesum lass' ich nicht, Allein Gott in der Höh' sei Ehr', Wie soll ich dich empfangen)*; many chorale-variations, preludes, fugues and toccatas, in MS; also 5 collections of 'Choralbearbeitungen' by other composers. His organ works were ed. by M. Seiffert in vols. 26 and 27 of 'Denkmäler deutscher Tonkunst' (with a biographical sketch). His *Praecepta der musikalischen Composition* was publ. at Leipzig, 1955, ed. by Peter Benary. —Cf. H.

Gehrmann, *J. G. Walther als Theoretiker,* in 'Vierteljahrsschrift für Musikwissenschaft' (1891); G. Schünemann, *J. G. Walther und H. Bokemeyer,* in 'Bach-Jahrbuch' (1933); O. Brodde, *J. G. Walther. Leben und Werk* (1937).

Walther, Johann Jakob, notable German violinist and composer; b. Witterda, near Erfurt, 1650; date and place of death unknown. He was concertmaster at the Electoral Court of Saxony in Dresden (from 1674), and Italian secretary, in charge of the correspondence with Rome, to the Elector of Mainz (from 1688); in 1693 he was designated as *Doctor.* He publ. *Scherzi da violino solo* with continuo (1676; reprinted in 'Das Erbe deutscher Musik' vol. 17); *Hortulus Chelicus, uni violino, duabus, tribus et quatuor subinde chordis simul sonantibus . . .* (1688; 2nd ed. as *Wohlgepflanzter Violinischer Lustgarten,* 1694). Reprints are found in A. Schering's 'Geschichte der Musik in Beispielen' (No. 239) and in 'Alte Meister' (No. 10); several violin sonatas ed. by G. Beckmann (1921). —Cf. J. W. von Wasielewski, *Die Violine und ihre Meister* (7th ed., 1927); G. Beckmann, *Das Violinspiel in Deutschland vor 1700* (1918); A. Moser, *Geschichte des Violinspiels* (1923).

Walther von der Vogelweide. See **Vogelweide.**

Walthew, Richard Henry, English composer and pedagogue; b. London, Nov. 4, 1872; d. East Preston, Sussex, Nov. 14, 1951. He studied with Parry at the Royal College of Music (1890-94); after a directorship of the Passmore Edwards Settlement Place (1900-04), he was appointed instructor of the opera class at the Guildhall School of Music; in 1907, became prof. of music at Queen's College; also conducted provincial orchestras. His works include two operettas: *The Enchanted Island* (London, May 8, 1900) and *The Gardeners* (London, Feb. 12, 1906); the cantatas: *Ode to a Nightingale* and *The Pied Piper of Hamelin;* a piano concerto; a piano quintet; a piano quartet; two piano trios; a violin sonata; vocal quartets with piano; songs. Author of *The Development of Chamber Music* (1909). —Cf. 'Cobbett's Cyclopedic Survey of Chamber Music' (London, 1930; vol. II, p. 566); K. H. Leech, *R. H. Walthew,* in 'Mus. Opinion' (Jan., 1952).

Walton, Sir **William (Turner),** eminent English composer; b. Oldham, Lancashire, March 29, 1902. He received his early education from his father, a music teacher; was sent to the Christ Church Cathedral Choir School at Oxford at the age of 10, and at 16 entered Christ Church College; studied under Sir Hugh Allen at Oxford, and also received advice from E. J. Dent, Busoni, and Ansermet. At the age of 17 he wrote a piano quartet. On June 12, 1923, his amusing and original work, *Façade,* for speaking voice and instruments, to poems by Edith Sitwell, created something of a sensation in London. However, the somewhat impish wit displayed in *Façade* is but one aspect of Walton's creative personality; in his later works, there is evident a deep emotional strain, a fine eloquence, and a definitely English melodic style; the sense of tonality is strong in the modern harmonic structure; and the formal design is invariably clear. Walton's temperament lends itself to great versatility; he is successful both in lighter music, as exemplified by his overtures *Portsmouth Point* and *Scapino,* and compositions of an epical character, such as the oratorio *Belshazzar's Feast.* His symphonic works show him as an inheritor of the grand Romantic tradition; his viola concerto and his violin concerto demonstrate his adroitness in modern instrumental writing. He wrote his 1st opera, *Troilus and Cressida,* at the age of 52. He was knighted in 1951. —Works: opera, *Troilus and Cressida* (London, Dec. 3, 1954); ballet, *The Quest* (1943); *Façade,* an 'entertainment' for declamation, flute, clarinet, saxophone, trumpet, cello, and percussion (London, June 12, 1923; revised in 1942, with an augmented orch.). For orch.: *Portsmouth Point,* overture (Zürich Festival of the International Society for Contemporary Music, June 22, 1926); *Siesta* (1926); *Sinfonia concertante* for piano and orch. (London, Jan. 5, 1928); viola concerto (London, Oct. 3, 1929); symph. No. 1 (London, Nov. 6, 1935); *Crown Imperial,* coronation march for George VI (1937); violin concerto (Cleveland, Dec. 7, 1939, Jascha Heifetz soloist); *Orb and Sceptre,* coronation march for Elizabeth II (1953); *Johannesburg Festival Overture* (Johannesburg, South Africa, Sept. 25, 1956); cello concerto (Boston, Piatigorsky soloist, Jan. 25, 1957); *Partita* (Cleveland, Jan. 30, 1958); 2 orchestral suites from *Façade* (also used as ballet scores): No. 1 (Siena Festival of the International Society for Contemporary Music, Sept. 14, 1928); No. 2 (N. Y., March 30, 1938). Vocal works: *Belshazzar's Feast,* oratorio for baritone, chorus, and orch. (Leeds Festival, Oct. 10, 1931); *In Honour of the City of London,* for chorus and orch. (Leeds Festival, 1937); *Te Deum* for the coronation of Queen Elizabeth II (London, June 2, 1953). Chamber music: string quartet (1918-19; Salzburg Festival of the International Society for Contemporary Music, Aug. 4, 1923); Toccata for violin and piano (1923); string quartet in A minor (1947); violin sonata (1949); also piano pieces; transcriptions for orch. of 6 pieces by Bach, arranged as a ballet suite under the title *The Wise Virgins* (1940); film music: *Escape Me Never* (1934), *As You Like It* (1936), *Stolen Life* (1939), *Major Barbara* (1941), *Henry V* (1944), *Hamlet* (1947), *Richard III* (1954), etc.; several suites have been drawn from these scores. —Cf. H. J. Foss, *William Walton,* in the 'Mus. Quarterly' (Oct., 1940); F. S. Howes, *The Music of William Walton,* 2 vols. (London, 1942 and 1943; 'Mus. Pilgrim' series); E. Evans, *William Walton,* in the 'Mus. Times' (1944); K. Avery, *William Walton,* in 'Music & Letters' (Jan., 1947).

Waltz, Gustavus, German bass; place and date of birth unknown; d. London about 1753; was in Handel's household in London. He appeared on the London stage in 1732 in Handel's *Acis and Galatea* and subsequently sang in Handel's oratorios. He is chiefly celebrated because of the reported acrid comment of Handel on Gluck: 'He knows no more of counterpoint than my cook Waltz.' —Cf. W. C. Smith, *Gustavus Waltz: Was He Handel's Cook?,* in *Concerning Handel* (London, 1948).

Wambach, Emile, composer; b. Arlon, Luxembourg, Nov. 26, 1854; d. Antwerp, May 6, 1924. He was a pupil of Benoit, Mertens, and Callaerts at the Antwerp Cons. In 1902 he was appointed inspector of the music schools in Belgium; in 1913 succeeded Jan Blockx as director of the Royal Flemish Cons. in Antwerp. His works include the Flemish opera *Nathans Parabel;* 2 oratorios, *Moses op den Nijl* and *Yolande;* cantata *Vlaanderland (Flanders)* for male chorus; *De Lente (Spring)* for female chorus with orch.; a symph. poem, *Aan de boorden van de Schelde (On the Banks of the Schelde);* sacred works; piano pieces; songs. —Cf. L. Vocht, *Levensbericht over E. Wambach,* in the 'Annuaire' of the Académie Royale de Belgique (vol. 118; 1952; with a list of works).

Wangemann (văhn'-gĕh-măhn), **Otto,** German music scholar; b. Loitz-on-the-Peene, Jan. 9, 1848; d. Berlin, Feb. 25, 1914. He studied with F. Kiel in Berlin; in 1886, settled there as church organist and singing teacher. He publ. *Grundriss der Musik-Geschichte* (1878); *Geschichte der Orgel* (1879; 3rd ed., 1887); *Geschichte des Oratoriums* (1880); also singing manuals for schools; a *Weihnachtsmusik* for solo voices, chorus, and orch.; school songs; piano pieces.

Wanhal (Vanhall), Johann Baptist, Bohemian composer; b. Nechanicz, Bohemia, May 12, 1739; d. Vienna, Aug. 26, 1813. His musical ability brought him the patronage of Countess Schaffgotsch, who enabled him to study in Vienna with Dittersdorf; another patron, Baron Riesch, sent him to Italy for further study. He settled in Vienna. An extremely prolific composer, he wrote a great number of piano pieces, which enjoyed considerable popularity among amateurs. He also composed an enormous amount of instrumental music (some 100 symphonies and as many string quartets); 26 Masses; 2 Requiems; 36 offertories. Among his published works are 12 symphonies for strings, 2 oboes, and 2 horns; 12 string quartets; 12 trios for 2 violins and cello; quartets (concerti) for piano and strings; quartets for piano, flute, violin, and cello; piano trios; 5 piano sonatas for 4 hands, and 6 for 2 hands; violin duos; 6 violin sonatas with piano; characteristic sonatas *(Militaire, The Battle of Würzburg, The Battle of Trafalgar)*; many piano sonatinas; 70 books of piano variations; fantasias, dances, and other piano pieces, fugues, preludes, etc., for organ; etc. —Cf. M. von Dewitz, *J. B. Vanhall, Leben und Klavierwerke* (dissertation; Munich, 1933); G. Wolters, *J. Wanhal als Sinfoniker* (dissertation; Cologne, 1933).

Wanless, John, English organist and composer; flourished early in the 17th century. He was organist at the Lincoln Cathedral between 1616 and 1625; only a few of his church works are extant, among them an anthem *Plead thou my cause.* His son, **Thomas Wanless** (d. 1721), was organist of York Minster from 1691 till 1695. He publ. a psalter, *The Metre Psalm-tunes* in 4 parts (London, 1702); composed a *York Litany.*

Wannenmacher (Latinized as **Vannius**), **Johannes,** German composer; b. Neuenburg on the Rhine; d. Interlaken, 1551. He was cantor at Bern, Switzerland, in 1510, and at Freiburg-im-Breisgau in 1514; because of his inclinations toward Lutheranism, he was obliged to leave Germany; settled in Interlaken in 1531 as town clerk, and remained there until his death. He was greatly esteemed in his time as a fine polyphonist; Glareanus cites a motet for 4 voices in the *Dodecachordon*. Wannenmacher's *An Wasserflüssen Babylon* for 3-6 voices was publ. in Ott's *Liederbuch* (1544); some German songs by him were publ. posthumously (Bern, 1553). —Cf. A. Geering, *Die Vokalmusik in der Schweiz zur Zeit der Reformation: Leben und Werke von Bartholomäus Frank, Johannes Wannenmacher, Cosmas Alder* (Aarau, 1933).

Warburg, Felix Moritz, patron of music; b. Hamburg, Jan. 14, 1871; d. New York, Oct. 20, 1937. He came to the U.S. in 1894, and became associated with the banking firm of Kuhn, Loeb & Co.; U.S. citizen, 1900. He participated in many musical activities as sponsor; was a member of the board of the Institute of Musical Art and (in the last two years of his life) of the Metropolitan Opera. He owned a quartet of Stradivarius instruments, and sponsored the concerts of the Stradivarius String Quartet.

Ward, Frank Edwin, American organist and composer; b. Wysox, Pa., Oct. 7, 1872; d. Wolfburo, N. H., Sept. 15, 1953. He studied at the N.Y. College of Music with J. P. Lawrence (organ) and S. A. Pearce (theory); was a student of MacDowell at Columbia Univ. (1898-1903); later became associate prof. of music there (1909-19); for 40 years (1906-46) was organist and choirmaster at the Church of the Holy Trinity, N.Y. His works include a Lenten cantata, *The Saviour of the World;* a Christmas cantata, *The Divine Birth; Ocean Rhapsody* for orch.; services; anthems; organ pieces; part-songs; also 2 string quartets and other chamber music.

Ward, John, English composer; place and date of birth unknown; d. before 1641. He was in the service of Sir Henry Fanshawe (d. 1616), to whom he dedicated *The First Set of English Madrigals to 3. 4. 5. and 6. parts apt both for Viols and Voyces. With a Mourning Song in memory of Prince Henry* (London, 1613). As a composer he is especially notable for his madrigals for 5 and 6 voices; he also wrote services and anthems; fancies for 4, 5, and 6 viols; and pieces for the virginals. His madrigals were reprinted in vol. XIX of 'The English Madrigal School.' —Cf. E. H. Fellowes, *The English Madrigal Composers* (1921).

Ward, John Milton, American musicologist; b. Oakland, Calif., July 6, 1917. He studied at the Univ. of Washington (M.M., 1942); New York Univ. (Ph. D., 1953, with the dissertation *The Vihuela de Mano and Its Music* [*1536-76*]); held the following teaching positions: instructor, Dept. of Literature and Fine Arts, Michigan State Univ. (1947-53); assistant (later associate) prof., Univ. of Illinois (1953-55); 1955, appointed associate prof., Harvard Univ.; 1958, prof. He publ. *The Dublin Virginal MS* (Wellesley, Mass., 1954); also *The Editorial Methods of Venegas de Henestrosa,* in 'Musica Disciplina' (1952); *Les Sources de la musique pour le clavier en Angleterre,* in 'La Musique instrumentale de la Renaissance' (Paris, 1955); and other articles in various publications.

Ward, Robert, American composer; b. Cleveland, Sept. 13, 1917. He studied at the Eastman School of Music, Rochester, N.Y., with Howard Hanson and Bernard Rogers, and at the Juilliard School, N. Y., with Frederick Jacobi (composition) and Albert Stoessel (conducting); also took a course with Aaron Copland at the Berkshire Music Center. He graduated from the Army Music School at Fort Meyer, Va.; composed the musical score for the Army revue, *The Life of Riley,* produced at Fort Riley; was bandleader of the 7th Infantry Division Band in the Pacific Theater. After the war, he graduated from the Juilliard School (1946); then taught there, and elsewhere in N. Y. He held Guggenheim Fellowships in 1949 and 1951. In 1955 he became president of the American Composers Alliance; in 1956 he was appointed managing editor of the Galaxy Music Corporation and Highgate Press. —Works: *Fatal Interview* for soprano and orch. (1937); *Ode* for orch. (1939); *Yankee Overture* (1940); symph. No. 1 (N. Y., May 10, 1941); *Adagio and Allegro* for orch. (1943); *Jubilation Overture* (Los Angeles, Nov. 21, 1946); symph. No. 2 (Washington, Jan. 25, 1948); *Concert Music* for orch. (1948); *Night Music,* for chamber orch. (1949); *Jonathon and the Gingery Snare,* for narrator, small orch., and percussion (Young People's Concert, N.Y. Philharmonic, Feb. 4, 1950); symph. No. 3 (Washington, March 31, 1950); *Fantasia* for brass choir and timpani (1953); *Euphony* for orch. (1954); *Pantaloon,* opera after Leonid Andreyev's play, *He Who Gets Slapped* (Juilliard School of Music, N. Y., May 17, 1956); chamber music: violin sonata (1950) and *Arioso and Tarantella,* for cello and piano (1954); choruses; piano pieces; songs. —Cf. 'American Composers Alliance Bulletin' (1955, No. 4).

Ware, Harriet, American pianist and composer; b. Waupun, Wis., Aug. 26, 1877. She received her musical instruction from her father, who was a professional musician and choral conductor; she then studied piano with Dr. William Mason in N.Y. and with Sigismund Stojowski in Paris; composition with Hugo Kaun in Berlin; in 1906 she returned to the United States. Her *Women's Triumphal March* was made the national song of the Federation of Women's Clubs in 1927; her symph. poem *The Artisan* was given by the N.Y. Symph. Orch. in 1929. Some of her songs *(Boat Song, Joy of the Morning, The Call of Radha, Stars, Sunlight Waltz Song,* etc.) have achieved considerable popularity. She also wrote the choral cycles, *Trees* and *Undine;* an operetta, *Waltz For Three;* piano pieces *(Mountain Pictures, Midnight Waltz,* etc.).

Wareing, Herbert Walter, English composer; b. Birmingham, April 5, 1857; d. Malvern, March 29, 1918. He studied at the Leipzig Cons. with Reinecke, Jadassohn, and Papperitz; upon his return to England he filled various positions as organist; in 1909 became prof. of piano at Malvern College, where he remained until his death. He wrote several operettas for children: *Princess Snowflake, The Court of Queen Summergold, A Garden of Japan, A Day in Roseland;* cantatas, *The Wreck of the Hesperus, The Angel Reapers, The Nativity, The Good Shepherd, New Year's Eve;* numerous choruses and solo songs; church services; piano pieces.

Warlich (văhr'-lih), **Reinhold von,** baritone; b. St. Petersburg, May 24, 1877; d. New York, Nov. 10, 1939. His father, a German musician resident in Russia, was an opera conductor in St. Petersburg, and Warlich received his training at home; then studied at the Hamburg Cons., in Florence, and in Cologne. He toured in Europe as a singer of German lieder, and was especially distinguished as an interpreter of Schubert, whose song cycles he gave in their entirety. He lived for some time in Canada; later was singing teacher in Paris and London; made concert tours in the U.S. from 1909, eventually settling in N.Y.

Warlock, Peter. See **Heseltine.**

Warnecke (văhr'-nĕh-kĕh), **(Johann Heinrich) Friedrich,** German double-bass player and pedagogue; b. Bodenteich, Nov. 19, 1856; d. Hamburg, March 1, 1931. He studied with Bontemps in Ülzen and with Walther in Hanover; was a member of various military bands (1874-89); then settled in Hamburg; from 1893 to 1924 he was a member of the Hamburg Philharmonic and prof. at the Hamburg Cons. He publ. *Das Studium des Kontrabass-Spiels* (2 parts; with German and English text); piano pieces and songs. Author of *'Ad infinitum.' Der Kontrabass, seine Geschichte und seine Zukunft. Probleme und deren Lösung zur Hebung des Kontrabass-Spiels* (1909) and *Der Kontrabass* (1929).

Warner, Harry Waldo, English viola player and composer; b. Northampton, Jan. 4, 1874; d. London, June 1, 1945. He studied violin with Alfred Gibson and theory with R. Orlando Morgan at the Guildhall School of Music; subsequently taught there (until 1920); while still a student, he wrote an opera, *The Royal Vagrants* (1900), which was performed by the opera class. When the London String Quartet was founded in 1907, he joined it as viola player, remaining with it until 1928. His chamber music received several prizes, including the $1000 E. S. Coolidge prize for a piano trio (1921) and a Cobbett prize for an earlier piano trio. His other works comprise 2 Phantasy Quartets (1906 and 1913); a *Folk-Song Phantasy* for string quartet (1917), *The Pixy Ring* for string quartet (1921); *3 Elfin Dances* (1905) for orch.; *Hampton Wick,* a tone picture for orch. (awarded $1000 in the Hollywood Bowl Competition, 1932; 1st performance, Cincinnati Symph. Orch., Nov. 30, 1934); *Suite in the Olden Style,* for string orch. (originally for string quartet; London, Sept. 22, 1928); piano pieces; many songs. —Cf. 'Cobbett's Cyclopedic Survey of Chamber Music' (London, 1930; vol. II, pp. 567-69).

Warner, Sylvia Townsend, English novelist and writer on music; b. London, Dec. 6, 1893. Apart from her well-known novels and books of poetry, she publ. valuable papers on music history; author of *The Point of Perfection in 16th Century Notation* (1919); was one of the editors of the collection 'Tudor Church Music.' She also composed a rhapsody for voice and string quartet, *Memorial;* a song cycle, *Children of the Earth;* etc.

Warnots, Henri, Belgian tenor and composer; b. Brussels, July 11, 1832; d. Saint-Josse-ten-Noode, Feb. 27, 1893. He studied at the Brussels Cons.; then sang in Paris and Strasbourg. In 1867, he became prof. at the Brussels Cons.; in 1870, established a music school in Saint-Josse-ten-Noode, where he remained until his death. His operetta, *Une Heure de mariage,* was produced in Strasbourg on Jan. 24, 1865.

Warren, Elinor Remick, American pianist and composer of songs; b. Los Angeles, Feb. 23, 1905. She was educated at the Westlake School for Girls, and at Mills College; publ. her first compositions while still in high school; later studied in N. Y. with Frank La Forge, Paolo Gallico, and Clarence Dickinson; appeared as pianist. —Works: *The Harp Weaver,* for women's chorus, baritone, harp, and orch.; *The Passing of King Arthur* for orch.; *Singing Earth,* song cycle for voice and piano (or orch.); many songs (*White Horses of the Sea, Children of the Moon, My Lady Lo Fu, We Two, Christmas Candle,* etc.).

Warren, George William, American organist and composer of sacred music; b. Albany, N.Y., Aug. 17, 1828; d. New York, March 17, 1902. He held positions as church organist in Albany (1846-60), in Brooklyn (1860-70), and at St. Thomas', N.Y. (from 1870 until his death). He publ. 'Warren's Hymns and Tunes, as Sung at St. Thomas's Church' (1888). He is remembered chiefly for his tune, *National Hymn,* to which *God of Our Fathers* is sung.

Warren, Leonard, American baritone; b. New York, April 21, 1911. The original family name was Varenov; it was Americanized as Warren when his father came from Russia to the U.S. His father was in the fur business in N.Y., and Leonard Warren helped him, while studying at the Greenwich House Music School. He won an audition with the Metropolitan Opera in 1938 and was granted a stipend to study in Milan. Returning to America, he made his début at the Metropolitan Opera on Jan. 13, 1939 as Paolo in *Simon Boccanegra.* He quickly advanced in the favor of the public; sang baritone roles in Verdi's operas with excellent success; also toured in South America and Canada. He appeared at La Scala, Milan, in 1953 as Rigoletto (one of his best roles). In the spring of 1958 he made a successful tour in Russia.

Warren, Richard Henry, American organist and composer; son of G. W. Warren; b. Albany, N.Y. Sept. 17, 1859; d. South Chatham, Mass., Dec. 3, 1933. He was organist and choirmaster in various churches in N.Y.; founded (1886) the Church Choral Society, which he conducted until 1895 and again from 1903 to 1907, producing many important works, including the American premières of choral compositions by Dvořák, Liszt, Gounod, Saint-Saëns, etc. Horatio Parker wrote his *Hora Novissima* for this society, and Warren brought it out on May 3, 1893. Among Warren's own compositions are the operettas *Igala* (1880), *All on a Summer's Day* (1882), *Magnolia* (1886), *The Rightful Heir* (1899); a 'romantic opera,' *Phyllis* (N.Y., May 7, 1900); a cantata, *Ticonderoga* (1894); services; anthems; songs.

Warren, Samuel Prowse, organist; b. Montreal, Feb. 18, 1841; d. New York, Oct. 7, 1915. He studied organ with Haupt in Berlin, piano with Gustav Schumann, and theory with Wieprecht. After filling various positions in N.Y. churches, he inaugurated a series of organ recitals, which were greatly appreciated, and created for him a reputation as one of the foremost concert organists in the U.S. He publ. many organ pieces and songs; also made excellent transcriptions for organ of works by Weber, Beethoven, Schumann, and Wagner.

Wartel (văhr-těhl'), **Pierre-François,** noted French singer and teacher; b. Versailles, April 3, 1806; d. Paris, Aug. 3, 1882. He studied at the Paris Cons. with Nourrit; was engaged as tenor at the Paris Opéra (1831-46), but became known chiefly as an experienced singing teacher; Christine Nilsson was one of his many famous pupils. He also gave song recitals, in which he performed songs by Schubert for the first time in France. His wife, **Atale Thérèse Annette Wartel** (*née* Adrien; b. Paris, July 2, 1814; d. there, Nov. 6, 1865), was a talented pianist; she also composed piano studies and other pieces.

Wasielewski (văh-sē-lěhf'-skē), **Wilhelm Joseph von,** eminent German music scholar; b. Gross-Leesen, near Danzig, June 17, 1822; d. Sondershausen, Dec. 13, 1896. He studied violin as a private pupil of Ferdinand David in Leipzig, and also had lessons with Mendelssohn (1843-45). He joined the Gewandhaus Orch. (until 1850); went to Düsseldorf, where he was concertmaster under Schumann (1850-52); then was choral conductor in Bonn (1852-55); in 1855 he settled in Dresden as a writer, in which capacity he greatly distinguished himself. He was music critic for the 'Signale' and wrote for the 'Leipziger Zeitung' and the 'Dresdner Journal'; in 1869 he became town music director in Bonn, remaining in that position until

1884, when he went to Sondershausen. —Writings: *Robert Schumann* (1858; 4th ed., 1906; English transl., 1871), with important supplementary matter in *Schumanniana* (1883); *Die Violine und ihre Meister* (1869; 2nd augmented ed., 1883; 7th ed., 1927); *Die Violine im 17. Jahrhundert und die Anfänge der Instrumentalkomposition* (1874; 2nd ed., 1905); *Geschichte der Instrumentalmusik im 16. Jahrhundert* (1878); *Beethoven* (1888; 2 vols.); *Das Violoncell und seine Geschichte* (1889; 3rd ed. by his son Waldemar, 1925; in English, 1894); *Carl Reinecke, sein Leben, Wirken und Schaffen* (Leipzig, 1892); and *Aus 70 Jahren,* memoirs (Stuttgart, 1897). To Waldersee's 'Sammlung musikalischer Vorträge' he contributed *Musikalische Fürsten vom Mittelalter bis zum Beginne des 19. Jahrhunderts* (1879) and *Goethes Verhältniss zur Musik* (1880).

Wassermann, Heinrich Joseph, German conductor and composer; b. Schwarzbach, near Fulda, April 3, 1791; d. Riehen, near Basel, Sept. 3, 1838. He was a pupil of Spohr; became an orchestral conductor in Switzerland. He wrote a *Thème original varié* for string quartet; a quartet for flute, violin, viola, and cello; *Air varié* for bassoon and string orch.; *Divertissement* (on the Tyrolian 'Alma-Lied') for violin and orch.; a number of orchestral dances; pieces for guitar.

Waters, Edward N(eighbor), American musicologist; b. Leavenworth, Kansas, July 23, 1906. He studied piano and theory at the Eastman School of Music (B.M., 1927); M.M. in musicology, 1928. In 1931 he joined the staff of the Music Division, Library of Congress, Washington, D. C., becoming assistant chief; president of the Music Library Association (1941-46); was program annotator for the concerts of the National Symph. Orch., Washington (1934-43); 1937-38, taught bibliography at the Catholic Univ. of Washington; contributed valuable papers to various musical periodicals; publ. a definitive biography of Victor Herbert (N. Y., 1955).

Watson, Henry, English composer; b. Burnley, Lancashire, April 30, 1846; d. Salford, Jan. 8, 1911. He studied with private teachers; then was organist in various churches. In 1867 he founded (with Henry Wilson) the Manchester Vocal Union, becoming its conductor in 1885 (after Wilson's death); also taught the choral class at the Royal College of Music, Manchester. In 1899 he presented his valuable library (some 30,000 vols.) to the Corporation of Manchester. He composed an opera, *Fair Rosine* (Manchester, 1882); *A Shakespearian Cantata; The Deliverance of Israel,* oratorio for solo voices, chorus, and orch.; many part-songs. See the article on him in the 'Mus. Times'(June, 1909).

Watson, William Michael, English composer and poet; b. Newcastle-on-Tyne, July 31, 1840; d. London, Oct. 3, 1889. He established the West End School of Music in London in 1883; composed a cantata, *Aladdin* (1885), part-songs, piano pieces, etc.

Watts, Wintter, American composer; b. Cincinnati, March 14, 1884. He studied at the Institute of Musical Art, N.Y.; in 1919 received the Morris Loeb Prize of $1000 for his symph. poem *Young Blood;* won the Pulitzer Prize in 1923, and the Prix de Rome, which enabled him to study at the American Academy in Rome (1923-25). He lived for some time in Europe, returning to N.Y. in 1931. Among his larger works are a *Bridal Overture* (1916), an orchestral suite, *Etchings* (1921), etc., but he is chiefly known as a composer of fine songs: *Wings of Night, Joy, With the Tide, Wild Tears, Alone;* a cycle of 9 songs to poems by Sara Teasdale, *Vignettes of Italy;* etc. —Cf. W. T. Upton, *Art-Song in America* (N.Y., 1930; pp. 182-97).

Waxman, Franz, composer; b. Königshütte, Germany, Dec. 24, 1906. He studied in Dresden and Berlin; went to the U.S. in 1934, and settled in Hollywood, where he took lessons with Arnold Schoenberg; became a successful composer for films; his musical score for *Sunset Boulevard* won the Academy Award for 1950; other works include a Sinfonietta for string orch. and timpani (1955); a fantasy on *Carmen* for violin and orch.; etc.

Weaver, Powell, American pianist and composer, b. Clearfield, Pa., June 10, 1890; d. Kansas City, Dec. 22, 1951. He studied organ with Pietro Yon in N.Y., and composition with Respighi in Rome. Returning to the U.S., he was engaged as accompanist to prominent singers; also gave organ recitals. —Works: for orch.: *Plantation Overture* (1925), *The Little Faun* (1925; Boston Women's Symph. Orch., April 14, 1929), *The Vagabond,* symph. poem (Minneapolis, March 6, 1931), *Dance of the Sand-Dune Cranes,* for piano and orch. (1941); choral works: *Boating Song, Spirit* *of God, Moon-Marketing, The Humming-Bird,* also a *Sabbath Evening Service* (Hebrew); chamber music: *An Ode,* for piano and strings, a violin sonata, etc.

Webb, Daniel, English writer on music; b. Taunton, 1735; d. Bath, Aug. 2, 1815. He publ. the important paper, *Observations on the Correspondence between Poetry and Music* (London, 1769; reprinted in his 'Miscellanies,' 1803).

Webb, Frank Rush, American organist and bandmaster; b. Covington, Ind., Oct. 8, 1851; d. Baltimore, Oct. 20, 1934. He studied at the New England Cons. in Boston; then was church organist in Indianapolis and piano teacher in Ohio; from 1883 to 1910, he was director of the School of Music in the Virginia Female Institute, Staunton, Va.; from 1883 to 1892, bandmaster of the Stonewall Brigade Band. He publ. nearly 200 pieces for military band; also much salon music for piano, aggregating to 108 op. numbers; church music; songs.

Webb, George James, organist and magazine editor; b. Rushmore Lodge, near Salisbury, England, June 24, 1803; d. Orange, N. J., Oct. 7, 1887. He settled in Boston in 1830, becoming organist of the Old South Church, a founder of the Boston Academy of Music in 1836, and president of the Handel and Haydn Society in 1840. In 1870 he settled in Orange, N. J., but continued musical activities in N. Y. as teacher. He edited two periodicals: 'The Musical Library' (1835-36), with L. Mason; and 'The Musical Cabinet' (1841-42), with T. B. Hayward; also brought out the 'Young Ladies' Vocal Class Book' (Boston, 1853); 'The Glee Hive' and 'The New Odeon' (both with L. Mason); and 'Cantica laudis' (N. Y., 1850; also with Mason); publ. *Vocal Technics* and *Voice Culture* (with C. G. Allen). His hymn tune, known simply as *Webb,* retains its popularity.

Webbe, Samuel, famous English composer of catches and glees; b. London, 1740; d. there, May 25, 1816. He began his career as a copyist for the London publisher Welcker, who enabled him to study music with the organist Barbandt; was appointed organist and choirmaster at the Chapel of the Portuguese Embassy in 1776, and later obtained a similar appointment at the Sardinian Embassy (holding both positions concurrently); from 1784 until his death he was secretary of the Catch Club, also librarian of the Glee Club (from 1787). In 1766, his canon *O that I had wings* won the prize of the Catch Club, and subsequently he carried off 26 other prizes with various catches and glees. Publ. 9 vols. of catches and glees (reprinted later with 3 additional vols.), a *Cecilian Ode* for 6 voices, a concerto for harpsichord, a *Divertissement* for wind band, and several collections of Masses and motets.

Webbe, Samuel, Jr., English composer, son of the preceding; b. London, 1770; d. there, Nov. 25, 1843. He was a pupil of his father, and also received instruction from Clementi. He wrote many glees and catches, obtaining several prizes from the Catch Club; also produced his musical comedy, *The Speechless Wife* (Covent Garden, May 22, 1794). He lived in Liverpool from 1798 until 1817; returned to London, where he taught at Logier's School of Music and served as organist at the Spanish Embassy. Besides glees, duets, hymn-tunes, organ voluntaries, sonatas for harpsichord, etc., he wrote *L'Amico del principiante* (28 short solfeggi) and *Harmony Epitomised, or Elements of the Thorough-bass;* also ed. 'Convito Armonico' (4 vols.; a collection of madrigals, glees, catches, canons, etc., by prominent composers).

Webber, Amherst, English composer; b. Cannes, France, Oct. 25, 1867; d. London, July 25, 1946. He studied in Oxford, Dresden, and Paris. His first professional occupation was that of an opera coach at Covent Garden in London and at the Metropolitan Opera in New York. He wrote a short comic opera *Fiorella* (London, June 7, 1905), and many songs to French and English words. His symphony had several performances in Europe and America.

Weber, Alain, French composer; b. Château-Thierry, Dec. 8, 1930; studied with Tony Aubin at the Paris Cons.; won 2nd prize in composition; in 1952 received the Premier Grand Prix de Rome. In his works he emulates Ravel and Honegger. He has written a ballet, *Le petit jeu* (Paris, 1953); concertino for flute and orch.; string quintet and many miniatures for various instruments.

Weber, Ben, American composer; b. St. Louis, July 23, 1916. He studied medicine at the Univ. of Illinois; then music at De Paul Univ.; held a Guggenheim Fellowship twice. From his early steps in composition he adopted an atonal melodic style and a highly coloristic harmonic idiom, while adhering to basic forms and shunning representational music. Works: ballet, *The Pool of Darkness,* for flute, violin, trumpet, bassoon, cello, and piano (1949); *Sinfonia* for cello and orch. (also cello and piano); *Symphony on Poems of William Blake* (N. Y., Oct. 28, 1952); violin concerto (1954); *Prelude and Passacaglia* for orch. (Louisville, Feb. 19, 1955); 2 pieces for string orch.; chamber music: *Pastorale and Scherzo* for woodwind instruments, fantasy for violin and piano, 2 violin sonatas, *Lyric Piece* for string quartet, *Pastorale* for violin and piano, *Variations* for violin, clarinet, cello, and piano, concertino for violin, clarinet, and cello, 5 pieces for cello and piano, divertimento for 2 solo cellos, *Chorale and Variations* for viola and piano, *Sonata da Camera* for violin and piano, concerto for piano solo, cello, and woodwind quintet, *Colloquy* for brass septet, serenade for harpsichord, flute, oboe, and cello, ballade for cello and piano, *Aubade* for flute, cello, and harp, 2 string quartets, 2 violin sonatas, 2 string trios, 2 dances for cello and piano; *Closing Piece* for organ solo; songs; piano pieces. —Cf. 'Bulletin of American Composers Alliance' (1955, No. 2).

Weber, Bernhard Anselm, German pianist and composer; b. Mannheim, April 18, 1766; d. Berlin, March 23, 1821. He studied with Abbé Vogler and Holzbauer; also took courses in theology and law at the Univ. of Heidelberg; then traveled as performer on the Xänorphica, a keyboard instrument invented by Röllig. In 1787 he became music director of Grossmann's opera troupe; went to Stockholm in 1790; in 1792 was appointed conductor of the Königstadt Theater in Berlin, remaining in this capacity after its union with the Italian Opera. A great admirer of Gluck, he was the first to introduce Gluck's operas in Berlin, and his own works closely followed Gluck's style. He produced in Berlin 2 of his operas: *Mudarra* (March 10, 1800) and *Die Wette* (Jan. 21, 1805). Some of his songs were popular for a time. —Cf. H. Fischer, *B. A. Weber* (dissertation; Berlin, 1923).

Weber, Bernhard Christian, German organist and composer; b. Wolferschwenda, Dec. 1, 1712; d. Tennstedt, Feb. 5, 1758. He settled in Tennstedt as town organist in 1732. Inspired by Bach's example, and at the instigation of Bach's pupil G. H. Noah, Weber composed for organ a work containing 24 preludes and fugues in all keys, and entitled it *Das wohltemperierte Klavier* (new ed. by Max Seiffert in the 'Neue Bachgesellschaft,' 1933).

Weber (vā'-běhr), **Carl Maria (Friedrich Ernst),** Freiherr **von,** celebrated German composer; the founder of the German Romantic school; b. Eutin, Oldenburg, Nov. 18, 1786; d. London, June 5, 1826. His father, Franz Anton von Weber (1734-1812), was an army officer and a good musical amateur, who played the violin and served as town musician in Eutin. It was his fondest wish to see one of his children become a great musician; Constanze Weber, Mozart's wife, was his niece (so that Carl Maria was Mozart's first cousin by marriage), and Mozart was constantly the family's ideal to follow. Carl Maria's mother was a singer of some ability; she died when he was 12 years old. Franz Anton von Weber led a wandering life as musical director of a traveling theatrical troupe, and he took his family with him. Although this mode of life interfered with Weber's regular education, it gave him practical knowledge of the stage, and stimulated his imagination as a dramatic composer. Weber's first teacher was his stepbrother Fritz, a pupil of Haydn; at Hildburghausen, where he found himself with his father's company in 1796, he received piano instruction from J. P. Heuschkel. The next year he was in Salzburg, where he attracted the attention of Michael Haydn, who taught him counterpoint. As his peregrinations continued, he was taught singing by Valesi (J. B. Wallishauser), and composition by J. N. Kalcher, in Munich (1798-1800); by that time he had already publ. his first work, 6 fughettas for piano (1798). At the age of 13, he wrote an opera, *Die Macht der Liebe und des Weins;* it was never performed, and the MS is lost. He also appeared as a pianist. Through a meeting with Aloys Senefelder, the inventor of lithography, he became greatly interested in engraving; still a mere boy, he acquired considerable skill in the process, and even worked out some improvements; engraved his variations for piano, op. 2, himself, in 1800. His father, too, became interested in the business possibilities of lithography, and set up a workshop with him in Freiberg, Saxony; the venture did not succeed, and Carl Maria turned again to music; wrote a 2-act opera, *Das Waldmädchen,* which was produced in Freiberg 6 days after his 14th birthday, on Nov. 24, 1800; performances followed in Chemnitz (Dec. 5, 1800) and, 4 years later, in Vienna. In 1801 the family was once more in Salzburg, where

Weber studied further with Michael Haydn, and wrote another opera, *Peter Schmoll und seine Nachbarn;* after a stay in Hamburg (1802), they proceeded to Augsburg (1803) and finally to Vienna. There, Weber made a serious study of the works of the great masters under the guidance of Abbé Vogler, at whose recommendation he secured the post of conductor of the Breslau City Theater (1804); in 1806 he became Musik-Intendant to Duke Eugen of Württemberg at Schloss Carlsruhe in Silesia; in Sept. 1807 he was engaged as private secretary to Duke Ludwig at Stuttgart, and music master to his children. This employment was abruptly terminated when Weber became innocently involved in a scheme of securing a ducal appointment for a rich man's son in order to exempt him from military service, and accepted a loan of money; as a result of the disclosure of this affair, Weber was arrested and kept in prison for 2 weeks, after which he was expelled from Stuttgart. He went to Darmstadt, where he rejoined his old teacher Abbé Vogler, for whom he did some editorial and analytic work in publishing an edition of Bach's chorales. On Sept. 16, 1810, Weber's opera *Silvana* was successfully presented in Frankfurt; on June 4, 1811, he brought out in Munich a new opera, *Abu Hassan.* In the meantime, he appeared as pianist, giving concerts in Frankfurt, Würzburg, Nuremberg, Bamberg, Weimar, Gotha, and other German towns. In 1813 he received his first important appointment, that of conductor of the German Opera in Prague; there he presented a distinguished repertory, which included Beethoven's *Fidelio;* traveled to Vienna to engage a company of singers; among them was Caroline Brandt, his future wife. His reputation as music director and composer rose considerably, and the King of Saxony called him to Dresden to take charge of the German Opera Theater there. He opened his Dresden season on Jan. 30, 1817; became friendly with Friedrich Kind, a Dresden lawyer and writer, and suggested to him the idea of writing a libretto on a typically German subject. They agreed on *Der Freischütz,* a fairy tale from J. A. Apel's and F. Laun's collection of ghost stories, *Gespensterbuch.* The composition of this work, which was to prove his masterpiece, occupied him fully 3 years; the overture was finished in May 1820; interrupting his work, he wrote (in 3 weeks) several musical numbers to *Preciosa,* a play in 4 acts with spoken dialogue; it was produced in Berlin on March 14, 1821; another stage work, *Die drei Pintos,* which Weber started at about the same time, was left unfinished. Finally, *Der Freischütz* was completed, and accepted for performance at the new Berlin Opera Theater. There existed an undercurrent of rivalry with Spontini, director of the Berlin Opera and an almost absolute master of operatic policy in Berlin; the challenge was that of rising German nationalism against the Italian-French tradition. Weber conducted the première on June 18, 1821; the work's success surpassed all expectations; the cause of new Romantic art was won; *Der Freischütz* was soon staged by all the major opera houses of Europe. In English, it was given first in London, on July 22, 1824; translations into other languages followed. Weber's next opera was *Euryanthe,* produced in Vienna, on Oct. 25, 1823, with only moderate success. Meanwhile, Weber's health was affected by incipient tuberculosis, and he was compelled to go to Marienbad for a cure (1824). He recovered sufficiently to begin the composition of *Oberon,* commissioned from him by Covent Garden, London; the English libretto was by J. R. Planché, based on a translation of C. M. Wieland's *Oberon.* Once more, illness interrupted Weber's progress on his work; he spent some time in Ems to recuperate, and then embarked on the voyage to England, early in 1826. He rehearsed the opera thoroughly, and conducted the première at Covent Garden on April 12, 1826, obtaining tremendous success with the London audience. Despite his greatly weakened condition, he conducted eleven more performances of *Oberon,* and participated also in various London concerts, playing for the last time a week before his death. He was buried in London; his remains were removed to Dresden on Dec. 15, 1844; on that occasion Richard Wagner delivered an oration and conducted a funeral march on motifs from *Euryanthe,* as well as a funeral ode for double chorus expressly written for the service. Weber's role in music history is epoch-making; in his operas, particularly in *Der Freischütz,* he opened the era of musical Romanticism, in decisive opposition to the established Italianate style. The highly dramatic and poetic portrayal of a German fairy-tale, with its aura of supernatural mystery, appealed to the public, whose imagination had been stirred by the emergent Romantic literature of the period. Weber's melodic genius and his mastery of the craft of composition made it possible for him to break with tradition and to start on a new path, at a critical time when individualism and naionalism began to emerge as sources of creative artistry. His instrumental works, too, possess a new quality which signalizes the transition from Classical to Romantic music. For piano he wrote pieces of extraordinary brilliance, introducing some novel elements in chord writing and passage work. He was himself an excellent pianist; his large hands gave him an unusual command of the keyboard—he could stretch the interval of a twelfth. Weber's influence on the development of German music was very great. The evolutionary link to Wagner's music drama is evident in the coloring of the orchestral parts in Weber's operas and in the adumbration of the principle of leading motifs. —A complete edition of Weber's works was undertaken in 1926 under the general editorship of H. J. Moser; only the following vols. were published: vols. I-II, early operas, ed. by A. Lorenz and W. Kaehler; vol. III, the Salzburg Mass, ed. by C. Schneider; *Preciosa,* ed. by L. K. Mayer. Previously unpublished works are found in L. Hirschberg's *Reliquienschrein des Meisters C. M. von Weber* (Berlin, 1827). A complete thematic catalogue of Weber's works was publ. by F. W. Jähns, *C. M. von Weber in seinen Werken* (Berlin, 1871).

WORKS

OPERAS: *Das Waldmädchen* (Freiberg, Nov. 24, 1800); *Peter Schmoll und seine Nachbarn* (Augsburg, March, 1803); *Rübezahl* (1805; unfinished); *Silvana* (Frankfurt, Sept. 16, 1810); *Abu Hassan* (Munich, June 4, 1811); *Preciosa* (Berlin, March 14, 1821); *Der Freischütz* (Berlin, June 18, 1821); *Die drei Pintos* (1821; unfinished; completed by Gustav Mahler after Weber's sketches and produced in Leipzig, Jan. 20, 1888); *Euryanthe* (Vienna, Oct. 25, 1823); *Oberon,* or *The Elf King's Oath* (London, April 12, 1826); incidental music to Gozzi's *Turandot* (1809), Moreto's *Donna Diana* (1817), Adolf Müllner's *König Yngurd* (1817), Theodor Hell's *Das Haus Anglade* (1818), Grillparzer's *Sappho* (1818), Gehe's *Heinrich IV* (1818), Rublack's *Lieb' um Liebe* (1818), Houwald's *Der Leuchtturm* (1820), Ludwig Robert's *Den Sachsensohn vermählet heute* (1822).

OTHER VOCAL WORKS: The cantata *Der erste Ton,* for declamation, chorus, and orch. (1808); op. 36, *In seiner Ordnung schafft der Herr,* for soli, chorus, and orch. (1812); op. 44, *Kampf und Sieg,* cantata on the battle of Waterloo (1815); *L'Accoglianza* for 6 solo voices, chorus, and orch. (1817); op. 58, *Jubel-Kantate* for soli, chorus, and orch. (1818); op. 61, *Natur und Liebe,* cantata for 2 sopranos, 2 tenors, and 2 basses, with piano (1818); other occasional cantatas; 2 Masses (E♭, G), also 2 offertories, for soli, chorus, and orch.; 6 part-songs for men's voices, op. 42 (to Th. Körner's *Leyer und Schwert;* achieved great popularity with students); 5 part-songs for men's chorus, op. 53b; 6 part-songs for men's chorus, op. 68; 5 scenes for soprano with orch. (op. 16, 'Il Momento s'avvicina'; op. 50, 'Misera me,' for *Atalia,* 1811; op. 51, 'Non paventar, mia vita,' for *Ines de Castro,* 1816; op. 52, 'Ah, se Edmondo fosse l'uccisor,' for Méhul's *Hélène,* 1815; op. 56, 'Was sag' ich? Schaudern macht mich der Gedanke,' for Cherubini's *Lodoiska*); op. 53, scena for tenor, double chorus, and orch., 'Signor, se padre sei,' for *Ines de Castro;* scena and aria for tenor, men's chorus, and orch., 'Qual altro attendi'; recitative, 'Doch welche Töne steigen jetzt hernieder,' for Spontini's *Olympie;* many songs (op. 13, 15, 23, 25, 29, 30, 41, 43, 46, 47, 54, 64, 66, 71, 80); 8 part-songs for mixed voices, with and without accompaniment; 6 canons for 3 and 4 voices; duets (op. 31); 10 Scotch folksongs arranged with accompaniment of flute, violin, cello, and piano.

INSTRUMENTAL WORKS. FOR ORCHESTRA: Op. 27, *Der Beherrscher der Geister,* overture (to the unfinished opera, *Rübezahl*); op. 59, *Jubel-Ouvertüre;* 2 symphonies, both in C major; march for wind instruments; waltz for wind instruments.—CONCERTED PIECES: 2 piano concertos (op. 11, C major; op. 32, E♭ major) and a *Konzertstück* in F major (op. 79); concertino for clarinet and orch. in E♭ major (op. 26) and 2 clarinet concertos (op. 73, F minor; op. 74, E♭ major); *Andante und Rondo* in C minor for bassoon and orch. (op. 35); concerto in F major for bassoon and orch. (op. 75); concertino in E minor for horn and orch. (op. 45); *Romanza siciliana* for flute and orch.; 6 variations on a German folksong for cello and orch.; Potpourri for cello and orch.; Andante and variations in D minor for cello and orch.; Adagio and Rondo for 'Harmonichord' and orchestra. —CHAMBER MUSIC: Op. 8, piano quartet in B♭ major; op. 13, 6 sonatas for violin and piano (F major, G major, D minor, E♭ major, A major, C major); op. 22, variations on a Norwegian theme for violin and piano, in D minor; op. 33, variations for clarinet and piano in B♭ major; op. 34, clarinet quintet in B♭ major; op. 48, *Duo concertant* in E♭ major for clarinet and piano; op. 63, piano trio in G minor. —FOR PIANO SOLO: 4 sonatas (op. 24, C major; op. 39, A♭ major; op. 49, D minor; op. 70, E minor); op. 1, *Sechs Fughetten;* op. 2, variations on an original theme; op. 4, *Douze Allemandes;* op. 5, variations on an Air de ballet from Vogler's *Castor et Pollux;* op. 6, variations on an air from Vogler's *Samori;* op. 7, variations on Bianchi's *Vien quà, Dorina,* op. 9, variations on an original theme; op. 12, *Momento capriccioso;* op. 21, *Grande Polonaise* in E♭ major; op. 28, variations on a theme from Méhul's *Joseph;* op. 40, variations on a Russian theme; op. 50, *Polonaise brillante* in E major; op. 53, caprice and variations on a theme from *Preciosa;* op. 55, variations on a Gypsy theme; op. 62, *Rondo brillant* in E♭ major; op. 65, *Aufforderung zum Tanz* (*Invitation to the Dance*; in 2 orchestral versions, by Berlioz and Weingartner, and in innumerable arrangements for various instruments); op. 72, *Polacca brillante* (arranged for piano and orch. by Liszt); op. 81, *Les Adieux,* fantasy; 6 *Écossaises; 18 Valses favorites de l'Impératrice de France.* —For Piano 4 Hands: Op. 3, *Sechs leichte Stücke;* op. 10, *Six sonates progressives et agréables;* op. 60, *Acht leichte Stücke.* A popular piece publ. under the title *Weber's Last Waltz* (or *Weber's Last Thought)* is a composition of K. G. Reissiger, not Weber.

Writings: An unfinished novel, criticisms, explanatory remarks on new works produced by him in Dresden, poems, etc., were publ. by Th. Hell as *Hinterlassene Schriften von C. M. von Weber* (3 vols.; Dresden, 1828; 2nd ed., 1850). A more complete and a better ed. is that of G. Kaiser, *Sämtliche Schriften von C. M. von Weber* (Berlin, 1908). R. Kleinecke publ. *Ausgewählte Schriften von K. M. von Weber* (Leipzig, 1892); a more recent collection was publ. by W. Altmann, *Weber's Ausgewählte Schriften* (Regensburg, 1928). *Ein Brevier* was ed. by H. Dünnebeil (Berlin, 1949).

BIBLIOGRAPHY —A. Biography: W. Neumann, *Weber. Eine Biographie* (Kassel, 1855); Max M. von Weber (son of the composer), *C. M. von Weber. Ein Lebensbild* (3 vols., Leipzig, 1864-66; English adaptation by J. P. Simpson as *Weber: The Life of an Artist,* 2 vols., London, 1865; new abridged ed. by R. Pechel, Berlin, 1912; still the standard biography); F. W. Jähns, *Weber. Eine Lebensskizze nach authentischen Quellen* (Leipzig, 1873); J. Benedict, *Weber* (London and N.Y., 1881; 5th ed., 1899; in the series 'Great Musicians'); L. Nohl, *Weber* (Leipzig, 1883); A. Reissmann, *Weber, sein Leben und seine Werke* (Berlin, 1886); H. Gehrmann, *Weber* (Berlin, 1899); G. Servières, *Weber* (Paris, 1906; new ed., 1925; in the series 'Musiciens célèbres'); H. von der Pfordten, *Weber* (Leipzig, 1919); A. Cœuroy, *Weber* (Paris, 1925; in the series 'Les Maîtres de la musique'; new ed., 1953); J. Kapp, *Weber. Eine Biographie* (Berlin, 1922; 5th revised ed., 1931); E. Kroll, *Weber* (Potsdam, 1934); L. P. and R. P. Stebbins, *Enchanted Wanderer: The Life of C. M. von Weber* (N. Y., 1940); W. Saunders, *Weber* (London and N.Y., 1940); H. J. Moser, *C. M. von Weber. Leben und Werk* (Leipzig, 1941; 2nd ed., 1955); P. Raabe, *Wege zu Weber* (Regensburg, 1942); W. Zentner, *C. M. von Weber. Sein Leben und sein Schaffen* (Olten, 1952); H. Schnoor, *Weber: Gestalt und Schöpfung* (Dresden, 1953); H. Dünnebeil, *Webers Leben und Wirken in chronologischen Tafeln* (Berlin, 1953); F. Grüniger, *C. M. von Weber: Leben und Werk* (Freiburg-im-Breisgau, 1954). See also Weber's *Autobiographische Skizze,* in Kaiser's ed. of Weber's *Sämtliche Schriften* (pp. 3-8). —B. Criticism, Appreciation: A. Jullien, *Weber à Paris en 1826* (Paris, 1877); G. F. Kaiser, *Beiträge zu einer Charakteristik Webers als Musikschriftsteller* (Leipzig, 1910); G. Servières, *Le 'Freischütz' de Weber* (Paris, 1913); W. Georgii, *Weber als Klavierkomponist* (dissertation; Halle, 1914); H. W. von Waltershausen, *Der Freischütz. Ein Versuch über die musikalische Romantik* (Munich, 1920); H. Allekotte, *Webers Messen* (Bonn, 1913); E. J. Dent, *A Weber Centenary,* in 'Music & Letters' (July, 1921); F. Hasselberg, *Der Freischütz. Friedrich Kinds Operndichtung und ihre Quellen* (Berlin, 1921); M. Degen, *Die Lieder von Weber* (Basel, 1923); A. Cœuroy, *Le Problème d'Euryanthe,* in 'Le Correspondent' (Oct. 25, 1923): A. Cœuroy, *Weber as Writer,* in the 'Mus. Quarterly' (Jan., 1925); E. Reiter, *Webers künstlerische Persönlichkeit aus seinen Schriften* (Leipzig, 1926); H. Abert, *Weber und sein 'Freischütz,'* in 'Jahrbuch der Musikbibliothek Peters' (1927; reprinted in Abert's *Gesammelte Schriften,* Halle, 1929); J. G. Prod'homme, *The Works of Weber in France,* in the 'Mus. Quarterly' (July, 1928); A. Sandt, *Webers Opern in ihrer Instrumentation* (Frankfurt, 1932); G. Kinsky, *Was Mendelssohn Indebted to Weber?* in the 'Mus. Quarterly' (April, 1933); G. Abraham, *Weber as Novelist and Critic* (ib., Jan., 1934); P. Listl, *C. M. von Weber als Ouvertürenkomponist* (dissertation; Würzburg, 1936); A. Einstein. *C. M. Weber,* in 'Music & Letters' (Jan., 1937); H. Schnoor, *W. auf dem Welttheater; ein Freischützbuch* (Dresden, 1942); P. R. Kirby, *Weber's Operas in London 1824 to 1826,* in the 'Mus. Quarterly' (July, 1946). Wagner's articles on Weber are found in vol. VII of his complete works (English transl., London,

1898); also in C. F. Glasenapp's *Wagner-Encyklopädie,* II, pp. 259-80 (Leipzig, 1891). —C. CORRESPONDENCE: L. Nohl, *Musiker-Briefe* (Leipzig, 1867; 2nd ed., 1873; English transl. by Lady Wallace as *Letters of Distinguished Musicians,* London, 1867); L. Nohl, *Mosaik für musikalisch-gebildete* (Leipzig, 1882); A. von Weber (grandson of the composer), *Reise-Briefe von Weber an seine Gattin Caroline* (Leipzig, 1886); E. Rudorff, *Briefe von Weber an Heinrich Lichtenstein* (Brunswick, 1900); G. Kaiser, *Webers Briefe an den Grafen Karl von Brühl* (Leipzig, 1911); L. Hirschberg, *77 bisher ungedruckte Briefe Webers* (Hildburghausen, 1926); G. Kinsky, *Ungedruckte Briefe Webers,* in the 'Zeitschrift für Musik' (1926).—D. WEBER AND HIS CONTEMPORARIES: J. C. Lobe, *Gespräche mit Weber,* in his *Fliegende Blätter für Musik* (Leipzig, 1853; reprinted in his *Consonanzen und Dissonanzen,* 1869); M. Runze, *Loewe und Weber,* in his *Loewe Redivivus* (Berlin, 1888); H. A. Krüger, *Pseudoromantik, Friedrich Kind und der Dresdener Liederkreis* (Leipzig, 1904); H. B. and C. O. E. Cox, *Leaves from the Journal of Sir G. Smart* (London, 1907); K. Huschke, *Webers Beziehungen zu Ludwig van Beethoven und Franz Schubert,* in 'Deutsche Revue' (May-June, 1919); E. Kroll, *E. T. A. Hoffmann und Weber,* in the 'Neue Musik-Zeitung' (1921); K. Huschke, *Spohr und Weber,* in 'Allgemeine Musik-Zeitung' (1934); E. Kroll, *Beethoven und Weber,* in 'Neues Beethoven-Jahrbuch' (Augsburg, 1935); O. Kroll, *Weber und Bärmann,* in the 'Neue Zeitschrift für Musik' (1936). —E. MISCELLANEOUS: R. Haas, *Ein Notizen-Buch C. M. von Webers aus Prag,* in 'Der Merker' (1916); A. Maecklenburg, *Der Fall Spontini-Weber,* in 'Zeitschrift für Musikwissenschaft' (1923-24); O. Hellinghaus, *Weber. Seine Persönlichkeit in seinen Briefen und Tagebüchern und in Aufzeichnungen seiner Zeitgenossen* (Freiburg-im-Breisgau, 1924); E. Kroll, *Weber. Sein Leben in Bildern* (Leipzig, 1936); F. Rapp, *Ein unbekanntes Bildnis Webers* (Stuttgart, 1937); G. Hausswald, ed., *Weber: Eine Gedenkschrift* (Dresden, 1951).

Weber, Franz, German organist and conductor; b. Cologne, Aug. 26, 1805; d. there Sept. 18, 1876. He studied with Bernhard Klein in Berlin; in 1838 was appointed organist of the Cologne Cathedral. He wrote a *Kriegsgesang der Rheinpreussen* for male chorus and orch.; publ. several song books ('Kommersbuch,' 'Turner-Liederbuch,' 'Des deutschen Soldaten Liederbuch,' etc.).

Weber, Friedrich August, German physician and composer; b. Heilbronn, Jan. 24, 1753; d. there, Jan. 21, 1806. He wrote numerous oratorios and cantatas with orch.; also symphonies, chamber music, piano sonatas for 4 hands; contributed articles on music to various journals.

Weber, Friedrich Dionys, Bohemian composer and writer on music; b. Velichov, Oct. 9, 1766; d. Prague, Dec. 25, 1842. He studied with Abbé Vogler; in 1811 was one of the founders of the Prague Cons., and its first director; among his pupils were Moscheles and Kalliwoda. He wrote several operas, 18 cantatas, a number of military marches, a sextet for 6 trombones, a sextet for 6 cornets, quartets for 4 cornets, variations for violin and cello, numerous popular quadrilles, *Ländler,* etc., for piano; publ. *Das Konservatorium der Musik zu Prag* (1817), *Allgemeine theoretisch-praktische Vorschule der Musik* (1828), *Theoretisch-praktisches Lehrbuch der Harmonie und des Generalbasses* (1830-41; 4 parts).

Weber, Georg Viktor, German ecclesiastic and choral conductor; b. Ober-Erlenbach, Feb. 25, 1838; d. Mainz, Sept. 24, 1911. He took holy orders in 1863; in 1866 was appointed music director and organist at the Cathedral of Mainz, where he presented fine concerts of a cappella music of the 15th and 16th centuries with his excellent choir. He was also an expert on organ building. He publ. *Manuale cantus ecclesiastici juxta ritum S. Rom. ecclesiae* (1878; 2nd ed., 1897); *Orgelbuch zum Mainzer Diocesan-Gesangbuch*(1880; 3rd ed., 1896); *Über Sprachgesang* (1883); *Über Orgeldispositionen* (1890); *Die Verbesserung der 'Medicaea'* (1901); articles in Böckeler's 'Gregorius-Blatt' and Haberl's 'Cäcilien-Kalender'; also Masses, motets, psalms, etc.

Weber (vā'-běhr), **Gottfried,** eminent German theorist and composer; b. Freinsheim, near Mannheim, March 1, 1779; d. Kreuznach, Sept. 21, 1839. He studied law at Heidelberg and Göttingen, and filled positions as judge in Mannheim (1802), Mainz (1814), and Darmstadt (1818); was appointed public prosecutor for the state of Hesse in 1832. He was an excellent amateur pianist, and also played the flute and the cello; conducted a musical society in Mannheim, and founded the Mannheim Cons.; in Mainz he was active as opera director; in 1824 began to publish the magazine 'Caecilia' and edited it until his death. He made a thorough study of the theoretical works of Marpurg, Kirnberger, Abbé Vogler, and others, and then brought out his important treatise, *Versuch einer geordneten Theorie der Tonsetzkunst* (3 vols., 1817-21; 2nd ed. in 4 vols., 1824; 3rd ed. in 4 vols., 1830-32), in which he introduced the now widely accepted symbols for designating the major keys with capital letters and minor keys with small letters, Roman figures for degrees of the scale, etc. It was publ. in English in Boston (1846) and London (1851). His other theoretical publications include *Über chronometrische Tempobezeichnung* (1817); *Beschreibung und Tonleiter der G. Weber'schen Doppelposaune* (1817); *Versuch einer praktischen Akustik der Blasinstrumente* (in Ersch and Gruber's 'Encyclopädie'); *Allgemeine Musiklehre zum Selbstunterrichte* (1822; 3rd ed., 1831; in English, Boston, 1842); *Über Saiteninstrumente mit Bünden* (in 'Berliner Musikzeitung,' 1825); *Die Generalbasslehre zum Selbstunterrichte* (1833); many essays for the 'Allgemeine musikalische Zeitung' and for his own paper, 'Caecilia.' He questioned the authenticity of Mozart's Requiem (in 'Caecilia,' 1826). As a composer, he wrote 3 Masses, a Requiem, and a Te Deum (all with orch.); variations for guitar and cello; some chamber music; part-songs.

Weber, Henry (George), American conductor; b. Berlin (of American parents), Dec. 9, 1900. He was brought to the U.S. in 1901, but returned to Europe for study in Vienna; subsequently attended the Univ. of Chicago. He conducted the Chicago Civic Opera Co. (1924-29); in 1940 became artistic director of the Chicago City Opera Co.; also conducted symph. concerts in Chicago. At various times he was in charge of music festivals in Chicago; also active on the radio.

Weber, Josef Miroslaw, Czech violinist and composer; b. Prague, Nov. 9, 1854; d. Munich, Jan. 1, 1906. He was taught by his father, and played violin in public as a child; then studied at the Prague Cons. He subsequently occupied posts as concertmaster in Sondershausen (1873-75), Darmstadt (1875), and Wiesbaden (until 1893); finally became concertmaster of the Court Opera in Munich, where he remained until his death. He wrote the operas *Der selige Herr Vetter* (Wiesbaden, 1894) and *Die neue Mamsell* (Munich, 1896); a ballet, *Die Rheinnixe* (Wiesbaden, 1884); a violin concerto; septet for violin, viola, cello, clarinet, bassoon, and 2 horns; a string quintet; etc.

Weber, Karl Gustav, Swiss composer; b. Münchenbuchsee, Oct. 30, 1845; d. Zürich, June 12, 1887. He studied at the Leipzig Cons. and with Tausig in Berlin; his symphonic poem *Zur Iliade* was presented by Liszt at the Beethoven Centennial Festival in 1870. In 1872 he settled in Zürich as church organist, teacher at the Cons., and choral conductor. He publ. a group of waltzes for piano 4 hands; piano quartet; piano trio; violin sonata; *Prinz Carneval,* an album of children's pieces; many choruses; choral arrangements of old German songs. For several years he was editor of the 'Schweizerische Musikzeitung.' — Cf. A. Schneider, *G. Weber* (Zürich, 1888); A. Steiner, *Gustav Weber* (Zürich, 1910).

Weber, Ludwig, German composer; b. Nuremberg, Oct. 13, 1891; d. Borken, June 30, 1947. Until 1925 he was a school teacher in Nuremberg, and was self-taught in music, except for some private instruction with Hermann Abendroth and Courvoisier. After occupying some minor posts as music teacher, he became conductor of the municipal chorus in Mülheim; associated himself with the musical youth movement, and wrote a number of choral and other works in the folksong manner.—Works: a symph. in B minor; *Hymnen an die Nacht* for chorus and orch.; a quintet for wind instruments; 2 string quartets; *Der Natur* for chorus and orch.; *Heilige Namen* for chorus and orch.; *Fröhlich soll meinem Herze* (4-16 voices unaccompanied); 3 one-act operas: *Midas, Christgeburt,* and *Totentanz.* —Cf. F. W. Herzog, *Ludwig Weber* (Wolfenbüttel, 1929); K. Ziebler, *Ludwig Weber* (1939).

Weber, Wilhelm, German choral conductor and composer; b. Bruchsal, Nov. 16, 1859; d. Augsburg, Oct. 14, 1918. After studying at the Stuttgart Cons. he went to Augsburg, where he taught at the Musikschule from 1884, becoming its director in 1905. From 1892 he was conductor of the 'Oratorienverein,' notable for its numerous German premières of works by foreign composers; he also conducted at various festivals in Germany. He publ. 2 books of *Landsknechtslieder* and other songs; choruses; piano pieces. Author of *Beethovens Missa solemnis* (1897; 2nd ed., 1903) and *Händels Oratorien, übersetzt und bearbeitet von F. Chrysander* (3 vols.; 1898; 1900; 1902).

Webern, Anton von, remarkable Austrian composer; b. Vienna, Dec. 3, 1883; d. Mittersill, Sept. 15, 1945 (accidentally killed by an American military policeman). He studied musicology with Guido Adler at the Univ. of Vienna (*Dr. phil.,* 1906, with a dissertation on Isaac's *Choralis Constantinus*); composition with Schoenberg, whose ardent disciple he became. From 1908 till 1914 he conducted theater orchestras in Vienna, in Prague, and in Germany. After the end of World War I he settled in Mödling, near Vienna, where he taught composition; was closely associated with the 'Society for Private Musical Performances' organized in Vienna by Schoenberg with the intention of promoting modern music without being exposed to reactionary opposition (music critics were not admitted to these performances); Webern supervised the programs during its existence (1918-21). He subsequently conducted the orch. of the workers' concerts and the workers' chorus in Vienna (1922-24); also appeared as guest conductor with the BBC orch. in London (1929) and in Barcelona (1932). Throughout World War II he remained in Vienna; after his son was killed in an air bombardment of a train in Feb. 1945, Webern and his wife fled from Vienna, and went to live with their married daughter in Mittersill, near Salzburg. He was mortally wounded by a member of the U. S. military police when he stepped out of the house in the evening, unaware of the curfew established by the U.S. occupation troops. Webern left relatively few works, and most of them are of short duration (the 4th of his Five Pieces for Orch., op. 10, scored for clarinet, trumpet, trombone, mandolin, celesta, harp, drum, violin, and viola, takes only 19 seconds to play); but in his music he achieves the utmost subtilization of expressive means. He adopted the 12-tone method of composition almost immediately after its definitive formulation by Schoenberg (1924), and extended the principle of nonrepetition of notes to tone colors, so that in some of his works (e.g., symph., op. 21) no instrument is allowed to play 2 successive thematic notes. Dynamic marks are also greatly diversified. Harmonic concepts are all but obliterated; counterpoint (always dissonant) is deprived of imitation or canon; single motifs are extremely brief, and stand out as individual particles or lyric ejaculations. The impact of these works on the general public and on the critics was usually disconcerting, and upon occasion led to violent demonstrations; however, the extraordinary skill and novelty of technique, as well as inherent poetic quality, made this music endure beyond the fashions of the times; performances of Webern's works multiplied after his death, and began to influence increasingly larger groups of modern musicians; Stravinsky acknowledged the use of Webern's methods in his latest works; jazz composers have professed to follow Webern's ideas of tone color; analytical treatises have been publ. in several languages. —Works: for orch.: Passacaglia, op. 1 (1908); *6 Orchestral Pieces,* op. 6 (Vienna, March 31, 1913); *5 Orchestral Pieces,* op. 10 (1913; Zürich Festival of the International Society for Contemporary Music, June 23, 1926); symph. for chamber orch., op. 21 (1928; N.Y., League of Composers, Dec. 18, 1929); *Variations,* op. 30 (1940); choral music: *Entflieht auf leichten Kähnen,* op. 2, for unaccompanied chorus (1908); 2 songs, to words by Goethe, op. 19, for chorus, celesta, guitar, violin, clarinet, and bass clarinet (1926); *Das Augenlicht* for chorus and orch., op. 26 (1935; London Festival, June 17, 1938); 2 cantatas, op. 29 and op. 31 (1940 and 1943); chamber music: 5 movements for string quartet, op. 5 (1909); *6 Bagatelles* for string quartet, op. 9 (1913); trio for violin, viola, and cello, op. 20 (1927); quartet for violin, clarinet, saxophone, and piano, op. 22 (1930); concerto for 9 instruments, op. 24 (Prague Festival, Sept. 4, 1935); string quartet, op. 28 (1938); *4 Pieces* for violin and piano, op. 7 (1910); *3 Little Pieces* for cello and piano, op. 11 (1914); variations for piano solo, op. 27 (1926); song cycles with instrumental accompaniment, op. 8, 13, 14, 15, 16, 17, 18; songs with piano accompaniment, op. 3, 4, 12, 23, 25; arrangements for orch. of Schubert's *Deutsche Tänze,* of Bach's *Ricercare a 6* from *Das musikalische Opfer;* publ. *Der Weg zur Komposition mit 12 Tönen* (Vienna, 1932); *Der Weg zur neuen Musik* (Vienna, 1933); edited a vol. of compositions from Isaac's *Choralis Constantinus* in the 'Denkmäler der Tonkunst in Österreich' (vol. 32). —Bibliography: E. Stein, *Anton von Webern,* in 'Chesterian' (Oct., 1923); W. Reich, *Anton von Webern,* in 'Die Musik' (1930); T. Wiesengrund-Adorno, *Berg and Webern — Schönberg's Heirs,* in 'Modern Music' (1931); a special issue of the Vienna magazine '23' (1934); H. Searle, *Webern's Last Works,* in the 'Monthly Mus. Record' (Dec., 1946); R. Leibowitz, *Schoenberg et son école* (Paris, 1947; English transl., N.Y., 1949); L. Rognoni, *Espressionismo e dodecafonia* (Turin, 1954); R. Craft, *Anton Webern,* in 'The Score' (Sept., 1955); R. Vlad, *Storia della dodecafonia* (Milan, 1958). See also the compendium, *Anton Webern, Dokumente, Bekenntnisse, Erkenntnisse, Analysen* (Vienna, 1955).

Webster, Beveridge, American pianist; b. Pittsburgh, May 30, 1908. He studied music with his father, who was director of the Pittsburgh Cons. of Music; at the age of 13, he was sent to Paris to study with Isidor Philipp at the Cons.; graduated in 1926, winning the Grand Prix for piano playing. He gave concerts in Europe; returned to the U.S. in 1934, and developed a successful concert career, appearing with major symph. orchestras; also continued to give concerts in Europe.

Wecker, Georg Kaspar, German organist and composer; b. Nuremberg, April 2, 1632; d. there, April 20, 1695. He studied organ with Erasmus Kindermann, and soon obtained a position as church organist in Nuremberg; his last appointment was at the Sebaldkirche there (1686-95). He also was a respected teacher; Johann Krieger and Pachelbel were among his pupils. Several of his sacred songs were publ. in hymn books in Nuremberg; 3 sacred choral works are reproduced in the 'Denkmäler der Tonkunst in Bayern' (vol. VI, 1).

Weckerlin, Jean-Baptiste-Théodore, eminent French music scholar and composer; b. Gebweiler, Alsace, Nov. 29, 1821; d. there, May 20, 1910. He was trained for his father's business of cotton-dyeing; but went over to music in 1844, studying under Ponchard (singing) and Halévy (composition) at the Paris Cons., producing a heroic symphony, *Roland,* for soli, chorus, and orch., in 1847; on leaving the Cons. in 1849, he gave music lessons, took part with Seghers in the direction of the Société Sainte-Cécile, which brought out some of his works; and achieved success in 1853 with a 1-act comic opera, *L'Organiste dans l'embarras* (100 performances at the Théâtre-Lyrique). This was followed by 2 comic operas in Alsatian dialect, *Die drifach Hochzitt im Bäsethal* (Colmar, 1863) and *D'r verhäxt' Herbst* (Colmar, 1879), and the 1-act opera *Après Fontenoy* (Théâtre-Lyrique, 1877). Meantime he had become an assistant librarian at the Paris Cons. (1869); in 1876 succeeded Félicien David as librarian, and in 1885 publ. a bibliographical catalogue; was also chosen librarian of the Société des Compositeurs, for whose bulletins he wrote important articles. He retired in 1909. He won distinction as a composer of grand choral works; also wrote choruses a cappella, songs, and a grand *Symphonie de la forêt,* for orch.; but his greatest achievement was the compilation of old French songs. His 'Échos du temps passé' (1853-55) and 'Souvenirs du temps passé' (1864) are collections of chansons, noëls, madrigals, etc., from the 12th-18th centuries; the 'Musiciana' (3 vols.; 1877, 1890, 1899) is a collection from rare and curious works on music, with anecdotes, etc.; other collections are 'Les Échos d'Angleterre' (1877; folksongs with piano); 'Chansons et rondes populaires' (children's songs with piano); 'Les Poètes français mis en musique' (1868); 'Chansons populaires des provinces de la France'; *L'ancienne chanson populaire en France* (1886); 'Chansons populaires du Pays de France' (2 vols.; 1903). A catalogue of his private library was publ. at Leipzig in 1910.

Weckmann (vek'-mahn), **Matthias,** German organist and composer; b. Niederdorla, near Mühlhausen, Thuringia, 1619; d. Hamburg, Feb. 24, 1674. He was the son of a schoolmaster; was a chorister in the Dresden court chapel, where he was a pupil of Heinrich Schütz. In 1637 he was sent to Hamburg for further study with Reinken, Jakob Praetorius, and H. Scheidemann, by whom he was trained in the organ method of Sweelinck. In 1641 he became organist for the crown prince in Dresden, and in 1642 was appointed to a similar post in Copenhagen; he returned in 1647 to Dresden, where he became a friend of J. J. Froberger; in 1655 he went to Hamburg as organist at the Jacobikirche, and there founded, with Christoph Bernhard, the 'Collegium musicum,' a concert-society for the performance of new works (it was discontinued after Weckmann's death). Weckmann's solo cantatas and choral works with instrumental accompaniment were publ. by Max Seiffert in the 'Denkmäler deutscher Tonkunst' (vol. 6); instrumental pieces and songs in the 'Erbe deutscher Musik' (series 2, vol. 4); 2 numbers are reproduced in A. Schering's 'Geschichte der Musik in Beispielen' (Nos. 212 and 213); etc. —Cf. M. Seiffert, *Matthias Weckmann und das Collegium Musicum in Hamburg,* in 'Sammelbände der Internationalen Musik-Gesellschaft' (II, 1900); G. Ilgner, *Matthias Weckmann. Sein Leben und seine Werke* (Wolfenbüttel, 1939).

Wedge, George (Anson), American organist and educator; b. Danbury, Conn., Jan. 15, 1890. He studied organ, piano, and composition at the Institute of Musical Art in N.Y.; subsequently occupied various teaching positions: at N.Y. Univ. (1920-27); at the Curtis Institute of Music, Philadelphia (1924-26); dean of the Institute of Musical Art and of the Juilliard School of Music (1938-46); director of the Juilliard

Summer School (1932-47). He publ. *Ear-training and Sight-singing* (1921); *Advanced Ear-training and Sight-singing* (1922); *Keyboard Harmony* (1924); *Rhythm in Music* (1927); *Applied Harmony,* in 2 vols. (1930-31); *The Gist of Music* (1936).

Weede, Robert, American baritone; b. Baltimore, Feb. 22, 1903. He studied singing with George Castelle in Baltimore; in 1927 won the competition of the National Federation of Music Clubs; received a scholarship of the Caruso Memorial Foundation, and went to Italy, where he studied with Oscar Anselmi in Milan. Returning to America, he was engaged as a radio singer. He was a member of the Metropolitan Opera in 1937-42 and 1944-45. In 1956 he obtained great success in the leading role of Frank Loesser's musical comedy *The Most Happy Fella.*

Weelkes, Thomas, English composer; b. c. 1575; d. London, Nov. 30, 1623. In 1597 he publ. a book of madrigals for 3-6 voices; in 1598, he publ. 'Balletts and Madrigals' for 5 voices, dedicated to Edward Darcy, Groom of the Privy Chamber; in 1600, he brought out two more books, containing madrigals for 5 and 6 voices; served as organist at the College of Winchester (1600-02). He was a friend of Morley, to whose collection 'The Triumphes of Oriana' (1601-03) he contributed a fine madrigal for 6 voices, *As Vesta was from Latmos Hill Descending.* In 1602 he was granted the degree of B. Mus. at the New College, Oxford, and was appointed organist of Chichester Cathedral. A subsequent publication was 'Ayres; or, Phantasticke Spirits for 3 voices' (1608; reprinted by Arkwright in the 'Old English Edition'). Weelkes was one of the greatest English madrigalists, possessing remarkable power in melodic characterization of the text; he occasionally used chromatic progressions in harmony that were well in advance of his time. He wrote a considerable amount of church music (services and anthems); also instrumental works (2 pavanes and other pieces, for 5 viols). His madrigals and other vocal works are reprinted in 'The English Madrigal School,' ed. by E. H. Fellowes (vols. 9-13); anthems in the series 'Tudor Church Music.' —Cf. E. H. Fellowes, *The English Madrigal Composers* (London, 1921; 2nd ed., 1948); D. M. Arnold, *Thomas Weelkes and the Madrigal,* in 'Music & Letters' (Jan., 1950).

Weerbecke (Weerbeke, Werbecke), Gaspar van, Flemish composer; b. Audenarde, Flanders, c. 1445. Pupil of Ockeghem; in 1472, organizer of the ducal court chapel at Milan, his singers including Josquin des Prez; from 1481 to 1489, singer in the papal chapel at Rome, a post he resumed from 1500 to 1509 after sojourns in Milan and Flanders; there is no trace of him after 1514. Masses, motets, and Lamentations by Weerbecke were publ. by Petrucci (1505-09). —Cf. G. Cesari, in the 'Rivista Musicale Italiana' (1922); G. Croll, *Gaspar van Weerbeke,* in 'Musica Disciplina' (vol. 6, 1952; with a list of works). See also G. Reese, *Music in the Renaissance* (N.Y., 1954, pp. 218-19).

Wegeler (vĕh'-gĕh-lĕhr), **Franz Gerhard,** German physician and music amateur; b. Bonn, Aug. 22, 1765; d. Coblenz, May 7, 1848. He was a practicing physician in Bonn and Coblenz, and knew Beethoven as a youth. With Ries, he publ. *Biographische Notizen über Ludwig van Beethoven* (1838; supplement, 1845; reprinted by A. Kalischer, 1906). —Cf. S. Ley, ed., *Beethoven als Freund der Familie Wegeler -v. Breuning* (Bonn, 1927).

Wegelius (vā-gā'-lē-ōōs), **Martin,** eminent Finnish composer and pedagogue; b. Helsinki, Nov. 10, 1846; d. there, March 22, 1906. He studied philosophy, taking his master's degree in 1869; studied music with Rudolph Bibl in Vienna (1870-71), and with Richter and Paul in Leipzig (1871-73); he went to Leipzig for further study in 1877-78. Returning to Finland, he became operatic coach at the Helsinki National Theater. In 1882 he was appointed director of the newly-founded Helsinki Cons., holding this post until his death. Under his guidance, the institution became one of the finest schools in Europe, with excellent teachers. Sibelius was one of the pupils of Wegelius; others were Järnefelt, Melartin, and Palmgren. Wegelius emphasized the cultivation of national Finnish music, and thus was mainly responsible for the magnificent development of Finland as a musical nation. —Works: overture *Daniel Hjort* (1872); *Divertissement à la hongroise* (1880); *Rondo quasi fantasia* for piano and orch. (1872); *Mignon,* 6 songs with orch., after Goethe's *Westöstlicher Diwan* (1875); a Christmas cantata (1877), a festival cantata, *The 6th of May* (1878); a violin sonata; piano pieces; songs. He publ. (in Swedish) a number of manuals and books on music history: *Lärobok i allmän musik-*

lära och analys (2 vols., 1888-89); *Hufvuddragen af den västerländska musikens historia* (3 vols., 1891-93); *Kurs i tonträffning* (3 vols., 1893-95); *Kurs i homofon sats* (2 vols., 1897-1905); etc.—Cf. K. T. Flodin, *Martin Wegelius* (in Swedish, Stockholm, 1916; in Finnish, Helsinki, 1922); *Martin Wegelius* (letters; 2 vols.; Helsinki, 1918-19); Arvi Karvonen, *Martin Wegelius,* in *Suomen Säveltäjiä,* ed. by Sulho Ranta (Helsinki, 1945; pp. 169-83).

Wehle, Gerhard Fürchtegott, German musicologist; b. Paramaribo, Dutch Guiana, Oct. 11, 1884. He studied in Germany, and settled in Berlin in 1907. He publ. *Die Kunst der Improvisation,* in 3 vols. (1925, 1926, 1932; 5th ed. of vol. 3, on organ improvisation, 1953); manuals on theory; composed much vocal music.

Wehle (vā'-lĕ), **Karl,** Bohemian pianist; b. Prague, March 17, 1825; d. Paris, June 3, 1883. Trained for a mercantile career, he abandoned it for music; studied piano with Moscheles at Leipzig and Kullak in Berlin; made extended tours to Asia, Africa, America, and Australia, but resided chiefly in Paris. He publ. a number of brilliant compositions for piano, among them a *Sérénade napolitaine,* an *Allegro à la hongroise,* 3 *Tarentelles,* 2 *Impromptus, Berceuse javanaise, Marche cosaque, Fête bohémienne, Un Songe à Vaucluse,* etc.

Wehrli (vĕhr'-lĕ), **Werner,** Swiss composer; b. Aarau, Jan. 8, 1892; d. Lucerne, June 27, 1944. He studied at the Zürich Cons. with Hegar and in Frankfurt with Knorr; wrote a number of 'festival operas' in a Romantic vein; cantatas and chamber music. His oratorio *Wallfahrt* (1939) enjoyed a modicum of success. His opera *Das heiss Eisen,* after Hans Sachs, was produced in Bern on Dec. 11, 1918.—G. H. Leuenberger, *Werner Wehrli,* in 'Schweizerische Musikzeitung' (May, 1952).

Weidig (vī'-dig), **Adolf,** American music teacher and composer; b. Hamburg, Nov. 28, 1867; d. Hinsdale, Ill., Sept. 23, 1931. He studied at the Hamburg Cons. with Bargheer (violin) and later with Hugo Riemann (theory); then in Munich with Rheinberger (composition). In 1892 he settled in Chicago; played the violin in the Chicago Symphony Orch. (1892-96); in 1898 joined the faculty of the American Cons. of Music; conducted his own works in Chicago, Minneapolis, and also in Germany. He was greatly esteemed as a teacher; publ. *Harmonic Material and its Uses* (1923); composed 2 symphonies; a symph. poem, *Semiramis; Drei Episoden* for orch.; a string quintet; 3 string quartets; a piano trio; songs.—See 'Dictionary of American Biography.'

Weidt (vīdt), **Lucy,** German soprano; b. Troppau, Silesia, 1880; d. Vienna, July 28, 1940. She studied piano and singing with her father, and then with Rosa Papier in Vienna, where she made her début as Elisabeth in 1904. She sang in Germany, appearing at the Wagner festival in 1908-10. On Nov. 18, 1910 she made her first American appearance as Brünnhilde in *Die Walküre,* at the Metropolitan Opera, N. Y.; after a season there, she sang in Italy (mostly in Wagnerian parts). In 1909 she married Baron Joseph von Urmenyi. Her voice was of unusual attractiveness and power, enabling her to perform Wagnerian parts with distinction.

Weigel, Eugene, American composer; b. Cleveland, Oct. 11, 1910. He was instructed in early years by his father, an organist; then studied violin at the Cleveland Institute of Music with Maurice Hewitt; composition with Arthur Shepherd at Western Reserve Univ. From 1929 to 1941 he was organist and choirmaster at a Franciscan church in Cleveland; in 1943 took a course of study with Hindemith at Yale; also studied viola with Hugo Kortschak; became 1st violist of the New Haven Symph. Orch., and director of music for Thomas More Chapel at Yale; B.M., Yale, 1946; in 1947 was appointed artist in residence at the Univ. of Illinois, as violist with the Walden String Quartet; participated in many performances by this quartet; was chairman of the theory dept. at the Univ. of Illinois Music School (1950-56); in 1956 appointed composer in residence and prof. at Montana State Univ.; held a Guggenheim Fellowship in 1954-55. Works: operas: *The Lion Makers,* a Hindu fable (1953), *The Mountain Child,* a ballad opera in one act (Montana State Univ., Missoula, July 29, 1958); for orch.: *Sonata for Strings* (1948), *Prairie Symphony* (1953); Requiem Mass for chorus and orch. (Univ. of Illinois, Urbana, March 27, 1956); quintet for clarinet and strings (1946); *Short, Slow, and Fast,* for woodwind quintet (1949); *3 Pieces for 4 Trombones* (1953); piano pieces and songs.

Weigl (vīgl), **Bruno,** writer on music and composer; b. Brno, June 16, 1881; d. there, Sept. 25, 1938. He studied with O. Kitzler and R. von Mojsisovics; publ. *Die Geschichte des Walzers, nebst einem Anhang über die moderne Operette* (1910), *Handbuch der Violoncell-Literatur* (1911; 3rd ed., 1929), *Harmonielehre* (2 vols.; 1925), and *Handbuch der Orgelliteratur* (1931); composed a comic opera, *Mandragola* (Brno, 1912); *Serenade* for orch.; *Fasching,* song cycle for baritone and orch.; many organ pieces.

Weigl (vīgl), **Joseph,** Austrian composer; b. Eisenstadt, March 28, 1766; d. Vienna, Feb. 3, 1846. His father, Joseph Franz Weigl (1740-1820), was a cellist in the service of Prince Esterházy with Haydn; his mother was a singer; he was a godson of Haydn. Brought up in a musical environment, he wrote an operetta, *Die unnützige Vorsicht,* at the age of 16 for a puppet show; Salieri accepted him as a pupil; he also studied with Albrechtsberger. He was assistant conductor to Salieri at the Vienna Court Theater from 1790 till 1823. Altogether, Weigl wrote 14 operas in Italian and 19 in German. The most successful were *La Principessa d'Amalfi* (Vienna, Jan. 12, 1794; Haydn described it as a masterpiece in a letter to Weigl after the performance) and *Die Schweizerfamilie* (Vienna, March 14, 1809; produced in Paris, Feb. 6, 1827 as *Emmeline, ou la famille suisse;* also staged in opera houses all over Europe until about 1900, when it disappeared from the repertory). The following operas by Weigl were produced in Vienna with varying success: *Il Pazzo per forza* (Nov. 14, 1788), *La Caffettiera bizzarra* (Sept. 15, 1790), *L'Amor marinaro* (Oct. 15, 1797); *Das Dorf im Gebürge* (April 17, 1798), *Die Uniform* (Feb. 15, 1805), *Vestas Feuer* (Aug. 10, 1805), *Kaiser Hadrian* (May 21, 1807), *Adrian von Ostade* (July 3, 1807), *Das Waisenhaus* (Oct. 4, 1808), *Nachtigall und Rabe* (April 20, 1818), *Margarethe von Anjou* (March 16, 1819), *Baals Sturz* (April 13, 1820), *König Waldemar* (May 11, 1821), *Edmund und Caroline* (Sept. 21, 1821), *Die eiserne Pforte* (Feb. 27, 1823). Three operas were produced at La Scala, Milan: *Cleopatra* (Dec. 19, 1807); *Il Rivale di se stesso* (April 18, 1808), and *L'Imboscata* (Nov. 8, 1815). Weigl also wrote 18 ballets; 2 oratorios; 22 cantatas; 11 Masses and other church music.—Cf. W. Neumann, *Joseph Weigl* (Kassel, 1855); A. Eisner-Eisenhof, *Joseph Weigl,* in the 'Rivista Musicale Italiana' (1904); W. Bollert, *Joseph Weigl und das deutsche singspiel,* in his *Aufsätze zur Musikgeschichte* (Bottrop, 1938); for details of productions of Weigl's operas, see A. Loewenberg's *Annals of Opera* (Cambridge, 1943; 2nd ed., Geneva, 1955).

Weigl (vīgl), **Karl,** composer; b. Vienna, Feb. 6, 1881; d. New York, Aug. 11, 1949. He studied piano with A. Door and theory with R. Fuchs at the Vienna Cons., graduating in 1902; later studied composition with Zemlinsky, and musicology with Guido Adler at the Vienna Univ. (Ph. D., 1903). Was a coach at the Vienna Opera (1904-06); in 1910 won the Beethoven Prize of the 'Gesellschaft der Musikfreunde' for a string quartet; and (1924) the prize of the City of Vienna for the symphonic cantata *World Festival.* In 1938 he settled in New York as a teacher. Weigl was a prolific composer; wrote 6 symphonies; several overtures; an orch. suite, *Tänze aus dem alten Wien* (1939; renamed *City That Was*); 8 string quartets, etc. His 1st symphony (1908) was published and performed in Zürich, 1910; most of his other works remain in manuscript.

Weigl (vīgl), **Thaddäus,** Austrian composer and publisher; brother of Joseph Weigl; b. Vienna, 1776; d. there, Feb. 10, 1844. He wrote the Singspiele, *Die Marionettenbude* (Vienna, March 17, 1795) and *Idoli* (Vienna, March 12, 1796); and 13 ballets. In 1801 he established in Vienna a publishing firm, which issued several works by Schubert. He retired in 1826.

Weil (vīl), **Hermann,** German baritone; b. Karlsruhe, May 29, 1877; d. (drowned in Blue Mountain Lake, N. Y.), July 6, 1949. He studied at the Cons. of Karlsruhe and in Frankfurt (with Adolf Dippel); made his début as Wolfram at Freiburg, Baden (Sept. 6, 1901); then appeared in Stuttgart and other German cities; also sang in Vienna, Brussels, Amsterdam, Milan, London, etc.; participated in the Bayreuth festivals every summer from 1909 till 1912. On Nov. 17, 1911 he made his first American appearance as Kurvenal in *Tristan und Isolde,* at the Metropolitan Opera, N. Y., under Toscanini. He remained with the Metropolitan until 1917, when he returned to Germany. He came back to the U. S. in 1938. The unusual compass (3 full octaves) of his voice enabled him to undertake bass as well as baritone parts; he had about 100 roles in his repertory; excelled in Wagnerian parts, and was also successful as a recital singer.

Weill (vīl), **Kurt**, outstanding composer of modern operas; b. Dessau, March 2, 1900; d. New York, April 3, 1950. He was a pupil of Albert Bing in Dessau; in 1918 studied for one semester at the Berlin Hochschule für Musik under Humperdinck and Krasselt. He was then engaged as opera coach in Dessau, and was also theater conductor at Lüdenscheid. In 1921 he moved to Berlin, and became a student of Busoni. Under the impact of new ideas in the theater, calling for bold portrayal of contemporary themes, and cultivating social satire, he began writing short operas in a modernistic manner: *Der Protagonist* (Dresden, March 27, 1926) and *Royal Palace* (Berlin, March 2, 1927). His next work was a 'Singspiel,' *Aufstieg und Fall der Stadt Mahagonny,* a satire on life in America, to a libretto by Bert Brecht. Its première was given at the Baden-Baden Festival on July 17, 1927; Weill subsequently remodeled the play, and it was presented in an extended version at Leipzig (March 9, 1930). He then wrote an opera buffa *Der Zar lässt sich photographieren* (Leipzig, Feb. 18, 1928). His first striking success came with a modernistic version of *The Beggar's Opera,* to a pungent libretto by Bert Brecht; it was staged under the title *Die Dreigroschenoper* in Berlin, on Aug. 31, 1928, and soon became the rage all over Germany; also produced in translations in Poland, Holland, Denmark, Hungary, Russia, France, and England; given in N. Y. on April 13, 1933, as *The Threepenny Opera;* Marc Blitzstein made a new libretto, versified in a modern American style, and in this form the work was presented for the first time at the Brandeis Univ. Festival, Waltham, Mass., on June 14, 1952. Other stage works by Weill produced in Germany were a school opera *Der Jasager* (1930), *Die Bürgschaft* (Berlin, March 10, 1932), and *Der Silbersee* (1933). After the establishment of the Nazi government, Weill and his wife, the actress and singer Lotte Lenya, who appeared in many of his musical plays, were driven out of Germany; he went to Paris, where he wrote an opera, *Marie galante* (1933), and to London, where he produced a satirical musical play, *A Kingdom for a Cow* (1935). In 1935 he settled in America, remaining there until his death. Quickly absorbing the modes and fashions of American popular music, he succeeded, with amazing fidelity, in creating American-flavored musical plays; this stylistic transition was facilitated by the fact that in his European productions he had already injected elements of American popular songs and jazz rhythms. His highly developed assimilative faculty enabled him to combine this Americanized idiom with the advanced techniques of modern music (atonality, polytonality, polyrhythms), and present the product in a pleasing and yet sophisticated and challenging manner. For the American theater he wrote the scores for the operas *Street Scene* (by Elmer Rice; N. Y., Jan. 9, 1947) and *Lost in the Stars* (by Maxwell Anderson; N. Y., Oct. 30, 1949); the musical comedies *Knickerbocker Holiday* (book and lyrics by Maxwell Anderson; Hartford, Conn., Sept. 26, 1938; contains the popular *September Song); Lady in the Dark* (by Moss Hart), and *One Touch of Venus* (by S. J. Perelman and Ogden Nash); music for *The Firebrand of Florence* (by E. J. Mayer and Ira Gershwin) and *A Flag Is Born* (by Ben Hecht); also for several films. He achieved a signal success with the production of his 'folk opera' *Down in the Valley* (Indiana Univ., Bloomington, July 15, 1948), based on Kentucky mountain songs; many performances were given all over the U. S. Other works include the ballet *Die sieben Todsünden* (1933); the radio cantata *Lindberghflug* (in collaboration with Bert Brecht; commemorating Lindbergh's transatlantic flight, 1927; Berlin, Dec. 5, 1929); *The Ballad of Magna Carta,* modern historical drama with text by Maxwell Anderson (Columbia network broadcast, Feb. 4, 1940); *Der neue Orpheus,* cantata; *Vom Tod im Walde,* ballade for bass voice and 10 wind instruments; *Recordare* for chorus a cappella; *Rilke-Lieder,* for voice with orch. For orch.: *Fantasie, Passacaglia und Hymnus* (1923) and *Quodlibet* (1924); *Frauentanz* for soprano, viola, flute, clarinet, horn, and bassoon (Salzburg Festival of the International Society for Contemporary Music, Aug. 6, 1924); concerto for violin and woodwind instruments (Zürich Festival, June 23, 1926); a string quartet and other chamber music; piano pieces; songs. A *Berliner Symphonie,* written in 1921 and regarded as lost, was rediscovered in 1958. —Cf. Paul Bekker, *Briefe an zeitgenössische Musiker* (1932); V. Thomson, *Most Melodious Tears,* in 'Modern Music' (Nov.-Dec., 1933); H. W. Heinsheimer, *Kurt Weill,* in 'Tomorrow' (March, 1948); H. Strobel, *Erinnerung an Kurt Weill,* in 'Melos' (May, 1950); D. Drew, *Topicality and the Universal: The Strange Case of Weill's 'Die Bürgschaft,'* in 'Music & Letters' (July, 1958). For details on performances of Weill's operas see A. Loewenberg, *Annals of Opera* (Cambridge, 1943; 2nd ed., Geneva, 1955).

Weinberg, Jacob, pianist and composer; b. Odessa, July 5, 1879; d. New York, Nov. 2, 1956. He studied at the Moscow Cons. with Igumnov (piano), S. Taneyev and Ippolitov-Ivanov (composition); was a private pupil of Leschetizky in Vienna (1910-11); taught piano at the Odessa Cons. (1915-21); then went to Palestine, where he stayed for 5 years (1921-26). In 1926 he came to the U. S.; taught piano at Hunter College and the N. Y. College of Music. He composed an opera on a modern Hebrew subject, *Hechalutz (The Pioneers)*; fragments were performed in Jerusalem, in a Hebrew transl., on April 4, 1925; the complete opera was performed in N. Y. on Nov. 25, 1934, under the title *The Pioneers of Israel*, in an English transl.; he also wrote the oratorios *Isaiah* (1948) and *The Life of Moses* (1952); *The Gettysburg Address*, ode for chorus and orch. (N. Y., 1936); *Sabbath Liturgy* for baritone, chorus, and organ; a piano concerto; a piano trio; a string quartet; a violin sonata; contributed essays on Russian music to the 'Mus. Quarterly' and other periodicals.

Weinberger (vīn'-bĕr-gĕr), **Jaromir**, notable Czech composer; b. Prague, Jan. 8, 1896. He studied with Křička and Hofmeister at the Prague Cons., then briefly with Max Reger in Berlin. In 1922 he visited the U. S., and taught for a semester at the Cons. of Ithaca, N. Y. Returning to Europe, he was active as conductor and teacher in Bratislava, Prague, Vienna, and also in Moscow; lived mostly in Prague until 1937, when he went to London; in 1939 he settled permanently in the U. S., living in St. Petersburg, Fla. Weinberger achieved sudden fame with the production of his opera in a popular Bohemian style, *Švanda dudák (Schwanda, the Bagpiper)*, at the Czech Opera in Prague, on April 27, 1927. Its success was immediate, and performances followed all over Europe in several languages; it was produced in German (as *Schwanda der Dudelsackpfeifer*) at the Metropolitan Opera, N. Y., on Nov. 7, 1931; the *Polka and Fugue* from this opera has become a popular number in the orchestral repertory. His other operas include *Die geliebte Stimme* (Munich, Feb. 28, 1931); *Lidé z Pokerflatu (The Outcasts of Poker Flat*, after Bret Harte; Brno, Nov. 19, 1932); *A Bed of Roses*, light opera (Prague, 1934); and *Wallenstein*, lyric tragedy after Schiller (Vienna, Nov. 18, 1937). He wrote for orch. *Marionette Overture* (1913), 6 Bohemian songs and dances (1929), *Under the Spreading Chestnut Tree*, variations and fugue (N. Y., Oct. 12, 1939); *Song of the High Seas* (N. Y., Nov. 9, 1940); *Lincoln Symphony* (Cincinnati, Oct. 17, 1941); *Czech Rhapsody* (Washington, D. C., Nov. 5, 1941); *A Bird's Opera* (Detroit, Nov. 13, 1941); *Préludes religieuses et profanes* (1953); *Ecclesiastes*, for soprano, baritone, mixed chorus, and organ (1945); other choral works; violin pieces; piano pieces; a song cycle of Jewish melodies; etc.

Weiner, Lazar, composer and conductor; b. Cherkassy, near Kiev, Oct. 27, 1897. He studied at the Kiev Cons.; at the age of 17, came to the U. S., where he took courses in composition in N. Y., with Frederick Jacobi, R. R. Bennett, and Joseph Schillinger; conducted various choral societies in N. Y. and Brooklyn. His works include the cantatas *Legend of Toil* (1933), *Man in the World* (1939), *Fight for Freedom* (1943), *To Thee, America* (1944); several Jewish ballets for the N. Y. stage; chamber music. His son, **Yehudi Weiner** (b. N. Y., June 1, 1929), a student of Richard Donovan at Yale, is a gifted composer; in 1952 he went to Rome on a stipend.

Weiner (vī'-ner), **Leo**, outstanding Hungarian composer; b. Budapest, April 16, 1885. He was a pupil of Hans Koessler at the Budapest Academy of Music, winning several prizes for excellence; in 1906 he won the 'Franz-Josef Jubiläumspreis,' which enabled him to study further in Germany and in Paris. Returning to Budapest, he became prof. at the Academy (1908); pensioned in 1949. In his works he adopted a characteristic Hungarian style, within the framework of Romanticism, stemming from Brahms. —Works: for orch.: *Scherzo* (1905); *Serenade* (Budapest, Oct. 22, 1906; his most successful work); *Carnival*, a humoresque (1907); *Katonásdi (Soldatenspiel*, 1924); *Hungarian Folk Dances* (1933); 3 divertimentos on old Hungarian tunes, for string orch. (1933, 1939, 1950); *Pastorale, phantasie et fugue*, for strings (1941); concertino for piano and orch.; chamber music: 3 string quartets (1908, 1922, 1949), string trio (1909), *Ballade* for clarinet and piano (1912), *Romanze* for cello and piano (1925), 2 violin sonatas; a number of piano pieces: *Változatok, Caprice, Miniatures;* 6 Hungarian peasant dances; *Lakodalmas* (wedding dance); children's pieces (1948); incidental music for Vörösmarty's play *Czongor and Tünde* (1913). He publ. didactic works on musical form (1911), on harmony (1917), and on analytical harmony (1944); arranged for orch. a number of Bach's works, of which the Toccata and Fugue in C major is widely performed.

Weingartner (vīn'-gart-nĕhr), **(Paul) Felix,** Edler **von Münzberg,** famous conductor, b. Zara, Dalmatia, June 2, 1863; d. Winterthur, Switzerland, May 7, 1942, After his father's death (1867), his mother moved to Graz, where Weingartner studied under W. A. Remy. As a pupil, he began to write piano pieces, songs, dramatic scenes with orch., etc., and publ. his early piano pieces at the age of 16. For these he received, on the recommendation of Brahms, a stipend from the state, enabling him to continue his studies at the Leipzig Cons. (1881-83) under Reinecke, Jadassohn, and Paul. Having graduated as winner of the Mozart prize, he went to Liszt, who recommended his opera *Sakuntala* for production at Weimar (March 23, 1884). Then began his brilliant career as conductor; he held positions in Königsberg (1884), Danzig (1885-87), Hamburg (1887-89), and Mannheim (1889-91). In 1891 he was engaged as 1st conductor at the Berlin Opera, and conductor of the symph. concerts of the Royal Orch. there; he left the Berlin Opera in 1898, but retained the conductorship of the symph. concerts; from 1898 to 1903 he also conducted the Kaim Orch. in Munich; extended tours with the Berlin orch. established his fame as one of the world's foremost conductors; at the same time he won a fine reputation as an ensemble player; formed the Weingartner Trio, with himself as pianist, R. Rettich as violinist, and H. Warnke as cellist, visiting the principal German cities. In 1908 he succeeded Mahler as director of the Vienna State Opera (until 1910) and conductor of the symph. concerts of the opera orch. From 1912 to 1914 he was in Hamburg as conductor of the Municipal Opera; from 1914 to 1919, conductor of the court orch. in Darmstadt, and director of the Darmstadt Cons. He was musical director of the Vienna Volksoper (1919-24), and conducted the Vienna Philharmonic until 1927, when he became director of the Basel Cons. and conductor of the concerts of the Allgemeine Musikgesellschaft there; was music director of the Vienna State Opera in 1935-36. He appeared as conductor with many European orchestras, and also in the U. S.; made his American début with the N. Y. Philharmonic on Feb. 10, 1905; then conducted the N. Y. Symph. Society (Jan.-March, 1906). He appeared as opera conductor with the Boston Opera Company on Feb. 12, 1912, conducting *Tristan und Isolde;* he and his 3rd wife, the mezzo-soprano Lucille Marcel, were engaged for a season with the same company in 1913. (His 1st wife was Marie Juillerat, whom he married in 1891; his 2nd wife was the Baroness Feodora von Dreifus, whom he married in 1903.) In 1936 he visited Japan; returning to Europe, he settled in Interlaken, Switzerland; established a summer conducting school; his classes attracted students from all parts of the world. His musical scholarship was very high. He was one of the editors of the complete works of Berlioz (from 1899) and of Haydn (from 1907); also edited Weber's *Oberon,* Wagner's *Der fliegende Holländer,* and Méhul's *Joseph.* Weingartner was a prolific composer; besides his early opera *Sakuntala,* he wrote several others: *Genesius* (Berlin, Nov. 15, 1892); *Orestes,* a trilogy (Leipzig, Feb. 15, 1902); *Kain und Abel* (Darmstadt, May 17, 1914); *Dame Kobold* (Darmstadt, Feb. 23, 1916); *Die Dorfschule* (Vienna, May 13, 1920); *Meister Andrea* (Vienna, May 13, 1920). For most of these he wrote his own librettos, and conducted the first performances. His orchestral works include 6 symphonies and the symph. poems *King Lear* and *Frühling;* he also wrote 5 string quartets; piano sextet (with double-bass); string quintet; quintet for clarinet, violin, viola, cello, and piano; octet for clarinet, horn, bassoon, 2 violins, viola, cello, and piano; 2 violin sonatas; a number of orchestral arrangements of piano works, including Beethoven's *Hammerklavier* sonata, op. 106, and Weber's *Aufforderung zum Tanz.* — Writings: *Die Lehre von der Wiedergeburt und das musikalische Drama* (1895); *Über das Dirigieren* (1895; 5th ed., 1913; a fundamental essay on conducting); *Bayreuth 1876-1896* (1897; 2nd ed., 1904); *Die Symphonie nach Beethoven* (1897; 4th ed., 1901; English transl., 1904); *Ratschläge für Aufführung der Sinfonien Beethovens* (1906; 3rd ed., 1928; English transl., 1908); *Ratschläge für Aufführung der Sinfonien Schuberts und Schumanns* (1918); *Ratschläge für Aufführung der Sinfonien Mozarts* (1923); *Musikalische Walpurgisnacht* (1907, a satirical comedy); *Akkorde* (1912; collected essays); *Bo Yin Ra* (1927); *Lebenserinnerungen* (vol. I, 1923; vol. II, 1929; English version as *Buffets and Rewards, a Musician's Reminiscences,* London, 1937); *Unwirkliches und Wirkliches* (1936); *Franz Liszt as Man and Artist,* in the 'Mus. Quarterly' (July, 1936); also a polemical pamphlet, *Erlebnisse eines kgl. Kapellmeisters in Berlin* (1912; an attack upon the Berlin intendancy; a rebuttal was publ. by A. Wolff, in *Der Fall Weingartner,* 1912). —Cf. E. Krause, *Felix Weingartner als schaffender Künstler* (Berlin, 1904); P. Riesenfeld, *Felix Weingartner. Ein kritischer Versuch* (Breslau, 1906); W. Hutschenruyter, *Levensschets en portret van Felix Weingartner* (Haarlem, 1906); Paul Stefan, *Gustav Mahlers Erbe* (Munich, 1908); J. C. Lustig, *Felix Weingartner. Persönlichkeiten* (Berlin, 1908); P. Raabe, *Felix Weingartner,* in 'Die Musik' (Jan., 1908); F. Günther, *Felix Weingartner* (1917); W. Jacob, *Felix Weingartner* (Wiesbaden, 1933); also 'Festschrift für Dr. Felix Weingartner' (for his 70th birthday; Basel, 1933).

Weinlig (vīn'-lih), **Christian Ehregott,** German organist and composer, b. Dresden, Sept. 30, 1743; d. there, March 14, 1813. He studied with Homilius, at the Kreuzschule; in 1767, organist at the Evangelical Church, Leipzig; in 1773, at Thorn; in 1780, accompanist at the Italian Opera, Dresden, and organist at the Frauenkirche; in 1785, succeeded his teacher Homilius as cantor of the Kreuzschule. He publ. sonatas for piano with flute and cello; brought out several oratorios; also light theater pieces.

Weinlig (vīn'-lih), **(Christian) Theodor,** noted German music theorist and teacher; nephew and pupil of preceding; b. Dresden, July 25, 1780; d. Leipzig, March 6, 1842. After a period of study under his uncle, he became a pupil of Stanislao Mattei in Bologna; returning to Dresden, he was cantor at the Kreuzschule (1814-17); in 1823, succeeded Schicht as cantor of the Thomasschule, Leipzig. He enjoyed high repute as a teacher of theory and composition; Richard Wagner was his pupil. His own works include a *Deutsches Magnificat* for soli, chorus, and orch.; vocalises; publ. a practical manual, *Theoretisch-praktische Anleitung zur Fuge, für den Selbstunterricht* (1845; 2d ed., 1852). —Cf. A. Kurz, *Geschichte der Familie Weinlig von 1580-1850* (Bonn, 1912); R. Roch, *Theodor Weinlig* (Leipzig, 1917).

Weinmann (vīn'-mahn), **Karl,** German musicologist, authority on church music; b. Vohenstrauss, Upper Palatinate, Dec. 22, 1873; d. Pielenhofen, near Regensburg, Sept. 26, 1929. He was a pupil of Haberl and Haller at the Kirchenmusikschule in Regensburg; after further study under Peter Wagner in Freiburg, Switzerland, he obtained the degree of *Dr. phil.* with the dissertation *Das Hymnarium Parisiense* (1905). After his ordination to the priesthood, he became prof. at the Kirchenmusikschule in Regensburg; in 1910 succeeded Haberl as its director; in 1917, he was made *Dr. theol.* He was editor of the 'Kirchenmusikalisches Jahrbuch' (from 1908), of 'Musica Sacra' (from 1911), and of the 'Cäcilienvereinsorgan' (from 1926). He ed. for Pustet (after the 'Editio vaticana') *Römisches Gradualbuch* (1909; 4th ed., 1928); *Graduale* (1910); *Kyriale* (1911); *Totenoffizium* (1912; 2nd ed., 1928); *Graduale parvum* (1913); *Römisches Vesperbuch mit Psalmenbuch* (1915); *Karwochenbuch* (1924); *Feier der heiligen Karwoche* (1925); *Sonntagsvesper und Komplet* (2nd ed., 1928). Was also ed. of the collection 'Kirchenmusik,' for which he wrote *Geschichte der Kirchenmusik* (1906; 4th ed., 1925; English transl., 1910; also transl. into French, Italian, Polish, and Hungarian), and monographs on Leonhard Paminger (1907) and Karl Proske (1909). Other writings include *Palestrinas Geburtsjahr* (Regensburg, 1915); *Stille Nacht, heilige Nacht: die Geschichte des Liedes zu seinem 100. Geburtstag* (1918; 2nd ed., 1920); *Das Konzil von Trient und die Kirchenmusik* (1919); *Zur Geschichte der Missa Papae Marcelli,* in 'Peters-Jahrbuch' (1916); etc. He publ. a new ed. of the 4th chapter of Tinctoris' *De inventione et usu musicae,* in the 'Riemann-Festschrift' (1909; also separately, 1917), and ed. the 'Peter Wagner-Festschrift' (1926).

Weinrich, Carl, American organist; b. Paterson, N.J., July 2, 1904. After graduation from N.Y. Univ. (B.A., 1927), he studied at the Curtis Institute of Music in Philadelphia (1927-30); also studied organ privately with Lynnwood Farnam and Marcel Dupré, and piano with Abram Chasins. In 1930 he became successor of Lynnwood Farnam as organist at the Holy Communion Church, N.Y.; taught organ at the Westminster Choir School, Princeton, N.J. (1934-40) and at Columbia Univ. (1942-52); in 1943, appointed director of music at the Princeton Univ. Chapel; was visiting lecturer at Harvard Univ. in 1950; appeared in numerous recitals; also with orchestras.

Weinstock, Herbert, American writer on music; b. Milwaukee, Wis., Nov. 16, 1905; educated in his native town; later took courses at the Univ. of Chicago. He publ. the following books: *Tchaikovsky* (1943; also publ. in French, Portuguese, Spanish, and German); *Handel* (1946; also in German); *Chopin: The Man and His Music* (1949; also in German); *Music as an Art* (1953); co-author, with Wallace Brockway, of *Men of Music* (1939; revised and enlarged, 1950) and *The*

Opera: A History of Its Creation and Performance (1941). Weinstock is an executive editor of Alfred A. Knopf, Inc., N. Y., publishers.

Weinwurm (vīn'-vŏŏrm), **Rudolf,** Austrian choral conductor; b. Schaidldorf-on-the-Thaja, April 3, 1835; d. Vienna, May 26, 1911. He was trained musically as a chorister in the Imperial Chapel, Vienna; conducted the Vienna Singakademie (from 1864) and the Männergesangverein (from 1866); in 1880 he became musical director of Vienna Univ. He publ. the manuals *Allgemeine Musiklehre* (1870); *Musikalische Lehrmittel* (1873); *Methodik des Gesangunterrichts* (1876); composed a *Deutsches Requiem* for male chorus a cappella, and one for female chorus with organ; also other church music.

Weinzierl (vīn'-tsērl), **Max,** Ritter **von,** conductor and composer, b. Bergstadtl, Bohemia, Sept. 16, 1841; d. Mödling, near Vienna, July 10, 1898. He served as conductor at various theaters in Vienna; from 1882, was chorusmaster of the Männergesangverein. He wrote the operas *Don Quixote* (Vienna, Feb. 15, 1879; with L. Roth), *Die weiblichen Jäger* (Vienna, May 5, 1880), *Moclemos* (Vienna, June 5, 1880), *Fioretta* (Prague, 1886), *Page Fritz* (Prague, 1889), *Der Schwiegerpapa* (Berlin, 1893); the oratorio *Hiob* (Vienna, 1870); the choral works with orch.: *Nachtgruss, Liedesweihe, Gesang der Nixen, Die Sphinx, Der Zigeuner, Donausage, Hubertus,* etc.; many male choruses a cappella.

Weinzweig, John Jacob, Canadian composer; b. Toronto, March 11, 1913. He studied at the Univ. of Toronto with Healey Willan and at the Eastman School, Rochester, with Bernard Rogers. In 1934 he organized the Univ. of Toronto Symph. Orch., and conducted it until 1937; then was appointed teacher of composition at the Toronto Cons. On Feb. 3, 1951, he organized the Canadian League of Composers, of which he is chairman. —Works: ballet: *The Red Ear of Corn* (Toronto, March 2, 1949); a symph. (1940); symph. poems: *The Enchanted Hill* (1938) and *A Tale of Tuamotu* (1939); *Spectre,* for kettledrums and strings (1928); violin concerto (1951); 2 string quartets (1937; 1946); divertimento No. 1, for flute and strings (1946); divertimento No. 2, for oboe and strings (1947); violin sonata (1941); cello sonata (1949); piano pieces; choruses: songs.

Weis, Flemming, Danish composer; b. Copenhagen, April 15, 1898. He studied organ in Copenhagen and composition in Leipzig. Returning to Denmark, he became active as music teacher. He wrote an oratorio, *Det forjættede Land (The Promised Land;* Copenhagen, Dec. 8, 1949); 2 symphonies (1946; 1948); a symph. poem, *In temporis vernalis* (1945); a serenade for wind quintet; 3 string quartets; *Diverterende musik,* for flute, violin, viola, and cello; other chamber music; choruses; songs.

Weis, Karel, Czech conductor and composer; b. Prague, Feb. 13, 1862; d. there, April 4, 1944. He studied violin at the Prague Cons.; also organ with Skuherský and composition with Fibich at the Organ School in Prague; subsequently filled various posts as organist and conductor in Prague and other towns in Bohemia. He devoted much of his time to collecting Bohemian folksongs, and publ. them in 15 vols. (1928-41). —Works: the operas *Viola,* after Shakespeare's *Twelfth Night* (Prague, Jan. 17, 1892), *Der polnische Jude* (Prague, March 3, 1901; very successful; produced in English at the Metropolitan Opera House, March 9, 1921), *Die Dorfmusikanten* (Prague, Jan. 1, 1905), *Der Revisor* (after Gogol; 1907), *Útok na mlýn* (after Zola's *L'Attaque du Moulin;* Prague, March 29, 1912), *Lešetínský kovář (The Blacksmith of Lešetín;* Prague, June 6, 1920); a symph.; a string quartet; piano pieces; songs. —Cf. L. Firkušný, *Karel Weis* (Prague, 1949).

Weisbach, Hans, German conductor; b. Glogau, July 19, 1885. He studied at the Hochschule für Musik in Berlin; then became an opera coach in Munich; subsequently conducted in various provincial towns in Germany; held the post of music director and conductor at Düsseldorf (1926-33); then conducted the Leipzig Radio Orch. (1933-39) and the Municipal Orch. of Vienna (1938-45); in 1947 he was appointed music director at Wuppertal. He made several appearances in London; also conducted in Russia.—Cf. C. Heinzen, *Hans Weisbach,* in 'Die Musik' (Feb., 1931).

Weisgall, Hugo, composer; b. Ivančice, Czechoslovakia, Oct. 13, 1912. His family settled in Baltimore in 1920; there he studied theory at the Peabody Cons. with Louis Cheslock; later with Roger Sessions in N.Y., and Rosario Scalero at the Curtis Institute, Philadelphia. He was a cultural attaché at the American embassy in Prague (1946-47); then returned to Baltimore, where he taught and lectured at various music schools; in 1951 founded the Baltimore Chamber Music Society; appeared as guest conductor in Baltimore, Washington, etc. —Works: operas: *Night* (1932), *Lillith* (1934), *The Tenor* (Baltimore, Feb. 11, 1952), *The Stronger,* after Strindberg (Westport, Conn., Aug. 9, 1952), *6 Characters in Search of an Author,* after Pirandello (1953-56); ballets: *Quest* (Baltimore, May 17, 1938), *One Thing Is Certain* (Baltimore, Feb. 25, 1939), *Outpost* (1947); *Overture in F* (London, July 29, 1943); *A Garden Eastward,* cantata for high voice and orch. (Baltimore, Jan. 31, 1953); *Soldier Songs* for baritone and orch. (1946); 2 *Choral Etudes* (1937, 1953); a number of songs. —Cf. G. Rochberg, *Hugo Weisgall,* in the 'Bulletin of American Composers Alliance' (1958, No. 2).

Weismann (vīs'-man), **Julius,** German composer; b. Freiburg-im-Breisgau, Dec. 26, 1879; d. Singen (Bodensee), Dec. 22, 1950. He studied in Munich with Rheinberger and Thuille; devoted himself mainly to the composition of operas, the most important of which was *Leonce und Lena* (Freiburg-im-Breisgau, June 21, 1925). Other operas: *Schwanenweiss,* after Strindberg (Duisburg, Sept. 29, 1923); *Ein Traumspiel* (Duisburg, 1925); *Regina del Lago* (Karlsruhe, 1928); *Die Gespenstersonate,* after Strindberg (Munich, Dec. 19, 1930); *Landsknechte* (Essen, 1936); *Die pfiffige Magd,* after Holberg (Leipzig, Feb. 11, 1939); a symph., *Über einem Grabe,* for chorus and orch.; *Fingerhütchen,* fairy ballad for baritone solo, female chorus, and orch.; *Macht hoch die Tür,* cantata; *Tanzfantasie* for orch.; a piano concerto; a violin concerto; much chamber music, including 2 piano trios, 2 violin sonatas, etc. —Cf. W. Thomas-San Galli, *Julius Weismann,* in vol. 2 of 'Monographien moderner Musiker' (Leipzig, 1907); F. Doldinger, *Julius Weismann,* in 'Neue Musikzeitschrift' (Dec., 1947); H. J. Moser, *Julius Weismann,* in 'Musica' (June, 1955).

Weismann, Wilhelm, German composer; b. Alfdorf, Sept. 20, 1900. He studied at the Stuttgart Cons. with Karg-Elert, and in Leipzig with M. Ludwig; in 1948 was appointed prof. at the Hochschule für Musik in Leipzig. He wrote a number of choral works, both secular and sacred; Italian and German madrigals; several piano suites in the Baroque style; publ. numerous arrangements of old vocal music; brought out *Das kleine Volksliederbuch;* also active as editor for German publishing firms.

Weiss, Adolph, American composer and bassoonist; b. Baltimore, Sept. 12, 1891 (of German parents). He studied piano, violin, and the bassoon; at the age of 16, was engaged as 1st bassoonist of the Russian Symph. Orch. of N. Y.; then played in the N. Y. Philharmonic under Mahler; for many years was with the N. Y. Symph. under Walter Damrosch. In the meantime he studied composition with Cornelius Rybner at Columbia Univ. In 1916 he joined the Chicago Symph. Orch. as bassoonist; studied theory with Adolf Weidig and Theodore Otterstrom there; then was bassoonist with the Rochester, N. Y., Orch. In 1925 he went to Europe to study with Arnold Schoenberg, whose influence was decisive in the formation of his musical style, which is in the 12-tone idiom. In 1931 he received a Guggenheim Fellowship. Returning to the U.S., he played in the San Francisco Symph. Orch.; then moved to Hollywood, where he settled. —Works: *Fantasie* for piano (1918); *I Segreti* for orch. (1922; Rochester, May 1, 1925); 3 string quartets (1925, 1926, 1932); chamber symph. for 10 instruments (1927); 12 preludes for piano (1927); *American Life,* 'Scherzoso Jazzoso' for large orch. (N. Y., Feb. 21, 1930); *Sonata da Camera* for flute and viola (1929); 7 songs for soprano and string quartet (1928); *The Libation Bearers,* choreographic cantata, for soloists, chorus, and orch. (1930); quintet for flute, oboe, clarinet, bassoon, and horn, a 12-tone piece (1931); piano sonata (1932); *Theme and Variations* for large orch. (1933); *Suite* for orch. (1938); *Petite Suite* for flute, clarinet, and bassoon (1939); violin sonata (1941); *Passacaglia* for horn and viola (1942); 10 pieces for low instrument and orch. (1943); *Ode to the West Wind* for baritone, viola, and piano (1945); *Protest* for 2 pianos (1945); sextet for flute, oboe, clarinet, bassoon, horn, and piano (1947); trio for clarinet, viola, and cello (1948); concerto for bassoon and string quartet (1949); *Pulse of the Sea,* an étude for piano (1950); concerto for trumpet and orch. (1952); trio for flute, violin, and piano (1955); 5 fantasies for violin and piano (1956); *Tone Poem* for brass and percussion (1957); *Rhapsody* for 4 French horns (1957); *Vade Mecum* for a group of wind instruments (1958). —Cf. W. Riegger, *Adolph Weiss and Colin McPhee,* in H. Cowell, ed., *American Composers on American Music* (Stanford Univ., 1933); 'Bulletin of American Composers Alliance' (1958, No. 3).

Weiss, Amalie. See **Joachim, Amalie.**

Weiss, Franz, viola player; b. Silesia, Jan. 18, 1778; d. Vienna, Jan. 25, 1830. When Prince Razumovsky formed his string quartet in Vienna (1808), Franz Weiss was engaged as viola player, with Schuppanzigh as 1st violin, Prince Razumovsky as 2nd violin, and Linke as cellist. Weiss composed some chamber music; *Variations brillantes* for violin and orch.; several piano sonatas; as a symph. for flute, bassoon, and trumpet; etc.

Weiss, Johann, Austrian hymnologist; b. St. Ruprecht-on-Raab, Styria, Nov. 20, 1850; d. there, Sept. 7, 1919. He studied theology; in 1881 appointed teacher of hymnology at the Graz Seminary; was organist at the Graz Cathedral (1884-91); from 1902 was co-editor of the 'Gregorianische Rundschau.' He publ. *Die musikalischen Instrumente in den heiligen Schriften des Alten Testaments* (1895).

Weiss, Julius, German violinist; b. Berlin, July 19, 1814; d. there, June 30, 1898. He studied with Henning; wrote music criticism; publ. instructive works for violin; was also active in music publishing.

Weiss, Sylvius Leopold, German lute player and composer; b. Breslau, Oct. 12, 1686; d. Dresden, Oct. 15, 1750. He learned to play the lute from his father; served as lutenist at the court of Düsseldorf (1706); then with Alexander Sobieski, Prince of Poland, in Rome (1708-14); and at Hesse-Kassel (1715-16). In 1717 he went to Dresden, where he remained for the rest of his life, with the exception of a few months in Berlin (1728). He was regarded as one of the greatest lute players of his time; in 1728, publ. a treatise on the lute. 6 of his suites are reprinted in vol. XII of the 'Reichsdenkmale' (Brunswick, 1939). —Cf. H. Neemann, *Die Lautenhandschriften von S. L. Weiss in der Bibliothek Dr. Werner Wolffheim, Berlin,* in 'Zeitschrift für Musikwissenschaft' (vol. 10; 1928); H. Neemann, *Die Lautenistenfamilie Weiss,* in 'Archiv für Musikforschung' (vol. 4; 1939).

Weissberg (vīs'-berg), **Yulia Lazarevna,** Russian composer; b. Orenburg, Dec. 25, 1878; d. Leningrad, March 1, 1942. She studied at the St. Petersburg Cons. with Rimsky-Korsakov, and married his son Andrey; in 1907 took a course with Max Reger in Germany; was a co-editor of the periodical 'Musikalnyi Sovremennik' (1915-17). — Works: operas: *Mermaid,* after Andersen (1923), *Gülnara* (1935), *The Dead Princess* (1937); 2 children's operas: *Little Rabbit's House* (1935) and *Geese and Swans* (1937); *The Twelve,* to the poem of Alexander Blok, for chorus and orch. (1928); symph. poem, *In the Night* (1929); *Sailor's Dance,* for orch. (1936); several song cycles for voice with instruments; children's choruses; a number of solo songs; transcriptions of folksongs.

Weisse, Hans, Austrian music theorist and composer; b. Vienna, March 31, 1892; d. New York, Feb. 10, 1940. He studied with Schenker and became an exponent of his theory. In 1931 he came to the U. S. and gave courses in theory at the Mannes Music School, in N. Y. He wrote mostly chamber music: 3 string quartets (1920-36); string sextet (1924); quintet for clarinet and strings (1928); octet for strings and winds (1929); concerto for flute, oboe, and harpsichord (1937); *Choral Partita,* for strings and winds (1938).

Weissenbäck (vī'-sĕn-bäk), **(Franz) Andreas,** Austrian choral conductor and composer; b. St. Lorenzen, Styria, Nov. 26, 1880. He studied in Graz; in 1899, entered the monastery at Klosterneuburg, near Vienna; became a Catholic priest in 1904; then took up musicology under Guido Adler at the Univ. of Vienna *(Dr. phil.,* 1912); was for many years choirmaster at Klosterneuburg. He was co-founder and co-editor of the review 'Musica Divina'; publ. *Sacra Musica,* a lexicon of Catholic church music (1937); collaborated in the 'Denkmäler der Tonkunst in Österreich'; contributed valuable papers to various publications, particularly on Gregorian Chant; also was an expert on church bells. He composed a German Mass for male chorus; publ. many sacred works; also a Mass for mixed chorus and 7 wind instruments, including 2 saxophones (first use of saxophones in liturgical music).

Weissheimer (vīs'-hī-mĕr), **Wendelin,** conductor and composer; b. Osthofen, Alsace, Feb. 26, 1838; d. Nuremberg, June 16, 1910. He studied at the Leipzig Cons. and later took lessons in composition with Liszt at Weimar. He was opera conductor at Würzburg, at Mainz, and at Strasbourg; then lived in various towns on the Rhine and in Bavaria. As a composer, he followed the Wagnerian vogue; wrote 2 music dramas, *Theodor Körner* (Munich, May 28, 1872) and *Meister Martin und seine Gesellen* (Karlsruhe, April 14, 1879); also 18 songs to words by Goethe; *5 Geistliche Sonette* for voice, flute, oboe, clarinet, and harmonium. His book of reminiscences, *Erlebnisse mit Richard Wagner, Franz Liszt und vielen anderen Zeitgenossen, nebst deren Briefen* (Stuttgart, 1898), quotes many letters from Wagner, with whom he maintained an intimate friendship.

Weissmann (vīs'-man), **Adolf,** German writer on music; b. Rosenberg, Silesia, Aug. 15, 1873; d. Saïda, near Haifa, April 23, 1929. He studied in Berlin, Breslau, Florence, etc.; *Dr. phil.,* 1914. He was critic for the 'Berliner Tageblatt' (1900-15) and from 1916 for the 'Berliner Zeitung am Mittag'; also wrote for German music magazines; went on a lecture tour in Palestine and died there. —Books: *Berlin als Musikstadt (1740-1911)* (1911); *G. Bizet* (1907; in the collection 'Die Musik,' ed. by Richard Strauss); *Chopin* (1912; 3rd ed., 1919); *Der Virtuose* (1918); *Die Primadonna* (1920); *Der klingende Garten. Impressionen über das Erotische in der Musik* (1920); the 3 preceding titles together as *Die Musik der Sinne* (1925); *Giacomo Puccini* (1922); *Die Musik in der Weltkrise* (1922; English transl. as *The Problems of Modern Music,* London, 1925); *Verdi* (1922); *Der Dirigent im 20. Jahrhundert* (1925); *Die Entgötterung der Musik* (1928; English transl., as *Music Come to Earth,* London, 1930). —Cf. E. Preussner, *Adolf Weissmann,* in 'Die Musik' (vol. 21; 1929).

Weissmann, Frieder, conductor; b. Langen, Germany, Jan. 23, 1898. He studied law and music at the Univ. of Munich; conducted at the Berlin State Opera (1920-25); then at Münster and Königsberg; was subsequently conductor of the Dresden Philharmonic (1927-31) and of the Berlin Symph. Orch. (1931-33); made a South American tour (1934-37); made his U.S. début with the Cincinnati Symph. Orch. during the season of 1937-38; was conductor of the Scranton, Pa., Philharmonic (1943-50); from 1950 conducted the Havana Philharmonic.

Weissmann, John (János), musicologist; b. Budapest, July 10, 1910. He studied at the Budapest Cons.; was opera coach at the Municipal Theater (1932-34); then assistant conductor there (1935-37). In 1937 he settled in London, where he attended classes of conducting at the Royal Academy of Music. Subsequently he devoted his attention mainly to musicology; has contributed numerous valuable essays to various periodicals; publ. a monograph on Goffredo Petrassi (Milan, 1957; in English); wrote the articles on Hungarian music and musicians for the 5th ed. of Grove's Dictionary (1954).

Weitzmann (vīts'-man), **Karl Friedrich,** noted German theorist and composer; b. Berlin, Aug. 10, 1808; d. there, Nov. 7, 1880. He studied violin with Henning and theory with Klein; later, at Kassel, was a pupil of Spohr and Hauptmann. He then held the post of concertmaster in Riga (1832-34), Reval (1834-36), and St. Petersburg (1836-46). After sojourns in Paris and London (1846-48), he settled in Berlin as a teacher of composition. He was an ardent disciple and friend of Wagner and Liszt; among his posthumous papers was found the original MS of a double fugue for piano by Wagner, with corrections in the handwriting of Weinlig (Wagner's teacher). The piece was publ. by E. Istel in 'Die Musik' (July, 1912). Weitzmann was an original thinker in his harmonic theories; made an investigation of the modulatory functions of the whole-tone scale, and interested Liszt in its use. He composed a 4th variation to Liszt's *Todtentanz.* A full exposition of his theories is found in a book by his American pupil, E. M. Bowman, *K. F. Weitzmann's Manual of Musical Theory* (N.Y., 1877). Weitzmann's theoretical works in German include *Der übermässige Dreiklang* (1853); *Der verminderte Septimenakkord* (1854); *Geschichte des Septimen-Akkordes* (1854); *Geschichte der Harmonie und ihrer Lehre* (in the 'Allgemeine musikalische Zeitung,' 1849); *Harmoniesystem* (1860); *Die neue Harmonielehre im Streit mit der alten* (1861); *Geschichte des Klavierspiels und der Klavierlitteratur* (1863, as Part III of the Lebert-Stark piano method; 2nd ed., 1879, printed separately, with an added *Geschichte des Klaviers*; in English, N.Y., 1894, with a biographical sketch by Otto Lessmann; 3rd German ed., Leipzig, 1899, as *Geschichte der Klaviermusik,* edited by Max Seiffert, with a supplement, *Geschichte des Klaviers,* by Otto Fleischer); *Der letzte der Virtuosen* (on Tausig; 1868); many essays in various musical periodicals. As a composer, he followed the fashionable Romantic trends; wrote the operas *Räuberliebe* (1834), *Walpurgisnacht* (1835), and *Lorbeer und Bettelstab* (1836), which he brought out in Reval; 3 books of *Valses nobles* for piano; Preludes and Modulations for piano, in 2 parts, 'Classic' and 'Romantic'; also wrote 2 books of ingenious canonic *Rätsel* for piano 4 hands, and 2 books of *Kontrapunkt-Studien* for piano.

Welch, Roy Dickinson, American pianist and music educator; b. Dansville, N.Y., Jan. 19, 1885; d. Princeton, N.J., Jan. 8, 1951. He studied at the Univ. of Michigan (B.A., 1909); then went to Berlin, where he took piano lessons from Josef Lhévinne (1910-12). From 1914 to 1935 he was chairman of the music dept. of Smith College, Northampton, Mass.; went to Europe on a Guggenheim Fellowship (1930-32); in 1935 was appointed chairman of the music dept. of Princeton

Univ. He publ. *The Study of Music in the American College* (Northampton, Mass., 1925) and *The Appreciation of Music* (N.Y., 1927; revised ed., 1945).

Weld, Arthur Cyril Gordon, American conductor; b. Boston, March 4, 1862; d. near West Point, N.Y., Oct. 11, 1914 (of apoplexy, while driving an automobile). He studied in Dresden, in Berlin, and in Munich. Upon returning to America, he became general director of the H. W. Savage Opera Co., and conducted the first performance of the famous musical comedy *Floradora* (N. Y., 1900). Some of his songs were publ.

Weldon, George, English conductor; b. Chichester, June 5, 1906. He studied at the Royal College of Music with Malcolm Sargent; conducted various provincial orchestras; traveled as guest conductor in North Africa, Turkey, and Yugoslavia. He was conductor of the Birmingham City Orch. from 1943 to 1950. —Cf. Donald Brook, *International Gallery of Conductors* (London, 1951; pp. 221-23).

Weldon, Georgina (*née* Thomas), English soprano; b. London, May 24, 1837; d. Brighton, Jan. 11, 1914. She took up singing after her marriage to Capt. Weldon in 1860, and did not appear in public until 1870. She organized an orphan asylum for the purpose of musical education, and also dabbled in music publishing. Special interest attaches to her because of her romantic friendship with Gounod, who during his London sojourn (1870-75) lived at her residence, and whom she assisted in training the 'Gounod Choir.' She translated his autobiography (which goes only as far as 1859) into English (1875). Their relationship deteriorated, leading to a legal entanglement in connection with her claims regarding the copyright of Gounod's choral works; she wrote numerous and highly acrimonious letters to the press, defending her stand. She also publ. some songs of her own (to French texts) and the didactic manuals *Hints for Pronunciation in Singing* (1872) and *Musical Reform* (1875).

Welitsch, Ljuba (real name, Velitchkova), Bulgarian soprano; b. Borisovo, near Varna, July 10, 1913. She played the violin as a child; then entered high school; subsequently took courses in philosophy at the Univ. of Sofia; then went to Vienna, where she studied voice with Lierhammer. She made her operatic début as Nedda in *I Pagliacci* at the Graz Opera (1936); from 1941 to 1943, sang in Hamburg and Berlin; in 1943-46, was in Munich. On June 11, 1944 she made her first appearance as Salome (later to become her most famous role) in Vienna, under the direction of Richard Strauss himself, on his 80th birthday. She made her début in London with the Vienna State Opera as Donna Anna in *Don Giovanni* on Sept. 20, 1947. Her American début, at the Metropolitan Opera House, N. Y., in *Salome* (Feb. 4, 1949) was greatly acclaimed. She remained a member of the Metropolitan Opera until 1952.

Wellek (věl'-lěk), **Albert,** Austrian musicologist; b. Vienna, Oct. 16, 1904. He studied at the Universities of Prague, Vienna, and Leipzig (*Dr. phil.,* Vienna, 1928), and the Prague Cons.; in 1933 he became assistant to Felix Krueger in the psychology dept. of the Univ. of Leipzig; in 1943 was appointed prof. of psychology at Breslau; subsequently at the Univ. of Mainz. From 1938 he was co-editor of the 'Neue psychologische Studien.' —Writings: *Das absolute Gehör und seine Typen* (Leipzig, 1938); *Typologie der Musikbegabung im deutschen Volke* (Munich, 1939); numerous articles on musical psychology in various German periodicals; *Quarter-Tones and Progress,* in the 'Mus. Quarterly' (April, 1926); etc.

Wellesz (věhl'-ěs), **Egon,** eminent Austrian composer and musicologist; b. Vienna, Oct. 21, 1885. He studied harmony with Carl Frühling, musicology with Guido Adler, and counterpoint and composition with Schoenberg; obtained the degree of *Dr. phil.* in 1908 with a thesis on Giuseppe Bonno, publ. in the 'Sammelbände der Internationalen Musik-Gesellschaft' (vol. XI, 1910). From 1911 to 1915 he taught music history at the Neues Conservatorium in Vienna; in 1913 was engaged as lecturer on musicology at the Univ. of Vienna, and was prof. there from 1930 to 1938, when the annexation of Austria by Nazi Germany compelled him to leave. He went to England and joined the music dept. of Oxford Univ., which in 1932 had conferred upon him the degree of Mus. Doc. *(hon. c.).* In 1943 he became lecturer in the history of music at Oxford Univ.; in 1946, appointed to the editorial board of the 'New Oxford History of Music,' to which he then contributed, and in 1948, elected Univ. Reader in Byzantine music at Oxford. In 1956-57 he lectured in the U.S. A scholar and a musician of extraordinary capacities, Wellesz has distinguished himself as an early disciple and biographer of Schoenberg, as a composer of highly complex musical scores, and as an authority on Byzantine music. —Works: operas: *Die Prinzessin Girnara* (Hanover,

May 15, 1921; revised version, Mannheim, Sept. 2, 1928); *Alkestis* (Mannheim, March 20, 1924); *Opferung des Gefangenen* (Cologne, April 10, 1926); *Scherz, List und Rache* (Stuttgart, March 1, 1928); *Die Bakchantinnen* (Vienna, June 20, 1931); *Incognita* (Oxford, Dec. 5, 1951); ballets: *Das Wunder der Diana* (Mannheim, March 20, 1924); *Persisches Ballet* (Donaueschingen, 1924); *Achilles auf Skyros* (Stuttgart, March 4, 1927); *Die Nächtlichen* (Berlin, Nov. 20, 1924); for orch.: 5 symphonies (1945, 1948, 1951, 1952, 1957); symph. poem, *Vorfrühling* (1912); *Festlicher Marsch* (1929); *Prosperos Beschwörungen,* after Shakespeare's *The Tempest* (1936-38); piano concerto (1935); chamber music: 7 string quartets; 2 pieces for clarinet and piano; suite for violin and piano; sonata for unaccompanied violin; sonata for unaccompanied cello; *Little Suite* for flute unaccompanied; octet for clarinet, bassoon, horn, and strings (1948); a number of piano pieces; vocal works: *Gebete der Mädchen zu Maria,* after Rilke, for soprano, chorus, and orch. (1909); cantata, *Mitte des Lebens,* for soprano, chorus, and orch. (1932); Mass, for chorus and organ (1934); Short Mass for chorus and chamber orch. (1937); several motets; *Proprium* (1953); arias for voice with orch.; 5 sonnets by Elizabeth Browning, for soprano and string quartet (1935); *The Leaden Echo and the Golden Echo,* for soprano, violin, clarinet, cello, and piano (1942); several song cycles. —Writings: *Cavalli und der Stil der venetianischen Oper (1640-60),* in Adler's 'Studien' I (1913); *Schönberg and Beyond,* in the 'Mus. Quarterly' (Jan., 1916); *Die Grundlagen der musikgeschichtlichen Forschung,* in 'Archiv für Musikwissenschaft' (1919); *Arnold Schönberg* (1921; English transl., 1925); *Der Beginn des musikalischen Barock und Die Anfänge der Oper in Wien* (1922); *Aufgaben und Probleme auf dem Gebiete der byzantinischen und orientalischen Kirchenmusik* (1923); *Byzantinische Musik* (1927); *Die neue Instrumentation* (2 vols.; 1928, 1929); *Eastern Elements in Western Chant* (Oxford, 1947); *A History of Byzantine Music and Hymnography* (Oxford, 1949); *Essays on Opera* (London, 1950); *The Origin of Schoenberg's Twelve-Tone System* (Washington, 1958); numerous essays on a variety of subjects in German and English periodicals. He edited Fux's *Costanza e Fortezza,* in the 'Denkmäler der Tonkunst in Österreich' (vol. 34-35); *Trésor de Musique Byzantine,* vol. I (Paris, 1934); *Die Hymnen des Sticherarium für September* (1936; vol. I of the 'Monumenta Musicae Byzantinae, Transcripta'); and vol. I of the *New Oxford History of Music,* 'Ancient and Oriental Music' (1957). —Cf. O. F. Beer, *Egon Wellesz und die Oper,* in 'Die Musik' (Sept., 1931); H. F. Redlich, *Egon Wellesz,* in the 'Mus. Quarterly' (Jan., 1940); R. Reti, *Egon Wellesz, Musician and Scholar,* in the 'Mus. Quarterly' (Jan., 1956).

Wels, Charles, pianist and composer; b. Prague, Aug. 24, 1825; d. New York, May 12, 1906. After studying in Prague, he went to America in 1849, and settled in N.Y.; filled various positions as church organist and teacher; retired in 1901. He composed about 170 op. numbers, including 5 Masses; a piano concerto; fantasias, other pieces, transcriptions, and arrangements for piano, 2 or 4 hands; several male quartets; songs.

Welsh, Thomas, English singer and composer; b. Wells, c. 1780; d. Brighton, Jan. 24, 1848. He was a chorister at Wells Cathedral, and a pupil of J. B. Cramer and Baumgarten. He made his opera début in London at the age of 12; after his voice changed he became a bass, and sang in oratorio. He was particularly distinguished as a vocal teacher; publ. *Vocal Instructor, or the Art of Singing Exemplified in 15 Lessons leading to 40 Progressive Exercises* (1825); piano sonatas; glees, duets, and part-songs; also wrote several musical pieces for the theater. His wife and pupil Mary Anne, *née* Wilson (1802-67), was a noted soprano who made her début at Drury Lane, Jan. 18, 1821, in Arne's *Artaxerxes.*

Welte, Michael, German manufacturer of musical instruments; b. Unterkirnach, Black Forest, Sept. 29, 1807; d. Freiburg-im-Breisgau, Jan. 17, 1880. Having served an apprenticeship with Josef Blessing, a maker of musical clocks, he established himself at Voehrenbach (1832); exhibited his first 'orchestrion' at Karlsruhe in 1849; later took his sons (Emil, Berthold, and Michael, Jr.) into partnership. His instruments obtained 1st prizes at London (1862), Paris (1867), Munich (1885), Vienna (1892), Chicago (1893), St. Louis (1904), Leipzig (1909), and Turin (1911); in 1872 the factory was removed to Freiburg-im-Breisgau. —His oldest son, **Emil Welte** (b. Voehrenbach, April 20, 1841; d. Norwich, Conn., Oct. 25, 1923), established a branch in N.Y. (1865); he improved the then newly invented paper roll (taking the place of the earlier wooden cylinders), and was the first to use it, in connection with a pneumatic action, in a large orchestrion built for Theiss' Alhambra Court (N.Y. City). A son of Berthold Welte, **Edwin** (b. Freiburg, 1875; d. there, Jan. 4, 1958), applied the paper roll to the piano, producing the 'Welte-Mignon Reproducing Piano' (first exhibited in Freiburg, 1904); the application of the same principle to the organ resulted in the invention of the 'Philharmonic Organ' (1912).

Wen Chung, Chou. See **Chou Wen Chung.**

Wendel, Ernst, German violinist and conductor; b. Breslau, March 26, 1876; d. Jena, May 20, 1938. He studied violin with Joachim in Berlin; theory with Bargiel. In 1896 he went to America, and was a member of the Chicago Symph. Orch. for 2 seasons; returning to Germany, was conductor of the 'Musikverein' in Königsberg (1898-1909); then conductor in Bremen, Berlin, Frankfurt, and Nuremberg. He composed *Das Grab im Busento* and *Das deutsche Lied,* both for men's chorus with orch.; also men's choruses a cappella and songs.

Wendland, Waldemar, German composer; b. Liegnitz, May 10, 1873; d. Zeitz, Aug. 15, 1947. He studied for a short time with Humperdinck, while acting as an assistant conductor at the Frankfurt Opera; then settled in Berlin. He wrote the operas *Das kluge Felleisen* (Magdeburg, 1909), *Das vergessene Ich* (Berlin, 1911), *Der Schneider von Malta* (Leipzig, 1812), *Peter Sukoff* (Basel, 1921), *Die vier Temperamente* (Freiburg, 1927), *Koreanisches Märchen* (Altenburg, May 11, 1946); several ballets; orchestral works; chamber music; about 200 songs.

Wendling, Johann Baptist, German flutist and composer; b. Alsace, c. 1720; d. Munich, Nov. 27, 1797. He was active in Mannheim as a flutist from 1754; accompanied Mozart to Paris in 1778; then was with the Mannheim court in Munich. He composed a number of flute concertos and other flute music. His wife, Dorothea Wendling (1737-1811), was an opera singer; Mozart wrote an aria for her.

Wendling, Karl, German pianist; b. Frankenthal, Nov. 14, 1857; d. Leipzig, June 20, 1918. He studied at the Leipzig Cons.; made a specialty of the Jankó keyboard, on which he became highly proficient; also taught piano at the Leipzig Cons.; publ. 'Meisterwerke aus der Etüden-Literatur' (4 books; in progressive order).

Wendt, Ernst Adolf, German pianist and composer; b. Schwiebus, Prussia, Jan. 6, 1806; d. Neuwied, Feb. 5, 1850. He was a pupil of Zelter in Berlin; then became instructor at the Teachers' Seminary there. He publ. variations for piano and orch.; a piano trio; a 4-hand piano sonata; a collection of his organ pieces was publ. by Karl Becker as *Wendt Album.*

Wennerberg, Gunnar, Swedish writer and composer; b. Linköping, Oct. 2, 1817; d. Leckö, Aug. 22, 1901. He studied at the Univ. of Upsala, and entered the Swedish Parliament. He learned music by himself; began to write songs for male voices, which became very successful in Sweden; publ. the collections 'Frihetssånger' (1847) and 'Gluntarne' (1849-51; reprinted, Upsala, 1949); also composed a Christmas oratorio, and settings of the Psalms of David for solo voices, chorus, and piano. His literary works were publ. in 4 vols. (1881-85). —Cf. S. Almquist, *Om Gunnar Wennerberg: hans tid och hans gärning* (Stockholm, 1917); C. F. Hennerberg, *Förteckning över G. Wennerbergs Tonverk* (Stockholm, 1918); G. Jeanson, *G. Wennerberg som Musiker* (Stockholm, 1929).

Wenzel (vĕn'-tsĕl), **Ernst Ferdinand,** German pianist and writer on music; b. Walddorf, near Löbau, Jan. 25, 1808; d. Bad Kösen, Aug. 16, 1880. A student of philosophy at Leipzig Univ., he also had private piano lessons with Fr. Wieck, became a fast friend of his fellow-pupil Schumann, and was a frequent contributor to the 'Neue Zeitschrift für Musik' during Schumann's editorship (till 1844). He was also an intimate friend of Mendelssohn; taught piano at the Leipzig Cons. from its foundation in 1843 until his death; the majority of English-speaking students there were in his classes, or had private instruction from him.

Wenzel, Leopold, Italian violinist, conductor, and composer; b. Naples, Jan. 31, 1847; d. Asnières, near Paris, Aug., 1925. He studied at the Cons. S. Pietro a Majella, Naples, but left it at the age of 13, traveling as a violinist in Greece, Turkey, Egypt, eventually going to Paris as theater conductor there. From 1889 to 1914 he was in London, conducting at the Empire Theatre and the Gaiety Theatre. He wrote about 20 ballets, the most successful being *Dream of Wealth, Katrina,* and *The Girl I Left behind Me;* the operettas *Le Chevalier Mignon* (Paris, 1884), *L'Élève du Conservatoire* (Paris, 1894); also many songs.

Wenzinger, August, Swiss cellist and music editor; b. Basel, Nov. 14, 1905. He studied cello in Basel; took a course in composition with Jarnach in Cologne (1927-29); then was orchestral cellist in Bremen and other German cities; in 1934 returned to Basel, where he gave concerts on the viola da gamba; was active in old music societies there. He publ. *Gambenübung* (2 vols.; 1935, 1938) and *Gambenfibel* (with Marianne Majer; 1943); edited Haydn's cello concerto in D major and Bach's unaccompanied suites for cello; publ. various papers in music magazines.

Werba, Erik, Austrian composer; b. Baden, near Vienna, May 23, 1918. He studied with J. Marx (theory), with Lach, Wellesz, and Schenk (musicology); *Dr. phil.*, 1940, Univ. of Vienna. In 1948 appointed prof. at the Vienna State Academy. He composed several Singspiele, chamber music, songs.

Werckmeister, Andreas, German organist and theorist; b. Beneckenstein, Nov. 30, 1645; d. Halberstadt, Oct. 26, 1706. He studied organ with his uncles, Christian and Victor; was organist at Hasselfelde (1664-74), at Quedlinburg (1675-96), and finally at Halberstadt, from 1696 to his death. He publ. the important treatise *Orgelprobe* . . . (1681; 2nd ed., 1698; 3rd ed., 1716; 4th ed., 1764; English transl. in 'Organ Institute Quarterly,' vol. 6, 1956); *Musicae mathematicae Hodegus curiosus, oder richtiger musikalisher Weg-Weiser* . . . (1686; 2nd ed., 1698); *Der edlen Music-Kunst Würde, Gebrauch und Missbrauch* . . . (1691); *Musikalische Temperatur* . . . (1691; the earliest treatise on equal temperament); *Hypomnemata musica, oder musikalisches Memorial* . . . (1697); *Die nothwendigsten Anmerckungen und Regeln wie der Bassus continuus . . . könne tractiret werden* . . . (1698); *Harmonologia musica, oder kurtze Anleitung zur musikalischen Composition* . . . (1702); *Organum Gruningense redivivum, oder kurtze Beschreibung des in der grüningischen Schloss-Kirchen berühmten Orgel-Wercks* . . . (1705); *Musikalische Paradoxal-Discourse* . . . (posthumous; 1707). A facsimile reprint of the *Orgelprobe* (ed. of 1698) was publ. in Kassel in 1927; the *Organum Gruningense* was republ. in Mainz, in 1932. —Cf. W. Serauky, *Andreas Werckmeister als Musiktheoretiker,* in the 'Max Schneider Festschrift' (Halle, 1935); R. Dammann, *Zur Musiklehre des Andreas Werckmeister,* in 'Archiv für Musikwissenschaft' (vol. 11; 1954).

Wermann, Friedrich Oskar, German organist and composer; b. Neichen, near Trebsen, April 30, 1840; d. Oberloschwitz, near Dresden, Nov. 22, 1906. He was a pupil of Fr. Wieck (piano); later of Reinecke, Hauptmann, and Richter at the Leipzig Cons. He occupied various positions as organist in Alsace, before settling in Dresden (1868) as teacher and church organist; also conducted the Lehrergesangverein there. He composed a Christmas fairy tale, *Die Wunderglocke;* a symph. poem, *König Witichis;* several overtures; a *Reformationskantate;* a *Passionskantate;* 2 Masses; several psalms for double chorus a cappella; numerous organ works; études for piano; part-songs.

Werner, Arno, German organist and musicologist; b. Prittitz, Weissenfels, Nov. 22, 1865; d. Bitterfeld, Feb. 15, 1955. He studied at the Royal Institute for Church-Music in Berlin (1889-90); in 1890 became municipal organist at Bitterfeld; in 1894 was appointed music teacher at the Gymnasium there, retiring in 1931; continued his activities as musicologist until his death; contributed articles to 'Die Musik in Geschichte und Gegenwart' (1953). —Writings: *Samuel und Gottfried Scheidt* (1900); *Geschichte der Kantorei-Gesellschaften im Gebiete des Kurfürstentums Sachsen* (1902); *Die Kantorei zu Bitterfeld* (1903); *Städtische und fürstliche Musikpflege in Weissenfels* . . . (1911); *Städtische und fürstliche Musikpflege in Zeitz* (1922); *Zur Geschichte der Kantorei in Zörbig* (1927); *Musikpflege in Stadt und Kreis Bitterfeld* (1931); *Vier Jahrhunderte im Dienste der Kirchenmusik. Geschichte der Kantoren, Organisten und Stadtpfeifer seit der Reformation* (1932); *Der deutsche Kantor* (1933); *Freie Musikgemeinschaften im mitteldeutschen Raum* (1940).

Werner, Eric, musicologist; b. Lundenberg, near Vienna, Aug. 1, 1901. He studied composition with Kornauth in Vienna, and Schreker and Busoni in Berlin; also took courses at the universities of Graz, Vienna, Prague, Berlin, Göttingen, and Strasbourg; *Dr. phil.* (1928); held teaching positions in Saarbrücken (1926-33) and Breslau (1935-38). In 1938 he settled in the U.S.; was engaged as lecturer at the Hebrew Union College, Cincinnati; prof., 1946; chairman of faculty at Hebrew Union School of Sacred Music, N.Y., 1948; since 1955 chairman of graduate department there. Received a Guggenheim Fellowship in 1957. He is an authority on Jewish and early Christian music; publ. *In the Choir Loft* (N.Y., 1957); *The Sacred Bridge* (London, 1958); contributed articles to the 'Mus. Quarterly' and other publications; composed a *Symphony-Requiem;* chamber music; various other pieces.

Werner, Gregor Joseph, Austrian music director and composer; b. 1695; d. Eisenstadt, March 3, 1766. In 1728 he was appointed Kapellmeister to Prince Esterházy at Eisenstadt (was succeeded after his death by Haydn). He wrote a number of works, including 40 Masses, 18 oratorios, instrumental pieces. His fugues for string quartet were arranged by Haydn. Modern reprints, ed. by E. F. Schmid, include *Hirtenkantate* (1934); *Hirtenmusik* (1934; 1938); *Kleine Hirtenmusik* (1940); *Pastorella in D;* works for 2 violins and harpsichord ed. by Fritz Stein in 'Das Erbe deutscher Musik' vol. 31; etc.

Werner, Heinrich, German composer; b. Kirchohmfeld, Oct. 2, 1800; d. Brunswick, May 3, 1833. His song *Haidenröslein* became a perennial favorite in Germany; he also publ. male quartets and light piano music. —Cf. Fr. Mecke, *Heinrich Werner* (dissertation; Bonn, 1913); P. Egert, *Festschrift zur Einweihung des Denkmals für Werner in Kirchohmfeld* (1913).

Werner, Johann Gottlob, German organist and teacher; b. Grossenhain, 1777; d. Chemnitz, July 19, 1822. After holding minor positions as organist in provincial towns, he was appointed cathedral organist and music director at Merseburg, but died 3 years later. He publ. organ methods which were much in use: *Orgelschule* (1805; Part II as *Lehrbuch, das Orgelwerk . . . kennen . . . zu lernen,* 1823; both often republ.); *Musikalisches ABC* for beginners on the piano (1806; often republ.); *Choralbuch zum holländischen Psalm- und Gesangbuch* (1814); *Choralbuch zu den neuern sächsischen Gesangbüchern* (Leipzig); *Versuch einer kurzen und deutlichen Darstellung der Harmonielehre* (2 parts, 1818, 1819); many chorale-preludes; 40 organ pieces for beginners; etc.

Werner, Josef, German cellist; b. Würzburg, June 25, 1837; d. Munich, Nov. 14, 1922. He studied at the Würzburg Cons.; became a teacher at the Munich Musikschule; publ. a *Praktische Violoncell-Schule* (with 7 supplements); *Der erste Anfang im Violoncellspiel;* several books of *Übungen für Violoncell;* numerous pieces for cello with piano; also a quartet for 4 cellos.

Werner, Theodor Wilhelm, German writer on music; b. Hanover, June 8, 1874; d. Salzburg, Dec. 6, 1957. He studied philology; then music with Draeseke and Noren in Dresden; musicology with Johannes Wolf in Berlin, Sandberger and Kroyer in Munich; *Dr. phil.,* 1917. He became instructor at Hanover; also wrote music criticism; from 1945 lived in Salzburg. He publ. *Musik in Frankreich* (1927); ed. works by G. Benda ('Denkmäler deutscher Tonkunst' vol. 64), Telemann ('Das Erbe deutscher Musik' vol. 6), and others; composed 2 symphonies; 2 string quartets; choruses.

Werrekoren (Verecoren, Werrecore), Hermann Mathias, 16th-century German composer. He was maestro di cappella in Milan (1538-55); his principal work is a descriptive composition for 4 voices a cappella entitled *Die Schlacht vor Pavia* (The Battle of Pavia), publ. in Schmeltzl's collection 'Guter seltzamer . . . teutscher Gesang . . .' (Nuremberg, 1544) and reprinted by Gardano in Venice in 1549 as *La Battaglia Taliana;* also publ. a book of motets for 4 voices (1555); various other motets were publ. in the collections of the period. Werrekoren was mistakenly identified with Matthäus Le Maistre by Fétis and Kade; research by Haberl, Elsa Bienenfeld, and Cecie Stainer demonstrated the fallacy of this assumption. —Cf. Haberl's articles in the 'Kirchenmusikalisches Jahrbuch' (1871 and 1873); Elsa Bienenfeld in the 'Sammelbände der Internationalen Musik-Gesellschaft' (1904-05).

Werrenrath, Reinald, American baritone; b. Brooklyn, Aug. 7, 1883; d. Plattsburg, N.Y., Sept. 12, 1953. He was a pupil of his father, a tenor; then studied with David Bispham and Herbert Witherspoon. He began his career as a concert singer; also in oratorio; made his operatic début on Feb. 19, 1919, at the Metropolitan Opera House, N.Y., as Silvio in *I Pagliacci,* and remained with the company until 1921; then devoted himself to teaching and concert singing; appeared in public for the last time at Carnegie Hall, N.Y., on Oct. 23, 1952. He edited 'Modern Scandinavian Songs' (2 vols.; Boston, 1925-26). He was married 3 times: to Ada Peterson (1909; divorced, 1927); to Verna True Nidig (1928; divorced, 1941); and to Frances M. Aston (1942).

Wersen, Louis G., American music educator; b. LaConner, Wash., Aug. 18, 1905. He took his B.A. in music at the State College of Washington (1927); M.A. (1938); Mus. Doc. at Waynesburg, Pa., College (1954); held numerous teaching posts in California; head of music education dept. of College of Puget Sound (1938-44); director, Division of Music Education, Philadelphia Public Schools (1944-55); conducted high school orchestras in Philadelphia and Urbana, Ill.; publ. *Rhythmic Foundation Through Drumming;* co-author of various songbooks.

Wert, Giaches de (Jakob van Wert), Flemish contrapuntist; b. Weert, between May 6 and Aug. 18, 1535; d. Mantua, May 6, 1596. He was a boy chorister in the retinue of Maria di Cardona, Marchesa della Padulla, and followed the household to Italy. At the age of 9 he entered the ducal choir at Novellara; while still a youth he joined the court chapel of the Duke of Mantua, who appointed him maestro di cappella in 1565. He held this position until his death, with an interval as vice-maestro at Novellara (1567-74); from 1565 to 1583 was also choirmaster of the Church of Santa Barbara in Mantua. He was a very industrious composer, and greatly esteemed by contemporary musicians; Palestrina praised him, and he was also mentioned favorably by Thomas Morley, Artusi, G. B. Doni, and Monteverdi. His compositions were included in many collections of sacred and secular music, beginning in 1558. He publ. 11 books of madrigals for 5 voices, one for 4 voices, and one for 5 and 6 voices; one book of canzonets, and 3 of motets for 5 and 6 voices; many other works are preserved in MS in European libraries. Modern reprints are found in S. Smith's 'Musica antiqua,' vol. I; Dehn's 'Sammlung älterer Musik,' vol. VI; Barclay Squire's 'Ausgewählte Madrigale,' No. 40; and Wüllner's 'Chorübungen' (new ed. by E. Schwickerath, Munich, 1931). —Cf. A.-M. Bautier-Regnier, *Jacques de Wert,* in the 'Revue Belge de Musicologie' (1950, nos. 1-2); G. Reese, *Music in the Renaissance* (N.Y., 1954; pp. 408-11); C. MacClintock, *Some Notes on the Secular Music of Giaches de Wert,* in 'Musica Disciplina' (vol. 10; 1956).

Wesembeek. See **Burbure de Wesembeek.**

Wesendonk, Mathilde (*née* Luckemeyer), German poetess, friend of Wagner; b. Elberfeld, Dec. 23, 1828; d. at her villa Traunblick, near Altmünster on the Traunsee, Austria, Aug. 31, 1902. Her first meeting with Wagner took place in Zürich, early in 1852, and soon developed into a deep friendship. She wrote the famous *Fünf Gedichte (Der Engel, Stehe still, Träume, Schmerzen, Im Treibhaus),* which Wagner set to music as studies for *Tristan und Isolde.* On May 19, 1848, she married **Otto Wesendonk** (b. March 16, 1815; d. Berlin, Nov. 18, 1896); in 1857 he gave Wagner the use of a beautiful house on his estate on Lake Zürich, where the 1st act of *Tristan und Isolde* was written, and the 2nd act sketched. —Cf. A. Heintz, *Meine Erinnerungen* (reminiscences of Mathilde Wesendonk), in the 'Allgemeine Musikzeitung' (Feb. 14, 1896); W. Golther, ed., *Richard Wagner an Mathilde Wesendonk. Tagebuchblätter und Briefe* (Berlin, 1904; many subsequent eds.; English transl., London, 1905); W. Golther, ed., *Briefe Richard Wagners an Otto Wesendonk* (Berlin, 8th printing, 1905; English transl., London, 1911); H. Bélart, *Richard Wagners Liebestragödie mit Mathilde Wesendonk* (Dresden, 1912); E. H. Müller von Asow, ed., *Johannes Brahms und Mathilde Wesendonk; ein Briefwechsel* (Vienna, 1943).

Wesley, Charles, English organist and harpsichord player; nephew of John Wesley; b. Bristol, Dec. 11, 1757; d. London, May 23, 1834. He was a pupil of Kelway and Boyce in London; then held various positions as church organist; publ. 'Six Concertos for the Organ or Harpsichord,' op. 1; anthems, hymns, etc.; 6 string quartets. He was the brother and teacher of Samuel Wesley. —Cf. R. Green, *Works of John and Charles Wesley —A Bibliography* (London, 1896).

Wesley, John, the founder of the Wesleyan Methodist Church; b. Epworth, June 17, 1703; d. London, March 2, 1791. He was educated at Christ Church, Oxford; in 1735 he came to America with his brother Charles to do missionary work, and 2 years later publ. his 1st 'Collection of Psalms and Hymns' (Charlestown, 1737). Returning to England, he spread the doctrine of Methodism and became famous as a preacher and writer. He has been called 'the father of Methodist hymnology.' —Cf. R. Green, *Works of John and Charles Wesley—A Bibliography* (London, 1896); J. T. Lightwood, *Methodist Music in the 18th Century* (London, 1927); J. L. Nuelsen, *John Wesley und das deutsche Kirchenlied* (Bremen, 1938).

Wesley, Samuel, English organist and composer; brother of Charles Wesley; nephew of John Wesley; b. Bristol, Feb. 24, 1766; d. London, Oct. 11, 1837. He studied with his brother, and began to compose at the age of 8; learned to play the violin as well as the organ. He publ. *Eight Lessons for the Harpsichord* when he was 11 (1777). Subsequently he developed his fine talent as an organist, and was generally regarded as the greatest performer and improviser of his time. Although he suffered from a skull injury as a result of a fall, which seriously interfered with his activities, he continued to give public concerts till the year of his death. He was an earnest student of the works of Bach, and did much to make them known in England. He wrote 11 organ concertos; voluntaries, preludes, and fugues for organ; 4 symphonies;

4 overtures; 2 string quartets; a string quintet; a trio for oboe, violin, and cello; a trio for 2 flutes and piano; much church music, including 4 Masses, motets, several services, anthems, and psalm-tunes; choral pieces; songs; vocal duets; a number of rondos for piano, based on popular songs and on operatic arias; also numerous glees, for 3 and 4 voices. —Cf. W. Winters, *An Account of the Remarkable Musical Talents of Several Members of the Wesley Family* (London, 1874); E. Wesley (his daughter), *Letters of Samuel Wesley to Mr. Jacobs . . ., relating to the Introduction into this Country of the Works of Bach* (London, 1875; 2nd ed., 1878); G. J. Stevenson, *Memorials of the Wesley Family* (London, 1876); J. T. Lightwood, *Samuel Wesley, Musician: The Story of His Life* (London, 1937).

Wesley, Samuel Sebastian, English organist and composer; natural son of Samuel Wesley; b. London, Aug. 14, 1810; d. Gloucester, April 19, 1876. He was a boy chorister at the Chapel Royal; from the age of 16 he held appointments as organist in London churches; 1832, organist of Hereford Cathedral; 1835, at Exeter Cathedral; 1842, at Leeds Parish Church; 1849, at Winchester Cathedral; 1865, at Gloucester Cathedral. He received the degrees of B. Mus. and D. Mus. at Oxford (1839). His works include 4 church services; 2 psalms; 27 anthems; several glees; an *Ode to Labour* (1864); pieces for organ; and songs. He publ. *A Few Words on Cathedral Music and the Musical System of the Church, with a Plan of Reform* (1849). —Cf. G. J. Stevenson, *Memorials of the Wesley Family* (London, 1876).

Wessel, Mark, American composer and teacher; b. Coldwater, Mich., March 26, 1894. He studied at Northwestern Univ. (Mus. Bac., 1917; Mus. M., 1918), and with Schoenberg in Vienna (1922); was awarded a Guggenheim Fellowship in 1930; also won a Pulitzer Scholarship. Returning to America, he became instructor at Northwestern Univ.; then was appointed to the faculty of the Univ. of Colorado. —Works: *Symphonie Concertante,* for horn, piano, and orch. (1929); symphony (1932); *Holiday,* for orch. (1932); *Song and Dance,* for orch. (1932); 2 piano concertos; concertino, for flute and chamber orch. (1928); *Ballade,* for violin, oboe, and string orch. (1931); sextet, for flute, oboe, horn, bassoon, clarinet, and piano (1928); violin sonata (1930); piano trio (1931); string quartet (1931); *Plains and Mountains,* for piano and string quartet (1937); 2 cello sonatas (1937, 1943); a sonatina for trumpet and piano (1942); piano pieces.

West, John Ebenezer, English organist and composer; b. London, Dec. 7, 1863; d. there, Feb. 28, 1929. He was a nephew of Ebenezer Prout, and studied with him at the Royal Academy of Music; was organist and choirmaster at various London churches; in 1884 was appointed to the editorial staff of Novello & Co. He wrote 2 cantatas, *The Healing of the Canaanite's Daughter* (1882) and *Seed-time and Harvest* (1892); several church services and anthems; an orchestral march, *Victoria, Our Queen;* organ music; publ. an important book, *Cathedral Organists* (London, 1899; new ed., 1921).

Westbrook, William Joseph, English organist and composer; b. London, Jan. 1, 1831; d. Sydenham, March 24, 1894. He was organist at several churches in London; in 1851 appointed to St. Bartholomew's, Sydenham, and held this post until his death. In 1862 he founded the periodical, 'Musical Standard' (with Hammond and Crowdy). He wrote an oratorio, *Jesus;* a cantata, *The Lord Is My Shepherd;* services, anthems, part-songs; sonatas and voluntaries for organ; several textbooks on the organ, etc.

Westergaard, Peter, American composer and teacher; b. Champaign, Ill., May 28, 1931. He studied at Harvard Univ. with Walter Piston (A.B., 1953) and at Princeton, with Roger Sessions (M.F.A., 1956); received a John Knowles Paine Travelling Fellowship (1953-54) and a Fulbright Student Grant (1956-57); was Fulbright Guest Lecturer at the Staatliche Hochschule für Musik in Freiburg-im-Breisgau, Germany (1958); then appointed instructor, Columbia Univ.—Works: 2 cantatas: *The Plot Against the Giant,* to words by Wallace Stevens (1957), and *A Refusal to Mourn the Death, by Fire, of a Child in London,* to words by Dylan Thomas (1958); *5 Sätze für kleines Orchester* (1958); chamber music.

Westerhout, Niccolò van. See **Van Westerhout.**

Westlake, Frederick, English pianist and composer; b. Romsey, Hampshire, Feb. 25, 1840; d. London, Feb. 12, 1898. He studied at the Royal Academy of Music with W. Macfarren (piano) and G. A. Macfarren (harmony); in 1862 was appointed to the faculty as piano teacher. He wrote several Masses, hymns, piano pieces, and a collection of part-songs, *Lyra Studentium.*

Westmorland, John Fane, Earl of (Lord Burghersh), English composer; b. London, Feb. 3, 1784; d. Apthorpe House, Northants, Oct. 16, 1859. He was in the British Army, fought in the Spanish campaign and in Egypt, attaining the rank of general in 1854; also occupied various diplomatic posts between wars. He studied music in Lisbon with Marcos Portugal (1809-12); was a founder of the Royal Academy of Music in London (1822). He wrote 7 Italian operas; the following were performed at his own palace in Florence (where he served as British Resident): *Fedra* (Nov. 17, 1824); *L'Eroe di Lancastro* (June 13, 1829); *Lo Scompiglio teatrale* (1830). Other works include several church services; some piano music; also a *Sinfonia in D* for orch. A list of his works is found in W. W. Cazelet's *The History of the Royal Academy of Music* (London, 1854).

Westphal, Rudolf (Georg Hermann), notable German music scholar; b. Oberkirchen, July 3, 1826; d. Stadthagen, July 11, 1892. He was a student of classical philology in Marburg; taught at the Univ. of Breslau (1858-62); then went to Moscow as teacher at a lyceum (1875-80); subsequently lived in Leipzig, Bückeburg, and Stadthagen. He wrote numerous learned papers on Greek music, and maintained that the Greeks employed polyphony, a theory that he himself eventually abandoned as untenable. —Writings: *Metrik der griechischen Dramatiker und Lyriker* (with Rossbach; 3 vols., 1854-65; 3rd ed. as *Theorie der musischen Künste der Hellenen,* 1885-89); *Die Fragmente und Lehrsätze der griechischen Rhythmiker* (1861); *System der antiken Rhythmik* (1865); *Geschichte der alten und mittelalterlichen Musik* (1865; unfinished; includes *Plutarch über die Musik,* 1864); *Theorie der neuhochdeutschen Metrik* (1870; 2nd ed., 1877); *Elemente des musikalischen Rhythmus mit besonderer Rücksicht auf unsre Opernmusik* (1872); *Allgemeine Theorie der musikalischen Rhythmik seit J. S. Bach* (1880); *Die Musik des griechischen Altertums* (1883); *Allgemeine Metrik der indo-germanischen und semitischen Völker auf Grundlage der vergleichenden Sprachwissenschaft* (1892; with addendum by R. Kruse, *Der griechische Hexameter in der deutschen Nachdichtung);* and *Metrik und Rhythmik des klassischen Hellenentums,* 2 vols. (1883-93). —Cf. H. Riemann, *Handbuch der Musikgeschichte,* Vol. I (1904).

Westrup, Jack Allan, English musicologist; b. London, July 26, 1904. He received his education at Dulwich College, London, and Balliol College, Oxford (B. Mus., 1926; M.A., 1929; D. Mus., 1944); assistant master at Dulwich College (1928-34); then became music critic of the London 'Daily Telegraph' (1934-39); editor of the 'Monthly Mus. Record' (1933-45). He was prof. of music at Birmingham Univ. (1944-47); in 1947 appointed prof. of music at Oxford Univ., succeeding Sir Hugh Allen. He edited Monteverdi's *Orfeo* (1925) and *L'Incoronazione di Poppea* (1927); is chairman of the editorial board of the *New Oxford History of Music,* to which he has contributed; publ. *Purcell,* in the 'Master Musicians' series (London, 1937); *Handel* (London, 1938) and *Liszt* (London, 1940), in the Novello series; *Sharps and Flats,* essays (London, 1940); *British Music* (London, 1943; new ed., 1949); *An Introduction to Musical History* (London, 1955). Edited Ernest Walker's *A History of Music in England* (3rd ed., Oxford, 1952).

Wettergren (*née* Palson), **Gertrud,** Swedish contralto; b. Eslöv, Feb. 17, 1897. She studied at the Stockholm Cons., and later in London; made her operatic début at the Royal Opera in Stockholm, 1922, and remained on its roster for 10 years. On Dec. 20, 1935, she appeared at the Metropolitan Opera House, as Amneris in *Aida;* remained with that company until the season of 1937-38; also sang with the Chicago City Opera (1936-38); made guest appearances at Covent Garden, London (1936 and 1939). She then returned to Sweden, as singer to the court. In 1925 she married Erik Wettergren (director of the National Museum of Stockholm).

Wetz, Richard, German composer and teacher; b. Gleiwitz, Feb. 26, 1875; d. Erfurt, Jan. 16, 1935. He studied with R. Hofmann in Leipzig and Thuille in Munich; in 1906 went to Erfurt as choral conductor and teacher; also taught in Weimar. He composed an opera, *Das ewige Feuer* (Düsseldorf, March 19, 1907); a *Kleist-Ouvertüre; Traumsommernacht,* for women's chorus and orch.; *Gesang des Lebens,* for male chorus and orch.; *Nicht geboren ist das Beste,* for mixed chorus and orch.; *Hyperion,* for baritone solo, chorus, and orch.; about 100 songs. He publ. monographs on Bruckner (1922), Liszt (1925), and Beethoven (1927; 2nd ed., 1933). A Richard Wetz Society was founded in Gleiwitz in 1943. —Cf. G. Armin, *Die Lieder von Richard Wetz* (Leipzig, 1911); E. L. Schellenberg, *Richard Wetz* (Leipzig, 1911; 2nd ed.; 1914); H. Polack, *Richard Wetz. Sein Werk* (Leipzig, 1935).

Wetzel, Justus Hermann, German composer and musicologist; b. Kyritz, March 11, 1879. He studied natural sciences, philosophy, and history of art (*Dr. phil.,* 1901); then took up music, and was teacher at the Riemann Cons. in Stettin (1905-07); settled in Berlin in 1910; taught at the Academy for Church- and School-Music (from 1925; prof., 1935). He composed about 400 songs; choral works; chamber music; piano pieces; edited and arranged several collections of German songs; publ. an analysis of Beethoven's violin sonatas; other publications are *Zur psychologischen Begründung des Rhythmus,* in the 'Riemann-Festschrift' (1909); *Elementartheorie der Musik* (Leipzig, 1911); *Die Liedformen,* in Martens' *Musikalische Formen in historischen Reihen* (1931); etc. —Cf. F. Welter, *Justus Hermann Wetzel* (Berlin, 1931; with list of works).

Wetzler, Hermann Hans, German-American conductor and composer; b. Frankfurt, Sept. 8, 1870; d. New York, May 29, 1943. He was brought to the U.S. as a child, but in 1882 returned to Germany, where he studied at Hoch's Cons. in Frankfurt with Clara Schumann (piano), Iwan Knorr (counterpoint), and Humperdinck (instrumentation). In 1892 he came to N.Y.; was church organist for several years; in 1903 he established the Wetzler Symph. Concerts, which had considerable success; Richard Strauss conducted a series of 4 concerts of his own works with the Wetzler group (Feb.-March, 1904), including the world première of the *Sinfonia Domestica.* In 1905 Wetzler went to Europe again; conducted opera in Hamburg (until 1908), Elberfeld (1908-09), Riga (1909-13), Halle (1913-15), Lübeck (1915-19), Cologne (1919-23); remained in Cologne until 1930; then went to Basel; returned to the U.S. in 1940. He composed an opera, *Die baskische Venus* (Leipzig, Nov. 18, 1928); incidental music to Shakespeare's *As You Like It* (1917); a symph. suite, *Visions* (1923); *Assisi,* legend for orch. written in commemoration of the 700th anniversary of the death of St. Francis of Assisi (won a prize of $1,000 in a competition sponsored by the Chicago North Shore Festival Association, Evanston, Ill.; 1925; first performed there, May 30, 1925); *Symphonic Dance in Basque Style* (1927; from his opera *Die baskische Venus*); *Symphonie Concertante,* for violin and orch. (1932); chamber music; choral works; songs. Publ. *Wege zur Musik,* a collection of his lectures (Zürich, 1938).

Weweler (věh'-věh-lěhr), **August,** German composer; b. Reike, Oct. 20, 1868; d. Detmold, Dec. 8, 1952. He studied at the Leipzig Cons. with Jadassohn and others; in 1898 settled in Detmold as a teacher. —Works: the operas *Dornröschen* (Kassel, 1903) and *Der grobe Märker* (Detmold, 1908); the oratorio *Die Sintflut* (Detmold, 1914); a ballet, *Des Malers Traumbild; Sankt Hubertus, Vom Bäuerlein, das Alles in Gold verwandelte,* and *Frau Musika in Freud und Leid* for declamation with chorus and piano; male choruses and piano pieces. Author of *Ave Musica! Das Wesen der Tonkunst und die modernen Bestrebungen* (1913; 2nd ed., 1919).

Weymarn, Pavel Platonovitch, Russian writer on music and composer; b. St. Petersburg, 1857; d. Narva, Sept. 22, 1905. He studied piano and theory at the St. Petersburg Cons.; in 1888-90 edited the music periodical 'Bayan'; publ. monographs on Napravnik (1889) and Cui (1897); was music critic for several Russian newspapers; collaborated in the Russian edition of Riemann's *Musik-Lexikon* (1904). He composed a string quartet and some piano pieces and songs.

Weyrauch (vī'-rowh), **August Heinrich von,** German song composer; b. Riga, April 30, 1788; date of death unknown. In 1824 he publ. (under his own name) a song, *Nach Osten* (words by Wetzel). About 1840 an anonymous Paris publisher reprinted it, with Schubert's name on the title page, as *Adieu* (French words by Bélanger); a piano transcription of it, also crediting the authorship to Schubert, was published by Döhler in Germany (1843); Schlesinger of Berlin reprinted the song, with a German transl. of the French text, as Schubert's in 1845; since then it has been reprinted many time, as Schubert's, by European and American publishers. —Cf. G. Nottebohm, *Thematisches Verzeichnis der im Druck erschienenen Werke von Franz Schubert* (Vienna, 1874; p. 254).

Weyse (vī'-sě), **Christoph Ernst Friedrich,** German-Danish composer; b. Altona, March 5, 1774; d. Copenhagen, Oct. 8, 1842. He was a pupil of his grandfather, a cantor at Altona; in 1789 he went to Copenhagen, where he studied with J. A. P. Schulz. In 1794 he was appointed organist at the Reformed Church; in 1805 became organist at the Fruekirke; in 1819 appointed court composer. Through the court conductor Kunzen he became interested in a movement for the establishment of a national school of Danish opera, for which his works (together with those of

Kuhlau) effectively prepared the way. —Works: operas (all performed in Copenhagen): *Sovedrikken (The Sleeping-Potion;* April 21, 1809); *Faruk* (Jan. 30, 1812); *Ludlams Hule (Ludlam's Cave;* Jan. 30, 1816); *Floribella* (Jan. 29, 1825); *Eventyr i Rosenborg Have (Adventure in Rosenborg Gardens;* May 26, 1827); *Balders Død (The Death of Baldur;* Nov. 23, 1832); *Festen paa Kenilworth* (after Walter Scott; Jan. 6, 1836); about 30 cantatas; *Miserere* for double chorus and orch.; *Te Deum* for chorus and orch.; 4 symphonies; preludes and fugues for organ; piano pieces (including sonatas and études); songs. He collected 100 Danish folksongs, of which he harmonized 59; they were published by his pupil A. P. Berggreen as '100 gamle Kämpevisemelodier' ('Old Ballad Melodies'). —Cf. A. P. Berggreen, *C. E. F. Weyse's Biographie* (Danish; Copenhagen, 1876); R. von Liliencron, *Weyse und die dänische Musik seit dem vorigen Jahrhundert,* in Raumer-Riehl's 'Historisches Taschenbuch' (Leipzig, 1878); W. Behrend, *Weyse und Kuhlau,* in 'Die Musik' (III, 22; 1904), J. P. Larsen, *Weyses Romancer og Sange* (Copenhagen, 1944).

White, Clarence Cameron, American Negro violinist and composer; b. Clarksville, Tenn., Aug. 10, 1880. He studied at the Oberlin Cons.; in London with Samuel Coleridge-Taylor, and in Paris with Laparra; won the Harmon Foundation Award and the Rosenwald Foundation Fellowship for composition; also the David Bispham Medal, for his opera *Ouanga,* to a libretto from a Haitian historic episode (1930-32; selections performed in Chicago, Nov. 13, 1932). His *Elegy* for orch. won the 1954 Benjamin Award for 'tranquil music' (New Orleans, March 16, 1954). He held various positions as violinist, in Boston and elsewhere; publ. technical exercises for violin; also *American Negro Folk Songs* (1928).

White, Eric Walter, English writer on music; b. Bristol, Sept. 10, 1905. He studied at Balliol College at Oxford; was a member of the Secretariat of the League of Nations (1929-33) and subsequently of the National Council of Social Service, London (1935-42), of the Council for the Encouragement of Music and Arts, London (1942-46), and of the Arts Council of Great Britain (from 1946). —Books: *Stravinsky's Sacrifice to Apollo* (London, 1930); *Stravinsky* (London, 1947); *Benjamin Britten* (London, 1948; new ed., 1954); *The Rise of English Opera* (London, 1951).

White, Felix Harold, English composer; b. London, April 27, 1884; d. there, Jan. 31, 1945. He was entirely self-taught, except for some piano lessons from his mother. His overture *Shylock* was performed in London in 1907; other works for orch. include the symph. poems *Astarte Syriaca* and *The Deserted Village,* a polonaise, 2 rhapsodies, etc.; he also wrote chamber music, choral works, about 250 songs, 60 part-songs, 80 piano pieces, etc. He publ. a *Dictionary of Musical Terms;* edited piano works of Scriabin for the Belaieff publ. firm.

White, John, American organist and composer; b. West Springfield, Mass., March 12, 1855; d. Bad Nauheim, July 18, 1902. He studied organ with Dudley Buck in N.Y. and August Haupt in Berlin; composition with Rheinberger in Munich. He was organist of the Church of the Ascension, N.Y., from 1887 to 1896; then went back to Germany. He publ. a *Missa solemnis,* a *Requiem,* a *Te Deum;* many Latin hymns for mixed chorus a cappella; and an oratorio, *Alpha and Omega.*

White, Mary Louisa, English composer and teacher; b. Sheffield, Sept. 2, 1866; d. London, Jan., 1935. She studied in London and dedicated herself to teaching music to beginners; developed the 'Letterless Method' for this purpose. She wrote several children's operettas *(Beauty and the Beast, The Babes in the Woods);* also piano pieces (some for 4 hands); songs.

White, Maude Valérie, English composer; b. Dieppe, France (of English parents), June 23, 1855; d. London, Nov. 2, 1937. She studied with W. S. Rockstro; entered the Royal Academy of Music in 1876, was elected Mendelssohn Scholar in 1879 (the first woman to win this honor), then continued her studies under Sir G. Macfarren; later with R. Fuchs in Vienna. She traveled extensively through Europe and South America; lived in London, and for some years in Florence. She wrote a number of attractive songs to English, German, French, and Italian texts; a vocal quintet to Heine's poem, *Du bist wie eine Blume;* an album of piano pieces, *Pictures from Abroad; Naissance d'amour,* for cello and piano; etc. Publ. her memoirs, *Friends and Memories* (London, 1914) and *My Indian Summer* (London, 1932).

White, Paul, American composer, violinist, and conductor; b. Bangor, Maine, Aug. 22, 1895. He studied at the New England Cons. of Music with Chadwick; then went to

Cincinnati, where he studied violin with Eugène Ysaÿe, at that time conductor of the Cincinnati Symph. Orch.; White then returned to Boston as violin teacher (1921-23); then went to Rochester as a member of the Rochester Philharmonic; studied conducting with Eugene Goossens; in 1929 was appointed associate conductor of the Rochester Civic Orch. —Works: for orch.: *Variations* (Bangor, April 20, 1925); symph. No. 1 (Rochester, March 28, 1934); *Pagan Festival Overture* (Rochester, April 28, 1936); *Four Spokes from the Hub* (Boston Pops, June 18, 1938); *Lake Spray* (Rochester, Nov. 22, 1939); *College Caprice* (1939); *Sea Chanty,* for harp and strings (Rochester, March 4, 1942); *Lake Placid Scenes* (1943); *Idyl* (1944); *Andante and Rondo,* for cello and orch. (1945); chamber music: a string quartet (1925); a violin sonata (1926); *Fantastic Dance,* for woodwinds (1922); also *5 Miniatures* for piano, including the popular *Mosquito Dance* (also for orch.)

White, Robert, one of the most important English composers of the 16th century; b. c. 1530; d. London, Nov., 1574. He studied music for several years, obtaining the degree of Mus. Bac. at Cambridge Univ. on Dec. 13, 1560; appointed Master of the choristers at Ely Cathedral in 1561, retaining this post until 1565; then master of the choristers at Westminster Abbey, from 1570. He composed Latin services and motets, English anthems, etc. —Modern eds. and a biography are found in 'Tudor Church Music' vol. V (1926).

White, William, English composer of the 17th century; d. c. 1660. He wrote music for viols; most of his MSS are preserved at Oxford. He wrote fantasies, pavans, and other court dance tunes. Apparently he was held in some esteem, for his name is mentioned by Simpson in his *Principles of Practicle Musick* (1665); also by Thomas Mace, in *Musick's Monument* (1676).

Whitehill, Clarence Eugene, American bass; b. Marengo, Iowa, Nov. 5, 1871; d. New York, Dec. 19, 1932. He studied with H.D. Phelps in Chicago; earned his living as a clerk in an express office, and also sang in churches; then went to Paris in 1896, where he studied with Giraudet and Sbriglia; he was the first American male singer to be engaged at the Opéra-Comique (1900); then was a member of Henry Savage's 'Grand English Opera Co.' at the Metropolitan Opera House in the autumn of 1900; went for further study to Stockhausen in Frankfurt, and from there to Bayreuth, where he studied the entire Wagner repertory with Cosima Wagner; after engagements in Germany, he became a member of the Cologne Opera (1903-08); then at the Metropolitan Opera House (1909-10); with the Chicago Opera Co. (1911-15), and again with the Metropolitan Opera (1914-32).

Whitehouse, William Edward, English cellist; b. London, May 20, 1859; d. there, Jan. 12, 1935. He first studied violin; then turned to the cello; was a pupil of Piatti at the Royal Academy of Music (1877-81); joined its faculty in 1882; also held teaching posts at Cambridge Univ. and other educational institutions. In 1889 he formed the London Trio with Achille Simonetti (violin) and Amina Goodwin (piano); toured with it in England, France, and Italy until its dissolution in 1904. He was an eminent teacher; among his pupils were Felix Salmond and Beatrice Harrison. He wrote a number of pieces for cello and piano *(Allegro perpetuo, Gedanken, Remembrance, Serenade,* etc.) and edited much 18th-century cello music. Publ. *Recollections of a Violoncellist* (London, 1930).

Whiteman, Paul, American conductor of popular music; b. Denver, Col., March 28, 1890, where his father was supervisor of music for the public schools. Played viola in the Denver Symph. Orch. and later in the San Francisco People's Symph. Orch.; in 1917-18 he was conductor of a 40-piece band in the U. S. Navy. He then formed a hotel orch. in Santa Barbara, Calif., and began to develop a style of playing known as 'symphonic jazz,' which soon made him famous. On Feb. 12, 1924, he gave a concert in Aeolian Hall, N. Y., at which he introduced Gershwin's *Rhapsody in Blue,* written for his orch. He gave other concerts throughout the U. S. and in 1926 made a tour in Europe. He established the Whiteman Awards, made annually for 'symphonic jazz' compositions written by Americans. Author of a book on *Jazz* (with M. M. McBride; N. Y., 1926), *How to Be a Bandleader* (with L. Lieber; N. Y., 1941), and *Records for the Millions* (N. Y., 1948).

Whithorne, Emerson, American composer; b. Cleveland, Sept. 6, 1884; d. Lyme, Conn., March 25, 1958. His name was Whittern; he had it legally changed in 1918 to Whithorne (the original family name of his paternal grandfather). He studied in Cleveland with J. H. Rogers; embarked on a musical career at the age of 15, and appeared as pianist on the Chautauqua circuit for 2 seasons. In 1904 he went to Vienna and took lessons with

Leschetizky (piano) and Robert Fuchs (composition). From 1905-07 he was a pupil of Artur Schnabel. In 1907 he married Ethel Leginska (q.v.), acting as her impresario in Germany until 1909; they were separated in 1912, and divorced in 1916. Between 1907 and 1915, Whithorne lived mainly in London as music critic; studied Chinese and Japanese music from materials in the British Museum, and wrote several pieces based on oriental tunes *(Adventures of a Samurai;* settings for *The Yellow Jacket; The Typhoon).* Returning to America, he became editor for the Art Publication Society of St. Louis, Mo. (1915-20); then settled in N. Y., and devoted himself entirely to composition; was active as a member of the League of Composers, N. Y. In his music, he assumed a militantly modernistic attitude; wrote several pieces in the fashionable 'machine music' style. —Works: for orch.: *The Rain* (Detroit, Feb. 22, 1913); *The Aeroplane* (Birmingham, England, Jan. 30, 1926; orchestral version of the piano piece written in 1920, one of the earliest examples of 'machine music'); *Saturday's Child,* to poems by Countee Cullen, for mezzo-soprano, tenor, and small orch. (N. Y., March 13, 1926); *New York Days and Nights* (Philadelphia, July 30, 1926; originally for piano); *Poem* for piano and orch. (Chicago, Feb. 4, 1927); *Fata Morgana,* symph. poem (N. Y., Oct. 11, 1928); incidental music to Eugene O'Neill's *Marco Millions* (1928); symph. No. 1 (1929; Cincinnati, Jan. 12, 1934); *The Dream Pedlar,* symph. poem (Los Angeles, Jan. 15, 1931); violin concerto (Chicago, Nov. 12, 1931); *Fandango* (N. Y., April 19, 1932); *Moon Trail,* symph. poem (Boston, Dec. 15, 1933); symph. No. 2 (Cincinnati, March 19, 1937); *Sierra Morena* (N. Y., May 7, 1938); also a piano quintet (N. Y., Dec. 19, 1926) and other chamber music, piano pieces, songs. —Cf. J. T. Howard, *Emerson Whithorne* (N. Y., 1929); R. Hammond, *Emerson Whithorne,* in 'Modern Music' (Jan.-Feb., 1931).

Whiting, Arthur Battelle, American composer and pianist; nephew of George E. Whiting; b. Cambridge, Mass., June 20, 1861; d. Beverly, Mass., July 20, 1936. He studied in Boston with Sherwood (piano), Maas (harmony), and Chadwick (composition). In 1883 he went to Munich for 2 years and took courses at the Cons. there with Rheinberger (composition) and others. He then lived in Boston until 1895, when he settled in N. Y.; from 1907, gave educational chamber music concerts at Yale, Harvard, Princeton, and Columbia; in 1911, inaugurated a series of concerts of early music, playing the harpsichord, other artists being Constance Edson (violin), Georges Barrère (flute), and Paul Kéfer (viola da gamba). He contributed papers on music to the 'Yale Review' and other publications. —Works: *Concert Overture* (Boston, Feb. 5, 1886); piano concerto (Boston, Nov. 16, 1888, composer soloist); *Fantasie,* for piano and orch. (Boston, March 5, 1897; composer soloist); suite for strings and 4 horns (Boston, March 13, 1891); *The Golden Cage—A Dance Pageant,* for small orch. (1926); a piano quintet; a string quartet; a piano trio; a violin sonata; etc.; a number of piano pieces: *6 Bagatelles, Suite moderne, 3 Characteristic Waltzes;* also *Melodious Technical Studies; Pianoforte Pedal Studies* (with text in English and German); 3 songs for soprano, to poems by Christina Rossetti; *Barrack Room Ballads* (Kipling) for baritone; musical settings from the *Rubáiyát of Omar Khayyám* for baritone; anthems; etc. —Cf. R. Hughes, *Contemporary American Composers* (Boston, 1900; pp. 283-91); D. G. Mason, *Arthur Whiting,* in the 'Mus. Quarterly' (Jan., 1937); D. G. Mason, *Music in My Time* (N. Y., 1938, pp. 65-80). See also 'National Cyclopedia of American Biography' (vol. XXVII, pp. 46-47).

Whiting, George Elbridge, American organist and composer; b. Holliston, Mass., Sept. 14, 1840; d. Cambridge, Mass., Oct. 14, 1923. He began to study with his brother Amos, a church organist, and played in public at the age of 13; at 17 he became organist of the North Congregational Church at Hartford; studied with George W. Morgan in N.Y.,; then went to England, where he became a pupil of W. T. Best of Liverpool (1863). Returning to America, he became organist at St. Joseph's in Albany, where the famous soprano Emma Albani sang in his choir. He then moved to Boston, where he was organist at King's Chapel; in 1874, he went to Berlin and studied harmony with Haupt and orchestration with Radecke. Settling finally in Boston, he taught the organ at the New England Cons. (until 1879, and again from 1883 to 1897). In the interim he was a teacher at the Cincinnati College of Music (1880-83). He was renowned as a teacher and composer of organ music; publ. *The Organist* (Boston, 1870) and *The First 6 Months on the Organ* (1871). He also wrote many sacred works: 2 Masses; Vesper Services; a *Te Deum;* the secular cantatas *The Tale of the Viking, Dream Pictures, March of the Monks of Bangor, Midnight, Henry of Navarre;* the 1-act opera *Lenora,* to an Italian libretto (1893); a symph.; an overture to Tennyson's *The Princess;* a piano concerto; a suite for cello and orch.; piano pieces; songs. —Cf. L. C. Elson, *The History of American Music* (N. Y., 1904; pp. 265-67).

Whitmer, Thomas Carl, American organist and composer; b. Altoona, Pa., June 24, 1873. He studied piano with C. Jarvis, organ with S. P. Warren, and composition with W. W. Gilchrist. He was director of the School of Music, Stephens College, Columbia, Mo. (1899-1909); director of music at the Pennsylvania College for Women, Pittsburgh (1909-16); organist and choirmaster of the Sixth Presbyterian Church, Pittsburgh (1916-32); then taught privately in N. Y.; 1953, living at La Grangeville, N. Y. He publ. *The Way of My Heart and Mind* (Pittsburgh, 1920) and *The Art of Improvisation: A Handbook of Principles and Methods* (N. Y., 1934; revised ed., 1941). —Compositions: *Poem of Life,* for piano and orch. (1914); *A Syrian Night,* ballet suite for orch. (Philadelphia Orch., Pittsburgh, Feb. 17, 1919); *When God Laughed,* for chorus a cappella (1932); *Radiations over a 13th Century Theme,* for string orch. (1935); *Supper at Emmaus,* choral suite (Pittsburgh, Feb. 21, 1939); cantata, *Chant Me the Poem that Comes from the Soul of America,* after Walt Whitman (Pittsburgh, Feb. 19, 1942); 1-act opera, *Oh, Isabel* (1951); chamber music; piano pieces; songs.

Whitney, Myron William, American bass singer; b. Ashby, Mass., Sept. 5, 1836; d. Sandwich, Mass., Sept. 19, 1910. He was a pupil of E. H. Frost in Boston, Randegger in London, and Vannucini in Florence. He sang in concert and oratorio in America and Great Britain; was a member of the Boston Ideal Opera Co. (1879) and the American Opera Co. (1885-86); retired in 1900. His son, **Myron Whitney,** Jr. (1872-1954), a baritone, traveled as joint artist with Melba and Nordica; for many years taught singing at the New England Cons., Boston. —Cf. H. C. Lahee, *Famous Singers of Today and Yesterday* (Boston, 1898; pp. 322-23).

Whitney, Robert, American conductor; b. Newcastle-on-the-Tyne, England (of an American father and an English mother), July 6, 1904. The family settled in Chicago, where he took music lessons with Rudolph Reuter (piano) and Leo Sowerby (composition); organized a quintet with his four sisters; in 1931, he began to study conducting with Eric De Lamarter; made his début as conductor in 1932, with the Chicago Civic Orch. In 1937 he was engaged as conductor of the Louisville Philharmonic (later renamed the Louisville Orch.). In 1948, at the suggestion of the Mayor of Louisville, Charles Farnsley, a music lover and champion of modernism, Whitney introduced a policy of presenting a new work at each concert. In April 1953, the Louisville Orch. obtained a grant of $400,000 from the Rockefeller Foundation for commissioning composers to write operatic and symphonic scores; about 130 world premières were given up to 1958, comprising works by foreign as well as American composers (Honegger, Milhaud, Malipiero, Petrassi, Krenek, Dallapiccola, Toch, Chávez, Villa-Lobos, Ginastera, Harris, Schuman, Thomson, Cowell, Piston, Sessions, Antheil, Creston, Mennin, and others). Among Whitney's own works are *Concerto Grosso* (1934); a symph. (1936); a *Sinfonietta* (1939); and *Sospiri di Roma* for chorus and orch. (1941). —Cf. Hope Stoddard, *Symphony Conductors of the U.S.A.* (N. Y., 1957; pp. 248-56).

Whittaker, William Gillies, English choral conductor and composer; b. Newcastle-on-the-Tyne, July 23, 1876; d. Orkney Islands, July 5, 1944. He studied organ and singing; conducted various choral societies in Newcastle and London; in 1929, appointed prof. at the Univ. of Glasgow. He edited *North Country Folk Tunes,* for voice and piano (2 vols.); *Oxford Choral Songs;* sonatas of John Blow; church cantatas of Bach; etc.; author of *Fugitive Notes on Certain Cantatas and the Motets of J. S. Bach* (London, 1924), *Class Singing* (London, 1925), *Collected Essays* (London, 1940); publ. *Time Exercises* for piano; received Carnegie Publication awards for his piano quintet, *Among the Northumbrian Hills,* and for his *A Lyke Wake Dirge,* for chorus and orch. (1924); also composed piano pieces and songs.

Whittall, Gertrude Clarke, American patron of music and literature; b. Bellevue, Neb., Oct. 7, 1867. Her maiden name was Clarke; she married Matthew John Whittall on June 4, 1906. In 1935 she donated to the Library of Congress, Washington, D.C., a quartet of Stradivari instruments—2 violins (including the famous 'Betts'), a viola, and a cello—together with 4 Tourte bows; she added another Stradivari violin (the 'Ward') and another Tourte bow in 1937. In 1936 she established an endowment fund in the Library of Congress to provide public concerts at which these instruments would be used, and in 1938 the Whittall Pavilion in the Library was built to house them and to serve other purposes in the musical life of the Library. In subsequent years, she continued to add to her gifts to the Library on behalf of both music and literature; one series enabled the Whittall Foundation to acquire many valuable autograph MSS of composers from Bach to Schoenberg, and in particular the finest single group of Brahms MSS gathered anywhere in the world. —Cf. W. D. Orcutt, *The Stradivari Memorial at Washington* (Washington, 1938); E. N. Waters, *Autograph Musical Scores . . . in the Whittall Foundation Collection* (Washington, 1951).

Whittlesey, Walter Rose, American librarian; b. Hartford, Conn., Jan. 5, 1861; d. Washington, D.C., April 9, 1936. Upon the opening of the new building of the Library of Congress (Sept. 1, 1897), he took charge of the musical copyright deposits which formed the basis of the present music collection; when O. G. Sonneck (q.v.) was appointed 1st chief of the Music Division, Whittlesey became his assistant; after Sonneck's resignation (1917) he was acting chief (until Dec. 31, 1921). He retired on June 30, 1932. He publ. *Catalogue of First Editions of Stephen C. Foster* (1915; with O. G. Sonneck).

Whythorne, Thomas, English song composer; b. c. 1528. He traveled abroad and acquired a liking for Italian (particularly Neapolitan) songs. Upon his return to London, he publ. a collection of 76 songs for 3, 4, and 5 voices, which was one of the earliest sets of secular vocal pieces publ. in England. In 1590 Whythorne brought out another collection, comprising 52 vocal duos. —Cf. Peter Warlock, *Thomas Whythorne: an Unknown Elizabethan Composer* (Oxford, 1927).

Wichmann, Hermann, German composer; b. Berlin, Oct. 24, 1824; d. Rome, Sept., 1905. He was a pupil of Taubert, Mendelssohn, and Spohr; lived most of his life in Berlin. —Works: 7 string quartets; a string quintet; a piano trio; a violin sonata; several piano sonatas; publ. a collection of essays, *Gesammelte Aufsätze* (2 vols.; 1884, 1887), and *Frohes und Ernstes aus meinem Leben* (Leipzig, 1898).

Wichtl, Georg, German violinist and composer; b. Trostberg, Feb. 2, 1805; d. Bunzlau, June 3, 1877. He studied in Munich; was a violinist and conductor in various orchestras in Silesia; wrote an opera, *Almaïda;* an oratorio, *Die Auferstehung und Himmelfahrt Jesu;* symphonies and overtures; a string quartet; 6 trios for 2 violins and cello; 3 trios for 3 violins; 6 duets for violin and cello; many instructive pieces for violin.

Wickede, Friedrich von, German composer; b. Dömitz-on-Elbe, July 28, 1834; d. Schwerin, Sept. 11, 1904. He studied with J. Vieth; held various government posts; composition was his avocation. He wrote 2 operas, *Ingo* and *Per aspera ad astra;* piano pieces; songs (which were praised by the critics).

Wickenhauser, Richard, Austrian composer; b. Brünn, Feb. 7, 1867; d. Vienna, July 1, 1936. He studied at the Leipzig Cons. with Jadassohn and Paul; won a state stipend in 1894 (awarded by Brahms and Hanslick); conducted choral societies in Brünn, Graz, and Vienna; from 1907 was conductor of the Vienna Singakademie. He publ. *Sang fahrender Schüler* for male chorus and orch.; a suite for string orch.; a violin sonata; a cello sonata; *10 Choralvorspiele* for organ; numerous male choruses a cappella and songs; also *Anton Bruckners Symphonien* (Leipzig, 1927).

Wickham, Florence, American contralto singer; b. Beaver, Pa., 1882. She studied in Philadelphia; then went to Germany, where she was a pupil of Franz Emerich in Berlin. After making appearances in Wiesbaden and Munich, she sang the role of Kundry in *Parsifal* in Henry W. Savage's touring opera troupe in America (1904-05). She was a member of the Metropolitan Opera Co. from 1909 to 1912. Subsequently she retired from the stage and took up composition; wrote an operetta, *Rosalynd,* after Shakespeare's *As You Like It* (1938); also songs; lived mostly in New York.

Widmann, Benedikt, German music pedagogue; b. Bräunlingen, near Donaueschingen, March 5, 1820; d. Frankfurt, March 4, 1910. He was active in musical instruction in Frankfurt; publ. several manuals: *Formenlehre der Instrumentalmusik* (1862); *Katechismus der allgemeinen Musiklehre* (2nd ed., 1879); *Grundzüge der musikalischen Klanglehre* (1868); *Praktischer Lehrgang für einen rationellen Gesangunterricht; Handbüchlein der Harmonie-, Melodie- und Formenlehre* (5th ed., 1889); *Generalbass-Übungen* (1859; 5th ed., 1893); *Die kunsthistorische Entwicklung des Männerchors* (1884); *Alberich Zwyssig als Komponist* (1905); etc.

Widmann, Erasmus, German composer and theorist; b. Hall, Württemberg, 1572; d. Rotenburg, Oct. 1634. After serving as cantor in Graz and Weickersheim, he became a schoolmaster at Rotenburg (1614). He wrote church music and some instrumental dance suites; publ. a treatise, *Praecepta musicae Latino-Germanica* (Nuremberg, 1615). —Cf. G. Reichert, *Erasmus Widmann: Leben und Werk* (Tübingen, 1940).

Widmann, Joseph Viktor, Swiss writer and journalist; b. Nennowitz, Moravia, Feb. 20, 1842; d. Bern, Nov. 6, 1911. He was brought to Switzerland as a child; became engaged in the literary profession; was well known as a dramatist; from 1880 he was literary editor of the 'Berner Bund'; wrote librettos. He was a friend of Brahms, and publ. *Johannes Brahms in Erinnerungen* (Berlin, 1898; new ed., Basel, 1947). —Cf. E. and M. Widmann, *Joseph Viktor Widmann* (2 vols.; 1922, 1924); M. Waser, *Josef Viktor Widmann* (Leipzig, 1927).

Widor (vē-dohr'), **Charles-Marie (-Jean-Albert),** distinguished French organist, pedagogue, and composer; b. Lyons, Feb. 21, 1844; d. Paris, March 12, 1937. His father, an Alsatian of Hungarian descent, was organist at the church of St.-François, Lyons; as a boy, Widor was a skillful improviser on the organ; studied later in Brussels under Lemmens (organ) and Fétis (composition). Still a youth, he was appointed organist at his father's church in Lyons (1860), and gained high repute by concerts in provincial French cities. In 1869 he obtained the important post of organist at St.-Sulpice in Paris, holding it for more than 60 years, retiring in 1934. On April 19, 1934, he played at St. Sulpice his *Pièce mystique,* composed at the age of 90. In 1890 he succeeded César Franck as prof. of organ at the Paris Cons.; in 1896 became prof. of counterpoint, fugue, and composition. He was active also as a music critic for 'L'Estafette' under the pen-name 'Aulétès'; also conducted the oratorio society 'Concordia.' In 1910 he was elected a member of the Institute, of which he became permanent secretary in 1913. He had many distinguished pupils, including Albert Schweitzer, with whom he collaborated in editing the first 5 vols. of a definitive 8-vol. ed. of J. S. Bach's organ works (brought out by G. Schirmer, N. Y.); also edited the collection 'L'Orgue moderne.' As a composer he wrote copiously in many forms, but is known best for his organ music, especially his 8 'symphonies' (suites); also the *Symphonie gothique* (op. 70) and the *Symphonie romaine* (op. 73). —Works: operas (all produced in Paris): *Maître Ambrose* (Opéra-Comique, May 6, 1886); *Les Pêcheurs de Saint-Jean* (Opéra-Comique, Dec. 26, 1905; his most successful opera); *Nerto* (Opéra, Oct. 27, 1924); incidental music to *Conte d'avril,* after Shakespeare's *Twelfth Night* (Odéon, Sept. 22, 1885); *Les Jacobites* (Nov. 21, 1885); etc.; a ballet, *La Korrigane* (Opéra, Dec. 1, 1880); symph. poem, *Une Nuit de Valpurgis* (London, April 19, 1888, composer conducting); 3 symphonies; a *Symphonie antique* (with organ and final chorus); *Sinfonia sacra* (with organ); *Ouverture espagnole;* 2 piano concertos; cello concerto; *Fantaisie* for piano and orch.; *Choral et variations* for harp and orch.; chamber music: 2 piano quintets; a string quartet; a piano trio; *Soirs d'Alsace* for piano trio; 2 violin sonatas; suite for cello and piano; cello sonata; *Trois Valses* for violin and piano; *Cavatina* for violin and piano; *Trois Pièces* for cello and piano; for piano: *Airs de ballet; La Prière; Caprice; Trois Valses; Impromptu; Six Morceaux; Prélude, andante et finale; Scènes de bal; Six Valses caractéristiques; Douze Feuillets d'album; Dans les bois; Romance; Suite polonaise;* suite in B minor; *Suite écossaise;* vocal music: Mass for 2 choirs and 2 organs; Psalm 83 for chorus and string quintet; Psalm 112 for 2 choirs, 2 organs, and orch.; *Tu es Petrus* for double chorus and organ; *Sacerdos et Pontifex* for chorus and organ; other church music; *Chant séculaire* for soprano, chorus, and orchestra; several song cycles, duets, choruses a cappella. He edited Berlioz's *Traité de l'instrumentation et d'orchestration modernes,* and wrote a supplement, *Technique de l'orchestre moderne* (1904; 2nd ed., 1906; in English, London, 1906 and 1946); publ. *La Musique grecque et les chants de l'Église latine,* in 'Revue des Deux Mondes' (1895); *Initiation musicale* (1923); *L'Orgue moderne* (1929); etc. —Cf. H. Reynaud, *L'Œuvre de Charles-Marie Widor* (Lyons, 1900); J. F. E. Rupp, *Charles-Marie Widor und sein Werk* (Bremen, 1912); Isidor Philipp, *Charles-Marie Widor,* in the 'Mus. Quarterly' (April, 1944).

Wiechowicz (vyā'-ho-vich), **Stanislaw,** Polish composer; b. Kroszyce, Nov. 27, 1893. He studied in Poland, Germany, and Russia; held various teaching posts in Poznan and later in Cracow. —Works: *Babie lato,* symph. poem (1922); *Chmiel,* symph. scherzo (1926); *Kasia,* folksong suite for orch. (1946); *Serenada polska* for orch. (1953); *Concerto 'Civita Vecchia'* for string orch. (1954); *Romantic Cantata* (1930); *Harvest Cantata* (1948); numerous choral works on Polish themes.

Wieck (vēk), **Alwin,** German pianist, son of Friedrich Wieck; b. Leipzig, Aug. 27, 1821; d. there, Oct. 21, 1885. He studied piano with his father, and violin with David; was a member of the Italian Opera orch. at St. Petersburg; then taught piano in Dresden. He publ. *Materialien zu F. Wiecks Pianoforte-Methodik* and *Vademecum perpetuum für den ersten Pianoforte-Unterricht nach F. Wiecks Methode;* also piano pieces.

Wieck (vēk), **Friedrich,** German pianist, father-in-law of Schumann; b. Pretzsch, near Torgau, Aug. 18, 1785; d. Loschwitz, near Dresden, Oct. 6, 1873. He studied theology at Wittenberg, and at the same time pursued musical studies in private; established a piano factory and a circulating music library in Leipzig, but gave up both in order to devote himself to teaching the piano, in which profession he had extraordinary success. Among his pupils were his daughters, Clara and Marie, Hans von Bülow, Fritz Spindler, Isidor Seiss, and Gustav Merkel. He was also Schumann's teacher, but opposed bitterly Schumann's marriage to Clara. He settled in Dresden in 1840. In 1843 Mendelssohn offered him a professorship at the newly established Leipzig Cons., but Wieck declined. Wieck's first wife (*née* Tromlitz) was the mother of Clara Schumann and Alwin; after her divorce she married Bargiel, the father of Woldemar Bargiel (q.v.); Marie Wieck was the daughter by Wieck's second wife, Clementine Fechner. He publ. 2 books of piano studies, and also *Clavier und Gesang* (1853; 3rd ed., 1878; also in English) and *Musikalische Bauernsprüche* (2nd ed. 1875, by Marie Wieck). —Cf. A. von Meichsner, *Friedrich Wieck und seine beiden Töchter Clara . . . und Marie* (Leipzig, 1875); A. Kohut, *Friedrich Wieck* (Dresden, 1887); V. Joss, *Friedrich Wieck und sein Verhältnis zu Robert Schumann* (Dresden, 1900); V. Joss, *Der Musikpädagoge Friedrich Wieck und seine Familie* (Dresden, 1902); Marie Wieck, *Aus dem Kreise Wieck-Schumann* (Dresden, 1912; 2nd augmented ed., 1914).

Wieck, Marie, German pianist, daughter of Friedrich Wieck; b. Leipzig, Jan. 17, 1832; d. Dresden, Nov. 2, 1916. She studied with her father; at the age of 11 made her début at a concert of her sister, Clara Schumann; appointed court pianist to the Prince of Hohenzollern in 1858; after tours of Germany, England, and Scandinavia, she settled in Dresden as a teacher of piano and singing; made prof. in 1914. Her last public appearance was with the Dresden Philharmonic Orch. in Nov., 1915, playing the Schumann concerto. She publ. piano pieces and songs; edited her father's *Pianoforte-Studien;* and wrote *Aus dem Kreise Wieck-Schumann* (1912; 2nd augmented ed., 1914).

Wiedebein (vē'-dĕ-bīn), **Gottlob,** German organist and conductor; b. Eilenstadt, July 27, 1779; d. Brunswick, April 17, 1854. After studying in Magdeburg, he settled in Brunswick as organist. He enjoyed a great reputation; Schumann sought his advice. He wrote some excellent lieder; was in correspondence with Beethoven, Schumann, and other composers; part of this correspondence was publ. in various German sources: 'Die Musik' (1911), 'Zeitschrift für Bücherfreunde' (1913), etc.

Wiedemann (vē'-deh-mahn), **Ernst Johann,** German composer and teacher; b. Hohengiersdorf, Silesia, March 28, 1797; d. Potsdam, Dec. 7, 1873. From 1818 to 1852 he was organist of the Roman Catholic Church in Berlin; founded and conducted 2 singing societies there; composed a *Te Deum* for soli, chorus, and orch., Masses, motets, and hymns.

Wiederkehr (vē'-der-kehr), **Jacob Christian Michael,** Alsatian composer; b: Strasbourg, April 28, 1739; d. Paris, April, 1823. From 1783 he was in Paris; played cello at the Concert Spirituel; bassoon at the Théâtre-Lyrique; trombone at the Opéra; taught singing at the Cons. (1795-1802). —Works: 12 *concertantes* for wind instruments; 2 quintets and 10 quartets for strings; 6 quintets for piano and wind instruments; 6 piano trios; 6 violin sonatas; etc.

Wiegand (vē'-gahnd), **(Josef Anton) Heinrich,** German bass; b. Fränkisch-Crumbach in the Odenwald, Sept. 9, 1842; d. Frankfurt, May 28, 1899. He studied voice privately in Paris; became a member of the opera at Zürich in 1870; then sang in Cologne, and from 1873 to 1877 was leading bass at Frankfurt. In 1877 he toured America with the Adams-Pappenheim troupe; then was in Leipzig (1878-82); sang at the Vienna Court Opera (1882-84); then was engaged at Hamburg. He also appeared in the *Nibelung* cycle in Berlin (1881) and London (1882).

Wiehmayer (vē'-mī-ĕr), **(Johann) Theodor,** German pianist; b. Marienfeld, Jan. 7, 1870; d. Starnberg, March 15, 1947. He studied at the Leipzig Cons. under Jadassohn (composition) and Reinecke (piano). After his début in Leipzig (1890) he undertook a successful tour in Sweden; then settled in Leipzig as a teacher, also giving concerts in other towns; 1902-06, teacher of piano in the Leipzig Cons.; from 1908 to 1925 at the Stuttgart Cons. Author of *Musikalische Rhythmik und Metrik* (1917) and *Musik-*

altsche Formenlehre in Analysen (1927); publ. technical studies for piano.

Wiel (vēl), **Taddeo,** Italian musicologist and composer; b. Oderzo, Treviso, Sept. 24, 1849; d. Venice, Feb. 17, 1920. He studied in Venice; became assistant librarian at San Marco; publ. valuable papers on Venetian music history: *I Codici contariniani ... nella R. Biblioteca di San Marco in Venezia* (1888); *I Teatri musicali veneziani del settecento* (1897); *Francesco Cavalli,* in the 'Mus. Antiquary' (Oct., 1912; also separately, Venice, 1914).

Wielhorsky (v'yehl-gohr'-skē), Count **Mikhail Yurievitch,** Russian patron of arts; b. Volynia, Nov. 12, 1788; d. Moscow, Sept. 9, 1856. His home in St. Petersburg was the gathering place of the most eminent musicians of the time. He was a friend of Glinka, but his suggestions as to the necessity of cuts in Glinka's opera, *Russlan and Ludmila,* were unfortunate. He publ. a string quartet and some songs, one of which, *Autrefois,* was arranged for piano by Liszt (1843). His brother, **Matvey Wielhorsky** (1794-1866), was a cellist; another brother, **Joseph** (1817-92), wrote piano pieces and songs (48 op. numbers).

Wieniawski (vyā-nyahv'-skē), **Adam Tadeusz,** Polish composer, nephew of Henri and Joseph Wieniawski; b. Warsaw, Nov. 27, 1879; d. Bydgoszcz, April 27, 1950. He studied in Warsaw with Melcer and Noskowski; then in Berlin with Bargiel, and in Paris with Vincent d'Indy, Fauré, and Gedalge. He fought in the French Army during World War I; returned to Warsaw in 1923; was appointed director of the Chopin School of Music in 1928. —Works: operas: *Megae* (Warsaw, Dec. 28, 1912); *Wyzwolony* (Warsaw, 1928); *Król Kochanek* (Warsaw, March 19, 1931); the ballets *Lalita* and *Le Festin chez Hérode* (1927); symph. poems *Kamaralmazan* (Paris, 1910) and *Princesse Baudour; Suite Polonaise* for orch. (1913); *Obrazki,* piano suite (also for orch.); arrangements of folksongs.

Wieniawski (vyā-nyahv'-skē), **Henryk (Henri),** famous Polish violinist; b. Lublin, July 10, 1835; d. Moscow, March 31, 1880. His mother, Regina Wolff-Wieniawska, was a talented pianist; on the advice of her brother, Eduard Wolff, pianist and composer who lived in France, she took Henryk to Paris, where he entered the Cons. at the age of 8, first in Clavel's class, and the following year, in the advanced class of Massart. At the age of 11 he graduated with 1st prize in violin, an unprecedented event in the annals of the Paris Cons. He gave his 1st concert in St. Petersburg on March 31, 1848, and played 3 more concerts there; then played in Finland and the Baltic provinces; after several successful appearances in Warsaw, he returned in 1849 to Paris, where he studied composition with Hippolyte Collet at the Cons., graduating (again with 1st prize) in 1850. He then traveled with his brother Joseph in Russia (1851-53); in 1859, appointed solo violinist to the Czar; taught at the newly founded St. Petersburg Cons. (1862-67); played the viola in the Ernst String Quartet. In 1872 he went on a tour of the U. S. with Anton Rubinstein; one of the featured works was Beethoven's *Kreutzer Sonata,* which they performed about 70 times. When Rubinstein returned to Europe, Wieniawski continued his American tour, which included California. He returned to Europe in 1874, gave several concerts with Rubinstein in Paris, and in the same year succeeded Vieuxtemps as prof. of violin playing at the Brussels Cons., resigning in 1877 owing to an increasingly grave heart condition; suffered a heart attack during a concert in Berlin in 1878, but still agreed to play several concerts in Moscow, where he remained until his death at the age of 44. He was married to Isobel Hampton, an Englishwoman; their youngest daughter Irene wrote music under the pen-name Poldowski (q.v.). He was undoubtedly one of the greatest violinists of the 19th century; he possessed a virtuoso technique and an extraordinary range of dynamics. He was equally distinguished as a chamber-music player. Many of his compositions are in the repertory of every violinist; of these the most famous are concerto in D minor; *Légende* for violin and orch.; *Souvenir de Moscou,* on Russian themes, for violin and orch.; and *Le Carnaval russe,* for violin and piano. Other works include (for violin and orch.): concerto in F♯ minor; *Polonaise; Scherzo-Tarentelle; Fantaisie brillante* (on themes from Gounod's *Faust*); *Polonaise brillante;* for violin and piano: *Caprice fantastique, Souvenir de Posen; Adagio élégiaque; Capriccio-Valse; Romance sans paroles et Rondo élégant;* 2 mazurkas; *Gigue; Études-Caprices* for 2 violins; etc. With his brother Joseph he wrote *Allegro de sonate* and *Grand duo polonais.* —Cf. A. Desfossez, *Henri Wieniawski: esquisse* (The Hague, 1856); J. Reiss, *Henryk Wieniawski* (Warsaw, 1931); I. Yampolski, *Henryk Wieniawski* (Moscow, 1955).

Wieniawski (vyā-nyahv'-skē), **Joseph,** Polish pianist and composer, brother of Henryk Wieniawski; b. Lublin, May 23, 1837;

d. Brussels, Nov. 11, 1912. He studied at the Paris Cons. with Zimmerman, Marmontel, and Alkan (piano), and LeCouppey (composition); in 1851 he went on tour with his brother, Henryk; studied with Liszt at Weimar (1855-56); and returned to Paris in 1857. In 1866 he settled in Moscow as a teacher at the Cons.; but soon established a piano school of his own, which flourished. In 1875-76 he was director of the Warsaw Music Society; then settled in Brussels, teaching at the Cons. He also made numerous concert tours throughout Europe. —Works: *Suite romantique,* for orch.; *Guillaume le Taciturne,* overture; a piano concerto; a string quartet; a piano trio; *Grand duo polonais,* for piano and violin (with his brother); a cello sonata; *Fantasia,* for 2 pianos; for piano solo: 4 polonaises; 5 waltzes; sonata in B minor; mazurkas; *Fantaisie et fugue; Sur l'Océan; Barcarole; Ballade; Notturno; Barcarole-Caprice, Romanze-Etüde,* etc.; also *24 Études de mécanisme et de style.* —Cf. L. Delcroix, *Joseph Wieniawski. Notices biographiques et anecdotiques* (Brussels, 1908).

Wieprecht (vē'-prĕht), **Friedrich Wilhelm,** German trombonist and inventor; b. Aschersleben, Aug. 8, 1802; d. Berlin, Aug. 4, 1872. He studied in Dresden and Leipzig, where he was already famous as a trombonist; lived in Berlin from 1824, at first as a violinist in the court orch., finally as director-general of all the Prussian military bands. He invented the bass tuba (1835, with the instrument-maker Moritz), the bathyphon, a sort of bass clarinet (1839, with Skorra), the 'piangendo' on brass instruments with pistons, and an improved contrabass bassoon; his claim of priority over Sax, in the invention of the saxhorns, was not upheld by the courts. —Cf. A. Kalkbrenner, *F. W. Wieprecht* (1888).

Wier, Albert Ernest, American music editor; b. Chelsea, Mass., July 22, 1879; d. Brooklyn, Sept. 8, 1945. He studied music at the New England Cons. and at Harvard Univ.; from 1900 was music ed. for various publishing firms in N. Y.; brought out a large number of collections and arrangements: *Whole World Music Series, The Pianist's Music Shelf, The Violinist's Music Shelf, Young Folks' Music Library, Radio Music Library,* etc.; also ed. 'The Macmillan Encyclopedia of Music and Musicians' (1938; withdrawn from circulation owing to an excessive number of demonstrable errors) and other reference works. Author of *The Piano, Its History . . . and Music* (N. Y., 1940).

Wiesengrund-Adorno, Theodor. See **Adorno.**

Wigglesworth, Frank, American composer; b. Boston, March 3, 1918. He studied at Bard College, at Columbia Univ. (B.S.), and at Converse College, Spartanburg, S.C. (M.A.); also took lessons from Luening and Cowell. He was in the Army Air Force during World War II; then taught at Columbia Univ. (1947-51) and Queens College (1954-55). In 1954 joined the faculty of the New School for Social Research, N. Y. Received the American Rome Prize (1951-54); editorial board chairman of 'New Music Edition' (1947-51). He is a great-nephew of Mrs. Elizabeth Sprague Coolidge. —Works: 2 symphonies (1957; 1958); *Creation,* for chorus and small orch. (1940); *New England Concerto,* for violin and strings (1941); *The Plunger,* for soprano, flute, viola, cello, and piano (1941); trio for flute, banjo, and harp (1942); *Jeremiah,* for baritone, chorus, and orch. (1942); *Sleep Becalmed,* for chorus and orch., after Dylan Thomas (1948); 3 movements for string orch. (1949); *Telesis,* for chamber orch. and percussion (1949); *Serenade for* flute, viola, and guitar (1952); brass quintet (1957).

Wihan (vē'-hahn), **Hans (Hanuš),** Czech cellist; b. Politz, near Braunau, Bohemia, June 5, 1855; d. Prague, May 3, 1920. He studied at the Prague Cons.; as a young man, he became instructor of cello at the Mozarteum, Salzburg; then was chamber musician in various courts in Germany; in 1880, became member of the private string quartet of King Ludwig of Bavaria, and frequently played at Wagner's soirées at Wahnfried; from 1888 prof. of cello at the Prague Cons. In 1891 he formed the 'Bohemian String Quartet,' selecting his four most talented pupils (Karel Hoffmann, Josef Suk, Oscar Nedbal, and Otto Berger); after Berger's retirement, owing to ill health, in 1897, Wihan himself took his place as cellist (until 1914); the Bohemian String Quartet for years enjoyed the highest reputation.

Wihtol (Vitols), Joseph, foremost Latvian composer; b. Volmar, July 26, 1863; d. Lübeck, April 24, 1948. He studied at the St. Petersburg Cons. (1880-86) with Rimsky-Korsakov; after graduation, was engaged as instructor there; succeeded Rimsky-Korsakov in 1908 as prof. of composition; among his students were Prokofiev and Miaskovsky. He was also music critic for the German daily 'St. Petersburger Zeitung.' In 1918 he left St. Petersburg; was for a season director of the Latvian Opera in Riga; in 1919 founded the

National Cons. there; many Latvian composers were his students. As the Soviet armies approached Riga (1944), Wihtol went to Germany, remaining there until his death. In his music he followed the harmonic practices of the Russian school, but often employed Latvian folksong patterns. Most of his works were publ. by Belaieff. —Works: a symphony (St. Petersburg, Dec. 17, 1887); *La Fête Ligho,* symph. tableau (1890); *Beverinas dziedonis (The Bard of Beverin),* for chorus and orch. (1891); *Ouverture dramatique* (1895); *Gaismas pils (The Castle of Light),* for chorus and orch. (1899); *Upe un cilvēka dzīve (River and Human Life),* for chorus (1903); *Spriditis,* Latvian fairy tale for orch. (1908); the cantatas *Song* (1908) and *Aurora Borealis* (1914); arrangements of 200 Latvian songs for voice and piano and for piano solo (2 books; 1906, 1919); many Latvian choral ballads; a string quartet; *10 Chants populaires lettons,* 'miniature paraphrases' for piano; songs. —Cf. O. Gravitis, *Latvian Composers* (Riga, 1955; in Russian; pp. 30-39).

Wijk, Arnold. See **Wyk, Arnold van.**

Wiklund, Adolf, Swedish composer and conductor; b. Langserud, June 5, 1879; d. Stockholm, April 3, 1950. He studied with J. Lindegren (composition) and R. Andersson (piano) at the Stockholm Cons.; was granted a state fellowship for study abroad; took lessons with James Kwast in Berlin (piano); was engaged as opera coach in Berlin; returning to Sweden in 1911, he became 2nd conductor of the Stockholm Opera; then led the Stockholm Court Orch. (1923-25) and the Concert Society (1925-38); also was guest conductor in London and Jena. He composed a symph. (1922); 2 piano concertos (1906; 1916); a *Konzertstück* for piano and orch. (1902); a symph. poem, *Sommarnatt och soluppgang* (1918); *Little Suite* for orch. (1928); *3 Pieces* for string orch. (1924); a violin sonata (1906); several albums of lyric pieces for piano; songs.

Wilbye, John, one of the greatest English madrigalists; b. Diss, Norfolk, 1574 (baptized March 7); d. Colchester, Sept., 1638. From 1595 until 1628 he was resident musician at Hengrave Hall, the home of Sir Thomas Kytson, near Bury St. Edmunds. After the death of Lady Kytson (1628), Wilbye settled in Colchester. He made frequent visits to London, where the Kytsons had a town house. His 1st book of madrigals (for 3, 4, 5, and 6 voices) appeared in 1598 (reprinted London, 1841); it contains 30 compositions; his 2nd book, containing 34 madrigals (also for 3 to 6 voices) came out in 1609 (reprinted London, 1846). To Leighton's 'Teares or Lamentations' (1614) he contributed 2 hymns, and for 'The Triumphes of Oriana' he wrote a 6-part madrigal, *The Lady Oriana.* His madrigals were reprinted in vols. VI and VII of 'The English Madrigal School.' —Cf. E. H. Fellowes, *The English Madrigal Composers* (1921; 2nd ed., 1948); H. Heurich, *John Wilbye in seinen Madrigalen* (Augsburg, 1931).

Wilckens, Friedrich, Austrian pianist and composer; b. Liezen, April 13, 1899. He studied piano with Lalewicz in Vienna and composition with Franz Schreker there and in Berlin (1916-20); in 1933 he settled in Seefeld. As a ballet pianist, he made 17 tours in the U.S. and 3 tours in South America. He wrote several ballets *(Himmel und Erde, Schwingender Tempel,* etc.), film music; various minor stage pieces.

Wilder, Alec, American composer; b. Rochester, N. Y., Feb. 17, 1907. He studied at the Eastman School of Music; active as composer for the theater and films, including a documentary film about Dr. Albert Schweitzer. He excels particularly in short operas scored for a limited ensemble of singers and instruments and suitable for performance in schools. —Works: operas: *The Lowland Sea* (1951) and *Sunday Excursion* (1953); *Kittiwake Island,* a musical comedy (1955); a ballet, *Juke Box* (1942); concerto for oboe, string orch., and percussion (1957); three woodwind quintets; a woodwind octet; piano pieces (*A Debutante's Dairy, Neurotic Goldfish, Walking Home in the Spring,* etc.); many songs.

Wilder (vil'-der), **(Jérôme Albert) Victor (van),** Belgian writer on music; b. Wetteren, near Ghent, Aug. 21, 1835; d. Paris, Sept. 8, 1892. He was a journalist; contributed articles to various publications in Paris, where he settled; wrote librettos; translated Wagner's texts into French, including *Der Ring des Nibelungen;* wrote *Mozart, l'homme et l'artiste* (Paris, 1880; English transl., 1908) and *Beethoven, sa vie et ses œuvres* (Paris, 1883).

Wildgans (vēld'-găns), **Friedrich,** Austrian composer; b. Vienna, June 5, 1913. He studied with J. Marx; taught at the Salzburg Mozarteum (1934-36); then played clarinet at the Vienna Opera; 1945-47, prof. at the Vienna State Academy of Music. He has written music in all genres, in an ultra-modern style, eventually adopting the 12-tone technique. —Works: opera, *Der Baum der Erkenntniss* (1935); choral symph. *Mayakovsky* (1946); *Sinfonia Austriaca;* 2 clarinet concertos; 3 piano sonatas; chamber music and choruses; author of *Entwicklung der Musik in Österreich im 20. Jahrhundert* (Vienna, 1950). In 1946 he married the Austrian soprano, Ilona Steingruber.

Wilhelm, Carl Friedrich, German choral composer; b. Schmalkalden, Sept. 5, 1815; d. there, Aug. 26, 1873. From 1839 to 1864 he was director of the Crefeld 'Liedertafel,' for which he composed many men's choruses, among them *Die Wacht am Rhein,* which became a national song of the Germans; it was first performed by the 'Liedertafel' on June 11, 1854, and first publ. in the 'Chorliedersammlung' of Erk and Greef (Essen, 1854). In 1860 he received the title of 'Royal Prussian Music Director'; in 1870 he was granted a pension of 3,000 marks. —Cf. K. Gollmick, *C. F. Wilhelm* (Frankfurt, 1848); W. Buchner, *C. F. Wilhelm* (Leipzig, 1874); G. Rogati, *Carl Wilhelm* (dissertation; Bonn, 1927).

Wilhelmj (vil-hĕhl'-mē), **August (Emil Daniel Ferdinand),** famous violin virtuoso; b. Usingen, Germany, Sept. 21, 1845; d. London, Jan. 22, 1908. He received his earliest instruction in music from his mother, who was an amateur pianist; then studied violin with Konrad Fischer, court musician at Wiesbaden; made his 1st appearance there as a child prodigy on Jan. 8, 1854. In 1861, at the recommendation of Liszt, he was sent to the Leipzig Cons., where he studied with Ferdinand David (violin), Hauptmann and Richter (theory); in 1864 he went to Frankfurt for an additional course with Raff; in 1865 he began his concert career, touring Switzerland; then played in Holland and England (1866), France and Italy (1867), Russia, Switzerland, France, and Belgium (1869), England, Scotland, and Ireland (1869-70); then traveled through Holland, Scandinavia, Germany, and Austria (1871-74), to England (1875-77), and America (1878), making a 4-year tour of the world to South America, Australia, and Asia (1878-82). In 1876 he was concertmaster of the Bayreuth orch. at the production of *Der Ring des Nibelungen.* For several years he lived chiefly at Biebrich-on-Rhine, where he established (with R. Niemann) a master school for violin playing. In 1886 he moved to Blasewitz, near Dresden; and in 1894 was appointed prof. of violin playing in the Guildhall School of Music, London. His first wife, whom he married in 1866, was Baroness Liphardt, a niece of Ferdinand David; in 1895 he married the pianist Mariella Mausch. He made a famous arrangement of Bach's Air from the orch. suite in D major which became known as the *Air on the G String* (Bach's original bore no such specification); also arranged Wagner's *Träume* for violin and orch.; wrote a cadenza to Beethoven's violin concerto; further composed for violin and orch. 2 *Konzertstücke* (No. 2, *In Memoriam), Alla Polacca,* and theme and variations (after 2 caprices of Paganini); *Romanze* for piano; songs. With James Brown he publ. *A Modern School for the Violin* (6 parts).—Cf. E. Frassinesi, *August Wilhelmj Violinista. Memorie* (Mirandola, 1913); E. Wagner, *Der Geigerkönig August Wilhelmj* (Homburg, 1928).

Wilhem (real name Bocquillon), **Guillaume-Louis,** French music educator; b. Paris, Dec. 18, 1781; d. there, April 26, 1842. The son of an army officer, he himself entered active service at the age of 12; but from 1795-1801 studied at the school of Liancourt, and then for 2 years in the Paris Cons. He taught music in the military school of Saint-Cyr; and in 1810 was appointed teacher of music at the Lycée Napoléon (later Collège Henri IV), occupying this position until death. The system of *enseignement mutuel* (mutual instruction), which had been introduced into the popular schools of France, attracted Wilhem's attention, and in 1815 he began to apply it in music teaching, with such marked success that in 1819 he was chosen to organize a system of music instruction for the primary schools in Paris, was appointed singing-teacher to the Polytechnique in 1820, and director of a Normal School of Music. In 1833 he conceived the idea of instituting regular reunions of the pupils in one grand chorus, to which he gave the name of 'Orphéon.' In 1835 he was made director general of music instruction in all primary schools of Paris, and was created a Chevalier of the Legion of Honor. Besides his school classes, he formed classes of adults, chiefly workingmen, in which the success of his system was equally conspicuous, and which later, under the name of 'Orphéons,' included several popular singing societies. He publ. numerous songs and choruses; also a collection of a cappella choruses, 'Orphéon,' in 5 (later 10) vols.; and 4 textbooks. —Cf. E. Niboyet, *Notice historique sur la vie et les ouvrages de G. L. B. Wilhem* (Paris, 1843); J. A. La Fage, *Notice sur Bocquillon-Wilhem* (Paris, 1845).

Wilke, Christian Friedrich Gottlieb, German organist and organ builder; b. Spandau,

March 13, 1769; d. Treuenbrietzen, July 31, 1848. He was organist in Spandau from 1791; in 1821, government expert on organ building. He publ. *Beiträge zur Geschichte der neuen Orgelbaukunst* (1846); *Über Wichtigkeit und Unentbehrlichkeit der Orgelmixturen* (1839).

Wilkes, Josué Teófilo, Argentine composer and musicologist; b. Buenos Aires, Jan. 8, 1883. He studied with Alberto Williams; in 1908 went to Europe for further study; took some lessons from Liapunov in St. Petersburg and also at the Schola Cantorum in Paris; returned to Argentina in 1914; for many years taught music in primary schools in Buenos Aires. He made a special study of Gregorian Chant; also transcribed and harmonized old colonial songs; composed 3 operas, *Nuit persane* (1916-20), *Por el cetro y la corona,* Byzantine tragedy after *Bajazet* of Racine (1924), *El Horoscopo* (after Calderón; 1926-27); a secular oratorio, *La Cautiva;* a symph. trilogy, *Humahuaca* (1911-14); a string octet; other chamber music; songs; *50 Canciones populares cuyanas* (arranged and harmonized), *Cancionero musical rioplatense* (Argentine dances); numerous magazine articles on Argentine music. With I. Guerrero Cárpena he publ. *Formas musicales rioplatenses . . .* (Buenos Aires, 1946).

Willaert (vil'-lahrt), **Adrian,** important Flemish composer; b. Bruges, c. 1490; d. Venice, Dec. 8, 1562. He went to Paris in 1514 to study law; was a pupil of Jean Mouton in music there; then traveled in Italy. He was in the service of Duke Alfonso I d'Este at Ferrara in 1522; in the spring of 1525 was attached to the court of Ippolito II d'Este, Archbishop of Milan. He became maestro di cappella at St. Mark's in Venice on Dec. 12, 1527; with the exception of 2 visits to Flanders (1542 and 1556), he remained in Venice, where he established a singing school, which flourished. Among his famous pupils were Zarlino, Cipriano de Rore, and Andrea Gabrieli; he is justly regarded as the founder of the great Venetian school of composition. The style of writing for 2 antiphonal choirs (prompted by the 2 opposed organs of St. Mark's Cathedral) was initiated by Willaert; he was one of the greatest masters of the madrigal and of the instrumental *ricercar;* also publ. motets, *canzone,* vesper psalms, and Masses. A complete edition of his works was begun by H. Zenck (5 vols. publ. by the American Institute of Musicology); Zenck also publ. *9 ricercari per sonar con tre stromenti* (Mainz, 1933); other reprints are found in Blume's 'Das Chorwerk' (ed. by Wiora and Hertzmann); in Attaignant's 'Treize livres de motets' (1550), reprinted by the Lyre-Bird Press (Paris, 1934); in Schering's 'Geschichte der Musik in Beispielen' (nos. 104, 105); in Tagliapietra's 'Antologia di musica antica e moderna' vol. I (*ricercari* arranged for piano); in Davison and Apel, 'Historical Anthology of Music' vol. I (nos. 113, 115); and in many other collections. —Cf. Ch. Carton, *Notice sur Adr. Willaert* (Bruges, 1849); E. Gregoir, *A. Willaert* (Antwerp, 1869); A. Averkamp, *Adrian Willaert,* in 'Tijdschrift der Vereeniging voor Nederlandsche Muziekgeschiedenis' (1922); H. Zenck, *Studien zu A. Willaert* (Leipzig, 1929); E. Hertzmann, *Adrian Willaert in der weltlichen Vokalmusik seiner Zeit* (Leipzig, 1931); Otto Gombosi, in 'Zeitschrift für Musikwissenschaft' (vol. XVI, 54); R. Lenaerts, *Notes sur Adrian Willaert* (Brussels, 1935). See also René Vannes, *Dictionnaire des musiciens* (Brussels, 1947); G. Reese, *Music in the Renaissance* (N. Y., 1954).

Willan, Healey, eminent organist and composer; b. Balham (Surrey), England, Oct. 12, 1880. He received his musical education at St. Saviour's Choir School, Eastbourne; was church organist in London until 1913, when he went to Canada as head of the theory dept. at the Royal Cons. in Toronto; was vice principal there (1920-36); in 1914 appointed lecturer and examiner at the Univ. of Toronto; 1937, prof. of music; retired in 1950; from 1932 was also organist of the Univ. of Toronto; founder and conductor of Tudor Singers (1934-39); greatly esteemed as pedagogue. —Works: 3 radio operas, commissioned and broadcast by the Canadian Broadcasting Corporation: *Transit through Fire* (March 8, 1942), *Brebeuf and his Brethren* (Sept. 26, 1943), *Deirdre* (April 20, 1946); symph. No. 1 (Toronto, Oct. 8, 1936); symph. No. 2 (Toronto, May 18, 1950); a piano concerto; *Agincourt Song,* for small orch.; a piano trio; 2 violin sonatas; several character pieces for piano; preludes and fugues for organ; other organ works; carols and hymn tunes; church services (Magnificats, Masses, etc.); motets a cappella; anthems with organ accompaniment; many other choral works; songs; arrangements of Canadian and British songs; school manuals.

Willeke, Willem, cellist; b. The Hague, Sept. 29, 1879; d. Pittsfield, Mass., Nov. 26, 1950. He studied cello in Holland; then was cellist in various German orchestras; also at the Vienna Opera (under Mahler). In 1907 he came to the U. S. and joined the Kneisel

Quartet, with which he remained until its disbandment in 1917; taught at the Institute of Musical Art, N. Y.; then was appointed director of the Berkshire Music Colony, in Pittsfield, Mass., where he remained until his death.

Willent-Bordogni (vi-lahn' bohr-doh'-ñē), **Jean-Baptiste-Joseph,** French bassoon virtuoso; b. Douai, Dec. 8, 1809; d. Paris, May 11, 1852. He studied with Delcambre at the Paris Cons.; played the bassoon in the orch. of the Théâtre Italien in Paris; married the daughter of the singing teacher Bordogni (1834) and added her name to his; taught at the Brussels Cons.; in 1848, was appointed to the faculty of the Paris Cons. He wrote a number of works for the bassoon, and publ. a method for it; also brought out 2 operas in Brussels: *Le Moine* (1844) and *Van Dyck* (1845).

Williams, Alberto, foremost Argentine composer; b. Buenos Aires, Nov. 23, 1862; d. there, June 17, 1952. He was a grandson of Benjamin Williams of Exeter, England; his maternal grandfather, Amancio Alcorta, was one of Argentina's early composers. Williams studied composition at the Paris Cons., with Guiraud, Durand, and Godard, piano with Mathias (a pupil of Chopin), and organ and counterpoint with César Franck. He returned to Argentina in 1889; founded the Alberto Williams Cons. in 1893; also organized branches in provincial towns of Argentina, numbering more than 100; founded a music publishing firm, 'La Quena' (also a music magazine of that title). He was the most prolific composer of Argentina; 112 op. numbers were publ. by 'La Quena.' The greatest influence in his music was that of César Franck, but modernistic usages are found in his application of whole-tone scales, parallel chord progressions, etc. In many of his works he used characteristic melorhythms of Argentina; composed a number of piano pieces in Argentinian song-and-dance forms (milongas, gatos, cielitos, etc.). He wrote 9 symphonies; the following were performed in Buenos Aires: No. 1 (Nov. 25, 1907); No. 2, *La Bruja de las montañas* (Sept. 9, 1910); No. 3, *La Selva sagrada* (Dec. 8, 1934); No. 4, *El Ataja-Caminos* (Dec. 15, 1935); No. 5, *El Corazón de la Muñeca* (Nov. 29, 1936); No. 6, *La Muerte del Cometa* (Nov. 26, 1937); No. 7, *Eterno reposo* (Nov. 26, 1937). Other orchestral works include several suites of Argentinian dances; he further composed 3 violin sonatas, a cello sonata, a piano trio; a great number of piano albums, the last of which was *En el parque,* which he wrote in the year of his death. He composed 136 opus numbers in all. He also publ. numerous didactic works and several books of poetry. A complete catalogue of his works is found in vol. 2 of 'Composers of the Americas' publ. by the Pan American Union, Washington, D.C. (1956; pp. 138-55).—Cf. Z. R. Lacoigne, *Alberto Williams; Músico argentino* (Buenos Aires, 1942); *Homenajes a Alberto Williams,* containing messages and opinions of musicians on the occasion of his 80th birthday (Buenos Aires, 1942); N. Slonimsky, *Alberto Williams: Father of Argentinian Music,* in 'Mus. America' (Jan. 10, 1942); V. A. Risolía, *Alberto Williams, curriculum vitae* (Buenos Aires, 1944).

Williams, Charles Francis Abdy, English writer on music; b. Dawlish, Devonshire, July 16, 1855; d. Milford, near Lymington, Feb. 27, 1923. While pursuing his studies at Trinity College, Cambridge, he played violin and viola in the orch. of the Cambridge Univ. Musical Society; then went to New Zealand, where he was church organist in Auckland; returning to England in 1881, he took the degree of Mus. Bac. at Oxford (1889) and Cambridge (1891); 1895-1901, was director of music at the Greek Theatre at Bradfield College, where he wrote choruses in ancient Greek modes for the productions of Greek tragedies. Retiring from teaching in 1901, he devoted himself to scholarly work; in 1904 he introduced the Solesmes system of performing plainchant at the priests' seminary in Capri, which won him recognition from the Pope. —Books: *A Short Historical Account of the Degrees in Music at Oxford and Cambridge* (1893); *Bach* (1900; new ed., 1934) and *Handel* (1901; new ed., 1935) in the series 'The Master Musicians'; *The Story of the Organ* (1903); *The Story of Notation* (1903); *The Story of Organ Music* (1905); *The Rhythm of Modern Music* (1909); *The Aristoxenian Theory of Musical Rhythm* (1911); essays on Greek music and plainchant in various journals.

Williams, Charles Lee, English organist and composer; b. Winchester, May 1, 1853; d. Gloucester, Aug. 29, 1935. He was a pupil of Dr. Arnold at the Cathedral of Winchester; from 1872 filled various posts as organist and choirmaster in Ireland and England; conducted several of the 'Three Choirs Festivals' held at Gloucester; after 1898 became active in the educational field. He composed the cantatas *Gethsemane, Bethany, A Harvest Song, A Dedication,* etc.; much church music; brought out (with H. G. Chance) a continuation (1895, covering the years 1864-94) of D. Lysons's *Origin and Progress of the Meeting of the Three Choirs of Gloucester, Worcester, and Hereford* . . . (1812, covering the years 1724-1811; supplemental vol. by John Amott in 1865, covering the years 1812-64); in 1931 brought out, with H. G. Chance and T. Hannan-Clark, a further continuation (covering the years 1895-1930) of the work, under the title *Annals of the Three Choirs.*

Williams, Christopher à Becket, English composer and writer on music; b. Dorchester, July 2, 1890; d. London, Nov. 3, 1956. He studied at Keble College, Oxford; was in the British army during World War I; subsequently traveled in Europe, Asia, and America; wrote 2 travel books, 3 novels, etc.; also contributed to musical periodicals. He composed several orchestral suites: *5 Impressions, Pepperpot Suite, Welsh Suite, Theme and Derivations* for strings, etc.; 3 violin sonatas; a cello sonata; 2 piano sonatas; several piano suites.

Williams, David Christmas, Welsh conductor and composer; b. Llanwrtyd, Sept. 12, 1871; d. there, March 21, 1926. He studied with J. Parry at the South Wales School of Music; conducted various music societies in Wales; wrote a cantata, *The Sands of Lavan,* which received a prize at Cardiff (1893); *The Battle of the Severn,* for chorus and orch.; *Psalms of Praise;* men's choruses; songs; piano piece.

Williams, Frederic Arthur, American pianist, composer, and pedagogue; b. Oberlin, Ohio, March 3, 1869; d. Cleveland, July 31, 1942. He studied piano and composition with W. G. Smith and others in Cleveland; subsequently occupied various teaching posts in Ohio. He wrote about 250 pieces for piano; also some songs. His technical publications for piano include *Wrist and Forearm Studies* and *Octave and Chord Studies.*

Williams, Harry Evan, American tenor; b. Mineral Ridge, Ohio, Sept. 7, 1867; d. Akron, Ohio, May 24, 1918. Originally he worked in a mine and steel mill; then studied singing in Cleveland and N. Y.; made his début at the Worcester, Mass., Festival of 1896, and then sang in oratorio at many other festivals; gave nearly 1000 recitals. He was one of the 1st American vocalists to introduce English translations in the regular concert repertory.

Williams, John Gerrard, English composer; b. London, Dec. 10, 1888; d. Oxted, Surrey, March 7, 1947. He was an architect by profession, but took some lessons in music from Richard Walthew, and soon began to compose; presented a concert of his works (chamber music, piano pieces, and songs) in London on March 27, 1922. He wrote a ballad opera, *Kate, the Cabin-Boy* (London, 1924); 2 operettas; a ballet, *The Wings of Horus* (1928); *3 Miniatures* and *Elegiac Rhapsody* for orch.; 2 string quartets; many songs and part-songs.

Williams, John M., American pianist and pedagogue; b. on a plantation in Washington County, Texas, Jan. 1, 1884. He studied in N. Y. and Chicago; since 1913 lectured on musical pedagogy to music teachers in the major cities of the U. S., Canada, England, and Scotland. His teaching material has had world-wide distribution, having been publ. in Great Britain, Australia, Cuba, and South America (Spanish editions). Some ten million copies of his various piano books have been sold. Among his teaching publications are the 'Grade by Grade' and 'Year by Year' books; 'Child's First Music Book' and 'Nothing Easier' or 'Adventures of Ten Little Fingers in Mother Goose Land'; also 'First Book for the Adult Beginner' (publ. also in a special Canadian ed.).

Williams, Joseph, English music publisher; he was the son of Lucy Williams, who established a printing shop at London in 1808. Joseph Williams continued the business; was succeeded in 1883 by his son, Joseph Benjamin Williams (who publ. some of his own pieces under the nom de plume of Florian Pascal); the business was incorporated as Joseph Williams, Ltd., in 1900. Upon the death of J. B. Williams, his son, Florian Williams, became head of the company. Joseph Williams, Ltd. specialized in publishing contemporary English music; also brought out Elizabethan works.—Cf. Florian Williams, *After Forty Years. Recollections of a Music Publisher,* in 'Mus. Opinion' (Feb.-Dec., 1940).

Williams, Ralph Vaughan. See **Vaughan Williams, Ralph.**

Williamson, John Finley, American choral conductor; b. Canton, Ohio, June 23, 1887. He studied singing with Witherspoon and Bispham in N. Y.; organ with Karl Straube in Leipzig. In 1921 he founded the Westminster Choir, and in 1926, the Westminster Choir School (later College) at Princeton,

N. J.; was its president until 1958, when he resigned. With his choir he gave 1000 concerts in America; also made 2 European tours; edited the 'Westminster Series' of choral music.

Willis, Henry, English organ builder; b. London, April 27, 1821; d. there, Feb. 11, 1901. As a youth he worked for John Gray (later Gray & Davidson), and still during his apprenticeship he invented the special manual and pedal couplers which he later used in his own instruments; from 1842 to 1845 he worked for Evans at Cheltenham, and in 1845 established his own business in London. He rebuilt the organ in the Gloucester Cathedral; exhibited a large organ at the Crystal Palace in 1851, which won the Council Medal, and was installed in the Winchester Cathedral; he subsequently was commissioned to build the great organ in St. George's Hall, Liverpool (1855). In 1878 he took his sons Vincent and Henry into partnership, adopting the firm name of 'Henry Willis & Sons'; he became generally known as 'Father Willis.' Willis himself regarded the organ in St. Paul's, which he built in 1891, as his masterpiece (77 speaking stops, 19 couplers). After the founder's death in 1901, his son Henry Willis became the head of the business, and soon took his son, also named Henry Willis, into partnership. They built the organ in the Liverpool Cathedral (167 speaking stops, 48 couplers) in 1912-14; this organ was the largest in the world at the time.

Willis Music Co., American music publishers. The business was founded by Charles H. Willis at Cincinnati in 1899, in association with his son William H. Willis. The firm became known as W. H. Willis & Co.; after absorption of G. B. Jennings & Co. in 1910 it was incorporated as the Willis Music Co. On July 1, 1919, the business was acquired by Gustave Schirmer of New York. The company specializes in educational publications.

Willis, Richard Storrs, American composer and writer on music; b. Boston, Feb. 10, 1819; d. Detroit, May 7, 1900. He was a brother of the poet Nathaniel Parker Willis; studied at Yale Univ., where he was president of the Beethoven Society (1837), for which he wrote choruses and instrumental pieces. He then went to Germany, and studied theory with Schnyder von Wartensee in Frankfurt and with Hauptmann in Leipzig. Returning to New York, he edited the periodical 'The Musical World' (1852-60); brought out a collection, 'Church Chorals and Choir Studies' (N. Y., 1850) and 'Our Church Music' (N. Y., 1856); also composed student songs and patriotic hymns, later collected as 'Waif of Song' and publ. in Paris in 1876.

Willmers, Rudolf, pianist and composer; b. Copenhagen, Oct. 31, 1821; d. Vienna, Aug. 24, 1878. His father, a Danish agriculturist, sent him to Germany at the age of 13 to study science, but Willmers turned to music; took lessons with Hummel for 2 years and with Fr. Schneider for a year; became a concert pianist and toured successfully in Germany and Austria; was much acclaimed in Paris and London (1846-47); in 1866 settled in Vienna. His technical specialty was the performance of 'chains of trills' for which he was famous. He wrote a number of brilliant piano solos: *Six études; Sérénade érotique* (for the left hand); *Sehnsucht am Meere; Un Jour d'été en Norvège; Deux études de concert (La Pompa di festa* and *La Danza delle Baccanti); Sonate héroïque; Tarantella giocosa; La Sylphide; Trillerketten; Aus der Geisterwelt,* tremolo-caprice; *Allegro symphonique;* he also composed some chamber music. —Cf. T. de L***, *Notice sur la vie et les travaux artistiques de R. Willmers,* in the 'Archives des Hommes du Jour' (Paris, April, 1847; also separately).

Willner, Arthur, pianist and composer; b. Teplice, Czechoslovakia, March 5, 1881. He studied at the Leipzig Cons. and in Munich. From 1904 to 1924 he taught at the Stern Cons. in Berlin; from 1924 to 1938, lived in Vienna; in 1938 settled in London. His list of works includes more than 100 op. numbers: a symph., a cello concerto, a piano concerto, 5 string quartets, 4 violin sonatas, 3 sonatinas for violin and piano, 4 piano sonatas and several character pieces, choral works, organ works, songs.

Willson, Meredith, American composer of popular music; b. Mason City, Iowa, May 18, 1902. He played the flute in a local orch. at the age of 11, and in 1916 was sent to N. Y., where he continued to study the flute with Georges Barrère. In 1919 he joined Sousa's band as flutist, touring with it until 1922. From 1923 to 1928 he was flutist in the N. Y. Philharmonic. He then entered the field of radio as conductor and composer. For the 30th anniversary of the San Francisco earthquake he composed his 1st symph. and conducted its première with the San Francisco Symph. Orch. on April 19, 1936; his 2nd symph. was presented by the Los Angeles Philharmonic on April 4, 1940. Other works include a symph. poem *The Jervis Bay* (1942); *Symphonic Variations on an American Theme;* an *O. O. McIntyre Suite* for orch. (San Francisco, 1936); also an *Anthem of the Atomic Age* for chorus; many pieces for band. Then he devoted himself mainly to popular music, with ever increasing success, culminating in the production of his musical revue, *The Music Man,* which opened on Broadway on Dec. 19, 1957. He also publ. an autobiography, *And There I Stood with My Piccolo* (N. Y., 1948) and *Eggs I Have Laid* (N. Y., 1955).

Willy. Pen name for **Gauthier-Villars.**

Wilm, Nicolai von, pianist and composer; b. Riga, March 4, 1834; d. Wiesbaden, Feb. 20, 1911. He studied with Plaidy, Hauptmann, and Richter at the Leipzig Cons.; then in 1857 went to Riga as theater conductor, and in 1860 proceeded to St. Petersburg, where he became instructor at the Imperial Nicolayevsky Institute; returned to Germany in 1875, and lived mostly in Dresden and Wiesbaden. A highly prolific composer (243 opus numbers), he is best known through his chamber music; wrote a string sextet, a string quartet, a piano trio, a cello sonata, 2 violin sonatas, a sonata for violin and harp; numerous pieces for piano solo: *Kleine Suite, Herbstfrüchte, Im russischen Dorf, Stimmungen, Dorf- und Waldidyllen, Musikalisches Dekameron;* etc.; for piano 4 hands: *Eine Nordlandfahrt, Reisebilder aus Schlesien, Musikalische Federzeichnungen, Kalendarium,* etc.; also variations and other pieces for 2 pianos; men's choruses; songs.

Wilms, Jan Willem, composer; b. Witzhelden, Schwarzburg-Sondershausen, March 30, 1772; d. Amsterdam, July 19, 1847. He received his early musical training from his father. In 1791 he went to Amsterdam, where he appeared as pianist and harpist. He composed 2 piano concertos, 2 flute concertos, 2 string quartets, 2 piano trios, 3 violin sonatas, 2 flute sonatas, a clarinet concerto; also 3 symphonies. He was the author of the Dutch national song *Wien Neerlandsch bloed door d'aderen vloeit* (1815).

Wilsing (vil'-zing), **Daniel Friedrich Eduard,** German composer; b. Hörde, near Dortmund, Oct. 21, 1809; d. Berlin, May 2, 1893. He was organist in Wesel from 1829 to 1834; then moved to Berlin. He composed an oratorio in 2 parts, *Jesus Christus* (produced in Bonn in 1889, by Wilsing's pupil, Arnold Mendelssohn); a *De profundis a* 16, which won the gold medal for art at Berlin; piano sonatas; songs.

Wilson, Domingo Santa Cruz. See **Santa Cruz Wilson, Domingo.**

Wilson, Grenville Dean, American composer; b. Plymouth, Conn., Jan. 26, 1833; d. Nyack, N. Y., Sept. 20, 1897. He was taught piano by his mother; then studied theory with A. W. Johnson in Boston; some of his piano pieces were publ. before he was 10 years old. In 1871 he was head of the music dept. of Rockland Institute, Nyack; in 1877 he organized the Nyack Symph. Society. He publ. 178 pieces, chiefly for piano, some of which were popular (*The Shepherd-boy, Wayside Chapel, Chapel in the Mountains, Moonlight on the Hudson, Voix du matin,* etc.).

Wilson, John, English lutenist and song writer; b. (probably in Faversham, Kent) April 5, 1595; d. London, Feb. 22, 1674. He was musically gifted; at the age of 19, wrote music for 'The Maske of Flowers.' According to some indications, he participated as a singer in a production of Shakespeare's *Much Ado About Nothing* (as 'Jacke Wilson'). In 1635 he was made one of the King's Musicians; was in favor with Charles I, whom he followed to Oxford during the civil war in 1644, and was made D. Mus. by Oxford Univ. on March 10, 1645; he was 'Musick Professor' there from 1656 until 1661. Upon the Restoration he resumed his post at court, and on Oct. 22, 1662 became successor of Henry Lawes as Gentleman of the Chapel Royal. He publ. *Psalterium Carolinum* (London, 1657), *Cheerfull Ayres or Ballads* (Oxford, 1660); wrote several songs to Shakespeare's words. Some of his songs were included in Playford's *Select Musicall Ayres and Dialogues* (1652, 1653), *Select Ayres and Dialogues* (1659), *Catch that catch can: or the Musical Companion* (1667), and *The Treasury of Musick* (1669). —Cf. E. R. Rimbault, *Who was 'Jacke Wilson,' the Singer of Shakespeare's Stage?* (London, 1846); E. F. Hart, *Caroline Lyrics and Contemporary Song-Books,* in 'Library' (London; June, 1953); V. H. Duckles, *The 'Curious' Art of John Wilson,* in 'Journal of the American Musicological Society' (Summer, 1954).

Wilson, Mortimer, American organist and composer; b. Chariton, Iowa, Aug. 6, 1876; d. New York, Jan. 27, 1932. He studied organ with Middelschulte in Chicago; composition with F. G. Gleason; in 1907 went to Leipzig to study with Max Reger. Returning to America in 1911, he became conductor of the Atlanta Philharmonic Orch. (until 1915); then taught at various music schools; settled in N. Y. He wrote 5 symphonies, an overture *New Orleans; Concerto Grosso* for strings; 2 piano trios; 3 violin sonatas; *Echoes from Childhood* and *Romance* for violin and piano; etc. Author of *The Rhetoric of Music* (Lincoln, Nebr., 1907) and *Harmonic and Melodic Technical Studies;* publ. 'A series of work tables prepared for students of harmony' (1921).

Wilson, Philip, English singer and music editor; b. Hove, Sussex, Nov. 29, 1886; d. London, July 26, 1924. After studying singing in London, he went to Australia in 1913 as a vocal teacher at the Sydney Cons.; returning to England in 1920, he gave historical recitals, especially of Elizabethan songs. With Peter Warlock (Philip Heseltine) he edited *English Ayres, Elizabethan and Jacobean,* and *Chromatic Tunes* of 1606; also edited *The Musical Proverbs* (London, 1924), from the Lekingfelde MS.

Wiltberger, August, German composer; brother of Heinrich Wiltberger; b. Sobernheim, April 17, 1850; d. Stuttgart, Dec. 2, 1928. He was engaged as music teacher in various towns in Alsace; wrote a number of sacred works; a secular cantata, *Barbarossas Erwachen;* chamber music; organ pieces; author of *Harmonielehre; zum Gebrauch in Lehrerbildungsanstalten* (1906; 3rd ed., 1912).

Wiltberger, Heinrich, German composer and teacher; brother of August Wiltberger; b. Sobernheim, Aug. 17, 1841; d. Colmar, May 26, 1916. He studied with his father, an organist; taught in various music schools in Alsace; his setting of Alsatian folksongs for male chorus were very popular. He also wrote a *Märchen* for string orch.; a Requiem; several Masses; brought out collections of Latin and German hymns; publ. *Der Gesangsunterricht in der Volksschule* (1907).

Winderstein (vĭn'-dĕr-shtīn), **Hans (Wilhelm Gustav),** German conductor; b. Lüneburg, Oct. 29, 1856; d. Giessen, June 23, 1925. He studied at the Leipzig Cons. with H. Schradieck (violin) and Richter (theory); also played in the Gewandhaus Orch. He conducted the concerts of the Philharmonic Societies of Nuremberg and Fürth (1890-93); then was conductor of the newly established Philharmonic Orch. at Munich, and of the Kaim Concerts (1893-96). In 1896 he organized the 'Winderstein Orch.' in Leipzig, which he conducted until 1919; from 1920 conducted summer concerts in Bad Nauheim. He composed a *Trauermarsch, Valse-Caprice,* and *Ständchen* for orch.; violin pieces; piano pieces.

Winding, August (Henrik), Danish pianist and composer; b. Taaro, March 24, 1835; d. Copenhagen, June 16, 1899. He studied with Gade; was appointed prof. at the Copenhagen Cons. in 1867; from 1891 till his death was its director. He composed a symphony; a *Nordische Ouvertüre;* a piano concerto; cadenzas to Beethoven's piano concertos and to many of Mozart's; a string sextet; piano quartet; 2 violin sonatas; many piano pieces *(Drei Fantasiestücke, Reisebilder, Ländliche Szenen, Studien und Stimmungen, Idyllen und Legenden, Albumblätter,* etc.); songs.

Windingstad, Ole, Norwegian conductor; b. Sandefjord, May 18, 1886. He graduated from the Oslo Cons. in 1902; then studied at the Leipzig Cons.; settled in America in 1913, and established the Scandinavian Symph. Orch., which he conducted until 1929; also conducted the Brooklyn Symph. Orch. (1930-32), the Knickerbocker Symph. Orch. in Albany, N. Y. (1937-39), the New Orleans Symph. Orch. (1940-44), and the Albany Symph. Orch. (1945-48). In 1929 he was decorated with the Norwegian Order of Saint Olaf. He composed a symphony (1913); a cantata, *The Skald of Norway* (1929); *The Tides,* for orch. (Albany, Feb. 13, 1938; composer conducting); many minor pieces.

Windsperger, Lothar, German composer; b. Ampfing, Oct. 22, 1885; d. Wiesbaden, May 29, 1935. He studied with R. Louis and others in Munich; from 1913, was in Mainz as artistic adviser to the music publisher B. Schott's Söhne. Among his works are a symphony; *Lumen amoris,* symph. fantasy; a piano concerto; a violin concerto; *Missa Symphonica;* Requiem; chamber music; piano pieces; organ pieces; songs.

Wingham, Thomas, English piano teacher and composer; b. London, Jan. 5, 1846; d. there, March 24, 1893. He studied with Sterndale Bennett at the Royal Academy of Music; became prof. of piano playing there in 1871; also served as church organist. He composed 2 Masses, motets, offertories, and other church music; also 4 symphonies; 6

overtures; *Concert-Capriccio* for piano and orch.; 2 string quartets; a septet for piano, strings, and wind instruments; songs.

Winkelmann, Hermann, German tenor; b. Brunswick, March 8, 1849; d. Vienna, Jan. 18, 1912. He started out as a piano maker, but became interested in singing; made a successful début at Sondershausen (1875), and then sang at Altenburg, Darmstadt, and Hamburg. His interpretation of Tannhäuser and Lohengrin (in special engagements at Vienna) induced Richter to recommend him to Wagner, who chose him to create Parsifal at Bayreuth (July 26, 1882). From 1883 to 1906, when he retired on a pension, he was one of the brightest stars of the Vienna Opera, where one of his most brilliant achievements was the performance of the role of Tristan (with Materna as Isolde) in the Vienna première (Oct. 4, 1883). In 1884 he sang in the U. S. at the Wagner festivals given by Theodore Thomas in New York, Boston, Philadelphia, Cincinnati, and Chicago.

Winkler, Alexander Adolfovitch, Russian composer and pianist; b. Kharkov, March 3, 1865; d. Leningrad, Oct., 1935. He studied with Duvernoy in Paris, and with Leschetizky (piano) and Navrátil (composition) in Vienna. Returning to Russia, he became a piano teacher in his native city (1890-96); in 1907 was appointed to the faculty of the St. Petersburg Cons. He composed an overture, *En Bretagne;* orchestral variations on a Russian folksong, and on a Finnish folksong; a string quintet; 3 string quartets; a piano quartet; a piano trio; a viola sonata; several albums of piano pieces; songs; also made arrangements for piano 4 hands of works by Glinka and Glazunov.

Winner, Septimus, American composer of popular music; b. Philadelphia, May 11, 1827; d. there, Nov. 22, 1902. He learned to play the violin; married at 20 and opened a music store in Philadelphia, where he began giving lessons on the violin, guitar, and banjo. In 1854 he wrote his best-known song, *Listen to the Mocking Bird,* selling the copyright for $5; in his lifetime the song sold 20 million copies. In 1862 he wrote *Give Us Back Our Old Commander: Little Mac, the People's Pride,* voicing a widespread sentiment for the return of Gen. McClellan; the song was regarded as subversive and Winner was arraigned, but soon released; later the song, slightly altered, was used for Grant's presidential campaign. Winner also wrote the song *Whispering Hope,* which became extremely popular. He was a pioneer in bringing music to the masses; wrote over 200 volumes of music, including many instructive works, for 23 different instruments, and made about 2,000 arrangements for violin and piano. He used the pen name Alice Hawthorne for many of his songs, including *Listen to the Mocking Bird.* —Cf. C. E. Claghorn, *The Mocking Bird: The Life and Diary of its Author, Sep. Winner* (Philadelphia, 1937).

Winter (vin'-ter), **Peter,** German composer; b. Mannheim (baptized Aug. 28), 1754; d. Munich, Oct. 17, 1825. He was a violinist in the Electoral orch. at the age of 11; studied with Abbé Vogler; in 1776 became music director at the court theater; went with the court to Munich in 1778; was appointed court conductor in 1798 and held this post until his death. In Munich he brought out a number of operas, of which the most important were: *Helena und Paris* (Feb. 5, 1782), *Der Bettelstudent* (Feb. 2, 1785), *Marie von Montalban* (Jan. 28, 1800), and *Colmal* (Sept. 15, 1809). Frequent leaves of absence from Munich enabled him to travel; in Venice he produced his operas *Catone in Utica* (1791), *I Sacrifizi di Creta* (1792), *I Fratelli rivali* (1793), and *Belisa* (1794). In Vienna he brought out *Das unterbrochene Opferfest* (June 14, 1796; his most successful opera; produced all over Europe), *Babylons Pyramiden* (Oct. 25, 1797), and *Das Labirint* (June 12, 1798); in Paris he produced his only French opera, *Tamerlan* (Sept. 14, 1802); in London, the Italian operas *La Grotta di Calipso* (May 31, 1803), *Il Trionfo dell' amor fraterno* (March 22, 1804), *Il Ratto di Proserpina* (May 3, 1804), and *Zaira* (Jan. 29, 1805); in Milan, *Maometto II* (Jan. 28, 1817), *I due Valdomiri* (Dec. 26, 1817), and *Etelinda* (March 23, 1817). He also wrote several ballets; 3 oratorios and 17 sacred cantatas for the Munich court chapel; 26 Masses and a vast amount of other church music; 9 symphonies (including the grand choral symph. *Die Schlacht*); overtures; 2 septets; 6 string quartets; 2 string quintets; concertos for clarinet, for bassoon, and other instruments with orch.; and a *Vollständige Singschule* in 3 parts. Some of his chamber music was republished by Riemann in the 'Denkmäler der Tonkunst in Bayern' (vols. XV and XVI; with a thematic catalogue). —Cf. V. Frensdorf, *Peter Winter als Opernkomponist* (dissertation; Erlangen, 1908); E. Löffler, *Die Messen Peter Winters* (Frankfurt, 1928).

Winter-Hjelm, Otto, Norwegian organist and composer; b. Christiania, Oct. 8, 1837; d. there, May 3, 1931. He studied with H. Kjerulf in Christiania, and with Kullak and Wüerst in Berlin. He was organist in the Trefoldighetskirke in Christiania from 1874 till 1921; wrote music criticism in the 'Aftenposten' (1887-1913). —Works: symph. No. 1 (Christiania, Sept. 27, 1862); symph. No. 2 (1862; first performed, Christiania, March 18, 1916); many choruses for men's voices; edited *50 Melodier til Hauges og Landstads Salmebøger* and *50 Salmemelodier* for piano; also church music. Publ. *Af Kristiania teaterliv i den seneste tid* (essays; Christiania, 1875).

Winterberger, Alexander, German pianist and composer; b. Weimar, Aug. 14, 1834; d. Leipzig, Sept. 23, 1914. He studied at the Leipzig Cons. (1848) and with Liszt. In 1861 he went to Vienna; in 1869, became piano prof. at the St. Petersburg Cons.; returned to Leipzig in 1872, and remained there as teacher and music critic. He publ. some piano pieces: *Alinen-Tänze* (waltzes, mazurkas, minuets, etc.), *Concert-Étude, Valse-Caprice, Concert-Adagio;* songs; German and Slavonic duets. —Cf. O. Foerster, *Alexander Winterberger. Seine Werke, sein Leben* (Hanover, 1905; with a list of works).

Winterfeld, Carl Georg August Vivigens von, German writer on music; b. Berlin, Jan. 28, 1784; d. there, Feb. 19, 1852. He studied law at the Univ. of Halle; then occupied juridical positions in Breslau and Berlin. He collected a valuable library of old music, which he donated to the Library of Berlin. —Publications: *Palestrina* (1832); *J. Gabrieli und sein Zeitalter* (1834; 3 vols); *Über K.Fr. Chr. Fasch's geistliche Gesangswerke* (1839); *Dr. Martin Luthers deutsche geistliche Lieder* (1840); *Der evangelische Kirchengesang und sein Verhältnis zur Kunst des Tonsatzes* (1843-47; 3 vols.); *Über Herstellung des Gemeinde- und Chorgesangs in der evangelischen Kirche* (1848); *Zur Geschichte heiliger Tonkunst* (2 parts; 1850, 1852); *Musiktreiben und Musikempfindungen im 16. und 17. Jahrhunderte* (1851); *Alceste . . . von Lulli, Händel und Gluck* (1851); *Allegorisch-poetische Festopern am Kaiserlichen Hofe zu Wien in der letzten Hälfte des 17. Jahrhunderts* (1852). —Cf. A. Prüfer, *Briefwechsel zwischen Carl von Winterfeld und Eduard Krüger* (Leipzig, 1898).

Winternitz, Emanuel, musicologist and authority on musical instruments; b. Vienna, Aug. 4, 1898. He studied at the universities of Vienna (1918-22) and Hamburg (1923); settled in the U. S.; lectured at Harvard Univ. (1938-41) and at Columbia Univ. (1947-48). In 1942 he was appointed keeper of the collection of musical instruments of the Metropolitan Museum of Art, N. Y.; in 1949, curator there, reorganizing the Crosby Brown Collection of musical instruments; received a Guggenheim Fellowship in 1946; since 1949, visiting lecturer at Yale Univ.; contributed numerous articles on musical instruments to the 'Bulletin' of the Metropolitan Museum. Publ. *Musical Autographs, from Monteverdi to Hindemith* (2 vols.; Princeton, N. J., 1955).

Wintzer, Richard, German composer; b. Nauendorf, near Halle, March 9, 1866; d. Berlin, Aug. 14, 1952. He studied painting, and also music (with Bargiel); lived mostly in Berlin, and was active as painter, composer, and music critic. He wrote 2 operas, *Die Willis* (1895) and *Marienkind* (1905); *Auf hohen Bergen,* for baritone solo, chorus, and orch.; some fine songs *(Ernste Gesänge, Kinderlieder, Sturmlieder);* piano pieces. He also publ. *Menschen von anderem Schlage* (1912) and an autobiography. —Cf. H. Killer, *Richard Wintzer, ein Leben zwischen den Künsten,* in 'Musik' (Berlin; March, 1941).

Wiora (vē-oh'-rah), **Walter,** musicologist; b. Katowice, Dec. 30, 1906. He studied musicology in Berlin with Abert, Blume, Gurlitt, Hornbostel, H. J. Moser, Schering, Schünemann, and J. Wolf. In 1936 he was appointed curator of the German Folk Music Archives in Freiburg-im-Breisgau; in 1942 lectured at the Univ. of Poznan; was in the German army; after 1945, returned to Freiburg and resumed his former post; 1958, succeeded Blume as prof. at Kiel Univ. He publ. a number of valuable treatises on German folk music: *Die angeblichen Volksmelodien bei Zuccalmaglio und Brahms* (dissertation, 1941); *Zur Frühgeschichte der Musik in den Alpenländern* (Basel, 1949); *Das echte Volkslied* (Heidelberg, 1950); *Europäischer Volksgesang: gemeinsame Formen in charakteristischen Abwandlungen* (Cologne, 1952); *Die rheinisch-bergischen Melodien bei Zuccalmaglio und Brahms* (Bad Godesberg, 1953); and *Europäische Volksmusik und abendländische Tonkunst,* vol. 1 in the series 'Die Musik im alten und neuen Europa' (Kassel, 1957; a work of fundamental significance). He also publ. a biography of Bruckner (Freiburg, 1952).

Wirén, Dag Ivar, prominent Swedish composer; b. Noraberg, Örebro, Oct. 15, 1905. He studied at the Stockholm Cons. with Oskar Lindberg and Ernst Ellberg; then in Paris with Leonid Sabaneyev. He returned to Sweden in 1934, and was music critic for the 'Svenska Morgonbladet' (1938-46); also participated in various activities of the Society of Swedish Composers. His music is cast in a neo-Classical vein, and it also embodies elements of purely Scandinavian inspiration. His first successful work was *Serenade* for strings (1937; also as a ballet, 1952); other works include the ballet *Oscarsbalen* (1949); the radio operas *Blått, gult, rött* (1940; inspired by Churchill's famous speech containing the phrase 'Blood, sweat, tears'), *Den glada patiencen* (1941); incidental music to Shakespeare's *Merchant of Venice* (1943); 4 symphonies (1932; 1939; 1944; 1952); *Little Suite* for orch. (1941); cello concerto (1936); violin concerto (1946); piano concerto (1950); 3 string quartets; a piano trio; a number of piano pieces. —Cf. M. Pergament, *Dag Wirén,* in 'Svenska tonsättare' (Stockholm, 1943; pp. 154-59).

Wirth (virt), **Emanuel,** violinist; b. Luditz, Bohemia, Oct. 18, 1842; d. Berlin, Jan. 5, 1923. He was a pupil of Kittl at the Prague Cons.; then taught at the Cons. of Rotterdam, and was concertmaster of the local orch.; succeeded Rappoldi as viola player in the Joachim String Quartet, in Berlin; subsequently formed his own trio, with R. Hausmann (cello) and H. Barth (piano), presenting numerous concerts in Germany.

Wirth, Friedrich Moritz, German writer on music; b. Euba, near Chemnitz, Sept. 14, 1849; d. Leipzig, April 26, 1917. He studied classical philology and philosophy at the Univ. of Leipzig, where he lived. His writings include *Drohender Untergang Bayreuths* (1887); *Wagner-Museum und Zukunft des Wagnertums* (1894); *Der Ring des Nibelungen als Wotandrama* (1912); *Parsifal in neuem Lichte* (1914); etc.

Wirth, Helmut, German musicologist and composer; b. Kiel, Oct. 10, 1912. He studied composition with R. Oppel, and musicology with Fritz Stein and Blume; *Dr. phil.,* 1937, at Kiel Univ., with the dissertation, *Joseph Haydn als Dramatiker* (Wolfenbüttel, 1940); from 1936, was active on the Hamburg Radio. He composed a *Goldoni Suite,* for chamber orch. (1939), an oboe sonata (1940), a harpsichord sonata (1946), many songs.

Wirth, Hermann Felix, Dutch music editor; b. Utrecht, May 6, 1885. He studied at the Univ. of Utrecht, and with Riemann in Leipzig (1906-07); *Dr. phil.,* Basel, 1910; subsequently lectured at the Univ. of Berlin; from 1918 taught music history at the Cons. of Brussels; for the 'Vereeniging voor nederlandsche Muziekgeschiedenis' he edited instrumental compositions by Dutch masters of the early 17th century (Amsterdam, 1913); also ed. a collection of early Dutch military marches (Berlin, 1914).

Wischnegradski, Ivan. See **Vyshnegradsky.**

Wise, Michael, English singer and composer; b. Wiltshire, c. 1648; d. Salisbury, Aug. 24, 1687. After an apprenticeship under Cooke at the Chapel Royal in London, he was appointed, at the age of 20, organist of Salisbury Cathedral; 1676, became Gentleman of the Chapel Royal; in 1687 he was appointed master of the choristers of St. Paul's Cathedral. He was killed by a watchman during a street dispute. He wrote anthems, church services, and catches; 6 of his anthems are included in Boyce's *Cathedral Music;* other pieces are found in various collections of the 17th century.

Wiske, C. Mortimer, American choral conductor; b. Bennington, Vt., Jan. 12, 1853; d. Lewiston, Maine, July 9, 1934. He studied piano and organ; was engaged by Theodore Thomas to drill the massed chorus (3000 voices) for the N. Y. May Festival of 1882, and was also chorusmaster during a series of Wagner festivals given by Thomas in the U. S. in 1884; subsequently conducted the N. Y. Chorus Society and various choruses in Paterson, N. J., and Newark.

Wissmer, Pierre, Swiss composer; b. Geneva, Oct. 30, 1915. He studied at the Paris Cons. with Roger-Ducasse, and at the Schola Cantorum with Daniel-Lesur; was on the staff of the Geneva Radio; subsequently divided his time between Geneva and Paris. He writes in the lucid neo-Classical style, and is particularly adept in writing for small instrumental groups. —Works: radio opera, *Marion ou la Belle au tricorne* (Geneva, Radio Suisse Romaine, April 16, 1947); comic opera, *Capitaine Bruno* (Geneva, Nov. 9, 1952); opéra-bouffe, *Léonidas ou la cruauté mentale* (Paris, Sept. 12, 1958); ballet, *Le beau dimanche* (1939; Geneva, March 20, 1944); *Naïades,* for narrator, soli, chorus, and orch. (Geneva, Jan. 21, 1942); 2 piano concertos (1937 and 1948); 2 symphonies (1938 and 1948);

Divertissement sur un choral, for 11 instruments (Geneva, Dec. 8, 1939); *Mouvement* for string orch. (Geneva, Feb. 1, 1940); violin concerto (Geneva, April 26, 1944); symph. suite, *Antoine et Cléopâtre* (Geneva, Oct. 2, 1946); overture, *La Mandrellina* (Geneva, April 16, 1952); 2 string quartets (1937 and 1949); *Sérénade* for oboe, clarinet, and bassoon (1938); sonatina for clarinet and piano (1941); sonatina for violin and piano (1946); piano sonata (1949); songs; choruses.

Wit, Paul de, Dutch cellist; b. Maestricht, Jan. 4, 1852; d. Leipzig, Dec. 10, 1925. In 1880 he founded (with O. Laffert) the 'Zeitschrift für Instrumentenbau'; opened a museum of musical instruments at Leipzig in 1886, but sold his collections to the Berlin Hochschule für Musik in 1888 and 1891; he then made a 3rd collection, which he sold in 1906 to Heyer of Cologne. Wit was a fine player on the viola da gamba, as well as a cellist. He publ.: *Geigenzettel alter Meister vom 16. bis zur Mitte des 19. Jahrhunderts* (1902; 2nd ed., 1910); *Weltadressbuch der gesammten Musikinstrumenten-Industrie* (1903; 8th ed., 1912); *Katalog des musikhistorischen Museums von P. de Wit* (1903).

Witassek, Johann Nepomuk August, Bohemian pianist and composer; b. Hořín, March 23, 1770; d. Prague, Dec. 7, 1839. The son of a schoolmaster, he received a good education; took music lessons with F. X. Dušek and J. A. Koželuch in Prague; succeeded Koželuch in 1814 as musical director at the Prague Cathedral; was appointed director of the School for Organists in Prague in 1830. He wrote an opera, *David,* brought out in Prague; 4 piano concertos; concertos for violin, for clarinet, and for bassoon; 6 string quartets; 4 violin sonatas; much church music.

Witek (vē'-tĕk), **Anton,** violinist; b. Saaz, Bohemia, Jan. 7, 1872; d. Winchester, Mass., Aug. 19, 1933. He studied violin with his father and with A. Bennewitz at the Prague Cons. From 1894 to 1910 he was concertmaster of the Berlin Philharmonic; in 1895, formed a duo with the Danish pianist Vita Gerhardt (1868-1925), whom he later married (1910). In 1910 he was engaged as concertmaster of the Boston Symph. Orch. (until 1918); from 1920 to 1925, was in Germany; then returned to America. After the death of his first wife (1925), he married the American violinist Alma Rosengrein. He publ. *Fingered Octaves* (1919).

Witherspoon, Herbert, American bass singer; b. Buffalo, N. Y., July 21, 1873; d. New York, May 10, 1935. He studied with Horatio Parker at Yale Univ., and also took lessons with MacDowell in N. Y. He then studied singing with Bouhy in Paris, Henry Wood in London, and G. B. Lamperti in Berlin. Returning to America, he made his concert début at New Haven (Oct. 21, 1895); made 5 tours of England as oratorio singer; his American opera début occurred at the Metropolitan Opera House as Titurel in *Parsifal* (Nov. 26, 1908); then devoted himself to teaching; in 1925 became president of the Chicago Musical College; 1931, president of the Cincinnati Cons. of Music; in 1933 he returned to N. Y., and in May, 1935, was chosen to succeed Gatti-Casazza as general manager of the Metropolitan Opera Co.; but he died suddenly of a heart attack. He publ. *Singing: A Treatise for Teachers and Students* (N. Y., 1925); *36 Lessons in Singing for Teacher and Student* (Chicago, 1930).

Witkowski (vit-kohf'-skē), **Georges-Martin,** French composer; b. Mostaganem, Algeria, Jan. 6, 1867 (of a French father and a Polish mother); d. Lyons, Aug. 12, 1943. He was educated at the military school of St.-Cyr; began music study with Vincent d'Indy at the Schola Cantorum; later left the army and settled in Lyons, where he founded the 'Société des Grands Concerts' in 1905 for the production of oratorios. In 1924 he was appointed director of the Lyons Cons. — Works: the opera *La Princesse lointaine* after Rostand (Paris, March 26, 1934); 2 symphonies (1900; 1910); *Poème de la maison,* for solo voices, chorus, and orch. (Lyons, Jan. 25, 1919); *Mon lac,* for piano and orch. (Lyons, Nov. 20, 1921); for voice and orch.: *4 Poèmes du Cœur Innombrable* (1925), *3 Poèmes de Ronsard* (1935), *Paysage rêvé* (1937); *Introduction et Danse* for violin and orch. (Paris, Oct. 10, 1937); a piano quintet (1897); a string quartet (1902); a violin sonata (1907). —Cf. M. Boucher, *G.-M. Witkowski,* in the 'Revue Musicale' (March, 1926).

Witt, Franz Xaver, German composer of church music; b. Walderbach, Feb. 9, 1834; d. Schatzhofen, Dec. 2, 1888. He studied with Proske and Schrems in Regensburg; took holy orders in 1856. In 1866 he established and edited the 'Fliegende Blätter für katholische Kirchenmusik' and 'Musica sacra'; in 1867 he founded the 'Allgemeiner deutscher Cäcilienverein' for the improvement of Catholic church music, which, while opposing the introduction of orchestral instruments into the church, helped to arouse interest in the great early masterpieces of church music. In his own early Masses, Witt employed the orch. Besides numerous Masses, he publ. 2 Requiems, many litanies, offertories, motets, and hymns (55 opus numbers); also some secular men's choruses; author of *Der Zustand der katholischen Kirchenmusik* (1865); *Über das Dirigieren der katholischen Kirchenmusik;* and *Das bayerische Kultusministerium* (1886). —Cf. A. Walter, *Dr. Franz Witt. Ein Lebensbild* (Regensburg, 1889; 2nd ed., 1906; includes a full list of works). A centennial vol. of his articles, *Ausgewählte Aufsätze zur Kirchenmusik . . .*, was brought out in Cologne (1934).

Witt, Friedrich, German violinist and composer; b. Hallenbergstetten, Württemberg, Nov. 8, 1770; d. Würzburg, 1837. He studied with Rosetti at Wallerstein; at 19, became 1st violin in the orch. of Prince von Oettingen; from 1802, was Kapellmeister at Würzburg, at first to the Prince-Bishop, then to the Grand Duke, finally to the city. It was Witt who composed the symphony in C, the so-called 'Jena Symphony,' attributed (falsely) to Beethoven (see H. C. Robbins Landon's article in the 'Music Review' for May 1957). Other works by Witt include the historical opera, *Palma* (Frankfurt, 1804); the comic opera *Das Fischerweib* (Würzburg, 1806); the oratorios *Der leidende Heiland* (Würzburg, 1802) and *Die Auferstehung Jesu;* Masses and cantatas; he publ. 9 symphonies, music for wind band, a septet for clarinet, horn, bassoon, and strings, a quintet for piano and winds, a flute concerto, etc.

Witt, Theodor de, German music editor and composer; b. Wesel, May 9, 1823; d. Rome, Dec. 1, 1855. He studied organ with his father. When Liszt visited Witt's native town, he became interested in the talented boy, and gave a concert for his benefit to enable him to study in Berlin (under Dehn). At 22, Witt developed tuberculosis, and was sent to Italy; there he made a detailed study of church music; edited the first 4 vols. of Breitkopf & Härtel's complete edition of Palestrina's works. His own works include a piano sonata and some vocal pieces.

Witte, Georg Hendrik, Dutch organist and composer; b. Utrecht, Nov. 16, 1843; d. Essen, Feb. 1, 1929. He studied at The Hague; then at the Leipzig Cons. with Moscheles and Plaidy (piano), Hauptmann and Reinecke (composition). In 1871 he was appointed conductor of the Musikverein at Essen, which post he held for 40 years, retiring in 1911. He wrote *Der Essener Musikverein 1838 bis 1913* (1913). His works include a cello concerto; a choral work, *An die Sonne;* a piano quartet; numerous piano pieces; also songs.

Wittgenstein, Count. See **Sayn-Wittgenstein-Berleburg.**

Wittgenstein, Paul, Austrian pianist; b. Vienna, Nov. 5, 1887. He was of a musical family; studied piano with Josef Labor and Leschetizky; made his 1st public appearance as pianist in 1913, in Vienna. He lost his right arm in World War I, at the Russian front; was prisoner of war in Omsk, Siberia; repatriated in 1916. He then developed an extraordinary technique for left hand alone, and performed a concerto specially composed for him by his teacher, Josef Labor. He subsequently commissioned left-hand piano concertos from Richard Strauss, Ravel, Prokofiev, and several other composers, of which he gave the world premières (except the Prokofiev concerto, which he found unsuitable). He appeared in the major musical centers in Europe; toured America in 1934; in 1939 settled in New York.

Witting, Karl, German violinist and composer; b. Jülich, Sept. 8, 1823; d. Dresden, June 28, 1907. He studied in Paris under A. Reichel; returned to Germany in 1855, living in Berlin, Hamburg, and Glogau, and finally settling in Dresden in 1861 as a teacher. He publ. a cello sonata, instructive pieces for violin and piano, a *Violinschule;* edited a collection, 'Die Kunst des Violinspiels' (8 books) and a collection of duets for 2 violins (4 books); wrote *Musikalisches Wörterbuch* (1887); *Geschichte des Violinspiels* (1900), and analyses for Breitkopf and Härtel's 'Konzertführer.'

Wodell, Frederick William, choral conductor and composer; b. London, Dec. 17, 1859; d. St. Petersburg, Fla., Feb. 13, 1938. He studied piano, voice, and composition with various teachers in London; settling in the U. S., he was for many years conductor of the People's Choral Union in Boston; also taught singing there. He composed a cantata, *The American Flag,* for tenor, baritone, men's chorus, and orch.; many anthems, songs, etc.; publ. *Choir and Chorus Conducting* (Philadelphia, 1901; 12th ed., 1931), and *How to Sing by Note* (1915).

Woehl (völ), **Waldemar,** German music editor and educator; b. Lipine, near Bethuen, Prussia, Aug. 31, 1902. He was brought up in Myslowitz; studied with his father, and later in Berlin at the Akademie für Kirchen- und Schulmusik, with Max Seiffert, Thiel, and Jöde; taught at the Folkwangschule in Essen; during World War II, led the Musikschule für Jugend und Volk in Villach, Austria; eventually settled in Soyen, Bavaria, as teacher and flute maker; started a movement for the restoration of vertical flutes (recorders). He publ. *Melodielehre* (Leipzig, 1929); *Klavierbuch für den Anfang* (Berlin, 1932); *Das Bach-Buch für Klavierspieler* (Berlin, 1932); 'Musik für Blockflöten' (4 vols.; Hanover, 1930-34); also a method, *Blockflötenschule* (1930), a *Kurze Spielanweisung für das Scheitholz* (1951); composed numerous pieces for the recorder, also for ensembles of recorders; edited much 18th-century chamber music.

Wohlfahrt, Franz, German piano pedagogue; son of Heinrich Wohlfahrt; b. Frauenpriesnitz, March 7, 1833; d. Gohlis, Feb. 14, 1884. He taught at Leipzig; publ. many piano studies, some of which have become standard exercises.

Wohlfahrt, Heinrich, German piano pedagogue; b. Kössnitz, near Apolda, Dec. 16, 1797; d. Connewitz, near Leipzig, May 9, 1883. He studied with Häser at Weimar; was cantor and tutor in Thuringian towns; taught at Jena and (from 1867) Leipzig. He publ. *Kinder-Klavierschule* (24 editions), *Der erste Klavierunterricht, Der Klavierfreund* (36 children's studies), *Klavierübungen, Grössere und rein praktische Elementar-Klavierschule, Schule der Fingermechanik, Anthologische Klavierschule, Theoretisch-praktische Modulationsschule* (English transl., Boston, 1878), *Vorschule der Harmonielehre, Wegweiser zum Componiren für Musik-Dilettanten* (English transl., Boston, 1859); also 3 children's sonatas; *Kleine Leute;* etc.

Wohlgemuth (vol'-geh-moot), **Gustav,** German composer and choral conductor; b. Leipzig, Dec. 2, 1863; d. there, March 2, 1937. He studied at the Leipzig Cons.; in 1891 founded the 'Leipziger Männerchor,' which he conducted for many years; later also conducted other choral societies in Leipzig; was editor (1907-26) of the 'Deutsche Sängerbundeszeitung'; publ. some 100 male choruses (some with orch.). —Cf. *Gustav Wohlgemuth, sein Leben und Wirken* (Leipzig, 1934), a collection of articles.

Woikowski-Biedau (voy-kohf'-skē bē'-dow), **Viktor Hugo von,** German composer; b. Nieder-Arnsdorf, near Schweidnitz, Sept. 2, 1866; d. Berlin, Jan. 1, 1935. He studied music with Wilhelm Berger in Berlin; was employed in the government statistics bureau; composed the operas *Helga* (Wiesbaden, 1904), *Der lange Kerl* (Berlin, 1906), and *Das Nothemd* (Dessau, 1913); 3 melodramas, *Jung Olaf, Der Todspieler,* and *Die Mette von Marienburg;* 4 ballads for baritone and orch., *Die Jüdin von Worms, Der Triumph des Lebens, Rahab, die Jerichonitin,* and *Jan van Jühren; Aus einem Menschenleben* for violin and piano; several song cycles (*Frühlingslieder, Lebensträume, Schiffslieder, Königslieder, Pagen-Balladen, Osterzauber, Des Sultans Gesetz,* etc.).

Woldemar, Michel, French violinist and composer; b. Orléans, Sept. 15, 1750; d. Clermont-Ferrand, Dec. 19, 1815. He studied with Lolli; for some years was conductor for a traveling theatrical troupe. By adding a 5th string *(c)* to the violin, he obtained an instrument that he called 'violon-alto,' because it included the viola range, and for which he wrote a concerto. He also publ. 3 violin concertos, a string quartet, duos for 2 violins and for violin and viola; *Sonates fantomagiques* for violin *(L'Ombre de Lolli, de Mestrino, de Pugnani, de Tartini);* 12 grand solos; *6 Rêves ou Caprices; Caprices ou études; Le nouveau Labyrinth pour violon,* followed by studies in double-stops; *Le nouvel Art de l'archet; Étude élémentaire de l'archet moderne;* variations on *Les Folies d'Espagne,* etc.; methods for violin, viola, and clarinet; also a system of musical stenography *(Tableau mélotachigraphique)* and a method of musical correspondence *(Notographie).*

Wöldike, Mogens, Danish organist and conductor; b. Copenhagen, July 5, 1897. He studied with Carl Nielsen; was organist and choirmaster in several Copenhagen churches; in 1937, became conductor of the radio madrigal chorus; toured with it in Scandinavia, England, and Italy. Also director for the series of records 'Masterpieces of Music before 1750' in collaboration with W. W. Norton & Co. and the Haydn Society of Vienna and Copenhagen. He publ. *Orgelkoraler til Kirkeaaret* (1943).

Wolf, Ernst Wilhelm, German composer; b. Grossenbehringen, near Gotha, 1735 (baptized Feb. 25); d. Weimar, 1792 (buried Dec. 1). In 1772 he became Kapellmeister to the music-loving Duchess of Saxe-Weimar, Anna Amalia. He wrote about 20 operas, of which the most successful were *Das Rosenfest* (Weimar, 1770) and *Die Dorfdeputierten* (Berlin, June 15, 1772). Other works include Passion oratorios and Easter cantatas; publ. 6 piano concertos; 4 quintets for piano, flute, violin, viola, and cello; 6 string quartets; 7 books of piano sonatas, each containing 6 numbers; in MS are 15 symphonies, 17 partitas, 12 piano concertos, and much chamber music. He also wrote *Kleine musikalische Reise* (1782) and *Musikalischer Unterricht* (1788; 2nd ed., 1804). —Cf. J. Brockt, *Ernst Wilhelm Wolf* (dissertation; Striegau, 1927).

Wolf, Ferdinand, Austrian writer on literature and music; b. Vienna, Dec. 8, 1796; d. there, Feb. 18, 1866, as librarian of the Imperial Library. His book *Über die Lais, Sequenzen und Leiche. Ein Beitrag zur Geschichte der rhythmischen Formen und Singweisen der Volkslieder und der volksmässigen Kirchen- und Kunstlieder im Mittelalter* (Heidelberg, 1841) is a valuable compendium.

Wolf (volf), **Hugo,** Austrian composer, one of the greatest masters of the modern song; b. Windischgraz, March 13, 1860; d. Vienna, Feb. 22, 1903. He studied piano and violin with his father, an amateur musician; then took lessons from Sebastian Weixler, a schoolmaster. In 1870 he was sent to Graz, where he entered a primary school, but left after a single semester, and was enrolled in the Seminary at the Benedictine monastery of St. Paul in Carinthia; in 1873 he went to a Gymnasium in Marburg; in 1875 he moved to Vienna, where he became a pupil at the Cons., studying piano with Wilhelm Schenner and harmony with Robert Fuchs. When Wagner visited Vienna in 1875, Wolf went to see him, bringing along some of his compositions; the fact that Wagner received him at all, and even said a few words of encouragement, gave Wolf great impetus towards further composition. But he was incapable of submitting himself to academic discipline, and soon difficulties arose between him and the Cons. authorities. He openly expressed his dissatisfaction with the teaching of Franz Krenn (who was also the teacher of Mahler), and was so impertinent to the director, Josef Hellmesberger, that he was expelled. In March, 1877, he returned to his native town, but after a few months at home, decided to go to Vienna again; there he managed to support himself by giving music lessons to children in the homes of friends. By that time he was composing diligently, writing songs to texts by his favorite poets—Goethe, Lenau, Heine. An unhappy encounter with Brahms, who advised him to study counterpoint before attempting to compose, embittered him, and he became determined to follow his own musical inclinations without seeking further advice. After a brief (and unsuccessful) employment as chorusmaster in Salzburg (1881), he secured in 1883 the position of music critic of the weekly 'Wiener Salonblatt.' He took this opportunity to indulge his professional frustration by attacking those not sympathetic with new trends in music; he poured invective of extraordinary virulence on Brahms, thus antagonizing the influential Hanslick and other admirers of Brahms. But he also formed a coterie of staunch friends, who had faith in his ability. Yet he was singularly unsuccessful in his repeated attempts to secure performances for his works. He submitted a string quartet to the celebrated Rosé Quartet, but it was rejected. Finally, Hans Richter accepted for the Vienna Philharmonic his symph. poem *Penthesilea,* but the public performance was a fiasco, and Wolf even accused Richter of deliberately sabotaging the work; later he reorchestrated the score, eliminating certain crudities of the early version. In 1887 he resigned as music critic of the 'Wiener Salonblatt' and devoted himself entirely to composition. He became convinced that he was creating the greatest masterpieces of song since Schubert and Schumann, and stated his conviction in plain terms in his letters. In historical perspective, his self-appraisal has proved remarkably accurate, but psychologists may well wonder whether Wolf was not consciously trying to give himself the needed encouragement by what must have seemed to him a wild exaggeration. However, a favorable turn in his fortunes came in 1889, when his 27 songs to words by Mörike and 10 songs to words by Eichendorff appeared in print. There followed 25 Goethe songs in 1890, and the album of exquisite songs after Heyse and Geibel, *Spanisches Liederbuch,* in 1891, as well as 6 songs to poems of Keller, *Alte Weisen.* The singer Ferdinand Jäger became a champion of Wolf's music, and gave repeated performances of his songs at the meetings of the Vienna Wagner-Verein. Soon Wolf's name became known in Germany; he presented concerts of his own works in Berlin, Darmstadt, Mannheim, and other musical centers. He completed the 1st part of his great cycle of 22 songs, *Italienisches Liederbuch,* in 1891, and composed the 2nd part (24 songs) in 5 weeks, in the spring of 1896. In 1897 he wrote the *3 Gedichte von Michelangelo*. While Wolf could compose songs with a facility and degree of excellence that were truly astounding, he labored painfully on his orchestral works. His early symph. was never completed, nor was a violin concerto; the work on *Penthesilea* took him a disproportionately long time. In 1895 he undertook the composition of his opera, *Der Corregidor,* to the famous tale by Alarcón, *El Sombrero de tres picos,* and, working feverishly, completed the vocal score with piano accompaniment in a few months. The orchestration took him a much longer time. *Der Corregidor* had its première in Mannheim on June 7, 1896, but it proved a disappointment. The opera was ineffective dramatically, and the orchestration was weak. Wolf subsequently revised the score, and in its new version *Der Corregidor* was brought out in Strasbourg on April 29, 1898. He never completed his 2nd opera, *Manuel Venegas* (also after Alarcón); fragments were presented in concert form on March 1, 1903. In the meantime, his fame grew. A Hugo Wolf-Verein was organized at Berlin in 1896, and did excellent work in furthering performances of Wolf's songs in Germany. Even more effective was the Hugo Wolf-Verein in Vienna, founded by Michael Haberlandt on April 22, 1897 (disbanded in 1906). Amidst these encouraging signs of recognition, tragedy struck. A supposed rebuke administered to Wolf by Mahler, at that time the newly appointed director of the Vienna Opera, who had been considering a performance of *Der Corregidor,* precipitated in him a mental breakdown. He declared to friends that Mahler had been relieved of his post, and that he, Wolf, was appointed director of the Vienna Opera in Mahler's stead. On Sept. 20, 1897, he was placed in a private mental institution; after a favorable remission, he was discharged (Jan. 24, 1898), and traveled in Italy and Austria. After his return to Vienna, symptoms of mental derangement manifested themselves in even greater degree. He attempted suicide by throwing himself into a lake, and then was committed to a state asylum at his own request. (A parallel with Schumann's case forcibly suggests itself.) He remained in confinement, gradually lapsing into complete irrationality. He died at the age of 42, and was buried near the graves of Schubert and Beethoven; a monument was unveiled on Oct. 20, 1904. — Wolf's significance in music history rests on his songs, about 300 in number, many of them publ. posthumously, and some still unpublished. The sobriquet 'the Wagner of the Lied' may well be justified in regard to involved contrapuntal texture and chromatic harmony, for Wolf accepted the Wagnerian idiom through natural affinity as well as by clear choice. The elaboration of the accompaniment, and the incorporation of the vocal line into the contrapuntal scheme of the whole, are Wagnerian traits. But with these external similarities, Wolf's dependence on Wagner's models ceases. In his intimate penetration of the poetic spirit of the text, Wolf appears a legitimate successor of Schubert and Schumann. Wolf's songs are symphonic poems in miniature, artistically designed and admirably arranged for voice and piano, the combination in which he was a master.

WORKS

FOR THE DRAMATIC STAGE: Incidental music to Ibsen's *Das Fest auf Solhaug* (Vienna, Nov. 21, 1891); *Der Corregidor,* 4-act comedy opera, after Alarcón's *El Sombrero de tres picos* (Mannheim, June 7, 1896; revised version, Strasbourg, April 29, 1898); *Manuel Venegas,* 3-act tragic opera, text after Alarcón's *El Niño de la Bola* (fragments performed in concert form, Mannheim, March 1, 1903). CHORAL WORKS: *6 geistliche a cappella Chöre* (1881; ed. by E. Thomas; arranged for men's voices by Max Reger); *Christnacht* for solo voices, chorus, and orch. (1886-89); *Elfenlied* for soprano solo, chorus, and orch. (1889-91); *Dem Vaterland* for male chorus and orch. (1890; many revisions). INSTRUMENTAL WORKS: string quartet in D minor (1878-84); *Penthesilea,* symph. poem after Kleist (1883-85); *Italienische Serenade* (1892; a transcription of the serenade in G major for string quartet, 1887); fragments from an early symph. in D minor and from a violin concerto. SONGS: *12 Lieder aus der Jugendzeit* (1888); *Lieder nach verschiedenen Dichtern,* 31 songs (1877-97); *Gedichte von Mörike,* 53 songs (1888); *Gedichte von Eichendorff,* 20 songs (1886-88); *Gedichte von Goethe,* 51 songs (1888-89); *Spanisches Liederbuch,* 44 songs after Geibel and Heyse (1889-90); *Italienisches Liederbuch,* 46 songs after Heyse, in 2 parts: 22 songs (1890-91), 24 songs (1896). 20 of the songs were orchestrated by Wolf; others by Max Reger. 40 previously unpublished songs, mostly of the earliest period, were publ. in Leipzig in 1936, in 4 vols. as *Nachgelassene Werke,* edited by R. Haas and H. Schultz; several piano pieces (mostly juvenilia) are in MS; 2 early piano sonatas remain incomplete. Wolf's collected writings were brought out by R. Batka and H. Werner as *Hugo Wolfs musikalische Kritiken* (Leipzig, 1911). A complete ed. of the songs was publ. by Peters (Leipzig, 1935).

BIBLIOGRAPHY—A. BIOGRAPHY: P. Müller, *Erinnerungen an Hugo Wolf*, in 'Die Musik' (March-April, 1903); M. Haberlandt, *Hugo Wolf. Erinnerungen und Gedanken* (Leipzig, 1903; 2nd ed., Darmstadt, 1911); E. Decsey, *Hugo Wolf* (4 vols., Berlin, 1903-06; new ed. in 1 vol., 1919; the standard work for facts and sources); P. Müller, *Hugo Wolf* (Berlin, 1904); E. Schmitz, *Hugo Wolf* (Leipzig, 1906); E. Newman, *Hugo Wolf* (London, 1907); M. Morold, *Hugo Wolf* (Leipzig, 1912; 2nd ed., 1920); H. Werner, *Hugo Wolf in Maierling* (Leipzig, 1913) and *Der Hugo Wolf-Verein in Wien* (Regensburg, 1922); G. Schur, *Erinnerungen an Hugo Wolf* (Regensburg, 1922); H. Werner, *Hugo Wolf in Perchtoldsdorf* (Regensburg, 1925) and *Hugo Wolf und der wiener akademische Wagner-Verein* (Regensburg, 1926); K. Grunsky, *Hugo Wolf* (Leipzig, 1928); B. B. Viterbi, *Hugo Wolf* (in Italian; Rome, 1931); H. Schouten, *Hugo Wolf: Mensch en Componist* (in Dutch; Amsterdam, 1935); A. von Ehrmann, *Hugo Wolf. Sein Leben in Bildern* (Leipzig, 1937); R. Litterscheid, *Hugo Wolf* (Potsdam, 1939); M. von Graedener-Hattingberg, *Hugo Wolf: vom Wesen und Werk des grössten Liedschöpfers* (Vienna and Leipzig, 1941; revised, 1953); A. von Ehrmann, *Johannes Brahms and Hugo Wolf: a Biographical Parallel*, in the 'Mus. Quarterly' (Oct., 1943); A. Orel, *Hugo Wolf* (Vienna, 1947); W. Reich, *Hugo Wolf-Rhapsodie* (Zürich, 1947); F. Walker, *Hugo Wolf: A Biography* (London, 1951); N. Loeser, *Wolf* (Haarlem, 1955). —B. CRITICISM, APPRECIATION: *Gesammelte Aufsäte über Hugo Wolf* (2 vols.; Vienna, 1898, 1899); E. von Hellmer, *Der Corregidor. Kritische und biographische Beiträge zu seiner Würdigung* (Vienna, 1900); K. Heckel, *Hugo Wolf in seinem Verhältnis zu Richard Wagner* (Munich, 1905); K. Grunsky, *Hugo Wolf-Fest in Stuttgart* (Stuttgart, 1906); R. Rolland, *Musiciens d'aujourd'hui* (1908; in English, N. Y., 1914); O. Bie, *Das deutsche Lied* (Berlin, 1926; pp. 199-246); V. O. Ludwig, *Mörike in der Lyrik von Hugo Wolf* (Bern and Leipzig, 1935); G. Bieri, *Die Lieder von Hugo Wolf* (Bern, 1935); A. Maecklenburg, *Hugo Wolf and Anton Bruckner*, in the 'Mus. Quarterly' (July, 1938); R. Hernried, *Hugo Wolf's 'Corregidor' at Mannheim*, in the 'Mus. Quarterly' (Jan., 1940); F. Walker, *The History of Wolf's Italian Serenade*, in the 'Mus. Review' (Aug., 1947). —C. CORRESPONDENCE: E. von Hellmer, *Hugo Wolfs Briefe an Emil Kauffmann* (Berlin, 1903); M. Haberlandt, *Hugo Wolfs Briefe an Hugo Faisst* (Stuttgart, 1904); P. Müller, *Ungedruckte Briefe von Hugo Wolf an Paul Müller*, in 'Jahrbuch Peters' (1904); H. Werner, *H. Wolfs Briefe an Oskar Grohe* (Berlin, 1905); E. von Hellmer, *Hugo Wolf. Eine Persönlichkeit in Briefen* (Leipzig, 1912; family letters); *Wolfs Briefe an Rosa Mayreder* (Vienna, 1921); H. Nonveiller, *Wolfs Briefe an Heinrich Potpeschnigg* (Stuttgart, 1923); H. Werner, *Wolfs Briefe an Henriette Lang* (Regensburg, 1923); H. Werner, *Some Unpublished Letters of Hugo Wolf*, in 'Monthly Mus. Record' (1927). —See also the *Hugo Wolf-Programme für alle Stimmlagen*, publ. by Peters (Leipzig, 1907); P. Müller, *H. Wolf. Verzeichnis seiner Werke* (Leipzig, 1908); K. Varges, *Der Musikkritiker, Hugo Wolf* (Magdeburg, 1934). An English transl. of the texts of all of Wolf's solo songs was publ. by Henry S. Drinker (N. Y., 1949).

Wolf, Johannes, eminent German musicologist; b. Berlin, April 17, 1869; d. Munich, May 25, 1947. He studied philology and musicology (with Philipp Spitta) at the Univ. of Berlin; also took courses at the Hochschule für Musik; taught music and conducted a choral society until 1896; then devoted several years to research work; in 1893, *Dr. phil.* in Leipzig; in 1902 became lecturer in musicology at Berlin Univ.; 1908, prof.; 1922, prof. emeritus; 1907-1927 also prof. of history of music at the Institut für Kirchenmusik; appointed curator of the collection of early music at the Royal Library in 1915; then was director of the music division there (1928-34). He was for many years president of the Deutsche Musikgesellschaft; with Oskar Fleischer he was co-editor of the 'Sammelbände der Internationalen Musik-Gesellschaft' (1899-1904). In 1943 he went to live in Gmein; in 1946, in Munich. He made a particular study of medieval music, and especially the history of notation. —Publications: *Geschichte der Mensural-Notation von 1250-1460 nach den theoretischen und praktischen Quellen* (3 parts, 1904; very important); *Deutsche Lieder des 15. Jahrhunderts* ('Liliencron-Festschrift,' 1910); *Handbuch der Notationskunde* (Part I, 1913; Part II, 1919); *Die Tonschriften* ('Jedermanns Bücherei,' 1924); *Kleine Musikgeschichte* (1925), with mus. examples in *Alte Sing- und Spielmusik* (1926-31; 2nd ed. in 1 vol., 1931; the examples only, as *Music of Earlier Times,* N. Y., 1950); *Zur Geschichte der Musikabteilung der Staatsbibliothek* (1930); *Altflämische Lieder des 14. und 15. Jahrhunderts* (Basel Kongress-Bericht, 1924); *L'Arte del biscanto da Jacopo da Bologna* ('Kroyer-Festschrift,' 1933); *Geschichte der Musik in allgemeinverständlicher Form* (3 vols.; Leipzig, 1925-29; 2nd ed. of vol. II, 1934); etc. For the 'Denkmäler deutscher Tonkunst' he ed. selected vocal works of Joh. Rud. Ahle (vol. V) and Rhaw's *Newe deutsche Geistliche Gesenge* (vol. XXXIV); for the 'Denkmäler der Tonkunst in Österreich,' Isaac's secular works (vols. XIV, 1, and XVI, 1); for the 'Vereeniging voor Nederlandsche Muziekgeschiedenis,' the complete works of Obrecht (from 1908; 30 vols.) and a collection of Dutch songs of the 16th century; also ed. the *Musica Practica* of Ramos de Pareja (Beiheft 2 of the Internationale Musik-Gesellschaft, 1901); the 'Squarcialupi Codex' (publ. posthumously, 1955); the publications of the Paul Hirsch Library, including Luther's *Deutsche Messe* (Kassel, 1934); *Musikalische Schrifttafeln* (Bückeburg, 1927); editor-in-chief of the *Corpus scriptorum de musica medii aevi* for the Berlin Academy. —A 'Joh. Wolf-Festschrift' was publ. in 1929, ed. by Lott, Osthoff, and Wolffheim. —Cf. Otto Gombosi, *Johannes Wolf,* in the 'Mus. Quarterly' (April, 1948); Otto Kinkeldey, *Johannes Wolf,* in the 'Journal of the American Musicological Society' (Spring, 1948).

Wolf, Ludwig, German pianist and composer; b. Frankfurt, 1804; d. Vienna, Aug. 6, 1859. He studied composition with Seyfried; was skillful both as pianist and violinist; composed 3 string quartets; a piano quartet; 4 string trios; many other works in MS.

Wolf, William, German pianist; b. Breslau, April 22, 1838; d. Berlin, Jan. 8, 1913. He studied with Th. Kullak; in 1881 established himself in Berlin as a teacher; contributed to musical periodicals; wrote *Musik-Ästhetik in kurzer und gemeinfasslicher Darstellung* (2 vols., 1895, 1906); a collection of essays appeared as *Gesammelte musikästhetische Aufsätze* (1894).

Wolf-Ferrari, Ermanno, opera composer; b. Venice, Jan. 12, 1876; d. there, Jan. 21, 1948. His mother was Italian; his father was a well-known German painter. Wolf-Ferrari was sent to Rome to study art, but became interested in opera, and decided to devote himself to music; accordingly, he was sent to Munich where he studied with Rheinberger (1893-95). In 1899 he returned to Venice, where his oratorio, *La Sulamite* was successfully performed. This was followed by the production of his first opera *Cenerentola* (1900). From 1902 to 1907 he was director of the Liceo Benedetto Marcello in Venice; then taught at the Salzburg Mozarteum; lived mostly in Neu-Biberg, near Munich; obtained his first success with the production of the comic opera *Le Donne curiose* (Munich, 1903); the next opera, *I quattro rusteghi* (Munich, 1906), was also well received; there followed his little masterpiece, *Il Segreto di Susanna,* a 1-act opera buffa in the style of the Italian 'verismo' (Susanna's secret being not infidelity, as her husband suspected, but indulgence in surreptitious smoking). Turning towards grand opera, he wrote *I Gioielli della Madonna (The Jewels of the Madonna);* it was brought out at Berlin in 1911, and soon became a repertory piece everywhere; he continued to compose, but his later operas failed to match the appeal of his early creations. —Works: Operas: *Cenerentola* (Venice, Feb. 22, 1900; in Bremen as *Aschenbrödel,* Jan. 31, 1902); *Le Donne curiose* (Munich, Nov. 27, 1903; in German as *Die neugierigen Frauen;* in Italian, N. Y., Jan. 3, 1912); *I quattro rusteghi* (Munich, March 19, 1906; in German as *Die vier Grobiane); Il Segreto di Susanna* (Munich, Dec. 4, 1909; in German as *Susannens Geheimnis;* in Italian, N. Y., March 14, 1911); *I Gioielli della Madonna* (Berlin, Dec. 23, 1911; in German as *Der Schmuck der Madonna;* in Italian, Chicago, Jan. 16, 1912; in English, as *The Jewels of the Madonna,* N.Y., Oct. 14, 1913); *L'Amore medico,* after Molière (Dresden, Dec. 4, 1913; in German, as *Der Liebhaber als Arzt;* in Italian, N. Y., Metropolitan Opera, March 25, 1914); *Gli Amanti sposi* (Venice, Feb. 19, 1925; *Veste di cielo* (Munich, April 21, 1927; in German as *Das Himmelskleid); Sly,* after the prologue to Shakespeare's *The Taming of the Shrew* (Milan, La Scala, Dec. 29, 1927; in Italian as *La Leggenda del dormiente risvegliato); La Vedova scaltra,* after Goldoni (Rome, March 5, 1931); *Il Campiello,* after Goldoni (Milan, Feb. 12, 1936); *La Dama boba,* after Lope de Vega (Milan, Feb. 1, 1939); *Gli dei a Tebe* (Hanover, June 5, 1943; in German as *Der Kuckuck in Theben);* also a revision of Mozart's *Idomeneo* (Munich, June 15, 1931). Other works: *La Sulamite,* biblical cantata (1899); *Talitha kumi,* mystery for solo voices, chorus, and orch. (1900); *La Vita nuova,* after Dante, oratorio (Munich,

Feb. 21, 1903; N. Y., Dec. 4, 1907); *Serenade* for string orch.; a *Kammersymphonie* (1901); *Idillio-concertino* for oboe, string orch., and 2 horns (Venice Festival, 1932); *Suite-concertino* for bassoon, string orch., and 2 horns (Rome, March 26, 1933); *Suite veneziana,* for orch. (1936); *Arabeschi* for orch. (1937); *Divertimento* for orch. (1938); *Kleines Konzert* for English horn and orch. (posthumous; Salzburg, Jan. 18, 1955); 2 violin sonatas; 2 piano trios; a string quartet; a piano quintet; piano pieces; songs. —Cf. H. Teibler, *Ermanno Wolf-Ferrari,* in vol. I of 'Monographien moderner Musiker' (Leipzig, 1906); E. L. Stahl, *Ermanno Wolf-Ferrari* (Salzburg, 1936); R. de Rensis, *Ermanno Wolf-Ferrari, la sua vita d'artista* (Milan, 1937); A. C. Grisson, *Ermanno Wolf-Ferrari: Lebensbeschreibung* (Regensburg, 1941); J. Ringo, *Ermanno Wolf-Ferrari; an Appreciation of His Work,* in 'Rivista Musicale Italiana' (July-Sept., 1949).

Wolfe, Jacques, American composer and teacher; b. Botoshan, Rumania, April 29, 1896. He was brought to the U. S. as a child; was educated in N. Y.; studied music at the Institute of Musical Art with Goetschius, Robinson, and Friskin (graduated in 1915). During World War I he was a clarinetist in the 50th Infantry Band; then was sent to North Carolina, where he studied Negro spirituals. Many of his songs are in the manner of spirituals; some of them acquired great popularity *(De Glory Road, Gwine to Hebb'n, Halleluja Rhythm, Short'nin' Bread,* etc.); he also wrote *Betsy's Boy, The Hand-Organ Man, Sailormen, British Children's Prayer;* wrote the music for Roark Bradford's play *John Henry* (N. Y., 1939); numerous choral works; piano pieces. 1958, living in Florida.

Wolfes, Felix, pianist and conductor; b. Hanover, Germany, Sept. 2, 1892. He studied at the Leipzig Cons. with Max Reger (theory) and R. Teichmüller (piano); later in Strasbourg with Pfitzner (composition); conducted opera at Breslau, Essen, and Dortmund (until 1933); then went to France; in 1938 came to the U. S. and was appointed assistant conductor at the Metropolitan Opera House; subsequently joined the faculty of the New England Cons. in Boston, as vocal teacher. He publ. piano scores of operas by Richard Strauss and Pfitzner; made adaptations of other operas.

Wolff, Albert (Louis), French conductor; b. Paris, Jan. 19, 1884. He studied at the Paris Cons.; in 1908 became chorusmaster at the Opéra-Comique, and was appointed conductor there in 1911; from 1919 to 1921 he was conductor of the French repertory at the Metropolitan Opera House; conducted the world première of his opera, *L'Oiseau bleu,* there on Dec. 27, 1919. In 1922 he succeeded Massenet as 1st conductor at the Opéra-Comique; from 1928 to 1934, conductor of the Concerts Lamoureux in Paris; from 1934 to 1940, of the Concerts Pasdeloup; toured in South America (1940-45); then returned to Paris; continued to conduct occasionally at the Opéra-Comique. —Cf. S. Wolff, *Albert Wolff, Doyen de l'Opéra-Comique,* in 'Le Guide du Concert et du Disque' (Oct. 3, 1958).

Wolff, Auguste (Désiré Bernard), French pianist and piano manufacturer; b. Paris, May 3, 1821; d. there, Feb. 3, 1887. He studied piano with Zimmerman at the Paris Cons. and composition with Halévy; after a few years of teaching, he joined the firm of the piano maker Camille Pleyel in 1852, succeeding him as head in 1855; the firm then became known as Pleyel-Wolff & Cie.

Wolff, Édouard, Polish pianist and composer; b. Warsaw, Sept. 15, 1816; d. Paris, Oct. 16, 1880. He studied in Warsaw with Zawadski (piano) and Elsner (composition); then was a piano pupil of Würfel in Vienna. In 1835 he settled in Paris, and became an esteemed teacher; he was a friend of Chopin, and imitated him in his piano music. He publ. 350 opus numbers for piano, among them several albums of études; a waltz, *La Favorite; Chansons polonaises originales; Tarentelle; Chansons bacchiques;* a piano concerto; also 30 celebrated duos for piano and violin (with de Bériot), and 8 more (with Vieuxtemps). His sister, **Regina Wolff,** a pianist, was the mother of Henryk Wieniawski.

Wolff, Erich, Austrian pianist; b. Vienna, Dec. 3, 1874; d. New York, March 20, 1913 (while on a concert tour). He studied in Vienna with Anton Door (piano); lived in Vienna, and (from 1906) in Berlin; became well known as an excellent accompanist of singers. A volume of 60 of his German songs was publ. posthumously, eliciting great praise. He also wrote a violin concerto and some chamber music.

Wolff, Ernst Victor, pianist and harpsichordist; b. Berlin, Aug. 6, 1889. He studied piano with Ph. Scharwenka in Berlin; musicology at the Univ. of Berlin; *Dr. phil.*

there with the dissertation *Robert Schumanns Lieder in ersten und späteren Fassungen* (Leipzig, 1914); was active in Germany as harpsichord player; lived mostly in Berlin until 1933; then went to London; in 1936 settled in N. Y. as teacher. Author of *With Reason and Rhyme* (New Haven, 1957).

Wolff, Hellmuth Christian, musicologist and composer; b. Zürich, May 23, 1906. He studied musicology in Berlin with Abert, Schering, Blume, and Sachs; 1932, *Dr. phil.* for his dissertation *Die venezianische Oper in der 2. Hälfte des 17. Jahrhunderts* (Berlin, 1937); from 1947, instructor of musicology at the Univ. of Leipzig; living in Halle. —Works: oboe concerto (1933); *Inferno 1944,* symph. poem (1946); piano concerto (1948); violin concerto (1948); several scenic oratorios *(Esther, Der Tod des Orpheus,* etc.); several string quartets; a violin sonata; a viola sonata; a cello sonata; choruses; song cycles; numerous editions of works by Handel, Telemann, J. J. Fux, J. G. Graun, etc. —Author of *Die Musik der alten Niederländer* (Leipzig, 1956); *Die Händel-Oper auf der modernen Bühne* (Leipzig, 1957).

Wolff, Hermann, German concert manager; b. Cologne, Sept. 4, 1845; d. Berlin, Feb. 3, 1902. He was a pupil of Franz Kroll and Wüerst; was editor of the 'Neue Berliner Musikzeitung' (1878-79); co-editor of the 'Musikwelt.' In 1881 he founded the Hermann Wolff Concert Management, which became famous; it was later styled H. Wolff & J. Sachs (until 1935). He also composed piano pieces and songs. —Cf. E. Stargardt-Wolff, *Wegbereiter grosser Musiker* (Berlin, 1954).

Wolff, Max, Austrian operetta composer; b. Moravia, Feb., 1840; d. Vienna, March 23, 1886. He studied music with Marx and Dessoff; became a successful composer of operettas, of which the following were produced in Vienna; *Die Pilger* (Sept. 6, 1872); *Die Porträt-Dame* (March 1, 1877); *Césarine* (Dec. 13, 1878).

Wolff, Werner, conductor and writer on music; b. Berlin, Oct. 2, 1883. He was the son of the concert manager Hermann Wolff (q. v.); studied with W. Klatte; was opera conductor in Vienna, Prague, Danzig, and Düsseldorf; from 1917 to 1932, conducted at the Hamburg Opera; in 1933, led the Wagner Memorial Festival in Venice, on the occasion of the semicentennial of Wagner's death. In 1938 he settled in the U. S.; was head of the music department at Tennessee Wesleyan College; in 1943 became director and conductor of the Chattanooga Opera Association; from 1950, columnist and music critic for the 'Chattanooga Daily Times.' He wrote the first full-length biography of Bruckner in English, *Anton Bruckner, Rustic Genius* (N. Y., 1942; revised German ed. as *Anton Bruckner: Genie und Einfalt,* Zürich, 1948); composed some symphonic and chamber music; piano pieces; songs.

Wolffers, Jules, American pianist, teacher, and music critic; b. Antwerp, Belgium, May 22, 1908. He attended school in London (1915-20); in 1922 came to the U. S. and settled in Boston; studied at the Boston English High School; piano with Hans Ebel; organ with Henry Gideon; theory and composition with Hugo Leichtentritt. He gave concerts in N. Y. and Boston; also piano-violin recitals with his wife, Harriet Elkind Wolffers; conducted choral groups and instrumental ensembles; associate conductor of the Civic Symph. Orch., Boston, 1947-50. He was appointed to the faculty of Boston Univ. in 1940; associate prof. of piano, 1953; administrative assistant to the Dean, 1954-57; 1957, chairman of the Division of Music (College of Music) of the Boston Univ. School of Fine and Applied Arts.

Wolffheim, Werner (Joachim), German musicologist; b. Berlin, Aug. 1, 1877; d. there, Oct. 26, 1930. While studying jurisprudence in Munich and Berlin (1895-98), he took courses in musicology with Sandberger and Fleischer; later studied with Kretzschmar and Johannes Wolf. With H. Springer and Max Schneider he was co-editor of 'Miscellanea bio-bibliographica' (supplement to Eitner's 'Quellen-Lexikon'); edited the piano concertos for Breitkopf & Härtel's complete ed. of Haydn's works, and prepared (with Kretzschmar) a new ed. of Spitta's life of Bach. He formed a valuable music library (catalogue in 2 vols.), which he sold in 1928-29.

Wolfinsohn, Wolfe, violinist and teacher; b. Cape Town, South Africa, Aug. 3, 1899. He studied at the Royal Academy of Music in London, graduating in 1917; settled in the U. S. in 1922; taught at the David Mannes Music School (1922-32); was 1st violinist of the Lenox String Quartet (1926-29); in 1929 founded the Stradivarius Quartet. In 1939 he settled in Boston as teacher and chamber music player.

Wölfl (Woelfl, Wölffl), Joseph, Austrian pianist and composer; b. Salzburg, Dec. 24, 1773; d. London, May 21, 1812. He was a pupil of Leopold Mozart and Michael Haydn; served as a chorister at the Salzburg Cathedral (1783-86); was then in Vienna (1790-92) and Warsaw (1793); again in Vienna from 1795; was considered Beethoven's rival as a pianist; brought out 4 operas with some success; married the actress Therese Klemm. Traveling through Germany, he gave numerous concerts as pianist, reaching Paris in 1801; there he settled for several years; produced 2 French operas and was acclaimed as a piano virtuoso. In 1805 he went to London, and almost immediately established himself in the favor of the public as pianist and teacher. He was, however, of an eccentric disposition, and became involved in all sorts of trouble. He died in obscurity at the age of 38. In his professional life, he emphasized the sensational element; gave fanciful titles to his works; named one of his piano sonatas *Ne plus ultra,* and claimed that it was the most difficult piece ever written. —Works: operas: *Der Höllenberg* (Vienna, Nov. 21, 1795), *Der Kopf ohne Mann* (Vienna, Dec. 3, 1798), *Das schöne Milchmädchen* (Vienna, Jan. 5, 1797), *Das trojanische Pferd* (Vienna, 1797), *L'Amour romanesque* (Paris, 1804), *Fernando, ou Les Maures* (Paris, 1805); the ballets *La Surprise de Diane* (London, Dec. 21, 1805) and *Alzire* (London, Jan. 27, 1807); 7 piano concertos, including *Le Calme* and *Concerto militaire;* other publ. compositions are 2 symphonies, 9 string quartets, 12 piano trios, 2 trios for 2 clarinets and bassoon; 42 violin sonatas; 58 piano sonatas; 24 sets of variations for piano; a *Méthode de piano* (with 100 studies); sonatas for 4 hands; waltzes, polonaises, rondos, fantasias, etc.; also songs. Some of his piano pieces were publ. in monthly issues, under the title *The Harmonic Budget* (London, 1810). —Cf. R. Duval, *Un Rival de Beethoven*: *Joseph Woelfl,* in the 'Rivista Musicale Italiana' (1898; also separately, Turin, 1898); R. Baum, *Joseph Wölfl. Leben, Klavierwerke, Klavierkammermusik und Klavierkonzerte* (Kassel, 1928).

Wolfram, Joseph Maria, Bohemian composer; b. Dobrzan, July 21, 1789; d. Teplitz, Sept. 30, 1839. He studied with J. A. Koželuch in Prague; moved to Vienna, as music teacher; then became a government official at Theusing, and mayor of Teplitz (1824). He brought out several successful operas: *Maja und Alpino* (Prague, May 24, 1826), *Der Bergmönch* (Dresden, March 14, 1830), *Das Schloss Candra* (Dresden, Dec. 1, 1832); a *Missa nuptialis* and some piano pieces and songs by him were published.

Wolfrum, Philipp, German musicologist and composer; b. Schwarzenbach am Wald, Dec. 17, 1854; d. Samaden, May 8, 1919. He was a pupil of Rheinberger and Wüllner in Munich; 1878-84, music teacher in Bamberg; from 1884, organist at Heidelberg Univ., where he also conducted several choral societies; became prof. of musicology there in 1898; *Dr. phil.* (Leipzig Univ., 1890) with the dissertation, *Die Entstehung und erste Entwickelung des deutschen evangelischen Kirchenliedes in musikalischer Beziehung. Dr. theol.* (honorary, Heidelberg Univ., 1910). Author of *Rhythmisch! Eine hymnologische Streitschrift* (1894; polemic directed against C. H. Cornill); *Schluss-Erwiderung auf die 'nichtrhythmischen' Auslassungen des Prof. C. H. Cornill in Heidelberg* (rebuttal in the polemics with Cornill; 1895); *Joh. Seb. Bach* (2 vols., 1906; 2nd ed. of vol. 1, 1910); *Die evangelische Kirchenmusik. Ihr Stand und ihre Weiterentwicklung* (1914); *Luther und Bach* (1917); *Luther und die Musik* (1918). Compositions: *Ein Weihnachtsmysterium,* a Christmas play, for chorus and orch. (1899); *Das grosse Hallelujah,* for male chorus and orch.; piano quintet; string quartet; piano trio; cello sonata; 3 organ sonatas; *Ballade* for piano; mixed choruses; edited 'Der evangelische Kirchenchor' (collection of 44 hymns) and 'Pfälzisches Melodienbuch.' —Cf. K. Hasse, *Philipp Wolfrum,* in the 'Zeitschrift für Musikwissenschaft' (vol. 2; 1919).

Wolfsohn, Juliusz, Polish pianist and composer; b. Warsaw, Jan. 7, 1880. He studied piano with Michalowski in Warsaw, Pugno in Paris, and Leschetizky in Vienna; in 1926 settled in the U. S. He composed a number of works based on Jewish melodies (*Jüdische Rhapsodie, Hebraic Suite,* etc.).

Wolfurt, Kurt von, German composer; b. Lettin, Sept. 7, 1880; d. Munich, Feb. 25, 1957. He belonged to the German Baltic nobility; was educated in St. Petersburg; then studied science at the univs. of Dorpat, Leipzig, and Munich; composition with Max Reger in Munich, where he settled; conducted opera in Strasbourg, Kottbus, and Stockholm; also pursued a business career as director of a paper manufacturing company in Latvia; lived mostly in Berlin and Munich; wrote music criticism; was lecturer at the Univ. of Göttingen (1945); visiting prof. at the Univ. of Johannesburg, South Africa (1949-52); in 1952 returned to Munich. —Works: operas: *Die Verwandlungen des Narren* (1900) and *Dame Kobold* (Kassel, March 14, 1940); *Faust,* after Goethe, for soprano, chorus, and orch.; *Lobgesang,* for men's chorus and orch.; *Hymnus,* for soprano, chorus, and orch.; *Gesang des Meeres,* symph. poem; *Concerto grosso;* piano concerto; chamber music; etc. He was the author of biographies of Mussorgsky (Stuttgart, 1927) and Tchaikovsky (Zürich, 1952). —Cf. special issue of the 'Zeitschrift für Musik' (Oct., 1940).

Wolgast, Johannes, German musicologist; b. Kiel, July 2, 1891; d. Leipzig, Oct. 24, 1932. He studied with Riemann, Straube, and Pembaur in Leipzig; was in the German army during World War I; after the Armistice, continued his studies with Schering and Abert in Berlin; *Dr. phil.,* 1923, with the dissertation, *Georg Böhm;* then taught at the Kirchenmusik-Institut in Leipzig and at the Leipzig Cons.; edited the collected works of Georg Böhm (2 vols.; 1927, 1932); compiled various useful catalogues; contributed articles to German musical magazines.

Wolkenstein, Oswald von, one of the last of the Minnesänger; b. Burg Wolkenstein, Grödener Tal (Tyrol), 1377; d. in his castle Burg Hauenstein, Aug. 2, 1445. He led an adventurous life, traveling through Russia, Persia, Greece, Spain, France, Italy (with King Ruprecht in 1401), etc. For several years (from 1415) he was in the service of King (later Emperor) Sigismund, whom he accompanied to the Council of Constance. The musical settings that he devised for his poems are notable for their genuine melodic quality; some of them are in 2-part and 3-part counterpoint; there are also examples of canonic imitation. His works were edited by Schatz and Koller for the 'Denkmäler der Tonkunst in Österreich' (vol. 18). —Cf. J. Beyrich, *Untersuchungen über den Stil Oswalds von Wolkenstein* (dissertation, Leipzig, 1910); W. Türler, *Stilistische Studien zu Oswald von Wolkenstein* (Heidelberg, 1920); C. W. Marold, *Kommentar zu den Liedern Wolkensteins* (dissertation, Göttingen, 1927); J. Schatz, *Sprache und Wortschatz Oswalds von Wolkenstein* (Vienna, 1930); A. Wolkenstein-Rodenegg, *Oswald von Wolkenstein* (Innsbruck, 1930); H. Loewenstein, *Wort und Ton bei Oswald von Wolkenstein* (dissertation, Königsberg, 1933); W. Salmen, *Werdegang und Lebensfülle des Oswald von Wolkenstein,* in 'Musica Disciplina' (1953).

Wollanck, Friedrich, German composer; b. Berlin, Nov. 3, 1782; d. there, Sept. 6, 1831. He was a lawyer and held a government position as counsellor of the city court in Berlin. His works include an opera, *Der Alpenhirt* (Berlin, 1811); a 'Liederspiel,' *Thibaut von Lowis;* 2 Masses; a Requiem and other church music; more than 100 songs; 33 part-songs; 3 string quartets; 2 string sextets; other chamber music; piano sonatas.

Wolle, John Frederick, American choral conductor and organist; b. Bethlehem, Pa., April 4, 1863; d. there, Jan. 12, 1933. After studying in Munich with Rheinberger (1884-85), he served as organist at the Moravian Church in Bethlehem (1885-1905) and in other churches; conducted choral societies in Harrisburg, York, and Lancaster; founded and led the Choral Union in Bethlehem (1882-92). On March 27, 1900, he inaugurated his most famous choral organization, the 'Bach Choir' (80 voices; greatly enlarged in subsequent decades) with the 1st complete American performance of Bach's Mass in B minor. Its concerts were interrupted during Wolle's absence from 1905 to 1911, when he was prof. of music at the Univ. of California, Berkeley; but were resumed upon his return to Bethlehem in 1911. —Cf. R. Walters, *The Bethlehem Bach Choir* (Boston, 1918); M. A. DeWolfe Howe, *'Venite in Bethlehem'—The Major Chord,* in the 'Mus. Quarterly' (April, 1942).

Wolle, Peter, 'Moravian' minister, bishop, and composer; b. New Herrnhut, St. Thomas, West Indies, Jan. 5, 1792; d. Bethlehem, Pa., Nov. 14, 1871. He was consecrated to the episcopacy on Sept. 26, 1845. He left several compositions; edited the 'Moravian Tune Book' (1836). One of his anthems, for double chorus with strings and organ, is included in the series, 'Music of the Moravians in America,' publ. by the N. Y. Public Library (1939). —Cf. A. G. Rau and H. T. David, *A Catalogue of Music by American Moravians* (Bethlehem, 1938).

Wollenhaupt, Hermann Adolf, German pianist and composer; b. Schkeuditz, near Leipzig, Sept. 27, 1827; d. New York, Sept. 18, 1863. He studied in Leipzig with Julius Knorr (piano) and Moritz Hauptmann (composition). In 1845 he settled in N. Y.; made a reputation as a concert pianist and teacher; in 1855 he toured in Europe. He wrote about 100 brilliant piano pieces, among them *Galop di bravura, Valses styriennes, Improvisation, Nocturne,* and *Scherzo brillante;* he also made numerous transcriptions and arrangements.

Wollgandt, Edgar, German violinist and teacher; b. Wiesbaden, July 18, 1880; d. Halle, Dec. 25, 1949. He studied violin with H. Heermann in Frankfurt; in 1903 became concertmaster of the Gewandhaus Orch., Leipzig; also was 1st violin of the Gewandhaus Quartet. He taught for many years in Leipzig, and in 1947 became prof. of the Musik Hochschule in Halle.

Wolpe, Stefan, composer; b. Berlin, Aug. 25, 1902, of Russian-Jewish and Austrian parentage. He studied with Paul Juon and Schreker at the State Academy of Music in Berlin; in 1933 went to Palestine; in 1938, settled in America, where he devoted himself to teaching and composing. His music shows traces of many successive influences: folk music, jazz, Hebrew and oriental melos, atonality, and modified 12-tone technique. —Works: the operas *Schöne Geschichten* (1927) and *Zeus und Elida* (1927, based on jazz rhythms); cantatas: *The Passion of Man* (1929), *On the Education of Man* (1930), *About Sport* (1931), *Israel and his Land* (1939), and *Unnamed Lands* (after Whitman, 1940); the ballet *The Man from Midian* (1942); much chamber music for various groups of instruments; *Quintet with Voice,* for baritone, horn, cello, harp, clarinet, and piano (N. Y., May 14, 1958). — Cf. M. Bauer, *Stefan Wolpe,* in 'Modern Music' (vol. 17; 1939).

Wolpert, Franz Alfons, German composer and theorist; b. Wiesentheid, Oct. 11, 1917. He studied in Regensburg (1937-39) with C. Thiel; then in Salzburg with Wolf-Ferrari (1939-41); was appointed teacher at the Mozarteum in 1941. —Works: song cycles to poems by Nietzsche, Eichendorff, Uhland, Lenau, Goethe, etc.; violin sonata; viola sonata; cello sonata; clarinet trio; 2 piano sonatas; 4 Shakespeare sonnets for voice and string trio; made arrangements for various instrumental combinations of Mozart's works; publ. *Neue Harmonik* (Berlin, 1950).

Wolstenholme, William, blind Engish organist and composer; b. Blackburn, Lancashire, Feb. 24, 1865; d. London, July 23, 1931. He entered the College for Blind Sons of Gentlemen in Worcester at the age of 9; studied with Dr. Done, the Cathedral organist there; Mus. Bac., Oxford, 1887; subsequently filled various posts as church organist in Blackburn, and (from 1902) in London. In 1908 he visited the U. S. — Works: *Lord Ullin's Daughter,* cantata; *Sir Humphrey Gilbert,* ballad for women's voices; *To Take the Air,* madrigal; suite in F for string orch.; about 100 compositions for organ; wind quintet; piano quartet; 2 string quartets; piano trio; violin sonata; piano pieces: *Impromptu-Polonaise, Marche humoresque, Fantasy-Intermezzo,* etc.; songs and part-songs. —Cf. F. H. Wood, *William Wolstenholme,* in the 'Mus. Times' (1931).

Woltmann, Frederick, American composer; b. Flushing, N. Y., May 13, 1908. He was educated at Brooklyn Polytechnic and Columbia Univ.; then studied at the Eastman School of Music, Rochester, N. Y., with Bernard Rogers and Howard Hanson (graduated in 1933). He received the American Prix de Rome in 1937, and studied with Pizzetti in Italy. —Works: *Dance of the Torch Bearers* for orch. (1932); *Poem for Flute and Orch.* (Rochester, Nov. 17, 1935); *Rhapsody for Horn and Orch.* (Rochester, Dec. 12, 1935); *Legend,* for cello and orch. (1936); *Songs for Autumn,* for soprano, baritone, and orch. (1937); piano concerto (1937); *The Pool of Pegasus,* symph. poem (1937); *From Dover Beach* (1938); *The Coliseum at Night,* symph. poem (1939); *Solitude,* for orch. (1942); *From 'Leaves of Grass,'* after Walt Whitman, for voice and orch. (1946); *Songs from a Chinese Lute,* for voice and 33 instruments (1936); scherzo for 8 wind instruments (1937); songs.

Wolzogen (vohl'-tsoh-gen), **Alfred,** Freiherr **von,** German writer on music; b. Frankfurt, May 27, 1823; d. San Remo, Jan. 14, 1883. From 1868 he was Intendant of the court theater at Schwerin. Author of *Über Theater und Musik* (Breslau, 1860); *Über die szenische Darstellung von Mozarts 'Don Giovanni'* (1860); *Wilhelmine Schröder-Devrient* (Leipzig, 1863); new German versions of Mozart's *Don Giovanni* and *Schauspieldirektor;* also articles in periodicals.

Wolzogen, Ernst, Freiherr **von,** German poet and musical journalist; son of Alfred von Wolzogen and half-brother of Hans von Wolzogen; b. Breslau, April 23, 1855; d. Munich, July 30, 1934. He studied at the Universities of Strasbourg and Leipzig. In 1901 he established in Berlin (with O. J. Bierbaum and F. Wedekind) the 'Überbrettl,' a kind of artistic cabaret for the production of dramatic pieces, pantomimes, poems with recitation and music, etc., most of them reflecting or satirizing contemporary German life; Oskar Straus provided most of the music, and Schoenberg contributed some of the numbers; 2 journals, 'Das moderne Brettl' and 'Bühne und Brettl,' were publ. for a year or so to promote the ideas of the enterprise; but the cabaret closed after 2 sensationally successful seasons. Ernst von Wolzogen publ. 2 books dealing with music: *Der Kraftmayr* (1897; humorous novel with Liszt as the central figure; English transl. as *Florian Mayr,* 1914) and *Ansichten und Aussichten* (1908; essays). — His wife, **Elsa Laura** (*née* Seemann von Mangern), became known as a singer, making a specialty of songs with lute accompaniment; with her husband she made a tour of the U. S. (1910-11); publ. 7 vols. of folksongs with lute accompaniment *(Meine Lieder zur Laute).* —Cf. A. Hertwig, *Ernst von Wolzogens 'Überbrettl' in Wort und Bild* (Berlin, 1901).

Wolzogen, Hans, Freiherr **von,** German writer on music and authority on Wagner; b. Potsdam, Nov. 13, 1848; d. Bayreuth, June 2, 1938. He studied mythology and comparative philology in Berlin (1868-71); then devoted himself to literature; in 1878, at Wagner's invitation, he became editor of the 'Bayreuther Blätter' and lived in Bayreuth most of his life. He popularized the term 'Leitmotif' (first used by F. W. Jähns, q. v.) in his *Motive in Wagners 'Götterdämmerung,'* publ. in the 'Musikalisches Wochenblatt' in 1887 (Wagner's preferred term was 'Grundthema'). His many writings include *Der Nibelungenmythos in Sage und Literatur* (1876); *Thematischer Leitfaden durch die Musik von R. Wagners Festspiel 'Der Ring des Nibelungen'* (1876; 4th ed. as *Erläuterungen zu R. Wagners Nibelungendrama,* 1878); *Die Tragödie in Bayreuth und ihr Satyrspiel* (1876; 5th ed., 1881); *Poetische Lautsymbolik. Psychische Wirkungen der Sprachlaute aus R. Wagners 'Ring des Nibelungen'* (1876; 3rd ed., 1897); *Grundlage und Aufgabe des allgemeinen Patronatvereins zur Pflege und Erhaltung der Bühnenfestspiele in Bayreuth* (1877); *Die Sprache in Wagners Dichtungen* (1877; 2nd ed., 1881); *R. Wagners Tristan und Isolde* (1880); *Unsre Zeit und unsre Kunst* (1881); *Was ist Stil? was will Wagner?* (1881); *Die Religion des Mitleidens* (1882); *Parsifal. Ein thematischer Leitfaden* (1882; 21st printing, 1914); *R. Wagners Heldengestalten erläutert* (2nd ed., 1886); *Wagneriana* (1888); *R. Wagner und die Tierwelt; auch eine Biographie* (1890, 3rd ed., 1910); *Wagners Lebensbericht* (1884; the original of *The Work and Mission of My Life,* publ. 1879 in the 'North American Review,' under Wagner's name); *Erinnerungen an R. Wagner* (1883); *Die Idealisierung des Theaters* (1885); *Grossmeister deutscher Musik* (1897); *Wagner-Brevier* (1904; in Strauss' series 'Die Musik'); *R. Wagner* (1905; in Remer's series 'Die Dichtung'); *Musikalisch-dramatische Parallelen* (1906); *E. T. A. Hoffmann und R. Wagner* (1906); *Aus R. Wagners Geisteswelt* (1908); *Kunst und Kirche* (1913); *E. T. A. Hoffmann, der deutsche Geisterseher* (1922); *Lebensbilder* (autobiographical; 1923); *Wagner und seine Werke* (1924); *Wohltäterin Musik* (1925); *Musik und Theater* (1929); edited Wagner's *Ausgewählte Schriften über Staat und Kunst und Religion* (1902; 3rd ed., 1914) and *Entwürfe zu 'Die Meistersinger,' 'Tristan und Isolde' und 'Parsifal'* (1907).

Wood, Charles, Irish organist and composer; b. Armagh, June 15, 1866; d. Cambridge, England, July 12, 1926. He studied at the Royal College of Music in London, and subsequently taught harmony there; received his Mus. Doc. degree, Cambridge, 1894. In 1924 he succeeded Stanford as prof. of music at Cambridge Univ. He wrote 6 string quartets (mostly in an Irish manner); vocal works with orch.: *Ode on Time* (1898), *Dirge for Two Veterans* (1901), *Song of the Tempest* (1902), *Ballad of Dundee* (1904); church music; edited a collection of Irish folksongs (1897).

Wood, David Duffie, blind American organist; b. Pittsburgh, March 2, 1838; d. Philadelphia, March 27, 1910. Having lost his eyesight by an accident at the age of 3, he was educated at the Penn. Institute for the Blind; from 1858 till his death he was instructor of music there. He was a fine organist; wrote anthems and songs. —Publ. *A Dictionary of Musical Terms, for the Use of the Blind* (Philadelphia, 1869).

Wood, Haydn, English violinist and composer; b. Slaithwaite, March 25, 1882. He entered the Royal College of Music in London at 15; studied there with Fernández Arbós (violin)and Stanford (composition); later studied with César Thomson in Brussels. A prolific composer, his works include 8 overtures, 8 rhapsodies for band, 18 orchestral suites, 31 entr'actes for orch., 12 violin solos, 2 flute pieces, 3 accordion solos, and about 200 songs. His *Phantasy Quartet* for strings received a Cobbett Prize.

Wood, Sir Henry J., eminent English conductor; b. London, March 3, 1869; d. Hitchin, Herts, Aug. 19, 1944. Of musical parentage, he was taught to play the piano by his mother; participated in family musicales from the age of 6; he was equally precocious on the organ; at the age of 10 he often acted as deputy organist, and gave organ recitals at the Fisheries Exhibition (1883) and at the Inventions Exhibition (1885). In 1886 he entered the Royal Academy of Music, where his teachers were Prout, Steggall, Macfarren, and Garcia; won 4 medals. In 1888 he brought out some of his songs; then composed light operas and cantatas. But soon his ambition crystallized in the direction of conducting; he traveled with an opera company in 1889; then became assistant conductor at the Savoy Theatre (1890); was engaged as conductor for various other operatic enterprises. On Oct. 6, 1895 he began the 1st series of Promenade concerts (the famous 'Proms') in Queen's Hall, London, with an orch. of about 100 members. Their success was so conspicuous that a new series of concerts was inaugurated on Jan. 30, 1897, under Wood's direction, and flourished from the beginning. In 1899 he founded the Nottingham Orch.; also was appointed conductor of the Wolverhampton Festival Choral Society (1900), of the Sheffield Festival (1902-11), and of the Norwich Festival (1908). In 1904 he conducted in N. Y. He was married to Olga Urusova, a Russian noblewoman, and became greatly interested in Russian music, which he performed frequently at his concerts. He adopted a Russian pseudonym, Paul Klenovsky, for his compositions and arrangements, and supplied an imaginary biography of his alter ego for use in program notes. His wife died in 1909, and Wood married Muriel Greatorex in 1911. He was knighted in 1911. In 1918 he was offered the conductorship of the Boston Symph. Orch. as successor to Muck, but declined. In 1923 he was appointed prof. of conducting and orchestral playing at the Royal Academy of Music. In 1925 he conducted in California; in 1926 received the degree of Mus. Doc. *(hon. c.)* from Oxford Univ. Wood continued to conduct the Promenade Concerts almost to the end of his life, presenting the last concert on July 28, 1944. Among his popular arrangements are Chopin's *Marche Funèbre,* some works by Bach, and the *Trumpet Voluntary* (mistakenly attributed to Purcell, but actually by Jeremiah Clarke). He publ. *The Gentle Art of Singing* (4 vols.; 1927-28) and *About Conducting* (London, 1945), and edited the *Handbook of Miniature Orchestral and Chamber Music Scores* for J. W. Chester & Co. (1937); wrote an autobiography, *My Life of Music* (London, 1938). — Cf. R. Newmarch, *Henry J. Wood,* in the 'Living Masters of Music' series (London, 1904); R. Hill and others, *Sir Henry Wood: Fifty Years of the 'Proms'* (London, 1944); J. Wood, *The Last Years of Henry J. Wood* (London, 1954; with a foreword by Sir Malcolm Sargent).

Wood, Mary Knight, American pianist and composer; b. Easthampton, Mass., April 7, 1857; d. Florence, Dec. 20, 1944. She studied in Boston with B. J. Lang and in N. Y. with Huss; married A. B. Mason and went to live in Florence, where she remained for many years until her death. She publ. about 30 songs, among them *Ashes of Roses, In Harbor,* and *Poppies.*

Wood, Thomas, English composer and author; b. Chorley, Lancashire, Nov. 28, 1892; d. Bures, Essex, Nov. 19, 1950. He was educated at Exeter College, Oxford; then studied at the Royal College of Music with Stanford; was music director at Tonbridge School (1919-24); lecturer and precentor at Exeter College (1924-29). His extensive travels took him to the Far East and to the Arctic; his familiarity with the sea was reflected in many of his compositions (for chorus and orch.), such as *40 Singing Seamen* (1925), *Master Mariners* (1927), *Merchantmen* (1934), and in *A Seaman's Overture* (for orch., 1927). He edited vol. II of the *Oxford Song Book* (1928; 3rd ed., 1937). His books include *Music and Boyhood* (1925) and the autobiographical *True Thomas* (1936); also publ. *Cobbers* (on his Australian tour of 1930-32), which became highly popular in England, and a sequel to it, *Cobbers Campaigning* (1940). —Cf. N. Coghill, *Thomas Wood,* in 'Music & Letters' (April, 1951).

Wood, William G., Irish organist; brother of Charles Wood; b. Armagh, Jan. 16, 1859; d. London, Sept. 25, 1895. He studied at the Royal Academy of Music in London; from 1886 till his death he was organist and music master at the Highgate Grammar School. He composed some fine organ music (3 canons, a sonata, *Fantasia and Fugue, Introduction and Allegro, Minuet and Trio,* etc.).

Woodbury (original name, Woodberry), **Isaac Baker,** American composer of songs and music editor; b. Beverly, Mass., Oct.

23, 1819; d. Charleston, S. C., Oct. 26, 1858. Originally a blacksmith, he took up music, going to Europe in 1838 for study in Paris and London; upon his return he settled in Boston as teacher. From 1850 to his death he was an editor of a New York music magazine publ. successively as 'American Monthly Musical Review,' 'Musical Pioneer,' etc. In 1852, he made another trip to Europe. His collection of sacred songs, 'The Dulcimer,' enjoyed great popularity; he also compiled a 'Collection of Church Music' for the Boston Music Educational Society (1842) and 'The Choral' (1845); publ. *Woodbury's Self-Instructor in Musical Composition and Thorough-Bass,* and many secular songs. —Cf. F. J. Metcalf, *American Writers and Compilers of Sacred Music* (1925). See also 'Dictionary of American Biography.'

Wood-Hill, Mabel, American composer; b. Brooklyn, March 12, 1870; d. Stamford, Conn., March 1, 1954. She was educated at Smith College and at Columbia Univ., where she studied composition with Rybner. She wrote songs and choruses; orchestrated pieces by Couperin *(Louis XIV Suite)* and Bach. Her pantomime, *The Adventures of Pinocchio,* was performed for the 1st time in N. Y. on April 13, 1931.

Woodhouse, George, English pianist; b. Cradley Heath, near Birmingham, Dec. 16, 1877; d. Southsea, Jan. 4, 1954. He studied in Birmingham and later took piano lessons with Leschetizky in Vienna. He established his own piano school in London; publ. *The Artist at the Piano* (London, 1910), *Creative Technique* (London, 1922), *From Keyboard to Music* (London, 1949), and *A Realistic Approach to Piano Playing* (London, 1953).

Woodman, Raymond Huntington, American organist and composer; b. Brooklyn, Jan. 18, 1861; d. there, Dec. 25, 1943. He studied piano with his father; theory with Dudley Buck; then went to Paris, where he took lessons in organ playing from César Franck (1888). He filled various posts as church organist and teacher in N. Y.; also taught theory and conducted a choral society in Brooklyn. He publ. about 150 compositions, among them anthems, organ pieces, piano pieces *(Romance, The Brook, Spring Song, Three Album-Leaves,* etc.); songs, of which *A Birthday* was especially successful.

Woods, Francis Cunningham, English organist and composer; b. London, Aug. 29, 1862; d. there, Sept. 21, 1929. He studied at the National Training School for Music under Sullivan, Prout, Stainer, and Cowen; after serving as organist at Brasenose College and Exeter College, was private organist to the Duke of Marlborough (1891-94); then prof. of organ and lecturer at Oxford Univ. (1890-95); in 1896 succeeded William G. Wood as organist and music master of the Highgate Grammar School, London. He composed *King Harold,* a 'historical cantata'; *Greyport Legend,* a ballad for baritone, men's chorus, and orch.; *Old May-Day,* cantata for women's voices and piano; *The Lords of Labor,* ode; some orchestral pieces; songs.

Woodworth, George Wallace, American choral conductor and music educator; b. Boston, Nov. 6, 1902. He was educated at Harvard Univ. (B. A., 1924; M. A., 1926); also studied at the Royal College of Music in London (1927-28). In 1925 he joined the staff of the music dept. at Harvard; prof. in 1948. In 1925 he became conductor of the Radcliffe Choral Society; in 1934, conductor of the Harvard Glee Club; and in 1940, Harvard Univ. organist and choirmaster for the Harvard Univ. Chapel, resigning all these posts in 1958 to devote himself to teaching. He conducted the Harvard-Radcliffe Chorus in a transcontinental tour in 1954, and the Harvard Glee Club on its European tour in 1956; led the Harvard-Radcliffe Chorus with the Boston Symph. in regular concerts during the seasons of 1943-44, 1951-52, and 1955-56; also in Tanglewood. He is the editor of 'Harvard-Radcliffe Choral Music' (G. Schirmer). He holds the honorary degree of Mus. Doc. (New England Cons., 1958); awarded Harvard Glee Club Medal (1958); Lowell Television Lecturer of Harvard Univ. (1959).

Wooldridge, Harry Ellis, English musicologist; b. Winchester, March 28, 1845; d. London, Feb. 13, 1917. While studying at Trinity College, Oxford (1860-64), he became deeply interested in painting and music; entered the Royal Academy of Fine Arts in 1865, at the same time beginning his researches regarding early music in the libraries of Oxford and London; from 1895 till his death he was Slade Prof. of Fine Arts at Oxford Univ. —Publ. *The English Metrical Psalter* (1890); *The Polyphonic Period,* being vols. I and II of the *Oxford History of Music* (1901, 1905; 2nd ed., revised by P. C. Buck, 1929-32); radically revised Chappell's *Popular Music of the Olden Time,* and publ. it under the title

Old English Popular Music (2 vols., 1893); also edited 'Early English Harmony' (2 vols., 1897, 1913; pieces from the 10th to 15th centuries); 'The Yattendon Hymnal' (1899; with R. Bridges); Purcell's sacred compositions (vols. XIII, XIV, and XVIII of Novello's ed. of Purcell's complete works).

Wooler, Alfred, American music teacher and composer; b. Shipley, Yorkshire, May 11, 1867; d. Lake Winola, Pa., Aug. 7, 1937. He settled in the U. S. as a youth, and studied at the Univ. of Pennsylvania; taught harmony at Scranton, Buffalo, and N. Y.; also conducted choral societies. He composed about 250 anthems, songs, and part-songs; also piano pieces.

Woolf, Benjamin Edward, American composer and music critic; b. London, Feb. 16, 1836; d. Boston, Feb. 7, 1901. He was taken to America in 1839 by his father, who taught him the elements of music, and various instruments; studied under W. R. Bristow (organ) in N. Y.; conducted theater orchestras in Boston, Philadelphia, and New Orleans; in 1870 he was music and drama critic for the Boston 'Globe,' later for the 'Saturday Evening Gazette,' and from 1895 for the Boston 'Herald.' He composed string quartets, piano trios, and other chamber music; the 'operatic comedietta' *Lawn Tennis, or Djakh and Djill* (Boston, 1880); the comic opera *Pounce & Co.* (Boston, 1883); and an operetta *Westward Ho!* (Boston, Dec. 31, 1894).

Woolhouse, Wesley S. B., English mathematician and writer on musical subjects; b. North Shields, May 6, 1809; d. London, Aug. 12, 1893. He was head assistant at the Nautical Almanach Establishment. Publ. *Essay on Musical Intervals, Harmonics, and the Temperament of the Musical Scale* (1835; new ed., 1888); *A Catechism of Music* (1843); *Treatise on Singing.* He owned a fine collection of violins.

Woollen, Russell, American composer; b. Hartford, Conn., Jan. 7, 1923. He studied for the priesthood; attended the Pius X school of Liturgical Music, N. Y.; in 1948 studied Gregorian Chant at the Benedictine Abbey at Solesmes. After his ordination as a priest, he was assigned to the Catholic Univ. of America, Washington, D. C., where he taught liturgical music; continued his studies in composition with Nicolas Nabokov in Baltimore (1949-51), with Nadia Boulanger in Paris (1951), and with Walter Piston at Harvard Univ. (1953-55), returning to his post at Catholic Univ. in 1955. —Works: *Missa causa nostrae laetitiae* (1949); sonata for piano duo (1950); sextet for clarinet, string quartet, and piano (1951); *Missa melismatica* (1951); 40 duets on *Au Clair de la lune* for recorders (1952); *Shakespeare Sonnets* for chorus a cappella (1952); piano quartet (1952); *Apotheosis to the Blessed Virgin* for chorus a cappella (1952); Mass No. 3 (1952); Holy Week Responsories for men's voices (1952-53); Mass in Major Modes (1953); quartet for flute and strings (1953); Toccata for orch. (1954-55); woodwind quintet (1955); piano trio (1956-57); *Missa simplex* (1956); Triptych for brass choir (1957); symph. No. 1 (1957-58); *Missa Domus aurea* (1957); *Summer Jubilee Overture* (Washington, D. C., June 26, 1958); motets; hymns; secular choruses; piano pieces; songs.

Woollett, Henri Édouard, French composer; b. (of English parentage) Le Havre, Aug. 13, 1864; d. there, Oct. 9, 1936. He studied in Paris with Pugno (piano) and Massenet (composition); returned to Le Havre, and established himself as a teacher; André Caplet was his student there. He also founded the Société d'Enseignement Musical, a free elementary music school, and the Schola Cantorum there (1920). —Works: *Pierrot amoureux,* a pantomime; *La Rose de Sharon,* 'poème lyrique' for orch.; *Petite Suite* for orch.; *De l'aube à la nuit* for vocal quartet and piano; 2 violin sonatas; a cello sonata; sonata for flute and piano; piano pieces *(Nocturnes et pastorales, Pièces intimes, À travers la vie,* etc.); songs. Author of *Petit traité de prosodie* (1903); *Histoire de la musique depuis l'antiquité jusqu'à nos jours* (4 vols., 1909-25); *Histoire de l'orchestration* (with Gabriel Pierné; in Lavignac's 'Encyclopédie'); *Un Mélodiste français, René Lenormand* (1930).

Wordsworth, William, English composer; b. London, Dec. 17, 1908. He studied with his father; then with Tovey at Edinburgh. He began to compose rather late in life, but compensated for it by a rapid development. His musical style is marked by a certain austerity of essential materials, and compactness of form. —Works: 4 symphonies (1936; 1944; 1948; 1954); a piano concerto (1946); 3 string quartets (1941; 1943; 1947); a piano quartet (1948); a violin sonata (1944); a cello sonata (1937); songs. —Cf. S. Bayliss, *William Wordsworth,* in the 'Chesterian' (April, 1950).

Work, Henry Clay, American composer of popular songs; b. Middletown, Conn., Oct. 1, 1832; d. Hartford, June 8, 1884. He was a printer by trade; entirely self-taught in music; his first success was *We are coming, Sister Mary;* other well-known songs are *Grandfather's Clock; Father, Come Home; Shadows on the Floor;* his Civil War song *Marching through Georgia* became celebrated; other songs of the Civil War were *Drafted into the Army; God Save the Nation; Song of a Thousand Years; Wake, Nicodemus; Kingdom Coming,* etc. —Cf. R. S. Hill, *The Mysterious Chord of Henry Clay Work,* in 'Notes' (March-June, 1953).

Wormser, André (Alphonse-Toussaint), French composer; b. Paris, Nov. 1, 1851; d. there, Nov. 4, 1926. He studied at the Paris Cons. with Marmontel (piano) and Bazin (theory); won 1st prize for piano in 1872, and the Grand Prix de Rome in 1875 with the cantata *Clytemnestre.* His most successful work was the pantomime or 'wordless opera' *L'Enfant prodigue* (Paris, June 14, 1890); also composed other stage works, orchestral works, men's choruses, songs, and piano pieces. —Cf. E. Newman, *A Musical Motley* (1919).

Wörner, Karl Heinrich, German musicologist; b. Waldorf, near Heidelberg, Jan. 6, 1910. He studied musicology in Berlin with Schünemann and Schering, and conducting with Julius Prüwer; received the degree of *Dr. phil.* at Berlin Univ. with the dissertation *Beiträge zur Geschichte des Leitmotivs in der Oper,* publ. in the 'Zeitschrift für Musikwissenschaft' (Dec., 1931); was critic for the 'B. Z. am Mittag'; then (1935-40) opera conductor at Stettin, Magdeburg, and Frankfurt. He was in the German Army during World War II; 1944-46, prisoner of war in the U. S. Returning to Germany in 1946, he was active as lecturer. From 1956 to 1958 he was on the staff of B. Schott's Söhne (Mainz); 1958, on the faculty of the Folkwangschule in Essen. Author of *Mendelssohn* (Wiesbaden, 1947); *Musik der Gegenwart* (Mainz, 1949); *Schumann* (Zürich, 1949); *Musiker-Worte* (Baden-Baden, 1949); *Geschichte der Musik* (Göttingen, 1954); *Neue Musik in der Entscheidung* (Mainz, 1954).

Woronoff, Wladimir, Russian-Belgian composer; b. St. Petersburg, Jan. 5, 1903. He studied in Berlin; later in Brussels, where he settled. —Works: *Le Masque de la mort rouge,* opera-ballet after Poe; *La Foule,* for bass solo, chorus, and orch.; *Suite de Bruxelles* for orch.; *Concert lyrique* for piano and orch.; *Invocation à Venus* for voice and string quartet; songs; etc.

Worp, Johannes, Dutch organist, composer, and arranger; b. Broek, Dec. 24, 1821; d. Groningen, April 21, 1891. He studied in Amsterdam, where he was active as church organist; then went to Leipzig, where he took a course with Moscheles; returning to Holland, he became organist at Groningen. He publ. valuable organ works and methods, which have gone through numerous editions: *De Melodieën der Evangelische Gezangen . . .,* for organ, piano, and chorus; *De Melodieën der Psalmen en Lof- en Bedezangen . . .,* for organ, piano, and chorus (20th printing, 1947); the manual, *Algemeene Muziekleer* (13th printing, 1932, revised by Sem Dresden); *Kleine Muziekleer* for schools; *Eerste en tweede Zangboekje* for schools; *De zingende Kinderwereld* (songs for children; many editions); *Volksliedjes uit het Land der Liefde;* etc.

Woržischek (Voříšek), Johann Hugo, Bohemian composer; b. Wamberg, Bohemia, May 11, 1791; d. Vienna, Nov. 19, 1825. He studied with his father and with Tomaschek in Prague, where he lived from 1801; in 1813 he went to Vienna and became known as a pianist; in 1818 he was appointed conductor of the Gesellschaft der Musikfreunde; having studied law, he obtained a post in the civil service in 1822 but abandoned it after a year, when he was made court organist. He composed symphonies, choral works with orch., a piano concerto, etc.; of more interest are his piano pieces, especially the *Rhapsodies* (1818) and *Impromptus* (1822), because Schubert was strongly influenced by them. A piano sonata in B minor (1820) shows kinship with Beethoven, whom he knew intimately. —Cf. W. Kahl, *Das lyrische Klavierstück Schuberts und seiner Vorgänger seit 1810,* in 'Archiv für Musikwissenschaft' (1921).

Wöss, Josef Venantius von, Austrian musicologist; b. Cattaro, Dalmatia, June 13, 1863; d. Vienna, Oct. 22, 1943. He received his first musical instruction from his mother and an uncle; studied composition at the Vienna Cons. with Franz Krenn; wrote music criticism for 'Musica Divina'; later in the editorial dept. of the 'Universal Edition,' for which he edited the collection 'Deutsche Meisterlieder.' He composed the operas *Lenzlüge* (Elberfeld, 1905) and *Flaviennes Abenteuer* (Breslau, 1910); *Heiliges Lied,* for male chorus and orch.; *Serenade,* for orch.; *Sakuntala,* overture; a piano sextet; sacred music (a *Te Deum* and 2 Masses); motets with orch.; songs *(Sulamith, 4 slawische Lieder, 4 orientalische Gesänge,* etc.). He made the piano scores of Mahler's *Das klagende Lied, Lied von der Erde,* and symphonies Nos. 3, 4, 8, and 9; edited Bruckner's symphonies; publ. *Die Modulation* (Vienna, 1921). His recollections of Bruckner were publ. in 'Gregoriusblatt' (1932).

Wöss, Kurt, Austrian conductor; b. Linz, May 2, 1914. He studied conducting with Felix Weingartner in Vienna; became a theater conductor there; from 1948 to 1956 conducted the Tonkünstlerorchester in Vienna; in 1956, appointed conductor of the Melbourne, Australia, Symph. Orch.

Wotquenne (vŏht-kĕhn'), **Alfred,** Belgian musicologist; b. Lobbes, Jan. 25, 1867; d. Antibes, France, Sept. 25, 1939. He studied at the Brussels Cons. with Mailly (organ), and Joseph Dupont and Gevaert (theory); from 1894 to 1919 was librarian, secretary, and inspector of studies at the Brussels Cons.; then moved to Antibes in southern France, where in 1921 he became maître de chapelle. —Publ. *Catalogue de la bibliothèque du Cons. Royal de Musique de Bruxelles* (vol. I, 1894; with a supplement, *Libretti d'opéras et d'oratorios italiens du XVIIe siècle,* 1901; II, 1902; III, 1908; IV, 1912; V, 1914); *Baldassare Galuppi* (1899; 2nd augmented ed., 1902, as *Baldassare Galuppi. Étude bibliographique sur ses œuvres dramatiques); Thematisches Verzeichnis der Werke von Chr. W. v. Gluck* (1904); *Catalogue thématique des œuvres de C. Ph. E. Bach* (1905); *Table alphabétique des morceaux mesurés contenus dans les œuvres dramatiques de Zeno, Metastasio et Goldoni* (1905); *Étude bibliographique sur le compositeur napolitain Luigi Rossi* (1909; with thematic catalogue). He prepared a card catalogue of 18,000 Italian 'cantate da camera' of the 18th century; edited 'Chansons italiennes de la fin du XVIe siècle' (canzonette *a* 4); continued the collections begun by Gevaert, 'Répertoire classique du chant français' and 'Répertoire français de l'ancien chant classique,' and edited a new collection, 'Répertoire Wotquenne' (4 vols. publ.); also ed. violin sonatas of Tartini, Veracini, and others; composed much sacred music. —The MSS of several important bibliographies in his collection were bought by the Library of Congress in 1929; these comprise *Répertoire des textes publiés par les éditeurs parisiens Ballard; Histoire musicale et chronologique du Théâtre de la Foire depuis 1680 jusqu'à 1762; Histoire du nouveau Théâtre-Italien à Paris (1718-1762);* etc. A large part of his private music library was also bought by the Library of Congress.

Wouters (voo-tär'), **(François) Adolphe,** Belgian organist and composer; b. Brussels, May 28, 1841; d. there, April 16, 1924. He studied at the Brussels Cons.; then taught piano there (1871-1920); from 1868 he was also organist at Notre-Dame-de-Finistère and maître de chapelle at Saint-Nicolas. He composed church music, men's choruses, technical studies and transcriptions for piano, etc.

Woyrsch, Felix von, composer and conductor; b. Troppau, Silesia, Oct. 8, 1860; d. Altona-Hamburg, March 20, 1944. He studied with A. Chevallier in Hamburg, but was chiefly self-taught. In 1894 he settled in Altona as conductor of the Kirchenchor, the Singakademie (from 1895), and the municipal symph. concerts and Volkskonzerte (from 1903); from 1895 to 1903 he was organist of the Friedenskirche, then of the Johanniskirche. —Compositions: Operas, *Der Pfarrer von Meudon* (Hamburg, 1886); *Der Weiberkrieg* (Hamburg, 1890); *Wikingerfahrt* (Nuremberg, 1896). For orch.: symph. prologue to *Divina Commedia; Skaldische Rhapsodie,* for violin and orch.; 2 symphonies; *3 Böcklin-Phantasien (Die Toteninsel, Der Eremit, Im Spiel der Wellen); Hamlet,* overture. Vocal works with orch.: *Da Jesus auf Erden ging,* a mystery play (Hamburg, Jan. 29, 1917; one of his best works); *Geburt Jesu, Deutscher Heerbann, Der Vandalen Auszug, Passions-Oratorium, Sapphische Ode an Aphrodite, Totentanz, Da lachte schön Sigrid, Wollt' er nur fragen, Edward.* Chamber music: piano quintet; string quartet. For piano: *3 Notturnos; 2 Walzer; Walzer* (4 hands); theme and variations; *4 Impromptus; Improvisationen; Metamorphosen.* He also composed song cycles *(Persische Lieder, Spanisches Liederbuch, 10 Rattenfängerlieder);* edited *Deutsche Volkslieder* (14th-16th centuries), and choral works of Heinrich Schütz for practical use (3 vols.).

Woytowicz, Boleslaw, Polish composer; b. Dunajowce Podolia, Dec. 5, 1899. In Warsaw he studied piano with Michalowski and composition with Statkowski and Maliszewski; also studied with Nadia Boulanger in Paris (1930-33). Returning from Paris, he became instructor at the Chopin Music School in Warsaw; won several prizes for his compositions. —Works: 2 symphonies (1938; 1945); several cantatas; a concert suite for orch.; a piano concerto (1932); various pieces for piano; songs.

Wrangel (vrăhn'-gĕl), **Vassily Georgievitch,** Baron, Russian composer; b. St. Petersburg, June 25, 1862; d. there, March 10, 1901. A functionary at the Ministry of Home Affairs, he was a musician by avocation; took several courses at the St. Petersburg Cons. His songs, many of which were publ., attracted singers by their artless melodic quality, and enjoyed some popularity for a time; he also wrote a ballet, *The Mikado's Daughter* (St. Petersburg, Dec. 1, 1897).

Wranitzky (vrah-nit'skē), **Anton,** violinist and composer; b. Neureisch, Moravia, June 13, 1761; d. Vienna, Aug. 6, 1820. He studied with his older brother Paul; also had lessons in Vienna with Albrechtsberger, Haydn, and Mozart. From 1794 he was Kapellmeister to Prince Lobkowitz at his castle in Bohemia, and later (1808) in Vienna. He wrote 15 violin concertos, and other concertos with several soloists; much chamber music; marches; dances; etc.

Wranitzky, Paul, violinist and composer; brother of Anton Wranitzky; b. Neureisch, Moravia, Dec. 30, 1756; d. Vienna, Sept. 28, 1808. After studying in various provincial towns of Moravia, he went to Vienna in 1776, where he was a pupil of Joseph Martin Kraus. In 1780 he became a member of Prince Esterházy's orch. at Eisenstadt; in 1785, became concertmaster of the Vienna Opera, and retained this position until his death. His opera *Oberon, König der Elfen* was given with excellent success in Vienna on Nov. 7, 1789; other operas and Singspiele by him produced in Vienna were *Rudolf von Felseck* (Oct. 6, 1792); *Merkur, der Heurat-Stifter* (Feb. 21, 1793); *Das Fest der Lazzaroni* (Feb. 4, 1794); *Die gute Mutter* (May 11, 1795); *Johanna von Montfaucon* (Jan. 25, 1799); *Der Schreiner* (July 18, 1799); *Mitgefühl* (April 21, 1804); *Die Erkenntlichkeit* (July 22, 1805). He also produced numerous ballets; wrote incidental music to several plays; composed a great deal of instrumental music, including 22 symphonies; 5 concertos for various instruments with orch.; 6 quintets; 47 string quartets; 12 quartets for flute and strings; 3 piano quartets; string trios; etc.

Wrede (vrā'-dĕ), **Ferdinand,** German pianist and composer; b. Brökel, Hanover, July 28, 1827; d. Frankfurt-on-the-Oder, Jan. 20, 1899. He studied with Marschner and Litolff; then was active as singing teacher and choral conductor; wrote men's choruses and songs.

Wrightson, Herbert James, composer and teacher; b. Sunderland, England, Dec. 20, 1869; d. West Lebanon, N. Y., Dec. 24, 1949. He studied at the Leipzig Cons. with Jadassohn and Reinecke. In 1897 he settled in the U. S.; taught in Philadelphia, Chicago, etc. His works include a symphony; 15 organ pieces; 29 piano pieces; 2 melodramas for speaker with music; 144 songs, of which nearly 100 were published. His hymns are included in various hymnals. He publ. *Elements of the Theory of Music* (Boston, 1921) and *Modern Classical Harmony;* contributed articles to the 'Mus. Quarterly,' 'Etude,' etc.

Wüerst (vü'-erst), **Richard (Ferdinand),** German composer; b. Berlin, Feb. 22, 1824; d. there, Oct. 9, 1881. He studied violin with Ferdinand David at the Leipzig Cons., where he also took lessons with Mendelssohn. He then taught at Kullak's Neue Akademie der Tonkunst in Berlin. As music critic for the 'Berliner Fremdenblatt' he exercised considerable influence; he was editor of the 'Neue Berliner Musikzeitung' (1874-75); publ. *Leitfaden der Elementartheorie der Musik* (1867; English transl. as *Elementary Theory of Music and Treatment of Chords,* Boston, 1893). As a composer, he was a follower of Mendelssohn. —Works: the operas *Der Rotmantel* (Berlin, 1848), *Vineta* (Bratislava, Dec. 21, 1862), *Eine Künstlerreise* (with Winterfeld; Berlin, 1868), *Faublas* (Berlin, 1873), *A-ing-fo-hi* (Berlin, Jan. 28, 1878), *Die Offiziere der Kaiserin* (Berlin, 1878); cantata *Der Wasserneck;* 3 symphonies; *Ein Märchen,* symph. fantasy; *Variations sur une chanson nègre de Kentucky,* for orch. (on Stephen Foster's *My Old Kentucky Home); Sous le balcon,* a serenade for string orch. with cello obbligato; *Russische Suite* for string orch. with violin obbligato; *Tanz der Mücken, Fliegen und Käfer,* an orchestral scherzo; piano trio; cello sonata; 3 string quartets; various violin pieces; songs; vocal duets and terzets.

Wüllner, Franz, German pianist, conductor, and composer; b. Münster, Jan. 28, 1832; d. Braunfels-on-the-Lahn, Sept. 7, 1902. He studied with Schindler (Beethoven's disciple and biographer) in Münster and Frankfurt. After further study in Berlin, Cologne, Brussels, Bremen, Hanover, and

Leipzig (where he also gave piano recitals), he went to Munich in 1854; was teacher at the Munich Cons. (1856-58); then municipal music director at Aachen (1858-64). He returned to Munich in 1864; succeeded Hans von Bülow as conductor of the Munich court theater in 1869; became 1st Kapellmeister in 1870. Under unfavorable conditions (against Wagner's wishes) he prepared and conducted the first performances of *Das Rheingold* (Sept. 22, 1869) and *Die Walküre* (June 26, 1870). In 1877 he became court conductor at Dresden; in 1882 Schuch was promoted to take his place; thereafter Wüllner conducted the Berlin Philharmonic (1883-84); and on Oct. 1, 1884, succeeded Hiller as director of the Cologne Cons., later becoming also municipal music director, which posts he held until his death. He was an excellent conductor in both opera and symph. concerts; directed the Lower Rhine Music Festivals in 1864, 1886, and 1890. He was highly esteemed as a teacher, and made a good name for himself as a composer; for the choral classes of the Munich School of Music he wrote the valuable and practical 'Chorübungen der Münchener Musikschule' (1867; new ed. by E. Schwickerath, Munich, 1931). —Works: vocal with orch.: *Die Flucht der heiligen Familie; Heinrich der Finkler; Deutscher Siegesgesang; Lied und Leben;* Psalm 98; Psalm 127; church music a cappella: 2 Masses; motets; *Miserere* for double chorus; *Stabat Mater* for double chorus; several secular choruses; chamber music; 2 piano sonatas and other piano pieces; songs. His additional recitatives to Weber's *Oberon* have been adopted in many German opera houses. —Cf. O. Klauwell, *Studien und Erinnerungen* (Langensalza, 1906); E. Wolff, ed., *Johannes Brahms im Briefwechsel mit Franz Wüllner* (Berlin, 1922; with a list of works); J. Wüllner, *Johannes Brahms in seiner Lebensfreundschaft mit Franz Wüllner,* in 'Die Musik' (March, 1942).

Wüllner, Ludwig, distinguished German singer; son of Franz Wüllner; b. Münster, Aug. 19, 1858; d. Berlin, March 19, 1938. He studied Germanic philology at the universities of Munich, Berlin, and Strasbourg, and took the degree of *Dr. phil.;* taught Germanic philology at the Akademie in Münster (1884-87), and sang occasionally in concert; his musical training began only in 1887, when he took a course of study at the Cologne Cons. A second change of vocation brought him to the Meiningen court theater, where he appeared as an actor of heroic parts in the spoken drama (1889-95); became friendly with Brahms, who commended his singing of German folksongs. In 1895 he gave song recitals in Berlin with such acclaim that he decided to devote himself mainly to lieder. He then made tours of all Europe, arousing tremendous enthusiasm; his first recital in N. Y. (Nov. 15, 1908) was a sensational success, and he followed it by one extensive tour of the U. S. and then another (1909-10). His peculiar distinction was his ability to give an actor's impersonation of the character of each song, introducing an element of drama on the concert stage. —Cf. F. Ludwig, *L. Wüllner. Sein Leben und seine Kunst* (Leipzig, 1931).

Wunderer, Alexander, Austrian oboist, composer, and teacher; b. Vienna, April 11, 1877; d. Zinkenbach, near St. Gilgen (Salzkammergut), Dec. 29, 1955. He taught the oboe and other wind instruments at the State Academy of Music in Vienna (1919-37); wrote chamber music; was co-author of a book on orchestration. After 1945 he taught oboe classes at the Salzburg Mozarteum.

Wunsch, Hermann, German composer; b. Neuss, Aug. 9, 1884; d. Berlin, Dec. 21, 1954. He studied in Düsseldorf and Cologne and later at the Hochschule für Musik in Berlin, where he subsequently taught (prof., 1945). He composed 6 symphonies, of which the 5th won the Schubert Memorial Prize (German section) of the Columbia Phonograph Co. contest (Schubert Centennial, 1928). Other works include the chamber operas *Bianca* (Weimar, May 22, 1927), *Don Juans Sohn* (Weimar, 1928), and *Franzosenzeit* (Schwerin, 1933); 2 Masses; *Südpolkantate* for chorus and orch.; *Helden* for chorus and orch. (Berlin, 1941); 3 violin concertos; concerto for piano and small orch.; *Kleine Lustspielsuite* for orch.; *Fest auf Monbijou,* suite for chamber orch.; *Erntelied,* a symph. with a concluding chorus.

Wünsch, Walther, ethnomusicologist; b. Gablonz, Bohemia, July 23, 1908. He studied musicology in Prague with Becking, and later in Vienna; then taught in Prague; was teacher in Graz until 1945; then moved to Gratkorn. He publ. *Die Geigentechnik der südslawischen Guslaren* (Brno, 1934); *Heldensänger in Südosteuropa* (Leipzig, 1937); various other essays on folk music in European periodicals.

Würfel, Wilhelm, pianist and composer; b. Planian, Bohemia, 1791; d. Vienna, April

22, 1852. After touring as concert pianist he became prof. at the Warsaw Cons. (1815); in 1826 became assistant conductor at the Kärthnertor Theater in Vienna. He composed an opera, *Rübezahl* (Vienna, March 10, 1825); a piano concerto; many other piano pieces in a bravura style.

Wurlitzer, Rudolph H., American instrument dealer; b. Cincinnati, Dec. 30, 1873; d. there, May 27, 1948. He was the son of the founder of the Wurlitzer Co. (established 1856); studied violin at the Cincinnati College of Music and later in Berlin with Emanuel Wirth. He became secretary-treasurer of the Wurlitzer Co. in 1899; later vice-president, and finally president. In 1929 the company purchased 64 string instruments from the Rodman Wanamaker Collection, including some fine specimens. Several richly illustrated catalogues of string instruments in the Wurlitzer Collection have been issued: *Old Master Violins, Violas, Violoncellos* (Cincinnati, 1915); *Masterpieces of the Great Violin Makers* (N. Y., 1917; 2nd ed., 1918); *Rare Violins, Violas, Violoncellos of the 17th, 18th, and 19th Centuries* (N. Y., 1931); *Rare Bows for Violin, Viola, Violoncello, by Makers of the 18th and 19th Centuries* (N. Y., 1931); *Rare Violas by Celebrated Makers of the 16th-19th Centuries* (N. Y., 1940).

Wurm, Marie, noted English pianist; b. Southampton, May 18, 1860; d. Munich, Jan. 21, 1938. She was of German extraction; went to study in Germany; was a pupil at the Stuttgart Cons., and later studied piano with Joseph Wieniawski, Raff, and Clara Schumann; then took up theory and composition in London with Stanford and Arthur Sullivan. She gave numerous recitals in London and in Germany; lived for some years as teacher in Hanover, and in 1911 moved to Berlin; in 1925, settled in Munich. Apart from her principal career, she also conducted orchestras; organized a women's orch. in Berlin (inaugural concert, Oct. 10, 1899); composed a number of works, including the opera *Die Mitschuldigen* (Leipzig, 1923); a piano concerto; a string quartet; a violin sonata; a cello sonata; a piano sonata; numerous piano pieces (*Valse de concert, Barcarolle, Sylph Dance, Suite,* gavottes, mazurkas, etc.); author of *Das ABC der Musik,* and *Praktische Vorschule zur Caland-Lehre* (1914). —Her sisters, **Adela** and **Mathilda,** changed their name to **Verne** (q. v.) and pursued their careers in England.

Würz, Anton, German composer and musicologist; b. Munich, July 14, 1903; studied with Sandberger at the Munich Univ.; was music critic of the 'Münchner Telegraph-Zeitung' (1927-45). His works include several song cycles, to words by Rilke, Eichendorff, etc.; a string quintet; 4 string quartets; a string trio; a violin sonata; a viola sonata; publ. numerous opera and operetta guide books for the Reclam ed.

Würz, Richard, German composer and pedagogue; b. Munich, Feb. 15, 1885; studied with Max Reger; then became active as music critic and teacher in Munich; publ. numerous songs and piano pieces; also didactic works; ed. and contributed to *Max Reger,* a collection of studies (4 vols.; Munich, 1920-23). —Cf. W. Zentner, *Richard Würz,* in 'Neue Musikzeitschrift' (Jan., 1950).

Wüst, Philipp, German conductor; b. Oppau, May 3, 1894; after 1919 was engaged as conductor and music director in Mannheim, Oldenburg, Breslau (1936-43), and Stuttgart (1943-45); in 1946 he settled in Saarbrücken as general music director.

Wustmann, Rudolf, German musicologist; b. Leipzig, Jan. 5, 1872; d. Bühlau, near Dresden, Aug. 15, 1916. He was the son of the bibliographer Gustav Wustmann; studied philology, history, and musicology (with Kretzschmar) at the Universities of Munich and Leipzig; was a teacher of academic subjects in Leipzig (1895-1900); later lived in Bolzano, Italy, and finally in Bühlau, devoting himself to philological and historical research. He publ. *Musikalische Bilder* (1907); *Musikgeschichte Leipzigs* (Leipzig, 1909; vol. I only, up to the middle of the 17th century; vols. II and III written by Schering); *J. S. Bachs Kantatentexte* (1913); *Die Hofweise Walthers von der Vogelweide* (Strasbourg, 1913); numerous articles in German musical periodicals.

Wyk (vīk), **Arnold van,** South African composer; b. Calvinia, Cape Province, April 26, 1916. He studied in London; worked with the B.B.C. (1939-44); then returned to South Africa as a member of the faculty of the Univ. of Cape Town. His compositions include *Southern Cross,* for orch. (1943); symph No. 1 (1944); *Christmas Oratorio* (1949); *Rhapsody* for orch. (Cape Town Festival, March 4, 1952); symph. No. 2 (Cape Town Festival, March 13, 1952); *5 Elegies* for string quartet (1941); the song cycle *Liefde en Verlatenheid* (Festival of the International Society for Contemporary Music, Haifa, May 31, 1954); string quartet No. 1 (1957). —Cf. H. Ferguson, *Arnold van Wyk: Recently Published Works,* in 'Tempo' (Summer, 1958).

Wylde, Henry, English conductor, composer, and educator; b. Bushey, Herts, May 22, 1822; d. London, March 13, 1890. He was the son of Henry Wylde, London organist and composer of glees. He studied piano with Moscheles and Cipriani Potter at the Royal Academy of Music; was active as church organist. In 1852 he founded in London the New Philharmonic Society, and conducted its concerts in cooperation with Berlioz, Lindpaintner, and Spohr for 3 seasons; took complete charge of its concerts in 1858 and conducted them until 1879. In 1861 he founded the London Academy of Music; supervised the building of St. George's Hall (1867) to house it; in 1863 became prof. of music there, retaining this post until his death. —Compositions: *Paradise Lost,* oratorio after Milton (London, May 11, 1853); piano concerto (London, April 14, 1852); songs; piano pieces. —Books: *The Science of Music* (1865); *Music in Its Art-Mysteries* (1867); *Modern Counterpoint in Major Keys* (1873); *Occult Principles of Music* (1881); *Music as an Educator* (1882); *The Evolution of the Beautiful in Sound* (1888).

Wyman, Addison P., American violinist and composer; b. Cornish, N. H., June 23, 1832; d. Washington, Pa., April 15, 1872. He was a violin teacher; founded a music school at Claremont, N. H., in 1869. Publ. popular piano pieces (166 op. numbers): *Silvery Waves, Woodland Echoes, Moonlight Musings, Music among the Pines,* etc.

Wyschnegradsky, Iwan. See **Vyshnegradsky.**

Wyzewa (vē-zŭ-văh'), **Théodore de** (real name Wyzewski), noted musicologist; b. Kalushin, Russian Poland, Sept. 12, 1862; d. Paris, April 17, 1917. In 1869 his parents settled in Châtellerault, France, where he received his education; in 1884 he founded in Paris, with Édouard Dujardin, the 'Revue wagnérienne,' which, until it ceased publication in 1888, did much to advance the cause of Wagner in France. His importance as a musicologist rests upon his researches concerning the life and work of Mozart, about whom he publ. new facts in *Recherches sur la Jeunesse de Mozart,* in the 'Revue des Deux Mondes' (1904-05), and in *W. A. Mozart. Sa Vie musicale et son Œuvre de l'enfance à la pleine maturité* (with G. de Saint-Foix; 2 vols., Paris, 1912; 3 more vols. added by Saint-Foix in 1937, in 1940, and in 1946). He also wrote *Littérature wagnérienne en France* (in 'Revue Politique et Littéraire,' Sept. 15, 1894) and *Beethoven et Wagner* (Paris, 1898; new ed., 1914), besides several books dealing with religion, art, and philosophy. Edited 20 piano sonatas of Clementi with a biographical notice (vol. I, Paris, 1917; vol. II, posthumous, brought out by Henry Expert).

X

Xanrof (zahn-rohf'), **Léon,** French composer of popular music; b. Paris, Dec. 9, 1867; d. there, May 17, 1953. His real name was Léon Fourneau; Xanrof is an anagram of its Latin equivalent *(fornax).* He was a lawyer by profession; from 1890 produced light stage pieces in the Paris theaters; the chansonette *Le Fiacre,* which he wrote for Yvette Guilbert, achieved great popularity. He also contributed music criticism to various Paris papers.

Xenakis, Yannis, Greek composer; b. Athens, May 29, 1922. He studied engineering, obtaining a diploma at the Athens Polytechnic Institute. In 1948 he went to Paris; studied architecture with Le Corbusier, and composition at the École Normale de Musique (with Honegger and Milhaud) and at the Cons. (with Messiaen). His early works reflect his interest in Greek folklore; he then wrote some music in the dodecaphonic technique; in 1952 he adopted a novel method of 'probabilistic' composition, based on a calculation of probabilities of recurrence of certain notes and rhythms. As an architect, he collaborated with Le Corbusier in the design of the Pavillon Philips at the 1958 World's Fair in Brussels; wrote parts of the *Poème Électronique* (with Varèse) for the exhibit. In 1956 he received a stipend of 12,000 Swiss francs from the Fondation Européenne de la Culture. —Works: *Métastasis,* for orch. (Donaueschingen, Oct. 15, 1955); *Pithoprakta* for string orch. (Munich, March 8, 1957); *Achorripsis,* for 21 instruments (Brussels, July 20, 1958).

Xyndas (ksün'-dahs), **Spyridon,** Greek composer; b. Corfu, June 8, 1812; d. Athens, Nov. 25, 1896. He studied in Italy, and appeared as a guitar player; composed many attractive popular Greek songs; several operas to Italian librettos *(Il Conte Giuliano, I due pretendenti,* etc.); also *The Parliamentary*

Candidate (Athens, March, 1888), which was probably the first opera with a Greek text. He became blind toward the end of his life.

Y

Yamada, Kôsçak, eminent Japanese composer and conductor; b. Tokyo, June 9, 1886. He studied at the Imperial Academy of Music in Tokyo; then in Berlin with Max Bruch (1909-13). Returning to Japan in 1914, he organized the Tokyo Philharmonic Orch. On Oct. 16, 1918, he conducted a program of Japanese music in Carnegie Hall, N. Y., including some of his own works *(Festival of Autumn, The Dark Gate, Flower of Madara,* and an *Oriental Suite);* appeared as guest conductor in the U. S. until 1921; in 1930, and again in 1933, he conducted in Russia; in 1937 he toured Europe. Most of his MSS were destroyed during the air raid on Tokyo on May 25, 1945; several scores have been restored from the extant orchestral parts. —Works: operas *Alladine et Palomides,* after Maeterlinck (1913), *The Depraved Heavenly Maiden* (1908; Tokyo, Dec. 3, 1929), *Ayame (The Sweet Flag;* Tokyo, Feb. 24, 1935), *The Black Ships* (Tokyo, 1940), *Yoake (The Dawn;* Nov. 28, 1940), *Hsiang Fei* (1946); cantatas: *Bonno-Koru* (Tokyo, Oct. 9, 1931) and *The Dawn of the Orient* (Tokyo, July 7, 1941); a symph. (Tokyo, Dec. 6, 1914); *Ode to Meiji* for chorus and orch. (Tokyo, April 26, 1925); *Homage to Showa,* symph. poem (Tokyo, May 13, 1939); *Kamikaze,* symph. suite (1944); chamber music; nearly 1,000 choral pieces and songs.

Yardumian, Richard, American composer; b. (of Armenian parents) Philadelphia, April 5, 1917; self-taught in music. His compositions reflect the spirit of Armenian folksongs and religious melodies. His *Armenian Suite* for orch. was performed for the 1st time by the Philadelphia Orch. on March 5, 1954. Other symph. works (also brought out by the Philadelphia Orch.) are *Desolate City* (April 6, 1945) and a violin concerto (March 30, 1951).

Yasser, Joseph, noted organist and musicologist; b. Lodz, Poland, April 16, 1893. He studied at the Moscow Cons. (graduated 1917), and became organ teacher there (1918-20); 1921, lecturer for the music dept. of the Siberian Board of Education; 1922, conducted a choral society in Shanghai; came to the U. S. and was organist of the Free Synagogue in N. Y. (1927-28); and at the Temple Rodeph Sholom, N. Y. (from 1929); held various positions in musicological societies. He publ. *A Theory of Evolving Tonality* (N. Y., 1932), in which he offered an ingenious hypothesis of the origin of the pentatonic and heptatonic scales; contributed a series of articles, *Medieval Quartal Harmony,* to the 'Mus. Quarterly' (April, July, 1937, and July, 1938; also publ. separately, N. Y., 1938); publ. many other articles and reviews.

Yon, Pietro Alessandro, eminent organist and composer; b. Settimo Vittone, Italy, Aug. 8, 1886; d. Huntington, L. I., N. Y., Nov. 22, 1943. He studied with Fumagalli at the Milan Cons.; winning a scholarship for piano, he continued his studies at the Turin Cons. (1901-04), and at the Santa Cecilia in Rome with Remigio Renzi (organ) and Sgambati (piano), graduating in 1905 with 1st prize; then was organist at St. Peter's, Rome (1905-07). In 1907 he emigrated to the U. S.; was organist at St. Francis-Xavier's, N. Y., from 1907 till 1919, and again from 1921 till 1926. In 1926 he was appointed organist of St. Patrick's Cathedral in N. Y.; became a U. S. citizen in 1921. He gave numerous organ recitals in Europe and the U. S. —Works: Mass in G major; *Messa Melodica* for chorus, string orch., horns, and organ; other Masses; *Jerusalem Surge,* motet for men's voices and orch.; other motets a cappella and with organ; oratorio *The Triumph of St. Patrick* (N. Y., April 29, 1934); many organ pieces; one of these, *Gesù Bambino* (1917), became very popular in numerous vocal and instrumental arrangements; other organ works are: *Concerto Gregoriano,* 3 sonatas, 2 rhapsodies, 12 divertimentos, *Natale in Sicilia, Preludio Pastorale, Toccata, Echo* (double canon); piano pieces *(Nena, Mountain Slopes, Alpine Nocturne, Rain);* songs *(Ave Maria, They Call Him Jesus, Christ Triumphant).*

Yonge (Young), Nicholas, English musician and editor; b. Lewes; d. London (buried Oct. 23), 1619; was a chorister at St. Paul's Cathedral. He translated and arranged a number of Italian madrigals, which he publ. in 2 books under the general title *Musica Transalpina* (1588; 1597). —Cf. A. Obertello, *Madrigali italiani in Inghilterra* (Milan, 1949).

York, Francis Lodowick, American organist and teacher; b. Ontonagon, Mich., March 9, 1861; d. there, Jan. 13, 1955. He studied piano in Boston and Detroit; in 1892 became a pupil of Guilmant in Paris (organ and composition); was piano and organ teacher at the State Normal Cons., Ypsilanti, Mich. (1896-1902); director of the Detroit Cons. (1902-27); in 1930, elected chairman of the board of the Detroit Institute of Mus. Art; Mus. Doc. *(hon. c.)*, Univ. of Michigan, 1922. He publ. a Te Deum, choruses, songs, and organ pieces; in MS, among other works, a comic opera, *The Inca.* Author of *Harmony Simplified* (1897; revised and enlarged ed., 1901) and *Counterpoint Simplified* (1907).

Yost, Gaylord, American violinist and composer; b. Fayette, Ohio, Jan. 28, 1888; d. Wauseon, Ohio, Oct. 10, 1958. He studied music in Toledo and Detroit; later with Issaye Barmas (violin) in Berlin; appeared in recitals in Europe and America; head of the violin dept. at Indiana College of Music, Indianapolis (1915-21); head of the violin dept. at the Pittsburgh Mus. Institute (1921-43). Founded the Yost String Quartet in 1925. In 1951, he became editor and publisher of the 'Fayette Review,' founded by his father; from 1954 to 1957 served as mayor of Fayette. He publ. *The Yost System* in 8 vols. (1932; an abridged ed. as *The Yost Violin Method,* in 3 vols.); also *Basic Principles of Violin Playing* (1940).

Yost, Michel, famous French clarinetist; b. Paris, 1754; d. there, July 5, 1786. He studied with Beer. Publ. 14 clarinet concertos; 30 quartets for clarinet and strings; 8 books of duos for clarinets; *Airs variés* for clarinet with viola and bass.

Youdin, Mikhail Alexeyevitch, Russian composer; b. St. Petersburg, Sept. 29, 1893; d. Kazan, Feb. 8, 1948. He studied at the St. Petersburg Cons., graduating in 1923; joined its staff as instructor in 1926. He went to Kazan in 1942, and taught at the Cons. there until his death. —Works: opera *Farida* (1943); cantata *Song of Spring and Joy* (Leningrad, Nov. 25, 1936); *Heroic Oratorio* (1937); *Poem 1926* for orch. (Leningrad, March 30, 1927); other symph. pieces; 2 string quartets; piano sonata; organ toccata; choruses; songs; arrangements of folksongs.

Youll, Henry, English composer; flourished c. 1600. He publ. *Canzonets to three voyces* (1608), a collection of 24 vocal pieces *(Slow, slow, fresh fount,* to Ben Jonson's words; *Pipe, shepherds, pipe;* etc.). It was republished in 'The English Madrigal School' (vol. XXVIII).

Youmans, Vincent, American composer of popular music; b. New York, Sept. 27, 1898; d. Denver, Colo., April 5, 1946. He studied engineering; then was active in business; enlisted in the U. S. Navy during World War I, and was in the entertainment unit at the Great Lakes Training Station; in 1918 he entered the field of music publishing in N. Y. In 1921, his musical comedy *Two Little Girls in Blue* was produced in N. Y.; there followed *Wildflower,* and the immensely successful *No, No, Nanette* (1925) containing the celebrated song *Tea for Two.* Other musical comedies were *A Night Out* (1925), *Oh! Please* (1926), *Hit the Deck* (1927), *Rainbow* (1928), *Great Day* (1929), and *Through the Years* (1932). In 1933 he went to Hollywood to complete his score for the film *Flying Down to Rio*; soon afterwards illness (tuberculosis) forced him to abandon further work. Among his songs, the following were hits: *Bambalina; I Want to Be Happy; Hallelujah; Sometimes I'm Happy; Great Day; Without a Song; Time on My Hands; Through the Years; Oh, Me, Oh, My, Oh, You; Carioca; Orchids in the Moonlight; Drums in My Heart; More Than You Know; Rise 'n' Shine.*

Young, Alexander, English tenor; b. London, Oct. 18, 1920. He studied in London and Naples; joined the Glyndebourne Opera Co., singing minor parts, then rising to prominence; obtained signal success as Tom Rakewell in Stravinsky's *The Rake's Progress,* and also distinguished himself as a Mozart singer; has given numerous recitals in England.

Young, Anthony, English organist and composer; b. c. 1685; d. after 1720. He was organist at various churches in London; wrote numerous songs; he is chiefly known as one of the composers falsely credited with the authorship of the tune of *God Save the King.*

Young, Cecilia, English singer; b. London, c. 1710; d. there, Oct. 6, 1789. She made her appearance at the Drury Lane Theatre on March 4, 1730; in 1735 was engaged by Handel for his opera company; married T. A. Arne on March 15, 1737; went with him to Dublin in 1742, and sang soprano parts in his works presented there *(Comus, Judgment of Paris, Alfred,* etc.). — Cf. W. H. Cummings, *Dr. Arne and 'Rule Britannia!'* (London, 1912).

Young, John Matthew Wilson, English organist and composer; b. Durham, Dec.

17, 1822; d. West Norwood, March 4, 1897. In 1850 he became organist of the Lincoln Cathedral, retiring shortly before his death. He composed a sacred cantata, *The Return of Israel to Palestine,* and numerous church services.

Young, Percy Marshall, English writer on music and composer; b. Northwich, Cheshire, May 17, 1912. He studied in Cambridge with E. J. Dent, and at Trinity College, Dublin (Mus. D.). Returning to England, he occupied various posts as teacher. His compositions include *On Eastnor Knoll* (after Masefield) for voice and orch.; *The Stolen Child* (after Yeats) for voice, women's chorus, and orch.; a *Fugal Concerto* for piano and orch.; *Au Moyen-âge* for viola and orch.; several suites for string orch. on themes from the 17th century; edited and arranged a *Pageant of England's Music* (1939), *Samuel Pepys Music Book* (16 pieces known to Pepys), arranged for recorder or voice (1942), *Carols for the 12 Days of Christmas* (50 carols; London, 1952). —Books: *Handel,* in the 'Master Musicians' series (London, 1947); *The Oratorios of Handel* (London, 1949); *Vaughan Williams,* in the 'Contemporary Composers' series (London, 1953); *A Critical Dictionary of Composers and Their Music* (London, 1954; in America as *Biographical Dictionary of Composers); Elgar, O. M.: A Study of a Musician* (London, 1955); *The Story of Song* (London, 1955); *Instrumental Music* (London, 1955); *In Search of Music* (essays; London, 1956); *Concerto* (London, 1957); *Symphony* (London, 1957); also biographies for young people, *Music Makers* (London, 1951; N. Y., 1953); *More Music Makers* (London, 1955); edited *Letters of Edward Elgar and Other Writings* (London, 1956).

Young, Polly (Mary), English singer; b. London, c. 1745; d. there, Sept. 20, 1799. She lived in Dublin with her aunt (Mrs. T. A. Arne), and made her début as a singer upon her return to London in 1762. In 1766 she married François-Hippolyte Barthélemon (q. v.); their daughter, Cecilia Maria (Mrs. Henslowe), was a talented musician.

Young, Victor, American pianist and composer; b. Bristol, Tenn., April 9, 1889. He studied piano with Isidor Philipp in Paris; toured in England and the U. S. as accompanist to prominent singers; held various teaching positions; was music director in Thomas A. Edison's Experimental Laboratory in West Orange, N. J., conducting tonal tests and making piano recordings under Edison's personal supervision (1919-27). He wrote the musical score for one of the earliest sound motion pictures, *In Old California;* composed some 300 film scores altogether. Other works: for orch.: *Scherzetto; Jeep; In the Great Smokies; Charm Assembly Line Ballet;* etc.; piano pieces (including *Under a Spanish Moon);* songs *(Gossip, Cuckoo Clock,* etc.).

Young, Victor, American composer of popular music; b. Chicago, Aug. 8, 1900; d. Palm Springs, Calif., Nov. 10, 1956. As a youth he was sent to Poland, where he studied violin at the Warsaw Cons., and made his début with the Warsaw Philharmonic. He returned to Chicago in 1914, and after further study, became active on the radio. In 1935 he went to Hollywood, where he wrote film music. Some of his songs became famous *(Sweet Sue, Street of Dreams, Can't We Talk It Over, My Romance, Ghost of a Chance, Love Letters, Golden Earrings, Stella by Starlight, My Foolish Heart, Song of Delilah,* etc.). Shortly before his death, he completed the musical score for the motion picture *Around the World in 80 Days* (1956).

Young, William, English violinist, flutist, and composer; date of birth unknown; d. London, Dec. 21, 1671. He was attached to the court of the Archduke Ferdinand Karl in Innsbruck, where he publ. a book of 30 *Sonate a 3, 4, 5 voci con allemande, corranti* . . . dedicated to the Archduke (1653). In 1660 he was a flutist in the private orch. of Charles II in London. The following year he also played the violin. Other pieces by Young include *Ayre, Almain and 2 Sarabands* in Playford's *Musick's Recreation on the Lyra Viol* (1652), and *Fantasies for 3 viols* in Playford's *Treasury of Musick* (1669); numerous MSS are in the Bodleian Library, Oxford; Gresham College, London; Corporation Music Library, Manchester; and in some private collections. —Cf. W. Gillies Whittaker, *The Concerted Music of William Young* (Oxford, 1931).

Youssoupoff, Prince **Nicolas,** Russian musical dilettante and writer on musical subjects; b. St. Petersburg, 1827; d. Baden-Baden, Aug. 3, 1891. He was a pupil of Vieuxtemps (violin), and was an eager collector of violin literature; had a private orch. in his palace in St. Petersburg, but lived abroad for many years. He composed a programmatic symph., *Gonzalvo de Córdova*, with violin obbligato; *Concerto symphonique* for violin and orch.; several pieces for violin and piano (*Féeries de la scène, Hallucination, Chant d'amour, Plainte, Saltimbanques*, etc.); publ. an interesting book on violin making, *Luthomonographie, historique et raisonnée* (Frankfurt, 1856; printed in French in Munich; subsequent editions, Paris) and *Musique sacrée suivie d'un choix de morceaux de chants d'église* (Paris, 1862, as vol. I of a projected *Histoire de la musique en Russie;* contains a valuable study of Russian neumes and examples of traditional chants). Themes from Youssoupoff's *Ballet d'Espagne* were used by Bériot for a group of 6 violin duets.

Yradier (ē-rah-dyehr'), **Sebastián**, Spanish composer; b. Sauciego, Álava, Jan. 20, 1809; d. Vitoria, Dec. 6, 1865. He composed theater music; after 1851 became singing master to the Empress Eugénie in Paris; for some time lived in Cuba. He publ. a number of melodious songs in a Spanish manner; one of them, *El Arreglito*, subtitled *Chanson havanaise*, was used by Bizet for the famous Habanera in *Carmen;* Bizet retained the key and the pattern of the accompaniment, making some changes in the melody to adjust it to French words. Yradier's other songs that became famous are *La Paloma* and *Ay Chiquita!* In Paris he publ. 2 collections, 'Écho d'Espagne' (8 songs) and 'Fleurs d'Espagne' (25 songs). —Cf. E. Istel, *Bizet und 'Carmen'* (Stuttgart, 1927); J. Tiersot, *Bizet and Spanish Music*, in the 'Mus. Quarterly' (Oct., 1927).

Yriarte, Tomás de, Spanish poet and musician; b. Orotava, Tenerife, Canary Islands, Sept. 18, 1750; d. Santa María, near Cádiz, Sept. 17, 1791. He was secretary at the Chancellery of State in Madrid and chief archivist at the Ministry of War. His literary works include a long didactic poem, *La Música* (Madrid, 1779; English transl., 1807). He composed 'tonadillas' and some vocal and instrumental music. —Cf. E. Cotarelo y Mori, *Yriarte y su época* (Madrid, 1897); J. Subirá, *El Compositor Yriarte y el cultivo español del melólogo*, 2 vols. (Madrid, 1949-50).

Ysaÿe (ē-zah-ē'), **Eugène**, famous Belgian violinist and conductor; b. Liège, July 16, 1858; d. Brussels, May 12, 1931. At the age of 5 he began to study violin with his father, a theater conductor; at the age of 7 he was enrolled at the Cons. of Liège as a pupil of Désiré Heynberg; then studied with Rodolphe Massart there; in 1867, obtained 2nd prize for violin playing (sharing it with Ovide Musin); in 1868, 1st prize for violin and chamber music. Still a very young boy, he played in his father's orchestras; in 1876 he was sent to Brussels to study with Henryk Wieniawski, and later was also a pupil of Vieuxtemps. After a sojourn in Bordeaux, he became concertmaster of Bilse's orch. in Berlin; appeared as soloist at Pauline Lucca's concerts in Cologne and Aachen; in Germany he met Anton Rubinstein, who took him to Russia, where he spent 2 winters; also toured Norway. In 1883 he settled in Paris, where he met César Franck, Vincent d'Indy, etc. and gave successful concerts; formed a duo with the pianist Raoul Pugno, and started a long series of concerts with him, establishing a new standard of excellence. In 1887 he married Louise Bourdeau; César Franck dedicated his violin sonata to him as a wedding present; Ysaÿe's interpretation of this work made it famous. In 1886 he was named prof. at the Cons. of Brussels (resigned in 1898); in 1886 he also organized the Ysaÿe Quartet (with Crickboom, Léon Van Hout, and Joseph Jacob); Debussy dedicated his string quartet to Ysaÿe's group, which gave its first performance at the Société Nationale, Paris, on Dec. 29, 1893. In 1889 he made successful appearances in England; on Nov. 16, 1894, he made his American début, playing the Beethoven violin concerto with the N. Y. Philharmonic, and created a sensation by his virtuosity. He revisited America many times, with undiminished acclaim. He began his career as a conductor in 1894 and established his own orch. in Brussels, the 'Société des Concerts Ysaÿe.' When the Germans invaded Belgium in 1914 he fled to London, where he remained during World War I. On April 5, 1918, he made his American début as conductor with the Cincinnati Symph. Orch., and also led the Cincinnati May Festival in that year. His success was so great that he was offered the permanent position as conductor of the Cincinnati Symph. Orch., which he held from 1918 to 1922. He then returned to Belgium and resumed leadership of the 'Société des Concerts Ysaÿe.' After the death of his 1st wife, he married, on July 9, 1927, an American pupil, Jeannette Dincin (b. Brooklyn, Aug. 26, 1902). —Ysaÿe's style of playing is best described as heroic; but his art was equally convincing in the expression of moods of exquisite delicacy and tenderness; his frequent employment of 'tempo rubato' produced an effect of elasticity without distorting the melodic line. Ysaÿe was also a composer. His works include 8 violin concertos; 6 violin sonatas; *Poème nocturne,* for violin, cello, and strings; *Les Harmonies du soir,* for string quartet and string orch.; divertimento for violin and orch.; *Méditation* for cello and string orch.; *Chant d'hiver* for violin and chamber orch.; *Trio de concert,* for 2 violins, viola, and orch.; *Amitié,* for 2 violins and orch. At the age of 70 he began the composition of an opera in the Walloon language, *Piér li Houïeu (Peter the Miner),* which was produced in Liège on March 4, 1931, in the presence of the composer, who was brought to the theater in an invalid's chair, suffering from the extreme ravages of diabetes, which had necessitated the amputation of his left foot. He began the composition of a 2nd Walloon opera, *L'Avierge di Pire (La Vierge de Pierre),* but had no time to complete it. —In 1937 Queen Elizabeth of Belgium inaugurated the annual Prix International Eugène Ysaÿe in Brussels; the first winner was the famous Russian violinist, David Oistrakh. —Cf. M. Pincherle, *Feuillets d'histoire du violon* (Paris, 1927); J. Quitin, *Eugène Ysaÿe: Étude biographique et critique* (Brussels, 1938); E. Christen, *Ysaÿe* (Geneva, 1946; 2nd ed., 1947); Antoine Ysaÿe and B. Ratcliffe, *Ysaÿe: His Life, Work and Influence* (London, 1947); Antoine Ysaÿe, *Eugène Ysaÿe: sa vie . . . d'après les documents receuillis par son fils* (Brussels, 1948; a considerably altered version of the preceding).

Ysaÿe, Théophile, Belgian pianist and composer; brother of Eugène Ysaÿe; b. Verviers, March 2, 1865; d. Nice, March 24, 1918. He was a pupil at the Liège Cons.; then studied at the Kullak Academy in Berlin, and also took lessons from César Franck in Paris; returning to Belgium, he became director of the Académie de Musique in Brussels; was noted as a fine ensemble player, and gave sonata recitals with his brother; during the latter's absence on tours, he also conducted the 'Société des Concerts Ysaÿe' in Brussels. After the invasion of Belgium in 1914, he went with his brother to London; when the Zeppelin air raids began, he left England and went to Nice, where he remained until his death. He was a prolific composer; his brother conducted a concert of Théophile's works in Brussels, on Nov. 6, 1904, including the premières of a symph. in F major (his best-known composition) and the symph. poem *Le Cygne.* Other works are: a piano concerto; symph. poems *(Les Abeilles, La Forêt et l'Oiseau); Fantaisie sur un thème populaire wallon,* for orch.; a piano quintet; piano pieces; a Requiem.

Yuon, Paul. See **Juon.**

Yurgenson, Peter. See **Jurgenson.**

Yussupov, Prince **Nicolai.** See **Youssoupoff.**

Yvain, Maurice, French composer of musical comedies; b. Paris, Feb. 12, 1891. Among his successful productions are *Ta bouche* (1922), *Pas sur la bouche* (1925), *Bouche à bouche* (1936), and film scores *(Rien qu'un baiser; J'ai tant d'amour,* etc.). He also produced a ballet, *Blanche neige* (Paris Opéra, Nov. 14, 1951).

Yzac. See **Isaac.**

Z

Zabaleta, Nicanor, Spanish harpist; b. San Sebastian, Jan. 7, 1907. He studied at the Madrid Cons.; in 1925, went to Paris to study with Marcel Tournier; toured in Europe, South America, and the U. S. He is noted for his efforts to increase the number of works available for the harp, both by bringing to light neglected compositions of old composers, and by prompting modern composers to write music for the harp. In 1958 he made a long European tour as soloist with leading orchestras.

Zabalza y Olaso, Don **Dámaso,** Spanish composer and pianist; b. Irurita, Navarra, Dec. 11, 1833; d. Madrid, Feb. 25, 1894. He studied with Mariano García; in 1858 settled in Madrid as a piano teacher at the National Cons. He publ. a number of piano pieces, many of which became very popular; also piano studies that were used at the Paris Cons., in Italy, and in Spain.

Zabel (tsăh'-bĕl), **Albert Heinrich,** German harpist; b. Berlin, 1830; d. St. Petersburg, Feb. 21, 1910. He studied at the Institut für Kirchenmusik in Berlin; toured Germany, Russia, England, and America with Gungl's orch.; solo harpist at the Royal Opera in Berlin (1848-51), and of the Imperial Ballet in St. Petersburg (from 1854). In 1862 he joined the staff of the newly-founded St. Petersburg Cons., and held that post until his death. He composed a harp concerto and numerous short pieces for the harp *(Élégie fantastique, Légende, Marguérite au rouet, Am Springbrunnen, Chanson du pêcheur, Warum?, Murmure de cascade,* etc.). Also publ. a harp method (in German, French, and English), and a pamphlet, *A Word to Composers about the*

Practical Employment of the Harp in the Orchestra (St. Petersburg, 1899; in Russian and German).

Zacconi (tsăh-kŏh'-nē), **Lodovico,** Italian music theorist; b. Pesaro, June 11, 1555; d. Fiorenzuola, near Pesaro, March 23, 1627. He was a pupil of Baccusi and A. Gabrieli in Venice; studied theology in Pavia, entered the Order of St. Augustine, and became maestro di cappella at the monastery of his order in Venice; was tenor singer in the court chapel at Graz (1585), and at Munich (1591-95); then returned to Venice. His chief work, *Prattica di Musica,* in 2 parts (Venice, 1592, 1619), contains treatises on mensural theory and counterpoint, detailed descriptions of contemporary musical instruments, and explanations for executing the ornaments in vocal polyphonic music. He also wrote 4 books of *Canoni musicali,* with comments and solutions (publ. by F. Vatielli, Pesaro, 1905); *Ricercari* for organ and 2 collections of examples of counterpoint are still in MS. His MS autobiography (written in 1626) is in the library of the Liceo Musicale, Bologna. —Cf. F. Chrysander, *L. Zacconi als Lehrer des Kunstgesanges,* in 'Vierteljahrsschrift für Musikwissenschaft' (vols. 7, 9, 10; 1891-94; with an epitome of the autobiography); F. Vatielli, *Un Musicista pesarese nel secolo XVI* (Pesaro, 1904); H. Kretzschmar, *L. Zacconis Leben auf Grund seiner Autobiographie,* in 'Jahrbuch der Musikbibliothek Peters' (1910); F. Vatielli, *Notizie su la vita e le opere di L. Zacconi* (Pesaro, 1912).

Zach, Johann, Czech composer; b. Czellakowitz, Bohemia, Nov. 13, 1699; date of death unknown. He was in Prague in 1724, studying with Czernohorsky; was court Kapellmeister in Mainz (1745-56). He composed church music and a number of concertos and other orchestral works, in a style resembling that of the Mannheim School. —Cf. K. M. Komma, *Johann Zach und die tschechischen Musiker im deutschen Umbruch des 18. Jahrhunderts* (dissertation; Kassel, 1938).

Zach, Max (Wilhelm), conductor and viola player; b. Lwów, Aug. 31, 1864; d. St. Louis, Feb. 3, 1921. He studied at the Vienna Cons. with Grün (violin), R. Fuchs (harmony), and Krenn (theory); from 1886 till 1907 was first violist in the Boston Symph. Orch., played the viola in the Adamowski Quartet, and conducted the Boston Pops (1887-97). In 1907 he was appointed conductor of the St. Louis Symph. Orch., and held this post until his death.

Zacharewitsch, Michael, Russian-English violinist; b. Ostrov, Aug. 26, 1879; d. London, Dec. 20, 1953. Through Tchaikovsky's financial assistance, Zacharewitsch was sent to study with Ševčik in Prague; later studied for a short time with Ysaÿe in Brussels. He went to London in 1903, and became a British subject in 1915; toured Australia, New Zealand, and South Africa. He wrote *The New Art of Violin Playing* (1934), and composed *Dunkirk — 1940* (1945), for violin and orch., as well as violin exercises.

Zachau (Zachow), Friedrich Wilhelm, German organist and composer; b. Leipzig, Nov. 19, 1663; d. Halle, Aug. 14, 1712. He studied with his father, who was town musician in Leipzig, and learned to play the organ, violin, oboe, and harpsichord. From 1684 to his death he was organist of the Liebfrauenkirche in Halle, where Handel studied with him as a boy. Max Seiffert publ. Zachau's works in the 'Denkmäler deutscher Tonkunst' (vols. 21, 22); organ pieces, chorale settings, etc., were publ. in Breitkopf & Härtel's 'Sammlung von Präludien, Fugen, etc.' and in 'Organum.'

Zádor, Eugen, Hungarian composer; b. Bátaszék, Nov. 5, 1894. He studied at the Vienna Cons. with Heuberger and in Leipzig with Max Reger (composition), also with Abert, Schering, and Volbach (musicology), becoming *Dr. phil.* with the dissertation, *Wesen und Form der symphonischen Dichtung von Liszt bis Strauss.* In 1921 he became teacher of composition at the New Vienna Cons.; came to the U. S. in 1939; settled in Hollywood as composer of film music. —Works: operas: *Diana* (Budapest, Dec. 22, 1923), *A holtak szigete* (*The Island of the Dead,* Budapest, March 29, 1928), *Rembrandt* (Budapest, 1930), *Azra* (Budapest, Feb. 15, 1936), *Christoph Columbus* (1939); a ballet, *A gépember* (*The Machine-Man;* 1934); for orch.: 4 symphonies (*Romantische Symphonie,* 1922; *Sinfonia tecnica,* 1931; *Tanzsymphonie,* 1936; *Children's Symphony,* 1941); *Bánk bán,* symph. poem (1918), *Variations on a Hungarian Folksong* (1928), *Ungarisches Capriccio* (1935), *Pastorale and Tarantella* (Chicago, Feb. 5, 1942), *Biblical Triptych* (Chicago, Dec. 9, 1943), *Elegie and Dance* (Philadelphia, March 12, 1954); Chamber Concerto for strings, 2 horns, and piano (1930); piano quintet (1933); songs. —Cf. Donald Tovey, *Essays in Musical Analysis* (vol. VI; London, 1939).

Zadora, Michael von, pianist and composer; b. New York (of Polish parents), June 14, 1882; d. there, June 30, 1946. He studied with his father; then at the Paris Cons. (1899), and later with Leschetizky and Busoni. He appeared first as a child prodigy; taught a master class at the Lwów Cons. (1911-12); then at the Institute of Musical Art in N. Y. (1913-14). He transcribed for piano several organ and violin works by Buxtehude and Bach; also composed piano pieces, songs, etc.

Zafred, Mario, Italian critic and composer; b. Trieste, Feb. 21, 1922. He studied with Pizzetti at the Santa Cecilia in Rome. Among his works are 5 symphonies, a *Canto della pace,* for viola and orch. (1951); several string quartets; 3 piano trios; concerto for 2 pianos. In 1949 he became music critic of the Roman daily 'L'Unità.' In conformity with his political philosophy, he employs a simplified idiom of modern music similar to that of Soviet composers. —Cf. G. Viozzi, *Mario Zafred,* in 'Diapason' (Milan, Oct.-Nov., 1951).

Zagiba, Franz, Slovak musicologist; b. Rosenau, Oct. 20, 1912. He studied music and Slavic philology in Bratislava, and later at the Univ. of Vienna; was director of the Musicological Institute at the Slovak Academy of Sciences and Arts, Bratislava (1942-45); in 1947 joined the staff of the Univ. of Vienna; in 1951 established the Austrian branch of the Chopin Society. He publ. *Die Musikdenkmäler der Franziskanerklöster in der Ostslowakei* (Prague, 1940); *Geschichte der slowakischen Musik* (vol. I, Bratislava, 1943; in Czech, with German summary); *Opernführer* (Bratislava, 1947); *Chopin und Wien* (Vienna, 1951); *Tschaikovskij, Leben und Werk* (Zürich, 1953); *Johann L. Bella (1843-1936) und das wiener Musikleben* (Vienna, 1955); numerous valuable articles dealing with music in Slovakia and historical developments in Slavic music.

Zagwijn (zag'-vine), **Henri,** Dutch composer; b. Nieuwer-Amstel, July 17, 1878. He had no formal education in music, but followed the trends of Impressionism, and wrote music in the modern French style. In 1916 he was appointed teacher at the Rotterdam Academy of Music; in 1918, founded (with Sem Dresden) the Society of Modern Composers in the Netherlands; later settled in The Hague. He was a follower of Rudolf Steiner's anthroposophic movement, and publ. a book, *De Muziek in het licht der anthroposophie* (1925); also publ. a biography of Debussy (The Hague, 1940). —Works: *Auferstehung,* an overture (1918); *Weihe-Nacht,* an orchestral prelude (1918); 2 concertantes for piano and orch. (1939; 1946); concertante for flute and orch. (1941); harp concerto (1948); *Nocturne* for wind instruments, harp, and celesta (1918); string sextet (1932); quintet for flute, violin, viola, cello, and harp (1937); *Pastorale* for flute, oboe, and piano (1937); *Mystère,* for harp and piano (1941); trio for flute, oboe, and clarinet (1944); trio for violin, viola, and cello (1946); *Cortège,* for brass and percussion (1948); quintet for flute, oboe, clarinet, horn, and bassoon (1948); trio for flute, oboe, and clarinet (1949); sonata for flute and harpsichord (1949); 2 string quartets; other chamber music; several albums of piano pieces; choral works; declamation for speaking voice with piano or other instrumental accompaniment; a number of songs; *Musik zur Eurhythmie* (6 books of piano pieces for eurhythmic exercises). —Cf. W. Paap, *Henri Zagwijn,* in 'Mens en Melodie' (Sept., 1948; Nov., 1954).

Zahn (tsan), **Johannes,** German composer and music scholar; b. Espenbach, Aug. 1, 1817; d. Neudettelsau, Feb. 17, 1895. He was a student of theology at Munich and Berlin; director of the teachers' seminary at Altdorf (1854-88). In 1875 he founded the periodical 'Siona' for liturgy and church music. He publ. a valuable work, *Die Melodien der deutschen evangelischen Kirchenlieder, aus den Quellen geschöpft und mitgetheilt* (6 vols., 1889-93); a *Sonntagsschulbuch für die lutherischen Gemeinden Nordamerikas* (1894); and various other scholarly and didactic works on church music.

Zaimov, Halik, Russian composer; b. Sultanovo, near Uralsk, Nov. 13, 1914; studied at the Moscow Cons. With Spadavecchia (q. v.) he wrote an opera, *Ak Buzat (The Magic Steed;* Ufa, Nov. 7, 1942); also composed a ballet, *Galima* (1955); 3 cantatas to Bashkir words; 2 string quartets; 24 preludes for piano.

Zajc, Ivan. See Zaytz, Giovanni von.

Zajic (zah'-yits), **Florian,** violinist; b. Unhoscht, Bohemia, May 4, 1853; d. Berlin, May 17, 1926. He studied at the Prague Cons.; then was a theater violinist in various German cities; in 1891, became violin teacher at the Stern Cons., Berlin; gave sonata recitals; publ. 30 études for violin, and a cadenza to the violin concerto by Brahms.

Zakharov (zah-ha'-rof), **Vladimir Grigorievitch,** Soviet composer of songs; b. Bogodukhov, on the Don Basin, Oct. 18, 1901; d. Moscow, July 13, 1956. He studied at the Rostov Cons.; after 1932, devoted himself mainly to the composition of mass songs, derived from the polyphonic essence of Russian folk music and employing asymmetric meters. Of these songs, *Two Falcons* and *Who can tell?* attained immense popularity in Russia. He received several prizes and was awarded the Order of Lenin.

Zamara, Antonio, Italian harpist; b. Milan, June 13, 1829; d. Hietzing, near Vienna, Nov. 11, 1901. He studied with Sechter in Vienna; for nearly 50 years was 1st harpist at the Kärntnertor Theater; for many years also was prof. at the Vienna Cons. He publ. a *Harfenschule* (4 books); a number of pieces for harp solo *(Barcarolle, La Rêveuse, Chant du berceau, L'Absence, Marche des Croates,* etc.); also pieces for harp and cello *(Élégie, L'Addio,* etc.) and transcriptions of operatic airs for 2 harps.

Zampieri, Giusto, Italian writer on music; b. Trieste, Nov. 6, 1879; d. Pavia, June 8, 1950. He was prof. of music history at the Cons. of Milan (1908-23); then at the Univ. of Pavia. He publ. *Il Pianoforte* (Milan, 1912), *F. Gafurio* (Pavia, 1925), and other books.

Zandonai (tsahn-doh-nah'-ē), **Riccardo,** Italian composer; b. Sacco, Trentino, May 28, 1883; d. Pesaro, June 5, 1944. He was a pupil of Gianferrari at Rovereto (1893-98); then studied with Mascagni at the Liceo Rossini in Pesaro. He graduated in 1902; for his final examination he composed a symph. poem for solo voices, chorus, and orch., *Il Ritorno di Odisseo.* He then turned to opera, which remained his favored genre throughout his career. His first opera was *Il Grillo del focolare,* based on *The Cricket on the Hearth* of Dickens, which was produced in Turin on Nov. 28, 1908, with excellent success. With his next opera, *Conchita,* after the novel *La Femme et le pantin* by Pierre Louÿs (Milan, Oct. 14, 1911), he established himself as an important Italian composer; the title role was created by the soprano Tarquinia Tarquini, whom Zandonai married in 1917. *Conchita* received its American première in San Francisco on Sept. 28, 1912; as *La Femme et le pantin* it was given at the Opéra-Comique, Paris, on March 11, 1929. Zandonai's reputation was enhanced by subsequent works, notably *Francesca da Rimini,* after Gabriele d'Annunzio (Turin, Feb. 19, 1914; Metropolitan Opera, N. Y., Dec. 22, 1916), but a previous opera, *Melenis* (Milan, Nov. 13, 1912), was unsuccessful. During World War I Zandonai participated in the political agitation for the return of former Italian provinces; wrote a student hymn calling for the redemption of Trieste (1915). His other operas were: *La Via della finestra* (Pesaro, July 27, 1919; revised version, Trieste, Jan. 18, 1923); *Giulietta e Romeo* (Rome, Feb. 14, 1922); *I Cavalieri di Ekebù* (Milan, March 7, 1925); *Giuliano* (Naples, Feb. 4, 1928); *Una Partita* (Milan, Jan. 19, 1933); and *La Farsa amorosa,* after Alarcón's *El Sombrero de tres picos* (Rome, Feb. 22, 1933). He further wrote the symph. poems *Primavera in Val di Sole* (1908), *Patria lontana* (1918), *Fra gli alberghi delle Dolomiti* (1932); *Concerto romantico* for violin and orch. (1921); *Concerto andaloso* for cello and small orch. (1937); *Rapsodia trentina* for orch. (1937); a *Messa da Requiem;* some chamber music. In 1939 he was appointed director of the Liceo Rossini in Pesaro, remaining there for the rest of his life. —Cf. V. Bonajuti Tarquini, *Riccardo Zandonai, nel ricordo dei suoi intimi* (Milan, 1951). See also *Bibliografia delle opere musicali di Riccardo Zandonai,* in 'Bollettino bibliografico musicale' (Dec., 1931).

Zandt, Marie Van. See **Van Zandt, Marie.**

Zanella (tsăh-nĕl'-lăh), **Amilcare,** Italian composer; b. Monticelli d'Ongina, Piacenza, Sept. 26, 1873; d. Pesaro, Jan. 9, 1949. He studied with Andreotti in Cremona, then with Bottesini at the Parma Cons., graduating in 1891. In 1892 he went to South America as pianist and opera conductor; returning to Italy in 1901, he organized his own orch., giving symph. concerts in the principal Italian cities and introducing his own works. He then was director of the Parma Cons. (1903-05); succeeded Mascagni as director of the Liceo Rossini in Pesaro in 1905, and held this post until 1939, when he was succeeded by Zandonai. His operas include *Aura* (Pesaro, Aug. 27, 1910); *La Sulamita* (Piacenza, Feb. 11, 1926); and *Il Revisore,* after Gogol (Trieste, Feb. 20, 1940). He also composed a symph.; 2 symph. poems, *Fede* and *Vita; Festa campestre, Danza paesana* etc. for orch.; *Fantasia e Fugato* (on 4 subjects) for piano and orch.; a nonet for strings, woodwind instruments, and piano; a piano trio; a number of piano pieces *(Due Leggende, Passero solitario, Canto d'anima, Ansia,* etc.). —Cf. A. Dioli and M. F. Nobili, *La Vita e l'arte di Amilcare Zanella* (Bergamo, 1941). A compendium, *Amilcare Zanella, artista, uomo, educatore,* was publ. in Ferrara in 1932.

Zanettini. See **Gianettini.**

Zang (tsahngk), **Johann Heinrich,** German organist and composer; b. Zella St. Blasii, near Gotha, April 13, 1733; d. Mainstockheim, Aug. 18, 1811. As a youth he was trained by Bach in Leipzig (for 2 years); composed and engraved *Die singende Muse am Main* (1776); wrote a *Kunst- und Handwerksbuch,* Part II of which is *Der vollkommene Orgelmacher, oder Lehre von der Orgel und Windprobe* (1804). In MS are church cantatas, organ trios, piano sonatas, etc.

Zanger (**Zangerus**), **Johannes,** music theorist; b. Weinbrück, Hungary, 1517; d. Brunswick, April 5, 1587. He was a pupil of Heinrich Finck, Arnold von Bruck, and others; became cantor in Brunswick in 1545; also rector and pastor. He publ. *Musicae practicae praecepta* (Leipzig, 1554). —Cf. H. J. Moser, *Johannes Zanger's Praecepta,* in 'Musica Disciplina' (vol. 5; 1951).

Zangius, Nikolaus, German organist and composer; b. c. 1570; d. Berlin, c. 1618. He was chamber musician in Brunswick (1597), church organist in Danzig (1602-05); then in Prague (1609), in Vienna, and finally in Berlin (from 1612). He composed a cappella choruses, motets, and a number of quodlibets. His *Cantiones sacrae* and 3-part German songs are reprinted in the 'Denkmäler der Tonkunst in Österreich' (vol. 87). —Cf. Joh. Sachs, *N. Zangius' weltliche Lieder* (dissertation; Vienna, 1934).

Zanten, Cornelie Van. See **Van Zanten.**

Zarate, Eliodoro Ortíz de, Chilean composer; b. Valparaiso, Dec. 29, 1865; d. Santiago, June 27, 1953. He studied in his native city; in 1885 won first prize offered by the Chilean government, and studied at the Milan Cons., graduating in 1888. Returning to Chile, he brought out his opera (to his own libretto in Italian), *La Fioraia di Lugano* (Santiago, Nov. 1, 1895), which was one of the earliest operas, if not the first, by a Chilean composer that was produced in Santiago.

Zaremba, Nikolai Ivanovitch, Russian composer and pedagogue; b. near Vitebsk, June 15, 1821; d. St. Petersburg, April 8, 1879. He studied in Berlin with Marx and others. When the St. Petersburg Cons. was founded in 1862, he was engaged as instructor of theory; in 1867 he succeeded Anton Rubinstein as director, but continued to teach composition; resigned in 1871, and spent several years abroad, returning to St. Petersburg shortly before his death. Although an extremely conservative musician and insignificant composer, he was a good teacher; Tchaikovsky was one of his pupils. Mussorgsky satirized Zaremba in his *Peepshow,* illustrating Zaremba's classical tastes by a mock quotation from Handel.

Zarembski, Jules de, Polish pianist and composer; b. Zhitomir, Feb. 28, 1854; d. there, Sept. 15, 1885. He studied in Vienna with Dachs and in Weimar with Liszt; in 1879 became prof. of piano at the Brussels Cons.; then returned to Russia. He publ. for piano several concert studies; *Suite polonaise; Ballade; Sérénade burlesque; Berceuse; À travers Pologne; Sérénade espagnole; Étrennes* (6 pieces); 2 sets of Polish dances for piano 4 hands.

Zarin, Marger, Latvian composer; b. Jaunpiebalg, May 24, 1910; studied with his father, an organist; then at the Cons. of Riga with Wihtol, graduating in 1936. From 1940 to 1950, conductor and musical director of the Latvian Art Theater. —Works: the operas *The Lord and the Gusli Player* (1939) and *Toward a New Shore* (Riga, July 20, 1955); *Song of Friendship* for soloists, chorus, and orch. (1948); *Festive Prologue,* for chorus with orch. (1950); cantata, *The Heroes of Valmier* (1950); piano concerto (1936); 3 *Legends,* for string quartet, flute, clarinet, and English horn; choruses on Latvian folk themes; many song cycles; incidental music to plays; arrangements of folksongs. —Cf. O. Gravitis, *Brief Biographies of Latvian Composers* (Riga, 1955; pp. 107-13).

Zarlino (tsahr-lē'-noh), **Gioseffo** (**Zarlinus Clodiensis**), important Italian music theorist and composer; b. Chioggia, March 22, 1517; d. Venice, Feb. 14, 1590. He entered the Franciscan order in 1539, and in 1541 went to Venice, where he became a pupil of Willaert. In 1565 he succeeded his fellow-pupil Cipriano de Rore as maestro di cappella at San Marco, holding this position until his death; also held the office of chaplain at San Severo. He was greatly esteemed not only as a teacher but also as a composer; indeed, Foscarini describes him as 'the famous regenerator of music in all Italy.' Most of Zarlino's MSS are lost; his extant works comprise *21 Modulationes 6 vocum* (Venice, 1566; edited by Zarlino's pupil, Usberti), *3 Lectiones pro mortuis* (part of a collection of motets *a* 4 by Cipriano de Rore and others; publ. by Scotto, Venice, 1563), and a Mass (MS in the library of the Liceo Filarmonico in Bologna). 2 motets *a* 5 were publ. by L. Torchi in 'L'Arte Musicale in Italia' (vol. I). —Zarlino's lasting significance lies in his theoretical works, particularly the *Istituzioni armoniche* (in 4 sections; Venice, 1558; republ. 1562, 1573), in which Zarlino treats the major and minor thirds as inversions within a fifth, and consequently, the major and minor triads as mutual mirror reflections of component intervals, thus anticipating the modern dualism of Rameau, Tartini, Hauptmann, and Riemann; also gives lucid and practical demonstrations of double counterpoint and canon, illustrated by numerous musical examples; while adhering to the system of 12 modes, he places the Ionian, rather than the Dorian mode, at the head of the list, thus pointing towards the emergence of the major scale as the preponderant mode; gives 10 rules for proper syllabification of the text in musical settings; suggests equal temperament for the tuning of the lute. In 1571 he publ. *Dimostrationi armoniche,* in the form of 5 dialogues between Willaert and his disciples and friends. Zarlino's theories were attacked, with a violence uncommon even for the polemical spirit of the age, by Vincenzo Galilei, one of his former pupils, in *Dialogo . . . della musica antica e della moderna* (Florence, 1581) and *Discorso intorno alle opere di Gioseffo Zarlino* (Florence, 1589). In reply to the first of Galilei's books, Zarlino publ. *Sopplimenti musicali* (Venice, 1588). Collected works of Zarlino (4 vols.), publ. in Venice in 1589, included, in addition to his former books, also a theological tract, *Trattato della pazienza.* —Cf. G. Ravagnan, *Elogio di G. Zarlino* (Venice, 1819); G. Caffi, *Narrazione della vita e delle opere del prete Gioseffo Zarlino* (Venice, 1836); G. Caffi, *Storia della musica sacra nella già cappella di San Marco in Venezia* (Venice, 1854; vol. I); H. Riemann, *Geschichte der Musiktheorie* (2nd ed., 1921); V. Bellenio, *Gioseffo Zarlino* (Chioggia, 1884); F. Högler, *Bemerkungen zu Zarlinos Theorie,* in the 'Zeitschrift für Musikwissenschaft' (vol. 9; 1926); H. Zenck, *Zarlinos 'Istituzioni armoniche' . . .,* ibid. (vol. 13; 1930). See also G. Reese, *Music in the Renaissance* (N. Y., 1954; pp. 376-79). —Books III-IV of the *Istituzioni armoniche* are publ. in English transl. in O. Strunk, *Source Readings in Music History* (N. Y., 1950).

Zarotus, Antonio, Italian music printer, active in Milan. He printed a 'Missale Romanum' dated April 26, 1476, in which he used for the first time movable types for the music (the type is in Gothic style). This incunabulum was publ. 6 months earlier than the 'Missale' of Ulrich Han (q. v.), at one time considered the earliest specimen of music printed from movable type. —Cf. Otto Kinkeldey, *Music and Music Printing in Incunabula,* in 'Papers' of the Bibliographic Society of America (1932).

Zarzycki (zahr-zits'-kē), **Alexander,** Polish pianist and composer; b. Lwów, Feb. 21, 1834; d. Warsaw, Nov. 1, 1895. He studied in Lwów and later in Paris (1856-61) with Reber; gave brilliant concerts in France, Germany, Austria, and Poland; was director of the Warsaw Music Society (1866-74). In 1879 he became director of the Warsaw Cons. He wrote effective piano pieces (nocturnes, mazurkas, waltzes, etc.); also a piano concerto; *Grande Polonaise* for piano with orch.; *Introduction et Cracovienne* for violin and orch.; *Suite polonaise* for orch.; *Mazourka* in G major for violin with orch. (very popular); also 2 albums of songs.

Zaslawsky, Georges, Russian-American conductor; b. Kiev, Feb. 15, 1880; d. New York, Jan. 28, 1953. He studied at the St. Petersburg Cons. with Auer (violin) and Liadov (composition). In 1922 he emigrated to the U. S.; made his début as conductor at a special concert in Carnegie Hall, N. Y., April 12, 1926; in 1927 founded and conducted a 'Beethoven Symph. Orch.' in N. Y., which was discontinued after a few concerts. He also conducted in South America.

Zavertal, Ladislao, Italian bandmaster (of Bohemian extraction); b. Milan, Sept. 29, 1849; d. Cadenabbia, Jan. 29, 1942. He was the son of the clarinetist Wenceslas Hugo Zavertal (1821-1899). After studying at home, he went to Treviso (where he produced an opera) and then to Milan (1869). In 1871 he went to Glasgow, where he conducted various orchestral groups; in 1881, became bandmaster of the Royal Artillery Band at Woolwich; from 1895 to 1905 he conducted Sunday band concerts in the Albert Hall, London, which enjoyed considerable popularity. He returned to Italy in 1906. He was a voluminous composer; wrote operas, symphonies, and band pieces; received various honors from the governments of England, Italy, Greece, Serbia, and Turkey. —Cf. A. Faraone, *Il Commendatore Ladislao Zavertal* (Treviso, 1929); H. G. Farmer, *Ladislao Zavertal: His Life and Work* (London, 1949); H. G. Farmer, *Cavaliere Zavertal and the Royal Artillery Band* (London, 1951).

Zay, (William) Henri, American singing teacher and composer; b. Findlay, Ohio, March 20, 1869; d. New York, Nov. 2, 1927. He studied at the Cleveland Cons. and at the Royal Academy of Music in London. Returning to the U. S., he established himself as a voice specialist, gradually evolving and perfecting his own method, publ. as *Practical Psychology of Voice and of Life* (N. Y., 1917; reprinted, 1945); composed *Cosmic Conception* for orch., and several song cycles.

Zaytz, Giovanni von (real name Ivan Zajc), Croatian composer; b. Fiume, Aug. 3, 1831; d. Zagreb, Dec. 16, 1914. He was trained by his father, a bandmaster in the Austrian army; then in Milan by Lauro Rossi. Returning to Fiume, he conducted the municipal band; then was theater conductor in Vienna (1862-70). Upon entering professional life, he changed his name to Giovanni von Zaytz. In 1870 he settled in Zagreb; was conductor of the Zagreb Opera (1870-89) and director of the Cons. there (until 1908). He composed about 1200 works of all descriptions (among them 20 operas), and was the author of the first Croatian national opera, *Nikola Šubrič Zrinski* (Zagreb, Nov. 4, 1876). He also wrote several Italian operas, of which *Amelia, ossia Il Bandito* (Fiume, April 14, 1860) enjoyed considerable popularity. Other operas and operettas (all produced by him in Vienna) are: *Mannschaft an Bord* (Dec. 15, 1863); *Fitzliputzli* (Nov. 5, 1864); *Die Lazzaroni vom Stanzel* (May 4, 1865); *Die Hexe von Boissy* (April 24, 1866); *Nachtschwärmer* (Nov. 10, 1866); *Das Rendezvous in der Schweiz* (April 3, 1867); *Das Gaugericht* (Sept. 14, 1867); *Nach Mekka* (Jan. 11, 1868); *Somnambula* (Jan. 25, 1868); *Schützen von Einst und Jetzt* (July 25, 1868); *Meister Puff* (May 22, 1869); and *Der gefangene Amor* (Sept. 12, 1874). In addition he wrote incidental music for 23 plays; 60 cantatas; 250 choral works, sacred and secular; 40 overtures; symphonic poems; more than 200 songs.

Zbinden, Julien-François, Swiss composer; b. Rolle, Nov. 11, 1917. He studied at the Cons. of Lausanne; then was a pupil of Marie Panthès (piano) and René Gerber (composition). After playing in jazz orchestras, he became pianist and assistant director at the Radio-Lausanne. —Works: piano concerto (1945); *Divertissement* for double-bass and orch. (1949); a symph. (Lausanne, Oct. 26, 1953); concertino for trumpet and strings (1946); septet (1948); wind trio (1949); sonatina for flute and piano (1945); jazz sonatina for piano (1949); concerto for piano and strings (1950-51). —Cf. H. Jaccard, *Initiation à la musique contemporaine: trois compositeurs vaudois: Raffaele d'Alessandro, Constantin Regamey, Julien-François Zbinden* (Lausanne, 1955).

Zecchi (tsek'-kee), **Adone,** Italian composer and conductor; b. Bologna, July 23, 1904; he studied composition with Franco Alfano at the Liceo Musicale in Bologna, graduating in 1926; in 1930 he established the Orchestra Bolognese da Camera, with which he gave concerts in Italy; then joined the staff of the Liceo Musicale, Bologna; also was active as music critic. His works comprise a *Partita* for orch. (1933), *Toccata, Ricercare e Finale* for orch. (1941), *Due Astrazioni in forma di fuga* for a small ensemble (Copenhagen Festival of the International Society for Contemporary Music, June 2, 1947); Requiem for chorus and orch. (1946); a piano trio and other chamber music.

Zecchi (tsek'-kee), **Carlo,** Italian pianist and conductor; b. Rome, July 18, 1903. He studied with Refice in Rome and with Artur Schnabel and Busoni in Berlin; began his concert career at 17; made a tour of the U. S. in 1931. In 1938 he became interested in conducting; appeared as conductor in Vienna, London, and Edinburgh; also taught at the Santa Cecilia in Rome.

Zech, Frederick, American pianist and composer; b. Philadelphia, May 10, 1858; d. San Francisco, Oct. 25, 1926. He was taken to San Francisco as a child, and studied piano there; later in Berlin with Kullak; subsequently (1880-82) taught at Kullak's 'Neue Akademie' there. Upon his return to San Francisco he held classes in advanced piano playing; in 1882-83 and 1902, organized and conducted symph. concerts there. His compositions comprise 2 operas, *La Paloma* and *Wa-Kin-Yon* or *The Passing of the Red Men;* 4 symphonies; 4 symph. poems: *The Eve of St. Agnes,* after Keats (1898), *Lamia,* after Keats (1902), *The Raven,* after Poe (1902), and *The*

Wreck of the Hesperus, after Longfellow (1909); 4 piano concertos; a violin concerto; a cello concerto; a piano quintet; 2 string quartets; a piano trio; 3 violin sonatas; a cello sonata; a flute sonata; 2 clarinet sonatas.

Zeckwer, Richard, German-American pianist and composer; b. Stendal, Prussia, April 30, 1850; d. Philadelphia, Dec. 30, 1922. He studied at the Leipzig Cons. with Moscheles (piano), Hauptmann, Richter, and Reinecke (composition). In 1870 he settled in Philadelphia as teacher and church organist. He composed 2 overtures *(Festival* and *Bride of Messina);* a number of songs; publ. *A Scientific Investigation of Piano-Touch* (1902). His son, **Camille Zeckwer** (b. Philadephia, June 26, 1875; d. Southampton, N. Y., Aug. 7, 1924), was educated by his father, studied composition in N. Y. with Dvořák, and later with Ph. Scharwenka in Berlin; returning to Philadelphia, he devoted most of his time to teaching. He composed a *Swedish Fantasy* for violin and orch.; piano concerto (performed by him with the Philadelphia Orch. in 1899, 1904, and 1914); *The New Day,* cantata (1914); *Sérénade mélancolique* for violin, cello, and piano; *Sohrab and Rustum,* symph. poem (Philadelphia, Feb. 4, 1916); piano pieces (prelude and fugue, a sonata, *Rapsodia fantastica,* etc.); choruses and songs. A 3-act opera, *Jane and Janetta,* was not produced.

Zehnder, Max, Swiss composer; b. Turgi, Canton Aargau, Nov. 17, 1901. He studied at the Zürich Cons. and later became a provincial teacher of music. Among his works are several cantatas; a toccata for orch.; a concerto for flute, oboe, and strings; vocal compositions.

Zeidman, Boris Isaacovitch, Russian composer; b. St. Petersburg, Feb. 10, 1908; studied with M. Steinberg at the St. Petersburg Cons. In 1939 he joined the faculty of the Cons. of Baku. —Works: operas: *The People's Wrath* (Baku, Dec. 28, 1941), *Son of the Regiment* (Baku, Feb. 23, 1955); a symphonietta (1943); 3 overtures on Azerbaijan themes (1949; 1950; 1951); viola concerto (1938); bassoon concerto (1938); cello concerto (1949); piano sonata; an album of 24 children's pieces for piano; songs.

Zeinally, Assaf, Azerbaijan composer; b. Derbent, April 2, 1909; d. Baku, Oct. 27, 1932. He studied trumpet and cello in Baku; made a study of folk music with Gadzhibekov; graduated from the Baku Cons. in 1931, and was appointed to its faculty, but he died a year later at the age of 23. He was a highly promising composer; wrote pieces based on Azerbaijan themes for 2 cellos, for violin and piano, for vocal duet, and for a piano trio; also many songs; a piano sonata; a children's suite for piano; 9 fugues for piano.

Zeisl, Eric, Austrian-American composer; b. Vienna, May 18, 1905. He studied at the State Academy of Music in Vienna; publ. his first songs at the age of 16; in 1934 received the Austrian State prize for a Requiem. He emigrated to America in 1939, and settled in Hollywood. —Works: the operas *Leonce und Lena* (Prague, 1937) and *Job* (1945-58); *Little Symphony* (Vienna Radio, May 30, 1937); *Passacaglia Fantasy* for orch. (Vienna, Nov. 4, 1937); *November,* suite for chamber orch. (N. Y., Jan. 25, 1941); *Cossack Dance* for orch. (Hollywood Bowl, Aug. 18, 1946); *Return of Ulysses,* suite for chamber orch. (Chicago, Nov. 17, 1948); *Requiem Ebraico;* 4 Songs for Wordless Chorus; *Sonata barocca* for piano (1949); *Brandeis Sonata* for violin and piano (1950); viola sonata; cello sonata; 2 string quartets; violin pieces; songs.

Zeisler (tsīs'-ler), **Fannie (Bloomfield),** noted pianist; b. Bielitz, Austrian Silesia, July 16, 1863; d. Chicago, Aug. 20, 1927. Her original name was Blumenfeld; it was changed to Bloomfield when the family settled in Chicago in 1868. Her first teachers there were Carl Wolfsohn and Bernhard Ziehn. She made her concert début in Chicago on Feb. 26, 1875; in 1878 she went to Vienna, where she studied with Leschetizky (1878-83). From 1883 until 1893 she played annually in the U. S.; in 1893 she made a tour of Germany and Austria, which established her reputation as one of the best woman-pianists; other European tours followed in 1894-95, 1898, 1902-03, 1911-12, and the spring of 1914. She then returned to Chicago; made her farewell appearance there on Feb. 25, 1925, in a special concert to mark her golden jubilee. On Oct. 18, 1885, she married Sigmund Zeisler, a Chicago lawyer. —See 'Dictionary of American Biography.'

Zelenka, Jan Dismas, Bohemian composer; b. Louňovice, Oct. 16, 1679; d. Dresden, Dec. 23, 1745. He received his general education in Prague; in 1710 he joined the court orch. in Dresden, playing the double-bass; then studied with Fux in Vienna and with Lotti in Italy (1716). In 1719 he returned to Dresden, where he became assistant to Heinichen, succeeding him in 1729; he was named court Kapellmeister in 1733. He was a prolific composer; wrote much church music, including 21 Masses, 3 Requiems, and many motets; 3 Italian oratorios, etc.; and a melodrama *De Sancto Venceslao;* also an interesting overture entitled *Hypocondria.* —Cf. M. Fürstenau, *Zur Geschichte der Musik und des Theaters am Hofe zu Dresden,* vol. II (Dresden, 1862); O. Schmid, *Musik am sächsischen Hofe,* Part VI (contains musical examples); K. M. Komma, *Johann Zach und die tschechischen Musiker im deutschen Umbruch des 18. Jahrhunderts* (dissertation; Kassel, 1938).

Zelenski (zhā-lĕn'-skē), **Wladislaw,** Polish composer and pedagogue; b. Grodkowice, near Cracow, July 6, 1837; d. Cracow, Jan. 23, 1921. He studied with Mirecki in Cracow, Krejči in Prague, and Reber in Paris. He returned to Poland in 1871; was theory teacher at the Warsaw Cons. (1872-81). In 1887 he organized the Cracow Cons., and remained its director until his death; he also taught piano and theory there. As a pedagogue, he enjoyed a very high reputation; among his pupils were Stojowski, Opienski, and Szopski. He publ. 2 music manuals. —Works: operas: *Konrad Wallenrod* (Lwów, Feb. 26, 1885), *Goplana* (Cracow, July 23, 1896), *Janek* (Lwów, Oct. 4, 1900), *Stara baśń* (Lwów, March 14, 1907); 2 symphonies; 2 overtures; piano concerto; 7 cantatas; 2 Masses; motets for men's voices; 2 violin sonatas; a piano trio; 2 string quartets; a string sextet; a piano quartet; 3 piano sonatas; about 80 songs to Polish words; a number of piano pieces *(Valse-caprice, Humoreske und Gavotte, Grand scherzo de concert, Grosse Polonaise, Moments d'un carnaval,* etc.); 25 preludes for organ. —Cf. F. Szopski, *W. Zeleński* (Warsaw, 1928); Z. Jachimecki, *Wladislaw Zeleński; zycie i twórczość, 1837-1921* (Cracow, 1952).

Zelinka, Jan Evangelista, Czech composer; b. Prague, Jan. 13, 1893. He studied music with his father, an organist, and later with J. B. Foerster, Suk, and Novák; wrote a number of works for the stage, including 4 operas: *Dceruška hostinského (The Tavern-keeper's Little Daughter;* Prague, Feb. 24, 1925), *Devatá louka (The Ninth Field;* Prague, Sept. 19, 1931), *Palicatý švec (The Stubborn Cobbler;* Prague, March 28, 1944), *Melusina* (Pilsen, April 15, 1950); ballets and incidental music; 3 cantatas; chamber music; songs.

Zelle, Friedrich, German musicologist; b. Berlin, Jan. 24, 1845; d. there, Sept. 10, 1927. He studied piano with Kullak, composition with Geyer and Bellermann; taught at the Humboldt Akademie in Berlin (1875-92) and later was director of the Berlin Realschule (1893-1915). He edited Hassler's *Lustgarten* (1887), J. W. Franck's *Choralkantate* (1890), and Keiser's opera *Jodelet* (1892); also Passions by Sebastiani and Theile for the 'Denkmäler deutscher Tonkunst' (vol. 17). —Writings: *Beiträge zur Geschichte der ältesten deutschen Oper: I, J. W. Franck* (1889), II, *Joh. Theile und N. A. Strungk* (1891), III, *J. Ph. Förtsch* (1893); *Die Singweisen der ältesten evangelischen Lieder* (1899, 1900); *Theorie der Musik* (1880); *Das erste evangelische Choralbuch* [Osiander, 1586] (1913); *Das älteste lutherische Hausgesangbuch* [the so-called *Färbefass-Enchiridion* of 1524] (1903); *Ballettstücke aus Keiserschen Opern* (1890).

Zeller (tsel'-ler), **Carl,** Austrian composer of operettas; b. St. Peter-in-der-Au, July 19, 1842; d. Baden, near Vienna, Aug. 17, 1898. He was an official in the Austrian Ministry of Education. Although following music only as an avocation, he became one of the most popular operetta composers of the day, winning extraordinary success with his *Der Vogelhändler* (Vienna, Jan. 10, 1891) and *Der Obersteiger* (Vienna, Jan. 5, 1894). Other successful operettas (all produced in Vienna) were *Joconde* (March 18, 1876), *Die Carbonari* (Nov. 27, 1880), *Der Vagabund* (Oct. 30, 1886), and *Der Kellermeister* (Dec. 21, 1901). —Cf. C. W. Zeller, *Mein Vater Karl Zeller* (St. Plöten, 1942).

Zellner (tsel'-ner), **Julius,** Austrian pianist and composer; b. Vienna, May 18, 1832; d. Mürzzuschlag, July 28, 1900. He was first engaged in a mercantile career, but abandoned it for music; became successful in Vienna as teacher and composer. —Works: 2 symphonies; *Melusine,* symph. suite; piano concerto; piano quartet; 3 piano trios; 2 cello sonatas; 2 violin sonatas; a number of piano pieces *(Adagio und Allegro appassionato; Zwei kleine Suiten; Zwei Sonatinen;* etc.); piano pieces 4 hands *(Drei deutsche Tänze,* etc.); also a puppet play, *Wasserkaspar.*

Zellner, Leopold Alexander, Austrian organist and music editor; b. Agram, Sept. 23,

1823; d. Vienna, Nov. 24, 1894. He studied with his father, organist of the Agram Cathedral; at 15 became a church organist; taught music in Vienna; founded and edited the 'Blätter für Theater, Musik und bildende Kunst' (1855-68). In 1868 he became prof. of harmony at the Vienna Cons.; wrote a method for the harmonium, and made improvements in its mechanism; publ. instructive pieces; also composed choruses and chamber music; ed. violin sonatas by Nardini and Vivaldi with additional piano parts. His lectures were publ. as *Vorträge über Akustik* (2 vols.; 1892) and *Vorträge über Orgelbau* (1893).

Zelter (tsel'-ter), **Carl Friedrich,** eminent German composer and teacher; b. Berlin, Dec. 11, 1758; d. there, May 15, 1832. The son of a mason, he was brought up in the same trade, but his musical inclinations soon asserted themselves; he studied organ, and at the age of 18 had a cantata of his composition performed in a church; then he became a pupil of K. F. C. Fasch and Kirnberger; was engaged as music director in Rellstab's 'Liebhaber-Konzerte'; in 1786 he brought out a funeral cantata on the death of Frederick the Great; in 1791 he joined the 'Singverein' (later 'Singakademie') conducted by Fasch, often acting as his deputy, and succeeding him in 1800. He was elected associate ('Assessor') of the 'Akademie' in 1806; prof. in 1809. In 1807 he organized a 'Ripienschule' for orchestral practice; and in 1809 he founded in Berlin the 'Liedertafel,' a pioneer men's choral society which became famous; similar organizations were subsequently formed throughout Germany, and later in America. Zelter composed about 100 men's choruses for the 'Liedertafel.' In 1822 he founded the Royal Institute for Church Music, of which he was director until his death (the Institute was later reorganized as the Akademie für Kirchen- und Schulmusik). Goethe greatly admired Zelter's musical settings of his poems, preferring them to Schubert's and Beethoven's; this predilection led to their friendship, which was reflected in a voluminous correspondence, *Briefwechsel zwischen Goethe und Zelter* (ed. in 6 vols. by F. W. Riemer, Berlin, 1833-34; ed. in 3 vols. by L. Geiger, Leipzig, 1906; ed. in 4 vols. by M. Hecker, Leipzig, 1913; English transl. by A. D. Coleridge, London, 1887). He publ. a biography of Fasch (Berlin, 1801). Zelter's autobiography was first publ. under the title, *C. F. Zelter. Eine Lebensbeschreibung nach autobiographischen Manuscripten,* edited by W. Rintel; then as *C. F. Zelter. Darstellungen seines Lebens* (Weimar, 1931). His songs are historically important, since they form a link between old ballad types and the new art of the lied, which found its flowering in Schubert and Schumann. Zelter's settings of Goethe's *König von Thule* and of *Es ist ein Schuss gefallen* became extremely popular. Other songs were publ. in collections of 12 each (1796 and 1801), followed by other albums: *Sämtliche Lieder, Balladen, Romanzen* (1810 et seq.), *Neue Sammlung* (1821), and *6 deutsche Lieder* (1827). New editions were brought out by Jöde (1930), Landshoff (1932), etc.; the cantatas *Johanna Sebus* and *Die Gunst des Augenblicks* were publ. by Müller-Blattau. —Cf. W. Bornemann, *Die Zeltersche Liedertafel in Berlin* (Berlin, 1851); L. Sieber, *C. F. Zelter und der deutsche Männergesang* (Basel, 1862); H. Kuhlo, *Geschichte der Zelterschen Liedertafel von 1809-1909* (Berlin, 1909); G. R. Kruse, *Zelter* (Leipzig, 1915); J. W. Schottländer, *Zelters Beziehungen zu den Komponisten seiner Zeit,* in 'Zeitschrift für Musikwissenschaft' (vol. XV); H. J. Moser, *Goethes Dichtung in der neueren Musik,* in the 'Goethe-Jahrbuch' (1931); J. Müller-Blattau, *Goethe und die Kantate,* in the 'Jahrbuch Peters' (1931); G. Schünemann, *C. F. Zelter, der Begründer der preussischen Musikpflege* (Berlin, 1932); G. Wittmann, *Das klavierbegleitete Sololied C. F. Zelters* (dissertation, Giessen, 1936); G. Schünemann, *C. F. Zelter: der Mensch und sein Werk* (Berlin, 1937); S. Holtzmann, ed., *C. F. Zelter im Spiegel seines Briefwechsel mit Goethe* (Weimar, 1957); W. Reich, ed., *C. F. Zelter, Selbstdarstellung,* a collection of documents (Zürich, 1958).

Zemlinsky, Alexander von, Austrian composer, conductor, and teacher; b. Vienna (of Polish parentage), Oct. 4, 1872; d. Larchmont, N. Y., March 16, 1942. He studied at the Vienna Cons. with Door (piano), Krenn, Robert Fuchs and J. N. Fuchs (composition); was encouraged by Brahms, who expressed a favorable opinion of his early chamber music. In 1900 he obtained the post of conductor of the Karlstheater in Vienna; in 1906 became conductor of the Vienna Volksoper; 1908, at the Vienna Opera. In 1909 he was engaged as conductor at the Mannheim Opera; from 1911 to 1927, conducted at the German Opera in Prague; also taught composition and conducting at the Prague College of Music. From 1927 to 1932 he was conductor of the Berlin State Opera; in 1933 returned to Vienna; also made guest appearances in Spain, Russia, etc. In 1938, he emigrated to the U. S. He was the teacher of Arnold Schoenberg, who married his sister. —Works: operas: *Sarema* (Munich, Oct. 10, 1897); *Es war einmal* (his most successful work; Vienna, Jan. 22, 1900, Mahler conducting); *Kleider machen Leute* (Vienna, Dec. 2, 1910); *Eine florentinische Tragödie* (Stuttgart, Jan. 30, 1917); *Der Zwerg* (Cologne, May 28, 1922); *Der Kreidekreis* (Zürich, Oct. 14, 1933). He also wrote several symphonies, of which the 1st won the Beethoven Prize of the Gesellschaft der Musikfreunde (Vienna, 1897); choruses, chamber music, piano pieces, and songs. —Cf. special issue of 'Der Auftakt' (Prague; vol. 1; 1921).

Zenatello, Giovanni, Italian tenor; b. Verona, Feb. 22, 1876; d. New York, Feb. 11, 1949. He studied in Verona, and for 2 years sang as a baritone in minor opera companies; then took lessons from Moretti in Milan, making his début as a tenor at the San Carlo Theater in Naples as Canio in *I Pagliacci* (May, 1901); from 1903 till 1907 was on the roster of La Scala, Milan, where he created the role of Pinkerton in Puccini's *Madama Butterfly* (Feb. 17, 1904); from 1905 he sang at Covent Garden, London, in several successive seasons; made his American début at Hammerstein's Manhattan Opera House, on Nov. 4, 1907, as Enzo Grimaldo in Ponchielli's *La Gioconda.* From 1909 till 1914 he was the leading tenor of the Boston Opera Co., except for the season of 1912-13, when he sang with the Chicago Opera Co.; also appeared with various opera companies in South America, Spain, and Russia. He retired from the stage in 1930; then settled in N. Y. as a singing teacher, maintaining a studio with his wife, the contralto Maria Gay (q. v.), whom he married in 1913. They trained many well-known singers, among them Lily Pons and Nino Martini.

Zenck, Hermann, German musicologist; b. Karlsruhe, March 19, 1898; d. Freiburg-im-Breisgau, Dec. 2, 1950. He studied with Ordenstein at the Karlsruhe Cons.; later in Heidelberg (with Kroyer), in Munich and Leipzig *(Dr. phil.,* 1924); then became assistant at the Institute for Musicology in Leipzig, where he also taught at the Cons. In 1932 he joined the faculty of the Univ. of Göttingen; in 1943, went to Freiburg-im-Breisgau as prof. at the Univ. there. He edited the periodical 'Musik und Volk'; was editor of works by Willaert (2 vols. publ. in 1937; vol. 3 in 1950); and Sixtus Dietrich (1942); also edited the *Megalynodia* of Praetorius (1934); Johann Schultz's *Musikalischer Lustgarten* (1937); Handel's Italian cantatas, etc. —Publications: *Marienklage und Osterspiel des Wolfenbüttler Codex* (Hamburg, 1927); *Sixtus Dietrich* (Leipzig, 1928); *Zarlinos Istitutioni harmoniche . . .,* in the 'Zeitschrift für Musikwissenschaft' (1930); many valuable articles. —Cf. W. Gerstenberg, *Hermann Zenck,* in 'Musikforschung' (vol. 4; 1951).

Zenger (tsen'-ger), **Max,** German composer and conductor; b. Munich, Feb. 2, 1837; d. there, Nov. 18, 1911. He studied in Munich and Leipzig; in 1860 became theater conductor in Regensburg; in 1869, musical director of the Munich Court Opera; then was court conductor at Karlsruhe (1872-78); conductor of the Munich Oratorio Society (1878-85) and other choral societies there. —Works: operas: *Die Foscari* (Munich, 1863), *Ruy Blas* (Mannheim, 1868), *Wieland der Schmied* (Munich, 1880; revised, 1894); *Eros und Psyche* (Munich, 1901); oratorio *Kain,* after Byron (Munich, 1867; often performed elsewhere in Germany); secular cantata *Die Heinzelmännchen;* 2 ballets for King Ludwig II of Bavaria, *Venus und Adonis* and *Les Plaisirs de l'île enchantée* (1881); 2 Gretchen scenes from *Faust* for soprano and small orch.; *Zwei Konzertstücke* for mixed chorus and string orch.; *Altgriechisches Liederspiel* for soprano solo, chorus, and orch.; *Die Kraniche des Ibikus,* melodrama with orch.; *Die deutsche Flotte* for men's chorus and orch.; a symph.; *Tragische Ouvertüre; Adagio concertante* for cello and orch.; a piano trio; a cello sonata; choruses; piano pieces; songs. He wrote the valuable *Entstehung und Entwicklung der Instrumentalmusik* (Langensalza, 1906) and *Geschichte der Münchener Oper* (posthumous; ed. by Th. Kroyer, 1923).

Zeno (tsā'-no), **Apostolo,** famous Italian opera librettist; b. Venice, Dec. 11, 1668; d. there, Nov. 11, 1750. In 1710 he founded the 'Giornale dei Letterati d'Italia'; in 1718 was appointed court poet at Vienna; returned to Venice in 1729. The total number of librettos written by him (some in collaboration with Pietro Pariati) is 71; they were collected and edited by Gasparo Gozzi as *Poesie drammatiche di Apostolo Zeno* (10 vols., Venice, 1744; reprinted in 11 vols. at Orléans, 1785-86). A man of great knowledge and culture, he was also an ardent numismatist; his large collection of coins was exhibited at Vienna in 1955. —Cf. A. Wotquenne, *Libretti d'opéras et d'oratorios italiens du XVIIme siècle* (Brussels, 1901);

A. Wotquenne, *Table alphabétique des morceaux mesurés contenus dans les oeuvres dramatiques de Zeno, Metastasio et Goldoni* (Leipzig, 1905; also in German); M. Fehr, *Apostolo Zeno und seine Reform des Operntextes* (dissertation, Zürich, 1912); O. G. Sonneck, *Catalogue of Opera Librettos Printed before 1800* (2 vols.; Washington, 1914); R. Giazotto, *Apostolo Zeno, Pietro Metastasio e la critica del settecento,* in 'Rivista Musicale Italiana' (1946).

Zepler (tsep'-ler), **Bogumil,** German composer; b. Breslau, May 6, 1858; d. Krummhübel im Riesengebirge, Aug. 17, 1918. He studied architecture in Berlin, then medicine at the Univ. of Breslau (M.D., 1884); later began the study of music with H. Urban in Berlin; attracted attention in 1891 with *Cavalleria Berolina,* a parody on Mascagni's *Cavalleria Rusticana;* wrote stage music for Ernst von Wolzogen's artistic cabaret, 'Überbrettl' (1901-02); also wrote a parody on Strauss' *Salome.* He further composed the comic operas *Der Brautmarkt zu Hira* (Berlin, 1892), *Der Vicomte von Letorières* (Hamburg, 1899), *Die Bäder von Lucca* (Berlin, 1905), *Monsieur Bonaparte* (Leipzig, 1911); several operettas *(Diogenes, Pick und Pocket, Die Liebesfestung,* etc.); a serious 1-act opera, *Nacht* (Bern, 1901); 2 pantomimes, *Die Galgenfrist* and *Die Geisterbraut;* songs *(Rokokolieder,* etc.). He was editor in Berlin of 'Musik für Alle' (from 1904).

Zerrahn, Carl, German-American conductor; b. Malchow, Mecklenburg, July 28, 1826; d. Milton, Mass., Dec. 29, 1909. He was a pupil of Fr. Weber at Rostock; studied further in Hanover and Berlin. After the German revolution of 1848, he emigrated to the U. S., settling in Boston; played the flute in the Germania Orch.; then became active as conductor. For 42 years (1854-96) he was conductor of the Handel and Haydn Society; also conducted the concerts of the Boston Philharmonic (1855-63) and of the Harvard Mus. Association (1865-82). From 1866 to 1897 he conducted the Worcester, Mass., Music Festivals. He was choral director for the famous Peace Jubilee Concerts in Boston in 1869 and 1872, and conducted the huge choruses assembled on these occasions. He taught harmony and singing at the New England Cons. (until 1898). —Cf. 'Dictionary of American Biography.'

Zeuner, Charles (real name Heinrich Christoph), German-American organist; b. Eisleben, Saxony, Sept. 20, 1795; d. (suicide) Philadelphia, Nov. 7, 1857. He studied in Erfurt. About 1830 he settled in Boston, where he became organist at Park Street Church; also organist of the Handel and Haydn Society (1830-37), and briefly its president (1838-39). He then went to Philadelphia, where he served as church organist. He composed one of the earliest American oratorios, *The Feast of Tabernacles* (Boston, May 3, 1837); publ. *Church Music, Consisting of New and Original Anthems, Motets and Chants* (1831); *The American Harp* (1832); *The Ancient Lyre,* a book of hymn tunes (1834 and several later eds.); *Organ Voluntaries* (1840); contributed to Lowell Mason's *Lyra Sacra* (1832); some of his compositions are also included in *The Psaltery,* ed. by Mason and Webb (1845). For an account of his suicide, see the 'New York Mus. Review and Gazette' for Nov. 14, 1857. —Cf. F. J. Metcalf, *American Writers and Compilers of Sacred Music* (1925). See also 'Dictionary of American Biography.'

Zeuner (tsoi'-ner), **Karl Traugott,** German pianist and composer; b. Dresden, April 28, 1775; d. Paris, Jan. 24, 1841. He studied with Türk in Halle and Clementi in Russia; gave concerts and taught in Paris, Vienna, St. Petersburg, and Dresden. He composed 2 piano concertos; 3 string quartets; variations on a Russian theme for piano, violin, and cello; polonaises, fantasias, etc., for piano; these pieces were much in vogue in his time.

Žganec (zhgăh'-nets), **Vinko,** Croatian musicologist and folksong collector; b. Vratišinci, Jan. 22, 1890. He studied at the Univ. of Zagreb; traveled in the countryside gathering native melodies, and published 5 albums of arrangements of these songs (1924 and 1950-51). In his analysis of the structure of Croatian songs, he applies modern methods of ethnomusicology.

Zhelobinsky, Valery Victorovitch, Russian composer; b. Tambov, Jan. 27, 1913; d. Leningrad, Aug. 13, 1946. He studied at the Tambov Music School; then entered the Leningrad Cons. as a student of Vladimir Shtcherbatchev (1928-32); in 1942 was appointed prof. at the Tambov Music School; then returned to Leningrad. —Works: operas: *Kamarinsky Muzhik* (Leningrad, Sept. 15, 1933), *Her Saint's Day* (Leningrad, Feb. 22, 1935), *Mother,* after Maxim Gorky (Leningrad, Dec. 30, 1938); operetta *The Last Ball* (Leningrad, March 30,

1939); 6 symphonies: I (1930); II, *To the Memory of Revolutionary Victims* (1932); III, *Dramatic Symphony* (Moscow, Dec. 17, 1939); IV (Moscow, May 30, 1943); V (1944); VI (1946); 3 piano concertos (1933, 1934, 1939); violin concerto (1934); *Romantic Poem* for violin and orch. (1939); 24 preludes for piano; 2 children's albums for piano; film music.

Zhiganov, Nazib, Russian composer; b. Uralsk, Jan. 15, 1911; was brought up in an orphan asylum; educated in a music school in Kazan; then studied with Litinsky in Moscow. In 1945 he was appointed director of the Kazan Cons.; was awarded the Order of Lenin in 1950. He composed several operas to librettos in the Tatar language: *Katchkyn* (Kazan, June 17, 1939); *Irek (Liberty;* Kazan, Feb. 24, 1940); *Altyntchetch (The Golden-Haired;* Kazan, July 12, 1941); *Ildar* (Kazan, Nov. 7, 1942); *Tulyak* (Kazan, July 27, 1945); *Namus (Honor;* Kazan, June 25, 1950); the ballet *Zugra* (Kazan, May 17, 1946); a symph.; a suite on Tatar folk themes; overtures; marches; piano pieces; film music.

Zhitomirsky, Alexander Matveyevitch, Russian composer; b. Kherson, May 23, 1881; d. Leningrad, Dec. 16, 1937. He studied violin and theory in Vienna; then at the St. Petersburg Cons. with Rimsky-Korsakov, Liadov, and Glazunov. In 1914 joined the staff of the Cons., as instructor of composition. —Works: *Heroic Poem,* for orch. (1933); violin concerto (1937); string quartet (1927); *Elegy* for cello and piano; several songs to Russian, Jewish, and French words.

Zhivotov, Alexey Semionovitch, Russian composer; b. Kazan, Nov. 14, 1904. He studied at the Leningrad Cons. with Tchernov and Vladimir Shtcherbatchev, graduating in 1930. During the seige of Leningrad (1941-42), he remained in the city and was awarded a medal for defense. In his earlier works he experimented with jazz in symph. music. His compositions include a number of patriotic overtures; incidental music to plays by Shakespeare, Sheridan, Lope de Vega, etc.; many songs and choruses.

Zhukovsky, Herman Leontievitch, Ukrainian composer; b. Radzivilovo, Volynya, Nov. 13, 1913; studied piano and composition at the Kiev Cons. (graduated in 1941). His opera *From the Bottom of My Heart* (Moscow, Jan. 16, 1951) was severely criticized by the Central Committee of the Communist Party for ideological and musical faults; he revised it radically, and the new version was approved. Other works include the operas *Marina* (Kiev, March 12, 1939) and *Honor* (1943); piano concerto (1938); violin concerto (1953); film music; mass songs.

Ziani (tsyah'-nē), **Marco Antonio,** Italian composer, nephew of Pietro Andrea Ziani; b. Venice, c. 1653; d. Vienna, Jan. 22, 1715. In 1700 he became vice Kapellmeister at the Vienna court; in 1712, Kapellmeister. He composed 45 operas and serenades, of which the following were produced in Vienna: *Il Giordano pio* (July 26, 1700); *Gli Ossequi della notte* (July 22, 1701); *Temistocle* (June 9, 1701); *La Fuga dell' invidia* (Nov. 15, 1701); *Il Romolo* (June 9, 1702); *Cajo Popilio* (June 9, 1704); *L' Ercole vincitore dell'invidia* (March 19, 1706); *Meleagro* (Aug. 16, 1706); *Chilonida* (April 21, 1709); *Il Campidoglio ricuperato* (July 26, 1709); *L'Atenaide* (with Negri and Caldara; Nov. 19, 1714). He also composed church music.

Ziani, Pietro Andrea, Italian organist and composer, uncle of Marco Antonio Ziani; b. Venice, c. 1620; d. Naples, Feb. 12, 1684. In 1669 he succeeded Cavalli as 2nd organist at San Marco, Venice; went to Naples in 1676; in 1677 he entered the service of Empress Eleonora at Vienna; pensioned in 1684. He wrote 23 operas, including *Le Fortune di Rodope, e di Damira* (Venice, Carnival of 1657), *L'Antigona delusa da Alceste* (Venice, Jan. 15, 1660), *La Congiura del vizio contra la virtù* (Vienna, Nov. 15, 1663), and *La Circe* (Vienna, June 9, 1665); oratorio, *Le Lagrime della Vergine* (Venice, 1662); *Sacrae laudes a* 5 (1659); sonatas for 3, 4, 5, or 6 instruments (1691); church music; etc.— Cf. H. Kretzschmar, *Weitere Beiträge zur Geschichte der venezianischen Oper,* in the 'Jahrbuch der Bibliothek Peters' (1910).

Zich, Jaroslav, Czech musicologist and composer; son of Otakar Zich; b. Prague, Jan. 17, 1912. He studied with his father as a youth; then with J. B. Foerster (1928-31); went to Charles Univ. in Prague (Ph. D., 1936); from 1937, on the staff of the Czechoslovak broadcasting organization. —Works: ballet, *U muziky* (*At the Dance;* 1940); *Letný host (Flying Guest;* 1931), set of songs with orch. or piano; *Romance helgolandská* (1931), recitation with orch.; a quintet for wind instruments; a string quartet; duo for violin and cello; *Variations and Fugue* for piano; songs.

Zich, Otakar, Czech composer and musicologist; father of Jaroslav Zich; b: Králové Městec, March 25, 1879; d. Ouběnice, near Benešov, July 9, 1934. He was educated at Charles Univ. in Prague (1897-1901; Ph.D., 1902); appointed lecturer there in 1911; in 1920, prof. of esthetics at Masaryk Univ. in Brno; in 1924 he again became a member of the staff of Charles Univ., where he remained until his death. —Works: opera: *Marlířský nápad (Painter's Whim;* Prague, March 11, 1910); *Vina (Guilt,* Prague, March 14, 1922); *Preciézky,* after Molière's *Les Précieuses ridicules* (Prague, May 11, 1926); also cantatas, song cycles, part-songs, etc. Compiled *Vojenský spěvník československý* (unaccompanied melodies; Prague, 1922). Author of books on musical esthetics and Bohemian folk music. —Cf. J. Hutter, *Otakar Zich a jeho 'Vina'* (Prague, 1922).

Zichy (zit'-chē), **Géza,** Count **Vasony-Keö,** Hungarian left-hand pianist and composer; b. Sztára Castle, July 22, 1849; d. Budapest, Jan. 14, 1924. He studied with R. Volkmann and Liszt. At the age of 14 he lost his right arm in a hunting accident, and, refusing to give up music, developed his left-hand technique to the point of virtuosity; also made arrangements for left hand. On several occasions he played in public with Liszt an arrangement of the *Rákóczy March* for 3 hands. From 1875 to 1918 he was president of the National Cons. in Budapest; was also intendant of the National Theater and Opera there (1890-94). He composed 3 operas, produced at Budapest: *A vár története* (*Castle Story;* May 16, 1888), *Alár* (April 11, 1896), *Roland mester* (Jan. 10, 1899), and a dramatic trilogy on the life of Rákóczi: *Nemo* (March 30, 1905), *Rákóczi Ferenz* (Jan. 30, 1909), and *Rodostó* (March 20, 1912); a ballet, *Gemma* (Prague, 1903); a cantata, *Dolores* (1889); a piano concerto (1902); a piano sonata; studies and piano pieces for the left hand alone; songs; etc. He publ. an autobiography, *Aus meinem Leben* (German ed., 3 vols., 1911-20).

Ziegler, Edward, American music critic and administrator; b. Baltimore, March 25, 1870; d. New York, Oct. 25, 1947. He was music critic of the N.Y. 'American' in 1902, of the N.Y. 'World' from 1903 to 1908, and of the N.Y. 'Herald' from 1908 to 1917; was administrative secretary of the Metropolitan Opera House (1917-20), and assistant general manager (from 1920).

Ziehn (tsēn), **Bernhard,** noted German-American music theorist and teacher; b. Erfurt, Jan. 20, 1845; d. Chicago, Sept. 8, 1912. He studied at the teacher's seminary in Erfurt; was for 3 years a school teacher in Mühlhausen, Thuringia; in 1868, emigrated to the U.S.; taught German, mathematics, and music theory at the German Lutheran School in Chicago (1868-71); subsequently became a private music teacher and established himself as a theorist; his 'enharmonic law,' built on the principle of functional equality of chords, is an original contribution to the theory of harmony. He was also an important teacher; John Alden Carpenter, among others, was his pupil. —Writings: *System der Übungen für Clavierspieler* (1881); *Ein Lehrgang für den ersten Clavierunterricht* (1881); *Harmonie- und Modulationslehre* (1887; 2nd ed., 1909; completely recast and publ. in English as *Manual of Harmony: Theoretical and Practical,* 1907; valuable for the choice and range of the examples); *Five- and Six-Part Harmonies* (1911; contains some 800 musical examples); *Canonical Studies; a New Technic in Composition* (1912; in both English and German); wrote a number of theoretical and polemical articles in German musical journals (particularly against Riemann); a collection of his articles (in German), ed. by J. Goebel, was publ. by the German-American Historical Society of Illinois, as *Gesammelte Aufsätze zur Geschichte und Theorie der Musik* (Chicago, 1927). —Cf. W . Sargeant, *Bernhard Ziehn, Precursor,* in the 'Mus. Quarterly' (April, 1933); H. J. Moser, *Bernhard Ziehn: der deutsch-amerikanische Musiktheoretiker* (Bayreuth, 1950). See also 'Dictionary of American Biography.'

Ziehrer (tsē'-rĕr), **Karl Michael,** Austrian bandleader and composer of operettas; b. Vienna, May 2, 1843; d. there, Nov. 14, 1922. Entirely self-taught in music, he organized in 1863 a dance orch., with which he made tours of Austria and Germany, introducing his own pieces; with an enlarged orch. (50 players) he established a regular series of popular concerts in Vienna, which met with great success; in 1907 he was appointed music director of the court balls. His fortunes declined with the fall of the Habsburg monarchy, and he died in want. He publ. nearly 600 marches and dances for orch. (some very popular: *Meeresleuchten, Evatöchter, Donauwalzer, Alt-Wien, Ziehrereien,* etc.) and produced in Vienna a number of operettas: *Wiener Kinder* (Feb. 19, 1881); *Mahomeds Paradies* (Feb. 26,

1866); *König Jerôme* (Nov. 28, 1878); *Ein Deutschmeister* (Nov. 30, 1888); *Der schöne Rigo* (May 24, 1898); *Die Landstreicher,* his best work (July 29, 1899); *Die drei Wünsche* (March 9, 1901); *Der Fremdenführer* (Oct. 11, 1902); *Der Schätzmeister* (Dec. 10, 1904); *Fesche Geister* (July 7, 1905); *Am Lido* (Aug. 31, 1907); *Ein tolles Mädel* (Nov. 8, 1907); *Der Liebeswalzer* (Oct. 24, 1908); *Die Gaukler* (Sept. 6, 1909); *Herr und Frau Biedermeier* (Oct. 5, 1910); *In 50 Jahren* (Jan. 7, 1911); *Fürst Casimir* (Sept. 13, 1913); *Der Husarengeneral* (Oct. 3, 1913); *Das dumme Herz* (Feb. 27, 1914); *Die verliebte Eskadron* (July 11, 1920).

Zielinski, Jaroslaw de, Polish pianist; b. Lubycza Królewska, Galicia, March 31, 1844; d. Santa Barbara, Calif., July 25, 1922. He studied piano with Mikuli in Lwów and Schulhoff in Vienna; in 1863, taking active part in the Polish revolution against Russia, he was severely wounded; came to the U.S. in 1864, enlisted in a Massachusetts regiment, and served to the end of the Civil War; subsequently was active as pianist and teacher in New York, Detroit, and Buffalo; eventually settled in Los Angeles, where he founded the Zielinski Trio Club. He publ. some graceful piano music *(Prelude, At the Spring, Gavotte, Minuet, Bourrée, Dreams,* mazurkas, etc.); author of *The Poles in Music* (in vol. 18 of 'The Century Library of Music').

Zika, Richard, Czech violinist and composer; b. Vsetín, Moravia, Jan. 9, 1897; d. Prague, Nov. 10, 1947. He studied with his father, and later took courses at the Prague Cons.; was 1st violinist in the Prague Quartet (1920-32), and then (1932-46) in the Ondříček Quartet; in 1946 became prof. at the Prague Academy of Musical Arts. He composed some quartet music.

Zilcher (tsil'-her), **Hermann,** German composer; b. Frankfurt, Aug. 18, 1881; d. Würzburg, Jan. 1, 1948. He studied piano with his father, Paul Zilcher, a music teacher; later at Hoch's Cons. in Frankfurt, with J. Kwast (piano), I. Knorr and B. Scholz (composition). From 1901 to 1905 he was in Berlin as concert pianist and teacher; 1905-08, taught piano at Hoch's Cons., Frankfurt; from 1908 to 1920, was prof. at the Akademie der Tonkunst in Munich; from 1920, director of the Würzburg Cons. and conductor of the symph. concerts there. He toured as pianist in Europe, and in the U. S. (1905, with Franz von Vecsey). —Works: incidental music for several Shakespearian plays: *As You Like It* (1917), *The Winter's Tale* (1919), *The Taming of the Shrew* (1926), and *A Comedy of Errors* (1934); the comic opera *Doktor Eisenbart* (Mannheim, 1922); *Liebesmesser,* oratorio (Strasbourg, 1913); 5 symphonies (No. 5, 1947; performed posthumously, Hamburg, Feb. 11, 1948); *An mein deutsches Land,* prelude for chorus and orch.; *Tanzphantasie* (produced as a ballet, Hamburg, 1933); *Rameau Suite,* for orch. (1934); double concerto for 2 violins and orch.; violin concerto; piano concerto; *Nacht und Morgen* for 2 pianos, orch., and kettledrums; chamber music; many piano pieces; about 150 songs; etc. —Cf. W. Altmann, *Hermann Zilcher,* in vol. II of 'Monographien moderner Musiker' (Leipzig, 1907); H. Oppenheim, *Hermann Zilcher* (Munich, 1921).

Zillig, Winfried, German conductor and composer; b. Würzburg, April 1, 1905. He studied with Schoenberg in Vienna and Berlin and has largely adopted the 12-tone method of composition; from 1928 to 1943 conducted opera in Oldenburg, Düsseldorf, Essen, etc.; 1947-51, conductor of the Hesse Radio. —Works: the operas *Rossknecht* (Düsseldorf, Feb. 11, 1933), *Das Opfer* (Hamburg, Nov. 12, 1937), *Die Windsbraut* (Leipzig, May 12, 1941), *Troilus und Cressida* (Düsseldorf, Feb. 3, 1951); *Chorfantasie* for chorus and orch. (Frankfurt, May 30, 1952); a cello concerto; several string quartets and other chamber music; songs; piano pieces.

Ziloti, Alexander. See Siloti.

Zimbalist, Efrem, violinist and composer; b. Rostov on the Don, Russia, April 9, 1889. He began to study the violin with his father, an orchestra conductor; from 1901 to 1907 he studied with Leopold Auer at the St. Petersburg Cons., graduating as winner of the gold medal and a scholarship of 1200 rubles. He made his European début in Berlin, on Nov. 7, 1907, and created a sensation; a month later he produced a similar effect in London, and within a year most of the music centers of Europe had heard and admired him. In 1911 he emigrated to the U.S. and made his American début with the Boston Symph. Orch. on Oct. 27, 1911, playing Glazunov's violin concerto (its 1st performance in the U.S.). In 1914 he married the singer Alma

Gluck (q. v.); his second wife, whom he married in 1943, was Mrs. Mary Louise Curtis Bok, founder of the Curtis Institute of Music in Philadelphia. Zimbalist toured in the Far East, as well as throughout Europe and the U.S. In 1941 he became director of the Curtis Institute. —Works: the opera *Landara* (Philadelphia, April 6, 1956); *Slavonic Dances,* for violin and orch.; *American Rhapsody,* for orch. (Chicago, March 3, 1936; revised version, Philadelphia, Feb. 5, 1943); *Portrait of an Artist,* symph. poem (Philadelphia, Dec. 7, 1945); a violin concerto; a string quartet; a violin sonata; *Concert Phantasy on Le Coq d'or* for violin and piano; *Sarasateana,* for violin and piano; songs; etc. He publ. *One Hour's Daily Exercises* for violin.

Zimmer, Friedrich August, German organist and music educator; b. Herrengosserstädt, Thuringia, Feb. 26, 1826; d. Berlin, Feb. 8, 1899. He studied in Weissenfels; then devoted himself to teaching; publ. *Elementarmusiklehre* (new ed. by G. Hecht, 1901), a *Violin-Schule,* and *Die Orgel* (1897). —His son, **Friedrich Zimmer** (b. Gardelegen, Sept. 22, 1855; d. Giessen, Dec. 5, 1919), was a student of theology, and prof. at the Univ. of Königsberg (until 1890); publ. numerous collections for schools, and books of Lutheran hymns; also composed choruses and songs for children. —Cf. W. Stölten, *Friedrich Zimmer, ein deutscher Volkserzieher* (1933).

Zimmerman, Louis, Dutch violinist and composer; b. Groningen, July 19, 1873; d. Amsterdam, March 6, 1954. He studied at the Leipzig Cons. with Hans Sitt and Carl Reinecke; also with Eugène Ysaÿe in Brussels. He was a member of the Concertgebouw Orch. in Amsterdam (1899-1904); taught violin at the Royal College of Music, London (1904-1910); then rejoined the Concertgebouw as its concertmaster, retiring in 1940. He wrote numerous violin pieces; also cadenzas for the violin concertos by Beethoven and Brahms.

Zimmerman, Pierre-Joseph-Guillaume, famous French piano teacher and composer; b. Paris, March 19, 1785; d. there, Oct. 29, 1853. The son of a Paris piano maker, he entered the Paris Cons. in 1798, studying under Boieldieu, Rey, Catel, and Cherubini; won 1st prize for piano in 1800, and for harmony in 1802; became piano prof. at the Cons. in 1816, and was pensioned in 1848. Among his many pupils were Alkan, Marmontel, Lacombe, Ambroise Thomas, and César Franck. —Works: opera *L'Enlèvement* (Opéra-Comique, Oct. 26, 1830); 2 piano concertos; a piano sonata; 24 études; etc. His chief work is the *Encyclopédie du Pianiste,* a complete method for piano, Part III of which is a treatise on harmony and counterpoint. —Cf. J. B. Labat, *Zimmerman et l'École française de piano* (Paris, 1865).

Zimmermann, Agnes, pianist and composer; b. Cologne, July 5, 1847; d. London, Nov. 14, 1925. She studied at the Royal Academy of Music in London with Potter and Ernst Pauer (piano), and Charles Steggall and G. Macfarren (composition); made her début at the Crystal Palace on Dec. 5, 1863; toured England and Germany, and won high repute as an interpreter of classical compositions. She edited the sonatas of Mozart and Beethoven, and the complete piano works of Schumann (for Novello). She was also a composer; wrote a piano trio; 3 violin sonatas; cello sonata; many piano pieces. —Cf. Lady Arbuthnot, *In Memoriam Agnes Zimmerman,* in the 'Mus. Times' (1926).

Zimmermann, Anton, Austrian composer; b. Pressburg, 1741; d. there, Oct. 8, 1781. Kapellmeister to Prince Batthyány, and organist at Pressburg Cathedral. —He publ. 9 sonatas for piano and violin; a piano concerto; *Die Belagerung von Valenciennes* for piano and violin; 6 string quartets; 6 violin duos; and the Singspiel *Andromeda und Perseus* (Vienna, Apri 23, 1781); other works in MS.

Zimmermann, Bernd Alois, German composer; b. Bliesheim, near Cologne, March 20, 1918. He studied in Cologne with Heinrich Lemacher and Philipp Jarnach; later with Fortner and Leibowitz in Darmstadt; returning to Cologne he became prof. at the Cons. there. His works include *Lob der Torheit,* for soloists, chorus, and orch. (1948); 4 symphonies (No. 4, composed 1947-53, was performed at the Strasbourg Festival of the International Society for Contemporary Music, June 13, 1958); violin concerto (Salzburg Festival of the International Society for Contemporary Music, June 26, 1952); oboe concerto (Donaueschingen Festival, Oct., 1952); sonata for unaccompanied viola (Donaueschingen Festival, Oct. 16, 1955); *Canto di Speranza,* for cello and chamber orch. (Darmstadt, Sept. 12, 1958); also a string trio (1944); a violin sonata (1950); *Konfigurationen,* 8 pieces for piano (1956); minor compositions of various kinds.

Zinck, Benedikt Friedrich, German composer; b. Husum, Holstein, May 23, 1743; d. Ludwigslust, Mecklenburg, June 23, 1801. He was a church organist; in 1783 became court musician at Ludwigslust. Among his works are several symphonies, harpsichord sonatas, chamber music.

Zinck, Harnak Otto Conrad, German composer, brother of Benedikt Friedrich Zinck; b. Husum, Holstein, July 2, 1746; d. Copenhagen, Feb. 15, 1832. He was organist in Hamburg; then joined his brother at Ludwigslust, but left in 1787 for Copenhagen, where he was church organist and teacher; there he produced an opera to a Danish text. *Selim og Mirza* (Copenhagen, Feb. 1, 1790); also composed several oratorios, instrumental music, etc.; publ. *Die nördliche Harfe* (Copenhagen, 1801; on Scandinavian music) and *Vorlesungen über Musik und ihre nützlichste Anwendung* (Copenhagen, 1813).

Zingarelli (tsin-gah-rel'-lē), **Nicola Antonio,** Italian composer; b. Naples, April 4, 1752; d. Torre del Greco, near Naples, May 5, 1837. He studied at the Cons. di Loreto, Naples, with Fenaroli and Speranza (composition); also studied violin. His first stage work, *I quattro pazzi,* was performed at the Cons. in 1768. After finishing school in 1769 he earned his living as a violin teacher. He spent much time traveling throughout Italy, supervising the production of his operas. In 1792 he was appointed maestro di cappella at the Cathedral of Milan; in 1794, at the Santa Casa in Loreto; and in 1804, at the Sistine Chapel in the Vatican, Rome. In 1811, for refusing to conduct a Te Deum to celebrate the birthday of Napoleon's son, the 'King of Rome,' he was imprisoned at Civitavecchia, and later transported to Paris by order of Napoleon, who set him at liberty and liberally paid him for a Mass written in Paris. As Fioravanti had meanwhile become maestro at St. Peter's, Zingarelli went to Naples, and in 1813 became director of the royal Collegio di Musica; in 1816 he succeeded Paisiello as maestro at the Naples Cathedral. He was renowned as a teacher; Bellini, Mercadante, Carlo Conti, Lauro Rossi, Morlacchi, and Sir Michael Costa were his students. His operas, interpreted by the finest singers of the time (Catalani, Crescentini, Grassini, Marchesi, and Rubinelli), were highly successful. His facility was such that he was able to write an opera in a week. He wrote 37 operas in all; of these the following were produced at La Scala, Milan: *Alsinda* (Feb. 22, 1785); *Ifigenia in Aulide* (Jan. 27, 1787); *La Morte di Cesare* (Dec. 26, 1790); *Pirro, re d'Epiro* (Dec. 26, 1791); *Il Mercato di Monfregoso* (Sept. 22, 1792); *La Secchia rapita* (Sept. 7, 1793); *Artaserse* (Dec. 26, 1793); *Giulietta e Romeo,* after Shakespeare (Jan. 30, 1796; his best known work; staged all over Europe, and also in N. Y., with considerable success, but disappeared from the repertory after Zingarelli's death); *Meleagro* (Jan., 1798); *Il Ritratto* (Oct. 12, 1799); *Clitennestra* (Dec. 26, 1800). Other operas: *Antigono* (Mantua, April 13, 1786); *Alzira* (Florence, Sept. 7, 1794); *Il Conte di Saldagna* (Venice, Dec. 26, 1794); *Orazi e Curiazi* (Naples, Nov. 4, 1795); *La Morte di Mitridate* (Venice, May 27, 1797); *Il Ratto delle Sabine* (Venice, Dec. 26, 1799); *Edipo a Colono* (Venice, Dec. 26, 1802); *La Distruzione di Gerusalemme* (Florence, Nov. 27, 1803); *L'Oracolo sannita* (Naples, Oct. 11, 1806); *Il Ritorno di Serse* (Modena, July 16, 1808); *Baldovino* (Rome, Feb. 11, 1811); *Berenice, regina d'Armenia* (Rome, Nov. 12, 1811). He further wrote a number of oratorios, among them *Pimmalione* (Naples, 1779), *Ero* (Milan, 1786), *Telemaco* (Milan, 1787), *Il Trionfo di David* (Naples, 1788), *Francesca da Rimini* (Rome, 1804), *Tancredi al sepolcro di Clorinda* (Naples, 1805), and *La Fuga in Egitto* (Naples, 1837); a vast amount of church music; the Cons. di Loreto contains 541 MSS by Zingarelli, in a collection known as 'Annuale di Zingarelli' (or 'Annuale di Loreto'), including a series of Masses for every day in the year; a 4-part Miserere 'alla Palestrina' (1827); 73 Magnificats, 28 Stabat Maters, 21 Credos, many Te Deums, motets, hymns, etc.; also solfeggi, arias, organ sonatas, some chamber music. —Cf. R. Liberatore, *Necrologia di N. Zingarelli* (Naples, 1837); A. Schmid, *Joseph Haydn und N. Zingarelli* (Vienna, 1847); F. Florimo in vol. II of *La Scuola musicale di Napoli* (Naples, 1880); S. di Giacomo, *Il fiero Zingarelli,* in 'Musica d'oggi' (June, 1923); P. Dotto, *N. Zingarelli,* in 'Musica d'oggi' (July, 1941).

Zingel (tsing'-el), **Rudolf Ewald,** German organist and composer; b. Liegnitz, Sept. 5, 1876; d. there, Feb. 20, 1944. He studied at the Hochschule für Musik in Berlin; then was active as church organist and choral conductor in Berlin and in Frankfurt-on-the-Oder. He wrote 2 operas, *Margot* (Frankfurt-on-the-Oder, 1902) and *Persepolis* (Rostock, 1909); an operetta, *Liebeszauber* (Stralsund, 1908); a symph. poem, *Freudvoll und liedvoll;* a secular oratorio,

Der wilde Jäger; several sacred cantatas for men's chorus and string orch.; numerous piano pieces and songs.

Zinkeisen (tsink'-ī-zen), **Konrad Ludwig Dietrich,** German violinist and composer; b. Hanover, June 3, 1779; d. Brunswick, Nov. 28, 1838. He was trained by his father, and by Rode at Wolfenbüttel; played 1st violin under Forkel at the Academic Concerts in Göttingen; in 1819 appointed chamber musician in the Brunswick court orch. He wrote 6 violin concertos, 4 orch. overtures, 3 string quartets; concertos for oboe, for clarinet, for basset horn, for bassoon, and various other pieces for solo instruments with orch.; music for military band; choral works.

Zipoli, Domenico, Italian composer and organist; b. Prato, Oct. 16, 1688; d. Córdoba, Argentina, Jan. 2, 1726. He went to Rome as a young man; was organist at the Jesuit Church there. His oratorios *Sant' Antonio di Padova* (1712) and *Santa Caterina, vergine e martire* (1714) were presented in Rome. In 1716 he publ. *Sonate d'intavolatura per organo e cimbalo.* He joined the Jesuit order at Seville in 1716, and in 1717 went to South America, where he became organist of the Jesuit Church in Córdoba, Argentina. Walsh of London reprinted parts of the *Sonate d'intavolatura* under the titles *Six Suits of Italian Lessons for the Harpsichord* and *Third Collection of Toccatas, Vollentarys and Fugues.* Modern reprints of Zipoli's pieces are found in Torchi's 'L'Arte Musicale in Italia' (vol. III), Farrenc's 'Trésor du pianiste' (vol. XI), Pauer's 'Alte Meister,' 'Raccolta Nazionale delle musiche italiane,' etc. —Cf. G. Pannain, *Le Origini e lo sviluppo dell' arte pianistica in Italia dal 1500 al 1730* (Naples, 1919); L. Ayestarán, *Domenico Zipoli, el gran compositor y organista romano del 1700 en el Rio de La Plata,* in 'Revista histórica' of the Museo Histórico Nacional (Montevideo, 1941; basic study establishing biographical facts); A. Salazar, *El Caso de Domenico Zipoli,* in 'Nuestra Musica' (Mexico, May, 1946; arguing against the identification of the immigrant organist Zipoli with the composer); V. de Rubertis, *Dove e quando nacque e morì Domenico Zipoli,* in 'Rivista Musicale Italiana' (April-June, 1951).

Zipp, Friedrich, German choral composer; b. Frankfurt, June 20, 1914; he studied in Berlin and at Hoch's Cons. in Frankfurt; then again in Berlin, with Armin Knab (composition); from 1938 occupied various teaching posts in Frankfurt. He publ. a number of cantatas, motets, song cycles, and various choral works; also piano pieces.

Zítek, Otakar, Czech writer on music and composer; b. Prague, Nov. 5, 1892. He studied composition with Novák at the Vienna Cons. and musicology with Adler and Graedener at the Univ. there; was music critic for the 'Hudební Revue' and 'Lidové Noviny' in Prague, and in 1920 taught operatic dramaturgy at the Cons. there; from 1921, stage director at the National Theater in Brno, and teacher at the Brno Cons. —Works: the operas *Vznesene srdce (The Exalted Heart;* 1918) and *Pád Petra Králence (The Downfall of Peter Králence;* Brno, March 23, 1923); a ballet *O růži,* after Wilde's *Birthday of the Infanta* (*On the Rose,* Pilsen, 1942); *Město,* symph. poem (1925); songs; etc. He also publ. a book, *The New Opera* (in Czech).

Zmeskall, Nikolaus, Baron **von Domanovecz,** Hungarian diplomat and musical amateur; b. 1759; d. Vienna, June 23, 1833. He was secretary of the Hungarian Chancellery in Vienna; was an intimate friend of Beethoven, who dedicated to him the string quartet op. 95. Zmeskall was also a composer in his own right; wrote 14 string quartets and other instrumental music. —Cf. A. Sandberger, *Beethovens Freund Zmeskall als Komponist,* in his *Gesammelte Aufsätze,* vol. II (1924); C. Pidoll, *Verklungenes Spiel: Erinnerungen des Herrn Nikolaus Zmeskall* (Innsbruck, 1949).

Znosko-Borovsky, Alexander Feodorovitch, Russian composer; b. Kiev, Feb. 27, 1908. He studied violin and composition in Kiev; was composer for films there (1931-42); then in the army (1942-45); in 1946 he returned to Kiev. —Works: ballet *Akpamyk* on Turkmenian themes (Ashkhabad, April 14, 1945); cantata, *Our Victory* (Kiev, May 8, 1946); a symph. poem, *Kiev* (Kiev, March 9, 1949); violin concerto (Kiev, Dec. 17, 1955); a string quartet on Ukrainian themes (1937); *In Turkmenia,* for string quartet (1942); sonata for unaccompanied violin (1950); Scherzo for 3 trombones (1938); songs; film music.

Zoeller (tsöl'-ler), **Carl,** composer; b. Berlin, March 28, 1840; d. London, July 13, 1889. He studied violin with Hubert Ries in Berlin; after traveling in Germany with various opera troupes as violinist, he went to London, settling there in 1873; in 1879, he became bandmaster of the 7th (Queen's

Own) Hussars. In England he often performed on the viola d'amore; published *The Viole d'Amour, Its Origin and History, and Art of Playing it.* He composed an operetta, *The Missing Heir,* and a serious music drama, *Mary Stuart of Fotheringay;* a violin concerto; songs.

Zoellner, Joseph, Sr., American violinist; b. Brooklyn, Feb. 2, 1862; d. Los Angeles, Jan. 24, 1950. During his parents' residence at Aschaffenburg he studied piano and violin there; returning to N. Y., he continued his violin studies; in 1882 he established a music school in Brooklyn (until 1903); then was in Stockton, Calif. (1903-06) and in Brussels (1907-12). During his stay in Belgium he organized, with 2 sons and a daughter, the Zoellner Quartet, giving performances in Belgium, and also traveling to Berlin and Paris. From 1912 till 1922, the family lived in N. Y.; in 1922 Zoellner founded with his children the Zoellner Cons. of Music in Los Angeles.

Zoilo, Annibale, Italian composer; b. Rome, c. 1537; d. Loreto, 1592. He was maestro di cappella at San Luigi dei Francesi from 1561 to 1566; at San Giovanni in Laterano from Jan., 1568, to June, 1570. In 1570 he became a singer in the Papal Choir, Rome (until 1581); then was at the Cathedral of Todi; returning to Rome, he entered the service of Cardinal Sirleto (until 1584); subsequently became maestro at the Santa Casa in Loreto (till June 30, 1592). In 1577 he and Palestrina were entrusted with the revision of the Roman Gradual *(Editio Medicaea).* He publ. *Madrigali a 4 e 5 voci* (Rome, 1563); a *Salve Regina* for 12 voices is in Constantini's 'Selectae Cantiones excellentissimorum auctorum' (Rome, 1614), and various compositions in other collections, publ. between 1567 and 1616. Masses and a 16-part *Tenebrae* are in MS (in the archives of the Papal Chapel); 4 madrigals for 5 voices are in Torchi's 'L'Arte Musicale in Italia' (vol. I). —Cf. R. Casimiri, *Anibale Zoilo e la sua famiglia: nuovi documenti biografici,* in 'Note d'Archivio' (Jan.-April, 1940).

Zöllner, Heinrich, German composer, son of Karl Friedrich Zöllner; b. July 4, 1854; d. Freiburg-im-Breisgau, May 4, 1941. He studied at the Leipzig Cons. under Reinecke, Jadassohn, Richter, and Wenzel. After serving a few years as music director at the Univ. of Dorpat, Russia, he settled in Cologne as choral conductor; in 1890 he was engaged as conductor of the Deutscher Liederkranz in N. Y.; in 1898 returned to Germany, and was choral director and prof. of composition at the Leipzig Cons. (1902-07); then was conductor at the Flemish Opera in Antwerp (1907-14); subsequently settled in Freiburg. —Works: the operas *Frithjof* (Cologne, 1884), *Die lustigen Chinesinnen* (Cologne, 1886), *Faust* (Munich, Oct. 19, 1887), *Matteo Falcone* (N. Y., 1894, *Der Überfall* (Dresden, Sept. 7, 1895), *Die versunkene Glocke* (Berlin, July 8, 1899; his best opera), *Der Schützenkönig* (Leipzig, 1903), *Zigeuner* (Stuttgart, 1912); the musical comedy *Das hölzerne Schwert* (Kassel, 1897); choral works with orch.: *Die Hunnenschlacht; Morgengesang im Kriege; Das Fest der Rebenblüte; Wanderers Sturmlied; Zum Lutherfeste; Kolumbus; Lied fahrender Schüler; Hymnus der Liebe; König Sigurd Ring's Brautfahrt; Indianischer Liebesgesang,* from 'Hiawatha'; *Die Meerfahrer; Heldenrequiem; Königsode; Zwei Sprüche; Heerschau; Bonifacius; Der deutsche Michel; Aventiure; Robespierre; Fahnenschwur; Totentanz; Talismane; Angelus; Die Leipziger Schlacht; Aus den Freiheitskriegen 1813-1814; Deutschland und seine Kinder; Die neue Welt;* etc.; for orch.: 3 symphonies; *Sommerfahrt,* for string orch.; *Elegie,* for violin and orch.; *Unter dem Sternenbanner,* overture; *Serenade* for flute and string orch.; chamber music; songs. He also publ. a poem, *Beethoven in Bonn. Ein Sang vom Rhein* (1898). —Cf. E. Segnitz, *Heinrich Zöllner,* in vol. II of 'Monographien moderner Musiker' (Leipzig, 1907).

Zöllner, Karl Friedrich, German choral conductor and composer; b. Mittelhausen, Thuringia, March 17, 1800; d. Leipzig, Sept. 25, 1860. He studied at the Thomasschule, Leipzig; became a vocal instructor and began writing male choruses; in 1833 he founded in Leipzig a 'Liedertafel' known as the 'Zöllner-Verein,' a male choral society modeled after Zelter's Berlin organization; after Zöllner's death, several choral societies were united to form the 'Zöllner-Bund.' Zöllner was one of the most successful German composers of part-songs for male choruses; he also wrote for mixed chorus, and songs with piano accompaniment. —Cf. R. Hänsch, *Der Liedermeister Karl Friedrich Zöllner* (Dresden, 1927).

Zöllner, Karl Heinrich, German composer; b. Öls, Silesia, May 5, 1792; d. Wandsbeck, near Hamburg, July 2, 1836. He toured Germany as an organist; for a while lived in Vienna; in 1833 settled in Hamburg. He wrote an opera, *Kunz von Kauffungen* (Vienna, March 27, 1826); a melodrama, *Ein Uhr;* publ. Masses, motets, psalms, part-songs, organ pieces, a piano sonata, piano pieces, etc.

Zolotarev (zŏh-lŏh-tăh-ryŏf'), **Vassily Andreyevitch,** Russian composer; b. Taganrog, March 7, 1873. He was a student at the court chapel in St. Petersburg, where he studied violin with Krasnoutsky, and composition with Balakirev and Liadov (graduated in 1892); then entered the St. Petersburg Cons., studying with Rimsky-Korsakov (graduated in 1900); received the Rubinstein Prize for his cantata *Paradise and Peri.* He then held numerous teaching positions: instructor of violin at the court chapel (1897-1900); teacher of composition at the Rostov Music School (1906-08); at the Moscow Cons. (1908-18), the Ekaterinodar Cons. (1912-24), the Odessa Cons. (1924-26), the Kiev Musico-Dramatic Institute (1926-31), the Sverdlovsk Music School (1931-33), and the Minsk Cons. (1933-41). In 1941 he settled in Moscow. In 1955 he was awarded the Order of Lenin. —Works: the operas *The Decembrists* (Moscow, Dec. 27, 1925) and *Ak-Gul,* on Uzbek themes (1942); ballet, *Lake Prince* (Minsk, Jan. 15, 1949); 6 symphonies: I (1902), II (1905; revised 1955), III (1935), IV (1936), V (1942), VI (1943); overture, *Fête villageoise; Rhapsodie hébraïque,* for orch.; symph. suites: *Moldavian Suite* (1926), *Uzbek Suite* (1931), *Tadzhik Suite* (1932), *White-Russian Suite* (1936); cello concerto (1943); 6 string quartets (1899, 1902, 1907, 1912, 1916, 1945); piano quintet (1904); string quintet (1904); piano trio (1905); violin sonata (1922); 2 piano sonatas (1903; 1919); many songs. He publ. a manual on the fugue (Moscow, 1932).

Zopff, Hermann, German music critic and composer; b. Glogau, June 1, 1826; d. Leipzig, July 12, 1883. He studied agriculture, then music (at the Stern Cons. in Berlin); founded an 'Opernakademie' and an 'Orchesterverein' in Berlin; in 1864, settled in Leipzig as co-editor of the 'Neue Zeitschrift für Musik,' becoming editor-in-chief in 1868. He publ. *Ratschläge für angehende Dirigenten* (1861; 3rd ed., 1922) and *Grundzüge einer Theorie der Oper* (Leipzig, 1868). His compositions include a symph. poem, *Wilhelm Tell; Drei Idyllen* for small orch.; *Gesangsstück* for cello and orch.; *Asträa, oder Das Evangelium der Tat* for solo voices, chorus, and orch.; piano pieces; male choruses; songs. His 2 operas, *Makkabäus* and *Mohammed,* were publ., but not produced.

Zoras, Leonidas, Greek conductor and composer; b. Sparta, March 8, 1905. He studied in Athens and Berlin; in 1940 was appointed conductor of the National Lyric Theater in Athens. Among his compositions are a symphony (1947); incidental music and ballet for *The Legend of Violanto* (1931); *Kleftic Dance,* for orch. (1934); *Legend,* for orch. (1936); suite for orch. (1947); concertino for violin and woodwind (1950); violin sonata (1950); piano pieces; songs.

Zschocher (tchŏh-hĕr), **Johann,** noted German piano pedagogue; b. Leipzig, May 16, 1821; d. there, Jan. 6, 1897. He was a pupil of Iwan Knorr, Th. Kullak, Henselt, and Liszt. In 1846 he founded the 'Zschocher'sches Musik-Institut' in Leipzig, which became a flourishing music school, still active in the 20th century.

Zsolt, Nándor, Hungarian violinist and composer; b. Esztergom, May 12, 1887; d. Budapest, June 25, 1936. He studied violin with Hubay in Budapest; in 1908 went to London, where he participated in chamber music concerts; returning to Budapest, he became a violin teacher. His piano quintet (1914) was awarded a prize. He also wrote a symph.; many violin pieces (*Valse Caprice, Berceuse, Enchaînée, Satyr et Dryade,* etc.). —Cf. Cyril Scott, *Nándor Zsolt,* in 'Monthly Mus. Record' (1915).

Zubiaurre (y Urionabarrenechea), Valentí, Spanish composer; b. Villa de Garay, Feb. 13, 1837; d. Madrid, Jan. 13, 1914. He was a chorister at Bilbao; at the age of 16 he undertook a voyage to South America; returning to Spain in 1866, he began to study music seriously with Hilarión Eslava. He wrote a considerable number of sacred works; then turned to opera; received 1st national prize with his opera *Fernando el Emplazado* (Madrid, May 12, 1871); in 1873, went to Rome on a government stipend; in 1875 was named 2nd maestro at the Royal Chapel in Madrid, and in 1878, succeeded Eslava as 1st maestro; in the same year he was appointed prof. at the Madrid Cons. His 2nd opera, *Ledia,* was produced with considerable success in Madrid, on April 22, 1877. He also composed several zarzuelas, a symph., a potpourri of Basque folksongs, choruses, etc.

Zucca, Mana. See **Mana-Zucca.**

Zuccalmaglio (tsook-kahl-mahl'-yō), **Anton Wilhelm Florentin von,** German collector of folksongs and writer on music; b. Waldbröl, April 12, 1803; d. Nachrodt, near Grüna, Westphalia, March 23, 1869. The son of a physician, who was a musical amateur, he learned music at home; contributed to the 'Neue Zeitschrift für Musik' during Schumann's editorship, under the pseudonyms Wilhelm von Waldbrühl and Dorfküster Wedel; publ. 2 collections of folksongs, in 1829 and 1836 (with E. Baumstark); then brought out (with A. Kretzschmer) the important compilation, *Deutsche Volkslieder mit ihren Originalweisen* (2 vols.; 1838; 1840). However, these songs are only partly authentic; a few melodies were composed by Zuccalmaglio himself; others were combined from various sources; the texts were frequently rearranged. Brahms made use of the collection for his arrangements of German folksongs. —Cf. M. Friedlaender, *Zuccalmaglio und das Volkslied,* in the 'Jahrbuch der Bibliothek Peters' (1918; also separately); W. Wiora, *Die Herkunft der Melodien in Kretzschmers und Zuccalmaglios Sammlung,* in the 'Beiheft' of the 'Jahrbuch für Volksliedforschung' (1941), revised and publ. as *Die rheinisch-bergischen Melodien bei Zuccalmaglio und Brahms* (Bad Godesberg, 1953).

Zuelli (tsoo-ehl'-lē), **Guglielmo,** Italian composer; b. Reggio Emilia, Oct. 20, 1859; d. Milan, Oct. 8, 1941. He studied with A. Busi and L. Mancinelli in Bologna; after teaching and conducting in various provincial towns, he became director of the Cons. in Palermo (1894-1911), of the Parma Cons. (1911-29), and of the Liceo Musicale of Alessandria, Piedmont (1929-33); then retired. —Works: the opera *La Fata del Nord* (Milan, May 4, 1884; Sonzogno prize); opera-ballet *Il Profeta di Korassan; Inno alla Notte* for solo voices, chorus, and orch.; 2 symphonies; *Un Saluto al mare,* symph. suite (its 3rd movement, *Festa delle sirene,* became extremely popular as a separate piece); *Il Canto del Coaro Romagnuolo* for orch.; a string quartet and minor pieces for strings; fugues for organ; songs; etc. Author of *Gioacchino Rossini: Pagine segrete* (Bologna, 1922). —Cf. G. Tebaldini, *Guglielmo Zuelli,* in 'Rivista Musicale Italiana' (1942).

Zulauf (tsoo'-lowf), **Ernst,** German conductor; b. Kassel, Feb. 15, 1876. He studied with Reinecke at the Leipzig Cons., and with Kretzschmar at the Univ. there *(Dr. phil.,* 1902); held various positions as opera coach and conductor at the Staatstheater in Wiesbaden; from 1946, lived on a pension in Wiesbaden. He wrote incidental music for various plays.

Zulauf, Max, Swiss musicologist; b. Bern, May 19, 1898. He studied with Ernst Kurth at the Univ. of Bern; Ph. D. with the dissertation *Die Harmonik J. S. Bachs* (Bern, 1927); taught at the Univ. of Bern (1933-48). He publ. *Der Musikunterricht in der Geschichte des bernischen Schulwesens von 1528-1798* (Bern, 1934).

Zumpe (tsoom'-pĕh), **Hermann,** German conductor and composer; b. Taubenheim, April 9, 1850; d. Munich, Sept. 4, 1903. He studied in Bautzen and Leipzig. In 1873 he joined Wagner at Bayreuth, aiding in the preparation of the performances of *Der Ring des Nibelungen;* then conducted opera in Salzburg, Würzburg, Magdeburg, Frankfurt, and Hamburg. After some years spent in teaching and composing, he was appointed court conductor in Stuttgart in 1891; in 1895 was called to Munich in a similar capacity; then was court conductor in Schwerin (1897-1900); returned to Munich in 1900 as 'Generalmusikdirektor.' —Works: the opera *Anahna* (Berlin, 1881); the operettas *Farinelli* (Hamburg, 1886), *Karin* (Hamburg, 1888), and *Polnische Wirtschaft* (Hamburg, 1889); overtures; songs. 2 operas were performed posthumously: *Sawitri* (completed by Rosseler; Schwerin, Sept. 8, 1907) and *Das Gespenst von Horodin* (Hamburg, 1910). —See the compendium, *H. Zumpe. Persönliche Erinnerungen nebst Mitteilungen aus seinen Tagebuchblättern und Briefen,* with an introduction by E. von Possart and a list of works (Munich, 1905).

Zumsteeg (tsoom'-shtāg), **Johann Rudolf,** German composer; b. Sachsenflur, Odenwald, Jan. 10, 1760; d. Stuttgart, Jan. 27, 1802. As a pupil of the Carlsschule (near Stuttgart), he was intimate with Schiller, who attended the same school. He studied cello and theory with the Kapellmeister Poli, whom he succeeded in 1792 as director of the Stuttgart Opera. He produced 8 operas at Stuttgart, of which the best was *Die Geisterinsel,* after Shakespeare's *The Tempest* (Nov. 7, 1798); among other operas were *Elbondokani, Zalaor,* and *Das Pfauenfest;* also wrote choruses to Schiller's *Die Räuber;* 21 church cantatas; a cello concerto; duos for cellos, and other instrumental music. But it is chiefly as a composer of ballades, the precursor of Loewe and Schubert, that he is historically important; he wrote 20 ballades for solo voice with piano accompaniment, including settings for Schiller's *Maria Stuart,* Bürger's *Lenore,* Goethe's *Colma,* etc. —Cf. T. F. K. Arnold, *J. R. Zumsteeg. Seine kurze Biographie* (Erfurt, 1810; with a list of works); L. Landshoff, *J. R. Zumsteeg: ein Beitrag zur Geschichte des Liedes und der Ballade* (dissertation; Berlin, 1902); A. Sandberger, *Zumsteeg und Schubert,* in the 'Münchner Allgemeine Zeitung' (July 15, 1906); H. von Hase, *J. R. Zumsteeg,* in 'Zeitschrift für Musikwissenschaft' (vol. 2; 1920); F. Szymichowski, *J. R. Zumsteeg als Komponist von Balladen und Monodien* (dissertation; Stuttgart, 1932). For an analysis of *Die Geisterinsel,* see T. F. K. Arnold, *Gallerie der berühmtesten Tonkünstler . . .* (part I, pp. 44-96).

Zur Mühlen, Raimund von, tenor singer; b. Livonia, Nov. 10, 1854; d. Steyning, Sussex, Dec. 9, 1931. He studied singing with Stockhausen in Frankfurt and with Bussine in Paris; then took a special course with Clara Schumann, who instructed him in the interpretation of songs by Schumann and Schubert; this gave him the foundation of his career. He had his greatest success in England, where he lived from 1905 until his death. It was he who introduced into London the 'song recital' *(Liederabend;* programs devoted exculsively to songs). He was also a fine teacher. —Cf. G. Newberry, *Raimund von Zur Mühlen,* in 'Music & Letters' (1932).

Zur Nieden, Albrecht, German composer; b. Emmerich, March 6, 1819; d. Duisburg, April 14, 1873. He studied theology in Bonn, and music with Fr. Schneider at Dessau. In 1850 he settled in Duisburg as choral conductor. He publ. the 'lyrico-dramatic song' *Die Sage von der Martinswand* for solo voices, chorus, and orch., and two more works of a similar nature, *Der blinde König* and *Das Grab im Busento;* also a *Deutscher Marsch* for piano 4 hands; songs.

Zuschnied (tsoo'-shnīt), **Karl,** German choral conductor; b. Oberglogau, Silesia, May 29, 1854; d. Weimar, Aug. 1, 1926. He studied piano and composition at the Stuttgart Cons.; then occupied various posts as choral conductor and teacher in Göttingen (1879-89), Minden (1889-97), and Erfurt (1897-1907); then was director of the Hochschule für Musik in Mannheim; retired in 1917. —Works: for chorus and orch.: *Hermann der Befreier; Lenzfahrt; Sängergebet; Deutschlands Erwachen; Die Zollern und das Reich; Unter den Sternen;* men's choruses; *Konzertstück* for violin and orch.; piano pieces; songs. He publ. *Theoretisch-praktische Klavierschule* and *Methodischer Leitfaden für den Klavierunterricht.*

Zuth (tsoot), **Josef,** Austrian guitarist and musicologist; b. Fischern, near Karlsbad, Nov. 24, 1879; d. Vienna, Aug. 30, 1932. He was in the civil service (1902-25), and began to study music late in life; learned to play the guitar; studied with R. Batka; attended classes in musicology under Adler and Koczirz at the Univ. of Vienna; *Dr. phil.,* 1919, with the dissertation *Simon Molitor und die wiener Gitarristik* (publ. 1920). He taught the guitar at the Volksschule Urania in Vienna (from 1919) and edited (from 1921) the 'Zeitschrift für die Gitarre' (in 1927 the title was changed to 'Musik im Haus'); edited many works for the guitar. —Publications: *R. Batkas Vorschule des Gitarren- und Lautenspiels* (1919); *Das künstlerische Gitarrenspiel* (1920); *Die Gitarre, Spezialstudien auf theoretischer Grundlage* (6 parts; 1920); *F. Carullis Gitarrenschule* (10 parts; 1921); *Volkstümliche Gitarrenschule* (1922); *Handbuch der Laute und Gitarre* (1926-28).

Zvonař (zvoh'-nahrzh), **Joseph Leopold,** Czech organist and theorist; b. Kublov, near Prague, Jan. 22, 1824; d. Prague, Nov. 23, 1865. He studied at the Prague School for Organists, and taught there from 1844; also served as church organist. He publ. the first treatise on harmony in the Czech language; contributed articles on Czech music to various publications; publ. a valuable collection of choral arrangements of national songs, *Hudební památky české* (4 vols.; 1862-64); composed *Der Ritt zum Elfenstein* for solo voices, chorus, and orch.; a Requiem; piano pieces *(Impromptu, Loreley,* etc.); men's choruses; songs. His opera *Záboj* remained unperformed.

Zweers (zwārs), **Bernard,** Dutch composer; b. Amsterdam, May 18, 1854; d. there, Dec. 9, 1924. He studied at the Amsterdam Cons., and later in Leipzig with Jadassohn; returning to Holland, he became prof. of theory at the Amsterdam Cons. (from 1895). He wrote 3 symphonies; a *Kroningscantate* for soprano, tenor, chorus, and orch.; *St. Nicolasfeest,* children's cantata; *Kosmos* (Psalm 104) for chorus and orch.; *Ons Hollandsch* for men's chorus and orch.; church music; songs. —Cf. H. Rutters, *Bernard Zweers,* in 'Mens en Melodie' (Dec., 1949).

Zweig, Fritz, conductor; b. Olomouc, Moravia, Sept. 8, 1893. He studied with Schoenberg in Vienna; then devoted himself to opera conducting; was on the staff of the Mannheim Opera (1912-14 and 1919-21); music director at Barmen-Elberfeld (1921-23); then conducted opera in Berlin (1923-33); at the German Opera in Prague (1934-38); then appeared in Paris and London; in 1940 emigrated to America; in 1942 settled in Hollywood as a teacher.

Zwintscher (tsvin'-cher), **Bruno,** German pianist; b. Ziegenhain, May 15, 1838; d. Oberlössnitz, near Dresden, March 4, 1905. He studied piano with Julius Otto in Dresden and with Moscheles in Leipzig; taught at the Leipzig Cons. from 1875 till 1896; then settled in Dresden as a successful piano teacher. He publ. *Technische Studien* (a continuation of Plaidy's manual; English transl. by C. H. Porter) and *Schule der Ornamentik* (also available in English).

Zwyssig (tsvis'-sig), **Alberich,** Swiss composer; b. Bauen, Nov. 17, 1808; d. in the Cistercian monastery at Mehrerau, Nov. 18, 1854. He entered the Order of the Cistercians in 1826 (giving up his real name, Joseph, for the monastic name Albreich); was Kapellmeister in the monasteries of Wettingen, Zug, Wurmbach, and (shortly before his death) Mehrerau. His *Schweizer Psalm* for men's chorus a cappella (1841) attained the popularity of a national hymn; he also wrote sacred and secular choruses a cappella and some church music with organ. —Cf. B. Widmann, *Alberich Zwyssig als Komponist* (Bregenz, 1905); H. Meng, *Alberich Zwyssig, 1808-1854; Gedenkschrift* (Wettingen, 1954).

BAKER'S BIOGRAPHICAL DICTIONARY of MUSICIANS

1971 SUPPLEMENT

by

NICOLAS SLONIMSKY

G. SCHIRMER
New York/London

Printed in U.S.A.
47131cx x244
Library of Congress Catalog Card No. 66-8001
ISBN 0-911320-63-6

1971 SUPPLEMENT
to
BAKER'S BIOGRAPHICAL DICTIONARY OF MUSICIANS

AARON — ABRAMSKY

A

Aaron, Pietro. Born in 1489 (not 1480).

Aav, Evald, Estonian composer; b. Reval, Feb. 22, 1900; d. there, March 21, 1939. He studied composition in Reval with Arthur Kapp; wrote mostly vocal music to words in the Estonian language. In 1928 he composed the first national Estonian opera, *The Vikings* (Tallinn, Sept. 8, 1928). In his style of composition he followed the model of Tchaikovsky.

Aavik, Juhan. Add to compositions: 2 symphonies; a cello concerto; a concerto for double-bass and orch.; publ. a history of Estonian music (4 vols., Stockholm, 1965-69).

Abaco, Joseph Marie Clément. The name of his father was Evaristo (not Evariste). Place of death, Arbizzano di Valpolicella (not Volpolicella). He composed (at least) 30 cello sonatas (not 29).

Abbado, Claudio, Italian conductor, brother of Marcello Abbado; b. Milan, June 26, 1933. He received his early training from his father; then enrolled in the Milan Cons., graduating in 1955 as pianist; in 1957 he studied conducting with Swarowsky in Vienna. In 1958 he won the Koussevitzky conducting prize in Tanglewood and in 1963 the Mitropoulos prize in New York. He rapidly established himself as a fine symphonic conductor; his guest appearances with the N. Y. Philharmonic and the Boston Symphony were acclaimed. He also conducted opera at La Scala in Milan. In 1971 he was engaged as permanent conductor of the Vienna Philharmonic.

Abbado, Marcello. Add to works: *Costruzioni* for 5 small orchestras (1964); double concerto for violin, piano and 2 chamber orchestras (1967); quadruple concerto for piano, violin, viola, cello and orch. (1969); 3 string quartets (1947, 1953, 1969). He was director of the Liceo Musicale in Piacenza (1958-66); in 1966 appointed director of the Rossini Cons. in Pesaro.

Abell, Arthur. Died in Hastings-on-Hudson, N. Y., Feb. 8, 1958.

Aber, Adolf. Died in London, May 21, 1960.

Abraham, Paul, Hungarian composer of light operas; b. Apatin, Nov. 2, 1892; d. Hamburg, May 6, 1960. He studied in Budapest and wrote chamber music before turning to light opera. His first successful operetta was *Victoria und ihr Husar* (Vienna, Dec. 23, 1930); his other popular productions were *Die Blume von Hawaii* (Leipzig, July 24, 1931) and *Ball im Savoy* (Vienna, Dec. 25, 1933). In 1938 Abraham went to the U.S., but suffered a mental breakdown, and was in 1955 committed to a sanitarium in Hamburg, where he died.

Abramsky, Alexander, Russian composer; b. Lutsk, Jan. 22, 1898. He studied with Miaskovsky at the Moscow Cons., graduating in 1926. Commissioned to do research work in Asian folklore, he traveled to Uzbekistan; wrote a music drama on native themes, *Laylikhon and Anarkhon* (Andizhan, Dec. 28, 1943). He also composed a piano concerto (1941); *Laconic Sonata* for piano solo; many choruses.

Abreu, José Antonio, Venezuelan composer; b. Valera, Venezuela, May 17, 1939. He studied with local teachers before going to Caracas, where he took courses with Vicente Emilio Sojo. His works follow the traditional line of tonal composition. They include *Sinfonieta Neoclásica,* 2 symphonies, a symphonic poem *Sancta et Inmaculata Virginitas; Tríptico* for 11 instruments; quintet for wind instruments; string quartet; choruses.

Absil, Jean. Continued as director of the Academy of Etterbeck until its closure in 1958; in 1962 was elected to the Royal Academy of Belgium. The full title of his musical comedy is *Fansou* (not *Fanson*) *ou le chapeau chinois.* Add to works: *Fantaisie concertante* for violin and piano (Brussels, May 12, 1959); 2nd violin concerto (1964); *Ballade* for piano left hand (1966); *Asymétries* for 2 pianos (1968); Symph. No. 4 (1969). Bibl.: R. de Guide, *Jean Absil, vie et œuvre* (Tournai, 1965).

Achron, Isidor. He was a brother of Joseph Achron.

Achron, Joseph. He and Isidor Achron were brothers. He settled in Hollywood in 1934 (not in 1939). Add bibl.: Ph. Moddel, *Joseph Achron* (Tel Aviv, 1966).

Adam de la Hale. He wrote *Le Jeu de Robin et de Marion* for the Anjou court in Naples (not for the Aragonese court, which was a Sicilian branch).

Adaskin, John. Died in Toronto, March 4, 1964.

Adler, Clarence. Died in New York, Dec. 24, 1969.

Adler, F. Charles. Died in Vienna, Feb. 16, 1959.

Adler, Samuel. In 1966 he was appointed professor of composition at the Eastman School of Music, Rochester. Add to works: opera, *The Outcasts of Poker Flat,* after Bret Harte (1959); 4 symphonies (1953, 1957, 1960, 1967); *Rhapsody* for violin and orch. (1961); string quartet No. 4 (1963); *Music for Eleven* for 6 woodwinds and 5 percussion instruments (1964); *7 Epigrams* for woodwind sextet (1966); *The Binding,* a biblical oratorio (1967); *5 Vignettes* for 12 trombones (1968); *City by the Lake,* a symphonic portrait of Rochester, N. Y. (1968); *A Whole Bunch of Fun,* secular cantata (1969); *From Out of Bondage,* cantata to a biblical text (Temple Sinai, Brookline, Mass., April 4, 1969); string quartet No. 5 (1969); 3 violin sonatas; sonata for unaccompanied cello; sacred choruses.

Admon-Gorochov, Jedidiah, Israeli composer; b. Ekaterinoslav, Russia, Dec. 5, 1894. He settled in Palestine as a child and studied music in Jerusalem; lived in the U.S. in 1923-27. His works, mostly for voices, are thematically derived from traditional Jewish cantillation. His chamber music is more cosmopolitan in nature.

Adolphus, Milton, American composer; b. New York, Jan. 27, 1913. In 1935 he moved to Philadelphia, where he studied composition with Rosario Scalero; was subsequently director of the Philadelphia Music Center; in 1938 he went to Harrisburg where he was engaged in an administrative capacity by the Department of Labor and Industry of the Commonwealth of Pennsylvania. Although he never practiced music vocationally, he is extremely prolific in composition. He wrote 13 symphonies (1930-54) and 26 string quartets (1935-64) as well as other pieces of symphonic and chamber music. Some of his works show a measure of sophisticated humor, exemplified by *Bitter Suite* for oboe, 4 clarinets and strings (1955) and *Petits fours* for cello and piano (1960). He also wrote a *United Nations Suite* for orch. (1962).

Adorno, Theodor. Died in Brig, Switzerland, Aug. 6, 1969. Add to books: *Klangfiguren* (Berlin, 1959).

Adriaensen, Emanuel (alternative spelling, **Emmanuel Adriaenssen**). Died in Antwerp in 1604; date of burial, Feb. 27, 1604.

Aeschbacher, Niklaus. In 1959 he was appointed music director and conductor of symph. concerts in Kiel; in 1964 he became music director at the Detmold Opera.

Aeschbacher, Walther. Died in Bern, Dec. 6, 1969.

Afanassiev, Nikolay Yakovlevitch. Exact date of birth, Jan. 12, 1821.

Agay, Dénes, Hungarian-American pianist, composer and arranger; b. Budapest, June 10, 1911. He studied at the Budapest Academy of Music, graduating in 1933. In 1939 he went to the U. S. and settled in New York as piano teacher. Since 1950, he is active mainly as editor of educational material for piano students; compiled several collections of piano music adapted for beginners (*Easy Classics to Moderns, The Young Pianist's Library,* etc.).

Agostini, Paolo. Year of birth, 1583 (not 1593).

Agostini, Pietro Simone. Died in Parma, Oct. 1, 1680. Born probably c. 1640 (not c. 1650).

Aguilar-Ahumada, Miguel, Chilean composer; b. Huara, Chile, April 12, 1931. He studied piano and composition at the Santiago Conservatory and later in Cologne, Germany. Returning to Chile he taught at the Conservatory of Concepción (1956-63). Under the influence of the German avant-garde, he adopted a fairly advanced atonal idiom. Works: *Obertura al Teatro Integral* for orch. (1954); *Septet* for wind instruments and double-bass (1954); *Sonatina Concertante* for clarinet and piano (1956); *Microscopía* for soprano and piano (1958); *Torre Eiffel* for soprano and instruments (1967); 5 piano sonatas and several electronic pieces.

Aguilera de Heredia, Sebastian. Died in 1627; date of interment, Dec. 16, 1627.

Ahrens, Joseph. Add to compositions: *Missa Dodekaphonica* (1966) in which Gregorian chant is combined with 12-tone melodic patterns.

Aitken, Hugh, American composer; b. New York, Sept. 7, 1924. He studied music with his father, a violinist, and his mother, a pianist; was a navigator in the U. S. Army Air Force during World War II. In 1946 he entered the Juilliard School of Music, N. Y., where he studied composition with Bernard Wagenaar and Vincent Persichetti; after graduation in 1950 he joined its faculty. His works include 5 cantatas, 4 partitas for various ensembles; a dance score *The Moirai* (New London, Aug. 18, 1961); a piano concerto; an oboe quintet; 8 pieces for wind quintet; a quartet for clarinet and strings; sacred choruses; *Montages* for solo bassoon; suite for solo bass; suite for solo clarinet; a number of piano pieces and songs. In 1971 he was appointed chairman of the Music Department of Peterson State College in Wayne, New Jersey.

Akimenko, Fyodor Stepanovitch. His real name was Yakimenko. Date of death, Jan. 3 (not 8), 1945. From 1886 to 1890 he was a student at the Court Chapel in St. Petersburg (not at the St. Petersburg Cons.); studied with Liadov and Rimsky-Korsakov at the St. Petersburg Cons. from 1895 to 1900. He was the first composition teacher of Stravinsky.

Akutagawa, Yasushi. Date of birth, July 12 (not July 10), 1925. Add to works: the opera *Kurai Kagami* (*Dark Mirror;* Tokyo, 1960); *Negative* for string orch. (1966); *Orpheus in Hiroshima,* television opera (1970).

Albanese, Licia. Did not live in Italy during World War II, but remained in the U. S. after her Metropolitan debut in 1940.

Albéniz, Isaac. Place of death, Cambo-les-Bains (not Cambo-Bains).

Albersheim, Gerhard, German-American pianist and musicologist; b. Cologne, Nov. 17, 1902. He studied at Vienna Univ.; emigrated to the U.S. in 1940. From 1953-56 he was on the staff of Univ. of Calif., Los Angeles; in 1956 appointed prof. at Calif. State College at Los Angeles. He began his career as an accompanist, playing for Lotte Lehmann, Elisabeth Schumann, Ezio Pinza and other eminent artists. He publ. *Zur Psychologie der Ton- und Klangeigenschaften* (Strasbourg, 1939); contributed numerous essays on musical esthetics to American and German publications.

Albert, Stephen, American composer; b. New York, Feb. 6, 1941. He studied composition privately with Elie Siegmeister (1956-58); then with Bernard Rogers at the Eastman School of Music in Rochester (1958-60), with Joseph Castaldo at the Philadelphia Musical Academy (1960-62) and with George Rochberg at the University of Pennsylvania (1963); was a Fellow of the American Academy in Rome in 1965-67; held a Guggenheim Fellowship in 1968-69. His works include *Illuminations* for 2 pianos, brass and percussion (1962); *Supernatural Songs* for soprano and chamber orchestra (1964); *Imitations* for string quartet (1964); *Winter Songs* for tenor and orchestra (1965); *Leaves from the Golden Notebook* for orchestra (1970). His style of composition is omnimodern, without overflowing into the crepuscular realm of tonal glossolalia; he accepts in his creative vocabulary even neo-classical and neo-romantic types of melody and harmony.

Albertsen, Per Hjort. Add to works: *Presentation,* overture (1958); *Concerto piccolo* for violin and amateur string orch. (1961).

Albicastro, Henricus, Swiss violinist and composer. His real name was Heinrich Weissenburg; he was born in Switzerland at an uncertain date; died about 1738 in Holland where he was a court musician. His works for string instruments were publ. in Amsterdam between 1700 and 1706; of these, 12 concertos *a 4,* a trio sonata and several violin sonatas with basso continuo are available in modern editions. See W. S. Newman, *The Sonata in the Baroque Era* (Chapel Hill, 1959; pp. 343-44).

Albrecht, Evgeny Karlovitch. He was not a professional conductor, but a violinist; was active also as a musical administrator.

Albrecht, Hans. Died in Kiel, Jan. 20, 1961. Cf. *Hans Albrecht in Memoriam,* ed. by W. Brennecke and H. Haase (Kassel, 1962).

Albrecht, Konstantin Karlovitch. Date of birth, Oct. 4, 1835 (not 1836).

Alderighi, Dante. Died in Rome, Dec. 12, 1968.

Aldrich, Putnam (Calder). Add to books: *Rhythm in 17th-century Italian Monody* (London, 1965).

Alemshah, Kourkene M., Armenian composer; b. Erevan, May 22, 1907; d. Detroit, Dec. 14, 1947. He studied in Milan with Pizzetti (1924-30); in 1931 he settled in Paris. He died during an American tour which he undertook as a choral conductor. His music is strongly permeated with Armenian melos, and the settings are impressionistic. Works: symph. poem *Légende* (Paris, June 19, 1932); symph. poem *La Bataille d'Avarayr* (Paris, June 2, 1934); *Danses populaires arméniennes* for orch. (Paris, June 2, 1934). A memorial festival of his music was presented in Paris on Feb. 19, 1950.

Alessandrescu, Alfred. Died in Bucharest, Feb. 18, 1959. Date of birth, Aug. 13 (not 14), 1893. See V. Tomescu, *Alfred Alessandrescu* (Bucharest, 1962).

Alessandri, Felice. Date of birth Nov. 24, 1747 (not 1742).

d'Alessandro, Rafaele. Died in Lausanne, March 17, 1959 (on his 48th birthday). Add to works: ballet *Isla persa* (1952); *Rumba* for orch. (1940); *Conga contrapuntique* for orch. (1941); *Tema variato* for orch. (1957); violin concerto (1941); flute concerto (1943); bassoon concerto (1955); concerto for oboe and strings (1958); 2 violin sonatas; sonata for bassoon and piano; sonatina for 2 flutes; sonata for flute, viola and piano; 24 piano preludes; 6 pieces for piano left hand.

Alexandrov, Anatoly Nikolayevitch, Russian pianist and composer; b. Moscow, May 25, 1888. He studied privately with Sergey Taneyev (1907-10); then at the Moscow Cons. with Igumnov (piano) and Vassilenko (composition), graduating in 1916. In 1923 he became prof. at the Moscow Cons. Alexandrov is particularly distinguished as a composer of piano music; he wrote 12 piano sonatas and many smaller works for the instrument; in his style, he follows the main line of Rachmaninoff and Scriabin. His other works include the operas, *Two Worlds* (1916); *Bela* (Moscow, Dec. 10, 1946); *Wild Bara* (Moscow, March 2, 1957); 4 string quartets (1914-54); *Romantic Suite* for orch. and chorus (1920); *Classical Suite* for orch. (1926); several song cycles; incidental music for theatrical plays.

Alfano, Franco. Correct the title, in column 2, line 1: *Ritratto,* not *Rittrato.*

Alferaky, Achilles Nikolayevitch. The spelling of his last name should be Alferaki. Exact date of death, Dec. 27, 1919 (not 1920).

Alfvén, Hugo. Died in Falum, May 8, 1960. The first Paris performance of his symph. poem *Midsommarvaka* took place on Oct. 25, 1920 (not 1925).

Aliabiev, Alexander Nikolayevitch. His patronymic was Alexandrovitch (not Nikolayevitch). Upon returning to Russia after 1812, he lived mostly in St. Petersburg and in Voronezh (not in Moscow, where he did not settle until 1823). He was exiled to Siberia not on express orders of the Czar, but by court decision. His 3 string quartets were written before he went into exile, and not in Siberia. *The Prisoner of the Caucasus* is a cantata (not an opera); it did not achieve wide popularity.

Ali Akbar Khan, Hindu instrumentalist; b. Shibpore, Bengal, April 14, 1922. He studied dhrupad, dhamar, khayal and sarod with his father; pakhawaj and tabla with his uncle. He founded the Ali Akbar College of Music in Calcutta in 1956; toured widely in Europe, America and Japan as a virtuoso; held the post of court musician in Jodhpur. He has written a number of new ragas. Several of his students achieved prominence as Indian instrumentalists in their own right.

Allen, Warren D. Died in Olympia, Washington, June 21, 1964.

Allende Sarón, (Pedro) Humberto. Died in Santiago, Aug. 16, 1959. The first performance of his violin concerto took place on Dec. 4 (not Nov. 27), 1942.

Allers, Franz, conductor; b. Prague, Aug. 6, 1905. He studied violin at the Prague Cons. and later in Berlin; was a member of the Berlin Philharmonic for a season; then conducted theater orchestras in Germany (1926-38). He left Germany in 1938 and conducted ballet in London, South America and Canada, eventually settling in the U. S. as conductor of musical shows on Broadway; also appeared as symphonic conductor in Europe and America.

Altschuler, Modest. Died in Los Angeles, Sept. 12, 1963.

Alwyn, William. Add to works: Symph. No. 2, 3 and 4 (1953, 1956, 1959); *Autumn Legend* for English horn and string orch. (1956); string trio (1963); clarinet sonata (1963).

Amar, Licco. Died in Freiburg-im-Breisgau, July 19, 1959.

Ambros, August Wilhelm. Place of birth, Vysoké Myto (not Mauth). The 2nd vol. of his *Geschichte der Musik* was revised by H. Reimann (not Riemann).

Ameller, André-Charles. Add to works: *Cyrnos,* opera (Nancy, April 6, 1962).

Amiot, Joseph-Marie. Name of the editor of his *Mémoires* was Roussier (not Rouffier).

Amirkhanian, Charles, American composer of Armenian extraction; b. Fresno, Calif. Jan. 19, 1945. Autodidact as composer, he began to experiment with the rhythmic potentialities of drums; wrote *Sonatina* for 4 bass-drums in polyrhythmic counterpoint (1963) and *Composition No. 1* for solo amplified ratchet (1965). His *Symphony* I (1965) is scored for 12 players and 200-odd non-musical objects, ranging from pitchpipes to pitchforks. In collaboration with the painter Ted Greer, Amirkhanian developed a radical system of notation in which visual images are transduced by performers into sound events. Representative of this inter-media genre are *Micah, the Prophet,* a cantata for 4 intoning males, 2 accordions, 2 drummers and 2 painters (1965); *Mooga Pook,* a tetraphallic action for dancers, realistically notated on graph paper (produced in San Francisco, Dec. 12, 1967); an alliteratively titled piece of concrete music, *Muse Ache* (near-homonym for Muzak) and an environmental western event *R. Wild Westly* (1970). He also evolved a genre of verbalized sound pieces, among them *Words* (1969), *Oratora Konkurso Rezulto: Autoro de la Jaro,* an Esperanto recitation (1970); *If In Is* (1971); *Spoffy Nene* (1971). In 1969 Amirkhanian became Sound Sensitivity Information Director of radio station KPFA in Berkeley, California.

Amirov, Fikret Dzhamil. The title of his symph. poem is *To the Memory of the Heroes of the Great National War* (not *Greek National War*). Add to works: opera *Sevil* (Baku, Dec. 25, 1953). He visited the U. S. in 1959 as a member of the Soviet delegation of composers under the auspices of the Program for Cultural Exchange. See D. Danilov, *Fikret Amirov* (Moscow, 1958).

Ammon, Blasius. Born in Hall (not in Imst), in 1558 (not 1560).

Amram, David Werner, American composer; b. Philadelphia, Nov. 17, 1930. He learned to play piano, trumpet and French horn; took courses at the Oberlin Cons.; after serving in the U. S. Army in Europe (1952-55), he studied composition with Vittorio Giannini in New York. He then began to compose prolifically and flexibly for theater, television, motion pictures and jazz bands; also played in various jazz combos. Among his works are a trio for saxophone, French horn and bassoon (1958); violin sonata (1960); Overture and Allegro for unaccompanied flute (1960); many jazz pieces. His 'Passover opera,' *The Final Ingredient* was produced on television, in New York, April 11, 1965. Other works include: *King Lear Variations,* for winds and percussion (1967); string quartet (1968); opera, *Twelfth Night* (1968); *Triple Concerto* for woodwinds, brass, jazz quintet and orch. (N. Y., Jan. 10, 1971). He publ. an autobiography *Vibrations: The Adventures and Musical Times of David Amram* (N. Y., 1968).

Amy, Gilbert, French composer; b. Paris, Aug. 29, 1936. He studied composition with Darius Milhaud and Olivier Messiaen. His principal works are *Œil de fumée* for soprano and piano (1955); *Variations* for 4 instruments (1956); *Cantate brève* to words by García Lorca (1957); *Mouvements* for 17 instruments (1958); *Alpha-Beth* for 6 wind instruments (1963); *Antiphonies* for 2 orch. (1963); *Triade* for orch. (1964); *Trajectoires* for violin and orch. (1966); *Cycle* for 6 percussion players (1967); *Chant* for orch. (Donaueschingen, Oct. 20, 1968); *Relais* for 5 brass instruments (1969). In his music he follows the baroque precepts of antiphony and concertante, but applies them in combination with modern serialism.

Ančerl, Karel, Czech conductor; b. Tucapy, April 11, 1908. He studied music with Alois Hába at the Prague Cons. and conducting with Talich and Scherchen. Subsequently, he was active as theater conductor in Prague (1931-33) and at the Prague Radio (1933-39). During the occupation of Czechoslovakia by Nazi troops, he was interned in a concentration camp. After the end of the war he served as musical director of the Prague Opera; was also in charge of the Prague Radio Orchestra and of the Czech Philharmonic. In 1965 he toured the United States and Canada with the Czech Philharmonic Orch. In 1970 he was appointed conductor of the Toronto Symphony Orchestra.

Anda, Géza. He became a Swiss citizen in 1955; lived mostly in Zürich, but continued concert tours in Europe and America.

Anderberg, Carl-Olof, Swedish composer; b. Stockholm, March 13, 1914. He studied composition with N. Broman in Stockholm, piano in Copenhagen and conducting with Weingartner in Salzburg. In 1956 he became director of the electronic music studio in Malmö. In his music he applies modern serial techniques while retaining the basic classical forms, even in electronic compositions. Works: *Episode,* chamber opera (1952); *Duo* for flute and piano (1958); *Triad* for solo violin (1959); *Transfers* for symphonic groups (1960); *Hexafoni* for 6 instruments (1963); *Execution* for piano, clarinet and percussion (1963); *Acroama I* and *Acroama II* for orch. (1965); piano concerto (1968).

Andersen, Karl August. Died in Oslo, Aug. 15, 1970.

Anderson, Emily, English musicologist; b. Galway, Ireland, March 17, 1891; d. London, Oct. 26, 1962. She studied music in Berlin; was employed in the British Foreign Office, but continued her musical research. The result of her effort was the publication of two monumental collections, translated and annotated by her: *Letters of Mozart and his Family* (3 vols., London, 1938) and *The Letters of Beethoven* (3 vols., London, 1962).

Anderson, Leroy, American composer of light music; b. Cambridge, Mass., June 29, 1908. He studied music at Harvard Univ., with Spalding, Ballantine and Piston (B.A., *magna cum laude,* 1929; M.A., 1930); played double-bass in the Harvard Univ. Orch.; later (1931-35) was its conductor. He developed a unique genre of sophisticated miniatures, which he wrote with considerable ingenuity and musical wit, in expert orchestral dress. Of these pieces, many have attained great popularity: *Jazz pizzicato, Jazz legato, Fiddle Faddle, Sleigh Ride, Blue Tango, The Syncopated Clock, The Typewriter, The Waltzing Cat,* etc. He also wrote a musical comedy *Goldilocks* (N. Y., Oct. 11, 1958).

Andreae, Volkmar. Died in Zürich, June 18, 1962.

Andrico, Michal. Add to works: 10 symphonies (1943-68); 9 symphoniettas (1945-65). He was prof. at the Bucharest Cons. from 1926 to 1959. For many years he served as accompanist to Georges Enesco.

Andriessen, Jurriaan. He studied with Aaron Copland at the Berkshire Center, Tanglewood, during the summers of 1949 and 1950. Add to works: *Berkshire Symphonies* (1949; produced as a ballet under the title *Jones Beach,* N. Y., March 12, 1950); flute concerto (1951); Symph. No. 2 (1962); Symph. No. 3 (1963); Symph. No. 4, *Aves,* after Aristophanes, with chorus (1963); also *Thai,* symph. rhapsody based on jazz tunes by King Phumiphon Aduldet of Thailand, written for a special performance during the King's visit in The Netherlands (The Hague, Oct. 25, 1960).

Andriessen, Willem. Died in Amsterdam, March 29, 1964.

Anet, Jean-Baptiste. Born in 1675 (baptized Jan. 2, 1676), not in 1661.

d'Angelo, Louis. Died in Jersey City, N.J., Aug. 9, 1958.

Anglès, Higini. Died in Rome, Dec. 8, 1969.

Anhalt, Istvan, Hungarian-Canadian composer; b. Budapest, April 12, 1919. He studied with Kodály at the Budapest Academy of Music, graduating in 1941; in 1946 went to Paris where he took lessons with Nadia Boulanger. He settled in Canada in 1949; was appointed to the faculty of music at McGill Univ. He developed a highly advanced style of composition, without abandoning classical forms or tonal organization. He is one of the pioneers in electronic music in Canada. Works: *Interludium* for strings, piano and kettledrums (1950); piano sonata (1951); piano trio (1953); *Fantasia* for piano (1954); violin sonata (1955); symphony (1958); *Cantata urbana* for voices and magnetic tape (1967).

Animuccia, Giovanni. Probable year of birth, 1514 (not 1500).

Anka, Paul, popular Canadian singer and composer; b. Ottawa, July 30, 1941, of Syrian parentage. He began improvising songs as a child; at the age of 15 he recorded his song *Diana,* to his own lyrics, and it became a substantial hit. He then embarked on a highly successful career as a ballad singer; acquired considerable musical ability, and wrote some 300 songs. In 1962 he incorporated himself to manage his growing fortune. He had his nose remodeled in 1958 for television appearances. He married Anne de Zogheb on Feb. 16, 1963.

Anna Amalia, Princess of Prussia. Date of death, Sept. 30 (not March 30), 1787.

Anrooy, Peter van. Died in The Hague Dec. 31, 1954. The date of composition of his orch. rhapsody *Piet Hein,* 1901 (not 1911).

Ansermet, Ernest. Died in Geneva, Feb. 20, 1969. Published *Les fondements de la musique dans la conscience humaine* (2 vols.; Neuchâtel, 1961), using mathematical formulations to prove the lack of validity in dodecaphony and other advanced techniques of composition.

Antegnati, Costanzo. He was baptized on Dec. 9, 1549. Date of death, Nov. 14 (not Nov. 16), 1624.

Antheil, George. Died in New York, Feb. 12, 1959. *Volpone* was produced on Jan. 9, 1953 (not 1954). *Zingareska* was first performed in Berlin on Nov. 21, 1922. He composed many film scores (not flute scores). His *Jazz Symphony* was revised for larger orch. in 1955 (first performed in the new version, N. Y., Dec. 14, 1960). He wrote 4 (not 2) violin sonatas, one of which (1923) requires the pianist to change to a set of drums for the last section of the piece. There is also a sonatina for violin and piano (1945). His posthumous cantata, *Cabeza de Vaca,* was produced on CBS Television on June 10, 1962.

Anton, Karl. Died in Weinheim, Feb. 21, 1956.

Antoniou, Theodor, Greek composer of advanced tendencies; b. Athens, Feb. 10, 1935. He studied composition with Yannis Papaioannou in Athens; in 1961 went to Munich where he continued his musical education with G. Bialas. He developed a mathematically oriented method of composition, following serial principles, intermingling dodecaphony, modality and folk-like motivic configurations. Works: piano sonata (1959); string quartet (1960); concerto for violin, piano, trumpet and orch. (1960); *Triptychon* for 5 instruments (1961); sonata for unaccompanied violin (1961); trio for flute, viola and cello (1961); concertino for piano and orch. (1962); *Antitheses* for orch. (1963); *Dialogues* for flute and guitar (1963); *Epilogue* for mezzo-soprano, speaker and 6 instruments (1963); *Jeux* for cello and string orch. (1963); *Mikrographien* for orch. (1964); *Kinesis ABCD* for 3 string orchestras (1966); *Events* for violin, piano and orch. (1968).

Apel, Willi. Add to books: *Gregorian Chant* (Bloomington, Indiana, 1957); 2nd edition of the *Harvard Dictionary of Music,* revised and enlarged (Cambridge, 1969).

Appia, Edmond, Italian Swiss violinist and conductor; b. Turin, May 7, 1894; d. Geneva, Feb. 12, 1961. He studied violin with Henri Marteau at the Cons. of Geneva, in Paris with Lucien Capet, and at the Brussels Cons. obtaining Premier Prix in 1920; toured Europe (1920-35); taught violin in Geneva and Lausanne. In 1935 he became a conductor of Radiodiffusion Suisse in Lausanne; in 1938 was appointed conductor of the Geneva Radio Orch. He also wrote articles on Swiss music for 'The Mus. Quarterly' and many European publications.

Applebaum, Louis, Canadian composer; b. Toronto, April 3, 1918. He studied with Healey Willan and Sir Ernest MacMillan in Toronto; later in New York with Roy Harris and Bernard Wagenaar; returned to Canada in 1949, where he became engaged in writing music for theatrical plays and films. Among his works are *Christmas Overture* (1951); a ballet suite *Dark of the Moon* (1953); 2 string quartets; songs.

Araja, Francesco. Exact date of birth, June 25, 1709.

Aranyi, Francis. Died in Seattle, May 5, 1966.

d'Aranyi, Yelly. Died in Florence, March 30, 1966. Correct spelling of first name should be Jelly (not Yelly). Add bibl.: J. Macleod, *The Sisters d'Aranyi* (London, 1969).

Arapov, Boris Alexandrovitch, Russian composer; b. St. Petersburg, Sept. 12, 1905. He studied at the Leningrad Cons. with Vladimir Stcherbatchev, graduating in 1930; subsequently joined its teaching staff. He spent several years in Central Asia, collecting and codifying native folk melodies; many of his works are based on Asian themes. He wrote a comic opera *Hodzha-Nasreddin* (1943); *Symphony in C* (1947); *Russian Suite* for orch. (1950); *Tadzhik Suite* for orch. (1938); *Free China,* symph. poem (Leningrad, Oct. 2, 1960); trio for clarinet, violin and piano, on Mongol themes (1942); piano pieces.

Arbatsky, Yury. Died in New Hartford, N. Y., Sept. 3, 1963.

Arcadelt, Jacob. Exact date of death, Oct. 14, 1568. See F. Lesure, *Notes et Documents,* in 'Revue de Musicologie' (Paris, Dec. 1961).

Archer, Violet, Canadian pianist and composer; b. Montreal, April 24, 1913. She studied piano and composition at the McGill Cons.; subsequently studied at Yale Univ. with Hindemith, and also had some lessons with Béla Bartók in N. Y. She taught at the North Texas State College (1950-53) and at the Univ. of Oklahoma (1953-61). In 1961 she returned to Canada; in 1962 she was appointed to the faculty of the Univ. of Alberta, Edmonton. Her music is tonally organized although she occasionally applies modified methods of composing with 12 tones. Works: Concerto for timpani and orch. (1939); *Britannia, a Joyful Overture* (1941); Symph. No. 1 (1946); piano concerto (1956); violin concerto (1959); *3 Sketches* for orch. (1961); *Sinfonia* (Edmonton, Oct. 24, 1970); sonata for clarinet and piano (1970); 2 string quartets; 2 string trios, 2 piano trios; numerous works for various chamber groups; choruses.

Arel, Bülent. In 1960 he began to cultivate electronic music. Add to works: *Mimiana,* ballet (1968).

Arensky, Anton Stepanovitch. Date of birth, July 12 (not Aug. 11), 1861. His piano trio is dedicated to the memory of the cellist Karl Davidov (q.v.), not of Tchaikovsky.

Argenta, Ataulfo. Died in Madrid, Jan. 21, 1958. Add bibl.: A. Fernandez-Cid, *Ataulfo Argenta* (Madrid, 1958).

Arizaga, Rodolfo, Argentinian composer; b. Buenos Aires, July 11, 1926. He studied composition with Luis Gianneo; went to Europe in 1950, and in 1954 settled in Paris where he had lessons with Olivier Messiaen and Nadia Boulanger. Upon his return to Argentina he became Secretary of the National Symph. Orch. in Buenos Aires. Works: *Martirio de Santa Olalla,* cantata to the text of García Lorca (1950-52; received the Municipal Prize of Buenos Aires); *Serenata* for orch. (1953); *Délires,* cantata after Rimbaud (1954-57); *Serranillas del Jaque* for orch. (1958); piano concerto (1963); *Música para Cristóbal Colón* for orch. (1966); 2 string quartets (1968 and 1969). He publ. the monographs *Manuel de Falla* (Buenos Aires, 1961) and *Juán José Castro* (Buenos Aires, 1963); also an *Enciclopedia de la música argentina* (Buenos Aires, 1970).

Arlen, Harold. He wrote the musicals *Bloomer Girl* (1944); *St. Louis Woman* (1946); *House of Flowers* (1954); *Jamaica* (1957). His film scores include *The Wizard of Oz* (1939). See: Edward Jablonski, *Happy with the Blues* (Garden City, 1961).

Armin, Georg. Died in Karlslunde Strand, Denmark, Feb. 16, 1963.

Armstrong, Louis, American Negro jazz trumpeter, familiarly known as "Satchmo" (for "Satchel Mouth," with reference to his spacious and resonant oral cavity); b. New Orleans, July 4, 1900; d. in New York, July 6, 1971. He lost both his parents at the age of 10 and was placed in a waifs' home; in 1922 went to Chicago, where he played cornet in King Oliver's Creole Jazz Band; in 1925 he organized his own band and rapidly earned fame; set an endurance record when he sounded high C on the trumpet 280 times in succession. His authentic swing style won admirers all over the world (including Russia), some critics hailing him as "The Einstein of Jazz." Although unlettered, he improvised and composed many songs which became swing classics, including *Satchel Mouth Swing, Wild Man Blues* and *Sugar Foot Stomp.* He wrote an autobiography, *Satchmo, My Life in New Orleans* (N. Y., 1954). See also R. Goffin, *Horn of Plenty, The Story of Louis Armstrong* (N. Y., 1947); H. Panassié, *Louis Armstrong* (Paris, 1947).

d'Arneiro, (José Augusto) Ferreira Veiga. Should be listed as **Arneiro, Ferreira da Veiga.** Exact date of death, July 7, 1903.

Arnell, Richard. Add to works: Symph. No. 5 (1957); puppet opera for television, *The Petrified Princess* (1959); *Food of Love,* overture (1968); multi-media spectacle *Combat Zone* (1969).

Arnold, Johann Gottfried. Date of birth, Feb. 1 (not Feb. 15), 1773.

Arnold, Karl. He was the son of Johann Gottfried Arnold. Date of birth, May 6, (not March 6), 1794; date of death, Nov. 11, 1877 (not 1873).

Arnold, Malcolm. Add to works: Symph. No. 3 (London, Dec. 2, 1957); Symph. No. 4 (London, Nov. 2, 1960); Symph. No. 5 (1961); Symph. No. 6 (1968).

Arrieu, Claude, French composer and pianist; b. Paris, Nov. 30, 1903. She studied piano with Marguerite Long, and composition at the Paris Cons. with Roger-Ducasse and Noël Gallon, graduating with Premier Prix in 1932. Among her many works are a music drama, *Noë* (Strasbourg, Jan. 29, 1950); comic operas *Cadet Roussel* (Marseille, Oct. 2, 1953); *La Cabine téléphonique* (Paris Radio, March 15, 1959) and *La Princesse de Babylone* (Reims, March 4, 1960); numerous scores of incidental music for radio; 2 violin concertos; a piano concerto; a flute concerto; chamber music; songs.

Arrigo, Girolamo, Italian composer; b. in Palermo, April 2, 1930. He studied composition at the Palermo Cons., and later in Paris; in 1964 he settled in Rome. His works include a string trio (1958); *Tre occasioni* for soprano and orch. (1959); *Quarta occasione* for tenor and small ensemble (1960); *Fluxus* for 9 instruments (1961); *Episodi* for soprano and 4 flutes (1963); *Thumos* for wind instruments and percussion (1964); *Shadows* for orch. (1966) and *Infrarosso* for 16 instruments (1967).

Arroyo, Martina, American soprano; b. in New York, Feb. 2, 1940. She made her debut at the age of 18; sang with the N. Y. Philharmonic and other orchestras as soloist. In 1965 she was called upon to substitute for Birgit Nilsson at the Metropolitan Opera as Aida, scoring spontaneous acclaim. This marked the beginning of a spectacular operatic career, and she has since made successful appearances in America and in Europe.

Artaria. Did not publish Beethoven's op. 131, but op. 130 and op. 133.

Asafiev, Boris Vladimirovitch. His ballet *The Flames of Paris* was produced on Nov. 7, 1932 (not June 23, 1923); *The Partisan Days,* on May 16 (not Sept. 12), 1937.

Ashkenazy, Vladimir, Russian pianist; b. Gorki, July 6, 1937. He studied with Oborin at the Moscow Cons.; at the age of 19 won the first prize at the Brussels International Competition under the auspices of Queen Elisabeth of Belgium (1956); he also won the Chopin International Prize in Warsaw (1955). His pianistic style combines the traditional romantic treatment of the old Russian school with the digital precision demanded for performance of modern music.

Ashley, Robert, American composer; b. Ann Arbor, Michigan, March 28, 1930. He studied music at the Univ. of Michigan (Mus. B., 1952) and The Manhattan School of Music (Mus. M., 1954); took post-graduate courses in psychoacoustics at the Univ. of Michigan (1957-60). In his independent composition, he pursues the ideal of 'total musical events' which absorbs gesticulation, natural human noises and the entire planetary environment. In 1961 he became cofounder of the ONCE group in Ann Arbor dedicated to such actions; from 1958 to 1966 he operated an electronic music studio in association with the composer Gordon Mumma; in 1970 was appointed co-director of the Center of Contemporary Music at Mills College, Oakland, Calif. Most of his works utilize electronic sounds; of these the following are notable for the totality of their envergure: *The Fourth of July* (1960); *Something* for clarinet, piano and tape (1961); *Detroit Divided* (1962); *Complete with Heat* (1962); *Kitty Hawk,* an 'anti-gravity piece' (1964); *Untitled Mixes* (1965); *Night Train* (1966); *The Trial of Anne Opie Wehrer and Unknown Accomplices for Crimes Against Humanity* (1968); *Purposeful Lady Slow Afternoon* (1968); *Illusion Models* for hypothetical computer (1970); several film scores: *The Image in Time* (1957); *The Bottleman* (1960); *Jenny and the Poet* (1964); *My May* (1965); *Overdrive* (1968); *Portraits, Self-Portraits and Still Lifes* (1969); *Battery Davis* (1970). He also composed music performable on traditional instruments, among them *Maneuvers for Small Hands* for piano (1961), quartet for any number of instruments (1965) and organ pieces.

Asola, Giovanni Matteo. Was born probably between 1524 and 1532. Acceded to the position of chaplain at the Church of S. Stefano in Verona in 1566.

Atanasov, Georgi. Date of birth, according to new style, May 18 (not May 6), 1881; place and date of death, Fasano (not Rome), Nov. 17 (not Nov. 1), 1931.

Attaignant, Pierre. Add to bibl.: D. Heartz, *Pierre Attaingnant, Royal Printer of Music* (Berkeley, Calif., 1969).

Atterberg, Kurt. First performances of his

6 symphonies were given in Stockholm on the following dates: No. 1 — Jan. 10, 1912, No. 2 — Feb. 11, 1912; No. 3 — Nov. 28, 1916; No. 4 — March 27, 1919; No. 5 — Jan. 6, 1923; No. 6 — Oct. 15, 1928. His 9th symphony was first performed in Stockholm, Feb. 26, 1957.

Attwood, Thomas. Date of death, March 28 (not 24), 1838, in London (not Chelsea).

Aubain, Jean, French composer; b. Bordeaux, Feb. 1, 1928. He studied with Tony Aubin at the Paris Cons.; received Premier Grand Prix de Rome with his cantata *Le Mariage forcé* in 1956. He has written much music for radio and television.

Aubert, Louis-François-Marie. Died in Paris, Jan. 9, 1968. Bibl.: Marcel Landowski and Guy Morançon, *Louis Aubert* (Paris, 1967).

Auda, Antoine. Died in Brussels, Aug. 19, 1964.

Auer, Max. Died in Vienna, Sept. 24, 1962.

Auric, Georges. In 1960 appointed director of the combined theaters of Grand Opéra and Opéra-Comique in Paris. Add to works: *Partita* for 2 pianos (1958); *Bal des Voleurs,* ballet (1959); *Suite Symphonique* (1960); *Imaginées I* for flute and piano (1969); *Doubles jeux* for 2 pianos (1970). Bibl.: Anton Goléa, *Georges Auric* (Paris, 1959).

Austin, Henry Richter. Died in Marblehead, Mass., May 13, 1961.

Austin, Larry, American avant-garde composer; b. Duncan, Oklahoma, Sept. 12, 1930. He studied at the North Texas State Univ., Denton (B.M. 1951; M.M. 1952); at Mills College with Darius Milhaud, and at the Univ. of California, Berkeley (1955-58) with Seymour Shifrin; in 1969 he took a course in computer-generated music systems at Stanford Univ. He was on the faculty of the Univ. of California at Berkeley (1956-58); in 1958, joined the Univ. of California at Davis (prof. of music, 1970). From 1967 to 1970 he was the editor of the progressive ultra-modern unperiodical avant-garde publication 'Source'. He has held several creative fellowships, among them one in Rome (1965). Most of his works are cast for mixed media in which theatrical, acoustical, and dynamic elements appear as manifestations of universal vitality. He makes use of traditional instruments as well as electronic, computerized and aleatory resources. In order to secure a maximum impact with a minimum of anarchy, he introduced the concept of coordinated improvisation, which he terms "Open Style." Works: woodwind quartet (1948); woodwind quintet (1949); brass quintet (1949); string trio (1952); *Concertino* for flute, trumpet and strings (1952); *Prosody* for orch. (1953); *Improvisations for Orchestra and Jazz Soloists* (1961); *Collage* for a variety of instruments (1963); *Continuum* for 2, 3, 4, 5, 6, or 7 instruments, (1964); *In Memoriam J. F. Kennedy* for band (1964); *Piano Variations* (1964); *A Broken Consort* for 7 instruments (1964); *Open Style for Orchestra and Piano Soloists* (1965); *The Maze: A Theater Piece in Open Style* (1967); *Catharsis: Open Style for Two Improvisation Ensembles, Tapes and Conductor* (1967; Oakland, Nov. 11, 1969); *Accidents* for prepared piano, magnetic tape mirrors, actions, and projections (1967); *Piano Set in Open Style* (1968); *Current* for clarinet and piano (1968); *The Magicians* for mixed media (1968); *Transmission One,* a video-audio electronic composition for color television (1969); *Agape,* a celebration for priests, musicians, actors and poets (Buffalo, Feb. 25, 1970); *Plastic Surgery* for electric piano, percussion, magnetic tape and film (N. Y., March 1, 1970).

Austin, William W., American musicologist; b. Lawton, Oklahoma, Jan. 18, 1920. He studied at Harvard Univ., obtaining his Ph.D. in 1951. In 1947, he was appointed to the faculty of Cornell Univ. In 1961-62 he was the recipient of a Guggenheim Fellowship. He publ. *Music of the 20th Century from late Debussy to late Stravinsky* (N. Y., 1966); contributed numerous articles to the 'Mus. Quarterly.'

Austral, Florence. Died in Sydney, May 15, 1968. Name of husband, John Amadeo (not Amadio). She returned to Australia after World War II.

Auteri-Manzocchi, Salvatore. Date of birth, Dec. 26 (not 25), 1845; date of death, Feb. 21 (not 22), 1924.

Aventinus, Johannes. Place of death, Regensburg (not Abensberg).

Avison, Charles. Baptized Feb. 16, 1709, old style, but 1710 new style (since prior to 1752, the year commenced in March). Add to bibl.: Ch. Cudworth, 'Avison of Newcastle' in 'The Musical Times' (London, May, 1970).

Avshalomov, Aaron. Died in New York, April 26, 1965.

Axman, Emil. Date of death, Jan. 25 (not Jan. 5), 1949.

Ayestarán, Lauro. Died in Montevideo, Uruguay, July 22, 1966. Add to publications: *El Folklore Musical Uruguayo* (Montevideo, 1967).

Ayrton, Edmund. He was baptized on Nov. 19, 1734; was born probably a day before.

Azmayparashvili, Shalva, Georgian conductor and composer; b. Tiflis, Jan. 7, 1903. He studied trumpet and kettledrums at the Tiflis Cons.; from 1938 to 1954 was conductor of the Tiflis Opera Theater. Works: opera, *The Village Elder* (Tbilisi, Jan. 21, 1951); musical comedy, *Times are Different* (Tbilisi, Feb. 12, 1952); symph. suite, *Pictures of Old Tiflis* (1941); a group of mass songs.

Aznavour, Charles (real name **Aznavurian**), French chansonnier; b. Paris, May 22, 1924. A son of an Armenian baritone from Tiflis, he received his early musical training at home; acted in Paris variety shows at the age of 5; learned to play the guitar. He made several American tours as a night club entertainer with a valuable French accent; also acted in films. He composed a great number of songs, of the genre of "tristesse chansons" and frustration ballads, among them the popular tunes *On ne sait jamais, Comme des étrangers* and *Ce jour tant attendu*. His operetta *Monsieur Carnaval* was produced in Paris on Dec. 17, 1965. He wrote an autobiography, entitled *Aznavour par Aznavour* (Paris, 1970).

B

Baaren, Kees van, Dutch composer; b. Enschede, Oct. 22, 1906; d. Oegstgeest, Sept. 2, 1970. He studied music theory with Willem Pijper and followed his impressionistic manner of composition. His early works are in the lyric tradition of Grieg; later he adopted a Debussyan style. However, he destroyed all his manuscripts in 1933 and started afresh in the direction of structural techniques, in particular the 12-tone method. Later he adopted an integral serial style, in which not only the 12 tones of the chromatic scale, but durations, dynamics and meters are organized according to a unifying thematic set. His works comprise a cantata *The Hollow Men,* after T. S. Eliot (1948); sextet for violin, wind instruments and double-bass (1952); *Sinfonia* (1957) and *Variazioni per Orchestra* (1959). He was director of the Amsterdam Music Academy (1948-53) and of the Cons. of Utrecht (from 1953 to his death).

Babadzhanian, Arnold, Armenian composer; b. Erevan, Jan. 22, 1921. He studied at the Erevan Cons., and later at the Moscow Cons., graduating as pianist in 1948. In 1950 he was appointed prof. at the Erevan Cons. His works include a piano concerto (1944); a violin concerto (1949); 2 string quartets; piano trio; several piano sonatas and other piano pieces; many choruses.

Babbitt, Milton. Add data: 1960, was named professor of music at Princeton Univ.; received N. Y. Music Critics Citation in 1949 and 1964; held a Guggenheim grant in 1961; elected member of the National Institute of Arts and Letters in 1965. He is the founder of the Council for the Electronic Music Center in Columbia Univ. and Princeton Univ. Babbitt is a pioneer of total serialism. His *3 Compositions for Piano* (1947) are based on 4 different note values; in *Composition for 12 Instruments* (1948) he serializes 12 different note values and 12 different time intervals between entries of the instruments. He later extended the principle of serialism to dynamic parameters and instrumental timbres. To describe the fractional combinations of the basic four forms of the tone-row, in which the series is subdivided into groups, used horizontally as melody and vertically as counterpoint, into 2 hexachords, 3 tetrachords and 4 trichords, he introduced the term 'Combinatoriality'; such symmetric parts of a tone-row he terms 'derivations.' His paper, 'Twelve-Tone Invariants as Compositional Determinants' ('The Mus. Quarterly,' April 1960) is fundamental to his theories. Add to works: wind quartet (1953); string quartet No. 1 (1954); string quartet No. 2 (1954); *2 Sonnets* for baritone and 3 instruments (1955); *Semi-Simple Variations* for piano (1956); *All Set* for jazz ensemble (1957); *Composition for Synthesizer* (1961); *Philomel* for soprano and magnetic tape (1964); *Ensembles for Synthesizer* (1964); *Relata I* for orch. (1965); *Correspondences* for string orch. and magnetic tape (1967); *Relata II* for orch. (1968); *Occasional Variations by Synthesizer* (1969). See A. Pike, 'The Ordering of the All-Combinatorial Source Set' ('Music Review,' 1962); R. Kostelanetz, *Milton Babbitt* ('Stereo Review,' April, 1969).

Babić, Konstantin, Serbian composer; b. Belgrade, Feb. 10, 1927. He studied in Belgrade; wrote a number of symphonic pieces in a neo-classical vein; of these, *Konzertna Intrada* (Belgrade, Sept. 30, 1955) is the most effective. His *Levačka Svita* (*Suite from Levač*) for mixed choir (1966) uses folkloric texts, but is nonetheless presented in 3 classical sections, *Passacaglia, Fuga* and *Toccata.*

Bacarisse, Salvador. Died in Paris, Aug. 7, 1963.

Baccaloni, Salvatore. Died in New York, Dec. 31, 1969.

Bacewicz, Grazyna. Died in Warsaw, Jan. 17, 1969. Add to works: radio opera, *Przygoda króla Artura* (*Adventures of King Arthur;* Warsaw, Nov. 10, 1958); *Muzyka* for strings, horn and percussion (Warsaw, Sept. 14, 1959); 7 violin concertos (1938, 1946, 1948, 1952, 1954, 1957, 1965); 2 cello concertos (1951, 1963); *Pensieri notturni* for 24 instruments (1961); *Concerto* for orch. (1962); *Musica in tre movimenti* for orch. (1965); 7 string quartets (1938, 1942, 1947, 1951, 1956, 1960, 1965); quartet for 4 cellos (1964); 5 violin sonatas (1945, 1946, 1948, 1949, 1951); 2 piano quintets (1952, 1965); a ballet, *Z chlopa król* (1953).

Bach, Johann Sebastian. Add to bibl.: G. von Dadelsen, *Beiträge zur Chronologie der Werke J. S. Bachs* (Trossingen, 1958); W. G. Whittaker, *The Cantatas of J. S. Bach, Sacred and Secular* (2 vols., London, 1959); E. Bodky, *The Interpretation of Bach's Keyboard Works* (Cambridge, Mass., 1960); H. Franck, *J. S. Bach: die Geschichte seines Lebens* (Berlin, 1960); A. Mendel, *Recent Developments in Bach Chronology,* in 'The Mus. Quarterly' (July, 1960); W. Neumann, *Bach: A Pictorial Biography* (N. Y., 1961); R. Steglich, *Tanzrhythmen in der Musik Johann Sebastian Bachs* (Wolfenbüttel, 1962); J. Day, *The Literary Background to Bach's Cantatas* (London, 1962); P. Aldrich, *On the Interpretation of Bach's Trills* in 'The Mus. Quarterly' (July, 1963); E. E. Buchet, *Jean-Sébastien Bach, l'œuvre et la vie* (Paris, 1963); I. Holst, *Bach* (London, 1965); K. Geiringer, *Johann Sebastian Bach* (N. Y., 1966); N. Carrell, *Bach the Borrower* (London, 1967); F. Blume, *Der junge Bach* (Wolfenbüttel, 1967); F. Smend, *Bach-Studien: Gesammelte Reden und Aufsätze* (Kassel, 1969).

Bach, Wilhelm Friedemann. Add to bibl.: Hans Franck, *Friedemann, der Sohn J. S. Bachs* (Berlin, 1963).

Bacharach, Burt, American composer of popular songs; b. Kansas City, May 12, 1928. He was raised in a cultural atmosphere (his father was a newspaper columnist). He played jazz piano in night clubs; then studied music seriously at McGill Univ. in Montreal; also attended courses of Darius Milhaud and Henry Cowell at the New School for Social Research in N. Y. From 1958 to 1961 he traveled with Marlene Dietrich as her accompanist. In 1962 he joined forces with the lyricist Hal David with felicitous results; together they produced such fine songs as *Reach Out for Me, Trains and Boats and Planes, Make It Easy on Yourself, Blue on Blue, Walk on By, Always Something There to Remind Me, What the World Needs Now is Love, Do You Know the Way to San Jose?, Raindrops Keep Fallin' on My Head, The Look of Love, I'll Never Fall in Love Again, Our Little Secret, She Likes Baseball.* He wrote the title songs for the films *What's New Pussycat?, Wives and Lovers, Alfie, Send Me No Flowers, Promise Her Anything* and *Butch Cassidy and the Sundance Kid.* With Hal David again as his lyricist, he produced the highly successful Broadway musical *Promises, Promises* (1968). He is married to the actress Angie Dickinson.

Bachelet, Alfred. *Un jardin sur l'Oronte* was produced on Nov. 3, 1932 (not Nov. 7, 1931).

Bachmann, Alberto Abraham. Died at Neuilly-sur-Seine, Nov. 24, 1963.

Bäck, Sven-Erik. In 1954 he was appointed conductor of the school orch. of the Swedish Broadcasting Corporation; since 1959, director of its school of music at Edsberg. Add to works: *Sinfonia per archi* (1951); *Sinfonia da Camara* (1955); violin concerto (1957); chamber operas *Tranfjädrarna* (*The Crane Feathers*), his most important work (Stockholm, Feb. 28, 1957); *The Feast* (1958) and *The Bird* (1960); *Ett Spel om Maria* (*A Play on Mary*), scenic oratorio (Stockholm, April 4, 1958); *Favola* for clarinet and percussion (1962); string quartet No. 3 (1963).

Backhaus, Wilhelm. Died at Villach, Austria, July 5, 1969.

Bacon, Ernst. Add to works: *Riolama,* a concerto in 10 short movements for piano and orch. (1964); *Nature,* a cantata cycle to words by Emily Dickinson (1964-68); *Spirits and Places* for organ, a cycle with geographic connotations (1966); 13 songs in cycle form to poems of A. E. Housman (1968-69); *Jehovah and the Ark,* ballet for children, adults, narrator and orch. (1968-70); *Saws,* various canons for voice and piano (1960-71); *The Last Invocation,* a requiem for chorus, orch. and piano (Syracuse, March 27, 1971). Add to publications: *Notes on the Piano* (Syracuse, 1963).

Badarzewska, Thekla. Probable year of birth, 1834 (not 1838). She publ. her notorious *Prière d'une vierge* (under the Polish title *Molitwa dziewicy*) in Warsaw in 1851, at the age of 17.

Badings, Henk. Add to works: *Cain and Abel,* electronic ballet for orchestra, magnetic tape and optical siren (The Hague, June 21, 1956); *Evolutions,* electronic ballet (Hannover, Sept. 28, 1958); *Genèse,* music for 5 oscillators on tracks of spatial sound (Brussels, Oct. 7, 1958; produced as ballet under the title *Der sechste Tag* at Innsbruck, Nov. 7, 1959; retitled *Mikrobiologisches,* and produced at Linz, Feb. 22, 1960); *Salto mortale,* opera for 5 voices with electronic accompaniment (Netherlands Television, Eindhoven, June 19, 1959); *The Woman of Andros,* electronic ballet with voices (Hannover, April 14, 1960); *Martin Korda, D. P.,* opera with electronic instruments (The Hague, June 15, 1960); Eighth Symphony (Hannover, Jan. 11, 1957); Ninth Symphony (Amsterdam, Dec. 17, 1960); Tenth Symphony (1961); Concerto for two violins and orch. (The Hague, Jan. 19, 1955); concerto for harp and wind instruments (1967); *Armageddon,* for amplified soprano, wind instruments and magnetic tape (1968).

Bailey, Parker. Since 1942 associated with the New York financial firm Davis, Polk & Wardwell. Was on the board of directors of the Edward MacDowell Association from 1954-62; on the board of the Society for the Publication of American Music from 1947-62.

Bainton, Edgar Leslie. Died in Sydney, Australia, Dec. 8, 1956.

Baird, Martha, American pianist; b. Madera, Calif., March 15, 1895; d. New York, Jan. 24, 1971. She studied at the New England Cons. and with Artur Schnabel in Berlin; appeared as soloist with Sir Thomas Beecham in London and Koussevitzky in Boston. In 1957 she married John D. Rockefeller, Jr. and became a benefactress of opera and concert music.

Bakala, Břetislav. Died in Brno, April 1, 1958.

Baker, Janet, British mezzo-soprano; b. York, England, Aug. 21, 1933. She studied in England; then at the Mozarteum in Salzburg; attended a master class of Lotte Lehmann; received the Queen's Prize from the Royal College of Music in 1959. She made her American debut in 1966, singing to tumultuous applause; her interpretations of classical opera parts received great acclaim from the public and praise from sophisticated critics. She also distinguished herself in modern operatic repertory, particularly in Britten's works. In 1970 she received the Order of Commander of the British Empire. See 'Current Biography' for June 1971.

Balakirev, Mily Alexeyevitch. Add bibl.: E. Garden, *Balakirev: A Critical Study of His Life and Music* (N. Y., 1967).

Balantchivadze, Andrey. Add to works: Symph. No. 2 (Tbilisi, April 25, 1959).

Bales, Richard. Add to works: 2 orchestral suites inspired by watercolors in the National Gallery of Art in Washington: *American Design* (Washington, May 26, 1957) and *American Chronicle* (Washington, May 23, 1965); numerous arrangements and orchestrations of 19th-century American songs and dances. See *Composers of the Americas,* vol. 15 (Washington, 1969).

Ballantine, Edward. Died in Martha's Vineyard, Mass., July 2, 1971.

Ballou, Esther Williamson, American composer; b. Elmira, N.Y., July 17, 1915. She studied at Bennington College, Vermont; at Mills College, Calif.; at the Juilliard School of Music, N.Y. and privately with Wallingford Riegger and Otto Luening. She is a member of the Music Department of the American Univ. in Washington, D.C. Works: Concertino for oboe and strings (1953); *Early American Portrait* for soprano and chamber orch. (1961); piano trio (1956); Suite for 10 wind instruments (1957); Sextet for brass and piano (1961); *Capriccio* for violin and piano (1963); 2 sonatas for 2 pianos (1943, 1959); *Beguine* for 2 pianos (1951); songs.

Baloković, Zlatko. Died in Venice, March 29, 1965.

Baltzell, Winton James. He was Assistant Editor of 'Etude' from 1897 (not from 1887).

Bamboschek, Giuseppe. Died in New York, June 24, 1969.

Banchieri, Adriano. Add to bibl.: H. J. Wilbert, *Die Messen des Adriano Banchieri* (Mainz, 1969).

Banks, Don, Australian composer; b. Melbourne, Oct. 25, 1923. He studied at the Melbourne Cons.; then in London, with Mátyás Seiber (1950) and in Florence with Luigi Dallapiccola (1953); eventually settled in London. In some of his works he uses the 12-tone method of composition. He wrote *Duo* for violin and cello (Salzburg Festival, 1952): violin sonata (Tel Aviv Festival, 1954); *Three Studies* for cello and piano (1954); violin concerto (London, Aug. 12, 1968); *Nexus* for orch. and jazz quintet (1971); *Divertimento* for flute and string trio; *Psalm 70* for soprano and chamber orch.; *Episode* for chamber orch., etc.

Barab, Seymour, American cellist; b. Chicago, Jan. 9, 1921. He began his career as a pianist; also played cello; was a cellist in the Cleveland Symphony Orch. and other orchestras; performed on the viola da gamba. He composed the comic operas, *Chanticleer* (1954), *The Rajah's Ruby* (1954) and *A Game of Chance* (1956); also music for films.

Baranović, Krešimir. He was director of the Belgrade Philharmonic from 1951 to 1961; conducted the Belgrade Opera from 1946 to 1962. His opera *Striženo-košeno* was first performed in Zagreb on May 4, 1932; his comic opera *Nevjesta od Cetingrada* (*The Bride from Cetingrad*) written in 1942, was produced on May 12, 1951 at the Belgrade Opera, under the direction of the composer. He also wrote a ballet *Kineska priča* (*Chinese Tale*), making use of the pentatonic scale (Belgrade, April 30, 1955); *Pjesma guslara* (*Song of the Minstrel*), orchestral rhapsody (Zagreb, Jan. 25, 1947); *Pan,* for narrator, voices and orch. (Belgrade, March 10, 1958); *Oblaci* (*The Clouds*), for mezzo-soprano and orch. (Belgrade, Oct. 31, 1964).

Barati, George. In 1968 he terminated his tenure as conductor of the Honolulu Symph. Orch. and settled in California; was appointed Executive Director of the Montalvo Center for the Arts in Saratoga, Calif. and conductor of the Santa Cruz County Symphony. Add to works: quartet for harpsichord, flute, oboe and double-bass (1964); *The Waters of Kane,* festival ode for chorus and orch. (Honolulu, Sept. 23, 1966); *Octet* for harpsichord, flute, oboe and string quintet (1966); *Festival Hula,* symph. dance (1969); *South Seas Suite* for guitar and orch. (1971); *Noelani,* opera on a Polynesian subject (1971).

Barbaja, Domenico. Place of birth, Milan (not Naples).

Barber, Samuel. The exact date of the first performance of his opera *Vanessa* at the Metropolitan Opera is Jan. 15, 1958. Add to works: *A Hand of Bridge,* one-act opera to a libretto by Gian Carlo Menotti, for 4 solo voices and chamber orch. (Festival of Two Worlds, Spoleto, Italy, June 17, 1959); *Toccata Festiva* for orch. (Philadelphia, Sept. 30, 1960); *Die Natali* for orch. (Boston Symph. Orch., Dec. 22, 1960); *Andromache's Farewell* for voice and orch. (1962; N. Y., April 4, 1963); piano concerto (Boston Symph. Orch., Lincoln Center, N. Y., Sept. 24, 1962, Erich Leinsdorf conducting, John Browning soloist; a striking modern work, spontaneously successful and acclaimed at many subsequent performances in Europe and America); *Antony and Cleopatra,* opera in 3 acts, after Shakespeare, commissioned for the opening of the new Metropolitan Opera Building in Lincoln Center, N. Y., and produced there on Sept. 16, 1966; *Despite and Still,* a song cycle (1969); *Fadograph from a Yestern Scene* for orch., after James Joyce's *Finnegans Wake* (Pittsburgh, Sept. 10, 1971); *The Lovers,* for baritone, chorus and orch., to words by Pablo Neruda (Philadelphia, Sept. 22, 1971).

Barbirolli, Sir John. Died in London, July 29, 1970. See Charles Reid, *John Barbirolli* (London, 1971).

Barblan, Otto. Add bibl.: E. Perini, *Otto Barblan* (Zürich, 1960).

Barbour, J. Murray. Died in Homestead, Pa., near Pittsburgh, Jan. 4, 1970.

Barenboim, Daniel, Israeli pianist and conductor; b. Buenos Aires, Argentina, Nov. 15, 1942. He studied with his mother and his father; made his debut in Buenos Aires at the age of 7; was taken to Salzburg when he was 9; studied piano there with Edwin Fischer and received first lessons in conducting with Igor Markevitch. In 1952 the family settled in Israel; his subsequent studies were with Nadia Boulanger in Paris and at Santa Cecilia in Rome, where he was one of the youngest students to receive a diploma in 1956. He made his American debut as pianist at Carnegie Hall on Jan. 20, 1957, playing Prokofiev's *First Piano Concerto* with Leopold Stokowski; gave his first U.S. solo recital in New York on Jan. 17, 1958; made several world tours. He began to conduct orchestras in 1962 and soon established himself as a professional conductor of high caliber. In his piano playing he subordinates romantic passion to classical balance of form and thematic content; his performances of the entire cycle of Beethoven sonatas are notable for technical proficiency and interpretative taste. On June 15, 1967 he married the English cellist Jacqueline DuPré.

Bark, Jan, Swedish composer; b. Härnösand, April 19, 1934. He studied at the Royal Academy of Music in Stockholm, taking courses in composition with Lars-Erik Larsson and Karl-Birger Blomdahl; he was initiated into ultra-modern music by György Ligeti in Stockholm and during his American trip in 1962 when he was associated with the avant-garde groups of San Francisco; in 1963 he traveled to the Far East. His works include *Lamento* for piano, percussion and double-bass (1962); *Pyknos* for orch. (1962); *Metakronismer* for orch. (1960); *Ost Funk* for 8 jazz musicians; *Eko* for news broadcaster and 5 tape recorders; and *Boca Chica* for radio orch.

Barlow, Fred, French composer; b. Mulhouse, Oct. 26, 1881; d. Paris, Jan. 3, 1951. He was of British parentage; studied engineering; then turned to music; took lessons in Paris with Jean Huré and Charles Koechlin. Works: *Sylvie,* comic opera (Paris, March 7, 1924); *La Grande Jatte,* ballet (Paris, July 12, 1950); *Gladys,* ballet (posthumous; Mulhouse, Jan. 7, 1956); several symph. suites; string quartet (1947); violin sonata; cello sonata; piano pieces; vocal compositions.

Barlow, Wayne. Add to works: *Wait for the Promise of the Father,* cantata (1968).

Barnes, Edward Shippen. Died in Idyllwild, Calif., Feb. 14, 1958. He was organist at the First Presbyterian Church in Santa Monica for 20 years before his death, and not at St. Stephen's Episcopal Church; prior to that he was organist at St. Stephen's Church in Philadelphia.

Barnett, John Francis. *The Raising of Lazarus* was first performed in London on June 18, 1873 (not in Hereford, 1876, which was a local première).

Baron, Maurice. Died at Oyster Bay, Long Island, N. Y., Sept. 5, 1964.

Barraqué, Jean, French composer; b. Paris, Jan 17, 1928. He studied with Jean Langlais and Olivier Messiaen; worked in the experimental laboratory of the Radiodiffusion Française in Paris, and elaborated a system of serial composition of his own. His major work, *Séquence* (1950-55), for soprano, piano, harp, violin, cello, glockenspiel, xylophone and percussion, is based on a 12-tone row, but the esthetic problems of coordination with the philosophy of the text and impressionistic distillation of instrumental colors constitute the main preoccupation of the music. Barraqué's other works include a piano sonata (1952), *Le Temps restitué* for voices and orchestra (1957) and *Au-délà du hasard* for voices and 4 instrumental groups (Paris, Jan. 26, 1960). Despite the deliberate caution of his process of composition, limited productivity and scarcity of completed works, Barraqué has gained a number of ardent champions, of whom the most enthusiastic is A. Hodeir, who devotes a whole chapter to Barraqué in his book *Since Debussy* (N. Y., 1961).

Barraud, Henry. Add to works: *Te Deum* for chorus and six instruments, to the memory of Koussevitzky (1955); *Symphony* for string orch. (1955); Symph. No. 3 (Boston, March 7, 1958); *Rapsodie cartésienne* for orch. (1959); *Rapsodie dionysienne* for orch. (1961); *Lavinia,* opera-buffa (Aix-en-Provence, July 20, 1961); *Divertimento* for orch. (1962); concerto for flute and strings (1963); *Symphonie concertante* for trumpet and string orch. (1965). He publ. a book, *La France et la musique occidentale* (Paris, 1956).

Barrios, Angel, Spanish composer; b. Granada, Jan. 4, 1882; d. Madrid, Nov. 27, 1964. Of a musical family (his father was a famous guitarist), he studied violin and played in bands as a child. He later studied theory with Conrado del Campo in Madrid and with Gedalge in Paris. At the same time, he perfected his guitar playing; formed a trio 'Iberia' and traveled in Europe playing Spanish popular music. He spent his declining years in Madrid. In collaboration with his teacher Conrado del Campo, he wrote a successful operetta *El Avapiés* (Madrid, 1919) and several zarzuelas: *La Suerte, La Romería, Seguidilla gitana, Castigo de Dios, En Nombre del Rey,* and *Lola se va a los puertos;* also numerous overtures and other orchestral pieces based on popular Spanish motives.

Barstow, Vera. Date of birth, June 3, 1891 (not 1893). In 1971 she was teaching piano privately in Long Beach, California.

Barth, Hans. Died in Jacksonville, Florida, Dec. 9, 1956.

Bartha, Dénes, Hungarian musicologist; b. Budapest, Oct. 2, 1908. He studied musicology at the University of Berlin (1926-30) with Blume, Sachs, Hornbostel and Schering; received his doctorate with the thesis 'Benedictus Ducis und Appenzeller' (Wolfenbüttel, 1930). Returning to Budapest he was active as lecturer at the Univ. there and as a music critic. He was visiting professor at Smith College (1964), Harvard Univ. summer school (1964-65), Cornell Univ. (1965-66). His learned publications include *Lehrbuch der Musikgeschichte* (Budapest, 1935; in Hungarian); *Franz Liszt* (Leipzig, 1936; in German); *Beethoven* (Budapest, 1939; in Hungarian); *Die ungarische Musik* (with Kodály, Budapest, 1943); *Anthologie der Musikgeschichte* (Budapest, 1948); *J. S. Bach* (Budapest, 1956); *Haydn als Opernkapellmeister* (with L. Somfai; Budapest-Mainz, 1960). He edited the compendious music encyclopedia, *Zenei Lexikon* (3 vols., Budapest, 1965).

Bartók, Béla. His 3rd piano concerto was virtually completed at the time of his death; only the last 17 bars were orchestrated by Tibor Serly. Its first performance took place in Philadelphia on Feb. 8, 1946. The manuscript of his early violin concerto (1908) was discovered in 1958, and first performed in Basel on May 30, 1958. Add to bibl.: Roswitha Traimer, *Béla Bartóks Kompositionstechnik dargestellt an seinen sechs Streichquartetten* (Regensburg, 1956); R. Pelzoldt, *Béla Bartók, Sein Leben im Bildern* (Leipzig, 1958); A. Fassett, *The Naked Face of Genius: Béla Bartók's American Years* (Boston, 1958); Willi Reich, ed., *Béla Bartók: Eigene Schriften und Erinnerungen der Freunde* (Basel, 1958); J. Uhde, *Béla Bartók* (Berlin, 1959); *Studia Memoriae Béla Bartók Sacra;* edited by Z. Kodály and L. Lajtha (N. Y., 1959); B. Szabolcsi, *Béla Bartók: Leben und Werk* (Leipzig, 1961); L. Lesznai, *Béla Bartók: sein Leben, seine Werke* (Leipzig, 1961); E. Helm, *Béla Bartók in Selbstzeugnissen und Bilddokumenten* (1965); E. Lendvai, *Duality and Synthesis in the Music of Béla Bartók,* in G. Kepes, *Module, Proportion, Symmetry, Rhythm* (N. Y., 1966); I. Martynov, *Béla Bartók* (Moscow, 1968); I. Nestyev, *Béla Bartók* (Moscow, 1969); J. Szegö, *Bartók Béla élete* (Budapest, 1969). Bartók's correspondence, ed. by J. Demeny, was publ. in German, under the title of *Ausgewählte Briefe* (Budapest, 1960); see also V. Bator, *The Béla Bartók Archives; History and Catalogue* (N. Y., 1964). A periodical, 'Documenta Bartókiana,' was publ. in Budapest from 1964. Material on Bartók's American travels may be found in H. W. Heinsheimer, *Best Regards to Aida* (N. Y., 1968).

Bartoletti, Bruno, Italian conductor; b. Sesto Fiorentino, June 10, 1926. He studied flute; was flutist in the orchestra of the Maggio Fiorentino; acted as a substitute conductor at these festivals with an instant acclaim, which was an auspicious beginning of his career. He was appointed conductor at the Lyric Opera in Chicago in 1964; in 1965 he became musical director at the Rome Opera; also made frequent appearances at the Teatro Colón in Buenos Aires. He excels equally in the classical Italian opera and the modern repertory; conducted many first performances.

Bartolozzi, Bruno, Italian composer; b. Florence, June 8, 1911. A concert violinist, he turned to composition late in life; studied with Dallapiccola, and followed him along the path of lyric dodecaphony. Works: Concerto for orch. (1952); *Sentimento del sogno* for soprano and orch. (1954); *Immagine* for women's voices and 17 instruments, to 2 poems by Rilke (1959); string quartet (1960); *Concertazione* for oboe and instruments (1966); Concerto for violin and strings with harpsichord (1968); *Tres recuerdos del cielo* for voice and instruments (1968). He wrote a book, *New Sounds for Woodwind* (in English; London, 1967), demonstrating the possibility of producing simultaneously several pitches on a single woodwind instrument.

Bartoš, Josef. Died in Prague, Oct. 27, 1952.

Baselt, Fritz (Friedrich Gustav Otto). Died in Frankfurt (not in Oels).

Basie, William ("Count"), American Negro bandleader, pianist and composer; b. Red Bank, N. J., Aug. 21, 1904. He played piano as a child; studied organ with Fats Waller; accompanied singers in vaudeville. He organized his own band in Kansas City; in 1936 moved to N. Y.; enlarged his original band emphasizing the rhythmic element in his arrangements; introduced female ballad singers as soloists. He made a tour of Europe in 1956; played a command performance for the Queen of England during his British tour in 1957.

Basiola, Mario, Italian baritone; b. Annico, July 12, 1892; d. there, Jan. 3, 1965. He studied in Rome; was engaged at the Metropolitan Opera in N. Y. (1925-32); at La Scala in Milan and at Rome (1933-38); also sang at Covent Garden, London (1939) and in Australia (1949); then returned to Italy and was active there as a teacher.

Bassett, Leslie, American composer; b. Hanford, Calif., Jan. 22, 1923. He studied piano played the trombone in jazz combos; was trombonist during his military service, playing in the 13th Armored Division Band. He then enrolled in Fresno, Calif., State College (B.A., 1947); later studied composition with Ross Lee Finney at the Univ. of Michigan (M.M., 1949; Dr.M., 1956); also took private lessons with Arthur Honegger and Nadia Boulanger in Paris in 1950. In 1952 he was appointed to the faculty of the Univ. of Michigan. He held the American Prix de Rome in 1961-63, and National Institute of Arts and Letters Award in 1964. In 1966 he received the Pulitzer Prize in Music for his *Variations for Orchestra.* In his music, he pursues the ideal of structural logic within the judicial limits of the modern school of composition, with some serial elements discernible in his use of thematic rhythms and motivic periodicity. His works include *Suite in G* for orch. (Fresno, Dec. 3, 1946); *Five Movements* for orch. (Rome, July 5, 1962); *Variations for Orchestra* (Rome, July 6, 1963; Philadelphia, Oct. 22, 1965; received the Pulitzer Prize in 1966); *Colloquy* for orch. (Fresno, May 23, 1969).

Bate, Stanley Richard. Died in London, Oct. 19, 1959.

Bathori, Jane, French mezzo-soprano; b. Paris, June 14, 1877; d. there, Jan. 21, 1970. After an active operatic career, she devoted herself to the cultivation of modern French music; sang first performances of works by Debussy, Ravel, Satie and Milhaud; gave numerous recitals in England. Returning to Paris, she limited herself to teaching. She published *Conseils sur le chant* (Paris, 1929) and *Sur l'Interprétation des mélodies de Claude Debussy* (Paris, 1953).

Baudo, Serge, French conductor; b. Marseille, July 16, 1927. He studied at the Paris Cons., conducting with Louis Fourestier, and theory with Jean Gallon and Noël Gallon; received Premier Prix as drummer (1948) and as conductor (1949). He was engaged as pianist and percussion player in the orchestra of the Concerts Lamoureux; then toured as opera conductor. In 1967 he was appointed musical director and conductor of the Orchestre de Paris.

Bautista, Julian. Died in Buenos Aires, July 8, 1961.

Bazelaire, Paul, French cellist and composer; b. Sedan, March 4, 1886; d. Paris, Dec. 11, 1958. He graduated from the Paris Cons. as a cellist at the age of 11, with the Premier Prix; after a concert career became prof. of cello at the Paris Cons. (1918-56); founded a unique ensemble of 50 cellos. Works: *Suite Française sur des chants populaires* for orch.; symph. poem *Cléopâtre* (Paris, Jan. 23, 1908); *Suite Grecque* for small orch. (1910); *Rapsodie dans le style russe* for cello and orch. (Paris, Feb. 2, 1941). He orchestrated Bach's six cello suites; publ. a teaching manual, *Pédagogie du violoncelle.*

Bazelon, Irwin, American composer; b. Evanston, Illinois, June 4, 1922. After graduation from DePaul Univ. of Chicago in 1945, he studied composition with Darius Milhaud at Mills College, Oakland, Calif. (1946-48) and with Ernest Bloch at Univ. of Calif., Berkeley (1947). He went to N. Y. in 1948 where he remained. His style of composition is marked by imaginative eclecticism; he regards music as a practical art. Works: suite for clarinet, cello and piano (1947); Ballet Suite for small ensemble (1949); *Concert Overture* (1952; revised 1960); *Movimento da Camera* for flute, bassoon, horn and harpsichord (1954); *Adagio and Fugue* for string orch. (1956); suite for small orch. (1956); Chamber Symphony for 7 instruments (1957); Symph. No. 1 (1960; Kansas City, Nov. 29, 1963); Symph. No. 2 (*Short Symphony;* Washington, Dec. 4, 1962); Symph. No. 3 for brass, percussion, piano and string sextet (1963); Symph. No. 4 (1965); Symph. No. 5 (1966); Symph. No. 6 (Kansas City, Nov. 17, 1970); *Fusions* for orch. (1965); *Ballet Centauri 17* for orch. (1960); *Suite for Merry Wives of Windsor* (1958); *Overture to The Taming of the Shrew* (1960); brass quintet (1963); *Excursion* for orch. (Kansas City, March 5, 1966); *Concerto for 14 Players* (N. Y., May 16, 1971); 2 string quartets; 3 piano sonatas; 5 Pieces for cello and piano, etc.

Beardslee, Bethany, American soprano; b. Lansing, Michigan, Dec. 25, 1927. She studied at Michigan State Univ. and at the Juilliard School of Music in New York; specialized in modern music; evolved an extraordinary technique with a flute-like ability to sound impeccably precise intonation; mastered the art of Sprechstimme, which enabled her to give fine renditions of such works as Schoenberg's *Pierrot Lunaire;* has distinguished herself also in vocal scores by Alban Berg, Anton von Webern, Stravinsky and Krenek.

Bécaud, Gilbert, French composer of popular songs; b. Toulon, Oct. 24, 1927. He studied at the Cons. of Nice; made his debut as a chansonnier in Versailles on Dec. 20, 1952, where he was featured as "Monsieur 100,000 volts." With this sobriquet, he launched a highly lucrative career as a performer of his own songs in music halls, and was accompanist to Edith Piaf on her American tours. He later tried his hand at serious music with a cantata *L'Enfant à l'Étoile* (Paris, Jan. 7, 1962) and *Opéra d'Aran* (Paris, Oct. 22, 1962).

Becerra Schmidt, Gustavo, Chilean composer; b. Temuco, Aug. 26, 1925. He studied piano and violin; then composition with Allende and Santa Cruz at the Cons. of Santiago; subsequently became prof. of harmony there. A prolific composer, he wrote an opera *Don Rodrigo* and numerous choral works; ballets; piano pieces.

Bechet, Sidney, American Negro jazz clarinetist and saxophonist; b. New Orleans, May 14, 1897; d. Garches, France, May 14, 1959. He traveled to Chicago where he played in various bands; in 1947 settled in Paris. In jazz he represented the romantic New Orleans school, playing in an expressively sentimental ballad style. See R. Munly, *Sidney Bechet* (Paris, 1959).

Beck, Conrad. Add to works: Symph. No. 7, surnamed *Aeneas-Silvius* (Zürich, Feb. 25, 1958); *Die Sonnenfinsternis,* cantata (Lucerne, Aug. 25, 1967); clarinet concerto (1968); *Fantasie* for orch. (1969).

Beck, John Ness, American composer; b. Warren, Ohio, Nov. 11, 1930. He studied composition at the Ohio State Univ. and subsequently taught harmony and theory there, resigning later to assume the management of a retail sheet music business in Columbus, Ohio. He wrote mainly sacred choral works, among them *Upon this Rock, Hymn for Our Time, Canticle of Praise, Hymn for Easter Day, Litany of Thanksgiving* and *Exhortation.* Other compositions include *5 Carol Fantasies* for piano (1970); sonata for flute and piano and pieces for concert band.

Beck, Thomas Ludvigsen. Died in Oslo, Sept. 9, 1963.

Becker, Gustave Louis. Died in Epsom, Surrey, England, Feb. 25, 1959.

Becker, John J. Died in Wilmette, Illinois, Jan. 21, 1961.

Beckett, Wheeler, American conductor; b. San Francisco, March 7, 1898; studied at Columbia Univ. and Univ. of California; took a course in conducting with Felix Weingartner in Basel (1928-30); served as organist and choirmaster at Grace Cathedral, San Francisco (1921-25); conducted Young People's Concerts with the San Francisco Symph. Orch. (1927-30); was conductor of the Richmond Symph. Orch. (1932-36); Boston Symph. Youth Concerts (1938-48); in 1957 organized the New York Youth Concerts; under the auspices of the State Dept., conducted in the Far East (1959-62). He composed an opera *Snow White;* an organ concerto; a symphony; church music; songs.

Beckmann, Johann Friedrich Gottlieb. Exact place and date of birth, Celle, Sept. 6, 1737.

Beckwith, John, Canadian composer; b. Victoria, B. C., March 9, 1927; studied piano at the Cons. of Toronto (1945-50); toured in Canada as pianist; then took courses in composition with Nadia Boulanger in Paris (1950-52). Works: *Music for Dancing,* for piano four hands (1948); *The Great Lakes Suite* for voices and instruments (1949); 5 pieces for trumpet, horn and trombone (1951); Suite for violin alone (1951); woodwind quartet (1951); *Montage* for orch. (1953); *3 Studies* for string trio (1956); *Mobiles,* six piano pieces (1959); *Concerto-Fantasy* for piano and orch. (1959); *Night Blooming Cereus,* chamber opera (Toronto radio, March 4, 1959; first stage performance, Toronto, April 5, 1960); *Circle with Tangents* for harpsichord and 13 solo strings (1968).

Bedford, David, English composer; b. London, Aug 4, 1937. He studied at the Royal Academy of Music, London, with Lennox Berkeley (1958-61); then went to Italy where he took lessons with Luigi Nono in Venice; subsequently spent some time in the Milan electronic studios. Works: *Concerto for 24 Instruments* (1960); *Piece II* for electronic instruments (1962); *+2, −2,* for orch. (1963); *Piece for Mo* for chamber ensemble (1963); *Music for Albion Moonlight* for soprano and chamber ensemble (1964); *The Great Birds* for 30-part chorus (1964); *Octet for 9* (1964); *A Dream of the Seven Lost Stars* for chorus and instruments (1965); *The Tentacles of the Dark Nebula* for tenor and solo strings (London, Sept. 22, 1969).

Beecham, Sir Thomas. Died in London, March 8, 1961. He publ. an exhaustive biography of Delius (London, 1959). Cf. C. Ried, *Thomas Beecham: an Independent Biography* (London, 1961).

Beecher, Carl Milton. Died in Portland, Oregon, Nov. 21, 1968.

Beeson, Jack Hamilton, American composer; b. Muncie, Indiana, July 15, 1921. He studied at the Eastman School of Music, Rochester, N. Y. with Burrill Phillips, Bernard Rogers and Howard Hanson; was composer in residence at the American Academy in Rome; did graduate work at Columbia Univ. and took private lessons with Béla Bartók in New York. Later he joined the staff of Columbia Univ. His works include the operas *Jonah* (1950), *Hello Out There* (N. Y., April 27, 1954), *The Sweet Bye and Bye* (N. Y., Nov. 22, 1957) and *Lizzie Borden* (N.Y., March 25, 1965); Symphony in A (1959). *Transformations* for orch. (1959); *Commemoration* for band (1960); 5 piano sonatas; viola sonata; many vocal works; *My Heart's in the Highlands,* television opera after a play by William Saroyan (National Educational Television Theater, March 17, 1970).

Beethoven, Ludwig van. The composer of the so-called Jena Symphony was proved (by H. C. Landon) to be Friedrich Witt (q.v.). Add to bibl.: Paul Nettl, *Beethoven und seine Zeit* (Hamburg, 1958); J. V. Cockshoot, *The Fugue in Beethoven's Piano Music* (London, 1959); R. Bory, *La vie et l'œuvre de Ludwig van Beethoven par image* (Paris, 1960); Emily Anderson, *The Letters of Beethoven* (3 vols.; highly meritorious, despite minor flaws and questionable renditions into English; London, 1962); L. G. Bachmann, *Beethoven contra Beethoven; Geschichte eines berühmten Rechtsfalles* (Munich, 1963); Ivan Mahaim, *Beethoven, Naissance et Renaissance des derniers quatuors* (2 vols., Paris, 1964; an original and informative investigation, including valuable biographical documentation on performers of Beethoven's chamber music). The name of the author of *Beethovens ferne und unsterbliche Geliebte* is Kaznelson (not Axnelson). Kenneth M. Stevens and William G. Hemenway argue convincingly that Beethoven's deafness was caused by cochlear otosclerosis ('American Medical Association Journal,' Aug., 1970). See also G. F. Marek, *Beethoven: Biography of a Genius* (N. Y., 1969); Martin Cooper, *Beethoven: The Last Decade* (with a medical appendix by E. Larkin; London, 1970); Joseph Schmidt-Görg and Hans Schmidt eds., *Ludwig van Beethoven* (N. Y., 1970; pictorial edition with commentaries). Other publications of some value are: W. Hess, *Beethoven* (Zürich, 1956); P. Mies, *Text Kritische Untersuchungen bei Beethoven* (Bonn, 1957); H. Unverricht, *Die Eigenschriften und die Originalausgaben von Werken Beethovens in ihrer Bedeutung für die moderne Textkritik* (Kassel, 1960); A. Tyson, *The Authentic English Editions of Beethoven* (London, 1963); J. Schmidt-Görg, *Beethoven: die Geschichte seiner Familie* (Bonn, 1964); L. Misch, *Neue Beethoven-Studien* (Bonn, 1967); J. Kerman, *The Beethoven Quartets* (N. Y., 1967). The claim advanced by J. A. Rogers in his book, *100 Amazing Facts About the Negro* (N. Y., c. 1930), that Beethoven was of African descent, made largely on iconographic grounds, was moderated by the author in his subsequent publication, *Most Famous People of African Descent,* in which he concedes legitimate dubiety on the subject.

Beglarian, Grant, American composer; b. in Georgia (Russia), Dec. 1, 1927. In his early childhood the family moved to Tehran, Iran. He emigrated to the U.S. in 1947; studied viola with Paul Doktor; then enrolled at the Univ. of Michigan, studying composition with Ross Lee Finney and musicology with Hans T. David; obtained his Dr. M. in 1957. He was on the faculty of the Army School of Music in Munich (1952-54); later played the viola with the Seventh Army Symph. Orch. in Europe. In 1969 he was appointed Dean of the School of Performing Arts at the Univ. of Southern California in Los Angeles. Works: *Symphony in Two Movements* (1950); *Divertimento* for orch. (1957); *Sinfonia* (1961); string quartet (1948); violin sonata (1949); cello sonata (1951); woodwind quintet (1966); choruses.

Behrens, Jack, American composer; b. Lancaster, Pennsylvania, March 25, 1935. He studied at the Juilliard School of Music in New York with Bergsma, Persichetti, and Mennin, obtaining his B.S. in composition in 1958; attended seminars of Kirchner and Sessions at Harvard Univ. (1968). He taught at the Univ. of Saskatchewan, Canada (1962-66); was teaching fellow at Harvard Univ. (1969-70). Works: *Introspection* for strings (1956); *Quarter- tone Quartet* (1960); *Declaration* for orch. (1964); *Pentad for vibraphone and piano* (1965); choruses; piano pieces.

Beiderbecke, Leon Bismark ('Bix'), American jazz trumpet player; b. Davenport, Iowa, March 10, 1903; d. New York, Aug. 6, 1931. His parents, emigrants from Germany, were amateur musicians. After studying music at home, he wandered off to New Orleans; later played in various jazz bands in Chicago, St. Louis and New York, until he finally became a member of Paul Whiteman's band. There he developed his distinctive style of lyric melancholy; also composed piano pieces in an impressionistic vein. A prey to alcohol, he succumbed at the age of 28. His life is the subject of a semi-fictional novel *Young Man With a Horn* by D. Baker (1938).

Beinum, Eduard van. Died in Amsterdam, April 13, 1959.

Bekku, Sadao, Japanese composer; b. Tokyo, May 24, 1922. He studied in Tokyo with Tomojiro Ikenouchi; went to Paris in 1951-54, where he took courses with Darius Milhaud, Olivier Messiaen and Jean Rivier. His works are couched in a neo-classical vein; some of them include authentic Japanese modalities. Works: trio for oboe, clarinet and bassoon (1953); flute sonata (1954); string quartet (1955); *Suite japonaise* for wind quintet (Tokyo, Sept. 30, 1955); *Deux Prières* for orch. (Tokyo, May 10, 1956); *Symphonietta* for string orch. (Tokyo, Nov. 27, 1959); Symph. No. 1 (Tokyo, Jan. 18, 1962); violin sonata (1967).

Belafonte, Harry (Harold George, Jr.), American folk singer; b. New York, March 1, 1927, of a Jamaican mother and Martinique father. As a youth he lived partly in New York, partly in Jamaica; worked as a janitor and a cart pusher in Manhattan. When his voice was discovered, he got singing jobs in Greenwich Village restaurants; acted the role of Joe in the film *Carmen Jones* (1954). From 1948 to 1957 he was married to the Negro child psychologist Frances Marguerite Byrd; his second marriage was to Julie Robinson. Belafonte's greatest success came as an interpreter of Calypso songs, which he performed with great dramatic power. He made numerous tours abroad.

Belaiev, Victor Mikhailovitch. Died in Moscow, Feb. 16, 1968.

Belcher, Supply, American hymn writer, dubbed "the Handel of Maine"; b. Stoughton, Mass., March 29 (April 9, new style), 1751; d. at Farmington, Maine, in 1836. He was a tavern keeper and original member (with Billings) of the Stoughton Musical Society. After service in the Revolutionary War under Washington, he went to Farmington, Maine. He published *The Harmony of Maine,* a collection of hymns, in 1794.

Bell, Donald, Canadian bass-baritone; b. South Burnaby, B. C., June 19, 1934. He studied at the Royal College of Music in London; made a brilliant debut in a concert at 20. In 1958 he went to Berlin where he made successful appearances at the Berlin State Opera; sang at the Bayreuth Festivals in 1958-61. He made his American debut as a soloist with the Philadelphia Orch. in Carnegie Hall, N. Y., in 1959; toured Russia in 1963. In 1964 he joined the staff of the Düsseldorf Opera Company.

Bellezza, Vincenzo, Italian conductor; b. Bitonto, Bari, Feb. 17, 1888; d. Rome, Feb. 8, 1964. He studied in Naples; became an opera conductor at various European theaters; was on the staff of the Metropolitan Opera in New York (1926-35).

Bellini, Vincenzo. Add bibl.: L. Orrey, *Bellini* (London, 1969); Herbert Weinstock, *Vincenzo Bellini: His Life and Operas* (N. Y., 1971).

Benatzky, Ralph. Died in Zürich, Oct. 16, 1957. Add to works: the operettas, *Die drei Musketiere* (1929); *Im weissen Rössl* (his most popular work; first performed in Berlin, Nov. 8, 1930); *Bezauberndes Fräulein* (1935); *Kleinstadtzauber* (1947); *Ein Liebestraum* (on Liszt's themes; 1951); *Don Juans Wiederkehr* (1953).

Bendl, Karl. Date of death, Sept. 20 (not Sept. 16), 1897.

Ben-Haim, Paul. Add to works: *Cello Concerto* (Limburg, Holland, Dec. 14, 1967).

Benjamin, Arthur. Died in London, April 9, 1960. The date of first performance of his opera *The Devil Take Her* is Dec. 1, 1931 (not Nov. 30, 1932). His posthumous opera, *Tartuffe,* was performed in London on Nov. 30, 1964.

Benjamin, William E., American composer; b. Montreal, Canada, Dec. 7, 1944. He attended McGill Univ. (1961-65) receiving his Mus. Bac. degree; studied composition with Istvan Anhalt; also took piano lessons at the Conservatoire de Musique de la Province de Quebec. In 1966 he enrolled at Princeton Univ., where his teachers were Milton Babbitt, Edward T. Cone, Peter Westergaard and James K. Randall; received the M.F.A. in 1968. In 1970 he was appointed instructor in music at Wellesley College. In his music he strives to fashion a rational multi-dimensional musical space, in which dynamics, rhythm and tonality are functional components in free serial arrangements. His works include *Mah Tovu* for mixed chorus a cappella (1965); *Variations for Four Players* (1967); *At Sixes* *and Sevens,* a sextet (1968); piano concerto (1970).

Bennard, George, American hymn composer; b. Youngstown, Ohio, Feb. 4, 1873; d. Reed City, Mich., Oct. 10, 1958. He served as a Salvation Army officer from 1892-1907; subsequently traveled as evangelist in the U.S. and Canada. He wrote a number of sacred songs, among them *God Bless our Boys, The Old Rugged Cross, Sweet Songs of Salvation.*

Bennett, Richard Rodney, English composer; b. Broadstairs, Kent, March 29, 1936. He took courses in composition at the Royal Academy of Music in London with Lennox Berkeley and Howard Ferguson, and in Paris with Boulez (1957-59). His music is influenced mainly by Béla Bartók, but he has also pursued serial methods. Works: string quartets No. 1 (1952), No. 2 (1953); Cantata for voice and percussion (1954); Sonatina for flute solo (1954); 4 Improvisations for solo violin (1955); 5 Pieces for orch. (1956); Concerto for horn and orch (1956); *The Approaches of Sleep* for 4 voices and 10 instruments (1959); *Journal* for orch. (1960); *Calendar* for chamber orch. (1960); *The Ledge,* one-act opera (1961); string quartet No. 3 (1960); *London Pastoral* for tenor and chamber orch. (1962); *Nocturnes* for chamber orch. (1962); *Aubade* for orch. (1964); string quartet No. 4 (1964); solo violin sonata (1964); *Conversations* for 2 flutes (1964); wind trio (1964); *The Mines of Sulphur,* 3-act opera (London, Feb. 24, 1965); Symph. No. 1 (London, Feb. 10, 1966); *A Penny for a Song,* comic opera (London, Oct. 31, 1967); Symph. No. 2, commissioned by the N. Y. Philharmonic (New York, Jan. 18, 1968); *Victory,* opera after the novel by Joseph Conrad (Royal Opera, Covent Garden, London, April 13, 1970).

Bennett, Robert Russell. Add to works: Concerto for violin, piano and orch. (Portland, Oregon, March 18, 1963).

Benoit, Peter. Add to bibl.: Floris van der Mueren, *Peter Benoit in het huidig perspectief* (Amsterdam, 1968).

Bentinelli, Bruno. Delete the entry; the name is a misprint for **Bettinelli, Bruno** (q.v.).

Bentzon, Niels Viggo. Add to works: *Torquilla,* oratorio (Aarhus, Oct. 23, 1961); *Faust II,* operatic trilogy (Kiel, Germany, June 21, 1964).

Benvenuti, Arrigo, Italian composer; b. Buggiano, Pistoia, May 2, 1925. He settled in Florence in 1945, where he studied advanced composition with Dallapiccola. He has adopted an ultra-modern style of composition, with serial techniques diversified by aleatory permissiveness. His works include *4 Studi* for 11 instruments (1961); *Polymérie* for orch. (1961); *Folia* for piano and string quartet (1963); *Débris* for 24 instruments (1964); *Pop Pourri* for 18 instruments (1967); electronic pieces.

Benzell, Mimi, American soprano; b. Bridgeport, Conn., April 6, 1922; d. Manhasset, Long Island, N. Y., Dec. 23, 1970. Her grandfather was a Jewish folksong singer in Russia before his emigration to America. She studied at the David Mannes Music School in New York; appeared at the Metropolitan Opera on Jan. 5, 1945 in the role of the Queen of the Night in *The Magic Flute;* in the next five years she sang about 20 different roles with the Metropolitan, including Gilda in *Rigoletto* and Mussetta in *La Bohème.* In 1949 she abandoned grand opera and became a popular singer in Broadway shows and in nightclubs.

Berberian, Cathy, American mezzo-soprano of Armenian descent; b. Attleboro, Mass. July 4, 1925. She studied singing and dance in the U.S. and in Italy; in 1950 she married the Italian composer Luciano Berio; separated in 1965. An ardent student of ultra-modern music, she has become a foremost exponent of the most complex works by the cosmopolitan avant-garde excelling in rhythmic precision and intonation.

Berg, Alban. Add to bibl.: K. Vogelsang, *Alban Berg: Leben und Werk* (Berlin, 1959); Willi Reich. ed., *Alban Berg, Bildnis im Wort* (Zürich, 1959); G. Ploebsch, *Alban Bergs Wozzeck* (Vienna, 1968).

Berg, Josef, Czech composer; b. Brno, March 8, 1927; d. there, Feb. 26, 1971. He studied at the Brno Cons.; wrote music for the radio and the films. Works: 3 symphonies (1950, 1952, 1955); piano cycle, *Brothers Karamazov* (1949); string quartet (1949); *Song of the Fatherland,* cantata (1952); *Fantasy* for 2 pianos (1962); nonet for 2 harps, piano, cembalo, bells, celesta, xylophone, vibraphone and magnetic tape (1963).

Berg, Natanaël. Died in Stockholm, Oct. 15, 1957. The title of his first opera is *Leila* (not *Lelia*).

Bergamo, Petar, Serbian composer; b.

Split, Feb. 27, 1930. He studied at the Music Academy in Belgrade; adopted a neo-classical method of composition. His overture entitled *Navigare necesse est* (Belgrade, Feb. 27, 1962) is one of his most characteristic pieces; his *Musica concertante* for orch. (Belgrade, Feb. 18, 1963) tends toward atonality. He further wrote two symphonies (1961, 1963); and *Concerto abbreviato* for clarinet solo (1966).

Berger, Arthur. Add to works: *Chamber Music* for 13 players (1956); Duo for clarinet and piano (1957); string quartet (1958). See J. Perkins, *Arthur Berger: the Composer as Mannerist,* in 'Perspectives of New Music' (Fall-Winter, 1966).

Berger, Jean. Date of birth, Sept. 27, 1909 (not 1901). He served in the U. S. Army during World War II; was member of the faculty at Middlebury College (1948-59); from 1959, teaching at the Univ. of Illinois at Urbana. Add to works: *Brazilian Psalm* for chorus (1941); 4 Sonnets for voice and string quartet (1941); *Vision of Peace* for chorus a cappella (1949); *Creole Overture* (1949); *Caribbean Concerto* for mouth harmonica and orch., possibly the first of its kind, written for Larry Adler, who gave its first performance, with the St. Louis Symph. Orch., on March 10, 1942.

Berger, Theodor. Add to works: *Homerische Symphonie* (1948); *La Parola* for orch. based on the sesquitone scale of alternating whole tones and semitones (1955); *Sinfonia Parabolica* (1956); *Symphonischer Triglyph,* on themes from Schubert's chamber music (1958); violin concerto (1963).

Bergh, Arthur. Died aboard the S.S. President Cleveland en route to Honolulu, Feb. 11, 1962.

Bergman, Erik. In 1963 he was appointed prof. at the Sibelius Academy of Music in Helsinki. Add to works: *Burla* for orch. (1948); *Rubaiyat* for male chorus and chamber orch. (1953); *Aton* for baritone, mixed chorus and orch. (1959); *Sela,* cantata (1961); *Faglarna* (*The Birds*) for baritone, chorus and percussion (1962). After study with Wladimir Vogel he adopted a modified 12-tone technique, which he used in *Tre aspetti d'una seria dodecafonica* (1957), *Simbolo* (1960) and *Concerto da camera* (1960).

Bergsma, William. Was on the faculty of the Juilliard School of Music, 1946-63; 1963, appointed director of the School of Music at the Univ. of Washington, Seattle. Add to works: concerto for wind quintet (1958); *Fantastic Variations* on a theme from *Tristan und Isolde* for viola and piano (Boston, March 2, 1961); *In Celebration: Toccata for the Sixth Day,* commissioned for the inaugural week concert of the Juilliard Orch. during the week of dedication of Philharmonic Hall in Lincoln Center for the Performing Arts, N.Y., and performed there on Sept. 28, 1962; *Confrontation* from the *Book of Job,* for chorus and 22 instruments (Des Moines, Iowa, Nov. 29, 1963); *Serenade, To Await the Moon* for chamber orch. (La Jolla, Calif., Aug. 22, 1965); violin concerto (Tacoma, Washington, May 18, 1966).

Bergt, Christian Gottlob August. Date of birth, June 17, 1771 (not 1772).

Berio, Luciano, Italian composer of avant-garde music; b. Oneglia, Oct. 24, 1925. He studied music with his father, an organist, and at the Milan Cons. with Ghedini (comp.) and Giulini (conducting); received a Koussevitzky Foundation Fellowship in 1952; took a summer course with Dallapiccola at the Berkshire Center in Tanglewood. Returning to Italy, he joined the staff of the Italian Radio; founded the Studio di Fonologia Musicale for experimental work on acoustics; edited the progressive magazine *Incontri Musicali.* His works, many of them written in a special optical notation, comprise: *2 pezzi* for violin and piano (1951); *5 Variazioni* for piano (1952); *Chamber Music* to poems by James Joyce for voice, clarinet, cello and harp (1952); *Variazioni* for chamber orch. (1953); *Mimomusique,* ballet (1953); *Nones* for orch. (1954); string quartet (1955); *Allelujah I* for orch. (1956); *Allelujah II* for 5 instrumental groups (1956-58); *Serenata* for flute and 14 instruments (1957); *Sequenza I* for flute solo (1958); *Tempi concertati* for chamber orch. (1959); *Differences* for 5 instruments and stereophonic tape (1959); *Circles,* to poems by E. E. Cummings, for voice, harp and percussion (1960); *Quaderni* for orch. (1960); *Sequenza II* for harp (1963); *Traces,* for voices and orch. (1964); *Chemins I, II, III,* for voices and orch. (1965, 1967, 1967); *Sequenza III* for female voice (1966); *Sequenza IV* for piano (1966); *Sequenza V* for trombone solo (1966); *Sincronie* for string quartet (1967); a number of scores for electronic instruments (*Mutazioni, Perspectives, Omaggio a Joyce, Momento,* etc.); *Sinfonia,* containing a movement based on remembered fragments of works by Mahler, Ravel, Richard Strauss, etc. (N. Y., Oct. 10, 1968); *Opera,* spectacle for mixed media (Santa Fe, Aug. 12, 1970);

Memory for Electronic Piano and Electronic Harpsichord (N. Y., March 12, 1971, with Berio and Peter Serkin at the respective electronic keyboards); *Prayer,* a speech sound event with magnetic tape accompaniment (N. Y., April 5, 1971). In 1965 Berio joined the faculty of the Juilliard School of Music in New York.

Bériot, Charles-Wilfride de. Born Feb. 21, 1833 (not 1883).

Berkeley, Lennox. Add to works: Symph. No. 2 (Birmingham, Feb. 24, 1959); *Castaway,* opera (Aldeburgh, England, June 3, 1967); Symph. No. 3 (Cheltenham, July 9, 1969).

Berkowitz, Ralph, American pianist and educator; b. New York City, Sept. 5, 1910. He studied at the Curtis Institute of Music, Philadelphia (1933-42); then was instructor at the Berkshire Music Center in Tanglewood; in 1947 was appointed Dean. He made tours as pianist and accompanist in America, Europe and in the Orient; publ. numerous piano arrangements; edited works by Bach, Haydn, Chopin, Debussy, etc. He also wrote a short opera *A Telephone Call* which was performed in Rio de Janeiro on Dec. 15, 1955.

Berlinski, Herman, German - American composer; b. Leipzig, Aug. 18, 1910; studied at the Leipzig Cons.; left Germany in 1933, and took lessons with Alfred Cortot (piano) and Nadia Boulanger (composition) in Paris. During World War II he joined the French Foreign Legion; eventually emigrated to the U. S. In his music he emphasizes the rhapsodic element of traditional Jewish cantillation, combining it with dodecaphonic techniques. Works: flute sonata (1941); violin sonata (1949); *Symphonic Visions* (1949); liturgical compositions: *Kaddish* (1953); *Avodat Shabbat* (1957); *Kiddush Ha-Shem* (1958); songs. See M. Kayden, *The Music of H. B.,* in the 'Bulletin of the American Composers Alliance' (1959, No. 3).

Bermudo, Juan. Add to bibl.: R. Stevenson, *Juan Bermudo* (The Hague, 1960).

Bernac, Pierre. Published *The Interpretation of French Song* (N. Y., 1970).

Bernard, Robert. Died in Paris, May 2, 1971.

Bernat, Robert, American composer; b; Johnstown, Pa., July 3, 1931. He has been active as a teacher and conductor. His *Passacaglia* for orch., "In Memoriam: John F. Kennedy," was brought out by the Pittsburgh Symph. Orch. on Nov. 25, 1966.

Berners, Lord. Place of birth Bridgnorth (not Bridgenorth). *Le Carrosse du Saint-Sacrement* was first produced in Paris on April 24, 1924 (not 1921).

Bernstein, Elmer, American composer of film, radio and television music; b. New York, April 4, 1922. Among his film scores are *The Ten Commandments, The Man with the Golden Arm* and *From the Terrace.* He writes music charged with emotional energy, marked by adroit modernistic turns and piquant rhythms.

Bernstein, Leonard. In 1958 he became the musical director and conductor of the N. Y. Philharmonic, the first American to hold this post; toured with it in Latin America (1958); in Russia and 17 other countries of Europe and Near East (1959); in Japan, Alaska and Canada (1960); etc. He resigned as musical director in the Spring 1969, but continued to lead occasional concerts as 'laureate conductor.' In the interim he launched on an active career as guest conductor of European symphony orchestras; shortly after the conclusion of Israel's six-day war, he conducted the Israel Philharmonic Orch. on Mt. Scopus in Jerusalem in a program of works by Mendelssohn and Mahler (July 9, 1967). Add to works: *Candide,* musical comedy after Voltaire (N. Y., Dec. 1, 1956); *West Side Story,* social music drama (Washington, Aug. 19, 1957; N. Y., Sept. 26, 1957; enormously successful; also produced as a motion picture); *Kaddish,* oratorio for narrator, chorus and orch. (Tel Aviv, Dec. 9, 1963); *Chichester Psalms* for chorus and orch. (commissioned by the Dean of Chichester, England, but first performed by the N. Y. Philharmonic, Leonard Bernstein conducting, July 14, 1965). For the opening, on Sept. 7, 1971, of the John F. Kennedy Center for the Performing Arts in Washington, he wrote a *Mass,* 'a theater piece' arranged for orch., chorus, a group of boy singers, dancers and dancer-singers, to a text partly consisting of the Roman Liturgy in Latin, partly in vernacular. — *Kid Songs* is the subtitle of the song cycle *I Hate Music,* and not a separate work. Bernstein publ. *The Joy of Music,* a collection of his television talks (N. Y., 1959; revised and amplified as *Young People's Concerts,* N. Y., 1970); *The Infinite Variety of Music* (N. Y., 1966). Bibl.: D. Ewen, *Leonard Bernstein: A Biography for Young People*

(N. Y., 1960); A. Holde, *Leonard Bernstein* (Berlin, 1961); J. Briggs, *Leonard Bernstein, The Man, His Work and His World* (Cleveland, 1961).

Berté, Heinrich. Born May 8, 1857 (not 1858).

Bertoni, Ferdinando (Gioseffo). Add to bibl.: I. Haas, *Ferdinando Bertoni: Leben und Instrumentalwerk* (Vienna, 1958).

Berutti, Arturo. Naturalized Argentine spelling, **Beruti.** Add his opera *Horrida Nox,* the first by a native to a Spanish libretto to be produced in Argentina (Buenos Aires, July 7, 1908). See E. M. Navarro, *San Juan en la Historia de la Música* (San Juan, Argentina, 1964).

Berwald, Franz. Date of death, April 3 (not 30), 1868. See R. Layton, *Berwald* (Stockholm, 1956; in English, London, 1959).

Besanzoni, Gabriella, Italian contralto; b. Rome, Sept. 20, 1890; d. there, July 8, 1962. She made her debut as a soprano in *Norma* in 1913; from 1915 appeared as mezzo-soprano and contralto in major opera houses all over the world, making her home principally in Rio de Janeiro, until her return to Italy and retirement in 1938. She was particularly famous in Italy as Carmen.

Besozzi, Alessandro. Carlo Besozzi died in Dresden, March 22, 1791.

Bessel, Vassili Vassilievitch. He was born on April 25, 1842 (not 1843); died March 1 (not March 4), 1907.

Besseler, Heinrich. Died in Leipzig, July 25, 1969. A Festschrift in his honor was published on his 60th birthday in 1960 by the Karl Marx Univ. in Leipzig, where he held professorship.

Bettinelli, Bruno. Add to works: operas *La Smorfia* (Como, Sept. 30, 1959); *Il Pozzo e il Pendolo* (after Poe; Bergamo, Oct. 24, 1967); *Count Down* (Milan, March 26, 1970); for orch.: *Preludio elegiaco* (1960); *Episodi* (1961); Concerto for two pianos and orch. (1962); piano concerto No. 2 (1968); *Varianti per orchestra* (1970); *Improvvisazione* for violin and piano (1968); *Improvvisazione* for guitar (1969).

Betts, Lorne M., Canadian composer; b. Winnipeg, Aug. 2, 1918. He studied composition with John Weinzweig in Toronto and also took summer courses in the U.S. with Ernst Krenek and Roy Harris. In 1952 he was appointed to the faculty of the Hamilton Cons. in Hamilton, Ontario. His works adhere to a neo-classical idiom. He wrote two one-act operas, *Riders to the Sea* (1955) and *The Woodcarver's Wife* (1961); *Sonata* for orch. (1949); Symph. No. 1 (1954); *Fantasia Canadiana* for orch. (1955); *Two Abstracts* for orch. (1961); Symph. No. 2 (1961) 2 piano concertos (1955; 1957); *Kanadario* for orch. (1966); *Variants* for orch. (1969); 2 string quartets; a string trio; quartet for flute, clarinet, bass clarinet and celesta; numerous songs and sacred choruses; piano pieces.

Beversdorf, Thomas. Add to works: *The Rock,* oratorio (1958); violin concerto (1959); Symph. No. 4 (1960); sonata for trumpet and piano (1962); *Variations* for orch. (1963); violin sonata (1963); flute sonata (1964); *Vision of Christ,* after a 14th-century sacred drama (Bucknell Univ., Lewisburg, Pa., May 1, 1971).

Beydts, Louis. Died at Caudéran, near Bordeaux (not in Bordeaux itself), Sept. 19 (not 16), 1953.

Beyschlag, Adolf. Date of death, Aug. 19 (not March 22), 1914.

Bezekirsky, Vassili. Died in East Windham, N. Y., Nov. 8, 1960.

Biaggi, Girolamo Alessandro. Born in Calcio, Bergamo (not Milan).

Bibalo, Antonio, Italian composer; b. in Trieste, Jan. 18, 1922, of Slovak descent (his family name was Bibalitsch). He studied piano at the Cons. of Trieste; during the disruption caused by the war he earned his living as a bar pianist and a sanitation worker. After the end of hostilities he took ship to Melbourne; in 1946 went to London, where he studied advanced composition with Elizabeth Lutyens. In 1952 he settled in Norway. He attracted the attention of the musical world with the production of his opera, after Henry Miller's story *The Smile at the Foot of the Ladder;* the original libretto was in Italian as *Sorrisi ai piedi d'una scala,* but it was produced in German under the name *Das Lächeln am Fusse der Leiter* at the Hamburg State Opera on April 6, 1965, with excellent success. Bibalo also wrote the ballet *Pinocchio* (1967); 2 symphonies; a piano concerto; a violin concerto and a number of piano pieces.

Bimboni, Alberto. Died in New York, June 18, 1960.

Binder, Abraham Wolfe. Died in New York, Oct. 10, 1966.

Binenbaum, Janco, Bulgarian-French composer; b. Adrianopol, Dec. 28, 1880; d. Chevreuse (Seine-et-Oise), France, Feb. 4, 1956. He studied in Munich with Rheinberger and others; was active as piano teacher in Germany and France, eventually settling in Chevreuse, where he remained until his death. He wrote a considerable amount of symphonic and chamber music in an impressionistic vein, colored with Balkan rhythms, none of which was published, and little ever performed. Nonetheless, Binenbaum found a number of sincere admirers of his works among music critics, among whom M. D. Calvocoressi was the most vocal.

Binet, Jean. Died in Trélex, Switzerland, Feb. 24, 1960.

Bing, Rudolph. First name Rudolf (not Rudolph). In 1971 he was given by Queen Elizabeth II the title of Knight Commander of the Order of the British Empire. In 1972 he resigned as general manager of the Metropolitan Opera.

Binkerd, Gordon, American composer and teacher; b. Lynch, Nebraska, May 22, 1916. He studied piano in South Dakota; composition with Bernard Rogers at the Eastman School of Music, Rochester, and with Walter Piston at Harvard Univ.; from 1949 to 1971, member of the faculty of the Univ. of Illinois; received a Guggenheim Fellowship in 1959. Works: Symph. No. 1 (Univ. of Illinois, Urbana, March 20, 1955); Symph. No. 2 (Univ. of Illinois, Urbana, April 13, 1957); Symph. No. 3 (N. Y., Jan. 6, 1961); Symph. No. 4 (St. Louis, Oct. 12, 1963; dismembered and reduced to a *Movement for Orchestra*); 2 string quartets; string trio; trio for clarinet, viola and cello; duo for flute and oboe; cello sonata; 3 songs for mezzo-soprano and string quartet; *Portrait Intérieur* for mezzo-soprano, violin and cello; piano sonata; *Entertainments* for piano; numerous sacred choruses; songs.

Biriotti, León, Uruguayan conductor and composer; b. Montevideo, Dec. 1, 1929. He studied oboe, theory and musicology; began to conduct experimentally without preliminary training; founded a string orchestra in Montevideo; conducted the instrumental group Juventudes Musicales of Uruguay. His works comprise 3 symphonies (1964, 1965, 1968); a *Suite* for violin and cello (1952); string sextet (1957); trio for oboe, clarinet and bassoon (1963); string quartet (1965); violin sonata (1967); songs and piano pieces.

Birkenstock, Johann Adam, German violinist and composer; b. Alsfeld, Feb. 19, 1687; d. Eisenach, Feb. 26, 1733. He studied with Fiorelli; was employed in the Kassel Court orch. (1709-30), and in 1730 went to Eisenach as kapellmeister. His sonatas for violin with basso continuo (Amsterdam, 1722) are included in various anthologies.

Birtwistle, Harrison, English composer; b. Accrington, Lancashire, July 15, 1934. He studied at the Royal Manchester College of Music, and later at the Royal Academy of Music in London. His compositions have been widely performed at European festivals of modern music. Works: *Refrains and Choruses* for wind quintet (1957); *Monody for Corpus Christi* for soprano solo, flute, violin and horn (1959); *The World is Discovered,* instrumental motet (1960; Festival of the International Society for Contemporary Music, Copenhagen, June 2, 1964); *Chorales* for orch. (1963); *Narration: The Description of the Passing of a Year* for a cappella choir (1964); *Précis* for piano solo; *Punch and Judy,* chamber opera (Edinburgh Festival, Aug. 22, 1968); *Nomos* for orch. (London, Aug. 23, 1968); *Medusa* for chamber orch. and percussion (London, Oct. 22, 1969; revised and produced in London on March 3, 1970); *Verses for Ensembles,* for 12 players forming interlocking groups of woodwinds, brass and percussion (London, Aug. 31, 1970).

Bismillah Khan, Indian virtuoso on the shehnai; b. Dumraon, March 21, 1916. He studied instrumental and vocal music; earned a great renown in India; appeared as soloist at the Commonwealth Arts Festival in London in 1965.

Bittner, Julius. Add bibl.: Ullrich Bittner, *Julius Bittner* (Vienna, 1969).

Bizet, Georges. His early symphony in C was discovered in the Bizet collection at the Paris Cons. in 1933, and was given its first performance anywhere by Felix Weingartner in Basel on Feb. 26, 1935; it rapidly became popular in concert repertory. Add to bibl.: Mina Curtiss, *Bizet and His World* (N. Y., 1958); W. Dean, *Georges Bizet: His Life and Work* (London, 1965).

Bjelinski, Bruno. Add to works *Simfonija Ljeta* (*Summer Symphony;* Zagreb, Oct. 15, 1956); *Serenade* for trumpet, piano, strings and percussion (1957); *Mediterranean Sin-*

fonietta (Zagreb, Dec. 9, 1959); operatic fairy-tale, *Pčelica Maja* (*Maya the Bee;* 1952); see K. Kovačević, *Hrvatski Kompozitori i Njihova Djela* (Zagreb, 1960).

Björling, Jussi. Died at Siarö, near Stockholm, Sept. 9, 1960. Date of birth, Feb. 2, 1911 (not 1907). The name of his second teacher was Tullio Voghiera (not Jullio Voghera).

Blacher, Boris. Add to works: *Rosamunde Floris,* opera (Berlin, Sept. 21, 1960); *Zwischenfälle bei einer Notlandung* (*Incidents at a Forced Landing*), a "reportage" for singers, instruments and electronic devices (Hamburg, Feb. 4, 1966); *200.000 Taler,* opera, after Scholom Aleichem (Berlin, Sept. 25, 1969). Cf. H. H. Stuckenschmidt, *Boris Blacher* (Berlin, 1964).

Black, Frank. Died in Atlanta, Georgia, Jan. 29, 1968.

Blackwood, Easley, American composer; b. Indianapolis, April 21, 1933. He studied piano in his home town; composition at the Berkshire Music Center (1948-50) and with Hindemith at Yale Univ. (1950); in 1954 received a Fulbright grant for study in France, and took courses with Nadia Boulanger in Paris; in 1958 was appointed to the faculty of the Univ. of Chicago. He attracted considerable attention with his brilliant 1st symphony (Boston, April 18, 1958) which received the first prize of the Koussevitzky Foundation. His 2nd symphony, commissioned by G. Schirmer, Inc., on the occasion of the firm's centenary in 1960, was first performed by the Cleveland Orch., George Szell conducting, on Jan. 5, 1961. His 3rd symphony was performed for the first time at a concert of American music presented at the Univ. of Chicago, March 7, 1965, by the Chicago Symph. Orch., Jean Martinon conducting. His other works comprise a viola sonata (1953); a chamber symphony (1955); string quartet No. 1 (1957); Concertino for 5 instruments (1959); string quartet No. 2 (1960); violin sonata (1960); clarinet concerto (1964); violin concerto (Bath, England, June 18, 1967); flute concerto (Dartmouth College, Hanover, N. H., July 28, 1968). His music is marked by impassioned romantic élan and is set in a highly evolved chromatic idiom. Blackwood is also an accomplished pianist, particularly notable for his performances of modern works of transcendental difficulty, such as the Concord Sonata of Ives and the 2nd piano sonata of Boulez.

Bláha-Mikeš, Záboj. Died in Prague, April 3, 1957.

Blanc, Giuseppe. Died in Santa Margherita Ligure, Dec. 7, 1969.

Bland, James A., American Negro song composer; b. Flushing, N.Y., Oct. 22, 1854; d. Philadelphia, May 5, 1911. He learned to play the banjo and joined a minstrel troupe, improvising songs in the manner of Negro spirituals. His most famous ballad, *Carry Me Back to Old Virginny,* was publ. in 1878; in 1940 it was designated the official song of the state of Virginia. From 1881 to 1901 Bland lived in England, enjoying excellent success as an entertainer, including a command performance for Queen Victoria, but he dissipated his savings and died in abject poverty.

Blažek, Zdeněk, Czech composer; b. Žarošice, May 24, 1905. He studied with Petrželka at the Brno Cons. and with Suk at the Prague Cons.; later became a teacher in Brno. Works: *Verchovina,* opera (1951; Brno, 1956); piano trio (1929); *Divertimento* for woodwind quartet (1946); string quintet (1949); 3 string quartets (1943, 1947, 1956).

Blazhkov, Igor, Ukrainian conductor and music scholar; b. Kiev, Sept. 23, 1936. He studied at the Kiev Cons., graduating in 1959; appeared as guest conductor in Moscow and Leningrad, specializing in modern music, including American works. From 1958 to 1962 he was assistant conductor of the Ukrainian State Orchestra in Kiev.

Blech, Leo. Died in Berlin, Aug. 24, 1958.

Bledsoe, Jules. Born on Dec. 29, 1898 (not 1902).

Bleichmann, Yuly Ivanovitch. Date of death, Jan. 8, 1910 (not Dec. 5, 1909).

Bleyle, Karl. Died in Stuttgart, June 5, 1969.

Bliss, Sir Arthur (Edward Drummond). Add to works: *The Lady of Shalott,* ballet (Berkeley, Cal., May 2, 1958). *Morning Heroes* was first performed on Oct. 22, (not Oct. 6), 1930. He wrote an autobiography, *As I Remember* (London, 1970).

Bliss, Philip Paul, American hymn writer; b. in a log cabin in the woods of Clearfield County, Pennsylvania, July 9, 1838; d. in a train wreck near Ashtabula, Ohio, Dec. 29, 1876. He was an itinerant minstrel, traveling with a mechanical melodeon and an old horse.

In 1864 he settled in Chicago, taught singing, and did some preaching. He publ. *Gospel Songs* (1874); *Gospel Hymns* (1875), all highly successful. Cf. R. G. McCutchan, *Our Hymnody* (N. Y., 1937).

Blitzstein, Marc. Died in Fort-de-France, Martinique, Jan. 22, 1964, from a brain injury sustained after a political altercation with a group of men in a bar. His opera on the subject of Sacco and Vanzetti, commissioned by the Ford Foundation for production by the Metropolitan Opera, remained unfinished.

Bloch, André. Died in Paris, Aug. 7, 1960. *Broceliande* (not *Brocellande*) is a "prélude féerique" in one act, not an opera; *Les maisons de l'éternité* was composed in 1930 (not 1945). Add *Suite palestinienne* for cello and orch. (his most successful instrumental work; Paris, Nov. 14, 1948).

Bloch, Ernest. Died in Portland, Oregon, July 15, 1959. Add to works: string quartet No. 5 (1956); 2nd piano quintet (1957); 2 suites for solo violin (1958); 3 suites for solo cello (1958); *Suite Modale* for flute solo and strings (1957). The world première of *Hiver-Printemps* took place in Geneva on Jan. 27, 1906.

Blom, Eric. Died in London, April 11, 1959. Add to books: *Classics, Major and Minor with Some Other Musical Ruminations* (London, 1958).

Blomdahl, Karl-Birger. Died in Kungsängen, June 14, 1968. (His ashes were strewn over the nearby Lake Mälaren.) Add to works: 2 choreographic suites for orch., *Sisyphos* (Stockholm, Oct. 20, 1954) and *Minotauros* (Stockholm, April 5, 1958); *I Speglarnas sal* (*In the Glass of Mirrors*), for soli, chorus and orch. (Stockholm, May 29, 1954); *Anabase* for baritone, narrator, chorus and orch. (Stockholm, Dec. 14, 1956); *Aniara,* futuristic opera to a story of interplanetary voyage (Stockholm, May 31, 1959); *Fioriture* for orch. (Cologne, June 17, 1960); *Der Herr von Hancken,* comic opera (Stockholm, Sept. 2, 1965); *Altisonans* for electronic instruments (Stockholm, Sept. 24, 1966).

Blum, Robert. Add to works: Symph. No. 5 for wind instruments and male chorus (1961); Symph. No. 6 (Zürich, Sept. 23, 1969).

Blume, Friedrich. Add bibl.: A. A. Abert and W. Pfannkuch, *Festschrift Friedrich Blume zum 70. Geburtstag* (Kassel, 1963).

Blumenfeld, Felix Michailovitch. Place of birth Kovalevka (not Kovalevska). Taught piano at the St. Petersburg Cons. from 1885 until 1918; at the Kiev Cons. from 1918 'til 1922; at the Moscow Cons. from 1922 (not from 1918) until his death.

Blumer, Theodor. Died in Berlin, Sept. 21, 1964. Date of birth, March 24, 1881 (not 1882).

Boatwright, McHenry, American Negro baritone; b. Tenile, Georgia, Feb. 29, 1928. He studied at the New England Cons. in Boston; made his concert debut in 1956; sang in London in 1962; was soloist with the N. Y. Philharmonic, Philadelphia Orch. and other orchestras in the U. S. He created the central role in Gunther Schuller's opera *The Visitation* (Hamburg, Oct. 12, 1968).

Boccherini, Luigi. He was invited to Madrid in 1769 (not 1796). Add to bibl.: *Thematic, Bibliographical and Critical Catalogue of the Works of Luigi Boccherini,* compiled by Yves Gérard (London, 1969).

Bockelmann, Rudolph. Died in Dresden, Oct 9. 1958. Correct first name Rudolf.

Boda, John, American composer; b. Boyceswille, Wisconsin, Aug. 2, 1922. He studied at the Eastman School of Music in Rochester, N. Y.; in 1946 joined the faculty of Florida State Univ. at Tallahassee. His *Sinfonia* was first performed in Knoxville, Tenn., on Dec. 6, 1960.

Bode, Rudolf, German acoustician and theorist of rhythmic gymnastics; b. Kiel, Feb. 3, 1881; d. Munich, Oct. 7, 1970. He studied physiology and philosophy at the Univ. of Leipzig, and music theory at the Leipzig Cons. After attending the Dalcroze Institute of Eurhythmics in Hellerau, he formulated a system of 'rhythmic gymnastics' and in 1911 founded a school in Munich with courses embodying Bode's body theories intended to achieve perfect physical and mental health. He publ. a number of books and essays on the subject: *Der Rhythmus und seine Bedeutung für die Erziehung* (Jena, 1920); *Ausdruckgymnastik* (Munich, 1922; in English as *Expressions-Gymnastic,* N. Y., 1931); *Musik und Bewegung* (Kassel, 1930); *Energie und Rhythmus* (Berlin, 1939). He also wrote a manual of piano study as a rhythmic muscular action, *Rhythmus und Anschlag* (Munich, 1933).

Bodin, Lars-Gunnar, Swedish composer; b. Stockholm, July 15, 1935. He studied composition with Lennart Wenström; became interested primarily in electronic music. His works include *My World is Your World* for organ and magnetic tape (1966); *Cybo I* and *Cybo II* for tape (1967); *From Any Point to Any Other Point* for tape (1968); and a television ballet, *Events-Happenings* (1971).

Bodky, Erwin. Died in Lucerne, Switzerland, Dec. 6, 1958. Add to publications: *The Interpretation of Bach's Keyboard Works* (Cambridge, Mass., 1960).

Boepple, Paul. Died in Brattleboro, Vermont, Dec. 21, 1970.

Boero, Felipe. Died in Buenos Aires, Aug. 9, 1958.

Boethius, Anicius Manlius Torquatus Severinus. Did not invent the Latin musical notation, but merely used Latin letters as indexes for traditional Greek notation. Cf. H. Potizon, *Boèce, théoricien de la musique grecque* (Paris, 1961).

Boetticher, Wolfgang, German musicologist; b. Bad Ems, Aug. 19, 1914. He studied at Berlin Univ. (1933-39); in 1948 joined the staff of Göttingen Univ. His publications include *Robert Schumann, Einführung in Persönlichkeit und Werk* (Berlin, 1941); *Orlando di Lasso und seine Zeit* (2 vols.; Kassel, 1958).

Bogdanov-Berezovsky, Valerian, Russian composer and musicologist; b. St. Petersburg, July 17, 1903; d. Moscow in June, 1971. He began his career as musical director for theatrical presentations; composed several ballets; 2 symphonies; a piano concerto; a violin concerto; chamber music and songs. He is the author of a number of valuable monographs on Russian composers and performers.

Bohnen, Michael. Died in Berlin, April 26, 1965. Born in Cologne (not Keulen), May 2, 1887 (not Jan. 23, 1886). Studied at the Cons. of Cologne (not Keulen).

Bois, Rob du, Dutch composer; b. Amsterdam, May 28, 1934. He studied law; as a composer he is mainly autodidact. His principal influences are Schoenberg and Berg; he also follows the ultra-modern techniques of the cosmopolitan avant-garde. Works: Septet for strings, woodwinds and piano (1960); piano concerto (1961); *Bewegungen* for piccolo and piano (1961); trio for flute, oboe and clarinet (1961); *Rondeaux* for piano and percussion (1962), *Spiel und Zwischenspiel* for recorder and piano (1962); *Chants et contrepoints* for wind quintet (1962); *Cercle* for piano, 9 wind instruments and percussion (1963); *Pastorale* for guitar (1963); *Une façon de dire que les hommes de cent vingt ans ne chantent plus* for soprano, piano and 4 percussion instruments (1963); quartet for oboe, violin, viola and cello (1964); *Rondeaux* for piano 4 hands and percussion (1964).

Boismortier, Joseph Bodin de, French composer; b. Perpignan, 1691; d. Paris, 1755. He wrote three operas: *Les voyages de l'Amour* (1736), *Don Quichotte* (1743) and *Daphnis et Chloé* (1747); several oratorios; chamber music; also suites of pieces for the musette: *Gentillesses* (1731; reprinted, Paris, 1920); *Divertissements de campagne* (1734); *Les loisirs du bercail* (1734).

Boisselot, Xavier, French composer and piano manufacturer; b. Montpellier, Dec. 3, 1811; d. Marseille, March 28, 1893. He studied with Fétis and Lesueur in Paris; received the Grand Prix de Rome in 1836; then went to Marseille where he joined the piano manufacturing company founded by his father.

Bok, Mary Louise Curtis, American patroness of music; b. Boston, Aug. 6, 1876; d. Philadelphia, Jan. 4, 1970. She inherited her fortune from Cyrus H. K. Curtis, founder of the Curtis Publishing Co. In 1924 she established in Philadelphia the Curtis Institute of Music and endowed it initially with a gift of $12.5 million in memory of her mother; the school had a faculty of the most distinguished American and European musicians, and it provided tuition exclusively on a scholarship basis; many talented composers and performers were its students. She was first married to Edward W. Bok in 1896; upon his death in 1930 she married Efrem Zimbalist, director of the Curtis Institute from 1941 to 1969. She purchased in England the famous Burrell Collection of Wagneriana and brought it to the U.S. Her honorary degrees include Hon. Dr. of Humane Letters, Univ. of Pennsylvania (1932), Hon. Mus. Doc., Williams College (1934), Order of Polonia Restituta (1932).

Bolcom, William, American composer; b. Seattle, May 26, 1938. He studied at the Univ. of Washington, at Mills College, at Stanford Univ. and at the Paris Cons. Works: *Dynamite Tonight,* 'opera for actors' (N.Y. Actors' Studio, Dec. 21, 1963); *Concerto-Serenade* for violin and strings (1964); *Oracles* for orch. (Seattle, May 2, 1965); *Ses-*

sion for 7 players (Berlin, May 12, 1965); *Fantasy-Sonata* for piano; 12 piano etudes; 8 string quartets.

Bombardelli, Silvije, Croatian conductor and composer; b. Split, March 3, 1916. He studied violin in Belgrade; returning to Split in 1945 he organized an orchestra, and also conducted opera. In his music he applies modernistic procedures, including modified serial techniques. Works: ballet *Stranac* (*The Stranger;* Split, Jan. 25, 1956); *Plameni Vjetar* (*The Flaming Wind*) for orch. and speaking chorus (Split, June 18, 1940); a symphony (Zagreb, Nov. 3, 1951); cantatas and choruses. See K. Kovačević, *Hrvatski Kompozitori i Njihova Djela* (Zagreb, 1960).

Bonaventura, Mario di, American conductor; b. Follensbee, W. Va., Feb. 20, 1924. He studied violin in New York; won an award of the N. Y. Philharmonic in Young Composers' Composition in 1941; served in the U.S. Army during World War II. In 1947 he went to Paris where he took courses in composition with Nadia Boulanger and conducting with Igor Markevitch. He was staff pianist of the Pasdeloup Orch. in Paris (1954-56); returning to the U.S. in 1957 he enrolled in the classes in modern music with Luigi Dallapiccola at Queens College. He was conductor of the Fort Lauderdale Symphony Orch. (1959-62); in 1962 he was appointed director of music at Hopkins Center at Dartmouth College in Hanover, N. H. In 1963 he inaugurated an ambitious series of summer festivals at Dartmouth College under the title 'Congregation of the Arts,' for which he commissioned works from noted American and European composers. During the first seven summer festivals the Congregation of the Arts presented 389 contemporary works, of which 147 were by American composers, with 38 world premières. Among composers in residence were Zoltán Kodály, Frank Martin, Boris Blacher, Hans Werner Henze, Ernst Krenek, Witold Lutoslawski, Luigi Dallapiccola, Roberto Gerhard, Walter Piston, Roger Sessions, Niels Viggo Bentzon, Carlos Chávez, Easley Blackwood, Elliott Carter, Aaron Copland, Henry Cowell, Ross Lee Finney, Alberto Ginastera, Peter Mennin and Vincent Persichetti.

Bond, Carrie Jacobs. *A Perfect Day* was not her first song; it was preceded by *Is My Dolly Dead?* She did not establish her own press, but was the proprietor of a music selling agency, and used the imprint Carrie Jacobs Bond & Son for her publications. She died in Glendale, California (not in Hollywood).

Bondon, Jacques, French composer; b. Boulbon (Bouches-du-Rhône), Dec. 6, 1927. He studied violin and painting in Marseille. In 1945 he went to Paris, where he took courses in composition with Kœchlin, Milhaud and Jean Rivier. After early experimentation with ultra-modern techniques he tergiversated to prudential modernism. He became associated with Martenot, and wrote a concerto for Ondes Martenot and orchestra (1955); also composed music for films and for the radio. Works: for orchestra: *La Coupole* (1954); *Le Taillis ensorcelé* (1954); *Suite indienne* (1958); *Musique pour un autre monde* (1962); *Concert de printemps* for trumpet, strings and percussion (1957); *Mélousine au rocher,* radio opera (Luxembourg, Oct. 30, 1969); *Le Soleil multicolore* for flute, harp and viola (1970); *Giocoso* for violin solo and string orch. (1970); *Lumières et formes animées* for string orch. (Paris, Oct. 6, 1970); opera *Ana et l'Albatros* (Metz, Nov. 21, 1970). See Jean Roy, *Musique française* (Paris, 1962; pp. 471-483).

Bonelli, Richard. Date of birth, Feb. 6, 1887 (not 1894). In 1970 he was living in Los Angeles.

Bononcini, Giovanni Maria. Add bibl.: W. Klenz, *G. M. Bononcini of Modena; a Chapter in Baroque Instrumental Music* (Durham, N. C., 1962).

Boone, Charles, American composer of the avant-garde; b. Cleveland, June 21, 1939. He studied with Karl Schiske at the Vienna Academy of Music (1960-61); took private lessons with Ernst Krenek and Adolph Weiss in Los Angeles (1961-63); attended Univ. of Southern Calif. (B.M., 1963) and San Francisco State College (M.A., 1968); served as chairman of the San Francisco Composers' Forum and coordinator of Mills College Performing Group and Tape Music Center. In his music he strives to create a sonic environment on purely structural lines, employing serial matrices, coloristic contrasts and spatial parameters of performing instruments, with resulting styles ranging from lyrical pointillism to static sonorism. He also avails himself of electronic resources. Works: *Icarus* for flute solo (1964); *Song of Suchness* for soprano, flute, piccolo, viola, piano and celesta (1964); *Parallels* for violin and piano (1964); *Oblique Formation* for flute and piano (1965); *Starfish* for a small ensemble (1966); *The Yellow Bird* for orch. (1967); *Constant Comment* for stereophonic tape (1967); *Shadow* for oboe solo, tape and orch. (1968); *The Edge of the Land* for orch. (1968); *Not Now* for clarinet solo (1969); *Quartet* for violin, clarinet, cello and piano (1970); *Zephyrus* for oboe and piano (1970); *Chinese Texts* for soprano and orch. (1970).

Boott, Francis. His bequest of $10,000 to Harvard Univ., made in April 1904, was increased through capital gains to $15,246 in 1960.

Borchard, Adolphe. Died in Paris, Dec. 13, 1967.

Borel-Clerc, Charles. Died in Cannes, April 9, 1959.

Borgioli, Dino. Died in Florence, Sept. 12, 1960.

Bori, Lucrezia. Died in New York, May 14, 1960.

Borodin, Alexander Porfirievitch. Date of birth, according to new style calendar, Nov. 12 (not Nov. 11), 1833. *Mazurka* was not a posthumous work; it was included in the series of paraphrases on *Chopsticks Waltz*, publ. in 1880. An English translation of S. Dianin's biography was publ. in 1963.

Borovsky, Alexander. Died in Waban, Mass., April 27, 1968.

Borresen, Hakon. Died in Copenhagen, Oct. 6, 1954.

Bortniansky, Dimitri Stepanovitch. Date of death, Oct. 10 (not Oct. 7), 1825.

Bortolotto, Mario, Italian physician and writer of music; b. Pordenone, Aug. 30, 1927. He published *Introduzione al lied romantico* (Milan, 1962) and *Fase seconda* (Milan, 1969) which aroused controversy; for polemical exchange that followed its publication see 'Nuova Rivista Musicale Italiana' (Sept.-Oct., 1969).

Boscovich, Alexander Uriah. Died in Tel-Aviv, Nov. 13, 1964.

Bosquet, Émile. Died in Uccle (Brussels), July 18, 1958.

Bosseur, Jean-Yves, French composer; b. Paris, Feb. 5, 1947. He studied privately with Stockhausen and Pousseur. His music is marked by experimentalization without specific serial procedures. Among his works there is a symph. suite, *Un arraché de partout* for brass, Hammond organ, 2 electric guitars, vibraphone, xylorimba, marimbaphone and percussion (Paris, March 22, 1968).

Bossi, Costante Adolfo, Italian composer; brother of Marco Enrico Bossi; b. Morbegno, Dec. 25, 1876; d. Milan, Jan. 4, 1953. He studied at the Milan Cons.; subsequently was prof. there (1914-41). He wrote an opera *La Mammola e l'eroe* (Milan, 1916); a Requiem (1920); numerous choruses and songs.

Bossi, Renzo. Died in Milan, April 2, 1965. The title of his third opera is *La Rosa rossa* (not *Rossa rossa*); it was first performed in Parma, Jan. 9, 1940.

Bostelmann, Otto, German-American composer; b. Hamburg, Aug. 22, 1907; settled in the U. S. in 1926. He studied with Wesley La Violette in Los Angeles; in 1957 organized the Bohemian Composers Group in Los Angeles. His works comprise 3 symphonies, 3 'crescendi' for orch.; much chamber music.

Boucourechliev, André, Bulgarian-French music critic; b. Sofia, July 28, 1925. He studied in Paris and settled there; in 1964 traveled in the U. S. He publ. a biography of Schumann (Paris, 1957; N. Y., 1959); and a pictorial biography of Chopin (N. Y., 1962); became a music critic; also composed music in an advanced idiom. For Beethoven's bicentennial he wrote *Ombres, Hommage à Beethoven* for string orch. (Toulouse, June 8, 1970).

Boughtón, Rutland. Died in London, Jan. 25, 1960.

Boulez, Pierre. He was visiting lecturer at Harvard Univ. in the spring of 1963; was guest conductor of the Cleveland Orch. on March 11, 1965. In 1969 his appointment as musical director was announced by the N. Y. Philharmonic, effective in Sept. 1971. Add to works: *Le Marteau sans Maître,* cantata for contralto, flute, viola, guitar, vibraphone and percussion (International Festival of the Society for Contemporary Music, Baden-Baden, June 18, 1955); *Poésie pour pouvoir,* spatial work for 2 orchestras conducted by 2 synchronized conductors (Donaueschingen Festival, Oct. 19, 1958, under the direction of Boulez and Hans Rosbaud); *Pli selon pli* for voice and orch. (Cologne, June 13, 1960); *Figures, Doubles, Prismes* for orch. (Brussels, Dec. 13, 1964, composer conducting); *Structures* for 2 pianos (book I, 1952; book II, 1961); piano sonata No. 3 (1957); *Éclats* for chamber orch. (Los Angeles, March 26, 1965, composer conducting); *Domaines* for solo clarinet and 21 instruments (1968). Add to writings: *Penser la musique aujourd'hui* (Paris, 1963; publ. in English as *Boulez on Music Today,* Cambridge Mass., 1970); *Relevés d'apprenti* (Paris, 1967; English translation as *Notes of an Apprenticeship,* N. Y., 1968). Bibl.: A. Goléa, *Rencontres avec Pierre Boulez* (Paris, 1958).

Boult, Sir Adrian Cedric. Publ.: *A Handbook on the Technique of Conducting* (London, 1968).

Bourguignon, Francis de. Died in Brussels, April 11, 1961.

Boutry, Roger, French pianist, conductor and composer; b. Paris, Feb. 27, 1932. He studied at the Paris Cons.; received first prize as pianist at the age of 16; first prize as conductor at 21; and the Premier Prix de Rome at 22. In 1963 he was awarded the Grand Prix Musical of the City of Paris. He embarked on a successful career as pianist; toured in Europe, Russia and Australia; as a conductor, he appeared with several orchestras in France; also conducted opera in Monte Carlo. Works: piano concerto (1954); *Rapsodie* for piano and orch. (1956); *Ouverture-Tableau* for orch. (1959); *Divertimento* for saxophone and orch. (1964); *Concerto-Fantaisie* for 2 pianos and orch. (Paris, Feb. 16, 1967); *Intermezzi* for chamber orch. (1970); a quartet for trombones; flute concerto; 2 sextets; *Pastels et Contours* for 5 harps; also didactic pieces for various instruments.

Bowen, Edwin York. Died in Hampstead, England, Nov. 23, 1961.

Boyd, Charles N. He was director of the Pittsburgh Musical (not Music) Institute from 1915 (not from 1925) to 1937.

Boykan, Martin, American pianist and composer; b. New York, April 12, 1931. He studied composition with Walter Piston at Harvard Univ., and also with Copland and Hindemith. As a pianist, he developed a remarkable technique entirely adequate for the most demanding contemporary compositions. As a composer he writes mostly chamber music. His works include 2 string quartets (1949, 1967); a flute sonata (1950); *Duo* for violin and piano (1951); a quintet for flute, piano and strings (1953); a *Chamber Concerto* (1970). In 1957 he was appointed to the faculty of Brandeis Univ.

Braein, Edvard, Norwegian composer; b. Kristiansund, Aug. 23, 1924. He studied at Oslo Cons. with Bjarne Brustad; played organ; then was conductor in Bergen; took private lessons with Jean Rivier in Paris (1950-51). Works: *Serenade* for clarinet, violin, viola and cello (1947); *Concert Overture* (1948); Symph. No. 1 (1950); *Serenade* for orch. (1952); Symph. No. 2 (1954); *Capriccio* for piano and orch. (1958); *Divertimento* for flute and chamber orch. (1959); *Divertimento* for clarinet, violin, viola and cello (1962); *Little Overture* (1962); string trio (1964); Symph. No. 3 (1967).

Braga, Francisco. Add to bibl.: *Exposição Comemorativa do Centenario do Nascimento de Francisco Braga* (Rio de Janeiro, 1968).

Braga, Gaetano. The English title of *Leggenda valacca* is *Angel's* (not *Angels'*) *Serenade;* the original version was for voice with cello (or violin) obbligato, not a cello solo.

Brahms, Johannes. Add bibl.: Hans Gál, *Johannes Brahms: Werk und Persönlichkeit* (Frankfurt, 1961; in English, N. Y., 1963).

Brailoiu, Constantin, Rumanian ethnomusicographer; b. Bucharest, Aug. 26, 1893; d. Geneva, Dec. 20, 1958. He studied in Austria and Switzerland; in 1928 founded the Archive of Folklore in Bucharest; also was a member of ethnomusical organizations in Geneva and Paris. Publications: *Esquisse d'une méthode de folklore musical* (Paris, 1930); *La musique populaire roumaine* (Paris, 1940); *Le folklore musical* (Zürich, 1948); *Le rythme aksak* (Paris, 1952); *La rythmique enfantine* (Brussels, 1956).

Brain, Dennis. Died in an automobile accident at Hatfield, Hertfordshire, Sept. 1, 1957.

Braithwaite, Warwick. Died in London, Jan. 18, 1971.

Brandukov, Anatol Andreyevitch. Born Dec. 22, 1856 (not Jan. 6, 1859).

Brant, Henry Dreyfus. Add to works: *'5 and 10¢ Store'* for violin, piano and kitchen ware (1932); *Origins,* percussion symphony (1952); *The Grand Universal Circus,* spatial theater piece (1956); *Mythical Beasts* for orch. (1958); *Conversations in an Unknown Tongue* for strings (1958); *Dialogue of the Jungle* for voices, whistles, sirens and percussion (1959); *Atlantis,* antiphonal symphony with chorus and narrator (1960); *The Fire Garden* for voices and instruments (1960); *Bird with Passenger* for viola d'amore with music boxes (1960); *Fire in Cities* for chorus, wind instruments and percussion (1961); *Violin Concerto with Lights,* for violin and 5 electric switches (1961); *Voyage Four,* 'spatial concert piece' (New Haven, Jan. 14, 1964); *Consort for True Violins,* scored for a consortium of assorted varisized violins (1968).

Branzell, Karin Maria. She taught in the Juilliard Summer School from 1946-1950; later was on the faculty at Adelphi College and at the Manhattan School of Music. In 1969 she moved to Altadena, California.

Brauel, Henning, German composer; b. Hannover, July 1, 1940. He studied piano and composition in Hannover, Salzburg and Stuttgart. His style is marked by structural cohesion within a framework of freely dissonant counterpoint. His *Sinfonische Paraphrasen on a Theme by Paganini* received a Stuttgart Municipal Prize (1968).

Braun, Karl. Died in Hamburg, April 19, 1960.

Breazul, George, Rumanian musicologist; b. Oltenien, Sept. 14, 1887; d. Bucharest, Aug. 3, 1961. He studied at the Bucharest Cons. with Castaldi and Kiriac, and in Berlin with Hornbostel, Sachs, Stumpf, Schünemann and Johannes Wolf. Upon return to Bucharest he organized a phonograph archive; publ. numerous articles dealing with Rumanian folklore; contributed to 'Die Musik in Geschichte und Gegenwart' and other reference works. A festschrift, in Rumanian, was publ. in his honor in 1966.

Brediceano, Tiberiu. Died in Bucharest, Dec. 19, 1968. He publ. valuable collections of Rumanian songs and dances, including 170 Rumanian folk melodies, 810 tunes of the Banat regions and 1000 songs of Transylvania.

Brehm, Alvin, American composer; b. New York, Feb. 8, 1925. He studied at the Juilliard School of Music and Columbia Univ.; played double-bass with various instrumental ensembles. Among his works are a *Divertimento* for brass trio, a set of variations for unaccompanied cello, and *Hephaestus,* an "extended overture" (1966).

Brehme, Hans. Died in Stuttgart, Nov. 10, 1957.

Breil, Joseph Carl. *The Legend* was first produced by the Metropolitan Opera in New York on March 12 (not April 4), 1919. He was not the first composer to write a motion picture score; Saint-Saëns wrote one in 1908; Walter Cleveland Simon wrote another in 1911.

Brenta, Gaston. Died in Brussels, May 30, 1969.

Bresnick, Martin, American composer; b. New York, Nov. 13, 1946. He studied with Arnold Franchetti at the Hartt College of Music in Hartford, Conn. and with Leland Smith and John Chowning at Stanford Univ.; received a Fulbright Fellowship for study in Vienna (1969-70); there he took courses in composition with Gottfried von Einem and Friedrich Cerha. Works: Trio for 2 trumpets and percussion (1966); string quartet (1968); *PCOMP,* a computer composition (Vienna, April 8, 1970); *Ocean of Storms* for orch. (1970); also music for films, including a computer score for the film *Pour* (Prague, March 5, 1970).

Bret, Gustave, French organist and composer; b. Brignoles, Aug. 30, 1875; d. Fréjus, April 16, 1969. He studied with Widor and d'Indy in Paris; wrote music criticism. He composed mostly church music.

Bretón y Hernández, Tomás. *Los Amantes de Teruel* was produced on Feb. 12, 1889 (not in 1899); *La Verbena de la Paloma,* properly a zarzuela rather than an opera, was produced Feb. 17, 1894 (not in 1897); *La Dolores* (not *Dolores*), also a zarzuela, was produced on March 16, 1895. The exact date of the first performance of *Tabaré,* Madrid, March 26, 1913.

Brian, Havergal. He wrote 32 symphonies, the last seven after the age of 90. He studied violin, cello and organ as a child with local teachers; left school at 12 to earn his living (his father's occupation was a potter's turner). At the same time he studied books on music theory; was self-taught as a composer; also learned French and German without an instructor. In 1904 he engaged in musical journalism; continued in this line until 1949. His list of works is as follows: Operas: *The Tigers,* to his own libretto (1916-18); *Turandot,* after Schiller, to a German libretto (1951); *The Cenci,* after Shelley (1953); *Doktor Faust,* to a German libretto, after Goethe (1956); *Agamemnon,* after Aeschylus, to a libretto in English (1957). Symphonies: No. 1, *The Gothic,* for vocal soloists, chorus, 4 mixed choirs, children's choir, 4 brass bands, and very large orch. (1919-22; first performed in London, June 24, 1961, with a semi-amateur group; first professional performance, London, Oct. 30, 1966); No. 2 (1931); No. 3 (1932); No. 4, *Das Siegeslied,* a setting of Psalm 68 in the Lutheran version, for soprano, double chorus and orch., with a German text (1933; London, July 3, 1967); No. 5, *Wine of Summer,* for baritone solo and orch. (1937; London, Dec. 11, 1969); No. 6, *Sinfonia Tragica* (1948; London, Sept. 21, 1966); No. 7 (1948; London, March 13, 1968); No. 8 (1949; London, Feb. 1, 1954); No. 9 (1951; London, March 22, 1958); No. 10 (1954; London, Nov. 3, 1958); No. 11 (1954; London, Nov. 5, 1959); No. 12 (1957; London, Nov. 5, 1959); No. 13 (1959); No. 14 (1960; London, May 10, 1970); No. 15 (1960); No. 16 (1960); No. 17 (1961); No. 18 (1961; London, Feb. 26, 1962); No. 19 (1961); No. 20 (1962); No. 21 (1963; London, May 10, 1970); No. 22, *Symphonia Brevis* (1965); No. 23 (1965); No. 24 (1965); No. 25 (1966); No. 26 (1966); No. 27 (1966); No. 28 (1967); No. 29 (1967); No. 30 (1967); No. 31 (1968); No. 32 (1968; London, Jan. 28, 1971). Concertos: violin concerto (1935; London, June 20, 1969); cello concerto (1964). Orchestral works: 4 English Suites (1899-1921); *For Valour,* concert overture (1902); *The Tinker's Wedding,* comedy overture (1948); *The Jolly Miller,* comedy overture (1952); *Concerto for Orchestra* (1964); *Legend: Ave atque Vale* (1968). Vocal works: *The Vision of Cleopatra,* for soli, chorus and orch. (1908); 21 songs for voice and piano; 40 part-songs; 7 unison songs for children. Bibl.: R. Nettel, *Ordeal by Music: The Strange Experience of Havergal Brian* (London, 1945); R. L. E. Foreman. ed., *Havergal Brian, A Collection of Essays* (London, 1969).

Brico, Antonia. In 1946 she settled in Denver as teacher and conductor; led the Denver Community Symph. Orch.

Bridgetower, George Auguste Polgreen, mulatto violinist; b. Biala, Poland, Feb. 29, 1780; d. London, Feb. 29, 1860 (on his 80th birthday). His father was an Abyssinian; his mother of Polish extraction. He studied with Giornovichi, and as a youth was in the retinue of the Prince of Wales in Brighton. He played in the violin section of the Haydn-Salomon London Concerts in 1791. His name is historically important because of his association with Beethoven; he gave the first performance, from manuscript, of the *Kreutzer Sonata,* with Beethoven himself at the piano, in Vienna on May 17, 1803. Beethoven spelled his name Brischdower. Bibl.: Betty Matthews, *George Polgreen Bridgetower,* in 'Music Review' (London, Feb. 1968).

Briegel, Wolfgang Carl, German organist and composer; b. Nuremberg, 1629; d. Darmstadt, Nov. 19, 1712. He was a court cantor in Gotha in 1650; court kapellmeister in Darmstadt (1671-1709). He wrote a great number of sacred works; also some vocal music for the stage. Cf. K. F. Hirschmann, *W. C. Briegel,* (Giessen, 1936); Elisabeth Noack, *W. C. Briegel: ein Barock-Komponist in seiner Zeit* (Berlin, 1963).

Britain, Radie. Add to works: *Radiation* for orch. (1955); *Cowboy Rhapsody* for orch. (1956); *Minha Terra* for orch. (1958); *Cosmic Mist Symph.* (1962); *Chipmunks* for woodwind, harp and percussion (1964); *Happyland,* operetta (1946); *Carillon,* opera (1952); *The Spider and the Butterfly,* operetta for children (1953); *Kuthara,* chamber opera (1960); numerous choral works and character pieces for piano; songs. Several of her works received prizes of the National Federation of Music Clubs, Texas Federation of Music Clubs, National League of American Penwomen and other organizations. After the lunar landing in 1969 she wrote a set of songs *Translunar Cycle,* and dedicated it to the National Aeronautics and Space Administration.

Britt, Horace. Died in Austin, Texas, Feb. 3, 1971.

Britten, Benjamin. Add to works: *Noye's Fludde,* one-act opera, after a medieval English miracle play (Aldeburgh, England, June 18, 1958); *Nocturne,* suite of songs with orch. to English poems (Leeds, England, Oct. 16, 1958); *Missa Brevis* for boys' voices and organ (London, July 22, 1959); *A Midsummer Night's Dream,* opera (Aldeburgh, June 11, 1960); *Cantata Academica* (Basel, July 1, 1960); *War Requiem* to the texts of the Latin Requiem Mass and 9 poems of the British poet Wilfred Owen, for chorus, soloists and orch. (one of Britten's finest creations; first performed at the rebuilt Coventry Cathedral on May 30, 1962, obtaining instant recognition; first American performance, by the Boston Symph. Orch. in Tanglewood, July 27, 1963); *Cantata Misericordium* (for the centenary of the International Red Cross; Geneva, Sept. 1, 1963); *Cello Symphony,* for cello and orch. (written for the Soviet cellist Rostropovitch, and first performed by him, with Britten conducting, in Moscow, March 12, 1964); four 'parables' for church performance: *Curlew River* (Aldeburgh, Eng., June 13, 1964); *The Burning Fiery Furnace* (Aldeburgh, June 9, 1966); *The Prodigal Son* (Aldeburgh, June 10, 1968); *Children's*

Crusade (St. Paul's Cathedral, London, May 19, 1969); *Suite* for harp (Aldeburgh, June 24, 1969); television opera *Owen Wingrave,* after Henry James (May 16, 1971; simultaneous production by the B.B.C. and its affiliated stations and the N.E.T. Opera Theater in New York). Add to bibl.: *Tribute to Benjamin Britten on his 50th Birthday* (a collection of articles; London, 1963); *Benjamin Britten: A Complete Catalogue of His Works* (N. Y., 1963); E. W. White, *Benjamin Britten: His Life and Operas* (new edition, London, 1970).

Brkanović, Ivan. Add to works: opera, *Zlato Zadra (The Gold of Zadar;* Zagreb, April 15, 1954); *Sarajevska Suita* for orch. (Zagreb, Jan. 20, 1958). See K. Kovačević, *Hrvatski Kompozitori i Njihova Djela* (Zagreb, 1960).

Brod, Max. Died in Tel Aviv, Dec. 20, 1968.

Broder, Nathan. Died in New York, Dec. 16, 1967. Add to publications: *The Collector's Bach* (Philadelphia, 1958: contains discography and biographical information); introductory essays to *The Great Operas of Mozart* (N. Y., 1962). Was president of the American Musicological Society (1962-64); adjunct prof. of music, Columbia Univ. (1959-62); received a Ford Foundation Grant for research in 1961; Executive Director, American section, International Inventory of Musical Sources (1961-65); since 1963, music editor, W. W. Norton & Co.; co-editor (with Paul Henry Lang) of *Contemporary Music in Europe, a Comprehensive Survey* (N. Y., 1965; a reprint of the semi-centennial issue of 'The Mus. Quarterly').

Brodsky, Adolf. Gave first performance of Tchaikovsky's Violin Concerto in Vienna on Dec. 4, 1881 (not 1882). After he settled in England he always spelled his first name Adolph.

Broekman, David. Died in New York, April 1, 1958.

Brogue, Roslyn, American composer; b. Chicago, Feb. 16, 1919. She studied languages at the Univ. of Chicago and music at Radcliffe College (Ph.D., 1947). In 1944 she married her private student, Ervin Henning (q.v.). Works: trio for oboe, clarinet and bassoon (1946); *Suite* for small orch. (1947); *Suite for Recorders* (1949); piano quartet (1949); string quartet (1951); trio for violin, clarinet and piano (1953); many songs with varied instrumental accompaniments. Her music follows dodecaphonic precepts.

Broman, Natanael. Died in Stockholm, Aug. 27, 1966.

Broman, Sten, Swedish composer; b. Uppsala, March 25, 1902. He studied at the German Music Academy in Prague attending a master class in violin playing with Henri Marteau; subsequently studied musicology with Curt Sachs in Berlin. From 1929 to 1951 he played the viola in various Swedish string quartets; also conducted orchestras in Sweden and Denmark; in 1946 he was appointed conductor of the Philharmonic Society in Malmö. His works, mostly in a neo-romantic vein, include four symphonies (1962, 1963, 1965, 1968), 3 suites for viola and piano (1935, 1937, 1942), 2 string quartets (1929, 1938), sextet for strings, percussion and piano (1963) and a ballet *Malmö Dances* (1952).

Brons, Carel, Dutch composer; b. Amsterdam, Jan. 1, 1931. He studied piano, organ and composition; in 1954 became engaged on the Radio Holland. Works: *Balletto* for wind quintet (1961); *Dialogues* for oboe and piano (1962); string quartet (1962); *Serenata* for flute solo (1963); *Mutazione* for wind quintet (1964); *Serenata* for oboe, clarinet and bassoon (1965).

Brooks, John Benson, American jazz pianist and composer; b. Houlton, Maine, Feb. 23, 1917. He attended John Cage's classes of modern music at the New School for Social Research, N.Y., and became immersed in dodecaphonic and aleatory lore. Moreover, he read books on astrology, numerology and epistemology. Using the techniques of horoscopes, ink-blot tests and extrasensory perception as catalytic agents to the imagination, he developed an individualized method of serial composition; by analogy with the principle of indeterminacy, he postulated that velocity of musical particles and their temporary positions at a given point cannot be both precisely determined, and followed this idea in his improvisations, with *ostinatos* as departures from randomness. He composed an *Alabama Concerto* and a number of jazz songs.

Brott, Alexander. Add to works: *Arabesques* for cello and orch. (1958); *Analogy in Anagram* for orch. (1959); *Three Astral Visions* for string orch. (1960); *Spheres in Orbit,* symph. suite (1961); *Three Acts for Four Sinners* for saxophone quartet (1961); *Three on a Spree* for harp, flute and oboe (1962); *Salvation Orgy* for brass quintet (1962); *World Sophisticate* for brass quintet (1962); *Triangle, Circle, Four Squares* for string orch.

(1963); *The Emperor's New Clothes* for orch. and narrator (Kingston, Ontario, Feb. 21, 1971).

Brown, Earle, American composer of the avant-garde; b. Lunenburg, Mass., Dec. 26, 1926. He studied the Schillinger System and expanded it to include aleatory processes; also devised an optical system of notation in which pitch, duration and dynamics are indicated by symbolic ideograms. In his pioneer work *In 25 Pages* (1953) he introduced the concept of 'open end' composition in which the performer is free to select the order of notated fragments of the piece. Works: *Folio Pieces* (1952); 2 octets for 8 magnetic tapes (1953, 1954); *Pentathis* for 9 instruments (1958); *Hodograph* for flute, piano, celesta, bells, vibraphone and marimba (1959); *Indices* for 12 players (1960); *Light Music* for electric lights, electronic equipment and variable numbers of instruments (1961); *Available Forms I* for 18 players (Darmstadt, Sept. 8, 1961); *Available Forms II* for 98 players and 2 conductors (1963); *Event: Synergy II* (1967) for a flexible ensemble up to 19 players and between one and two conductors, with no two performances identical in content, nor rehearsals similar to public presentations. He also composed normal music for cello.

Brown, Howard Mayer, American musicologist; b. Los Angeles, April 13, 1930. He studied at Harvard Univ. with Walter Piston (composition), Otto Gombosi (musicology) and others (B.A., 1951; M.A., 1954; Ph.D., 1959); continued his study in Vienna (1951-53); held a Guggenheim Fellowship in Florence (1963-64). He taught at Wellesley College (1958-60); in 1960 he was appointed to the faculty of the Univ. of Chicago. Publications: *Music in the French Secular Theater, 1400-1550* (Cambridge, Mass., 1963); *Instrumental Music Printed Before 1600: A Bibliography* (Cambridge, Mass., 1965); contributed a number of articles to music magazines.

Brown, Rayner, American composer; b. Des Moines, Iowa, Feb. 23, 1912; studied at the Univ. of Southern California, obtaining his M. Mus. in 1946; became active as church organist and teacher in Los Angeles. Works: 3 symphonies (1952, 1957, 1958); concerto for organ and orchestra (1959); piano quartet (1947); string quartet (1953); 2 woodwind quintets (1955, 1957); brass quintet (1957); 2 flute sonatas (1944, 1959); 3 fugues for 5 flutes (1952); trio for flute, clarinet and viola (1957); 12 sonatinas for organ; piano sonata, etc.

Browning, John, brilliant American pianist; b. Denver, May 22, 1933. He made his professional debut in Denver at the age of 10; then went to Los Angeles where he studied with Lee Pattison, and to New York where he enrolled in the Juilliard School of Music as a student of Rosina Lhévinne. He received the Steinway Centennial Award in 1954 and the Leventritt Award in 1955; in 1956 won the first award at the Queen Elisabeth Competition in Brussels. He attracted wide attention on Sept. 24, 1962, when he was soloist with the Boston Symph. Orch. at Lincoln Center, New York, in the world première of the piano concerto by Samuel Barber, commissioned by G. Schirmer, Inc., in celebration of the firm's 100th anniversary.

Brownlee, John. Died in New York, Jan. 10, 1969.

Brubeck, David (Dave), American pianist and jazz improviser; brother of Howard Brubeck; b. Concord, California, Dec. 6, 1920. He played piano in jazz bands as a boy; then took lessons with Milhaud at Mills College, and with Schoenberg in Los Angeles. During World War II he was assigned to a band in Europe; after demobilization, he organized a highly successful band of his own. In his half-improvised compositions he employs a contrapuntal idiom combining elements of jazz with baroque textures. He wrote the oratorio *Truth Has Fallen* for the opening of the new Midland, Michigan, Center for the Arts, May 1, 1971.

Brubeck, Howard, American composer, brother of David Brubeck; b. Concord, California, July 11, 1916. After studying with Darius Milhaud and others, he devoted himself to teaching; was chairman of the Music Department at Palomar Jr. College in La Mesa, California. Works: *Elizabethan Suite* for chamber orch. and women's chorus (1944); *California Suite* for orch. (1945); *Overture to the Devil's Disciple* (1954); *Four Dialogues for Jazz Combo and Orchestra* (San Diego, Aug. 1, 1956); *The Gardens of Versailles,* suite for orch. (1960); woodwind quintet (1950); choruses; piano pieces; arrangements for jazz combo and orch. on David Brubeck's themes.

Bruchollerie, Monique de la, French pianist; b. Paris, April 20, 1915. She studied with Isidor Philipp; graduated from the Paris Cons. at the age of 13; toured widely as a concert pianist; also was active as a teacher. In 1964 she made a bold proposal to modernize the piano as a performing instrument by constructing a crescent-shaped keyboard to facilitate simultaneous playing in high treble and low bass. She further proposed to install electronic controls enabling the pianist to activate a whole chord by striking a single key. See 'Time' Magazine for April 30, 1965.

Bruči, Rudolf, Serbian composer; b. Zagreb, March 30, 1917. He studied in Vienna with Uhl; returning to Serbia, became teacher and opera conductor in Novi Sad. In his works he employs polytonal and atonal devices, culminating in free dodecaphony. Works: *Maskal,* symph, suite (1955); Concerto for Orch. (Belgrade, Nov. 25, 1959); *Čovek je vidik bez kraja,* cantata (Belgrade, Dec. 21, 1961); *Srbija,* cantata (Belgrade, May 24, 1962); *Sinfonia lesta* (received the Grand Prix at the Queen Elisabeth of Belgium Competition in Brussels, 1965); *Sinfonietta* for strings (1965); *Salut au monde,* oratorio (1967).

Bruckner, Anton. Add to bibl.: W. Abendroth, *Bruckner: Eine Bibliographie* (Munich, 1958); E. Doernberg, *The Life and Symphonies of Anton Bruckner* (London, 1960); R. Simpson, *The Essence of Bruckner* (Philadelphia, 1968); H. H. Schönzeler, *Bruckner* (N. Y., 1970).

Bruhns, Nicolaus, German violinist, organist and composer; b. Schwabstedt, 1665; d. Husum, March 29, 1697. He studied with Buxtehude in Lübeck; was organist in Copenhagen, and from 1689 in Husum. He was also an experienced violinist. He wrote 12 church cantatas, and a number of organ pieces. See H. Kölsch, *Nicolaus Bruhns* (Kassel, 1958).

Brun, Alphonse, German-Swiss violinist; b. Frankfurt, Oct. 25, 1888; d. Bern, March 27, 1963. He studied in Zürich and Berlin; in 1912 settled in Bern, where he organized a renowned string quartet; also was active as teacher.

Brun, Fritz. Died in Grosshöchstetten, Switzerland, Nov. 29, 1959.

Brunswick, Mark. Died in London, May 26, 1971. Was chairman of the music department of N. Y. City College from 1946 to 1965. He left unfinished an opera, *The Master Builder.*

Bruscantini, Sesto, Italian bass singer; b. Civitanova, Dec. 10, 1919. He studied law; then went to Rome for vocal instruction; sang small opera parts in Italy. Advancing rapidly in his new career, he formed a repertory of 130 roles in 108 operas; particularly excelled as a basso buffo. He appeared in England, U.S., Japan and in Scandinavia with excellent success.

Brustad, Bjarne. Add to works: 5 symphonies (1948, 1951, 1953, 1967, 1967); 3 violin sonatas (1950, 1956, 1958); violin concerto No. 4 (1961).

Bucci, Mark, American composer; b. New York, Feb. 26, 1924. He studied with Jacobi and Giannini at the Juiliard School of Music and with Copland at the Berkshire Music Center, Tanglewood; adopted a pragmatic method of composition in a strong rhythmic style, in modern but tonal harmonies, particularly effective in his stage works. Works: one-act operas, *The Boor* (after Chekhov; N. Y., Dec. 29, 1949); *The Dress* (N. Y., Dec. 8, 1953); *Sweet Betsy from Pike* (N. Y., Dec. 8, 1953); *The Thirteen Clocks* (N. Y., Dec. 29, 1953); *Tale for a Deaf Ear* (Tanglewood, Aug. 5, 1957); *The Hero* (Educational Television, N. Y., Sept. 24, 1965). *His Concerto for a Singing Instrument* was first performed as a *Concerto for Kazoo* by the N. Y. Philharmonic, Leonard Bernstein conducting, on March 26, 1960, with Anita Darian as a kazoo virtuoso.

Bucht, Gunnar, Swedish composer; b. Stockholm, Aug. 5, 1927. He studied at Uppsala Univ.; took a course in composition with Karl-Birger Blomdahl; later in Germany with Carl Orff and in Italy with Goffredo Petrassi. Works: string quintet (1950); *Introduction and Allegro* for string orch. (1950); *Meditation* for piano and orch. (1950); piano sonata (1951); string quartet (1951); Symph. No. 1 (1952); Symph. No. 2 (1953); Symph. No. 3 (1954); cello concerto (1954); *Symphonic Fantasy* (1955); *Divertimento* for orch. (1956); *Tronkrävarna,* opera after Ibsen (Stockholm, Sept. 10, 1966).

Buckner, Milton (Milt), American jazz pianist; b. St. Louis, July 10, 1915. He played in Lionel Hampton's band; popularized the 'locked-hands' technique of parallel block chords; perfected the rigid rhythmical patterns in the blues style; used the Hammond organ for the first time in jazz.

Budd, Harold, American composer; b. Los Angeles, May 24, 1936. He studied composition, acoustics and esthetics with Gerald Strang and Aurelio de la Vega at San Fernando Valley State College, California (B.A., 1963) and at the Univ. of Southern California with Ingolf Dahl (M.Mus., 1966); in 1968 he was appointed to the faculty of the California Institute of the Arts. In the interim he earned his living as a jazz musician. His compositions are mostly for mixed media, some of them modular, capable of being choreographed one into another; some are mere verbalizations of the mode of performance in a frequently benumbing, stultifying, mesmerizing or fantasist manner. These works are *Analogies from Rothko* for orch. (1964); *The Sixth This Year* for orch. (1967); *September Music* (1967); *November* (1967; displayed as a painting at the Museum of Contemporary Crafts in New York); *Black Flowers,* a 'quiet chamber ritual for 4 performers,' to be staged in semi-darkness on the threshold of visibility and audibility (1968); *Intermission Piece,* to be played at random with the "amplitude spectrum barely audible" during intermission, with the audience "physically or conceptually, absent" (1968; Hartford, Conn., Jan. 28, 1970); *One Sound,* for string quartet glissando (1968); *Mangus Colorado* for amplified gongs (1969; Buffalo, Feb. 4, 1970); *Lovely Thing* for piano, telling the player "select a chord — if in doubt call me (in lieu of performance) at 213-662-7819 for spiritual advice" first realized performance. Memphis, Tenn., Oct. 23. 1969); *Lovely Thing* for strings (1969); *California 99* (1969); *The Candy-Apple Revision* (1970).

Bughici, Dumitru, Rumanian composer; b. Jassy, Nov. 14, 1921. He studied composition in his native town, and later at the Cons. of Leningrad (1950-55). In 1955 he became prof. of the Bucharest Cons. Among his works are a symphonic poem *Evocare* (1956); *Poemul primaveri* (*Spring Poem*) for violin and orch. (1950); *Poemul burcuriei* (*Poem of Joy*) for orch. (1962); various violin and piano pieces.

Bull, Ole Bornemann. Add to bibl.: I. Bull, *Ole Bull Returns to Pennsylvania* (N. Y., 1961).

Bumbry, Grace (Ann), American Negro singer; b. St. Louis, Jan. 4, 1937. She sang in church choirs as a child; in 1955 went to Northwestern Univ. to study voice with Lotte Lehmann, and continued her lessons with her in California. She made her professional debut in London in 1959; then made a spectacular appearance as Amneris at the Paris Opéra. In 1962 she appeared as Carmen with a French operatic troupe visiting Japan. Her greatest triumph came when she was selected by Wieland Wagner to sing Venus in *Tannhäuser* at the Bayreuth Festival (July 23, 1961), the first Negro to sing this role. She subsequently performed this role several times, including an appearance with the Lyric Opera of Chicago in 1963.

Bunin, Vladimir Vasilievitch. Died in Moscow, March 23, 1970.

Burada, Theodor, Rumanian violinist and folklorist; b. Jassy, Oct. 3, 1839; d. there, Feb. 17, 1923. He studied in Rumania and at the Paris Cons. His significance lies in his pioneer work connected with Rumanian folklore and codifying folk melodies and popular ballads. He also wrote some violin music.

Burco, Ferruccio, precocious Italian conductor; b. Milan, April 5, 1939; killed in an automobile accident near Ostuni, April 27, 1965. Phenomenally gifted, he was trained by his mother, a singer, and on May 30, 1943, at the age of 4, conducted an orchestra in Milan, by memorizing gestures to give cues. With his father acting as his manager, he was exhibited throughout Italy; in 1948 he was brought to the U.S. and conducted a concert at Carnegie Hall, N.Y.; also led sympathetic symphonic groups in Philadelphia, Detroit, Boston, Chicago, Los Angeles and San Francisco. At a special opera performance at the Triborough Stadium at Randalls Island in New York, he conducted *Cavalleria rusticana,* with his mother singing the role of Santuzza. During his American tour he weighed only 82 pounds. His subsequent development failed to do justice to his fantastic beginnings, and at the time of his death he was the leader of an itinerant provincial Italian band.

Burian, Emil František. Died in Prague, Aug. 9, 1959.

Burian, Karl. Add to bibl.: E. F. Burian, *Karl Burian* (Prague, 1948).

Burk, John N. Died in Boston, Sept. 6, 1967.

Burkhard, Willy. Add to bibl.: Ernst Mohr, *Willy Burkhard: Leben und Werk* (Zürich, 1957).

Burleigh, Henry Thacker. Joined St. George's Church in 1894 (not 1892). He did not compose *Deep River* but arranged it for voice and piano, altering the middle section to the extent that it became practically his own work.

Burney, Charles. Add bibl.: Roger Lonsdale, *Dr. Charles Burney: a Literary Biography* (London, 1965).

Burt, Francis, English composer; b. London, April 28, 1926. He studied at the Royal Academy of Music with Howard Ferguson (1948-51) and at the Hochschule für Musik in Berlin with Boris Blacher (1951-54); was awarded the German Mendelssohn Scholarship; went for further study to Rome; in 1956 he received a stipend from the Fondation européenne de la Culture; from 1957 lived mostly in Vienna. Works: string quartet (1953); *Iambics* for orch. (1955); *Music for Two Pianos* (1955); *The Skull,* cantata for tenor and orch. (1956); *Duo* for clarinet and piano (1956); *Bavarian Gentians* for vocal quartet and piano (1957); *Espressione orchestrale* (1959); *Volpone,* opera after Ben Jonson (1960); *The Golem,* ballet (1962); *Fantasmagoria* for orch. (1963).

Buschkötter, Wilhelm. Died in Berlin, May 12, 1967.

Bush, Alan Dudley. He joined the Communist Party in 1935 and simplified his musical language to make it more accessible to proletarian masses. Most of his operas are produced in East Germany. Date of first performance of his Symph. No. 1, July 24 (not Aug. 24), 1942; *Fantasia on Soviet Themes* was first performed in London on July 27 (not Aug. 27), 1945; *The Winter Journey,* on Dec. 14 (not Dec. 12), 1946. Add to works: operas: *The Men of Blackmoor* (Weimar, Nov. 18, 1956); *Guayana Johnny* (Leipzig, Dec. 11, 1966); *Joe Hill,* on the subject of the execution of the labor agitator Joe Hill in Salt Lake City on Nov. 19, 1915 (East Berlin, Sept 29, 1970); *Third Symphony,* subtitled *Byron Symphony* (1960).

Busoni, Ferruccio Benvenuto. Add to bibl.: Augusta Cottlow, *My Years with Busoni,* in 'The Mus. Observer,' June 1925; Heinz Meyer, *Die Klaviermusik Ferruccio Busonis* (Zürich, 1969); H. H. Stuckenschmidt, *Ferruccio Busoni, Zeittafel eines Europäers* (Zürich, 1967; in English, *Ferruccio Busoni, Chronicle of a European,* London, 1970).

Busser, Henri-Paul. Safely passed his 99th birthday on Jan. 16, 1971. He married the French opera singer Yvonne Gall in 1958. See 'Qui est qui en France' for 1971-72.

Bussotti, Sylvano, Italian composer of the avant-garde; b. Florence, Oct. 1, 1931. He studied music and painting, combining both arts in the audio-visual notation of his music; verbalization and pictorial illustrations are integral parts in his compositions. He applies a wide range of media, from serial techniques to aleatory discursions. His works include *Torso,* a song cycle for voice and orch. (1960); *Memoria* for baritone, chorus and orch. (1962); *Fragmentations* for harp (1962); and *La Passion selon Sade,* his crowning achievement, which makes use of theatrical effects, diagrams, drawings, surrealistic illustrations, etc., with thematic content evolving from a dodecaphonic nucleus, allowing great latitude for free interpolations, and set in an open-end form in which fragments of the music are recapitulated at will, until the players are mutually neutralized. The unifying element of the score is the recurrent motive D-Es-A-D-E, spelling the name De Sade, interwoven with that of B-A-C-H. The first production of *La Passion selon Sade* took place in Palermo on Sept. 5, 1965. Among Bussotti's other conceits are *5 Pieces for David Tudor,* in which the dedicatee wears thick gloves to avoid hitting single and potentially melodious tones on the keyboard.

Bustabo, Guila. In 1964 she moved to Innsbruck, as teacher at the Conservatory there.

Bustini, Alessandro, Italian composer; b. Rome, Dec. 24, 1876; d. there, June 23, 1970. He studied at the Santa Cecilia Academy with Sgambati (piano), Renzi (organ) and Falchi (composition), graduating in 1897. He was subsequently appointed to the faculty of Santa Cecilia, and was its president from 1952 to 1964. His works, all written in the traditional Italian manner, include the opera *Maria Dulcis* (Rome, April 15, 1902); 2 symphonies (1899 and 1909); *Le tentazioni,* a symph. poem (1914); *Le stagioni* for violin and chamber orch. (1934); 2 string quartets; songs; piano works.

Butting, Max. Add to works: opera, *Plautus im Nonnenkloster* (Leipzig, Oct. 3, 1959); wrote 9 symphonies; in his 9th symph. (1956) he applied the 12-tone method of composition.

C

Caamaño, Roberto, Argentinian pianist and composer; b. Buenos Aires, July 7, 1923. He studied in Buenos Aires; then became an instructor of sacred music; toured as a concert pianist. From 1960-64 he was artistic director of the Teatro Colón of Buenos Aires. Works: 2 string quartets (1945, 1946); *Variaciones Americanas* for orch. (1954); piano concerto (Inter-American Festival of Music, Washington, April 18, 1958); piano quintet (1962); choral pieces.

Caba, Eduardo, Bolivian composer; b. Potosí, Oct. 13, 1890; d. La Paz, March 3, 1953. He was educated in Buenos Aires; then went to study with Turina in Spain; in 1942 he settled in La Paz. His ballets and other music are inspired by the pentatonic structure of Bolivian folksongs.

Cacioppo, George, Canadian composer; b. Monroe, Michigan, Sept. 24, 1927. He studied with Ross Lee Finney at the Univ. of Michigan; received his M.A. in composition in 1952; then worked in Tanglewood, studying with Leon Kirchner. In 1960 he attended classes of Roberto Gerhard, then a visiting prof. at the Univ. of Michigan. Cacioppo was a co-founder of the ONCE Festival concerts in Ann Arbor in 1960. His technique partakes of serialism of the Schoenbergian credo while studiously avoiding the chronic chromaticism of atonal writing. Verbalization is an integral part of all of his music; aleatory principles are expressed in 'open end' forms. Works: *Pianopieces* for any number of pianos with their realizations on tape sounding synchronously or non-synchronously and lasting any practical, or impractical length of time; *Holy Ghost Vacuum, or America Faints,* for electric organ (Ann Arbor, March 29, 1966, composer at the manuals). See *Apteryx Papers* by G. Cacioppo quoted in full in 'Canavanguard' (Don Mills, Ontario, 1967).

Cage, John. Add to works: *Concert* for piano and orch. (N. Y., May 15, 1958); *Music for Amplified Toy Pianos* (Wesleyan Univ., Middletown, Conn., Feb. 25, 1960); *Cartridge Music* (Cologne, Oct. 6, 1960); *Atlas Eclipticalis* for orch. (Montreal, Aug. 3, 1961); *O'OO",* an idempotent "to be performed in any way by anyone" (Tokyo, Oct. 24, 1962); also other works for ad libitum ensembles (tacet). He publ. a book of surrealist essays and lectures, *Silence* (Middletown, Conn., 1961); *A Year from Monday* (Middletown, Conn., 1967); and *Notations* (N. Y., 1969). A detailed annotated catalogue of his works was publ. by Edition Peters (N. Y., 1962). Bibl.: *John Cage,* a collection of essays edited by Richard Kostelanetz (N. Y., 1970).

Caldara, Antonio. Died Dec. 26 (not 28), 1736. See Mario Rinaldi, *Contributo alla futura biografia di Antonio Caldara* ('Rivista Musicale Italiana,' Sept.-Oct. 1970).

Calligaris, Sergio, Argentinian pianist; b. Tosario, Argentina, of Italian parents, Jan. 22, 1941. He made his concert debut in Rosario at 13; then studied with Jorge Fanelli in Buenos Aires; in 1964 went to America and studied with Arthur Loesser at the Cleveland Institute of Music, receiving an artist's diploma in 1966; taught there for an academic season; then went to Italy, where he studied with Guido Agosti at the Santa Cecilia Academy in Rome (1967-69); in 1970 was appointed to the piano faculty of the California State College in Los Angeles. His playing is distinguished by a romantic élan and virtuoso technique.

Calloway, Cab, American jazz singer; b. Rochester, N.Y., Dec. 25, 1907. He became a proponent of Scat singing, characterized by nonsense syllabization and rapid glossolalia with the melodic line largely submerged under an asymmetric inundation of rhythmic heterophony. He led bands and appeared in the movies. He also compiled a *Hepster's Dictionary,* listing jazz terms (1938).

Campagnoli, Bartolommeo. Place of birth, Cento di Ferrara (not Cento, near Bologna).

Campos-Parisi, Hector, Puerto Rican composer; b. Ponce, Oct. 1, 1922. He studied at the New England Cons. in Boston, with Nadia Boulanger in Paris and with Copland at Tanglewood; returning to Puerto Rico he developed energetic activities as composer, poet, journalist, music critic, educator, television commentator and concert manager. Works: *Incidente,* ballet (1948); *Music for 3 violins* (1949); string quartet (1950); *Versiculos* for viola unaccompanied (1950); *Melos,* ballet (1952); *Divertimento del Sur* for flute, clarinet and strings (1953); *Annunciation,* cantata (1954); *Juan Bobo,* ballet (1957); *Madrigales* for contralto and strings (1959); *Rapsodia elegiaca,* in memoriam Villa-Lobos (1960); *Duo Tragico* for piano and orch. (1965); piano sonata; sonatina for violin and piano; choruses; songs.

Camps, Pompeyo, Argentine composer; b. Paraná, Oct. 27, 1924. After playing piano in bands in his native town, he settled in Buenos Aires in 1947; studied with Jaime Pahissa and adopted Pahissa's "intertonal system" of convertible counterpoint. In 1964 he modified this technique by incorporating serial procedures. He is also active as a music critic. Works: *La Pendiente,* opera in 1 act (1959); *Ballad of the Reading Gaol* (1964) for men's choir, narrator and orch.; *Sinfónia para un Poeta* for baritone and orch. (obtained first municipal prize of Buenos Aires in 1967); *Tríptico Arcáico* for flute, viola, cello and guitar (1961); *Danzas* for percussion (1966); songs; piano pieces.

Camussi, Ezio. Died in Milan, Aug. 11, 1956.

Cannon, Philip, English composer; b. Paris, Dec. 21, 1929, of English-French parentage. He was educated in England; studied composition with Imogen Holst; then at the Royal College of Music, London, with Gordon Jacob. He subsequently took lessons with Hindemith. After graduation from the Royal College, he was appointed lecturer on music at the Univ. of Sydney, Australia; in 1952 he joined the staff of the Royal College of Music, London. His style of composition is neo-romantic, but adheres to classical forms, preserving a clear sense of tonality. Works. *Morvoren,* opera on a Cornish legend (London, July 15, 1964); 2 Rhapsodies for piano (1943); string quartet No. 1 (1944); string trio (1945); *Fantasia* for string quartet (1946); *In the Time of the Breaking of Nations,* after Thomas Hardy, for voice and piano quintet (1945); sextet for flute, oboe and string quartet (1946); Sinfonietta for chamber orch. (1947); *Symphonic Study: Spring* for orch. (1949); *Song to Delight* for women's chorus and strings (1950); *Galop Parisien* for 2 pianos (1950); Sinfonietta for strings (1952); *Cinq Chansons de Femme* for soprano and harp (1952); *L'Enfant s'amuse,* suite for piano (1954); *Sonatine Champêtre* for piano (1959); Sonata for 2 pianos (1960); *Son of Science,* cantata for the Machine Age, for chorus, tenor, piano, percussion and strings (Aylesbury, Dec. 2, 1961); *Fanfare to Youth* for 8 trumpets (1963); string quartet No. 2 (1964); *Kai-kaus* (*A Persian Suite*) for a chamber group (1965).

Cantelli, Guido. Date of death, Nov. 24 (not Nov. 23), 1956. Made his American debut with the NBC Symph. Orch. on Jan. 15, 1949 (not 1948).

Canteloube de Malaret, Marie-Joseph. Died in Paris, Nov. 4, 1957.

Capdevielle, Pierre. Died in Bordeaux, July 9, 1969. Add to works: *Fille de l'homme,* lyric tragedy (Paris Radio, Nov. 9, 1967).

Capuana, Franco, Italian conductor; b. Fano, Sept. 29, 1894; d. Naples, Dec. 10, 1969. He studied in Naples: began his career as opera conductor in 1915; from 1930 to 1937 he was music director of the Teatro San Carlo in Naples. He specialized in Verdi and Wagner, and also produced a number of modern operas.

Carapetyan, Armen, American musicologist of Persian origin; b. Isfahan, Oct. 11, 1908. He studied philosophy in Paris and New York; musicology at Harvard Univ. In 1945 he organized the American Institute of Musicology, with headquarters in Rome and Cambridge, Mass.; edited valuable collections, among them *Corpus Mensurabilis Musicae, Corpus Scriptorum de Musica, Musicological Studies and Documents;* contributed numerous articles, mainly on the music of the Renaissance, to American and European periodicals.

Cardew, Cornelius, English composer of the avant-garde; b. Winchcombe, Gloucester, May 7, 1936. He was a chorister at Canterbury Cathedral until puberty; then studied composition with Howard Ferguson, at the Royal Academy of Music in London (1953-57); played piano and cello. In 1957 he went to Cologne and worked at the electronic studio there; was assistant to Karlheinz Stockhausen (1958-60) whose *Carré* for 4 orchestras, 4 choruses and 4 conductors was produced with Cardew's collaboration. Returning to England in 1960, he organized concerts of experimental music; in 1963-65 he was in Italy and studied with Goffredo Petrassi in Rome. In 1966 he was elected Fellow of the Royal Academy of Music in London. His compositions are preponderantly latitudinarian and disestablishmentarian, replete with unpremeditated verbalization. But he also wrote explicitly performable music. His works include string trio (1957); *Arrangement* for orch. (1960); *First Movement for String Quartet* (1962); *Volo Solo* for any instrument (1965); *Three Winter Potatoes* for piano solo (1965), and *Schooltime Compositions,* scored for 'matrices arranged around vocal sounds, triangles, newspapers, balloons, noise, desire, keyboard, with many people working' (Focus Opera Group, London, March 11, 1968).

Carey, Bruce. Died in Hamilton, Ontario, May 8, 1960.

Carey, Francis Clive Savill. Died in London, April 30, 1968.

Carlstedt, Jan, Swedish composer; b. Stockholm, June 15, 1926. He studied composition with Lars-Erik Larsson at the Royal Academy of Music in Stockholm (1948-52), and later in England and Italy. Returning to Stockholm he became active in furthering the cause of modern music. He writes mostly instrumental music in classical forms. Works: Symph. No. 1 (1954); Symph. No. 2 (1969), dedicated to the memory of Martin Luther King; 3 string quartets (1952, 1966, 1967);

sonata for 2 violins (1956); sonata for solo violin (1959); *Sinfonietta* for 5 wind instruments (1959); *Divertimento* for oboe and strings (1962).

Carmichael, Hoagy, American jazz pianist and composer; b. Bloomington, Indiana, Nov. 11, 1899. He played in various bands as a youth; later formed his own band with Benny Goodman and others. Although unable to read or write music, he composed a number of melodious songs of considerable sentimental impact; of these *Stardust* became famous. Other songs are *Lazy River, Rocking Chair, Georgia on My Mind.* Cf. H. C. and Stephen Longstreet, *Sometimes I Wonder: the Story of Hoagy Carmichael* (N.Y., 1965).

Carner, Mosco. Add to books: *Puccini: A Critical Biography* (London, 1958).

Carneyro, Claudio. Died in Oporto, Oct. 18, 1963.

Carolan, Turlough. Add to bibl.: D. O'Sullivan, *Carolan: The Life, Times and Music of an Irish Harper* (London, 1958).

Carr, Arthur, American pianist and composer; b. Pontiac, Michigan, Feb. 29, 1908. He studied theory with David Stanley Smith and Richard Donovan at Yale Univ.; piano with Bruce Simonds; composition with Halsey Stevens at the Univ. of S. Calif. (Mus. M., 1947). In 1942-46 he served as bandleader in the U. S. Army. His works include a symph. poem *Desire* (1932); a comic opera *Captain Jupiter* (1939); a *Celtic Rondo* for orch. (1941); *Thème varié* for string quartet; piano pieces; songs. He made several tours in America and in Europe as a pianist and accompanist.

Carreño, Inocente, Venezuelan composer; b. Porlamar, Dec. 28, 1919. He studied French horn, clarinet, piano and theory in Caracas; graduated in composition in 1946; subsequently became engaged in pedagogical work; also played the French horn in the Caracas Symph. Orch. and conducted choruses. His works include a symphonic poem, *El Pozo* (1946); *Concerto* for horn and strings (1958); *Sinfonieta Satírica* for 11 instruments (1965); chamber music and choruses.

Carrillo, Julián. Died in Mexico City, Sept. 9, 1965.

Carroll, Walter. Died in Manchester, England, Oct. 9, 1955.

Carse, Adam von Ahn. Died in Great Missenden, Bucks., Nov. 2, 1958.

Carter, Elliott Cook. About 1955 he changed his style radically, adopting the method of serialization of intervals and dynamics. Was prof. of composition at Yale Univ. (1960-62); in 1963 was composer-in-residence at the American Academy in Rome. Add to works: 2nd string quartet (1960; received a Pulitzer Prize and the New York Music Critics Circle Award; was also elected as the most important work of the year by the International Rostrum of Composers); *Double Concerto* for harpsichord and piano with two chamber orchestras (N. Y., Sept. 6, 1961); piano concerto (Boston, Jan. 6, 1967); *Concerto for Orchestra* (N. Y. Philharmonic, N. Y., Feb. 5, 1970). Bibl.: E. Carter, *Shoptalk by an American Composer* in 'The Mus. Quarterly' (April, 1960).

Carvalho, Eleazar. He was conductor of the St. Louis Symph. Orch. from 1963 until 1969; introduced numerous modern works in its repertory, much to the discomfiture of the financial backers of the orchestra. In 1969 he was appointed conductor of the Hofstra Univ. Orch., in Hempstead, N. Y., enjoying a liberal esthetic environment. He is the husband of the avant-garde composer and pianist Jocy de Oliveira.

Carver, Robert, Scottish composer; b. 1487; d. after 1546. He was a Monk of Scone Abbey; developed a melismatic style of composition; wrote masses on the medieval song, *L'Homme armé* and many motets, one of them in 19 independent parts. He is regarded as an equal of Dunstable in melodic and rhythmic excellence. Vol. 1 of his collected works was publ. by the American Institute of Musicology, ed. by Denis Stevens, in 1959.

Casabona, Francisco, Brazilian composer and pedagogue; b. São Paulo, Oct. 16, 1894. He studied in Brazil and in Italy; attended classes of Alessandro Longo (piano), Camillo de Nardis (theory) and Giovanni Barbieri (composition) at the Cons. of Naples. Returning to Brazil, he became prof. of the São Paulo Cons. In his music, Casabona follows an Italianate expressive style, excelling equally in vocal and instrumental works. He wrote the comic operas *Godiamo la Vita* (Rome, 1917) and *Principessa dell'Atelier* (Naples, 1918); the symph. poems *Nero* (1915), *Crepúsculo Sertanejo* (1926), and *Noite de São João* (1934); Sinfonia No. 1 (1937); Sinfonia No. 2 (1940); *La Fable d'Einstein* for orch.

(1946); *Maracatú,* Afro-Brazilian dance (1964); violin sonata; piano pieces in the Brazilian idiom; choruses and songs.

Casadesus, Robert. The first performance of his concerto for two pianos and orch. took place in Warsaw in 1934; he played it with his wife, accompanied by the N. Y. Philharmonic on Nov. 25, 1940 (not April 3, 1950).

Casals, Pablo. He conducted the world première of his Christmas oratorio, *El Pesebre* (*The Manger*) in Acapulco, Mexico, Dec. 17, 1960. Add to bibl.: *Joys and Sorrows, Reflections* as told to Albert E. Kahn (N. Y., 1970). On Dec. 29, 1970 he gloriously passed his 94th birthday, the only musician in all history to continue his professional activities as conductor and player well into the tenth decade of his life.

Casanova, André, French composer; b. Paris, Oct. 12, 1919. He studied law as well as music; took lessons with René Leibowitz and others in Paris. His music is cast in a neo-classical framework, with some atonal deviations. Works: Symph. No. 1 (1949); Symph. No. 2 (Nice, Feb. 20, 1971); *Capriccio* for oboe and chamber orch. (1960); *Anamorphoses* for orch. (Strasbourg, June 21, 1963); *La clé d'argent,* lyric drama (1965); trumpet concerto (1966); *Le Bonheur dans le crime,* opera (1969).

Casanovas, Narciso. Exact date of birth, Nov. 17, 1747.

Casella, Alfredo. *La favola d'Orfeo* (not *di Orfeo*) was first performed on Sept. 6 (not Nov. 6), 1932. *Le couvent sur l'eau* (Paris, April 23, 1914) is a symph. suite from the ballet, *Il convento veneziano,* produced at La Scala, Milan, Feb. 7, 1925. Add bibl.: F. d'Amico & G. M. Gatti, editors, *Alfredo Casella* (Milan, 1958).

Cash, Johnny, American popular singer of partly Indian descent (1/4 Cherokee); b. in a railroad shack near Kingsland, Arkansas, Feb. 26, 1932. He worked as a water boy in a farmer's family; sang Baptist hymns in church; at the age of 17 won $5.00 at a local amateur talent contest. In 1950 he enlisted in the U.S. Air Force; served in Germany returning to the U.S. in 1954. He learned to play the guitar while in the service; in 1955 began a series of appearances on the radio and various country circuits specializing in Country-Western music, and soon began to compose his own songs, both lyrics and tunes. He could never learn to read the notes, which was of no importance to his professional life. The subjects of his songs concern the miseries of common folks as well as prison life. His most popular songs are *Folsom Prison Blues* and *I Walk the Line.*

Cassadó, Gaspar. Died in Madrid, Dec. 24, 1966.

Castaldi, Alfonso, Rumanian composer and conductor; b. Maddalone, Italy, April 23, 1874; d. Bucharest, Aug. 6, 1942. He studied in Naples; in 1901 became prof. at the Bucharest Cons. He was the first Rumanian composer to employ modern harmonies in his works. His style of composition combines Italian and German characteristics. Works: symph. poems, *Thalassa* (1906), *Marsyas* (1907), *L'Eroe senza gloria* (1925); numerous choruses. Castaldi was greatly esteemed as a pedagogue; many Rumanian composers were his pupils, among them Alfred Alessandrescu, Ion Nonno Otescu, Dimitrie Cuclin, Gheorghe Dumitrescu and Ion Dumitrescu.

Castaldo, Joseph, American composer; b. New York, Dec. 23, 1927. He studied in New York; was a clarinetist; enrolled in the Santa Cecilia Academy in Rome. Returning to the U.S. he took composition lessons with Giannini and Persichetti. Among his works are a string quartet; *Epigrams* for piano and orch.; *Flight,* a cantata; *Dichotomy* for woodwind quintet; *Epiphonia* for orch. In 1966 he was appointed President of the Philadelphia Music Academy.

Castelnuovo-Tedesco, Mario. Died in Los Angeles, March 16, 1968. Add to list of works: *Il Mercante di Venezia,* opera after Shakespeare's *The Merchant of Venice,* to his own Italian libretto; it won first prize at the International Competition of La Scala and was first performed at the Maggio Musicale, Florence, on May 25, 1961; *All's Well That Ends Well,* opera after Shakespeare (1959); *Saul,* biblical opera (1960); *The Importance of Being Earnest,* after Oscar Wilde, chamber opera (1962); *The Song of Songs,* scenic oratorio (Hollywood, Aug. 7, 1963); numerous pieces for guitar including *Les Guitares bien temperées* (24 preludes and fugues for 2 guitars, 1962) and a concerto for 2 guitars and orch. (1962); 3rd string quartet (1964); *Tobias and the Angel* (from the Book of Tobit), scenic oratorio (1965); Sonatina for flute and guitar (1965). *Variazioni sinfoniche* for violin and orch. was first performed by the N. Y. Philharmonic on April 9, 1930 (not in Rome, Dec. 19, 1930). *The Princess and the Pea* is not an opera but an overture with a narrator. The first performance of *Aucassin* *et Nicolette* took place in Florence on June 2, 1952.

Castéra, René de. Place of death, Angoume (not Angoumi).

Castiglioni, Niccolò, Italian pianist and composer; b. Milan, July 17, 1932. He studied composition with Ghedini at the Milan Cons.; had a successful career as a concert pianist. Works: *Tropi* for 6 players (1959); *Après-lude* for orch. (1959); *Disegni* for chamber orch. (1960); *Gymel* for flute and piano (1960); *Rondels* for orch. (1961); *Consonante* for chamber orch. (1962); *Synchronie* for orch. (1963); *A Solemn Music,* solo cantata for soprano and chamber orch., after Milton's poem (1963); *Masques* for 12 instruments, a bouillabaisse of polytonally combined melodic particles of familiarly remembered tunes (1968). Castiglioni cultivates a wide range of avant-garde techniques.

Castilla, Alberto, Colombian composer; b. Bogotá, April 9, 1883; d. Ibague, June 10, 1937. He studied engineering; was at one time connected with the government of Colombia. In 1898 he settled in Tolima, where he founded a music school. He wrote a number of songs, some of which achieved popularity. In 1954 the Colombian government issued a postage stamp in his honor.

Castro, José María. Died in Buenos Aires, Aug. 2, 1964.

Castro, Juan José. Died in Buenos Aires, Sept. 3, 1968. Place of birth, Avellaneda, in the province of Buenos Aires (not Buenos Aires itself). From 1956 to 1960 he was conductor of the Orquesta Sinfónica Nacional in Buenos Aires. Add to works: Symph. No. 5 (1956); *Suite introspectiva* for orch. (1961); violin concerto (Washington, May 11, 1965). Add to bibl.: R. Arizaga, *J. J. Castro* (Buenos Aires, 1963).

Caudella, Edoardo. Died April 11, 1924 (not April 11, 1923). Add to works: 2 violin concertos (1913, 1918); the operas *Olteanca* (Jassy, March 8, 1880); *Hatmanul Baltag* (Bucharest, March 1, 1884); *Fata razesului* (Bucharest, March 2, 1893).

Cavos, Catterino. Exact date of birth, Oct. 30, 1775. See R.-Aloys Mooser, *Un musicista veneziano in Russia: Catterino Cavos,* in 'Nuova Rivista Musicale Italiana' (Jan-Feb., 1969).

Cazden, Norman. Add to works: quintet for oboe and strings (1960); *Woodland Valley Sketches* for orch. (1961); *Adventure* for orch. (1963); a Chamber Concerto for clarinet and strings (1965); *Elizabethan Suite* No. 1 for brass quintet (1965); *Elizabethan Suite* No. 2 for string quartet (1965); woodwind quintet (1966); piano trio (1969). See *Composers of the Americas,* vol. 15 (Washington, 1969).

Ceccato, Aldo, Italian conductor; b. Milan, Feb. 18, 1934. He studied at the Cons. of Milan, and at the Academy of Music in Berlin. In 1969 he won first prize in the International Competition of Italian Radio for young conductors. He made his American debut with the N. Y. Philharmonic on Nov. 5, 1970 with excellent success. There followed engagements in England and Canada. He was also invited to conduct opera productions at Covent Garden in London.

Ceely, Robert Paige, American composer; b. Torrington, Conn., Jan. 17, 1930. He studied music at the New England Cons. of Music (B. Mus. in Composition, 1954), Mills College (M. A. 1961); attended classes at Princeton Univ. In 1965 he was appointed to the faculty of the New England Cons. of Music in Boston. Works: string trio (1953); *Music for Ten Instruments* (1963); *Strati* for magnetic tape (1963); *Logs,* a duet for double-basses (1968); *Spectrum* for chamber group and magnetic tape (1969); *Hymn* for double-bass and cello (1970).

Ceremuga, Josef, Czechoslovak composer; b. Ostrava-Kunčice, June 14, 1930. He studied composition with Řidký, Alois Hába and Dobiáš in Prague; wrote a symph.; a violin concerto; a piano concerto (Teplice, Jan. 21, 1963); ballad-opera, *Juraj Čup* (Prague, April 27, 1963).

Cererols, Joan, Catalan composer; b. Martorell, Sept. 9, 1618; d. Montserrat, Aug. 28, 1676. In 1636 he entered the Monastery of Montserrat; studied organ and violin there. He wrote a great number of sacred vocal works. The Monastery of Montserrat publ. in its series *Música Instrumental,* his Psalms and Vespers (vol. I, 1930), masses (vol. II, 1931) and villancicos (vol. III, 1932), edited by Dom David Pujol.

Cerha, Friedrich, Austrian composer; b. Vienna, Feb. 17, 1926. He studied violin with Vasa Prihoda and composition with Alfred Uhl; took courses in musicology at the Univ. of Vienna. Upon graduation he became active in the modernistic movement as violinist, conductor and composer. In 1958 he organized in Vienna a concert ensemble 'Die Reihe' devoted to modern music. In 1960 he became director of the electronic studios at the Vienna Music Academy. His music pursues the aim of "atomization of thematic materials" as a means toward total integration of infinitesimal compositional quantities, with minimal variations of successive temporal units. Works: *Espressioni fondamentali* for orch. (Berlin, Nov. 17, 1960); *Relazioni fragili* for harpsichord and chamber orchestra (Vienna, May 16, 1960); *Enjambements* for 6 performers (Paris, March 7, 1962); *Mouvements* for chamber orchestra (Berlin, March 16, 1962); *Intersecazioni* for violin and orch. (1961); *Phantasma 63* for chamber ensemble (Vienna, May 25, 1963); *Spiegel I—VI* (1964; *Deux éclats en reflexion* for violin and piano (1956); piano pieces.

Černušák, Gracian. Died in Brno, Oct. 13, 1961.

Chabrier, Emmanuel. Add bibl.: Rollo Myers, *Emmanuel Chabrier and His Circle* (London, 1969).

Chailley, Jacques, French musicologist; b. Paris, March 24, 1910. He studied comp. with Nadia Boulanger, Delvincourt and Busser; musicology with Pirro; taught at the Paris Cons. and at the Sorbonne. Publications: *Histoire musicale du moyen âge* (Paris, 1950; new ed. 1969); *La Musique mediévale* (Paris, 1951); *Précis de Musicologie* (Paris, 1958); *40,000 Ans de Musique* (Paris, 1961; translated into English under the title *40,000 Years of Music: Man in Search of Music,* N. Y., 1964); *The Magic Flute, Masonic Opera* (in English translation, N. Y., 1971). He composed a ballet *La Dame à la Licorne* (1953); several oratorios; a symphony; chamber music; piano pieces.

Chailly, Luciano, Italian composer; b. Ferrara, Jan. 19, 1920. He studied in Bologna and then with Renzo Bossi in Milan; in 1948 took courses with Hindemith in Salzburg. In 1962 he was appointed head of the Rome Television. He composes in a communicative neo-classical idiom with some dodecaphonic incrustations and electronic effects. He wrote the operas *Ferrovia Sopraelevata* (Bergamo, Oct. 1, 1955); *Il Canto del Cigno* (Bologna, Nov. 16, 1957); *Una Domanda di matrimonio,* after Chekhov (Milan, May 22, 1957); *La Riva delle Sirti* (Monte Carlo, March 1, 1959); *Procedura penale* (Como, Sept. 30, 1959); *Il Mantello,* surrealist opera (Florence, May 11, 1960); *Era proibita* (Milan, March 5, 1963); *L'Idiota,* after Dostoyevsky (Rome, Feb. 14, 1970). He also composed music for television.

Chajes, Julius. On Jan. 11, 1970 he celebrated his 30th season as conductor of the Jewish Community Center Orch. in Detroit by the first performance of his new symphonic *Scherzo.*

Chamlee, Mario. Died in Hollywood, Cal., Nov. 13, 1966.

Champagne, Claude. Died in Montreal, Dec. 21, 1965.

Chanler, Theodore Ward. Died in Boston, July 27, 1961.

Charles, Ray, black jazz singer and pianist; b. Albany, Georgia, Sept. 23, 1930. His real nan.e was Ray Charles Robinson, but he changed it to avoid confusion with the boxer Sugar Ray Robinson. He lost his sight in childhood; was educated at the St. Augustine School for the Blind in Florida, where he learned to play clarinet and alto saxophone. His style of performance incorporates 'soul music' of Gospel songs, syncopated urban sound and country balladry. He was twice arrested on narcotics charges (1955 and 1961) but rehabilitated himself. In 1964 he made a world tour.

Charpentier, Jacques, French composer; b. Paris, Oct. 18, 1933. He studied piano and composition with Olivier Messiaen and Tony Aubin; traveled to India where he made a thorough study of Indian music; several of his works contain thematic allusions to Indian ragas. Works: *Symphonie brève* (1958); Concerto for Ondes Martenot and orch. (1960); *72 Etudes karnatiques* for piano (1960); *Quatuor de forme liturgique* for 4 trombones (1960); *La Croisade des pastoreaux,* oratorio for chorus and percussion (1964); *Sinfonia sacra* for string orch. (1965); *Prélude pour la Genèse* for string orch. (1968); *La Femme et son ombre,* mimodrama (Bezançon, Sept. 5, 1968); *Shive Natoraja* (3rd Symphony; Paris, March 2, 1969); *Gavambodi* for saxophone and piano (1969); quartet for Ondes Martenot (1969).

Charpentier, Raymond, French music critic and composer; b. Chartres, Aug. 14, 1880; d. Paris, Dec. 27, 1960. He studied with André Gedalge; in 1910 he became music critic of various Paris periodicals. Among his compositions are *Trois Esquisses symphoniques,* 2 string quartets, a wind quintet, a piano quartet, a viola sonata; also choral works.

Chase, Gilbert. Add data: U.S. Cultural Attaché in Lima, Peru, and Buenos Aires (1951-55); Director, School of Music, Univ.

of Oklahoma (1955-57); U.S. Cultural Attaché in Belgium (1958-60); Prof. of Music, Tulane Univ., New Orleans (1960-66); Editor of the *Yearbook for Inter-American Musical Research* from 1965. In 1971, made his home in Italy. Add to publications: *The American Composer Speaks: A Historical Anthology* (N. Y., 1966); *Music in Latin America* (with Gerard Béhague; N. Y., 1972).

Chasins, Abram. He publ. the books, *Speaking of Pianists* (N. Y., 1958) and *The Van Cliburn Legend* (N. Y., 1959).

Chausson, Ernest. See Jean Gallois, *Ernest Chausson: l'Homme et son œuvre* (Paris, 1967).

Chauvet, Charles-Alexis, French organist and composer; b. Marines (Seine-et-Oise), July 7, 1837; d. Argentan (Orne), Jan. 28, 1871. He studied organ and composition at the Paris Cons.; in 1869 he was appointed to the important post of chief organist at the Trinité in Paris. He published numerous organ works and piano pieces adaptable for teachers, students and performers.

Chavarri, Eduardo López. Died in Valencia, Spain, Oct. 28, 1970. Date of birth, Jan. 31, 1871 (not 1875).

Chávez, Carlos. In 1958-59 he was Charles Eliot Norton Lecturer at Harvard Univ.; his lectures were publ. in book form under the title, *Musical Thought* (Cambridge, Mass., 1960). Add to works: opera, *Panfilo and Lauretta,* first produced in English (N. Y. May 9, 1957); then revised and produced in a Spanish version, as *El Amor propiciado* (Mexico City, Oct. 28, 1959); Symph. No. 6 (N. Y., May 7, 1964); *Resonancias* for orch. (Mexico City, Sept. 18, 1964); *Elatio* for orch. (Mexico City, July 15, 1967); *Discovery* for orch. (Aptos, Calif., Aug. 24, 1969); *Clio,* symph. ode (Houston, Texas, March 23, 1970). In his instrumental pieces under the generic title *Invention* (No. 1, for piano, 1958; No. 2, for string trio, 1965; No. 3, for harp, 1967) he introduces an inductive method of thematic illation in which each musical phrase is the logical consequent of the one immediately preceding it. His *Sinfonia de Antigona,* derived from his ballet, *Antigona,* was first performed in this symphonic version in Mexico City on Dec. 15, 1933. His early symphony was written in 1918 (not 1919). He was in Europe in 1922-23; in the U.S., 1923-24, 1926-28, 1932, 1935-36, and regularly in subsequent years. Bibl.: R. G. Morillo, *Carlos Chávez, vida y obra* (Buenos Aires, 1960).

Chenoweth, Wilbur, American pianist, organist and composer; b. Tecumseh, Nebraska, June 4, 1899. He studied piano with Sigismund Stojowski and Alexander Lambert in N. Y.; organ and comp. with Pietro Yon. In 1938 he moved to Los Angeles. He composed numerous effective piano pieces (*Concert Waltz; Cortege); choruses (Of The Father's Love Begotten; God of Comfort; Noel, Noel, Bells are Ringing; Rise, Men Courageous*); songs (*Vocalise, The Arrow and The Song*). Among his works in larger forms is *Fiesta* for piano and orch. (also for two pianos).

Cherbuliez, Antoine-Élisée. Died in Zürich, Oct. 15, 1964.

Cherubini, Luigi. Add to bibl.: Basil Deane, *Cherubini* (London, 1965).

Chevillard, Camille. He was assistant conductor of the Lamoureux Concerts in 1897 (not from 1886 to 1897) and succeeded Lamoureux as conductor in 1898 (not 1897), having married his daughter.

Chiari, Giuseppe, Italian composer of extreme avant-garde tendencies; b. Florence, Sept. 26, 1926. He studied piano; organized a group 'Musica e Segno' in association with Sylvano Bussotti; participated in the festival 'Fluxus' in Wiesbaden (1962), in avant-garde manifestations in New York (1964) and at the Centre de Musique in Paris (1965). Eventually he returned to Florence, where he owned a clothing store. In his productions he follows the most latitudinarian and disestablishmentarian trends of metadadaistic fragmentationarianism both in tonal and verbal structures. He publ. *Musica senza contrappunto,* a varitype anthology of disjected observations (Rome, 1969). In it he launched the slogan 'Musica gestuale,' which deals with audio-visual and tactile events, volitional as well as aleatory. His works include: *Intervalli* for piano (1956); *Per arco* for cello (1962); *Teatrino* for actor-pianist, rubber dolls, alarm clocks and a handsaw (1963); *Don't Trade Here* for action theater (1965).

Chihara, Paul, American composer of Japanese descent; b. Seattle, July 9, 1938. After the outbreak of the war, his family was relocated, among many other Japanese Americans, to Minadoka, Idaho. He studied piano as a child; took courses in English literature at the Univ. of Washington (B.A., 1960) and at Cornell Univ. (M.A., 1961); then went to Europe, where he studied composition with Nadia Boulanger in Paris (1962-63); and with Ernst Pepping in West Berlin (1965-66);

in the interim he obtained his A.M.D., at Cornell Univ. (1965). In 1966 he joined the music faculty of the Univ. of California, Los Angeles; traveled to Japan for research in 1967. In his music he utilizes advanced forms of serial techniques, occasionally extending them to aleatory procedures. In his choral compositions he follows the time-honored polyphonic methods of the Renaissance. Works: viola concerto (1965); string quartet (1965); *Tree Music* for 3 violas and 3 trombones (1966); *Branches* for 2 bassoons and percussion (1966); *Magnificat* for treble voices (1966); *The 90th Psalm,* a choral cantata (1966); *Nocturne* for 24 solo voices (1966); *Redwood* for viola and percussion (1967); *Willow, Willow* for bass flute, tuba and percussion (1968); *Rain Music,* a tape collage using brewery noises, commissioned by Rainier Breweries in Seattle (1968); *Forest Music* for orch. (1968; Los Angeles, May 2, 1971); *Driftwood* for violin, 2 violas and cello (1969); *Logs XVI* for amplified string bass and magnetic tape (1970).

Childs, Barney, American composer; b. Spokane, Washington, Feb. 13, 1926. He studied sporadically and intermittently with Leonard Ratner, Carlos Chávez, Aaron Copland and Elliott Carter; obtained a B.A. degree in English from the Univ. of Nevada, (1949); M.A. from Oxford Univ. as a Rhodes Scholar (1955); and Ph.D. at Stanford Univ., both in English and in Music (1959). He taught English at the Univ. of Arizona (1956-65); was Dean of Deep Springs College (1965-69). In 1969-71 he taught theory at Wisconsin College Cons. in Milwaukee. Not overly concerned with public tastes and current fashions of cosmopolitan styles in music he cultivates indeterminate structures. An exceptionally prolific composer he has written two symphonies (1954, 1956); 7 string quartets (1951-68); 5 wind quintets (1951-69); violin sonata (1950); sonata for solo clarinet (1951); *Concerto da camera* for trumpet and woodwinds (1951); trio for flute, oboe, and clarinet (1952); quartet for clarinet and strings (1953); sonata for bassoon and piano (1953); *Four Involutions* for solo English horn (1955); *Five Considerations* for solo French horn (1955); *7 Epigrams* for soprano and clarinet (1955); *Concerto* for English horn, strings, harp and percussion (1955); 2nd violin sonata (1956); quartet for bassoons (1958); sonata for solo oboe (1958); brass trio (1959); flute sonata (1960); sonata for solo trombone (1961); 6 pieces under the generic title *Interbalances* (1941-64) for various groups; *Take 5* for 5 instruments (1962); *Stances* for flute and silence (1963); quartet for flute, oboe, double-bass and percussion (1964); *Music for Double-bass and Friend* (1964); *6 Events* for band (1965); *Music for Piano and Strings* (1965); *Jack's New Bag* for 10 players (1966); *The Golden Bubble* for contrabass sarrusophone and percussion (1967); nonet (1967); *Operation Flabby Sleep* for any instruments (1968); *Music for 6 tubas* (1969); *Keet Seel* for chorus a cappella (1970); concerto for clarinet and orch. (1970).

Chisholm, Erik. Died in Rondebosch, South Africa, June 8, 1965. His book, *The Operas of Leoš Janáček* was publ posthumously (N. Y., 1971).

Chopin, (François-) Frédéric. The weight of evidence seems to indicate that he was born on March 1, 1810, the date given out by Chopin himself in his letter of acceptance of membership in the Polish Literary Society in Paris in 1833; the date of Feb. 22, 1810 is contained in the certificate of baptism, but appears to be an error. See A. Hedley, *Selected Correspondence of F. Chopin* (London, 1962).

Chorbajian, John, American composer; b. New York, June 2, 1936. He studied composition with Vittorio Giannini at the Manhattan School of Music, obtaining his M.M. in 1959. Subsequently he became active as a teacher of piano and music theory in New York. • His works include: violin sonata (1956); *Antigone,* one-act opera (1959); *The Magic of Music,* scene for mime with orchestra (1960); *The Crucifixion,* cantata for mixed chorus and orch. (1962); *The Swing* for children's chorus, flute and piano (1966); numerous choral pieces.

Chotzinoff, Samuel. Died in New York, Feb. 9, 1964. His autobiography, under the title *Day's at the Morn* and his book, *A Little Night Music* were publ. posthumously in 1964.

Chou, Wen-chung. Born on May 16, 1923, according to the lunar calendar in the Chinese Year of the Boar, which corresponds to June 29 (not July 28), 1923 of the Western calendar.

Christou, Jani, Greek composer; b. Heliopolis, Egypt, Jan. 9, 1926; died in an automobile accident, near Athens, Jan. 8, 1970. He studied philosophy at King's College in Cambridge, England, and took music lessons with Hans Redlich in Letchworth; then studied with Lavagnino in Siena, Italy. In 1956 he settled on the island of Chios, with frequent sojourns in Athens. As a composer, he developed a highly original style, dynamic and lyric in essence, with a superstructure of asymmetrical rhythmic patterns. Works: *Phoenix Music* for orchestra (1949); First Symphony (1950; London, April 29, 1951); Mass for mixed chorus, brass and percussion (1953); *Six Songs* for voice and orchestra, to poems by T. S. Eliot (1957; originally for voice and piano); *Patterns and Permutations* for orch. (1960; Athens, March 11, 1963); *Toccata* for piano and orch. (1962); *Tongues of Fire,* Pentecost oratorio (Oxford, June 27, 1964); *The Strychnine Lady,* for mixed media (Athens, April 8, 1967). In his last compositions he extended the field of music to embrace a totality of human and metaphysical expression, for which he designed a surrealistic graphic notation, indicating a 'psychoid factor' by the Greek letter psi, aleatory practices by a pair of dice, a sudden stop by a dagger, etc. His score *Enantiodromia* (1968), in such a graphic notation, is reproduced in the avant-garde publication 'Source' (No. 6, 1969). Christou's 'conceptual' work *Epicycle* (1968) is 'open-ended,' and may take a chiliad or a hebdomad, a nanosecond or a quindecillion of non-zero moments to perform.

Christov, Dimiter, Bulgarian composer; b. Sofia, Oct. 2, 1933. He studied composition with Goleminov at the Sofia Cons.; subsequently taught there. Among his works are a symphony (Sofia, Oct. 15, 1959); a symphonietta; several orchestral suites; chamber music.

Ciconia, Jean. Died in Padua (not in Padula).

Cigna, Gina. She taught at the Royal Cons. in Toronto from 1953 to 1957.

Cikker, Jan, Czech composer; b. Banska Bystrica, July 29, 1911. He studied composition with Jaroslav Křička and Vitězslav Novák. In 1951 he was appointed prof. of music of the Cons. of Bratislava. He devoted himself mostly to the theater; composed the operas *Juro Jánošík* (Bratislava, Nov. 10, 1954); *Beg Bajazid* (Bratislava, Feb. 16, 1957); and *Resurrection,* after Tolstoy (Prague, May 18, 1962; written in a highly tense, atonal and romantically expressive modern idiom); *Mr. Scrooge,* after Dickens, produced in a German version under the title, *Abend, Nacht und Morgen* (Kassel, Oct. 5, 1963).

Cilèa, Francesco. He was director of the Majella Cons. in Naples until 1935. Cf. T. d'Amico, *Francesco Cilèa* (Milan, 1960).

Cimara, Pietro. Died in Milan, Oct. 1, 1967.

Ciortea, Tudor, Rumanian composer; b. Brasov, Nov. 15, 1903. He studied in Brussels with Joseph Jongen, in Paris with Paul Dukas and Nadia Boulanger and in Bucharest with Ion Nonna Oteșcu. In 1947 he was appointed prof. of the Bucharest Cons. In his music he follows the models of French Impressionist composers; his songs to texts by Rumanian poets have a fine lyric quality. He wrote much chamber music: a violin sonata (1946); a cello sonata (1948); 2 string quartets (1952, 1954); a piano quintet (1958); a flute sonata (1960); 2 piano sonatas; 2 piano suites on Rumanian folk themes.

Cirino, Giulio, Italian bass singer; b. Rome, Feb. 15, 1880; d. there, Feb. 26, 1970. He made his opera debut in Rome in 1903; subsequently sang at La Scala in Milan; was on the roster of the Teatro Colón in Buenos Aires from 1909 to 1923; retired from the stage in 1935. He was particularly successful in buffo roles, in the Italian repertory; but he also sang in Wagner's operas.

Claflin, (Alan) Avery, American composer; b. Keene, N. H., June 21, 1898. He studied law and banking and pursued a business career. He also took music courses at Harvard Univ. and in Europe; attracted attention by his amusing choral piece, a fiscal madrigal entitled *Lament for April 15,* to the text in toto of an Internal Revenue tax form. Among his other works are the operas *Hester Prynne* (after *The Scarlet Letter* of Hawthorne), of which scene II of Act II was performed at Hartford on Dec. 15. 1934; *The Fall of Usher* (not performed); *La Grande Bretèche,* on Balzac's story (CBS radio, Feb. 3, 1957); *Uncle Tom's Cabin* (1961-64); 2 symphonies; *Teen Scenes* for strings (1955); *Pop Concert Concerto* for piano and orch. (1958); piano trio and other chamber music.

Clark, Edward. Died in London, April 29, 1962.

Clarke, Henry Leland. In 1959 appointed prof. of the Univ. of Washington, Seattle.

Clarke, Hugh Archibald. His father's name was James Paton (not Peyton) Clarke.

Clarke, James Peyton. Second Christian name, Paton (not Peyton). Both St. George's Church and St. Mary's Episcopal Chapel, where he served, were in Glasgow (not in Edinburgh). He settled in Elora (not Ellora);

came to Toronto in 1845 (not in 1841); was not prof. in Upper Canada Univ. (there was no such institution in Toronto).

Clarke, Rebecca. In 1970 she was living in New York after abandoning her career as composer and performer.

Clementi, Aldo, Italian composer of avant-garde tendencies; b. Catania, May 25, 1925. He studied with Petrassi, Maderna and others; then took summer courses in Darmstadt, adopting serialistic techniques. His works include *Collage 1,* 'musical action' for the stage (1959); *Collage 2* for electronic instruments (1960); *Ideogrammi* I and II for orch. (1959); *Informel* I and II for chamber ensemble (1962); *Intavolature* for harpsichord (1963); *Informal III* for orch. (1966).

Cleva, Fausto, Italian conductor; b. Trieste, May 17, 1902; d. Athens (collapsed while conducting), Aug. 6, 1971. He studied in Milan; began his conducting career as a youth; in 1920 emigrated to the U. S.; became an American citizen in 1931. He was chorusmaster and later conductor of the Metropolitan Opera until 1942; then was conductor of the San Francisco Opera Co. (1942-44 and 1949-55); then again with the Metropolitan Opera. In 1971 he was presented with a gold cigarette case by the directors of the Metropolitan Opera on the occasion of his 50th anniversary as a regular member, since the age of 18, of the Metropolitan conducting staff.

Cleve, Halfdan. Died in Oslo, April 6, 1951.

Cliburn, Van (Harvey Lavan, Jr.), American pianist; b. Shreveport, Louisiana, July 12, 1934; studied piano with his mother; then with Rosina Lhévinne at the Juilliard School of Music, N. Y., graduating in 1954. He made his debut with the Houston Symph. Orch. at the age of 13; appeared with the N. Y. Philharmonic in 1954; toured as a concert pianist in the U. S. He became suddenly famous when he won the Tchaikovsky Prize in Moscow in 1958, the first American to score such a triumph in Russia. where he became a prime favorite. Upon his return to New York he received a hero's welcome in a street parade. In 1964 he made his debut as orchestral conductor. His playing combines a superlative technique with a genuine romantic sentiment; this style is particularly effective in the music of Tchaikovsky and Rachmaninoff. See A. Chasins: *The Van Cliburn Legend* (N. Y., 1959).

Clifton, Chalmers. Died in New York, June 19, 1966.

Clokey, Joseph Waddell. Died in Covina, California, Sept. 14, 1960.

Clough-Leighter, Henry. He died on Sept. 15 (not Sept. 25), 1956.

Cluytens, André. Died in Neuilly, near Paris, June 3, 1967.

Cluzeau-Mortet, Luis, Uruguayan composer; b. Montevideo, Nov. 16, 1889; d. there, Sept. 28, 1957. He studied piano and theory with his maternal grandfather, who was the first Uruguayan to receive a prize at the Paris Cons. Cluzeau-Mortet played piano and the viola in radio bands in Montevideo and composed industriously. His music is marked by romantic influences, with occasional excursions into prudential modernism. All of his orchestral works were first performed by the Radio orch. SODRE, in Montevideo, of which he was a member. Among them are *Llanuras* (Oct. 14, 1944); *Rancherío* (Aug. 2, 1947); *Artigas* (Aug. 13, 1955); *Sinfonía del Este* (unfinished; a movement *La Laguna negra* was played on Aug. 16, 1958, as a posthumous act of homage); he further wrote a *Fantasía Concerto* for piano and chamber orch.; *4 Ritmos criollos* for string quartet; *Bagatelas criollas* for 4 flutes; songs and piano pieces. A complete catalogue of his works is found in Vol. 14 of the series *Compositores de América* (Washington, D. C., 1968).

Coates, Albert. He made his American debut on Dec. 30, 1920 (not 1921).

Coates, Eric. Died in Chichester, Dec 21, 1957.

Cobbett, Walter Wilson. A supplementary 3rd volume of Cobbett's *Cyclopedic Survey of Chamber Music* was publ. in London, 1963.

Cockshott, Gerald Wilfred, English composer; b. Bristol, Nov. 14, 1915. He took courses in English literature at the Univ. of Bristol; was head of the English Dept. at Whittingehame College, Brighton (1948-64) and at Ifield Grammar School, Crawley, Sussex (from 1965). He studied composition privately with Vaughan Williams; became active primarily as a writer on musical subjects. His music is transparently tonal, and is impressed with melorhythms of English folksongs; but its simplicity is of a sophisticated nature. Works: one-act operas *Apollo and Persephone* (1952) and *A Faun in the Forest* (1958); Symph. in B minor (1949); *Serenade* for flute and string orch. (1952); *Maddermarket Suite* for orch. (1953); *Divertimento* for orch. (1960); *3 Pieces on Appalachian Folk Tunes* for cello and piano (1962); Duo for clarinet and bassoon on a Handel theme (1964); songs; carols; choruses; numerous arrangements of American, English, French-Canadian, Danish and Dutch songs.

Coerne, Louis Adolphe. *Zenobia* was not the first opera by an American composer to be produced in Europe; it was preempted by William Legrand Howland's *Sarrona,* given in Bruges on Aug. 3, 1903.

Cogan, Robert, American composer; b. Detroit, Feb. 2, 1930. He studied at the Univ. of Michigan (M. M., 1952), at the Berkshire Music Center (1953) and at Princeton Univ. (1953-56); attended Philipp Jarnach's seminar in Hamburg (1958-60). Works: string quartet (1950); *Fantasia* for orch. (1951); viola sonata (1953); string trio No. 1 (1955); string trio No. 2 (1959); *Sounds and Variants* for piano (1961); *Spaces and Cries* for 5 brass instruments (1964); *Whirl . . ds I* for voice, 44 instruments and a microphonist, to words by the composer (1967).

Cohen, Harriet. Died in London, Nov. 13, 1967. She was not created Dame, but received the order of Dame Commander of the British Empire. Her book of memoirs, entitled *A Bundle of Time,* was published posthumously in London in 1967.

Cohn, Arthur. He publ. 2 books: *The Collector's Twentieth-Century Music in the Western Hemisphere* (N.Y., 1961) and *Twentieth-Century Music in Western Europe* (N. Y., 1965); also *Musical Quizzical* (77 puzzles; N.Y., 1970; dedicated 'to the most sagacious and needle-witted musician I know').

Coker, Wilson, American composer; b. Pinckneyville, Illinois, Nov. 26, 1928. He studied at the St. Louis Institute of Music; then at Yale Univ. In 1971 he was chairman of the Music Dept. at Fresno State College. He publ. a book on esthetics, *Music and Meaning* (1971). Compositions: 2 string quartets (1949, 1954); *Duo Concertante* for trumpet and harpsichord (1951); woodwind quintet (1955); *Analogies* for orch. (1957); Symph. No. 1 (1958); Concertino for bassoon and string trio (1959); *Lyric Statement* for orch. (1960); *Declarative Essay* for orch. (1960); *Overture Giocosa* (1961).

Cole, Nat "King" (Nathaniel Adams Coles), black American pianist and singer; b. Montgomery, Alabama, March 17, 1917; d. Santa Monica, Cal., Feb. 15, 1965. He worked as jazz pianist in Los Angeles night clubs; in 1939 formed the original King Cole Trio (piano, guitar, bass); then turned to singing. He was the first Negro artist to acquire a sponsor on a radio program; also had a brief series on television. He created a distinct style of velvet vocalization and satin softness in the rendition of intimate, brooding and sentimental songs. His appeal was universal; his tours in South America, Europe, the Middle East and Orient attracted great multitudes of admirers who knew him by his recordings. The sole exception was his native state; at his concert in Birmingham, Alabama, on April 10, 1956, he was attacked by six white men and suffered a minor back injury.

Coleman, Ornette, black American jazz alto saxophonist and composer; b. Ft. Worth, Texas, March 19, 1930. He was autodidact; served his apprenticeship playing in carnival and 'rhythm and blues' bands. His own studies of harmony and theory led him to develop a distinctive style in which the improvisational melodic line is independent of the pre-assigned harmonic scheme. He also writes concert music in a respectable modernistic idiom.

Colgrass, Michael (Charles), American composer; b. Chicago, April 22, 1932. He studied at the Univ. of Illinois (Mus. B., 1956); attended classes at the Berkshire Music Center in Tanglewood (1952-54). His principal teachers were Darius Milhaud, Lukas Foss, Wallingford Riegger and Ben Weber. A percussion player by profession, he was employed in various ensembles in N. Y. In his own music, percussion plays a significant melorhythmic role. He also studied theater arts, including special techniques of the Commedia dell' Arte of the Piccolo Teatro of Milan and physical training for actors at the Polish Theater Laboratory; wrote drama and poetry. He received the Guggenheim Fellowship Awards in 1964 and 1968; was a beneficiary of several other grants as well. Works: *Chamber Music* for 4 drums and string quartet (1954); percussion quintet (1955); *Divertimento* for 8 drums, piano and strings (1960); *Rhapsody* for clarinet, violin and piano (1962); *Light Spirit* for flute, viola, guitar and percussion (1963); *Sea Shadow* for orch. (1966); *As Quiet As* for orch. (1966); *New People,* song cycle for mezzo-soprano, viola and piano (1969); *The Earth's a Baked Apple* for chorus and orch. (1969).

Collaer, Paul. Add to books: *A History of Modern Music* (amplified edition of *La Musique moderne,* N.Y., 1963).

Collette, Buddy, black American jazz flutist and composer; b. Los Angeles, Calif., Aug. 6, 1922. He studied composition with Ernest Kanitz. He played flute with Henry Mancini, Quincy Jones and Benny Carter bands; appeared at the San Remo Festival, Italy, in 1962. He favors the West Coast jazz style in an eloquently cool technique; his song *Blue Sands* has become a jazz standard.

Coltrane, John William, black American tenor saxophonist; b. Hamlet, North Carolina, Sept. 23, 1926; d. Huntington, Long Island, N.Y., July 17, 1967. He studied at the Ornstein School of Music, Philadelphia; played in the bands of Dizzy Gillespie, Johnny Hodges, Miles Davis and Thelonious Monk. His style is marked by a vital rhythmic drive, at the same time maintaining leisurely phraseology of the melodic line.

Comissiona, Sergiu, Rumanian conductor; b. Bucharest, June 16, 1928. He studied violin and theory in Bucharest; conducting with Constantin Silvestri. He was one of the principal conductors of the Rumanian State Opera and the Bucharest Philharmonic; subsequently conducted the Haifa Symph. Orch. (1959); was guest conductor with the London Philharmonic (1960-63), the Stockholm Philharmonic (1964-66), Berlin Radio Symph. Orch. (1965-67); also was guest conductor with major symphony orchestras in the U.S. In 1969 he was appointed musical director and conductor of the Baltimore Symph. Orch.

Commette, Édouard. Died in Lyons, April 21, 1967.

Connolly, Justin Riveagh, English composer; b. London, Aug. 11, 1933. He studied composition with Peter Racine Fricker at the Royal College of Music in London; held a Harkness Fellowship at Yale Univ. (1963-65); was instructor in music theory there in 1965-66. Returning to London, he joined the faculty of his alma mater; was also at various times engaged as conductor. He associated himself with the avant-garde; was greatly influenced by new American methods, particularly the theory of combinatoriality of Milton Babbitt and the practice of metrical modulation of Elliott Carter; beginning with 1968 he made use of electronic sound. His works are often arranged in sets unified by a generic title and a numerical rubric; they include several *Triads* (i. e., trios): *Triad I* for trumpet, viola and piano; *Triad II* for double-bass, piano and percussion; *Triad III* for oboe, viola and cello; *Triad IV* for flute, two percussion instruments and recorded sounds; *Triad V* for clarinet, viola and cello. Another set bears the general title *Obbligati: I* for 13 players; *II* for flute, clarinet, violin, cello and electronics; *III* for 20 players. Other works are: *Poems of Wallace Stevens: I* for soprano and 7 players; *II* for soprano, flute and piano; *III* for soprano, piano and electronics; 2 compositions entitled *Tesserae: I* for oboe and harpsichord; *II* for flute and piano; *Phases-Phrases* for 48 solo players; *Antiphonies* for 36 players; *Cinquepaces* for brass quintet; *M-piriform* (with reference to the piriform muscle of the thigh) for soprano, flute, violin and electronic instruments. He also wrote an overture *Rebus* for the 95th birthday of Havergal Brian in 1971, constructed on rhythmic figures of 5 and 19 units as factors of 95.

Constantinesco, Paul. Died in Bucharest, Dec. 20, 1963. Add to works: opera, *Pana Lesnea* (Bucharest, June 27, 1956).

Conus, Julius. Exact date of birth, Feb. 1, 1869; died at Malenki, Ivanov District (not in Moscow) on Jan. 3, 1942.

Conus, Sergey, Russian pianist and composer, son of Julius Conus; b. Moscow, Oct. 18, 1902. He studied music with his father, with his uncle, Leo Conus, and with Oskar Riesemann. In 1920 he went to Paris where he studied piano with Cortot and Isidor Philipp; then lived in Serbia, Bulgaria and Poland. He was again in France from 1937 to 1949, and in Morocco from 1949 to 1959; in 1959 settled in America; taught piano at the Boston Cons. His compositions are mostly for piano (24 preludes, many miniatures, a piano concerto); he also wrote a symphony. His style is characteristically Russian, closely resembling that of Rachmaninoff.

Converse, Frederick Shepherd. His opera, *The Pipe of Desire,* was first performed at the Metropolitan Opera on March 18, 1910 (not 1909).

Cooke, Arnold. Add to works: clarinet concerto (1955); oboe sonata (1957); violin concerto (1958); clarinet sonata (1959); Suite for 3 clarinets (1959); *Jabez and the Devil,* ballet (1961); clarinet quintet (1962); *Variations on a Theme of Dufay* for orch. (1966); Symph. No. 2 (1963); Symph. No. 3 (1967); piano quintet (1970).

Cooke, Deryck, English musicologist; b. Leicester, Sept. 14, 1919. He studied piano privately and composition at Cambridge Univ. with Patrick Hadley and Robin Orr, earning his B.A. in 1940, M.A. in 1943, and Mus. B. in 1947. From 1947 to 1959 he was a member of the music staff of the BBC; after 1959, devoted most of his time to writing on music and broadcasting. He attracted considerable attention by his scholarly and congenial arrangement of Mahler's unfinished Tenth Symphony, which he completed using authentic fragments from Mahler's sketch; this version was approved by Alma Mahler, the composer's widow. It was first performed at a BBC Henry Wood Promenade Concert in the Albert Hall, London, on Aug. 13, 1964, with Berthold Goldschmidt conducting the London Symph. Orch. Cooke is the author of *The Language of Music* (London, 1959) and *Mahler 1860-1911* (BBC centenary booklet, 1960). He contributed Part I to vol. X of the *New Oxford History of Music;* also wrote reviews for 'The Listener,' weekly publication of the BBC.

Cooke, James Francis. Died in Philadelphia, March 3, 1960.

Cooley, Spade (Donnell), American country fiddler, once renowned as 'King of Western Swing'; b. in a storm cellar under a shack near Saddle Paddle Creek, Oklahoma, Dec. 17, 1910; d. Oakland, Cal., Nov. 23, 1969, while on a furlough from the Calif. State Medical Facility at Bakersfield, the minimum security state prison where he was confined from 1961 for the murder of his wife Ella Mae. Cooley was one-quarter Cherokee Indian; he joined the cowboy star Roy Rogers in Hollywood in his act, and acquired the nickname 'Spade' after a spectacular poker game during which he filled several successive flushes in spades. He replenished his financial resources from these winnings, and went into the real estate business. He is credited with the authorship of the song *Shame, Shame on You.*

Cooper, Emil. Died in New York, Nov. 16, 1960.

Coopersmith, Jacob Maurice. Died in Washington, May 12, 1968.

Copland, Aaron. He was head of the Composition Dept. at the Berkshire Music Center at Tanglewood from 1940 to 1965, and from 1957 to 1965 was chairman of the faculty. His film score for *The Heiress* won an Academy Award. On July 4, 1964, he was awarded the Medal of Freedom by the U.S. Government. He studied composition and orchestration with Nadia Boulanger (not harmony and counterpoint, which he had studied previously with Rubin Goldmark in N.Y.). Delete the indefinite article in *A Lincoln Portrait,* as it does not appear in the title page of the printed score (but most orchestral program books list the work as *A Lincoln Portrait); Music for Radio* was not renamed *Saga of the Prairie;* the latter was its subtitle. *Danzón Cubano* did not win the New York Critics Award for 1947; it was the *Third Symphony* that won it. *Five Kings* was incidental music for a play, not a motion picture. *Quiet City* was music for a play, not for a film. The date of first performance of *Fanfare for the Common Man* is March 12 (not 14), 1943. Add to works: *Old American Songs* for voice and orch. (2 sets; 1950, 1952); *Piano Fantasy* (1957); *Nonet* for strings (1960; Georgetown, D. C., March 2, 1961); *Connotations* for orch., written entirely in the 12-tone technique (first performed, as a commissioned work, in Philharmonic Hall, Lincoln Center, N.Y., at its inauguration, Sept. 23, 1962); *Dance Panels* in 7 movements, ballet (Munich, Dec. 3, 1963); *Music for a Great City,* symph. suite descriptive of life in New York City (London, May 26, 1964; composer conducting the London Symph.); *Inscape* for orch., commissioned by the N.Y. Philharmonic (first performance at the Univ. of Mich., Ann Arbor, Sept. 13, 1967, Leonard Bernstein conducting the N.Y. Philharmonic). Add to publications: *Copland on Music* (N.Y., 1960); *The New Music 1900-1960,* revised and enlarged edition (N. Y., 1968). See special issue of 'Tempo' (London, 1970-71) devoted to Copland on the occasion of his 70th birthday.

Coppola, Piero. Died in Lausanne, March 13, 1971.

Cordero, Roque. He adopted the dodecaphonic idiom in 1948. Add to works: Symph. No. 2 (1956); string quartet (1960); cello sonata (1962); violin concerto (1962).

Cordon, Norman. Died in Chapel Hill, N. C., March 1, 1964.

Corelli, Franco, Italian tenor; b. Ancona, April 8, 1923. He learned to sing by imitating great voices on the phonograph; advanced rapidly in his career after a modest debut in Spoleto in 1952. He sang at La Scala, Milan, in 1953; made his first appearance at the Metropolitan Opera in New York on Jan. 27, 1961; thenceforth made successful tours all over the world.

Corigliano, John, American violinist; b. New York, Aug. 28, 1901. He studied with

Leopold Auer in New York; gave violin recitals; in 1935 he was appointed assistant concert master of the New York Philharmonic, and in 1943 concertmaster; he resigned his position in 1966 and joined the San Antonio Symphony in the same capacity.

Corigliano, John, American composer; son of the violinist John Corigliano; b. New York, Feb. 16, 1938. He studied at Columbia Univ. with Otto Luening (B.A., 1959), with Vittorio Giannini at the Manhattan School of Music, and privately with Paul Creston. He was subsequently employed as script writer for radio station WQXR in New York and as assistant director for musical television shows there; later he was in charge of the music section at WBAI. He held the Guggenheim Fellowship in 1968-69. His style of composition shows a fine capacity for lyrical expression, and an incisive sense of rhythm, in the generic tradition of Béla Bartók and Prokofiev. Despite the dissonant freedom of his polyphonic writing, his music retains a firm tonal anchorage. Works: *Kaleidoscope* for two pianos (1959); *Pastorale* for cello and piano (1958); *Fern Hill* for chorus and orch. to words by Dylan Thomas (N.Y., Dec. 19, 1961); violin sonata (1963; received first prize in the Spoleto Festival Competition of 1964); *The Cloisters,* a cycle of songs (1965); *Elegy* for orch. (San Francisco, June 1, 1966); *Tournaments Overture* (1967); piano concerto (San Antonio, Texas, April 5, 1968); *Poem in October* for tenor and 8 instruments (1969); incidental music for Molière's *Le Malade imaginaire,* Sheridan's *The Rivals,* Sophocles' *Oedipus Rex,* Brecht's *Galileo;* also special scores for the New York Shakespeare Festival of 1970. He arranged Bizet's *Carmen* for singers, rock and pop groups, Moog Synthesizer and instruments, issued on record under the title *The Naked Carmen.*

Corner, Philip, American composer; b. New York, April 10, 1933. He studied piano; began composing autogenetically at 13, gestated a 3-minute piano piece in 9 months; learned to play the trombone. In 1955 he went to Paris where he took a course in musical philosophy with Olivier Messiaen; spent a year in Korea studying Oriental calligraphy in order to apply it to the needs of graphic music notation. In 1958 he turned to serial music, but mitigated its stern doctrines by aleatory indeterminacy; he often composes works after their first performances so as to avoid the stigma of premeditation. The titles of his compositions show a surrealistic flavor: *Passionate Expanse of the Law, Certain Distilling Processes, Expressions in Parallel, Air Effect,* and *Music Reserved Until Now.* In his *Punishment Piece,* using the naked strings of a grand piano, musical material is determined by tossing spotted transparent paper on the manuscript. In 1965 he composed a timeless piece for indefinitely prolonged chanting on a single note. In 1968 he verbalized a work with the injunction: 'One anti-personnel type CBU bomb will be thrown into the audience,' publ. in 'Source' (No. 6, Sacramento, Calif., 1969), but never performed.

Correa de Araujo, Francisco. Date and place of death, Segovia, Feb., 1655. He was organist in Seville (1599-1636), in Jaén (1636-40) and in Segovia (1640-54). See Robert Stevenson, *Francisco Correa de Arauxo* ('Revista Musical Chilena,' Jan.-March, 1968).

Cortes, Ramiro, American composer of Mexican extraction; b. Dallas, Texas, Nov. 25, 1933. He studied with Henry Cowell in New York and at the Univ. of Southern California with Halsey Stevens and Ingolf Dahl. From 1956 to 1958 he was in Rome on a Fulbright Fellowship Award; there he studied with Petrassi. Returning to America in 1959 he took lessons with Roger Sessions at Princeton Univ. Works: *Elegy* for flute and piano (1952); *Divertimento* for flute, clarinet and bassoon (1953); piano quintet (1953); piano sonata (1954; awarded Steinway Centennial prize); *Sinfonia Sacra* for orch. (1954; received George Gershwin Memorial Award; N. Y. Philharmonic, April 9, 1955; revised in 1959); *Night Music* for chamber orch. (1954; received first prize of Broadcast Music Incorporated Awards); *Yerma,* symph. portrait after a play by García Lorca (1955); *Xochitl* for orch. (1955; Hollywood, April 22, 1956); Chamber Concerto for cello solo and 12 wind instruments (1958; first prize of Broadcast Music Incorporated Awards); symphony (1953-58); *Sinfonia breve* (1955-58); string quartet (1958); piano trio (1959); *Prometheus,* opera in one act (1960).

Cortot, Alfred (Denis). Died in Lausanne, June 15, 1962.

Cosma, Viorel, Rumanian musicologist; b. Timişoara, March 30, 1923. He studied composition with Mihail Jora, Ion Dumitrescu, Paul Constantinesco, Theodor Rogalski; musicology with Zeno Vancea. He was active as a choral conductor and teacher; then devoted himself mainly to music criticism; publ. several valuable monographs on Rumanian musicians (Ciprian Porumbescu, Ion Ivanovici, and others). He compiled a uniquely useful biographical dictionary of Rumanian composers and musicologists, *Muzicien Români Lexicon* (Bucharest, 1965; revised and augmented edition, 1970).

Cossetto, Emil, Croatian composer; b. Trieste, Oct. 12, 1918. He studied in Zagreb. His compositions, based mostly on patriotic themes, include *Borbena Kantata* (*Cantata of the Struggle,* 1947), inspired by the wartime resistance in Yugoslavia; *Zagreb Cantata* (Zagreb, May 7, 1950); *Konjanik,* a 'cavalcade' for men's voices and orch. (Zagreb, Dec. 9, 1957); numerous choruses.

Cossotto, Fiorenza, Italian contralto; b. Crescentino, Vercelli, near Turin, April 22, 1935. She studied at the Turin Cons.; sang at La Scala as a student; at the Vienna State Opera, in Covent Garden, London, in Paris, in South America, and in Russia. She made her American debut in 1964 at the Lyric Opera in Chicago; was soloist in Verdi's *Requiem* in N. Y. with the orchestra of the Teatro alla Scala during its American visit in 1967. In 1968 she sang Amneris at her Metropolitan Opera debut. Among her most successful roles was that of Santuzza in *Cavalleria Rusticana.* She is married to the Italian bass Ivo Vinco.

Cotapos, Acario, Chilean composer; b. Valdivia, April 30, 1889; d. Santiago, Nov. 22, 1969. He studied music in Santiago; in 1916 went to New York where he took lessons with 10 teachers, among them Ernest Bloch. He lived in France until 1936; then went to Spain to work in defense of the Loyalists during the Spanish Civil War; in 1939 he returned to Chile. An experimenter by nature, he adopted an advanced quasi-serial technique of monothematic mottoes of 8 or more notes. He wrote a music drama *Voces de Gesta* (1933); several symphonic preludes; a string quartet; piano pieces.

Cottlow, Augusta. Her memoir, *My Years with Busoni,* was published in 'The Musical Observer' (not 'The Musician'), in an issue of June, 1925.

Coulthard, Jean, Canadian pianist and composer; b. Vancouver, Feb. 10, 1908. She studied piano with her mother; in 1929 went to London where she studied composition with Vaughan Williams; returning to Vancouver, she took lessons with Arthur Benjamin; also at various times was a student of Schoenberg, Darius Milhaud and Copland. In 1947 she joined the staff of the newly created department of music at the Univ. of British Columbia. Works: *Canadian Fantasy* for orch. (1939); *Song of the Sea,* overture (1942); Symph. No. 1 (1950); violin concerto (1959); piano concerto (1963); 2 string quartets; cello sonata; oboe sonata; *4 Bizarre Dances* for violin and piano; *Sonata-Rhapsody* for viola and piano; song cycles.

Coward, Noël. He was knighted in 1970.

Cowell, Henry Dixon. Died in Shady, New York, Dec. 10, 1965. Add to works: 12th symph. (Houston, March 28, 1960); 13th symph. surnamed *Madras Symphony* (Madras, India, March 3, 1959); 14th symph. (Washington, April 27, 1961); 15th symph. (N. Y., Nov. 5, 1962); 16th symph. (*Icelandic Symphony;* Reykjavik, March 21, 1963); 17th symph. (1963); 18th symph. (1964); 19th symph. (1965); Concerto for koto and orch. (N.Y., Dec. 18, 1964). See Hugo Weisgall, *The Music of Henry Cowell* in the 'Mus. Quarterly' (Oct. 1959).

Cowles, Cecil Marion. Died in New York, March 28, 1968.

Cowles, Walter Ruel. Died in Tallahassee, Florida, Dec. 8, 1959.

Crabbé, Armand. Date of birth, April 23, 1883 (not 1884); date of death, July 24 (not Sept. 14), 1947.

Craft, Marcella. Died in Riverside, Cal., Dec. 12, 1959.

Craft, Robert. Collaborated with Igor Stravinsky on 6 volumes of a catechumenical and discursive nature: *Conversations with Igor Stravinsky* (N. Y., 1959); *Memories and Commentaries* (N. Y., 1960); *Expositions and Developments* (N. Y., 1962); *Dialogues and a Diary* (N. Y., 1963); *Themes and Episodes* (N. Y., 1967); *Retrospections and Conclusions* (N. Y., 1969). Resentful of frequent referral to him as a musical Boswell, Craft insists that his collaboration with Stravinsky was more akin to that between the Goncourt brothers, both acting and reacting to an emerging topic of discussion, with Stravinsky evoking his colorful ancient memories in careful, yet lapidary English, or fluent French, rich in linguistic esoterica mainly derived from Stravinsky's cultural legacy of Greek and Latin studies, spiced with unrestrained discourtesies towards professional colleagues on the American scene, and Craft reifying the material with an often analeptic bulimia of quaquaversal literary, psychological, physiological and culinary references in a flow of impeccably ordered dialogue.

Crawford, Robert M. Died in New York, March 12, 1961.

Creston, Paul. Did not study theory, but only organ playing, with Yon; was autodidact in composition. Add to works: 1st violin concerto (1956; Detroit, Jan. 14, 1960); 2nd violin concerto (Los Angeles, Nov. 17, 1960); Suite for cello and piano (1956); *Lydian Ode* for orch. (1956); *Pre-Classic Suite* for orch. (New Orleans, April 3, 1958); Concerto for accordion and orch. (1958); *Janus* for orch. (Denver, July 17, 1959); *Isaiah's Prophecy,* a Christmas oratorio (1961); *Pavane Variations* for orch. (La Jolla, Calif., Aug. 21, 1966); *Chthonic Ode,* an "homage to Henry Moore" (Detroit, April 6, 1967); *Concerto* for 2 pianos and orch. (Montevallo, Alabama, Nov. 18, 1968). He publ. a book, *Principles of Rhythm* (N. Y., 1964).

Crist, Bainbridge. Died in Barnstable, Mass., Feb. 7, 1969. Correct the title of the violin piece to *Abhisarika* (not *Abisharika).*

Crosby, Bing (Harry), American vocalist and song stylist; b. Tacoma, Washington, May 3, 1903. A perfervid reader of the comic strip 'The Bingville Bugle' he was nicknamed Bing in school. He was a drummer in dance bands; in 1926 settled in Los Angeles and became a singer. He made his mark on the radio and in the movies; his success grew; he used his limited vocal resources to striking advantage by a cunning projection of deep thoracic mock-sentimental undertones. He holds an honorary degree of Doctor of Music from Gonzaga Univ. which he intermittently attended in his youth. His brother, Bob Crosby, is a bandleader; his four sons are also in show business as crooners. See Ted Crosby, *The Story of Bing Crosby* (N.Y., 1937; 2nd ed., 1946); Barry Ulanov, *The Incredible Crosby* (N.Y., 1947).

Cross, Lowell Merlin, American composer and electro-musicologist; b. Kingsville, Texas, June 24, 1938. He studied mathematics and music at Texas Technological College, graduating in 1963; then entered the Univ. of Toronto, Canada, obtaining his M.A. in musicology in 1968; attended classes of Marshall McLuhan in environmental technology there; took a course in electronic music with Myron Schaeffer and Gustav Ciamaga. In 1968 he was active at the Tape Music Center at Mills College as artistic director; in 1970 served as resident programmer for Experiments in Art and Technology at Expo '70 in Osaka, Japan, and guest consultant in electronic music at the National Institute of Design in Ahmedabad, India; in 1971 was appointed Artist-in-Residence at the Center for New Performing Arts, Univ. of Iowa. Eschewing any preliminary serial experimentation, Cross espoused a cybernetic totality of audio-visual, electronic and theatrical arts. His works include *4 Random Studies* for tape (1961); *0.8 Century* for tape (1962); *Eclectic Music* for flute and piano (1964); *Antiphonies* for tape (1964); *After Long Silence* for soprano and quadraphonic tape (1964); *3 Etudes* for tape (1965); *Video I* and *Video II* for variable media, including tape, audio system, oscilloscope and television (1965-68); *Musica Instrumentalis* for acoustical stereophonic instruments, monochrome and polychrome television (1965-68); *Video III,* for television and a phase-derived audio system (1968); *Electro-Acustica* for instruments, a laser deflection system, television and a phase-derived audio system (1970-71). The notation of his audio-visual compositions consists of color photographs of television images resulting from the programmed manipulation of sound-producing mechanisms in the acoustical space. (See his technical paper, *Audio/Video/Laser,* publ. in 'Source,' Sacramento, Calif., No. 8, 1970). He compiled a valuable manual, *A Bibliography of Electronic Music* (Toronto, 1967). As a pioneer in astromusicology, he created the selenogeodesic score *Lunar Laser Beam* (broadcast as a salutatory message on Nicolas Slonimsky's 77th birthday, April 27, 1971, purportedly via Leningrad, the subject's birthplace, the Sea of Tranquillity on the moon and the Ciudad de la Nuestra Señora Reina de Los Angeles in California).

Cross, Ronald, American musicologist; b. Fort Worth, Texas, Feb. 18, 1929. He studied at Guilmant Organ School in N. Y., at Centenary College of Louisiana and at N. Y. Univ. (Ph.D., 1961). In 1955 he received a Fulbright Fellowship to travel in Italy. In 1959 he was appointed to the faculty of Notre Dame College of Staten Island. He wrote a number of choral pieces; also chamber music; edited the collected works of Matthaeus Pipelare; contributed articles to musicological journals.

Crumb, George, American composer; b. Charleston, West Virginia, Oct. 24, 1929. He studied at the Mason College of Music in Charleston, at the Univ. of Illinois in Urbana, (M. M., 1953), at the Univ. of Michigan, where he was a student in composition of Ross Lee Finney (D. M. A., 1959); also took a course with Boris Blacher at the Hochschule für Musik in Berlin (1955-56).

He received grants from the Rockefeller (1965), Guggenheim (1967), and Coolidge Foundations (1970); received the National Institute of Arts and Letters Award in 1967, and the Pulitzer Prize in 1968. He was a member of the faculty at the Univ. of Colorado (1959-65); in 1965 was appointed to the staff of the School of Music of the Univ. of Pennsylvania. He was visiting composer at Tanglewood in the summer of 1970. In his music he preserves the formalities of the classical type of composition, making use of consecrated Baroque forms but filling them with modern devices; he attaches thematic importance to percussion. Works: string quartet (1954); sonata for solo cello (1955); *Variazioni* for orch. (1959); *Night Music I* for soprano, piano and percussion (1963); *Four Nocturnes (Night Music II)* for violin and piano (1964); *Madrigals,* Book I for soprano, vibraphone and double-bass (1965); *Madrigals,* Book II for soprano, alto flute and percussion (1965); *Eleven Echoes of Autumn 1965* for violin, alto flute, clarinet and piano (1966); *Echoes of Time and The River: Four Processionals for Orchestra* (Chicago, May 26, 1967; received the Pulitzer Prize for 1968); *Songs, Drones and Refrains of Death* for baritone, electric guitar, electric double-bass, electric piano and percussion, to poems by Federico García Lorca (1968); *Madrigals,* Book III for soprano, harp and percussion (1969); *Madrigals,* Book IV for soprano, flute, harp, double-bass and percussion (1969); *Night of the Four Moons* for alto flute, banjo, electric cello and percussion (1969); *Black Angels: 13 Images from the Darkland* for electric string quartet (1970); *Ancient Voices of Children* for soprano, boy soprano and 7 instrumentalists, to words by Federico García Lorca (Coolidge Festival of Chamber Music, Washington, Oct. 31, 1970; highly acclaimed).

Cuclin, Dimitri. He wrote 18 symphonies in all, between 1910 and 1967 (No. 1, 1910; No. 2, 1938; No. 3, 1942; No. 4, 1944; No. 5, 1947; No. 6, 1948; No. 7, 1948; No. 8, 1948; No. 9, 1949; No. 10, 1949; No. 11, 1950; No. 12, 1951; No. 13, 1951; No. 14, 1952; No. 15, 1954; No. 16, 1959; No. 17, 1965; No. 18, 1967). For a complete list of his works, see Viorel Cosma, *Muzicien Români Lexicon* (Bucharest, 1965; rev. ed., 1970).

Cugat, Xavier, Spanish-American band leader; b. Barcelona, Jan. 1, 1900. As a youth he came to the U.S.; studied violin with Franz Kneisel; played at concerts with Caruso; then became a cartoonist for the Los Angeles 'Times.' In 1928 he organized a dance orch.; led a combo with his niece, the actress Margo, as a dancer. In 1933 he was engaged as band leader of the Hotel Astoria in N.Y.; played numerous engagements at hotels and night clubs, achieving popularity by his astute arrangements of Latin American dances; invented a congat (a crossbreed of bongos and a conga). He was married to the singers Carmen Castillo (1929-45), Lorraine Allen (1946-50) and Abbe Lane (1952-63). He publ. an autobiography, *The Rumba is My Life* (N. Y., 1949).

Cui, César Antonovitch. Date of death, March 26 (not 24), 1918.

Culp, Julia. Died in Amsterdam, Oct. 13, 1970.

Cumberworth, Starling, American composer; b. Remson Corners, Ohio, July 25, 1915; studied at the Cleveland Institute of Music with Herbert Elwell and Arthur Shepherd; then at Yale Univ. with Quincy Porter and Paul Hindemith (M.M., 1948) and at the Eastman School of Music, Rochester, with Bernard Rogers and Howard Hanson (Ph.D., 1956). In 1956 he joined the staff of the Cleveland Music School Settlement. Among his works are an opera *Home Burial* (1955); 2 string quartets; suite for oboe and piano; suite for flute and piano; violin sonata; trio for violin, clarinet and piano.

Curtin, Phyllis, American soprano; b. Clarksburg, West Virginia, Dec. 3, 1922. She studied with Olga Avierino in Boston; sang with the New England Opera Co.; then was a member of the N. Y. City Opera; made successful appearances at the Teatro Colón in Buenos Aires (1959) and at the Vienna State Opera (1960-61). She made her debut with the Metropolitan Opera Co. on Nov. 4, 1961. Among her most successful roles is Salome; she also sang leading parts in first performances of several American operas.

Curtiss, Mina. Add to publications: *Bizet and His World* (N. Y., 1958).

Cziffra, György, Hungarian pianist; b. Budapest, Sept. 5, 1921. His musical education was interrupted by World War II when he was in the Hungarian Army. He played in cafes and cabarets before engaging on a serious career as a concert pianist. After the abortive Hungarian revolt of 1956 he went to Paris; made numerous successful tours in Europe. He is most successful in the romantic repertory, which he interprets in a peculiarly free manner, often disregarding the tradition in favor of coloristic and rhythmic effects.

D

Dahl, Ingolf. Died in Frutigen, near Bern, Switzerland, Aug. 7, 1970. Add to works: piano quartet (1957); *Sonata Pastorale* for piano (1960); *Serenade* for 4 flutes (1960); *Sinfonietta* for concert band (1961); piano trio (1962); *Aria Sinfonica* (Los Angeles, April 15, 1965).

Dahms, Walter. In 1935 he went to Lisbon, Portugal, adopted an operatic-sounding lusitanized nom de machine à écrire, making use of 60% of the letters in his original surname, chopped two lustra off his age and continued to publish books in German, among them biographies of *Paganini* (1960), *Liszt* (1961) and *Wagner* (1962), while steadfastly declining to admit his true identity.

Dallapiccola, Luigi. Add to works: *Canti di Liberazione* for mixed chorus and orch. (Cologne, June 16, 1960); *Parole di San Paolo* for voice and instruments (Washington, Oct. 30, 1964); *Odysseus,* opera (Berlin, Sept. 29, 1968, to a German libretto; in Italian, Milan, 1969); *Sicut umbra* for mezzo-soprano and 12 instruments (Washington, Oct. 30, 1970).

Dalley-Scarlett, Robert. Died in Brisbane, July 31, 1959.

Damase, Jean-Michel. Add to works: *Colombe,* lyric comedy (Bordeaux, May 5, 1961); piano concerto (Paris, Feb. 6, 1963).

Damrosch, Walter Johannes. His comic opera *The Dove of Peace* was first performed on Oct. 15, 1912 in Philadelphia (not in New York). He conducted the first American performance of *Parsifal* in New York, March 3, 1886 (not 1896).

Dan, Ikuma. Add to works: Symph. No. 4 (Kanagawa, Oct. 13, 1965).

Daniel, Oliver, American music critic and editor; b. De Pere, Wisconsin, Nov. 24, 1911. He studied piano in Amsterdam and Berlin; taught at the Boston Cons. (1936-38) and at Marot College, Thompson, Conn. (1939-42). In 1942 he joined the Columbia Broadcasting System as music director of its educational division; 1944-46, was with the American Broadcasting Co. as supervisor of serious music. Returning to the C.B.S. (1947-54) he continued to produce musical programs; in 1955-58 produced and narrated 'New Ideas in Music' for the radio station WNYC devoted entirely to modern works. He was editor of the American Composers' Alliance (1951-54); in 1954 became Director of the Concert Music Administration of Broadcast Music, Inc., continuing in this post in 1971. He was co-founder, with Leopold Stokowski, of the Contemporary Music Society in 1952; represented the U.S. at the International Music Council of UNESCO (1958, 1961, 1964, 1967, 1969, 1971); contributed to 'Saturday Review' and other publications; edited the collections, *The Harmony of Maine, Down East Spirituals* and *The Music of William Billings.*

Daniélou, Alain, French musicologist; b. Paris, Oct. 4, 1907. He devoted himself to the study of Asian and African music; lived mostly in India; lectured at the Univ. of Benares (1949-54); was director of research in Madras (1954-56), at the Institute of Indology in Pondichery (1956-59); in 1959 was appointed instructor at the École Française d'Extrême Orient in Paris; from 1960, member of the International Music Council of UNESCO. Publications: *Northern Indian Music* (2 vols.; Calcutta, 1949, 1953); *Traité de musicologie comparée* (Paris, 1959); supervised numerous phonograph recordings of Asian music.

Daniels, Mabel. Died in Boston, March 10, 1971.

Dankevitch, Konstantin. Add to works: *Nazar Stodolya,* opera (Kharkov, May 28, 1960).

Dannreuther, Edward. Complete name **Edward George Dannreuther.**

Darré, Jeanne-Marie, French pianist; b. Givet, July 30, 1905. She studied with Marguerite Long and Isidor Philipp in Paris; after numerous concerts in France and elsewhere in Europe, she made a successful series of tours in the U. S., appearing with major American orchestras. A virtuoso in a grand manner, she produced a sensation by playing several piano concertos on a single night.

Dart, Thurston. Died in London, March 6, 1971. From 1964 he was King Edward Prof. of Music at King's College at the Univ. of London.

Davico, Vincenzo. Died in Rome, Dec. 8, 1969. The exact date of the first perf. of *La Principessa prigioniera* is Sept. 29, 1940. Add to works: *Requiem per la morte d'un povero* (1950).

David, Ferdinand. Date of death, July 18 (not July 14), 1873. The name of the author of the monograph on David is J. Eckardt (not Eckhardt).

David, Gyula, Hungarian composer; b. Budapest, May 6, 1913. He studied with Kodály; became a professional conductor and taught at the Music Academy in Budapest. He composes in a traditional neo-classical vein; among his works are 3 symphonies (1947, 1957, 1960); viola concerto (1950); Sinfonietta (1961); 2 wind quintets; a string quartet; a number of scores of incidental music for theatrical plays.

David, Hans Theodore. Died in Ann Arbor, Mich., Oct. 30, 1967.

David, Johann Nepomuk. Add to works: Symph. No. 6 (1954); No. 7 (1956); 2nd violin concerto (1957); *Melancholia*, for viola and chamber orch. (1958); *Magische Quadrate*, a symph. fantasy on serial principles (1959); *Spiegelkabinett*, waltzes for orch. (1960); Sonata for 3 cellos (1962); Symph. No. 8 (Stuttgart, No. 21, 1965). See R. Klein, *J. N. David* (Vienna, 1964); H. H. Stuckenschmidt, *J. N. David* (Wiesbaden, 1965).

David, José, French composer, son of the singer Léon David; b. Sables-d'Olonne, Jan. 6, 1913. He entered the Paris Cons. in 1933; studied with Fauchet, Jacques de la Presle and Henri Busser; also took organ lessons with Marcel Dupré and music history with Maurice Emmanuel. He was mobilized in 1939 and served in the artillery regiment of the French Army during World War II. After the armistice he returned to Paris. His works include: *Impressions de Vendée* for piano (1944; also for orch.); *La Ballade de Florentin Prunier* for voice, violin, cello and piano (1947); *Symphonie* for Ondes Martenot and orch. (1948); ballet, *Jacquet le Prioux* (1950). He collaborated with Nicolas Obouhov in *Traité d'Harmonie Tonale et Atonale* (Paris, 1947).

David, Léon, French tenor; b. Sables-d'Olonne, Dec. 18, 1867; d. there, Oct. 27, 1962. He studied singing at the Cons. of Nantes and later at the Paris Cons.; made his debut at the Opéra-Comique in Paris in 1892; appeared subsequently in Brussels, Monte Carlo, Marseille, Bordeaux, Cairo, Lisbon, Bucharest, etc. He was prof. of singing at the Paris Cons. from 1924 to 1938.

Davidovsky, Mario, Argentinian composer; b. Buenos Aires, March 4, 1934. He studied there with Ernesto Epstein and others; went to the U.S. in 1958; held two consecutive Guggenheim Fellowships (1960-62); worked in the electronic music center of Columbia Univ. and Princeton Univ.; in 1964 was a guest lecturer at the school of music at the Univ. of Michigan. He received a Rockefeller Grant in 1965. Works: string quartet No. 1 (1954); clarinet quintet (1956); *Nonet* (1957); concerto for strings and percussion (1957); string quartet No. 2 (1958); *Suite Sinfónica para el Payaso* (1958); *Serie Sinfónica* (1959); *Planos* for orch. (1961); 2 *Studies* for electronic sound (1961, 1962); *Contrasts* for strings and electronic sound (1962); 6 pieces under the generic title *Synchronisms* for different instrumental groups (1963-70); his *Synchronisms No. 6* for piano and electronic sound was awarded the 1971 Pulitzer Prize.

Davidson, Harold Gibson. Died in Glendale, California, Dec. 14, 1959.

Davies, Peter Maxwell, English composer; b. Manchester, Sept. 8, 1934. He studied at the Royal Manchester College of Music; in 1957 went to Rome to study with Goffredo Petrassi; from 1959-62 he was Director of Music at Cirencester Grammar School; in 1962 went to the U. S. and studied with Roger Sessions at Princeton Univ. In his music he effects a non-eclectic synthesis of disparate styles and idioms, ranging from Renaissance polyphony to serial organization; in some of his works he also applies precepts of controlled improvisation. Works: Sonata for trumpet and piano (1955); 5 Pieces for piano (1956); *Alma Redemptoris Mater* for wind sextet (1957); *St. Michael,* sonata for 17 wind instruments (1957); *Prolation* for orch. (1958); *Ricercar and Doubles* for 8 instruments (1959); 5 motets for a cappella chorus (1959); *O Magnum Mysterium,* cycle of carols and instrumental sonatas (1960); string quartet (1961); *Te Lucis ante Terminum,* cycle of carols with instrumental sonatas (1961); settings of Giacomo Leopardi for soprano, contralto and chamber ensemble (1961); *Sinfonia* for chamber orch. (1962); 2 Fantasias on *In nomine of John Taverner* for orch. (1962; 1964); *Veni sancte Spiritus* for soloists, chorus and orch. (1962); *Shakespeare Music,* a set of dances for 11 instruments (1963); 5 Motets for voices, chorus and instruments (1964); *Revelation and Fall* for soprano and chamber orch. (1968); *Eight Songs for a Mad King* (George III) for voice and instruments (London, April 22, 1969); *Vesalii Icones,* for solo cello, wind instruments and piano, in 14 movements, after 14 anatomical drawings by Vesalius (London,

Dec. 9, 1969). Cf. R. Henderson, *Peter Maxwell Davies,* in the 'Mus. Times' (Oct. 1961).

Davis, Colin, English conductor; b. Weybridge, Surrey, Sept. 25, 1927. He played the clarinet in various orchestras in London; at the same time did national service in the Household Cavalry. He studied academic musical subjects at the Royal College of Music in London, but was entirely autodidact in conducting, which he learned from printed manuals. He showed his mettle in 1952 when he was called upon to lead a concert performance of *Don Giovanni* unexpectedly for the suddenly indisposed Otto Klemperer, and displayed fine fettle again as a substitute for the ailing Sir Thomas Beecham in 1960 at the Glyndebourne Festival. Rapidly advancing in his career, he became assistant conductor of the BBC Scottish Orch. in Glasgow (1957-59); then was principal conductor at Sadler's Wells Opera in London. In 1967 he was appointed chief conductor of the BBC Symph. Orch., and in 1971 musical director of the Royal (Covent Garden) Opera. He made his entrance on the American scene with the Minneapolis Symph. Orch. in 1961, and subsequently conducted concerts with the New York Philharmonic, the Boston Symph., the Philadelphia Orch., the Los Angeles Philharmonic, etc. In 1968 he made his Metropolitan Opera debut in New York in a performance of Benjamin Britten's *Peter Grimes;* also appeared as guest conductor in major musical centers on the continent, including Russia, and in Canada. In 1965 he was created Commander of the Order of the British Empire. A scholar as well as a musician, Davis impresses his audiences and professional critics by the clarity of his interpretations and a studied absence of histrionics on the podium.

Davis, Ivan, American pianist; b. Electra, Texas, Feb. 4, 1932. He studied piano with Silvio Scionti at North Texas State Univ. in Denton and later at the Academy of St. Cecilia in Rome with Carlo Zecchi. He also took private lessons with Vladimir Horowitz beginning in 1961. He obtained first prizes at Busoni Competition in Bolzano (1958), at Casella Competition at Naples (1958), and at the Franz Liszt Competition in New York (1960). He appeared as soloist with the N. Y. Philharmonic, Boston Symphony Orch., Philadelphia Orch., Chicago Symphony, London Symphony, Concertgebouw in Amsterdam, etc. In 1970 he was artist in residence at the Univ. of Miami at Coral Gables, Florida.

Davis, Miles Dewey, American jazz band leader; b. Alton, Illinois, May 25, 1926. He played trumpet as a youth; joined Billy Eckstine's band in 1946; led two bands in N. Y. in 1948, playing the French horn as well as trumpet. He developed a characteristic staccato bebop style, changing it later to a cantabile "cool" manner; was hailed by critics as true lyricist of romantic jazz.

Davison, Archibald Thompson. Died in Brant Rock, Cape Cod, Mass., Feb. 6, 1961. His honorary degrees included also those of Litt. D. from Washington Univ. (1953) and L. H. D. from Temple Univ. (1955). He was associate editor, with Thomas W. Surette, of a multi-volume Concord Series, for which he made numerous arrangements. Was organist and choirmaster of Harvard Univ. from 1910 until 1940, but never taught organ at Harvard. Was conductor of the Harvard Glee Club until 1933 (not 1934). The date of publication of Vol. I of *The Historical Anthology of Music* is 1946 (not 1947); revised edition was published in 1949 (not 1950). Add to books: *Harvard University Hymn Book* (with E. C. Moore, 1926); *Choral Conducting* (1945). Add bibl.: *Essays on Music in Honor of Archibald Thompson Davison by His Associates* (Cambridge, Mass., 1957).

Debussy, (Achille-) Claude. Entered the Paris Cons. on Aug. 25, 1872, when he was only 10 years old, and not at the age of 11. Add to bibl.: E. Vuillermoz, *Claude Debussy* (Geneva, 1957); E. Lockspeiser, ed., *Lettres inédites à André Caplet, 1908-1914* (Monaco, 1957); J. L. Pasteur Vallery-Radot, *Tel était Claude Debussy* (with letters to the author; Paris, 1958); Y. Tiénot & O. d'Estrade-Guerra, *Debussy: l'homme, son œuvre, son milieu* (Paris, 1961); M. Dietschy, *La Passion de Claude Debussy* (Neuchâtel, 1962); E. Lockspeiser, *Debussy: His Life and Mind,* (2 vols.; London, 1962, 1965); F. Lesure, editor, *Claude Debussy, Textes et Documents inédits,* a special issue of 'Revue de musicologie' (Paris, 1962); A. Goléa, *Claude Debussy* (Paris, 1965); E. Weber, editor, *Debussy et l'évolution de la musique au XXe siècle* (Paris, 1965); E. Hardeck, *Untersuchungen zu den Klavierliedern Claude Debussys* (Regensburg, 1967); Stefan Jarocinski, *Debussy, Impressionnisme et symbolisme* (Paris, 1970; translated from Polish).

Decoust, Michel, French composer; b. Paris, Nov. 19, 1936. He studied at the Paris Cons. with Olivier Messiaen and others; received Premier Second Grand Prix de Rome (1963). His works include *Mouvement* for strings and percussion (1964); *Études* for flutes and cellos (1966); *Polymorphée* for orch. (Royan, April 1, 1967); *Instants-Stabiles* for a chamber ensemble (1967).

Defauw, Désiré. Died in Gary, Indiana, July 25, 1960. Was conductor of the Gary Symph. Orch. from 1950 to 1958.

Dehn, Siegfried Wilhelm. The 2nd ed. of his *Theoretisch-praktische Harmonielehre* was publ. in 1860 (not in 1858).

Deis, Carl. Died in New York, July 24, 1960.

De Jong, Conrad, American composer; b. Hull, Iowa, Jan. 13, 1934. He studied trumpet at North Texas State Univ. in Denton, Texas, majoring in music education; received his B.M. Ed. in 1954; later studied composition with Bernhard Heiden at Indiana Univ. in Bloomington, obtaining his M. M. in 1959. He was appointed to the music faculty of Wisconsin State Univ. at River Falls in 1959. His works include *Unicycle* for harpsichord (1960); *3 Studies* for brass septet (1960); *Music for Two Tubas* (1961); *Essay* for brass quintet (1963); string trio (1964); *Fun and Games* for any instrument with piano (1966); *Aanraking (Contact)* for solo trombone (1969); *Hist Whist* for soprano, flute, viola and percussion (1969); *Grab Gab* for tuba ensemble (1970); *Peace on Earth* for unison chorus and organ (1970).

De Koven, Henry Louis Reginald. *Oh Promise Me* was not written for the London performance of *Robin Hood,* but composed in Vienna in 1888, and published as a separate song in 1889. It was introduced into *Robin Hood* shortly after its première in 1890.

Dela, Maurice, French Canadian composer and organist; b. Montreal, Sept. 9, 1919. He studied organ and composition in Montreal. His works, couched in an ingratiating romantic idiom, comprise a Ballade for piano and orch. (1945); piano concerto (1950); *Ronde* for soprano and orch. (1949); *Les Fleurs de Glais* for narrator and orch. (1951); Concertino for piano and orch. (1962); *Sonatine romantique* for violin and piano (1944); *Petite suite maritime* for wind quintet (1946); 2 string quartets; arrangements of folksongs of Quebec province.

Delage, Maurice. Died in Paris, Sept. 19, 1961.

Delannoy, Marcel. Died in Nantes, Sept. 14, 1962. Add to works: Symph. No. 2 (Paris, March 9, 1958). *Le Fou de la Dame* was first performed in concert form in Paris on Nov. 9, 1928.

Delden, Lex van. See **Van Delden, Lex.**

Delgadillo, Luis A. Died in Managua, Nicaragua, in 1955.

Delius, Frederick. His full baptismal name was Fritz Albert Theodor. He officially married Jelka Rosen in 1903 (not in 1897). Add to bibl.: Sir Thomas Beecham, *Frederick Delius* (London, 1959); Gloria Jahoda, *The Road to Samarkand: Frederick Delius and His Music* (N. Y., 1969).

Della Ciaia, Azzolino Bernardino. Exact date of death, Jan. 15, 1755.

Della Corte, Andrea. Died in Turin, March 12, 1968.

Deller, Alfred, English countertenor; b. Margate, May 30, 1912. He studied voice with his father; began singing as a boy soprano, later developing the alto range. He sang in the choirs of the Canterbury Cathedral (1940-47) and at St. Paul's in London. In 1948 he formed his own vocal and instrumental ensemble, the Deller Consort, acting as conductor and soloist in a repertory of old English music. This unique enterprise led to a modest revival of English madrigals and other songs of the Renaissance.

Dello Joio, Norman. First performance of his *Ricercari* was given on Dec. 19, 1946 (not 1945). Add to works: opera, *Blood Moon* (San Francisco, Sept. 18, 1961); *Fantasy and Variations* for piano and orch. (Cincinnati, March 9, 1962); *Antiphonal Fantasy on a Theme of Vincenzo Albrici,* for organ, brasses and strings (1966); *Mass,* for chorus, brass and organ (1968); *Songs of Abélard* for band and optional voice (1969); *Evocations* for chorus and orch. (Tampa, Florida, Oct. 2, 1970, composer conducting). See Edward Downes, *The Music of Norman Dello Joio* in the 'Mus. Quarterly' (April 1962).

Delmar, Dezso, Hungarian-American composer; b. Timișoara, July 14, 1891. He studied piano with Béla Bartók and theory with Kodály at the Royal Academy of Music in Budapest, graduating in 1913; concurrently took courses in jurisprudence, obtaining a lawyer's degree. He served in the Austro-Hungarian Army in World War I; after demobilization, he devoted himself entirely to music. He came to the U. S. in 1922; lived in New York until 1929, then moved to Los Angeles; in 1946 settled in Sacramento, California, as a teacher of piano and theory. His works include a symphony (1949); *Hungarian Sketches* for orch. (1947); 3 string quartets, a string trio, a violin sonata, etc., choral music; many piano pieces and songs. His works reflect the melorhythmic modalities of Hungarian folk music.

Del Tredici, David, American composer; b. Cloverdale, Calif., March 16, 1937. He studied composition with Seymour Shifrin at the Univ. of California at Berkeley (B.A., 1959); at Princeton Univ. with Roger Sessions (M.F.A., 1964); later joined the faculty of Harvard Univ. In his music he plies a modified dodecaphonic course in a polyrhythmic context, without necessarily eschewing tonality. Works: *Six Songs* to texts of James Joyce for voice and piano (1959); string trio (1959); *The Last Gospel* for amplified rock group, chorus and orch. (1967); *The Lobster Quadrille,* ballet sequence from the opera *Alice in Wonderland* (London, Nov. 25, 1969); *Syzygy* for soprano and 18 instruments (N. Y., July 7, 1968).

Demarquez, Suzanne, French composer; b. Paris, July 5, 1899; d. there, Oct. 23, 1965. She studied at the Paris Cons.; composed mostly chamber music; publ. the valuable monographs *André Jolivet* (Paris, 1958); *Manuel de Falla* (Paris, 1963; in English, Philadelphia, 1968); *Hector Berlioz* (Paris, 1969).

Demessieux, Jeanne. Died in Paris, Nov. 11, 1968.

Demian, Wilhelm, Rumanian composer and conductor; b. Brasov, June 9, 1910. He studied in Vienna (1929-33). In 1948 he became conductor of the Philharmonic of Cluj, and later at the Hungarian State Opera there (1952); taught at the Cluj Cons. since 1950. His music is set in a distinct classical style following the contrapuntal and harmonic models of the new German school. Among his works are a symphony (1947); a piano concerto (1953); a violin concerto (1955); chamber music, songs.

Demuth, Norman. Died in Chichester, England, April 21, 1968. Add to writings: *French Piano Music: A Survey with Notes on its Performance* (London, 1959).

Dendrino, Gherase, Rumanian composer and conductor; b. Bucharest, Sept. 3, 1901. He studied at the Bucharest Cons. with Kiriac and Castaldi; became conductor of the State Operetta Theater in Bucharest. He wrote mostly light operas; of these, *Lysistrata* (Bucharest, Dec. 15, 1960) was particularly successful on the Rumanian stage.

Denis, Didier, French composer; b. Paris, Nov. 5, 1947. He studied at the Paris Cons. with Henri Challan, Marcel Bitsch, Olivier Messiaen and Jean Rivier, graduating in 1968. His works include a trio for flute, clarinet and bassoon (1966); *Fugue indoue* for two groups of percussion instruments (1968); *Chants de Tse Yeh* for piano and 12 instruments (1969); *Puzzle* for voice, Spanish guitar and percussion (1970).

Denisov, Edison Vasilievitch, Soviet composer; b. Tomsk, April 6, 1929. He was named after Thomas Alva Edison by his father, an electrical engineer. He studied mathematics at Moscow Univ., graduating in 1951, and composition at the Moscow Cons. with Shebalin and Rakov. An experimenter by nature, he wrote instrumental works of an empirical genre; of these the most typical is *Crescendo e diminuendo* for harpsichord and string instruments (first performed at the Zagreb Festival on May 14, 1967, and two days later by the N.Y. Philharmonic). Other works are: Variation for piano (1952); *Improvviso* for violin and piano (1953); piano trio (1954); trio for violin, clarinet and bassoon (1957); *Sinfonietta* on Tadzhik themes (1957); sonata for 2 violins (1958); *Musica* for 11 wind instruments and timpani (1961); *Canti di Catulli* for voice and 3 trombones (1962); *The Sun of the Incas,* a cantata to words by Gabriela Mistral (1964); Symphony for 2 string orchestras (1964). He also wrote an opera, *Ivan the Soldier* (1959).

Densmore, Frances. Died in Red Wing, Minnesota, June 5, 1957.

Dent, Edward Joseph. Died in London, Aug. 22, 1957.

De Pablo, Luis, Spanish composer; b. Bilbao, Jan. 28, 1930. He studied music in Madrid. A follower of serial techniques, he does not exclude tonality; his instrumental works *Movil* and *Radial* contain quasi-tonal complexes in a dodecaphonic framework. His *Cesuras* for a double trio of woodwinds and strings, first performed at the First Festival of American and Spanish Music in Madrid on Oct. 22, 1964, emphasizes the expressive connotations of thematic silences. He publ. *Aproximación a una estética de la música contemporánea* (Madrid, 1968).

Déré, Jean. Died in Sainte-Suzanne (Mayenne), Dec. 6, 1970.

De Rensis, Raffaello, Italian music critic; b. Casacalenda, Campobasso, Nov. 17, 1880; d. Rome, Nov. 3, 1970. He founded a weekly magazine 'Musica' in 1908; wrote music criticism in daily newspapers. He publ. a number of monographs: *Il Cantore del popolo, B. Gigli* (Rome, 1934); *F. Faccio e Verdi* (Milan, 1934); *Ottorino Respighi* (Turin, 1935); *E. Wolf-Ferrari* (Milan, 1937); *A. Boito* (Florence, 1942); *U. Giordano e R. Leoncavallo* (Siena, 1949); *F. Cilèa* (Palmi, 1950); also a collection of essays, *Musica vista* (Milan, 1960).

De Reszke, Jean. Add bibl.: P. G. Hurst, *Jean de Reszke: 40 Years of Opera, 1874-1914* (London, 1958).

De Rose, Peter, American composer of popular music; b. New York, March 10, 1900; d. there, April 24, 1953. After desultory musical education, he formed a radio team, 'The Sweethearts of the Air,' with May Singhi Brown, whom he married. He gained fame with a piano piece entitled *Deep Purple;* it was introduced in an orchestral version by Paul Whiteman (N. Y., May 10, 1934) and subsequently converted into a saccharine ballad with lachrymose lyrics, which became a commercial hit. Other lucrative songs by De Rose are *The Lamp is Low* (derived from a malformed fragmentation of Ravel's *Pavane*) and *As Years Go By,* a sentimentalized misinterpretation of Brahms' *Hungarian Dance No. 4.*

Deshevov, Vladimir. Died in Leningrad, Oct. 27, 1955.

Des Marais, Paul, American composer; b. Menominee, Michigan, June 23, 1920; was taken to Chicago as an infant; studied there with Leo Sowerby; then with Nadia Boulanger in Cambridge, Mass., and with Walter Piston at Harvard Univ. (B.A., 1949; M.A., 1953). He received the Lili Boulanger prize (1947-48); Boott prize in composition from Harvard Univ. (1949); John Knowles Paine Traveling Fellowship (1949-51); joined the staff of Univ. of California, Los Angeles, in 1960; received the Institute of Creative Arts Award there in 1964-65. His early music was oriented toward neo-classicism, with pandiatonic excrescences in harmonic structures; in 1959 he evolved a decaphonic idiom using series of no more than 10 notes, while preserving a free, not necessarily non-tonal, style of writing. Works: Mass a cappella (1949); 2 piano sonatas (1947; 1952); *Theme and Changes* for harpsichord (1953); Motet for mixed voices, cellos and double - basses (1959); *Psalm 121* for chorus a cappella (1959); *Capriccio* for 2 pianos, percussion and celesta (1962; Los Angeles, March 18, 1963); *Epiphanies,* chamber opera with intervening film sequences (1964-68). In 1970-73 he held the Thorne Music Fund award to enable him to work on his project on the sounds produced by underwater mammals as a foundation of musico-marine electronic and acoustical works.

Desormière, Roger. Died in Paris, Oct. 25, 1963.

Dešpalj, Pavle, Croatian composer; b. Blato na Korčuli, June 18, 1934. He studied with Šulek in Zagreb; played violin in the Zagreb Philharmonic; also did some conducting; made symph. arrangements of Bach's works. As a composer, he deployed a non-atonal quasi-serialistic modus of composition, while outwardly adhering to classical forms. Works: *Variations* for chamber orch. (1957); violin concerto (1960); concerto for alto saxophone and string orch. (1963).

Des Prez, Josquin. The probable year of birth is 1440, rather than 1450. See Claudio Sartori's article in 'Annales musicologiques' (1956). Add to bibl.: H. Osthoff, *Josquin Desprez* (2 vols.; Tutzing, 1962, 1965).

Dessau, Paul. Add to works: symph. triptych, *In Memoriam Bertolt Brecht* (1957); *Symph. Variations* on themes of J. S. Bach and K. Ph. Em. Bach (1963); *Puntila,* opera (East Berlin, Nov. 15, 1966); *Geschäftsbericht,* "minimal opera" of 600 seconds duration (Leipzig, April 29, 1967); *Meer der Stürme,* symph. poem (East Berlin, Oct. 14, 1967).

Destouches, Franz (Seraph) von. Date of death, Dec. 10 (not 9), 1844.

Déthier, Edouard. Died in New York, Feb. 19, 1962.

Déthier, Gaston-Marie. Died in New York, May 26, 1958.

Dettmer, Roger (Christian), American music critic; b. Cincinnati, Aug. 2, 1927. He practiced piano, clarinet and drums before puberty; precociously produced, directed and starred in a school pageant-drama at ten; then took up music seriously at the Univ. of Cincinnati (1945-47), at Columbia Univ. (1948) and Univ. of Michigan (B.A., 1950); also studied composition privately with Vittorio Giannini. He composed sundry pieces for piano and other instruments, mostly in B flat major, but destroyed the manuscripts. Relieved of the composing itch, he engaged in musical journalism. In 1953 he became music and theater editor of 'Chicago Today' (formerly 'Chicago Herald-American,' 'The Chicago American' and 'Chicago's American'); contributed to various publications in the U.S., Europe and Japan; was instructor in the Rockefeller Foundation course for the training of music critics at the Univ. of Southern California, Los Angeles (1965-68); lectured widely; also was active in music management.

Deutsch, Otto Erich. Died in Vienna, Nov. 23, 1967. A Festschrift, *Otto Erich Deutsch zum 80. Geburtstag,* was publ. in Vienna in 1963.

Devčić, Natko. Add to works: opera, *Labinska Vjestica* (*The Witch of Labin;* Zagreb, Dec. 25, 1957); Concertino for violin and chamber orch. (1958). See K. Kovačević, *Hrvatski Kompozitori i Njihova Djela* (Zagreb, 1960).

Deyo, Felix. Died in Baldwin, N. Y., June 21, 1959.

Deyo, Ruth Lynda. Died in Cairo, March 4, 1960.

Diaghilev, Sergei Pavlovitch. Add to bibl.: Boris Kochno, *Diaghilev and the Ballets Russes* (N. Y., 1970).

Diamond, David. Add to works: *World of Paul Klee,* orch. suite (Portland, Oregon, Feb. 15, 1958); Symph. No. 8 (N. Y., Oct. 26, 1961); Nonet for 3 violins, 3 violas and 3 cellos (1962); *This Sacred Ground,* for chorus, male voice and orch. (Buffalo, Nov. 17, 1963). His Symph. No. 5 and piano concerto were performed for the first time by the N. Y. Philharmonic on April 28, 1966.

Dianda, Hilda, Argentinian composer; b. Córdoba, April 13, 1925. She studied in Europe with Scherchen and Malipiero; in 1958-62 worked at the Radiodiffusion Française in Paris. Upon returning to Argentina she devoted herself to composition and organization of concerts of ultra-modern music. Works: 3 string quartets (1947, 1960, 1962); *Concertante* for cello and chamber orch. (1952); trio for flute, oboe and bassoon (1953); wind quintet (1957); *Díptico* for 16 instruments (1962); *Núcleos* for string orch., 2 pianos and percussion (1964); electronic music.

Dianin, Sergey Alexandrovitch, Russian writer on music; b. St. Petersburg, Dec. 26, 1888; d. in the village of Davidovo, Vladimir district, Oct. 26, 1968. A son of Borodin's assistant in chemistry, he became a mathematician by profession; having access to Borodin's archives, he published 4 vols. of Borodin's letters (Moscow, 1928, 1936, 1949, 1950) and a biography *Borodin, Life, Materials, Documents* (Moscow, 1955; 2nd ed., 1960; in English, London, 1963).

Dichter, Misha, American pianist; b. in Shanghai, China, of Russian parents, Sept. 27, 1945. He was raised in Los Angeles; at the age of 15 he won a contest of the Music Educators National Conference, Western Division. He subsequently appeared as soloist with young symphonic groups. He entered the Univ. of California, Los Angeles, where he enrolled in a master class conducted by Rosina Lhévinne; later joined her class at the Juilliard School of Music in New York. In 1966 he entered the Tchaikovsky piano competition in Moscow and won 2nd prize, with great popular acclaim among Russian audiences. This marked the beginning of a highly successful career, with numerous appearances in America and in Europe. Dichter's natural predilections lie in the romantic repertory; his playing possesses a fine emotional appeal.

Dickinson, Clarence. Died in New York, Aug. 2, 1969.

Dickinson, George Sherman. Died in Chapel Hill, North Carolina, Nov. 6, 1964.

Dickinson, Helen Adell. Died in Tucson, Arizona, Aug. 25, 1957.

Dickinson, Peter, English composer; b. Lytham St. Annes, Lancashire, Nov. 15, 1934. Of a musical family, he studied piano and began to compose early in life. He entered the Univ. of Cambridge; after obtaining his M.A. Degree in music there, he went to the U.S. on a Rotary Foundation Fellowship, and studied with Bernard Wagenaar at the Juilliard School of Music, N.Y. (1958-60). Returning to England, he became lecturer at the College of St. Mark and St. John, London. In his music he combines the esoteric techniques of serialism with pragmatic considerations for performance. Works: *Postlude on Adeste Fideles* for organ (1954); *Jesus Christ is Risen Today* for chorus a cappella (1955); Sonatina for flute and piano (1955); *4 W. H. Auden Songs* for voice and piano (1956); *Variations* for piano (1957); *5 Blake Songs* for tenor, horn, clarinet and bassoon (1957); string quartet (1958); *Air* for solo flute (1958); *Monologue* for string orch. (1959); *A Dylan Thomas Song Cycle* for baritone and piano (1959); *Study in Pianissimo* for organ (1959); *Fantasia* for solo violin (1959); *Vitalitas,* ballet (1960); violin sonata (1961); 4 Duos for flute and cello (1962); trio for flute, oboe and harpsichord (1962); *5 Forgeries* for piano duet (1963); *5 Diversions* for keyboard instruments (1963); *Carillon* for organ (1964); *The Judas Tree,* a musical drama for speakers, singers, chorus and chamber orch. (London, May 27, 1965). See R. Norrington, *Peter Dickinson* in the 'Mus. Times' (Feb. 1965).

Diémer, Louis. Pronunciation of his last name should be d'ya-mär' with the final letter sounded fully.

Diether, Jack, American musicologist; b. Vancouver, British Columbia, Feb. 26, 1919. He was educated at the Univ. of British Columbia; served in the Canadian Army and Air Force during World War II. In 1955 he settled in the U. S.; was employed at Pickwick Bookshop in Hollywood and at G. Schirmer's Music Store in New York. In the meantime he wrote for music magazines, concentrating on the clarification of obscure periods in the lives and works of Bruckner and Mahler; contributed valuable articles to the organ of the Bruckner Society of America, 'Chord and Discord,' of which he became the editor in 1969; wrote annotations for orchestra programs and for phonograph records. His valuable article 'Notes on Some Mahler Juvenilia' (in 'Chord and Discord,' Vol. 3, No. 1, 1969) settles some moot questions regarding Mahler's early development.

Diller, Angela. Died in Stamford, Conn., April 30, 1968.

Dimov, Bojidar, Bulgarian composer; b. Lom, Jan. 31, 1935. He studied composition with Vesselin Stoyanov in Sofia; in 1958 went to Vienna where he enrolled at the Music Academy and took courses with Karl Schiske. His works include *Incantations* for soprano, flute, trumpet, viola and harp; *Komposition I* for piano; *5 Haikus* for soprano, alto and piano; *Komposition II* for string quartet; *Komposition III* for orch.; minor pieces. In his music, he follows the precepts of Anton von Webern, striving to obtain a maximum expression from a minimum of structural material.

Dinicu, Grigoras, Rumanian composer of light music; b. Bucharest, April 3, 1889; d. there, March 28, 1949. A member of a family of musicians, he studied violin with Carl Flesch who taught at the Bucharest Cons. in 1902. At his graduation in 1906, Dinicu played a violin piece of his own based on popular Rumanian rhythms, *Hora Staccato.* Jascha Heifetz made a virtuoso arrangement of it in 1932. Subsequently Dinicu played in hotels, restaurants, night clubs and cafés in Bucharest, and in Western Europe. Apart from *Hora Staccato* he composed numerous other pieces of light music in the gypsy and Rumanian manner. Cf. Viorel Cosma, *Figuri de Lautari* (Bucharest, 1960; pp. 189-229).

Di Stefano, Giuseppe, Italian tenor; b. Catania, July 24, 1921. He studied in Milan; sang at La Scala (1946-47); made a successful debut at the Metropolitan Opera, N. Y., in 1948 with numerous re-engagements; also appeared in Mexico (1952). He is equally adept in lyric and dramatic roles; besides his Italian repertoire, he performed leading tenor parts in French and Russian operas.

Doane, William Howard, American hymn writer; b. Preston, Conn., Feb. 3, 1832; d. South Orange, N. J., Dec. 24, 1915. He served as a clerk and later entered manufacturing business. He composed more than 2000 gospel songs and a Christmas cantata, *Santa Claus.* His hymn *Pass Me Not* was popular. Cf. R. G. McCutchan, *Our Hymnody* (N. Y., 1937).

Dobronić, Antun. Add to works: Symphony No. 5, subtitled *Emphatic Symphony* (1949; Zagreb, March 18, 1954). See K. Kovačević, *Hrvatski Kompozitori i Njihova Djela* (Zagreb, 1960).

Dobrowen, Issay Alexandrovitch. Date of birth, Feb. 27, 1891 (not 1893). His real name was Barabeitchik; his orphaned mother was adopted by Israil Dobrovel; Issay Dobrowen changed his legal name Dobrovel to Dobrowein, and later to Dobrowen. He studied at the Nizhny-Novgorod Cons. as a small child (1896-1900) before entering the Moscow Conservatory.

Dobrowolski, Andrzej, Polish composer; b. Lwow, Sept. 9, 1921. He studied organ, singing and clarinet in Warsaw, and composition in Cracow with Malawski; became active as music teacher in Warsaw. His works include a symphony; concerto for bassoon and orchestra; a trio for oboe, clarinet and bassoon; piano music and songs.

Dodds, Johnny, American Negro jazz clarinetist; b. New Orleans, April 12, 1892; d. Chicago, Aug. 8, 1940. He was a member of the King Oliver Creole Jazz Band with Louis Armstrong; played in the Hot Five; advanced to Hot Seven; excelled in the blues style. In his last years he formed the Johnny

Dodds Washboard Band. See G. E. Lambert, *Johnny Dodds* (N.Y., 1961).

Dodds, Warren (Baby), American Negro drummer, brother of Johnny Dodds; b. New Orleans, Dec. 24, 1898; d. Chicago, Feb. 14, 1959. He played on showboats; joined the King Oliver Creole Band. He was praised by the cognoscenti as a rhythmician of versatile gifts. His autobiography 'as told to Larry Gara' was publ. posthumously in Los Angeles, 1959.

Dodge, Charles, American composer; b. Ames, Iowa, June 5, 1942. He studied composition with Philip Bezanson at the Univ. of Iowa (B. A., 1964); with Darius Milhaud at Aspen Summer School (1961); Gunther Schuller and Arthur Berger at the Berkshire Music Center in Tanglewood (1964) and with Jack Beeson, Chou Wen-chung, Otto Luening, and Vladimir Ussachevsky at Columbia Univ. (M. A., 1966). He subsequently was on the faculty of Columbia and Princeton Univ., teaching electronic music; received numerous commissions, grants and awards, including one from the Koussevitzky Foundation in 1969. He composes in an empirical manner, following serial ideas; in most of his works he makes use of electronic media. He wrote *Folia* for 7 instruments and percussion (1963); *Rota* for orch. (1966); *Changes* for electronic tape with the aid of a digital computer storing a succession of numbers made audible by an analog converter (first performed at the Coolidge Festival, Washington, Oct. 31, 1970).

Dohnányi, Ernst von. Died in New York, Feb. 9, 1960. His orchestral work, *Variations on a Nursery Song,* was first performed in Berlin on Feb. 17, 1914 (not 1916). His first symphony in F major is a student work without an opus number; ditto *Zrinyi Overture.* Add to bibl.: *Ernst von Dohnányi: Message to Posterity* (Jacksonville, Florida, 1960).

Doire, René, French composer and conductor; b. Evreux, June 13, 1879; d. Paris, July 9, 1959. He studied in Rouen and later in Paris with Widor and Vincent d'Indy; then was engaged as bandleader in the casinos of various French spas. He composed a one-act opera *Morituri* (1903); a cycle of songs, *Reflets de Jeunesse* for voice and piano, or orch. (1902); *Vision d'Espagne* for violin and orch. (1916); violin sonata (1918); *Dramatico* for piano and orch. (1923); songs.

Doktor, Paul, Austrian-American violist; b. Vienna, March 28, 1919. He studied with his father, Karl Doktor, violinist of the renowned Busch String Quartet; graduated as a violinist at the State Academy of Music in Vienna in 1938, but subsequently changed to viola, and in 1942 received the first prize for viola at the International Music Competition in Geneva. He left Vienna in 1938; from 1939-47 was solo violist of the Lucerne Orch.; emigrated to the U. S. in 1947. He founded the Rococo Ensemble in New York and the New York String Sextet; edited several collections of viola music for G. Schirmer, Inc. (*Solos for the Viola Player,* Schubert's Arpeggione Sonata, 2 Sonatas by Brahms, Mozart's Duets for violin and viola, etc.). He has taught at the Univ. of Michigan, Ann Arbor (1948-51); at the Mozarteum in Salzburg (1952-58); at Colorado College, Colorado Springs (summers, 1957-62); Indiana Univ., Bloomington, Indiana (1963); appeared frequently as a viola virtuoso in America and in Europe.

Dolmetsch, Arnold. Add bibl.: M. Dolmetsch, *Personal Recollections of Arnold Dolmetsch* (London, 1957).

Dolukhanova, Zara, Russian mezzo-soprano of Armenian extraction; b. Moscow, March 5, 1918. She studied with private teachers; joined the Moscow Radio staff in 1944; was awarded the Lenin Prize in 1966. A lyric singer, she excels in the romantic Russian repertoire. In 1959 she made her first American tour enjoying great acclaim; she toured America again in 1970.

Donalda, Pauline. Died in London, Oct. 22, 1970.

Donati, Pino, Italian composer; b. Verona, May 9, 1907. He studied violin; then took composition lessons with G. C. Paribeni. He wrote two operas: *Corradino lo Svevo* (Verona, April 4, 1931) and *Lancillotto del Lago* (Bergamo, Oct. 2, 1938); also chamber music. In 1958 he went to the U. S. as music consultant for the Chicago Lyric Opera.

Donato, Anthony. Add to works: *Improvisation* for orch. (1956); piano trio (1959); opera, *The Walker Through Walls* (Evanston, Illinois, Feb. 26, 1965, composer conducting); sonata for clarinet and piano (1966); *Centennial Ode* for orch., commissioned by the Nebraska State Centennial (Omaha, Dec. 11, 1967); *Improvisation* for orch. (Kansas City, May 3, 1969); *Discourse* for flute and piano (1969). He publ. *Preparing Music Manuscript* (Englewood Cliffs, N. J., 1963). See 'Composers of the Americas,' vol. 15 (Washington, 1969).

Donatoni, Franco, Italian composer; b. Verona, June 9, 1927. He studied with Pizzetti in Rome; in 1955 became instructor at the Cons. of Milan. He became dedicated to the experimental type of composition with the application of serial and aleatory techniques. Works: *Divertimento* for violin and chamber orch. (1954); *Divertimento* II for strings (1962); 4 string quartets (1956-63); *Per orchestra* (1963).

Donington, Robert. Published *The Interpretation of Early Music* (N. Y., 1963); *Wagner's Ring and Its Symbols* (London, 1963).

Donizetti, Gaetano. He did not study architecture or literature. *Enrico di Borgogna* was not his first opera, but rather the first one to be produced; it was preceded by *Il Pigmalione,* which had its modern revival in Bergamo on Oct. 13, 1960. *Il Falegname di Livonia* was not his next opera; two operas intervened: *Una Follia* (1818) and *I piccoli Virtuosi ambulanti* (1819). He did not obtain exemption from military service owing to the success of his opera *Zoraide di Granata,* but at least a year earlier, thanks to the intercession of an influential noblewoman. He was not married to Virginia Vasselli for 14 years, but only for 9 years (married on June 1, 1828; she died on July 30, 1837). He did not leave Milan for Paris in anger following the censorship of his production of *Poliuto,* for he was not in Milan, but in Naples, from where he sailed directly for Genoa and Marseille. He did not write an opera called *Adelasia,* which must be an error for *Adelia,* produced in Rome on Feb. 11, 1841. *Caterina Cornaro* was neither Donizetti's last work (it was written in 1842-43) nor his last work to be produced. It was, however, his last work to be staged during his lifetime; other posthumous works were *Rita* produced in 1860, *Gabriella di Vergy* (1869) and *Le Duc d'Albe* (1882). The opera listed as *Pietro il Grande, Czar delle Russie* is better known under the title *Il Falegname di Livonia. I Voti dei Studditi* is not an opera, but a cantata. The title *Alahor in Granata* should be changed to *Alahor di Granata.* There is no proof that Donizetti composed an opera called *Il Castello degli invalidi,* and if he did, the date Feb. 27, 1826 of its production in Palermo cannot be substantiated. The common title for the opera listed as *Gli esiliati in Siberia* is *Otto Mesi in due ore.* The first performance of *L'Esule di Roma* at the Teatro San Carlo, Naples, was given on Jan. 1 (not 2) 1828. The correct title of the next opera is *Alina, Regina di Golconda* (rather than *La Regina di Golconda*). *Il Castello di Kenilworth* should be corrected to *Elisabetta al Castello di Kenilworth.* The first performance of *Il Diluvio universale* took place in Naples on Feb. 28, 1830 (not March 6, 1830). A cantata called *Il Ritorno desiderato,* which may be identical with *Il fausto Ritorno,* may have been performed in Naples in August (but not on July 31), 1830, as a ceremonial piece to celebrate the return of Francesco I and Isabella Maria from Spain. The exact date of the first performance of *La Romanziera e l'uomo nero,* given as June 18, 1831, cannot be established. The correct date for the first production of *Maria Stuarda* in Naples is Oct. 18 (not 19), 1834. *Roberto Devereux* is the proper title for the opera listed as *Roberto d'Evereux Conte d'Essex,* but it was also known at various times as *Il Conte d'Essex.* Rectify *Catarina Cornaro* to *Caterina Cornaro* at the end of the list of Donizetti's operas. In the bibliography, the statement that Zavadini's compendium is a greatly detailed biography is misleading, because it consists largely of Donizetti's correspondence. On the other hand, Zavadini's book, *G. Donizetti: vicende della sua vita e catalogo* does not contain any letters, as mistakenly asserted in the bibliography. For thorough elucidation of all these imbroglios see H. Weinstock, *Donizetti and the World of Opera in Italy, Paris and Vienna in the First Half of the 19th Century* (N. Y., 1964).

Donostia, José Antonio de. Died in Lecaroz, Navarra, Aug. 30, 1957.

Donovan, Richard Frank. Died in Middletown, Conn., Aug. 22, 1970.

Doran, Matt, American composer; b. Covington, Kentucky, Sept. 1, 1921. He studied at the Univ. of Southern California with Ernst Toch; also with Hanns Eisler and Gail Kubik in Los Angeles; orchestration with Cailliet. His works include 2 symphonies; a string quartet; a woodwind quintet; a clarinet sonata; a flute sonata; a trio for oboe, violin and viola; many songs and piano pieces. His short opera, *The Committee,* satirizing music college examinations, was produced in Corpus Christi, Texas, on May 25, 1955, and received a spate of performances elsewhere.

Dorati, Antal. He conducted the Minneapolis Symph. Orch. from 1949 to 1960; B.B.C. Orch. in London from 1963 to 1966. In 1966 he was appointed musical director of the Stockholm Philharmonic; in 1970 was engaged as conductor of the National Symph. Orch. in Washington, while continuing his tenure with the Stockholm Philharmonic.

Add to works: Symphony in 5 movements (Minneapolis, March 18, 1960, composer conducting).

Doret, Gustave. His opera *Les Armaillis* was first performed in Paris on Oct. 23 (not Nov. 8). 1906.

Dorian, Frederick. Add to writings: *Commitment to Culture* (Pittsburgh, 1964). His book *The Musical Workshop* appeared in Spanish (Buenos Aires, 1961) and in French (Paris, 1962); *The History of Music in Performance* was publ. in Japanese (Tokyo, 1964), and also in Braille Edition (Division for the Blind, The Library of Congress, Washington, D. C., 1965).

Dorsey, James (Jimmy), American clarinet and saxophone player, brother of Thomas Dorsey; b. Shenandoah, Pa., Feb. 29, 1904; d. New York, June 12, 1957. He played clarinet in school bands, and at one time led a band of his own; later joined his brother's group, rapidly climbing the ladder of commercial success, epitomized in the film 'The Fabulous Dorseys' (1947).

Dorsey, Thomas (Tommy), American trombonist and band leader, brother of James Dorsey; b. Mahoney Plains, Pa., Nov. 19, 1905; d. Greenwich, Conn., Nov. 26, 1956. He played trumpet and other instruments in school bands; then took up the trombone and developed a virtuoso technique using a unique method of convex breathing that enabled him to maintain miraculously long passages *legato*. His brother regularly played the clarinet and alto saxophone in his band from 1953 on. A film 'The Fabulous Dorseys' (1947) bears eloquent testimony to the brothers' fame.

Doubrava, Jaroslav, Czech composer; b. Chrudim, April 25, 1909; d. Prague, Oct. 2, 1960. He studied with Otakar Jeremiáš; became active in theater music and on the radio. Works: 3 symphonies (1938, 1944, 1958); opera, *A Midsummer Night's Dream,* after Shakespeare (1945); *Partizanský Pochod,* symph. poem glorifying the resistance against the Nazi occupation (1945); the opera *Balada o lásce* (posthumous; Prague, June 21, 1962); several ballets; chamber music.

Dougherty, Celius, American pianist and composer; b. Glenwood, Minnesota, May 27, 1902. He studied piano and composition at the Univ. of Minnesota with Donald Ferguson, and later at Juilliard School in N. Y. with Rubin Goldmark (comp.) and Josef Lhévinne (piano). He became a highly successful accompanist and toured with many celebrated singers. He published a number of songs some of which became popular in recitals (*Weathers, Song for Autumn, Five American Sea-Chanties, A Minor Bird, The First Christmas, Green Meadows, Hush'd Be the Camps Today, Love in the Dictionary, Portrait Primavera, The Stranger, Upstream, Seven Songs* to texts of E. E. Cummings, etc.). He also wrote an opera *Many Moons,* based on a story of James Thurber, which was first performed at Vassar College on Dec. 6, 1962.

Dounias, Minos, musicologist; b. Cetate, Rumania, Sept. 26, 1900, of Greek parents; d. Athens, Oct. 20, 1962. He studied violin; musicology at the Univ. of Berlin with Abert and Schering; publ. a dissertation, *Die Violinkonzerte Giuseppe Tartinis* (Berlin, 1935). In 1936 he settled in Athens as music critic.

Dowland, John. Traveled on the continent in 1594-95, visiting Wolfenbüttel, Kassel, Nuremberg, Genoa, Florence and Venice, but never studied with Marenzio.

Dowland, Robert. Born in 1591 (not 1586). Exact date of death, Nov. 28, 1641. See Cecil Hill, *John Dowland,* in the 'Mus. Times' (Nov. 1963).

Downes, Edward, American music historian, son of Olin Downes; b. Boston, August 12, 1911. He studied at Columbia Univ. (1929-30), Univ. of Paris (1932-33), Univ. of Munich (1934-36, 1938); Ph.D. Harvard Univ., 1958. In 1960 became program annotator of the New York Philharmonic; also radio commentator for Metropolitan Opera broadcasts. He publ. *Adventures in Symphonic Music* (N. Y., 1943); contributed articles to various publications.

Downes, Edward (Thomas), English conductor; b. Aston (Birmingham), June 17, 1924. He studied at the Univ. of Birmingham (1941-44) taking B.A. in music; and at the Royal College of Music, London (1944-46), studying horn, theory and composition. In 1948 was awarded the Carnegie Scholarship which he used for taking a course in conducting with Hermann Scherchen. His first professional post as conductor was with the Carl Rosa Opera (1951); in 1952 he became a staff conductor of Covent Garden Opera in London, with which he conducted every work in the repertory, including the complete Ring of the Nibelung cycle; in 1969 he left the Covent Garden staff as a regular member in order to devote himself to symphonic conducting, but continued to fill in occasional opera engagements. He conducted the world première of Richard Rodney Bennett's opera *Victory* (April 13, 1970). He also conducted the world premières of Havergal Brian's 14th and 21st symphonies with the London Symph. Orch. on May 10, 1970. Edward Downes is the author of translations of Russian opera librettos into English, notably *Katerina Izmailova* by Shostakovich.

Dragoi, Sabin. Died in Bucharest, Dec. 31, 1968.

Dragon, Carmen, American conductor of light music; b. Antioch, Calif., July 28, 1914. He studied in Los Angeles; organized and conducted orchestral groups; made adipose arrangements of popular works; filled engagements at the Hollywood Bowl and other open-air places, supplying desirable musical fare for the listening pleasure of contented people.

Dresden, Sem. Died in The Hague, July 31, 1957.

Driessler, Johannes. *Gaudia Mundana* was first performed in Frankfurt on March 1, 1953 (not 1952).

Drinker, Henry S. Died in Merion, Pennsylvania, March 9, 1965. He founded the Drinker Library of Choral Music, which he eventually donated to the Free Library of Philadelphia.

Drozdov, Anatol Nikolaievitch. Exact dates: b. Oct. 23, 1883; d. Sept. 10, 1950.

Dubensky, Arcady. Died in Tenafly, New Jersey, Oct. 14, 1966.

Dubois, Pierre-Max, French composer; b. Graulhet (Tarn), March 1, 1930. He studied at the Cons. in Tours, obtaining a prize in piano at the age of 15; later studied composition with Darius Milhaud at the Paris Cons. His works include *Impressions foraines* for orch. (1951); *Divertissement* for saxophone and orch. (1952); *Sérénades* for bassoon and orch. (1953); *Capriccio* for violin and orch. (1954); *Concertstück* for saxophone and piano (1955); violin concerto (Strasbourg, June 20, 1957); cello concerto (1958); concerto for saxophone and string orch. (1959); Symph. No. 1, subtitled *Drame pour Epidaure* (1960); *Le Docteur OX,* ballet-bouffe, after Jules Verne (Lyon, Feb. 23, 1964); quartet for 4 French horns (1961); quartet for 4 flutes (1961); quartet for 4 trombones (1961); *Concerto italien* for 2 pianos and orch. (1962); *Concerto* for violin, piano and orch. (Besançon, Sept. 15, 1963); quartet for 4 clarinets (1962); Symph. No. 2 *(Symphonie-Sérénade)* for strings (1964); *Musique pour un Western,* for orch. (1964); *Cover Girls,* a choreographic spectacle (1965); *Concerto ironico* for bassoon and orch. (1968).

Duckles, Vincent Harris, American musicologist and librarian; b. Boston, Sept. 21, 1913. He studied at Columbia Univ. and at the Univ. of Calif., Berkeley (Ph.D., 1953); in 1947, appointed Head of the Music Library, Univ. of Calif., at Berkeley; prof. of music there, 1960 He specializes in 17th-century English song literature; music bibliography; history of musical scholarship. He has held 2 Fulbright Fellowships (1950; Cambridge, 1957; Univ. of Göttingen); a Grant-in-Aid from the American Council of Learned Societies (1964; Florence). He publ. a valuable manual, *Music Reference and Research Materials: an Annotated Bibliography* (N.Y., 1964); contributed numerous articles to 'Die Musik in Geschichte und Gegenwart,' 'Acta Musicologica,' etc.

Dufallo, Richard (pronounced DuFAHlo), American clarinetist and conductor; b. East Chicago, Indiana, Jan. 30, 1933. He studied at the American Cons. of Music in Chicago; played clarinet as a youngster. Subsequently he studied composition with Lukas Foss at the Univ. of Calif., Los Angeles; in 1957 he joined the Improvisation Chamber Ensemble organized by Foss, and showed an exceptional talent for controlled improvisation in the ultra-modern manner. In 1965 he joined Lukas Foss as Associate Conductor of the Buffalo Philharmonic. He also was guest conductor with the Pittsburgh Symph. Orch.; attended a conducting seminar with William Steinberg and a course in conducting with Pierre Boulez in Basel in the summer of 1969. In 1967 he went to Japan and other Asian countries as Assistant Tour Conductor with the N. Y. Philharmonic. He has a natural flair for new music, but he has also been praised for his interpretations of the classical symphonic repertory.

Dufourcq, Norbert. Edited *Larousse de la Musique* (2 vols., Paris, 1957).

Duke, Vernon. See **Dukelsky, Vladimir.**

Dukelsky, Vladimir. Died in Santa Monica, Cal., Jan. 16, 1969. He published *Listen Here! A Critical Essay on Music Depreciation* (N. Y., 1963). See Igor Stravinsky, *A Cure for V. D.,* in the unperiodical magazine 'Listen' (Sept. 1964).

Dumesnil, René. Died in Paris, Dec. 24, 1967.

Dumler, Martin G. Died in Cincinnati, Oct. 19, 1958.

Dunayevsky, Isaak. Place of birth, Lokhvitza (not Lokhvita).

Dunstable, John. Probable date of birth, between 1380 and 1390, rather than 1370.

DuPré, Jacqueline, English cello player; b. Oxford, Jan. 26, 1945. The Gallic name of her family dates back to the Norman times. Both her parents were musicians; her mother even wrote a ballet score. Jacqueline DuPré studied cello at the Guildhall School of Music in London and later with Paul Tortelier in Paris, in Switzerland with Casals, and with Rostropovitch in Moscow. She owns the famous 'Davidov cello' made by Stradivarius in 1712. She made her American debut in New York on May 14, 1965, with electrifying success playing Elgar's *Cello Concerto,* eliciting rapturous reviews from the critics. On June 15, 1967 she married the Israeli pianist Daniel Barenboim, and she became converted to Judaism. She stands 5′9″. Her husband calls her Smiley.

Dupré, Marcel. Died in Meudon, near Paris, May 30, 1971.

Dupuis, Albert. Died in St. Josse-ten-Noodey, Belgium, Sept. 19, 1967.

Durand, Jacques. Place of death, Bel-Ébat (not Bel-Etat).

Durey, Louis. Add to works: Concertino for piano, wind instruments, double-bass and timpani (1969); *Obsession* for wind instruments, harp, double-bass and percussion (1970).

Durme, Jef van, Belgian composer; b. Kemseke, May 7, 1907. He studied with Alpaerts in Brusssels and with Alban Berg in Vienna. His works comprise an opera *Remous* (Brussels, 1935), 6 symphonies, 2 piano concertos, a violin concerto, 5 string quartets, etc.

Dushkin, Samuel. Born Dec. 13, 1891 (not 1897).

Dussek (Dušek), Johann Ladislaus. The Czech form of the name is Dusík (not Dušek); Christian names, in Czech, Jan Ladislav. The name of his teacher was Špinar (not Spenar).

Dutilleux, Henri. Add to works: Second Symphony (Boston, Dec. 11, 1959); *Cinq Métaboles* for orch. (Cleveland, Jan. 14, 1965); *Tout un monde lointain* for cello and orch. (Aix-en-Provence, July 25, 1970).

Duvosel, Seraphien Lieven. Died in Sint-Martens-Lutern, Belgium, April 20, 1956.

Dux, Claire. Died in Chicago, Oct. 8, 1967.

Dvarionas, Balis, Lithuanian composer; b. Liepaia, June 19, 1904. He studied at the Leipzig Cons. with Teichmüller (piano) and Karg-Elert (composition). In 1926 he went to Kaunas and taught piano there; 1933 he became prof. at the Lithuanian Cons. in Vilna; also conducted the Lithuanian Philharmonic Orchestra there. Among his works are a symphony (1947); a violin concerto (1948; received a State Prize); a piano concerto (1958) and a number of choral works. He wrote the music for the national anthem of the Lithuanian Soviet Socialist Republic (1950).

Dvořáček, Jiří, Czechoslovak composer; b. Vamberk, June 8, 1928. He studied organ and composition at the Prague Cons.; composed a symph. (1953); *Sonata Capricciosa* for violin and piano (1956); *Ex Post* for piano and orch. (Prague, Feb. 16, 1964); the opera, *The Isle of Aphrodite* (Dresden, Feb. 13, 1971, with a German libretto).

Dvořák, Antonin. Op. number of Symphony in C minor, is 3 (not 31); that of Symphony in B^b, is 4 (not 41). Add to bibl.: J. Burghauser, *Antonin Dvořák: Thematic Catalogue, Bibliography, and Survey of Life and Work* (in Czech, German and English, Prague, 1960); J. Clapham, *Antonin Dvořák: Musician and Craftsman* (N. Y., 1966); Gervase Hughes, *Dvořák: His Life and Music* (N. Y., 1967).

Dyer, Louise (Mrs. Louise B. M. Hanson), patroness of music and publisher; b. Melbourne, Australia, July 16, 1890; d. Monaco, Nov. 9, 1962. She established in Monaco an important publishing enterprise, L'Oiseau-Lyre (The Lyre-Bird Press), financing it entirely out of her own resources. The Lyre-Bird Press has issued a great number of unpublished or obscure works of medieval and Renaissance French music.

Dylan, Bob, American folk singer; b. Duluth, Minnesota, May 24, 1941. His real name was Robert Zimmermann, but he changed it to Dylan out of admiration for the poet Dylan Thomas. Possessed by wanderlust he rode freight trains across the country; played guitar and crooned in the coffee houses of New York. He also improvised songs to his own lyrics. His nasalized country-type semi-Western style and his self-haunted soft guitar strumming captured the imagination not only of untutored adolescents but also of certified cognoscenti in search of convincing authenticity. In 1966 he broke his neck in a motorcycle accident which forced him to interrupt his charismatic career for two years. In 1970 he was awarded an honorary doctorate from Princeton Univ., the first such honor given to a popular singer innocent of all academic training. A group of militants in the Students for a Democratic Society adopted the name 'Weathermen' after a line from Dylan's song *Subterranean Homesick Blues,* 'You don't need a weatherman to know which way the wind blows.' The Weathermen claimed credit for several bombings in New York City during 1969 and 1970. See: Daniel Kramer, *Bob Dylan* (N. Y., 1967); Bob Dylan, *Tarantula* (N. Y., 1971).

Dyson, Sir George. Died in Winchester, England, Sept. 29, 1964.

Dzegelenok, Alexander Michailovitch. Died in Moscow, Jan. 31, 1969.

Dzerzhinsky, Ivan Ivanovitch. Date of birth, April 9 (not April 21), 1909. Add to works: opera, *A Man's Destiny* (Moscow, Sept 30, 1961).

E

Earhart, Will. Died in Los Angeles, April 23, 1960. Cf. C. V. Buttelman, ed., *Will Earhart: Teacher, Philosopher, Humanitarian* (Washington, 1962).

Eaton, John, American composer; b. Bryn Mawr, Pa., March 30, 1935. He received his A. B. and M. F. A. degrees from Princeton Univ., where he studied composition with Milton Babbitt, Edward Cone and Roger Sessions; subsequently held three American Prix de Rome awards and two Guggenheim grants. In his works he avails himself of all resources of modern music, including serial techniques, microtones and electronic media. In several of his scores he makes use of the Syn-Ket (a portable electronic synthesizer built by the Roman sound engineer named Ketoff) and of the Syn-Mill (an electric generator based on a design of Robert Moog and built specially for Eaton by Edward Miller). Works: three operas: *Ma Barker* (1957); *Heracles* (broadcast in an Italian version from Rome, Feb. 14, 1970; first stage performance, in English, scheduled for the opening of the Indiana Univ. Opera House, Bloomington, Oct. 16, 1971); *Myshkin,* television opera after Dostoyevsky's novel *The Idiot* (1970); *Holy Sonnets of John Donne* for orch. and soprano solo (1957); *Piano Variations* (1958); trumpet sonata (1958); string quartet (1959); *3 Epigrams* for clarinet and piano (1960); *Concert Music* for solo clarinet (1961); *Concert Piece* for magnetic tape and jazz ensemble (1962); *Soliloquy* for Syn-Ket (1967); *Vibrations* for woodwinds with quarter-tone scordatura (1967); *Thoughts on Rilke* for solo soprano, Syn-Ket and Syn-Mill (1967); *Duet* for Syn-Ket and Moog Synthesizer (1968); *Mass* for soprano, clarinet, 3 Syn-Kets, Moog synthesizer and Syn-Mill, commissioned by the Koussevitzky Foundation, and first performed at the Coolidge concert at the Library of Congress in Washington on Oct. 31, 1970.

Ebel, Arnold. Died in Berlin, March 4, 1963.

Eben, Petr, Czech composer; b. Zamberk, Jan. 22, 1929. He studied at the Prague Cons., graduating in 1954. He was active as a pianist and teacher; composed an organ concerto (1954); wind quartet (1951); a suite for cello and piano (1955); piano concerto (1961); numerous choruses and songs.

Echaniz, José, Cuban pianist; b. Havana, June 4, 1905; d. Pittsford, N. Y., Dec. 30, 1969. He studied piano in Havana; appeared as soloist with major American orchestras, receiving praise for his brilliant interpretations. In 1944 he joined the staff of the Eastman School of Music in Rochester. He also served as conductor of the Grand Rapids Symph. Orchestra.

Eckhardt-Gramatté, Sophie Carmen. She settled in Winnipeg, Canada, in 1954, and changed her first name to the Russian diminutive, Sonia.

Eckstein, Pavel, Czech musicologist; b. Opava, April 27, 1911. He studied jurisprudence at Charles Univ. in Prague, graduating in 1935; received his musical education there. During the German occupation (1941-45) he was in a concentration camp in Lodz, Poland, but survived and returned to Prague where he became active as organizer of music festivals, editor and writer on music.

Eckstine, William Clarence (Billy), American Negro jazz singer and bandleader; b. Pittsburgh, July 8, 1914. He worked in night clubs as a crooner; formed a band of his own in 1944, proselytizing for bebop, in association with such bop figures as Dizzy Gillespie and Miles Davis; later became successful as a balladeer of cool jazz.

Eddy, Nelson. Died in Miami Beach, Florida, March 6, 1967.

Edelmann, Johann Friedrich. Date of birth, May 5 (not May 6), 1749. See Rita Benton, *J. F. Edelmann, a musical victim of the French Revolution,* in the 'Mus. Quarterly' (April 1964).

Eder, Helmut. Add to works: opera, *Oedipus* (1960); opera *Der Kardinal* (1962); 3 symphonies (1952, 1960, 1962); piano concerto (1958); violin concerto (1964); oboe concerto (1964).

Edwards, Clara. The words of her song *By the Bend of the River* are not by her, but by Bernhard Haig.

Eeden, Jean-Baptiste van den. Exact dates of first performances of his operas are: *Numance* (Antwerp, Feb. 2, 1898); *Rhéna* (Brussels, Feb. 15, 1912).

Egge, Klaus. Add to works: Symph. No. 3 (1957); Symph. No. 4 (Detroit, March 28, 1968); Symph. No. 5 (1969).

Eggen, Arne. Place of death, Baerum, suburb of Oslo (not Drammen).

Eggen, Erik. Died in Ringsaker, Norway, June 7, 1957.

Egk, Werner. Add to works: *Die Verlobung in San Domingo,* opera (Munich, Nov. 27, 1963); *17 Days & 4 Minutes,* burlesque opera (1969); *Casanova in London,* ballet (Munich, Nov. 23, 1969).

Ehlers, Alice. Date of birth, April 16, 1887 (not 1890).

Ehrenberg, Carl Emil Theodor. Died in Munich, Feb. 26, 1962.

Ehrling, Sixten. He made guest appearances with the Minneapolis Symph. Orch., Los Angeles Philharmonic and the Philadelphia Orch. In 1963 he was appointed music director and conductor of the Detroit Symph. Orchestra.

Eichner, Ernst. Add to bibl.: Marianne Reissinger, *Die Sinfonien Ernst Eichners* (Wiesbaden, 1970).

Einem, Gottfried von. Add to works: *Das Stundenlied,* choral suite with orch. (Hamburg, March 1, 1959); *Philadelphia Symphony,* commissioned by the Philadelphia Orchestra (first performed in Vienna, Nov. 14, 1961; the Philadelphia performance followed on Nov. 9, 1962).

Eisler, Hanns. Died in Berlin, Sept. 6, 1962. Add to bibl.: Hanns Eisler, *Reden und Aufsätze* (Leipzig, 1961); I. Nestyev, *Hanns Eisler and His Songs* (Moscow, 1962); N. Notowicz, *Hanns Eisler Quellennachweise* (Leipzig, 1966).

Eisma, Will, Dutch composer; b. Sungailiat, Indonesia, May 13, 1929. He studied violin at the Rotterdam Cons.; joined the Rotterdam Philharmonic as a violinist; then studied with Petrassi at the Accademia S. Cecilia in Rome, graduating in 1961. His music is based on tropes in the framework of the 12-tone technique. Among his works are 3 concertos for orch. (1958-1960); concerto for 2 violins and orch. (1961); chamber music.

Eitler, Esteban. Died in Santiago, Chile, Feb., 1960.

Ekier, Jan, Polish pianist and composer; b. Cracow, Aug. 29, 1913. He studied composition with Sikorski; became a concert pianist. Among his works is a suite, *Melodies in Color,* for mixed chorus and orch. to words from folk songs in Polish, Russian, German, French and English (1951).

Eklund, Hans, Swedish composer; b. Stockholm, July 1, 1927. He studied composition with Lars-Erik Larsson; in his music he applies Baroque techniques in a fairly advanced idiom. Works: 3 symphonies (1958, 1964, 1968); *Symphonic Dances* (1953); *Chamber Music No. 1* for cello and string orch. (1955); *Chamber Music No. 2* for trumpet and instruments (1956); *Chamber Music No. 3* for violin and chamber orch. (1957); *Bocetos españoles* for chamber orch. (1961); *Toccata* for orch. (1966); numerous minor pieces.

El-Dabh, Halim. Add to works: *Tahmela,* symph. poem (Cairo, Jan. 22, 1960); *Ballet of Lights* (Cairo, before the Sphinx, July 23, 1960); *Opera Flies,* on the story of the Kent State Univ. killings of 1969, the 'flies' in the title being an ironically bitter reference to the student victims (Washington, May 5, 1971).

Elgar, Sir **Edward (William).** His oratorio *The Light of Life* was first performed in Worcester in 1896 (not 1890). Add to bibl.: Michael Kennedy, *Portrait of Elgar* (London, 1968); Michael Hurd, *Elgar* (London, 1969).

Elías, Manuel Jorge de, Mexican composer; b. in Mexico City, June 5, 1939. He studied piano with his father Alfonso de Elías and conducting with Luis Herrera de la Fuente; later attended courses in modern music with Karlheinz Stockhausen. In 1968 he was appointed assistant conductor of the Orquesta Sinfónica Nacional in Mexico City. In his music he combines traditional instrumentation with tone-clusters and aleatory passages. Works: *Sinfonietta* (1958-61); *Elegía heroica,* symph. poem (1967); *Vitral No. 1* for orch. (1962); *Vitral No. 2* for chamber orch. and magnetic tape (1967); *Vitral No. 3* for orch. (1969); numerous pieces for chamber ensemble, for chorus and for piano. See 'Composers of the Americas,' vol. 15 (Washington, 1969).

Elizalde, Federico. Date of birth, Dec. 12, 1908 (not 1907).

Elkus, Albert Israel. Died in Oakland, Calif., Feb. 19, 1962.

Ellington, Edward Kennedy ("Duke" Ellington). Add to bibl.: P. Gammond, *Duke Ellington, His Life and Music* (London, 1958); S. Dance, *The World of Duke Ellington* (N. Y., 1970). In 1971 he toured Russia.

Ellis, Don, American trumpet player, arranger and composer; b. Los Angeles, July 25, 1934. He studied composition at Boston Univ. with Gardner Read and later at the Univ. of Calif., Los Angeles, with John Vincent. He took trumpet lessons with 7 teachers in Boston, New York and Los Angeles; was first trumpet player with the National Symph. Orch., Washington; then with numerous bands in Boston and New York; subsequently formed his own band. In his compositions and arrangements he boldly introduces nonbinary meters and asymmetrical rhythms. His major work is *Contrasts for Two Orchestras and Trumpet* (1965).

Elman, Mischa. Died in New York, April 5, 1967.

Eloy, Jean-Claude, French composer; b. Mont-Saint-Aignan (Seine-Maritime), June 15, 1938. He studied in Paris with Darius Milhaud and in Basel with Pierre Boulez. From his earliest works he adopted the advanced techniques of serialism; his main influences are Boulez, Varèse and Webern; there is an extreme miniaturization in his instrumental music. He composed *Équivalences* (1963) and *Faisceaux-Diffractions* (1970), both for chamber orch. In 1965 he visited the U. S.

Emmett, Daniel Decatur. Add to bibl.: Hans Nathan, *Dan Emmett and the Rise of Early Negro Minstrelsy* (Norman, Oklahoma, 1962).

Enacovici, Georg. Died in Bucharest, Jan. 26, 1965.

Enesco (Enescu), Georges. His posthumous symph. poem *Vox Maris,* written shortly before his death, was performed for the first time in Bucharest on Sept. 10, 1964. The first performances of his *Rapsodie Roumaine No. 1* and *Rapsodie Roumaine No. 2* took place in Bucharest on March 8, 1903 (not Feb. 7, 1908).

Engel, A. Lehman. Add to works: *Overture: Jackson* (Jackson, Miss., Feb. 13, 1961); *The Shoebird,* ballet (Jackson, Miss., April 20, 1968). He publ. an autobiography, *The Bright Day* (N. Y., 1956); an instruction book, *Planning and Producing the Musical Show* (N. Y., 1957; revised, 1966); an essay, *The American Musical Theater: A Consideration* (N. Y., 1967); edited a collection, *Three Centuries of Choral Music: Renaissance to Baroque* (N. Y., 1939-56). The title of his ballet is *Transitions* (not *Traditions*). For a detailed list of his works for the theater, see Walter Rigdon, ed., *Who's Who of the American Theater* (N. Y., 1966).

Engel, Hans. Died in Marburg, May 15, 1970.

Engelmann, Hans Ulrich, German composer; b. Darmstadt, Sept. 8, 1921. He had piano lessons while in high school; after the end of the disrupting war, he took courses in composition with Wolfgang Fortner in Heidelberg (1945-49); in 1948-50 he attended the classes of René Leibowitz and Ernst Krenek in Darmstadt; enrolled at the Univ. of Frankfurt (1946-52) in the classes of musicology (with Gennrich and Osthoff) and philosophy (with Adorno); in 1952, received his Dr. phil. with a thesis on Béla Bartók's *Mikrokosmos* (publ. Würzburg, 1953). Parallel to these pursuits, he took courses in architecture. In 1949 he held a Harvard Univ. stipend at the Salzburg Seminar in American Studies; was active in radio programming, composition for films and for the theater; spent a season in Iceland (1953-54); then was theater composer in Darmstadt (1954-61). In 1969 he was appointed instructor at the Musikhochschule in Frankfurt. His early works are impregnated by chromaticism with an impressionistic tinge; rhythmically his music is affected by jazz techniques. Under the influence of Leibowitz and Krenek he adopted the 12-tone method of composition, expanding it into a sui generis "field technique" of total serialism, in which rhythms and instrumental timbres are organized systematically. In his theater music he utilizes aleatory devices, musique concrète, and electronic sonorities. Works: *Klangstück* for violin and piano (1947); *Concerto* for cello and string orch. (1948); *Doktor Fausts Höllenfahrt,* chamber opera (Hamburg, Jan. 11, 1951); *Orchester-Fantasie* (1951); string quartet (1953); *Komposition in 4 Teilen* (1953; his first work in the 12-tone technique); *Partita* for 3 trumpets, percussion and strings (1953); *Integrale* for saxophone and piano (1954); *Strukturen* for chamber orch. (1954); *Atlantische Ballade* for voices, strings and percussion (1955); *Die Mauer,* dramatic cantata, after Langston Hughes (radio production, Hamburg, Oct. 4, 1955; stage première, Darmstadt, March 21, 1960); *Metall,* "chronicle" for soloists, chorus and orch. (1958); *Permutazioni* for flute, oboe, clarinet and bassoon (1959); *Ezra Pound Music* for chamber orch. (1959); *Der Verlorene Schatten,* opera (1960); *Trias* for piano, orch. and magnetic tape (1962); *Noche de Luna,* ballet (Lübeck, June 1, 1965); *Duplum* for 2 pianos (1965); *Manifest vom Menschen,* oratorio (1966); *Capricciosi* for orch. (1967); *Der Fall Van Damm,* radio opera (Cologne, June 7, 1968); *Sinfonies* for orch. (1968); *Ophelia,* music for action theater *(Hannover,* Feb. 1, 1969); *Drei Kreise* for orch. groups (1970).

English, Granville. Died in New York, Sept. 1, 1968.

Enriquez, Manuel, Mexican composer; b. Ocotlán, June 17, 1926. He studied violin and composition in Guadalajara; entered the Juilliard School of Music in N. Y. in 1955, and studied violin with Ivan Galamian, and composition with Peter Mennin. Returning to Mexico, he became a teacher of composition at the National Cons. of Music. As a composer, he has adopted a constructivist idiom, employing graphic optical notation. His works include Symph. No. 1 (1957); 2 violin concertos (1955, 1966); 2 string quartets (1959, 1967); *Obertura lírica* for orch. (1963); *Pentamúsica* for 5 wind instruments (1963); *Transición* for orch. (1965); *Trayectorías* for orch. (1967); *Ixamatl* for orch. (1969); *5 Plus 2* for flute, viola, trombone, piano and percussion (1969); *Concierto para 8* (1969); *Díptico I* for flute and piano (1969). See 'Composers of the Americas,' vol. 15 (Washington, 1969).

Eppert, Carl. Died in Milwaukee, Oct. 1, 1961. Wrote 7 symphonies (not 4).

Epstein, David M., American composer; b. New York, Oct. 3, 1930. He was educated at the New England Cons. of Music (M. Mus., 1953); at Brandeis Univ. (M. F. A., 1954), and Princeton Univ. (Ph.D., 1968); also studied composition privately with Darius Milhaud, and conducting with Max Rudolf, Izler Solomon and George Szell; appeared as conductor with the Cleveland Orch. and in Europe. In 1965 he was appointed prof. of music at the Massachusetts Institute of Technology in Cambridge, Mass. Works: *Movement* for orch. (1953); *Excerpts from a Diary,* song cycle (1953); piano trio (1953); *The Seasons,* song cycle, to poems by Emily Dickinson (1956); symphony (1958); piano variations (1961); string trio (1964); *Sonority-Variations* for orch. (1968); music for films.

Erb, Donald, American composer; b. Youngstown, Ohio, Jan. 17, 1927. He played the trumpet in dance bands and in the U. S. Navy; attended Kent State Univ. (B.S., 1950), the Cleveland Institute of Music (M.M., 1953) and Indiana Univ. (D.M., 1964); was a member of the music faculty at the Cleveland Institute of Music (1953-61), at Indiana Univ. (1961-64), at Bowling Green State Univ. (1964-65), at Case Institute of Technology (1965-67); composer-in-residence with the Dallas Symph. Orch. (1968-69); held fellowships and awards from Ford Foundation (1962-63), Guggenheim (1965-66); and National Council on the Arts (1967-68); in the summer of 1968 he headed the composition workshop at the Centennial Alaska Festival. His music combines classical structural elements with ultramodern serial and aleatory techniques. Works: *Dialogue* for violin and piano (1958); string quartet No. 1 (1960); *Spacemusic* for symphonic band (1963); *Hexagon* for 6 instruments (1963); *Antipodes* for string quartet and 4 percussion instruments (1963); *Symphony of Overtures* (Indiana Univ., Bloomington, Feb. 11, 1965); trio for violin, electric guitar and cello (1966); *Concerto* for solo percussion and orch. (Detroit, Dec. 29, 1966); *Reconnaissance* for violin, string bass, piano, percussion and 2 electronic setups (1967); *Christmas Music* for orch. (Cleveland, Dec. 21, 1967); *The Seventh Trumpet* for orch. (Dallas, April 5, 1969); *Basspiece* for string bass and 4 tracks of prerecorded string bass (1969); *Klangfarbenfunk I* for orch., rock band and electronic sounds (Detroit, Oct. 1, 1970).

Erbse, Heimo. Add to works: *Julietta,* opera semiseria (Salzburg, Aug. 17, 1959).

Erdmann, Eduard. Died in Hamburg, June 21, 1958.

Erickson, Robert, American composer; b. Marquette, Mich., March 7, 1917. He studied music with Wesley La Violette at the Chicago Cons.; with Ernst Krenek at Hamline Univ. in St. Paul (B. A., 1943); in 1950, attended a seminar in composition under Roger Sessions at the Univ. of Calif., Berkeley; in 1966 held a Guggenheim Fellowship. In 1967 he was appointed prof. of composition at the Univ. of Calif., San Diego. In his music he explores electronic and serial techniques. Works: *Introduction and Allegro* for orch. (Minneapolis, March 11, 1949); piano sonata (1948); string quartet No. 1 (1950); piano trio (1953); *Divertimento* for flute, clarinet and strings (1953); *Fantasy* for cello and orch. (1953), string quartet No. 2 (1956); *Variations* for orch. (1957); *Duo* for violin and piano (1959); *Chamber Concerto* (1960); *Toccata* for piano (1962); *Concerto* for piano and 7 instruments (1963); *Sirens and Other Flyers* for orch. (1965); *Piece for Bells and Toy Pianos* (1965); *Ricercar a 5* for trombone and tape (1966); *Scapes,* a 'contest for 2 groups' (1966); *Birdland* for electronic tape (1967); *Ricercar a 3* for solo double-bass and electronic tape (1967); *Cardenitas,* dramatic aria for singer, mime, conductor, 7 musicians and stereophonic prerecorded tape (1968); *Pacific Sirens,* for instruments and tape (1969); *General Speech* for trombone (1969).

d'Erlanger, Rodolphe, French musicologist; b. Boulogne-sur-Seine, 1872; d. Sidi-Bou-Sadi, Tunisia, Oct. 29, 1932. He lived most of his life in Tunisia; collected Arab folk songs; selected and edited treatises on music by Arab scholars of the 10th - 16th centuries, which were published in 6 vols. (1930, 1935, 1938, 1939, 1949, 1959).

Ernesaks, Gustav, Estonian composer; b. Chariu, Dec. 12, 1908. He studied composition at the Tallinn Cons. with Arthur Kapp; then was active as a choral conductor. He wrote the music drama *Tormida Rand* (*Stormy Coast;* Tallinn, Sept. 29, 1949), and a comic opera *Bridegrooms* (1960); also many mass songs in Estonian.

Erpf, Hermann. Died in Stuttgart, Oct. 17, 1969.

Escobar, Luis Antonio. Add to works: *Sinfonía Cero* (1955); *Sinfonía X* (1955); piano concerto (1959); *Juramento a Bolívar* for male chorus and orch. (1964); *Little Symphony* (Washington, May 7, 1965).

Escobar-Budge, Roberto, Chilean composer; b. Santiago, May 11, 1926. He studied composition in Santiago with René Amengual and Alfonso Letelier; was active as a music critic. His works include a wind quintet (1957); *Diferencias Sinfónicas* for orch. (1962); *Los Bisontes,* symph. suite (1964); nonet (1965); *Cuarteto Estructural* for strings (1965); *Sinfonía Valparaíso* (1967); *Incógnita* for harpsichord, trumpet, bassoon, cello and percussion (1967); choruses; piano pieces.

Escudier, Léon. Born Sept. 17, 1816 (not 1821); his brother, **Marie Escudier,** was born on June 29, 1809 (not 1819); died on April 18 (not 17), 1880.

Eshpai, Andrey, Soviet composer, son of Yakov Eshpai; b. Kozmodemiansk, May 15, 1925. He studied with Aram Khatchaturian in Moscow; during the war he acted as a translator from German. In his music he makes use of folk motives of the Mari nation from which he descended. Works: 2 symphonies (1959, 1962); piano concerto (1954); violin concerto (1956); several symph. suites; choruses. He is also successful as composer of popular songs.

Eshpai, Yakov, Russian composer of Mari extraction; b. near Zvenigorodsk, Nov. 11, 1890; d. Moscow, Feb. 20, 1963. He studied violin and singing in Kazan, and later at the Moscow Cons. He publ. important collections of national songs of the Ural region, particularly of the Mari ethnic group; also wrote vocal and instrumental music on native themes.

Esplá, Oscar. Add to works: *Sinfonía Aitana* (Madrid, Oct. 31, 1964); *Nochebuena del Diablo,* scenic cantata (Madrid, Oct. 21, 1967). Bibl.: A. Iglesias, *Oscar Esplá* (Madrid, 1960).

Esser, Heinrich. Add bibl.: Karl-Josef Müller, *Heinrich Esser als Komponist* (Mainz, 1969).

Estes, Charles E. Died in Dover, New Hampshire, Sept. 16, 1968.

Estévez, Antonio, Venezuelan composer; b. Calabozo, Jan. 3, 1916. He studied composition in Caracas with Vicente Emilio Sojo; played the oboe in the Caracas Symph. Orch. At the age of 50 he became interested in electronic music and obtained a scholarship from the Venezuelan National Institute of Culture and Fine Arts to study electronic techniques in Paris. Works: *Suite Llanera* for orch.

(1942); *Cantata Criolla* for voices and orch. (1954); choruses; piano pieces and a group of electronic works under the title *Cosmovibrafonía.*

Etler, Alvin Derald. Was on the staff of the Univ. of Illinois from 1947 to 1949; since 1949 teaching at Smith College. Add to works: *Triptych* for orch. (1961); Concerto for wind quintet and orch. (Tokyo, Oct. 18, 1962); brass quintet (1962); string quartet No. 1 (1963); string quartet No. 2 (1965); concerto for string quartet and orch. (1967).

Eulenburg, Kurt. He safely passed his 92nd birthday on Feb. 22, 1971.

Evangelisti, Franco, Italian composer of avant-garde convictions; b. Rome, Jan. 21, 1926. He studied in Rome and, with Genzmer, in Darmstadt; experimented with electronic music in the studios of Cologne and Warsaw. Works: *4!* for violin and piano (1954); *Variazioni* for orch. (1955); *Incontri di fasce sonore* for magnetic tape (1957); *Ordini* for orch. (1958); *Campi integrati* for magnetic tape (1959); *Proporzioni* for flute solo (1960); *Aleatorio* for chamber orch. (1960); *Spazio a 5* for voices and percussion (1961); *Random or not Random* for orch. (1962).

Evans, Ian Ernest Gilmore Green (Gil), Canadian jazz pianist and bandleader; b. Toronto, May 13, 1912. He went to California as a youth and had a band of his own in Stockton (1933-38); then moved to N. Y.; made arrangements of popular songs utilizing non-jazz instruments; became a proponent of bebop style of rhythmic swing; his version of *Boplicity* is a milestone of cool jazz. Moving toward increasingly complex modernity, he applied polyharmonic and polyrhythmic procedures in his arrangements.

Evett, Robert, American composer; b. Loveland, Colorado, Nov. 30, 1922. He studied with Roy Harris in Colorado Springs; settled in Washington as writer and composer. Works: cello concerto (1954); *Variations* for clarinet and orch. (1955); piano concerto (1957); Symph. No. 1 (1960); concerto for harpsichord and orch. (Washington, April 25, 1961); sonata for cello and harpsichord (1955); viola sonata (1958); piano quartet (1961); sonata for oboe and harpsichord (1964); Symph. No. 2, *Billy Ascends* for voices and orch., to the text by Melville (Washington, May 7, 1965); *The Windhover,* a concerto for bassoon and orch. (5th Inter-American Music Festival, Washington, May 20, 1971); songs; piano pieces.

Evseyev, Sergey Vassilievitch. Died on March 16 (not June), 1956.

Ewald, Victor Vladimirovitch, Russian composer; b. St. Petersburg, Nov. 27, 1860; d. Leningrad, April 26, 1935. He studied engineering; from 1895 to 1915 was prof. at the Institute of Civil Engineering. Music was his avocation; he played the cello and the French horn; took part in Belaieff's quartet evenings and wrote a number of chamber music works; of these, his brass quintet and a symphony for 5-part brass choir are still popular. After the Revolution he continued his primary profession as a civil engineer and instructor; also was active as an ethnomusicologist and participated in the expeditions in the North of European Russia collecting folk songs. His daughter Zinaida (1894-1942) continued his work in folklore and publ. several collections of Russian songs, in collaboration with her husband Evgeny Gippius (b. 1903).

Ewen, David. His 75th book, *New Encyclopedia of the Opera,* a radical revision of *Encyclopedia of the Opera* (first publ. in 1955), was issued in 1971. Statistically, Ewen has written and publ. more books on music than anyone, living or dead; has fiinancially harvested a maximum in the field. Some of his publications have been translated into 17 languages. Titles (not including all the revisions published with the amplificatory modifier 'New'): *Complete Book of the American Musical Theater* (N. Y., 1958; extremely valuable; brought up to date as *The New Complete Book of the American Musical Theater,* 1970); *Encyclopedia of Concert Music* (N. Y., 1959); *The World of Jerome Kern* (N. Y., 1960); *Leonard Bernstein* (N. Y., 1960; revised 1967); *History of Popular Music* (N. Y., 1961); *The Story of America's Musical Theater* (N.Y., 1961; revised 1969); *Ewen's Lighter Classics in Music* (N. Y., 1961); *David Ewen Introduces Modern Music* (N. Y., 1962; revised in 1969); *The Book of European Light Opera* (N. Y., 1962); *Popular American Composers* (N. Y., 1962); *The Complete Book of Classical Music* (N.Y., 1963); *The Life and Death of Tin Pan Alley* (N. Y., 1964); *American Popular Songs: From the Revolutionary War to the Present* (N. Y., 1966); *Great Composers: 1300-1900* (N. Y., 1966); *The World of 20th-Century Music* (N. Y., 1968); *Composers Since 1900* (N. Y., 1969); *George Gershwin: His Journey to Greatness* (N. Y., 1970; originally publ. in 1956 under the main title *A Journey to*

Greatness, but enlarged and completely rewritten); *Great Men of American Popular Songs* (N. Y., 1970); *Composers of Tomorrow's Music* (N. Y., 1971); also publ. a number of books for young people (on Gershwin, Bernstein, Haydn, Irving Berlin, Toscanini, Johann Strauss, Jerome Kern, Richard Rodgers and Cole Porter). He rewrote, revised and expanded the *Milton Cross Encyclopedia of Great Composers* (N. Y., 1960). Revised editions of *The Book of Modern Composers,* originally publ. in 1943, appeared as *The New Book of Modern Composers* in 1960 and 1967. He further edited *The World of Great Composers* (Englewood Cliffs, N. J., 1962).

Expert, Henry. Vols. IV, V, VII, VIII, IX, and X of his collection of Renaissance music contain works publ. in vol. I of *Les Maîtres Musiciens* . . . and thus are not separate publications.

Eybler, Joseph. Born on Feb. 8, 1765 (not 1764).

F

Fachiri, Adila. Died in Florence, Dec. 15, 1962.

Falk, Richard. Died in New York, March 3, 1949. Born April 29, 1878 (not 1886),

Falla, Manuel de. His posthumous opera *La Atlántida* was completed by Ernesto Halffter and produced at La Scala, Milan, on June 18, 1962. The first performance, in concert form, of *El retablo de Maese Pedro* took place in Seville (not in Madrid) on March 23, 1923 (not in 1919); a private stage performance was given in the salon of Princesse de Polignac, in Paris, on June 25, 1923; first public stage performance, Paris, Nov. 13, 1923, under the composer's direction. Add to bibl.: Suzanne Demarquez, *Manuel de Falla* (Paris, 1963; also in English, Philadelphia, 1968); J. J. Vinegra y Lasso de la Vega, *Vida intima de Manuel de Falla* (Cadiz, 1966); A. Saeardia, *Vida y obra de Manuel de Falla* (Madrid, 1967).

Fano, Guido Alberto. Died in Tauriano di Spilimbergo (Udine), Aug. 14, 1961.

Farkas, Ferenc. Add to works: *Cantus Pannonicus,* cantata to the Latin verses of the 15th-century Hungarian archbishop Janus Pannonius (Budapest, April 3, 1959).

Farmer, Henry George. Died in Law, Lanarkshire, Dec. 30, 1965.

Farrar, Geraldine. Died in Ridgefield, Conn., March 11, 1967.

Farrell, Eileen, American soprano; b. Willimantic, Connecticut, Feb. 13, 1920. Her parents were vaudeville singers; she received her early vocal training with Merle Alcock in New York, and later studied with Eleanor McLellan. In 1940 she sang on the radio; in 1947-48 made a U. S. tour as a concert singer; toured South America in 1949. Her song recital in New York on Oct. 24, 1950 was enthusiastically acclaimed and secured for her immediate recognition. She was soloist in Beethoven's Ninth Symphony with Toscanini and the NBC Symph. Orch.; also appeared many times with the N. Y. Philharmonic. In 1958 she joined the San Francisco Opera Co. and in 1959 became a member of the Lyric Opera of Chicago. On Dec. 6, 1960, she made a successful debut with the Metropolitan Opera Co., N. Y., in Gluck's *Alcestis.* Her voice is remarkable for its projective power and indefatigability.

Farrow, Norman D., Canadian baritone; b. Regina, May 6, 1916. He studied at the Juilliard School of Music and at N. Y. Univ.; took voice lessons with Mack Harrell and others; was one of the organizers of the Bach Aria Group. He toured as soloist with choral ensembles; in 1960 he was engaged as artist-in-residence at Southern Methodist Univ. in Dallas.

Fauchet, Paul Robert, French composer; b. Paris, June 27, 1881; d. there, Nov. 12, 1937. He studied at the Paris Cons., and later taught harmony there; also was the Maître de Chapelle of the Saint-Pierre de Chaillot in Paris. He wrote a number of sacred works, but is remembered mainly for his *Symphonie* for band, the earliest example of a classical symphony written for the medium (1936); it even had some modern instances; its *Scherzo* is profusely enmeshed with whole-tone scales.

Fauré, Gabriel-Urbain. Add to bibl.: E. Vuillermoz, *Gabriel Fauré* (Paris, 1960; also in English, Philadelphia, 1969). The first performance of *Prométhée* took place on Aug. 27 (not Aug. 1), 1900.

Fay, Maud, American soprano; b. San Francisco, April 18, 1879; d. there, Oct. 7, 1964. She studied in Dresden; became a member of the Munich opera (1906-16); appeared in Covent Garden, London, in 1910, and with the Thomas Beecham Opera Co. in

1914. After the outbreak of World War I she returned to America; sang with the Metropolitan Opera in 1916; also appeared with the Chicago Opera Co. She was particularly distinguished in Wagnerian roles.

Feather, Leonard, British-American writer on music, expert on jazz; b. London, Sept. 13, 1914. He studied at St. Paul School in London; in 1935 he came to the U. S.; naturalized in 1948. He held various jobs as an arranger, lyricist, advisor for jazz festivals, radio commentator and lecturer; specialized in the field of jazz and folk music; publ. *Inside Be-bop* (N. Y., 1949); a compendious *Encyclopedia of Jazz* (N. Y., 1955), which he supplemented by *New Encyclopedia of Jazz* (1960); and *Encyclopedia of Jazz in the 60's* (1966). He makes his home in Hollywood.

Feicht, Hieronim. Died in Warsaw, March 31, 1967.

Feinberg, Samuel Evgenievitch. Died in Moscow, Oct. 23, 1962.

Fekete, Zóltan. The acute accent should be placed on a (not on o) in Zoltán.

Feld, Jindřich, Czech composer; b. Prague, Feb. 19, 1925. He studied violin with his father; composition at the Prague Cons., graduating in 1952. Among his works are *Furiant* for symph. orch. (1950); Concerto for orch. (1951); flute concerto (1954); Rhapsody for violin and orch. (1955); much chamber music in a neo-baroque manner.

Feldman, Morton, American composer of the avant-garde; b. New York, Jan. 12, 1926. He studied piano with Vera Maurina-Press and composition with Wallingford Riegger and Stefan Wolpe. Profoundly impressed by the abstract expressionism of modern painting, he evolved a congenial set of musical concepts and introduced an element of predetermined indeterminacy into the performance of his music. Accordingly, he indicates only an approximation of the notes to be played in a musical 'action,' specifying the instrumental range (high, medium, low) and the number of notes per time unit in any voluntary or involuntary rhythmic distribution. He uses graphic optical notation optionally, transcribing it into traditional score for practical performance. His works include several sets of instrumental pieces, with subsets designated by Roman numerals: *Durations I-V; Extensions I-V; Projections I-V; Vertical Thoughts I-V; Intermissions I-VI; Structures I-II; Intervals* for baritone and instruments; *Eleven Instruments* for 11 instruments; *Two Instruments* for cello and French horn; pieces for piano solo, piano 3 hands, piano 4 hands. 2 pianos, 4 pianos; *Last Pieces* for piano solo; *Numbers* for 9 instruments; *Journey to the End of the Night* for soprano and 4 wind instruments; ballet *Ixion;* cantata, *The Swallows of Salangan* for mixed chorus and 16 instruments; *The Straits of Magellan* for 7 instruments; *Atlantis* for chamber orch.; *De Kooning* for piano, violin, cello, French horn and percussion; *For Franz Kline* for soprano, violin. cello. French horn, chimes and piano; *Rabbi Akiba* for soprano and 10 instruments; *Mme. Press Died Last Week at 90* (St. Paul de Vence, July 20, 1970, Lukas Foss conducting); *The Viola in My Life* for viola and 6 instrumentalists (1970).

Fellerer, Karl Gustav. Add to books: *Einführung in die Musikwissenschaft* (Hamburg, 1956). Edited *Beiträge zur Musikgeschichte der Stadt Essen* (Cologne, 1955); *Beiträge zur Geschichte der Musik am Niederrhein* (Cologne, 1956). A *Festschrift* was publ. to honor him on his 60th birthday (Regensburg, 1962).

Felsenstein, Walter, Austrian opera director; b. Vienna, May 30, 1901. He studied music in Graz; was opera intendant in Mannheim (1924-25); Basel (1927-29); Freiburg-im-Breisgau (1929-32); Cologne (1932-34); Frankfurt (1934-36); Zürich (1938-40) and in Berlin (1940-47). In 1947 he became director of the Komische Oper in East Berlin, bringing it to a high point of excellence. He visited the U.S. in the spring of 1971 on a lecture tour illustrated by films of his productions.

Felumb, Svend Christian. Resigned as conductor of the Tivoli Orch. in Copenhagen in 1962.

Ferand, Ernest T. First name should be spelled Ernst.

Fere, Vladimir Georgievitch, Russian composer and ethnomusicologist; b. Kamyshin, in the Saratov district, May 20, 1902. He studied piano with Goldenweiser and composition with Glière and Miaskovsky in Moscow. In 1936 he went to Frunze, Kirgizia; composed (in collaboration with Vlasov) a number of operas based on materials by native composers, among them *Golden Girl* (Frunze, May 1, 1937); *Moon Beauty* (Frunze, April 15, 1939); *For People's Happiness* (Frunze, May 1, 1941); *Patriots* (Frunze, Nov. 6, 1941); *Son of the People* (Frunze, Nov. 8, 1947); *On the Shores of*

Issyk-Kul (Frunze, Feb. 1, 1951). Returning to Moscow, he continued to promote the cause of Kirghiz music; also wrote a symphony *Kirgizstan* and some other music on Central Asian themes.

Ferguson, Donald Nivison. Add to books: *Music as Metaphor; The Elements of Expression* (Minneapolis, 1960); *Image and Structure in Chamber Music* (Minneapolis, 1964).

Ferrari, Gabriella. First name should be spelled Gabrielle.

Ferrari-Trecate, Luigi. Died in Rome, April 17, 1964. Place of birth, Alessandria (not Alexandria). The exact date of the first performance of *Bellinda e il mostro* (in the final version, *La Bella e il mostro*) is March 20, 1926. The opera *Il rè Orso* (properly *L'Orso rè*) was produced at La Scala, Milan, Feb. 8, 1950 (not 1949); Add opera, *Buricchio* (Bologna, Nov. 5, 1948).

Février, Henri. Died in Paris, July 6, 1957.

Fiala, George, Russian-Canadian composer; b. Kiev, March 31, 1922. He studied at the Kiev Cons. (1939-41) with Revutsky, Liatoshinsky and others. When the Germans occupied Kiev in 1942, he went to Berlin, where he continued his studies despite wartime difficulties. In 1945 he moved to Brussels, where he took lessons with Léon Jongen. In 1949 he emigrated to Canada, settling in Montreal. Beginning with a romantically colored Russian type of composition, Fiala went through a neo-classical phase, and after 1961 adopted the dodecaphonic method and other serial procedures. Works: piano concerto (1946); *Symph. in E minor* (1950); Capriccio for piano and orch. (1962); *Shadows of Our Forgotten Ancestors,* symph. poem (1962); *Ukrainian Suite* for cello and piano (1948); woodwind quintet (1948); trio for oboe, cello and piano (1948); woodwind octet (1948); 2 saxophone quartets (1955, 1961); string quartet (1956); quartet for 4 cellos (1957); piano quartet (1957); *Australian Suite* for piano (1960); cello sonata (1970). See '34 Biographies of Canadian Composers,' issued by the Canadian Broadcasting Corporation (1964).

Fields, James, American pianist; b. Los Angeles, Nov. 1, 1948. He studied piano with Ethel Leginska and Victor Aller; appeared in public as a child. In 1965 he won a debut grant of the Young Musicians Foundation in California, which catapulted him into a promising concert career at the age of sixteen.

Figner, Nicolay Nicolayevitch. Born in Nikiforovka, in the Kazan government (not in St. Petersburg), Feb. 10, 1857. Add bibl.: *Nicolay Figner: Recollections, Letters, Materials* (Leningrad, 1968).

Figueredo, Carlos, Venezuelan composer; b. Valencia, Aug. 15, 1910. He studied with Vicente Emilio Sojo at the Caracas School of Music graduating in 1947. For 7 years (1948-55) he was on the staff of the Venezuelan Embassy in Paris. He writes in a moderately modern idiom. Among his works are 4 symphonies, a string quartet, a violin sonata and choruses.

Filiasi, Lorenzo. Died in Rome, July 30, 1963.

Filleul, Henri. Died at Saint-Omer, May 1, 1959; he spelled his first name Henry (not Henri). St. Omer is in France (not in Belgium, as erroneously stated).

Finagin, Alexei Vassilievitch. Died in Leningrad, Feb. 4, 1942. Date of birth, March 16 (not March 17), 1890.

Fine, Irving. Died in Boston, Aug. 23, 1962. Add to works: *Symphony* (Boston, March 23, 1962).

Finke, Fidelio Fritz. Died in Dresden, June 12, 1968.

Finney, Ross Lee. Add to works: Symph. No. 1 (1943); Symph. No. 2 (Ann Arbor, Michigan, May 8, 1960); *Variations* for orch. (1962); *Still Are New Worlds,* for narrator, chorus, orch. and tape (1963); Symph. No. 3 (Philadelphia, March 6, 1964).

Fischer, Edwin. Died in Zürich, Jan. 24, 1960.

Fischer, Wilhelm. Died in Vienna, Feb. 27, 1962.

Fischer, William Gustavus, American hymn writer; b. Baltimore, Oct. 14, 1835; d. Philadelphia, Aug. 13, 1912. He sang in a Baltimore German church; was a bookbinder by trade and a choral conductor by avocation; then entered the retail piano business and, under its imprint, Gould & Fischer, printed a number of Sunday-school leaflets. Of his songs, *Coming to the Cross,* first sung at a National Camp meeting at Hamilton, Mass., June 22, 1870, is the best known. Cf. R. G. McCutchan, *Our Hymnody* (N. Y., 1937).

Fišer, Luboš (pronounced Fisher), Czech composer; b. Prague, Sept. 30, 1935. He studied at the Prague Cons. and at the Academy of Music and Dramatic Arts. He wrote a successful opera *Lancelot* (Prague, May 19, 1961); two symphonies (1956, 1960); a string quartet; sextet for flute, oboe, clarinet, horn, bassoon and piano; a violin sonata; 4 piano sonatas; a symphonic suite, *15 Prints After Dürer's Apocalypse* (Prague, May 15, 1966; shared Third Prize at the Prague Spring Competition in 1966); *Report* for orch. (1971).

Fisher, Stephen D., American composer; b. Albany, N. Y., May 27, 1940. He studied at the New England Cons. in Boston with Billy Jim Layton and Daniel Pinkham; received a BMI Student Composers Award in 1960. Works: *Involution* for piccolo, trumpet and harpsichord (1963); *Music for 9 Instruments* (1963); string quartet (1964).

Fiume, Orazio, Italian composer; b. Monopoli, Jan. 16, 1908. He studied piano and theory in Palermo and Naples; was later a student of Pizzetti (composition) and Molinari (conducting) in Rome. He taught harmony at the Cons. of Parma (1941-51), at Milan (1951-59), Pesaro (1959-60) and in 1961 became director of the Cons. of Trieste. His music follows the tradition of expansive Italian romanticism. He wrote an opera *Il Tamburo di panno* (Rome, April 12, 1962); 2 concertos for orch. (1945, 1956); cantata *Ajace* (1940); songs.

Flagello, Nicolas, American composer of Italian extraction; b. New York, March 15, 1928. He studied piano, violin, cello and oboe; obtained his M. M. from the Manhattan School of Music in 1950; then went to Italy where he took lessons with Ildebrando Pizzetti at the St. Cecilia Academy in Rome; received his Mus. D. degree there in 1956. Returning to the U. S., he joined the staff of the Manhattan School of Music. He toured as accompanist to Tito Schipa, Richard Tucker and other singers; played violin, viola and oboe in various orchestras; in 1960-61 served as assistant conductor at the Chicago Lyric Opera. His music exhales an uninhibited lyrical sentiment in the finest Italianate tradition and is animated in rapid passages by an impetuous flow of kinetic energy; his contrapuntal and harmonic lines are invariably lucid. Flagello writes in a modern idiom with a prudential application of non-toxic dissonances. Works: *Lyra* for 6 brass instruments (1945); *Beowulf,* symph. poem (1949); piano concerto No. 1 (1950); *Mirra,* opera in 3 acts (1953); *The Wig,* one-act opera (1953); piano concerto No. 2 (1955); violin concerto (1956); *Rip Van Winkle,* children's operetta (1957); *Missa sinfonica* for orch. without voices (1957); *The Sisters,* one-act opera (1958; N. Y., Feb. 23, 1961); *Concerto* for string orch. (1959); *The Judgment of St. Francis,* one-act opera (1959; N. Y., March 18, 1966); *Divertimento* for piano and percussion (1960); *Capriccio* for cello and orch. (1961); *Burlesca* for flute and guitar (1961); piano concerto No. 3 (1962); *Concertino* for piano, brass and timpani (1963); violin sonata (1963); *Lautrec,* ballet suite (1965); Symphony No. 1 (1967; N. Y., April 23, 1971); *Passion of Martin Luther King* for soloists, orch. and chorus (1968); *Te Deum for Mankind* for chorus (1968); *The Piper of Hamelin,* children's opera to Flagello's own libretto (1970).

Flagstad, Kirsten. Died in Oslo, Dec. 7, 1962.

Flament, Édouard. Died in Bois-Colombes (Seine), Dec. 27, 1958.

Flanagan, William, American composer; b. Detroit, Aug. 14, 1923; d. New York, Aug. 31, 1969 (found dead in his apartment, a victim of an overdose of barbiturates). He studied composition at the Eastman School of Music, Rochester, N. Y., with Burrill Phillips and Bernard Rogers; then at the Berkshire Music Center in Tanglewood with Arthur Honegger, Arthur Berger and Aaron Copland; also, in N. Y., with David Diamond. Concurrently, he became engaged in musical journalism; was a reviewer for the N. Y. 'Herald Tribune' (1957-60). His style of composition is characterized by an intense pursuit of an expressive melodic line, projected on polycentric but firmly tonal harmonies. Works: one-act opera *Bartleby,* after Melville's short story (1952-57; N. Y., Jan. 24, 1961); *A Concert Ode for orch.* (1951; Detroit, Jan. 14, 1960); *A Concert Overture* (N. Y., Dec. 4, 1959); *Divertimento for Classical Orchestra* (1948; Toledo, Ohio, Jan. 9, 1960); *Notations* for large orch. (1960); *Chapter from Ecclesiastes,* for mixed chorus and string quintet (N. Y., March 21, 1963); *Narrative for Orchestra* (Detroit, March 25, 1964); *Divertimento* for string quartet (1947); *Chaconne* for violin and piano (1948); *Passacaglia* for piano (1947); piano sonata (1950); song cycles. He wrote background music for

Edward Albee's plays *The Sandbox* (1961) and *The Ballad of the Sad Café* (1963). See articles on Flanagan in the 'Bulletin of the American Composers Alliance' (Sept. 1961).

Fleisher, Edwin A. Died in Philadelphia, Jan. 9, 1959.

Fleisher, Leon. His right hand became inoperative in 1964 owing to an intractable psychosomatic ailment; unable to continue his career as a pianist, he turned to conducting. In 1968 he was appointed conductor of the Annapolis Symphony. In 1970 he conducted concerts of classical music in New York, receiving fine critical notices. He is on the staff of the Peabody Cons. in Baltimore.

Fleming, Robert, Canadian pianist and composer; b. Prince Albert, Saskatchewan, Nov. 12, 1921. He studied at the Royal College of Music in London with Arthur Benjamin (piano) and Herbert Howells (composition). After service in the Canadian Air Force in World War II he continued his musical education at the Toronto Cons. with Healey Willan and others. He subsequently joined the staff of the National Film Board of Canada and devoted his energies mainly to composing for films. Works: *Around the House,* suite for orch. (1942); *Kaleidoscope* for orch. (1949); *Westland* for orch. (1950); *Shadow on the Prairie,* symph. suite (1953); *Recollections* for violin and strings (1954). *Summer Suite* for orch. (1958); *Short and Simple,* suite for strings and piano (1959); brass quintet (1962); *Maritime Suite* for woodwinds, strings and harp (1962); piano concerto (1963); songs.

Flesch, Karl. Add bibl.: *The Memoirs of Carl Flesch,* ed. by Hans Keller and C. F. Flesch (London, 1958).

Fletcher, Grant. In 1970 he was appointed to the staff of the Arizona State Univ. at Tempe. Add to works: opera, *The Sack of Calabasas* (1964; excerpts performed in Phoenix, Arizona, April 6, 1964); *Glyphs* for orch. (1968); *Diaphony* for symph. band (1968); *Uroboros* for a percussion ensemble (1969); Symph. No. 2 (1970).

Flores, Bernal, Costa Rican composer; b. San José, July 28, 1937. After acquiring the rudiments of music in Costa Rica he came to the U.S. and enrolled at the Eastman School of Music in Rochester (M.M., 1962; Ph.D. 1964). Returning to Costa Rica, he became prof. at the Cons. of San José. Works: Symph. No. 1 for strings (1965); Symph. No. 2 (1966); Concerto for piano, percussion and orch. (1963); clarinet concerto (1968); piano pieces; songs.

Florio, Caryl. The title of his second opera is *Uncle Tom's Cabin* (not *Uncle Tom*).

Flosman, Oldřich, Czech composer; b. Plzen, April 5, 1925. He was educated at the Prague Cons.; wrote mostly chamber music: string quartet; wind quintet; a suite for nonet; sonata for clarinet and piano; also concertos for clarinet and bassoon; theater music.

Flower, Sir Newman. Died in Dorset, March 12, 1964.

Floyd, Carlisle. Add operas: *Wuthering Heights* (Santa Fe, July 16, 1958); *The Passion of Jonathan Wade* (N. Y., Oct. 11, 1962); *The Sojourner and Mollie Sinclair* (Raleigh, N. Carolina, Dec. 2, 1963); *Markheim* (New Orleans, March 31, 1966); *Of Mice and Men,* after John Steinbeck's novel (Seattle, Jan. 22, 1970).

Flury, Richard. Died in Solothurn, Switzerland, Dec. 23, 1967.

Foerster, Josef Bohuslav. The spelling of his 4th opera should be *Nepřemožení.*

Fomin, Evstigney Ipatovitch. The manuscript score of his opera *The Americans* (the title refers to Russians in Alaska) was not discovered in 1940; the vocal score was publ. as early as 1893.

Fongaard, Björn, Norwegian composer; b. Oslo, March 2, 1919. He studied at the Oslo Cons. with Bjarne Brustad; later took a course in advanced techniques with Karl Andersen. He also began to experiment with fractional intervals. His total output numbers 340 polyphonic studies in tonality, 12 piano sonatinas, 44 experimental piano pieces, and much instrumental music. Fascinated by science, he wrote a symph. poem, *Uran 235,* glorifying the energy of the fissionable isotope (1963); *Galaxies* for three specially designed quarter-tone guitars (1966); *Kosmos* for strings and percussion (1968). Other works are: *Orafoni* for male speaking chorus, strings and percussion (1964); *Orchestra Antiphonalis* (1968); *Sonata* for a single tam-tam, electronically metamorphosed (1968); *Vision* for strings (1968). Fongaard is renowned as a guitar virtuoso and is professor of guitar playing at the Cons. of Oslo.

Forbes, Elliot, American choral conductor and music educator; b. Cambridge, Mass.,

Aug. 30, 1917. He studied at Harvard Univ. (B.A., 1941; M.A., 1947); also took courses at Mozarteum in Salzburg (1937). He subsequently joined the staff of the Music Dept. of Princeton Univ. (1947-57). In 1958 he was appointed prof. of Harvard Univ. and conductor of the Harvard Glee Club and Radcliffe Choral Society; conducted the Harvard Glee Club in a tour around the world in 1961 and the Harvard-Radcliffe Chorus in a North American tour in 1964. In 1965 he taught at the Berkshire Music Center in Tanglewood. He is the editor of the revision of Thayer's *Life of Beethoven* (Princeton, 1964), of *Harvard-Radcliffe Choral Music* and the *Harvard Song Book* (Boston, 1965).

Fornerod, Aloys, Swiss violinist and composer; b. Montet-Cudrefin (Vaud), Nov. 16, 1890; d. Fribourg, Switzerland, Jan. 8, 1965. He studied violin and theory at the Cons. of Lausanne and at the Schola Cantorum in Paris. Returning to Switzerland, he was a member of the Lausanne Symph. Orch.; in 1954 he was appointed director of the Fribourg Cons. As a composer, he followed the French modern style, in the spirit of fin-de-siècle impressionism. Works: *Geneviève,* one-act comic opera (Lausanne, May 20, 1954); *Te Deum* for soloists, chorus and orch. (1955); *Hymne à la Très Sainte Trinité* for chorus and brass (1961); *Le Voyage de printemps,* symph. suite (1943); piano concerto (1944); violin sonata (1925); concerto for 2 violins and piano (1927); cello sonata (1934); choruses and songs. He publ. *Les Tendances de la musique moderne* (Lausanne, 1924); was for 40 years a critic in 'La Tribune de Lausanne.'

Fortner, Wolfgang. He revised the previous two versions of his opera to García Lorca's play (*Der Wald* and *Die Bluthochzeit*); also wrote an opera on another play by Lorca, *In seinem Garten liebt Don Perlimplin Belison* (Schwetzingen, May 10, 1962). Add to works: *Triplum* for 3 pianos and orch. (International Festival for Contemporary Music, Prague, Oct. 4, 1967); *Immagini* for strings with optional sopranos (1967); *Marginalien* for orch. (1969). In 1961 he taught a master class in composition at the Berkshire Music Center at Tanglewood; he visited the U.S. again in 1968. Bibl.: H. Lindlar, ed., *Wolfgang Fortner* (Rodenkirchen, 1960).

Foss, Lukas. From 1963 to 1970 he was musical director and conductor of the Buffalo Philharmonic Orch.; revolutionized its repertory by introducing ultra-modern scores. In his own compositions he abandoned his erstwhile neo-classical idiom and adopted novel techniques, including an element of 'controlled improvisation.' Add to works: *Symphony of Chorales,* based on Bach's chorales (Pittsburgh, Oct. 24, 1958); *Introductions and Goodbyes,* miniature opera (N. Y., May 6, 1960); *Time Cycle,* suite for soprano and orch. in 4 movements to texts by Auden, Housman, Kafka and Nietzsche with intercalative improvisations by a combo of clarinet, cello, percussion and piano (N. Y., Oct. 21, 1960; won the N. Y. Music Critics' Award); *Echoi,* for piano, percussion, clarinet and cello, in 4 parts, with the application of stochastic techniques controlled by the drummer striking the anvil to redirect the musical happening, banging on the strings of the piano to stop the pianist, and similar unconventional practices and mutual urgings (first performed, N. Y., Nov. 11, 1963, with Foss presiding at the piano); *Elytres* (Elytra, protective exterior wings in certain insects) for solo flute, two solo violins, distant violins, pitchless percussion, harp, vibraphone and piano, making use of piano strings tapped by mallets, with spatial parameters intrinsic to the conception of the ensemble (Los Angeles, Dec. 8, 1964); *Phorion* for strings, electronic organ, amplified harpsichord and amplified harp, interchangeable with electric guitar, with thematic material derived from the prelude of Bach's E major *Partita* for solo violin (hence the title "carried off"; first performed N. Y., April 27, 1967); *Concert* for cello and orch. (N. Y., March 5, 1967, Rostropovitch soloist); *Geod* for orch. divided into 4 groups, and conceived as a musical action "without an end, without development, without rhetoric" (Hamburg, Dec. 6, 1969, composer conducting); *Paradigm* for mixed media (N. Y., March 19, 1970); MAP (acronym for Men At Play), a musical game for 5 instrumentalists and electronic tape containing generative information for deoxyribonucleic thematic replication (1970).

Foster, Fay. Died in Bayport, N. Y., April 17, 1960.

Foster, Lawrence, American conductor; b. Los Angeles, Oct. 23, 1941. He made his first conducting appearance with the Young Musicians Foundation Debut Orch. in 1960. At the age of 24 he was appointed assistant conductor of the Los Angeles Philharmonic Orch.; in 1966 received the Koussevitzky Memorial Conducting Prize at the Berkshire Music Festival in Tanglewood, Mass. In 1969 he became a regular guest conductor of the Royal Philharmonic Orchestra of London. In

1970 he was appointed conductor-in-chief of the Houston Symphony Orch. He is particularly notable for his dynamic interpretations of modern works, but has also been acclaimed for his precise and intelligent presentations of the classical and romantic repertory.

Fouret, Maurice, French composer; b. St.-Quentin, Nov. 28, 1888; d. Paris, Jan. 22, 1962. He studied with Ravel, Charpentier and Busser. He composed several symph. poems on exotic subjects, among them *Aladdin* (Paris, Nov. 28, 1920), *Danse de Sita* (1922); the ballets *Le Rustre imprudent* (1931), *La jeune fille aux joues roses* (1934); a group of symph. suites inspired by Alsatian folklore; songs.

Fox, Virgil (Keel), American organist; b. Princeton, Illinois, May 3, 1912. He studied with Wilhelm Middelschulte in Chicago; then in Paris with Marcel Dupré. He embarked on an international career, performing in Westminster Abbey and in the greatest cathedrals of the continent; also gave organ recitals. From 1946 to 1964 he was organist at Riverside Church in New York. See 'Current Biography' (Jan. 1964).

Fradkin, Frederick. Died in New York, Oct. 3, 1963. First name Fredric (not Frederick).

Fraenkel, Wolfgang, German-American composer; b. Berlin, Oct. 10, 1897. He studied violin, piano and theory at the Klindworth-Scharwenka Cons. in Berlin; at the same time practiced law; was a judge in a Berlin court until the advent of the Nazi regime in 1933; was interned at the Sachsenhausen concentration camp; released in 1939; went to Shanghai where he taught at the National Cons. of Music; later lived in Nanking. In 1947 he settled in Los Angeles; was employed as a music copyist in film studios. His name attracted attention in 1965 when he received the first prize of the International Competition of the City of Milan for his *Symphonische Aphorismen.* Other works include an opera *Der brennende Dornbusch* (1924); flute concerto (1930); *Der Wegweiser,* cantata (1931); *Filippo,* a children's story for narrator and orch. (1948); 5 string quartets; violin sonata; viola sonata; cello sonata; piano pieces; songs.

Frager, Malcolm, American pianist; b. St. Louis, Jan. 15, 1935. He studied languages at Columbia Univ.; majored in Russian, graduating in 1957. He studied piano with Carl Friedberg in New York (1949-55); received various prizes in the U.S. In 1960 he won the Queen Elisabeth of Belgium International Competition, which marked the beginning of his world-wide career; he was particularly successful in Russia.

Françaix, Jean. Add to works: *L'Horloge de Flore,* suite for oboe and orch. (Philadelphia, March 31, 1961); *La Princesse de Clèves,* opera (Rouen, Dec. 11, 1965); flute concerto (Schwetzingen, May 13, 1967); violin concerto (1970); quartet for English horn, violin, viola and cello (1971).

Francescatti, Zino. His father was a violinist (not a cellist).

Franck, César (-Auguste). The first performance of *Variations Symphoniques* took place on May 1, 1886 (not 1885). Add to bibl.: W. Mohr, *César Franck* (Tutzing, 1969); Laurence Davies, *César Franck and His Circle* (Boston, 1970).

Franckenstein, Clemens von. Place of death, Hechendorf (not Munich).

Franco, Johan. Add to works: *Saga of the Sea* for carillon (1970).

François, Samson, French pianist; b. Frankfurt, son of the French consul there, May 18, 1924; d. Paris, Oct. 22, 1970. He received a prize at the Nice Cons. at the age of 11; studied in Paris with Alfred Cortot. He traveled widely as a concert pianist; made his American debut in 1947; played again in N. Y. in 1960 and 1961. In 1964 he made a concert tour of China, He was particularly noted for his interpretations of Debussy.

Frankel, Benjamin. Add to works: *Bagatelles* for 11 instruments (1959); *Serenata concertante* for piano trio and orch. (1962); Symph. No. 2 (Cheltenham, July 13, 1962); Symph. No. 3 (1965); Symph. No. 4 (London, Dec. 18, 1966); Symph. No. 5 (1967); Symph. No. 6 (London, March 23, 1969); Symph. No. 7 (London, June 4, 1970); *Overture to a Ceremony* (1970).

Franklin, Aretha, black "soul" singer; b. Memphis, Tenn., March 25, 1942. Her father was a Baptist preacher; the family settled in Detroit where he established a pastorate; his church became a hearth of gospel songs and evangelical group singing. At 18 Aretha Franklin went to New York where she quickly attracted attention; her singing at the Newport Jazz Festival in 1963 led to numerous important and lucrative engagements; the sales of her recordings skyrocketed to the million mark. In 1967 she toured Europe; in 1968 she made a sensation with her "soul" version of *The Star-Spangled Banner* at the ill-fated Democratic Convention in Chicago.

Fränzl, Ignaz. Add bibl.: Roland Würtz, *Ignaz Fränzl* (Mainz, 1970).

Freed, Isadore. Died at Rockville Centre, Long Island, N. Y., Nov. 10, 1960.

Freedman, Harry, Polish-Canadian oboist and composer; b. Lodz, April 5, 1922. He was taken to Canada as an infant, and his family settled in Winnipeg. He studied clarinet and oboe at the Toronto Cons.; then was engaged as the English horn player in the Toronto Symph. Orch. Works: *Matinée Suite* for orch. (1951-55); *Fantasia and Dance* for violin and orch. (1955); *Images,* symph. suite on 3 Canadian paintings (1958); Symph. No. 1 (1960; Washington, April 23, 1961).

French, Jacob. Exact date of birth, Stoughton, Mass., July 15, 1754; died at Simsbury, Conn., in May, 1817. He was co-founder (with William Billings) of the Stoughton Mus. Society, in 1774; fought at the battle of Bunker Hill in the Revolutionary War; was one of the few survivors of the Cherry Valley Massacre. After the war he became a singing teacher, retiring in 1814.

Freni, Mirella, Italian soprano; b. Modena, Feb. 27, 1935. She made her debut as Micaela in *Carmen* in Modena in 1955. An early marriage interrupted her career. She sang in Holland in 1960 and at La Scala in Milan in 1963. In 1965 she joined the Metropolitan Opera in New York. Her early successes were as a soubrette but she soon assumed full stature singing principal parts in the Italian repertory.

Frescobaldi, Girolamo. It is unlikely, indeed incredible, that 30,000 people attended his first perf. at St. Peter's; the exaggeration is due to early biographers; the actual number of those in attendance can only be conjectured without any evidential support.

Freund, Marya. Died in Paris, May 21, 1966.

Fribec, Krešimir, Croatian composer; b. Daruvar, May 24, 1908. He studied in Zagreb; adopted a nationalistic style of composition; wrote mostly vocal music. Works: *Povratak,* poem for baritone and orch. (1951); *Bijele Noći,* song cycle with orch. (1953); *Vibracije,* ballet pantomime (1955); the operas *Sluga Jernej* (Zagreb, Feb. 12, 1952); *Romeo and Juliet* (Zagreb, June 21, 1955); *Krvava Svadba* (*Blood Wedding;* 1956). See K. Kovačević, *Hrvatski Kompozitori i Njihova Djela* (Zagreb, 1960).

Fricker, Herbert Austin. He was conductor of the Mendelssohn Choir of Toronto from 1917 to 1942.

Fricker, Peter Racine. In 1964 he went to Santa Barbara, Cal. as visiting prof. at the Univ. of California; in 1970 he became chairman of the music dept. there. Add to works: Suite for recorders (1956); *The Death of Vivien,* radio opera (1956); Suite for harpsichord (1957); cello sonata (1957); *A Vision of Judgment,* oratorio (Leeds, Oct. 13, 1958); octet for wind and string instruments (1958); *14 Aubades* for piano (1958); *Comedy Overture* (1958); *Toccata* for piano and orch. (1959); *Serenade No. 1* for 6 instruments (1959); *Serenade No. 2* for flute, oboe and piano (1959); Symph. No. 3 (London, Nov. 8, 1960); 12 studies for piano (1961); *O Longs Désirs,* song cycle for soprano and orch. (1964); *Commissary Report* for men's voices (1965); *4 Dialogues* for oboe and piano (1965); *5 Canons* for 2 flutes and 2 oboes (1966); *Fantasy* for viola and piano (1966); Symph. No. 4, *'In Memoriam Mátyás Seiber'* (Cheltenham, Feb. 14, 1967); *3 Scenes* for orch. (Santa Barbara, Feb. 26, 1967); *7 Counterpoints* for orch. (Pasadena, Oct. 21, 1967); *Refrains* for solo oboe (1968); *Magnificat* for soloists, chorus and orch. (Santa Barbara, May 27, 1968); *Concertante No. 4* for flute, oboe, violin and strings (Santa Cruz, Cal. Feb. 25, 1969); *Some Superior Nonsense* for tenor, flute, oboe and harpsichord (Santa Barbara, Feb. 26, 1969); *Serenade No. 3* for saxophone quartet (1969); *3 Arguments* for bassoon and cello (1969); *Paseo* for guitar (1969); *The Roofs* for coloratura soprano and percussion (1970).

Fricsay, Ferenc. Died in Basel, Feb. 20, 1963. He had made his home in Switzerland in 1952, while continuing his activities as conductor in Europe and America.

Fried, Oskar. Exact date of death, Moscow, July 5, 1941.

Friedheim, Arthur. Add to books: *Life and Liszt: The Recollections of a Concert Pianist* (N. Y., 1961).

Friedman, Ken, American avant-garde composer; b. New London, Conn., Sept. 19,

1939. He was mostly self-taught in music theory; became associated with Richard Maxfield who initiated him into the arcana of ultra modern music. Friedman developed feverish activities in intellectual and musical fields; edited ephemeral magazines; directed an underground radio program 'Garnisht Kigele' in Mt. Carroll, Illinois; was a founder of the avant-garde group 'Fluxus'; gave seminars on surrealism; edited an anti-periodical in Boston; contributed to the National Underground Review in N. Y.; was a member of the board of Nameless Newsprint; Artist-in-Residence at Unitarian Universalist Church in Ventura, California; member of the faculty of the Free University of Berkeley; general manager of Something Else Press. As an avant-garde artist and designer he has exhibited his products in Brno, Nice, Cologne, Copenhagen, Trieste and San Diego; staged happenings and audio-visual events in California, announcing himself as 'The Truly Incredible Friedman.' Most of his works are verbal exhortations to existentialist actions, e.g., *Scrub Piece* (scrubbing a statue in a public square), *Riverboat Brawl* (starting a brawl in a riverboat at Disneyland), *Goff Street* (a 'theft event,' transplanting a street sign), *Come Ze Revolution* (chanting pseudo-Greek songs), *Watermelon* (splitting a watermelon with a karate blow), etc. He also composed a *Quiet Sonata* (1969) for 75 truncated guitar fingerboards with no strings attached.

Friedman, Richard, American composer; b. in New York, Jan. 6, 1944. He received his formal education in exact sciences, specializing in electronics. He worked at the Intermedia Electronic Music Studio at N. Y. Univ. (1966 - 68), in collaboration with Morton Subotnick; prepared electronic tape pieces, mostly of scientific inspiration: *Lumia Mix* (1967); *Crescent* (1967); and *To The Star Messenger* (1968), a melodrama depicting the discovery of the moons of Jupiter by Galileo. Another piece of the period was *Alchemical Manuscript* (1968), inspired by the arcane lore of the searchers for the philosopher's stone. In 1968 Friedman moved to California; worked with the Music Department of the radio station KPFA in Berkeley; arranged numerous broadcasts of electronic materials, notably *Serenade* for viola on tape and *Four-Pole Neuro-Magnet with Double Cross,* composed in 1970. Taking advantage of the techniques of amplification, Friedman was able to create a sound of an orchestra of violas with a single viola player. In most of his works he applies the avant-garde philosophy of tonal frugality, limiting his resources to a few notes. Apart from his radio work, he conducted information/media performances at the San Francisco Museum of Art under the general title 'Outside / Inside' utilizing closed circuit television, inflatable structures and sculptures activated by light beams.

Frijsh, Povla. Died in Blue Hill, Maine, July 10, 1960. Date of birth, Aug. 3, 1881, at Aarhus (not Marstal), Denmark. Her real name was Paula Frisch.

Friml, Rudolf. Born on Dec. 2 (not Dec. 7), 1879. His original family name was Frimel. He energetically passed his 91st birthday in Los Angeles in 1970 without palpable diminution of his vital functions.

Friskin, James. Died in New York, March 16, 1967.

Froidebise, Pierre. Died in Liège, Oct. 28, 1962.

Fromm, Andreas. Born in Plänitz (not Pänitz); died in the Strahov (not Strahow) monastery in Prague on Oct. 16, 1683.

Frotscher, Gotthold. Died in Berlin, Sept. 30, 1967.

Frotzler, Carl. Died in Stockerau, July 8, 1960.

Frühbeck de Burgos, Rafael, Spanish conductor of German parentage; b. Burgos, Sept. 15, 1933. He studied violin and piano at the Bilbao Cons. and later at the Cons. of Madrid and at the Hochschule für Musik in Munich. In 1959 he was appointed musical director of the Bilbao Symph. Orch., the youngest musician to lead an orchestra in Spain. In 1962 he was appointed conductor of the Orquesta Nacional in Madrid. In the meantime he toured as guest conductor in the European music centers. In 1968-70 he was guest conductor with major orchestras in the United States.

Frumerie, (Per) Gunnar (Fredrick) de. Add to works: clarinet concerto (1958); trumpet concerto (1959); oboe concerto (1961); piano quartet No. 2 (1963); flute concerto (1969).

Fryklund, Lars Axel Daniel. Died in Hälsingborg, Aug. 25, 1965.

Fuchs, Joseph, American violinist; b. New York, April 26, 1900. He graduated from the Institute of Musical Art in New York in 1918; was concertmaster of the Cleveland Orch. (1926-40); joined the faculty of the Juilliard School of Music in 1946. In the meantime he continued his career as a concert violinist; toured Europe in 1954, South America in 1957, and Russia in 1965.

Fuchs, Viktor, Austrian opera singer and teacher; b. Vienna, Jan. 19, 1891; d. Los Angeles, Sept. 14, 1966. He studied voice with Franz Steiner; sang both tenor and baritone parts; made his operatic debut in Breslau in 1912. From 1918-38 he taught at the Vienna Cons. In 1938 he went to the U. S. and settled in Hollywood as a vocal teacher. He publ. a manual, *The Art of Singing and Voice Technique* (London, 1962).

Fukushima, Kazuo, Japanese composer; b. Tokyo, April 11, 1930. Autodidact in composition, he became determined to effect an esthetic and idiomatic synthesis between the traditional Japanese style of court music and the serial organization of western modernism. In 1963 he received a traveling fellowship of the Japan Society of New York. His works include *Kadha Hi-Haku (The Flying Spirit)* for chamber orch.; *Tsuki-shiro (The Moon Spirit)* for string orch.; *Hi-Kyo* for flute, strings and percussion; *3 Pieces from Chu-U* for flute and piano; etc.

Fuleihan, Anis. Died in Stanford, Calif., Oct. 11, 1970. Went to Tunis in 1962 under the auspices of the State Dept.; in 1963 organized the Orchestre Classique de Tunis. Add to works: opera, *Vasco* (1960); *Toccata* for piano and orch. (1960); *Islands* symph. suite (1961); piano concerto No. 3 (1963); cello concerto (1963); viola concerto (1963); violin concerto No. 2 (1965); string quartets No. 4 and No. 5; horn quintet; clarinet quintet; violin sonata; viola sonata; cello sonata; piano sonatas No. 5-11; symph. No. 2 (N. Y., Feb. 16, 1967, composer conducting).

Futterer, Carl, Swiss composer; b. Basel, Feb. 21, 1873; d. Ludwigshafen, Nov. 5, 1927. He studied to be a lawyer; then began taking lessons in composition with Hans Huber; wrote operas and other works but kept them hidden until late in life. His comic opera *Don Gil mit den grünen Hosen* (1915) was produced in Freiburg-im-Breisgau in 1922; another opera *Der Geiger von Gmünd* (1917) was produced in Basel in 1921. He further wrote a sinfonietta (1917); octet (1921); quartet for oboe, clarinet, horn and bassoon (1921); trio for clarinet, cello and piano (1924); piano trio (1927); violin sonata (1927); piano concerto (1927).

Fux, Johann Joseph. Add bibl.: J. H. Van den Meer, *Johann Josef Fux als Opernkomponist* (3 vols.: Bilthoven, 1961); E. Wellesz, *Fux* (London, 1965).

G

Gaburo, Kenneth, American composer; b. Somerville, N. J., July 5, 1927. He studied composition with Bernard Rogers at the Eastman School of Music, Rochester, and at the Academy of St. Cecilia in Rome with Goffredo Petrassi. Works: *The Snow Queen,* 3-act opera (Lake Charles, Louisiana, May 5, 1952); *The Widow,* 1-act opera (Urbana, Illinois, Feb. 26, 1961); *On A Quiet Theme,* for orch. (1952); *4 Inventions* for clarinet and piano (1953); *Music for 5 Instruments* (1954); a set of 3 *Ideas and Transformations* for pairs of strings (1955); string quartet No. 1 (1956); *Line Studies* for 4 instruments (1957); *Antiphony I* for 3 string groups and electronic sound; *Antiphony II* for piano and electronic sound; *Antiphony III* for singers and electronic sound; *Two* for mezzo-soprano, alto flute and double bass (1963); *The Flow of E,* based on a synthesized vowel *e* and its electronic transformations (1965); *Inside,* a quartet for one double-bass player (1969); electronic score for the play *The Hydrogen Jukebox;* other theater music; choruses; piano pieces; songs.

Gade, Jacob. Died in Copenhagen, Feb. 21, 1963. Bibl.: Karl Bjarnjof, *Tango Jalousie* (Copenhagen, 1969).

Gadzhibekov, Uzeir. Date of performance of his opera *Arshin Mal Alan,* according to new style calendar, Nov. 7 (not Oct. 25), 1913. *Kyor-Oglu* was produced in Baku on April 30 (not Jan. 13), 1937.

Gagnebin, Henri. Add to publ.: *Musique, mon beau souci: Réflexions sur mon métier* (Paris, 1968).

Galindo, Blas. Add to works: Symph. No. 2 (1957; shared 1st prize at the Caracas Festival, 1957); Symph No. 3 (Washington, April 30, 1961).

Gall (Galle), Yvonne, French soprano; b. Paris, March 6, 1885. She studied at the Paris Cons.; made her debut at the Paris Opéra in 1908; later sang also at the Opéra-Comique. She rapidly rose on the operatic horizon and was regarded as one of the greatest prime donne in France. She was a member of the Chicago Opera in 1918-20; toured all over Europe; then retired and taught voice at the Paris Cons. In 1958 she married the composer Henri Busser.

Galla-Rini, Anthony, American accordionist and composer; b. Manchester, Conn., Jan. 18, 1904. He learned music from his father, a bandmaster; toured the U. S. and Canada since the age of 6, playing accordion, cornet, mandolin, piccolo, oboe, French horn, contrabassoon, euphonium and sarrusophone, as well as several other instruments. He was the first accordionist to appear with an orchestra in a concerto of his own composition (Oklahoma City, Nov. 15, 1941); invented many technical improvements for his instrument; was the first to omit the fifth in the dominant-seventh row. In 1921 he introduced the 160-bass system in an extended left-hand range model. He publ. a number of transcriptions of classical and popular music for accordion.

Galli-Curci, Amelita. Died in La Jolla, Calif., Nov. 26, 1963.

Gallo, Fortune. Died in New York, March 28, 1970.

Gallon, Jean. Died in Paris, June 23, 1959.

Gallon, Noël. Died in Paris, Dec. 26, 1966.

Galuppi, Baldassare. Did not visit St. Petersburg in 1743; was there from 1765 (not 1766) until 1768.

Gange, Fraser. Died in Baltimore, July 1, 1962.

Ganz, Rudolph. Publ.: *Rudolph Ganz Evaluates Modern Piano Music* (N. Y., 1968).

Garaguly, Carl. He left the Stockholm Philharmonic in 1953; then was conductor of the Bergen, Norway, Philharmonic (1953-58); was guest conductor in Denmark and Holland after 1960.

Garant, Serge, Canadian composer; b. in Quebec City, Sept. 22, 1928. He studied piano and clarinet in Sherbrooke and composition in Montreal with Claude Champagne. In 1951 he went to Paris to take a course in musical analysis with Olivier Messiaen. Returning to Canada he founded the modern group 'Musique de notre temps' in Montreal, dedicated to the presentation of new European and American music. He subsequently joined the music faculty of the Univ. of Montreal. His works include *Anerca* for soprano and 8 instruments, to words of two Eskimo poems (1961); *Cage d'Oiseau* for soprano and piano (1962).

Garbuzov, Nikolai Alexandrovitch. Died in Moscow, May 3, 1955.

Garden, Mary. Died in Aberdeen, Scotland, Jan. 4, 1967. Born on Feb. 20, 1874 (not 1877).

Garner, Errol, American jazz pianist and song writer; b. Pittsburgh, June 15, 1921. Completely untutored and unlettered, he composed tunes extemporaneously, singing and accompanying himself at the piano, with an amanuensis to put down the notes. He also played drums and slap bass. His nervous rubato style won acclaim from the cognoscenti and jazz aficionados; he made a European tour in 1958. Among his own songs, the plangent *Misty* achieved great popularity.

Garrido, Pablo, Chilean composer and musicologist; b. Valparaiso, March 26, 1905. Early in his musical career he joined progressive causes in music and in politics; gave the first concert of jazz in Chile in 1923; settled in Santiago as conductor, lecturer and musical organizer. Works: *Rapsodia Chilena* for piano and orch. (1938); piano concerto (1950); *Fantasia Antillana* for cello and orch. (1950); *13x13* for string quartet (1951); *La Sugestión,* chamber opera (Santiago, Oct. 18, 1961); *El Guerrillero,* ballet (1963). He publ. a valuable monograph, *Biografía de la Cueca* (Santiago, 1942).

Garrido-Lecca, Celso, Peruvian composer; b. Piura, March 9, 1926. He studied in Lima with Rodolfo Holzmann. Later he went to Santiago, Chile, where he worked with Domingo Santa Cruz. Returning to Peru, he engaged in music criticism. At the same time he began to compose. His one-movement symphony was first performed at the 2nd Inter-American Music Festival in Washington on April 22, 1961. Of his chamber music, a *Divertimento* for woodwind quintet merits mention. In most of his works he uses a modified 12-tone idiom.

Garrison, Mabel. Died in New York, Aug. 20, 1963.

Gauthier, Eva. Died in New York, Dec. 26, 1958.

Gebhard, Heinrich. Died in North Arlington, N. J., May 5, 1963. His book, *The Art of Pedaling,* was publ. posthumously, with an introduction by Leonard Bernstein, who was one of his students (N. Y., 1963).

Gedda, Giulio Cesare, Italian conductor and composer; b. in Turin, April 16, 1899; d. Callegno, near Turin, Sept. 7, 1970. He studied composition with Alfano in Turin; played cello and organ; began conducting in 1932; lived mostly in Turin. He wrote an opera *L'amoroso fantasma* (Turin, 1931); a cello concerto, a concerto for 4 saxophones, piano, strings and percussion (1954); chamber music. He ended his days in a mental asylum.

Gedda, Nicolai, Swedish tenor; b. Stockholm, July 11, 1925, of Russian-Swedish extraction. (His real name was Ustinov). He studied in Stockholm, where he made his debut in 1952; in 1953 appeared in Paris and London; in 1957 was engaged by the Metropolitan Opera in N.Y.; sang the role of Anatol in Samuel Barber's opera *Vanessa* (1958); also appeared in Salzburg.

Gedzhadze, Irakly, Georgian composer; b. Mtskheta, Oct. 26, 1925. He studied with Matchavariani at the Cons. of Tbilisi; graduated in 1957. His works include the opera *Sunrise* (Tbilisi, Nov. 23, 1961); *Lake Palestomi,* symph. poem (1956); piano pieces.

Geiringer, Karl. In 1962 he was appointed prof. at the Univ. of California, Santa Barbara. A festschrift, 'Studies in 18th-century Music: A Tribute to Karl Geiringer on his 70th Birthday,' edited by H. C. Robbins Landon and Roger E. Chapman, was publ. in his honor (N. Y., 1967). Add to books: *Johann Sebastian Bach: The Culmination of an Era* (N. Y., 1966).

Gelbrun, Artur, Polish-born Israeli composer; b. Warsaw, July 11, 1913. He studied violin at the Warsaw Cons. and composition with Alfredo Casella in Rome; conducting with Hermann Scherchen in Switzerland. He concertized as a violinist; in 1946 devoted himself mainly to conducting and composing. Eventually he settled in Israel; joined the staff of the Academy of Music in Tel Aviv as prof. of composition and conducting. Works: Sonatina for 2 violins (1944); string trio (1945); *Esquisse* for flute and harp (1946); *Chant des Lamentations,* cantata (1951); Symph. No. 1 (1958); Symph. No. 2 (1961); cello concerto (1962); *Piccolo Divertimento* for orch. (1963); *Concerto Fantasia* for flute, harp and strings (1963); *Le Livre du Feu,* cantata (1964); *Miadoux,* ballet (1968); *Prologue à Décameron,* ballet (1968); string quartet (1969); *Partita* for clarinet solo (1969); *Miniature* for bassoon solo (1969).

Gelineau, Joseph, French composer of sacred music and editor; b. Champ-sur-Layon (Maine-et-Loire), Oct. 31, 1920. At age of 21 he entered the Order of Jesuits; studied organ and composition at the École César Franck in Paris; also obtained a doctorate in theology. He publ. *Chant et Musique dans le Culte Chrétien* (Paris, 1962); composed *Missa Plebs Sancta* (1960), psalms, etc.; translated and set to music the Psalmody of the Bible of Jerusalem.

Gelinek, Joseph. Place of birth, near Beroun (not Beraun).

Geminiani, Francesco. Was not the author of the first published violin method. The treatise, which appeared in vol. V of Prelleur's *The Modern Musick Master . . .* under Geminiani's name, was an edited republication of an earlier violin method titled *Volens Nolens,* originally publ. in London in 1695. Cf. David D. Boyden, *Geminiani and the First Violin Tutor* in 'Acta Musicologica' (Feb. 1960).

Gennrich, Friedrich. Died in Langen (Hessen), Sept. 22, 1967. Add to books: *Die Wimpfener Fragmente der Hessischen Landesbibliothek* (Darmstadt, 1958); *Der musikalische Nachlass der Troubadours* (Darmstadt, 1960).

Gentele, Goeran, Swedish opera manager; b. Stockholm, Sept. 20, 1917. He served 3 years in the Swedish army; studied political science at Stockholm Univ. and art at the Sorbonne in Paris. He also played the violin and piano as a child. He began his theatrical career as an actor at the Royal Dramatic Theater in Stockholm (1941-46); then was stage director there (1946-52) and at the Royal Opera (1952-63). He also directed and produced films. In 1963 he was appointed head of the Royal Opera in Stockholm. In 1970 he was engaged as general manager of the Metropolitan Opera House in New York as successor to Rudolf Bing, effective June 1972.

Genzmer, Harald. Add to works: Symph. No. 1 (1957; revised 1970).

Georgescu, Georges. Died in Bucharest, Sept. 1, 1964. Conducted the N. Y. Philharmonic during the season 1926-27 (not 1930). Was guest conductor in the U. S. again in 1960-61.

Georgiades, Thrasybulos. Add to books: *Musik und Rhythmus bei den Griechen; Zum Ursprung der abendländischen Musik*

(Hamburg, 1958), revised and enlarged version of *Greek Music, Verse, Dance* (N. Y., 1956).

Georgiadis, Georges, Greek pianist and composer; b. Salonika, Sept. 8, 1912. He studied piano and composition at the Cons. of Athens; in 1943 was appointed prof. of piano there. His music, in a traditional mold, is inspired chiefly by Greek folk resources. Works: Symphony in E minor, surnamed *De la Paix* (1960); concertino for piano and orch. (1959); two violin sonatas; songs; many piano pieces; incidental music for *Demeter and Persephone, Medea,* etc.

Georgii, Walter. Died in Tübingen, Feb. 23, 1967.

Gerelli, Ennio, Italian conductor and composer; b. Cremona, Feb. 12, 1907; d. there, Oct. 5, 1970. He studied at the Cons. of Bologna; conducted ballet and opera in Italy; was on the staff of La Scala in Milan (1935-40); in 1961 he founded the Camerata di Cremona. He wrote a ballet, *Il Gioco dei grandi* (1942) and some chamber music.

Gerhard, Roberto. Died in Cambridge, England, Jan. 5, 1970. Add to works: Nonet (1956); Symph. No. 2 (London, Oct. 28, 1959); Symph. No. 3, *Collages,* for orch. and magnetic tape (London, Feb. 8, 1961); *Concert for Eight* (London, May 17, 1962); string quartet No. 2 (1962); *Hymnody* for wind ensemble, percussion and 2 pianos (London, May 23, 1963); *The Plague,* oratorio (London, April 1, 1964); *Concerto for Orchestra* (world première, B. B. C. Orch., Boston, Mass., April 25, 1965); *Epithalamion* for orch. (Valdagno, Italy, Sept. 17, 1966); Symph. No. 4 (N. Y., Dec. 14, 1967); *Leo* for 10 players (Dartmouth College, Hanover, N. H., Aug. 23, 1969); His Violin Concerto was first performed at the Maggio Musicale in Florence on June 16 (not May), 1950.

Gerhardt, Elena. Died in London, Jan. 11, 1961.

Gerlach, Theodor. His opera *Liebeswogen* was produced in Bremen on Nov. 7, 1903 (not 1904). *Das Seegespenst* was not a new opera, but a revised version of *Liebeswogen,* and it was first produced in Altenburg on April 24, 1914.

Gerschefski, Edwin. Add to works: *Workout* for 2 violins and 2 violas (1970).

Gershfeld, David, Moldavian composer; b. Bobrinets, Aug. 28, 1911. He studied music in Odessa; in 1940 became director of the Kishinev Cons. He has written the first Moldavian opera, *Grozovan* (Kishinev, June 9, 1956); also wrote another Moldavian opera *Aurelia,* on a subject from World War II (Kishinev, April 26, 1959).

Gershwin, George. Date of birth, Sept. 26 (not Sept. 28), 1898. The 3 piano preludes were written in 1926 (not 1936); *Cuban Overture* was composed in 1932 (not 1934); first performance, in N. Y. Aug. 16, 1932. Add his variations for piano and orch. on his song *I Got Rhythm* (1934). Add to bibl.: M. Armitage, *George Gershwin, Man and Legend* (N. Y., 1958); David Ewen, *George Gershwin, His Journey to Greatness* (N. Y., 1970; a radical revision of his previous book on Gershwin, publ. in 1956).

Gerster, Ottmar. Died in Leipzig, Aug. 31, 1969.

Gesensway, Louis. Add to works: duo for oboe and guitar (1959); duo for viola and bassoon (1960); *Ode to Peace* for orch. (Philadelphia, April 15, 1960); *The Great Boffo and His Talking Dog,* for small orch. (Philadelphia, Feb. 27, 1961); *Divertimento* for flute, 2 violins and viola (1969); duo for violin and cello (1970); *Commemoration Symphony* (Philadelphia, Feb. 25, 1971). In 1971 he retired as member of the first violin section of the Philadelphia Orch.

Ghedini, Giorgio Federico. Died in Nervi, March 25, 1965. Add to works: opera, *La Via della Croce* (Venice, April 9, 1961).

Gheluwe, Leon van, Belgian composer; b. Wanneghem-Lede, Sept. 15, 1837; d. Ghent, July 14, 1914. He studied in Ghent with Gevaert and others; became prof. at the Cons. of Ghent in 1869, and later was director of the École de Musique in Bruges. He wrote a Flemish opera *Philippine van Vlaanderen* (Brussels, 1876) and a number of songs.

Ghent, Emmanuel, American composer; b. Montreal, Canada, May 15, 1925. He studied bassoon and music theory at McGill Univ.; also took courses in psychology and psychoanalysis; eventually settled in New York as a practicing psychiatrist. In 1964, with the aid of an engineer, he constructed the Polynome, a device capable of accurate reproduction of multiple rhythms by click signals transmitted to a performer's ear through a tiny earphone; applied this instrument in several of his compositions. Works: *Movement* for wind quintet (1944); *3 Duos* for flutes (1944); *Lament* for string quartet (1958); quartet for flute, oboe, clarinet and bassoon (1960); *2 Duos* for flute and clarinet (1962); *Dance Movement* for trumpet and string quartet (1962); *Entelechy* for viola and piano (1963); *Triality I* and *II* for violin, trumpet and bassoon in conjunction with the Polynome (1964); brass quintet (1965).

Ghiaurov, Nicolai, Bulgarian bass singer; b. Velimgrad, Sept. 13, 1929. He studied violin and piano in Bulgaria; then went to Moscow where he received his vocal training. He made his debut in Sofia as Don Basilio in *The Barber of Seville* in 1956; then appeared in Moscow (1958) and at La Scala in Milan (1959). He soon established himself as a fine singer; his quality of voice is that of basso cantante. He made an excellent impression in his appearances in New York in 1967.

Ghione, Franco. Died in Rome, Jan. 19, 1964. Born Aug. 26, 1886 (not 1889).

Giannini, Vittorio. Died in New York, Nov. 28, 1966. Add to works: *Sinfonia* (Symph. No. 3; Cincinnati, April 6, 1951); Symph. No. 4 (N. Y., May 27, 1960); opera *The Harvest* (Chicago, Nov. 25, 1961); *Rehearsal Call,* opera buffa (N. Y., Feb. 15, 1962); *The Servant of Two Masters,* opera (posthumous, N. Y., March 9, 1967).

Gibbs, Cecil Armstrong. Died in Chelmsford, May 12, 1960.

Gideon, Miriam. In 1971 she was appointed visiting prof. of the College of the City of New York.

Giegling, Franz. In the title of his dissertation, correct *italianischen* to *italienischen.*

Gieseking, Walter, Add to writings: *So wurde ich Pianist* (Wiesbaden, 1963).

Gigli, Beniamino. Died in Rome, Nov. 30, 1957. His debut took place at Rovigo (not Rovigno).

Gilardi, Gilardo. Died in Buenos Aires, Jan. 16, 1963.

Gilbert, L. Wolfe, American songwriter; b. Odessa, Russia, Aug. 31, 1886; d. Beverly Hills, Calif., July 12, 1970. His family went to Philadelphia when he was an infant; at 14 he went to New York and sang in vaudeville, burlesque theaters and nightclubs; he also toured as an entertainer with John L. Sullivan, the prize fighter. In 1912 he wrote his first hit song, *Waitin' for the Robert E. Lee.* He settled in Hollywood in 1929, where he formed his own publishing company. He composed some 250 songs, of which several became perennial favorites: *Ramona* (written for a motion picture in 1927); *Peanut Vendor, Down Yonder,* and *Lucky Lindy,* inspired by Lindbergh's transatlantic flight of 1927.

Gilbert, Sir William Schwenck. Technically speaking, he did not die of drowning, but of a cardiac arrest following his successful rescue of an amateur girl swimmer who herself nearly drowned in the pool at his estate.

Gillespie, John Birks ("Dizzy"), American jazz player, trumpeter and bandleader; b. Cheraw, South Carolina, Oct. 21, 1917. He played with Cab Calloway before forming his own band. He was the reputed generator, c. 1940, of the bebop style of group improvisation emphasizing the main beat with a striking ictus (bop).

Gil-Marchex, Henri. Died in Paris, Nov. 22, 1970.

Ginastera, Alberto. Add to works: piano concerto (Washington, April 22, 1961); *Cantata para América Mágica,* for soprano and percussion ensemble of 53 instruments (Washington, April 30, 1961); violin concerto (N. Y., Oct. 3, 1963); *Don Rodrigo,* opera (Buenos Aires, July 24, 1964); *Bomarzo,* cantata (Washington, Nov. 1, 1964); *Concerto per corde* (Caracas, Venezuela, May 14, 1966); opera, *Bomarzo* (first stage performance, Washington, D.C., May 19, 1967); *Estudios sinfónicos* (Vancouver, Canada, March 31, 1968); cello concerto (Dartmouth College, Hanover, N. H., July 7, 1968); *Beatrix Cenci,* opera for the opening season at the Kennedy Center for Performing Arts, Washington, Sept. 10, 1971. He received an honorary doctor's degree in music from Yale Univ. in 1968.

Giovannelli, Ruggiero. Proper spelling of first name, **Ruggero.** He was nominated director of the cappella of San Luigi de' Francesi on Aug. 6, 1583 (not in 1587).

Glanville-Hicks, Peggy. Add to works: the operas, *The Glittering Gate* (N. Y., May 14, 1959) and *Nausicaa* (Athens, Aug. 19, 1961).

Glazunov, Alexander Konstantinovitch. His Saxophone Concerto was written in collaboration with Sigurd Rascher (not with Petiot), and first performed by Rascher in Nykoping, Sweden, on Nov. 25, 1934. His Symph. No. 7 was first performed on Jan.

3, 1903 (not Nov. 15, 1902). The first performance of the violin concerto took place in St. Petersburg, with Leopold Auer as soloist, on March 4, 1905; Elman's performance in London, on Oct. 17, 1905, was the first outside Russia.

Gleason, Harold. Add to books: *Music in America,* an anthology (in collaboration with W. T. Marrocco; N. Y., 1964).

Glière, Reinhold Moritzovitch. Additional dates of first performances: ballets, *Chrysis* (Moscow, Nov. 30, 1912); *Cleopatra* (Moscow, Jan. 11, 1926); *Comedians* (Moscow, April 5, 1931); *The Bronze Knight* (Leningrad, March 14, 1949); Symph. No. 1 (Moscow, Jan. 3, 1903); *The Sirens,* symph. poem (Moscow, Jan. 30, 1909); Symph. No. 3, *Ilya Murometz* (Moscow, March 23, 1912); *Cossacks of Zaporozh* (Odessa, Dec. 23, 1925); harp concerto (Moscow, Nov. 23, 1938); concerto for coloratura soprano and orch. (Moscow, May 12, 1943); cello concerto (Moscow, Feb. 18, 1947). Add to works: *Leily and Medzhnun,* opera (Tashkent, July 18, 1940); *Rachel,* one-act opera after Maupassant's *Mademoiselle Fifi* (Moscow, April 19, 1947); *Ghulsara,* Uzbek opera (Tashkent, Dec. 25, 1949).

Glinka, Michael. Add to works: ballet, *Chao-Kang* (1828-1831).

Gluck, Christoph Willibald. Add to bibl.: A. A. Abert, *G. W. Gluck* (Munich, 1959); *The Collected Correspondence and Papers of C. W. Gluck* (London, 1962); Patricia Howard, *Gluck and the Birth of Modern Opera* (N. Y., 1964).

Gnazzo, Anthony J., American avant-garde composer; b. New Britain, Conn., April 21, 1936. He studied music theory at Brandeis Univ. (M. F. A., 1965; Ph. D., 1970); mathematics at the Univ. of Hartford (B. A., 1963); served in the U. S. Navy (1957-61); attended 21 Navy schools and took courses in technology, data processing and allied subjects; was instructor in electronic system design at the Univ. of Toronto (1965-66); lecturer in music at Mills College (1967-69); in 1969 appointed design consultant and equipment technician in the electronics laboratory at Calif. State College at Hayward; also worked as computer programmer. His compositions are notated in the form of geometric graphs with verbal instructions and rhetorical interjections, e.g. 'Music, is it? Eh? It IS!!! But! Music? Yes, Music!' His 'theater pieces' are graphic scenarios with action indicated by circles, curves and vectors. His *Canned Music* (1969) is a sticker inscribed, 'Caution—Caution—Caution—This Can Has Been Filled with Extremely Loud Sound for 45 Minutes! Open With Care!' He also designed a piece entitled *Four-Letter Words* in surrealistically drawn phallic shapes. Among his literary productions are intermittent dialogues and 'manifolds' for the theater, e.g. *Inevitably Plastic* (1969) and *Experience Counter Experience* (1970).

Gnecchi, Vittorio. Died Feb. 1 (not Feb. 5), 1954. His article *Telepatia Musicale* was publ. in the Feb. - March 1909 (not May 1908) issue of the 'Rivista Italiana Musicale.'

Gnessin, Mikhail Fabianovitch. Date of death, May 5 (not May 6), 1957.

Goedicke, Alexander Fedorovitch. Died in Moscow, Aug. 9, 1957.

Goehr, Alexander, English composer; son of Walter Goehr; b. Berlin, Aug. 10, 1932; studied at the Royal Manchester College of Music and at the Paris Cons. He began to compose prolifically from an early age, adopting a severe atonal style of polyphonic writing, tending toward integral serialism. Works: piano sonata (1952); *Fantasies* for clarinet and piano (1955); *Fantasia* for orch. (1955); *Narration,* to words of Blake, for voice and piano (1955); string quartet (1958); *The Deluge,* cantata (1958); *Sutter's Gold,* cantata (1960); *Hecuba's Lament,* cantata (1960); suite for flute, clarinet, horn, violin, viola, cello and harp (1961); *Four Songs from the Japanese* for soprano and orch. (1961); violin concerto (1962); *Arden muss sterben,* opera (Hamburg, March 5, 1967); *Naboth's Vineyard,* dramatic madrigal after a biblical story for singers, piano duet, flute, clarinet, trombone, violin and double-bass (London, July 16, 1968); symphony (London, May 9, 1970); *Shadowplay,* 'music theater' after Plato's *Republic,* for 5 instruments (London, July 8, 1970); Concerto for 11 instruments (Brussels, Jan. 25, 1971).

Goehr, Walter. Died in Sheffield, England, Dec. 4, 1960.

Goetze, Walter W. Died in Berlin, March 24, 1961.

Gold, Ernest, Austrian-American composer; b. Vienna, July 13, 1921. He studied piano and violin at home (his father was an amateur musician); in 1938 emigrated to the U. S.; studied harmony in N. Y. with Otto Cesana. He began writing songs in a popular vein; of these, *Practice Makes Perfect* became a hit. At the same time he composed in classical forms; to this category belong his *Pan American Symphony,* piano concerto, string quartet and piano sonata. In 1946 he went to Hollywood as an arranger; took lessons with George Antheil; then was commissioned to write film scores; among them the following were very successful: *The Defiant Ones, On the Beach, Exodus* (Academy Award, 1960); *Judgment at Nuremberg* (1961); *It's a Mad, Mad, Mad World* (1963). In 1950 he married the singer Marni Nixon.

Goldberg, Albert, American music critic; b. Shenandoah, Iowa, June 2, 1898. He studied at the Chicago Musical College (1920-22); taught there (1924-26); appeared as pianist and conductor; was music critic of the Chicago 'Herald Examiner' (1925-36) and of the Chicago 'Tribune' (1943-46). In 1947 he was appointed music critic of the Los Angeles 'Times.'

Goldberg, Theo. He settled in Vancouver, Canada, in 1954.

Goldenweiser, Alexander Borissovitch. Died in Moscow, Nov. 26, 1961.

Goldman, Richard Franko. He publ. *Harmony of Western Music* (N. Y., 1965). In 1968 he was appointed director of the Peabody Cons. of Music in Baltimore.

Goldstein, Mikhail, Russian violinist and composer; b. Odessa, Nov. 8, 1917. He was a violin prodigy before entering the Moscow Cons., where he studied violin with Yampolsky, composition with Miaskovsky and conducting with Saradzev. During the war (1941-45) he was active in the Soviet Army entertainment corps. In 1946 he returned to Odessa. In 1948 he perpetrated a hoax by claiming the discovery of the 21st symphony allegedly written in 1810 by a mythical Russian musician Ovsianiko-Kulikovsky; a doctoral dissertation on it was written by the Soviet musicologist Valerian Dovzhenko. The work was widely performed in the Soviet Union and recorded. When Goldstein admitted his deception and declared that the symphony was in fact his own composition, he was attacked in the Soviet press as an impostor trying to appropriate an authentic work of historical importance. In eclipse as a result of this episode, Goldstein left Russia in 1964; lived in East Berlin; in 1967 went to Israel and taught violin at the Musical Academy in Jerusalem. In 1969 he settled in Hamburg, where he resumed his primary career as a concert violinist; contributed articles to 'Die Musik in Geschichte und Gegenwart' and other German publications. His works include, apart from the 'Ovsianiko-Kulikovsky' score, 4 symphonies (1934, 1936, 1944, 1945); 2 violin concertos (1936, 1939); violin sonata (1935); sonata for violin and viola (1946); 12 Preludes for 2 violins (1964); pedagogical pieces for violin.

Goleminov, Marin. Add to works: opera *Ivailo* (Sofia, Feb. 13, 1959); operatic fairy tale, *The Golden Bird* (Sofia, Dec. 20, 1961).

Golschmann, Vladimir. Resigned from the St. Louis Symph. Orch. in 1958; was conductor of the Denver Symph. Orch. in 1964-70.

Golyscheff, Jefim, Russian-German-Brazilian composer and painter; b. Kherson, Sept. 20, 1895. He studied music and art in Odessa; in 1909 he went to Germany, where he remained until 1933; subsequently went to France; in 1957 settled in São Paulo, Brazil, where he devoted himself chiefly to painting in the abstract expressionist manner. Golyscheff played a historical role in the development of the 12-tone method of composition; he used themes of 12 different notes as early as 1914 in a string quartet; his string trio, published in Berlin in 1925, contains passages described as 'Zwölftondauer-Komplexen.' See H. Eimert, *Atonale Musiklehre* (Leipzig, 1924; reprinted under the title *Zwölftontechnik,* Wiesbaden, 1954).

Gomólka, Mikolaj (Nicolas). See M. Perz, *Mikolaj Gomólka* (Warsaw, 1969).

González-Zuleta, Fabio, Colombian composer; b. Bogotá, Nov. 2, 1920. He studied organ and composition at the Bogotá Cons.; after graduation became a member of its faculty; in 1957 was appointed its director. Works: Symph. No. 1 (1956); violin concerto (1958); Symph. No. 2 (1959); piano trio (1955); trio for flute, violin and viola (1955); suite for wind quintet (1956); clarinet sonata (1958); *Quintetto Abstracto* for wind instruments (1960); sonata for double-bass and piano (1960).

Goodman, Alfred, German-American composer (real name Guttmann); b. Berlin, March 1, 1920. He studied at the Berlin Cons.; in 1939 went to England, and in 1940 settled in America; was in the U. S. Army during World War II. In 1946 he was arranger with several dance bands; at the same time he studied with Henry Cowell and Otto

Luening at Columbia Univ., receiving his B. S. in 1952 and his M. A. in 1953. In 1960 he returned to Germany. Works: *The Audition,* one-act opera (Athens, Ohio, July 27, 1954); 2 symphonies; choral and chamber music. He published a music lexicon, *Von A-Z* (Munich, 1971).

Goodson, Katharine. Died in London, April 14, 1958.

Goossens, Sir **Eugene.** Died in London, June 13, 1962.

Gordeli, Otar, Georgian composer; b. Tbilisi, Nov. 18, 1928. He studied composition with Andrey Balantchivadze; later took courses at the Moscow Cons., graduating in 1955. In 1959 he was appointed instructor at the Cons. of Tbilisi. In his music he applies resources of native folk songs; his polyphonic structure is considerably advanced. Among his works are a piano concerto (1952); cantata *The Seasons,* for narrator, boys' chorus and chamber orch. (1955); Concertino for flute and orch. (1958); *Festive Overture* (1959); *Georgian Dance* for orch. (1961); film music; jazz pieces.

Gordon, Gavin Muspratt. Died in London, Nov. 18, 1970.

Górecki, Henryk, Polish composer; b. Czernica, Dec. 6, 1933. He studied with Boleslaw Szabelski in Katowice. His works reflect an experimental turn, while retaining classical forms. Among them, the most important are Toccata for 2 pianos (1955); sonata for 2 violins (1957); *Symphonia 1959* for string orchestra with percussion; *Instrumental Ensemble* for 15 players; *Musique polonaise ancienne* for orch. (Warsaw, Sept. 24, 1969).

Gostuški, Dragutin, Serbian composer; b. Belgrade, Jan. 3, 1923. He studied in Belgrade, where he was subsequently engaged as a music critic. His works include a symph. poem, *Belgrade* (Belgrade, June 11, 1951); *Concerto accelerato* for violin and orch. (Belgrade, Nov. 14, 1961); a fantastic ballet, *Remis* (1955; first stage performance, Zagreb, May 15, 1963); chamber music; piano pieces; songs.

Gotovac, Jakov. Add to works: *Stanac,* opera (Zagreb, Dec. 6, 1959); *Dalmaro,* opera-legend (Zagreb, Dec. 20, 1964).

Gotthelf, Felix. Place of birth, Mönchen-Gladbach, near Düsseldorf (not near Munich).

Gottlieb, Jack, American composer; b. New Rochelle, N.Y., Oct. 12, 1930. He studied with Karol Rathaus at Queens College and Irving Fine at Brandeis Univ.; at the Berkshire Music Center in Tanglewood with Boris Blacher and Aaron Copland and at the Univ. of Illinois with Burrill Phillips and Robert Palmer. In 1958 he was appointed general musical assistant to Leonard Bernstein in charge of organization of programs of the New York Philharmonic. Works: quartet for 3 clarinets and bass clarinet (1952); string quartet (1954); *Twilight Crane* for woodwind quintet (1961); *Pieces of Seven,* overture (Jacksonville, Florida, Oct. 23, 1962); piano sonata (1960); *Song of Loneliness,* cycle of 7 songs for baritone and piano (1962).

Gottschalk, Louis (Moreau). Add to bibl.: V. Loggins, *Where the World Ends: The Life of Louis Moreau Gottschalk* (Baton Rouge, 1958). His journals were republished in English under the title *Notes of a Pianist* (N.Y., 1964).

Goudimel, Claude. A more probable date of birth is 1510 (not 1505).

Gould, Glenn. Did not fancy, countenance or compose jazz. The misguided statement regarding his alleged predilection for American popular music or his participation in jazzmen's activities, in public or in private, was intended to apply to Friedrich Gulda (q.v.). Gould composed several pieces of chamber music and a chorus with piano accompaniment to his own words, *So You Want to Write a Fugue* (1964).

Gould, Morton. Add to works: *Declaration* for orch., chorus and 2 speakers (Washington, Jan. 20, 1957); *Venice* for double orch. and brass bands (Seattle, May 2, 1967).

Grabner, Hermann. Died in Bolzano, Italy, July 3, 1969.

Grabovsky, Leonid, Ukrainian composer; b. Kiev, Jan. 28, 1935. He studied at the Kiev Cons. with Revutsky and Liatoshinsky, graduating in 1959. His music is marked by modern tendencies, making use of dissonant counterpoint and asymmetric polyrhythmic combinations. Works: *Intermezzo* for orch. (1958); string quartet (1958); *4 Ukrainian Songs* for chorus and orch. (1959; awarded first prize at the Young Composers' Festival in Moscow, 1962); sonata for unaccompanied violin (1959); *Symphonic Frescoes* (1961).

Gradenwitz, Peter. Add to books: *Music and Musicians in Israel* (Tel Aviv, 1959); *Wege zur Musik der Gegenwart* (Stuttgart, 1963).

Graetzer, Guillermo, Austrian - Argentine composer; b. Vienna, Sept. 5, 1914. He studied in Vienna with Paul A. Pisk; in 1930 moved to Buenos Aires, devoting himself mainly to educational activities; also edited musical anthologies. Works: *Concierto para Orquesta* (1939); *La Parábola* for orch. (1947); *Sinfonía Brevis* (1951); *Concierto de Cámara* (1953); cello concerto (1957); chamber music; piano pieces; songs.

Graf, Max. Died in Vienna, June 23, 1958.

Graffman, Gary. Date of birth, Oct. 14 (not Oct. 19), 1928.

Gräflinger, Franz. Died in Bad Ischl, Austria, Sept. 9, 1962.

Grainger, Percy Aldridge. Died in White Plains, N. Y., Feb. 20, 1961. *Irish Tune from County Derry* was written in 1909 (not 1911); *Shepherd's Hey,* in 1913 (not 1914); *Colonial Song* in 1913 (not 1914). In a modest way, he was a pioneer of electronic music; as early as 1937 he wrote a quartet for Theremins, notating the pitch by zigzags and curves.

Granados, Enrique. Add to bibl.: F. Vicens, *Enrique Granados* (Barcelona, 1958).

Granichstaedten, Bruno. Died in New York, May 20, 1944.

Grassi, Eugène. Exact date of death, June 8, 1941.

Graudan, Nikolai, Russian-American cellist; b. Libau, Sept. 5, 1896; d. Moscow, Aug. 9, 1964. He studied cello with Abbiate at the St. Petersburg Cons.; subsequently was instructor there; left Russia in 1922 and went to Germany; was first cellist of the Berlin Philharmonic (1926-35). In 1935 he went to London, and in 1938 to the U. S.; from 1939-44 was first cellist of the Minneapolis Orch.; in 1944-50 lived in New York; in 1950 settled in Los Angeles; gave duo recitals with his wife, the pianist Joanna Freudberg; was member of the Festival Quartet; taught at Black Mountain College, Santa Barbara Academy of the West, at Aspen and at the Univ. of California, Los Angeles. In 1964 he went to Moscow for a visit, and died there. He edited 6 Vivaldi cello sonatas with the realization of the piano part; arranged several Chopin pieces for cello and piano.

Graveure, Louis. Died in Los Angeles, April 27, 1965.

Gray, Donald, American publisher; b. New Rochelle, N. Y., May 25, 1903; d. Stamford, Conn. Oct. 21, 1969. He studied at Dartmouth College, graduating in 1924; joined the music publishing house founded by his father H. Willard Gray; succeeded him as president in 1951. He published many works by American composers, among them Aaron Copland, Leo Sowerby and Philip James.

Graziani, Bonifazio, Italian composer of church music; b. Marino, 1605; d. Rome, June 15, 1664; held the post as maestro di cappella in Rome; composed much sacred music publ. in 1652-78.

Green, John, American composer and conductor of popular music; b. New York, Oct. 10, 1908. He studied economics at Harvard Univ. (A.B., 1928); music theory with W. R. Spalding; piano with Ignace Hilsberg. He settled in Hollywood in 1942; became arranger for Guy Lombardo; wrote songs; among them, *Body and Soul* (1931) and *I Cover the Waterfront* (1933) became popular; conducted many motion picture scores and received Academy awards for *Easter Parade* (1948), *An American in Paris* (1951) and *West Side Story* (1961); also arranged and conducted music for television. He was conductor of the Los Angeles Philharmonic Promenade Concerts (1959-63) and guest conductor of other orchestras in the U.S.

Greenberg, Noah, American conductor and musicologist; b. New York, April 9, 1919; d. there, Jan. 9, 1966. He studied music privately; served in the U.S. Merchant Marine (1944-49); organized choruses in New York. In 1952 he founded in N. Y. the choral society Pro Musica Antiqua specializing in Renaissance music; revived the medieval liturgical music dramas *The Play of Daniel* (1958) and *The Play of Herod* (1963); traveled with his ensemble in Europe in 1960 and 1963. He held a Guggenheim Fellowship in 1955 and the Ford Fellowship in 1960 and 1962.

Greene, Maurice. He died on Dec. 1, 1755 (not 1775).

Greenfield, Edward, English writer on music; b. Westcliff-on-Sea, Essex, July 30, 1928. He studied law at Cambridge Univ. (1949-

52); joined the staff of the 'Manchester Guardian' as phonograph record critic in 1955, and became its music critic in 1964. He was a regular broadcaster for B.B.C. from 1957; contributed to 'The Gramophone' and other music journals. He was joint author (with Denis Stevens and Ivan March) of the multi-volume 'Stereo Record Guide.' He publ. a monograph, *Puccini: Keeper of the Seal* (London, 1958).

Gregor, Čestmír, Czech composer; b. Brno, May 14, 1926. He studied at the Brno Cons.; wrote 2 programmatic symphonies, subtitled *The Glory of Our Life* (1950) and *Land and People* (1953); piano concerto (1958); chamber music.

Gretchaninov, Alexander Tikhonovitch. The first performance of his opera *Dobrinya Nikititch* took place in Moscow on Oct. 27 (not Oct. 17), 1903.

Grétry, André Ernest Modeste. Add to bibl.: *La Correspondance générale de Grétry* (Brussels, 1962).

Grevillius, Nils. Died in Mariefred, Sweden, Aug. 15, 1970.

Grieg, Edvard Hagerup. Add to bibl.: H. J. Hurum, *I Edvard Griegs verden* (Oslo, 1960).

Griffis, Elliot, American pianist and composer; b. Boston, Jan. 28, 1893; d. Los Angeles, June 8, 1967. He studied at Yale School of Music with Horatio Parker and at the New England Cons. with Chadwick; held numerous educational posts as teacher of piano and theory; appeared in recitals; eventually settled in Los Angeles. His music is set in ingratiatingly romantic colors. He also publ. several volumes of verse. Works: *Paul Bunyan, Colossus,* symph. poem (1926-34); Symph. No. 1 (1931); *Fantastic Pursuit,* for strings (1941); *Port of Pleasure,* one-act opera (Los Angeles, June 29, 1963); semi-classical piano pieces.

Grofé, Ferde. Add to works: *San Francisco Suite* for orch. (San Francisco, April 23, 1960); *Niagara Falls Suite* for orch. (Buffalo, Feb., 1961); *World's Fair Suite* for orch. (N. Y., April 22, 1964); *Virginia City: Requiem for a Ghost Town,* symph. poem (Virginia City, Nevada, Aug. 10, 1968).

Grossmann, Ferdinand, Austrian conductor; b. Tulln, July 4, 1887; d. Vienna, Dec. 5, 1970. He studied music in Linz; later took a course in conducting with Weingartner in Vienna. In 1923 he founded a Volkskonservatorium in Vienna; in 1946 organized the Chamber Chorus of the Vienna Academy of Music and toured with it in Europe and America. He was also a composer; wrote a *German Mass* a cappella (1952) and some chamber music.

Grout, Donald Jay. Add to books: *A History of Western Music* (N. Y., 1960).

Groven, Eivind. Add to works: *In the Hospital at Night* for soprano, harp and strings (1946); *Faldafeykir* for orch. (1967). He publ. a valuable treatise on Eskimo melodies in Alaska, *Eskimomelodier fra Alaska* (1955).

Gruenberg, Louis. Died in Los Angeles, June 9, 1964. Add to works: *Americana,* suite for orch. (1945); opera, *Anthony and Cleopatra* (1940-60); *A Song of Faith,* spiritual rhapsody for speaker, voices, chorus, orch. and a dance group (1952-62). *Green Mansions* was produced on Oct. 17 (not Sept. 7), 1937.

Grümmer, Paul. Died in Zug, Switzerland, Oct. 30, 1965.

Grunwald, Hugo. Died on Oct. 2 (not Oct. 3), 1956.

Gruppe, Paulo Mesdag. Publ. a book, *A Reasonable and Practical Approach to the Cello* (Univ. of Illinois, Urbana, Ill., 1964).

Guarino, Carmine, Italian composer; b. Rovigo, Oct. 1, 1893; d. Genoa, June 5, 1965. He studied violin and composition at the Cons. of Naples. His first opera *Madama di Challant,* set in a Verdian tradition, was produced there on March 9, 1927, attracting favorable comments. He was also the composer of the first Italian radio opera, *Cuore di Wanda* (Radio Italiano, Dec. 20, 1931). Other works for the stage comprise an operetta *Gaby* (San Remo, March 20, 1924); a musical fable, *Tabarano alla Corte di Nonesiste* (1931); one-act opera *Balilla* (Rome, March 7, 1935); one-act opera *Sogno di un mattino d'autunno* (Cluj, Rumania, March 30, 1936); and a ballet *El Samet, il silenzioso* (1958).

Guarnieri, Camargo. His middle name is Mozart. Add to works: violin concerto No. 2 (Rio de Janeiro, June 2, 1956).

Guba, Vladimir, Ukrainian composer; b. Kiev, Dec. 22, 1938. He studied at the Kiev Cons. with Liatoshinsky; became interested in modern techniques of composition; applied the 12-tone method in his piano pieces *Deformation* and *Echo* (1961); also wrote a series of 30 piano pieces, *In the World of*

Childhood, and a cycle of 24 piano pieces, *Sonorous Exhibits.*

Guerrero, Francisco. Born in 1528 (probably on St. Francis Day, Oct. 4), not in 1527. See R. Stevenson, *Spanish Cathedral Music in the Golden Age* (Berkeley/Los Angeles, 1961).

Guerrini, Guido. Died in Rome, June 14, 1965. A catalogue of his works and an appreciation were publ. for his 70th birthday in Rome in 1961. His opera *Enea* was produced in Rome on Feb. 11 (not March 7), 1953.

Guézec, Jean-Pierre, French composer; b. Dijon, Aug. 29, 1934; d. Paris, March 9, 1971. He enrolled at the Paris Cons. where he attended classes of Olivier Messiaen, Darius Milhaud and Jean Rivier; received Premier Prix in 1963; joined the faculty of the Paris Cons. in 1969. Works: *Suite pour Mondrian* for orch. (1962); *Architectures* for 15 instruments (1964); *Formes* for orch. (1966); *Textures enchainées* for 13 wind instruments (1967); *Assemblages* for 28 instruments (1967); string trio (1968); *Reliefs polychromés* for chorus (1969); *Couleurs juxtaposées* for 2 percussion groups (1969).

Guido d'Arezzo. Putative date of birth, 997, rather than 990. Date of death uncertain; the precise date, May 17, 1050, is without foundation.

Guillaume, Eugène, Belgian composer; b. Namur, June 29, 1882; d. Brussels, Dec. 17, 1953. He studied organ at the Brussels Cons. and composition at the Cons. of Liège. He joined the staff of the Brussels Cons. in 1921. He composed 2 symphonies; symph. poems *Wallonia, Versailles, Fantaisie romantique, Au Cinéma,* etc.; a viola concerto; *Poème* for cello and orch.; chamber music.

Gulda, Friedrich. He liked to play in jazz groups, and composed jazz pieces, a hobby erroneously attributed to Glenn Gould (q.v.).

Gura, Hermann. Died in Bad Wiessee, Bavaria, Sept. 13, 1944.

Guridi, Jesús. Died in Madrid, April 7, 1961.

Gurlitt, Wilibald. Died in Freiburg-im-Breisgau, Dec. 15, 1963. He was editor of the first 2 vols. (1959; 1961) of the 12th edition of Hugo Riemann's *Musik-Lexikon.*

Gürsching, Albrecht, German oboist and composer; b. Nuremberg, Sept. 9, 1934. He studied composition in Stuttgart with Karl Marx and in Munich with Günter Bialas; was engaged as oboist in various ensembles. His works include a concerto for oboe, viola and strings (1961); *Rondo* for violin and string quartet (1963); 2 string quartets (1964); quartet for oboe and string trio (1964); symph. for small orch. (1964).

Gutchë, Gene (real name Romeo E. Gutsche), American composer; b. Berlin, July 3, 1907. He studied in Germany, then went to the U. S., where he undertook additional academic work at the Univ. of Minnesota with Donald Ferguson and at the Univ. of Iowa with Philip Greeley Clapp (Ph.D., 1953); held two Guggenheim Fellowships (1961, 1964). His music is marked by a fairly advanced idiom and a neo-romantic treatment of programmatic subject matter. In some of his orchestral works he applies fractional tones by dividing the strings into two groups tuned at slightly differing pitches. Works: Symph. No. 1 (Minneapolis, April 11, 1950); Symph. No. 2 (1950-54); Symph. No. 3 (1952); *Rondo Capriccioso* (1953; N. Y., Feb. 19, 1960; with the application of fractional tones); piano concerto (Minneapolis, June 19, 1956); cello concerto (1957); Symph. No. 4 (1960; Albuquerque, March 8, 1962); Symph. No. 5 for strings (Chautauqua, July 29, 1962); *Timpani Concertante* (Oakland, Calif., Feb. 14, 1962); violin concerto (1962); *Genghis Khan,* symph. poem (Minneapolis, Dec. 6, 1963); *Rites in Tenochtitlán* for small orch. (St. Paul, Jan. 26, 1965); *Gemini* for orch., with microtones (Minneapolis, July 26, 1966); *Classic Concerto* for orch. (St. Paul, Nov. 11, 1967); *Epimetheus* USA for orch. (Detroit, Nov. 13, 1969); 4 string quartets; 3 piano sonatas; choruses. See: 'Composers of the Americas' vol. 15 (Washington, 1969).

Guthrie, Woody, American folk-singer (full name **Woodrow Wilson Guthrie**); b. Okemah, Oklahoma, July 14, 1912; d. New York, Oct. 3, 1967. His father was a prize fighter and a professional guitar player. The family suffered adversity during the depression; Woody Guthrie took to the road; performed in saloons and at labor meetings, improvising songs of social significance. Later he joined Pete Seeger and others in a group known as Almanac Singers; publ. the books *Bound for Glory* and *American Folksong.* Although not a trained singer, Guthrie acquired fame as an impassionate balladeer of disadvantaged Americans. Ignoring for the moment his freely professed radical convictions, the U. S. Government bestowed upon him in 1966 an award of merit as 'a poet of the American landscape.' His career was cut short in 1957 when he contracted Huntington's chorea, which incapacitated him. His son Arlo Guthrie (b. New York, July 10, 1947) carried on Woody Guthrie's tradition as a folk singer; became famous for his ballad *Alice's Restaurant,* which is also the title of a motion picture in which he starred as himself, getting busted.

Gutiérrez, Gonzalo, Spanish organist and composer; b. about 1540; d. Granada, 1605. He was appointed organist at the Cathedral of Granada in 1569, and held his post until his death. Cf. José Lopez Calo, *La Música en la Catedral de Granada en el Siglo XVI* (Granada, 1963; vol. I, pp. 205-210; vol. II includes several of his works).

Gutman, Robert W., American writer on music; b. New York, Sept. 11, 1925. He studied at N. Y. Univ. (B.A., 1945; M.A., 1948); his principal teacher in musicology was Curt Sachs. In 1957 he was appointed to the faculty of the Univ. of the State of N. Y. He contributed essays to music magazines; publ. a searching and original biographical analysis of Wagner, *Richard Wagner: The Man, His Mind and His Music* (N. Y., 1968; German translation, Munich, 1970; French translation, 1971).

Guzikov, Michal Jozef. Date of birth, according to new style calendar, Sept. 14 (not Sept. 2), 1806. He was born near Mohilev, Russia (not Szklow, Poland).

Gysi, Fritz. Died in Zürich, March 5, 1967.

H

Haan, Willem de, Dutch composer; b. Rotterdam, Sept. 24, 1849; d. Berlin, Sept. 26, 1930. He studied at the Leipzig Cons.; in 1876 became conductor in Darmstadt; in 1923 moved to Berlin. He wrote an opera *Die Kaiserstochter* (Darmstadt, Feb. 1, 1885) and much choral music.

Haarklou, Johannes. Add to bibl.: F. Benestad, *Johannes Haarklou, Mannen og verket* (Oslo, 1961).

Haas, Joseph. Died in Munich, March 31, 1960. Add to works: *Deutsche Kindermesse* (1958), *Marienkantate* (1959).

Haase, Hans. Was not appointed editor of 'Die Musik in Geschichte und Gegenwart' but remained a member of its editorial staff. He publ. *Jobst vom Brandt* (dissertation).

Hába, Alois. Retired as prof. of the Univ. of Prague in 1953. Add to works: Nonet No. 3 (1953); string quartet No. 11, in sixth-tones (1953); string quartet No. 12, in quarter-tones (1960); string quartet No. 13, dodecaphonic (1960); violin concerto (1954; Prague, Feb. 17, 1963).

Hadley, Henry (Kimball). He was associate conductor of the N. Y. Philharmonic from 1920 to 1927 (not 1915 to 1922). He conducted the first performance of his Symph. No. 5, *Connecticut,* at Norfolk Festival on June 2, 1935 (not 1934). The world première of *The Culprit Fay* took place in Grand Rapids on May 28 (not Oct. 30), 1909.

Hadzhiev, Parashken, Bulgarian composer; b. Sofia, April 14, 1912. He studied with his father, an opera conductor, and with Pantcho Vladigerov; later was a student in composition of Josef Marx in Vienna. Returning to Sofia, he was appointed prof. of the Sofia Cons. As a composer, he is at his best in music for the theater. Works: musical fairy tale *There Was a Time* (Sofia, April 11, 1957); a comic opera *Lud gidia* (*Madcap;* Sofia, Nov. 15, 1959); a ballet *Silver Slippers* (Varna, March 20, 1962) and a tragic opera on a national Bulgarian subject, *Albena* (Varna, Nov. 2, 1962). Another opera, *A July Night,* was produced in Plovdiv, Feb. 16, 1965.

Hadzidakis, Manos, Greek composer; b. Xanthi, Macedonia, Oct. 23, 1925. He wrote piano pieces in an advanced idiom, recalling Prokofiev; then turned to film music. He is the composer of the famous theme song in the film released in America under the title *Never on Sunday* (original Greek title, *Children of Piraeus*).

Hageman, Richard. Died in Beverly Hills, Calif., March 6, 1966.

Hahn, Reynaldo. Exact date of first performance of *La Colombe de Buddha,* March 21, 1921; *Le Marchand de Venise* was produced on March 25 (not March 29), 1935.

Haieff, Alexei. In 1968 he was appointed composer-in-residence at the Univ. of Utah. Add to works: Symph. No. 2 (Boston, April 11, 1958); Symph. No. 3 (New Haven, April 11, 1961); *Eclogue* for harp and strings (1963); cello sonata (1965); *Éloge* for chamber orch. (1967).

Haitink, Bernard, Dutch conductor; b. Amsterdam, March 4, 1929. He studied violin, and played in orchestras; in 1955 he was appointed conductor of the Radio Orch. in Amsterdam; toured with it in Italy and Germany. He was guest conductor of the Concertgebouw Orch. during its American tour in 1961, and upon return to Holland, was appointed its permanent conductor. In 1962 he toured with it in Japan. He also made guest appearances with the Hallé Orch. of Manchester, London Philharmonic Orch., BBC Symph. Orch., Berlin Philharmonic and Los Angeles Philharmonic.

Hales, Hubert (James). Died in Cromer, England, July 13, 1965.

Halffter, Cristóbal, Spanish composer, nephew of Ernesto and Rodolfo Halffter; b. Madrid, March 24, 1930. He studied with Conrado del Campo and Alexandre Tansman; in 1962 he became prof. of composition at the Madrid Cons. His works include *Antífona* (1952); *Concertino for String Orchestra* (1960); *Formantes* for 2 pianos (1961); *Cantata in Exspectatione Resurrectionis Domini* (1962); *Espejos* for 3 percussion groups and electronic tape (1963); *Sinfonia* for 3 instrumental groups (1963); string quartet (1970); ballet, *Anillos* (Lyon, April 13, 1971). He adopts the combinatory method of composition in which melodic elements and meter are part of a serial progression.

Halffter, Ernesto. He completed and orchestrated Manuel de Falla's *Atlántida* (Milan, June 18, 1962).

Hall, Pauline. Died in Oslo, Jan. 23, 1969.

Hallnäs, Hilding. He wrote six symphonies in all: No. 1, *Sinfonia pastorale* (1944; Göteborg, March 22, 1945); No. 2, *Sinfonia notturna* (1946; Göteborg, March 4, 1948); No. 3, *Little Symphony* for strings (1948; Göteborg, Oct. 3, 1948); No. 4, *Metamorfose Sinfonische* (1950-51; Göteborg, April 17, 1952); No. 5, *Sinfonia aforistica* (1962; Göteborg, Jan. 24, 1963); No. 6, *Musica intima* (1966; Malmö, Nov. 7, 1967). Other works to be added are: piano concerto (1956); 2 flute concertos (1957, 1962); *Concerto* for string orch. and percussion (1959); piano trio (1960); *Epitaph* for string orch. (1963); *Rapsodia* for chamber orch. and soprano (1963); *A Greek Saga* for orch. (1967-68); *Momenti bucolichi* for oboe solo and orchestra (1969); *Horisont och linjespel* for string orch. (1969).

Halvorsen, Leif. Died in Oslo, Dec. 28, 1959.

Ham, Albert. *Little Jack Horner* is not his tune, but he made a popular arrangement of it.

Hamal, Jean-Noël. Add to bibl.: M. de Smet, *Jean-Noël Hamal (1709-1778), chanoine impérial et Directeur de la Musique de la Cathédrale Saint-Lambert de Liège: Vie et Œuvre* (Brusssels, 1959).

Hambourg, Mark. Died in Cambridge, England, Aug. 26, 1960.

Hambraeus, Bengt, Swedish organist and composer; b. Stockholm, Jan. 29, 1928. He studied at Uppsala Univ. (M. A. 1956). In 1957 he joined the music staff of the Swedish Broadcasting Corp.; in 1968 became its music director; was also active as organist and teacher. He took courses in modern techniques in Darmstadt; became one of the pioneers of electronic music in Scandinavia. In his works he combines the constructivism of the cosmopolitan avant-garde with the linear polyphony of medieval modality. Works: *Diptychon* for flute, oboe, viola, celesta and harpsichord (1952); *Spectrogram* for voice and orch. (1953); *Crystal Sequence* for voice and instruments (1954); *Segnali* for string quintet (1956); pieces for acoustical and electronic sounds, including *Rota* (1957), *Transition and Transfiguration* (1956-66); *Mikrogram* for instruments (1961); *Fresque Sonore* for soprano and instruments (1967); etc. In 1971 he made a lecture tour of the U.S.

Hamerik, Ebbe. Died in Copenhagen, Aug. 15, 1951 (drowned in Kattegat).

Hamilton, Iain. He was prof. of music at Duke Univ., North Carolina (1962-71); in 1971 appointed to the staff of City Univ. in New York. Add to works: Concerto for jazz trumpet and orch. (1958); *Sinfonia* for 2 orchestras (1959); *Ecossaise* for orch (1959); cello sonata (1959); piano concerto (1960; revised, 1967); sextet for flute, 2 clarinets, violin, cello and piano (1962); *Sonatas and Variants* for 10 wind instruments (1963); *Sonata notturna* for horn and piano (1965); string quartet No. 2 (1965); *Sonata for Five,* for wind quintet (1966); *Agamemnon,* opera in 2 acts (1967-69); *The Royal Hunt of the Sun,* opera in 2 acts (1967-69); *Circus* for 2 trumpets and orch. (1969); *Voyage* for horn and orch. (1970); *Alastor* for orch. (1970).

Hammerstein, Oscar. The Olympia Music Hall was built in 1895, not 1899.

Hammerstein, Oscar II. Died in Highland Farms, Doylestown, Penn., Aug. 23, 1960.

Hammond, John Hays Jr. Died in New York, Feb. 12, 1965.

Hampton, Lionel, American jazz pianist and band leader; b. Louisville, Kentucky, Dec. 4, 1913. He played drums in Chicago night clubs; then moved to Los Angeles where he formed a band of his own. He achieved commercial success by simplifying the rhythmic formula of jazz, accentuating the main beat, accelerating the tempo and amplifying instrumental sonorities to a maximum of aural toleration; but sometimes he plays tunes at a relatively low speed. He was a pioneer in introducing the vibraphone into jazz bands; he is the originator of the 'trigger-finger' method of piano playing (2 forefingers drumming upon a single note *prestissimo*). Beginning in 1956 he made several successful European tours.

Handel, Georg Friedrich. His youthful duel with Mattheson (if it took place at all) was fought with swords, not pistols. The reference to Händel's letters in 'Musica d'oggi' of Jan. 1933 (not Dec. 1932) is to Rolli's comments concerning Handel, not to Handel's own letters edited by Rolli. Add to bibliography: W. Serauky, *G. F. Händel: Sein Leben, sein Werk* (Kassel, 1958); E. Flessa, *Ombra mai fu: Die Händel Chronik des Johann Christopher Smith* (Biberbach, 1958); Paul Nettl, *G. F. Händel* (Berlin, 1958); J. M. Müller-Blattau, *G. F. Händel: Der Wille zur Vollendung* (Mainz, 1959); W. Dean, *Handel's Dramatic Oratorios and Masques* (London, 1959); Richard Friedenthal, *G. F. Händel in Selbstzeugnissen und Bilddokumenten* (Hamburg, 1959); M. Nicolescu, *Händel* (Bucharest, 1959); W. C. Smith and C. Humphries, *Handel: A Descriptive Catalogue of the Early Editions* (London, 1960); H. B. Dietz, *Die Chorfuge bei G. F. Händel* (Tutzing, 1961); W. Rockwitz and H. Steffens, *G. F. Händel, Persönlichkeit, Umwelt, Vermächtnis* (Leipzig, 1962); K. Sarre, *Händel Bibliographie* (Leipzig, 1963); H. W. Shaw, *A Textual and Historical Companion to Handel's Messiah* (London, 1965); W. C. Smith, *A Handelian's Notebook* (London, 1965); Paul Henry Lang, *Handel* (N. Y., 1965; highly valuable, both historically and biographically); M. Szentkuthny, *Händel* (Budapest, 1967); John Tobin, *Handel's Messiah* (London, 1969); W. Dean, *Handel and the Opera Seria* (Berkeley, Calif., 1969).

Handschin, Jacques. Add bibl.: *In Memoriam Jacques Handschin* (Strasbourg, 1962).

Handy, William Christopher. Died in New York, March 28, 1958.

Hannikainen, Tauno. Died in Helsinki, Oct. 12, 1968.

Hanon, Charles-Louis. Born at Renescure, near Dunkerque (not at Rem-sur-l'Aire), July 2, 1819 (not 1820).

Hanson, Howard. In 1961-62 conducted the Eastman School Philharmonia Orch. in Portugal, Spain, Switzerland, France, Luxembourg, Belgium, Sweden, Greece, Cyprus, Syria, Egypt, Lebanon, Turkey, Germany, Poland and Russia, under the auspices of the State Department. In 1964 resigned as Director of the Eastman School of Music. Add to works: *Mosaics* for orch. (Cleveland, Jan. 23, 1958); *Song of Human Rights,* cantata (Washington, Dec. 10, 1963); symph. No. 6 (N. Y., Feb. 29, 1968). He publ. a manual, *Harmonic Materials of Modern Music: Resources of the Tempered Scale* (N. Y., 1960).

Haraszti, Emile. Died in Paris, Dec. 27, 1958.

Harbison, John, American composer; b. Orange, N. J., Dec. 20, 1938. He studied piano, violin, viola, and also conducting; took courses in composition at Harvard Univ. (B. A., 1960) and at Princeton Univ. with Roger Sessions (M. F. A., 1963). In 1969 he was appointed assistant prof. of music at the Massachusetts Institute of Technology. His works include a *Sinfonia* for violin and double orch. (1963); *Confinement* for a chamber ensemble (1965); violin concerto (1967); *Serenade* for six players (1968); piano trio (1969).

d'Harcourt, Marguerite. Died in Paris, Aug. 2, 1964.

Harewood, 7th Earl of, **George Henry Hubert Lascelles,** British music editor and organizer; b. Cambridge, Feb. 7, 1923. He was educated at Eton and King's College, Cambridge, served as Capt., Grenadier Guards in World War II; wounded and taken prisoner in 1944. He was founder and editor of magazine *Opera* (1950-53); Chairman of the Music Advisory Committee, British Council from 1956; Artistic Director of the Edinburgh International Festival 1961-64; Chancellor, Univ. of York since 1962. He edited Kobbé's *Complete Opera Book* (1954).

Harline, Leigh. Died in Long Beach, Calif., Dec. 10, 1969.

Harling, William Franke. Died in Sierra Madre, Calif., Nov. 22, 1958. *Deep River* had its first performance in Lancaster, Penn., on Sept. 18, 1926 (before the N. Y. performance).

Harrell, Mack. Died in Dallas, Jan. 29, 1960.

Harris, Roy. Was prof. of composition of Indiana Univ., Bloomington (1957-60); then at the Inter-American Univ., San Germán, Puerto Rico (1960-61); in 1961, appointed to the faculty of the Univ. of California, Los Angeles. Add to works: *Abraham Lincoln Walks at Midnight,* for soprano, piano and orch. (Pittsburgh, 1953); *Fantasy* for piano and orch. (Hartford, Nov. 17, 1954); *Give Me the Splendid Silent Sun,* for baritone and orch., to words by Walt Whitman (Washington, April 27, 1961); *Canticle to the Sun,* for coloratura soprano and chamber orch., after St. Francis (Washington, Sept. 21, 1961); 8th Symph. (San Francisco, Jan 17, 1962); 9th Symph. (Philadelphia, Jan. 18, 1963); *Epilogue to Profiles in Courage: J. F. K.,* for orch. (Los Angeles, May 10, 1964); *Jubilation* for chorus, brasses and piano (San Francisco, May 16, 1964); *Horn of Plenty* for orch. (Beverly Hills, Calif., June 14, 1964); *Duo* for cello and piano (1964); *Rhythms and Spaces* for string orch. (an orchestral version of his 3rd string quartet; N.Y., April 7, 1965); *Abraham Lincoln Symphony* (10th Symph.) for chorus, brass and two amplified pianos (Long Beach, Cal., April 14, 1965); symph. No. 11 (N. Y., Feb. 8, 1968); Symph. No. 12, commissioned by Marquette Univ., and written in commemoration of the 300th anniversary of Marquette's exploration of the Midwest (partial performance, Milwaukee, Feb. 24, 1968).

Harrison, Beatrice. Died in Smallfield, Surrey, March 10, 1965.

Harrison, George, English rock 'n' roll singer; member of the celebrated group 'The Beatles'; b. Liverpool, Feb. 25, 1943. Like his co-Beatles, he had no formal musical education and learned to play the guitar by osmosis and acclimatization. Not as extrovert as John Lennon (q.v.), not as exhibitionistic as Paul McCartney (q.v.), and not as histrionic as Ringo Starr (q.v.), he was not as conspicuously projected into public consciousness as his comrades-in-rock. Yet he exercised a distinct influence on the character of the songs that The Beatles sang. He became infatuated with the mystical lore of India; sat at the feet of a hirsute guru; introduced the sitar into his rock arrangements. He is the author of *Something,* one of the greatest successes of The Beatles. When the group broke up in 1970. Harrison proved sufficiently talented to impress his individual image in his own music; he also collaborated on songs of social consciousness with Bob Dylan. Bibl.: Hunter Davies, *The Beatles,* 'the authorized biography' (N. Y., 1968).

Harrison, Jay (parental name Smolens), American music critic and editor; b. New York, Jan. 25, 1927. He studied music with Philip James at N.Y. Univ. (A.B., 1948); joined the staff of N.Y. Univ. after graduation (1948). He was music critic for the N.Y. 'Herald Tribune' (1948-61); editor of 'Musical America' (1962-64).

Harrison, Julius Allen Greenway. Died in London, April 5, 1963.

Harrison, Lou. Add to works: *Simfony from Simfonies* in free style (1956); *Koncerto por la Violono kun perkuta orkestro* (N. Y., Nov. 19, 1959); *Symphony on G* (Oakland, Calif., Feb. 8, 1966); *Young Caesar,* puppet opera (Aptos, Calif., Aug. 21, 1971).

Harrison, May. Died in South Nutfield, Surrey, June 8, 1959.

Hartmann, Carl. Died in Munich, May 30, 1969.

Hartmann, Karl Amadeus. Died in Munich, Dec. 5, 1963. Add to works: Symph. No. 7 (Hamburg, March 15, 1959); Symph. No. 8 (Cologne, Jan. 25, 1963); *Kammerkonzert* for clarinet, string quartet and string orch. (posthumous; Zürich, June 17, 1969). The exact date of the first performance of his Symph. No. 4 in Munich, is April 2, 1948.

Haskil, Clara. Died in Brussels, Dec. 7, 1960. See R. Wolfensberger, *Clara Haskil* (Bern, 1961).

Hasse, Karl. Died in Dresden, July 31, 1960.

Hassell, Jon, American composer of the avant-garde; b. Memphis, Tenn., March 22, 1937. He was trained as a trumpet player; studied composition with Bernard Rogers at the Eastman School of Music in Rochester, N. Y. (B. M., 1969; M. M. 1970). Progressing away from traditional arts, he took courses in advanced electronic techniques with Karlheinz Stockhausen and Henri Pousseur in Cologne (1965-67); returning to the U. S. was composer-in-residence and performer at the Center for Creative and Performing Arts in Buffalo (1967-69). In 1969 he moved to New York City to pursue independent activities in music and in sculpture. His works include *Music for Vibraphones* (1965); *Blackboard Piece with Girls and Loops* for 2 girls and 2 pitch-producing blackboards (N. Y., March 26, 1968); *Superball* for 4 players, with hand-held magnetic tape heads (Ithaca, Oct. 29, 1969); *Goodbye Music* for mixed media (Buffalo, May 4, 1969); also sound sculptures: *Map 1* and *Map 2* for hand-held magnetic playback heads, designed to explore potential sounds (exhibited in Buffalo, as sculptures, 1969); and *Elemental Warnings* (1969).

Hasselmans, Louis. Died in San Juan, Puerto Rico, Dec. 27, 1957.

Hatze, Josip, Croatian composer; b. Split, March 21, 1879; d. there, Jan. 30, 1959. He studied with Mascagni in Italy. He belongs to a generation of Yugoslav composers entirely influenced by Italian music. He wrote the operas *Povratak* (*The Return;* Zagreb, March 21, 1911); *Adel i Mara* (Zagreb, March 1, 1933); many songs.

Haubenstock-Ramati, Roman, Polish composer of experimental music; b. Cracow, Nov. 27, 1919. He studied composition with Malawski and Koffler. In 1947-50 he was music director of Radio Cracow; then went to Israel where he was director of the Music Library in Tel-Aviv; subsequently lived in Paris, where he was connected with the Studio of Musique Concrète. In 1957 he settled in Vienna. His early works were written in the neo-baroque style, but about 1957 he adopted serial techniques with the application of exotic and electronic sonorities. Works: *Ricercari* for string trio (1950); *Blessings* for voice and 9 players (1952); *Recitativo and Aria* for cembalo and orch. (1954); *Papageno's Pocket-Size Concerto* for orch. and glockenspiel (1955); *Les Symphonies de Timbres* for orch. (1957); *Chants et Prismes* for orch. (1957); *Sequences* for violin and orch. in 4 groups (1958); *Interpolation,* a 'mobile' for flute solo (1958); *Liaisons,* a 'mobile' for vibraphone and marimbaphone (1959); *Petite Musique de Nuit,* a 'mobile' for orch. (1959); *Mobile for Shakespeare* for voice and 6 players (1960); *Credentials or "Think, Think Lucky"* for speech-voice and 8 players (1960); *Jeux* for 6 percussion groups (1961); *Vermutungen über ein dunkles Haus* for 3 orchestras (1963); *Amerika,* opera after Kafka's novel (Berlin, Oct. 8, 1966).

Haubiel, Charles. In 1971 he lived in Los Angeles. Add to works: *Sunday Costs Five Pesos,* Mexican folk-opera in one act (Charlotte, N.C., Nov. 6, 1950).

Haudebert, Lucien. Died in Paris, Feb. 24, 1963.

Hauer, Josef Matthias. Died in Vienna, Sept. 22, 1959. Add to works: *Die schwarze Spinne,* opera (Vienna, May 23, 1966; posthumous). Bibl.: Monika Lichtensfeld, *Untersuchungen zur Theorie der Zwölftontechnik bei J. M. Hauer* (Regensburg, 1964).

Haug, Hans. Died in Lausanne, Sept. 15, 1967.

Hauptmann, Moritz. Add bibl.: P. Rummenhöller, *Moritz Hauptmann als Theoretiker* (Wiesbaden, 1963).

Havelka, Svatopluk, Czech composer; b. Vrbice, Silesia, May 2, 1925. He studied violin and piano; took composition lessons with K. B. Jirák; eventually settled in Ostrava. Among his works are a cantata *Spring* (1949); 2 *Pastorales* for orch. (1948, 1951); several suites for chamber orch.; a symph. (1956); a cantata, *Heptameron* (Prague, March 25, 1964); theater and film music.

Hawkins, Coleman, American saxophone player; b. St. Joseph, Mo. Nov. 21, 1904; d. New York, May 19, 1969. He followed the traditional style of bebop, using slap-tongue effects and a trilling vibrato, but soon developed a distinctive manner with a broad dynamic range and a fine bel canto quality. He joined the Kansas City 'Jazz Hounds' in 1921; later became a member of Henderson's band in New York; toured in England and France in 1934-39; then returned to America.

Haydn, (Franz) Joseph. Add to bibl.: L. Nowak, *Joseph Haydn: Leben, Bedeutung, und Werk* (Zürich, 1959); D. Barth and M. Somfai, *Haydn als Opernkapellmeister* (Mainz, 1960); H. Seeger, *Joseph Haydn* (Leipzig, 1961); Anthon van Hoboken, *Discrepancies in Haydn Biographies* (Washington, D.C., 1962); G. A. Greisinger, *Joseph Haydn* (Madison, Wisconsin, 1963); Alan Tyson and H. C. Robbins Landon, *Who Composed Haydn's Op. 3?* in the 'Mus. Times' (July, 1964); *J. Haydn: Gesammelte Briefe und Aufzeichnungen* (Kassel, 1965).

Haydon, Glen. Died at Chapel Hill, North Carolina, May 8, 1966.

Hayton, Leonard George (Lennie), American jazz pianist, arranger and conductor; b. New York, Feb. 13, 1908; d. Palm Springs, Calif., April 24, 1971. He played piano in various jazz groups in New York; then went to California, where he was music director for Metro-Goldwyn-Mayer and for the 20th Century-Fox Film Corporation. He composed several semi-classic instrumental numbers and orchestrated scores for films. He married the black singer Lena Horne in 1948, and was acting as song arranger for her.

Haywood, Charles. Add to publ.: *A Treasury of World Folksongs* (N. Y., 1965). A new edition, revised and enlarged, of his *Bibliography of North American Folklore and Folksongs* was publ. in 2 vols. (N.Y., 1961).

Headington, Christopher, English composer and pianist; b. London, April 28, 1930. He studied piano and composition at the Royal Academy of Music, London; also took private lessons with Benjamin Britten. Works: *Variations* for piano and orch. (1950); cello sonata (1950); *Introduction and Allegro* for chamber orch. (1951); string quartet (1953); piano sonata (1956); *Chanson de l'éternelle tristesse,* ballet (1957); violin concerto (1959); Sonatina for oboe and piano (1960); Sonatina for unaccompanied flute (1960); Toccata for piano (1962); *Towards a Pindaric Ode* for soprano, mezzo-soprano and piano (1965); *Capriccio* for viola and piano (1965); film music; choruses.

Heartz, Daniel, American musicologist; b. Exeter, New Hampshire, Oct. 5, 1928. He studied at the Univ. of New Hampshire (A.B., 1950) and at Harvard Univ. (A.M., 1951; Ph.D., 1957). In 1957-60 he was on the faculty of the Univ. of Chicago; from 1960, at the Univ. of California, Berkeley. He publ. a valuable monograph, *Pierre Attaingnant, Royal Printer of Music* (Berkeley, Calif., 1969).

Hedley, Arthur, English musicologist; b. Shiremoor, near Newcastle-upon-Tyne, Nov. 12, 1905; d. Birmingham, Nov. 8, 1969. He studied French literature at the Federal Univ. of Durham (1923-27) and music with W. G. Whittaker at Newcastle. An ardent Chopinist, he learned the Polish language to be able to study Chopin documentation in the original; publ. a biography, *Chopin* (London, 1947); edited *Selected Correspondence of Chopin* (London, 1962); helped to dispel cumulative misconceptions and deceptions relating to Chopin's life; was instrumental in exposing the falsity of the notorious Potocka-Chopin correspondence produced by Mme. Czernicka (who killed herself in 1949 on the 100th anniversary of Chopin's death, after the fraudulence of her claims was irrefutably demonstrated by Hedley at the Chopin Institute in Warsaw). Hedley's Chopinolatry was carried to the point of fetishism; he acquired Chopin's cuff-links and a lead pencil; proved the authenticity of Chopin's silk waistcoat which came to light in Paris.

Heiden, Bernhard, German - American composer; b. Frankfurt, Aug. 24, 1910. He learned to play piano, clarinet and violin at home; studied composition with Hindemith in Berlin (1929-33). He emigrated to America in 1935, settling in Detroit, where he became active as conductor and arranger. In 1946 he was engaged as prof. of composition at Indiana Univ., Bloomington. His music is neo-classical in general outline, and his contrapuntal idiom follows Hindemith's percepts. Works: 2 symphonies (1938, 1954); Concerto for small orch. (Detroit, Dec. 6, 1949); *Euphorion,* for orch. (1949); *Memorial* for orch. (N.Y., Oct. 4, 1956); *Sinfonia* for woodwind quintet (1949); quintet for horn and string quartet (1952); sonata for saxophone and piano (1937); 3 string quartets (1947, 1951, 1964); sonata for horn and piano (1954); violin sonata (1954); sonatina for clarinet and piano (1955); *The Darkened City,* opera (Indiana Univ., Bloomington, Feb. 23, 1963); 2 piano sonatas; choruses.

Heider, Werner, German composer; b. Furth, Jan. 1, 1930. He studied in Nuremberg and Munich, and became active as pianist, conductor and composer. Among his works are *Glimpses* for soprano, piano and orch. (1958); *Choreographie* for clarinet and jazz band (1961); *Konturen* for violin and orch. (1962); *Konflikte* for percussion and orch. (1963). In his music he emphasizes structural factors, in which thematic elements follow serial organization.

Heinitz, Wilhelm. Died in Hamburg, March 31, 1963.

Heinroth, Charles. Died in Southampton, Long Island, N. Y., Jan. 8, 1963. He was the first to broadcast organ music over the radio.

Heinsheimer, Hans (Walter). Add book: *Best Regards to Aida* (N. Y., 1968).

Hekking, Gérard. Date of birth, Aug. 22 (not Aug. 12), 1879.

Helfer, Walter. Died in New Rochelle, N. Y., April 16, 1959.

Helfman, Max. Died in Dallas, Texas, Aug. 9, 1963.

Heller, Hans Ewald. Died in New York, Oct. 1, 1966.

Helm, Everett. He publ. *Composer, Performer, Public: A Study in Communication* (Florence, 1970, in English).

Helms, Hans G., German composer; b. Teterow, Mecklenburg, June 8, 1932. He studied literature and comparative philology; in 1957 settled in Cologne; worked on various speech problems in connection with recordings. His compositions exploit the musical possibilities of the speaking voice; of these, *Golem,* 'polemics for 9 vocal soloists' has been widely performed at modern music festivals in Germany. Other works are *Daidalos* for 4 solo singers and a group of speaking and listening pieces *Geschichte von Yahud* (1963).

Helps, Robert, American pianist and composer; b. Passaic, New Jersey, Sept. 23, 1928. He studied at the Juilliard School of Music in New York with Abby Whiteside (piano) and Roger Sessions (composition). He occupied teaching posts at Princeton Univ., the San Francisco Cons. of Music, Stanford Univ. and the Univ. of California at Berkeley. In 1970 he was on the staff of the New England Cons. of Music. His natural pianism helps Helps to write idiomatically for his instrument. Works: *Fantasy* for piano (1952); Symph. No. 1 (1955); piano trio (1957); *Image* for piano (1958); *Recollections* for piano (1959); *Portrait* for piano (1960); *Cortège* for orch. (1963); *Serenade* in 3 parts: (1) *Fantasy* for violin and piano (2) *Nocturne* for string quartet (3) *Postlude* for piano, violin, and horn (1964); piano concerto (1966); *Saccade* for piano 4-hands (1967); *Quartet* for piano solo, divided into 4 equal parts, each numbering 22 keys (1971).

Hemel, Oscar van, Dutch composer; b. Antwerp, Aug. 3, 1892. He studied with Willem Pijper in Amsterdam, but began to compose rather late in life. His style adheres to a romantic concept of dramatic expression without interfering with contrapuntal and harmonic coherence. In his later works he applied the 12-tone method of composition. He wrote 4 symphonies (1934-58), a violin concerto (1944), 4 string quartets, clarinet quintet, an opera *Viviane,* and many choral pieces.

Henderson, Ray, American composer of popular songs; b. Buffalo, Dec. 1, 1896; d. Greenwich, Conn., Dec. 31, 1970. He studied music at the Univ. of Southern Calif.; played the organ in churches and piano in jazz groups in Buffalo; then went to New York as a song plugger in Tin Pan Alley, and soon began writing songs of his own. His first success was *Georgette* (1922); this was followed by *Sonny Boy* which he wrote for Al Jolson's early talkie *The Singing Fool*; subsequent hits were *You're the Cream in My Coffee, Button Up Your Overcoat; Alabamy Bound, Hold Everything, Three Cheers,* etc.; some of these songs were written in collaboration with B. G. DeSylva. Unlike most of Broadway composers, Henderson could read and write music; he even took private lessons with Benjamin Britten. His film biography *The Best Things in Life are Free* was made in 1966.

Hendl, Walter. In 1964 he was appointed successor to Howard Hanson as Director of the Eastman School of Music, Rochester, N. Y.

Hendrix, Jimi (James Marshall), black American rock 'n' roll musician; b. Seattle, Nov. 27, 1942; d. London, Sept. 18, 1970, from suffocation from vomiting while unconscious as a result of an overdose of barbiturates. He rose to fame as a singer-guitarist whose erotic body movements underscored the sexual implications of his lyrics. He produced a sensation by his performance of an electronically amplified version of *The Star Spangled Banner* at the Woodstock Festival in August, 1969. His popularity in England was enhanced by his appearance at the Isle of Wight Festival in August, 1970.

Henning, Ervin Arthur, American composer; b. Marion, South Dakota, Nov. 22, 1910, of German immigrant parents. He studied music in Chicago with Roslyn Brogue, whom he subsequently married. In 1944 he entered New England Cons. in Boston, graduating in 1946. He writes mostly for chamber music combinations; in his later works he adopted the 12-tone method of composition. Works: quintet for flute, horn, violin, viola and cello (1946); *Partita* for string quartet (1948); Suite for viola concertante, 2 violins and cello (1950); *Divertimento* for unaccompanied bassoon (1950); trio for clarinet, viola and piano (1959); piano sonata (1959); pieces for recorders;

arrangements of Bach for various woodwind ensembles.

Henry, Harold. Died in Orangeburg, N. Y., Oct. 15, 1956.

Henry, Leigh Vaughan. Died in London, March 8, 1958.

Henry, Pierre, French composer of the avant-garde; b. Paris, Dec. 9, 1927. He studied with Nadia Boulanger and Olivier Messiaen; in 1942 joined the Groupe de Recherche de Musique Concrète organized by Pierre Schaeffer; collaborated with him in the composition of *Symphonie pour un Homme Seul* (1950) and the experimental opera *Orphée 53* (1953); wrote the score for the ballet *Die Reise* (1962).

Henze, Hans Werner. Place of birth Gütersloh (not Güttersloh). Symph. No. 1 was first performed in its entirety in Bad Pyrmont on Aug. 25, 1948; revised version, in Berlin, April 9, 1964. *Anrufung Apolls,* first performed as a ballet in Wiesbaden, Oct. 28, 1951, was incorporated into Symph. No. 3 as its first movement. Add to works: *Undine,* ballet (London, Oct. 27, 1958); *L'Usignolo dell' Imperatore,* pantomime after Andersen (Venice, Sept. 16, 1959); *Der Prinz von Homburg,* opera (Hamburg, May 22, 1960); *Elegie für junge Liebende,* chamber opera (Schwetzingen, May 20, 1961; in English, as *Elegy for Young Lovers,* which is the original title of the text by W. H. Auden from which the German libretto was made, Glyndebourne, July 13, 1961); *Novae de infinito laudes,* cantata (Venice, April 24, 1963); Symph. No. 4 (West Berlin, Oct. 9, 1963); Symph. No. 5 (N. Y., May 16, 1963); *Los Caprichos,* fantasia for orch. (1963; Duisburg, April 6, 1967); *Cantata della Fiaba estrema* (Zürich, Feb. 26, 1965); *Der junge Lord,* comic opera (Berlin, April 7, 1965); *Ein Landarzt,* monodrama for baritone and orch. (Berlin, Oct. 13, 1965); *Tancredi,* ballet (Vienna, May 14, 1966); *Die Bassariden,* 'opera seria' with an Intermezzo, after Euripides, to the libretto of W. H. Auden and Chester Kallman (Salzburg, Aug. 6, 1966); *Doppio Concerto* for oboe, harp and strings (Zürich, Dec. 2, 1966); *Fantasia* for strings (1966; Berlin, April 1, 1967); *Telemanniana* for orch., on themes of Telemann (Berlin, April 4, 1967); concerto for double-bass and orch. (Chicago, Nov. 2, 1967); *Moralities,* scenic cantatas after Aesop, to texts by W. H. Auden (Cincinnati May Festival, May 18, 1968); piano concerto No. 2 (Bielefeld, Sept. 29, 1968); *Versuch über Schweine* for baritone and chamber orch. (London, Feb. 14, 1969; the title refers to the insulting term applied by reactionaries to the rebellious Berlin students); Symph. No. 6 (Havana, Nov. 19, 1969); *El Cimarrón* for baritone, flute, guitar and percussion, to texts from *The Autobiography of a Runaway Slave* by Esteban Montejo (Aldeburgh Festival, June 22, 1970); *Compases para Preguntas ensimismadas* for viola and 22 players (Basel, Feb. 11, 1971); opera, *Il difficile percorso verso la casa di Natascha Ungeheuer* (Rome, May 17, 1971). Henze's oratorio, *Das Floss der Medusa,* produced in Hamburg on Dec. 9, 1968, with Henze on the podium, was aborted midway through the performance, when the chorus refused to sing when a red flag was hoisted on the stage, causing Henze to remark that revolution was more important than performances of new compositions. Bibl.: Klaus Geitel, *H. W. Henze* (Berlin, 1970).

Hercigonja, Nikola, Croatian composer; b. Vinkovcim, Feb. 19, 1911. He studied in Zagreb; in 1950 became a prof. of the Music Academy in Belgrade. In his music he follows a general trend of realistic composition, inspired by national folk songs. Works: *Vječni Žid u Zagrebu* (*The Wandering Jew in Zagreb*), musical burlesque (1942); *Gorski Vijenac (Mountain Wreath),* opera-oratorio (Belgrade, Oct. 19, 1957); *Planetarium,* scenic action for voices, speaking chorus and orch. (1960); numerous choruses.

Herman, Jerry, American composer of popular music; b. New York, July 10, 1933. He played piano by ear but never learned to read music. He studied drama at the Univ. of Miami; then became a script writer for television in N. Y. Later he devoted himself entirely to musical comedies, for which he wrote both lyrics and music. His shows *Parade* (1960) and *Milk and Honey* (1961) were fairly successful; but he made his greatest hit with the production of *Hello, Dolly!* (N. Y., Jan. 16, 1964), which had the longest run in the history of Broadway shows, closing on Dec. 26, 1970. A comparable success was achieved by his next musical *Mame,* which opened in New York on May 24, 1966.

Hernández-López, Rhazes, Venezuelan composer and musicologist; b. Petare, June 30, 1918. He studied in Caracas with Vicente Emilio Sojo and Juan Bautista Plaza. Apart from composition, he engaged in teaching and radio work. In his series of piano pieces under the title *Casualismo* he applies the 12-tone method of composition. Other works include

Las Torres Desprevenidas, symph. poem (1951); *Sonorritmo* for orch. (1953); *Mérida, Geografía Celeste,* symph. suite (1958); *Expansión Tres* for orch. (1965); *Tres Dimensiones* for strings (1967); *Cuadros* for flute, violin, viola, cello and harp (1950); *Viola Sonata* (1952); *Tres Espacios* for violin, cello and piano (1965); *Horizontal* for flute and strings (1966); piano pieces; songs.

Hérold, Louis-Joseph-Ferdinand. He spelled his last name **Herold,** without an accent.

Herrmann, Hugo. Died in Stuttgart, Sept. 7, 1967.

Hertzmann, Erich. Died in New York, March 3, 1963.

Hess, Myra. Died in London, Nov. 25, 1965.

Heymann, Werner Richard. Died in Munich, May 30 ,1961.

Hickmann, Hans Robert Hermann. Died in Blandford Forum, Dorset, England, Sept. 4, 1968. Add to publications: *Musikgeschichte in Bildern,* vol. 2, on Egypt (Leipzig, 1962).

Higgins, Richard C. (Dick), American composer; b. Cambridge, England, March 15, 1938. He was taken to America as a child; studied piano in Worcester, Mass.; composition and mycology with John Cage in N. Y. Eventually he moved to California. A militant promoter of radical ideas in art, he joined the mushrooming avant-garde groups; participated in staging 'happenings' across the country; was a co-founder of 'Fluxus' (1961); organized 'Something Else Press' (1964) with the aim of publishing something else. Not averse to academic activities, he joined the faculty of the California Institute of the Arts in Los Angeles. In his productions he pursues the objective of total involvement, in which music is verbalized in conceptual designs without reification, or expressed in physical action; the ultimate in this direction is achieved by his work *The Thousand Symphonies* (1968) in which the composer shoots machine-gun bullets through manuscript paper; his Symph. No. 585, shot by a sergeant of the army at the composer's behest, was distributed in holographs in No. 6 of the avant-garde magazine 'Source' (1969) under the subtitle 'The Creative Use of Police Resources.' Other major compositions include: *Graphis,* 146 works for varying groups (1958); *Musical Processes,* a cycle of 5 pieces for indeterminate ensembles (1960); *Constellations and Constributions* for multimedia (1959-60); *Symphoniae Sacrae,* conceptual works without a definite realization (1961); *In Memoriam,* a 164-part canon (1961); *The Peaceable Kingdom,* spoken opera with bells (1961); *Danger Musics,* a cycle of 43 conceptual pieces (1961-63); *Litany* for 5 pianos and tape recorder (1962-68); *Requiem for Wagner the Criminal Mayor* for tape recorder (1962); *Lavender Blue,* opera (1963); *Egg* for magnetic tape (1967); *Sophocles I and II,* fatal pieces for piano (1970). He publ. *foew&ombwhnw,* 'a grammar of the mind and a phenomenology of love and a science of the arts as seen by a stalker of the wild mushroom' (N. Y., 1969). His Zodiac parameter is Aries with the Sun in Pisces.

Hill, Alfred. Died in Darlinghurst, New South Wales, Oct. 30, 1960.

Hill, Edward Burlingame. Died in Francestown, N. H., July 9, 1960.

Hill, Richard S. Died in Naples, Florida, Feb. 7, 1961.

Hiller, Ferdinand. Add to bibl.: R. Seitz, ed.; *Aus Ferdinand Hillers Briefwechsel,* in 2 vols. (Cologne, 1958; 1961).

Hilsberg, Alexander. Died in Camden, Maine, Aug. 10, 1961.

Hilsberg, Ignace, Polish-American pianist; b. Warsaw, July 20, 1894. He studied at St. Petersburg Cons. with Isabelle Vengerova, Essipova, and Dubassov, graduating in 1917. After the Revolution he taught in Tomsk in Siberia and in Harbin, Manchuria. In 1920 he went to China, where he gave a series of concerts, including a command performance for Sun Yat-sen in Peking. In 1922 he taught at the Cons. of Athens, Greece. In 1923 he went to America. In 1925 he won the prestigious Lewisohn piano contest in New York, which enabled him to give concerts; he was soloist with the Boston Symph. and other orchestras. In 1936 he settled in Hollywood; played piano for sound films; taught at the Univ. of Calif. in Los Angeles. In 1969 he moved to San Diego as a teacher. In his interpretations he represents the time-honored Russian tradition, combining romantic expressiveness with technical virtuosity.

Hindemith, Paul. Died in Frankfurt, Dec. 28, 1963. Add to works: *Pittsburgh Symphony* (Pittsburgh, Jan. 30, 1959, composer conducting); Sinfonietta in E (Louisville, March 1, 1960); opera *Das lange Weihnachtsmahl* (Mannheim, Dec. 17, 1961);

Concerto for organ and orch. (N.Y., April 26, 1963, composer conducting); Mass for mixed choir a cappella (Vienna, Nov. 12, 1963). The date of the first performance of *Hin und Zurück* in Baden-Baden is July 17 (not July 15), 1927. Add to bibl.: H. L. Schilling, *Paul Hindemith's Cardillac* (Würzburg, 1962); H. Boatwright, *Paul Hindemith as a Teacher,* in the 'Mus. Quarterly' (July 1964); two valuable iconographic collections: *Paul Hindemith: Zeugnis in Bildern* (Mainz, 1961) and *Paul Hindemith: die letzten Jahre; ein Zeugnis in Bildern* (Mainz, 1965).

Hines, Jerome (real name Heinz), American bass singer; b. Los Angeles, Nov. 8, 1921. After studying chemistry at the Univ. of California, Los Angeles, he turned to singing; took voice lessons with Gennaro Curci; sang minor operatic roles in Los Angeles and San Francisco. He was employed as a chemist during World War II. On Nov. 21, 1946 he made his debut at the Metropolitan Opera House in N. Y. in a minor part, but created a very fine impression, and was assigned the title role in *Boris Godunov* (Feb. 11, 1954). He scored a great personal triumph when he sang the role in the Russian language in the Bolshoi Theater in Moscow (Oct. 23, 1962).

Hinrichsen, Max. Died in London, Dec. 17, 1965.

Hinrichsen, Walter. Died in New York, July 21, 1969.

Hinze-Reinhold, Bruno, German pianist; b. Danzig, Oct. 20, 1877; d. Weimar, Dec. 26, 1964. He studied at the Leipzig Cons.; taught piano at the Stern Cons. in Berlin (1901-13). In 1913 he moved to Weimar; was director of the State Music School (1916-49); then retired, but continued his activity as private piano teacher. He publ. a pedagogical manual *Technische Grundbegriffe eines natürlichen neuzeitlichen Klavierspiels.*

Hirao, Kishio. Died in Tokyo, Dec. 15, 1953.

Hirt, Fritz. Died in Chigny-sur-Morges, Switzerland, Jan. 5, 1970.

Hoboken, Anthony van. A *Festschrift* in his honor was publ. on his 75th birthday, ed. by J. Schmidt-Görg (Mainz, 1962).

Hochreiter, Emil, Austrian composer; b. Debreczin, Hungary, Dec. 27, 1871; d. Vienna, Aug. 3, 1938. He studied jurisprudence and music; composed mainly sacred choruses; also some symphonic overtures in a traditional romantic manner. During his sojourn of many years in Novo Mesto he collected Slovenian eucharistic songs, some of which he publ. in anthologies.

Hoddinott, Alun. Add to works: *Variants* for orch. (London, Nov. 2, 1966).

Hodeir, André, French music critic and jazz enthusiast; b. Paris, Jan. 22, 1921. He studied at the Paris Cons. with Messiaen and others; in 1954 founded The Jazz Group of Paris. He publ. several essays on jazz; edited the periodical 'Jazz Hot' (1947-50). In his writings he offers bold theories and startling evaluations; his book *Since Debussy* (N. Y., 1961) aroused much controversy on account of its iconoclastic attitude toward recognized modern composers and immoderate praise of putative young geniuses.

Hodges, Johnny (John Cornelius), American saxophonist; b. Cambridge, Mass. July 25, 1906; d. New York, May 11, 1970. He took saxophone lessons from Sidney Bechet; joined the Duke Ellington Band in 1928, remaining with it for the rest of his career, except for a period of 5 years when he had his own band. He became famous for his unabashed swinging style in the 1930's, but later developed a lyrical melodious mode which remained the principal characteristic of his playing.

Hodkinson, Sydney P., Canadian composer; b. Winnipeg, Jan. 17, 1934. He played the clarinet in bands; studied composition at the Eastman School of Music in Rochester, N. Y., with Louis Mennini and Bernard Rogers; later took courses with Elliott Carter, Roger Sessions and Milton Babbitt at Princeton Univ. (1960); then enrolled at the Univ. of Michigan as a student of Leslie Bassett and Ross Lee Finney (Mus. D., 1968). He was on the faculty of the Univ. of Virginia (1958-63) and of Ohio Univ. (1963-68); in 1968 appointed to the staff of the School of Music at the Univ. of Michigan; served as resident composer in Minneapolis (1970-71). In his music he pursues advanced techniques employing serial and aleatory resources. Works: *Lyric Impressions* for orch. (1956); *Threnody* for orch. (1957); *Two Studies* for string quartet (1958); *Structures* for percussion ensemble (1958); *Stanzas* for piano trio (1959); *Dynamics* for orch. (1960); *Lament for Guitar and Two Lovers,* a theatrical action (1962); *Five Absurdities* for 5 trombones (1963); *Mosaic* for brass quintet (1964); *Caricatures* for orch. (1966); *Armistice,* a truce for dancers and musicians (1966);

Interplay, a histrionic controversy for 4 musicians (1966); *Dissolution of the Serial* for piano and one instrument (1967); string quartet for 5 players (1967); *Fresco,* a mural for orch. (1968); *Organasm,* a scenario for organ soloist and assistants (1968); *Flux* for chamber orch. (1968); *Funks,* improvisation for 7 jazzmen (1969); *Another Man's Poison* for brass quintet (1970); *Valence* for chamber orch. (1970); pieces for various groups under the generic title *Drawings* (1969-70).

Hoffmann, Richard, Austrian-American composer; b. Vienna, April 20, 1925. He studied violin and harmony in Vienna as a child; was in New Zealand from 1935 until 1947; graduated from the Auckland Univ. College in 1945. He settled in the U. S. in 1947; studied composition with Arnold Schoenberg, and subsequently became his amanuensis and secretary. In 1954 he joined the faculty of the Oberlin Cons. of Music. He developed a sui generis serial technique, in which intervals, meters, rhythms, timbres and dynamics are systematically organized, while the tone-row is not necessarily dodecaphonic. His works include a string quartet (1947); trio for piano, violin and bass clarinet (1948); piano quartet (1950); *Fantasy and Fugue, in Memoriam Arnold Schoenberg,* for orch., in which the subject is a single reiterated note in five different dynamics (1951); piano concerto (1954); cello concerto (1956-59); pieces for piano solo; choruses; song cycles.

Hofman, Shlomo, Polish-Israeli composer and musicologist; b. Warsaw, April 24, 1909. He studied at the Warsaw Cons., graduating in 1934; then went to Paris where he studied composition with Roger-Ducasse, Charles Koechlin and Darius Milhaud (1937-38). He subsequently settled in Palestine; in 1954 became lecturer in musicology at the Israel Academy of Music in Tel-Aviv. Among his works are an oboe concerto (1950); a Hebrew cantata *Tawashih* (1960); a quintet for clarinet and strings (1945); several song titles. He publ. a valuable thesis, *L'Œuvre de Clavecin de François Couperin Le Grand* (Paris, 1961): a polyglot *Dictionary of Musical Terms* (Jerusalem, 1955); *The Music of Israel* (1959); *La Musique Arabe en Israel* (1963), etc.

Hofmann, Leopold, Austrian composer; b. Vienna, Aug. 14, 1738; d. there, March 17, 1793. He studied piano and violin; held posts as choirmaster in Vienna churches; also served as court organist. He wrote much church music; a number of instrumental concertos and chamber works, highly competent technically but lacking in invention and polyphonic strength. The article by Hermine Prohaszka in 'Die Musik in Geschichte und Gegenwart' gives a detailed list of his published and unpublished works.

Hofstetter, Romanus, German cleric and composer; was monk in the monastery of Armorbach, near Miltenberg ca. 1750. He published 12 string quartets under his own name and, more importantly, is the true author of six string quartets commonly attributed to Haydn as his op. 3. See Alan Tyson and H. C. Robbins Landon, *Who Composed Haydn's Op. 3?* in the 'Mus. Times' (July 1964).

Hoiby, Lee. Add to works: *The Scarf,* one-act opera after Chekhov (Spoleto, June 20, 1958); *Beatrice,* opera, after Maeterlinck (Louisville, Oct. 23, 1959); *Natalia Petrovna,* opera after Turgenev (N. Y., Oct. 8, 1964); *Summer and Smoke,* opera after a play by Tennessee Williams (St. Paul, Minn., June 19, 1971).

Holbrooke, Josef. Died in London, Aug. 5, 1958.

Holde, Artur. Died in New York City, June 23, 1962. Place of birth, Rendsburg (not Randzburg).

Holewa, Hans, Swedish composer; b. Vienna, May 26, 1905. He studied music in Vienna; in 1937 went to Stockholm, where he established himself as a pianist and pedagogue. In 1949 he joined the staff of the Swedish Broadcasting Corp. In his music he adopted a modified method of 12-tone composition. Works: Symphony (1948); Sonata for cello solo (1952); string trio (1959); quintet for clarinet, cello, trombone, percussion and piano (1962); *Concertino* for viola and 11 string instruments (1966).

Holiday, Billie (Lady Day), American Negro jazz singer; b. Baltimore, April 7, 1915; d. New York, July 17, 1959. She sang in Harlem night clubs; was discovered by Benny Goodman and appeared with his band; also with Count Basie, Artie Shaw and others; toured Europe (1954, 1958). She used her distinctive vocal endowments to create a synthesis of primitive emotionalism and sophisticated urbanity; her singing of the blues established a nostalgic trend through recordings. She publ. (with some professional journalistic help) an autobiography, *Lady Sings the Blues* (N. Y., 1956).

Holliger, Heinz, Swiss oboist and composer; b. Langenthal, May 21, 1939. He studied oboe and piano in Bern and Paris; composition with Veress in Bern and with Boulez in Paris. He won several international prizes as an oboe player, and toured in Europe and America as a virtuoso; several Swiss composers wrote special works for him. In his own music he follows in the footsteps of Webern. Works: *Himmel und Erde,* cantata for tenor, flute, harp, violin, viola and cello (1961); *Studie* for soprano, oboe, cello and harpsichord (1962); *Improvisationen* for oboe, harp and 12 string instruments (1963); sonata for unaccompanied oboe (1956); sonata for oboe and piano (1957); *Der magische Tänzer,* dodecaphonic chamber opera for 2 men and 2 marionettes (Basel, April 26, 1970); *Pneuma* for winds, percussion, organ (Donaueschingen, Oct. 18, 1970).

Hollingsworth, John. Died in London, Dec. 29, 1963.

Holmboe, Vagn. Add to works: 10 string quartets (1949-69); *Requiem for Nietzsche* (1964); Symph. No. 9 (1968).

Holyoke, Samuel. Add to bibl.: J. L. Willhide, *Samuel Holyoke, American Music-Educator* (Los Angeles, 1954).

Homs, Joaquin, Catalan composer; b. Barcelona, Aug. 22, 1906. He studied cello; began to compose late in life. He took lessons in music theory with Roberto Gerhard (1931-37); formed a constructivist style with thematic contents partly based on Catalan melorhythms. Works: 7 string quartets (1938-68); Duo for flute and clarinet (1936); wind quintet (1940); concertino for piano and strings (1946); sextet (1959).

Honegger, Arthur. *Chota Roustaveli* was first performed on May 5 (not May 14), 1946. Add to bibl.: Willi Reich, ed. *Arthur Honegger, Nachklang: Schriften, Photos, Dokumente* (Zürich 1957); Jacques Feschotte, *Arthur Honegger: L'Homme et son œuvre* (Paris, 1966). Honegger's book, *Je suis compositeur* (1951) was publ. in English as *I Am a Composer* (London, 1966).

Hood, Mantle, American musicologist; b. Springfield, Illinois, June 24, 1918. He studied at the Univ. of Calif., Los Angeles (A.B., 1951; M.A., 1952); then at the Univ. of Amsterdam (Ph.D., 1954). In 1954 he joined the staff of U.C.L.A. In 1956-57 he traveled to Indonesia on a Ford Foundation Fellowship. In 1961 he was appointed Director of the Institute of Ethnomusicology at U.C.L.A. He contributed numerous valuable articles on Oriental music to various learned journals and musical encyclopedias; made arrangements of Indonesian melodies. He is also a composer; his works include a symph. poem, *Vernal Equinox* (1955); woodwind trio (1950); 6 Duets for soprano and alto recorder (1954); piano pieces; etc.

Hoof, Jef van, Belgian composer; b. Antwerp, May 8, 1886; d. there, April 24, 1959. He studied composition at the Antwerp Cons. with Gilson, Mortelmas and Huybrechts; composed three operas: *Tycho-Brahe* (1911), *Meivuur* (1916) and *Jonker Lichthart* (1928); 5 symphonies (1938, 1941, 1945, 1951, 1956); choruses; lieder; piano pieces. His style of composition is neo-romantic, with a penchant for expansive sonorities.

Hoogstraten, Willem van. Died in Tutzing, Germany, Sept. 12, 1965.

Hopkins, John Henry, American hymn writer; b. Pittsburgh, Oct. 28, 1820; d. Troy, N. Y., Aug. 13, 1891. He was a preacher; published *Carols, Hymns and Songs* (1862). His anthem, *We Three Kings of Orient Are,* is perennially popular as a Christmas carol. Cf. R. G. McCutchan, *Our Hymnody* (N. Y., 1937).

Hopkinson, Francis. Correct name of his instrument is Bellarmonic; it was not a measuring device, but a set of steel bells. Cf. G. E. Hastings, *The Life and Works of Francis Hopkinson* (Chicago, 1926).

Hoppin, Richard Hallowell, American musicologist; b. Northfield, Minn., Feb. 22, 1913. He studied piano at the École Normale de Musique in Paris (1933-35); musicology at Harvard Univ. (M.A., 1938; Ph.D., 1952). He was on the music faculty of the Univ. of Texas, Austin (1949-61); in 1961, appointed prof. of music at Ohio State Univ. In 1959-60 he was the recipient of a Guggenheim Fellowship. He edited the important collection, *The Cypriot-French Repertory of the Manuscript Torino* (4 vols., Rome, 1960-63); contributed numerous articles to scholarly musical publications.

Horký, Karel. Add to works: *Jed z Elsinoru (The Poison from Elsinor),* opera, freely derived from *Hamlet* (Brno, Nov. 11, 1969).

Horne, Lena, American Negro singer; b. Brooklyn, June 30, 1917. She sang in supper clubs in New York and in Las Vegas; became popular in cafe society, and invited praise by her earthy and husky voice capable of considerable depth of expression. She publ. an autobiography *In Person, Lena Horne* (N.Y., 1950).

Horne, Marilyn, American soprano; b. Bradford, Penna., Jan. 16, 1934. She studied voice with William Vennard at the Univ. of Southern Calif.,; also attended master classes of Lotte Lehmann. She made her opera debut in Gelsenkirchen, Germany in 1957. Returning to the U.S., she sang the demanding part of Marie in Berg's *Wozzeck* with the San Francisco Opera Co. (Oct. 4, 1960). In 1969 she toured Italy; sang in Stravinsky's *Oedipus Rex* at La Scala in Milan (March 13, 1969). She made her Metropolitan Opera debut in N. Y. on March 3, 1970. She is married to the conductor Henry Lewis.

Horowitz, Vladimir. He received his early training in piano with Sergei Tarnowsky (1914-19), before he began to study with Felix Blumenfeld. After 12 years of self-imposed retirement, he reappeared on the concert stage at Carnegie Hall, N.Y., May 9, 1965, with sensational emotional acclaim.

Horst, Anthon van der. Died in Hilversum, March 7, 1965.

Horton, Austin Asadata Dafora, Nigerian composer; b. Freetown, Sierra Leone, West Africa, Aug. 4, 1890; d. New York, March 4, 1965. As a youth, he became deeply interested in African folk dance festivals and studied the culture of many African tribes. He then went to Europe and organized a dance group in Germany. He settled in the U.S. in 1921, devoting himself to the propagation of African art, coaching singers, dancers and drummers for performance of African dances. He utilized authentic African melorhythms in several of his stage spectacles for which he also arranged the musical score. Of these, *Kykunkor, the Witch,* produced at the Unity Theatre Studio in N.Y. on May 7, 1934, attracted considerable attention. He also produced a dance drama *Tunguru.*

Hovhaness, Alan. Add to works: opera, *The Blue Flame* (San Antonio, Texas, Dec. 15, 1959); *Arjuna,* symph. poem (Madras, Feb. 1, 1960); Symph. No. 16 for strings and Korean percussion instruments (Seoul, Korea, Jan. 26, 1963); *Spirit of the Avalanche,* opera (Tokyo, Feb. 15, 1963); Symph. No. 17 (*Symphony for Metal Orch.;* Cleveland, Oct. 23, 1963); *Wind Drum,* dance - drama (Union College, Gatlinburg, Tenn., Aug. 23, 1964); *Meditation on Zeami,* symph. poem (N. Y., Oct. 5, 1964); *Ukiyo-Floating World,* symph. poem (Salt Lake City, Jan. 30, 1965); *Pilate,* chamber opera (Pepperdine College, Los Angeles, Calif., June 26, 1966); *The Holy City* for orch. (Portland, Maine, April 11, 1967); *The Travelers,* operatic scene (Foothill College, Calif., April 22, 1967); *To Vishnu,* symph. poem (N. Y., June 2, 1967); *And God Created Great Whales* for humpback whale solo (on tape) and orch. (N. Y., June 11, 1970). He traveled to Japan in 1960; to France and Germany in 1961; to Russia in 1965.

Howard, John Tasker. Died in West Orange, N. J., Nov. 20, 1964.

Howe, Mary. Died in Washington, Sept. 14, 1964.

Howells, Herbert Norman. His piano concerto was first performed on July 10, 1914 (not in 1913).

Hrisanide, Alexandru, Rumanian composer; b. Petrila, June 15, 1936. He studied at the Bucharest Cons. with Paul Constantinescu, Tudor Ciortea, Zeno Vancea, Mihail Jora and Alfred Mendelsohn. In 1965 he won the annual award of the Lili Boulanger Memorial Fund for his *Inventions* for cello and piano and his clarinet sonata. His other works include *Passacaglia* for orch. (1959); Concerto for Orch. (1964); violin sonata; flute sonata; clarinet sonata; trio for violin, viola and bassoon (1963); choruses.

Hristić, Stevan. Died in Belgrade, Aug. 21, 1958.

Hubbell, Frank Allen, American conductor, arranger and composer; b. Denver, Colorado, May 9. 1907. He was taken to California as a child and studied music at the Univ. of Southern Calif., and conducting with Albert Coates and Vladimir Bakaleinikov. In 1946 he organized the Los Angeles Symphonette. He also appeared as guest conductor with other orchestras in California. His orchestral compositions are mostly arrangements of Western country ballads.

Huber, Hans. Date of first performance of *Der Simplicius,* Feb. 22 (not Nov. 22), 1912.

Huber, Klaus, Swiss composer; b. Bern, Nov. 30, 1924. He studied with Willy Burkhard at the Zürich Cons. and with Boris Blacher in Berlin. Among his works are *Oratio Mechtildis* for contralto and chamber orch. (Strasbourg Festival, June 9, 1958) and a cantata for voice and four instruments, *Des Engels Anredung an die Seele* (Rome, June 13, 1959). He also wrote chamber music for various combinations and sacred choral works.

Huber, Kurt. He was beheaded in Munich, not in Berlin.

Huehn, Julius. Died in Rochester, N. Y., June 8, 1971. Date of birth Jan. 12, 1908 (not 1910).

Hughes, Edwin. Died in New York, July 17, 1965.

Hüllmandel, Nicolas-Joseph, Alsatian clavecinist and composer; b. Strasbourg, May 23, 1756; d. London, Dec. 19, 1823. He was a son of Michel Hüllmandel, organist at the Strasbourg Cathedral; served as a choir boy there under F. X. Richter; subsequently went to Hamburg to study under C. Ph. E. Bach. In 1776 he settled in Paris as teacher of piano and the glass harmonica. After the French Revolution he emigrated to London where he remained until his death. He publ. there a manual, *Principles of Music, Chiefly Calculated for the Pianoforte* (1795). His keyboard music was praised by Mozart. His sonatas and suites for piano (some with violin obbligato) were publ. in Paris (1773-95); in London he ceased to compose. See Rita Benton, *N. J. Hüllmandel* in 'Revue de Musicologie,' (Dec. 1961).

Huneker, James Gibbons. Add to bibl.: A. T. Schwab, *James Gibbons Huneker: Critic of the Seven Arts* (Stanford, Calif., 1963).

Hungerford, Bruce, Australian pianist; b. Korumburra, Victoria, Nov. 24, 1922. He received his education in Melbourne; studied piano with Ignaz Friedman in Sydney (1944), and later with Ernest Hutcheson at the Juilliard School of Music in New York (1945-47); took private lessons with Myra Hess in New York between 1948 and 1958, and also with Carl Friedberg from 1948 to 1955. He gave his first piano recital in New York in 1951; was in Europe from 1958 to 1967; conducted master classes in Bayreuth (1959-66); toured in Australia and the Middle East. He is acclaimed as a foremost interpreter of Beethoven. Apart from virtuoso technique, he possesses an extraordinary mastery of dynamic gradations and self-consistent musical phraseology. Hungerford has also gained recognition as a color photographer and archeologist, specializing in Egyptology.

Hunt, Jerry, American composer; b. Waco, Texas, Nov. 30, 1943. He studied piano at North Texas State Univ.; self-taught in composition. In 1967 he was appointed to the faculty of Southern Methodist Univ. He has been active as a technical consultant for recording studios through the Audio-Visual Studio Ensemble, founded in Dallas in 1964. His works, all of them involving electronic techniques include six pieces under the generic title *Helix,* each capable of performance by a varying number of players; *Preparallel* for orchestral group (1964); *Autotransform glissando* for instruments with electronics (1969); *Infrasolo* in 8 versions for 8 different instrumental groups (1969).

Hünten, Franz. Add to bibl.: Gerd Zöllner, *Franz Hünten: Sein Leben und sein Werk* (Cologne, 1959).

Huré, Jean. His saxophone piece is not a concerto, but an *Andante. Le Bois sacré* is not an opera, but a ballet; it was produced at the Opéra Comique in Paris on June 28, 1921.

Hurum, Alf. He left Norway in 1929; was in Berlin, Rome and Paris until 1933; then went back to Honolulu where he devoted himself mainly to painting.

Husa, Karel. In 1970 he was prof. at Cornell Univ. Add to works: *Mozaïques* for orch. (Hamburg, Nov. 7, 1961, composer conducting); *Serenade* for woodwind quintet, strings, harp and xylophone (1964); string quartet No. 3 (Pulitzer Prize 1969).

I

Ibert, Jacques. Died in Paris, Feb. 5, 1962. Bibl.: G. Michel, *Jacques Ibert, l'homme et son œuvre* (Paris, 1968).

Ikonomov, Boyan. Add to works: *Concertino* for piano and string orch. (1939); Symph. No. 3 (1955).

Iliev, Constantin, Bulgarian composer and conductor; b. Sofia, March 9, 1924. He studied composition with Pantcho Vladigerov in Sofia and with Alois Hába in Prague. Returning to Bulgaria, he conducted orchestras in Rusa and Varna, and in 1956 was appointed conductor of the Sofia Philharmonic; he also toured Russia. As a composer, he elaborated a highly advanced harmonic idiom, adroitly exploiting the asymmetric Balkan rhythms and orientalistic melismas to recreate the aura of folkloric authenticity. In this manner is written his opera *The Master of Boyan* (Sofia, Oct. 3, 1962). He also composed 5 symphonies (1947, 1951, 1954, 1957, 1959); 4 string quartets and other chamber music. However, it is primarily as a conductor that he is known in Bulgaria and elsewhere.

Ilitsch, Daniza. Died in Vienna, Jan. 15, 1965. Born Feb. 21, 1914 (not 1919).

Ilyinsky, Alexander Alexandrovitch. Died on Feb. 23, 1920 (not in 1919).

Imbrie, Andrew. Add to works.: violin concerto (San Francisco, April 22, 1958); symph. poem, *Legend* (San Francisco, Dec. 9, 1959); opera, *Three Against Christmas* (Berkeley, Calif., Dec. 3, 1964); Symph. No. 1 (San Francisco, May 11, 1966).

d'Indy, Vincent. *Jour d'été à la montagne,* op. 61, was first performed on Feb. 18, 1906 (not 1905). *Le Chant de la Cloche* was produced in its operatic form in Brussels on Nov. 21 (not Dec. 22), 1912.

Infante, Manuel. Died in Paris, April 21, 1958.

Inghelbrecht, Désiré Émile. Died in Paris, Feb. 14, 1965.

Ioannidis, Iannis, Greek composer; b. Athens, June 8, 1930. He studied piano in Athens; organ and composition in Vienna. In his music he adopts atonality without strict adherence to the 12-tone method. Works: piano sonata (1959); string quartet (1961); *Triptych* for orch. (1962); *Duo* for violin and piano (1962).

Ipavec, Benjamin, Slovenian composer; b. St. Jurij, Dec. 24, 1829; d. Graz, Dec. 20, 1909. He studied medicine in Vienna and became a professional physician, with music as an avocation. He publ. several collections of Slovenian songs; also composed a number of Lieder in a romantic vein.

Ipuche-Riva, Pedro, Uruguayan composer; b. Montevideo, Oct. 26, 1924. He studied at the Cons. of Montevideo, and later in Paris with Jean Rivier and Nöel Gallon. Returning to Uruguay, he unfolded energetic activities as a music critic, lecturer, teacher and radio commentator. Works: *Concerto Grosso* for strings (1959); *Sinfonietta* (1960); symph. poem, *El Arból Solo* (1961); 2 symphonies (1962, 1965); cello concerto (1962); sacred choruses; chamber music; piano pieces.

Ireland, John. Died in Washington, England, June 12, 1962. Place of birth, Bowdon (not Bowden). Add to bibl.: John Longmire, *John Ireland: Portrait of a Friend* (London, 1969).

Irino, Yoshiro. Add to works: *Double Concerto* for violin, piano and orch. (1955); *Music* for violin and cello (1959); *Music* for cembalo, percussion and strings (1963); string trio (1965).

Irrgang, Heinrich Bernhard, German organist; b. Zduny, July 23, 1869; d. Berlin, April 8, 1916. He was a church organist and teacher in Berlin; composed organ music and songs.

Isaac, Heinrich. Add to bibl.: Frank A. d'Accone, *Heinrich Isaac in Florence: New and Unpublished Documents,* in the 'Mus. Quarterly' (Oct. 1963).

Ishii, Kan. Add to works: *Sinfonia Ainu* for soprano, chorus and orch. (1959); viola sonata (1960). He compiled a valuable collection of Japanese folksongs publ. in 6 volumes.

Ishii, Maki, Japanese composer; brother of Kan Ishii; b. Tokyo, May 28, 1936. He studied at the Hochschule für Musik in Berlin with Boris Blacher and Josef Rufer, graduating in 1961. His works include *7 Stücke* for small orch. (1961); *4 Bagatellen* for violin and piano (1961); *Transitions* for small orch. (1962); *Aphorisms* for strings, percussion and piano (1963).

Isserlis, Julius. Died in London, July 23, 1968.

Ištvan, Miloslav, Czech composer; b. Olomouc, Sept. 2, 1928. He studied at the Brno Cons. with Jaroslav Kvapil; subsequently became a teacher there. Among his works are a concerto for horn, piano and string orch. (1950); a symph. (1952); a *Winter Suite* for strings, piano and percussion (1956); Partita for flute, clarinet and bassoon (1957); piano concerto (1958); violin concerto (1963); *Dodekameron* for orch. (1964); piano pieces and songs. In 1963 he joined the so-called Creative Group A of Czechoslovakia, dedicated to the exploration of all modern methods of composition 'uninhibited by puritanically limited didactical regulations.'

Iturbi, Amparo. Died in Beverly Hills, Calif., April 21, 1969.

Ivanov, Georgi, Bulgarian composer; b. Sofia, Aug. 23, 1924. He studied composition with Pipkov in Sofia and with Shaporin in Moscow. His works include a symph. poem, *Legend of the Lopian Forest* (Sofia, Feb. 15, 1951); a symph. poem, *The Mutiny on the S. S. Nadezhda* (1956); a symph. (Sofia, June 22, 1960); *Divertimento* for clarinet, violin, harpsichord and chamber orch. (1963).

Ivanov-Radkevitch, Nicolay Pavlovitch. Died in Moscow, Feb. 4, 1962.

Ivanovici. First name Ion. He was born in 1845 (not 1848); died in Bucharest, Sept. 29, 1902 (not April 1, 1905). He played the flute and clarinet in a military band in Galatz, and in 1880 became band leader there. In the same year he wrote his famous waltz *Valurile Dunării* (*The Waves of the Danube*). He participated in the Paris Exposition of 1889, conducting a band of 116 musicians. In 1900 he was appointed Inspector of Military Music in Rumania. His published compositions, mostly dances for band, comprise 150 numbers. See Viorel Cosma, *Ivanovici* (Bucharest, 1958).

Ives, Burl (Icle Ivanhoe), American folk singer; b. Hunt Township, Jasper County, Illinois, June 14, 1909. He studied briefly at N. Y. Univ.; traveled through the U. S. and Canada as an itinerant handyman, supplementing his earnings by singing and playing the banjo. He then became a dramatic actor, and appeared on the stage and in films, gave concerts of folk ballads accompanying himself on the guitar. He publ. an autobiography, *Wayfaring Stranger* (N. Y., 1948) and the anthologies, *The Burl Ives Songbook* (1953) and *Burl Ives Book of Irish Songs* (1958).

Ives, Charles Edward. The strip of wood is used in the 2nd movement (not last movement) of the *Concord Sonata.* First performance of the 3rd Symph. took place in N. Y. on April 5, 1946 (not May 5, 1947). His 4th symph. was performed in its entirety for the first time in New York on April 26, 1965, Leopold Stokowski conducting the American Symph. Orch. It was awarded a special citation by the New York Music Critics' Circle. Add to bibl.: J. Kirkpatrick, *A Temporary Mimeographed Catalogue of the Music Manuscripts and Related Materials of Charles Edward Ives* (New Haven, 1960); S. R. Charles, *The Use of Borrowed Materials in Ives' Second Symphony,* in 'Music Review' (May, 1967); D. Marshall, *Charles Ives' Quotations: Manner or Substance?* in 'Perspectives of New Music,' (Spring-Summer, 1968); J. Bernlef and R. de Leeuw, *Charles Ives* (Amsterdam, 1969); Dominique-René de Lerma, *Charles Edward Ives, 1874-1954: A Bibliography of His Music* (Kent, Ohio, 1970).

J

Jackson, Mahalia, black American singer; b. New Orleans, Oct. 26, 1911. She went to Chicago and was employed as a hotel maid; sang in Baptist churches; operated a beauty salon; owned a flower shop. She revealed an innate talent for expressive hymn singing, and soon was in demand for conventions and political meetings. She steadfastly refused to appear in night clubs. In 1952 she made a triumphant European tour; other successful appearances followed. She publ. her autobiography as a 'soul singer' under the title *Movin' On Up* (N. Y., 1966).

Jacobs, Arthur, English music critic, lexicographer, opera librettist and translator; b. Manchester, June 14, 1922. He studied at Oxford Univ. From 1947 to 1952 he was music critic for the 'Daily Express' and has since then written articles for a number of publications. From 1960 to 1971 he was an associate editor of the London monthly 'Opera.' In 1952 he publ. a book on Gilbert and Sullivan. He then became deeply involved in musical lexicography; compiled an uncommonly intelligent compact reference work, *A New Dictionary of Music* (London, 1958; 2nd ed., 1967; reprints with revisions, 1968, 1970). In 1964 Jacobs was appointed lecturer in music history at the Royal Academy of Music, London; was visiting prof. at the Univ. of Illinois (1967); at the Univ. of Calif., Santa Barbara (1969) and at Temple Univ. in Philadelphia (1970, 1971); toured Australia and Russia. An innate linguist, he has mastered Russian, as well as German, French, Italian and Spanish; has translated with admirable fidelity to the syllabic and musical values of the originals, some 20 operas, among them Tchaikovsky's *The Queen of Spades,* Schoenberg's *Erwartung* and Alban Berg's *Lulu;* wrote the libretto of Nicholas Maw's opera *One Man Show* (London, 1964). Several of these translations have been adopted by the Covent Garden Opera (from 1968 renamed the Royal Opera) and Sadler's Wells Opera in London. In 1971 he was appointed editor of 'Music Yearbook' publ. in London.

Janáček, Leoš. Add to bibl.: H. Richter, *L. J.* (Leipzig, 1958); J. Vogel, *L. J.: Leben und Werk* (Prague, 1958; in English, London, 1962); B. Stedron, *The Works of L. J.* (Prague, 1959); J. Rocek, *L. J.* (Leipzig, 1962); Hans Hollander, *L. J.: His Life and Work* (N. Y., 1963); Erik Chisholm, *The Operas of Leoš Janáček* (N. Y., 1971).

Janequin, Clément. Putative year of birth, 1475 (not 1485).

Jankélévitch, Vladimir. Add to books: *Le Nocturne: Fauré, Chopin et la Nuit; Satie et le Matin* (Paris, 1957).

Janssen, Herbert. Died in New York, June 3, 1965.

Járdányi, Pál. Died in Budapest, July 29, 1966.

Jarecki, Tadeusz. Died in New York, April 29, 1955.

Jarnach, Philipp. His redaction of Busoni's opera *Doktor Faust* was first produced in Dresden (not in Berlin).

Järnefelt, Armas. Died in Stockholm, June 23, 1958.

Jarre, Maurice, French composer; b. Lyon, Sept. 13, 1924. He studied electrical engineering at Lyon; in 1944 went to Paris and began to study music. Works: *Mouvements en relief* for orch.; *Polyphonies concertantes* for piano, trumpet, percussion and orch.; *Passacaille,* in memory of Honegger (Strasbourg Festival, June 15, 1956); *Mobiles* for violin and orch. (Strasbourg Festival, June 20, 1961). He became a successful film composer; won the Academy Award for his emotional score to *Dr. Zhivago* (1966). See Jean Roy, *Musique française* (Paris, 1962).

Jeanneret, Albert, Swiss violinist, composer and educator; b. La Chaux-de-Fonds, Feb. 7, 1886. He studied violin with Andreas Moser at the Hochschule für Musik in Berlin and with Henri Marteau at the Geneva Cons., graduating with the Premier Prix de Virtuosité in 1909; subsequently joined the staff of the Jaques-Dalcroze Institute of Eurhythmics in Hellerau. In 1919 he went to Paris where he founded a school of rhythmic gymnastics and organized a children's orchestra. In 1939 he returned to Switzerland and settled in Vevey, where he led a children's orchestra similar to the one he had in Paris. About the same time he became a follower of the Moral Rearmament Movement. On July 21, 1968 he received (and subsequently published) a telepathic message from his brother, the architect Le Corbusier (Charles Édouard Jeanneret), who had died three years before, urging him to continue his pursuits of functional art. In accordance with these ideas, which he shared with his brother, Jeanneret wrote some 25 'symphonies enfantines' for children's orchestra, employing 'bruits humanisés' produced by graduated bottles partially filled with water at different levels, metal pipes, wooden boxes, etc.; a *Suite pittoresque* for 3 violins, and choruses for Moral Rearmament meetings. See Pierre Meylan, *Albert Jeanneret et les 'bruits humanisés'* in 'Revue Musicale de Suisse Romande' (March, 1971).

Jelinek, Hanns. Died in Vienna, Jan. 27, 1969.

Jemnitz, Alexander. Died in Balatonfüred, Aug 8, 1963.

Jenko, Davorin, Slovenian composer; b. Dvorje, Nov. 9, 1835; d. Ljubljana, Nov. 25, 1914. He studied jurisprudence and music in Trieste and Vienna; was a choral conductor in Belgrade (1871-1902); then settled in Ljubljana. He was the composer of the first Serbian operetta *Vračara* (*The Fortune Teller;* Belgrade, May 3, 1882), a musical comedy *Dido* (Belgrade, June 19, 1892) and many choral works. The melody of the royal Serbian national anthem was taken from one of Jenko's choruses.

Jenks, Alden Ferriss, American composer; b. Harbor Beach, Michigan, Aug. 10, 1940. He studied at Yale Univ. (B.A., 1962) and at the Univ. of California in Berkeley (M.A., 1968); also attended seminars with Karlheinz Stockhausen at the Univ. of California, Davis (1966-67). In 1968 he organized in Berkeley a group called 'Deus ex Machina' which gave performances of acoustical and electronic music with human and mechanical participants. His productions fall into three categories: (1) written scores that can be performed by untutored players (2) electronic music on magnetic tape and (3) conceptual composition that exists only in verbalized instructions. Inventory: *Expedition* for orch. (1964); *The Exterminator* for double chorus and individual speaking, shouting, laughing and occasionally singing voices (1965); *Quasar* for brass and percussion (1966); *Chez Elle* for magnetic tape (1968); *Q.E.D.* for amplified autoharp, amplified metal wastebasket, modulated spoken material and slide projector (1969); *Emissions,* a duet for 3 World War II shortwave receivers and a gesticulating lecturer whose discourse is inaudible (1969); *The Magic Pillow Show* for mixed media (1970); music for experimental films.

Jensen, Ludvig Irgens. Died in Enna, Sicily, April 11, 1969.

Jeppesen, Knud. A Festschrift, *Natalica musicologica: Knud Jeppesen, septuagenario, collegis oblata,* co-edited by Søren Sørensen and Bjørn Hjelmborg was publ. in Copenhagen in 1962.

Jeremiáš, Otakar. Died in Prague, March 5, 1962.

Jeritza, Maria. Did not divorce Winfield Sheehan. He died.

Jesinghaus, Walter, Swiss violinist and composer; b. Genoa, July 13, 1902; d. Ticino, Sept. 18, 1966. He studied violin in Milan and Lugano; gave concerts as a child virtuoso. In 1918 he went to Zürich to study academic music subjects with Andreae and Jarnach; later enrolled at the Basel Cons.; in 1921-25 was active as theater conductor in Germany; in 1925 he settled in Lugano. He wrote several operas (*Tartuffe, Sœur Béatrice, Belinda e il mostro, La luna e la città*); also a *Symphonia choralis* and much chamber music including a number of pieces for viola d'amore. See D. Poli, *Walter Jesinghaus* (Bologna, 1929).

Jessel, Leon, German operetta composer; b. Stettin, Jan. 22, 1871; d. Berlin, Jan. 4, 1942. He began his career as a theater conductor in Germany, then produced numerous operettas, some of which enjoyed considerable popular success, among them *Die beiden Husaren* (Berlin, 1913), *Schwarzwaldmädel* (1917), *Verliebte Frauen* (1920), *Die Postmeisterin* (1921), *Schwalbenhochzeit* (1921), *Des Königs Nachbarin* (1924), *Die Luxuskabine* (1929), *Junger Wein* (1933), *Die goldene Mühle* (1940).

Jiménez-Mabarak, Carlos, Mexican composer; b. Tacuba, Jan. 31, 1916. He received his education in Santiago, Chile; in 1932 went to Europe and studied musicology with Charles Van Den Borren in Brussels; then took courses with René Leibowitz in Paris. Returning to Mexico he joined the staff of the National Cons. in Mexico City. Works: one-act opera *Misa de Seis* (Mexico City, June 21, 1962); Symph. No. 1 (1945); *Balada del Venado y la Luna* for orch. (1948); *Balada Mágica* for orch. (1951); *Balada de los Quetzales* for orch. (1953); concerto for piano and percussion (1961); symph. in one movement (1962); choruses.

Jirák, Karel Boleslav. Add to works: string quartets No. 4, 5, 6, 7 (1949, 1951, 1958, 1960); trio for oboe, clarinet and bassoon (1956).

Jirko, Ivan, Czech composer; b. Prague, Oct. 7, 1926. After a period of study at the Prague Cons., he became a psychiatrist; wrote a cantata, *Land Most Beautiful* (1950), and a group of romantic ballads.

Joachim, Otto, German-Canadian violist and composer; b. Düsseldorf, Oct. 13, 1910. He studied violin with his father; in 1933 left Germany and traveled in the Far East; lived mostly in China. In 1941 he settled in Montreal; founded the Société de Musique de Notre Temps; played first viola in the Montreal Symph. Orch. In his music he follows serial principles. Works: *Asia,* symph. poem (1939); *Concertante No. 1* for solo violin, percussion and strings (1956); *Concertante No. 2* for string orch. (1961); string quartet (1956); *Interlude* for 4 saxophones (1960); Nonet for strings, winds and piano (1960); *Divertimento* for 5 wind instruments (1962); *Expansion* for flute and piano (1962); *Music for 4 viols* (1962); piano pieces.

Jochum, Georg Ludwig. Died in Mülheim-an-der-Ruhr, Nov. 1, 1970.

Jöde, Fritz. Died in Hamburg, Oct. 19, 1970. Bibl.: R. Stapelberg, ed., *Fritz Jöde: Leben und Werk* (Wolfenbüttel, 1957).

Johanos, Donald, American conductor; b. Cedar Rapids, Iowa, Feb. 10, 1928. He studied violin with André de Ribaupierre and Cecil Burleigh at the Eastman School of Music, Rochester, N.Y.; conducting with Eugene Ormandy, George Szell, Eduard van Beinum and Otto Klemperer (1955-57). He conducted in Altoona and Johnstown, Pennsylvania; joined the Dallas symph. orch. as associate conductor in 1957. In 1961 he was appointed resident conductor there and in the fall of 1962 became its music director. He appeared as guest conductor with the Philadelphia Orch., the Concertgebouw in Amsterdam, in Pittsburgh, Minneapolis, etc. One of the few American-born conductors in charge of a major symph. orch., he received encomiums from music critics, usually accorded only to foreign luminaries.

Johansen, David Monrad. Add to works: piano concerto (1955); *Epigrams,* on Norwegian motives (1961).

Johansen, Gunnar, Danish-American pianist; b. Copenhagen, Jan. 21, 1906. He studied piano with Victor Schiøler; later in Berlin with Frederic Lamond, Edwin Fischer and Egon Petri. From 1924 to 1929 he toured Europe as a concert pianist; then lived in California. In 1939 he joined the faculty of the Univ. of Wisconsin in Madison as Artist-in-Residence, a title that was specially created for him. An early admirer of Busoni, he devoted himself to the propaganda of his music. In March 1966 he presented a Busoni Centennial Commemorative program at the Univ. of Wisconsin including Busoni's piano concerto and *Fantasia Contrappuntistica.* He recorded for Artist Direct Records the complete piano works of Busoni and his Bach transcriptions; the complete piano works of Liszt and complete clavier works of Bach. Johansen produced a sensation of seismic proportions on Jan. 14, 1969, when he played with the Philadelphia Orch. in New York the piano version of Beethoven's violin concerto at 30 ½ hours' notice. Johansen is also a composer. He wrote 2 piano concertos (1930, 1970); *East-West,* cantata for wordless women's voices, piano, 3 woodwinds and percussion (1944); 31 piano sonatas (1941-51); and 246 piano sonatas improvised directly on the keyboard and recorded on tape (1952-70). A scholar as well as a musician, Johansen translated from Danish into English George Brandes's biography of Kierkegaard.

Johnsen, Halvard, Norwegian composer; b. Hamburg, June 27, 1916. He went to Norway as a youth; studied flute and composition at the Oslo Cons.; appeared as a concert flutist, and played flute in the General Staff military band. He wrote 9 symphonies (1949, 1953, 1957, 1959, 1960, 1961, 1962, 1965, 1968); 2 violin concertos (1958, 1967); wind quintet with vibraphone (1965); *Canzona* for Janissary orchestra (1968); trumpet concerto (1967); two string quartets; choral music.

Johnson, Edward. Died in Guelph, Ontario, April 20, 1959. Date of birth, Aug. 22, 1878 (not 1881).

Johnson, Hall, black American choral leader, composer and arranger; b. Athens, Georgia, June 2, 1887; d. New York, April 30, 1970. He studied at the Univ. of Atlanta and at the Univ. of Southern California in Los Angeles; also took courses with Percy Goetschius in New York. In 1925 he formed the Hall Johnson Choir, with which he gave numerous concerts; in 1936 he organized the Negro Chorus of Los Angeles. In 1951 he toured Germany and Austria with his chorus under the auspices of the U.S. State Department. He composed choral music and made arrangements for the films and television.

Johnson, Horace. Died in Tucson, Arizona, May 30, 1964.

Johnson, Lockrem. He was chairman of the music department at the Cornish School in Seattle (1962-69). Add to works: Symph. No. 1 (Seattle, Dec. 2, 1966).

Johnson, William Geary (Bunk), black American jazz trumpeter; b. New Orleans, Dec. 27, 1879; d. New Iberia, La., July 7, 1949. As a youth he played trumpet with Dixieland bands; toured with minstrel shows, circus troupes and numerous jazz aggregations. He lost all his teeth due to the ravages of pyorrhea and had to stop playing; rediscovered by 'hot jazz' aficionados, he was fitted with dentures and resumed his career, enjoying belated fame in a revival of Dixieland music.

Johnston, Benjamin, American avant-garde composer; b. Macon, Georgia, March 15, 1926. He was educated at the College of William and Mary (A.B., 1949), at the Cincinnati Cons. of Music (M. Mus., 1950), and at Mills College (M.A., 1952). Later he joined the faculty of the Univ. of Illinois, Urbana. In 1959 he received a Guggenheim Fellowship. His works include *Celebration* for solo piano; *Duo* for flute and string bass; *9 Variations for string quartet; Knocking Piece* for percussion; *Night,* cantata (1955); *Gambit for Dancers and Orch.* (1959); *Sonata for Microtonal Piano* (1965); *Quintet for Groups* (1966) and a memorial piece, *Ci gît Satie* for the Swingle singers (1966).

Jokl, Otto. Died in New York, Nov. 13, 1963. Name of teacher, Hermann Grädener (not Brädener).

Jolas, Betsy, French composer of American parentage; b. Paris, Aug. 5, 1926. She went to America in 1939; studied at Bennington College (B.A., 1946); returned to Paris in 1946 and took courses with Olivier Messiaen at the Paris Cons. In her music she applies constructivistic methods in neo-Baroque forms and quasi-serial techniques. Works: *Figures* for 9 instruments (1956); *Mots* for 5 voices and 8 instruments (1963); *Quatuor* for coloratura soprano, violin, viola and cello (1964); *J.D.E.* for 14 instruments (1966); *D'un Opéra de Voyage* for 22 instruments (1967); *Quatre Plages* for string orch. (1968); *États* for violin and percussion

(1969); *Winter Music* for organ and chamber orch. (1970).

Jolivet, André. Add to works: Symph. No. 2 (Berlin, Oct. 3, 1959); *Controversia* for oboe and harp (1970).

Jonas, Maryla. Died in New York, July 3, 1959.

Jones, Alton, American pianist; b. Fairfield, Nebraska, Aug. 3, 1899; d. New York, Jan. 2, 1971. He studied at Drake Univ. (B.M., 1919) and at the Institute of Musical Art in New York, graduating in 1921. He made his concert debut in N. Y. in 1924; was a soloist with the N. Y. Philharmonic in 1949; gave his last N. Y. recital in 1955. He taught at the Juilliard School of Music from 1921 until his death; his reputation as a pedagogue was high; many American pianists were his pupils.

Jones, Charles, Canadian composer; b. Tamworth, June 21, 1910. He studied at the Juilliard School of Music in N.Y., where he later became a faculty member. Works: Suite for strings (1937); Symph. No. 1 (1939); *Galop* for orch. (1940); *Cassation* for orch. (1949); Symph. No. 2 (1957); *Suite after a Notebook of 1762* for orch. (1957); Symph. No. 3 (1962); Concerto for 4 violins and orch. (1963); symph. in 5 short movements (1965); 5 string quartets (1936-61); sonatina for violin alone (1938); sonatina for violin and piano (1942); *Threnody* for viola unaccompanied (1947); *Sonata a tre* (1952); *Epiphany* for speaker and 4 instruments (1952); violin sonata (1958); *The Seasons,* a cantata (1959); *Sonata piccola* for piccolo and harpsichord (1961); 2 piano sonatas; sonata for 2 pianos (1957); *Keyboard Book* for harpsichord (1953); *Toccata* for piano; *Ballade* for piano.

Jones, Daniel. Add to works: *The Knife,* opera (London, Dec. 2, 1963).

Jones, Edward. Date of birth, March 29 (not April 2), 1752; called "Bardd y Brenin" (not "Bardy Brenin"). Add to bibl.: T. Ellis, *Edward Jones, Bardd y Brenin* (1957).

Jones, Kelsey, Canadian composer; b. South Norwalk, Conn., June 17, 1922. In 1945 he moved to Montreal. He studied in Toronto with Sir Ernest MacMillan and Healey Willan; also took lessons with Nadia Boulanger in Paris. In 1951 he obtained his D. Mus. from the Univ. of Toronto; subsequently was appointed to the faculty of the McGill Univ. in Montreal. He follows the neo-classical type of composition and writes mostly in traditional Baroque forms. Works: *Suite* for flute and strings (1954); *Four Pieces for Recorders* (1955); *Sonata da Camera* for flute, oboe and harpsichord (1957); *Rondo* for solo flute (1963); choral pieces.

Jones, Parry, Welsh operatic tenor; b. Blaina, Monmouthshire, Feb. 14, 1891; d. London, Dec. 26, 1963. He studied in London, in Italy and in Germany; made his debut as tenor in 1914; toured widely in Europe and America. He was principal tenor at the Covent Garden Opera House until 1955; sang tenor parts in many modern operas, including Alban Berg's *Wozzeck.*

Jones, Quincy Delight, Jr., American pianist, trumpeter, bandleader and composer; b. Chicago, March 14, 1933. He studied hot trumpet in Seattle and in Boston; joined Lionel Hampton's band; toured with Dizzy Gillespie in the Near East; traveled in Europe (1957-60). His songs and arrangements (*Kingfish, Stockholm Sweetnin', Evening in Paris,* etc.) are sophisticated realizations of swing patterns.

Jones, 'Spike' (Lindley Armstrong), American band leader; b. Long Beach, Calif., Dec. 14, 1911; d. Los Angeles, May 1, 1965. He played drums as a boy; then led a school band. On July 30, 1942 he made a recording of a satirical song *Der Führer's Face,* featuring a Bronx-cheer razzer; toured the U.S. with his band, The City Slickers, which included a washboard, a Smith and Wesson pistol, anti-bug Flit guns in E flat, doorbells, anvils, hammers to break glass, and a live goat trained to bleat rhythmically. Climactically, he introduced the Latrinophone (a toilet seat strung with catgut). With this ensemble he launched a Musical Depreciation Revue. He retired in 1963 when the wave of extravaganza that carried him to the crest of commercial success had subsided.

Jongen, Léon. Died in Brussels, Nov. 18, 1969.

Jonsson, Josef Petrus. Died in Norrköping, Sweden, May 9, 1969.

Joplin, Janis, American rock and blues singer; b. Port Arthur, Texas, Jan. 19, 1943; d. Hollywood, Oct. 4, 1970, of an overdose of heroin. After several attempts at formal education she held sporadic jobs as barroom singer in Austin and Los Angeles. In 1966 she joined the band of Travis Rivers in San Francisco; made a profound impression by her passionate wailing in a raspy voice; her appearances in such esoteric emporia as Psychedelic Supermarket in Boston, Kinetic Playground in Chicago, Whisky A-Go-Go in Los Angeles and Fillmore East in New York established her reputation as an uninhibited representative of the young generation. She was arrested in Tampa, Florida, in 1969 for having hurled porcine epithets at a policeman, which further endeared her with her public. On the more positive side, the Southern Comfort Distillery Co. presented her with a fur coat in recognition for the publicity she gave the firm by her habitual consumption of a quart of Southern Comfort at each of her appearances, brandishing the bottle conspicuously so as to display the brand name on its label. Her extraordinary ability to inject religious passion even into a commercial theme is illustrated by a song she composed, 'Oh Lord, Won't You Buy Me a Mercedes-Benz?'

Joplin, Scott, black American pianist; b. Texarkana, Nov 24, 1868; d. New York, April 4, 1917. He played in various emporiums in St. Louis and in Chicago before coming to New York. He is acknowledged as the chief proponent of the classical type of ragtime playing, characterized by an emphatic bass, arpeggiated chords, incisive tonic-dominant harmonies and rapidly articulated passages in the treble. He composed a number of ragtime songs, among them *Maple Leaf Rag* and *Wall Street Rag*. He was also a pioneer in player-piano recordings.

Jordan, Mary. Died in San Antonio, Texas, May 15, 1961.

Jordan, Sverre. Add to works: *Concerto romantico* for horn and orch. (1957); *Concerto Piccolo* for piano and orch. (1963); violin concerto (1966); two piano trios; string quartet; two violin sonatas; sonatina for flute and piano.

Josten, Werner. Died in New York, Feb. 6, 1963. Add to works: *Serenade* for small orch. (Cleveland, Dec. 20, 1934); *Rhapsody* for orch. (1957). *Concerto Sacro* was composed in 1925 (not in 1927); it was performed for the first time in N. Y., March 27, 1929. Symph. suite from *Batouala* was first performed at Smith College, Northampton, on Nov. 10, 1963, under the title *Suite nègre*. The first performance of the ballet *Joseph and His Brethren* took place in N. Y., March 9, 1936; as a symph. suite, in Philadelphia, May 15, 1939; *Endymion* was first performed as a symph. suite in N. Y., Oct. 28, 1936. See *Werner Josten, 1885-1963, A Summary of His Compositions With Press Reviews* (N. Y., 1964).

Joubert, John. Add to works: *Silas Marner,* opera (Cape Town, May 20, 1961); symph. (1956); *North Country Overture* (1958); piano concerto (1958); string trio (1958); Octet for clarinet, bassoon, horn, string quartet and double-bass (1960); *Sinfonietta* for chamber orch. (1962); *Leaves of Life,* ballad-cantata (1962); *Urbs beata,* cantata for tenor and baritone soli, chorus and orch. (St. George's Cathedral, Cape Town, Nov. 26, 1963); *The Holy Mountain,* a canticle for chorus and two pianos (1963); *Sonata a cinque* for recorder, 2 violins, cello and harpsichord (1963); *The Choir Invisible,* choral symphony (Halifax, England, May 18, 1968). His carols, *Torches* and *There is no Rose,* achieved wide popularity.

Joy, Geneviève, French pianist; b. Bernaville, Oct. 4, 1919. She studied at the Paris Cons. with Yves Nat (piano), Jean and Noël Gallon (theory); received Premier Prix in piano in 1941. In 1945 she married the composer Henri Dutilleux. She specialized in modern music; gave numerous first performances of piano works by French composers, some of them written especially for her.

Juilliard, Augustus D. He was born not in Canton, Ohio, but at sea, during his parents' voyage in a sailing vessel from Burgundy to America; the family eventually settled in Canton, Ohio.

Jurovský, Simon. Died in Prague, Nov. 8, 1963.

Juzeliunas, Julius, Lithuanian composer; b. Zeimelis, Feb. 20, 1916. He studied at the Kaunas Cons., graduating in 1948; subsequently taught there. His works include a ballet *On the Seashore* (Vilna, May 10, 1953); 2 symphonies (1948, 1949); concerto for tenor and orch. (1954); opera, *The Rebels* (1957); *African Sketches* for orch. (1961); *Poem-Concerto* for strings (1961); chamber music; choruses.

K

Kabalevsky, Dmitri Borisovitch. His opera *Nikita Vershinin* was produced in Moscow on Nov. 26, 1955. Add to works: *Requiem* (Moscow, Feb. 9, 1963); cello concerto No. 2 (1964); opera, *The Sisters* (1969); oratorio, *A Letter to the 30th Century* (1970). Bibl.: L. Danilevitch, *Creative Work of D. B. Kabalevsky* (Moscow, 1963).

Kabeláč, Miloslav. Add to works: Symphonies No. 3 (1957); No. 4 (1958); No. 5

(1960); No. 6 (1961); cantata, *Mysterium Času* (*Mystery of Time;* 1957); suite for saxophone and piano (1959).

Kačinkas, Jeronimas, Lithuanian composer and conductor; b. Viduklé, April 17, 1907. He studied with his father, a church organist; then at the State Music School in Klaipeda and at the Cons. of Prague with Jaroslav Kříčka and Alois Hába. Returning to Lithuania, he became conductor of the Klaipeda Symph. Orch. (1932-38); in 1938 was appointed music director for the Lithuanian Radio in Kaunas; during World War II conducted the Vilna Philharmonic; left Vilna in 1944; from 1945 to 1949 lived in a Displaced Persons Camp in Augsburg, Germany. In 1949 he settled in the U. S., teaching in Boston. His music reflects the influences of Scriabin and French Impressionists. Among his works are a trumpet concerto; 2 string quartets; sacred choruses; piano pieces.

Kadosa, Paul. Add to works: Symph. No. 3 (1957); Symph. No. 4 (1960); Symph. No. 5 (1961); Symph. No. 6 (Budapest, Aug. 19, 1966); piano concerto No. 2 (1938); piano concerto No. 3 (1955). The title of his opera is *Adventure in Huszt* (not *Hoszt*); it was produced in Budapest on Dec. 22, 1951.

Kagel, Mauricio, composer of advanced modern music; b. Buenos Aires, Dec. 24, 1931. He studied in Buenos Aires; in 1957, settled in Cologne, Germany. He evolved a highly complex system of composition in which serial organization of notes, intervals and rhythms is supplemented by aleatory techniques derived from the use of linguistic permutations in several languages, random patterns of lights and shadows on exposed photographic film, etc. Works: a string sextet (1953; revised in 1957); *Traummusik* for instruments and musique concrète (1954); *Anagrama* for speaking chorus, 4 vocalists and chamber ensemble (1958); *Transición I* for electronic sounds (1958); *Transición II* for piano, percussion and two magnetic tapes (1959); *Pandora's Box* for magnetic tape (1961); *Sonant* for electric guitar, harp, double-bass and 20 instruments (1961); *Sur scène* for 6 participants in mixed media, with musicians instructed to interfere with actors and singers (concert performance, Radio Bremen, May 6, 1962). For the Beethoven bicentennial in 1970, he produced a surrealistic film *Ludwig van,* in the manner of 'instrumental theater,' with the application of sound collages of thematic fragments of Beethoven's works and satirical references to commercialized anniversary festivals. See Dieter Schnebel, *Mauricio Kagel: Musik, Theater, Film* (Cologne, 1970).

Kagen, Sergius, Russian-American pianist and composer; b. St. Petersburg, Aug. 22, 1909; d. New York, March 1, 1964. He went to Berlin in 1921; emigrated to the U.S. in 1925; studied at the Juilliard School of Music, N. Y., graduating in 1930; later joined its faculty. He wrote an opera *Hamlet* (Baltimore, 1962); piano pieces and vocal works; edited *40 French Songs* (2 vols.; N.Y., 1952).

Kahl, Willi. Died in Cologne, Oct. 3, 1962.

Kahn, Erich Itor. Add to bibl.: R. Leibowitz and K. Wolff, *Erich Itor Kahn, un grand représentant de la musique contemporaine* (Paris, 1958).

Kahn, Otto Hermann. Add to bibl.: M. J. Matz, *The Many Lives of Otto Kahn* (N. Y., 1963).

Kahowez, Günter, Austrian composer; b. Vöcklabruck, Dec. 4, 1940. He studied at the Bruckner Cons. in Linz and later at the Vienna Music Academy with Karl Schiske. With neo-classical precepts as points of departure, he rapidly progressed in the direction of modern serialism. Works: wind quintet (1959); string quartet (1960); *Klangrhythmen* for piano (1962); *Flächengitter* for flute solo (1962); *Megalyse* for electronic instruments (1962); *Duale* for clarinet and guitar (1963); *Schichtungen* for orch. (1963); *Ouverture & Pantomime* for orch. (1964); *Kleine Serenade* for 2 melody instruments and piano (1965).

Kaiser, Alfred. Born Feb. 29 (not March 1), 1872; died Bournemouth (not London), Oct. 1 (not Oct. 2), 1917. During World War I he changed his name to De Keyser to escape the odium attached to the Kaiser of Germany.

Kalabis, Viktor, Czech composer; b. Červený Kostelec, Feb. 27, 1923. He studied composition at the Prague Cons. and at the Academy of Arts there, graduating in 1952; subsequently became music director on the Prague radio. He wrote a cello concerto (1951); *Classic Nonet* (1956); a symph. (1957); a violin concerto (1959); *Sinfonia Pacis* (1960); 2 string quartets; choruses.

Kalafati, Vassili Pavlovitch. Exact date of death, Jan. 30, 1942.

Kallmann, Helmut, Canadian librarian and musicologist; b. Berlin, Aug. 7, 1922. He studied music with his father; left Germany in 1939 for London. In 1940 he was sent to Canada; was interned in refugee camps; upon release took music courses at the Univ. of Toronto, graduating in 1949. In 1951 he became music librarian for the Canadian Broadcasting Corporation. He publ. a valuable *Catalogue of Canadian Composers* (Toronto, 1952) and *A History of Music in Canada 1534-1914* (Toronto, 1960); collaborated in various publications dealing with Canadian composers.

Kálmán, Emmerich (Imre). *Ein Herbstmanöver* was first performed in Hungarian, in Budapest on Feb. 22, 1908.

Kalnins, Alfreds. Bibl.: J. Vitolins, *Alfreds Kalnins, a monograph* (in Latvian; Riga, 1968).

Kalomiris, Manolis. Died in Athens, April 3, 1962. Add to works: Symph. No. 3, for narrator and orch. (1955); *Palamas Symphony* for voice and orch., to texts by the Greek poet Palamas (Athens, Jan. 22, 1956); opera, *Constantin Palaeologus* (Athens, Aug. 12, 1962).

Kaminski, Heinrich. Add to bibl.: I. Samson, *Das Vokalschaffen von Heinrich Kaminski, mit Ausnahme der Opern* (Frankfurt, 1956).

Kanitz, Ernst. Changed his first name to Ernest to distinguish himself from a homonymous Vienna concert manager. Retired from the Univ. of Southern Calif. in 1959; then taught at Marymount College, Palos Verdes, Calif. (1960-64). Add to works: one-act operas: *Kumana* (1953); *Room No. 12* (1958); *Royal Auction* (1958); *The Lucky Dollar* (1959); *Perpetual* (1960); for orch.: *Concerto Grosso* (1949); *Concert Piece* for trumpet and orch. (1951); *Intermezzo Concertante* for alto saxophone and symph. band (1953); concerto for chamber orch. (1957); bassoon concerto (San Francisco, April 8, 1964); *Sinfonia Seria* (St. Louis, Oct. 17, 1964); Symph. No. 2 (1965; San Francisco, Dec. 11, 1968); chamber music: *Dance Sonata* for flute, clarinet, trumpet, bassoon and piano (1932); sonata for violin and cello (1947); Divertimento for viola and cello (1949); *Notturno* for flute, violin and viola (1950); string trio (1951); *Sonata breve* for violin, cello and piano (1952); *Sonata Californiana* for alto saxophone and piano (1952); sonata for cello unaccompanied (1956); sonatina for viola and piano (1958); Suite for a brass quintet (1960); vocal works: *Cantata 1961* for mixed chorus and 2 pianos (1961); *Visions at Twilight* for flute, string quintet, piano and women's voices in unison (1962); also *Little Concerto* for unaccompanied saxophone (Chicago, Dec. 15, 1970).

Kanner-Rosenthal, Hedwig. Died in Asheville, North Carolina, Sept. 5, 1959.

Kapp, Julius. Died in Sonthofen, March 18, 1962. Place of birth, Seelbach (not Steinbach).

Kapp, Villem, Estonian composer; nephew of Arthur Kapp, first cousin of Eugen Kapp; b. Suure-Jöani, Sept. 7, 1913; d. Tallinn, March 24, 1964. He studied music at the Tallinn Cons.; from 1944 was prof. of composition there. He wrote in an expansive romantic style rooted in folksong; his opera *Lembitu* (Tallinn, Aug. 23, 1961) glorifies Estes Lembitu, the leader of the Estonian struggle against the invading Teutonic crusaders in 1217. He also wrote two symphonies, chamber music and choral pieces. Bibl.: Helga Tönson, *Villem Kapp* (Tallinn, 1967).

Kappel, Gertrude. Died in Munich, April 3, 1971.

Karajan, Herbert von. Add data: He made his conducting début with the orch. of the Vienna Music Academy as a student on Dec. 17, 1928; conducted opera at the Ulm Stadttheater (1929-34); then was conductor of the Aachen Opera (1934-38); was engaged to conduct at the Berlin State Opera in 1938; inaugurated his season there with *Fidelio* on Sept. 30, 1938, but continued his tenure at the Aachen Opera until 1941. His second marriage to a woman with an undeniable Jewish grandparent created difficulties for him, even though he was a member in good standing of the National Socialist Party from 1935; however, he continued to conduct sporadic performances at the Berlin State Opera until its destruction in an air raid in 1944. After a lengthy process of de-Nazification, he was judged by the Allied occupying forces in Austria as sufficiently fumigated of Nazi impurities to be allowed to conduct at the Salzburg Festival in 1948; in the same year he was appointed conductor of the Vienna Symph. Orch. He subsequently conducted at La Scala in Milan as musical director of the German repertoire and at Bayreuth. In 1954 he succeeded Furtwängler as conductor of the Berlin Philharmonic, retaining this post until 1968; concurrently was artistic director of the Vienna State Opera (1957-64). Bibl.: Ernst Haeussermann, *Herbert von Karajan* (Gütersloh, 1968); Christian Spiel, editor, *Anekdoten um Herbert von Karajan* (Berlin, 1970).

Karel, Rudolf. The English title of his opera *Smrt kmotřička* should be *Godmother Death* (not *Godmother's Death*); it was produced in Brno (not in Prague).

Karg-Elert, Sigfrid. Karg means 'avaricious' (not 'coffin'). Add bibl.: Walter Kwasnik, *S. Karg-Elert: Sein Leben und Werk in heutiger Sicht* (1971).

Karkoff, Maurice Ingvar, Swedish composer; b. Stockholm, March 17, 1927. He studied composition with Lars-Erik Larsson at the Royal Academy of Music in Stockholm; took courses with Nadia Boulanger and André Jolivet in Paris (1957) and with Wladimir Vogel in Switzerland (1959-61) His technique is based on the serial method of composition, but he adheres to classical forms. Works: 3 symphonies (1950-58); violin concerto (1956); string quartet (1957); cello concerto (1957); trombone concerto (1958); *Variations* for orch. (1961); *Metamorphoses* for orch. (1967); *3 Episodes* for clarinet, cello and piano (1968); *Sinfonietta* (1969).

Kasemets, Udo, Estonian-born Canadian composer; b. Tallinn, Nov. 16, 1919. He studied at the Tallinn Cons., at the Stuttgart State Academy of Music and in Darmstadt. In 1951 he settled in Canada as organist, accompanist and teacher; later became music critic for the Toronto 'Daily Star.' His early works reflect his Estonian provenance, as exemplified by his string trio on Estonian folk tunes (1953). Later he espoused dodecaphony according to the strict Schoenbergian doctrine; to this period belongs his *Sonata da Camera* for cello solo (1955); violin concerto (1956); string quartet (1957); wind quintet (1957); *Four for Four* for soprano and string trio (1958); and *Sinfonietta* (1959). Beginning in 1960, he progressed towards total serialism; became editor of 'Canavangard,' an annotated catalogue of works by Canadian avant-garde composers. In his advanced idiom he wrote *Haiku* for voice, flute, cello and piano, to Japanese texts (1961); *Squares* for piano duet (1962); *Trigon* for 1 or 3 or 9 or 27 performers, a multi-dimensional score in which thematic information is provided by a deoxyribonucleic matrix (1963); *Communications,* a cybernetic manifestation for singular or plural singers, speakers, instrumentalists or dancers of an indeterminate duration (1963); *Cumulus* for any solo instruments or ensemble and 2 tape recorders, the score consisting of 9 segments to be played in any order (1964); *Timepiece* for a performer using any singular or plural instruments of an indeterminate duration (1964); *Cascando* for 1 to 128 performers (1965); *5PP,* 5 performance pieces for painters, actors, audiences, tasters, smellers, touchers, poets and composers (1966); *Calceolaria,* time - space variations on a floral theme (1966); *Contactics,* a choreography for musicians and audience (1966); *Variations on Variations on Variations* for singers, instrumentalists and 4 loudspeakers (1966); *Octagonal Octet and/or Ode* for 8 or fewer performers (1967).

Kässmeyer, Moritz. Last name should be spelled **Kässmayer;** exact date of birth, March 20, 1831.

Kastle, Leonard. Add to works: television opera, *Deseret* (NBC Opera Co., N. Y., Jan. 1, 1961).

Katchen, Julius. Died in Paris, April 29, 1969.

Kates, Stephen, American cellist; b. New York, May 7, 1943. He studied at the Juilliard School of Music; in 1963 won a honorable mention and a medal of merit at the International Cello Competition in Budapest; appeared at the Young People's Concerts with the N.Y. Philharmonic under Leonard Bernstein; in 1964 toured Europe with the Pittsburgh Symph. Orch.; then went to study with Gregor Piatigorsky in Los Angeles. In 1965 he won a debut grant of the Young Musicians Foundation in California.

Katz, Israel J., American musicologist; b. New York, July 21, 1930. He studied at the Univ. of Calif., Los Angeles, with Klaus P. Wachsmann and Boris Kremenliev, earning his B.A. in 1956 and Ph.D. in 1967. He specialized in Jewish and Spanish music; publ. a monograph, *Judeo-Spanish Traditional Ballads from Jerusalem* (2 vols., Brooklyn, 1971); contributed scholarly articles to the 'Encyclopedia Judaica,' 'Ethnomusicology' and other publications.

Kaufman, Louis. He settled in Hollywood; played violin solos for the soundtrack of some 500 motion pictures.

Kaufmann, Harry. Died in Beverly Hills, Calif., Aug. 22, 1961. Correct spelling: **Kaufman** (not Kaufmann).

Kaufmann, Helen. She was born on Feb. 2, 1887 (not 1882).

Kaufmann, Walter. Add to works: *A Hoosier Tale,* opera (Bloomington, Indiana, July 30, 1966).

Kaul, Oskar. Died in Unterwössen, July 17, 1968.

Kay, Hershy, American composer and arranger; b. Philadelphia, Nov. 17, 1919. He studied at the Curtis Institute of Music in Philadelphia; then went to N. Y.; orchestrated Leonard Bernstein's musical comedies *On the Town* (1944) and *Candide* (1956). He made numerous arrangements for Balanchine's ballet company, among them *Concert* (1956) from Chopin's music. His original ballet, *Western Symphony,* was produced by Balanchine with the N. Y. City Ballet Co. on Sept. 7, 1954, and was included in its Russian tour in 1962.

Kay, Ulysses Simpson. Add to works: one-act opera *The Juggler of Our Lady* (1956; New Orleans, Feb. 23, 1962); string quartet No. 3 (1961); *Fantasy Variations* for orch. (1963); *Umbrian Scene* for orch. (New Orleans, March, 31, 1964); *Inscriptions from Whitman* for chorus and orch. (Atlantic City, April 26, 1964); *Markings,* symph. essay dedicated to the memory of Dag Hammarskjöld (Rochester, Michigan, Aug. 18, 1966); *Aulos* for flute and chamber orch. (Bloomington, Indiana, Feb. 21, 1971).

Kazandzhiev, Vasil, Bulgarian composer; b. Rusa, Sept. 10, 1934. He studied with Vladigerov; wrote a symph.; a trumpet concerto; a violin concerto; many minor pieces.

Keats, Donald, American composer; b. New York, May 27, 1929. He studied piano at the Manhattan School of Music; composition at Yale Univ. with Quincy Porter and Paul Hindemith (Mus. B., 1949) and at Columbia Univ. with Otto Luening, Douglas Moore and Henry Cowell (M.A., 1953); musicology with Alfred Einstein and Leo Schrade at Yale and with Paul Henry Lang at Columbia. Subsequently he obtained a Ph.D. in composition from the Univ. of Minnesota. In 1954 he received a Fulbright Grant for study in Germany, and took lessons with Philipp Jarnach in Hamburg. In 1957 he joined the staff of Antioch College. In 1964-65 he held a Guggenheim Fellowship; lives in Italy. Works: clarinet sonata (1948); string trio (1949); *Divertimento* for winds and strings (1949); *The Hollow Men* for chorus and instruments (1955); string quartet No. 1 (1956); *Variations* for piano (1956); Symph. No. 1 (1959); piano sonata (1960); *The Naming of Cats* for chorus (1961); Symph. No. 2 (*Elegiac Symphony;* Kansas City, April 28, 1964); string quartet No. 2 (1965).

Kee, Piet, Dutch organist; b. Zaandam, Aug. 30, 1927. He studied organ with his father Cor Kee; graduated as pianist and organist from the Amsterdam Cons. in 1948; gave numerous recitals in Holland; eventually was appointed organist of St. Laurens Church in Alkmaar and prof. of the Muzieklyceum in Amsterdam. He composed a number of organ pieces; made arrangements of hymns and folksongs.

Keene, Christopher, American conductor; b. Berkeley, Calif., Dec. 21, 1946. He studied piano and cello; took courses at the Univ. of California, in Berkeley, majoring in history in 1963. While still a student he organized an opera company, with which he staged several modern works including the West Coast première of Henze's *Elegy for Young Lovers;* was guest conductor of the Spoleto Festivals in the summers of 1968, 1969 and 1971. Concurrently, he was musical director of the American Ballet Company, for which he wrote a ballet of his own, *The Consort* (1970). In 1970 he joined the conducting staff of the New York City Opera as the winner of the Julius Rudel Award; made a brilliant debut in Ginastera's opera *Don Rodrigo;* on March 12, 1971, conducted the world première of Menotti's opera, *The Most Important Man;* on Aug. 12, 1971 he conducted the posthumous world première of the opera *Yerma* by Villa-Lobos, with the Santa Fe Opera Co. At his New York appearances he was enthusiastically acclaimed by the critics as one of the brightest precocious talents in the profession. In April 1971 he distinguished himself with the N. Y. City Opera by a highly competent performance of *La Traviata,* and later conducted also at the Metropolitan Opera. These accomplishments are all the more remarkable since he never took a regular course in conducting, but learned to lead orchestras by instinctual instrumental navigation.

Keilberth, Joseph. Died in Munich, July 20, 1968.

Keiser, Reinhard. The number of his stage works written for the Hamburg Opera is 116 (not 126) and, of these, only 77 are genuine operas; the rest are singspiele and interludes.

Kelberine, Alexander. The date of his death is indeterminate; he committed suicide by swallowing sleeping pills between Jan. 27, 1940, when he played his last concert in New York (in a program containing pieces only in minor keys and concluding with Liszt's Todtentanz) and Jan. 30, 1940, when his body was discovered in his apartment. He was married to the pianist Jeanne Behrend.

Keldorfer, Victor. Died in Vienna, Jan. 28, 1959.

Kelemen, Milko. About 1953 he radically changed his style of composition, adopting serial procedures and experimenting with aleatory potentialities. Works: piano concerto (Zagreb, Dec. 22, 1953): *Koncertantne Improvizacije* for strings (Zagreb, Oct. 10, 1955); bassoon concerto (Zagreb, April 11, 1956); *Igre (Games)*, song cycle for baritone and strings (Zagreb, Sept. 29, 1956); *Concerto Giocoso* for chamber orch. (Zagreb, Jan. 4, 1957); violin concerto (Zagreb, April 19, 1957); *Simfonijska Muzika 57* (Zagreb, June 4, 1958); Concertino for double-bass and strings (Zagreb, Oct. 21, 1959); *Changeant* for cello and orch. (1968); *Floreal* for chamber orch. (Coolidge Festival, Washington, Oct. 30, 1970); opera, *Opsadno Stanje (The Siege)*, after a novel by Camus (Zagreb, May 9, 1971). See K. Kovačevič, *Hrvatski Kompozitori i Njihova Djela* (Zagreb, 1960).

Keller, Hermann. Died in Freiburg-im-Breisgau, Aug. 17, 1967, in an automobile accident.

Kellogg, Clara Louise. Born July 9 (not July 12), 1842.

Kelly, Robert. Add to works and amplify data: *The White Gods,* opera in 3 acts on the Aztec impression of the conquistadores (1966; partial first performance, Univ. of Illinois, Urbana, July 3, 1966); Symph. No. 2 (1958); concerto for violin. cello and orch. (Univ. of Illinois, Urbana, March 8, 1961); Symph. No. 3, *Emancipation Symphony* (Washington, D.C., Feb. 5, 1963); *An American Diptych* for orch. (Austin, Texas, April 26, 1963); *Colloquy* for chamber orch. (Chicago, April 17, 1965); violin concerto (1968); chamber music: 2 string quartets (1944, 1952); viola sonata (1950); violin sonata (1952); sonata for trombone and piano (1952); sonata for oboe and harp (1955); quintet for clarinet and strings (1956); cello sonata (1958); *Toccata* for marimba and percussion (1959); *Triptych* for cello and piano (1962); choruses; songs; band music.

Kelterborn, Rudolf, Swiss composer; b. Basel, Sept. 3, 1931. He studied with Jacques Handschin, Willy Burkhard, Boris Blacher and Wolfgang Fortner. In 1960 he became instructor at the Music Academy in Detmold, Germany; was also active as conductor. In his music he applies serial organization in which quantitative values of duration form a recurrent progression; the changes of tempi are also subject to serialization. Both melody and harmony are derived from a basic tone-row, with the dissonant intervals of minor 2nd and major 7th as mainstays. Works: *Suite* for woodwinds, percussion and strings (1954); *Concertino* for violin and chamber orch. (1954); Sonata for 16 solo strings (1955); *Metamorphosen* for piano (1956); *5 Fantasien* for flute, cello and harpsichord (1958); *7 Bagatellen* for wind quintet (1958); *Canto Apassionato* for orch. (1959); Concertino for piano, percussion and strings (1959); *Metamorphosen* for orch. (1960); *Cantata profana* for baritone, chorus and 13 instruments (1960); *Ewige Wiederkehr,* cantata for mezzo-soprano, flute and string trio (1960); cello concerto (1962); *Esquisses* for harpsichord and percussion (1962); *Meditationen* for 6 wind instruments (1962); *Kammersonate* for flute, oboe, string trio and harpsichord (1963); *Kaiser Jovian,* opera (Karlsruhe, March 4, 1967); Symph. No. 1 (Vienna, April 26, 1968). He publ. a book. *Stilistische Mannigfaltigkeit in der zeitgenossischen Musik* (Amriswill, 1958). Cf. Ernst Mohr, *Zur Kompositionstechnik Rudolf Kelterborns* in 'Musica' (May 1960).

Kemp, Barbara. Died in Berlin, April 17, 1959. Date of birth, Dec. 12, 1881 (not 1886); place of birth Cochem (not Kochem).

Kenins, Talivaldis, Canadian composer; b. Liepaja, Latvia, April 23, 1919. He studied at the Paris Cons. with Tony Aubin and Olivier Messiaen. In 1951 he settled in Canada; in 1952 was appointed to the faculty of the Royal Cons. of Toronto. Works: string quartet (1948); septet (1949); cello sonata (1950); Duo for piano and orch. (1951); piano trio (1952); violin sonata (1954); *Diversions on a Gypsy Song* for cello and piano (1958); piano quartet (1958); symph. for chamber orch. (1959); *Divertimento* for clarinet and piano (1960); piano sonata; choruses.

Kenton, Stanley Newcomb (Stan), American jazz band leader, composer and pianist; b. Wichita, Kansas, Feb. 19, 1912. He spent his youth in California; began arranging and composing at the age of 16; in 1941 he organized his own band; in 1950 toured with an orch., including strings, and instituted a type of 'progressive jazz' by discovering such devices as whole-tone scales and consecutive major 9th-chords; however, his style of playing varied, according to arrangers he used at each particular time. He dabbled in theoretical speculation, and took a course in the Schillinger System of Composition.

Kerman, Joseph, American musicologist; b. London, England (of American parents), April 3, 1924. He studied musicology at Princeton Univ. with Oliver Strunk (Ph.D., 1950). In 1951 he was appointed to the staff of the Univ. of California at Berkeley. His Ph.D. thesis, *The Elizabethan Madrigal: A Comparative Study* was publ. in the series 'American Musicological Society Studies and Documents' (N.Y., 1962); he also publ. *Opera as Drama* (N. Y., 1956) and *The Beethoven Quartets* (N. Y., 1967).

Kern, Jerome (David). Returned to New York in 1904 (not 1907).

Kertesz, Istvan, Hungarian conductor; b. Budapest, Aug. 28, 1929. He studied at the Academy of Music in Budapest and at Santa Cecilia, Rome (1958); was conductor at Györ (1953-55), at the Budapest Opera (1955-57) and of the London Symph. Orch. (1965-68).

Kestenberg, Leo. Died in Tel Aviv, Jan. 14, 1962.

Ketèlbey, Albert William, English composer of light music; b. Birmingham, Aug. 9, 1875; d. Cowes, Isle of Wight, Nov. 26, 1959. He was of remote Danish origin. Precociously gifted in music, he wrote a piano sonata at the age of 11, and played it at the Worcester Town Hall; Elgar heard it and praised it. At the age of 13, he competed for a Trinity College scholarship, and was installed as Queen Victoria Scholar; at 16 he obtained the post of organist at St. John's Church at Wimbledon; at 20 began tours as conductor of a musical comedy troupe. For some years he was music director of Columbia Gramophone Co. and music editor at Chappell's Music Publishing Company. Among his works are a quintet for woodwinds and piano, a string quartet, *Caprice* for piano and orch., a comic opera *The Wonder Worker,* etc. He achieved fame with a series of remarkably popular instrumental pieces on exotic subjects (*In a Persian Market, In a Monastery Garden, Sanctuary of the Heart. In a Chinese Temple Garden,* etc.). He also publ. many small pieces under various pseudonyms.

Ketting, Otto, Dutch composer; b. The Hague, Sept. 3, 1935. He played trumpet in the Hague Philharmonic; began to compose for brass instruments. In his symphonic scores he often applies the 12-tone technique of composition. Works: *Intrada Festiva* for brass and percussion (1956); *Due Canzoni* for orch. (1957); Concertino for 2 trumpets (1958); Variations on a Dutch folksong for clarinet, bassoon and piano (1958); a symph. (1959); Concertino for jazz quintet and orch. (1960); piano pieces in the dodecaphonic technique.

Khandoshkin, Ivan. Date of death, according to Gregorian calendar, March 28 (not March 16), 1804.

Khatchaturian, Aram. The name of his wife is Makarova (q.v.), not Markarova. Add to works: *Concerto-Rhapsody* for violin and orch. (Moscow, Nov. 3, 1962). Add to bibl.: I. Martynov, *Aram Khatchaturian* (Moscow, 1956); G. Schneerson, *Aram Khatchaturian* (Moscow, 1958); G. Khubov, *Aram Khatchaturian* (Moscow, 1962).

Khatchaturian, Karen, Soviet composer; nephew of Aram Khatchaturian; b. Moscow, Sept. 19, 1920. He studied at the Moscow Cons. with Litinsky; during World War II served in the entertainment division of the Red Army. He resumed his studies in 1945 at the Moscow Cons. with Shebalin, Shostakovitch and Miaskovsky. His music is distinguished by formal elegance and rhythmic power. Among his works are a symph. (Moscow, March 12, 1955); several overtures; a number of symph. suites; a violin sonata; a cello sonata; songs.

Khrennikov, Tikhon. His 2nd symph. was first performed on Jan. 10 (not 14), 1943. Add to works: violin concerto (Moscow, Oct. 21, 1959); operetta, *100 Devils* (Moscow, May 16, 1963); *White Nights,* 'musical chronicle' (Moscow, Nov. 3, 1967); piano concerto No. 2 (1970). Cf. V. Kukharsky, *Tikhon Khrennikov* (Moscow, 1957).

Kielland, Olva. First name **Olav** (not Olva). Add to works: *Concerto grosso Norvegese* (1952); Symph. No. 2 (1961); Symph. No. 3 (1966). See: Bjarne Kortsen, *Contemporary Norwegian Orchestral Music* (Bergen, 1969; pp. 244-282).

Kienzl, Wilhelm. Died Oct. 3 (not Oct. 19), 1941.

Kiepura, Jan. Died in Rye, New York, Aug. 15, 1966. His American debut took place in Chicago in 1931; his engagement with the Metropolitan Opera came 7 years later.

Kiladze, Grigory Varfolomeyevitch. Died in Tbilisi, April 3, 1962.

Kilar, Wojciech, Polish composer; b. Lwow, July 17, 1932. He studied piano and composition with Boleslaw Woytowicz in Katowice, and later took lessons with Nadia Boulanger in Paris. Of an experimental turn of mind, he made use of serial techniques, while retaining essential classical forms. Of his works, the most important are *Little Overture* (1955); Symph. No. 1 for strings (1955); Symph. No. 2 (*Concertante*) for piano and orch. (1956); *Béla Bartók in Memoriam* for violin, wind instruments and percussion (1957); Concerto for 2 pianos and percussion (1958); *Mask of the Red Death,* ballet after Poe (1961); *Herbsttag,* for soprano and string quartet, to words by Rilke (1962).

Kilenyi, Edward, Sr. Died in Tallahassee, Florida, Aug. 15, 1968.

Killmayer, Wilhelm. Add to works: *Lauda* for chorus (1968); *Sinfonie 'Folgi'* (Hannover, Feb. 9, 1971).

Kilpinen, Yriö. Died in Helsinki, March 2, 1959. Correct spelling of the first name, Yrjö (not Yriö). Add bibl.: M. Pulkkinen, *Yrjö Kilpinen: Gedruckte Kompositionen* (Helsinki, 1960).

Kim, Earl, American composer; b. Dinuba, Calif., Jan. 6, 1920. He studied at the Univ. of Calif., Berkeley (M.A. 1952); was associate prof. at Princeton Univ. (1952-67) and subsequently on the staff of Harvard Univ. His works include *Dialogues* for piano and orch. (1959); *They are Far Out,* for soprano, violin, cello and percussion (1966); *Gooseberries, She Said,* for soprano, 5 instruments and percussion (1968); *Letter Found Near a Suicide,* a song cycle; and *Exercises en Route,* a multi-media composition. He received in 1971 the Brandeis Univ. Creative Arts Award.

Kimball, Jacob, Jr. Add to bibl.: G. Wilcox, *Jacob Kimball, Jr.: His Life and Works* (Los Angeles, 1957).

Kinkeldey, Otto. Died in Orange, New Jersey, Sept. 19, 1966. Add to bibl.: Ch. Seeger, ed., *A Musicological Offering to Otto Kinkeldey Upon the Occasion of his 80th Birthday* (Philadelphia, 1960).

Kinsky, Georg. Vol. III of his catalogue of the Heyer collection was never published, and remains in manuscript.

Kipnis, Igor, American harpsichordist; son of the singer Alexander Kipnis; b. Berlin, Sept. 27, 1930. He studied at Westport, Conn., School of Music and at Harvard Univ. (A.B., 1952); after holding various jobs as music director for radio programs, he devoted himself to the study of the harpsichord, achieving a fine reputation both as scholar and performer; gave concerts on the harpsichord; toured in America and in Europe; taught at the Berkshire Music Center (1964-67); lectured widely on the subject of proper interpretation of Baroque music; made numerous recordings; edited collections of music for the harpsichord.

Kirchner, Leon. Add to works: string quartet No. 2 (1958); concerto for violin, cello, 10 instruments and percussion (1960); piano concerto No. 2 (Seattle, Oct. 28, 1963); string quartet No. 3, with electronic sounds (awarded the Pulitzer Prize for 1967). In 1961 he was appointed prof. of composition at Harvard Univ.; in 1970 was visiting prof. at the Univ. of Calif., Los Angeles.

Kirigin, Ivo. Add to works: Symph. No. 1 (1950); cantata *Pjesma o Zemliji* (*Song of the Land;* 1952); *Kameni Horizonti* (*Stone Horizons;* Zagreb, March 16, 1955); 5 movements for strings (1958).

Kirkpatrick, John. Change 'graduated in 1926' to 'flunked out in 1926' (in classics). Studied music in Paris in winter and summer (not only in summer). He spent 10 years (not 2) studying the *Concord Sonata.* Compiled an annotated and exhaustive catalogue of works of Charles Ives (New Haven, 1960).

Kirnberger, Johann Philipp. Vol. I of *Die Kunst des reinen Satzes in der Musik* was publ. in 1771 (not 1774).

Kisielewski, Stefan, Polish composer; b. Warsaw, March 7, 1911. He studied in Warsaw with Sikorski; was prof. of composition at the State School of Music in Cracow (1945-49); was also active as music editor and journalist. He composed 2 symphonies; several overtures; chamber music; piano pieces.

Kitt, Eartha, black American singer of popular songs; b. in the town named North, South Carolina, Jan. 26, 1928. She moved to Brooklyn and began to sing in various establishments in New York. In 1948 she went to Paris where she attracted attention as an exotic chanteuse. She excelled particularly in earthy, passion-laden songs delivered in an ostentatiously low-key monotone; produced a sensation by her rendition of *Monotonous*. She has also appeared as a motion picture actress in roles of abandoned women. Her autobiography *Thursday's Child*, arranged for public consumption by journalistic hands, was publ. in N. Y. in 1956.

Klafsky, Anton Maria. Died in Baden, near Vienna, Jan. 1, 1965.

Klami, Uuno. Died in Helsinki, May 29, 1961.

Klebe, Giselher. Add to works: opera, *Die tödlichen Wünsche* (Düsseldorf, June 14, 1959); opera *Alkmene* (Berlin, Sept. 25, 1961); opera buffa, *Figaro lässt sich scheiden* (Hamburg, June 28, 1963); *Stabat Mater* for soloists, chorus and orch. (Valdagno, Oct. 24, 1964); comic opera, *Jakobowsky und der Oberst* (Hamburg, Nov. 2, 1965); fairy-tale opera, *Das Märchen von der schönen Lilie* (Schwetzingen, May 15, 1969); *Das Testament*, ballet-symphony (Symph. No. 4) for orch. and 2 pianos tuned a quarter-tone apart (Wiesbaden, April 30, 1971).

Kleiber, Erich. Bibl.: J. Russell, *Erich Kleiber: A Memoir* (London, 1957).

Klein, Lothar, American composer; b. Hannover, Germany, Jan. 27, 1932. He came to the U.S. as a child; studied music at the Univ. of Minnesota; in 1958-60 took courses in composition with Josef Rufer at the Free Univ. of Berlin. Returning to the U.S. he joined the staff of the Univ. of Texas, Austin. His music is basically tonal; its esthetical premises are both neo-classical and neo-romantic. In his more abstract compositions he applies various species of serialism. **Works:** Symph. No. 1 (1955); Concerto for 4 winds and orch. (St. Paul, Minnesota, Nov. 8, 1958); *Symmetries* for orch., 4 sets (1959, 1960, 1962, 1964); *Appassionato* for orch. (1959, Dallas, Feb. 8, 1965); *Trio Concertante* for solo strings and orch., in memory of Hemingway, Camus and President Kennedy (Hamburg, Germany, Nov. 11, 1964); Symph. No. 2 (1965); cantatas; chamber music for various combinations; song cycles.

Kleinheinz, Franz Xaver. His opera *Harald* was produced in Budapest on March 22, 1814 (not in Ofen; not in 1914).

Klemperer, Otto. He publ. *Erinnerungen an Gustav Mahler* (Zürich, 1960) and *Minor Recollections* (London, 1964).

Klose, Margarete, German contralto; b. Berlin, Aug. 6, 1902; d. there, Dec. 14, 1968. She studied music at the Klindworth-Scharwenka Cons. in Berlin; made her debut in Ulm in 1927; then sang in Mannheim (1928-31) and finally at the Berlin State Opera, where she obtained a decisive popular and musical success; she continued her active career until her 60th year; sang in Italy, England and the U.S. She was particularly praised for her Wagnerian contralto roles.

Klusák, Jan, Czech composer; b. Prague, April 18, 1934. He studied with Jaroslav Řídký and Pavel Bořkovec. Among his works are 3 symphonies (1956, 1959, 1960); Concertino for flute and strings (1955); Concerto grosso (1957); Concertino for 8 instruments (1960); *Images* for 12 wind instruments (1960); 2 string quartets (1956, 1962). In 1964 he completed an opera on the subject of Kafka's novel *The Trial*. In this opera, and in his songs on Kafka's texts, he applies dodecaphonic and serial techniques.

Knapp, Phoebe Palmer, American hymn writer; b. New York, 1839; d. Poland Springs, Maine, July 10, 1908. She and her husband, the founder of the Metropolitan Life Insurance Company, supported much philanthropic work as members of the Methodist Episcopal Church. She wrote both verse and music; her most popular hymn is *Assurance* (1873). Cf. R. G. McCutchan, *Our Hymnody* (N. Y., 1937).

Knappertsbusch, Hans. Died in Munich, Oct. 25, 1965.

Knipper, Lev Konstantinovitch. Add to works: Symph. No. 14 (Moscow, Feb. 15, 1956, composer conducting); symph. poem, *To a War Comrade* (Moscow, Feb. 23, 1958); *Tales of the Soil*, symph. suite (Moscow, Oct. 16, 1960); *Letters to Friends*, symph. suite (1961); Sinfonietta for an ensemble of violas and cellos (1961); *Concerto-Monologue* for cello, 7 brass instruments and kettledrums (1962); *Little Concerto* for violin and strings (1963); *Saga*, symph. poem for cello, chorus and orch. (1963).

Knittl, Karl. He became administrative director of the Prague Cons. in 1902; did not succeed Dvořák, who held the post of artistic director. *Lied von der Glocke* is a cantata, not a symphonic work.

Knoch, Ernst. Died in New York, March 20, 1959.

Kobald, Karl. Died in Germany, Oct. 12, 1957.

Koch, Caspar Petrus. Died in Pittsburgh, April 3, 1970.

Koch, (Sigurd Christian) Erland von. Add to works: 2 piano concertos (1950, 1962); cello concerto (1951); *Musica malinconica* for string orch. (1952); saxophone concerto (1958); *Concerto piccolo* for soprano, alto saxophone and string orch. (1962); *Fantasia concertante* for violin and orch. (1964); 6 string quartets; piano pieces; songs.

Koch, Karl, Austrian organist and composer of sacred music; b. Biberwier, Tyrol, Jan. 29, 1887. He studied religion and music at a theological seminary in Brixen; took courses in conducting with Max Springer at the Musical Academy in Vienna. In 1926 he settled in Innsbruck as choral conductor. He wrote a number of sacred choruses and much organ music; a symphony *Aus den Bergen* (1942), a string quartet; 2 piano sonatas; publ. a manual, *Harmonielehre* (Vienna, 1948). See Wilhelm Isser, *Karl Koch: Das Bild eines zeitgenössischen Komponisten* (Innsbruck, 1969).

Kocian, Jaroslav. Date of death, March 7 (not March 8), 1950. Last name should have an acute accent on A (Kocián).

Kodály, Zoltán. Died in Budapest, March 6, 1967. On Dec. 18, 1959, he married Sarolta Péczely, a student (b. 1940). In 1965 he visited the U.S. as a lecturer. Add to works: *Symphony in C* (Lucerne, Aug. 16, 1961). Did not write a viola concerto (1947), nor a concerto for string quartet (1947). Went to high school in Nagyszombat (not Magyszombat). His book *Folk Music of Hungary,* was publ. in English (N. Y., 1960). Add bibl.: L. Eösze, *Zoltán Kodály: His Life and Work* (in English; Budapest, 1962); Percy M. Young, *Zoltán Kodály* (London, 1964).

Koeberg, Frits Ehrhardt Adriaan. Died in The Hague, Nov. 9, 1961.

Koechlin, Charles. Place of death, Canadel (not Canaden).

Koetsier, Jan, Dutch conductor and composer; b. Amsterdam, Aug. 14, 1911. He studied in Berlin; began his career as conductor in Holland; settled in Germany in 1947. He wrote 3 symphonies; several instrumental concertos; an opera, *Franz Hals.*

Koffler, Josef. He was shot by the Nazis, with his wife and child, in Wieliczka, near Cracow, during a street roundup of Jews in 1943.

Kohn, Karl, American pianist and composer; b. Vienna, Aug. 1, 1926; settled in the U. S. in 1939; studied at Harvard Univ. with Walter Piston, Irving Fine and Randall Thompson (B.A., 1950; M.A., 1955). In 1956 he traveled in Finland on a Fulbright grant; upon return to the U. S. taught piano and theory at Pomona College, California. His style of composition veers toward the integral chromaticism of dodecaphony but in his works for school performance he makes concessions to tonality. Works: *Sinfonia Concertante* for piano and orch. (1951); Overture for string orch. (Helsinki, April 17, 1956); *Castles and Kings,* symph. suite for children (1958); string trio (1949); piano quartet (1952); wind quintet (1955); violin sonata (1956); quartet for horns (1957); *Divertimento* for flute, oboe, clarinet and bassoon (1959); *3 Scenes* for orch. (1960); *Serenade* for wind quintet and piano (1961); *Capriccios* for harp, cello, flute, clarinet and piano (1962); *Concerto mutabile* for piano and orch. (1962; San Francisco, March 8, 1964); *Little Suite* for wind quintet (1963); *Sonata da camera* for alto flute, clarinet and piano (1964); *Introductions and Parodies* for clarinet, French horn, bassoon, string quartet and piano (Pasadena, Calif., Nov. 15, 1970); 2 sonatinas, *Rhapsody* and *Partita* for piano; choruses; songs.

Kohoutek, Ctirad, Czech composer; b. Zábřeh, March 18, 1929. He studied at the Brno Cons.; in 1953 became an instructor there. He wrote the symph. poems *February 1948* (1953) and *Munich* (1953) and other works of political connotations; viola concerto (1952); violin concerto (1958); string quartet (1959); *Sinfonietta* (Brno, March 10, 1964).

Kohs, Ellis B. He publ. *Music Theory, a Syllabus for Teacher and Student* (2 vols.; N. Y., 1961); *Musical Form* (N. Y., 1968). Add to works: opera *Amerika* (1969; abridged concert version produced in Los Angeles; May 19, 1970); *Studies in Variation,* in 4 parts: for woodwind quintet, for piano quartet, for piano solo, for unaccompanied violin (1962); Sonata for snare-drum and piano (1966); Suite for cello and piano (1970).

Kokkonen, Joonas, Finnish composer; b. Idensalmi, Nov. 13, 1921. He studied at the

Sibelius Academy of Music in Helsinki; upon graduation engaged in composing and teaching. He wrote 3 symphonies (1960, 1961, 1967); *Sinfonia da camera* (1962); *Opus sonorum* for orch. (1964); 2 string quartets; piano quintet; minor pieces. His music is constructivistic, with a succession of motives ordered by acoustical rather than formal logic.

Kollmann, August Friedrich Christoph. Exact date of birth, March 21, 1756.

Kolneder, Walter. Add to writings: *Anton Webern: Einführung in Werk und Stil* (Rodenkirchen, 1961; in English, as *Anton Webern: An Introduction to His Works,* Los Angeles, 1968); *Antonio Vivaldi* (Wiesbaden, 1965; in English, Berkeley, Calif., 1970).

Kolodin, Irving. Add to books: *The Continuity of Music: a History of Influence* (N.Y., 1968).

Komorzynski, Egon. Died in Vienna, March 16, 1963.

Kondorssy, Leslie. Last name, **Kondorossy** (not Kondorssy). *Night in the Puszta* was produced in Cleveland on June 28, 1953; *The Voice* was produced in concert form in Cleveland, on May 15, 1954. Add to works: *The Midnight Duel,* lyric drama (Cleveland, radio performance, March 20, 1955); radio opera, *The String Quartet* (Cleveland, May 8, 1955); trombone concerto (1958); trumpet concerto (1959); harp concerto (1961); *The Fox,* opera (Cleveland, Jan. 28, 1961); operas *The Baksis* (1960-64) and *Nathan the Wise* (1961-64).

Konjović, Petar. Died in Belgrade, Oct. 1, 1970. His opera *Knez od Zete* was produced May 25, 1929 (not 1939); title of his other opera is *Vilin Veo* (not *Vilin Vee*).

Kono, Kristo, Albanian composer; b. Tirana, July 17, 1907. He studied at the Milan Cons.; wrote the first national Albanian operetta *The Dawn* (1954); also an opera, *Flowers of Memories* (1959) and many choruses.

Koole, Arend. Left South Africa in 1964; in the same year appointed prof. of music history at the Univ. of Southern Calif., Los Angeles.

Korn, Peter Jona, German-American composer; b. Berlin, March 30, 1922; left Germany as a child in 1933; studied in England (1934-36); lived in Jerusalem (1936-39); in 1941 emigrated to the U. S., settling in Los Angeles. His teachers in composition were Edmund Rubbra in London, Stefan Wolpe in Jerusalem, Hanns Eisler and Ernst Toch in Los Angeles; he also attended Schoenberg's classes at the Univ. of Calif., Los Angeles (1942) and studied the technique of composition for films with Ingolf Dahl and Miklós Rózsa. The resulting style ultimately adopted by Korn is that of pragmatic romanticism marked by polycentric tonality in the framework of strong rhythmic counterpoint. His works comprise an opera *Heidi* (1961-63); 3 symphonies (1946, 1952, 1956); *Variations* on a tune from *Beggar's Opera,* for orch. (Louisville, Oct. 1, 1955); *Tom Paine Overture* (1950; Malmö, Sweden, Dec. 8, 1959, composer conducting); *In Medias Res,* symph. overture (1953); *Rhapsody* for oboe and strings (1952); concertino for horn and double string orch. (1952); saxophone concerto (1956); cello sonata (1949); oboe sonata (1949); horn sonata (1953); string quartet No. 1 (1950); *Serenade* for 4 horns (1957); *Passacaglia and Fugue* for 8 horns (1952): string quartet No. 2 (1963): *Quintettino* for flute, clarinet, bassoon, cello and piano (1964).

Kornauth, Egon. Died in Vienna, Oct. 28, 1959.

Körner, Christian Gottfried. Add to bibl.: W. Seifert, *C. G. Körner: ein Musikästhetiker der deutschen Klassik* (Regensburg, 1960).

Korngold, Erich Wolfgang. The title of his 4th opera is *Das* (not *Die*) *Wunder der Heliane.*

Kortchmarev, Klimenty Arkadyevitch. Died in Moscow, April 7, 1958.

Korte, Oldřich František, Slovak composer; b. Šal, April 26, 1926. He studied in Prague; wrote mostly in miniature forms; his *Praise for Death* scored for piccolo and glockenspiel (1948) is characteristic of his experimental music. His symph. drama, *The Floating Flutes* (1949-51), attracted attention. By profession, he is a journalist and a writer of film scripts.

Kortsen, Bjarne, Norwegian musicologist; b. Haugesund, July 4, 1930. He studied music and electrical engineering; was employed by the Norwegian railways for 3 years while studying musicology at the Univ. of Oslo (M.A., 1962); later studied at the Univ. of Glasgow (Ph.D., 1964), at the Univ. of Cologne, and at the Musik-Hochschule in Berlin. He publ. a number of valuable books in

Norwegian, German and English: *Fartein Valen, Life and Music* (3 vols.; Oslo, 1965); *Modern Norwegian Chamber Music* (Haugesund, 1965); *Contemporary Norwegian Orchestral Music* (West Berlin, 1969); *Chamber Music Works by Johan Svendsen* (Bergen, 1971).

Kosakoff, Reuven, American pianist and composer; b. New Haven, Conn., Jan. 8, 1898. He studied at Yale Univ. and at Juilliard School of Music in N. Y.; then went to Berlin as a private piano student of Artur Schnabel. He has written several biblical cantatas; 2 Sabbath services; a piano concerto on Hebrew themes (Pittsburgh, March 24, 1941); a symph. suite, *Jack and the Beanstalk* (New Haven, April 22, 1944).

Koschat, Thomas. The title of the monograph on him should be *Der Sänger Kärnthens* (not *Kärnthners).*

Koshetz, Nina. Died in Santa Ana, Calif., May 14, 1965.

Kosma, Joseph. Died in La Roche-Guyon, near Paris, Aug. 7, 1969. The title of his ballet is *L'Ecuyère* (not *Lecuyère).* Add to works: ballet *Le Pierrot de Montmartre* (1952); comic operas, *Les Chansons de Bilitis* (1954); *Un amour électronique* (Paris, 1962); *La Révolte des canuts* (Lyon, 1964); *Les Hussards* (Lyon, Oct. 21, 1969).

Kostić, Dušan, Yugoslav composer; b. Zagreb, Jan. 23, 1925. He studied at the Music Academy in Belgrade; later took a course in conducting with Scherchen. He incorporated neo-classical, impressionistic and serial techniques in his music; also wrote occasional pieces on national folk themes. Works: 2 symphonies (1957, 1961); symph. poem *Contrasts* (1954); *Crnogorska suita* for orch. (1957); *Sonata amorosa* for violin and piano (1957); opera-buffa, *Majstori su prvi ljudi* (Belgrade, April 23, 1962); *Kragujevac,* symph. poem for voices and orch., commemorating the execution of the schoolboys at Kragujevac in 1941 by the Nazi occupation forces (Belgrade, Feb. 5, 1962); choruses; songs; piano pieces.

Kostić, Vojislav, Serbian composer; b. Belgrade, Sept. 21, 1931. He studied in his native city; adopted a sophisticated style of utilitarian music. His *Karakteri* for clarinet, piano and 18 percussion instruments (1958) had numerous performances in Yugoslavia. He also wrote a *Divertimento* for wind quintet; a suite for bassoon and piano; and *Ciganska priča (Gypsy Tale)* for male chorus and chamber orch., to Gypsy texts (1964).

Kotoński, Wlodzimierz, Polish composer; b. Warsaw, Aug. 23, 1925. He studied music with Rytel and Szeligowski at the Warsaw Cons., graduating in 1951; from 1956-58 was music consultant for the documentary film center in Warsaw. His early works are derived from native music; his style then changed to neo-classicism, and finally to constructivism. Works: *Poème* for orch. (1949); *Quartettino* for 4 horns (1950); *Danses montagnardes* (1950); *Prelude and Passacaglia* for orch. (1953); 6 miniatures for clarinet and piano (1957); *Musique de chambre* for 21 percussion instruments (Warsaw Festival, Oct. 2, 1958); *Musique en rélief* for sextuple orchestral ensemble (Darmstadt, Sept. 5, 1959); *Etude concrète* for a single stroke of cymbals electronically metamorphosed (Darmstadt, July 9, 1960); *Concerto per quattro* (1960); *Canto* for 18 instruments (1961); *Pezzo* for flute and piano (1962); *Pour 4,* for clarinet, trombone, piano and cello (1968); *Actions* for electronic sound (Cracow, June 5, 1969).

Kotzwara, Franz. He was engaged in Dublin as a viola player (not as a violinist).

Kouguell, Arkadie, Russian-American pianist and composer; b. Simferopol, Dec. 25, 1898. He studied at the St. Petersburg Cons. From 1928 to 1948 he lived in Beirut; then in Paris. In 1952 he settled in New York as piano teacher. Works: *Impressions of Damascus* for orch. (1930); *Rapsodie tartare* for orch. (1947); piano concerto (1930): piano concerto for left hand (1934); cello concerto (1950); concertino for trombone and piano (1956); *Bédouin Dance* for an ensemble of 60 cellos (1932); 2 string quartets; 3 piano sonatas; violin sonata; 2 cello sonatas; suites for various chamber groups.

Kounadis, Arghyris, Greek composer; b. Constantinople, Feb. 14, 1924; moved to Athens in his infancy; studied piano at home and jurisprudence at the Univ. of Athens; at the same time began to compose. In 1958 he went to Freiburg, Germany, where he studied composition with Wolfgang Fortner; became interested in the theater; wrote incidental music for Greek plays produced at Epidaurus (1958, 1960, 1961). In his instrumental works he follows the dodecaphonic technique. Of these, his *Chorikon* for orchestra was performed by the Berlin Philharmonic on May 15, 1962. This was followed by another symph. work in the same manner, *Triptychon* (1964).

Koutzen, Boris. Died at Mount Kisco, N.Y., Dec. 10, 1966.

Koval, Marian Victorovitch. Died in Moscow, Feb. 15, 1971.

Kovařovic, Karel. The title of his first opera, *Ženichové* (not *Ženiohové*); title of his 2nd ballet, *Pohádka o nalezeném štěstí.*

Kox, Hans, Dutch composer; b. Arnhem, May 19, 1930. He studied with Henk Badings; adopted a neo-classical idiom, with occasional resort to the 12-tone method of composition. Works: *Concertante Music* for horn, trumpet and trombone with orch. (1956); *Amphion* for 2 narrators, brass and percussion (1958); Concerto for Orchestra (1959); a symph. (1959); violin sonata (1961); piano concerto (1962); violin concerto (1963); concerto for 2 violins and orch. (1964); *Cyclofonie* for orch. (1964); *Paraklesis* for orch. (1964); pieces for violin, for string quartet and for organ in a 31-tone system.

Koyama, Kiyoshige, Japanese composer; b. Nagano, Jan. 15, 1914. He studied composition with Komei Abe; wrote a number of works in a Japanese national style, among them *Shinano-Bayashi* for orch. (Tokyo, June 3, 1946); *Kobiki-Uta* for orch. (Tokyo, Oct. 3, 1957); Symph. suite *Nomen,* for a Noh play (Tokyo, Dec. 5, 1959); *Ubusuna* for koto and other Japanese instruments (1962); *Ainu no Uta* for string orch. (Tokyo, May 23, 1964).

Kraft, William, American composer; b. Chicago, Sept. 6, 1923. He studied composition with Otto Luening and musicology with Paul Henry Lang at Columbia Univ. In his music he adopts pragmatic techniques containing elements of neo-classicism, impressionism and jazz, seasoned by a prudential application of serial procedures. As the principal drummer with the Los Angeles Philharmonic since 1962 and a virtuoso on all genera of instruments percussion, friction and concussion, he assigns important parts to the percussion section in his scores. Works: violin sonata (1951); string quartet (1954); *Nonet* for brass and percussion (1958); *Theme and Variations* for percussion quartet (1958); *3 Miniatures* for percussion and orch. (Los Angeles, Feb. 14, 1959); *Variations on a Folksong* for orch. (1960); Symph. for strings and percussion (1961); *Concerto Grosso* (1962; San Diego, Calif., March 22, 1963); *Concerto for 4 Percussion Soloists and Orchestra* (1964); *Momentum* for 8 percussionists (1966); *Encounters* for unaccompanied tuba (1966); *Contextures: Riots — Decade '60* (Los Angeles, April 4, 1968); *Triangles: a Concerto for percussion and 10 instruments* (1968); *Games: Collages No. 1 and No. 2* for wind instruments and percussion (1969); *Mobiles* for 10 instruments (1970).

Kramer, A. Walter. Died in New York, April 8, 1969.

Krapf, Gerhard, German-American organist and composer; b. Meissenheim-bei-Lahr, Dec. 12, 1924. He studied piano and organ in Karlsruhe; was in the German army during World War II and prisoner of war in Russia; upon release he went to America; studied composition with Paul A. Pisk at the Univ. of Redlands, Calif., graduating in 1951; then held positions as church organist and teacher of theory in Michigan, Missouri, Wyoming, etc. He has written a number of organ pieces and choral works.

Krásová, Marta, Czech contralto; b. Protovin, March 16, 1901; d. Vráz, near Beroun, Feb. 20, 1970. She studied voice in Prague and Vienna; made her debut in Bratislava in 1924; subsequently joined the National Theater in Prague; made highly successful guest appearances in Hamburg, Dresden, Madrid, Paris, Moscow and Warsaw; toured the United States in 1938-39. In 1935 she married the Czech composer Karel Boleslav Jirák. She achieved distinction in the principal parts in national Czech operas; was also notable as a Wagnerian singer.

Kreger, James, American violoncellist; b. Nashville, Tennessee, March 30, 1947. He received his early musical training taking piano lessons with local teachers. In 1965 the family moved to Beverly Hills, Calif., where he studied cello with Gabor Rejto; in 1966 he went to New York and enrolled at the Juilliard School of Music as a student of Leonard Rose and Harvey Shapiro. He also took courses at the Michigan State Univ., and played the cello in a student orchestra in Tanglewood. On March 16, 1971 he gave an auspicious recital in New York, eliciting high praise from hardened music critics.

Krein, Alexander Abramovitch. Place of death, Staraya Ruza, near Moscow (not Moscow itself).

Krein, Grigory Abramovitch. Died in Komarovo, near Leningrad, Jan. 6, 1955. Date of birth, March 18, 1879 (not April 15, 1880).

Kreisler, Fritz. Died in New York, Jan. 29, 1962. The name of his teacher was Jacques Auber (not Auer). At the age of 6 he was sent to study with Jacob Dont; then studied with Hellmesberger in Vienna (1882-85) and Massart in Paris (1885-87).

Kreissle von Hellborn, Heinrich. He was born on Jan. 19, 1822 (not 1812).

Krejčí, Iša. Died in Prague, March 6, 1968.

Kremlev, Yuly Anatolievitch, Russian musicologist and composer; b. Essentuki, June 19, 1908; d. in Leningrad, Feb. 19, 1971. He studied at the Leningrad Cons.; devoted himself mainly to musical biography; publ. monographs on Chopin (Moscow, 1949; revised ed. 1960), Grieg (Moscow, 1958) and Debussy (Moscow, 1964) and essays on esthetics. He also wrote a symphony, several piano sonatas and songs.

Krenek, Ernst. In 1963 he was awarded the Grand Prize of Austria. He became an American citizen in 1954; settled in Palm Springs, Calif. Add to works: *Ausgerechnet und verspielt,* comic opera (Vienna, June 27, 1962); *Der goldene Bock,* fantastic chamber opera (Hamburg, June 16, 1964, composer conducting); *Spass mit Karten,* ballet (1957); *Kette, Kreis und Spiegel,* symph. poem (1957); *Spiritus Intelligentiae, Sanctus* for voices and electronic sounds (1957); *Hexaeder,* 6 pieces for chamber ensemble (1958); *Missa duodecim tonorum* for mixed chorus and organ (1958); *Sestina* for soprano and small ensemble (1958); *Quaestio Temporis* for chamber orch. (Hamburg. Sept. 30, 1960); *La Corona,* cantata (1959); *From Three Make Seven,* for chamber orch. (1961); *5 + 1 (Alpbach Quintet;* 1962); opera *Das kommt davon, oder Wenn Sardakai auf Reisen geht (That's What Happened,* or, *If Sardakai Goes Traveling),* to his own libretto (Hamburg State Opera, June 27, 1970). Add to publications: *Gedanken Unterwegs* (Munich, 1959). His violin concerto was first performed in Dessau on Jan. 5, 1925 (not 1924). Bibl.: F. Saathen, *Ernst Krenek, Ein Essay* (Munich, 1959); Lothar Knessl, *Ernst Krenek* (Vienna, 1967).

Křička, Jaroslav. Died in Prague, Jan. 23, 1969.

Krieger, Armando, Argentine composer; b. Buenos Aires, May 7, 1940. He studied composition with Alberto Ginastera; gave piano concerts in programs of advanced modern music. In his compositions he adopts a serial technique in which rhythmic, melodic and harmonic elements follow a predetermined formula of contrasts. He has written a symph. for strings; a cantata; a concerto for two pianos and orch., etc.

Krieger, Edino, Brazilian composer; b. Brusque (Santa Catarina), March 17, 1928. He studied music with his father Aldo Krieger, director of the local Cons., and H. J. Koellreutter. In 1948 he studied with Aaron Copland at the Berkshire Music Center in Tanglewood; then at the Juilliard School of Music, N.Y., with Peter Mennin; also with Ernst Krenek in Brazil in 1952 and with Leonard Berkeley in London. He adopted the dodecaphonic method of composition, but in 1953 turned toward neoclassicism with national allusions. To the first period belong his *Epigramas* for piano; Sonatina for flute and piano; *Música de Câmara* for flute, trumpet, violin and timpani and *Melopeia* for voice, viola, oboe, saxophone and trombone; to the second, *Abertura sinfonica;* string quartet; 2 piano sonatas; *Concertante* for piano and orch.; *Fantasia* for orch; *Divertimento* for string orch.; *Brasiliana* for viola and orch.; and 4-hand piano sonata. However, he applies dodecaphonic techniques in his Brazilian work *Chôro* for flute and string orch. and in *Variações elementares* for chamber orch. (1965).

Krips, Josef. Was conductor of the San Francisco Symph. Orch. (1963-69); also guest conductor of the N.Y. Philharmonic and other American and European orchestras.

Křivinka, Gustav, Czech composer; b. Doubravice, April 24, 1928. He studied violin and composition in Brno, graduating in 1954 from the Brno Cons. He wrote 2 symphonies; 2 violin concertos; 2 piano concertos; several song cycles; chamber music.

Kroeger, Karl, American composer; b. Louisville, Kentucky, April 4, 1932. He studied music at the Univ. of Louisville and Univ. of Illinois; then moved to New York, where he became head of the Americana Collection of the New York Public Library's Music Division. In 1964 he was appointed composer-in-residence at the Univ. of Oregon. He has written symphonic and chamber music in a neo-classical manner.

Krohn, Ernst C., American musicologist; b. New York, Dec. 23, 1888. He settled in St. Louis in 1898; studied piano with his father and with Ottmar Moll, attaining a modicum of virtuosity; gave recitals and taught piano in various schools in St. Louis from 1909 to 1963; also composed songs and piano pieces. He was co-founder of the Bach Society of St. Louis in 1942. Publications: *A Century of Missouri Music* (St. Louis, 1924); *The History of Music: an Index to the Literature Available in a Selected Group of Musicological Publications* (St. Louis, 1952).

Krohn, Ilmari (Henrik Reinhold). Died in Helsinki, April 25, 1960.

Krombholc, Karlo, Hungarian - Serbian composer; b. Budapest, Dec. 20, 1905. He studied at the Vienna Academy of Music; was active as a concert pianist from 1927 to 1939; in 1945 he went to Yugoslavia and settled in Novi Sad as piano teacher. His works are influenced mainly by Béla Bartók, with ethnic modalities gadrooned by atonal extrapolations. Typical of these is his extensive piano work *Sazvezda* (*Constellation*; 1969). He also wrote orchestral works based on Hungarian and Balkan folk tunes.

Kromolicki, Joseph. Died in Berlin, Oct. 11, 1961.

Kroyer, Theodor. Place of death, Wiesbaden (not Cologne).

Krstič, Peter. Died in Belgrade, Jan. 21, 1957. First name Petar (not Peter). Title of his opera is *Zulumćar* (not *Zalumcar*); it was produced in Belgrade on Nov. 23, 1927.

Krul, Eli, Polish-American composer; b. Pabianice, Jan. 1, 1926; studied at the Hochschule für Musik in Munich (1945-49). In 1950 he settled in New York. His works include a string quartet (1958); *O Come, Let Us Sing* for chorus and organ (1960); *Alleluia* for chorus a cappella (1962), etc.

Krumpholtz, Johann Baptist. He was born in Budenice, near Zlonice (not Zlonice, near Prague).

Krupa, Gene, American jazz drummer; b. Chicago, Jan. 15, 1909. He joined a jazz band when still in his adolescence; made his first recording at 18, playing a battery of percussion which included the bass drum. In 1935 he became Benny Goodman's drummer and scaled the heights of the swing world; had his own band which he led intermittently from 1938 on. He toured Europe and the Orient and became internationally famous. A largely fictional film. 'The Gene Krupa Story,' was produced in 1959.

Kruyf, Ton de, Dutch composer; b. Leerdam, Oct. 3, 1937. He studied violin; self-taught in composition. In 1958 he adopted serial techniques. Works: *Sinfonietta* for strings (1958); *Mouvements Symphoniques* (1959); quartet for flute, violin, trumpet and bassoon (1960); Sonatina for flute and piano (1960); *Sgrafitti* for piano (1960); string quartet (1962); *Einst dem Grau . . .* for mezzo-soprano and chamber ensemble, after Paul Klee (1964); sonata for cello unaccompanied (1964).

Kubelík, Rafael. Was music director of the Covent Garden Opera, London (1955-58); in 1961 appointed conductor and music director of the Bavarian Radio Orch. in Munich; toured with it in Europe in 1962; was guest conductor in the U. S. in 1965. In 1972 he was appointed Music Director of the Metropolitan Opera in an artistic collaboration with the new general manager of the company, Goeran Gentele.

Kubik, Gail. In 1970 he joined the faculty of Scripps College, Claremont, Calif. Add to works: Symph. No. 2 (1955); Symph. No. 3 (1956); sonatina for clarinet and piano (1959); *Divertimento* No. 1 (1959); *Divertimento* No. 2 (1959); *Scenes for Orchestra* (1963); *A Record of Our Time,* 'a protest piece' for chorus, narrator, soloists and orch. (1970); *Divertimento* for piano, violin, and cello (1971). Kubik is the composer of the famous score for the animated film cartoon *Gerald McBoing-Boing* (1950; received the Motion Picture Academy Award, and also the British Film Institute Award) which launched a vogue of twangy rhinogenic tunes in popular music.

Kucharz, Johann Baptist. He studied at the Jesuit College in Königsgratz (not (Königgrätz).

Kunc, Božidar, Croatian-American pianist and composer; b. Zagreb, July 18, 1903; d. Detroit, April 1, 1964. He received his academic training at the Music Academy in Zagreb; in 1950 emigrated to the U. S. He was a brother of the singer Zinka Milanov. Works: *Poljima,* cycle of piano pieces (1931); *Mlado Lisce,* cycle of piano pieces (1933); piano concerto (Zagreb, April 27, 1934, composer soloist); 4 piano sonatas (1936-41); 2 violin concertos (1950, 1954); *3 Episodes* for piano and string orch. (1956); several symphonies; a string quartet; a piano trio; a piano quartet; songs. His music reveals some impressionistic traits. See K. Kovačević, *Hrvatski Kompozitori i njihova djela* (Zagreb, 1960).

Kupferman, Meyer, American composer; b. New York, July 3, 1926. He attended Queens College; in 1951 joined the staff of Sarah Lawrence College. His works include 4 symphonies, 5 string quartets, *Cycle of Infinities* (a number of pieces for various ensembles); *Concertino* for 11 brass instruments; *Sonata on Jazz Elements* for piano; *Tunnel of Love* for jazz combo (N. Y., May 22, 1971); several short operas: *In a Garden* (N. Y., Dec. 29, 1949); *The Curious Fern,* and *Voices for a Mirror* (both produced in N. Y. on June 5, 1957) and *Draagenfut Girl* (Bronx, N. Y., May 8, 1958).

Kurka, Robert, American composer of Czech descent; b. Cicero, Illinois, Dec. 22, 1921; d. New York City, Dec. 12, 1957. He studied violin with Kathleen Parlow and Hans Letz; composition with Otto Luening and Darius Milhaud; received a Guggenheim Fellowship in 1951 and 1952. His opera *The Good Soldier Schweik,* completed shortly before his untimely death of leukemia, was produced with extraordinary success at the New York City Center on April 23, 1958, and has since been widely performed in America and in Europe. His other works include 2 symphonies; serenade for chamber orch.; violin concerto; concerto for 2 pianos, string orch. and trumpet; concerto for marimba and orch.; *Ballad* for French horn and strings; 5 string quartets; piano trio; 4 violin sonatas; piano pieces; choruses.

Kurtág, György, Hungarian composer; b. Lugos (Rumania), Feb. 19, 1926. He studied piano and composition in Budapest, with Veress, Farkas, Kadosa and Leo Weiner. He writes mostly instrumental music, in a neo-classical idiom. Among his works are a viola concerto; a string quartet; a wind quintet; and a suite for violin and cimbalom.

Kurz, Selma. She was born on Nov. 15, 1874 (not 1875).

Kusevitsky, Moshe. Died at Kings Point, Long Island, N. Y., Aug. 23, 1966.

Kutev, Filip. In 1951 he became the leader of the Bulgarian ensemble of popular songs and dances, which he brought up to a high point of virtuosity; toured with it in Europe (1958) and in the U. S. (1963).

Kutschera, Elsa, Austrian operatic soprano; b. Vienna, June 1, 1867; d. there, Dec. 29, 1945. She studied with Pauline Viardot-Garcia and Padilla; sang in Berlin in 1892; made U. S. tours in 1895 and 1915.

Kuyper, Elisabeth. Died in Lugano, Feb. 26, 1953.

Küzdö, Victor. Died in Glendale, Calif., Feb. 24, 1966. According to his death certificate, he was 106 years old when he died, and was born on Sept. 18, 1859 (not 1869).

Kuznetzov, Konstantin Alexeyevitch. Died in Moscow on May 25, 1953 (not July, 1953).

Kvapil, Jaroslav. Died in Brno, Feb. 18, 1958.

Kvernadze, Alexander, Georgian composer; b. Signahi, Georgia, June 29, 1928. He studied with Andrey Balantchivadze at the Cons. of Tbilisi, graduating in 1953. Works: piano concerto (1950); violin concerto (1956); *Dance-Fantasy* for orch. (1959); a symphony (1961); violin pieces; film music.

L

Labey, Marcel. Died in Nancy, Nov. 25, 1968.

Labia, Maria. Died at Malcesine del Garda, Feb. 10, 1953.

Labunski, Felix. Retired from the College of Music of the Univ. of Cincinnati in 1964. Add to works: *Symphonic Dialogues* (Cincinnati, Feb. 9, 1961).

Lach, Robert. Died in Salzburg, Sept. 11, 1958.

Lachner, Ignaz. His opera *Die Regenbrüder* was produced on May 20, 1839 (not 1939).

Lacombe, Louis (Brouillon). The second name is **Trouillon** (not Brouillon). Add to bibl.: E. Jongleux, *Un grand musicien méconnu: Louis Lacombe* (Bourges, 1935).

Laderman, Ezra, American composer; b. New York, June 29, 1924. He studied at Brooklyn College and at Columbia Univ. with Otto Luening and Douglas Moore (composition) and Paul Henry Lang (musicology); received 3 Guggenheim grants. Works: the operas *Jacob and the Indians* (Woodstock, N. Y., July 26, 1957); *Sarah,* television opera (N. Y., Nov. 30, 1958); *Goodbye to the Clown* (N. Y., May 22, 1960); *The Hunting* *of the Snark,* children's opera after Lewis Carroll (N. Y., March 25, 1961); *Galileo Galilei,* opera oratorio for television (N. Y., May 14, 1967); *Magic Prison* for two narrators and orch. (N. Y., June 12, 1967); a symphony; *Concerto for Orchestra;* violin concerto; *Celestial Bodies* for flute and strings; *Double Helix* for flute, oboe, and strings; *Nonet* for wind instruments; *Octet* for wind instruments; 2 piano sonatas. He also wrote the score for the film *The Eleanor Roosevelt Story* which won an Oscar. His cantata *And David Wept* was produced by CBS Television in N. Y. on April 10, 1971.

Laistner, Max, German musician; b. Stuttgart, Feb. 16, 1853; d. London, July 3, 1917. He settled in London where he founded the first German Glee Club; wrote a number of choral works. His arrangement of Chopin's 'Minute Waltz' is included in the anthology, *13 Transcriptions of Chopin's Waltz in D-flat, Op. 64,* edited by D. M. Garvelmann (N. Y., 1969).

Lajtha, László. Died in Budapest, Feb. 16, 1963. Add to works: Symph. No. 6 (Brussels, Dec. 12, 1960); Symph. No. 7 (Paris, April 26, 1958); Symph. No. 8 (Budapest, May 21, 1960); Symph. No. 9 (posthumous; Paris, May 2, 1963).

Lake, George Ernest, English organist and composer; b. London, May 29, 1854; d. there, March 15, 1893. He served as church organist in London and Edinburgh; wrote anthems and hymns; also a musical comedy, *Sweepstakes* (London, May 21, 1891).

Lalo, Charles. Died in Paris, April 1, 1953.

LaMarchina, Robert, American cellist and conductor; b. New York, Sept. 3, 1928. He studied cello with his father; appeared as a wunderkind in public; continued his studies with Gregor Piatigorsky and Emanuel Feuermann; in 1944 played in the N.B.C. Symphony under Toscanini; later joined the Los Angeles Philharmonic; sporadically conducted orchestras near and around Los Angeles; ultimately became primarily a conductor. In 1967 he was engaged as conductor of the Honolulu Symphony Orchestra.

La Montaine, John, American composer; b. Oak Park, Illinois, March 17, 1920. He studied piano with Rudolph Ganz in Chicago and in Rochester, at the Eastman School of Music, with Howard Hanson and Bernard Rogers; at the Juilliard School, New York, with Bernard Wagenaar, and with Nadia Boulanger. He received 2 Guggenheim Fellowships in composition (1959 and 1960); in 1962 served as Composer in Residence at the American Academy in Rome; was visiting prof. at the Eastman School of Music in 1964-65. He received the Pulitzer Prize for his piano concerto in 1959. Works: piano concerto (Washington, Nov. 25, 1958); *Jubilant Overture; Colloquy* for string orch.; Symph. No. 1; *From Sea to Shining Sea* for orch.; *Novellis, Novellis,* a Christmas pageant opera (Washington Cathedral, Dec. 24, 1961); *The Shepherdes Playe,* opera television production (Washington, Dec 24, 1967); *Erode the Great,* cantata (Washington, Dec. 30, 1969); also *Birds of Paradise* for piano and orch.; *Te Deum; Songs of the Rose of Sharon* for soprano and orch.; cello sonata; string quartet; organ pieces; songs.

Lamote de Grignon, Ricard. Died in Barcelona, Feb. 5, 1962.

Lampe, Walther, German pianist, composer and pedagogue; b. Leipzig, April 28, 1872; d. Munich, Jan. 23, 1964. He studied piano with Clara Schumann; composition with Knorr in Frankfurt and with Humperdinck in Berlin; was prof. of piano at the Munich Academy of Music from 1920 to 1937. His edition of Mozart piano sonatas (2 vols., Munich, 1954), according to the original manuscripts, is valuable. Among his works are piano pieces and songs.

Lancen, Serge Jean Mathieu, French composer and pianist; b. Paris, Nov. 5, 1922. He studied at the Paris Cons. with Aubin, Büsser and Noël Gallon. During World War II he went to Switzerland; returning to Paris he continued his studies; obtained Premier Prix de Rome for composition in 1949. Works: *La mauvaise conscience,* chamber opera (Paris, Jan. 4, 1964); *Les Prix,* ballet (Bordeaux, March 13, 1954); piano concerto (1947); concerto for mouth harmonica written for Larry Adler (1955); concerto for double-bass and orch. (1960); *Manhattan Symphony* (1962); *Concert à six* for 6 clarinets (1962); light pieces for radio: *Cadence, Promenade, Bahamas, Brazilia, En route for Monte-Carlo, Suite Gastronomique, Futilités;* also *Marche triomphale* commissioned by the convention of the League against Rheumatism (Amsterdam, June 15, 1955).

Landau, Siegfried. Add to works: *The Sons of Aaron,* opera on a biblical subject (Scarsdale, N. Y., Feb. 28, 1959).

Landon, H. C. Robbins. Add to books: *Beethoven, Documents and Pictures* (N. Y.,

1970); *Essays on the Viennese Classical Style* (N. Y., 1970).

Landowska, Wanda. Died in Lakeville, Conn., Aug. 16, 1959. A collection of her articles was publ. posthumously under the title *Landowska on Music,* edited and translated by Denise Restout and Robert Hawkins (N.Y., 1964).

Landowski, Marcel. Add to works: *Le Ventriloque,* lyric comedy (Paris, Feb. 8, 1957); *Les Adieux,* one-act lyric drama (Paris, Oct. 8, 1960); *L'Orage,* symph. poem (1961); *L'Opéra de poussière,* opera in two acts (Avignon, Oct. 25, 1962); *Les Notes de nuit* for narrator and orch. (Boulogne, Dec. 16, 1962); piano concerto No. 2 (Paris, Feb. 28, 1964); Symph. No. 2 (Strasbourg, June 24, 1965); Symph. No. 3 (1965); concerto for flute and string orch. (1968). See A. Goléa, *Marcel Landowski: L'Homme et son œuvre* (Paris, 1969).

Landowski, W. L. Died in Paris, April 18, 1959.

Landré, Guillaume (Louis Frédéric). Died in Amsterdam, Nov. 6, 1968. Add to works: Symph. No. 4 (Stockholm, June 5, 1956); clarinet concerto (Amsterdam, June 25, 1959) *Jean Levecq,* opera (Amsterdam, June 16, 1965); *La Symphonie pastorale,* opera (Rouen, March 31, 1968).

Lane, Eastwood. Died in Central Square, Oswego County, N. Y., Jan. 22, 1951.

Lane, Louis, American conductor; b. Eagle Pass, Texas, Dec. 25, 1923. He studied at the Univ. of Texas, the Eastman School of Music and at the Berkshire Music Center in Tanglewood. In 1947 he won a competition to become apprentice conductor to George Szell, the musical director of the Cleveland Orch.; in 1956 he was appointed assistant conductor to Szell. In 1959 he was appointed regular conductor of the Akron, Ohio Symph. Orch. In addition, he appeared as guest conductor with the Chicago Symph. Orch. and with the Detroit Symph. Orch. During the tour of the Cleveland Orch. in Europe, including Russia, in 1965, he conducted concerts in several European countries. He has generally been commended for his workmanlike competence in leading a varied repertory of orchestral works.

Lang, Margaret Ruthven. She safely passed her 103rd birthday on Nov. 27, 1970.

Lang, Paul Henry. Resigned as music critic of the N. Y. 'Herald Tribune' in 1963. In 1970 he retired from Columbia University. Add to publications: *A Pictorial History of Music* (with O. Bettmann; N. Y., 1960); edited *The Creative World of Mozart* (N.Y., 1963); edited (with Nathan Broder) *Contemporary Music in Europe, a Comprehensive Survey* (N.Y., 1965; a reprint of the semicentennial issue of the 'Mus. Quarterly'). He publ. an important bio-musical volume, *George Frideric Handel* (N. Y., 1965).

Lang, Walter. Died in Baden, Switzerland, March 17, 1966.

Lange, Hans. Died in Albuquerque, New Mexico, Aug. 13, 1960. Conducted Albuquerque Symph. Orch. from 1951 to 1958.

Lanza, Mario. Died in Rome, Oct. 7, 1959.

La Prade, Ernest. Died in Sherman, Conn. April 20, 1969.

La Presle, Jacques de. Died in Paris, May 6, 1969.

Laquai, Reinhold. Died in Oberrieden, Oct. 3, 1957.

Lara, Agustín, Mexican composer of popular songs; b. Tlacotalpán, Oct. 14, 1900; d. Mexico City, Nov. 5, 1970. He learned to play piano by ear; earned his living as an entertainer in a Mexican house of tolerance, where he wrote his first successful song *Rosa;* an encounter with a woman who impulsively slashed his face during an altercation, inspired him to write a paean to womanhood, *Morucha,* which acquired great popularity. His other songs that became famous are *Tus Pupilas, Gotas de Amor,* and the most famous, *Mujer.*

Lara-Bareiro, Carlos, Paraguayan composer; b. Capiatá, March 6, 1914. He played in the boy scout band conducted by his father; then studied violin in Asunción and in Rio de Janeiro; during his stay in Brazil he also took lessons in composition and conducting. Returning to Paraguay in 1951 he organized in Asunción the Symph. Orch. of the Association of Musicians of Paraguay. Eventually he moved to Buenos Aires. His works reflect the modes and moods of Paraguayan folk music. He wrote several symphonic suites on Paraguayan themes and a piano concerto.

Laredo, Jaime, Bolivian violinist; b. Cochabamba, June 7, 1941. He was sent to the U. S. as a child; studied with Josef Gingold in Cleveland and with Ivan Galamian at the Curtis Institute in Philadelphia. In 1959, a week before his 18th birthday, he won the International Music Competition in Brussels under the auspices of Queen Elisabeth of Belgium among 37 contestants; this was the beginning of a brilliant career; he has since appeared as soloist with orchestras in Europe and America with fine success. The Bolivian government issued in his honor a series of airmail stamps with his picture, bearing the notes A, D, C in the treble clef, spelling his name in Latin notation (La-Re-Do).

La Rotella, Pasquale, Italian composer and conductor; b. Bitonto, Feb. 26, 1880; d. Bari, March 20, 1963. He studied in Naples; was choral conductor at the Bari Cathedral (1902-13); from 1934-49, taught at the Liceo Musicale there; toured Italy as opera conductor. His works include the operas *Ivan* (Bari, Jan. 20, 1900); *Dea* (Bari, April 11, 1903); *Fasma* (Milan, Nov. 28, 1908); *Corsaresca* (Rome, Nov. 13, 1933); *Manuela* (Nice, March 4, 1948); and much sacred music.

Larrocha, Alicia de, Spanish pianist; b. Barcelona, May 23, 1923. She studied piano with Frank Marshall and theory with Ricardo Lamote de Grignon. She made her first public appearance at the age of 5; was soloist with the Orquesta Sinfónica of Madrid at the age of 11. In 1940 she launched her career in earnest; from 1947 made extensive concert tours in Europe and America. Her interpretations of Spanish music have evoked universal admiration for their authentic quality, but she has also been exuberantly praised by sober-minded critics for her impeccable taste and exquisitely polished technique in classical works. She enjoys a fine reputation as a pedagogue; conducts regular classes at the Academia Marshall in Barcelona.

LaRue, (Adrian) Jan (Pieters), American musicologist; b. in Kisaran, Sumatra, July 31, 1918, of native American parentage (his ancestor was a French Huguenot who fled first to the Palatinate and then came to America, landing in Massachusetts in 1670; La Rue's parents spent three years in Indonesia where his father served as a botanist and developed a basic budding process used on rubber trees). He studied at Harvard Univ. (Ph.D., 1952) and at Princeton Univ.; taught at Wellesley College; in 1957 became prof. at N. Y. Univ. His dual specialties are 18th-century music and style analysis. He prepared a thematic catalogue of about 10,000 entries on symphonies and instrumental concertos of the classic period; contributed to various publications a number of original articles bringing informing light on obscure subjects. His most important papers include: *Native Music in Okinawa* ('Mus. Quarterly,' April 1946); *The Okinawan Notation System* ('Journal of the American Musicological Society,' 1951); *Die Datierung von Wasserzeichen im 18. Jahrhundert* (*'Kongress-Bericht,'* Mozart-Jahr, 1956; also in English, *Watermarks and Musicology,* in 'Acta Musicologica,' 1961); *Bifocal Tonality; An Explanation for Ambiguous Baroque Cadences* ('Essays on Music in Honor of Archibald T. Davison,' Cambridge, Mass., 1957); *Harmonic Rhythm in the Beethoven Symphonies* ('Music Review,' 1957); *Significant and Coincidental Resemblance between Classical Themes* ('Journal of American Musicological Society,' 1961). He publ. *Guidelines for Style Analysis* (N. Y., 1970); was editor of the *Report of the Eighth Congress of the International Musicological Society, New York 1961* (Kassel, 1961); co-editor of the Festschrift for Otto Erich Deutsch (Kassel, 1963) and of the Festschrift for Gustave Reese (N. Y., 1965). His dissertation, *The Okinawan Classical Songs,* is scheduled for publication by the Harvard Univ. Press (1973). In 1966-68 he was president of the American Musicological Society.

La Rue, Pierre de. The number of his known Masses is 33; wrote motets and chansons, not madrigals. He was born, in all probability, between 1455 and 1460.

Lassus, Roland de. Add to bibl.: H. Leuchtmann, *Die musikalischen Wortausdeutungen in den Motetten des Magnum Opus Musicum von Orlando di Lasso* (Strasbourg, 1959).

Latilla, Gaetano. Date of birth, Jan. 21 (not Jan. 12), 1711; date of death, Jan. 15, 1788 (not 1791).

Lattuada, Felice. Died in Milan, Nov. 2, 1962. Add to works: opera *Caino* (Milan, Jan. 10, 1957).

Laub, Ferdinand. Date of death, March 18 (not March 17), 1875.

Lauber, Joseph. Date of birth, Dec. 27 (not 25), 1864; date of death May 28 (not 27), 1952.

Lauro, Antonio, Venezuelan guitarist and composer; b. Ciudad Bolívar, Aug. 3, 1917. He studied in Caracas; became a proficient guitar player; was soloist in the first performance of his guitar concerto (Caracas, July 25, 1956). He wrote many pieces for guitar, a choral symph. poem *Cantacharo,* several symph. suites, choruses and songs.

Lavalle-García, Armando, Mexican composer; b. Ocotlán, Jalisco, Nov. 23, 1924. He studied violin and theory at the National Cons. of Music in Mexico City; became a violinist in the National Symph. Orch. of Mexico. A competent musician, he writes in a fairly effective modern style. Among his works are a symph. poem *Mi Viaje* (1950); viola concerto (1965); violin concerto (1966); violin sonata (1966); oboe sonata (1967); and a trio for oboe, cello and bassoon accompanied by percussion (1969).

Lavista, Mario, Mexican composer; b. Mexico City, April 3, 1943. He studied harmony with Rodolfo Halffter; attended classes and seminars of Karlheinz Stockhausen and Henri Pousseur in Darmstadt and Cologne. Upon return to Mexico he joined the faculty of the National Cons. of Music in Mexico City. He writes in a decidedly modern manner employing constructivist techniques and electronic devices. Among his works are *Sinfonía Modal* (1965); *Ondina* for orch. (1966); *Divertimento* for wind instruments (1968); *Diacronía* for string quartet (1969); *Kronos* for alarm clocks, loudspeakers and magnetic tapes with an indeterminate chronometric duration from 5 to 1,440 minutes (1969).

Lavry, Marc. Died in Haifa, March 20, 1967. Add to works: *Tamar and Judah,* opera in the form of a series of cantillations with homophonic instrumental accompaniment (1958; first performed, in concert form, at the Jewish Arts Festival of Congregation Rodeph Sholom in New York, March 22, 1970).

Lawton, Dorothy. Died in Bournemouth, England, Feb. 19, 1960. Returned to England in 1946 (not 1945).

Layton, Billy Jim, American composer; b. Corsicana, Texas, Nov. 14, 1924. He studied at the New England Cons. with Carl McKinley, graduating in 1948; then at Yale Univ. with Quincy Porter and at Harvard Univ. with Walter Piston. He won the American Prix de Rome in 1954; returned to U. S. in 1957; appointed member of faculty at Harvard in 1960. Works: *An American Portrait,* a symph. overture; *3 Dylan Thomas Poems* for mixed choir and brass sextet; string quartet; piano pieces.

Lazarof, Henri, Bulgarian-American composer; b. Sofia, April 12, 1932. He left Bulgaria in 1948 for Palestine, and studied composition with Paul Ben-Haim in Jerusalem; then took courses with Goffredo Petrassi at Santa Cecilia in Rome (1955-57). He received a study fellowship from Brandeis Univ., where he studied with Harold Shapero (1957-59); subsequently became a member of the faculty at the Univ. of Calif., Los Angeles. His music is marked by formal solidity; in his later works he applies serial techniques. Works: piano concerto (1957); *Piccola Serenata* for orch. (Boston, June 14, 1959); viola concerto (Monaco, Feb. 20, 1962; 1st prize at the International Competition of Monaco); concerto for piano and 20 instruments (Milan Radio, May 28, 1963); *Odes* for orch. (1963); *Concertino da camera* for woodwind quintet (1959); *Tempi Concertati,* a double concerto for violin, viola and chamber orch. (1964); 2 string quartets (1956, 1962); string trio (1957); sonata for violin solo (1958); *Inventions* for viola and piano (1962); *Asymptotes* for flute and vibraphone (1963); *Quantetti* (a telescoped title for 'Quattro Canti per Quartetto di pianoforte') scored for 4 pianos (1964); *Structures Sonores* for orch. (1966; received first International Prize of the City of Milan, La Scala Award); *Rhapsody* for violin and piano (1966); *Espaces* for 10 instruments (1966); *Octet* for wind instruments (1967); *Mutazione* for orch. (1967); Concerto for cello and orch. (1968; Oslo, Norway, Sept. 12, 1969); *Omaggio* chamber concerto for 19 players (1968); *Divertimenti* for 5 players (1969); *Textures* for piano and 5 ensembles (1970); *Continuum* for strings (1970).

Lear, Evelyn, American soprano; b. New York, Jan. 18, 1930. She studied voice at Hunter College and later at the Juilliard School of Music. In 1957 she went to Berlin on a Fulbright grant and studied there at the Hochschule für Musik. In 1958 she was engaged by the Deutsche Staatsoper in Berlin; in 1962 she sang the role of Lulu in Alban Berg's unfinished opera in Vienna. Returning to America she sang Marie in Berg's *Wozzeck* at the Chicago Lyric Opera in 1966. She made her Metropolitan Opera debut in the first performance of Marvin David Levy's opera *Mourning Becomes Electra* on March 16, 1967. She continued her appearances in Europe, both in classical and in modern repertory, earning for herself a firm reputation as a dramatic singer and interpretive artist. She is married to the American baritone Thomas Stewart.

Lebert, Siegmund. His real name was Sigmund Levi (not Levy); he was born on Dec. 12, 1821 (not 1822).

Lebeuf, Abbé Jean. Place of death, Paris (not Auxerre).

Le Caine, Hugh, Canadian acoustician; b. Port Arthur, Ontario, May 27, 1914. He held a B.Sc. degree at Queen's Univ., Kingston, Ontario in 1938 and M.Sc. in 1939; obtained his Ph.D. in nuclear physics from the Univ. of Birmingham, England, in 1952; cooperated with the first Canadian Electronic Music Studio at the Univ. of Toronto in 1959, and at McGill Univ. in Montreal in 1964; exhibited electronic music instruments at Expo '67 in Montreal. He contributed papers on electronic music to various scholarly journals; realized a number of electronic compositions for the radio and television studios in Toronto and Montreal, among them *Dripsody* (1959), *Alchemy* (1964) and *Perpetual Motion* for data systems computer (1970).

Leclair, Jean Marie. Add to bibl.: G. Nutting, *J.-M. Leclair,* in the 'Mus. Quarterly' (Oct. 1964).

Lecuna, Juan, Venezuelan composer; b. Valencia, Carabobo, Nov. 20, 1894; d. Rome, April 15, 1954. He studied in Caracas; later went to the U.S.; took lessons with Gustave Strube in Baltimore. He also engaged in diplomatic service, and during the last years of his life was a member of the Venezuelan legation at the Vatican. He wrote a *Suite Venezolana* for 4 guitars; a string quartet; a piano concerto and a suite of 4 Venezuelan dances for piano.

Lecuona, Ernesto. Died in Santa Cruz de Tenerife, Canary Islands, Nov. 29, 1963.

Ledbetter, Huddie (Leadbelly), American Negro folk singer and guitarist; b. Mooringsport, Louisiana, 1888; d. N.Y., Dec. 6, 1949. He never had an education but possessed a genuine talent for folksong singing. He was jailed for murder in 1918; released in 1925; served another term for attempted homicide (1930-34) and for assault (1939-40). After release, he played and sang in night clubs. The authenticity of his performance gives him a historic niche in folksong history. A cult arose around his name after his death; the 'hootenanny' movement was much influenced by his style.

Le Duc, Simon, French composer; b. about 1745; d. Paris, Jan. 20, 1777. He studied violin with Gaviniès; made his debut as a soloist on Sept. 8, 1763 at the Concert Spirituel in Paris. He subsequently became active as a composer of instrumental music and a publisher. His works comprise 3 symphonies, a *Symphonie Concertante* and concertante string trios with orchestra. See Barry S. Brook, *Simon Le Duc l'ainé, a French Symphonist at the time of Mozart,* in the 'Mus. Quarterly' (Oct. 1962).

Leedy, Douglas, American composer; b. Portland, Oregon, March 3, 1938. He studied at Pomona College (B.A., 1959) and at the Univ. of California, Berkeley (M.A., 1962). He played the French horn in the Oakland, Calif., Symph. Orch. and at the San Francisco Opera (1961-65); 1965-66 held a U.S. grant for study in Poland; was on the faculty of the Univ. of California, Los Angeles (1967-70). He cultivates avant-garde methods of electronic application to mixed media. His works include: *Exhibition Music* (1965; continued indefinitely); *Decay,* theater piece for piano, Wagner tuba and tape (1965); *Antifonia* for brass quartet (1965); *Usable Music I for Very Small Instruments with Holes* (1966); *Usable Music II* for brass (1966); *Teddy Bears Picnic,* audiotactile electronic theater piece (1968); *Ave Maris Stella* for soprano, instrumental trio, organ and electronic sound (1968); *88 is Great,* theater piece for many-handed piano (1968); *The Electric Zodiac,* electronic music (1969); *Entropical Paradise: Six Sonic Environments* for electronic recordings (1970); *Gloria* for soprano, chorus and instruments (1970).

Lees, Benjamin, American composer; b. Harbin, Manchuria, Jan. 8, 1924, of Russian parents. He was brought to the U. S. as an infant; studied piano in San Francisco and Los Angeles; served in the U. S. Army (1942-45); then enrolled at the Univ. of Southern Calif., Los Angeles, studying theory, harmony and composition with Halsey Stevens, Ingolf Dahl and Ernst Kanitz; also took private lessons with George Antheil. In 1955 he received a Guggenheim Fellowship for travel in Europe, and in 1956 a Fulbright Fellowship for Finland. His compositions are marked by the classical solidity of form and polyphonic texture; his predilection is for purely instrumental music. Works: Sonata for 2 pianos (N. Y., Nov. 8, 1952); *Profile for Orchestra* (1952); string quartet No. 1 (1952); *Declamations* for string orch. and piano (1953); Symph. No. 1 (1953); *Fantasia* for piano (1954); violin sonata (1954); *Kaleidoscopes* for piano (1954); *Toccata* for piano (1953); string quartet No. 2 (1955); piano concerto No. 1 (Vienna, April 26, 1956); Symph. No. 2 (Louisville, Dec. 3, 1958); *Concerto for Orchestra* (1959); violin concerto (1960); *Visions of Poets,* dramatic cantata (1961); concerto for oboe and orch. (1963); *Concerto* for string quartet and orch. (Kansas City, Jan. 19, 1965); piano concerto No. 2 (1966; Boston, March 15, 1968); Symph. No. 3 (Detroit, Jan. 16, 1969); *Medea of Corinth* for vocal quartet and woodwind quintet (1970).

Leeuw, Ton de, Dutch composer; b. Rotterdam, Nov. 16, 1926. He studied composition in Paris with Messiaen and Thomas de Hartmann; became interested in musical folklore; made a tour of India in 1961 to collect materials. His main interests, however, lie in the field of experimental music. Among his principal works, *Ombres,* for orch. with a large percussion section, was performed at the Amsterdam Festival of Contemporary Music on June 8, 1963. His opera, *De Droom (The Dream),* was produced at the Holland Festival (Amsterdam, June 16, 1965).

LeFanu, Nicola, British composer, daughter of Elizabeth Maconchy; b. Wickham Bishops, Essex, April 28, 1947. She studied music at St. Hilda's College, Oxford (B.A., 1968); also took private lessons with Goffredo Petrassi in Italy and with Thea Musgrave and Peter Maxwell Davies in England. Although she scrutinized her mother's works with great interest, she never had formal instruction from her. Brought up in an extremely cultured and sophisticated environment (her father William LeFanu is well known in the literary world), she absorbed the seemingly conflicting and quaquaversal musical influences with elegance and ease; her own style of composition is that of median vigesimosecular modernism, without prejudice even in regard to overt triadic harmonies. In 1970 she won first prize at the BBC National Competition for her *Variations* for oboe quartet (1968). Her other works include *Soliloquy* for oboe solo (1965); *Preludio* for chamber orch. (1967); *Chiaroscuro* for piano (1969); *Quartettsatz* for string quartet (1970); quintet for clarinet and strings (1970).

Leftwich, Vernon, American composer; b. London, June 19, 1881. He studied piano, organ and composition at the Guildhall School of Music in London; emigrated to the U.S.; settled in Los Angeles. His instrumental music is evolved in modern polyphony with firm tonal foundation. Works: *Cremation of Care,* symph. poem (1929); *Sunken Ships* for orch. (1939); cello concerto (1941); *Seven Ages of Man* for baritone and orch. (1942); 4 symph. suites; *Musical Forum* for 9 instruments; string quartet; piano quartet; string quintet; several pieces for brass quintet; cello sonata; choruses; songs; piano pieces.

Leginska, Ethel. Died in Los Angeles, Feb. 26, 1970.

Legrand, Michel, French composer of popular music; b. Paris, Feb. 24, 1932. He entered the Paris Cons. at the age of 11; still a student, began making professional jazz arrangements; wrote for radio, television and the cinema. His inventive score for the motion picture *Les Parapluies de Cherbourg* (1965), written throughout in sing-song fashion, enjoyed merited critical applause.

Lehár, Franz. Add to bibl.: *Katalog der Bühnenwerke von Franz Lehár* (Vienna, 1955); B. Grun, *Gold and Silver: The Life and Times of Franz Lehár* (London, 1970).

Lehmann, Hans Ulrich, Swiss composer; b. Biel, May 4, 1937. He studied cello in Biel and music theory in Zürich; took courses in advanced composition at seminars of Pierre Boulez and Karlheinz Stockhausen in Basel (1960-63). In 1964 he was appointed to the faculty of the Musik-Akademie in Basel; from 1969, teaching music theory at the Univ. of Zürich. As a composer, he adheres to progressive neo-classicism with serial connotations. Works: *Structures transparentes* for piano, viola and clarinet (1961); *Quanti I* for flute and chamber ensemble (1962); *Régions pour un flûtiste* (1963); *Episoden* for wind quintet (1964); *Mosaik* for clarinet (1964); *Komposition für 19,* for a chamber group (1965); *Spiele* for oboe and harp (1965); *Rondo* for voice and orch. (1967); *Instants* for piano (1968); *Konzert* for 2 wind instruments and strings (1969); *Régions III* for clarinet, trombone and cello (1970); *Monodie* for a wind instrument (1970).

Lehmann, Lotte. The title of her autobiography is *Anfang und Aufstieg* (not *Aufsteig*). She publ. a book of reminiscences, *Five Operas and Richard Strauss* (N.Y., 1964). Bibl.: B. W. Wessling, *Lotte Lehmann, mehr als eine Sängerin* (Salzburg, 1969).

Leibowitz, René. He publ. (in collaboration with Konrad Wolff) *Erich Itor Kahn, un grand représentant de la musique contemporaine* (Paris, 1958); composed *Espagnols à Venise,* opéra-bouffe (Grenoble, Jan. 27, 1970).

Leigh, Walter. Add place of birth: London.

Leighton, Kenneth, English composer; b. Wakefield, Yorkshire, Oct. 2, 1929. He enrolled at the Queen's College, Oxford, to study classics and music (B. Mus., 1951); later took courses with Goffredo Petrassi in Rome. In 1956 he was appointed lecturer in composition at the Univ. of Edinburgh; in 1960, was made a Doctor of Music in the Univ. of Oxford. Works: *Symphony for Strings* (1965); 2 piano concertos; violin concerto; cello concerto; concerto for viola, harp, timpani and strings; 2 string quartets; piano quintet; *Fantasia contrappuntistica* for piano; 2 violin sonatas; a number of sacred cantatas and other choral music.

Leinsdorf, Erich. Was conductor of the Boston Symph. Orch. from 1962 till 1969.

Lemacher, Heinrich. Died in Cologne, March 16, 1966.

Lemit, William, French ethnomusicologist; b. Paris, Dec. 15, 1908; d. there (by suicide), Aug. 21, 1966. He was entirely autodidact in music; traveled through the French countryside collecting popular songs. He publ. several song anthologies of French children's rhymes, among them *La Vie du garçon* (1950); *Les Jeux chantés enfantins du folklore français* (1957).

Lennon, John (Winston), English rock 'n' roll singer, guitarist, poet and instinctive composer, member of the celebrated rock group 'The Beatles'; b. Liverpool, Oct. 9, 1940, during a German air raid on the city. He was educated by an aunt after his parents became separated; played the mouth organ as a child; later learned the guitar; was encouraged to become a musician by the conductor of a Liverpool-Edinburgh bus. Emotionally rocked over by Elvis Presley's animal magnetism he became infatuated with American popular music. With three other rock-crazed Liverpudlians, Paul McCartney, George Harrison and Stuart Sutcliffe, he formed a pop combo. Inspired by the success of a local group, 'The Crickets,' Lennon hit upon the name 'The Beatles' which possessed the acoustical ring of the coleopterous insect, beetle, and the rock-associated beat. 'The Beatles' opened at the pseudo-exotic Casbah Club in Liverpool in 1959; soon moved to the more prestigious Cavern Club, where they co-opted Pete Best as a drummer. In 1960 they played in Hamburg, scoring a gratifyingly vulgar success with the beer-sodden customers by their loud, electrically amplified sound. Back in England, 'The Beatles' crept on to fame. In 1961 they were taken up by a pre-cognitive promoter Brian Epstein who launched an extensive publicity campaign to put them over the footlights. Sutcliffe died of a brain hemorrhage in 1962. Pete Best left the group and was replaced by Richard Starkey, whose 'nom-de-beatle' became Ringo Starr. The quartet opened at the London Palladium in 1963 and drove the youthful audience to a frenzy, a scene that was to be repeated in America, in Europe, in Japan and in Australia. After a period of shocked recoil, the British establishment acknowledged the beneficent contribution of 'The Beatles' to British art and the Exchequer. In 1965 Queen Elizabeth II bestowed upon them the Order of the British Empire. Although American in origin, the type of popular music plied by John Lennon and 'The Beatles' as a group, has a peculiarly English folk-like flavor. The meter is square; the main beat is accentuated; syncopation is at a minimum; the harmony is modal, with a lowered subdominant in major keys as a constantly present feature; a propensity for plagal cadences and a proclivity for consecutive triadic progressions create at times an almost hymnal mood. But professional arrangers employed by 'The Beatles' invest their bland melodies in raucous dissonances; electronic amplification makes the music of 'The Beatles' the loudest in the world. The lyrics, most of them written by John Lennon and Paul McCartney, are distinguished by suggestive allusions, sensuous but not flagrantly erotic, anarchistic but not destructive, cynical but also humane. There are covert references to psychedelic drugs. 'The Beatles' produced four highly original films: *A Hard Day's Night, Help!, Yellow Submarine* and *Let It Be.* The most successful individual songs in the Beatles' repertory are: *Love Me Do, I Want to Hold Your Hand, Can't Buy Me Love, Ticket to Ride, Day Tripper, All My Loving, I Wanna Be Your Man, And I Love Her, Eight Days a Week, Yesterday, Michelle, Eleanor Rigby, With a Little Help from My Friends, Sergeant Pepper's Lonely Hearts Club Band, Magical Mystery Tour, Lady Madonna, All My Loving, You're Going to Lose That Girl, Norwegian Wood, Good Day Sunshine, Hey Jude;* also title songs of the films. Bibl.: Hunter Davies, *The Beatles,* 'the authorized biography' (N.Y., 1968).

Leo, Leonardo. Add to bibl.: G. A. Pastore, *Leonardo Leo* (Galatina, 1957).

Leoncavallo, Ruggiero. First name, Ruggero, rather than Ruggiero, although the latter is widely used in printed editions of his works. The title of his famous opera is *Pagliacci* (not *I Pagliacci*).

Leonhardt, Gustav, Dutch organist and harpsichord player; b. 'sGraveland, May 30,

1928; studied in Holland and Switzerland; toured widely in Europe; made 6 tours in America as performer and lecturer. He edited collections of keyboard music; publ. a controversial thesis, *The Art of Fugue —Bach's Last Harpsichord Work* (The Hague, 1952).

Leonova, Darya Mikhailovna. She was born in Vyshny-Volotchok (not Tver). Exact date of birth, March 9, 1829. Add to bibl.: V. Yakovlev, *D. M. Leonova* (Moscow, 1950).

Leplin, Emanuel, American composer; b. San Francisco, Oct. 3, 1917. He studied violin with Georges Enesco; conducting with Pierre Monteux; composition with Roger Sessions. He was a violinist in the San Francisco Symph. Orch. from 1946 to 1954, when he was stricken with paralytic polio. In spite of this handicap, he continued to compose. Works: *Galaxy* for 2 cellos and orch. (1942); *Cosmos* for violin and orch. (1949); 2 symph. poems, *Landscapes* and *Skyscrapers* (San Francisco, May 5, 1960); a symph. (San Francisco, Jan. 3, 1962); 3 string quartets; chamber music for various instrumental combinations; piano pieces.

Le Roux, Maurice, French composer and conductor; b. Paris, Feb. 6, 1923. He studied with Messiaen at the Paris Cons.; then worked at the electronic studios of the Radiodiffusion Française. In his music he adopts serial procedures. In 1952 he embarked on a conductor's career. Works: *Le Petit Prince,* ballet (1950); *Sables,* ballet (1956); *Le Cercle des Métamorphoses* for orch. (1953); *Trois visages* for trumpet and piano; *Pièces dodécaphoniques* for piano; songs. He publ. *Introduction à la Musique contemporaine* (Paris, 1947); *Claudio Monteverdi* (Paris, 1951).

Lesur, Daniel. Add to works: *Andrea del Sarto,* opera (Marseille, Jan. 24, 1969).

Letz, Hans. Died in Hackensack, New Jersey, Nov. 14, 1969.

Lev, Ray. Died in New York, May 20, 1968.

Levy, Burt, American composer; b. Brooklyn, Aug. 5, 1936. He studied composition with George Rochberg, Salvatore Martirano and others; received degrees from the Univ. of Oregon and Temple Univ. in Philadelphia. He joined the faculty of the Univ. of Illinois in Urbana. His works are an experimental variety. In *Orbs with Flute* he applies such effects as slapping keys, pitchless clacks, tongue blocking the embouchure hole, etc.

Levy, Ellis, American violinist and composer; b. Indianapolis, Oct. 23, 1887. He studied violin with Emile Sauret in Berlin and with Eugene Ysaÿe and César Thomson in Brussels. Returning to the U.S. in 1910, he joined the St. Louis Symph. Orch. as assistant concert master, retiring in 1936; then settled in Los Angeles. He wrote a number of lightweight violin pieces (*The Gypsy, Waltz Serenade, Rain Drops, The Ghost Dance,* etc.); *March Triumphal* for 4 violins and piano (1918); *A Woodland Story,* children's suite for piano (1921); *Night in the Desert* for orch. (Los Angeles, Feb. 7, 1930); publ. a manual, *Modern Violin Technique* (Los Angeles, 1940).

Lévy, Ernst. Add to works: Symph. No. 14 (Basel, Jan. 20, 1964).

Levy, Frank, American composer, son of Ernst Lévy; b. Paris, Oct. 15, 1930. He went to America with his father; studied at the Juilliard School of Music in New York (B.S., 1951) and at the Univ. of Chicago (M.A., 1954); studied cello with Leonard Rose and Janos Starker in New York; was cellist in various orchestras. His compositions include *Ricercar* for 4 celli (1958); sonata for unaccompanied cello (1959); *Quintet* for flute and strings (1959); bassoon concerto (1961); trio for clarinet, horn and bassoon (1961); sonata for bassoon and piano (1963); *Fantasy* for tuba, harp, timpani and strings (1965); choruses and solo songs.

Lévy, Lazare. Died in Paris, Sept. 20, 1964.

Levy, Marvin David, American composer; b. Passaic, N.J., Aug. 2, 1932. He studied composition with Philip James at N.Y. Univ., and with Otto Luening at Columbia Univ.; was awarded an American Prix de Rome and a Guggenheim fellowship. He showed a particular disposition towards the musical theater; wrote the one-act operas *Sotoba Komachi* (N.Y., April 7, 1957); *The Tower* (Santa Fe, Aug. 2, 1957); and *Escorial* (N.Y., May 4, 1958). In 1961 he was commissioned to write an opera for the Metropolitan Opera at Lincoln Center, N.Y., to a libretto from O'Neill's play *Mourning Becomes Electra.* It was produced at the Metropolitan on March 17, 1967; although critical reception was indecisive, the opera was retained in the repertory for several seasons, a signal honor to an American composer. His other works include a string quartet

(1955); *Rhapsody* for violin, clarinet and harp (1956); *Chassidic Suite* for French horn and piano (1956); a Christmas oratorio, *For the Time Being* (1959); *Caramoor Festival Overture* (1959); a symphony (1960); *Sacred Service* for the Park Avenue Synagogue in N. Y. (1964); piano concerto (Chicago, Dec. 3, 1970). In his vocal and instrumental writing Levy adopts an expressionistic mode along atonal lines, in an ambience of prudentially dissonant harmonies vivified by a nervously asymmetric rhythmic pulse.

Lévy, Michel-Maurice. Died in Paris, Jan. 24, 1965.

Lewenthal, Raymond, American pianist; b. San Antonio, Texas, Aug. 29, 1926. He was taken to Hollywood as a child; learned to read music; studied piano with local teachers. He then enrolled at the Juilliard School of Music in N. Y., as a student of Olga Samaroff; continued his studies in Europe with Alfred Cortot; spent a year in Rio de Janeiro as a piano teacher. Returning to the U.S., he devoted himself to the propaganda of piano music by neglected romantic composers, among them Thalberg, Hummel and Henselt, whose works he performed at his recitals. Particularly meritorious is his redemption from undeserved oblivion of the voluminous output of Charles-Valentin Alkan. He edited a collection of Alkan's piano works for G. Schirmer, Inc.

Lewis, Henry, black American conductor; b. Los Angeles, Oct. 16, 1932. He learned to play piano and string instruments as a child; at the age of 16 was engaged as double-bass player in the Los Angeles Philharmonic; from 1955-59 played the double-bass in the 7th Army Symph. Orch. overseas, and also conducted it in Germany and in Holland. Returning to the U.S., he founded the Los Angeles Chamber Orch.; in 1963 traveled with it in Europe under the auspices of the State Dept.; subsequently was guest conductor with the Los Angeles Philharmonic and the American Symph. Orch. in N. Y. In 1968 he was appointed conductor and music director of the New Jersey Symph. Orch. in Newark, the first Negro to head a state orchestral organization. On this post he succeeded in increasing the number of annual concerts to more than a hundred; conducted it also in New York. Lewis is married to the soprano singer Marilyn Horne.

Lewis, John Aaron, American jazz pianist, composer and band leader; b. La Grange, Illinois, May 3, 1920. He served in the U. S. Army during World War II; enrolled in the Manhattan School of Music, N. Y.; became an arranger. In 1952 he organized the Modern Jazz Quartet, with the proclaimed aim of effecting the coalition of serious and popular music in the modern rhythmic manner.

Ley, Salvador. Add to works: *Lera,* opera in 2 acts (1959); *Danza exotica* for piano (1959); Suite for flute and piano (1962); *Concertante* for viola and string orch. (1962); *Toccatina* for piano (1965); *Introduction and Movement* for unaccompanied cello (1965).

Lhévinne, Rosina. She gloriously passed her 91st birthday on March 28, 1971.

Lhotka, Fran. Died in Zagreb, Jan. 26, 1962.

Liadov, Anatol Konstantinovitch. He died not in Novgorod itself, but on his estate of Polynovka, in the district of Novgorod.

Liapunov, Sergey Mikhailovitch. Did not study with Tchaikovsky; became sub-director of the Imperial Choir in 1894 (not 1884). His Symph. No. 1 was composed in 1887 (not 1901) and was first performed in St. Petersburg on April 23, 1888; the Berlin performance, under Liapunov's direction, took place on Jan. 15 (not Jan. 28), 1907. Add to works: Symph. No. 2 (1910-17; Leningrad, Dec. 28, 1950). His *12 études d'exécution transcendante,* all in sharp keys, were written in emulation of Liszt's similarly titled studies in flat keys. Cf. M. Shifman, *S. M. Liapunov* (Moscow, 1960).

Liatoshinsky, Boris Nikolayevitch. Died in Kiev, April 15, 1968.

Liberace, Walter (Wladziu Valentino), popular American pianist of Italian-Polish parentage; b. West Allis, Wisconsin, May 16, 1919. He received rudimentary musical training from his father, a French horn player. Encouraged by Paderewski, he began to study piano; played at night clubs, billed as Walter Busterkeys. In 1940 he moved to New York; evolved a facile repertoire of semi-classical arrangements; made a synthesis of the first movement of Beethoven's *Sonata quasi una fantasia* and Rachmaninoff's Prelude in C sharp minor, taking advantage of the fact that both works are in the same key. He prospered; made lucrative inroads on television; built a home in California with a piano-shaped swimming pool. Inspired by a movie on Chopin, he placed a candelabra on the piano at his concerts; this decorative object identified him as a Romantic pianist, an impression enhanced by the dress suit of white silk mohair he habitually wears. In 1959 he won a suit for defamation of character against the London 'Daily Mirror' and its columnist W. Connor (Cassandra) who suggested in print that Liberace was a deviate.

Lichey, Reinhold. Died in Plaue, Germany, Dec. 5, 1957.

Lidholm, Ingvar. Add to works: *Ritornello* for orch. (1955); *Mutanza* for orch. (1959); *Motus-Colores* for orch. (1960); *Poesis* for orch. (1963); *Holländarn (The Dutchman)*, television opera after Strindberg (first broadcast over the Swedish television network on Dec. 10, 1967).

Lídl, Václav, Czech composer; b. Brno, Nov. 5, 1922. He studied at the Brno Cons., graduating in 1948; devoted himself principally to composing for the films. However, he took time off to write a *Romantic Sonata* for violin and piano; 2 string quartets; a Divertimento for flute, clarinet and bassoon; children's choruses.

Liebermann, Rolf. Add to works: *Les Échanges,* for 52 industrial machines, recorded on tape (Lausanne, April 24, 1964). In 1959 he became intendant of the Hamburg State Opera, and in 1962 its artistic director. In this post he instituted a courageous program of commissioned works from avant-garde composers (among them Krenek, Schuller, Penderecki and Menotti). Concurrently, he was program director of the North German Radio and West Berlin Radio. In addition to these positions, he was named director of the Paris Opéra effective as of 1973. Eclipsing by far his reputation as a composer, Liebermann became one of the most renowned and ablest administrators in the field of musical theater.

Lieberson, Goddard. In 1964 he was named president of the Record Industry Association of America; continued as head of Columbia Records, Inc.

Liebling, Estelle. Died in New York, Sept. 25, 1970. Date of birth, April 21, 1880 (not 1884).

Lieurance, Thurlow. Died in Boulder, Colorado, Oct. 9, 1963.

Ligeti, György, Hungarian composer of the avant-garde; b. Dicsöszentmarton, Transylvania, May 28, 1923. He studied composition with Sándor Veress and Ferenc Farkas at the Budapest Music Academy (1945-49) and became instructor there (1950-56). In 1956 he left Budapest; worked in the Studio for Electronic Music in Cologne (1957-58); in 1959 was appointed instructor at the International Courses for New Music in Darmstadt; in 1961 was visiting prof. of composition at the Stockholm Music Academy; eventually settled in Vienna. After a period of composing in a cosmopolitan neo-classical manner, he determinedly swerved in the direction of experimental music. His works have been widely performed at international festivals of modern music; the most important among them are: *Artikulation* for electronic sounds (1958); *Apparitions* for orch. (1958-59); *Atmosphères* for orch. (1961); *Volumina* for organ (1961-62); *Aventures* for 3 singers and 7 instruments (1962); *Nouvelles Aventures* for soprano and 7 instruments (1962-65); *Requiem* for soprano, mezzo-soprano, 2 choruses and orch. (1963-65; Stockholm, March 14, 1965; *Kyrie* from it was used in the film *2001: A Space Odyssey*); cello concerto (Berlin, April 19, 1967); *Lontano* for orch. (Donaueschingen, Oct. 22, 1967); 10 pieces for wind quintet (Malmö, Jan. 19, 1969); *Chamber Concerto* for 13 instruments (Ottawa, April 2, 1970). His *Poème Symphonique* for 100 metronomes, running at different speeds, was performed at the Buffalo Festival of The Arts Today on March 4, 1965, and created a sensation. See Erkki Salmenhaara, *György Ligeti* (1969).

Lincke, Paul. Place of death Klausthal-Zellerfeld (not Zellernfeld). The musical quotation on the postage stamp in his honor is from his operetta *Berliner Luft* (not from *Glow-Worm*).

Lind, Jenny. Her London debut took place on May 4 (not March 4) 1847. Add to bibl.: G. D. Schultz, *Jenny Lind, the Swedish Nightingale* (Philadelphia, 1962).

Lioncourt, Guy de. Died in Paris, Dec. 24, 1961.

Lipatti, Dinu. He died of lymphogranulomatosis, not of rheumatoid arthritis.

Lipkin, Malcolm, English composer; b. Liverpool, May 2, 1932. He studied at the Royal College of Music, London, specializing in piano; subsequently studied composition with Mátyás Seiber. Works: violin concerto No. 1 (1951-52); *Dramatic Overture* (1955); *Movement* for strings (1957); piano concerto (1957); violin concerto No. 2 (1962); *Pastorale* for horn and strings

(1963); string quartet (1951); trio for flute, violin and piano (1957); violin sonata (1957); suite for flute and cello (1961); string trio (1964); 4 piano sonatas; songs.

Lisinski, Vatroslav. Bibl: L. Zupanović, *Vatroslav Lisinski* (Zagreb, 1969).

Liška, Zdeněk, Czech composer; b. Smečno, March 16, 1922. He studied at the Prague Cons.; since 1945 active as composer for the State Studios of Documentary Films. For the Czechoslovak spectacle, 'Laterna Magica,' he wrote a violin concerto in a modern virtuoso manner. This concerto, first performed in Leningrad on Dec. 5, 1960, was a featured work in the presentation of 'Laterna Magica' in New York in the summer of 1964.

Lissenko, Nikolai Vitalievitch. Born in Grinki (not Grilki).

List, Emanuel. Died in Vienna, June 21, 1967.

List, Kurt, Austrian-American musician; b. Vienna, June 21, 1913; d. Milan, Nov. 16, 1970. He studied music at the Vienna Academy of Music (M.A. 1936) and at the Univ. of Vienna (Ph.D. 1938); also took private lessons with Alban Berg (1932-35) and Anton von Webern (1935-38). He went to the U.S. in 1938; became active in the field of recording; wrote music criticism. After World War II he returned to Europe and lived mostly in Italy. His string quartet and a wind quintet were performed in New York; he also wrote two unperformed operas, *Der Triumph des Todes* and *Mayerling,* stylistically influenced by Richard Strauss.

Liszt, Franz. Rectify the typographical error on p. 966, col. 1, line 8: *Weihnachtsbaum,* not *Weinachtsbaum.* Add to bibl.: J. Rousselot, *Franz Liszt* (London, 1960); C. Rostand, *Liszt* (Paris, 1960); P. Rehberg, *Franz Liszt: die Geschichte seines Lebens, Schaffens und Wirkens* (Zürich, 1961); W. G. Armando, *Franz Liszt: eine Biographie* (Hamburg, 1961); J. Hankiss, *Wenn Liszt ein Tagebuch geführt hätte* (Budapest, 1961); M. Bagby, *Liszt's Weimar* (N.Y., 1961); A. Leroy, *Franz Liszt* (Lausanne, 1967); Alan Walker, ed., *Franz Liszt, The Man and His Music* (N. Y., 1970); C. V. Lachmund, *Mein Leben mit Franz Liszt* (Eschwege, 1970).

Litinsky, Genrik (Heinrich), Soviet composer; b. Lipovetz, March 17, 1901. He studied composition with Glière at the Moscow Cons., graduating in 1928; subsequently taught there (1928-43); among his students were Khrennikov, Zhiganov, Arutunian and other Soviet composers. In 1945 he went to Yakutsk as an ethnomusicologist; in collaboration with native Siberian composers he produced the first national Yakut operas, based on authentic folk melorhythms and arranged in contemporary harmonies according to the precepts of Socialist Realism: *Nurgun Botur* (Yakutsk, June 29, 1947), *Sygy Kyrynastyr* (Yakutsk, July 4, 1947), and *Red Shaman* (Yakutsk, Dec. 9, 1967). He wrote three Yakut ballets: *Altan's Joy* (Yakutsk, June 19, 1963); *Field Flower* (Yakutsk, July 2, 1947); *Crimson Kerchief* (Yakutsk, Jan. 9, 1968). Other works include: Symphony (1928); *Dagestan Suite* for orch. (1931); trumpet concerto (1934); *Festive Rhapsody* for orch. (1966); 12 string quartets (1923-61); string octet (1944); 12 concert studies for cello (1967); 12 concert studies for trumpet and piano (1968); 15 concert studies for oboe and piano (1969). He published the valuable manuals. *Problems of Polyphony* (3 vols., 1965, 1966, 1967), ranging from pentatonic to dodecaphonic patterns and from elementary harmonization to polytonality; also *Formation of Imitation in the Strict Style* (1970). In 1964 he was named People's Artist of the Yakut Soviet Socialist Republic and of the Tatar Soviet Socialist Republic; he also holds honorary degrees in fine arts from the Russian Soviet Socialist Republic and the Chuvash Soviet Socialist Republic.

Liviabella, Lino. Died in Parma, Oct. 21, 1964. Was director of the Cons. of Pesaro from 1953 to 1959; in 1959 appointed director of the Parma Cons.

Lobo, Duarte. He was not identical with the person of the same name baptized on Sept. 19, 1565; his date of birth must therefore remain uncertain. See Manuel Joaquim, *20 libros de música polifónica* (Lisbon, 1953; pp. 58-59).

Lockspeiser, Edward. Edited *Claude Debussy: Lettres inédites à André Caplet, 1908-1914* (Monaco, 1957); publ. *Debussy: His Life and Mind* (2 vols.; London, 1962, 1965).

Lockwood, Anna, composeress of the militant avant-garde; b. Christchurch, New Zealand, July 29, 1939. She studied at Canterbury Univ. in New Zealand; then went to London, where she took courses with Peter Racine Fricker at the Royal College of Music; subsequently attended classes at the Musikhochschule in Cologne and at the Electronic Music Center in Bilthoven, Holland.

In 1968 she gave non-lectures at the Anti-University of London. With her husband, Harvey Matusow, she undertook a series of experiments in total art, including aural, oral, visual, tactile, gustatory and olfactory demonstrations and sporadic transcendental manifestations; of these, the most remarkable was the summoning (in German) of Beethoven's ghost at a séance held in London on Oct. 3, 1968, with sound recorded on magnetic tape, which in playback revealed some surprisingly dissonant music of apparently metapsychic origin, tending to indicate that Beethoven was essentially an avant-garde composer (the tape was not released in order to avoid unanswerable controversy); the séance was preceded by the burning of a combustible piano and of an inflammable microphone. Anna Lockwood also experimented with surgical piano transplants. Her other works, some of them consisting of controlled glossolalia and notated optically on graphic paper, are *À Abélard, Héloïse* for mezzo-soprano and 10 instruments (1962); *Aspects of a Parable* for baritone and 12 instruments (1963); *Love Field,* for tape, a lament for John F. Kennedy, with reference to the name of the Dallas Airport (1964); *Glass Concert I* (1967); *Glass Concert II,* scored for sheets of armour plate glass, spotlight bulbs, wine glasses, milk bottles, glass curtains, fluorescent tubes, glass mobiles and other vitreous objects (1969; blueprint and directions publ. in 'Source' No. 5); *Dark Touch* for tactile-aural equipment (1970); *Gentle Grass,* a ritual for 6 players (1970); *Humm,* for 70 or more hummers (1971); *Bus Trip,* a moving event with food, free love and realistic sound effects (1971); *River Archives,* an anthology of sounds from world rivers (1971).

Loeb, John Jacob, American composer of popular songs; b. Chicago, Feb. 18, 1910; d. Valley Stream, Long Island, N.Y., March 2, 1970. He began writing songs for Broadway shows and jazz bands at the age of 18. Among his best-known songs are *Sweetie Pie, Boo Hoo, Seems Like Old Times, Masquerade* and *Reflections in the Water.*

Loeffler, Charles Martin. Date of 1st performance of *La Villanelle du Diable,* April 11 (not April 2), 1902.

Loesser, Arthur. Died in Cleveland, Jan. 4, 1969.

Loesser, Frank. Died in New York, July 28, 1969.

Logar, Mihovil, Croatian composer; b. Fiume, Oct. 6, 1902. He studied in Prague with K. B. Jirák and J. Suk. In 1927 he returned to Belgrade and became prof. of composition at the Belgrade Musical Academy. A highly prolific composer, he writes in all genres, employing a restrained modern idiom. Works: the operas *Pokondirena Tikva* (*Middle-Class Noblewoman;* Belgrade, Oct. 20, 1956); *Četrdesetprva* (*The Year of 1941;* Sarajevo, Feb. 10, 1961); ballet *Zlatna ribica* (*Goldfish,* after Pushkin's tale; Belgrade, Nov. 11, 1953); *4 Scenes from Shakespeare,* incidental music for orch. (1954); *Rondo rustico* for orch. (1945); violin concerto (1954); clarinet concerto (1956); *Vatra* (*Fire*), cantata (Belgrade, Sept. 27, 1960); *Kosmonauti,* concert overture in honor of the Soviet cosmonauts (Belgrade, June 8, 1962); *Sinfonia italiana* (Belgrade, Nov. 24, 1964); *Doppio Concerto* for clarinet and French horn (Belgrade, April 5, 1968).

Logothetis, Anestis, Bulgarian painter and composer of Greek extraction; b. Burgas, Oct. 27, 1921. He studied art at the State Academy in Vienna and exhibited in Vienna galleries a series of polymorphic graphs capable of being performed as music by optional instrumental groups. The titles of these graphs indicate a preoccupation with scientific concepts: Cycloid, Culmination, Coordination, Expansion-Contraction, Impulse (quantitative), Impulse (qualitative), Interpolation, Catalyzation, Parallax, Texture-Structure, Concatenation, Centrifugal. His score *Anastasis,* an experimental stage piece for speakers, singers, tapes, films, instrumentalists and television (1971), typifies his ideas of total environmental art.

Lombardo, Carmen, Canadian-born American song writer and saxophone player; b. London, Ontario, July 16, 1903; d. North Miami, Florida, April 17, 1971. He was a brother of Guy Lombardo and played the saxophone in his band from 1929 when it was formed until the year of his death. His lush saxophone tone contributed greatly to the emotional euphony of the Lombardo sound and his vibrato was most ingratiating. He was also a composer; among his popular hits are such tunes as *Seems Like Old Times, Sailboat in the Moonlight, Powder Your Face With Sunshine* and the lachrymose classic *Boo Hoo.*

Lombardo, Guy, Canadian-born American bandleader; b. London, Ontario, June 19, 1902, of Italian parents. With his brother Carmen Lombardo, the saxophone player, he organized a dance band, 'The Royal Canadians' and took it to the U.S. in 1924; two other brothers, Lebert and Victor, were also members of the band. The band rapidly rose to success on the commercial wave of pervasive sentimentality; in 1928 it was publicized as the purveyor of 'the sweetest music this side of Heaven.' The rendition of *Auld Lang Syne* by the Guy Lombardo Band at the Waldorf-Astoria Hotel in N. Y. at New Year's Eve celebrations every winter from 1929 to 1962 (with the exception of 1959) became a nostalgic feature. In his arrangements, Guy Lombardo cultivates unabashed emotionalism; in his orchestrations all intervallic interstices are well filled, and saxophones are tremulous with vibrato. The result is a velvety, creamy, but not necessarily oleaginous harmoniousness, which possesses an irresistible appeal to the obsolescent members of the superannuated generation of the 1920's.

London, George. In 1971 he was appointed general director of the Los Angeles Music Center Opera Association.

Long, Marguerite. Died in Paris, Feb. 13, 1966. She was born on Nov. 13, 1874 (not 1878); her 90th birthday was widely celebrated in 1964. Add publications: *Au Piano avec Claude Debussy* (Paris, 1960); *Au Piano avec Gabriel Fauré* (Paris, 1963). See Janine-Weil, *Marguerite Long: une vie fascinante* (Paris, 1969).

Loomis, Clarence. Died in Aptos, Calif., July 3, 1965. Taught piano and organ at New Mexico Highlands Univ. (1945-55); in 1960 settled in Aptos, Calif., as a private teacher. Add to works: operas: *The White Cloud* (1935), *Revival* (1943), *The Captive Woman* (1953); for orch.: *Gargoyles,* symphonic prelude (1936); *Gaelic Suite* for strings (1953); *Fantasy* for piano and orch. (1954); *Macbeth* (1954); *The Passion Play* for chorus and orch.; 2 string quartets (1953, 1963); cantata, *Song of the White Earth* (1956); numerous sacred choruses; *Susanna Don't You Cry,* a stage extravaganza (1939); piano suites; songs; organ pieces.

Lopatnikov, Nikolai. He spells his last name **Lopatnikoff.** Symph. No. 1 was first performed in Karlsruhe, on Jan. 8, 1929 (not in Königsberg in 1930, which was a later performance); piano concerto No. 1 was first performed in Cologne on Nov. 3, 1925; piano concerto No. 2, in Düsseldorf, Oct. 16, 1930. The piano concerto performed at the Vienna Festival was No. 2 (not No. 1); the C.B.S. Symph. performance of the piano concerto No. 2 (Nov. 27, 1946) was its first American performance, but not world première. Add to works: *2 Russian Nocturnes* for orch. (1945); concerto for 2 pianos and orch. (Pittsburgh, Nov. 7, 1958); *Music for Orchestra* (Louisville, Jan. 14, 1959); string quartet No. 3 (1956); *Danton,* opera (1931-33; excerpts performed by the Pittsburgh Symph. Orch., March 25, 1967). In 1968 he resigned as prof. at the Technological Institute in Pittsburgh.

Lorenzo, Leonardo de. Died in Santa Barbara, Calif., July 27, 1962.

Lourié, Arthur (Vincent). Died in Princeton, N.J., Oct. 13, 1966. Add to works: *The Blackamoor of Peter the Great,* opera (1961); *The Mime* for solo clarinet (1956); *Concerto da Camera* for violin solo and string orch. (1957). See C. Camajani, *The Music of Arthur Lourié,* in 'Ramparts' (Menlo Park, Calif., Jan. 1965).

Lowens, Irving, American musicologist, librarian and music critic; b. New York, Aug. 19, 1916. He studied at Teachers College, Columbia Univ. (B.S. in Music, 1939); Univ. of Maryland (Ph.D. in American Civilization, 1965). In 1962 he was recipient of travel grant to Germany given by the American Council of Learned Societies. Publications: *The Hartford Harmony: a Selection of American Hymns from the Late 18th and Early 19th Centuries* (Hartford, 1953); *Music and Musicians of Early America* (N.Y., 1964); *Music in America* (N. Y., 1965); *A Bibliography of American Songsters Published Before 1821* (Worcester, Mass., 1966); *Source Readings in American Music History* (N. Y., 1966).

Lowry, Robert, American hymn writer; b. Philadelphia, March 12, 1826; d. Plainfield, N. J., Nov. 25, 1899. He was a Baptist preacher and studied music in his middle age. His most popular hymn tune is *Something for Jesus.* Cf. R. G. McCutchan, *Our Hymnody* (N. Y., 1937).

Lowtzky, Hermann, Russian composer; b. Kamenetz-Podolsk, June 20, 1871; d. Zürich, Dec. 8, 1957. He studied law, philosophy and music; went to St. Petersburg in 1899 and enrolled in Rimsky-Korsakov's class at the Conservatory there. He moved to Switzerland in 1910. His music preserves the Russian elements of style and idiom. Among his published works are the opera *Lucretia* to his own libretto (Kiev, Dec. 18, 1912);

piano trio (1905); and a cantata *Paradies und Peri*. In manuscript are an opera *Mozart* and *Kol Nidre* for cello and orch.

Loy, Max, German conductor and composer; b. Nuremberg, June 18, 1913. He studied piano and composition in Nuremberg; was conductor of the Nuremberg Opera (1938-44 and 1948-65); traveled as pianist and accompanist. He received his Ph.D. in 1937 with the dissertation *Die Aesthetik der komischen Oper*. In 1965 he was guest conductor in Los Angeles and elsewhere in the U.S.; also conducted in Japan. He composed a piano concerto, 5 string quartets, a piano quintet and songs.

Lualdi, Adriano. He was music critic of the 'Giornale d'Italia' (1936-42); director of the Florence Cons. from 1947 (not 1949) to 1956. His opera *Le Nozze di Haura,* composed in 1908, had a concert performance over the Radio Italiano on Oct. 19, 1939, and its first stage production in Rome on April 17, 1943. *Le Furie d'Arlecchino* was produced in Milan on May 10, 1915 (not in Buenos Aires); *La Rosa di Saron* was composed in 1915 (not in 1927) and was first performed on the same bill with *Le Furie d'Arlecchino* (Milan, May 10, 1915). *Il Cantico* is an alternative title of *La Rosa di Saron. Lumawig* (not *Lumavig*) *e la Saetta* is a mimodrama (not an opera). Add to works: *La Luna dei Caraibi,* one-act opera after O'Neill (Rome, Jan. 29, 1953).

Lubin, Napoleone Antonio Eugenio. Delete article; identical with Saint-Luban (q.v.).

Luboshutz, Léa. Died in Philadelphia, March 18, 1965. Date of birth, Feb. 22, 1885 (not 1887).

Luboshutz, Pierre. Died in Rockport, Maine, April 17, 1971. Born June 17, 1891 (not 1894); his wife, Genia Nemenoff, was born Oct. 23, 1905 (not 1908). From 1962 to 1968, they headed the Piano Dept. at Michigan State Univ.; then returned to New York.

Lucier, Alvin, American composer; b. Nashua, N.H., May 14, 1931. He studied theory with Quincy Porter at Yale Univ. and with Arthur Berger, Irving Fine and Harold Shapero at Brandeis Univ.; also took a course with Lukas Foss at Tanglewood. He spent two years in Rome on a Fulbright Scholarship. Returning to America in 1962, he was appointed to the faculty at Brandeis Univ. In his works he exploits serial and electronic techniques. Among them are *Music* for solo performer (1965), derived from amplified electroencephalographic waves, which activate percussion instruments; *Whistlers,* depicting magnetic disturbances in the ionosphere; *Shelter 999,* amplifications of minisounds in the immediate environment with parietal filters; *Music for High Structures; Chambers,* derived from the noises of displaced objects; *Vespers,* produced by acoustic orientation by means of echolocation; *The Only Talking Machine of Its Kind in the World,* for mixed media, featuring electronic ventriloquy (1969). He wrote a computer controlled environmental work for the Pepsi Cola Pavilion of Expo '70 in Osaka, Japan, a sound mosaic, with hundreds of tape recorders; also a biographical composition for oboe, accompanied by the Atlantic Ocean, a chest of drawers and the Federal Bureau of Investigation (1970). In 1970 he resigned from Brandeis Univ. and joined the staff of Wesleyan University.

Ludikar, Pavel. Died in Vienna, Feb. 19, 1970.

Ludwig, Christa, German soprano; b. Berlin, March 16, 1928. Both her parents were professional singers, and she took her first music lessons with her mother. She began her career as a contralto; appeared in opera in Darmstadt (1952-54), in Hannover (1954-55), in Vienna (1955), in Berlin, Hamburg, Rome and Milan. In 1959 she sang for the first time at the Metropolitan Opera in New York.

Luening, Otto. Add to works: *Sonority Canon* for 4 solo flutes accompanied by 33 flutes on tape (N. Y., May 15, 1962).

Lully, Jean-Baptiste. Add to bibl.: J. Eppelsheim, *Das Orchester in den Werken J. B. Lullys* (Tutzing, 1961).

Lund, Signe. Died in Oslo, April 6, 1950.

Lundquist, Torbjörn, Swedish composer; b. Stockholm, Sept. 30, 1920. He studied composition with Dag Wirén; was active as pianist and conductor. In his music he follows the romantic tradition of Sibelius; during his travels in the north he collected songs of Lapland, which he used in heterophonic counterpoint in some of his works. He also experimented with ultra-modern techniques of "organized spontaneity." Works: Symph. No. 1 (1956); Symph. No. 2 (1968); *Concerto da Camera* for accordion and orch. (1965); *Combinazioni* for violin and percussion (1966); *Concerto Sinfonico* for piano and orch. (1967); *Teamwork,* for wind quintet (1967); *Evoluzione* for strings (1968); *Confrontation* for orch. (1968); *Sound on Sound* for speaker, piano and stereophonic orch. (1969); *Stereogram III* for electric guitar, xylorimba, and concert accordion (1969); *Quatre Rondeaux* for wind quartet and piano (1969).

Lunetta, Stanley G., American avant-garde composer; b. Sacramento, Calif., June 5, 1937. He received his B.A. at Sacramento State College and completed graduate work at the Univ. of California, Davis, where he studied composition with Larry Austin, Jerome Rosen and Richard Swift; also took a course with Karlheinz Stockhausen when he lectured at Davis. In 1963 he formed the New Music Ensemble devoted to contemporary music. His works explore the potentialities of electronic media; a major project is to build a computer capable of independent creative composition, both in ultra-modern and infra-classical fields. His pieces, most of them for mixed media characterized by disestablishmentarian latitudinarianism, include *A Piece for Bandoneon and Strings* (1966); *Funkart* for mixers, lights and audio-visual input material (1967); *TA-TA* for chorus with mailing tubes (Santa Barbara, Calif., May 15, 1969); *I Am Definitely Not Running for Vice President* for photo-cells, modulators and 4 governors (1967); *TWOMANSHOW,* an evening of environmental theater (1968); *Spider-Song,* a comic-book and a situation (in collaboration with Larry Austin, first demonstrated in N.Y., Dec. 17, 1968); *Mr. Machine* for flute and electronics (1969) and an epithalamium for a married percussionist couple (1970). He is (1971) the editor of the hyper-modern music magazine 'Source' published (where else?) in California.

Lupi, Roberto. Died in Rome, April 17, 1971.

Lutkin, Peter Christian. In 1883 he became instructor in piano and organ at Northwestern Univ., Evanston, Illinois; from 1895 to 1928 was Dean of the School of Music there; also taught church music at the Garrett Biblical Institute at Evanston (1915-28).

Lutoslawski, Witold. In the summer of 1962 he was invited to give a course in composition at the Berkshire Music Center in Tanglewood; in the summer of 1966 he was composer-in-residence at Dartmouth College, Hanover, N.H. The date of first performance of his *Triptyque Silésien,* Warsaw, Dec. 2, 1951. Add to works: *Variations Symphoniques* (Cracow, June 17, 1939); *Symphonie* (Katowice, April 6, 1948); *Overture* for strings (Prague, Nov. 9, 1949); *Musique Funèbre* for string orch., dedicated to the memory of Béla Bartók, and thematically based on a dodecaphonic concatenation of tritones (Katowice, March 26, 1958); *Jeux vénitiens* for orch. (Venice, April 24, 1961); *Paroles tissés* for tenor and orch. (Aldeburgh Festival, June 20, 1965, composer conducting); Symph. No. 2 (1967); *Livre pour Orchestre* (1968); cello concerto (London, Oct. 14, 1970, Mstislav Rostropovitch soloist). Beginning with *Jeux vénitiens,* Lutoslawski adopts a decisively ultra-modernistic technique, including serial and aleatory procedures, making use of graphic notation. Bibl.: S. Jarociński, *Witold Lutoslawski,* in *Polish Music* (Warsaw, 1965, in English; pp. 191-199); Ove Nordwall, *Lutoslawski* (Stockholm, 1968).

Lutyens, Elizabeth. She spells her first name **Elisabeth** (not **Elizabeth**). Add to works: *Essence of our Happiness* for tenor, chorus and orch. (London, Sept. 8, 1970) to words by Abu Yasid, Donne and Rimbaud.

Luzzaschi, Luzzasco. Add to bibl.: A. Einstein, *The Italian Madrigal* (Princeton, 1949).

Lybbert, Donald, American composer; b. Cresco, Iowa, Feb. 19, 1923. He studied at the Univ. of Iowa (B.M., 1946); at Columbia Univ. with Elliott Carter and Otto Luening (M.A., 1950); and with Nadia Boulanger at Fontainebleau, France (1961). He is associate prof. of music at Hunter College, N.Y. His style of composition is evolved from firm classical foundations, but he applies dodecaphonic and other serial techniques; without abandoning central tonality, he refrains from using key signatures; his rhythmic patterns are asymmetrical but his polymetry maintains a strong common denominator. Works: operas *Monica* (Amsterdam, Nov. 2, 1952) and *Scarlet Letter* (1965); *Introduction and Toccata* for brass and piano (1955); trio for clarinet, horn and bassoon (1957); chamber sonata for horn, viola and piano (1958); *Leopardi Canti,* song cycle for soprano, flute, viola and bass clarinet (1959); *Sonorities* for 11 instruments (1960); *Sonata brevis* for piano (1962); *Praeludium* for brass and percussion (1962); 2 piano sonatas; choral pieces; song cycles.

Lyman, Howard Wilder. In 1971, having safely passed his 92nd birthday, he was living in retirement in Herkimer, New York.

Lynn, George, American choral conductor and composer; b. Edwardsville, Penna., Oct. 5, 1915. He studied composition with Roy Harris at Westminster Choir College, organ with Carl Weinrich and conducting with John Finley Williamson. In 1964 he succeeded Williamson as director of Westminster Choir College and conductor of Westminster Choir. His works include a symph,; a piano concerto; *Gettysburg Address* for baritone solo, chorus and orch.; *Greek Folksong Rhapsody* for contralto, chorus and orch.; 3 Sacred Symphonies for chorus; 3 string quartets; 30 organ pieces; 40 songs; about 130 choruses. He is editor of Westminster Choir Series, publ. by G. Schirmer, Inc.

Lyon, David. English composer; b. Walsall, Staffordshire, Dec. 29, 1938. He was educated in London. His compositions include a string quartet (1962); *Divertimento* for small orch. (1963); piano concerto (1964); *Partita* for solo horn (1964); *Dance Prelude* for small orch. (1964).

Lyons, James, American music critic and editor; b. Peabody, Mass., Nov. 24, 1925. At the age of 16 he lost sections of two left-hand fingers in a factory accident while operating a machine which stamped corners for Monopoly game boxes. This put an end to any musical career as a performer. He subsequently took courses at Boston Univ. with Karl Geiringer and at the New England Cons. with Warren Storey Smith; wrote music criticism for the 'Boston Post,' 'Boston Globe' and 'Boston Evening Transcript'; contributed articles to various music magazines. Majoring in journalism, he won in 1947 the prestigious gold medal awarded by the American Newspaper Publishers Association 'for advancement of the daily newspaper in public service'; also in 1947 received a B.S. from Boston Univ. He then went to Florida as staff writer and later editorial page editor on the 'Miami Herald.' In 1952 he settled in New York and returned to music, writing regularly for the N. Y. 'Herald Tribune' (1953-62); served as assistant editor of 'Musical America' (1953-55); in 1957 became editor and publisher of 'The American Record Guide'; made it the standard journal in its field. He studied psychology at N. Y. Univ. obtaining his M.A. in 1964; later taught psychology there. He also engaged in a profound study of the music of India and the Orient; in 1966 was elected board chairman of the Society for Asian Music. From 1967 he was regular program annotator for the Boston Symph. Orch.; received the ASCAP-Deems Taylor Award for this work in 1968. In 1968-72 he was trustee of the National Academy of Recording Arts and Sciences. He is co-author (with John Tasker Howard) of *Modern Music* (N. Y., 1957). In his critical essays and annotations, Lyons achieves a blend of modern American journalism with a scholarly communication of the purely technical and stylistic elements of music.

M

Maazel, Lorin. Appointed music director and conductor of the Cleveland Orchestra, effective in the 1972-73 season.

MacArdle, Donald Wales. Died in Littleton, Colo., Dec. 23, 1964.

MacDermid, James G. Died in Brooklyn, Aug. 16, 1960.

MacDowell, Edward Alexander. He enrolled at the Paris Cons. as auditor in Savard's class on Oct. 18, 1876; admitted as a regular student on Feb. 8, 1877, and withdrew on Sept. 30, 1878. He studied piano with Marmontel in 1877-79 (not 1876-78) and solfège with Marmontel's son in 1877. He married Marian Nevins in New York on July 9, 1884, 12 days before the home ceremony at Shaw Farm in Waterford, Conn. His *Indian Suite* was first performed in New York on Jan. 23, 1895, before its Boston performance.

Machabey, Armand. Died in Paris, Aug. 31, 1966.

Machado, Augusto. Date of death, March 26 (not 24), 1924.

Machl, Tadeusz. Polish composer; b. Lwow, Oct. 22, 1922. He studied in Cracow with Malawski (composition) and Rutkowski (organ). Among his works are 4 symphonies (1947, 1948, 1949, 1954); 3 concertos for organ and orch. (1950, 1952, 1953); *Lyric Suite* for orch. (1955); chamber music; song cycles.

Machlis, Joseph. American music historian and pedagogue; b. Riga, Latvia, Aug. 11, 1906; was brought to the U.S. as an infant. He studied at the College of the City of N.Y. (B.A., 1927), and at the Institute of Musical Art of the Juilliard School (Teachers Diploma, 1927); also held an M.A. in English literature from Columbia Univ. (1938). In 1938 he was appointed to the music faculty at Queens College of the City Univ. of N.Y. He publ. 2 well-written and scholarly manuals, *The Enjoyment of Music* (N.Y., 1955;

revised edition, 1963) and *Introduction to Contemporary Music* (N.Y., 1961); also *American Composers of Our Time* for young people (N.Y., 1963) and *Getting to Know Music* for high-school students (N.Y., 1966). He translated a number of operatic librettos for the NBC Opera Company (*Rigoletto, La Traviata, Fidelio, La Bohème, Cavalleria Rusticana,* Prokofiev's *War and Peace,* etc.); *Boris Godunov, Tosca* and Manuel de Falla's *Atlántida* for other opera companies. He is the author of a novel *57th Street* about the 'concert industry' (N. Y., 1970), published under the phonetically palindromic pseudonym George Selcamm.

Mackerras, Charles. He conducted in Australia (not Austria).

Maclean, Quentin Stuart Morvaren. Died in Toronto, July 9, 1962.

MacMillan, Sir **Ernest Campbell.** He was conductor of the Mendelssohn Choir in Toronto from 1942 to 1957; director of Toronto Cons. from 1926 to 1942 (not 1952); dean, faculty of music, Univ. of Toronto, from 1926 to 1952.

Maconchy, Elizabeth. Add to works: 3 one-act operas: *The Sofa,* to a libretto by Ursula Vaughan Williams (London, Dec. 13, 1959); *The Departure* (London, Dec. 16, 1962); *The Three Strangers* after Thomas Hardy (London, June 5, 1968); *The Birds,* operatic extravaganza after Aristophanes (London, June 5, 1968); *The Jesse Tree,* church masque (Dorchester Abbey, Oct. 7, 1970); instrumental music: *Reflections* for oboe, clarinet, viola and harp (1960); *Serenata Concertante* for violin and orch. (1962); quintet for clarinet and strings (1963); *Variazioni concertanti* for oboe, clarinet, bassoon, horn and strings (1965); *Sonatina* for harpsichord (1965); *An Essex Overture* (1966); *6 Pieces* for solo violin (1966); string quartet No. 8 (1966); *3 Cloudscapes* for orch. (1968); *Preludio, Fugato and Finale* for piano duet (1968); *Samson at the Gates of Gaza* for chamber orch. (1969); string quartet No. 9 (1969); *Duo* for clarinet and viola (1969); *3 Settings of Gerard Manley Hopkins* for soprano and chamber orch. (1969).

Madatov, Grigori Yakovlevitch, Russian flutist and composer; b. Baku, April 2, 1898. He studied at the Moscow Cons. Upon graduation, he taught flute playing in Baku (1920-37) and at the Cons. of Tbilisi (1938-44). In 1947 he joined the staff of the Musical Pedagogical Institute in Moscow. He wrote a number of pieces for flute suitable as teaching material.

Maddy, Joseph Edgar. Died in Traverse City, Michigan, April 18, 1966.

Madeira, Jean (née Browning), American contralto; b. Centralia, Illinois, Nov. 14, 1924. She studied piano with her mother, and was regarded as a child prodigy; at the age of 12, she was piano soloist with the St. Louis Symph. Orch.; took vocal lessons in St. Louis; then studied both piano and voice at the Juilliard School, N. Y. Subsequently she became a member of the Chautauqua Opera Co., and the San Carlo Opera Co. In 1953 she sang minor roles at the Metropolitan Opera; went to Europe; sang Carmen with the Vienna State Opera on Sept. 18, 1955, obtaining extraordinary success; on March 17, 1956 she appeared as Carmen with the Metropolitan Opera, N. Y., and this role became one of her best. Her European tours included appearances at Covent Garden, La Scala, Paris Opéra and Bayreuth. She was married to Francis Madeira on June 17, 1947.

Maderna, Bruno. Exact date of birth, April 21, 1920. After 1950 he lived mostly in West Germany; naturalized as a German citizen in 1963. Add to works: *Œdipe-Roi,* electronic ballet (Monte Carlo, Dec. 31, 1970); *Juilliard Serenade* for chamber orch. and taped sounds (N. Y., Jan. 31, 1971, Maderna conducting).

Maelzel, Johannes Nepomuk. Died on board the brig Otis in the harbor of La Guiara, Venezuela, en route to Philadelphia on July 21 (not July 31), 1838. (The brig landed in Philadelphia on July 30, 1838.)

Magaloff, Nikita, Russian-Swiss pianist; b. St. Petersburg, Feb. 8, 1912. His family left Russia after the Revolution; he enrolled in the Paris Cons. as a student of Isidor Philipp; graduated with Premier Prix at the age of 17. In 1939 he settled in Switzerland; in 1947 made his first American tour; also toured South America, South Africa, etc. In 1949 he was appointed 'professeur de virtuosité' at the Cons. of Geneva. He is renowned for his lyrico-dramatic interpretations of Chopin, with lapidary attention to detail. He is also a composer; he wrote a piano toccata; sonatina for violin and piano; songs; cadenzas for Mozart's piano concertos.

Mager, Jörg, German music theorist and pioneer in electronic music; b. Eichstätt, Nov. 6, 1880; d. Aschaffenburg, April, 1939. After completing his university studies, he became interested in electronic reproduction of sounds; constructed several instruments capable of producing microtonal intervals by electronic means, which he named Sphärophon, Elektrophon and Partiturophon; he was also active in visual music for film. He publ. *Vierteltonmusik* (Aschaffenburg, 1916) and *Eine neue Epoche der Musik durch Radio* (Berlin, 1924).

Maggini, Giovanni Paolo. Date of birth, Nov. 29, 1579 (not Aug. 25, 1580).

Maggioni, Aurelio Antonio, Italian composer; b. Milan, April 8, 1908. He studied at the Milan Cons.; graduated as a pianist (1926) and composer (1933). He subsequently taught music theory in Parma (1938), in Florence (1939-51), in Milan (1952-54), in Lima, Peru (1954-59) and again in Milan from 1959. He wrote the opera *Il Gioco di Soleima* (Bergamo, 1955); during his stay in Peru he composed a *Suite incaica* for orch., making use of indigenous themes; also a mandatory amount of chamber music and minor pieces, all set in a competent Italianate style.

Mahaim, Ivan, Swiss physician, amateur violinist and writer on music; b. Liège, June 25, 1897; d. Lausanne, Dec. 3, 1965. He studied violin with Alfred Pochon in Lausanne; held the post of associate prof. in cardiology at the Univ. of Lausanne. He publ. a highly valuable 2-vol. edition, *Beethoven, Naissance et Renaissance des Derniers Quatuors* (Paris, 1964); contributed many articles on Beethoven to various publications.

Mahler, Gustav. A realization of his Symph. No. 10 (by Deryck Cooke) was broadcast over BBC from London for the first time, Dec. 19, 1960. The title originally given by Mahler to his Symph. No. 3 was *Ein Sommermorgentraum* (not *Die Fröhliche Wissenschaft*). Its first complete performance was given in Krefeld on June 9 (not 12), 1902. Add to bibl.: Willi Reich, ed., *Gustav Mahler: Im eigenen Wort, im Wort der Freunde* (Zürich, 1958); T. Adorno, *Mahler: eine musikalische Physiognomik* (Frankfurt, 1960); S. Vestdijk, *Gustav Mahler* (The Hague, 1960); N. Cardus, *Gustav Mahler: His Mind and His Music* (vol. I; London, 1965); Heinrich Kralik, *Gustav Mahler* (Vienna, 1968); Jack Diether, *Notes on Some Mahler Juvenilia* (in 'Chord and Discord,' Vol. 3, No. 1, 1969); Kurt Blaukopf, *Gustav Mahler, oder Zeitgenosse der Zukunft* (Vienna, 1969).

Mahrenholz, Christhard. A collection of his articles, *Musicologica et liturgica: Gesammelte Aufsätze von Christhard Mahrenholz,* edited by K. F. Müller, was publ. in Kassel in 1960, as an homage on his 60th birthday.

Maison, René. Died in Mont-Dore, France, July 15, 1962.

Majeske, Daniel, American violinist; b. Detroit, Sept. 17, 1932. He began studying violin at the age of 4 and at 16 appeared as soloist with the Detroit Symphony Orchestra; continued his studies at the Curtis Institute in Philadelphia with Ivan Galamian. In 1955 he joined the violin section of the Cleveland Orchestra; in 1969 he was named its concertmaster. He appeared as a soloist with major American orchestras; in 1965 he was appointed to the faculty of the Cleveland Music School Settlement. He owns the 'Marquis de Riviera' Stradivarius violin of 1718.

Major, Ervin. Died in Budapest. Oct. 10, 1967.

Makeba, Miriam, black South African singer; b. Prospect, near Johannesburg, March 4, 1932. She sang in a mission choir in Pretoria; then joined an itinerant minstrel show. She first attracted attention when she sang the leading part in the African opera *King Kong* (Johannesburg, Feb. 2, 1959). In 1959 she went to the U.S.; appeared in New York night clubs and on television; testified at the United Nations on racist policies of South Africa; made a successful tour of Europe; also traveled to Ethiopia and Kenya as a representative of Negro art. See 'Current Biography' (June 1965).

Makedonski, Kiril, Macedonian composer; b. Bitol, Jan. 19, 1925. After completing his academic schooling in Skoplje, he studied with Krst Odak at the Music Academy in Zagreb; later continued his composition studies with Brkanović in Sarajevo, and in Ljubljana with Škerjanc. He is the composer of the first national Macedonian opera *Goce* (Skoplje, May 24, 1954); his second opera was *Tsar Samuil* (Skoplje, Nov. 5, 1968). He also wrote 4 symphonies; chamber music and a number of choruses. His idiom follows the fundamental vocal and harmonic usages of the Russian National School. See Branko Karakaš, *Muzicki Stvaraoci u Makedoniji* (Belgrade, 1970; pp. 68-70).

Maksimović, Rajko, Serbian composer; b. Belgrade, July 27, 1935. He studied at the Academy of Music in Belgrade; later joined its faculty; also took a post-graduate course at Princeton Univ. His style of composition combines formal neo-classicism with serial procedures and ethnic Balkan thematics. Among his works are *Muzika posta-janja* based on an atonally treated motive B-A-C-H (Belgrade, July 20, 1965); *Partita concertante* for violin and strings (1965); *Kad su živi zavideli mrtvima* (*When the Living Envied the Dead*), cantata to texts from medieval Serbian chronicles (Belgrade, April 21, 1964); *Three Haiku* for female choir and chamber orch., with the application of aleatory devices (Zagreb, May 16, 1967). See Vlastimir Peričić, *Muzički Stvaraoci u Srbiji* (Belgrade, 1969; pp. 238-43).

Malawski, Artur. Add bibl.: B. Schäffer, editor, *Artur Malawski: zycie i twórczość* (Cracow, 1969).

Maleingreau, Paul de. Died in Brussels, Jan. 12, 1956. Correct form of last name, **Malengreau.**

Malek, Viktor, Czech composer; b. Velká Polana. Dec. 20, 1922. He studied music with his father at home; then enrolled at the Prague Cons. graduating in 1946. He subsequently became a symphonic and operatic conductor; also composed operas.

Malherbe, Edmond Paul Henri. Died in Corbeil-Essonnes (Seine-et-Oise), March 7, 1963.

Malipiero, Gian Francesco. His early opera *Sogno d'un tramonto d'autunno,* composed in 1914, was brought to first performance 50 years later, on the Milan Radio. Oct. 4, 1963. His Symph. No. 2 was first performed on Jan. 25, 1937 (not 1936); *Antonio e Cleopatra* was first performed on May 4 (not June 4), 1938; piano concerto No. 4 was first performed in Turin, on the radio. on Jan. 28, 1951 (not in N. Y., March 29, 1951). *Il Figliuol prodigo* and *Venere prigioniera* were produced on May 14 (not May 11), 1957. The exact date of the first performance of *La Cena,* Rochester, N.Y., April 25, 1929. *Stradivario* was first performed in Florence, June 20, 1949 (not Feb. 28, 1951 in Lisbon). Add to works: piano concerto No. 5 (1958); *Serenata mattutina* for 10 instruments (1959); *Concerto di concerti* for baritone, violin and orch. (1960); *Serenata* for bassoon and chamber orch. (1961); *Sinfonia per Antigenida* (1962); *Abracadabra* for baritone and orch. (1962): *Il Capitan Spavento,* one-act opera (Naples, March 16, 1963); *Don Giovanni,* one-act opera after Pushkin (Naples, Sept. 22, 1963); violin concerto No. 2 (1963); Symph. No. 8 (1964); *Il Marescalco,* opera in 2 acts (1964); *Le Metamorfosi di Bonaventura,* fantastic opera in 3 parts (Venice, Sept. 5, 1966); Symph. No. 9 (1966); piano concerto No. 6, subtitled 'delle machine' (Rome, Feb. 5, 1966); *Don Tartufo bacchettone,* opera (1966; Venice, Jan. 20, 1970); Symph. No. 10 (1967); flute concerto (1968); Symph. No. 11, subtitled 'delle cornamuse' (1970). A collection of his articles was publ. under the title *Il Filo d'Arianna* in Turin, 1966. See Everett Helm, *Gian Francesco Malipiero: An Introduction* ('Soundings,' No. 1, Cardiff, Autumn, 1970).

Malkin, Joseph. Died in New York, Sept. 1, 1969.

Malkin, Manfred. Died in New York, Jan. 8, 1966.

Malko, Nikolay Andreyevitch. Died in Sydney, Australia, June 23, 1961.

Malotte, Albert Hay. Died in Los Angeles, Nov. 16, 1964.

Mamangakis, Nikos, Greek composer; b. Rethymnon, Crete, March 3, 1929. He studied in Germany with Carl Orff and Harald Genzmer; adopted a serial method of composition. Among his published works are *Constructions* for an optional ensemble of instruments (1961); *Monolog* for cello (1962); *Cassandra* for soprano and chamber orch. (1963); *Antagonismi* for cello, xylophone and percussion (1964); *Tetraktis* for string quartet; *Erotokritos* for 5 instruments and 3 voices.

Mana-Zucca. Born on Dec. 25, 1887 (not 1890).

Mancini, Henry, American composer of film and television music; b. Cleveland, April 16, 1924, of Italian parents. He took piccolo lessons from his father. a member of the Sons of Italy band in Aliquippa, Pennsylvania. After playing in dance bands, he studied at Carnegie Institute in Pittsburgh and at the Juilliard School of Music, N. Y. He further studied composition in Los Angeles with Castelnuovo-Tedesco, Ernst Krenek and Alfred Sendrey. In 1952 he became a composer for Universal-International film studios, and in 1958 began writing background music for television. His jazzy theme for the Peter Gunn series placed him at once as one of the most adroit composers of melodramatic music; he won 5 television awards and several Academy awards for film scores.

Mandić, Josef. Died in Prague, Oct. 5, 1959. Add to works: opera, *Mirjana* (Olomouc, Feb. 20, 1937).

Mann, Alfred, American musicologist; b. Hamburg, Germany, April 28, 1917. He emigrated to the U.S. at an early age; studied at the Curtis Institute of Music in Philadelphia, graduating in 1942; later took courses in musicology at Columbia Univ. (Ph.D., 1955). In 1947 he was appointed prof. of music at Rutgers Univ. in Newark, N.J. Publications: *Die Lehre vom Kontrapunkt* (Celle, 1938); *Steps to Parnassus* (English edition of J. J. Fux's *Gradus ad Parnassum;* N.Y., 1943; new edition, under the title *The Study of Counterpoint,* N.Y., 1965); *The Study of Fugue* (New Brunswick, 1958); numerous articles in the 'Mus. Quarterly' and other scholarly journals.

Mannes, David. Died in New York, April 25, 1959.

Mannes, Leopold Damrosch. Died at Martha's Vineyard, Cape Cod, Mass., Aug. 11, 1964.

Mannino, Franco, Italian pianist, composer and conductor; b. Palermo, April 25, 1924. He studied piano with R. Silvestri and composition with V. Mortari at the St. Cecilia Academy in Rome, graduating in 1940; toured as pianist in Europe, America and Africa. He wrote the operas *Vivi* (Naples, March 28, 1957); *Il Diavolo in giardino* (Palermo, Feb. 28, 1963); *Il Quadro delle meraviglie* (Rome, April 24, 1963); *Le Notti della paura* (radio opera, broadcast from Rome, May 24, 1963); *La Speranza* (Trieste, Feb. 14, 1970); ballet, *Mario e il mago* (Milan, La Scala, Feb. 25, 1956); and a *Sinfonia Americana* for orch. (Florence, Nov. 11, 1956). After 1952, he was active mainly as opera conductor; in 1969 was appointed music director of the Teatro San Carlo in Naples. His operas and other works are written in a traditional melodramatic Italian style, diversified by occasional modernistic procedures.

Mansfield, Purcell James. Died in London, Sept. 22, 1968.

Manski, Dorothée. Died in Atlanta, Georgia, Feb. 24, 1967.

Mantovani, Annunzio Paolo, Italian conductor of popular music; b. Venice, Nov. 15, 1905. He went to London as a youth; studied at the Trinity College of Music there; became a British subject in 1933. He formed an orchestra of his own in Birmingham at the age of 18; then led bands in hotels and in theaters. His ingratiatingly harmonious orchestral arrangements made his name famous; the 'Mantovani sound' became a byword with sedentary music lovers seeking relaxation and listening pleasure an as antidote to the dramatic enervation of hazardous modern living and raucous popular music.

Manzoni, Giacomo, Italian composer; b. Milan, Sept. 26, 1932. He studied in Messina and in Milan; in 1958 became music critic of 'Unità' and in 1962 was engaged as instructor at the Milan Cons. His opera *Atomtod* (Milan, March 25, 1965), depicting the apocalyptic scenes after the ultimate atomic war, attracted much attention. He also wrote instrumental music.

Maragno, Virtú, Argentinian composer; b. Santa Fé, March 18, 1928. He studied in Buenos Aires and later in Rome with Goffredo Petrassi. Returning to Argentina, he became active as a choral conductor and teacher. He writes in a distinctly modernistic vein, leaning toward serial techniques. Works: *Triste y Danza* for small orch. (1947); *Divertimento* for wind quintet (1952); *Scherzo Sinfónico* (Buenos Aires, June 16, 1953); Concertino for piano and 14 instruments (1954); 2 string quartets (1958, 1961); *Expresión* for double orch. and percussion (Rome, June 23, 1961); *Intensidad y Espacio* for orch. (1962); *Composición I* for voices, instruments and magnetic tape (Buenos Aires, Oct. 5, 1962); music for the theater; film scores; choruses; songs.

Marazzoli, Marco. Born in 1619 (not c. 1600).

Marcelli, Nino. Died in San Diego, Calif., Aug. 16, 1967.

Marcello, Benedetto. Born Aug. 9 (not July 24), 1686.

Marcoux, Vanni. Died in Paris, Oct. 21, 1962.

Maréchal, Maurice. Died in Paris, April 19, 1964.

Marenzio, Luca. Add bibl.: D. Arnold, *Marenzio* (London, 1965).

Margaritis, Loris, Greek pianist; b. Aigion, Aug. 15, 1895; d. Athens, Sept. 27, 1953. He began his career as an infant prodigy; studied in Berlin and Munich. When his early promise failed to materialize, he returned to Greece in 1915, and became an instructor at the Cons. of Salonika.

Marić, Ljubica, Serbian composer; b. Kragujevac, March 18, 1909. She studied with J. Suk and Alois Hába in Prague; developed an intensely atonal and rhythmically complex style of composition; cultivated mainly chamber music; wrote a string quartet; a wind quintet; a trio for clarinet, trombone and double-bass in quarter-tones; a violin sonata; a cantata *Pesme prostora* (Belgrade, Dec. 8, 1956); *Passacaglia* for orch. (Belgrade, April 21, 1958); several works designated as "melodic recitations"; piano pieces. At the same time she experimented with modern realizations of ancient Byzantine chants; to this group belong *Muzika oktoiha* for orch. (Belgrade, Feb. 28, 1959); *Byzantine Concerto* for piano and orch. (Belgrade, June 4, 1963); *Ostinato super tema octoicha* for chamber orch. (1963); *Symphonia octoicha* (1964). See V. Peričić, *Muzički Stvaraoci u Srbiji* (Belgrade, 1969; pp. 251-62).

Marie, Gabriel. Place of death, Puigcerda, Catalonia.

Marinov, Ivan, Bulgarian composer; b. Sofia, Oct. 17, 1928. He studied with Stoyanov at the Sofia Cons.; then became conductor of the People's Opera in Plovdiv. He wrote a symph. poem *The Day of Elijah* (1956); many choruses and scores for theatrical performances.

Marliave, Joseph de, French writer on music; b. Toulouse, Nov. 16, 1873; killed in battle at Verdun, Aug. 24, 1914. He wrote a valuable monograph, *Les Quatuors de Beethoven,* which was publ. posthumously in Paris in 1917 and reprinted, with a preface by Gabriel Fauré, in 1925. He was the husband of the pianist Marguerite Long.

Maros, Rudolf, Hungarian composer; b. Stachy, Jan. 19, 1917. He studied with Kodály; in 1950 became prof. of the Music Academy in Budapest. In his early works he followed the national tradition of Kodály; then began to experiment with serial techniques. To the first period belong his ballet *The Wedding at Ecser;* a string quartet; a string trio; a bassoon concerto and *Musica leggiera* for wind quintet: in the second category are *Ricercare* for orch. (1957), *5 Studies* for orch. (1960) and the ballet *Ballad of the Miners* (1960).

Marpurg, Friedrich Wilhelm. Part I of *Die Kunst das Clavier zu spielen* was publ. in Berlin in 1750; part II appeared in 1761.

Marrocco, William Thomas. Add to books: *Music in America,* an anthology (in collaboration with Harold Gleason; N. Y., 1964).

Marsh, Robert Charles, American music critic; b. Columbus, Ohio, Aug. 5, 1924. He studied journalism at Northwestern Univ. (B.S., 1945) and philosophy (A.M., 1946); held a doctorate in education at Harvard (1951). Synchronously he took courses in music theory with Robert Palmer at Cornell Univ. (1946-47) and propaedeutics of music history with Hindemith at Harvard (1949-50); studied musicology with Thurston Dart and theory of criticism with H. S. Middleton at Cambridge, England (1955-56). He held teaching positions at the Univ. of Illinois (1947-49); Chicago City Junior College (1950-51); Univ. of Kansas City (1951-52); State Univ. of New York (1953-54) and Univ. of Chicago (1956-58). He became music critic with the Chicago 'Sun Times' in 1956; contributed articles on music to various literary publications and philosophical journals; edited *Logic and Knowledge of Bertrand Russell* (1956); publ. *Toscanini and the Art of Orchestral Performance* (Philadelphia, 1956; revised as *Toscanini and the Art of Conducting,* 1962); also a book on the Cleveland Orchestra (1967). In his newspaper criticisms, Marsh adopts a metaphorical language in vivid images, giving free rein to his personal evaluations of composers and performers.

Marsick, Armand. Died in Brussels, April 30, 1959.

Marteau, Henri. Add to bibl.: B. Marteau, *Henri Marteau, Siegeszug einer Geige* (Tutzing, 1971).

Martin, Frank. Add to works: *Le Mystère de la Nativité,* oratorio (Geneva, Dec. 24, 1959); *Monsieur de Pourceaugnac,* opera (Geneva, April 23, 1963); cello concerto (Basel, Jan. 27, 1967). Add bibl.: B. Billeter, *Frank Martin, Ein Aussenseiter der neuen Musik* (Basel, 1970).

Martinelli, Giovanni. Died in New York, Feb. 2, 1969.

Martino, Donald, American composer; b. Plainfield, New Jersey, May 16, 1931. He studied music at Princeton Univ. and in Florence. In his music he adopts the principle of serial composition based on arithmetical permutations. Among his works are a *Set for Clarinet;* quartet for clarinet and strings; *5 Fragments* for oboe and double-bass; woodwind quintet; pieces for piano solo. His trio for violin, clarinet and piano was performed at the Amsterdam Festival of Contemporary Music on June 13, 1963.

Martinon, Jean. Born Jan. 10 (not Jan. 18), 1910. He was musical director of the City of Düsseldorf from 1960 to 1963; conductor of the Chicago Symph. Orch., from 1963 to 1969. Add to works: cello concerto (Hamburg, Jan. 24, 1965); *Altitudes,* for orch. (Chicago, Dec. 30, 1965, composer conducting).

Martinu, Bohuslav. Died in Liestal, Switzerland, Aug. 28, 1959. Symph. No. 5 had its world première in Prague, May 27, 1947; the N. Y. performance on Jan. 24, 1948, was the American première. Date of first performance of *Fantaisies symphoniques,* Boston, Jan. 7 (not Jan. 9), 1955. The opera *Voják a tanečnice* (not *Tenečnice*) was first performed in Brno on May 5, 1928. *Les Larmes* (not *Lames*) *du couteau* (*The Tears of a Knife,* not *The Knife's Edge*), composed in 1928, was never performed. *Journée de bonté* (correct title *Semaine de bonté*) was left unfinished. *Hry o Marii* was first performed in Brno, Feb. 23, 1935 (not in 1934). *Hlas lesá* is a radio opera originally broadcast in Prague on Oct. 6, 1935. The English title of *Divadlo za bránou* is *Suburban* (not *Surburban*) *Theater;* it was first performed in Brno on Sept. 20, 1936. *Comedy on a Bridge* (original title, *Veselohra na mostě*) is a radio opera (first performed in Prague, on March 18, 1937). Correct title of the opera *Juliette* is *Julietta.* The ballet *Istar* was produced in Prague on Sept. 11, 1924 (not 1922). The ballet *Who is the most Powerful in the World?* was produced in Brno on Jan. 31, 1925; the ballet *Revolt* was produced in Prague on Feb. 11, 1928. *Špalíček* had its première in Prague on Sept. 19, 1933 (not 1932); it was revived and produced in a new version in Prague on April 2, 1949. Add to works: ballet, *The Strangler* (New London, Conn., Aug. 15, 1948); *Intermezzo* for orch. (Louisville Orch., Carnegie Hall, N. Y.. Dec. 29, 1950); *Suite on the Frescoes of Piero della Francesca* for orch. (Salzburg, Aug. 28, 1956); *Fantasia Concertante* for piano and orch. (Berlin, Jan 31, 1959); *Estampes,* symph. suite (Louisville, Feb. 4, 1959); *Parables,* symph. suite (Boston, Feb. 13, 1959); *Mirandolina,* opera (Prague, May 17, 1959); *Ariadne,* opera (Gelsenkirchen, March 2, 1961); *The Greek Passion,* oratorio (Zürich, June 9, 1961); *Prophecy of Isaiah,* oratorio (Jerusalem, April 2, 1963); *Alexander bis,* opera buffa (Mannheim, Feb. 18, 1964). Add to bibl.: Z. Zouhar, editor, *Bohuslav Martinu* (Brno, 1957); M. Šafránek, *Bohuslav Martinu: His Life and Works* (London, 1962); H. Halbreich, *Bohuslav Martinu* (Zürich, 1968).

Martirano, Salvatore, American composer; b. Yonkers, N. Y., Jan. 12, 1927. He studied piano and composition at the Oberlin Cons. of Music (B.M., 1951); then at the Eastman School of Music, Rochester, N. Y., with Bernard Rogers (M.M., 1952); later went to Italy where he took courses with Luigi Dallapiccola at the Cherubini Cons. of Music in Florence (1952-54). He served 14 months in the U. S. Marine Corps; played clarinet and cornet with the Parris Island Marine Band; received an honorable discharge with rank of Private First Class in 1946. From 1956-59 he held a fellowship to the American Academy in Rome, and in 1960 received a Guggenheim Fellowship and the American Academy of Arts and Letters Award. In 1968 he joined the faculty of the Univ. of Illinois at Urbana. He writes in a progressive avant-garde idiom, applying the quaquaversal techniques of vigesimosecular radical modernism in the ambience of total musical action. His works include the following: *Sextet* for wind instruments (1949); *Prelude* for orch. (1950); *Variations* for flute and piano (1950); string quartet No. 1 (1951); *The Magic Stones,* chamber opera after Decameron (Oberlin Cons. April 24, 1952); *Piece for Orchestra* (1952); violin sonata (1952); *Contrasto* for orch. (1954); *Chansons Innocentes* for soprano and piano (1957); *O,O,O,O, That Shakespeherian Rag* for mixed chorus and instrumental ensemble (1958); *Cocktail Music* for piano (1962); *Octet* (1963); *Underworld* for 4 actors, 4 percussion instruments, 2 double-basses, tenor saxophone and tape (1965); *Ballad* for amplified nite-club singer and instrumental ensemble (1966); *L's.G.A.* for a gas-masked politico, helium bomb, 3-16mm movie projectors and tape (1968); *The Proposal* for tapes and slides (1968); *Action Analysis* for 12 people, Bunny and controller (1968); *Selections* for alto flute, bass clarinet, viola and cello (1970).

Marvin, Frederick, American pianist; b. Los Angeles, June 11, 1923. He studied voice with his mother and appeared as a boy soprano on the radio; made his debut as a concert pianist in Los Angeles at the age of 16; then studied with Rudolf Serkin at the Curtis Institute of Music in Philadelphia. During World War II he worked as a musical therapist in U.S. Army hospitals; resuming his career after 1945 he gave concerts in the U.S.; made his first European tour in 1954. He did research in Spain on the works of Antonio Soler; discovered a number of his keyboard sonatas in manuscript; edited 6 vols. of Soler's music, including an important *Fandango.*

Marx, Joseph. Died in Graz, Sept. 3, 1964. Cf. E. Werba, *Joseph Marx: Eine Studie* (Vienna, 1964).

Mason, Colin. Died in London, Feb. 6, 1971. He was the music critic of the 'Daily Telegraph' from 1964; editor of 'Tempo' from 1962; edited the revised edition of Cobbett's *Cyclopedic Survey of Chamber Music* (London, 1963).

Massenet, Jules. Add to bibl: James Harding, *Massenet* (N. Y., 1971).

Masson, Gérard, French composer; b. Paris, Aug. 12, 1936. He took courses in advanced techniques with Stockhausen, Pousseur and Earle Brown, working along the lines of serial methods and acoustical coordination of sonorous blocs; experienced profound influence of the theory and practice of Varèse's 'organized sound.' His music is marked by strict constructivism, enlivened by lyric exoticism. Works: *Piece* for 14 instruments and percussion (1964); *Dans le Deuil des Vagues I* for 14 instruments (Royan Festival, April 1, 1967); *Ouest I* for 10 instruments (Vienna, April 25, 1968); *Dans le Deuil des Vagues II* for orch. (London, Nov. 20, 1968); *Ouest II* for voice and instruments (Paris, April 26, 1971). Stravinsky, who had an opportunity to examine some of Masson's scores, commended him in one of his last published interviews.

Matchavariani, Alexey Davidovitch. Add to works: *Hamlet,* opera (1964); *Knight in a Tiger's Skin,* ballet (1965).

Mather, Bruce, Canadian composer; b. Toronto, May 9, 1939. He studied in Toronto with Oskar Morawetz and John Weinzweig and in Paris with Darius Milhaud and Olivier Messiaen; subsequently entered Stanford Univ. (B.A., 1964) and the Univ. of Toronto (M.A., 1967). He is a lecturer on music at McGill Univ. in Montreal. He writes in neoclassical forms, but his idiom is tinged with acrid atonality. Works: *Venice* for soprano, clarinet, cello and piano (1957); *Concerto* for piano and chamber orch. (Aspen, Colo., Aug. 20, 1958, composer soloist); *Etude* for solo clarinet (1962); *Symphonic Ode* (Toronto, March 28, 1965); *Ombres* for orch. (1968); piano pieces; songs.

Mathias, Franz Xaver, Alsatian church musician; b. Dinsheim, July 16, 1871; d. Strasbourg, Feb. 2, 1939. He studied in Germany with Hugo Riemann; was organist at the Strasbourg Cathedral (1898-1908); then prof. of sacred music at the Univ. of Strasbourg. Among his works the best known is the oratorio *Mystère de Joseph,* containing an instrumental *Ballet égyptien.* He also wrote an oratorio of gigantic dimensions, *Urbem Virgo tuam serva* for two choruses (with the assistance of a 'crowd' of many voices); 28 cantatas; several Masses; psalms; motets; many organ pieces; publ. a manual of accompaniment of Gregorian Chant.

Mathis, Edith, Swiss soprano; b. Lucerne, Feb. 11, 1938. She studied in Zürich; made her operatic debut at the age of 18; was subsequently engaged at the Cologne Opera (1959); at the Salzburg Festival (1960) and in Glyndebourne (1962). In 1963 she joined the staff of the Berlin Opera; in 1964-65 was at the Hamburg State Opera.

Matičić, Janez, Slovenian composer; b. Ljubljana, June 3, 1926. He studied in Paris and worked in the electronic studios of the Radiodiffusion française; wrote numerous works using the resources of musique concrète. He also composed music in a traditional manner: a symph. (1953); songs; piano pieces.

Matsushita, Shin-ichi, Japanese composer; b. Osaka, Oct. 1, 1922. He studied in Japan; adopted an advanced cosmopolitan idiom. Works: *Correlazioni per 3 Gruppi* (1958); *Composizione da Camera per 8* (1958); *Le Croître Noir* for chorus, electronic instruments, piano, harp, percussion and concrete noises (Osaka, Nov. 14, 1959); *Canzona da Sonare* for piano and percussion (1960); *Successioni* for chamber orch. (1962); *Musique* for soprano and string quartet (Osaka, Sept. 14, 1964); *Fresque Sonore* for 7 instruments (1964).

Mattfeld, Julius. Died in New York, July 31, 1968. Add to books: *A Handbook of American Operatic Premières, 1731 - 1962* (Detroit, 1963).

Matthews, (Harvey) Alexander. His first Christian name is **Harry** (not Harvey). In 1971 he safely passed his 92nd birthday.

Matton, Roger, Canadian composer; b. Granby, Quebec, May 18, 1929. He studied at the Cons. of Montreal and with Nadia Boulanger in Paris. Returning to Canada in 1957, he became prof. of composition at Laval Univ. in Quebec City. Works: *Pax,* symph. suite (1950); *L'Horoscope,* choreographic suite (1958); *Concerto* for 2 pianos and orch. (1964); choral works.

Matys, Jiří, Czech composer; b. Bakov, Oct. 27, 1927. He studied at the Brno Cons., graduating in 1947. Among his works is a symph. (1951); 2 string quartets; a wind quintet; a quartet for 4 violins; several song cycles.

Matzenauer, Margarete. Died in Van Nuys, California, May 19, 1963.

Matzka, George, German-American violinist and composer; b. Coburg, Oct. 31, 1825; d. New York, June 15, 1883. He was a member of the N. Y. Philharmonic, and its conductor in 1876. He wrote overtures, choruses and some chamber music.

Mauersberger, Rudolf, German choral conductor and composer; b. Mauersberg, Jan. 29, 1889; d. Dresden, Feb. 22, 1971. He studied piano with Teichmüller, organ with Straube and music theory with Krehl at the Leipzig Cons. He held posts as choral conductor and organist in Aachen and Eisenach (1919-30); in 1930 went to Dresden; became a foremost proponent of choral singing methods in the classical tradition. He composed a number of liturgical works, mostly for chorus a cappella; also a *Dresdner Requiem* (1948), commemorating the destruction of Dresden in the air raid of March 1945.

Maunder, John Henry, British composer of sacred oratorios and hymns; b. London, 1858; d. there in 1920. He studied at the Royal Academy of Music in London; was organist in several London churches; also acted as piano accompanist. He began as a composer by writing an operetta, *Daisy Dingle* (1885); later devoted himself exclusively to oratorios, of which *The Martyrs* (Oxford, May 25, 1894), *Penitence, Pardon and Peace* and *From Olivet to Calvary* became perennial favorites in church performances well into the twentieth century.

Maury, Lowndes, American composer; b. Butte, Montana, July 7, 1911. He earned his B.A. degree in music at the Univ. of Montana in 1931; went to Los Angeles where he studied composition with Wesley La Violette and Schoenberg; became active in Hollywood as pianist, arranger and teacher. Works: violin sonata, *In Memory of the Korean War Dead* (1952); *Proud Music of the Storm,* cantata to words by Walt Whitman (1953); *Night Life* for cello and piano (1956); *Passacaglia* for string orch. (1959); *Springtime Digressions* for piano, flute and string quintet (1961); *Man is My Song,* cantata (1963); *Speculations* for piano and 3 string instruments (1964); *Summer of Green,* rhapsody for alto flute and string orch. (1964); *Scène de Ballet* for piccolo and string quartet (1965).

Maw, Nicholas, English composer; b. Grantham, Lincolnshire, Nov. 5, 1935. He played clarinet and piano; studied composition with Lennox Berkeley at the Royal Academy of Music in London (1955-58) and with Nadia Boulanger in Paris (1958-59). In his music he makes use of serial methods of composition without abandoning the principle of tonality. Works: *8 Chinese Lyrics* for mezzo-soprano (1956); flute sonatina (1957); *Requiem* for female choir, soprano, contralto, string trio and string orch. (1957); *Nocturne* for mezzo-soprano and orch. (1958); *6 Chinese Songs* for contralto and piano (1959); *5 Epigrams* for chorus a cappella (1960); *Chamber Music* for flute, clarinet, horn, bassoon and piano (1962); *Scenes and Arias* for solo voices and orch. (1962); *One-Man Show,* opera-buffa (London, Nov. 12, 1964); *Sinfonia* (Newcastle-upon-Tyne, May 1, 1966); *The Rising of the Moon,* opera (Glyndebourne, July 19, 1970). See Susan Bradshaw. *Nicholas Maw,* in the 'Mus. Times' (Sept. 1962).

Maxfield, Richard (**Vance**), American avant-garde composer; b. Seattle, Washington, Feb. 2, 1927; d. (by self-defenestration from a hotel room), Los Angeles, June 27, 1969. He studied at the Univ. of California, Berkeley, with Roger Sessions, and at Princeton Univ. with Milton Babbitt; also took courses with Ernst Krenek and Luigi Dallapiccola. He became deeply engaged in acoustical engineering and electronics; taught experimental music at the New School for Social Research in New York and at the San Francisco State College; contributed essays to avant-garde publications; two of them, in free verse, were published in *Contemporary Composers on Contemporary Music,* edited by Elliott Schwartz and Barney Childs (N. Y., 1967). His own works are for the most part designed for electronic instruments; typical of these is *Night Music,* produced by interaction of an oscilloscope and magnetic tape intended to evoke the antiphonal chirping of birds and humming of insects on a summer night; his *Cough Music,* with sonic materials obtained from coughs and other bronchial sound effects recorded during a modern dance recital and electronically arranged in a piece of tussive polyphony, was performed for the first time as the opening number in an audio-visual spectacle, 'Musical Essays in Time, Space and Sound' by the Division of Adult Education of the Cooper Union for the Advancement of Science and Art in New York City on Jan. 13, 1961.

Mayer, William, American composer; b. New York, Nov. 18, 1925. He studied at Yale Univ. and the Mannes College of Music; took lessons in composition with Roger Sessions and Felix Salzer. His most successful compositions are for the theater and the radio. Works: *The Greatest Sound Around,* short children's opera (1954); *Hello World!* ("a musical trip around the world"), children's opera for narrator, orch. and audience participation (N. Y., Nov. 10, 1956); *One Christmas Long Ago,* one-act opera (Philadelphia, Dec. 12, 1964); *Brief Candle,* "micro-opera" (1964); *The Snow Queen,* ballet (1963); *Andante for Strings* (1955); *Hebraic Portrait* for orch. (1957); *Overture for an American* (1958); *Two Pastels* for orch. (1960); *Country Fair* for brass trio (1962); *Elegy* for brass quintet (1964); *Octagon* for piano and orch. (N. Y., American Symphony, William Masselos soloist, Leopold Stokowski conducting, March 21, 1971); many choruses (*The Passionate Shepherd to His Love, The Nymph's Reply to the Passionate Shepherd, Corinna's Going A-Maying,* etc.); string quartet and other chamber music; piano sonata; children's pieces for piano; songs.

Mayer-Mahr, Moritz. Born Jan. 17 (not Jan. 7), 1869.

Mayer-Reinach, Albert. Died in Örebro, Sweden, Feb. 25, 1954.

Mayer-Serra, Otto. Died in Mexico City, March 19, 1968.

Mayuzumi, Toshiro. Add to works: *Phonologie symphonique* (Tokyo, May 28, 1957); *Nirvana Symphony* (Tokyo, April 2, 1958); *U-So-Ri,* oratorio (Tokyo, June 12, 1959); *Mandala-Symphonie* (Tokyo, March 27, 1960); *Bunraku* for cello solo (1960); *Music with Sculpture* for winds (Pittsburgh, June 29, 1961); *Prelude* for string quartet (1961); *Bugaku,* ballet (N. Y., March 20, 1963); *Samsara,* symph. poem (Tokyo, June 12, 1962); *Texture* for band (Pittsburgh, June 10, 1962); *Essay in Sonorities* (Osaka, Jan. 21, 1963); *Fireworks* for band (Pittsburgh, June 13, 1963); *Pratidesana,* Buddhist cantata (Kyoto, Sept. 5, 1963); *The Ritual Overture* for band (Pittsburgh, July 2, 1964); *The Birth of Music,* symph. poem (Tokyo, Oct. 10, 1964); symph. poem, *Showa Tempyo Raku* (*Old and Present Music;* Tokyo, Oct. 31, 1970).

Mazas, Jacques-Féréol. Date of death, Aug. 25 (not Aug. 26), 1849.

Mazzoleni, Ettore. Died in Toronto, as a result of an automobile accident, June 1, 1968.

McCabe, John, English pianist and composer; b. Liverpool, April 21, 1939, of mixed Scottish-Irish stock on his father's side and of German-Scandinavian-Spanish ancestry on his mother's. He played piano, violin and cello as a child and, according to family lore, composed 13 symphonies and an opera before puberty. He studied composition with Thomas Pitfield at Manchester Univ. (Mus. B., 1960); at the Royal Manchester College of Music and in Munich with Harald Genzmer; was pianist in residence at Univ. College in Cardiff (1965-68); then settled in London, devoting himself to composition and musical journalism. Works: *Movements* for clarinet, violin and cello (1964); Symph. No. 1 (1965); *Concertante* for harpsichord and chamber ensemble (1965); piano concerto No. 1 (1966); string trio (1966); *Nocturnal* for piano quintet (1966); *Dance Movements* for horn, violin and piano (1967); *Rounds* for brass quintet (1967); cantata *Aspects of Whiteness* for mixed chorus and piano (1967); *Concertante Music* for orch. (1968); *Metamorphoses* for harpsichord and orch. (1968); sonata for clarinet, cello and piano (1969); quartet for oboe and string trio (1969); *The Lion, the Witch and the Wardrobe,* children's opera (1969); piano concerto No. 2 (1970); Symph. No. 2 (1970). He also wrote *Miniconcerto* for organ, percussion and 485 penny-whistles (1966); *This Town's a Corporation Full of Crooked Streets,* an entertainment for speaker, tenor, children's chorus, mixed chorus and instrumental ensemble (1969); many piano pieces, organ works and choruses.

McCartney, John Paul, English rock 'n' roll singer and composer; member of the famous Liverpudlian quartet 'The Beatles'; b. Liverpool, June 18, 1942. He picked out chords on a family piano (his father was an amateur ragtime player), and at puberty began playing a left-handed guitar. He is the only 'Beatle' who attended college and studied English literature. Fascinated by Elvis Presley, he tried to emulate the spirit of American rock 'n' roll *à l'anglaise*. He joined John Lennon and George Harrison in the Casbah Club in Liverpool in 1959; this fruitful and fantastically lucrative association with them, and later with Ringo Starr, continued until the breakup of the group in 1970 when McCartney went to the High Court to end the partnership and asked for an accounting of assets and income. Endowed with an authentic poetic gift, McCartney infused a literary quality into the lyrics used by 'The Beatles,' fashioning them in archaic English prosody, which in combination with the modal harmony of the arrangements, imparted a somewhat distant quality to their products. Like his co-Beatles, McCartney went through a period of transcendental meditation when he sat at the feet of a hirsute Indian guru, but his British common sense soon overrode this metaphysical infatuation. See Hunter Davies, *The Beatles,* 'the authorized biography' (N. Y., 1968).

McCorkle, Donald Macomber. He publ. a valuable source book, *Moravian Music in Salem: A German-American Heritage* (Winston-Salem, N. C., 1958).

McCormack, John. Add to bibl.: R. Foxall, *John McCormack* (N. Y., 1964).

McCutchan, Robert Guy, American choral conductor and hymnologist; b. Mount Ayr, Iowa, Sept. 13, 1877; d. Claremont, Calif., May 15, 1958. He was active as music educator and choral conductor in the schools and churches of Iowa, Kansas and Indiana; made a thorough study of American hymnals and publ. a valuable compilation, *Our Hymnody* (Nashville, 1937; 2nd ed. 1942; contains detailed biographical information on American hymn composers); also *Hymn Tune Names: Their Sources and Significance* (Nashville, 1957).

McDonald, Susann, American harpist; b. Rock Island, Illinois, May 26, 1935. She studied with Marcel Grandjany in N. Y., and with Lily Laskine in Paris; received Premier Prix de harpe at the Paris Cons. (1955). She made her American debut in Los Angeles in 1956; then gave concerts in New York (1959), in Europe and in South America; conducted harp classes at the Univ. of Southern Calif. in Los Angeles from 1967; also at the Univ. of Arizona and at the Calif. State College at Los Angeles. She is noted for her interpretations of contemporary music and her complete command of modern harp techniques.

McDowell, John Herbert, American composer; b. Washington, D.C., Dec. 21, 1926. He studied at Colgate Univ. (B.A., 1948) and at Columbia Univ. with Otto Luening, Jack Beeson and Roger Goeb (M.A., 1957); held a Guggenheim Fellowship in 1962. He has written about 400 works; since 1962 devoted his energies chiefly to music for the theater and dance; has been active as theater director, actor and choreographer. His works include a cantata, *Good News From Heaven* (1957); *Four Sixes and a Nine* for orch. (1959); *Accumulation* for 35 flutes, strings and percussion (1964); 100-odd pieces for dance, among them *Insects and Heroes* (1961); *From Sea to Shining Sea,* an homage to Ives (1965); *Dark Psalters* (1968).

McEwen, Sir John Blackwood. He studied at the Royal Academy (not College) of Music; was principal there, and succeeded MacKenzie in that capacity.

McHugh, Jimmy, American composer of popular songs; b. Boston, July 10, 1894; d. Beverly Hills, May 22, 1969. He was a rehearsal accompanist for the Boston Opera Company before embarking on composition. He moved to New York in 1921. His first Broadway show was *Blackbirds of 1928* which included his greatest hit song *I Can't Give you Anything but Love, Baby.* In 1930 he went to Hollywood and began to write for the films; one of his most famous songs of the period was *South American Way.* During the war he wrote the inspirational song *Comin' in on a Wing and a Prayer.* He was awarded a Presidential Certificate of Merit for his work on War Bonds. He also received honorary doctor's degrees from Harvard Univ., Georgetown Univ. and Holy Cross College.

McKay, George Frederick. Died at Stateline, Nevada, Oct. 4, 1970. He retired from the Univ. of Washington School of Music in 1968.

McKinley, Carl. Died in Boston, July 24, 1966.

McKuen, Rod, lucky American minstrel and lyricist; b. Oakland, Calif., April 29, 1933; ran away from his previously broken home at the age of 11; bummed as logger, rod man, roping calves and dogging bulls in and out of rodeo shows; became a disc jockey and a script writer in a psychological warfare unit during the Korean war. Returning to the U.S., he appeared as a folksy balladeer in San Francisco night clubs; obtained a music theory book and learned to write tunes; supported himself by playing supporting roles in otherwise unsupportable bit parts in the movies; eked out a posh living by crashing parties and gorging himself on choice comestibles. He became a roving poet, dispensing a plethora of facile country style songs with monosyllabic assonances for rhymes and a simple appeal of scenes of non-obscene free love against an artificially flavored pastoral landscape. His first anthology of verse, *An Autumn Came,* was a failure, but he stumbled into a poetic bonanza with the commercially issued volumes *Stanyan Street* and *Listen to the Warm.* He never indentured himself to an agent, and so was able to reap a lucrative harvest of success, blandly chanting, 'I have no special bed, I give myself to those who offer love.'

McPhee, Colin. Died in Los Angeles, Jan. 7, 1964.

Medins, Janis. Died in Stockholm, March 4, 1966.

Méfano, Paul, French composer; b. Basra, Iraq, March 6, 1937. He studied at the Paris Cons. with Dandelot, Messiaen, Martenot and Milhaud; attended seminars of Boulez, Stockhausen and Pousseur in Basel. He received a grant of the Harkness Foundation for residence in the U.S. (1966-68) and in Berlin (1968-69). In his music he pursues a constructivist style, with an emphasis on rhythmic percussion and electronic sound; the influences of Stravinsky and Varèse are particularly in evidence. Works: *Incidences* for orch. and piano (1960); *Paraboles* for soprano and chamber ensemble (Paris, Jan. 20, 1965); *Interférences* for a chamber group (1966); *Lignes* for bass voice, brass, percussion, bassoon and amplified double-bass (1968); *Aurélia* for 3 choruses, 3 orchestras and 3 conductors (1968); *La Cérémonie* for voices, instrumental groups and speaking choruses (1970); *Intersection,* electronic piece for 2 generators and ring modulartor (1971).

Mehta, Mehli, Indian violinist and conductor, father of Zubin Mehta; b. Bombay, Sept. 25, 1908. He studied violin in Bombay and at the Trinity College in London, obtaining his licentiate there in 1929. In 1935 he founded the Bombay Symph. Orch.; in 1942 organized the Bombay String Quartet. He was assistant concertmaster of the Hallé Orch. in Manchester from 1955 to 1959; then settled in the U. S. In 1964 he became conductor of the orchestra of the Univ. of Calif., Los Angeles.

Mehta, Zubin, Indian conductor, son of Mehli Mehta; b. Bombay, April 29, 1936. He received his early musical training from his father; in 1954 he went to Vienna where he studied conducting with Hans Swarowsky. In 1958 he won an international competition for young conductors in Liverpool, England. In 1959 he was engaged as guest conductor of the Vienna Philharmonic, and subsequently conducted in Canada, France, England, Switzerland, Italy, Hungary, Rumania, Czechoslovakia, Poland and Russia. Developing with prodigious rapidity, he became the youngest conductor ever to lead a major symphony orchestra when at the age of 24 he was appointed associate conductor of the Los Angeles Philharmonic, and its music director in Dec., 1961. In 1962 he became concurrently conductor of the Montreal Symphony Orchestra. His romantic approach to conducting, combined with a superlative technical ability, have contributed to his spectacular success with audiences in Europe and America. He is especially appreciated in Israel, where he made frequent appearances.

Meitus, Yuli Sergeyevitch. Add to works: *The Purloined Happiness,* opera (Lwow, Sept. 11, 1960); *The Brothers Ulyanov,* opera (Ufa, Nov. 25, 1967).

Melachrino, George Miltiades, English band leader; b. London, May 1, 1909; d. there, June 18, 1965. He studied at the Trinity College of Music; formed his own band; then launched a new group, the Melachrino Strings, which he imbued with black-velvet coloration that made the 'Melachrino sound' a byword among music lovers. He could play every instrument except harp and piano.

Melani, Jacopo. Exact date of death, Aug. 19, 1676.

Melba, Nellie. Melba toast is a crisp, thinly-sliced toasted bread, patented in 1929 by Bert Weil (1890-1965), president of the Devonsheer Melba Corporation. Add to bibl.: J. Wechsberg, *Red Plush and Black Velvet: The Story of Melba and her Times* (Boston, 1961).

Melichar, Alois, Austrian music critic; b. Vienna, April 18, 1896. He studied theory at the Vienna Academy of Music with Josef Marx (1917-20) and at the Hochschule für Musik in Berlin with Schreker (1920-23). In 1923-26 he was in the Caucasus where he collected materials on Caucasian folk songs; from 1927-33 was active as conductor in Berlin; from 1946-49 was in charge of Vienna radio broadcasts of modern music. In his compositions he follows the safe footpath of Reger, Pfitzner and Graener; he wrote a symph. poem *Der Dom* (1934); *Rhapsodie über ein schwedisches Volkslied* (1939); *Lustspiel-Ouvertüre* (1942); lieder; film music. As a music critic, he acquired notoriety by his vicious attacks on modern composers. His books written in this virulent polemical manner include *Die unteilbare Musik* (Vienna, 1952); *Musik in der Zwangsjacke* (Vienna, 1958) and *Schönberg und die Folgen* (Vienna, 1960.)

Melik-Pashayev, Alexander, Russian conductor; b. Tiflis, Georgia, Oct. 23, 1905; d. Moscow, June 18, 1964. He studied at the Leningrad Cons. (1928-30); began his career in Tiflis as opera conductor; from 1931, was at the Bolshoi Theater in Moscow. For his productions of Russian and Italian operas he received 2 Stalin Prizes, in 1942 and 1943.

Melis, Carmen. Died in Longone al Segrino, Italy, Dec. 19, 1967.

Melkikh, Dmitri Mikheyevitch. Died in Moscow, Feb. 22, 1943. He wrote 3 symphonies (1925, 1933, 1938), 4 string quartets, etc.

Mellers, Wilfrid Howard. Add to books: *Music in a New Found Land: Themes and Developments in the History of American Music* (N. Y., 1965); *Harmonious Meetings: A Study of the Relationships between English Music, Poetry and Theatre c. 1600-1900* (London, 1965); *Caliban Reborn: Renewal in Twentieth-Century Music* (N. Y., 1967).

Mellnäs, Arne, Swedish composer; b. Stockholm, Aug. 30, 1933. He studied with Lars-Erik Larsson and Karl-Birger Blomdahl; later he took courses with Boris Blacher and György Ligeti, specializing in electronic music. Among his works are *Collage* for orch. (1962); *Tombola* for chamber ensemble (1962); *Per caso* for chamber ensemble (1963); *Aura* for orch. (1964); *Gestes Sonores* for any ensemble (1964); *Sick Transit* for instruments and tape (1965); *Intensity 6, 5* for tape (1966; dedicated to the memory of Edgar Varèse, containing electronically modified quotations from Varèse's piece for solo flute, *Density 21.5*); *Drones* for jazz combo (1967); an opera *Minibuff* for two singers and tape (1967); *Conglomerat* for electronic music (1967); *Eufoni* for electronic music (1969); *Monotrem* for electronics (1969); *Far Out,* electronic composition with texts (1970); *Capricorn Flakes* for piano, harpsichord and vibraphone (1970); *Splinters* for electronic music (1970); *Schizofoni* for singular or plural pianos (1971).

Melton, James. Died in New York, April 21, 1961. Studied at Vanderbilt College with Gaetano de Luca (not Giuseppe de Luca).

Menager, Laurent, Luxembourg composer; b. Luxembourg, Jan. 10, 1835; d. there, Feb. 7, 1902. He was a song composer and a respected pedagogue. A postage stamp was issued in his honor by the Government of Luxembourg in 1951.

Menasce, Jacques de. Died in Gstaad, Switzerland, Jan. 28, 1960.

Mendelsohn, Alfred, Rumanian composer; b. Bucharest, Feb. 17, 1910; d. there, May 9, 1966. He studied in Vienna with Joseph Marx, Franz Schmidt and others (1928-31); in Bucharest with Jora. From 1944-54 he was conductor of the Rumanian Opera in Bucharest; in 1949 was appointed prof. at the Bucharest Cons. An exceptionally prolific composer, he produced a great amount of highly competent, technically accomplished music. Influenced primarily by the programmatic romanticism of the Vienna School, he also probed the potentialities of motivic structures, suggesting the serial concepts of modern constructivists, while remaining faithful to basic tonalitarianism. Works: the ballets *Harap Alb* (*The White Moor;* 1949); *Calin* (1956); the oratorios *1907* (dealing with the 1907 peasant uprising in Rumania; Bucharest, March 21, 1957), *1917* (on the Russian Revolution; 1956), *Glasul lui Lenin (The Voice of Lenin;* Bucharest, Nov. 2, 1957); 8 symphonies (1945-61); symph. poems *Prăbusirea Doftanei* (*Doftana's Assault;* 1949), *Eliberarea* (*Liberation;* 1954), *Va înflori acel armindean* (*The May Tree Will Blossom;* 1961). *Schite dobrogene* (*Dobrudjan Sketches;* 1961); chamber symph. (1961); 2 piano concertos (1946, 1949); cello concerto (1950); 2 violin concertos (1952, 1957); concertino for harp and strings (1955); *Divertimento* for horn and strings (1957); organ concerto (1959); 9 string quartets (1930-60); piano quintet (1953); harp quintet (1955); string sextet (1957); piano trio (1959); 4 violin sonatas; song cycles; piano pieces.

Mendelssohn, Felix. Add to bibl.: Hans C. Worbs, *Felix Mendelssohn-Bartholdy: Wesen und Wirken im Spiegel von Selbsterzeugnissen* *und Berichten der Zeitgenossen* (Leipzig, 1958); H. E. Jacob, *Felix Mendelssohn und seine Zeit* (Frankfurt, 1959); Eric Werner, *Felix Mendelssohn, a New Image of the Composer and His Age* (N. Y., 1963); G. Friedrich, *Die Fugenkomposition in Mendelssohns Instrumentalwerk* (Bonn, 1969); S. Grossmann-Vendrey, *Felix Mendelssohn-Bartholdy und die Musik der Vergangenheit* (Regensberg, 1969); Willi Reich, *Felix Mendelssohn im Spiegel eigener Aussagen und zeitgenössischer Dokumente* (Zürich, 1970).

Mendelssohn, Felix Robert. He was a lateral, not direct descendant (grand-grandnephew) of Felix Mendelssohn.

Mengelberg, Kurt Rudolf. Died in Monte Carlo, Oct. 12, 1959.

Mennin, Peter. Was director of the Peabody Cons. in Baltimore (1959-63). In 1963, appointed president of the Juilliard School of Music. Add to works: Symph. No. 7, subtitled *Variation Symphony* (Cleveland, Jan. 23, 1964); *Canto for Orchestra* (1964); *Pied Piper of Hamelin* for narrator and orch., to the poem of Robert Browning (Cincinnati, May 2, 1969); *Symphonic Movements* (Minneapolis, Jan. 21, 1971; later performed also under the title *Sinfonia*).

Menotti, Gian Carlo. Add to works: *Labyrinth,* television opera to Menotti's own libretto (N. Y., March 3, 1963); *Death of the Bishop of Brindisi,* dramatic cantata with the text by the composer (Cincinnati, May 18, 1963); *Le dernier sauvage,* opera buffa, originally with an Italian libretto by Menotti, produced at the Opéra-Comique in Paris in a French translation (Oct. 21, 1963; produced in English at the Metropolitan Opera, New York, Jan. 23, 1964); *Martin's Lie,* chamber opera to Menotti's text (Bath, England, June 3, 1964); *Help, Help, the Globolinks!,* 'an opera in one act for children and those who like children' to words by Menotti, with electronic effects (Hamburg, Dec. 19, 1968); *Triplo Concerto a Tre,* triple concerto in 3 movements (N. Y., Oct. 6, 1970); *The Most Important Man,* opera to his own libretto, commissioned by the N. Y. City Opera (N. Y., March 12, 1971). He also wrote a play without music, *The Leper* (Tallahassee, Florida, April 22, 1970). Bibl.: Robert Tricoire, *Gian Carlo Menotti, l'Homme et son œuvre* (Paris, 1966).

Menuhin, Yehudi. Add bibl.: N. Wymer, *Yehudi Menuhin* (London, 1961); Eric Fenby, *Menuhin's House of Music* (London, 1969).

Mercure, Pierre. Died in an ambulance between Avallon and Auxerres, France, on Jan. 29, 1966, after an automobile crash while driving from Paris to Lyon. Add to works: *Divertimento* for solo string quartet and string orch. (1957); *Triptique* for orch. (1959); *Incandescence,* ballet music for synthetic electronic sounds on magnetic tape (1961); *Structures métalliques,* metallic sonorities on tape (1961); *Répercussions* for triple magnetic tapes (1961); *Psaume pour abri,* radiophonic cantata for narrator, electronic music, orch. and 2 choirs (Montreal, May 15, 1963).

Merikanto, Aarre. Died in Helsinki, Sept. 28, 1958. Date of birth, June 29 (not July 29), 1893.

Merö, Yolanda. Died in New York, Oct. 17, 1963.

Merriman, Nan (Katherine-Ann), American mezzo-soprano; b. Pittsburgh, April 28, 1920. She studied with Alexia Bassian in Hollywood; made her debut as soloist with the NBC Symph. Orch. under Toscanini on July 25, 1943; appeared subsequently with numerous other orchestras in Europe and America, in Beethoven's *Missa Solemnis,* Mahler's *Lied von der Erde,* etc. She excels in songs by Mahler, Debussy, Ravel and Manuel de Falla.

Mersenne, Marin. Add to bibl.: *Marin Mersenne: Correspondance,* ed. by C. de Waard (Paris, 1959).

Messiaen, Olivier. Add to works: *Chronochromie* for orch. (Donaueschingen, Oct. 16, 1960); *La Transfiguration de notre Seigneur Jésus Christ,* in 13 movements for voices and orch. to words from the New Testament, St. Thomas Aquinas and the Catholic liturgy, scored for mixed chorus in 10 parts, 7 instrumental soloists and orchestra with a large percussion section (Gulbenkian Festival, Lisbon, June 7, 1969). Add to bibl.: A. Goléa, *Rencontres avec Olivier Messiaen* (Paris, 1961).

Mester, Jorge, American conductor; b. Mexico City, April 10, 1935, of Hungarian parents. He attended an American school in Mexico City and later a military academy in Hollywood. In 1952 he enrolled at the Juilliard School of Music as a student in conducting with Jean Morel, graduating in 1958. He also attended conducting classes with Leonard Bernstein in Tanglewood; at 22 was appointed to the Juilliard faculty. In 1959-60 he was music director of the St. Louis Philharmonic Orch.; in 1961-62 was musical director of the Greenwich Village Symph.

Orch. in N. Y. In 1965 he became musical director for the parodisitic P.D.Q. Bach Series at Lincoln Center; in 1965-66 conducted orchestras in Japan, Germany, Switzerland and Italy. In 1967 he was engaged as musical director and conductor of the Louisville Symph. Orch.; in 1967-71 appeared as guest conductor with the Los Angeles Philharmonic, Pittsburgh Symph. Orch., New Orleans Philharmonic, Philadelphia Orch., Cincinnati Symph. Orch. and the Boston Symph. Orch.; also conducted opera and ballet at the Spoleto summer festivals. In 1969 he was appointed music director of the Aspen Music Festival. He is the recipient of the Naumburg award for excellence, competence and elegance in his performances (1968). Equally at home in the classical and modern repertory, in symphonic music and in opera, Mester's interpretations are marked by a rhapsodic sense of color combined with a precision of technical detail.

Messner, Joseph. Died in Salzburg, Feb. 23, 1969.

Metallov, Vassili Mikhailovitch. Died in Moscow, June 1, 1926 (not 1927).

Meulemans, Arthur. Died in Brussels, June 29, 1966.

Meyer, Leonard B., American musicologist and writer on esthetics; b. New York, Jan. 12, 1918. He studied philosophy and composition at Columbia Univ. (M.A. in music, 1948) and humanities at the Univ. of Chicago (Ph.D., 1954); also took private lessons in composition with Stefan Wolpe and Aaron Copland. In 1946 he was appointed to the staff of the Univ. of Chicago; in 1961, chairman of the Music Dept. He publ. an important book dealing with the problems of communication and cultural contexts in the human response to music, *Emotion and Meaning in Music* (Chicago, 1956) and *The Rhythmic Structure of Music* (with Grosvenor Cooper; Chicago, 1960); also contributed valuable articles to various scholarly journals.

Meyer-Beer, Kathi. Correct form of last name is **Meyer-Baer.**

Meyerbeer, Giacomo. Vol. I of his correspondence and diaries was publ. by the Academy of Arts in Berlin, edited by Heinz Becker (Berlin, 1960).

Meyer-Eppler, Werner, Dutch - German physicist and pioneer in electronic music; b. Antwerp, April 30, 1913; d. Bonn, July 8, 1960. He studied physics and mathematics in Cologne and Bonn. In 1949 he joined the faculty of the Bonn University, working on communication theory. He published a valuable treatise, *Musik, Raumgestaltung und Elektroakustik* (Mainz, 1955).

Meyerowitz, Jan. Add to works: one-act opera *Port Town* to the libretto by Langston Hughes (Berkshire Music Center, Tanglewood, Aug. 4, 1960); opera, *Godfather Death* (1961); ballet *Homage to Hieronymus Bosch* (Marseille, 1961); *Flemish Overture — Homage to Pieter Breughel,* symph. poem (Cleveland, Dec. 3, 1959); concerto for flute and orch. (1962); concerto for oboe and orch. (1963); *Die Doppelgängerin,* opera (Hannover, Jan. 29, 1967).

Meylan, Pierre, Swiss musicologist and editor; b. Lucens (Vaud), Oct. 22, 1908. He studied philology at the Universities of Lausanne, Halle and Leipzig, and piano in Lausanne. In 1933 he began his career as a musical journalist and writer, specializing in the problem of literary sources of musical works. He publ. *Les écrivains et la musique* (2 vols.; Lausanne, 1944, 1952); edited the collections *Richard Strauss: Anecdotes et Souvenirs* (Lausanne, 1951); *Les plus belles lettres de Mozart* (Lausanne, 1956). He is editor-in-chief of 'Revue Musicale de Suisse Romande.'

Miaskovsky, Nikolai Yakovlevitch. The world première of Symph. No. 13 was given in Winterthur, Switzerland, Oct. 16, 1934 (not in Chicago); Symph. No. 16 is in F major (not D minor); Symph. No. 17, in G-sharp minor (not C-sharp minor); Symph. No. 21 is subtitled *Symphonie-Fantaisie* (not *Symphonie-Fantasie*); *Salutatory Overture* was first performed on Dec. 21 (not 20), 1939. Symph. No. 25 was performed for the first time on March 6 (not March 15), 1947. Symph. No. 26 was not unperformed; it had its first performance in Moscow, Dec. 28, 1948. Add to bibl.: S. Shlifstein, ed., *Miaskovsky, Articles, Letters, Reminiscences* (2 vols.; Moscow, 1959).

Michelangeli, Arturo Benedetti, Italian pianist; b. Brescia, Jan. 5, 1920. He was trained by his father; gave recitals as a child; won the International Piano Contest in Geneva in 1939. He served in the Italian Air Force during World War II; after the war he devoted himself mainly to teaching. Resuming his concert career with grand éclat, and repeatedly toured Europe and America with enormous acclaim. His playing combines a superb modern technique with a quasi-romantic type of interpretation without being outré.

Middleton, Hubert Stanley, British organist and music educator; b. Windsor, May 11, 1890; d. London, Aug. 13, 1959. He studied at the Royal Academy of Music in London and at the Univ. of Cambridge (M.A., 1920). He was appointed organist and director of music at Trinity College, Cambridge, in 1931; also taught at the Royal Academy of Music in London. His specialty was cathedral music. He himself composed a certain number of anthems and organ pieces. He was greatly esteemed as an educator, and his teaching methods exercised profound influence on his students, many of whom became educators in their own right.

Mieg, Peter, Swiss composer; b. Lenzburg, Sept. 5, 1906. He studied piano and theory in Basel; took courses in literature and archeology in Paris; received his Ph.D. in Zürich for a dissertation on art. He subsequently studied composition with Frank Martin; simultaneously was active as a professional painter. His works comprise a string trio (1937); 2 string quartets (1938, 1945); concerto for 2 pianos and orch. (1941); ballet, *Daphne* (1945); 2 piano concertos (1947, 1961); violin concerto (1949); *Concerto Veneziano* for string orch. (1955); concerto for oboe and orch. (1957); *Sinfonie* (1958); concerto for flute and string orch. (1962); several piano sonatas and other piano pieces; songs.

Mignan, Édouard-Charles-Octave, French organist and composer; b. Paris, March 17, 1884; d. there, Sept. 17, 1969. He studied at the Paris Cons. with Widor (organ) and Paul Vidal (composition); was church organist at Orléans and later on at the Madeleine in Paris. He wrote a number of melodious orchestral suites, a symphony, sacred choruses, numerous motets and organ pieces.

Migot, Georges. Add to works: *Cantate de la Vie meilleure* (Paris, Jan. 29, 1959); *La Passion* for chorus and orch. (Hilversum, March 27, 1959); *Nuit pascale et Résurrection,* oratorio (Paris, March 28, 1959); *Symphonie* (Bésançon, Sept. 7, 1961).

Mihalovici, Marcel. Add to works: *Les Jumeaux,* opera (Brunswick, Germany, Jan. 23, 1963).

Mihály, András, Hungarian composer; b. Budapest, Nov. 6, 1917. He studied with Kadosa; became a prof. of chamber music at the Music Academy in Budapest. He composes in the neo-classical idiom; among his works are 2 string quartets (1947, 1960); cello concerto (1953); *Fantasy* for wind quintet and string orch. (1956); violin concerto (1959); a number of didactic pieces.

Mikuli, Karl. Date of birth, Oct. 20, 1819 (not 1821).

Milde, Hans Feodor von. Place of birth, Petronell (not Petronek).

Miletić, Miroslav, Croatian violinist and composer; b. Sisak, Aug. 22, 1925. He studied in Zagreb; organized there the renowned Pro Arte String Quartet, specializing in performances of modern music. Works: operas, *Hasanaginica* and *Der Fall Ruženka;* radio-opera *Auvergnanski Senatori* (1957); *Vision,* television ballet (1958); suite for string orch. (1955); violin concerto (1958); viola concerto (1959); symph. (1959); *Rhapsodic Variations* for violin and piano (1962); 4 string quartets; violin sonata; *Proportions* for 6 instruments; *Lamentation* for viola and magnetic tape; piano pieces; Croatian songs arranged for recorder.

Milford, Robin. Died in Lyme Regis, Dec. 29, 1959.

Milhaud, Darius. His Symph. No. 5 was first performed on the Turin Radio on Oct. 16, 1953 (not 1955). His opera *David* was written to celebrate not the foundation of Jerusalem, but its establishment as the capital of Judaea. *Le Pauvre Matelot* was composed in 1926 (not 1916). Add to works: piano concerto No. 5 (N.Y., June 25, 1956); Symph. No. 9 (Fort Lauderdale, Florida, March 29, 1960); *Aubade* for orch. (Oakland, March 14, 1961); Symph. No. 10 (Portland, Oregon, April 4, 1961); Symph. No. 11 (1961); Symph No. 12 *(Rural;* Davis, California, Feb. 16, 1962); *Murder of a Great Chief of State* for orch. (to the memory of John F. Kennedy; Oakland, Dec. 3, 1963); *Pacem in terris,* choral symph. (Paris, Dec. 20, 1963); string septet (Washington, Oct. 31, 1964); *La Mère Coupable,* opera to a libretto by Madeleine Milhaud after Beaumarchais (Geneva, June 13, 1966); *Musique pour Prague* for orch. (1966); piano quartet (1966); *Musique pour l'Indiana* for orch. (Indianapolis, Oct. 29, 1966); *Musique pour Lisbonne* for orch. (1966); *Musique pour Nouvelle Orléans* (announced for performance by the New Orleans Symph. Orch. for March 12, 1968, but cancelled and performed for the first time in Aspen, Colorado, Aug. 11, 1968, with Milhaud conducting); *Cantate de Psaumes* (Paris, May 2, 1968);

Musique pour l'Univers Claudelien (Aix-en-Provence, July 30, 1968); piano trio (1968); *Stanford Serenade* (Stanford, May 24, 1970); *Musique pour Graz* (Graz, Nov. 24, 1970); *Six Danses en trois mouvements* for 2 pianos (Paris, Dec. 17, 1970); *Saint Louis, Roi de France,* opera-oratorio to the poem of Paul Claudel (1970-71), with interpolations from 13th-century texts selected and adapted by Henri Doublier. Milhaud's teacher of fugue and composition was Widor; he studied conducting (not composition) with Vincent d'Indy; did not study orchestration with Paul Dukas, but rather played in the first violin section of the student orchestra of the Paris Cons. which Dukas conducted. Add bibl.: Antonio Braga, *Darius Milhaud* (Naples, 1969).

Miller, Glenn, American trombonist and band leader; b. Clarinda, Iowa, March 1, 1904; perished in a plane during the war on a flight from England to France, Dec. 16, 1944. He studied at the Univ. of Colorado; went to N. Y. in 1930; in 1935 joined Ray Noble's band. He then went to Joseph Schillinger to study orchestration; began experimenting with special effects, combining clarinets with saxophones in the same register; the resultant sound became the Glenn Miller hallmark. At the outbreak of World War II, he assembled a large band and flew to England where he played for the American Air Force. A motion picture, 'The Glenn Miller Story,' was produced in 1953.

Millöcker, Karl. Date of birth, April 29 (not May 29), 1842.

Mills-Cockell, John, Canadian composer; b. in Toronto, May 19, 1943. He studied composition and electronic music at the Univ. of Toronto and at the Royal Cons. of Music there. In 1966 he developed, in collaboration with the writer Blake Parker, artist Michael Hayden and designer Dick Zander, a method of composition and performance called Intersystems; joined the rock bands 'Kensington Market' in Toronto and 'Hydroelectric Streetcar' in Vancouver, utilizing the Moog Synthesizer; in 1970 organized his own band 'Syrinx,' a trio including electric hand drums, electric saxophone and Moog Synthesizer. He also wrote electronic music for films. His works include *Canonic Variations* for prepared piano, bassoon and stereo tape; a wind quartet; *Reverberations* for solo trombone and 2 stereo tape loops; numerous pieces for mixed media, among them *Journey Tree, Father of Light, Apaloosa-Pegasus, Hollywood Dream Trip,* and *Gold Rush.*

Milner, Anthony, English composer; b. Bristol, May 13, 1925. He studied with Herbert Fryer and R. O. Morris at the Royal College of Music, London, and privately with Mátyás Seiber. He taught at Morley College in London (1947-62); appointed to the staff of Royal College of Music, London, in 1962. In 1965 he was appointed lecturer, Univ. of London, King's College. Works: *Variations* for orch. (1958); *Divertimento* for string orch. (1961); *April Prologue* for orch. (1961); *Sinfonia pasquale* for string orch. (1963); symph. (1964); cantatas: *Salutatio Angelica* (1948), *The City of Desolation* (1955), *St. Francis* (1956), *The Water and the Fire* (1961); quartet for oboe and strings (1953); string quartet (1964); quintet for wind instruments (1964); sacred choruses a cappella; song cycles. He publ. *Harmony for Class Teaching* (2 vols.; 1950).

Mimaroglu, Ilhan Kemaleddin, Turkish composer and musicologist; b. Istanbul, March 11, 1926. He studied law at the Univ. of Ankara; traveled to the U.S. on a Rockefeller Fellowship in 1955; took courses at Columbia Univ. with Jack Beeson, Chou Wen-chung and Vladimir Ussachevsky; also received some advice from Edgar Varèse. Under the auspices of the Turkish-American Univ. Association he lectured on modern music in Turkey; publ. several monographs in connection with the U.S. Information Agency (*Sounds of America, Jazz as an Art, 11 Contemporary Composers, A History of Music*). Works: *Parodie sérieuse* for string quartet (1947); 4 pieces for clarinet and piano (1952); *Pièces sentimentales* for piano (1957); *Pièces futiles* for clarinet and cello (1958); *Bagatelles* for piano (1959); *Trio 1961* for clarinet, violin and piano (1961); *2 x e.e.* for vocal quartet, on poems of e.e. cummings (1963); *Conjectus I* for 3 instruments (1964); *Music* for 4 bassoons and cello (1964); *Trenodia* for piano (1965). He also wrote compositions for electronic instruments: *Rhapsody for Clarinet and Clarinet* (1963), *3 Visual Studies* (1964), *Le Tombeau d' Edgar Poe* (1964), *Anacolutha* (1965).

Mingus, Charlie, American jazz musician; b. Nogales, Arizona, April 22, 1922. He played the bass fiddle in various combos; composed jazz pieces with sophisticated titles, such as *Pithecantropus Erectus* and many mock-sentimental ballads. See *Beneath the Underdog; His World as Composed by Mingus* (dictated autobiography, edited by Nel King; N. Y., 1971).

Minkus, (Aloysius) Ludwig, Austrian composer; b. Vienna, March 23, 1826; d. after 1891 (place and date unknown). He was a violinist by profession; in 1850 he went to Russia; served as music supervisor at the Bolshoi Theater in Moscow (1866-72); in 1872 went to St. Petersburg where he became ballet composer for the Imperial Theaters. His undistinguished but easily choreographable music found lasting favor with Russian balletmasters and balletomanes; his ballets are firmly embedded in the repertory of Soviet theaters as well. His most popular scores, the best of which may be charitably compared with diluted Delibes, include *La Fiammetta* (1863), *Don Quixote* (1869) and *La Bayadère* (1877). He left Russia after the termination of his contract with the Imperial Theaters in 1891; all efforts to find out where and when he died have remained fruitless.

Mirovitch, Alfred, Russian-American pianist; b. St. Petersburg, May 4, 1884; d. Whitefield, N. M., Aug. 3, 1959. He graduated from the St. Petersburg Cons. with the first prize in piano as a student of Anna Essipova in 1909; began his concert career in 1911; made 9 world tours; made his American debut in 1921. He conducted master classes in piano at the Juilliard School of Music, N. Y. (1944-52); then joined the faculty of Boston Univ. He edited, for G. Schirmer, Inc., a number of collections of classical piano music for students: *Early Classics for the Piano; Introduction to Piano Classics* (3 vols. for different grades); *Introduction to the Romantics; Introduction to the Study of Bach* (2 vols.); *Introduction to Chopin* (2 vols.); also edited piano pieces by Russian composers; wrote original piano compositions (*Spring Song, Toccata,* etc.).

Mirzoyan, Edvard, Armenian composer; b. Gori, Georgia, May 12, 1921. He studied music in Erevan, and later in Moscow. In 1948 he became prof. at the Erevan Cons. In his music he follows a lucid neo-classical style, while his thematic materials are of native Armenian provenance. He wrote a string quartet (1947); the cantatas *Soviet Armenia* (1948) and *Lenin* (in collaboration with Arutunian, 1950); a symph. for strings (1962, his strongest composition); songs. The characteristic melorhythms of Armenian folk music are omnipresent in his works.

Misch, Ludwig, German-American musicologist; b. Berlin, June 13, 1887; d. New York, April 22, 1967. He studied music theory with Max Friedlaender at the Univ. of Berlin; simultaneously took courses in law, obtaining his doctor's degree in Heidelberg in 1911. He was music critic for the 'Allgemeine Musikzeitung' (1909-13); conducted theater orchestras in Berlin, Essen and Bremen. From 1921 to 1933 he was music critic of the 'Berliner Lokalanzeiger.' Under the Nazi regime he conducted a Jewish Madrigal Choir in Berlin until he was sent to a concentration camp. In 1947 he emigrated to New York, where he became active as organist and musicologist. He publ. the valuable books *Johannes Brahms* (Berlin, 1922); *Beethoven-Studien* (Berlin, 1950; also in English, in an enlarged edition, Norman, Oklahoma, 1953); translated and annotated (with Donald W. MacArdle) *New Beethoven Letters* (Norman, Oklahoma, 1957).

Mischakov, Mischa. Resigned as concertmaster of the Detroit Symph. Orch. in 1968. His original name was Mischa Fischberg; inasmuch as there was a prolixity of Russian-Jewish violinists named Fischberg playing in American orchestras, he decided to change it by adding the Russian ending 'koff' to his first name, which in itself is a Russian diminutive for Michael. He retained the spelling Mischakoff; the version Mischakov may be phonetically justified, but is improper. He owns two Stradivarius violins.

Misón, Luis. Date of death, Feb. 13, 1776 (not 1766).

Misra, Mahapurush, Indian virtuoso on the tabla; b. Calcutta, Jan. 1, 1933. He studied with eminent swamis and gurus; toured in Europe in 1959 and in the U.S. in 1961.

Mitchell, Donald. Died in Binghampton, N. Y., Aug. 17, 1971. Add to books: *Gustav Mahler: The Early Years* (N. Y., 1958); *The Language of Modern Music* (London, 1963).

Mitchell, Dwike, American jazz pianist; b. Jacksonville, Florida, Feb. 14, 1930. He studied at the Philadelphia Music Academy; formed a duo with the French horn player and bassist Willie Ruff, a Yale Univ. graduate, and together they played in night clubs with complete popular acceptance despite their academic education and ability to read music. In 1959 they gave impromptu sessions of jazz music in Russia, overcoming Soviet coolness for hot jazz and arousing unrestrained enthusiasm among the young Soviet audiences.

Mitchell, Howard. In 1969 he resigned as conductor of the National Symphony Orch. in Washington.

Mitropoulos, Dimitri. Died in Milan, Nov. 2, 1960.

Mittelmann, Norman, Canadian baritone; b. Winnipeg, May 25, 1932. He studied with Martial Singher at the Curtis Institute in Philadelphia, and with Lotte Lehmann in Santa Barbara, Calif. He was a member of the staff of the Toronto Opera. On Oct. 28, 1961 he made his debut in a minor role at the Metropolitan Opera.

Mittler, Franz. Died in Munich, Dec. 28, 1970.

Miyoshi, Akira, Japanese composer; b. Tokyo, Jan. 10, 1933. He studied in Tokyo and later in Paris. His works include a sonata for flute, cello and piano (1955); *Trois Mouvements symphoniques* (1960); 2 string quartets (1961, 1967); *Duel* for soprano and orch. (1964); Concerto for Orchestra (1964); violin concerto (1965).

Mizelle, John, American avant-garde composer; b. in Stillwater, Oklahoma, June 14, 1940. He studied at the Sacramento State College (B.A., 1965) and at the Univ. of California in Davis (M.A., 1967) where he took courses with Larry Austin, Jerome Rosen, Karlheinz Stockhausen, Richard Swith, and David Tudor. He later joined the staff at Davis as Associate prof. in music. He is a professional trombone player and a member of the New Music Ensemble. In his music he affects technological associations; uses graphic notation. Works: *Piano Opus* (1966); *Light Sculpture* (1967); *Radial Energy I* (1967); *Mass for Voices and Electronics* (1967); *Tangential Energy II* (1968); *Wave Forms* (1968).

Moevs, Robert W., American composer; b. La Crosse, Wisconsin, Dec. 2, 1921. He studied at Harvard Univ. (A. B., 1942); after service as a pilot in the U. S. Air Force, he took courses with Nadia Boulanger (1946-51); then returned to Harvard, studying with Walter Piston. He was a Fellow at the American Academy in Rome (1952-55); later joined the music faculty at Harvard. His music is marked by sonorous exuberance and rhythmic impulsiveness; his use of percussion is plangent. He favors ornamental variation forms. Works: *14 Variations for Orchestra* (Boston, April 6, 1956); *Symphony in Three Movements* (Cleveland, April 10, 1958); *Attis* for orch. with chorus and tenor solo (Boston, Feb. 12, 1960); *Et Occidentem Illustra* (Boston Symph., Feb. 24, 1967); piano sonata; *Cantata Sacra;* string quartet; sonata for violin unaccompanied.

Moffo, Anna, American soprano; b. Wayne, Pennsylvania, June 27, 1932, of Italian parentage. She studied voice at the Curtis Institute of Music in Philadelphia; later went to Italy on a Fulbright fellowship studying at the Accademia di Santa Cecilia in Rome. She made her debut in Rome and, progressing rapidly in her career, was engaged at La Scala, Milan, at the Vienna State Opera and in Paris. Returning to America, she sang with the Chicago Lyric Opera; on Nov. 14, 1957 made her debut at the Metropolitan Opera in N. Y. as Violetta, obtaining a gratifying success; she continued to sing regularly at the Metropolitan Opera, earning a stellar reputation for both her singing and acting ability.

Mohaupt, Richard. The first performance of his opera *Der grüne Kakadu* was given in Hamburg on Sept. 16, 1958 (not Jan. 1958).

Moiseiwitsch, Benno. Died in London, April 9, 1963. Cf. M. Moiseiwitsch, *Benno Moiseiwitsch* (London, 1965).

Mokranjac, Vasilije, Serbian composer; b. Belgrade, Sept. 11, 1923. He was brought up in a musical environment (his father was a cellist, a nephew of the famous Serbian composer Stevan Mokranjac). He studied piano and composition at the Belgrade Academy of Music; his early works are romantic in style, but he gradually began experimenting with serial techniques, while safeguarding the basic tonal and even triadic connotations. Works: Symph. No. 1 (Belgrade, Feb. 2, 1962); Symph. No. 2 (Belgrade, April 1, 1966); Symph. No. 3 (Belgrade, Oct. 25, 1968); *Dramatic Overture* (1950); *Concertino* for piano, string orch. and two harps (Belgrade, March 15, 1960); chamber music; piano pieces; incidental music for dramatic plays. See Vlastimir Peričić, *Muzički Stvaraoci u Srbiji* (Belgrade, 1969).

Mokrejs, John, American pianist, composer and teacher of Czech descent; b. Cedar Rapids, Iowa, Feb. 10, 1875; d. there, Nov. 22, 1968. He studied piano with Leopold Godowsky and theory with Adolph Weidig at the American Cons. of Music in Chicago; was active as piano teacher in New York; from 1945 to 1966 lived in Los Angeles; then returned to Cedar Rapids. His compositions include an opera, *Sohrab and Rustum;* an operetta *The Mayflower;* an *American Cantata* (on the life of Abraham Lincoln); a piano trio; a string quartet; songs. He is best known, however, for his teaching pieces for piano: *Valcik (Little Waltz), Boutade, Bird Rondo, Day in Summer, Indian Dance, Har-*

vest Moon, Military Nocturne, Moravian Lullaby, Carillon and *Rainbow Pieces.* He also publ. instruction books: *Lessons in Sight Reading* (Chicago, 1909); *Lessons in Harmony* (N. Y., 1913); *Natural Counterpoint* (Chicago, 1941).

Mokroussov, Boris Andreyevitch. Died in Moscow, March 27, 1968.

Moldenhauer, Hans. Add to books: *The Death of Anton Webern* (N. Y., 1961).

Molinari Pradelli, Francesco, Italian conductor; b. Bologna, July 4, 1911. He studied in Bologna and in Rome. In 1946 he conducted at La Scala in Milan; in 1951 he was guest conductor in London; also conducted opera at San Carlo, Naples; from 1957 led successful opera performances in San Francisco and Los Angeles. He is particularly renowned for his interpretations of Wagner and Puccini.

Momigny, Jérôme-Joseph de. Add to bibl.: Albert Palm, *Jérôme-Joseph de Momigny* (Paris, 1957).

Mompou, Federico. He visited the United States in 1970.

Mondonville, Jean-Joseph Cassanea de. Made his first appearance at the Concert Spirituel, Paris, in 1734 (not 1737).

Monfred, Avenir H. de, composer of Franco-Russian ancestry; b. St. Petersburg, Sept. 17, 1903. He studied piano, organ and composition at the St. Petersburg Cons., graduating in 1922. In 1924 he went to Paris and studied with Vincent d'Indy at the Schola Cantorum (1925-27); also took private lessons with Ravel. He was subsequently connected with various cinematic enterprises in Paris; was active as arranger for several radio networks in New York. He promulgated an interesting theory of composition, 'Diatonic Polymodality'; expounded it in detail in his book, *The New Diatonic Modal Principle of Relative Music* (N.Y., 1970). His works include 2 symphonies (1955, 1957); a symph. poem *Vienna, 1850* (1941); a ballet *Suite New-yorkaise* (Monte Carlo, Nov. 19. 1956); symph. suite *Manhattan Sketches* (1958); *Rapsodie Juive* for orch. (1926); a string quartet (1939); 3 violin sonatas (1922, 1926, 1947); cello sonata (1938); many pieces for piano and for organ; choruses.

Moniuszko, Stanislaw. Add to bibl.: Jan Prosnak, *Stanislaw Moniuszko* (Cracow, 1968).

Monk, Thelonious ('**Sphere**'), American Negro jazz pianist; b. Rocky Mount, North Carolina, Oct. 10, 1918. He was named after his father; Thelonious Monk is his real name. He played in various bands in New York making use of a special 'stride' style, with single notes on the strong beats, and accented chords on off-beats, which became the mark of bebop. In his improvisations Monk uses dissonant progressions; composed a number of pieces for his jazz combo, among them *Off Minor, Evidence, Epistrophy, Blue Monk* and *Crepuscle With Nelly.* He made a successful tour of Japan in 1963 and gave concerts in Europe in 1964. See 'Current Biography' (Oct. 1964).

Monsigny, Pierre-Alexandre. Place of birth Fauquembergues (not Franquembergues).

Montagu-Nathan, Montagu. Died in London, Nov. 15, 1958.

Monteux, Pierre. Died in Hancock, Maine, July 1, 1964.

Monteverdi, Claudio. Add to bibl.: R. Roche, *Monteverdi* (Paris, 1959).

Montsalvatge, Bassols Xavier, Catalan composer; b. Gerona, March 11, 1912. He studied with Morera and Pahissa; in 1936 received the Pedrell prize for his *Pequeña suite burlesca* for violin and woodwinds; subsequently wrote songs and piano pieces; also ballets. In 1949, he composed a *Sinfonia mediterránea.*

Moog (pronounced **Mohg**), **Robert A.,** American electric engineer, inventor of the Moog music synthesizer; b. Flushing, N. Y., May 23, 1934. He attended the Bronx High School of Science (1948-52), Queens College (1952-55), Columbia Univ. (1955-57) and Cornell Univ. (1957-65); received his B.S. in Physics from Queens College (1957); B.S. in electrical engineering from Columbia Univ. (1957); Ph. D. in Engineering Physics from Cornell Univ. (1965). He established The R. A. Moog Co. in 1954 for the purpose of perfecting electronic musical instruments; introduced components of electronic music synthesizers in 1964; the company was incorporated in 1968, with the office at Trumansburg, N. Y. His synthesizer which has colloquially been dubbed as 'The Moog' rapidly acquired popularity. Although even pre-Moog electronic generators could synthesize tone-colors, the 'Moog' has achieved a high degree of vitality, which made it an artistic musical medium. The 1969 'Moog' has a manual of 5½ octaves, with the keys responding to the touch of the fingers, enabling the player to secure an extended spectrum of dynamic gradations. As the technology of the 'Moog' continued to improve, there arose a whole generation of 'Moog' virtuosos; among these Walter Carlos earned enviable fame for his colorful renditions of Bach's keyboard music in a manner which was popularized as 'switched-on Bach.'

Moór, Emanuel. Died Oct. 20 (not Oct. 21), 1931. His wife, Winifred Christie, died in London, Feb. 8, 1965. Add bibl.: Max Pirani, *Emanuel Moór* (London, 1959; with a preface by Pablo Casals).

Moor, Karel. *Viy* was first produced on July 14 (not Dec. 26), 1903.

Moore, Douglas Stuart. Died at Greenport, L. I., N. Y., July 25, 1969. Retired from Columbia Univ. in 1962. Add to works: operas *The Wings of the Dove* (N. Y., Oct. 12, 1961) and *Carrie Nation* (Univ. of Kansas, Lawrence, Kansas, April 28, 1966).

Moore, Gerald. Add to books: *Am I Too Loud?* (N.Y., 1962).

Moore, Thomas. Died near Devizes, Wilts (not in Dublin).

Mooser, R.-Aloys. Died in Geneva, Aug. 24, 1969. His mother was a Russian. He was organist at the French church in St. Petersburg (1896-1909). Add to publ.: *Visage de la musique contemporaine, 1957-1961* (Paris, 1962).

Morales, Olallo Juan Magnus. Exact date of death, April 29 (not May), 1957.

Moran, Robert Leonard, American composer of the avant-garde; b. Denver, Jan. 8, 1937. He studied piano; went to Vienna in 1958, where he took lessons in 12-tone composition with Hans Erich Apostel. Returning to America, he enrolled at Mills College, where he attended seminars of Luciano Berio and Darius Milhaud (M.A., 1963). At the same time he painted in the manner of abstract expressionism. In 1959 he toured Sweden as pianist in programs of hypermodernistic compositions. His music is written in graphic notation, and is animated by surrealistic imagination and Satiesque wit. Works: *Eclectic Boogies* for 13 percussionists (N. Y., Jan. 14, 1965); *Interiors* for any instrumental ensemble (San Francisco, April 2, 1965); *Within the Momentary Illumination* for 2 harps, electric guitar, timpani and brass (Tokyo, Dec. 1, 1965); *L'Après-midi du Dracoula* for any group of instruments capable of producing sounds (1966); *Elegant Journey with Stopping Points of Interest* for orch. (1967); *Smell Piece for Mills College* for frying pans and foods (Mills College, Nov. 20, 1967; originally intended to produce a conflagration sufficiently thermal to burn down the college); *Scream Kiss No. 1* for harpsichord and stereophonic tape (1968); *Let's Build a Nut House,* opera in memory of Paul Hindemith (San Jose, April 19, 1969); *Titus* for amplified automobile and players (1969); *39 Minutes for 39 Autos,* environmental work for 30 skyscrapers, 39 auto horns, Moog synthesizer and players, employing 100,000 persons, directed from atop Twin Peaks in San Francisco, and making use of autos, airplanes, searchlights and local radio and television stations (San Francisco, Aug. 20, 1969); *Silver and the Circle of Messages* for chamber orch. (San Francisco, April 24, (1970); *Hallelujah,* 'a joyous phenomenon with fanfares' for marching bands, drum and bugle corps, church choirs, organs, carillons, rock 'n' roll bands, television stations, automobile horns and any other sounding implements, commissioned by Lehigh Univ. for the city of Bethlehem, Pennsylvania, with the participation of its entire population of 72,320 inhabitants (staged in Bethlehem, April 23, 1971).

Moravec, Ivan, Czech pianist; b. Prague, Nov. 9, 1930. He studied at the Prague Cons.; graduated in 1948 gaining the first prize in piano playing. He subsequently toured in Europe with considerable success. He made his American debut with the Cleveland Orch., Jan. 30, 1964.

Morawetz, Oscar. Add to works: Symph. No. 1 (1953); *Overture to a Fairy Tale* (1956); Symph. No. 2 (Toronto, Feb. 2, 1960); piano concerto (Montreal, April 23, 1963); *Capriccio* for orch. (1960); trio for flute, oboe and harpsichord (1961); *From the Diary of Anne Frank,* for soprano and orch. (Toronto, May 26, 1970); 3 string quartets; duo for violin and piano; violin sonata. His *Serenade* for strings was publ. under the title *Divertimento.* Cf. '34 Biographies of Canadian Composers' issued by the Canadian Broadcasting Co. (Montreal, 1964).

Morel, François d'Assise. Add to works: symph. poems, *Rituel de l'espace* (1959); *Boréal* (1959); *Le Mythe de La Roche percée* (1961); *L'Étoile noire* (1962); *Symphonie* for brass (1956); *Spirale* for chamber orch. (1956); *Rythmologue* for percussion ensemble (1957); brass quintet (1962); *Beat-*

nik for jazz band (1959); *Jazz Baroque Suite* (1960); *Symphonies* for jazz band (1963).

Morelli, Carlo. Died in Mexico City, May 12, 1970. He sang with the San Carlo Opera at the City Center, New York (1940-49); in 1949 settled in Mexico.

Morelli, Giuseppe, Italian conductor; b. Rome, Aug. 2, 1907. He served as a choir boy in St. Peter's in Rome and studied at the St. Cecilia Cons., obtaining his diploma in composition in 1930. He subsequently took a course in conducting with Bernardino Molinari; rapidly earned the reputation as a fine opera conductor; in Italy he has had engagements with the Rome Opera, in Naples, Palermo, Parma, Bologna, and Venice. He also appeared as an opera conductor in Paris, Madrid, Vienna, Brussels, Amsterdam, West Berlin, in Scandinavia and Japan. He made a successful American debut as conductor at the New York City Opera in 1970. His specialty is the Italian repertory, but he has also been acclaimed for his interpretations of the German, French, and Russian operatic masterworks.

Morgan, Russ, American jazz trombonist and band leader; b. Scranton, Pa., April 29, 1904; d. Las Vegas, Aug. 7, 1969. A son of a coal-mine foreman, he worked the mines from the age of 9; learned piano from his mother; then studied the trombone. In 1923 he formed his first band The Scranton Sirens. Later he went to New York and became an arranger for John Philip Sousa. Subsequently he played in nightclubs and theaters; in 1936 he formed a band to assist Rudy Vallee on his radio show. He endeared himself with radio audiences and jazz bands by the emotional use of the waah-waah mute on the trombone, obtaining effective contrasts in the mellow style of "sweet jazz."

Morlacchi, Francesco. His opera *Colombo* was produced, in Genoa, on June 21, 1828 (not 1823).

Moroi, Makoto, Japanese composer, son of Saburo Moroi; b. Tokyo, March 12, 1930. He studied with his father; graduated from Tokyo Academy of music in 1952. Works: *Développements raréfiants* for soprano and chamber group (Karuizawa, July 12, 1957); *Suite Concertante* for violin and orch. (Kyoto, Sept. 7, 1963); *Cinq Epigrammes* for 7 instruments (Tokyo, Feb. 29, 1964); several cycles of piano pieces.

Morris, Harold. Died in New York City, May 6, 1964.

Mortensen, Finn, Norwegian composer; b. Oslo, Jan. 6, 1922. He studied composition with Klaus Egge, and later took a course with Niels-Viggo Bentzon in Copenhagen. In his instrumental works he follows a modified 12-tone method supplemented by the devices of permutation and thematic rotation. His works include a symphony (1953); *Evolution* for orch. (1961); *Tone Colors* for orch. (1962); piano concerto (1963); a number of solo pieces for various instruments: flute sonata (1953); clarinet sonatina (1957); viola sonatina (1959); bassoon fantasy (1959); sonatina for oboe and piano (1959); sonata for violin and piano (1959); piano quartet (1960); and 12 short 12-tone piano pieces for children (1964).

Mortensen, Otto, Danish composer; b. Copenhagen, Aug. 18, 1907. He studied piano, organ and composition at the Cons. of Copenhagen; in 1939 went to Paris where he studied with Darius Milhaud. In 1942 he joined the staff of the Cons. of Copenhagen. He composes mostly vocal music; among his instrumental works are: string quartet (1937); quartet for flute, violin, cello and piano (1938); wind quintet (1944); oboe sonata (1947); piano concerto (1948); symph. (1957).

Morton, 'Jelly Roll' (Ferdinand Joseph La Menthe), American jazz pianist; b. Gulfport, Louisiana, Sept. 20, 1885; d. Los Angeles, July 10, 1941. He was pianist in various bands in New Orleans from 1902 to 1912; then played in St. Louis, California, Chicago and New York. He represented the so-called "Creole" school of piano playing, direct successor of Dixie ragtime, marked by precision of metric accent and sharp syncopation in the melody. See A. Lomax, *Mr. Jelly Roll* (N. Y., 1950).

Moser, Hans Joachim. Died in Berlin, Aug. 14, 1967. Add to books: *Die Tonsprachen des Abendlandes: 10 Essais als Wesenkunde der europäischen Musik* (Berlin, 1960); *Musik in Zeit und Raum* (Berlin, 1960); *Orgelromantik* (Ludwigsburg, 1961).

Moser, Rudolf. Died in a fall, while mountain climbing near St. Moritz, Aug. 20, 1960.

Moss, Lawrence, American composer; b. Los Angeles, Nov. 18, 1927. He studied music at Pomona College, Univ. of Calif., Los Angeles, Eastman School of Music in Rochester and Univ. of Southern Calif. (Ph.D., 1957). In 1956-59 he taught at Mills College; in 1959 received a Guggenheim Fellowship for travel in Italy; in 1960 appointed to the faculty of Yale Univ. His stylistic usages tend to polycentric tonality, with sporadic application of serial techniques. Works: *Suite* for orch. (1950); *Fantasia* for piano (1952); trio for flute, violin and cello (1953); *Song of Myself,* to Whitman's words, for baritone and chamber ensemble (1957); string quartet (1958); violin sonata (1959).

Mottu, Alexandre, Swiss pianist, organist and composer; b. Geneva, June 11, 1883; d. there, Nov. 24, 1943. He studied organ with Otto Barblan in Geneva; piano with Teresa Carreño in Berlin. He was appointed prof. of piano and organ at the Cons. of Geneva in 1907. His works include various pieces for piano, violin and organ, and much choral music.

Moulaert, Raymond. Died in Brussels, Jan. 18, 1962.

Mozart, Wolfgang Amadeus. Add to bibl.: Erich Schenk, *W. A. Mozart: Eine Biographie* (Vienna, 1955; in English, N. Y., 1959); O. Schneider & A. Algatzy, *Mozart: Handbuch* (Vienna, 1962); W. A. Bauer & Otto Erich Deutsch, *Mozart: Briefe und Aufzeichnungen* (vol. 1, Kassel, 1962); Otto Erich Deutsch, ed., *Mozart: Dokumente seines Lebens* (Munich, 1963; also in English, Palo Alto, Calif., 1965); Brigid Brophy, *Mozart the Dramatist* (a Freudian interpretation; N. Y. 1964); S. Sadie, *Mozart* (London, 1965); R. B. Moberly, *Three Mozart Operas* (N. Y., 1968); Jean & Brigitte Massin, *W. A. Mozart* (Paris, 1970).

Mshvelidze, Shalva, Georgian composer; b. Tbilisi, May 28, 1904. He studied at the Tbilisi Cons., graduating in 1931; traveled in the Caucasus and collected samples of native folk songs and dances. In 1942 he became prof. of composition at the Tbilisi Cons.; also was active as conductor of popular ensembles. His works comprise the operas: *Legend of Tariel* (Tbilisi, Feb. 25, 1946); *The Grandmaster's Right Hand* (Tbilisi, June 3, 1961); oratorio *Caucasus* (1947); 3 symphonies (1942, 1944, 1953); symph. poems: *Azar* (1933), *Zviadauri* (1940), *Mindia* (1949), *Youngling and Tiger* (1962); chamber music; songs.

Muczynski, Robert. Add to works: *Galena, A Town* for orch. (1958); trumpet trio (1959); *Dovetail Overture* (1959); *3 Designs* for 3 timpani (1960); *Statements* for percussion (1961); 3 Preludes for unaccompanied flute (1962).

Mueller von Asow, Erich Hermann. Died in Berlin, June 4, 1964.

Muffat, Georg. Place of birth, Megève, is in Savoy (not in Alsace). Add to bibl.: W. Kolneder, *Georg Muffat: Zur Aufführungspraxis* (1970).

Müller, Paul. Add to bibl.: F. Jakob, *Paul Müller: Biographie und Werkverzeichnis* (Zürich, 1963).

Müller von Kulm, Walter. Died in Basel, Oct. 2, 1967.

Mumma, Gordon, American avant-garde composer; b. Framingham, Mass., March 30, 1935. He studied piano and French horn at the Univ. of Michigan; began experimenting with electronic music at the age of 19, composing music and sound effects for an experimental theater in Ann Arbor. In 1957 he joined Robert Ashley and the artist Milton Cohen in a revolutionary theatrical art based on projected images; this developed into an esthetic medium called "Manifestations: Light and Sound" and later "Space Theatre;" in 1964 Mumma, Cohen and Ashley gave a memorable presentation of the Space Theatre at the Biennial Exhibition in Venice, becoming pioneers in the electronic light-show. With the development of transistor circuitry in electronics, Mumma began a serious study of its technology. In 1961 Mumma became a founder of the annual contemporary music festival in Ann Arbor called ONCE. Working at the Institute of Science and Technology in Ann Arbor, he developed a skill in seismology; made a study of tape recordings of earthquakes and underground nuclear explosions. In 1966 he joined the Merce Cunningham Dance Company and moved to New York; formed an ensemble called the Sonic Arts Union, which made two European tours. He gave courses in electronic circuitry at Brandeis Univ. (1966-67) and at the Univ. of Illinois in Urbana (1969-70); designed the Sound Modifier Console for the Pepsi Cola Pavilion at EXPO 70 in Osaka, Japan; developed a process of "cybersonic" control of acoustical and electronic media. He also applied computer techniques to composition. His works for magnetic tape include *Vectors* (1959); *Densities* (1959); *Sinfonia* for 12 instruments with tape (1960); *Mirrors* (1960); *Meanwhile, a Twopiece* for percussion and tape (1961); *Epoxy* (1962); *Megaton for William Burroughs* (1963); *Le Corbusier* for orch., organ, tape and cybersonic concertante (1965). Instrumental works: *A Quarter of Fourpiece* for four instruments (1963); a group of pieces with the punning titles *Very Small Size Mograph, Medium Size Mograph, Large Size Mograph* (1962-64) for piano and instruments; *Mesa* for cybersonic bandoneon with electronic accompaniment (1966; his most significant work); *Diastasis, As in Beer* for two cybersonic guitars with electronic accompaniment (1967); *Swarmer* for violin, concertina, musical saw and cybersonic modifiers (1968); *Communication in a Noisy Environment* (produced in Automation House, New York, by Intermedia Institute, Nov. 19, 1970); also a number of works with the generic title *Conspiracy* for digital computer and several performers intended to illustrate a democratic society in which the living enjoy civil rights on a par with computers.

Munch, Charles. Died in Richmond, Va., Nov. 6, 1968, on an American tour of the Orchestre de Paris, founded by him in Paris after retirement from the conductorship of the Boston Symph. Orch. in 1962. Add that he studied conducting in Paris with Alfred Szendrei (Sendrey) from 1933 to 1940.

Münch, Ernst, Alsatian organist and choral conductor; b. Niederbronn, Dec. 31, 1859; d. Strasbourg, April 1, 1928. He was appointed organist at St. Wilhelm (St. Guillaume) Church in Strasbourg in 1882, where he founded a choir which attained a great renown for its performance of Bach's cantatas and passions; Albert Schweitzer served as organist at these performances. His son, Fritz Münch (b. Strasbourg, June 2, 1890), succeeded him as conductor of the St. Wilhelm Choir in 1924; his second son, Charles Münch (Munch), became a celebrated conductor; his third son was Hans Münch.

Muradeli, Vano Ilitch. Died in Tomsk, Siberia, Aug. 14, 1970. Add to works: *October,* opera (Moscow, April 22, 1964).

Murray, Bain. In 1970 he was associate prof. of music at the Cleveland State Univ.

Musgrave, Thea, Scottish composer; b. Edinburgh, May 27, 1928. She studied composition at the Univ. of Edinburgh and in Paris with Nadia Boulanger; attended courses at the Berkshire Center in Tanglewood in the summer of 1958. In 1970 she was visiting prof. at the Univ. of California, Santa Barbara. The diatonic lyricism of the initial period of her creative evolution soon gave way to increasingly chromatic constructions, eventually systematized into serial organization. She has described her compositions as 'dramatic-abstract' in form, because though they contain no program they reveal some unusual dramatic traits. Works: *A Tale for Thieves,* ballet (1953); *Four Madrigals* for unaccompanied chorus (1953); *A Suite o' Bairnsangs* for voice and piano (1953); *Cantata for a Summer's Day* for vocal quartet, speaker, flute, clarinet, string quartet and double-bass (1954); *Song of the Burn* for unaccompanied chorus (1954); *The Abbot of Drimock,* chamber opera in one act (1955); *5 Love Songs* for tenor and guitar (1955); *Divertimento* for string orch. (1957); string quartet (1958); *Obliques* for orch. (1958); *A Song for Christmas* for voice and piano (1958); *Scottish Dance Suite* for orch. (1959); *Triptych* for tenor and orch. (1959); *Colloquy* for violin and piano (1960); trio for flute, oboe, and piano (1960); *Monologue* for piano (1960); *Serenade* for flute, clarinet, harp, viola and cello (1961); *Perspectives* for orch. (1961); Chamber Concerto No. 1 for 9 instruments (1962); *The Phoenix and the Turtle* for chorus and orch. (1962); *Marko the Miser,* 'a tale for children to mime, sing and play' (1962); *Sinfonia* (1963); *The Five Ages of Man* for chorus and orch. (1964); *The Decision,* opera in 3 acts (1964; London, Nov. 30, 1967); *Excursions* for piano duet (1965); *Festival Overture* (1965); Chamber Concerto No. 2 for 5 instruments (1966); Chamber Concerto No. 3 for 8 instruments (1966); *Nocturnes and Arias* for orch. (1966); *Variations* for brass band (1966); *Sonata for Three* for flute, violin and guitar (1966); *Impromptu No. 1* for flute and oboe (1967); *Concerto for Orchestra* (1967); *Memento Creatoris* for unaccompanied chorus (1967); *Music* for horn and piano (1967); clarinet concerto (London, Feb. 5, 1969; a deft, chic virtuoso piece, requiring the soloist to promenade among members of the orchestra); *Beauty and the Beast,* ballet for chamber orch. and electronic tape (1968-69; London, Nov. 19, 1969); *Soliloquy No. 1* for guitar and electronic tape (1969); *Night Music* for chamber orch. (1969); *Memento Vitae* for orch. (1969-70); *Elegy* for viola and cello (1970); *Impromptu No. 2* for flute, oboe and clarinet (1970); *From One to Another* for viola and electronic tape (1970).

Musicescu, Gavriil, Rumanian composer of sacred music and folksong arranger; b. Ismail, March 20, 1847; d. Jassy, Dec. 21, 1903. He studied at the Cons. of Jassy and later at the St. Petersburg Cons. In 1872 he was appointed prof. at the Jassy Cons., and became its director in 1901. He composed mainly choral music for the Orthodox Church; published a manual for vocal teachers (Jassy, 1877). His arrangements of Rumanian folksongs have an authentic flavor, thanks to his skill in finding suitable harmonizations of intervallically peculiar melodic patterns. Bibl.: G. Breazul, *G. Musicescu* (Bucharest, 1962).

Musin, Ovide. He did not study at the Paris Cons., but at the Cons. of Liège, and it was there that he won the gold medal at the age of 15; followed Léonard to Paris only for private coaching.

Mussolini, Romano, Italian jazz pianist; son of Il Duce; b. Carpena, Forli, Sept. 26, 1927. With the rest of Mussolini's family he lived in Ischia after the war; picked up accordion and piano; became a professional jazz band leader in Rome.

Mycielski, Zygmunt, Polish composer and musicologist; b. Przeworsk, Aug. 17, 1907. He studied in Cracow and later in Paris with Nadia Boulanger and Paul Dukas. In 1929-36 was a member of the Society of Young Polish Composers in Paris. After the end of World War II he became active as a journalist in Poland; edited the principal Polish music magazine 'Ruch Muzyczny.' His works, written in a modern idiom, contain elements of Polish national music; but dodecaphonic usages are also encountered. His principal compositions are: *Lamento di Tristano* for small orch., in memory of Szymanowski (1937); 2 symphonies (1947, 1960); *Portrait of a Muse* for recitation, mixed chorus and 15 instruments (1947); piano concerto (1954).

Myers, Rollo. Edited an anthology, *Twentieth Century Music* (London, 1960); publ. *Emmanuel Chabrier and His Circle* (London, 1969).

Mysliveczek, Joseph. *Il Bellerofonte* was produced on Jan. 20 (not Jan. 29), 1767. *Armida* was produced in Lucca, Aug. 15, 1778, before its Milan performance.

N

Nabokov, Nicolas. In 1964 he was appointed cultural counselor for West Berlin Music Festival. His *Ode* was produced in Paris (not in Monte Carlo). His opera *The Holy Devil* was produced in a revised and amplified version in Cologne, under the title *Der Tod des Grigori Rasputin,* on Nov. 27, 1959. Add to works: Symph. No. 3, *A Prayer* (N.Y., Jan. 4, 1968).

Nadel, Arno. Perished in Auschwitz in March, 1943.

Napoli, Jacopo. In 1962 he was appointed Director of the Cons. of Milan.

Narayana Menon, Yatakke Kurupath, Indian virtuoso on the veena; b. New Delhi, June 27, 1911. He specialized in comparative musicology; was for many years, director of the All India Radio; made many European tours as performer and lecturer.

Nardini, Pietro. Was in Stuttgart in 1762-65 (not 1753-67). Schubart praised him, not Schobert.

Nasidze, Sulkhan, Georgian composer; b. Tbilisi, March 17, 1927. He studied at the Tbilisi Cons., graduating in 1955. His music is imbued with Georgian melorhythms and set in a fairly advanced idiom. Works: symph. (1957); 2 piano concertos (1955, 1961); string quartet (1956); piano trio (1958); piano pieces; choruses.

Nastasijević, Svetomir, Serbian composer; b. Gornje Milanovec, April 1, 1902. He studied engineering and architecture; at the same time he learned to play the violin; wrote music criticism and publ. 2 manuals on music theory. His works include the music drama, *Medjuluško Blago (The Treasure of the Medjuluzje;* Belgrade, March 4, 1937); *Đurad Branković,* national opera from medieval Serbian history (Belgrade, June 12, 1940); several symphonic poems and choruses. In his operas, he adopts the Wagnerian system of leitmotives. See V. Peričić, *Muzički Stvaraoci u Srbiji* (Belgrade, 1969; pp. 342-50).

Nathan, Isaac. Add to bibl.: Catherine Mackerras, *The Hebrew Melodist; A Life of Isaac Nathan* (Sydney, 1963).

Nazareth, Ernesto, Brazilian pianist and composer of dance music and songs; b. Rio de Janeiro, March 20, 1863; d. there, Feb. 4, 1934. He was a pioneer in fostering a national Brazilian type of composition, writing pieces in European forms with Brazilian melorhythmic inflections, pointedly entitled *Fado brasileiro, Tango brasileiro, Valsa brasileira, Marcha brasileira,* etc.; he also composed original dances in the rhythms of samba and chôro. In his declining years he became totally deaf. A detailed list of his works was compiled by Mercedes Reis Pequeno for the series of *Composers of the Americas,* Vol. X (Washington, 1964).

Nef, Albert. Died in Bern, Dec. 6, 1966.

Negrea, Martian, Rumanian composer; b. Vorumloc, Jan. 9, 1893. He studied in Vienna with Franz Schmidt and Mandyczewski (1918-21). Returning to Rumania he became prof. of composition in Cluj (1921-41). Later he taught at the Bucharest Cons. His music is marked by a romantic quality; almost all of his compositions are programmatic in intent and folkloric in content. Thematically, he applies elements of Transylvanian melorhythms. Works: opera, *Marin Pescarul* (Cluj, Oct. 3, 1934); *Rapsodia romana,* No. 1 for orch. (1938); *Rapsodia romana,* No. 2 for orch. (1950); *Prin Muntii Apuseni* (*In the West Carpathians*), symph suite (1952); *Recrutul* (*The Recruit*), symph. poem (1953); *Sinfonia primăverii* (*Spring Symphony,* 1956); choruses and songs. He also publ. several manuals for music schools.

Nejedlý, Vít. Died Jan. 1, 1945 (not Dec. 30, 1944).

Nejedlý, Zdeněk. Died in Prague, March 9, 1962. Was minister of education from 1948 to 1953; then deputy premier (not vice-president).

Nelhybel, Vaclav, Czech composer; b. Polanka, Sept. 24, 1919. He studied composition and conducting at the Prague Cons., then lived in Switzerland. In 1957 he settled in N.Y. where he became active as composer and conductor. His music is couched in linear modal counterpoint, in which thematic notes, rhythms and intervals become serially organized. The harmonic idiom is of a freely dissonant texture, with all melorhythmic components gravitating towards tonal centers. Works: 3 ballets: *Fêtes de Feux* (1942); *In the Shadow of a Lime Tree* (1946); *The Cock and the Hangman* (1946); opera *A Legend* (1954); for orch.: *Ballade* (1946); *Etude symphonique* (1949); *3 Movements* for strings (1949); *3 Modes* (1952); *Sinfonietta Concertante* (1960); viola concerto (1962); *Passacaglia* (1965); *Houston Concerto* (1967); chamber music: 2 string quartets; 3 woodwind quintets; 3 organa for 4 bassoons (1948); quartet for horns (1957); 2 brass quintets (1961, 1965); 9 clarinet trios (1963); *Quintetto concertante* (1965); choruses; *103 Short, Short Pieces* for piano.

Nelson, Oliver E., American composer and arranger; b. St. Louis, June 4, 1932. He studied piano, saxophone, taxidermy, dermatology and embalming; interrupting his courses in mortuary science, he took private lessons in composition with Elliott Carter in New York and George Tremblay in Los Angeles; then devoted himself chiefly to composing, conducting and arranging. Among his works are *Divertimento* for 10 woodwind instruments (1962); *Soundpiece for Jazz Orchestra* (1964); *Patterns* for orch. (1965); *A Study in 5/4* for wind ensemble (1966); concerto for xylophone, marimba and vibes (1967); *Jazzhattan Suite* for jazz combo (1967). In 1967 he moved to Hollywood, where he specialized in writing music for educational films.

Nelson, Robert U., American musicologist; b. Brush, Colorado, Sept. 16, 1902. He studied at the Univ. of Calif., Berkeley (A.B., 1923); later worked with Gaston Déthier and Percy Goetschius at the Institute of Musical Art, N.Y. (diplomas in piano and organ, 1925), and with Walter Piston and Willi Apel at Harvard Univ. (M.A., 1937; Ph.D., 1944). He also studied composition with Gustav Holst and Eugene Zador. From 1925 to 1937 he was member of faculty at Washington State Univ.; in 1938 became instructor at the Univ. of Calif., Los Angeles; prof. since 1955. He publ. a valuable study, *The Technique of Variation* (Berkeley, California, 1948); contributed numerous articles to music magazines.

Nerini, Émile. Died in Paris, March 22, 1967.

Nestyev, Israel. The 1957 edition of his biography of Prokofiev was publ. in English with a foreword by Nicolas Slonimsky (Stanford, California, 1961).

Nettl, Bruno. In 1958 he was appointed Librarian at the Univ. of Detroit. Add to publications: *Reference Materials in Ethnomusicology* (Detroit, 1961); *Theory and Method in Ethnomusicology* (N.Y., 1964).

Nettl, Paul. A bio-bibliographical brochure, *Ein Musikwissenschaftler in Zwei Welten: Die musikwissenschaftlichen und literarischen Arbeiten von Paul Nettl,* compiled by Thomas Atcherson, was publ. as a Festschrift in Vienna, 1962.

Neuhaus, Heinrich, eminent Russian pianist and pedagogue; b. Kiev, March 30, 1888; d. Moscow, Oct. 10, 1964. He studied in Vienna; became prof. of the Moscow Cons. in 1922. Among his students was Sviatoslav Richter. Neuhaus publ. a manual *The Art of Piano Playing* (Moscow, 1958).

Neukomm, Sigismund Ritter von. See L. H. Correa de Azevedo, *S. Neukomm, an Austrian Composer in the New World,* in the 'Mus. Quarterly' (Oct. 1959).

Neumann, Věroslav, Czech composer; b. at Citoliby, near Louny, May 27, 1931. He studied theory with Jaroslav Řídký at the Prague Cons. Among his works are a triptych *Panorama of Prague* for baritone and orch. (1962), a *Peace Symphony* (1964) and a television opera *The Little Chimney* (1965).

Nevin, Ethelbert. Studied singing and piano with Franz Böhme (not von Boehme). His lessons with Stephen Austin Pearce (1880-81) were conducted by correspondence (Pearce was then resident in New York). In Boston (1881-82) he studied with Benjamin J. Lang (piano) and Stephen A. Emery (harmony). Did not study with Hans von Bülow, but only auditioned for him. In Berlin, he studied with Karl Klindworth (piano) and Karl Bial (composition).

Neway, Patricia, American soprano; b. Brooklyn, Sept. 30, 1919. She studied at the Mannes College of Music in N. Y. After several appearances in minor roles, she achieved her first significant success as Magda in Menotti's opera *The Consul* (Philadelphia, March 1, 1950); appeared in another Menotti opera, *Maria Golovin,* at the Brussels World's Fair on Aug. 20, 1958. Her repertoire includes parts in operas by Alban Berg, Benjamin Britten and other modern composers; in all these works she shows her profound understanding of the contemporary idiom.

Newcomb, Ethel. Died in Whitney Point, N. Y., July 3, 1959. Born in 1875 (not 1879).

Newman, Alfred, American composer; b. New Haven, March 17, 1901; d. Hollywood, Feb. 17, 1970. He studied piano with Sigismund Stojowski and composition with Rubin Goldmark; also attended a Schoenberg seminar at the Univ. of California, Los Angeles. He began his career as a pianist in vaudeville shows; in 1930 went to Hollywood and devoted himself entirely to composition for the motion pictures; wrote 300-odd scores, 44 of which were nominated for awards of the Motion Picture Academy, and 8 were winners; among his most successful were *All About Eve, The Egyptian* and *Love Is a Many-Splendored Thing.* Stylistically he followed an eclectic type of median romanticism, mimicking the most popular works of Tchaikovsky, Rachmaninoff, Wagner and Liszt, and amalgamating these elements in an iridescent free fantasia.

Newman, Ernest. Died in Tadworth, Surrey, July 7, 1959. His real name was William Roberts; he assumed his nom de plume to symbolize an "earnest new man." A collection of his essays was publ. under the title *Testament of Music* (London, 1963). See Vera Newman, *Ernest Newman, a Memoir* (London, 1963).

Newman, William S. Held a Guggenheim Fellowship (1960-61) for research on sonata literature; publ. the valuable books: *The Sonata in the Baroque Era* (Chapel Hill, 1959); *The Sonata in the Classic Era* (Chapel Hill, 1963); *The Sonata Since Beethoven* (Chapel Hill, 1969); edited *8 Sonatas by Minor Classic Masters* (Chicago, 1965).

Newmark, John, Canadian pianist; b. Bremen, Germany, June 12, 1904. He studied in Leipzig; made a career as an accompanist; traveled all over the world with celebrated singers, violinists and cellists, among them Kathleen Ferrier, Elisabeth Schumann, Richard Tucker, George London, Szymon Goldberg and Maurice Eisenberg. He settled in Montreal.

Newsom, Hugh Raymond, American concert manager and composer; b. Cawnpore, India, Dec. 20, 1891. He was brought to America as an infant, and spent his childhood in Iowa, where he studied music with Alexander Rommel at the German College in Mount Pleasant, Iowa. He subsequently entered the Oberlin Cons. of Music, where he studied theory with Arthur Heacox; later he had some lessons with George Chadwick at the New England Cons. in Boston. He became engaged as a concert manager; lived mostly in New York and San Francisco, eventually settling in Baltimore. In 1937 he married the harpist Marjorie Brunton. In the meantime he composed prolifically, but his music had few performances. In his style of composition he adheres to romanticism, not without some coloristic touches of impressionistic harmonies. He emphasizes the clarity of texture and the natural melodiousness of the vocal line. His works include an oratorio-drama *The Divine Tragedy,* the choral trilogy *The Holy Birth,* the sacred oratorios *The Miracles, Trial Before Pilate, The Psalms of David;* a *Requiem; The King Arthur Suite* for orch.; *Night Pictures* for harp and orch.; a harp concerto (N. Y., Nov. 6, 1968; Mrs. Newsom soloist); many character pieces and *Etudes* for piano and song cycles, of which *Songs of Love and Death* to poems by Edna St. Vincent Millay are notable for their expressive settings and harmonious sonorities.

Ney, Elly. Died in Tutzing, Germany, March 31, 1968.

Nezhdanova, Antonina, Russian soprano; b. Krivaya Balka, near Odessa, July 29, 1873; d. Moscow, June 26, 1950. She studied at the Moscow Cons.; in 1902 joined the staff of the Bolshoi Theater. She was equally successful as a lyric, dramatic and coloratura soprano; her range extended to high G. In 1912 she made an appearance as Gilda in *Rigoletto* at the Grand Opéra in Paris. Her best roles were Tatiana in *Eugene Onegin;* Marguerite in *Faust* and Elsa in *Lohengrin.* In 1943 she became prof. of voice at the Moscow Cons.

Nicholls, Agnes. Died in London. Sept. 21, 1959.

Nichols, Ernest Loring ('Red'), American cornetist and band leader; b. Ogden, Utah, May 8, 1905; d. Las Vegas, June 28, 1965. He received his early training from his father, a clarinet player; joined various bands in New York; then cut a swath in the world of popular music with his own band, 'Red Nichols and his Five Pennies' (actually, the number of 'Pennies' was ten); among his players were Jimmy Dorsey, Benny Goodman and Glenn Miller. A maudlin motion picture, 'The Five Pennies' was made in 1959 and catapulted Red Nichols into top ranks of jazzmen. But scholarly exegetes, particularly in European hermeneutics, lamented the commercialization of his style, giving preference to his earlier, less slick, jazzification.

Niculescu, Stefan, Rumanian composer and musicologist; b. Moreni (Ploesti), July 31, 1927. He studied at the Bucharest Cons. with Milhail Jora, Ion Dumitrescu, Theodor Rogalski and others; has written mostly chamber music in a neo-classical style. He has contributed a number of musicological articles to Rumanian music publications. In 1963 he was appointed to the staff of the Bucharest Cons. In his music he follows the structural technique of modified serialism, exemplified in the orchestra scores *Hétéromorphie* (1967) and *Unisonos* (1970).

Nielsen, Carl (August). Died Oct. 3 (not Oct. 2), 1931. Add to bibl.: R. Simpson, *Sibelius and Nielsen* (London, 1965); D. Fog, *Carl Nielsen, Kompositioner; en bibliografi* (Copenhagen, 1965); A. M. Telmanyi, *Mit Barndomschjem* (Copenhagen, 1965); *Carl Nielsen: Centenary Essays* (London, 1966).

Nigg, Serge. Add to works: violin concerto (Paris, May 27, 1960); *Hieronymus Bosch Symphony* (Strasbourg, June 21, 1960); *Fulgur* for band, percussion, 2 harps, piano, celesta and tubular chimes (Paris, Oct. 9, 1969).

Nikolais, Alwin, American choreographer, stage director and composer of electronic ballet scores; b. Southington, Conn., Nov. 25, 1912. He studied piano; played in movie houses for the silent films. In 1929 he began to study dance with a pupil of Mary Wigman; became director of the Hartford Parks Marionette Theater and later chairman of the dance dept. of the Hartt School of Music in Hartford. In 1942-46 he served in military counterintelligence in Europe; then studied with Hanya Holm in New York. In 1948 he joined the dance faculty of the Henry Street Settlement and in 1949 became co-director of the Henry Street Playhouse in N. Y. His principal choreographic innovation is the technique of body extension by tubular projections and disks attached to the head, upper and nether limbs, so that a biped dancer becomes a stereogeometrical figure; often in his productions clusters of dancers form primitivistic ziggurats. His production of extra-terrestrial creatures in Menotti's children's opera *Help, Help, the Globolinks!* was acclaimed for its imaginative quality at its première at the Hamburg State Opera (Dec. 19, 1968).

Nikolov, Lazar, Bulgarian composer; b. Burgas, Aug. 26, 1922. He studied composition with Vladigerov; later began investigating the potentialities of ultra-modern music, and formed an idiom melodically verging on atonality, and harmonically on polytonality. He was soloist in his 1st piano concerto (Rusa, Nov. 21, 1949). The works that followed, all in increasingly complex musical language, were: *Concerto for String Orchestra* (Rusa, Nov. 30, 1951); violin concerto (Varna, March 25, 1955); sonata for 2 pianos (1952); 1st symph. (Varna, Feb. 16, 1956); violin sonata (1954); 2nd piano concerto (Sofia, Feb. 28, 1963); viola sonata (1955); 3 piano sonatas (1950, 1951, 1956); piano quintet (1959); 2nd symph. with 2 pianos (1961); flute sonata (1962); clarinet sonata (1962); cello sonata (1962).

Nilius, Rudolf, Austrian conductor; b. Vienna, March 23, 1883; d. Bad Ischl, Dec. 31, 1962. He studied cello; was a member of the Vienna Philharmonic (1904-12); conducted the Tonkünstlerorchester in Vienna (1912-21). In 1921 he founded in Vienna the Philharmonic Chamber Orch. Concerts.

Nilsson, Birgit, Swedish dramatic soprano; b. West Karup, Sweden, May 17, 1918. She studied singing in Stockholm. In 1947 she joined the Royal Opera; sang Elsa at the Bayreuth Festival in 1954, and Isolde in 1957 and 1959; she also appeared at La Scala, Milan. She made her U.S. debut at the Hollywood Bowl on Aug. 9, 1956; sang Wagnerian roles with the San Francisco Opera and the Chicago Lyric Opera. In London she sang Brünnhilde in a complete cycle of Wagner's tetralogy in 1957. She made her long-delayed debut with the Metropolitan Opera as Isolde in N.Y., on Dec. 18, 1959; her American career was thenceforward assured.

Nilsson, Bo, Swedish composer of ultramodern tendencies; b. Skelleftea, May 1, 1937. Largely autodidact, he experimented with new techniques of serial composition and electronic sonorities. His *Frequencies* (1955) for piccolo, flute, percussion, guitar, xylophone, vibraphone and double-bass, had frequent performances at European festivals of modern music; *Moments of Time* for ten woodwind instruments (1957) also enjoyed momentary success. He further wrote *Quantities* for piano (1958); *Audiograms* for electronic generators (1959); *A Prodigal Son* for contralto, alto flute and a chamber ensemble (1959) and *Reactions* for percussion quartet (1960).

Nixon, Roger, American composer; b. Tulare, California, Aug. 8, 1921. He studied clarinet with a local teacher; in 1940 attended a seminar in composition with Arthur Bliss at the Univ. of California, Berkeley, and in 1941 with Ernest Bloch. In 1942-46 he was in the U.S. Army; returned to Berkeley in 1947, studying with Roger Sessions (Ph.D., 1952); in the summer of 1948 took private lessons with Schoenberg. Subsequently he joined the staff of San Francisco State College. A prolific composer, he writes in a consistent modern idiom anchored in fluctuating tonality and diversified by atonal protuberances. His music is marked by distinctly American melorhythms; his miniature opera, *The Bride Comes to Yellow Sky,* is an exemplar of adroit modernistic Westernism fashioned in a non-ethnomusicological manner. Works: string quartet No. 1 (1949); *Air for Strings* (1952); violin concerto (1956); *The Wine of Astonishment,* cantata for baritone solo and mixed chorus (1960); *Reflections* for symphonic band (1962); *Elegiac Rhapsody* for viola and orch. (1962); *Three Dances* for orch. (1963); *Nocturne* for symph. band (1965); opera, *The Bride Comes to Yellow Sky* (Eastern Illinois Univ., Feb. 20, 1968; revised and performed by the San Francisco State College Opera Workshop, March 22, 1969); viola concerto (San Francisco, April 29, 1970); *A Solemn Processional* for symph. band (San Francisco, May 9, 1971); various pieces of chamber music; choruses; songs; piano pieces.

Nobre, Marlos, Brazilian composer; b. Recife, Feb. 18, 1939. He studied piano and theory with local teachers; in 1960 went to Rio de Janeiro where he took lessons with H. J. Koellreutter; later studied with Camargo Guarnieri in São Paulo and with Alberto Ginastera in Buenos Aires; further received instruction with Olivier Messiaen and Luigi Dallapiccola; took a course in electronic music with Vladimir Ussachevsky at Columbia Univ. Despite a somewhat quaquaversal efflux of styles and idioms to which he was exposed during his student days, he succeeded in forming a strongly individual manner of musical self-expression, in which sonorous and structural elements are effectively combined with impressionistic, pointilistic and serial techniques, supplemented by prudential aleatory procedures. He is one of the few contemporary Latin American composers who does not disdain the use of native melorhythmic inflections, resulting in ingratiating harmoniousness. Works: *Concertino* for piano and strings (1959); sonata for viola solo (1963); *Divertimento* for piano and orch. (1963); *Rhythmic Variations* for piano and percussion (1963); *Ukrínmakrinkrín* for soprano, wind instruments and piano, to a text derived from primitive Brazilian, Negro and Indian rituals (1964); *Sonata breve* for piano (1966); *Canticum instrumentale* for flute, harp, piano and timpani (1968); *Rhythmetron* for percussion (1968); *Convergencies* for orch. (1968); wind quintet (1968); *Tropicale* for flute, clarinet, piano and percussion (1968); Toccata for viola and piano (1968); *Concerto breve* for piano and orch. (1969; his most significant work, frequently performed); *Ludus instrumentalis* for chamber orch. (1969); *Biosfera* for string orch. (1970); *Mosaico* for orch. (1970); *Sonancias* for piano and percussion (1971).

Nolte, Ewald Valentin, American music educator; b. Utica, Nebraska, Sept. 21, 1909. He studied music with Albert Noelte (not related to Nolte) at Northwestern Univ., Evanston, Illinois (M. Mus. 1945; Ph.D., 1954), and with Paul Hindemith and Leo Schrade (1950-51) at Yale Univ. His professional career was devoted mainly to education and to conducting church choruses. From 1944 to 1964 he was on the music faculty of Northwestern Univ.; in 1964 was appointed Director of the Moravian Music Foundation. He has published a series of anthologies *Music for Young Americans;* arranged American folk songs; supplied accompaniments to hymns; composed choral sacred music.

Nono, Luigi. Add to works: *Il Canto sospeso* for solo voices, chorus and orch, to texts from letters by young men and women condemned to death by the Fascists (Cologne, Oct. 24, 1956); *Intolleranza 1960,* scenic action' with radical anti-atomic connotations (Venice, April 13, 1961; evoked a riot in the hall, when a group of neo-Fascists began showering the audience with leaflets from the balcony, denouncing Nono as an acknowledged member of the Italian Communist Party and protesting against the alleged contamination of Italian music by alien dodecaphony); *Sarà dolce tacere* for 8 solo voices to texts from 'La Terra e la Morte' by Cesare Pavese (Washington, Feb. 17, 1961); music for the documentary play *The Representative,* by Peter Weiss dealing with the trial of Nazi guards (Frankfurt, Oct. 19, 1965); *A Floresta e jovem e chea de vida,* oratorio to texts from pronouncements by Angolan guerrilla fighters (1966); *Per Bastiana* for electronic tape and 3 orchestral groups (1967); *Voci destroying Muros* for voices and instruments in mixed media, with a machine gun pointed towards the audience (1970); *A Spectre Rises Over Europe,* to words from the Communist Manifesto, for voice and orch. (Cologne, Feb. 11, 1971). Nono is married to Schoenberg's daughter Nuria.

Nordal, Jon, Icelandic composer; b. Reykjavik, March 6, 1926. He studied in Iceland; then in Zürich, Paris and Rome. Adopting the neo-classical method of composition, he wrote a *Concerto grosso* (1950); *Sinfonietta seriosa* (1954); Concerto for piano and orch. (1957); *Adagio* for flute, harp, piano and strings (1965).

Nordheim, Arne, Norwegian composer; b. Larvik, June 20, 1931. He studied at the Cons. of Oslo with Karl Andersen and Bjarne Brustad; in 1955 he went to Paris where he absorbed innovating techniques. Returning to Oslo he joined the avant-garde circles; experimented in pointillistic tone color; adopted a motivic method of melorhythmic structures without formal development. In 1968 he visited the U.S. as a lecturer and composer. Works: *Evening Land,* song cycle for soprano and chamber orch. (1957); *Canzona per orchestra* (1960); *Katharsis,* choreographic suite for orch. with electronic sounds (1962); *Partita* for viola, harpsichord, and percussion (1963); *Epitaffio* for orch. and magnetic tape (1963); *Evolution* for electronic sound (1966); *Colorations* for organ, percussion and magnetic tape (1967); *Solitaire* for electronic tape (1968). See Bjarne Kortsen, *Contemporary Norwegian Orchestral Music* (Bergen, 1969; pp. 300-315).

Nordica, Lillian. Date of birth Dec. 12 (not May 12), 1857, as per genealogical register in *A History of Farmington, Franklin County, Maine* (Farmington, 1885, p. 545). Name of teacher, John O'Neill (not O'Neal). Nordica began separation proceedings from her husband in 1884 (not 1883). The world tour during which she died was not announced by her as a 'farewell tour.' Add to bibl.: Ira Glackens, *Yankee Diva; Lillian Nordica and the Golden Days of Opera* (N.Y., 1963).

Noren, Heinrich Gottlieb. His real name was Heinrich Suso Johannes Gottlieb; in 1916 he added his wife's maiden name Noren to his own. Date of birth is Jan. 5 (not Jan. 6), 1861. It was not Richard Strauss himself but his callous publishers who instituted a lawsuit to prevent publication of Noren's *Kaleidoskop,* in which the last variation, dedicated 'to a famous contemporary,' included thematic materials from *Ein Heldenleben.* Exact date of the first performance of *Kaleidoskop* is Dresden, July 1, 1907.

Norena, Eide. Died in Switzerland, Nov. 19, 1968.

Nørgaard, Per, Danish composer; b. Copenhagen, July 13, 1932. He studied with Holmboe in Denmark and Nadia Boulanger in Paris. His music is experimental in nature, adhering to dodecaphony and other serial methods. His works include *Konstellationen* for 12 string instruments, or 12 sets of instruments (Copenhagen, Nov. 3, 1958) and an opera, *Labyrinth* (Copenhagen, Sept. 2, 1967). About 1960 he abandoned conventional serialism in favor of metrical modulation and pitch pointillism; adopted a graphic notation in a free aleatory interchange of tone colors and rhythms. In this manner are written his *Fragment VI* for 6 orchestral groups (1961); the scenic oratorio *Dommen (The Judgment)*; *Nocturnes* for soprano, piano and 19 instruments, to Chinese texts; *Iris* for orch. (Copenhagen, May 19, 1967).

North, Alex, American composer and conductor; b. Chester, Pa., Dec. 4, 1910. He studied at the Curtis Institute in Philadelphia and at the Juilliard School of Music in New York; also took lessons with Ernst Toch and Aaron Copland. He began his career as a composer for documentary films and gradually established himself as a film composer of dramatic and effective music; wrote the scores for *Death of a Salesman, Viva Zapata!, A Streetcar Named Desire, The Bad Seed, The Sound and the Fury, Spartacus, The Misfits, Cleopatra, The Agony and the Ecstasy* and *Who's Afraid of Virginia Woolf?;* music for television. His song *Unchained Melody* has acquired great popularity. Apart from these lucrative tasks, he has written grand symphonies, modernistic concertos and unorthodox cantatas. His works of this elevated nature include: *Rhapsody* for piano and orch. (N. Y., Nov. 11, 1941); *Revue* for clarinet and orch. (N. Y., Nov. 20, 1946, Benny Goodman soloist, Leonard Bernstein conducting); Symph. No. 1 (1947); *Morning Star Cantata* (N. Y., May 18, 1947); *Little Indian Drum* for narrator and orch. (N. Y., Oct. 19, 1947); *Negro Mother Cantata* (N. Y., May 17, 1948); *Holiday Set* for orch. (Saratoga, N. Y., July 10, 1948); Symph. No. 2 (1968); Symph. No. 3 (1971; incorporating parerga & paralipomena left over from the score originally written for the film *2001, a Space Odyssey,* but not used).

North, Roger, English musician; b. Tostock, Suffolk, Sept. 3, 1653; d. Rougham, March 1, 1734. He was a solicitor; rose to be named Attorney-General to King James II; music was his avocation. He publ. *Memoires of Musick* and *Musicall Gramarian,* containing comments on the musical mores of his era. Bibl.: J. Wilson, ed., *Roger North on Music; Being a Selection from his Essays Written During the Years c. 1695-1728* (London, 1959).

Novák, Johann Baptist, Slovenian composer; b. Ljubljana, 1756; d. there, Jan. 29, 1833. He served as a government clerk and at the same time studied music; was music director of the Philharmonic Society in Ljubljana (1808-25), and gave concerts as a singer and violinist. A close contemporary of Mozart, he composed in a Mozartean manner. His historical importance lies in his incidental music to *Figaro,* a play in the Slovenian language based on the same comedy by Beaumarchais that served for Mozart's great opera. Novák's music forms a striking parallel to Mozart's procedures and yet contains some original traits. See Dragotin Cvetko's article, *J. B. Novák—Ein slowenischer Anhanger Mozarts,* in 'Bericht über den internationalen Musikwissenschaftlichen Kongress Wien,' Mozartjahr, 1956.

Novák, Vítězslav. Date of the first performances of *Signorina Gioventù* and *Nikotina,* Feb. 10, 1929 (not March 8, 1930). The first performance of *De Profundis* took place on Oct. 9 (not Nov. 20), 1941. Bibl.: Bohumir Štedron, *Vítězslav Novák v obrazech* (Prague, 1967); Vladimir Lebl, *Vítězslav Novák,* in English (Prague, 1968).

Novello-Davies, Clara. The exact place and date of birth of her son, **Ivor Novello,** Cardiff, Jan. 15, 1893.

Nowowiejski, Felix. The spelling of the last name should be **Nowowjejski.** See Jan Boehm, *F. Nowowjejski* (Olsztyn, 1968).

Nystedt, Knut. Add to works: *Symphony for Strings* (1950); *The Seven Seals* for orch. (1960); 4 string quartets (1939, 1948, 1956, 1966); *The Moment* for soprano, celesta and percussion (1962); *Collocations* for orch. (1963). In 1969 he visited the U.S. as a composer in residence at Berea College, Kentucky.

Nystroem, Gösta. Died in Sarö, near Göteborg, Aug. 10, 1966. The following are the dates of first performances of his four symphonies: *Sinfonia breve* (Göteborg, Oct. 19, 1932); *Sinfonia espressiva* (Göteborg, Feb. 18, 1937); *Sinfonia del mare* (Stockholm, March 24, 1949); *Sinfonia Shakespeareana* (Göteborg, Nov. 5, 1952). Add to works: *Concerto ricercante* for piano and orch. (1959); *Herr Arnes Penningar,* opera based on a novel by Selma Lagerlöf (Göteborg, Jan. 6, 1961); *Sinfonia seria* (Stockholm, Oct. 9, 1963); *Sinfonia tramontana* (Stockholm, Oct. 30, 1966).

O

Oboussier, Robert. His collection of critical reviews, *Berliner Musik-Chronik 1930-38* was publ. posthumously in 1969.

Obradović, Aleksandar, Serbian composer; b. Bled, Aug. 22, 1927. He studied in Belgrade with Logar and in London with Berkeley. He spent a year (1966-67) in the U.S. working mainly with electronic musical instruments. Formally, his music adheres to the architectonic classical design with strongly discernible tonal centers, but he boldly experiments with atonal thematics and polytonal harmonies; in several of his works he applies explicit dodecaphonic formulas. Works: Symph. No. 1 (Belgrade, June 20, 1952); Symph. No. 2 (Belgrade, Jan. 22, 1965); Symph. No. 3 (*Mikrosimfonija*) for orch. and stereo tape (1967); *Plameni Vjetar* (*Flaming Wind*), song cycle for baritone and orch. (Belgrade, Jan. 13, 1959); Concerto for clarinet and strings (Belgrade, March 26, 1959); *Sym-*

phonic Epitaph for speaker, mixed chorus and orch. (Belgrade, May 21, 1959); *Scherzo in modo dodecafonico* for orch. (Belgrade, May 24, 1962); *Epitaf H* for orch. and tape (Berlin, Oct. 6, 1965); *Electronic Toccata and Fugue* for stereo-magnetic tape (Belgrade, Oct. 11, 1967). See V. Peričić, *Muzički Stvaraoci u Srbiji* (Belgrade, 1969; pp. 351-63).

Obrecht, Jacob. Apparently not identical with the student of the same name who was admitted to the Univ. of Louvain in 1470, since his father's baptismal name was different. Therefore, there is no proof that he was born in 1452; 1450 or 1451 are the alternative dates. See G. Reese, *Music of the Renaissance* (2nd edition, N.Y., 1959; p. 186, footnote 8).

Obretenov, Svetoslav, Bulgarian composer; b. Provadia, Nov. 25, 1909. He studied at the Sofia Cons.; was active as choral conductor. He has written mostly for chorus; his oratorio *The Partisans* was performed for the first time in Sofia on June 25, 1949. See V. Krstev, *Svetoslav Obretenov* (Sofia, 1959).

Ockeghem, Johannes. Born c. 1425 (not 1430), probably in Termonde (Dendermonde).

O'Connell, Charles. Died in New York, Sept. 1, 1962.

Oetting, William H. Died in Pittsburgh, Oct. 29, 1969.

Offenbach, Jacques. Add to bibl.: A. Decaux, *Offenbach, Roi du Second Empire* (Paris, 1958).

Ogdon, John (Andrew Howard), English pianist; b. Manchester, Jan. 27, 1937. He studied at the Royal Manchester College of Music; made appearances in recitals and as soloist with orchestras. In 1962 he won the world's most prestigious contest, the Tchaikovsky Competition in Moscow. A man of massive physique, he handles the piano with masculine power, but is also capable of the finest quality of lyricism. In 1965 he made his first American tour.

Ohana, Maurice, French composer and pianist; b. Gibraltar, June 6, 1914. He studied piano with Lazare Lévy in Paris and Casella in Rome; composition with Daniel Lesur. He settled in Paris and became one of the directors of the Club Français du Disque. His works include a *Sonate monodique* for piano; a guitar concerto; *Portraits de Don Quichotte* for orch. and narrator, etc.

O'Hara, Geoffrey. Died in St. Petersburg, Florida, Jan. 31, 1967.

Ohlsson, Garrick, American pianist; b. Bronxville, N. Y., April 3, 1948. He entered the preparatory division of the Juilliard School of Music in 1961 as a student of Sascha Gorodnitzki; in 1968 he enrolled in the master class of Rosina Lhévinne. He came to public notice in 1969 when he won the international Busoni competition in Bolzano and the Montreal contest for pianists. A giant leap in his career was made when he became the first American pianist to win the prestigious quinquennial Chopin International Piano Competition in Warsaw in 1970, contending against topnotch Polish and Russian performers. A Polish writer described Ohlsson as a 'bear-butterfly' for his ability to traverse the entire spectrum of 18 dynamic degrees discernible on the modern pianoforte, from the thundering fortississimo to the finest pianississimo,with reference also to his height (6 foot, 4 inches), weight (225 lbs.) and stretch of hands (an octave and a fifth in the left hand and an octave and a fourth in the right hand). His interpretations are marked by a distinctive Americanism, technically flawless, objective and free of romantic narcissism.

Oistrakh, David Feodorovitch. Add bibl.: I. Yampolsky, *David Oistrakh* (Moscow, 1964).

Oistrakh, Igor. Exact date of birth, Odessa, April 27, 1931.

Olah, Tiberiu, Rumanian composer; b. Arpasel, Jan. 2, 1928. He studied in Cluj, then went to Russia where he studied at the Moscow Cons. (1949-54). Returning to Rumania, he became instructor of composition at the Bucharest Cons. In his own compositions, Olah adopts a strong contrapuntal style, with some excursions into the atonal domain and dodecaphonic organization. Works: Symphony (1955); the cantatas *Prind visele aripi (Dreams become Reality,* 1959); *Constelatia omului (The Galaxy of Man)* to texts by Mayakovsky (1960); string quartet (1951); trio for violin, clarinet and piano (1952); sonata for solo clarinet (1963); piano pieces.

Olczewska, Maria. Died in Klagenfurt, Austria, May 17, 1969. Correct spelling of last name **Olszewska.**

Oldberg, Arne. Died in Evanston, Illinois, Feb. 17, 1962.

Oldman, Cecil Bernard. Died in London, Oct. 7, 1969.

Olds, Gerry, American composer; b. Cleveland, Feb. 26, 1933. He studied at the Cleveland Institute and at the Chicago Cons. (M.A., 1957). His works include a *Short Symphony* (1956); violin concerto (1957); Toccata for string orch. (1958); wind quintet (1958); 2nd Symph. in one movement (1958); string trio (1959) and piano concerto (1960).

Olenin, Alexander Alexeyevitch. Exact date of death, Moscow, Feb. 15, 1944.

Olénine d'Alheim, Marie. Died in Moscow, Aug. 27, 1970, at the age of 100. In 1949 she joined the French Communist party; in 1959 went back to Russia.

Oliveira, Jocy de, Brazilian pianist and avant-garde composer; b. Curitiba-Parana, Brazil, on April 11, 1936, of French and Portuguese origin. She studied piano in São Paulo with J. Kliass and in Paris with Marguerite Long; received a fellowship from the Pan American Union to study composition in the U.S.; obtained her M.A. at Washington Univ. at St. Louis in 1968. She appeared as a piano soloist with major orchestras in Europe and America, specializing in modern repertory; in 1966 she played the piano part in Stravinsky's *Capriccio* in St. Louis, under Stravinsky's direction. As a composer, she occupies the aphelion of ultra-modernism, experimenting in electronic, environmental, theatrical, cinematic and television media, as exemplified by *Probabilistic Theater* I, II and III for musicians, actors, dancers, television and traffic conductor, and other environmental manifestations. Her *Polinteracões I, II, III* present the culmination of 'total music', concerned with happenings in socio-theatrical situations and programmed as a synesthetic action, including the specifics of illumination and spatial parameters such as inflatable floors and movable panels, and involving the visual, aural, tactile, gustatory and olfactory senses, with an anatomic chart serving as a score for guidance of plural or singular participants, supplemented by a phonemic table indicating the proper verbalization of vocal parts. (Complete score and illustrations are reproduced in 'Source,' No. 7, Sacramento, California, 1970.) A performance of *Polinteracões* was attempted on the occasion of the Catalytic Celebration of the 10th Anniversary Festival of the New Music Circle in St. Louis on April 7, 1970, but was interrupted halfway through the proceedings by the management as a noisy, noisome nuisance. Jocy de Oliveira is also active in belles-lettres; she wrote a socio-logical fantasy *O 3° Mundo (The Third World;* a utopian, optimistic vision of the future); a controversial play, *Apague meu (Spotlight)*, first produced in São Paulo in 1961; poetical works, etc. She also composed a number of advanced Sambas, precipitating the vogue of the Brazilian 'bossa nova.' She is the wife of the Brazilian conductor Eleazar Carvalho.

Oliver, Joseph ('King'), black American jazz band leader; b. on a plantation near Abend, Louisiana, May 11, 1885; d. Savannah, Georgia, April 8, 1938. He played cornet in a school brass band; took odd jobs; performed in the New Orleans red light district. His distinctive improvisation of jazz breaks fascinated the listeners; riding the wave of success, he formed his own King Oliver Creole Jazz Band, specializing in 'gully-low' New Orleans music which he projected with an insistent rhythmic stress. His name remains as one of the most potent figures in the annals of jazz.

Oliveros, Pauline, American avant-garde composer; b. Houston, May 30, 1932. She received the rudiments of musical education from her mother and grandmother; studied composition at the Univ. of Houston (1949-52), at San Francisco State College (1954-56), and privately with Robert Erickson. In 1967 she joined the faculty of the Univ. of California at San Diego. As a composer, she cultivates total music in mixed media, often with whimsical intent. She is a frequent participant at avant-garde events. She is active as instructor in group improvisation; she has also tutored psychiatric patients (1965-67). Works: *Trio* for flute, piano and page turner (1961); *Outline* for flute, percussion and string bass (1963); *Duo* for accordion and bandoneon with optional mynah bird obbligato, see-saw version (1964); *Variation for Sextet* (1964); *Pieces of Eight* for wind octet, cash register and magnetic tape (1965); *Rock Symphony* for electronic tape (1965); *Seven Sets of Mnemonics* for multimedia (1965); *Bye Bye Butterfly* for oscillators, amplifiers, and assorted tapes (1965); *Participle Dangling in Honor of Gertrude Stein* for tape, mobile and work crew (1966); *Engineer's Delight* for piccolo and 7 conductors (1967); *Evidence for Computing Bimolecular and Termolecular Mechanism in the Hydrochlorination of Cyclohexene,* for inter-media (1968); *Double-Basses at 20 Paces* (1968); *The Dying Alchemist* for multi-media (1968); *Night Jar* for viola d'amore (1968); *The Wheel of Fortune,* improvisation suggested by the trump cards of the Tarot deck (1969); *One Sound* for string quartet, an invariant quadritone monody; *Apple Box Orchestra with Bottle Chorus* (1970). As a member of the militant feminist group SCUM (Society for Cutting Up Men), she prefers the egalitarian designation Ms in place of the more customary Miss or Mrs..

d'Ollone, Max. Died in Paris, May 15, 1959.

Olsen, Poul Rovsing, Danish composer; b. Copenhagen, Nov. 4, 1922. He studied at the Copenhagen Cons. and later with Nadia Boulanger in Paris. Returning to Copenhagen, he studied ethnomusicology and traveled to Greenland in search of materials. Among his works are *Variations symphoniques* (1953); a piano concerto (1954); *Sinfonia* (1958); *Passacaglia* for flute, violin, cello and piano (1960); piano sonata; cello sonata; songs. He also composed an opera *Belisa* (1964) and several ballets.

Olsson, Otto Emanuel. Died in Stockholm, Sept. 1, 1964.

Ondříček, Emanuel. Died in Boston, Dec. 30, 1958.

Ondříček, Franz. Date of birth, April 29, 1857 (not 1859); date of death, April 12 (not April 13), 1922.

Oosterzee, Cornelie van, Dutch composer; b. Batavia, Java, Aug. 16, 1863; d. Berlin, Aug. 8, 1943. She studied in Berlin, and settled there in 1890; her opera *Das Gelöbnis* was produced in Weimar on May 1, 1910.

Orbón, Julián. Add to works: *Partita* for harpsichord, string quartet, vibraphone, celesta and harmonium (1964).

Orchard, William Arundel. Died at sea, near Sydney, Australia, April 7, 1961.

Ordoñez, Carlos, Austrian composer of Spanish extraction; b. Vienna, April 19, 1734; d. there, Sept. 6, 1786. He was employed as a clerk, but studied violin and performed successfully at chamber music concerts. He wrote numerous singspiele and much instrumental music, some of which was publ. still in his lifetime. His singspiel *Diesmal hat der Mann den Willen* was performed in Vienna on April 22, 1778; his marionette opera *Alceste* was introduced by Haydn in Esterház in 1775. He developed an excellent métier, and several of his symphonies possessed enough merit to be misattributed to Haydn. For further details see H. C. Robbins Landon's article on Ordoñez in 'Die Musik in Geschichte und Gegenwart.'

Orefice, Giacomo. Pronunciation: accent on the 2nd syllable (not on the 3rd).

Orel, Alfred. Died in Vienna, April 11, 1967. A Festschrift in honor of his 70th birthday was publ. in Vienna in 1960.

Orff, Carl. Add to works: *Comoedia de Christi Resurrectione,* Easter cantata (Munich, March 31, 1956); *Oedipus der Tyrann,* musical play after Sophocles (Stuttgart, Dec. 11, 1959); *Ludus de nato infante mirificus,* a nativity play (Stuttgart, Dec. 11, 1960); *Prometheus,* opera (Stuttgart, March 24, 1968). See I. Kiekert, *Die musikalische Form in den Werken Carl Orffs* (Regensburg, 1957); A. Liess, *Carl Orff: His Life and His Music* (N. Y., 1966).

Orlov, Nikolay Andreyevitch. Died in Grantown-on-Spey, Scotland, May 31, 1964.

Ornstein, Leo. Date of birth Dec. 11, 1892 (not 1895).

Orr, Robin, Scottish composer; b. Brechin, June 2, 1909. He studied organ and theory at the Royal College of Music in London and at Cambridge Univ. (1929-32). He subsequently studied composition with Edward J. Dent in London, with Alfredo Casella in Siena and with Nadia Boulanger in Paris. In 1938 he returned to Cambridge as organist of St. John's college; was lecturer at Cambridge Univ. (1947-50) and at the Royal College of Music in London (1950-56). In 1956 he was appointed prof. of music in the Univ. of Glasgow. His works include *Symphony in One Movement* (London, Dec 12, 1963); *Full Circle,* opera (Perth, Scotland, April 10, 1968); *Divertimento* for chamber orch.; string quartet, choral music. He edited 'The Kelvin Series of Scots Songs.'

Orrego Salas, Juan. In 1961 was appointed prof. of composition at Indiana Univ., Bloomington; also became Director of the Latin American Music Center, newly established there. Add to works: Symph. No. 3 (1961); *Psalms* for narrator and wind orch. (1962); concerto for wind orch. (1964); *Concerto a Tre* for violin, cello, piano and orch. (Washington, May 7, 1965); *Sonata a Quattro* for flute, oboe, harpsichord and double-bass (1964); *Alboradas* for piano, harpsichord, percussion and female chorus (1964); *America, no invocamos tu nombre en vano,* cantata (1965); *Palabras de Don Quijote* for baritone and chamber orch. (Coolidge Festival, Washington, D.C., Oct. 31, 1970).

Osghian, Petar, Serbian composer; b. Dubrovnik, April 27, 1932. He studied in Belgrade; adopted a free neo-romantic style of composition. Works: *Poema eroico* for orch. (Belgrade, Dec. 8, 1959); *Symphoniette* for strings (Belgrade, Dec. 20, 1960); Concerto for Orchestra (Belgrade, Feb. 25, 1964); *Sigogis* for orch. (Zagreb, May 12, 1967); *Meditation* for 2 pianos; numerous other piano pieces.

Osthoff, Helmuth. A Festschrift was publ. in Tutzing in 1961 to honor his 65th birthday, and another for his 70th birthday.

Otaño, (José María) Nemesio. Died April 29, 1956 (not 1957).

Oudrid (y Segura), Cristóbal. Born Feb. 7, 1825 (not 1829); died March 12 (not March 15), 1877.

Oulibishev, Alexander Dimitrievitch. He spelled his name **Oulibicheff.** Date of death, Feb. 5 (not Feb. 10), 1858. He settled in Nizhny-Novgorod in 1841 (not 1830).

Overton, Hall, American composer; b. Bangor, Michigan, Feb. 23, 1920. He studied piano at the Chicago Musical College; served in the U.S. Army overseas (1942-45) and learned to play jazz. In 1947 he settled in N.Y.; studied composition with Persichetti at the Juilliard School of Music, N.Y., graduating in 1951; subsequently took lessons with Wallingford Riegger and Darius Milhaud. At the same time he began to play jazz piano professionally. His works include the operas, *The Enchanted Pear Tree,* after Boccaccio's *Decameron* (Juilliard School of Music, N. Y., Feb. 7, 1950); *Pietro's Petard* (1963); *Huckleberry Finn,* after Mark Twain (Juilliard American Opera Center, N. Y., May 20, 1971); 2 symphonies (1955, 1962); 2 string quartets; string trio; piano pieces; songs.

Ozawa, Seiji, Japanese conductor; b. Hoten, Sept. 1, 1935. He studied piano, composition and conducting at the Toho School of Music in Tokyo graduating in 1959. He was employed as a salesman for a Japanese motor scooter company; went to Italy to promote its sales, and scooted to Paris, where he studied conducting with Eugène Bigot; later he took a course in conducting with Herbert von Karajan in Berlin. In 1960 Leonard Bernstein engaged him as an assistant conductor of the New York Philharmonic, and Ozawa made an auspicious debut at Carnegie Hall on April 14, 1961. Immediately afterwards he accompanied Bernstein and the New York Philharmonic to Japan. He was invited to conduct a Japanese orchestra in Tokyo, but the initial concert had to be cancelled when trouble developed between him and the players who objected to being commanded in an imperious manner by one of their own countrymen. In the meantime he advanced significantly in the esteem of American audiences; was engaged as a guest conductor with the Chicago Symphony Orch. in 1964, and in 1965 was appointed permanent conductor of the Toronto Symphony Orch., with which he toured Europe. In 1969 he was appointed conductor and music director of the San Francisco Symphony Orchestra. He is praised equally for his impassioned interpretation of romantic symphonies, for his authentic polyphonic scanning of the classics, as well as for his precision and rhythmical impetus in ultra-modern scores.

P

Pacini, Giovanni. His opera *Annetta e Lucinda* was first performed in Milan (not in Venice).

Paganini, Niccolò. Add to bibl.: R. de Saussine, *Paganini* (Milan, 1958); M. Codignola, *Arte e magia di Niccolò Paganini* (Milan, 1960); W. G. Armando, *Paganini: eine Biographie* (Hamburg, 1960); D. F. Botti, *Paganini e Parma* (Parma, 1961); P. Berri, *Paganini: Documenti e testimonianze* (Genoa, 1962); L. Day, *Paganini of Genoa* (London, 1966).

Page, Kate Stearns. Died in New York, Jan. 19, 1963.

Pahissa, Jaime. Died in Buenos Aires, Oct. 27, 1969. His opera *Marianela* (not *Marianella*) was produced on March 31, 1923 (not 1925).

Pakhmutova, Alexandra, Soviet composer; b. Stalingrad, Nov. 9, 1929. She studied at the Moscow Cons. with Shebalin, graduating in 1953. Her music is unpretentious and melodious; its thematic resources are derived from Russian folksongs. Her most successful work is a concerto for trumpet and orch. (Moscow, June 11, 1955); she also wrote songs, some of which became popular.

Paik, Nam June, Korean-American composer of the foremost avant-garde; b. Seoul,

July 20, 1932. He studied at the Univ. of Tokyo and in Germany; took courses in composition with Thrasybulos Georgiades in Munich and with Wolfgang Fortner in Freiburg-im-Breisgau; did experimental work at the Electronic Music Studio in Cologne (1958-60); attended the summer seminars for new music at Darmstadt (1957-61). In his creative evolution he pursues the objective of total music as the sum of integrated synesthetic experiences, involving walking, talking, dressing, undressing, drinking, smoking, moving furniture, all sorts of quaquaversal commotion, soft or loud noises, etc., so that any human, or inhuman, action becomes a musical event by sheer power of volition or by force of the ontological imperative. Demolition of upright pianos and other destructible musical instruments is an important part in Paik's concert programs. Paik is a familiar figure at international happenings; he has attracted newspaperwide attention by his duo recitals with the topless cellist Charlotte Moorman in which he plays the role of a surrogate cello, with his spinal column, denuded, serving as the fingerboard for her cello bow while his skin provides an ample area for intermittent pizzicati. Works: *Ommaggio a Cage,* for piano demolition, breakage of eggs, painting of hands in jet black, etc. with tape-recorded accompaniment in the highest decibel range (Düsseldorf, Nov. 13, 1959); *Etude for Pianoforte* (1960); *Simple* (1961); *Symphony for 20 Rooms* (1962); *Variations on a Theme of Saint-Saëns* for cello and piano, performing fragments of *Le Cygne,* while the cellist is instructed to dive into an oil drum filled with water (N.Y., Aug. 25, 1965, composer at the piano, Charlotte Moorman in the oil drum); *Opéra Sextronique* (1967); *Opéra Electronique* (1968); *Performable Music,* wherein the player is told to make a cut not less than 10 centimeters on his left arm with a razor; other compositions calling for similar mayhem; also an impractical command, with or without music, *Creep Into the Vagina of a Whale.* The Los Angeles earthquake of Feb. 9, 1971 (magnitude 6.5 on the Richter Scale) forms the finale of Paik's *Third Symphony.*

Palange, Louis Salvador, American conductor, composer and arranger, of Italian descent; b. Oakland, Cal., Dec. 17, 1917. He played the clarinet and bassoon in school bands; in 1936 went to Los Angeles, where he took lessons with Wesley La Violette; also attended classes at the Univ. of California. During World War II he served in the U.S. Navy and conducted the U.S. Naval Training Station Orch. in San Diego; in 1953 founded the Los Angeles Philharmonic Band; in 1955 he became conductor of the Beach Cities Symph. Orch. In 1962 he organized the West Coast Opera Co.; in 1965 formed the Southeast Symph. Continuing to accumulate orchestral positions, he assumed in 1967 the direction of 3 more orchestras: Downey Symph. Orch., Hollywood-Wilshire Symph. Orch. and the Metropolitan Symph. Orch.; in 1968 he added the Senior Citizens Symph. Orch. of Los Angeles to the list; was also musical director of the Music Teachers Assn. of California Concerts Orch. (1965-69); guest conductor of Inglewood Philharmonic, San Gabriel Valley Symph. Orch., Burbank Symph. Orch. and Sacramento Honor Orch., etc., etc., etc. His works include: *Symphony in Steel* for band (Los Angeles, March 8, 1941); *Evangeline* for orch. (Washington, March 2, 1945); Symphony No. 1 (*Invasion Symphony,* 1946); *Classical Trio* for flute, violin and viola (1950); a violin concerto (1950); string quartet (1950); *Hollywood Panorama,* tone poem (Burbank, Sept. 21, 1952); *A Romantic Piano Concerto* (Cleveland, May 13, 1954); *Poker Deck Ballet Suite* for orch. (Redondo Beach, Cal., Dec. 9, 1960, composer conducting); *Symphony in E minor* (Los Angeles, March 22, 1968).

Palau, Manuel. Died in Valencia, Feb. 18, 1967. Add to bibl.: F. J. L. Tello, *La obra pianistica de Manuel Palau* (Valencia, 1956).

Palisca, Claude Victor, American musicologist; b. Fiume, Nov. 24, 1921. He came to the U. S. in 1930; attended public schools in N. Y. and Florida; studied composition at Queens College with Karol Rathaus (B.A., 1943) and at Harvard Univ. with Walter Piston and Randall Thompson (composition) and with Otto Kinkeldey, Gombosi and Davison (musicology); obtained his M.A. in 1948; Ph.D. in 1954. He was a member of the faculty at the Univ. of Illinois, Urbana, from 1953-59; in 1959 joined the staff of Yale Univ. He held the John Knowles Paine Traveling Fellowship (1949-50); Fulbright Grant for Italy (1950-52); Guggenheim Fellowship (1960-61). Publications: *Girolamo Mei: Letters on Ancient and Modern Music to Vincenzo Galilei and Giovanni Bardi* (Rome, 1960); *17th-Century Science and the Arts* (with others; Princeton, 1961); *Musicology* (with others; Englewood Cliffs, N. J., 1963); *Baroque Music* (N. Y., 1970).

Panizza, Ettore. Died in Buenos Aires, Nov. 27, 1967.

Panufnik, Andrzej. Add to works: *Sinfonia Sacra* (Monaco, Aug. 12, 1964); *Epitaph for the Victims of Katyn* (N.Y., Nov. 17, 1968); *Universal Prayer,* a setting of Alexander Pope's poem for 4 solo voices, three harps, organ and choir (first performance at the Cathedral Church of St. John the Divine, N. Y., Leopold Stokowski conducting, May 24, 1970).

Papaioannou, Iannis, Greek composer; b. Kavala, Jan. 5, 1910. He studied at the Athens Cons., and later went to Paris where he took lessons with Honegger. In 1953 he received a prize at the Queen Elisabeth International Competition in Brussels. Returning to Greece, he was appointed prof. of composition at the Athens Cons. In his music he adopted a neoclassical style; later he added serial procedures. Works: 5 symphonies (1946, 1951, 1953, 1962, 1964); symphonic poems: *The Corsair* (1940), *Poem of the Forest* (1942), *Mating of Souls* (1947), *Pygmalion* (1951), *Hellas* (1956); quartet for flute, clarinet, guitar and cello (1962); trio for oboe, clarinet and bassoon (1962); *Archaic* for 2 guitars (1962); string trio (1963); piano pieces; songs.

Papandopulo, Boris. Add to works: *Rona,* opera (Rijeka, May 25, 1956); *8 Studies* for piano (1956); viola sonata (1956); opera *Marulova Pisan* (Split, Aug. 14, 1970), a 'solemn musical play' dedicated to the town of Split and dealing with the siege of a neighboring town by the Turks ca. 1500 and its liberation by Spalatines. In his works of the last period, such as his *Dodekafonski Concert* for 2 pianos (1961), he adopts 12-tone techniques. See Kovačević, *Hrvatski Kompozitori i Njihova Djela* (Zagreb, 1960).

Papineau-Couture, Jean, Canadian composer; b. Outremont, Quebec, Nov. 12, 1916. He studied at the New England Cons. in Boston with Quincy Porter and later at the Longy School in Cambridge, Mass., with Nadia Boulanger. Returning to Canada, he joined the music faculty of Montreal Univ. In his music he applies serial methods without sacrificing basic tonality. Works: Concerto grosso (1953); *Symphonie* (1948); violin concerto (1951); *Poème* for orch. (1952); *5 Pièces concertantes* for various instrumental ensembles (1957-63); chamber music; choruses.

Parker, Charlie, nicknamed 'Yardbird' or 'Bird' (real Christian names, Charles Christopher), American Negro saxophonist; b. Kansas City, Aug. 29, 1920; d. New York, March 12, 1955. With Dizzy Gillespie he organized an aggressively percussive combo whose modus operandi became known as rebop, bebop, and eventually, simply bop. A brilliant improviser, Parker became a virtuoso performer on the alto saxophone; he was almost equally proficient on the tenor sax. At the age of 15, he became a narcotics addict and could never be completely rehabilitated. His best period was between 1941 and 1950. He made his last appearance a week before his death. Some of his improvised compositions, under such whimsical titles as *Yardbird Suite* and *Ornithology* (with reference to his ornithological nickname) were published. See R. G. Reisner. *Bird: the Legend of Charles Parker* (N.Y., 1962).

Parlow, Kathleen. Died in Oakville, Ontario, Aug. 19, 1963.

Parris, Herman M., American physician and composer; b. Ekaterinoslav, Russia, Oct. 30, 1903; was brought to America in 1905, the family settling in Philadelphia. He studied medicine at the Jefferson Medical College, Maryland, obtaining his M.D. in 1926. He received his musical training at the Univ. of Pennsylvania, graduating in 1921. Works: four symphonies (1946, 1947, 1949, 1952); 8 piano concertos (one each year between 1946 and 1953); 4 string quartets (1946, 1948, 1960, 1964); 22 piano sonatas (at least one each year between 1946 and 1965); 115 piano preludes (on the average of 5 a year between 1946 and 1967); *Hebrew Rhapsody* for orch. (1949); 4 rhapsodies for brass ensemble (1949); *Rhapsody No. 2* for orch., subtitled *Heart* (1950); *Images* for brass octet (1950); *Lament* for string orch., dedicated to the memory of Olin Downes (1956); viola sonata; cello sonata; 2 violin sonatas; songs. His orchestral piece entitled *Hospital Suite,* portraying events in the sick room, brought out, congenially so, by the Doctors' Orchestral Society (N.Y., May 13, 1948), attracted considerable attention in medical circles.

Parris, Robert, American composer; b. Philadelphia, May 21, 1924. He studied composition with Peter Mennin at the Juilliard School of Music, N.Y. (1946-48); at Tanglewood with Ibert (1950) and Copland (1951) and in Paris with Honegger (1952-53). He settled in Washington; in 1963 was appointed to the faculty of George Washington Univ. His music is distinguished by strong formal structure and tonal cohesion; when pragmatically justifiable, he applies serialistic techniques with deliberate circumspection.

His composition that had the greatest repercussion was a percussion piece, Concerto for 5 kettledrums and orch. (1955; Washington, March 25, 1958). Other works are: sextet for brass (1948); *Night* for baritone, clarinet and string quartet (1951); symphony (1952); piano concerto (1954); viola concerto (1956); quintet for flute, oboe, bassoon, violin and cello (1957); violin concerto (1959); *The Raids: 1940* for soprano, violin and piano (1960); *Lamentations and Praises* for 8 instruments and percussion (1962); viola concerto (5th Inter-American Music Festival, Washington, May 20, 1971); violin sonata; viola sonata; sonatina for flute, oboe, clarinet, horn and bass; 2 string quartets; 2 string trios; trio for clarinet, cello and piano; songs.

Parrish, Carl. Died as a result of an automobile accident in Valhalla, N.Y., Nov. 27, 1965.

Parry, Sir Charles Hubert Hastings. He studied at Eton (not Eaton).

Partch, Harry, American composer; b. Oakland, California, June 24, 1901. Largely autodidact, he began experimenting with instruments capable of producing fractional intervals, which led him to the formulation of a 43-tone scale; he expounded his findings in his book, *Genesis of a Music* (1949). Among new instruments constructed by him are elongated violas, a chromelodeon, kitharas with 72 strings, harmonic canons with 44 strings, boos (made of giant Philippine bamboo reeds), cloud-chamber bowls, blow-boys (a pair of bellows with an attached automobile horn), etc. Seeking intimate contact with American life, he wandered across the country; collected indigenous expressions of folkways, inscriptions on public walls, etc. for texts in his productions. Works: *8 Hitchhiker Inscriptions from a California Highway Railing* and *U.S. Highball, a Musical Account of a Transcontinental Hobo Trip* for chorus and instruments (both performed for the first time in Carnegie Chamber Hall, N.Y., April 22, 1944); *The Letter, a Depression Message from a Hobo Friend*, for voices and instrumental ensemble (1944); *Oedipus*, music drama (Mills College, Oakland, Calif., March 14, 1952); *The Bewitched,* a dance satire (Univ. of Illinois, Urbana, Ill., March 26, 1957); *Revelation in the Courthouse Park,* a musical tragedy (Univ. of Illinois, Urbana, April 11, 1961); *Water, Water*, an American ritual (Univ. of Ill., March 9, 1962). See Peter Yates, *Genesis of a Music* in 'High Fidelity' (July 1963).

Patterson, Franklin Peale. Died in New Rochelle, N. Y., July 6, 1966.

Pattison, Lee. Died in Claremont, Calif., Dec. 22, 1966.

Paulson, Gustaf. Died in Hälsingborg, Sweden, Dec. 17, 1966.

Paumgartner, Bernhard. Died in Salzburg, July 26, 1971. He publ. an autobiographical memoir *Erinnerungen* (Salzburg, 1969).

Paunović, Milenko, Serbian composer; b. Šajkaš, Nov. 28, 1889; d. Belgrade, Oct. 1, 1924. He studied in Leipzig with Max Reger and Hugo Riemann; became a choral conductor in Novi Sad. In his music he followed Wagnerian concepts, and wrote several music dramas to his own texts. He also composed a *Yugoslav Symphony* (Ljubljana, March 17, 1924).

Payne, John, American composer; b. New York, May 23, 1941. He studied psychology at Brown Univ. (B.A., 1962); played in jazz bands. Bypassing the traditional forms of conventional modernism, he devoted his energies to total environmental art. He collaborated with Carol Law and Charles Amirkhanian in producing a live-electronic theater event *Ode to Gravity* (San Francisco, Sept. 21, 1968); staged the audience participation happenings *Thursday Mix* (San Francisco, March 27, 1969, a Thursday) and *Friday Mix* (San Francisco, May 2, 1969, a Friday). He also programmed a number of electronic scores, among them *Elevator Music* and *Toot le fromage,* making use of inchoate concrete noises.

Pechner, Gerhard, German baritone; b. Berlin, 1903; d. New York, Oct. 21, 1969. He made his first appearance as an opera singer in Berlin in 1927; was compelled to leave Germany in 1933; from 1933 till 1939 he was on the staff of the German Opera House in Prague. In 1940 he was engaged by the San Francisco Opera, and in 1941 made his debut at the Metropolitan Opera in New York. He particularly distinguished himself in Wagnerian roles.

Pedrollo, Arrigo. Died in Vicenza, Dec. 23, 1964.

Pelletier, Wilfred. Correct form of first name, **Wilfrid.**

Penderecki (pronounced Pen-deh-rétz-key), **Krzysztof** (pronounced Krzhýsh-tof), foremost Polish composer of the 20th-century avant-garde; b. Debica, Nov. 23, 1933. He studied music theory with Arthur Malawski and Stanislaw Wiechowicz at the Superior School of Music in Cracow, matriculating in 1958; after graduation he taught there; then went to West Germany; in 1970 visited the U.S. After a few works of an academic nature, he developed a hyper-modern technique of composition in a highly individual style, in which no demarcation line is drawn between consonances and dissonances, tonal or atonal melody, traditional or innovating instrumentation; an egalitarian attitude prevails towards all available resources of sound. While Penderecki's idiom is naturally complex, he does not disdain tonality, even in its overt triadic forms. In his creative evolution, he has bypassed orthodox serial procedures; his music follows an athematic course, in constantly varying metrical and rhythmic patterns. He utilizes an entire spectrum of modern sonorities, expanding the domain of tone to unpitched elements, making use of such effects as shouting, hissing and verbal ejaculations in vocal parts, at times reaching a climax of aleatory glossolalia; tapping, rubbing or snapping the fingers against the body of an instrument; striking the piano strings by mallets, etc. For this he designed an optical notation, with symbolic ideograms indicating the desired sound; thus a black isosceles triangle denotes the highest possible pitch; an inverted isosceles triangle, the lowest possible pitch; a black rectangle for a sonic complex of white noise within a given interval; vertical lines tied over by an arc for arpeggios below the bridge of a string instrument; wavy lines of varying amplitudes for extensive vibrato; curvilinear figures for aleatory passages; dots and dashes for repetitions of a pattern; sinusoidal oscillations for quaquaversal glissandos, etc. He applies these modern devices to religious music, including masses in the orthodox Roman Catholic ritual. — Works: *Strophes* for soprano, narrator and 10 instruments (Warsaw, Sept. 17, 1959); *Emanacje* for 2 orchestras of string instruments (1959); *Wymiary czasu i ciszy* (*Dimensions of Time and Silence*) for wordless chorus, strings and percussion (Warsaw, Sept. 18, 1960); string quartet No. 1 (1960); *Anaklasis* for string instruments and percussion (Baden-Baden, Oct. 22, 1960); *Tren pamieci ofiarom Hiroszimy* (*Threnody in Memory of Victims of Hiroshima*) for 52 string instruments, Penderecki's most impressive and most frequently performed work, rich in dynamic contrasts and ending on a tone-cluster of two octavefuls of icositetraphonic harmony (Warsaw, May 31, 1961); *Psalmus* for electronic instruments (1961); *Stabat Mater* for 3 choruses a cappella (1961); *Polymorphia* for 48 string instruments (Hamburg, April 16, 1962); *Psalmy Dawida* for mixed chorus and percussion (Cracow, June 26, 1962); *Canon* for 52 string instruments and magnetic tape (Warsaw, Sept. 20, 1962); *Fluorescences* for orch. (Baden-Baden, Oct. 21, 1962); *Cantata in Honorem Almae Matris* for chorus and orch. (1964); *Mensura Sortis* for 2 pianos (1964); *Sonata* for cello and orch. (1964); *Capriccio No. 1* for oboe and strings (1965); *Passio et Mors Domini Nostri secundum Lucam* (Münster Cathedral, March 30, 1966, a specially commissioned work); *De Natura Sonoris* for string orch. (Royan, April 7, 1966); *Dies Irae* (Cracow, April 14, 1967; also performed two days later at a commemorative service at the site of the Nazi concentration camp at Oświecim-Brzezinka); *Capriccio No. 2* for violin and orch. (Donaueschingen, April 22, 1967); *Pittsburgh Overture* for wind ensemble (1967); *Concerto* for violino grande, a specially constructed instrument with 5 strings (Östersund, Sweden, July 1, 1967; revised version, Hanover, N.H.. Aug. 4, 1968); *Die Teufel von Loudun* (*The Devils of Loudun*), music drama dealing with a furor uterinus among nuns of Loudun struck by a multifutuent incubus personified by a neighboring monastic youth (Hamburg, June 20, 1969); string quartet No. 2 (1970); *Utrenja* (*Morning Prayer*) for 2 choruses, 5 soloists and percussion, to a text in old Slavonic (Altenberg Cathedral, April 8, 1970); *Kosmogonia* for chorus and orch., commissioned by the United Nations (N. Y., Oct. 24, 1970); *Auferstehung Christi,* Easter oratorio (Altenberg Cathedral, May 28, 1971).

Pentland, Barbara, Canadian pianist and composer; b. Winnipeg, Jan. 2, 1912. She studied at the Juilliard School of Music, N.Y., with Frederick Jacobi and Bernard Wagenaar, graduating in 1939; took courses with Aaron Copland at the Berkshire Music Center in Tanglewood (1941-42). In 1942 she was appointed instructor at the Toronto Cons. In 1949 she moved to Vancouver, where she was on the faculty of the Music Dept. of the Univ. of British Columbia until 1963. In her compositions, after an initial period of eclecticism, she accepted the Schoenbergian method as best suited to her aspirations. Works: 4 symphonies (1948-59); violin concerto (1942); *Weekend Overture* for winds, percussion and piano (1949); concerto for piano and strings (1956); piano quartet (1939); cello sonata (1943); violin sonata (1946); octet for wind instruments (1950);

3 string quartets (1943, 1953, 1970); Duo for viola and piano (1960); *Canzona* for flute, oboe and harpsichord (1961). See '34 Biographies of Canadian Composers' publ. by the Canadian Broadcasting Co. (Montreal, 1964).

Pépin, Clermont. There is an acute accent on é in his name. Add to works: *Le Rite du Soleil Noir,* symph. poem (1955); Symph. No. 2 (1957); *Monologue* for orch. (1961); *Nombres* for 2 pianos and orch. (1962); string quartet No. 3 (1959); string quartet No. 4, subtitled *Hyperboles* (1960); piano trio (1959); *Hymn to the North Wind,* cantata for tenor and orch. (1960); 3 toccatas for piano; *Les Quasars* for chorus and orch. (Montreal, Feb. 7, 1967); songs. See '34 Biographies of Canadian Composers' publ. by the Canadian Broadcasting Co. (Montreal, 1964).

Pepöck, August. Died in Gmunden, Sept. 5, 1967.

Peragallo, 'Mario. The title of his opera is *Ginevra* (not *Ginerva*) *degli Almieri.*

Perceval, Julio, Argentinian composer; b. Brussels, July 17, 1903; d. (in a traffic accident) in Santiago, Chile, Sept. 7, 1963. He studied organ at the Brussels Cons.; subsequently with Marcel Dupré in Paris. Emigrating to Argentina in 1926, he became active as organist in Buenos Aires; then was prof. of organ playing at the Univ. of Cuyo (1939-59). In 1959 he went to Chile where he taught at the National Cons. of Santiago. He composed a number of songs and organ pieces; also some chamber music.

Pereira-Salas, Eugenio. Add to books: *Historia de la música en Chile (1850-1900)* (Santiago, 1957).

Pergament, Moses. Add to works: piano concerto (1951); *Concerto* for 2 violins and orch. (1954); cello concerto (1955); *Abram,* opera (1957); sonata for flute and piano (1957); *Pezzo intimo* for 16 solo cellos (1957); *Fyra dikter* for soprano and orch. (1965); *Arstider,* song cycle for baritone and orch. (1968).

Peri, Jacopo. He was born in Rome (not in Florence).

Peričić, Vlastimir, Serbian composer and musicologist; b. Vršac, Dec. 7, 1927. He studied in Vienna with Uhl; became active as a pedagogue in Belgrade; publ. manuals on harmony and form. Works: string quartet (1950); *Symphonic Movement* (Belgrade, Oct. 14, 1952); *Fantasia quasi una sonata* for violin and piano (1954); *Sinfonietta* for strings (Zagreb, Nov. 13, 1957); piano pieces. He compiled a valuable reference work on Serbian composers, *Muzički Stvaraoci u Srbiji* (Belgrade, 1969).

Perkins, Francis Davenport. Died in New York, Oct. 8, 1970.

Perkins, John MacIvor, American composer and pedagogue; b. St. Louis, Aug. 2, 1935. He studied music at Harvard Univ. (B.A., 1958), and at Brandeis Univ. (M.F.A., 1962); also took lessons with Nadia Boulanger in Paris and with Roberto Gerhard and Edmund Rubbra in London. He was instructor in music at the Univ. of Chicago (1962-64); lecturer on music at Harvard Univ. (1965-70). In 1970 he was appointed head of the music dept. of Washington Univ. in his native St. Louis. His major works include *Canons* for 9 instruments (1957); *Three Miniatures* for string quartet (1960); *Variations* for flute, clarinet, trumpet, piano and percussion (1962); *Music for 13 Players* (1964); *Music for Orchestra* (1965); choral works and piano pieces.

Perle, George. Add to works: *Monody I* for flute (1960); *Monody II* for double-bass (1962); *Solo Partita* for violin and viola (1965); cello concerto (1966); string quartet No. 5 (1967); string quartet No. 6 (1969).

Perlea, Jonel. Died in New York, July 29, 1970. He suffered a heart attack in 1957 and a stroke in 1958 as a result of which he lost the use of his right arm, but continued to conduct with his left hand. In 1969 he led concerts for the Bucharest Philharmonic.

Perosi, Lorenzo. Add bibl.: M. Rinaldi, *Lorenzo Perosi* (Rome, 1967).

Perotin. Putative dates of life: born between 1155 and 1160; died between 1200 and 1205. See Hans Tischler, *The Motet in 13th-Century France* (New Haven, 1942).

Perrin, Pierre. Year of birth, closer to 1620 than to 1616.

Persichetti, Vincent. Add to works: 7 Serenades for piano (1928-52); 11 piano sonatas (1939-65); 6 piano sonatinas (1950-54); Symph. No. 7 (St. Louis, Oct. 24, 1959); piano concerto (Dartmouth College, Aug. 2, 1964); *Winter Cantata* for women's chorus, flute and marimba (1964); *Parable* for solo flute (1965); Symph. No.

8 (Berea, Ohio, Oct. 29, 1967); *The Creation,* oratorio (N. Y., April 17, 1970); *Janiculum,* symphony (Philadelphia, March 5, 1971). choruses to words by E. E. Cummings. He publ. a manual *Twentieth-Century Harmony: Creative Aspects and Practice* (N. Y., 1961); contributed essays on modern idioms and techniques to various music periodicals.

Persinger, Louis. Died in New York, Dec. 31, 1966.

Pertile, Aureliano, Italian operatic tenor; b. Montagnara, Nov. 9, 1885; d. Milan, Jan. 11, 1952. He made his debut in 1911; was for a season (1921-22) a member of the Metropolitan Opera, N.Y.; then at La Scala, Milan (1922-37); also sang in London. After retirement, he settled down in Milan as voice teacher.

Petin, Nikola, Serbian composer; b. Belgrade, Dec. 19, 1920. He studied with Slavenski and others; became teacher at Novi Sad. His music is romantically colored. Among his works are *3 Symphonic Portraits: Hamlet, Ophelia, Polonius; Symphonia brevis; Ballade* for bassoon and piano; incidental music for the theater.

Petrassi, Goffredo. Add to works: *Estri* for chamber orch. (Dartmouth College, Hanover, N. H., Aug. 2, 1967); *Beatitudines,* oratorio in memory of Martin Luther King (Fiuggi, July 17, 1969).

Petrauskas, Kipras. Died in Vilna, Jan. 17, 1968.

Petri, Egon. Died in Berkeley, Calif., May 27, 1962.

Petrov, Andrey, Soviet composer; b. Leningrad, Sept. 2, 1930. He studied at the Leningrad Cons. with Evlakhov. When still a student he wrote a number of works that were successfully performed: the ballets *The Magic Apple Tree* (Leningrad, Nov. 8, 1953); *The Stationmaster* (after Pushkin; Leningrad, May 9, 1955); symph. poem *Radda and Loiko* (after Maxim Gorky; Leningrad, Dec. 12, 1954); a song cycle with orch., *For Peace* (Leningrad, Dec. 20, 1951); *Pioneer Suite* for orch. (1951; quite successful); *Sport Suite* for orch., written for the International Festival of Democratic Youth in Bucharest (1953). Other works include a song cycle *Simple Songs* (1956) and a ballet *The Shores of Hope* (1959). In his music Petrov maintains an ambiance of lyric melodiousness and harmonious simplicity.

Petrov, Ivan, Russian operatic bass; b. Irkutsk, Feb. 23, 1920. He made his debut at the Bolshoi Theater, Moscow, in 1943; his most celebrated interpretation is in the title role of *Boris Godunov,* inviting a comparison with Shaliapin.

Petrov, Ossip Afanassievitch. Born Nov. 15, 1806 (not 1807). Died March 11 (not March 14), 1878.

Petrović, Radomir, Yugoslav composer; b. Belgrade, May 13, 1923. He studied in Belgrade, and subsequently became active as a teacher there. His works are in a classical tradition, but he often makes use of national thematic elements; of these, his *Moto sinfonico* (Belgrade, March 3, 1959) is the most successful.

Petrovics, Emil, Hungarian composer; b. Nagybecskerek, Feb. 9, 1930. He studied composition with R. Sugár and with Ferenc Farkas in Budapest. In 1960 he became conductor of the National Theater in Budapest. His satirical one-act opera, *C'est la guerre* (Budapest, Aug, 17, 1961) obtained considerable success in Hungary, and was also performed in Paris. Other works are *Lysistrata,* a 'concert opera' (1962); *Crime and Punishment,* opera after Dostoyevsky (Budapest, Oct. 26, 1969); a flute concerto; string quartet and other chamber music.

Petrželka, Vilém. Died in Brno, Jan. 10, 1967.

Pettersson, Gustaf Allan, Swedish composer; b. Västra Ryd, Sept. 19, 1911. He studied composition with Karl-Birger Blomdahl in Stockholm. In 1950 he went to Paris where he took private lessons with René Leibowitz and Arthur Honegger. Upon return to Sweden, he played the viola in the Stockholm Philharmonic (1939-51). A prolific composer, he wrote 9 symphonies (1951-1970); 3 concertos for string orch. (1950, 1956, 1957); 7 sonatas for 2 violins; a concerto for violin and string quartet; songs, etc. His style of composition is that of Scandinavian romanticism.

Pfitzner, Hans (Erich). Add to bibl.: J. Müller-Blattau, *Hans Pfitzner: Lebensweg und Schaffensernte* (Frankfurt, 1969).

Philip, Achille, French composer; b. Arles, Oct. 12, 1878; d. Béziers (Hérault), Nov. 12, 1959. He studied at the Paris Cons. with Guilmant (organ) and Vincent d'Indy (composition); from 1905 to 1950 taught organ at the Schola Cantorum in Paris. He wrote an opera *L'or du Menhir* (Rouen, 1934); the symphonic poems, *Les Djinns* (1913); *Dans un parc enchanté* (1917) and *Nymphes et Naiades* (1920); a number of sacred works; chamber music; songs.

Phillips, Montague Fawcett. Died in Esher, England, Jan. 4, 1969.

Phillips, Philip, American hymn writer; b. on a farm in Chautauqua County, N.Y., Aug. 13, 1834; d. Delaware, Ohio, June 25, 1895. He sang in a choir as a child; was a cheesemaker by trade; then traveled as an itinerant singer; published gospel song books. His best known hymn is *Home of the Soul.* Cf. R. G. McCutchan, *Our Hymnody,* (N.Y., 1937).

Piaf, Edith, French chanteuse; b. Paris, Dec. 19, 1915; d. there, Oct. 11, 1963. Her real name was Giovanna Gassion; she took her first name from Edith Cavell, Belgian nurse shot by the Germans in World War I. Her childhood was tragic; she was abandoned by her mother, an Italian café singer; traveled with her father, a circus contortionist, taking part in his act as an acrobat. She then became a street singer in Paris, earning the nickname Piaf (Parisian argot for sparrow) on account of her ragged and emaciated appearance. She was befriended by a cabaret owner; when he was murdered she was held by the French police as a material witness. During the war and German occupation she entertained French prisoners in Germany; as a result, she was accused of collaboration, but was exonerated. In 1964 she made her first American tour. Although untutored, she developed a type of ballad singing that was infused with profound sentiment and expressive artistry. eliciting enthusiastic response from nightclub audiences and sophisticated music critics alike. She composed chansonettes, among which *La Vie en rose* became popular; publ. a book of memoirs *Au Bal de la Chance* (Paris, 1958).

Piastro, Michel. Died in New York, April 10, 1970.

Piatigorsky, Gregor. Born April 17 (not April 20), 1903. He publ. an autobiography, *Cellist* (N.Y., 1965).

Picchi, Silvano, Argentine composer; b. Pisa, Italy, Jan. 15, 1922. His family emigrated to Argentina while he was a child; he studied composition with Constantino Gaito, Alberto Ginastera, Arturo Luzzatti, Gilardo Gilardi and Floro M. Ugarte in Buenos Aires. He is the music critic of 'La Prensa' in Buenos Aires. Works: *Suite irreverente* for orch. (1949); *Musica para caballos* for orch. (1952); piano concerto (Buenos Aires, July 23, 1967); violin concerto (Buenos Aires, Aug. 12, 1968); *Discantus* for guitar and bassoon (1968); *Euè,* funeral chant for string orch. on an African theme (Buenos Aires, March 18, 1969).

Pierre, Constant. *Le Concert Spirituel, 1725-1790,* was not publ. in 1900, but remained in manuscript.

Pierson, Henry Hugh. Title of opera, *Contarini* (not *Contrarini*).

Pijper, Willem. Add bibl.: W. C. M. Kloppenburg, *Thematisch-bibliografische Catalogus van de Werken van Willem Pijper* (Amsterdam, 1960).

Pimsleur, Solomon, American pianist and composer; b. Paris, Sept. 19, 1900, of Austrian-Jewish parents; d. New York, April 22, 1962. He was taken to the U.S. as an infant in 1903; studied piano privately; took music courses at Columbia Univ., but graduated in English literature (M.A., 1923); also studied with Rubin Goldmark. He gave numerous piano recitals in the U.S. His compositions, in a romantically flavored and technically competent idiom, include an *Ode to Intensity,* a "symphonic ballad" (N.Y., Aug. 14, 1933); an *Overture to Disillusionment;* a *Meditative Nocturne* for orch.; 3 string quartets; a piano trio; a piano quintet; a violin sonata; a cello sonata; many piano pieces with imaginative titles *(Impulsive Sonata, Tranquil Sonata, Reflective Sonata, Mournful Prelude and Melodious Fugue,* etc.); a *Shakespearean Sonnet Symphony* for chorus and orch. His projected opera, *Diary of Anne Frank,* remained unfinished.

Pineda Duque, Roberto, Colombian composer; b. El Santuario, Aug. 29, 1910. He studied in Paris; occupied various teaching posts in Colombia; also conducted band concerts. He composed much religious music and short symphonic works. His *Preludio Sinfónico* had performances in America and in Europe.

Pinkham, Daniel. Add to works: Symph. No. 1 (1960); *Catacoustical Measures,* composed to test the acoustics at Lincoln Center in New York (1962); Symph. No. 2 (Lansing, Michigan, Nov. 23, 1963); *Signs of the Zodiac* for speaker and orch. (1964); *Eclogue* for flute, harpsichord and handbells (1965); violin concerto (1968).

Pipelare, Matthaeus, Flemish composer; b. about 1450; d. about 1512. He was active in Antwerp; was engaged as master of the choirboys in 's-Hertogenbosch (1498-1500). His style has a certain affinity to that of Pierre de la Rue. His extant works include 9 masses and a number of motets and chansons. Cf. R. Cross, *The Life and Works of Matthaeus Pipelare,* in 'Musica disciplina' (1963).

Pipkov, Lubomir. Add to bibl.: K. Iliev, *Lubomir Pipkov* (Sofia, 1958).

Pirogov, Alexandr Stepanovitch, Russian operatic bass; b. Moscow, July 4, 1899; d. there, June 18, 1964. He was engaged as a member of the Bolshoi Theater in 1924, and appeared in leading roles in Russian repertoire.

Pironkov, Simeon, Bulgarian composer; b. Lom, June 18, 1927. He studied with Stoyanov at the Sofia Cons., graduating in 1952; subsequently became active as a composer for films. Among his works the most important is a *Symphony for Strings* (1960).

Pisk, Paul Amadeus. Resigned from the Univ. of Texas in 1962; joined the staff of Washington Univ., St. Louis, in 1963.

Piston, Walter. Middle name **Hamor.** Retired from Harvard Univ. in 1960. In Paris he studied also with Paul Dukas at the École Normale de Musique (1925). Was for a time a draftsman for Boston Elevated Railway. Add to works: viola concerto (Boston, March 7, 1958); Concerto for 2 pianos and orch. (1959); *Three New England Sketches* for orch. (Worcester, Mass., Music Festival, Oct. 23, 1959); violin concerto No. 2 (Pittsburgh, Oct. 28, 1960); Symph. No. 7 (Philadelphia, Feb. 10, 1961; received a Pulitzer Prize); *Symphonic Prelude* (Cleveland, April 20, 1961); *Lincoln Center Festival Overture* (N.Y., Sept. 25, 1962); *Capriccio* for harp and string orch. (1963; Washington, 3rd Inter-American Music Festival, May 8, 1965); Symph. No. 8 (Boston, March 5, 1965); *Variations* for cello and orchestra (N.Y., March 2, 1967, with Rostropovitch as soloist); clarinet concerto (Dartmouth College, Hanover, N.H., Aug. 6, 1967); *Ricercare* for orch. (N. Y., March 7, 1968); 3 pieces for flute, clarinet and bassoon; (1926); flute sonata (1930); suite for oboe and piano (1931); piano trio (1935); violin sonata (1939); *Interlude* for viola and piano (1942); quintet for piano and string quartet (1949); duo for viola and cello (1949); quintet for horn and woodwinds (1956); sextet for stringed instruments (1964); piano quartet (1964); 5 string quartets (1933, 1935, 1947, 1951, 1962). Beginning about 1965, and particularly in his Symph. No. 8 and *Variations* for cello and orch., Piston decisively adopts, for the first time in his distinctly non-atonal music, an explicit 12-tone system of composition in building and developing his thematic materials.

Pizzetti, Ildebrando. Died in Rome, Feb. 13, 1968. Add to works: *Il Calzare d'argento,* sacred play (Milan, La Scala, March 23, 1961); *Clitennestra,* music drama (La Scala, Milan, March 1, 1965). Add to bibl.: M. LaMorgia, *La città d'annunziana a Ildebrando Pizzetti: saggi e note* (Milan, 1958).

Plamenac, Dragan. A festschrift in his honor, was published in Pittsburgh in 1969 under the title *Essays in Musicology,* edited by Gustave Reese and R. J. Snow.

Platti, Giovanni. Exact date of birth, July 9, 1697 (not 1690). Add bibl.: Fausto Torrefranca, *G. B. Platti e la sonata moderna* (Milan, 1963).

Plaza, Juan Bautista, Venezuelan composer; b. Caracas, July 19, 1898; d. there, Jan. 1, 1964. He went to Rome in 1920 to study at the Pontifical Institute of Sacred Music; upon returning to Venezuela, became organist of the Cathedral of Caracas. He wrote a number of sacred choral works; also the symph. poems, *El Picacho abrupto, Vigilia, Campanas de Pascua, Las Horas,* etc.; a *Fuga criolla* for orch.; a *Sonatina venezolana* for piano; songs.

Pleshakov, Vladimir, American pianist; b. Shanghai, of Russian parents, Oct. 4, 1934. He studied piano with Russian teachers in Shanghai; in 1949 went to Australia, enrolling in the New South Wales State Conservatorium in Sydney where he took piano lessons with Alexander Sverjensky and attended master classes of Eugene Goossens, graduating in 1953. In 1955 he emigrated to America; entered the Medical School at the Univ. of California, Berkeley, obtaining his A.B. in medical sciences in 1958; contributed research papers to medical journals. Turning back to music, he took piano lessons with Adolph Baller in Palo Alto (1964-66); in 1968 he entered Stanford Univ. as a graduate music student; in 1970 was a Ph.D. candidate. He became particularly interested in the history of piano manufacture, and made a thorough investigation of the mechanism of pianos of the period between 1770 and 1810. In 1969 he became a member of the faculty of the Nueva Day School in Menlo Park. He joined the Society of Forgotten Music, founded by Vernon Duke, and gave piano recitals featuring works by neglected composers; in particular he helped to rescue from undeserved oblivion the piano music of Joseph Wölfl, F. M. Rust, Paul Dukas, Ernest Chausson and Nikolai Medtner.

Pochon, Alfred. Died in Lutry, Switzerland, Feb. 26, 1959.

Podešva, Jaromír, Czech composer; b. Brno, March 8, 1927. He studied at the Brno Cons.; later taught there. He has written several symph. works on programmatic subjects, among them a symph. poem, *The Path of the Fatherland* (1953); numerous choral cycles; 3 string quartets; a sextet for 2 violins, viola, cello, horn and clarinet; *Poetic Trio* for violin, cello and piano; a group of piano pieces entitled *Rhapsodietti.*

Pokorný, Franz Xaver, Czech composer; b. Königstadt (Mestec Kralove), Dec. 20, 1728; d. Regensburg, July 2, 1794. He joined the court orchestra in Oettingen-Wallerstein in 1753; then went to Mannheim, where he studied with Stamitz, Holzbauer and Richter, returning to Wallerstein after a few months. In 1767 he became a court musician in Thurn and Taxis. In the light of recent research, Pokorný appears as a pioneer in symphonic writing; fully 165 symphonies have been discovered that are probably his; they are all written in a characteristic style of the Mannheim School. See J. Murray Barbour, *Pokorný Vindicated* in the 'Mus. Quarterly' (Jan., 1963).

Polacco, Giorgio. Died in New York, April 30, 1960.

Poldowski. Born March 18, 1879 (not May 16, 1880).

Polignac, Armande de. Died in Neauphle-le-Vieux (Seine-et-Oise), April 29, 1962.

Pollack, Ben, American drummer and bandleader; b. Chicago, June 22, 1903; d. (suicide by hanging) at Palm Springs, Calif., June 7, 1971. He was a drummer with a New Orleans band; in 1924 he organized his own group, with 16-year-old Benny Goodman as clarinetist and Glenn Miller as trombonist and arranger; later he engaged Harry James as trumpeter; he himself presided at the drums. With this stellar personnel he cut a deep swath through the jazzland and was dubbed 'The Father of Swing.' When his career declined, he entered entertainment business; ran a restaurant in Hollywood; later managed a night club in Palm Springs. He left a suicide note, explaining his act by despondency over personal and financial problems.

Pollak, Robert. Died in Brunnen, Switzerland, Sept. 7, 1962.

Pollini, Francesco (Giuseppe). Born on Mar. 25, 1762 (not 1763).

Polovinkin, Leonid. Died Feb. 8 (not Feb. 2), 1949.

Poniatowski, Josef. Place of death, Chislehurst (not Chiselhurst).

Poniridis, Georges. Add to compositions: *Petite Symphonie* (1956); flute sonata (1956); string quartet (1959); clarinet sonata (1962); quartet for oboe, clarinet, bassoon and xylophone (1962); trio for xylophone, clarinet and bassoon (1962); trio for flute, oboe and clarinet (1962).

Pons, Charles. Born Dec. 7 (not Dec. 8), 1870. Died March 16 (not April), 1957.

Popov, Alexander, Bulgarian composer; b. Kolarovgrad, July 14, 1927. He studied composition with Stoyanov; played viola in the orchestra of the National Opera in Sofia. He writes mostly chamber music; his suite for string quartet with string orch. (1962) follows the classical model.

Popov, Gavriil Nikolayevitch. Add to works: *Symph. No. 6* (Moscow, Jan. 23, 1970).

Popovici, Doru, Rumanian composer; b. Resita (Banat), Feb. 17, 1932. He studied at the Bucharest Cons. with Mihail Jora, Paul Constantinesco, Theodor Rogalski and others. Works: operas: *Prometheus* (1958; Bucharest, Dec. 16, 1964); *Mariana Pineda* (Bucharest, Dec. 22, 1966); Symph. No. 1 (1962); Symph. No. 2 (1966); Symph. No. 3 (1968).

Poradowski, Stefan Boleslaw. Died in Posnan, July 6, 1967.

Porrino, Ennio. Died in Rome, Sept. 25, 1959.

Porter, Cole. Died in Santa Monica, Calif., Oct. 15, 1964. Date of birth, June 9, 1892 (not 1893).

Porter, Quincy. Died in Bethany, Conn., Nov. 12, 1966. Add to works: Symph. No. 2

(Louisville. Jan. 14, 1964); string quartets No. 9 (1955) and No. 10 (1965).

Porumbescu, Ciprian, Rumanian composer; b. Sipote, Oct. 14, 1853; d. Stupca, Bukovina, July 6, 1883. After preliminary studies in Rumania, he went to Vienna where he became a student of Bruckner; published a collection of "social songs of Rumanian students" (Vienna, 1880); composed an operetta *Cral Nou (The New King)* to a Rumanian libretto and many songs. His death at the age of 29 deprived Rumania of the country's first national composer, but he is greatly revered as such. The town of Stupca where he died has been renamed Ciprian Porumbescu, and his name is attached to the official designation of several Rumanian conservatories.

Poueigh. Jean. Died at Olivet (Loiret), Oct. 14, 1958.

Poulenc, Francis. Died in Paris, Jan. 30, 1963. First performance of *Les Mamelles de Tirésias* took place on June 3 (not June 10), 1947. Add to works: *La voix humaine,* one-act opera (Paris, Feb. 9, 1959); *Gloria,* for soprano, chorus and orch. (Boston, Jan. 20, 1961); *La Dame de Monte Carlo,* lyric scene for voice and orch. (Paris, Dec. 5, 1961); *Sept Répons des Ténèbres,* posthumous work for orch. (N.Y., April 11, 1963). Cf. *Moi et mes amis, confidences recueillies par Stéphanie Audel* (Paris, 1963).

Pourtalès. Guy de. Died in Lausanne, June 12, 1941. He was born in Berlin (not in Geneva) but lived most of his life in his castle near Geneva. His complete name was Guido James de Pourtalès.

Pousseur, Henri, Belgian composer of the ultra-modern school; b. Malmédy, July 23, 1929. He studied in Brussels; had private lessons in composition with André Souris and Pierre Boulez; was a member of the avant-garde group of composers 'Variation' in Liège. His music is greatly influenced by Anton von Webern. Works: *3 Chants sacrés* for soprano and string trio (1951); *Seismogrammes* for magnetic tape (1953); *Symphonies* for 15 solo instruments (1955); *Quintet* to the memory of Webern (1955); *Mobile* for two pianos (1958); *Couleurs croisées* for soprano and tape (1967), representing a series of crypto-musical variations on the Negro Liberation song, *We Shall Overcome; Croisées des couleurs croisées* (an intensified sequel to *Couleur croisées*) for soprano, tape recorders, two pianos and two radio receivers dialed aleatorily, to texts from Indian and Negro materials and political speeches (N. Y., Nov. 29, 1970); several scores for electronic instruments. He publ. *Fragments théoriques sur la musique expérimentale* (Brussels, 1970).

Powell, Earl (Bud), American pianist and composer; b. New York, Sept. 27, 1924; d. there, Aug. 1, 1966. He played in night clubs; became a vigorous exponent of the bop style, but suffered a succession of nervous breakdowns; from 1947 to 1959 was mostly in mental hospitals. The titles of his songs reflect his inner disturbances: *Hallucinations, Oblivion, Glass Enclosure.*

Powell, John. Died in Charlottesville, Virginia, Aug. 15, 1963. Add to works: *Virginia Symphony* (Richmond, Nov. 5, 1951).

Powell, Mel. Add to works: *Miniatures* for baroque ensemble (1957); *Filigree Setting* for string quartet (1958); *2 Prayer Settings* for tenor, oboe and 3 strings (1962); *Cantilena* for soprano, violin and electronic tape (1970); other electronic pieces.

Pozdro, John Walter, American composer; b. Chicago, August 14, 1923. He studied at the American Cons. in Chicago, at Northwestern Univ. and at the Eastman School of Music (with Howard Hanson and Bernard Rogers), graduating in 1958 with a Ph.D. in composition. He subsequently joined the faculty of the Univ. of Kansas. His works include 3 symphonies (1949, 1958, 1959); *A Cynical Overture* (1953); quintet for wind instruments and piano (1947); 2 string quartets (1947, 1948); sextet for flute and strings (1948); quintet for woodwinds (1951); *Trilogy* for clarinet, bassoon, trumpet and piano (1960); *Rondo Giojoso* for string orch. (1964); 3 piano sonatas (1947, 1963, 1964).

Praetorius, Michael. The imprints of *Syntagma Musicum* are: vol. I, part 1, Wolfenbüttel, 1614; vol. I, part 2. Wittenberg, 1615; vol. II, Wolfenbüttel, 1618 (appendix 1620); vol. III, Wolfenbüttel, 1618 (not 1619).

Pratella, Francesco Balilla. *L'aviatore Dro* was first performed in Lugo on Nov. 4 (not Sept. 4), 1920.

Preger, Leo. Died in Ajaccio, Corsica, Dec. 25, 1965.

Preobrazhensky, Anton Viktorovitch. Exact date and place of birth, Syzran, Feb. 28, 1870.

Presley, Elvis, popular American ballad singer; b. Tupelo, Miss., Jan. 8, 1935. He was employed as a mechanic and furniture repairman in his early youth; picked up guitar playing in his leisure hours; sang cowboy ballads on the radio and at social gatherings. With the advent of rock 'n' roll he suddenly revealed himself as the prime genius of the genre. He captivated multitudes of adolescents by the hallucinogenic monotone of his vocal delivery rhythmically enhanced by measured pelvic oscillations (hence the invidious appellation 'Elvis the Pelvis'); made recordings that sold in the millions of copies; appeared as an actor in sentimental motion pictures. His art was the prime inspiration of the famous Liverpudlian quartet, 'The Beatles.'

Prêtre, Georges, French conductor; b. Waziers, Aug. 14, 1924. He studied at Douai and in Paris; in 1946 made his debut at the Opéra-Comique; also conducted the Pasdeloup Concerts. In 1965 he made an American tour; appeared as guest conductor with the Philadelphia Orch. By temperament, he is an ebullient interpreter of romantic music indulging in eloquent bodily movements and projecting musical rhetorics with an imperious hand; but he can be superlatively restrained in classical repertory.

Previn, André, American pianist, conductor and composer; b. Berlin, April 6, 1929, of Jewish parents. He went to the U.S. in 1939 and studied composition in Los Angeles with Castelnuovo-Tedesco; at the age of 17 he began writing music for films. After service in the U.S. Army (1950-52), he toured as a pianist; also played in jazz groups. A versatile musician, Previn embarked on a successful conducting career; was music director of the Houston Symph. Orch. (1967-68), and in 1968 was engaged as principal conductor of the London Symph.; also continued to appear as a concert pianist. He composed the scores for the films *Bad Day at Black Rock* (1955), *The Subterraneans,* a documentary on beatniks (1960) and *Two for the Seesaw* (1962); adapted Borodin's music from the opera *Prince Igor* for the ballet *Kismet* (1955); arranged the musicals *Irma La Douce* (1963) and *My Fair Lady* (1964). On Feb. 26, 1970, Mia Farrow, the actress, bore him in London the twin boys named Matthew Phineas and Sacha Villiers, of whom Previn readily acknowledged paternity; he married her on Sept. 10, 1970, after the dissolution of his marriage to the singer Dory Langdon.

Prey, Hermann, German baritone; b. Berlin, July 11, 1929. He studied at the Berlin Hochschule für Musik; in 1952 won the first prize in a singing contest organized by the U.S. Army and went on an American tour. Returning to Europe, he sang in Vienna, Berlin, Munich and at La Scala in Milan; appeared as Wolfram in *Tannhäuser* with the Metropolitan Opera, N.Y. He is successful also on the concert stage.

Price, Leontyne, black American soprano; b. Laurel, Mississippi, Feb. 10, 1927. She studied at Central State College at Wilberforce, Ohio, and at the Juilliard School of Music, N.Y. (1949-52), with Florence Page Kimball. She achieved her first successes in the role of Bess in Gershwin's opera *Porgy and Bess,* which she sang on tour in the U.S. in 1952-54 and in Europe in 1955. In 1956 she gave concerts in India. In 1957 she joined the San Francisco Opera Co.; was also a member of the Lyric Opera in Chicago. In 1958 she sang *Aida* at the Vienna State Opera, and in 1960 she appeared in the same role at La Scala, Milan, with exceptional acclaim. On Jan. 27, 1961, she made her debut with the Metropolitan Opera Co., N.Y., as Leonora in *Il Trovatore;* subsequently sang the principal parts in *Madama Butterfly, Don Giovanni, Turandot* and *La Fanciulla del West* with unfailing musical, theatrical and popular success. She married the baritone William C. Warfield in 1952. On July 4, 1964 she was awarded the Medal of Freedom by the U.S. Government.

Prieberg, Fred K., German writer on music; b. Berlin, June 3, 1928. He took music courses at the Univ. of Freiburg-im-Breisgau; settled in Baden-Baden. He published a number of informative books on modern music, among them *Musik des technischen Zeitalters* (Zürich, 1956); *Lexikon der neuen Musik* (Freiburg, 1958); *Musica ex machina* (Berlin, 1960).

Příhoda, Váša. Died in Vienna, July 26, 1960; born Aug. 22 (not Aug. 24), 1900.

Primrose, William. He has not been knighted; received the Order of Commander of British Empire. He was violist of the Festival Piano Quartet, not String Quartet.

Pringsheim, Klaus. He was director of the Tokyo Chamber Symph. Orch. from 1941 to 1944 (not 1946). He wrote a Concerto for Orchestra in C (Tokyo, Oct. 13, 1935), not a piano concerto, nor *Symph. Concert Piece.* In 1971 he was still actively engaged in Tokyo as critic and conductor.

Profeta, Laurentiu, Rumanian composer; b. Bucharest, Jan. 14, 1925. He studied with Paul Constantinesco and Alfred Mendelsohn at the Bucharest Cons. and later at the Moscow Cons. (1954-56). His music is marked by rhapsodic expansiveness in romantically rich harmonies. His works include *Poemul Patriei (Poem of Fatherland)* for orch. (1952); *Carnival* for two pianos (1957); numerous choral pieces. He is also active as a musical journalist.

Prokofiev, Sergey Sergeyevitch. He began the composition of *Ondine* in March 1904, even before he went to study with Glière, and finished it in 1907. After his Russian tour of 1927, Prokofiev visited Russia again in 1929; made another concert tour in December 1932 before finally settling in Moscow. His cantata for the 20th anniversary of the October Revolution was finally brought to a performance on April 5, 1966 in Moscow, but not in its entirety; the section which used a text from Stalin was omitted. *Hamlet,* op. 77, is not a symph. suite from a film score, but incidental music for the Shakespeare play; it was first performed in connection with the opening of the Leningrad Drama Theater on May 15, 1938. The first unabridged performance of the opera *The Flaming Angel* took place in Paris on Nov. 25, 1954; its stage première was given in Venice on Sept. 14, 1955. After the unsuccessful private presentation of the opera *Story of a Real Man* in Leningrad in 1948, it was revived posthumously at the Bolshoi Theater in Moscow on Oct. 8, 1960. The cello concerto in E minor, op. 58, was revised and performed for the first time in Moscow on Feb. 18, 1952, as cello concerto No. 2, but subsequently renamed *Sinfonia-Concertante* and renumbered op. 125; this final version was first performed posthumously in Copenhagen on Dec. 9, 1954. Add to works: *Egyptian Nights,* incidental music for scenes from Shakespeare, Shaw and Pushkin (1933); music for films: *Lermontov* (1941), *Tonya* (1942), *Kotovsky* (1942), *Partisans in the Ukrainian Steppes* (1942). Add to bibl.: F. Streller, *Prokofiev* (Leipzig, 1960); C. Samuel, *Prokofiev* (Paris, 1960); L. Gakkel, *Piano Works of S. Prokofiev* (Moscow, 1960); I. V. Nestyev and G. Edelman, eds., *Sergey Prokofiev, Articles and Materials* (Moscow, 1962); L. Berger, ed., *Traits of Prokofiev's Style* (Moscow, 1962); M. Hofmann, *Prokofiev* (Paris, 1963); L. and E. Hanson, *Prokofiev, The Prodigal Son* (London, 1964); S. Slonimsky, *The Symphonies of Prokofiev* (Leningrad, 1964); S. Shlifshtein, ed. *Prokofiev,* album of pictures annotated in Russian and English (Moscow, 1965); V. Serov, *S. Prokofiev, a Soviet Tragedy* (N. Y., 1968). The 2nd ed. of I. Nestyev's biography of Prokofiev (1957) was published in English with a foreword by Nicolas Slonimsky (Stamford, Calif., 1961).

Prota-Giurleo, Ulisse. Add to publications: *I Teatri di Napoli nel '600; la commedia e le maschere* (Naples, 1962).

Provenzale, Francesco. Exact date of death, Sept. 6, 1704.

Puccini, Giacomo. The first American performance of *Manon Lescaut* took place on Aug. 29 (not July 29), 1894. Add to bibl.: E. Greenfield, *Puccini: Keeper of the Seal* (London, 1958); C. Sartori, *Puccini* (Milan, 1958); M. Carner, *Puccini* (London, 1958); W. Sandelewski, *Puccini* (Cracow, 1963).

Purcell, Henry. Add to bibl.: *Henry Purcell, 1659-1695; Essays on His Music,* edited by Imogen Holst (London, 1959); F. B. Zimmerman, *Henry Purcell: an Analytical Catalogue of His Music* (N. Y., 1963); F. B. Zimmerman, *Henry Purcell, His Life and Times* (N.Y., 1967).

Q

Quiroga, Manuel. Died in Pontevedra, Spain, April 19, 1961.

R

Rabinof, Benno, American violinist; b. New York, of Russian-Jewish parents, Oct. 11, 1910. He studied privately with Victor Küzdö, Franz Kneisel and Leopold Auer. He made his debut in 1927, playing the Tchaikovsky violin concerto with members of the N.Y. Philharmonic conducted by Leopold Auer. In 1930 he played Glazunov's concerto, with Glazunov himself leading the Boston Symph. Orch. as guest conductor. With his wife, the pianist Sylvia Smith-Rabinof, he has traveled extensively in Europe and America, in Israel, Turkey, etc. In 1959 he received a 1734 Stradivarius violin as a gift from a wealthy admirer.

Rabinovitch, David, Russian musicologist; b. Kharkov, Aug. 8, 1900. He studied piano at the St. Petersburg Cons. with Essipova, and first appeared in public at the age of 13; then entered classes in composition with Glière and piano with Igumnov at the Moscow Cons., graduating in 1930. He subsequently abandoned his concert career as pianist, and devoted himself to musicology, specializing in monographs on Soviet composers. He publ. *D. Shostakovitch, Composer* (Moscow, 1959, in an English translation); *Portraits of Pianists* (Moscow, 1962); numerous articles in Soviet music periodicals.

Rachmaninoff, Sergey Vassilievitch. Add to the list of works: *Variations on a Theme by Corelli* for piano, op. 42. The first complete performance of his piano concerto No. 2 took place on Nov. 9 (not Oct. 27), 1901.

Rachmilovich, Jacques. Died on board the S.S. Giacomo, en route to Italy, Aug. 7, 1956, and was buried at sea.

Radenković, Milutin, Serbian composer; b. Mostar, April 6, 1921. He studied at the Belgrade Music Academy, where he subsequently became a teacher; also active as music critic. His works are couched in a neo-classical idiom; of these, the most significant are *Concertino* for piano and orch. (1958) and *Dramatic Overture* (1960); he also composed chamber music; 2 piano sonatas; piano etudes and preludes; song cycles.

Radić, Dušan, Serbian composer; b. Sombor, April 10, 1929. He studied in Paris with Milhaud and Messiaen; at first adopted a neoclassical method of composition; later began to employ sharply dissonant counterpoint. Works: *Symphoniette* (1954); *Spisak (The Catalogue),* 13 sketches for 13 performers (Belgrade, March 17, 1954); *Balada o mesecu lutalici (Ballad of the Erring Moon),* ballet (Belgrade, Oct. 19, 1960); Concertino for clarinet and strings; piano quintet; several cantatas; songs; theater music. See V. Peričić, *Muzički Stvaraoci u Srbiji* (Belgrade, 1969; pp. 407-21).

Radica, Ruben, Slovenian composer; b. Split, May 19, 1931. He studied with Kelemen in Zagreb, with Frazzi in Siena and with Leibowitz in Paris. In 1963 he was appointed to the faculty of the Music Academy in Zagreb. He belongs to the avant-garde of Slovenian music; in 1961 he adopted the 12-tone method of composition. Works: *Concerto grosso* (1957); *4 Dramatic Epigrams* for piano and string quartet (1959); *Concerto abbreviato* for cello and orch. (1960); *Lyrical Variations* for strings (1961); *Choreographic Music* for orch. (1962).

Radovanović, Vladan, Serbian composer; b. Belgrade, Sept. 5, 1932. He studied at the Music Academy in Belgrade. His early works are set in a neo-classical style; later he annexed ultra-modern techniques, including electronic effects. His *Urklang* for mezzo-soprano and chamber orch. (Belgrade, March 14, 1962) deploys a counterpoint of instrumental colors, with the soloist singing wordlessly. Similarly wordless is his suite, *Chorales, Intermezzi e Fuga* for women's chorus (Belgrade, May 16, 1962). His experimental period includes such innovative works as *Sphaeroön* in 26 vocal parts, singing detached vowels (Belgrade, March 14, 1962) and *Pentaptych,* suite for voice and 6 instruments (Belgrade, April 22, 1964). See V. Peričić, *Muzički Stvaraoci u Srbiji* (Belgrade, 1969; pp. 422-29).

Radziwill, Anton Heinrich. Died April 7 (not April 8), 1833.

Rago, Alexis, Venezuelan composer; b. Caracas, May 25, 1930. He studied in Caracas and later at the Peabody Cons. in Baltimore; then went for further studies to Vienna and Rome, where he took courses in piano and composition. Returning to Venezuela he became Director of the Cons. of the state of Aragua. Works: *Tres Escenas de Ritos Prohibidos* for piano (1959); *Autantepuy,* symph. poem (1962); *5 Instantes* for orch. (1968); *Mítica de Sueños y Cosmogonías* for wind quintet (commissioned by the 4th Inter-American Festival in Washington, and performed there on June 25, 1968); *Guri,* symph. poem on indigenous themes (1968); *Sincronismos, Audio-Sonorrítmicos* (1969); several piano suites; songs.

Raichl, Miroslav, Czech composer; b. Náchod, Feb. 2, 1930. He studied in Prague, graduating in 1953 from the Academy of Musical Arts there. He wrote an opera *Fuente Ovejuna* after Lope de Vega (1957); 2 symphonies (1955, 1960); a cello concerto (1956); chamber music.

Raimondi, Gianni, Italian tenor; b. Bologna, April 17, 1923. He made his debut in 1947 in Bologna; appeared at La Scala, Milan as Alfredo in *La Traviata,* with Maria Callas as Violetta. In 1957 he made his first American tour; in 1965 made his debut with the Metropolitan Opera in New York. He is particularly impressive in the Italian repertory.

Rainier, Priaulx. Add to works: cello concerto (London, Sept. 3, 1964); *Aequora Lunae,* symph. suite (Cheltenham, July 18, 1967).

Raisa, Rosa. Died in Los Angeles, Sept. 28, 1963.

Raitchev, Alexander, Bulgarian composer; b. Lom, April 11, 1922. He studied with Pantcho Vladigerov in Sofia; later took courses in Budapest. His music is marked by bright colors and clear tonal harmonies. Works: symphony-cantata, *He Will Never Die* (1952); oratorio, *Friendship* (1954); *Sonata-Poem* for violin and orch. (1955); symph. poem, *The New Prometheus* (1958); operetta, *The Orchid's Glory* (Sofia, March 6, 1963).

Rajičič, Stanojlo. Correct form of last name, **Rajičić.** Add to works: opera, *Simonida* (Sarajevo, May 24, 1957); symph. in G (1959); *Magnovenja,* song cycle for mezzo soprano and orch. (1964); *Symphony in E* (Symph. No. 6; 1967). See V. Peričić, *Muzički Stvaraoci u Srbiji* (Belgrade, 1969; pp. 430-52).

Ralf, Richard, German composer; b. Karlsruhe, Sept. 30, 1897. He studied piano as a child with his father, the choirmaster at the Karlsruhe Opera; later attended the Scharwenka Cons. in Berlin, graduating in 1914. Drafted into the German Army, he suffered a severe shell shock at the French front; returning to Berlin, he studied composition with Hugo Kaun. He was active as a composer and arranger for radio and motion pictures; wrote the score for the German release of the film *Battleship Potemkin* (1925). In 1936 he was forced by the Nazi government to give up his professional activities on account of the Jewish origin of his wife. In 1946 he emigrated to the U.S., eventually settling in Los Angeles. His music follows the florid and emotional trend of post-Wagnerian romanticism; he excels mainly in the instrumental genre. Works: *Transcendental,* ballet (1921); violin sonata (1923); string quartet (1924); violin concerto (1925); *Brothers Arise,* cantata (1959); *Symphonic Songs* for mezzo-soprano and orch. (1968).

Rameau, Jean-Philippe. Vol. XVII of his collected works is in 2 parts: Part I contains *Pygmalion* and *Les Surprises de l'Amour;* Part II, *Anacréon* and *Les Sybarites.* Vol. XVIII contains only *Naïs.* The last vol. of the series appeared in 1924 (not 1914). Add to bibl.: J. Malignon, *Rameau* (Paris, 1960); H. Charlier, *J. Ph. Rameau* (Lyon, 1960); Sr. M. M. Keane. *The Theoretical Writings of J. Ph. Rameau* (Washington, 1961).

Ramovš, Primož, Slovenian composer; b. Ljubljana, March 20, 1921. He studied with Slavko Osterc, and later went to Italy where he became a student of Alfredo Casella. Returning to Ljubljana, he was appointed Librarian of the Slovenian Academy of Sciences and Arts. His style of composition is neo-classical. distinguished by great contrapuntal skill and ingenious handling of dissonant sonorities. Works: 3 symphonies (1941, 1943, 1948); sinfonietta (1951); 2 piano concertos (1948, 1949); concerto for 2 pianos and orch. (1949); *Concerto piccolo* for bassoon and string orch. (1958); concertino for trumpet and orch. (1960); concerto for violin and viola with orch. (1961); *Koncertantna glasba* for timpani and orch. (1961; his most remarkable work); *Antiparallels* for orch. (Zagreb, May 15, 1967); 2 clarinet sonatas; sonatina for horn and piano; sonatina for harp; trio for oboe, clarinet and bassoon; trio for 2 violins and viola; piano pieces; choruses; songs.

Ramsey, Robert, English organist and madrigalist; b. about 1595. He took his Mus. B. at Cambridge in 1616; was organist of Trinity College (1628-44) and Master of the Children (1637-44). He wrote numerous church services. anthems and madrigals, which remained in manuscript until 1962, when an *Evening Service* and some madrigals were published in England. See E. Thompson, *Robert Ramsey* in the 'Mus. Quarterly' (April, 1963).

Rands, Bernard, English composer; b. Sheffield, March 2, 1935. He studied at Univ. College, Bangor, N. Wales, specializing in composition; traveled on a Univ. of Wales Fellowship to Italy where he took lessons with Roman Vlad in Rome and with Luigi Dallapiccola in Florence; also consulted with Luciano Berio on problems of electronic music. Returning to England in 1961, he joined the staff of Univ. College, Bangor. Works: *3 Aspects* for piano (1959); *Quartet Music* for violin, viola, cello and piano (1959); *4 Compositions* for violin and piano (1959); *Tre Espressioni* for piano (1960); *Refractions* for 24 players, each manning several instruments (1961); *Actions for 6* for flute viola, cello, harp and 2 percussion players, each of the latter commanding an arsenal of 20-odd pieces of battery (1963); *Espressione IV* for 2 pianos (1964); *Formants* for harp solo (1965).

Ránki, György. Acute accent on á in the last name. Add to works: opera *Pomádé király uj ruhája* (after Andersen's *The Emperor's New Clothes;* Budapest, June 6, 1953); wind quintet (1958); *1514,* symph. poem for piano and orch. (1959), depicting the Hungarian peasant rebellion of 1514.

Rankl, Karl. Died in Salzburg, Sept. 6, 1968.

Ranta, Sulho. Died in Helsinki, May 5, 1960.

Raphael, Günther. Died in Herford, Oct. 19, 1960.

Ratner, Leonard Gilbert, American musicologist and composer; b. Minneapolis, July 30, 1916. He studied composition with Arnold Schoenberg at the Univ. of Calif., Los Angeles, and musicology with Manfred Bukofzer and Albert Elkus at Berkeley (Ph.D., 1947). He also had composition lessons with Ernest Bloch and Frederick Jacobi. In 1947 he was appointed to the staff of Stanford Univ.; held a Guggenheim Fellowship in 1962-63. Works: chamber opera, *The Necklace;* a symph.; an overture, *Harlequin;* 2 string quartets; violin sonata; cello sonata; piano sonata; etc. Books: *Music: The Listener's Art* (N.Y., 1957); *Harmony: Structure and Style* (N.Y., 1962).

Rattenbach, Augusto, Argentine composer; b. Buenos Aires, Feb. 5, 1927. After a study of elementary music theory in Argentina, he went to Hamburg where he learned modern techniques. Most of his mature compositions are in a serial idiom, with the formative elements determined in advance. Works: piano concerto (1956); *Passacaglia* (1957); wind quintet (1957); ballet, *Un Episodio Vulgar* (1961); *Serenata* for flute, clarinet, trumpet and cello (1962); *Obstinaciones* for orch. (1965); a series of *Microvariaciones* for various ensembles.

Raugel, Félix. Still active in France in 1971, in his 90th year, as a musicologist and a critic.

Ravel, Maurice. Add to bibl.: R. de Fragny, *Maurice Ravel* (Lyon, 1960); R. H. Myers, *Ravel: Life and Works* (London, 1960); H. H. Stuckenschmidt, *Maurice Ravel: Variationen über Person und Werk* (Frankfurt, 1966; in English, Philadelphia, 1968); P. Petit, *Ravel* (Paris, 1970). The 4-hand version of *Ma mère l'Oye* was first played on April 20, 1910 (not 1920). The names of children who performed it were Christine (not Christina) Verger and Germaine Durant (not Duramy). The first performance of *Rapsodie espagnole* took place on March 15 (not March 19), 1908.

Rawsthorne, Alan. Died in Cambridge, England, July 24, 1971. Add to the list of works: violin sonata (1959); piano trio (1962); *Concerto for Ten Instruments* (1962); cello concerto (London, April 6, 1966); quintet for clarinet, horn, violin, cello and piano (1970).

Ray, Don Brandon, American conductor and composer; b. Santa Maria, Calif., June 7, 1926. He studied composition with John Vincent at the Univ. of Calif., Los Angeles (B.A., 1948) and with Ernst Kanitz at the Univ. of Southern Calif.; conducting with Roger Wagner and Richard Lert. In 1960 he was engaged as conductor of the Committee on The Arts (COTA) Symph. Orch. and Chorale in the San Fernando Valley. Impelled by intellectual and musicological curiosity, he has searched for neglected works by acknowledged masters; gave the first known performance outside Russia of Tchaikovsky's oratorio *To Joy* (Van Nuys, Calif., Nov. 1, 1969), written to the same Schiller text that Beethoven used in the *Ninth Symphony.* As a composer, Ray wrote numerous anthems and Protestant church services; incidental music to theatrical plays.

Razumovsky, Andrey Kyrillovitch. He was not a regular second violinist in his quartet, but took part in it only upon occasion; the permanent second violin player was Louis Sina (See E. Hanslick, *Geschichte des Concertwesens in Wien,* p. 204). **Razumovsky's palace burned down on Dec. 31, 1814 (not in** 1815).

Razzi, Fausto, Italian composer; b. Rome, May 4, 1932. He studied piano and composition with Goffredo Petrassi; wrote music for various instrumental and choral combinations.

Read, Gardner. Add to works: *Los Dioses aztecos,* a suite of 7 movements for percussion ensemble (1959); *The Prophet,* oratorio (1960); *Jeux des timbres* for orch. (1960-63); *5 Polytonal Studies* for piano (1961-64); *Chants d'Auvergne* for chorus and instruments (1962); *Petite Suite* for recorders and harpsichord (1963); Symph. No. 4 (Cincinnati, Jan. 30, 1970). He publ. *Music Notation: a Manual of Modern Practice* (Boston, 1964).

Rebikov, Vladimir Ivanovitch. Date of death, Aug. 4 (not Dec. 1), 1920. Date of first performance of *Christmas Tree,* Nov. 1 (not Oct. 31), 1903.

Rebner, Adolf. Died in Baden-Baden, June 18, 1967.

Redlich, Hans Ferdinand. Died in Manchester, England, Nov. 27, 1968.

Redman, Harry Newton. Died in Boston, Dec. 26, 1958.

Reed, Peter Hugh, American music critic and journalist; b. Washington, June 14, 1892; d. Wingdale, N. Y., Sept. 25, 1969. He studied voice in Italy, preparing for an operatic career, which was frustrated when he entered the U.S. Army in World War I and was gassed. His speaking voice was, however, unimpaired; he became a pioneer of radio reviews of phonograph records. In 1935 he founded 'The American Music Lover,' a monthly magazine devoted to serious music on records; in 1944 the name was changed to 'The American Record Guide.' Reed remained its editor and publisher until 1957.

Refardt, Edgar. Died in Basel, March 3, 1968.

Regamey, Constantin. Add to works: *Autographs* for chamber orch. (1962); *4 x 5,* concerto for 4 quintets (Basel, May 28, 1964).

Reger, Max. *Suite,* op. 103a, is for violin and piano (not flute and piano). Op. 82, for piano solo, is in 4 volumes containing 35 (not only 22) pieces. Clarinet sonatas, op. 49 are in A-flat major and F-sharp minor (not A and F minor). Op. 96 is for 2 pianos (not 1 piano, 4 hands). Op. 89 comprises 4 sonatinas. in E minor, D major. F major and A minor respectively. The transcriptions of Albert's overture to *Esther* and Hugo Wolf's *Italian Serenade* and *Penthesilea* (a symph. poem, not overture) are for piano 4 hands, not for piano solo. Add the following to the list of works: Op. 91, 7 sonatas for unaccompanied violin; op. 131a, 6 preludes and fugues for unaccompanied violin; Op. 131b, 3 Duos for 2 violins; Op. 133, piano quartet in A minor; Op. 141a, *Serenade,* in G major for flute, violin and cello; Op. 141b, *Trio* in D minor for violin, viola and cello; Op. 143, *Träume am Kamin,* 12 pieces for piano solo; Op. 146, clarinet quintet in A major; without op. number, piano quintet in C minor.

Reich, Steve, American composer; b. New York, Oct. 3, 1936. He studied philosophy at Cornell Univ. (B.A. 1957) and composition at the Juilliard School of Music (1958-61) and at Mills College, with Luciano Berio and Darius Milhaud (M.A. 1963). He moved back to New York in 1965; formed a performing ensemble with Arthur Murphy and Jon Gibson; in 1970 made a trip to Ghana to study African drumming. His music explores the potentialities of mixed media, electronics and ethnic resources. His works include: *Pitch Charts* for an instrumental ensemble (1963); *Music for Piano and Tapes* (1964); *Livelihood* for tape (1965); *It's Gonna Rain* for tape (1965); *Come Out* for tape (1966); *Melodica* for tape (1966); *Reed Phase* for a reed instrument and tape (1966); *Piano Phase* for two pianos (1967); *My Name Is* for several performers, tape recorders and audience (1967); *Violin Phase* for violin and tape (1967); *Pendulum Music* for microphone, amplifiers, speakers and performers (1968); *Pulse Music* for the phase shifting pulse gate, an electronic device built by Reich (1969); *Four Log Drums* for four log drums and phase shifting pulse gate (1969); *Four Organs* for four electric organs and maracas (1970). He also composed music for films. In his career he consciously avoided teaching jobs of an academic nature.

Reich, Willi. He edited *Arthur Honegger Nachklang: Schriften, Photos, Dokumente.* (Zürich, 1957); *Gustav Mahler im eigenen Wort, im Wort der Freunde* (Zürich, 1958); *Felix Mendelssohn im Spiegel eigener Aussagen und zeitgenössischer Dokumente* (Zürich, 1970).

Reif, Paul, Czech-American composer; b. Prague, March 23, 1910. He started his musical career as a child violinist; then studied composition with Richard Stöhr and Franz Schmidt, and conducting with Franz Schalk and Bruno Walter; also had lessons with Richard Strauss. He wrote operettas; one of his songs, from the musical revue *Strassenmusik* (Vienna, 1934) became extremely popular under the title *Isle of Capri.* In March, 1940, he left Vienna, and arrived in New York, by way of Norway and Haiti, in 1941. In 1942 he joined the U.S. Intelligence Corps; while with the U.S. Army in North Africa he set to music the soldiers' song *Dirty Gertie from Bizerte,* which was introduced by Josephine Baker in Algiers in April, 1943. Upon his discharge in 1945 he was awarded the Croix de Guerre and the Purple Heart. Returning to the U.S., he was active as an arranger in Hollywood; wrote a number of lightweight pieces (*Petticoat Waltz, Dream Concerto,* etc.); also several song cycles, among them *5 Finger Exercises,* to poems by T. S. Eliot; *Reverence for Life* and *Monsieur le Pélican* as a tribute to Albert Schweitzer; etc. His larger works comprise *Triple City* for chorus and brass ensemble (N.Y., April 16, 1963); *Requiem to War* for mixed chorus and percussion (N.Y., May 20, 1963);

Birches, to Robert Frost's words, for voice and orch. (N.Y., Feb. 2, 1965); *Letter from a Birmingham Jail* for mixed chorus and piano, to words by Martin Luther King, Jr. (Howard Univ., Washington, D.C., March 2, 1965); *Philidor's Defense* for chamber orch., inspired by the famous Philidor chess opening: 1. P-K4, P-K4; 2. N-KB3, P-Q3 (N. Y., April 10, 1965); the operas, *Mad Hamlet* (1965) and *Portrait in Brownstone* (1965); *Pentagram* for piano (1969).

Reimann, Aribert, German pianist and composer; b. Berlin, March 4, 1936. He studied with Blacher and Pepping; then took music courses at the German Academy in Rome; subsequently became active as accompanist. He composed a *Quasimodo Cantata;* an opera *Traumspiel* after Strindberg; a cello concerto; *Nenia* for women's voices (Sprechstimme) and orch. (1968); *Inanes,* monologue for soprano and orch. (Berlin, Jan. 8, 1969); *Loqui* for orch. (Saarbrücken, Dec. 5, 1969); *Vogelscheuchen,* ballet (Berlin, Oct. 7, 1970); *Melusine,* opera (Schwetzinger, April 29, 1971).

Reiner, Fritz. Died in New York, Nov. 15, 1963.

Reiner, Karel. Add to works: trio for flute, bass clarinet and percussion (1964); quartet for 4 clarinets (1966); *Concerto* for bass clarinet and orch. (1966); brass quintet (1968); *Prolegomena* for string quartet (1968). In his works he applies a modified 12-tone technique.

Reinken, Jan Adams. Did not study with J. Sweelinck (who died before Reinken was born), but possibly with Sweelinck's son. Reinken went with his father to Holland at the age of 14; returned to Hamburg a few years later. *Hortus Musicus* is scored for 2 violins, viola da gamba (not viola) and bass.

Reiss, Jósef Wladyslaw. Died in Cracow, Feb. 22, 1956.

Reizenstein, Franz. Died in London, Oct. 15, 1968. Add to works: piano concerto No. 2 (London, June 7, 1961).

Rellstab, (Heinrich Friedrich) Ludwig. He edited 'Iris im Gebiete der Tonkunst' from 1830 to 1841 (not 1839-41).

Remenkov, Stefan, Bulgarian composer; b. Silistra, April 30, 1923. He studied with Stoyanov at the Sofia Cons. and later took a course with Khatchaturian at the Moscow Cons. He has written several symph. suites; 2 piano sonatas; a violin sonata; a piano concerto.

Rémy, Guillaume, Belgian violinist; b. Ougrée, Aug. 26, 1856; d. Nantes, France, June 16, 1932. He studied at the Cons. of Liège; graduated in 1873 sharing the first prize with Ysaÿe; continued his studies under Massart at the Paris Cons.; awarded first prize in 1878. Settling in Paris, he became concertmaster of the Colonne Orch., frequently apearing as a soloist. From 1885 to 1930 he was prof. at the Paris Cons.; played recitals with Saint-Saëns and Gabriel Fauré at the piano. He also formed a string quartet. During the last years of his life he was head of the violin department of the American Cons. at Fontainebleau.

Respighi, Ottorino. Did not study with Max Bruch. *La Fiamma* was produced on Jan. 23 (not Jan. 24), 1934. Add to bibl.: Elsa Respighi. *Ottorino Respighi: His Life Story* (in English; London, 1962).

Rethberg, Elisabeth. Real name Sättler (not Sattler).

Reuchsel, Amédée. Died in Montereau (Loire), July 10, 1931.

Reuchsel, Maurice. Died in Lyon, July 12, 1968.

Reutter, Hermann. First performance of the opera *Ballade der Landstrasse* took place in Göttingen on Jan. 25, 1948 under the title *Der Weg nach Freundschaft* (not in Stuttgart on July 21, 1952); the name *Ballade der Landstrasse* is the subtitle. Add to works: *Der Tod des Empedokles,* scenic concerto in one act (Schwetzinger, May 29, 1966); *Der grosse Kalender,* oratorio (1970). In 1971 he traveled as visiting prof. in the U.S. and Japan.

Révész, Géza. Died in Amsterdam, Aug. 19, 1955.

Reyer, Louis-Étienne-Ernest. The title of opera, *Erostrate* (not *Erostate*).

Reynolds, Roger, American composer; b. Detroit, July 18, 1934. He studied engineering at the Univ. of Michigan (B.S.E., 1957) and composition (M.M., 1961); spent a year in Cologne on a Fulbright Grant for work on electronic music (1962); was in Paris in 1963 and in Italy on a Guggenheim Fellowship, in 1964-65. In his early scores he used serial methods, but later expanded his resources to include the entire spectrum of multi-media expression, enhanced by the mathematical concepts of sets and matrices and Gestalt psychology. In 1960 he was one of the founders of the avant-garde festival ONCE in Ann Arbor, Michigan. In 1966 he went to Japan at the invitation of the Institute of Current World Affairs. In 1969 he staged there the festival Cross Talk Intermedia, featuring experimental works by Japanese and American composers. In 1970 he joined the faculty of the Univ. of California in San Diego. Reynolds uses graphic notation in his scores suggesting the desired sounds by pictorial shapes. Works: *Epigram and Evolution* for piano (1959); *Sky,* a song cycle for soprano, alto flute, bassoon and harp, to Japanese Haiku poems (1960); *Wedge* for chamber orch. (1961); *Acquaintances* for flute, double-bass and piano (1961); 4 Etudes for flute quartet (1961); *Mosaic* for flute and piano (1962); *The Emperor of Ice Cream,* his major work, to a poem of Wallace Stevens, scored for 8 voices, piano, percussion and double-bass (1962); *A Portrait of Vanzetti* for narrator, wind instruments, percussion and magnetic tape (1963); *Graffiti* for orch. (1964); *Fantasy* for pianists (1964); *Quick are the Mouths of Earth* for chamber orch. (1965); *Ambages* for solo flute (1965); *Masks* for orch. and mixed chorus, to a text by Melville (1965); *Blind Men* for mixed choir, brass, percussion and slide projection, to a text by Melville (1966); *Threshold* for orch. (1967); . . . *between* . . . for chamber orch. and electronics (1968); *Traces* for piano, flute, cello, tapes and electronics (1969); *Ping,* inspired by a story of Samuel Beckett, scored for flute, (multiphonic), piano (motorized by agitating of strings), harmonium, bowed cymbal and tam-tam, electronic sound distribution, film, ring modulator, 35 slides and magnetic tape (1969); *I/O* (for 'In and Out'), for 9 female vocalists, 9 male mimes, 2 flutes, clarinet, electronics and projections (1969) based on a concept of Buckminster Fuller with relation to the synergetic antonyms of the opposite sexes.

Reynolds, Verne, American horn player and composer; b. Lyons, Kansas, July 18, 1926. He studied composition at the Cincinnati Cons. (B.M., 1950); at the Univ. of Wisconsin with Cecil Burleigh (M.M., 1951) and at the Royal College of Music in London with Herbert Howells. He played the horn in the Cincinnati Symph. Orch., and in the Rochester Philharmonic; appointed prof. of horn at the Eastman School of Music. Works: violin concerto (1951); overture, *Saturday with Venus* (1953); *The Hollow Men* for baritone. male chorus, brass choir and percussion (1954); *Music for 5 Trumpets* (1957); *Serenade* for 13 winds (1958); *Toccata, Arioso and Passacaglia* for orch. (1958); 48 Etudes for horn (1959); *Celebration Overture* for orch. (1960); *Partita* for horn and piano (1961); sonata for flute and piano (1962); Suite for 4 horns (1962); Suite for brass quintet (1963); woodwind quintet (1964); *Serenade* for horn and strings (1966); string quartet (1967); *Concertare I* for brass quintet and percussion (1968); *Concertare II* for trumpet and strings (1968); Sonata for tuba and piano (1968); *Concertare III* for woodwind quintet and piano (1969); Sonata for horn and piano (1970); 48 etudes for trumpet (1970); violin sonata (1970); *Concertare IV* for brass quintet and piano (1971); *Scenes* for wind instruments and percussion (1971). He has made many transcriptions for various instrumental combinations of works by Handel, Kreutzer, J. J. Fux, Schumann, etc.

Rheinberger, Josef (Gabriel). Add bibl.: Hans-Josef Irmen, *G. J. Rheinberger als Antipode des Cäcilianismus* (Regensburg, 1970).

Ricci, Ruggiero. Born July 24, 1918 (not 1920); made his first appearance in San Francisco at the age of 10 (not 8).

Ricordi & Co., G. Add to bibl.: C. Sartori, *Casa Ricordi, 1808-1958: profilo storico* (Milan, 1958).

Rider-Kelsey, Corinne. Her Covent Garden debut took place on July 2 (not July 7), 1908.

Rídký, Jaroslav, Czech composer; b. Františkov, near Liberec, Aug. 25, 1897; d. Poděbrady, Aug. 14, 1956. He studied composition at the Prague Cons. with Jaroslav Křička and E. B. Foerster; simultaneously studied the harp; was first harpist in the Prague Philharmonic (1924-38); later became its conductor. He taught theory at the Prague Cons. (1928-48); in 1948 was appointed prof. of composition at the Music Academy in Prague. His works include 7 symphonies (1924, 1925, 1927, 1928, 1933, 1935, 1938); violin concerto (1926); 2 cello concertos (1930, 1940); piano concerto (1932); cantatas *Winter Tale* (1936) and *To My Fatherland* (1941); *Serenade* for strings (1941); 2 nonets; clarinet quintet; 5 string quartets; piano trio; violin sonata; 2 cello sonatas; piano pieces; choruses.

Ridout, Godfrey. Add to works: *Cantiones Mysticae* for soprano and orch. (1953); *Fall Fair* for orch. (1961); *In Memoriam Anne Frank,* cantata (Toronto, March 14, 1965).

Riegger, Wallingford. Died in New York, April 2, 1961. Add to works: *Quintuple jazz* (Iowa City, May 20, 1959); *Variations* for violin and orch. (Louisville, April 1, 1959).

Riemann, Hugo. A completely revised edition of his *Musik-Lexikon* was publ. in 3 vols. in 1959-65 under the editorship of Wilibald Gurlitt; an exceptionally valuable supplement was publ. in 1972, with numerous new biographical entries, detailed amplifications of previous articles and gratifying rectifications of long stagnant wrong dates, unimpeachably documented by birth and death certificates from official registries.

Ries, Ferdinand. Born in Godesberg (not Bonn). His father was born in Bonn on Nov. 10, 1755 (not 1775) and died in Godesberg, Nov. 1, 1846.

Riezler, Walter. Died in Munich, Jan. 22, 1965.

Riisager, Knudaage. Add works: Symph. No. 1 (Copenhagen, July 17, 1926); Symph. No. 2 (Copenhagen, March 5, 1927); *T-DOXC,* mechanical poem for orch. (Copenhagen, Sept. 3, 1927); *Benzin,* ballet (Copenhagen, Dec. 26, 1930); *Primavera,* concert overture (Copenhagen, Jan. 31, 1935); Symph. No. 3 (Copenhagen, Nov. 21, 1935); *Slaraffenland* (*Fool's Paradise*), ballet (Copenhagen, Nov. 25, 1936); concerto for trumpet and strings (London, June 20, 1938); concertino for saxophone and chamber orch. (Warsaw, April 15, 1939); Symph. No. 4 (Copenhagen, Oct. 24, 1940); *Qarrtsiluni,* ballet on Eskimo themes (Copenhagen, Feb. 21, 1942); *Tivoli-Tivoli,* symph. suite (Copenhagen, Aug. 15, 1943); *Summer Rhapsody* for orch. (Copenhagen, Jan. 30, 1944); *Phoenix,* ballet (Copenhagen, May 12, 1946); *Etude,* ballet on Czerny exercises (Copenhagen, Jan. 15, 1948); Symph. No. 5 (Copenhagen, Nov. 21, 1950); violin concerto (Copenhagen, Oct. 11, 1951); *Sinfonia serena* for strings and kettledrums (Salzburg, June 24, 1952). Bibl.: Sigurd Berg, *K. Riisagers Kompositioner* (Copenhagen, 1967), an annotated catalogue of works.

Riley, John, American composer and cellist; b. Altoona, Pennsylvania, Sept. 17, 1920. He studied cello and composition in the U.S., and also in London; received his Mus. B. at the Eastman School of Music, Rochester, in 1951; studied composition on a Fulbright Grant with Arthur Honegger in Paris (1952-53); at Yale Univ. with Quincy Porter (Mus. M., 1955). His works include a *Rhapsody* for cello and orch. (1951); *Apostasy* for orch. (1954); *Fantasy* for oboe and string orch. (1955); Sinfonietta (1955); 2 string quartets (1954, 1959).

Riley, Terry, American composer; b. Colfax, California, June 24, 1935. He studied at the Univ. of California at Berkeley with Seymour Shifrin, William Denny and Robert Erikson, obtaining his M.A. in composition in 1961; went to Europe and played piano and saxophone in cabarets in Paris and in Scandinavia. In 1970 he was initiated in San Francisco as a disciple of Pandit Pran Nath, the North Indian singer, and followed him to India. In his music Riley explores the extremes of complexity and gymnosophistical simplicity. His ascertainable works include *Spectra* for 6 instruments (1959), string trio (1961), and *In C,* for orchestra, notated in fragments to be played any number of times at will in the spirit of aleatory latitudinarianism, all within the key of C major, with an occasional F sharp providing a *trompe l'oreille* effect; it was first performed in San Francisco, May 21, 1965. His other compositions are *Poppy Nogoods Phantom Band* (1966), *A Rainbow in Curved Air* (1968), and *Genesis '70,* a ballet (1970). Riley's astrological signs are Sun in Cancer (euphemistically known in Southern California as Moon's Children so as to exorcise middle-aged fear of malignancy), Scorpio Rising and Aries Moon.

Ringer, Alexander L., American musicologist; b. Berlin, Feb. 3, 1921, of Dutch parentage. He attended the Hollander Cons. in Berlin; in 1939 went to Amsterdam where he studied composition with Henk Badings. In 1946 he emigrated to the U.S.; was on the staff of City College of N.Y. (1948-52), Univ. of Pennsylvania (1952-55), Univ of Calif., Berkeley (1955-56) and Univ. of Oklahoma (1956-58). In 1958 he was appointed to the faculty of the Univ. of Illinois, Urbana. Publications: *The Chasse: Historical and Analytical Bibliography of a Musical Genre* (Ann Arbor, Michigan Univ. Microfilm, 1955); *Western Man and His Music,* in *The Cultural Heritage of the Twentieth Century* ('Pennsylvania Literary Review,' Philadelphia, 1956); numerous articles in the 'Mus. Quarterly' and 'Saturday Review.'

Ringo, (Henry) James, American music critic and composer; b. St. Louis, March 4, 1926. He studied there with local teachers; then entered the Juilliard School of Music, N. Y., where his teachers were Vittorio Giannini and Frederick Jacobi (composition), Alton Jones (piano) and Robert Tangeman (musicology); gained a B.S. there in 1949; then took lessons with Darius Milhaud and Olivier Messiaen in Paris; received an M.A. in composition from Mills College, Oakland, Calif. in 1951. He composed several scores of incidental music for the theater; his instrumental works include *5 Pieces* from *Le Trésor d'Orphée* for string orch. (1948); string trio (1949); sonata for cello solo (1950); two books of *Portraits* for piano (1951, 1954). He has contributed to many periodicals; won the ASCAP-Deems Taylor Award prize for articles on music in 1969.

Ristić, Milan, Serbian composer; b. Belgrade, Aug. 31, 1908. He studied in Belgrade with Slavenski and in Prague with Alois Hába. A prolific composer, he writes mostly instrumental music; his style ranges from neo-romantic grandiosity to economic neo-classicism, from epically declamatory diatonicism to expressionistically atonal melos. Some of his works are written in an explicit dodecaphonic technique; in some, he makes use of quarter-tones. His output includes 6 symphonies (1941, 1951, 1961, 1966, 1967, 1968); violin concerto (1944); piano concerto (1954); *Suite giocosa* for orch. (1956); *Symphonic Variations* (1957); *Burleska* for orch. (1957); *7 Bagatelles* for orch. (1959); Concerto for orch. (1963); clarinet concerto (1964); 2 string quartets; wind quintet; septet; violin sonata; viola sonata; 24 fugues for various instrumental combinations; a suite for 4 trombones in quarter-tones. See V. Peričić, *Muzički Stvaraoci u Srbiji* (Belgrade, 1969; pp. 453-73).

Rivier Jean. Add to works: Symph. No. 6, *Les Présages* (Paris, Dec. 11, 1958); Symph. No. 7, *Les Contrastes* (Paris, Jan. 9, 1962); oboe concerto (Paris, Jan. 16, 1969).

Robertson, Leroy. Died in Salt Lake City, July 25, 1971. He retired as chairman of the music dept. of the Univ. of Utah in 1963. Add to works: piano concerto (Salt Lake City, Nov. 30, 1966).

Robeson, Lila. Died in Euclid, Ohio, Dec. 7, 1960.

Rochberg, George. He studied composition (not piano) with Szell and Mannes; previously studied composition with Hans Weisse (1939). Received the Gershwin Memorial Award in 1952 (not 1953). Joined Theodore Presser Co. in 1951 (not 1955). Add to the list of works: Symph. No. 2 (Cleveland, Feb. 26, 1959); *Time-Span*, symph. movement (St. Louis, Oct. 22, 1960); Symph. No. 3 for solo voices, chamber chorus, double chorus and orch., constituting a mosaic of metamorphosed but recognizable citations from works by Schütz, Bach, Mahler and Ives, treated as 'objets trouvés' (N. Y., Nov. 24, 1970).

Rode, (Jacques-) Pierre. Beethoven wrote for him not the *Romance*, op. 50, but the G major sonata, op. 96, which Rode performed with Archduke Rudolph in Vienna, on Dec. 29, 1812.

Rodgers, Richard. Add the musicals: *The Sound of Music* (N.Y., Nov. 16, 1959) to a libretto dealing with the Trapp family singers (extremely successful); produced also as a motion picture (1965); *No Strings* (1962); *Do I Hear a Waltz?* (1965). He wrote the musical score for the television series, *Winston Churchill: The Valiant Years* (1960-61); *Two by Two*, musical revue on the subject of Noah's Ark (N.Y., Nov. 10, 1970). Exact place of his birth is Hammels Station, Long Island, N.Y., not New York City itself.

Rodriguez, Felipe. Born in Madrid, May 1, 1759; died there in May, 1814.

Rodzinski, Artur. Died in Boston, Nov. 27, 1958. Date of birth, Jan. 1, 1892 (not 1894).

Rogalski, Theodor, Rumanian composer and conductor; b. Bucharest, April 11, 1901; d. Zürich, Feb. 2, 1954. He studied at the Bucharest Cons. with Castaldi and Cuclin; at the Leipzig Cons. with Karg-Elert (1920-22); and in Paris with Vincent d'Indy (1922-25). Returning to Rumania, he was music director of the Bucharest Radio (1939-44) and chief conductor of the Bucharest State Philharmonic (1950-54). His *Trei dansuri romîneşti (3 Rumanian Dances;* Bucharest, May 27, 1951) attained great popularity and had numerous performances in Europe and America. His other works include *2 Capricci* for orch. (1932); a string quartet (1925); violin pieces and songs. His music is permeated with the spirit of Rumanian folklore, while his harmony and orchestration reveal impressionistic traits.

Roger-Ducasse, Jean-Jules Aimable. Date of death, July 19 (not July 20), 1954. Taught at the Paris Cons. from 1935 to 1945 (not 1940). *Le Cœur de l'eau* and *Noëls des roses* are songs (not piano pieces). His *Symphonie sur la Cathédrale de Reims* was never completed. Add to bibl.: *Catalogue de l'œuvre de Roger-Ducasse* (Bordeaux, 1955).

Rogers, Bernard. Died in Rochester, N.Y., May 24, 1968.

Rogister, Jean, Belgian composer; b. Liège, Oct. 25, 1879; d. there, March 20, 1964. He studied violin and composition at the Liège Cons. In 1900 he became prof. there; organized his own Quatuor de Liège, in which he played the viola. A prolific composer, he wrote a *Requiem* (Liège, March 24, 1945); 3 symphonies; *Divertissement symphonique;* symph. poems, *Le Destin, Paysage, La lune et les peupliers; Fantaisie burlesque* for orch.; *Ouverture romantique; Suite ardennaise* for orch.; *Symphonie intime* for 8 instruments; 8 string quartets; *The Bells,* cantata for soprano and 8 instruments; wind quintet; *Dialogue des Pédants* for clarinet and bassoon; quintet for old instruments (clavecin, 2 quintons, viola d'amore and viola da gamba); viola concerto; cello concerto; trombone concerto; *Fantaisie concertante* for viola and orch.; many pieces for cello and piano; choruses; songs. His style of composition follows the precepts of César Franck, but he also injects into his music some impressionistic sonorities.

Rohan, Jindřich, Czech conductor; b. Prague, May 14, 1919. He studied at the Prague Cons.; conducted various professional groups in Prague, devoting himself chiefly to the symphonic repertory of classical Czech music. In 1960 he was appointed to the board of the Academy of Musical Arts in Prague as instructor in conducting.

Roig, Gonzalo, Cuban conductor and composer; b. Havana, July 20, 1890; d. there, June 13, 1970. He played violin in theater orchestras; in 1922 organized the Orquesta Sinfónica de la Habana. He also wrote zarzuelas, among which *Cecilia Valdés* enjoyed considerable success. In 1912 he wrote the song *Quiereme mucho,* which became a popular hit.

Roland-Manuel, Alexis. Died in Paris, Nov. 1, 1966.

Rollin, Jean, French composer; b. Paris, Aug. 3, 1906. He studied composition at the Paris Cons. with Noël Gallon and musicology with Pirro and Masson. His works include *Concerto* for piano and strings (1947); violin concerto (1950); concerto for double-bass and orch. (1951); 2 symphonies (1953, 1958); the opera, *Gringouê* (1965); chamber music; songs.

Roncaglia, Gino. Died in Modena, Nov. 27, 1968.

Ronnefeld, Peter, German composer and conductor; b. Dresden, Jan. 26, 1935; d. Kiel, Aug. 6, 1965. He studied with Blacher in Berlin and Messiaen in Paris; was chorus conductor at the Vienna Opera (1957-59); then was active in Kiel. As a conductor he specialized in modern music, but he also excelled in the romantic repertory; his own opera *Die Ameise* (Düsseldorf, Oct. 21, 1961) had a fine reception. His early death was lamented.

Rorem, Ned. His opera, *A Childhood Miracle,* was produced on May 10, 1955 (not 1952). Add to works; Symph. No. 3 (N.Y., April 19, 1959); *Eagles,* symph. poem (Philadelphia, Oct. 23, 1959); trio for flute, cello and piano (1960); *Lovers,* a 'narrative' for harpsichord, oboe, cello and percussion (1964); *Sun* for orch. (N.Y., July 1, 1967). He publ. a series of entertaining and overtly personal books: *Paris Diary* (N.Y., 1966); *New York Diary* (N.Y., 1967); *Critical Affairs: A Composer's Journal* (N.Y., 1970).

Rosbaud, Hans. Died in Lugano, Dec. 29, 1962.

Rosen, Jerome. Add to works: concerto for saxophone and orch. (Sacramento, Jan. 24, 1958); quintet for clarinet and strings (1959).

Rosenberg, Hilding (Constantin). The title of his opera is *De tva Konungadöttrarna* (not *De tva Kungadöttrarna*); the subtitle of his Symph. No. 3 is *De fyra livseldrarna* (not *tidsaldrarna*). Add to works: 12 string quartets (1920-57); opera, *Portrait* (after Gogol; Stockholm, March 22, 1956); quintet for wind instruments (1959); sonata for solo flute (1959); *Riflessioni* No. 1, 2, 3 for string orch. (1960); sonata for solo clarinet (1960); *Metamorfosi Sinfonichi* (1963). In his later works he applies a modified form of the 12-tone technique.

Rosenbloom, Sydney. Died in East London, South Africa, July 22, 1967.

Rosenboom, David, American composer of the avant-garde; b. Fairfield, Iowa, Sept. 9, 1947. He studied piano with his mother; also played violin, viola, trumpet and drums. He attended the Univ. of Illinois where he took courses in composition with Salvatore Martirano and Gordon Binkerd; worked with Lejaren Hiller in the Experimental Music Studio there (1965-67). In 1967 he became an associate at the Center of the Creative and Performing Arts of the State

Univ. of N.Y. at Buffalo. In 1968-69 he served as artistic coordinator for the Electric Ear mixed-media series at the Electric Circus in New York. In 1970 he participated in research in neurophysics and biofeedback systems at the State Univ. of N. Y. at Stony Brook; invented a portable computer for sound synthesis systems. With this esthetic background, his music was bound to be experimental in nature; however, he also composed in classical forms. His scores are notated in diagrams and engineering blueprints, with special symbols for dynamics, tempi, etc. Works: *Contrasts* for violin and orch. (1963); septet for strings, brass and piano (1964); sextet for bassoon, flute and string quartet (1965); trio for clarinet, trumpet and string bass (1966); *Caliban Upon Setebos,* after Robert Browning, for orch. (1966); *The Thud, Thud, Thud, of Suffocating Blackness* for saxophone, electric cello, piano, celesta, percussion, tape and lights (1966); *Percussion Village* for drums (1966); *mississippippississim* for 33 musicians, speaker and tape (1968); *She Loves Me, She Loves Me Not . . .*, a theater piece (1968); *Urboui* for electronic tape and film (1968); *And Come Up Dripping* for oboe and analog computer (1968); *How Much Better If Plymouth Rock Had Landed On The Pilgrims* for electronic and traditional instruments (1969); *Ecology of the Skin,* a demonstration in biofeedback experience with audience participation (1970). His Zodiac sign is Virgo.

Rosenfeld, Paul. Analects from his articles have been publ. as *Musical Impressions,* selections from his writings (N. Y., 1970).

Rosenman, Leonard, American composer; b. Brooklyn, Sept. 7, 1924. He studied with local teachers; later took courses with Roger Sessions, Luigi Dallapiccola and briefly with Arnold Schoenberg. His main mundane occupation is that of a movie composer; he wrote the scores for such commercially notable films as *East of Eden, Rebel Without a Cause* and *The Chapman Report* (dealing with sexual statistics); also compiled music for television programs, among them *The Defenders* and *Marcus Welby, M.D.* But he is also the composer of a number of highly respectable and even elevated musical works, among them a violin concerto and the challenging score *Foci* for 3 orchestras. His *Threnody on a Song of K. R.* (written to the memory of the composer's wife Kay Rosenman), a set of orchestral variations on her original melody, was performed by the Los Angeles Philharmonic, under the composer's direction, on May 6, 1971.

Rosenthal, Harold, English music editor and critic; b. London, Sept. 30, 1917. He received his B.A. degree from the Univ. of London in 1940; served in the British Army during World War II; in 1950 launched, with Earl of Harewood, the magazine 'Opera' and became its editor in 1953; also issued 'Opera Annuals' (1954-60). He was archivist of the Royal Opera House, Covent Garden (1950-56); contributed to many European and American music journals. His publications include: *Sopranos of Today* (London, 1956); *Two Centuries of Opera at Covent Garden* (London, 1958); *A Concise Oxford Dictionary of Opera* (with John Warrack; London, 1964). He also edited *The Mapleson Memoires* (London, 1965). In 1964 he undertook a lecture tour of the U.S.

Rosenthal, Manuel. Add to works: *Aeolus* for wind quintet and strings (1970).

Rosier, Carl, Netherlandish organist and composer; b. Liège, Dec., 1640; d. Cologne, Dec., 1725. He was a practical musician; served as organist at the Cologne Cathedral and City Hall (1699-1725); wrote much sacred music; publ. 14 sonatas for oboe witn violins (Amsterdam, 1700). Cf. Ursel Niemöller, *Carl Rosier, Kölner Dom- und Ratskapellmeister* (Cologne, 1957).

Rosing, Vladimir, Russian-American tenor and opera director; b. St. Petersburg, Jan. 23, 1890; d. Los Angeles, Nov. 24, 1963. He studied voice with Jean de Reszke; made his debut as tenor in St. Petersburg in 1912; gave a successful series of song recitals in programs of Russian songs in London between 1913 and 1921. In 1923 he was appointed director of the opera department at the Eastman School of Music in Rochester, N.Y.; founded an American Opera Co. which he directed in a series of operatic productions in the English language. In 1939 he went to Los Angeles as organizer and artistic director of the Southern California Opera Association. He staged several pageants: *The California Story* in Hollywood Bowl in 1950; *The Oregon Story* in 1959; *The Kansas Story* in 1960. In the interim he directed several operas at the N.Y. City Center.

Rosowsky, Salomo, Jewish-American music scholar and composer; b. Riga, Latvia, March 15, 1878; d. New York, July 30, 1962. He studied law at the Univ. of Kiev, and composition at the St. Petersburg Cons. with Liadov, Rimsky-Korsakov and Glazunov. He was a co-founder of the Society for Jewish Folk Music in St. Petersburg in 1909; in 1920 he went back to Riga, and organized there the first Jewish Cons. of Music; in 1925 he emigrated to Palestine. He settled in New York in 1947, devoting himself mainly to the music of biblical times, culminating in the publication of an important volume, *The Cantillation of the Bible* (N.Y., 1957). His compositions include a piano trio (1909) and several scores of incidental music for plays in Yiddish.

Rossellini, Renzo. Add to works: *La Guerra,* one-act opera to his own libretto (Rome, Feb. 25, 1956); *Il Vortice,* opera (Naples, Feb. 8, 1958); *Uno Sguardo del Ponte,* opera after Arthur Miller's play (Rome, March 11, 1961); *Ut Unum Sint,* for orch. (Miami, Oct. 20, 1963); *L'Avventuriere,* opera (Monte Carlo, Feb. 2, 1968).

Rossi, Salomone. Born in 1570 (not in 1587).

Rossini, Gioacchino (Antonio). Add to works: *Ciro in Babilonia,* opera (Ferrara, 1812); *Stabat Mater* (1832). Rectify the spelling, *Bianca e Falliero* (not *Faliero*). The correct date of the first performance of *L'Equivoco stravagante* is Oct. 26 (not 29), 1811. Rossini entered the Liceo Comunale of Bologna on Feb. 28, 1806, when he was actually 14 (not 15) years old, since it was a day before his putative birthday, Feb. 29, which did not exist in 1806, it not being a bissextile year. It is incorrect to say that he 'abandoned his study of counterpoint with Mattei when an opportunity presented itself for the composition of an opera,' for the opportunity of writing an opera *(Il Cambiale di matrimonio)* was first presented after he had already relinquished his studies. There is no reason for asserting that 'Benelli failed to keep the terms of his contract.' Rather, it was Rossini himself who did not observe them, having never completed the promised opera. It is unlikely that Rossini earned only 7,000 pounds during his 5 months in London; in all probability he received many times as much, as he commanded high fees for his concerts sponsored by nobility, and his income was further augmented by fees for accompanying singers at recitals in private British homes. The French Revolution of 1830 did not invalidate Rossini's agreement with the court of the deposed king Charles X; the pension of 6,000 francs was not granted him in 1835 but was provided for in the contract with Charles X, validated in the Paris courts because Charles X had signed it in person. The name of his second wife was Olympia Descuilliers (not Desguilliers). She married Rossini on Aug. 16 (not 21), 1846. Rossini was not operated on in Paris in 1843 for gallstones, but apparently underwent a corrective surgical treatment of the urinary tract for gonorrhea. Add to bibl.: F. Schlitzer, *Rossini e Siena e altri scritti rossiniani* (Siena, 1958); R. Bacchelli, *Rossini e esperienze rossiniane* (Milan, 1959); P. Ingerslev-Jensen, *Rossini* (Copenhagen, 1959); H. Weinstock, *Rossini* (N. Y., 1968).

Rosslavetz, Nikolay Andreyevitch. Died in Moscow, Aug. 23, 1944.

Rostand, Claude, French writer on music; b. Paris, Dec. 3, 1912; d. Villejuif, Oct. 11, 1970. He studied with N. Dufourck. In 1958 he organized a modern music society in Paris, 'Musique d'aujourd'hui.' Publications: *L'œuvre de Gabriel Fauré* (Paris, 1945); *Richard Strauss* (Paris, 1949); *La Musique française contemporaine* (Paris, 1952); dialogues with Milhaud, Poulenc, Markevitch and others; biographies of Brahms (2 vols., Paris, 1954-55), Liszt (Paris, 1960); Hugo Wolf (Paris, 1967) and Webern (1969); *Dictionnaire de la Musique Contemporaine* (Lausanne, 1970).

Rostropovitch, Mstislav Leopoldovitch. Add bibl.: Tatyana Gaidamovich, *Mstislav Rostropovitch* (Moscow, 1969).

Rota, Nino. Add to works: opera-buffa, *La Notte di un Nevrastenico* (Turin, Nov. 19, 1959); *La Visita meravigliosa* (Palermo, Feb. 6, 1970), opera.

Roth, Feri. Died in Los Angeles, May 7, 1969. He organized the Roth Quartet in 1926; it was not connected with the Budapest Quartet. From 1946 to his death he was prof. of music at the Univ. of California, Los Angeles.

Rousseau, Jean-Jacques. The existence of the 1767 Geneva edition of his *Dictionnaire de musique* cannot be proved; first known edition, Paris, 1768.

Roussel, Albert. Add to bibl.: Basil Deane, *Albert Roussel* (London, 1961); Dom Angelico Surchamp, *Albert Roussel: l'Homme et son œuvre* (Paris, 1967).

Roy, Klaus George. He wrote only one opera; *Sterlingman* is the title of a revised version of *The Easter Guest.*

Royce, Edward. Died in Stamford, Conn., July 7, 1963.

Rózsa, Miklós. Add to works: piano concerto (Los Angeles, April 6, 1967).

Rubbra, Edmund. Add to works: Symph. No. 8 (London, Jan. 5, 1971).

Rubsamen, Walter (Howard). Add to publications: *Chanson and Madrigal, 1480-1530* (with D. Heartz and H. M. Brown; Cambridge, Mass., 1964); article, *Justiniane or Viniziane of the 15th Century* in 'Acta Musicologica' (1957); *Mr. Seedo, Ballad Opera and the Singspiel* in 'Miscelánea en Homenaje a Mons. Higinio Anglés' (Barcelona, 1958-61); *The Earliest French Lute Tablature,* in 'Journal of the American Musicological Society' (1958); *Unifying Techniques in Selected Masses of Josquin and La Rue: A Stylistic Comparison,* in 'Proceedings of the Josquin Festival Conference' (1971). He edited *Opera Omnia* of Pierre de La Rue for the American Institute of Musicology; *Puer natus est* of Jacobus Regnart (N. Y., 1968) and a German 16th-century *Magnificat on Christmas Carols* (N. Y., 1971). In 1965 he was appointed chairman of the music dept. at the Univ. of California, Los Angeles.

Rudel, Julius, American conductor; b. Vienna, March 6, 1921. He studied at the Vienna Academy of Music; in 1938 emigrated to the U.S. (naturalized citizen, 1944). In 1943 he made his American debut as conductor of the N.Y. City Opera; in 1957 became its music director. He also appeared as guest conductor of the Philadelphia Orch. and of several operatic companies; received numerous awards from American cultural organizations. In 1961 the Austrian government bestowed on him honorary insignia for arts and sciences. In 1965 he was named to the Lincoln Center Council. He championed the cause of American opera; gave first performances of several new stage works by American composers. He also translated operatic libretti into English. See 'Current Biography' for July 1965.

Rudzinski, Witold. Add to works: *Janko muzykant,* opera (Bytom, June 20, 1953); *Komendant Paryza,* opera (Poznan, 1960); *Deux portraits des Femmes* for soprano and string quartet (1960).

Rufer, Josef. He publ. an annotated catalog of Schoenberg's works, *Das Werk Arnold Schönbergs* (Kassel, 1959); also in English, *The Works of Arnold Schoenberg* (London, 1962).

Ruff, Willie, American jazz musician; b. Sheffield, Alabama, Jan. 9, 1931. One of the small number of jazz players with a college diploma, he studied at Yale Univ. (M.M., 1954); played the French horn and string bass. He formed a duo with another educated jazz player, the pianist Dwike Mitchell, and together they filled a series of highly successful engagements in de luxe night clubs. In 1959 they gave jazz concerts in Russia, triumphantly overriding Soviet scruples regarding jazz and scoring a popular success.

Ruggles, Carl. Organized the Winona Symph. Orch. in Winona, Minnesota (not in Minneapolis); conducted it for 5 years. An orchestral version of his piano suite *Evocations* was first performed in N. Y., Feb. 3, 1971. He serenely passed his 95th birthday in 1971, living on in his chosen Vermont, while his music was being revived in concert hall and on records showing extraordinary vitality and relevance.

Rupnik, Ivan, Serbian composer; b. Belgrade, Aug. 29, 1911. He studied in Ljubljana; later in Vienna with Alban Berg. His early works are in a neo-romantic vein, with expressionistic overtones; later he abjured modern devices and began writing music for the masses, in conformity with socialist ideology. His cantata, *Song of Dead Proletarians,* which he conducted in Belgrade on Dec. 4, 1947, is an epitome of programmatic realism. He further wrote a symphony, several overtures (*Romantic Overture, Youth Overture*), ethnic symphonic works (*Musical Impressions from Istria, A Peasant Evening Party*) and a *Hymn of Peace.*

Rusca, Francesco, Italian composer of church music; was Maestro di Cappella of the Como Cathedral from 1659 until 1699. He wrote about 100 masses, psalms, cantatas, etc., in a highly developed polyphonic style, containing as many as 16 independent vocal and instrumental parts. His 5 keyboard toccatas are included in Vol. III of *I Classici* (Como, 1961).

Rusconi, Gerardo, Italian composer; b. Milan, Feb. 1, 1922. He studied at the Cons. of Parma; began his career as a composer by writing light music for the stage, radio and the films; then undertook more serious genres of music. Works: *La moglie di Lot* for soprano, horn and piano (1962); *Instantanee sonore* for piano (1964); *Concerto breve* for horn and strings (1965); *Tre musiche* for flute and piano (1967); *Attraction* for piano solo (1967); *Moments* for orch. in memory of Martin Luther King (1968); *L'Appuntamento,* one-act opera (1971); numerous transcriptions and harmonizations of popular songs.

Rush, Loren, American composer; b. Fullerton, Calif., Aug. 23, 1935. He studied piano, bassoon and the double-bass; played the bassoon in the Oakland Symphony and the double-bass in the Richmond Symphony; also was a drummer. He studied composition with Robert Erickson at San Francisco State College (B.A., 1957); upon graduation organized the Loren Rush Jazz Quartet; enrolled at the Univ. of California at Berkeley studying composition with Andrew Imbrie, Seymour Shifrin, William Denny and Charles Cushing (M.A., 1960). He applies a whole spectrum of modern techniques, including serialism, spatial distribution, controlled improvisation and pointillistic exoticism. His works include *Five Japanese Poems* for soprano, flute, clarinet, viola and piano (1959); *Serenade* for violin and viola (1960); *Mandala Music,* improvisation for a group, inspired by the Oriental geometrization of the Cosmos and an important symbol in Jungian psychology (1962); *Hexahedron* for piano, notated on all six surfaces of a large cube (1964); *Nexus 16* for chamber orch. (1964); *soft music, HARD MUSIC* for two amplified pianos (1969); *The Cloud Messenger* for orch. (1970). In 1971 he received a Guggenheim Fellowship and a National Institute of Arts and Letters Award.

Russo, William Joseph, American composer; b. Chicago, June 25, 1928. He played trombone in various jazz bands; was orchestrator for Stan Kenton; then struck out on his own, and formed a band. Simultaneously with his activities in the popular music field, he undertook a serious study of real music and wrote symphonies. His 2nd symph., subtitled *Titans,* was performed by the N. Y. Philharmonic on April 19, 1959. Jazz rhythms animate his symphonic music, while learned counterpoint dignifies many of his jazz pieces.

Russolo, Luigi. Died Feb. 4 (not Feb. 6), 1947. He was also a remarkable painter of impressionist tendencies.

Ruyneman, Daniel. Died in Amsterdam, July 25, 1963. Add to works: *Symphonie 1953* (Utrecht, March 14, 1956).

Rychlík, Jan, Czech composer; b. Prague, April 27, 1916; d. there, Jan. 20, 1964. He studied at the Cons. of Prague, graduating in 1946. A practical musician, he played in dance orchestras; became an authority on jazz; experimented with modern techniques; was active also as music critic. Works: *Partita giocosa* for band (1947); trio for clarinet, trumpet and bassoon (1948); Serenade for 3 double-basses (1951); *Etudes* for English horn and piano (1953); string trio (1954); *Chamber Suite* for string quartet (1955); *Suite-Burlesque* for clarinet solo (1956); *Serenade* for 8 wind instruments (1957).

Rydman, Kari, Finnish composer; b. Helsinki, Oct. 15, 1936. He studied music, art, theology and psychology at the Univ. of Helsinki; later lived in Iceland and Sweden; adopted an advanced idiom of composition, while adhering to classical forms. His *Symphony of the Modern Worlds,* commissioned by the Swedish Broadcasting Corp. (1968) contains assorted ethnic and popular sources, including blues, beat rhythms, political songs and the Chinese Communist anthem, *Dong Fang Hong (The East is Red).* He also wrote chamber music and film scores.

Ryelandt, Joseph. Died in Bruges, June 29, 1965.

Rysanek, Leonie, Austrian soprano; b. Vienna, Nov. 14, 1926. She studied at the Vienna Cons. with Rudolf Grossmann, whom she later married. After a debut in Innsbruck (1949) she sang at Saarbrücken (1950-52) and at the Munich State Opera (1952-54). She joined the Vienna State Opera in 1954, and appeared also at La Scala in Milan, Covent Garden in London, and the Paris Opéra. In 1954 she sang for the first time at the Metropolitan Opera in New York, joining its staff on a permanent basis in 1959; appeared numerous times at the Bayreuth Festival. Her younger sister **Lotte Rysanek** (b. Vienna, March 18, 1928) has attained a fine reputation in Vienna as a lyric soprano.

Rzewski, Frederic, American avant-garde composer; b. Westfield, Mass., April 13, 1938, of Polish parentage. He attended Harvard Univ. (1954-58) and Princeton Univ. (1958-60); was active in modern music circles in Italy (1960-62) where he stayed on a Fulbright scholarship; subsequently he received a Ford Foundation grant which enabled him to spend two years in Berlin (1963-65); in the interim he played concerts with the topless cellist Charlotte Moorman; returning to Rome, he formed there the group 'Musica Electronica Viva.' As a composer, he pursues the vision of positivistic anti-music. His works, mostly in free association for fluid ensembles with aleatory interludes, include *Composition for Two* (1964); *Zoologischer Garten* (1965), *Nature morte* (1965), and his magnum opus, a score of 'collective music,' *Spacecraft* (1967). His *Plan for Spacecraft* was publ. in 'Source' (No. 3, 1968).

S

Sabata, Victor de. Died in Santa Margherita Ligure, Dec. 11, 1967.

Sabin, Robert, American music critic and editor; b. Rochester, Feb. 21, 1912; d. New York, May 17, 1969. He studied at the Eastman School of Music in Rochester before going to New York; was editor of 'Musical America' (1945-50); edited the 9th edition of Oscar Thompson's *International Cyclopedia of Music and Musicians* (1964).

Sachs, Curt. Died in New York, Feb. 5, 1959.

Sachse, Leopold. Died in Englewood, N. J., April 4, 1961.

Sacks, Stuart, American composer: b. Albany, N.Y., Feb. 28, 1941. He studied at Boston Univ. with Hugo Norden; developed a neo-romantic style couched in emotional tonality. The CBS Television network presented on April 11, 1965, in N.Y., performances of his *Saul* for mezzo-soprano, oboe, percussion and strings and *Poème* for violin and piano. His other works include an overture; *Arioso* for strings; *Divertissement* for winds and strings; *Elegy* for solo cello and orch.

Saenz, Pedro, Argentine composer; b. Buenos Aires, May 4, 1915. He studied piano with Alberto Williams, and theory with Arturo Palma. In 1948 he went to Paris where he took lessons with Arthur Honegger, Darius Milhaud and Jean Rivier. Returning to Buenos Aires he occupied numerous teaching and administrative posts in educational institutions. Works: *Movimientos sinfónicos* (1963); piano quintet; violin sonatas; string trio; *Divertimento* for oboe and clarinet, etc.

Saerchinger, César. Died in Washington, Oct. 10, 1971.

Saeverud, Harald. Add to works: *Minnesota Symphony* (Minneapolis, Oct. 18, 1958); Concerto for bassoon and orch. (1963); Symph. No. 9 (Bergen, June 12, 1966).

Sagaev, Dimiter, Bulgarian composer; b. Plovdiv, Feb. 27, 1915. He studied at the Sofia Cons. with Vladigerov and Stoyanov. His compositions include a ballet *The Knight of Madar;* 3 symph. dances; symph. poem *Sofia;* several symph. suites on regional folk motives; violin concerto; chamber music for various instrumental groups; songs.

Saint-Luban, Léon de. Correct spelling of the name is **Saint-Lubin.** He was solo violinist at the Josephstadt Theater in Vienna beginning in 1823 (not 1827).

Saint-Requier, Léon. Died in Paris, Oct. 1, 1964.

Saint-Saëns, Camille. His *Introduction et Rondo Capriccioso* was performed shortly after its composition in 1863; the Paris performance of Nov. 6, 1913 was that of the arrangement for violin and piano made by Bizet. Add to bibl.: James Harding, *Saint-Saëns and his Circle* (London, 1965).

Salas Viú, Vicente. Died in Santiago, Sept. 2, 1967.

Salazar, Adolfo. Died in Mexico City, Sept. 27, 1958.

Sales, Pietro Pompeo. Exact date of death, Nov. 21, 1797. Probable date of birth, 1729 (not 1719). Was in Augsburg in 1760; in Stuttgart in 1766-69; in Koblenz from 1770 (not from 1768).

Saleski, Gdal. Died in Los Angeles, Oct. 8, 1966.

Salmanov, Vadim, Russian composer; b. St. Petersburg, Nov. 17, 1912. He studied piano with his father; theory with Akimenko; composition at the Leningrad Cons. with Gnessin and Shostakovitch; in 1952 he was appointed prof. there. His early works are marked by broad Russian melodism, with the harmonic structure following the models of Prokofiev and Shostakovitch; during his last period he adopted more advanced techniques; his violin sonata (1962) is written in the 12-tone idiom. Works: piano concerto (1947); Symph. No. 1 (1952); *Poetic Pictures,* symph. suite (1955); *The Twelve,* oratorio to the text by Alexander Blok (1957); Symph. No. 2 (1959). Cf. M. Aranovsky, *V. N. Salmanov* (Leningrad, 1960).

Salzedo, Carlos. Died in Waterville, Maine, Aug. 17, 1961.

Salzman, Eric, American composer and musicologist; b. New York, Sept. 8, 1933. He studied composition at Columbia Univ., with Otto Luening, Vladimir Ussachevsky, William Mitchell and Jack Beeson (B.A., 1954) and at Princeton Univ. with Roger Sessions and Milton Babbitt (M.F.A., 1956); in addition he took courses in musicology with Oliver Strunk, Arthur Mendel and Nino Pirotta. In 1957 he went to Europe on a Fulbright Fellowship to study with Goffredo Petrassi in Rome; also attended courses of Karlheinz Stockhausen at Darmstadt. Returning to the U.S., he became a music critic for the N.Y. Times (1958-62) and for the N.Y. Herald Tribune (1963-66). In 1966 he was appointed assistant prof. of music at Queens College. In his compositions he follows the most advanced techniques in mixed media. Works: string quartet (1955); flute sonata (1956); *Partita* for solo violin (1958); *Inventions* for orch. (1959); *The Owl and the Cuckoo,* for soprano, guitar and chamber ensemble (1963); *Verses and Cantos* for 4 voices and instruments, with electronic extensions (N.Y., Nov. 30, 1967); *Larynx Music,* magnetic tape piece for dance (1968); *Feedback,* 'environment piece' for magnetic tape and film (1968); aleatory pieces for electronic and mixed media under the general title *The Electric Ear* for performance at the Electric Circus in Greenwich Village in New York. He publ. *An Introduction to Twentieth Century Music* (N.Y., 1967).

Samazeuilh, Gustave. Died in Paris, Aug. 4, 1967.

Saminsky, Lazare. Died in Port Chester, N.Y., June 30, 1959.

Sammarco, (Giuseppe) Mario. Date of birth, Dec. 13, 1868 (not 1873).

Samosud, Samuil, Russian opera conductor; b. Odessa, May 14, 1884; d. Moscow, Nov. 6, 1964. He conducted opera in Leningrad (1917-36); then moved to Moscow, conducting at Bolshoi Theater (1936-43) and at the Stanislavsky Musical Theater (1943-50); also appeared as a symph. conductor.

Sams, Eric, English music critic; b. London, May 3, 1926. He was educated at Cambridge Univ.; became active in broadcasting and in musical journalism; contributed regularly to 'The Musical Times'; pub. valuable monographs, *The Songs of Hugo Wolf* (London, 1961) and *Songs of Robert Schumann* (London, 1969).

Samuel, Gerhard, German-American conductor; b. Bonn, April 20, 1924. He studied violin as a child; his family emigrated to America in 1938. He performed menial jobs as a dishwasher and shoe salesman in New York before winning a scholarship at the Eastman School of Music in Rochester, N.Y.; there he studied conducting with Hermann Gerhard and composition with Howard Hanson (B.A., 1945); also played violin with the Rochester Philharmonic (1941-45). In 1945 he enrolled at Yale Univ., studying composition with Paul Hindemith (M.M., 1947); attended for two summers the conducting sessions with Koussevitzky at the Berkshire Music Center in Tanglewood. From 1949 to 1959 he was violinist and assistant conductor of the Minneapolis Symph. Orch.; from 1959 to 1970 he conducted the Oakland Symph. Orch. In 1970 he was appointed associate conductor of the Los Angeles Philharmonic. In his interpretations he strives for a dynamic equilibrium of massed sonorities, supported by a lapidary precision of details. Latitudinarian in his musical tastes, he includes in his programs works by the extreme avant-garde composers.

Samuel-Rousseau, Marcel. The reference should be directed to Rousseau, Marcel (not to Rousseau, Marcel Samuel).

Sandby, Herman. Died in Copenhagen, Dec. 14, 1965. Place of birth, Kundby, near Holbaek (not Sandby).

Sanders, Robert L. Add to works: cantata, *Song of Myself,* to Walt Whitman's words (Brooklyn, April 19, 1970).

Sandvik, Ole Mörk. In 1971 he observed his 96th birthday in Oslo in reasonably good health; continued his activities in various fields of scholarly research.

Sanjuán, Pedro. Add to works: *Symphonic Suite* (Washington, May 9, 1965).

Sankey, Ira David, American hymn writer; b. Edinburgh, Pennsylvania, Aug. 28, 1840; d. Brooklyn, N.Y., Aug. 13, 1908. He sang at Sunday School conventions; became famous as an evangelical singer appearing with the preacher Dwight L. Moody. He publ. *Sacred Songs and Solos* (1873) and *My Life and the Story of the Gospel Hymns* (1905). Of his songs, *I Am Praying for You* became widely popular. Cf. R. G. McCutchan, *Our Hymnody* (N.Y., 1937).

Sanromá, Jesús María. Date of birth, Nov. 7, 1902 (not 1903).

Santa Cruz Wilson, Domingo. In 1965 he toured the U.S. as lecturer on Latin American music. Add to works: *Canciones del Mar,* song cycle (1955); *Endechas* for tenor and 8 instruments (1957); string quartet No. 3 (1959); wind quintet (1960); Symph. No. 3, with contralto solo (Washington, May 9, 1965); Symph. No. 4 (1968).

Santoro, Claudio. Add to works: Symph. No. 5 (Rio de Janeiro, March 28, 1956); No. 6 (Paris, May 1, 1963); No. 7, surnamed

Brasilia (1960); No. 8 (1963); 2 violin concertos (1951, 1958); 3 piano concertos (1953, 1959, 1960); cello concerto (1961; Washington, May 12, 1965); string quartets No. 4 (1955); No. 5 (1957); No. 6 (1963); *5 Esboços* for orch. (1965); flute sonata; oboe sonata; trumpet sonata; 24 piano preludes; violin sonatas No. 4 and 5; cello sonatas No. 3 and 4. The world première of his *Symphony of Peace* (No. 4) took place in Rio de Janeiro on Oct.. 30, 1954. Since 1960, Santoro has resumed composition in serial techniques; typical of this period is his *Antistruktur* for harp and cello (1970).

Sapelnikov, Vassily. Born Nov. 2, 1867 (not 1868).

Saperstein, David, American composer; b. New York, March 6, 1948. He studied at the Juilliard School of Music, and took courses with Elliott Carter, Walter Piston and Vincent Persichetti at the Dartmouth College Summer Sessions (1963-64), and with Milton Babbitt at Princeton Univ., receiving his A.B. degree in 1969. In 1970 he enrolled in the graduate school at Brandeis Univ. His works, written in an advanced idiom, include wind quintet (1963); *Duo* for violin and percussion (1965); brass quartet (1966); *Etudes* for piano (1967); *Composition* for violin and tape (1968); *Variations* for 8 instruments (1969); *Bagatelle* for piano (1969); *Sextet* (1970).

Saperton, David. Died in Baltimore, July 5, 1970.

Sarai, Tibor, Hungarian composer; b. Budapest, May 10, 1919. He studied composition with Kadosa; became prof. at the Music Academy in Budapest. His music is romantic in nature. Among his works are a *Spring Concerto* for orch. (1955); a string quartet (1959); songs and choruses.

Sarasate, Pablo de. He played for Queen Isabella at the age of 12 (not 10). She did not present him with a Stradivarius violin; he purchased it out of his own resources in 1866.

Sargeant, Winthrop. Studied composition (not violin) with Albert Elkus in San Francisco and with Karl Prohaska in Vienna. His violin teachers were Arthur Argiewicz in San Francisco and Lucien Capet in Paris. He publ. a 'personal memoir,' *In Spite of Myself* (N.Y., 1970), in which he recounts with astonishing candor a series of his sexual and musical frustrations.

Sargent, Sir (Harold) Malcolm (Watts). Died in London, Oct. 3, 1967. Place of birth, Ashford, Kent (not London). See Charles Reid. *Malcolm Sargent: A Biography* (N.Y., 1970).

Sari, Ada, Polish soprano; b. Wadowice, near Cracow, June 29, 1886; d. Ciechocinek, July 12, 1968. Her real name was Jadwiga Szajerowa. She studied in Milan; after appearances in Rome, Naples, Trieste and Parma, she joined the staff of the Warsaw Opera; made extensive tours in Europe, in South America and in the U.S. Eventually she returned to Warsaw, devoting herself mainly to teaching.

Sarly, Henry. Died in Brussels, Dec. 3, 1954.

Sartori, Claudio. Add to publ.: *Puccini* (Milan, 1958); *Casa Ricordi, 1808-1958: profilo storico* (Milan, 1958); *Le Musiche della Cappella del Duomo di Milano* (Florence, 1958).

Sás, Andrés. Died in Lima, Peru, Aug. 1967.

Satie, Erik. His piano piece *Vexations* was performed 840 times consecutively by 5 pianists working in shifts, day and night in New York, from 6:00 p.m., Sept. 9, 1963 to 12:40 p.m., Sept. 10, 1963.

Sato, Keijiro, Japanese composer; b. Tokyo, June 6, 1927. He studied medicine and music; composed miniatures in modernistic style; his *Calligraphy* for piano was performed at the Vienna Festival of the International Society for Contemporary Music on June 17, 1961.

Sauguet, Henri. His real name is Henri-Pierre Poupard; he assumed his mother's maiden name, Sauguet. The title of his opera is *La Gageure* (not *Gageuse) imprévue*. Add to works: *Suite Royale* for harpsichord solo (1962); *Symphonie de marches* (Paris, June 4, 1966).

Sauret, Émile. He married Teresa Carreño in June 1873 (not 1872); they were divorced in 1876 (not 1877).

Sawallisch, Wolfgang, German conductor; b. Munich, Aug. 26, 1923. He studied piano and composition at the Cons. of Munich, graduating in 1946. He made his conducting debut in Augsburg in 1947; subsequently occupied posts as music director in Aachen (1953-57), Wiesbaden (1957-59) and Cologne (1959-63). In 1964 he toured the U.S.

with the Vienna Philharmonic. Specializing in opera, he achieved one of his finest successes in the Wagnerian repertory, conducting in Bayreuth since 1957.

Scacciati, Bianca, Italian soprano; b. Florence, July 3, 1894; d. Brescia, Oct. 15, 1948. She studied in Milan; made her debut there as Marguerite in *Faust* in 1917. She rapidly asserted herself as one of the most impressive dramatic sopranos in Italy; sang for many seasons at La Scala, Milan; also made successful appearances at Covent Garden, London, at the Paris Opéra and at the Teatro Colón in Buenos Aires. She was particularly noted for her interpretation of the title role of Puccini's *Turandot.*

Scarlatesco, Ion, Rumanian composer; b. Bucharest, 1872; d. there, Sept. 19, 1922. A versatile musician, he began his career as pianist; also wrote plays and was active as music critic and harmony teacher. He composed about 50 ballads for voice and piano; a string quartet; a *Rumanian Rhapsody* for orch.; several other pieces in the Rumanian style, among which *Bagatelle* for violin became popular.

Scarlatti, Alessandro. Add to bibl.: M. Fabbri, *Alessandro Scarlatti e il principe Ferdinand de Medici* (Florence, 1961).

Scarmolin, (Anthony) Louis. Died in New Jersey, July 13, 1969.

Schaefer, Theodor, Czech composer; b. Telč, Jan. 23, 1904. He studied in Brno and at the Prague Cons. with Vitězslav Novák. Works: violin concerto (1933); piano concerto (1943); *Diathema* for viola and orch. (1956); *Diathema* for orch. (1958); symph. (Brno, March 11, 1964); 3 string quartets; wind quintet; songs.

Schaeffer, Pierre, French acoustician and inventor; b. Nancy, Aug. 14, 1910. Working in a Paris radio studio he conceived the idea of a musical montage composed of random sounds, and, on April 15, 1948, formulated the theory of 'musique concrète.' When the magnetic tape was perfected, Schaeffer made ingenious use of it by rhythmic acceleration and deceleration, changing the pitch and dynamics and modifying the nature of the instrumental timbre. He made several collages of elements of 'concrete music,' among them *Concert de bruits* (1948) and (with Pierre Henry) *Symphonie pour un Homme Seul* (1950) and an experimental opera *Orphée 53* (1953); he also wrote *Variation sur une flûte mexicaine* (1949). He publ. *A la recherche de la musique concrète* (Paris, 1952) and *Traité des objets sonores* (Paris, 1966). Bibl.: Marc Pierret, *Entretiens avec Pierre Schaeffer* (Paris, 1969).

Schafer, R. Murray, Canadian composer; b. Sarnia, Ontario, July 18, 1933. He studied at the Royal Cons. of Music in Toronto with John Weinzweig; spent several years in England. Returning to Canada in 1962, he became associated with the Canadian Broadcasting Corp., arranging festivals of modern music and conducting experimental sessions using electronic, serial and aleatory techniques. He has developed a sui generis system of topological transmutation, exemplified by his electronic score *The Son of Heldenleben* (first performed in Montreal on Nov. 13, 1968), in which he imaginatively distorted the thematic materials of *Ein Heldenleben* by Richard Strauss, retaining the essential motivic substance of the parent work. Among his original compositions are *Canzoni for Prisoners* for small orch. (1962); *Invertible Material* for orch. (1963); *Untitled Composition* for orch. (1963); *Statement in Blue* for youth orch., in aleatory notation (1964); *Loving* for mixed media (1965); *Gita,* electronic piece for chorus, brass ensemble and tape (Lenox, Mass., Aug. 10, 1967); *No Longer Than Ten Minutes* for orch. (the title derives from the stipulation of the maximum length of the piece commissioned by the Toronto Symph. Orch., and performed by it on Feb. 16, 1971).

Schäffer, Boguslaw, Polish composer; b. Lwow, June 6, 1929. He studied composition in Cracow with Arthur Malawski; musicology at the Jagello Univ. in Cracow with Jachimecki. His early works are based on Polish folk music; later he turned towards constructivistic types of composition; devised a graphic notation indicating intensity of sound, proportional lengths of duration and position of notes in melodic and contrapuntal lines using methods of analytic geometry; in some of his scores he applies polychromatic optical notation. Works: *Nocturne* for string orch. (1953); *Quattro Movimenti* for piano and orch. (1958); *Tertium Datur* for clavichord and a chamber orch. (1958); *Monosonata* for 24 string instruments (1959); *Equivalenze sonore* for percussion ensemble (1959); *Concerto breve* for cello and orch. (1959); *Topofonica* for 40 instruments (1960); *Concerto per sei e tre* for instrumental ensemble (1960); *Scultura per orchestra* (1960); *Musica per Cembalo e strumenti* (1961); *Kody* for chamber orch. (1961); *Musica Ipsa* for orch. (1961); *4 Essays* for string trio (1961); violin concerto (1964); *Symphony* for electronic instruments (1965); *Przeslanie* for cello and 2 pianos (1965); *Assemblage* for magnetic tape (1966); *Cantata* for 60 voices and orch. (1966). He publ. several informative books in the Polish language: *Maly Informator Muzyki XX wieka* (Cracow, 1958); *Nowa Muzyka* (Cracow, 1958); *Klasycy dodekafonii* (2 vols., Cracow, 1961, 1964) and *Leksykon Kompozytorów* XX *wieka* (2 vols.; Cracow, 1963, 1965).

Scharrer, Irene. Died in London, Jan. 11, 1971.

Schat, Peter, Dutch composer; b. Utrecht, June 5, 1935. He studied music at Utrecht and The Hague, and later took private lessons with Mátyás Seiber in London. From his earliest steps in composition, he adopted the serial method; he also experimented with electronic sonorities. Works: septet (1956); octet (1958); *Mosaics* (1959); *Cryptogramen* for baritone and orch. (1959); *Concerto da Camera* (1960); *Improvisations and Symphonies* for wind quintet (1960); *Entelechie* for 5 instrumental groups (1960); *Labyrinth,* theatrical spectacle in mixed media (Amsterdam, June 23, 1966).

Schauffler, Robert Haven. Died in New York, Nov. 24, 1964.

Scheidt, Samuel. Add to bibl.: E. Gessner, *Samuel Scheidts Geistliche Konzerte: Ein Beitrag zur Geschichte der Gattung* (Berlin, 1961).

Schein, Johann Hermann. Add to bibl.: A. Adrio, *Johann Hermann Schein* (Berlin, 1959).

Schenck, Jean (Johann). He was born in Amsterdam (baptized June 3, 1660), not in Elberfeld, not on Feb. 20, 1656. See K. H. Pauls, in 'Die Musikforschung' 1962, pp. 157-171 and 1966, pp. 288-289.

Schenk, Erich. A Festschrift, edited by O. Wessely, was publ. in honor of his 60th *birthday* (Vienna, 1962). His book, *W. A. Mozart: Eine Biographie* (Vienna, 1955) was publ. in English (N. Y., 1959).

Scherchen, Hermann. Died in Florence, June 12, 1966. Made his American debut as a conductor with the Philadelphia Orch., Oct. 30, 1964.

Schibler, Armin. Add to works: *Concerto* for percussion and orch. (Zürich, Jan. 6, 1961); *Blackwood & Co.,* burlesque opera (Zürich, June 3, 1962); *Media in vita,* symph. oratorio (Zürich, April 26, 1963); *Metamorphoses Ebrietatis,* symph. poem (Montreux, Switzerland, Sept. 6, 1966).

Schickele, Peter, American composer; b. Ames, Iowa, July 17, 1935. He studied at the Juilliard School of Music, with Vincent Persichetti and William Bergsma. After quaquaversal professional gyrations, he rocketed to rock 'n' roll fame in the rollicking role of a roly-poly character P.D.Q. Bach, the mythical composer of such outrageous travesties as *The Civilian Barber, Gross Concerto for Divers Flutes* (featuring a nose flute and a wienerwhistle to be eaten during the performance), *Concerto for Piano vs. Orchestra, Iphigenia in Brooklyn, The Seasonings, Pervertimento for Bagpipes, Bicycles & Balloons,* etc., perpetrated in a clever pseudo-Baroque style.

Schidlowsky, León, Chilean composer; b. Santiago, July 21, 1931. He studied at the Universidad de Chile; then in Germany (1952-55). Returning to Chile, he organized an avant-garde group 'Tonus' for the propagation of new techniques of composition. In 1965 he was appointed to the faculty of the Conservatorio Nacional de Música in Santiago. In his works he adopts a serial technique, extending it into the fields of rhythms and intensities; beginning with 1964 he superadded aleatory elements using graphic notation. Works: piano trio (1955); *Cantata negra* for contralto, piano, xylophone and percussion (1957); *Triptico* for orch. (1959); *La Noche de Cristal* for tenor, male chorus and orch., dedicated to the martyrdom of Jews on the Nazi "crystal night" (1961); *Cuarteto Mixto* for flute, clarinet, violin and cello (1966); *Nueva York* for orch., dedicated to 'my brothers in Harlem' (1966); *Visiones* for 12 string instruments (1967); wind quintet (1968).

Schifrin, Lalo (Boris), American composer; b. Buenos Aires, June 21, 1932. He studied music at home with his father who was concertmaster at the Teatro Colón; took composition lessons with the Argentinian dodecaphonist Juan Carlos Paz. In 1950 he went to Paris where he attended the classes of Olivier Messiaen. He became interested in jazz and represented Argentina at the International Jazz Festival in Paris in 1955; returning to Buenos Aires he formed his own jazz band adopting the bebop style of swing. In 1958 he went to New York as arranger for Xavier Cugat; then was pianist with Dizzy Gillespie's band (1960-62); composed for it several exotic melodies, such as *Manteca, Con Alma* and *Night in Tunisia;* the latter he expanded into an orchestral work, *Tunisian Fantasy.* In 1963 he wrote a ballet *Jazz Faust.*

In 1964 he went to Hollywood, where he rapidly found his métier as composer for the films and television; among his motion picture scores are *The Liquidator, The Fox* and *The Cincinnati Kid.* He also experimented with applying the jazz idiom to religious texts, as, for instance, in his *Jazz Suite on Mass Texts.* He achieved his greatest popular success with the theme-motto for the television series *Mission: Impossible,* in 5/4 time, for which he received two 'Grammy' awards. His adaptation of modern techniques into mass media placed him in the enviable position of being praised by professional musicians. His oratorio, *The Rise and Fall of the Third Reich* featuring realistic excerpts and incorporating an actual recording of Hitler's speech in electronic amplification was brought out at the Hollywood Bowl on Aug. 3, 1967. His other works include a suite for trumpet and brass orch. (1961); *The Ritual of Sound* for 15 instruments (1962); *Pulsations* for electronic keyboard, jazz band and orch. (Los Angeles, Jan. 21, 1971).

Schillinger, Joseph. Was active in Leningrad from 1922 (not 1926) to 1928. Came to U.S. in 1928 (not 1929).

Schillings, Max von. Died July 24 (not July 23), 1933.

Schindler, Anton Felix. Place of birth, Medlov (not Meedl), in the district of Olomouc.

Schiøler, Victor. Died in Copenhagen, Feb. 17, 1967.

Schiøtz, Aksel. He publ. *The Singer and His Art* (N.Y., 1969).

Schipa, Tito. Died in New York, Dec. 16, 1965.

Schippers, Thomas. In 1970 he succeeded Max Rudolf as music director of the Cincinnati Symphony Orchestra.

Schirmer, Gustave, 3rd. Died in Palm Beach, Florida, May 28, 1965.

Schiske, Karl. Died in Vienna, June 16, 1969. Add bibl.: Karlheinz Roschitz, *Karl Schiske* (Vienna, 1970).

Schiuma, Alfredo. Died in Buenos Aires in 1963.

Schlesinger, Adolf Martin. Born in Berlin, Oct. 4, 1769; d. there, Nov. 11, 1838. Founded his business not later than 1795, although the name of the firm was not used until 1821.

Schlesinger, Maurice Adolf. Exact dates: b. Oct. 3, 1797; d. Feb. 25, 1871. Was publishing in Paris at least as early as 1822.

Schloezer, Boris de. Died in Paris, Oct. 7, 1969.

Schmid, Ernst Friedrich. Died in Augsburg, Jan. 20. 1960.

Schmidt, William, American composer; b. Chicago, March 6, 1926. He moved to Los Angeles in 1952 and studied composition with Halsey Stevens and Ingolf Dahl at the Univ. of Southern California; at the same time was active as jazz arranger. He composed a *Concerto Breve for Brass and Band* (1957); pieces for orch. and numerous works for various chamber ensembles: 6 bassoon duets (1957); *Serenade* for tuba and piano (1958); *Rondino* for trombone and piano (1959); viola sonata (1959); woodwind quintet (1959); *Percussive Rondo* for percussion quartet (1957); etc.

Schmidt-Isserstedt, Hans, German conductor; b. Berlin, May 5, 1900. He studied composition with Franz Schreker; then devoted himself mainly to conducting. After a series of appointments as opera conductor in Germany he was engaged at the Hamburg State Opera in 1935; was conductor of the Staatsoper in Berlin in 1943; conducted at Glyndebourne in 1958, and in London, at Covent Garden, in 1962. In 1963 he made his American debut as symphonic conductor.

Schminke, Oscar Eberhard. Died in Liberty, N.Y., Feb. 22, 1969.

Schmitz, Eugen. Died in Leipzig, July 10, 1959. He was born in Neuburg (not Neuberg).

Schnabel, Artur. Add to publ.: *My Life and Music* (London, 1961).

Schneerson, Grigory Mikhailovitch, Russian musicologist and critic; b. Eniseisk, Siberia, March 13, 1901. He studied piano at the Moscow Cons. with Medtner and Igumnov. In 1931 he joined the International Music Bureau in Moscow; from 1939 to 1948 was in charge of the Music Dept. of the VOKS (All-Union Society for Cultural Relations with Foreign Nations); from 1948 to 1961 was head of the foreign section of 'Sovietskaya Musica,' and from 1954 to 1966 edited the bibliographic series 'Foreign Literature of Music.' A gifted linguist, he mastered all European languages and undertook a study of Chinese. In his polemical writings he attacks the extreme manifestations of

Western modernism with vitriolic scorn and devastating sarcasm, but he preserves scholarly impartiality in his monographs on foreign music. Books (all publ. in Moscow): *Musical Culture in China* (1952); *Aram Khatchaturian* (1957; also in English, 1959); *Music, Living and Dead* (in praise of the state of music in the nations of the Socialist bloc, and in condemnation of Western trends, 1960; revised and mitigated, 1964); *Ernst Busch* (1962; revised, 1964); *French Music of the 20th Century* (1964; revised, 1970).

Schneider, Max. Died in Halle, May 5, 1967.

Schoeck, Othmar. *Das Wandbild* is a pantomime (not an opera); op. 40, *Lebendig begraben* (not *vegraben*).

Schoemaker, Maurice. Died in Brussels, Aug. 24, 1964.

Schoenberg, Arnold. His incomplete oratorio *Die Jakobsleiter* was performed for the first time in Vienna, on June 16, 1961. *Verklärte Nacht* was first performed in Vienna on March 18, 1902; *Serenade,* op. 24 was first performed in Donaueschingen (not in Vienna) on July 20, 1924. Add to bibl.: E. Stein, ed. *Arnold Schönberg, Briefe* (Mainz, 1958); J. C. Paz, *Arnold Schönberg: El fin de la era tonal* (Buenos Aires, 1958); Karl H. Wörner, *Gotteswort und Magie: die Oper Moses und Aron* (Heidelberg, 1959); M. Kassler, *The Decision of Arnold Schoenberg's Twelve-Note-Class-System and Related Systems* (Princeton, 1961); Georg Krieger, *Schönbergs Werke für Klavier* (1968); Reinhold Brinkmann, *Arnold Schönberg: Drei Klavierstücke Op. 11* (1969); René Leibowitz, *Schoenberg* (Paris, 1969); Willi Reich, *Arnold Schönberg, oder Der Konservative Revolutionär* (Vienna, 1969). For a complete survey of Schoenberg's works, see the annotated catalogue compiled by Josef Rufer, *Das Werk Arnold Schönbergs* (Kassel, 1959; also in English).

Scholes, Percy Alfred. The 10th edition of *The Oxford Companion to Music* was edited by John Owen Ward (N.Y., 1970).

Schollum, Robert, Austrian composer, musicologist and critic; b. Vienna, Aug. 22, 1913. He studied piano and organ at the Vienna Music Academy; composition with Joseph Marx. After World War II he settled in Linz as organist and educator. In 1959 he was appointed prof. of singing at the Vienna Academy of Music. He wrote 3 symphonies; a violin concerto; a one-act opera *Der Biedermann Elend;* an octet in 8 sketches (received the Austrian State Prize in 1961); chamber music; songs.

Schönbach, Dieter, German composer; b. Stolp-Pommern, Feb. 18, 1931. He studied at the Freiburg Hochschule für Musik with Wolfgang Fortner; in 1958 he was appointed music director at the municipal theater in Bochum. His style of composition is neoclassical, with pragmatic application of modified dodecaphony. His *Canticum Psalmi Resurrectionis* was performed at the International Festival of Contemporary Music in Rome on June 13, 1959.

Schonberg, Harold C. He publ. *The Great Pianists* (N.Y., 1963); *Lives of the Great Composers* (N.Y. 1970). In 1971 he was awarded the Pulitzer Prize 'for distinguished criticism.'

Schott, Bernhard. Founded his firm in 1770 (not 1773). Born in Eltville (baptized Aug. 19, 1748); died in Heidesheim, in the Mainz district (not in Mainz itself), April 26, 1809 (not 1817). Dates of Franz Philipp Schott are: b. July 30, 1811; d. May 8, 1874.

Schrade, Leo. Died in Spéracédès (French Alps), Sept. 21, 1964. He was Charles Eliot Norton Lecturer at Harvard (1962-63); his lectures were publ. under the title, *Tragedy in the Art of Music* (Cambridge, Mass., 1964); also publ. *W. A. Mozart* (Munich, 1964). Add to bibl.: *Music and History: Leo Schrade on the Occasion of his 60th Birthday* (Cologne, 1963).

Schuh, Willi. Add to books: *Umgang mit Musik* (Zürich, 1970).

Schulhoff, Erwin. His oratorio *The Communist Manifesto* was performed posthumously in Prague, on April 5, 1962.

Schuller, Gunther. In 1957 he launched the slogan 'Third Stream' combining the improvisatory elements of jazz with classical forms in a discrete synthesis of disparate entities. From 1964-66 he was associate prof. at Yale Univ.; in 1966 became President of The New England Cons. in Boston; from 1965 he was also head of the composition department at the Berkshire Music Center in Tanglewood. Add to works: *Seven Studies on Themes of Paul Klee* for orch. (Minneapolis, Nov. 27, 1959); *Spectra* for orch. (N. Y., Jan. 15, 1960); *Variants,* a ballet (N. Y., Jan. 4, 1961); *Contrasts* for orch. (Donaueschingen, Oct. 22, 1961); piano concerto (Cincinnati, Oct. 29, 1962); Symph. No. 1 (Dallas,

Texas, Feb. 8, 1965); *American Triptych: Three Studies in Texture,* for orch. (New Orleans, March 9, 1965, composer conducting); *The Visitation,* opera (Hamburg, Oct. 12, 1966); *Diptych* for brass quintet and orch., symphonic amplification of the original brass quintet (Boston, March 31, 1967); *Triplum* for orch. (N.Y., June 28, 1967); *Concerto* for double-bass and orch. (N.Y., June 27, 1968); *The Fisherman and His Wife,* children's opera after a Grimm fairy-tale (Boston, May 8, 1970). He publ. a manual, *Horn Technique* (N. Y., 1962) and a very valuable source book, *Early Jazz: Its Roots and Musical Development* (N. Y., 1968).

Schulthess, Walter. Died in Zürich, June 23, 1971. His wife, Stefi Geyer, was a violinist, not a pianist.

Schuman, William Howard. He was President of Lincoln Center, N.Y., from 1962 to 1969, after resignation as President of the Juilliard School of Music. The first performance of his *Night Journey* took place at Cambridge, Mass, on May 1, 1947 (not Feb. 17, 1948). Add to works: Symph. No. 7 (Boston, Oct. 21, 1960); *Song of Orpheus* for cello and orch. (N.Y., Sept. 26, 1962); Symph. No. 8 (N.Y., Oct. 4, 1962); Symph. No. 9, subtitled *Le Fosse Ardeatine,* in memory of Italian civilians murdered by the Germans in a cave in Rome in retaliation for resistance activities (Philadelphia, Jan. 10, 1969); *In Praise of Shahn,* canticle for orch., in memory of the American painter Ben Shahn (N.Y., Jan. 30, 1970).

Schumann, Clara. Add to bibl.: R. Pitron, *Clara Schumann* (Paris, 1961).

Schumann, Robert. He heralded Chopin's genius in 1831 (not in 1834); his later endorsements were semantically not of a heralding nature. Op. 113 is for piano and viola (or violin); op. 132 is for clarinet (or violin), piano and viola. Add to bibl.: A. Boucourechliev, *Robert Schumann in Selbstzeugnissen und Bilddokumenten* (Hamburg, 1958); L. B. Plantinga, *Schumann as Critic* (New Haven, 1967); T. A. Brown, *The Aesthetics of Robert Schumann* (N. Y., 1968); Eric Sams, *The Songs of Robert Schumann* (London, 1969).

Schumann, Walter, American composer of applied music; b. New York, Oct. 8, 1913; d. Minneapolis, Aug. 21, 1958. He studied law and music at the Univ. of Southern California in Los Angeles; became associated with radio shows and composed music for films; wrote an opera, *John Brown's Body* (Los Angeles, Sept. 21, 1953). He contributed the famous ominously syncopated theme to the television serial *Dragnet,* based on the initial three notes of the minor scale.

Schuppanzigh, Ignaz. Did not take his quartet on tour when he left Vienna in 1815. The fire in Razumovsky's Palace was conflagrated on Dec. 31, 1814 (not 1815). Was director of the German opera in 1828 (not 1928).

Schuricht, Carl. Died in Corseaux-sur-Vevey, Switzerland, Jan. 7, 1967.

Schürmann, Gerard, English composer; b. Kertosono, Indonesia, Jan. 19, 1928. He studied piano with his mother; at the outbreak of the war in the Pacific in 1941 he was sent to England; studied piano with Kathleen Long at the Royal College of Music in London, and composition with Alan Rawsthorne. At the same time he served as a Netherlands Cultural Attaché to Great Britain. In 1951 he was appointed conductor at the Dutch Radio in Hilversum; in 1953 he returned to England and devoted himself mainly to composition. His music is set in an advanced neo-Baroque style with application of serial techniques. Works: 2 string quartets (1948, 1964); *Intrada* for strings (1950); *Nine Poems of Blake,* a song cycle (1955); wind quintet (1963); *Fantasia* for cello and piano (1965); *Chuench'i* for voice and orch. (1967); *Six Studies of Francis Bacon* for orch. (1968); sonatina for flute and piano (1968); *Serenade* for solo violin (1969); *Variants* for chamber orch. (1970); piano concerto (1970).

Schuster, Joseph. Died in Los Angeles, Feb. 16, 1969.

Schütz, Franz, Austrian organist; b. Vienna, April 15, 1892; d. there, May 19, 1962. He was on the staff of the Cons. of the Gesellschaft der Musikfreunde in Vienna from 1921; gave organ recitals; composed organ pieces.

Schütz, Heinrich. Add to bibl.: H. J. Moser, *Heinrich Schütz: His Life and Work* (translated from 2nd rev. ed. by Carl G. Pfatteicher; St. Louis, 1959); H. H. Eggebrecht, *Heinrich Schütz, Musicus poeticus* (Göttingen, 1959); G. Kirchner, *Der Generalbass bei Heinrich Schütz* (Kassel, 1960); W. S. Huber, *Motivsymbolik bei Heinrich Schütz* (Kassel, 1961).

Schützendorf, Guido. Died in Germany, April, 1967.

Schuyt, Nico, Dutch composer; b. Alkmaar, Jan. 2, 1922. He studied composition with Bertus van Lier; did not begin to compose until he was 25 years old. His works include *Sonata a tre* for oboe, bassoon and piano (1954); *Reveil* for orch. (1955); *Corteggio* for orch. (1958); *Sonata per orchestra* (1964); a ballet, *De Kast van de oude Chinees (The Old Chinese Cupboard)*; a school opera, *De Varkenshoeder* (*The Little Pig Boy*); choruses; piano pieces.

Schwann, William, American organist and musicographer; b. Salem, Illinois, May 13, 1913. He studied at the Louisville, Kentucky, School of Music at the Univ. of Louisville (A.B., 1935). He began his musical career as an organist and choir director in Louisville churches (1930-35); then went to Boston, where he studied organ with E. Power Biggs; also attended classes of Hugo Leichtentritt, Wallace Woodworth and A. T. Merritt at Harvard Univ.; wrote music criticism. In 1939 he set up a retail shop of phonograph records in Cambridge; in 1949 he launched his 'Schwann Record Catalog.' In 1953 the title was changed to 'Schwann Long Playing Record Catalog'. In 1971 he added 8-track cartridge tape and cassette tape listings under the new title 'Schwann Record and Tape Guide.' He also publishes a semi-annual 'Supplementary Record & Tape Guide,' an annual 'Children's Record Catalog,' an annual 'Country and Western Record & Tape Catalog' and a quadrennial 'Artist Issue' which lists classical music indexed alphabetically by the names of performing artists. The 'Schwann Catalog' is generally regarded as the most authoritative and the most comprehensive compilation of its kind.

Schwarz, Boris. He publ. *Music and Musical Life in Soviet Russia 1917-1970* (N. Y., 1971).

Schwarz, Vera, soprano; b. Zagreb, July 10, 1889; d. Vienna, Dec. 4, 1964. She studied voice and piano in Vienna; appeared in operettas there; went to Hamburg in 1914 and to Berlin in 1917; toured in South America. In 1939 she went to Hollywood where she became a vocal instructor; in 1948 she returned to Austria; gave courses at the Mozarteum in Salzburg. Her best roles were Carmen and Tosca.

Schweitzer, Albert. Died in his jungle hospital at Lambaréné, Gabon, Sept. 4, 1965, at the age of 90. Cf. Charles R. Joy, ***Albert Schweitzer, an Anthology*** **(N.Y., 1965);** Werner Picht, *The Life and Thought of Albert Schweitzer* (N.Y., 1965).

Schwieger, Hans. In 1938-41 he was conductor at Columbia, S.C. (not Columbus).

Sciammarella, Valdo, Argentine composer; b. Buenos Aires, Jan. 20, 1924. He studied composition with Julián Bautista; subsequently engaged in pedagogy. In 1965 he was appointed head of the Music Department at the National School of Fine Arts in Buenos Aires. He wrote a one-act lyric comedy*Marianita Limena* (Buenos Aires, Nov. 11, 1957); *Variaciones Concertantes* for piano and orch. (1952); *Scherzino* for oboe, clarinet and bassoon (1956); piano pieces; several scores of incidental music for theatrical plays.

Scott, Charles Kennedy. Died in London, July 2, 1965.

Scott, Cyril Meir. Died in Eastbourne, Dec. 31, 1970. Date of first performance of his piano concerto, May 15, 1915. Started on his U.S. tour in 1920 (not 1921); was soloist in his piano concerto with the Philadelphia Orch. on Nov. 5, 1920. Symph. No. 2 was converted into *Three Symphonic Dances,* and no longer exists as a separate work. Add to works: *Christmas Overture* (London, Nov. 13, 1906); *La Princesse Maleine,* symph. poem (London, Aug. 22, 1907); Symph. No. 3, *The Muses* (1939); violin concerto (Birmingham, Jan. 27, 1928); cello concerto (1937); 2nd piano concerto (1950); *Irish Serenade* for string orch. (1951); 2nd piano trio (1955); trio for flute, cello and piano (1957-61); sonata for flute and piano (1961); *Sinfonietta* (1962). Shortly before his death he publ. a book of memoirs, *Bone of Contention* (London, 1969).

Scott, Francis George, Scottish composer; b. Hawick, Roxburghshire, Jan. 25, 1880; d. Glasgow, Nov. 6, 1958. He studied humanities at the Univ. of Edinburgh; later at Durham Univ. (B.M., 1909); also took theory lessons with a local organist. As a composer, he cultivated Scottish art-music; publ. a number of songs at his own expense; of these the most significant are *Scottish Lyrics* (5 vols., 1921-39). His more ambitious works include *The Ballad of Kynd Kittok* for baritone and orch.; *Lament for the Heroes* for string orch.; and a concert overture, *Renaissance* (Glasgow, Jan. 14, 1939). Scott had a number of ardent admirers in England, among them the poet Hugh MacDiarmid and the composer Kaikhosru Sorabji, who in their exhuberant encomiums place him in the ranks of Schubert and Schumann as a song writer.

Scott, Tom. Died in New York City, Aug. 12, 1961.

Scriabin, Alexander Nikolayevitch. Add bibl.: Faubion Bowers, *Scriabin: A Biography of the Russian Composer* (2 vols., Palo Alto, 1969).

Scriabine, Marina, Russian-French music scholar and composer; daughter of Scriabin; b. Moscow, Jan. 30, 1911. After her father's death, she lived with her mother in Kiev and Moscow; when her mother died, she went to Belgium to live with her maternal grandmother; in 1927 she settled in Paris. She studied at the École Nationale des Arts Décoratifs and designed art posters; studied music theory with René Leibowitz. In 1950 she joined the Radioffusion française and worked in electronic techniques; composed a *Suite radiophonique* (1951); also a ballet *Bayalett* (1952) and some chamber music. In 1967 she received a doctorate in esthetics for her thesis, *Représentation du temps et de l'Intemporalité dans les arts plastiques figuratifs.* She publ. *Problèmes de la musique moderne* (in collaboration with her uncle, Boris de Schloezer; Paris, 1959; also in Spanish, 1960); *Le Langage Musical* (Paris, 1963); *Le Miroir du Temps* (Paris, 1973). She contributed the biographical entry on Scriabin for the *Encyclopédie de la Musique,* publ. by Fasquelle (Paris, 1961).

Sculthorpe, Peter, Australian composer; b. Launceston, Tasmania, April 29, 1929. He studied music at the Univ. of Melbourne, obtaining his B.M. degree in 1951. In his music he utilizes Indonesian, Japanese and aboriginal Australian modalities. His works include 4 orchestral scores entitled *Sun Music* (1965-67); *The Fifth Continent,* incorporating prerecorded sounds of Australian primitive instruments; *Love 200* for orch. (Sydney, Feb. 14, 1970); a series of compositions under the generic title *Irkanda* for various instrumental groups; *Tabuh Tabuhan* for wind quintet and percussion; 7 string quartets; sonata for viola and percussion; piano pieces; choral works; also a musical farce, *Ulterior Motifs.*

Searle, Humphrey. In 1964-65 he was on the faculty of Stanford Univ., Calif. Add to works: *The Diary of a Madman,* one-act opera, after Gogol (Berlin Music Festival, Oct. 3, 1958); *The Great Peacock,* ballet (1958); Symph. No. 2 (1958); *3 Movements* for string quartet (1959); Symph. No. 3 (Edinburgh, Sept. 3, 1960); Symph. No. 4 (Birmingham, England, Nov. 8, 1962); *Burn-Up* for speaker and instruments (1962); *Dualities,* ballet (1963); *The Photo of the Colonel,* opera (Frankfurt, Germany, June 3, 1964); Symph. No. 5 (Manchester, Oct. 7, 1964); *Scherzi* for orch. (1964); *Hamlet,* opera to a libretto in German (Hamburg, March 5, 1968). He publ. *Ballet Music: an Introduction* (London, 1958).

Seedo (Sydow), German musician active in London between 1720 and 1736; d. Potsdam, c. 1754. He was one of the earliest composers of English ballad-operas in London; contributed airs to a number of operatic and choreographic productions in Drury-Lane, London (*The Boarding-School, The Devil of a Duke, The Judgment of Paris, The Lottery,* etc.). Cf. Walter H. Rubsamen, *Mr. Seedo, Ballad Opera, and the Singspiel,* in *Miscelánea en Homenaje a Monseñor Higinio Anglés,* vol. II (Barcelona, 1958-61).

Seeger, Pete, American folk singer; son of Charles Seeger; nephew of the poet Alan Seeger; b. New York, May 3, 1919. After a brief study of social sciences at Harvard Univ., he became a traveling singer; formed two folksong groups, 'Almanac Singers' and 'Weavers'; served in the U.S. Army in 1942-45, and entertained U.S. troops in the Pacific. In 1963 he undertook a world-wide tour visiting Australia and many countries in Europe, including Russia where he was spectacularly successful. He publ. a manual, *How to Play the 5-String Banjo* (1948) and compiled several songbooks.

Segovia, Andrés. Date of birth Feb. 21 (not Feb. 17), 1893; the corrected date is confirmed by Segovia's birth certificate and his own corroborative statement. A commemorative plaque was affixed in 1969 to the house where he was born in Linares, honoring him as the 'hijo predilecto de la ciudad.'

Sehlbach, Oswald Erich, German composer; b. Wuppertal-Barmen, Nov. 18, 1898. He studied at the Leipzig Cons.; in 1928 was appointed to the faculty of the Folkwang-Schule in Essen as prof. of music theory. He wrote the operas *Die Stadt* (Krefeld, Feb. 1, 1935); *Galilei* (Essen, Feb. 10, 1937) and *Signor Caraffa* (Duisburg, March 19, 1938); 2 symphonies; sinfonietta for string orch.; piano concerto; concertino for flute and orch.; choral works; chamber music.

Seiber, Mátyás. Died in an automobile accident in Johannesburg, Sept. 25, 1960. Add to works: *The Invitation,* ballet (London, Dec. 30, 1960).

Seidel, Toscha. Died in Rosemead, Calif., Nov. 15, 1962.

Semkow, Georg (Jerzy), Polish conductor; b. Radomsko, Oct. 12, 1928. He studied at the Cracow Cons.; in 1950 was apprenticed to Eugene Mravinsky, conductor of the Leningrad Philharmonic; also conducted opera at the Bolshoi Theater in Moscow. In the meantime he continued studies in conducting with Tullio Serafin in Rome and Bruno Walter in Vienna. After serving as conductor of the National Polish Opera in Warsaw he received the conductorship of the Royal Opera House in Copenhagen. In the interim, he was guest conductor with numerous European orchestras; toured Japan with the London Philharmonic Orch. He made his U.S. debut in 1968 with the Boston Symph. Orch.; there followed appearances with the N.Y. Philharmonic, Chicago Symph. Orch., Cleveland Orch., etc. A conductor of the romantic school, he gives impassioned performances of the Vienna classics, Russian and Polish compositions; he is also adept in precise projections of modern scores.

Senaillé, Jean Baptiste. Although the spelling Senaillé is widely used, he signed his name Senallié, as did his father; contemporary editions of his music invariably use the form Senallié. Date of death, Oct. 15 (not Oct. 8), 1730.

Senart, Maurice. Died in Paris, May 23, 1962.

Sendrey, Albert. Add to works: *Bohème A-Go-Go,* rock 'n' roll opera on motives from Puccini's *La Bohème* (1971).

Senesino, Francesco. His voice was mezzo-soprano (not soprano).

Serafin, Tullio. Died in Rome, Feb. 2, 1968.

Serauky, Walter. Died in Leipzig, Aug. 20, 1959.

Serebrier, José, Uruguayan-American conductor and composer; b. Montevideo, Dec. 3, 1938. He began to conduct at the age of 12; received two Guggenheim Fellowships as composer. In 1950 settled in the U.S. Works: Symph. No. 1 (Houston, 1957); *Poema Elegiaco* (N. Y., Oct. 7, 1963); *Colores mágicos,* variations for harp and chamber orch. with 'Synchrona' images (5th Inter-American Music Festival, Washington, May 20, 1971).

Serendero-Proust, David, Chilean composer and conductor; b. Santiago, July 28, 1934. He studied violin and composition at the National Cons. of Music in Santiago; then went to Germany where he studied conducting in Stuttgart. In 1967 he was appointed conductor of the Orquesta Sinfónica de Chile in Santiago. As a composer, he follows the line of median modernism. Works: string trio (1952); *Duo heterogéneo* for flute and clarinet (1953); *El Ensayo,* a melodrama for soprano and 14 instruments (1962); *Estratos* for orch. (Mexico City, March 28, 1969, composer conducting).

Seress, Rezsö, Hungarian composer of popular songs; b. Budapest, Nov. 3, 1899; d. there, Jan. 12, 1968. He earned his living by playing piano and singing in restaurants and nightclubs; acquired fame in 1936 by his song *Gloomy Sunday,* which was banned in Hungary and several other countries because its ineffable sadness precipitated a wave of Sunday suicides among the young. Seress jumped out of a window from the second floor of his Budapest apartment on Jan. 8, 1968 (a Monday, not a Sunday), and died 4 days later.

Serini, Giovanni Battista, Italian composer; b. Cremona, c. 1724; date and place of death unknown. He was in the service of Robert d'Arcy, British ambassador in Venice (1744-46); subsequently was court musician in Bückeburg (1750-56). A collection of his instrumental and vocal works was found in the library at York Minster. Three keyboard sonatas are included in vol. 29 of *I Classici della Musica Italiana.* See Jack Pilgrim, *A Note on G. B. Serini* in the 'Mus. Times' (London, Aug. 1964).

Serkin, Peter, American pianist, son of Rudolf Serkin: b. New York, July 24, 1947. He made his public debut at the age of 10 as a student of his father, and at the age of 14 appeared with his father in Mozart's Concerto for 2 pianos and orch. with the Cleveland Orch. (April 19, 1962); then he started on a promising career of his own, specializing in ultra-modern music.

Serocki, Kazimierz. Add to works: *Episodes* for strings and 3 percussion groups (1959); *Segmenti* for 12 wind instruments, 6 string instruments, piano, celesta, harpsichord, harp, guitar, mandoline and 58 percussion instruments (1961).

Sessions, Roger. Symph. No. 4 was first performed in Minneapolis, Jan. 2, 1960. Add to works: Symph. No. 5 (Philadelphia, Feb. 7, 1964); opera, *Montezuma* (West Berlin, April 19, 1964); *Divertimento* for orch.

(Honolulu, Jan. 9, 1965); Symph. No. 6 (Newark, Nov. 19, 1966); Symph. No. 7 (Ann Arbor, Michigan, Oct. 1, 1967); Symph. No. 8 (N.Y., May 2, 1968); *Rhapsody for Orchestra* (Baltimore, March 18, 1970). He publ. *Questions About Music* (Cambridge, Mass., 1970).

Séverac, Déodat de. Date of birth, July 20, 1872 (not 1873).

Sevitzky, Fabien. Died in Athens, Greece, Feb. 2, 1967. Born Sept. 29, 1891 (not 1893).

Shaliapin, Feodor Ivanovitch. Add to bibl.: *An Autobiography as Told to Maxim Gorky* (N.Y., 1967); Jean Goury, *Fédor Chaliapine: Iconographie, Biographie, Discographie* (Paris, 1969).

Shankar, Rávi, Indian sitarist and composer; b. Benares, April 7, 1920. He was trained by his brother, Uday Shankar, and began his career as a musician and a dancer. He then engaged in a serious study of the Indian classical instrument, sitar, and in time became a great virtuoso on it. As a consequence of the growing infatuation with Oriental arts in Western countries, he suddenly became popular, and his concerts were greeted with reverential awe by youthful multitudes. This popularity increased a thousandfold when he was annexed by 'The Beatles' as a guest artist, placing him on the pedestal usually reserved for untutored guitar strummers. As a composer he distinguished himself by several film scores, including the famous *Pather Panchali;* he also wrote the film scores for *Kabulliwallah* and *Anuradha.* For the Tagore Centenary he wrote a ballet *Samanya Kshati,* based on Tagore's poem of the same name; it was produced in New Delhi on May 7, 1961. He publ. a memoir, *My Music, My Life* (N. Y., 1968).

Shapey, Ralph. Add to works: *Rituals* for orch. (Chicago, May 12, 1966); *Invocation—Concerto* for violin and orch. (N.Y., May 24, 1968).

Shaporin, Yuri Alexandrovitch. Died in Moscow, Dec. 9, 1966. Date of birth, Nov. 8, 1887 (not 1889). See S. Levit, *Y. A. Shaporin* (Moscow, 1964); Ivan Martynov, *Yuri Shaporin* (Moscow, 1966).

Shaw, Artie (real name Arthur Arshawsky), American clarinetist and band leader; b. New York, May 23, 1910. He played clarinet in bands as a boy; became a proponent of swing, attaining enormous popularity. Later he turned intellectual and publ. a quasi-autobiographical novel *The Trouble with Cinderella* (N.Y., 1952); went to live in Spain as a gesture of abdication from success. He was consecutively married to several famous motion picture stars, including Lana Turner and Ava Gardner; was married also to the sex authoress Kathleen Winsor.

Shaw, Martin. Died in Southwald, Sussex, Oct. 24, 1958.

Shchedrin, Rodion, Soviet composer; b. Moscow, Dec. 16, 1932. He studied at the Moscow Cons. with Shaporin, graduating in 1955. He developed an individual style distinguished by impulsive rhythm, broad melodic flow and sonorous harmonies; he excels particularly in theatrical music. His ballet *The Humpback Horse* (1955) has become a repertory piece in the Soviet Union; he also wrote an opera, *Not For Love Alone* (1964). Other works include a piano concerto (Moscow, June 10, 1954, composer soloist); *Chimes* for orch., commissioned by the N.Y. Philharmonic (N.Y., Jan. 11, 1968); piano quintet; three string quartets; a suite for clarinet and piano; many songs. He made an ingenious arrangement of fragments from Bizet's *Carmen* as a ballet suite, scored for strings and percussion, which he wrote for his wife, the ballerina Maya Plisetskya (1968).

Shearing, George Albert, English jazz pianist; b. London, Aug. 13, 1919. He was blind from birth; for several years he played piano in a blind band; then transferred himself to the U.S. and organized a quintet, with vibraphone, guitar, drums and bass; close harmony arrangements became the Shearing combo mark. He composed famous tunes, among them *Lullaby of Birdland.*

Shebalin, Vissarion Yakovlevitch. Died in Moscow, May 29, 1963. Add to works: *Sun Over the Steppes,* opera (Moscow, June 9, 1958); Symph. No. 5 (Moscow, Oct. 9, 1962). The total number of his string quartets is nine.

Shekhter, Boris Semionovitch. Died in Moscow, Dec. 16, 1961.

Sheridan, Frank. Died in New York, April 15, 1962.

Shifrin, Seymour J., American composer; b. New York, Feb. 28, 1926. He studied music at Columbia Univ. (M.A., 1949), and privately with William Schuman and Darius Milhaud. In 1952 he was appointed to the faculty of the Univ. of Calif., Berkeley. He held a Guggenheim Fellowship in composition twice, in 1956 and 1959. His works include 4 string quartets; a chamber symph.; *Satires of Circumstances,* for soprano and instruments; a cello sonata; *3 Pieces for Orchestra* (Minneapolis, Jan. 8, 1960); several song cycles.

Shimizu, Osamu. Add to works: operas, *The Charcoal Princess* (Osaka, Nov. 1, 1956); *The Man Who Shoots at the Blue Sky* (Osaka, Nov. 26, 1956); *Violoncellist Gauche* (Osaka, Oct. 11, 1957); *The Singing Skeleton* (Osaka, March 15, 1962); *The Banishment* (Osaka, Nov. 18, 1964); comic opera *Muko Erabi (The Marriage Contest;* Tokyo, March 14, 1969); historic opera, *Daibutsu-Kaigen* (on the inauguration of the great bronze statue of Buddha on April 9, 752 A.D.; produced in Tokyo, Oct. 2, 1970). the ballets, *The Earth* (1957); *Fire on the Plain* (1962); *Olympic Hymn* for chorus and orch. for the opening of the Olympic Games in Japan (Tokyo, Oct. 10, 1964); Symph. No. 2 (1957); Symph. No. 3 (1960); quartet for koto and strings; *Esquisses* for 3 kotos; about 300 choruses; songs.

Shindo, Tak, American composer; b. Sacramento, Calif. of Japanese parentage, Nov. 11, 1922. He studied music at the Univ. of Southern Calif., orchestration with Miklós Rózsa. As a musicologist he specialized in Japanese music. He became active as composer and arranger in various motion picture studios in Hollywood.

Shirinsky, Vassily Petrovitch. Died in Moscow, Aug. 16, 1965.

Shostakovitch, Dmitri Dmitrievitch. He was awarded the Order of Hero of Socialist Labor on the occasion of his 60th birthday in 1966. The ballet *The Limpid Brook* was first performed in Leningrad on April 4, (not June 4) 1935. Symph. No. 3 was first performed in Leningrad on Jan. 21, 1930 (not on Nov. 6, 1931). The première of *The Song of the Forests* took place in Leningrad on Nov. 15, 1949 (not in Moscow, Nov. 26, 1949). Symph. No. 4, composed in 1936, but withdrawn by the composer, was finally performed for the first time in Moscow on Jan. 20, 1962. His opera *Lady Macbeth of the District of Mtzensk* was performed for the first time under the changed name *Katerina Izmailova* at its Moscow production on Jan. 24, 1934. He revised the opera in 1962. Add to works: *Moskva Tcheryomushki,* operetta (Moscow, Jan. 24, 1959); cello concerto No. 1 (Leningrad, Oct. 4, 1959); string quartet No. 7 (1960); *Pictures of the Past,* a song cycle (1960); string quartet No. 8 (1960); Symph. No. 12, *The Year 1917,* dedicated to the memory of Lenin (1960; Leningrad, Oct. 1, 1961); Symph. No. 13 for orch., chorus and solo bass, to words by Evtushenko (1961; Moscow, Dec. 18, 1962; aroused controversy on account of the text recalling the massacre of Jews in Kiev by the Nazis and containing a warning against residual anti-Semitism in Soviet Russia); *Overture* on Russian and Kirghiz themes (1963); music for the film *Hamlet* (1963); string quartet No. 9 (1964); string quartet No. 10 (1964); *The Execution of Stepan Razin* for orch., mixed choir and bass, to words by Evtushenko (1964; Moscow, Dec. 28, 1964); *5 Songs* to texts from the Moscow comic magazine *Crocodile* (1965); string quartet No. 11 (1966); *Foreword to My Collected Works and a Brief Meditation About this Foreword* for bass voice and orch. (1966); cello concerto No. 2 (1966; Moscow, Sept. 25, 1966); *7 Songs* to words by Alexander Blok, vocal-instrumental suite for soprano, violin, cello and piano (1967); *Spring, Spring,* song to words by Pushkin (1967); violin concerto No. 2 (Moscow, Sept. 26, 1967); *Prelude* for orch., to the memory of the heroes of the Battle of Stalingrad (1967); *October,* symph. poem (Moscow, Sept. 26, 1967); music for the film *Sophie Perovskaya,* depicting the life and execution of one of the assassins of the Czar Alexander II (1967); string quartet No. 12, based on a 12-tone subject, being the first overt use of thematic dodecaphony by Shostakovitch (1968); violin sonata (1968); Symph. No. 14, for soprano, bass and chamber orch., in 11 sections, to texts by Federico García Lorca, Apollinaire, Rilke, and Wilhelm Küchelbecker (1969; Leningrad, Sept. 29, 1969); *Fidelity,* 8 ballads for male chorus (1970); music for the film *King Lear* (1970); string quartet No. 13 (1970). Add to bibl.: D. Rabinovitch, *Dmitri Shostakovitch, Composer* (Foreign Languages Publ. House, in English, Moscow, 1959); G. Ordzhonokidze, compiler, *Dmitri Shostakovitch,* collection of articles (Moscow, 1967).

Shtogarenko, Andrei, Ukrainian composer; b. Noviye Kaidaki, near Ekaterinoslav, Oct. 15, 1902. He studied at the Kharkov Cons., graduating in 1936. During World War II he worked in Turkmenia. In 1954 he was appointed director of the Kiev Cons. Virtually all of his music is devoted to Ukrainian subjects. Works: Symph. cantata, *My Ukraine* (1943); *Partisan Sketches* for orch. (1957); *The Dawn of Communism Has Come* for chorus, vocal soloists and orch. (1957); a choral symph., *Lenin Walks the Planet* (1958); several symph. suites; choruses.

Shulman, Alan. Date of birth, June 4 (not June 14), 1915. Delete 2nd symph.; the place and date (Great Neck, May 25, 1958) of its alleged première refers to a second performance of *Top Brass.* The suite for cello was composed in 1950 (not 1956). After 1960 he wrote mainly teaching pieces. In 1961 he became the cellist in the newly founded Philharmonic Trio.

Shure, Leonard, American pianist; b. Los Angeles, April 10, 1910. He studied in Berlin with Artur Schnabel; returning to the U.S. in 1933, he taught at the New England Cons. of Music; then was engaged at the School of Music of the Univ. of Texas in Austin. His manner of playing is sweepingly romantic and subjective. Although his primary activity was that of a teacher, he continues to give intermittent recitals.

Sibelius, Jean. Add to bibl.: S. Parmet, *The Symphonies of Sibelius: A Study in Musical Appreciation* (London, 1959; transl. from his 1955 monograph); H. E. Johnson, *Jean Sibelius* (N.Y., 1959); E. Tanzberger, *J. Sibelius* (Wiesbaden, 1962).

Sicilianos, Yorgo, Greek composer; b. Athens, Aug. 29, 1922. He studied law at the Univ. of Athens and music at the Cons. there, graduating in 1951. He then went to Rome where he studied with Pizzetti at the Santa Cecilia Academy. In 1955 he obtained a Fulbright Scholarship and went to Harvard Univ. for a year's study with Walter Piston: he also took courses with Boris Blacher in Tanglewood and with Vincent Persichetti at the Juilliard School of Music in New York. Upon his return to Athens, he held various posts with the Hellenic Broadcasting Institute. His music is neo-classical in formal outline, atonal and polytonal in harmonic idiom; in his later works he makes use of serial techniques. Compositions: *Prelude and Dance* for orch. (Athens Radio, Sept. 1, 1948); *The Revelation of the Fifth Seal,* symph. poem (Athens, May 11, 1952); string quartet No. 1 (1952); concertino for 5 wind instruments and string orch. (Rome, June 9, 1953); *Concerto for Orchestra* (Athens, Nov. 28, 1954); string quartet No. 2 (1955); Symph. No. 1 (N. Y. Philharmonic, Dimitri Mitropoulos conducting, March 1, 1958); string quartet No. 3 (1957-62); *Tanagra,* a ballet for 2 pianos and percussion (Athens, April 21, 1958; orch. version, Athens, Feb. 5, 1962); *Iphigenia in Tauris,* incidental music to Euripides' play (Epidaurus, June 15, 1958); *Bacchantes,* orch. suite from a ballet after Euripides (Athens, Jan. 11, 1960); incidental music to *Hercules furens,* after a play of Euripides (Epidaurus, 1960); *Synthesis* for double string orch. and percussion (Athens, Nov. 26, 1962).

Siegmeister, Elie. In 1966 he was appointed composer-in-residence at Hofstra Univ. in Long Island. Add to works: *The Mermaid in Lock No. 7* (Pittsburgh, July 10, 1958); *Cordura Suite* for orch. (Indianapolis, Nov. 28, 1959); flute concerto (1960); string quartet No. 2 (1960); 3-act opera *The Plough and the Stars* (St. Louis, May 15, 1963); sextet for brass and percussion (1965); *Fantasy and Soliloquy* for cello solo (1965); piano sonata No. 2 (1965); violin sonata No. 3 (1966); *I Have a Dream* for baritone, chorus, narrator and piano, to words from Martin Luther King's speech (1967); *The Face of War* for baritone and orch. to words by Langston Hughes (1968); *Contrasts* for bassoon and piano (1970); *Five Fantasies of the Theater* (1970). He publ. a manual, *Harmony and Melody* (2 vols.; Belmont, Calif., 1965-66).

Siepi, Cesare. Made his debut in 1941 as Sparafucile (not as Rigoletto).

Sigubjörnsson, Thorkell, Icelandic composer; b. Reykjavik, July 16, 1938. He went to America and took courses in electronic music at the Univ. of Illinois. Returning to Reykjavik he founded there a modern group 'Musica Nova.' In his works he combines traditional modalities with electronics. Among his compositions are *Flökt* for orch. (1962); *Capricer* for piano and orch. (1968); piano pieces; songs.

Sills, Beverly, American soprano; b. Brooklyn, May 25, 1929. Her real name was Belle Silverman; at the age of three she appeared on the radio as Bubbles. At the age of 12 she began to study music seriously, singing with Estelle Liebling and piano with Paolo Gallico. From acting soap-operas on the radio she gradually progressed to grand opera; appeared with the Philadelphia Civic Opera, and the N.Y. City Opera. On July 7, 1956 she created the role of Baby Doe in Douglas Moore's folk opera *The Ballad of Baby Doe,* at Central City, Colorado. Eventually she launched a brilliantly successful career; appeared at La Scala in Milan; at the Teatro Colón in Buenos Aires, and other famous opera houses; was acclaimed by the most fastidious European and American critics as a stellar diva of the first magnitude.

Silva, Luigi. Died in New York, Nov. 29, 1961.

Silva, Oscar da. Died in Oporto, March 6, 1958.

Silverstein, Joseph, American violinist; b. Detroit, March 21, 1932. He studied with his father and with Efrem Zimbalist at the Curtis Institute of Music in Philadelphia; later with Joseph Gingold and Mischa Mischakoff. He played in the Houston Orch., Denver Orch. and the Philadelphia Orch. In 1955 he joined the Boston Symph. Orch., and in 1961 was appointed its concertmaster. He also appeared as soloist.

Silvestri, Constantin, Rumanian conductor; b. Bucharest, May 31, 1913; d. London, Feb. 23, 1969. He studied composition with Georges Enesco; toured as pianist; then was engaged as conductor of the Bucharest Philharmonic (1946-55); also conducted the Bucharest Opera. In 1961 he went to England, where he became the principal conductor of the Bournemouth Symphony Orchestra.

Silvestrov, Valentin, Ukrainian composer; b. Kiev, Sept. 30, 1937. He studied with Liatoshinsky at the Kiev Cons.; began to compose in a boldly experimental idiom of Western provenance; wrote piano pieces in the strict 12-tone technique. Although severely reprimanded in the press, he was not forcibly restrained from continuing to write music in a modernistic manner. Works: for piano: *Variations* (1958), sonatina (1959), sonata (1960), *Signals* (1962), *Serenade* (1962), piano quintet (1961); *Quartetto piccolo* for string quartet (1961); trio for flute, trumpet and celesta (1962). Some of his compositions had their world premières at European festivals of modern music.

Simić, Borivoje, Serbian conductor and composer; b. Belgrade, Nov. 1, 1920. He studied in Belgrade and became a choral conductor of the Belgrade Radio. His music is modernistic in nature and eclectic in its materials, making use of a dissonant counterpoint and jazz. His *Movimento dinamico* (Belgrade, Sept. 30, 1955) is characteristic in this respect.

Simon, Alicia. Died in Lodz, May 23, 1957. She was prof. at the Univ. of Lodz from 1945.

Simon, Anton. Born Aug. 5, 1850 (not 1851); died in St. Petersburg, Feb. 1, 1916 (not 1918).

Simpson, George Elliott. Died in Kansas City, Oct. 8, 1958.

Simpson, Robert. He obtained his Mus. D. degree at Durham Univ. in 1951 (not 1952); joined the staff of the B.B.C. also in 1951. The first performance of his Symph. No. 1, in one continuous movement, was given by the Danish State Radio Orch. in Copenhagen on June 11, 1953. Add to works: Symph. No. 2 (1955; Cheltenham Festival, July 16, 1957); Symph. No. 3 (1962; Birmingham, March 14, 1963); Symph. No. 4 (1971); *Variations and Fugue* for recorder and string quartet (1958); violin concerto (1959; Birmingham, Feb. 25, 1960); piano concerto (Cheltenham Festival, July 14, 1967); trio for clarinet, cello and piano (1967); quintet for clarinet and strings (1968). He publ. in addition to his basic monograph on Nielsen (1952), *The Essence of Bruckner* (London, 1967) and 3 B.B.C. booklets: *Bruckner and the Symphony* (1963), *Sibelius and Nielsen* (1965); *Beethoven's Symphonies* (1970); also edited *The Symphony* (2 vols.; London, 1967).

Simrock, Nikolaus. Born in Mainz, Aug. 23, 1751 (not 1752); died in Bonn, June 12, 1832 (not 1833). Was a member of the Electoral Orch. in Bonn until the spring of 1794. During Beethoven's lifetime Simrock's catalogue listed 85 Beethoven works, including original compositions, reprints and arrangements.

Sims, Ezra, American composer; b. Birmingham, Alabama, Jan. 16, 1928. He studied at the Birmingham Cons. of Music (1945-48), with Quincy Porter at Yale Univ. (B.M., 1952) and with Darius Milhaud and Leon Kirchner at Mills College (M.A., 1955). He subsequently settled in Cambridge, Mass. His music incorporates experimental techniques, including microtones and electronic collage. Works: *Chamber Cantata on Chinese Poems* (1954); cello sonata (1957); string quartet No. 1 (1959); *Sonate Concertanti* for 'demountable octet,' consisting of 5 sonatinas for oboe, viola, cello and bass, and 5 sonatas for 2 string quartets (1961-62); string quartet No. 2 (1962); *Octet* for strings in quartertones and sixth-tones (1964); *Antimatter* for magnetic tape collage (1968); *Real Toads,* musique concrète (1970); *More Overture and Another Interlude* for tape collage with musique concrète (1970).

Sinatra, Frank (Francis Albert), popular American singer; b. Hoboken, N.J., Dec. 12, 1915, of immigrant Italian parents. He sang in a glee club in school; appeared on amateur radio shows. Inspired by the tone production of Tommy Dorsey's trombone playing, he evolved, by convex inhalation from a corner of the mouth, a *sui generis* 'mal canto' in *sotto voce* delivery, employing a Caruso-like *coup-de-glotte* at climactic points. This mode of singing, combined with an engagingly slender physique, stirred the young females of the World War II era to fainting frenzy at his performances. Sinatra's press agents were quick to exploit the phenomenon, dubbing him 'Swoonlight Sinatra.' He eventually overcame his anesthetic appeal and became a successful baritone crooner; like most of his colleagues, he never learned to read music. He revealed an unexpected dramatic talent as a movie actor, eliciting praise from astonished cinema critics. In 1971 he announced his decision to retire from the entertainment world, so as to be able to devote his energies to transcendental meditation on the problems of life. See E. J. Kahn, *The Voice: The Story of an American Phenomenon* (N .Y., 1947).

Skinner, Ernest M. Died in Duxbury, Mass., Nov. 27, 1960.

Sklavos, Georges, Greek composer; b. Brailov, Rumania, of Greek parents, Aug. 20, 1888. He studied with Armand Marsick at the Athens Cons.; was appointed instructor there in 1913. He devoted himself chiefly to the musical theater. Works: operas: *Lestenitza* (Athens, March 14, 1947), *Kassiani* (Oct. 30, 1959), *Amphitryon* (1960); symph. poems: *L'Aigle* (1922); ethnically colored orchestral pieces: *Fantaisie crétoise, Noces insulaires, Suite arcadienne;* choruses; songs.

Škroup, Franz. *Libušin snatek (Libusa's Marriage)* was produced in its entirety on April 11, 1850; only the 3rd act was performed on Nov. 6, 1835.

Skrowaczewski, Stanislaw. From 1946 began to give increasing attention to his career as symph. conductor. He led the Wroclaw Philharmonic (1946-47), the Katowice Philharmonic Orch. (1949-54) and the Warsaw Philharmonic (1957-59). He made his U.S. debut with the Cleveland Orch. on Dec. 4, 1958; was guest conductor with the Cincinnati Symph. Orch., Pittsburgh Symph. Orch. and the N.Y. Philharmonic (1958-60); also conducted in South America. In 1960 he was appointed conductor and music director of the Minneapolis Symph. Orch., renamed in 1970 as Minnesota Orchestra.

Slavický, Klement, Czech composer; b. Tovačov. Sept. 22, 1910. He studied at the Prague Cons. with K. B. Jirák. Works: *Fantasy* for piano and orch. (1931); string quartet (1933); *Sinfonietta* (1941); *Rhapsodic Variations* for orch. (1953); chamber music; educational pieces for children.

Slezak, Leo. His book *Rückfall* was publ. in 1940 (not 1930).

Slobodskaya, Oda, Russian soprano; b. Vilna, Nov. 28, 1889; d. London, July 30, 1970. She studied voice at the St. Petersburg Cons.; made her opera debut in Petrograd in 1918. In 1922 she went to Paris; in 1931 settled in London, where she appeared as a music hall singer under the pseudonym Odali Careno for a few seasons; in 1932 sang Venus in *Tannhäuser* at Covent Garden; in the interim she appeared at La Scala in Milan and at the Teatro Colón in Buenos Aires.

Slonimsky, Nicolas. In 1962-63, traveled in Russia, Poland, Yugoslavia, Bulgaria, Rumania, Greece and Israel under the auspices of the State Dept. In 1964, appointed Lecturer in Music at the Univ. of Calif., Los Angeles; was retired in 1967, ostensibly for superannuation and recessive infantiloquy, but continued to agitate. Add to compositions: *Möbius Strip Tease* for soprano and tenor, a unilateral perpetual rondo in a linearly dodecaphonic vertically consonant counterpoint, notated on Möbius bands rotated around the singers' heads (world première at the Arrière-Garde Coffee Concert, with the composer at the piano obbligato, Univ. of Calif., Los Angeles, May 5, 1965). Add to publications: *Music Since 1900,* 4th ed., greatly enlarged (N. Y., 1971). For a complete list of works, see *Composers of America,* vol. 15 (Washington. 1969). He contributed a valuable research paper *Sex and the Music Librarian* to a symposium of the Music Library Association (Chapel Hill, N. C., Feb. 2, 1968; delivered by proxy).

Slonimsky, Sergey, Soviet composer, nephew of Nicolas Slonimsky; b. Leningrad, Aug. 12, 1932. He studied with Boris Arapov and Orest Evlakhov at the Leningrad Cons., graduating in 1955. In 1958 he was appointed instructor in theory there. His style of composition is in the tradition of Soviet modernism, evolving towards considerable complexity of texture and boldness of idiom. Works: *Carnival Overture* (1957); symph. (Leningrad, March 11, 1962); *Songs of Freedom,* on Russian folk motives for mezzo-soprano, baritone and piano (1957; orchestral version, 1962); suite for viola and piano (1959); sonata for unaccompanied violin (1961); piano sonata (1963); *Concerto buffo* for chamber orch. (Leningrad, April 28, 1966); *Virineya,* music drama (Leningrad, Sept. 30, 1967); *Antiphones* for string quartet, in non-tempered tuning and 'ambulatory' counterpoint, with the performers instructed to walk about the hall and the stage while playing (1969); *Farewell to a Friend,* a vocal scene for high voice and piano (1970); *Icarus,* ballet (Moscow, May 30, 1971).

Smallens, Alexander. He retired in 1958 and went to live in Taormina, Sicily.

Smalley, Roger, English composer; b. Swinton, near Manchester, July 26, 1943. He studied at the Royal College of Music in London with Antony Hopkins (piano) and Peter Racine Fricker (composition); later attended courses in new music with Stockhausen in Cologne. In 1967, he became Artist-in-Residence at King's College, Cambridge. In 1970 he formed a new ensemble called 'Intermodulation' to promote socially unacceptable music. In this antagonistic manner he wrote *Strata* for 15 string players (1970) and *Beat Music* for 55 players (London, Aug. 12, 1971). But he also composed an austere *Missa Brevis.*

Smareglia, Antonio. Add bibl.: Silvio Benco, *Ricordi di Antonio Smareglia* (1968).

Smetáček, Václav, Czech conductor; b. Brno, Sept. 30, 1906. He studied oboe at the Prague Cons.; was first oboist in the Czech Philharmonic Orch. (1930-33); also studied composition with Jaroslav Křička at Charles Univ. in Prague. In 1934 he embarked on his chief career as conductor; led the choral society Hlahol in Prague; then enlarged his activities into the field of opera and symphonic music; has made numerous appearances as guest conductor all over Europe, in America and in Japan.

Smetana, Bedřich. Add bibl.: Brian Large, *Smetana* (N. Y., 1970).

Smeterlin, Jan, Polish pianist; b. Bielsko, Poland, Feb. 7, 1892; d. London, Jan. 18, 1967. He was a child prodigy; made his first concert appearance at the age of 8; toured widely as a concert pianist, eventually settling in London. He was praised for his congenially romantic interpretations of Chopin's music.

Smith, Bessie (Elizabeth), black 'blues' singer; b. Chattanooga, Tennessee, April 15, 1895; d. in an automobile accident, Sept. 26, 1937, on a highway outside Clarksdale, Miss., of injuries aggravated by a delay in sending a segregated negritudinal ambulance. Born in a wretchedly poor family, she joined the 'Rabbit Foot Minstrels' and developed a style of singing that rapidly brought her fame. Her first record, *Down Hearted Blues,* sold 800,000 copies in 1923, and she was billed as the 'Empress of the Blues.' Although entirely untutored, she was able to sing with precise intonation and syllabify the text with perfect clarity; she developed a consummate art of melismatic ornamentation against a background of constantly shifting harmonies. Bibl.: Carman Moore, *Somebody's Angel Child* (N. Y., 1969).

Smith, Carleton Sprague. Resigned as Chief of the Music Division of the N.Y. Public Library in 1959.

Smith, Leland, American composer; b. Oakland, Calif., Aug. 6, 1925. He studied composition at Mills College with Darius Milhaud (1941-43) and at Univ. of California, Berkeley, with Roger Sessions (1946-48), obtaining his A.B. and M.A. degrees; also took courses in musicology there with Manfred Bukofzer. He subsequently attended classes of Olivier Messiaen at the Paris Cons. (1948-49). In 1950 he was appointed to the music faculty of the Univ. of California at Berkeley; other posts included Mills College (summer classes between 1951 and 1961) and Univ. of Chicago (1952-58). In 1958 he joined the faculty at Stanford Univ.; became a professor in 1968. His style of composition is that of liberal vigesimosecular modernism marked by a discriminate application of eclectic idioms, not excluding triadic usages. Works: sonata for trumpet and piano (1947); trio for flute, cello and piano (1947); trio for violin, trumpet and clarinet (1948); *Divertimento No. 1* for 5 instruments (1949); Symph. No. 1 (1951); woodwind quintet (1951); Sonata for Heckelphone (or viola) and piano (1954); *Santa Claus,* opera in 5 scenes on the libretto by E. E. Cummings (1955); *Concerto for Orchestra* (1956); quintet for bassoon and strings (1956); *Divertimento No. 2* for chamber orch. (1957); *3 Pacifist Songs* (1960); wind trio (1960); quartet for horn, violin, cello and piano (1961); *Orpheus* for guitar, harp and harpsichord (1967); *Machines of Loving Grace* for computer, bassoon and narrator (1970). He publ. *Handbook of Harmonic Analysis* (Stanford, 1963).

Smith, Moses, American music critic; b. Chelsea, Mass., March 4, 1901; d. Boston, July 27, 1964. He studied law at Harvard Univ. (graduated 1924) and also music. He was music critic of the 'Boston American' (1924-34) and of the 'Boston Evening Transcript' (1934-39); then was appointed music director of the Columbia Phonograph Co. (1939-42). In 1947 he published a controversial biography of Koussevitzky, who brought a libel suit for a million dollars against Smith and his publisher, claiming that the book described him as "generally incompetent, brutal to the musicians and a poseur." The suit, however, was dismissed.

Smith, William O., American composer; b. Sacramento, California, Sept. 22, 1926. He studied clarinet and took courses in composition with Darius Milhaud at Mills College, Oakland, Calif., and with Roger Sessions at the Univ. of Calif., Berkeley (M.A., 1952). He taught clarinet in various institutions in Calif.; in 1960 received a Guggenheim Fellowship. Works: Suite for clarinet, flute and trumpet (1947); *Serenade* for flute, violin, trumpet and clarinet (1947); *Schizophrenic Scherzo* for clarinet, trumpet, saxophone and trombone (1947); clarinet sonata (1948); *Concertino* for trumpet and jazz instruments (1948); quintet for clarinet and string quartet (1950); string quartet (1952); *Capriccio* for violin and piano (1952); suite for violin and clarinet (1952); *Divertimento* for jazz instruments (1956); concerto for clarinet and combo (1957); trio for clarinet, violin and piano (1957); quartet for clarinet, violin, cello and piano (1958); 5 pieces for clarinet alone (1958); *Quadrodram* for clarinet, trombone, piano, percussion, dancer and film (Seattle, Dec. 9, 1970).

Smolensky, Stepan Vassilievitch. First name properly Stefan (not Stepan). Place of death. Vasilsursk, near Nizhny-Novgorod (not Kazan).

Smyth, Ethel. Add to bibl.: C. St. John, *Ethel Smyth: A Biography* (N.Y., 1959).

Sobolewski, Eduard de. Full name. Friedrich Eduard. He died May 17 (not May 18), 1872.

Socor, Matei, Rumanian composer and conductor; b. Jassy, Sept. 28, 1908. He studied with Castaldi at the Bucharest Cons. (1927-29) and at Leipzig Cons. with Karg-Elert. Works: *Passacaglia* for cello and orch. (1944); violin concerto (1955); the oratorio *Stejarul din Borzesti (Oaks of Borzesti)*; mass choruses.

Sokoloff, Nicolai. Died in La Jolla, Calif., Sept. 25, 1965. He habitually spelled his first name Nikolai.

Solares, Enrique, Guatemalan pianist and composer; b. Guatemala City, July 11, 1910. He studied piano with Salvador Ley in Guatemala, with Ernst Bacon in San Francisco and with Alfredo Casella in Rome; composition with Ricardo Castillo in Guatemala, Raymond Moulart in Brussels and Jaroslav Křička in Prague. In 1948 he entered the diplomatic service of Guatemala while continuing his musical activities. His *Partita Clásica* received a prize at the Central American Competition in 1947. He further wrote a string quartet; guitar pieces; choruses.

Sollberger, Harvey, American flutist and composer; b. Cedar Rapids, Iowa, May 11, 1938. He studied composition with Philip Bezanson at the Univ. of Iowa and with Jack Beeson and Otto Luening at Columbia Univ. (M.A. 1964). In 1965-71 he was on the staff of Columbia Univ. In his music he employs an imaginatively applied serial method. Works: Trio for flute, cello and piano (1961); *Grand Quartet* for flutes (1962); *Solos* for violin and 5 instruments (1962); *Two Oboes Troping* (1963); *Chamber Variations* for 12 players and conductor (1964); *Musica Transalpina* for soprano, baritone and 6 players (1965).

Solti, Georg. He made his first appearance as conductor at the Metropolitan Opera, N. Y., on Dec. 17, 1960. His appointment as music director of the Los Angeles Philharmonic, effective for 1961-62, collapsed when the orchestra board refused to grant him full powers of engaging guest conductors and other artists. He was music director of the Royal Opera at Covent Garden, London from 1961 to 1971. In 1969 he was appointed conductor of the Chicago Symph. Orch. In 1971 he accepted the post of conductor of the Orchestre Symphonique de Paris, to be filled synchronously with his Chicago duties. In addition to all these positions, he was named Musical Counselor of the Paris Grand Opéra, effective as of 1973. Regarded as a foremost conductor of Wagner's operas, he is also praised for his impeccable interpretations of symphonic masterpieces and his sovereign ability to elicit the finest nuances of tone color from the orchestra.

Soltys, Adam. Died in Lwow, July 6, 1968.

Soltys, Miecyslaw. First name should be spelled Mieczyslaw.

Somer, Hilde, Austrian-American pianist; b. Vienna, Feb. 11, 1930. She studied piano with her mother; appeared in public as a child prodigy; in 1938 was taken to the U.S.; at the age of 14, she enrolled at the Curtis Institute of Music in Philadelphia as a student of Rudolf Serkin, and also took private lessons with Moritz Rosenthal, Wanda Landowska and Claudio Arrau. Soon she embarked on an energetic career in recital and with orchestras in Europe and America. While preserving her native sentiment for the Viennese classics, she boldly plunged into the world of modern music, with a special predilection for American and Latin American composers. She gave world premières of piano concertos by John Corigliano, Jr. (San Antonio, April 5, 1968) and Antonio Tauriello (Washington, June 30, 1968). Her greatest distinction is her fervent revival of Scriabin for whose music she has a peculiarly intimate affinity; she was the first pianist to make a tour of concerts playing Scriabin's music with the accompaniment of moving colored lights and shadows projected onto a screen and imaginatively modulated according to Scriabin's own synesthetic associations of sound and color.

Somers, Harry Stewart. Add to works: piano sonata No. 5 (1957); string quartet No. 3 (1959); *Lyric* for orch (1960); *5 Concepts* for orch. (1962); symph. for winds, brass and percussion (1962); *Stereophony* for orch. (Toronto, March 19, 1963); *The House of Atreus,* ballet (Ottawa, Jan. 13, 1964); *12 Miniatures* for soprano, flute, cello and harpsichord (1964); *Picasso Suite* for orch. (Saskatoon, Canada, Feb. 28, 1965); *Louis Riel,* historical opera (Toronto, Sept. 23, 1967).

Somis, Giovanni Battista. The 2 volumes of *Sonate,* op. 1 and op. 2 are not by him, but by his brother Lorenzo Giovanni Somis.

Sommer, Vladimír, Czech composer; b. Dolní Jiřetín, near Most, Feb. 28, 1921. He studied at the Prague Cons.; became an arranger on the radio. His most ambitious work is a *Vocal Symphony* to texts by Dostoyevsky, Kafka and Cesare Pavese (Prague, March 12, 1963). Other works are: violin concerto (1950); piano concerto (1951); string quartet (1955).

Sonnleithner, Joseph von. Eliminate the nobility particle von. He was never ennobled. Exact date of birth, March 3, 1766 (not 1765).

Sontag, Henriette. Add bibliography: Frank Russell, *Queen of Song, The Life of Henriette Sontag, Countess de Rossi* (N.Y., 1964).

Sorabji, Kaikhosru. About 1950 he wrote his *Opus Archimagicum* for piano, a work of enormous proportions. About the same time he prohibited public performances of any of his works.

Soriano, Alberto, Uruguayan composer; b. Santiago del Estero, Argentina, Feb. 5, 1915. He studied violin in Bahia, Brazil; in 1937 went to Montevideo, where he settled. In his music he makes use of South American melorhythms, while retaining fundamental classical forms. Works: piano concerto (1952); guitar concerto No. 1 (1952); *Sinfonietta* for guitar, cello, bassoon and flute (1952); *4 Rituales sinfónicos* (1953); *Divertimento* for bassoon and string orch. (1954); cello sonata (1955); violin concerto (1956); guitar concerto No. 2 (1957); violin sonata (1959); piano trio (1961); *Canticos sinfónicos a la Revolución de Cuba* (1961); Concertino for cello and orch. (1961); *Pastoral de Sibiu* for flute and orch. (1962); *Tríptico de Praga* for orch. (1962); *Tiempo sinfónico para los caidos en Buchenwald* (1962).

Souris, André. Died in Paris, Feb. 12, 1970. He was director of the Brussels Cons. from 1949 till his death.

Souster, Tim, English composer of the extreme avant-garde; b. Bletchley, Buckinghamshire, Jan. 29, 1943. He studied music theory at New College in Oxford; in 1963 attended courses in new music given by Stockhausen and Berio in Darmstadt. Back in England, he became one of the most articulate exponents of serial, aleatory and combinatorialitarian ideas, in which electronic media are employed in conjunction with acoustical performances by humans; he expounded these ideas in his writings in 'The Listener,' 'Tempo' and other progressive publications. In 1969 he was a co-founder of the Intermodulation Group, with the aim of presenting works by congenial composers and experimenters. In 1969-71 he was composer in residence at King's College in Cambridge. His works include *Songs of the Seasons* for soprano and viola (1965); *Poem in Depression* for soprano, flute, viola, cello and piano (1965); *Parallels* for 2 percussion players (1966); *Metropolitan Games* for piano duet (1967); *Titus Groan Music* for wind quintet, electronics and magnetic tape (1969); *Chinese Whispers* for percussion and 3 electronic synthesizers (1970); *Waste Land Music* for soprano saxophone, modulated piano, modulated organ and electronic synthesizer (London, July 14, 1970); *Triple Music II* for 3 orchestras (London, Aug. 13, 1970).

Souzay, Gérard (real name, Gérard Marcel Tisserand), French baritone; b. Angers,

Dec. 8, 1920. He studied with Vanni-Marcoux and others at the Paris Cons.; specialized in French art songs and German lieder, but also earned distinction as interpreter of operatic parts, among them Count Almaviva in Mozart's *Le Nozze di Figaro* and Golaud in Debussy's *Pelléas et Mélisande.* He made his American debut as an opera singer in 1960 with the New York City Opera; on Jan. 21, 1965, he appeared with the Metropolitan Opera in N. Y. as Count Almaviva.

Sowande, Fela, Nigerian composer; b. Oyo, Nigeria, May 29, 1905; studied music in Lagos; then went to London where he played in a combo in night clubs; at the same time he took courses at London Univ. and Trinity College of Music. He served in the Royal Air Force during World War II. In 1944 he composed an *African Suite* for strings; returned to Nigeria in 1953; in 1957 he received a grant from the State Dept. to travel in the U.S.; was again in the U.S. in 1961, on a Rockefeller grant, and on June 1, 1961 conducted a group of members of the New York Philharmonic in Carnegie Hall in a program of his own compositions, among them a *Nigerian Folk Symphony.* Upon returning to Nigeria, he joined the staff of the Univ. College at Ibadan. In his music he pursues the goal of cultural integration of native folk material with western art forms.

Sowerby, Leo. Died in Port Clinton, Ohio, July 7, 1968. In 1962 he resigned as organist and choirmaster of the Cathedral of St. James', Chicago, and as prof. at the American Cons. of Music in Chicago. In the same year he was named director of the College for Church Musicians at the National Cathedral in Washington, D.C. Add to the list of works: piano concerto with soprano obbligato (Chicago, Jan. 17, 1917); 1st cello concerto (Chicago, Jan. 17, 1917); 2nd cello concerto (N.Y., April 2, 1935); piano concerto in F (Chicago, March 6, 1920); piano concerto No. 2 (Boston, Nov. 30, 1936); *Medieval Poem* for organ and orch. (Chicago, April 20, 1926). *From the Northland* was composed in 1922-23 (not in 1927) and first performed in Rome on May 27, 1924.

Spadavecchia, Antonio. Add to works: opera *Yukki* (1970).

Spaeth, Sigmund. Died in New York, Nov. 11, 1965. Add to books: *50 Years of Music* (N.Y., 1959).

Spalding, Walter Raymond. Died in Cambridge, Mass., Feb. 10, 1962.

Spelman, Timothy Mather. Died in Florence, Italy, Aug. 21, 1970.

Spencer, Émile-Alexis-Xavier, French composer; b. Brussels, May 24, 1859; d. Nanterre (Seine), May 24, 1921. He studied piano in Brussels; in 1881 went to Paris where he found his métier as a composer for vaudeville; was credited with about 4,000 chansonettes, which were popularized by famous singers, among them Yvette Guilbert. His chanson *Jambes de bois* was used by Stravinsky in *Pétrouchka* under the impression that it was a folk song; when Spencer brought an action for infringement on his authorship, Stravinsky agreed to pay him part of the royalties for performances.

Spilka, František. His opera *Stará práva* was produced in Prague on June 10, 1917 (not May 10, 1907).

Spisak, Michal. Died in Paris, Jan. 29, 1965.

Spitalny, Phil, American conductor of popular music; b. Odessa, Russia, Nov. 7, 1889; d. Miami, Florida, Oct. 11, 1970. He emigrated to the United States in 1905; played clarinet in various bands. In 1934 he conceived the idea of organizing an instrumental ensemble consisting only of girls of nubile age and engaging exterior; in 1935 he inaugurated the radio program 'Hour of Charm' with his group. In 1937 he won the award of merit of the Radio Committee of the Women's National Exposition of Arts and Industries. With the advent of television, Spitalny's radio program fell into terminal desuetude, and he went to Florida. He was also an amateur composer; made arrangements of amorous songs, among them *The Kiss I Can't Forget.*

Spitzmueller, Alexander. Died in Paris, Nov. 12, 1962.

Spohr, Ludwig (Louis). Add to bibl.: Dorothy M. Mayer, *The Forgotten Master: The Life and Times of Louis Spohr* (London, 1959).

Spontini, Gasparo (Luigi Pacifico). The first name is Gaspare, not Gasparo.

Spross, Charles Gilbert. Died in Poughkeepsie, Dec. 23, 1961.

Squire, William Henry. Died in London, March 17, 1963.

Srebotnjak, Alojz, Slovenian composer; b. Postojna, April 27, 1931. He studied in Ljubljana, Siena, Rome and London. In a few years he went through several avatars undergoing transitions from neo-classicism to expressionism to serialism. Works: *Fantasia notturna* for 3 violins, clarinet and harp (1956); *Sinfonietta in due tempi* (1958); *Ekstaza smrti (Ecstasy of Death)* for baritone, French horn and orch. (1961); *Monologi* for flute, oboe, French horn, timpani and strings (1962); *Antifona* for orch. (1964); *Microsongs* for voice and 13 instruments (1964); 3 Sonatinas for violin and piano (1957, 1966, 1968); *Episodes* for orch. (1967); songs; film music.

Stabile, Mariano, Italian baritone; b. Palermo, May 12, 1888; d. Milan, Jan. 11, 1968. He studied voice at the Santa Cecilia Academy in Rome, and made his debut in Palermo in 1909. For a number of seasons he sang in provincial opera houses in Italy. The turning point in his career came when he was engaged by Toscanini to sing Falstaff in Verdi's opera at La Scala (Dec. 26, 1921). He triumphed and the role became his major success; he sang it more than a thousand times. He was also noted as the interpreter of the part of Rigoletto. He retired from the stage in 1960.

Stainov, Petko. Add bibl.: V. Krstev, *Petko Stainov* (Sofia, 1957).

Starer, Robert. Add to works: concerto for viola, strings and percussion (Geneva, July 3, 1959); *Concerto* for violin, cello and orch. (Pittsburgh, Oct. 11, 1968).

Starker, Janos, Hungarian-American cellist; b. Budapest, July 5, 1924. He made his first appearance as a soloist at the age of ten. After graduating from the Budapest Academy of Music, he was first cellist at the Budapest Opera. He left Hungary in 1946; settled in the U.S. in 1948; held the positions of first cellist in the Dallas Symph. Orch., the Metropolitan Opera Orch. and the Chicago Symph. Orch. In 1958 he was appointed prof. at Indiana Univ. in Bloomington. He toured widely in Europe and America in solo recitals.

Starr, 'Ringo' (real name **Richard Starkey**), English drummer, member of the celebrated Liverpudlian vocal quartet The Beatles; b. Liverpool, July 7, 1940 (delivered by forceps on account of his enormous puerperal bulk). His nickname 'Ringo' originated from his ostentatious habit of wearing several rings on each of his fingers. As an adolescent, he performed menial jobs, as a messenger boy for British railways, a barman on a boat, etc. A sickly boy, he spent several years in hospitals to cure an effusion on the lung, but he played drums in ward bands. He spontaneously evolved a rhythmic technique of an overwhelming animal vitality. In 1962, Ringo Starr joined The Beatles; his association with them continued until the dissolution of the group in 1970. His histrionic ability in handling the drums became the most striking visual feature in the beatlophonic ritual, contributing much to mass frenzy that attended their shows wherever The Beatles went. See Hunter Davies, *The Beatles,* 'the authorized biography,' (N.Y., 1968).

Staryk, Steven, Canadian-American violinist of Ukrainian parentage; b. Toronto, April 28, 1932. He studied with 15 different teachers before and after enrolling in the Royal Cons. of Music in Toronto; at the age of 24 he became concertmaster of the Royal Philharmonic Orch. of London; then concertmaster of the Concertgebouw Orch. of Amsterdam (1960) and of the Chicago Symph. (1963); also taught at the Amsterdam Cons. As a soloist he appeared all over Europe, Canada, the U.S. and in Japan. In 1969 he was appointed prof. at the Oberlin College Cons. in Ohio. A musician of broad culture, he is equally adept in the classical Baroque repertory and in ultra-modern American and Canadian music.

Štědroň, Bohumír. Add to books: *The Works of Leoš Janáček* (Prague, 1959).

Stein, Fritz. Died in Berlin, Nov. 14, 1961.

Steinbauer, Othmar, Austrian violinist and composer; b. Vienna, Nov. 6, 1895; d. Altenburg, Sept. 5, 1962. He studied violin at the Vienna Music Academy; founded the Chamber Concert Society of Vienna, playing and conducting works of the modern Viennese school. He publ. a theoretical treatise, *Das Wesen der Tonalität* (Munich, 1928). In 1938 he founded the Musikschule der Stadt Wien. After 1945 he devoted himself mainly to manufacturing new instruments; constructed a violin specially adapted for easy performance by amateurs. His own music is quite conservative.

Steinberg, Michael, American music critic; b. Breslau, Oct. 4, 1928. He went to England in 1939 and to the U.S. in 1943; studied music at Princeton Univ. (A.B., 1949, M.F.A., 1951); then was in Italy (1952-54). Returning to America, he taught music courses at Princeton Univ., Hunter College, Manhattan

School of Music, Univ. of Saskatchewan, Smith College, Brandeis Univ., Boston Univ. and (from 1968) at the New England Cons. of Music. In 1964 he was appointed music critic of the Boston *Globe.* His criticisms, aggressively sharp and utterly disrespectful of the most sacrosanct musical personalities, aroused periodical outbursts of indignation among outraged artists, aggrieved managers and chagrined promoters. In 1969, the Boston Symphony Orch. players petitioned the management to banish him from attendance of their concerts. His other honors and distinctions include an honorary Doctor of Music degree from the New England Cons. of Music (1966) and an appointment to the Music Advisory Panel of the National Endowment for the Arts and Humanities (1970).

Steinberg, William. He was conductor of the Boston Symph. Orch. from 1969 till 1972; continued as musical director of the Pittsburgh Symph. Orch.

Steingruber, Ilona. Died in Vienna, Dec. 10, 1962.

Steinhardt, Milton. He undertook a complete edition of works by Jacobus Vaet in 'Denkmäler der Tonkunst in Österreich' (Graz/Vienna, vols. 98, 100, 103/104, 108/109).

Stenberg, Jordan, American avant-garde composer of Swedish and Spanish extraction; b. Fresno, Cal., May 31, 1947. He studied music theory with Robert Moran at the San Francisco Cons. and worked on electronic problems with Robert Ashley at Mills College. In his compositions he aims at creating an organic expression of cosmic philosophy as formalized by his deep reading of Russian theosophists and Indian psychologists. His zodiacal parameters are Sun in Gemini, moon in Scorpio, with Libra rising. His works include *88 Fog-Horn Seconds,* recording actual fog-horns on electronic tape (1967); *A Snail's Progress in a Goldfish Bowl* for string glissandi within a definite integral of white sound (1968); *Music for 4 Horse-Drawn Carriages* a literal equestrian exercise (1968); *Mind Over Matter,* film opera for voices and instruments (1969); *Extension Chords,* to be performed by nomadic bands on the desert floor during a lunar eclipse or at the winter solstice (1970); *A Stitch in Time* for 11 acoustical sources (1970); *The Clock Struck One,* opera-play for voices, instruments and dervish dancers (1970); *Circles, Lines, Planes,* a choreographed acoustical dance notated in the form of an enneagram, to be produced in a canyon by 9 bagpipers and 9 x 9 buglers (1970). He has also written music for flower conservatories to stimulate the growth of timid plants.

Stephanescu, George, Rumanian composer; b. Bucharest, Dec. 13, 1843; d. there, April 24, 1925. He studied in Bucharest, and at Paris Cons. with Ambroise Thomas and Auber (1867-71). He was voice teacher at the Bucharest Cons. (1872-1909). Stephanescu was the composer of the first Rumanian symph. work based on national themes *Uvertura nationala* (1876) and of the first symph. written by a Rumanian (1869). He also wrote many choruses and solo songs to Rumanian texts.

Stephani, Hermann. Died in Marburg, Dec. 3, 1960.

Sternberg, Erich Walter. Born on May 31, 1891 (not 1898).

Steuermann, Eduard. Died in New York, Nov. 11, 1964.

Stevenson, Robert. Add to books: *La Música en la Catedral de Sevilla, 1478-1606; documentos para su estudio* (Los Angeles, 1954); *Cathedral Music in Colonial Peru* (Lima, 1959); *The Music of Peru: Aboriginal and Viceroyal Epochs* (Washington, 1960); *Juan Bermudo* (The Hague, 1960); *Spanish Music in the Age of Columbus* (The Hague, 1960); *Music Instruction in Inca Land* (Baltimore, 1960); *Spanish Cathedral Music in the Golden Age* (Berkeley, Calif., 1961); *Mexico City Cathedral Music, 1600-1750* (Washington, 1964); *La Müsica Colonial en Colombia* (Cali, 1964); *Protestant Church Music in America* (N. Y., 1966); *Music in Aztec and Inca Territory* (Berkeley, Calif., 1968); *Renaissance and Baroque Musical Sources in the Americas* (Washington, 1970).

Stevenson, Ronald, English composer; b. Blackburn, Lancashire, March 6, 1928, of Scottish and Welsh ancestry. He studied piano as a child; began to compose at 14; took courses in composition at the Royal Manchester College at 17. In 1955 he went to Italy on a scholarship granted by the Italian government; studied at the Santa Cecilia Academy in Rome. Returning to England, he was appointed lecturer at Edinburgh Univ. (in the Extra-Mural Dept.) in 1962; was on the music staff at the Univ. of Cape Town, South Africa, in 1963-65. A fervent intellectual, he contributed cultured articles to 'The Listener' and other adult publications; engaged in a thoroughgoing bio-musical tome on Busoni, with whose art he felt a particular kinship; publ. a book, *Western Music: an Introduction* (London, 1971). In his own works, he adheres to neo-Baroque polyphony; a formidable exemplar is his *Passacaglia on DSCH* for piano, a brobdingnagian set of variations in 3 parts, 80 minutes long, derived from the initial D and the first three letters of the name of Dmitri Shostakovitch, in German notation (D; S = Es = E flat; C; H = B), first performed by Stevenson himself in Cape Town, Dec. 10, 1963. Other works include: *Anger Dance* for guitar (1965); *Triptych* on themes from Busoni's opera *Doktor Faust,* for piano and orch. (piano concerto No. 1; Edinburgh, Jan. 6, 1966, composer soloist); *Scots Dance Toccata* for orch. (Glasgow, July 4, 1970); *Peter Grimes Fantasy* for piano, on themes from Britten's opera (1971); *Duo-Sonata* for harp and piano (1971); piano concerto No. 2 (1972); numerous settings for voice and piano and for chorus of Scottish folk songs; transcriptions of works of Purcell, Bach, Chopin, Berlioz, Busoni, Paderewski, Delius, Britten, Alban Berg, Pizzetti, Percy Grainger, etc.

Stewart, Reginald. In 1962, he became head of the piano department and artist-in-residence at the Music Academy of the West in Santa Barbara, California.

Stewart, Thomas, American baritone; b. San Saba, Texas, Aug. 29, 1928. He studied electric engineering in Waco; later went to New York where he became a student of Mack Harrell at the Juilliard School of Music. He sang at the N. Y. City Opera and in Chicago; in 1967 went to Germany on a Fulbright grant and was engaged by the Deutsche Staatsoper in Berlin; in the interim he made appearances at Covent Garden, London. He sang at the Wagner Festival in Bayreuth in 1960, and at the Salzburg Festival in 1967. He made his Metropolitan Opera debut in N. Y., on March 9, 1966 as Ford in *Falstaff*. He also sang the roles of Don Giovanni, Escamillo and Iago. He is married to the American soprano Evelyn Lear.

Stibilj, Milan, Slovenian composer; b. Ljubljana, Nov. 2, 1929. He studied with Kelemen and adopted an advanced idiom of composition, exploring the techniques of integral organization of musical parameters. Works: *Concertantna glasba* for French horn and orch. (1958); *Vrtnica i slavček* (*The Nightingale and the Rose*), symph. poem (1961); choruses.

Stiedry, Fritz. Died in Zürich, Aug 9, 1968.

Still, Robert, English composer; b. London, June 10, 1910; d. Bucklebury, Reading, Jan. 13, 1971. He was educated at Eton College (1923-28) and Oxford Univ. (1929-32); later took courses in musicology at the Royal College of Music in London (1932-33). He served with the Royal Artillery during World War II; began to compose in earnest only after the war. He was also interested in psycho-analysis and publ. an essay on Mahler from the Freudian point of view. His works include 4 symphonies (1954, 1956, 1960, 1964); violin concerto (1969); piano concerto (1970) and 5 string quartets, as well as minor pieces.

Still, William Grant. Add to works: *Highway No. 1, U.S.A.,* one-act opera (Miami, May 13, 1963).

Stock, David F., American composer, b. Pittsburgh, June 3, 1939. He studied trumpet; then enrolled at the Carnegie Institute of Technology in Pittsburgh where he took courses in composition with Nikolai Lopatnikoff and musicology with Frederick Dorian. He subsequently obtained his M.F.A. (1963) at Brandeis Univ. studying advanced composition with Arthur Berger and Harold Shapero; played trumpet in various orchestras. His works include *Divertimento* for orch. (1957); *Capriccio* for small orch. (1963); *Symphony in One Movement* (1963); quintet for clarinet and strings (1966); *Flashback* for chamber ensemble (1968).

Stockhausen, Karlheinz. He developed energetic missionary activities in behalf of new music as a lecturer and master of avant-garde ceremonies; conducted summer seminars for the Ferienkurse für Musik in Darmstadt, attracting auditors from many countries; made a lecture tour of Canadian and American universities in 1958; was visiting professor at the Univ. of California, Davis, in 1966-67; gave highly successful public lectures in England in 1969; monitored performances of his music at the '70 Expo in Osaka, Japan; publ. numerous guiding articles dealing with new musical techniques. He is a pioneer in the concept of 'time-space' composition and performances, marked by controlled aleatory procedures, and adding the vectorial (i. e., directional) parameter to the four traditional aspects of serial music (pitch, duration, timbre and dynamics), with instrumentalists and vocalists, or loudspeakers in electronic works, placed in different parts of the concert hall. Add to works: *Der Gesang der Jünglinge,* to a text composed of disjected verbal particles from the Book of Daniel, dealing with the ordeal of 3 monotheistic Hebrew youths in the Babylonian fiery furnace, scored for 5 groups of loudspeakers surrounding the audience (first performed at the Radio Studio in Cologne, May 30, 1956); *Gruppen,* spatial work for 3 chamber orchestras and 3 conductors beating 3 different tempi (Cologne, March 24, 1959); *Kontakte* for electronic instruments, piano and percussion (Cologne, June 11, 1960); *Carré* for 4 orchestras, 4 choruses and 4 conductors (Hamburg, Oct. 28, 1960); *Zyklus* for one percussionist (1961); *Momente* for soprano, 4 choruses (singing, speaking, whispering, screaming, laughing, stamping, clapping, etc.), 13 instrumentalists and percussion (Cologne, May 21, 1962; extended and revised, 1965); *Mikrophonie I* and *II* (1964, 1965); *Stimmung* for 6 singers (1967); *X,* for dancers (1967), autogenetically producing sounds by activating eggshells placed on the floor or piano wires strung across the stage; *Hymnen,* electronic piece (Cologne, Nov. 30, 1967); *Aus den Sieben Tagen,* for optional instruments (1968), written out in graphic notation with verbal instructions, such as 'play a tone in the certainty that you have plenty of time and space'; *Telemusik* for an instrumental ensemble and electronic instruments (Warsaw, Sept. 23, 1968); *Plus-Minus* for clarinet, trombone, cello and 3 pianos (Warsaw, Sept. 25, 1968); *Kurzwellen* for 5 performers (1969); *Prozession* for tamtam, viola, electronium, piano and microphone (1969); *Opus 1970,* a Beethoven bicentennial piece for multi-media, using raw materials from Beethoven's works, and including a reading of the Heiligenstadt Testament (1970); *Mantra* for 2 pianos (Donaueschingen, Oct. 18, 1970).

Stockhoff, Walter William, American composer; b. St. Louis, Nov. 12, 1876, of German parentage; d. there, April 1, 1968. He was largely autodidact, and began to compose early in life. In his music he was influenced mainly by German romantic composers, but his thematic material is distinctly American. In some of his early piano music he made use of modernistic devices, such as the whole-tone scale, cadential triads with the added sixth, etc. Busoni wrote an enthusiastic article about Stockhoff (1915) in which he describes him as one of the most original composers of America. The orchestral version of Stockhoff's piano suite *To The Mountains* was performed for the first time, under the title *American Symphonic Suite* in Frankfurt, Germany, on Dec. 10, 1924. Several of his piano works and some chamber music were publ. by Breitkopf & Härtel. Other works include *5 Dramatic Poems* for orch. (1943); a piano sonata; *Metamorphoses* for piano, etc.

Stoessel, Albert (Frederic). Walter Damrosch was not his father-in-law; the maiden name of Stoessel's wife was Julia Pickard.

Stöhr, Richard. Died in Montpelier, Vermont, Dec. 11, 1967. Add bibl.: H. Sittner, *Richard Stöhr, Mensch, Musiker, Lehrer* (Vienna, 1964).

Stojowski, Sigismund. Born May 14 (not April 8), 1869.

Stoker, Richard, English composer; b. Castleford, Yorkshire, 1938. He studied composition with Eric Fenby and later with Lennox Berkeley at the Royal Academy of Music in London and with Nadia Boulanger in Paris. In his music he cultivates the 12-tone technique but derives it tonally from the quintal cycle of scales. Otherwise he adheres to classical forms. As a believer in the universality of the arts, he writes utilitarian music for dilettantes, amateurs, musicasters and children. Works: trio for flute, oboe and clarinet (1960); *Festival Suite* for trumpet and piano (1961); clarinet sonata (1961); wind quintet (1962); *Miniature Spring Trio* (1963); sextet for wind and strings (1963); violin sonata (1964); piano trio (1965); *Three Miniature Quartets* (1966); and an opera *Johnson Preserv'd* (London, July 4, 1967).

Stolz, Robert. Born Aug. 25, 1880 (not 1882). Add to operettas: *Trauminsel* (Bregenz, July 21, 1962); *Früjahrs-Parade* (Vienna, March 25, 1964).

Stone, Kurt, German-American musicologist; b. Hamburg, Germany, Nov. 14, 1911. He studied music in Hamburg and Copenhagen; came to New York in 1938, and entered the field of music publishing; held editorial positions with the Associated Music Publishers and G. Schirmer, Inc.; contributed knowledgeable articles on modern music and composers to various periodicals. He also edited reprints of old music, among them *Parthenia* (N. Y., 1951).

Storchio, Rosina, Italian soprano; b. Venice, May 19, 1876; d. Milan, July 24, 1945. She studied in Mantua and made her debut at 16. On Feb. 17, 1904, she created the title role in the world première of *Madama Butterfly* at La Scala in Milan. After a series of tours in South America and in Europe, she was briefly engaged at the Chicago Opera (1920-21); then retired from the stage. She was paralyzed during the last years of her life as a result of an apoplectic stroke.

Stout, Alan, American composer; b. Baltimore, Nov. 26, 1932. He studied at the Peabody Cons. of Music in Baltimore, with Henry Cowell; obtained his M.A. degree in composition at the Univ. of Washington in Seattle. In 1963 he joined the faculty of the School of Music at Northwestern Univ. An industrious composer, he has written 100-odd identifiable works, among them 4 symphonies, choral pieces, chamber music and songs, all couched in a non-aggressive, prudentially dissonant but harmonious vigesimosecular idiom.

Stoyanov, Veselin, Bulgarian composer; b. Shumen, April 20, 1902; d. Sofia, June 29, 1969. He studied piano in Sofia; composition in Vienna with Franz Schmidt. In 1937 he was appointed prof. at the Sofia Musical Academy. He wrote the operas *Kingdom of Women* (Sofia, April 5, 1935) and *Salammbo* (Sofia, May 22, 1940); a symph.; 2 piano concertos; a violin concerto; 3 string quartets.

Stradella, Alessandro. Add bibl.: R. Giazotto, *Vita di Alessandro Stradella* (2 vols., Milan, 1962).

Straesser, Ewald. A more common form of the spelling of his last name is Strässer. Cf. A. Strässer, *Ewald Strässer* (Stuttgart, 1936).

Strassburg, Robert, American music educator and composer; b. New York, Aug. 30, 1915. He studied composition with Marion Bauer at N. Y. Univ.; then enrolled in Harvard Univ. (M.A., 1950). He subsequently lived in Miami; was conductor and founder of the All-Miami Youth Symph. (1957-60). In 1961 he joined the faculty of the Univ. of Judaism in Los Angeles; from 1966 he was also on the faculty of California State College. His works include *Four Biblical Statements* for string orch. (1946); *Fantasy and Allegro* for violin and orch. (1947); *Torah Sonata* for piano (1950); folk opera *Chelm* (1956); *Tropal Suite* for string orch. (1967).

Stratas, Teresa (real name, **Anastasia Strataki**), Canadian soprano of Greek extraction; b. Toronto, May 26, 1938. She studied at the Cons. of Toronto; made her début with the Toronto Opera as Mimi in *La Bohème* on Oct. 16, 1958; won the Metropolitan Opera Auditions and appeared with the Metropolitan, N.Y., on Oct. 28, 1959. She also gave solo recitals.

Strauss, Franz. Date of death, May 31 (not June 2), 1905.

Strauss, Johann, Sr. Add to bibl.: H. Jacob, *Johann Strauss, Vater und Sohn: Die Geschichte einer musikalischen Weltherrschaft* (Bremen, 1960).

Strauss, Johann, Jr. His first engagement was at Dommayer's restaurant (not Donmayer's) in Hietzing (not Heitzing).

Strauss, Richard. The date of first performance of *Symphonia Domestica,* March 21 (not 31), 1904. *Parergon zur Symphonia Domestica* was first performed in Dresden, on Oct. 16, 1925 (not in Leipzig on Oct. 29, 1925, which was a later performance). Date of first performance of *Burleske* for piano and orch., Eisenach, June 21, 1890, Strauss conducting, Eugen d'Albert soloist. Add to bibl.: I. Fabian, *Richard Strauss* (Budapest, 1962); N. Del Mar, *Richard Strauss: A Critical Commentary on His Life and Works* (2 vols.; I, London, 1962; II, Philadelphia, 1969); A. Jefferson, *The Operas of Richard Strauss in Britain, 1910-1963* (London, 1963); Lotte Lehmann, *Five Operas and Richard Strauss* (N.Y., 1964); W. Mann, *Richard Strauss: A Critical Study of the Operas* (London, 1964); G. Marek, *Richard Strauss: The Life of a Non-Hero* (N. Y., 1967). The 1952 edition of *Richard Strauss und Hugo von Hofmannsthal: Briefwechsel* was later published in English under the title *A Working Friendship: The Correspondence between Richard Strauss and Hugo von Hofmannsthal* (London, 1961).

Stravinsky, Feodor Ignatievitch. Born near Retchitza, in the district of Minsk (not in Tchernigov), on June 20 (not June 15), 1843. Died in St. Petersburg (not in Wildungen, whence he was brought back to Russia on Oct. 28, 1902, in dying condition), Dec. 4 (not Dec. 3), 1902. See S. Stark, *Essay on F. I. Stravinsky,* in the 'Annals of the Imperial Theaters' (St. Petersburg, 1903-04).

Stravinsky, Igor (Feodorovitch). Died in New York, April 6, 1971. His body was flown to Venice and buried in the Russian corner of the cemetery island of San Michele, according to the Greek Orthodox ritual; his *Requiem Canticles* was performed at the ceremony, conducted by Robert Craft. In 1962, at the invitation of the Union of Soviet Composers, he visited Russia for the first time in 48 years; conducted concerts in Moscow and Leningrad. Correct title in French of his 1937 ballet is *Jeu* (not *Jeux*) *de cartes.* Symphony in E^b major was first performed in St. Petersburg on Feb. 5 (not Jan. 22), 1908; *Le Faune et la bergère* was first performed at the same concert on Feb. 5 (not Feb. 29), 1908. The opera *Renard* was first performed in Paris on May 18 (not June 3), 1922. *Agon* is not strictly speaking a serial work; it is basically tonal, but contains serial elements in 12-tone motives in some variations; the number of dancers (12) has no dodecaphonic implications. Add to works: *Epitaphium for Prince Max of Fürstenberg* for flute, clarinet and harp (Donaueschingen, Oct. 17, 1959); *Movements for Piano and Orchestra* (N.Y., Jan. 10, 1960); *Monumentum pro Gesualdo di Venosa ad CD Annum,* an instrumental surrealization of 3 madrigals by Gesualdo (Venice, Sept. 27, 1960); *A Sermon, A Narrative, and A Prayer,* triptych for contralto, tenor, speaker, chorus and orch. (Basel, Feb. 23, 1962); *Noah and the Flood,* biblical spectacle, narrated, mimed, sung and danced (NBC television broadcast, N.Y., June 14, 1962); *Elegy for J.F.K.* for baritone, 2 clarinets and corno di bassetto (Los Angeles, April 6, 1964); *Abraham and Isaac,* sacred ballad for baritone and chamber orch. to Hebrew words (Jerusalem, Aug. 23, 1964); *Variations (Aldous Huxley in Memoriam)* for orch. (Chicago, April 17, 1965); *Introitus (T.S. Eliot in Memoriam)* for male chorus, harp, piano, timpani, tam-tams, solo viola and double-bass (Chicago, April 17, 1965); *Requiem Canticles* for vocal quartet, chorus and orch. (Princeton, Oct. 8, 1966). With Robert Craft, Stravinsky publ. 6 vols. of revelatory autobiographical dialogues: *Conversations with Igor Stravinsky* (N.Y., 1958); *Memories and Commentaries* (N.Y., 1959); *Expositions and Developments* (N.Y., 1962); *Dialogues and a Diary* (N.Y., 1963); *Themes and Episodes* (N.Y., 1967); and *Retrospections and Conclusions* (N.Y., 1969). Add to bibl.: Roman Vlad, *Stravinsky* (Rome, 1958; in English, London, 1960); Robert Siohan, *Stravinsky* (Paris, 1959; in English, London, 1966); Friedrich Herzfeld, *Igor Stravinsky* (Berlin, 1961); Paul Henry Lang, ed., *Stravinsky: A New Appraisal of His Work* (N.Y., 1963); Boris Yarustovsky, *Stravinsky* (Moscow, 1963); Nicolas Nabokov, *Igor Stravinsky* (Berlin, 1964); Eric Walter White, *Stravinsky, The Composer and His Works* (Berkeley, Calif., 1966; 2nd enlarged printing, 1969); A. Boucourechliev, ed., *Stravinsky* (Paris, 1968); Arnold Dobrin, *Igor Stravinsky, His Life and Time* (London, 1970). Stravinsky's sketches for *Le Sacre du Printemps* were publ. in facsimile in London in 1969.

Strayhorn, William (Billy), American Negro jazz pianist and composer; b. Dayton, Ohio, Nov. 29, 1915; d. New York, May 30, 1967. He studied music in Pittsburgh; joined Duke Ellington's band as lyricist and arranger in 1939. Many songs credited to Ellington *(Chelsea Bridge, Perfume Suite, Such Sweet Thunder, A Drum is a Woman,* etc.) are in fact products of a mutually beneficial musical symbiosis, with Ellington suggesting the initial idea, mood and character and Strayhorn doing the actual writing, often using Ellington's quasi-impressionistic techniques (e.g., modal harmonies, whole-tone scales, etc.). Strayhorn's own acknowledged songs, *Lush Life, Take the 'A' Train* and others, are jazz standards.

Strimer, Joseph. Died in New York, Jan. 1962.

Stringfield, Lamar. Died in Asheville, Jan. 21, 1959.

Strobel, Heinrich. Died in Baden-Baden, Aug. 18, 1970.

Stroe, Aurel, Rumanian composer; b. Bucharest, May 5, 1932. He studied at the Bucharest Cons. with Martian Negrea, Ion Dumitrescu and Rogalski. Works: trio for oboe, clarinet and bassoon (1953); string quartet (1955); concerto for string orch. (1950); *Uvertura Burlesca* (1961); etc.

Stuckenschmidt, Hans Heinz. Add to publ.: *Schöpfer der neuen Musik; Portraits und Studien* (Frankfurt, 1958); J.N. David (Wiesbaden, 1965); *Maurice Ravel: Variationen über Person und Werk* (Frankfurt, 1966); *Ferruccio Busoni, Zeittafel eines Europäers* (Zürich, 1967; in English, *Ferruccio Busoni, Chronicle of a European,* London, 1970): *Twentieth Century Music,* in English (N. Y., 1969); *Germany and Central Europe,* as part of the series 'Twentieth Century Composers' (London, 1970).

Styne, Jule, American composer of popular music; b. London, England, Dec. 31, 1905. His original name was Jules Stein. He was taught piano by his parents; taken to the U.S. at the age of 8; appeared with the Chicago Symph. Orch. as a child prodigy; subsequently studied at the Chicago Musical College. However, he did not pursue a concert career; in 1942 he went to Hollywood and rapidly established himself as a successful composer of musical comedies; wrote the scores of *High Button Shoes* (1947); *Gentlemen Prefer Blondes* (1949); *Bells are Ringing* (1956); *Gypsy,* to the life story of the striptease artist Gypsy Rose Lee (1959); and *Funny Girl,* a musical biography of the singer Fanny Brice (1965). He also wrote music for the films.

Subotnick, Morton, American avant-garde composer; b. Los Angeles, April 14, 1933. He studied music at the Univ. of Denver; then at Mills College with Darius Milhaud. He subsequently taught at Mills College; was in charge of the Intermedia Program at the School of Arts at N. Y. Univ.; also directed exhibits at the Electric Circus in Greenwich Village in New York. In 1969 he was appointed Associate Dean and Director of Electronic Music at the School of Music at the California Institute of the Arts in Los Angeles. His fortissimo lies in multi-media theatrical presentations, with emphasis on electronic devices. His works include four pieces for mixed media under the all-embracing title *Play!; The Tarot* for 10 instruments and tape; *Concert* for woodwind quintet, 2 film projectors, electronic sounds and 12 spotlights; *Music for 12 Elevators; Lamination* for orch. and electronic sounds; *The Wild Bull* for electronic music synthesizer; incidental music for the plays *Galileo, The Balcony* and *The Caucasian Chalk Circle.*

Such, Percy Frederick. Died in New York, Feb. 16, 1959.

Suchoň, Eugen. Add to works: *Svatopluk,* historical opera (Bratislava, March 10, 1960).

Suckling, Norman. Was lecturer in French language and literature at King's College, Newcastle-upon-Tyne in the Federal Univ. of Durham from 1943 till 1970. His compositions include *Introduction and Scherzo* for string quartet (1923); *Ode* for violin and piano (1925); *A Vision of Avalon,* chamber opera (1928); *A Cycle of Shakespeare Sonnets* for tenor, violin and piano (1928); violin sonata (1928); *Man in the Beginning,* ballet (1934); *Berceuse élégiaque* for clarinet and piano, to commemorate a pet kitten, and written for the composer's first wife (1943); *Pastorale saugrenue* for flute and bassoon (1944); *Variations on a Theme of Rameau* for flute and piano (1947); many songs to words by English poets. He contributed articles on English and French composers to 'The Listener' and other publications.

Suda, Stanislav. Date of death, Sept. 2 (not Aug. 28), 1931.

Sugár, Rezsö, Hungarian composer; b. Budapest, Oct. 9, 1919. He studied with Kodály; became prof. of composition at the Budapest Cons.; wrote mostly chamber music; also a patriotic oratorio *Hunyadi* (1952). He is highly regarded as a pedagogue; publ. a number of didactic pieces for young musicians.

Suk, Josef (1874-1935). Add bibl.: Jan M. Kvet, *Josef Suk v obrazech* (Prague, 1964); Ratibor Budis, ed., *Josef Suk* (Prague, 1965); Jiři Berkovec, *Josef Suk* (Prague, 1969).

Suk, Josef, Czech violinist, grandson of the composer Josef Suk and great-grandson of Dvořák; b. Prague, Aug. 8, 1929. He studied at the Prague Cons. (1944-50) with Jaroslav Kocian; after graduation he embarked on a highly successful concert career in all parts of the world; made his American debut as soloist with the Cleveland Orch., Jan. 23, 1964.

Sulek, Stjepan. Diacritical sign missing: Šulek. Add to works: *Koriolan,* music drama (Zagreb, Oct. 12, 1958); concerto for bassoon and orch. (1958); Symph. No. 5 (1963); piano concerto No. 3 (1963). See K. Kovačević, *Hrvatski Kompozitori i Njihova Djela* (Zagreb, 1960); K. Šipuš, *Stjepan Šulek* (Zagreb, 1961).

Supervia, Conchita. Born on Dec. 8, 1895 (not 1899).

Susskind, Walter. From 1956 to 1965 he was conductor of the Toronto Symph. Orch.

Suter, Robert, Swiss composer; b. St. Gallen, Jan. 30, 1919. He studied in Basel; in 1950 was appointed to the staff of the Musik-Akademie there. Works: *Petite Suite* for orch. (1953); *Lyrische Suite* for chamber orch. (1959); *Suite* for violin and viola (1942); string quartet (1952); *Divertimento* for oboe, clarinet and bassoon (1955); *Sonatine* for clarinet and piano (1957); *4 Etudes* for wind quintet (1962); *Sonata per orchestra* (Basel, Feb. 22, 1968); *Epitaffio* for woodwinds, percussion and strings (Lucerne, Aug. 7, 1968); *3 Nocturnes* for viola and orch. (Basel, March 19, 1970); numerous choruses and songs with instrumental accompaniment.

Sutermeister, Heinrich. Add to works: *Seraphine,* opera-buffa after Rabelais (Zürich, June 10, 1959); piano concerto No. 3 (Hamburg, Sept. 30, 1963); *Madame Bovary,* opera (Zürich, May 26, 1967); *Serenade for Montreux* for chamber orch. (Montreux, Sept. 17, 1970).

Sutherland, Joan, Australian soprano; b. Sydney, Nov. 7, 1926. She received her early vocal training in Australia; in 1951 she went to London where she studied voice with Clive Carey at the Royal College of Music. She was then engaged at Covent Garden, obtaining a signal success as Lucia on Feb. 17, 1959; in 1961 she made her first appearance in the

U.S., scoring tremendous critical acclaim. She excels in the Italian bel canto repertory, but the extraordinary flexibility of her voice makes her interpretations of dramatic parts equally fine. See R. Braddon, *Joan Sutherland* (London, 1962).

Svanholm, Set. Died in Saltsjoe-Duvnaes, Oct. 4, 1964.

Svendsen, Johan (Severin). Add to bibl.: Bjarne Kortsen, *Chamber Music Works by Johan Svendsen* (Bergen, 1971).

Svoboda, Tomáš, Czech composer; b. Paris, Dec. 6, 1939, of Czech parents (his father was a renowned mathematician, Antonín Svoboda). The family returned to Prague in 1946; he studied piano privately and composition with Hlobil, Kabeláč and Dobiáš at the Prague Cons., graduating in 1959. In 1964 he left Czechoslovakia and settled in the U.S. In 1970, appointed member of the faculty at Portland State Univ., Oregon. His music is marked by broad melodic lines in economically disposed harmonies; there are elements of serialism in chromatic episodes. Works: Symph. No. 1 (Prague, Sept. 7, 1957); Symph. No. 2 (1964-65); Symph. No. 3 (1965); trio for piano, oboe and bassoon (1962); *Řezanička,* dance for string orch. (1962); *Classical Sonatina* for oboe and piano (1962); *Etude* for chamber orch. (1963); *Ballade* for bassoon and piano (1963); viola sonata (1963); Suite for bassoon, strings and harpsichord (1963); *Ballet Etudes* for 7 instruments (1963); *Chamber Concertino* for harp and chamber orch. (1964); *Suite* for mezzo-soprano and orch. (1964).

Swain, Freda. Date of birth, Oct. 31 (not Oct. 13), 1902.

Swan, Alfred (Julius). Died in Haverford, Pa., Oct. 2, 1970.

Swanson, Howard. Add to works: Symph. No. 3 (N.Y., March 1, 1970).

Swarthout, Gladys. Died near Florence, July 8, 1969.

Swift, Richard, American composer; b. Middlepoint, Ohio, Sept. 24, 1927. He studied at the Univ. of Chicago (M.A. 1956); then became a member of the faculty of the Univ. of California at Davis; was appointed chairman of the music dept. there in 1963. In his compositions he applies a variety of functional serial techniques, including electronic and aleatory devices, while preserving the external forms of Baroque music. Works: *A Coronal* for orch. (Louisville, April 14, 1956); *Serenade Concertante* for piano and wind quintet (1956); sonata for clarinet and piano (1957); trio for clarinet, cello and piano (1957); concerto for piano and chamber ensemble (1961); *Extravaganza* for orch. (1962); *The Trial of Tender O'Shea,* one-act opera (Univ. of Calif., Davis, Aug. 12, 1964); *Thrones* for alto flute, and double-bass (1966); *Tristia* for orch. (Oakland, Calif., April 20, 1968); violin concerto (Oakland, Calif., May 28, 1968); symphony (1970); 3 string quartets (1955, 1958 and 1964); 2 works for 3 instruments entitled *Music for a While;* 8 works for different instrumental groups, or solos entitled *Stravaganza,* and 3 works under the generic title *Domains* for voice, instruments and percussion; 25 sets of incidental music for the theater, including musique concrète and electronic sounds.

Swoboda, Henry, Czech-American conductor; b. Prague, Oct. 29, 1897; studied music with Zemlinsky and Talich; received his Ph.D. at the German University of Prague. From 1921 to 1923 he was assistant conductor at the Prague Opera; then conducted in Germany; from 1931 to 1938 was conductor with the Prague Radio. In 1938 he settled in the U.S.; was music director and conductor of Concert Hall and Westminster Recording Companies (1948-51); toured extensively as guest conductor in Europe and South America; conducted in Ankara, Teheran and Athens in 1962-63 under the auspices of the State Dept.; 1962-64, conducted the Harvard-Radcliffe Orch. In 1964 he was appointed conductor of the Univ. Orch. and director of the Opera Workshop at the Univ. of Texas, Austin.

Sychra, Antonín, Czech musicologist; b. Boskovice, June 9, 1918; d. Prague, Oct. 20, 1969. He studied music in Brno and Prague; settling in Prague, he publ. a number of scholarly monographs on esthetics; also taught music history at the Charles Univ. in Prague. Publications: *Estetika Dvořákovy symfonické tvorby* (Prague, 1959); *Leoš Janáček* (Prague, 1956).

Sydeman, William, American composer; b. New York, May 8, 1928. He studied at Mannes College with Felix Salzer; later with Roger Sessions and Goffredo Petrassi, at Tanglewood. In 1959 he joined the faculty of Mannes College, N.Y. His style of composition stems primarily from Mahler and Berg, and tends towards atonal expressionism invigorated by spasmodic percussive rhythms in asymmetrically arranged meters. His works include *Orchestral Abstractions* (1958; N.Y.,

Jan. 10, 1962); *Study for Orchestra* (1959); concertino for oboe, piano and string orch. (1956); divertimento for 8 instruments (1957); *Concerto da Camera No. 1* for violin and chamber orch. (1959); *Concerto da Camera No. 2* for violin and chamber orch. (1960); *Chamber Concerto* for piano, 2 flutes and string quartet (1961); *7 Movements* for septet (1960); 2 woodwind quintets (1955, 1959); *Westbrook Quintet* for clarinet, horn, double-bass, piano and percussion (1959); string quartet (1955); quartet for clarinet, violin, trumpet and double-bass (1955); quartet for oboe and strings (1961); *The Affections,* suite for trumpet and piano (1965); *Malediction,* for tenor, a speaking actor, string quartet and electronic tape, to words from Laurence Sterne's *Tristam Shandy* (N. Y., Feb. 5, 1971); numerous other works for various instrumental ensembles.

Sykes, James Andrews, American pianist; b. Atlantic City, N. J., July 10, 1908. He studied at Princeton (A.B., 1930) and at the Univ. of Rochester (A.M., 1933); subsequently held teaching positions in Colorado College (1935-46) and Colgate Univ. (1947-53); 1953, appointed prof. at Dartmouth College. He toured West Germany (1954); South America (1960); Greece, Turkey, Malaysia, Vietnam, Pakistan, Iran, Lebanon, as an American Specialist for the State Dept. (1965); also Japan (1965). He specializes in modern American piano music.

Symonds, Norman A., Canadian composer; b. Nelson, British Columbia, Dec. 23, 1920. He served in the Canadian Navy during World War II; then participated in various jazz groups. His works include a *Concerto Grosso* for jazz quintet and orch. (1958); *Bordello Ballad* for jazz octet (1957); *Perspectives* for jazz octet (1962); *Boy Meets Girl* for chorus and percussion (1964).

Szabelski, Boleslaw, Polish composer; b. Radoryz, Dec. 3, 1896. He studied with Szymanowski and Statkowski at the Warsaw Cons.; was active as composer and organist. After 1945 he taught composition and organ in Katowice. His works include 4 symphonies (1926, 1934, 1954, 1956); *Aphorisms* for orch. (1962); flute concerto (1965); chamber music.

Szabó, Ferenc. Died in Budapest, Nov. 4, 1969. Add to works: oratorio, *Feltámádt a tenger* (*The Sea is Rising;* Budapest, June 15, 1955); ballet, *Ludas Matyi* (Budapest, May 16, 1960). He also composed a cycle of piano pieces, *Melodies of Liberation* (1949).

Szabolcsi, Bence. Add to books: *The Twilight of Ferenc Liszt* (in English; Budapest, 1959); *A Concise History of Hungarian Music* (in English; Budapest, 1964).

Szalonek, Witold, Polish composer; b. Czechowice, Silesia, March 2, 1927. He studied composition with Boleslaw Woytowicz in Katowice; then taught there. Among his works are a *Suite kurpiowska* for contralto and 9 instruments based on folk songs of the region of Kurpie (1955; Rome Festival, June 14, 1959); *Symphonic Satire;* a triptych *Wyzania* for chorus, speaking voice and chamber orch; songs.

Szeligowski, Tadeusz. Died in Poznan, Jan. 10, 1963.

Szell, George. Died in Cleveland, July 30, 1970.

Szendrei, Aladár. The title of his opera is *Der* (not *Das*) *türkisenblaue Garten.* Add to books: *David's Harp: A Popular History of the Music in Biblical Times* (N. Y., 1964); *Music in Ancient Israel* (1969); *The Music of the Jews in the Diaspora* (1969). In 1962 he was appointed prof. of Jewish music at the Univ. of Judaism, Los Angeles; retained this post in 1971. All his books were publ. under his naturalized American name, **Sendrey.**

Szervánsky, Endre. Date of birth, Dec. 27, 1911 (not Jan. 1, 1912). Add to works: string quartet No. 2 (1957); 6 pieces for orch. (1958). In these and later works he applies modified serial techniques.

Szeryng, Henryk, Polish violinist; b. Warsaw, Nov. 22, 1918. He studied with Willy Hess and Karl Flesch in Berlin, and with Jacques Thibaud in Paris. In 1933 he went to America; in 1948 he was engaged as prof. at the Cons. of Mexico City, while continuing his career as a concert violinist in Europe and America.

Szigeti, Joseph. He publ. *A Violinist's Notebook* (London, 1965); *Szigeti on the Violin: Improvisations on a Violinist's Themes* (N. Y., 1969). A monograph on him was publ. in Russian: Y. L. Soroker, *Joseph Szigeti* (Moscow, 1968).

Szymanowski, Karol. Exact date of first performance of *Hagith,* May 13, 1922. Symph. No. 3, in one movement, subtitled *Song of the Night,* was performed for the first time anywhere in London, Albert Coates conducting, on Oct. 24, 1921. *Symphonie Concertante* was performed prior to the Warsaw and Paris performances in Poznan, on Oct. 9, 1932, with the composer at the piano. *Stabat Mater* was completed in 1926 (not in 1929) and first performed in Warsaw on Jan. 11, 1929. The group of 12 songs are Kurpian (not Kuprian). Add to works: *Mandragora,* pantomime (Warsaw, June 15, 1920). Add to bibl.: J. M. Chomiński, *Studia nad twórczością Karola Szymanowskiego* (Cracow, 1969).

T

Tajčević, Marko, Serbian composer; b. Osijek, Jan. 29, 1900. He studied in Zagreb, Prague and Vienna; in 1945 was appointed prof. at the Belgrade Music Academy. He is primarily a folklore composer, and is at his best in choral works derived from regional folksongs. His *7 Balkan Dances* for piano are brilliant stylizations of Serbian melorhythms.

Takemitsu, Toru, Japanese composer; b. Tokyo, Oct. 8, 1930. He studied composition with Yosuji Kiyose. In 1951 he organized in Tokyo an avant-garde group, 'Experimental Laboratory,' with the aim of combining traditional Japanese music with modernistic serial techniques. His *Requiem* for string orch. (Tokyo, June 20, 1958) attracted considerable attention in Japan and also had performances in Germany and in the U.S. His other works include 3 pieces for strings under the generic title *Le Son Calligraphie* (1958-60); *Solitude Sonore* for orch. (Tokyo, Nov. 9, 1958); *Uninterrupted Rests* for piano (1959); *Masque* for 2 flutes (1959); *Landscape* for string quartet (1960); *Piano-Distance* for piano solo (1961); *Ki No Kyoku* (*Music of the Trees*) for orch. (1961); *Sacrifice* for flute, lute, ancient cymbals and vibraphone (1962); *Coral Island* for soprano and orch. (1963); *The Dorian Horizon* for strings (1966); *November Steps,* symph. sketch (N. Y., Nov. 9, 1967); *Eucalyptus* for flute, oboe, harp and strings (Tokyo, Nov. 16, 1970).

Taktakishvili, Otar. Add to works: *Mindia,* opera (Tbilisi, July 23, 1961).

Talich, Václav. Died in Beroun, March 16, 1961.

Talma, Louise. Add to works: *The Alcestiad,* opera (Frankfurt, Germany, March 1, 1962).

Tamberg, Eino, Estonian composer; b. Tallinn, May 27, 1930. He studied in Tallinn; promoted Socialist Realism in his music, mostly choral. His opera, *The House of Iron* (Tallinn, July 15, 1965), glorifies the revolutionary spirit of Estonian proletarian patriots.

Taneyev, Alexander Sergeyevitch. He was not an uncle of Sergey Taneyev, but a distant relative several times removed.

Taneyev, Sergey Ivanovitch. Place of death: Dyudkovo, Zvenigorodsk District (not Moscow). His Symph. in C minor was composed in 1896-97 (not in 1902); first performed under the direction of Glazunov in St. Petersburg, April 2, 1898. His treatise *Podvizhnoy Kontrapunkt Strogavo Pisma* was publ. in English as *Convertible Counterpoint in the Strict Style* (Boston, 1962). He was not a nephew of Alexander Taneyev, but a distant relative several times removed.

Tappert, Wilhelm. In the subtitle of his *Wagner-Lexikon,* the 6th word should be *höhnende* (not *höhnede*).

Tardos, Béla, Hungarian composer; b. Budapest, June 21, 1910; d. there, Nov. 18, 1966. He studied with Kodály; was engaged in editorial and publishing work and at the same time composed choral music for mass singing, employing the modalities of Hungarian folksongs. Among his works is a wind octet (1935); piano concerto (1954); a symph. in memory of the victims of Fascism (1961); *Laura,* comic opera (performed posthumously in Debrecen, Dec. 11, 1966); teaching pieces.

Tate, Phyllis (Margaret Duncan). Add to works: *The Lodger,* opera (London, July 14, 1960).

Tauriello, Antonio, Argentinian composer; b. Buenos Aires, March 20, 1931. He studied piano with Walter Gieseking and composition with Alberto Ginastera; still a youth, he was engaged to conduct opera and ballet at the Teatro Colón, Buenos Aires. His music is neo-classical in its general mold. Works: piano concerto (1952); *Serenade* for orch. (1957); *Ricercare* for orch. (1963); *Transparencies* for 6 instrumental groups (Washington, D.C., 3rd Inter-American Music Festival, May 12, 1965); piano concerto (Washington, D.C., 4th Inter-American Music Festival, June 30, 1968).

Tavener, John, British composer; b. London, Jan. 28, 1944. He studied with Lennox Berkeley at the Royal Academy of Music; also took a course with the Australian composer David Lumsdaine. Among the formative influences of his creative evolution were medieval hymnology and Indian transcendentalism; his technical equipment is, by contrast, ultra-modern, including combinatorial serialism and electronic generation of sound. Works (all first performed in London): *The Cappemakers,* a dramatic cantata for two narrators, 10 soloists, male chorus and chamber orch. (Jan. 14, 1964); *3 Holy Sonnets* for baritone and chamber orch., to texts from John Donne (1964); *Cain and Abel,* dramatic cantata for soloists and chamber orch. (Oct. 22, 1966); *The Whale,* dramatic cantata for narrator, soloists, chorus and orch. (Jan. 24, 1968); *Grandma's Footsteps* for chamber group (March 14, 1968); *Introit for March 27th* for soprano, contralto, chorus and orch. (March 27, 1968); *Chamber Concerto* for chamber orch. (June 12, 1968); *3 Surrealist Songs* for mezzo-soprano, tape, piano and percussion (1968); *In Alium* for soprano, orch. and tape (Aug. 12, 1968); *A Celtic Requiem,* dramatic cantata for soloists, children's choir, chorus and orch. (July 16, 1969); *Coplas* for chorus, soloists and tape (July 9, 1970); *Nomine Jesu* for 5 male speaking voices, mezzo-soprano, chorus, two alto flutes, organ and harpsichord (Aug. 14, 1970).

Taylor, (Joseph) Deems. Died in New York, July 3, 1966. His opera *The King's Henchman* was produced on Feb. 17, 1927 (not 1926). The title of his one-act opera is *The Dragon* (not *Dragoon*).

Tchaikovsky, Boris. Add to works: piano concerto (1969); violin concerto (1970).

Tchaikovsky, Modest. Born in Alapaevsk, Perm district (not in St. Petersburg), May 13, 1850.

Tchaikovsky, Piotr Ilyitch. His orchestration of Sophie Menter's *Ungarische Zigeunerweisen* is not lost; a microfilm of the score of the original manuscript is in the Library of Congress in Washington.

Tcherepnin, Alexander Nikolayevitch. His mother was a niece of Alexander Benois, not a sister. Add to works: piano concerto No. 4 (1947; retitled *Fantaisie*); Symph. No. 4 (Boston, Dec. 5, 1958); *Symphony-Prayer* (Chicago, Aug. 19, 1960); piano concerto No. 5 (West Berlin, Oct. 13, 1963, composer soloist); *Serenade* for string orch. (1964); *Vom Spass und Ernst,* folksong cantata for voice and strings (1964); piano concerto No. 6 (1965); *Suite for Harpsichord* (1966); *Sonata da Chiesa* for viola da gamba and organ (1966); *The Story of Ivan the Fool,* cantata with a narrator (London, Dec. 24, 1968). He publ. an *Anthology of Russian Music* (with English and German texts, Bonn, 1966). Bibl.: Willi Reich, *Alexander Tcherepnin* (Bonn, 1961, in German; French translation, Paris, 1962); N. Slonimsky, *Alexander Tcherepnin, Septuagenarian,* in 'Tempo' (London, Jan. 1969).

Tcherepnin, Ivan, American composer, son of Alexander Tcherepnin; b. Paris, Feb. 5, 1943. He received his early musical education with his father in France; then followed him to the U.S., where he entered Harvard Univ., graduating in 1964; also attended courses with Karlheinz Stockhausen and Henri Pousseur in Cologne, and with Pierre Boulez in Darmstadt; studied electronic techniques in Toronto in 1966; returned to Harvard for graduate studies as a pupil of Randall Thompson and Leon Kirchner. In 1968 he went to Oakland, Calif. and worked with David Tudor and Anthony Gnazzo at Mills College; collaborated in numerous productions of electronic works. Once again at Harvard, he obtained his M.A. degree in 1969. In 1970 he was engaged as instructor in theory of composition at the San Francisco Cons. of Music and also at Stanford Univ. Works: *Suite progressive pentatonique* for flute, cello and timpani (1959); *Deux Entourages sur un thème Russe* for Ondes Martenot, percussion and piano (1961); *Four Pieces from Before* for piano (1962); *Mozartean Suite* for flute, clarinet and bassoon (1962); *Reciprocals* for flute, clarinet and bassoon (1962); *Cadenzas in Transition* for flute, clarinet and piano (1963); *Beginnings* for piano (1963); *Work Music* for electric guitar, French horn, clarinet and cello (1965); *Sombres Lumières* for flute, guitar and cello (1965); *Wheelwinds* for 9 wind instruments (1966); *AC-DC* for percussion, 3 tape machines, 2 ring modulators and oscillators (1967); *Rings* for string quartet and ring modulators (1968); *Summer Music* for brass sextet (1970); *Light Music With Water* for 4 instrumental groups, 4 sound-activated strobe lights, electronic accessories and prepared tape (1970); also electronic music for films.

Tcherepnin, Serge, American composer, son of Alexander Tcherepnin; b. Paris, Feb. 2, 1941. He studied violin as a child; was taken to the U.S. in 1949; received his training in theory with his father; then took courses with Karlheinz Stockhausen and Pierre Boulez in Darmstadt. He pursued his regular academic education at Harvard Univ. where he studied with Walter Piston, Leon Kirchner and Billy Jim Layton, obtaining his B.A. in 1964. In

1966 he went to Milan to study electronic techniques. His works include a string trio, a string quartet, piano pieces and film music.

Tchesnokov, Pavel Grigorievitch, Russian composer; b. near Voskresensk, Oct. 24, 1877; d. Moscow, March 14, 1944. He studied at the Moscow Cons. with Vassilenko, graduating in 1917; also took courses with Sergey Taneyev and Ippolitov-Ivanov. He devoted himself exclusively to choral composition, both secular and sacred; was from 1920 prof. of choral conducting at the Moscow Cons. He publ. a manual for choral singing (Moscow, 1940).

Teed, Roy, English pianist and composer; b. Herne Bay, Kent, May 18, 1928. He studied composition with Lennox Berkeley at the Royal Academy in London; also obtained a diploma in piano. Works: piano concerto (1952); *Festival Suite* for cello and string orch. (1958); *Introduction and Scherzo* for flute, oboe and piano (1960); *So Blest a Day,* a Christmas cantata (1960); *The Pied Piper* for chorus (1961); quartet for flute and strings (1961); *Around the Town,* a comedy march (1962); *The Jackdaw of Rheims,* a narrative cantata (1964); numerous part-songs and carols.

Templeton, Alec. Died in Greenwich, Conn., March 28, 1963.

Tenschert, Roland. Died in Vienna, April 3, 1970.

Terhune, Anice. Died in Pompton Lakes, New Jersey, Nov. 9, 1964.

Tessier, Roger, French composer; b. Nantes, Jan. 14, 1939. He received his education in Nantes and Paris. His works, mostly for small instrumental groups include a string trio (1964), *Concerto da camera* (1965), *5 Etudes* for wind instruments, piano, percussion and harp (1965) and *Suite concertante* for flute, piano and strings (1969).

Thayer, Alexander Wheelock. A redaction of his *Life of Beethoven,* prepared by Elliot Forbes, was publ. in 1963.

Theodorakis, Mikis (Michael George), Greek composer; b. Chios, July 29, 1925. He studied at the Athens Cons.; composed melodies in the authentic spirit of modern Greek folksongs; wrote music for productions of ancient Greek tragedies, among them *Oedipus Tyrannos.* He achieved international success with the musical score for the film *Zorba the Greek.* At the same time he was actively engaged in politics. In 1963 he was chosen chairman of the Greek United Democratic Left Party; in 1964 he was elected a member of the Greek Parliament and joined the Communist Party. After the military coup of 1967 he was arrested and held on a farm near Corinth; later was sent to Zatouna, in the central Peloponnesus; there he wrote the music for the film Z dealing with the police murder of the Socialist politician Gregory Lambrakis in Salonika in 1963. The film and the music were greatly acclaimed in Europe and America, and the fate of Theodorakis became a cause célèbre. Yielding to pressure from the international public opinion, the Greek government freed Theodorakis in 1970, and he went to Paris; in July 1970 he was a participant in the Congress at the United Nations World Youth Assembly in New York. Bibl.: J. Coubard, *Mikis Theodorakis* (Paris, 1969).

Theodorini, Helena. She was born on March 25, 1857 (not 1862). Exact date of death, Feb. 27 (not March), 1926. She made her debut in La Scala, Milan, on March 20, 1880 (not 1883). In 1964 the Rumanian government issued a postage stamp in her honor bearing her stage portrait. Cf. O. Cosma, *Elena Teodorini* (Bucharest, 1962).

Thomas, John Charles. Died in Apple Valley, California, Dec. 13, 1960.

Thomas, Michael Tilson, American conductor; b. Hollywood, Dec. 21, 1944. A grandson of Boris and Bessie Thomashefsky, founders of the Yiddish Theater in New York, he was brought up in a cultural atmosphere; studied composition with Ingolf Dahl at the Univ. of Southern California; concurrently took courses in chemistry. His conducting career began when he led concerts at the Ojai Music Festival (1967-69); was also assistant to Pierre Boulez at the Bayreuth Opera. In 1969 he was appointed associate conductor of the Boston Symph. Orch., the youngest ever to receive such a distinction. He was catapulted into public notice spectacularly on Oct. 22, 1969, when he was called upon to conduct the second part of the New York concert of the Boston Symph. Orch., substituting for the regular conductor William Steinberg who was taken suddenly ill. Thomas received on that occasion an enthusiastic critical acclaim; his subsequent appearances with the Boston Symph. Orch. confirmed his exceptional gifts as conductor. In 1971 he was engaged as music director of the Buffalo Philharmonic, combining this post with his regular duties in Boston.

Thompson, John Sylvanus. Died in Tucson, Arizona, March 1, 1963.

Thompson, Randall. Add to works: *Ode to the Virginian Voyage,* for chorus and orch. (Jamestown, Va., April 1, 1957); *Requiem* for double chorus a cappella (Berkeley, Calif., May 22, 1958); *The Passion According to Saint Luke,* oratorio (Boston, March 28, 1965).

Thompson, Will Lamartine, American hymn writer; b. East Liverpool, Ohio, Nov. 7, 1847; d. there, Sept. 20, 1909. He studied music at the Boston Cons.; wrote a number of religious and patriotic songs. His best known hymn is *Softly and Tenderly Jesus is Calling.* Cf. R. G. McCutchan, *Our Hymnody* (N.Y., 1937).

Thomson, George. Served as secretary to the Board of Trustees for the Encouragement of Arts and Manufactures in Scotland from 1780 to 1839 (not to 1830) for 59 years (not 50). Add to bibl.: Cecil Hopkinson and C. B. Oldman, *Thomson's Collections of National song* (Edinburgh Bibliographical Society Transactions, 1940 and 1954).

Thomson, Virgil. Was organist at King's Chapel in 1923-24 (not 1922-23). He composed the score for the film *Voyage to America,* for the U.S. Pavilion at the N.Y. World's Fair (1964). Add to works: *Missa pro Defunctis* (State Univ. College of Education, Potsdam, N.Y., May 14, 1960); *The Feast of Love,* for baritone and orch. (Washington, Nov. 1, 1964); opera, *Lord Byron* (1970). He publ. an autobiography calmly titled *Virgil Thomson* (N. Y. 1967) and a book of national historic criticism, *American Music Since 1910* (N. Y., 1971). Bibl.: K. O. Hoover and John Cage, *Virgil Thomson: His Life and Music* (N. Y., 1959).

Thorborg, Kerstin. Died in Hedemora, Sweden, April 12, 1970.

Thorne, Francis, American composer; b. in Bay Shore, Long Island, N. Y., June 23, 1922. Of a cultural heritage (his maternal grandfather was the opera expert Gustave Kobbé), he absorbed musical impressions crouching under the grand piano while his father, a banker, played ragtime; at puberty, sang in a school chorus; entering Yale Univ., he was a member of the varsity rowboat team, as a prelude to service in the U.S. Navy during World War II. Returning from the wars, he joined the stock-brokerage firm of Harris, Upham & Co. as a customers' man, but soon defected and joined various N. Y. jazz groups as pianist; then went to Italy; took lessons in advanced composition with David Diamond in Florence; divided his leisure between the banks of the Arno and Hudson Rivers. Impressed and distressed by the inhumanly impecunious condition of middle-aged atonal composers, he established an eleemosynary Thorne Music Fund drawing on the natural wealth of his family, and disbursed munificent grants to those who qualify, among them Stefan Wolpe, Ben Weber, Lou Harrison, Lester Trimble, John Cage and David Diamond. Thorne's own music shares with that of his beneficiaries a determined vigesimosecular spirit, with a prudential dissonant technique servicing the conceptual abstractions and titular paronomasia of their compositions. Works: Symph. No. 1 (1961); *Elegy* for orch. (1963); *Burlesque Overture* (1964); Symph. No. 2 (1964); *Rhapsodic Variations* for piano and orch. (1965); piano concerto (1966); *Gemini Variations* for viola, double-bass and orch. (1968); *Sonar Plexus* for electric guitar and orch. (1968); *Chamber Deviation I* for clarinet, double-bass and percussion (1968); Symph. No. 3 for percussion and strings (1969); *Antiphonies* for wind instruments and percussion (1970); *Chamber Deviation II* for brass quintet, guitar and percussion (1971).

Thornhill, Claude, American pianist and band leader; b. Terre Haute, Indiana, Aug. 10, 1909; d. Caldwell, N.J., July 1, 1965. He received regular academic training at the Cincinnati Cons. and at the Curtis Institute of Music in Philadelphia; was arranger for Benny Goodman and others; in 1940 organized a band of his own. Because of his uncommon musical literacy, he was able to impress plausible novelties on his arrangements (e.g., contrapuntal use of French horn passages).

Tibbett, Lawrence. Died in New York, July 15, 1960. Made his last appearance with the Metropolitan Opera on March 24, 1950, as Ivan in *Khovanshchina.*

Tierney, Harry, American composer of popular music; b. Perth Amboy, N.J., May 21, 1895; d. New York, March 22, 1965. He studied piano and planned a concert career; then turned to composition of popular songs; wrote many numbers for the Ziegfeld Follies. His musical shows *Irene* (N.Y., Nov. 18, 1919), *Up She Goes* (N.Y., Nov. 6, 1922) and *Kid Boots* (N.Y., Dec. 31, 1923) were quite successful, but they were eclipsed by the fame of his *Rio Rita* (N.Y., Feb. 2, 1927). His early song *M-i-s-s-i-s-s-i-p-p-i* (1916) flooded the nation.

Tijardović, Ivo. Add to works: *Marco Polo,* opera (Zagreb, Dec. 3, 1960).

Tikotsky, Evgeny Karlovitch. Died in Minsk, Nov. 24, 1970.

Tillyard, Henry Julius Wetenhall. Died in Cambridge, England, Jan. 2, 1968.

Tiomkin, Dmitri, composer of film music; b. St. Petersburg, May 10, 1894; studied piano at the St. Petersburg Cons. with Isabelle Vengerova; left Russia in 1921; lived in Berlin. He began his career as a concert pianist in Europe; came to America in 1925; after a few years in New York, settled in Hollywood, where he became a highly successful composer of film music. He received an Academy Award for best score and best theme song of *High Noon* (1952); was also the recipient of awards of merit, scrolls of appreciation, plaques of recognition, golden globes, etc. He published a dictated autobiography under the title *Please Don't Hate Me* (N. Y., 1959).

Tippett, Michael. Was knighted in 1966. Add to works: *King Priam,* opera (Coventry, May 29, 1962); *Concerto for Orchestra* (Edinburgh, Aug. 26, 1963); *The Vision of St. Augustine,* cantata (London, Jan. 19, 1966); *The Shires Suite* for chorus and orch. (London, July 8, 1970); *The Knot Garden,* opera to his own libretto (London, Dec. 2, 1970). See A. Milner, *The Music of Michael Tippett* in 'The Mus. Quarterly' (Oct. 1964); Ian Kemp, editor, *Michael Tippett: A Symposium on His 60th Birthday* (London, 1965).

Tircuit, Heuwell (Andrew), American composer, percussion player and music critic; b. Plaquemine, Louisiana, Oct. 18, 1931. He was trained in a Gregorian Boys' Choir; played drums at the age of 9; studied piano and theory at Louisiana State Univ.; took courses in musicology with John Ohl of Northwestern Univ. (M.M., 1964); served in U.S. Army Bands (1954-56). In 1956 he went to Japan; played percussion in Japanese orchestras and wrote music criticism for the 'Asahi Evening News' and the 'Japan Times.' Returning to the U.S. in 1963, he served as asst. music critic of the 'Chicago American' and later critic for music and dance of the 'San Francisco Chronicle.' In his compositions, he cultivates a disestablishmentarian latitudinarianism uncircumscribed by doctrinaire precepts, in a communicative vigesimosecular idiom; as a professional drummer he makes liberal use in his music of a broad variety of percussionable objects, including oriental bells, wood blocks and cymbals; he successfully essays a compatible westernization of Japanese modalities; preserves a cogent polythematic illation in organizing his sonorous materials, and revives in a modern way the traditional dichotomy of classical binary forms. Works: *The Lonely People,* a ballet (1950); string quartet No. 1 (1953); trumpet sonata (1954); sonata for harp solo (1957); string quartet No. 2 (1957); *Argument,* for dance (1959); *Manga,* suite of 7 symph. sketches (1959); cello concerto (1960); *A Singing of Instruments* (1960); string trio (1960); violin sonata (1960); viola sonata (1961); *Erotica I* for alto flute solo (1961); *Cassation* for cello and wind quintet (1961); *Knell* for 27 solo flutes and percussion (1962); *Odoru Katachi* (*Dance Patterns*) for solo percussion and orch. (1962); *Chronological Variations* for orch. (1963); a cycle of 6 orchestral concertos (1966-72); *Fool's Dance* for solo percussionist and orch. (1967); flute sonata (1968); Concerto for percussionist and orch. (his most ambitious work; Chicago, July 6, 1969); *Erotica II* for solo percussionist (1970); Concerto for violin and 10 wind instruments (1971); *Erotica III* for solo cello (1971); also 3 extensive cantatas of significant subject matter: No. 1, in Japanese, dealing with birth (1959); No. 2, an Epithalamium, with an optional children's chorus representing the prospective family (1962); No. 3, on the existence of God (1967).

Tischer, Gerhard. Died in Starnberg, Dec. 1, 1959.

Tischler, Hans, Austrian-American musicologist; b. Vienna, Jan. 18, 1915. He studied piano with Paul Wittgenstein; composition with Richard Stöhr and Franz Schmidt; musicology with Robert Lach, Egon Wellesz and Robert Haas at Vienna Univ. (Ph. D., 1937). He left Austria in 1938, settling in the U.S.; continued his musicological studies with Leo Schrade at Yale Univ. (Ph. D., 1942). He taught music theory at West Virginia Wesleyan College (1945-47) and at Roosevelt Univ. in Chicago (1947-65). In 1965 he was appointed prof. of music at Indiana Univ., Bloomington. In 1964-65 he held a Guggenheim Fellowship. Publications: *The Perceptive Music Listener* (N.Y., 1955); *Practical Harmony* (Boston, 1964); edited *A Complete Edition of the Earliest Motets* (Rome, 1966); *A Complete Edition of the Parisian Two-Part Organa* (Rome, 1966); contributed articles to the 'Mus. Quarterly' and European periodicals.

Tishchenko, Boris, Soviet composer; b. Leningrad, March 23, 1939. He studied composition at the Leningrad Cons. with Salmanov, Voloshinov and Evlakhov, graduating in 1962; later took courses with Shostakovitch. In his works he demonstrates a strong rhythmic power and polyphonic mastery; his musical style is greatly advanced without overstepping the bounds of tonality. Works: piano variations (1955); sonata for unaccompanied violin (1957); violin concerto (1958); string quartet (1959); *Lenin Lives,* cantata (1959); symph. (1961); piano concerto (1962); ballet *The Twelve,* after Alexander Blok (Leningrad, Dec. 31, 1964); cello concerto (Leningrad, Feb. 5, 1966).

Tisne, Antoine, French composer; b. Lourdes, Nov. 29, 1932. He studied with Darius Milhaud and Jean Rivier at the Paris Cons., obtaining Premier Second Grand Prix de Rome in 1962. His works include Symph. No. 1 (1960); 3 piano concertos (1958, 1961, 1963); *À une ombre* for 22 players (1963); violin sonata (1963); string quartet (1963); cello sonata (1964); *Visions des temps immémoriaux* for Ondes Martenot, piano, and percussion (1965); *Caractères* for 10 wind instruments (1965); flute concerto (1965); cello concerto (1965); Symph. No. 2 (1966); *Cosmogonies* for 3 orchestras (Paris, Dec. 10, 1968); *Disparates* for wind quintet (1968); *Elégie* for double-bass and piano (1969); *Séquences pour un rituel* for string orch. (1969); *Hommage à Calder* for clavecin (1969).

Toch, Ernst. Died in Los Angeles, Oct. 1, 1964. Add to works: *Peter Pan,* fairy tale for orch. (Seattle, Feb. 13, 1956); *3 Improvisations* for violin, viola and cello (1963); Symph. No. 5 (Boston, March 13, 1964); *Symphony for strings* (1964); *3 pantomimes* for orch. (1964); quartet for oboe, clarinet, bassoon and viola (1964); *Enamored Harlequin,* a puppet show (1964); 3 solo pieces for violin, for viola and for cello (1964).

Toduţa, Sigismund, Rumanian composer; b. Simeria, May 17, 1908. He studied in Cluj and later at the Santa Cecilia Academy in Rome (1936-38) with Pizzetti (composition) and Casella (piano). Returning to Rumania, he became an instructor at the Cluj Cons., and in 1962 became its director. His music is distinguished by a flowing romantic melody in large rhapsodic sonorities. He wrote 5 symphonies (1954, 1955, 1957, 1961, 1963); flute sonata (1952); cello sonata (1952); violin sonata (1953); oboe sonata (1956); opera, *Manole* (1943-47).

Toebosch, Louis, Dutch composer; b. Maastricht, March 28, 1916. He studied organ; became active as church organist and choir leader in Breda where he settled in 1940. He won a prize at the International Organ Improvisation Competition at Haarlem in 1951. His music combines the polyphonic style of the Renaissance with modern techniques; he applies the 12-tone method of composition even in his sacred music. Principal works: *Breda Suite* for orch. (1948); *Christmas Cantata* (1959); *Missa 12 Apostolorum* (1961); *Philippica Moderata,* written for the 50th anniversary of scientific research of the Philips Co., for mixed chorus, contralto, baritone and orch. (1963).

Tokatyan, Armand. Died in Pasadena, Calif., June 12, 1960. Born (of Armenian descent), Feb. 12, 1896 (not 1899). He made his Metropolitan début on Nov. 19, 1922 (not Feb. 14, 1923) as Turiddu in a concert version of *Cavalleria Rusticana.*

Toldrá, Eduardo. Died in Barcelona, May 31, 1962.

Tollefsen, Carl H. Died in Brooklyn, N. Y., Dec. 10, 1963.

Tolstoy, Dmitri Alexeyevitch, Soviet composer, son of the writer Alexey Tolstoy; b. Berlin, Jan. 20, 1923. He went to Russia with his father after temporary emigration; studied at the Leningrad Cons., graduating in 1947; took courses in composition with Shebalin in Moscow and Shostakovitch in Leningrad. Works: *Poem About Leningrad* for orch. (1953); *Spring Victory,* cantata (1946); *Masquerade,* opera (Moscow, Jan. 17, 1956); *Mariuta,* opera (Perm, Dec. 30, 1960); 3 piano sonatas; 12 preludes for piano; many songs.

Tomasi, Henri. Died in Paris, Jan. 13, 1971. Add to the list of works: *Jabadao,* choreographic symph. poem (Paris, Jan. 10, 1960); *Symphonie du tiers monde* (Paris, Feb. 18, 1968); *Chant pour le Vietnam,* symph. poem for wind band and percussion (Paris, Dec. 7, 1969); cello concerto (Paris, Jan. 21, 1970).

Toni, Alceo. Died in Milan, Dec. 4, 1969.

Torkanowsky, Werner, German-American conductor, b. Berlin, March 30, 1926. He studied music with his mother; went to Palestine after 1933; emigrated to the U.S. in 1948. He began his musical career as a violinist; was a member of the Pittsburgh

Symph. Orch.; appeared as soloist with Robert Shaw Collegiate Chorale Orch. In 1955 he joined the master class of Pierre Monteux in Maine; subsequently conducted at the Spoleto Festivals. In 1963 he was engaged by the New Orleans Philharmonic Symph. Orch. as music director and conductor.

Tosar, Hector. Add to works: *Stray Birds,* triptych for baritone and 11 instruments, to the text by Rabindranath Tagore (Washington, May 11, 1965).

Toscanini, Arturo. Add to bibl.: Patrick Cairns (Spike) Hughes, *The Toscanini Legacy: A Critical Study of Arturo Toscanini's Performances of Beethoven, Verdi, and Other Composers* (London, 1959); Luciana Frassati, *Il Maestro Arturo Toscanini e il suo mondo* (Turin, 1967).

Tours, Frank E. Died in Santa Monica, Calif., Feb. 2, 1963.

Toyama, Yuzo, Japanese composer; b. Tokyo, May 10, 1931. He studied at the Tokyo Academy of Music graduating in 1952, and in Vienna (1958-60). He writes mostly instrumental music. His works include: *Rhapsody* for orch. (1960); *Divertimento* for orch. (1961); and violin concerto (1963).

Toye, (John) Francis. Died in Florence, Oct 31, 1964.

Tozzi, Giorgio, American bass singer of Italian descent; b. Chicago, Jan. 8, 1923. He studied in Italy, and after touring as a concert singer, sang at La Scala in Milan. In 1955 he was engaged at the Metropolitan Opera in New York; made a fine impression as Figaro in *Le Nozze di Figaro* and Don Basilio in *Il Barbiere de Siviglia.* He achieved spectacular success in the role of Hans Sachs in the film of *Die Meistersinger,* produced for German television by the Hamburg State Opera in 1969.

Traetta, Tommaso (Michele Francesco Saverio). Add to bibl.: F. Casavola, *Tommaso Traetta di Bitonto* (Bari, 1957).

Trambitsky, Victor Nikolayevitch. Died in Leningrad, Aug. 13, 1970. He moved to Sverdlovsk in 1930 (not in 1925). *Orlena* was produced in Sverdlovsk on Nov. 13, 1934 (not 1935). His opera *The Laceworker Nastia* was produced in Leningrad in 1963.

Trautwein, Friedrich, German electrical engineer; b. Würzburg, Aug. 11, 1888; d. Düsseldorf, Dec. 21, 1956. He was trained in engineering; was an instructor in musical acoustics at the Berlin Musikhochschule. In 1930 he constructed an electronic musical instrument which became known, after the first syllable of his name, as Trautonium. Hindemith wrote a concerto for it. Trautwein contributed numerous articles on electronic music to German periodicals.

Tregian, Francis, English musician; b. 1574; d. London, 1619. He was a recusant, and fled England to escape persecution; was attached to Catholic dignitaries in Douai and in Rome. Returning to England to settle his father's estate, he was convicted in 1609, remaining in prison until his death. His significance for English music lies in the fact that he was the scribe of the Fitzwilliam Virginal Book and of 2 manuscripts containing more than 2000 motets, madrigals, etc., some of them possibly of his own composition. Cf. Elizabeth Cole, *In Search of Francis Tregian,* in 'Music & Letters' (Jan. 1952).

Tremblay, Gilles, Canadian composer; b. Arvida, Quebec, Sept. 6, 1932. He studied at the Cons. of Montreal with Germaine Malépart (piano) and Claude Champagne (composition); then went to Paris where he took courses with Olivier Messiaen, Yvonne Loriod, Andrée Vaurabourg, and Maurice Martenot; worked with the Groupe de Récherches Musicales at the Paris Radio. Upon returning to Canada he joined the staff of the Conservatoire du Quebec in Montreal. An adept of constructivism, he uses optical notation in his scores. Works: *Phases* for piano (1956); *Réseaux* for piano (1958); *Cantique de Durées* for 7 instrumental formations (Paris, March 24, 1963); *Champs I* for piano, marimba, vibraphone and percussion (1965); *Kékoba* for vocal trio and percussion (Montreal, April 5, 1967); sonorization of the Quebec Pavilion at Expo '67 in Montreal, for an icositetrastereophonic electro-acoustical system (1967); *Souffles* (*Champs II*) for wind ensemble, piano and percussion (Montreal, March 21, 1968); *Vers* (*Champs III*) for 9 instruments and percussion (Stratford Festival, Ontario, Aug. 2, 1969); *Le Sifflement des vents porteurs de l'amour* for flute and percussion (1971).

Trimble, Lester, American composer; b. Bangor, Wisconsin, Aug. 29, 1923. He studied composition with Nikolai Lopatnikoff at the Carnegie Institute of Technology in Pittsburgh and later took private lessons in Paris with Darius Milhaud and Arthur Honegger; subsequently was appointed to the faculty of the Univ. of Maryland. Works: 2 string quartets (1950, 1955); Symphony (1951); sextet for woodwinds, horn and piano (1952); violin concerto (1955); *Closing Piece* for orch. (1957); *5 Episodes* for orch. (1961); *Kennedy Concerto* for chamber orch. (1964); *In Praise of Diplomacy and Common Sense* for baritone, percussion, male speaking chorus and 2 speaking soloists (1965); *Solo for a Virtuoso* for solo violin (1971); songs.

Trudić, Božidar, Serbian composer; b. Smederevska Palanka, March 24, 1911. He studied with Slavenski; became a teacher in Sarajevo. His music is inspired by Serbian folksongs, but the harmonic treatment is often modernistic. Among his works are a cantata *1804* (Sarajevo, Dec. 26, 1956); a violin concerto (1951); cello concerto (1963); 2 symphonies (1954, 1957); choruses and songs.

Trunk, Richard. Died in Herrsching am Ammersee, June 2, 1968.

Tsfasman, Alexander Naumovitch. Died in Moscow, Feb. 20, 1971.

Tsouyopoulos, Georges, Greek composer; b. Athens, Oct. 11, 1930. He received his early training in Athens and Milan; then went to Zürich to study with Hindemith. In 1962 he settled in Munich. Works: *Sinfonietta da Camera* for 8 instruments (1955); *Serenata* for soprano, flute, guitar and viola (1957); *Due Madrigali* for soprano and orch. (1957); *Tre Frammenti* for chorus and orch. (1958); *Due Toccate* for piano (1958); *Music for Percussion* (1959); 2 string quartets; vocal pieces. His early compositions are neo-classical in style; later he adopted serial methods. In his latest works he departs still farther from orthodoxy, determinedly pursuing the goal of structural indeterminacy.

Tua, Teresina. Died in Rome, Oct. 29, 1955.

Tucker, Richard. His real name was Reuben Ticker. Date of birth, Brooklyn, Aug. 28, 1913 (not 1914).

Tudor, David, American avant-garde pianist and aleatory composer; b. Philadelphia, Jan. 20, 1926. He studied organ with William Hawke, piano with Irma Wolpe and composition with Stefan Wolpe. He played the organ in St. Mark's Church in Philadelphia (1938-43) and at Swarthmore College (1944-48); these ecclesiastical services to the contrary notwithstanding, he instinctively inclined towards modern experimentation and developed a hyper-modern virtuoso technique as a quaquaversal hyperdactyl pianist; earned an awesome reputation by his performance of the nearly insurmountable 2nd piano sonata of Pierre Boulez (N. Y., Dec. 17, 1950), which he memorized video-mentally from the score. Composers of indeterminate music in optical notation flocked to him for congenial reification of their works. He became the unique collaborator, animator and divinator of the recondite practices of John Cage, and was the first to unplay John Cage's monumental tacit piece *4'33"* (Woodstock, N. Y., Aug 29, 1952); was also unheard in it in Cologne, Germany, and elsewhere, obtaining vociferous acclaim. In audible performance he often applies special piano techniques; thus in playing *Five Piano Pieces for David Tudor* by Sylvano Bussotti, he puts on thick gloves to make sure that only tone clusters are possible. In addition, he mastered the Argentine instrument, the Bandoneon, and performed compositions specially written for him and it. In 1970 he was one of the overseers of the design of the Pepsi-Cola Pavilion for the Project of Experiments in Art and Technology, Inc., at the Expo '70 in Osaka, Japan. As a composer he contributed the following innovative works: *Fluorescent Sound* (Stockholm, Sept. 13, 1964); *Bandoneon —!* (factorial bandoneon, idempotentially multiplied ad infinitum); *Reunion* (in collaboration with the painter Marcel Duchamp and others); *Rainforest,* for dancers; and, in collaboration with John Cage, *Talk I* (Ann Arbor, Mich., Sept. 19, 1965) and *Fontana Mix* for bass drum and electronic circuits (Brandeis Univ., Waltham, Mass., April Fools' Day, 1967). Some of his biographers and annotators claim for him a direct descent, possibly through a morganatic line, from Henry Tudor (Henry VIII) or from one of the decapitated lovers of the beheaded Queen Anne Boleyn. Since Henry VIII himself dabbled in 'aleatorick musick,' David Tudor's own preoccupation with tonal indeterminacy may be a recessive royal trait.

Tulindberg, Erik, Finnish composer; b. in Lillkyro, Feb. 22, 1761; d. Abo (Turku), Sept. 1, 1814. He studied academic disciplines at the Abo Academy, obtaining the degree of Magister Philosophiae in 1782; was subsequently a municipal functionary in Abo. Music was his avocation; he learned to play the violin; owned a large library, including works of Mozart, Haydn and Boccherini; in 1797 he was elected member of the Swedish Academy of Music. He wrote a violin concerto and 6 string quartets in the traditional style of the Viennese School. His works show a respectable ability, and he is entitled to a place in music history as the first professional composer of Finland.

Turchi, Guido. Add to works: *Il buon soldato Svajk,* opera (Milan, April 6, 1962).

Turner, Robert Comrie. Add to works: symph. for strings (1962); *Phoenix and the Turtle* for mezzo-soprano and chamber orch. (Vancouver, Aug. 23, 1964).

Tusler, Robert Leon, American musicologist; b. Stoughton, Wisconsin, April 1, 1920; studied piano and organ at Friends' Univ., Wichita, Kansas (B.M., 1947); musicology at the Univ. of Calif., Los Angeles (M.A., 1952); then at the Univ. of Utrecht, Holland, with Smijers and Reeser, on a Fulbright Scholarship (1956-58). In 1958 he joined the music faculty of Univ. of Calif., Los Angeles. His writings include *The Style of J. S. Bach's Chorale Preludes* (Berkeley, Univ. of Calif., 1956); *The Organ Music of Jan Pieterszoon Sweelinck* (Bilthoven, 1958). He contributed articles to the 'Mus. Quarterly' and other scholarly periodicals.

Tzvetanov, Tzvetan, Bulgarian composer; b. Sofia, Nov. 6, 1931. He studied with Vladigerov at the Sofia Cons., where he subsequently became an instructor. Among his works the most significant is *The Great Beginning,* cantata (1962); he also wrote chamber music and songs.

Tzybin, Vladimir Nikolayevitch, Russian composer; b. Ivanovo-Voznesensk, 1877; d. Moscow, May 31, 1949. He played flute in the orch. of the Bolshoi Theater in Moscow from 1896 to 1907 and from 1921 to 1929. From 1907 to 1920 he was first flutist at the Imperial Opera of St. Petersburg. He composed 2 operas: *Flengo* (1918) and *Tale of the Dead Princess and Seven Heroes* (1947); publ. several collections of flute pieces. He was esteemed as a pedagogue.

U

Unger, Heinz, German-Canadian conductor; b. Berlin, Dec. 14, 1895; d. Toronto, Feb. 25, 1965. He studied in Berlin and Munich; was active as a choral conductor in Berlin until the advent of the Nazi regime in 1933. He then went to Russia; was conductor of the Leningrad Radio Orch. (1934-36). After a sojourn in England, he settled in Canada in 1948 and acquired a great renown as conductor of the Toronto Symph. Orch. He publ. an account of his conducting experiences in Russia under the title *Hammer, Sickle and Baton* (London, 1939).

Unger, Hermann. Died in Cologne, Dec. 31, 1958.

Unger, Max. Died in Zürich, Dec. 1, 1959.

Upton, William Treat. Died in Adelphi, Maryland, Jan. 19, 1961.

Uribe-Holguín, Guillermo. His symphonies Nos. 4-7 were first performed in Bogotá on the following dates: No. 4 (April 13, 1956); No. 5 (Oct. 26, 1956); No. 6 (April 5, 1957); No. 7 (July 20, 1957). He also wrote a historical symph. poem, *Conquistadores* (Bogotá, April 3, 1959).

Ursprung, Otto. Died in Schöndorf-am-Ammersee, Sept. 14, 1960.

Usandizaga, José María. Add to bibl.: Jesús María de Arozamena, *José María Usandizaga y la bella época donostiarra* (San Sebastian, 1969).

Ustvolskaya, Galina, Soviet composer; b. Petrograd, July 17, 1919. She studied with Shostakovitch at the Leningrad Cons., graduating in 1947. Her early music was marked by a romantic Russian manner; later she progressed toward greater melodic diversity and harmonic complexity; in some of her chamber music she applies dodecaphonic procedures. Works: *Stepan Razin's Dream,* for bass and orch. (Leningrad, Feb. 10, 1949); *A Man from the Tall Mountain,* for voices and orch. (Leningrad, May 22, 1952); Symph with voices (1955); *Heroic Deed,* symph. poem (1957); piano concerto (1947); octet for 4 violins, 2 oboes, piano and kettledrums (1951); string quartet; 3 piano sonatas; violin sonata; cello sonata; etc.

V

Vacek, Miloš, Czech composer; b. Horní Roveň, June 20, 1928. He studied organ and composition at the Prague Cons., graduating in 1951; devoted himself primarily to theater and film music; some of his scores for the Prague Puppet Theater became popular. Works: an opera, *Jan Zelivský;* ballets, *Wind in the Hair, The Last Dandelion, Meteor* and *Decameron; Sinfonietta; Rebel Rhapsody* for orch.; *Pastorella* for piccolo and wind quintet; other chamber music.

Vaet, Jacobus. His birthplace is not certain; it may be Courtrai or Harlebeke. He was a tenor in the Flemish Chapel of Charles V in 1550. A complete edition of his work was undertaken by M. Steinhardt in 'Denkmäler der Tonkunst in Österreich' (Graz/Vienna, vols. 98, 100, 103/104, 108/109). See also 'Addenda to the Biography of Jacobus Vaet,' by M. Steinhardt in *The Commonwealth of Music* (N.Y., 1964) and his paper, 'The Missa Si me tenes: a Problem of Authorship' in *Aspects of Medieval and Renaissance Music* (N.Y., 1965).

Valen, Fartein. Add to bibl.: B. Kortsen, *Studies of Form in Fartein Valen's Music* (Oslo, 1962); idem, *Melodic Structure and Thematic Unity in Fartein Valen's Music* (2 vols., Glasgow, 1963); idem, *Fartein Valen, Life and Music* (3 vols., Oslo, 1965).

Valentin, Erich. 1964, appointed director of the State Hochschule für Musik in Munich.

Vancea, Zeno, Rumanian composer and musicologist; b. Vasiova (Banat), Oct. 8, 1900. He studied at the Cluj Cons. and later in Vienna with Ernst Kanitz (1921-26). He occupied various teaching posts, and in 1949 was appointed prof. at the Bucharest Cons. In 1954 he became the editor of the most important Rumanian musical monthly 'Muzica.' Vancea belongs to the national school of Rumanian composers; in his music he makes use of native folksong patterns without direct quotations from popular melodies. Harmonically, he adopts many procedures of western modern music. Among his works are a ballet, *Priculiciul* (1932); Sinfonietta (1949); *Ouverture,* subtitled *A Summer Day in a Collective Farm* (1951): *Burlesque* for orch. (1959); *Symphonic Triptych* (1959); *Concerto* for chamber orchestra (1961); 2 string quartets; many choruses and songs.

Van Delden, Lex, Dutch composer; b. Amsterdam, Sept. 10, 1919. He studied medicine, music and literature; was active as music critic. Works: 7 symphonies (1951, 1953, 1956, 1957, 1959, 1963, 1964); harp concerto (1951); *Introduzione ed Allegro* for violin, piano and orch. (1951); trumpet concerto (1956); concerto for 2 oboes and orch. (1959); piano concerto (1960); concerto for 2 string orchestras (1961); *Piccola musica concertata* for chamber orch. (1963).

Van Den Borren, Charles (-Jean-Eugène). Died in Brussels, Jan. 14, 1966.

Vanni-Marcoux. See **Marcoux.**

Van Vactor, David. Add to works: violin concerto (Knoxville, April 10, 1951); Symph. No. 2 (Pittsburgh, April 3, 1959); woodwind quintet (1959); octet for brass (1963); *Suite on Chilean Folk Themes* for orch. (1963); *Sinfonia breve* (Indianapolis, Oct. 30, 1966); *Economy Band No. 1* for trumpet, trombone and percussion (1966); *Economy Band No. 2* for horn, tuba and percussion (1969); *Walden* for chorus and orch. to texts from Thoreau's *Walden* (Knoxville, March 1, 1970). The idiom of his music is medium modern, set in sophisticatedly enhanced tonalities and sparked with ingenious inventions.

Van Vechten, Carl. Died in New York, Dec. 21, 1964.

Varèse, Edgar. Died in New York, Nov. 6, 1965. Date of birth, Dec. 22, 1883 (not 1885). *Arcana* was first performed by the Philadelphia Orch., Leopold Stokowski conducting, April 8, 1927. Add to works: *Etude pour Espace* for chorus, 2 pianos and percussion (N. Y., April 20, 1947, composer conducting); *Nocturnal* for soprano, chorus of bass voices, orch., piano and percussion, to words from *House of Incest* by Anaïs Nin (N. Y., May 1, 1961). See Chou Wen-chung, *Varèse: A Sketch of the Man and His Music* ('The Mus. Quarterly,' April, 1966); Fernand Ouellette, *Edgar Varèse* (Paris, 1966; in English, N. Y., 1968); Georges Charbonnier, *Entretiens avec Edgard Varèse* (Paris, 1970).

Varga, Ovidiu, Rumanian composer; b. Pascani, Oct. 5, 1913. He studied violin and composition in Jassy; subsequently became prof. at the Bucharest Cons. He excels in vocal music; has written several cantatas on patriotic subjects; a concerto for string orch. and percussion (1957); many mass songs and instrumental pieces.

Varlamov, Alexander Egorovitch. Add bibl.: Natalya Listova, *Alexander Varlamov* (Moscow, 1968).

Varro, Marie-Aimée, French pianist; b. Brunoy, Feb. 18, 1915; d. Neuchâtel, Sept. 14, 1971. She studied piano at the Paris Cons., obtaining the Premier Prix; she subsequently worked with Robert Casadesus and Alfred Cortot; completed her advanced studies with Emil von Sauer in Vienna who gave her indications for authentic interpretation of Liszt's piano works which he had received from Liszt himself. In her own career, she specialized in the works of the great romantic composers, particularly Schumann, Chopin, Liszt and Brahms. She gave recitals in Europe and America; also appeared as soloist with major orchestras.

Varviso, Silvio, Swiss conductor; b. Zürich, Feb. 26, 1924. He studied piano and conducting at the Zürich Cons.; was conductor at St. Gallen (1946-50); at the Basel Stadttheater (1950-58); guest conductor at the Berlin Opera (1958-61); then with the San Francisco Opera (1959-61); made his Metropolitan Opera debut in N. Y. in 1961. He was conductor of the Stockholm Opera from 1965-72; in 1972 appointed musical director of the Stuttgart Opera.

Varvoglis, Mario. Died in Athens, July 30, 1967.

Vassilenko, Sergey Nikiforovitch. The title of his third opera is *Buran* (name of the protagonist, not the word meaning blizzard). Both this opera and *The Great Canal* were written in collaboration with the Uzbek musician, Mukhtar Ashrafi.

Vatielli, Francesco. Date of birth, Jan. 1, 1877 (not Dec. 31, 1876).

Vaughan Williams, Ralph. Correct title, *On Wenlock Edge* (not *Wenleck Edge*). Add bibl.: J. Day, *Vaughan Williams* (London, 1961); A. E. Dickinson, *Vaughan Williams* (London, 1963); M. Kennedy, *The Works of Ralph Vaughan Williams* (London, 1964); Ursula Vaughan Williams, *R.V.W.: A Biography of Ralph Vaughan Williams* (London, 1964); M. Hurd, *Vaughan Williams* (London, 1970).

Vecsei, Desider Josef. Died in Hollywood, March 1, 1966.

Vega, Aurelio de la, Cuban-American composer; b. Havana, Nov. 28, 1925. He studied in Havana; went to America in 1947 and served as cultural attaché at the Cuban Consulate in Los Angeles; there he took composition lessons with Ernst Toch. At first he cultivated Cuban melorhythms but soon adopted modernistic methods. In 1960 he was appointed to the faculty of San Fernando Valley State College. Works: piano trio (1949); *Soliloquio* for viola and piano (1950); *Obertura a una Farsa Seria* (Havana, April 28, 1951); *Leyenda del Ariel Criollo* for cello and piano (1953); *Elegía* for strings (London, Nov. 16, 1954); string quartet (1957); wind quintet (1959); trio for flute, oboe and clarinet (1960); *Sinfonía en cuatro partes* (Interamerican Music Festival, Washington, D.C., April 30, 1961); *Structures* for piano and string quartet (1962); *Coordinates* for magnetic tape (1963); *Analigus* for orch. (1966); piano music; songs.

Vega, Carlos. Died in Buenos Aires, Feb. 10, 1966.

Velasco-Llanos, Santiago, Colombian composer; b. Cali, Jan. 28, 1915. He studied in Cali with Antonio María Valencia, and later with Domingo Santa Cruz and Pedro Humberto Allende in Santiago, Chile. Returning to Colombia, he was appointed Director of the Cali Cons. Works: *Sinfonia breve* (1947); *Sinfonietta* (1966); *Bambuco jocoso* for orch. (1967); 2 string quartets; piano pieces; choruses; songs.

Vennard, William D., American voice teacher; b. Bloomington, Illinois, Jan. 31, 1909; d. Los Angeles, Jan. 10, 1971. He was a graduate of Northwestern Univ. and the American Cons. of Music in Chicago. In 1946 he joined the faculty of the Univ. of Southern Calif. in Los Angeles. He was a prolific writer of articles for professional journals, including 'American Music Teacher,' 'Journal of Speech and Hearing' and 'Folia Phoniatrica.' He publ. the manuals *Singing, the Mechanism and the Technique* and *Developing Voices;* he also appeared as a singer at various functions in California.

Veprik, Alexander Moiseyevitch. Died in Moscow, Oct. 13, 1958.

Verdi, (Fortunino) Giuseppe (Francesco). A definitive *vita* in 4 vols. by Franco Abbiate, *Giuseppe Verdi,* was publ. by Ricordi in Milan in 1959. Add to bibl.: P. Petit, *Verdi* (Paris, 1958); M. Mila, *Il melodramma di Verdi* (Milan, 1960); Frank Walker, *The Man Verdi* (N. Y., 1962); G. Martin, *Verdi, His Music, Life and Times* (N. Y., 1963); C. Osborne, *The Complete Operas of Verdi* (N. Y., 1970).

Veremans, Renaat. Died in Antwerp, June 5, 1969.

Verevka, Grigory, Ukrainian composer; b. Bereznia, Tchernigov district, Dec. 25, 1895; d. Kiev, Oct. 21, 1964. He was a boy chorister in Tchernigov; then studied at the Kiev Institute of Music and Drama; became engaged in choral conducting. He wrote a number of choruses which entered general repertory; made choral arrangements of nearly 100 revolutionary songs.

Verheyden, Edward, Belgian composer; b. Antwerp, Oct. 8, 1878; d. there, April 10, 1959. He studied violin in Antwerp and Brussels; then turned to composition. He wrote the operas *Heibieke* (1908) and *De Geest* (1924); symphonic works; lieder and choruses.

Vermeulen, Matthijs. Died in Laren, Holland, July 29, 1967. Add to works: Symph. No. 6 (Utrecht, Nov. 29, 1959).

Verrall, John. Add to works: *Nonette* for string quartet and wind quintet (1970).

Vetter, Walther. Died in Berlin, April 1, 1967.

Viardot-García, Pauline. Add to bibl.: April FitzLyon, *The Price of Genius: A Life of Pauline Viardot* (London, 1964).

Vickers, Jon, Canadian tenor; b. Prince Albert, Saskatchewan, Oct. 29, 1926. He studied at the Toronto Cons.; went to London where he sang at Covent Garden; in the summer of 1958 appeared as Siegmund in *Die Walküre* at the Wagner Festival in Bayreuth, creating a fine impression; in 1959 was with the Vienna State Opera; made his début at the Metropolitan Opera, as Canio in *Pagliacci* on Jan. 17, 1960; from then on advanced rapidly to the front ranks as a Wagnerian Heldentenor.

Vidu, Ion, Rumanian composer; b. Minerau (Banat), Dec. 14, 1863; d. Lugoj (Banat), Feb. 7, 1931. He studied in Jassy; became choral conductor in Lugoj. He wrote a great number of choruses in a distinct native style, but harmonized his melodies according to German models; many of his arrangements have become repertory pieces in Rumania.

Vieru, Anatol, Rumanian composer; b. Jassy, June 8, 1926. He studied at the Bucharest Cons., and later at the Moscow Cons., where he was a student of Khatchaturian. From his earliest years he began to compose in a relatively advanced idiom, without losing contact with the characteristic melorhythmic patterns of Rumanian folksongs. Very interesting in this respect is his oratorio *Miorita* (1957), after a Rumanian folk tale, in which he applies serial procedures to folklike materials. His Concerto for cello and orchestra, written in an original manner combining neo-classical and impressionistic traits, received the first prize in a Geneva competition (1962). His other works include a Suite for string orch. (1946); concertino for violin and orch. (1952); Concerto for orch. (1954); 2 string quartets (1956); quintet for strings and clarinet (1958); piano pieces; choruses.

Villa-Lobos, Heitor. Died in Rio de Janeiro, Nov. 17, 1959. *Chôros No. 12* was first performed by the Boston Symph. Orch. in Cambridge, Mass., (not in Boston), on Feb. 21 (not Feb. 23), 1945. *Chôros No. 10* was not the score used for the Paris production under the title *Jurupary. Bachianas Brasileiras No. 1* was first performed in Rio de Janeiro, Sept. 12 (not 22), 1932, conducted by Burle Marx (not by Villa-Lobos). *Bachianas Brasileiras No. 2* is scored for chamber orch. (not for 8 cellos and soprano). The exact date of first performance of *Bachianas Brasileiras No. 3* is Feb. 19, 1947, Villa-Lobos conducting, in N. Y. Add to works: *Bachianas Brasileiras No. 9* for strings (1945); Concerto for mouth harmonica and orch. (1955; Cartagena, Colombia, June 5, 1961); *Yerma,* opera after Federico García Lorca (1955; produced posthumously, in Spanish, in Santa Fe, Aug. 12, 1971). Add to bibl.: A. M. di Giacomo, *Villa-Lobos, alma sonora do Brasil* (S. Paulo, 1960); J. C. de Muricy, *Villa-Lobos* (Rio de Janeiro, 1961).

Vincent, John. In 1964 traveled in South America as conductor and lecturer under the auspices of the State Dept. Retired as prof. of music at the Univ. of California, Los Angeles, in 1969. Add to works: *Symphonic Poem after Descartes* (Philadelphia, March 20, 1959); *La Jolla Concerto* for chamber orch. (La Jolla, Calif., July 19, 1959); *Consort* for piano and strings (1960); *Benjamin Franklin Suite* for orch. and glass harmonica obbligato (based on the string quartet attributed to Benjamin Franklin; Philadelphia, March 24, 1963); *Rondo-Rhapsody* (Washington, May 9, 1965); Symph. No. 2 (1965); *The Phoenix, Fabulous Bird,* symph. poem (Phoenix, Arizona, Feb. 21, 1966); *Primeval Void,* one-act opera, to his own libretto (1969); *Stabat Mater,* for chorus (1969).

Viola, P. Anselm, Catalan composer; b. Teruel, July, 1738; d. Montserrat, Jan. 25, 1798. He was a monk at Montserrat; wrote much instrumental music of surprising excellence in a fine baroque style. His *Concerto* for 2 oboes, 2 horns, violins and cello obbligato is included in vol. II of *Música Instrumental,* publ. by the Monastery of Montserrat in 1936, edited by Dom David Pujol.

Viski, Janos, Hungarian composer; b.Kolozsvár, June 10, 1906; d. Budapest, Jan. 16, 1961. He studied with Kodály; in 1940 became prof. of composition at the Music Academy in Budapest. Most of his music is permeated with Hungarian melorhythms, and set in classical forms. Works: *2 Hungarian Dances* (1938); *Enigma,* symph. poem (1939); violin concerto (1946); piano concerto (1952); cello concerto (1959).

Vitalis, George. Died in Athens, April 27, 1959.

Vivaldi, Antonio. Exact date of birth, March 4, 1678. Add to bibl.: Marc Pincherle,

Vivaldi, Genius of the Baroque (translated from French; N. Y., 1962); *Vivaldi, Catalogo numerico-tematico* (Milan, 1968); Walter Kolneder, *Antonio Vivaldi: Leben und Werk* (Wiesbaden, 1965; also in English, London, 1970).

Vlad, Roman. Add to works: *Il Dottore di vetro,* radiophonic opera (Rome, Feb. 26, 1960). He publ. a monograph on Stravinsky (Turin, 1958; in English, London, 1960; 2nd revised ed., 1967).

Vladigerov, Alexander, Bulgarian conductor, son of Pantcho Vladigerov; b. Sofia, Aug. 4, 1933. He studied with his father and also took music courses in Russia. As a conductor, he toured in Poland, Rumania and Russia; returning to Bulgaria he was appointed conductor of the symph. orch. in Rusa. He also composed a number of orchestral pieces, among them *A Rumanian Dance* (1961).

Vladigerov, Pantcho. Born in Zürich (not Shumen), on March 13 (not March 18), 1899, in a geminal parturition. Distrustful of Bulgarian puerperal skill, his mother sped to Zürich with alacrity when she learned that she was going to have a multiple birth. Pantcho's non-identical twin brother Luben, a violinist, was born 16 hours earlier than Pantcho, on the previous day, March 12, 1899. Add to works: *The Legend of the Lake,* ballet (1946); Symph. No. 1 (1939); Symph. No. 2 (1949); piano concertos No. 2 (1930), No. 3 (1937), No. 4 (1953), No. 5 (1963). He also arranged Dinicu's *Hora Staccato* for orch. Bibl.: E. Pavlov, *Pantcho Vladigerov: a Monograph* (Sofia, 1961).

Vlasov, Vladimir Alexandrovitch, Russian composer and ethnomusicologist; b. Moscow, Jan. 7, 1903. He studied violin at the Moscow Cons.; was active as a teacher. In 1936 he traveled to Frunze, Kirgizia, where he diligently went about collecting authentic songs of the natives. In collaboration with Vladimir Fere, similarly intentioned, he wrote a number of operas based on Kirgiz national melorhythms supplied by local musicians. These operas were subsequently produced in Frunze and at the ethnic festivals in Moscow. They include: *Golden Girl* (Frunze, May 1, 1937); *Moon Beauty* (Frunze, April 15, 1939); *For People's Happiness* (Frunze, May 1, 1941); *Patriots* (Frunze, Nov. 6, 1941); *Son of the People* (Frunze, Nov. 8, 1947); *On the Shores of Issyk-Kul* (Frunze, Feb. 1, 1951); *The Witch,* radio opera (1961). Returning to Moscow, Vlasov occupied various administrative positions; publ. articles on Kirgiz folk music. He also wrote a cello concerto (1963); 3 string quartets and a variety of minor pieces and songs.

Vlijmen, Jan van, Dutch composer; b. Rotterdam, Oct. 11, 1935. He studied at the Utrecht Cons. with Kees van Baaren; from his very first steps in composition he adopted the dodecaphonic method, and continued to apply it to most of his music. In 1961 he was appointed Director of the Amersfoort School of Music. He is also active as a pianist. Works: string quartet (1955); quintet for wind instruments (1958); *Costruzione* for 2 pianos (1960); *Serie per 6 strumenti* (1960); *Mythos* for mezzo-soprano and 9 instruments (1962); *Gruppi* for 20 instruments (1962); *Spostamenti* for orch. (1963); *Serenata I* for 12 percussion instruments (1964); *Serenata II* for flute and 4 instrumental groups (1964).

Vogel, Adolf. Died in Vienna, Dec. 20, 1969. Date of birth, Aug. 18, 1897 (not 1895).

Vogel, Wladimir. Title of work, *Spiegelungen* (not *Spielungen*). Add to works: *Meditationen über die Totenmaske von Amedeo Modigliani,* cantata (Lugano, Switzerland, March 31, 1962); *Die Flucht,* dramatic oratorio (Zürich, Nov. 8, 1966); cantata *Gli Spaziali* for speakers, vocalists and orch., to words from the writings of Leonardo da Vinci, *Autour de la Lune* by Jules Verne and utterances of the American astronauts (1970). See Hans Oesch, *Wladimir Vogel; sein Weg zu einer neuen musikalischen Wirklichkeit* (Bern, 1967).

Volkmann, Hans. Died in Dresden, Dec. 26, 1946.

Volkmann, Robert. His complete name is Friedrich Robert Volkmann.

Volkonsky, Andrey, Soviet composer; b. Geneva, of Russian parents of princely nobility, Feb. 14, 1933. He studied piano with Lipatti and composition with Nadia Boulanger in Paris. In 1948 he went to Russia, and studied at the Moscow Cons. with Shaporin (1950-54). His cantata, *The Image of the World* (Moscow, May 8, 1953), and his *Concerto for Orchestra* (Moscow, June 10, 1954) are in the impressionistic style; but beginning with his piano quintet (1955) he deployed a set of increasingly aggressive modernistic procedures in atonal and polytonal idioms. As a result, he was publicly reprimanded by the Union of Soviet Composers; for several years none of his works were performed; his first composition heard after this hiatus was *The Lament of Shaza* for soprano and small orch. (Moscow, May 12, 1965).

Voloshinov, Victor, Soviet composer; b. Kiev, Oct. 17, 1905; d. Leningrad, Oct. 22, 1960. He studied composition with Stcherbatchev at the Leningrad Cons.; later became a prof. there. He wrote the operas *Glory* (1939) and *Stronger than Death* (1942); several symph. suites on Central Asian themes; chamber music; songs; incidental music for the theater. He enjoyed great renown as a pedagogue; many Soviet composers were his students.

Vomáčka, Boleslav. Died in Prague, March 1, 1965.

Vrionides, Christos. Died in Yaphank, Long Island, N.Y., Dec. 31, 1961.

Vuataz, Roger. Add to works: *Monsieur Jabot,* one-act opera-buffa (Geneva, Nov. 28, 1958); *Tipilizoïp,* radiophonic play (1959); *Le Fleuve,* radiophonic fresco (1960); *Solitude,* ballet (1962); *Suite d'après Rembrandt* for harpsichord (1958); *Estampes genevoises,* symph. suite (1959).

Vučković, Vojislav, Serbian composer; b. Pirot, Oct. 18, 1910; d. Belgrade (killed by German police), Dec. 25, 1942. He studied in Prague with J. Suk and Zděnek Nejedlý. Returning to Belgrade in 1934, he displayed energetic activity as composer, conductor, publicist and writer on economic subjects; publ. pamphlets on materialistic interpretation of music in the light of Marxist dialectics. He was in the resistance movement during the German occupation, and was killed by the Nazis in the street. His works include 2 symphonies; a symph. poem, *Burevesnik* (*Stormy Petrel;* 1942; Belgrade, Dec. 25, 1944); a *Heroic Oratorio* (1942; Cetinje, Sept. 5, 1951); chamber music; choruses. After a period of composition in the expressionistic manner (including the application of quartertones) he abruptly changed his style out of ideological considerations to programmatic realism. See V. Peričić, ed., *Vojislav Vučković, Umetnik i borac* (2 vols., Belgrade, 1968).

Vuillermoz, Émile. Died in Paris, March 2, 1960.

Vukdragović, Mihailo, Serbian composer; b. Okučani, Sept. 8, 1900. He studied in Prague; in 1927 returned to Belgrade and was active as conductor and pedagogue. He wrote several works in impressionistic style before embracing the esthetics of socialist realism. Works: symph. poem *Put u pobedu* (*Road to Victory;* Belgrade, Oct. 19, 1945); cantata *Vezilja slobode* (*Champion of Freedom;* Belgrade, Jan. 5, 1948); cantata for bass, speaker, chorus and orch., *Srbija* (*Serbia;* Niš, July 6, 1961). See V. Peričić, *Muzički Stvaraoci u Srbiji* (Belgrade, 1969; pp. 582-90).

Vycpálek, Ladislav. Died in Prague, Jan. 9, 1969.

W

Wagenaar, Bernard. Died in York, Maine, May 19, 1971.

Wagner, Cosima. Date of birth, Dec. 24 (not Dec. 25), 1837. Add to bibl.: Alice Hunt Sokoloff, *Cosima Wagner, Extraordinary Daughter of Franz Liszt* (N. Y., 1969).

Wagner, Joseph Frederick. In 1960 settled in Hollywood; 1961 appointed prof. at Pepperdine College in Los Angeles. Add to works: *Symphonic Transitions* for concert band (1958); *Patterns of Contrast* for wind quartet (1959); *Sonata of Sonnets* for voice and piano (1961); concerto for organ, brass and percussion (1963); *Fantasy Sonata* for harp solo (1963); *Merlin and Sir Boss,* symph. tale for concert band based on *A Connecticut Yankee* by Mark Twain (1963); *American Ballad Set* for chorus a cappella (1963); *Preludes and Toccata* for harp, violin and cello (1964); concerto for harp and orch. (1964); *New England Sampler,* one-act opera (Los Angeles, Feb. 26, 1965); *Concert Piece* for violin and cello (1966); *A Festive Fanfare* for band (1968); *Fantasy and Fugue* for woodwind quintet (1968); *Three Charades* for brass quintet (1968); *12 Concert Preludes* for organ (1969); *Three Browning Love Songs* for voice and piano (1970). Add to books: *Band Scoring* (N. Y., 1960).

Wagner, (Wilhelm) Richard. Add to bibl.: J. Bertram, *Mythos, Symbol, Idee in Richard Wagners Musikdramen* (Hamburg, 1957); O. Daube, *Richard Wagners Lehrjahre aus den erhaltenen Dokumenten* (Cologne, 1960); J. M. Stein, *Richard Wagner and the Synthesis of the Arts* (Detroit, 1960); O. J. Hartmann, *Die Esoterik im Werk Richard Wagners* (Freiburg, 1960); H. Barth, *Internationale Wagner Bibliographie* (Bayreuth, 1961); R. Donington, *Wagner's Ring and Its Symbols* (London, 1963); E. Zuckerman, *The First*

Hundred Years of Wagner's Tristan (N. Y., 1964); R. Gutman, *Richard Wagner: The Man, His Life, and His Music* (N. Y., 1968).

Wagner, Roger, American choral conductor; b. LePuy, France, Jan. 16, 1914. He studied organ with Marcel Dupré; settled in Los Angeles in 1937; studied philosophy and French literature at the Univ. of Calif. and at the Univ. of Southern Calif., Los Angeles; studied orchestration with Lucien Caillet and conducting with Bruno Walter. In 1948 he founded the Roger Wagner Chorale, and toured with it in the U.S., Canada and Latin America. In 1965 he organized the Los Angeles Master Chorale and Sinfonia Orchestra, which opened its inaugural season on Jan. 27, 1965. He occupies the post of Director of Choral Music at the Univ. of Calif., Los Angeles; is also head of the Music Dept. at Marymount College in Palos Verdes, Calif. He has published numerous choral arrangements.

Wagner, Siegfried. Add bibl.: Zdenko von Kraft, *Der Sohn: Siegfried Wagners Leben und Umwelt* (1969).

Wagner-Régeny, Rudolf. Died in Berlin, Sept. 18, 1969. His setting for *A Midsummer Night's Dream* was produced on June 6, 1935 (not 1934). Add to works: the operas, *Prometheus* (Kassel, Sept. 12, 1959) and *Das Bergwerk zu Falun* (Salzburg, Aug. 16, 1961). Bibl.: *Rudolf Wagner-Régeny: Begegnungen, Biographische Aufzeichnungen, Tagebücher und sein Briefwechsel mit Caspar Neher* (Berlin, 1968).

Waldrop, Gid, American composer; b. on a ranch in Haskell County, Texas, Sept. 2, 1919. He studied at the Eastman School of Music in Rochester, N.Y. (Ph. D., 1952). He was editor of the 'Musical Courier' (1954-58). In 1961 he was appointed Assistant to the President of the Juilliard School of Music; in 1963 became Dean. He wrote a trio for viola, clarinet and harp (1939); *Lydian Trumpeter* for trumpet and piano (1946); a symph. (1952); choruses.

Walker, Frank. Died (suicide) in Tring, England, March 4, 1962. He studied telegraphy; in 1926 went to Rio de Janeiro as a representative of the Western Telegraph Co. From 1931-1943 he was in London; 1944-45, in Naples and later in Vienna. Add to books: *The Man Verdi* (London, 1962).

Waller, Thomas ('Fats'), American jazz pianist; b. New York, May 21, 1904; d. Kansas City, Dec. 15, 1943 (en route from Los Angeles to New York). He learned piano at home; played in cabarets from the age of 15 in N.Y. and Chicago; in 1934 organized a recording group of 6 jazz players. He improvised, or composed, with the aid of an amanuensis, a number of catchy tunes (*Ain't Misbehavin', Honeysuckle Rose,* etc.).

Walter, Arnold. His positions were: Director of Music, Upper Canada College, Toronto (1937-43); Director of Senior School, Royal Cons., Toronto (1945-52); Director of Music Faculty, Univ. of Toronto (from 1952).

Walter, Bruno. Died in Beverly Hills, Calif., Feb. 17, 1962. He publ. *Von der Musik und vom Musizieren* (Frankfurt, 1959; in English, N. Y., 1961). Add bibl.: *Briefe 1894-1962,* edited by Lotte Walter-Lindt (1969).

Walter, Friedrich Wilhelm. Died in Heidelberg, Nov. 4, 1956.

Walton, Sir **William (Turner).** Add to works: *Fanfare* for the Queen's entrance at the NATO Parliamentary Conference (London, June 5, 1959); Symph. No. 2 (Edinburgh, Sept. 2, 1960); *Gloria* for vocal soloists, mixed chorus and orch. (Liverpool, Nov. 24, 1961); *A Song for the Lord Mayor's Table* for soprano and piano (London, July 18, 1962); *Variations on a Theme by Hindemith* for orch. (London, March 8, 1963); *The Twelve* for chorus and organ (Oxford, May 16, 1965); *Missa Brevis* for double mixed chorus and organ (Coventry, April 10, 1966); *The Bear,* an extravaganza in one act (Aldeburgh Festival, June 3, 1967); *Capriccio Burlesco* for orch. (N. Y., Dec. 7, 1968); *Improvisations on an Impromptu of Britten* for orch. (San Francisco, Jan. 14, 1970). Add bibl.: F. Howes, *The Music of William Walton* (London, 1965).

Walzel, Leopold Matthias, Austrian composer; b. Vienna, Nov. 29, 1902; d. there, June 9, 1970. A lawyer by profession, he also studied music at the Univ. of Vienna; composed 5 symphonies, an opera *Salamis,* a piano quartet, an octet, 2 quintets and several song cycles.

Ward, Robert. Add to works: the operas, *The Crucible* (N.Y., Oct. 26, 1961) and *The Lady from Colorado* (Central City, Colorado, July 3, 1964; received the Pulitzer Prize).

Ware, Harriet. Died in New York, Feb. 9, 1962.

Warfield, William, Negro baritone; b. Helena, Arkansas, Jan. 20, 1920. He studied at the Eastman School of Music, Rochester, N.Y., graduating in 1946; sang in opera and musical comedy; gave his first N.Y. song recital on March 19, 1950, with excellent critical acclaim. He subsequently toured Europe in the role of Porgy in the production of Gershwin's *Porgy and Bess.* He married the soprano Leontyne Price in 1952.

Waring, Fred M., popular American conductor; b. Tyrone, Pa., June 9, 1900. He trained choruses; formed a group called 'The Pennsylvanians,' which became very popular on the radio. He is the chairman of the board of the Waring Manufacturing Co., producing the widely used Waring Blenders.

Warren, Leonard. Died in New York City, March 4, 1960, during the performance of *La Forza del destino,* on the stage of The Metropolitan Opera House. His real name was Warenoff (not Varenov).

Warren, Raymond, English composer; b. Western Super Mare, Nov. 7, 1928. He studied with Robin Orr at Cambridge Univ. (1949-52) and later took lessons with Michael Tippett and Lennox Berkeley; received his Mus.B. at Cambridge Univ. (1952); in 1955 was appointed Lecturer in Music at Belfast Univ. Works: *The Lady of Ephesus,* one-act chamber opera (Belfast, Feb. 16, 1959); *Finn and the Black Hag,* children's opera after an Irish folk tale (Belfast, Dec. 11, 1959); *The Passion,* oratorio (Belfast, Feb. 19, 1962); *Graduation Ode,* comic opera (Belfast, Nov. 17, 1963); Symph. No. 1 (1965); chamber music and songs.

Washburn, Robert, American composer; b. Bouckville, New York, July 11, 1928. He attended the State College of Potsdam, N. Y., where he received his M.S. He served in the U.S. Air Force (1950-54) and later studied composition at the Eastman School of Music in Rochester, N. Y., with Bernard Rogers. He also took a summer course at Aspen with Darius Milhaud. In 1954 he was appointed prof. of music at the State College of Education at Potsdam, N. Y. Works: Symph. No. 1 (1959); *Synthesis* for orch. (1960); *St. Lawrence Overture* (1962); Sinfonietta for string orch. (1964); *Serenade* for strings (1966); *Symphonic Essay* (1967); *North Country Overture* (1969); *Blue Lake Overture* (1970); chamber music.

Watts, André, American pianist; b. in a U.S. Army camp in Nuremberg, June 20, 1946, as a legitimate son of a Hungarian mother and a black American soldier. His parents were divorced in 1962. He studied in Philadelphia; attracted national attention at 16 as soloist with Leonard Bernstein's Young People's Concert televised on Jan. 15, 1963; since then played to tumultuous applause in America and in Europe. On Aug. 14, 1971, he gave a highly successful recital in his native Nuremberg.

Watts, Wintter. Died in Brooklyn, Nov. 1, 1962.

Waxman, Franz. Died in Los Angeles, Feb. 24, 1967. Add to works: oratorio *Joshua* (Dallas, May 23, 1959).

Wayditch, Gabriel (full name, **Baron Gabriel Wajditsch Verbovac von Dönhoff**), Hungarian-American composer; b. Budapest, Dec. 28, 1888; d. New York, July 28, 1969. He studied piano with Emil Sauer and composition with Hans Koessler at the Budapest Academy of Music. In 1907 he emigrated to the U.S.; lived mostly in New York. He wrote 14 lengthy operas to his own libretti in Hungarian, dealing mostly with oriental or religious subjects; of these only one, *Horus,* was performed, at the composer's expense, in Philadelphia, on Jan. 5, 1939. The longest opera, *Sahara,* in 8 acts, requires 6½ hours to perform; the shortest, *The Caliph's Magician,* in one act, takes 2 hours. The other operas are: *Opium Dreams, Buddha, Jesus Before Herod, Maria Magdalena, Maria Tesztver, Nereida, The Heretics, The Catacombs, Anthony of Padua, The Venus Dwellers, Neptune's Daughter.*

Weber, Alain. Add to works: wind quintet (1955); *Sextuor* for clarinets (1956); *Voie unique,* chamber opera (1960); *Exergues,* suite for strings (1961); *Symphonie* (1961); *Sonate* for harp and oboe (1961); *Concertino* for piano and orch. (1963); *Variations* for 12 instruments (1965); *Midjaay,* symph. poem (1966); *Palindromes* for bassoon and piano (1967); *Commentaires concertants* for flute and orch. (1968); *Concerto* for trombones and orch. (1969); *Solipsisme* for orch. (1969); *Syllepse* for chamber orch. (1970).

Weber, Ben. Add to works: *Rapsodie Concertante* for viola and orch. (1957); *Chamber Fantasy* for small orch. (1959); piano concerto (1961).

Weber, Carl Maria (Friedrich Ernst). His *Konzerstück* is in F minor (not F major). Add to bibl.: J. Warrack, *Carl Maria von Weber* (N. Y., 1968).

Weber, Margrit, Swiss pianist; b. Ebnat-Kappel, Feb. 24, 1924. She studied organ in

Zürich; was employed as an organist at the age of 15; then devoted herself chiefly to the piano. She toured Europe in concert recitals presenting many new works; in 1956 and in 1965 she played in the U.S. and Canada. She was the soloist in the first performances of piano concertos by Martinu and Alexander Tcherepnin, and of Stravinsky's *Movements*.

Webern, Anton von. It is incorrect to state that in his last works, counterpoint is deprived of imitation or canon; quite to the contrary, motivic imitation, precise as to interval, is fundamental, and appears even more emphatically in his last opus numbers; canons in inversion and augmentation are important features. Melodically and harmonically, the intervals of the major 7th and minor 9th are stressed, while the 12-tone row retains its governing function. Add to bibl.: Hans Moldenhauer, *The Death of Anton Webern* (N.Y., 1961); W. Kolneder, *Anton Webern: Einführung in Werk und Stil* (Rodenkirchen, 1961; in English, Berkeley, 1967); Claude Rostand, *Anton Webern: L'Homme et son oeuvre* (Paris, 1969). Stenograms of lectures delivered by Webern in a private home in Vienna in 1932-33 were edited by Willi Reich and publ. in English under the title *The Path to the New Music* (1965); facsimile reproductions from Webern's sketchbooks were publ. with a commentary by Ernst Krenek and a foreword by Hans Moldenhauer (N. Y., 1969).

Wedge, George (Anson). Died in Barbados, Oct. 31, 1964.

Weelkes, Thomas. Add bibl.: David Brown, *Thomas Weelkes: A Biographical and Critical Study* (1969).

Weigl, Karl. His Fifth Symphony was performed for the first time posthumously, N. Y., Oct. 27, 1968.

Weinberger, Jaromir. Died in St. Petersburg, Florida, Aug. 8, 1967 (suicide by overdose of sedative drugs). Studied with Max Reger in Leipzig (not Berlin); never lived in London, nor in Moscow; was never engaged as conductor; did not compose a song cycle of Jewish melodies.

Weiner, Leo. Died in Budapest, Sept. 13, 1960.

Weinstock, Herbert. Add to books: *Donizetti and the World of Opera in Italy, Paris and Vienna in the First Half of the 19th Century* (N.Y., 1963). *Rossini* (N.Y., 1968); *Vincenzo Bellini: His Life and Operas* (N.Y., 1971).

Weintraub, Eugene, American publisher; b. Stalnoye, Russia, March 10, 1904. His family settled in the U.S. when he was an infant; he studied violin with Victor Küzdö, and conducting at the Juilliard School in N.Y. In 1940 he entered the field of music publishing; was director of Am-Rus Music Corp., in charge of Soviet music distribution in America. He obtained the highest rental fee in history by charging $10,000 for the first American performance of Shostakovitch's Symph. No. 8 (1944). In 1950 he established the Weintraub Music Co., specializing in works by modern American composers.

Weinzweig, John Jacob. Add to works: *Wine of Peace* for soprano and orch. (1957); *Symphonic Ode* (1958); *Divertimento No. 3* for bassoon and string orch. (1959); *Divertimento No. 5* for trumpet, trombone and wind ensemble (1961); string quartet No. 3 (1962); woodwind quintet (1964); clarinet quartet (1965). See '34 Biographies of Canadian Composers' publ. by the Canadian Broadcasting Co. (Montreal, 1964).

Weisbach, Hans. Died in Wuppertal, April 23, 1961.

Weisgall, Hugo. Add to works: *Purgatory,* opera in one act to the text of W. B. Yeats (Library of Congress, Washington, Feb. 17, 1961); *Athaliah,* opera (N. Y., Feb. 17, 1964); *Nine Rivers from Jordan,* opera (N. Y., Oct. 9, 1968).

Weiss, Adolph. Died in Van Nuys, Calif., Feb. 21, 1971.

Weissberg, Yulia Lazarevna. *The Twelve* for chorus and orch. was composed in 1925 (not 1928); performed for the first time in Leningrad, May 12, 1926.

Weissenbäck, (Franz) Andreas. Died in Vienna, March 14, 1960.

Weldon, George. Died in Cape Town, South Africa, Aug. 17, 1963.

Welk, Lawrence, popular American conductor of entertainment music; b. Strasburg, North Dakota, March 11, 1903. He received his training in California; in 1955 he began a series of television concerts which became increasingly popular, thanks to his skillful selection of programs containing a varied mixture of semi-classical pieces, western American ballads and Slavic folk-dance tunes. His use of an accordion section in his arrangements, steadfast rhythmic beat and sentimentalized tempi impart to his renditions a rudimentary sound quality that makes him a favorite with undiscriminating audiences. He publ. (with outside help) an autobiography, *Wunnerful, Wunnerful!* (N. Y., 1971), radiating euphoria.

Wellesz, Egon. Add to works: violin concerto (Vienna, Jan. 19, 1962); quintet for clarinet and strings (1959); Symph. No. 6 (Nuremberg, June 1, 1966). Add to books: *Die Hymnen der Ostkirche* (Kassel, 1962). Cf. R. Schollum, *Egon Wellesz* (Vienna, 1964).

Wennerberg, Gunnar. Date of death, Aug. 24 (not Aug. 22), 1901. Place of death, Läckö (not Leckö).

Werle, Lars Johan, Swedish composer; b. Gävle, June 23, 1926. He studied with Sven-Erik Bäck (composition) and Carl-Allan Moberg (musicology) at Uppsala Univ.; held positions at the Swedish Broadcasting Corporation and as instructor at the National School of Music Drama in Stockholm. In his music he employs an amiably modern idiom, stimulating to the untutored ear, while retaining the specific gravity of triadic tonal constructions. His two operas, *Dream of Therese,* after Zola's novel (Stockholm, May 26, 1964) and *Resan (The Voyager;* Hamburg, March 2, 1969) were received with unquestioning approbation. He also wrote *Pentagram* for string quartet (1959); *Sinfonia da camera* (1960); and *Zodiak,* ballet (1966).

Werner, Eric. Add to books: *Mendelssohn: A New Image of the Composer and his Age* (N.Y., 1963).

Westrup, Jack Allan. With F. L. Harrison, he edited the 'Collins Music Encyclopedia' (London, 1959); American ed., as 'The New College Encyclopedia of Music' (N.Y., 1960).

Wetzel, Justus Hermann. In 1970, was living in retirement in Überlingen.

Whear, Paul William, American composer; b. Auburn, Indiana, Nov. 13, 1925. He studied with Wayne Barlow at the Eastman School of Music, Rochester, N.Y., and with Gardner Read at Boston Univ. In 1960 he became chairman of the Music Dept. at Doane College, Crete, Nebraska. His principal works include a violin concerto (1950); the symphonic poems, *Proemion* (1949) and *St. Joan* (1951); a cantata *The Ten Commandments* (1955); *Renaissance Suite* for orch. (1958); 3 string quartets; choruses.

White, Clarence Cameron. Died in New York, June 30, 1960.

White, John S. (real name, Hans Schwarzkopf), opera director, linguist; b. Vienna, March 4, 1910; studied at the Univ. of Vienna, at the Sorbonne in Paris, and in Perugia, specializing in romance and Germanic languages, art and music history. He came to the U.S. in 1938; served in the U.S. Army during World War II; lectured at the New School for Social Research in N. Y.; pursued widely diversified studies ranging from philosophy to literature, and from psychoanalysis to equestrianism; is co-founder and treasurer of the American Dressage Institute, a haute école which trains exhibition horses to perform intricate gaits. White published analytical studies, *Georg Büchner, or the Suffering Through the Father* and *Psyche and Tuberculosis: The Libido Organization of Franz Kafka; Renaissance Cavalier* (on Baldassare Castiglione; N.Y., 1959). In 1946 he joined the administrative staff of the N. Y. City Opera; then became its managing director.

White, Michael, American composer; b. Chicago, March 6, 1931. He studied at the Chicago Musical College and at the Juilliard School of Music, N. Y., with Peter Mennin. In 1963 he received a Guggenheim Fellowship and lived in Italy. Works: *Fantasy* for orch. (1957); *Suite* for orch. (1959); *Gloria* for chorus and orch. (1960); *The Diary of Anne Frank* for soprano and orch. (1960); *Prelude and Ostinato* for string orch. (1960); *The Dybbuk,* opera (1960-62); *Sleep, Little Lord* for children's chorus and strings (1961); many choruses a cappella; piano sonata; songs.

White, William C., American bandleader and march composer; b. Utah, Sept. 29, 1881; d. Tenafly, New Jersey, Sept. 30, 1964. He studied violin at the New England Cons. in Boston and later at the Institute of Musical Arts in N.Y., graduating in 1914. He served for many years as principal of the Army Music School on Governors Island and led the 321st Army Band. He composed several marches, among them the popular *American Doughboy;* publ. *A History of Military Music in America; Military Band Arranging,* and *Tone Building and Intonation Studies for Military Bands.*

Whiteman, Paul. Died in Doylestown, Pennsylvania, Dec. 29, 1967.

Whitmer, Thomas Carl. Died in Poughkeepsie, N.Y., May 30, 1959.

Whittaker, Howard, American composer; b. Lakewood, Ohio, Dec. 19, 1922. He studied with Herbert Elwell in Cleveland; in 1948 was appointed director of the Cleveland Music School Settlement. He has written a piano concerto, 2 string quartets, a piano sonata, works for organ and songs. His *Two Murals for Orchestra,* inspired by paintings of Orozco, was performed for the first time by the Cleveland Orch. on March 31, 1960. In most of his works he applies modified serial procedures, but refuses to abandon tonality.

Whittall, Gertrude Clarke. Died in Washington, D.C., June 29, 1965.

Whythorne, Thomas. His autobiography, discovered ca. 1950, was published in Oxford in 1961 in his original phonetic spelling, and reprinted in modern spelling in 1963, ed. by J. M. Osborn.

Wickham, Florence. Died in New York, Oct. 20, 1962. Born in 1880 (not 1882).

Wiechowicz, Stanislaw. Died in Cracow, May 12, 1963.

Wielhorsky, Mikhail Yurievitch. Joseph Wielhorsky was his distant relative (not a brother).

Wieniawski, Henryk (Henri). Date of death, April 12 (not March 31), 1880. Cf. J. W. Reiss, *H. Wieniawski* (Cracow, 1962).

Wikmanson, Johan, Swedish organist and composer; b. Stockholm, Dec. 28, 1753; d. there, Jan. 16, 1800. He was trained as an engineer, but also studied music; played organ in Stockholm churches; took composition lessons with J. M. Kraus. He wrote 5 string quartets; 2 piano sonatas; songs. His style closely approximates that of Haydn. Cf. G. S. Möner, *J. Wikmanson* (Stockholm, 1952).

Wildberger, Jacques, Swiss composer; b. Basel, Mar. 1, 1922. He studied composition with Wladimir Vogel; became instructor at the Basel Musical Academy. In his works he adopts the principles of serialism with underlying mathematical interrelationships of notes, intervals and rhythms. Works: Quartet for flute, clarinet, violin and cello (1952); trio for oboe, clarinet and bassoon (1953); *Tre Mutazioni* for chamber orch. (1953); *Intensio-Centrum-Remissio* for orch. (1958); *Zeitebenen* for 8 instruments (1958); *Musik* for 22 solo strings (Vienna, June 13, 1961); oboe concerto (1963); *Épitaphe pour Évariste Galois,* 'documented action' for soprano, baritone, speaking chorus, speakers, orch. and magnetic tape (Basel, May 20, 1964); *Mouvements* for orch. (1964); choral works.

Wilder, Alec. The title of his piano piece is *A Debutante's Diary* (not *Dairy*).

Wilderer, Johann Hugo von, German composer; b. in Bavaria, ca. 1670; d. Mannheim, 1724. He studied with Legrenzi in Venice; was court organist in Düsseldorf and Mannheim. He wrote operas to Italian libretti; of these, *La Forza del Giusto* had a modicum of success. He also composed sacred music. See G. Steffen, *Johann Hugo Wilderer* (Cologne, 1960).

Wildgans, Friedrich. Died in Mödling, near Vienna, Nov. 7, 1965.

Willan, Healey. Died in Toronto, Feb. 16, 1968.

Williams, John T., American composer; b. Flushing, N. Y., Feb. 8, 1932. He studied piano with Rosina Lhévinne at the Juilliard School of Music in New York; then moved to Los Angeles where he took composition lessons with Mario Castelnuovo-Tedesco. In his instrumental music he adopts a modified serial method of composition; he also writes for jazz. His works include an *Essay for Strings* (1966) and various pieces of chamber music.

Williams, Spencer, American composer of popular music; b. New Orleans, Oct. 14, 1889; d. New York, July 14, 1965. He played piano in night clubs in New Orleans, Chicago and New York; began to write songs in the slow rhythmic manner of the New Orleans blues. In 1932 he went to Europe for a prolonged stay; lived in Paris, London and Stockholm; returned to the U.S. in 1957. His most famous song was *Basin Street Blues;* later he wrote other songs on the blues theme in a faster tempo: *Arkansas Blues, Mississippi Blues, Royal Garden Blues.* His *Mahogany Hall Stomp* became a perennial favorite.

Williamson, John Finley. Died in Toledo, Ohio, May 28, 1964.

Williamson, Malcolm, Australian composer; b. Sydney, Nov. 21, 1931. He studied with Eugene Goossens at the Sydney Cons.; in 1950 went to Europe; studied composition with Elisabeth Lutyens in London. Untutored, he mastered the organ and was employed as church organist in England. After a period of using the most advanced serial methods in his compositions, he returned to harmonic simplicity. Works: *Santiago de Espada,* overture; piano concertos No. 1 (1958), No. 2 (1961), No. 3 (1962); *Fons Amoris* for organ (1955); *Elevamini* for orch. (1956); 3 piano sonatas (1955, 1957,

1958); concerto for organ and orch. (1961); *Symphony for Voices* a cappella (1962); *Our Man in Havana,* opera after Graham Greene's novel (London, July 2, 1963); *Variations* for cello and piano (1964); *The Display,* ballet, a dance symphony in 4 movements (Adelaide Festival, March 14, 1964); *Sinfonietta* (1965); *The Happy Prince,* children's opera after Oscar Wilde (Farnham, May 22, 1965); violin concerto (Bath, England, June 15, 1965, Yehudi Menuhin soloist); *Concerto Grosso* (London, Aug. 28, 1965); *Symphonic Variations* (Edinburgh, Sept. 9, 1965); *Julius Caesar Jones,* opera for children's voices with 3 adults (London, Jan. 4, 1966); *Sun Into Darkness,* ballet, (London, April 13, 1966); *The Violins of Saint-Jacques,* opera (London, Nov. 29, 1966); *The Moonrakers,* cassation for audience and orch. or piano (Brighton, April 22, 1967); *Dunstan and the Devil,* chamber opera (Cookham, May 19, 1967); *Knights in Shining Armour,* cassation for audience and piano (Brighton, April 19, 1968); *The Snow Wolf,* cassation for audience and piano (Brighton, April 30, 1968); *The Growing Castle,* chamber opera for 4 singers, piano, harpsichord, tubular chimes and drums, after Strindberg's *Dream Play* (commissioned for the Dynevor Festival, and first performed there Aug. 13, 1968, with the composer alternately at the piano and at the harpsichord); Symph. No. 2 (Bristol, Oct. 29, 1969).

Willman, Allan, American composer and pianist; b. Hinckley, Illinois, May 11, 1909. He studied at the Chicago Musical College (M.M., 1930); then took lessons with Nadia Boulanger in Paris (1935). In 1936 he joined the faculty of the Univ. of Wyoming. His works include *Idyl* for orch. (1930); *Solitude* for orch. (1930; Boston Symph., April 20, 1936); *A Ballade of the Night* for voice and string quartet (1936); numerous piano pieces and songs.

Willner, Arthur. Died in London, April 7, 1959.

Willson, Meredith. Add to books: *But He Doesn't Know the Territory* (descriptive of the origin of his musical, *The Music Man;* N.Y., 1959).

Wilson, Richard, American composer; b. Cleveland, May 15, 1941. He studied piano and cello in Cleveland; entered Harvard College in 1959, where he studied composition with Robert Moevs (A.B. 1963, magna cum laude); subsequently took courses in music theory at Rutgers Univ. (M.A. 1966). In 1966 he was appointed associate prof. of music at Vassar College. His works include *Suite* for 5 players (1963); trio for oboe, violin and cello (1964); *Fantasy and Variations* for chamber orchestra (1965); *Concert Piece* for violin and piano (1967); *A Dissolve* for women's voices a cappella (1968); *Light in Spring Poplars* for mixed voices a cappella (1968); string quartet (1968); *Music for Violin and Cello* (1969); quartet for flutes, double-bass and harpsichord (1969); *Initiation* for orch. (Newburgh, N. Y., April 11, 1970).

Wimberger, Gerhard, Austrian composer; b. Vienna, Aug. 30, 1923. He studied in Salzburg; later conducted the Mozarteum there. He wrote several comic operas: *Schaubundengeschichte* (Mannheim, 1954); *Der Handschuh* (Frankfurt, 1955); *La Battaglia* (Schwetzingen, 1960); also *Kantate vom Sport* (1953); concerto for piano and 15 string instruments (1955); *Divertimento* for string orch. (1956); *Loga-Rhythmen* for orch. (1956); *Figuren und Phantasien* for orch. (1957); *Risonanze* for 3 orchestral groups (Berlin, Jan. 31, 1968); *Ars Amatoria,* to texts from Ovid, for voices, chorus, jazz combo and orch. (Vienna, Feb. 7, 1969).

Windingstad, Ole. Died in Kingston, N. Y., June 3, 1959.

Winkler, Alexander Adolfovitch. Died in Besançon (not in Leningrad), Aug. 6 (not Oct.), 1935.

Winkler, Peter K., American composer; b. Los Angeles, Jan. 26, 1943. He studied at the Univ. of California in Berkeley (A.B., 1964) and at Princeton Univ. (M.A., 1966). His works include *Etude* for 2 horns (1964); string quartet (1967); *Praise of Silence* for soprano, chorus, instruments and tape (1969); incidental music for plays, radio and television.

Winograd, Arthur, American cellist and conductor; b. New York, April 22, 1920. He studied at the New England Cons. (1937-40) and at the Curtis Institute (1940-41); played the cello in the Boston Symphony (1940-41) and in the NBC Symph. Orch. (1942-43); then was a member of the Juilliard String Quartet; joined the faculty of the Juilliard School of Music (1946-55) and later began to conduct. He was the conductor of the Birmingham, Alabama Symph. Orch. (1960-64); in 1964 he was appointed conductor and music director of the Hartford, Conn. Symph. Orch.

Winternitz, Emanuel. Publ.: *Musical Instruments and their Symbolism in Western Art* (N. Y., 1967).

Wirén, Dag Ivar. Add to works: Symph. No. 5 (1964).

Wissmer, Pierre. Add to works: 2nd violin concerto (1954); Symph. No. 3 (1955); guitar concerto (1957); clarinet concerto (1961); trumpet concerto (1961); Symph. No. 4 (1962); Symph. No. 5 (1969); *Le Quatrième mage,* oratorio (Paris, Oct. 14, 1969).

Wittgenstein, Paul. Died in Manhasset, Long Island, N.Y., March 3, 1961.

Woldemar, Michel. Date of birth, June 17 (not Sept. 15), 1750.

Wolf, Arthur William, American choral conductor and educator; b. Rochester, N.Y., May 21, 1905. He studied singing in New York with Coenraad Bos; choral conducting with Günther Ramin in Leipzig and with Bruno Kittel in Berlin. In 1941 he settled in Hollywood; became dean of the School of Music of the California Institute of the Arts; also wrote music criticism. He was Musical Director of NBC's 'Voice of the Cathedral' (1949-1951); also conducted the first televised oratorio (Los Angeles, 1949).

Wolf, Hugo. Place of birth Windisch-Gräz (not Windischgraz). Add to bibl.: E. Sams, *The Songs of Hugo Wolf* (N. Y., 1962); Rita Egger, *Die Deklamationsrhythmik Hugo Wolfs in historischer Sicht* (Tutzing, 1963).

Wolfe, Stanley, American music educator and composer; b. Brooklyn, Feb. 7, 1924. After service in the U.S. Army during World War II, he enrolled at the Juilliard School of Music in New York, studying composition with William Bergsma, Vincent Persichetti and Peter Mennin (B.S., 1952; M.S., 1955); then joined its faculty; in 1963 was appointed director of the Juilliard Extension Division. Since 1969, adjunct prof. of music at the Lincoln Center campus of Fordham Univ. Works.: *Adagio* for woodwind quintet (1948); Symph. No. 1 (1954); Symph. No. 2 (1955); *Three Profiles* for piano (1955); *Lincoln Square Overture* (1957); Symph. No. 3 (Albuquerque, Nov. 18, 1959); Symph. No. 4 (Albuquerque, Dec. 7, 1966); *Variations* for orch. (1967); Symph. No. 5 (N. Y., April 2, 1971).

Wolfes, Felix. Died in Boston, March 28, 1971.

Wolff, Albert (Louis). Died in Paris, Feb. 20, 1970. Succeeded Messager (not Massenet) as conductor at the Opéra-Comique.

Wolff, Christian, American composer of the avant-garde; b. Nice, France, March 8, 1934; came to the U.S. in 1941. He studied piano in New York; took lessons in composition with John Cage. He studied classical languages at Harvard Univ.; received his Ph.D. in comparative literature in 1963. In 1962 he was appointed instructor in Greek and Latin at Harvard. He evolved a curiously static method of composition, using drastically restricted numbers of pitches. His only structural resources became arithmetical progressions of rhythmic values and the expressive use of rests. He used 3 different pitches in his *Duo* for violin and piano; 4 different pitches in the *Trio* for flute, cello and trumpet (1951); 9 in a piano piece called *For Piano I.* Beginning in 1957 he introduced into his works various degrees of free choice; sometimes the players are required to react to the musical activities of their partners according to unforeseen cues. Works: Trio for flute, cello and trumpet (1951); *Nine* for 9 instruments (1951); *For 6 or 7 Players* (1959); *Summer* for string quartet (1961); *Duo for Violinist and Pianist* (1961); *For 5 or 10 Players* (1962); *In Between Pieces,* for 3 players (1963); *For 1, 2 or 3 People* (1964); Septet, for any instruments (1964); piano pieces, entitled *For Pianist, For Piano I, For Piano II, Duo for Pianists I and II,* for 2 pianos, 4 hands; *Duet I,* for piano, 4 hands; *Duet II,* for piano and horn.

Wolff, Ernst Victor. Died in East Lansing Aug. 21, 1960. Joined the Michigan State faculty in 1947.

Wolff, Werner. Died in Rüschlikon, Switzerland, Nov. 23, 1961. Retired from Chattanooga Opera Association in 1959.

Wolffers, Jules. From 1961 to 1964 was in New Zealand; then went to California. In 1971 he was teaching piano in San Jose.

Wolfsohn, Juliusz. Died in New York in 1944. Settled in the U.S. in 1933 (not in 1926).

Wood, Haydn. Died in London, March 11, 1959.

Wood, Sir Henry J. Add to bibl.: Reginald Pound, *Sir Henry Wood: A Biography* (1969).

Wood, Hugh, English composer; b. Parbold, near Wigan, Lancashire, June 27, 1932. He studied composition with Anthony Milner, Iain Hamilton and Mátyás Seiber. In 1962 he joined the staff of the Royal Academy of Music, London. His works include trio for flute, viola and piano (1961); 2 string quartets (1962, 1970); *Scenes from Comus* for soprano, tenor and orch. (1965); quintet for clarinet, horn, violin, cello and piano (1967); cello concerto (London, Aug. 26, 1969).

Wood, Joseph, American composer; b. Pittsburgh, May 12, 1915. He studied with Bernard Wagenaar at the Juilliard School, N.Y., graduating in 1949, and with Otto Luening at Columbia Univ., (M.A., 1950). In 1950 he was appointed prof. in composition at the Oberlin Cons. of Music in Ohio. His works include an opera *The Mother* (1945); 3 symphonies (1939, 1952, 1958); piano trio (1937); viola sonata (1938); string quartet (1942); violin sonata (1947); piano quintet (1956); *Divertimento* for piano and chamber orch. (1959); choruses; incidental music for theatrical plays; piano pieces; songs. His music is couched in a modern romantic vein; upon occasion he applies serial techniques.

Woodbury, Arthur, American composer; b. Kimball, Nebraska, June 20, 1930. He studied at the Univ. of Idaho (B.S., 1951; M.M., 1955); also attended the Univ. of California, Berkeley (1957-58). A bassoon player by profession, he was a member of various orchestras; also played the saxophone. In 1963 he joined the staff of the Univ. of California, Davis. His early works are written in a traditional modern idiom; later he branched out as a composer of experimental music, cultivating electronic and aleatory techniques. Works: woodwind quartet (1955); *Symphony* (1958); *Autobiography: Patricia Belle,* for soprano, electronic instruments and an amplified chamber ensemble (1968); *Remembrances* for violin, saxophone and vibraphone (1968); *Recall,* a theater piece (1969); *An Evening of the Music of Neil Jansen, A Put-on,* for tape, utilizing the Moog synthesizer (1969); *Werner Vonbrawnasaurus Rex* for tape, slide guitar, electric piano and music synthesizer (1970).

Woodworth, George Wallace. Died in Cambridge, Mass., July 18, 1969. He publ. *The World of Music* (Cambridge, Mass., 1964).

Wooldridge, David, English conductor and writer on music; b. Seal, Kent, Aug. 24, 1927. After service in the Royal Navy he entered the Royal Academy of Music and Trinity College of Music in London (B.M., 1952), studying violin with David Martin, piano with Henry Geehl, theory with William Lovelock and choral conducting with Charles Kennedy Scott. Progressing rapidly as conductor, he was apprenticed to Erich Kleiber at Royal Opera House, Covent Garden in 1952; was later assistant to Clemens Krauss at the Vienna State Opera; in 1954-55 conducted at the Bavarian State Opera in Munich; in 1961-65 he held the post of music director and conductor of the National Orch. of Lebanon in Beirut; in 1968-69 was in charge of the Opera Workshop at Indiana Univ. in Bloomington, obtaining his M.M. degree there in 1969. In 1970 he was appointed orchestra director at Grinnell College, Iowa. He publ. *Conductor's World* (London, 1970). He is a grandson of the English musicologist Henry Ellis Wooldridge and godson of Rachmaninoff.

Wordsworth, William. Add to works: Sinfonietta (1958); Symph. No. 5 (1960); cello concerto (1963); string quartet No. 4 (1950), No. 5 (1955), No. 6 (1964); *Highland Overture* (1964); *A Song of Praise* for chorus and orch. (1956); 2nd cello sonata (1959).

Wörner, Karl Heinrich. Died in Heiligenkirchen, near Detmold, Aug. 11, 1969. Add to publ.: *Gotteswort und Magie; die Oper 'Moses und Aron' von Arnold Schönberg* (Heidelberg, 1959); *Das Zeitalter der thematischen Prozesse in der Geschichte der Musik* (1969); *Die Musik in der Geistesgeschicte* (1970).

Wouters, (François) Adolphe. Date of birth, May 28, 1849 (not 1841).

Wuorinen, Charles, American composer; b. New York, June 9, 1938. He studied piano at home; composition at Columbia Univ. with Otto Luening. He worked as an accompanist; sang countertenor parts in choral groups; served as a recording engineer; taught at Columbia Univ. (from 1964-71). At the age of 16 he received a N. Y. Philharmonic Young Composers Award; several other awards and grants followed, among them the Lili Boulanger Memorial Award (1960). His mode of composition reposes on strictly rational formal principles, while his materials are discriminately derived from available modern resources and incorporate serialistic procedures. He has written 3 symphonies; 3 chamber concertos; other chamber music of varied contents; choruses; electronic pieces. Other works include *Orchestral and Electronic Exchanges* (1965) combining pre-recorded music with a live performance; *Time's Encomium* for electronic media produced through the Mark II Synthesizer (1969; received the Pulitzer Prize); piano sonata (1969); *1851: A Message to Denmark Hill,* for baritone, flute, cello and piano (1970); *Variations* for unaccompanied cello (1970); *A Song to the Lute in Musicke* for voice and piano (1970).

Würz, Richard. Died in Munich, Feb. 2, 1965.

Wykes, Robert, American composer; b. Aliquippa, Penna., May 19, 1926. He studied at the Eastman School of Music (M.M., 1950) and at the Univ. of Illinois (Dr. of Mus. Arts, 1955). Trained as a flute player, he was a member of the St. Louis Symph. Orch. (1963-65). In 1965 he was appointed prof. of music at Washington Univ., St. Louis. Works: piano quintet (1959); *Density III* for orch. (1961); *Horizons* for small orch. (1964); *Wave Forms and Pulses* for orch. (1964); *The Shape of Time* for orch. (1965); *4 American Indian Lyrics* for chorus; also music for documentary films.

Wyner, Yehudi, American composer, son of Lazar Weiner (whose name he phonetically changed to Wyner); b. Calgary, Canada, June 1, 1929. He followed his parents to the U. S.; enrolled in the Juilliard School of Music in N. Y., graduating in 1946; then entered Yale Univ. where his principal teacher was Richard Donovan; obtained his A.B. in 1950; B. Mus., 1951; M. Mus., 1953; in the interim he also acquired the M.A. degree from Harvard Univ. After occupying several temporary teaching posts, he joined the staff of Yale Univ. in 1963; was appointed chairman of the music dept. there in 1969. He held the Guggenheim Fellowship in 1960. His music is expressively vigesimosecular in its structural sobriety and melorhythmic aggressiveness; his serial techniques, anchored in tritones and major sevenths, are mitigated by a certain combinatorial harmoniousness; formally, he follows neo-Baroque practices. Works: *Dance Variations* for wind octet (1953); piano sonata (1954); *Concerto Duo* for violin and piano (1957); *3 Informal Pieces* for violin and piano (1961); *Friday Evening Service* for cantor, chorus and organ (1963); *Torah Service* (1966); *Da Camera* for piano and orch. (1967).

Wyss, Niklaus, Swiss conductor; b. Zürich, Nov. 5, 1936. He studied piano and violin in Zürich; conducting in Brussels and Rome. He is active mainly in Italy, Switzerland and Holland.

Wyttenbach, Jürg, Swiss pianist and composer; b. Bern, Dec. 2, 1935. He studied in Bern with Veress and later in Paris. In 1962 he became prof. of piano at the Bern Cons. He won several prizes as pianist. He wrote a piano concerto (1959); sonata for oboe solo (1961); incidental music for plays; songs and choruses.

X

Xenakis, Yannis. Alternate spelling of the first name, **Iannis.** Born in Braila, Rumania (not in Athens), of Greek parents; moved to Greece at the age of 10. He published a comprehensive volume dealing with aleatory and stochastic (probabilistic) methods of composition, *Musiques formelles* (Paris, 1963; in English, N. Y., 1971). Add to works: *Duel,* a game for two orchestras (1959); *Syrmos* (*Chain of Events*) for 18 strings (1959); *Analogiques* for 9 string instruments and magnetic tape (1959); *Herma* (*Foundation*) for piano solo (1961); *ST/48—1,240162* (ST=Stochastic; 48=number of players; 1=1st work for this contingent; 240162=24 January 1962, date on which the work was calculated by the IBM 7090 electronic brain in Paris as programmed probabilistically by Xenakis); *ST/10—1,080262* (ST=Stochastic; 10=number of players; 1=1st work for this contingent; 080262=8 February 1962, date on which this work was electronically calculated); *Morsima-Amorsima* (Morsima=that which comes by Fate; Amorsima=that which does not come by Fate) for 10 players (1962); *Amorsima-Morsima* for piano, violin cello and double-bass (1962); *Atrees* (*Law of Necessity*) for 10 players (1962; written in homage to Blaise Pascal, the founder of the calculus of probabilities, and calculated by the 7090 computer, with some license); *Polla ta Dhina* ('Many are the wonders') for children's chorus and small orch. to a text of Sophocles (1962); *Stratégie,* game for two orchestras, a stochastic match with the winning orchestra adjudged by points (Venice Festival, April 23, 1963); *Eonta* (neuter plural of the present participle of the verb 'to be' in the Ionian dialect, the title being in Cypriot syllabic characters of Creto-Mycenean origin) for piano, 2 trumpets and 2 trombones (1964); *Hiketides* (*The Suppliants*) for 50 women's voices, percussion and 10 instruments, after Aeschylus (1964); *Akrata* (*Pure*) for 16 wind instruments (1965; Oxford, June 28, 1966); *Terretektorh* (*Action of Construction*) for 88 players scattered among the audience (Royan Festival of Contemporary Music, April 3, 1966); *Nomos Alpha* (*Law Alpha*) for cello solo (1966); *Nomos Gamma* for orch. and percussion (Royan Festival, April 3, 1969); *Kraanerg* (*Perfection of Energy*), ballet (Ottawa, June 2, 1969); *Synaphai* for piano and orch. (1971).

Y

Yamada, Kosaku. Died in Tokyo, Dec. 29, 1965. Preferred spelling of his first name is Kôsçak.

Yamash'ta, Stomu (really **Yamashita, Tsutomu**), Japanese virtuoso percussionist and composer; b. Kyoto, March 10, 1947. He was trained in music by his father; played piano as an infant; began to practice drums before puberty; as an adolescent joined the percussion section of the Kyoto Philharmonic and Osaka Philharmonic; synchronously he carried on with sports of all descriptions; won the speed skating championship of Japan for his age group. At 16 he went to London for further study, and at 17 to the U.S. as a scholarship student at Interlochen Arts Academy, Michigan; continued his musical education in Boston, N. Y. and Chicago. He developed a fantastic degree of equilibristic agility in manipulating more than a hundred drums, chimes, wood blocks and assorted oriental bells and gongs, reeling around at 360° from the center of a circle of percussionable objects. He also perfected special techniques, such as rolling snare-drums with one hand. As a composer, he cultivates a vigesimosecular quasi-aleatory idiom based on controlled improvisation within suspended tempi. Among his original works are a ballet, *Fox* (1968); *Hito* for trio of any instruments (1970); *Prisms* for solo percussion (1970); *Nenbutsu* for solo percussion (1970); *As Expanding As* for chamber ensemble (1971); *Red Buddha* for chamber ensemble (1971).

Yardumian, Richard. Add to works: piano concerto (Philadelphia, Jan. 3, 1958); Symph. No. 1 (Philadelphia, Dec. 1, 1961); Symph. No. 2 (*Psalms*) for orch. and contralto (Philadelphia, Nov. 13, 1964).

Yarustovsky, Boris, Soviet musicologist; b. Moscow, May 14, 1911. He studied at the Moscow Cons. where he later became a prof. of musicology. He publ. books on Tchaikovsky, essays on Soviet composers, a monograph on Stravinsky (1963), etc. In 1959 he was a delegate of the Union of Soviet Composers to the United States. His book on Russian opera was publ. in a German translation, *Die Dramaturgie der klassischen russischen Oper* (1957).

Yashiro, Akio, Japanese composer; b. Tokyo, Sept. 10, 1929. He studied piano with Leonid Kreutzer and composition with Saburo Moroi; graduated from the Tokyo Academy of Music in 1951; then went to Paris where he took courses with Nadia Boulanger and Olivier Messiaen. Works: string quartet (1955); symphony (Tokyo, June 9, 1958); sonata for 2 flutes and piano (1958); cello concerto (Tokyo, June 24, 1960); piano concerto (Tokyo, Nov. 5, 1967).

Yasser, Joseph. Add bibl.: 'Joseph Yasser: An Annotated Bibliography of his Selected Writings and Lectures,' compiled by Albert Weisser for The Jewish Liturgical Music Society of America (N. Y., 1970).

Yavorsky, Boleslav, Russian pianist and music theorist; b. Saratov, June 22, 1877; d. Kharkov, Nov. 26, 1942. He studied piano and composition with Taneyev in Moscow; in 1906 founded a People's Cons. there. From 1916-1921 he taught at the Kiev Cons.; then went to Moscow. His theory of aural gravitation as the determining factor of the formation of modes is embodied in his publications *Structure of Musical Speech* (Moscow, 1908), *Exercises in Schematic Formation of Modal Rhythm* (Moscow, 1915) and several monographs. He was also active in the field of general musical education, and his methods influenced Soviet practice in pedagogy. Vol. 1 of the collected edition of his articles and letters was published in Moscow in 1964.

Young, Douglas, English composer; b. London, June 18, 1947. He studied at the Royal College of Music with Anthony Milner (composition) and Anthony Hopkins (piano) in 1966. He composes mostly instrumental music. Works: *Sonata for horn and piano* (1965); *Sonnet* for orch. (1967); *Sonata* for violin, viola and cello (1968); *The Listeners,* ballet (London, Dec. 13, 1969); piano pieces for children.

Young, La Monte, American composer of the avant-garde; b. Bern, Idaho, Oct. 14, 1935. He studied at the Univ. of Calif., Los Angeles (1956-57) and at Berkeley (1957-60); took a course in advanced composition with Karlheinz Stockhausen at Darmstadt in 1959. Still a student, he plunged deep into experimental music; lectured on guerrilla warfare (with electronic realization) at the

New School for Social Research in N.Y. (1961); also presented a 'Poem for Chairs, Tables and Benches' (ibidem). His works include two stage spectacles for voice, gong and strings: *The Tortoise Droning Selected Pitches From the Holy Numbers for the Two Black Tigers, the Green Tiger and the Hermit* (N.Y., Oct. 30, 1964) and *The Tortoise Recalling the Drone of the Holy Numbers as They Were Revealed in the Dreams of the Whirlwind and the Obsidian Gong, Illuminated by the Sawmill, the Green Sawtooth Ocelot, and the High-Tension Line Stepdown Transformer* (N.Y., Dec. 12, 1964); a number of piano pieces (many performed in Europe and the Orient). He edited *An Anthology* (N.Y., 1963), containing music, poetry and art, his own contribution being a straight line in India ink on a 3 x 5 filing card, composed in 1960. In his working schedule he follows a circadian period of 26 hours, rising two hours later every passing day.

Young, Percy Marshall. Add to books: *Music and its Story* (London, 1960); *The Choral Tradition: An Historical and Analytical Survey from the 16th Century to the Present Day* (London, 1962); *Zoltán Kodály* (London, 1964); *The Bachs* (N. Y., 1970).

Young, Victor. Died in Ossining, N. Y., Sept. 2, 1968.

Ysaÿe, Eugène. The title of his 2nd opera in the Walloon dialect is *L'Avierge di Piér* (not *Pire*).

Yuasa, Joji, Japanese composer; b. Koriyama, Aug. 12, 1929. He studied composition in the 'experimental workshop' in Japan. In 1968 he received the Japan Society Fellowship for travel in Europe and the U.S. In 1969 he was one of the organizers of the 'Cross Talk Festival' in Tokyo and Osaka. In his works he adopts the most advanced multimedia techniques. Works: *Projection* for 7 players (1955); *Cosmos Haptic* for piano (1957); *Projection Topologic* for piano (1959); *Projection Esemplastic* for piano (1961); *Aoi no Ue,* musique concrète (1961); *Interpenetration* for two flutes (1963); *Projection Esemplastic* for electronic media (1964); *Kansoku* for voices (1965); *Projection* for violoncello and piano (1967); *Projection* for several kotos and orch. (1967); *Projection* for electric guitars (1968); *Projection* for string quartet (1970); *Triplicity* for contrabass (1970); *Questions* for chorus (1971).

Yun, Isang, Korean composer; b. Tong Young, Sept. 17, 1917. He studied music in Korea (1935-37) and in Japan (1941-43); in 1955 went to Berlin and took courses in composition with Boris Blacher and Josef Rufer. In his works he combines modern serialism with oriental modalities, with the scoring vivified by impressionistic color. His career was dramatically interrupted on June 17, 1967, when he and his wife were abducted from West Berlin by security agents of South Korea and secretly flown to Seoul to stand trial for sedition; he was sentenced to life imprisonment and his wife to 3 years in jail; this high-handed action aroused indignation in the free world. Twenty-four composers signed a protest and the West German government threatened to cut its economic aid to South Korea in retaliation for illegal acts committed on West German territory. Yielding to the universal demands for justice, the South Korean government freed Yun and his wife in March 1969, and they returned to Germany. Yun's most significant works are two short operas to librettos after oriental fairy tales: *Der Traum des Liu-Tung* (Berlin, Sept. 25, 1965) and *Die Witwe des Schmetterlings* (completed by him in his Seoul prison cell and produced in absentia in Bonn on Dec. 9, 1967); he also wrote *Musik* for 7 instruments (1959); *Colloides sonores* for string orch. (1961); *Fluctuations* for orch. (1964); *Nore* for cello and piano (1964); *Réak* for orch. (1966); *Images* for flute, oboe, violin and cello (1968); *Riul* for clarinet and piano (1968).

Yvain, Maurice. Died in Paris, July 28, 1965.

Z

Zabel, Albert Heinrich. Born in Berlin, Feb. 22, 1834 (not 1830); d. St. Petersburg, Feb. 16 (not Feb. 21) 1910.

Zabrack, Harold, American pianist and composer; b. St. Louis, June 30, 1929. He studied piano with Rudolph Ganz at the Chicago Musical College (M.M., 1951); composition with Nadia Boulanger at Fontainebleau. In 1955-57 he held a Fulbright grant for travel in Europe; gave concerts in West Germany. Returning to St. Louis, he became active as concert pianist and teacher. He is associate prof. of music at Webster College, Missouri. Works: *Piano Variations* (1959); 2 Duets for viola and oboe (1961); piano sonata (1964); piano concerto No. 1 (St. Louis, April 5, 1964, composer soloist); piano concerto No. 2 (1965).

Zach, Johann. Died at Bruchsal in 1773.

Zádor, Eugen. In the U.S. he spells his name Eugene Zador. Settled in Hollywood not mainly as a composer for films but as an orchestrator of motion picture scores (more than 120) by other composers. His *Variations on a Hungarian Folksong* was composed in 1926 (not 1928); first performed, Vienna, Feb. 9, 1927. The full title of his third opera is *X-mal Rembrandt* (referring to the multiple copies of Rembrandt's self-portraits passed as genuine); it was first performed in Gera, May 24, 1930. The opera *Christoph Columbus* was produced in New York on Oct. 8, 1939. Add to works: *Divertimento* for strings (1955); *Fugue-Fantasia* for orch. (1958); *Suite for Brass* (1961); *Rhapsody* for orch. (Los Angeles, Feb. 5, 1961); *Christmas Overture* (1961); *Cantata technica* (1961); *Scherzo domestico* for chorus (1961); *The Remarkable Adventure of Henry Bold,* for narrator and orch. (Beverly Hills, Calif., Oct. 24, 1963); *Variations on a Merry Theme* for orch. (1963; Birmingham, Alabama, Jan. 12, 1965); *The Virgin and the Fawn,* one-act opera (Los Angeles, Oct. 24, 1964); *5 Contrasts for Orchestra* (Philadelphia, Jan. 8, 1965); *Suite for 8 celli* (1966); *The Magic Chair,* one-act opera (Baton Rouge, Louisiana, May 14, 1966); concerto for trombone and orch. (Rochester, Michigan, July 20, 1967); *The Scarlet Mill,* one-act opera (Brooklyn, Oct. 26, 1968); *Rhapsody* for cimbalom and orch. (Los Angeles, Nov. 2, 1969); *Music for Clarinet and Strings* (St. Louis, June 26, 1970); *Studies for Orchestra* (Detroit, Nov. 12, 1970); *Fantasia Hungarica* for double-bass and orch. (1970). His opera *Revisor* (*Inspector General*), after Gogol, written in 1928, which had lain fallow for 43 years, was finally brought to performance for the first time in Los Angeles, on June 11, 1971.

Zafred, Mario. Date of birth, March 2 (not Feb. 21), 1922. Add to works: opera *Wallenstein* (Rome, 1965).

Zagwijn, Henri. Died at The Hague, Oct. 23, 1954.

Zarlino, Gioseffo. Add to bibl.: R. Flury, *Gioseffo Zarlino als Komponist* (Winterthur, 1962).

Zbar, Michel, French composer; b. Clermont-Ferrand, April 24, 1942. He studied at the Paris Cons. with Olivier Messiaen and Tony Aubin graduating in 1967; also worked with Pierre Schaeffer at the Groupe de Recherches Musicales of the Paris Radio. In 1968 he won the competition for the Prix de Rome with his *Tragédie d'Hamlet.* Other works include *Tropismes* for violin and orch. (1969); *Incandescences* for soprano, speaker and orch. (1970).

Zbinden, Julien-François. Add to works: *Jazzific* for jazz band and strings (1958); *Ballade* for bassoon and orch. (1961); *Concerto breve* for cello and orch. (1962); violin concerto (1964).

Zdravković, Živojin, Serbian conductor; b. Belgrade, Nov. 24, 1914. He studied music theory at the Belgrade Music Academy and conducting with Talich in Prague. He conducted the Belgrade Radio Orch. (1948-51); was assistant conductor of the Belgrade Philharmonic (1951-61); in 1961 became its music director. In the 1960's he toured as guest conductor in the Near East, South America, Brazil and the U.S.

Zeerleder, Niklaus, Swiss cleric and theorist; b. Bern, July 5, 1628; d. Kirchberg, July 5, 1691. He was cantor in Bern, and later in Kirchberg. He publ. a singing instruction book, *Musica figuralis oder Kurtze Gründliche Underweysung der Sing Kunst* (Bern, 1658).

Zeisl, Eric. Died in Los Angeles, Feb. 18, 1959.

Zelenka, Istvan, Hungarian composer; b. Budapest, July 30, 1936. He studied music in Budapest and later took a course with Hanns Jelinek in Vienna; in 1962 he went to Geneva where he became an acoustical engineer. His works, all in an experimental style, with the application of serial and electronic techniques, include a chamber opera, *Ein Zwischenspiel* (1960); *Conversionen* for 3 string quartets, piano, harmonium and harpsichord (1961); *Décors* for chamber orch. (1962); *Biais* for chamber orch., spatially and serially divided into 3 autochthonic groups (1963); *Hommage à Joan Miró* for orch. (1965).

Zeljenka, Ilja, Czech composer; b. Bratislava, Dec. 21, 1932. He studied music in Bratislava with Jan Cikker. His early works reflect his interest in folklore; he also wrote a melodrama *Oswieczym,* dealing with the tragedy of the notorious concentration camp. In his instrumental works he developed a serial method in which the tone-row does not necessarily govern the thematic content. Among his compositions are 2 symphonies, 2 piano quintets; film music.

Zemlinsky, Alexander von. Date of birth, Oct. 14, 1871 (not Oct. 4, 1872).

Zhukovsky, Herman Leontievitch. Add to works: *Forest Song,* ballet (Moscow, May 1, 1961).

Zillig, Winfried. Died in Hamburg, Dec. 17, 1963. Add to works: *Das Verlöbnis,* opera (Linz, Austria, Nov. 23, 1963). He publ. *Variationen über neue Musik* (Munich 1959); *Die neue Musik: Linien und Porträts* (Munich, 1963).

Zimbalist, Efrem. Retired as director of the Curtis Institute of Music in 1961.

Zimmermann, Agnes. Date of birth, July 5, 1845 (not 1847).

Zimmermann, Bernd Alois. Died in Königsdorf, Aug. 10, 1970 (suicide). Add to works: *Dialoge* for 2 pianos and orch. (Cologne, Dec. 5, 1960); *Die Soldaten* (Cologne, Feb. 15, 1965); concerto for cello and orch. (Strasbourg, April 8, 1968); *Stille und Umkehr* for orch. (Nuremberg, March 19, 1971).

Zinnen, Jean-Antoine, Luxembourg composer; b. Neuenbourg, April 25, 1827; d. Neuilly-sur-Seine, May 16, 1898. He was the composer of the National Hymn of Luxembourg (1864); wrote several operettas. In 1881 he went to Paris. After his death, his remains were brought to Luxembourg. A postage stamp in his honor was issued in 1950.

Zítek, Otakar. Died in Bratislava, April 29, 1955.

Živković, Milenko, Serbian composer; b. Belgrade, May 25, 1901; d. there, June 29, 1964. He studied law in Belgrade and music at the Leipzig Cons. with Grabner and at the Schola Cantorum in Paris with Vincent d'Indy. Returning to Belgrade he taught at the Academy of Music until 1960. A follower of the national school of composition, he wrote music permeated with ethnic Balkan melorhythms. His works include: *Symphonic Prologue* (Belgrade, April 16, 1935); *Zelena Godina* (*Green Year*), folk ballet scenes for orch. (Belgrade, April 27, 1937); several suites of Yugoslav dances for piano and numerous choruses.

Zolotarev, Vassily Andreyevitch. Died in Moscow, May 25, 1964. Taught at the Ekaterinodar Cons. from 1918 to 1924 (not 1912-24).

Zukerman, Pinchas, Israeli violinist; b. Tel Aviv, July 16, 1948. He went to America as a youth and studied with Ivan Galamian. On April 3, 1971. he made an auspicious New York debut. His playing is distinguished by an innate emotional élan and a modern virtuoso technique.

Zukofsky, Paul, American violinist; b. Brooklyn Heights, N. Y., Oct. 22, 1943. Reared in an acutely intellectual environment (his father was a poet who experimented in highly complex verbal forms), he began playing the violin at the age of 4 on a quarter-size instrument; was soloist with the New Haven Symph. at the age of 8. At 16 he entered the Juilliard School of Music where he studied with Ivan Galamian. From his earliest years he was fascinated by ultra-modern music and developed maximal celerity, dexterity and alacrity in manipulating special techniques, and in effect transforming the violin into a multi-media instrument beyond its normal capacities. In 1969 he inaugurated in New York a concert series, 'Music for the Twentieth Century Violin,' performing works often requiring acrobatic coordination. His repertory includes all 4 violin sonatas by Charles Ives, the violin concertos by William Schuman and Roger Sessions, *Capriccio* by Penderecki, etc. As violin instructor, he held the post of 'Creative Associate' at the Buffalo Center of the Creative and Performing Arts; also taught at the Berkshire Music Center in Tanglewood and at the New England Cons. of Music. In 1970 his father published a novel, *Little,* dealing with the trials and triumphs of a violin wunderkind.

Zumbro, Nicholas, American pianist; b. Murfreesboro, Tenn., Sept. 25, 1935. He studied with Johana Harris in Nashville, and later with Rosina Lhévinne at the Juilliard School in New York, obtaining his M.A. in 1960. He began his career with a successful American tour in 1963.

Zundel, John, German-American hymn writer; b. Hochdorf, Germany, Dec. 10, 1815; d. Cannstadt, Germany, July, 1882. He was organist and bandmaster in St. Petersburg, Russia; went to America in 1847 where he became organist at Central Methodist Episcopal Church in New York. He went back to Germany in 1877. In America he edited the 'Monthly Choir and Organ Journal'; was also one of the compilers, in association with Henry Ward Beecher, of the *Plymouth Collection* (1855). He wrote the celebrated hymn *Love Divine,* also known as *Beecher* or *Zundel;* it is included in *Zundel's Christian Heart Songs* (1870). Cf. R. G. McCutchan, *Our Hymnody* (N.Y., 1937).

Zuschnied, Karl. Correct spelling of last name, **Zuschneid.**

Zverev, Vasily Ivanovitch, Russian composer; b. Moscow, July 20, 1904. He studied composition at the Moscow Cons. with Gnessin and Shebalin, graduating in 1935. In 1949 he was appointed editor of the State Music Publishing Edition. He wrote 2 symphonies (1934, 1937); a flute concerto (1946); *Rhapsody* for clarinet and orch. (1947); chamber music with emphatic participation of the flute.

Zwyssig, Alberich. Correct the typographical error in line 6: monastic name Alberich (not Albreich).

Zykan, Otto M., Austrian pianist and composer; b. Vienna, April 29, 1935. He studied piano and composition at the Vienna Academy of Music; in 1958, won first prize at the Darmstadt Competition for young pianists and started on a successful concert career, specializing in modern music. His own compositions reveal a strong influence of Anton von Webern, but he does not exclude tonal and even triadic combinations and accepts formal periodicity in structure. Works: string quartet (1956); *Loblied der Kreaturen,* cantata (1961); *3 Sätze* for percussion, wind instruments and piano (1962).

REFERENCE - NOT TO BE
TAKEN FROM THIS ROOM